THE COMPLETE GENEVA BIBLE

WITH APOCRYPHA

1560 81 Books

OLD TESTAMENT

NEW TESTAMENT

AUTHENTIC VERSION

EXTENSIVE MARGINAL ANNOTATIONS

TABLE OF CONTENTS

THE
OLD TESTAMENT

THE FIRST BOOK OF MOSES, CALLED

[a]GENESIS

1

1 God created the heaven and the earth. 3 The light and the darkness, 8 The firmament, 9 He separateth the water from the earth. 16 He createth the sun, the moon, and the stars. 21 He createth the fish, birds, beasts, 26 He createth man, and giveth him rule over all creatures, 29 And provideth nurture for man and beast.

1 In the [b]beginning [1]God created the heaven and the earth. **2** And the earth was [c,d]without form and void, and [e]darkness was upon the [f]deep, and the Spirit of God [g]moved upon the [h]waters. **3** Then God said, [2]Let there be light: And there was [i]light. **4** And God saw the light that it was good, and God separated [j]the light from the darkness. **5** And God called the Light, Day, and the darkness he called Night [k]So the evening and the morning were the first day. **6** Again God said, [3]Let there be a [l]firmament in the midst of the waters, and let it separate the waters from the waters. **7** Then God made the firmament, and separated the waters, which were [m]under the firmament, from the waters which were [4]above the firmament: and it was so. **8** And God called the firmament, [n]Heaven So the evening and the morning were the second day. **9** God said again, [5]Let the waters under the heaven be gathered into one place, and let the dry land appear: and it was so. **10** And God called the dry land, Earth, and he called the gathering together of the waters, Seas: and God saw that it was good. **11** Then God said, [o]Let the earth bud forth the bud of the herb, that seedeth seed, the fruitful tree, which beareth fruit according to his kind, which hath his seed in itself upon the earth: and it was so. **12** And the earth brought forth the bud of the herb, that seedeth seed according to his kind, also the tree that beareth fruit, which hath his seed in itself according to his kind: and God [p]saw that it was good. **13** So the evening and the morning were the third day. **14** And God said, [6]Let there be [q]lights in the firmament of the heaven, to [r]separate the day from the night, and let them be for [s]signs, and for seasons, and for days, and years. **15** And let them be for lights in the firmament of the heaven to give light upon the earth: and it was so. **16** God then made two great [t]lights: the greater light to [u]rule the day, and the lesser light to rule the night: he made also the stars. **17** And God set them in the firmament of the heaven, to shine upon the earth, **18** And to [7]rule in the day, and in the night, and to separate the light from the darkness: and God saw that it was good. **19** So the evening and the morning were the fourth day. **20** Afterward God said, Let the waters bring forth in abundance every [v]creeping thing that hath [w]life: and let the fowl fly upon the earth in the [x]open firmament of the heaven. **21** Then God created the great whales, and everything living and moving, which the [y]waters brought forth in abundance according to their kind, and every feathered fowl according to his kind: and God saw that it was good. **22** Then God [z]blessed them, saying, Bring forth fruit and multiply, and fill the waters in the seas, and let the fowl multiply in the earth. **23** So the evening and the morning were the fifth day. **24** Moreover God said, Let the earth bring forth the [aa]living thing according to his kind, cattle, and that which creepeth, and the beast of the earth according to his kind, and it was so. **25** And God made the beast of the earth according to his kind, and the cattle according to his kind, and every creeping thing of the earth according to his kind: and God saw that it was good. **26** Furthermore God said, [8,ab]Let us make man in our [ac]image according to our likeness, and let them rule over the fish of the sea, and over the fowl of the heaven, and over the beasts, and over all the earth, and over everything that creepeth and moveth on the earth. **27** Thus God created the man in his image: in the image of God created he him: he created them [9]male and female. **28** And God [ad]blessed them, and God said to them, [10]Bring forth fruit, and multiply, and fill the earth, and subdue it, and rule over the fish of the sea, and over the fowl of the heaven, and over every beast that moveth upon the earth. **29** And God said, Behold, I have given unto you [ae]every herb bearing seed, which is upon all the earth, and every tree, wherein is the fruit of a tree bearing seed: [11]that shall be to you for meat. **30** Likewise to every beast of the earth, and to every fowl of the heaven, and to everything that moveth upon the earth, which hath life in itself, every green herb shall be for meat, and it was so. **31** [12]And God saw all that he had made, and lo, it was very good So the evening and the morning were the sixth day.

2

2 God resteth the seventh day, and sanctifieth it. 15 He setteth man in the garden. 22 He createth the woman. 24 Marriage is ordained.

1 Thus the heavens and the earth were finished, and all the [a]host of them. **2** For in the seventh day God ended his work which he had made, [1]and the seventh day he [b]rested from all his work, which he had made. **3** So God blessed the seventh day, and [c]sanctified it, because that in it he had rested from all his work, which God created and made. **4** These are the [d]generations of the heavens and of the earth, when they were created, in the day, that the Lord God made the earth and the heavens, **5** And every [e]plant of the field, before it was in the earth, and every herb of the field, before it grew, for the Lord God had not caused it to [f]rain upon the earth, neither was there a man to till the ground, **6** But a mist went up from the earth, and watered all the earth. **7** The Lord God also [g]made the man [h]of the dust of the ground, and breathed in his face breath of life, [2]and the man was a living soul. **8** And the Lord God planted a garden Eastward in [i]Eden, and there he put the man whom he had made. **9** (For out of the ground made the Lord God to grow every tree pleasant to the sight, and good for meat: the [j]tree of life also in the midst of the garden, [k]and the tree of knowledge of good and of evil. **10** And out of Eden went a river to water the garden, and from thence it was

---

GEN. 1

- **a.** TITLE - This word signifieth the beginning and generation of the creatures.
- **b.** Gen. 1:1 First of all, and before that any creature was, God made heaven and earth of nothing.
- **c.** Gen. 1:2 As a rude lump and without any creature in it: for the waters covered all.
- **d.** Gen. 1:2 Or, waste.
- **e.** Gen. 1:2 Darkness covered the deep waters, for as yet the light was not created.
- **f.** Gen. 1:2 Hebrew, face of the deep.
- **g.** Gen. 1:2 He maintained this confused heap by his secret power.
- **h.** Gen. 1:2 Hebrew, face of the waters.
- **i.** Gen. 1:3 The light was made before either Sun or Moon was created: therefore we must not attribute that to the creatures that are God's instruments, which only appertaineth to God.
- **j.** Gen. 1:4 Hebrew, between the light, and between the darkness.
- **k.** Gen. 1:5 Hebrew, so was the evening, so was the morning.
- **l.** Gen. 1:6 Or, spreading over, and air.
- **m.** Gen. 1:7 As the sea and rivers, from those waters that are in the clouds, which are upheld by God's power, lest they should overwhelm the world.
- **n.** Gen. 1:8 That is, the region of the air, and all that is above us.
- **o.** Gen. 1:11 So that we see it is the only power of God's word that maketh the earth fruitful, which else naturally is barren.
- **p.** Gen. 1:12 This sentence is so oft repeated, to signify that God made all his creatures to serve to his glory, and to the profit of man: but for sin they were accursed, yet to the elect, by Christ they are restored, and serve to their wealth.
- **q.** Gen. 1:14 By the lights he meaneth the Sun, the Moon, and the Stars.
- **r.** Gen. 1:14 Which is the artificial day, from the Sun rising, to the going down.
- **s.** Gen. 1:14 Of things appertaining to natural and political orders and seasons.
- **t.** Gen. 1:16 To wit, the Sun and the Moon, and here he speaketh, as man judgeth by his eye: for else the Moon is less than the planet Saturn.
- **u.** Gen. 1:16 To give it sufficient light, as instruments appointed for the same, to serve to man's use.
- **v.** Gen. 1:20 As fish and worms which slide, swim, or creep.
- **w.** Gen. 1:20 Hebrew, the soul of life.
- **x.** Gen. 1:20 Hebrew, face of the firmament.
- **y.** Gen. 1:21 The fish and fowls had both one beginning, wherein we see that nature giveth place to God's will, forasmuch as the one sort is made to fly about in the air, and the other to swim beneath in the water.
- **z.** Gen. 1:22 That is, by the virtue of his word he gave power to his creatures to engender.
- **aa.** Gen. 1:24 Hebrew, soul of life.
- **ab.** Gen. 1:26 God commanded the water and the earth to bring forth other creatures: but of man he saith, Let us make: signifying, that God taketh counsel with his wisdom and virtue, purposing to make an excellent work above all the rest of his creation.
- **ac.** Gen. 1:26 This image and likeness of God in man is expounded, Eph. 4:24, where it is written that man was created after God in righteousness and true holiness, meaning by these two words, all perfection, as wisdom, truth, innocence, power, etc
- **ad.** Gen. 1:28 The propagation of man is the blessing of God, Ps. 128.
- **ae.** Gen. 1:29 God's great liberality to man, taketh away all excuse of his ingratitude.

GEN. 1

- **1.** Ps. 33:6 - Ps.136:5 - Acts 14:15 - Acts 17:24
- **2.** Herb. 11:3
- **3.** Ps. 33:6 - Ps. 136:5 - Jer.10:12 - Jer.51:15
- **4.** Ps. 148.4
- **5.** Ps.89:11 - Ps.136:6 - Job 38:4
- **6.** Ps. 136:7 - Deut. 4:19
- **7.** Jer. 31:35
- **8.** Gen.5:1 - Gen.9:6 - 2 Cor. 11:7 - Col. 3:10
- **9.** Matt. 19:4
- **10.** Gen. 8:17 - Gen. 9:1
- **11.** Gen. 9:3
- **12.** Exod. 31:17 - Mark 7:37

GEN. 2

- **a.** Gen. 2:1 That is, the innumerable abundance of creatures in heaven and earth.
- **b.** Gen. 2:2 For he had now finished his creation, but his providence still watcheth over his creatures, and governeth them.
- **c.** Gen. 2:3 Appointed it to be kept holy, that man might therein consider the excellency of his works and God's goodness toward him.
- **d.** Gen. 2:4 Or, the original and beginning.
- **e.** Gen. 2:5 Or, tree, as Gen. 21:15.
- **f.** Gen. 2:5 God only openeth the heavens and shutteth them, he sendeth drought and rain according to his good pleasure.
- **g.** Gen. 2:7 Or, formed.
- **h.** Gen. 2:7 He showeth whereof man's body was created, to the intent that man should not glory in the excellency of his own nature.
- **i.** Gen. 2:8 This was the name of a place, as some think in Mesopotamia, most pleasant and abundant in all things.
- **j.** Gen. 2:9 Which was a sign of the life received of God.
- **k.** Gen. 2:9 That is, of miserable experience, which came by disobeying God.

divided, and became into four heads. **11** The name of one is Pishon: the same compasseth the whole land of [l]Havilah, where is gold. **12** And the gold of that land is good: there is [m]Bdellium, and the Onyx stone. **13** And the name of the second river is Gihon: the same compasseth the whole land of [n]Cush. **14** And the name of the third river is [o]Hiddekel: this goeth toward the East side of [p]Ashshur: and the fourth river is [q]Parah) **15** Then the Lord God took the man, and put him into the garden of Eden, that he might [r]dress it, and keep it. **16** And the Lord God [s]commanded the man, saying, [t]Thou shalt eat freely of every tree of the garden, **17** But of the tree of knowledge of good and evil, thou shalt not eat of it: for [u]in the day that thou eatest thereof, thou shalt die the [v]death. **18** Also the Lord God said, It is not good that the man should be himself alone: I will make him an help [w]meet for him. **19** So the Lord God formed of the earth every beast of the field, and every fowl of the heaven, and brought them unto the [x]man to see how he would call them: for howsoever the man named the living creature, so was the name thereof. **20** The man therefore gave names unto all cattle, and to the fowl of the heaven, and to every beast of the field: but for Adam found he not an helper meet for him. **21** Therefore the Lord God caused an heavy sleep to fall upon the man, and he slept: and he took one of his ribs, and closed up the flesh in stead thereof. **22** And the rib which the Lord God had taken from the man, [y]made he a [z]woman, and brought her to the man. **23** Then the man said, [3]This now is bone of my bones, and flesh of my flesh She shall be called [aa]woman, because she was taken out of the man. **24** [4]Therefore shall man leave [ab]his father and his mother, and shall cleave to his wife, and they shall be one flesh. **25** And they were both naked, the man and his wife, and they were not [ac]ashamed.

3

1 The woman seduced by the serpent, 6 enticeth her husband to sin. 8 They both flee from God. 14 They three are punished. 15 Christ is promised. 19 Man is dust. 22 Man is cast out of Paradise.

1 Now the serpent was more [a]subtle than any beast of the field, which the Lord God had made: and he [b]said to the woman, Yea, hath God indeed said, ye shall not eat of every tree of the garden? **2** And the woman said unto the serpent, We eat of the fruit of the trees of the garden. **3** But of the fruit of the tree which is in the midst of the garden, God hath said, Ye shall not eat of it, neither shall ye touch it, [c]lest ye die. **4** Then the [1]serpent said to the woman, Ye shall not [d,e]die at all, **5** But God doth know that when ye shall eat thereof, your eyes shall be opened, and ye shall be as gods, [f]knowing good and evil. **6** So the woman (seeing that the tree was good for meat, and that it was pleasant to the eyes, and a tree to be desired, to get knowledge) took of the fruit thereof, and did [2]eat, and gave also to her husband with her, and he [g]did eat. **7** Then the eyes of them both were opened, and they [h]knew that they were naked, and they sewed fig tree leaves together, and made themselves [i]breeches. **8** Afterward they heard the voice of the Lord God walking in the garden in the [j]cool of the day, and the man and his wife [k]hid themselves from the presence of the Lord God among the trees of the garden. **9** But the Lord God called to the man, and said unto him, Where art thou? **10** Who said, I heard thy voice in the garden and was afraid: because I was [l]naked, therefore I hid myself. **11** And he said, Who told thee that thou wast naked? Hast thou eaten of the tree whereof I commanded thee that thou shouldest not eat? **12** Then the man said, The woman which thou [m]gavest to be with me, she gave me of the tree, and I did eat. **13** And the Lord God said to the woman, Why hast thou done this? And the woman said, [n]The serpent beguiled me, and I did eat. **14** Then the Lord God said to the serpent, [o]Because thou hast done this, thou art cursed above all cattle, and above every beast of the field: upon thy belly shalt thou go, and [p]dust shalt thou eat all the days of thy life. **15** I will also put enmity between [q]thee and the woman, and between thy seed and her seed He shall break thine [r]head, and thou shalt [s]bruise his heel. **16** Unto the woman he said, I will greatly increase thy [t]sorrows, and thy conceptions In sorrow shalt thou bring forth children, and thy desire shall be subject to thine husband, and he shall [3]rule over thee. **17** Also to Adam he said, Because thou hast obeyed the voice of thy wife, and hast eaten of the tree, (whereof I commanded thee, saying, Thou shalt not eat of it) [u]cursed is the earth for thy sake: in sorrow shalt thou eat of it all the days of thy life. **18** [v]Thorns also and thistles shall it bring forth to thee, and thou shalt eat the herb of the field. **19** In the sweat of thy face shalt thou eat bread till thou return to the earth: for out of it wast thou taken, because thou art dust, and to dust shalt thou return. **20** (And the man called his wife's name Eve, because she was the mother of all living) **21** Unto Adam also and to his wife did the Lord God [w]make coats of skins, and clothed them. **22** And the Lord God said, [x]Behold, the man is become as one of us, to know good and evil And now lest he put forth his hand, and [y]take also of the tree of life, and eat, and live forever, **23** Therefore the Lord God sent him forth from the garden of Eden, to till the earth, whence he was taken. **24** Thus he cast out the man, and at the East side of the garden of Eden he set the Cherubims, and the blade of a sword shaken, to keep the way of the tree of life.

4

1 The generation of mankind. 3 Cain and Abel offer sacrifice. 8 Cain killeth Abel. 23 Lamech a tyrant encourageth his fearful wives. 26 True religion is restored.

1 Afterward the man knew Eve his wife which [a]conceived and bare Cain, and said, I have obtained a man [b]by the Lord. **2** And again she brought forth his brother Abel, and Abel was a keeper of sheep, and Cain was a tiller of the ground. **3** And in process of time it came to pass, that Cain brought an [c]oblation unto the Lord of the fruit of the ground. **4** And [1]Abel also himself brought of the firstfruits of his sheep, and of the fat of them, and the Lord had respect unto Abel, and to his offering, **5** But unto Cain and to his offering he had no [d]regard: wherefore Cain was exceedingly wroth and his countenance fell down. **6** Then the Lord said unto Cain, Why art thou wroth? and why is thy countenance cast down? **7** If thou do well, shalt thou not be [e]accepted? and if thou doest not well, sin lieth at the [f]door: also unto thee his [g]desire shall be subject, and thou shalt rule over him. **8** Then Cain spake unto Abel his brother. And [2]when they were in the field, Cain rose up against Abel his brother, and slew him. **9** Then the Lord said unto Cain, Where is Abel thy brother? Who answered, I cannot tell [h]Am I

---

l. Gen. 2:11 Which Havilah is a country joining to Persia Eastward, and inclineth toward the West.
m. Gen. 2:12 Or, precious stone, or pearl. Pliny saith it is the name of a tree.
n. Gen. 2:13 Or, Ethiopia.
o. Gen. 2:14 Or, Tigris.
p. Gen. 2:14 Or, Assyria.
q. Gen. 2:14 Or, Euphrates.
r. Gen. 2:15 God would not have man idle, though as yet there was no need to labor.
s. Gen. 2:16 So that man might know there was a sovereign Lord, to whom he owed obedience.
t. Gen. 2:16 Hebrew, eating thou shalt eat of.
u. Gen. 2:17 Or, whensoever.
v. Gen. 2:17 By this death he meaneth the separation of man from God, who is our life and chief felicity: and also that our disobedience is the cause thereof.
w. Gen. 2:18 Hebrew, before him.
x. Gen. 2:19 By moving them to come and submit themselves to Adam.
y. Gen. 2:22 Hebrew, built.
z. Gen. 2:22 Signifying that mankind was perfect, when the woman was created, which before was like an imperfect building.
aa. Gen. 2:23 Or, Manness, because she cometh of man: for in Hebrew Ish is man, and Ishah the woman.
ab. Gen. 2:24 So that marriage requireth a greater duty of us toward our wives, than otherwise we are bound to show to our parents.
ac. Gen. 2:25 For before sin entered, all things were honest and comely.

GEN. 2

1. Exod. 20:11 - Exod. 31:17 - Deut 5.14 - Herb 4:4
2. 1 Cor. 15:45
3. 1 Cor. 11:8
4. Matt 19:5 - Mark 10:7 - 1Cor. 6:16 - Eph. 5:31

GEN. 3

a. Gen. 3:1 As Satan can change himself into an Angel of light, so did he abuse the wisdom of the serpent to deceive man.
b. Gen. 3:1 God suffered Satan to make the serpent his instrument and to speak in him.
c. Gen. 3:3 In doubting of God's threatenings she yielded to Satan.
d. Gen. 3:4 This is Satan's chiefest subtlety, to cause us not to fear God's threatenings.
e. Gen. 3:4 Hebrew, die the death.
f. Gen. 3:5 As though he should say, God doth not forbid you to eat of the fruit, save that he knoweth that if ye should eat thereof, ye should be like to him.
g. Gen. 3:6 Not so much to please his wife, as moved by ambition at her persuasion.
h. Gen. 3:7 They began to feel their misery, but they sought not to God for remedy.
i. Gen. 3:7 Hebrew, things to gird about them to hide their privities.
j. Gen. 3:8 Or, wind.
k. Gen. 3:8 The sinful conscience fleeth God's presence.
l. Gen. 3:10 His hypocrisy appeareth in that he hid the cause of his nakedness, which was the transgression of God's commandment.
m. Gen. 3:12 His wickedness and lack of true repentance appeareth in this that he burdeneth God with his fault, because he had given him a wife.
n. Gen. 3:13 Instead of confessing her sin, she increaseth it by accusing the serpent.
o. Gen. 3:14 He asked the reason of Adam and his wife, because he would bring them to repentance, but he asketh not the serpent, because he would show him no mercy.
p. Gen. 3:14 As a vile and contemptible beast, Isa. 65:25.
q. Gen. 3:15 He chiefly meaneth Satan, by whose motion and craft the serpent deceived the woman.
r. Gen. 3:15 That is, the power of sin and death.
s. Gen. 3:15 Satan shall sting Christ and his members, but not overcome them.
t. Gen. 3:16 The Lord comforteth Adam by the promise of the blessed seed, and also punisheth the body for the sin which the soul should have been punished for; that the spirit having conceived hope of forgiveness, might live by faith.
u. Gen. 3:17 The transgression of God's commandment was the cause that both mankind and all other creatures were subject to the curse.
v. Gen. 3:18 These are not the natural fruits of the earth, but proceed of the corruption of sin.
w. Gen. 3:21 Or, gave them knowledge to make themselves coats.
x. Gen. 3:22 By this derision he reproacheth Adam's misery, whereinto he was fallen by ambition.
y. Gen. 3:22 Adam deprived of life, lost also the sign thereof.

GEN. 3

1. 2Cor. 11:13
2. 1Tim. 2:14
3. 1Cor. 14:34

GEN. 4

a. Gen. 4:1 Man's nature, the estate of marriage, and God's blessing were not utterly abolished through sin, but the quality or condition thereof was changed.
b. Gen. 4:1 That is, according to the Lord's promise, as Gen. 3:15, some read, To the Lord, as rejoicing for the son which she had born, whom she would offer to the Lord as the firstfruits of her birth.
c. Gen. 4:3 This declareth that the father instructed his children in the knowledge of God, and also how God gave them sacrifices to signify their salvation, albeit they were destitute of the sacrament of the tree of life.
d. Gen. 4:5 Because he was an hypocrite, and offered only for an outward show without sincerity of heart.
e. Gen. 4:7 Both thou and thy sacrifice shall be acceptable to me.
f. Gen. 4:7 Sin shall still torment thy conscience.
g. Gen. 4:7 The dignity of the firstborn is given to Cain over Abel.
h. Gen. 4:9 This is the nature of the reprobate when they are reproved of their hypocrisy, even to neglect God and despite him.

my brother's keeper? **10** Again he said, What hast thou done? the [i]voice of thy brother's blood crieth unto me, from the earth. **11** Now therefore thou art cursed [j]from the earth, which hath opened her mouth to receive thy brother's blood from thine hand. **12** When thou shalt till the ground, it shall not henceforth yield unto thee her strength: a [k]vagabond and a runagate shalt thou be in the earth. **13** Then Cain said to the Lord, [l,m]My punishment is greater than I can bear. **14** Behold, thou hast cast me out this day from [n]the earth, and from thy face shall I be hid, and shall be a vagabond, and a runagate in the earth, and whosoever findeth me shall slay me. **15** Then the Lord said unto him, Doubtless whosoever slayeth Cain, he shall be [o]punished seven fold And the Lord set a [p]mark upon Cain, lest any man finding him, should kill him. **16** Then Cain went out from the presence of the Lord, and dwelt in the land of Nod toward the East side of Eden. **17** Cain also knew his wife, which conceived and bore Enoch: and he built a [q]city, and called the name of the city by the name of his son, Enoch. **18** And to Enoch was born Irad, and Irad begat Mehujael, and Mehujael begat Methushael, and Methushael begat Lamech. **19** And Lamech took to him [r]two wives: the name of the one was Adah, and the name of the other Zillah. **20** And Adah bare Jabal, who was the [s]father of such as dwell in the tents, and of such as have cattle. **21** And his brother's name was Jubal, who was the father of all that play on the harp and [t]organs. **22** And Zillah also bore Tubal-Cain, who wrought cunningly every craft of brass and of iron: and the sister of Tubal-Cain was Naamah. **23** Then Lamech said unto his wives, Adah and Zillah, Hear my voice, ye wives of Lamech; hearken unto my speech: [u]for I would slay a man in my wound, and a young man to mine hurt. **24** If Cain shall be avenged sevenfold, truly Lamech [v]seventy times sevenfold. **25** And Adam knew his wife again, and she bare a son, and she called his name Seth: for God, said she, hath appointed me another seed for Abel, because Cain slew him. **26** And to the same Seth also there was born a son, and he called his name Enosh Then began men to [w]call upon the name of the Lord.

5

The genealogy. 5 The age and death of Adam. 6 His succession unto Noah and his children. 24 Enoch was taken away.

1 This is the [a]book of the generations of Adam In the day that God created Adam, in the [b]likeness of God made he him, **2** Male and female created he them, and blessed them, and called their name [c]Adam in the day that they were created. **3** Now Adam lived an hundred and thirty years, and begat a child in his own [d]likeness after his image, and called his name Seth. **4** [1]And the days of Adam, after he had begotten Seth, were eight hundred years, and he begat sons and daughters. **5** So all the days that Adam lived, were nine hundred and thirty years, and he died. **6** And [e]Seth lived an hundred and five years, and begat Enosh. **7** And Seth lived after he begat Enosh, eight hundred and seven years, and begat sons and daughters. **8** So all the days of Seth were [f]nine hundred and twelve years: and he died. **9** Also Enosh lived ninety years, and begat Cainan. **10** And Enosh lived after he begat Cainan, eight hundred and fifteen years, and begat sons and daughters. **11** So all the days of Enosh were nine hundred and five years: and he died. **12** Likewise Cainan lived seventy years, and begat Mahalalel. **13** And Cainan lived, after he begat Mahalalel, eight hundred and forty years, and begat sons and daughters. **14** So all the days of Cainan were nine hundred and ten years: and he died. **15** Mahalalel also lived sixty and five years, and begat Jared. **16** Also Mahalalel lived, after he begat Jared, eight hundred and thirty years, and begat sons and daughters. **17** So all the days of Mahalalel were eight hundred ninety and five years: and he died. **18** And Jared lived an hundred sixty and two years, and begat Enoch. **19** Then Jared lived, after he begat Enoch, eight hundred years, and begat sons and daughters. **20** So all the days of Jared were nine hundred sixty and two years: and he died. **21** [2]Also Enoch lived sixty and five years, and begat Methuselah. **22** And Enoch [g]walked with God, after he begat Methuselah, three hundred years, and begat sons and daughters. **23** So all the days of Enoch were three hundred sixty and five years. **24** And Enoch walked with God, and he was no more seen: for [h]God took him away. **25** Methuselah also lived an hundred eighty and seven years, and begat Lamech. **26** And Methuselah lived, after he begat Lamech, seven hundred eighty and two years, and begat sons and daughters. **27** So all the days of Methuselah were nine hundred sixty and nine years, and he died. **28** Then Lamech lived an hundred eighty and two years, and begat a son, **29** And called his name, Noah, saying, This same shall [i]comfort us concerning our work and sorrow of our hands, as touching the earth, which the Lord hath cursed. **30** And Lamech lived, after he begat Noah, five hundred ninety and five years, and begat sons and daughters. **31** So all the days of Lamech were seven hundred seventy and seven years: and he died. **32** And Noah was five hundred years old And Noah begat Shem, Ham and Japheth.

6

3 God threateneth to bring the flood. 5 Man altogether corrupt. 6 God repenteth that he made him. 18 Noah and his are preserved in the Ark, which he was commanded to make.

1 So when men began to be multiplied upon the earth, and there were daughters born unto them, **2** Then the [a]sons of God saw the daughters [b]of men that they were [c]fair, and they took them wives of all that they [d]liked. **3** Therefore the Lord said, My spirit shall not always [e]strive with man, because he is but flesh, and his days shall be an [f]hundred and twenty years. **4** There were [g]giants in the earth in those days: yea, and after that the sons of God came unto the daughters of men, and they had borne them children, these were mighty men, which in old time were men of [h]renown. **5** When the Lord saw that the wickedness of man was great in the earth, and all the imaginations of the thoughts of his [1]heart were only evil [i]continually, **6** Then it [j]repented the Lord, that he had made man in the earth, and he was sorry in his heart. **7** Therefore the Lord said, I will destroy from the earth the man, whom I have created, from man [k]to beast, to the creeping thing, and to the fowl of the heaven: for I repent that I have made them. **8** But Noah [l]found grace in the eyes of the Lord. **9** These are the [m]generations of Noah: Noah was a just and upright man in his time: and Noah walked with God. **10** And Noah begat three sons, Shem, Ham and Japheth. **11** The earth also was corrupt before God: for the earth was filled with [n]cruelty. **12** Then God looked upon the earth, and behold, it was corrupt: for all flesh had corrupted his way upon the earth. **13** And God said unto Noah, [o]An end of all flesh is come before me: for the earth is filled with [p]cruelty [q]through them: and behold, I will destroy them with the earth. **14** Make thee an Ark of [r]pine trees: thou shalt make [s]cabins in the Ark, and shalt pitch it within and without with pitch. **15** And [t]thus shalt thou make it: the length of the Ark shall be three hundred cubits, the breadth of it fifty cubits, and the height of it thirty cubits. **16** A window shalt thou make in the Ark, and in a cubit shalt thou finish it above, and the door of the Ark shalt thou set in the side thereof: thou shalt make it with the [u]low, second, and third

---

i. Gen. 4:10 God revengeth the wrongs of his Saints, though none complain: for the iniquity itself crieth for vengeance.
j. Gen. 4:11 The earth shall be a witness against thee, which mercifully received that blood which thou most cruelly sheddest.
k. Gen. 4:12 Thou shalt never have rest: for thine heart shall be in continual fear and care.
l. Gen. 4:13 He burdeneth God as a cruel judge because he did punish him so sharply.
m. Gen. 4:13 Or, my sin is greater than can be pardoned.
n. Gen. 4:14 Hebrew, from off the face of.
o. Gen. 4:15 Not for the love he bare to Cain, but to suppress murder.
p. Gen. 4:15 Which was some visible sign of God's judgment, that others should fear thereby.
q. Gen. 4:17 Thinking thereby to be sure, and to have less occasion to fear God's judgments against him.
r. Gen. 4:19 The lawful institution of marriage, which is, that two should be one flesh, was first corrupted in the house of Cain by Lamech.
s. Gen. 4:20 Or, first inventor.
t. Gen. 4:21 Or, flutes, and pipes.
u. Gen. 4:23 His wives seeing that all men hated him for his cruelty, were afraid, therefore he braggeth that there is none so lusty that were able to resist, although he were already wounded.
v. Gen. 4:24 He mocked at God's sufferance in Cain, jesting as though God would suffer none to punish him and yet give him license to murder others.
w. Gen. 4:26 In these days God began to move the hearts of the godly to restore religion, which a long time by the wicked had been suppressed.

GEN. 4
1. Heb. 11:4
2. Matt. 23:35 -1John 3:11 - Jude 11

GEN. 5
a. Gen. 5:1 Or, rehearsal of the stock.
b. Gen. 5:1 Read Gen. 1:26.
c. Gen. 5:2 By giving them both one name, he noteth the inseparable conjunction of man and wife.
d. Gen. 5:3 As well concerning his creation, as his corruption.
e. Gen. 5:6 He proveth Adam's generation by them which came of Seth, to show which is the true Church, and also what care God had over the same from the beginning, in that he continued ever his graces toward it by a continual succession.
f. Gen. 5:8 The chief cause of long life in the first age, was the multiplication of mankind, that according to God's commandment at the beginning the world might be increased with people, which might universally praise him.
g. Gen. 5:22 That is, he led an upright and godly life.
h. Gen. 5:24 To show that there was a better life prepared, and to be a testimony of the immortality of souls and bodies. As to inquire where he became, is mere curiosity.
i. Gen. 5:29 Lamech had respect to the promise, Gen. 3:15, and desired to see the deliverer which should be sent, and yet saw but a figure thereof, he also spake this by the spirit of prophecy because Noah delivered the Church and preserved it by his obedience.

GEN. 5
1. 1Chron. 1:1
2. Heb. 11:5

GEN. 6
a. Gen. 6:2 The children of the godly, which began to degenerate.
b. Gen. 6:2 Those that came of wicked parents, as of Cain.
c. Gen. 6:2 Having more respect to their beauty and to worldly considerations, than to their manners and godliness.
d. Gen. 6:2 Or, had chosen.
e. Gen. 6:3 Because man could not be won by God's lenity and long sufferance whereby he strove to overcome him, he would no longer stay his vengeance.
f. Gen. 6:3 Which term God gave man to repent before he would destroy the earth, 1 Pet. 3:20.
g. Gen. 6:4 Or, tyrants.
h. Gen. 6:4 Which usurped authority over others, and did degenerate from that simplicity, wherein their fathers lived.
i. Gen. 6:5 Hebrew, every day.
j. Gen. 6:6 God doth never repent, but he speaketh after our capacity, because he did destroy him, and in that as it were did disavow him to be his creature.
k. Gen. 6:7 God declareth how much he detesteth sin, seeing the punishment thereof extendeth to the brute beasts.
l. Gen. 6:8 God was merciful unto him.
m. Gen. 6:9 Or, history.
n. Gen. 6:11 Meaning, that all were given to the contempt of God, and oppression of their neighbors.
o. Gen. 6:13 Or, I will destroy mankind.
p. Gen. 6:13 Or, oppression and wickedness.
q. Gen. 6:13 Hebrew, from the face of them.
r. Gen. 6:14 Hebrew, Gopher.
s. Gen. 6:14 Hebrew, nests.
t. Gen. 6:15 Or, of this measure.
u. Gen. 6:16 That is, of three heights, as appeareth in the figure.

room. **17** And I, behold, I will bring a flood of waters upon the earth to destroy all flesh, wherein is the breath of life under heaven: all that is in the earth shall perish. **18** But with thee will I [v]establish my covenant, and thou shalt go into the Ark, thou, and thy sons, and thy wife, and thy sons' wives with thee. **19** And of every living thing of all flesh two of every sort shalt thou cause to come into the Ark, to keep them alive with thee: they shall be male and female. **20** Of the fowls, after their kind, and of the cattle after their kind, of every creeping thing of the earth after his kind, two of every sort shall come unto thee, that thou mayest keep them alive. **21** And take thou with thee of all meat that is eaten: and thou shalt gather it to thee, that it may be meat for thee and for them. **22** [2]Noah therefore did according unto all that God commanded him: even [w]so did he.

7

1 Noah and his enter into the Ark. 20 The flood destroyeth all the rest upon the earth.

1 And the Lord said unto Noah, Enter thou and all thine house into the Ark: for thee have I seen [1,a]righteous before me in this [b]age. **2** Of every [c]clean beast thou shalt take to thee by sevens, the male and his female: but of unclean beasts by couples, the male and his female. **3** Of the fowls also of the heaven by sevens, male and female, to keep seed alive upon the whole earth. **4** For seven days hence I will cause it rain upon the earth forty days, and forty nights, and all the substance that I have made, will I destroy from off the earth. **5** [2]Noah therefore did according to all that the Lord commanded him. **6** And Noah was six hundred years old, when the flood of waters was upon the earth. **7** So Noah entered and his sons, and his wife, and his sons' wives with him into the Ark, because of the waters of the flood. **8** Of the clean beasts, and of the unclean beasts, and of the fowls, and of all that creepeth upon the earth, **9** There [d]came two and two unto Noah into the Ark, male and female, as God had commanded Noah. **10** And so after seven days, the waters of the flood were upon the earth. **11** In the six hundredth year of Noah's life, in the [e]second month, the seventeenth day of the month, in the same day were all the [f]fountains of the great deep broken up, and the windows of heaven were opened, **12** And the rain was upon the earth forty days and forty nights. **13** In the selfsame day entered Noah with Shem, and Ham and Japheth, the sons of Noah, and Noah's wife, and the three wives of his sons with them into the Ark. **14** They and every beast after his kind, and all cattle after their kind, and everything that creepeth and moveth upon the earth after his kind, and every fowl after his kind, even every bird of every feather. **15** For they came to Noah into the Ark, two and two, [g]of all flesh wherein is the breath of life. **16** And they entering in, came male and female of all flesh, as God had commanded him: and the Lord [h,i]shut him in. **17** Then the flood was forty days upon the earth, and the waters were increased, and bare up the Ark, which was lifted up above the earth. **18** The waters also waxed strong, and were increased exceedingly upon the earth, and the Ark went upon the waters. **19** The waters [j]prevailed so exceedingly upon the earth, that all the high mountains, that are under the whole heaven, were covered. **20** Fifteen cubits upward did the waters prevail, when the mountains were covered. **21** Then all flesh perished that moved upon the earth, both fowl and cattle and beast, and everything that creepeth and moveth upon the earth, and every man. **22** Everything in whose nostrils the spirit of life did breathe, whatsoever they were in the dry land, they died. **23** So [k]he destroyed everything that was upon the earth, from man to beast, to the creeping thing, and to the fowl of the heaven: they were even destroyed from the earth And Noah only [l]remained, and they that were with him in the Ark. **24** And the waters prevailed upon the earth an hundred and fifty days.

8

13 The flood ceaseth. 16 Noah is commanded to come forth of the Ark with his. 20 He sacrificeth to the Lord. 22 God promiseth that all things should continue in their first order.

1 Now God [a]remembered Noah and [b]every beast, and all the cattle that were with him in the Ark: therefore God made a wind to pass upon the earth, and the waters ceased. **2** The fountains also of the deep and the windows of heaven were stopped, and the rain from heaven was restrained. **3** And the waters returned from above the earth, going and returning: and after the end of the hundred and fiftieth day the waters abated. **4** And in the [c]seventh month, in the seventeenth day of the month, the Ark [d]rested upon the mountains of [e]Ararat. **5** And the waters were going and decreasing until the [f]tenth month: in the tenth month, and in the first day of the month, were the tops of the mountains seen. **6** So [g]after forty days, Noah opened the window of the Ark which he had made, **7** And sent forth a raven, which went out, going forth and returning, until the waters were dried up upon the earth. **8** Again he sent a dove from him, that he might see if the waters were diminished from off the earth. **9** But the dove found no rest for the sole of her foot: therefore she returned unto him into the Ark (for the waters were upon the whole earth) and he [h]put forth his hand, and received her, and took her to him into the Ark. **10** And he abode yet another seven days, and again he sent forth the dove out of the Ark. **11** And the dove came to him in the evening, and lo in her [i]mouth was an [j]olive leaf that she had plucked: whereby Noah knew that the waters were abated from off the earth. **12** Notwithstanding, he waited yet another seven days, and sent forth the dove, which returned not again unto him anymore. **13** And in the six hundred and one year, in the first day of the [k]first month, the waters were dried up from off the earth: and Noah removed the covering of the Ark, and looked, and behold, the upper part of the ground was dry. **14** And in the second month, in the seven and twentieth day of the month, was the earth dry. **15** Then God spake to Noah, saying, **16** [l]Go forth of the Ark, thou, and thy wife, and thy sons, and thy sons' wives with thee. **17** Bring forth with thee every beast that is with thee, of all flesh, both fowl and cattle, and everything that creepeth and moveth upon the earth, that they may breed abundantly in the earth, [1]and bring forth fruit and increase upon the earth. **18** So Noah came forth, and his sons, and his wife, and his sons' wives with him. **19** Every beast, every creeping thing, and every fowl, all that moveth upon the earth, after their kinds, went out of the Ark. **20** Then Noah [m]built an altar to the Lord, and took of every clean beast, and of every clean fowl, and offered burnt offerings upon the altar. **21** And the Lord smelled a [n,o]savor of rest, and the Lord said in his heart, I will henceforth curse the ground no more for man's cause: for the [2]imagination of man's heart is evil, even from his youth: neither will I smite anymore all things living, as I have done. **22** Hereafter [p]seed time and harvest, and cold and heat, and Summer and Winter, and day and night shall not cease, so long as the earth remaineth.

9

1 The confirmation of marriage. 2 Man's authoritiy over all creatures. 3 Permission of meats. 6 The power of the sword. 14 The rainbow is the sign of God's promise. 21 Noah is drunk, and mocked of his son, whom he curseth. 29 The age and death of Noah.

1 And God [a]blessed Noah and his sons, and said to them, [1]Bring forth fruit, and multiply, and replenish the earth. **2** Also the [b]fear of you, and the dread of you shall be upon every beast of the earth, and upon every fowl of the heaven, upon all that moveth on the earth, and upon all the fishes of the sea: into your hand are they delivered. **3** Everything [c]that moveth and liveth, shall be meat for you: as the [2]green herb, have I given you all things. **4** [3,d]But flesh with the life

---

v. Gen. 6:18 To the intent that in this great enterprise and mockings of the whole world, thou mayest be confirmed, that thy faith fail not.
w. Gen. 6:22 That is, he obeyed God's commandment in all points without adding or diminishing.

GEN. 6
1. Gen. 8:21 - Matt. 15:19 **2.** Heb. 11:7

GEN. 7
a. Gen. 7:1 In respect of the rest of the world, and because he had a desire to serve God and live uprightly.
b. Gen. 7:1 Or, generation.
c. Gen. 7:2 Which might be offered in sacrifice, whereof six were for breed, and the seventh for sacrifice.
d. Gen. 7:9 God compelled them to present themselves to Noah, as they did before to Adam, when he gave them names, Gen. 2:19.
e. Gen. 7:11 Which was about the beginning of May, when all things did most flourish.
f. Gen. 7:11 Both the waters in the earth did overflow, and also the clouds poured down.
g. Gen. 7:15 Every living thing that God would have to be preserved on earth, came into the Ark to Noah.
h. Gen. 7:16 So that God's secret power defended him against the rage of the mighty waters.
i. Gen. 7:16 Or, shut it upon him.
j. Gen. 7:19 Hebrew, waxed very mighty.
k. Gen. 7:23 That is, God.
l. Gen. 7:23 Learn what it is to obey God only, and to forsake the multitude, 1 Pet. 3:20.

GEN. 7
1. 1Pet. 2:5 **2.** Matt. 24:37 -Luke 27:26 - 1Pet. 3:20

GEN. 8
a. Gen. 8:1 Not that God forgetteth his at any time, but when he sendeth succor then he showeth that he remembereth them.
b. Gen. 8:1 If God remember every brute beast, what ought to be the assurance of his children?
c. Gen. 8:4 Which contained part of September, and part of October.
d. Gen. 8:4 Or, stayed.
e. Gen. 8:4 Or, Armenia.
f. Gen. 8:5 Which was the month of December.
g. Gen. 8:6 Hebrew, at the end of forty days.
h. Gen. 8:9 It is like that the raven did fly to and fro, resting on the Ark, but came not into it, as the dove that was taken in.
i. Gen. 8:11 Or, bill.
j. Gen. 8:11 Which was a sign that the waters were much diminished: for the olives grow not on the high mountains.
k. Gen. 8:13 Called in Hebrew Abib, containing part of March and part of April.
l. Gen. 8:16 Noah declareth his obedience, in that he would not depart out of the Ark without God's express commandment, as he did not enter in without the same: the Ark being a figure of the Church, wherein nothing must be done without the word of God.
m. Gen. 8:20 For sacrifices which were as an exercise of their faith, whereby they used to give thanks to God for his benefits.
n. Gen. 8:21 Or, sweet savor.
o. Gen. 8:21 That is, thereby he showeth himself appeased and his anger to rest.
p. Gen. 8:22 The order of nature destroyed by the flood, is restored by God's promise.

GEN. 8
1. Gen. 1:22 - Gen. 9:1 **2.** Gen. 6:5 - Matt. 15:12

GEN. 9
a. Gen. 9:1 God increased them with fruit, and declared unto them his counsel as touching the replenishing of the earth.
b. Gen. 9:2 By the virtue of this commandment beasts rage not so much against man as they would, yea, and many serve to his use thereby.
c. Gen. 9:3 By this permission man may with a good conscience use the creatures of God for his necessity.
d. Gen. 9:4 That is, living creatures, and the flesh of beasts that are strangled: and hereby all cruelty is forbidden.

thereof, I mean, with the blood thereof, shall ye not eat. **5** [e]For surely I will re-
quire your blood, wherein your lives are: at the hands of every beast will I require
it: and at the hand of man, even at the hand of a man's [f]brother will I require the
life of man. **6** Who so [4]sheddeth man's blood, [g]by man shall his blood be shed:
[5]for in the [h]image of God hath he made man. **7** But bring ye forth fruit and
multiply: grow plentifully in the earth, and increase therein. **8** God spake also to
Noah and to his sons with him, saying, **9** Behold, I, even I establish my [i]cove-
nant with you, and with your [j]seed after you, **10** And with every living creature
that is with you, with the fowl, with the cattle, and with every beast of the earth
with you, from all that go out of the Ark, unto every beast of the earth. **11** [6]And
my covenant will I establish with you, that from henceforth all flesh shall not be ro-
oted out by the waters of the flood, neither shall there be a flood to destroy the ear-
th anymore. **12** Then God said, This is the token of the covenant which I make
between me and you, and between every living thing that is with you unto perpe-
tual generations. **13** I have set my [k]bow in the cloud, and it shall be for a sign
of the covenant between me and the earth. **14** And when I shall cover the earth
with a cloud, and the bow shall be seen in the cloud, **15** Then will I remember
my [l]covenant which is between me and you, and between every living thing in all
flesh, and there shall be no more waters of a flood to destroy all flesh. **16** The-
refore the bow shall be in the cloud, that I may see it, and remember the everla-
sting covenant between God and every living thing, in all flesh that is upon the
earth. **17** God said yet to Noah, [m]This is the sign of the covenant, which I have
established between me and all flesh that is upon the earth. **18** Now the sons of
Noah going forth of the Ark, were Shem and Ham and Japheth And Ham is the fa-
ther of Canaan. **19** These are the three sons of Noah, and of them was the whole
earth [n]overspread. **20** [o]Noah also began to be an husbandman, and planted a
vineyard. **21** And he drunk of the wine, and was [p]drunken, and was uncovered
in the midst of his tent. **22** And when Ham the father of [q]Canaan saw the nake-
dness of his father, [r]he told his two brethren without. **23** Then took Shem and
Japheth a garment, and put it upon both their shoulders, and went backward and
covered the nakedness of their father with their faces backward: so they saw not
their father's nakedness. **24** Then Noah awoke from his wine, and knew what his
younger son had done unto him, **25** And said, [s]Cursed be Canaan: a [t]servant of
servants shall he be unto his brethren. **26** He said moreover, Blessed be the Lord
God of Shem, and let Canaan be his [u]servant. **27** God [v,w]persuade Japheth, that
he may dwell in the tents of Shem, and let Canaan be his servant. **28** And Noah
lived after the flood three hundred and fifty years. **29** So all the days of Noah
were nine hundred and fifty years: and he died.

10

1 The increase of mankind by Noah and his sons. 10 The beginning of cities, countries, and nations.

1 Now these are the [a]generations of the sons of Noah, Shem, Ham and Ja-
pheth: unto whom sons were born after the flood. **2** The sons of Japheth were
Gomer, and Magog, and [b]Madai, and Javan, and Tubal, and Meshech, and Ti-
ras. **3** And the sons of Gomer, Ashkenaz, and Riphath, and Togarmah. **4** Also
the sons of Javan, Elishah and Tarshish, Kittim, and Dodanim. **5** Of these were
the [c]isles of the Gentiles divided in their lands, every man after his tongue, and
after their families in their nations. **6** Moreover, the sons of Ham were [d]Cush,
and Mizraim, and Put, and Canaan. **7** And the sons of Cush, Seba and Havilah,
and Sabtah, and Raamah, and Sabtechah: also the sons of Raamah were Sheba
and Dedan. **8** And Cush begat Nimrod, who began to be [e]mighty in the ear-
th. **9** He was a mighty hunter before the Lord Wherefore it is said, [f]As Nimrod the
mighty hunter before the Lord. **10** And the beginning of his kingdom was Babel
and Erech, and Accad, and Calneh, in the land of [g]Shinar. **11** Out of that land
came Assyria, and built Nineveh, and the [h]city Rehoboth, and Calah: **12** Resen
also between Nineveh and Calah: this is a great city. **13** And Mizraim begat
[i]Ludim, and Anamim, and Lehabim, and Naphtuhim. **14** Pathrusim also, and
Casluhim (out of whom came the Philistines) and [j]Caphtorims. **15** Also Cana-
an begat Sidon his firstborn, and Heth, **16** And Jebusi, and Emori, and Girga-
shi, **17** And Hivi, and Arki, and Sini, **18** And Arvadi, and Zemari, and Hama-
thi: and afterward were the families of the Canaanites spread abroad. **19** Then
the border of the Canaanites was from Sidon, as thou comest to Gerar until Gaza,
and as thou goest unto Sodom and Gomorrah, and Admah, and Zeboiim, even
unto Lasha. **20** These are the sons of Ham according to their families, accor-
ding to their tongues in their countries, and in their nations. **21** Unto [k]Shem
also the father of all the sons of [l]Eber, and elder brother of Japheth were children
born. **22** [1]The sons of Shem were Elam and Asshur, and Arphaxad, and Lud, and
Aram. **23** And the sons of Aram, Uz and Hul, and Gether, and Mash. **24** Also
Arphaxad begat Salah, and Salah begat Eber. **25** Unto Eber also were born two
sons: the name of the one was Peleg: for in his days was the earth [m]divided: and his
brother's name was Joktan. **26** Then Joktan begat Almodad, and Sheleph, and
Hazarmaveth, and Jerah, **27** And Hadoram, and Uzal, and Diklah, **28** And
Obal, and Abimael, and Sheba, **29** And Ophir, and Havilah, and Jobab: all these
were the sons of Joktan. **30** And their dwelling was from Mesha, as thou goest up
to Sephar, a mount of the East. **31** These are the sons of Shem, according to their
families, according to their tongues in their countries and nations. **32** These are
the families of the sons of Noah, after their generations among their people: and
[n]out of these were the nations divided in the earth after the flood.

11

6 The building of Babel was the cause of the confusion of tongues. 10 The age and generation of Shem unto Abram. 31 Abram's departure from Ur with his father Terah, Sarai and Lot. 32 The age and death of Terah.

1 Then the whole earth was of one language and one speech. **2** And [a]as
[b]they went from the [c]East, they found a plain in the land of [d]Shinar, and there they
abode. **3** And they said one to another, Come, let us make brick and burn it in
the fire, so they had brick for stone, and slime had they instead of mortar. **4** Also
they said, Go to, let us [e]build us a city and a tower, whose top may reach unto
the heaven, that we may get us a name, lest we be scattered upon the whole ear-
th. **5** But the Lord [f]came down, to see the city and tower which the sons of men
built. **6** And the Lord said, [g]Behold, the people is one, and they all have one lan-
guage, and this they begin to do, neither can they now be stopped from whatsoe-
ver they have imagined to do. **7** Come on, [h]let us go down, and [i]there confound
their language, that everyone perceive not another's speech. **8** So the Lord scatte-
red them from thence upon all the earth, and they left off to build the city. **9** The-
refore the name of it was called [j]Babel, because the Lord did there confound the
language of all the earth: from thence then did the Lord scatter them upon all the
earth. **10** [1]These are the generations [k]of Shem: Shem was an hundred years old,
and begat Arphaxad two years after the flood. **11** And Shem lived after he begat
Arphaxad five hundred years, and begat sons and daughters. **12** Also Arphaxad
lived five and thirty years, and begat Salah. **13** And Arphaxad lived after he begat

---

e. Gen. 9:5 That is, I will take vengeance for your blood.
f. Gen. 9:5 Or, neighbor.
g. Gen. 9:6 Not only by the magistrate, but oft times God raiseth up one murderer to kill another.
h. Gen. 9:6 Therefore to kill man is to deface God's image, and so injury is not only done to man, but also to God.
i. Gen. 9:9 To assure you that the world shall be no more destroyed by a flood.
j. Gen. 9:9 The children which are not yet born, are comprehended in God's covenant made with their fathers.
k. Gen. 9:13 Hereby we see that signs or sacraments ought not to be separate from the word.
l. Gen. 9:15 When men shall see my bow in the heaven, they shall know that I have not forgotten my covenant with them.
m. Gen. 9:17 God doth repeat this the oftener, to confirm Noah's faith so much the more.
n. Gen. 9:19 This declareth what was the virtue of God's blessing, when he said, increase and bring forth, Gen. 1:28.
o. Gen. 9:20 Or, Noah began again.
p. Gen. 9:21 This is set before our eyes to show what an horrible thing drunkenness is.
q. Gen. 9:22 Of whom came the Canaanites that wicked nation, who were also cursed of God.
r. Gen. 9:22 In derision and contempt of his father.
s. Gen. 9:25 He pronounceth as a Prophet the curse of God against all them that honor not their parents: for Ham and his posterity were accursed.
t. Gen. 9:25 That is, a most vile slave.
u. Gen. 9:26 Or, their.
v. Gen. 9:27 Or, enlarge, or cause to return.
w. Gen. 9:27 He declareth that the Gentiles, which came of Japheth, and were separated from the Church, should be joined to the same by the persuasion of God's Spirit, and preaching of the Gospel.

GEN. 9

1.	Gen. 2:28 - Gen. 8:17	**4.**	Matt.26:52 - Rev. 13:10
2.	Gen. 1:29	**5.**	Gen.1:27
3.	Lev. 17:14	**6.**	Isa.54:9

GEN. 10

a. Gen. 10:1 These generations are here recited, partly to declare the marvelous increase in so small a time, and also to set forth their great forgetfulness of God's grace towards their fathers.
b. Gen. 10:2 Of Madai and Javan came the Medes, and Greeks.
c. Gen. 10:5 The Jews so call all countries which are separated from them by sea, as Greece, Italy, etc, which were given to the children of Japheth, of whom came the Gentiles.
d. Gen. 10:6 Of Cush and Mizraim came the Ethiopians and Egyptians.
e. Gen. 10:8 Meaning, a cruel oppressor and tyrant.
f. Gen. 10:9 His tyranny came into a proverb as hated both of God and man: for he passed not to commit cruelty even in God's presence.
g. Gen. 10:10 For there was another city in Egypt, called also Babel.
h. Gen. 10:11 Or, the streets of the city.
i. Gen. 10:13 Of Lud came the Lydians.
j. Gen. 10:14 Or, the Cappadocians.
k. Gen. 10:21 In his stock the Church was preserved: therefore Moses leaveth off speaking of Japheth and Ham, and entreateth of Shem more at large.
l. Gen. 10:21 Of whom came the Hebrews or Jews.
m. Gen. 10:25 This division came by the diversity of languages, as appeareth, Gen. 11:9.
n. Gen. 10:32 Or, of these came divers nations.

GEN. 10

1. 1 Chron. 1:17

GEN. 11

a. Gen. 11:2 In the year one hundred and thirty after the flood.
b. Gen. 11:2 To wit, Nimrod and his company.
c. Gen. 11:2 That is, from Armenia where the Ark stayed.
d. Gen. 11:2 Which was afterward called Chaldea.
e. Gen. 11:4 They were moved with pride and ambition, thinking to prefer their own glory to God's honor.
f. Gen. 11:5 Meaning, that he declared by effect, that he knew their wicked enterprise: for God's power is everywhere, and doth neither ascend nor descend.
g. Gen. 11:6 God speaketh this in derision, because of their foolish persuasion and enterprise.
h. Gen. 11:7 He speaketh as though he took counsel with his own wisdom and power: to wit, with the Son and holy Ghost: signifying the greatness and certainty of the punishment.
i. Gen. 11:7 By this great plague of the confusion of tongues appeareth God's horrible judgment against man's pride and vain glory.
j. Gen. 11:9 Or, confusion.
k. Gen. 11:10 He returneth to the genealogy of Shem, to come to the history of Abram, wherein the Church of God is described, which is Moses' principle purpose.
l. Gen. 11:27 He maketh mention first of Abram, not because he was the firstborn, but for the history which properly appertaineth unto him. Also Abram at the confusion of

Salah, four hundred and three years, and begat sons and daughters. **14** And Sa-
lah lived thirty years, and begat Eber. **15** So Salah lived after he begat Eber four
hundred and three years, and begat sons and daughters. **16** Likewise Eber lived
four and thirty years, and begat Peleg. **17** So Eber lived after he begat Peleg four
hundred and thirty years, and begat sons and daughters. **18** And Peleg lived
thirty years, and begat Reu. **19** [2]And Peleg lived after he begat Reu two hundred
and nine years, and begat sons and daughters. **20** Also Reu lived two and thirty
years, and begat Serug. **21** So Reu lived after he begat Serug two hundred and
seven years, and begat sons and daughters. **22** Moreover Serug lived thirty years,
and begat Nahor. **23** And Serug lived after he begat Nahor two hundred years,
and begat sons and daughters. **24** And Nahor lived nine and twenty years, and
begat Terah. **25** So Nahor lived after he begat Terah, an hundred and nineteen
years, and begat sons and daughters. **26** [3]So Terah lived seventy years, and begat
Abram, Nahor, and Haran. **27** Now these are the generations of Terah: Terah
begat [l]Abram, Nahor, and Haran: and Haran begat Lot. **28** Then Haran died
before Terah his father in the land of his nativity, in Ur of [m]the Chaldeans. **29** So
Abram and Nahor took them wives The name of Abram's wife was Sarai, and
the name of Nahor's wife Milcah, the daughter of Haran, the father of Milcah,
and the father of [n]Iscah. **30** But Sarai was barren, and had no child. **31** Then
[o]Terah took Abram his son, and Lot the son of Haran his son's son, and Sarai his
daughter-in-law, his son Abram's wife: and they departed together from Ur of the
Chaldeans, to [4]go into the land of Canaan, and they came to [p]Haran, and dwelt
there. **32** So the days of Terah were two hundred and five years, and Terah died
in Haran.

12

1 Abram by God's commandment goeth to Canaan. 3 Christ is promised. 7 Abram buildeth Altars for exercise and declaration of his faith among the infidels. 10 Because of the dearth he goeth into Egypt. 15 Pharaoh taketh his wife, and is punished.

1 For the Lord had said unto Abram, [1,a]Get thee out of thy country, and
from thy kindred, and from thy father's house unto [b]the land that I will show
thee. **2** And I will make of thee a great nation, and will bless thee, and make
thy name great, and thou shalt be a [c]blessing. **3** I will also bless them that bless
thee, and curse them that curse thee, and in thee shall all families of the earth be
blessed. **4** So Abram departed, even as the Lord spake unto him, and Lot went
with him, (and Abram was seventy and five years old, when he departed out of
Haran) **5** Then Abram took Sarai his wife, and Lot his brother's son, and all
their substance that they possessed, and the [d]souls that they had gotten in Ha-
ran, and they departed to go to the land of Canaan, and to the land of Canaan
they came. **6** So Abram [e]passed through the land unto the place of Shechem,
and unto the [f]plain of Moreh (and the [g]Canaanite was then in the land) **7** And
the Lord appeared unto Abram, and said, Unto thy seed will I give this land And
there built he [h]an altar unto the Lord, which appeared unto him. **8** Afterward
removing [i]thence unto a mountain Eastward from Bethel, he pitched his tent ha-
ving Bethel on the West side, and Ai on the East, and there he built an [j]altar unto
the Lord, and called on the Name of the Lord. **9** [k]Again Abram went forth
going and journeying toward the South. **10** Then there came a [l]famine in the
land: therefore Abram went down into Egypt to sojourn there: for there was a
great famine in the land. **11** And when he drew near to enter into Egypt, he
said to Sarai his wife, Behold now, I know that thou art a fair woman to look
upon: **12** Therefore it will come to pass that when the Egyptians see thee, they
will say, She is his wife: so will they kill me, but they will keep thee alive. **13** Say,
I pray thee, that thou art my [m]sister, that I may fare well for thy sake, and that my
[n]life may be preserved by thee. **14** Now when Abram was come into Egypt, the
Egyptians beheld the woman: for she was very fair. **15** And the Princes of Pha-
raoh saw her, and commended her unto Pharaoh: so the woman was [o]taken into
Pharaoh's house: **16** Who entreated Abram well for her sake, and he had sheep,
and beeves, and he asses, and menservants, and maidservants, and she asses, and
camels. **17** But the Lord [p]plagued Pharaoh and his house with great plagues,
because of Sarai Abram's wife. **18** Then Pharaoh called Abram, and said, Why
hast thou done this unto me? Wherefore diddest thou not tell me, that she was thy
wife? **19** Why saidest thou, She is my sister, that I should take her to be my wife?
Now therefore behold thy wife, take her and go thy way. **20** And Pharaoh gave
men [q]commandment concerning him: and they conveyed him forth and his wife,
and all that he had.

13

1 Abram departeth out of Egypt. 4 He calleth upon the Name of the Lord. 11 Lot departeth from him. 13 The wickedness of the Sodomites. 14 The promise made to Abram is renewed. 18 Abram buildeth an altar to the Lord.

1 Then [a]Abram went up from Egypt, he and his wife, and all that he had, and
Lot with him toward the South. **2** And Abram was very rich in cattle, in silver
and in gold. **3** And he went on his journey from the South toward [b]Bethel, to the
place where his tent had been at the beginning, between Bethel and Ai, **4** Unto
the place of the [1]altar, which he had made there at the first: and there Abram
called on the Name of the Lord. **5** And Lot also, who went with Abram, had
sheep, and cattle and tents, **6** So that the land could not [c]bear them, that they
might dwell together: for their [2]substance was great, so that they could not dwell
together. **7** Also there was debate between the herdsmen of Abram's cattle, and
the herdsmen of Lot's cattle, (and the [d]Canaanites and the Perizzites dwelleth at
that time in the land.) **8** Then said Abram unto Lot, Let there be no [e]strife, I
pray thee, between thee and me, neither between mine herdsmen and thine herd-
smen: for we be brethren. **9** Is not the whole land before thee? depart I pray
thee from me: if thou wilt [f]take the left hand, then I will go to the right: or if
thou go to the right hand, then I will take the left. **10** So when Lot lifted up
his eyes, he saw that all the plain of Jordan was watered everywhere (for before
the Lord destroyed Sodom and Gomorrah, it was as the [g]garden of the Lord like
the land of Egypt, as thou goest unto Zoar.) **11** Then Lot chose unto him all
the plain of Jordan, and took his journey from the East: and they departed the
[h]one from the other. **12** Abram dwelled in the land of Canaan, and Lot abode
in the cities of the plain, and pitched his tent even unto Sodom. **13** Now the
men of Sodom were wicked and exceeding [i]sinners against the Lord. **14** Then
the Lord said unto [j]Abram, (after that Lot was departed from him) Lift up thine
eyes now, and look from the place where thou art, Northward, and Southward,
and Eastward, and Westward: **15** For all [3]the land which thou seest, will I give
unto thee, and to thy seed [k]forever, **16** And I will make thy seed as the dust of
the earth: so that if a man can number the dust of the earth, then shall thy seed be
numbered. **17** Arise, walk through the land, in the length thereof, and breadth
thereof: for I will give it unto thee. **18** Then Abram removed his tent, and came
and dwelled in the plain of Mamre, which is in Hebron, and built there an altar
unto the Lord.

14

12 In the overthrow of Sodom Lot is taken prisoner. 16 Abram delivereth him. 18 Melchizedek cometh to meet him. 23 Abram would not be enriched by the king of Sodom.

1 And in the days of Amraphel king of [a]Shinar, Arioch king of Ellasar, Che-
dorlaomer king of Elam, and Tidal king of the [b]nations: **2** These men made war

---

tongues, was 48 years old, for in the destruction of Sodom he was 99. And it was destroyed 52 years after the confusion of tongues.

- **m.** Gen. 11:28 Hebrew, Casdim.
- **n.** Gen. 11:29 Some think that this Iscah was Sarai.
- **o.** Gen. 11:31 Albeit the oracle of God came to Abram, yet the honor is given to Terah, because he was the father.
- **p.** Gen. 11:31 Which was a city of Mesopotamia.

GEN. 11

1. 1 Chron. 1:17
2. 1Chron. 1:26 - Josh. 24:2
3. Josh. 24:2
4. Josh. 24:2 - Neh. 9:7 - Judg. 5:7 - Acts 7:4

GEN. 12

- **a.** Gen. 12:1 From the flood to this time were four hundred twenty and three years.
- **b.** Gen. 12:1 In appointed him no certain place, he proveth so much more his faith and obedience.
- **c.** Gen. 12:2 The world shall recover by thy seed, which is Christ, the blessing which they lost in Adam.
- **d.** Gen. 12:5 Meaning, as well servants as cattle.
- **e.** Gen. 12:6 He wandered to and fro in the land before he could find a settling place: thus God exerciseth the faith of his children.
- **f.** Gen. 12:6 Or, oak grove.
- **g.** Gen. 12:6 Which was a cruel and rebellious nation, by whom God kept his in continual exercise.
- **h.** Gen. 12:7 It was not enough for him to worship God in his heart, but it was expedient to declare by outward profession his faith before men, whereof this altar was a sign.
- **i.** Gen. 12:8 Because of the troubles that he had among that wicked people.
- **j.** Gen. 12:8 And so served the true God, and renounced all idolatry.
- **k.** Gen. 12:9 Thus the children of God may look for no rest in this world, but must wait for the heavenly rest and quietness.
- **l.** Gen. 12:10 This was a new trial of Abram's faith: whereby we see that the end of one affliction is the beginning of another.
- **m.** Gen. 12:13 By this we may learn not to use unlawful means, nor to put others in danger to save ourselves, read verse 20, albeit it may appear that Abram feared not so much death, as that if he should die without issue, God's promise should not have taken place: wherein appeared a weak faith.
- **n.** Gen. 12:13 Hebrew, that my soul may live.
- **o.** Gen. 12:15 To be his wife.
- **p.** Gen. 12:17 The Lord took the defense of this poor stranger against a mighty king: and as he is ever careful over his, so did he preserve Sarai.
- **q.** Gen. 12:20 To the intent that none should hurt him either in his person or goods.

GEN. 12

1. Acts 7:3

GEN. 13

- **a.** Gen. 13:1 His great riches gotten in Egypt, hindreth him not to follow his vocation.
- **b.** Gen. 13:3 He calleth the place by that name which was after given unto it, Gen. 28:19.
- **c.** Gen. 13:6 This incommodity came by their riches, which brake friendship and as it were the bound of nature.
- **d.** Gen. 13:7 Who seeing their contention, might blaspheme God and destroy them.
- **e.** Gen. 13:8 He cutteth off the occasion of contention: therefore the evil ceaseth.
- **f.** Gen. 13:9 Abram resigneth his own right to buy peace.
- **g.** Gen. 13:10 Which was in Eden, Gen. 2:10.
- **h.** Gen. 13:11 This was done by God's providence, that only Abram and his seed might dwell in the land of Canaan.
- **i.** Gen. 13:13 Lot thinking to get paradise, found hell.
- **j.** Gen. 13:14 The Lord comforted him, lest he should have taken thought for the departure of his nephew.
- **k.** Gen. 13:15 Meaning, a long time, and till the coming of Christ as Exod. 12:14 and 21:6; Deut. 15:17, and spiritually this is referred to the true children of Abram, born according to the promise, and not according to the flesh, which are heirs of the true land of Canaan.

GEN. 13

1. Gen. 12:7
2. Gen. 36:7
3. Gen. 12:7 - Gen. 15:7,11 - Gen. 26.4 - Deut. 34:4

with Bera king of Sodom, and with Birsha king of Gomorrah, Shinab king of Ad-
mah, and Shemeber king of Zeboiim, and the king of Bela, which is Zoar. **3** All
these [c]joined together in the valley of [d]Siddim, which is the [e]salt Sea. **4** Twelve
years were they subject to Chedorlaomer, but in the thirteenth year they rebel-
led. **5** And in the fourteenth year came Chedorlaomer, and the kings that were
with him, and smote the [f]Rephaims in Ashteroth Karnaim, and the Zuzims in
Ham, and the Emims in [g]Shaveh Kiriathaim, **6** And the Horites in their mount
Seir, unto the plain of El Paran, which is by the wilderness. **7** And they retur-
ned and came to En Mishpat, which is Kadesh, and [h]smote all the country of the
Amalekites, and also the Amorites that dwelled in Hazezon Tamar. **8** Then went
out the king of Sodom, and the king of Gomorrah, and the king of Admah, and
the king of Zeboiim, and the king of Bela, which is Zoar: and they joined battle
with them in the valley of Siddim, **9** To wit, with Chedorlaomer king of Elam,
and Tidal king of nations, and Amraphel king of Shinar, and Arioch king of Ella-
sar: four kings against five. **10** Now the [i]valley of Siddim was full of slime pits,
and the kings of Sodom and Gomorrah fled and [j]fell there: and the residue fled
to the mountain. **11** And they took all the substance of Sodom and Gomorrah,
and all their vittles and went their way. **12** They [k]took Lot also Abram's brother's
son and his substance (for he dwelt at Sodom) and departed. **13** Then came one
that had escaped, and told Abram the Hebrew, which dwelt in the plain of Mamre
the Amorite, brother of Eshcol, and brother of Aner, which were [l]confederate with
Abram. **14** When Abram heard that his brother was taken, he [m]brought forth
of them that were born and brought up in his house, three hundred and eighteen,
and pursued them unto Dan. **15** Then he and his servants divided themselves
against them by night, and smote them, and pursued them unto Hobah, which is
on the left side of [n]Damascus, **16** And he recovered all the substance, and also
brought again his brother Lot, and his goods, and the women also and the peo-
ple. **17** After that he returned from the slaughter of Chedorlaomer and of the
kings that were with him, came the King of Sodom forth to meet him in the valley
of Shaveh, which is the [1]King's dale. **18** And [2]Melchizedek King of Salem [o]brou-
ght forth bread and wine: and he was a Priest of the most high God. **19** There-
fore he [p]blessed him, saying, Blessed art thou, Abram, of God most high, Possessor
of heaven and earth, **20** And blessed be the most high God, which hath delive-
red thine enemies into thine hand. [3]And Abram gave him tithes of all. **21** Then
the king of Sodom said to Abram, Give me the [q]persons, and take the goods to
thyself. **22** And Abram said to the king of Sodom, [r]I have lifted up mine hand
unto the Lord the most high God possessor of heaven and earth, **23** [s]That I will
not take of all that is thine, so much as a thread or shoe latchet, lest thou shouldest
say, I have made Abram rich, **24** [t]Save only that, which the young men have ea-
ten, and the parts of the men which went with me, Aner, Eshcol, and Mamre: let
them take their parts.

15

1 The Lord is Abram's defense and reward. 6 He is justified by faith. 13 The servitude and deliverance out of Egypt is declared. 18 The land of Canaan is promised the fourth time.

1 After these things, the [a]word of the Lord came unto Abram in a [1]vi-
sion, saying, Fear not, Abram, I am thy buckler, and thine exceeding [2]great
reward. **2** And Abram said, [b]O Lord God, what wilt thou give me, seeing I go
childless, and the steward of mine house is this Eliezer of Damascus? **3** Again
Abram said, Behold, to me thou hast given no seed: wherefore lo, a servant of
mine house shall be mine heir. **4** Then behold, the word of the Lord came unto
him, saying, This man shall not be thine heir, but one that shall come out of thine
own bowels, he shall be thine heir. **5** Moreover he brought him forth and said,
[3]Look up now unto heaven, and tell the stars if thou be able to number them:
and he said unto him, So shall thy seed be. **6** And Abram [4]believed the Lord,
and he counted that to him for righteousness. **7** Again he said unto him, I am
the Lord, that brought thee out of [5]Ur, of the Chaldeans, to give thee this land
to inherit it. **8** And he said, O Lord God, [c]Whereby shall I know that I shall
inherit it? **9** Then he said unto him, Take me an heifer of three years old, and
a she goat of three years old, and a ram of three years old, a turtle dove also and
a pigeon. **10** So he took all these unto him, and [d]divided them in the midst,
and laid every piece one against another: but the birds divided he not. **11** Then
fowls fell on the carcasses, and Abram drove them away. **12** And when the sun
went down, there fell an heavy sleep unto Abram: and lo, [e]a very fearful darkness
fell upon him. **13** Then he said to Abram, [6]Know for a surety, that thy seed
shall be a stranger in a land that is not theirs, [7,f]four hundred years, and shall ser-
ve them: and they entreat them evil. **14** Notwithstanding, the nation whom
they shall serve, will I judge: and afterward shall they come out with great sub-
stance. **15** But thou shalt go unto thy fathers in peace, and shalt be buried in a
good age. **16** And in the [g]fourth generation they shall come hither again: for the
[h]wickedness of the Amorites is not yet full. **17** Also when the sun went down,
there was a darkness: and behold, a smoking furnace, and a firebrand, which went
between those pieces. **18** [8]In that same day the Lord made a covenant with
Abram, saying, Unto thy seed have I given this land: [9]from the river of Egypt unto
the great river [i]Euphrates. **19** Then Kenites, and the Kenezzites, and the Kad-
monites, **20** And the Hittites, and the Perizzites, and the Rephaims, **21** The
Amorites also, and the Canaanites, and the Girgashites, and the Jebusites.

16

3 Sarai being barren giveth Hagar to Abram. 4 Which conceiveth and despiseth her dame: 6 And being ill handled, fleeth. 7 The Angel comforteth her. 11, 12 The name and manners of her son. 13 She calleth upon the Lord, whom she findeth true.

1 Now [a]Sarai Abram's wife bore him no children, and she had a maid an
Egyptian, Hagar by name. **2** And Sarai said unto Abram, Behold now, the Lord
hath [b]restrained me from childbearing, I pray thee go in unto my maid: [c]it may be
that I shall [d]receive a child by her And Abram obeyed the voice of Sarai. **3** Then
Sarai Abram's wife took Hagar her maid the Egyptian, after Abram had dwel-
led ten years in the land of Canaan, and gave her to her husband Abram for his
wife. **4** And he went in unto Hagar, and she conceived: and when she saw that
she had conceived, her dame was [e]despised in her eyes. **5** Then Sarai said to
Abram, [f]Thou doest me wrong, I have given my maid into thy bosom, and she se-
eth that she hath conceived, and I am despised in her eyes: the Lord judge between
me and thee. **6** Then Abram said to Sarai, Behold, thy maid is in thine [g]hand: do
with her as it pleaseth thee Then Sarai dealt roughly with her: wherefore she fled
from her. **7** But the [h]Angel of the Lord found her beside a fountain in the way of
Shur, **8** And he said, Hagar Sarai's maid, whence comest thou? and whither wilt
thou go? And she said, I flee from my dame Sarai. **9** Then the Angel of the Lord
said to her, [i]Return to thy dame, and humble thyself under her hands. **10** Again
the Angel of the Lord said unto her, I will so greatly increase thy seed, that it shall
not be numbered for multitude. **11** Also the Angel of the Lord said unto her,
See, thou art with child, and shalt bear a son, and shalt call his name Ishmael: for
the Lord hath heard thy tribulation. **12** And he shall be a [j]wild man: his hand
shall be against every man, and every man's hand against him, [1]and [k]he shall dwell
in the presence of all his brethren. **13** Then she called the name of the Lord that
spake unto her, Thou God lookest on me: for she said, [l]Have I not also here looked
after him that seeth me? **14** [2]Wherefore the Well was called, [m]Beer Lahai Roi:

GEN. 14

- **a.** Gen. 14:1 That is, of Babylon: by kings here, meaning, them that were governors of cities.
- **b.** Gen. 14:1 Of a people gathered of divers countries.
- **c.** Gen. 14:3 Ambition is the chief cause of wars among princes.
- **d.** Gen. 14:3 Or, of the labored fields.
- **e.** Gen. 14:3 Called also the dead sea, or the lake Asphaltite, near unto Sodom and Gomorrah.
- **f.** Gen. 14:5 Or, giants.
- **g.** Gen. 14:5 Or, plain.
- **h.** Gen. 14:7 Or, destroyed.
- **i.** Gen. 14:10 And afterward was overwhelmed with water, and so was called the salt sea.
- **j.** Gen. 14:10 Or, were discomfited.
- **k.** Gen. 14:12 The godly are plagued many times with the wicked: therefore their company is dangerous.
- **l.** Gen. 14:13 God moved them to join with Abram, and preserveth him from their idolatry and superstitions.
- **m.** Gen. 14:14 Or, armed.
- **n.** Gen. 14:15 Hebrew, Dammesck.
- **o.** Gen. 14:18 For Abram and his soldiers' refection, and not to offer sacrifice.
- **p.** Gen. 14:19 In that Melchizedek fed Abram, he declared himself to represent a king, and in that he blessed him, the high Priest.
- **q.** Gen. 14:21 Hebrew, souls.
- **r.** Gen. 14:22 Or, I have sworn.
- **s.** Gen. 14:23 Hebrew, If I take from thee a thread, etc. Read 1 Sam. 14:45.
- **t.** Gen. 14:24 He would not that his liberality should be hurtful to others.

GEN. 14

1. 2Sam. 18:18
2. Heb. 7:1
3. Heb. 7:8

GEN. 15

- **a.** Gen. 15:1 Or, the Lord spake to Abram.
- **b.** Gen. 15:2 His fear was not only lest he should not have children, but lest the promise of the blessed seed should not be accomplished in him.
- **c.** Gen. 15:8 This is a particular motion of God's Spirit, which is not lawful for all to follow, in asking signs: but was permitted to some by a peculiar motion, as to Gideon and Hezekiah.
- **d.** Gen. 15:10 This was the old custom in making covenants, Jer. 34:18, to the which God added these conditions, that Abram's posterity should be as torn in pieces, but after they should be coupled together: also that it should be assaulted, but yet delivered.
- **e.** Gen. 15:12 Hebrew, a fear of great darkness.
- **f.** Gen. 15:13 Counting from the birth of Isaac to their departure out of Egypt: Which declareth that God will suffer his to be afflicted in this world.
- **g.** Gen. 15:16 Or, after four hundred years.
- **h.** Gen. 15:16 Though God suffer the wicked for a time, yet his vengeance falleth upon them, when the measure of their wickedness is full.
- **i.** Gen. 15:18 Hebrew, Perath.

GEN. 15

1. Num. 12:6
2. Ps. 16:6
3. Rom. 4:18
4. Rom.4:3 - Gal.3:6 - James 2:23 - Gen. 11:28
5. Gen. 11:28
6. Acts 7:6
7. Exod. 12:40
8. Gen. 12:7 - Gen. 13:5 - Gen. 26:4 - Deut. 4:5
9. 1Kings 4:21 - 2Chron. 9:26

GEN. 16

- **a.** Gen. 16:1 It seemeth that she had respect to God's promise, which could not be accomplished without issue.
- **b.** Gen. 16:2 She faileth in binding God's power to the common order of nature, as though God could not give her children in her old age.
- **c.** Gen. 16:2 Or, peradventure.
- **d.** Gen. 16:2 Hebrew, be built by her.
- **e.** Gen. 16:4 This punishment declareth what they gain that attempt anything against the word of God.
- **f.** Gen. 16:5 Hebrew, mine injury is upon thee.
- **g.** Gen. 16:6 Or, power.
- **h.** Gen. 16:7 Which was Christ, as appeareth verse 13 and Gen. 18:17.
- **i.** Gen. 16:9 God rejecteth none estate of people in their misery, but sendeth them comfort.
- **j.** Gen. 16:12 Or, fierce and cruel, or; as a wild ass.
- **k.** Gen. 16:12 That is, the Ishmaelites shall be a peculiar people by themselves, and not a portion of another people.
- **l.** Gen. 16:13 She rebuketh her own dullness and acknowledgeth God's graces, who was present with her everywhere.
- **m.** Gen. 16:14 Or, the well of the living, and seeing me.

lo, it is between Kadesh and Bered. **15** And Hagar bare Abram a son, and Abram called his son's name which Hagar bare, Ishmael. **16** And Abram was four score and six years old when Hagar bare him Ishmael.

17

5 Abram's name is changed to confirm him in the promise. 8 The land of Canaan is the fifth time promised. 12 Circumcision instituted. 15 Sarai is named Sarah. 18 Abraham prayeth for Ishmael. 19 Isaac is promised. 23 Abraham and his house are circumcised.

1 When Abram was ninety years old and nine, the Lord appeared to Abram, and said unto him, I am God [a]all sufficient, [1]walk before me, and be thou [b]upright, **2** And I will make my covenant between me and thee, and I will multiply thee exceedingly. **3** Then Abram fell on his face, and God talked with him, saying, **4** Behold, I make my covenant with thee, and thou shalt be a [c]father of many nations, **5** Neither shall thy name anymore be called Abram, but thy name shall be [d]Abraham: [2]for a father of many nations have I made thee. **6** Also I will make thee exceedingly fruitful, and will make nations of thee, yea, Kings shall proceed of thee. **7** Moreover, I will establish my covenant between me and thee, and thy seed after thee in their generations, for an [3]everlasting covenant, to be God unto thee, and to thy seed after thee. **8** And I will give thee and thy seed after thee the land, wherein thou art a stranger, even all the land of Canaan, for an everlasting possession, and I will be their God. **9** Again God said unto Abraham, Thou also shalt keep my covenant, thou, and thy seed after thee in their generations. **10** [e]This is my covenant which ye shall keep between me and you, and thy seed after thee, [4]Let every man-child among you be circumcised: **11** That is, ye shall circumcise the [f]foreskin of your flesh, and it shall be a [5]sign of the covenant between me and you. **12** And every man-child of eight days old among you, shall be circumcised in your generations, as well he that is born in thine house, as he that is bought with money of any stranger, which is not of thy seed. **13** He that is born in thine house, and he that is bought with thy money, must needs be circumcised: so my covenant shall be in your flesh for an everlasting covenant. **14** But the uncircumcised [g]man-child, in whose flesh the foreskin is not circumcised, even that person shall be cut off from his people, because he hath broken my covenant. **15** Afterward God said unto Abraham, Sarai thy wife shalt thou not call Sarai, but [h]Sarah shall be her name. **16** And I will bless her, and will also give thee a son of her, yea, I will bless her, and she shall be the mother of nations: Kings also of people shall come of her. **17** Then Abraham fell upon his face, and [i]laughed, and said in his heart, Shall a child be born unto him, that is an hundred years old? and shall Sarah that is ninety years old, bear? **18** And Abraham said unto God, Oh, that Ishmael might live in thy sight. **19** Then God said, [6]Sarah thy wife shall bear thee a son indeed, and thou shalt call his name Isaac: and I will establish my covenant with him for an [j]everlasting covenant, and with his seed after him. **20** And as concerning Ishmael, I have heard thee: lo, I have blessed him, and will make him fruitful, and will multiply him [k]exceedingly: twelve princes shall he beget, and I will make a great nation of him. **21** But my covenant will I establish with Isaac, which Sarah shall bear unto thee, the next [7]year at this season. **22** And he left off talking with him, and God went up from Abraham. **23** Then Abraham took Ishmael his son, and all that were born in his house, and all that was bought with his money, that is, every man-child among the men of Abraham's house, and [l]he circumcised the foreskin of their flesh in that selfsame day, as God had commanded him. **24** Abraham also himself was ninety years old and nine, when the foreskin of his flesh was circumcised. **25** And Ishmael his son was thirteen years old, when the foreskin of his flesh was circumcised. **26** The selfsame day was Abraham circumcised, and Ishmael his son: **27** And all the men of his house both born in his house, and bought with money of the stranger, were circumcised with him.

18

2 Abraham receiveth three Angels into his house. 10 Isaac is promised again. 12 Sarah laugheth. 18 Christ is promised to all nations. 19 Abraham taught his family to know God. 21 The destruction of Sodom is declared unto Abraham. 23 Abraham prayeth for them.

1 Again the Lord [1]appeared unto him in the [a]plain of Mamre, as he sat in his tent door about the heat of the day. **2** And he lifted up his eyes, and looked: and lo, three [b]men stood by him, and when he saw them, he ran to meet them from the tent door, and bowed himself to the ground. **3** And he said, [c]Lord, if I have now found favor in thy sight, go not, I pray thee, from thy servant. **4** Let a little water, I pray you, be brought, and [d]wash your feet, and rest yourselves under the tree. **5** And I will bring a morsel of bread, that you may comfort your hearts, afterward ye shall go your ways: for therefore are ye [e]come to your servant And they said, Do even as thou hast said. **6** Then Abraham made haste into the tent unto Sarah, and said, Make ready at once three [f]measures of fine meal, knead it, and make cakes upon the hearth. **7** And Abraham ran to the beasts, and took a tender and good calf, and gave it to the servant, who hasted to make it ready. **8** And he took butter and milk, and the calf which he had prepared, and set before them, and stood himself by them under the tree: and [g]they did eat. **9** Then they said unto him, Where is Sarah thy wife? And he answered, Behold, she is in the tent. **10** And he said, [1]I will certainly come again unto thee according to the time of [h]life: and lo, Sarah thy wife shall have a son: and Sarah heard in the tent door, which was behind him. **11** (Now Abraham and Sarah were old and stricken in age, and it ceased to be with Sarah after the manner of women.) **12** Therefore Sarah [i]laughed within herself, saying, After I am waxed old, [3]and my lord also, shall I have lust? **13** And the Lord said unto Abraham, Wherefore did Sarah thus laugh, saying, Shall I certainly bear a child, which am old? **14** (Shall anything be [4,j]hard to the Lord? as the time appointed will I return unto thee, even according to the time of life, and Sarah shall have a son.) **15** But Sarah denied, saying, I laughed not: for she was afraid And he said, [k]It is not so: for thou laughedst. **16** Afterward, the men did rise up from thence, and looked toward Sodom: and Abraham went with them to bring them on the way. **17** And the [l]Lord said, Shall I hide from Abraham that thing which I do, **18** Seeing that Abraham shall be indeed a great and a mighty nation, and [5]all the nations of the earth shall be blessed in him? **19** For I know him [m]that he will command his sons and his household after him, that they keep the way of the Lord to do righteousness and judgment, that the Lord may bring upon Abraham, that he hath spoken unto him. **20** Then the Lord said, Because the cry of Sodom and Gomorrah is great, and because their sin is exceedingly grievous, **21** I will [n]go down now, and see whether they have done altogether according to that [o]cry, which is come unto me: and if not, that I may know. **22** And the men turned thence, and went toward Sodom: but Abraham stood yet before the Lord. **23** Then Abraham drew near, and said, Wilt thou also destroy the righteous with the wicked? **24** If there be fifty righteous within the city, wilt thou destroy and not spare the place for the fifty righteous that are therein? **25** Be it far from thee from doing this thing, to slay the righteous with the wicked: and that the righteous should be even as the wicked, be it far from thee Shall not the Judge of all the world [p]do right? **26** And the Lord answered, If I shall find in Sodom [q]fifty righteous within the city, then will I spare all the place for their sakes. **27** Then Abraham answered and said, Behold now, I have begun to speak unto my Lord, and I am [r]but dust and ashes, **28** If there shall lack five of fifty righteous, wilt thou destroy all the city for five? And he said, If I find there five and forty, I will not destroy it. **29** And he yet spake to him again, and said, What if there shall be found forty there? Then he answered, I will not do it for forty's sake. **30** Again he said, Let not my Lord now be angry that I speak, What if thirty be found there? Then he said, I will not do it, if I find thirty there. **31** Moreover he said, Behold now, I have begun to speak unto my Lord, What if twenty be found there? And he answered, I will not destroy it for twenty's sake. **32** Then he said, Let not my Lord be now angry, and I will speak

---

GEN. 16

1. Gen. 25:!8
2. Gen. 24:62

GEN. 17

- **a.** Gen. 17:1 Or, Almighty.
- **b.** Gen. 17:1 Or, without hypocrisy.
- **c.** Gen. 17:4 Not only according to the flesh, but of a far greater multitude by faith, Rom. 4:17.
- **d.** Gen. 17:5 The changing of his name is a seal to confirm God's promise unto him.
- **e.** Gen. 17:10 Circumcision is called the covenant, because it signifieth the covenant, and hath the promise of grace joined unto it: which phrase is common to all Sacraments.
- **f.** Gen. 17:11 That privy part is circumcised, to show that all that is begotten of man is corrupt, and must be mortified.
- **g.** Gen. 17:14 Albeit women were not circumcised, yet were they partakers of God's promise: for under the mankind all was consecrated, and here is declared, that whosoever contemneth the sign, despiseth also the promise.
- **h.** Gen. 17:15 Or, dame, or princess.
- **i.** Gen. 17:17 Which proceeded of a sudden joy, and not of infidelity.
- **j.** Gen. 17:19 The everlasting Covenant is made with the children of the Spirit: and with the children of the flesh is made the temporal promise, as was promised to Ishmael.
- **k.** Gen. 17:20 Hebrew, greatly, greatly.
- **l.** Gen. 17:23 They were well instructed which obeyed to be circumcised without resistance: which thing declareth that masters in their houses ought to be as preachers to their families, that from the highest to the lowest they may obey the will of God.

GEN. 17

1. Gen. 5:22
2. Rom. 4:17
3. Gen. 13:16
4. Acts 7:8
5. Rom. 4:11
6. Gen. 18:10 - Gen. 21:2
7. Gen. 21:2

GEN.18

- **a.** Gen. 18:1 Or, oak grove.
- **b.** Gen. 18:2 That is, three Angels in man's shape.
- **c.** Gen. 18:3 Speaking to one of them in whom appeared to be most majesty, for he thought they had been men.
- **d.** Gen. 18:4 For men used because of the great heat to go bare footed in those parts.
- **e.** Gen. 18:5 As sent of God, that I should do my duty to you.
- **f.** Gen. 18:6 Hebrew, Seim.
- **g.** Gen. 18:8 For as God gave them bodies for a time, so gave he them the faculties thereof, to walk, to eat and drink, and such like.
- **h.** Gen. 18:10 That is, about this time when she shall be alive, or when the child shall come into this life.
- **i.** Gen. 18:12 For she rather had respect to the order of nature, than believed the promise of God.
- **j.** Gen. 18:14 Or, hid.
- **k.** Gen. 18:15 Hebrew, No.
- **l.** Gen. 18:17 Jehovah the Hebrew word which we call Lord, showeth that this Angel was Christ: for this word is only applied to God.
- **m.** Gen. 18:19 He showeth that fathers ought both to know God's judgments, and to declare them to their children.
- **n.** Gen. 18:21 God speaketh after the fashion of men: that is, I will enter into judgment with good advice.
- **o.** Gen. 18:21 For our sins cry for vengeance, though none accuse us.
- **p.** Gen. 18:25 Hebrew, do judgment.
- **q.** Gen. 18:26 God declareth that his judgments were done with great mercy, forasmuch as all were so corrupt, that not only fifty but ten righteous men could not be found there, and also that the wicked are spared for the righteous' sake.
- **r.** Gen. 18:27 Hereby we learn, that the nearer we approach unto God, the more doth our miserable estate appear, and the more are we humbled.

but this [s]once, What if ten be found there? And he answered, I will not destroy it
for ten's sake. **33** And the Lord went his way, when he had left communing with
Abraham, and Abraham returned unto his place.

19

3 Lot receiveth two Angels into his house. 4 The filthy lusts of the Sodomites. 16 Lot is delivered. 14 Sodom is destroyed. 26 Lot's wife is made a pillar of salt. 33 Lot's daughters lie with their father, of whom came Moab and Ammon.

1 And in the evening there came two [a]Angels to Sodom: and Lot sat at the
gate of Sodom, and Lot saw them, and rose up to meet them, and he bowed him-
self with his face to the ground. **2** And he said, See my lords, I pray you turn
in now into your servant's house, and tarry all night, and [1]wash your feet, and ye
shall rise up early and go your ways Who said, Nay, but we will abide in the street
all night. **3** Then [b]he pressed upon them earnestly, and they turned in to him,
and came to his house, and he made them a feast, and did bake unleavened bread,
and they [c]did eat. **4** But before they went to bed, the men of the city, even the
men of Sodom compassed the house round about, from the young even to the old,
[d]all the people from all quarters. **5** Who crying unto Lot said to him, Where
are the men, which came to thee this night? bring them out unto us, that we may
know them. **6** Then Lot went out at the door unto them, and shut the door after
him, **7** And said, I pray you, my brethren, do not so wickedly. **8** Behold now,
I have two [e]daughters, which have not known man: them will I bring out now
unto you, and do them as seemeth you good: only unto these men do nothing:
[f]for therefore are they come under the shadow of my roof. **9** Then they said,
Away hence: and they said, He is come alone as a stranger, and shall he judge
and rule? we will now deal worse with thee than with them So they pressed sore
upon Lot [2]himself, and came to break the door. **10** But the men put forth their
hand, and pulled Lot into the house to them, and shut to the door. **11** Then
they smote the men that were at the door of the house, with blindness, both small
and great, so that they were weary in [g]seeking the door. **12** Then the men said
unto Lot, Whom hast thou yet here? either son-in-law, or thy sons or thy dau-
ghters, or whatsoever thou hast in the city, bring it out of this place. **13** For
[h]we will destroy this place, because the [3]cry of them is great before the Lord, and
the Lord hath sent us to destroy it. **14** Then Lot went out and spake unto his
sons-in-law, which [i]married his daughters, and said, Arise, get you out of this pla-
ce: for the Lord will destroy the city, but he seemed to his sons-in-law, as thou-
gh he had mocked. **15** And when the morning arose, the Angels hasted Lot,
saying, Arise, take thy wife and thy two daughters [j]which are here, lest thou be
destroyed in the punishment of the city. **16** And as he [k]prolonged the time,
the men caught both him and his wife, and his two daughters by the hands (the
Lord being merciful unto him) and they brought him forth, and set him without
the city. **17** And when they had brought them out, the Angel said, Escape for
thy life: [l]look not behind thee, neither tarry thou in all the plain: escape into the
mountain, lest thou be destroyed. **18** And Lot said unto them, Not so, I pray
thee, my Lord. **19** Behold now, thy servant hath found grace in thy sight, and
thou hast magnified thy mercy, which thou hast showed unto me in saving my life:
and I cannot escape in the mountain, lest some evil take me, and I die. **20** See
now this city hereby to flee unto, which is a little one: Oh let me escape thither: is
it not a [m]little one, and my soul shall live? **21** Then he said unto him, Behold, I
have received [n]thy request also concerning this thing, that I will not overthrow this
city, for the which thou hast spoken. **22** Haste thee, save thee there: for I can
do [o]nothing till thou come thither Therefore the name of the city was called [p]Zo-
ar. **23** The sun did rise upon the earth, when Lot entered into Zoar. **24** Then
the Lord [4]rained upon Sodom and upon Gomorrah, brimstone and fire from the
Lord out of heaven, **25** And overthrew those cities, and all the plain, and all
the inhabitants of the cities, and that grew upon the earth. **26** Now his wife
behind him looked back, and she became a [q]pillar of salt. **27** And Abraham
rising up early in the morning went to the place, where he had stood before the
Lord, **28** And looking toward Sodom and Gomorrah, and toward all the land of
the plain, behold, he saw the smoke of the land mounting up as the smoke of a fur-
nace. **29** But yet when God destroyed the cities of the plain, God thought upon
Abraham, and sent Lot out from the midst of the destruction, when he overthrew
the cities, wherein Lot dwelled. **30** Then Lot went up out of Zoar, and dwelt in
the mountain with his two daughters for he [r]feared to tarry in Zoar, but dwelt in
a cave, he and his two daughters. **31** And the elder said unto the younger, Our
father is old, and there is not a man in the [s]earth, to come in unto us after the
manner of all the earth. **32** Come, we will make our father [t]drink wine, and lie
with him, that we may preserve seed of our father. **33** So they made their father
drink wine that night, and the elder went and lay with her father: but he perceived
not, neither when she lay down, neither when she rose up. **34** And on the mor-
row the elder said to the younger, Behold, yester night lay I with my father: let us
make him drink wine this night also, and go thou and lie with him, that we may
[u]preserve seed of our father. **35** So they made their father drink wine that night
also, and the younger arose, and lay with him: but he perceived it not, when she
lay down, neither when she rose up. **36** Thus were [v]both the daughters of Lot
with child by their father. **37** And the elder bare a son, and she called his name
Moab: the same is the father of the [w]Moabites unto this day. **38** And the youn-
ger bare a son also, and she called his name [x]Ben-Ammi: the same is the father of
the Ammonites unto this day.

20

1 Abraham dwelleth as a stranger in the land of Gerar. 2 Abimelech taketh away his wife. 3 God reproveth the king, 9 and the king Abraham. 14 Sarah is restored with great gifts. 17 Abraham prayeth, and the king and his are healed.

1 Afterward Abraham departed thence toward the South country and dwel-
led between Kadesh and [a]Shur, and sojourned in Gerar. **2** And Abraham said
of Sarah his wife, [b]She is my sister Then Abimelech king of Gerar sent and took
Sarah. **3** But God came to Abimelech in a dream by night, and said to him,
Behold, [c]thou art but dead, because of the woman, which thou hast taken: for
she is a man's wife. **4** (Notwithstanding Abimelech had not yet come near her)
And he said, Lord, wilt thou slay even [d]the righteous nation? **5** Said not he unto
me, She is my sister? yea, and she herself said, He is my brother: with an upright
[e]mind, and [f]innocent hands have I done this. **6** And God said unto him by a
dream, I know that thou diddest this even with an upright mind, and I [g]kept thee
also that thou shouldest not sin against me: therefore suffered I thee not to touch
her. **7** Now then deliver the man his wife again: for he is a [h]Prophet, and he [i]shall
pray for thee, that thou mayest live: but if thou deliver her not again, be sure that
thou shalt die the death, thou, and all that thou hast. **8** Then Abimelech rising
up early in the morning, called all his servants, and told all these things [j]unto them,
and the men were sore afraid. **9** Afterward Abimelech called Abraham, and said
unto him, What hast thou done unto us? and what have I offended thee, that thou
hast brought on me, and on my [k]kingdom this great sin? thou hast done things
unto me that ought to be done. **10** So Abimelech said unto Abraham, What
sawest thou that thou hast done this thing? **11** Then Abraham answered, Becau-
se I thought thus, Surely the [l]fear of God is not in this place, and they will slay me
for my wife's sake. **12** Yet in very deed she is my [m]sister: for she is the daughter of

---

s. Gen. 18:32 If God refused not the prayer for the wicked Sodomites, even to the sixth request, how much more will he grant the prayers of the godly for the afflicted Church?

GEN. 18

1. Heb. 13:2
2. Gen. 17:19,21 - Gen. 21:2 - Rom. 9:9
3. 1Pet. 3:6
4. Zech. 8:6
5. Gen. 12:3 - Gen. 22:18

GEN. 19

a. Gen. 19:1 Wherein we see God's provident care in preserving his: albeit he revealeth not himself to all alike: for Lot had but two Angels, and Abraham three.
b. Gen. 19:3 That is, he prayed them so instantly.
c. Gen. 19:3 Not for that they had necessity, but because the time was not yet come that they would reveal themselves.
d. Gen. 19:4 Nothing is more dangerous than to dwell where sin reigneth: for it corrupteth all.
e. Gen. 19:8 He deserveth praise in defending his guests, but he is to be blamed in seeking unlawful means.
f. Gen. 19:8 That I should preserve them from all injury.
g. Gen. 19:11 Hebrew, finding.
h. Gen. 19:13 This proveth that the Angels are ministers, as well to execute God's wrath, as to declare his favor.
i. Gen. 19:14 Or, should marry.
j. Gen. 19:15 Hebrew, which are found.
k. Gen. 19:16 The mercy of God striveth to overcome man's slowness in following God's calling.
l. Gen. 19:17 He willed him to flee from God's judgments, and not to be sorry to depart from that rich country, and full of vain pleasures.
m. Gen. 19:20 Though it be little, yet it is great enough to save my life: wherein he offendeth in choosing another place than the Angel had appointed him.
n. Gen. 19:21 Hebrew, thy face.
o. Gen. 19:22 Because God's commandment was to destroy the city, and to save Lot.
p. Gen. 19:22 Which before was called Bela, Gen. 14:2.
q. Gen. 19:26 As touching the body only: and this is a notable monument of God's vengeance to all them that passed that way.
r. Gen. 19:30 Having before felt God's mercy, he durst not provoke him again by continuing among the wicked.
s. Gen. 19:31 Meaning in the country, which the Lord had now destroyed.
t. Gen. 19:32 For except he had been overcome with wine, he would never have done that abominable act.
u. Gen. 19:34 Hebrew, keep alive.
v. Gen. 19:36 Thus God permitted him to fall most horribly in the solitary mountains, whom the wickedness of Sodom could not overcome.
w. Gen. 19:37 Who as they were born in most horrible incest, so were they and their posterity vile and wicked.
x. Gen. 19:38 That is, son of my people: signifying that they rather rejoiced in their sin, than repented for the same.

GEN. 19

1. Gen. 18:4
2. Pet. 2:7
3. Gen. 18:20
4. Deut. 29:23 -Isa. 13:19 - Jeur. 50:40 -Ezek. 16:49 - Hos. 11:8 - Amos 4:11 - Luke 17:29 - Jude 7

GEN. 20

a. Gen. 20:1 Which was toward Egypt.
b. Gen. 20:2 Abraham had now twice fallen into this fault: such is man's frailty.
c. Gen. 20:3 So greatly God detesteth the breach of marriage.
d. Gen. 20:4 The infidels confessed that God would not punish but for just occasion: therefore, whensoever he punisheth, the occasion is just.
e. Gen. 20:5 As one falling by ignorance, and not doing evil of purpose.
f. Gen. 20:5 Not thinking to do any man harm.
g. Gen. 20:6 God by his holy Spirit retaineth them that offend by ignorance, that they fall not into greater inconvenience.
h. Gen. 20:7 That is, one, to whom God revealeth himself familiarly.
i. Gen. 20:7 For the prayer of the godly is of force towards God.
j. Gen. 20:8 Hebrew, in their ears.
k. Gen. 20:9 The wickedness of the King bringeth God's wrath upon the whole realm.
l. Gen. 20:11 He showeth that no honesty can be hoped for, where the fear of God is not.
m. Gen. 20:12 By sister, he meaneth his cousin germaine, and by daughter, Abraham's niece, Gen. 11:29, for so the Hebrews use these words.
n. Gen. 20:15 Or, is at thy commandment.
o. Gen. 20:16 Such an head, as with whom thou mayest be preserved from all dangers.

my father, but not the daughter of my mother, and she is my wife. **13** Now when God caused me to wander out of my father's house, I said then to her, This is thy kindness that thou shalt show unto me in all places where we come, [1]Say thou of me, He is my brother. **14** Then took Abimelech sheep and beeves, and men servants, and women servants, and gave them unto Abraham, and restored him Sarah his wife. **15** And Abimelech said, Behold, my land is [n]before thee, dwell where it pleaseth thee. **16** Likewise to Sarah he said, Behold, I have given thy brother a thousand pieces of silver: behold, he is the [o]veil of thine eyes to all that are with thee, and to all others: and she was [p]thus reproved. **17** Then Abraham prayed unto God, and God healed Abimelech and his wife, and his women servants: and they bare children. **18** For the Lord [q]had shut up every womb of the house of Abimelech, because of Sarah Abraham's wife.

21

3 Isaac is born. 9 Ishmael mocketh Isaac. 14 Hagar is cast out with her son. 17 The Angel comforteth Hagar. 32 The covenant between Abimelech and Abraham. 33 Abraham called upon the Lord.

1 Now the Lord visited Sarah, as he had said, and did unto her [1]according as he had promised. **2** For [2]Sarah conceived, and bare Abraham a son in his [a]old age, at the same season that God told him. **3** And Abraham called his son's name that was born unto him, which Sarah bare him, Isaac. **4** Then Abraham circumcised Isaac his son, when he was eight days old, [3]as God had commanded him. **5** So Abraham was an hundred years old, when his son Isaac was born unto him. **6** Then Sarah said, God hath made me to rejoice: all that hear, will rejoice with me. **7** Again she said, [b]Who would have said to Abraham, that Sarah should have given children suck? for I have borne him a son in his old age. **8** Then the child grew and was weaned: and Abraham made a great feast the same day that Isaac was weaned. **9** And Sarah saw the son of Hagar the Egyptian (which she had borne unto Abraham) [c]mocking. **10** Wherefore she said unto Abraham, [4]Cast out this bondwoman and her son: for the son of this bondwoman shall not be heir with my son Isaac. **11** And this thing was very grievous in Abraham's sight, because of his son. **12** But God said unto Abraham, Let it not be grievous in thy sight for the child, and for thy bondwoman: in all that Sarah shall say unto thee, hear her voice: for in Isaac shall thy seed be [d]called. **13** As for the son of the bondwoman, I will make him [e]a nation also, because he is thy seed. **14** So Abraham arose up early in the morning and took bread, and a bottle of water, and gave it unto Hagar putting it on her shoulder, and the child also, and [f]sent her away: who departing, wandered in the wilderness of Beersheba. **15** And when the water of the bottle was spent, she cast the child under a certain tree. **16** Then she went and sat her over against him afar off about a bow shoot: for she said, I will not see the death of the child And she sat down over against him, and lift up her voice, and wept. **17** Then God [g]heard the voice of the child, and the Angel of God called to Hagar from heaven, and said unto her, What aileth thee, Hagar? fear not, for God hath heard the voice of the child where he is. **18** Arise, take up the child, and hold him in thine hand: for I will make him a great people. **19** And God [h]opened her eyes, and she saw a well of water: so she went and filled the bottle with water, and gave the boy drink. **20** So God was [i]with the child, and he grew and dwelt in the wilderness, and was an [j]archer. **21** And he dwelt in the wilderness of Paran, and his mother took him a wife out of the land of Egypt. **22** And at the same time Abimelech and Phichol his chief captain spake unto Abraham, saying, God is with thee in all that thou doest. **23** Now therefore swear unto me here by God, that thou wilt not [k]hurt me, nor my children, nor my children's children: thou shalt deal with me, and with the country, where thou hast been a stranger, according unto the kindness that I have showed thee. **24** Then Abraham said, I will [l]swear. **25** And Abraham rebuked Abimelech for a well of water, which Abimelech's servants had violently taken away. **26** And Abimelech said, [m]I know not who hath done this thing: also thou toldest me not, neither heard I of it but this day. **27** Then Abraham took sheep and beeves, and gave them unto Abimelech: and they two made a covenant. **28** And Abraham set seven lambs of the flock by themselves. **29** Then Abimelech said unto Abraham, What mean these seven lambs, which thou hast set by themselves? **30** And he answered, Because thou shalt receive of mine hand these seven lambs, that it may be a witness unto me, that I have dug this well. **31** Wherefore the place is called [n]Beersheba, because there they both swear. **32** Thus made they a [o]covenant at Beersheba: afterward Abimelech and Phichol the chief captain rose up, and turned again unto the land of the Philistines. **33** And Abraham planted a grove in Beersheba, and [p]called there on the Name of the Lord, the everlasting God. **34** And Abraham was a stranger in the Philistine's land a long season.

22

1,2 The faith of Abraham is proved in offering his son Isaac. 3 Isaac is a figure of Christ. 20 The generations of Nahor Abraham's brother of whom cometh Rebekah.

1 And after these things God did [1]prove Abraham, and said unto him, Abraham Who answered, [a]Here am I. **2** And he said, Take now thine only son Isaac whom thou lovest, and get thee unto the land of [b]Moriah, and [c]offer him there for a burnt offering upon one of the mountains, which I will show thee. **3** Then Abraham rose up early in the morning, and saddled his ass, and took two of his servants with him, and Isaac his son, and clove wood for the burnt offering, and rose up and went to the place, which God had told him. **4** Then the third day Abraham lifted up his eyes, and saw the place afar off, **5** And said unto his servants, Abide you here with the ass: for I and the child will go yonder and worship, and [d]come again unto you. **6** Then Abraham took the wood of the burnt offering, and laid it upon Isaac his son, and he took the fire in his hand, and the knife: and they went both together. **7** Then spake Isaac unto Abraham his father, and said, My father And he answered, Here am I, my son And he said, Behold the fire and the wood, but where is the lamb for the burnt offering? **8** Then Abraham answered, My son, God will [e]provide him a lamb for a burnt offering: so they went both together. **9** And when they came to the place which God had showed him, Abraham built an altar there, and couched the wood, and [f]bound Isaac his son, [2]and laid him on the altar upon the wood. **10** And Abraham stretching forth his hand, took the knife to kill his son. **11** But the Angel of the Lord called unto him from heaven, saying, Abraham, Abraham And he answered, Here am I. **12** Then he said, Lay not thine hand upon the child, neither do anything unto him: for now I [g]know that thou fearest God, seeing for my sake [h]thou hast not spared thine [i]only son. **13** And Abraham lifting up his eyes, looked and behold, there was a ram behind him caught by the horns in a bush: then Abraham went and took the ram, and offered him up for a burnt offering in the stead of his son. **14** And Abraham called the name of that place [j]Jehovah Jireh: as it is said this day, In the mount will the Lord [k]be seen. **15** And the Angel of the Lord cried unto Abraham from heaven the second time, **16** And said, [3]By [l]myself have I sworn (saith the Lord) because thou hast done this thing, and hast not spared thine only son, **17** Therefore will I surely bless thee, and will greatly multiply thy seed, as the stars of the heaven, and as the sand which is upon the sea shore, and thy seed shall possess the [m]gate of his enemies. **18** [4]And in thy seed shall all the nations of the earth be blessed, because thou hast obeyed my voice. **19** Then turned Abraham again unto his servants, and they rose up, and went together to Beersheba: and Abraham dwelt at Beersheba. **20** And after these things one told Abraham, saying, Behold Milcah, she hath also born children unto thy brother Nahor: **21** To wit, Huz his eldest son, and Buz his brother, and Kemuel the father of [n]Aram, **22** And Chesed, and Hazo, and Pildash, and Jidlaph, and Bethuel. **23** And Bethuel begat Rebekah: these eight did Milcah bear to Nahor, Abraham's brother. **24** And his [o]concubine called Reumah, she bare also Tebah, and Gaham, and Thahash and Maachah.

---

p. Gen. 20:16 God caused this heathen King to reprove her because she dissembled, seeing that God had given her an husband as her veil and defense.
q. Gen. 20:18 Had taken away from them the gift of conceiving.

GEN. 20
1. Gen. 12:13

GEN. 21
a. Gen. 21:2 Therefore the miracle was greater.
b. Gen. 21:7 She accuseth herself of ingratitude, that she did not believe the Angel.
c. Gen. 21:9 He derided God's promise made to Isaac, which the Apostle calleth persecution, Gal. 4:29.
d. Gen. 21:12 The promised seed shall be counted from Isaac, and not from Ishmael, Rom. 9:7; Heb. 11:18.
e. Gen. 21:13 The Ishmaelites shall come of him.
f. Gen. 21:14 True faith renounceth all natural affections to obey God's commandment.
g. Gen. 21:17 For his promise sake made to Abraham; and not because the child had discretion and judgment to pray.
h. Gen. 21:19 Except God open our eyes, we can neither see, nor use the means which are before us.
i. Gen. 21:20 As touching outward things God caused him to prosper.
j. Gen. 21:20 Or, shot in the bow, and was an hunter.
k. Gen. 21:23 Hebrew, deal falsely with me, or lie.
l. Gen. 21:24 So that it is a lawful thing to take an oath in matters of importance, for to justify the truth, and to assure others of our sincerity.
m. Gen. 21:26 Wicked servants do many evils unknown to their masters.
n. Gen. 21:31 Or, well of the oath, or of seven, meaning lambs.
o. Gen. 21:32 Thus we see that the godly, as touching outward things may make peace with the wicked that know not the true God.
p. Gen. 21:33 That is, he worshipped God in all points of true Religion.

GEN. 21
1. Gen. 17:19 - Gen. 18:10
2. Matt. 1:2 - Acts 7:8 - Gal. 4:23 Heb. 11:11
3. Gen.17:12
4. Gal. 4:30

GEN. 22
a. Gen. 22:1 Hebrew, Lo, I.
b. Gen. 22:2 Which signifieth the fear of God, in the which place he was honored: and Solomon afterward built the Temple.
c. Gen. 22:2 Herein stood the chiefest point of his tentation, seeing he was commanded to offer up him in whom God had promised to bless all the nations of the world.
d. Gen. 22:5 He doubted not, but God would accomplish his promise, though he should sacrifice his son.
e. Gen. 22:8 The only way to overcome all tentation, is to rest upon God's providence.
f. Gen. 22:9 For it is like that his father had declared to him God's commandment, whereunto he showed himself obedient.
g. Gen. 22:12 That is, by thy true obedience thou hast declared thy lively faith.
h. Gen. 22:12 Or, and hast not withheld thine only son from me.
i. Gen. 22:12 Hebrew, thy son, thy only son.
j. Gen. 22:14 Or, the Lord will see or provide.
k. Gen. 22:14 The name is changed, to show that God doth both see and provide secretly for his, and also evidently is seen, and felt in time convenient.
l. Gen. 22:16 Signifying, that there is no greater than he.
m. Gen. 22:17 Or, holds.
n. Gen. 22:21 Or, of the Syrians.
o. Gen. 22:24 Concubine is oftentimes taken in the good part for those women which were inferior to the wives.

GEN. 22
1. Heb. 11:17
2. James 2:21
3. Ps. 105:9 - Luke 1:73 - Heb. 6:13
4. Gen. 12:3 - Gen. 18:8 - Acts 3:25 - gal. 3:8

23 *2 Abraham laments the death of Sarah. 4 He buyeth a field to bury her, ofthe Hittites. 13 The equity of Abraham. 19 Sarah is buried in Machpelah.*

1 When Sarah was an hundred twenty and seven years old ([a]so long lived she.) **2** Then Sarah died in Kirjath Arba: the same is Hebron in the land of Canaan And Abraham came to mourn for Sarah and to weep for her. **3** Then Abraham [b]rose up from the sight of his corpse, and talked with the [c]Hittites, saying, **4** I am a stranger, and a foreigner among you: give me a possession of burial with you, that I may bury my dead out of my sight. **5** Then the Hittites answered Abraham, saying unto him, **6** Hear us, my lord: thou art a prince [d]of God among us: in the chiefest of our sepulchers bury the dead: none of us shall forbid thee his sepulcher, but thou mayest bury thy dead therein. **7** Then Abraham stood up, and bowed himself before the people of the land of the Hittites. **8** And he communed with them, saying, If it be [e]your mind, that I shall bury my dead out of my sight, hear me, and entreat for me to Ephron the son of Zohar, **9** That he would give me the cave of [f]Machpelah, which he hath in the end of his field: that he would give it me for as much [g]money as it is worth, for a possession to bury in among you. **10** (For Ephron dwelt among the Hittites) Then Ephron the Hittite answered Abraham in the audience of all the Hittites that [h]went in at the gates of his city, saying, **11** No, my Lord, hear me: the field give I thee and the cave that therein is, I give it thee: even in the presence of the sons of my people give I it thee to bury thy dead. **12** Then Abraham [i]bowed himself before the people of the land, **13** And spake unto Ephron in the audience of the people of the country, saying, Seeing thou wilt give it, I pray thee, hear me, I will give the price of the field: receive it of me, and I will bury my dead there. **14** Ephron then answered Abraham, saying unto him, **15** My lord, hearken unto me: the land is worth four hundred [j]shekels of silver: what is that between me and thee? bury therefore thy dead. **16** So Abraham hearkened unto Ephron, and Abraham weighed to Ephron the silver, which he had named, in the audience of the Hittites, even four hundred silver shekels of current money among merchants. **17** So the field of Ephron which was in Machpelah, and over against Mamre, even the field and the cave that was therein, and all the trees that were in the field, which were in all the borders round about, was made sure **18** Unto Abraham for a possession, in the sight of the Hittites, even of all that [k]went in at the gates of his city. **19** And after this, Abraham buried Sarah his wife in the cave of the field of Machpelah over against Mamre: the same is Hebron in the land of Canaan. **20** Thus the field, and the cave that is therein, was made sure unto Abraham for a possession of burial [l]by the Hittites.

24 *2 Abraham causeth his servant to swear to take a wife for Isaac in his own kindred. 12 The servant prayeth to God. 33 His fidelity toward his master. 50 The friends of Rebekah commit the matter to God. 58 They ask her consent, and she agreeth.*

1 Now Abraham was old, and [a]stricken in years, and the Lord had blessed Abraham in all things. **2** Therefore Abraham said unto his eldest servant of his house, which had the rule over all that he had, [1,b]Put now thine hand under my thigh, **3** And I will make thee [c]swear by the Lord God of the heaven, and God of the earth, that thou shalt not take a wife unto my son of the daughters of the Canaanites among whom I dwell: **4** But thou shalt go unto my [d]country, and to my kindred, and take a wife unto my son Isaac. **5** And the servant said to him, What if the woman will not come with me to this land? shall I bring thy son again unto the land from whence thou camest? **6** To whom Abraham answered, Beware that thou bring not my son [e]thither again. **7** The Lord God of heaven, who took me from my father's house, and from the land where I was born, and that spake unto me, and that swear unto me, saying, [2]Unto thy seed will I give this land, he shall send his Angel before thee, and thou shalt take a wife unto my son from thence. **8** Nevertheless if the woman will not follow thee, then shalt thou be [f]discharged of this mine oath: only bring not my son thither again. **9** Then the servant put his hand under the thigh of Abraham his master, and sware to him for this matter. **10** So the servant took ten camels of the camels of his master, and departed: (for he had all his master's goods in his hand:) and so he arose, and went to [g]Aram Naharaim, unto the [h]city of Nahor. **11** And he made his camels to [i]lie down without the city by a well of water, at eventide about the time that the women come out to draw water. **12** And he said, O [j]Lord God of my master Abraham, I beseech thee, [k]send me good speed this day, and show mercy unto my master Abraham. **13** Lo, I stand by the well of water while the men's daughters of this city come out to draw water. **14** [l]Grant therefore that the maid, to whom I say: Bow down thy pitcher, I pray thee, that I may drink: if she say, Drink, and I will give thy camels drink also: may be she that thou hast ordained for thy servant Isaac: and thereby shall I know that thou hast showed mercy on my master. **15** And now yet he had left speaking, behold, [m]Rebekah came out, the daughter of Bethuel, son of Milcah the wife of Nahor Abraham's brother, and her Pitcher upon her shoulder. **16** (And the maid was very fair to look upon, a virgin and unknown of man) and she [n]went down to the well, and filled her pitcher and came up. **17** Then the servant ran to meet her, and said, Let me drink, I pray thee, a little water of thy pitcher. **18** And she said, Drink [o]sir: and she hasted, and let down her pitcher upon her hand and gave him drink. **19** And when she had given him drink, she said, I will draw water for thy camels also until they [p]have drunken enough. **20** And she poured out her pitcher into the trough speedily, and ran again unto the well to draw water, and she drew for all his camels. **21** So the man wondered at her, and held his peace, to know whether the Lord had made his journey prosperous or not. **22** And when the camels had left drinking, the man took a golden [q,r]abillement of [s]half a shekel weight, and two bracelets for her hands, of ten shekels weight of gold: **23** And he said, Whose daughter art thou? tell me, I pray thee, Is there room in thy father's house for us to lodge in? **24** Then she said to him, I am the daughter of Bethuel the son of Milcah whom she bare unto Nahor. **25** Moreover she said unto him, We have litter also and provender enough, and room to lodge in. **26** And the man bowed himself and worshipped the Lord, **27** And said, Blessed be the Lord God of my master Abraham, which hath not withdrawn his mercy [t]and his truth from my master: for when I was in the way, the Lord brought me to my master's brethren's house. **28** And the maid ran and told them of her mother's house according to these words. **29** Now Rebekah had a brother called Laban, and Laban ran unto the man to the well. **30** For when he had seen the earrings and bracelets in his sister's hands, and when he heard the words of Rebekah his sister, saying, Thus said the man unto me, then he went to the man, and lo, [u]he stood by the camels at the well. **31** And he said, Come in thou blessed of the Lord: wherefore standest thou without, seeing I have prepared the house, and room for the camels? **32** Then the man came into the house, and [v]he unsaddled the [w]camels, and brought litter and provender for the camels, and water to wash his feet, and the men's feet that were with him. **33** Afterward the meat was set before him: but he said, I [x]will not eat, until I have said my message And he said: Speak on. **34** Then he said, I am Abraham's servant, **35** And the Lord hath [y]blessed my master wonderfully, that he is become great: for he hath given him sheep, and beeves, and silver, and gold, and men servants, and maid servants, and camels, and asses. **36** And Sarah my master's wife hath borne a son to my master, when she was old, and unto him hath he given all that he hath. **37** Now my master made me swear, saying, Thou shalt not take a wife to my son of the daughters of the [z]Canaanites, in whose land I dwell: **38** But thou shalt go unto my [aa]father's house and to my kindred, and take a wife unto my son. **39** Then I said unto my master, What if the woman will not follow me? **40** Who answered me, The Lord, before who I walk, will send his Angel with thee, and prosper thy journey, and thou shalt take a wife for my son of my kindred and my father's house. **41** Then shalt thou be discharged of [ab]mine oath, when thou comest to my kindred: and if they give thee not one, thou shalt be free from mine oath. **42** So

GEN. 23

a. Gen. 23:1 Hebrew, the years of the life of Sarah.
b. Gen. 23:3 That is, when he had mourned: so the godly may mourn, if they pass not measure, and the natural affection is commendable.
c. Gen. 23:3 Hebrew, sons of Heth.
d. Gen. 23:6 That is, godly or excellent: for the Hebrews so speak of all things that are notable, because all excellency cometh of God.
e. Gen. 23:8 Hebrew, in your soul.
f. Gen. 23:9 Or, double cave, because one was within another.
g. Gen. 23:9 Hebrew, in full silver.
h. Gen. 23:10 Meaning, all the citizens and inhabitants.
i. Gen. 23:12 To show that he had them in good estimation and reverence.
j. Gen. 23:15 The common shekel is about 20 pence, so then 400 shekels mount to 33 pound 6 shillings and 8 pence after 5 shilling sterling the ounce.
k. Gen. 23:18 Or, citizens.
l. Gen. 23:20 That is, all the people confirmed the sale.

GEN. 24

a. Gen. 24:1 Hebrew, come into days.
b. Gen. 24:2 Which ceremony declared, the servant's obedience towards his master, and the master's power over the servant.
c. Gen. 24:3 This showeth that an oath may be required in a lawful cause.
d. Gen. 24:4 He would not that his son should marry out of the godly family: for the inconveniences that come by marrying with the ungodly are set forth in sundry places of the Scriptures.
e. Gen. 24:6 Lest he should lose the inheritance promised.
f. Gen. 24:8 Hebrew, innocent.
g. Gen. 24:10 Or, Mesopotamia, or, Syria of the two floods: to wit, of Tigris and Euphrates.
h. Gen. 24:10 That is, to Haran.
i. Gen. 24:11 Hebrew, to bow their knees.
j. Gen. 24:12 He groundeth his prayer upon God's promise made to his master.
k. Gen. 24:12 Or, cause me to meet.
l. Gen. 24:14 The servant moved by God's spirit desired to be assured by a sign, whether God prospered his journey or no.
m. Gen. 24:15 God giveth good success to all things that are undertaken for the glory of his name and according to his word.
n. Gen. 24:16 Here is declared that God ever heareth the prayers of his, and granteth their requests.
o. Gen. 24:18 Hebrew, my Lord.
p. Gen. 24:19 Hebrew, have made an end of drinking.
q. Gen. 24:22 Or, earring.
r. Gen. 24:22 God permitted many things both in apparel and other things which are now forbid: specially when they appertain not to our mortification.
s. Gen. 24:22 The golden shekel is here meant and not that of silver.
t. Gen. 24:27 He boasteth not his good fortune (as do the wicked) but acknowledgeth that God hath dealt mercifully with his master in keeping promise.
u. Gen. 24:30 For he waited on God's hand, who had now heard his prayer.
v. Gen. 24:32 To wit, Laban.
w. Gen. 24:32 The gentle entertainment of strangers used among the godly fathers.
x. Gen. 24:33 The fidelity that servants owe to their masters, causeth them to prefer their master's business to their own necessity.
y. Gen. 24:35 To bless, signifieth here to enrich, or increase with substance, as the text in the same verse declareth.
z. Gen. 24:37 The Canaanites were accursed, and therefore the godly could not join with them in marriage.
aa. Gen. 24:38 Meaning among his kinsfolk, as verse 40.

I came this day to the well, and said, O Lord, the God of my master Abraham, if thou now prosper my [ac]journey which I go, **43** Behold, [3]I stand by the well of water when a virgin cometh forth to draw water, and I say to her, Give me, I pray thee, a little water of thy pitcher to drink, **44** And she said to me, Drink thou, and I will also draw for thy camels, let her be the wife, which the Lord hath [ad]prepared for thy master's son. **45** And before I had made an end of speaking in mine [ae]heart, behold, Rebekah came forth and her pitcher on her shoulder, and she went down to the well, and drew water Then I said unto her, Give me drink, I pray thee. **46** And she made haste, and took down her pitcher from her shoulder, and said, Drink, and I will give thy camels drink also So I drank, and she gave the camels drink also. **47** Then I asked her, and said, Whose daughter art thou? And she answered, The daughter of Bethuel Nahor's son, whom Milcah bare unto him Then I put the abillement upon her face, and the bracelets upon her hands: **48** [af]And I bowed down and worshipped the Lord, and blessed the Lord God of my master Abraham, which had brought me the [ag]right way to take my master's brother's daughter unto his son. **49** Now therefore, if ye will deal [ah]mercifully and truly with my master, tell me: and if not, tell me, that I may turn me to the [ai]right hand or to the left. **50** Then answered Laban and Bethuel, and said, [aj]This thing is proceeded of the Lord: we cannot therefore say unto thee, neither evil nor good. **51** Behold, Rebekah is [ak]before thee, take her and go, that she may be thy master's son's wife, even as the Lord hath [al]said. **52** And when Abraham's servant heard their words, he bowed himself toward the earth unto the Lord. **53** Then the servant took forth jewels of silver, and jewels of gold, and raiment, and gave to Rebekah: also unto her brother and to her mother he gave gifts. **54** Afterward they did eat and drink, both he, and the men that were with him, and tarried all night, and when they rose up in the morning, he said, [4]Let me depart unto my master. **55** Then her brother and her mother answered, Let the maid abide with us, at the least [am]ten days: then shall she go. **56** But he said unto them, Hinder you me not, seeing the Lord hath prospered my journey: send me away, that I may go to my master. **57** Then they said, We will call the maid, and ask [an]her consent. **58** And they called Rebekah, and said unto her: Wilt thou go with this man? And [ao]she answered, I will go. **59** So they let Rebekah their sister go, and her nurse, with Abraham's servant and his men. **60** And they blessed Rebekah, and said unto her, Thou art our sister, grow into thousand thousand's, and thy seed possess the [ap]gate of his enemies. **61** Then Rebekah arose, and her maids, and rode upon the camels, and followed the man, and the servant took Rebekah and departed. **62** Now Isaac came from the way of [5]Beer Lahai Roi, (for he dwelt in the South country.) **63** And Isaac went out to [aq]pray in the field toward the evening: who lift up his eyes and looked, and behold, the camels came. **64** Also Rebekah lift up her eyes, and when she saw Isaac, she lighted down from the camel. **65** (For she had said to the servant, Who is yonder man, that cometh in the field to meet us? and the servant had said, It is my master) So she took [ar]a veil, and covered her. **66** And the servant told Isaac all things, that he had done. **67** Afterward Isaac brought her into the tent, of Sarah his mother, and he took Rebekah, and she was his wife, and he loved her: So Isaac was [as]comforted after his mother's death.

25

1 Abraham taketh Keturah to wife, and getteth many children. 5 Abrahamgiveth all his goods to Isaac. 8 He dieth. 12 The genealogy of Ishmael. 25 The birth of Jacob and Esau.

1 Now Abraham had taken [a]him another wife called Keturah, **2** Which bare him Zimran, and Jokshan, and Medan, and Midian, and Ishbak, and Shuah. **3** And Jokshan, begat Sheba, and Dedan: [1]And the sons of Dedan were Asshurim, and Letushim, and Leummim. **4** Also the sons of Midian were Ephah, and Epher, and Hanoch, and Abidah, and Eldaah, all these were the sons of Keturah. **5** And Abraham gave [b]all his goods to Isaac. **6** But unto the [c]sons of the [d]concubines, which Abraham had, Abraham [e]gave gifts, and sent them away from Isaac his son (while he yet lived) Eastward to the East country. **7** And this is the age of Abraham's life, which he lived, an hundred seventy and five years. **8** Then Abraham yielded the spirit, and died in a good age, an old man, and of great years, and was [f]gathered to his people. **9** And his sons Isaac and Ishmael buried him in the cave of Machpelah, in the field of Ephron son of Zohar the Hittite, before Mamre, **10** Which [2]field Abraham bought of the Hittites, where Abraham was buried with Sarah his wife. **11** And after the death of Abraham God blessed Isaac his son, [3]and Isaac dwelt by Beer Lahai Roi. **12** Now these are the [4]generations of Ishmael Abraham's son, whom Hagar the Egyptian Sarah's handmaid bare unto Abraham. **13** And these are the names of the sons of Ishmael, name by name, according to their kindreds: the [g]eldest son of Ishmael was Nebajoth then Kedar, and Adbeel, and Mibsam, **14** And Mishma, and Dumah, and Massa, **15** Hadar, and Tema, Jetur, Naphish, and Kedemah. **16** These are the sons of Ishmael, and these are their names, by their towns and by their castles: to wit, twelve princes of their nations. **17** (And these are the years of the life of Ishmael, an hundred thirty and seven years, and he yielded up the spirit, and died, and was gathered unto his [h]people.) **18** And they dwelt from Havilah unto Shur, that is towards Egypt, as thou goest to Asshur Ishmael [i]dwelt [j]in the presence of all his brethren. **19** Likewise these are the generations of Isaac Abraham's son Abraham begat Isaac. **20** And Isaac was forty years old, when he took Rebekah to wife, the daughter of Bethuel the [k]Aramite of Padan Aram, and sister to Laban the Aramite. **21** And Isaac prayed unto the Lord for his wife, because she was barren: and the Lord was entreated of him, and Rebekah his wife conceived. **22** But the children [l]strove together within her: therefore she said, Seeing it is so, why am I [m]thus? wherefore she went [n]to ask the Lord. **23** And the Lord said to her, Two nations are in thy womb, and two manner of people shall be divided out of thy bowels, and the one people shall be mightier than the other, and the [5]elder shall serve the younger. **24** Therefore when her time of deliverance was fulfilled, behold, twins were in her womb. **25** So he that came out first was red, and he was all over as rough as a garment, and they called his name Esau. **26** [6]And afterward came his brother out, and his hand held Esau by the heel, therefore his name was called Jacob Now Isaac was threescore years old when Rebekah bare them. **27** And the boys grew, and Esau was a cunning hunter, and [o]lived in the fields: but Jacob was a [p]plain man, and dwelt in tents. **28** And Isaac loved Esau, for [q]venison was his meat, but Rebekah loved Jacob. **29** Now Jacob sod pottage, and Esau came from the field and was weary. **30** Then Esau said to Jacob, [r]Let me eat, I pray thee, of that pottage so red, for I am weary Therefore was his name called Edom. **31** And Jacob said, Sell me even now thy birthright. **32** And Esau said, Lo, I am almost dead, what is then this [s]birthright to me? **33** Jacob then said, Swear to me even now And he swear to him, [7]and [t]sold his birthright unto Jacob. **34** Then Jacob gave Esau bread and pottage of lentils: and he did eat and drink, and rose up, and went his way: So Esau contemned his birthright.

26

1 God provideth for Isaac in the famine. 3 He reneweth his promise. 9 The King blameth him for denying his wife. 14 The Philistines hate him for his riches. 15 Stop his wells. 16 And drive him away. 24 God comforteth him.

1 And there was a famine in the [a]land besides the first famine that was in the days of Abraham Wherefore Isaac went to Abimelech King of the Philistines unto Gerar. **2** For the Lord appeared unto him, and said, [b]Go not down into Egypt, but abide in the land which I shall show thee. **3** Dwell in this land, and I will be with thee, and will bless thee: for to thee, and to thy seed I will give all these [1]countries, and I will perform the oath which I swear unto Abraham thy

---

ab. Gen. 24:41 Which by mine authority I caused thee to make.
ac. Gen. 24:42 Or, way.
ad. Gen. 24:44 Or, showed.
ae. Gen. 24:45 Signifying that this prayer was not spoken by the mouth, but only meditated in his heart.
af. Gen. 24:48 He showeth what is our duty, when we have received any benefit of the Lord.
ag. Gen. 24:48 Hebrew, in the way of truth.
ah. Gen. 24:49 If you will freely and faithfully give your daughter to my master's son.
ai. Gen. 24:49 That is, that I may provide elsewhere.
aj. Gen. 24:50 So soon as they perceive that it is God's ordinance they yield.
ak. Gen. 24:51 Or, at thy commandment.
al. Gen. 24:51 Or, ordained.
am. Gen. 24:55 Hebrew, days, or ten.
an. Gen. 24:57 This showeth that parents have not authority to marry their children without consent of the parties.
ao. Gen. 24:58 Hebrew, her mouth.
ap. Gen. 24:60 That is, let it be victorious over his enemies: which blessing is fully accomplished in Jesus Christ.
aq. Gen. 24:63 This was the exercise of the godly fathers to meditate God's promises, and to pray for the accomplishment thereof.
ar. Gen. 24:65 The custom was that the spouse was brought to her husband, her head being covered, in token of shamefastness and chastity.
as. Gen. 24:67 Or, had left mourning for his mother.

GEN. 24

1. Gen. 47:29
2. Gen. 12:7 - Gen. 13:15 - Gen. 15:18 - Gen. 26:4
3. Gen. 24:13
4. Gen. 24:56,59
5. Gen. 16:14 - Gen. 25:11

GEN. 25

a. Gen. 25:1 While Sarah was yet alive.
b. Gen. 25:5 Hebrew, all that he had.
c. Gen. 25:6 For by the virtue of God's word he had not only Isaac, but begat many more.
d. Gen. 25:6 Read Gen. 22:24.
e. Gen. 25:6 To avoid the dissention that else might have come because of the heritage.
f. Gen. 25:8 Hereby the ancients signified that man by death perished not wholly but as the souls of the godly lived after in perpetual joy, so the souls of the wicked in perpetual pain.
g. Gen. 25:13 Hebrew, firstborn.
h. Gen. 25:17 Which dwelt among the Arabians, and were separate from the blessed seed.
i. Gen. 25:18 Or, his lot fell.
j. Gen. 25:18 He meaneth that his lot fell to dwell among his brethren as the Angel promised, Gen. 16:12.
k. Gen. 25:20 Or, Syrian of Mesopotamia.
l. Gen. 25:22 Or, hurt one another.
m. Gen. 25:22 That is, with child, seeing one shall destroy another.
n. Gen. 25:22 For that is the only refuge in all our miseries.
o. Gen. 25:27 Hebrew, a man of the field.
p. Gen. 25:27 Or, simple and innocent.
q. Gen. 25:28 Hebrew, venison in his mouth.
r. Gen. 25:30 Or, feed me quickly.
s. Gen. 25:32 The reprobate esteem not God's benefits except they feel them presently, and therefore they prefer present pleasures.
t. Gen. 25:33 Thus the wicked prefer their worldly commodities to God's spiritual graces: but the children of God do the contrary.

GEN. 25

1. 1Chron. 1:32
2. Gen. 23:16
3. Gen. 16:14 - Gen. 24:62
4. 1Chron. 1:20
5. Rom. 9:12
6. Hos. 11:3 - Matt. 1:2
7. Heb. 12:16

GEN. 26

a. Gen. 26:1 In the land of Canaan.
b. Gen. 26:2 God's providence always watcheth to direct the ways of his children.

father. **4** Also I will cause thy seed to multiply as the stars of heaven, and will give unto thy seed all these countries: and in thy seed shall all the nations of the earth be [2]blessed, **5** Because that Abraham [c]obeyed my voice and kept mine [d]ordinance, my commandments, my statutes, and my laws. **6** So Isaac dwelt in Gerar. **7** And the men of the place asked him of his wife, and he said, She is my sister: for he [e]feared to say, she is my wife, lest, said he, the men of the place should kill me, because of Rebekah, for she was beautiful to the eye. **8** So after he had been there a long time, Abimelech King of the Philistines looked out at a window, and lo, he saw Isaac [f]sporting with Rebekah his wife. **9** Then Abimelech called Isaac, and said, Lo, she is of a surety thy wife, and why saidest thou, She is my sister? To whom Isaac answered, Because I thought this, It may be that I shall die for her. **10** Then Abimelech said, Why hast thou done this unto us? one of the people had almost lain by thy wife, so shouldest thou have brought [g]sin upon us. **11** Then Abimelech charged all his people, saying, He that toucheth this man, or his wife, shall die the death. **12** Afterward Isaac sowed in that land, and found in the same year an [h]hundredfold by estimation: and so the Lord blessed him. **13** And the man waxed mightily, and [i]still increased, till he was exceeding great. **14** For he had flocks of sheep, and herds of cattle, and a mighty household: therefore the Philistines had [j]envy at him, **15** Insomuch that the Philistines stopped, and filled up with earth all the wells, which his father's servants dug in his father Abraham's time. **16** Then Abimelech said unto Isaac, Get thee from us, for thou art mightier than we a great deal. **17** Therefore Isaac departed thence and pitched his tent in the [k]valley of Gerar, and dwelt there. **18** And Isaac returning, dug the wells of water, which they had dug in the days of Abraham his father, for the Philistines had stopped them after the death of Abraham, and he gave them the same names, that his father gave them. **19** Isaac's servants then dug in the valley and found there a well of [l]living water. **20** But the herdsmen of Gerar did strive with Isaac's herdsmen, saying, The water is ours, therefore called he the name of the well [m]Esek, because they were at strife with him. **21** Afterward they dug another well, and strove for that also, and he called the name of it [n]Sitnah. **22** Then he removed thence, and dug another well, for which they strove not: therefore called he the name of it [o]Rehoboth, and said, Because the Lord hath now made us room, we shall increase upon the earth. **23** So he went up thence to Beersheba. **24** And the Lord appeared unto him the same night, and said, I am the God [p]of Abraham thy father: fear not, I am with thee, and will bless thee, and multiply thy seed for my servant Abraham's sake. **25** Then he built an [q]altar there, and called upon the Name of the Lord, and there spread his tent: where also Isaac's servants dug a well. **26** Then came Abimelech to him from Gerar, and Ahuzzath one of his friends, and Phichol the captain of his army. **27** To whom Isaac said, Wherefore come ye to me, seeing ye hate me and have put me away from you? **28** Who answered, We saw certainly that the Lord was with thee, and we thought thus, Let there be now an oath between us, even between us and thee, and let us make a covenant with thee. **29** [r]If thou shalt do us no hurt, as we have not touched thee, and as we have done unto thee nothing but good, and sent thee away in peace: thou now, the blessed of the Lord, do this. **30** Then he made them a feast, and they did eat and drink. **31** And they rose up betimes in the morning, and swear one to another: then Isaac let them go, and they departed from him in peace. **32** And that same day Isaac's servants came and told him of a well, which they had dug, and said unto him, We have found water. **33** So he called it [s]Shebah: therefore the name of the city is called [t]Beersheba unto this day. **34** Now when Esau was forty years old, he took to wife Judith, the daughter of Beeri an Hittite, and Basemath the daughter of Elon an Hittite also. **35** And they [3]were [u]a grief of mind to Isaac and to Rebekah.

27

8 Jacob getteth the blessing from Esau by his mother's counsel. 38 Esau by weeping moveth his father to pity him. 41 Esau hateth Jacob and threateneth his death. 43 Rebekah sendeth Jacob away.

1 And when Isaac was old, and his eyes were dim (so that he could not see) he called Esau his eldest son, and said unto him, My son And he answered him, [a]I am here. **2** Then he said, Behold, I am now old, and know not the day of my death. **3** Wherefore now, I pray thee take thine instruments, thy quiver and thy bow, and get thee to the field, that thou mayest [b]take me some venison. **4** Then make me savory meat, such as I love, and bring it me that I may eat, and that my [c]soul may bless thee, before I die. **5** (Now Rebekah heard, when Isaac spake to Esau his son) and Esau went into the field to hunt for venison, and to bring it. **6** Then Rebekah spake unto Jacob her son, saying, Behold, I have heard thy father talking with Esau thy brother, saying, **7** Bring me venison, and make me savory meat, that I may eat and bless thee before the Lord, afore my death. **8** Now therefore, my son, hear my voice in that which I command thee. **9** [d]Get thee now to the flock, and bring me thence two good kids of the goats, that I may make pleasant meat of them for thy father, such as he loveth. **10** Then thou shalt bring it to thy father, and he shall eat, to the intent that he may bless thee before his death. **11** But Jacob said to Rebekah his mother, Behold, Esau my brother is rough, and I am smooth. **12** My father may possibly feel me, and I shall seem [e]to him as a [f]mocker: so shall I bring a curse upon me, and not a blessing. **13** But his mother said unto him, [g,h]Upon me be thy curse, my son: only hear my voice, and go and bring me them. **14** So he went and set them, and brought them to his mother: and his mother made pleasant meat, such as his father loved. **15** And Rebekah took fair clothes of her elder son Esau, which were in her house, and clothed Jacob her younger son: **16** And she covered his hands and the smooth of his neck with the skins of the kids of the goats. **17** Afterward she put the pleasant meat and bread, which she had prepared, in the hand of her son Jacob. **18** And when he came to his father, he said, My father Who answered, I am here: who art thou, my son? **19** And Jacob said to his father, [i]I am Esau thy firstborn, I have done as thou badest me, arise, I pray thee: sit up and eat of my venison, that thy soul may bless me. **20** Then Isaac said unto his son, How hast thou found it so quickly my son? Who said, Because the Lord thy God brought it to mine hand. **21** Again said Isaac unto Jacob, Come near now, that I may feel thee, my son, whether thou be that my son Esau, or not. **22** Then Jacob came near to Isaac his father, and he felt him and said, The [j]voice is Jacob's voice, but the hands are the hands of Esau. **23** (For he knew him not, because his hands were rough as his brother Esau's hands: wherefore he blessed him.) **24** Again he said, Art thou that my son Esau? Who answered, [k]Yea. **25** Then said he, Bring it me hither, and I will eat of my son's venison, that my soul may bless thee And he brought it to him, and he ate: also he brought him wine, and he drank. **26** Afterward his father Isaac said unto him, Come near now, and kiss me, my son. **27** And he came near and kissed him Then he smelled the savor of his garments, and blessed him, and said, Behold, the smell of my son is as the smell of a field, which the Lord hath blessed. **28** [1]God give thee therefore of the dew of heaven, and the fatness of the earth, and plenty of wheat and wine. **29** Let people be thy servants, and nations bow down unto thee: be Lord over thy brethren, and let thy mother's children honor thee, cursed be he that curseth thee, and blessed be he that blesseth thee. **30** And when Isaac had made an end of blessing Jacob, and Jacob was scarce gone out from the presence of Isaac his father, then came Esau his brother from his hunting, **31** And he also prepared savory meat, and brought it to his father, and said unto his father, Let my father arise, and eat of his son's venison, that thy soul may bless me. **32** But his father Isaac said unto him, Who art thou? And he answered, I am thy son, even thy firstborn Esau. **33** Then Isaac was [l]stricken with a marvelous great fear, and said, Who and where is he that hunted venison, and brought it me, and I have eaten [m]of all before thou camest? and I have blessed him, therefore he shall be blessed. **34** When Esau heard the words of his father, he cried out with a great cry and bitter, out of measure, and said unto his father, Bless me, even me also, my father. **35** Who answered, Thy brother came with subtlety, and hath taken away thy blessing. **36** Then he said, Was he not justly called [n]Jacob? for he hath deceived me these two times: he took my birthright, and lo, now hath he taken my blessing Also he said, Hast thou not reserved a blessing for me? **37** Then Isaac answered, and said unto Esau, Behold, I have made him [o]thy lord, and all his brethren have I made his servants: and with wheat and wine have I furnished him, and unto thee now what shall I do, my son? **38** Then

---

c. Gen. 26:5 He commendeth Abraham's obedience, because Isaac should be the more ready to follow the like: for as God made this promise of his free mercy, so doth the confirmation thereof proceed of the same fountain.
d. Gen. 26:5 Hebrew, my keeping.
e. Gen. 26:7 Whereby we see that fear and distrust is found in the most faithful.
f. Gen. 26:8 Or showing some familiar sign of love, whereby it might be known that she was his wife.
g. Gen. 26:10 In all ages men were persuaded that God's vengeance should light upon wedlock breakers.
h. Gen. 26:12 Or, an hundred measures.
i. Gen. 26:13 Hebrew, he went forth going and increasing.
j. Gen. 26:14 The malicious envy always the graces of God in others.
k. Gen. 26:17 The Hebrew word signifieth a flood, or valley, where water at any time runneth.
l. Gen. 26:19 Or, springing.
m. Gen. 26:20 Or, contention, strife.
n. Gen. 26:21 Or, hatred.
o. Gen. 26:22 Or, largeness, room.
p. Gen. 26:24 God assureth Isaac against all fear by rehearsing the promise made to Abraham.
q. Gen. 26:25 To signify that he would serve none other God, but the God of his father Abraham.
r. Gen. 26:29 The Hebrews in swearing begin commonly with If, and understand the rest, that is, that God shall punish him that breaketh the oath: here the wicked show that they are afraid lest that come to them which they would do to others.
s. Gen. 26:33 Or, oath.
t. Gen. 26:33 Or, the well of the oath.
u. Gen. 26:35 Or, disobedient and rebellious.

GEN. 26

1. Gen. 13:15 - Gen. 15:18
2. Gen. 12:3 - Gen. 15:18 - Gen. 18:18 - Gen. 22:18 - Gen. 28:14
3. Gen. 27:46

GEN. 27

a. Gen. 27:1 Hebrew, Lo, I.
b. Gen. 27:3 Hebrew, hunt.
c. Gen. 27:4 The carnal affection, which he bare to his son made him forget that which God spake to his wife, Gen. 25:23.
d. Gen. 27:9 This subtlety is blameworthy because she should have tarried till God had performed his promise.
e. Gen. 27:12 Hebrew, before his eyes.
f. Gen. 27:12 Or, as though I would deceive him.
g. Gen. 27:13 Or, I will take the danger on me.
h. Gen. 27:13 The assurance of God's decree made her bold.
i. Gen. 27:19 Although Jacob was assured of this blessing by faith: yet he did evil to seek it by lies, and the more because he abuseth God's name thereunto.
j. Gen. 27:22 This declareth that he suspected something, yet God would not have his decree altered.
k. Gen. 27:24 Hebrew, I am.
l. Gen. 27:33 In perceiving his error, by appointing his heir against God's sentence pronounced before.
m. Gen. 27:33 Or, sufficiently.
n. Gen. 27:36 In Gen. 25, he was so called because he held his brother by the heel, as though he would overthrow him: and therefore he is here called an overthrower, or deceiver.
o. Gen. 27:37 For Isaac did this as he was the minister and Prophet of God.
p. Gen. 27:38 Or, I am also (thy son).
q. Gen. 27:40 Because thine enemies shall be round about thee.

Esau said unto his father, Hast thou but one blessing, my father? bless me, [p]even
me, also my father: and Esau lifted up his voice, and [2]wept. **39** Then Isaac his
father answered, and said unto him, Behold, the fatness of the earth shall be thy
dwelling place, and thou shalt have of the dew of heaven from above. **40** And
[q]by thy word shalt thou live, and shalt be thy brother's [r]servant But it shall come
to pass, when thou shalt get the mastery, that thou shalt break his yoke from thy
neck. **41** Therefore Esau hated Jacob, because of the blessing, wherewith his fa-
ther blessed him And Esau thought in his mind, [3]The days of mourning for my
father will come shortly, [s]then I will slay my brother Jacob. **42** And it was told
to Rebekah of the words of Esau her elder son, and she sent and called Jacob her
younger son, and said unto him, Behold, thy brother Esau [t]is comforted against
thee, meaning to kill thee: **43** Now therefore my son, hear my voice: arise, and
flee thou to Haran to my brother Laban, **44** And tarry with him a while until
thy brother's fierceness be swaged, **45** And till thy brother's wrath turn away
from thee, and he forget the things, which thou hast done to him: then will I
send and take thee from thence: why should I be [u]deprived of you both in one
day? **46** Also Rebekah said to Isaac, [4]I am weary of my life, for the daughters of
Heth If Jacob take a wife of the [v]daughters of Heth like these of the daughters of
the land, [w]what availeth it me to live?

28

1 Isaac forbiddeth Jacob to take a wife of the Canaanites. 6 Esau taketh a wife of the daughters of Ishmael against his father's will. 12 Jacob in the way to Haran seeth a ladder reaching to heaven. 14 Christ is promised.

1 Then Isaac called Jacob and [a]blessed him, and charged him, and said unto
him, take not a wife of the daughters of Canaan. **2** Arise, [1]get thee to [2]Padan
Aram to the house of Bethuel thy mother's father, and thence take thee a wife of the
daughters of Laban thy mother's brother. **3** And God all [b]sufficient bless thee,
and make thee to increase, and multiply thee, that thou mayest be a multitude of
people, **4** And give thee the blessing of Abraham, even to thee and to thy seed
with thee, that thou mayest inherit the land (wherein thou art a [c]stranger,) which
God gave unto Abraham. **5** Thus Isaac sent forth Jacob, and he went to Padan
Aram unto Laban son of Bethuel the Aramite, brother to Rebekah, Jacob's and
Esau's mother. **6** When Esau saw that Isaac had blessed Jacob, and sent him to
Padan Aram, to fetch him a wife thence, and given him a charge when he blessed
him, saying, Thou shalt not take a wife of the daughters of Canaan, **7** And that
Jacob had obeyed his father and his mother, and was gone to Padan Aram: **8** Also
Esau seeing that the daughters of Canaan displeased Isaac his father, **9** Then
went Esau to Ishmael, and took [d]unto the wives which he had, Mahalath the dau-
ghter of [e]Ishmael Abraham's son, the sister of Nebajoth, to be his wife. **10** Now
Jacob departed from Beersheba, and went to Haran, **11** And he came unto a
certain place, and tarried there all night because the sun was down, and took of the
stones of the place, and laid under his head and slept in the same place. **12** Then
he dreamed, and behold, there stood a [f]ladder upon the earth, and the top of it re-
ached up to heaven: and lo, the Angels of God went up and down by it. **13** [3]And
behold, the Lord stood above it, and said, I am the Lord God of Abraham thy fa-
ther, and the God of Isaac: the land, upon the which thou sleepest, [g]will I give thee
and thy seed. **14** And thy seed shall be as the dust of the earth, and thou shalt
spread abroad [4]to the West, and to the East, and to the North, and to the South,
and in thee and in thy seed shall all the [5]families of the earth be blessed. **15** And
lo, I am with thee, and will keep thee whithersoever thou goest, and will bring thee
again into this land: for I will not forsake thee until I have performed that, that I
have promised thee. **16** Then Jacob awoke out of his sleep and said, Surely the
Lord is in this place, and I was not aware. **17** And he was [h]afraid, and said, How
fearful is this place! this is none other but the house of God, and this is the gate of
heaven. **18** Then Jacob rose up early in the morning, and took the stone that he
had laid under his head, and [i]set it up as [6]a pillar, and poured oil upon the top of
it. **19** And he called the name of that place [j]Bethel: notwithstanding the name
of that city was at the first called Luz. **20** Then Jacob vowed a vow, saying, If
[k]God will be with me, and will keep me in this journey which I go, and will give
me bread to eat, and clothes to put on: **21** So that I come again unto my father's
house in safety, then shall the Lord be my God. **22** And this stone, which I have
set up as a pillar, shall be God's house: and of all that thou shalt give me, will I give
the tenth unto thee.

29

13 Jacob cometh to Laban and serveth seven years for Rachel. 23 Leah brought to his bed instead of Rachel. 27 He serveth seven years more for Rachel. 31 Leah conceiveth and beareth four sons.

1 Then Jacob [a]lift up his feet and came into the [b]East country. **2** And as he
looked about, behold, there was a well in the field, [c]and lo, three flocks of sheep
lay thereby (for at that well were the flocks watered) and there was a great stone
upon the well's mouth. **3** And thither were all the flocks gathered, and they rol-
led the stone from the well's mouth, and watered the sheep, and put the stone again
upon the well's mouth in his place. **4** And Jacob said unto them, My [d]brethren,
whence be ye? And they answered, We are of Haran. **5** Then he said unto them,
Know ye Laban the son of Nahor? Who said, We know him. **6** Again he said
unto them, [e]Is he in good health? And they answered, He is in good health, and
behold, his daughter Rachel cometh with the sheep. **7** Then he said, Lo, it is
yet high day, neither is it time that the cattle should be gathered together: water
ye the sheep and go feed them. **8** But they said, We may not, until all the flocks
be brought together, and till men roll the stone from the well's mouth, that we
may water the sheep. **9** While he talked with them, Rachel also came with her
father's sheep, for she kept them. **10** And as soon as Jacob saw Rachel the dau-
ghter of Laban his mother's brother, and the sheep of Laban his mother's brother,
then came Jacob near, and rolled the stone from the well's mouth, and watered the
flock of Laban his mother's brother. **11** And Jacob kissed Rachel, and lifted up
his voice and wept. **12** (For Jacob told Rachel, that he was her father's [f]brother,
and that he was Rebekah's son) then she ran and told her father. **13** And when
Laban heard tell of Jacob his sister's son, he ran to meet him, and embraced him
and kissed him, and brought him to his house: and he told Laban [g]all these thin-
gs. **14** To whom Laban said, Well, thou art my [h]bone and my flesh, and he abo-
de with him the space of a month. **15** For Laban said unto Jacob, Though thou
be my brother, shouldest thou therefore serve me for nought? tell me, what shall
be thy wages? **16** Now Laban had two daughters, the elder called Leah, and the
younger called Rachel. **17** And Leah was [i]tender eyed, but Rachel was beautiful
and fair. **18** And Jacob loved Rachel, and said, I will serve thee seven years for
Rachel thy younger daughter. **19** Then Laban answered, It is better that I give
her thee, than that I should give her to another man: abide with me. **20** And
Jacob served seven years for Rachel, and they seemed unto him but a [j]few days, be-
cause he loved her. **21** Then Jacob said to Laban, Give me my wife, that I may go
in to her: for my [k]term is ended. **22** Wherefore Laban gathered together all the
men of the place, and made a feast. **23** But [l]when the evening was come, he took
Leah his daughter, and brought her to him, and he went in unto her. **24** And
Laban gave his maid Zilpah to his daughter Leah, to be her servant. **25** But
when the morning was come, behold, it was Leah Then said he to Laban, Whe-
refore hast thou done thus to me? did not I serve thee for Rachel? wherefore then
hast thou beguiled me? **26** And Laban answered, It is not the [m]manner of this
place, to give the younger before the elder. **27** Fulfill seven years for her, and we
will also give thee this for the service, which thou shalt serve me yet seven years
more. **28** Then Jacob did so, and fulfilled her seven years, so he gave him Rachel
his daughter to be his wife. **29** Laban also gave to Rachel his daughter, Bilhah his
maid to be her servant. **30** So entered he in to Rachel also, and loved also Rachel
more than Leah, and served him yet seven years more. **31** When the Lord saw
that Leah was despised, he [n]made her [o]fruitful: but Rachel was barren. **32** And
Leah conceived and bare a son, and she called his name Reuben: for she said,

---

r. Gen. 27:40 Which was fulfilled in his posterity the Idumeans: who were tributaries for a time to Israel, and after came to liberty.
s. Gen. 27:41 Hypocrites only abstain from doing evil for fear of men.
t. Gen. 27:42 He hath good hope to recover his birthright by killing thee.
u. Gen. 27:45 For the wicked son will kill the godly: and the plague of God will afterward light on the wicked son.
v. Gen. 27:46 Which were Esau's wives.
w. Gen. 27:46 Hereby she persuaded Isaac to agree to Jacob's departing.

GEN. 27

1. Heb. 11:20
2. Heb. 11:17
3. Oboad. 10
4. Gen. 26:35

GEN. 28

a. Gen. 28:1 This second blessing was to confirm Jacob's faith, lest he should think that his father had given it without God's motion.
b. Gen. 28:3 Or, almighty.
c. Gen. 28:4 The godly fathers were put in mind continually, that they were but strangers in this world: to the intent they should lift up their eyes to the heavens where they should have a sure dwelling.
d. Gen. 28:9 Or, beside his wives.
e. Gen. 28:9 Thinking hereby to have reconciled himself to his father, but all in vain: for he taketh not away the cause of the evil.
f. Gen. 28:12 Christ is the ladder whereby God and man are joined together, and by whom the Angels minister unto us: all graces by him are given unto us, and we by him ascend into heaven.
g. Gen. 28:13 He felt the force of this promise only by faith: for all his lifetime he was but a stranger in this land.
h. Gen. 28:17 He was touched with a godly fear and reverence.
i. Gen. 28:18 To be a remembrance only of the vision showed unto him.
j. Gen. 28:19 Or, house of God.
k. Gen. 28:20 He bindeth not God under this condition, but acknowledgeth his infirmity, and promiseth to be thankful.

GEN. 28

1. Hos. 12:12
2. Gen. 24:10
3. Gen. 35:1 - Gen. 48:3
4. Deut. 12:20 - Deut. 19:14
5. Gen. 12:8 - Gen. 18:18 - Gen. 22:18 - Gen. 26:4
6. Gen. 31:13

GEN. 29

a. Gen. 29:1 That is, he went forth on his journey.
b. Gen. 29:1 Hebrew, to the land of the children of the East.
c. Gen. 29:2 Thus he was directed by the only providence of God, who brought him also to Laban's house.
d. Gen. 29:4 It seemeth that in those days the custom was to call even strangers, brethren.
e. Gen. 29:6 Or, he is in peace? by the which word the Hebrews signify all prosperity.
f. Gen. 29:12 Or, nephew.
g. Gen. 29:13 That is, the cause why he departed from his father's house, and what he saw in the way.
h. Gen. 29:14 That is, of my blood and kindred.
i. Gen. 29:17 Or, blear-eyed.
j. Gen. 29:20 Meaning, after that the years were accomplished.
k. Gen. 29:21 Hebrew, my days are full.
l. Gen. 29:23 The cause why Jacob was deceived was, that in old time the wife was covered with a veil, when she was brought to her husband in sign of chastity and shamefastness.
m. Gen. 29:26 He esteemed more the profit that he had of Jacob's service, than either his promise of the manner of the country, though he alleged custom for his excuse.
n. Gen. 29:31 Hebrew, opened her womb.

Because the [p]Lord hath looked upon my tribulation, now therefore mine husband will [q]love me. **33** And she conceived again and bare a son, and said, Because the Lord heard that I was hated, he hath therefore given me this son also, and she called his name Simeon. **34** And she conceived again and bare a son, and said, Now at this time will my husband keep me company, because I have borne him three sons: therefore was his name called Levi. **35** Moreover she conceived again and bare a son, saying, Now will I [r]praise the Lord: [1]therefore she called his name Judah, and [s]left bearing.

30

4,9 Rachel and Leah being both barren, give their maids unto their husband, and they bare him children. 15 Leah giveth mandrakes to Rachel that Jacob might lie with her. 27 Laban is enriched for Jacob's sake. 34 Jacob is made very rich.

1 And when Rachel saw that she bare Jacob no children, Rachel envied her sister, and said unto Jacob, Give me children, or else I die. **2** Then Jacob's anger was kindled against Rachel, and he said, Am I in [a]God's stead, which hath withholden from thee the fruit of the womb? **3** And she said, Behold my maid Bilhah, go in to her, and she shall bear upon my [b]knees, and [c]I shall have children also by her. **4** Then she gave him Bilhah her maid to wife, and Jacob went in to her. **5** So Bilhah conceived and bare Jacob a son. **6** Then said Rachel, God hath given sentence on my side, and hath also heard my voice, and hath given me a son: therefore called she his name, Dan. **7** And Bilhah Rachel's maid conceived again, and bare Jacob the second son. **8** Then Rachel said, With [d]excellent wrestlings have I [e]wrestled with my sister, and have gotten the upper hand: and she called his name, Naphtali. **9** And when Leah saw that she had left bearing, she took Zilpah her maid, and gave her Jacob to wife. **10** And Zilpah Leah's maid bare Jacob a son. **11** Then said Leah, [f]A company cometh: and she called his name, Gad. **12** Again Zilpah Leah's maid bare Jacob another son. **13** Then said Leah, Ah, blessed am I, for the daughters will bless me, and she called his name Asher. **14** Now Reuben went in the days of the wheat harvest, and found [g]mandrakes in the field, and brought them unto his mother Leah Then said Rachel to Leah, Give me, I pray thee, of thy son's mandrakes. **15** But she answered her, Is it a small matter for thee to take mine husband, except thou take my son's mandrakes also? Then said Rachel, Therefore he shall sleep with thee this night for thy son's mandrakes. **16** And Jacob came from the field in the evening, and Leah went out to meet him, and said, Come in to me, for I have [h]bought and paid for thee with my son's mandrakes: and he slept with her that night. **17** And God heard Leah and she conceived, and bare unto Jacob the fifth son. **18** Then said Leah, God hath given me my reward, because I gave my [i]maid to my husband, and she called his name Issachar. **19** After, Leah conceived again, and bare Jacob the sixth son. **20** Then Leah said, God hath endowed me with a good dowry: now will mine husband dwell with me, because I have borne him six sons: and she called his name Zebulun. **21** After that, she bare a daughter, and she called her name Dinah. **22** And God remembered Rachel, and God heard her, [j]and opened her womb. **23** So she conceived and bare a son, and said, God hath taken away my [k]rebuke. **24** And she called his name Joseph, saying, The Lord will give me yet another son. **25** And as soon as Rachel had borne Joseph, Jacob said to Laban, Send me away that I may go unto my place and to my country. **26** Give me my wives and my children, for whom I have served thee, and let me go: for thou knowest what service I have done thee. **27** To whom Laban answered, If I have now found favor in thy sight, tarry: I have [l]perceived that the Lord hath blessed me for thy sake. **28** Also he said, Appoint unto me thy wages, and I will give it thee. **29** But he said unto him, Thou knowest, what service I have done thee, and in what taking thy cattle hath been [m]under me. **30** For the little, that thou haddest before I came, is increased into a multitude: and the Lord hath blessed thee [n]by my coming: but now when shall [o]I travail for mine own house also? **31** Then he said, What shall I give thee? And Jacob answered, Thou shalt give me nothing at all: if thou wilt do this thing for me, I will return, feed, and keep thy sheep. **32** I will pass through all thy flocks this day, and [p]separate from them all the sheep with little spots and great spots, and all [q]black lambs among the sheep, and the great spotted, and little spotted among the goats: [r]and it shall be my wages. **33** So shall my [s]righteousness answer for me hereafter, when it shall come for my reward before thy face, and everyone that hath not little or great spots among the goats, and black among the sheep, the same shall be [t]theft with me. **34** Then Laban said, Go to, would God it might be according to thy saying. **35** Therefore [u]he took out the same day the he goats that were parti-colored and with great spots, and all the she goats with little and great spots, and all that had white in them, and all the [v]black among the sheep, and put them in the keeping of his sons. **36** And he set three days journey between himself and Jacob And Jacob kept the rest of Laban's sheep. **37** Then Jacob [w]took rods of green poplar, and of hazel, and of the chestnut tree, and pilled white strakes in them, and made the white appear in the rods. **38** Then he put the rods, which he had pilled, in the gutters and watering troughs, when the sheep came to drink, before the sheep: (for they were in heat, when they came to drink.) **39** And the sheep [x]were in heat before the rods, and afterward brought forth young of parti-color, and with small and great spots. **40** And Jacob parted these lambs, and turned the faces of the flock towards those lambs parti-colored, and all manner of black, among the sheep of Laban: so he put his own flock by themselves, and put them not with Laban's flock. **41** And in every ramming time of the [y]stronger sheep, Jacob laid the rods before the eyes of the sheep in the gutters, that they might conceive before the rods. **42** But when the sheep were feeble, he put them not in: and so the feebler were Laban's, and the stronger Jacob's. **43** So the man increased exceedingly, and had many flocks, and maid servants, and men servants, and camels, and asses.

31

1 Laban's children murmur against Jacob. 3 God commandeth him to return to his country. 13, 14 The care of God for Jacob. 19 Rachel stealeth her father's idols. 23 Laban followeth Jacob. 44 The covenant between Laban and Jacob.

1 Now he heard the [a]words of Laban's sons, saying, Jacob hath taken away all that was our father's, and of our father's goods hath he gotten all this honor. **2** Also Jacob beheld the countenance of Laban, [b]that it was not towards him as in times past: **3** And the Lord had said unto Jacob, Turn again into the land of thy fathers, and to thy kindred, and I will be with thee. **4** Therefore Jacob sent and called Rachel and Leah to the field unto his flock. **5** Then said he unto them, I see your father's countenance, that it is not towards me [c]as it was wont, and the [d]God of my father hath been with me. **6** And ye know that I have served your father with all my might, **7** But your father hath deceived me, and changed my wages [e]ten times: but God suffered him not to hurt me. **8** If he thus said, The spotted shall be thy wages, then all the sheep bare spotted: and if he said thus, the parti-colored shall be thy reward, then bare all the sheep parti-colored. **9** Thus hath [f]God taken away your father's [g]substance, and given it me. **10** For in ramming time I lifted up mine eyes and saw in a dream, and behold, the he goats leaped upon the she goats, that were parti-colored with little and great spots spotted. **11** And the Angel of God said to me in a dream, Jacob And I answered, Lo, I am here. **12** And he said, Lift up now thine eyes, and see all the he goats leaping upon the she goats that are parti-colored, spotted with little and great spots: for I have seen all that Laban doeth unto thee. **13** [h]I am the God of Bethel, where thou [1]anointedst the pillar, where thou vowedst a vow unto me Now arise, get thee out of this country and return unto the land where thou wast born. **14** Then answered Rachel and Leah, and said unto him, Have we any more portion and inheritance in our father's house? **15** Doth not he count us as strangers? for he hath [i]sold us, and hath eaten up and consumed our money. **16** Therefore all the riches, which God hath taken from our father, is ours and our children's: now then whatsoever God hath said unto thee, do it. **17** Then Jacob rose up, and set his sons and his wives

---

o. Gen. 29:31 This declareth that oft times they which are despised of men, are favored of God.
p. Gen. 29:32 Hereby appeareth, that she had recourse to God in her affliction.
q. Gen. 29:32 For children are a great cause of mutual love between man and wife.
r. Gen. 29:35 Or, confess.
s. Gen. 29:35 Hebrew, stood from bearing.

GEN. 29
1. Matt. 1:2

GEN. 30
a. Gen. 30:2 It is only God that maketh barren and fruitful, and therefore I am not in fault.
b. Gen. 30:3 I will receive her children on my lap, as though they were mine own.
c. Gen. 30:3 Hebrew, I shall be built.
d. Gen. 30:8 Hebrew, wrestlings of God.
e. Gen. 30:8 The arrogancy of man's nature appeareth in that she contemneth her sister, after she hath received this benefit of God to bear children.
f. Gen. 30:11 That is, God doth increase me with a multitude of children: for so Jacob doth expound this name Gad, Gen. 49:19.
g. Gen. 30:14 Which is a kind of herb whose root hath a certain likeness of the figure of a man.
h. Gen. 30:16 Hebrew, buying I have bought.
i. Gen. 30:18 Instead of acknowledging her fault, she boasteth as if God had rewarded her therefore.
j. Gen. 30:22 Or, made her fruitful.
k. Gen. 30:23 Because fruitfulness came of God's blessing, who said Increase and multiply: barrenness was counted as a curse.
l. Gen. 30:27 Or, tried by experience.
m. Gen. 30:29 Or, with me.
n. Gen. 30:30 Hebrew, at my feet.
o. Gen. 30:30 The order of nature requireth that everyone provide for his own family.
p. Gen. 30:32 Or, separate thou.
q. Gen. 30:32 Or, rid.
r. Gen. 30:32 That which shall hereafter be thus spotted.
s. Gen. 30:33 God shall testify for my righteous dealing by rewarding my labors.
t. Gen. 30:33 Or, counted theft.
u. Gen. 30:35 Or, Laban.
v. Gen. 30:35 Or, red or brown.
w. Gen. 30:37 Jacob herein used no deceit: for it was God's commandment as he declareth in Gen. 31:9, 11.
x. Gen. 30:39 Or, received.
y. Gen. 30:41 As they which took the ram about September and brought forth about March: so the feebler in March, and lamb in September.

GEN. 31
a. Gen. 31:1 The children uttered in words that which the father dissembled in heart, for the covetous think that whatsoever they cannot snatch, is plucked from them.
b. Gen. 31:2 Hebrew, and lo, not be with him, as yesterday, and ere yesterday.
c. Gen. 31:5 Hebrew, as yesterday and before yesterday.
d. Gen. 31:5 The God whom my father worshipped.
e. Gen. 31:7 Or, many times.
f. Gen. 31:9 This declareth that the thing, which Jacob did before, was by God's commandment, and not through deceit.
g. Gen. 31:9 Or, cattle.
h. Gen. 31:13 This Angel was Christ which appeared to Jacob in Bethel: and hereby appeareth he had taught his wives the fear of God: for he talketh as though they knew this thing.
i. Gen. 31:15 For they were given to Jacob in recompence of his service, which was a kind of sale.

upon camels. **18** And he carried away all his flocks, and all his substance which he had gotten, to wit, his riches, which he had gotten in Padan Aram, to go to Isaac his father unto the land of Canaan. **19** When Laban was gone to sheer his sheep, then Rachel stole her father's [j]idols. **20** Thus Jacob [k]stole away the heart of Laban the Aramite: for he told him not that he fled. **21** So fled he with all that he had, and he rose up, and passed the [l]river, and set his face toward mount Gilead. **22** And the third day after was it told Laban, that Jacob fled. **23** Then he took his [m]brethren with him and followed after him seven days journey, and [n]overtook him at mount Gilead. **24** And God came to Laban the Aramite in a dream by night, and said unto him, Take heed that thou speak not to Jacob [o]ought save good. **25** Then Laban overtook Jacob, and Jacob had pitched his tent in the mount: and Laban also with his brethren pitched upon mount Gilead. **26** Then Laban said to Jacob, What hast thou done? [p]thou hast even stolen away mine heart and carried away my daughters as though they had been taken captives with the sword. **27** Wherefore diddest thou flee so secretly and steal away from me, and diddest not tell me, that I might have sent thee forth with mirth and with songs, with timbrell and with harp? **28** But thou hast not suffered me to kiss my sons and my daughters: now thou hast done foolishly in doing so. **29** I am [q]able to do you evil: but the [r]God of your father spake unto me yesternight, saying, Take heed that thou speak not to Jacob ought save good. **30** Now though thou wentest thy way, because thou greatly longedst after thy father's house, yet wherefore hast thou stolen my gods? **31** Then Jacob answered, and said to Laban, Because I was afraid, and thought that thou wouldest have taken thy daughters from me. **32** But with whom thou findest thy gods, [s]let him not live Search thou before our brethren what I have of thine, and take it to thee, (but Jacob wist not that Rachel had stolen them.) **33** Then came Laban into Jacob's tent, and into Leah's tent, and into the two maid's tents, but found them not So he went out of Leah's tent, and entered into Rachel's tent. **34** (Now Rachel had taken the idols, and put them in the camel's [t]litter and sat down upon them) and Laban searched all the tent, but found them not. **35** Then said she to her father, [u]My Lord, be not angry that I cannot rise up before thee: for the custom of women is upon me: so he searched, but found not the idols. **36** Then Jacob was wroth, and chode with Laban: Jacob also answered and said to Laban, What have I trespassed? what have I offended, that thou hast pursued after me? **37** Seeing thou hast searched all my stuff, what hast thou found of all thine household stuff? put it here before my brethren and thy brethren, that they may judge between us both. **38** This twenty years I have been with thee: thine ewes and thy goats have not [v]cast their young, and the rams of thy flock have I not eaten. **39** [w]Whatsoever was torn of beasts, I brought it not unto thee, but made it good myself: [2]of mine hand diddest thou require it, were it stolen by day, or stolen by night. **40** I was in the day consumed with heat, and with frost in the night, and my [x]sleep departed from mine eyes. **41** Thus have I been twenty years in thine house, and served thee fourteen years for thy two daughters, and six years for thy sheep, and thou hast changed my wages ten times. **42** Except the God of my father, the God of Abraham, and the [y]fear of Isaac had been with me, surely thou haddest sent me away now empty: but God beheld my tribulation, and the labor of mine hands, and rebuked thee yesternight. **43** Then Laban answered, and said unto Jacob, These daughters are my daughters, and these sons are my sons, and these sheep are my sheep, and all that thou seest, is mine, and what can I do this day unto these my daughters, or to their sons which they have borne? **44** Now therefore [z]come let us make a covenant, I and thou, which may be a witness between me and thee. **45** Then took Jacob a stone, and set it up as a pillar: **46** And Jacob said unto his brethren, Gather stones: who brought stones, and made a heap, and they did eat there upon the heap. **47** And Laban called it [aa]Jegar Sahadutha, and Jacob called it [ab]Galeed. **48** For Laban said, This heap is witness between me and thee this day: therefore he called the name of it Galeed. **49** Also he called it [ac]Mizpah, because he said, The Lord [ad]look between me and he, when we shall be [ae]departed one from another. **50** If thou shalt vex my daughters, or shalt take [af]wives beside my daughters: there is no man with us, behold, God is witness between me and thee. **51** Moreover Laban said to Jacob, Behold this heap, and behold the pillar, which I have set between me and thee. **52** This heap shall be witness, and the pillar shall be witness, that I will not come over this heap to thee, and that thou shalt not pass over this heap and this pillar unto me for evil. **53** The God of Abraham, and the God of [ag]Nahor, and the God of their father be judge between us: but Jacob sware by the [ah]fear of his father Isaac. **54** Then Jacob did offer a sacrifice upon the mount, and called his brethren to eat [ai]bread, and they did eat bread, and tarried all night in the mount. **55** And early in the morning Laban rose up and kissed his sons, and his daughters, and [aj]blessed them, and Laban departing, went unto his place again.

32

1 God comforteth Jacob by his Angels. 9, 10 He prayeth unto God confessing his unworthiness. 13 He sendeth presents unto Esau. 24, 28 He wrestled with the Angel who nameth him Israel.

1 Now Jacob went forth on his journey, and [1]the Angels of God met him. **2** And when Jacob saw them, he said, [a]This is God's host: and he called the name of the same place [b]Mahanaim. **3** Then Jacob sent messengers before him to Esau his brother, unto the land of Seir into the country of Edom. **4** To whom he gave commandment, saying, Thus shall ye speak to my [c]lord Esau: thy servant Jacob saith thus, I have been a stranger with Laban, and tarried unto this time. **5** I have beeves also and asses, sheep, and men servants, and women servants, and have sent to show my lord, that I may find grace in thy sight. **6** So the messengers came again to Jacob, saying, We came unto thy brother Esau, and he also cometh against thee and four hundred men with him. **7** Then Jacob was [d]greatly afraid, and was sore troubled, and divided the people that was with him, and the sheep, and the beeves, and the camels into two companies. **8** For he said, If Esau come to the one company and smite it, the other company shall escape. **9** Moreover Jacob said, O God of my father Abraham, and God of my father Isaac, Lord, which [2]saidst unto me, Return unto thy country, and to thy kindred, and I will do thee good. **10** I am not [e]worthy of the least of all the mercies, and all the truth, which thou hast showed unto thy servant: for with my [f]staff came I over this Jordan, and now have I gotten two bands. **11** I pray thee, Deliver me from the hand of my brother, from the hand of Esau: for I fear him, lest he will come and smite me, and the [g]mother upon the children. **12** And thou saidest, I will surely do to thee good, and make thy seed as the sand of the sea, which cannot be numbered for multitude. **13** And he tarried there that same night and took of that which came to hand, a [h]present for Esau his brother: **14** Two hundred she goats, and twenty he goats, two hundred ewes and twenty rams: **15** Thirty milch camels with their colts, forty kine, and ten bullocks, twenty she asses, and ten foals. **16** So he delivered them into the hand of his servants, every drove by themselves, and said unto his servants, Pass before me, and put a space between drove and drove. **17** And he commanded the foremost, saying, If my brother Esau meet thee, and ask thee, saying, Whose servant art thou? And whither goest thou? and whose are these before thee? **18** Then thou shalt say, They be thy servant Jacob's: it is a present sent unto my lord Esau: and behold, he himself also is behind us. **19** So likewise commanded he the second and the third, and all that followed the droves, saying, After this manner, ye shall speak unto Esau, when ye find him. **20** And ye shall say moreover, Behold, thy servant Jacob cometh after us (for he thought, I [i]will appease his wrath with the present that goeth before me, and afterward I will see his face: it may be that he will [j]accept me.) **21** So went the present before him: but he tarried that night with the company. **22** And he rose up the same night, and took his two wives, and his two maids, and his eleven children, and went over the ford Jabbok. **23** And he took them, and sent them over the river, and sent over that he had. **24** Now when Jacob was left himself alone, there wrestled a [k]man with him unto the breaking of the day. **25** And he saw that he could not [l]prevail against him: therefore he touched the hollow of his thigh, and the hollow of Jacob's thigh was loosed, as he wrestled with him. **26** And he said, Let me go, for the morning appeareth Who answered, I [3]will not let thee go, except thou bless me. **27** Then said he unto him, What is thy name? And he said, Jacob. **28** And said he, [4]Thy name shall be called Jacob no more, but Israel: because thou hast had [m]power with God, thou shalt also prevail with men. **29** And Jacob demanded, saying, Tell me, I pray thee, thy name And he said, Wherefore now dost

---

j. Gen. 31:19 For so the word here signifieth, because Laban calleth them gods, verse 30.
k. Gen. 31:20 Or, went away privily from Laban.
l. Gen. 31:21 Or, Euphrates.
m. Gen. 31:23 Or, kinsfolks and friends.
n. Gen. 31:23 Or, joined with him.
o. Gen. 31:24 Hebrew, from good to evil.
p. Gen. 31:26 Or, conveyed thyself away privily.
q. Gen. 31:29 Hebrew, power is in mine hand.
r. Gen. 31:29 He was an Idolater, and therefore would not acknowledge the God of Jacob for his God.
s. Gen. 31:32 Or, let him die.
t. Gen. 31:34 Or, straw, or saddle.
u. Gen. 31:35 Hebrew, let not anger be in the eyes of my Lord.
v. Gen. 31:38 Or, been barren.
w. Gen. 31:39 Hebrew, the torn, or taken by prey.
x. Gen. 31:40 Or, I slept not.
y. Gen. 31:42 That is, the God whom Isaac did fear, and reverence.
z. Gen. 31:44 His conscience reproved him of his misbehavior toward Jacob, and therefore moved him to seek peace.
aa. Gen. 31:47 Or, the heap of witness.
ab. Gen. 31:47 The one named the place in the Syrian tongue, and the other in the Hebrew tongue.
ac. Gen. 31:49 Or, watch tower.
ad. Gen. 31:49 To punish the trespasser.
ae. Gen. 31:49 Or, hid.
af. Gen. 31:50 Nature compelleth him to condemn that vice, whereunto through covetousness he forced Jacob.
ag. Gen. 31:53 Behold, how the idolaters mingle the true God with their feigned gods.
ah. Gen. 31:53 Meaning, by the true God whom Isaac worshipped.
ai. Gen. 31:54 Or, meat.
aj. Gen. 31:55 We see that there is ever some seed of the knowledge of God in the hearts of the wicked.

GEN. 31

1. Gen. 28:18
2. Exod. 22:12

GEN. 32

a. Gen. 32:2 He acknowledgeth God's benefits: who for the preservation of his, sendeth hosts of Angels.
b. Gen. 32:2 Or, tents.
c. Gen. 32:4 He reverenced his brother in worldly things, because he chiefly looked to be preferred to the spiritual promise.
d. Gen. 32:7 Albeit he was comforted by the Angels, yet the infirmity of the flesh doth appear.
e. Gen. 32:10 Hebrew, I am less than all thy mercies.
f. Gen. 32:10 That is, poor and without all provision.
g. Gen. 32:11 Meaning, he will put all to death. This proverb cometh of them which kill the bird together with his young ones.
h. Gen. 32:13 Not distrusting God's assistance, but using such means as God had given him.
i. Gen. 32:20 He thought it no loss to depart with these goods, to the intent he might follow the vocation whereunto God called him.
j. Gen. 32:20 Hebrew, receive my face.
k. Gen. 32:24 That is, God in form of man.
l. Gen. 32:25 For God assaileth his with the one hand, and upholdeth them with the other.
m. Gen. 32:28 God gave Jacob both power to overcome, and also the praise of the victory.

thou ask my name? and he blessed him there. **30** And Jacob called the name of the place, Peniel: for, said he, I have seen God face to face, and [n]my life is preserved. **31** And the sun rose up to him as he passed Peniel, and he [o]halted upon his thigh. **32** Therefore the children of Israel eat not of the sinew which shrank in the hollow of the thigh, unto this day: because he touched the sinew that shrank in the hollow of Jacob's thigh.

33

4 Esau and Jacob meet and are agreed. 11 Esau receiveth his gifts. 19 Jacob buyeth a possession, 20 And buildeth an altar.

1 And as Jacob lifted up his eyes, and looked, behold, Esau came, and with him four hundred men: and he [a]divided the children to Leah, and unto Rachel, and to the two maids. **2** And he put the maids, and their children foremost, and Leah, and her children after, and Rachel and Joseph hindermost. **3** So he went before them and [b]bowed himself to the ground seven times, until he came near to his brother. **4** And Esau ran to meet him, and embraced him, and fell on his neck, and kissed him, and they wept. **5** And he lifted up his eyes, and saw the women, and the children, and said, Who are these with thee? And he answered, They are the children whom God of his grace hath given thy servant. **6** Then came the maids near, they and their children, and [c]bowed themselves. **7** Leah also with her children came near and made obeisance: and after Joseph and Rachel drew near, and did reverence. **8** Then he said, What meanest thou by all this drove, which I met? Who answered, I have sent it, that I may find favor in the sight of my lord. **9** And Esau said, I have enough, my brother: keep that thou hast to thyself. **10** But Jacob answered, Nay, I pray thee, if I have found grace now in thy sight, then receive my present at my hand: for [d]I have seen thy face, as though I had seen the face of God, because thou hast accepted me. **11** I pray thee take my [e]blessing, that is brought thee: for God hath had mercy on me, and therefore I have all things: for he [f]compelled him, and he took it. **12** And he said, Let us take our journey and go, and I will go before thee. **13** Then he answered him, My lord knoweth, that the children are tender, and the ewes and kine with young under mine hand: and if they should overdrive them one day, all the flock would die. **14** Let now my lord go before his servant, and I will drive softly, according to the pace of the cattle, which is before me, and as the children be able to endure, until [g]I come to my lord unto Seir. **15** Then Esau said, I will leave then some of my folk with thee And he answered, What needeth this? let me find grace in the sight of my lord. **16** So Esau returned, and went his way that same day unto Seir. **17** And Jacob went forward toward Succoth, and built him an house, and made booths for his cattle: therefore he called the name of the place [h]Succoth. **18** Afterward, Jacob came safe to Shechem a city, which is in the land of Canaan, when he came from [i]Padan Aram, and pitched before the city. **19** And there he bought a parcel of ground, where he pitched his tent, at the hand of the sons of Hamor Shechem's father, for an hundred [j]pieces of money. **20** And he set up there an altar, and called [k]it, The mighty God of Israel.

34

1 Dinah is ravished. 8 Hamor asketh her in marriage for his son. 22 The Shechemites are circumcised at the request of Jacob's sons and the persuasion of Hamor. 25 The whoredome is revenged.

1 Then Dinah the daughter of Leah, which she bare unto Jacob, [a]went out to see the daughters of that country. **2** Whom when Shechem the son of Hamor the Hivite lord of that country saw, he took her, and lay with her, and [b]defiled her. **3** So his heart clave unto Dinah the daughter of Jacob: and he loved the maid, and [c]spake kindly to the maid. **4** Then said Shechem to his father Hamor, saying, [d]Get me this maid to wife. **5** (Now Jacob heard that he had defiled Dinah his daughter, and his sons were with his cattle in the field: therefore Jacob held his peace, until they were come.) **6** Then Hamor the father of Shechem went out unto Jacob to commune with him. **7** And when the sons of Jacob were come out of the field and heard it, it grieved the men, and they were very angry, because he had wrought [e]villany in Israel, in that he had lain with Jacob's daughter: [f]which thing ought not to be done. **8** And Hamor communed with them, saying, The soul of my son: Shechem longeth for your daughter, [g]give her him to wife, I pray you. **9** So make affinity with us, give your daughters unto us, and take our daughters unto you. **10** And ye shall dwell with us, and the land shall be before you, dwell, and do your business in it, and have your possessions therein. **11** Shechem also said unto her father and unto her brethren, [h]Let me find favor in your eyes, and I will give whatsoever ye shall appoint me. **12** [i]Ask of me abundantly both dowry, and gifts, and I will give as ye appoint me, so that ye give me the maid to wife. **13** Then the sons of Jacob answered, Shechem and Hamor his father, talking deceitfully, because he had defiled their sister: **14** And they said unto them, [j]We cannot do this thing, to give our sister to an uncircumcised man: for that were a [k]reproof unto us. **15** But in this we will consent unto you, if ye will be as we are, that every man child among you be [l]circumcised, **16** Then will we give our daughters to you, and we will take your daughters to us, and will dwell with you, and be one people. **17** But if ye will not hearken unto us to be circumcised, then will we take our daughter and depart. **18** Now their words pleased Hamor, and Shechem Hamor's son. **19** And the young man deferred not to do the thing because he loved Jacob's daughter: he was also the [m]most set by of all his father's house. **20** Then Hamor and Shechem his Son went unto the [n]gate of their city, and communed with the men of their city, saying, **21** These men are [o]peaceable with us: and that they may dwell in the land, and do their affairs therein (for behold, the land hath room enough for them) let us take their daughters to wives, and give them our daughters. **22** Only herein will the men consent unto us for to dwell with us, and to be one people, if all the men children among us be circumcised as they are circumcised. **23** Shall not [p]their flocks and their substance and all their cattle be ours? only let us consent herein unto them and they will dwell with us. **24** And unto Hamor, and Shechem his son hearkened all that went out of the gate of his city: and all the men children were circumcised, even all that went out of the gate of his city. **25** And on the third day (when they were sore) two of the sons of Jacob, [q]Simeon and Levi, Dinah's brethren took either of them his sword and went into the city boldly, and [1]slew [r]every male. **26** They slew also Hamor and Shechem his son with the [s]edge of the sword, and took Dinah out of Shechem's house, and went their way. **27** Again, the other sons of Jacob came upon the dead, and spoiled the city, because they had defiled their sister. **28** They took their sheep and their beeves, and their asses, and whatsoever was in the city and in the fields. **29** Also they carried away captive and spoiled all their goods, and all their children and their wives, and all that was in the houses. **30** Then Jacob said to Simeon and Levi, Ye have troubled me, and made me [t]stink among the inhabitants of the land, as well the Canaanites, as the Perizzites, and I being few in number, they shall gather themselves together against me, and slay me, and so shall I, and my house be destroyed. **31** And they answered, Should he abuse our sister as a whore?

35

1 Jacob at God's commandment goeth up to Bethel built an altar. 2 He reformeth his household. 5 God maketh the enemies of Jacob afraid. 8 Deborah dieth. 12 The land of Canaan is promised him. 18 Rachel dieth in labor. 22 Reuben lieth with his father's concubine.

1 Then [a]God said to Jacob, Arise, go up to Bethel and dwell there, and make there an altar unto God, that appeared unto thee, [1]when thou fleddest from Esau thy brother. **2** Then said Jacob unto his household and to all that were with him, Put away the strange gods that are among you, and [b]cleanse yourselves, and change your garments: **3** For we will rise and go up to Bethel, and I will make an altar there unto God, which heard me in the day of my tribulation, and was with me in the way which I went. **4** And they gave unto Jacob all the strange gods, which were in their hands, and all their [c]earrings which were in their ears, and Jacob

---

n. Gen. 32:30 Or, my soul is delivered.
o. Gen. 32:31 The faithful to overcome their tentations, that they feel the smart thereof, to the intent that they should not glory, but in their humility.

GEN. 32
1. Gen. 48:16
2. Gen. 31:13
3. Hos. 12:4
4. Gen. 35:10

GEN. 33
a. Gen. 33:1 That if the one part were assailed, the other might escape.
b. Gen. 33:3 By this gesture he partly did reverence to his brother, and partly prayed to God to mitigate Esau's wrath.
c. Gen. 33:6 Jacob and his family are the image of the Church under the yoke of tyrants which for fear are brought to subjection.
d. Gen. 33:10 In that that his brother embraced him so lovingly, contrary to his expectation, he accepted it as a plain sign of God's presence.
e. Gen. 33:11 Or, gift.
f. Gen. 33:11 By earnest entreaty.
g. Gen. 33:14 He promised that which (as seemeth) his mind was not to perform.
h. Gen. 33:17 Or, tent.
i. Gen. 33:18 Or, Mesopotamia.
j. Gen. 33:19 Or, lambs, or money so marked.
k. Gen. 33:20 He calleth the sign, the thing which it signifieth, in token that God had mightily delivered him.

GEN. 34
a. Gen. 34:1 This example teacheth us that too much liberty is not to be given to youth.
b. Gen. 34:2 Hebrew, humbled her.
c. Gen. 34:3 Hebrew, spake to the heart of the maid.
d. Gen. 34:4 This proveth that the consent of parents is requisite in marriage, seeing the very Infidels did also observe it as a thing necessary.
e. Gen. 34:7 Or, folly.
f. Gen. 34:7 Hebrew, and it shall not be so done.
g. Gen. 34:8 Or, marriage.
h. Gen. 34:11 Or, grant my request.
i. Gen. 34:12 Hebrew, multiply greatly the dowry.
j. Gen. 34:14 They made the holy ordinance of God a means to compasse their wicked purpose.
k. Gen. 34:14 As it is abomination for them that are baptized to join with Infidels.
l. Gen. 34:15 Their fault is the greater in that they make religion a cloak for their craft.
m. Gen. 34:19 Or, most honorable.
n. Gen. 34:20 For the people used to assemble there, and justice was also ministered.
o. Gen. 34:21 Thus many pretend to speak for a public profit, when they only speak for their own private gain and commodity.
p. Gen. 34:23 Thus they lack no kind of persuasion, which prefer their own commodities before the commonwealth.
q. Gen. 34:25 For they were the chief of the company.
r. Gen. 34:25 The people are punished with their wicked princes.
s. Gen. 34:26 Hebrew, mouth of the sword.
t. Gen. 34:30 Or, to be abhorred.

GEN. 34
1. Gen. 49:6

GEN. 35
a. Gen. 35:1 God is ever at hand to succor his in their troubles.
b. Gen. 35:2 That by this outward act they should show their inward repentance.
c. Gen. 35:4 For therein was some sign of superstition, as in tablets and Agnus deis.

hid them under an oak, which was by Shechem. **5** Then they went on their
journey, and the [d]fear of God was upon the cities that were round about them: so
that they did not follow after the sons of Jacob. **6** So came Jacob to Luz, which
is in the land of Canaan: (the same is Bethel) he and all the people that were with
him. **7** And he built there an altar, and [2]had called the place, The God of Bethel,
because that God appeared unto him there, when he fled from his brother. **8** But
Deborah Rebekah's nurse died, and was buried beneath Bethel under an oak: and
he called the name of it [e]Allon Bachuth. **9** Again God appeared unto Jacob,
after he came to Padan Aram, and blessed him. **10** Moreover God said unto
him, Thy name is Jacob: thy name shall be no more called Jacob, but [3]Israel shall
be thy name: and he called his name Israel. **11** And God said unto him, I am
God [f]all-sufficient: grow, and multiply: a nation and a multitude of nations shall
spring of thee, and kings shall come out of thy loins. **12** Also I will give the
land, which I gave to Abraham and Isaac, unto thee: and unto thy seed after thee
will I give that land. **13** So God [g]ascended from him in the place where he had
talked with him. **14** And Jacob set up a pillar in the place where he talked with
him, a pillar of stone, and poured drink offerings thereon: also he poured oil the-
reon. **15** And Jacob called the name of that place where God spake with him,
Bethel. **16** Then they departed from Bethel, and when there was [h]about half a
day's journey of ground to come to Ephrath, Rachel travailed, and in travailing she
was in peril. **17** And when she was in the pains of her labor, the midwife said
unto her, Fear not, for thou shalt have this son also. **18** Then as she was about to
yield up the ghost (for she died) she called his name Ben-Oni, but his father called
him Benjamin. **19** Thus [4]died Rachel and was buried in the way to Ephrath,
which is Bethlehem. **20** And Jacob set a [i]pillar upon her grave: This is the pillar
of Rachel's grave unto this day. **21** Then Israel went forward, and pitched his
tent beyond Migdal Eder. **22** Now when Israel dwelt in that land, Reuben went
and [j]lay [5]with Bilhah his father's concubine, and it came to Israel's ear And Jacob
had twelve sons. **23** The sons of Leah: Reuben Jacob's eldest son, and Simeon,
and Levi, and Judah, and Issachar, and Zebulun: **24** The sons of Rachel; Jose-
ph, and Benjamin: **25** And the sons of Bilhah Rachel's maid: Dan and Naphta-
li: **26** And the sons of Zilpah Leah's maid: Gad and Asher These are the sons of
Jacob, which were born him in Padan Aram. **27** Then Jacob came unto Isaac his
father unto Mamre a city of Kirjath Arbah: that is Hebron, where Abraham and
Isaac were strangers. **28** And the days of Isaac were an hundred and fourscore ye-
ars. **29** And Isaac gave up the ghost and died, and was [6]gathered unto his people,
being old and full of days: and his sons Esau and Jacob buried him.

36

2 The wives of Esau. 7 Jacob and Esau are rich. 9 The genealogy of Esau. 24 The finding of mules.

1 Now these are [a]the generations of Esau, which is Edom. **2** Esau took his
wives of the [b]daughters of Canaan: Adah the daughter of Elon an Hittite and Aho-
libamah the daughter of Anah, the daughter of Zibeon an Hivite. **3** And took
Basemath Ishmael's daughter, sister of Nebajoth. **4** And [1]Adah bare unto Esau,
Eliphaz: and Basemath bare Reuel, **5** Also Aholibamah bare Jeush, and Jaalam,
and Korah: these are the sons of Esau which were born to him in the land of Ca-
naan. **6** So Esau took his wives and his sons, and his daughters, and all the souls
of his house, and his flocks, and all his cattle, and all his substance, which he had
gotten in the land of Canaan, and [c]went into another country from his brother
Jacob. **7** For their riches were so great, that they could not dwell together, and
the land, wherein they were strangers, could not receive them because of their
flocks. **8** [2]Therefore dwelt Esau in mount Seir: this Esau is Edom. **9** So these
are the generations of Esau father of [d]Edom in mount Seir: **10** These are the
names of Esau's sons: [3]Eliphaz, the son of Adah, the wife of Esau, and Reuel the
son of Basemath, the wife of Esau. **11** And the sons of Eliphaz were Teman,
Omar, Zepho, and Gatam, and Kenaz. **12** And Timna was concubine to Eli-
phaz Esau's son, and bare unto Eliphaz, Amalek: these be the sons of Adah Esau's
wife. **13** And these are the [e]sons of Reuel: Nahath, and Zerah, Shammah, and
Mizzah: these be the sons of Basemath Esau's wife. **14** And these were the sons
of Aholibamah the daughter of Anah, [f]daughter of Zibeon Esau's wife: for she bare
unto Esau, Jeush, and Jaalam, and Korah. **15** These were [g,h]Dukes of the sons of
Esau the sons of Eliphaz, the firstborn of Esau Duke Teman, Duke Omar, Duke
Zepho, Duke Kenaz, **16** Duke Korah, Duke Gatam, and Duke Amalek: these
are the Dukes that came of Eliphaz in the land of Edom: these were the [i]sons of
Adah. **17** And these are the sons of Reuel Esau's son: Duke Nahath, Duke Zerah,
Duke Shammah, Duke Mizzah: these are the Dukes that came of Reuel in the land
of Edom: these are the [j]sons of Basemath Esau's wife. **18** Likewise these were
the sons of Aholibamah Esau's wife: Duke Jeush, Duke Jaalam, Duke Korah: these
Dukes came of Aholibamah, the daughter of Anah Esau's wife. **19** These are the
children of Esau, and these are the Dukes of them: This Esau is Edom. **20** [4]The-
se are the sons of Seir the Horite, which [k]inhabited the land before Lotan, and Sho-
bal, and Zibeon, and Anah, **21** And Dishon, and Ezer, and Dishan: these are the
Dukes of the Horites, the sons of Seir in the land of Edom. **22** And the sons of
Lotan were, Hori and Hemam, and Lotan's sister was Timna. **23** And the sons of
Shobal were these: Alvan, and Manahath, and Ebal, Shepho, and Onam. **24** And
these are the sons of Zibeon: Both Ajah, and Anah: this was Anah that found [l]mu-
les in the wilderness, as he fed his father Zibeon's asses. **25** And the children of
Anah were these: Dishon and Aholibamah, the daughter of Anah. **26** Also these
are the sons of Dishon: Hemdan, and Eshban, and Ithran, and Cheran. **27** The
sons of Ezer are these: Bilhan, and Zaavan, and Akan. **28** The sons of Dishan
are these, Uz, and Aran. **29** These are the Dukes of the Horites: Duke Lotan,
Duke Shobal, Duke Zibeon, Duke Anah, **30** Duke Dishon, Duke Ezer, Duke
Dishan: these be the Dukes of the Horites, after their Dukedoms in the land of
Seir. **31** And these are the [m]Kings that reigned in the land of Edom, before the-
re reigned any King over the children of Israel. **32** Then Bela the son of Beor
reigned in Edom, and the name of his city was Dinhabah. **33** And when Bela
died, Jobab the son of Zerah of Bozrah reigned in his stead. **34** When Jobab
also was dead, Husham of the land of Temani reigned in his stead. **35** And after
the death of Husham, Hadad the son of Bedad, which slew Midian in the field of
Moab, reigned in his stead, and the name of his city was Avith. **36** When Hadad
was dead, then Samlah of Masrekah reigned in his stead. **37** When Samlah was
dead, Saul of [n]Rehoboth by the river, reigned in his stead. **38** When Saul died,
Baal-Hanan the son of Achbor reigned in his stead. **39** And after the death of
Baal-Hanan the son of Achbor, Hadar reigned in his stead, and the name of his
city was Pau: and his wife's name Mehetabel the daughter of Matred, the [o]daughter
of Mezahab. **40** Then these are the names of the Dukes of Esau according to
their families, their places, and by their names: Duke Timnah, Duke Alvah, Duke
Jetheth. **41** Duke Aholibamah, Duke Elah, Duke Pinon, **42** Duke Kenaz,
Duke Teman, Duke Mibzar, **43** Duke Magdiel, Duke Iram: these be the Dukes
of Edom, according to their habitations, in the land of their inheritance This Esau
is the father of [p]Edom.

37

2 Joseph accuseth his brethren. 5 He dreameth and is hated of his brethren. 28 They sell him to the Ishmaelites. 34 Jacob bewaileth Joseph.

1 Jacob now dwelt in the land, wherein his father was a stranger, in the land of
Canaan. **2** These are the [a]generations of Jacob when Joseph was seventeen years
old, he kept sheep with his brethren, and the child was with the sons of Bilhah, and
with the sons of Zilpah, his father's wives, And Joseph brought unto their father
their evil [b,c]saying. **3** Now Israel loved Joseph more than all his sons, because he
begat him in his old age and he made him a coat of many [d]colors. **4** So when his
brethren saw that their father loved him more than all his brethren, then they hated
him, and could not speak peaceably unto him. **5** And Joseph [e]dreamed a dre-
am, and told his brethren, who hated him so much the more. **6** For he said unto
them, Hear, I pray you this dream which I have dreamed. **7** Behold now, we were
binding sheaves in the midst of the field: and lo, my sheaf arose and also stood upri-
ght, and behold, your sheaves compassed round about, and did reverence to my
sheaf. **8** Then his brethren said to him, What, shalt thou reign over us, and rule

---

d. Gen. 35:5 Thus, notwithstanding the inconvenience that came before, God delivered Jacob.
e. Gen. 35:8 Or, oak of lamentations.
f. Gen. 35:11 Or, almighty.
g. Gen. 35:13 As God is said to descend when he showeth some sign of his presence: so he is said to ascend when vision is ended.
h. Gen. 35:16 The Hebrew word signifieth as much ground as one may go from baite to baite, which is taken for half a day's journey.
i. Gen. 35:20 The ancient fathers used this ceremony to testify their hope of the resurrection to come, which was not generally revealed.
j. Gen. 35:22 This teacheth that the fathers were not chosen for their merits, but by God's only mercies, whose election by their faults was not changed.

GEN. 35

1. Gen. 28:13
2. Gen. 28:19
3. Gen. 32:28
4. Gen. 48:7
5. Gen. 49:4
6. Gen. 23:8

GEN. 36

a. Gen. 36:1 This genealogy declareth that Esau was blessed temporally, and that his father's blessing took place in worldly things.
b. Gen. 36:2 Besides those wives whereof is spoken, Gen. 26:34.
c. Gen. 36:6 Herein appeareth God's providence, which causeth the wicked to give place to the godly, that Jacob might enjoy Canaan according to God's promise.
d. Gen. 36:9 Or, the edomites.
e. Gen. 36:13 Or, nephews.
f. Gen. 36:14 Or, niece.
g. Gen. 36:15 Or, chief men.
h. Gen. 36:15 If God's promises be so sure towards them which are not of his household, how much more will he perform the same to us?
i. Gen. 36:16 Or, nephews.
j. Gen. 36:17 Or, nephews.
k. Gen. 36:20 Before that Esau did there inhabit.
l. Gen. 36:24 Who not contented with those kinds of beasts, which God had created, found out the monstrous generation of mules between the Ass and the mare.
m. Gen. 36:31 The wicked rise up suddenly to honor, and perish as quickly: but the inheritance of the children of God continueth ever, Ps. 102:28.
n. Gen. 36:37 Which city is by the river Euphrates.
o. Gen. 36:39 Or, niece.
p. Gen. 36:43 Of Edom came the Idumeans.

GEN. 36

1. 1Chron. 1:35
2. josh. 24:4
3. 1Chron. 1:35
4. 1Chron. 1:38

GEN. 37

a. Gen. 37:2 That is, the story of such things as came to him and his family, as Gen. 5:1.
b. Gen. 37:2 Or, slander.
c. Gen. 37:2 He complained of the evil words and injuries which they spake and did against him.
d. Gen. 37:3 Or, pieces.
e. Gen. 37:5 God revealed to him by a dream what should come to pass.
f. Gen. 37:8 The more that God showed himself favorable to his, the more doth the malice of the wicked rage against them.

us? or shalt thou have altogether dominion over us? And they [f]hated him so much the more, for his dreams, and for his words. **9** Again he dreamed another dream, and told it his brethren, and said, Behold, I have had one dream more, and behold, the Sun and the Moon and eleven stars did reverence to me. **10** Then he told it unto his father and to his brethren, and his father [g]rebuked him, and said unto him, What is this thy dream, which thou hast dreamed? shall I, and thy mother, and thy brethren come indeed and fall on the ground before thee? **11** And his brethren envied him, but his father [h,i]noted the saying. **12** Then his brethren went to keep their father's sheep in Shechem. **13** And Israel said unto Joseph, Do not thy brethren keep in Shechem? come and I will send thee to them. **14** And he answered him, I am here Then he said unto him, Go now, see whether it be well with thy brethren, and how the flocks prosper, and bring me word again: so he sent him from the vale of Hebron, and he came to Shechem. **15** Then a man found him: for lo, he was wandering in the field, and the man asked him, saying, what seekest thou? **16** And he answered, I seek my brethren: tell me, I pray thee, where they keep sheep. **17** And the man said, they are departed hence: for I heard them say, Let us go unto Dothan Then went Joseph after his brethren, and found them in Dothan. **18** And when they saw him afar off, even before he came at them, they [j]conspired against him for to slay him. **19** For they said one to another, Behold, this [k]dreamer cometh. **20** Come now therefore, and let us slay him, and cast him into some pit, and we will say, A wicked beast hath devoured him: then we shall see, what will come of his dreams. **21** [1]But when Reuben heard that, he delivered him out of their hands, and said, [l]Let us not kill him. **22** Also Reuben said unto them, Shed not blood, but cast him into this pit that is in the wilderness, and lay no hand upon him Thus he said, that he might deliver him out of their hand, and restore him to his father. **23** Now when Joseph was come unto his brethren, they stripped Joseph out of his coat, his parti-colored coat that was upon him. **24** And they took him, and cast [m]him into a pit, and the pit was empty, without water in it. **25** Then they sat them down to eat bread: and lift up their eyes and looked, and behold, there came a company of Ishmaelites from Gilead, and their camels laden with spicery, and [n]balm, and myrrh, and were going to carry it down into Egypt. **26** Then Judah said to his brethren, What availeth it, if we slay our brother, though we keep his blood secret? **27** Come and let us [2]sell him to the Ishmaelites, and let not our hands be upon him: for he is our brother, and our flesh: and his brethren obeyed. **28** Then the [o]Midianites' merchant men passed by, and they drew forth, and lift Joseph out of the pit, and sold Joseph to the Ishmaelites for twenty pieces of silver: who brought Joseph into Egypt. **29** Afterward Reuben returned to the pit, and behold, Joseph was not in the pit: then he rent his clothes, **30** And returned to his brethren, and said, The child is not yonder, and I, whither shall I go? **31** And they took Joseph's coat, and killed a kid of the goats, and dipped the coat in the blood. **32** So they sent that parti-colored coat, [p]and they brought it unto their father, and said, This have we found: see now, whether it be thy son's coat, or no. **33** Then he knew it, and said, It is my son's coat: a wicked beast hath [3]devoured him: Joseph is surely torn in pieces. **34** And Jacob rent his clothes, and put sackcloth about his loins, and sorrowed for his son a long season. **35** Then all his sons and his daughters arose up to comfort him, but he would not be comforted, but said, [q]Surely I will go down into the grave unto my son mourning: so his father wept for him. **36** And the Midianites sold him into Egypt unto Potiphar [r]an Eunuch of Pharaoh's and his [s]chief steward.

38

2 The marriage of Judah. 7, 9 The trespass of Er and Onan, and the vengeance of God that came thereupon. 18 Judah lieth with his daughter-in-law Tamar. 24 Tamar is judged to be burnt for whoredom. 29, 30 The birth of Perez and Zerah.

1 And at that time [a]Judah went down from his brethren, and turned into a man called Hirah an Adullamite. **2** And Judah saw there a daughter of a man called [1]Shua a [b]Canaanite: and he took her to wife, and went into her. **3** So she conceived and bare a son, and he called his name Er. **4** [2]And she conceived again and bare a son, and she called his name Onan. **5** Moreover she bare yet a son, whom she called Shelah: and Judah was at Chezib when she bare him. **6** Then Judah took a wife to Er his firstborn son, whose name was Tamar. **7** [3]Now Er the firstborn of Judah was wicked in the sight of the Lord: therefore the Lord slew him. **8** And Judah said to Onan, Go in unto thy brother's wife, and do the office of a kinsman unto her, and raise [c]up seed unto thy brother. **9** And Onan knew that the seed should not be his: therefore when he went in unto his brother's wife, he spilled it on the ground, lest that he should give seed to his brother. **10** And it was wicked in the eyes of the Lord, which he did: wherefore he slew him also. **11** Then Judah said to Tamar his daughter-in-law, [d]Remain a widow in thy father's house, till Shelah my son grow up (for he thought thus, Lest he die as well as his brethren,) So Tamar went and dwelt in her father's house. **12** And in process of time also the daughter of Shua Judah's wife died Then Judah, when he [e]had left mourning, went up to his sheepshearers to Timnah, he, and his neighbor Hirah the Adullamite. **13** And it was told Tamar, saying, Behold, thy father-in-law goeth up to Timnath, to shear his sheep. **14** Then she put her widow's garments off from her, and covered her with a veil, and wrapped herself, and sat down in [f]Pethah-enam which is by the way to Timnah, because she saw that Shelah was grown, and she was not given unto him to wife. **15** When Judah saw her, he judged her an whore: for she had covered her face. **16** And he turned to the way towards her, and said, Come, I pray thee, let me lie with thee, (for he [g]knew not that she was his daughter-in-law.) And she answered, What wilt thou give me for to lie with me? **17** Then said he, I will send thee a kid of the goats from the flock, and she said, Well, if thou wilt give me a pledge, till thou send it. **18** Then he said, What is the pledge that I shall give thee? And she answered, Thy signet and thy [h]cloak and thy staff that is in thine hand So he gave it her, and lay by her, and she was with child by him. **19** Then she rose, and went and put her veil from her and put on her widow's raiment. **20** Afterward Judah sent a kid of the goats by the hand of his [i]neighbor the Adullamite, for to receive his pledge from the woman's hand: but he found her not. **21** Then asked he the men of the place, saying, Where is the whore, that sat in Enaim by the wayside? and they answered, There was no whore there. **22** He came therefore to Judah again, and said, I cannot find her, and also the men of the place said, There was no whore there. **23** Then Judah said, Let her take it to her, lest we be [j,k]shamed: behold, I sent this kid, and thou hast not found her. **24** Now after three months, one told Judah, saying, Tamar thy daughter-in-law hath played the whore, and lo, with playing the whore, she is great with child Then Judah said, Bring ye her forth and let her be [l]burnt. **25** When she was brought forth, she sent to her father-in-law, saying, By the man, unto whom these things pertain, am I with child: and said also, Look I pray thee, whose these are, the seal, and the cloak, and the staff. **26** Then Judah knew them, and said, She is [m]more righteous than I: for she hath done it because I gave her not to Shelah my son So he lay with her [n]no more. **27** Now, when the time was come that she should be delivered, behold, there were twins in her womb. **28** And when she was in travail, the one put out his hand: and the midwife took and bound a red thread about his hand, saying, this is come out first. **29** But when he [o]plucked his hand back again, lo, his brother came out, and the midwife said, How hast [p]thou broken the breach upon thee? and his name was called [4]Perez. **30** And afterward came out his brother that had the red thread about his hand, and his name was called Zerah.

39

1 Joseph sold to Potiphar. 2 God prospereth him. 7 Potiphar's wife tempteth him. 13, 20 He is accused and cast in prison. 23 God showeth him favor.

1 Now Joseph was brought down into Egypt: and Potiphar [a]an Eunuch of Pharaoh's (and his chief steward an Egyptian) bought him at the hand of the Ishmaelites, which had brought him thither. **2** And the [b]Lord was with Joseph, and he was a man that prospered and was in the house of his master the Egyptian. **3** And his master saw that the Lord was with him, and that the Lord made all that he did to prosper in his hand. **4** So Joseph found favor in his sight,

---

g. Gen. 37:10 Not despising the vision, but seeking to appease his brethren.
h. Gen. 37:11 Or, kept diligently.
i. Gen. 37:11 He knew that God was author of the dream, but he understood not the meaning.
j. Gen. 37:18 The holy Ghost covereth not men's faults, as do vain writers, which make vice virtue.
k. Gen. 37:19 Or, master of dreams.
l. Gen. 37:21 Hebrew, let us not smite his life.
m. Gen. 37:24 Their hypocrisy appeareth in this that they feared man more than God: and thought it was not murder, if they shed not his blood: or else had an excuse to cover their fault.
n. Gen. 37:25 Or, rosen, turpentine, or treacle.
o. Gen. 37:28 Moses writing according to the opinion of them which took the Midianites and Ishmaelites to be both one, doth here confound their names: as also appeareth, verse 36 and Gen. 39:1, or else he was first offered to the Midianites, but sold to the Ishmaelites.
p. Gen. 37:32 To wit, the messengers which were sent.
q. Gen. 37:35 Or, I will mourn for him so long as I live.
r. Gen. 37:36 Which word doth not always signify him that is gelded, but also him that is in some high dignity.
s. Gen. 37:36 Or, captain of the guard.

GEN. 37
1. Gen. 42:22
2. Ps. 105:17
3. Gen. 44:28

GEN. 38
a. Gen. 38:1 Moses describeth the genealogy of Judah, because the Messiah should come of him.
b. Gen. 38:2 Which affinity notwithstanding was condemned of God.
c. Gen. 38:8 This order was for the preservation of the stock, that the child begotten by the second brother should have the name and inheritance of the first: which is in the new Testament abolished.
d. Gen. 38:11 For she could not marry in any other family so long as Judah would retain her in his.
e. Gen. 38:12 Hebrew, was comforted.
f. Gen. 38:14 Or, in the door of the fountain, or, where were two ways.
g. Gen. 38:16 God had wonderfully blinded him that he could not know her by her talk.
h. Gen. 38:18 Or, tyre of thine head.
i. Gen. 38:20 That his wickedness might not be known to others.
j. Gen. 38:23 Hebrew, in contempt.
k. Gen. 38:23 He feareth man more than God.
l. Gen. 38:24 We see that the Law, which was written in man's heart, taught them that whoredom should be punished with death: albeit no law, as yet was given.
m. Gen. 38:26 That is, she ought rather to accuse me than I her.
n. Gen. 38:26 For the horror of the sin condemned him.
o. Gen. 38:29 Their heinous sin was signified by this monstrous birth.
p. Gen. 38:29 Or the separation between thee and thy brother.

GEN. 38
1. 1Chron. 2:3
2. Num. 26:19
3. Num. 26:19
4. 1Chron. 2:4
5. Matt. 1:3

GEN. 39
a. Gen. 39:1 Read Gen. 37:36.
b. Gen. 39:2 The favor of God is the fountain of all prosperity.

and served him: and made him [c]ruler of his house, and put all that he had in his hand. **5** And from that time that he had made him ruler over his house and over all that he had, the Lord [d]blessed the Egyptian's house for Joseph's sake: and the blessing of the Lord was upon all that he had in the house, and in the field. **6** Therefore he left all that he had in Joseph's hand, [e]and took account of nothing, that was with him, save only of the bread, which he did eat And Joseph was a fair person, and well favored. **7** Now therefore after these things, his master's wife cast her eyes upon Joseph, and said, [f]Lie with me. **8** But he refused and said to his master's wife, Behold, my master knoweth not what he hath in the house with me, but hath committed all that he had to mine hand. **9** There is no man greater in this house than I: neither hath he kept anything from me, but only thee, because thou art his wife: how then can I do this great wickedness and so sin against [g]God? **10** And albeit she spake to Joseph day by day, yet he hearkened not unto her, to lie with her, or to be in her company. **11** Then on a certain day Joseph entered into the house to do his business: and there was no man of the household in the house. **12** Therefore she caught him by his garment, saying, Sleep with me: but he left his garment in her hand and fled, and got him out. **13** Now when she saw that he had left his garment in her hand, and was fled out, **14** She called unto the men of her house, and told them, saying, Behold, he hath brought in an Hebrew unto us [h]to mock us: who came in to me for to have slept with me: but I [i]cried with a loud voice. **15** And when he heard that I lift up my voice and cried, he left his garments with me, and fled away, and got him out. **16** So she laid up his garment by her, until her lord came home. **17** Then she told him [j]according to these words, saying, The Hebrew servant, which thou hast brought unto us, came into me, to mock me. **18** But as soon as I lift up my voice and cried, he left his garment with me, and fled out. **19** Then when his master heard the words of his wife, which she told him, saying, After this manner did thy servant to me, his anger was kindled. **20** And Joseph's master took him and put him in [k,l]prison, in the place, where the king's prisoners lay bound: and there he was in prison. **21** But the Lord was with Joseph, and [m]showed him mercy, and got him favor in the sight of the [n]master of the prison. **22** And the keeper of the prison committed to Joseph's hand all the prisoners that were in the prison, and [o]whatsoever they did there, that did he. **23** And the keeper of the prison looked unto nothing that was under his hand, seeing that the Lord was with him: for whatsoever he did, the Lord made it to prosper.

40

8 The interpretation of dreams is of God. 12, 19 Joseph expoundeth the dreams of the two prisoners. 23 The ingratitude of the butler.

1 And after these things, the butler of the King of Egypt and his baker offended their Lord the King of Egypt. **2** And Pharaoh was angry against his two [a]Officers, against the chief butler, and against the chief baker. **3** Therefore he put them in ward in his chief steward's house, in the prison and place where [b]Joseph was bound. **4** And the chief steward gave Joseph charge over them, and he served them: and they continued a season in ward. **5** And they both dreamed a dream, either of them his dream in one night, [c]each one according to the interpretation of his dream, both the butler and the baker of the King of Egypt, which were bound in the prison. **6** And when Joseph came in unto them in the morning, and looked upon them, behold, they were sad. **7** And he asked Pharaoh's officers, that were with him in his master's ward, saying, Wherefore [d]look ye so sadly today? **8** Who answered him, We have dreamed each one a dream, and there is none to interpret the same Then Joseph said unto them, [e]Are not interpretations of God? tell them me now. **9** So the chief butler told his dream to Joseph, and said unto him, In my dream, behold, a vine was before me, **10** And in the vine were three branches, and as it budded, her flower came forth: and the clusters of grapes waxed ripe. **11** And I had Pharaoh's cup in mine hand, and I took the grapes, and wrung them into Pharaoh's cup, and I gave the cup into Pharaoh's hand. **12** Then Joseph said unto him, This [f]is the interpretation of it: the three branches are three days. **13** Within three days shall Pharaoh lift up thine head, and restore thee unto thine [g]office, and thou shalt give Pharaoh's cup into his hand after the old manner, when thou wast his butler, **14** But have me in remembrance with thee, when thou art in good case, and show mercy, I pray thee unto me, and [h]make mention of me to Pharaoh, that thou mayest bring me out of this house. **15** For I was stolen away by theft out of the land of the Hebrews, and here also have I done nothing, wherefore they should put me [i]in the dungeon. **16** And when the chief baker saw that the interpretation was good, he said unto Joseph, Also me thought in my dream that I had three [j]white baskets on mine head. **17** And in the uppermost basket there was of all manner bakemeats for Pharaoh: and the birds did eat them out of the basket upon mine head. **18** Then Joseph answered, and said, [k]This is the interpretation thereof: The three baskets are three days: **19** Within three days shall Pharaoh take thine head from thee, and shall hang thee on a tree and the birds shall eat thy flesh from off thee. **20** And so the third day, which was Pharaoh's [l]birthday, he made a feast unto all his servants: and he lifted up the head of the chief butler, and the chief baker among his servants. **21** And he restored the chief butler unto his butlership, who gave the cup into Pharaoh's hand. **22** But he hanged the chief baker, as Joseph had interpreted unto them. **23** Yet the chief butler did not remember Joseph, but forgot him.

41

26 Pharaoh's dreams are expounded by Joseph. 40 He is made ruler over all Egypt. 45 Joseph's name is changed. 50 He hath two sons Manasseh and Ephraim.

1 And [a]two years after, Pharaoh also [b]dreamed, and behold, he stood by a river. **2** And lo, there came out of the river seven [c]goodly kine and fat-fleshed, and they fed in a [d]meadow. **3** And lo, seven other kine came up after them out of the river, evil favored and lean fleshed, and stood by the other kine upon the brink of the river. **4** And the evil favored and lean fleshed kine did eat up the seven well favored and fat kine: so Pharaoh awoke. **5** Again he slept, and dreamed the [e]second time: and behold, seven ears of corn grew upon one stalk, rank and goodly. **6** And lo, seven thin ears, and blasted with the East wind, sprang up after them. **7** And the thin ears devoured the seven rank and full ears, then Pharaoh awaked, and lo it was a dream. **8** Now when the morning came, his spirit was [f]troubled: therefore he sent and called all the soothsayers of Egypt, and all the wise men thereof, and Pharaoh told them his dreams: but [g]none could interpret them to Pharaoh. **9** Then spake the chief butler unto Pharaoh, saying, I [h]call to mind my faults this day. **10** Pharaoh being angry with his servants, put me in ward in the chief steward's house, both me, and the chief baker. **11** Then we dreamed a dream in one night both I, and he: we dreamed each man according to the interpretation of his dream. **12** And there was with us a young man, an Hebrew, servant unto the chief steward, whom when we told, he declared our dreams to [i]us, to everyone he declared according to his dream. **13** And as he declared unto us, so it came to pass: for he restored me to mine office, and hanged him. **14** [j]Then sent Pharaoh, and called [j]Joseph and they brought him hastily out of prison, and he shaved him, and changed his raiment, and came to Pharaoh. **15** Then Pharaoh said to Joseph, I have dreamed a dream, and no man can interpret it, and I have heard say of thee, that when thou hearest a dream, thou canst interpret it. **16** And Joseph answered Pharaoh, saying, [k]Without me God shall [l]answer for the wealth of Pharaoh. **17** And Pharaoh said unto Joseph: In my dream, behold, I stood by the bank of the river: **18** And lo, there came up out of the river seven fat fleshed, and well favored kine and they fed in the meadow. **19** Also lo, seven other kine came up after them poor and very [m]evil favored kine, and lean fleshed: I never saw the like in all the land of Egypt, for evil favored. **20** And the lean and the evil favored kine did eat up the first seven fat kine. **21** And when they [n]had eaten them up: it could not be known that they had eaten them, but they were still as evil favored, as they were at the beginning: so did I awake. **22** Moreover I saw in my dream, and behold, seven ears sprang out of one stalk, full and fair. **23** And lo, seven ears withered, thin, and blasted with the East wind, sprang up after them. **24** And the thin ears devoured the seven good ears Now

---

c. Gen. 39:4 Because God prospered him: and so he made religion to serve his profit.
d. Gen. 39:5 The wicked are blessed by the company of the godly.
e. Gen. 39:6 For he was assured that all things should prosper well: therefore he ate and drank and took no care.
f. Gen. 39:7 In this word he declareth the sum whereunto all her flatteries did tend.
g. Gen. 39:9 The fear of God preserved him against her continual tentations.
h. Gen. 39:14 Or, to do us villainy and shame.
i. Gen. 39:14 This declareth that where incontinence is, thereunto is joined extreme impudency and craft.
j. Gen. 39:17 Or, after this manner.
k. Gen. 39:20 Hebrew, in the prison house.
l. Gen. 39:20 His evil intreatment in the prison may be gathered of Ps. 105:18.
m. Gen. 39:21 Hebrew, inclined mercy unto him.
n. Gen. 39:21 Or, lord.
o. Gen. 39:22 That is, nothing was done without his commandment.

GEN. 40

a. Gen. 40:2 Or, eunuchs, the word signifieth them, that were in high estate, or them that were gelded.
b. Gen. 40:3 God worketh many wonderful means to deliver his.
c. Gen. 40:5 That is, every dream had his interpretation, as the thing afterward declared.
d. Gen. 40:7 Hebrew, why are your faces evil?
e. Gen. 40:8 Cannot God raise up such as shall interpret such things?
f. Gen. 40:12 He was assured by the spirit of God, that his interpretation was true.
g. Gen. 40:13 Hebrew, place.
h. Gen. 40:14 He refused not the means to be delivered, which he thought God had appointed.
i. Gen. 40:15 Or, in the pit.
j. Gen. 40:16 That is made of white twigs, or as some read, baskets full of holes.
k. Gen. 40:18 He showeth that the ministers of God ought not to conceal that, which God revealeth unto them.
l. Gen. 40:20 Which was an occasion to appoint his officers, and so to examine them that were in prison.

GEN. 41

a. Gen. 41:1 Hebrew, at the end of two years of days.
b. Gen. 41:1 This dream was not so much for Pharaoh, as to be a means to deliver Joseph, and to provide for God's Church.
c. Gen. 41:2 Or, fair to behold.
d. Gen. 41:2 Or, staggie place.
e. Gen. 41:5 All these means God used to deliver his servant, and to bring him into favor and authority.
f. Gen. 41:8 This fear was enough to teach him that this vision was sent of God.
g. Gen. 41:8 The wise of the world understand not God's secrets, but to his servants his will is revealed.
h. Gen. 41:9 He confesseth his fault against the king before he speak of Joseph.
i. Gen. 41:12 Read Gen. 40:5.
j. Gen. 41:14 The wicked seek to the Prophets of God in their necessity, whom in their prosperity they abhor.
k. Gen. 41:16 As though he would say, if I interpret thy dream it cometh of God, and not of me.
l. Gen. 41:16 Hebrew, answer peace.
m. Gen. 41:19 Hebrew, naught.
n. Gen. 41:21 Hebrew, were gone into their inward parts.

I have told the soothsayers, and none can declare it unto me. **25** Then Joseph
answered Pharaoh, [o]Both Pharaoh's dreams are one God hath showed Pharaoh
what he is about to do. **26** The seven good Kine are seven years, and the seven
good ears are seven years: this is one dream. **27** Likewise the seven thin and
evil favored kine, that came out after them, are seven years: and the seven empty
ears blasted with the East wind, are seven years of famine. **28** This is the thing
which I have said unto Pharaoh, that God hath showed unto Pharaoh, what he is
about to do. **29** Behold, there come seven years of great [p]plenty in all the land of
Egypt. **30** Again, there shall arise after them seven years of famine, so that all the
plenty shall be forgotten in the land of Egypt, and the famine shall consume the
land: **31** Neither shall the plenty [q]be known in the land, by reason of this famine
that shall come after, for it shall be exceeding great. **32** And therefore the dream
was doubled unto Pharaoh the second time, because the thing is established by
God, and God hasteth to perform it. **33** Now therefore let Pharaoh [r]provide for
a man of understanding and wisdom, and set him over the land of Egypt. **34** Let
Pharaoh make and appoint officers over the land, and take up the fifth part of the
land of Egypt in the seven plenteous years. **35** Also let them gather all the food
of these good years that come, and lay up corn under the hand of Pharaoh for food,
in the cities, and let them keep it. **36** So the food shall be for the provision of the
land, against the seven years of famine, which shall be in the land of Egypt, that the
land perish not by famine. **37** And the saying pleased Pharaoh and all his servan-
ts. **38** Then said Pharaoh unto his servants, Can we find such a man as this, in
whom is the [s]Spirit of God? **39** Then Pharaoh said to Joseph, Forasmuch as God
hath showed thee all this, there is no man of understanding, or wisdom like unto
thee. **40** [2]Thou shalt be over mine house, and at thy [t,u]word shall all my people
be armed, only in the king's throne will I be above thee. **41** Moreover Pharaoh
said to Joseph, Behold, I have set thee over all the land of Egypt. **42** And Pha-
raoh took off his [v]ring from his hand, and put it upon Joseph's hand, and arrayed
him in garments of fine linen, and put a golden chain about his neck. **43** So he
sat him upon the [w]best chariot that he had, save one: and they cried before him,
[x]Abrech, and placed him over all the land of Egypt. **44** Again Pharaoh said unto
Joseph, I am Pharaoh, and without thee shall no man lift up his hand or his foot
in the land of Egypt. **45** And Pharaoh called Joseph's name [y]Zaphnath-Paane-
ah: and he gave him to wife Asenath the daughter of Poti-Pherah [z]Prince of On:
then went Joseph abroad in the land of Egypt. **46** And Joseph was [aa]thirty ye-
ars old when he stood before Pharaoh King of Egypt: and Joseph departing from
the presence of Pharaoh, went throughout all the land of Egypt. **47** And in the
seven plenteous years the earth [ab]brought forth store. **48** And he gathered up
all the food of the seven plenteous years, which were in the land of Egypt, and
laid up the food in the cities: the food of the field, that was round about every
city, laid he up in the same. **49** So Joseph gathered wheat, like unto the sand
of the sea in multitude out of measure, until he left numbering: for it was wi-
thout number. **50** Now unto Joseph were born [3]two sons (before the year of
famine came) which Asenath the daughter of Poti-Pherah prince of On bare unto
him. **51** And Joseph called the name of the firstborn Manasseh: for God, said
he, hath made me forget all my labor and all my [ac]father's household. **52** Also he
called the name of the second, Ephraim: For God, said he, hath made me fruitful
in the land of my affliction. **53** So the seven years of the plenty that was in the
land of Egypt were ended. **54** [4]Then began the seven years of famine to come,
according as Joseph had said: and the famine was in all lands, but in all the land
of Egypt was [ad]bread. **55** At the length all the land of Egypt was famished, and
the people cried unto Pharaoh for bread And Pharaoh said unto all the Egyptians,
Go to Joseph: what he saith to you, do ye. **56** When the famine was upon all the
land, Joseph opened all places, wherein the store was, and sold unto the Egyptians:
for the famine waxed sore in the land of Egypt. **57** And all the countries [ae]came
to Egypt to buy corn of Joseph, because the famine was sore in all lands.

42

3 Joseph's brethren come into Egypt to buy corn. 7 He knoweth them, and tryeth them. 24 Simeon is put in prison. 34 The others go to fetch Benjamin.

1 Then [a]Jacob saw that there was [b]food in Egypt, and Jacob said unto his sons,
Why [c]gaze ye one upon another? **2** And he said, Behold, I have heard that the-
re is food in Egypt, [1]Get you down thither, and buy us food thence, that we may
live and not die. **3** So went Joseph's ten brethren down to buy corn of the Egyp-
tians. **4** But Benjamin Joseph's brother, would not Jacob send with his brethren:
for he said, Lest death should [d]befall him. **5** And the sons of Israel came to buy
food among them that came: for there was famine in the land of Canaan. **6** Now
Joseph was governor of the land, who sold to all the people of the land: then Jose-
ph's brethren came, and bowed their faces to the ground before him. **7** And when
Joseph saw his brethren, he knew them, and [e]made himself strange toward them,
and spake to them roughly, and said unto them, Whence come ye? Who answered,
Out of the land of Canaan, to buy vittles. **8** (Now Joseph knew his brethren, but
they knew not him. **9** And Joseph remembered the [2]dreams, which he dreamed
of them) and he said unto them, Ye are spies, and are come to see the [f]weakness of
the land. **10** But they said unto him, Nay, my lord, but to buy vittles thy servan-
ts are come. **11** We are all one man's sons: we mean truly, and thy servants are
no spies. **12** But he said unto them, Nay, but ye are come to see the weakness of
the land. **13** And they said, We thy servants, are twelve brethren, the sons of one
man in the land of Canaan: and behold, the youngest is this day with our father,
and one [g]is not. **14** Again Joseph said unto them, This is it that I spake unto
you, saying, Ye are spies. **15** Hereby ye shall be proved: [h]by the life of Pharaoh,
ye shall not go hence, except your youngest brother come hither. **16** Send one of
you which may fetch your brother, and ye shall be kept in prison, that your words
may be proved, whether there be truth in you, or else by the life of Pharaoh ye are
but spies. **17** So he put them in ward three days. **18** Then Joseph said unto
them the third day, This do, and live: for I [i]fear God. **19** If ye be true men, let
one of your brethren be bound in your prison house, and go ye, carry food for the
famine of your houses: **20** [3]But bring your younger brother unto me, that your
words may be tried, and that ye die not: and they did so. **21** And they said one
to another, [j]We have verily sinned against our brother, in that we saw the angui-
sh of his soul, when he besought us, and we would not hear him: therefore is this
trouble come upon us. **22** And Reuben answered them, saying, Warned I not
you, saying, [4]Sin not against the child, and ye would not hear? and lo, his [k]blood
is now required. **23** (And they were not aware that Joseph understood them:
for he [l]spake unto them by an interpreter.) **24** Then he turned from them, and
[m]wept, and turned to them again, and communed with them, and took Simeon
from among them, and bound him before their eyes. **25** So Joseph commanded
that they should fill their sacks with wheat, and put every man's money again in his
sack, and give them vittles for the journey: and thus did he unto them. **26** And
they laid their vittles upon their asses, and departed thence. **27** And as one of
them opened his sack for to give his ass provender in the Inn, he espied his money:
for lo, it was in his sack's mouth. **28** Then he said unto his brethren, My mo-
ney is restored: for lo, it is even in my sack And their heart [n]failed them, and they
were [o]astonished, and said one to another, What is this, that God hath done unto
us? **29** And they came unto Jacob their father unto the land of Canaan, and told
him all that had befallen them, saying, **30** The man who is lord of the land, spa-
ke roughly to us, and put us in prison as spies of the country. **31** And we said
unto him, We are true men, and are no spies. **32** We be twelve brethren, sons of
our father: one [p]is not, and the youngest is this day with our father in the land of
Canaan. **33** Then the lord of the country said unto us, Hereby shall I know if
ye be true men: Leave one of your brethren with me, and take food for the famine
of your houses, and depart, **34** And bring your youngest brother unto me, that
I may know that ye are no spies, but true men: so will I deliver you your brother,
and ye shall occupy in the land. **35** And as they emptied their sacks, behold,
every man's bundle of money was in his sack: and when they and their father saw
the bundles of their money, they were afraid. **36** Then Jacob their father said to
them, Ye have robbed me of my children: Joseph is not, and Simeon is not, and ye
will take Benjamin: all these things [q]are against [r]me. **37** Then Reuben answered
his father, saying, Slay my two sons, if I bring him not to thee again: deliver him
to mine hand, and I will bring him to thee again. **38** But he said, My son shall
not go down with you: for his brother is dead, and he is left alone: if death come

---

o. Gen. 41:25 Both his dreams tend to one end.
p. Gen. 41:29 Or, abundance and saturity.
q. Gen. 41:31 Or, they shall remember no more the plenty.
r. Gen. 41:33 The office of a true Prophet is not only to show the evils to come, but also the remedies for the same.
s. Gen. 41:38 None should be preferred to honor that have not gifts of God meet for the same.
t. Gen. 41:40 Hebrew, mouth.
u. Gen. 41:40 Some read, the people shall kiss thy mouth, that is shall obey thee in all things.
v. Gen. 41:42 Or, his signet.
w. Gen. 41:43 Hebrew, second chariot.
x. Gen. 41:43 In sign of honor: which word some expound, tender father, or father of the king, or kneel down.
y. Gen. 41:45 Or, the expounder of secrets.
z. Gen. 41:45 Or, priest.
aa. Gen. 41:46 His age is mentioned both to show that his authority came of God, and also that he suffered imprisonment and exile twelve years and more.
ab. Gen. 41:47 Hebrew, made for gatherings.
ac. Gen. 41:51 Notwithstanding that his father's house was the true Church of God: yet the company of the wicked and prosperity caused him to forget it.
ad. Gen. 41:54 Or, food.
ae. Gen. 41:57 Or, came to Egypt to Joseph.

GEN. 41

1. Ps. 105:20
2. Ps. 105.21 - Acts 7:10
3. Gen. 46:20 - Gen. 48:5
4. Ps. 105.16

GEN. 42

a. Gen. 42:1 This story showeth plainly that all things are governed by God's providence for the profit of his Church.
b. Gen. 42:1 Or, corn.
c. Gen. 42:1 As men destitute of counsel.
d. Gen. 42:4 Hebrew, should meet him.
e. Gen. 42:7 This dissembling is not to be followed, nor any particular facts of the fathers not approved by God's word.
f. Gen. 42:9 Hebrew, nakedness, or, filthiness.
g. Gen. 42:13 Or, is dead.
h. Gen. 42:15 The Egyptians which were idolaters, used to swear by their king's life: but God forbiddeth to swear by any but him: yet Joseph dwelling among the wicked smelleth of their corruptions.
i. Gen. 42:18 And therefore am true and just.
j. Gen. 42:21 Affliction maketh men to acknowledge their faults, which otherwise they would dissemble.
k. Gen. 42:22 God will take vengeance upon us, and measure us with our own measure.
l. Gen. 42:23 Hebrew, an interpreter between them.
m. Gen. 42:24 Though he showed himself rigorous, yet his brotherly affection remained.
n. Gen. 42:28 Hebrew, went out.
o. Gen. 42:28 Because their conscience accused them of their sin, they thought God would have brought them to trouble by this money.
p. Gen. 42:32 Or, cannot be found.
q. Gen. 42:36 Or, light upon me.
r. Gen. 42:36 For they seemed not to be touched with any love toward their brethren which increased his sorrow: and partly as appeareth he suspected them for Joseph.

unto him by the way which ye go, then ye shall bring my gray head with sorrow unto the grave.

43

13 Jacob suffereth Benjamin to depart with his children. 14 Simeon is delivered out of prison. 30 Joseph goeth aside and weepeth.

1 Now great [a]famine was in the land. **2** And when they had eaten up the vittles, which they had brought from Egypt, their father said unto them, Turn again and buy us a little food. **3** And Judah answered him, saying, The man charged us by an oath, saying, [1]Never see my face, except your brother be with you. **4** If thou wilt send our brother with us, we will go down, and buy thee food. **5** But if thou wilt not send him, we will not go down: for the man said unto us, [2]Look me not in the face, except your brother be with you. **6** And Israel said, Wherefore dealt ye so evil with me, as to tell the man, whether ye had yet a brother or no? **7** And they answered, The man asked straightly of [b]ourselves and of our kindred, saying, Is your father yet alive? have ye any brother? And we told him according to [c]these words: could we know certainly that he would say, Bring your brother down? **8** Then said Judah to Israel his father, Send the boy with me, that we may rise and go, and that we may live, and not die, both we, and thou, and our children. **9** I will be surety for him: of mine hand shalt thou require him [3]If I bring him not to thee, and set him before thee, [d]then let me bear the blame forever. **10** For except we had made this tarrying, doubtless by this we had returned the second time. **11** Then their father Israel said unto them, If it must needs be so now, do thus: take of the best fruits of the land in your vessels, and bring the man a present, a little rosin, and a little honey, [e]spices and myrrh, nuts, and almonds: **12** And take [f]double money in your hand, and the money, that was brought again in your sacks' mouths carry it again in your hand, lest it were some oversight. **13** Take also your brother and arise, and go again to the man. **14** And [g]God Almighty give you mercy in the sight of the man, that he may deliver you your other brother, and Benjamin: but I shall be [h]robbed of my child, as I have been. **15** Thus the men took this present, and took twice so much money in their hand with Benjamin, and rose up, and went down to Egypt, and stood before Joseph. **16** And when Joseph saw Benjamin with them, he said [i]to his steward, Bring these men home and kill meat, and make ready: for the men shall eat with me at noon. **17** And the men did as Joseph bade, and brought the men unto Joseph's house. **18** Now when the men were brought into Joseph's house, they were [j]afraid, and said, Because of the money, that came in our sack's mouths at the first time, are we brought, that he may [k]pick a quarrel against us, and [l]lay something to our charge, and bring us in bondage and our asses. **19** Therefore came they to Joseph's steward, and communed with him at the door of his house, **20** And said, O sir, [4]we came indeed down hither at the first time to buy food, **21** And as we came to an Inn and opened our sacks, behold, every man's money was in his sack's mouth, even our money in full weight, but we have brought it in our hands. **22** Also other money have we brought in our hands to buy food, but we cannot tell, who put our money in our sacks. **23** And he said, [m]Peace be to you, fear not: [n]your God, and the God of your father hath given you that treasure in your sacks, I had your money: and he brought forth Simeon to them. **24** So the man led them into Joseph's house, and gave them water to wash their feet, and gave their asses provender. **25** And they made ready their present against Joseph came at noon, (for they heard say, that they should eat bread there.) **26** When Joseph came home, they brought the present into the house to him, which was in their hands, and bowed down to the ground before him. **27** And he asked them of their [o]prosperity, and said, Is your father the old man, of whom ye told me, in good health? is he yet alive? **28** Who answered, Thy servant our father is in good health, he is yet alive: and they bowed down, and made obeisance. **29** And he lifting up his eyes, beheld his brother Benjamin, his [p]mother's son, and said, Is this your younger brother of whom ye told me? And he said, God be merciful unto thee, my son. **30** And Joseph made haste (for his [q]affection was inflamed toward his brother, and sought where to weep) and entered into his chamber and wept there. **31** Afterward he washed his face, and came out, and refrained himself, and said, Set on [r]meat. **32** And they [s]prepared for him by himself, and for them by themselves, and for the Egyptians, which did eat with him, by themselves, because the Egyptians might not eat bread with the Hebrews: for that was an [t]abomination unto the Egyptians. **33** So they sat before him: the eldest according unto his age, and the youngest according unto his youth: and the men marveled among themselves. **34** And they took meats from before him, and sent to them: but Benjamin's meat was five times so much as any of theirs: and they drank, [u]and had of the best drink with him.

44

15 Joseph accuseth his brother of theft. 33 Judah offereth himself to be servant for Benjamin.

1 Afterward he commanded his steward, saying, Fill the men's sacks with food, as much as they can carry, and put every man's money in his sack's mouth. **2** And [a]put my cup, I mean, the silver cup, in the sack's mouth of the youngest, and his corn money And he did according to the commandment that Joseph gave him. **3** And in the [b]morning the men were sent away, they, and their asses. **4** And when they went out of the city not far off, Joseph said to his steward, Up, follow after the men: and when thou dost overtake them, say unto them, Wherefore have ye rewarded evil for good? **5** Is not that the cup wherein my lord drinketh? [c]and in the which he doth divine and prophesy? ye have done evil in so doing. **6** And when he overtook them, he said these words unto them. **7** And they answered him, Wherefore saith my lord such words? God forbid that thy servants should do such a thing. **8** Behold, the money which we found in our sacks' mouths, we brought again unto thee out of the land of Canaan: how then should we steal out of thy lord's house silver or gold? **9** With whomsoever of thy servants it be found, let him die, and we also will be my lord's bondmen. **10** And he said, Now then let it be according unto your words: he with whom it is found, shall be my servant, and ye shall be [d]blameless. **11** Then at once every man took down his sack to the ground, and everyone opened his sack. **12** And he searched, and began at the eldest, and left at the youngest: and the cup was found in Benjamin's sack. **13** Then they [e]rent their clothes, and laded every man his ass, and went again into the city. **14** So Judah and his brethren came to Joseph's house (for he was yet there) and they fell before him on the ground. **15** Then Joseph said unto them, What act is this, which ye have done? know ye not that such a man as I, can divine and prophesy? **16** Then said Judah, What shall we say unto my lord? what shall we speak? and how can we justify ourselves? [f]God hath found out the wickedness of thy servants: behold, we are servants to my lord, both we, and he, with whom the cup is found. **17** But he answered, God forbid, that I should do so, but the man, with whom the cup is found, he shall be my servant, and go ye in peace unto your father. **18** Then Judah drew near unto him, and said, Oh my lord, let thy servant now speak a word in my lord's ears, and let not thy wrath be kindled against thy servant: for thou art even [g]as Pharaoh. **19** My lord asked his servants, saying, [1]Have ye a father, or a brother? **20** And we answered my lord, We have a father that is old, and a young [h]child, which he begat in his age: and his brother is dead, and he alone is left of his mother, and his father loveth him. **21** Now thou saidest unto thy servants, Bring him unto me, that I may [i]set mine eye upon him. **22** And we answered my lord, The child cannot depart his father: for if he leave his father, his father would die. **23** Then saidest thou unto thy servants, [2]Except your younger brother come down with you, look in my face no more. **24** So when we came unto thy servant our father, and showed him what my lord had said, **25** And our father said unto us, Go again, buy us a little food. **26** Then we answered, We cannot go down, but if our youngest brother [j]go with us, then will we go down: for we may not see the man's face, except our youngest brother be with us. **27** Then thy servant my father said unto us, Ye know that my [k]wife bare me two sons. **28** And the one went out from me, and I said, Of a surety he is torn in [3]pieces, and I saw him not since. **29** Now ye take this also away from me: if death take him, then [l]ye shall bring my gray head in sorrow to the grave. **30** Now therefore, when I come to thy servant my father, and the child be not with us (seeing that his [m]life dependeth

---

GEN. 42

1. Acts. 7:12
2. Gen. 37:5
3. Gen. 35:5
4. Gen. 37:21

GEN. 43

a. Gen. 43:1 This was a great tentation to Jacob to suffer so great famine in that land where God had promised to bless him.
b. Gen. 43:7 Or, of our estate and condition.
c. Gen. 43:7 Hebrew, to the mouth of these words: that is, that thing which he asked us.
d. Gen. 43:9 Hebrew, I will sin to thee.
e. Gen. 43:11 Or, sweet smells.
f. Gen. 43:12 When we are in necessity or danger, God forbiddeth not to use all honest means to better our estate and condition.
g. Gen. 43:14 Our chief trust ought to be in God, and not in worldly means.
h. Gen. 43:14 He speaketh these words not so much of despair, as to make his sons more careful to bring again their brother.
i. Gen. 43:16 Or, to the ruler of his house.
j. Gen. 43:18 So the judgment of God pressed their conscience.
k. Gen. 43:18 Hebrew, roll himself upon us.
l. Gen. 43:18 Hebrew, cast himself upon us.
m. Gen. 43:23 Or, you are well.
n. Gen. 43:23 Notwithstanding the corruptions of Egypt, yet Joseph taught his family to fear God.
o. Gen. 43:27 Hebrew, peace.
p. Gen. 43:29 For they two only were born of Rachel.
q. Gen. 43:30 Hebrew, bowels.
r. Gen. 43:31 Hebrew, bread.
s. Gen. 43:32 To signify his dignity.
t. Gen. 43:32 The nature of the superstitious is to condemn all others in respect of themselves.
u. Gen. 43:34 Sometimes this word signifieth to be drunken, but here it is meant, that they had enough, and drank of the best wine.

GEN. 43

1. Gen. 42:20
2. Gen. 42:20
3. Gen. 44.32
4. Gen. 42:3

GEN. 44

a. Gen. 44:2 We may not by this example use any unlawful practices, seeing God hath commanded us to walk in simplicity.
b. Gen. 44:3 Hebrew, the morning shone.
c. Gen. 44:5 Because the people thought he could divine, he attributeth to himself that knowledge: or else he feigneth that he consulted with soothsayers for it: Which simulation is worthy to be reproved.
d. Gen. 44:10 Hebrew, innocent.
e. Gen. 44:13 To signify how greatly the thing displeased them, and how sorry they were for it.
f. Gen. 44:16 If we see no evident cause of our affliction, let us look to the secret counsel of God, who punisheth us justly for our sins.
g. Gen. 44:18 Equal in authority or, next unto the king.
h. Gen. 44:20 Hebrew, child of his old age.
i. Gen. 44:21 Or, that I may see him.
j. Gen. 44:26 Hebrew, be with us.
k. Gen. 44:27 Rachel bare to Jacob, Joseph and Benjamin.
l. Gen. 44:29 Ye shall cause me to die for sorrow.
m. Gen. 44:30 Hebrew, his soul is bound to his soul.

on the child's life.) **31** Then when he shall see that the child is not come, he will
die: so shall thy servants bring down the gray head of thy servant our father with
sorrow to the grave. **32** Doubtless thy servant became surety for the child to my
father, and, [4]If I bring him not unto thee again, then I will bear the blame unto
my father forever. **33** Now therefore, I pray thee, let me thy servant abide for the
child, as a servant to my lord, and let the child go up with his brethren. **34** For
[n]how can I go up to my father: if the child be not with me, unless I would see the
evil that shall come on my father.

45

1 Joseph maketh himself known to his brethren. 8 He showeth that all was done by God's providence. 18 Pharaoh commandeth him to send for his father. 24 Joseph exhorteth his brethren to concord.

1 Then Joseph could not refrain himself before all that stood by him, but
he cried, [a]Have forth every man from me And there tarried not one with him,
while Joseph uttered himself unto his brethren. **2** And he wept, and cried, so
that the Egyptians heard: the house of Pharaoh heard also. **3** Then Joseph said
unto his brethren, I am Joseph: doth my father yet live? But his brethren could
not answer him, for they were astonished at his presence. **4** Again, Joseph said
to his brethren, Come near, I pray you, to me And they came near And he said,
[1]I am Joseph your brother, whom ye sold into Egypt. **5** Now therefore be not
[b]sad, neither grieved with yourselves, that ye sold me hither: [2]For God did send
me before you for your preservation. **6** For now two years of famine have been
through the land, and five years are behind, wherein neither shall be earing nor
harvest. **7** Wherefore God sent me before you to preserve your posterity in this
land, and to save you alive by a great deliverance. **8** Now then you sent not me
hither, but [c]God, who hath made me a father unto Pharaoh, and lord of all his
house, and ruler throughout all the land of Egypt. **9** Haste you and go up to
my father, and tell him, Thus saith thy son Joseph, God hath made me lord of
all Egypt: come down to me, tarry not. **10** And thou shalt dwell in the land of
Goshen, and shalt be near me, thou and thy children, and thy children's children,
and thy sheep, and thy beasts, and all that thou hast. **11** Also I will nourish thee
there (for yet remain five years of famine) lest thou perish through poverty, thou
and thy household, and all that thou hast. **12** And behold, your eyes do see, and
the eyes of my brother Benjamin, that [d]my mouth speaketh to you. **13** There-
fore tell my father of all mine honor in Egypt, and of all that ye have seen, and
make haste, and bring my father hither. **14** Then he fell on his brother Benja-
min's neck, and wept, and Benjamin wept on his neck. **15** Moreover, he kis-
sed all his brethren, and wept upon them: and afterward his brethren talked with
him. **16** And the [e]tidings came to Pharaoh's house, so that they said, Joseph's
brethren are come: and it pleased Pharaoh well, and his servants. **17** Then Pha-
raoh said to Joseph, Say to thy brethren, This do ye, laid your beasts and depart,
go to the land of Canaan, **18** And take your father, and your household, and
come to me, and I will give you the [f]best of the land of Egypt, and ye shall eat of
the [g]fat of the land. **19** And I command thee, Thus do ye, take you chariots out
of the land of Egypt for your children, and for your wives, and bring your father
and come. **20** Also [h]regard not your stuff: for the best of all the land of Egypt is
yours. **21** And the children of Israel did so: and Joseph gave them chariots ac-
cording to the commandment of Pharaoh: he gave them vittles also for the jour-
ney. **22** He gave them all, none except, change of raiment: but unto Benjamin
he gave three hundred pieces of silver, and five suits of raiment. **23** And unto his
father [i]likewise he sent ten he asses laden with the best things of Egypt, and ten she
asses laden with wheat, and bread and meat for his father by the way. **24** So sent
he his brethren away, and they departed: and he said unto them, [j]Fall not out by
the way. **25** Then they went up from Egypt, and came unto the land of Cana-
an, unto Jacob their father, **26** And told him, saying, Joseph is yet alive, and he
also is governor over all the land of Egypt, and Jacob's heart [k]failed: for he believed
them not. **27** And they told him all the words of Joseph, which he had said unto
them: but when he saw the chariots, which Joseph had sent to carry him, then the
spirit of Jacob their father revived. **28** And Israel said, I have enough: Joseph my
son is yet alive: I will go and see him yet I die.

46

2 God assureth Jacob of his journey into Egypt. 27 The number of his family when he went into Egypt. 29 Joseph meeteth his father. 34 He teacheth his brethren what to answer to Pharaoh.

1 Then Israel took his journey with all that he had, and came to Beersheba,
and [a]offered sacrifice unto the God of his father Isaac. **2** And God spake unto
Israel in a vision by night, saying, Jacob, Jacob Who answered, I am here. **3** Then
he said, I am God, the God of thy father, fear not to go down into Egypt: for I
will there make of thee a great nation. **4** I will [b]go down with thee into Egypt,
and I will also [c]bring thee up again, and Joseph shall [d]put his hand upon thine
eyes. **5** Then Jacob rose up from Beersheba: and the sons of Israel carried Jacob
their father, and their children, and their wives in the chariots, which Pharaoh had
sent to carry him. **6** And they took their cattle, and their goods, which they had
gotten in the land of Canaan, and came into Egypt, both [1]Jacob and all his seed
with him. **7** His sons and his sons' sons with him, his daughters, and his sons'
daughters, and all his seed brought he with him into Egypt. **8** And these are the
names of the children of Israel, which came into Egypt, even Jacob and his sons:
[2]Reuben, Jacob's firstborn. **9** And the sons of Reuben: Hanoch, and Pallu, and
Hezron, and Carmi. **10** And the sons of [3]Simeon: Jemuel, and Jamin, and Ohad,
and Jachin, and Zohar, and Shaul the son of a Canaanitish woman. **11** Also the
sons of [4]Levi: Gershon, Kohath, and Merari. **12** Also the sons of [5]Judah: Er, and
Onan, and Shelah, and Perez, and Zerah: (but Er and Onan died in the land of
Canaan.) And the sons of Perez were Hezron and Hamul. **13** Also the sons of
[6]Issachar: Tola, and Puvah, and Job, and Shimron. **14** Also the sons of Zebulun:
Sered, and Elon, and Jahleel. **15** These be the sons of Leah, which she bare unto
Jacob in Padan Aram, with his daughter Dinah All the [e]souls of his sons and his
daughters were thirty and three. **16** Also the sons of Gad: Ziphion, and Haggi,
Shuni, and Ezbon, Eri, and Arodi, and Areli. **17** Also the sons of [7]Asher: Jimnah,
and Ishuah, and Isui, and Beriah, and Serah their sister And the sons of Beriah: and
Heber, Malchiel. **18** These are the children of Zilpah, whom Laban gave to Leah
his daughter: and these she bare unto Jacob, even sixteen souls. **19** The sons of
Rachel Jacob's wife were Joseph, and Benjamin. **20** And unto Joseph in the land
of Egypt were born Manasseh, and Ephraim, which [8]Asenath the daughter of Po-
ti-Pherah prince of On bare unto him. **21** Also the sons of [9]Benjamin: Belah,
and Becher, and Ashbel, and Gera, Naaman, Ehi, and Rosh, Muppim, and Hup-
pim, and Ard. **22** These are the sons of Rachel, which were born unto Jacob,
fourteen souls in all. **23** Also the sons of Dan: Hushim. **24** Also the sons of
Naphtali: Jahzeel, and Guni, and Jezer, and Shillem. **25** These are the sons of
Bilhah, which Laban gave unto Rachel his daughter, and she bare these unto Jacob,
in all seven souls. **26** All the [10]souls, that came with Jacob into Egypt, which
came out of his [f]loins (besides Jacob's sons' wives) were in the whole, threescore
and six souls. **27** Also the sons of Joseph, which were born him in Egypt, were
two souls: so that all the souls of the house of Jacob, which came into Egypt, are
seventy. **28** Then he sent Judah before him unto Joseph, to [g]direct his way unto
Goshen, and they came into the land of Goshen. **29** Then Joseph [h]made ready
his chariot, and went up to Goshen to meet Israel his father, and presented himself
unto him, and fell on his neck and wept upon his neck a [i]good while. **30** And
Israel said unto Joseph, Now let me die since I have seen thy face, and that thou
art yet alive. **31** Then Joseph said to his brethren, and to his father's house, I will
go up and show Pharaoh, and tell him, My brethren and my father's house, which
were in the land of Canaan, are come unto me. **32** And the men are [j]sheepher-
ders, and because they are sheepherders, they have brought their sheep and their
cattle, and all that they have. **33** And if Pharaoh call you, and ask you, What
is your trade? **34** That ye shall say, Thy servants are men occupied about catt-
le, from our childhood even unto this time, both we and our fathers: that ye may
dwell in the land of Goshen: for every sheep keeper is an [k]abomination unto the
Egyptians.

47

7 Jacob cometh before Pharaoh, and telleth him his age. 11 The land of Goshen is given him. 22 The idolatrous priests have living of the King. 28 Jacob's age when he dieth.

---

n. Gen. 44:34 Meaning, he had rather remain their prisoner, than to return and see his father in heaviness.

GEN. 44

1. Gen. 42:13,16
2. Gen. 43:3
3. Gen. 37:33
4. Gen. 43:9

GEN. 45

a. Gen. 45:1 Not that he was ashamed of his kindred, but that he would cover his brethren's fault.
b. Gen. 45:5 This example teacheth that we must by all means comfort them, which are truly humbled and wounded for their sins.
c. Gen. 45:8 Albeit God detest sin, yet he turneth man's wickedness to serve to his glory.
d. Gen. 45:12 That is, that I speak in your own language, and have none interpreter.
e. Gen. 45:16 Hebrew, voice.
f. Gen. 45:18 The most plentiful ground.
g. Gen. 45:18 The chiefest fruits and commodities.
h. Gen. 45:20 Hebrew, let not your eyes spare your vessel.
i. Gen. 45:23 Or, he sent as much, to wit, silver as verse 22, and ten asses.
j. Gen. 45:24 Seeing he had remitted the fault done toward him, he would not that they should accuse one another.
k. Gen. 45:26 As one between hope and fear.

GEN. 45

1. Acts 7:13
2. Gen. 50:20

GEN. 46

a. Gen. 46:1 Whereby he both signifieth, that he worshipped the true God, and also that he kept in his heart the possession of that land from whence present necessity drove him.
b. Gen. 46:4 Conducting thee by my power.
c. Gen. 46:4 In thy posterity.
d. Gen. 46:4 Shall shut thine eyes when thou diest: which appertained to him that was most dearest, or chief of the kindred.
e. Gen. 46:15 Or, persons.
f. Gen. 46:26 Hebrew, thighs.
g. Gen. 46:28 Or, to prepare him a place.
h. Gen. 46:29 Hebrew, bound his chariot.
i. Gen. 46:29 Hebrew, yet, or still.
j. Gen. 46:32 He was not ashamed of his father and kindred, though they were of base condition.
k. Gen. 46:34 God suffereth the world to hate his, that they may forsake the filth of the world, and cleave to him.

GEN. 46

1. Josh. 24:4 - Ps. 105:23 - Isa. 52:4
2. Exod. 1:2 - Exod. 6:24 - Num.26:5 - 1Chron. 5:1
3. Exod. 6:15 - 1Chron. 5:1
4. 1Chron. 6:1
5. 1Chron. 2:3 - 1Chron. 9:21 - Gen. 38:3
6. 1Chron. 7:1
7. 2Chron. 7:30
8. Gen. 41:50
9. 1Chron. 7:6 - 1Chron. 8:1
10. Deut. 10:25

1 Then came Joseph and told Pharaoh, and said, My father, and my brethren, and their sheep, and their cattle, and all that they have, are come out of the land of Canaan, and behold, they are in the land of Goshen. **2** And Joseph took part of his brethren, even [a]five men, and presented them unto Pharaoh. **3** When Pharaoh said unto his brethren, What is your trade? And they answered Pharaoh, Thy servants are shepherds, both we and our fathers. **4** They said moreover unto Pharaoh, For to sojourn in the land are we come: for thy servants have no pasture for their sheep, so sore is the famine in the land of Canaan, Now therefore, we pray thee: let thy servants dwell in the land of Goshen. **5** Then spake Pharaoh to Joseph, saying, Thy father and thy brethren are come unto thee. **6** The [b]land of Egypt is before thee: in the best place of the land make thy father and thy brethren to dwell: let them dwell in the land of Goshen: and if thou knowest that there be men of activity among them, make them rulers over my cattle. **7** Joseph also brought Jacob his father, and set him before Pharaoh And Jacob [c]saluted Pharaoh. **8** Then Pharaoh said unto Jacob, [d]How old art thou? **9** And Jacob said unto Pharaoh, The whole time of my [1]pilgrimage is an hundred and thirty years: few and evil have the days of my life been, and I have not attained unto the years of the life of my fathers, in the days of their pilgrimages. **10** And Jacob [e]took leave of Pharaoh, and departed from the presence of Pharaoh. **11** And Joseph placed his father, and his brethren, and gave them possession in the land of Egypt, in the best of the land, even in the land of [f]Rameses, as Pharaoh had commanded. **12** And Joseph nourished his father, and his brethren, and all his father's household with bread [g]even to the young children. **13** Now there was no bread in all the land; for the famine was exceeding sore: so that the land of Egypt, and the land of Canaan were [h]famished by reason of the famine. **14** And Joseph gathered all the money, that was found in the land of Egypt, and in the land of Canaan, for the corn which they bought, and [i]Joseph laid up the money in Pharaoh's house. **15** So when money failed in the land of Egypt, and in the land of Canaan, then all the Egyptians came unto Joseph and said, Give us bread: for why should we die before thee? for our money is spent. **16** Then said Joseph, Bring your cattle, and I will give you for your cattle, if your money be spent. **17** So they brought their cattle unto Joseph, and Joseph gave them bread for the horses, and for the flocks of sheep, and for the herds of cattle, and for the asses: so he fed them with bread for all their cattle that year. **18** But when the year was ended, they came unto him the second year, and said unto him, We will not hide from my lord, that since our money is spent, and my lord hath the herds of the cattle, there is nothing left in the sight of my lord, but our bodies and our ground. **19** Why shall we perish in thy sight, both we and our [j]land? buy us and our land for bread, and we and our land will be bound to Pharaoh: therefore give us seed, that we may live and not die, and that the land go not to waste. **20** So Joseph bought all the land of Egypt for Pharaoh: for the Egyptians sold every man his ground, because the famine was sore upon them: so the land became Pharaoh's. **21** And he [k]removed the people unto the cities, [l]from one side of Egypt even to the other. **22** Only the land of the Priests bought he not: for the Priests had an ordinary of Pharaoh, and they did eat their ordinary, which Pharaoh gave them: wherefore they sold not their ground. **23** Then Joseph said unto the people, Behold, I have bought you this day, and your land for Pharaoh: lo, here is seed for you: sow therefore the ground. **24** And of the increase ye shall give the fifth part unto Pharaoh, and four parts shall be yours for seed of the field, and for your meat, and for them of your households, and for your children to eat. **25** Then they answered, Thou hast saved our lives: let us find grace in the sight of my lord, and we will be Pharaoh's servants. **26** Then Joseph made it a law over the land of Egypt unto this day, that Pharaoh should have the fifth part, [m]except the land of the Priests only, which was not Pharaoh's. **27** And Israel dwelt in the land of Egypt, in the country of Goshen: and they had their possessions therein, and grew and multiplied exceedingly. **28** Moreover, Jacob lived in the land of Egypt seventeen years, so the whole age of Jacob was an hundred forty and seven years. **29** Now when the time drew near that Israel must die, he called his son Joseph, and said unto him, If I have now found grace in thy sight, [2]put thine hand now under my thigh, and deal mercifully and truly with me: bury me not, I pray thee, in Egypt. **30** But when I shall [n]sleep with my fathers, thou shalt carry me out of Egypt, and bury me in their burial And he answered, I will do as thou hast said. **31** Then he said, swear unto me And he sware unto him And Israel [o]worshipped towards the bed's head.

48

1 Joseph with his two sons visiteth his sick father. 3 Jacob rehearseth God's promise. 5 He receiveth Joseph's sons as his. 19 He preferreth the younger.

1 Again after this, one said to Joseph, Lo, thy father is sick: then he took with him his [a]two sons, Manasseh and Ephraim. **2** Also one told Jacob, and said, Behold thy son Joseph is come to thee, and Israel took his strength unto him and sat upon the bed. **3** Then Jacob said unto Joseph, God [b]almighty appeared unto me at [1]Luz in the land of Canaan, and blessed me, **4** And said unto me, Behold, I will make thee fruitful, and will multiply thee, and will make a great number of people of thee, and will give this land unto thy seed after thee for an [c]everlasting possession. **5** And now thy [2]two sons, Manasseh and Ephraim, which are born unto thee in the land of Egypt before I came to thee into Egypt, shall be mine, as Reuben and Simeon are mine. **6** But thy lineage, which thou hast begotten after them, shall be thine: they shall be called after the names of their brethren in their inheritance. **7** Now when I came from Padan, Rachel [3]died upon mine hand in the land of Canaan, by the way when there was but half a day's journey of ground to come to Ephrath: and I buried her there in the way to Ephrath: the same is Bethlehem. **8** Then Israel beheld Joseph's sons and said, Whose are these? **9** And Joseph said unto his father, They are my sons, which [d]God hath given me here Then he said, I pray thee, bring them to me, that I may bless them: **10** (For the eyes of Israel were dim for age, so that he could not well see) Then he caused them to come to him, and he kissed them and embraced them. **11** And Israel said unto Joseph, I had not thought to have seen thy face: yet lo, God hath showed me also thy seed. **12** And Joseph took them away from his knees, and did reverence [e]down to the ground. **13** Then took Joseph them both, Ephraim in his right hand toward Israel's left hand, and Manasseh in his left hand toward Israel's right hand, so he brought them unto him. **14** But Israel stretched out his right hand, and laid it on [f]Ephraim's head which was the younger, and his left hand upon Manasseh's head (directing his hands of purpose) for Manasseh was the elder. **15** [4]Also he blesseth Joseph, and said, The God, before whom my fathers, Abraham and Isaac did walk, the God which hath fed me all my life long, unto this day, bless thee. **16** The [g]Angel, which hath delivered me from all evil, bless the children, and let my [h]name be named upon them, and the name of my fathers Abraham and Isaac, that they may grow as fish into a multitude in the midst of the earth. **17** But when Joseph saw that his father laid his right hand upon the head of Ephraim, it [i]displeased him: and he stayed his father's hand to remove it from Ephraim's head to Manasseh's head. **18** And Joseph said unto his father, Not so, my father: for this is the eldest: put thy right hand upon his head. **19** But his father refused, and said, I know well, my son, I know well: he shall be also a people, and he shall be great likewise: but his younger brother shall be greater than he, and his seed shall be full of nations. **20** So he blessed them that day, and said, In thee Israel shall bless, and say, God make thee as [j]Ephraim and as Manasseh, and he set Ephraim before Manasseh. **21** Then Israel said unto Joseph, Behold, I die, and God shall be with you, and bring you again unto the land of [k]your fathers. **22** Moreover, I have given unto thee one portion above thy brethren, which [l]I got out of the hand of the Amorite by my [5]sword and by my bow.

49

1 Jacob blesseth all his sons by name. 10 He telleth them that Christ shall come out of Judah. 29 He will be buried with his fathers. 33 He dieth.

1 Then Jacob called his sons, and said, Gather yourselves together, that I may tell you what shall come to you in the [a]last days. **2** Gather yourselves together, and hear, ye sons of Jacob, and hearken unto Israel your father. **3** Reuben mine eldest son, thou art my [b]might, and the beginning of my strength, [c]the excellency of dignity, and the excellency of power: **4** Thou wast light as water: thou shalt not be excellent, because [1]thou wentest up to thy father's bed: [d]then diddest thou defile

---

GEN. 47

- **a.** Gen. 47:2 That the king might be assured they were come, and see what manner of people they were.
- **b.** Gen. 47:6 Joseph's great modesty appeareth in that he would enterprise nothing without the king's commandment.
- **c.** Gen. 47:7 Hebrew, blessed.
- **d.** Gen. 47:8 Hebrew, how many days are the years of thy life?
- **e.** Gen. 47:10 Hebrew, blessed.
- **f.** Gen. 47:11 Which was a city in the country of Goshen, Exod. 1:11.
- **g.** Gen. 47:12 Some read, that he fed them as little babes, because they could not provide for themselves against that famine.
- **h.** Gen. 47:13 Hebrew, brought to an extremity, or at their wit's end.
- **i.** Gen. 47:14 Wherein he both declareth his fidelity toward the King, and his mind free from covetousness.
- **j.** Gen. 47:19 For except the ground be tilled and sown, it perisheth, and is as it were dead.
- **k.** Gen. 47:21 By this changing they signified that they had nothing of their own, but received all of the king's liberality.
- **l.** Gen. 47:21 Hebrew, end of the border.
- **m.** Gen. 47:26 Pharaoh in providing for Idolatrous priests, shall be a condemnation to all them which neglect the true ministers of God's word.
- **n.** Gen. 47:30 Hereby he protested that he died in the faith of his fathers, teaching his children to hope for the promised land.
- **o.** Gen. 47:31 He rejoiced that Joseph had promised him, and setting himself up upon his pillow, praised God. Read 1 Chron. 29:10.

GEN. 47

- **1.** Heb. 11:9,13
- **2.** Gen. 24:2

GEN. 48

- **a.** Gen. 48:1 Joseph more esteemeth that his children should be received into Jacob's family, which was the Church of God, than to enjoy all the treasures of Egypt.
- **b.** Gen. 48:3 Or, all sufficient.
- **c.** Gen. 48:4 Which is true in the carnal Israel unto the coming of Christ, and in the spiritual forever.
- **d.** Gen. 48:9 The faithful acknowledge all benefits come of God's free mercies.
- **e.** Gen. 48:12 Hebrew, his face to the ground.
- **f.** Gen. 48:14 God's judgments is oft times contrary to man's, and he preferreth that, which man despiseth.
- **g.** Gen. 48:16 This Angel must be understood of Christ, as Gen. 31:13 and 32:1.
- **h.** Gen. 48:16 Let them be taken as my children.
- **i.** Gen. 48:17 Joseph faileth in binding God's grace to the order of nature.
- **j.** Gen. 48:20 In whom God's graces should manifestly appear.
- **k.** Gen. 48:21 Which they had by faith in the promise.
- **l.** Gen. 48:22 By my children whom God spared for my sake.

GEN. 48

- **1.** Gen. 28:13
- **2.** Gen. 41:50
- **3.** Gen. 35:19
- **4.** Heb. 11:21
- **5.** Gen. 34:25

GEN. 49

- **a.** Gen. 49:1 When God shall bring you out of Egypt, and because that he speaketh of the Messiah, he nameth it the last days.Gen. 49:3 Begotten in my youth.

my bed, thy dignity is gone. **5** Simeon and Levi, brethren in evil, [e]the instrumen-
ts of cruelty are in their habitations. **6** Into their secret let not my soul come: my
[f]glory be not thou joined with their assembly: for in their wrath they slew a [g]man,
and in their self-will they dug down a wall. **7** Cursed be their wrath, for it was
fierce, and their rage, for it was cruel: I will [h]divide them in Jacob, and scatter them
in Israel. **8** Thou Judah, thy brethren shall praise thee: thy hand shall be in the
neck of thine enemies: thy father's son shall [i]bow down before unto thee. **9** Ju-
dah as a Lion's whelp shalt thou come up from the spoil, my son He shall lie down
and couch a Lion, and as a Lioness: [j]Who shall stir him up? **10** The [k]Sceptre
shall not depart from Judah, nor a Lawgiver from between his feet, until [l]Shiloh
come, and the people shall be gathered unto him. **11** He shall bind his Ass foal
unto the [m]vine, and his ass's colt unto the best vine He shall wash his garment in
wine, and his cloak in the blood of grapes. **12** His eyes shall be red with wine,
and his teeth white with milk. **13** Zebulun shall dwell by the seaside, and he
shall be an haven for ships: and his border shall be unto Sidon. **14** Issachar shall
be [n,o]a strong ass, couching down between two burdens: **15** And he shall see that
rest is good, and that the land is pleasant, and he shall bow his shoulder to bear, and
shall be subject unto tribute. **16** Dan [p]shall judge his people as one of the tribes
of Israel. **17** Dan shall be a [q]serpent by the way, an adder by the path, biting the
horse heels, so that his rider shall fall backward. **18** [r]O Lord, I have waited for
thy salvation. **19** Gad, a host of men shall overcome him, but he shall overcome
at the last. **20** Concerning Asher, his [s]bread shall be fat, and he shall give pleasu-
res for a king. **21** Naphtali shall be a hind let go, giving [t]goodly words. **22** Jo-
seph shall be [u]a fruitful bough, even a fruitful bough by the well side: the [v]small
boughs shall turn upon the wall: **23** [w]And the archers grieved him, and shot
against him, and hated him. **24** But his bow abode strong, and the hands of his
arms were strengthened, by the hands of the mighty God of Jacob, of whom was
the feeder appointed by the [x]stone of Israel, **25** Even by the God of thy father,
who shall help thee, and by the almighty, who shall bless thee with heavenly bles-
sings from above, with blessings of the deep that lieth beneath, with blessings of the
breasts, and of the womb. **26** The blessings of thy father shall be [y]stronger than
the blessings of mine elders: unto the end of the hills of the world they shall be on
the head of Joseph, and on the top of the head of him that was [z]separated from
his brethren. **27** Benjamin shall raven as a wolf: in the morning he shall devour
the prey, and at night he shall divide the spoil. **28** All these are the twelve tribes
of Israel, and thus their father spake unto them, and blessed them: every one of
them blessed he with a several blessing. **29** And he charged them and said unto
them, I am ready to be gathered unto my people: [2]bury me with my fathers in the
cave, that is in the field of Ephron the Hittite, **30** In the cave that is in the field
of Machpelah, besides Mamre in the land of Canaan: which cave Abraham bought
with the field of Ephron the Hittite for a possession to bury in. **31** There they
buried Abraham and Sarah his wife: there they buried Isaac and Rebekah his wife:
and there I buried Leah. **32** The purchase of the field and the cave that is the-
rein, was bought of the children of Heth. **33** Thus Jacob made an end of giving
charge to his sons, and [aa]plucked his feet into the bed, and gave up the ghost, and
was gathered to his people.

50

1 Jacob is buried. 19 Joseph forgiveth his brethren. 23 He seeth his children's children. 26 He dieth.

1 Then Joseph fell upon his father's face and wept upon him, and kissed
him. **2** And Joseph commanded his servants the [a]physicians to embalm his fa-
ther, and the physicians embalmed Israel. **3** So forty days were accomplished
(for so long did the days of them that were embalmed last) and the Egyptians
bewailed him [b]seventy days. **4** And when the days of his mourning were past,
Joseph spake to the house of Pharaoh, saying, If I have now found favor in your
eyes, speak, I pray you, in the ears, of Pharaoh, and say, **5** My father made me
[1]swear saying, Lo, I die, bury me in my grave, which I have made me in the
land of Canaan: now therefore let me go, I pray thee, and bury my father, and I
will come again. **6** Then Pharaoh said, Go up and bury thy father, [c]as he made
thee to swear. **7** So Joseph went up to bury his father, and with him went all
the servants of Pharaoh, both the elders of his house, and all the elders of the
land of Egypt, **8** Likewise all the house of Joseph, and his brethren, and his fa-
ther's house: only their children, and their sheep, and their cattle left they in the
land of Goshen. **9** And there went up with him both chariots and horsemen:
and they were an exceeding great company. **10** And they came to [d]Goren Atad,
which is beyond Jordan, and there they made a great and exceeding sore lamen-
tation: and he mourned for his father seven days. **11** And when the Canaani-
tes the inhabitants of the land saw the mourning in Goren Atad, they said, This
is a great mourning unto the Egyptians: wherefore the name thereof was called
[e]Abel Mizraim, which is beyond Jordan. **12** So his sons did unto him, accor-
ding as he had commanded them: **13** [2]For his sons carried him into the land
of Canaan, and buried him in the cave of the field of Machpelah, which cave
[3]Abraham bought with the field, to be a [f]place to bury in, of Ephron the Hit-
tite beside Mamre. **14** Then Joseph returned into Egypt, he and his brethren,
and all that went up with him to bury his father, after that he had buried his fa-
ther. **15** And when Joseph's brethren saw that their father was dead, they said, [g]It
may be that Joseph will hate us, and will pay us again all the evil which we did unto
him. **16** Therefore they sent unto Joseph, saying, Thy father commanded befo-
re his death, saying, **17** Thus shall ye say unto Joseph, Forgive now, I pray thee,
the trespass of thy brethren, and their sin: for they rewarded thee evil And now, we
pray thee, forgive the trespass of the servants of thy father's [h]God And Joseph wept,
when [i]they spake unto him. **18** Also his brethren came unto him, and fell down
before his face, and said, Behold, we be thy servants. **19** To whom Joseph said,
[4]Fear not: for [j]am not I under [k]God? **20** When ye thought evil against me, God
disposed it to good, that he might bring to pass, as it is this day, and save much pe-
ople alive. **21** Fear not now therefore, I will nourish you, and your children: and
he comforted them, and spake [l]kindly unto them. **22** So Joseph dwelt in Egypt,
he, and his father's house: and Joseph lived an [m]hundred and ten years. **23** [5]And
Joseph saw Ephraim's children, even unto the third generation: also the sons of
Machir the son of Manasseh were brought upon Joseph's knees. **24** And Joseph
said unto his brethren, [6]I am ready to die, and God will surely visit you, and bring
you out of this land, unto the land which he sware unto Abraham, unto Isaac, and
unto Jacob. **25** And Joseph took an oath of the children of Israel, saying, [7,n]God
will surely visit you, and ye shall carry my bones hence. **26** So Joseph died, when
he was an hundred and ten years old: and they embalmed him, and put him in a
chest in Egypt.

---

b. Gen. 49:3 If thou hadst not lost thy birthright by thine offense.
c. Gen. 49:4 Or, it ceased to be my bed.
d. Gen. 49:5 Or, their swords were instruments of violence.
e. Gen. 49:6 Or, tongue: meaning that he neither consented to them in word nor thought.
f. Gen. 49:6 The Shechemites, Gen. 34:26.
g. Gen. 49:7 For Levi had no part, and Simeon was under Judah, Josh. 19:1, till God gave them the place of the Amalekites, 1 Chron. 4:43.
h. Gen. 49:8 As was verified in David and Christ.
i. Gen. 49:9 His enemies shall so fear him.
j. Gen. 49:10 Or, Kingdom.
k. Gen. 49:10 Which is Christ the Messiah, the giver of prosperity who shall call the Gentiles to salvation.
l. Gen. 49:11 A country most abundant with vines and pastures is promised him.
m. Gen. 49:14 Hebrew, an ass of great bones.
n. Gen. 49:14 His force shall be great, but he shall want courage to resist his enemies.
o. Gen. 49:16 Shall have the honor of a tribe.
p. Gen. 49:17 That is, full of subtlety.
q. Gen. 49:18 Seeing the miseries that his posterity should fall into, he bursteth out in prayer to God to remedy it.
r. Gen. 49:20 He shall abound in corn and pleasant fruits.
s. Gen. 49:21 Overcoming more by fair words than by force.
t. Gen. 49:22 Hebrew, a son of increase.
u. Gen. 49:22 Hebrew, daughters.
v. Gen. 49:23 As his brethren when they were his enemies, Potiphar and others.
w. Gen. 49:24 That is God.
x. Gen. 49:26 Inasmuch as he was more near to the accomplishment of the promise, and it had been more often confirmed.
y. Gen. 49:26 Either in dignity, or when he was sold from his brethren.
z. Gen. 49:33 Whereby is signified how quietly he died.

GEN. 49

1. Gen. 32:22 - 1Chron. 5:1
2. Gen. 47:30

GEN. 50

a. Gen. 50:2 He meaneth them that embalmed the dead and buried them.
b. Gen. 50:3 They were more excessive in lamenting than the faithful.
c. Gen. 50:6 The very infidels would have oaths performed.
d. Gen. 50:10 Or, the corn floor of Atad.
e. Gen. 50:11 Or, the lamentation of the Egyptians.
f. Gen. 50:13 Or, a possession.
g. Gen. 50:15 An evil conscience is never fully at rest.
h. Gen. 50:17 Meaning, that they which have one God should be joined in most sure love.
i. Gen. 50:17 Or, the messenger.
j. Gen. 50:19 Or, am I in God's stead, meaning to take vengeance.
k. Gen. 50:19 Who by the good success seemeth to remit it, and therefore it ought not to be revenged by me.
l. Gen. 50:21 Hebrew, to their heart.
m. Gen. 50:22 Who, notwithstanding he bare rule in Egypt about fourscore years, yet was joined with the church of God in faith and religion.
n. Gen. 50:25 He speaketh this by the spirit of prophecy, exhorting his brethren to have full trust in God's promise for their deliverance.

GEN. 50

1. Gen. 47:29
2. Acts 7:26
3. Gen. 23:16
4. Gen.45:5
5. Num.32:39
6. Heb.11:22
7. Exod.13:19

THE SECOND BOOK OF MOSES, CALLED

EXODUS

1

2 The children of Jacob that came into Egypt. 8 The new Pharaoh op-
presseth them. 12 The providence of God toward them. 15 The King's
commandment to the midwives. 22 The sons of the Hebrews are commanded to be
cast into the river.

1 Now [1,a]these are the names of the children of Israel, which came into Egypt
(every man and his household came thither with Jacob) **2** Reuben, Simeon, Levi,
and Judah, **3** Issachar, Zebulun, and Benjamin, **4** Dan, and Naphtali, Gad,
and Asher. **5** So all the [b]souls, that came out of the loins of Jacob, were [2]seventy
souls: Joseph was in Egypt already. **6** Now Joseph died and all his brethren, and
that whole generation. **7** And the [3]children of Israel [c]brought forth fruit and in-
creased in abundance, and were multiplied, and were exceeding mighty, so that the
[d]land was full of them. **8** Then there rose up a new King in Egypt, who [e]knew
not Joseph. **9** And he said unto his people, Behold, the people of the children of
Israel are greater, and mightier than we. **10** Come, let us work wisely with them,
lest they multiply, and it come to pass, that if there be war, they join themselves also
unto our enemies, and fight against us, and [f,g]get them out of the land. **11** The-
refore did they set taskmasters over them, to keep them under with burdens: and
they built the cities Pithom and Raamses for the [h]treasures of Pharaoh. **12** But
the more they vexed them, the more they multiplied and grew: therefore [i]they
were more grieved against the children of Israel. **13** Wherefore the Egyptians
by cruelty caused the children of Israel to serve. **14** Thus they made them weary
of their lives by sore labor in clay and in brick, and in all work in the field, with
all manner of bondage, [j]which they laid upon them most cruelly. **15** Moreover
the King of Egypt commanded the midwives of the Hebrew women (of which
the one's name was [k]Shiphrah, and the name of the other Puah) **16** And said,
When ye do the office of a midwife to the women of the Hebrews, and see them
on their [l]stools, if it be a son, then ye shall kill him: but if it be a daughter, then let
her live. **17** Notwithstanding the midwives feared God, and did not as the King
of Egypt commanded them, but preserved alive the men children. **18** Then the
King of Egypt called for the midwives, and said unto them, Why have ye done
thus, and have preserved alive the men children? **19** And the midwives answered
Pharaoh, Because the Hebrew [m]women are not as the women of Egypt: for they are
lively, and are delivered ere the midwives come at them. **20** God therefore pro-
spered the midwives, and the people multiplied, and were very mighty. **21** And
because the midwives feared God, therefore he [n]made them houses. **22** Then
Pharaoh charged all his people, saying, Every man-child that is born, [o]cast ye into
the river, but reserve every maid-child alive.

2

2 Moses is born and cast into the flags. 5 He is taken up of Pharaoh's dau-
ghter and kept. 12 He killeth the Egyptian. 15 He fleeth and marrieth a
wife. 23 The Israelites cry unto the Lord.

1 Then there went a [a]man of the house of Levi, and took to wife a daughter
of Levi. **2** And the woman conceived and bare a son: and when she saw that
he was fair, [1]she hid him three months. **3** But when she could no longer hide
him, she took for him an ark made of reed, and daubed it with slime and with
pitch, and [b]laid the child therein, and put it among the bulrushes by the river's
brink. **4** Now his sister stood afar off, to wit what would come of him. **5** Then
the daughter of Pharaoh came down to wash her in the river, and her maidens
walked by the river's side: and when she saw the ark among the bulrushes, she sent
her maid to fetch it. **6** Then she opened it, and saw it was a child, and behold,
the babe wept: so she had compassion on it, and said, This is one of the Hebrews'
children. **7** Then said his sister unto Pharaoh's daughter, Shall I go and call unto
thee a nurse of the Hebrew women to nurse thee the child? **8** And Pharaoh's
daughter said to her, Go So the maid went and called the [c]child's mother. **9** To
whom Pharaoh's daughter said, Take this child away, and nurse it for me, and I will
reward thee Then the woman took the child, and nursed him. **10** Now the child
grew, and she brought him unto Pharaoh's daughter, and he was as her son, and
she called his name Moses, because, said she, I drew him out of the water. **11**
And in those days, when Moses was [d]grown, he went forth unto his brethren, and
looked on their burdens: also he saw an Egyptian smiting an Hebrew one of his
brethren. **12** And he looked [e]round about, and when he saw no man, he [f]slew
the Egyptian, and hid him in the sand. **13** Again he came forth the second day,
and behold two Hebrews strove: and he said unto him that did the wrong, Whe-
refore smitest thou thy fellow? **14** And he answered, Who made thee a man
of authority, and a judge over us? Thinkest thou to kill me, as thou killedst the
Egyptian? Then Moses [g]feared and said, Certainly this thing is known. **15** Now
Pharaoh heard this matter, and sought to slay Moses: therefore Moses fled from
Pharaoh, and dwelt in the land of Midian, and he sat down by a well. **16** And
the [h]Priest of Midian had seven daughters, which came and drew water, and filled
the troughs, for to water their father's sheep. **17** Then the shepherds came and
drove them away: but Moses rose up, and [i]defended them, and watered their she-
ep. **18** And when they came to Reuel their [j]father, he said, How are ye come so
soon today? **19** And they said, A man of Egypt delivered us from the hand of the
shepherds, and also drew us water enough, and watered the sheep. **20** Then he
said unto his daughters, And where is he? why have ye so left the man? [k]call him
that he may eat bread. **21** And Moses agreed to dwell with the man: who gave
unto Moses Zipporah his daughter: **22** And she bare a son, [2]whose name he cal-
led Gershom: for he said, I have been a stranger in a strange land. **23** Then in
process of time, the King of Egypt died, and the children of Israel sighed for the
bondage and [l]cried: and their cry for the bondage came up unto God. **24** Then
God heard their moan, and God remembered his covenant with Abraham, Isaac,
and Jacob. **25** So God looked upon the children of Israel, and God [m]had respect
unto them.

3

1 Moses keepeth sheep, and God appeareth unto him in a bush. 10 He
sendeth him to deliver the children of Israel. 14 The name of God.

1 When Moses kept the sheep of Jethro his father-in-law, Priest of Midian,
and drove the flock to the [a]back side of the desert, and came to the [b]Mountain
of God, [c]Horeb, **2** Then the Angel of the Lord appeared unto him [1]in a flame

---

EXOD. 1

- **a.** Exod. 1:1 Moses describeth the wonderful order that God observeth in performing his promise to Abraham, Gen. 15:14.
- **b.** Exod. 1:5 Or, persons.
- **c.** Exod. 1:7 Or, did grow.
- **d.** Exod. 1:7 He meaneth the country of Goshen.
- **e.** Exod. 1:8 He considered not how God had preserved Egypt for Joseph's sake.
- **f.** Exod. 1:10 Into Canaan, and so we shall lose our commodity.
- **g.** Exod. 1:10 Or, go up out of the land.
- **h.** Exod. 1:11 Or, corn and provision.
- **i.** Exod. 1:12 The more that God blesseth his, the more doth the wicked envy them.
- **j.** Exod. 1:14 Hebrew, wherewith they served themselves of them by cruelty.
- **k.** Exod. 1:15 These seem to have been the chief of the rest.
- **l.** Exod. 1:16 Or, seats whereupon they sat in travail.
- **m.** Exod. 1:19 Their disobedience herein was lawful, but their dissembling evil.
- **n.** Exod. 1:21 That is, God increased the families of the Israelites by their means.
- **o.** Exod. 1:22 When tyrants cannot prevail by craft, they burst forth into open rage.

EXOD. 1

- **1.** Gen. 46:8
- **2.** Gen. 26:7 / Deut. 10:22
- **3.** Acts 7:17

EXOD. 2

- **a.** Exod. 2:1 This Levite was called Amram, who married Jochebed, Exod. 6:20.
- **b.** Exod. 2:3 Committing him to the providence of God, whom she could not keep from the rage of the tyrant.
- **c.** Exod. 2:8 Man's counsel cannot hinder that, which God hath determined shall come to pass.
- **d.** Exod. 2:11 That is, was forty years old, Acts 7:23.
- **e.** Exod. 2:12 Hebrew, thus and thus.
- **f.** Exod. 2:12 Being assured that God had appointed him to deliver the Israelites, Acts 7:25.
- **g.** Exod. 2:14 Though by his fear he showed his infirmity, yet faith covered it, Heb. 11:27.
- **h.** Exod. 2:16 Or, prince.
- **i.** Exod. 2:17 Hebrew, saved them.
- **j.** Exod. 2:18 Or, grandfather.
- **k.** Exod. 2:20 Wherein he declared a thankful mind, which would recompense the benefit done unto his.
- **l.** Exod. 2:23 God humbleth his by afflictions, that they should cry unto him, and receive the fruit of his promise.
- **m.** Exod. 2:25 He judgeth their causes or acknowledged them to be his.

EXOD. 2

- **1.** Num. 26:59 / 1 Chron. 23:13 / Acts 7:20 / Heb. 11:23
- **2.** Exod. 18:3

EXOD. 3

- **a.** Exod. 3:1 Or, far within the desert.
- **b.** Exod. 3:1 It was so called after the law was given.
- **c.** Exod. 3:1 Called also Sinai.
- **d.** Exod. 3:2 This signifieth that the Church is not consumed by the fire of affliction, because God is in the midst thereof.

of fire out of the midst of a [d]bush, and he looked, and behold, the bush burned
with fire, and the bush was not consumed. **3** Therefore Moses said, I will turn
aside now, and see this great sight, why the bush burneth not. **4** And when the
[e]Lord saw that he turned aside to see, God called unto him out of the midst of
the bush, and said, Moses, Moses And he answered, I am here. **5** Then he said,
Come not hither, [f]put thy shoes off thy feet: for the place whereon thou standest
is [g]holy ground. **6** Moreover he said, [2]I am the God of thy father, the God of
Abraham, the God of Isaac, and the God of Jacob Then Moses hid his face: for
he was [h]afraid to look upon God. **7** Then the Lord said, I have surely seen the
trouble of my people, which are in Egypt, and have heard their cry, because of their
[i]taskmasters: for I know their sorrows. **8** Therefore I am come down to deliver
them out of the hand of the Egyptians, and to bring them out of that land into
a good land and a large, into a land that [j]floweth with milk and honey, even into
the place of the Canaanites, and the Hittites, and the Amorites, and the Perizzites,
and the Hivites, and the Jebusites. **9** [k]And now lo, the cry of the children of Isra-
el is come unto me, and I have also seen the oppression wherewith the Egyptians
oppress them. **10** Come now therefore, and I will send thee unto Pharaoh, that
thou mayest bring my people the children of Israel out of Egypt. **11** But Mo-
ses said unto God, Who am [l]I, that I should go unto Pharaoh, and that I should
bring the children of Israel out of Egypt? **12** And he answered, [m]Certainly I will
be with thee: and this shall be a token unto thee, that I have sent thee, After that
thou hast brought the people out of Egypt, ye shall serve God upon this moun-
tain. **13** Then Moses said unto God, Behold, when I shall come unto the chil-
dren of Israel, and shall say unto them, The God of your fathers hath sent me unto
you: if they say unto me, What is his Name? what shall I say unto them? **14** And
God answered Moses, I [n]AM THAT I AM Also he said, Thus shalt thou say unto
the children of Israel, I AM hath sent me unto you. **15** And God spake fur-
ther unto Moses, Thus shalt thou say unto the children of Israel, The Lord God
of your fathers, the God of Abraham, the God of Isaac, and the God of Jacob
hath sent me unto you: this is my Name forever, and this is my memorial unto
all ages. **16** Go and gather the Elders of Israel together, and thou shalt say unto
them, The Lord God of your fathers, the God of Abraham, Isaac, and Jacob appe-
ared unto me, and said, [o]I have surely remembered you, and that which is done
to you in Egypt. **17** Therefore I did say, I will bring you out of the affliction of
Egypt unto the land of the Canaanites, and the Hittites, and the Amorites, and the
Perizzites, and the Hivites, and the Jebusites, unto a land that floweth with milk
and honey. **18** Then shall they obey my voice, and thou and the Elders of Israel
shall go unto the King of Egypt, and say unto him, The Lord God of the Hebrews
hath [p]met with us: we pray thee now therefore, let us go three days' journey in the
wilderness, that we may [q]sacrifice unto the Lord our God. **19** But I know, that
the King of Egypt will not let you go, but by strong hand. **20** Therefore will I
stretch out mine hand and smite Egypt with all my wonders, which I will do in the
midst thereof: and after that shall he let you go. **21** And I will make this people
to be favored of the Egyptians: so that when ye go, ye shall not go empty. **22** [3,r]
For every woman shall ask of her neighbor, and of her [s]that sojourneth in her hou-
se, jewels of silver and jewels of gold and raiment, and ye shall put them on your
sons, and on your daughters, and shall spoil the Egyptians.

4

3 Moses' rod is turned into a serpent. 6 His hand is leprous. 9 The water of the river is turned into blood. 14 Aaron is given to help Moses. 21 God hardeneth Pharaoh. 25 Moses' wife circumciseth her son.

1 Then Moses answered, and said, [a]But lo, they will not believe me, nor
hearken unto my voice: for they will say, The Lord hath not appeared unto
thee. **2** And the Lord said unto him, What is that in thine hand? And he answe-
red, A rod. **3** Then said he, Cast it on the ground So he cast it on the ground,
and it was turned into a serpent: and Moses fled from it. **4** Again the Lord said
unto Moses, Put forth thine hand, and take it by the tail Then he put forth his
hand and caught it, and it was turned into a rod in his hand. **5** Do this [b]that
they may believe, that the Lord God of their fathers, the God of Abraham, the
God of Isaac, and the God of Jacob hath appeared unto thee. **6** And the Lord
said furthermore unto him, Thrust now thine hand into thy bosom And he thrust
his hand into his bosom, and when he took it out again, behold his hand was [c]le-
prous as snow. **7** Moreover he said, Put thine hand into thy bosom again So he
put his hand into his bosom again, and plucked it out of his bosom, and behold,
it was turned again as his other flesh. **8** So shall it be, if they will not believe
thee, neither obey [d]the voice of the first sign, yet shall they believe for the voice of
the second sign. **9** But if they will not yet believe these two signs, neither obey
unto thy voice, then shalt thou take of the [e]water of the river, and pour it upon
the dry land: so the water which thou shalt take out of the river, shall be turned
to blood upon the dry land. **10** But Moses said unto the Lord, Oh my Lord, I
am not eloquent, [f]neither at any time have been, nor yet since thou hast spoken
unto thy servant: but I am [g]slow of speech and slow of tongue. **11** Then the
Lord said unto him, Who hath given the mouth to man? or who hath made the
dumb, or the deaf, or him that seeth, or the blind? have not I the Lord? **12** The-
refore go now, and [1]I will be with thy mouth, and will teach thee what thou shalt
say. **13** But he said, Oh my Lord, send, I pray thee, by the [h]hand of him, whom
thou [i]shouldest send. **14** Then the Lord was [j]very angry with Moses, and said,
Do not I know Aaron thy brother the Levite, that he himself shall speak? for lo, he
cometh also forth to meet thee, and when he seeth thee, he will be glad in his he-
art. **15** Therefore thou shalt speak unto him, and [k]put the words in his mouth,
and I will be with thy mouth, and with his mouth, and will teach you what ye ou-
ght to do. **16** And he shall be thy spokesman unto the people: and he shall be,
even he shall be as thy mouth, and thou shalt be to him as [2,l]God. **17** Moreover
thou shalt take this rod in thine hand, wherewith thou shalt do miracles. **18**
Therefore Moses went and returned to Jethro his father-in-law, and said unto him,
I pray thee, let me go, and return to my [m]brethren, which are in Egypt, and see
whether they be yet alive Then Jethro said to Moses, Go in peace. **19** (For the
Lord had said unto Moses in Midian, Go, return to Egypt: for they are all dead
which [n]went about to kill thee.) **20** Then Moses took his wife and his sons, and
[o]put them on an ass, and returned toward the land of Egypt, and Moses took the
[p]rod of God in his hand. **21** And the Lord said unto Moses, When thou art
entered and come into Egypt again, see that thou do all the wonders before Pha-
raoh, which I have put in thine hand: but I will [q]harden his heart, and he shall
not let the people go. **22** Then thou shalt say to Pharaoh, Thus saith the Lord,
Israel is my son, even my [r]firstborn. **23** Wherefore I say to thee, Let my son go,
that he may serve me: if thou refuse to let him go, behold, I will slay thy son, even
thy firstborn. **24** And as he was by the way in the Inn, the Lord met him, and
[s]would have killed him. **25** Then Zipporah took a sharp knife, and [t]cut away the
foreskin of her son, and cast it at his feet, and said, Thou art indeed a bloody hu-
sband unto me. **26** So [u]he departed from him Then she said, O bloody husband
(because of the circumcision). **27** Then the Lord said unto Aaron, Go meet
Moses in the wilderness And he went and met him in the [v]Mount of God, and
kissed him. **28** Then Moses told Aaron all the words of the Lord, who had sent
him, and all the signs wherewith he had charged him. **29** So went Moses and
Aaron, and gathered all the elders of the children of Israel. **30** And Aaron told all
the words, which the Lord had spoken unto Moses, and he did the miracles in the
sight of the people. **31** And the [w]people believed, and when they heard that the
Lord had visited the children of Israel, and had looked upon their tribulation, they
bowed down, and worshipped.

5

1 Moses and Aaron do their message unto Pharaoh, who oppresseth the people of Israel more and more. 20 They cry out upon Moses and Aaron therefore, and Moses complaineth unto God.

1 Then afterward Moses and Aaron went and said to [a]Pharaoh, Thus saith the
Lord God of Israel, Let my people go, that they may [b]celebrate a feast unto me
in the wilderness. **2** And Pharaoh said, Who is the Lord, that I should hear his

---

e. Exod. 3:4 Whom he calleth the Angel, verse 2.
f. Exod. 3:5 Resign thyself up to me, Ruth 4:7; Josh. 5:15.
g. Exod. 3:5 Because of my presence.
h. Exod. 3:6 For sin causeth man to fear God's justice.
i. Exod. 3:7 Whose cruelty was intolerable.
j. Exod. 3:8 Most plentiful of all things.
k. Exod. 3:9 He heard before, but now he would revenge it.
l. Exod. 3:11 He doth not fully disobey God, but acknowledgeth his own weakness.
m. Exod. 3:12 Neither fear thine own weakness, nor Pharaoh's tyranny.
n. Exod. 3:14 The God which ever have been, am, and shall be: the God almighty, by whom all things have their being, and the God of mercy, mindful of my promise, Rev. 1:8.
o. Exod. 3:16 Hebrew, in visiting have visited.
p. Exod. 3:18 Or, appeared unto us.
q. Exod. 3:18 Because Egypt was full of idolatry, God would appoint them a place where they should serve him purely.
r. Exod. 3:22 This example may not be followed generally: though at God's commandment they did it justly, receiving some recompense of their labors.
s. Exod. 3:22 Or, in whose house she sojourneth.

EXOD. 3

1. Acts 7:30
2. Matt. 22:32 / Acts 7:32
3. Exod. 11:2 / Exod. 12:35

EXOD. 4

a. Exod. 4:1 God beareth with Moses' doubting, because he was not altogether without faith.
b. Exod. 4:5 This power to work miracles was to confirm his doctrine, and to assure him of his vocation.
c. Exod. 4:6 Or, white as snow.
d. Exod. 4:8 Or, the words confirmed by the first sign.
e. Exod. 4:9 Because these three signs should be sufficient witnesses to prove that Moses should deliver God's people.
f. Exod. 4:10 Hebrew, from yesterday, and ere yesterday.
g. Exod. 4:10 Hebrew, heavy of mouth.
h. Exod. 4:13 Or, ministry.
i. Exod. 4:13 That is, the Messiah: or some other, that is more meet than I.
j. Exod. 4:14 Though we provoke God justly to anger, yet he will never reject his.
k. Exod. 4:15 Thou shalt instruct him what to say.
l. Exod. 4:16 Meaning, as a wise counselor and full of God's spirit.
m. Exod. 4:18 Or, kinsfolk, and lineage.
n. Exod. 4:19 Hebrew, sought thy soul.
o. Exod. 4:20 Hebrew, caused them to ride.
p. Exod. 4:20 Whereby he wrought the miracles.
q. Exod. 4:21 By receiving my spirit and delivering him unto Satan to increase his malice.
r. Exod. 4:22 Meaning, most dear unto him.
s. Exod. 4:24 God punished him with sickness for neglecting his Sacrament.
t. Exod. 4:25 This act was extraordinary: for Moses was sore sick, and God even then required it.
u. Exod. 4:26 Or, the Angel.
v. Exod. 4:27 Or, Horeb.
w. Exod. 4:31 So that Moses had now experience of God's promise that he should have good success.

EXOD. 4

1. Matt. 10:19 / Matt. 12:22
2. Exod. 7:1

EXOD. 5

a. Exod. 5:1 Faith overcometh fear, and maketh men bold in their vocation.
b. Exod. 5:1 And offer sacrifice.

voice, and let Israel go? I know not the Lord, neither will I let Israel go. **3** And
they said, [c]We worship the God of the Hebrews: we pray thee, let us go three
days' journey in the desert, and sacrifice unto the Lord our God, lest [d]he bring
upon us the pestilence or sword. **4** Then said the King of Egypt unto them,
Moses and Aaron, why cause ye the people to cease from their works? get you to
your burdens. **5** Pharaoh said furthermore, Behold, much people is now in the
land, and ye [e]make them leave their burdens. **6** Therefore Pharaoh gave com-
mandment the same day unto the taskmasters of the people, and to their [f]officers,
saying, **7** Ye shall give the people no more straw, to make brick ([g]as in time past)
but let them go and gather them straw themselves. **8** Notwithstanding lay upon
them the number of brick, which they made in time past, diminish nothing there-
of: for they be idle, therefore they cry, saying, Let us go to offer sacrifice unto our
God. **9** [h]Lay more work upon the men, and cause them to do it, and let them
not regard [i]vain words. **10** Then went the taskmasters of the people and their of-
ficers out, and told the people, saying, Thus saith Pharaoh, I will give you no more
straw. **11** Go yourselves, get ye straw where ye can find it, yet shall nothing of
your labor be diminished. **12** Then were the people scattered abroad throughout
all the land of Egypt, for to gather stubble instead of straw. **13** And the taskma-
sters hasted them, saying, Finish your day's work [j]every day's task, as ye did when ye
had straw. **14** And the Officers of the children of Israel, which Pharaoh's taskma-
sters had set over them, were beaten, and demanded, Wherefore have ye not fulfil-
led your task in making brick yesterday and today, as in times past? **15** Then the
officers of the children of Israel came and cried unto Pharaoh, saying, Wherefore
dealest thou thus thy servants? **16** There is no straw given to thy servants, and
they say unto us, Make brick: and lo, thy servants are beaten, and [k]thy people is
blamed. **17** But he said, [l]Ye are too much idle: therefore ye say, Let us go to of-
fer sacrifice to the Lord. **18** Go therefore now and work: for there shall no straw
be given you, yet shall ye deliver the whole tale of brick. **19** Then the officers of
the children of Israel [m]saw themselves in an evil case, because it was said, Ye shall
diminish nothing of your brick, nor of every day's task. **20** And they met Mo-
ses and Aaron, which stood in their way as they came out from Pharaoh. **21** To
whom they said, The Lord look upon you and judge: for ye have made our savor to
[n]stink before Pharaoh and before his servants, in that ye have [o]put a sword in their
hand to slay us. **22** Wherefore Moses returned to the Lord, and said, Lord, why
hast thou afflicted this people? wherefore hast thou thus sent me? **23** For since
I came to Pharaoh to speak in thy name, he hath vexed this people, and yet thou
hast not delivered thy people.

6

8 God reneweth his promise of deliverance of the Israelites. 9 Moses speaketh to the Israelites, but they believe him not. 10 Moses and Aaron are sent again unto Pharaoh.

1 Then the Lord said unto Moses, Now shalt thou see, what I will do unto
Pharaoh: for by a strong hand shall he let them go, and even [a]be constrained to
drive them out of his land. **2** Moreover God spake unto Moses, and said unto
him, I am the Lord, **3** And I appeared unto Abraham, to Isaac, and to Jacob by
the Name of [b]Almighty God, but by my Name [c]Jehovah was I not known unto
them. **4** Furthermore as I made my covenant with them to give them the land
of Canaan, the land of their pilgrimage, wherein they were strangers: **5** So I
have also heard the groaning of the children of Israel, whom the Egyptians keep
in bondage, and have remembered my covenant. **6** Wherefore say thou unto
the children of Israel, I am the Lord, and I will bring you out from the burdens
of the Egyptians, and will deliver you out of their bondage, and will redeem you
in a stretched out arm, and in great [d]judgments. **7** Also I will [e]take you for
my people, and will be your God: then ye shall know that I the Lord your God
bring you out from the burdens of the Egyptians. **8** And I will bring you into
the land which I [f]sware that I would give to Abraham, and to Isaac, and to Jacob,
and I will give it unto you for a possession: I am the Lord. **9** So Moses told the
children of Israel thus: but they hearkened [g]not unto Moses, for anguish of spirit
and for cruel bondage. **10** Then the Lord spake unto Moses, saying, **11** Go
speak to Pharaoh King of Egypt, that he let the children of Israel go out of his
land. **12** But Moses spake before the Lord, saying, Behold, the children of Israel
hearken not unto me, how then shall Pharaoh hear me, which am of [h]uncircumci-
sed lips? **13** Then the Lord spake unto Moses and unto Aaron, and charged them
to go to the children of Israel and to Pharaoh King of Egypt, to bring the children
of Israel out of the land of Egypt. **14** These be the heads [i]of their father's hou-
ses: the [1]sons of Reuben the firstborn of Israel are Hanoch and Pallu, Hezron and
Carmi: these are the families of Reuben. **15** [2]Also the sons of Simeon: Jemuel
and Jamin, and Ohad, and Jachin, and Zohar, and Shaul the son of a Canaaniti-
sh woman: these are the families of Simeon. **16** [3]These also are the names of
the sons of Levi in their generations: Gershon and Kohath and Merari (and the
years of the life of Levi were an hundred [j]thirty and seven years). **17** The sons of
Gershon were Libni and Shimi by their families. **18** [4]And the sons of Kohath,
Amram and Izhar, and Hebron, and Uzziel (and Kohath lived an hundred thirty
and three years). **19** Also the sons of Merari were Mahli and Mushi: these are the
families of Levi their kindreds. **20** And Amram took Jochebed his [k]father's sister
to his wife, and she bare him Aaron and [5]Moses (and Amram lived an hundred
thirty and seven years). **21** Also the sons of Izhar: [l]Korah, and Nepheg, and Zi-
chri. **22** And the sons of Uzziel: Mishael, and Elzaphan, and Zithri. **23** And
Aaron took Elisheba daughter of Amminadab, sister of [m]Nahshon to his wife, whi-
ch bare him Nadab, and Abihu, Eleazar and Ithamar. **24** Also the sons of Korah:
Assir, and Elkanah and Abiasaph: these are the families of the Korahites. **25** And
Eleazar Aaron's son took him one of the daughters of Putiel to his wife, which bare
him [6]Phinehas: these are the principal fathers of the Levites throughout their fami-
lies. **26** These are Aaron and Moses to whom the Lord said, Bring the children
of Israel out of the land of Egypt, according to their [n]armies. **27** These are that
Moses, and Aaron, which spake to Pharaoh King of Egypt, that they might bring
the children of Israel out of Egypt. **28** And at that time when the Lord spake
unto Moses in the land of Egypt, **29** When the Lord, I say, spake unto Moses,
saying, I am the Lord, speak thou unto Pharaoh the King of Egypt all that I say
unto thee. **30** Then Moses said before the Lord, Behold, I am of [o]uncircumcised
lips, and how shall Pharaoh hear me?

7

3 God hardeneth Pharaoh's heart. 10 Moses and Aaron do the miracles of the serpent, and the blood: and Pharaoh's sorcerers do the like.

1 Then the Lord said to Moses, Behold, I have made thee [a]Pharaoh's [b]God,
and Aaron thy brother shall [c]be thy Prophet. **2** Thou shalt speak all that I com-
manded thee: and Aaron thy brother shall speak unto Pharaoh, that he suffer the
children of Israel to go out of his land. **3** But I will harden Pharaoh's heart, and
multiply my miracles, and my wonders in the land of Egypt. **4** And Pharaoh
shall not hearken unto you, that I may lay mine hand upon Egypt, and bring out
mine armies, even my people, the children of Israel out of the land of Egypt, by
great [d]judgments. **5** Then the Egyptians shall know that I am the Lord, when
I stretch forth mine hand upon Egypt, and bring out the children of Israel from
among them. **6** So Moses and Aaron did as the Lord commanded them, even so
did they. **7** (Now Moses was [e]fourscore years old, and Aaron fourscore and three,
when they spake unto Pharaoh.) **8** And the Lord had spoken unto Moses and
Aaron, saying, **9** If Pharaoh speak unto you, saying, Show a miracle for you, then
thou shalt say unto Aaron, Take thy rod, and cast it before Pharaoh, and it shall be
turned into a [f]serpent. **10** Then went Moses and Aaron unto Pharaoh, and did
even as the Lord had commanded, and Aaron cast forth his rod before Pharaoh and
before his servants, and it was turned into a serpent. **11** Then Pharaoh also called
for the wise men and [g]sorcerers: and those charmers also of Egypt did in like man-
ner with their enchantments. **12** For they cast down every man his rod, and they
were turned into serpents: but Aaron's rod devoured their rods. **13** So Pharaoh's
heart was hardened, and he hearkened not to them, as the Lord had said. **14**
The Lord then said unto Moses, Pharaoh's heart is [h]obstinate, he refuseth to let the

---

c. Exod. 5:3 Or, God hath met us.
d. Exod. 5:3 Hebrew, Lest he meet us with pestilence.
e. Exod. 5:5 As though ye would rebel.
f. Exod. 5:6 Which were of the Israelites, and had charge to see them do their work.
g. Exod. 5:7 Hebrew, yesterday and ere yesterday.
h. Exod. 5:9 The more cruelly that tyrants rage, the nearer is God's help.
i. Exod. 5:9 Of Moses and Aaron.
j. Exod. 5:13 Hebrew, the work of a day in his day.
k. Exod. 5:16 Or, thy people the Egyptians are in fault.
l. Exod. 5:17 Hebrew, idle, ye are idle.
m. Exod. 5:19 Or, looked sad on them, which said.
n. Exod. 5:21 Read Gen. 34:30.
o. Exod. 5:21 It is a grievous thing to the servants of God to be accused of evil, specially of their brethren, when they do as their duty requireth.

EXOD. 6

a. Exod. 6:1 Hebrew, in a strong hand.
b. Exod. 6:3 Or, all sufficient.
c. Exod. 6:3 Whereby he signifieth that he will perform indeed that which he promised to their fathers: for this name declareth that he is constant and will perform his promise.
d. Exod. 6:6 Or, plagues.
e. Exod. 6:7 He meaneth, as touching the outward vocation, the dignity whereof they lost afterward by their rebellion: but as for election to life everlasting, it is immutable.
f. Exod. 6:8 Hebrew, Lift up mine hand.
g. Exod. 6:9 So hard a thing it is to show true obedience under the cross.
h. Exod. 6:12 Or barbarous and rude in speech: and by this word (uncircumcised) is signified the whole corruption of man's nature.
i. Exod. 6:14 This genealogy showeth of whom Moses and Aaron came.
j. Exod. 6:16 For he was 42 years old, when he came into Egypt, and there lived 94.
k. Exod. 6:20 Which kind of marriage was after in the law forbidden, Lev. 18:12.
l. Exod. 6:21 Moses and he were brothers' children, whose rebellion was punished, Num. 16:1.
m. Exod. 6:23 Who was a prince of Judah, Num. 1:7.
n. Exod. 6:26 For their families were so great, that they might be compared to armies.
o. Exod. 6:30 The disobedience both of Moses and of the people, showeth that their deliverance came only of God's free mercy.

EXOD. 6

1. Gen. 46:9 / Num. 26:5 / 1 Chron. 5:8
2. 1 Chron. 4:24
3. Num. 3:17 / 1 Chron. 6:1 / 1 Chron. 23:6
4. Num. 26:57 / 1 Chron. 6:1 / 1 Chron. 23:6
5. Exod. 2:2 / Num. 26:59
6. Num. 25:18

EXOD. 7

a. Exod. 7:1 Or, a God to Pharaoh.
b. Exod. 7:1 I have given thee power and authority to speak in my name and to execute my judgments upon him.
c. Exod. 7:1 Or, shall speak for thee (before Pharaoh.)
d. Exod. 7:4 To strengthen Moses' faith, God promiseth again to punish most sharply the oppression of his Church.
e. Exod. 7:7 Moses lived in affliction and banishment forty years before he enjoined his office to deliver God's people.
f. Exod. 7:9 Or, dragon.
g. Exod. 7:11 It seemeth that these were Jannes and Jambres: read 2 Tim. 3:8, so ever the wicked maliciously resist the truth of God.
h. Exod. 7:14 Or, heavy and dull.

people go. **15** Go unto Pharaoh in the morning, (lo, he will come forth unto the water) and thou shalt stand and meet him by [i]the river's brink, and the rod, which was turned into a serpent, shalt thou take in thine hand. **16** And thou shalt say unto him, The Lord God of the Hebrews hath sent me unto thee, saying, Let my people go that they may serve me in the wilderness: and behold, hitherto thou wouldest not hear. **17** Thus saith the Lord, In this thou shalt know that I am the Lord: behold, I will smite with the rod that is in mine hand upon the water that is in the river, and it shall be turned into blood. **18** And the fish that is in the river shall die, and the river shall stink, and it shall [j]grieve the Egyptians to drink of the water of the river. **19** The Lord then spake to Moses, Say unto Aaron, Take thy rod, and stretch out thine hand over the waters of Egypt, over their streams, over their rivers, and over their ponds, and over all pools of their waters, and they shall be [k]blood, and there shall be blood throughout the land of Egypt, both in vessels of wood, and of stone. **20** So Moses and Aaron did even as the Lord commanded: [1]and he lift up the rod, and smote the water that was in the river in the sight of Pharaoh, and in the sight of his servants: and [2]all the water that was in the river, was turned into blood. **21** And the [l]fish that was in the river died, and the river stank: so that the Egyptians could not drink of the water of the river: and there was blood throughout the land of Egypt. **22** And the enchanters of Egypt did [m]likewise with their sorceries: and the heart of Pharaoh was [n]hardened: so that he did not hearken unto them, as the Lord hath said. **23** Then Pharaoh returned, and went again into his house, [o]neither did this yet enter into his heart. **24** All the Egyptians then dug round about the river for waters to drink: for they could not drink of the water of the river. **25** And this [p]continued fully seven days after the Lord had smitten the river.

8

6 Frogs are sent. 13 Moses prayeth, and they die. 17 Lice are sent, whereby the sorcerers acknowledge God's power. 24 Egypt is plagued with noisome flies. 30 Moses prayeth again.

1 Afterward the Lord said unto Moses, Go unto Pharaoh, and tell him, Thus saith the Lord, Let my people go, that they may serve me. **2** And if thou wilt not let them go, behold, I will smite all thy country with [a]frogs: **3** And the river shall crawl full of frogs, which shall go up and come into thine house, and into thy chamber, where thou sleepest, and upon thy bed, and into the house of thy servants, and upon thy people, and into thy ovens, and [b]into thy kneading troughs. **4** Yea, the frogs shall climb up upon thee, and on thy people, and upon all thy servants. **5** Also the Lord said to Moses, Say thou unto Aaron, Stretch out thine hand with thy rod upon the streams, upon the rivers, and upon the ponds, and cause frogs to come up upon the land of Egypt. **6** Then Aaron stretched out his hand upon the waters of Egypt, and the [c]frogs came up and covered the land of [d]Egypt. **7** And the sorcerers did likewise with their sorceries, and brought frogs up upon the land of Egypt. **8** Then Pharaoh called for Moses and Aaron, and said, [e]Pray ye unto the Lord, that he may take away the frogs from me, and from my people, and I will let the people go, that they may do sacrifice unto the Lord. **9** And Moses said unto Pharaoh, [f]Concerning me, even [g]command when I shall pray for thee, and for thy servants, and for thy people, to destroy the frogs from thee and from thine houses, that they may remain in the river only. **10** Then he said, Tomorrow And he answered, Be it [h]as thou hast said, that thou mayest know, that there is none like unto the Lord our God. **11** So the frogs shall depart from thee, and from thine houses, and from thy servants, and from thy people: only they shall remain in the river. **12** Then Moses and Aaron went out from Pharaoh: and Moses cried unto the Lord concerning the frogs, which he had [i]sent unto Pharaoh. **13** And the Lord did according to the saying of Moses: So the frogs [j]died in the houses, in the towns, and the fields. **14** And they gathered them together by heaps, and the land stank of them. **15** But when Pharaoh saw that he had rest given him, he [k]hardened his heart, and hearkened not unto them, as the Lord had said. **16** Again the Lord said unto Moses, Say unto Aaron, Stretch out thy rod, and smite the dust of the earth, that it may be turned to [l]lice throughout all the land of Egypt. **17** And they did so: for Aaron stretched out his hand with his rod, and smote the dust of the earth: and lice came upon man and upon beast: all the dust of the earth was lice throughout all the land of Egypt. **18** Now the enchanters assayed likewise with their enchantments to bring forth lice, but they [m]could not So the lice were upon man and upon beast. **19** Then said the enchanters unto Pharaoh, This is [n]the finger of God But Pharaoh's heart remained obstinate, and he hearkened not unto them, as the Lord had said. **20** Moreover the Lord said to Moses, Rise up early in the morning, and stand before Pharaoh (lo, he will come forth unto the water) and say unto him, Thus saith the Lord, Let my people go, that they may serve me. **21** Else, if thou wilt not let my people go, behold, I will send [o]swarms of flies both upon thee, and upon thy servants, and upon thy people, and into thine houses: and the houses of the Egyptians shall be full of swarms of flies, and the ground also whereon they are. **22** But the land of Goshen, where my people are, will I cause to be [p]wonderful in that day, so that no swarms of flies shall be there, that thou mayest know that I am the Lord in the midst of the [q]earth. **23** And I will make a deliverance of my people from thy people: tomorrow shall this miracle be. **24** And the Lord did so: for there came [r]great swarms of flies into the house of Pharaoh, and into his servants' houses, so that through all the land of Egypt, the earth was corrupt by the swarms of flies. **25** Then Pharaoh called for Moses and Aaron, and said, Go, do sacrifice unto your God in this land. **26** And Moses answered, It is not meet to do so: for then we should offer unto the Lord our God that, which is an [s]abomination unto the Egyptians Lo, can we sacrifice the abomination of the Egyptians before their eyes, and they not stone us? **27** Let us go three days' journey in the desert, and sacrifice unto the Lord our God, [1]as he hath commanded us. **28** And Pharaoh said, I will let you go, that ye may sacrifice unto the Lord your God in the wilderness: but [t]go not far away, pray for me. **29** And Moses said, Behold, I will go out from thee, and pray unto the Lord, that the swarms of flies may depart from Pharaoh, from his servants, and from his people tomorrow: but let Pharaoh from henceforth [u]deceive no more, in not suffering the people to sacrifice unto the Lord. **30** So Moses went out from Pharaoh and prayed unto the Lord. **31** And the Lord did according to the saying of Moses, and the swarms of flies departed from Pharaoh, from his servants, and from his people, and there remained not one. **32** Yet Pharaoh [v]hardened his heart at this time also, and did not let the people go.

9

3 The moraine of beasts. 10 The plague of botches and sores. 23 The horrible hail, thunder, and lightning. 26 The land of Goshen ever is excepted. 27 Pharaoh confesseth his wickedness. 33 Moses prayeth for him. 35 Yet he is obstinate.

1 Then the Lord said unto Moses, Go to Pharaoh, and tell him, Thus saith the Lord God of the Hebrews, Let my people go, that they may serve me. **2** But if thou refuse to let them go, and wilt yet hold them still, **3** Behold, the hand of the Lord is upon thy flock which is in the field: for upon the horses, upon the asses, upon the camels, upon the cattle, and upon the sheep shall be a [a]mighty great moraine. **4** And the Lord shall do [b]wonderfully between the beasts of Israel, and the beasts of Egypt: so that there shall nothing die at all, that pertaineth to the children of Israel. **5** And the Lord appointed a time, saying, Tomorrow the Lord shall finish this thing in this land. **6** So the Lord did this thing on the morrow, and all the cattle of Egypt died: but of the cattle of the children of Israel died not one. **7** Then Pharaoh [c]sent, and behold, there was not one of the cattle of the Israelites dead: and the heart of Pharaoh was obstinate, and he did not let the people go. **8** And the Lord said to Moses and to Aaron, Take your handful of [d]ashes of the furnace, and Moses shall sprinkle them toward the heaven in the sight of Pharaoh, **9** And they shall be turned to dust in all the land of Egypt: and it shall be as a scab breaking out into blisters upon man, and upon beast throughout all the land of Egypt. **10** Then they took ashes of the furnace, and stood before Pharaoh: and Moses sprinkled them toward the heaven, and there came [a] [e]scab breaking out into blisters upon man, and upon beast. **11** And the sorcerers could not stand before Moses, because of the scab: for the scab was upon the enchanters and upon all the Egyptians. **12** And the Lord hardened the heart of Pharaoh, and he hearkened not unto them, [1]as the Lord had said unto Moses. **13** Also the Lord said unto Moses, Rise up early in the morning, and stand before Pharaoh,

---

i. Exod. 7:15 To wit, the river Nile.
j. Exod. 7:18 Or, they shall be weary, and abhor to drink.
k. Exod. 7:19 The first plague.
l. Exod. 7:21 To signify that it was a true miracle, and that God plagued them in that which was most necessary for the preservation of life.
m. Exod. 7:22 In outward appearance, and after that the seven days were ended.
n. Exod. 7:22 Hebrew, was made strong.
o. Exod. 7:23 Hebrew, he set not his heart at all thereunto.
p. Exod. 7:25 Or seven days accomplished.

EXOD. 7
1. Exod. 17:5 **2.** Ps.78:44

EXOD. 8
a. Exod. 8:2 There is nothing so weak, that God cannot cause to overcome the greatest power of man.
b. Exod. 8:3 Or, upon thy dough, or into thine ambries.
c. Exod. 8:6 The second plague.
d. Exod. 8:6 But Goshen, where God's people dwelt, was excepted.
e. Exod. 8:8 Not love, but fear causeth the very Infidels to seek unto God.
f. Exod. 8:9 Hebrew, have this honor over me.
g. Exod. 8:9 Or, speak plain unto me.
h. Exod. 8:10 Hebrew, according to thy word.
i. Exod. 8:12 Or, laid upon.
j. Exod. 8:13 In things of this life God oft times heareth the prayers of the just for the ungodly.
k. Exod. 8:15 Or, made his heart heavy.
l. Exod. 8:16 The third plague.
m. Exod. 8:18 God confounded their wisdom and authority in a thing most vile.
n. Exod. 8:19 They acknowledged that this was done by God's power and not by sorcery, Luke 11:20.
o. Exod. 8:21 Or, a multitude of venomous beasts as serpents, etc.
p. Exod. 8:22 Or, I will separate.
q. Exod. 8:22 Or, land of Egypt.
r. Exod. 8:24 The fourth plague.
s. Exod. 8:26 For the Egyptians worshipped divers beasts, as the ox, the sheep and such like which the Israelites offered in sacrifice, which thing the Egyptians abhorred to see.
t. Exod. 8:28 So the wicked prescribe unto God's messengers how far they shall go.
u. Exod. 8:29 He could not judge his heart, but yet he charged him to do this unfeignedly.
v. Exod. 8:32 Where God giveth not faith, no miracles can prevail.

EXOD. 8
1. Exod. 3:18

EXOD. 9
a. Exod. 9:3 The fifth plague.
b. Exod. 9:4 He shall declare his heavenly judgment against his enemies, and his favor toward his children.
c. Exod. 9:7 Into the land of Goshen, where the Israelites dwelled.
d. Exod. 9:8 Or, embers.
e. Exod. 9:10 The sixth plague.
f. Exod. 9:14 So that thine own conscience shall condemn thee of ingratitude and malice.

and tell him, Thus saith the Lord God of the Hebrews, Let my people go that they may serve me. **14** For I will at this time send my plagues upon [f]thine heart, and upon thy servants, and upon thy people, that thou mayest know that there is none like me in all the earth. **15** For now I will stretch out mine hand, that I may smite thee and thy people with the pestilence: and thou shalt perish from the earth. **16** And indeed, [2]for this cause have [g]I appointed thee, to [h]show my power in thee, and to declare my [i]name throughout all the world. **17** Yet thou exaltest thyself against my people, and lettest them not go. **18** Behold, tomorrow this time I will cause to rain a mighty great hail, such as was not in Egypt since the foundation thereof was laid unto this time. **19** Send therefore now, and [j]gather the cattle, and all that thou hast in the field: for upon all the men, and the beasts, which are found in the field, and not brought home, the hail shall fall upon them, and they shall die. **20** Such then as feared the word of the Lord among the servants of Pharaoh, made his servants and his cattle flee into the houses. **21** But such as [k]regarded not the [l]word of the Lord, left his servants, and his cattle in the field. **22** And the Lord said to Moses, Stretch forth thine hand toward heaven, that there may be hail in all the land of Egypt, upon man, and upon beast, and upon all the herbs of the field in the land of Egypt. **23** Then Moses stretched out his rod toward heaven, and the Lord sent thunder and [m]hail, and [n]lightning upon the ground: and the Lord caused hail to rain upon the land of Egypt. **24** So there was hail, and fire mingled with the hail, so grievous, as there was none throughout all the land of Egypt, since [o]it was a nation. **25** And the hail smote throughout all the land of Egypt all that was in the field, both man and beast: also the hail smote all the trees of the field and brake to pieces all the trees of the field. **26** Only in the land of Goshen (where the children of Israel were) was no hail. **27** Then Pharaoh sent and called for Moses and Aaron, and said unto them, I [p]have now sinned: the Lord is righteous, but I and my people are wicked. **28** Pray ye unto the Lord (for it is enough) that there be no more [q]mighty thunders, and hail, and I will let you go, and ye shall tarry no longer. **29** Then Moses said unto him, As soon as I am out of the city, I will spread mine hands unto the Lord, and the thunder shall cease, neither shall there be any more hail, that thou mayest know that [3]the earth is the Lord's. **30** As for thee and thy servants, I know [r]afore I pray, ye will fear before the face of the Lord God. **31** (And the flax, and the barley were smitten: for the barley was eared, and the flax was bolled. **32** But the wheat and the rye were not smitten, for they were [s]hid in the ground.) **33** Then Moses went out of the city from Pharaoh, and spread his hands to the Lord, and the thunder and the hail ceased, neither rained it upon the earth. **34** And when Pharaoh saw that the rain and the hail and the thunder were ceased, he sinned again, and hardened his heart, both he, and his servants. **35** So the heart of Pharaoh was hardened: neither would he let the children of Israel go, as the Lord had said [t]by Moses.

10

7 Pharaoh's servants counsel him to let the Israelites depart. 13 Grasshoppers destroy the country. 16 Pharaoh confesseth his sin. 22 Darkness is sent.

1 Again the Lord said unto Moses, Go to Pharaoh, [1]for I have hardened his heart, and the heart of his servants, that I might work these [a]my miracles in the midst of his realm, **2** And that thou mayest declare in the [b]ears of thy son, and of thy son's son, what things I have done in Egypt, and my miracles, which I have done among them: that ye may know that I am the Lord. **3** Then came Moses and Aaron unto Pharaoh, and they said unto him, Thus saith the Lord God of the Hebrews, How long wilt thou refuse [c]to humble thyself before me? Let my people go, that they may serve me. **4** But if thou refuse to let my people go, behold, tomorrow will I bring [d]grasshoppers into thy coasts. **5** And they shall cover the face of the earth, that a man cannot see the earth: and they shall eat the residue which remaineth unto you, and hath escaped from the hail: and they shall eat all your trees that bud in the field. **6** And they shall fill thine houses, and all thy servants' houses, and the houses of all the Egyptians, as neither thy fathers, nor thy fathers' fathers have seen, since the time they were upon the earth unto this day So he returned, and went out from Pharaoh. **7** Then Pharaoh's servants said unto him, How long shall he be [e]an [f]offence unto us? let the men go, that they may serve the Lord their God: wilt thou first know that Egypt is destroyed? **8** So Moses and Aaron were brought again unto Pharaoh, and he said unto them, Go, serve the Lord your God, but who are they that shall go? **9** And Moses answered, We will go with our young, and with our old, with our sons, and with our daughters, with our sheep, and with our cattle will we go: for we must celebrate a feast unto the Lord. **10** And he said unto them, Let [g]the Lord so be with you, as I will let you go and your children: [h]behold, for evil is before your face. **11** It shall not be so: now go ye that are men, and serve the Lord: for that was your desire Then they were thrust out from Pharaoh's presence. **12** After, the Lord said unto Moses, Stretch out thine hand upon the land of Egypt for the grasshoppers, that they may come upon the land of Egypt, and eat all the herbs of the land, even all that the hail had left. **13** Then Moses stretched forth his rod upon the land of Egypt: and the Lord brought an East wind upon the land all that day, and all that night: and in the morning the East wind brought the [i]grasshoppers. **14** So the grasshoppers went up upon all the land of Egypt, and [j]remained in all quarters of Egypt: so grievous Grasshoppers, like to these were never before, neither after them shall be such. **15** For they covered all the face of the earth, so that the land was dark: and they did eat all the herbs of the land, and all the fruits of the trees, which the hail had left, so that there was no green thing left upon the trees, nor among the herbs of the field throughout all the land of Egypt. **16** Therefore Pharaoh called for [k]Moses and Aaron in haste, and said, I have sinned against the Lord your God, and against you. **17** And now forgive me my sin only this once, and pray unto the Lord your God, that he may take away from me this death only. **18** Moses then went out from Pharaoh, and prayed unto the Lord. **19** And the Lord turned a mighty strong West wind, and took away the grasshoppers, and violently cast them into the [l]red Sea, so that there remained not one grasshopper in all the land of Egypt. **20** But the Lord hardened Pharaoh's heart, and he did not let the children of Israel go. **21** Again the Lord said unto Moses, Stretch out thine hand toward heaven, that there may be upon the land of Egypt darkness, even darkness that may be [m]felt. **22** Then Moses stretched forth his hand toward heaven, and there was a [n]black darkness in all the land of Egypt three days. **23** No man saw another, neither rose up from the place where he was for three days: but all the children of Israel had light where they dwelt. **24** Then Pharaoh called for Moses, and said, Go serve the Lord: only your sheep and your cattle shall abide, and your children shall go with you. **25** And Moses said, Thou must give us also sacrifices, and burnt offerings that we may do sacrifice unto the Lord our God. **26** Therefore our cattle also shall go with us: there shall not an [o]hoof be left, for thereof must we take to serve the Lord our God: neither do we know [p]how we shall serve the Lord, until we come thither. **27** (But the Lord hardened Pharaoh's heart, and he would not let them go.) **28** And Pharaoh said unto him, Get thee from me: look thou see my face no more: for whensoever thou comest in my sight, thou shalt [q]die. **29** Then Moses said, Thou hast said well: from henceforth will I see thy face no more.

11

1 God promiseth their departure. 2 He willeth them to borrow their neighbors' jewels. 3 Moses was esteemed of all save Pharaoh.

1 Now the Lord had said unto Moses, yet will I bring one plague more upon Pharaoh, and upon Egypt, after that, he will let you go hence: when he letteth you go, he shall [a]at once chase you hence. **2** Speak thou now to the people, that every man [b]require of his neighbor, and every woman of her neighbor, [1]jewels of silver, and jewels of gold. **3** And the Lord gave the people favor in the sight of the Egyptians: also Moses was very great in the land of Egypt, in the sight of Pharaoh's servants, and in the sight of the people. **4** And Moses said, Thus saith the Lord, [2]About midnight will I go out into the midst of Egypt. **5** And all the firstborn in the land of Egypt shall die, from the firstborn of Pharaoh that sitteth on his throne, unto the firstborn of the maid servant, that is at [c]the mill, and all the firstborn of beasts. **6** Then there shall be a great cry throughout all the land of Egypt, such as was never none like, nor shall be. **7** But against none of the children of Israel shall a dog move his tongue, neither against man nor beast, that ye may know that the Lord putteth a difference between the Egyptians and Israel. **8** And all these thy servants shall come down unto me, and fall before me, saying, Get thee

---

g. Exod. 9:16 Or, set thee up.
h. Exod. 9:16 Or, to show thee.
i. Exod. 9:16 That is, that all the world may magnify my power in overcoming thee.
j. Exod. 9:19 Here we see though God's wrath be kindled, yet there is a certain mercy showed even to his enemies.
k. Exod. 9:21 Hebrew, set not his heart to.
l. Exod. 9:21 The word of the minister is called the word of God.
m. Exod. 9:23 The seventh plague.
n. Exod. 9:23 Hebrew, fire walked.
o. Exod. 9:24 Or, since it was inhabited.
p. Exod. 9:27 The wicked confess their sins to their condemnation, but they cannot believe to obtain remission.
q. Exod. 9:28 Hebrew, voice of God.
r. Exod. 9:30 Meaning, that when they have their request, they are never the better, though they make many fair promises, wherein we see the practices of the wicked.
s. Exod. 9:32 Or, late sown.
t. Exod. 9:35 Hebrew, by the hand of Moses.

EXOD. 9

1. Exod. 4:21
2. Rom. 9:17
3. Ps. 24:1

EXOD. 10

a. Exod. 10:1 Or, in his presence, or among them.
b. Exod. 10:2 The miracles should be so great, that they should be spoken of for ever: where also we see the duty of parents toward their children.
c. Exod. 10:3 The end of affliction is, to humble ourselves with true repentance under the hand of God.
d. Exod. 10:4 Or, locusts.
e. Exod. 10:7 Or, snare.
f. Exod. 10:7 Meaning, the occasion of all these evils: so are the godly ever charged as Elijah was by Ahab.
g. Exod. 10:10 That is, I would the Lord were no more affectioned toward you, than I am minded to let you go.
h. Exod. 10:10 Punishment is prepared for you. Some read, Ye intend some mischief.
i. Exod. 10:13 The eighth plague.
j. Exod. 10:14 Or, he caused them to remain.
k. Exod. 10:16 The wicked in their miseries seek to God's ministers for help, albeit they hate and detest them.
l. Exod. 10:19 The water seemed red, because the sand or gravel is red: the Hebrews called it the Sea of bulrushes.
m. Exod. 10:21 Because it was so thick.
n. Exod. 10:22 The ninth plague.
o. Exod. 10:26 The ministers of God ought not to yield one iota to the wicked, as touching their charge.
p. Exod. 10:26 That is, with what beasts, or how many.
q. Exod. 10:28 Though before he confessed Moses just, yet again his own conscience he threateneth to put him to death.

EXOD. 10

1. Exod. 4:2

EXOD. 11

a. Exod. 11:1 Without any condition, but with haste and violence.
b. Exod. 11:2 Or, borrow.
c. Exod. 11:5 From the highest to the lowest.
d. Exod. 11:8 That is, under thy power and government.

out, and all the people that [d]are at thy feet, and after this will I depart So he went out from Pharaoh very angry. 9 And the Lord said unto Moses, Pharaoh shall not hear you, [e]that my wonders may be multiplied in the land of Egypt. 10 So Moses and Aaron did all these wonders before Pharaoh: but the Lord hardened Pharaoh's heart, and he suffered not the children of Israel to go out of his land.

12

1 The Lord instituteth the passover. 26 The fathers must teach their children the mystery thereof. 29 The firstborn are slain. 31 The Israelites are driven out of the land. 35 The Egyptians are spoiled. 37 The number that departeth out of Egypt.

1 Then the Lord spake to Moses and to Aaron in the land of Egypt, saying, 2 This [a]month shall be unto you the beginning of months: it shall be to you the first [b]month of the year. 3 Speak ye unto all the congregation of Israel, saying, In the tenth of this month let every man take unto him a lamb, according to the house of the [c]fathers, a lamb for an house. 4 And if the household be too little for the lamb, he shall take his neighbor, which is next unto his house, according to the number of the persons: every one of you, according to his [d]eating shall make your count for the lamb. 5 Your lamb shall be without blemish, a male of a year old: ye shall take it of the lambs, or of the kids. 6 And ye shall keep it until the fourteenth day of this month: then [e]all the multitude of the congregation of Israel shall kill it [f]at even. 7 After, they shall take of the blood, and strike it on the two posts, and on the upper doorpost of the houses where they shall eat it. 8 And they shall eat the flesh that same night, roast with fire, and unleavened bread: with sour herbs they shall eat it. 9 Eat not thereof raw, boiled nor sodden in water, but roast with fire, both his [g]head, his feet, and his purtenance. 10 And ye shall reserve nothing of it unto the morning: but that, which remaineth of it unto the morrow shall ye burn with fire. 11 And thus shall ye eat it, Your loins girded, your shoes on your feet, and your staves in your hands, and ye shall eat it in haste: for [h]it is the Lord's Passover. 12 For I will pass through the land of Egypt the same night, and will smite all the firstborn in the land of Egypt, both man and beast, and I will execute judgment upon all the [i]gods of Egypt, I am the Lord. 13 And the blood shall be a token for you upon the houses where ye are: so when I see the blood, I will pass over you, and the plague shall not be upon you to destruction, when I smite the land of Egypt. 14 And this day shall be unto you a [j]remembrance: and ye shall keep it an holy feast unto the Lord, throughout your generations: ye shall keep it holy by an ordinance [k]forever. 15 Seven days shall ye eat unleavened bread, and in any case ye shall put away leaven the first day out of your houses: for whosoever eateth leavened bread from the first day until the seventh day, that person shall be cut off from Israel. 16 And in the first day shall be an holy [l]assembly: also in the seventh day shall be an holy assembly unto you: no work shall be done in them, save about that which every man must eat: that only may ye do. 17 Ye shall keep also the feast of unleavened bread: for that same day I will bring your armies out of the land of Egypt: therefore ye shall observe this day, throughout your posterity, by an ordinance forever. 18 [1]In the first month and the fourteenth day of the month at [m]even, ye shall eat unleavened bread unto the one and twentieth day of the month at even. 19 Seven days shall no leaven be found in your houses: for whosoever eateth leavened bread, that person shall be cut off from the Congregation of Israel: whether he be a stranger, or born in the land. 20 Ye shall eat no leavened bread: but in all your habitations shall ye eat unleavened bread. 21 Then Moses called all the Elders of Israel, and said unto them, Choose out and take you for every of your households a lamb, and kill the Passover. 22 And take [2]a bunch of hyssop, and dip it in the blood that is in the basin, and strike the [n]lintel, and the [o]door cheeks with the blood that is in the basin, and let none of you go out at the door of the house, until the morning. 23 For the Lord will pass by to smite the Egyptians: and when he seeth the blood upon the lintel and on the two door cheeks, the Lord will pass over the door, and will not suffer the [p]destroyer to come into your houses to plague you. 24 Therefore shall ye observe this thing as an ordinance, both for thee and thy sons forever. 25 And when ye shall come into the [q]land, which the Lord will give you, as he hath promised, then ye shall keep this [r]service. 26 [3]And when your children ask you, What service is this ye keep? 27 Then ye shall say, It is the sacrifice of the Lord's Passover, which passed over the houses of the children of Israel in Egypt, when he smote the Egyptians, and preserved our houses Then the people [s]bowed themselves and worshipped. 28 So the children of Israel went, and did as the Lord had commanded Moses and Aaron: so did they. 29 Now at [4]midnight, the Lord [t]smote all the firstborn in the land of Egypt, from the firstborn of Pharaoh that sat on his throne, unto the firstborn of the captive that was in prison, and all the firstborn of beasts. 30 And Pharaoh rose up in the night, he, and all his servants, and all the Egyptians: and there was a great cry in Egypt: for there was [u]no house where there was not one dead. 31 And he called to Moses and to Aaron by night, and said, Rise up, get you out from among my people, both ye, and the children of Israel, and go serve the Lord as ye have said. 32 Take also your sheep and your cattle as ye have said, and depart, and [v]bless me also. 33 And the Egyptians did force the people, because they would send them out of the land in haste: for they said, We die all. 34 Therefore the people took their dough before it was leavened, even their dough bound in clothes upon their shoulders. 35 And the children of Israel did according to the saying of Moses, and they asked of the Egyptians [5]jewels of silver and jewels of gold, and raiment. 36 And the Lord gave the people favor in the sight of the Egyptians: and they [w]granted their request: so they spoiled the Egyptians. 37 Then the [6]children of Israel took their journey from [x]Rameses to Succoth about six hundred thousand men of foot, besides children. 38 And [y]a great multitude of sundry sorts of people went out with them, and sheep, and beeves, and cattle in great abundance. 39 And they baked the dough which they brought out of Egypt, and made unleavened cakes: for it was not leavened, because they were thrust out of Egypt, neither could they tarry, nor yet prepare themselves vittles. 40 So the dwelling of the children of Israel, while they dwelled in Egypt, was [7]four hundred and thirty years. 41 And when the [z]four hundred and thirty years were expired, even the selfsame day departed all the hosts of the Lord out of the land of Egypt. 42 It is a night to be kept holy to the Lord, because he brought them out of the land of Egypt: this is that night of the Lord, which all the children of Israel must keep throughout their generations. 43 Also the Lord said unto Moses and Aaron, This is the Law of the Passover: [aa]no stranger shall eat thereof. 44 But every servant that is bought for money, when thou hast circumcised him, then shall he eat thereof. 45 A stranger or an hired servant shall not eat thereof. 46 [8]In one house shall it be eaten: thou shalt carry none of the flesh out of the house, [9]neither shall ye break a bone thereof. 47 All the Congregation of Israel shall observe it. 48 But if a stranger dwell with thee, and will observe the passover of the Lord, let him circumcise all the males, that belong unto him, and then let him come and observe it, and he shall be as one that is born in the land: for none uncircumcised person shall eat thereof. 49 One [ab]law shall be to him that is born in the land, and to the stranger that dwelleth among you. 50 Then all the children of Israel did as the Lord commanded Moses and Aaron: so did they. 51 And the selfsame day did the Lord bring the children of Israel out of the land of Egypt by their armies.

13

The firstborn are offered to God. 3 The memorial of their deliverance. 6 The institution of the Passover. 8, 14 An exhortation to teach their children to remember this deliverance. 17 Why they are led by the wilderness. 19 The bones of Joseph. 21 The pillar of the cloud and of the fire.

1 And the Lord spake unto Moses, saying, 2 [1]Sanctify unto me all the firstborn: that is, every one that first openeth the womb among the children of Israel, as well of man as of beast: for it is mine. 3 Then Moses said unto the people, [2]Remember this day in the which ye came out of Egypt, out of the [a]house of [b]bondage: for by a mighty hand the Lord brought you out from thence: therefore no leavened bread shall be [c]eaten. 4 This day come ye out in the month of [d]Abib. 5 Now when the Lord hath brought thee into the land of the Canaanites, and Hittites, and Amorites, and Hivites, and Jebusites, (which he sware unto thy fathers, that he would give thee, a land flowing with milk and honey) then thou shalt keep

---

e. Exod. 11:9 God hardeneth the hearts of the reprobate, that his glory thereby might be the more set forth, Rom. 9:17.

EXOD. 11

1. Exod. 3:32 / Exod. 3:35 **2.** Exod. 12:29

EXOD. 12

a. Exod. 12:2 Called Nisan, containing part of March, and part of April.
b. Exod. 12:2 As touching the observation of feasts: as for other policies, they reckoned from September.
c. Exod. 12:3 As the fathers of the household had great or small families.
d. Exod. 12:4 He shall take so many as are sufficient to eat the lamb.
e. Exod. 12:6 Everyone his house.
f. Exod. 12:6 Hebrew, between the two evenings, or twilight.
g. Exod. 12:9 That is, all that may be eaten.
h. Exod. 12:11 The lamb was not the Passover, but signified it, as sacraments are not the thing itself, which they do represent, but signify it.
i. Exod. 12:12 Or, princes, or Idols.
j. Exod. 12:14 Of the benefit received for your deliverance.
k. Exod. 12:14 That is, until Christ's coming: for then ceremonies had an end.
l. Exod. 12:16 Or, calling together of the people to serve God.
m. Exod. 12:18 For in old time so they counted, beginning the day at Sunset till the next day at the same time.
n. Exod. 12:22 Or, transom, or upper door post.
o. Exod. 12:22 Or, two side posts.
p. Exod. 12:23 The Angel sent of God to kill the firstborn.
q. Exod. 12:25 The land of Canaan.
r. Exod. 12:25 Or, ceremony.
s. Exod. 12:27 They gave God thanks for so great a benefit.
t. Exod. 12:29 The tenth plague.
u. Exod. 12:30 Of those houses, wherein any firstborn was, either of men or beasts.
v. Exod. 12:32 Pray for me.
w. Exod. 12:36 Or, lent them.
x. Exod. 12:37 Which was a city in Goshen, Gen. 47:11.
y. Exod. 12:38 Which were strangers, and not born of the Israelites.
z. Exod. 12:41 From Abraham's departing from Ur in Chaldea unto the departing of the children of Israel from Egypt are 430 years.
aa. Exod. 12:43 Except he be circumcised, and only profess your religion.
ab. Exod. 12:49 They that are of the household of God, must be all joined in one faith and religion.

EXOD. 12

1. Lev. 23:5 / Num. 28:16
2. Heb. 21:28
3. Josh. 4:6
4. Exod. 11:4
5. Exod 3:12 / Exod. 11:2
6. Num. 32:3 / Josh 24:6
7. Gen. 15:13 / Acts 7:6 / Gal. 3:17
8. Num. 9:12
9. John. 29:36

EXOD. 13

a. Exod. 13:3 Hebrew, house of servants.
b. Exod. 13:3 Where they were in most cruel slavery.
c. Exod. 13:3 To signify that they had not leisure to leaven their bread.
d. Exod. 13:4 Containing part of March and part of April, when corn began to ripe in that country.
e. Exod. 13:6 Both the seventh and the first day were holy, as Exod. 12:16.

this service in this month. **6** Seven days shalt thou eat unleavened bread, and the [e]seventh day shall be the feast of the Lord. **7** Unleavened bread shall be eaten seven days, and there shall no leavened bread be seen with thee, nor yet leaven be seen with thee in all thy quarters. **8** And thou shalt show thy son [f]in that day, saying, This is done, because of that which the Lord did unto me, when I came out of Egypt. **9** And it shall be a sign unto thee [g]upon thine hand, and for a remembrance between thine eyes, that the Law of the Lord may be in thy mouth: for by a strong hand the Lord brought thee out of Egypt. **10** Keep therefore this ordinance in his season appointed from year to year. **11** And when the Lord shall bring thee into the land of the Canaanites, as he sware unto thee and to thy fathers, and shall give it thee, **12** [3]Then shalt thou set apart unto the Lord all that first openeth the womb: also everything that first doth open the womb, and cometh forth of thy beast: the males shall be the Lord's. **13** But every [h]first foal of an [i]ass, thou shalt redeem with a lamb: and if thou redeem him not, then shalt thou break his neck: likewise also the firstborn of man among thy sons shalt thou [j]buy out. **14** And when thy son shall ask thee [k]tomorrow, saying, What is this? thou shalt then say unto him, With a mighty hand the Lord brought us out of Egypt, out of the house of bondage. **15** For when Pharaoh was hard hearted against our departing, the Lord then slew all the firstborn in the land of Egypt, from the firstborn of man even to the firstborn of beast: therefore I sacrifice unto the Lord all the males that first open the womb, but all the firstborn of my sons I redeem. **16** And it shall be as a token upon thine hand, and as [l]frontlets between thine eyes, that the Lord brought us out of Egypt by a mighty hand. **17** Now when Pharaoh had let the people go, God carried them not by the way of the Philistines' country, [m]though it were nearer: (for God said, Lest the people repent when they [n]see war, and turn again to Egypt). **18** But God made the people to go about by the way of the wilderness of the red sea: and the children of Israel went up [o]armed out of the land of Egypt. **19** (And Moses took the bones of Joseph with him: for he had made the children of Israel swear, saying, [4]God will surely visit you, and ye shall take my bones away hence with you.) **20** [5]So they took their journey from Succoth, and camped in Etham in the edge of the wilderness. **21** [6]And the Lord went before them by day in a pillar of a [p]cloud to lead them the way, and by night in a pillar of fire to give them light, that they might go both by day and by night. **22** [7]He took not away the pillar of the cloud by day, nor the pillar of fire by night from before the people.

14

4, 8 Pharaoh's heart is hardened, and pursueth the Israelites. 11 The Israelites stricken with fear, murmur against Moses. 13 Moses doth encourage them. 21 He divideth the Sea. 23, 27 The Egyptians follow and are drowned.

1 Then the Lord spake unto Moses, saying, **2** Speak to the children of Israel, that they [a]return and camp before [b]Pi Hahiroth, between Migdol and the Sea, over against [1]Baal Zephon: about it shall ye camp by the Sea. **3** For Pharaoh will say of the children of Israel, They are tangled in the land: the wilderness hath shut them in. **4** And I will harden Pharaoh's heart that he shall follow after you: so I will [c]get me honor upon Pharaoh, and upon all his host: the Egyptians also shall know that I am the Lord: and they did so. **5** Then it was told the king of Egypt, that the people fled: and the heart of Pharaoh and of his servants was turned against the people, and they said, Why have we this done, and have let Israel go out of our service? **6** And he made ready his chariots, and took his people with him, **7** And took six hundred chosen chariots, and [d]all the chariots of Egypt, and captains over every one of them. **8** (For the Lord had hardened the heart of Pharaoh king of Egypt, and he followed after the children of Israel: but the children of Israel went out with an [e]high hand.) **9** [2]And the Egyptians pursued after them, and all the horses and chariots of Pharaoh, and his horsemen and his host overtook them camping by the Sea, beside Pi Hahiroth, before Baal Zephon. **10** And when Pharaoh drew nigh, the children of Israel lift up their eyes, and behold, the Egyptians marched after them, and they were sore [f]afraid: wherefore the children of Israel cried unto the Lord. **11** And they said unto Moses, Hast thou brought us to die in the wilderness, because there were no graves in Egypt? wherefore hast thou served us thus, to carry us out of Egypt? **12** Did not we tell thee this thing in Egypt, saying, Let [g]us be in rest, that we may serve the Egyptians? for it had been better for us to serve the Egyptians, than that we should die in the wilderness. **13** Then Moses said to the people, Fear ye not, stand still, and behold [h]the salvation of the Lord which he will show to you this day For the Egyptians whom ye have seen this day, ye shall never see them again. **14** The Lord shall fight for you: therefore [i]hold you your peace. **15** And the Lord said unto Moses, Wherefore [j]cryest thou unto me? speak unto the children of Israel, that they go forward: **16** And lift thou up thy rod, and stretch out thine hand upon the Sea and divide it, and let the children of Israel go on dry ground through the midst of the Sea. **17** And I, behold, I will harden the heart of the Egyptians, that they may follow them, and I will get me honor upon Pharaoh, and upon all his host, upon his chariots, and upon his horsemen. **18** Then the Egyptians shall know that I am the Lord, when I have gotten me honor upon Pharaoh, upon his chariots, and upon his horsemen. **19** (And the Angel of God, which went before the host of Israel, removed, and went behind them: also the pillar of the cloud went from before them, and stood behind them, **20** And came between the camp of the Egyptians and the camp of Israel: it was both a cloud and darkness, yet gave it [k]light by night, so that all the night long the one came not at the other.) **21** And Moses stretched forth his hand upon the Sea, and the Lord caused the Sea to run back by a strong East wind all the night, and made the Sea dry land: for the waters were [3]divided. **22** Then the [4]children of Israel went through the midst of the Sea upon the dry ground, and the waters were a wall unto them on their right hand, and on their left hand. **23** And the Egyptians pursued and went after them to the midst of the Sea, even all Pharaoh's horses, his chariots, and his horsemen. **24** Now, in the morning [l]watch, when the Lord looked unto the host of the Egyptians, out of the fiery and cloudy pillar, he struck the host of the Egyptians with fear. **25** For he took off their chariot wheels, and they drove them with [m]much ado: so that the Egyptians every one said, I will flee from the face of Israel: for the Lord fighteth for them against the Egyptians. **26** Then the Lord said to Moses, Stretch thine hand upon the Sea, that the waters may return upon the Egyptians, upon their chariots and upon their horsemen. **27** Then Moses stretched forth his hand upon the Sea, and the Sea returned to his force early in the morning, and the Egyptians fled against it: but the Lord [n]overthrew the Egyptians in the midst of the Sea. **28** So the water returned and covered the chariots, and the horsemen, even all the host of Pharaoh that came into the Sea after them: there remained not one of them. **29** But the children of Israel walked upon dry land through the midst of the Sea, and the waters were a wall unto them on their right hand, and on their left. **30** Thus the Lord saved Israel the same day out of the hand of the Egyptians, and Israel saw the Egyptians dead upon the Sea bank. **31** And Israel saw the mighty [o]power, which the Lord showed upon the Egyptians: so the people feared the Lord, and believed the Lord, and his [p]servant Moses.

15

1, 20 Moses with the men and women sing praises unto God for their deliverance. 23 The people murmur. 25 At the prayer of Moses the bitter waters are sweet. 26 God teacheth the people obedience.

1 Then [a]sang Moses and the children of Israel this song unto the Lord, and said in this manner, I will sing unto the Lord: for he hath triumphed gloriously: the horse and him that rode upon him hath he overthrown in the Sea. **2** The Lord is my strength, and [b]praise, and he is become my salvation He is my God, and I will [c]prepare him a tabernacle: he is my father's God, and I will exalt him. **3** The Lord is a [d]man of war, his [e]Name is Jehovah. **4** Pharaoh's chariots and his host hath he cast into the sea: his chosen captains also were drowned in the red Sea. **5** The depths have covered them, they sank to the bottom as a stone. **6** Thy [f]right hand, O Lord, is glorious in power: thy right hand, O Lord, hath bruised the enemy. **7** And in thy great glory thou hast overthrown them that rose against

---

f. Exod. 13:8 When thou dost celebrate the feast of unleavened bread.
g. Exod. 13:9 Thou shalt have continual remembrance thereof, as thou wouldest of a thing that is in thine hand, or before thine eyes.
h. Exod. 13:13 Hebrew, that first cometh forth.
i. Exod. 13:13 This is also understood of the horse and other beasts which were not offered in sacrifice.
j. Exod. 13:13 By offering a clean beast in sacrifice, Lev. 12:6.
k. Exod. 13:14 Or, hereafterwards.
l. Exod. 13:16 Or, signs of remembrance.
m. Exod. 13:17 Or, because.
n. Exod. 13:17 Which the Philistines would have made against them by stopping them the passage.
o. Exod. 13:18 That is, not privily, but openly and as the word doth signify, set in order by five and five.
p. Exod. 13:21 To defend them from the heat of the sun.

EXOD. 13
1. Exod. 22:29 / Exod. 34:19 / Lev. 27.26 / Num. 3:13 / Num. 8:16 / Luke 2:23
2. Exod. 23:23
3. Exod. 22:29 / Exod. 34:19 / Ezek. 44:30
4. Gen. 50:22 / Josh. 24:30
5. Num. 33:6
6. Num. 14:14 / Deut. 1:33 / Ps. 78:14 / 1Cor. 10:1
7. Neh. 9:19

EXOD. 14
a. Exod. 14:2 From toward the country of the Philistines.
b. Exod. 14:2 So the Sea was before them, mountains on either side, and the enemies at their back: yet they obeyed God, and were delivered.
c. Exod. 14:4 By punishing his obstinate rebellion.
d. Exod. 14:7 Josephus writeth, that besides those chariots there were 50,000 horsemen, and 80,000 footmen.
e. Exod. 14:8 With great joy and boldness.
f. Exod. 14:10 They which a little before in their deliverance rejoiced, being now in danger, are afraid and …
g. Exod. 14:12 Such is the impatience of the flesh, that it cannot abide God's appointed time.
h. Exod. 14:13 Or, deliverance.
i. Exod. 14:14 Only put your trust in God without grudging or doubting.
j. Exod. 14:15 Thus in tentations faith fighteth against the flesh, and crieth with inward groanings to the Lord.
k. Exod. 14:20 The cloud showeth light to the Israelites, but to the Egyptians it was darkness, so that their two hosts could not join together.
l. Exod. 14:24 Which was about the three last hours of the night.
m. Exod. 14:25 Or, heavily.
n. Exod. 14:27 So the Lord by the water saved his, and by the water drowned his enemies.
o. Exod. 14:31 Hebrew, hand.
p. Exod. 14:31 That is, the doctrine which he taught them in the Name of the Lord.

EXOD. 14
1. Num. 33:7
2. Josh. 24:6
3. Josh. 4:23 / Ps. 114:3
4. Ps. 78:13 / 1 Cor. 10:1 / Heb. 11:29

EXOD. 15
a. Exod. 15:1 Praising God for the overthrow of his enemies, and their deliverance.
b. Exod. 15:2 Or, the occasion of my song of praise.
c. Exod. 15:2 To worship him therein.
d. Exod. 15:3 In battle he overcometh ever.
e. Exod. 15:3 Ever constant in his promise.
f. Exod. 15:6 Or, power.

[g]thee: thou sentest forth thy wrath, which consumed them as the stubble. **8** And
by the blast of thy nostrils the waters were gathered, the floods stood still as an
heap, the depths congealed together in the [h]heart of the Sea. **9** The enemy said,
I will pursue, I will overtake them, I will divide the spoil, [i]my lust shall be sati-
sfied upon them, I will draw my sword, mine hand shall destroy them. **10** Thou
blewest with thy wind, the sea covered them, they sank as lead in the mighty wa-
ters. **11** Who is like unto thee, O Lord, among the [j]gods! Who is like thee so glo-
rious in holiness, [k]fearful in praises, doing wonders! **12** Thou stretchedst out thy
right hand, the earth swallowed them. **13** Thou wilt by thy mercy carry this pe-
ople, which thou deliveredst, thou wilt bring them in thy strength unto thine holy
[l]habitation. **14** The people shall hear and be afraid: sorrow shall come upon the
inhabitants of Philistia. **15** Then the dukes of Edom shall be amazed, and trem-
bling shall come upon the great men of Moab: all the inhabitants of Canaan shall
wax faint hearted. **16** [1]Fear and dread shall fall upon them: because of the [m]grea-
tness of thine arm, they shall be still as a stone, till thy people pass, O Lord: till this
people pass, which thou hast purchased. **17** Thou shalt bring them in, and plant
them in the mountain of thine [n]inheritance, which is the place that thou hast pre-
pared, O Lord, for to dwell in, even the sanctuary, O Lord, which thine hands shall
establish. **18** The Lord shall reign forever and ever. **19** For Pharaoh's horses
went with his chariots and horsemen into the sea, and the Lord brought the waters
of the sea upon them: but the children of Israel went on dry land in the midst of
the sea. **20** And Miriam the Prophetess, sister of Aaron, took a timbrel in her
hand, and all the women came out after her with timbrels and [o]dances. **21** And
Miriam [p]answered the men, Sing ye unto the Lord: for he hath triumphed gloriou-
sly: the horse and his rider hath he overthrown in the sea. **22** Then Moses brou-
ght Israel from the red sea, and they went out into the wilderness of [q]Shur: and
they went three days in the wilderness, and found no waters. **23** And when they
came to Marah, they could not drink of the waters of Marah, for they were bitter:
therefore the name of the place was called [r]Marah. **24** Then the people murmu-
red against Moses, saying, What shall we drink? **25** And he cried unto the Lord,
and the Lord showed him a tree, which when he had cast into the waters, the wa-
ters were sweet: there he made them an ordinance and a law, and there [s]he proved
them, **26** And said, If thou wilt diligently hearken, O Israel, unto the voice of
the Lord thy God, and wilt do that which is [t]right in his sight, and wilt give ear
unto his commandments, and keep all his ordinances, then will I put none of these
diseases upon thee, which I brought upon the Egyptians: for I am the Lord that
healeth thee. **27** [2]And they came to Elim, where were twelve fountains of water,
and seventy [u]palm trees, and they camped there by the waters.

16

1 The Israelites come to the desert of Sin, and murmur against Moses and Aaron. 13 The Lord sendeth Quails and Manna. 23 The Sabbath is sanctified unto the Lord. 27 The seventh day Manna could not be found. 32 It is kept for a remembrance to the posterity.

1 Afterward all the Congregation of the children of Israel departed
from Elim, and came to the wilderness of [a]Sin, (which is between Elim and Si-
nai) the fifteenth day of the second month after their departing out of the land
of Egypt. **2** And the whole Congregation of the children of Israel murmured
against Moses, and against Aaron in the wilderness. **3** For the children of Israel
said to them, Oh that we had died by the hand of the Lord in the land of Egypt,
when we sat by the flesh [b]pots, when we ate bread our bellies full: for ye have
brought us out into this wilderness, to kill this whole company with famine. **4**
Then said the Lord unto Moses, Behold, I will cause bread to rain from heaven to
you, and the people shall go out, and gather [c]that that is sufficient for every [d]day,
that I may prove them, whether they will walk in my law or no. **5** But the six-
th day they shall prepare that, which they shall bring home, and it shall be twice
as much as they gather daily. **6** Then Moses and Aaron said unto all the chil-
dren of Israel, At even ye shall know, that the Lord brought you out of the land
of Egypt: **7** And in the morning ye shall see the glory of the Lord: [e]for he hath
heard your grudgings against the Lord: and what are we that ye have murmured
against us? **8** Again, Moses said, At even shall the Lord give you flesh to eat, and
in the morning your fill of bread: for the Lord hath heard your murmurings, which
ye murmur against him: for what are we? your murmurings are not against us, but
against the [f]Lord. **9** And Moses said to Aaron, Say unto all the Congregation of
the children of Israel, Draw near before the Lord: for he hath heard your murmu-
rings. **10** Now as Aaron spake unto the whole Congregation of the children of
Israel, they looked toward the wilderness, and behold, the glory of the Lord appe-
ared [1]in a cloud. **11** (For the Lord had spoken unto Moses, saying, **12** I have
heard the murmurings of the children of Israel: tell them therefore, and say, [g]At
even ye shall eat flesh, and in the morning ye shall be filled with bread, and ye shall
know that I am the Lord your God.) **13** And so at even the [2]quails came and co-
vered the camp: and in the morning the dew lay round about the host. **14** [3]And
when the dew that was fallen was ascended, behold, a small round thing was upon
the face of the wilderness, small as the hoary frost upon the earth. **15** And when
the children of Israel saw it, they said one to another, It is [h]Manna, for they wist
not what it was And Moses said unto them, [4]This is the bread which the Lord hath
given you to eat. **16** This is the thing which the Lord hath commanded: gather
of it every man according to his eating, [i]an omer for [j]a man according to the num-
ber of your persons: every man shall take for them which are in his tent. **17** And
the children of Israel did so, and gathered, some more, some less. **18** And when
they did measure it with an omer, [5]he that had gathered much, had nothing over,
and he that had gathered little, had no [k]lack: so every man gathered according to
his eating. **19** Moses then said unto them, Let no man reserve thereof till mor-
ning. **20** Notwithstanding, they obeyed not Moses: but some of them reserved
of it till morning, and it was full of worms, and [l]stank: therefore Moses was angry
with them. **21** And they gathered it every morning, every man according to his
eating: for when the heat of the sun came, it was melted. **22** And the sixth day
they gathered [m]twice so much bread, two omers for one man: then all the rulers
of the Congregation came and told Moses. **23** And he answered them, This is
that which the Lord hath said, Tomorrow is the rest of the holy Sabbath unto the
Lord: bake that today which ye will bake, and seethe that which ye will seethe,
and all that remaineth, lay it up to be kept till the morning for you. **24** And
they laid it up till the morning, as Moses bade, and it stank not, neither was there
any worm therein. **25** Then Moses said, Eat that today: for today is the Sabbath
unto the Lord: today ye shall not [n]find it in the field. **26** Six days shall ye gather
it, but in the seventh day is the Sabbath: in it there shall be none. **27** Notwith-
standing, there [o]went out some of the people in the seventh day for to gather, and
they found none. **28** And the Lord said unto Moses, How long refuse ye to keep
my commandments, and my laws? **29** Behold, how the Lord hath given you the
Sabbath: therefore he giveth you the sixth day bread for two days: tarry therefore
every man in his place: let no man go out of his place the seventh day. **30** So the
people rested the seventh day. **31** And the house of Israel called the name of it
Manna, and it was like [p]to coriander seed, but white: and the taste of it was like
unto wafers made with honey. **32** And Moses said, This is that which the Lord
had commanded, Fill an omer of it, to keep it for your posterity: that they may see
the bread wherewith I have fed you in wilderness, when I brought you out of the
land of Egypt. **33** Moses also said to Aaron, Take a [q]pot and put an omer full of
Manna therein, and set it before the Lord to be kept for your posterity. **34** As
the Lord commanded Moses, so Aaron laid it up before the [r]Testimony to be
kept. **35** And the children of Israel did eat Manna [6]forty years, until they came
unto a land inhabited: they did eat Manna until they came to the borders of the
land of Canaan. **36** The omer is the tenth part of the [s]Ephah.

17

1 The Israelites come into Rephidim, and grudge for water. 6 Water is given them out of the rock. 11 Moses holdeth up his hands, and they overcome the Amalekites. 15 Moses buildeth an altar to the Lord.

1 And all the Congregation of the children of Israel departed from the wilder-
ness of Sin, by their journeys at the [a]commandment of the Lord, and camped in
[b]Rephidim, where was no water for the people to drink. **2** [1]Wherefore the people

---

g. Exod. 15:7 Those, that are enemies to God's people, are his enemies.
h. Exod. 15:8 Or, in the depth of the sea.
i. Exod. 15:9 Hebrew, my soul shall be filled.
j. Exod. 15:11 For so oftentimes the Scripture calleth the mighty men of the world.
k. Exod. 15:11 Which oughtest to be praised with all fear and reverence.
l. Exod. 15:13 That is, into the land of Canaan: or into mount Zion.
m. Exod. 15:16 Or, for thy great power.
n. Exod. 15:17 Which was mount Zion, where afterward the Temple was built.
o. Exod. 15:20 Signifying their great joy: which custom the Jews observed in certain solemnities, Judg. 11:34 and 11:21, but it ought not to be a cloak to cover our wanton dances.
p. Exod. 15:21 By singing the like song of thanksgiving.
q. Exod. 15:22 Which was called Etham, Num. 33:8.
r. Exod. 15:23 Or, bitterness.
s. Exod. 15:25 That is, God, or Moses in God's name.
t. Exod. 15:26 Which is, to do that only that God commanded.
u. Exod. 15:27 Or, date trees.

EXOD. 15
1. Deut. 2:25 / Josh. 2:9
2. Num. 33:9

EXOD. 16
a. Exod. 16:1 This is the eighth place wherein they had camped, there is another place called Zin, which was the 33rd place wherein they camped: and is also called Kadesh, Num. 33:36.
b. Exod. 16:3 So hard a thing is it to the flesh not to murmur against God when the belly is pinched.
c. Exod. 16:4 Hebrew, the portion of a day in his day.
d. Exod. 16:4 To signify, that they should patiently depend upon God's providence from day to day.
e. Exod. 16:7 He gave them not Manna because they murmured, but for his promise sake.
f. Exod. 16:8 He that contemneth God's ministers, contemneth God himself.
g. Exod. 16:12 Or, in the twilight.
h. Exod. 16:15 Which signifieth a part, portion, or gift: also meat prepared.
i. Exod. 16:16 Which containeth about a pottle of our measure.
j. Exod. 16:16 Hebrew, for an head.
k. Exod. 16:18 God is a rich feeder of all, and none can justly complain.
l. Exod. 16:20 No creature is so pure, but being abused it turneth to our destruction.
m. Exod. 16:22 Which portion should serve for the Sabbath and the day before.
n. Exod. 16:25 God took away the occasion from their labor, to signify how holy he would have the Sabbath kept.
o. Exod. 16:27 Their infidelity was so great, that they did expressly against God's commandment.
p. Exod. 16:31 In form and figure, but not in color, Num.11:7.
q. Exod. 16:33 Of this vessel, read Heb. 9:4.
r. Exod. 16:34 That is, the Ark of the covenant, to wit, after that the Ark was made.
s. Exod. 16:36 Which measure contained about ten pottels.

EXOD. 16
1. Exod. 13:21
2. Num. 11:3 / Ps. 78:24
3. John. 6:30 / 1 Cor. 10:3
4. 2 Cor. 8:15
5. Josh. 5:12 / Neh. 5:15

EXOD. 17
a. Exod. 17:1 Hebrew, at the mouth.

contended with Moses, and said, Give us water, that we may drink And Moses said
unto them, Why contend ye with me? wherefore do ye [c]tempt the Lord? **3** So the
people thirsted there for water, and the people murmured against Moses, and said,
Wherefore hast thou thus brought us out of Egypt, to kill us, and our children, and
our cattle with thirst? **4** And Moses cried unto the Lord, saying, What shall I do
to this people? for they be almost ready to [d]stone me. **5** And the Lord answered
to Moses, Go before the people, and take with thee of the Elders of Israel: and thy
rod wherewith thou [2]smotest the river, take in thine hand, and go: **6** [3]Behold, I
will stand there before thee upon the rock in Horeb, and thou shalt smite on the
rock, and water shall come out of it, that the people may drink And Moses did so
in the sight of the Elders of Israel. **7** And he called the name of the place [e]Mas-
sah and [f]Meribah, because of the contention of the children of Israel, and becau-
se they had tempted the Lord, saying, Is the [g]Lord among us, or no? **8** [4]Then
came [h]Amalek and fought with Israel in Rephidim. **9** And Moses said to Joshua,
Choose us out men, and go fight with Amalek: tomorrow I will stand on the top
of the [i]hill with the rod of God in mine hand. **10** So Joshua did as Moses bade
him, and fought with Amalek: and Moses, Aaron, and Hur, went up to the top of
the hill. **11** And when Moses held up his hand, Israel prevailed: but when he let
his hand [j]down, Amalek prevailed. **12** Now Moses' hands were heavy: therefore
they took a stone and put it under him, and he sat upon it: and Aaron and Hur
stayed up his hands, the one on the one side, and the other on the other side: so
his hands were steady until the going down of the sun. **13** And Joshua discomfi-
ted Amalek and his people with the edge of the sword. **14** And the Lord said to
Moses, Write this for a remembrance [k]in the book, and [l]rehearse it to Joshua: for
[5]I will utterly put out the remembrance of Amalek from under heaven. **15** (And
Moses built an altar, and called the name of it [m]Jehovah Nissi.) **16** Also he said,
[n]The Lord hath sworn, that he will have war with Amalek from generation to
generation.

18

1 Jethro cometh to see Moses his son-in-law. 8 Moses telleth him of the wonders of Egypt. 9 Jethro rejoiceth and offereth sacrifice to God. 21 What manner of men officers and judges ought to be. 24 Moses obeyeth Jethro's counsel in appointing officers.

1 When Jethro the [1]Priest of Midian, Moses' father-in-law, heard all that
God had done for Moses, and for Israel his people, and how the Lord had brought
Israel out of Egypt, **2** Then Jethro the father-in-law of Moses, took Zipporah
Moses' wife, (after he had [a]sent her away) **3** And her two sons, (whereof the one
was called [2]Gershom: for he said, I have been an alien in a strange land: **4** And
the name of the other was Eliezer: for the God of my father, said he, was mine help,
and delivered me from the sword of Pharaoh). **5** And Jethro Moses' father-in-
law came with his two sons, and his wife unto Moses into the wilderness, where
he camped by the [b]mount of God. **6** And he [c]said to Moses, I thy father-in-law
Jethro am come to thee, and thy wife and her two sons with her. **7** And Moses
went out to meet his father-in-law, and did obeisance, and kissed him, and each
asked other of his [d]welfare: and they came into the tent. **8** Then Moses told his
father-in-law all that the Lord had done unto Pharaoh, and to the Egyptians for
Israel's sake, and all the travail that had come unto them by the way, and how
the Lord delivered them. **9** And Jethro rejoiced at all the goodness, which the
Lord had showed to Israel, and because he had delivered them out of the hand of
the Egyptians. **10** Therefore Jethro said, [e]Blessed be the Lord who hath delive-
red you out of the hand of the Egyptians, and out of the hand of Pharaoh: who
hath also delivered the people from under the hand of the Egyptians. **11** Now
I know that the Lord is greater than all the gods: for as they have dealt [3]proudly
with them, so are they [f]recompensed. **12** Then Jethro Moses' father-in-law took
burnt offerings and sacrifices, to offer unto God And Aaron and all the Elders of
Israel came to eat bread with Moses' father-in-law [g]before God. **13** Now on the
morrow, when Moses sat to judge the people, the people stood about Moses from
morning unto even. **14** And when Moses' father-in-law saw all that he did to the
people, he said, What is this that thou doest to the people? why sittest thou thyself
alone, and all the people stand about thee from morning unto even? **15** And
Moses said unto his father-in-law, Because the people come unto me to seek
[h]God. **16** When they have a matter, they come unto me, and I judge between
one and another, and declare the ordinances of God, and his laws. **17** But Moses'
father-in-law said unto him, The thing which thou doest, is not well. **18** Thou
both [i]weariest thyself greatly, and this people that is with thee: for the thing is too
heavy for thee: [4]thou art not able to do it thyself alone. **19** Hear now my [j]voice,
(I will give thee counsel, and God shall be with thee) be thou for the people to
[k]Godward, and report thou the causes unto God, **20** And admonish them of the
ordinances, and of the laws, and show them the way, wherein they must walk, and
the work that they must do. **21** Moreover, provide thou among all the people
[l]men of courage, fearing God, men dealing truly, hating covetousness: and appoint
such over them to be rulers over thousands, rulers over hundreds, rulers over fifties,
and rulers over tens. **22** And let them judge the people at all seasons: but every
great matter let them bring unto thee, and let them judge all small causes: so shall
it be easier for thee, when they shall bear the burden with thee. **23** If thou do this
thing, (and God so command thee) both thou shalt be able to endure, and all this
people shall also go quietly to their place. **24** So Moses [m]obeyed the voice of his
father-in-law, and did all that he had said: **25** And Moses chose men of courage
out of all Israel, and made them heads over the people, rulers over thousands, rulers
over hundreds, rulers over fifties, and rulers over tens. **26** And they judged the
people at all seasons, but they brought the hard causes to Moses: for they judged
all small matters themselves. **27** Afterward Moses [n]let his father-in-law depart,
and he went into his country.

19

1 The Israelites come to Sinai. 5 Israel is chosen from among all other nations. 8 The people promise to obey God. 12 He that toucheth the hill, dieth. 16 God appeareth unto Moses upon the mount in thunder and lightning.

1 In the [a]third month, after the children of Israel were gone out of the
land of Egypt, the same [b]day came they into the wilderness of Sinai. **2** For they
departed from Rephidim, and came to the desert of Sinai, and camped in the wil-
derness, even there Israel camped before the mount. **3** [1]But Moses went up unto
God, for the Lord had called out of the mount unto him, saying, Thus shalt thou
say to the house of [c]Jacob, and tell the children of Israel. **4** [2]Ye have seen what
I did unto the Egyptians, and how I carried you upon [d]eagle's wings, and have
brought you unto me. **5** Now therefore [3]if ye will hear my voice indeed, and
keep my covenant, then ye shall be my chief treasure above all people, [4]though all
the earth be mine. **6** Ye shall be unto me also a kingdom of [5]Priests, and an holy
nation These are the words which thou shalt speak unto the children of Israel. **7**
Moses then came and called for the Elders of the people, and proposed unto them
all these things, which the Lord commanded him. **8** And the people answered
all together, and said, [6]All that the Lord hath commanded, we will do And Mo-
ses reported the words of the people unto the Lord. **9** And the Lord said unto
Moses, Lo, I come unto thee in a thick cloud, that the people may hear while I
talk with thee, and that they may also believe thee forever (For Moses had told the
words of the people unto the Lord.) **10** Moreover the Lord said unto Moses, Go
to the people, and [e]sanctify them today and tomorrow, and let them wash their
clothes. **11** And let them be ready on the third day: for the third day the Lord
will come down in the sight of all the people upon mount Sinai: **12** And thou
shalt set marks unto the people round about, saying, Take heed to yourselves, that
ye go not up to the [7]mount, nor touch the border of it, whosoever toucheth the
mount, shall surely die. **13** No hand shall touch it, but he shall be stoned to de-
ath, or stricken through with darts: whether it be beast or man, he shall not live:
when the [f]horn bloweth long, they shall come up [g]into the mountain. **14** Then
Moses went down from the mount unto the people, and sanctified the people,

---

b. Exod. 17:1 Moses here noteth not every place where they camped, as Num. 33, but only those places, where some notable thing was done.
c. Exod. 17:2 Why distrust you God? why look ye not for succor of him without murmuring against us?
d. Exod. 17:4 How ready the people are for their own matters to slay the true Prophets, and how slow they are to revenge God's cause against his enemies and false Prophets.
e. Exod. 17:7 Or, tentation.
f. Exod. 17:7 Or, strife.
g. Exod. 17:7 When in adversity we think God to be absent, then we neglect his promise, and make him a liar.
h. Exod. 17:8 Who came of Eliphaz, son of Esau, Gen. 36:12.
i. Exod. 17:9 That is, Horeb, which is also called Sinai.
j. Exod. 17:11 So that we see how dangerous a thing it is to faint in prayer.
k. Exod. 17:14 In the book of the Law.
l. Exod. 17:14 Hebrew, put it in the ears of Joshua.
m. Exod. 17:15 That is, the Lord is my banner as he declared by holding up his rod and his hands.
n. Exod. 17:16 Hebrew, the hand of the Lord upon the throne.

EXOD. 17
1. Num. 20:4
2. Exod. 7:20
3. Num. 2:9 / Ps. 78:15 / Ps. 105:41 / 1 Cor. 10:4
4. Deut. 25:17
5. Num. 24:20 / 1Sam. 15:3

EXOD. 18
a. Exod. 18:2 It may seem that he sent her back for a time to her father for her impatience, lest she should be a let to his vocation, which was so dangerous, Exod. 4:25.
b. Exod. 18:5 Horeb is called the mount of God, because God wrought many miracles there. So Peter calleth the mount where Christ was transfigured, the holy mount: for by Christ's presence it was holy for a time, 2 Pet. 1:18.
c. Exod. 18:6 That is, he sent messengers to say unto him.
d. Exod. 18:7 Hebrew, of peace.
e. Exod. 18:10 Whereby it is evident that he worshipped the true God, and therefore Moses refused not to marry his daughter.
f. Exod. 18:11 For they that drowned the children of the Israelites, perished themselves by water.
g. Exod. 18:12 They ate in that place, where the sacrifice was offered: for part was burnt, and the rest eaten.
h. Exod. 18:15 That is, to know God's will, and to have justice executed.
i. Exod. 18:18 Hebrew, thou wilt faint and fall.
j. Exod. 18:19 Or, counsel.
k. Exod. 18:19 Judge thou in hard causes, which cannot be decided but by consulting with God.
l. Exod. 18:21 What manner of men ought to be chosen to bear office.
m. Exod. 18:24 Godly counsel ought ever to be obeyed, though it come of our inferiors, for to such God oftentimes giveth wisdom to humble them that are exalted, and to declare that one member hath need of another.
n. Exod. 18:27 Read the occasion, Num. 10:29.

EXOD. 18
1. Exod. 2:16
2. Exod. 2:22
3. Exod. 1:10, 16,22 / Exod. 5:7 / Exod. 14:8
4. Deut. 1:9

EXOD. 19
a. Exod. 19:1 Which was in the beginning of the month Sivan, containing part of May, and part of June.
b. Exod. 19:1 That they departed from Rephidim.
c. Exod. 19:3 God called Jacob, Israel: therefore the house of Jacob and the people of Israel signify only God's people.
d. Exod. 19:4 For the Eagle by flying high, is out of danger, and by carrying her birds rather on her wings than in her talons declareth her love.
e. Exod. 19:10 Teach them to be pure in heart, as they show themselves outwardly clean by washing.
f. Exod. 19:13 Or, trumpet.

and they washed their clothes. **15** And he said unto the people, Be ready on
the third day, and come not at your [h]wives. **16** And the third day, when it was
morning, there was thunders and lightnings, and a thick cloud upon the mount,
and the sound of the trumpet exceeding loud, so that all the people that was in the
camp was afraid. **17** Then Moses brought the people out of the tents to meet
with God, and they stood in the nether part of the mount. **18** [8]And mount Si-
nai was all on smoke, because the Lord came down upon it in fire, and the smoke
thereof ascended, as the smoke of a furnace, and all the mount [i]trembled exceedin-
gly. **19** And when the sound of the trumpet blew long, and waxed louder and
louder, Moses spake, and God answered him by [j]voice. **20** (For the Lord came
down upon mount Sinai on the top of the mount) and when the Lord called Mo-
ses up into the top of the mount, Moses went up. **21** Then the Lord said unto
Moses, Go down, charge the people, that they break not their bounds, to go up to
the Lord to gaze, lest many of them perish. **22** And let the [k]Priests also which
come to the Lord be sanctified, lest the Lord [l]destroy them. **23** And Moses said
unto the Lord, The people cannot come up into the mount Sinai: for thou hast
charged us, saying, Set marks on the mountain, and sanctify it. **24** And the Lord
said unto him, Go, get thee down, and come up thou, and Aaron with thee: but
let not the [m]Priests and the people break their bounds to come up unto the Lord,
lest he destroy them. **25** So Moses went down unto the people, and told them.

20

2 The Commandments of the first Table. 13 The Commandments of the second. 18 The people afraid are comforted by Moses. 23 Gods of silver and gold are again forbidden. 24 Of what sort the altar ought to be.

1 Then God [a]spake all these words, saying, **2** [1]I am the Lord thy God,
which have brought thee out of the land of Egypt, out of the house of [b]bonda-
ge. **3** Thou shalt have none other gods [c]before me. **4** [2]Thou shalt make thee
no graven image, neither any similitude of things that are in heaven above, neither
that are in the earth beneath, nor that are in the waters under the earth. **5** Thou
shalt not [d]bow down to them, neither serve them: for I am the Lord thy God, a
[e]jealous God, visiting the iniquity of the fathers upon the children, upon the third
generation and upon the fourth of them that hate me: **6** And showing mercy
unto [f]thousands to them that love me, and keep my commandments. **7** [3]Thou
shalt not take the Name of the Lord thy God in [g]vain: for the Lord will not hold
him guiltless that taketh his Name in vain. **8** Remember the Sabbath day, [h]to
keep it holy. **9** [4]Six days shalt thou labor, and do all thy work, **10** But the se-
venth day is the Sabbath of the Lord thy God: in it thou shalt not do any work,
thou, nor thy son, nor thy daughter, thy manservant, nor thy maid, nor thy beast,
nor thy stranger that is within thy [i]gates. **11** [5]For in six days the Lord made the
heaven and the earth, the sea, and all that in them is, and rested the seventh day:
therefore the Lord blessed the seventh day, and hallowed it. **12** [6]Honor thy [j]fa-
ther and thy mother, that thy days may be prolonged upon the land, which the
Lord thy God giveth thee. **13** [7]Thou shalt not [k]kill. **14** Thou shalt not [l]com-
mit adultery. **15** Thou shalt not [m]steal. **16** Thou shalt not bear false [n]witness
against thy neighbor. **17** [8]Thou shalt not [o]covet thy neighbor's house, neither
shalt thou covet thy neighbor's wife, nor his manservant, nor his maid, nor his ox,
nor his ass, neither anything that is thy neighbor's. **18** And all the people [p]saw
the thunders: and the [q]lightnings, and the sound of the trumpet, and the moun-
tain smoking, and when the people saw it, they fled and stood afar off, **19** And
said unto Moses, [9]Talk thou with us, and we will hear: but let not God talk with
us, lest we die. **20** Then Moses said unto the people, Fear not: for God is come
to [r]prove you, and that his fear may be before you, that ye sin not. **21** So the
people stood afar off, but Moses drew near unto the darkness where God was. **22**
And the Lord said unto Moses, Thus thou shalt say unto the children of Israel, Ye
have seen that I have talked with you from heaven. **23** Ye shall not make there-
fore with me gods of silver, nor gods of gold: you shall make you none. **24** [10]An
altar of earth thou shalt make unto me, and thereon shalt offer thy burnt offerings,
and [11]thy peace offerings, thy sheep, and thine oxen: in all places, where I shall put
the remembrance of my Name, I will come unto thee, and bless thee. **25** [12]But
if thou wilt make me an altar of stone, thou shalt not build it of hewn stones: for
if thou lift up thy tool upon them, thou hast polluted [s]them. **26** Neither shalt
thou go up by steps unto mine altar, that thy [t]filthiness be not discovered thereon.

21

Temporal and civil ordinances appointed by God touching servitude, murders, and wrongs: the observation whereof doth not justify a man, but are given to bridle our corrupt nature, which else would break out into all mischief and cruelty.

1 Now these are the laws, which thou shalt set before them: **2** [1]If thou
buy an Hebrew servant, he shall serve six years, and in the seventh he shall go out
free for [a]nothing. **3** If he [b]came himself alone, he shall go out himself alone: if
he were married, then his wife shall go out with him. **4** If his master hath given
him a wife and she hath borne him sons or daughters, the wife and her children
shall be her [c]master's, but he shall go out himself alone. **5** But if the servant say
thus, I love my master, my wife and my children, I will not go out free, **6** Then
his master shall bring him unto the [d]Judges, and set him to the [e]door, or to the
post, and his master shall bore his ear through with an awl, and he shall serve him
[f]forever. **7** Likewise if a man [g]sell his daughter to be a servant, she shall not go
out as the menservants do. **8** If she please not her master, who hath betrothed
her to himself, then shall [h]he cause to buy her: he shall have no power to sell her
to a strange people, seeing he [i]despised her. **9** But if he hath betrothed her unto
his son, he shall deal with her [j]according to the custom of the daughters. **10** If
he take [k]him another wife, he shall not diminish her food, her raiment, and re-
compense of her virginity. **11** And if he do not these [l]three unto her, then shall
she go out free, paying no money. **12** [2]He that smiteth a man, and he die, shall
die the death. **13** And if a man hath not laid wait, but [m]God hath offered him
into his hand, then I will appoint thee a place whither he shall flee. **14** But if a
man come presumptuously upon his neighbor to slay him with guile, [3]thou shalt
take him from mine [n]altar, that he may die. **15** Also he that smiteth his father
or his mother, shall die the death. **16** And he that stealeth a man, and selleth
him, if it be found with him, shall die the death. **17** [4]And he that curseth his
father or his mother, shall die the death. **18** When men also strive together,
and one smite another with a [o]stone, or with the fist, and he die not but lieth in
bed. **19** If he rise again and walk without upon his staff, then shall he that smote
him go [p]quit, save only he shall bear his charges [q]for his resting, and shall pay for
his healing. **20** And if a man smite his servant, or his maid with a rod, and he
die under his hand, he shall be surely punished. **21** But if he continue a day or
two days, he shall not [r]be punished: for he is his money. **22** Also if men strive
and hurt a woman with child, so that her child depart from her and [s]death follow
not, he shall be surely punished, according as the woman's husband shall appoint
him, or he shall pay as the [t]Judges determine. **23** But if death follow, then thou
shalt pay life for life. **24** [u,5]Eye for eye, tooth for tooth, hand for hand, foot for
foot, **25** Burning for burning, wound for wound, stripe for stripe. **26** And if
a man smite his servant in the eye, or his maid in the eye, and hath perished it, he
shall let him go free for his eye. **27** Also if he smite [v]out his servant's tooth, or his

---

g. Exod. 19:13 Or, toward.
h. Exod. 19:15 But give yourselves to prayer and abstinence, that you may at this time attend only upon the Lord, 1 Cor. 7:5.
i. Exod. 19:18 God used these fearful signs, that his law should be had in greater reverence, and his majesty the more feared.
j. Exod. 19:19 He gave authority to Moses by plain words, that the people might understand him.
k. Exod. 19:22 Or, rulers.
l. Exod. 19:22 Or, break out upon them.
m. Exod. 19:24 Neither dignity nor multitude have authority to pass the bounds that God's word prescribeth.

EXOD. 19

1. Acts 7:38
2. Deut. 29:2
3. Deut. 5:2
4. Deut. 10:14 / Ps. 24:1
5. 1 Pet. 2:9 / Rev. 1:6
6. Exod. 24:3 / Deut. 5:27 / Deut. 26:17 / Josh. 21:16
7. Heb. 12:20 / Deut. 4:11

EXOD. 20

a. Exod. 20:1 When Moses and Aaron were gone up, or had passed the bounds of the people, God spake thus out of the mount Horeb, that all the people heard.
b. Exod. 20:2 Or, servants.
c. Exod. 20:3 To whose eyes all things are open.
d. Exod. 20:5 By this outward gesture, all kinds of service and worship to idols is forbidden.
e. Exod. 20:5 And will be revenged on the contemners of mine honor.
f. Exod. 20:6 So ready is he rather to show mercy than to punish.
g. Exod. 20:7 Either by swearing falsely or rashly by his Name, or by contemning it.
h. Exod. 20:8 Which is by meditating the spiritual rest, by hearing God's word, and resting from worldly travails.
i. Exod. 20:10 Or, city.
j. Exod. 20:12 By the parents also is meant all that have authority over us.
k. Exod. 20:13 But love and preserve thy brother's life.
l. Exod. 20:14 But be pure in heart, word and deed.
m. Exod. 20:15 But study to save his goods.
n. Exod. 20:16 But further his good name, and speak truth.
o. Exod. 20:17 Thou mayst not so much as wish his hinderance in anything.
p. Exod. 20:18 Or, heard.
q. Exod. 20:18 Hebrew, fire brands.
r. Exod. 20:20 Whether you will obey his precepts as you promised, Exod. 19:8.
s. Exod. 20:25 Hebrew, it, that is, the stone.
t. Exod. 20:26 Which might be by his stooping or flying abroad of his clothes.

EXOD. 20

1. Deut. 5:6 / Ps. 81.10
2. Lev. 26:1 / Ps. 97:7
3. Lev. 19:12 / Deut. 5:11 / Matt. 5:33
4. Exod. 23:12 / Ezek. 20:12
5. Gen. 2:2
6. Deut. 5:16 / Matt. 15:4 / Eph. 6:2
7. Matt. 5:21 / Rom. 7:7
8. Deut. 5:24 / Deut. 18:16 / Heb. 12:18
9. Exod. 27:8 / Exod. 38:7
10. Lev. 3:1
11. Deut. 27:5 / Josh 8:31

EXOD. 21

a. Exod. 21:2 Paying no money for his liberty.
b. Exod. 21:3 Not having wife nor children.
c. Exod. 21:4 Till her time of servitude was expired which might be the seventh year or the fiftieth.
d. Exod. 21:6 Hebrew, gods.
e. Exod. 21:6 Where the judges sat.
f. Exod. 21:6 That is, to the year of Jubilee, which was every fiftieth year.
g. Exod. 21:7 Constrained either by poverty, or else to the intent that the master should marry her.
h. Exod. 21:8 By giving another money to buy her of him.
i. Exod. 21:8 Or, deflowered her.
j. Exod. 21:9 That is, he shall give his dowry.
k. Exod. 21:10 For his son.
l. Exod. 21:11 Neither marry her himself, nor give another money to buy her, nor bestow her upon his son.
m. Exod. 21:13 Though a man be killed at unawares, yet it is God's providence that it should so be.
n. Exod. 21:14 The holiness of the place ought not to defend the murderer.
o. Exod. 21:18 Either far off him or near.
p. Exod. 21:19 By the civil Justice.
q. Exod. 21:19 Or, losing of his time.
r. Exod. 21:21 By the civil magistrate, but before God he is a murderer.
s. Exod. 21:22 Of the mother or child.
t. Exod. 21:22 Or, arbiters.
u. Exod. 21:24 The execution of this law only belonged to the magistrate, Matt. 5:38.
v. Exod. 21:27 So God revengeth cruelty in the most least things.

maid's tooth, he shall let him go out free for his tooth. **28** If an ox gore a man
or a woman that he die, the [6]ox shall be [w]stoned to death, and his flesh shall not
be eaten, but the owner of the ox shall go quite. **29** If the ox were wont to push
in times past, and it hath been [x]told his master, and he hath not kept him, and
after he killeth a man or a woman, the ox shall be stoned, and his owner shall die
also. **30** If there be set to him a [y]sum of money, then he shall pay the ransom of
his life, whatsoever shall be laid upon him. **31** Whether he hath gored a son, or
gored a daughter, he shall be judged after the same manner. **32** If the ox gore a
servant or a maid, he shall give unto their master thirty [z]shekels of silver, and the
ox shall be stoned. **33** And when a man shall open a well, or when he shall dig
a pit and cover it not, and an ox or an ass fall therein, **34** The owner of the pit
shall [aa]make it good, and give money to the owner thereof, but the dead beast shall
be his. **35** And if a man's ox hurt his neighbor's ox that he die, then they shall
sell the live ox, and divide the money thereof, and the dead ox also they shall di-
vide. **36** Or if it be known that the ox hath used to push in times past, and his
master hath not kept him, he shall pay ox for ox, but the dead shall be his own.

22

1 Of theft. 5 Damage. 7 Lending. 14 Borrowing. 16 Enticing of maids. 18 Witchcraft. 20 Idolatry. 21 Support of strangers, widows, and fatherless. 25 Usury. 28 Reverence to Magistrates.

1 If a man steal an [a]ox or a sheep, and kill it or sell it, he shall restore five
oxen for the ox, [1]and four sheep for the sheep. **2** If a thief be found [b]breaking
up, and be smitten that he die, no blood shall be shed for him. **3** But if it be [c]in
the daylight, [d]blood shall be shed for him: for he should make full restitution: if he
had not wherewith, then should he be sold for his theft. **4** If the theft be found
[e]with him alive, (whether it be ox, ass, or sheep) he shall restore the double. **5**
If a man do hurt field, or vineyard, and put in his beast to feed in another man's
field, he shall recompense of the best of his own field, and of the best of his own
vineyard. **6** If fire break out, and catch in the thorns, and the stacks of corn, or
the standing corn, or the field be consumed, he that kindled the fire shall make
full restitution. **7** If a man deliver his neighbor money or stuff to keep, and it
be stolen out of his house, if the thief be found, he shall pay the double. **8** If the
thief be not found, then the master of the house shall be brought unto the [f]Judges
to swear, whether he hath [g]put his hand unto his neighbor's good, or no. **9** In
all manner of trespass, whether it be for oxen, for ass, for sheep, for raiment, or for
any manner of lost thing which another challengeth to be his, the cause of both
parties shall come before the judges, and whom the Judges condemn, he shall pay
the double unto the neighbor. **10** If a man deliver unto his neighbor to keep ass,
or ox, or sheep, or any beast, and it die, or be [h]hurt, or taken away by enemies, and
no man see it, **11** [i]An oath of the Lord shall be between them twain, that he hath
not put his hand unto his neighbor's good, and the owner of it shall take the oath,
and he shall not make it good: **12** [2]But if it be stolen from him, he shall make
restitution unto the owner thereof. **13** If it be torn in pieces, he shall bring [j]re-
cord, and shall not make that good, which is devoured. **14** And if a man borrow
ought of his neighbor, and it be hurt, or else die, the owner thereof not being by,
he shall surely make it good. **15** If the owner thereof be by, he shall not make it
good: for if it be an hired thing, it [k]came for his hire. **16** [3]And if a man entice a
maid that is not betrothed, and lie with her, he shall endow her, and take her to his
wife. **17** If her father refuse to give her to him, he shall pay money according to
the dowry of virgins. **18** Thou shalt not suffer a witch to live. **19** Whosoever
lieth with a beast, shall die the death. **20** [4]He that offereth unto any gods, save
unto the Lord only, shall be slain. **21** [5]Moreover, thou shalt not do injury to a
stranger, neither oppress him: for ye were strangers in the land of Egypt. **22** [6]Ye
shall not trouble any widow, nor fatherless child. **23** If thou vex or trouble such,
and so he call and cry unto me, I will surely hear his cry. **24** Then shall my wra-
th be kindled, and I will kill you with the sword, and your [l]wives shall be widows,
and your children fatherless. **25** [7]If thou lend money to my people, that is, to
the poor with thee, thou shalt not be as an usurer unto him: ye shall not oppress
him with usury. **26** If thou take thy neighbor's raiment to pledge, thou shalt re-
store it unto him before the sun go down. **27** For that is his covering only, and
this is his garment for his skin: wherein shall he sleep? therefore when he [m]crieth
unto me, I will hear him: for I am merciful. **28** [8]Thou shalt not rail upon the
Judges, neither speak evil of the ruler of thy people. **29** Thine [n]abundance and
thy liquor shalt thou not keep back. [9]The firstborn of thy sons shalt thou give
me. **30** Likewise shalt thou do with thine oxen and with thy sheep: seven days
it shall be with his dam, and the eighth day thou shalt give it me. **31** Ye shall be
an holy people unto me, [10]neither shall ye eat any flesh that is torn of beasts in the
field: ye shall cast it [o]to the dog.

23

2 Not to follow the multitude. 13 Not to make mention of the strange gods. 14 The three solemn feasts. 20, 23 The Angel is promised to lead his people. 25 What God promiseth if they obey him. 29 God will cast out the Canaanites by little and little, and why.

1 Thou shalt not [a]receive a false tale, neither shalt thou put thine hand
with the wicked, to be a [b]false witness. **2** Thou shalt not follow a multitude to
do evil, neither [c]agree in a controversy [d]to decline after many and overthrow the
truth. **3** Thou shalt not esteem a poor man in his cause. **4** If thou meet thine
enemy's ox, or his ass going astray, thou shalt [e]bring him to him again. **5** If thou
see thine enemy's [f]ass lying under his burden, wilt thou cease to help him? thou
shalt help him up again with it. **6** Thou shalt not overthrow the right of the poor
in his suit. **7** Thou shalt keep thee far from a false matter, thou shalt not slay the
[g]innocent and the righteous: for I will not justify a wicked man. **8** [1]Thou shalt
take no gift: for the gift blindeth the [h]wise, and perverteth the words of the righte-
ous. **9** Thou shalt not oppress a stranger: for ye know the [i]heart of a stranger,
seeing ye were strangers in the land of Egypt. **10** [2]Moreover, six years thou shalt
sow thy land, and gather the fruits thereof. **11** But the seventh year thou shalt
let it rest and lie still, that the poor of thy people may eat, and what they leave, the
beasts of the field shall eat In like manner thou shalt do with thy vineyard, and
with thine olive trees. **12** [3]Six days thou shalt do thy work, and in the seventh
day thou shalt rest, that thine ox, and thine ass may rest, and the son of thy maid,
and the stranger may be refreshed. **13** And ye shall take heed to all things that I
have said unto you: and ye shall make [j]no mention of the name of other gods, nei-
ther shall it be heard out of thy mouth. **14** Three times shalt thou keep a feast
unto me in the year. **15** Thou [4]shalt keep the feast of [k]unleavened bread: thou
shalt eat unleavened bread seven days, as I commanded thee, in the season of the
month of Abib: for in it thou camest out of Egypt: and [5]none shall appear before
me empty. **16** The [l]feast also of the harvest of the first fruits of thy labors, whi-
ch thou hast sown in the field: and the [m]feast of gathering fruits in the end of the
year, when thou hast gathered in thy labors out of the field. **17** These three times
in the year shall all thy men children appear before the Lord Jehovah. **18** Thou
shalt not offer the blood of my sacrifice with [n]leavened bread: neither shall the fat
of my sacrifice remain until the morning. **19** [6]The first of the firstfruits of thy
land, thou shalt bring into the house of the Lord thy God: yet shalt thou not seethe
a kid in his [o]mother's milk. **20** [7]Behold, I send an Angel before thee, to keep
thee in thy way, and to bring thee to the place which I have prepared. **21** Beware
of him, and hear his voice, and provoke him not: for he will not spare your misde-
eds, because my [p]name is in him. **22** But if thou hearken unto his voice, and do
all that I speak, then I will be an enemy unto thine enemies, and will afflict them
that afflict thee. **23** For mine Angel [8]shall go before thee, and bring thee unto
the Amorites, and the Hittites, and the Perizzites, and the Canaanites, the Hivites,
and the Jebusites, and I will destroy them. **24** Thou shalt not bow down to their
gods, neither serve them, nor do after the works of them: but [q,9]utterly overthrow
them, and break in pieces their images. **25** For ye shall serve the Lord your God,
and he shall bless thy [r]bread and thy water, and I will take all sickness away from

---

w. Exod. 21:28 If the beast be punished, much more shall the murderer.
x. Exod. 21:29 Or, testified to his.
y. Exod. 21:30 By the next of the kindred of him that is so slain.
z. Exod. 21:32 Read Gen. 23:15.
aa. Exod. 21:34 This law forbiddeth not only not to hurt, but to beware lest any be hurt.

EXOD. 21

1. Lev. 25:39 / Deut. 15:12 / Jer. 34:14
2. Lev. 24:17
3. Deut. 12:3
4. Lev. 22:9 / Prov. 20:20 / Matt. 15:4 / Mark 7:10
5. Lev. 24:20 / Deut. 19:21 / Matt. 5:38
6. Gen. 9:5

EXOD. 22

a. Exod. 22:1 Either [a] great beast of the herd, or a small beast of the flock.
b. Exod. 22:2 Breaking an house to enter in, or undermining.
c. Exod. 22:3 Hebrew, when the sun riseth upon him.
d. Exod. 22:3 He shall be put to death that killeth him.
e. Exod. 22:4 Hebrew, in his hand.
f. Exod. 22:8 Hebrew, gods.
g. Exod. 22:8 That is, whether he hath stolen.
h. Exod. 22:10 Hebrew, broken.
i. Exod. 22:11 They should swear by the Name of the Lord.
j. Exod. 22:13 He shall show some part of the beast, or bring in witnesses.
k. Exod. 22:15 He that hired it shall be free by paying the hire.
l. Exod. 22:24 The just plague of God upon the oppressors.
m. Exod. 22:27 For cold and necessity.
n. Exod. 22:29 Thine abundance of thy corn, oil and wine.
o. Exod. 22:31 And so have nothing to do with it.

EXOD. 22

1. 2 Sam. 1:26
2. Gen. 31:39
3. Deut. 12:28
4. Deut. 13:13-15
5. Lev. 19:33
6. Zech. 7:10
7. Lev. 25:37 / Deut. 23:19 / Ps. 15:5
8. Acts 25:5
9. Exod. 13:2-12 /Exod. 34:19
10. Lev. 22:8 / Ezek. 44:31

EXOD. 23

a. Exod. 23:1 Or, report a false tale.
b. Exod. 23:1 Or, cruel.
c. Exod. 23:2 Hebrew, answer.
d. Exod. 23:2 Do that which is godly, though few do favor it.
e. Exod. 23:4 If we be bound to do good to our enemy's beast, much more to our enemy himself, Matt. 5:44.
f. Exod. 23:5 If God command to help up our enemy's ass under his burden, will he suffer us to cast down our brethren with heavy burdens?
g. Exod. 23:7 Whether thou be magistrate or art commanded by the magistrate.
h. Exod. 23:8 Hebrew, seeing.
i. Exod. 23:9 For in that that he is a stranger, his heart is sorrowful enough.
j. Exod. 23:13 Neither by swearing by them nor speaking of them, Ps. 16:4; Eph. 5:3.
k. Exod. 23:15 That is, Easter, in remembrance that the Angel passed over and spared the Israelites, when he slew the firstborn of the Egyptians.
l. Exod. 23:16 Which is Whitsuntide, in token that the Law was given 50 days after they departed from Egypt.
m. Exod. 23:16 This is the feast of Tabernacles, signifying that they dwelled 40 years under the tents or the Tabernacles in wilderness.
n. Exod. 23:18 No leavened bread shall be there in thine house.
o. Exod. 23:19 Meaning, that no fruits should be taken before just time: and hereby are bridled all cruel and wanton appetites.
p. Exod. 23:21 I will give him mine authority, and he shall govern you in my name.
q. Exod. 23:24 God commandeth his not only not to worship idols, but to destroy them.
r. Exod. 23:25 That is, all things necessary for this present life.

the midst of thee. **26** [10]There shall none cast their fruit, nor be barren in thy land, the number of thy days will I fulfill. **27** I will send my [s]fear before thee, and will destroy all the people among whom thou shalt go: and I will make all thine enemies turn their backs unto thee: **28** And I will send [11]hornets before thee, which shall drive out the Hivites, the Canaanites, and the Hittites from thy face. **29** I will not cast them out from thy face in one year, lest the land grow to a wilderness, and the beasts of the field multiply against thee. **30** By little and little I will drive them out from thy face, until thou increase, and inherit the land. **31** And I will make thy coasts from the red sea unto the sea [t]of the Philistines, and from the [u]desert unto the [v]River: for I will deliver the inhabitants of the land into your hand, and thou shalt drive them out from thy face. **32** [12]Thou shalt make no covenant with them, nor with their gods: **33** Neither shall they dwell in the land, lest they make thee sin against me: for if thou serve their gods, surely it shall be thy [w,13]destruction.

24

3 The people promise to obey God. 4 Moses writeth the civil Laws. 9, 13 Moses returneth into the mountain. 14 Aaron and Hur have the charge of the people. 18 Moses was forty days and forty nights in the mountain.

1 Now he had [a]said unto Moses, Come up to the Lord, thou, and Aaron, Nadab, and Abihu, and seventy of the Elders of Israel, and ye shall worship afar off. **2** And Moses himself alone shall come near to the Lord, but they shall not come near, neither shall the people go up with him. **3** [b]Afterward Moses came and told the people all the words of the Lord, and all the [c]Laws: and all the people answered with one voice, and said, [1]All the things which the Lord hath said, will we do. **4** And Moses wrote all the words of the Lord and rose up early, and set up an [2]altar [d]under the mountain, and twelve pillars according to the twelve tribes of Israel. **5** And he sent young [e]men of the children of Israel, which offered burnt offerings of beeves, and sacrificed peace offerings unto the Lord. **6** Then Moses took half of the blood, and put it in basins, and half of the blood he sprinkled on the altar. **7** After, he took the [f]book of the covenant, and read it in the audience of the people: who said, All that the Lord hath said, we will do, and be obedient. **8** Then Moses took the [3]blood, and sprinkled it on the people, and said, Behold the [g]blood of the covenant, which the Lord hath made with you concerning all these things. **9** Then went up Moses, and Aaron, Nadab, and Abihu, and seventy of the Elders of Israel. **10** And they [h]saw the God of Israel, and under his feet was as it were a [i]work of a Sapphire stone, and as the very heaven when it is clear. **11** And upon the nobles of the children of Israel he [j]laid not his hand: also they saw God, and [k]did eat and drink. **12** And the Lord [l]said unto Moses, Come up to me into the mountain, and be there, and I will give thee [m]tables of stone, and the Law, and the Commandment, which I have written, for to teach [n]them. **13** Then Moses rose up, and his minister Joshua, and Moses went up into the mountain of God, **14** And said unto the Elders, Tarry us here until we come again unto you: and behold, Aaron and Hur are with you: whosoever hath any matters, let him come to them. **15** Then Moses went up to the mount, and the cloud covered the mountain, **16** And the glory of the Lord abode upon mount Sinai, and the cloud covered [o]it six days: and the seventh day he called unto Moses out of the midst of the cloud. **17** And the sight of the glory of the Lord was like [p]consuming fire on the top of the mountain, in the eyes of the children of Israel. **18** And Moses entered into the midst of the cloud, and went up to the mountain and Moses was in the [4]mount forty days and forty nights.

25

2 The voluntary gifts for the making of the Tabernacle. 10 The form of the Ark. 17 The Mercy seat. 23 The Table. 31 The Candlestick. 40 All must be done according to the pattern.

1 Then the Lord spake unto Moses, saying, **2** [a]Speak unto the children of Israel that they receive an offering for me: of [1]every man, whose heart giveth it freely, ye shall take the offering for me. **3** And this is the offering which ye shall [b]take of them, gold and silver, and brass, **4** And [c]blue silk, and purple, and scarlet, and fine linen and goat's hair, **5** And ram's skins colored red, and the skins of badgers, and the wood [d]Shittim, **6** Oil for the light, spices for [e]anointing oil, and for the perfume of sweet savor. **7** Onyx stones, and stones to be set in the [2]Ephod, and in the [3]breastplate. **8** Also they shall make me a [f]Sanctuary, that I may dwell among them. **9** According to all that I show thee, even so shall ye make the form of the Tabernacle, and the fashion of all the instruments thereof. **10** They shall make also an [4]Ark of Shittim wood, two cubits and an half long, and a cubit and an half broad, and a cubit and an half high. **11** And thou shalt overlay it with pure gold, within and without shalt thou overlay it, and shalt make upon it a [g]crown of gold round about. **12** And thou shalt cast four rings of gold for it, and put them in the four [h]corners thereof: that is, two rings shall be on the one side of it, and two rings on the other side thereof. **13** And thou shalt make bars of Shittim wood, and cover them with gold. **14** Then thou shalt put the bars in the rings by the sides of the Ark, to bear the Ark with them. **15** The bars shall be in the rings of the Ark: they shall not be taken away from it. **16** So thou shalt put in the Ark the [i]Testimony, which I shall give thee. **17** Also thou shalt make a [j,k]Mercy seat of pure gold, two cubits and an half long and a cubit and an half broad. **18** And thou shalt make two Cherubims of gold: of work beaten out with the hammer shalt thou make them at the two ends of the Mercy seat. **19** And the one Cherub shalt thou make at the one end, and the other Cherub at the other end: of the matter of the Mercy seat shall ye make the Cherubims, on the two ends thereof. **20** And the Cherubims shall stretch their wings on high, covering the Mercy seat with their wings and their faces one to another: to the Mercy seatward shall the faces of the Cherubims be. **21** And thou shalt put the Mercy seat above upon the Ark, and in the Ark thou shalt put the Testimony, which I will give thee. **22** And there I will [l]declare myself unto thee, and from above the Mercy seat [5]between the two Cherubims, which are upon the Ark of the Testimony, I will tell thee all things which I will give thee in commandment unto the children of Israel. **23** [6]Thou shalt also make a Table of Shittim wood, of two cubits long, and one cubit broad, and a cubit and a half high: **24** And thou shalt cover it with pure gold, and make thereto a crown of gold round about. **25** Thou shalt also make unto it a border of [m]four fingers round about: and thou shalt make a golden crown round about the border thereof: **26** After, thou shalt make for it four rings of gold, and shalt put the rings in the four corners that are in the four feet thereof. **27** Over against the border shall the rings be for places for bars to bear the Table. **28** And thou shalt make the bars of Shittim wood, and shalt overlay them with gold, that the Table may be borne with them. **29** Thou shalt make also [n]dishes for it, and incense cups for it, and coverings for it, and goblets, wherewith it shall be covered, even of fine gold shalt thou make them. **30** And thou shalt set upon the Table Showbread before me continually. **31** [7]Also thou shalt make a candlestick of pure gold: of [o]work beaten out with the hammer shall the Candlestick be made, his shaft, and his branches, his bowls, his knops: and his flowers shall be of the same. **32** Six branches also shall come out of the sides of it: three branches of the candlestick out of the one side of it, and three branches of the Candlestick out of the other side of it. **33** Three bowls like unto almonds, one knop and one flower in one branch: and three bowls like almonds in the other branch, one knop and one flower: so throughout the six branches that come out of the Candlestick. **34** And in the shaft of the Candlestick shall be four bowls like unto almonds, his knops and his flowers. **35** And there shall be a knop under two branches made thereof: and a knop under two branches made thereof: and a knop under two branches made thereof, according to the six branches coming out of the Candlestick. **36** Their knops and their branches shall be thereof: all this shall be one beaten work of pure gold. **37** And thou shalt make the seven lamps thereof: and the lamps thereof shalt thou put thereon, to give light toward that that is before it. **38** Also the snuffers and snuffdishes thereof shall be of pure gold. **39** Of a [p]talent of fine gold shalt thou make it with all these instruments. **40** [8]Look therefore that thou make them after their fashion, that was showed thee in the mountain.

---

s. Exod. 23:27 I will make them afraid at thy coming and send mine Angel to destroy them, as Exod. 35:2.
t. Exod. 23:31 Called the Sea of Syria.
u. Exod. 23:31 Of Arabia called desert.
v. Exod. 23:31 To wit, Ephraim.
w. Exod. 23:33 Hebrew, offense or snare.

EXOD. 23

1. Deut. 16:19
2. Lev. 25:3 - Lev. 26:43 - Deut. 15:1
3. Exod. 20:8 - Deut. 5:13
4. Exod. 13:3 - Exod. 34:18
5. Deut. 16:16
6. Exod. 34:26 - Deut. 14:22
7. Exod. 33:2 - Deut. 7:22
8. Exod. 33:2 - Deut. 7:21 - Josh. 24:12
9. Deut. 7:25
10. Deut. 7:14
11. Josh. 24:12
12. Exod. 34:15 / Deut. 7:2
13. Deut. 7:16 - Josh. 23.13

EXOD. 24

a. Exod. 24:1 When he called him up to the mountain to give him the Laws, beginning at Exod. 20, hitherto.
b. Exod. 24:3 When he had received these laws in mount Sinai.
c. Exod. 24:3 Hebrew, judgments.
d. Exod. 24:4 Or, at the foot of the mountain.
e. Exod. 24:5 For as yet the Priesthood was not given to Levi.
f. Exod. 24:7 Or, the book of the Law.
g. Exod. 24:8 Which blood signifieth that the covenant broken cannot be satisfied without blood shedding.
h. Exod. 24:10 As perfectly as their infirmities could behold his majesty.
i. Exod. 24:10 Hebrew, brick work.
j. Exod. 24:11 He made them not afraid, nor punished them.
k. Exod. 24:11 That is, rejoiced.
l. Exod. 24:12 The second time.
m. Exod. 24:12 Signifying the hardness of our hearts, except God do write his laws therein by his Spirit, Jer. 31:33; Ezek. 11:19; 2 Cor. 3:3; Heb. 8:10 and 10:16.
n. Exod. 24:12 To wit, the people.
o. Exod. 24:16 Or, him.
p. Exod. 24:17 The Lord appeareth like devouring fire to carnal men: but to them that he draweth with his Spirit, he is like pleasant Sapphire.

EXOD. 24

1. Exod. 19:8
2. Exod. 20:24
3. 1 Pet. 1:2 /Heb. 9:20
4. Exod. 34:28 / Deut. 9:9

EXOD. 25

a. Exod. 25:2 After the moral and judicial law he giveth them the ceremonial law that nothing should be left to man's invention.
b. Exod. 25:3 For the building and use of the Tabernacle.
c. Exod. 25:4 Or, yellow.
d. Exod. 25:5 Which is thought to be a kindle of Cedar, which will not rot.
e. Exod. 25:6 Ordained for the Priests.
f. Exod. 25:8 A place both to offer sacrifice, and to hear the Law.
g. Exod. 25:11 Or, a circle and a border.
h. Exod. 25:12 Or, feet.
i. Exod. 25:16 The stone tables, the rod of Aaron and Manna which were a testimony of God's presence.
j. Exod. 25:17 Or, covering: or propitiatory.
k. Exod. 25:17 There God appeared mercifully unto them: and this was a figure of Christ.
l. Exod. 25:22 Or, will appoint with thee.
m. Exod. 25:25 Or, an hand broad.
n. Exod. 25:29 To set the bread upon.
o. Exod. 25:31 It shall not be molten, but beaten out of the lump of gold with the hammer.

26

1 The form of the Tabernacle and the appertinences. 33 The places of the Ark, of the Mercy seat, of the Table, and of the Candlestick.

1 Afterward thou shalt make the Tabernacle with ten curtains of fine twined linen and blue silk, and purple, and scarlet: and in them thou shalt make Cherubims of [a]broidered work. **2** The length of one curtain shall be eight and twenty cubits, and the breadth of one curtain four cubits: every one of the curtains shall have one measure. **3** Five curtains shall be coupled one to another: and the other five curtains shall be coupled one to another. **4** And thou shalt make strings of blue silk upon the edge of the one curtain, which is in the selvedge [b]of the coupling: and likewise shalt thou make in the edge of the other curtain in the selvedge, in the second coupling. **5** Fifty strings shalt thou make in one curtain, and fifty strings shalt thou make in the edge of the curtain, which is in the [c]second coupling: the strings shall be one right against another. **6** Thou shalt make also fifty [d]taches of gold, and couple the curtains one to another with the taches, and it shall be one [e]Tabernacle. **7** Also thou shalt make curtains of goats' hair, to be a [f]covering upon the Tabernacle, thou shalt make them to the number of eleven curtains. **8** The length of a curtain shall be thirty cubits, and the breadth of a curtain four cubits: the eleven curtains shall be of one measure. **9** And thou shalt couple five curtains by themselves, and the six curtains by themselves: but thou shalt double the [g]sixth curtain upon the forefront of the covering. **10** And thou shalt make fifty strings in the edge of one curtain in the selvedge of the coupling, and fifty strings in the edge of the other curtain in the second coupling. **11** Likewise thou shalt make fifty [h]taches of brass, and fasten them on the strings, and shalt couple the covering together that it may be one. **12** And the [i]remnant that resteth in the curtains of the covering, even the half curtain that resteth, shall be left at the backside of the Tabernacle. **13** That the cubit on the one side, and the cubit on the other side of that which is left in the length of the curtains of the covering may remain on either side of the Tabernacle to cover it. **14** Moreover, for that covering thou shalt make a [j]covering of rams' skins dyed red, and a covering of [k]badgers' skins above. **15** Also thou shalt make boards for the Tabernacle of Shittim wood to stand up. **16** Ten cubits shall be the length of a board, and a cubit and an half cubit the breadth of one board. **17** Two tenons shall be in one board set in order as the feet of a Ladder, one against another: thus shalt thou make for all the boards of the Tabernacle. **18** And thou shalt make boards for the Tabernacle, even twenty boards on the South side, even full South. **19** And thou shalt make forty [l]sockets of silver under the twenty boards, two sockets under one board for his two tenons, and two sockets under another board for his two tenons. **20** In like manner on the other side of the Tabernacle toward the North side shall be twenty boards, **21** And their forty sockets of silver, two sockets under one board, and two sockets under another board. **22** And on the side of the Tabernacle, toward the West, shalt thou make six boards. **23** Also two boards shalt thou make in the corners of the Tabernacle in the two sides. **24** Also they shall be [m]joined beneath, and likewise they shall be joined above to a ring: thus shall it be for them two: they shall be for the two corners. **25** So they shall be eight boards having sockets of silver, even sixteen sockets, that is, two sockets under one board, and two sockets under another board. **26** Then thou shalt make five bars of Shittim wood for the boards of one side of the Tabernacle. **27** And five bars for the boards of the other side of the Tabernacle: also five bars for the boards of the side of the Tabernacle toward the West side. **28** And the middle bar shall go through the midst of the boards, from end to end. **29** And thou shalt cover the boards with gold, and make their rings of gold, for places for the bars, and thou shalt cover the bars with gold. **30** [1]So thou shalt rear up the Tabernacle, according to the fashion thereof, which was showed thee in the Mount. **31** Moreover, thou shalt make a veil of blue silk, and purple, and scarlet, and fine twined linen, thou shalt make it of broidered work with Cherubims. **32** And thou shalt hang it upon four pillars of Shittim wood covered with gold, (whose [n]hooks shall be of gold) standing upon four sockets of silver. **33** Afterward thou shalt hang the veil [o]on the hooks, that thou mayest bring in thither, that is, within the veil, the Ark of the Testimony: and the veil shall make you a separation between the Holy place and the [p]most holy place. **34** Also thou shalt put the Mercy seat upon the Ark of the Testimony in the most Holy place. **35** And thou shalt set the Table [q]without the veil, and the Candlestick over against the Table on the South side of the Tabernacle, and thou shalt set the Table on the North side. **36** Also thou shalt make an [r]hanging for the door of the Tabernacle of blue silk, and purple, and scarlet, and fine twined linen wrought with needle. **37** And thou shalt make for the hanging five pillars of Shittim, and cover them with gold: their heads shall be of gold, and thou shalt cast five sockets of brass for them.

27

1 The Altar of the burnt offering. 9 The courts of the Tabernacle. 20 The lamps continually burning.

1 Moreover thou shalt make the [a]Altar of Shittim wood, five cubits long and five cubits broad (the altar shall be four square) and the height thereof three cubits. **2** And thou shalt make it horns in the four corners thereof: the horns shall be of [b]itself, and thou shalt cover it with brass. **3** Also thou shalt make his ash pans for his ashes, and his besoms, and his basins, and his flesh-hooks, and his [c]censers: thou shalt make all the instruments thereof of brass. **4** And thou shalt make unto it a grate, like network of brass: also upon that [d]grate shalt thou make four brazen rings upon the four corners thereof. **5** And thou shalt put it under the compass of the altar beneath, that the grate may be in the midst of the altar. **6** Also thou shalt make bars for the altar, bars, I say, of Shittim wood, and shalt cover them with brass. **7** And the bars thereof shall be put in the rings, the which bars shall be upon the two sides of the altar to bear it. **8** Thou shalt make the altar hollow between the boards: as God showeth thee in the mount, so shall they make it. **9** Also thou shalt make the [e]court of the Tabernacle in the South side, even full South: the court shall have curtains of fine twined linen, of an hundred cubits long, for one side, **10** And it shall have twenty pillars, with their twenty sockets of brass: the heads of the pillars, and their [f]fillets shall be silver. **11** Likewise on the North side in length there shall be hangings of an hundred cubits long, and the twenty pillars thereof with their twenty sockets of brass: the heads of the pillars and the fillets shall be silver. **12** And the breadth of the court, on the West side shall have curtains of fifty cubits, with their ten pillars, and their ten sockets. **13** And the breadth of the court, Eastward full East, shall have [g]fifty cubits. **14** Also hangings of fifteen cubits shall be on the one [h]side with their three pillars and their three sockets. **15** Likewise on the other side shall be hangings of fifteen cubits, with their three pillars and their three sockets. **16** And in the gate of the court shall be a veil of twenty cubits of blue silk, and purple, and scarlet, and fine twined linen wrought with needle, with the four pillars thereof and their four sockets. **17** All the pillars of the court shall have fillets of silver round about, with their heads of silver, and their sockets of brass. **18** The length of the court shall be an hundred cubits, and the breadth fifty [i]at either end, and the height five cubits, and the hangings of fine twined linen, and their sockets of brass. **19** All the vessels of the Tabernacle for all manner service thereof, and all the [j]pins thereof, and all the pins of the court shall be brass. **20** And thou shalt command the children of Israel, that they bring unto thee pure oil olive [k]beaten for the light, that the lamps may always [l]burn. **21** In the Tabernacle of the Congregation without the veil, which is before the Testimony, shall Aaron and his sons dress them from evening to morning before the Lord, for a statute forever unto their generations, to be observed by the children of Israel.

28

1 The Lord calleth Aaron and his sons to the Priesthood. 4 Their garments. 13, 29 Aaron entereth into the Sanctuary in the name of the children of Israel. 30 Urim and Thummim. 38 Aaron beareth the iniquity of the Israelites' offerings.

1 And cause thou thy brother Aaron to come unto thee, and his sons with him, from among the children of Israel, that he may serve me in the Priest's office: I mean, Aaron, Nadab, and Abihu, Eleazar, and Ithamar Aaron's sons. **2** Also thou shalt make holy garments for Aaron thy brother, [a]glorious and

---

p. Exod. 25:39 This was the talent weight of the Temple, and weighed 120 pounds.

EXOD. 25

1. Exod. 35:5
2. Exod. 28:4
3. Exod. 28:15
4. Exod. 37:1
5. Num. 7:89
6. Exod. 37:10
7. Exod. 37:17
8. Heb. 8:5
9. Acts 7:44

EXOD. 26

a. Exod. 26:1 That is, of most cunning or fine work.
b. Exod. 26:4 On the side that the curtains might be tied together.
c. Exod. 26:5 In tying together both the sides.
d. Exod. 26:6 Or, hooks.
e. Exod. 26:6 Or, partition.
f. Exod. 26:7 Lest rain and weather should mar it.
g. Exod. 26:9 That is, five on the one side, and five on the other, and the sixth should hang over the door of the Tabernacle.
h. Exod. 26:11 Or, hooks.
i. Exod. 26:12 For these curtains were two cubits longer than the curtains of the Tabernacle so that they were wider by a cubit on both sides.
j. Exod. 26:14 To be put upon the covering that was made of goats' hair.
k. Exod. 26:14 This was the third covering of the Tabernacle.
l. Exod. 26:19 Or, brass pieces, wherein were the mortises for the tenons.
m. Exod. 26:24 The Hebrew word signifieth twins: declaring that they should be so perfect and well joined as was possible.
n. Exod. 26:32 Some read, heads of the pillars.
o. Exod. 26:33 Hebrew, Under the hooks: meaning that it should hang downward from the hooks.
p. Exod. 26:33 Whereinto the high Priest only entered once a year.
q. Exod. 26:35 Meaning, in the holy place.
r. Exod. 26:36 This hanging or veil was between the holy place, and there where the people were.

EXOD. 26

1. Exod. 25:9,40 / Heb. 8:5 / Acts 7:44

EXOD. 27

a. Exod. 27:1 For the burnt offering.
b. Exod. 27:2 Of the same wood and matter not fastened unto it.
c. Exod. 27:3 Or, fire pans.
d. Exod. 27:4 Hebrew, net.
e. Exod. 27:9 This was the first entry into the Tabernacle, where the people abode.
f. Exod. 27:10 They were certain hoops or circles for to beautify the pillar.
g. Exod. 27:13 Meaning, curtains of fifty cubits.
h. Exod. 27:14 Of the door of the court.
i. Exod. 27:18 Hebrew, fifty in fifty.
j. Exod. 27:19 Or, stakes, wherewith the curtains were fastened to the ground.
k. Exod. 27:20 Such as cometh from the olive, when it is first pressed or beaten.
l. Exod. 27:20 Or, ascend up.

EXOD. 28

a. Exod. 28:2 Whereby his office may be known to be glorious and excellent.

beautiful. 3 Therefore thou shalt speak unto all [b]cunning men, whom I have filled with the spirit of wisdom, that they make Aaron's garments to [c]consecrate him, that he may serve me in the Priest's office. 4 Now these shall be the garments, which they shall make, a breastplate, and an [d]Ephod, and a robe, and a broidered coat, a mitre, and a girdle: so these holy garments shall they make for Aaron thy brother, and for his sons, that he may serve me in the Priest's office. 5 Therefore they shall take gold, and blue silk, and purple, and scarlet, and fine linen. 6 And they shall make the Ephod of gold, blue silk, and purple, scarlet, and fine twined linen of broidered work. 7 The two shoulders thereof shall be joined together by their two edges: so shall it be closed. 8 And the [e]embroidered girdle of the same Ephod, which shall be upon him, shall be of the selfsame work and stuff, even of gold, blue silk, and purple, and scarlet, and fine twined linen. 9 And thou shalt take two Onyx stones, and grave upon them the names of the children of Israel. 10 Six names of them upon the one stone, and the six names that remain, upon the second stone, according to [f]their generations. 11 Thou shalt cause to grave the two stones according to the names of the children of Israel, by a graver of signets that worketh and graveth in stone, and shalt make them to be set and embossed in gold. 12 And thou shalt put the two stones upon the shoulders of the Ephod, as stones of [g]remembrance of the children of Israel: for Aaron shall bear their names before the Lord upon his two shoulders for a remembrance. 13 So thou shalt make bosses of gold, 14 And two chains of fine gold [h]at the end, of wreathen work shalt thou make them, and shalt fasten the wreathen chains upon the bosses. 15 Also thou shalt make the breastplate of [i]judgment with broidered work: like the work of the Ephod shalt thou make it: of gold, blue silk, and purple, and scarlet, and fine twined linen shalt thou make it. 16 [j]Foursquare it shall be and double, an hand breadth long and an hand breadth broad. 17 Then thou shalt set it full of places for stones, even four rows of stones: the order shall be this, a [k]ruby, a topaz, and a [l]carbuncle in the first row. 18 And in the second row thou shalt set an [m]emerald, a sapphire, and a [n]diamond. 19 And in the third row a turquoise, an agate, and an Hematite. 20 And in the fourth row [o]a chrysolite, an onyx, and a jasper: and they shall be set in gold in their embossments. 21 And the stones shall be according to the names of the children of Israel, twelve, according to their names, graven as signets, every one after his name, and they shall be for the twelve tribes. 22 Then thou shalt make upon the breastplate two chains at the ends, of wreathen work of pure gold. 23 Thou shalt make also upon the breastplate two rings of gold, and put the two rings on [p]the two ends of the breastplate. 24 And thou shalt put the two wreathen chains of gold in the two rings in the ends of the breastplate. 25 And the other two ends of the two wreathen chains, thou shalt fasten in the two embossments, and shalt put them upon the shoulders of the Ephod upon the foreside of it. 26 Also thou shalt make two rings of gold, which thou shalt put in the [q]two other ends of the breastplate, upon the border thereof, toward the inside of the Ephod. 27 And two other rings of gold thou shalt make, and put them on the two sides of the Ephod, beneath in the forepart of it over against the coupling of it upon the broidered girdle of the Ephod. 28 Thus shall they bind the breastplate by his rings unto the rings of the Ephod, with a lace of blue silk, that it may be fast upon the broidered girdle of the Ephod, and that the breastplate be not loosed from the Ephod. 29 So Aaron shall [r]bear the names of the children of Israel in the breastplate of judgment upon his heart, when he goeth into the holy place for a remembrance continually before the Lord. 30 Also thou shalt put in the breastplate of judgment, the [s]Urim and the Thummim, which shall be upon Aaron's heart, when he goeth in before the Lord, and Aaron shall bear the judgment of the children of Israel upon his heart before the Lord continually. 31 And thou shalt make the robe of the Ephod altogether of blue silk. 32 And the hole for his head shall be in the midst of it, having an edge of woven work round about the collar of it: so shall it be as the collar of an habergeon, that it rent not. 33 And beneath upon the skirts thereof, thou shalt make pomegranates of blue silk, and purple, and scarlet round about the skirts thereof, and bells of gold between them round about: 34 That is, a golden bell and a pomegranate, a golden bell and a pomegranate round about upon the skirts of the robe. 35 So shall it be upon Aaron, when he ministereth, and his sound shall be heard when he goeth into the holy place before the Lord, and when he cometh out, and he shall not die. 36 Also thou shalt make a plate of pure gold, and grave thereon, as signets are graven, [t]HOLINESS TO THE LORD. 37 And thou shalt put it on a blue silk lace, and it shall be upon the mitre, even upon the forefront of the mitre shall it be. 38 So shall it be upon Aaron's forehead, that Aaron may [u]bear the iniquity of the offerings, which the children of Israel shall offer in all their holy offerings: and it shall be always upon his forehead, to make them acceptable before the Lord. 39 Likewise thou shalt embroider the fine linen coat, and thou shalt make a mitre of fine linen, but thou shalt make a girdle of needle work. 40 Also thou shalt make for Aaron's sons coats, and thou shalt make them girdles, and bonnets shalt thou make them for glory and comeliness. 41 And thou shalt put them upon Aaron thy brother, and on his sons with him, and shalt anoint them, and [v]fill their hands, and sanctify them, that they may minister unto me in the Priest's office. 42 Thou shalt also make them linen breeches to cover their privities: from the loins unto the thighs shall they reach. 43 And they shall be for Aaron and his sons, when they come into the Tabernacle [w]of the Congregation, or when they come unto the altar to minister in the holy place, that they [x]commit not iniquity, and so die This shall be a law forever unto him, and to his seed after him.

29

1 The manner of consecrating the Priests. 38 The continual sacrifice. 45 The Lord promiseth to dwell among the children of Israel.

1 This thing also shalt thou do unto them, when thou consecratest them to be my Priests, [1]Take a young calf, and two rams without blemish, 2 And unleavened bread, and cakes unleavened tempered with oil, and wafers unleavened anointed with oil: (of fine wheat flour shalt thou make them). 3 Then thou shalt put them in one basket, and [a]present them in the basket with the calf and the two rams, 4 And shalt bring Aaron and his sons unto the door of the Tabernacle of the Congregation, and wash them with water. 5 Also thou shalt take the garments, and put upon Aaron the tunicle, and the [b]robe of the Ephod, and the Ephod, and the breastplate, and shalt close them to him with the broidered girdle of the Ephod. 6 Then thou shalt put the mitre upon his head, and shalt put the holy [2]crown upon the mitre. 7 And thou shalt take the anointing [3]oil, and shalt pour upon his head and anoint him. 8 And thou shalt bring his sons, and put coats upon them. 9 And shalt gird them with girdles, both Aaron and his sons: and shalt put the bonnets on them, and the Priest's office shall be theirs for a perpetual law: thou [4]shalt also [c]fill the hands of Aaron, and the hands of his sons. 10 After, thou shalt present the calf before the Tabernacle of the congregation, [5]and Aaron and his sons shall [d]put their hands upon the head of the calf. 11 So shalt thou kill the calf before the Lord, at the door of the Tabernacle of the Congregation. 12 Then thou shalt take of the blood of the calf, and put it upon the horns of the Altar with thy finger, and shalt pour all the rest of the blood at the foot of the Altar. 13 [6]Also thou shalt take all the fat that covereth the inwards, and the caul, that is on the liver, and the two kidneys, and the fat that is upon them, and shalt burn them upon the Altar. 14 But the flesh of the calf, and his skin, and his dung shalt thou burn with fire without the host: it is a [e]sin offering. 15 Thou shalt also take one ram, and Aaron and his sons shall put their hands upon the head of the ram. 16 Then thou shalt kill the ram, and take his blood, and sprinkle it round about upon the Altar, 17 And thou shalt cut the ram in pieces, and wash the inwards of him and his legs, and shalt put them upon the pieces thereof, and upon his head. 18 So thou shalt burn the whole ram upon the Altar: for it is a burnt offering unto the Lord [f]for a sweet savor: it is an offering made by fire unto the Lord. 19 And shalt thou take the other ram, and Aaron and his sons shall put their hands upon the head of the ram. 20 Then shalt thou kill the ram, and take of his blood, and put it [g]upon the lap of Aaron's ear, and upon the lap of the right ear of his sons, and upon the thumb of their right hand, and upon the great toe of their right foot, and shalt sprinkle the blood upon the altar round about. 21 And thou shalt take of the blood that is [h]upon the Altar, and of the anointing oil, and shalt sprinkle it upon Aaron, and upon his garments, and upon his sons, and upon the garments of his sons with him: so he shall be hallowed, and his clothes, and his sons, and the garments of his sons with him. 22 Also thou shalt take of the rams the fat and the rump, even the fat that covereth the inwards, and the caul of the liver, and the two kidneys, and the fat that is upon them, and the right shoulder, (for it is the [i]ram of consecration). 23 And one loaf of bread, and one cake of bread tempered with oil, and one wafer, out of the basket of the unleavened bread that is before the Lord: 24 And thou shalt put all this in the hands of Aaron, and in the hands of his sons, and shalt shake them to and fro before the Lord. 25 Again, thou shalt receive them of their hands, and burn them upon the altar besides the burnt offering for a sweet savor before the Lord: for this is an offering made by fire

---

b. Exod. 28:3 Hebrew, wise in heart.
c. Exod. 28:3 Which is to separate him from the rest.
d. Exod. 28:4 A short and straight coat without sleeves, put upmost upon his garments to keep them close unto him.
e. Exod. 28:8 Which went about his upmost coat.
f. Exod. 28:10 As they were in age, so should they be graven in order.
g. Exod. 28:12 That Aaron might remember the Israelites to Godward.
h. Exod. 28:14 Of the bosses.
i. Exod. 28:15 It was so called, because the high Priest could not give sentence in judgment without that on his breast.
j. Exod. 28:16 The description of the breastplate.
k. Exod. 28:17 Or, Sardius.
l. Exod. 28:17 Or, Emerald.
m. Exod. 28:18 Or, Carbuncle.
n. Exod. 28:18 Or, Jasper.
o. Exod. 28:20 Hebrew, Tarshish.
p. Exod. 28:23 Which are upmost toward the shoulder.
q. Exod. 28:26 Which are beneath.
r. Exod. 28:29 Aaron shall not enter into the holy place in his own name, but in the name of all the children of Israel.
s. Exod. 28:30 Urim signifieth light, and Thummim perfection: declaring that the stones of the breastplate were most clear, and of perfect beauty: by Urim also is meant knowledge, and Thummim holiness, showing what virtues are required in the Priests.
t. Exod. 28:36 Holiness appertaineth to the Lord: for he is most holy, and nothing unholy may appear before him.
u. Exod. 28:38 Their offerings could not be so perfect, but some fault would be therein: which sin the high Priest bare, and pacified God.
v. Exod. 28:41 That is, consecrate them, by giving them things to offer and thereby admit them to their office.
w. Exod. 28:43 Or, of witness.
x. Exod. 28:43 In not hiding their nakedness.

EXOD. 29

a. Exod. 29:3 To offer them in sacrifice.
b. Exod. 29:5 Which was next under the Ephod.
c. Exod. 29:9 Or, consecrate them.
d. Exod. 29:10 Signifying that the sacrifice was also offered for them, and that they did approve it.
e. Exod. 29:14 Hebrew, sin, 2 Cor. 5:21.
f. Exod. 29:18 Or, savor of rest, which causeth the wrath of God to cease.
g. Exod. 29:20 Meaning the soft and nether part of the ear.
h. Exod. 29:21 Wherewith the Altar must be sprinkled.

unto the Lord. **26** Likewise thou shalt take the breast of the ram of the consecration, which is for Aaron, and shalt shake it to [j]and fro before the Lord, and it shall be thy part. **27** And thou shalt sanctify the breast of the shaken offering, and the shoulder of the [k]heave offering, which was shaken to and fro, and which was heaved up of the ram of the consecration which was for Aaron, and which was for his sons. **28** And Aaron and his sons shall have it by a statute forever, of the children of Israel: for it is an heave offering, and it shall be an heave offering of the children of Israel, of their [l]peace offerings, even their heave offering to the Lord. **29** And the holy garments which appertain to Aaron, shall be his sons' after him, to be anointed therein, and to be consecrated therein. **30** That son that shall be Priest in his stead, shall put them on seven days, when he cometh into the Tabernacle of the Congregation to minister in the holy place. **31** So thou shalt take the ram of the consecration, and seethe his flesh in the holy place. **32** [7]And Aaron and his sons shall eat the flesh of the ram, and the bread that is in the basket, at the door of the Tabernacle of the Congregation. **33** So they shall eat these things, [m]whereby their atonement was made, to consecrate them, and to sanctify them: but a stranger shall not eat thereof, because they are holy things. **34** Now if ought of the flesh of the consecration, or of the bread remain unto the morning, then thou shalt burn the rest with fire: it shall not be eaten, because it is an holy thing. **35** Therefore shalt thou do thus unto Aaron and unto his sons, according to all things which I have commanded thee: seven days shalt thou [n]consecrate them. **36** And shalt offer every day a calf for a sin offering, for [o]reconciliation: and thou shalt cleanse the Altar, when thou hast offered upon it for reconciliation, and shalt anoint it to sanctify it. **37** Seven days shalt thou cleanse the Altar and sanctify it, so the Altar shall be most holy: and whatsoever toucheth the Altar, shall be holy. **38** [8]Now this is that which thou shalt present upon the altar: even two lambs of one year old, day by day continually. **39** The one lamb thou shalt present in the morning, and the other lamb thou shalt present at even. **40** And with the one lamb, a [p]tenth part of fine flour mingled with the fourth part of an [q]Hin of beaten oil, and the fourth part of an Hin of wine for a drink offering. **41** And the other lamb thou shalt present at even: thou shalt do thereto according to the offering of the morning, and according to the drink offering thereof, to be a burnt offering for a sweet savor unto the Lord. **42** This shall be a continually burnt offering in your generations at the door of the Tabernacle of the Congregation before the Lord, where I will [r]make appointment with you, to speak there unto thee. **43** There I will appoint with the children of Israel, and the place shall be sanctified by my [s]glory. **44** And I will sanctify the Tabernacle of the Congregation and the Altar: I will sanctify also Aaron and his sons to be my Priests, **45** And I will [9]dwell among the children of Israel, and will be their God. **46** Then shall they know that I am the Lord their God, that brought them out of the land of Egypt, that I might dwell among them: [t]I am the Lord their God.

30

The Altar of incense. 13 The sum that the Israelites should pay to the Tabernacle. 28 The brazen laver. 33 The anointing oil. 34 The making of the perfume.

1 Furthermore thou shalt make an Altar [a]for sweet perfume, of Shittim wood thou shalt make it. **2** The length thereof a cubit, and the breadth thereof a cubit, (it shall be foursquare) and the height thereof two cubits: the horns thereof shall be [b]of the same. **3** And thou shalt overlay it with fine gold, both the top thereof, and the sides thereof round about, and his horns: also thou shalt make unto it [c]a crown of gold round about. **4** Besides this thou shalt make under this crown two golden rings on either side: even on every side shalt thou make them, that they may be as places for the bars to bear it withal. **5** The which bars thou shalt make of Shittim wood, and shalt cover them with gold. **6** After thou shalt set it [d]before the veil, that is near the Ark of the Testimony, before the Mercy seat that is upon the Testimony, where I will appoint with thee. **7** And Aaron shall burn thereon sweet incense every morning: when he [e]dresseth the lamps thereof, shall he burn it. **8** Likewise at even, when Aaron setteth up the lamps thereof, he shall burn incense: this perfume shall be perpetually before the Lord, throughout your generations. **9** Ye shall offer no [f]strange incense thereon, nor burnt sacrifice, nor offering, neither pour any drink offering [g]thereon. **10** And Aaron shall make reconciliation upon the horns of it once in a year with the blood of the sin offering in the day of reconciliation: once in the year shall he make reconciliation upon it throughout your generations: this is most holy unto the Lord. **11** Afterward the Lord spake unto Moses, saying, **12** [1]When thou takest the sum of the children of Israel after their number, then they shall give every man [h]a redemption of his life unto the Lord, when thou tellest them, that there be no plague among them when thou countest them. **13** This shall every man give, that goeth into the number, half a shekel, after the [i]shekel of the Sanctuary: ([2]a shekel is twenty gerahs) the half shekel shall be an offering to the Lord. **14** All that are numbered from twenty years old and above, shall give an offering to the Lord. **15** The rich shall not pass, and the poor shall not diminish from half a shekel, when ye shall give an offering unto the Lord, [j]for the redemption of your lives. **16** So thou shalt take the money of the redemption of the children of Israel, and shalt put it unto the use of the Tabernacle of the Congregation, that it may be a memorial unto the children of Israel before the Lord, for the redemption of your lives. **17** Also the Lord spake unto Moses, saying, **18** Thou shalt also make a Laver of brass, and his foot of brass to wash, and shalt put it between the Tabernacle of the Congregation and the Altar, and shalt put water therein. **19** For Aaron and his sons shall [k]wash their hands, and their feet thereat. **20** When they go into the Tabernacle of the Congregation, or when they go unto the Altar to minister, and to make the perfume of the burnt offering to the Lord, they shall wash themselves with water, lest they die. **21** So they shall wash their hands and their feet that they die not: and this shall be to them an ordinance [l]forever, both unto him and to his seed throughout their generations. **22** Also the Lord spake unto Moses, saying, **23** Take thou also unto thee principal spices: of the most pure myrrh five hundred [m]shekels, of sweet cinnamon half so much, that is, two hundred and fifty, and of sweet [n]calamus, two hundred, and fifty: **24** Also of Cassia five hundred, after the shekel of the Sanctuary, and of oil olive an [3]Hin. **25** So thou shalt make of it the oil of holy ointment, even a most precious ointment after the art of the Apothecary: this shall be the oil of holy ointment. **26** And thou shalt anoint the [o]Tabernacle of the Congregation therewith, and the Ark of the Testimony: **27** Also the Table, and all the instruments thereof, and the Candlestick, with all the instruments thereof, and the altar of incense: **28** Also the altar of burnt offering with all his instruments, and the laver and his foot. **29** So thou shalt sanctify them, and they shall be most holy: all that shall touch them, shall be holy. **30** Thou shalt also anoint Aaron and his sons, and shalt consecrate them, that they may minister unto me in the Priest's office. **31** Moreover thou shalt speak unto the children of Israel, saying, This shall be an holy anointing oil unto me, throughout your generations. **32** None shall anoint [p]man's flesh therewith, neither shall ye make any composition like unto it: for it is holy, and shall be holy unto you. **33** Whosoever shall make the like ointment, or whosoever shall put any of it upon [q]a stranger, even he shall be cut off from his people. **34** And the Lord said unto Moses, Take unto thee these spices, pure myrrh and [r]clear gum and galbanum, these odors with pure frankincense of each like weight: **35** Then thou shalt make of them perfume composed after the art of the apothecary, mingled together, pure and holy. **36** And thou shalt beat it to powder, and shalt put it before the Ark of the Testimony in the tabernacle of the congregation, where I will make appointment with thee: it shall be unto you most holy. **37** And ye shall not make unto you any composition like this perfume, which thou shalt make: it shall be unto thee holy for the [s]Lord. **38** Whosoever shall make like unto that to smell thereto, even he shall be cut off from his people.

31

2 God maketh Bezalel and Aholiab meet for his work. 13 The Sabbath day is the sign of our sanctification. 18 The Tables written by the finger of God.

1 And the Lord spake unto Moses, saying, **2** Behold, I [a]have called by name Bezalel the son of Uri, the son of Hur, of the tribe of Judah, **3** Whom I have filled with the Spirit of God, in wisdom, and in understanding, and in knowledge, and in all [b]workmanship: **4** To find out curious works to work in gold,

---

i. Exod. 29:22 Which is offered for the consecration of the high Priest.
j. Exod. 29:26 This sacrifice the Priest did move toward the East, West, North, and South.
k. Exod. 29:27 So called because it was not only shaken to and fro, but also lifted up.
l. Exod. 29:28 Which were offerings of thanksgiving to God for his benefits.
m. Exod. 29:33 That is, by the sacrifices.
n. Exod. 29:35 Hebrew, fill their hands.
o. Exod. 29:36 To appease God's wrath that sin may be pardoned.
p. Exod. 29:40 That is, an Omer, read Exod. 16:16.
q. Exod. 29:40 Which is about a pint.
r. Exod. 29:42 Or, declare myself to you.
s. Exod. 29:43 Because of my glorious presence.
t. Exod. 29:46 It is I the Lord, that am their God.

EXOD. 29
1. Lev. 9:2
2. Exod. 28:36
3. Exod. 30:25
4. Exod. 28:41
5. Lev. 1:4
6. Lev. 3:3

EXOD. 30
a. Exod. 30:1 Upon the which the sweet perfume was burnt, verse 34.
b. Exod. 30:2 Of the same wood and matter.
c. Exod. 30:3 Or, a circle and border.
d. Exod. 30:6 That is, in the Sanctuary, and not in the holiest of all.
e. Exod. 30:7 Meaning, when he trimmeth them, and refresheth the oil.
f. Exod. 30:9 Otherwise made them this, which is described.
g. Exod. 30:9 But it must only serve to burn perfume.
h. Exod. 30:12 Whereby he testified that he redeemed his life which he had forfeit, as is declared by David, 2 Sam. 24:1.
i. Exod. 30:13 This shekel valued two common shekels: and the gerah valued about 12 pence after five shillings sterling the ounce of silver.
j. Exod. 30:15 That God should be merciful unto you.
k. Exod. 30:19 Signifying, that he that cometh to God, must be washed from all sin and corruption.
l. Exod. 30:21 So long as the Priesthood shall last.
m. Exod. 30:23 Weighing so much.
n. Exod. 30:23 It is a kind of reed of a very sweet savor within, and it is used in powders and odors.
o. Exod. 30:26 All things which appertain to the Tabernacle.
p. Exod. 30:32 Neither at their burials nor otherwise.
q. Exod. 30:33 Either a stranger or an Israelite, save only the Priests.
r. Exod. 30:34 In Hebrew, Sheheleth: which is a sweet kind of gum and shineth as the nail.
s. Exod. 30:37 Only dedicated to the use of the Tabernacle.

EXOD. 30
1. Num. 1:2,5
2. Lev. 27:25 / Num. 3:47 / Ezek. 45:12
3. Exod. 29:40

EXOD. 31
a. Exod. 31:2 I have chosen and made meet, Exod. 35:30.
b. Exod. 31:3 This showeth that handicrafts are the gifts of God's spirit, and therefore ought to be esteemed.

and in silver, and in brass, **5** Also in the art to set stones, and to carve in timber, and to work in all manner of workmanship. **6** And behold, I have joined him with Aholiab the son of Ahisamach of the tribe of Dan, and in the hearts of all that are [c]wise hearted, have I put wisdom to make all that I have commanded thee: **7** That is, the Tabernacle of the Congregation, and the Ark of the Testimony, and the Mercy seat that shall be thereupon, with all instruments of the Tabernacle: **8** Also the Table and the instruments thereof, and the [d]pure Candlestick with all his instruments, and the Altar of perfume: **9** Likewise the Altar of burnt offering with all his instruments, and the Laver with his foot: **10** Also the garments of the ministration, and the holy garment for Aaron the Priest, and the garments of his sons, to minister in the Priest's office, **11** And the [e]anointing oil, and sweet perfume for the Sanctuary according to all that I have commanded thee, shall they do. **12** Afterward the Lord spake unto Moses, saying, **13** Speak thou also unto the children of Israel, and say, [f]Notwithstanding keep ye my Sabbaths: for it is a sign between me and you in your generations, that ye may know that I the Lord do sanctify you. **14** [1]Ye shall therefore keep the [g]Sabbath: for it is holy unto you: he that defileth it, shall die the death: therefore whosoever worketh therein, the same person shall be even cut off from among his people. **15** Six days shall men work, but in the seventh day is the Sabbath of the holy rest to the Lord: whosoever doeth any work in the Sabbath day, shall die the death. **16** Wherefore the children of Israel shall keep the Sabbath, that they may observe the [h]rest throughout their generations for an everlasting Covenant. **17** It is a sign between me and the children of Israel forever: [2]for in six days the Lord made the heaven and the earth, and in the seventh day [i]he ceased and rested. **18** Thus (when the Lord had made an end of communing with Moses upon mount Sinai) [3]he gave him two Tables [j]of the Testimony, even tables of stone, written with the finger of God.

32

4 The Israelites impute their deliverance to the calf. 14 God is appeased by Moses' prayer. 19 Moses breaketh the Tables.

1 But when the people saw, that Moses tarried long ere he came down from the mountain, the people gathered themselves together against Aaron, and said unto him, Up, [a]make us gods to go before us: for of this Moses (the man that brought us out of the land of Egypt) we know not what is become of him. **2** And Aaron said unto them, [b]Pluck off the golden earrings, which are in the ears of your wives, of your sons, and of your daughters, and bring them unto me. **3** Then all the people plucked from [c]themselves the golden earrings, which were in their ears, and they brought them unto Aaron. **4** [1]Who received them at their hands, and fashioned it with the graving tool, and made of it a [d]molten calf: then they said, [2]These be thy gods, O Israel, which brought thee out of the land of Egypt. **5** When Aaron saw that, he made an Altar before it: and Aaron proclaimed, saying, Tomorrow shall be the holy day of the Lord. **6** So they rose up the next day in the morning, and offered burnt offerings, and brought peace offerings: also [3]the people sat them down to eat and drink, and rose up to play. **7** Then the Lord said unto Moses, [4]Go get thee down: for thy people which thou hast brought out of the land of Egypt, hath corrupted their ways. **8** They [e]are soon turned out of the way, which I commanded them: for they have made them a molten calf, and have worshipped it, and have offered thereto, saying, [5]These be thy gods, O Israel, which have brought thee out of the land of Egypt. **9** Again the Lord said unto Moses, [6]I have seen this people, and behold, it is a stiff-necked people. **10** Now [f]therefore let me alone, that my wrath may wax hot against them, for I will consume them: but I will make of thee a mighty people **11** [7]But Moses prayed unto the Lord his God, and said, O Lord, why doth thy wrath wax hot against thy people, which thou hast brought out of the land of Egypt, with great power and with a mighty hand? **12** [8]Wherefore shall the Egyptians [g]speak, and say, He hath brought them out maliciously for to slay them in the mountains, and to consume them from the earth? turn from thy fierce wrath, and [h]change thy mind from this evil toward thy people. **13** Remember [i]Abraham, Isaac, and Israel thy servants, to whom thou swarest by thine own self, and saidest unto them, [9]I will multiply your seed, as the stars of heaven, and all this land, that I have spoken of, will I give unto your seed, and they shall inherit it forever. **14** Then the Lord changed his mind from the evil, which he threatened to do unto his people. **15** So Moses returned and went down from the mountain with the two Tables of the Testimony in his hand: the tables were written on both their sides, even on the one side and on the other were they written. **16** And these Tables were the work of God, and [j]this writing was the writing of God graven in the Tables. **17** And when Joshua heard the noise of the people, as they shouted, he said unto Moses, There is a noise of war in the host. **18** Who answered, It is not the noise of them that have the victory, nor the noise of them that are overcome: but I do hear the noise of singing. **19** Now, as soon as he came near unto the host, he saw the calf and the dancing: so Moses' wrath waxed hot, and he cast the Tables out of his hands, and brake them in pieces beneath the mountain. **20** [10]After, he took the calf, which they had made, and burned it in the fire, and ground it unto powder, and strowed it upon the water, and made the children of Israel [k]drink of it. **21** Also Moses said unto Aaron, What did this people unto thee, that thou hast brought so great a sin upon them? **22** Then Aaron answered, Let not the wrath of my Lord wax fierce: Thou knowest this people, that they are even set on mischief. **23** And they said unto me, Make us gods to go before us: for we know not what is become of this Moses (the man that brought us out of the land of Egypt). **24** Then I said to them, Ye that have gold, pluck it off: and they brought it me, and I did cast it into the fire, and thereof came this calf. **25** Moses therefore saw that the people were [l]naked (for Aaron had made them naked unto their shame among their enemies) **26** And Moses stood in the gate of the camp, and said, Who pertaineth to the Lord? let them come to me And all the sons of Levi gathered themselves unto him. **27** Then he said unto them, Thus saith the Lord God of Israel: Put every man his sword by his side, go to and fro, from gate to gate, through the host, and [m]slay every man his brother, and every man his companion, and every man his neighbor. **28** So the children of Levi did as Moses had commanded: and there fell of the people the same day about three thousand men. **29** (For Moses had said, Consecrate your hands unto the Lord this day, even every man upon his [n]son, and upon his brother, that there may be given you a blessing this day.) **30** And when the morning came, Moses said unto the people, Ye have committed a grievous crime: but now I will go up to the Lord, if I may pacify him for your sin. **31** Moses therefore went again unto the Lord, and said, Oh, this people have sinned a great sin, and have made them gods of gold. **32** Therefore now if thou pardon their sin, thy mercy shall appear: but if thou wilt not, I pray thee, raise me [o]out of thy book, which thou hast written. **33** Then the Lord said to Moses, Whosoever hath sinned against me, I will put him out of my [p]book. **34** Go now therefore, bring the people unto the place which I commanded thee: behold, mine Angel shall go before thee, but yet in the day of my visitation I will visit their sin upon them. **35** [q]So the Lord plagued the people, because they caused Aaron to make the calf which he made.

33

2 God promiseth to send an Angel before his people. 4 They are sad because the Lord denieth to go up with them. 9 Moses talketh familiarly with God. 13 He prayeth for the people.

1 Afterward the Lord said unto Moses, Depart, [a]go up from hence, thou, and the people (which thou hast brought up out of the land of Egypt) unto the land which I sware unto Abraham, to Isaac, and to Jacob, saying, [1]Unto thy seed will I give it. **2** And [2]I will send an Angel before thee, and will cast out the Canaanites, the Amorites, and the Hittites, and the Perizzites, the Hivites, and the Jebusites, **3** To a land, I say, that floweth with milk and honey: for I will not go up with thee, [3]because thou art a stiff-necked people, lest I consume thee in the way. **4** And when the people heard this evil tidings, they sorrowed, and no man put on his best raiment. **5** (For the Lord had said unto Moses, Say unto the children of Israel, Ye are a stiff-necked people, I will come suddenly upon thee and consume thee: therefore now put thy costly raiment from thee, that I may know [b]what to do unto thee.) **6** So the children of Israel laid their good raiment from them, after Moses came down from the mount Horeb. **7** Then Moses took his

---

c. Exod. 31:6 I have instructed them, and increased their knowledge.
d. Exod. 31:8 So called, because of the cunning and art used therein, or because the whole was beaten out of the piece.
e. Exod. 31:11 Which only was to anoint the Priests and the instruments of the tabernacle, and not to burn.
f. Exod. 31:13 Though I command these works to be done, yet will I not that you break my Sabbath days.
g. Exod. 31:14 God repeateth this point because the whole keeping of the law standeth in the true use of the Sabbath, which is to cease from our works, and to obey the will of God.
h. Exod. 31:16 Or, Sabbath.
i. Exod. 31:17 From creating his creatures, but not from governing and preserving them.
j. Exod. 31:18 Whereby he declared his will to his people.

EXOD. 31

1. Exod. 20:8 - Ezek. 20:12
2. Gen. 31 - Gen. 22
3. Deut. 9:10

EXOD. 32

a. Exod. 32:1 The root of Idolatry is, when men think that God is not at hand, except they see him carnally.
b. Exod. 32:2 Thinking that they would rather forego idolatry, than to resign their most precious jewels.
c. Exod. 32:3 Such is the rage of idolaters, that they spare no cost to satisfy their wicked desires.
d. Exod. 32:4 They smelled of their leaven of Egypt, where they saw calves, oxen and serpents worshipped.
e. Exod. 32:8 Whereby we see what necessity we have to pray earnestly to God, to keep us in his true obedience, and to send us good guides.
f. Exod. 32:10 God showeth that the prayers of the godly stay his punishment.
g. Exod. 32:12 Or, blaspheme.
h. Exod. 32:12 Or, repent.
i. Exod. 32:13 That is, thy promise made to Abraham.
j. Exod. 32:16 All these repetitions show how excellent a thing they defrauded themselves of by their idolatry.
k. Exod. 32:20 Partly to despite them of their idolatry, and partly that they should have none occasion to remember it afterward.
l. Exod. 32:25 Both destitute of God's favor, and an occasion to their enemies to speak evil of their God.
m. Exod. 32:27 This fact did so please God, that he turned the curse of Jacob against Levi to a blessing, Deut. 33:9.
n. Exod. 32:29 In revenging God's glory we must have no respect to person, but put off all carnal affection.
o. Exod. 32:32 So much he esteemed the glory of God, that he preferred it even to his own salvation.
p. Exod. 32:33 I will make it known that he was never predestinated in mine eternal counsel to life everlasting.
q. Exod. 32:35 This declareth how grievous a sin idolatry is, seeing that at Moses' prayer God would not fully remit it.

EXOD. 32

1. Ps. 106:19
2. 1Kings 12:28
3. 1 Cor. 10:7
4. Deut. 9:12
5. 1 Kings. 12:28
6. Exod. 33:3 / Deut. 9:!3
7. Ps. 106:23
8. Num. 14:13
9. Gen. 12:7 / Gen 15:7 / Gen. 48:16
10. Deut. 9:21

EXOD. 33

a. Exod. 33:1 The land of Canaan was compassed with hills: so they that entered into it, must pass up by the hills.
b. Exod. 33:5 That either I may show mercy, if thou repent, or else punish thy rebellion.

tabernacle, and pitched it without the host far off from the host, and called it [c]Ohel-moed And when any did seek to the Lord, he went out unto the Tabernacle of the Congregation, which was without the host. **8** And when Moses went out unto the Tabernacle, all the people rose up, and stood every man at his tent door, and looked after Moses, until he was gone into the Tabernacle. **9** And as soon as Moses was entered into the Tabernacle, the cloudy pillar descended and stood at the door of the Tabernacle, and the Lord talked with Moses. **10** Now when all the people saw the cloudy pillar stand at the Tabernacle door, all the people rose up, and worshipped every man in his tent door. **11** And the Lord spake unto Moses, [d]face to face, as a man speaketh unto his friend After he turned again into the host, but his servant Joshua the son of Nun a young man, departed not out of the Tabernacle. **12** Then Moses said unto the Lord, See, thou sayest unto me, Lead this people forth, and thou hast not showed me whom thou wilt send with me: thou hast said moreover, I know thee by [e]name, and thou hast also found grace in my sight. **13** Now therefore, I pray thee, if I have found favor in thy sight, show me now thy way, that I may know thee, and that I may find grace in thy sight: consider also that this nation is thy people. **14** And he answered, My [f,g]presence shall go with thee, and I will give thee rest. **15** Then he said unto him, If thy presence go not with us, carry us not hence. **16** And wherein now shall it be known, that I and thy people have found favor in thy sight? shall it not be when thou goest with us? so I, and thy people shall have preeminence before all the people that are upon the earth. **17** And the Lord said unto Moses, I will do this also that thou hast said: for thou hast found grace in my sight, and I know thee by name. **18** Again he said, I beseech thee, show me thy [h]glory. **19** And he answered, I will make all my [i]good go before thee, and I will [j]proclaim the Name of the Lord before thee: [4]for I will show [k]mercy to whom I will show mercy, and will have compassion on whom I will have compassion. **20** Furthermore he said, Thou canst not see my face, for there shall no man see me, and [l]live. **21** Also the Lord said, Behold, there is a place by [m]me, and thou shalt stand upon the rock: **22** And while my glory passeth by, I will put thee in a cleft of the rock, and will cover thee with mine hand while I pass by. **23** After I will take away mine hand, and thou shalt see my [n]back parts: but my face shall not be seen.

34

1 The Tables are renewed. 6 The description of God. 12 All fellowship with idolaters is forbidden. 18 The feasts. 28 Moses is 40 days in the mount. 30 His face shineth, and he covereth it with a veil.

1 And the Lord said unto Moses, [1]Hew thee two Tables of stone, like unto the first, and I will write upon the Tables the words that were in the first Tables, which thou brakest in pieces. **2** And be ready in the morning, that thou mayest come up early unto the mount of Sinai, and [a]wait there for me in the top of the mount. **3** But let no man come up with thee, neither let any man be seen throughout all the mount; neither let the sheep nor cattle feed [b]before this mount. **4** Then Moses hewed [c]two Tables of stone like unto the first, and rose up early in the morning, and went up unto the mount of Sinai, as the Lord had commanded him, and took in his hand two Tables of stone. **5** And the Lord descended in the cloud, and stood with him there, and proclaimed the name of the Lord. **6** So the Lord passed before his face, and [d]cried, The Lord, the Lord, strong, merciful, and gracious, slow to anger, and abundant in goodness and truth. **7** Reserving mercy for thousands, forgiving iniquity, and transgression and sin, and not [e]making the wicked innocent, [2]visiting the iniquity of the fathers upon the children, and upon children's children, unto the third and fourth generation. **8** Then Moses made haste and bowed himself to the earth, and worshipped, **9** And said, O Lord, I pray thee, If I have found grace in thy sight, that the Lord would now go with us ([f]for it is a stiff-necked people) and pardon our iniquity and our sin, and take us for thine inheritance. **10** And he answered, Behold, [3]I will make a covenant before all thy people, and will do marvels, such as have not been done in all the world, neither in all nations: and all the people among whom thou art, shall see the work of the Lord: for it is a terrible thing that I will do with thee. **11** Keep diligently that which I command thee this day: Behold, I will cast out before thee the Amorites, and the Canaanites, and the Hittites, and the Perizzites, and the Hivites, and the Jebusites. **12** [4]Take heed to thyself, that thou make no compact with the inhabitants of the land whither thou goest, lest they be the cause of [g]ruin among you: **13** But ye shall overthrow their altars, and break their images in pieces, and cut down their [h]groves, **14** (For thou shalt bow down to none other god, because the Lord, whose Name is [5]Jealous, is a jealous God.) **15** Lest thou make a [6]compact with the inhabitants of the land, and when they go a whoring after their gods, and do sacrifice unto their gods, some man call thee, and thou [7]eat of his sacrifice. **16** And lest thou take of their [8]daughters unto thy sons, and their daughters go a whoring after their gods, and make thy sons go a whoring after their gods. **17** Thou shalt make thee no gods of [i]metal. **18** The feast of [9]unleavened bread shalt thou keep: seven days shalt thou eat unleavened bread, as I commanded thee, in the time of the [10]month of Abib: for in the month of Abib thou camest out of Egypt. **19** [11]Every male that first openeth the womb, shall be mine: also all the firstborn of thy flock shall be reckoned mine, both of beeves and sheep. **20** But the first of the ass thou shalt buy out with a lamb: and if thou redeem him not, then thou shalt break his neck: all the firstborn of thy sons shalt thou redeem, and none shall appear before me [j,12]empty. **21** [13]Six days shalt thou work, and in the seventh day thou shalt rest: both in earing time, and in the harvest thou shalt rest. **22** [14]Thou shalt also observe the feast of weeks in the time of the firstfruits, of wheat harvest, and the feast of gathering fruits in [k]the end of the year. **23** [15]Thrice in a year shall all your men children appear before the Lord Jehovah God of Israel. **24** For I will cast out the nations before thee and enlarge thy coasts, so that no man shall [l]desire thy land, when thou shalt come up to appear before the Lord thy God thrice in the year. **25** [16]Thou shall not offer the blood of my sacrifice with leaven, neither shall ought of the sacrifice of the feast of Passover be left unto the morning. **26** The first ripe fruits of thy land thou shalt bring unto the house of the Lord thy God: yet shalt thou not [m]seethe a kid in his mother's milk. **27** And the Lord said unto Moses, Write thou these words: for after the tenor of [17]these words I have made a covenant with thee and with Israel. **28** So he was there with the Lord [n]forty days and forty nights, and did neither eat bread nor drink water, and he wrote in the Tables [18]the words of the covenant, even the [o]Ten commandments. **29** So when Moses came down from mount Sinai, the two Tables of the Testimony were in Moses' hand, as he descended from the mount: (now Moses wist not that the skin of his face shone bright, after that God had talked with him). **30** And Aaron and all the children of Israel looked upon Moses, and behold, the skin of his face shone bright, and they were [p]afraid to come near him. **31** But Moses called them: and Aaron and all the chief of the congregation returned unto him: and Moses talked with them. **32** And afterward all the children of Israel came near, and he charged them with all that the Lord had said unto him in mount Sinai. **33** So Moses made an end of communing with them, [19]and had put a covering upon his face. **34** But, when Moses came [q]before the Lord to speak with him, he took off the covering until he came out: then he came out, and spake unto the children of Israel that which he was commanded. **35** And the children of Israel saw the face of Moses, how the skin of Moses' face shone bright: therefore Moses put the covering upon his face, until he went to speak with God.

35

2 The Sabbath. 5 The free gifts are required. 21 The readiness of the people to offer. 30 Bezalel and Aholiab are praised of Moses.

1 Then Moses assembled all the Congregation of the children of Israel, and said unto them, These are the words which the Lord hath commanded, that ye should do them: **2** [1]Six days thou shalt work, but the seventh day shall be unto you the holy [a]Sabbath of rest unto the Lord: whosoever doeth any work therein, shall die. **3** Ye shall kindle no fire throughout all your habitations upon the Sabbath day. **4** Again, Moses spake unto all the Congregation of the children of Israel, saying, This is the thing which the Lord commandeth, saying, **5** Take

---

c. Exod. 33:7 That is, the Tabernacle of the Congregation: so called, because the people resorted thither, when they should be instructed of the Lord's will.
d. Exod. 33:11 Most plainly and familiarly of all others, Num. 12:7,8; Deut. 34:10.
e. Exod. 33:12 I care for thee and will preserve thee in this thy vocation.
f. Exod. 33:14 Hebrew, face.
g. Exod. 33:14 Signifying that the Israelites should excel through God's favor all other people, verse 16.
h. Exod. 33:18 Thy face, thy substance, and thy majesty.
i. Exod. 33:19 My mercy and fatherly care.
j. Exod. 33:19 Read Exod. 34:6,7.
k. Exod. 33:19 For finding nothing in man that can deserve mercy, he will freely save his.
l. Exod. 33:20 For Moses saw not his face in full majesty, but as man's weakness could bear.
m. Exod. 33:21 In mount Horeb.
n. Exod. 33:23 So much of my glory as in this mortal life thou art able to see.

EXOD. 33
1. Gen. 12:7
2. Exod. 23:27 / Josh. 24:11 / Deut. 7:22
3. Exod. 3:19 / Deut. 9:13
4. Rom. 9:15

EXOD. 34
a. Exod. 34:2 Hebrew, stand to me.
b. Exod. 34:3 Or, about.
c. Exod. 34:4 Or, polished.
d. Exod. 34:6 This ought to be referred to the Lord, and not to Moses proclaiming: as Exod. 33:19.
e. Exod. 34:7 Hebrew, not making innocent.
f. Exod. 34:9 Seeing the people are thus of nature, the rulers have need to call upon God that he would always be present with his Spirit.
g. Exod. 34:12 If thou follow their wickedness, and pollute thyself with their idolatry.
h. Exod. 34:13 Which pleasant places they chose for their idols.
i. Exod. 34:17 As gold, silver, brass, or anything that is molten: And herein is condemned all manner of idols, whatsoever they be made of.
j. Exod. 34:20 Without offering something.
k. Exod. 34:22 Which was in September, when the sun declined which in the count of political things they called the end of the year.
l. Exod. 34:24 God promiseth to defend them and theirs, which obey his commandment.
m. Exod. 34:26 Read Exod. 23:1; Deut. 14:21.
n. Exod. 34:28 This miracle was to confirm the authority of the law, and ought no more to be followed than other miracles.
o. Exod. 34:28 Or, words.
p. Exod. 34:30 Read 2 Cor. 3:7.
q. Exod. 34:34 Which was in the Tabernacle of the congregation.

EXOD. 34
1. Deut. 10:1
2. Deut. 5:9 / Jer. 32:18
3. Deut. 5:2
4. Deut. 7:2
5. Exod.. 20:5
6. 1Cor. 8:10
7. Exod. 23:32 / Deut. 7:2,3
8. 1 Kings 11:2
9. Exod. 23:15
10. Exod. 13:4
11. Exod. 13:2 / Exod. 22:29 / Ezek. 44:30
12. Exod. 22:29 / Ezek. 44:30
13. Exod. 23:25
14. Exod. 23:12
15. Exod. 23:15
16. Deut. 16:16 / Exod. 23:14,17
17. Exod. 23:18
18. Exod. 24:18 / Deut. 9:9
19. Deut. 4:23
20. 2Cor. 3:13

EXOD. 35
a. Exod. 35:2 Wherein ye shall rest from all bodily work.

from among you an offering unto the Lord: whosoever is of a [2]willing heart, let
him bring this offering to the Lord, namely gold, and silver and brass: **6** Also
blue silk, and purple, and scarlet, and fine linen, and goats' hair, **7** And rams'
skins dyed red, and badgers' skins with Shittim wood: **8** Also oil for light, and
spices for the anointing oil, and for the sweet incense, **9** And onyx stones, and
stones to be set in the Ephod, and in the breastplate. **10** And all the wise [b]hearted
among you, shall come and make all that the Lord hath commanded: **11** That
is, the [3]Tabernacle, the pavilion thereof, and his covering, and his taches, and his
boards, his bars, his pillars, and his sockets, **12** The Ark, and the bars thereof:
the Mercy seat, and the veil that [c]covereth it, **13** The Table, and the bars of it,
and all the instruments thereof, and the showbread: **14** Also the Candlestick of
light and his instruments, and his lamps with the oil for the light: **15** [4]Likewise
the Altar of perfume and his bars, and the anointing oil, and the sweet incense,
and the veil of the door at the entering in of the Tabernacle, **16** The [5]Altar of
burnt offering with his brazen grate, his bars and all his instruments, the laver and
his foot, **17** The hangings of the court, his pillars and his sockets, and the veil of
the gate of the court, **18** The pins of the Tabernacle, and the pins of the court
with their cords, **19** The [d]ministering garments to minister in the holy place,
and the holy garments of Aaron the Priest, and the garments of his sons, that they
may minister in the Priest's office. **20** Then all the Congregation of the children
of Israel departed from the presence of Moses. **21** And every one, whose heart
[e]encouraged him, and every one, whose spirit made him willing, came and brought
an offering to the Lord, for the work of the Tabernacle of the Congregation, and
for all his uses, and for the holy garments. **22** Both men and women, as many
as were free hearted, came and brought [f]taches and earrings, and rings, and bra-
celets, all were jewels of gold: and every one that offered an offering of gold unto
the Lord: **23** Every man also, which had blue silk, and purple, and scarlet, and
fine linen and goats' hair, and rams' skins dyed red, and badgers' skins, brought
them. **24** All that offered an oblation of silver and of brass, brought the offe-
ring unto the Lord: and every one, that [g]had Shittim wood for any manner work
of the ministration, brought it. **25** And all the women that were [h]wise-hearted,
did spin with their hands, and brought the spun work, even the blue silk, and the
purple, the scarlet, and fine linen. **26** Likewise all the women, [i]whose hearts
were moved with knowledge, spun goats' hair. **27** And the rulers brought onyx
stones, and stones to be set in the Ephod, and in the breastplate: **28** Also spice,
and oil for light, and for the [6]anointing oil, and for the sweet perfume. **29** Every
man and woman of the children of Israel, whose hearts moved them willingly to
bring for all the work which the Lord had commanded them to make [j]by the hand
of Moses, brought a free offering unto the Lord. **30** Then Moses said unto the
children of Israel, Behold, [7]the Lord hath called by name Bezalel the son of Uri, the
son of Hur of the tribe of Judah, **31** And hath filled him [k]with an excellent spirit
of wisdom, of understanding, and of knowledge, and in all manner work, **32** To
find out curious works, to work in gold, and in silver, and in brass, **33** And in
graving stones to set them, and in carving of wood, even to make any manner of
fine work. **34** And he hath put in his heart that he may teach other: both he, and
Aholiab the son of Ahisamach of the tribe of Dan: **35** Them hath he filled with
wisdom of heart to work all manner [l]of cunning [8]and broidered, and needle work:
in blue silk, and in purple, in scarlet, and in fine linen and weaving, even to do all
manner of work and subtle inventions.

36

5 The great readiness of the people. 8 The curtains made. 19 The coverings. 20 The boards. 31 The bars, 35 and the veil.

1 Then wrought Bezalel, and Aholiab, and all [a]cunning men, to whom the
Lord gave wisdom, and understanding, to know how to work all manner work
for the service of the [b]Sanctuary, according to all that the Lord had comman-
ded. **2** For Moses had called Bezalel, and Aholiab, and all the wise-hearted men,
in whose hearts the Lord had given wisdom, even as many as their hearts encou-
raged to come unto that work to work it. **3** And they received of Moses all the
offering which the children of Israel had brought for the work of the service of
the Sanctuary, to make it: also [c]they brought still unto him free gifts every mor-
ning. **4** So all the wise men, that wrought all the holy work, came every man
from his work which they wrought, **5** And spake to Moses, saying, The people
bring too [d]much, and more than enough for the use of the work, which the Lord
hath commanded to be made. **6** Then Moses gave a commandment, and they
caused it to be proclaimed throughout the host, saying, Let neither man nor wo-
man prepare any more work for the oblations of the Sanctuary So the people were
stayed from offering. **7** For the stuff they had, was sufficient for all the work to
make it, and too much. **8** [1]All the cunning men therefore among the workmen,
made for the Tabernacle ten curtains of fine twined linen, and of blue silk, and
purple, and scarlet: [e]Cherubims of broidered work made they upon them. **9** The
length of one curtain was twenty and eight cubits, and the breadth of one curtain
four cubits: and the curtains were all of one size. **10** And he coupled five curtains
together, and another five coupled he together. **11** And he made strings of blue
silk by the edge of one curtain, in the selvedge of the coupling: likewise he made
on the side of the other curtain in the selvedge in the second coupling. **12** [2]Fi-
fty strings made he in the one curtain, and fifty strings made he in the edge of the
other curtain, which was in the second coupling: the strings were set one against
another. **13** After, he made fifty [f]taches of gold, and coupled the curtains one to
another with the taches: so was it one Tabernacle. **14** Also he made curtains of
goats' hair for the [g]covering upon the Tabernacle: he made them to the number
of eleven curtains. **15** The length of one curtain had thirty cubits, and the bre-
adth of one curtain four cubits: the eleven curtains were of one size. **16** And he
coupled five curtains by themselves, and six curtains by themselves. **17** Also he
made fifty strings upon the edge of one curtain in the selvedge in the coupling,
and fifty strings made he upon the edge of the other curtain in the second cou-
pling. **18** He made also fifty taches of brass to couple the covering that it mi-
ght be one. **19** And he made a [h]covering upon the pavilion of rams' skins dyed
red, and a covering of badgers' skins above. **20** Likewise he made the boards
for the Tabernacle, of Shittim wood to [i]stand up. **21** The length of a board was
ten cubits, and the breadth of one board was a cubit and an half. **22** One bo-
ard had two tenons, set in order as the feet of a ladder, one against another: thus
made he for all the boards of the Tabernacle. **23** So he made twenty boards for
the South side of the Tabernacle, even full South. **24** And forty sockets of silver
made he under the twenty boards, two sockets under one board for his two te-
nons, and two sockets under another board for his two tenons. **25** Also for the
other side of the Tabernacle toward the North, he made twenty boards. **26** And
their forty sockets of silver, two sockets under one board, and two sockets under
another board. **27** Likewise toward [j]the West side of the Tabernacle he made six
boards. **28** And two boards made he in the corners of the Tabernacle for either
side, **29** And they were [3]joined beneath, and likewise were made sure above
with a ring: thus he did to both in both corners. **30** So there were eight boards,
and their sixteen sockets of silver, under every board two sockets. **31** After,
he made [4]bars of Shittim wood, five for the boards in the one side of the Taber-
nacle, **32** And five bars for the boards in the other side of the Tabernacle, and
five bars for the boards of the Tabernacle on the side toward the West. **33** And
he made the middle bar to shoot through the boards, from the one end to the
other. **34** He overlaid also the boards with gold, and made their rings of gold for
places for the bars, and covered the bars with gold. **35** Moreover he made a [k]veil
of blue silk and purple, and of scarlet, and of fine twined linen: with Cherubims of
broidered work made he it: **36** And made thereunto four pillars of Shittim, and
overlaid them with gold: whose [l]hooks were also of gold, and he cast for them four
sockets of silver. **37** And he made an [m]hanging for the Tabernacle door, of blue
silk, and purple, and scarlet, and fine twined linen, and needle work, **38** And the
five pillars of it with their hooks, and overlaid their chapiters, and their [n]fillets with
gold, but their five sockets were of brass.

37

1 The Ark. 6 The Mercy seat. 10 The Table. 17 The Candlestick. 25 The altar of incense.

1 After this, Bezalel made the [1]Ark of Shittim wood, two cubits and an half
long, and a cubit and an half broad, and a cubit and an half high: **2** And over-
laid it with fine gold within and without, and made a [a]crown of gold to it round
about, **3** And cast for it four rings of gold for the four corners of it: that is, two
rings for the one side of it, and two rings for the other side thereof. **4** Also he
made bars of Shittim wood, and covered them with gold, **5** And put the bars in
the rings by the sides of the Ark, to bear the Ark. **6** And he made the [2]Mercy
seat of pure gold: two cubits and an half was the length thereof, and one cubit
and an half the breadth thereof. **7** And he made two Cherubims of gold, upon
the two ends of the Mercy seat: even of work beaten with the hammer made he

---

b. Exod. 35:10 Read Exod. 28:3.
c. Exod. 35:12 Which hanged before the Mercy seat that it could not be seen.
d. Exod. 35:19 Such as appertain to the service of the Tabernacle.
e. Exod. 35:21 Hebrew, lifted him up.
f. Exod. 35:22 Or, hooks.
g. Exod. 35:24 Hebrew, with whom was found.
h. Exod. 35:25 Which were witty and expert.
i. Exod. 35:26 That is, which were good spinners.
j. Exod. 35:29 Using Moses as a minister thereof.
k. Exod. 35:31 Or, with the spirit of God.
l. Exod. 35:35 Pertaining to graving, or carving, or such like.

EXOD. 35
1. Exod. 20:9
2. Exod. 25:2
3. Exod. 26:31
4. Exod. 30:1
5. Exod. 27:1
6. Exod. 30:23
7. Exod. 31:2
8. Exod. 26:1

EXOD. 36
a. Exod. 36:1 Hebrew, wise in heart.
b. Exod. 36:1 By the Sanctuary he meaneth all the Tabernacle.
c. Exod. 36:3 Meaning, the Israelites.
d. Exod. 36:5 A rare example and notable to see the people so ready to serve God with their goods.
e. Exod. 36:8 Which were little pictures with wings in the form of children.
f. Exod. 36:13 Or, hooks.
g. Exod. 36:14 Or, pavilion.
h. Exod. 36:19 These two were about the covering of goats' hair.
i. Exod. 36:20 And to bear up the curtains of the Tabernacle.
j. Exod. 36:27 Or, toward the Sea, which was the Sea called Mediterranean, Westward from Jerusalem.
k. Exod. 36:35 Which was between the Sanctuary and the Holiest of all.
l. Exod. 36:36 Or, heads.
m. Exod. 36:37 Which was between the court and the Sanctuary.
n. Exod. 36:38 Or, graven borders.

EXOD. 36
1. Exod. 26: 3,4
2. Exod. 26:10
3. Exod. 26:24
4. Exod. 25:28 / Exod. 30:4,5

EXOD. 37
a. Exod. 37:2 Like battlements.
b. Exod. 37:8 Of the selfsame matter that the Mercy seat was.
c. Exod. 37:12 Or, four fingers.
d. Exod. 37:24 Read Exod. 25:39.

them. **8** One Cherub on the one end, and another Cherub on the other end:
[b]of the Mercy seat made he the Cherubims, at the two ends thereof. **9** And the
Cherubims spread out their wings on high, and covered the Mercy seat with their
wings and their faces were one towards another: toward the Mercy seat were the
faces of the Cherubims. **10** Also he made the Table of Shittim wood: two cubits
was the length thereof and a cubit the breadth thereof, and a cubit and an half the
height of it. **11** And he overlaid it with fine gold, and made thereto a crown of
gold round about. **12** Also he made thereto a border of an [c]hand breadth round
about, and made upon the border a crown of gold round about. **13** And he cast
for it four rings of gold, and put the rings in the four corners that were in the four
feet thereof. **14** Against the border were the rings, as places for the bars to bear
the Table. **15** And he made the bars of Shittim wood, and covered them with
gold to bear the Table. **16** [3]Also he made the instruments for the Table of pure
gold: dishes for it, and incense cups for it, and goblets for it, and coverings for it,
wherewith it should be covered. **17** Likewise he made the Candlestick of pure
gold: of work beaten out with the hammer made he the Candlestick: and his shaft,
and his branch, his bowls, his knops, and his flowers were of one piece. **18** And
six branches came out of the sides thereof: three branches of the Candlestick out
of the one side of it, and three branches of the Candlestick out of the other side
of it. **19** In one branch three bowls made like almonds, a knop and a flower:
and in another branch three bowls made like almonds, a knop and a flower: and
so throughout the six branches that proceeded out of the Candlestick. **20** And
upon the Candlestick were four bowls after the fashion of almonds, the knops
thereof and the flowers thereof. **21** That is, under every two branches a knop
made thereof, and a knop under the second branch thereof, and a knop under the
third branch thereof, according to the six branches coming out of it. **22** Their
knops and their branches were of the same: it was all one [4]beaten work of pure
gold. **23** And he made for it seven lamps with the snuffers, and snuffdishes the-
reof of pure gold. **24** Of a [d]talent of pure gold made he it with all the instru-
ments thereof. **25** Furthermore he made the [5]perfume altar of Shittim wood:
the length of it was a cubit, and the breadth of it a cubit (it was square) and two
cubits high, and the horns thereof were of the same. **26** And he covered it with
pure gold, both the top and the sides thereof round about, and the horns of it, and
made unto it a crown of gold round about. **27** And he made two rings of gold
for it, under the crown thereof in the two corners of the two sides thereof, to put
bars in for to bear it therewith. **28** Also he made the bars of Shittim wood, and
overlaid them with gold. **29** And he made the holy [6]anointing oil, and the sweet
pure incense after the apothecary's art.

38

1 The altar of burnt offerings. 8 The brazen Laver. 9 The Court. 24 The sum of that the people offered.

1 Also he made the altar of the burnt offering of [1]Shittim wood: five cu-
bits was the length thereof, and five cubits the breadth thereof: it was square and
three cubits high. **2** And he made unto it horns in the four corners thereof: the
horns thereof were of the same, and he overlaid it with brass. **3** Also he made
all the instruments of the altar: the [a]ashpans, and the besoms and the basins, the
fleshhooks, and the [2]censers: all the instruments thereof made he of brass. **4** Mo-
reover, he made a brazen grate wrought like a net to the Altar, under the compass
of it beneath in the [b]midst of it. **5** And cast four rings of brass for the four ends
of the grate to put bars in. **6** And he made the bars of Shittim wood, and cove-
red them with brass. **7** The which bars he put into the rings on the sides of the
altar to bear it withal, and made it [3]hollow within the boards. **8** Also he made
the laver of brass, and the foot of it of brass of the [c]glasses of the women that
did assemble and came together at the door of the Tabernacle of the Congrega-
tion. **9** Finally, he made the court on the South side full South: the hangings of
the court were of fine twined linen, having an hundred cubits. **10** Their pillars
were twenty, and their brazen sockets twenty: the hooks of the pillars and their
fillets were of silver. **11** And on the North side the hangings were an hundred
cubits: their pillars twenty, and their sockets of brass twenty, the hooks of the pil-
lars, and their fillets of silver. **12** On the west side also were hangings of fifty
cubits, their ten pillars with their ten sockets: the hooks of the pillars, and their
fillets of silver. **13** And toward the East side, full East were hangings of fifty cu-
bits. **14** The hangings of the one side were fifteen cubits, their three pillars, and
their three sockets: **15** [4]And of the other side of the court gate on both sides were
hangings of fifteen cubits, with their three pillars and their three sockets. **16** All
the hangings of the court round about were of fine twined linen. **17** But the
sockets of the pillars were of brass: the hooks of the pillars and their fillets of
silver, and the covering of their chapiters of silver: and all the pillars of the court
were hooped about with silver. **18** He made also the hanging of the gate of the
court of needle work, blue silk, and purple, and scarlet, and fine twined linen even
twenty cubits long, and five cubits in height and breadth, [d]like the hangings of the
court. **19** And their pillars were four with their four sockets of brass: their hooks
of silver, and the covering of the chapiters, and their fillets of silver. **20** But all
the [5]pins of the Tabernacle and of the court round about were of brass. **21** These
are the parts of the Tabernacle, I mean, of the Tabernacle of the Testimony, which
was appointed by the commandment of Moses for the office of the [e]Levites, by the
hand of Ithamar son to Aaron the Priest. **22** So Bezalel the son of Uri, the son
of Hur of the tribe of Judah, made all that the Lord commanded Moses. **23** And
with him Aholiab son of Ahisamach of the tribe of Dan, a [f]cunning workman and
an embroiderer, and a worker of needle work in blue silk, and in purple, and in
scarlet, and in fine linen. **24** All the gold that was occupied in all the work wrou-
ght for the holy place (which was the gold of the offering) was nine and twenty
talents and seven hundred and thirty shekels, according to the shekel of the San-
ctuary. **25** But the silver of them that were numbered in the Congregation, was
an hundred talents, and a thousand seven hundred seventy and five shekels, after
the shekel of the Sanctuary. **26** A [g]portion for a man, that is, half a shekel after
the shekel of the Sanctuary, for all them that were numbered from twenty years
old and above, among six hundred thousand, and three thousand, and five hun-
dred and fifty men. **27** Moreover there were an hundred talents of silver, to cast
the sockets of the Sanctuary, and the sockets of the veil: an hundred sockets of an
hundred talents, a talent for a socket. **28** But he made the hooks for the pillars
of a thousand seven hundred and seventy and five shekels, and overlaid their cha-
piters, and made fillets about them. **29** Also the brass of the offering was seventy
[h]talents, and two thousand, and four hundred shekels. **30** Whereof he made the
sockets to the door of the Tabernacle of the Congregation, and the brazen altar, and
the brazen grate which was for it, with all the instruments of the Altar. **31** And
the sockets of the court round about, and the sockets for the court gate, and all the
[6]pins of the Tabernacle, and all the pins of the court round about.

39

1 The apparel of Aaron and his sons. 32 All that the Lord commanded was made, and finished. 43 Moses blesseth the people.

1 Moreover they made [a]garments of ministration to minister in the San-
ctuary of blue silk, and purple, and scarlet: they [1]made also the holy garments for
Aaron, as the Lord had commanded Moses. **2** So he made the Ephod of gold,
blue silk, and purple, and scarlet, and fine twined linen. **3** And they did beat the
gold into thin plates, and cut it into wires, to work it in the blue silk and in the
purple, and in the scarlet, and in the fine linen, with broidered work. **4** For the
which they made shoulders to couple together: for it was closed by the two edges
thereof. **5** And the broidered girdle of his Ephod that was upon him, was of the
same stuff, and of like work: even of gold, of blue silk, and purple, and scarlet,
and fine twined linen, as the Lord had commanded Moses. **6** And they wrou-
ght [2]two Onyx stones closed in ouches of gold, and graved, as [b]signets are graven,
with the names of the children of Israel. **7** And put them on the shoulders of
the Ephod, as stones for a [3]remembrance of the children of Israel, as the Lord
had commanded Moses. **8** Also he made the breastplate of broidered work like
the work of the Ephod: to wit, of gold, blue silk, and purple, and scarlet, and fine
twined linen. **9** They made the breast plate double, and it was square an hand
breadth long, and an hand breadth broad: it was also double. **10** And they fil-
led it with four rows of stones The order was thus, a Ruby, a Topaz, and a Car-
buncle in the first row. **11** And in the second row an Emerald, a Sapphire, and
a Diamond: **12** Also in the third row [c]a Turquoise, an Agate, and an Hemati-
te: **13** Likewise in the fourth row a Chrysolite, an Onyx, and a Jasper: closed
and set in ouches of gold. **14** So the stones were according to the names of the
children of Israel, even twelve [d]after their names, graven like signets, every one
after his name, according to the twelve tribes. **15** After, they made upon the
breastplate chains at the ends, of wreathen work and pure gold. **16** They made
also two bosses of gold, and two gold rings, and put the two rings in the two cor-
ners of the breastplate. **17** And they put the two wreathen chains of gold in the
two rings, in the corners of the breastplate. **18** Also the two other ends of the
two wreathen chains they fastened in the two bosses, and put them on the shoul-
ders of the Ephod, upon the forefront of it. **19** Likewise they made two rings of
gold, and put them in the two other corners of the breastplate upon the edge of
it, which was on the inside of the Ephod. **20** They made also two other golden
rings, and put them on the two sides of the Ephod, beneath on the foreside of it,

---

EXOD. 37

1. Exod. 25:10
2. Exod. 25:17
3. Exod. 25:29
4. Exod. 25:31
5. Exod. 30:1-4
6. Exod. 30:33-39

EXOD. 38

a. Exod. 38:3 Or, fire pans.
b. Exod. 38:4 So that the gridiron or grate was half so high as the altar, and stood within it.
c. Exod. 38:8 R. Kimbi saith, that the women brought their looking glasses, which were of brass or fine metal, and offered them freely unto the use of the Tabernacle: which was a bright thing and of great majesty.
d. Exod. 38:18 Hebrew, over against.
e. Exod. 38:21 That the Levites might have the charge thereof, and minister in the same, as did Eleazar and Ithamar, Num. 3:4.
f. Exod. 38:23 Or, a graver, or carpenter, Exod. 36:4.
g. Exod. 38:26 Or, half a shekel.
h. Exod. 38:29 Read the weight of a talent, Exod. 25:39.

EXOD. 38

1. Exod. 27:1
2. Exod. 27:3
3. Exod. 27:8
4. Exod. 27:14
5. Exod. 29:17
6. Exod. 17:15

EXOD. 39

a. Exod. 39:1 As coverings for the Ark, the Candlestick, the Altars and such like.
b. Exod. 39:6 That is, of very fine and curious workmanship.
c. Exod. 39:12 Or, a ligure, which stone authors write that it cometh of the urine of the beast called Lynx.
d. Exod. 39:14 That is, every tribe had his name written on a stone.

and over against his coupling above the broidered girdle of the Ephod. **21** Then they fastened the breastplate by his rings unto the rings of the Ephod, with a lace of blue silk that it might be fast upon the broidered girdle of the Ephod, and that the breastplate should not be loosed from the Ephod, as the Lord had commanded Moses. **22** Moreover, he made the robe of the [e]Ephod of woven work, altogether of blue silk. **23** And [f]the hole of the robe was in the midst of it, as the collar of an habergeon, with an edge about the collar, that it should not rent. **24** And they made upon the skirt of the robe pomegranates, of blue silk and purple, and scarlet, and fine linen twined. **25** They made also [4]bells of pure gold, and put the bells between the pomegranates upon the skirts of the robe round about between the pomegranates. **26** A bell and a pomegranate, a bell and a pomegranate round about the skirts of the robe to minister in, as the Lord had commanded Moses. **27** After, they made coats of fine linen, of woven work for Aaron and for his sons. **28** And the mitre of fine linen, and goodly bonnets of fine linen, and linen [5]breeches of fine twined linen. **29** And the girdle of fine twined linen, and of blue silk, and purple, and scarlet, even of needle work, as the Lord had commanded Moses. **30** Finally, they made the plate for the holy crown of fine gold, and wrote upon it a superscription like to the graving of a signet, [6]HOLINESS TO THE LORD. **31** And they tied unto it a lace of blue silk to fasten it on high upon the mitre, as the Lord had commanded Moses. **32** Thus was all the work of the Tabernacle, even of the [7]Tabernacle of the Congregation finished: and the children of Israel did according to all that the Lord had commanded Moses: so did they. **33** Afterward they brought the Tabernacle unto Moses, the Tabernacle and all his instruments, his taches, his boards, his bars, and his pillars, and his sockets, **34** And the covering of rams' skins, dyed red, and the coverings of badgers' skins, and the [g]covering veil. **35** The Ark of the testimony, and the bars thereof, and the Mercy seat. **36** The Table, with all the instruments thereof, and the showbread. **37** The pure Candlestick, the lamps thereof, even the Lamps [h]set in order, and all the instruments thereof, and the oil for light: **38** Also the golden Altar and the anointing oil, and the sweet incense, and the hanging of the Tabernacle door, **39** The brazen Altar with his grate of brass, his bars and all his instruments, the Laver and his foot. **40** The curtains of the court with his pillars, and his sockets, and the hanging to the court gate, and his cords, and his pins, and all the instruments of the service of the Tabernacle, called the Tabernacle of the Congregation. **41** Finally, the ministering garments to serve in the Sanctuary, and the holy garments for Aaron the Priest, and his sons' garments to minister in the Priest's office. **42** According to every point that the Lord had [i]commanded Moses, so the children of Israel made all the work. **43** And Moses beheld all the work, and behold they had done it as the Lord had commanded: so had they done: and Moses [j]blessed them.

40

The Tabernacle with the appertinences is reared up. 34 The glory of the Lord appeareth in the cloud covering the Tabernacle.

1 Then the Lord spake unto Moses, saying, **2** In the [a]first day of the first month in the very first of the same month shalt thou set up the Tabernacle, called the Tabernacle of the Congregation: **3** And thou shalt put therein the Ark of the Testimony, and cover the Ark with the veil. **4** Also thou shalt bring in the [b]Table, and set it in order as it doth require: thou shalt also bring in the Candlestick, and light his lamps. **5** And thou shalt set the incense Altar [c]of gold before the Ark of the Testimony; and put the [d]hanging at the door of the Tabernacle. **6** Moreover, thou shalt set the burnt offering Altar before the door of the Tabernacle, called the Tabernacle of the Congregation. **7** And thou shalt set the Laver between the Tabernacle of the Congregation and the Altar, and put water therein. **8** Then thou shalt appoint the court round about, and hang up the hanging at the court gate. **9** After, thou shalt take the anointing oil, and anoint the Tabernacle, and all that is therein, and hallow it with all the instruments thereof, that it may be holy. **10** And thou shalt anoint the Altar of the burnt offering, and all his instruments, and shalt sanctify the Altar, that it may be an altar most holy. **11** Also thou shalt anoint the Laver, and his foot, and shalt sanctify it. **12** Then thou shalt bring Aaron and his sons unto the door of the Tabernacle of the Congregation, and wash them with water. **13** And thou shalt put upon Aaron the holy garments, and shalt anoint him, and sanctify him, that he may minister unto me in the Priest's office. **14** Thou shalt also bring his sons and clothe them with garments. **15** And shalt anoint them as thou didst anoint their father, that they may minister unto me in the Priest's office: for their anointing shall be a sign, that the Priesthood [e]shall be everlasting unto them throughout their generations. **16** So Moses did according to all that the Lord had commanded him; so did he. **17** [1]Thus was the Tabernacle reared up the first day of the first month in [f]the second year. **18** Then Moses reared up the Tabernacle and fastened his sockets, and set up the boards thereof, and put in the bars of it, and reared up his pillars. **19** And he spread the covering over the Tabernacle, and put the covering of that covering on high above it, as the Lord had commanded Moses. **20** And he took and put the [g]Testimony in the Ark, and put the bars in the rings of the Ark, and set the Mercy seat on high upon the Ark. **21** He brought also the Ark into the Tabernacle, and hanged up the [2]covering veil, and covered the Ark of the Testimony, as the Lord had commanded Moses. **22** Furthermore he put the Table in the Tabernacle of the Congregation in the North side of the Tabernacle, without the veil, **23** And set the bread in order before the Lord, as the Lord had commanded Moses. **24** Also he put the Candlestick in the Tabernacle of the Congregation, over against the Table toward the South side of the Tabernacle. **25** And he [h]lighted the lamps before the Lord, as the Lord had commanded Moses. **26** Moreover, he set the golden Altar in the Tabernacle of the Congregation before the veil, **27** And burnt sweet incense thereon, as the Lord had commanded Moses. **28** Also he hanged up the veil at the [i]door of the Tabernacle. **29** After, he set the burnt offering Altar without the door of the Tabernacle, called the Tabernacle of the Congregation, and offered the burnt offering and the sacrifice thereon, as the Lord had commanded Moses. **30** Likewise he set the Laver between the Tabernacle of the Congregation and the Altar, and poured water therein to wash with. **31** So Moses and Aaron, and his sons washed their hands and their feet thereat. **32** When they went into the Tabernacle of the Congregation, and when they approached to the Altar, they washed, as the Lord had commanded Moses. **33** Finally, he reared up the court round about the Tabernacle and the Altar, and hanged up the veil at the court gate: so Moses finished the work. **34** [3]Then the cloud covered the Tabernacle of the Congregation, and the glory of the Lord filled the Tabernacle. **35** So Moses could not enter into the Tabernacle of the Congregation, because the cloud abode thereon, and the glory of the Lord filled the Tabernacle. **36** Now when the cloud ascended up from the Tabernacle, the children of Israel went forward in all their journeys. **37** But if the cloud ascended not, then they journeyed not till the day that it ascended. **38** For [j]the cloud of the Lord was upon the Tabernacle by day, and fire was in it by night in the sight of all the house of Israel, throughout all their journeys.

---

e. Exod. 39:22 Which was next under the Ephod.
f. Exod. 39:23 Where he should put through his head.
g. Exod. 39:34 So called, because it hanged before the mercy seat and covered it from sight, Exod. 35:12.
h. Exod. 39:37 Or, which Aaron dressed and refreshed with oil every morning, Exod. 30:7.
i. Exod. 39:42 Signifying that in God's matters man may neither add, nor diminish.
j. Exod. 39:43 Praised God for the people's diligence, and prayed for them.

EXOD. 39
1. Exod. 31:10 / Exod. 35:29
2. Exod. 28:9
3. Exod. 28:12
4. Exod. 28:33
5. Exod. 28:41
6. Exod. 28:36
7. Exod. 27:21

EXOD. 40
a. Exod. 40:2 After that Moses had been 40 days, and 40 nights in the mount, that is, from the beginning of August to the tenth of September, he came down, and caused this work to be done: which being finished, was set up in Abib, which month containeth half March and half April.
b. Exod. 40:4 Read Exod. 26:35.
c. Exod. 40:5 That is, the altar of perfume, or to burn incense on.
d. Exod. 40:5 This hanging or veil was between the Sanctuary and the court.
e. Exod. 40:15 Till both the Priesthood and the ceremonies should end, which was at Christ's coming.
f. Exod. 40:17 After they came out of Egypt, Num. 7:1.
g. Exod. 40:20 That is, the Tables of the law, Exod. 31:18 and 34:29.
h. Exod. 40:25 Or, set up.
i. Exod. 40:28 Between the Sanctuary and the court.
j. Exod. 40:38 Thus the presence of God preserved and guided them night and day, till they came to the land promised.

EXOD. 40
1. Num. 7:1
2. Exod. 35:12
3. Num. 9:15 / 1 Kings 8:20

THE THIRD BOOK OF MOSES, CALLED

[a]LEVITICUS

1 *1 Of burnt offerings for particular persons. 3, 10, and 14 The manner to offer burnt offerings as well of bullocks, as of sheep and birds.*

1 Now the [b]Lord called Moses, and spake unto him out of the Tabernacle of the Congregation, saying, **2** Speak unto the children of Israel, and thou shalt say unto them, If any of you offer a sacrifice unto the Lord, ye shall offer your sacrifice of [c]cattle, as of beeves and of the sheep. **3** [1]If his sacrifice be a burnt offering of the herd, he shall offer a male without blemish, presenting him of his own voluntary will at the door of the [d]Tabernacle of the Congregation before the Lord. **4** And he shall put his hand upon the head of the burnt offering, and it shall be accepted [e]to the Lord, to be his atonement. **5** And [f]he shall kill the bullock before the Lord, and the Priests Aaron's sons shall offer the blood, and shall sprinkle it round about upon the [g]altar, that is by the door of the Tabernacle of the Congregation. **6** Then shall he slay the burnt offering, and cut it in pieces. **7** So the sons of Aaron the Priest shall put fire upon the altar, and lay the wood in order upon the fire. **8** Then the Priests Aaron's sons shall lay the parts in order, the head and the [h]caul upon the wood that is in the fire which is upon the altar. **9** But the inwards thereof and the legs thereof he shall wash in water, and the Priest shall burn all on the altar: for it is a burnt offering, an oblation made by fire, for a sweet savor [i]unto the Lord. **10** And if his sacrifice for the burnt offering be of the flocks (as of the sheep, or of the goats) he shall offer a male without blemish. **11** [j]And he shall kill it on the North side of the altar [k]before the Lord, and the Priests Aaron's sons shall sprinkle the blood thereof round about upon the altar. **12** And he shall cut it in [l]pieces, separating his head and his [m]caul, and the Priest shall lay them in order upon the wood that lieth in the fire which is on the altar: **13** But he shall wash the inwards, and the legs with water, and the Priest shall offer the whole and burn it upon the altar: for it is a burnt offering, an oblation made by fire for a sweet savor unto the Lord. **14** And if his sacrifice be a burnt offering to the Lord of the fowls, then shall he offer his sacrifice of the turtledoves, or of the young pigeons. **15** And the Priest shall bring it unto the altar, and [n]wring the neck of it asunder, and burn it on the altar: and the blood thereof shall be [o]shed upon the side of the altar. **16** And he shall pluck out his maw with his feathers, and cast them beside the altar on the [p]East part in the place of the ashes. **17** And he shall cleave it with his wings, but not divide it asunder: and the Priest shall burn it upon the altar upon the wood that is in the fire: for it is a burnt offering, an oblation made by fire for a sweet savor unto the Lord.

2 *1 The meat offering is after three sorts of fine flour unbaked. 4 Of bread baked.*

1 And when any will offer a [a]meat offering unto the Lord, his offering shall be of fine flour, and he shall pour oil upon it, and put incense thereon. **2** And shall bring it unto Aaron's sons the Priests, and [b]he shall take thence his handful of the flour, and of the oil with all the incense, and the Priest shall burn it for a [c]memorial upon the altar: for it is an offering made by fire for a sweet savor unto the Lord. **3** But the remnant of the meat offering shall be Aaron's and his sons': for it is [d]most holy of the Lord's offerings made by fire. **4** If thou bring also a meat offering baked in the oven, it shall be an unleavened cake of fine flour mingled with oil, or an unleavened wafer anointed with oil. **5** But if thy [e]meat offering be an oblation of the frying pan, it shall be of fine flour unleavened, mingled with oil. **6** And thou shalt part it in pieces, and pour oil thereon: for it is a meat offering. **7** And if thy meat offering be an oblation made in the caldron, it shall be made of fine flour with oil. **8** After, thou shalt bring the meat offering (that is made of these things) unto the Lord, and shalt present it unto the Priest, and he shall bring it to the altar, **9** And the Priest shall take from the meat offering a [1]memorial of it, and shall burn it upon the altar: for it is an oblation [2]made by fire for a sweet savor unto the Lord. **10** But that which is left of the meat offering, shall be Aaron's and his sons': for it is most holy of the offerings of the Lord made by fire. **11** All the meat offerings which ye shall offer unto the Lord, shall be made without leaven: for ye shall neither burn leaven nor honey in any offering of the Lord made by fire. **12** In the oblation of the firstfruits ye shall offer [f]them unto the Lord, but they shall not be burnt [g]upon the altar for a sweet savor, **13** (All the meat offerings also shalt thou season with [3]salt, neither shalt thou suffer the salt of the [h]covenant of thy God to be lacking from thy meat offering, but upon all thine oblations thou shalt offer salt.) **14** If then thou offer a meat offering of thy firstfruits unto the Lord, thou shalt offer for thy meat offering of thy firstfruits [4]ears of corn dried by the fire, and wheat beaten out of [i]the green ears. **15** After, thou shalt put oil upon it, and lay incense thereon: for it is a meat offering. **16** And the Priest shall burn the memorial of it, even of that, that is beaten, and of the oil of it with all the incense thereof: for it is an offering unto the Lord made by fire.

3 *The manner of peace offerings, and beasts for the same. 17 The Israelites may not eat fat nor blood.*

1 Also if his oblation be a [a]peace offering, if he will offer of the drove (whether it be male or female) he shall offer such as is without blemish, before the Lord. **2** And shall put his hand upon the head of his offering, and kill it at the door of the Tabernacle of the Congregation: and Aaron's sons the Priests shall sprinkle the blood upon the altar round about. **3** So he shall offer [b]part of the peace offering, as a sacrifice made by fire unto the Lord, even the [1]fat that covereth the inwards, and all the fat that is upon the inwards. **4** He shall also take away the two kidneys, and the fat that is on them, and upon [c]the flanks, and the caul on the liver with the kidneys. **5** And Aaron's sons shall burn it on the altar, with the burnt offering, which is upon the wood, that is on the fire: this is a sacrifice made by fire for a sweet savor unto the Lord. **6** Also if his oblation be a peace offering unto the Lord out of the flock, whether it be [d]male or female, he shall offer it without blemish. **7** If he offer a Lamb for his oblation, then he shall bring it before the Lord. **8** And lay his hand upon the head of his offering, and shall kill it before the Tabernacle of the Congregation, and Aaron's sons shall sprinkle the blood thereof round about upon the altar. **9** After, of the peace offerings he shall offer [e]an offering made by fire unto the Lord: he shall take away the fat thereof, and the rump altogether, hard by the back bone, and the fat that covereth the inwards, and all the fat that is upon the inwards. **10** Also he shall take away the two kidneys, with the fat that is upon them, and upon the [2]flanks, and the caul upon the liver with the kidneys. **11** Then the Priest shall burn it upon the altar, as the meat of an offering made by fire unto the Lord. **12** Also if his offering be a goat, then shall he offer it before the Lord, **13** And shall put his hand upon the head of it, and kill it before [f]the Tabernacle of the Congregation, and the sons of Aaron shall sprinkle the blood thereof upon the altar round about. **14** Then he shall offer

---

LEV. 1

- **a.** TITLE - Because in this book is chiefly entreated of the Levites, and of things pertaining to their office.
- **b.** Lev. 1:1 Hereby Moses declareth that he taught nothing to the people but that which he received of God.
- **c.** Lev. 1:2 So they could offer of none other sort, but of those which were commanded.
- **d.** Lev. 1:3 Meaning, within the court of the Tabernacle.
- **e.** Lev. 1:4 Hebrew, to him.
- **f.** Lev. 1:5 The Priest or Levite.
- **g.** Lev. 1:5 Of the burnt offering, Exod. 27:1.
- **h.** Lev. 1:8 Or, the body of the . . ., or the fat.
- **i.** Lev. 1:9 Or a savor of rest, which pacifieth the anger of the Lord.
- **j.** Lev. 1:11 Read verse 5.
- **k.** Lev. 1:11 Before the altar of the Lord.
- **l.** Lev. 1:12 Hebrew, into his pieces.
- **m.** Lev. 1:12 Or, fat.
- **n.** Lev. 1:15 The Hebrew word signifieth to pinch off with the nail.
- **o.** Lev. 1:15 Or, strained or pressed.
- **p.** Lev. 1:16 On the side of the court gate in the pans which stood with ashes, Exod. 17:3.

LEV. 1

1. Exod. 29:10

LEV. 2

- **a.** Lev. 2:1 Because the burnt offering could not be without the meat offering.
- **b.** Lev. 2:2 The Priest.
- **c.** Lev. 2:2 To signify that God remembereth him that offereth.
- **d.** Lev. 2:3 Therefore none could eat of it but the Priest.
- **e.** Lev. 2:5 Which is a gift offered to God to pacify him.
- **f.** Lev. 2:12 That is, fruits, which were sweet as honey, ye may offer.
- **g.** Lev. 2:12 But reserved for the Priests.
- **h.** Lev. 2:13 Which they were bound (as by covenant) to use all sacrifices, Num. 18:19; 2 Chron. 13:5; Ezek. 43:24, or it meaneth a sure and pure covenant.
- **i.** Lev. 2:14 Or, full ears: for the word signifieth a fruitful field. Read 2 Chron. 26:10 in the note 2.

LEV. 2

1. Lev. 2:2
2. Exod. 29:18
3. Mark. 9:49
4. Lev. 23:14

LEV. 3

- **a.** Lev. 3:1 A sacrifice of thanksgiving offered for peace and prosperity, either generally or particularly.
- **b.** Lev. 3:3 One part was burnt, another was to the Priests, and the third to him that offered.
- **c.** Lev. 3:4 Or, the which kidneys are near the flank.
- **d.** Lev. 3:6 In the peace offering it was indifferent to offer either male or female, but in the burnt offering only the male: so here can be offered no birds, but in the burnt offering they might: all there was consumed with fire, and in the peace offering put apart.
- **e.** Lev. 3:9 The burnt offering was wholly consumed, and of the offering made by fire only the inwards, etc. were burnt: the

thereof his offering, even an offering made by fire unto the Lord, the fat that covereth the inwards, and all the fat that is upon the inwards. **15** Also he shall take away the two kidneys, and the fat that is upon them, and upon the flanks, and the caul upon the liver with the kidneys. **16** So the Priest shall burn them upon the altar, as the meat of an offering made by fire for a sweet savor: [3]all the fat is the Lord's. **17** This shall be a perpetual ordinance for your generations, throughout all your dwellings, so that ye shall eat neither [g]fat nor [4]blood.

4

1 The offering for sins done of ignorance. 3 For the Priest, the Congregation, the ruler, and private man.

1 Moreover, the Lord spake unto Moses, saying, **2** Speak unto the children of Israel, saying, If [a]any shall sin through [b]ignorance, in any of the commandments of the Lord, (which ought not to be done) but shall do contrary to any of them, **3** If [c]the Priest that is anointed do sin (according to the sin of the people) then shall he offer, for his sin which he hath sinned, a young bullock without blemish unto the Lord for a sin offering, **4** And he shall bring the bullock unto the door of the Tabernacle of the Congregation before the Lord, and shall put his hand upon the bullock's head, and [d]kill the bullock before the Lord. **5** And the Priest that is anointed, shall take of the bullock's blood, and bring it into the Tabernacle of the Congregation. **6** Then the Priest shall dip his finger in the blood, and sprinkle of the blood seven times before the Lord, before the veil of the [e]Sanctuary. **7** The Priest also shall put some of the blood before the Lord, upon the horns of the altar of sweet incense, which is in the [f]Tabernacle of the Congregation, then shall he pour [1]all the rest of the blood of the bullock at the foot of the altar of burnt offering, which is at the door of the Tabernacle of the Congregation. **8** And he shall take away all the fat of the bullock for the sin offering: to wit, the fat that covereth the inwards, and all the fat that is about the inwards. **9** He shall take away also the two kidneys, and the fat that is upon them, and upon the flanks, and the caul upon the liver with the kidneys, **10** As it was taken away from the bullock of the peace offerings, and the Priest shall burn them upon the altar of burnt offering. **11** [2]But the skin of the bullock, and all his flesh, with his head, and his legs, and his inwards, and his dung shall he bear out. **12** So he shall carry the whole bullock out of the [3]host unto a clean place, where the ashes are poured, and shall burn him on the wood in the fire: where the ashes are cast out, shall he be burnt. **13** And if the [g]whole Congregation of Israel shall sin through ignorance, and the thing be [4]hid from the eyes of the multitude, and have done against any of the commandments of the Lord which should not be done, and have offended: **14** When the sin which they have committed shall be known, then the Congregation shall offer a young bullock for the sin, and bring him before the Tabernacle of the Congregation. **15** And the [h]Elders of the Congregation shall put their hands upon the head of the bullock before the Lord, and [i]he shall kill the bullock before the Lord. **16** Then the Priest that is anointed, shall bring of the bullock's blood into the Tabernacle of the Congregation, **17** And the Priest shall dip his finger in the blood, and sprinkle it seven times before the Lord, even before the veil. **18** Also he shall put some of the blood upon the horns of the altar, which is before the Lord, that is in the Tabernacle of the Congregation: then shall he pour all the rest of the blood at the foot of the altar of burnt offering, which is at the door of the Tabernacle of the Congregation, **19** And he shall take all his fat from him, and [j]burn it upon the altar. **20** And the Priest shall do with his bullock, as he did with the bullock for his sin: so shall he do with this: so the Priest shall make an atonement for them, and it shall be forgiven them. **21** For he shall carry the bullock without the host, and burn him as he burned the first bullock: for it is an offering for the sin of the Congregation. **22** When a ruler shall sin, and do through ignorance against any of the commandments of the Lord his God, which should not be done, and shall offend, **23** If one show unto him his sin, which he hath committed, then shall he bring for his offering an [k]he goat without blemish, **24** And shall lay his hand upon the head of the he goat, and kill it in [l]the place where he should kill the burnt offering before the Lord: for it is a sin offering. **25** Then the Priest shall take of the blood of the sin offering with his finger, and put it upon the horns of the burnt offering altar, and shall pour the rest of his blood at the foot of the burnt offering altar, **26** And shall burn all his fat upon the altar, as the fat of the peace offering: so the Priest shall make [m]an atonement for him, concerning his sin, and it shall be forgiven him. **27** Likewise if any of the [n]people of the land shall sin through ignorance in doing against any of the commandments of the Lord, which should not be done, and shall offend, **28** If one show him his sin which he hath committed, then he shall bring for his offering, [o]a she goat without blemish for his sin which he hath committed. **29** [p]And he shall lay his hand upon the head of the sin offering, and slay the sin offering in the place of burnt offering. **30** Then the Priest shall take of the blood thereof with his finger, and put it upon the horns of the burnt offering altar, and pour all the rest of the blood thereof at the foot of the altar, **31** And shall take away all his fat, as the fat of the peace offerings is taken away, and the Priest shall burn it upon the altar for a [5]sweet savor unto the Lord, and the Priest shall make an atonement for him, and it shall be forgiven him. **32** And if he bring a lamb for his sin offering, he shall bring a female without blemish. **33** And shall lay his [q]hand upon the head of the sin offering, and he shall slay it for a sin offering in the place where he should kill the burnt offering. **34** Then the Priest shall take of the blood of the sin offering with his finger, and put it upon the horns of the burnt offering altar, and shall pour all the rest of the blood thereof at the foot of the altar. **35** And he shall take away all the fat thereof, as the fat of the lamb of the peace offerings is taken away: then the Priest shall burn it upon the altar [r]with the oblations of the Lord made by fire, and the Priest shall make an atonement for him concerning his sin that he hath committed, and it shall be forgiven him.

5

1 Of him that testifieth the truth. 4 Of him that voweth rashly. 15 Of him that by ignorance withdraweth anything dedicated to the Lord.

1 Also if [a]any have sinned, that is, [b]if he have heard the voice of an oath, and he can be a witness, whether he hath seen or [c]known of it, if he do not utter it, he shall bear his iniquity: **2** Either if one touch any unclean thing, whether it be a carrion of an unclean beast, or a carrion of unclean cattle, or a carrion of unclean creeping things, and is not ware of it, yet he is unclean, and hath offended: **3** Either if he touch any uncleanness of man (whatsoever uncleanness it be, that he is defiled with) and is not ware of it, and after cometh to the knowledge of it, he hath sinned: **4** Either if any [d]swear and pronounce with his lips to do evil, or to do good (whatsoever it be that a man shall pronounce with an oath) and it be hid from him, and after knoweth that he hath offended in one of these points, **5** When he hath sinned in any of these [e]things, then he shall confess that he hath sinned therein. **6** Therefore shall he bring his trespass offering unto the Lord for his sin which he hath committed, even a female from the flock, be it a lamb or a she goat for a sin offering, and the Priest shall make an atonement for him concerning his sin. **7** But [f]if he be not able to bring a sheep, he shall bring for his trespass which he hath committed, two turtledoves, or two young pigeons unto the Lord, one for a sin offering, and the other for a burnt offering. **8** So he shall bring them unto the Priest, who shall offer the sin offering first, and [1]wring the neck of it asunder, but not pluck it clean off. **9** After he shall sprinkle of the blood of the sin offering upon the side of the altar, and the rest of the blood shall be [g]shed at the foot of the altar: for it is a sin offering. **10** Also he shall offer the second for a burnt offering [h]as the manner is: so shall the Priest [i]make an atonement for him (for his sin which he hath committed) and it shall be forgiven him. **11** But if he [2]be not able to bring two turtledoves, or two young pigeons, then he that hath sinned, shall bring for his offering the tenth part of an [j]Ephah of fine flour for a sin offering, he shall put none [k]oil thereto, neither put any incense thereon: for it is a sin offering. **12** Then shall he bring it to the Priest, and the Priest shall take his handful of it for the [3]remembrance thereof, and burn it upon the altar [4]with the offerings of the Lord made by fire: for it is a sin offering. **13** So the Priest shall make an atonement for him, as touching his sin, that he hath committed in one of these points, and it shall be forgiven him: and the remnant shall be the Priest's, as the meat offering. **14** And the Lord spake unto Moses, saying, **15** If any person transgress and sin through ignorance [l]by taking away things consecrated unto the Lord, he shall then bring for his trespass offering unto the Lord a ram without blemish out

---

shoulder and breast, with the two jaws and the maw were the Priest's, and the rest his that offered.

- **f.** Lev. 3:13 Meaning, at the north side of the Altar, Lev. 1:1.
- **g.** Lev. 3:17 By eating fat, was meant to be carnal, and by blood eating, was signified cruelty.

LEV. 3

- **1.** Exod. 29:22
- **2.** Lev. 3:4
- **3.** Lev. 7:25
- **4.** Gen. 9:4 / Lev. 17:4

LEV. 4

- **a.** Lev. 4:2 Hebrew, a soul.
- **b.** Lev. 4:2 That is, of negligence or ignorance, specially in the ceremonial law: for otherwise the punishment for crime is appointed according to the transgression, Num. 15:22.
- **c.** Lev. 4:3 Meaning, the high Priest.
- **d.** Lev. 4:4 Hereby confessing that he deserved the same punishment which the beast suffered.
- **e.** Lev. 4:6 Which was between the Holiest of all, and the Sanctuary.
- **f.** Lev. 4:7 Which was in the court: meaning by the Tabernacle the Sanctuary: and in the end of this verse it is taken for the court.
- **g.** Lev. 4:13 The multitude excuseth not the sin, but if all have sinned, they must all be punished.
- **h.** Lev. 4:15 For all the people could not lay on their hands: therefore it was sufficient that the Ancients of the people did it in the name of all the Congregation.
- **i.** Lev. 4:15 Or, the Priest.
- **j.** Lev. 4:19 Or, make a perfume with it.
- **k.** Lev. 4:23 Or, the male goat of the fold.
- **l.** Lev. 4:24 That is, the Priest shall kill it; for it was not lawful for any out of that office to kill the beast.
- **m.** Lev. 4:26 Wherein he represented Jesus Christ.
- **n.** Lev. 4:27 Or, private person.
- **o.** Lev. 4:28 Or, the female of the goats.
- **p.** Lev. 4:29 Read verse 24.
- **q.** Lev. 4:33 Meaning, that the punishment of his sin should be laid upon that beast, or, that he had received all things of God, and offered this willingly.
- **r.** Lev. 4:35 Or, besides the burnt offerings, which were daily offered to the Lord.

LEV. 4

- **1.** Lev. 5:9
- **2.** Exod. 29:14 / Num. 19:5
- **3.** Heb. 13:12
- **4.** Lev. 5:2-4
- **5.** Exod. 29:18

LEV. 5

- **a.** Lev. 5:1 Hebrew, a soul.
- **b.** Lev. 5:1 Or, if the judge hath taken an oath of any other.
- **c.** Lev. 5:1 Whereby it is commanded to bear witness to the truth, and disclose the iniquity of the ungodly.
- **d.** Lev. 5:4 Or, vow rashly without just examination of the circumstances, and not knowing what shall be the issue of the same.
- **e.** Lev. 5:5 Which have been mentioned before in this Chapter.
- **f.** Lev. 5:7 Hebrew, if his hand cannot touch, meaning for his poverty.
- **g.** Lev. 5:9 Or, poured.
- **h.** Lev. 5:10 Or, according to the Law.
- **i.** Lev. 5:10 Or, declare him to be purged of that sin.
- **j.** Lev. 5:11 Which was about a pottle.
- **k.** Lev. 5:11 As in the meat offering, Lev. 2:1.

of the flock, worth two shekels of silver [m]by thy estimation after the shekel of the Sanctuary, for a trespass offering. **16** So he shall restore that wherein he hath offended, in taking away of the holy thing, and shall put the fifth part more thereto, and give it unto the Priest: so the Priest shall make an atonement for him with the ram of the trespass offering, and it shall be forgiven him. **17** Also if any sin and [5]do against any of the Commandments of the Lord, which ought not to be done, and know not, and [n]sin and bear his iniquity, **18** Then shall he bring a ram without blemish out of the flock, in thy estimation worth [6]two shekels for a trespass offering unto the Priest: and the Priest shall make an atonement for him concerning his [o]ignorance wherein he erred, and was not ware: so it shall be forgiven him. **19** This is the trespass offering for the trespass committed against the Lord.

6

6 The offering for sins which are done willingly. 9 The law of the burnt offerings. 13 The fire must abide evermore upon the altar. 14 The law of the meat offering. 20 The offerings of Aaron, and his sons.

1 And the Lord spake unto Moses, saying, **2** If any sin and commit a trespass against the Lord, and deny unto his neighbor that which was taken him to keep, or that which was put to him[a]of trust, or doth by [b]robbery, or by violence oppress his neighbor, **3** Or hath found that which was lost, and denieth it, and sweareth falsely, [1]for any of these things that a man doeth, wherein he [c]sinneth: **4** When, I say, he thus sinneth and trespasseth, he shall then restore the robbery that he robbed, or the thing taken by violence which he took by force, or the thing which was delivered him to keep, or the lost thing which he found, **5** Or for whatsoever he hath sworn falsely, he shall both restore it in the whole [2]sum, and shall add the fifth part more thereto, and give it unto him to whom it pertaineth, the same day that he offereth for his trespass. **6** Also he shall bring for his trespass unto the Lord, a ram without blemish out of the [3]flock in thy estimation worth two shekels for a trespass offering unto the Priest. **7** And the Priest shall make an atonement for him before the Lord, and it shall be forgiven him, whatsoever thing he hath done, and trespassed therein. **8** Then the Lord spake unto Moses, saying, **9** Command Aaron and his sons, saying, This is the [d]law of the burnt offering, (it is the burnt offering because it burneth upon the altar all the night unto the morning, and the fire burneth on the altar). **10** And the Priest shall put on his linen garment, and shall put on his linen breeches upon [e]his flesh, and take away the ashes when the fire hath consumed the burnt offering upon the altar, and he shall put them beside the [f]altar. **11** After, he shall put off his garments, and put on other raiment, and carry the ashes forth without the host unto a clean place. **12** But the fire upon the altar shall burn thereon and never be put out: wherefore the Priest shall burn wood on it every morning, and lay the burnt offering in order upon it, and he shall burn thereon the fat of the peace offerings. **13** The fire shall ever burn upon the altar, and never go out. **14** [4]Also this is the law of the meat offering, which Aaron's sons shall offer in the presence of the Lord, before the altar. **15** He shall even take thence his handful of fine flour of the meat offering and of the oil, and all the incense which is upon the meat offering, and shall burn it upon the altar for a sweet savor, as a [5]memorial therefore unto the Lord: **16** But the rest thereof shall Aaron and his sons eat: it shall be eaten without leaven in the holy place: in the court of the Tabernacle of the Congregation they shall eat it. **17** It shall not be [g]baked with leaven: I have given it for their portion of mine offering made by fire: for it is as the sin offering, and as the trespass offering. **18** All the males among the children of Aaron shall eat of it: It shall be a statute forever in your generations concerning the offerings of the Lord made by fire: [6]whatsoever toucheth them shall be holy: **19** Again the Lord spake unto Moses, saying, **20** This is the offering of Aaron and his sons, which they shall offer unto the Lord in the day when he is anointed: the tenth part of an [7]Ephah of fine flour, for a meat offering [h]perpetual: half of it in the morning, and half thereof at night. **21** In the frying pan it shall be made with oil: thou shalt bring it fried, and shalt offer the [i]baked pieces of the meat offering for a sweet savor unto the Lord. **22** And the Priest that is [j]anointed in his stead, among his sons shall offer it: It is the Lord's ordinance forever, it shall be burnt altogether. **23** For every meat offering of the Priest shall be burnt altogether, it shall not be eaten. **24** Furthermore, the Lord spake unto Moses, saying, **25** Speak unto Aaron, and unto his sons, and say, This is the Law of the sin offering, In the place where the burnt offering is killed, shall the sin offering be killed before the Lord, for it is most holy. **26** The Priest that offereth this sin offering, shall eat it: in the holy place shall it be eaten, in the court of the Tabernacle of the Congregation. **27** Whatsoever shall touch the flesh thereof shall be holy: and when there droppeth of the blood thereof upon a [k]garment, thou shalt wash that whereon it droppeth in the holy place. **28** Also the earthen pot that it is sodden in, shall be broken, but if it be sodden in a brazen pot, it shall both be scoured and washed with [l]water. **29** All the males among the Priests shall eat thereof, for it is most holy. **30** [8]But no sin offering, whose blood is brought into the Tabernacle of the Congregation, to make reconciliation in the holy place, shall be eaten, but shall be burnt with [m]fire.

7

1 The law of the trespass offering. 11 Also of the peace offering. 23 The fat and the blood may not be eaten.

1 Likewise this is the law of the [a]trespass offering, it is most holy. **2** In the place [b]where they kill the burnt offering, shall they kill the trespass offering, and the blood thereof shall he sprinkle round about upon the altar. **3** All the fat thereof also shall [c]he offer, the rump, and the fat that covered the inwards. **4** After, he shall take away the two kidneys, with the fat that is on them and upon the flanks, and the caul on the liver with the kidneys. **5** Then the Priest shall burn them upon the altar, for an offering made by fire unto the Lord: this is a trespass offering. **6** All the males among the Priests shall eat thereof, it shall be eaten in the holy place for it is most holy. **7** As the sin offering is, so is the trespass offering, one [d]law serveth for both: [e]that wherewith the Priest shall make atonement, shall be his. **8** Also the Priest that offereth any man's burnt offering, shall have the skin of the burnt offering which he hath offered. **9** And all the meat offering that is baked in the oven, and that is dressed in the pan, and in the frying pan, shall be the Priest's that offereth it. **10** And every meat offering mingled with oil, and that is [f]dry, shall pertain unto all the sons of Aaron, to all alike. **11** Furthermore, this is the law of the peace offerings, which he shall offer unto the Lord. **12** If he offer it to [g]give thanks, then he shall offer for his thanks offering, unleavened cakes mingled with oil, and unleavened wafers anointed with oil, and fine flour fried with the cakes mingled with oil. **13** He shall offer also his offering with cakes of leavened bread, for his peace offerings, to give thanks. **14** And of all the sacrifice he shall offer one cake for an heave offering unto the Lord, and it shall be the Priest's that sprinkled the blood of the peace offerings. **15** Also the flesh of the peace offerings, for thanksgiving, shall be eaten the same day that it is offered: he shall leave nothing thereof until the morning. **16** But if the sacrifice of his offering be a [h]vow, or a free offering, it shall be eaten the same day that he offereth his sacrifice: and so in the morning the residue thereof shall be eaten. **17** But as much of the offered flesh as remaineth unto the third day, shall be burnt with fire. **18** For if any of the flesh of his peace offerings be eaten in the third day, he shall not be accepted that offereth it, neither shall it be reckoned unto him, but shall be an abomination: therefore the person that eateth of it shall [i]bear his iniquity. **19** The flesh also that toucheth any unclean [j]thing, shall not be eaten, but burnt with fire: but [k]of this flesh all that be clean shall eat thereof. **20** But if any eat of the flesh of the peace offerings that pertaineth to the Lord, having his [1]uncleanness upon him, even the same person shall be cut off from his people. **21** Moreover, when any toucheth any unclean thing, as the uncleanness of man, or of an unclean beast, or of any filthy abomination, and eat of the flesh of the peace offerings, which pertaineth unto the Lord, even that person shall be cut off from his people. **22** Again the Lord spake unto Moses, saying, **23** Speak unto the children of Israel, and say, [2]Ye shall eat no fat of beeves, nor of sheep, nor of goats. **24** Yet the fat of the dead beast, and the fat of that, which is torn with beasts, shall be occupied to any use, but ye shall not eat of it. **25** For whosoever eateth the fat of the beast, of the which ye shall offer an offering made by fire to the Lord, even the person that eateth, shall be cut off from his people. **26** Neither [3]shall ye eat any blood, either of fowl, or of beast in all your dwellings. **27** Every person that eateth any blood, even the same person shall be cut off from his people. **28** And the Lord talked with Moses, saying, **29** Speak unto the children of Israel, and say, He that offereth his peace offerings unto the Lord, shall bring his gift unto the Lord of his peace offerings. **30** His [l]hands shall bring the offerings of the Lord made

---

l. Lev. 5:15 As touching the firstfruits or tithes, due to the Priests and Levites.
m. Lev. 5:15 By the estimation of the Priest, Lev. 27:12.
n. Lev. 5:17 That is, afterward remembereth that he hath sinned when his conscience doth accuse him.
o. Lev. 5:18 Else if his sin against God come of malice, he must die, Num. 15:30.

LEV. 5

1. Lev. 1:16
2. Lev. 5:7
3. Lev. 2:2
4. Lev. 4:35
5. Lev. 4:2
6. Exod. 30:13

LEV. 6

a. Lev. 6:2 To bestow, and occupy for the use of him that gave it.
b. Lev. 6:2 By any guile, or unlawful means.
c. Lev. 6:3 Wherein he cannot but sin: or, wherein a man accustometh to sin by perjury or such like thing.
d. Lev. 6:9 That is, the ceremonies which ought to be observed therein.
e. Lev. 6:10 Upon his secret parts, Exod. 28:43.
f. Lev. 6:10 In the ash pans appointed for that use.
g. Lev. 6:17 Or, kneaded with leaven and after baked.
h. Lev. 6:20 So oft as the high Priest shall be elected and anointed.
i. Lev. 6:21 Or, fried.
j. Lev. 6:22 His son that shall succeed him.
k. Lev. 6:27 Meaning, the garment of the Priest.
l. Lev. 6:28 Which was in the laver, Exod. 30:18.
m. Lev. 6:30 Out of the camp, Lev. 4:12.

LEV. 6

1. Num. 5:6
2. Num. 5:7
3. Lev. 5:15
4. Lev. 2:1 / Num. 15:4
5. Lev. 2:9
6. Exod. 29:37
7. Exod. 29:37
8. Lev. 4:5 / Heb. 13:11

LEV. 7

a. Lev. 7:1 Which is for the smaller sins, and such as are committed by ignorance.
b. Lev. 7:2 At the court gate.
c. Lev. 7:3 The high Priest.
d. Lev. 7:7 The same ceremonies, notwithstanding that this word trespass signifieth less than sin.
e. Lev. 7:7 Meaning, the rest which is left and not burnt.
f. Lev. 7:10 Because it had no oil nor liquor.
g. Lev. 7:12 Peace offerings contain a confession and thanksgiving for a benefit received, and also a vow, and free offering to receive a benefit.
h. Lev. 7:16 If he makes a vow to offer: for else the flesh of the peace offerings must be eaten the same day.
i. Lev. 7:18 The sin wherefore he offered shall remain.
j. Lev. 7:19 After it be sacrificed.
k. Lev. 7:19 Of the peace offering that is clean.
l. Lev. 7:30 And should not send it by another.

by fire: even the fat with the breast shall he bring, that the breast may be [4]shaken to and fro before the Lord. **31** Then the Priest shall burn the fat upon the Altar, and the breast shall be Aaron's and his sons'. **32** And the right shoulder shall ye give unto the Priest for an heave offering, of your peace offerings. **33** The same that offereth the blood of the peace offerings, and the fat among the sons of Aaron, shall have the right shoulder for his part. **34** For the breast shaken to and fro, and the shoulder lifted up, have I taken of the children of Israel, even of their peace offerings, and have given them unto Aaron the Priest and unto his sons by a statute forever from among the children of Israel. **35** This is the [m]anointing of Aaron, and the anointing of his sons, concerning the offerings of the Lord made by fire, in the day when he presented them to serve in the Priest's office unto the Lord. **36** The which portions the Lord commanded to give them in the day that he anointed them from among the children of Israel, by a statute forever in their generations. **37** This is also the law of the burnt offering, of the meat offering, and of the sin offering, and of the trespass offering, and of the [n]consecrations, and of the peace offerings, **38** Which the Lord commanded Moses in the mount Sinai, when he commanded the children of Israel to offer their gifts unto the Lord in the wilderness of Sinai.

8

12 The anointing of Aaron, and his sons, with the sacrifice concerning the same.

1 Afterward the Lord spake unto Moses, saying, **2** [1]Take Aaron and his sons with him, and the garments, and the [2]anointing oil, and a bullock for the sin offering, and two rams, and a basket of unleavened bread, **3** And assemble all the company at the door of the Tabernacle of the Congregation. **4** So Moses did as the Lord had commanded him, and the company was assembled at the door of the Tabernacle of the Congregation. **5** Then Moses said unto the company, [3]This is the thing which the Lord hath commanded to do. **6** And Moses brought Aaron and his sons, and washed them with water, **7** And put upon him the coat, and girded him with a girdle, and clothed him with the robe, and put the Ephod on him, which he girded with the broidered girdle of the Ephod, and bound it unto him therewith. **8** And he put the breastplate thereon, and put in the breastplate [4]the Urim and the Thummim. **9** Also he put the miter upon his head, and put upon the miter on the forefront the golden plate, and the [a]holy crown, as the Lord hath commanded Moses. **10** (Now Moses had taken the anointing oil, and anointed the [b]Tabernacle, and all that was therein, and sanctified them, **11** And sprinkled thereof upon the altar seven times, and anointed the altar and all his instruments, and the laver, and his foot, to sanctify them.) **12** [5]And he poured of the anointing oil upon Aaron's head, and anointed him to sanctify him. **13** After, Moses brought Aaron's sons, and put coats upon them, and girded them with girdles, and put bonnets upon their heads, as the Lord had commanded Moses. **14** [6]Then he brought the bullock for the sin offering, and Aaron and his sons put their hands upon the head of the bullock for the sin offering. **15** And Moses slew him, and took the blood, which he put upon the horn of the [c]Altar round about with his finger, and purified the altar, and poured the rest of the blood at the foot of the altar: so he sanctified [d]it, to make reconciliation upon it. **16** Then he took all the fat that was upon the inwards, and the caul of the liver, and the two kidneys with their fat, which Moses burned upon the altar. **17** But the bullock and his [e]hide, and his flesh, and his dung, he burnt with fire without the host as the Lord had commanded Moses. **18** Also he brought the ram for the burnt offering, and Aaron and his sons put their hands upon the head of the ram. **19** So Moses killed it, and sprinkled the blood upon the altar round about, **20** And Moses cut the ram in pieces, and burnt the head with the pieces, and the fat, **21** And washed the inwards and the legs in water: so Moses burnt the ram every whit upon the Altar: for it was a burnt offering for a sweet savor, which was made by fire unto the Lord, as the Lord had commanded Moses. **22** [7]After, he brought the other ram, the ram of consecrations, and Aaron and his sons laid their hands upon the head of the ram, **23** Which Moses [f]slew, and took of the blood of it, and put it upon the lap of Aaron's right ear, and upon the thumb of his right hand, and upon the great toe of his right foot. **24** Then Moses brought Aaron's sons, and put of the blood on the lap of their right ears, and upon the thumbs of their right hands, and upon the great toes of their right feet, and Moses sprinkled the rest of the blood upon the Altar round about. **25** And he took the fat and the rump, and all the fat that was upon the inwards, and the caul of the liver, and the two kidneys with their fat, and the right shoulder. **26** Also he took of the basket of the unleavened cake, and a cake of oiled bread, and one wafer, and put them on the fat, and upon the right shoulder. **27** So he put [8]all in Aaron's hands, and in his sons' hands, and shook it to and fro before the Lord. **28** After, Moses took them out of their hands, and burnt them upon the altar for a burnt offering: for these were consecrations for a sweet savor, which were made by fire unto the Lord. **29** Likewise Moses took the breast of the ram of consecrations, and shook it to and fro before the Lord: for it was Moses' [9]portion as the Lord had commanded Moses. **30** Also Moses took of the anointing oil, and of the blood which was upon the Altar, and sprinkled it upon Aaron, upon his garments, and upon his sons, and on his sons' garments with him: so he sanctified Aaron, his garments, and his sons, and his sons' garments with him. **31** Afterward Moses said unto Aaron and his sons, Seethe the flesh at the door of the [g]Tabernacle of the Congregation, and there [10]eat it with the bread that is in the basket of consecrations, as I commanded, saying, Aaron and his sons shall eat it. **32** But that which remaineth of the flesh and of the bread, shall ye burn with fire. **33** And ye shall not depart from the door of the Tabernacle of the Congregation seven days, until the days of your consecrations be at an end: [11]for seven days, said the Lord, shall he [h]consecrate you, **34** As [i]he hath done this day: so the Lord hath commanded to do, to make an atonement for you. **35** Therefore shall ye abide at the door of the Tabernacle of the Congregation, day and night, seven days, and shall keep the watch of the Lord, that ye die not: for so I am commanded. **36** So Aaron and his sons did all things which the Lord had commanded by the [j]hand of Moses.

9

8 The first offerings of Aaron. 12 Aaron blesseth the people. 23 The glory of the Lord is showed. 24 The fire cometh from the Lord.

1 And in the [a]eighth day Moses called Aaron and his sons, and the Elders of Israel: **2** [1]Then he said unto Aaron, Take thee a young calf for a [b]sin offering, and a ram for a burnt offering, both without blemish, and bring them before the Lord. **3** And unto the children of Israel thou shalt speak, saying, Take ye an he goat for a sin offering, and a calf, and a lamb, both of a year old, without blemish for a burnt offering: **4** Also a bullock, and a ram for peace offerings, to offer before the Lord, and a meat offering mingled with oil: for today the Lord will appear unto you. **5** Then they brought that which Moses commanded before the Tabernacle of the Congregation, and all the assembly drew near, and stood before the [c]Lord. **6** (For Moses had said, This is the thing, which the Lord commanded that ye should do, and the glory of the Lord shall appear unto you.) **7** Then Moses said unto Aaron, Draw near to the Altar, and offer thy sin offering, and thy burnt offering, and make an atonement for [d]thee and for the people: offer also the offering of the people, and make an atonement for them, as the Lord hath commanded. **8** Aaron therefore went unto the altar, and killed the calf of the sin offering, which was for himself. **9** And the sons of Aaron brought the blood unto him, and he dipped his finger in the blood, and put it upon the horns of the Altar, and poured the rest of the blood at the foot of the Altar. **10** But the fat and the kidneys, and the caul of the liver of the sin offering, he [e]burnt unto the Altar, as the Lord had commanded Moses. **11** The flesh also and the hide he burnt with fire without the host. **12** After, he slew the burnt offering, and Aaron's sons brought unto him the blood, which he sprinkled round about the Altar. **13** Also they brought the burnt offering unto him with the pieces thereof, and the head, and he burnt them upon the Altar. **14** Likewise he did wash the inwards and the legs, and [f]burnt them upon the burnt offering on the Altar. **15** Then he offered the people's offering and took a goat, which was the sin offering for the people, and slew it: and offered it for sin, as the first: **16** So he offered the burnt offering, and prepared it, according to the manner. **17** He presented also the meat offering, and filled his hand thereof, [2]and beside the burnt sacrifice of the morning he burnt this upon the altar. **18** He slew also the bullock, and the ram for the peace offerings, that was for the people, and Aaron's sons brought unto him the blood, which he sprinkled upon the Altar round about. **19** With the fat of the bullock, and of the ram, the rump, and that which covereth the inwards, and the kidneys, and the caul of the liver. **20** So they laid the fat upon the breasts, and he burnt the fat upon the Altar. **21** But the [g]breasts and the right shoulder Aaron shook to and fro before the Lord, as the Lord had commanded Moses. **22** So Aaron lift up his hand toward the people, and blessed them, and [h]came down from offering of the sin offering, and the burnt offering, and the peace offerings. **23** After, Moses

---

m. Lev. 7:35 That is, his privilege, reward and portion.
n. Lev. 7:37 Which sacrifice was offered when the Priests were consecrated, Exod. 29:22.

LEV. 7

1. Lev. 15:5
2. Lev. 3:17
3. Gen. 9:4 / Lev. 17:14
4. Exod. 29:24

LEV. 8

a. Lev. 8:9 So called, because this superscription, Holiness to the Lord, was graven in it.
b. Lev. 8:10 That is, the Holiest of all, the Sanctuary and the court.
c. Lev. 8:15 Of the burnt offering.
d. Lev. 8:15 To offer for the sins of the people.
e. Lev. 8:17 In other burnt offerings, which are not of consecration, or offering for himself, the Priest hath the skin, Lev. 7:8.
f. Lev. 8:23 Moses did this because that the Priests were not yet established in their office.
g. Lev. 8:31 At the door of the court.
h. Lev. 8:33 Hebrew, fill your hands.
i. Lev. 8:34 Or, as I have done.
j. Lev. 8:36 By commission given to Moses.

LEV. 8

1. Exod. 28:14
2. Exod. 30:24
3. Exod. 29:30
4. Exod. 28:30
5. Ps. 33:2
6. Exod. 33:2
7. Exod. 29:1 / Lev. 9:2
8. Exod. 29:31
9. Exod. 29:24
10. Exod. 29:26
11. Exod. 29:32 / Lev. 24:9
12. Exod. 29:35

LEV.9

a. Lev. 9:1 After their consecration: for the seven days before, the Priests were consecrated.
b. Lev. 9:2 Aaron entereth into the possession of the Priesthood: and offereth the four principal sacrifices, the burnt offering, the sin offering, the peace offerings, and the meat offering.
c. Lev. 9:5 Before the Altar where his glory appeared.
d. Lev. 9:7 Read for the understanding of this peace, Heb. 4:5 and 7:27.
e. Lev. 9:10 That is, he laid them in order, and so they were burnt when the Lord sent down fire.
f. Lev. 9:14 All this must be understood of the preparation of the sacrifices which were burnt after, verse 24.
g. Lev. 9:21 Of the bullock and the ram.
h. Lev. 9:22 Because the altar was near the Sanctuary, which was the upper end, therefore he is said to come down.

and Aaron went into the Tabernacle of the Congregation, and came out, and [i]blessed the people, and the glory of the Lord appeared to all the people. **24** [3]And there came a fire out from the Lord, and consumed upon the Altar the burnt offering and the fat: which when all the people saw, they [j]gave thanks, and fell on their faces.

10

2 Nadab and Abihu are burnt. 6 Israel mourneth for them. 9 The Priests are forbidden wine.

1 But [1]Nadab and Abihu, the sons of Aaron, took either of them his censor, and put fire therein, and put incense thereupon, and offered [a]strange fire before the Lord, which he had not commanded them. **2** Therefore a fire went out from the Lord, and devoured them: so they died before the Lord. **3** Then Moses said unto Aaron, This is it that the Lord spake, saying, I will be [b]sanctified in them that come near me, and before all the people I will be glorified: but Aaron held his peace. **4** And Moses called Mishael and Elzaphan the sons of Uzziel, the uncle of Aaron, and said unto them, Come near, carry your [c]brethren from before the Sanctuary out of the host. **5** Then they went, and carried them in their coats out of the host, as Moses had commanded. **6** After, Moses said unto Aaron and unto Eleazar, and Ithamar his sons, [d]Uncover not your heads, neither rent your clothes, lest ye die, and lest wrath come upon all the people: but let your brethren, all the house of Israel bewail the burning which the Lord hath [e]kindled. **7** And go not ye out from the door of the Tabernacle of the Congregation lest ye die: for the anointing oil of the Lord is upon you: and they did according to Moses' commandment. **8** And the Lord spake unto Aaron, saying, **9** Thou shalt not drink wine nor [f]strong drink, thou, nor thy sons with thee, when ye come into the Tabernacle of the Congregation, lest ye die: this is an ordinance forever throughout your generations, **10** That ye may put difference between the holy and the unholy, and between the clean and the unclean, **11** And that ye may teach the children of Israel all the statutes which the Lord hath commanded them by the [g]hand of Moses. **12** Then Moses said unto Aaron and unto Eleazar and to Ithamar his sons that were left, Take the meat offering that remaineth of the offerings of the Lord made by fire, and eat it without leaven beside the altar: for it is most holy: **13** And ye shall eat it in the holy place, because it is thy duty and thy son's duty of the offerings of the Lord made by fire: for so I am commanded. **14** Also the [2]shaken breast and the heave shoulder shall ye eat in a [h]clean place: thou, and thy sons, and thy [i]daughters with thee: for they are given as thy [j]duty and thy son's duty, of the peace offerings of the children of Israel. **15** The heave shoulder, and the shaken breast shall they bring with the offerings made by fire of the fat, to shake it to and fro before the Lord, and it shall be thine and thy sons with thee by a law forever, as the Lord hath commanded. **16** And Moses sought the goat that was offered for sin, and lo, it was burnt: therefore he was angry with Eleazar and Ithamar the sons of Aaron, which were [k]left alive, saying, **17** Wherefore have ye not eaten the sin offering in the holy place, seeing it is most Holy? and God hath given it you, to bear the iniquity of the Congregation, to make an atonement for them before the Lord. **18** Behold, the blood of it was not brought within the holy place: ye should have eaten it in the holy place, [3]as I commanded. **19** And Aaron said unto Moses, Behold, this day [l]have they offered their sin offering, and their burnt offering before the Lord, and such things as thou knowest are come unto me: If I had eaten the sin offering today, should it have been accepted in the sight of the Lord? **20** So when Moses heard it, he was [m]content.

11

1 Of beasts, fishes and birds, which be clean, and which be unclean.

1 After, the Lord spake to Moses and to Aaron, saying unto them, **2** Speak unto the children of Israel, and say, [1]These are the beasts which ye [a]shall eat, among all the beasts that are on the earth. **3** Whatsoever parteth the [b]hoof, and is cloven footed, and cheweth the cud, among the beasts, that shall ye eat: **4** But of them that chew the cud, or divide the hoof only, of them ye shall not eat: as the camel, because he cheweth the cud, and divideth not the hoof, he shall be unclean unto you. **5** Likewise the coney, because he cheweth the cud, and divideth not the hoof, he shall be unclean to you. **6** Also the hare, because he cheweth the cud, and divideth not the hoof, he shall be unclean to you. **7** And the swine, because he parteth the hoof, and is cloven footed, but cheweth not the cud, he shall be unclean to you. **8** Of their [c]flesh shall ye not eat, and their carcass shall ye not touch: for they shall be unclean to you. **9** These shall ye eat, of all that are in the waters: whatsoever hath fins and scales in the waters, in the seas, or in the rivers, them shall ye eat. **10** But all that have not fins nor scales in the seas, or in the rivers, of all that [d]moveth in the waters, and of all [e]living things that are in the waters, they shall be an abomination unto you. **11** They, I say, shall be an abomination to you: ye shall not eat of their flesh, but shall abhor their carcass. **12** Whatsoever hath not fins nor scales in the waters, that shall be abomination unto you. **13** These shall ye have also in abomination among the fowls, they shall not be eaten, for they are an abomination, the eagle, and the [f]goshawk, and the osprey: **14** Also the vulture, and the kite after his kind, **15** Also the ravens after their kind: **16** The ostrich also, and the night-crow, and the [g]seamew, and the hawk after his kind. **17** The little owl also, and the cormorant, and the great owl: **18** Also the [h]redshank, and the pelican, and the swan: **19** The stork also, the heron after his kind, and the lapwing and the bat: **20** Also every fowl that creepeth and goeth upon all four, such shall be an abomination unto you. **21** Yet these shall ye eat: of every fowl that creepeth, and goeth upon all four which [i]have their feet and legs all of one to leap withal upon the earth. **22** Of them ye shall eat these, the grasshopper after his kind, and the [j]solean after his kind, the hargol after his kind, and the hagab after his kind. **23** But all other fowls that creep and have four feet, they shall be abomination unto you. **24** For by such ye shall be polluted: whosoever toucheth the carcass, shall be unclean unto the evening. **25** Whosoever also [k]beareth of their carcass, shall wash his clothes, and be unclean until even. **26** Every beast that hath claws divided, and is [l]not cloven footed, nor cheweth the cud, such shall be unclean unto you: everyone that toucheth them, shall be unclean. **27** And whatsoever goeth upon his paws among all manner beasts that goeth on all four, such shall be unclean unto you: who so doth touch their carcass, shall be unclean until the even. **28** And he that beareth their carcass, shall wash his clothes, and be unclean until the even: for such shall be unclean unto you. **29** Also these shall be unclean to you among the things that creep and move upon the earth, the weasel, and the mouse, and the [m],[n]frog, after his kind: **30** Also the rat, and the lizard, and the chameleon, and the stellio, and the mole. **31** These shall be unclean to you among all that creep: whosoever doth touch them when they be dead, shall be unclean until the even. **32** Also whatsoever any of the dead carcasses of them doth fall upon, shall be unclean, whether it be vessel of wood, or raiment, or [o]skin, or sack: whatsoever vessel it be that is occupied, it shall be put in the water as unclean until the even, and so be purified. **33** But every earthen vessel, wherein any of them falleth, whatsoever is within it shall be unclean, and [2]ye shall break it. **34** All meat also that shall be eaten, if any such water come upon it, shall be unclean: and all drink that shall be drunk in all such vessels shall be unclean. **35** And everything that their carcass fall upon, shall be unclean: the furnace or the pot shall be broken: for they are unclean, and shall be unclean unto you. **36** Yet the fountains and wells where there is plenty of water shall be clean: but that which [p]toucheth their carcasses, shall be unclean. **37** And if there fall of the dead carcass upon any seed, which useth to be sown, it shall be unclean. **38** But if any [q]water be poured upon the seed, and there fall of the dead carcass thereon, it shall be unclean unto you. **39** If also any beast, whereof ye may eat, die, he that toucheth the carcass thereof, shall be unclean until the even. **40** And he that eateth of the carcass of it, shall wash his clothes, and be unclean until the even: he also that beareth the carcass of it, shall wash his clothes, and be unclean until the even. **41** Every creeping thing therefore that creepeth upon the earth, shall be an abomination, and not be eaten. **42** Whatsoever goeth upon the breast, and whatsoever goeth upon all four, or that hath many feet among all creeping things that creep upon the earth, ye shall not eat of them, for they shall be abomination. **43** Ye shall not pollute yourselves with anything that creepeth, neither make yourselves unclean with them, neither defile yourselves thereby: ye shall not, I say, be defiled by them. **44** For I am the Lord your God: be sanctified therefore, and be [r]holy, for I am holy, and defile not

---

i. Lev. 9:23 Or prayed for the people.
j. Lev. 9:24 Or, gave a shout for joy.

LEV. 9

1. Exod. 29:1
2. Exod. 29:38
3. Gen. 4:4 / 1 Kings 18:38 / 2 Chron. 7:1

LEV. 10

a. Lev. 10:1 Not taken of the altar, which was sent from heaven, and endured till the captivity of Babylon.
b. Lev. 10:3 I will punish them that serve me otherwise than I have commanded, not sparing the chief, that the people may fear and praise my judgments.
c. Lev. 10:4 Or, cousins.
d. Lev. 10:6 As though ye lamented for them, preferring your carnal affection to God's just judgment, Lev. 19:18; Deut. 14:1.
e. Lev. 10:6 In destroying Nadab and Abihu the chief, and menacing the rest, except they repent.
f. Lev. 10:9 Or, drink that maketh drunk.
g. Lev. 10:11 Or, commission.
h. Lev. 10:14 Or, where is no uncleanness.
i. Lev. 10:14 For the breast and shoulders of the peace offerings might be brought to their families, so that their daughters might eat of them, as also of the offerings of firstfruits, the firstborn, and the Easter lamb, Read Lev. 22:12,13.
j. Lev. 10:14 Or, right or portion.
k. Lev. 10:16 And not consumed as Nadab and Abihu.
l. Lev. 10:19 That is, Nadab and Abihu.
m. Lev. 10:20 Moses bare with his infirmity, considering his great sorrow, but doth not leave an example to forgive them that maliciously transgress the commandment of God.

LEV. 10

1. Num. 3:4 / Num. 26:61 / 1 Chron. 24:2
2. Exod. 29:24
3. Lev. 6:26

LEV. 11

a. Lev. 11:2 Or, whereof ye may eat.
b. Lev. 11:3 He noteth four sorts of beasts, some chew the cud only, and some have only the foot cleft: others neither chew the cud, nor have the hoof cleft: the fourth both chew the cud and have the hoof divided, which may be eaten.
c. Lev. 11:8 God would that hereby for a time they should be discerned as his people from the Gentiles.
d. Lev. 11:10 As little fish engendered of the slime.
e. Lev. 11:10 As they which come of generation.
f. Lev. 11:13 Or, gryphon, as it is in the Greek.
g. Lev. 11:16 Or, cuckoo.
h. Lev. 11:18 Or, porphyrio.
i. Lev. 11:21 Or, have no bowings on their feet.
j. Lev. 11:22 These were certain kinds of grasshoppers, which are not now properly known.
k. Lev. 11:25 Out of the camp.
l. Lev. 11:26 Or, hath not his foot cloven in two.
m. Lev. 11:29 The green frog that sitteth on the bushes.
n. Lev. 11:29 Or, crocodile.
o. Lev. 11:32 As a bottle or bag.
p. Lev. 11:36 So much of the water as toucheth it.
q. Lev. 11:38 He speaketh of seed that is laid to sleep before it be sown.
r. Lev. 11:44 He showeth why God did choose them to be his people, 1 Pet. 1:15.

yourselves with any creeping thing that creepeth upon the earth. **45** For I am the Lord that brought you out of the land of Egypt, to be your God, and that you should be holy, for I am holy. **46** This is the law of beasts, and of fowls, and of every living thing that moveth in the waters, and of every thing that creepeth upon the earth: **47** That there may be a difference between the unclean and clean, and between the beast that may be eaten, and the beast that ought not to be eaten.

12

2 A law how women should be purged after their deliverance.

1 And the Lord spake unto Moses, saying, **2** Speak unto the children of Israel, and say, When a woman hath brought forth seed, and borne a man-child, she shall be unclean [a]seven days, like as she is unclean when she is put apart for her [b,1]disease. **3** ([2]And in the eighth day the foreskin of the children's flesh shall be circumcised.) **4** And she shall continue in the blood of her purifying three [c]and thirty days: she shall touch no [d]hallowed thing, nor come into the [e]Sanctuary, until the time of her purifying be out. **5** But if she bear a maid-child, then she shall be unclean two [f]weeks, as when she hath her disease: and she shall continue in the blood of her purifying threescore and six days. **6** Now when the days of her purifying are out (whether it be for a son or for a daughter) she shall bring to the Priest a lamb of one year old for a burnt offering, and a young pigeon or a turtledove for a sin offering, unto the door of the [g]Tabernacle of the Congregation, **7** Who shall offer it before the Lord, and make an atonement for her: so she shall be purged of the issue of her blood: this is the law for her that hath borne a male or female. **8** But if she [h]be not able to bring a lamb, she shall bring two [3]turtles, or two young pigeons: the one for a burnt offering, and the other for a sin offering: and the Priest shall make an atonement for her: so she shall be clean.

13

2 What considerations the Priests ought to have in judging the leprosy, 29 the black spot, or scab, 47 and the leprosy of the garment.

1 Moreover the Lord spake unto Moses and to Aaron, saying, **2** The man that shall have in the skin of his flesh a swelling or a scab, or a white spot, so that in the skin of his flesh [a]it be like the plague of leprosy, then he shall be brought unto Aaron the Priest, or unto one of his sons the Priests, **3** And the Priest shall look on the sore in the skin of his flesh: if the hair in the sore be turned into white, and the sore seen to be [b]lower than the skin of his flesh, it is a plague of leprosy: therefore the Priest shall look on him, and [c]pronounce him unclean. **4** But if the white spot be in the skin of his flesh, and seem not to be lower than the skin, nor the hair thereof be turned unto white, then the Priest shall shut up him that hath the plague, seven days. **5** After, the Priest shall look upon him the seventh day: and if the plague seem [d]to him to abide still, and the plague grow not in the skin, the Priest shall shut him up yet seven days more. **6** Then the Priest shall look on him again the seventh day, and if the plague [e]be dark, and the sore grow not in the skin, then the Priest shall [f]pronounce him clean, for it is a scab: therefore he shall wash his clothes, and be clean. **7** But if the scab grow more in the skin, after that he is seen of the Priest for to be purged, he shall be seen of the Priest yet again. **8** Then the Priest shall consider, and if the scab [g]grow in the skin, then the Priest shall pronounce him [h]unclean: for it is leprosy. **9** When the plague of leprosy is in a man, he shall be brought unto the Priest, **10** And the Priest shall see him: and if the swelling be white in the skin, and have made the hair white, and there be raw flesh in the swelling, **11** It is an old leprosy in the skin of his flesh: and the Priest shall pronounce him unclean, and shall not shut him up, for he is unclean. **12** Also if the leprosy [i]break out in the skin, and the leprosy cover all the skin of the plague, from his head even to his feet, wheresoever the Priest looketh, **13** Then the Priest shall consider: and if the leprosy cover all his flesh, he shall pronounce the plague to be [j]clean, because it is all turned into whiteness: so he shall be clean. **14** But if there be raw flesh on him when he is seen, he shall be unclean. **15** For the Priest shall see the raw flesh, and declare him to be unclean: for the raw flesh is [k]unclean, therefore it is the leprosy. **16** Or if the raw flesh change and be turned into white, then he shall come to the Priest, **17** And the Priest shall behold him: and if the sore be changed into white, then the Priest shall pronounce the plague clean, for it is clean. **18** The flesh also in whose skin there is [l]a boil, and is healed **19** And in the place of the boil there be a white swelling, or a white spot somewhat reddish, it shall be seen of the Priest. **20** And when the Priest seeth it, if it appear lower than the skin, and the hair thereof be changed into white, the Priest then shall pronounce him [m]unclean: for it is a plague of leprosy, broken out in the boil. **21** But if the Priest look on it, and there be no white hairs therein, and if it be not lower than the skin, but be darker, then the Priest shall shut him up seven days. **22** And if it spread abroad in the flesh, the Priest shall pronounce him unclean, for it is a sore. **23** But if the spot continue in his place, and grow not, it is a burning boil: therefore the Priest shall declare him to be clean. **24** If there be any flesh, in whose skin there is an hot burning, and the quick flesh of the burning have a [n]white spot, somewhat reddish or pale, **25** Then the Priest shall look upon it: and if the hair in that spot be changed into white, and it appear lower than the skin, it is a leprosy broken out in the burning: therefore the Priest shall pronounce him unclean: for it is the plague of leprosy. **26** But if the Priest look on it, and there be no white hair in the spot, and be no lower than the other skin, but be darker, then the Priest shall shut him up seven days. **27** After, the Priest shall look on him the seventh day: if it be grown abroad in the skin, then the Priest shall pronounce him unclean: for it is the plague of leprosy. **28** And if the spot abide in his place, not growing in the skin, but is dark, it is a [o]rising of the burning: the Priest shall therefore declare him clean: for it is the drying up of the burning. **29** If also a man or a woman hath a sore on the head or in the beard, **30** Then the Priest shall see the sore: and if it appears lower than the skin, and there be in it a small yellow [p]hair, then the Priest shall pronounce him unclean: for it is a black spot, and leprosy of the head or of the beard. **31** And if the Priest look on the sore of the black spot, and if it seem not lower than the skin, nor have any black hair in it, then the Priest shall shut up him that hath the sore of the black spot, seven days. **32** After, in the seventh day the Priest shall look on the sore: and if the black spot grow not, and there be in it no yellow hair, and the black spot seem not lower than the skin, **33** Then he shall be shaven, but the place of the black spot shall he not shave: but the Priest shall shut up him that hath black spot, seven days more. **34** And the seventh day the Priest shall look on the black spot: and if the black spot grow not in the skin, nor seem lower than the other skin, then the Priest shall cleanse him, and he shall wash his clothes, and be clean. **35** But if the black spot grow abroad in the flesh after his cleansing, **36** Then the Priest shall look on it, and if the black spot grow in the skin, the Priest shall not [q]seek for the yellow hair: for it is unclean. **37** But if the black spot seem to him to abide, and that black hair grow therein, the black spot is healed, he is clean, and the Priest shall declare him to be clean. **38** Furthermore if there be any white spots in the skin of the flesh of man or woman, **39** Then the Priest shall consider: and if the spots in the skin of their flesh be somewhat dark and white withal, it is but a white spot broken out in the skin: therefore he is clean. **40** And the man whose hair is fallen off his head, and is bald, is clean. **41** And if his head lose the [r]hair on the forepart, and be bald before, he is clean. **42** But if there be in the bald head, or in the bald forehead a white reddish sore, it is a leprosy springing in his bald head, or in his bald forehead. **43** Therefore the Priest shall look upon it, and if the rising of the sore be white reddish in his bald head, or in his bald forehead, appearing like leprosy in the skin of the flesh, **44** He is a leper and unclean: therefore the Priest shall pronounce him altogether unclean: for the sore is in his head. **45** The leper also in whom the plague is, shall have his clothes [s]rent, and his head bare, and shall put a covering upon his [t]lips, and shall cry, I am unclean, I am unclean. **46** As long as the disease shall be upon him, he shall be polluted, for he is unclean: he shall dwell alone, [1]without the camp shall his habitation be. **47** Also the garment that the plague of leprosy is in, whether it be a woolen garment or a linen garment, **48** Whether it be in the warp or in the woof of linen or of woolen, either in a skin, or in anything made of skin, **49** And if the sore be green or somewhat reddish in the garment or in the skin, or in the warp or in the woof, or in anything that is made of [u]skin, it is a plague of leprosy, and shall be showed unto the Priest. **50** Then the Priest shall see the plague, and shut up it that hath the plague, seven days, **51** And shall look on the plague the seventh day: if the plague grow in the garment or in the warp, or in the woof, or in the skin, or in anything that is made of skin, that plague is a fretting leprosy and unclean. **52** And he shall burn the garment, or the warp, or the woof, whether it be woolen or linen, or anything that is made of skin, wherein the plague is: for it is a fretting leprosy, therefore it shall be burnt in the fire. **53** If the Priest yet see that

---

LEV. 11

1. Gen. 7:2 / Deut. 14:1 / Acts 10:14
2. Lev. 6:28

LEV. 12

a. Lev. 12:2 So that her husband for that time could not resort to her.
b. Lev. 12:2 Or, flowers.
c. Lev. 12:4 Besides the first seven days.
d. Lev. 12:4 As sacrifice, or such like.
e. Lev. 12:4 That is, into the court gate, till after forty days.
f. Lev. 12:5 Twice so long as if she bare a man-child.
g. Lev. 12:6 Where the burnt offerings were wont to be offered.
h. Lev. 12:8 Hebrew, if her hand find not the worth of a lamb.

LEV. 12

1. Lev. 15:19
2. Luke 1:21 / John 7:22
3. Luke 2:24

LEV. 13

a. Lev. 13:2 That it may be suspected to be the leprosy.
b. Lev. 13:3 That is, shrunken in, and be lower than the rest of the skin.
c. Lev. 13:3 Hebrew, shall pollute him.
d. Lev. 13:5 Hebrew, in his eyes.
e. Lev. 13:6 As having the skin drawn together, or blackish.
f. Lev. 13:6 Hebrew, shall cleanse him.
g. Lev. 13:8 Or, be spread abroad.
h. Lev. 13:8 As touching his bodily disease: for his disease was not imputed to him for sin before God, though it were the punishment of sin.
i. Lev. 13:12 Or, bud.
j. Lev. 13:13 For it is not that contagious leprosy that infecteth, but a kind of scurvy, which hath not the flesh raw as the leprosy.
k. Lev. 13:15 That is, declareth that the flesh is not found, but is in danger to be leprous.
l. Lev. 13:18 Or, impostume.
m. Lev. 13:20 None were exempted, but if the Priest pronounced him unclean, he was put out from among the people: as appeareth by Mary the prophetess, Num. 12:14, and by king Uzziah, 2 Chron. 26:20.
n. Lev. 13:24 If he have a white spot in the place where the burning was, and was after healed.
o. Lev. 13:28 Or, swelling.
p. Lev. 13:30 Which was not wont to be there, or else smaller than in any other part of the body.
q. Lev. 13:36 He shall not care whether the yellow hair be there or no.
r. Lev. 13:41 By sickness, or any other inconvenience.
s. Lev. 13:45 In sign of sorrow and lamentation.
t. Lev. 13:45 Either in token of mourning, or for fear of infecting others.
u. Lev. 13:49 Whether it be garment, vessel, or instrument.
v. Lev. 13:53 But abide still in one place, as verse 37.
w. Lev. 13:55 But remain as it did before.

the plague [v]grow not in the garment, or in the woof, or in whatsoever thing of skin
it be, 54 Then the Priest shall command them to wash the thing wherein the
plague is, and he shall shut it up seven days more. 55 Again the Priest shall look
on the plague, after it is washed: and if the plague have not changed his [w]color,
though the plague spread no further, it is unclean: thou shalt burn it in the fire, for
it is a fret inward, [x]whether the spot be in the bare place of the whole, or in part
thereof. 56 And if the Priest see that the plague be darker, after that it is washed,
he shall cut it out of the garment, or out of the skin, or out of the warp, or out of
the woof. 57 And if it appear still in the garment or in the warp, or in the woof,
or in anything made of skin, it is a spreading leprosy: thou shalt burn the thing
wherein the plague is, in the fire. 58 If thou hast washed the garment, or the
warp, or the woof, or whatsoever thing of skin it be, if the plague be departed the-
refrom, then shall it be washed [y]the second time, and be clean. 59 This is the law
of the plague of leprosy in a garment of woolen or linen, or in the warp, or in the
woof, or in anything of skin, to make it clean or unclean.

14

1 The cleansing of the leper, 34 And of the house that he is in.

1 And the Lord spake unto Moses, saying, 2 [1]This is the [a]law of
the leper in the day of his cleansing: that is, he shall be brought unto the
Priest, 3 And the Priest shall go out of the camp, and the Priest shall consider
him: and if the plague of leprosy be healed in the leper, 4 Then shall the Priest
command to take for him that is cleansed, two [b]sparrows alive and [c]clean, and ce-
darwood and a scarlet lace, and hyssop. 5 And the Priest shall command to kill
one of the birds over [d]pure water in an earthen vessel. 6 After, he shall take the
live sparrow with the cedarwood, and the scarlet lace, and the hyssop, and shall dip
them and the living sparrow in the blood of the sparrow slain, over the pure wa-
ter. 7 And he shall sprinkle upon him, that must be cleansed of his leprosy, seven
times, and cleanse him, and shall [e]let go the live sparrow into the broad
field. 8 Then he that shall be cleansed, shall wash his clothes, and shave off all his
hair, and wash himself in water, so he shall be clean: after that shall he come into
the host, and shall tarry without his tent seven days. 9 So in the seventh day he
shall shave off all his hair both his head and his beard, and his eyebrows: even all
his hair shall be shaven, and shall wash his clothes, and shall wash his flesh in water:
so he shall be clean. 10 Then in the eighth day he shall take two he lambs wi-
thout [f]blemish, and an ewe lamb of a year old without blemish, and three-tenth
deals of fine flour for a meat offering, mingled with oil, [g]and a pint of oil. 11 And
the Priest that maketh him clean shall bring the man which is to be made clean,
and those things, before the Lord, at the door of the Tabernacle of the Congrega-
tion. 12 Then the Priest shall take one lamb, and offer him for a trespass offering,
and the pint of oil, and [2]shake them to and fro before the Lord. 13 And he shall
kill the lamb in the place where the [3]sin offering and the burnt offering are slain,
even in the holy place: for as the sin offering is the Priest's, so is the trespass offe-
ring: for it is most holy. 14 So the Priest shall take of the blood of the trespass
offering, and put it upon the lap of the right ear of him that shall be cleansed, and
upon the thumb of his right hand, and upon the great toe of his right foot. 15 The
Priest shall also take of the pint of oil, and pour it into the palm of his left
hand, 16 And the Priest shall dip his [h]right finger in the oil that is in his left
hand, and sprinkle of the oil with his finger seven times before the Lord. 17 And
of the rest of the oil that is in his hand, shall the Priest put upon the lap of the right
ear of him that is to be cleansed, and upon the thumb of his right hand, and upon
the great toe of his right foot, [i]where the blood of the trespass offering was
put. 18 But the remnant of the oil that is in the Priest's hand, he shall pour upon
the head of him that is to be cleansed: so the Priest shall make an atonement for
him before the Lord. 19 And the Priest shall offer the burnt offering, and make
an atonement for him that is to be cleansed of his uncleanness: then after shall he
kill the burnt offering. 20 So the Priest shall offer the burnt offering and the
meat offering upon the Altar: and the Priest shall make an atonement for him: so
he shall be clean. 21 But if he be poor, and not [j]able, then he shall bring one
lamb for a trespass offering to be shaken, for his reconciliation, and a [k]tenth deal
of fine flour mingled with oil, for a meat offering, with a pint of oil. 22 Also two
turtledoves, or two young pigeons, as he is able, whereof the one shall be a sin
offering, and the other a burnt offering, 23 And he shall bring them the eighth
day for his cleansing unto the Priest at the door of the Tabernacle of the Congrega-
tion before the Lord. 24 Then the Priest shall take the lamb of the trespass offe-
ring, and the pint of oil, and the Priest shall [l]shake them to and fro before the
Lord. 25 And he shall kill the lamb of the trespass offering, and the Priest shall
take of the blood of the trespass offering, and put it upon the lap of his right ear
that is to be cleansed, and upon the thumb of his right hand, and upon the great
toe of his right foot. 26 Also the Priest shall pour of the oil into the palm of his
own [m]left hand. 27 So the Priest shall with his right finger sprinkle of the oil that
is in his left hand, seven times before the Lord. 28 Then the Priest shall put of
the oil that is in his hand, upon the lap of the right ear of him that is to be cleansed,
and upon the thumb of his right hand, and upon the great toe of his right foot:
upon the place [n]of the blood of the trespass offering. 29 But the rest of the oil
that is in the Priest's hand, he shall put upon the head of him that is to be cleansed,
to make an atonement for him before the Lord. 30 Also he shall present one of
the turtledoves, or of the young pigeons, [o]as he is able. 31 Such, I say, as he is
able, the one for a sin offering, and the other for a burnt offering, [p]with the meat
offering: so the Priest shall make an atonement for him that is to be cleansed before
the Lord. 32 This is the [q]Law of him which hath the plague of leprosy, who is
not able in his cleansing to offer the whole. 33 The Lord also spake unto Moses
and to Aaron, saying, 34 When ye be come unto the land of Canaan which I
give you in possession, if I [r]send the plague of leprosy in an house of the land of
your possession, 35 Then he that owneth the house shall come and tell the
Priest, saying, Me think there is like a plague of leprosy in the house. 36 Then
the Priest shall command them to empty the house before the Priest go into it to
see the plague, that all that is in the house be not made unclean, and then shall the
Priest go in to see the house. 37 And he shall mark the plague: and if the plague
be in the walls of the house, and that there be [s]deep spots, greenish or reddish, whi-
ch seem to be lower than the wall. 38 Then the Priest shall go out of the house
to the door of the house, and shall cause to shut up the house seven days. 39 So
the Priest shall come again the seventh day: and if he see that the plague be increa-
sed in the walls of the house, 40 Then the Priest shall command them to take
away the stones wherein the plague is, and they shall cast them into a [t]foul place
without the city. 41 Also he shall cause to scrape the house within round about,
and pour the dust, that they have pared off, without the city in [u]an unclean pla-
ce. 42 And they shall take other stones, and put them in the places of those sto-
nes, and shall take other mortar, to plaster the house with. 43 But if the plague
come again and break out in the house, after that he hath taken away the stones,
and after that he hath scraped and plastered the house, 44 Then the Priest shall
come and see: and if the plague grow in the house, it is a fretting leprosy in the
house: it is therefore unclean. 45 And he shall [v]break down the house, with the
stones of it, and the timber thereof, and all the [w]mortar of the house, and he shall
carry them out of the city unto an unclean place. 46 Moreover he that goeth into
the house all the while that it is shut up, he shall be unclean until the even. 47 He
also that sleepeth in the house shall wash his clothes: he likewise that eateth in the
house, shall wash his clothes. 48 But if the Priest shall come and see, that the
plague hath spread no further in the house, after the house be plastered, the Priest
shall pronounce the house clean, for the plague is healed. 49 Then shall he take
to purify the house, two sparrows, and cedarwood, and [x]scarlet lace, and hys-
sop. 50 And he shall kill one sparrow over pure water in an earthen ves-
sel, 51 And shall take the cedarwood, and the hyssop, and the scarlet lace with
the live Sparrow, and dip them in the blood of the slain Sparrow, and in the pure
water, and sprinkle the house seven times: 52 So shall he cleanse the house with
the blood of the sparrow, and with the pure water, and with the live sparrow, and
with the cedarwood, and with the hyssop, and with the scarlet lace. 53 Afterward
he shall let go the live sparrow out of the [y]town into the [z]broad fields: so shall he
make atonement for the house, and it shall be clean. 54 This is the law for every
plague of leprosy and [4]black spot, 55 And of the leprosy of the garment, and of
the house, 56 And of the [aa]swelling, and of the scab, and of the white
spot. 57 This is the law of the leprosy, to teach [ab]when a thing is unclean, and
when it is clean.

---

x. Lev. 13:55 Or, whether it be in any bare place before, or behind.
y. Lev. 13:58 To the intent he might be sure that the leprosy was departed, and that all occasion of infection might be taken away.

LEV. 13

1. Nun. 5:2 / 2 Kings 15:5

LEV. 14

a. Lev. 14:2 Or, the ceremony which shall be used in his purgation.
b. Lev. 14:4 Or, little birds.
c. Lev. 14:4 Of birds which were permitted to be eaten.
d. Lev. 14:5 Running water, or of the fountains.
e. Lev. 14:7 Signifying, that he that was made clean, was set at liberty, and restored to the company of others.
f. Lev. 14:10 Which hath no imperfection in any member.
g. Lev. 14:10 This measure in Hebrew, is called Log, and contained six eggs in measure.
h. Lev. 14:16 Hebrew, the finger of his right hand.
i. Lev. 14:17 Hebrew, upon the blood of the trespass offering.
j. Lev. 14:21 Hebrew, his hand cannot take it.
k. Lev. 14:21 Which is an Omer, read Exod. 16:16.
l. Lev. 14:24 Or, shall offer them as the offering that is shaken to and fro.
m. Lev. 14:26 Hebrew, into the palm of the Priest's left hand.
n. Lev. 14:28 Or, where the blood of the trespass offering was put, as verse 17.
o. Lev. 14:30 Whether of them he can get.
p. Lev. 14:31 Or, besides the meat offering.
q. Lev. 14:32 This order is appointed for the poor man.
r. Lev. 14:34 This declareth that no plague nor punishment cometh to man without God's providence and his sending.
s. Lev. 14:37 Or, blackness, or hollow streaks.
t. Lev. 14:40 Or, polluted.
u. Lev. 14:41 Where carrions were cast, and other filth, that the people might not be therewith infected.
v. Lev. 14:45 That is, he shall command it to be pulled down, as verse 40.
w. Lev. 14:45 Or, dust.
x. Lev. 14:49 It seemeth that this was a lace or string to bind the hyssop to the wood, and so was made a sprinkle: the Apostle to the Hebrews calleth it scarlet wool, Heb. 9:19.
y. Lev. 14:53 Hebrew, city.
z. Lev. 14:53 Hebrew, on the face of the field.
aa. Lev. 14:56 Or, rising.
ab. Lev. 14:57 Hebrew, in the day of the unclean, and in the day of the clean.

LEV. 14

1. Matt. 8:2 / Mark 1:40 / Luke 5:12
2. Exod. 29:24
3. Lev. 7:17
4. Lev. 13:30

15

8, 19 The manner of purging the unclean issues both of men and women. 31 The children of Israel must be separate from all uncleanness.

1 Moreover the Lord spake unto Moses, and to Aaron, saying, **2** Speak unto the children of Israel, and say unto them, Whosoever hath an issue from his [a]flesh, is unclean, because of his issue. **3** And this shall be his uncleanness in his issue, when his flesh avoideth his issue, or if his flesh be stopped from his issue, this is [b]his uncleanness. **4** Every bed whereon he lieth that hath the issue, shall be unclean, and everything whereon he sitteth, shall be unclean. **5** Whosoever also toucheth his bed, shall wash his clothes, and wash himself in water, and shall be unclean until the even. **6** And he that sitteth on any thing, whereon he sat that hath the issue, shall wash his clothes, and wash himself in water, and shall be unclean until the even. **7** Also he that toucheth the flesh of him that hath the issue, shall wash his clothes, and wash himself in water, and shall be unclean until the even. **8** If he also that hath the issue, spit upon him that is clean, [c]he shall wash his clothes, and wash himself in water, and shall be unclean until the even. **9** And what [d]saddle soever he rideth upon, that hath the issue, shall be unclean, **10** And whosoever toucheth any thing that was under him, shall be unclean until the even: and he that beareth those things, shall wash his clothes, and wash himself in water, and shall be unclean until the even. **11** Likewise whomsoever he toucheth that hath the issue (and hath not washed his hands in water) shall wash his clothes, and wash himself in water, and shall be unclean until the even. **12** [1]And the vessel of earth that he toucheth, which hath the issue, shall be broken: and every vessel of wood shall be rinsed in water. **13** But if he that hath an issue, be [e]cleansed of his issue, then shall he count him seven days for his cleansing, and wash his clothes, and wash his flesh in pure water: so shall he be clean. **14** Then the eighth day he shall take unto him two turtledoves, or two young pigeons, and come before the Lord at the door of the Tabernacle of the Congregation, and shall give them unto the Priest, **15** And the Priest shall make of the one of them a sin offering, and of the other a burnt offering: so the Priest shall make an atonement for him before the Lord for his issue. **16** Also if any man's issue of seed depart from him, he shall wash all his [f]flesh in water, and be unclean until the even. **17** And every garment, and every skin whereupon shall be issue of seed, shall be even washed with water, and be unclean unto the even. **18** If he that hath an issue of seed do lie with a woman, they shall both wash themselves with water, and be unclean until the even. **19** Also when a woman shall have an issue, and her issue in her [g]flesh shall be blood, she shall be put apart seven days: and whosoever toucheth her, shall be unclean until the even. **20** And whatsoever she lieth upon in [h]her separation, shall be unclean, and everything that she sitteth upon, shall be unclean. **21** Whosoever also toucheth her bed, shall wash his clothes, and wash himself with water, and shall be unclean unto the even. **22** And whosoever toucheth anything that she sat upon, shall wash his clothes, and wash himself in water, and shall be unclean until the even: **23** So that whether he toucheth her bed, or anything whereon she hath sat, he shall be unclean unto the even. **24** And if a man lie with her, and the flowers of her separation [i]touch him, he shall be unclean seven days, and all the whole bed whereon he lieth, shall be unclean. **25** Also when a woman's issue of blood runneth long time besides the time of her [j]flowers, or when she hath an issue longer than her flowers, all the days of the issue of her uncleanness she shall be unclean, as in the time of her flowers. **26** Every bed whereon she lieth (as long as her issue lasteth) shall be to her as the [k]bed of her separation: and whatsoever she sitteth upon, shall be unclean, as her uncleanness when she is put apart. **27** And whosoever toucheth these things, shall be unclean, and shall wash his clothes, and wash himself in water, and shall be unclean unto the even. **28** But if she be cleansed of her issue, then she shall [l]count her seven days, and after, she shall be clean. **29** And in the eighth day she shall take unto her two turtles, or two young pigeons, and bring them unto the Priest at the door of the Tabernacle of the Congregation. **30** And the Priest shall make of the one a sin offering, and of the other a burnt offering, and the Priest shall make an atonement for her before the Lord, for the issue of her uncleanness. **31** Thus shall ye [m]separate the children of Israel from their uncleanness, that they die not in their uncleanness, if they defile my Tabernacle that is among them. **32** This is the law of him that hath an issue, and of him from whom goeth an issue of seed whereby he is defiled: **33** Also of her that is sick of her flowers, and of him that hath a running issue, whether it be man or woman, and of him that lieth with her which is unclean.

16

2 The Priest might not at all times come into the most holy place. 8 The scapegoat. 14 The purging of the Sanctuary. 17 The cleansing of the Tabernacle. 21 The Priest confesseth the sins of the people. 29 The feast of cleansing sins.

1 Furthermore the Lord spake unto [1]Moses, after the death of the two sons of Aaron, when they came to offer before the Lord, and died: **2** And the Lord said unto Moses, Speak unto Aaron thy brother, [2]that he come not at [a]all times into the holy place within the veil, before the Mercy seat, which is upon the Ark, that he die not, for I will appear in the cloud upon the Mercy seat. **3** After this sort shall Aaron come into the Holy place: even with a young bullock for a sin offering, and a ram for a burnt offering. **4** He shall put on the holy linen coat, and shall have linen breeches upon his [b]flesh, and shall be girded with a linen girdle, and shall cover his head with a linen miter, these are the holy garments: therefore shall he wash his flesh in water, when he doth put them on. **5** And he shall take of the Congregation of the children of Israel, two he goats for a sin offering, and a ram for a burnt offering. **6** Then Aaron shall offer the bullock for his sin offering, [3]and make an atonement for himself, and for his house. **7** And he shall take the two he goats, and present them before the Lord at the door of the Tabernacle of the Congregation. **8** Then Aaron shall cast lots over the two he goats: one lot for the Lord, and the other for the [c]Scapegoat. **9** And Aaron shall offer the goat, upon which the Lord's lot shall fall, and make him a sin offering. **10** But the goat, on which the lot shall fall to be the Scapegoat, shall be presented alive before the Lord, to make reconciliation by him, and to let him go (as a Scapegoat) into the wilderness. **11** Thus Aaron shall offer the bullock for his sin offering, and make a reconciliation for himself, and for his house, and shall kill the bullock for his sin offering. **12** And he shall take a censer full of burning coals from off the altar before the Lord, and his hand full of sweet incense beaten small, and bring it within the [d]veil, **13** And shall put the incense upon the fire before the Lord, that the [e]cloud of the incense may cover the Mercy seat that is upon [f]the Testimony: so he shall not die. **14** And he shall [4]take of the blood of the bullock, [5]and sprinkle it with his finger upon the Mercy seat [g]Eastward: and before the Mercy seat shall he sprinkle of the blood with his finger seven times. **15** Then shall he kill the goat that is the people's sin offering, and bring his blood within the veil and do with that blood, as he did with the blood of the bullock, and sprinkle it upon the Mercy seat, and before the Mercy seat. **16** So he shall purge the Holy place from the uncleanness of the children of Israel, and from their trespasses of all their sins: so shall he do also for the Tabernacle of the Congregation [h]placed with them, in the midst of their uncleanness. **17** [6]And there shall be no man in the Tabernacle of the Congregation, when he goeth in to make an atonement in the Holy place, until he come out, and have made an atonement for himself, and for his household, and for all the Congregation of Israel. **18** After, he shall go out unto the [i]altar that is before the Lord, and make a reconciliation upon it, and shall take of the blood of the bullock, and of the blood of the goat, and put it upon the horns of the Altar round about. **19** So shall he sprinkle of the blood upon it with his finger seven times, and cleanse it, and hallow it from the uncleanness of the children of Israel. **20** When he hath made an end of purging the Holy place, and the Tabernacle of the Congregation, and the Altar, then he shall bring the live goat: **21** And Aaron shall put both his hands upon the head of the live goat, and confess over him all the iniquities of the children of Israel, and all their trespasses in all their sins, putting them [j]upon the head of the goat, and shall send him away (by the hand of a man appointed) into the wilderness. **22** So the goat shall bear upon him all their iniquities into [k]the land that is not inhabited, and he shall let the goat go into the wilderness. **23** After, Aaron shall come into the Tabernacle of the Congregation, and put off the linen clothes, which he put on when he went into the Holy place, and leave them there. **24** He shall wash also his flesh with water in [l]the holy place, and put on his own raiment, and come out, and make his burnt offering and the burnt offering of the people, and make an atonement for himself, and for the people. **25** Also the fat of the sin offering shall he burn upon the altar. **26** And he that carried forth the goat called the Scapegoat, shall wash his clothes, and wash his flesh in water, and after that shall come into the host. **27** Also the bullock

---

LEV. 15

a. Lev. 15:2 Whose seed either in sleeping, or else of weakness of nature issueth at his secret part.
b. Lev. 15:3 Of the thing wherefore he shall be unclean.
c. Lev. 15:8 Of whom the unclean man did spit.
d. Lev. 15:9 The word signifieth everything whereon a man rideth.
e. Lev. 15:13 That is, be restored to his old state, and be healed thereof.
f. Lev. 15:16 Meaning, all his body.
g. Lev. 15:19 Or, secret part.
h. Lev. 15:20 That is, when she hath her flowers, whereby she is separate from her husband, from the Tabernacle and from touching of any holy thing.
i. Lev. 15:24 If any of her uncleanness did only touch him in the bed: for else the man that companied with such a woman, should die, Lev. 20:18.
j. Lev. 15:25 Hebrew, separation.
k. Lev. 15:26 Shall be unclean as the bed whereon she lay when she had her natural disease.
l. Lev. 15:28 After the time that she is recovered.
m. Lev. 15:31 Seeing that God required of his purity and cleanness: we cannot be his, except our filth and sins be purged with the blood of Jesus Christ, and so we learn to detest all sin.

LEV. 15

1. Lev. 2:28

LEV. 16

a. Lev. 16:2 The high Priest entered into the Holiest of all but once a year even in the month of September.
b. Lev. 16:4 Or, privities.
c. Lev. 16:8 In Hebrew it is called Azazel, which some say, is a mountain near Sinai, whither this goat was sent, but rather it is called the Scapegoat, because it was not offered, but sent into the desert, as verse 11.
d. Lev. 16:12 The Holiest of all.
e. Lev. 16:13 Or, the smoke.
f. Lev. 16:13 Or, the Ark.
g. Lev. 16:14 That is, on the side which was toward the people: for the head of the Sanctuary stood Westward.
h. Lev. 16:16 Placed among them which are unclean.
i. Lev. 16:18 Whereupon the sweet incense and perfume was offered.
j. Lev. 16:21 Herein this goat is a true figure of Jesus Christ, who beareth the sins of the people, Isa. 53:9.
k. Lev. 16:22 Hebrew, the land of separations.
l. Lev. 16:24 In the court where was the Laver, Exod. 30:18.

for the burnt offering, and the goat for the sin offering (whose blood was brought to make a reconciliation in the Holy place) shall one [7]carry out without the host to be burnt in the fire, with their skins, and with their flesh, and with their dung. **28** And he that burneth them shall wash his clothes, and wash his flesh in water, and afterward come into the host. **29** So this shall be an ordinance forever unto you: the tenth day of the [m]seventh month, ye shall [n]humble your souls, and do no work at all, whether it be one of the same country, or a stranger that sojourneth among you. **30** For that [8]day shall the Priest make an atonement for you to cleanse you: ye shall be clean from all your sins before the Lord. **31** This shall be a [o]Sabbath of rest unto you, and you shall humble your souls by an ordinance forever. **32** And the Priest [p]whom he shall anoint, and whom he shall consecrate (to minister in his father's stead) shall make the atonement, and shall put on the linen clothes and holy vestments, **33** And shall purge the holy Sanctuary and the Tabernacle of the Congregation, and shall cleanse the altar, and make an atonement for the Priests and for all the people of the Congregation. **34** And this shall be an everlasting ordinance unto you to make an atonement for the children of Israel for all their sins [9]once a year: and as the Lord commanded Moses, he did.

17

All sacrifices must be brought to the door of the Tabernacle. 7 To devils they may not offer. 10 They may not eat blood.

1 And the Lord spake unto Moses, saying, **2** Speak unto Aaron, and to his sons, and to all the children of Israel, and say unto them, This is the thing which the Lord hath [a]commanded, saying, **3** Whosoever he be of the house of Israel that [b]killeth a bullock, or lamb, or goat in the host, or that killeth it out of the host, **4** And bringeth it not unto the door of the Tabernacle of the Congregation to offer an offering unto the Lord before the Tabernacle of the Lord, [c]blood shall be imputed unto that man: he hath shed blood, wherefore that man shall be cut off from among his people. **5** Therefore the children of Israel shall bring their offerings, which they would offer [d]abroad in the field, and present them unto the Lord at the door of the Tabernacle of the Congregation by the Priest, and offer them for peace offerings unto the Lord. **6** Then the Priest shall sprinkle the blood upon the Altar of the Lord before the door of the Tabernacle of the Congregation, and burn the fat for a [1]sweet savor unto the Lord. **7** And they shall no more offer their offerings unto [e]devils, after whom they have gone a [f]whoring: this shall be an ordinance forever unto them in their generations. **8** Also thou shalt say unto them, Whosoever he be of the house of Israel, or of the strangers which sojourn among them, that offereth a burnt offering or sacrifice, **9** And bringeth it not unto the door of the Tabernacle of the Congregation to offer it unto the Lord, even that man shall be cut off from his people. **10** Likewise whosoever he be of the house of Israel: or of the strangers that sojourn among them, that eateth any blood, I will even set [g]my face against that person that eateth blood, and will cut him off from among his people. **11** For the life of the flesh is in the blood, and I have given it unto you to offer upon the altar, to make an atonement for your souls: for this blood shall make an atonement for the soul. **12** Therefore I said unto the children of Israel, None of you shall eat blood: neither the stranger that sojourneth among you, shall eat blood. **13** Moreover whosoever he be of the children of Israel, or of the strangers that sojourn among them, which by hunting taketh any beast or fowl that may be [h]eaten, he shall pour out the blood thereof, and cover it with dust: **14** For the life of all flesh is his blood, it is joined with his life: therefore I said unto the children of Israel, [2]Ye shall eat the blood of no [i]flesh: for the life of all flesh is the blood thereof: whosoever eateth it, shall be cut off. **15** And every person that eateth it which dieth alone, or that which is torn with beasts, whether it be one of the same country or a stranger, he shall both wash his clothes, and wash himself in water, and be unclean unto the even: after he shall be [j]clean. **16** But if he wash them not, nor wash his [k]flesh, then he shall bear [l]his iniquity.

18

3 The Israelites ought not to follow the manners of the Egyptians and Canaanites. 6 The marriages that are unlawful.

1 And the Lord spake unto Moses, saying, **2** Speak unto the children of Israel, and say unto them, I am the Lord your God. **3** After the [a]doings of the land of Egypt, wherein ye dwelt, shall ye not do: and after the manner of the land of Canaan, whither I will bring you, shall ye not do, neither walk in their ordinances. **4** But do after my judgments, and keep mine ordinances, to walk therein: I am the Lord your God. **5** Ye shall keep therefore my statutes, and my judgments, [1]which if a man do, he shall then live in them: [b]I am the Lord. **6** None shall come near to any of the kindred of his flesh to [c]uncover her shame: I am the Lord. **7** Thou shalt not uncover the shame of thy father, nor the shame of thy mother, for she is thy mother, thou shalt not discover her shame. **8** [2]The shame of thy father's [d]wife shalt thou not discover: for it is thy father's shame. **9** Thou shalt not discover the shame of thy [e]sister, the daughter of thy father, or the daughter of thy mother, whether she be born at home or born without: thou shalt not discover their shame. **10** The shame of thy son's daughter, or of thy daughter's daughter, thou shalt not, I say, uncover their shame: for it is thy [f]shame. **11** The shame of thy father's wife's daughter, begotten of thy father (for she is thy sister) thou shalt not, I say, discover her shame. **12** [3]Thou shalt not uncover the [g]shame of thy father's sister: for she is thy father's kinswoman. **13** Thou shalt not discover the shame of thy mother's sister: for she is thy mother's kinswoman. **14** Thou shalt not uncover the shame of thy [h]father's brother: that is, thou shalt not go in to his wife, for she is thine [i]aunt. **15** [4]Thou shalt not discover the shame of thy daughter-in-law: for she is thy son's wife: therefore shalt thou not uncover her shame. **16** [5]Thou shalt not discover the shame of thy [j]brother's wife: for it is thy brother's shame. **17** Thou shalt not discover the shame of the wife and of her daughter, neither shalt thou take her son's daughter, nor her daughter's daughter, to uncover her shame: for they are thy kinsfolks, and it were wickedness. **18** Also thou shalt not take a wife with her sister, during her life to [k]vex her, in uncovering her shame upon her. **19** [6]Thou shalt not also go unto a woman to uncover her shame, as long as she is put [l]apart for her disease. **20** Moreover, thou shalt not give thy self to thy neighbor's wife by carnal copulation, to be defiled with her. **21** [7]Also thou shalt not give thy [m]children to [n]offer them unto [o]Molech, neither shalt thou defile the Name of thy God: for I am the Lord. **22** Thou shalt not lie with the male as one lieth with a woman: for it is abomination. **23** [8]Thou shalt not also lie with any beast to be defiled therewith, neither shall any woman stand before a beast, to lie down thereto: for it is [p]abomination. **24** Ye shall not defile yourselves in any of these things: for in all these the Nations are defiled which I will cast out before you: **25** And the land is defiled: therefore I will [q]visit the wickedness thereof upon it, and the land [r]shall vomit out her inhabitants. **26** Ye shall keep therefore mine ordinances, and my judgments, and commit none of these abominations, as well he that is of the same country, as the stranger that sojourneth among you. **27** (For all these abominations have the men of the land done, which were before you, and the land is defiled: **28** And shall not the land spew you out if ye defile it, as it [s]spewed out the people that were before you?) **29** For whosoever shall commit any of these abominations, the persons that do so, shall [t]be cut off from among their people. **30** Therefore shall ye keep mine ordinances, that ye do not any of the abominable customs, which have been done before you, and that ye defile not yourselves therein: for I am the Lord your God.

---

m. Lev. 16:29 Which was Tishri, and answereth to part of September, and part of October.
n. Lev. 16:29 Meaning, by abstinence and fasting, Num. 25:7.
o. Lev. 16:31 Or a rest which ye shall keep most diligently.
p. Lev. 16:32 Whom the Priest shall anoint by God's commandment to succeed in his father's room.

LEV. 16

1. Lev. 10:1,2
2. Exod. 30:10 / Heb. 9:7
3. Heb. 9:7
4. Heb. 9:13 / Heb. 10:4
5. Lev. 1:5
6. Luke 1:10
7. Lev. 6:30 / Heb. 15:11
8. Lev. 23:7
9. Exod. 30:10 / Heb. 9:7

LEV. 17

a. Lev. 17:2 Lest they should practice that idolatry, which they had learned among the Egyptians.
b. Lev. 17:3 To make a sacrifice of offering thereof.
c. Lev. 17:4 I do as much abhor it as though he had killed a man, as Isa. 66:3.
d. Lev. 17:5 Wheresoever they were moved with foolish devotion to offer it.
e. Lev. 17:7 Meaning, whatsoever is not the true God, 1 Cor. 10:10; Ps. 95:5.
f. Lev. 17:7 For idolatry is spiritual whoredom, because faith toward God is broken.
g. Lev. 17:10 I will declare my wrath by taking vengeance on him, as Lev. 20:3.
h. Lev. 17:13 Which the law permitteth to be eaten, because it is clean.
i. Lev. 17:14 Or, living creature.
j. Lev. 17:15 Or, counted clean.
k. Lev. 17:16 Or, himself.
l. Lev. 17:16 Or, the punishment of his sin.

LEV. 17

1. Exod. 29:18 / Lev. 4:31
2. Gen. 9:4

LEV. 18

a. Lev. 18:3 Ye shall preserve yourselves from these abominations following, which the Egyptians and Canaanites use.
b. Lev. 18:5 And therefore ye ought to serve me alone, as my people.
c. Lev. 18:6 That is, to lie with her, though it be under title of marriage.
d. Lev. 18:8 Which is thy stepmother.
e. Lev. 18:9 Either by father or mother, born in marriage or otherwise.
f. Lev. 18:10 They are her children whose shame thou hast uncovered.
g. Lev. 18:12 Or, secrets.
h. Lev. 18:14 Which thine uncle doth discover.
i. Lev. 18:14 Hebrew, thy father's brother's wife.
j. Lev. 18:16 Because the idolaters, among whom God's people had dwelt and should dwell, were given to these horrible incests, God chargeth his to beware of the same.
k. Lev. 18:18 By seeing thine affliction more bent to her sister than to her.
l. Lev. 18:19 Or while she hath her flowers.
m. Lev. 18:21 Hebrew, of thy seed.
n. Lev. 18:21 Or, to make them pass.
o. Lev. 18:21 Which was an idol of the Ammonites, unto whom they burned and sacrificed their children, 2 Kings 23:10. This seemed to be the chief and principal of all idols: and as the Jews write, was of a great stature, and hollow within, having seven places or chambers within him: one was to receive meal that was offered: another turtle doves: the third, a sheep: the fourth, a ram: the fifth a calf: the sixth an ox: the seventh a child. This idol's face was like a calf: his hands were ever stretched out to receive gifts: his priests were called Chemarim, 2 Kings 23:5; Hos. 10:5; Zeph. 1:4.
p. Lev. 18:23 Or, confusion.
q. Lev. 18:25 I will punish the land where such incestuous marriages and pollutions are suffered.
r. Lev. 18:25 He compareth the wicked to evil humors and surfeiting, which corrupt the stomach, and oppress nature, and therefore must be cast out by vomit.
s. Lev. 18:28 Both for their wicked marriages, unnatural copulations, idolatry or spiritual whoredom with Molech and such like abominations.
t. Lev. 18:29 Either by the civil sword or by some plague that God will send upon such.

LEV. 18

1. Ezek. 20:11 / Rom. 10:5 / Gal. 3:12
2. Lev. 20:11
3. Lev. 20:19 / Lev. 20:20
4. Lev. 20:12
5. Lev. 20:21
6. Lev. 20:18
7. Lev. 20:2 / 2 Kings 23:10
8. Lev. 20:15

19 *A repetition of sundry Laws and Ordinances.*

1 And the Lord spake unto Moses, saying, **2** Speak unto all the Congregation of the children of Israel, and say unto them, [1]Ye shall be [a]holy, for I the Lord your God am holy. **3** Ye shall fear every man his mother and his father, and shall keep my Sabbath: for I am the Lord your God. **4** Ye shall not turn unto idols, nor make you molten gods: I am the Lord your God. **5** And when ye shall offer a peace offering unto the Lord, ye shall offer it [b]freely. **6** [2]It shall be eaten the day ye offer it, or on the morrow: and that which remaineth until the third day, shall be burnt in the fire. **7** For if it be eaten the third day, it shall be unclean, it shall not be [c]accepted. **8** Therefore he that eateth it, shall bear his iniquity, because he hath defiled the hallowed thing of the Lord, and that person shall be cut off from his people. **9** [3]When ye reap the harvest of your land, ye shall not reap every corner of your field, neither shalt thou gather the [d]gleanings of thy harvest. **10** Thou shalt not gather the grapes of thy vineyard clean, neither gather every grape of thy vineyard, but thou shalt leave them for the poor and for the stranger: I am the Lord your God. **11** Ye shall not steal, neither [e]deal falsely, neither lie one to another. **12** [4]Also ye shall not swear by my Name falsely, neither shalt thou defile the Name of thy God: I am the Lord. **13** Thou shalt not do thy neighbor [f]wrong, neither rob him [5]The workman's hire shall not abide with thee until the morning. **14** Thou shalt not curse the deaf, [6]neither put a stumbling block before the blind, but shalt fear thy God: I am the Lord. **15** Ye shall not do unjustly in judgment: [7]Thou shalt not favor the person of the poor, nor honor the person of the mighty, but thou shalt judge thy neighbor justly. **16** Thou shalt not [g]walk about with tales among thy people: Thou shalt not [h]stand against the blood of thy neighbor: I am the Lord. **17** Thou shalt not hate thy brother in thine heart, but thou shalt plainly rebuke thy neighbor, [i]and suffer him not to sin. **18** Thou shalt not avenge, nor be mindful of wrong against the children of thy people, [8]but shalt love thy neighbor as thyself: I am the Lord. **19** Ye shall keep mine ordinances Thou shalt not let thy cattle gender with [j]others of divers kinds Thou shalt not sow thy field with mingled seed, neither shall a garment of divers things, as of linen and woolen come upon thee. **20** Whosoever also lieth and meddleth with a woman that is a bondmaid, affianced to a husband, and not redeemed, nor freedom given her, [k]she shall be scourged, but they shall not die, because she is not made free. **21** And he shall bring for his trespass offering unto the Lord, at the door of the Tabernacle of the Congregation, a ram for a trespass offering. **22** Then the Priest shall make an atonement for him with the ram of the trespass offering before the Lord, concerning his sin which he hath done, and pardon shall be given him for his sin which he hath committed. **23** Also when ye shall come into the land, and have planted every tree for meat, ye [l]shall count the fruit thereof as uncircumcised: three years shall it be uncircumcised unto you: it shall not be eaten: **24** But in the fourth year all the fruit thereof shall be holy to the praise of the Lord. **25** And the fifth year shall ye eat of the fruit of it, that it may [m]yield to you the increase thereof: I am the Lord your God. **26** Ye shall not eat the flesh with the [n]blood: ye shall not use witchcraft, nor [o]observe times. **27** [9]Ye shall not [p]cut round the corners of your heads, neither shalt thou [q]mar the tufts of thy beard. **28** [10]Ye shall not cut your flesh for the [r]dead, nor make any print of a [s]mark upon you: I am the Lord. **29** Thou shalt not make thy daughter common, to cause her to be a [t]whore, lest the land also fall to whoredom, and the land be full of wickedness. **30** Ye shall keep my Sabbaths, and reverence my Sanctuary: I am the Lord. **31** Ye shall not regard them that work with spirits, [11]neither Soothsayers: ye shall not seek to them to be defiled by them, I am the Lord your God. **32** Thou shalt [u]rise up before the hoary head, and honor the person of the old man, and dread thy God: I am the Lord. **33** And if a stranger sojourn with thee in your land, ye shall not [v]vex him. **34** [12]But the stranger that dwelleth with you, shall be as one of yourselves, and thou shalt love him as thyself: for ye were strangers in the land of Egypt: I am the Lord your God. **35** Ye shall not do unjustly in judgment, in [w]line, in weight, or in measure. **36** [13]You shall have just balances, true weights, a true [x]Ephah, and a true Hin, I am the Lord your God, which have brought you out of the land of Egypt. **37** Therefore shall ye observe all mine ordinances, and all my judgments, and do them: I am the Lord.

20 *2 They that give of their seed to Molech, must die. 6 They that have recourse to sorcerers. 10 The man that committeth adultery, 11 incest, or fornication with the kindred or affinity. 24 Israel a peculiar people to the Lord.*

1 And the Lord spake unto Moses, saying, **2** Thou shalt say also to the children of Israel, [1]Whosoever he be of the children of Israel, or of the strangers that dwell in Israel, that giveth his children unto [a]Molech, he shall die the death, the people of the land shall stone him to death. **3** And I will [b]set my face against that man and cut him off from among his people, because he hath given his children unto Molech, for to defile my Sanctuary, and to pollute mine holy Name. **4** And if the [c]people of the land hide their eyes, and wink at that man when he giveth his children unto Molech, and kill him not, **5** Then will I set my face against that man, and against his family, and will cut him off, and all that go a whoring after him to commit whoredom with Molech, from among their people. **6** If any turn after such as work with spirits, and after soothsayers to go a [d]whoring after them, then will I set my face against that person, and will cut him off from among his people. **7** Sanctify yourselves therefore, [2]and be holy, for I am the Lord your God. **8** Keep ye therefore mine ordinances, and do them: I am the Lord which doth sanctify you. **9** [3]If there be any that curseth his father or his mother he shall die the death, seeing he hath cursed his father and his mother, [e]his blood shall be upon him. **10** [4]And the man that committeth adultery with another man's wife, because he hath committed adultery with his neighbor's wife, the adulterer and the adulteress shall die the death. **11** And the man that lieth with his father's wife, because he hath uncovered his father's [5]shame, they shall both die: their blood shall be upon them. **12** Also the man that lieth with his daughter-in-law, they both shall die the death, they have wrought [f]abomination, their blood shall be upon them. **13** [6]The man also that lieth with the male, as one lieth with a woman, they have both committed abomination: they shall die the death, their blood shall be upon them. **14** Likewise he that taketh a wife and her mother, [g]committeth wickedness: they shall burn him and them with fire, that there be no wickedness among you. **15** [7]Also the man that lieth with a beast, shall die the death, and ye shall slay the beast. **16** And if a woman come to any beast, and lie therewith, then thou shalt kill the woman and the beast: they shall die the death, their blood shall be upon them. **17** Also the man that taketh his sister, his father's daughter, or his mother's daughter, and seeth her shame, and she seeth his shame, it is villainy: therefore they shall be cut off in the sight [h]of their people, because he that uncovered his sister's shame, he shall bear his iniquity. **18** [8]The man also that lieth with a woman having her [i]disease, and uncovereth her shame, and openeth her fountain, and she open the fountain of her blood, they shall be even both cut off from among their people. **19** Moreover, thou shalt not uncover the shame of thy mother's sister, [9]nor of thy father's sister: because he hath uncovered his [j]kin, they shall bear their iniquity. **20** Likewise the man that lieth with his father's brother's wife, and uncovereth his uncle's shame: they shall bear their iniquity, and shall die [k]childless. **21** So the man that taketh his brother's wife, committeth filthiness, because he hath uncovered his brother's [l]shame, they shall be childless. **22** Ye shall keep therefore all mine [10]ordinances and all my judgments, and do them, that the land whither I bring you to dwell therein, [11]spew you not out. **23** Wherefore ye shall not walk in the manners of this nation which I cast out before you: for they have committed all these things, [12]therefore I abhorred them. **24** But I have said unto you, Ye shall inherit their land, and I will give it unto you to possess it, even a land that [m]floweth with milk and honey: I am the Lord your God, which have separated you from other people. **25** [13]Therefore shall ye put difference between clean beasts and unclean, and between unclean fowls and clean, neither shall ye [n]defile your fowls with beasts and fowls, nor with any creeping thing, that the ground bringeth forth, which I have separated from you as unclean. **26** Therefore shall ye be [14]holy unto me: for I the Lord am holy,

---

LEV. 19

- **a.** Lev. 19:2 That is, void of all pollution, idolatry, and superstition both of soul and body.
- **b.** Lev. 19:5 Of your own accord.
- **c.** Lev. 19:7 To wit, of God.
- **d.** Lev. 19:9 Or, gatherings and leavings.
- **e.** Lev. 19:11 In that which is committed to your credit.
- **f.** Lev. 19:13 Or, oppress him by violence.
- **g.** Lev. 19:16 As a slanderer, backbiter, or quarrel picker.
- **h.** Lev. 19:16 By consenting to his death, or conspiring with the wicked.
- **i.** Lev. 19:17 Hebrew, suffer not sin upon him.
- **j.** Lev. 19:19 As a horse to leap an ass, or a mule a mare.
- **k.** Lev. 19:20 Hebrew, a beating shall be, some read, they shall be beaten.
- **l.** Lev. 19:23 It shall be unclean as that thing, which is not circumcised.
- **m.** Lev. 19:25 Or, that God may multiply.
- **n.** Lev. 19:26 Whether it be strangled, or otherwise.
- **o.** Lev. 19:26 To measure lucky or unlucky days.
- **p.** Lev. 19:27 As did the Gentiles in sign of mourning.
- **q.** Lev. 19:27 Or, cut, or tear.
- **r.** Lev. 19:28 Hebrew, soul or person.
- **s.** Lev. 19:28 By whipping your bodies or burning marks therein.
- **t.** Lev. 19:29 As did the Cyprians, and Locrians.
- **u.** Lev. 19:32 In token of reverence.
- **v.** Lev. 19:33 Or, do him wrong.
- **w.** Lev. 19:35 As in measuring the ground.
- **x.** Lev. 19:36 By these two measures he meaneth all others. Of Ephah, read Exod. 16:36, and of Hin, Exod. 29:40.

LEV. 19

1. Lev. 11:44 / Lev. 20:7 / 1 Pet. 1:16
2. Lev. 7:16
3. Lev. 23:22
4. Exod. 20:7 / Deut. 5:11 / Matt. 5:34
5. Deut. 24:14,15 / Deut. 4:14
6. Deut. 27:18
7. Exod. 23:3 / Deut. 1:17 / Deut 16:19 / Prov. 24:23 / James 2:2
8. Matt. 5:43 / Rom. 13:9 / Gal. 5:14 / James 2:8
9. Lev. 21:5
10. Deut. 14:1
11. 1Sam. 28:8
12. Exod. 22:21
13. Prov. 11:1 / Prov. 16:11 / Prov. 20:10

LEV. 20

- **a.** Lev. 20:2 By Molech he meaneth any kind of idol, Lev. 18:21.
- **b.** Lev. 20:3 Read Lev. 17:10 and 18:21.
- **c.** Lev. 20:4 Though the people be negligent to do their duty, and defend God's right, yet he will not suffer wickedness to go unpunished.
- **d.** Lev. 20:6 To esteem sorcerers or conjurers is spiritual whoredom, or idolatry.
- **e.** Lev. 20:9 He is worthy to die.
- **f.** Lev. 20:12 Or, confusion.
- **g.** Lev. 20:14 It is an execrable and detestable thing.
- **h.** Lev. 20:17 Hebrew, in the eyes of the children of their people.
- **i.** Lev. 20:18 Or, flowers.
- **j.** Lev. 20:19 Hebrew, flesh.
- **k.** Lev. 20:20 They shall be cut off from their people, and their children shall be taken as bastards, and not counted among the Israelites.
- **l.** Lev. 20:21 Read Lev.18:16.
- **m.** Lev. 20:24 Full of abundance of all things.
- **n.** Lev. 20:25 By eating them contrary to my commandment.

LEV. 20

1. Lev. 18:21
2. Lev. 11:44 / 1 Pet. 1:16
3. Exod. 21:17 / Prov. 20:20 / Matt. 15:4
4. Deut. 22:22 / John 8:4,5
5. Lev. 28:8 / Deut. 22:30
6. Lev. 18:22
7. Lev. 18:23
8. Lev. 18:19
9. Lev. 18:12,13

and I have separated you from other people that ye should be mine. 27 [15]And if a man or woman have a spirit of divination, or soothsaying in them, they shall die the death: they shall stone them to death, their blood shall be upon them.

21

2 For whom the Priests may lament. 6 How pure the Priests ought to be, both in themselves, and in their family.

1 And the Lord said unto Moses, Speak unto the Priests the sons of Aaron, and say unto them, Let none be [a]defiled by the dead among his people, 2 But by his kinsman that is near unto him: to wit, by his mother, or by his father, or by his son, or by his daughter, or by his brother, 3 Or by his sister a [b]maid, that is near unto him, which had not had an husband: for her [c]he may lament. 4 He shall not lament for the [d]Prince among his people, to pollute himself. 5 They shall not make [1]bald parts upon their head, nor shave off the locks of their beard, nor make any cuttings in their flesh. 6 They shall be holy unto their God, and not pollute the Name of their God: for the sacrifices of the Lord made by fire, and the bread of their God they do offer: therefore they shall be holy. 7 They shall not take to wife an whore, or [e]one polluted, neither shall they marry a woman divorced from her husband: for such one is holy unto his God. 8 Thou shalt [f]sanctify him therefore, for he offereth the [g]bread of thy God: he shall be holy unto thee: for I the Lord which sanctify you, am holy. 9 If a Priest's daughter fall to play the whore, she polluteth her father: therefore shall she be burnt with fire. 10 Also the high Priest among his brethren, (upon whose head the anointing oil was poured, and hath consecrated his hand to put on the garments) shall not [h]uncover his head nor rent his clothes. 11 Neither shall he go to any [i]dead body, nor make himself unclean by his father or by his mother, 12 Neither shall he go out of the [j]Sanctuary, nor pollute the holy place of his God: for the [k]crown of the anointing oil of his God is upon him: I am the Lord. 13 Also he shall take a maid unto his wife: 14 But a widow, or a divorced woman, or a polluted, or an harlot, these shall he not marry, but shall take a maid of his own [l]people to wife: 15 Neither shall he defile his [m]seed among his people: for I am the Lord which sanctify him. 16 And the Lord spake unto Moses, saying, 17 Speak unto Aaron, and say, Whosoever of thy seed in their generations hath any blemishes, shall not prease to offer the bread of his God: 18 For whosoever hath any blemish, shall not come near: as a man blind or lame, or that hath [n]a flat nose, or that hath any [o]misshapen member, 19 Or, a man that hath a broken foot, or a broken hand, 20 Or, is crookbacked, or blear-eyed, [p]or hath a blemish in his eye, or be scurvy, or scabbed, or hath his stones broken. 21 None of the seed of Aaron the Priest that hath a blemish, shall come near to offer the sacrifices of the Lord made by fire, having a blemish: he shall not prease to offer the [q]bread of his God. 22 The bread of his God, even of the [r]most holy, and [s]of the holy shall he eat: 23 But he shall not go in unto the [t]veil, nor come near the altar, because he hath a blemish, lest he pollute my Sanctuaries: for I am the Lord that sanctify them. 24 Thus spake Moses unto Aaron, and to his sons, and to all the children of Israel.

22

3 Who ought to abstain from eating the things that were offered. 19 What oblation should be offered.

1 And the Lord spake unto Moses, saying, 2 Speak unto Aaron, and to his sons, that they be [a]separated from the holy things of the children of Israel, and that they pollute not mine holy name in those things, which they hallow unto me: I am the Lord. 3 Say unto them, Whosoever he be of all your seed among your generations after you, that [b]toucheth the holy things which the children of Israel hallow unto the Lord, having his uncleanness upon him, even that person shall be cut off from my sight, I am the Lord. 4 [1]Whosoever also of the seed of Aaron is a leper, or hath a running issue, he shall not eat of the holy things until he be clean: and who so toucheth any that is [c]unclean by reason of the dead, or a man whose issue of seed runneth from him, 5 Or the man that toucheth any creeping thing, whereby he may be made unclean, or a man by whom he may take uncleanness, [d]whatsoever uncleanness he hath, 6 The person that hath touched such, shall therefore be unclean until the even, and shall not eat of the holy things, [e]except he have washed his flesh with water. 7 But when the Sun is down, he shall be clean, and shall afterward eat of the holy things: for it is his [f]food. 8 [2]Of a beast that dieth, or is rent with beasts, whereby he may be defiled, he shall not eat: I am the Lord. 9 Let them keep therefore mine ordinance, lest they bear their sin for it, and die for it, if they defile it: I the Lord sanctify them. 10 There shall no [g]stranger also eat of the holy thing, neither [h]the guest of the Priest, neither shall an hired servant eat of the holy thing: 11 But if the Priest buy any with money, he shall eat of it, also he that is born in his house: they shall eat of his meat. 12 If the Priest's daughter also be married unto a [i]stranger, she may not eat of the holy offerings. 13 Notwithstanding if the Priest's daughter be a widow or divorced, and have no child, but is returned unto her father's house, she shall eat of her father's bread, as she did in her [3]youth: but there shall no stranger eat thereof. 14 If a man eat of the holy thing unwittingly, he shall put the [j]fifth part thereunto, and give it unto the Priest with the hallowed thing. 15 So shall they not defile the holy things of the children of Israel, which they offer unto the Lord, 16 Neither cause the people to bear the iniquity of their [k]trespass, while they eat their holy thing: for I the Lord do hallow them. 17 And the Lord spake unto Moses, saying, 18 Speak unto Aaron, and to his sons, and to all the children of Israel, and say unto them, Whosoever he be of the house of Israel, or of the strangers in Israel, that will offer his sacrifice for all their vows, and for all their free offerings, which they use to offer unto the Lord for a burnt offering, 19 Ye shall offer of your free mind a male without blemish of the beeves, of the sheep, or of the goats. 20 Ye shall not offer anything that hath a blemish: for that shall not be acceptable for you. 21 [4]And whosoever bringeth a peace offering unto the Lord to accomplish his vow, or for a free offering of the beeves, or of the sheep, his free offering shall be perfect, no blemish shall be in it. 22 Blind, or broken, or maimed, or having a [l]wen, or scurvy, or scabbed: these shall ye not offer unto the Lord, nor make an offering by fire of these upon the Altar of the Lord. 23 Yet a bullock, or a sheep that hath any [5]member superfluous, or lacking, such mayest thou present for a free offering, but for a vow it shall not be accepted. 24 Ye shall not offer unto the Lord that which is bruised or crushed, or broken, or cut away, neither shall ye make an offering thereof in your land, 25 Neither [m]of the hand of a stranger shall ye offer the bread of your God of any of these, because their corruption is in them, there is a blemish in them: therefore shall they not be accepted for you. 26 And the Lord spake unto Moses, saying, 27 When a bullock, or a sheep, or a goat shall be brought forth, it shall be even seven days under his dam: and from the eighth day forth it shall be accepted for a sacrifice made by fire unto the Lord. 28 As for the cow or the ewe, ye shall not [6]kill her, and her young both in one day. 29 So when ye will offer a thank offering unto the Lord, ye shall offer willingly. 30 The same day shall it be eaten, ye shall leave [7]none of it to the morrow: I am the Lord. 31 Therefore shall ye keep my Commandments and do them: for I am the Lord. 32 Neither shall ye [n]pollute my holy Name, but I will be hallowed among the children of Israel I the Lord sanctify you, 33 Which have brought you out of the land of Egypt, to be your God: I am the Lord.

23

2 The feasts of the Lord. 3 The Sabbath. 5 The Passover. 6 The feast of unleavened bread. 10 The feast of firstfruits. 16 Whitsuntide. 24 The feast of blowing trumpets. 34 The feast of Tabernacles.

1 And the Lord spake unto Moses, saying, 2 Speak unto the children of Israel, and say unto them, The feasts of the Lord which ye shall call the holy [a]assemblies, even these are my feasts. 3 [1]Six days [b]shall work be done, but in the seventh day shall be the Sabbath of rest, an holy [c]convocation: ye shall do no work therein, it is the Sabbath of the Lord, in all your dwellings. 4 These are the feasts of the Lord, and holy convocations, which ye shall proclaim in their [d]seasons. 5 In the first month and in the fourteenth day of the month at evening shall be the Passover of the Lord. 6 And on the fifteenth day of this month shall be the feast [2]of unleavened bread unto the Lord: seven days ye shall eat unleavened bread. 7 In the first day ye shall have an holy convocation: ye shall do no [e]servile

---

10. Lev. 18:26
11. Lev. 18:25
12. Deut. 9:5
13. Lev. 11:2,3 / Deut. 14:4
14. Lev. 20:7
15. Deut. 18:11 / 1Sam. 25:7

LEV. 21

a. Lev. 21:1 By touching the dead, lamenting, or being at their burial.
b. Lev. 21:3 For being married she seemed to be cut off from his family.
c. Lev. 21:3 Hebrew, he may be defiled.
d. Lev. 21:4 The Priest was permitted to mourn for his next kindred only.
e. Lev. 21:7 Which hath an evil name or is defamed.
f. Lev. 21:8 Thou shalt count them holy and reverence them.
g. Lev. 21:8 The showbread.
h. Lev. 21:10 He shall use no such ceremonies as the mourners observed.
i. Lev. 21:11 Or, to the houses of the dead.
j. Lev. 21:12 To go to the dead.
k. Lev. 21:12 For by his anointing he was preferred to the other Priests and therefore could not lament the dead, lest he should have polluted his holy anointing.
l. Lev. 21:14 Not only of his tribe, but of all Israel.
m. Lev. 21:15 By marrying any unchaste or defamed woman.
n. Lev. 21:18 Which is deformed or bruised.
o. Lev. 21:18 As not of equal proportion, or having in number more or less.
p. Lev. 21:20 Or that hath a web or pearl.
q. Lev. 21:21 As the showbread, and meat offerings.
r. Lev. 21:22 As of sacrifice for sin.
s. Lev. 21:22 As of the tenths and firstfruits.
t. Lev. 21:23 Into the Sanctuary.

LEV. 21

1. Lev. 19:27

LEV. 22

a. Lev. 22:2 Meaning, that the Priests abstain from eating, so long as they are polluted.
b. Lev. 22:3 To eat thereof.
c. Lev. 22:4 By touching any dead thing, or being at burial of the dead.
d. Lev. 22:5 Hebrew, according to all his uncleanness.
e. Lev. 22:6 Or, until.
f. Lev. 22:7 Or, bread.
g. Lev. 22:10 Which is not of the tribe of Levi.
h. Lev. 22:10 Some read, the servant which had his ear bored, and would not go free, Exod. 21:6.
i. Lev. 22:12 Who is not of the Priest's kindred.
j. Lev. 22:14 He shall give that and a fifth part over.
k. Lev. 22:16 For if they did not offer for their error, the people by their example might commit the like offense.
l. Lev. 22:22 Or, wart.
m. Lev. 22:25 Ye shall not receive any imperfect thing of a stranger, to make it the Lord's offering: which he calleth the bread of the Lord.
n. Lev. 22:32 For whosoever doth otherwise than God commandeth polluted his Name.

LEV. 22

1. Lev. 15:2
2. Exod. 12:21 / Ezek. 45:31
3. Lev. 10:14
4. Deut. 15:21
5. Lev. 21:12
6. Deut. 22:6
7. Lev. 7:15

LEV. 23

a. Lev. 23:2 Or, convocations.
b. Lev. 23:3 Or, ye may work.
c. Lev. 23:3 Or, assembly.
d. Lev. 23:4 For the Sabbath was kept every week, and these others were kept but once every year.

work therein. **8** Also ye shall offer sacrifice made by fire unto the Lord seven days, and in the [f]seventh day shall be an holy convocation: ye shall do no servile work therein. **9** And the Lord spake unto Moses, saying, **10** Speak unto the children of Israel, and say unto them, When ye be come into the land which I give unto you, and reap the harvest thereof, then ye shall bring [g]a sheaf of the firstfruits of your harvest unto the Priest, **11** And he shall shake the sheaf before the Lord, that it may be acceptable for you: the morrow after the [h]Sabbath, the Priest shall shake it. **12** And that day when ye shake the sheaf, shall ye prepare a lamb without blemish of a year old, for a burnt offering unto the Lord: **13** And the meat offering thereof shall be two [i]tenth deals of fine flour mingled with oil, for a sacrifice made by fire unto the Lord of sweet savor: and the drink offering thereof the fourth part [j]of an Hin of wine. **14** And ye shall eat neither bread nor parched corn, nor [k]green ears until the selfsame day that ye have brought an offering unto your God: this shall be a Law forever in your generations and in all your dwellings. **15** Ye shall count also to you from the morrow after the [l]Sabbath, even from the day that ye shall bring the sheaf of the shake offering, seven [m]Sabbaths, they shall be complete. **16** Unto the morrow after the seventh Sabbath shall ye number fifty days: then ye shall bring a new meat offering unto the Lord. **17** Ye shall bring out of your habitations bread for the shake offering: they shall be two loaves of two tenth deals of fine flour, which shall be baken with [n]leaven for firstfruits unto the Lord. **18** Also ye shall offer with the bread seven lambs without blemish of one year old, and a young bullock and two rams: they shall be for a burnt offering unto the Lord, with their meat offerings and their drink offerings, for a sacrifice made by fire of a sweet savor unto the Lord. **19** Then ye shall prepare an he goat for a sin offering, and two lambs of one year old for peace offerings. **20** And the Priest shall shake them to and fro with the bread of the firstfruits before the Lord, and with the two lambs: they shall be holy to the Lord, for the [o]Priest. **21** So ye shall proclaim the same day, that it may be an holy convocation unto you: ye shall do no servile work therein: it shall be an ordinance forever in all your dwellings, throughout your generations. **22** [3]And when you reap the harvest of your land, thou shalt not rid clean the corners of thy field when thou reapest, neither shalt thou make any aftergathering of thy harvest, but shalt leave them unto the poor and to the stranger, I am the Lord your God. **23** And the Lord spake unto Moses, saying, **24** Speak unto the children of Israel, and say, In the [p]seventh month, and in the first day of the month shall ye [q]have a Sabbath, for the remembrance of [r]blowing the trumpets, an holy convocation. **25** Ye shall do no servile work therein, but offer sacrifice made by fire unto the Lord. **26** And the Lord spake unto Moses, saying, **27** The [4]tenth also of this seventh month, shall be a day of reconciliation: it shall be an holy convocation unto you, and ye shall [s]humble your souls, and offer sacrifice made by fire unto the Lord. **28** And ye shall do no work that same day: for it is a day of reconciliation, to make an atonement for you before the Lord your God. **29** For every person that humbleth not himself that same day, shall even be cut off from his people. **30** And every person that shall do any work that same day, the same person also will I destroy from among his people. **31** Ye shall do no manner work therefore: this shall be a law forever in your generations, throughout all your dwellings. **32** This shall be unto you a Sabbath of rest, and ye shall humble your souls: in the ninth day of the month at even, from [t]even to even shall ye [u]celebrate your Sabbath. **33** And the Lord spake unto Moses, saying, **34** Speak unto the children of Israel, and say, [5]In the fifteenth day of this seventh month shall be for seven days the feast of Tabernacles unto the Lord. **35** In the first day shall be an holy convocation: ye shall do no servile work therein. **36** Seven days ye shall offer [6]sacrifice made by fire unto the Lord, and in the eighth day shall be an holy convocation unto you, and ye shall offer sacrifices made by fire unto the Lord: it is the [v]solemn assembly, ye shall do no servile work therein. **37** These are the feasts of the Lord (which ye shall call holy convocations) to offer sacrifice made by fire unto the Lord, as burnt offering, and meat offering, [w]sacrifice, and drink offerings, every one upon his day, **38** Beside the Sabbaths of the Lord, and beside your gifts, and beside all your vows, and beside all your free offerings, which ye shall give unto the Lord. **39** But in the fifteenth day of the seventh month, when ye have gathered in the fruit of the land, ye shall keep an holy feast unto the Lord seven days: in the first day shall be a [x]Sabbath: likewise in the eighth day shall be a Sabbath. **40** And ye shall take you in the first day the fruit of goodly trees, branches of palm trees, and the boughs of [y]thick trees, and willows of the brook, and shall rejoice before the Lord your God seven days. **41** So ye shall keep this feast unto the Lord seven days in the year, by a perpetual ordinance through your generations: in the seventh month shall you keep it. **42** Ye shall dwell in booths seven days: all that are Israelites born, shall dwell in booths, **43** That your posterity may know that I have made the children of Israel to dwell in [z]booths, when I brought them out of the land of Egypt: I am the Lord your God. **44** So Moses declared unto the children of Israel the feasts of the Lord.

24

The oil for the lamps. 5 The showbread. 14 The blasphemer shall be stoned. 17 He that killeth shall be killed.

1 And the Lord spake unto Moses, saying, **2** [a]Command the children of Israel that they bring unto thee pure oil olive beaten, for the light, to cause the lamps to burn continually. **3** Without the veil [b]of the Testimony, in the Tabernacle of the Congregation, shall Aaron dress them, both even and morning before the Lord always: this shall be a law forever through your generations. **4** He shall dress the lamps upon the [1]pure Candlestick before the Lord perpetually. **5** Also thou shalt take fine flour, and bake twelve [2]cakes thereof: two [c]tenth deals shall be in one cake. **6** And thou shalt set them in two rows, six in a row upon the pure table before the Lord. **7** Thou shalt also put pure incense upon the rows, that [d]instead of the bread it may be for a remembrance, and an offering made by fire unto the Lord. **8** Every Sabbath he shall put them in rows before the Lord evermore, receiving them of the children of Israel for an everlasting Covenant. **9** [3]And the bread shall be Aaron's and his sons', and they shall eat it in the holy place: for it is most holy unto him of the offerings of the Lord made by fire by a perpetual ordinance. **10** And there went [e]out among the children of Israel the son of an Israelitish woman, whose father was an Egyptian: and this son of the Israelitish woman, and a man of Israel strove together in the host. **11** So the Israelitish woman's son [f]blasphemed the Name of the Lord, and cursed, and they brought him unto Moses (his mother's name also was Shelomith, the daughter of Dibri of the tribe of Dan) **12** And they [4]put him in ward, till he told them the mind of the Lord. **13** Then the Lord spake unto Moses, saying, **14** Bring the blasphemer without the host, and let all that heard him, [5]put their hands upon his head, and let all the Congregation stone him. **15** And thou shalt speak unto the children of Israel, saying, Whosoever curseth his God, shall [g]bear his sin. **16** And he that blasphemeth the Name of the Lord, shall be put to death: all the Congregation shall stone him to death: as well the stranger, as he that is born in the land: when he blasphemeth the Name of the Lord, let him be slain. **17** [6]He also that [h]killeth any man, he shall be put to death. **18** And he that killeth a beast, he shall restore it, [i]beast for beast. **19** Also if a man cause any blemish in his neighbor: as he hath done, so shall it be done to him: **20** [7]Breach for breach, eye for eye, tooth for tooth: such a blemish as he hath made in any, such shall be repaid to him. **21** And he that killeth a beast, shall restore it: but he that killeth a man, shall be slain. **22** Ye shall have one [8]law: it shall be as well for the stranger as for one born in the country, for I am the Lord your God. **23** Then [j]Moses told the children of Israel, and they brought the blasphemer out of the host, and stoned him with stones: so the children of Israel did as the Lord had commanded Moses.

25

2 The Sabbath of the seventh year. 8 The Jubilee in the fiftieth year. 14 Not to oppress their brethren. 23 The sale and redeeming of lands, houses and persons.

1 And the Lord spake unto Moses in mount Sinai, saying, **2** Speak unto the children of Israel, and say unto them, When ye shall come into the land which I give you, the [1]land shall [a]keep Sabbath unto the Lord. **3** [b]Six years thou shalt sow thy field, and six years thou shalt cut thy vineyard, and gather the fruit

---

e. Lev. 23:7 Or, bodily labor, save about that which one must eat, Exod. 22:16.
f. Lev. 23:8 The first day of the feast and the seventh were kept holy: in the rest they might work, except any feast were intermeddled, as the feast of unleavened bread, the fifteenth day, and the feast of sheaves the sixteenth day.
g. Lev. 23:10 Or, an Omer, read Deut. 24:19; Ruth 2:15; Ps. 129:7.
h. Lev. 23:11 That is, the second Sabbath of the Passover.
i. Lev. 23:13 Which is, the fifth part of an Ephah, or two Omers: read Exod. 16:16.
j. Lev. 23:13 Read Exod. 29:40.
k. Lev. 23:14 Or, full ears.
l. Lev. 23:15 That is the seventh day after the first Sabbath of the Passover.
m. Lev. 23:15 Or, weeks.
n. Lev. 23:17 Because the Priest should eat them, as Lev. 7:13, and they should not be offered to the Lord upon the altar.
o. Lev. 23:20 That is, offered to the Lord, and the rest should be for the Priests.
p. Lev. 23:24 That is, about the end of September.
q. Lev. 23:24 Or, an holy day to the Lord.
r. Lev. 23:24 Which blowing was to put them in remembrance of the manifold feasts that were in that month, and of the Jubilee.
s. Lev. 23:27 By fasting and prayer.
t. Lev. 23:32 Which containeth a night and a day: yet they took it but for their natural day.
u. Lev. 23:32 Hebrew, rest your Sabbath.
v. Lev. 23:36 Or, a day wherein the people are stayed from all work.
w. Lev. 23:37 Or, peace offering.
x. Lev. 23:39 Or, a solemn feast.
y. Lev. 23:40 Or, of boughs thick with leaves.
z. Lev. 23:43 In the wilderness, forasmuch as they would not credit Joshua and Caleb, when they returned from spying the land of Canaan.

LEV. 23

1. Exod. 20:9,10
2. Exod. 12:15 / Num. 28:17
3. Lev. 19:9 / Deut. 24:19
4. Lev. 19:29,30 / Num. 29:7
5. Num. 29:12 / John 7:2,37
6. Exod. 29:18

LEV. 24

a. Lev. 24:2 Read Exod. 27:20.
b. Lev. 24:3 Which veil separated the holiest of all, where was the Ark of the Testimony from the Sanctuary.
c. Lev. 24:5 That is, two Omers, read Exod. 16:16.
d. Lev. 24:7 For it was burnt every Sabbath, when the bread was taken away.
e. Lev. 24:10 Meaning, out of his tent.
f. Lev. 24:11 By swearing or despiting God.
g. Lev. 24:15 Shall be punished.
h. Lev. 24:17 Hebrew, smiteth the soul of any man.
i. Lev. 24:18 Hebrew, soul for soul.
j. Lev. 24:23 Because the punishment was not yet appointed by the law for the blasphemer, Moses consulted with the Lord, and told the people what God commanded.

LEV. 24

1. Exod. 31:8
2. Exod. 25:30
3. Exod. 29:48 / Lev. 8:31 / Matt. 12:1,5
4. Num. 25:34
5. Deut. 13:9 / Deut. 17:7
6. Exod. 21:12/Deut. 19:4,11
7. Exod. 21:24 / Deut. 19:21 / Matt. 5:38
8. Exod. 12:49

LEV. 25

a. Lev. 25:2 Hebrew, shall rest a rest.

thereof. **4** But the seventh year shall be a Sabbath of rest unto the land: it shall be
the Lord's Sabbath: thou shalt neither sow thy field nor cut thy vineyard. **5** That
which groweth of its [c]own accord of thy harvest, thou shalt not reap, neither gather
the grapes that thou hast left [d]unlabored: for it shall be a year of rest unto the
land. **6** And the [e]rest of the land shall be meat for you, even for thee and for thy
servant, and for thy maid, and for thy hired servant, and for the stranger that
sojourneth with thee: **7** And for thy cattle, and for the beasts that are in thy land,
shall all the increase thereof be meat. **8** Also thou shalt number seven [f]Sabbaths
of years unto thee, even seven times seven years: and the space of the seven Sabba-
ths of years will be unto thee nine and forty years. **9** [g]Then thou shalt cause to
blow the trumpet of the Jubilee in the tenth day of the seventh month: even in the
day of the reconciliation shall ye make the trumpet blow throughout all your
land. **10** And ye shall hallow that year, even the fiftieth year, and proclaim liberty
in the land to all the [h]inhabitants thereof: it shall be the Jubilee unto you, and ye
shall return every man unto his [i]possession, and every man shall return unto his
family. **11** This fiftieth year shall be a year of Jubilee unto you: ye shall not sow,
neither reap that which groweth of itself, neither gather the grapes thereof that are
left unlabored. **12** For it is the Jubilee, it shall be holy unto you: ye shall eat of
the increase thereof out of the field. **13** In the year of this Jubilee, ye shall return
every man unto his possession. **14** And when thou sellest ought to thy neighbor,
or buyest at thy neighbor's hand, ye shall [j]not oppress one another. **15** But accor-
ding to the number of [k]years after the Jubilee, thou shalt buy of thy neighbor: also
according to the number of the years of the revenues, he shall sell unto
thee. **16** According to the multitude of years, thou shalt increase the price there-
of, and according to the fewness of years thou shalt abate the price of it: for the
number of [l]fruits doth he sell unto thee. **17** Oppress not ye therefore any man
his neighbor, but thou shalt fear thy God: for I am the Lord your God. **18** Whe-
refore ye shall obey mine ordinances, and keep my laws, and do them, and ye shall
dwell in the land [m]in safety. **19** And the land shall give her fruit, and ye shall eat
your fill, and dwell therein in safety. **20** And if ye shall say, What shall we eat the
seventh year, for we shall not sow, nor gather in our increase? **21** I will [n]send my
blessing upon you in the sixth year, and it shall bring forth fruit for three ye-
ars. **22** And ye shall sow the eighth year, and eat of the old fruit until the ninth
year: until the fruit thereof come ye shall eat the old. **23** Also the land shall not
be sold to be [o]cut off from the family: for the land is mine, and ye be but strangers
and sojourners with me. **24** Therefore in all the land of your possession ye shall
[p]grant a redemption of the land. **25** If thy brother be impoverished, and sell his
possession, then his redeemer shall come, even his near kinsman, and buy out that,
which his [q]brother sold. **26** And if he have no redeemer, but [r]hath gotten and
found to buy it out, **27** Then shall he [s]count the years of his sale, and restore the
overplus to the man, to whom he sold it: so shall he return to his posses-
sion. **28** But if he cannot get sufficient to restore to him, then that which is sold,
shall remain in the hand of him that hath bought it, until the year of the Jubilee:
and in the Jubilee it shall come [t]out, and he shall return unto his posses-
sion. **29** Likewise if a man sell a dwelling house in a walled city, he may buy it
out again within a whole year after it is sold: within a year may he buy it
out. **30** But if it be not bought out within the space of a full year, then the house
that is in the walled city, shall be stablished, [u]as cut off from the family, to him that
bought it, throughout his generations: it shall not go out in the Jubilee. **31** But
the houses of villages which have no walls round about them, shall be esteemed as
the field of the country: they may be bought out again, and shall [v]go out in the
Jubilee. **32** Notwithstanding, the cities of the Levites, and the houses of the cities
of their possession, may the Levites redeem [w]at all seasons. **33** And if a man pur-
chase of the Levites, the house that was sold, and the city of their possession shall
go out in the Jubilee: for the houses of the cities of the Levites are their possession
among the children of Israel. **34** But the field of the [x]suburbs of their cities shall
not be sold: for it is their perpetual possession. **35** Moreover, if thy brother be
impoverished, and [y]fallen in decay with thee, thou shalt relieve him, and as a stran-
ger and sojourner, so shall he live with thee. **36** [2]Thou shalt take no usury of
him, nor vantage, but thou shalt fear thy God, that thy brother may live with
thee. **37** Thou shalt not give him thy money to usury, nor lend him thy vittles
for increase. **38** I am the Lord your God, which have brought you out of the
land of Egypt, to give you the land of Canaan, and to be your God. **39** [3]If thy
brother also that dwelleth by thee be impoverished, and be sold unto thee, thou
shalt not compel him to serve as a bond servant, **40** But as an hired servant, and
as a sojourner he shall be with thee: he shall serve thee unto the year of Jubi-
lee. **41** Then shall he depart from thee, both he and his children with him, and
shall return unto his family, and unto the possession of his fathers shall he re-
turn: **42** For they are my servants, whom I brought out of the land of Egypt:
they shall not [z]be sold as bondmen are sold. **43** [4]Thou shalt not rule over him
cruelly, but shalt fear thy God. **44** Thy bond servant also, and thy bondmaid,
which thou shalt have, shall be of the heathen that are round about you: of them
shall ye buy servants and maids. **45** And moreover, of the children of the stran-
gers that are sojourners among you, of them shall ye buy, and of their families that
are with you which they begat in your land: these shall be your [aa]posses-
sion. **46** So ye shall take them, as inheritance for your children after you to pos-
sess them by inheritance, ye shall use their labors forever: but over your brethren
the children of Israel ye shall not rule one over another with cruelty. **47** If a
sojourner or a stranger dwelling by thee [ab]get riches, and thy brother by him be
impoverished, and sell himself unto the stranger or sojourner dwelling by thee, or
to the stock of the stranger's family, **48** After that he is sold, he may be bought
out: one of his brethren may buy him out. **49** Or his uncle, or his uncle's son
may buy him out, or any of the kindred of his flesh among his family, may redeem
him: either if he can [ac]get so much, he may buy himself out. **50** Then he shall
reckon with his buyer from the year that he was sold to him, unto the year of Jubi-
lee: and the money of his sale shall be according to the number of [ad]years: accor-
ding to the time of an hired servant shall he be with him. **51** If there be many
years behind, according to them shall he give again for his deliverance, of the mo-
ney that he was bought for. **52** If there remain but few years unto the year of
Jubilee, then he shall count with him, and according to his years give again for his
redemption. **53** He shall be with him year by year as an hired servant: he shall
not rule cruelly over him in thy [ae]sight. **54** And if he be not redeemed thus, he
shall go out in the year of Jubilee, he, and his children with him. **55** For unto me
the children of Israel are servants, they are my servants whom I have brought out
of the land of Egypt: I am the Lord your God.

26

1 Idolatry forbidden. 3 A blessing to them that keep the commandments. 14 The curse to them that break them. 42 God promiseth to remember his covenant.

1 Ye shall make you none idols nor graven image, neither rear you up any [1]pil-
lar, neither shall ye set [a]any image of stone in your land to bow down to it: for I am
the Lord your God. **2** Ye shall keep my Sabbaths, and [2]reverence my Sanctuary:
I am the Lord. **3** [3]If ye walk in mine ordinances, and keep my commandments,
and do them, **4** I will then send you [b]rain in due season, and the land shall yield
her increase, and the trees of the field shall give their fruit. **5** And your threshing
shall reach unto the vintage, and the vintage shall reach unto sowing time, and
you shall eat your bread in plenteousness, and dwell in your land safely. **6** And
I will send peace in the land, and ye shall sleep, and none [4]shall make you afraid:
also I [c]will rid evil beasts out of the land, and the [d]sword shall not go through your
land. **7** Also ye shall chase your enemies, and they shall fall before you upon
the sword. **8** [5]And five of you shall chase an hundred, and an hundred of you
shall put ten thousand to flight, and your enemies shall fall before you upon the
sword. **9** For [e]I will have respect unto you, and make you increase, and multi-
ply you, and [f]stablish my covenant with you. **10** Ye shall eat also old store, and
carry out old because of the new. **11** [6]And I will set my [g]Tabernacle among you,
and my soul shall not loathe you. **12** Also I will walk among you, and I will be
your God, and ye shall be my people. **13** I am the Lord your God which have
brought you out of the land of Egypt, that ye should not be their bondmen, and
I have broken the [h]bonds of your yoke, and made you go upright. **14** [7]But if ye
will not obey me, nor do all these commandments, **15** And if ye shall despise
mine ordinances, either if your soul abhor my laws, so that ye will not do all my
Commandments, but break my [i]Covenant, **16** Then will I also do this unto
you, I will appoint over you [j]fearfulness, a consumption, and the burning ague to

---

b. Lev. 25:3 The Jews began the count of this year in September: for then all the fruits were gathered.
c. Lev. 25:5 By reason of the corn that fell out of the ears the year past.
d. Lev. 25:5 Or, which thou hast separated from thyself, and consecrated to God for the poor.
e. Lev. 25:6 That which the land bringeth forth in her rest.
f. Lev. 25:8 Or, weeks.
g. Lev. 25:9 In the beginning of the 50th year was the Jubilee, so called, because the joyful tidings of liberty were publicly proclaimed by the sound of a cornet.
h. Lev. 25:10 Which were in bondage.
i. Lev. 25:10 Because the tribes should neither have their possessions or families diminished nor confounded.
j. Lev. 25:14 By deceit, or otherwise.
k. Lev. 25:15 If the Jubilee to come be near, thou shalt sell better cheap: if it be far off, dearer.
l. Lev. 25:16 And not the full possession of the land.
m. Lev. 25:18 Or, boldly without fear.
n. Lev. 25:21 Hebrew, I will command.
o. Lev. 25:23 It could not be sold forever, but must return to the family in the Jubilee.
p. Lev. 25:24 Ye shall sell it on condition that it may be redeemed.
q. Lev. 25:25 Or, kinsman.
r. Lev. 25:26 Hebrew, his hand hath gotten.
s. Lev. 25:27 Abating the money of the years past, and paying for the rest of the years to come.
t. Lev. 25:28 From his hand that bought it.
u. Lev. 25:30 That is, forever, read verse 23.
v. Lev. 25:31 Or, return.
w. Lev. 25:32 Hebrew, forever.
x. Lev. 25:34 Where the Levites kept their cattle.
y. Lev. 25:35 In Hebrew it is, if his hand shake: meaning, if he stretch forth his hand for help as one in misery.
z. Lev. 25:42 Unto perpetual servitude.
aa. Lev. 25:45 For they shall not be bought out at the Jubilee.
ab. Lev. 25:47 Hebrew, his hand take hold.
ac. Lev. 25:49 If he be able.
ad. Lev. 25:50 Which remain yet to the Jubilee.
ae. Lev. 25:53 Thou shalt not suffer him to entreat him rigorously, if thou know it.

LEV. 25
1. Exod. 23:10
2. Exod. 22:25 / Deut. 23:19 / Prov. 28:8 / Ezek. 18:8 / Ezek 22:12
3. Exod. 21:2 / Deut. 15:12 / Jer. 34:14
4. Eph. 6:9 / Col. 4:1

LEV. 26
a. Lev. 26:1 Or, stone having any imagery.
b. Lev. 26:4 By promising abundance of earthly things, he stirreth the mind to consider the rich treasures of the spiritual blessings.
c. Lev. 26:6 Hebrew, will cause the evil beast to cease.
d. Lev. 26:6 Ye shall have no war.
e. Lev. 26:9 Hebrew, I will turn unto you.
f. Lev. 26:9 Perform that which I have promised.
g. Lev. 26:11 I will be daily present with you.
h. Lev. 26:13 I have set you at full liberty, whereas before ye were as beasts tied in bands.
i. Lev. 26:15 Which I made with you in choosing you to be my people.
j. Lev. 26:16 Or, an hasty plague.

consume the eyes, and make the heart heavy, and you shall sow your seed in vain: for your enemies shall eat it: **17** And I will set [k]my face against you, and ye shall fall before your enemies, and they that hate you, shall reign over you, [8]and ye shall flee when none pursueth you. **18** And if ye will not for these things obey me, then will I punish you [l]seven times more, according to your sins, **19** And I will break the pride of your power, and I will make your heaven as [m]iron, and your earth as brass: **20** And your [n]strength shall be spent in vain: neither shall your land give her increase, neither shall the trees of the land give their fruit. **21** And if ye walk [o]stubbornly against me, and will not obey me, I will then bring seven times more plagues upon you, according to your sins. **22** I will also send wild beasts upon you, which shall [p]spoil you, and destroy your cattle, and make you few in number: so your [q]highways shall be desolate. **23** Yet if by these ye will not be reformed by me, but walk stubbornly against me, **24** Then will I also walk [9]stubbornly against you, and I will smite you yet seven times for your sins: **25** And I will send a sword upon you, that shall avenge the quarrel of my Covenant: and when ye are gathered in your cities, I will send the pestilence among you, and ye shall be delivered into the hand of the enemy. **26** When I shall break the [r]staff of your bread, then ten women shall bake your bread in one [s]oven, and they shall deliver your bread again by weight, and ye shall eat, but not be satisfied. **27** Yet if ye will not for this obey me, but walk against me stubbornly, **28** Then will I walk stubbornly in mine anger against you, and I will also chastise you seven times more according to your sins. **29** [10]And ye shall eat the flesh of your sons, and the flesh of your daughters shall ye devour. **30** I will also destroy your high places, and [11]cut away your images, and cast your carcasses upon the [t]bodies of your idols, and my soul shall abhor you. **31** And I will make your cities desolate, and bring your Sanctuary unto naught, and [u]will not smell the savor of your sweet odors. **32** I will also bring the land unto a wilderness, and your enemies which dwell therein, shall be astonished thereat. **33** Also I will scatter you among the heathen, and [v]will draw out a sword after you, and your land shall be waste, and your cities shall be desolate. **34** Then shall the land enjoy her [12]Sabbaths, as long as it lieth void, and ye shall be in your enemies' land: then shall the land rest, and enjoy her Sabbaths. **35** All the days that it lieth void, it shall rest, because it did not rest in your [w]Sabbaths, when ye dwelt upon it. **36** And upon them that are left of you, I will send even a [x]faintness into their hearts in the land of your enemies, and the sound of a leaf shaken shall chase them, and they shall [y]flee as fleeing from a sword, and they shall fall, no man pursuing them. **37** They shall fall also one upon another, as before a sword, though none pursue them, and ye shall not be able to stand before your enemies: **38** And ye shall perish among the heathen, and the land of your enemies shall eat you up. **39** And they that are left of you, shall pine away for their iniquity, in your enemies' lands, and for the iniquities of their fathers shall they pine away with [z]them also. **40** Then they shall confess their iniquity, and the wickedness of their fathers for their trespass, which they have trespassed against me, and also because they have walked stubbornly against me. **41** Therefore I will walk stubbornly against them, and bring them into the land of their enemies: so then their uncircumcised hearts shall be humbled, and then they shall [aa]willingly bear the punishment of their iniquity. **42** Then I will remember my Covenant with Jacob, and my Covenant also with Isaac, and also my Covenant with Abraham will I remember, and will remember the land. **43** [ab]The land also in the mean season shall be left of them, and shall enjoy her Sabbaths while she lieth waste without them, but they shall willingly suffer the punishment of their iniquity, because they despised my Laws, and because their soul abhorred mine ordinances. **44** Yet notwithstanding this, when they shall be in the land of their enemies, [13]I will not cast them away, neither will I abhor them, to destroy them utterly, nor to break my Covenant with them: for I am the Lord their God: **45** But I will remember for them the [ac]Covenant of old, when I brought them out of the land of Egypt in the sight of the heathen, that I might be their God: I am the Lord. **46** These are the Ordinances, and the Judgments, and the Laws, which the Lord made between him, and the children of Israel, in mount [ad]Sinai by the hand of Moses.

27

2 Of divers vows, and the redemption of the same. 28 A thing separate from the use of man, cannot be sold nor redeemed, but remained to the Lord.

1 Moreover, the Lord spake unto Moses, saying, **2** Speak unto the children of Israel, and say unto them, If any man shall make a vow of [a]a person unto the Lord, by [b]thy estimation, **3** Then thy estimation shall be thus: a male from twenty years old unto sixty years old shall be by thy estimation even fifty [c]shekels of silver, after the shekel of the Sanctuary. **4** But if it be a female, then thy valuation shall be thirty shekels. **5** And from five years old to twenty years old, thy valuation shall be for the male twenty shekels, and for the female ten shekels. **6** But from a [d]month old unto five years old, thy price of the male shall be five shekels of silver, and thy price of the female, three shekels of silver. **7** And from sixty years old and above, if he be a male, then thy price shall be fifteen shekels, and for the female ten shekels. **8** But if he be poorer [e]than thou hast esteemed him, then shall he present himself before the Priest, and the Priest shall value him, according to the ability of him that vowed, so shall the Priest value him. **9** And if it be a [f]beast, whereof men bring an offering unto the Lord, all that one giveth of such unto the Lord, shall be holy. **10** He shall not alter it nor change it, a good for a bad, nor a bad for a good: and if he change beast for beast, then both this and that, which was changed for it, shall be [g]holy. **11** And if it be any unclean beast, of which men do not offer a sacrifice unto the Lord, he shall then present the beast before the Priest. **12** And the Priest shall value it, whether it be good or bad: and as thou valuest it, which art the Priest, so shall it be. **13** But if he will buy it again, then he shall give the fifth part of it more above thy valuation. **14** Also when a man shall dedicate his house to be holy unto the Lord, then the Priest shall value it, whether it be good or bad, and as the Priest shall price it, [h]so shall the value be. **15** But if he that sanctified it, will redeem his house, then he shall give thereto the fifth part of money more than thy estimation, and it shall be his. **16** If also a man dedicate to the Lord any ground of his inheritance, then shalt thou esteem it according to the [i]seed thereof, an [j]Homer of barley seed shall be at fifty shekels of silver. **17** If he dedicate his field immediately from the year of Jubilee, it shall be worth as thou dost esteem it. **18** But if he dedicate his field after the Jubilee, then the Priest shall reckon him the money according to the years that remain unto the year of Jubilee, and it shall be abated by thy estimation. **19** And if he that dedicateth it, will redeem the field, then he shall put the fifth part of the price, that thou esteemedst it at, thereunto, and it shall remain his. **20** And if he will not redeem the field, but the Priest [k]sell the field to another man, it shall be redeemed no more. **21** But the field shall be holy to the Lord, when it goeth out in the Jubilee, as a field [l]separate from common uses: the possession thereof shall be the Priest's. **22** If a man also dedicate unto the Lord a field which he hath bought, which is not of the ground of his inheritance, **23** Then the Priest shall set the price to him, as [1]thou esteemest it, unto the year of Jubilee, and he shall give [m]thy price the same day, as a thing holy unto the Lord. **24** But in the year of Jubilee, the field shall return unto him, of whom it was bought: to him I say, whose inheritance the land was. **25** And all the valuation shall be according to the shekel of the [2]Sanctuary: a shekel containeth twenty gerahs. **26** [3]Notwithstanding the firstborn of the beasts, because it is the Lord's firstborn, none shall dedicate such, be it bullock, or sheep: For it is the [n]Lord's. **27** But if it be an unclean beast, then he shall redeem it by thy valuation, and give the fifth part more thereto: and if it be not redeemed, then it shall be sold, according to thy estimation. **28** [4]Notwithstanding, nothing separate from the common use that a man doth separate unto the Lord of all that he hath (whether it be man or beast, or land of his inheritance) may be sold nor redeemed: for everything separate from the common use is most holy unto the Lord. **29** Nothing separate from the common use, which shall be separate from man, shall be redeemed, but [o]die the death. **30** Also all the tithe of the land both of the seed of the ground, and of the fruit of the trees is the Lord's: it is holy to the Lord. **31** But if a man will redeem any of his tithe, he shall add the [p]fifth part thereto. **32** And every tithe of bullock, and of sheep, and of all that goeth under the [q]rod, the tenth shall be holy unto the Lord. **33** He shall not look if it be good or bad, neither shall he change it: else if he change it, both it, and that it was changed withal, shall be holy, and it shall not be redeemed. **34** These are the Commandments which the Lord commanded by Moses unto the children of Israel in Mount Sinai.

---

k. Lev. 26:17 Read Lev.17:10.
l. Lev. 26:18 That is, more extremely.
m. Lev. 26:19 Ye shall have drought and barrenness, Hag. 1:10.
n. Lev. 26:20 Or, labor.
o. Lev. 26:21 Or as some read, by fortune, imputing my plagues to chance and fortune.
p. Lev. 26:22 Of your children, 2 Kings 17:25.
q. Lev. 26:22 Because none dare pass thereby for fear of beasts.
r. Lev. 26:26 That is, the strength, whereby the life is sustained, Ezek. 4:16 and 5:16.
s. Lev. 26:26 One oven shall be sufficient for ten families.
t. Lev. 26:30 Or, carrions.
u. Lev. 26:31 I will not accept your sacrifices.
v. Lev. 26:33 Signifying that no enemy can come without God's sending.
w. Lev. 26:35 Which I commanded you to keep.
x. Lev. 26:36 Or, cowardness.
y. Lev. 26:36 As if their enemies did chase them.
z. Lev. 26:39 Forasmuch as they are culpable of their fathers' faults, they shall be punished as well as their fathers.
aa. Lev. 26:41 Or, pray for their sin.
ab. Lev. 26:43 While they are captives, and without repentance.
ac. Lev. 26:45 Made to their forefathers.
ad. Lev. 26:46 Fifty days after they came out of Egypt.

LEV. 26
1. Exod. 20:4 / Deut. 5:8 / Ps. 97:7
2. Lev. 19:30
3. Deut. 28:1
4. Job. 11:19
5. Josh. 23:19
6. Ezek. 37:16 / 2Cor. 6:16
7. Deut. 28:15 / Lam. 2:17 / Mal. 2:2
8. Prov. 28:1
9. 2 Sam. 22:37 / Ps. 8:16
10. Deut. 28:35
11. 2Chron. 34:7
12. Lev. 25:2
13. Deut. 4:31 / Rom. 11:26

LEV. 27
a. Lev. 27:2 As of his son or his daughter.
b. Lev. 27:2 Which art the Priest.
c. Lev. 27:3 Read the value of the Shekel, Exod. 30:13.
d. Lev. 27:6 He speaketh of those vows whereby the fathers dedicated their children to God which were not of such force; but they might be redeemed from them.
e. Lev. 27:8 If he be not able to pay after thy valuation.
f. Lev. 27:9 Which is clean, Lev. 11:2.
g. Lev. 27:10 That is, consecrated to the Lord.
h. Lev. 27:14 Hebrew, so shall it stand.
i. Lev. 27:16 Valuing the price thereof according to the seed that is sown, or by the seed that it doth yield.
j. Lev. 27:16 Homer is a measure containing ten Ephahs, read of Ephah, Exod. 16:16, 36.
k. Lev. 27:20 For their own necessity or godly uses.
l. Lev. 27:21 That is, which dedicate to the Lord with a curse to him that doth turn it to his private use, Num. 21:2; Deut. 13:15; Josh. 9:17.
m. Lev. 27:23 The Priest's valuation.
n. Lev. 27:26 It was the Lord's already.
o. Lev. 27:29 It shall remain without redemption.
p. Lev. 27:31 Besides the value of the thing itself.
q. Lev. 27:32 All that which is numbered: that is, every tenth as he falleth by tally without exception or respect.

LEV. 27
1. Lev. 27:11
2. Exod. 30:13 / Num. 3:47 / Ezek. 45:12
3. Exod. 13:2 / Exod. 22:19 / Num. 3:23
4. Josh. 6:19

THE FOURTH BOOK OF MOSES, CALLED

[a]NUMBERS

1 *2 Moses and Aaron with the twelve princes of the tribes are commanded of*
the Lord to number them that are able to go to war. 49 The Levites are
exempted for the service of the Lord.

1 The Lord spake again unto Moses in the wilderness of [b]Sinai, in the Ta-
bernacle of the Congregation, in the first day of the [c]second month, in the se-
cond year after they were come out of the land of Egypt, saying, **2** [1]Take ye
the sum of all the Congregation of the children of Israel, after their families and
households of their fathers, with the number of their names: to wit, all the males,
[d]man by man: **3** From twenty years old and above, all that go forth to the war
in Israel: thou and Aaron shall number them throughout their armies. **4** And
with you shall be [e]men of every tribe, such as are the heads of the house of their
fathers. **5** And these are the names of the men that shall [f]stand with you, of
the tribe of Reuben, Elizur, the son of Shedeur: **6** Of Simeon, Shelumiel the
son of Zurishaddai: **7** Of Judah, Nahshon the son of Amminadab: **8** Of Issa-
char, Nethanel the son of Zuar: **9** Of Zebulun, Eliab, the son of Helon: **10** Of
the children of Joseph: of Ephraim, Elishama the son of Ammihud: of Manas-
seh, Gamaliel, the son of Pedahzur: **11** Of Benjamin, Abidan the son of Gide-
oni: **12** Of Dan, Ahiezer, the son of Ammishaddai: **13** Of Asher, Pagiel, the
son of Ocran: **14** Of Gad, Eliasaph the son of Deuel: **15** Of Naphtali, Ahira
the son of Enan. **16** These were famous in the Congregation, [g]princes of the
tribes of their fathers, and heads over thousands in Israel. **17** Then Moses and
Aaron took these men which are expressed by their names. **18** And they called
all the Congregation together in the first day of the second month, who declared
[h]their kindred by their families, and by the houses of their fathers according to the
number of their names, from twenty years old and above, man by man. **19** As
the Lord had commanded Moses, so he numbered them in the wilderness of Si-
nai. **20** So were the sons of [i]Reuben Israel's eldest son by their generations, by
their families, and by the houses of their fathers according to the number of their
names, man by man, every male from twenty years old and above, as many as [j]went
forth to war: **21** The number of them, I say, of the tribe of Reuben, was six and
forty thousand, and five hundred. **22** Of the sons of Simeon by their genera-
tions, by their families, and by the houses of their fathers, the sum thereof by the
number of their names, man by man, every male from twenty years old, and abo-
ve, all that went forth to war: **23** The sum of them, I say, of the tribe of Simeon
was nine and fifty thousand and three hundred. **24** Of the sons of Gad by their
generations, by their families, and by the houses of their fathers, according to the
number of their names, from twenty years old and above, all that went forth to
war: **25** The number of them, I say, of the tribe of Gad was five and forty thou-
sand, and six hundred and fifty. **26** Of the sons of Judah by their generations, by
their families, and by the houses of their fathers, according to the number of their
names, from twenty years old and above, all that went forth to war: **27** The num-
ber of them, I say, of the tribe of Judah, was three score and fourteen thousand, and
six hundred. **28** Of the sons of Issachar by their generations, by their families,
and by the houses of their fathers, according to the number of their names, from
twenty years old and above, all that went forth to war: **29** The number of them
also of the tribe of Issachar was four and fifty thousand, and four hundred. **30**
Of the sons of Zebulun by their generations, by their families, and by the houses
of their fathers, according to the number of their names, from twenty years old
and above: all that went forth to war: **31** The number of them also of the tribe
of Zebulun was seven and fifty thousand and four hundred. **32** Of the sons of
Joseph, namely of the sons of Ephraim by their generations, by their families, and
by the houses of their fathers, according to the number of their names, from twen-
ty years old and above, all that went forth to war: **33** The number of them also
of the tribe of Ephraim was forty thousand and five hundred. **34** Of the sons
of Manasseh by their generations, by their families and by the houses of their fa-
thers, according to the number of their names, from twenty years old and above,
all that went forth to war: **35** The number of them also of the tribe of Manasseh
was two and thirty thousand and two hundred. **36** Of the sons of Benjamin by
their generations, by their families, and by the houses of their fathers, according
to the number of their names, from twenty years old and above, all that went for-
th to war: **37** The number of them also of the tribe of Benjamin was five and
thirty thousand and four hundred. **38** Of the sons of Dan by their generations,
by their families, and by the houses of their fathers, according to the number of
their names, from twenty years old and above, all that went forth to war: **39** The
number of them also of the tribe of Dan was three score and two thousand, and
seven hundred. **40** Of the sons of Asher by their generations, by their families,
and by the houses of their fathers, according to the number of their names, from
twenty years old and above, all that went forth to war: **41** The number of them
also of the tribe of Asher was one and forty thousand and five hundred. **42** Of
the children of Naphtali, by their generations, by their families, and by the houses
of their fathers, according to the number of their names, from twenty years old
and above, all that went to the war: **43** The number of them also of the tribe
of Naphtali was three and fifty thousand, and four hundred. **44** These are the
[k]sums which Moses, and Aaron numbered, and the Princes of Israel, the twelve
men which were every one for the house of their fathers. **45** So this was all the
sum of the sons of Israel, by the houses of their fathers, from twenty years old and
above, all that went to the war in Israel. **46** And all they were in number six
hundred and three thousand five hundred and fifty. **47** But the Levites, after
the tribes of their fathers were not numbered among [l]them. **48** For the Lord
had spoken unto Moses, and said, **49** Only thou shalt not number the tribe of
Levi, neither take the sum of them among the children of Israel. **50** But thou
shalt appoint the Levites over the Tabernacle of the Testimony, and over all the
instruments thereof, and over all things that belong to it: they shall bear the Ta-
bernacle, and all the instruments thereof, and shall minister in it, and shall [m]dwell
round about the Tabernacle. **51** And when the Tabernacle goeth forth, the Le-
vites shall take it down: and when the Tabernacle is to be pitched, the Levites shall
set it up: for the [n]stranger that cometh near, shall be slain. **52** Also the children
of Israel shall pitch their tents every man in his camp, and every man under his
standard throughout their armies. **53** But the Levites shall pitch round about
the Tabernacle of the Testimony, lest vengeance [o]come upon the Congregation of
the children of Israel, and the Levites shall take the charge of the Tabernacle of the
Testimony. **54** So the children of Israel did according to all that the Lord had
commanded Moses: so did they.

2 *2 The order of the tents, and the names of the Captains of the Israelites.*

1 And the Lord spake unto Moses, and to Aaron, saying, **2** [a]Every
man of the children of Israel shall camp by his standard, and under the ensign of
their father's house: far off, about the Tabernacle of the Congregation shall they
pitch. **3** On the East side toward the rising of the sun, shall they of the stan-
dard of the host of Judah pitch according to their armies: and Nahshon the son
of Amminadab shall be [b]captain of the sons of Judah. **4** And his host and the
number of them were seventy and four thousand and six hundred. **5** Next unto
him shall they of the tribe [c]of Issachar pitch, and Nethanel the son of Zuar shall
be the captain of the sons of Issachar: **6** And his host and the number thereof
were four and fifty thousand, and four hundred. **7** Then the tribe of Zebulun,
and Eliab the son of Helon captain over the sons of Zebulun: **8** And his host and
the number thereof seven and fifty thousand and four hundred: **9** The whole
number of the [d]host of Judah are an hundred fourscore and six thousand, and four

---

NUM. 1

a. TITLE So called because of the diversity and multitude of numberings which are here chiefly contained, both of men's names and places.
b. Num. 1:1 In that place of the wilderness that was near to mount Sinai.
c. Num. 1:1 Which contained part of April, and part of May.
d. Num. 1:2 Hebrew, by their heads.
e. Num. 1:4 That is, the chiefest man of every tribe.
f. Num. 1:5 And assist you when ye number the people.
g. Num. 1:16 Or captains, and governors.
h. Num. 1:18 In showing every man his tribe, and his ancestors.
i. Num. 1:20 These are the names of the twelve tribes, as first of Reuben.
j. Num. 1:20 Or, as were able to bear weapons.
k. Num. 1:44 Or, full count.
l. Num. 1:47 Which were warriors, but were appointed to the use of the Tabernacle.
m. Num. 1:50 Hebrew, camp.
n. Num. 1:51 Whosoever is not of the tribe of Levi.
o. Num. 1:53 By not having due regard to the Tabernacle of the Lord.

NUM. 1

1. Exod. 30:12

NUM. 2

a. Num. 2:2 In the twelve tribes were four principle standards, so that every three tribes had their standard.
b. Num. 2:3 Or, prince.
c. Num. 2:5 Judah, Issachar, and Zebulun the sons of Leah were of the first standard.
d. Num. 2:9 Of them which were contained under that name.

hundred according to their armies: they shall first set forth. **10** On the South side shall be the standard of the host [e]of Reuben according to their armies: and the captain over the sons of Reuben shall be Elizur the son of Shedeur. **11** And his host and the number thereof, six and forty thousand and five hundred. **12** And by him shall the tribe of Simeon pitch, and the captain over the sons of Simeon shall be Shelumiel the son of Zurishaddai: **13** And his host, and the number of them, nine and fifty thousand and three hundred. **14** And the tribe of Gad, and the captain over the sons of Gad shall be Eliasaph the son of [f]Deuel: **15** And his host and the number of them were five and forty thousand, six hundred and fifty. **16** All the number of the camp of Reuben were an hundred and one and fifty thousand, and four hundred and fifty according to their armies, and they shall set forth in the second place. **17** Then the Tabernacle of the Congregation shall go with the host of the Levites, in the [g]midst of the camp as they have pitched, so shall they go forward, every man in his order, according to their standards. **18** [h]The standard of the camp of Ephraim shall be toward the West according to their armies: and the captain over the sons of Ephraim shall be Elishama the son of Ammihud: **19** And his host and the number of them were forty thousand and five hundred. **20** And by him shall be the tribe of Manasseh and the captain over the sons of Manasseh, shall be Gamaliel the son of Pedahzur: **21** And his host and the number of them were two and thirty thousand and two hundred. **22** And the tribe of Benjamin, and the captain over the sons of Benjamin shall be Abidan, the son of Gideoni: **23** And his host, and the number of them were five and thirty thousand and four hundred. **24** All the number of the camp of Ephraim were an hundred and eight thousand and one hundred according to their armies, and they shall go in the third place. **25** The standard of the host of [i]Dan shall be toward the North according to their armies: and the captain over the children of Dan shall be Ahiezer the son of Ammishaddai: **26** And his host and the number of them were two and threescore thousand and seven hundred. **27** And by him shall the tribe of Asher pitch, and the captain over the sons of Asher shall be Pagiel the son of Ocran. **28** And his host and the number of them were one and forty thousand, and five hundred. **29** Then the tribe of Naphtali, and the captain over the children of Naphtali shall be Ahira the son of Enan: **30** And his host and the number of them were three and fifty thousand and four hundred. **31** All the number of the host of Dan was an hundred and seven and fifty thousand and six hundred: they shall go hindmost with their standards. **32** These are the [j]sums of the children of Israel by the houses of their fathers, all the number of the host, according to their armies, six hundred and three thousand, five hundred and fifty. **33** But the Levites were not numbered among the children of Israel, as the Lord had commanded Moses. **34** And the children of Israel did according to all that the Lord had commanded Moses: so they pitched according to their [k]standards, and so they journeyed every one with his families, according to the houses of their fathers.

3

6 The charge and office of the Levites. 12, 35 Why the Lord separated the Levites for himself. 16 Their number, families, and captains. 40 The firstborn of Israel is redeemed by the Levites. 47 The overplus is redeemed by money.

1 These also were the [a]generations of Aaron and Moses, in the day that the Lord spake with Moses in mount Sinai. **2** So these are the names of the sons of Aaron, [1]Nadab the firstborn, and Abihu, Eleazar, and Ithamar. **3** These are the names of the sons of Aaron the anointed Priests, whom Moses did [2]consecrate to minister in the Priest's office. **4** [3]And Nadab and Abihu died [b]before the Lord, when they offered [4]strange fire before the Lord in the wilderness of Sinai, and had no children: but Eleazar and Ithamar served in the Priest's office in the [c]sight of Aaron their father. **5** Then the Lord spake unto Moses, saying, **6** Bring the tribe of Levi, and [d]set them before Aaron the Priest that they may serve him, **7** And take the charge with him, even the charge of the whole Congregation, [e]before the Tabernacle of the Congregation to do the service of the Tabernacle. **8** They shall also keep all the instruments of the Tabernacle of the Congregation, and have the charge of the children of Israel to do the service of the Tabernacle. **9** And thou shalt give the Levites unto Aaron and to his [f]sons: for they are given him freely from among the children of Israel. **10** And thou shalt appoint Aaron and his sons to execute their Priest's office: and the [g]stranger that cometh near, shall be slain. **11** Also the Lord spake unto Moses, saying, **12** Behold, I have even taken the Levites from among the children of Israel: for all the firstborn that openeth the matrice among the children of Israel, and the Levites shall be mine, **13** Because all the firstborn are mine: for the same day, that I smote all the firstborn in the land of Egypt, [5]I sanctified unto me all the firstborn in Israel, both man and beast: mine they shall be: I am the Lord. **14** Moreover, the Lord spake unto Moses in the wilderness of Sinai, saying, **15** Number the children of Levi after the houses of their fathers, in their families: every male from a month old and above shalt thou number. **16** Then Moses numbered them according to the word of the Lord, as he was commanded. **17** And these were the sons of Levi by their names, [6]Gershon, and Kohath, and Merari. **18** Also these were the names of the sons of Gershon by their families: Libni and Shimei. **19** The sons also of Kohath by their families: Amram and Izehar, Hebron, and Uzziel. **20** And the sons of Merari by their families: Mahli and Mushi These are the families of Levi, according to the houses of their fathers. **21** Of Gershon came the family of the Libnites and the family of the Shimites: these are the families of the Gershonites. **22** The sum whereof ([h]after the number of all the males from a month old and above) was counted seven thousand and five hundred. **23** The families of the Gershonites shall pitch behind the Tabernacle Westward. **24** The captain and [i]ancient of the house of the Gershonites shall be Eliasaph the son of Lael. **25** And the charge of the sons of Gershon in the Tabernacle of the Congregation, shall be the [j]Tabernacle, and the pavilion, the covering thereof, and the veil of the door of the Tabernacle of the Congregation, **26** And the hanging of the court, and the veil of the door of the court which is near the Tabernacle, and near the Altar round about, and the cords of it for all the service thereof. **27** And of Kohath came the family of the Amramites, and the family of the Izharites, and the family of the Hebronites, and the family of the Uzzielites: these are the families of the Kohathites. **28** The number of all the males from a month old and above, was eight thousand and six hundred, having the [k]charge of the Sanctuary. **29** The families of the sons of Kohath shall pitch on the South side of the Tabernacle. **30** The captain and ancient of the house and families of the Kohathites shall be Elizaphan the son of Uzziel: **31** And their charge shall be the [l]Ark, and the Table, and the Candlestick, and the altars, and the instruments of the Sanctuary that they minister with, and the veil, and all that serveth thereto. **32** And Eleazar the son of Aaron the Priest shall be [m]chief captain of the Levites, having the oversight of them that have the charge of the Sanctuary. **33** Of Merari came the family of the Mahlites, and the family of the Mushites: these are the families of Merari. **34** And the sum of them, according to the number of all the males, from a month old and above was six thousand and two hundred. **35** The captain and the ancient of the house of the families of Merari shall be Zuriel the son of Abihail: they shall pitch on the Northside of the Tabernacle. **36** And in the charge and custody of the sons of Merari shall be [n]the boards of the Tabernacle, and the bars thereof, and his pillars, and his sockets, and all the instruments thereof, and all that serveth thereto, **37** With the pillars of the court round about, with their sockets, and their pins and their cords. **38** Also on the forefront of the Tabernacle toward the East, before the Tabernacle I say, of the Congregation Eastward shall Moses and Aaron and his sons pitch, having the charge of the Sanctuary, [o]and the charge of the children of Israel: but the stranger that cometh near shall be slain. **39** The whole sum of the Levites, which Moses and Aaron numbered at the commandment of the Lord throughout their families, even all the males from a month old and above, was two and twenty [p]thousand. **40** And the Lord said unto Moses, Number all the firstborn that are males among the children of Israel from a month old and above, and take the number of their names. **41** And thou shalt take the Levites to me [q]for all the firstborn of the children of Israel (I am the Lord) and the cattle of the Levites for all the firstborn of the cattle of the children of Israel. **42** And Moses numbered, as the Lord commanded him, all the firstborn of the children of Israel. **43** And all the firstborn males rehearsed by name (from a month old and above) according to their number were two and twenty thousand, two hundred seventy and three. **44** And the Lord spake unto Moses, saying, **45** Take the Levites for all the firstborn of the children of Israel, and the cattle of the Levites for their cattle, and the Levites shall be mine, (I am the Lord.) **46** And for the redeeming of the two hundred seventy and three, (which are more than the Levites) of the firstborn of the children of Israel, **47** Thou shalt also take five shekels for every person: after the weight of the Sanctuary shalt thou take it: [7]the shekel containeth twenty gerahs. **48** And thou shalt give the money, wherewith the odd number of them is redeemed, unto Aaron and to his sons. **49** Thus Moses took the redemption of them that were redeemed, being more than the Levites: **50** Of

---

e. Num. 2:10 Reuben and Simeon, the sons of Leah, and Gad the son of Zilpah her maid, were of the second standard.
f. Num. 2:14 Or, Reuel.
g. Num. 2:17 Because it might be in equal distance from each one, and all indifferently have recourse thereunto.
h. Num. 2:18 Because Ephraim and Manasseh supplied the place of Joseph their father, they are taken to be Rachel's children, so they and Benjamin make the third standard.
i. Num. 2:25 Dan and Naphtali the sons of Bilhah Rachel's maid with Asher the son of Zilpah make the fourth standard.
j. Num. 2:32 Which were of twenty years and above.
k. Num. 2:34 For under every one of the four principal standards were divers signs to keep every band.

NUM. 3

a. Num. 3:1 Or, families and kindreds.
b. Num. 3:4 Or, before the Altar.
c. Num. 3:4 Whiles their father lived.
d. Num. 3:6 Offer them unto Aaron for the use of the Tabernacle.
e. Num. 3:7 Which appertained to the executing of the high Priest's commandment, to the oversight of the people, and the service of the Tabernacle.
f. Num. 3:9 Aaron's sons the Priests served in the Sanctuary in praying for the people and offering sacrifice: the Levites served for the inferior uses of the same.
g. Num. 3:10 Any that would minister not being a Levite.
h. Num. 3:22 Only numbering the male children.
i. Num. 3:24 Or, father.
j. Num. 3:25 Their charge was to carry the covering and hangings of the Tabernacle.
k. Num. 3:28 Doing every one his duty in the Sanctuary.
l. Num. 3:31 The chief things within the Sanctuary were committed to the Kohathites.
m. Num. 3:32 Or, prince of princes.
n. Num. 3:36 The woodwork and the rest of the instruments were committed to their charge.
o. Num. 3:38 That none should enter into the Tabernacle contrary to God's appointment.
p. Num. 3:39 So that the firstborn of the children of Israel were more by 273, as verse 43.
q. Num. 3:41 So that now the Levites should satisfy unto the Lord for the firstborn of Israel, save for the 273 which were more than the Levites, for whom they paid money.
r. Num. 3:50 Or the two hundred seventy and three, which were more than the Levites.

the [r]firstborn of the children of Israel took he the money: even a thousand three hundred three score and five shekels, after the shekel of the Sanctuary. **51** And Moses gave the money of them that were redeemed, unto Aaron and to his sons according to the word of the Lord, as the Lord had commanded Moses.

4

5 The offices of the Levites, when the host removed. 6 The number of the three families of Kohath, Gershon, and Merari.

1 And the Lord spake unto Moses, and to Aaron, saying, **2** Take the sum of the sons of Kohath from among the sons of Levi, after their families, and houses of their fathers, **3** From [a]thirty years old and above, even until fifty years old all that enter into the assembly to do the work in the Tabernacle of the Congregation. **4** This shall be the office of the sons of Kohath in the Tabernacle of the Congregation about the holiest of all. **5** When the host removeth, then Aaron and his sons shall come and take down[b] the covering veil, and shall cover the Ark of the Testimony therewith. **6** And they shall put thereon a covering of badger's skins, and shall spread upon it a cloth altogether of blue silk, and put to [c]the bars thereof: **7** And upon the [1]table of show bread, they shall spread a cloth of blue silk, and put thereon the dishes, and the incense cups and goblets, and coverings to cover it [d]with, and the bread shall be thereon continually. **8** And they shall spread upon them a covering of scarlet, and cover the same with a covering of badger's skins, and put to the bars thereof. **9** Then they shall take a cloth of blue silk, and cover the [2]candlestick of light with his lamps, and his snuffers, [3]and his snuffdishes, and all the oil vessels thereof, which they occupy about it. **10** So they shall put it, and all the instruments thereof in a covering of badger's skins, and put it upon the [e]bars. **11** Also upon the golden [f]altar they shall spread a cloth of blue silk, and cover it with a covering of badger's skins, and put to the bars thereof. **12** And they shall take all the instruments of the ministry, wherewith they minister in the Sanctuary, and put them in a cloth of blue silk, and cover them with a covering of badger's skins, and put them on the bars. **13** Also they shall take away the ashes from the [g]altar, and spread a purple cloth upon it, **14** And shall put upon it all the instruments thereof, which they occupy about it, the censers, the fleshhooks, and the besoms, and the basins, even all the instruments of the altar: and they shall spread upon it a covering of badger's skins, and put to the bars of it. **15** And when Aaron and his sons have made an end of covering the [h]Sanctuary, and all the instruments of the Sanctuary, at the removing of the host, afterward the sons of Kohath shall come to bear it, but they shall not [i]touch any holy thing lest they die This is the charge of the sons of Kohath in the Tabernacle of the Congregation. **16** And to the office of Eleazar the son of Aaron the Priest pertaineth the oil for the light, and the [4]sweet incense, and the [j]daily meat offering, and the [5]anointing oil with the oversight of all the Tabernacle, and of all that therein is, both in the Sanctuary, and in all the instruments thereof. **17** And the Lord spake unto Moses and to Aaron, saying, **18** Ye shall not [k]cut off the tribe of the families of the Kohathites from among the Levites: **19** But thus do unto them that they may live and not die, when they come near to the most holy things: let Aaron and his sons come and appoint [l]them, every one to his office, and to his charge. **20** But let them not go in, to see when the Sanctuary is folden up, lest they die. **21** And the Lord spake unto Moses, saying, **22** Take also the sum of the sons of Gershon, every one by the houses of their fathers, throughout their families: **23** From thirty years old and above until fifty years old shalt thou number them, all that [m]enter into the assembly for to do service in the Tabernacle of the Congregation. **24** This shall be the service of the families of the Gershonites to serve and to bear. **25** They shall bear the curtains of the Tabernacle, and the Tabernacle of the Congregation, his covering, and the covering of badger's skins, that is on high upon it, and the veil of the [n]door of the Tabernacle of the Congregation. **26** The curtains also of the court, and the veil of the entering in of the gate of the court, [o]which is near the Tabernacle and near the altar round about, with their cords: and all the instruments for their service, and all that is made for them: so shall they serve. **27** At the commandment of Aaron and his sons shall all the service of the sons of the Gershonites be done, in all their charges and in all their service, and ye shall appoint them to keep all their charges. **28** This is the service of the families of the sons of the Gershonites in the Tabernacle of the Congregation, and their watch shall be under the [p]hand of Ithamar the son of Aaron the Priest. **29** Thou shalt number the sons of Merari by their families, and by the houses of their fathers. **30** From thirty years old and above, even unto fifty years old shalt thou number them, all that enter into the assembly, to do the service of the Tabernacle of the Congregation. **31** And this is their office and charge according to all their service in the Tabernacle of the Congregation: the [6]boards of the Tabernacle with the bars thereof, and his pillars, and his sockets, **32** And the pillars round about the court, with their sockets and their pins, and their cords with all their instruments, even for all their service: and by [q]name ye shall reckon the instruments of their office and charge. **33** This is the service of the families of the sons of Merari, according to all their service in the Tabernacle of the Congregation under the hand of Ithamar the son of Aaron the Priest. **34** Then Moses and Aaron and the princes of the Congregation numbered the sons of the Kohathites, by their families and by the houses of their fathers, **35** From thirty years old and above, even unto fifty years old, all that enter into the assembly for the service of the Tabernacle of the Congregation. **36** So the [r]numbers of them throughout their families were two thousand, seven hundred and fifty. **37** These are the numbers of the families of the Kohathites, all that serve in the Tabernacle of the Congregation, which Moses and Aaron did number according to the commandment of the Lord by the [s]hand of Moses. **38** Also the numbers of the sons of Gershon throughout their families and houses of their fathers, **39** From thirty years old and upward, even unto fifty years old: all that enter into the assembly for the service of the Tabernacle of the Congregation. **40** So the numbers of them by their families, and by the houses of their fathers were two thousand six hundred and thirty. **41** These are the numbers of the families of the sons of Gershon: of all that [t]did service in the Tabernacle of the Congregation, whom Moses and Aaron did number according to the commandment of the Lord. **42** The numbers also of the families of the sons of Merari by their families, and by the houses of their fathers, **43** From thirty years old and upward, even unto fifty years old: all that enter into the assembly for the service of the Tabernacle of the Congregation. **44** So the numbers of them by their families were three thousand, and two hundred. **45** These are the sums of the families of the sons of Merari, whom Moses and Aaron numbered according to the commandment of the Lord, by the hand of Moses. **46** So all the numbers of the Levites, which Moses, and Aaron, and the princes of Israel numbered by their families and by the houses of their fathers, **47** From thirty years old and upward, even to fifty years old, every one that came to do [u]his duty, office, service and charge in the Tabernacle of the Congregation. **48** So the number of them were eight thousand five hundred and four score. **49** According to the [v]commandment of the Lord by the hand of Moses did Aaron number them, every one according to his service, and according to his charge Thus were they of that tribe numbered, as the Lord commanded [w]Moses.

5

2 The leprous and the polluted shall be cast forth. 6 The purging of sin. 15 The trial of the suspect wife.

1 And the Lord spake unto Moses, saying, **2** Command the children of Israel that they [1]put out of the host every leper, and every one that hath [2]an issue, and whosoever is defiled by [3]the dead. **3** Both male and female shall ye put out: [a]out of the host shall ye put them, that they defile not their [b]tents among whom I dwell. **4** And the children of Israel did so, and put them out of the host, even as the Lord had commanded Moses, so did the children of Israel. **5** And the Lord spake unto Moses, saying, **6** Speak unto the children of Israel, [4]When a man or woman shall commit any sin [c]that men commit, and transgress against the Lord, when that person shall trespass, **7** Then they shall confess their sin which they have done, and shall restore the damage thereof [5]with his principal, and put the fifth part of it more thereto, and shall give it unto him, against whom he hath trespassed. **8** But if the [d]man have no kinsman, to whom he should restore the damage, the damage shall be restored to the Lord for the Priest's use, besides the ram of the atonement, whereby he shall make atonement for him. **9** And every offering of all the [e]holy things of the children of Israel, which they bring unto the

---

NUM. 3

1. Exod. 6:23
2. Exod. 28:3
3. Lev. 10:1,2 / Num. 26:61 / 1 Chron. 24:2
4. Lev. 10:1,2
5. Exod. 13:1 / Exod. 34:19 / Lev. 27:26 / Num. 8:16 / Luke 2:23
6. Gen. 46:11 / Exod. 6:66 / Num. 26:57 / 1 Chron. 6:1 / 1 Chron. 23:6
7. Exod. 30:13 / Lev. 27:25 / Num. 18:16 / Ezek. 45:12

NUM. 4

a. Num. 4:3 The Levites were numbered after three sorts, first at a month old when they were consecrated to the Lord, next at 25 years old when they were appointed to serve in the Tabernacle, and 30 years old to bear the burdens of the Tabernacle.
b. Num. 4:5 Which divided the Sanctuary from the holiest of all.
c. Num. 4:6 That is, put them upon their shoulders to carry it: for the bars of the Ark could never be removed.
d. Num. 4:7 Meaning, to cover the bread.
e. Num. 4:10 The Hebrew word signifieth an instrument made of two staves or bars.
f. Num. 4:11 Which was to burn incense, read Exod. 30:1.
g. Num. 4:13 Of the burnt offering.
h. Num. 4:15 That is, in folding up the things of the Sanctuary, as the Ark, etc.
i. Num. 4:15 Before it be covered.
j. Num. 4:16 Which was offered at morning and evening.
k. Num. 4:18 Committing by your negligence that the holy things be not well wrapped, and so they by touching thereof perish.
l. Num. 4:19 Showing what part every man shall bear.
m. Num. 4:23 Which were received into the company of them that ministered in the Tabernacle of the Congregation.
n. Num. 4:25 Which veil hanged between the Sanctuary and the court.
o. Num. 4:26 Which court compassed both the Tabernacle of the Congregation and the altar of burnt offering.
p. Num. 4:28 Under the charge and oversight.
q. Num. 4:32 Ye shall make an inventory of all the things, which ye commit to their charge.
r. Num. 4:36 Hebrew, the numbered of them.
s. Num. 4:37 God appointing Moses to be the minister and executor thereof.
t. Num. 4:41 Which were of competent age to serve therein, that is between 30 and 50.
u. Num. 4:47 Whosoever of the Levites that had any manner of charge in the Tabernacle.
v. Num. 4:49 Hebrew, according to the mouth, or word.
w. Num. 4:49 So that Moses neither added, nor diminished, from that which the Lord commanded him.

NUM. 4

1. Exod. 25:15 / Exod. 25:30
2. Exod. 25:31
3. Exod. 25:38
4. Exod. 30:34,35
5. Exod. 30:23,25
6. Exod. 26:25

NUM. 5

a. Num. 5:3 Or, in a place out of the host.
b. Num. 5:3 There were three manner of tents: of the Lord, of the Levites, and of the Israelites.
c. Num. 5:6 Commit any fault willingly.
d. Num. 5:8 If he be dead to whom the wrong is done, and also have no kinsman.
e. Num. 5:9 Or, things offered to the Lord, as firstfruits, etc.

Priest, shallbe [6]his. 10 And every man's hallowed things shall be his: that is, whatsoever any man giveth the Priest, it shall be his. 11 And the Lord spake unto Moses, saying, 12 Speak unto the children of Israel, and say unto them, If any man's wife [f]turn to evil, and commit a trespass against him, 13 So that another man lie with her fleshly, and it be hid from the eyes of her husband, and kept close, and yet she be defiled, and there be no witness against her, neither she taken with the manner, 14 [g]If he be moved with a jealous mind, so that he is jealous over his wife, which is defiled, or if he have a jealous mind, so that he is jealous over his wife, which is not defiled, 15 Then shall the man bring his wife to the Priest, and bring her offering with her, the tenth part of an Ephah of barley meal, but he shall not pour [h]oil upon it, nor put incense thereon: for it is an offering of jealousy, an offering for a remembrance, calling the sin to [i]mind. 16 And the Priest shall bring her, and set her before the Lord. 17 Then the Priest shall take [j]the holy water in an earthen vessel, and of the dust that is in the floor of the Tabernacle, even the Priest shall take it and put it into the water. 18 After the Priest shall set the woman before the Lord, and uncover the woman's head, and put the offering of the memorial in her hands: it is the jealousy offering, and the Priest shall have bitter and [k]cursed water in his hand, 19 And the Priest shall charge her by an oath, and say unto the woman, If no man have lain with thee, neither thou hast turned to uncleanness from thine husband, be free from this bitter and cursed water. 20 But if thou hast turned from thine husband, and so art defiled, and some man hath lain with thee besides thine husband, 21 (Then the Priest shall charge the woman with an oath of cursing, and the Priest shall say unto the woman:) The Lord make thee to be [l]accursed, and detestable for the oath among the people, and the Lord cause thy thigh to [m]rot, and thy belly to swell: 22 And that this cursed water may go into thy bowels, to cause thy belly to swell, and thy thigh to rot Then the woman shall answer, [n]Amen, Amen. 23 After, the Priest shall write these curses in a book, and shall [o]blot them out with the bitter water, 24 And shall cause the woman to drink the bitter and cursed water, and the cursed water turned into bitterness shall enter into her. 25 Then the Priest shall take the jealousy offering out of the woman's hand, and shall shake the offering before the Lord, and offer it upon the altar. 26 And the Priest shall take an handful of the offering for a [p]memorial thereof, and burn it upon the [q]altar, and afterward make the woman drink the water. 27 When he hath made her drink the water, if she be defiled and have trespassed against her husband, then shall the cursed water, turned into bitterness, enter into her, and her belly shall swell, and her thigh shall rot, and the woman shall be accursed among her people. 28 But if the woman be not defiled, but be [r]clean, she shall be free, and shall conceive and bear. 29 This is the law of jealousy, when a wife turneth from her husband and is defiled, 30 Or, when a man is moved with a jealous mind, being jealous over his wife, then shall he bring the woman before the Lord, and the Priest shall do to her according to all this law, 31 And the man shall be [s]free from sin, but this woman shall bear her iniquity.

6

2 The law of the consecration of the Nazirites. 24 The manner to bless the people.

1 And the Lord spake unto Moses, saying, 2 Speak unto the children of Israel, and say unto them, When a man or a woman doth separate themselves to vow a vow of a [a]Nazirite, to separate himself unto the Lord, 3 He shall abstain from wine and strong drink, and shall drink no sour wine nor sour drink, nor shall drink any liquor of grapes, neither shall eat fresh grapes nor dried. 4 As long as his abstinence endureth, shall he eat nothing that is made of the wine of the vine, neither the kernels nor the husk. 5 While he is separated by his vow, the [1]razor shall not come upon his head, until the days be out, in the which he separateth himself unto the Lord, he shall be holy, and shall let the locks of the hair of his head grow. 6 During the time that he separateth himself unto the Lord, he shall come at no [b]dead body: 7 He shall not make himself unclean at the death of his father or mother, brother, or sister: for the consecration of his God is upon [c]his head. 8 All the days of his separation he shall be holy to the Lord. 9 And if any die suddenly by him, or he beware, then the [d]head of his consecration shall be defiled, and he shall shave his head in the day of his cleansing: in the seventh day he shall shave it. 10 And in the eighth day he shall bring two turtles, or two young pigeons to the Priest, at the door of the tabernacle of the Congregation. 11 Then the Priest shall prepare the one for a sin offering, and the other for a burnt offering, and shall make an atonement for him, because he sinned by [e]the dead: so shall he hallow his head the same day. 12 And he shall [f]consecrate unto the Lord the days of his separation, and shall bring a lamb of a year old for a trespass offering, and the first [g]days shall be void: for his consecration was defiled. 13 This then is the law of the Nazirite: when the time of his consecration is out, he shall come to the door of the tabernacle of the Congregation, 14 And he shall bring his offering unto the Lord, an he lamb of a year old without blemish, for a burnt offering, and a she lamb of a year old without blemish, for a sin offering, and a ram without blemish, for peace offerings, 15 And a basket of unleavened bread, of [2]Cakes of fine flour, mingled with oil, and wafers of unleavened bread anointed with oil, with their meat offering, and their drink offerings: 16 The which the Priest shall bring before the Lord, and make his sin offering and his burnt offering. 17 He shall prepare also the ram for a peace offering unto the Lord, with the basket of unleavened bread, and the Priest shall make his meat offering, and his drink offering. 18 And [3]the Nazirite shall shave the head [h]of his consecration at the door of the Tabernacle of the Congregation, and shall take the hair of the head of his consecration, and [i]put it in the fire which is under the peace offering. 19 Then the Priest shall take the sodden shoulder of the ram, and an unleavened cake out of the basket, and a wafer unleavened, and put them upon the hands of the Nazirite, after he hath shaven his consecration. 20 And the Priest shall [4]shake them to and fro before the Lord: this is an holy thing for the Priest [j]besides the shaken breast, and besides the heave shoulder: so afterward the Nazirite may drink wine. 21 This is the law of the Nazirite, which he hath vowed, and of his offering unto the Lord for his consecration, [k]besides that that he is able to bring: according to the vow which he vowed, so shall he do after the law of his consecration. 22 And the Lord spake unto Moses, saying, 23 Speak unto Aaron and to his sons, saying, Thus shall ye [l]bless the children of Israel, and say unto them, 24 The Lord bless thee, and keep thee, 25 The Lord make his face shine upon thee, and be merciful unto thee, 26 The Lord lift up his countenance upon thee, and give thee peace. 27 So they shall put my [m]Name upon the children of Israel, and I will bless them.

7

2 The heads or princes of Israel offer at the setting up of the Tabernacle. 10 And at the dedication of the Altar. 19 God speaketh to Moses from the Mercy seat.

1 Now when Moses had finished the setting up of the Tabernacle, and [1]anointed it and sanctified it, and all the instruments thereof, and the altar with all the [a]instruments thereof, and had anointed them, and sanctified them, 2 Then the [b]princes of Israel, heads over the houses of their fathers, (they were the princes of the tribes, who were over them that were numbered) offered, 3 And brought their offering before the Lord, six [c]covered chariots, and twelve oxen: one chariot for two princes, and for every one an ox, and they offered them before the Tabernacle. 4 And the Lord spake unto Moses, saying, 5 Take these of them, that they may be to do the [d]service of the Tabernacle of the Congregation, and thou shalt give them unto the Levites, to every man according unto his office. 6 So Moses took the chariots and the oxen, and gave them unto the Levites: 7 Two chariots and four oxen he gave to the sons of Gershon, according unto their [e]office. 8 And four chariots and eight oxen he gave to the sons of Merari, according unto their office, under the hand of Ithamar the son of Aaron the Priest. 9 But to the sons of Kohath he gave none, [f]because the charge of the Sanctuary belonged to them, which they did bear upon their shoulders. 10 The princes also offered in the [g]dedication for the altar in the day that it was anointed: then the princes offered their offering before the altar. 11 And the Lord said unto Moses, One prince one day, and another prince another day, shall offer their offering, for the dedication of the altar. 12 So then on the first day did Nahshon the son of Amminadab of the tribe of Judah offer his offering. 13 And his offering was a

---

f. Num. 5:12 By breaking the band of marriage, and playing the harlot.
g. Num. 5:14 Hebrew, If the spirit of jealousy come upon him.
h. Num. 5:15 Only in the sin offering, and so this offering of jealousy were neither oil nor incense offered.
i. Num. 5:15 Or, making the sin known, and not purging it.
j. Num. 5:17 Which also is called the water of purification or sprinkling, read Num. 19:9.
k. Num. 5:18 It was so called by the effect, because it declared the woman to be accursed, and turned to her destruction.
l. Num. 5:21 Both because she had committed so heinous a fault, and forsware herself in denying the same.
m. Num. 5:21 Hebrew, to fall.
n. Num. 5:22 That is, be it so, as thou wishest, as Ps. 41:23; Deut. 27:15.
o. Num. 5:23 Shall wash the curses, which are written, into the water in the vessel.
p. Num. 5:26 Or, perfume.
q. Num. 5:26 Where the incense was offered.
r. Num. 5:28 Or, innocent.
s. Num. 5:31 The man might accuse his wife upon suspicion, and not be reproved.

NUM. 5
1. Lev. 13:3
2. Lev. 15:2
3. Lev. 21:1
4. Lev. 6:3
5. Lev. 6:5
6. Lev. 10:12

NUM. 6
a. Num. 6:2 Which separated themselves from the world, and dedicated themselves to God: which figure was accomplished in Christ.
b. Num. 6:6 As at burials, or mournings.
c. Num. 6:7 In that he suffered his hair to grow, he signified that he was consecrated to God.
d. Num. 6:9 Which long hair is a sign that he is dedicated to God.
e. Num. 6:11 By being present where the dead was.
f. Num. 6:12 Beginning at the eighth day, when he is purified.
g. Num. 6:12 So that he shall begin his vow anew.
h. Num. 6:18 In token that his vow is ended.
i. Num. 6:18 For the hair which was consecrated to the Lord, might not be cast into any profane place.
j. Num. 6:20 Or, with the breast.
k. Num. 6:21 At the least he shall do this, if he be able to offer no more.
l. Num. 6:23 That is, pray for them.
m. Num. 6:27 They shall pray in my Name for them.

NUM. 6
1. Judg. 13:5 / 1 Sam. 1:11
2. Lev. 2:15
3. Acts 21:24
4. Exod. 29:27

NUM. 7
a. Num. 7:1 Or, vessels.
b. Num. 7:2 Or, captains.
c. Num. 7:3 Like horse litters, to keep the things that were carried in them from weather.
d. Num. 7:5 That is, to carry things and stuff in.
e. Num. 7:7 For their use to carry with.
f. Num. 7:9 The holy thing of the Sanctuary must be carried upon their shoulders and not drawn with oxen, Num. 4:15.
g. Num. 7:10 That is, when the first sacrifice was offered thereupon by Aaron, Lev. 9:1.

silver charger of an hundred and thirty shekels weight, a silver bowl of seventy
shekels, after the shekel of the Sanctuary, both full of fine flour, mingled with oil,
for a [2]meat offering, **14** An incense cup of gold of ten shekels, full of incen-
se, **15** A young bullock, a ram, a lamb of a year old for a burnt offering, **16** An
he goat for a sin offering, **17** And for peace offerings, two bullocks, five rams,
five he goats, and five lambs of a year old: this was the offering of Nahshon the son
of Amminadab. **18** The second day Nethanel, the son of Zuar, prince of the tri-
be of Issachar did offer. **19** Who offered for his offering a silver charger of an
hundred and thirty shekels weight, a silver bowl of seventy shekels, after the shekel
of the Sanctuary, both full of fine flour, mingled with oil, for a meat offe-
ring, **20** An incense cup of gold of ten shekels, full of incense, **21** A young
bullock, a ram, a lamb of a year old for a burnt offering, **22** An he goat for a sin
offering, **23** And for peace offerings two bullocks, five rams, five he goats, five
lambs of a year old: this was the offering of Nethanel the son of Zuar. **24** The
third day Eliab the son of Helon prince of the children of Zebulun offe-
red. **25** His offering was a silver charger of an hundred and thirty shekels weight,
a silver bowl of seventy shekels, after the shekel of the Sanctuary, both full of fine
flour, mingled with oil, for a meat offering, **26** A golden incense cup of ten
shekels, full of incense, **27** A young bullock, a ram, a lamb of a year old for a
burnt offering, **28** An he goat for a sin offering, **29** And for peace offerings,
two bullocks, five rams, five he goats, five lambs of a year old: this was the offering
of Eliab the son of Helon. **30** The fourth day Elizur the son of Shedeur prince
of the children of Reuben offered. **31** His offering was a silver charger of an hun-
dred and thirty shekels weight, a silver bowl of seventy shekels, after the shekel of
the Sanctuary, both full of fine flour, mingled with oil, for a meat offering, **32** A
golden incense cup of ten shekels, full of incense, **33** A young bullock, a ram, a
lamb of a year old for a burnt offering, **34** An he goat for a sin offering, **35** And
for a peace offering, two bullocks, five rams, five he goats, and five lambs of a year
old: this was the offering of Elizur the son of Shedeur. **36** The fifth day Shelu-
miel the son of Zurishaddai, prince of the children of Simeon offered. **37** His
offering was a silver charger of an hundred and thirty shekels weight, a silver bowl
of seventy shekels: after the shekel of the Sanctuary, both full of fine flour, mingled
with oil, for a meat offering, **38** A golden incense cup of ten shekels, full of in-
cense, **39** A young bullock, a ram, a lamb of a year old for a burnt offe-
ring, **40** An he goat for a sin offering, **41** And for a peace offering, two bul-
locks, five rams, five he goats, five lambs of a year old: this was the offering of
Shelumiel the son of Zurishaddai. **42** The sixth day Eliasaph the son of Deuel
prince of the children of Gad offered. **43** His offering was a silver charger of an
hundred and thirty shekels weight, a silver bowl of seventy shekels, after the shekel
of the Sanctuary, both full of fine flour, mingled with oil, for a meat offe-
ring, **44** A golden incense cup of ten shekels, full of incense, **45** A young bul-
lock, a ram, a lamb of a year old for a burnt offering, **46** An he goat for a sin
offering, **47** And for a peace offering, two bullocks, five rams, five he goats, five
lambs of a year old: this was the offering of Eliasaph the son of Deuel. **48** The
seventh day Elishama the son of Ammihud prince of the children of Ephraim offe-
red. **49** His offering was a silver charger of an hundred and thirty shekels weight,
a silver bowl of seventy shekels, after the shekel of the Sanctuary, both full of fine
flour, mingled with oil, for a meat offering, **50** A golden incense cup of ten
shekels, full of incense, **51** A young bullock, a ram, a lamb of a year old for a
burnt offering, **52** An he goat for a sin offering, **53** And for a peace offering,
two bullocks, five rams, five he goats, five lambs of a year old: this was the offering
of Elishama the son of Ammihud. **54** The eighth day offered Gamaliel the son
of Pedahzur, prince of the children of Manasseh. **55** His offering was a silver
charger of an hundred and thirty shekels weight, a silver bowl of seventy shekels,
after the shekel of the Sanctuary, both full of fine flour, mingled with oil, for a meat
offering, **56** A golden incense cup of ten shekels, full of incense, **57** A young
bullock, a ram, a lamb of a year old for a burnt offering, **58** An he goat for a sin
offering, **59** And for a peace offering, two bullocks, five rams, five he goats, five
lambs of a year old: this was the offering of Gamaliel the son of Pedahzur. **60**
The ninth day Abidan the son of Gideoni prince of the children of Benjamin offe-
red. **61** His offering was a silver charger of an hundred and thirty shekels weight,
a silver bowl of seventy shekels, after the shekel of the Sanctuary, both full of fine
flour, mingled with oil, for a meat offering, **62** A golden incense cup of ten
shekels, full of incense, **63** A young bullock, a ram, a lamb of a year old for a
burnt offering, **64** An he goat for a sin offering, **65** And for a peace offering,
two bullocks, five rams, five he goats, five lambs of a year old: this was the offering
of Abidan the son of Gideoni. **66** The tenth day Ahiezer the son of Ammishad-
dai, prince of the children of Dan offered. **67** His offering was a silver charger of
an hundred and thirty shekels weight, a silver bowl of seventy shekels, after the
shekel of the Sanctuary, both full of fine flour, mingled with oil, for a meat offe-
ring, **68** A golden incense cup of ten shekels, full of incense, **69** A young
bullock, a ram, a lamb of a year old for a burnt offering, **70** An he goat for a sin
offering, **71** And for a peace offering, two bullocks, five rams, five he goats, five
lambs of a year old: this was the offering of Ahiezer the son of Ammishaddai. **72**
The eleventh day Pagiel the son of Ocran, prince of the children of Asher offe-
red. **73** His offering was a silver charger of an hundred and thirty shekels weight,
a silver bowl of seventy shekels, after the shekel of the Sanctuary, both full of fine
flour, mingled with oil, for a meat offering, **74** A golden incense cup of ten
shekels, full of incense, **75** A young bullock, a ram, a lamb of a year old for a
burnt offering, **76** An he goat for a sin offering, **77** And for a peace offering,
two bullocks, five rams, five he goats, five lambs of a year old: this was the offering
of Pagiel the son of Ocran. **78** The twelfth day Ahira the son of Enan, prince of
the children of Naphtali offered. **79** His offering was a silver charger of an hun-
dred and thirty shekels weight, a silver bowl of seventy shekels, after the shekel of
the Sanctuary, both full of fine flour, mingled with oil, for a meat offering, **80** A
golden incense cup of ten shekels, full of incense, **81** A young bullock, a ram, a
lamb of a year old for a burnt offering, **82** An he goat for a sin offering, **83** And
for peace offerings, two bullocks, five rams, five he goats, five lambs of a year old,
this was the offering of Ahira the son of Enan. **84** This was the [h]dedication of the
Altar by the princes of Israel, when it was anointed, twelve chargers of silver, twelve
silver bowls: twelve incense cups of gold, **85** Every charger containing an hun-
dred and thirty shekels of silver, and every bowl seventy: all the silver vessel contai-
ned two thousand and four hundred shekels, after the shekel of the San-
ctuary. **86** Twelve incense cups of gold full of incense, containing ten shekels
every cup, after the shekel of the Sanctuary: and the gold of the incense cups was
an hundred and twenty shekels. **87** All the bullocks for the burnt offering were
twelve bullocks, the rams twelve, the lambs of a year old twelve, with their meat
offerings, and twelve he goats for a sin offering. **88** And all the bullocks for the
peace offerings were four and twenty bullocks, the rams sixty, the he goats sixty, the
lambs of a year old sixty: this was the dedication of the Altar, after that it was [i]a-
nointed. **89** And when Moses went into the [j]tabernacle of the Congregation to
speak with God, he heard the voice of one speaking unto him from the Mercy seat,
that was upon the Ark of the Testimony [k]between the two Cherubims, and he spa-
ke unto him.

8

2 The order of the lamps. 6 The purifying and offering of the Levites. 24 The age of the Levites when they are received to service, and when they are dismissed.

1 And the Lord spake unto Moses, saying, **2** Speak unto Aaron, and say
unto him, When thou lightest the lamps, the seven lamps shall give light toward
the [a]forefront of the Candlestick. **3** And Aaron did so, lighting the lamps the-
reof toward the forefront of the Candlestick, as the Lord had commanded Mo-
ses. **4** And this was the work of the Candlestick, even of gold beaten out with
the hammer, both the shaft, and the flower thereof [1]was beaten out with the ham-
mer: [b]according to the pattern which the Lord had showed Moses, so made he
the Candlestick. **5** And the Lord spake unto Moses, saying, **6** Take the Levi-
tes from among the children of Israel, and purify them. **7** And thus shalt thou
do unto them, when thou purifiest them, Sprinkle [c]water of purification upon
them, and let them shave all their flesh, and wash their clothes: so they shall be
clean. **8** Then they shall take a young bullock with his meat offering of fine
flour, mingled with oil, and another young bullock shalt thou take for a sin offe-
ring. **9** Then thou shalt bring the Levites before the Tabernacle of the Congrega-
tion, and assemble [d]all the Congregation of the children of Israel. **10** Thou shalt
bring the Levites also before the Lord, and the [e]children of Israel shall put their
hands upon the Levites. **11** And Aaron shall offer the Levites before the Lord, as
a shake offering of the children of Israel, that they may execute the service of the
Lord. **12** And the Levites shall put their hands upon the heads of the bullocks,
and make thou the one a sin offering, and the other a burnt offering unto the Lord,
that thou mayest make an atonement for the Levites. **13** And thou shalt set the
Levites before Aaron and before his sons, and offer them as a shake offering to the
Lord. **14** Thus thou shalt separate the Levites from among the children of Isra-
el, and the Levites shall be [2]mine. **15** And afterward shall the Levites go in, to
serve in the Tabernacle of the Congregation, and thou shalt purify them, and offer
them as a shake offering. **16** For they are freely given [3]unto me from among the
children of Israel, for [f]such as open any womb: for all the firstborn of the children
of Israel have I taken them unto me. **17** [4]For all the firstborn of the children of
Israel are mine, both of man and beast: since the day that I smote every firstborn in
the land of Egypt, I sanctified them for myself. **18** And I have taken the Levites
for all the firstborn of the children of Israel, **19** And have given the Levites as a
gift unto Aaron, and to his sons from among the children of Israel, to do the servi-
ce of the [g]children of Israel in the Tabernacle of the Congregation, and to make an

---

h. Num. 7:84 This was the offering of the princes, when Aaron did dedicate the Altar.
i. Num. 7:88 By Aaron.
j. Num. 7:89 That is, the Sanctuary.
k. Num. 7:89 According as he had promised, Exod. 25:22.

NUM. 7
1. Exod. 40:18
2. Lev. 2:1

NUM. 8
a. Num. 8:2 To that part which is over against the Candlestick, Exod. 25:37.
b. Num. 8:4 And not set together of divers pieces.
c. Num. 8:7 In Hebrew it is called the water of sin, because it is made to purge sin, as Num. 19:9.
d. Num. 8:9 That thou mayest do this in presence of them all.
e. Num. 8:10 Meaning, certain of them in the name of the whole.
f. Num. 8:16 That is, they that are the firstborn.
g. Num. 8:19 Which service the Israelites should else do.
h. Num. 8:19 Because the Levites go into the Sanctuary in their name.
i. Num. 8:22 In their presence, to serve them.

atonement for the children of Israel, that there be no plague among the children of Israel, when the children of Israel come near unto the [h]Sanctuary. **20** Then Moses and Aaron and all the Congregation of the children of Israel did with the Levites, according unto all that the Lord had commanded Moses concerning the Levites: so did the children of Israel unto them. **21** So the Levites were purified, and washed their clothes, and Aaron offered them as a shake offering before the Lord, and Aaron made an atonement for them, to purify them. **22** And after that, went the Levites in to do their service in the Tabernacle of the Congregation, [i]before Aaron and before his sons: as the Lord had commanded Moses concerning the Levites, so they did unto them. **23** And the Lord spake unto Moses, saying, **24** This also belongeth to the Levites: from five and twenty years old and upward, they shall go in, to execute their office in the service of the Tabernacle of the Congregation. **25** And after the age of fifty years, they shall cease from executing the [j]office, and shall serve no more. **26** But they shall minister [k]with their brethren in the Tabernacle of the Congregation, to keep things committed to their charge, but they shall do no service: thus shalt thou do unto the Levites touching their charge.

9

2 The Passover is commanded again. 13 The punishment of him that kepeth not the Passover. 15 The cloud conducteth the Israelites through the wilderness.

1 And the Lord spake unto Moses in the wilderness of Sinai, in the first month of the second year, after they were come out of the land of Egypt, saying, **2** The children of Israel shall also celebrate the [1]Passover at the time appointed thereunto. **3** In the fourteenth day of this month at [2]even, ye shall keep it in his due season: according to [a]all the ordinances of it, and according to all the ceremonies thereof shall ye keep it. **4** Then Moses spake unto the children of Israel, to celebrate the Passover. **5** And they kept the Passover in the fourteenth day of the first month at even in the wilderness of Sinai: according to all that the Lord had commanded Moses, so did the children of Israel. **6** And certain men were defiled [b]by a dead man, that they might not keep the Passover the same day: and they came before Moses and before Aaron the same day. **7** And those men said unto him, We are defiled by a dead man: wherefore are we kept back that we may not [c]offer an offering unto the Lord in the time thereunto appointed among the children of Israel? **8** Then Moses said unto them, Stand still, and I will hear what the Lord will command concerning you. **9** And the Lord spake unto Moses, saying, **10** Speak unto the children of Israel, and say, If any among you, or of your posterity shall be unclean by the reason of a corpse, or be in a long journey, [d]he shall keep the Passover unto the Lord. **11** In the fourteenth day of the [e]second month at even they shall keep it: with unleavened bread, and sour herbs shall they eat it. **12** They shall leave none of it unto the morning, [3]nor break any bone of it: according to all the ordinance of the Passover shall they keep it. **13** But the man that is clean and is not in a [f]journey, and is negligent to keep the Passover, the same person shall be cut off from his people: because he brought not the offering of the Lord in his due season, that man shall bear his [g]sin. **14** And if a stranger dwell among you, and will keep the Passover unto the Lord, as the ordinance of the Passover, and as the manner thereof is, so shall he do: [4]ye shall have one law both for the stranger, and for him that was born in the same land. **15** [5]And when the Tabernacle was reared up, a cloud covered the Tabernacle, namely, the Tabernacle of the Testimony: and at even there was upon the Tabernacle, as the [h]appearance of fire until morning. **16** So it was alway: the cloud covered it by day, and the appearance of fire by night. **17** And when the cloud was taken up from the Tabernacle, then afterward the children of Israel journeyed: and in the place where the cloud abode, there the children of Israel pitched their tents. **18** At the [i]commandment of the [j]Lord the children of Israel journeyed, and at the commandment of the Lord they pitched: as long as the cloud abode upon the Tabernacle, [6]they [k]lay still. **19** And when the cloud tarried still upon the Tabernacle a long time, the children of Israel kept the [l]watch of the Lord, and journeyed not. **20** So when the cloud abode [m]a few days upon the Tabernacle, they abode in their tents according to the commandment of the Lord: for they journeyed at the commandment of the Lord. **21** And though the cloud abode upon the Tabernacle from even unto the morning, yet if the cloud was taken up in the morning, then they journeyed: whether by day or by night the cloud was taken up, then they journeyed. **22** Or if the cloud tarried two days, or a month, or a year upon the Tabernacle, abiding thereon, the children of Israel [7]abode still, and journeyed not: but when it was taken up, they journeyed. **23** At the commandment of the Lord they pitched, and at the commandment of the Lord they journeyed, keeping the watch of the Lord at the commandment of the Lord by the [n]hand of Moses.

10

2 The use of the silver trumpets. 11 The Israelites depart from Sinai. 14 The captains of the host are numbered. 30 Hobab refuseth to go with Moses his son-in-law.

1 And the Lord spake unto Moses, saying, **2** Make thee two trumpets of silver: of an [a]whole piece shalt thou make them, that thou mayest use them for the assembling of the Congregation, and for the departure of the camp. **3** And when they shall blow with them, all the Congregation shall assemble to thee, before the door of the Tabernacle of the Congregation. **4** But if they blow with one, then the Princes, or heads over the thousands of Israel shall come unto thee. **5** But if ye blow an alarm, then the camp of them that pitch on the [b]East part, shall go forward. **6** If ye blow an alarm the second time, then the host of them that lie on the [c]South side, shall march: for they shall blow an alarm when they remove. **7** But in the assembling the Congregation, ye shall blow without an alarm. **8** And the sons of Aaron the Priest shall [d]blow the trumpets, and ye shall have them as a law forever in your generations. **9** And when ye go to war in your land against the enemy that vexeth you, ye shall blow an alarm with the trumpets, and ye shall be remembered before the Lord your God, and shall be saved from your enemies. **10** Also in the day of your [e]gladness, and in your feast days, and in the beginning of your months, ye shall also blow the trumpets [f]over your burnt sacrifices, and over your peace offerings, that they may be a remembrance for you before your God: I am the Lord your God. **11** And in the second year, in the second month, and in the twentieth day of the month, the cloud was taken up from the Tabernacle of the Testimony. **12** And the children of Israel departed on their [g]journeys out of the desert of Sinai, and the cloud rested in the wilderness of Paran. **13** So they [h]first took their journey at the commandment of the Lord by the hand of Moses. **14** [1]In the first place went the standard of the host of the children of Judah according to their armies: and [2]Nahshon the son of Amminadab was over his band. **15** And over the band of the tribe of the children of Issachar was Nethanel the son of Zuar. **16** And over the band of the tribe of the children of Zebulun was Eliab the son of Helon. **17** When the Tabernacle was taken down, then the sons of Gershon and the sons of Merari went forward bearing [i]the Tabernacle. **18** After, departed the standard of the host of Reuben, according to their armies, and over his band was Elizur the son of Shedeur. **19** And over the band of the tribe of the children of Simeon was Shelumiel the son of Zurishaddai. **20** And over the band of the tribe of the children of Gad was Eliasaph the son of Deuel. **21** The Kohathites also went forward and [j]bare the [3]Sanctuary, and the [k]former did set up the Tabernacle against they came. **22** Then the standard of the host of the children of Ephraim went forward according to their armies, and over his band was Elishama the son of Ammihud. **23** And over the band of the tribe of the sons of Manasseh was Gamaliel the son of Pedahzur. **24** And over the band of the tribe of the sons of Benjamin was Abidan the son of Gideoni. **25** Last, the standard of the host of the children of Dan marched, [l]gathering all the hosts according to their armies: and over his band was Ahiezer the son of Ammishaddai. **26** And over the band of the tribe of the children of Asher was Pagiel the son of Ocran. **27** And over the band of the tribe of the children of Naphtali was Ahira the son of Enan. **28** [m]These were the removings of the children of Israel according to their armies, when they marched. **29** After, Moses said unto [n]Hobab the son of Reuel the Midianite, the father-in-law of Moses, We go into the place, of which the Lord said, I will give it you Come thou with us, and we will do thee good: for the Lord hath promised good unto Israel. **30** And he answered him, I will not go: but I will depart to mine own country, and to my kindred. **31** Then he said, I pray thee, leave us not: for thou knowest our camping places in the wilderness: therefore thou mayest be [o]our guide. **32** And if thou go

---

j. Num. 8:25 Such office as was painful, as to bear burdens and such like.
k. Num. 8:26 In singing Psalms, instructing, counseling and keeping the things in order.

NUM. 8

1. Exod. 25:18
2. Num. 3:45
3. Num. 3:9
4. Exod. 13:2 / Luke 2:23

NUM. 9

a. Num. 9:3 Even in all points as the Lord hath instituted it.
b. Num. 9:6 By touching a corpse, or being at the burial.
c. Num. 9:7 Or, celebrate the Passover the fourteenth day of the first month.
d. Num. 9:10 And cannot come where the Tabernacle is, when others keep it.
e. Num. 9:11 So that the unclean, and they that are not at home, have a month longer granted unto them.
f. Num. 9:13 When the Passover is celebrated.
g. Num. 9:13 Or, punishment of his sin.
h. Num. 9:15 Like a pillar, read Exod. 13:22.
i. Num. 9:18 Hebrew, mouth.
j. Num. 9:18 Who taught them what to do by the cloud.
k. Num. 9:18 Hebrew, camped.
l. Num. 9:19 They waited when the Lord would signify either their departure, or their abode by the cloud.
m. Num. 9:20 Hebrew, days of number.
n. Num. 9:23 Under the charge and government of Moses.

NUM. 9

1. Exod. 12:1 / Lev. 23:5 / Num. 28:16 / Deut. 16:2
2. Exod. 12:6 / Deut. 16:6
3. Exod. 12:46 / John 19:36
4. Exod. 12:49
5. Exod. 40:34
6. 1 Cor. 10:1
7. Exod. 40:36,37 / Num. 9:18

NUM. 10

a. Num. 10:2 Or, of work beaten out with the hammer.
b. Num. 10:5 That is, the host of Judah and they that are under his ensign.
c. Num. 10:6 Meaning, the host of Reuben.
d. Num. 10:8 So that only the Priests must blow the trumpets, so long as the Priesthood lasted.
e. Num. 10:10 When ye rejoice that God hath removed any plague.
f. Num. 10:10 Or, when ye offer burnt offerings.
g. Num. 10:12 Or, in keeping this order in their journeys.
h. Num. 10:13 From Sinai to Paran, Num. 33:1.
i. Num. 10:17 With all the appertainances thereof.
j. Num. 10:21 Upon their shoulders.
k. Num. 10:21 The Merarites and Gershonites.
l. Num. 10:25 Leaving none behind, nor any of the former that fainted in the way.
m. Num. 10:28 This was the order of their host when they removed.
n. Num. 10:29 Some think that Reuel, Jethro, Hobab, and Keni were all one: Kimhi saith, that Reuel was Jethro's father: so Hobab was Moses' father-in-law, see Exod. 2:18, 3:1, 4:18, 18:1, and Judg. 4:11.
o. Num. 10:31 Hebrew, eyes unto us.
p. Num. 10:33 Mount Sinai, or Horeb.

with us, what goodness the Lord shall show unto us, the same will we show unto thee. **33** So they departed from the [p]mount of the Lord, three days' journey: and the Ark of the covenant of the Lord went before them in the three days' journey, to search out a resting place for them. **34** And the cloud of the Lord was upon them by day, when they went out of the camp. **35** And when the Ark went forward, Moses said, [q,4]Rise up Lord, and let thine enemies be scattered, and let them that hate thee, flee before thee. **36** And when it rested, he said, Return, O Lord, to the [r]many thousands of Israel.

11

1 The people murmureth, and is punished with fire. 4 The people lusteth after flesh. 6 They loathe Manna. 11 The weak faith of Moses. 16 The Lord divided the burden of Moses to seventy of the Ancients. 31 The Lord sendeth quails. 33 Their lust is punished.

1 When the people became [a]murmurers, [b]it displeased the Lord: and the Lord heard it, therefore his wrath was kindled, and the fire of the Lord burnt among them, and [1]consumed the utmost part of the host. **2** Then the people cried unto Moses: and when Moses prayed unto the Lord, the fire was quenched. **3** And he called the name of the place [c]Taberah, because the fire of the Lord burnt among them. **4** And a number of [d]people that was among them, fell a lusting, and [e]turned away, and the children of Israel also wept, and said, Who shall give us flesh to eat? **5** We remember the fish which we did eat in Egypt for [f]nought, the cucumbers, and the pepons, and the leeks, and the onions, and the garlic. **6** But now our soul is [g]dried away, we can see nothing but this Manna. **7** (The Manna also was as [2]coriander seed, and his color like the color of [h]bdellium. **8** The people went about and gathered, and ground it in mills, or beat it in mortars, and baked it in a cauldron, and made cakes of it, and the taste of it was like unto the taste of fresh oil. **9** And when the dew fell down upon the host in night, the Manna fell with it.) **10** Then Moses heard the people weep throughout their families, every man in the door of his tent, and the wrath of the Lord was grievously kindled: also Moses was grieved. **11** And Moses said unto the Lord, Wherefore hast thou [i]vexed thy servant? and why have I not found [j]favor in thy sight, seeing thou hast put the charge of all this people upon me? **12** Have I [k]conceived all this people? or have I begotten them, that thou shouldest say unto me, Carry them in thy bosom (as a nurse beareth the sucking child) unto the [l]land, for the which thou swarest unto their fathers? **13** Where should I have flesh to give unto all this people? for they weep unto me, saying, Give us flesh that we may eat. **14** I am not able to bear all this people alone, for it is too heavy for me. **15** Therefore if thou deal thus with me, I pray thee, if I have found favor in thy [m]sight, kill me, that I behold not my misery. **16** Then the Lord said unto Moses, Gather unto me seventy men of the Elders of Israel, whom thou knowest, that they are the Elders of the people, and governors over them, and bring them unto the Tabernacle of the Congregation, and let them stand there with thee. **17** And I will come down, and talk with thee there, [n]and take of the Spirit, which is upon thee, and put upon them, and they shall bear the burden of the people with thee: so thou shalt not bear it alone. **18** Furthermore thou shalt say unto the people, [o]Be sanctified against tomorrow, and ye shall eat flesh: for you have wept in the ears of the Lord, saying, Who shall give us flesh to eat? for we were better in Egypt: therefore the Lord will give you flesh, and ye shall eat. **19** Ye shall not eat one day nor two days, nor five days, neither ten days, nor twenty days, **20** But a whole month, until it come out at your nostrils, and be loathsome unto you, because ye have [p]contemned the Lord, which is [q]among you, and have wept before him, saying, Why came we hither out of Egypt? **21** And Moses said, Six hundred thousand footmen are there of the people, [r]among whom I am: and thou sayest, I will give them flesh, that they may eat a month long. **22** Shall the sheep and the beeves be slain for them to find them? either shall all the fish of the Sea be gathered together for them to suffice them? **23** And the Lord said unto Moses, Is [3]the Lord's hand shortened? thou shalt see now whether my word shall come to pass unto thee, or no. **24** So Moses went out, and told the people the words of the Lord, and gathered seventy men of the Elders of the people, and set them round about the Tabernacle. **25** Then the Lord came down in a cloud, and spake unto him, and [s]took of the Spirit that was upon him, and put it upon the seventy Ancient men: and when the Spirit rested upon them, then they prophesied, and did not [t]cease. **26** But there remained two of the men in the host: the name of the one was Eldad, and the name of the other Medad, and the Spirit rested upon them, (for they were of them that were written, and went not out unto the Tabernacle) and they prophesied in the host. **27** Then there ran a young man, and told Moses, and said, Eldad and Medad do prophesy in the host. **28** And Joshua the son of Nun the servant of Moses one of his [u]young men answered and said, My lord Moses, [v]forbid them. **29** But Moses said unto him, Enviest thou for my sake? yea, would God that all the Lord's people were Prophets, and that the Lord would put his spirit upon them. **30** And Moses returned into the host, he and the Elders of Israel. **31** Then there went forth a wind from the Lord, and [4]brought quails from the sea, and let them fall upon the camp, a day's journey on this side, and a day's journey on the other side, round about the host, and they were about two cubits above the earth. **32** Then the people arose, all that day, and all the night, and all the next day, and gathered the quails: he that gathered the least, gathered ten [w]Homers full, and they spread them abroad for their use round about the host. **33** While the flesh was yet between their teeth, before it was chewed, even the wrath of the Lord was kindled against the people, and the Lord [5]smote the people with an exceeding great plague. **34** So the name of the place was called, [x]Kibroth Hattaavah: for there they buried the people that fell a lusting. **35** From Kibroth Hattaavah the people took their journey to Hazeroth, and abode at Hazeroth.

12

1 Aaron and Miriam grudge against Moses. 10 Miriam is stricken with leprosy, and healed at the prayer of Moses.

1 Afterward Miriam and Aaron [a]spake against Moses, because of the woman of Ethiopia whom he had married (for he had married [b]a woman of Ethiopia.) **2** And they said, What? hath the Lord spoken but only by Moses? hath he not spoken also by us? and the Lord heard this. **3** (But Moses was a very [c]meek man above all the men that were upon the earth.) **4** And by and by the Lord said unto Moses, and unto Aaron, and unto Miriam, come out ye three unto the Tabernacle of the Congregation: and they three came forth. **5** Then the Lord came down in the pillar of the cloud, and stood in the door of the Tabernacle, and called Aaron and Miriam, and they both came forth. **6** And he said, Hear now my words, If there be a Prophet of the Lord among you, I will be known to him by a [d]vision, and will speak unto him by dream. **7** My servant Moses is not so, who is faithful [e]in all mine house, **8** Unto him will I speak [1]mouth to mouth, and by vision, and not in dark words, but he shall [f]see the similitude of the Lord Wherefore then were ye not afraid to speak against my servant, even against Moses? **9** Thus the Lord was very angry with them, and departed. **10** Also the cloud departed from the [g]Tabernacle: and behold, Miriam was leprous like snow: and Aaron looked upon Miriam, and behold, she was leprous. **11** Then Aaron said unto Moses, Alas, my lord, I beseech thee, lay not the sin upon us, which we have foolishly committed, and wherein we have sinned. **12** Let her not, I pray thee, be as one [h]dead, of whom the flesh is half consumed, when he cometh out of his mother's womb. **13** Then Moses cried unto the Lord, saying, O God, I beseech thee, heal her now. **14** And the Lord said unto Moses, If her father had [i]spit in her face, should she not have been ashamed seven days? let her be [2]shut out of the host seven days, and after she shall be received. **15** So Miriam was shut out of the host seven days, and the people removed not, till Miriam was brought in again.

13

4 Certain men are sent to search the land of Canaan. 24 They bring of the fruit of the land. 31 Caleb comforteth the people against the discouraging of the other spies.

1 Then afterward the people removed from Hazeroth, and pitched in the wilderness of [a]Paran. **2** And the Lord spake unto Moses, saying, **3** [b]Send thou men out to search the land of Canaan which I give unto the children of Israel:

---

q. Num. 10:35 Declare thy might and power.
r. Num. 10:36 Hebrew, to the ten thousand thousands.

NUM. 10
1. Num. 2:3
2. Num. 1:7
3. Num. 4:4
4. Ps. 68:1,2

NUM. 11
a. Num. 11:1 Hebrew, as unjust complainers.
b. Num. 11:1 Hebrew, it was evil in the ears of the Lord.
c. Num. 11:3 Or, burning.
d. Num. 11:4 Which were of those strangers that came out of Egypt with them, Exod. 12:38.
e. Num. 11:4 From God.
f. Num. 11:5 For a small price, or good cheap.
g. Num. 11:6 For the greedy lust of flesh.
h. Num. 11:7 Which is a white pearl, or precious stone.
i. Num. 11:11 Or, evil intreated.
j. Num. 11:11 Or, wherein have I displeased thee?
k. Num. 11:12 Am I their father, that none may have the charge of them but I?
l. Num. 11:12 Of Canaan promised by an oath to our fathers.
m. Num. 11:15 I had rather die than to see my grief and misery thus daily increase by their rebellion.
n. Num. 11:17 I will distribute my spirit among them, as I have done to thee.
o. Num. 11:18 Prepare yourselves that ye be not unclean.
p. Num. 11:20 Or, cast him off, because ye refused Manna, which he appointed as most meet for you.
q. Num. 11:20 Who leadeth and governeth you.
r. Num. 11:21 Of whom I have the charge.
s. Num. 11:25 Or, separated, verse 17.
t. Num. 11:25 From that day the spirit of prophecy did not fail them.
u. Num. 11:28 Or, a young man whom he had chosen from his youth.
v. Num. 11:28 Such blind zeal was in the Apostles, Mark 9:38; Luke 9:44.
w. Num. 11:32 Of Homer, read Lev. 27:16, also it signifieth an heap, as Exod. 8:14; Judg. 15:16.
x. Num. 11:34 Or, graves of lust.

NUM. 11
1. Ps. 78:21
2. Exod. 16:31 / Ps. 78:24 / John 6:31
3. Isa. 50:2 / Isa. 59:1
4. Exod. 16:13 / Ps. 78:26,27
5. Ps. 78:31

NUM. 12
a. Num. 12:1 Or, murmured.
b. Num. 12:1 Zipporah Moses' wife was a Midianite, and because Midian bordered on Ethiopia, it is sometimes in the Scriptures comprehended under this name.
c. Num. 12:3 And so bare with their grudging, although he knew them.
d. Num. 12:6 These were the two ordinary means.
e. Num. 12:7 In all Israel which was his Church.
f. Num. 12:8 So far as any man was able to comprehend, which he calleth his back parts, Exod. 33:23.
g. Num. 12:10 From the door of the Tabernacle.
h. Num. 12:12 As a child that cometh out of his mother's belly dead, having as it were but the skin.
i. Num. 12:14 In his displeasure.

NUM. 12
1. Exod. 33:11
2. Lev. 13:46

of every tribe of their fathers shall ye send a man, such as are all rulers among
them. **4** Then Moses sent them out of the wilderness of Paran at the command-
ment of the Lord: all those men were [c]heads of the children of Israel. **5** Also their
names are these: of the tribe of Reuben, Shammua the son of Zaccur: **6** Of the
tribe of Simeon, Shaphat the son of Hori: **7** Of the tribe of Judah, Caleb the son
of Jephunneh: **8** Of the tribe of Issachar, Igal the son of Joseph: **9** Of the tribe
of Ephraim, [d]Hoshea the son of Nun: **10** Of the tribe of Benjamin, Palti the son
of Raphu: **11** Of the tribe of Zebulun, Gaddiel the son of Sodi: **12** Of the tri-
be of Joseph, to wit, of the tribe of Manasseh, Gaddi the son of Susi: **13** Of the
tribe of Dan, Ammiel the son of Gemalli: **14** Of the tribe of Asher, Sethur the
son of Michael: **15** Of the tribe of Naphtali, Nahbi the son of Vophsi: **16** Of
the tribe of Gad, Geuel the son of Machi. **17** These are the names of the [e]men,
which Moses sent to spy out the land: and Moses called the name of Hoshea the
son of Nun, Joshua. **18** So Moses sent them to spy out the land of Canaan,
and said to them, Go up this way toward the South, and go up into the [f]moun-
tains. **19** And consider the land what it is, and the people that dwell therein,
whether they be strong, or weak, either few or many. **20** Also what the land is
that they dwell in, whether it be [g]good or bad: and what cities they be, that they
dwell in, whether they dwell in tents, or in walled towns. **21** And what the land
is: whether it be fat or lean, whether there be trees therein, or not And be of good
courage, and bring of the fruit of the land (for then was the time of the first ripe
grapes.) **22** So they went up, and searched out the land, from the wilderness of
[h]Zin unto Rehob, to go to Hamath. **23** And they ascended toward the South,
and came unto Hebron, where were Ahiman, Sheshai, and Talmai, the sons of
[i]Anak And [j]Hebron was built seven years before Zoan in Egypt. **24** [1]Then they
came to the river of Eshcol, and cut down thence a branch with one cluster of gra-
pes, and they bare it upon a bar between two, and brought of the pomegranates
and of the figs. **25** That place was called the [k]river Eshcol, because of the cluster
of grapes, which the children of Israel cut down thence. **26** Then after forty days
they turned again from searching of the land. **27** And they went and came to
Moses and to Aaron, and unto all the Congregation of the children of Israel, in
the wilderness of [l]Paran, to Kadesh, and brought to them, and to all the Congre-
gation tidings, and showed them the fruit of the land. **28** And they told [m]him,
and said, We came unto the land whither thou hast sent us, and surely it floweth
with [2]milk and honey: and here is of the fruit of it. **29** Nevertheless the people
be strong that dwell in the land, and the cities are walled and exceeding great: and
moreover, we saw the [n]sons of Anak there. **30** The Amalekites dwell in the South
country, and the Hittites, and the Jebusites, and the Amorites dwell in the moun-
tains, and the Canaanites dwell by the sea, and by the coasts of Jordan. **31** Then
Caleb stilled the people [o]before Moses, and said, Let us go up at once, and possess
it: for undoubtedly we shall overcome it. **32** But the men that went up with
him, said, We be not able to go up against the people: for they are stronger than
we. **33** So they brought up an evil report of the land which they had searched
for the children of Israel, saying, The land which we have gone through to search
it out, is a land that [p]eateth up the inhabitants thereof: for all the people that we
saw in it, are men of great stature. **34** For there we saw giants, the sons of Anak,
which come of the giants, so that we seemed in our sight like grasshoppers: and so
we were in their sight.

14

2 The people murmur against Moses. 10 They would have stoned Caleb and Joshua. 23 Moses pacifieth God by his prayer. 45 The people that would enter into the land contrary to God's will, are slain.

1 Then all the Congregation lifted up their voice, and cried: and the [a]people
wept that night, **2** And all the children of Israel murmured against Moses and
Aaron: and the whole assembly said unto them, Would God we had died in the
land of Egypt, or in this wilderness: would God we were dead. **3** Wherefore now
hath the Lord brought us into this land to fall upon the sword? our wives and our
children shall be [b]a prey: were it not better for us to return into Egypt? **4** And
they said one to another, Let us make a captain and return into Egypt. **5** Then
Moses and Aaron [c]fell on their faces before all the assembly of the Congregation
of the children of Israel. **6** And Joshua the son of Nun, and Caleb the son of
Jephunneh two of them that searched the land, [d]rent their clothes, **7** And spake
unto all the assembly of the children of Israel, saying, The land which we walked
through to search it, is a very good land. **8** If the Lord love us, he will bring
us into this land, and give it us, which is a land that floweth with milk and ho-
ney. **9** But rebel not ye against the Lord, neither fear ye the people of the land: for
they are but [e]bread for us: their shield is departed from them, and the Lord is with
us, fear them not. **10** And all the multitude said, [f]Stone them with stones: but
the glory of the Lord appeared in the Tabernacle of the Congregation before all the
children of Israel. **11** And the Lord said unto Moses, How long will this people
provoke me, and how long will it be ere they believe me, for all the signs which I
have showed among them? **12** I will smite them with the pestilence and destroy
them, and will make thee a greater nation and mightier than they. **13** But Moses
said unto the Lord, [1]When the Egyptians shall hear it, (for thou broughtest this
people by thy power from among them) **14** Then they shall say to the inhabi-
tants of the land, (for they have heard, that thou Lord, art among this people, and
that thou, Lord, art seen [g]face to face, and that thy cloud standeth over them, and
that thou [2]goest before them, by daytime in a pillar of a cloud, and in a pillar of
fire by night.) **15** That thou wilt kill this people as [h]one man: so the heathen
which have heard the fame of thee, shall thus say, **16** Because the Lord was not
[3]able to bring this people into the land which he sware unto them, therefore hath
he slain them in the wilderness. **17** And now, I beseech thee, let the power of
my Lord be great, according as thou hast spoken, saying, **18** The Lord is [4]slow
to anger, and of great mercy, and [5]forgiving iniquity and sin, but not making the
wicked innocent, and [6]visiting the wickedness of the fathers upon the children, in
the third and fourth generation: **19** Be merciful, I beseech thee, unto the ini-
quity of this people, according to thy great mercy, and as thou hast forgiven this
people from Egypt, even until now. **20** And the Lord said, I have forgiven [i]it,
according to thy request. **21** Notwithstanding, as I live, all the earth, shall be fil-
led with the glory of the Lord. **22** For all those men which have seen my glory,
and my miracles which I did in Egypt, and in the wilderness, and have tempted
me this [j]ten times, and have not obeyed my voice, **23** Certainly they shall not see
the land, whereof I sware unto their fathers: neither shall any that provoke me, see
it. **24** But my servant [7]Caleb, because he had another [k]spirit, and hath followed
me still, even him will I bring into the land, whither he went, and his seed shall
inherit it. **25** Now the Amalekites and the Canaanites [l]remain in the valley: whe-
refore turn back tomorrow, and get you into the [m]wilderness, by the way of the red
sea. **26** After, the Lord spake unto Moses and to Aaron, saying, **27** [8]How long
shall I suffer this wicked multitude to murmur against me? I have heard the mur-
murings of the children of Israel, which they murmur against me. **28** Tell them,
As I [9]live (saith the Lord) I will surely do unto you, even as ye have spoken in mine
ears. **29** Your carcasses shall fall in this wilderness, and all you that were [10]coun-
ted through all your numbers, from twenty years old and above, which have mur-
mured against me, **30** Ye shall not doubtless come into the land, for the which
I [11]lifted up mine hand, to make you dwell therein, save Caleb the son of Jephun-
neh, and Joshua the son of Nun. **31** But your children (which ye said should
be a prey) them will I bring in, and they shall know the land which ye have refu-
sed: **32** But even your carcasses shall fall in this wilderness. **33** And your chil-
dren shall [n]wander in the wilderness forty years, and shall bear your [o]whoredoms,
until your carcasses be wasted in the wilderness. **34** After the number of the days
in the which ye searched out the land, even forty days, [12]every day for a year, shall
you bear your iniquity, for [13]forty years, and ye [p]shall feel my breach of promi-
se. **35** I the Lord have said, Certainly I will do so to all this wicked company that
are gathered together against me: for in this wilderness they shall be consumed, and
there they shall die. **36** And the men which Moses had sent to search the land
(which when they came again, made all the people to murmur against him, and
brought up a slander upon the land.) **37** Even those men that did bring up that
vile slander upon the land, [14]shall die by a plague before the Lord. **38** But Joshua
the son of Nun, and Caleb the son of Jephunneh, of those men that went to search
the land, shall live. **39** Then Moses told these sayings unto all the children of
Israel, and the people sorrowed greatly. **40** [15]And they rose up early in the mor-
ning, and got them up into the top of the mountain, saying, Lo, we be ready to
go up to the place which the Lord hath promised: for we have [q]sinned. **41** But

---

NUM. 13

- **a.** Num. 13:1 That is, in Rithmah, which was in Paran, Num. 33:18.
- **b.** Num. 13:3 After the people had required it of Moses, as it is in Deut. 1:22, then the Lord spake to Moses so to do.
- **c.** Num. 13:4 Or, rulers.
- **d.** Num. 13:9 Or, Joshua.
- **e.** Num. 13:17 Which in number were twelve, according to the twelve tribes.
- **f.** Num. 13:18 Or, his country.
- **g.** Num. 13:20 Plentiful or barren.
- **h.** Num. 13:22 Which was in the wilderness of Paran.
- **i.** Num. 13:23 Which were a kind of giants.
- **j.** Num. 13:23 Declaring the antiquity thereof: also Abraham, Sarah, Isaac and Jacob were buried there.
- **k.** Num. 13:25 Or, the valley of Eshcol, that is, of grapes.
- **l.** Num. 13:27 Called also Kadesh Barnea.
- **m.** Num. 13:28 That is, Moses.
- **n.** Num. 13:29 Ahiman, Sheshai, and Talmai, whom Caleb slew afterward, Josh. 11:21, 22.
- **o.** Num. 13:31 Or, murmuring against Moses.
- **p.** Num. 13:33 The giants were so cruel, that they spoiled and killed one another and those that came to them.

NUM. 13

- **1.** Deut. 1:24
- **2.** Exod. 33:3

NUM. 14

- **a.** Num. 14:1 Such as were afraid at the report of the ten spies.
- **b.** Num. 14:3 To our enemies the Canaanites.
- **c.** Num. 14:5 Lamenting the people, and praying for them.
- **d.** Num. 14:6 For sorrow, hearing their blasphemy.
- **e.** Num. 14:9 We shall easily overcome them.
- **f.** Num. 14:10 This is the condition of them that would persuade in God's cause, to be persecuted of the multitude.
- **g.** Num. 14:14 Hebrew, eye to eye.
- **h.** Num. 14:15 So that none shall escape.
- **i.** Num. 14:20 In that he destroyed not them utterly, but left their posterity and certain to enter.
- **j.** Num. 14:22 That is, sundry times and often.
- **k.** Num. 14:24 A meek and obedient spirit, and not rebellious.
- **l.** Num. 14:25 And lie in wait for you.
- **m.** Num. 14:25 For I will not defend you.
- **n.** Num. 14:33 The word signifieth to be shepherds, or to wander like shepherds to and fro.
- **o.** Num. 14:33 Your infidelity and disobedience against God.
- **p.** Num. 14:34 Whether my promise be true or no.
- **q.** Num. 14:40 They confess they sinned by rebelling against God, but consider not they offended in going up without God's commandment.
- **r.** Num. 14:44 They could not be stayed by any means.

NUM. 14

- **1.** Exod. 32:12
- **2.** Exod. 13:21
- **3.** Deut. 9:28
- **4.** Exod. 34:6 / Ps. 103:8
- **5.** Ps. 10:3
- **6.** Exod. 20:5 / Exod. 34:7
- **7.** Josh. 14:6
- **8.** Ps. 106:26
- **9.** Num. 26:65 / Num. 32:10
- **10.** Deut. 1:35
- **11.** Gen. 14:22
- **12.** Ezek. 4:6
- **13.** Ps. 95:10
- **14.** 1 Cor. 10:10 / Heb. 3:10,17 / Jude 5
- **15.** Deut. 1:41

Moses said, Wherefore transgress ye thus the commandment of the Lord? it will
not so come well to pass. **42** Go not up, (for the Lord is not among you) lest ye
be overthrown before your enemies. **43** For the Amalekites and the Canaanites
are there before you, and ye shall fall by the sword: for inasmuch as ye are turned
away from the Lord, the Lord also will not be with you. **44** Yet they presumed
[r]obstinately to go up to the top of the mountain: but the Ark of the covenant of
the Lord, and Moses departed not out of the camp. **45** Then the Amalekites and
the Canaanites, which dwelt in that mountain, came down and smote them, [16]and
consumed them unto Hormah.

15

2 The offering which the Israelites should offer when they came into the land of Canaan. 32 The punishment of him that brake the Sabbath.

1 And the Lord spake unto Moses, saying, **2** Speak unto the children of
Israel, and say unto them, [1]When ye be come into the [a]land of your habitations
which I give unto you, **3** And will make an offering by fire unto the Lord, a bur-
nt offering or a sacrifice [b,2]to fulfill a vow, or a free offering, or in your feasts to
make a [3]sweet savor unto the Lord, of the herd or of the flock, **4** Then [4]let him
that offereth his offering unto the Lord, bring a meat offering of a tenth deal of fine
flour, mingled with the fourth part of an [c]Hin of oil. **5** Also thou shalt prepare
the fourth part of an Hin of wine to be poured on a lamb appointed for the burnt
offering, or any offering. **6** And for a ram thou shalt for a meat offering, prepare
two tenth deals of fine flour, mingled with the third part of an Hin of oil. **7** And
for a [d]drink offering thou shalt offer the third part of an Hin of wine, for a sweet
savor unto the Lord. **8** And when thou preparest a bullock for a burnt offering,
or for a sacrifice to fulfill a vow or a peace offering to the Lord, **9** Then let him
offer with the bullock a meat offering of [e]three tenth deals of fine flour, mingled
with half an Hin of oil. **10** And thou shalt bring for a drink offering half an Hin
of wine, for an offering made by fire of a sweet savor unto the Lord. **11** Thus
shall it be done for a bullock, or for a ram, or for a lamb, or for a kid. **12** Ac-
cording to the number [f]that ye prepare to offer, so shall ye do to everyone accor-
ding to their number. **13** All that are born of the country, shall do these things
thus, to offer an offering made by fire of sweet savor unto the Lord. **14** And if a
stranger sojourn with you, or whosoever be among you in your generations, and
will make an offering by fire of a sweet savor unto the Lord, as ye do, so he shall
do. **15** [5]One ordinance shall be both for you of the Congregation, and also for
the stranger that dwelleth with you, even an ordinance forever in your generations:
as you are, so shall the stranger be before the Lord. **16** One law and one manner
shall serve both for you and for the stranger that sojourneth with you. **17** And
the Lord spake unto Moses, saying, **18** Speak unto the children of Israel, and say
unto them, When ye be come into the land, to the which I bring you, **19** And
when ye shall eat of the bread of the land, ye shall offer an heave offering unto the
Lord. **20** Ye shall offer up a cake of the first of your [g]dough for an heave offering:
[6]as the heave offering of the barn, so ye shall lift it up. **21** Of the first of your
dough ye shall give unto the Lord an heave offering in your generations. **22** And
if ye [h]have erred, and not observed all these commandments, which the Lord hath
spoken unto Moses, **23** Even all that the Lord hath commanded you by the hand
of Moses, from the first day that the Lord commanded Moses, and hence forward
among your generations: **24** And if so be that ought be committed ignorantly
of the [i]Congregation, then all the Congregation shall give a bullock for a burnt of-
fering, for a sweet savor unto the Lord, with the meat offering and drink offering
thereto, according to the [7]manner, and an he goat for a sin offering. **25** And the
Priest shall make an atonement for all the Congregation of the children of Israel,
and it shall be forgiven them: for it is ignorance: and they shall bring their offering
for an offering made by fire unto the Lord, and their sin offering before the Lord
for their ignorance. **26** Then shall be forgiven all the Congregation of the chil-
dren of Israel, and the stranger that dwelleth among them: for all the people were
in ignorance. **27** [8]But if any one person sin through ignorance, then he shall
bring a she goat of a year old for a sin offering. **28** And the Priest shall make
an atonement for the ignorant person, when he sinneth by ignorance before the
Lord, to make reconciliation for him: and it shall be forgiven him. **29** He that
is born among the children of Israel, and the stranger that dwelleth among them,
shall have both one law, who so doth sin by ignorance. **30** But the person that
doeth ought [j]presumptuously, whether he be born in the land, or a stranger, the
same blasphemeth the Lord: therefore that person shall be cut off from among his
people, **31** Because he hath despised the word of the Lord, and hath broken his
commandment: that person shall be utterly cut off: his [k]iniquity shall be upon
him. **32** And while the children of Israel were in the wilderness, they found a
man that gathered sticks upon the Sabbath day. **33** And they that found him
gathering sticks, brought him unto Moses and to Aaron, and unto all the Con-
gregation, **34** And they put him [9]ward: for it was not declared what should be
done unto him. **35** Then the Lord said unto Moses, This man shall die the de-
ath: and let all the multitude stone him with stones without the host. **36** And
all the Congregation brought him without the host, and stoned him with stones,
and he died, as the Lord had commanded Moses. **37** And the Lord spake unto
Moses, saying, **38** Speak unto the children of Israel, and bid them that they
[10]make them fringes upon the borders of their garments throughout their gene-
rations, and put upon the fringes of the borders a ribbon of blue silk. **39** And
ye shall have the fringes that when ye look upon them, ye may remember all the
commandments of the Lord, and do them: and that ye seek not after your own
heart, nor after your own eyes, after the which ye go a [l]whoring; **40** That ye may
remember and do all my commandments, and be holy unto your God. **41** I am
the Lord your God, which brought you out of the land of Egypt to be your God:
I am the Lord your God.

16

1 The rebellion of Korah, Dathan, and Abiram. 31 Korah and his company perisheth. 41 The people the next day murmur. 49 14,700 are slain for murmuring.

1 Now [1]Korah the son of Izhar, the son of Kohath, the son of Levi [a]went apart
with Dathan, and Abiram the son of Eliab, and On the son of Peleth, the sons of
Reuben: **2** And they rose up [b]against Moses, with certain of the children of Isra-
el, two hundred and fifty captains of the assembly, [2]famous in the Congregation,
and men of renown, **3** Who gathered themselves together against Moses, and
against Aaron, and said unto them, [c]Ye take too much upon you, seeing all the
Congregation is holy, [d]every one of them, and the Lord is among them: wherefore
then lift ye yourselves above the Congregation of the Lord? **4** But when Moses
heard it, he fell upon his face, **5** And spake to Korah and unto all his company,
saying, Tomorrow the Lord will show who is his, and who is holy, and who ought
to approach near unto him: and whom he hath [e]chosen, he will cause to come
near to him. **6** This do therefore, Take you censers, both Korah and all his com-
pany, **7** And put fire therein, and put incense in them before the Lord tomorrow:
and the man whom the Lord doth choose, the same shall be holy: [f]ye take too much
upon you, ye sons of Levi. **8** Again Moses said unto Korah, Hear, I pray you, ye
sons of Levi. **9** Seemeth it a small thing unto you, that the God of Israel hath
separated you from the multitude of Israel, to take you near to himself, to do the
service of the Tabernacle of the Lord, and to stand before the Congregation, and to
minister unto them? **10** He hath also taken thee to [g]him, and all thy brethren,
the sons of Levi with thee, and seek ye the office of the Priest also? **11** For whi-
ch cause, thou, and all thy company are gathered together against the Lord: and
what is Aaron, that ye murmur against him? **12** And Moses sent to call Dathan,
and Abiram the sons of Eliab: who answered, We will not come up. **13** Is it a
small thing that thou hast brought us out [h]of a land that floweth with milk and
honey, to kill us in the wilderness, except thou make thyself lord and ruler over us
also? **14** Also thou hast not brought us unto a land that floweth with milk and
honey, neither given us inheritance of fields and vineyards: wilt thou [i]put out the
eyes of these men? we will not come up. **15** Then Moses waxed very angry, and
said unto the Lord, [3]Look not unto their offering: I have not taken so much as an
ass from them, neither have I hurt any of them. **16** And Moses said unto Korah,
Be thou and all thy company [j]before the Lord: both thou, they, and Aaron tomor-
row. **17** And take every man his censer, and put incense in them, and bring ye
every man his censer before the Lord, two hundred and fifty censers: thou also and
Aaron, every one his censer. **18** So they took every man his censer, and put fire
in them, and laid incense thereon, and stood in the door of the Tabernacle of the
Congregation with Moses and Aaron. **19** And Korah gathered all the [k]multitude
against them unto the door of the Tabernacle of the Congregation: then the glory
of the Lord appeared unto all the Congregation. **20** And the Lord spake unto
Moses and to Aaron, saying, **21** Separate yourselves from among this Congre-
gation, that I may consume them at once. **22** And they fell upon their faces and
said, O God, the God of the spirits [l]of all flesh, hath not one man only sinned, and

---

16. Deut. 1:44

NUM. 15

- **a.** Num. 15:2 Into the land of Canaan.
- **b.** Num. 15:3 Or, separate.
- **c.** Num. 15:4 Read Exod. 29:40.
- **d.** Num. 15:7 The liquor was so called, because it was poured on the thing that was offered.
- **e.** Num. 15:9 Or, three Omers.
- **f.** Num. 15:12 Every sacrifice of beasts must have their meat offering and drink offering according to this proportion.
- **g.** Num. 15:20 Which is made of the first corn ye gather.
- **h.** Num. 15:22 As by oversight or ignorance, read Lev. 4:2, 13.
- **i.** Num. 15:24 Some read, from the eyes of the Congregation, that is, which is hid from the Congregation.
- **j.** Num. 15:30 Hebrew, with an high hand, that is, in contempt of God.
- **k.** Num. 15:31 He shall sustain the punishment of his sin.
- **l.** Num. 15:39 By leaving God's commandments and following your own fantasies.

NUM. 15

- **1.** Lev. 23:10
- **2.** Lev. 22:21
- **3.** Lev. 2:1
- **4.** Exod. 29:18
- **5.** Exod. 12:49 / Num. 9:14
- **6.** Lev. 23:4
- **7.** Lev. 4:1
- **8.** Lev. 4:27
- **9.** Lev. 24:12
- **10.** Deut. 22:12 / Matt. 23:5

NUM. 16

- **a.** Num. 16:1 Or, took others with him.
- **b.** Num. 16:2 Or, before Moses.
- **c.** Num. 16:3 Or let it suffice you: meaning, to have abused them thus long.
- **d.** Num. 16:3 All are alike holy: therefore none ought to be preferred above others: thus the wicked reason against God's ordinance.
- **e.** Num. 16:5 To be the Priest and to offer.
- **f.** Num. 16:7 He layeth the same to their charge justly, wherewith they wrongfully charged him.
- **g.** Num. 16:10 To serve in the Congregation, as in the verse before.
- **h.** Num. 16:13 Thus they spake contemptuously, preferring Egypt to Canaan.
- **i.** Num. 16:14 Wilt thou make them that searched the land, believe that they saw not that which they saw?
- **j.** Num. 16:16 At the door of the Tabernacle.
- **k.** Num. 16:19 All that were of their faction.

wilt thou be wroth with all the Congregation? **23** And the Lord spake unto Moses, saying, **24** Speak unto the Congregation, and say, Get you away from about the Tabernacle of Korah, Dathan, and Abiram. **25** Then Moses rose up, and went unto Dathan and Abiram, and the Elders of Israel followed him. **26** And he spake unto the Congregation, saying, Depart, I pray you, from the tents of these wicked men, and touch nothing of theirs, lest ye perish [m]in all their sins. **27** So they got them away from the Tabernacle of Korah, Dathan, and Abiram on every side: and Dathan and Abiram came out and stood in the door of their tents, with their wives, and their sons, and their little children. **28** And Moses said, Hereby ye shall know that the Lord hath sent me to do all these works: for I have not done them of mine own [n]mind. **29** If these men die the common death of all men, or if they be visited after the visitation of all men, the Lord hath not sent me. **30** But if the Lord make [o]a new thing, and the earth open her mouth, and swallow them up with all that they have, and they go down quick into [p,q]the pit: then ye shall understand that these men have provoked the Lord. **31** And as soon as he had made an end of speaking all the words, even the ground clave asunder that was under them, **32** And the earth [4]opened her mouth, and swallowed them up with their families, and all the men that were with Korah, and all their goods. **33** So they and all that they had, went down alive into the pit, and the earth covered them: so they perished from among the Congregation. **34** And all Israel that were about them, fled at the cry of them: for they said, Let us flee, lest the earth swallow us up. **35** But there came out a fire from the Lord, and consumed the two hundred and fifty men that offered the incense. **36** And the Lord spake unto Moses, saying, **37** Speak unto Eleazar the son of Aaron the Priest, that he take up the censers out of the burning, and scatter the fire beyond the altar: for they are hallowed, **38** The censers, I say, of these sinners, that destroyed [r]themselves: and let them make of them broad plates for a covering of the Altar: for they offered them before the Lord, therefore they shall be holy, and they shall be a [s]sign unto the children of Israel. **39** Then Eleazar the Priest took the brazen censers, which they that were burnt had offered, and made broad plates of them for a covering of the Altar. **40** It is a remembrance unto the children of Israel, that no stranger which is not of the seed of Aaron, come near to offer incense before the Lord, that he be not like [t]Korah and his company, as the Lord said to him by the hand of Moses. **41** But on the morrow all the multitude of the children of Israel murmured against Moses and against Aaron, saying, Ye have killed the people of the Lord. **42** And when the Congregation was gathered against Moses and against Aaron, then they [u]turned their faces toward the tabernacle of the Congregation: and behold, the cloud covered it, and the glory of the Lord appeared. **43** Then Moses and Aaron were come before the Tabernacle of the Congregation. **44** And the Lord spake unto Moses, saying, **45** Get you up from among this Congregation: for I will consume them quickly: then they fell upon their faces. **46** And Moses said unto Aaron, Take the censer and put fire therein of the [v]Altar, and put therein incense, and go quickly unto the Congregation, and make an atonement for them: for there is wrath gone out from the Lord: the plague is begun. **47** Then Aaron took as Moses commanded him, and ran into the midst of the Congregation, and behold, the [w]plague was begun among the people, and he put incense, and made an atonement for the people. **48** And when he stood between the dead, and them that were alive, the [x]plague was stayed. **49** So they died of this plague fourteen thousand and seven hundred, beside them that died in the conspiracy of Korah. **50** And Aaron went again unto Moses before the door of the Tabernacle of the Congregation, and the plague was stayed.

17

2 The twelve rods of the twelve princes of the tribes of Israel. 8 Aaron's rod buddeth, and beareth blossoms, 10 For a testimony against the rebellious people.

1 And the Lord spake unto [a]Moses, saying, **2** Speak unto the children of Israel, and take of every one of them a rod, after the house of their fathers, of all their princes according to the family of their fathers, even twelve rods: and thou shalt write every man's name upon his rod. **3** And write Aaron's name upon the rod of Levi: for every rod shall be for the head of the house of their fathers. **4** And thou shalt put them in the Tabernacle of the Congregation, before the Ark of the testimony, [1]where I will declare myself to you. **5** And the man's rod, whom I [b]choose, shall blossom: and I will make cease from me the grudgings of the children of Israel, which grudge against you. **6** Then Moses spake unto the children of Israel, and all their Princes gave him a rod, one rod for every prince, according to the houses of their fathers, even twelve rods, and the rod [c]of Aaron was among their rods. **7** And Moses laid the rods before the Lord in the Tabernacle of the Testimony. **8** And when Moses on the morrow went into the Tabernacle of the Testimony, behold, the rod of Aaron [d]for the house of Levi was budded, and brought forth buds, and brought forth blossoms, and bare ripe almonds. **9** Then Moses brought out all the rods from before the Lord unto all the children of Israel: and they looked upon them, and took every man his rod. **10** After, the Lord said unto Moses, [2]Bring Aaron's rod again before the Testimony to be kept for a token to the rebellious children, and thou shalt cause their [e]murmurings to cease from me, that they die not. **11** So Moses did as the Lord had commanded him: so did he. **12** And the children of Israel spake unto Moses, saying, Behold, [f]we are dead, we perish, we are all lost: **13** Whosoever cometh near or approacheth to the Tabernacle of the Lord, shall die: shall we be consumed and die?

18

1, 7 The office of Aaron and his sons, 2 With the Levites. 8 The Priest's part of the offerings. 20 God is their portion. 26 The Levites have their tithes, and offer the tenths thereof to the Lord.

1 And the Lord said unto Aaron, Thou, and thy sons, and thy father's house with thee, shall bear [a]the iniquity of the Sanctuary: both thou and thy sons with thee shall bear the iniquity of your Priest's office. **2** And bring also with thee thy brethren of the tribe of Levi of the family of thy father which shall be joined with thee, and minister unto thee: but thou and thy sons with thee shall minister before the Tabernacle of the Testimony: **3** And they shall [b]keep my charge, even the charge of all the Tabernacle: but they shall not come near the instruments of the Sanctuary, nor to the altar, lest they die, both they and you. **4** And they shall be joined with thee, and keep the charge of the Tabernacle of the Congregation for all the service of the Tabernacle: and no [c]stranger shall come near unto you: **5** Therefore shall ye keep the charge of the Sanctuary, and the charge of the Altar: so there shall fall no more wrath upon the children of Israel. **6** For lo, I have [1]taken your brethren the Levites from among the children of Israel, which as a gift of yours, are given unto the Lord, to do the service of the Tabernacle of the Congregation. **7** But thou, and thy sons with thee shall keep your Priest's office for all things of the Altar, and within the veil: therefore shall ye serve: for I have made your Priest's office [d]an office of service: therefore the stranger that cometh near shall be slain. **8** Again the Lord spake unto Aaron, Behold, I have given thee the keeping of mine [e]offerings, of all the hallowed things of the children of Israel: unto thee have I given them for the anointing's sake, and to thy sons for a perpetual ordinance. **9** This shall be thine of the most holy things, reserved from [f]the fire: all their offering of all their meat offering, and of all their sin offering, and of all their trespass offering, which they bring unto me, that shall be most holy unto thee, and to thy sons. **10** In the most [g]holy place shalt thou eat it: every male shall eat of it: it is holy unto thee. **11** This also shall be thine: the heave offering of their gift, with all the shake offerings of the children of Israel, I have given them unto thee, and to thy sons and to thy [h]daughters with thee, to be a duty forever: all the clean in thine house shall eat of it. **12** All the [i]fat of the oil, and all the fat of the wine, and of the wheat, which they shall offer unto the Lord for their firstfruits, I have given them unto thee. **13** And the first ripe of all that is in their land, which they shall bring unto Lord shall be thine: all the clean in thine house shall eat of it. **14** [2]Everything separate from the common use in Israel shall be thine. **15** All that first openeth the [3]matrix of any flesh, which they shall offer unto the Lord of man or beast, shall be thine: but the firstborn of man shalt thou redeem, and the firstborn of the unclean beast shalt thou redeem. **16** And those that are to be redeemed, shalt thou redeem from the age of a month, according to thy estimation, for the money of five shekels, after the shekel of the Sanctuary, [4]which is twenty gerahs. **17** But the firstborn of a cow, or the firstborn of a sheep, or the firstborn of a goat shalt thou not [j]redeem: for they are holy: thou shalt sprinkle their blood at the altar, and thou shalt burn their fat: it is a sacrifice made by fire for a sweet savor unto the Lord. **18** And the flesh of them shall be thine, [5]as the shake breast, and as the right shoulder shall be thine. **19** All the heave offerings of the holy things which the children of Israel shall offer unto the Lord, have I given thee, and thy sons, and thy daughters with thee, to be a duty

---

l. Num. 16:22 Or, of every creature.
m. Num. 16:26 With them that have committed so many sins.
n. Num. 16:28 I have not forged them of mine own brain.
o. Num. 16:30 Or, show a strange sight.
p. Num. 16:30 Or, hell.
q. Num. 16:30 Or, deep and dark places of the earth.
r. Num. 16:38 Which were the occasion of their own death.
s. Num. 16:38 Of God's judgments against rebels.
t. Num. 16:40 Who presumed above his vocation.
u. Num. 16:42 Or fled, to wit, Moses and Aaron.
v. Num. 16:46 For it was not lawful to take any other fire, but of the altar of burnt offering, Lev. 10:1.
w. Num. 16:47 God had begun to punish the people.
x. Num. 16:48 God drew back his hand and ceased to punish them.

NUM. 16
1. Num. 27:3 / Jude 11 **2.** Num. 26:9 **3.** Gen. 44:3 **4.** Num. 17:3 / Deut. 11:6 / Ps. 106:17

NUM. 17
a. Num. 17:1 While he was in the door of the Tabernacle.
b. Num. 17:5 To be the chief Priest.
c. Num. 17:6 Though Joseph's tribe was divided into two in the distribution of the land, yet here it is but one and Levi maketh a tribe.
d. Num. 17:8 To declare that God did choose the house of Levi to serve him in the Tabernacle.
e. Num. 17:10 Grudging that Aaron should be high Priest.
f. Num. 17:12 The Chaldea text describeth thus their murmuring: We die by the sword, the earth swalloweth us up, the pestilence doth consume us.

NUM. 17
1. Exod. 25:21 **2.** Heb. 9:4

NUM. 18
a. Num. 18:1 If you trespass in anything concerning the ceremonies of the Sanctuary of your office, you shall be punished.
b. Num. 18:3 That is, the things which are committed to thee, or, which thou dost enjoin them.
c. Num. 18:4 Which was not of the tribe of Levi.
d. Num. 18:7 Or, gift.
e. Num. 18:8 As the firstfruit, firstborn, and the tenths.
f. Num. 18:9 That which was not burned should be the Priest's.
g. Num. 18:10 That is, in the Sanctuary, between the court and the Holiest of all.
h. Num. 18:11 Read Lev. 10:14.
i. Num. 18:12 That is, the chiefest, or the best.
j. Num. 18:17 Because they are appointed for sacrifice.
k. Num. 18:19 That is, sure, stable, and incorruptible.
l. Num. 18:20 Of Canaan.
m. Num. 18:22 To serve therein: for the Levites are put in their place.

forever: it is a perpetual covenant [k]of salt before the Lord, to thee, and to thy seed with thee. **20** And the Lord said unto Aaron, Thou shalt have none inheritance in their [l]land: neither shalt thou have any part among them: [6]I am thy part and thine inheritance among the children of Israel. **21** For behold, I have given the children of Levi all the tenth in Israel for an inheritance, for their service which they serve in the Tabernacle of the Congregation. **22** Neither shall the children of Israel any more [m]come near the Tabernacle of the Congregation, lest they sustain sin, and die. **23** But the Levites shall do the service in the Tabernacle of the Congregation, and they shall bear [n]their sin: it is a law forever in your generations, that among the children of Israel they possess none inheritance. **24** For the tithes of the children of Israel, which they shall offer as an offering unto the Lord, I have given the Levites for an inheritance, therefore I have said unto them, Among the children of Israel ye shall possess none inheritance. **25** And the Lord spake unto Moses, saying, **26** Speak also unto the Levites, and say unto them, When ye shall take of the children of Israel the tithes, which I have given you of them for your inheritance, then shall ye take an heave offering of that same for the Lord, even the tenth part of the tithe. **27** And your heave offering shall be reckoned unto you, as the [o]corn of the barn, or as the abundance of the winepress. **28** So ye shall also offer an heave offering unto the Lord of all your tithes, which ye shall receive of the children of Israel, and ye shall give thereof the Lord's heave offering to Aaron the Priest. **29** Ye shall offer of all your [p]gifts all the Lord's heave offerings: of all the [q]fat of the same shall ye offer the holy things thereof. **30** Therefore thou shalt say unto them, When ye have offered the fat thereof, then it shall be counted unto the Levites, as the increase of the corn floor, or as the increase of the winepress. **31** And ye shall eat it in all [r]places, ye, and your households: for it is your wages for your service in the Tabernacle of the Congregation. **32** And ye shall [s]bear no sin by the reason of it, when ye have offered the fat of it: neither shall ye pollute the holy [t]things of the children of Israel, lest ye die.

19

2 The sacrifice of the red cow. 9 The sprinkling water. 11 He that toucheth the dead. 14 The man that dieth in a tent.

1 And the Lord spake to Moses, and to Aaron, saying, **2** [a]This is the ordinance of the Law, which the Lord hath commanded, saying, Speak unto the children of Israel that they bring thee a red cow without blemish, wherein is no spot, upon the which never came yoke. **3** And ye shall give her unto Eleazar the Priest, that he may bring her [1]without the host, and cause her to [b]be slain before his face. **4** Then shall Eleazar the Priest take of her blood with his [2]finger, and sprinkle it before the Tabernacle of the Congregation seven times, **5** And cause the cow to be burnt in his sight: with her [3]skin, and her flesh, and her blood, and her dung shall he burn her. **6** Then shall the Priest take cedar wood, and hyssop, and scarlet lace, and cast them in the midst of the fire where the cow burneth. **7** Then shall the [c]Priest wash his clothes, and he shall wash his flesh in water, and then come into the host, and the Priest shall be unclean unto the even. **8** Also he that [d]burneth her, shall wash his clothes in water, and wash his flesh in water, and be unclean until even. **9** And a man, that is clean, shall take up the ashes of the cow, and put them without the host in a clean place: and it shall be kept for the Congregation of the children of Israel for [e]a sprinkling water: it is a sin offering. **10** Therefore he that gathereth the ashes of the cow, shall wash his clothes, and remain unclean until even: and it shall be unto the children of Israel, and unto the stranger that dwelleth among them, a statute forever. **11** He that toucheth the dead body of any man, shall be unclean even seven days. **12** He shall purify himself [f]therewith the third day, and the seventh day he shall be clean: but if he purify not himself the third day, then the seventh day he shall not be clean. **13** Whosoever toucheth the corpse of any man that is dead, and purgeth not himself, defileth the Tabernacle of the Lord, and that person shall be [g]cut off from Israel, because the sprinkling water was not sprinkled upon him: he shall be unclean, and his uncleanness shall remain still upon him. **14** This is the law, When a man dieth in a tent, all that come into the tent, and all that is in the tent, shall be unclean seven days. **15** And all the vessels that be open, which have no [h]covering fastened upon them, shall be unclean. **16** Also whosoever toucheth one that is slain with a sword in the field, or a dead person, or a bone of a dead man, or a grave, shall be unclean seven days. **17** Therefore for an unclean person, they shall take of the burnt ashes of the [i]sin offering, and [j]pure water shall be put thereto in a vessel. **18** And a [k]clean person shall take hyssop, and dip it in the water, and sprinkle it upon the tent, and upon all the vessels, and on the persons that were therein, and upon him that touched the bone, or the slain, or the dead, or the grave. **19** And the clean person shall sprinkle upon the unclean the third day, and the seventh day, and he shall purify himself the seventh day, and [l]wash his clothes, and wash himself in water, and shall be clean at even. **20** But the man that is unclean, and purifieth not himself, that person shall be cut off from among the Congregation, because he hath defiled the Sanctuary of the Lord: and the sprinkling water hath not been sprinkled upon him: therefore shall he be unclean. **21** And it shall be a perpetual law unto them, that he that sprinkleth the sprinkling water, shall wash his clothes: also he that toucheth the sprinkling water, shall be unclean until even. **22** And whatsoever the unclean person toucheth shall be unclean: and the person that toucheth [m]him, shall be unclean until the even.

20

1 Miriam dieth. 2 The people murmur. 8 They have water out of the rock. 14 Edom denieth the Israelites passage. 25, 28 The death of Aaron in whose room Eleazar succeedeth.

1 Then the children of Israel came with the whole Congregation to the desert of Zin in the first [a]month, and the people abode at Kadesh: where [b]Miriam died, and was buried there. **2** But there was no water for the Congregation, and they [c]assembled themselves against Moses and against Aaron. **3** And the people chode with Moses, and spake, saying, Would God we had perished [1]when our brethren died before the Lord. **4** [2]Why have ye thus brought the Congregation of the Lord unto this wilderness, that both we and our cattle should die there? **5** Wherefore now have ye made us to come up from Egypt, to bring us into this miserable place, which is no place of seed, nor figs, nor vines, nor pomegranates? neither is there any water to drink. **6** Then Moses and Aaron went from the assembly unto the door of the Tabernacle of the Congregation, and fell upon their faces: and the glory of the Lord appeared unto them. **7** And the Lord spake unto Moses, saying, **8** Take the [d]rod, and gather thou and thy brother Aaron the Congregation together, and speak ye unto the rock before their eyes, and it shall give forth his water, and thou shalt bring them water out of the rock: so thou shalt give the Congregation and the beasts drink. **9** Then Moses took the rod from before the Lord, as he had commanded him. **10** And Moses and Aaron gathered the Congregation together before the rock: and Moses said unto them, Hear now ye rebels: [e]shall we bring you water out of this rock? **11** Then Moses lift up his hand, and with his rod he smote the rock twice, and the water came out abundantly: so the Congregation, and their beasts drank. **12** Again, the Lord spake unto Moses, and to Aaron, Because ye believed me not, to [f]sanctify me in the presence of the children of Israel, therefore ye shall not bring this Congregation into the land which I have given them. **13** This is the water of [g]Meribah, because the children of Israel strove with the Lord, and he [h]was sanctified in them. **14** Then Moses sent messengers from Kadesh unto the king of [i]Edom, saying, Thus saith thy brother Israel, Thou knowest all the travail that we have had, **15** How our fathers went down into Egypt, and we dwelt in Egypt a long time, where the Egyptians handled us evil and our fathers. **16** But when we cried unto the Lord, he heard our voice, and sent an Angel, and hath brought us out of Egypt, and behold, we are in the city Kadesh, in thine utmost border. **17** I pray thee that we may pass through thy country: we will not go through the fields nor the vineyards, neither will we drink of the water of the wells: we will go by the [j]king's way, and neither turn to the right hand nor to the left, until we be past thy borders. **18** And Edom answered him, [k]Thou shalt not pass by me, lest I come out against thee with the sword. **19** Then the children of Israel said unto him, We will go up by the highway: and if I and my cattle drink of thy water, I will then pay for it: I will only (without any harm) go through on my feet. **20** He answered again, Thou shalt not go through Then [l]Edom came out against him with much people, and with a mighty power. **21** Thus Edom denied to give Israel passage through

---

n. Num. 18:23 If they fail in their office, they shall be punished.
o. Num. 18:27 As acceptable as the fruit of your own ground or vineyard.
p. Num. 18:29 Which ye have received of the children of Israel.
q. Num. 18:29 Read verse 12.
r. Num. 18:31 As in verse 11.
s. Num. 18:32 Ye shall not be punished therefore.
t. Num. 18:32 The offerings which the Israelites have offered to God.

NUM. 18

1. Num. 3:45
2. Lev. 27:28
3. Exod. 13:2 / Exod. 22:29 / Lev. 27:26 / Num. 3:13
4. Exod. 30:13 / Lev. 27:25 / Num. 3:47 / Ezek. 45:12
5. Exod. 29:26 / Lev. 7:30
6. Deut. 10:9 / Deut. 18:2 / Josh. 13:14,33 / Exod. 44:28

NUM. 19

a. Num. 19:2 According to this law and ceremony ye shall sacrifice the red cow.
b. Num. 19:3 By another Priest.
c. Num. 19:7 Meaning, Eleazar.
d. Num. 19:8 The inferior Priest who killed her, and burned her.
e. Num. 19:9 Or, the water of separation because they that were separate for their uncleanness, were sprinkled therewith and made clean, Num. 8:7. It is also called holy water, because it was ordained to an holy use, Num. 1:17.
f. Num. 19:12 With the sprinkling water.
g. Num. 19:13 So that he should not be esteemed to be of the holy people. But as a polluted and excommunicated person.
h. Num. 19:15 Hebrew, a covering of cloth.
i. Num. 19:17 Of the red cow burnt for sin.
j. Num. 19:17 Water of the fountain or river.
k. Num. 19:18 One of the priests which is clean.
l. Num. 19:19 Because he had been among them that were unclean: or, else had touched the water, as verse 21.
m. Num. 19:22 That is, unclean.

NUM. 19

1. Heb. 13:11
2. Heb. 9:13
3. Exod. 29:24 / Lev. 4:11,18

NUM. 20

a. Num. 20:1 This was forty years after their departure from Egypt.
b. Num. 20:1 Moses and Aaron's sister.
c. Num. 20:2 Another rebellion was in Raphidim, Exod. 17, and this was in Kadesh.
d. Num. 20:8 Wherewith thou diddest miracles in Egypt, and didst divide the sea.
e. Num. 20:10 The punishment which followed hereof, declared that Moses and Aaron believed not the Lord's promise, as appeareth, verse 12.
f. Num. 20:12 That the children of Israel should believe, and acknowledge my power, and so honor me.
g. Num. 20:13 Or, strife and contention, Num. 27:14.
h. Num. 20:13 By showing himself almighty and maintaining his glory.
i. Num. 20:14 Because Jacob or Israel was Esau's brother, who was called Edom.
j. Num. 20:17 Or, highway.
k. Num. 20:18 Or, come not.
l. Num. 20:20 Or, the Edomites.

his country: wherefore Israel [m]turned away from him. 22 And when the children of Israel with all the Congregation departed from [3]Kadesh, they came unto mount Hor. 23 And the Lord spake unto Moses and to Aaron in the mount Hor near the coast of the land of Edom, saying, 24 Aaron shall be [n]gathered unto his people: for he shall not enter into the land, which I have given unto the children of Israel, because ye [o]disobeyed my commandment at the water of [p]Meribah. 25 Take [4]Aaron and Eleazar his son, and bring them up into the mount Hor, 26 And cause Aaron to put off his garments, and put them upon Eleazar his son: for Aaron shall be gathered to his fathers, and shall die there. 27 And Moses did as the Lord had commanded: and they went up into the mount Hor, in the sight of all the Congregation. 28 And Moses put off Aaron's clothes, and put them upon Eleazar his son: [5]so Aaron died there in the top of the mount: and Moses and Eleazar came down from off the mount. 29 When all the Congregation saw that Aaron was dead, all the house of Israel [q]wept for Aaron thirty days.

21

3 Israel vanquisheth king Arad. 6 The fiery serpents are sent for the rebellion of the people. 24, 33 Sihon and Og are overcome in battle.

1 When [1]King Arad the Canaanite, which dwelt toward the South, heard tell that Israel came by the [a]way of the spies, then fought he against Israel, and took of them prisoners. 2 So Israel vowed a vow unto the Lord, and said, If thou wilt deliver and give this people into mine hand, then I will utterly destroy their cities. 3 And the Lord heard the voice of Israel, and delivered them the Canaanites: and they utterly destroyed them and their cities, and called the name of the place [b,2]Hormah. 4 After they departed from the mount Hor by the way of the Red Sea, to [c]compass the land of Edom: and the people were sore grieved because of the way. 5 And the people spake against God, and against Moses, saying, Wherefore have ye brought us out of Egypt, to die in the wilderness, for here is neither bread nor water, and our soul [3]loatheth this light [d]bread. 6 [4]Wherefore the Lord sent [e]fiery serpents among the people, which stung the people: so that many of the people of Israel died. 7 Therefore the people came to Moses, and said, We have sinned: for we have spoken against the Lord, and against thee: pray to the Lord, that he take away the serpents from us: and Moses prayed for the people. 8 And the Lord said unto Moses, Make thee a fiery serpent, and set it up for a [f]sign, that as many as are bitten, may look upon it, and live. 9 [5]So Moses made a serpent of brass, and set it up for a sign: and when a serpent had bitten a man, then he looked to the serpent of brass, and [g]lived. 10 [6]And the children of Israel departed thence, and pitched in Oboth. 11 And they departed from Oboth, and pitched [h]in Ije Abarim, in the wilderness, which is before Moab on the East side. 12 They removed thence, and pitched upon the river of Zared. 13 Thence they departed, and pitched on the other side of Arnon, which is in the wilderness, and cometh out of the coasts of the Amorites: (for Arnon is the border of Moab, between the Moabites and the Amorites), 14 Wherefore it shall be spoken in the [i]book of the battles of the Lord, [j]what thing he did in the red sea, and in the rivers of Arnon, 15 And at the stream of the rivers that goeth down to the dwelling of Ar, and lieth upon the border of Moab. 16 And from thence they turned to Beer: the same is the well where the Lord said unto Moses, Assemble the people, and I will give them water. 17 Then Israel sang this song, Rise up [k]well, [l]sing ye unto it. 18 The princes dug this well, the captains of the people dug it, even the [m]lawgiver, with their staves And from the wilderness they came to Mattanah, 19 And from Mattanah to Nahaliel, and from Nahaliel to Bamoth, 20 And from Bamoth in the valley, that is in the plain of Moab, to the top of Pisgah, that looketh toward Jeshimon. 21 Then Israel sent messengers unto Sihon, king of the Amorites, saying, 22 [7]Let me go through thy land: we will not turn aside into the fields, nor into the vineyards, neither drink of the waters of the wells: we will go by the king's way, until we be past thy country. 23 [8]But Sihon gave Israel no license to pass through his country, but Sihon assembled all his people, and went out against Israel into the wilderness, and he came to Jahaz, and fought against Israel. 24 [9]But Israel smote him with the edge of the sword, and conquered his land, from Arnon unto [n]Jabbok, even unto the children of Ammon, for the border of the children of Ammon was [o]strong. 25 And Israel took all these cities, and dwelt in all the cities of the Amorites in Heshbon, and in all the [p]villages thereof. 26 For [q]Heshbon was the city of Sihon the king of the Amorites, which had fought beforetime against the king of the Moabites, and had taken all his land out of his hand, even unto Arnon. 27 Wherefore they that speak in proverbs, say, Come to Heshbon, let the city of Sihon be built and repaired, 28 For [r]a fire is gone out of Heshbon, and a flame from the city of Sihon, and hath consumed Ar of the Moabites, and the lords of Bamoth in Arnon. 29 Woe be to thee, Moab: O people of [s]Chemosh, thou art undone: he hath suffered his sons to be pursued, and his daughters to be in captivity to Sihon the king of the Amorites. 30 Their [t]empire also is lost from Heshbon unto Dibon, and we have destroyed them unto Nophah, which reacheth unto Medeba. 31 Thus Israel dwelt in the land of the Amorites. 32 And Moses sent to search out Jazer, and they took the towns belonging thereto, and rooted out the Amorites that were there. 33 [10]And they turned, and went up toward Bashan: and Og the king of Bashan came out against them, he, and all his people, to fight at Edrei. 34 Then the Lord said unto Moses, Fear him not: for I have delivered him into thine hand, and all his people, and his land: [11]and thou shalt do to him as thou diddest unto Sihon the king of the Amorites, which dwelt at Heshbon. 35 They smote him therefore, and his sons, and all his people, until there was none left him: so they conquered his land.

22

5 King Balak sendeth for Balaam to curse the Israelites. 12 The Lord forbiddeth him to go. 22 The Angel of the Lord meeteth him, and his ass speaketh. 38 Balaam protesteth that he will speak nothing, but that which the Lord putteth in his mouth.

1 After, the children of Israel departed and pitched in the plain of Moab on the [a]other side of Jordan from Jericho. 2 Now Balak the son of Zippor saw all that Israel had done to the Amorites. 3 And the Moabites were sore afraid of the people, because they were many, and Moab [b]fretted against the children of Israel. 4 Therefore Moab said unto the [c]Elders of Midian, Now shall this multitude lick up all that are round about us, as an ox licketh up the grass of the field: and Balak the son of Zippor was King of the Moabites at that time. 5 [1]He sent messengers therefore unto Balaam the son of Beor to Pethor (which is by the [d]river of the land of the children of his folk) to call him, saying, Behold, there is a people come out of Egypt, which cover the face of the earth, and lie over against me. 6 Come now therefore, I pray thee, and curse me this people (for they are stronger than I) so it may be that I shall be able to smite them, and to drive them out of the land: for I know that he, whom thou blessest, is blessed, and he whom thou cursest, shall be cursed. 7 And the Elders of Moab, and the Elders of Midian departed, having [e]the reward of the soothsaying in their hand, and they came unto Balaam, and told him the words of Balak. 8 Who answered them, Tarry here this night, and I will give you an answer, as the Lord shall say unto me So [f]the princes of Moab abode with Balaam. 9 Then God came unto Balaam, and said, What men are these with thee? 10 And Baalam said unto God, Balak the son of Zippor king of Moab hath sent unto me, saying, 11 Behold, there is a people come out of Egypt, and covereth the face of the earth: come now, curse them for my sake: so it may be that I shall be able to overcome them in battle, and to drive them out. 12 And God [g]said unto Balaam, Go not thou with them, neither curse the people, for they are blessed. 13 And Balaam rose up in the morning, and said unto the princes of Balak, Return unto your land: for the Lord hath refused to give [h]me leave to go with you. 14 So the princes of Moab rose up, and went unto Balak, and said, Balaam hath refused to come with us. 15 Balak yet sent again more princes, and more honorable than they, 16 Who came to Balaam, and said to him, Thus saith Balak the son of Zippor, [i]Be not thou stayed, I pray thee, from coming unto me. 17 For I will promote thee unto great honor, and will do whatsoever thou

---

m. Num. 20:21 To pass by another way.
n. Num. 20:24 Read Gen. 25:8.
o. Num. 20:24 Or, rebelled.
p. Num. 20:24 Or, strife.
q. Num. 20:29 Or, mourned.

NUM. 20
1. Num. 12:33
2. Exod. 17:2
3. Num. 33:35
4. Num. 33:38 / Deut. 32:50
5. Deut. 10:6 / Deut. 32:50

NUM. 21
a. Num. 21:1 By that way which their spies, that searched the dangers found to be most safe.
b. Num. 21:3 Or, destruction.
c. Num. 21:4 For they were forbidden to destroy it, Deut. 2:5.
d. Num. 21:5 Meaning, Manna, which they thought did not nourish.
e. Num. 21:6 For they that were stung therewith, were so inflamed with the heat thereof, that they died.
f. Num. 21:8 Or, upon a pole.
g. Num. 21:9 Or, recovered.
h. Num. 21:11 Or, in the heaps of Abarim, or hills.
i. Num. 21:14 Which seemeth to be the book of the Judges, or as some think, a book which is lost.
j. Num. 21:14 Or, (How God destroyed) Waheb (the city) with a whirlwind and the valley of Arnon.
k. Num. 21:17 Or, spring.
l. Num. 21:17 Ye that receive the commodity thereof, give praise for it.
m. Num. 21:18 Moses and Aaron heads of the people only smote the rock with the rod or staff, which gave water as a well that were deep digged.
n. Num. 21:24 The river.
o. Num. 21:24 For the people were tall and strong like giants, Deut. 2:20.
p. Num. 21:25 Hebrew, daughters.
q. Num. 21:26 For if it had been the Moabites, the Israelites might not have possessed it, Deut. 2:9.
r. Num. 21:28 Meaning, war.
s. Num. 21:29 Chemosh was the idol of the Moabites, 1 Kings 11:33, who was not able to defend his worshippers, which took the idol for their father.
t. Num. 21:30 Hebrew, light.

NUM. 21
1. Num. 33:40
2. Judg. 1:27
3. Num. 11:6
4. 1 Cor. 10:9
5. 2 Kings 18:4 / Job 3:14
6. Num. 33:43
7. Deut. 2:26 / Judg. 11:19
8. Deut. 29:7
9. Josh. 12:2 / Ps. 135:11 / Amos 2:9
10. Deut. 3:1 / Deut. 29:7
11. Ps. 135:11

NUM. 22
a. Num. 22:1 Being at Jericho, it was beyond Jordan: but where the Israelites were, it was on this side.
b. Num. 22:3 Or, was vexed.
c. Num. 22:4 Which were the heads and governors.
d. Num. 22:5 To wit, Euphrates, upon the which stood this city Pethor.
e. Num. 22:7 Thinking to bribe him with gifts to curse the Israelites.
f. Num. 22:8 Whom before he called Elders: meaning the governors, and after calleth them servants: that is, subjects to their king.
g. Num. 22:12 He warned him by a dream, that he should not consent to the king's wicked request.
h. Num. 22:13 Else he showed himself willing, covetousness had so blinded his heart.
i. Num. 22:16 The wicked seek by all means to further their naughty enterprises, though they know that God is against them.
j. Num. 22:19 Because he tempted God to require him contrary to his commandment, his petition was granted, but it turned to his own condemnation.

sayest unto me: come therefore, I pray thee, curse me this people. **18** And Balaam answered, and said unto the servants of Balak, [2]If Balak would give me his house full of silver and gold, I cannot go beyond the word of the Lord my God, to do less or more. **19** But now, I pray you, tarry here this night, that I may wit, what the Lord will say unto me [j]more. **20** And God came unto Balaam by night, and said unto him, If the men come to call thee, rise up, and go with them: but only what thing I say unto thee, that shalt thou do. **21** So Balaam rose up early, and saddled his ass, and went with the princes of Moab. **22** And the wrath of God was kindled, because he [k]went: and the Angel of the Lord stood in the way to be against him, as he rode upon his ass, and his two servants were with him. **23** And [3]when the ass saw the Angel of the Lord stand in the way, and his sword drawn in his hand, the ass turned out of the way, and went into the field, but Balaam smote the ass to turn her into the way. **24** [l]Again the Angel of the Lord stood in a path of the vineyards, having a wall on the one side, and a wall on the other. **25** And when the ass saw the Angel of the Lord, she thrust herself unto the wall, and dashed Balaam's foot against the wall: wherefore he smote her again. **26** Then the Angel of the Lord went further, and stood in a narrow place, where was no way to turn, either to the right hand, or to the left. **27** And when the ass saw the Angel of the Lord, she [m]lay down under Balaam: therefore Balaam was very wroth, and smote the ass with a staff. **28** Then the Lord [n]opened the mouth of the ass, and she said unto Balaam, What have I done unto thee, that thou hast smitten me now three times? **29** And Balaam said unto the ass, Because thou hast mocked me: I would there were a sword in mine hand, for now would I kill thee. **30** And the ass said unto Balaam, Am not I thine ass, which thou hast ridden upon [o]since thy first time unto this day? have I used at any time, to do thus unto thee? Who said, Nay. **31** And the Lord [p]opened the eyes of Balaam, and he saw the Angel of the Lord standing in the way with his sword drawn in his hand: then he bowed himself, and fell flat on his face. **32** And the Angel of the Lord said unto him, Wherefore hast thou now smitten thine ass three times? behold, I came out to withstand thee, because thy [q]way is not straight before me. **33** But the ass saw me, and turned from me now three times: for else, if she had not turned from me, surely I had even now slain thee, and saved her alive. **34** Then Balaam said unto the Angel of the Lord, I have sinned: for I wist not that thou stoodest in the way [r]against me: now therefore if it displease thee, I will turn [s]home again. **35** But the Angel said unto Balaam, Go with the men: but [t]what I say unto thee, that shalt thou speak So Balaam went with the princes of Balak. **36** And when Balak heard that Balaam came, he went out to meet him unto a city of Moab, which is in the [u]border of Arnon, even in the utmost coast. **37** Then Balak said unto Balaam, Did not I send for thee to call thee? Wherefore camest thou not unto me? am I not able indeed to promote thee unto honor? **38** And Balaam made answer unto Balak, Lo, I am come unto thee, and can I now say [v]anything at all? the word that God putteth in my mouth that shall I speak. **39** So Balaam went with Balak, and they came unto the city of [w]Huzoth. **40** Then Balak offered bullocks, and sheep, and sent thereof to Balaam, and to the princes that were with him. **41** And on the morrow Balak took Balaam and brought him up into the high places of [x]Baal, that thence he might see the utmost part of the people.

23

1 Balaam causeth seven altars to be built. 5 God teacheth him what to answer. 8 Instead of cursing he blesseth Israel. 19 God is not like man.

1 And Balaam said unto Balak, Build me here seven altars, and prepare me here seven bullocks, and seven rams. **2** And Balak did as Balaam said, and [a]Balak and Balaam offered on every altar a bullock and a ram. **3** Then Balaam said unto Balak, Stand by thy burnt offering, and I will go, if so be that the Lord will come and meet me: and whatsoever he showeth me, I will tell thee: so he [b]went forth alone. **4** And God [c]met Balaam, and Balaam said unto him, I have prepared seven altars, and have offered upon every altar a bullock and a ram. **5** And the Lord [d]put an answer in Balaam's mouth, and said, Go again to Balak, and say on this wise. **6** So when he turned unto him, lo, he stood by his burnt offering, he, and all the princes of Moab. **7** Then he uttered his [e]parable, and said, Balak the king of Moab hath brought me from [f]Aram out of the mountains of the East, saying, Come, curse Jacob for my sake: come, and [g]detest Israel. **8** How shall I curse, where God hath not cursed? or how shall I detest, where the Lord hath not detested? **9** For from the top of the rocks I did see him, and from the hills I did behold him: lo, the people shall dwell by themselves, and shall not be reckoned among the [h]nations. **10** Who can tell the [i]dust of Jacob, and the number of the fourth part of Israel? Let me [j]die the death of the righteous, and let my last end be like his. **11** Then Balak said unto Balaam, What hast thou done unto me? I took thee to curse mine enemies, and behold, thou hast blessed them altogether. **12** And he answered, and said, Must I not take heed to speak that, which the Lord hath put in my mouth? **13** And Balak said unto him, Come, I pray thee, with me unto another place, whence thou mayest see them, and thou shalt see but the utmost part of them and shalt not see them all: therefore curse them out of that place for my sake. **14** And he brought him into [k]Zophim to the top of Pisgah, and built seven altars, and offered a bullock and a ram on every altar. **15** After, he said unto Balak, Stand here by thy burnt offering, and I will meet the Lord yonder. **16** And the Lord met Balaam, and [1]put an answer in his mouth, and said, Go again unto Balak, and say thus. **17** And when he came to him, behold, he stood by his burnt offering, and the princes of Moab with him: so Balak said unto him, What hath the Lord said? **18** And he uttered his parable, and said, Rise up Balak, and hear: hearken unto me, thou son of Zippor. **19** [l]God is not as man, that he should lie, neither as the son of man, that he should repent: hath he said, and shall he not do it? and hath he spoken, and shall he not accomplish it? **20** Behold, I have received commandment to bless: for he hath blessed, and I cannot alter it. **21** He seeth none iniquity in Jacob, nor seeth no transgression in Israel: the Lord his God is with him, and the [m]joyful shout of a King is among them. **22** God brought them out of Egypt: their strength is as an unicorn. **23** For there is no sorcery in Jacob, nor soothsaying in Israel, [n]according to this time it shall be said of Jacob and of Israel, What hath God wrought? **24** Behold, the people shall rise up as a lion, and lift up himself as a young lion: he shall not lie down, till he eat of the prey, and till he drink the blood of the slain. **25** Then Balak said unto Balaam, Neither curse, nor bless them at all. **26** But Balaam answered, and said unto Balak, Told not I thee, saying, All that the Lord speaketh, that must I do? **27** Again Balak said unto Balaam, Come, I pray thee, I will bring thee unto another [o]place, if so be it will please God, that thou mayest thence curse them for my sake. **28** So Balak brought Balaam unto the top of Peor, that looketh toward Jeshimon. **29** Then Balaam said unto Balak, Make me here seven altars, and prepare me here seven bullocks, and seven rams. **30** And Balak did as Balaam had said, and offered a bullock and a ram on every altar.

24

5 Balaam prophesieth of the great prosperity that should come unto Israel. 17 Also of the coming of Christ. 20 The destruction of the Amalekites, and of the Kenites.

1 When Balaam saw that it pleased the Lord to bless Israel, then he went not, [1]as certain times before, to set divinations, but set his face toward the [a]wilderness. **2** And Balaam lift up his eyes, and looked upon Israel, which dwelt according to their tribes, and the Spirit of God came upon him, **3** [2]And he uttered his parable, and said, Balaam the son of Beor hath said, and the man whose eyes [b]were shut up, hath said, **4** He hath said which heard the words of God, and saw the vision of the Almighty, and [c]falling in a trance had his eyes opened: **5** How goodly are thy tents, O Jacob, and thine habitations, O Israel! **6** As the valleys are they stretched forth, as gardens by the river's side, as the [d]aloe trees, which the Lord hath planted, as the cedars beside the waters. **7** The [e]water droppeth out of his bucket, and his seed shall be in many waters, and his King shall be higher than [f]Agag, and his kingdom shall be exalted. **8** God brought him out of Egypt: his strength shall be as an unicorn: he shall eat the nations his enemies, and bruise their bones, and shoot them through with his arrows. **9** [3]He coucheth, and lieth down as a young Lion, and as a Lion: Who shall stir him up? blessed is he that blesseth thee, and cursed is he that curseth thee. **10** Then Balak was very angry with Balaam, and [g]smote his hands together: so Balak said unto Balaam, I

---

k. Num. 22:22 Moved rather with covetousness than to obey God.
l. Num. 22:24 The second time.
m. Num. 22:27 Or, fell.
n. Num. 22:28 Gave her power to speak.
o. Num. 22:30 Since thou hast been my master.
p. Num. 22:31 For whose eyes the Lord doth not open, they can neither see his anger, nor his love.
q. Num. 22:32 Both thy heart is corrupt, and thine enterprise wicked.
r. Num. 22:34 Or, before me, or to meet me.
s. Num. 22:34 Hebrew, I will return to me.
t. Num. 22:35 Because his heart was evil, his charge was renewed, that he should not pretend ignorance.
u. Num. 22:36 Near the place where the Israelites camped.
v. Num. 22:38 Of myself I can speak nothing: only what God revealeth, that will I utter, seem it good or bad.
w. Num. 22:39 Or, of streets: or, a populous city.
x. Num. 22:41 Where the idol Baal was worshipped.

NUM. 22
1. Josh. 24:9
2. Num. 24:13
3. 2 Pet. 2:16 / Jude 11

NUM. 23
a. Num. 23:2 For among the Gentiles the kings oft times used to sacrifice, as did the Priests.
b. Num. 23:3 Or, went up higher.
c. Num. 23:4 Appeared unto him.
d. Num. 23:5 Taught him what to say.
e. Num. 23:7 Or, prophecy.
f. Num. 23:7 Or, Syria.
g. Num. 23:7 Cause that all may hate and detest them.
h. Num. 23:9 But shall have religion and laws apart.
i. Num. 23:10 The infinite multitude, as the dust of the earth.
j. Num. 23:10 The fear of God's judgment caused him to wish to be joined to the household of Abraham: thus the wicked have their consciences wounded when they consider God's judgments.
k. Num. 23:14 Or, into the field of them that spied: to wit, lest the enemy should approach.
l. Num. 23:19 God's enemies are compelled to confess that his government is just, constant, and without change or repentance.
m. Num. 23:21 They triumph as victorious kings over their enemies.
n. Num. 23:23 Considering what God shall work this time for the deliverance of his people, all the world shall wonder.
o. Num. 23:27 Thus the wicked imagine of God, that that which he will not grant in one place, he will do it in another.

NUM. 23
1. Num. 22:35

NUM. 24
a. Num. 24:1 Where the Israelites camped.
b. Num. 24:3 His eyes were shut up before in respect of the clear visions which he saw after: some read, were open.
c. Num. 24:4 Though he lay as in a sleep, yet the eyes of his mind were open.
d. Num. 24:6 Or, tents.
e. Num. 24:7 His prosperity and posterity shall be very great.

sent for thee to curse mine enemies, and behold, thou hast blessed them now three times. **11** Therefore now flee unto thy place: I thought surely to promote thee unto honor, but lo, the [h]Lord hath kept thee back from honor. **12** Then Balaam answered Balak, Told I not also thy messengers, which thou sentest unto me, saying, **13** If Balak would give me his house full of silver and gold, I cannot pass the commandment of the Lord, to do either good or bad of mine own mind? what the Lord shall command, that same will I speak. **14** And now behold, I go unto my people: come, I will [i,j]advertise thee what this people shall do to thy folk in the latter days. **15** And he uttered his parable, and said Balaam the son of Beor hath said, and the man whose eyes were shut up hath said, **16** He hath said that heard the words of God, and hath the knowledge of the most High, and saw the vision of the Almighty, and falling in a trance had his eyes opened: **17** I shall see him, but not now: I shall behold him, but not near: there shall come a [k]Star of Jacob, and a Scepter shall rise of Israel and shall smite the [l]coasts of Moab, and destroy all the sons of [m]Sheth. **18** And Edom shall be possessed, and Seir shall be a possession to their enemies: but Israel shall do valiantly. **19** He also that shall have dominion shall be of Jacob, and shall destroy the remnant of the [n]city. **20** And when he looked on Amalek, he uttered his parable, and said, Amalek was the [o]first of the nations: but his latter end shall come to destruction. **21** And he looked on the [p]Kenites, and uttered his parable, and said, Strong is thy dwelling place, and [q]put thy nest in the rock: **22** Nevertheless, [r]the Kenite shall be spoiled, until Asshur carry thee away captive. **23** Again he uttered his parable, and said, Alas, [s]who shall live when God doeth this? **24** The ships also shall come from the coasts of [t]Kittim, and subdue Asshur, and shall subdue Eber, and [u]he also shall come to destruction. **25** Then Balaam rose up, and went and returned to his place: and Balak also went his way.

25

2 The people committeth fornication with the daughters of Moab. 9 Phinehas killeth Zimri and Cozbi. 11 God maketh his covenant with Phinehas. 17 God commandeth, to kill the Midianites.

1 Now while Israel abode in [1]Shittim, the people began to commit whoredom with the [a]daughters of Moab: **2** Which called the people unto the sacrifice of their gods, and the people ate, and bowed down to their gods. **3** And Israel [b]coupled himself unto Baal of Peor: wherefore the wrath of the Lord was kindled against Israel: **4** And the Lord said unto Moses, [2]Take all the heads of the people and hang them up [c]before the Lord [d]against the Sun, that the indignation of the Lord's wrath may be turned from Israel. **5** Then Moses said unto the Judges of Israel, Everyone slay his [e]men that were joined unto Baal of Peor. **6** And behold, one of the children of Israel came and brought unto his brethren a Midianitish woman in the sight of Moses, and in the sight of all the Congregation of the children of Israel, [f]who wept before the door of the Tabernacle of the Congregation. **7** [3]And when Phinehas the son of Eleazar the son of Aaron the Priest saw it, he rose up from the midst of the Congregation, and took a [g]spear in his hand, **8** And followed the man of Israel into the tent, and thrust them both through: to wit, the man of Israel, and the woman, [h]through her belly: so the plague ceased from the children of Israel. **9** [4]And there died in that plague four and twenty thousand. **10** Then the Lord spake unto Moses, saying, **11** [5]Phinehas the son of Eleazar, the son of Aaron the Priest, hath turned mine anger away from the children of Israel, while he [i]was zealous for my sake among them: therefore I have not consumed the children of Israel in my jealousy. **12** Wherefore say to him, Behold, I give unto him my covenant of peace. **13** And he shall have it, and his seed after him, even the covenant of the Priest's office forever, because he was zealous for his God, and hath made an [j]atonement for the children of Israel. **14** And the name of the Israelite thus slain, which was killed with the Midianitish woman, was Zimri the son of Salu, prince [k]of the family of the Simeonites. **15** And the name of the Midianitish woman that was slain, was Cozbi the daughter of Zur, who was head over the people of his father's house in Midian. **16** Again the Lord spake unto Moses, saying, **17** [6]Vex the Midianites, and smite them: **18** For they trouble you with their [l]wiles, wherewith they have beguiled you as concerning Peor, and as concerning their sister Cozbi daughter of a prince of Midian, which was slain in the day of the plague because of Peor.

26

2 The Lord commandeth to number the children of Israel in the plain of Moab, from twenty years old and above. 57 The Levites and their families. 64 None of them that were numbered in Sinai go into Canaan, save Caleb and Joshua.

1 And so after the [a]plague, the Lord spake unto Moses, and to Eleazar the son of Aaron the Priest, saying, **2** Take the number of all the Congregation of the children of Israel, [1]from twenty years old and above, throughout their father's houses, all that go forth to war in Israel. **3** So Moses and Eleazar the Priest spake unto them in the plain of Moab, by Jordan [b]toward Jericho, saying, **4** From twenty years old and above ye shall number the people, as the Lord [2]had commanded Moses, and the children of Israel, when they came out of the land of Egypt. **5** [3]Reuben the firstborn of Israel: the children of Reuben were: Hanoch, of whom came the family of the Hanochites, and of Pallu the family of the Palluites: **6** Of Hezron, the family of the Hezronites: of Carmi, the family of the Carmites. **7** These are the families of the Reubenites: and they were in number three and forty thousand, seven hundred and thirty. **8** And the sons of Pallu, Eliab. **9** And the sons of Eliab, Nemuel, and Dathan and Abiram: this Dathan and Abiram were famous in the Congregation, [4]and strove against Moses and against Aaron in the [c]assembly of Korah, when they strove against the Lord. **10** And the earth opened her mouth, and swallowed them up with Korah, when the Congregation died, what time the fire consumed two hundred and fifty men, who were [d]for a sign. **11** Notwithstanding, all the sons of Korah died not. **12** And the children of Simeon after their families were: Nemuel, of whom came the family of the Nemuelites: of Jamin, the family of the Jaminites: of Jachin the family of the Jachinites: **13** Of Zerah, the family of the Zarhites: of Shaul, the family of the Shaulites. **14** These are the families of the Simeonites: two and twenty thousand, and two hundred. **15** The sons of Gad after their families were: Zephon, of whom came the family of the Zephonites: of Haggi, the family of the Haggites: of Shuni, the family of the Shunites: **16** Of Ozni the family of the Oznites: of Eri, the family of the Erites: **17** Of Arod, the family of the Arodites: of Areli, the family of the Arelites. **18** These are the families of the sons of Gad, according to their numbers forty thousand and five hundred. **19** The sons of Judah, Er and Onan, but Er and Onan died in the land of [e]Canaan. **20** So were the sons of Judah after their families: of Shelah came the family of the Shelanites: of Perez, the family of the Parzites, of Zerah, the family of the Zarhites. **21** And the sons of [5]Perez were: of Hezron, the family of the Hezronites: of Hamul the family of the Hamulites. **22** These are the families of Judah, after their numbers, seventy and six thousand and five hundred. **23** The sons of Issachar after their families were: Tola, of whom came the family of the Tolaites: of Puah, the family of the Punites: **24** Of Jashub the family of the Jashubites: of Shimron the family of the Shimronites. **25** These are the families of Issachar, after their numbers, threescore and four thousand and three hundred. **26** The sons of Zebulun, after their families were: of Sered, the family of the Sardites: of Elon, the family of the Elonites: of Jahleel, the family of the Jahleelites. **27** These are the families of the Zebulunites, after their numbers threescore thousand and five hundred. **28** The sons of Joseph after their families were: Manasseh and Ephraim. **29** The sons of Manasseh were of [6]Machir, the family of the Machirites: and Machir begat Gilead: of Gilead came the family of the Gileadites. **30** These are the sons of Gilead: of Jeezer, the family of the Jeezerites, of Helek, the family of the Helekites. **31** Of Asriel the family of the Asrielites: of Shechem, the family of Shechemites. **32** Of Shemida, the family of the Shemidaites: of Hepher, the family of the Hepherites. **33** And [7]Zelophehad the son of Hepher had no sons but daughters: and the names of the daughters of Zelophehad were Mahlah, and Noah, Hoglah, Milcah and Tirzah. **34** These are the families of Manasseh, and the number of them, two and fifty thousand and seven hundred. **35** These are the sons of Ephraim after their families: of Shuthelah came the family of the Shuthalhites: of Becher, the family of the Bachrites: of Tahan, the family of the Tahanites. **36** And these are the sons of Shuthelah: of Eran, the family of the Eranites. **37** These are the families of the sons of Ephraim after their numbers two and forty thousand and five hundred: these are the sons of Joseph after their families. **38** These are the sons of Benjamin after their families: of

---

f. Num. 24:7 Which name was common to the kings of Amalek.
g. Num. 24:10 In token of anger.
h. Num. 24:11 Thus the wicked burden God when they cannot compass their wicked enterprises.
i. Num. 24:14 Hebrew, counsel.
j. Num. 24:14 He gave also wicked counsel to cause the Israelites to sin, that thereby God might forsake them, Num. 31:16.
k. Num. 24:17 Meaning, Christ.
l. Num. 24:17 That is, the princes.
m. Num. 24:17 He shall subdue all that resist: for of Sheth came Noah, and of Noah all the world.
n. Num. 24:19 Of the Edomites.
o. Num. 24:20 The Amalekites first made war against Israel, as Num. 14:45.
p. Num. 24:21 Or, Midianites.
q. Num. 24:21 Make thyself as strong as thou canst.
r. Num. 24:22 Or, thou Kain shalt.
s. Num. 24:23 Some read, Oh who shall not perish when the enemy that is, Antichrist, shall set himself up as God?
t. Num. 24:24 The Grecians and Romans.
u. Num. 24:24 Meaning, Eber, or the Jews for rebelling against God.

NUM. 24

1. Num. 23:3,15
2. Num. 23:7,18
3. Gen. 49:9

NUM. 25

a. Num. 25:1 With the women.
b. Num. 25:3 Worshipped the idol of the Moabites, which was in the hill Peor.
c. Num. 25:4 Or, to the Lord.
d. Num. 25:4 Openly in the sight of all.
e. Num. 25:5 Let him see execution done of them that are under his charge.
f. Num. 25:6 Repenting that they had offended God.
g. Num. 25:7 Or, javelin.
h. Num. 25:8 Or, in her tent. Chalde and Greek, in her secrets.
i. Num. 25:11 He was zealous to maintain my glory.
j. Num. 25:13 He hath pacified God's wrath.
k. Num. 25:14 Hebrew, of the house of the father.
l. Num. 25:18 Causing you to commit both corporal and spiritual fornication by Balaam's counsel, Num. 31:16; Rev. 2:14.

NUM. 25

1. Num. 35:49
2. Deut. 4:3 / Josh. 22:17
3. Ps. 106:30
4. 1 Cor. 10:8
5. Ps. 106:30
6. Num. 31:2

NUM. 26

a. Num. 26:1 Which came for their whoredom and idolatry.
b. Num. 26:3 Where the river is near to Jericho.
c. Num. 26:9 In that rebellion whereof Korah was head.
d. Num. 26:10 That is, for an example that others should not murmur and rebel against God's ministers.
e. Num. 26:19 Before Jacob went into Egypt, Gen. 38:3,7,10 and 46:12.

Bela came the family of the Belaites: of Ashbel, the family of the Ashbelites: of Ahiram, the family of the Ahiramites: **39** Of Shupham, the family of the Shuphamites; of Hupham the family of the Huphamites. **40** And the sons of Bela, were Ard and Naaman; of Ard came the family of the Ardites, of Naaman the family of the Naamites. **41** These are the sons of Benjamin after their families, and their numbers, five and forty thousand and six hundred. **42** These are the sons of Dan after their families: of Shuham came the family of the Shuhamites: these are the families of Dan after their households. **43** All the families of the Shuhamites were after their numbers, threescore and four thousand, and four hundred. **44** The sons of Asher after their families were of Jimna, the families of the Jimnites: of Jesui, the family of the Jesuites: of Beriah, the family of the Beriites. **45** The sons of Beriah were: of Heber, the family of the Heberites: of Malchiel, the family of the Malchielites. **46** And the name of the daughter of Asher was Serah. **47** These are the families of the sons of Asher after their numbers three and fifty thousand and four hundred. **48** The sons of Naphtali, after their families were: of Jahzeel, the families of the Jahzeelites: of Guni, the family of the Gunites. **49** Of Jezer, the family of the Jezerites: of Shillem, the family of the Shillemites. **50** These are the families of Naphtali according to their households, and their number, five and forty thousand and four hundred. **51** These are the [f]numbers of the children of Israel: six hundred and one thousand seven hundred and thirty. **52** And the Lord spake unto Moses, saying, **53** Unto these the land shall be divided for an inheritance, according to the number of [g]names. **54** [8]To many thou shalt give the more inheritance, and to few thou shalt give less inheritance: to every one according to his number shall be given his inheritance. **55** Notwithstanding, the land shall be [9]divided by lot: according to the names of the tribes of their fathers they shall inherit: **56** According to the lot shall the possession thereof be divided between many and few. **57** [10]These also are the numbers of the Levites, after their families: of Gershon came the family of the Gershonites: of Kohath, the family of the Kohathites: of Merari, the family of the Merarites. **58** These are the families of Levi, the family of the Libnites: the family of the Hebronites: the family of the Mahlites: the family of the Mushites: the family of the Korathites: and Kohath begat Amram. **59** And Amram's wife was called [11]Jochebed the daughter of Levi, which was born unto Levi in Egypt: and she bare unto Amram Aaron, and Moses, and Miriam their sister. **60** And unto Aaron were born Nadab, and Abihu, Eleazar, and Ithamar. **61** [12]And Nadab and Abihu died, because they offered strange fire before the Lord. **62** And their numbers were three and twenty thousand, all males from a month old and above, for they were not numbered among the children of Israel, because there was none inheritance given them among the children of Israel. **63** These are the numbers of Moses and Eleazar the Priest which numbered the children of Israel in the plain of Moab, near Jordan, toward Jericho. **64** And among these there was not a man of them, [h]whom Moses and Aaron the Priest numbered, when they told the children of Israel in the wilderness of Sinai. **65** For the Lord said unto them, [13]They shall die in the wilderness: so there was not left a man of them, save Caleb the son of Jephunneh, and Joshua the son of Nun.

27

1 The Law of the heritage of the daughters of Zelophehad. 12 The land of promise showed unto Moses. 16 Moses prayeth for a governor unto the people. 18 Joshua is appointed in his stead.

1 Then came the daughters of [1]Zelophehad, the son of Hepher, the son of Gilead, the son of Machir, the son of Manasseh, of the family of Manasseh, the son of Joseph (and the names of his daughters were these, Mahlah, Noah, and Hoglah, and Milcah, and Tirzah) **2** And stood before Moses, and before Eleazar the Priest, and before the Princes, and all the assembly at the door of the Tabernacle of the Congregation, saying, **3** Our father [2]died in the wilderness, and he was not among the assembly of them that were assembled against the Lord in the company of Korah, but died in his [a]sin, and had no sons. **4** Wherefore should the name of our father be taken away from among his family, because he hath no son? give us a possession among the brethren of our father. **5** Then Moses brought their [b]cause before the Lord. **6** And the Lord spake unto Moses, saying, **7** The daughters of Zelophehad speak right: thou shalt give them a possession to inherit among their father's brethren, and shalt turn the inheritance of their father unto them. **8** Also thou shalt speak unto the children of Israel, saying, If a man die and have no son, then ye shall turn his inheritance unto his daughter. **9** And if he have no daughter, ye shall give his inheritance unto his brethren. **10** And if he have no brethren, ye shall give his inheritance unto his father's brethren. **11** And if his father have no brethren, ye shall give his inheritance unto his next kinsman of his family, and he shall possess it: and this shall be unto the children of Israel a law of [c]judgment, as the Lord hath commanded Moses. **12** Again the Lord said unto Moses, [3]Go up into this mount of Abarim, and behold the land which I have given unto the children of Israel. **13** And when thou hast seen it, thou shalt be gathered unto thy people also, [4]as Aaron thy brother was gathered. **14** For ye were [5]disobedient unto my word in the desert of Zin, in the strife of the assembly to sanctify me in the waters before their eyes: [6]That is the water of [d]Meribah in Kadesh in the wilderness of Zin. **15** Then Moses spake unto the Lord, saying, **16** Let the Lord God of the [e]spirits of all flesh appoint a man over the Congregation, **17** Who may [f]go out and in before them, and lead them out and in, that the Congregation of the Lord be not as sheep, which have not a shepherd. **18** And the Lord said unto Moses, Take thee Joshua the son of Nun, in whom is the Spirit, and [g]put thine hands upon him, **19** And set him before Eleazar the Priest, and before all the Congregation, and give him a charge in their sight, **20** And [h]give him of thy glory, that all the Congregation of the children of Israel may obey. **21** And he shall stand before Eleazar the Priest, who shall ask counsel for him [7]by the [i]judgment of Urim before the Lord: at his word they shall go out, and at his word they shall come in, both he, and all the children of Israel with him, and all the Congregation. **22** So Moses did as the Lord hath commanded him, and he took Joshua, and set him before Eleazar the Priest, and before all the Congregation. **23** Then he put his hands upon him, and gave him a [j]charge, as the Lord had spoken by the hand of Moses.

28

4 The daily sacrifice. 9 The sacrifice of Sabbath. 11 Of the Month, 16 Of the Passover, 26 Of the firstfruits.

1 And the Lord spake unto Moses, saying, **2** Command the children of Israel, and say unto them, Ye shall observe to offer unto me in their due season mine offering, and [a]my bread for my sacrifices made by fire for a sweet savor unto me. **3** Also thou shalt say unto them, [1]This is the offering made by fire which ye shall offer unto the Lord, two lambs of a year old, without spot daily, for a continual burnt offering. **4** One lamb shalt thou prepare in the morning, and the other lamb shalt thou prepare at even. **5** [2]And the tenth part of an Ephah of fine flour for a [3]meat offering mingled with the fourth part of an [4]Hin of beaten oil. **6** This shall be a daily burnt offering, as was made in the mount Sinai for a sweet savor: it is a sacrifice made by fire unto the Lord. **7** And the drink offering thereof the fourth part of an Hin for one lamb: in the holy place cause to pour the drink offering unto the Lord. **8** And the other lamb thou shalt prepare at even: as the meat offering of the morning, and as the drink offering thereof shalt thou prepare this [b]for an offering made by fire of sweet savor unto the Lord. **9** But on the Sabbath day ye shall offer two lambs of a year old, without spot, and two [c]tenth deals of fine flour for a meat offering mingled with oil, and the drink offering thereof. **10** This is the burnt offering of every Sabbath, beside the [d]continual burnt offering, and drink offering thereof. **11** And in the beginning of your months, ye shall offer a burnt offering unto the Lord, two young bullocks, and a ram, and seven lambs of a year old, without spot, **12** And three tenth deals of fine flour for a meat offering mingled with oil for one bullock, and two tenth deals of fine flour for a meat offering, mingled with oil for one ram, **13** And a tenth deal of fine flour mingled with oil for a meat offering unto one lamb, for a burnt offering of sweet savor: it is an offering made by fire unto the Lord. **14** And their [e]drink offerings shall be half an Hin of wine unto one bullock, and the third part of an Hin unto a ram, and the fourth part of an Hin unto a lamb: this is the burnt offering of every month, throughout the months of the year. **15** And one he goat for a sin offering unto the Lord shall be prepared, besides the continual burnt offering, and his drink offering. **16** [5]Also the fourteenth day of the first month is the Passover of the Lord. **17** And in the fifteenth day of the same month is the feast: seven days shall unleavened bread be eaten. **18** In the [6]first day shall be an holy [f]convocation, ye shall do no servile work therein. **19** But ye shall offer a sacrifice made by fire for a burnt offering unto the Lord, two young bullocks, one ram, and seven lambs of a year old: see that they be without blemish. **20** And

---

f. Num. 26:51 This is the third time that they are numbered.
g. Num. 26:53 Or, persons.
h. Num. 26:64 Wherein appeareth the great power of God, that so wonderfully increased his people.

NUM. 26

1. Num. 1:3
2. Num. 1:1
3. Gen. 46:8 / Exod. 6:14 / 1 Chron. 5:1
4. Num. 16:1
5. Gen. 46:12
6. Josh. 17:2
7. Num. 27:1
8. Num. 33:54
9. Josh. 11:23 / Josh. 14:2
10. Exod. 6:16-19
11. Exod. 2:2 / Exod. 6:20
12. Lev. 10:2 / Num. 3:4 / 1 Chron. 24:2
13. Num. 14:28,29 / 1 Cor. 20:5,6

NUM. 27

a. Num. 27:3 According as all men die, for as much as they are sinners.
b. Num. 27:5 That is, their matter to be judged, to know what he should determine, as he did all hard matters.
c. Num. 27:11 Meaning, an ordinance to judge by.
d. Num. 27:14 Or, strife.
e. Num. 27:16 Who as he hath created, so he governeth the hearts of all men.
f. Num. 27:17 That is, govern them and do his duty, as 2 Chron. 1:10.
g. Num. 27:18 And so appoint him governor.
h. Num. 27:20 Commend him to the people as meet for the office and appointed by God.
i. Num. 27:21 According to his office: signifying that the civil magistrate could execute nothing but that which he knew to be the will of God.
j. Num. 27:23 How he should govern himself in his office.

NUM. 27

1. Num. 26:33 / Num. 36:11 / Josh. 17:3
2. Num. 14:35 / Num. 26:64,65
3. Deut. 32:40
4. Num. 20:24
5. Num. 20:10
6. Exod. 17:7
7. Exod. 28:30

NUM. 28

a. Num. 28:2 By bread he meaneth all manner of sacrifice.
b. Num. 28:8 The meat offering and drink offering of the evening sacrifice.
c. Num. 28:9 Of the measure Ephah.
d. Num. 28:10 Which was offered every day at morning and at evening.
e. Num. 28:14 That is, the wine that shall be poured upon the sacrifice.
f. Num. 28:18 Or, solemn assembly.

their meat offering shall be of fine flour mingled with oil: three tenth deals shall
ye prepare for a bullock, and two tenth deals for a ram: 21 One tenth deal shalt
thou prepare for every lamb, even for the seven lambs. 22 And an he goat for a
sin offering, to make an atonement for you. 23 Ye shall prepare these beside the
burnt offering in the morning, which is a continual burnt sacrifice. 24 After this
manner ye shall prepare throughout all the seven days, for the [g]maintaining of the
offering made by fire for a sweet savor unto the Lord: it shall be done beside the
continual burnt offering and drink offering thereof. 25 And in the seventh day
ye shall have an holy convocation, wherein ye shall do no servile work. 26 Also
in the day of your firstfruits, when ye bring a new meat offering unto the Lord, ac-
cording to your [h]weeks ye shall have an holy convocation: and ye shall do no servile
work in it: 27 But ye shall offer a burnt offering for a sweet savor unto the Lord,
two young bullocks, a ram, and seven lambs of a year old, 28 And their meat
offering of fine flour mingled with oil, three tenth deals unto a bullock, two tenth
deals to a ram, 29 And one tenth deal unto every lamb throughout the seven
lambs, 30 And an he goat to make an atonement for you: 31 (Ye shall do this
besides the continual burnt offering, and his meat offering:) [i]see they be without
blemish, with their drink offerings.

29

1 Of the three principal feasts of the seventh month, to wit, the feast of trumpets, 7 The feast of reconciliation, 12 And the feast of Tabernacles.

1 Moreover, in the first day of the [a]seventh month ye shall have an holy con-
vocation: ye shall do no servile work therein: [1]it shall be a day of blowing the tru-
mpets unto you. 2 And ye shall make a burnt offering for a sweet savor unto the
Lord: one young bullock, one ram, and seven lambs of a year old, without blemi-
sh. 3 And their meat offering shall be of fine flour mingled with oil, three tenth
deals unto the bullock, and two tenth deals unto the ram, 4 And one tenth deal
unto the lamb, for the seven lambs, 5 And an he goat for a sin offering to make
an atonement for you, 6 Beside the burnt offering of the [b]month, and his meat
offering, and the continual [c]burnt offering, and his meat offering and the drink
offerings of the same according to their manner, for a sweet savor: it is a sacrifice
made by fire unto the Lord. 7 [2]And ye shall have in the tenth day of the seventh
month, an holy [d]convocation: and ye shall [3]humble yourselves, and shall not do
any work therein. 8 But ye shall offer a burnt offering unto the Lord for a sweet
savor: one young bullock, a ram, and seven lambs of a year old: see they be wi-
thout blemish. 9 And their meat offering shall be of fine flour mingled with oil,
three tenth deals to a bullock, and two tenth deals to a ram, 10 One tenth deal
unto every lamb, throughout the seven lambs, 11 An he goat for a sin offering,
(beside the sin offering to make the atonement, and the continual [e]burnt offering
and the meat offering thereof) and their drink offerings. 12 And in the fifteenth
day of the seventh month, ye shall have an holy [f]convocation: ye shall do no ser-
vile work therein, but ye shall keep a feast unto the Lord seven days. 13 And ye
shall offer a burnt offering for a sacrifice made by fire of sweet savor unto the Lord,
thirteen young bullocks, two rams, and fourteen lambs of a year old: they shall
be without blemish. 14 And their meat offering shall be of fine flour mingled
with oil, three tenth deals unto every bullock of the thirteen bullocks, two tenth
deals to either of the two rams, 15 And one tenth deal unto each of the fourteen
lambs, 16 And one he goat for a sin offering, beside the continual burnt offe-
ring, his meat offering, and his drink offering. 17 And the [g]second day ye shall
offer twelve young bullocks, two rams, fourteen lambs of a year old without ble-
mish, 18 With their meat offering and their drink offerings for the bullocks, for
the rams and for the lambs according to their number, after the manner, 19 And
an he goat for a sin offering, (beside the continual burnt offering and his meat
offering) and their drink offerings. 20 Also the third day ye shall offer eleven
bullocks, two rams and fourteen lambs of a year old without blemish, 21 With
their meat offering and their drink offerings, for the bullocks, for the rams, and
for the lambs, after their number, according to the [h]manner, 22 And an he goat
for a sin offering, beside the continual burnt offering, and his meat offering, and
his drink offering. 23 And the fourth day ye shall offer ten bullocks, two rams,
and fourteen lambs of a year old without blemish. 24 Their meat offering and
their drink offerings, for the bullocks, for the rams, and for the lambs according to
their number after the manner, 25 And an he goat for a sin offering, beside the
continual burnt offering, his meat offering and his drink offering. 26 In the fi-
fth day also ye shall offer nine bullocks, two rams, and fourteen lambs of a year old
without blemish, 27 And their meat offering, and their drink offerings for the
bullocks, for the rams, and for the lambs according to their number, after the man-
ner, 28 And an he goat for a sin offering, beside the continual burnt offering,
and his meat offering and his drink offering. 29 And in the sixth day ye shall
offer eight bullocks, two rams, and fourteen lambs of a year old without blemi-
sh, 30 And their meat offering, and their drink offerings for the bullocks, for the
rams, and for the lambs according to their number, after the manner, 31 And an
he goat for a sin offering, beside the continual burnt offering, his meat offering and
his drink offerings. 32 In the seventh day also ye shall offer seven bullocks, two
rams and fourteen lambs of a year old without blemish, 33 And their meat offe-
ring, and their drink offerings for the bullocks, for the rams, and for the lambs ac-
cording to their number, after their manner, 34 And an he goat for a sin offering,
beside the continual burnt offering, his meat offering and his drink offering. 35
In the eighth day, ye shall have [4]a solemn assembly: ye shall do no servile work
therein, 36 But ye shall offer a burnt offering, a sacrifice made by fire for a sweet
savor unto the Lord, one bullock, one ram, and seven lambs of a year old without
blemish, 37 Their meat offering and their drink offerings for the bullock, for the
ram, and for the lambs according to their number, after the manner, 38 And an
he goat for a sin offering, beside the continual burnt offering, and his meat offe-
ring, and his drink offering. 39 These things ye shall do unto the Lord in your
feasts, beside your [i]vows, and your free offerings, for your burnt offerings, and for
your meat offerings, and for your drink offerings, and for your peace offerings.

30

3 Concerning vows. 4 The vow of the maid, 7 Of the wife, 10 Of the widow or divorced.

1 Then Moses spake unto the children of Israel according to all that the Lord
had commanded [a]him. 2 Moses also spake unto the heads of the tribes [b]con-
cerning the children of Israel, saying, This is the thing which the Lord hath com-
manded, 3 Whosoever voweth a vow unto the Lord, or sweareth an oath to
bind [c]himself by a bond, he shall not [d]break his promise, but shall do according
to all that proceedeth out of his mouth. 4 If a woman also vow a vow unto the
Lord, and bind herself by a bond, being in her father's house, in the time of her
youth, 5 And her father hear her vow and bond, wherewith she hath bound her-
self, and her father hold his [e]peace concerning her, then all her vows shall stand
and every bond, wherewith she hath bound herself, shall stand. 6 But if her
[f]father disallow her the same day that he heareth all her vows and bonds, whe-
rewith she hath bound herself, they shall not be of value, and the Lord will forgive
her, because her father disallowed her. 7 And if she have an husband when she
voweth or [g]pronounceth ought with her lips, wherewith she bindeth herself, 8 If
her husband heard it, and holdeth his peace concerning her, the same day he he-
areth it, then her vow shall stand, and her bonds wherewith she bindeth herself
shall stand in effect. 9 But if her husband disallow her the same day that he he-
areth it, then shall he make her vow which she hath made, and that that she hath
pronounced with her lips, wherewith she bound [h]herself, of none effect: and the
Lord will forgive her. 10 But every vow of a widow, and of her that is divorced
(wherewith she hath bound herself) shall stand in [i]effect with her. 11 And if she
vowed in her husband's [j]house, or bound herself straightly with an oath, 12 And
her husband hath heard it, and held his peace concerning her, not disallowing
her, then all her vows shall stand, and every bond, wherewith she bound herself,
shall stand in effect. 13 But if her husband disannulled them the same day that
he heard them, nothing that proceeded out of her lips concerning her vows or
concerning [k]her bonds, shall stand in effect: for her husband hath disannulled
them: and the Lord will forgive her. 14 So every vow, and every oath or bond,
made to [l]humble the soul, her husband may stablish it, or her husband may bre-
ak it. 15 But if her husband hold his peace concerning her from [m]day to day,
then he stablisheth all her vows and all her bonds which she hath made: he hath

---

g. Num. 28:24 Hebrew, bread.
h. Num. 28:26 In counting seven weeks from the Passover to Whitsuntide, as Lev. 23:15.
i. Num. 28:31 Hebrew, they shall be to you.

NUM. 28

1. Exod. 29:38
2. Exod. 16:36
3. Lev. 2:1
4. Exod. 29:40
5. Exod. 12:18 / Exod. 23:15 / Lev. 23:5
6. Lev. 23:7

NUM.29

a. Num. 29:1 Which containeth part of September, and part of October.
b. Num. 29:6 Which must be offered in the beginning of every month.
c. Num. 29:6 Which is for morning and evening.
d. Num. 29:7 Which is the feast of reconciliation.
e. Num. 29:11 That is, offered every morning and evening.
f. Num. 29:12 Meaning, the feast of the Tabernacles.
g. Num. 29:17 The second day of the feast of Tabernacles.
h. Num. 29:21 According to the ceremonies appointed thereunto.
i. Num. 29:39 Beside the sacrifices that you shall vow or offer of your own minds.

NUM. 29

1. Lev. 23:24
2. Lev. 16:30,31 / Lev. 23:27
3. Lev. 16:29
4. Lev. 23:36

NUM. 30

a. Num. 30:1 Hebrew, Moses.
b. Num. 30:2 Because they might declare them to the Israelites.
c. Num. 30:3 Hebrew, his soul.
d. Num. 30:3 Hebrew, violate his word.
e. Num. 30:5 For in so doing he doth approve her.
f. Num. 30:6 By not approving or consenting to her vow.
g. Num. 30:7 Either by oath, or solemn promise.
h. Num. 30:9 For she is in subjection to her husband, and can perform nothing without his consent.
i. Num. 30:10 For they are not under the authority of the man.
j. Num. 30:11 Her husband being alive.
k. Num. 30:13 Hebrew, the bonds of her soul.
l. Num. 30:14 To mortify herself by abstinence or other bodily exercise.
m. Num. 30:15 And warn her not the same day that he heareth it, as verse 9.
n. Num. 30:16 Not the same day he heard them, but some day after, the sin shall be imputed to him and not to her.

NUM. 31

a. Num. 31:3 As he had commanded, Num. 25:17, declaring also that the injury done against his people is done against him.
b. Num. 31:6 For his great zeal that he bare to the Lord, Num. 25:13.
c. Num. 31:8 The false prophet who gave counsel how to cause the Israelites to offend their God.
d. Num. 31:10 Or, palaces and gorgeous buildings.
e. Num. 31:12 As the women and little children.
f. Num. 31:15 As though he said, ye ought to have spared none.
g. Num. 31:16 For worshipping of Peor.

confirmed them because he held his peace concerning her the same day that he
heard them. 16 But if he [n]break them after that he hath heard them, then shall
he bear her iniquity. 17 These are the ordinances which the Lord commanded
Moses, between a man and his wife, and between the father and his daughter, being
young in her father's house.

31

8 Five Kings of Midian and Balaam are slain. 18 Only the maids are reserved alive. 27 The prey is equally divided. 50 A present given of Israel.

1 And the Lord spake unto Moses, saying, 2 [1]Revenge the children of Israel
of the Midianites, and afterward shalt thou be [2]gathered unto thy people. 3 And
Moses spake to the people, saying, Harness some of you unto war, and let them go
against Midian, to execute the vengeance of the Lord [a]against Midian. 4 A thou-
sand of every tribe throughout all the tribes of Israel shall ye send to the war. 5 So
there were taken out of the thousands of Israel, twelve thousand prepared unto war,
of every tribe a thousand. 6 And Moses sent them to the war, even a thousand of
every tribe, and sent them with [b]Phinehas the son of Eleazar the Priest to the war:
and the holy instruments, that is, the trumpets to blow were in his hand. 7 And
they warred against Midian, as the Lord had commanded Moses, and slew all the
males. 8 They slew also the kings of Midian among them that were slain: [3]Evi,
and Rekem, and Zur, and Hur, and Reba, five kings of Midian, and they slew
[c]Balaam the son of Beor with the sword. 9 But the children of Israel took the
women of Midian prisoners, and their children, and spoiled all their cattle, and all
their flocks, and all their goods. 10 And they burnt all their cities, wherein they
dwelt, and all their [d]villages with fire. 11 And they took all the spoil, and all the
prey both of men and beasts. 12 And they brought the [e]captives and that which
they had taken, and the spoil unto Moses and to Eleazar the Priest, and unto the
Congregation of the children of Israel, into the camp in the plain of Moab, which
was by Jordan toward Jericho. 13 Then Moses and Eleazar the Priest, and all the
princes of the Congregation went out of the camp to meet them. 14 And Mo-
ses was angry with the captains of the host, with the captains over thousands, and
captains over hundreds, which came from the war and battle. 15 And Moses said
unto them, What? have ye saved all the [f]women? 16 Behold, [4]these caused the
children of Israel through the [5]counsel of Balaam to commit a trespass against the
Lord, [g]as concerning Peor, and there came a plague among the Congregation of the
Lord. 17 Now therefore, [6]slay all the males among the [h]children, and kill all the
women that have known man by carnal copulation. 18 But all the women-chil-
dren that have not known carnal copulation, keep alive for yourselves. 19 And
ye shall remain without the host seven days, all that have killed any person, [7]and
all that have touched any dead, and purify both yourselves and your prisoners the
third day and the seventh. 20 Also ye shall purify every garment and all that is
made of skins, and all work of goats' hair, and all things made of wood. 21 And
Eleazar the Priest said unto the men of war, which went to the battle, This is the
ordinance [i]of the law which the Lord [8]commanded Moses. 22 As for gold, and
silver, brass, iron, tin, and lead: 23 Even all that may abide the fire, ye shall make
it go through the fire, and it shall be clean: yet, it shall be [j]purified with [9]the wa-
ter of purification: and all that suffereth not the fire, ye shall cause to pass by the
[k]water. 24 Ye shall wash also your clothes the seventh day, and ye shall be clean:
and afterward ye shall come into the host. 25 And the Lord spake unto Moses,
saying, 26 Take the sum of the prey that was taken, both of persons and of cattle,
thou and Eleazar the Priest, and the chief fathers of the Congregation. 27 And
divide the prey [l]between the soldiers that went to the war, and all the Congrega-
tion. 28 And thou shalt take a tribute unto the Lord of the [m]men of war, which
went out to battle: one person of five hundred, both of the persons, and of the bee-
ves, and of the asses, and of the sheep. 29 Ye shall take it of their half, and give it
unto Eleazar the Priest, as an heave offering of the Lord. 30 But of the half of the
children of Israel thou shalt take [n]one, taken out of fifty, both of the persons, of the
beeves, of the asses, and of the sheep, even of all the cattle, and thou shalt give them
unto the Levites, which have the charge of the Tabernacle of the Lord. 31 And
Moses and Eleazar the Priest did as the Lord had commanded Moses. 32 And
the booty, to wit, the rest of the prey which the men of war had spoiled, was six
hundred seventy and five thousand sheep, 33 And seventy and two thousand
beeves, 34 And threescore and one thousand asses, 35 And two and thirty
thousand persons in all, of women that had [o]lain by no man. 36 And the half,
to wit, the part of them that went out to war, touching the number of sheep, was
three hundred seven and thirty thousand, and five hundred. 37 And the [p]Lord's
tribute of the sheep was six hundred seventy and five. 38 And the beeves were six
and thirty thousand, whereof the Lord's tribute was seventy and two. 39 And the
asses were thirty thousand and five hundred, whereof the Lord's tribute was three-
score and one: 40 And [q]of persons sixteen thousand, whereof the Lord's tribute
was two and thirty persons. 41 And Moses gave the tribute of the Lord's offering
unto Eleazar the Priest, as the Lord had commanded Moses. 42 And of the [r]half
of the children of Israel, which Moses divided from the men of war, 43 (For
the half that pertained unto the congregation, was three hundred thirty and se-
ven thousand sheep and five hundred, 44 And six and thirty thousand bee-
ves, 45 And thirty thousand asses, and five hundred, 46 And sixteen thou-
sand persons.) 47 Moses, I say, took of the half that pertained unto the [s]children
of Israel, one taken out of fifty, both of the persons, and of the cattle, and gave
them unto the Levites, which have the charge of the Tabernacle of the Lord, as the
Lord had commanded Moses. 48 Then the captains which were over thousands
of the host, the captains over the thousands, and the captains over the hundreds
came unto Moses: 49 And said to Moses, Thy servants have taken the sum of
the men of war which are under [t]our authority, and there lacketh not one man of
us. 50 [u]We have therefore brought a present unto the Lord, what every man
found of Jewels of gold, bracelets, and chains, rings, earrings, and ornaments of the
legs, to make an atonement for our souls before the Lord. 51 And Moses and
Eleazar the Priest took the gold of them, and all wrought jewels, 52 And all the
gold of the offering that they offered up to the Lord (of the captains over thousands
and hundreds) was sixteen thousand seven hundred and fifty shekels. 53 (For
the men of war had spoiled, every man for [v]himself.) 54 And Moses and Eleazar
the Priest took the gold of the captains over the thousands, and over the hundreds,
and brought it into the Tabernacle of the Congregation, for a [w]memorial of the
children of Israel before the Lord.

32

2 The request of the Reubenites and Gadites, 16 and their promise unto Moses. 20 Moses granteth their request. 33 The Gadites, Reubenites, and half the tribe of Manasseh, conquer and build cities on this side Jordan.

1 Now the children of [a]Reuben, and the children of Gad had an exceeding
great multitude of cattle: and they saw the land of Jazer, and the land of [b]Gilead,
that it was an apt place for cattle. 2 Then the children of Gad, and the children of
Reuben came, and spake unto Moses and to Eleazar the Priest, and unto the Princes
of the Congregation, saying, 3 The land of Ataroth, and Dibon, and Jazer, and
Nimrah, and Heshbon, and Elealeh, and Shebam, and Nebo, and Beon, 4 Whi-
ch country the Lord smote before the Congregation of Israel; is a land meet for
cattle, and thy servants have cattle: 5 Wherefore, said they, if we have found gra-
ce in thy sight, let this land be given unto thy servants for a possession, and bring us
not over Jordan. 6 And Moses said unto the children of Gad, and to the children
of Reuben, Shall your brethren go to war, and ye tarry here? 7 Wherefore now
[c]discourage you the heart of the children of Israel to go over into the land, which
the Lord hath given them? 8 Thus did your fathers, when I sent them from Ka-
desh Barnea to see the land. 9 For [1]when they went up even unto the [d]river of
Eshcol, and saw the land, they discouraged the heart of the children of Israel, that
they would not go into the land, which the Lord had given them. 10 And the
Lord's wrath was kindled the same day, and he did swear, saying, 11 [e]None of
the men that came out of Egypt, [2]from twenty years old and above, shall see the
land for the which I sware unto Abraham, to Isaac, and to Jacob, because they have
not [f]wholly followed me: 12 Except Caleb the son of Jephunneh the Kenizzite,
and Joshua the son of Nun: for they have constantly followed the Lord. 13 And
the Lord was very angry with Israel, and made them wander in the wilderness for-
ty years, until all the generation that had done [g]evil in the sight of the Lord, was
consumed. 14 And behold, ye are risen up in your father's stead as an increase of
sinful men still to augment the fierce wrath of the Lord toward Israel. 15 For if
ye turn away from following him, he will yet again leave the people in the wilder-
ness, and [h]ye shall destroy all this folk. 16 And they went near to him, and said,
We will build sheepfolds here for our sheep, and for our cattle, and cities for our
children. 17 But we ourselves will be ready armed to go before the children of
Israel, until we have brought them unto their [i]place: but our children shall dwell in
the defensed cities, because of the inhabitants of the land. 18 We will not return

---

h. Num. 31:17 That is, all the men-children.
i. Num. 31:21 Or, contained in the law.
j. Num. 31:23 The third day and before it be molten.
k. Num. 31:23 It shall be washed.
l. Num. 31:27 The prey is first divided equally among all.
m. Num. 31:28 Of the prey that falleth to the soldiers.
n. Num. 31:30 The Israelites which had not been at war, of every fiftieth paid one to the Lord: and the soldiers one of every five hundredth.
o. Num. 31:35 Hebrew, not known the bed of man.
p. Num. 31:37 This is the portion that the soldiers gave to the Lord.
q. Num. 31:40 Meaning, of the maids, or virgins which had not companied with man.
r. Num. 31:42 Of that part which was given unto them in dividing the spoil.
s. Num. 31:47 Which had not been at war.
t. Num. 31:49 Hebrew, under our hands.
u. Num. 31:50 The captains by the free offering acknowledge the great benefit of God in preserving his people.
v. Num. 31:53 And gave no portion to their captains.
w. Num. 31:54 That the Lord might remember the children of Israel.

NUM. 31

1. Num. 25:17
2. Num. 27:13
3. Josh. 13:21
4. Num. 25:2
5. 2 Pet. 2:15
6. Judg. 21:11
7. Num. 19:11
8. Num. 19:12
9. Num. 19:9

NUM. 32

a. Num. 32:1 Reuben came of Leah, and Gad of Zilpah her handmaid.
b. Num. 32:1 Which mountain was so named of the heap of stones that Jacob made as a sign of the covenant between him and Laban, Gen. 31:47.
c. Num. 32:7 Hebrew, break.
d. Num. 32:9 Or, valley.
e. Num. 32:11 Hebrew, if any of the men.
f. Num. 32:11 Or, persevered and continued.
g. Num. 32:13 Because they murmured, neither would believe their report, which told the truth as concerning the land.
h. Num. 32:15 By your occasion.

unto our houses, until the children of Israel have inherited, every man his inheritance. **19** Neither will we inherit with them beyond Jordan and on that side, because our inheritance is fallen to us on this side Jordan Eastward. **20** [3]And Moses said unto them, If ye will do this thing, and go [j]armed before the Lord to war: **21** And will go every one of you in harness over Jordan before the Lord, until he have cast out his [k]enemies from his sight: **22** And until the land be subdued before the Lord, then ye shall return and be innocent toward the Lord, and toward Israel: and this land shall be your possession [l]before the Lord. **23** But if ye will not do so, behold, ye have sinned against the Lord, and be sure, that your sin [m]will find you out. **24** Build you then cities for your children, and folds for your sheep, and do that ye have spoken. **25** Then the children of Gad and the children of Reuben spake unto Moses, saying, Thy servants will do as my lord commandeth: **26** Our children, our wives, our sheep, and all our cattle shall remain there in the cities of Gilead, **27** But [4]thy servants will go every one armed to war before the Lord for to fight, as my lord saith. **28** So concerning them, Moses [n]commanded Eleazar the Priest, and Joshua the son of Nun, and the chief fathers of the tribes of the children of Israel. **29** And Moses said unto them, If the children of Gad and the children of Reuben will go with you over Jordan, all armed to fight before the Lord, then when the land is subdued before you, ye shall give them the land of Gilead for a possession: **30** But if they will not go over with you armed, then they shall have their possessions among you in the land of Canaan. **31** And the children of Gad, and the children of Reuben answered, saying, As the [o]Lord hath said unto thy servants, so will we do. **32** We will go armed before the Lord into the land of Canaan: that the possession of our inheritance may be to us on this side Jordan. **33** [5]So Moses gave unto them, even to the children of Gad, and to the children of Reuben, and to half the tribe of Manasseh the son of Joseph, the kingdom of Sihon king of the [p]Amorites, and the kingdom of Og king of Bashan, the land with the cities thereof and coasts, even the cities of the country round about. **34** Then the children of Gad built Dibon, and Ataroth, and Aroer, **35** And Atroth, Shophan, and Jazer, and Jogbehah, **36** And Beth Nimrah, and Beth Haran, defensed cities: also sheepfolds. **37** And the children of Reuben built Heshbon, and Elealeh, and Kirjathaim, **38** And Nebo, and Baal Meon, and turned their names, and Shibmah: and gave other names unto the cities which they built. **39** And the children of [6]Machir the son of Manasseh went to Gilead, and took it, and put out the Amorites that dwelt therein. **40** Then Moses gave Gilead unto Machir the son of Manasseh, and he dwelt therein. **41** [7]And Jair the son of Manasseh went and took the small towns thereof, and called them [q]Havoth Jair. **42** Also Nobah went and took Kenath, with the villages thereof, and called it Nobah after his own name.

33

8 Two and forty journeys of Israel are numbered. 52 They are commanded to kill the Canaanites.

1 These are the [a]journeys of the children of Israel, which went out of the land of Egypt, according to their bands under the hand of Moses and Aaron. **2** And Moses wrote their going out by their journeys, according to the commandment of the Lord: so these are the journeys of their going out. **3** Now they [1]departed from Rameses the first month, even the fifteenth day of the first month, on the morrow after the Passover: and the children of Israel went out with an high hand in the sight of all the Egyptians. **4** (For the Egyptians buried all their firstborn, which the Lord had smitten among them: upon their [b]gods also the Lord did execution.) **5** And the children of Israel removed from Rameses, and pitched in Succoth. **6** And they departed from [2]Succoth, and pitched in Etham, which is in the edge of the wilderness. **7** And they removed from Etham, and turned again unto [c]Pi Hahiroth, which is before Baal Zephon, and pitched before Migdol. **8** And they departed from before Hahiroth, and [3]went through the midst of the Sea into the wilderness, and went three days' journey in the wilderness of Etham, and pitched in Marah. **9** And they removed from Marah, and came unto [4]Elim, and in Elim were twelve fountains of water, and seventy palm trees, and they pitched there. **10** And they removed from Elim, and camped by the red sea. **11** And they removed from the red Sea, and lay in the [5]wilderness of Sin. **12** And they took their journey out of the wilderness of Sin, and set up their tents in Dophkah. **13** And they departed from Dophkah, and lay in Alush. **14** And they removed from Alush, and lay in [6]Rephidim, where was no water for the people to drink. **15** And they departed from Rephidim, and pitched in the [7]wilderness of Sinai. **16** And they removed from the desert of Sinai, and pitched in [8]Kibroth Hattaavah. **17** And they departed from Kibroth Hattaavah, and lay at [9]Hazeroth. **18** And they departed from Hazeroth, and pitched in Rithmah. **19** And they departed from [10]Rithmah, and pitched at Rimmon Perez. **20** And they departed from Rimmon Perez, and pitched in Libnah. **21** And they removed from Libnah, and pitched in Rissah. **22** And they journeyed from Rissah, and pitched in Kehelathah. **23** And they went from Kehelathah, and pitched in mount Shepher. **24** And they removed from mount Shepher, and lay in Haradah. **25** And they removed from Haradah, and pitched in Makheloth. **26** And they removed from Makheloth, and lay in Tahath. **27** And they departed from Tahath, and pitched in Terah. **28** And they removed from Terah, and pitched in Mithkah. **29** And they went from Mithkah, and pitched in Hashmonah. **30** And they departed from Hashmonah, and lay in Moseroth. **31** And they departed from Moseroth, and pitched in Bene Jaakan. **32** And they removed from Bene Jaakan, and lay in Hor Hagidgad. **33** And they went from Hor Hagidgad, and pitched in Jotbathah. **34** And they removed from Jotbathah, and lay in Abronah. **35** And they departed from Abronah, and lay in Ezion Geber. **36** And they removed from Ezion Geber, and pitched in the [11]wilderness of Zin, which is Kadesh. **37** And they removed from Kadesh, and pitched in mount Hor, in the edge of the land of Edom. **38** ([12]And Aaron the Priest went up into mount Hor, at the commandment of the Lord and died there, in the fortieth year after the children of Israel were come out of the land of Egypt, in the first day of the [d]fifth month. **39** And Aaron was an hundred and three and twenty years old, when he died in mount Hor.) **40** And [13]King Arad the Canaanite, which dwelt in the South of the land of Canaan, heard of the coming of the children of Israel. **41** And they departed from mount [14]Hor, and pitched in Zalmonah. **42** And they departed from Zalmonah, and pitched in Punon. **43** And they departed from Punon, and pitched in Oboth. **44** [15]And they departed from Oboth, and pitched in Ije Abarim, in the borders of Moab. **45** And they departed from Ijim, and pitched in Dibon Gad. **46** And they removed from Dibon Gad, and lay in Almon Diblathaim. **47** And they removed from Almon Diblathaim, and pitched in the mountains of Abarim before Nebo. **48** And they departed from the mountains of Abarim, and pitched in the [e]plain of Moab by Jordan toward Jericho. **49** And they pitched by Jordan, from Beth Jesimoth unto [16]Abel Shittim, in the plain of Moab. **50** And the Lord spake unto Moses in the plain of Moab, by Jordan toward Jericho, saying, **51** Speak unto the children of Israel, and say unto them, [17]When ye are come over Jordan to enter into the land of Canaan, **52** Ye shall then drive out all the inhabitants of the land before you, and destroy all their [f]pictures, and break asunder all their images of metal, and pluck down all their high places, **53** And ye shall possess the land and dwell therein: for I have given you the land to possess it. **54** And ye shall inherit the land by lot, according to your families: [18]to the more ye shall give more inheritance, and to the fewer the less inheritance Where the lot shall fall to any man, that shall be his: according to the tribes of your fathers shall ye inherit. **55** But if ye will not drive out the inhabitants of the land before you, then those which ye let remain of them, shall be [g,19]pricks in your eyes, and thorns in your sides, and shall vex you in the land wherein ye dwell. **56** Moreover, it shall come to pass, that I shall do unto you, as I thought to do unto them.

34

3 The coasts and borders of the land of Canaan. 17 Certain men are assigned to divide the land.

1 And the Lord spake unto Moses, saying, **2** Command the children of Israel, and say unto them, When ye come into the land of Canaan, this is the [a]land that shall fall unto your inheritance: that is, the land of Canaan with the coasts thereof. **3** [1]And your South quarter shall be from the wilderness of Zin to the borders of Edom: so that your South quarter shall be from the salt Sea coast Eastward **4** And the border shall compass you from the South to [b]Maaleh Akrabbim, and reach to Zin, and go out from the South to Kadesh Barnea: thence it shall stretch to Hazar Addar, and go along to Azmon. **5** And the border shall compass from Azmon unto the [c]river of Egypt, and shall go out to the

---

i. Num. 32:17 In the land of Canaan.
j. Num. 32:20 Before the Ark of the Lord.
k. Num. 32:21 That is, the inhabitants of the land.
l. Num. 32:22 The Lord will grant you this land which ye require, Josh. 1:15.
m. Num. 32:23 Ye shall assuredly be punished for your sin.
n. Num. 32:28 Moses gave charge that his promise made to the Reubenites, and others, should be performed after his death, so that they brake not theirs.
o. Num. 32:31 This is attributed to the Lord, which his messenger speaketh.
p. Num. 32:33 The Amorites dwelled on both sides of Jordan: but here he maketh mention of them that dwelt on this side: and Josh. 10:12, he speaketh of them that inhabited beyond Jordan.
q. Num. 32:41 That is, the villages of Jair.

NUM. 32
1. Num. 13:24
2. Num. 14:28,29
3. Josh. 1:13
4. Josh. 4:12
5. Deut. 3:12 / Josh. 13:8 / Josh. 22:4
6. Gen. 50:23
7. Deut. 3:14

NUM. 33
a. Num. 33:1 From whence they departed, and whither they came.
b. Num. 33:4 Either meaning their idols, or their men of authority.
c. Num. 33:7 At the commandment of the Lord, Exod. 14:2.
d. Num. 33:38 Which the Hebrews call Ab, and answereth to part of July and part of August.
e. Num. 33:48 Or, field.
f. Num. 33:52 Which were set up in their high places to worship.
g. Num. 33:55 Or, knives.

NUM. 33
1. Exod. 12:37
2. Exod. 13:19
3. Exod. 15:22
4. Exod. 16:27
5. Exod. 15:1
6. Exod. 17:1
7. Exod. 19:1
8. Num. 11:34
9. Num. 11:35
10. Num. 13:1
11. Num. 20:22
12. Num. 20:25 / Deut. 32:50
13. Num. 21:1
14. Num. 11:4,10
15. Num. 21:11
16. Num. 25:1
17. Deut. 7:2 / Josh. 11:11,12
18. Num. 26:53,54
19. Josh. 23:13 / Judg. 2:3

NUM. 34
a. Num. 34:2 Meaning, the description of the land.
b. Num. 34:4 Or, ascending up of scorpions.
c. Num. 34:5 Which was Nilus, or as some think, Rhinocotura.
d. Num. 34:6 Which is called Mediterranean.
e. Num. 34:7 Which is a mountain near Tyre and Sidon, and not that Hor in the wilderness where Aaron died.

sea. **6** And your West quarter shall be [d]the great sea: even that border shall be your West coast. **7** And this shall be your North quarter, ye shall mark out your border from the great sea unto mount [e]Hor. **8** From mount Hor ye shall point out till it come unto Hamath, and the end of the coast shall be at Zedad. **9** And the coast shall reach out to Ziphron, and go out at Hazar Enan, this shall be your North quarter. **10** And ye shall mark out your East quarter from Hazar Enan to Shepham. **11** And the coast shall go down from Shepham to Riblah, and from the East side of Ain: and the same border shall descend and go out at the side of the sea of [f]Chinnereth Eastward. **12** Also that border shall go down to Jordan, and leave at the salt sea: this shall be your land with the coasts thereof round about. **13** Then Moses commanded the children of Israel, saying, This is the land which ye shall inherit by lot, which the Lord commanded to give unto nine tribes, and half the tribe. **14** [2]For the tribe of the children of Reuben, according to the households of their fathers, and the tribe of the children of Gad, according to their fathers' households, and half the tribe of Manasseh have received their inheritance. **15** Two tribes and an half tribe have received their inheritance on this side of Jordan toward Jericho full East. **16** Again the Lord spake to Moses, saying, **17** These are the names of the men which shall divide the land unto you: [3]Eleazar the Priest, and Joshua the son of Nun. **18** And ye shall take also a [g]prince of every tribe to divide the land. **19** The names also of the men are these: Of the tribe of Judah, Caleb the son of Jephunneh. **20** And of the tribe of the sons of Simeon, Shemuel the son of Ammihud. **21** Of the tribe of Benjamin, Elidad the son of Chislon. **22** Also of the tribe of the sons of Dan, the prince Bukki, the son of Jogli. **23** Of the sons of Joseph: of the tribe of the sons of Manasseh, the prince Hanniel the son of Ephod. **24** And of the tribe of the sons of Ephraim, the prince Kemuel, the son of Shiphtan. **25** Of the tribe also of the sons of Zebulun, the prince Elizaphan, the son of Parnach. **26** So of the tribe of the sons of Issachar, the prince Paltiel, the son of Azzan. **27** Of the tribe also of the sons of Asher, the prince Ahihud, the son of Shelomi. **28** And of the tribe of the sons of Naphtali, the prince Pedahel, the son of Ammihud. **29** These are they, whom the Lord commanded to [h]divide the inheritance unto the children of Israel, in the land of Canaan.

35

2 Unto the Levites are given cities and suburbs. 11 The cities of refuge. 16 The law of murder. 30 For one man's witness shall no man be condemned.

1 And the Lord spake unto Moses in the plain of Moab by Jordan, toward Jericho, saying, **2** [1]Command the children of Israel, that they give unto the [a]Levites of the inheritance of their possession, [b]cities to dwell in: ye shall give also unto the Levites the suburbs of the cities round about them. **3** So they shall have the cities to dwell in, and their suburbs shall be for their cattle, and for their substance, and for all their beasts. **4** And the suburbs of the cities, which ye shall give unto the Levites, from the wall of the city outward shall be a thousand cubits round about. **5** And ye shall measure without the city of the East side, [c]two thousand cubits: and of the South side, two thousand cubits: and of the West side, two thousand cubits: and of the North side, two thousand cubits: and the city shall be in the midst: this shall be the measure of the suburbs of their cities. **6** And of the cities which ye shall give unto the Levites, [2]there shall be six cities for refuge, which ye shall appoint, that he which killeth, may flee thither: and to them ye shall add two and forty cities more. **7** All the cities which ye shall give to the Levites, shall be eight and forty cities: them shall ye give with their suburbs. **8** And concerning the cities which ye shall give, of the possession of the children of Israel: of many ye shall take more, and of few ye shall take less: everyone shall give of his cities unto the Levites, according to his inheritance, which he inheriteth. **9** And the Lord spake unto Moses, saying, **10** Speak unto the children of Israel, and say unto them, [3]When ye be come over Jordan into the land of Canaan, **11** Ye shall appoint you cities, to be cities of refuge for you, that the slayer, which slayeth any person unawares, may flee thither. **12** And these cities shall be for you a refuge from thy [d]avenger, that he which killeth, die not, until he stand before the Congregation in judgment. **13** And of the cities which ye shall give, six cities shall ye have for refuge. **14** Ye shall appoint three [e]on this side Jordan, and ye shall appoint three cities in the land of [4]Canaan which shall be cities of refuge. **15** These six cities shall be a refuge for the children of Israel, and for the stranger, and for him that dwelleth [f]among you, that everyone which killeth any person unawares, may flee thither. **16** [5]And if one [g]smite another with an instrument of iron that he die, he is a murderer, and the murderer shall die the death. **17** Also if he smite him by casting a [h]stone, wherewith he may be slain, and he die, he is a murderer, and the murderer shall die the death. **18** Or if he smite him with an hand weapon of wood, wherewith he may be slain, if he die, he is a murderer, and the murderer shall die the death. **19** The revenger of the blood himself shall slay the murderer: when he meeteth him, he shall slay him. **20** But if he thrust him [6]of hate, or hurl at him by laying of wait, that he die, **21** Or smite him through enmity with his hand, that he die, he that smote him shall die the death: for he is a murderer: the revenger of the blood shall slay the murderer when he meeteth him. **22** But if he pushed him [i]unadvisedly, and [7]not of hatred, or cast upon him [j]anything, without laying of wait, **23** Or any stone (whereby he might be slain), and saw him not, or caused it to fall upon him, and he die, and was not his enemy, neither sought him any harm, **24** Then the Congregation shall judge between the slayer and the [k]avenger of blood according to these laws. **25** And the Congregation shall deliver the slayer out of the hand of the avenger of blood, and the Congregation shall restore him unto the city of his refuge, whither he was fled: and he shall abide there unto the death of the [l]high Priest, which is anointed with the holy oil. **26** But if the slayer come without the borders of the city of his refuge, whither he was fled, **27** And the revenger of blood find him without the borders of the city of his refuge, and the revenger of blood slay the [m]murderer, he shall be guiltless, **28** Because he should have remained in the city of his refuge, until the death of the high Priest: and after the death of the high Priest, the slayer shall return unto the land of his possession. **29** So these things shall be a [n]law of judgment unto you, throughout your generations in all your dwellings. **30** Whosoever killeth any person, the Judge shall slay the murderer, through [8]witnesses: but [9]one witness shall not testify against a person to cause him to die. **31** Moreover ye shall take no recompense for the life of the murderer, which is [o]worthy to die: but he shall be put to death. **32** Also ye shall take no recompense for him that is fled to the city of his refuge, that he should come again, and dwell in the land, before the death of the high Priest. **33** So ye shall not pollute the land wherein ye shall dwell: for [p]blood defileth the land: and the land cannot be [q]cleansed of the blood that is shed therein, but by the blood of him that shed it. **34** Defile not therefore the land which ye shall inhabit, for I dwell in the midst thereof: For I the Lord dwell among the children of Israel.

36

6 An order for the marriage of the daughters of Zelophehad.

1 Then [a]the chief fathers of the family of the sons of Gilead, the son of Machir, the son of Manasseh, of the families of the sons of Joseph, came, and spake before Moses, and before the princes, the chief fathers of the children of Israel, **2** And said, [1]The Lord commanded [b]my lord to give the land to inherit by lot to the children of Israel: and my lord was commanded by the Lord, to give the inheritance of Zelophehad our brother unto his daughters. **3** If they be married to any of the sons of the other tribes of the children of Israel, then shall their inheritance be taken away from the inheritance of our fathers, and shall be put unto the inheritance of the tribe whereof they shall be: so shall it be taken away from the lot of our inheritance. **4** Also when the [c]Jubilee of the children of Israel cometh, then shall their inheritance be put unto the inheritance of the tribe whereof they shall be: so shall their inheritance be taken away from the inheritance of the tribe of our fathers. **5** Then Moses commanded the children of Israel, according to the word of the Lord, saying, The tribe of the sons of Joseph have said [d]well. **6** This is the thing that the Lord hath commanded, concerning the daughters of Zelophehad, saying, They shall be wives, to whom they think best, only to the family of the tribe of their father shall they marry: **7** So shall not the inheritance of the children of Israel remove from tribe to tribe, for every one of the children of Israel shall join himself to the inheritance of the tribe of

---

f. Num. 34:11 Which in the Gospel is called the lake of Gennesaret.
g. Num. 34:18 One of the heads or chief men of every tribe.
h. Num. 34:29 And be judges over every piece of ground that should fall to any by lot, to the intent that all things might be done orderly and without contention.

NUM. 34

1. Josh. 15:1
2. Num. 32:33 / Josh.14:2,3
3. Josh. 19:51

NUM. 35

a. Num. 35:2 Because they had no inheritance assigned them in the land of Canaan.
b. Num. 35:2 God would have them scattered through all the land, because the people might be preserved by them in the obedience of God and his Law.
c. Num. 35:5 So that in all were three thousand, and in the compass of these two thousand, they might plant and sow.
d. Num. 35:12 Meaning, from the next of the kindred, who ought to pursue the cause.
e. Num. 35:14 Among the Reubenites, Gadites, and half the tribe of Manasseh, Deut. 4:41.
f. Num. 35:15 Hebrew, among them.
g. Num. 35:16 Wittingly, and willingly.
h. Num. 35:17 That is, with a big and dangerous stone: in Hebrew, with a stone of his hand.
i. Num. 35:22 Or, suddenly.
j. Num. 35:22 Hebrew, instrument.
k. Num. 35:24 That is, his next kinsman.
l. Num. 35:25 Under this figure is declared, that our sins could not be remitted, but by the death of the high Priest Jesus Christ.
m. Num. 35:27 By the sentence of the Judge.
n. Num. 35:29 A law to judge murders done either of purpose, or unadvisedly.
o. Num. 35:31 Which purposely hath committed murder.
p. Num. 35:33 Or, murder.
q. Num. 35:33 So God is mindful of the blood wrongfully shed, that he maketh his dumb creatures to demand vengeance thereof.

NUM. 35

1. Josh. 21:2
2. Deut. 4:41 / Josh. 20:2 / Josh. 21:3
3. Exod. 21:13 / Deut. 19:2 / Josh. 10:2
4. Josh. 20:7
5. Exod. 21:14
6. Deut. 19:11
7. Exod. 21:13
8. Deut. 17:6 / Deut. 9:15
9. Matt. 18:16 / 2 Cor. 13:1

NUM. 36

a. Num. 36:1 It seemeth that the tribes contended who might marry these daughters to have their inheritance: and therefore the sons of Joseph proposed the matter to Moses.
b. Num. 36:2 Meaning, Moses.
c. Num. 36:4 Signifying that at no time it could return, for in the Jubilee all things returned to their own tribes.
d. Num. 36:5 For the tribe could not have continued, if the inheritance which was the maintenance thereof should have been alienated to others.

his fathers. **8** And every daughter that possesseth any [e]inheritance of the tribes of the children of Israel, shall be wife unto one of the family of the tribe of her father: that the children of Israel may enjoy every man the inheritance of their fathers. **9** Neither shall the inheritance go about from tribe to tribe: but every one of the tribes of the children of Israel shall stick to his own inheritance. **10** As the Lord commanded Moses, so did the daughters of Zelophehad. **11** For [2]Mahlah, Tirzah, and Hoglah, and Milcah, and Noah the daughters of Zelophehad were married unto their father's brother's sons, **12** They were wives to certain of the families of the sons of Manasseh the son of Joseph: so their inheritance remained in the tribe of the family of their father. **13** These are the [f]commandments and laws which the Lord commanded by the hand of Moses, unto the children of Israel in the plain of Moab, by Jordan toward Jericho.

---

e. Num. 36:8 When there is no male to inherit.
f. Num. 36:13 Touching the ceremonial and judicial laws.

NUM. 36
1. Num. 27:1 / Josh. 17:3 **2.** Num. 27:1

THE FIFTH BOOK OF MOSES, CALLED

[a]DEUTERONOMY

---

1 *2 A brief rehearsal of things done before, from Horeb unto Kadesh Barnea. 32 Moses reproveth the people for their incredulity. 44 The Israelites are overcome by the Amorites because they fought against the commandment of the Lord.*

1 These be the words which Moses spake unto all Israel, on [b]this side Jordan in the wilderness, in the plain, [c]over against the red sea, between Paran and Tophel, and Laban, and Hazeroth, and Dizahab. **2** There are eleven days' journey from [d]Horeb unto Kadesh Barnea, by the way of mount Seir. **3** And it came to pass in the first day of the eleventh month, in the fortieth year that Moses spake unto the children of Israel according unto all that the Lord hath given him in commandment unto them. **4** After that he had slain [e,1]Sihon the King of the Amorites which dwelt in Heshbon, and Og king of Bashan, which dwelt at Ashtaroth in Edrei. **5** On this side Jordan at the land of Moab [f]began Moses to declare this law, saying, **6** The Lord our God spake unto us in [g]Horeb, saying, Ye have dwelt long enough in this mount, **7** Turn you and depart, and go unto the mountain of the Amorites, and unto all places near thereunto in the plain, in the mountain, or in the valley: both Southward, and to the Sea side to the land of the Canaanites, and unto Lebanon: even unto the great river, the river [h]Perah. **8** Behold, I have set the land before you: go in and [2]possess that land which the Lord sware, unto your fathers, Abraham, Isaac, and Jacob, to give unto them and unto their seed after them. **9** And I spake [i]unto you the same time, saying, I am not able to bear you myself alone: **10** The Lord your God hath [j]multiplied you: and behold, ye are this day as the stars of heaven in number: **11** (The Lord God of your fathers make you a thousand times so many more as ye are, and bless you, as he hath promised you,) **12** How can I alone [k]bear your cumbrance and your charge, and your strife? **13** Bring you men of wisdom and of understanding, and [l]known among your tribes, and I will make them rulers over you: **14** Then he answered me and said, the thing is good that thou hast commanded us to do. **15** So I took the chief of your tribes, [m]wise and known men, and made them rulers over you, captains over thousands, and captains over hundreds, and captains over fifty, and captains over ten, and officers among your tribes. **16** And I charged your Judges that same time, saying, Hear the controversies between your brethren, and [3]judge righteously between every man and his brother, and the stranger that is with him. **17** Ye shall have no respect of person in judgment, [4]but shall hear the small as well as the great: ye shall not fear the face of man: for the judgment is [n]God's: and the cause that is too hard for you, bring unto me, and I will hear it. **18** Also I commanded you the same time all the things which ye should do. **19** Then we departed from Horeb, and went through all that great and terrible wilderness (as ye have seen) by the way of the mountain of the Amorites, as the Lord our God commanded us: and we came to Kadesh Barnea. **20** And [o]I said unto you, Ye are come unto the mountain of the Amorites, which the Lord our God doth give unto us. **21** Behold, the Lord thy God hath laid the land before thee: go up and possess it, as the Lord the God of thy fathers hath said unto thee: fear not, neither be discouraged. **22** [p]Then ye came unto me everyone, and said, We will send men before us, to search us out the land, and to bring us word again, what way we must go up by, and unto what cities we shall come. **23** So the saying pleased me well, and I took twelve men of you, of every tribe one. **24** [5]Who departed, and went up into the mountain, and came unto the [q]river Eshcol, and searched out the land. **25** And took of the fruit of the land in their hand, and brought it unto us, and brought us word again, and [r]said, It is a good land, which the Lord our God doth give us. **26** Notwithstanding, ye would not go up, but were disobedient unto the commandment of the Lord your God, **27** And murmured in your tents, and said, Because the Lord [s]hated us, therefore hath he brought us out of the land of Egypt, to deliver us into the hand of the Amorites, and to destroy us. **28** Whither shall we go up, our [t]brethren have discouraged our hearts, saying, The people are greater, and taller than we: the cities are great and walled up to heaven: and moreover we have seen the sons of the [6]Anakims there. **29** But I said unto you, Dread not, nor be afraid of them. **30** The Lord your God, [u]who goeth before you, he shall fight for you, according to all that he did unto you in Egypt before your eyes, **31** And in the wilderness, where thou hast seen how the Lord thy God bare thee, as a man doth bear his son, in all the way which ye have gone, until ye came unto this place. **32** Yet for all this ye did not believe the Lord your God, **33** [7]Who went in the way before you, to search you out a place to pitch your tents in, in fire by night, that ye might see what way to go, and in a cloud by day. **34** Then the Lord heard the voice of your words, and was wroth, and sware, saying, **35** [8]Surely there shall not one of these men of this forward generation, see that good land, which I sware to give unto your fathers, **36** Save Caleb the son of Jephunneh: he shall see it, [9]and to him will I give the land that he hath trodden upon, and to his children, because he hath constantly followed the Lord. **37** [10]Also the Lord was angry with me for your sakes, saying, [11]Thou also shalt not go in thither, **38** But Joshua the son of Nun which standeth [v]before thee, he shall go in thither: encourage him: for he shall cause Israel to inherit it. **39** Moreover, your [w]children, which ye said should be a prey, and your sons, which in that day had no knowledge between good and evil, they shall go in thither, and unto them will I give it, and they shall possess it. **40** But as for you, turn back, and take your journey into the wilderness by the way of the red Sea. **41** Then ye answered and said unto me, We have sinned against the Lord,

---

DEUT. 1

a. TITLE - That is, a second law: so called, because the Law which God gave in mount Sinai, is here repeated, as though it were a new Law: and this book is a commentary or exposition of the ten commandments.
b. Deut. 1:1 In the country of Moab.
c. Deut. 1:1 So that the wilderness was between the Sea and this plain of Moab.
d. Deut. 1:2 In Horeb, or Sinai, forty years before this the Law was given: but because all that were then of age and judgment were now dead, Moses repeateth the same to the youth which either then were not born, or had not judgment.
e. Deut. 1:4 By these examples of God's favor, their minds are prepared to receive the Law.
f. Deut. 1:5 The second time.
g. Deut. 1:6 In the second year and second month, Num. 10:11.
h. Deut. 1:7 Or, Euphrates.
i. Deut. 1:9 By the counsel of Jethro my father-in-law, Exod. 18:19.
j. Deut. 1:10 Not so much by the course of nature, as miraculously.
k. Deut. 1:12 Signifying how great a burden it is, to govern the people.
l. Deut. 1:13 Whose godliness and uprightness is known.
m. Deut. 1:15 Declaring what sort of men ought to have a public charge, read Exod. 18:31.
n. Deut. 1:17 And you are his Lieutenants.
o. Deut. 1:20 So that the fault was in themselves, that they did not sooner possess the inheritance promised.
p. Deut. 1:22 Read Num. 13:13
q. Deut. 1:24 Or, valley of the cluster of grapes.
r. Deut. 1:25 To wit, Caleb, and Joshua: Moses preferreth the better part to the greater, that is, two to ten.
s. Deut. 1:27 Such was the Jews' unthankfulness, that they counted God's especial love, hatred.
t. Deut. 1:28 The other ten, not Caleb and Joshua.
u. Deut. 1:30 Declaring that to renounce our own force, and constantly to follow our vocation, and depend on the Lord, is the true boldness, and agreeable to God.
v. Deut. 1:38 Which ministreth unto thee.
w. Deut. 1:39 Which were under twenty years old, as Num. 14:31.

[x]we will go up, and fight, according to all that the Lord our God hath commanded us: and ye armed you every man to the war, and were ready to go up into the mountain. **42** But the Lord said unto me, Say unto them, Go not up, neither fight, (for I am [y]not among you) lest ye fall before your enemies. **43** And when I told you, ye would not hear, but rebelled against the commandment of the Lord, and were presumptuous, and went up into the mountain. **44** Then the Amorites which dwelt in that mountain came out against you, and chased you (as bees used to do) and destroyed you in Seir, even unto Hormah. **45** And when ye came again, ye wept before the Lord, but the Lord would not [z]hear your voice, nor incline his ears unto you. **46** So ye abode in Kadesh a long time, according to the time that ye had remained before.

2

4 Israel is forbidden to fight with the Edomites, 9 Moabites, 19 and Ammonites. 23 Sihon King of Heshbon.

1 Then [a]we turned, and took our journey into the wilderness, by the way of the red Sea, as the Lord spake unto me: and were compassed mount Seir [a] [b]long time. **2** And the Lord spake unto me, saying, **3** Ye have compassed this mountain long enough: turn you Northward. **4** And warn thou the people, saying, Ye shall go through the [c]coast of your brethren the children of Esau, which dwell in Seir, and they shall be afraid of you: take ye good heed therefore. **5** Ye shall not provoke them: for I will not give you of their land so much as a foot breadth, [1]because I have given mount Seir unto Esau for a possession. **6** Ye shall buy meat of them for money to eat, and ye shall also procure water of them for money to drink. **7** For the Lord thy God hath [d]blessed thee in all the works of thine hand: he knoweth thy walking through this great wilderness, and the Lord thy God hath been with thee this forty years, and thou hast lacked nothing. **8** And when we were departed from our brethren the children of Esau which dwelt in Seir: through the way of the [e]plain, from Elath, and from Ezion Geber, we turned and went by the way of the wilderness of Moab. **9** Then the Lord said unto me, Thou shalt not [f]vex Moab, neither provoke them to battle: for I will not give thee of their land for a possession, because I have given Ar unto the children [g]of Lot for a possession. **10** The [h]Emims dwelt therein in times past, a people great and many, and tall, as the Anakims. **11** They also were taken for giants as the Anakims: whom the Moabites call Emims. **12** The [2]Horites also dwelt in Seir before time, whom the children of Esau chased out and destroyed them before them, and dwelt in their stead: as Israel shall do unto the land of his possession, which the Lord hath given them. **13** Now rise up, said I, and get you over the river Zered: and we went over the river [3]Zered. **14** The [i]space also wherein we came from Kadesh Barnea, until we were come over the river Zered, was eight and thirty years, until all the generation of the men of war were wasted out from among the host, as the Lord sware unto them. **15** For indeed the [j]hand of the Lord was against them, to destroy them from among the host, till they were consumed. **16** So when all the men of war were consumed and dead from among the people: **17** Then the Lord spake unto me, saying, **18** Thou shalt go through Ar the coast of Moab this day: **19** And thou shalt come near over against the children of Ammon: but shalt not lay siege unto them, nor move war against them: for I will not give thee of the land of the children of Ammon any possession: for I have given it unto the children of Lot for a possession. **20** That also was taken for a land [k]of giants: for giants dwelt therein afore time, whom the Ammonites called Zamzummims: **21** A people that was great, and many, and tall, as the Anakims: but the Lord destroyed them before them, and they succeeded them in their inheritance, and dwelt in their stead: **22** As he did to the children of Esau which dwell in Seir, when he destroyed the Horites before them, and they possessed them, and dwelt in their stead unto this day. **23** And the Avim which dwelt in Hazarim even unto [l]Azzah, the Caphtorims which came out of Caphtor destroyed them, and dwelt in their stead. **24** Rise up therefore, said the Lord: take your journey, and pass over the river Arnon: behold, I have given into thy hand Sihon, the [m]Amorite, King of Heshbon, and his land: begin to possess it, and provoke him to battle. **25** This day will I [n]begin to send thy fear and thy dread, upon all people under the whole heaven, which shall hear thy fame, and shall tremble and quake before thee. **26** Then I sent messengers out of the wilderness of Kedemoth unto Sihon King of Heshbon, with words of peace, saying, **27** [4]Let me pass through thy land: I will go by the highway: I will neither turn unto the right hand nor to the left. **28** Thou shalt sell me meat for money, for to eat, and shalt give me water for money for to drink: only I will go through on my foot, **29** (As the [o]children of Esau which dwell in Seir, and the Moabites which dwell in Ar, did unto me) until I be come over Jordan, into the land which the Lord our God giveth us. **30** But Sihon the King of Heshbon would not let us pass by him: for the Lord thy God had [p]hardened his spirit, and made his heart obstinate, because he would deliver him into thine hand, as appeareth this day. **31** And the Lord said unto me, Behold, I have begun to give Sihon and his land before thee: begin to possess and inherit his land. **32** [5]Then came out Sihon to meet us, himself with all his people to fight at Jahaz. **33** But the Lord our God delivered him [q]into our power, and we smote him, and his sons, and all his people. **34** And we took all his cities the same time, and destroyed every city, men, and [r]women, and children: we let nothing remain. **35** Only the cattle we took to ourselves, and the spoil of the cities which we took. **36** From Aroer, which is by the bank of the river of Arnon, and from the city that is upon the river, even unto Gilead: there was not one city that escaped us: for the Lord our God delivered up all [s]before us. **37** Only unto the land of the children of Ammon thou camest not, nor unto any place of the [t]river Jabbok, nor unto the cities in the mountains, nor unto whatsoever the Lord our God forbade us.

3

3 Og King of Bashan is slain. 11 The bigness of his bed. 18 The Reubenites and Gadites are commanded to go over Jordan armed before their brethren. 21 Joshua is made captain. 27 Moses is permitted to see the land, but not to enter, albeit he desired it.

1 Then we turned, and went up by the way of Bashan: [1]and Og King of Bashan [a]came out against us, he and all his people to fight at Edrei. **2** And the Lord said unto me, Fear him not, for I will deliver him, and all his people, and his land into thine hand, and thou shalt do unto him as thou diddest unto [2]Sihon King of the Amorites, which dwelt at Heshbon. **3** So the Lord our God delivered also unto our hand, [3]Og the King of Bashan, and all his people: and we smote him, until none was left him alive. **4** And we took all his cities the same time, neither was there a city which we took not from them, even three score cities, and all the country of Argob, even the kingdom of Og in Bashan. **5** All these cities were fenced with high walls, gates and bars, beside [b]unwalled towns a great many. **6** And we overthrew them, as we did unto Sihon King of Heshbon, destroying every city, with men, [c]women, and children. **7** But all the cattle and the spoil of the cities we took for ourselves. **8** Thus we took at that time out of the hand of two Kings of the Amorites, the land that was on this side Jordan from the river of Arnon unto mount Hermon: **9** (Which Hermon the Sidonians call Sirion, but the Amorites call it Senir) **10** All the cities of the plain, and all Gilead, and all Bashan unto Salcah, and Edrei, cities of the kingdom of Og in Bashan. **11** For only Og King of Bashan remained of the remnant of the Giants, [d]whose bed was a bed of iron: is it not at Rabbath among the children of Ammon? the length thereof is nine cubits, and four cubits the breadth of it, after the cubit of a man. **12** And this land which we possessed at that time, from Aroer, which is by the river Arnon, and half mount Gilead, [4]and the cities thereof, gave I unto the Reubenites and Gadites. **13** And the rest of Gilead, and all Bashan, the kingdom of Og, gave I unto the half tribe of Manasseh: even all the country of Argob with all Bashan, which is called, The land of giants. **14** Jair the son of Manasseh took all the country of Argob, unto the coasts of Geshuri, and of Maachathi: and called them after his own name, Bashan, [5]Havoth Jair unto [e]this day. **15** And I gave part of Gilead unto Machir. **16** And unto the Reubenites and Gadites I gave the rest of Gilead, and unto the river of Arnon, half the river and the borders, even unto the

---

x. Deut. 1:41 This declareth man's nature, who will do that which God forbiddeth, and will not do that which he commendeth.
y. Deut. 1:42 Signifying that man hath no strength, but when God is at hand to help him.
z. Deut. 1:45 Because ye rather showed your hypocrisy, than true repentance: rather lamenting the loss of your brethren, than repenting for your sins.

DEUT. 1

1. Num. 21:24
2. Gen. 15:18 / Gen. 17:7,8
3. John 7:24
4. Lev. 19:15 / Deut. 16:19 / 1 Sam. 16:7 / Prov. 24:23 / James 2:2
5. Num. 13:24
6. Num. 13:29
7. Exod. 13:11
8. Num. 14:23
9. Josh. 14:6
10. Num. 20:12 / Num. 27:14
11. Deut. 3:26 / Deut. 4:21 / Deut. 34:4

DEUT. 2

a. Deut. 2:1 They obeyed, after that God had chastised them.
b. Deut. 2:1 Eight and thirty years, as verse 14.
c. Deut. 2:4 This was the second time: for before they had caused the Israelites to return, Num. 20:21.
d. Deut. 2:7 And given thee means, wherewith thou mayest make recompense: also God will direct thee by his providence, as he hath done.
e. Deut. 2:8 Or, wilderness.
f. Deut. 2:9 Or, besiege.
g. Deut. 2:9 Which were the Moabites and Ammonites.
h. Deut. 2:10 Signifying that as these giants were driven out for their sins: so the wicked when their sins are ripe, cannot avoid God's plagues.
i. Deut. 2:14 He showeth hereby, that as God is true in his promise, so his threatenings are not in vain.
j. Deut. 2:15 His plague and punishment to destroy all that were twenty years old and above.
k. Deut. 2:20 Who called themselves Rephaims: that is, preservers, or physicians to heal and reform vices: but were indeed Zamzummims, that is, wicked and abominable.
l. Deut. 2:23 Or, Gaza.
m. Deut. 2:24 According to his promise made to Abraham, Gen. 15:21.
n. Deut. 2:25 This declareth that the hearts of men are in God's hands either to be made faint, or bold.
o. Deut. 2:29 Because neither entreaty nor examples or others could move him, he could not complain of his just destruction.
p. Deut. 2:30 God in his election and reprobation doth not only appoint the ends, but the means tending to the same.
q. Deut. 2:33 Hebrew, before us.
r. Deut. 2:34 God had cursed Canaan, and therefore he would not that any of the wicked race should be preserved.
s. Deut. 2:36 Or, into our hand.
t. Deut. 2:37 Or, ford.

DEUT. 2

1. Gen. 36:3
2. Gen. 36:29
3. Num. 21:12
4. Num. 21:21,22
5. Num. 21:23

DEUT. 3

a. Deut. 3:1 Therefore beside the commandment of the Lord, they had just occasion of his part to fight against him.
b. Deut. 3:5 As villages and small towns.
c. Deut. 3:6 Because this was God's appointment, therefore it may not be judged cruel.
d. Deut. 3:11 The more terrible that this giant was, the greater occasion had they to glorify God for the victory.
e. Deut. 3:14 Meaning, when he wrote this history.
f. Deut. 3:16 Which separateth the Ammonites from the Amorites.

river [f]Jabbok, which is the border of the children of Ammon: **17** The plain also and Jordan, and the borders from Chinnereth even unto the sea of the plain, to wit, the salt Sea [g]under the springs of Pisgah Eastward. **18** And I commanded [h]you the same time, saying, The Lord your God hath given you this land to possess it: ye shall go over armed before your brethren the children of Israel, all men of war. **19** Your wives only, and your children, and your cattle (for I know that ye have much cattle) shall abide in your cities, which I have given you, **20** Until the Lord have given rest unto your brethren as unto you, and that they also possess the land, which the Lord your God hath given them beyond Jordan: then shall ye [6]return every man unto his possession, which I have given you. **21** [7]And I charged Joshua the same time, saying, Thine eyes have seen all that the [i]Lord your God hath done unto these two Kings: [8]so shall the Lord do unto all the kingdoms whither thou goest. **22** Ye shall not fear them: for the Lord your God, he shall fight for you. **23** And I besought the Lord the same time, saying, **24** O Lord God, thou hast begun to show thy servant thy greatness and thy mighty hand: for where is there a God in heaven or in earth, that can [j]do like thy works, and like thy [k]power? **25** I pray thee let me go over and see the good land that is beyond Jordan, that goodly [l]mountain, and Lebanon. **26** But the Lord was angry with me for your sakes, and would not hear me: and the Lord said unto me, Let it suffice thee, speak no more unto me of this matter. **27** Get thee up into the top of Pisgah, and [m]lift up thine eyes Westward, and Northward, and Southward, and Eastward, and behold it with thine eyes, for thou shalt not go over this Jordan: **28** But charge Joshua, and encourage him, and bolden him: for he shall go before this people, and he shall divide for inheritance unto them, the land which thou shalt see. **29** So we abode in the valley over against Beth Peor.

4

1 An exhortation to observe the law without adding thereto or diminishing. 6 Therein standeth our wisdom. 9 We must teach it to our children. 15 No image ought to be made to worship. 26 Threatenings against them that forsake the Law of God. 37 God chose the seed because he loved their fathers.

1 Now therefore hearken, O Israel, unto the ordinances and to the laws which I teach you to [a]do, that ye may live and go in, and possess the land, which the Lord God of your fathers giveth you. **2** [1]Ye shall [b]put nothing unto the word which I command you, neither shall ye [c]take ought there from, that ye may keep the commandments of the Lord your God which I command you. **3** Your [d]eyes have seen what the Lord did because of Baal Peor, for all the men that followed Baal Peor, the Lord thy God hath destroyed every one from among you. **4** But ye that did [e]cleave unto the Lord your God, are alive every one of you this day. **5** Behold, I have taught you ordinances, and laws, as the Lord my God commanded me, that ye should do even so within the land whither ye go to possess it. **6** Keep them therefore, and do them: for that is your [f]wisdom, and your understanding in the sight of the people, which shall hear all these ordinances, and shall say, [g]Only this people is wise, and of understanding, and a great nation. **7** For what nation is so great, unto whom the gods come so near unto them, as the Lord our God is, [h]near unto us, in all that we call unto him for? **8** And what nation is so great, that hath ordinances and laws so righteous, as all this Law, which I set before you this day? **9** But take heed to thyself, and [i]keep thy soul diligently, that thou forget not the things which thine eyes have seen, and that they depart not out of thine heart, all the days of thy life: but teach them thy sons, and thy sons' sons: **10** Forget not the day that thou stoodest before the Lord thy God in Horeb, when the Lord said unto me, Gather me the people together, and I will cause them to hear my words, that they may learn to fear me all the days that they shall live upon the earth, and that they may teach their children: **11** Then came you near and [2]stood under the mountain, and the mountain [j]burnt with fire unto the midst of heaven, and there was darkness, clouds and mist. **12** And the Lord spake unto you out of the midst of the fire, and ye heard the voice of the words, but saw no similitude, save a voice. **13** Then he declared unto you his covenant which he commanded you to [k]do, even the ten [l]commandments, and wrote them upon two Tables of stone. **14** And the Lord commanded me that same time, that I should teach you ordinances and laws, which ye should observe in the land, whither ye go, to possess it. **15** Take therefore good heed unto your [m]selves: for ye saw no [n]image in the day that the Lord spake unto you in Horeb out of the midst of the fire: **16** That ye corrupt not yourselves, and make you a graven image, or representation of any figure: whether it be the likeness of male or female, **17** The likeness of any beast that is on earth, or the likeness of any feathered fowl that flieth in the air: **18** Or the likeness of anything that creepeth on the earth, or the likeness of any fish that is in the waters beneath the earth, **19** And lest thou lift up thine eyes unto heaven, and when thou seest the sun and the moon and the stars with all the host of heaven, shouldest be driven to worship them and serve them, which the Lord thy God hath [o]distributed to all people under the whole heaven. **20** But the Lord hath taken you and brought you out of the [p]iron furnace, out of Egypt to be unto him a people and inheritance, as appeareth this day. **21** And the Lord was angry with me for your words, and sware that I should not go over Jordan, and that I should not go in unto that good land, which the Lord thy God giveth thee for an inheritance. **22** For I must die in this land, and shall not go over Jordan: but [q]ye shall go over, and possess that good land. **23** Take heed unto yourselves, lest ye forget the covenant of the Lord your God which he made with you, and lest ye make you any graven image, or likeness of anything, as the Lord thy God hath charged thee. **24** For the Lord thy God is a [r]consuming fire, and a jealous God. **25** When thou shalt beget children and children's children, and shalt have remained long in the land, if ye [s]corrupt yourselves, and make any graven image, or likeness of anything, and work evil in the sight of the Lord thy God, to provoke him to anger, **26** I [t]call heaven and earth to record against you this day, that ye shall shortly perish from the land, whereunto ye go over Jordan to possess it: ye shall not prolong your days therein, but shall utterly be destroyed. **27** And the Lord shall [u]scatter you among the people, and ye shall be left few in number among the nations, whither the Lord shall bring you: **28** And there ye shall serve gods: even the work of man's hand, wood, and stone, which neither see, nor hear, nor eat, nor smell. **29** But if from thence thou shalt seek the Lord thy God, thou shalt find him, if thou seek him with all thine [v]heart, and with all thy soul. **30** When thou art in tribulation, and all these things are come upon thee, [w]at the length, if thou return to the Lord thy God, and be obedient unto his voice, **31** (For the Lord thy God is a merciful God) he will not forsake thee, neither destroy thee, nor forget the covenant of thy fathers, which he [x]sware unto them. **32** For inquire now of the days that are past, which were before thee, since the day that God created man upon the earth, and [y]ask from the one end of heaven unto the other, if there came to pass such a great thing as this, or whether any such like thing hath been heard. **33** Did ever people hear the voice of God speaking out of the midst of a fire, as thou hast heard, and lived? **34** Or hath God assayed to go and take him a nation from among nations, by [z]tentations, by signs, and by wonders, and by war, and by a mighty hand, and by a stretched out arm, and by great fear, according unto all that the Lord your God did unto you in Egypt before your eyes? **35** Unto thee it was showed, that thou mightest [aa]know that the Lord he is God, and that there is none but he alone. **36** Out of heaven he made thee hear his voice to instruct thee, and upon earth he showed thee his great fire, and thou heardest his voice out of the midst of the fire. **37** And because [ab]he loved thy fathers, therefore he chose their seed after them, and hath brought thee out of Egypt in his sight by his mighty power, **38** To thrust out nations greater and mightier than thou, before thee, to bring thee in, and to give thee their land for inheritance: as appeareth this day. **39** Understand therefore this day, and consider in thine heart, that the Lord he is God in heaven above, and upon the earth beneath: there is none other. **40** Thou shalt keep therefore his ordinances, and his commandments which I command thee this day, that it may [ac]go well with thee, and with thy children after thee, and that thou mayest prolong thy days upon the earth, which the Lord thy God giveth thee forever. **41** Then Moses separated

---

g. Deut. 3:17 Or, at Asdoth-Pisgah.
h. Deut. 3:18 That is, the Reubenites, Gadites, and half Manasseh, as Num. 32:28.
i. Deut. 3:21 So that the victories came not by your own wisdom, strength or multitude.
j. Deut. 3:24 He speaketh according to the common and corrupt speech of them which attribute that power unto idols that only appertaineth unto God.
k. Deut. 3:24 Or, wonders.
l. Deut. 3:25 He meaneth Zion, where the Temple should be built, and God honored.
m. Deut. 3:27 As before he saw by the spirits of prophecy the good mountain which was Zion: so here his eyes were lifted up above the order of nature to behold all the plentiful land of Canaan.

DEUT. 3

1. Num. 21:35 / Deut. 29:7
2. Num. 21:24
3. Num. 21:33
4. Num. 32:33
5. Num. 32:41
6. Josh. 22:4
7. Num. 27:18,19,23
8. Josh. 15 / Josh. 10:8,25

DEUT. 4

a. Deut. 4:1 For this doctrine standeth not in bare knowledge, but in practice of life.
b. Deut. 4:2 Think not to be more wise than I am.
c. Deut. 4:2 God will not be served by halves, but will have full obedience.
d. Deut. 4:3 God's judgments executed upon other idolaters ought to serve for our instruction, read Num. 25:3,4.
e. Deut. 4:4 And were not idolaters.
f. Deut. 4:6 Because all men naturally desire wisdom, he showeth how to attain unto it.
g. Deut. 4:6 Or, surely.
h. Deut. 4:7 Helping us, and delivering us out of all dangers, as 2 Sam. 7:23.
i. Deut. 4:9 He addeth all these words, to show that we can never be careful enough to keep the law of God and to teach it to our posterity.
j. Deut. 4:11 The Law was given with fearful miracles, to declare both that God was the author thereof, and also that no flesh was able to abide the rigor of the same.
k. Deut. 4:13 God joineth this condition to his covenant.
l. Deut. 4:13 Or, words.
m. Deut. 4:15 Hebrew, souls.
n. Deut. 4:15 Signifying, that destruction is prepared for all them that make any image to represent God.
o. Deut. 4:19 He hath appointed them for to serve man.
p. Deut. 4:20 He hath delivered you out of most miserable slavery and freely chosen you for his.
q. Deut. 4:22 Moses' good affection appeareth in that he being deprived of such an excellent treasure, doth not envy them that must enjoy it.
r. Deut. 4:24 To those that come not unto him with love and reverence, but rebel against him, Heb. 12:29.
s. Deut. 4:25 Meaning hereby all superstition and corruption of the true service of God.
t. Deut. 4:26 Though men would absolve you, yet the insensible creatures shall be witnesses of your disobedience.
u. Deut. 4:27 So that his curse shall make his former blessings of none effect.
v. Deut. 4:29 Not with outward show or ceremony, but with a true confession of thy faults.
w. Deut. 4:30 Hebrew, in the latter days.
x. Deut. 4:31 To certify them the more of the assurance of their salvation.
y. Deut. 4:32 Man's negligence is partly cause, that he knoweth not God.
z. Deut. 4:34 By so manifest proofs that none could doubt thereof.
aa. Deut. 4:35 He showeth the cause why God wrought these miracles.
ab. Deut. 4:37 Freely, and not of their deserts.
ac. Deut. 4:40 God promiseth reward not for our merits, but to encourage us, and to assure us that our labor shall not be lost.

three cities on this side of Jordan toward the sun rising: **42** That the slayer should flee thither, which had killed his neighbor at unawares, and hated him not in time past, might flee, I say, unto one of those cities, and live: **43** That is, [3]Bezer in the wilderness, in the plain country of the Reubenites: and Ramoth in Gilead among the Gadites: and Golan in Bashan among them of Manasseh. **44** So this is the law which Moses set before the children of Israel. **45** These are the [ad]witnesses, and the ordinances, and the laws which Moses declared to the children of Israel after they came out of Egypt. **46** On this side Jordan, in the valley over against Beth Peor, in the land of Sihon King of the Amorites, which dwelt at Heshbon, whom Moses and the children of Israel [4]smote, after they were come out of Egypt: **47** And they possessed his land, and the land of [5]Og King of Bashan, two Kings of the Amorites, which were on this side Jordan toward the sun rising: **48** From Aroer, which is by the bank of the river Arnon, even unto mount Sion, which is Hermon, **49** And all the plain from Jordan Eastward, even unto [ae]the Sea of the plain, under the [6]springs of Pisgah.

5

5 Moses is the mean between God and the people. 6 The Law is repeated. 23 The people are afraid at God's voice. 29 The Lord wisheth that the people would fear him. 32 They must neither decline to the right hand nor left.

1 Then Moses called all Israel, and said unto them, Hear, O Israel, the ordinances and the laws which [a]I propose to you this day, that ye may learn them, and take heed to observe them. **2** [1]The Lord our God made a covenant with us in Horeb. **3** The Lord [b]made not this covenant with our fathers only, but with us, even with us all here alive this day. **4** The Lord talked with you [c]face to face in the Mount, out of the midst of the fire. **5** (At that time I stood between the Lord and you, to declare unto you the word of the Lord: for ye were afraid at the sight of the fire, and went not up into the mount) and he said, **6** [2]I am the Lord thy God, which have brought thee out of the land of Egypt, from the house of [d]bondage. **7** Thou shalt have none [e]other gods before my face. **8** Thou shalt make thee no graven image or any likeness of that that is in heaven above, or which is in the earth beneath, or that is in the waters under the earth. **9** Thou shalt neither bow thyself unto them, nor serve them: for [3]I the Lord thy God am a [f]jealous God, visiting the iniquity of the fathers upon the children, even unto the third and fourth generation of them that hate me: **10** And showing mercy unto thousands of them that [g]love me, and keep my commandments. **11** Thou shalt not take the Name of the Lord thy God in vain: for the Lord will not hold him guiltless that taketh his Name in vain. **12** Keep the Sabbath day to sanctify it, as the Lord thy God hath commanded thee. **13** Six days [h]thou shalt labor, and shalt do all thy work: **14** But the seventh day is the Sabbath of the Lord thy God: thou shalt not do any work therein, thou, nor thy son, nor thy daughter, nor thy manservant, nor thy maid, nor thine ox, nor thine ass, neither any of thy cattle, nor the stranger that is within thy gates: that thy manservant and thy maid may rest as well as thou. **15** For, remember that thou wast a servant in the land of Egypt, and that the Lord thy God brought thee out thence by a mighty hand, and a stretched out arm: therefore the Lord thy God commanded thee to observe the Sabbath day. **16** [i]Honor thy father and thy mother, as the Lord thy God hath commanded thee, that thy days may be prolonged, and that it may go well with thee upon the land, which the Lord thy God giveth thee. **17** [4]Thou shalt not kill. **18** [5]Neither shalt thou commit adultery. **19** [6]Neither shalt thou steal. **20** Neither shalt thou bear false witness against thy neighbor. **21** [7]Neither shalt [j]thou covet thy neighbor's wife, neither shalt thou desire thy neighbor's house, his field, nor his manservant, nor his maid, his ox, nor his ass, nor ought that thy neighbor hath. **22** These words the Lord spake unto all your multitude in the mount of the midst of the fire, the cloud and the darkness, with a great voice, and [k]added no more thereto: and wrote them upon two tables of stone, and delivered them unto me. **23** And when ye heard the voice out of the midst of the darkness, (for the mountain did burn with fire) then ye came to me, all the chief of your tribes, and your Elders: **24** And ye said, Behold, the Lord our God hath showed us his glory and his greatness, and [8]we have heard his voice out of the midst of the fire: we have seen this day that God doth talk with man, and he [9]liveth. **25** Now therefore, why should we die? for this great fire will consume us: if we hear the voice of the Lord our God anymore, we shall die. **26** For what [l]flesh was there ever that heard the voice of the living God speaking out of the midst of the fire as we have, and lived? **27** Go thou near and hear all that the Lord our God saith: and declare thou unto us all that the Lord our God saith unto thee: [10]and we will hear it, and do it. **28** Then the Lord heard the voice of your words, when ye spake unto me: and the Lord said unto me, I have heard the voice of the words of this people, which they have spoken unto thee: they have well said, all that they have spoken. **29** Oh [m]that there were such an heart in them to fear me, and to keep all my commandments always: that it might go well with them, and with their children forever. **30** Go, say unto them, Return you into your tents. **31** But stand thou here with me, and I will tell thee all the commandments, and the ordinances, and the laws, which thou shalt teach them: that they may do them in the land which I give them to possess it. **32** Take heed therefore, that ye do as the Lord your God hath commanded you: [n]turn not aside to the right hand nor to the left. **33** But walk in all the ways which the Lord your God hath commanded you, that ye may [o]live, and that it may go well with you: and that ye may prolong your days in the land which ye shall possess.

6

1 An exhortation to fear God, and keep his commandments, 5 Which is, to love him with all thine heart. 7 The same must be taught to the posterity. 16 Not to tempt God. 25 Righteousness is contained in the Law.

1 These now are the commandments, ordinances, and [a]laws, which the Lord your God commanded me to teach you, that ye might do them in the land whither ye go to possess it: **2** That thou mightest [b]fear the Lord thy God, and keep all his ordinances, and his commandments which I command thee, thou, and thy son, and thy son's son all the days of thy life, even that thy days may be prolonged: **3** Hear therefore, O Israel, and take heed to do it, that it may go well with thee, and that ye may increase mightily [c]in the land that floweth with milk and honey, as the Lord God of thy fathers hath promised thee. **4** Hear, O Israel, The Lord our God is Lord only, **5** And [1]thou shalt love the Lord thy God with all thine heart, and with all thy soul, and with all thy might. **6** [2]And these words which I command thee this day, shall be in thine heart. **7** And thou shalt [d]rehearse them continually unto thy children, and shalt talk of them when thou tarriest in thine house, and as thou walkest by the way, and when thou liest down, and when thou risest up: **8** And thou shalt bind them for a sign upon thine hand, and they shall be [e]as frontlets between thine eyes. **9** Also thou shalt write them upon the [f]posts of thine house, and upon thy gates. **10** And when the Lord thy God hath brought thee into the land, which he sware unto thy fathers Abraham, Isaac, and Jacob, to give to thee, with great and goodly cities which thou buildedst not, **11** And houses full of all manner of goods which thou filledst not, and wells dug which thou dug not, vineyards and olive trees which thou plantedst not, and when thou hast eaten and art full, **12** [g]Beware lest thou forget the Lord, which brought thee out of the land of Egypt, from the house of bondage: **13** Thou shalt fear the Lord thy God, and serve him, and shalt [h]swear by his Name. **14** Ye shall not walk after other gods, after any of the gods of the people which are round about you. **15** (For the Lord thy God is a jealous God among you:) lest the wrath of the Lord thy God be kindled against thee, and destroy thee from the face of the earth. **16** Ye shall not [i]tempt the Lord your God, as ye did tempt him in Massah: **17** But ye shall keep diligently the commandments of the Lord your God, and his testimonies and his ordinances, which he hath commanded thee. **18** And thou shalt do that which is right and good in the [j]sight of the Lord: that thou mayest prosper, and that thou mayest go in, and possess that good land which the Lord sware unto thy fathers, **19** To cast out all thine enemies before thee, as the Lord hath said. **20** When [k]thy son shall ask thee in time to come, saying, What mean these testimonies, and ordinances, and Laws, which the Lord our God hath commanded you? **21** Then shalt thou say unto thy son, We were Pharaoh's bondmen in Egypt: but the Lord brought us out of Egypt with a mighty

---

ad. Deut. 4:45 The articles and points of the covenant.
ae. Deut. 4:49 That is, the salt sea.

DEUT. 4

1. Deut. 12:32
2. Exod. 19:18
3. Josh. 20:8
4. Num. 21:24 / Deut. 1:4
5. Num. 21:33 / Deut. 3:3
6. Deut. 3:17

DEUT. 5

a. Deut. 5:1 Hebrew, I speak in your ears.
b. Deut. 5:3 Some read, God made not this covenant, that is, in such ample forth and with such signs and wonders.
c. Deut. 5:4 So plainly that ye need not to doubt thereof.
d. Deut. 5:6 Or, servant.
e. Deut. 5:7 God bindeth us to serve him only, without superstition and idolatry.
f. Deut. 5:9 That is, of his honor, not permitting it to be given to others.
g. Deut. 5:10 The first degree to keep the commandments, is to love God.
h. Deut. 5:13 Meaning, since God permitteth six days to our labors, that we ought willingly to dedicate the seventh to serve him wholly.
i. Deut. 5:16 Not for a show, but with true obedience, and due reverence.
j. Deut. 5:21 He speaketh not only of that resolute will, but that there be no motion or affection.
k. Deut. 5:22 Teaching us by his example to be content with his word, and add nothing thereto.
l. Deut. 5:26 Or, man.
m. Deut. 5:29 He requireth of us nothing but obedience, showing also that of ourselves we are unwilling thereunto.
n. Deut. 5:32 Ye shall neither add nor diminish, Deut. 4:2.
o. Deut. 5:33 As by obedience, God giveth us all felicity: so of disobeying God proceed all our miseries.

DEUT. 5

1. Exod. 19:5,6
2. Exod. 20:2 / Lev. 26:1 / Ps. 97:7,9
3. Exod. 34:7 / Jer. 32:18
4. Matt. 5:21
5. Luke 18:20
6. Rom. 13:9
7. Rom. 7:7
8. Exod. 19:19
9. Deut. 4:33
10. Exod. 20:19

DEUT. 6

a. Deut. 6:1 Or, judgments.
b. Deut. 6:2 A reverent face and love of God is the first beginning to keep God's commandments.
c. Deut. 6:3 Which hath abundance of all things appertaining to man's life.
d. Deut. 6:7 Some read, thou shalt whet them upon thy children: to wit, that they may print them more deeply in memory.
e. Deut. 6:8 Or, signs of remembrance.
f. Deut. 6:9 That when thou entrest in, thou mayest remember them.
g. Deut. 6:12 Let not wealth and ease cause thee forget God's mercies, whereby thou wast delivered out of misery.
h. Deut. 6:13 We must fear God, serve him only, and confess his Name, which is done by swearing lawfully.
i. Deut. 6:16 By doubting of his power, refusing lawful means, and abusing his graces.
j. Deut. 6:18 Here he condemneth all man's good intentions.
k. Deut. 6:20 God requireth not only that we serve him all our life, but also that we take pains that our posterity may set forth his glory.

hand. **22** And the Lord showed signs and wonders great and evil upon Egypt, upon Pharaoh, and upon all his household before our eyes, **23** And [l]brought us out from thence, to bring us in, and to give us the land which he sware unto our fathers. **24** Therefore the Lord hath commanded us, to do all these ordinances, and to fear the Lord our God, that it may go ever well with us, and that he may preserve us alive at this present. **25** Moreover, this shall be our [m]righteousness before the Lord our God, if we take heed to keep all these commandments, as he hath commanded us.

7

1 The Israelites may make no covenant with the Gentiles. 5 They must destroy the idols. 8 The election dependeth on the free love of God. 19 The experience of the power of God ought to confirm us. 25 To avoid all occasion of idolatry.

1 When the Lord thy God shall bring thee into the land whither thou goest to possess it, [1]and shall root out many nations before thee: the Hittites, and the Girgashites, and the Amorites, and the Canaanites, and the Perizzites, and the Hivites, and the Jebusites, seven nations greater and mightier than thou, **2** And the Lord thy God shall give them [a]before thee, then thou shalt smite them: thou shalt utterly destroy them: thou shalt make no [2]covenant with them, nor have compassion on them, **3** Neither shalt thou make marriages with them, neither give thy daughter unto his son, nor take his daughter unto thy son. **4** For [b]they will cause thy son to turn away from me, and to serve other gods: then will the wrath of the Lord wax hot against you, and destroy thee suddenly. **5** But thus ye shall deal with them, [c]Ye shall overthrow their altars, and break down their pillars, and ye shall cut down their groves, and burn their graven images with fire. **6** [3]For thou art an holy people unto the Lord thy God, [4]the Lord thy God hath chosen thee, to be a precious people unto himself, above all people that are upon the earth. **7** The Lord did not set his love upon you, nor chose you, because ye were more in number than any people: for ye were the fewest of all people: **8** But because the Lord [d]loved you, and because he would keep the oath which he had sworn unto your fathers, the Lord hath brought you out by a mighty hand, and delivered you out of the house of bondage from the hand of Pharaoh King of Egypt. **9** That thou mayest know, [e]that the Lord thy God, he is God, the faithful God, which keepeth covenant and mercy unto them that love him and keep his commandments, even to a thousand generations, **10** And rewardeth [f]them to their face that hate him, to bring them to destruction: he will not defer to reward him that hateth him, to his face. **11** Keep thou therefore the commandments, and the ordinances, and the laws, which I command thee this day to do them. **12** For if ye hearken unto these laws, and observe and do them, then the Lord thy God shall keep with thee the covenant, and the [g]mercy which he sware unto thy fathers. **13** And he will love thee, and bless thee, and multiply thee: he will also bless the fruit of thy womb, and the fruit of thy land, thy corn and thy wine, and thine oil, and the increase of thy kine, and the flocks of thy sheep in the land, which he sware unto thy fathers to give thee. **14** Thou shalt be blessed above all people: [5]there shall be neither male nor female barren among you, nor among your cattle. **15** Moreover, the Lord will take away from thee all infirmities, and will put none of the evil diseases of [6]Egypt (which thou knowest) upon thee, but will send them upon all that hate thee. **16** Thou shalt therefore consume all people which the Lord thy God shall give thee: [h]thine eye shall not spare them, neither shalt thou serve their gods, for that shall be thy [7]destruction. **17** If thou say in thine heart, These nations are more than I, how can I cast them out? **18** Thou shalt not fear them, but remember what the Lord thy God did unto Pharaoh, and unto all Egypt: **19** The great [i]tentations which thine eyes saw, and the signs and wonders, and the mighty hand and stretched out arm, whereby the Lord thy God brought thee out: so shall the Lord thy God do unto all the people, whose face thou fearest. **20** [8]Moreover, the Lord thy God will send [j]hornets among them until they that are left, and hide themselves from thee, be destroyed. **21** Thou shalt not fear them: for the Lord thy God is among you, a God mighty and dreadful. **22** And the Lord thy God will root out these nations before thee by little and little: thou mayest not consume them at once, lest the [k]beasts of the field increase upon thee. **23** But the Lord thy God shall give them before thee, and shall destroy them with a mighty destruction, until they be brought to naught. **24** And he shall deliver their Kings into thine hand, and thou shalt destroy their name from under heaven: there shall no man be able to stand before thee, until thou hast destroyed them. **25** The graven images of their gods shall ye [9]burn with fire, and covet not the silver and gold, that is on them, nor take it unto thee, lest thou [l]be snared therewith: for it is an abomination before the Lord thy God. **26** Bring not therefore abomination into thine house, lest thou be accursed like it, but utterly abhor it, and count it most abominable: for it is [10]accursed.

8

1 God humbleth the Israelites to try what they have in their heart. 5 God chastiseth them as his children. 14 The heart ought not to be proud of God's benefits. 19 The forgetfulness of God's benefits causeth destruction.

1 Ye shall keep all the commandments which I command thee this day, for [a]to do them: that ye may live, and be multiplied, and go in, and possess the land which the Lord sware unto your fathers. **2** And thou shalt remember all the way which the Lord thy God led thee this forty years in the wilderness, for to humble thee, and to [b]prove thee, to know what was in thine heart, whether thou wouldest keep his commandments or no. **3** Therefore he humbled thee, and made thee hungry, and fed thee with Manna, which thou knewest not, neither did thy fathers know it, that he might teach thee that man lived not by [c]bread only, but by every word that proceedeth out of the mouth of the Lord, doth a man live. **4** Thy raiment waxed not old upon thee, neither did thy foot [d]swell those forty years. **5** Know therefore in thine heart, that as a man nurtureth his son, so the Lord thy God [e]nurtureth thee. **6** Therefore shalt thou keep the commandments of the Lord thy God, that thou mayest walk in his ways, and fear him. **7** For the Lord thy God bringeth thee into a good land, a land in the which are rivers of water and fountains, and [f]depths that spring out of valleys and mountains: **8** A land of wheat and barley, and of vineyards, and fig trees, and pomegranates: a land of oil, olive and honey: **9** A land wherein thou shalt eat bread without scarcity, neither shalt thou lack anything therein: a land [g]whose stones are iron, and out of whose mountains thou shalt dig brass. **10** And when thou hast eaten and filled thyself, thou shalt [h]bless the Lord thy God for the good land, which he hath given thee. **11** Beware that thou forget not the Lord thy God, not keeping his commandments and his laws, and his ordinances, which I command thee this day: **12** Lest when thou hast eaten and filled thyself, and hast built goodly houses and dwelt therein, **13** And thy beasts, and the sheep are increased, and thy silver and gold is multiplied, and all that thou hast is increased; **14** Then thine heart [i]be lifted up and thou forget the Lord thy God, which brought thee out of the land of Egypt, from the house of bondage, **15** Who was thy guide in that great and terrible wilderness (wherein were fiery serpents, and scorpions and drought, where was no water, [1]who brought forth water for thee out of the rock of flint: **16** Who fed thee in the wilderness with [2]Manna, which thy fathers knew not) to humble thee, and to prove thee, that he might do thee good at the latter end. **17** Beware lest thou say in thine heart, My power, and the strength of mine own hand hath prepared me this abundance. **18** But remember the Lord thy God: for it is he which [j]giveth thee power to get substance to establish his covenant which he sware unto thy fathers, as appeareth this day. **19** And if thou forget the Lord thy God, and walk after other gods, and serve them, and worship them, I [k]testify unto you this day, that ye shall surely perish. **20** As the nations which the Lord destroyeth before you, so ye shall perish, because ye would not be obedient unto the voice of the Lord your God.

9

1 God doth not them good for their own righteousness, but for his own sake. 7 Moses putteth them in remembrance of their sins. 17 The two Tables are broken. 26 Moses prayeth for the people.

1 Hear, O Israel, Thou shalt pass over Jordan [a]this day, to go in and to possess nations greater and mightier than thyself, and cities great and walled up to heaven, **2** A people great and tall, even the children of the Anakims, whom thou

---

l. Deut. 6:23 Nothing ought to move us more to true obedience than the great benefits which we have received of God.
m. Deut. 6:25 But because none could fully obey the law, we must have our recourse to Christ to be justified by faith.

DEUT. 6
1. Matt. 22:37 / Mark 12:29,34 / Luke 13:27
2. Deut. 11:18

DEUT. 7
a. Deut. 7:2 Into thy power.
b. Deut. 7:4 Or, any of them.
c. Deut. 7:5 God would have his service pure without all idolatrous ceremonies and superstitions, Deut. 22:3.
d. Deut. 7:8 Freely, finding no cause in you more than in others so to do.
e. Deut. 7:9 And so put difference between him and idols.
f. Deut. 7:10 Meaning, manifestly, or in this life.
g. Deut. 7:12 This covenant is grounded upon his free grace: therefore in recompensing their obedience, he hath respect to his mercy and not to their merits.
h. Deut. 7:16 We ought not to be merciful, where God commandeth severity.
i. Deut. 7:19 Or, plagues, or trials, Deut. 29:3; as Exod. 15:25 and Exod. 16:4.
j. Deut. 7:20 There is not so small a creature, which I will not arm to fight on thy side against them.
k. Deut. 7:22 So that it is your commodity that God accomplish not his promise so soon as you would wish.
l. Deut. 7:25 And be enticed to idolatry.

DEUT. 7
1. Deut. 31:8
2. Exod. 23:32 / Exod. 34:12
3. Deut. 14:2 / Deut. 26:18,19
4. Exod. 19:5 / 2 Pet. 2:9
5. Exod. 23:26
6. Exod. 9:14 / Exod. 15:26
7. Exod. 23:33
8. Exod. 23:28 / Josh. 24:12
9. Deut. 12:3 / Exod. 23:24
10. Josh. 7:1,21
11. Deut. 13:17

DEUT. 8
a. Deut. 8:1 Showing that it is not enough to hear the word, except we express it by example of life.
b. Deut. 8:2 Which is declared in afflictions, either by patience, or by grudging against God's visitation.
c. Deut. 8:3 Man liveth not by meat only, but by the power of God, which giveth it strength to nourish us.
d. Deut. 8:4 As they that go barefooted.
e. Deut. 8:5 So that his afflictions are signs of his fatherly love toward us.
f. Deut. 8:7 Or, meres.
g. Deut. 8:9 Where there are mines of metal.
h. Deut. 8:10 For to receive God's benefits, and not to be thankful, is to contemn God in them.
i. Deut. 8:14 By attributing God's benefits to thine own wisdom and labor, or to good fortune.
j. Deut. 8:18 If things concerning this life, proceed only of God's mercy: much more spiritual gifts and life everlasting.
k. Deut. 8:19 Or, take to witness the heaven and the earth, as Deut. 4:26.

DEUT. 8
1. Num. 20:11
2. Exod. 16:15

knowest, and of whom thou hast [b]heard say, Who can stand before the children of
Anak? **3** Understand therefore that this day the Lord thy God is he which [c]goe-
th over before thee as a consuming fire: he shall destroy them, and he shall bring
them down before thy face: so thou shalt cast them out and destroy them suddenly,
as the Lord hath said unto thee. **4** Speak not thou in thine heart (after that the
Lord thy God hath cast them out before thee) saying, For my [d]righteousness the
Lord hath brought me in, to possess this land: but for the wickedness of these na-
tions, the Lord hath cast them out before thee. **5** For thou entrust not to inherit
their land for thy righteousness, or for their upright heart, but for the wickedness
of those nations, the Lord thy God doth cast them out before thee, and that he mi-
ght perform the word which the Lord thy God sware unto thy fathers, Abraham,
Isaac, and Jacob. **6** Understand therefore, that the Lord thy God giveth thee not
this good land to possess it for thy righteousness: for thou art a [e]stiff-necked pe-
ople. **7** Remember and forget not, how thou provokedst the Lord thy God to
anger in the wilderness: [f]since the day that thou didst depart out of the land of
Egypt, until ye came into this place, ye have rebelled against the Lord. **8** Also in
Horeb ye provoked the Lord to anger, so that the Lord was wroth with you, even
to destroy you. **9** When I was gone up into the mount, to receive the Tables of
stone, the Tables, I say, of the Covenant, which the Lord made with you: and [1]I
abode in the mount forty days and forty nights, and I neither ate bread nor yet
drank water: **10** [2]Then the Lord delivered me two tables of stone, written with
the [g]finger of God, and in them was contained according to all the words which
the Lord had said unto you in the mount out of the midst of the fire, in the day
of the assembly. **11** And when the forty days and forty nights were ended, the
Lord gave me the two tables of stone, the tables, I say, of the covenant. **12** And
the Lord said unto me, [3]Arise, get thee down quickly from hence: for thy people
which thou hast brought out of Egypt, have [h]corrupt their ways: they are soon
turned out of the way which I commanded them, they have made them a molten
image. **13** Furthermore the Lord spake unto me, saying, I have seen this peo-
ple, and behold, it is a stiff-necked people. **14** [i]Let me alone, that I may destroy
them, and put out their name from under heaven, and I will make of thee a mi-
ghty nation and greater than they be. **15** So I returned, and came down from the
mount (and the mount burnt with fire, and the two Tables of the Covenant were in
my two hands.) **16** Then I looked, and behold, ye had sinned against the Lord
your God: for ye had made you a molten calf, and had turned quickly out of the
[j]way which the Lord had commanded you. **17** Therefore I took the two Tables,
and cast them out of my two hands, and brake them before your eyes. **18** And
I fell down before the Lord, forty days, and forty nights, as before: I neither ate
bread nor drank water, because of all your sins which ye had committed, in doing
wickedly in the sight of the Lord, in that ye provoked him unto wrath. **19** (For
I was afraid of the wrath and indignation, wherewith the Lord was moved against
you, even to destroy you) yet the Lord heard me at that time also. **20** Likewi-
se the Lord was very angry with Aaron, even to [k]destroy him: but at that time I
prayed also for Aaron. **21** And I took your sin, I mean the calf which ye had
made, and burnt him with fire, and stamped him and ground him small, even
unto very dust: and I cast the dust thereof into the river, that descended out of
the [l]mount. **22** Also [4]in Taberah, and in [5]Massah, [6]and in Kibroth Hattaavah
ye provoked the Lord to anger. **23** Likewise when the Lord sent you from Ka-
desh Barnea, saying, Go up, and possess the land which I have given you, then ye
[m]rebelled against the commandment of the Lord your God, and believed him not,
nor hearkened unto his voice. **24** Ye have been rebellious unto the Lord, since
the day that I knew you. **25** Then I fell down before the Lord [n]forty days, and
forty nights, as I fell down before, because the Lord had said that he would destroy
you. **26** And I prayed unto the Lord, and said, O Lord God, destroy not thy
people and thine inheritance, which thou hast redeemed through thy greatness,
whom thou hast brought out of Egypt by a mighty hand. **27** [o]Remember thy
servants Abraham, Isaac, and Jacob: look not to the stubbornness of this people,
nor to their wickedness, nor to their sin, **28** Lest the country whence thou brou-
ghtest them, say, [7]Because the Lord was not able to bring them into the land which
he promised them, or because he hated them, he carried them out to slay them in
the wilderness. **29** Yet they are thy people, and thine inheritance, which thou
broughtest out by thy mighty power, and by thy stretched out arm.

10

5 The second Tables put in the Ark. 8 The tribe of Levi is dedicated to the service of the Tabernacle. 12 What the Lord requireth of his. 16 The circumcision of the heart. 17 God regardeth not the person. 21 The Lord is the praise of Israel.

1 In the same time the Lord said unto me, [1]Hew thee two tables of stone
like unto the first, and come up unto me into the mount, and make thee an Ark
of wood, **2** And I will write upon the tables, the words that were upon the first
Tables, which thou breakest, and thou shalt put them in the Ark. **3** And I made
an Ark of [a]Shittim wood, and hewed two tables of stone like unto the first, and
went up into the mountain, and the two Tables in mine hand. **4** Then he wrote
upon the Tables according to the first writing, (the ten commandments, which the
Lord spake unto you in the mount out of the midst of the fire, in the day of the
[b]assembly) and the Lord gave them unto me. **5** And I departed and came down
from the Mount, and put the Tables in the Ark which I had made: and there they
be, as the Lord commanded me. **6** And the children of Israel took their journey
from Beeroth of the children of Jaakan, to [c]Moserah, where Aaron died, and was
buried, and Eleazar his son became Priest in his stead. **7** From thence they de-
parted unto Gudgodah, and from Gudgodah to Jotbathah, a land of running wa-
ters. **8** The same time the Lord separated the tribe of Levi to bear the Ark of the
Covenant of the Lord, and to stand before the Lord, to [d]minister unto him, and to
bless in his Name unto this day. **9** Wherefore Levi hath no part nor inheritance
with his brethren: for the Lord is his [e]inheritance, as the Lord thy God hath promi-
sed him. **10** And I tarried in the mount, as at the first time, forty days and forty
nights, and the Lord heard me at that time also, and the Lord would not destroy
thee. **11** But the Lord said unto me, Arise, go forth in the journey before the
people, that they may go in and possess the land, which I sware unto their fathers
to give unto them. **12** And now, Israel, what doth the Lord thy God [f]require of
thee, but to fear the Lord thy God, to walk in all his ways, and to love him, and to
serve the Lord thy God with all thine heart, and with all thy soul? **13** That thou
keep the commandments of the Lord and his ordinances, which I command thee
this day, for thy wealth? **14** Behold, heaven, and the heaven of heavens is the
Lord's thy God, and the [2]earth, with all that therein is. **15** [g]Notwithstanding,
the Lord set his delight in thy fathers to love them, and did choose their seed after
them, even you above all people, as appeareth this day. **16** [h]Circumcise therefore
the foreskin of your heart, and harden your necks no more. **17** For the Lord your
God is God of gods, and Lord of lords, a great God, mighty and terrible, which
accepteth no [3]persons, nor taketh reward: **18** Who doeth right unto the father-
less and widow, and loveth the stranger, giving him food and raiment. **19** Love
ye therefore the stranger: for ye were strangers in the land of Egypt. **20** [4]Thou
shalt fear the Lord thy God: thou shalt serve him, and thou shalt cleave unto him,
and [i]shalt swear by his Name. **21** He is thy praise, and he is thy God, that hath
done for thee these great and terrible things, which thine eyes have seen. **22** Thy
fathers went down into Egypt [5]with seventy persons, and now the Lord thy God
hath made thee, as the [6]stars of the heaven in multitude.

11

1 An exhortation to love God, and keep his law. 10 The praises of Canaan. 18 To meditate continually the word of God. 19 To teach it unto the children. 26 Blessing and cursing.

1 Therefore thou shalt love the Lord thy God and shalt keep that, which he
commandeth to be kept: that is, his ordinances, and his laws and his command-
ments always. **2** And [a]consider this day (for I speak not to your children, which
have neither known nor seen) the chastisements of the Lord your God, his great-
ness, his mighty hand, and his stretched out arm, **3** And his signs, and his acts,
which he did in the midst of Egypt, unto Pharaoh the King of Egypt and unto all
his land: **4** And what he did unto the host of the Egyptians, unto their horses,
and to their chariots, when he caused the waters of the red Sea to overflow them, as
they pursued after you, and the Lord destroyed them unto this day: **5** And [b]what
he did unto you in the wilderness, until ye came unto this place: **6** And what he
did unto Dathan and Abiram the sons of Eliab the son of Reuben, when the earth
opened her mouth, and swallowed them with their households, and their tents,

---

DEUT. 9

a. Deut. 9:1 Meaning, shortly.
b. Deut. 9:2 By the report of the spies, Num. 13:26.
c. Deut. 9:3 To guide thee and govern thee.
d. Deut. 9:4 Man of himself can deserve nothing but God's anger, and if God spare any it cometh of his great mercy.
e. Deut. 9:6 Like stubborn oxen which will not endure their master's yoke.
f. Deut. 9:7 He proveth by the length of time, that their rebellion was most great and intolerable.
g. Deut. 9:10 That is, miraculously, and not by the hand of men.
h. Deut. 9:12 So soon as man declineth from the obedience of God, his ways are corrupt.
i. Deut. 9:14 Signifying that the prayers of the faithful are a bar to stay God's anger that he consume not all.
j. Deut. 9:16 That is, from the Law: wherein he declareth what is the cause of our perdition.
k. Deut. 9:20 Whereby he showeth what danger they are in, that have authority and resist not wickedness.
l. Deut. 9:21 Horeb, or Sinai.
m. Deut. 9:23 At the return of the spies.
n. Deut. 9:25 Whereby is signified that God requireth earnest continuance in prayer.
o. Deut. 9:27 The godly in their prayers ground on God's promise, and confess their sins.

DEUT. 9

1. Exod. 24:18 / Exod. 34:28
2. Exod. 31:18
3. Exod. 32:7
4. Num. 11:1,3
5. Exod. 17:7
6. Num. 11:34
7. Num. 14:16

DEUT. 10

a. Deut. 10:3 Which wood is of long continuance.
b. Deut. 10:4 When you were assembled to receive the Law.
c. Deut. 10:6 This mountain was also called Hor, Num. 20:28.
d. Deut. 10:8 That is, to offer sacrifice, and to declare the Law to the people.
e. Deut. 10:9 So God turned the curse of Jacob, Gen. 49:7, unto blessing.
f. Deut. 10:12 For all our sins and transgressions God requireth nothing but to turn to him and obey him.
g. Deut. 10:15 Although he was Lord of heaven and earth, yet would he choose none but you.
h. Deut. 10:16 Cut off all your evil affections, Jer 4:4.
i. Deut. 10:20 Read Deut. 6:13.

DEUT. 10

1. Exod. 34:1
2. Ps. 24:1
3. 2 Chron. 19:7 / Rom. 2:11
4. Deut. 6:13 / Matt. 4:10
5. Gen. 46:27 / Exod. 1:5
6. Gen. 15:5

DEUT. 11

a. Deut. 11:2 Ye, which have seen God's graces with your eyes, ought rather to be moved, than your children, which have only heard of them.
b. Deut. 11:5 As well concerning his benefits, as his corrections.
c. Deut. 11:6 Hebrew, was at their feet.

and all their substance that [c]they had in the midst of all Israel. **7** For your eyes have seen all the great acts of the Lord which he did. **8** Therefore shall ye keep [d]all the commandments, which I command you this day, that ye may be strong, and go in and possess the land whither ye go to possess it: **9** Also that ye may prolong your days in the land, which the Lord sware unto your fathers, to give unto them and to their seed, even a land that floweth with milk and honey. **10** For the land whither thou goest to possess it, is not as the land of Egypt, from whence ye came, where thou sowedst thy seed, and wateredst it with thy [e,f]feet as a garden of herbs: **11** But the land whither ye go to possess it, is a land of mountains and valleys, and drinketh water of the rain of heaven. **12** This land doth the Lord thy God care for: the eyes of the Lord thy God are always upon it, from the beginning of the year, even unto the end of the year. **13** If ye shall hearken therefore unto my commandments, which I command you this day, that ye love the Lord your God and serve him with all your heart, and with all your soul, **14** I also will give rain unto your land in due time, [g]the first rain and the latter, that thou mayest gather in thy wheat, and thy wine, and thine oil. **15** Also I will send grass in thy fields for thy cattle, that thou mayest eat, and have enough. **16** But beware lest your heart [h]deceive you, and lest ye turn aside, and serve other gods, and worship them. **17** And so the anger of the Lord be kindled against you, and he shut up the heaven, that there be no rain, and that your land yield not her fruit, and ye perish quickly from the good land, which the Lord giveth you. **18** Therefore shall ye lay up these my words in your heart and in your soul, and [1]bind them for a sign upon your hand, that they may be as a frontlet between your eyes, **19** And ye shall [2]teach them your children, speaking of them when thou sittest in thine house, and when thou walkest by the way, and when thou liest down, and when thou risest up. **20** And thou shalt write them upon the posts of thine house, and upon thy gates, **21** That your days may be multiplied, and the days of your children, in the land which the Lord sware unto your fathers to give them, as long as [i]the heavens are above the earth. **22** For if ye keep diligently all these Commandments, which I command you to do: that is, to love the Lord your God, to walk in all his ways, and to cleave unto him, **23** Then will the Lord cast out all these nations before you, and ye shall possess great nations and mightier than you. **24** [3]All the places whereon the soles of [j]your feet shall tread, shall be yours: your coast shall be from the wilderness and from Lebanon, and from the River even the river Perath, unto the uttermost [k]Sea. **25** No man shall stand against you: for the Lord your God shall cast the fear and dread of you upon all the land that ye shall tread upon, as he hath said unto you. **26** Behold, I set before you this day a blessing and a curse: **27** [4]The blessing, if ye obey the commandments of the Lord your God, which I command you this day: **28** And the [5]curse, if ye will not obey the Commandments of the Lord your God, but turn out of the way, which I command you this day, to go after other gods which ye have not [l]known. **29** When the Lord thy God therefore hath brought thee into the land, whither thou goest to possess it, then thou shalt put the [6]blessing upon mount Gerizim, and the curse upon mount Ebal. **30** Are they not beyond Jordan on that part, [m]where the Sun goeth down in the land of the Canaanites, which dwell in the plain over against Gilgal, beside [n]the grove of Moreh? **31** For ye shall pass over Jordan, to go in to possess that land which the Lord your God giveth you, and ye shall possess it, and dwell therein. **32** Take heed therefore that ye [7]do all the commandments and the laws, which I set before you this day.

12

3 To destroy the idolatrous places. 5, 8 To serve God where he commandeth, and as he commandeth, and not as men fantasize. 19 The Levites must be nourished. 31 Idolaters burnt their children to their gods, to add nothing to God's word.

1 These are the ordinances and the laws, which ye shall observe and do in the land, (which the Lord God [a]of thy fathers giveth thee to possess it) as long as ye live upon the earth. **2** [1]Ye shall utterly destroy all the places wherein the nations which ye shall possess, served their gods upon the high mountains, and upon the hills, and under every green tree. **3** [2]Also ye shall overthrow their altars, and break down their pillars, and burn their [b]groves with fire: and ye shall hew down the graven images of their gods, and abolish their names out of that place. **4** Ye shall [c]not do so unto the Lord your God, **5** But ye shall seek the place which the Lord your God shall [3]choose out of your tribes, to put his Name there, and there to dwell, and thither thou shalt come, **6** And ye shall bring thither your burnt offerings, and your sacrifices, and your tithes, and the [d]offering of your hands, and your vows, and your free offerings, and the firstborn of your kine and of your sheep. **7** And there ye shall eat [e]before the Lord your God, and ye shall rejoice in all that ye put your hand unto, both ye, and your households, because the Lord thy God hath blessed thee. **8** Ye shall not do after all these things that we do [f]here this day: that is, every man whatsoever seemeth him good in his own eyes. **9** For ye are not yet come to rest, and to the inheritance which the Lord thy God giveth thee. **10** But when ye go over Jordan, and dwell in the land, which the Lord your God hath given you to inherit, and when he hath given you [g]rest from all your enemies round about, and ye dwell in safety, **11** When there shall be a place which the Lord your God shall choose, to cause his name to dwell there, thither shall ye bring all that I command you: your burnt offerings, and your sacrifices, your tithes, and the offering of your hands, and all your [h]special vows which ye vow unto the Lord: **12** And ye shall rejoice before the Lord your God, ye, and your sons and your daughters, and your servants, and your maidens, and the Levite that is within your gates: [4]for he hath no part nor inheritance with you. **13** Take heed that thou offer not thy burnt offerings in every place that thou seest: **14** But in the place which the Lord shall [i]choose in one of thy tribes, there thou shalt offer thy burnt offerings, and there thou shalt do all that I command thee. **15** Notwithstanding thou mayest kill and eat flesh in all thy gates, whatsoever thine heart desireth, according to the [j]blessing of the Lord thy God which he had given thee: both the unclean and the clean may eat thereof, [k]as of the roebuck, and of the hart. **16** Only ye shall not eat the blood, but pour it upon the earth as water. **17** Thou mayest not eat within thy gates the [l]tithe of thy corn, nor of thy wine, nor of thine oil, nor the firstborn of thy kine, nor of thy sheep, neither any of thy vows which thou vowest, nor thy free offerings, nor the offering of thine hands, **18** But thou shalt eat it before the Lord thy God, in the place which the Lord thy God shall choose, thou and thy son, and thy daughter, and thy servant, and thy maid, and the Levite that is within thy gates: and thou shalt rejoice before the Lord thy God, in all that thou puttest thine hand to. **19** Beware, that thou forsake not the Levite, as long as thou livest upon the earth. **20** When the Lord thy God shall enlarge thy border, as [5]he hath promised thee, and thou shalt say, I will eat flesh (because thine heart longeth to eat flesh) thou mayest eat flesh, whatsoever thine heart desireth. **21** If the place which the Lord thy God hath chosen to put his Name there, be far from thee, then thou shalt kill of thy bullocks, and of thy sheep which the Lord hath given thee, as I have commanded thee, and thou shalt eat in thy gates, whatsoever thine heart desireth. **22** But as the roebuck, and the hart is eaten, so shalt thou eat them: both the unclean and the clean shall eat of them alike. **23** Only be [m]sure that thou eat not the blood: for the blood [n]is the life, and thou mayest not eat the life with the flesh. **24** Therefore thou shalt not eat it, but pour it upon the earth as water. **25** Thou shalt not eat it, that it may go well with thee, and with thy children after thee, when thou shalt do that which is right in the sight of the Lord: **26** But thine [o]holy things which thou hast, and thy vows thou shalt take up, and come unto the place which the Lord shall choose. **27** And thou shalt make thy burnt offerings of the flesh, and of the blood upon the altar of the Lord thy God, and the blood of thine offerings shall be poured upon the altar of the Lord thy God, and thou shalt eat the flesh. **28** Take heed, and hear all these words which I command thee, that it may go [p]well with thee, and with thy children after thee forever, when thou doest that which is good and right in the sight of the Lord thy God. **29** When the Lord thy God shall destroy the nations before thee, whither thou goest to possess them, and thou shalt possess them and dwell in their land, **30** Beware, lest thou be taken in [q]snare after them, after that they be destroyed before thee, and lest thou ask after their gods, saying, How did these nations serve their gods, that I may do so likewise? **31** Thou shalt not do so unto the Lord thy God: for all abomination, which the Lord hateth, have they done unto their gods: for they have [r]burned both their sons and their daughters with fire to their gods. **32** Therefore whatsoever I command you, take heed you do it: [6]thou shalt put nothing thereto, nor take ought therefrom.

- **d.** Deut. 11:8 Because ye have felt both his chastisements and his benefits.
- **e.** Deut. 11:10 Or, labor.
- **f.** Deut. 11:10 As by making gutters for the waters to come out of the river Nile to water the land.
- **g.** Deut. 11:14 In the seed time, and toward harvest.
- **h.** Deut. 11:16 By devising to yourselves foolish devotions according to your own fantasies.
- **i.** Deut. 11:21 As long as the heavens endure, 2 Pet. 3:10,12.
- **j.** Deut. 11:24 This was accomplished in David's and Solomon's time.
- **k.** Deut. 11:24 Called Mediterranean.
- **l.** Deut. 11:28 He reproveth the malice of men which leave that which is certain to follow that which is uncertain.
- **m.** Deut. 11:30 Meaning, in Samaria.
- **n.** Deut. 11:30 Or, plain.

DEUT. 11

1. Deut. 6:6,8
2. Deut. 4:10 / Deut. 6:7
3. Josh. 1:3
4. Deut. 28:2 / Deut. 30:1
5. Deut. 28:15
6. Deut. 27:13 / Josh. 8:33
7. Deut. 5:32

DEUT. 12

- **a.** Deut. 12:1 Whereby they are admonished to seek none other God.
- **b.** Deut. 12:3 Wherein they sacrificed to their idols.
- **c.** Deut. 12:4 Ye shall not serve the Lord with superstitions.
- **d.** Deut. 12:6 Meaning, the firstfruits.
- **e.** Deut. 12:7 Where his Ark shall be.
- **f.** Deut. 12:8 Not that they sacrificed after their fantasies, but that God would be served more purely in the land of Canaan.
- **g.** Deut. 12:10 It had not been enough to conquer, except God had maintained them in rest under his protection.
- **h.** Deut. 12:11 Or, that which ye choose out for your vows.
- **i.** Deut. 12:14 As was declared ever by the placing of the Ark, as in Shiloh 243 years, or as some write more than 300 years, and in other places till the temple was built.
- **j.** Deut. 12:15 As God hath given thee power and ability.
- **k.** Deut. 12:15 Everyone might eat at home as well the beast appointed for sacrifice, as the other.
- **l.** Deut. 12:17 Meaning, whatsoever was offered to the Lord, might not be eaten, but where he had appointed.
- **m.** Deut. 12:23 Hebrew, be strong or constant.
- **n.** Deut. 12:23 Because the life of beasts is in their blood.
- **o.** Deut. 12:26 That which thou wilt offer in sacrifice.
- **p.** Deut. 12:28 God by promise bindeth himself to do good to them that obey his word.
- **q.** Deut. 12:30 By following their superstitions and idolatries, and thinking to serve me thereby.
- **r.** Deut. 12:31 They thought nothing too dear to offer to their idols.

DEUT. 12

1. Deut. 7:5
2. Judg. 2:2
3. 1 Kings 8:29 / 2 Chron. 6:5 / 2 Chron. 7:12,16
4. Deut. 10:9
5. Gen. 28:14 / Deut. 19:8
6. Deut. 4:2 / Josh. 1:7 / Prov. 30:6 / Rev. 22:18

13

5 The enticers to idolatry must be slain, seem they never so holy. 6 So near of kindred or of friendship. 12 Or great in multitude or power.

1 If there arise among you a Prophet or a dreamer of [a]dreams, (and give thee
a sign or wonder, 2 And the sign and the wonder, which he hath told thee, come
to pass) saying, [b]Let us go after other gods, which thou hast not known, and let
us serve them, 3 Thou shalt not hearken unto the words of the prophet, or unto
that dreamer of dreams: for the Lord your God [c]proveth you, to know whether
you love the Lord your God with all your heart, and with all your soul. 4 Ye shall
walk after the Lord your God and fear him, and shall keep his commandments,
and hearken unto his voice, and ye shall serve him, and cleave unto him. 5 But
that Prophet, or that dreamer of dreams, he shall [d]be slain, because he hath spoken
to turn you away from the Lord your God (which brought you out of the land of
Egypt, and delivered you out of the house of bondage) to thrust thee out of the
way, wherein the Lord thy God commanded thee to walk: so shalt thou take the
evil away forth of the midst of thee. 6 If [e]thy brother, the son of thy mother, or
thine own son, or thy daughter, or the wife, that lieth in thy bosom, or thy friend,
which is as thine own [f]soul, entice thee secretly, saying, Let us go and serve other
gods, (which thou hast not known, thou I say, nor thy fathers) 7 Any of the gods
of the people which are round about you, near unto thee or far off from thee, from
the one end of the earth unto the other: 8 Thou shalt not consent unto him,
nor hear him, neither shall thine eye pity him, nor show mercy, nor keep him se-
cret: 9 But thou shalt even kill him: [g]thine hand shall be first upon him to put
him to death, and then the hands of the people. 10 And thou shalt stone him
with stones, that he die (because he hath gone about to thrust thee away from the
Lord thy God, which brought thee out of the land of Egypt: from the house of
bondage) 11 [1]That all Israel may hear and fear, and do no more any such wicke-
dness as this among you. 12 If thou shalt hear say (concerning any of thy cities,
which the Lord thy God hath given thee to dwell in) 13 [h]Wicked men are gone
out from among you, and have drawn away the inhabitants of their city, saying,
Let us go and serve other gods, which ye have not known, 14 Then [i]thou shalt
seek, and make search and inquire diligently: and if it be true, and the thing cer-
tain, that such abomination is wrought among you, 15 Thou shalt even slay the
inhabitants of that city with the edge of the sword: destroy it utterly, and all that
is therein, and the cattle thereof with the edge of the sword, 16 And [j]thou shalt
gather all the spoil of it into the midst of the street thereof, and burn with fire the
city and all the spoil thereof every whit, unto the Lord thy God: and it shall be an
heap forever, it shall not be built again. 17 And there shall cleave nothing of the
[k]damned thing to thine hand, that the Lord may turn from the fierceness of his
wrath, and show thee mercy, and have compassion on thee, and multiply thee as he
hath sworn unto thy fathers: 18 When thou shalt obey the voice of the Lord thy
God, and keep all his commandments which I command thee this day: that thou
do that which is right in the eyes of the Lord thy God.

14

1 The manners of the Gentiles in marking themselves for the dead, may not be followed. 4 What meats are clean to be eaten, and what not. 29 The tithes for the Levites, stranger, fatherless, and widow.

1 Ye are the children of the Lord your God, [1]Ye shall not cut yourselves, nor
make you any baldness between your eyes for the dead. 2 [2]For thou art an holy
people unto the Lord thy God, and the Lord hath chosen thee to be a [a]precious
people unto himself, above all the people that are upon the earth. 3 Thou shalt
eat no manner of abomination. 4 [b]These are the beasts, which ye shall eat, the
beef, the sheep, and the goat, 5 The hart, and the roebuck, and the bugle, and
the wild goat, and the unicorn, and the wild ox, and the Chamois. 6 And every
beast that parteth the hoof, and cleaveth the cleft into two claws, and is of the be-
asts that cheweth the cud, that shall ye eat. 7 But these ye shall not eat, of them
that chew the cud, and of them that divide and cleave the hoof only: the camel,
nor the hare, nor the coney: for they chew the cud, but divide not the hoof, the-
refore they shall be unclean unto you: 8 Also the swine, because he divideth
the hoof: and cheweth not the cud, shall be unclean unto you: ye shall not eat of
their flesh, nor touch their dead carcasses. 9 [3]These ye shall eat, of all that are
in the waters: all that have fins and scales shall ye eat. 10 And whatsoever hath
no fins nor scales, ye shall not eat: it shall be unclean unto you. 11 Of all clean
birds ye shall eat. 12 But these are they whereof ye shall not eat: the eagle nor
the goshawk, nor the osprey, 13 Nor the glede, nor the kite, nor the vulture,
after their kind, 14 Nor all kind of ravens, 15 Nor the ostrich, nor the night
crow, nor the [c]seamew, nor the hawk after her kind, 16 Neither the little owl,
nor the great owl, nor the redshank, 17 Nor the pelican, nor the swan, nor the
cormorant: 18 The stork also, and the heron in his kind, nor the lapwing, nor
[4]the bat. 19 And every creeping thing that flieth, shall be unclean unto you:
it shall not be eaten. 20 But of all clean fowls ye may eat. 21 Ye shall eat of
nothing that [d]dieth alone, but thou shalt give it unto the [e]stranger that is within
thy gates, that he may eat it: or thou mayest sell it unto a stranger: for thou art an
holy people unto the Lord thy God Thou shalt not [5]seethe a kid in his mother's
milk. 22 Thou shalt [f]give the tithe of all the increase of thy seed, that cometh
forth of the field year by year. 23 And thou shalt eat before the Lord thy God (in
the place which he shall choose to cause his Name to dwell there) the tithe of thy
corn, of thy wine, and of thine oil, and the firstborn of thy kine, and of thy she-
ep, that thou mayest learn to fear the Lord thy God always. 24 And if the way
be too long for thee, so that thou art not able to carry it, because the place is far
from thee, where the Lord thy God shall choose to set his name, [g]when the Lord
thy God shall bless thee, 25 Then shalt thou make it in money, and [h]take the
money in thine hand, and go unto the place which the Lord thy God shall cho-
ose. 26 And thou shalt bestow the money for whatsoever thine heart desireth:
whether it be ox, or sheep, or wine, or strong drink, or whatsoever thine heart de-
sireth: [i]and shalt eat it there before the Lord thy God, and rejoice, both thou, and
thine household. 27 And the Levite that is within thy gates, shalt thou not for-
sake: for he hath neither part nor inheritance with thee. 28 At the end of three
years thou shalt [j]bring forth all the tithes of thine increase of the same year, and
lay it up within thy gates. 29 Then the Levite shall come, because he hath no
part nor inheritance with thee, and the stranger, and the fatherless, and the widow,
which are within thy gates, and shall eat, and be filled, that the Lord thy God may
bless thee in all the work of thine hand which thou doest.

15

1 The year of releasing of debts. 5 God blesseth them that keep his commandments. 7 To help the poor. 12 The freedom of servants. 19 The firstborn of the cattle must be offered to the Lord.

1 At the term of seven years thou shalt make a freedom, 2 And this is the
manner of the freedom: every [a]creditor shall quit the loan of his hand which he
hath lent to his neighbor: he shall not ask it again of his neighbor, nor of his
brother: for the year of the Lord's freedom is proclaimed. 3 Of a stranger thou
mayest require it: but that which thou hast with thy brother, thine hand shall re-
mit: 4 [b]Save when there shall be no poor with thee: for the Lord shall bless thee
in the land, which the Lord thy God giveth thee, for an inheritance to possess
it. 5 So that thou hearken unto the voice of the Lord thy God, to observe and
do all these commandments, which I command thee this day. 6 For the Lord thy
God hath blessed thee, as he hath promised thee: and [1]thou shalt lend unto many
nations, but thou thyself shalt not borrow, and thou shalt reign over many nations,
and they shall not reign over thee. 7 If one of thy brethren with thee be poor [c]wi-
thin any of thy gates in thy land, which the Lord thy God giveth thee, thou shalt
not harden thine heart, nor shut thine hand from thy poor brother: 8 [2]But thou
shalt open thine hand unto him, and shalt lend him sufficient for his need which
he hath. 9 Beware that there be not a wicked thought in thine heart, to say, The
seventh year, the year of freedom is at hand: therefore [d]it grieveth thee to look on
thy poor brother, and thou givest him nought, and he cry unto the Lord against
thee, so that sin be in thee: 10 Thou shalt give him, and [e]let it not grieve thine
heart to give unto him: for because of this the Lord thy God shall bless thee in all
thy works, and in all that thou puttest thine hand to. 11 [f]Because there shall be
ever some poor in the land, therefore I command thee, saying, Thou shalt [g]open
thine hand unto thy brother, to thy needy, and to thy poor in thy land. 12 [3]If thy
brother an Hebrew sell himself to thee, or an Hebrewess, and serve thee six years,
even in the seventh year thou shalt let him go free from thee: 13 And when thou
sendest him out free from thee, thou shalt not let him go away empty, 14 But
shalt [h]give him a liberal reward of thy sheep, and of thy corn, and of thy wine: thou

---

DEUT. 13

- **a.** Deut. 13:1 Which sayeth that he hath things revealed unto him in dreams.
- **b.** Deut. 13:2 He showeth whereunto the false prophets tend.
- **c.** Deut. 13:3 God ordaineth all these things that his may be known.
- **d.** Deut. 13:5 Being convicted by testimonies, and condemned by the judge.
- **e.** Deut. 13:6 All natural affections must give place to God's honor.
- **f.** Deut. 13:6 Whom thou lovest as thy life.
- **g.** Deut. 13:9 As the witness is charged, Deut. 17:7.
- **h.** Deut. 13:13 Hebrew, children of Belial.
- **i.** Deut. 13:14 Which art appointed to see faults punished.
- **j.** Deut. 13:16 Signifying that no idolatry is so execrable, nor more grievously to be punished, than of them which once professed God.
- **k.** Deut. 13:17 Of the spoil of that idolatrous and cursed city, Read Deut. 7:26 and Josh. 7:11.

DEUT. 13

1. Deut. 17:13

DEUT. 14

- **a.** Deut. 14:2 Therefore thou oughtest not to follow the superstition of the Gentiles.
- **b.** Deut. 14:4 This ceremonial Law instructed the Jews to seek a spiritual pureness, even in their meat and drink.
- **c.** Deut. 14:15 Or, cuckoo
- **d.** Deut. 14:21 Because their blood was not shed, but remaineth in them.
- **e.** Deut. 14:21 Which is not of thy religion.
- **f.** Deut. 14:22 The tithes were ordained for the maintenance of the Levites, which had none inheritance.
- **g.** Deut. 14:24 When he shall give thee ability.
- **h.** Deut. 14:25 Or, bind up.
- **i.** Deut. 14:26 After the Priest hath received the Lord's part.
- **j.** Deut. 14:28 Besides the yearly tithes that were given to the Levites, these were laid up in store for the poor.

DEUT. 14

1. Lev. 19:28
2. Deut. 7:6 / Deut. 26:18,19
3. Lev. 11:9
4. Lev. 11:19
5. Exod. 23:19 / Exod. 34:25

DEUT. 15

- **a.** Deut. 15:2 He shall only release his debtors, which are not able to pay for that year.
- **b.** Deut. 15:4 For if thy debtor be rich, he may be constrained to pay.
- **c.** Deut. 15:7 Or, any of thy cities.
- **d.** Deut. 15:9 Hebrew, thine eye is evil.
- **e.** Deut. 15:10 Hebrew, let not thine heart be evil.
- **f.** Deut. 15:11 To try your charity, Matt. 26:11.
- **g.** Deut. 15:11 Thou shalt be liberal.
- **h.** Deut. 15:14 In token that thou dost acknowledge the benefit which God hath given thee by his labors.

shalt give him of that wherewith the Lord thy God hath blessed thee. **15** And remember that thou wast a servant in the land of Egypt, and the Lord thy God delivered thee: therefore I command thee this thing today. **16** And if he say unto thee, I will not go away from thee, because he loveth thee and thine house, and because he is well with thee, **17** [4]Then shalt thou take an awl, and pierce his ear through against the door, and he shall be thy servant [i]forever: and unto thy maid servant thou shall do likewise. **18** Let it not grieve thee, when thou lettest him go out free from thee: for he hath served thee six years, which is the double worth of [j]an hired servant: and the Lord thy God shall bless thee in all that thou doest. **19** [5]All the firstborn males that come of thy cattle, and of thy sheep, thou shalt sanctify unto the Lord thy God [k]Thou shalt do no work with thy firstborn bullock, nor shear thy firstborn sheep. **20** Thou shalt eat it before the Lord thy God year by year, in the place which the Lord shall choose, both thou, and thine household. **21** [6]But if there be any blemish therein, as if it be lame, or blind, or have any evil fault, thou shalt not offer it unto the Lord thy God, **22** But shalt eat it within thy gates: the unclean, and the clean shall eat it alike, [l]as the roebuck, and as the hart. **23** Only thou shalt not eat the blood thereof, but pour it upon the ground as water.

16

1 Of Easter. 10 Whitsuntide, 13 And the feast of tabernacles. 18 What officers ought to be ordained. 21 Idolatry forbidden.

1 Thou shalt keep the month of [a]Abib, and thou shalt celebrate the Passover unto the Lord thy God: for in the month of Abib the Lord thy God brought thee out of Egypt by night. **2** Thou shalt therefore [b]offer the Passover unto the Lord thy God, of sheep and bullocks [1]in the place where the Lord shall choose to cause his Name to dwell. **3** Thou [2]shalt eat no leavened bread with it: but seven days shalt thou eat unleavened bread therewith, even the bread of [c]tribulation: for thou camest out of the land of Egypt in haste: that thou mayest remember the day when thou camest out of the land of Egypt, all the days of thy life. **4** And there shall be no leaven seen with thee in all thy coasts seven days long: neither shall there remain the night any of the flesh until the morning which thou offeredst the first day at even. **5** Thou mayest [d]not offer the Passover within any of the gates, which the Lord thy God giveth thee: **6** But in the place which the Lord thy God shall choose to place his Name, there thou shalt offer the [e]Passover at even, about the going down of the sun, in the season that thou camest out of Egypt. **7** And thou shalt roast and eat it in the place which the Lord thy God shall choose, and shalt return on the morrow, and go unto thy tents. **8** Six days shalt thou eat unleavened bread, and the seventh day shall be a solemn assembly to the Lord thy God: thou shalt do no work therein. **9** Seven weeks shalt thou [f]number unto thee, and shalt begin to number the seven weeks, when thou beginnest to put the sickle to the corn: **10** And thou shalt keep the feast of weeks unto the Lord thy God, [g]even a free gift of thine hand, which thou shalt give unto the Lord thy God, as the Lord thy God hath blessed thee. **11** And thou shalt rejoice before the Lord thy God, thou and thy son, and thy daughter, and thy servant, and thy maid, and the Levite that is within thy gates, and the stranger, and the fatherless, and the widow, that are among you, in the place which the Lord thy God shall choose to place his Name there, **12** And thou shalt remember that thou wast a servant in Egypt: therefore thou shalt observe and do these ordinances. **13** Thou shalt [h]observe the feast of the Tabernacles seven days, when thou hast gathered in thy corn, and thy wine. **14** And thou shalt rejoice in thy feast, thou and thy son, and thy daughter, and thy servant, and thy maid, and the Levite, and the stranger, and the fatherless, and the widow, that are within thy gates. **15** Seven days shalt thou keep a feast unto the Lord thy God in the place which the Lord shall choose: when the Lord thy God shall bless thee in all thine increase, and in all the works of thine hands, thou shalt in any case be glad. **16** [3]Three times in the year shall all the males appear before the Lord thy God in the place which he shall choose: in the feast of the unleavened bread, and in the feast of the weeks, and in the feast of the Tabernacle: and they shall not appear before the Lord empty. **17** Every man shall give according to the gift of his [i]hand, and according to the blessing of the Lord thy God, which he hath given thee. **18** [j]Judges and officers shalt thou make thee in all thy cities, which the Lord thy God giveth thee, throughout the tribes: and they shall judge the people with righteous judgment. **19** Wrest not thou the Law, nor respect any person, neither take reward: for the reward blindeth the eyes of the wise, and perverteth the words of the just. **20** That which [k]is just and right shalt thou follow, that thou mayest live, and possess the land which the Lord thy God giveth thee. **21** Thou shalt plant thee no grove of any trees near unto the Altar of the Lord thy God, which thou shalt make thee. **22** Thou shalt set thee up no [l]pillar, which thing the Lord thy God hateth.

17

2 The punishment of the idolater. 9 Hard controversies are brought to the Priest and the Judge. 12 The contemner must die. 15 The election of the King, 16 and 17 What things he ought to avoid, etc.

1 Thou shalt offer unto the Lord thy God no bullock nor sheep wherein is [a,1]a blemish or any evil favored thing: for that is an abomination unto the Lord thy God. **2** If there be found among you in any of thy cities, which the Lord thy God giveth thee, man or [b]woman that hath wrought wickedness in the sight of the Lord thy God, in transgressing his covenant, **3** And hath gone and served other gods, and worshipped them: as the sun, or the moon, or any of the host of heaven, which I have not [c]commanded, **4** And it be told unto thee, and thou hast heard it, then shalt thou inquire diligently: and if it be true, and the thing certain, that such abomination is wrought in Israel, **5** Then shalt thou bring forth that man, or that woman (which hath committed that wicked thing) unto thy gates, whether it be man or woman, and shalt stone them with stones, till they die. **6** [2]At the mouth [d]of two or three witnesses shall he that is worthy of death, die: but at the mouth of one witness, he shall not die. **7** The hands of the [e]witnesses shall be first upon him, to kill him: and afterward the hands of all the [f]people: so thou shalt take the wicked away from among you. **8** If there rise a matter too hard for thee in judgment between blood and blood, between plea and plea, between plague and plague, in the matter of controversy within thy gates, then shalt thou arise, and go up unto the place which the Lord thy God shall choose, **9** And thou shalt come unto the Priests of the Levites, and unto the [g]Judge that shall be in those days, and ask, and they shall show thee the sentence of judgment, **10** And thou shalt do according to that thing, which they of that place (which the Lord hath chosen) show thee, and thou shalt observe to do according to all that they inform thee. **11** According to the Law, which they shall teach thee, and according to the judgment which they shall tell thee, shalt [h]thou do: thou shalt not decline from the thing which they shalt show thee, neither to the right hand, nor the left. **12** And that man that will do presumptuously, not hearkening unto the Priest (that standeth before the Lord thy God to [i]minister there) or unto the Judge, that man shall die, and thou shalt take away evil from Israel. **13** So all the people shall hear and fear, and do no more presumptuously. **14** When thou shalt come unto the land which the Lord thy God giveth thee, and shalt possess it, and dwell therein, if thou say, I will set a king over me, like as all the nations that are about me, **15** Then thou shalt make him King over thee, whom the Lord thy God shall choose: from among thy brethren shalt thou make a King over thee: thou [j]shalt not set a [k]stranger over thee which is not thy brother. **16** In any wise he shall not prepare him many horses, nor bring the people again to [l]Egypt, for to increase the number of horses, seeing the Lord hath said unto you, Ye shall henceforth go no more again that way. **17** Neither shall he take him many wives, lest his heart [m]turn away, neither shall he gather him much silver and gold. **18** And when he shall sit upon the throne of his Kingdom, then shall he write him this [n]law repeated in a book, by the [o]Priest of the Levites. **19** And it shall be with him, and he shall read therein all days of his life, that he may learn to fear the Lord his God, and to keep all the words of this Law, and these ordinances to do them: **20** That his heart be not lifted up above his [p]brethren, and that he turn not from the commandment, to the

---

i. Deut. 15:17 To the year of Jubilee, Lev. 25:40.
j. Deut. 15:18 For the hired servant served but three years, and he six.
k. Deut. 15:19 For they are the Lord's.
l. Deut. 15:22 Thou shalt as well eat them, as the roe buck, and other wild beasts.

DEUT. 15

1. Deut. 28:12
2. Matt. 5:42 / Luke 6:24
3. Exod. 21:2 / Jer. 34:24
4. Exod. 21:6
5. Exod. 34:19
6. Deut. 17:1

DEUT. 16

a. Deut. 16:1 Read Exod. 13:4.
b. Deut. 16:2 Thou shalt eat the Easter lamb.
c. Deut. 16:3 Which signified that affliction, which thou hadst in Egypt.
d. Deut. 16:5 This was chiefly accomplished, when the Temple was built.
e. Deut. 16:6 Which was instituted to put them in remembrance of their deliverance out of Egypt: and to continue them in the hope of Jesus Christ, of whom this lamb was a figure.
f. Deut. 16:9 Beginning at the next morning after the Passover, Lev. 23:15; Exod. 13:4.
g. Deut. 16:10 Or, as thou art able, willingly.
h. Deut. 16:13 That is, the 15th day of the seventh month, Lev. 23:34.
i. Deut. 16:17 According to the ability that God hath given him.
j. Deut. 16:18 He gave authority to that people for a time to choose themselves magistrates.
k. Deut. 16:20 The magistrate must constantly follow the tenor of the Law, and in nothing decline from justice.
l. Deut. 16:22 Or, image

DEUT. 16

1. Deut. 12:5
2. Exod. 12:14,15
3. Exod. 23:15 / Exod. 34:23

DEUT. 17

a. Deut. 17:1 Thou shalt not serve God for fashion's sake, as hypocrites do.
b. Deut. 17:2 Showing that the crime cannot be excused by the frailty of the person.
c. Deut. 17:3 Whereby he condemneth all religion and serving of God which God hath not commanded.
d. Deut. 17:6 Hebrew, of two witnesses or three witnesses.
e. Deut. 17:7 Whereby they declared that they testifieth the truth.
f. Deut. 17:7 To signify a common consent to maintain God's honor and true religion.
g. Deut. 17:9 Who shall give sentence as the Priests counsel him by the Law of God.
h. Deut. 17:11 Thou shalt obey their sentence that the controversy may have an end.
i. Deut. 17:12 So long as he is the true minister of God, and pronounceth according to his word.
j. Deut. 17:15 Or, mayest not.
k. Deut. 17:15 Who is not of thy nation, lest he change true religion into idolatry, and bring thee to slavery.
l. Deut. 17:16 To revenge their injuries, and to take them of their best horses, 1 Kings 10:28.
m. Deut. 17:17 From the Law of God.
n. Deut. 17:18 Meaning, the Deut..
o. Deut. 17:18 He shall cause it to be written by them, or he shall write it by their example.
p. Deut. 17:20 Whereby is meant, that Kings ought so to love their subjects as nature bindeth one brother to love another.

DEUT. 17

1. Deut. 15:21
2. Num. 35:30 / Deut. 19:15 / Matt. 18:16 / 1 Cor. 13:2

right hand or to the left, but that he may prolong his days in his kingdom, he and
his sons in the midst of Israel.

18

3 The portion of the Levites. 6 Of the Levites coming from another place. 9 To avoid the abominations of the Gentiles. 15 God will not leave them without a true Prophet.

1 The Priests of the Levites, and all the tribe of Levi [1]shall have no part nor
inheritance with Israel, [2]but shall eat the offerings of the Lord made by fire, and his
[a]inheritance. **2** Therefore shall they have no inheritance among their brethren:
for the Lord is their inheritance, as he hath said unto them. **3** And this shall be
the Priest's duty of the people, that they which offer sacrifice, whether it be bul-
lock or sheep, shall give unto the Priest the [b]shoulder, and the two cheeks, and
the maw. **4** The firstfruits also of thy corn, of thy wine, and of thine oil, and the
first of the fleece of thy sheep shalt thou give him. **5** For the Lord thy God hath
chosen him out of all thy tribes, to stand and minister in the Name of the Lord,
him, and his sons forever. **6** Also when a Levite shall come out of any of thy ci-
ties of all Israel, where he remained, and come with [c]all the desire of his heart unto
the place, which the Lord shall choose, **7** He shall then minister in the Name
of the Lord his God, as all his brethren the Levites, which remain there before the
Lord. **8** They shall have like portions to eat [d]beside that which cometh of the
sale of his patrimony. **9** When thou shalt come into the land which the Lord
thy God giveth thee, thou shalt not learn to do after the abominations of those na-
tions. **10** Let none be found among you that maketh his son or his daughter to
[e,3]go thorough the fire, or that useth witchcraft, or a regarder of times, or a marker
of the flying of fowls, or a sorcerer, **11** Or [4]a charmer, or that counseleth with
spirits, or a soothsayer, or that [5]asketh counsel at the dead. **12** For all that do
such things are abomination unto the Lord, and because of these abominations
the Lord thy God doth cast them out before thee. **13** Thou shalt be [f]upright
therefore with the Lord thy God. **14** For these nations which thou shalt possess,
hearken unto those that regard the times, and unto sorcerers: [g]as for thee, the Lord
thy God hath not [h]suffered thee so. **15** [6]The Lord thy God will raise up unto
thee a [i]Prophet like unto me, from among you, even of thy brethren: unto him
ye shall hearken. **16** According to all that thou desiredst of the Lord thy God in
Horeb, in the day of the assembly, when thou saidest, [7]Let me hear the voice of my
Lord God no more, nor see this great fire anymore, that I die not. **17** And the
Lord said unto me, They have well spoken. **18** [8]I will raise them up a Prophet
from among their brethren like unto thee, and will put my words in his [j]mouth,
and he shall speak unto them all that I shall command him. **19** And whosoever
will not hearken unto my words, which he shall speak in my Name, I will [k]require
it of him. **20** But the Prophet that shall presume to speak a word in my name,
which I have not commanded him to speak, or that speaketh in the name of other
gods, even the same Prophet shall die. **21** And if thou think in thine heart, How
shall we know the word which the Lord hath not spoken? **22** When a Prophet
speaketh in the Name of the Lord, if the thing [l]follow not nor come to pass, that is
the thing which the Lord hath not spoken, but the Prophet hath spoken it presu-
mptuously: thou shalt not therefore be afraid of him.

19

2 The franchised towns. 14 Not to remove thy neighbor's bounds. 16 The punishment of him that beareth false witness.

1 When the Lord thy God [1]shall root out the nations, whose land the Lord
thy God giveth thee, and thou shalt possess them, and dwell in their cities, and in
their houses, **2** [2]Thou shalt separate three cities for thee, in the midst of thy land
which the Lord thy God giveth thee to possess it. **3** Thou shalt [a]prepare thee
the way, and divide the coasts of the land, which the Lord thy God giveth thee to
inherit, into three parts, that every [b]manslayer may flee thither. **4** This also is the
cause wherefore the manslayer shall flee thither, and live: who so killeth his neigh-
bor ignorantly, and hated him not in time passed: **5** As he that goeth unto the
wood with his neighbor to hew wood, and his hand striketh with the axe to cut
down the tree, if the head slip from the helve, and hit his neighbor that he dieth,
the same [c]shall flee unto one of the cities, and live, **6** Lest the [3]avenger of the
blood follow after the manslayer while his heart is chafed, and overtake him, be-
cause the way is long, and slay him, although he be not [d]worthy of death, because
he hated him not in time passed. **7** Wherefore I commanded thee, saying, Thou
shalt appoint out three cities for thee. **8** And when the Lord thy God [e]enlargeth
thy coasts (as he hath sworn unto thy fathers) and giveth thee all the land which he
promised to give unto thy fathers. **9** (If thou keep all these commandments to
do them, which I command thee this day: to wit, that thou love the Lord thy God,
and walk in his ways forever) [4]then thou shalt add three cities more for thee besi-
des those three, **10** That no innocent blood be shed within thy land, which the
Lord thy God giveth thee to inherit, [f]lest blood be upon thee. **11** But if a man
hate his neighbor, and lay wait for him, and rise against him, and smite any man
that he die, and flee unto any of these cities, **12** Then the [g]Elders of his city shall
send and fet him thence, and deliver him to the hands of the avenger of the blood,
that he may die. **13** Thine [h]eye shall not spare him, but thou shalt put away the
cry of innocent blood from Israel, that it may go well with thee. **14** Thou shalt
not remove thy neighbor's mark, which they of old time have set in thine inheri-
tance, that thou shalt inherit in the land, which the Lord thy God giveth thee to
possess it. **15** [5]One witness shall not rise against a man for any trespass, or for
any sin, or for any fault that he offendeth in, [6]but at the mouth of two witnesses,
or at the mouth of three witnesses, shall the matter be stablished. **16** If a false
witness rise up against a man to accuse him of trespass, **17** Then both the men
which strive together, shall stand before the [i]Lord, even before the Priests and the
Judges, which shall be in those days. **18** And the Judges shall make diligent in-
quisition: and if the witness be found false, and hath given false witness against
his brother, **19** [7]Then shall ye do unto him as he had thought to do unto his
brother: so thou shalt take evil away forth of the midst of thee. **20** And the rest
shall hear this, and fear, and shall henceforth commit no more any such wickedness
among you. **21** Therefore thine eye shall have no compassion, but [8]life for life,
eye for eye, tooth for tooth, hand for hand, foot for foot.

20

3 The exhortation of the Priest when the Israelites go to battle. 5 The exhortation of the officers showing who should go to battle. 10 Peace must be first proclaimed. 19 The trees that bear fruit must not be destroyed.

1 When [a]thou shalt go forth to war against thine enemies, and shalt see horses
and chariots, and people more than thou, be not afraid of them: for the Lord thy
God is with thee, which brought thee out of the land of Egypt. **2** And when ye
are come near unto the battle, then the Priest shall come forth to speak unto the
people, **3** And shall say unto them, Hear, O Israel, ye are come this day unto
battle against your enemies: [1]let not your hearts faint, neither fear, nor be amazed,
nor a dread of them. **4** For the Lord your God [b]goeth with you, to fight for you
against your enemies, and to save you. **5** And let the officers speak unto the pe-
ople, saying, What man is there that hath built a new house, and hath not [c]dedi-
cated it, let him go and return to his house, lest he die in the battle, and another
man dedicate it. **6** And what man is there that hath planted a vineyard, and hath
not [d]eaten of the fruit? let him go to return again unto his house, lest he die in the
battle, and another eat the fruit. **7** And what man is there that hath betrothed a
wife, and hath not taken her? let him go and return again unto his house, lest he
die in battle, and another man take her. **8** And let the officers speak further unto
the people, and say, [2]Whosoever is afraid and faint hearted, let him go and return
unto his house, lest his brethren's heart faint like his heart. **9** And after that the
officers have made an end of speaking unto the people, they shall make captains of
the army to govern the people. **10** When thou comest near unto a city to fight
against it, [3]thou shalt offer it peace. **11** And if it answer thee again [e]peaceably,
and open unto thee, then let all the people that is found therein, be tributaries
unto thee, and serve thee. **12** But if it will make no peace with thee, but make
war against thee, then shalt thou besiege it. **13** And the Lord thy God shall deli-
ver it into thine hands, and thou shalt smite all the males thereof with the edge of
the sword. **14** Only the women, [4]and the children, and the cattle, and all that
is in the city, even all the spoil thereof shalt thou take unto thyself, and shalt eat
the spoil of thine enemies, which the Lord thy God hath given thee. **15** Thus
shalt thou do unto all the cities, which are a great way off from thee, which are not

---

DEUT. 18

- **a.** Deut. 18:1 That is, the Lord's part of his inheritance.
- **b.** Deut. 18:3 The right shoulder, Num. 28:18.
- **c.** Deut. 18:6 Meaning, to serve God unfainedly, and not to seek ease.
- **d.** Deut. 18:8 Not constrained to live of himself.
- **e.** Deut. 18:10 Signifying they were purged by this ceremony of passing between two fires.
- **f.** Deut. 18:13 Without hypocrisy or mixture or false religion.
- **g.** Deut. 18:14 Hebrew, but thou not so.
- **h.** Deut. 18:14 Hebrew, given or appointed.
- **i.** Deut. 18:15 Meaning, a continual succession of Prophets, till Christ the end of all Prophets come.
- **j.** Deut. 18:18 Which promise is not only made to Christ, but to all that teach in his name, Isa. 59:21.
- **k.** Deut. 18:19 By executing punishment upon him.
- **l.** Deut. 18:22 Under this sure note he compriseth all the other tokens.

DEUT. 18

1. Num. 18:20
2. Deut. 10:9 / 1 Cor. 9:13
3. Lev. 18:21
4. Lev. 20:27
5. 1 Sam. 28:7
6. Acts 7:37
7. Exod. 20:19
8. Josh. 1:45 / Acts 3:21

DEUT. 19

- **a.** Deut. 19:3 Make an open and ready way.
- **b.** Deut. 19:3 Which killeth against his will, and bare no hatred in his heart.
- **c.** Deut. 19:5 That murder be not committed upon murder.
- **d.** Deut. 19:6 Or, cannot be judged to death.
- **e.** Deut. 19:8 When thou goest over Jordan to possess the whole land of Canaan.
- **f.** Deut. 19:10 Lest thou be punished for innocent blood.
- **g.** Deut. 19:12 The Magistrates.
- **h.** Deut. 19:13 Then whosoever pardoneth murder, offendeth against the word of God.
- **i.** Deut. 19:17 God's presence is where his true ministers are assembled.

DEUT. 19

1. Deut. 12:29
2. Exod. 21:13 / Num. 35:9,11 / Josh. 20:2
3. Num. 35:12
4. Josh. 20:7
5. Deut. 17:9 / Matt. 18:6 / John 8:17
6. 2 Cor. 13:1 / Heb. 13:21
7. Prov. 19:5
8. Exod. 21:13 / Lev. 24:20 / Matt. 5:38

DEUT. 20

- **a.** Deut. 20:1 Meaning, upon just occasion: for God permitteth not his people to fight when it seemeth good to them.
- **b.** Deut. 20:4 Is present to defend you with his grace and power.
- **c.** Deut. 20:5 For when they entered first to dwell in an house, they gave thanks to God, acknowledging that they had that benefit by his grace.
- **d.** Deut. 20:6 The Hebrew word signifieth to make common or profane, Lev. 19:25.
- **e.** Deut. 20:11 If it accept peace.
- **f.** Deut. 20:15 For God had appointed that the Canaanites should be destroyed, and made the Israelites executors of his will, Deut. 7:1.

of the cities of these [f]nations here. **16** But of the cities of this people, which the Lord thy God shall give thee to inherit, thou shalt save no person alive, **17** But shalt utterly destroy them, to wit, the Hittites, and the Amorites, the Canaanites, and the Perizzites, the Hivites, and the Jebusites: as the Lord thy God hath commanded thee, **18** That they teach you not to do after all their abominations, which they have done unto their gods, and so ye should sin against the Lord your God. **19** When thou hast besieged a city long time, and made war against it to take it, destroy not the trees thereof, by smiting an axe into them: for thou mayest eat of them: therefore thou shalt not cut them down to further thee in the siege, (for the [g]tree of the field is man's life). **20** Only those trees which thou knowest are not for meat, those shalt thou destroy and cut down, and make forts against the city that maketh war with thee until thou subdue it.

21

2 Inquisition for murder. 11 Of the woman taken in war. 15 The birthright cannot be changed for affection. 18 The disobedient child. 23 The body may not hang all night.

1 If one be found [a]slain in the land, which the Lord thy God giveth thee to possess it, lying in the field, and it is not known who hath slain him, **2** Then thine Elders and thy Judges shall come forth, and measure unto the cities that are round about him that is slain: **3** And let the Elders of that city, which is next unto the slain man, take out of the drove an heifer that hath not been put to labor, nor hath drawn in the yoke. **4** And let the Elders of that city bring the heifer unto a [b]stony [c]valley, which is neither eared, nor sown, and strike off the heifer's neck there in the valley. **5** Also the Priests the sons of Levi (whom the Lord thy God hath chosen to minister, and to bless in the Name of the Lord) shall come forth, and by their word shall all strife and plague be tried. **6** And all the Elders of that city that came near to the slain man, shall wash their hands over the heifer that is beheaded in the valley: **7** And shall testify, and say, Our hands have not shed this blood, neither have our eyes seen it. **8** [d]O Lord, be merciful unto thy people Israel, whom thou hast redeemed, and lay no innocent blood to the charge of thy people Israel, and the blood shall be forgiven them. **9** So shalt thou take away the cry of innocent blood from thee, when thou shalt do that which is right in the sight of the Lord. **10** When thou shalt go to war against thine enemies, and the Lord thy God shall deliver them into thine hands, and thou shalt take them captives, **11** And shalt see among the captives a beautiful woman, and hast a desire unto her, and wouldest take her to thy wife, **12** Then thou shalt bring her home to thine house, [e]and she shall shave her head, and pare her nails, **13** And she shall put off the garment that she was taken in, and she shall remain in thine house, [f]and bewail her father and her mother a month long: and after that shalt thou go in unto her, and marry her, and she shall be thy [g]wife. **14** And if thou have no favor unto her, then thou mayest let her go whither she will, but thou shalt not sell her for money, nor make merchandise of her, because thou hast humbled her. **15** If a man have two wives, one loved and another [h]hated, and they have born him children, both the loved and also the hated: if the firstborn be the son of the hated, **16** Then when the time cometh, that he appointeth his sons to be heirs of that which he hath, he may not make the son of the beloved firstborn [i]before the son of the hated, which is the firstborn: **17** But he shall acknowledge the son of the hated for the firstborn, and give him [j]double portion for all that he hath: for he is the first of his strength, and to [k]him belongeth the right of firstborn. **18** If any man have a son that is stubborn and disobedient, which will not hearken unto the voice of his father, nor the voice of his [l]mother, and they have chastened him, and he would not obey them, **19** Then shall his father and his mother take him, and bring him out unto the Elders of his city, and unto the gate of the place where he dwelleth, **20** And shall say unto the Elders of his city, This our son is stubborn and disobedient, and he will not obey our admonition: he is a rioter, and a drunkard. **21** Then all the men of his city shall [m]stone him with stones unto death: so thou shalt take away evil from among you, that all Israel may hear it, and fear. **22** If a man also have committed a trespass worthy of death, and is put to death, and thou hangest him on a tree, **23** His body shall not remain [n]all night upon the tree, but thou shalt bury him the same day: for the [1]curse of God is on him that is hanged Defile not therefore thy land which the Lord thy God giveth thee to inherit.

22

2 He commandeth to have care of our neighbor's goods. 5 The woman may not wear man's apparel, nor man the woman's. 6 Of the dam and her young birds. 8 Why they should have battlements. 9 Not to mix divers kinds together. 13 Of the wife not being found a virgin. 23 The punishment of adultery.

1 Thou [1]shalt not see thy brother's ox nor his sheep go astray, and [a]withdraw thyself from them, but shalt bring them again unto thy brother. **2** And if thy brother be not [b]near unto thee, or if thou know him not, then thou shalt bring it into thine house, and it shall remain with thee, until thy brother seek after it, then shalt thou deliver it to him again: **3** In like manner shalt thou do with his [c]ass, and so shalt thou do with his raiment, and shalt so do with all lost things of thy brother, which he hath lost: if thou hast found them, thou shalt not withdraw thyself from them. **4** Thou shalt not see thy brother's ass nor his ox fall down by the way, and withdraw thyself from them, but shalt lift them up with him. **5** The [d]woman shall not wear that which pertaineth unto the man, neither shalt a man put on woman's raiment: for all that do so, are abomination unto the Lord thy God. **6** If thou find a bird's nest in the way, in any tree, or on the ground whether they be young or eggs, and the dam sitting upon the young, or upon the eggs, [e]thou shalt not take the dam with the young, **7** But shalt in any wise let the dam go, and take the young to thee, that thou mayest prosper and prolong thy days. **8** When thou buildest a new house, thou shalt make a battlement on thy roof, that thou lay not blood upon thine house, if any man fall thence. **9** Thou shalt not [f]sow thy vineyard with divers kinds of seeds, lest thou defile the increase of the seed which thou hast sown, and the fruit of the vineyard. **10** Thou shalt not plow with an ox and an ass together. **11** Thou shalt not wear a garment of divers sorts, as of woolen and linen together. **12** [2]Thou shalt make thee fringes upon the four quarters of thy vesture, wherewith thou coverest thyself. **13** If a man take a wife, and when he hath lain with her, hate her, **14** And lay [g]slanderous things unto her charge, and bring up an evil name upon her, and say, I took this wife, and when I came to her, I found her not a maid, **15** Then shall the father of the maid and her mother take and bring the signs of the maid's virginity unto the Elders of the city to the gate. **16** And the maid's father shall say unto the Elders, I gave my daughter unto this man to wife and he hateth her: **17** And lo, he layeth slanderous things unto her charge, saying, I found not thy daughter a maid: lo, these are the tokens of my daughter's virginity: and they shall spread the [h]vesture before the Elders of the city. **18** Then the Elders of the city shall take that man and chastise him, **19** And shall condemn him in an hundred shekels of silver, and give them unto the father [i]of the maid, because he hath brought up an evil name upon a maid of Israel: and she shall be his wife, and he may not put her away all his life. **20** But if this thing be true, that the maid be not found a virgin, **21** Then shall they bring forth the maid to the door of her father's house, and the men of her city shall stone her with stones to death: for she hath wrought folly in Israel, by playing the whore in her father's house: so thou shalt put evil away from among you. **22** [3]If a man be found lying with a woman married to a man, then they shall die even both twain: to wit, the man that lay with the wife, and the wife: so thou shalt put away evil from Israel. **23** If a maid be betrothed unto a husband, and a man find her in the town and lie with her, **24** Then shall ye bring them both out unto the gates of the same city, and shall stone them with stones to death: the maid because she cried not, being in the city, and the man, because he hath [j]humbled his neighbor's wife: so thou shalt put away evil from among you. **25** But if a man find a betrothed maid in the field and force her, and lie with her, then the man that lay with her, shall die alone: **26** And unto the maid thou shalt do nothing, because there is in the maid no [k]cause of death: for as when a man riseth against his neighbor and woundeth him to death, so [l]is this matter. **27** For he found her in the fields: the betrothed maid cried, and there was no man to succor her. **28** [4]If a man find a maid that is not betrothed, and

---

g. Deut. 20:19 Some read, For man shall be instead of the tree of the field, to come out in the siege against thee.

DEUT. 20

1. Deut. 28:7
2. Judg. 7:3
3. Num. 21:21 / Deut. 2:26
4. Josh. 8:2

DEUT. 21

a. Deut. 21:1 This law declareth how horrible a thing murder is, seeing that for one man whole country shall be punished, except remedy be found.
b. Deut. 21:4 Or, rough.
c. Deut. 21:4 That the blood shed of the innocent beasts in a solitary place, might make them abhor the fact.
d. Deut. 21:8 This was the prayer, which the Priests made in the audience of the people.
e. Deut. 21:12 Signifying that her former life must be changed before she could be joined to the people of God.
f. Deut. 21:13 As having renounced parents and country.
g. Deut. 21:13 This only was permitted in the wars, otherwise the Israelites could not marry strangers.
h. Deut. 21:15 This declareth that the plurality of wives came of a corrupt affection.
i. Deut. 21:16 Or, while the son of the hated liveth.
j. Deut. 21:17 As much as to two of the others.
k. Deut. 21:17 Except he be unworthy, as was Reuben Jacob's son.
l. Deut. 21:18 For it is the mother's duty also to instruct her children.
m. Deut. 21:21 Which death was also appointed for blasphemers and idolaters: so that to disobey the parents is most horrible.
n. Deut. 21:23 For God's Law by his death is satisfied, and nature abhorreth cruelty.

DEUT. 21

1. Gal. 3:13

DEUT. 22

a. Deut. 22:1 As though thou sawest it not.
b. Deut. 22:2 Showing that brotherly affection must be showed, not only to them that dwell near unto us, but also to them which are far off.
c. Deut. 22:3 Much more art thou bound to do for thy neighbor's person.
d. Deut. 22:5 For that were to alter the order of nature, and to despite God.
e. Deut. 22:6 If God detests cruelty done to little birds, how much more to man, made according to his image?
f. Deut. 22:9 The tenor of this Law, is to walk in simplicity, and not to be curious of new inventions.
g. Deut. 22:14 That is, be an occasion that she is slandered.
h. Deut. 22:17 Meaning, the sheet, wherein the signs of her virginity were.
i. Deut. 22:19 For the fault of the child redoundeth to the shame of the parents: therefore he was recompensed when she was faultless.
j. Deut. 22:24 Or, defiled.
k. Deut. 22:26 Or, no sin worthy of death.
l. Deut. 22:26 Meaning, that the innocent cannot be punished.
m. Deut. 22:30 He shall not lie with his stepmother, meaning hereby all other degrees forbidden, Lev. 18.

DEUT. 22

1. Exod. 23:4
2. Num. 15:38
3. Lev. 20:20
4. Exod. 22:16

take her, and lie with her, and they be found, **29** Then the man that lay with her, shall give unto the maid's father fifty shekels of silver: and she shall be his wife, because he hath humbled her: he can not put her away all his life. **30** No man shall [m]take his father's wife, nor shall uncover his father's skirt.

23

1 What men ought not to be admitted to office. 9 What they ought to avoid when they go to war. 15 Of the fugitive servant. 17 To flee all kinds of whoredom. 19 Of usury. 21 Of vows. 24 Of the neighbor's vine and corn.

1 None that is hurt by bursting, or that hath his privy member cut off, [a]shall enter into the Congregation of the Lord. **2** [b]A bastard shall not enter into the Congregation of the Lord: even to his tenth generation shall he not enter into the Congregation of the Lord. **3** [1]The Ammonites and the Moabites shall not enter into the Congregation of the Lord: even to their tenth generation shall they not enter into the Congregation of the Lord forever, **4** Because they [c]met you not with bread and water in the way, when ye came out of Egypt, and [2]because they hired against thee Balaam the son of Beor, of Pethor in Aram-naharaim, to curse thee. **5** Nevertheless, the Lord thy God would not hearken unto Balaam, but the Lord thy God turned the curse to a blessing unto thee, because the Lord thy God loved thee. **6** Thou [d]shall not seek their peace, nor their prosperity all thy days forever. **7** Thou shalt not abhor an Edomite: for he is thy brother, neither shalt thou abhor an Egyptian, because thou wast a stranger in his land. **8** The children that are begotten [e]of them in their third generation, shall enter into the Congregation of the Lord. **9** When thou goest out with the host against thine enemies, keep thee then from all wickedness. **10** If there be among you any that is unclean by that which cometh to him by night, he shall go out of the host, and shall not enter into the host, **11** But at even he shall wash himself with water, and when the sun is down, he shall enter into the host. **12** Thou shalt have a place also without the host, whither thou shalt [f]resort, **13** And thou shalt have a paddle among thy weapons, and when thou wouldest sit down without, thou shalt dig therewith, and returning, thou shalt [g]cover thine excrements. **14** For the Lord thy God walketh in the midst of thy camp to deliver thee, and to give thee thine enemies before thee: therefore thine host shall be holy, that he see no filthy thing in thee, and turn away from thee. **15** Thou shalt not [h]deliver the servant unto his master, which is escaped from his master unto thee. **16** He shall dwell with thee, even among you, in what place he shall choose, in one of thy [i]cities where it liketh him best: thou shalt not vex him. **17** There shall be no whore of the daughters of Israel, neither shall there be a whore keeper of the sons of Israel. **18** Thou shalt neither bring the [j]hire of a whore, nor the price of a dog into the house of the Lord thy God for any vow: for even both these are abomination unto the Lord thy God. **19** [3]Thou shalt not give to usury to thy brother: as usury of money, usury of meat, usury of anything that is put to usury. **20** Unto a [k]stranger thou mayest lend upon usury, but thou shalt not lend upon usury unto thy brother, that the Lord thy God may [l]bless thee in all that thou settest thine hand to, in the land whither thou goest to possess it. **21** When thou shalt vow a vow unto the Lord thy God, thou shalt not be slack to pay it: for the Lord thy God will surely require it of thee, and so it should be sin unto thee. **22** But when thou abstainest from vowing, it shall be no sin unto thee. **23** That which is gone out of thy lips, thou shalt [m]keep and perform, as thou hast vowed it willingly unto the Lord thy God: for thou hast spoken it with thy mouth. **24** When thou comest unto [n]thy neighbor's vineyard, then thou mayest eat grapes at thy pleasure, as much as thou wilt: but thou shalt put none in thy [o]vessel. **25** When thou comest unto thy neighbor's corn, [4]thou mayest pluck the ears with thine hand, but thou shalt not move a sickle to thy neighbor's corn.

24

1 Divorcement is permitted. 5 He that is newly married is exempted from war. 6 Of the pledge. 14 Wages must not be retained. 16 The good must not be punished for the bad. 17 The care of the stranger, fatherless, and widow.

1 When a man taketh a wife, and marrieth her, if so be she find no favor in his eyes, because he hath espied some filthiness in her, [a]then let him write her a bill of divorcement, and put it in her hand, and send her out of his house. **2** And when she is departed out of his house, and gone her way, and marry with another man, **3** And if the latter husband hate her, and write her a letter of divorcement, and put it in her hand, and send her out of his house, or if the latter man die which took her to wife: **4** Then her first husband, which sent her away, may not take her again to be his wife, after that she is [b]defiled: for that is abomination in the sight of the Lord, and thou shalt not cause the land to sin, which the Lord thy God doth give thee to inherit. **5** When a man taketh a new wife, he shall not go a warfare, [c]neither shall be charged with any business, but shall be free at home one year, and rejoice with his wife, which he hath taken. **6** No man shall take the nether nor the upper [d]millstone to pledge: for this gage is his living. **7** If any man be found stealing any of his brethren of the children of Israel, and maketh merchandise of him, or selleth him, that thief shall die: so shalt thou put evil away from among you. **8** Take heed of the [1]plague of leprosy, that thou observe diligently, and do according to all that the Priests of the Levites shall teach you: take heed ye do as I commanded them. **9** Remember what the Lord thy God did unto [2]Miriam by the way after that ye were come out of Egypt. **10** When thou shalt ask again of thy neighbor anything lent, thou shalt not go [e]into his house to fet his pledge. **11** But thou shalt stand without, and the man that borrowed it of thee, shall bring the pledge out of the doors unto thee. **12** Furthermore if it be a poor body, thou shalt not sleep with his pledge, **13** But shalt restore him the pledge when the sun goeth down, that he may sleep in his raiment, and bless thee: and it shall be righteousness unto thee [f]before the Lord thy God. **14** Thou shalt not oppress an hired servant that is needy and poor, neither of thy brethren nor of the stranger that is in thy land within thy gates. **15** [3]Thou shalt give him his hire for his day, neither shall the sun go down upon it: for he is poor, and therewith sustaineth his life: lest he cry against thee unto the Lord, and it be sin unto thee. **16** [4]The fathers shall not be put to death for the children, nor the children put to death for the fathers, but every man shall be put to death for his own sin. **17** Thou shalt not pervert the right of the [g]stranger, nor of the fatherless, nor take a widow's raiment to pledge. **18** But remember that thou wast a servant in Egypt, and how the Lord thy God delivered thee thence Therefore I command thee to do this thing. **19** [5]When thou cuttest down thine harvest in thy field, and hast forgotten a sheaf in the field, thou shalt not go again to fet it, but it shall be for the stranger, for the fatherless, and for the widow: that the Lord thy God may bless thee in all the works of thine hands. **20** When thou [h]beatest thine olive tree, thou shalt not go over the boughs again, but it shall be for the stranger, for the fatherless, and for the widow. **21** When thou gatherest thy [i]vineyard, thou shalt not gather the grapes clean after thee, but they shall be for the stranger, for the fatherless, and for the widow. **22** And remember that thou wast [j]a servant in the land of Egypt: therefore I command thee to do this thing.

25

3 The beating of the offenders. 5 To raise up seed to the kinsmen. 11 In what case a woman's hand must be cut off. 13 Of just weights and measures. 19 To destroy the Amalekites.

1 When there shall be strife between men, and they shall come unto judgment, [a]and sentence shall be given upon them, and the righteous shall be justified, and the wicked condemned, **2** Then if so be the wicked be worthy to be beaten, the judge shall cause him to lie down, [b]and to be beaten before his face, according to his trespass unto a certain number. **3** [c]Forty stripes shall he cause him to have, and not past, lest if he should exceed and beat him above that with many stripes, thy brother should appear despised in thy sight. **4** [1]Thou shalt not muzzle the ox that treadeth out the corn. **5** [2]If brethren dwell together, and one of them die and have no son, the wife of the dead shall not marry without, that is, unto a stranger, but his [d]kinsman shall go in unto her, and take her to wife, and do the kinsman's office to her. **6** And the firstborn which she beareth, shall succeed in the name of his brother which is dead, that his name be not put out of Israel. **7** And if the man will not take his kinswoman, then let his kinswoman go up to the gate

---

DEUT. 23

a. Deut. 23:1 Either to bear office, or to marry a wife.
b. Deut. 23:2 This was to cause them to live chastely, that their posterity might not be rejected.
c. Deut. 23:4 Hereby he condemneth all that further not the children of God in their vocation.
d. Deut. 23:6 Thou shalt have nothing to do with them.
e. Deut. 23:8 If the fathers have renounced their idolatry, and received circumcision.
f. Deut. 23:12 For the necessities of nature.
g. Deut. 23:13 Meaning hereby that his people should be pure both in body and soul.
h. Deut. 23:15 This is meant of the heathen, who fled for their masters' cruelty, and embraced the true religion.
i. Deut. 23:16 Hebrew, gates.
j. Deut. 23:18 Forbidding hereby that any gain gotten of evil things should be applied to the service of God, Mic. 2:7.
k. Deut. 23:20 This was permitted for a time for the hardness of their hearts.
l. Deut. 23:20 If thou show thy charity to thy brother, God will declare his love toward thee.
m. Deut. 23:23 If the vow be lawful and godly.
n. Deut. 23:24 Being hired for to labor.
o. Deut. 23:24 To bring home to thine house.

DEUT. 23

1. Neh. 1:31
2. Num. 22:5,6
3. Exod. 22:24 / Lev. 25:36
4. Matt. 12:1

DEUT. 24

a. Deut. 24:1 Hereby God approveth not that light divorcement, but permitteth it to avoid further inconvenience, Matt. 19:7.
b. Deut. 24:4 Seeing that by dimitting her, he judged her to be unclean and defiled.
c. Deut. 24:5 That they might learn to know one another's conditions, and so afterward live in godly peace.
d. Deut. 24:6 Not anything whereby a man getteth his living.
e. Deut. 24:10 As though thou wouldest appoint what to have, but shalt receive what he may spare.
f. Deut. 24:13 Though he would be unthankful, yet God will not forget it.
g. Deut. 24:17 Because the world did least esteem these sorts of people, therefore God hath most care over them.
h. Deut. 24:20 Or, gatherest thine olives.
i. Deut. 24:21 Or, the grapes of thy vineyard.
j. Deut. 24:22 God judged them not mindful of his benefit, except they were beneficial unto others.

DEUT. 24

1. Lev. 13:2
2. Num. 12:20
3. Lev. 10:13
4. 2 Kings 14:6 / 2 Chron. 25:4 / Jer. 31:29,30 / Ezek. 18:20
5. Lev. 19:9 / Lev. 23:22

DEUT. 25

a. Deut. 25:1 Whether there be a plaintiff or none, the magistrates ought to try our faults, and punish according to the crime.
b. Deut. 25:2 When the crime deserveth not death.
c. Deut. 25:3 The Jews of superstition afterward took one away, 2 Cor. 11:24.
d. Deut. 25:5 Because the Hebrew word signifieth not the natural brother, and the word that signifieth a brother, is taken

unto the Elders, and say, My kinsman refuseth to raise up unto his brother a name
in Israel: he will not do the office of a kinsman unto me. **8** Then the Elders of
the city shall call him, and commune with him: if he stand and say, I will not take
her, **9** Then shall his kinswoman come unto him in the presence of the Elders,
and loose his shoe from his foot, and spit in his face, and answer, and say, So shall
it be done unto that man that will not build up his brother's house. **10** And his
name shall be called in Israel, The house of him whose shoe is put off. **11** [e]When
men strive together, one with another, if the wife of the one come near, for to rid
her husband out of the hands of him that smiteth him, and put forth her hand, and
take him by his privities, **12** Then thou shalt cut off her hand: thine eye shall not
spare her. **13** Thou shalt not have in thy bag two manner of [f]weights, a great and
a small: **14** Neither shalt thou have in thine house divers [g]measures, a great and a
small: **15** But thou shalt have a right and just weight: a perfect and a just measu-
re shalt thou have, that thy days may be lengthened in the land, which the Lord thy
God giveth thee. **16** For all that do such things, and all that do unrighteously,
are abomination unto the Lord thy God. **17** [3]Remember what Amalek did unto
thee by the way, when ye were come out of Egypt: **18** How he met thee by the
way, and smote the hindmost of you, all that were feeble behind thee, when thou
wast fainted and weary, and he feared not God. **19** Therefore, when the Lord thy
God hath given thee rest from all thine enemies round about in the land which the
Lord thy God giveth thee for an inheritance to possess it, then thou shalt put out
the [h]remembrance of Amalek from under heaven: forget not.

26

3 The offering of the firstfruits. 5 What they must protest when they offer them. 12 The tithe of the first year. 13 Their protestation in offering it. 19 To what honor God preferreth them which acknowledge him to be their Lord.

1 Also when thou shalt come into the land which the Lord thy God giveth
thee for inheritance, and shalt possess it, and dwell therein, **2** [a]Then shalt thou
take of the first of all the fruit of the earth, and bring it out of the land that the Lord
thy God giveth thee, and put it in a basket, and go unto the place which the Lord
thy God shall choose, to [b]place his name there. **3** And thou shalt come unto the
Priest, that shall be in those days, and say unto him, I acknowledge this day unto
the Lord thy God, that I am come unto the country which the Lord sware unto our
fathers for to give us. **4** Then the Priest shall take the basket out of thine hand,
and set it down before the altar of the Lord thy God. **5** And thou shalt answer
and say before the Lord thy God, A [c]Syrian was my father, who being ready to pe-
rish for hunger, went down into Egypt, and sojourned there with a small company
and grew there unto a nation great, mighty [d]and full of people. **6** And the Egyp-
tians vexed us, and troubled us, and laded us with cruel bondage. **7** But when we
[e]cried unto the Lord God of our fathers, the Lord heard our voice, and looked on
our adversity, and on our labor, and on our oppression: **8** And the Lord brought
us out of Egypt in a mighty hand, and stretched out arm, with great terribleness,
both in signs and wonders. **9** And he hath brought us into this place, and hath
given us this land, even a land that floweth with milk and honey. **10** And now,
lo, I have [f]brought the firstfruits of the land, which thou, O Lord, hast given me,
and thou shalt set it before the Lord thy God, and worship before the Lord thy
God: **11** And thou shalt rejoice in all the good things which the Lord thy God
hath given unto thee, and to thine [g]household, thou and the Levite, and the stran-
ger that is among you. **12** When thou hast made an end of tithing all the tithes
of thine increase, the third year, which is the year of tithing, and hast given it unto
the Levite, to the stranger, to the fatherless, and to the widow, that they may eat
within thy gates, and be satisfied, **13** Then thou shalt [h]say before the Lord thy
God, I have brought the hallowed thing out of mine house, and also have given it
to the Levites and to the strangers, to the fatherless and to the widow, according
to all thy [1]commandments which thou hast commanded me: I have [i]transgressed
none of the commandments, nor forgotten them, **14** I have not eaten thereof
in my [j]mourning, nor suffered ought to perish [k]through uncleanness, nor given
ought thereof for the dead, but have hearkened unto the voice of the Lord my God:
I have done [l]after all that thou hast commanded me. **15** Look down from thine
holy habitation, even from heaven, and bless thy people Israel, and the land which
thou hast given us (as thou swarest unto our fathers) the land that floweth with
milk and honey. **16** This day the Lord thy God doth command thee to do these
ordinances and laws: keep them therefore, and do them with [m]all thine heart, and
with all thy soul. **17** Thou hast set up the Lord this day to be thy God, and to
walk in his ways, and to keep his ordinances, and his commandments, and his laws,
and to hearken unto his voice. **18** [n]And the Lord hath set thee up this day, to be
a [2]precious people unto him (as he hath promised thee) and that thou shouldest
keep all his commandments. **19** And to make thee [3]high above all nations (whi-
ch he hath made) in praise, and in name, and in glory, [4]and that thou shouldest be
an holy people unto the Lord thy God, as he hath said.

27

2 They are commanded to write the law upon stones for a remembrance. 5 Also to build an altar. 13 The cursings are given on mount Ebal.

1 Then Moses with the Elders of Israel [a]commanded the people, saying, Keep
all the commandments, which I command you this day. **2** And when ye shall
pass [1]over Jordan unto the land which the Lord thy God giveth thee, thou shalt
set thee up great stones, and plaster them with plaster, **3** [b]And shalt write upon
them all the words of this Law, when thou shalt come over, that thou mayest
go into the land which the Lord thy God giveth thee: a land that floweth with
milk and honey, as the Lord God of thy fathers hath promised thee. **4** Therefore
when ye shall pass over Jordan, ye shall set up these stones, which I command you
this day in mount Ebal, and thou shalt plaster them with plaster. **5** [2]And the-
re shalt thou build unto the Lord thy God an altar, even an altar of stones: thou
shalt lift none [c]iron instrument upon them. **6** Thou shalt make the altar of the
Lord thy God of whole stones, and offer burnt offerings thereon unto the Lord
thy God. **7** And thou shalt offer peace offerings, and shalt eat there and rejoice
before the Lord thy God: **8** And thou shalt write upon the stones all the words
of this Law, [d]well and plainly. **9** And Moses and the Priests of the Levites, spa-
ke unto all Israel, saying, Take heed and hear, O Israel: this day thou art become
the people of the Lord thy God. **10** Thou [e]shalt hearken therefore unto the
voice of the Lord thy God, and do his commandments and his ordinances, whi-
ch I command thee this day. **11** And Moses charged the people the same day,
saying, **12** These shall stand upon mount Gerizim, to bless the people when ye
shall pass over Jordan: Simeon, and Levi, and Judah, and Issachar, and [f]Joseph, and
Benjamin. **13** And these shall stand upon mount Ebal, to [g]curse: Reuben, Gad,
and Asher, and Zebulun, Dan, and Naphtali. **14** And the Levites shall answer
and say unto all the men of Israel with a loud voice, **15** Cursed be the man that
shall make any carved or molten [h]image, which is an abomination unto the Lord,
the work of the hands of the craftsman, and putteth it in a secret place: And all
the people shall answer and say: So be it. **16** Cursed be he that [i]curseth his fa-
ther and his mother: And all the people shall say: So be it. **17** Cursed be he that
removeth his neighbor's [j]mark: And all the people shall say: So be it. **18** Cursed
be he that maketh the [k]blind go out of the way: And all the people shall say: So be
it. **19** Cursed be he that hindereth the right of the stranger, the fatherless, and
the widow: And all the people shall say: So be it. **20** Cursed be he that lieth with
his father's wife: for he hath uncovered his father's [l]skirt: And all the people shall
say: So be it. **21** Cursed be he that lieth with any beast: And all the people shall
say: So be it. **22** Cursed be he that lieth with his sister, the daughter of his father,
or the daughter of his mother: And all the people shall say: So be it. **23** Cur-
sed be he that lieth with his [m]mother-in-law: And all the people shall say: So be
it. **24** Cursed be he that smiteth his neighbor [n]secretly: And all the people shall
say: So be it. **25** [3]Cursed be he that taketh a reward to put to death innocent
blood: And all the people shall say: So be it. **26** [4]Cursed be he that confirmeth
not all the words of this Law, to do them: And all the people shall say: So be it.

---

also for a kinsman: it seemeth that it is not meant that the natural brother should marry his brother's wife, but some other of the kindred that was in that degree which might marry.

e. Deut. 25:11 This law importeth that godly shamefastness be preserved: for it is an horrible thing to see a woman past shame.
f. Deut. 25:13 Hebrew, stone and stone.
g. Deut. 25:14 Hebrew, Ephah and Ephah, read Exod. 12:6.
h. Deut. 25:19 This was partly accomplished by Saul, about 450 years afterward.

DEUT. 25

1. 1 Cor. 9:9 / 1 Tim. 5:18
2. Ruth 4:3 / Matt. 22:24 / Mark 12:19 / Luke 20:28
3. Exod. 17:4

DEUT. 26

a. Deut. 26:2 By this ceremony they acknowledged that they received the land of Canaan as a free gift of God.
b. Deut. 26:2 To be called upon, served and worshipped spiritually, Deut. 12:5.
c. Deut. 26:5 Meaning, Jacob, who served 20 years in Syria.
d. Deut. 26:5 Only by God's mercy, and not by their fathers' deservings.
e. Deut. 26:7 Alleging the promises made unto our fathers, Abraham, Isaac, and Jacob.
f. Deut. 26:10 In token of a thankful heart, and mindful of this benefit.
g. Deut. 26:11 Signifying that God giveth us not goods for ourselves only, but for their uses also which are committed to our charge.
h. Deut. 26:13 Without hypocrisy.
i. Deut. 26:13 Of malice and contempt.
j. Deut. 26:14 Or, for any necessity.
k. Deut. 26:14 By putting them to any profane use.
l. Deut. 26:14 As far as my sinful nature would suffer: for else, as David and Paul say, there is not one just, Ps. 24:3; Rom. 3:10.
m. Deut. 26:16 With a good and simple conscience.
n. Deut. 26:18 Signifying that there is a mutual bond between God and his people.

DEUT. 26

1. Deut. 14:27
2. Deut. 7:6 / Deut. 14:2
3. Deut. 4:7 / Deut. 28:1
4. Deut. 7:6 / Deut. 14:2

DEUT. 27

a. Deut. 27:1 As God's minister and charged with the same.
b. Deut. 27:3 God would that his Law should be set up in the borders of the land of Canaan, that all that looked thereon might know that the land was dedicated to his service.
c. Deut. 27:5 The altar should not be curiously wrought, because it should continue but for a time: for God would have but one altar in Judah.
d. Deut. 27:8 That everyone may well read it, and understand it.
e. Deut. 27:10 This condition hath bound thee unto, that if thou wilt be his people, thou must keep his laws.
f. Deut. 27:12 Meaning, Ephraim and Manasseh.
g. Deut. 27:13 Signifying, that if they would not obey God for love, they should be made to obey for fear.
h. Deut. 27:15 Under this he containeth all the corruptions of God's service, and the transgression of the first Table.
i. Deut. 27:16 Or, contemneth: and this appertaineth to the second Table.
j. Deut. 27:17 He condemneth all injuries and extortions.
k. Deut. 27:18 Meaning, that helpeth not and counselleth not his neighbor.
l. Deut. 27:20 In committing villiany against him, Lev. 20:11; Deut. 22:30; Ezek. 22:10.
m. Deut. 27:23 Meaning, his wife's mother.
n. Deut. 27:24 For God that seeth in secret, will revenge it.

28

1 The promises to them that obey the Commandments. 15 The threatenings to the contrary.

1 If [1]thou shalt obey diligently the voice of the Lord thy God, and observe and do all his commandments, which I command thee this day, then the Lord thy God will [a]set thee on high above all the nations of the earth. **2** And all these blessings shall come on thee, and [b]overtake thee, if thou shalt obey the voice of the Lord thy God. **3** Blessed shalt thou be in the [c]city, and blessed also in the field. **4** Blessed shall be the fruit [d]of thy body, and the fruit of thy ground, and the fruit of thy cattle, the increase of thy kine, and the flocks of thy sheep. **5** Blessed shall be thy basket and thy dough. **6** Blessed shalt thou be when thou [e]comest in, and blessed also when thou goest out. **7** The Lord shall cause thine enemies that rise against thee, to fall before thy face: they shall come out against thee one way, and shall flee before thee [f]seven ways. **8** The Lord shall command the blessing to be with thee in thy store houses, and in all that thou settest thine [g]hand to, and will bless thee in the land which the Lord thy God giveth thee. **9** The Lord shall make thee an holy people unto himself, as he hath sworn unto thee, if thou shalt keep the commandments of the Lord thy God, and walk in his ways, **10** Then all people of the earth shall see that the Name of the Lord is [h]called upon over thee, and they shall be afraid of thee. **11** And the Lord shall make thee plenteous in goods, in the fruit of thy body, and in the fruit of thy cattle, and in the fruit of thy ground, in the land which the Lord swore unto thy fathers, to give thee. **12** The Lord shall open unto thee his good treasure, even the [i]heaven to give rain unto thy land in due season, and to bless all the work of thine hands: and [2]thou shalt lend unto many nations, but shalt not borrow thyself. **13** And the Lord shall make thee the head, and not the [j]tail, and thou shalt be above only, and shalt not be beneath, if thou obey the commandments of the Lord thy God which I command thee this day, to keep and to do them. **14** But thou shalt not decline from any of the words, which I command you this day, either to the [3]right hand or to the left, to go after other gods to serve them. **15** [4]But if thou wilt not obey the voice of the Lord thy God, to keep and to do all his commandments, and his ordinances, which I command thee this day, then all these curses shall come upon thee, and overtake thee. **16** Cursed shalt thou be in the town, and cursed also in the field. **17** Cursed shall thy basket be, and thy [k]dough. **18** Cursed shall be the fruit of thy body, and the fruit of thy land, the increase of thy kine, and the flocks of thy sheep. **19** Cursed shalt thou be when thou comest in, and cursed also when thou goest out. **20** The Lord shall send upon thee cursing, trouble, and [l]shame, in all that which thou settest thine hand to do, until thou be destroyed, and perish quickly, because of the wickedness of thy works, whereby thou hast forsaken me. **21** The Lord shall make the pestilence cleave unto thee, until he hath consumed thee from the land, whither thou goest to possess it. **22** [5]The Lord shall smite thee with a consumption, and with the fever, and with a burning ague, and with fervent heat, and with the sword, and with [m]blasting, and with the mildew, and they shall pursue thee until thou perish. **23** And thine heaven that is over thine head, shall be [n]brass, and the earth that is under thee, iron. **24** The Lord shall give thee for the rain of thy land, dust and ashes: even from [o]heaven shall it come down upon thee, until thou be destroyed. **25** And the Lord shall cause thee to fall before thine enemies: thou shalt come out one way against them, and shalt flee seven ways before them, and shalt be [p]scattered through all the kingdoms of the earth. **26** And thy [q]carcass shall be meat unto all fowls of the air, and unto the beasts of the earth, and none shall fray them away. **27** The Lord will smite thee with the botch of Egypt, and with the hemorrhoids, and with the scab, and with the itch, that thou canst not be healed. **28** And the Lord shall smite thee with madness, and with blindness, and with atoning of heart. **29** Thou shalt also grope at noon days, as the [r]blind gropeth in darkness, and shalt not prosper in thy ways: thou shalt never but be oppressed with wrong, and be powled evermore, and no man shall succor thee. **30** Thou shalt betroth a wife, and another man shall lie with her: thou shalt build an house, and shalt not dwell therein: thou shalt plant a vineyard, and shalt not [s]eat the fruit. **31** Thine ox shall be slain before thine eyes, and thou shalt not eat thereof: thine ass shall be violently taken away before thy face, and shall not be restored to thee: thy sheep shall be given unto thine enemies, and no man shall rescue them for thee. **32** Thy sons and thy daughters shall be given unto another people, and thine eyes [t]shall still look for them, even till they fall out, and there shall be no power in thine hand. **33** The fruit of thy land and all thy labors shall a people which thou knowest not, eat, and thou shalt never but suffer wrong, and violence always: **34** So that thou shalt be mad for the sight which thine eyes shall see. **35** The Lord shall smite thee in the knees, and in the thighs, with a sore botch, that thou canst not be healed: even from the sole of the foot unto the top of thine head. **36** The Lord shall bring thee and thy [u]King (which thou shalt set over thee) unto a nation, which neither thou nor thy fathers have known, and there thou shalt serve other gods: even wood and stone, **37** And thou shalt [6]be a wonder, a proverb and a common talk among all people, whither the Lord shall carry thee. **38** Thou shalt carry out much seed into the field, and shalt gather but little in: for the grasshoppers shall destroy it. **39** [7]Thou shalt plant a vineyard, and dress it, but shalt neither drink of the wine, nor gather the grapes: for the worms shall eat it. **40** Thou shalt have Olive trees in all thy coasts, but shalt not anoint thyself with the oil: for thine olives shall [v]fall. **41** Thou shalt beget sons and daughters, but shalt not have them: for they shall go into captivity. **42** All thy trees and fruit of thy land [w]shall the grasshopper consume. **43** The stranger that is among you, shall climb above thee up on high, and thou shalt come down beneath alow. **44** He shall lend thee, and thou shalt not lend him: he shall be the head, and thou shalt be the tail. **45** Moreover, all these curses shall come upon thee, and shall pursue thee and overtake thee, till thou be destroyed, because thou obeyedst not the voice of the Lord thy God, to keep his commandments, and his ordinances, which he commanded thee: **46** And they shall be upon [x]thee for signs and wonders, and upon thy seed forever, **47** Because thou servedst not the Lord thy God with joyfulness, and with a good heart, for the abundance of all things. **48** Therefore thou shalt serve thine enemies which the Lord shall send upon thee, in hunger and in thirst, and in nakedness, and in need of all things: and he shall put a yoke of iron upon thy neck until he have destroyed thee. **49** The Lord shall bring a nation upon thee from far, even from the end of the world, flying swift as an eagle: a nation whose tongue thou shalt not understand: **50** A nation of a [y]fierce countenance, which will not regard the person of the old, nor have compassion of the young. **51** The same shall eat the fruit of thy cattle, and the fruit of thy land, until thou be destroyed, and he shall leave thee neither wheat, wine, nor oil, neither the [z]increase of thy kine, nor the flocks of thy sheep, until he have brought thee to naught. **52** And he shall besiege thee in all thy cities, until thine high and strong walls fall down, wherein thou trustedst in all the land: and he shall besiege thee in all thy [aa]cities throughout all thy land, which the Lord thy God hath given thee. **53** [8]And thou shalt eat the fruit of thy body, even the flesh of thy sons and thy daughters, which the Lord thy God hath given thee, during the siege and straitness wherein thine enemies shall enclose thee: **54** So that the man (that is tender and exceeding dainty among you,) [9]shall be grieved at his brother, and at his wife that lieth in his bosom, and at the remnant of his children, which he hath yet left, **55** For fear of giving unto any of them of the flesh of his children, whom he shall eat, because he hath nothing left him in that siege, and straitness, wherewith thine enemy shall besiege thee in all thy cities. **56** The tender and dainty [ab]woman among you, which never would venture to set the sole of her foot upon the ground (for her softness and tenderness) shall be grieved at her husband that lieth in her bosom, and at her son, and at her daughter, **57** And at her [ac]afterbirth (that shall come out from between her feet) and at her children, which she shall bear: for when all things lack, she shall eat them secretly, during the siege and straightness wherewith thine enemy shall besiege thee in thy cities. **58** If thou wilt not keep and do [ad]all the words of the Law (that are written in this book) and fear this glorious and fearful Name, THE LORD THY GOD, **59** Then the Lord will make thy plagues wonderful, and the plagues of thy seed, even great plagues, and of long continuance, and sore diseases and of long durance. **60** Moreover, he will bring upon thee all the diseases of Egypt, whereof thou wast afraid, and they shall cleave unto thee. **61** And every sickness, and every plague, which is not [ae]written in the book of this Law, will the Lord heap upon thee, until thou be destroyed. **62** And ye shall be left few in number, where ye were as the [10]stars of heaven in multitude, because thou wouldest not obey the voice of the Lord thy God. **63** And as the Lord hath rejoiced over you, to do you good, and to multiply you, so he will rejoice over you, to destroy you, and bring you to naught, and ye shall be rooted out of the land, whither thou goest to possess it. **64** And the Lord shall [af]scatter thee among all people from the one end of the world unto the other, and there thou shalt serve other gods, which thou hast not known, nor thy fathers, even wood and

---

DEUT. 27

1. Josh. 4:1
2. Exod. 20:25 / Josh. 8:31
3. Ezek. 22:12
4. Gal. 3:10

DEUT. 28

a. Deut. 28:1 He will make thee the most excellent of all people.
b. Deut. 28:2 When thou thinkest thyself forsaken.
c. Deut. 28:3 Thou shalt live wealthily.
d. Deut. 28:4 Thy children and succession.
e. Deut. 28:6 All thine enterprises shall have good success.
f. Deut. 28:7 Meaning, many ways.
g. Deut. 28:8 God will bless us, if we do our duty, and not be idle.
h. Deut. 28:10 In that he is thy God, and thou art his people.
i. Deut. 28:12 For nothing in the earth is profitable but when God sendeth his blessings from heaven.
j. Deut. 28:13 Or, the lowest
k. Deut. 28:17 Or, store.
l. Deut. 28:20 Or, rebuke.
m. Deut. 28:22 Or, drought.
n. Deut. 28:23 It shall give thee no more moisture than if it were of brass.
o. Deut. 28:24 Or, out of the air as dust raised with wind.
p. Deut. 28:25 Some read, thou shalt be a terror and fear, when they shall hear how God hath plagued thee.
q. Deut. 28:26 Thou shalt be cursed both in thy life and in thy death: for the burial is a testimony of the resurrection which sign for thy wickedness thou shalt lack.
r. Deut. 28:29 In things most evident and clear thou shalt lack discretion and judgment.
s. Deut. 28:30 Hebrew, make it common.
t. Deut. 28:32 When they shall return from their captivity.
u. Deut. 28:36 As he did Manasseh, Jehoiakim, Zedekiah and others.
v. Deut. 28:40 Or, be shaken before they be ripe.
w. Deut. 28:42 Under one kind he containeth all the vermin, which destroy the fruits of the land: and this is an evident token of God's curse.
x. Deut. 28:46 God's plagues be evident signs that he is offended with thee.
y. Deut. 28:50 Or, barbarous, cruel or impudent.
z. Deut. 28:51 Or, firstborn of thy bullock.
aa. Deut. 28:52 Or, gates.
ab. Deut. 28:56 As came to pass in the days of Joram king of Israel, 2 Kings 6:20, and when the Romans besieged Jerusalem.
ac. Deut. 28:57 Hunger shall so bite her, that she shall be ready to eat her child before it be delivered.
ad. Deut. 28:58 For he that offendeth in one, is guilty of all, James 2:10.
ae. Deut. 28:61 Declaring, that God hath infinite means to plague the wicked, besides them that are ordinary or written.

stone. **65** Also among these nations thou shalt find no rest, neither shall the sole of thy foot have rest: for the Lord shall give thee there a trembling heart, and looking to return till thine eyes fall out, and a sorrowful mind. **66** And thy life shall [ag]hang before thee, and thou shalt fear both night and day, and shalt have none assurance of thy life. **67** In the morning thou shalt say, Would God it were evening, and at the evening thou shalt say, Would God it were morning, for the fear of thine heart, which thou shalt fear, and for the sight of thine eyes, which thou shalt see. **68** And the Lord shall bring thee into Egypt again with [ah]ships by the way, whereof I said unto thee, Thou shalt see it no more again: and there ye shall sell yourselves unto your enemies for bondmen and bondwomen, and there shall be no buyer.

29

2 The people are exhorted to observe the commandments. 10 The whole people from the highest to the lowest are comprehended under God's covenant. 19 The punishment of him that flattereth himself in his wickedness. 24 The cause of God's wrath against his people.

1 These are the [a]words of the covenant which the Lord commandeth Moses to make with the children of Israel, in the land of Moab, beside the covenant which he had made with them in [b]Horeb. **2** And Moses called all Israel, and said unto them, Ye have seen all that the Lord did before your eyes in the land of Egypt unto Pharaoh and unto all his servants, and unto all his land, **3** The [c]great tentations which thine eyes have seen, those great miracles and wonders: **4** Yet the Lord hath not [d]given you an heart to perceive, and eyes to see, and ears to hear, unto this day. **5** And I have led you forty years in the wilderness: your clothes are not waxed old upon you, neither is thy shoe waxed old upon thy foot. **6** Ye have eaten no [e]bread, neither drunk wine, nor strong drink, that ye might know how that I am the Lord your God. **7** After, ye came unto this place, and Sihon King of Heshbon, and Og King of Bashan came out against us unto battle, and we slew them, **8** And took their land, and gave it for an inheritance unto the Reubenites, and to the Gadites, and to the half tribe of Manasseh. **9** [1]Keep therefore the words of this covenant and do them, that ye may prosper in all that ye shall do. **10** Ye stand this day everyone of you before the Lord your [f]God: your heads of your tribes, your Elders and your officers, even all the men of Israel: **11** Your children, your wives, and thy stranger that is in thy camp, from the hewer of thy wood, unto the drawer of thy water, **12** That thou shouldest [g]pass into the covenant of the Lord thy God, and into his oath which the Lord thy God maketh with thee this day, **13** For to establish thee this day a people unto himself, and that he may be unto thee a God, as he hath said unto thee, and as he hath sworn unto thy fathers, Abraham, Isaac, and Jacob. **14** Neither make I this covenant and this oath with you only, **15** But as well with him that standeth here with us this day before the Lord our God, as with him [h]that is not here with us this day. **16** For ye know, how we have dwelt in the land of Egypt, and how we passed through the midst of the nations, which ye passed by. **17** And ye have seen their abominations and their idols (wood and stone, silver and gold) which were among them, **18** That there should not be among you man nor woman, nor family, nor tribe, which should turn his heart away this day from the Lord our God, to go and serve the gods of these nations, and that there should not be among you [i]any root that bringeth forth [2]gall and wormwood, **19** So that when he heareth the words of this curse, he [j]bless himself in his heart, saying, I shall have peace, although I walk according to the stubbornness of mine own heart, thus adding [k]drunkenness to thirst. **20** The Lord will not be merciful unto him, but then the wrath of the Lord and his jealousy shall smoke against that man, and every curse that is written in this book, shall light upon him, and the Lord shall put out his name from under heaven. **21** And the Lord shall separate him unto evil out of all the tribes of Israel, according unto all the curses of the covenant, that is written in the book of this Law. **22** So that the [l]generation to come, even your children, that shall rise up after you, and the stranger that shall come from a far land, shall say, when they shall see the plagues of this land, and the diseases thereof, wherewith the Lord shall smite it: **23** (For all that land shall burn with brimstone and salt: it shall not be sown, nor bring forth, nor any grass shall grow therein, like as in the overthrowing of [3]Sodom and Gomorrah, Admah, and Zeboiim, which the Lord overthrew in his wrath and in his anger.) **24** Then shall all nations say, [4]Wherefore hath the Lord done thus unto this land? how fierce is this great wrath? **25** And they shall answer, Because they have forsaken the covenant of the Lord God of their fathers, which he had made with them, when he brought them out of the land of Egypt, **26** And went and served other gods and worshipped them: even gods which they knew not, and [m]which had given them nothing, **27** Therefore the wrath of the Lord waxed hot against this land, to bring upon it every curse that is written in this book. **28** And the Lord hath rooted them out of their land in anger, and in wrath, and in great indignation, and hath cast them into another land, as appeareth this day. **29** The [n]secret things belong to the Lord our God, but the things revealed belong unto us, and to our children forever, that we may do all the words of this Law.

30

1 Mercy showed when they repent. 6 The Lord doth circumcise the heart. 11 All excuse of ignorance is taken away. 15, 19 Life and death is set before them. 20 The Lord is their life which obey him.

1 Now when all these things shall come upon thee, either the blessing or the curse which I have set before thee, and thou shalt [a]turn into thine heart, among all the nations whither the Lord thy God hath driven thee, **2** And shalt return unto the Lord thy God, and obey his voice in all that I command thee this day: thou, and thy children with all thine [b]heart and with all thy soul, **3** Then the Lord thy God will cause thy captives to return, and have compassion upon thee, and will return, to gather thee out of all the people where the Lord thy God hath scattered thee. **4** Though thou werest cast unto the utmost part of [c]heaven, from thence will the Lord thy God gather thee, and from thence will he [d]take thee, **5** And the Lord thy God will bring thee into the land which thy fathers possessed, and thou shalt possess it, and he will show thee favor, and will multiply thee above thy fathers. **6** And the Lord thy God will [e]circumcise thine heart, and the heart of thy seed, that thou mayest love the Lord thy God with all thine heart, and with all thy soul, that thou mayest live. **7** And the Lord thy God will lay all these curses upon thine enemies, and on them that hate thee, and that persecute thee. **8** [f]Return thou therefore, and obey the voice of the Lord, and do all his commandments, which I command thee this day. **9** And the Lord thy God will make thee plenteous in every work of thine hand, in the fruit of thy body, and in the fruit of thy cattle, and in the fruit of the land for thy wealth: for the Lord will turn again, and [g]rejoice over thee to do thee good, as he rejoiced over thy fathers, **10** Because thou shalt obey the voice of the Lord thy God, in keeping his commandments and his ordinances, which are written in the book of this law, when thou shalt return unto the Lord thy God with all thine heart and with all thy soul. **11** For this commandment which I command thee this day, is [h]not hid from thee, neither is it far off. **12** It is not in heaven, that thou shouldest say, [1]Who shall go up for us to heaven, and bring it us, and cause us to hear it, that we may do it? **13** Neither is it beyond the [i]sea, that thou shouldest say, Who shall go over the sea for us, and bring it us, and cause us to hear it, that we may do it? **14** But the [j]word is very near unto thee: even in thy mouth, and in thine heart, for to [k]do it. **15** Behold, I have set before thee this day life and good, death and evil, **16** In that I command thee this day, [l]to love the Lord thy God, to walk in his ways, and to keep his commandment, and his ordinances, and his laws, that thou mayest [m]live, and be multiplied, and that the Lord thy God may bless thee in the land, whither thou goest to possess it. **17** But if thine heart turn away, so that thou wilt not obey, but shalt be seduced and worship other gods, and serve them, **18** I pronounce unto you this day, that ye shall surely perish, ye shall not prolong your days in the land, whither thou passest over Jordan to possess it. **19** [2]I call heaven and earth

---

af. Deut. 28:64 Signifying that it is a singular gift of God to be in a place whereas we may worship God purely, and declare our faith and religion.
ag. Deut. 28:66 Or, thou shall be in doubt of thy life.
ah. Deut. 28:68 Because they were unmindful of that miracle, when the Sea gave place for them to pass through.

DEUT. 28

1. Lev. 26:3
2. Deut. 15:6
3. Josh. 23:6
4. Lev. 26:14 / Lam. 2:17 / Mal. 2:2
5. Lev. 26:16
6. Jer. 24:9 / Jer. 25:9 / 1 Kings 9:7
7. Mic. 6:15 / Hag. 1:6
8. Lev. 26:29 / 2 Kings 6:29 / Lam. 4:10
9. Deut. 15:9
10. Deut. 10:22

DEUT. 29

a. Deut. 29:1 That is, the articles, or conditions.
b. Deut. 29:1 At the first giving of the law, which was forty years before.
c. Deut. 29:3 The proofs of my power.
d. Deut. 29:4 He showeth that it is not in man's power to understand the mysteries of God, if it be not given him from above.
e. Deut. 29:6 Made by man's art, but Manna, which is called the bread of Angels.
f. Deut. 29:10 Who knoweth your hearts, and therefore ye may not think to dissemble with him.
g. Deut. 29:12 Alluding to them, that when they made a sure covenant, divided a beast in twain, and passed between the parts divided, Gen. 15:10.
h. Deut. 29:15 Meaning, their posterity.
i. Deut. 29:18 Such sin, as the bitter fruit thereof might choke and destroy you.
j. Deut. 29:19 Or, flatter.
k. Deut. 29:19 For as he that is thirsty desireth to drink much, so he that followeth his appetites, seeketh by all means, and yet cannot be satisfied.
l. Deut. 29:22 God's plagues upon them that rebel against him, shall be so strong, that all ages shall be astonished.
m. Deut. 29:26 Or, which had not given them a land to possess.
n. Deut. 29:29 Moses hereby proveth their curiosity, which seek those things that are only known to God: and their negligence that regard not that, which God hath revealed unto them, as the Law.

DEUT. 29

1. Deut. 4:6 / 1 Kings 2:3
2. Acts 8:23
3. Gen. 19:24,25
4. 1 Kings 9:8 / Jer. 22:8

DEUT. 30

a. Deut. 30:1 By calling to remembrance, both his mercies and plagues.
b. Deut. 30:2 In true repentance is none hypocrisy.
c. Deut. 30:4 Even to the world's end.
d. Deut. 30:4 And bring thee into thy country.
e. Deut. 30:6 God will purge all thy wicked affections, which thing is not in thine own power to do.
f. Deut. 30:8 If we will have God to work in us with his holy Spirit, we must turn again to him by repentance.
g. Deut. 30:9 He meaneth not that God is subject to these passions, to rejoice, or to be sad: but he useth this manner of speech to declare the love that he beareth unto us.
h. Deut. 30:11 The Law is so evident that none can pretend ignorance.
i. Deut. 30:13 By heaven and the sea he meaneth places most far distant.
j. Deut. 30:14 Even the law and the Gospel.
k. Deut. 30:14 By faith in Christ.
l. Deut. 30:16 So that to love and obey God, is only life and felicity.
m. Deut. 30:16 He addeth these promises to signify that it is for our profit that we love him, and not for his.
n. Deut. 30:19 That is, love and obey God: which thing is not in man's power, but God's Spirit only worketh it in his elect.

to record this day against you, that I have set before you life and death, blessing
and cursing: therefore [n]choose life, that both thou and thy seed may live, **20** By
loving the Lord thy God, by obeying his voice, and by cleaving unto him: for he is
thy life, and the length of thy days, that thou mayest dwell in the land which the
Lord sware unto thy fathers, Abraham, Isaac, and Jacob, to give them.

31

2, 7 Moses preparing himself to die, appointeth Joshua to rule the people. 9 He giveth the law to the Levites, that they should read it to the people. 19 God giveth them a song as a witness between him and them. 23 God confirmeth Joshua. 29 Moses showeth them that they will rebel after his death.

1 Then Moses went and spake these words unto all Israel, **2** And said unto
them, I am an hundred and twenty years old this day: I [a]can no more go out and
in: also the Lord hath said unto me, [1]Thou shalt not go over this Jordan. **3** The
Lord thy God he will go over before thee: he will destroy these nations before thee,
and thou shalt possess them [2]Joshua, he shall go before thee, as the Lord hath
said. **4** And the Lord shall do unto them, as he did to [3]Sihon and to Og kings of
the Amorites, and unto their land whom he destroyed. **5** And the Lord shall give
them [b]before you, that ye may do unto them according unto every [4]command-
ment which I have commanded you. **6** Pluck [c]up your hearts therefore, and be
strong: dread not, nor be afraid of them: for the Lord thy God himself doth go with
thee: he will not fail thee, nor forsake thee. **7** And Moses called Joshua, and said
unto him in the sight of all Israel, Be [d]of a good courage and strong: for thou shalt
go with this people unto the land which the Lord hath sworn unto their fathers, to
give them, and thou shalt give it them to inherit. **8** And the Lord himself doth
[e]go before thee: he will be with thee: he will not fail thee, neither forsake thee: fear
not therefore, nor be discomforted. **9** And Moses wrote this Law, and delive-
red it unto the Priests the sons of Levi (which bare the Ark of the covenant of the
Lord) and unto all the Elders of Israel. **10** And Moses commanded them, saying,
[5]Every seventh year [6]when the year of freedom shall be in the feast of the Taberna-
cles: **11** When all Israel shall come to appear [f]before the Lord thy God, and the
place which he shall choose, thou shalt read this Law before all Israel that they may
hear it. **12** Gather the people together: men, and women, and children, and thy
stranger that is within thy gates, that they may hear, and that they may learn, and
fear the Lord your God, and keep and observe all the words of this Law, **13** And
that their children which [g]have not known it, may hear it, and learn to fear the
Lord your God, as long as ye live in the land, whither ye go over Jordan to pos-
sess it. **14** Then the Lord said unto Moses, Behold, thy days are come, that thou
must die: Call Joshua, and stand ye in the Tabernacle of the Congregation that I
may give him a [h]charge So Moses and Joshua went, and stood in the Tabernacle of
the Congregation. **15** And the Lord appeared in the Tabernacle in the pillar of a
[i]cloud: and the pillar of the cloud stood over the door of the Tabernacle. **16** And
the Lord said unto Moses, Behold, thou shalt sleep with thy fathers, and this peo-
ple will rise up, and go a whoring after the gods of a strange land (whither they go
to dwell therein) and will forsake me: and break my covenant which I have made
with them. **17** Wherefore my wrath will wax hot against them at that day, and I
will forsake them, and will [j]hide my face from them: then they shall be consumed,
and many adversities and tribulations shall come upon them: so then they will say,
Are not these troubles come upon me, because God is not with me? **18** But I will
surely hide my face in that day, because of all the evil which they shall commit, in
that they are turned unto other gods. **19** Now therefore write ye this [k]song for
you, and teach it the children of Israel: put it in their mouths, that this song may
be my witness against the children of Israel. **20** For I will bring them into the
land (which I sware unto their fathers) that floweth with milk and honey: and they
shall eat and fill themselves, and wax fat: [l]then shall they turn unto other gods, and
serve them, and contemn me, and break my covenant. **21** And then when many
adversities and tribulations shall come upon them, this song shall [m]answer them
to their faces as a witness: for it shall not be forgotten out of the mouths of their
posterity: for I know their imagination, which they go about even now, before I
have brought them into the land which I sware. **22** Moses therefore wrote this
song the same day, and taught it the children of Israel. **23** And God gave Joshua
the son of Nun a charge, and said, [7]Be strong and of a good courage: for thou shalt
bring the children of Israel into the land, which I sware unto them, and I will be
with thee. **24** And when Moses had made an end of writing the words of this
Law in a book until he had finished them, **25** Then Moses commanded the Le-
vites, which bare the Ark of the covenant of the Lord, saying, **26** Take the book
of this Law, and put ye it in the side of the Ark of the covenant of the Lord your
God, that it may be there for a [n]witness against thee. **27** For I know thy rebel-
lion and thy stiff neck: behold, I being yet alive with you this day, ye are rebellious
against the Lord: how much more then after my death? **28** Gather unto me all
the Elders of your tribes, and your [o]officers, that I may speak these words in their
audience, and call heaven and earth to record against them. **29** For I am sure
that after my death, ye will utterly be corrupt and turn from the way which I have
commanded you: therefore evil will come upon you at the length, because ye will
commit evil in the sight of the Lord, by provoking him to anger through the [p]work
of your hands. **30** Thus Moses spake in the audience of all the Congregation of
Israel the words of this song, until he had ended them.

32

The song of Moses containing 7 God's benefits toward the people, 15 and their ingratitude toward him. 20 God menaceth them, 21 and speaketh of the vocation of the Gentiles. 46 Moses commandeth to teach the Law to the children. 49 God forewarneth Moses of his death.

1 Hearken, ye [a]heavens, and I will speak: and let the earth hear the words of
my mouth. **2** My [b]doctrine shall drop as the rain, and my speech shall still as the
dew, as the shower upon the herbs, and as the great rain upon the grass. **3** For
I will publish the Name of the Lord: give ye glory unto our God. **4** Perfect is
the work of the [c]mighty God: for all his ways are judgment God is true, and wi-
thout wickedness: just and righteous is he. **5** They have corrupted themselves
toward him by their vice, not being his children, but a froward and crooked gene-
ration. **6** Do ye so reward the Lord, O foolish people and unwise? is not he thy
father, that hath bought thee? he hath [d]made thee, and proportioned thee. **7** Re-
member the days of old: consider the years of so many generations: ask thy father,
and he will show thee: thine Elders, and they will tell thee. **8** When the most
high God divided to the nations their inheritance, when he separated the sons of
Adam, he appointed the borders of the [e]people, according to the number of the
children of Israel. **9** For the Lord's portion is his people: Jacob is the lot of his
inheritance. **10** He found him in the land of the wilderness, in a waste and roa-
ring wilderness: he led him about, he taught him, and kept him as the apple of his
eye. **11** As an eagle stirreth up her nest, [f]fluttereth over her birds, stretcheth out
her wings, taketh them and beareth them on her wings, **12** So the Lord alone
led him, and there was no [g]strange god with him. **13** He carried him up to the
high places of the [h]earth, that he might eat the fruits of the fields, and he caused
him to suck [i]honey out of the stone, and oil out of the hard rock: **14** Butter of
kine, and milk of sheep with fat of the lambs, and rams fed in Bashan, and goa-
ts, with the fat of the grains of wheat: and the red [j]liquor of the grape hast thou
drunk. **15** But he that should have been [k]upright, when he waxed fat, spurned
with his heel: thou art fat, thou art gross, thou art laden with fatness: therefo-
re he forsook God that made him, and regarded not the strong God of his sal-
vation. **16** They provoked him with [l]strange gods: they provoked him to an-
ger with abominations. **17** They offered unto devils, not to God, but to gods
whom they knew not: [m]new gods that came newly up, whom their fathers feared
not. **18** Thou hast forgotten the mighty God, that begat thee, and hast forgotten
God that formed thee. **19** The Lord then saw it, and was angry, for the provoca-
tion of his [n]sons and of his daughters. **20** And he said, I will hide my face from
them: I will see what their end shall be: for they are a froward generation, children
in whom is no faith. **21** They have moved me to jealousy with that which is not
God: they have provoked me to anger with their vanities: [1]and I will move them to
jealousy with those which are no [o]people: I will provoke them to anger with a foo-
lish nation. **22** For fire is kindled in my wrath, and shall burn unto the bottom

---

DEUT. 30

1. Rom. 10:6
2. Deut. 4:26

DEUT. 31

- **a.** Deut. 31:2 I can no longer execute mine office.
- **b.** Deut. 31:5 Into your hands.
- **c.** Deut. 31:6 Or, be of good courage.
- **d.** Deut. 31:7 For he that must govern the people, hath need to be valiant to repress vice, and constant to maintain virtue.
- **e.** Deut. 31:8 Signifying that man can never be of good courage, except he be persuaded of God's favor and assistance.
- **f.** Deut. 31:11 Before the Ark of the covenant, which was the sign of God's presence, and the figure of Christ.
- **g.** Deut. 31:13 Which were not born when the law was given.
- **h.** Deut. 31:14 Or, commandment.
- **i.** Deut. 31:15 In a cloud that was fashioned like a pillar.
- **j.** Deut. 31:17 That is, I will take my favor from them: as to turn his face toward us, is to show us his favor.
- **k.** Deut. 31:19 To preserve you and your children from idolatry, by remembering God's benefits.
- **l.** Deut. 31:20 For this is the nature of flesh, no longer to obey God, than it is under the rod.
- **m.** Deut. 31:21 That these evils are come upon them, because they forsook me.
- **n.** Deut. 31:26 Of thine infidelity, when thou shalt turn away from the doctrine contained therein.
- **o.** Deut. 31:28 As governors, judges and magistrates.
- **p.** Deut. 31:29 By idolatry, and worshipping images, which are the work of your hands.

DEUT. 31

1. Num. 20:12 / Deut. 3:26
2. Num. 27:18
3. Num. 21:24
4. Deut. 7:2
5. Neh. 8:1
6. Deut. 15:1
7. Josh. 1:6

DEUT. 32

- **a.** Deut. 32:1 As witness of this people's ingratitude.
- **b.** Deut. 32:2 He desireth that he may speak to God's glory, and that the people, as the green grass, may receive the dew of his doctrine.
- **c.** Deut. 32:4 The Hebrew word is rock, noting that God only is mighty, faithful and constant in his promise.
- **d.** Deut. 32:6 Not according to the common creation, but he hath made thee a new creature by his Spirit.
- **e.** Deut. 32:8 When God by his providence divided the world, he lent for a time that portion to the Canaanites, which should after be an inheritance for all his people Israel.
- **f.** Deut. 32:11 To teach them to fly.
- **g.** Deut. 32:12 Or, god of strange nations.
- **h.** Deut. 32:13 Meaning, of the land of Canaan, which was high in respect of Egypt.
- **i.** Deut. 32:13 That is, abundance of all things even in the very rocks.
- **j.** Deut. 32:14 Hebrew, blood.
- **k.** Deut. 32:15 He showeth what is the principal end of our vocation.
- **l.** Deut. 32:16 By changing his service for their superstitions.
- **m.** Deut. 32:17 Scripture calleth new, whatsoever man inventeth, be the error never so old.
- **n.** Deut. 32:19 He calleth them God's children, not to honor them, but to show them from what dignity they are fallen.
- **o.** Deut. 32:21 Which I have not favored, nor given my law unto them.

of hell, and shall consume the earth with her increase, and set on fire the foundations of the mountains. **23** I will spend plagues upon them: I will bestow mine arrows upon them. **24** They shall be burnt with hunger, and consumed with heat, and with bitter destruction: I will also send the teeth of beasts upon them, with the venom of serpents creeping in the dust. **25** The sword shall [p]kill them without, and in the chambers fear: both the young man and the young woman, the suckling with the man of gray hair. **26** I have said, I would scatter them abroad: I would make their remembrance to cease from among men, **27** Save that I feared the fury of the enemy, lest their adversaries should [q]wax proud, and lest they should say, Our high hand and not the Lord hath done all this. **28** For they are a nation void of counsel, neither is there any understanding in them. **29** Oh that they were wise, then they would understand this: they would [r]consider their latter end. **30** How should one chase a thousand, and two put ten thousand to flight, except their strong God had sold them, and the Lord had [s]shut them up? **31** For their god is not as our God, even our enemies being judges. **32** For their vine is of the vine of Sodom, and of the vines of Gomorrah: their grapes are grapes of gall, their clusters be bitter. **33** Their [t]wine is the poison of dragons, and the cruel gall of asps. **34** Is not this laid in store with me, and sealed up among my treasures? **35** [2]Vengeance and recompense are mine: their foot shall slide in due time: for the day of their destruction is at hand, and the things that shall come upon them, make haste. **36** For the Lord shall judge his people, and [u]repent toward his servants, when he seeth that their power is gone, and none [v]shut up in hold nor left abroad. **37** When men shall say, Where are their gods, their mighty God, in whom they trusted, **38** Which did eat the fat of their sacrifices, and did drink the wine of their drink offering? let them rise up, and help you: let him be your refuge. **39** Behold now, for I, I am he, and there is no gods with me: [3]I kill, and give life: I wound, and I make whole: neither is there any that can deliver out of mine hand. **40** For [w]I lift up mine hand to heaven, and say, I live forever. **41** If I whet my glittering sword, and mine hand take hold on judgment, I will execute vengeance on mine enemies, and will reward them that hate me. **42** I will make mine arrows drunk with blood, (and my sword shall eat flesh) for the blood of the slain, and of the captives, when I begin to take vengeance of the enemy. **43** [4]Ye nations, praise his people: for he will avenge the [x]blood of his servants, and will execute vengeance upon his adversaries, and will be merciful unto his land, and to his people. **44** Then Moses came and spake all the words of this song in the audience of the people, he and [y]Hoshea the son of Nun. **45** When Moses had made an end of speaking all these words to all Israel, **46** Then he said unto them, [5]Set your hearts unto all the words which I testify against you this day, that ye may command them unto your children, that they may observe and do all the words of this Law. **47** For it is no [z]vain word concerning you, but it is your life, and by this word ye shall prolong your days in the land, whither ye go over Jordan to possess it. **48** [6]And the Lord spake unto Moses the selfsame day, saying, **49** Go up into the mountain of Abarim, unto the mount Nebo, which is in the land of Moab, that is over against Jericho: and behold the land of Canaan, which I give unto the children of Israel for a possession, **50** And die in the mount which thou goest up unto, and thou shalt be [7]gathered unto thy people, [8]as Aaron thy brother died in mount Hor, and was gathered unto his people, **51** Because ye [9]trespassed against me among the children of Israel, at the waters aaof Meribah, at Kadesh in the wilderness of Zin: for ye absanctified me not among the children of Israel. **52** Thou shalt therefore see the land before thee, but shalt not go thither, I mean, into the land which I give the children of Israel.

33

1 Moses before his death blesseth all the tribes of Israel. 26 There is no god like to the God of Israel: 29 Nor any people like unto his.

1 Now this is the [a]blessing wherewith Moses the man of God blessed the children of Israel before his death, and said, **2** The Lord came from Sinai, and rose up from Seir unto them, and appeared clearly from mount Paran, and he came with ten [b]thousands of Saints, and at his right hand a fiery Law for them. **3** Though he love the people, yet [c]all thy Saints are in thine hands: and they are humbled at [d]thy feet, to receive thy words. **4** Moses commanded us a Law for an [e]inheritance of the Congregation of Jacob. **5** Then [f]he was among the [g]righteous people, as King, when the heads of the people, and the tribes of Israel were assembled. **6** Let [h]Reuben live, and not die, though his men be a small number. **7** And thus he blessed Judah, and said, Hear, O Lord, the voice of Judah, and bring him unto his people: his hands shall be [i]sufficient for him, if thou help him against his enemies. **8** And of Levi he said, Let thy [1]Thummim and thine Urim be with thine Holy one, whom thou didst prove in Massah, and didst cause him to strive at the waters of Meribah. **9** Who said unto his father and to his mother, [j]I have not seen him, neither knew he his brethren, nor knew his own children: for they observed thy word, and kept thy Covenant. **10** They shall teach Jacob thy judgments, and Israel thy Law: they shall put incense before thy face, and the burnt offering upon thine Altar. **11** Bless, O Lord, his substance, and accept the work of his hands: [k]smite through the loins of them that rise against him, and of them that hate him, that they rise not again. **12** Of Benjamin he said, The beloved of the Lord shall [l]dwell in safety by him: the Lord shall cover him all the day long, and dwell between his shoulders. **13** And of Joseph he said, Blessed of the Lord is his land for the sweetness of heaven, for the dew, and for the [m]depth lying beneath, **14** And for the sweet increase of the Sun, and for the sweet increase of the Moon, **15** And for thy sweetness of the top of the ancient mountains, and for the sweetness of the old hills, **16** And for the sweetness of the earth, and abundance therefore: and the good will of him that dwelt in the [n]bush, shall come upon the head of Joseph, and upon the top of the head of him that was [2]separated from his brethren. **17** His beauty shall be like his firstborn bullock, and his [o]horns as the horns of an unicorn: with them he shall smite the people together, even the ends of the world: these are also the ten thousands of Ephraim, and these are the thousands of Manasseh. **18** And of Zebulun he said, Rejoice, Zebulun, in thy [p]going out, and thou Issachar in thy tents. **19** They shall call the people unto the [q]mountain: there they shall offer the sacrifices of righteousness: for [r]they shall suck of the abundance of the sea, and of the treasures hid in the sand. **20** Also of Gad he said, Blessed be he that enlargeth Gad: he dwelleth as a lion, that catcheth for his prey the arm with the head. **21** And he looked to himself at the beginning, because there was a portion of the [s]Law-giver hid: yet he shall come with the heads of the people, to execute the justice of the Lord, and his judgments with Israel. **22** And of Dan he said, Dan is a lion's whelp: he shall leap from Bashan. **23** Also of Naphtali he said, O Naphtali, satisfied with favor, and filled with the blessing of the Lord, possess [t]the West and the South. **24** And of Asher he said, Asher shall be blessed with children: he shall be acceptable unto his brethren, and shall dip his foot in oil. **25** Thy shoes shall be [u]iron and brass, and thy strength shall continue as long as thou livest. **26** There is none like God, O righteous people, which rideth upon the heavens for thine help, and on the clouds in his glory. **27** The eternal God is thy refuge, and under his arms thou art forever: he shall cast out the enemy before thee, and will say, Destroy them. **28** Then Israel [v]the fountain of Jacob shall dwell alone in safety in a land of wheat and wine: also his heavens shall drop the dew. **29** Blessed art thou, O Israel: who is like unto thee, O people saved by the Lord, the shield of thine help, and which is the sword of thy glory? therefore [w]thine enemies shall be in subjection to thee, and thou shalt tread upon their high places.

34

1 Moses seeth all the Land of Canaan. 5 He dieth. 8. Israel weepeth. 9 Joshua succeedeth in Moses' room. 10 The praise of Moses.

1 Then Moses went from the plain of Moab up into mount [a]Nebo unto the top of Pisgah that is over against Jericho: and the Lord showed him [1]all the land of Gilead, unto Dan, **2** And all Naphtali and the land of Ephraim and Manasseh, and all the land of Judah, unto the utmost [b]sea: **3** And the South, and the plain

---

p. Deut. 32:25 They shall be slain both in the field and at home.
q. Deut. 32:27 Rejoicing to see the godly afflicted, and attributing that to themselves, which is wrought by God's hand.
r. Deut. 32:29 They would consider the felicity, that was prepared for them, if they had obeyed God.
s. Deut. 32:30 Or, delivered them to their enemies.
t. Deut. 32:33 The fruits of the wicked are as poison, detestable to God, and dangerous for man.
u. Deut. 32:36 Or, change his mind.
v. Deut. 32:36 When neither strong nor weak in a manner remain.
w. Deut. 32:40 That is, I swear, read Gen. 14:12.
x. Deut. 32:43 Whether the blood of God's people be shed for their sins or trial of their faith, he promiseth to revenge it.
y. Deut. 32:44 Or, Joshua.
z. Deut. 32:47 For I will perform my promise unto you, Isa. 55:10.
aa. Deut. 32:51 Or, of strife.
ab. Deut. 32:51 Ye were not earnest and constant to maintain mine honor.

DEUT. 32
1. Rom. 10:19
2. Rom. 12:19 / Heb. 10:30
3. 1 Sam. 2:6
4. Rom. 15:10
5. Deut. 6:6 / Deut. 11:18
6. Num. 27:12
7. Gen. 25:8
8. Num. 20:25,28 / Num. 3:38
9. Num. 20:12,13 / Num. 27:14

DEUT. 33
a. Deut. 33:1 This blessing containeth not only a simple prayer, but an assurance of the effect thereof.
b. Deut. 33:2 Meaning, infinite Angels.
c. Deut. 33:3 Hebrew, his Saints, that is, the children of Israel.
d. Deut. 33:3 As thy disciples.
e. Deut. 33:4 To us and our successors.
f. Deut. 33:5 Or, Moses.
g. Deut. 33:5 Or, Israel.
h. Deut. 33:6 Reuben shall be one of the tribes of God's people, though for his sin his honor be diminished, and his family but small.
i. Deut. 33:7 Signifying, that he should hardly obtain Jacob's promises, Gen. 49:8.
j. Deut. 33:9 He preferred God's glory to all natural affection, Exod. 32:29.
k. Deut. 33:11 He declareth that the ministers of God have many enemies, and therefore have need to be prayed for.
l. Deut. 33:12 Because the Temple should be built in Zion, which was in the tribe of Benjamin, he showeth that God should dwell with him there.
m. Deut. 33:13 Or, fountains.
n. Deut. 33:16 Which was God appearing unto Moses, Exod. 3:2.
o. Deut. 33:17 Or, strength.
p. Deut. 33:18 In thy prosperous voyages upon the Sea, Gen. 49:13.
q. Deut. 33:19 Or, mount Zion.
r. Deut. 33:19 The tribe of Zebulun.
s. Deut. 33:21 So the portion of the Gadites, and others on this side Jordan was God's, though it was not so known.
t. Deut. 33:23 Meaning, near the sea.
u. Deut. 33:25 Thou shalt be strong, or thy country full of metal. It seemeth that Simeon is left out, because he was under Judah, and his portion of his inheritance, Josh. 19:9.
v. Deut. 33:28 Who was plentiful in issue as a fountain.
w. Deut. 33:29 Thine enemies for fear shall lie and fain to be in subjection.

DEUT. 33
1. Exod. 28:30
2. Gen. 49:26

DEUT. 34
a. Deut. 34:1 Which was a part of mount Abarim, Num. 27:12.
b. Deut. 34:2 Called, Mediterranean.

of the valley of Jericho, the city of palm trees, unto Zoar. **4** And the Lord said
unto him, [2]This is the land which I sware unto Abraham, to Isaac and to Jacob,
saying, I will give it unto thy seed: I have caused thee to see it with thine eyes, but
thou shalt not go over thither. **5** So Moses the servant of the Lord died there in
the land of Moab, according to the word of the Lord. **6** And [c]he buried him in a
valley in the land of Moab over against Beth Peor, but no man knoweth of his se-
pulcher unto [d]this day. **7** Moses was now an hundred and twenty years old when
he died, his eye was not dim, nor his natural force abated: **8** And the children of
Israel wept for Moses in the plain of Moab thirty days: so the days of weeping and
mourning for Moses were ended. **9** And [e]Joshua the son of Nun was full of the
spirit of wisdom: for Moses had put his hands upon him And the children of Israel
were obedient unto him, and did as the Lord had commanded Moses. **10** But
there arose not a Prophet since in Israel like unto Moses (whom the Lord knew
[f]face to face.) **11** In all the miracles and wonders which the Lord sent him to do
in the land of Egypt before Pharaoh and before all his servants, and before all his
land, **12** And in all that mighty [g]hand and all that great fear, which Moses wrou-
ght in the sight of all Israel.

c. Deut. 34:6 To wit, the Angel of the Lord, Jude 9.
d. Deut. 34:6 That the Jews might not have occassion thereby to commit Idolatry.
e. Deut. 34:9 Hereby appeareth the favor of God, that leaveth not his Church destitute of a governor.
f. Deut. 34:10 Unto whom the Lord did reveal himself so plainly, as Exod. 33:11.
g. Deut. 34:12 Meaning, the power of God working by Moses in the wilderness.

DEUT. 34
1. Deut. 3:27
2. Gen. 12:7 / Gen. 13:15

THE BOOK OF JOSHUA

1

2 The Lord encourageth Joshua to invade the land. 4 The borders and limits of the land of the Israelites. 5 The Lord promiseth to assist Joshua, if he obey his word. 11 Joshua commandeth the people to prepare themselves to pass over Jordan, 12 and exhorteth the Reubenites to execute their charge.

1 Now after the [a]death of Moses the servant of the Lord, the Lord spake unto
Joshua the son of Nun, Moses' minister, saying, **2** Moses my servant is dead:
now therefore arise, go over this Jordan, thou, and all this people, unto the land
which I give them, that is, to the children of Israel. **3** [1]Every place that the sole
of your foot shall tread upon, have I given you, as I said unto Moses. **4** [2]From
the [b]wilderness and this Lebanon even unto the great river, the river [c]Perath: all
the land of the [d]Hittites, even unto the great [e]Sea toward the going down of the
sun, shall be your coast. **5** There shall not a man be able to withstand thee all the
days of thy life: as I was with Moses, so will I be with thee: [3]I will not leave thee,
nor forsake thee. **6** [4]Be strong and of a good courage: for unto this people shalt
thou divide the land for an inheritance, which I swore unto their fathers to give
them. **7** Only be thou strong, and [f]of a most valiant courage, that thou mayest
observe and do according to all the Law which Moses my servant hath commanded
thee: [5]thou shalt not turn away from it to the right hand, nor to the left, that thou
mayest [g]prosper whithersoever thou goest. **8** Let not this book of the Law depart
out of thy mouth, but meditate therein day and [h]night, that thou mayest observe
and do according to all that is written therein: for then shalt thou make thy way
prosperous, and then shalt thou [i]have good success. **9** Have not I commanded
thee, saying, Be strong and of a good courage, fear not, nor be discouraged? for I
the Lord thy God will be with thee whithersoever thou goest. **10** Then Joshua
commanded the officers of the people, saying, **11** Pass through the host, and
command the people, saying, Prepare you victuals: for [j]after three days ye shall pass
over this Jordan, to go in to possess the land, which the Lord your God giveth you
to possess it. **12** And unto the Reubenites, and to the Gadites, and to half the
tribe of Manasseh spake Joshua, saying, **13** [6]Remember the word, which Moses
the servant of the Lord commanded you, saying, The Lord your God hath given
you rest, and hath given you this [k]land. **14** Your wives, your children, and your
cattle shall remain in the land which Moses gave you [l]on this side Jordan: but ye
shall go over before your brethren armed, all that be men of war, and shall help
them, **15** Until the Lord have given your brethren rest as well as to you, and un-
til they also shall possess the land, which the Lord your God giveth them: then shall
ye return unto the land of your possession, and shall possess it, which land Moses
the Lord's [m]servant gave you on this side Jordan toward the sun rising. **16** Then
they answered Joshua, saying, All that thou hast commanded us, we will do, and
whithersoever thou sendest us, we will go. **17** As we obeyed Moses in all things,
[n]so will we obey thee: only the Lord thy God be with thee, as he was with Mo-
ses. **18** Whosoever shall rebel against thy commandment, and will not obey thy
words in all that thou commandest him, let him be put to death: only be strong
and of good courage.

2

1 Joshua sendeth men to spy Jericho, whom Rahab hideth. 11 She confesseth the God of Israel. 12 She requireth a sign for her deliverance. 21 The spies return to Joshua with comfortable tidings.

1 Then Joshua the son of Nun sent out of [a]Shittim two men to spy secret-
ly, saying, Go view the land, and also Jericho, and they went, and [1]came into an
[b]harlot's house, named Rahab, and lodged there. **2** Then report was made to the
King of Jericho, saying, Behold, there came men hither tonight, of the children
of Israel, to spy out the country. **3** And the king of Jericho sent unto Rahab
saying, [c]Bring forth the men that are come to thee, and which are entered into
thine house: for they be come to search out all the land. **4** (But the woman had
taken the two men, and hid them.) Therefore said she thus, There came men unto
me, but I wist not whence they were. **5** And when they shut the gate in the
dark, the men went out, whither the men went, I wot not: follow ye after them
quickly, for ye shall overtake them. **6** (But she had brought them up to the [d]ro-
of of the house, and hid them with the stalks of flax, which she had spread abro-
ad upon the roof.) **7** And certain men pursued after them, the way to Jordan,
unto the fords, and as soon as they which pursued after them, were gone out, they
shut the gate. **8** And before they were asleep, she came up unto them upon the
roof, **9** And said unto the men, I know that the Lord hath given you the land,
and that the [e]fear of you is fallen upon us, and that all the inhabitants of the land
faint because of you. **10** For we have heard how the Lord [2]dried up the water of
the red Sea [3]before you when ye came out of Egypt, and what you did unto the two
kings of the Amorites, that were on the other side Jordan, unto [4]Sihon and to Og,
whom ye utterly destroyed: **11** And when we heard it, our hearts [f]did faint, and
there remained no more [g]courage in any because of you: for [h]the Lord your God,
he is the God in heaven above, and in earth beneath. **12** Now therefore, I pray
you, swear unto me by the Lord, that as I have showed you mercy, ye will also show
mercy unto my father's house, and give me a true token, **13** And that ye will save

JOSH. 1
a. Josh. 1:1 The beginning of this book dependeth on the last chapter of Deut. which was written by Josh. as a preparation to his history.
b. Josh. 1:4 Of Zin, called Kadesh and Paran.
c. Josh. 1:4 Or, Euphrates.
d. Josh. 1:4 Meaning, the whole land of Canaan.
e. Josh. 1:4 Called Mediterranean.
f. Josh. 1:7 Or, grow stronger and stronger.
g. Josh. 1:7 He showeth wherein consisteth true prosperity, even to obey the word of God.
h. Josh. 1:8 Showing that it was not possible to govern well, without continual study of God's word.
i. Josh. 1:8 Or, govern wisely.
j. Josh. 1:11 Meaning, from the day that this was proclaimed, Josh. 3:2.
k. Josh. 1:13 Which belonged to Sihon the king of the Amorites, and Og king of Bashan.
l. Josh. 1:14 Or, beyond Jordan from Jericho.
m. Josh. 1:15 By your request, but yet by God's secret appointment, Deut. 33:21.
n. Josh. 1:17 They do not only promise to obey him so long as God is with him: but to help to punish all that rebel against him.

JOSH. 1
1. Josh. 14:9
2. Deut. 11:24
3. Heb. 13:5
4. Deut. 31:23
5. Deut. 3:32 / Deut. 28:14
6. Num. 32:20

JOSH. 2
a. Josh. 2:1 Which place was in the plain of Moab near unto Jordan.
b. Josh. 2:1 Or, taverner's house, or hostess.
c. Josh. 2:3 Though the wicked see the hand of God upon them, yet they repent not, but seek how they may by their power and policy resist his working.
d. Josh. 2:6 Meaning, upon the house: for then their houses were flat above, so that they might do their business thereupon.
e. Josh. 2:9 For so God promised, Deut. 28:7; Josh. 5:1.
f. Josh. 2:11 Or, melted.
g. Josh. 2:11 Or, spirit.

alive my father and my mother, and my brethren, and my sisters, and all that they have: and that ye will deliver our [i]souls from death. **14** And the men answered her, [j]Our life for you to die, if ye utter not this our business: and when the Lord hath given us the land, we will deal mercifully and truly with thee. **15** Then she let them down by a cord through the window: for her house was upon the town wall, and she dwelt upon the wall. **16** And she said unto them, Go you into the [k]mountain, lest the pursuers meet with you, and hide yourselves there three days, until the pursuers be returned: then afterward may ye go your way. **17** And the men said unto her, [l]We will be blameless of this thine oath which thou hast made us swear. **18** Behold, when we come into the land, thou shalt bind this cord of red thread in the window, whereby thou lettest us down, and thou shalt bring thy father and thy mother, and thy brethren, and all thy father's household home to thee. **19** And whosoever then doth go out at the doors of thine house into the street, [m]his blood shall be upon his head, and we will be guiltless: but whosoever shall be with thee in the house, his blood shall be on our head, if any hand touch him: **20** And if thou utter this our [n]matter, we will be quit of thine oath, which thou hast made us swear. **21** And she answered, According unto your words, so be it: then she sent them away, and they departed, and she bound the [o]red cord in the window. **22** And they departed, and came into the mountain, and there abode three days, until the pursuers were returned: and the pursuers sought them throughout all the way, but found them not. **23** So the two men returned, and descended from the mountain, and passed [p]over, and came to Joshua the son of Nun, and told him all things that came unto them. **24** Also they said unto Joshua, Surely the Lord hath delivered into our hands all the land: for even all the inhabitants of the country faint because of us.

3

3 Joshua commandeth them to depart when the Ark removeth. 7 The Lord promiseth to exalt Joshua before the people. 9 Joshua's exhortation to the people. 16 The waters part asunder while the people pass.

1 Then Joshua rose very early, and they removed from Shittim, and came to [a]Jordan, he, and all the children of Israel, and lodged there before they went over. **2** And after [b]three days, the officers went throughout the host, **3** And commanded the people, saying, When ye see the Ark of the covenant of the Lord your God and the Priests of the Levites bearing it, ye shall depart from your place, and go after it. **4** Yet shall there be a space between you and it, about [c]two thousand cubits by measure: ye shall not come near unto it, that ye may know the way, by the which ye shall go: for ye have not gone this way in times past. **5** (Now Joshua had said unto the people, [1]Sanctify yourselves: for tomorrow the Lord will do wonders among you.) **6** Also Joshua spake unto the Priests, saying, Take up the Ark of the covenant, and go over before the people: so they took up the Ark of the covenant, and went before the people. **7** Then the Lord said unto Joshua, This day will I begin to magnify thee in the sight of all Israel, which shall know, [2]that as I was with Moses, so will I be with thee. **8** Thou shalt therefore command the Priests that bear the Ark of the covenant, saying, When ye are come to the brink of the waters of Jordan, ye shall stand still [d]in Jordan. **9** Then Joshua said unto the children of Israel, Come hither, and hear the words of the Lord your God. **10** And Joshua said, [e]Hereby ye shall know that the living God is among you, and that he will certainly cast out before you the Canaanites, and the Hittites, and the Hivites, and the Perizzites, and the Girgashites, and the Amorites, and the Jebusites. **11** Behold, the Ark of the covenant of the Lord of all the world passeth before you into Jordan. **12** Now therefore take from among you [f]twelve men out of the tribes of Israel, out of every tribe a man. **13** And as soon as the soles of the feet of the Priests (that bear the Ark of the Lord God the Lord of all the world) shall stay in the waters of Jordan, the waters of Jordan shall be cut off: for the waters that come from above, [3]shall stand still upon an heap. **14** Then when the people were departed from their tents to go over Jordan, the Priests bearing the [4]Ark of the covenant, went before the people. **15** And as they that bare the Ark, came unto Jordan, and the feet of the Priests that bare the Ark were dipped in the brink of the water, ([5]for Jordan useth to fill all his [g]banks all the time of harvest) **16** Then the waters that came down from above, stayed and rose upon an heap, and departed far from the city of Adam that was beside Zaretan: but the waters that came down toward the Sea of the wilderness, even the salt Sea, failed and were cut off: so the people went right over against Jericho. **17** But the Priests that bare the Ark of the covenant of the Lord, stood dry within Jordan [h]ready prepared, and all the Israelites went over dry, until all the people were clean gone over through Jordan.

4

2 God commandeth Joshua to set up twelve stones in Jordan. 18 The waters return to their old course. 20 Other twelve stones are set upon Gilgal. 21 This miracle must be declared to posterity.

1 And when all the people were wholly gone [1]over Jordan (after the Lord had spoken unto Joshua, saying, **2** Take you twelve men out of the people out of every tribe a man, **3** And command you them, saying, Take you hence out of the midst of Jordan, out of the place where the Priests stood in a [a]readiness, twelve stones, which ye shall take away with you, and leave them in the [b]lodging, where you shall lodge this night) **4** Then Joshua called the twelve men, whom he had prepared of the children of Israel, out of every tribe a man, **5** And Joshua said unto them, Go over before the Ark of the Lord your God, even through the midst of Jordan, and take up every man of you a stone upon his shoulder according unto the number of the tribes of the children of Israel, **6** That this may be a sign among you, that when your [c]children shall ask their fathers in time to come, saying, What meant you by these stones? **7** Then ye may answer them, That the waters of Jordan were cut off before the Ark of the Covenant of the Lord: for when it passed through Jordan, the waters of Jordan were cut off: therefore these stones are a memorial unto the children of Israel forever. **8** Then the children of Israel did even so as Joshua had commanded, and took up twelve stones out of the midst of Jordan as the Lord had said unto Joshua, according unto the number of the tribes of the children of Israel, and carried them away with them unto the lodging, and laid them down there. **9** And Joshua set up [d]twelve stones in the midst of Jordan, in the place where the feet of the Priests, which bare the Ark of the Covenant stood, and there have they continued unto this day. **10** So the Priests, which bare the Ark, stood in the midst of Jordan, until everything was finished that the Lord had commanded Joshua to say unto the people, according to all that Moses charged Joshua: then the people hasted and went over. **11** When all the people were clean passed over, the Ark of the Lord went over also, and the Priests [e]before the people. **12** [2]And the sons of Reuben, and the sons of Gad, and half the tribe of Manasseh went over before the children of Israel armed, as Moses had charged them. **13** Even forty thousand prepared for war, went before the [f]Lord unto battle, into the plain of Jericho. **14** That day the Lord magnified Joshua in the sight of all Israel, and they [g]feared him, as they feared Moses all the days of his life. **15** And the Lord spake unto Joshua, saying, **16** Command the Priests that bear the [h]Ark of the testimony, to come up out of Jordan. **17** Joshua therefore commanded the Priests, saying, Come ye up out of Jordan. **18** And when the Priests that bare the Ark of the Covenant of the Lord, were come up out of the midst of Jordan, and as soon as the soles of the Priests' feet were set on the dry land, the waters of Jordan returned unto their place, and flowed over all the banks thereof, as they did before. **19** So the people came up out of Jordan the tenth day of the [i]first month, and pitched in Gilgal, in the East side of Jericho. **20** Also the twelve stones, which they took out of Jordan, did Joshua pitch in Gilgal. **21** And he spake unto the children of Israel, saying, When your children shall ask their fathers in time to come, and say, What mean these stones? **22** Then ye shall show your children, and say, Israel came over this Jordan on dry land: **23** For the Lord your God dried up the waters of Jordan before you, until ye were gone over as the Lord your God did the red Sea, [3]which he dried up before us, till we were gone over, **24** That all the people of the [j]world may know that the hand of the Lord is mighty, that ye might fear the Lord your God continually.

---

h. Josh. 2:11 Herein appeareth the great mercy of God, that in this common destruction he would draw a most miserable sinner to repent, and confess his Name.
i. Josh. 2:13 Or, lives.
j. Josh. 2:14 We warrant you on pain of our lives.
k. Josh. 2:16 Which was near unto the city.
l. Josh. 2:17 We shall be discharged of our oath if thou dost perform this condition that followeth: for so shalt thou and thine be delivered.
m. Josh. 2:19 He shall be guilty of his own death.
n. Josh. 2:20 So that others should think to escape by the same means.
o. Josh. 2:21 Or, scarlet colored.
p. Josh. 2:23 To wit, the river Jordan.

JOSH. 2
1. Heb. 11:31 / James 2:25
2. Exod. 14:21,22
3. Josh. 4:23
4. Num. 21:24

JOSH. 3
a. Josh. 3:1 Which according to the Hebrews was in March, and about 40 days after Moses' death.
b. Josh. 3:2 Which time was given for to prepare them victuals, Josh. 1:11.
c. Josh. 3:4 Or, a mile.
d. Josh. 3:8 Even in the channel where the stream had run, as verse 17.
e. Josh. 3:10 By this miracle in dividing the water.
f. Josh. 3:12 Which should set up twelve stones in remembrance of the benefit.
g. Josh. 3:15 Because the river was accustomed at this time to be full, the miracle is so much the greater.
h. Josh. 3:17 Either tarrying till the people were past, or as some read, sure, as though they had been upon the dry land.

JOSH. 3
1. Lev. 20:7 / Num. 11:18 / Josh. 7:13 / James 16:5
2. Josh. 1:5
3. Ps. 114:3
4. Acts 7:45
5. 1 Chron. 12:15

JOSH. 4
a. Josh. 4:3 As Josh. 3:17.
b. Josh. 4:3 Meaning, the place where they should camp.
c. Josh. 4:6 God commandeth that not only we ourselves profit by this wonderful work, but that our posterity may know the cause thereof and glorify his Name.
d. Josh. 4:9 Besides the twelve stones which were carried by the tribes and set up in Gilgal.
e. Josh. 4:11 Meaning, in the presence or sight of the people.
f. Josh. 4:13 That is, before the Ark.
g. Josh. 4:14 Or, reverenced him.
h. Josh. 4:16 Because the Ark testified God's presence, and the Tables of the Law contained therein, signified God's will toward his people.
i. Josh. 4:19 Called Abib or Nisan, containing part of March and part of April.
j. Josh. 4:24 God's benefits serve for a further condemnation to the wicked, and stir up his to reverence him, and obey him.

JOSH. 4
1. Deut. 27:2
2. Num. 32:27,29
3. Exod. 14:21,22

5 *1 The Canaanites are afraid of the Israelites. 2 Circumcision is commanded the second time. 10 The passover is kept. 12 Manna ceaseth. 13 The Angel appeareth unto Joshua.*

1 Now when all the Kings of the [a]Amorites, which were beyond Jordan Westward, and all the Kings of the Canaanites which were by the Sea, heard that the Lord had dried up the waters of Jordan before the children of Israel until they were gone over, their hearts fainted: and there was no courage in them anymore because of the children of Israel. 2 That same time the Lord said unto Joshua, [1]Make thee sharp knives, [b]and return, and circumcise the sons of Israel the second time. 3 Then Joshua made him sharp knives, and circumcised the sons of Israel in [c]the hill of the foreskins. 4 And this is the cause why Joshua circumcised all the people, even the males that came out of Egypt, because all the men of war were dead in the wilderness by the way after they came out of Egypt. 5 For all the people that came out, were circumcised: but all the people that were born in the wilderness by the way after they came out of Egypt, were [d]not circumcised. 6 For the children of Israel walked forty years in the wilderness, till all the people of the men of war that came out of Egypt, were consumed, because they obeyed not the voice of the Lord: unto whom the Lord sware that he would not show them the land, [2]which the Lord had sworn unto their fathers, that he would give us, even a land that floweth with milk and honey. 7 So their sons whom he raised up in their stead, Joshua circumcised: for they were uncircumcised, because they circumcised them not by the way. 8 And when they had made an end of circumcising all the people, they abode in the places in the camp till they [e]were whole. 9 After, the Lord said unto Joshua, This day I have taken away the [f]shame of Egypt from you: wherefore he called the name of that place, Gilgal, unto this day. 10 So the children of Israel abode in Gilgal, and kept the feast of the Passover the fourteenth day of the month at even, in the plain of Jericho. 11 And they did eat of the corn of the land, on the morrow after the Passover, unleavened bread, and parched corn in the same day. 12 And the Manna ceased on the morrow after they had eaten of the corn of the land, neither had the children of Israel Manna anymore, but did eat of the fruit of the land of Canaan that year. 13 And when Joshua was by Jericho, he lift up his eyes and looked: and behold, there stood a [3]man against him, having a sword drawn in his hand: and Joshua went unto him, and said unto him, Art thou on our side, or on our adversaries? 14 And he said, Nay, but as a captain of the host of the Lord am I now come: then Joshua fell on his face to the earth, and [g]did worship, and said unto him, What saith the Lord unto his servant? 15 And the captain of the Lord's host said unto Joshua, [4]Loose thy shoe of thy foot: for the place whereon thou standest, is holy: and Joshua did so.

6 *2 The Lord instructeth Joshua what he should do as touching Jericho. 6 Joshua commandeth the Priests and warriors what to do. 20 The walls fall. 22 Rahab is saved. 24 All is burnt save gold and metal. 26 The curse of him that buildeth the city.*

1 Now Jericho was [a]shut up, and [b]closed, [c]because of the children of Israel, none might go out nor enter in. 2 And the Lord said unto Joshua, Behold, I have given into thine hand Jericho and the king thereof, and the strong men of war. 3 All ye therefore that be men of war, shall compass the city, in going round about the city [d]once: thus shall you do six days: 4 And seven Priests shall bear seven trumpets of [e]rams' horns before the Ark: and the seventh day ye shall compass the city seven times, and the Priests shall blow with the trumpets, 5 And when they make a long blast with the ram's horn, and ye hear the sound of the trumpet, all the people shall shout with a great shout: then shall the wall of the city fall down flat, and the people shall ascend up, every man straight before him. 6 Then Joshua the son of Nun called the Priests and said unto them, Take up the Ark of the Covenant, and let seven Priests bear seven trumpets of rams' horns before the Ark of the Lord. 7 But he said unto the people, [f]Go and compass the city: and let him that is armed go forth before the Ark of the Lord. 8 And when Joshua had spoken unto the people, the seven priests bare the seven trumpets of rams' horns, and went forth before the Ark of the Lord, and blew with the trumpets, and the ark of the Covenant of the Lord followed them. 9 And the men of arms went before the priests and blew the trumpets: then the [g]gathering host came after the Ark, and they went and blew the trumpets. 10 (Now Joshua had commanded the people, saying, Ye shall not shout, neither make any noise with your voice, neither shall a word proceed out of your mouth, until the day that I say unto you, Shout, then shall ye shout.) 11 So the Ark of the Lord compassed the city, and went about it [h]once: then they returned into the host, and lodged in the camp. 12 And Joshua rose early in the morning, and the Priests bare the Ark of the Lord: 13 Also seven Priests bare seven trumpets of rams' horns, and went before the Ark of the Lord, and going blew with the trumpets: and the men of arms went before them, but the [i]gathering host came after the Ark of the Lord, as they went and blew the trumpets. 14 And the second day they compassed the city once, and returned into the host: thus they did six days. 15 And when the seventh day came, they rose early, even with the dawning of the day, and compassed the city after the same manner [j]seven times: only that day they compassed the city seven times. 16 And when the Priests had blown the trumpets the seventh time, Joshua said unto the people, Shout: for the Lord hath given you the city. 17 And the city shall be [k]an execrable thing, both it, and all that are therein, unto the Lord: only Rahab the harlot shall live, she, and all that are with her in the house: for [1]she hid the messengers that we sent. 18 Notwithstanding, be ye ware of the execrable thing, lest ye make yourselves execrable, and in taking of the [2]execrable thing, make also the host of Israel execrable, and trouble it. 19 But all silver, and gold, and vessels of brass, and iron shall be [l]consecrate unto the Lord, and shall come into the Lord's treasury. 20 So the people shouted, when they had blown trumpets: for when the people had heard the sound of the trumpets, they shouted with a great shout: and the [3]wall fell down flat: so the people went up into the city, every man straight before him: and they took the city. 21 And they utterly destroyed all that was in the cities both man and woman, young, and old, and ox, and sheep, and ass with the edge of the sword. 22 But Joshua had said unto the two men that had spied out the country, Go into the harlot's house, and bring out thence the woman, and all that she hath, [4]as ye swore to her. 23 So the young men that were spies, went in and brought out Rahab, and her father, and her mother, and her brethren, and all that she had: also they brought out all her family, and put them [m]without the host of Israel. 24 After, they burnt the city with fire, and all that was therein: only the silver and the gold, and the vessels of brass and iron, they put unto the treasure of the [n]house of the Lord. 25 So Joshua saved Rahab the harlot, and her father's household, and all that she had, and she [o]dwelt in Israel, even unto this day, because she had hid the messengers, which Joshua sent to spy out Jericho. 26 And Joshua swore at that time, saying, Cursed be the man before the Lord, that riseth up, and buildeth the city Jericho: [p]he shall lay the foundation thereof in his eldest son, and in his youngest son shall he set up the gates of it. 27 So the Lord was with Joshua, and he was famous through all the world.

7 *1 The Lord is angry with Achan. 4 They of Ai put the Israelites to flight. 6 Joshua prayeth to the Lord. 16 Joshua inquireth out him that sinned, and stoneth him and all his.*

1 But the children of Israel committed a trespass in the [a]excommunicate thing: for [1]Achan the son of Carmi, the son of Zabdi, the son of Zerah of the tribe of Judah, took of the excommunicate thing: wherefore the wrath of the Lord was kindled against the children of Israel. 2 And Joshua sent men from Jericho to [b]Ai, which is beside Beth Aven, on the East side of Bethel, and spake unto them, saying, Go up, and view the country And the men went up and viewed Ai, 3 And returned to Joshua, and said unto him, Let not all the people go up, but let as it were two or three thousand men go up, and smite Ai, and make not all the people to labor thither, for they are few. 4 So there went up thither of the people about three thousand men, and they fled before the men of Ai. 5 And the [c]men of Ai smote of them upon a thirty and six men: for they chased them from before the gate unto Shebarim, and smote them in the going down: wherefore the hearts of the people melted away like water. 6 Then Joshua rent his clothes, and fell to the earth upon his face before the Ark of the Lord, until the eventide, he,

---

JOSH. 5

- **a.** Josh. 5:1 The Amorites were on both sides of Jordan, whereof two kings were slain already on the side toward Moab.
- **b.** Josh. 5:2 For now they had left it off, about 40 years.
- **c.** Josh. 5:3 Gilgal was so called, because they were there circumcised.
- **d.** Josh. 5:5 For they looked daily to remove at the Lord's commandment, which thing they that were new circumcised, could not do without great danger.
- **e.** Josh. 5:8 For their sore was so grievous, that they were not able to remove.
- **f.** Josh. 5:9 By bringing you into this promised land, contrary to the wicked opinion of the Egyptians: or the foreskin whereby you were like to the Egyptians.
- **g.** Josh. 5:14 In that that Josh. worshippeth him, he acknowledgeth him to be God: and in that that he calleth himself the Lord's captain, he declareth himself to be Christ.

JOSH. 5

1. Exod. 4:25
2. Num. 14:23
3. Exod. 23:23
4. Exod. 3:5 / Ruth 4:7 / Acts 7:33

JOSH. 6

- **a.** Josh. 6:1 That none could go out.
- **b.** Josh. 6:1 That none could come in.
- **c.** Josh. 6:1 For fear of the Israelites.
- **d.** Josh. 6:3 Every day one.
- **e.** Josh. 6:4 That the conquest might not be assigned to man's power, but to the mercy of God, which with most weak things can overcome that which seemeth most strong.
- **f.** Josh. 6:7 This is chiefly meant by the Reubenites, Gadites, and half the tribe of Manasseh.
- **g.** Josh. 6:9 Meaning, the rearward, wherein was the standard of the tribe of Dan, Num. 10:25.
- **h.** Josh. 6:11 For that day.
- **i.** Josh. 6:13 The tribe of Dan was so called, because it marched last and gathered up whatsoever was left of others.
- **j.** Josh. 6:15 Beside every day once for the space of six days.
- **k.** Josh. 6:17 That is appointed wholly to be destroyed.
- **l.** Josh. 6:19 And therefore cannot be put to any private use, but must be first molten, and then serve for the Tabernacle.
- **m.** Josh. 6:23 For it was not lawful for strangers to dwell among the Israelites, till they were purged.
- **n.** Josh. 6:24 Meaning, the Tabernacle.
- **o.** Josh. 6:25 For she was married to Salmon prince of the tribe of Judah, Matt. 1:5.
- **p.** Josh. 6:26 He shall build it to the destruction of all his stock, which thing was fulfilled in Hiel of Bethel, 1 Kings 16:34.

JOSH. 6

1. Josh. 2:4
2. Lev. 27:21 / Num. 21:2 / Deut. 13:15-17
3. Heb. 11:30
4. Josh. 2:14 / Heb. 11:31

JOSH. 7

- **a.** Josh. 7:1 In taking that which was commanded to be destroyed.
- **b.** Josh. 7:2 This was a city of the Amorites: for there was another so called among the Amorites, Jer. 49:3. The first Ai is called Aiath, Isa. 10:28.
- **c.** Josh. 7:5 God would by this overthrow make them more earnest to search out and punish the sin committed.

and the Elders of Israel, and put dust upon their heads. **7** And Joshua said, Alas, O Lord God, wherefore hast thou brought this people over Jordan, to deliver us into the hand of the Amorites, and to destroy us? would God we had been content to dwell on the [d]other side Jordan. **8** Oh Lord what shall I say, when Israel turn their backs before their enemies? **9** For the Canaanites, and all the inhabitants of the land shall hear of it, and shall compass us, and destroy our name out of the earth: and what wilt thou do unto thy mighty [e]Name? **10** And the Lord said unto Joshua, Get thee up: wherefore liest thou thus upon thy face? **11** Israel hath sinned, and they have transgressed my covenant, which I commanded them: for they have even taken of the excommunicate thing, and have also stolen, and dissembled also, and have put it even with their own stuff. **12** Therefore the children of Israel cannot stand before their enemies: but have turned their backs before their enemies, because they be execrable: neither will I be with you anymore, except ye [f]destroy the excommunicate from among you. **13** Up therefore, sanctify the people, and say, Sanctify yourselves against tomorrow: for thus saith the Lord God of Israel, There is an execrable thing among you, O Israel, therefore ye cannot stand against your enemies, until ye have put the [g]execrable thing from among you. **14** In the morning therefore ye shall come according to your tribes, and the tribe which the Lord taketh, shall come according to the families: and the family which the Lord shall take, shall come by the households: and the household which the Lord shall take, shall come man by man. **15** And he that is [h]taken with the excommunicate thing, shall be burnt with fire, he, and all that he hath, because he hath transgressed the covenant of the Lord, and because he hath wrought folly in Israel. **16** So Joshua rose up early in the morning, and brought Israel by their tribes: and the tribe of Judah was taken. **17** And he brought the families of Judah, and took the family of the Zarhites, and he brought the family of the Zarhites, man by man, and Zabdi was taken. **18** And he brought his household, man by man, and Achan the son of Carmi, the son of Zabdi, the son of Zerah of the tribe of Judah was taken. **19** Then Joshua said unto Achan, My son, I beseech thee, give glory to the Lord God of Israel, and [i]make confession unto him, and show me now what thou hast done: hide it not from me. **20** And Achan answered Joshua, and said, Indeed I have sinned against the Lord God of Israel, and thus, and thus have I done. **21** I saw among the spoil a goodly [j]Babylonish garment, and two hundred shekels of silver, and a wedge of gold of fifty shekels weight, and I covered them, and took them: and behold, they lie hid in the earth in the midst of my tent, and the silver under it. **22** Then Joshua sent messengers, which ran unto the tent, and behold, it was hid in his tent, and the silver under it. **23** Therefore they took them out of the tent, and brought them unto Joshua, and unto all the children of Israel, and laid them before the Lord. **24** Then Joshua took Achan the [k]son of Zerah, and the silver, and the garment, and the [l]wedge of gold, and his [m]sons, and his daughters, and his oxen, and his asses, and his sheep, and his tent, and all that he had: and all Israel with him, brought them unto the valley of Achor. **25** And Joshua said, [n]In as much as thou hast troubled us, the Lord shall trouble thee this day: and all Israel threw stones at him, and burned them with fire, and stoned them with stones. **26** And they cast upon him a great heap of stones unto this day: and so the Lord turned from his fierce wrath: therefore he called the name of that place, The valley of Achor, unto this day.

8

3 The siege, 19 and winning of Ai. 29 The king thereof is hanged. 30 Joshua setteth up an Altar. 32 He writeth the Law upon stones, 35 and readeth it to all the people.

1 After, the Lord said unto Joshua, [1]Fear not, neither be thou faint hearted: take all the men of war with thee and arise, go up to Ai: behold, I have given into thine hand the king of Ai, and his people, and his city, and his land. **2** And thou shalt do to Ai and to the king thereof, as thou didst unto [2]Jericho and to the king thereof: nevertheless the spoil thereof and the [3]cattle thereof shall ye take unto you for a prey: thou shalt lie in wait against the city on the [a]back side thereof. **3** Then Joshua arose, and all the men of war to go up against Ai: and Joshua chose out thirty thousand strong men, and valiant, and sent them away by night. **4** And he commanded them, saying, Behold, ye [b]shall lie in wait against the city on the back side of the city: go not very far from the city, but be ye all in a readiness. **5** And I and all the people that are with me, will approach unto the city: and when they shall come out against us, as they did at the first time, then will we flee before them. **6** For they will come out after us, till we have brought them out of the city: for they will say, They flee before us as at the first time: so we will flee before them. **7** Then you shall rise up from lying in wait and [c]destroy the city: for the Lord your God will deliver it into your hand. **8** And when ye have taken the city, ye shall set it on fire: according to the commandment of the Lord shall ye do: behold, I have charged you. **9** Joshua then sent them forth, and they went to lie in wait, and abode between Bethel and Ai, on the West side of Ai: but Joshua lodged that night [d]among the people. **10** And Joshua rose up early in the morning, and [e]numbered the people: and he and the Elders of Israel went up before the people against Ai. **11** Also all the men of war that were with him went up and drew near, and came against the city, and pitched on the North side of Ai: and there was a valley between them and Ai. **12** And he took about five thousand men, [f]and set them to lie in wait between Bethel and Ai on the West side of the city. **13** And the people set all the host that was on the North side against the city, and the liars in wait on the West, against the city: and Joshua went the same night into the [g]midst of the valley. **14** And when the king of Ai saw it, then the men of the city hasted and rose up early, and went out against Israel to battle, he and all his people, at the time appointed, before the plain: for he knew not that any lay in wait against him on the back side of the city. **15** Then Joshua and all Israel [h]as beaten before them, fled by the way of the wilderness. **16** And all the people of the city were called together to pursue after them: and they pursued after Joshua, and were drawn away out of the city, **17** So that there was not a man left in Ai, nor in Bethel, that went not out after Israel: and they left the city open, and pursued after Israel. **18** Then the Lord said unto Joshua, [i]Stretch out the spear that is in thine hand, toward Ai: for I will give it into thine hand: and Joshua stretched out the spear that he had in his hand, toward the city. **19** And they that lay in wait, arose quickly out of their place, and ran as soon as he had stretched out his hand, and they entered into the city, and took it, and hasted, and set the city on fire. **20** And the men of Ai looked behind them, and saw it: for lo, the smoke of the city ascended up [j]to heaven, and they had no [k]power to flee this way or that way: for the people that fled to the wilderness, turned back upon the pursuers. **21** When Joshua and all Israel saw that they that lay in wait, had taken the city, and that the smoke of the city mounted up, then they turned again and slew the men of Ai. **22** Also the [l]other issued out of the city against them: so were they in the midst of Israel, these being on the one side, and the rest on the other side: and they slew them, so that they let none of them [4]remain nor escape. **23** And the King of Ai they took alive, and brought him to Joshua. **24** And when Israel had made an end of slaying all the inhabitants of Ai in the field, that is, in the wilderness where they chased them, and when they were all fallen on the edge of the sword, until they were consumed, all the Israelites returned unto Ai, and [m]smote it with the edge of the sword. **25** And all that fell that day, both of men and women, were twelve thousand, even all the men of Ai. **26** For Joshua drew not his hand back again which he had stretched out with the spear, until he had utterly destroyed all the inhabitants of Ai. **27** [5]Only the cattle and the spoil of this city, Israel took for a prey unto themselves, according unto the word of the Lord, which he commanded Joshua. **28** And Joshua burnt Ai, and made it an heap [n]forever, and a wilderness unto this day. **29** And the king of Ai he hanged on a tree, unto the evening And as soon as the sun was down, Joshua commanded [o]that they should take his carcass down from the tree, and cast it at the entering of the gate of the city, and [6]lay thereon a great heap of stones, that remaineth unto this day. **30** Then Joshua built an altar unto the Lord God of Israel, in mount Ebal, **31** As Moses the servant of the Lord had commanded the children of Israel, as it is written in the [7]book of the Law of Moses, an altar of whole stone, over which no man had lift an iron: and they offered thereon burnt offerings unto the Lord, and sacrificed peace offerings. **32** Also he wrote there upon the stones, a [p]rehearsal of the Law of Moses, which he wrote in the presence of the children of Israel. **33** And all Israel (and their Elders, and officers and their Judges stood on this side of the Ark, and on that side, before the Priests of the Levites, which bare the Ark of the covenant of the Lord) as well the stranger, as he that is born in the country: half of them were over against mount Gerizim, and half of them over against mount Ebal, [8]as Moses the servant of the Lord had commanded before, that they should bless the children of Israel. **34** Then afterward he read all the words of the Law, the blessings and cursings, according to all that is written in the book of the Law. **35** There was not a word of all that Moses had commanded,

---

d. Josh. 7:7 This infirmity of his faith showeth how we are inclined of nature to distrust.
e. Josh. 7:9 When thine enemies shall blaspheme thee and say, that thou wast not able to defend us from them.
f. Josh. 7:12 Then to suffer wickedness unpunished, is to refuse God willingly.
g. Josh. 7:13 Meaning, the man that took of the thing forbidden.
h. Josh. 7:15 That is found guilty, either by lots, or by the judgment of Urim, Num. 27:21.
i. Josh. 7:19 By declaring truth: for God is glorified when the truth is confessed.
j. Josh. 7:21 Such a rich garment as the states of Babylon did wear.
k. Josh. 7:24 Or, nephew.
l. Josh. 7:24 Some read a plate: others, a rod, and some a tongue.
m. Josh. 7:24 This judgment only appertaineth to God, and to whom he will reveal it, to man he had commanded not to punish the child for the father's fault, Deut. 24:16.
n. Josh. 7:25 He declareth that this is God's judgment because he had offended, and caused others to be slain.

JOSH. 7

1. Josh. 22:20 / 1 Chron. 2:7

JOSH. 8

a. Josh. 8:2 Meaning, on the West side, as verse 9.
b. Josh. 8:4 God would not destroy Ai by miracle, as Jericho, to the intent that other nations might fear the power and policy of his people.
c. Josh. 8:7 Or, drive out (the inhabitants) of the city.
d. Josh. 8:9 With the rest of the army.
e. Josh. 8:10 That is, viewed or mustered them, and set them in array.
f. Josh. 8:12 He sent these few, that the others which lay in ambush might not be discovered.
g. Josh. 8:13 To the intent that they in the city might the better discover his army.
h. Josh. 8:15 As they which feigned to flee for fear.
i. Josh. 8:18 Or, lift up the banner, to signify when they shall invade the city.
j. Josh. 8:20 Or, toward the heavens.
k. Josh. 8:20 Or, place.
l. Josh. 8:22 Which came out of the ambush.
m. Josh. 8:24 For the fire, which they had before set in the city, was not to consume it, but to signify unto Josh. that they were entered.
n. Josh. 8:28 That it could never be built again.
o. Josh. 8:29 According as it was commanded, Deut. 21:23.
p. Josh. 8:32 Meaning, the ten commandments, which are the sum of the whole Law.

which Joshua read not before all the Congregation of Israel, [9]as well before the [q]women and the children, as the stranger that was conversant among them.

9

1 Divers Kings assemble themselves against Joshua. 3 The craft of the Gibeonites. 15 Joshua maketh a league with them. 23 For their craft they are condemned to perpetual slavery.

1 And when all the Kings that [a]were beyond Jordan, in the mountains and in the valleys, and by all the coasts of the [b]great Sea over against Lebanon (as the Hittites, and the Amorites, the Canaanites, the Perizzites, the Hivites, and the Jebusites) heard thereof, **2** They gathered themselves together, to fight against Joshua, and against Israel with one [c]accord. **3** [1]But the inhabitants of Gibeon heard what Joshua had done unto Jericho, and to Ai. **4** And therefore they wrought craftily: for they went, and feigned themselves ambassadors, and took old sacks upon their asses, and old bottles for wine, both rent and [d]bound up, **5** And old shoes and clouted upon their feet: also the raiment upon them was old, and all their provision of bread was dried, and molded. **6** So they came unto Joshua into the host to Gilgal, and said unto him, and unto the men of Israel, We be come from a far country: now therefore make a league with us. **7** Then the men of Israel said unto the [e]Hivites, It may be that thou dwellest among us, how then can I make a league with thee? **8** And they said unto Joshua, We are thy servants Then Joshua said unto them, Who are ye, and whence come ye? **9** And they answered him, From a very far country thy servants are come for [f]the Name of the Lord thy God: for we have heard his fame and all that he hath done in Egypt, **10** And all that he hath done to the two kings of the Amorites that were beyond Jordan, to Sihon king of Heshbon, and to Og king of Bashan, which were at Ashtaroth. **11** Wherefore our Elders, and all the inhabitants of our country spake to us, saying, Take vittles [g]with you for the journey, and go to meet them, and say unto them, We are your servants: now therefore make ye a league with us. **12** This our [h]bread we took it hot with us for victuals out of our houses, the day we departed to come unto you: but now behold, it is dried, and it is molded. **13** Also these bottles of wine which we filled, were new, and lo, they be rent, and these our garments and our shoes are old, by reason of the exceeding great journey. **14** And the [i]men accepted their tale concerning their victuals, and counseled not with the mouth of the Lord. **15** So Joshua made peace with them, and made a league with them, that he would suffer them to live: also the Princes of the Congregation swore unto them. **16** But at the end of three days, after they had made a league with them, they heard that they were their neighbors, and that they dwelt among them. **17** And the children of Israel took their [j]journey, and came unto their cities the third day, and their cities were Gibeon, and Chephirah, and Beeroth and Kirjath Jearim. **18** And the children of Israel slew them not, because the Princes of the Congregation had sworn unto them by the Lord God of Israel: wherefore all the Congregation [k]murmured against the Princes. **19** Then all the Princes said unto all the Congregation, We have sworn unto them by the Lord God of Israel: now therefore we may not touch them. **20** But this we will do to them, and let them live, lest the wrath be upon us, because of the [l]oath which we swore unto them. **21** And the Princes said unto them again, Let them live, but they shall hew wood, and draw water unto all the Congregation, as the Princes appoint them. **22** Joshua then called them, and talked with them, and said, Wherefore have ye beguiled us, saying, We are very far from you, when ye dwell among us? **23** Now therefore ye are accursed, and there shall none of you be freed from being bondmen, and hewers of wood, and drawers of water for [m]the house of my God. **24** And they answered Joshua, and said, Because it was told thy servants, that the Lord thy God had [2]commanded his servant Moses to give you all the land, and to destroy all the inhabitants of the land out of your sight, therefore we were exceeding sore afraid for our lives at the presence of you, and have done this thing: **25** And behold now, we are in thine hand: do as it seemeth good and right in thine eyes to do unto us. **26** Even so did he unto them, and delivered them out of the [n]hand of the children of Israel, that they slew them not. **27** And Joshua appointed them that same day to be hewers of wood, and drawers of water for the Congregation, and for the [o]altar of the Lord unto this day, in the place which he should choose.

10

1 Five kings make war against Gibeon whom Joshua discomfiteth. 11 The Lord rained hailstones and slew many. 12 The Sun standeth at Joshua's prayer. 26 The five kings are hanged. 29 Many more cities and kings are destroyed.

1 Now when Adoni Zedek king of Jerusalem had heard how Joshua had taken Ai and had destroyed it, ([1]for as he had done to Jericho and to the king thereof, so he had done to [2]Ai and to the king thereof) and how the inhabitants of Gibeon had made peace with Israel, and were among them, **2** Then they feared exceedingly: for Gibeon was a great city, as one of the royal cities: for it was greater than Ai, and all the men thereof were mighty. **3** Wherefore [a]Adoni Zedek king of Jerusalem sent unto Hoham king of Hebron, and unto Piram king of Jarmuth, and unto Japhia king of Lachish, and unto Debir king of Eglon, saying, **4** Come up unto me, and help me, that we may smite Gibeon: for they have made peace with Joshua and with the children of Israel. **5** Therefore the five kings of the Amorites, the king of Jerusalem, the king of Hebron, the king of Jarmuth, the king of Lachish, and the king of Eglon, gathered themselves together, and went up, they with all their hosts, and besieged Gibeon, and made [b]war against it. **6** And the men of Gibeon sent unto Joshua, even to the host to Gilgal, saying, Withdraw not thine hand from thy servants: come up to us quickly, and save us, and help us: for all the kings of the Amorites, which dwell in the mountains, are gathered together against us. **7** So Joshua ascended from Gilgal, he, and all the people of war with him, and all the men of might. **8** And the Lord said unto Joshua, [c]Fear them not: for I have given them into thine hand: none of them shall stand against thee. **9** Joshua therefore came unto them suddenly: for he went up from Gilgal all the night. **10** And the Lord discomfited them before Israel, and slew them with a great slaughter at Gibeon, and chased them along the way that goeth up to Beth Horon, and smote them to Azekah, and to Makkedah. **11** And as they fled from before Israel, and were in the going down to Beth Horon, the Lord cast down great stones from heaven upon them, until Azekah, and they died: they were more that died with the [d]hailstones, than they whom the children of Israel slew with the sword. **12** Then spake Joshua to the Lord, in the day when the Lord gave the Amorites before the children of Israel, and he said in the sight of Israel, [3]Sun, stay thou in Gibeon, and thou Moon, in the valley of Aijalon. **13** And the Sun abode, and the moon stood still, until the people avenged themselves upon their enemies: (is not this written in the book of [e]Jasher?) so the Sun abode in the midst of the heaven, and hasted not to go down for a whole day. **14** And there was no day like that before it, nor after it, that the Lord heard the voice of a man: for the Lord [f]fought for Israel. **15** After, Joshua returned, and all Israel with him unto the camp to Gilgal: **16** But the five kings fled and were hid in a cave at Makkedah. **17** And it was told Joshua, saying, The five kings are found hid in a cave at Makkedah. **18** Then Joshua said, Roll great stones upon the mouth of the cave, and set men by it for to keep them. **19** But stand ye not still: follow after your enemies, and [g]smite all the hindmost, suffer them not to enter into their cities: for the Lord your God hath given them into your hand. **20** And when Joshua and the children of Israel had made an end of slaying them with an exceeding great slaughter till they were consumed, and the rest that remained of them were entered into walled cities, **21** Then all the people returned to the camp, to Joshua at Makkedah in [h]peace: no man moved his tongue against the children of Israel. **22** After, Joshua said, Open the mouth of the cave, and bring out these five kings unto me forth of the cave. **23** And they did so, and brought out those five kings unto him forth of the cave, even the king of Jerusalem, the king of Hebron, the king of Jarmuth, the king of Lachish, and the king of Eglon. **24** And when they had brought out those kings unto Joshua, Joshua called for all the men of Israel, and said unto the chief of the men of war, which went with him, Come near, set your feet upon the [i]necks of these kings, and they came near, and set their feet upon their necks. **25** And Joshua said unto them, Fear not, nor be faint hearted, but be strong and of a good courage: for thus will the Lord do to all your enemies, against whom ye fight. **26** So then Joshua smote them, and slew them, and hanged them on five trees, and they hanged still upon the trees until the evening. **27** And at the going down of the sun, Joshua gave commandment, that

---

q. Josh. 8:35 So neither young nor old, man nor woman, were exempted from hearing the word of the Lord.

JOSH. 8

1. Deut. 1:29 / Deut. 7:18
2. Josh. 6:21
3. Deut. 20:14
4. Deut. 7:2
5. Num. 31:22,26 / Josh. 8:2
6. Josh. 7:25,26
7. Exod. 20:25 / Deut. 27:5
8. Deut. 11:29 / Deut. 27:12,13
9. Deut. 31:12,13

JOSH. 9

a. Josh. 9:1 In respect of the plain of Moab.
b. Josh. 9:1 The main sea called Mediterranean.
c. Josh. 9:2 Hebrew, one mouth.
d. Josh. 9:4 Because they were all worn.
e. Josh. 9:7 For the Gibeonites and the Hivites were all one people.
f. Josh. 9:9 Even the idolaters for fear of death will pretend to honor the true God, and receive his religion.
g. Josh. 9:11 Hebrew, in your hand.
h. Josh. 9:12 The wicked lack no art, nor spare no lies to set forth their policy, when they will deceive the servants of God.
i. Josh. 9:14 Some think that the Israelites ate of their victuals, and so made a league with them.
j. Josh. 9:17 From Gilgal.
k. Josh. 9:18 Fearing lest for their fault the plague of God should have light upon them all.
l. Josh. 9:20 This doth not establish rash oaths, but showeth God's mercy toward his, which would not punish them for their fault.
m. Josh. 9:23 For the uses of the Tabernacle and of the temple when it shall be built.
n. Josh. 9:26 Who were minded to put them to death for fear of God's wrath.
o. Josh. 9:27 That is, for the service of the Temple, as verse 23.

JOSH. 9

1. 2 Sam. 21:1
2. Deut. 7:1

JOSH. 10

a. Josh. 10:3 That is, Lord of justice: so tyrants take to themselves glorious names, when indeed they be very enemies against God and all justice.
b. Josh. 10:5 So envious the wicked are, when any depart from their hand.
c. Josh. 10:8 Lest Josh. should have thought that God had sent this great power against him for his unlawful league with the Gibeonites, the Lord here strengtheneth him.
d. Josh. 10:11 So we see that all things serve to execute God's vengeance against the wicked.
e. Josh. 10:13 Some read the book of the righteous, meaning Moses: the Chaldea text readeth in the book of the Law, but it is like that it was a book thus named, which is now lost.
f. Josh. 10:14 By taking away the enemies' hearts and destroying them with hail stones.
g. Josh. 10:19 Hebrew, cut off all their train or tail.
h. Josh. 10:21 Or in safety, so that none gave them as much as an evil word.
i. Josh. 10:24 Signifying what should become of the rest of God's enemies, seeing that kings themselves were not spared.

they should take [4]them down off the trees, and cast them into the cave (wherein they had been hid) and they laid great stones upon the cave's mouth, which remain until this day. **28** And that same day Joshua took Makkedah and smote it with the edge of the sword, and the king thereof destroyed he with them, and [j]all the souls that were therein, he let none remain: for he did to the king of Makkedah, as he had done unto the king of Jericho. **29** Then Joshua went from Makkedah, and all Israel with him unto Libnah, and fought against Libnah. **30** And the Lord gave it also and the king thereof into the hand of Israel: and he smote it with the edge of the sword, and all the [k]souls that were therein: he let none remain in it: for he did unto the king thereof, as he had done unto the king of Jericho. **31** And Joshua departed from Libnah, and all Israel with him unto Lachish, and besieged it, and assaulted it. **32** And the Lord gave Lachish into the hand of Israel, which took it the second day, and smote it with the edge of the sword, and all the souls that were therein, according to all as he had done to Libnah. **33** Then Horam king of Gezer came up to help Lachish: but Joshua smote him and his people, until none of his remained. **34** And from Lachish Joshua departed unto Eglon, and all Israel with him, and they besieged it, and assaulted it. **35** And they took it the same day, and smote it with the edge of the sword, and all the souls that were therein he utterly destroyed the same day, according to all that he had done to Lachish. **36** Then Joshua went up from Eglon, and all Israel with him unto Hebron, and they fought against it. **37** And when they had taken it, they smote it with the edge of the sword, and the king thereof, and all the cities thereof, and all the souls that were therein: he left none remaining, according to all as he had done to Eglon: for he destroyed it utterly, and all the souls that were therein. **38** So Joshua returned, and all Israel with him to Debir, and fought against it. **39** And when he had taken it, and the king thereof, and all the city thereof, they smote them with the edge of the sword, and utterly destroyed all the souls that were therein, he let none remain: as he did to Hebron, so he did to Debir, and to the king thereof, as he had also done to Libnah, and to the king thereof. **40** So Joshua smote all the hill countries, and the South countries, and the valleys, and the [l]hillsides, and all their kings, and let none remain, but utterly destroyed every soul, as the Lord God of Israel had commanded. **41** And Joshua smote them from Kadesh Barnea even unto Gaza, and all the country of Goshen, even unto Gibeon. **42** And all these kings, and their land did Joshua take at [m]one time, because the Lord God of Israel fought for Israel. **43** Afterward, Joshua and all Israel with him returned unto the camp in [n]Gilgal.

11

1 Divers kings and cities, and countries overcome by Joshua. 15 Joshua did all that Moses had commanded him. 20 God hardeneth the enemies' hearts that they might be destroyed.

1 And when Jabin king of Hazor had heard this, then he [a]sent to Jobab king of Madon, and to the king of Shimron, and to the king of Achshaph, **2** And unto the kings that were by the North in the mountains and plains toward the South side of [b]Chinneroth, and in the valleys, and in the borders of Dor Westward, **3** And unto the Canaanites, both by East, and by West, and unto the Amorites, and Hittites, and Perizzites, and Jebusites in the mountains, and unto the Hivites, under [c]Hermon in the land of Mizpah. **4** And they came out, and all their hosts with them, many people, as the sand that is on the seashore, for multitude, with horses and chariots exceeding many. **5** So all these kings met together, and came and pitched together at the waters of Merom, for to fight against Israel. **6** Then the Lord said unto Joshua, Be not afraid for them: for tomorrow about this time will I deliver them all slain before Israel: thou shalt [d]hough their horses, and burn their chariots with fire. **7** Then came Joshua and all the men of war with him, against them, by the waters of Merom suddenly, and fell upon them. **8** And the Lord gave them into the hand of Israel: and they smote them, and chased them unto great Sidon, and unto [e]Misrephoth, and unto the valley of Mizpah Eastward, and smote them until they had none remaining of them. **9** And Joshua did unto them as the Lord bade him: he houghed their horses, and burnt their chariots with fire. **10** At that time also Joshua turned back, and took Hazor, and smote the King thereof with the sword: for Hazor beforetime was the head of all those kingdoms. **11** Moreover they smote all the [f]persons that were therein with the edge of the sword, utterly destroying all, leaving none alive, and he burnt Hazor with fire. **12** So all the cities of those kings, and all the kings of them did Joshua take, and smote them with the edge of the sword, and utterly destroyed them, [1]as Moses the servant of the Lord had commanded. **13** But Israel burnt none of the cities that stood still in their [g]strength, save Hazor only, that Joshua burnt. **14** And all the spoil of these cities and the cattle, the children of Israel took for their prey, but they smote every [h]man with the edge of the sword until they had destroyed them, not leaving one alive. **15** As the Lord [2]had commanded Moses his servant, so did Moses [3]command Joshua, and so did Joshua, he left nothing undone of all that the Lord had commanded Moses. **16** So Joshua took all this land of the mountains, and all the South, and all the land of Goshen, and the low country, and the plain, and the [i]mountain of Israel, and the low country of the same, **17** From the mount [j]Halak, that goeth up to Seir, even unto [k]Baal Gad in the valley of Lebanon, under mount Hermon: and all their kings he took, and smote them, and slew them. **18** Joshua made war [a] long time with all those Kings, **19** Neither was there any city that made peace with the children of Israel, [4]save those Hivites that inhabited Gibeon: all others they took by battle. **20** For it came of the Lord, to [l]harden their hearts that they should come against Israel in battle, to the intent that they should destroy them utterly, and show them no mercy, but that they should bring them to nought, as the Lord had commanded Moses. **21** And that same season came Joshua, and destroyed the Anakims out of the mountains: as out of Hebron, out of Debir, out of Anab, and out of all the mountains of Judah, and out of all the mountains of Israel: Joshua destroyed them utterly with their cities. **22** There was no Anakim left in the land of the children of Israel, only in Gaza, [m]in Gath, and in Ashdod were they left. **23** So Joshua took the whole land, according to all that the Lord had said unto Moses: and Joshua gave it for an inheritance unto Israel, [5]according to their portions through their tribes: then the land was at rest without war.

12

1, 7 What kings Joshua and the children of Israel killed on both sides of Jordan. 24 Which were in number thirty and one.

1 And these are the Kings of the land, which the children of Israel smote and possessed their land on the [a]other side Jordan toward the rising of the sun, from the river Arnon, unto mount Hermon, and all the plain Eastward. **2** [1]Sihon king of the Amorites, that dwelt in Heshbon, having dominion from Aroer, which is beside the river of Arnon, and from the middle of the river, and from half Gilead unto the river of Jabbok, in the border of the children of Ammon. **3** And from the plain unto the sea of Chinneroth Eastward, and unto the sea of the [b]plain, even the salt sea Eastward, the way to Beth Jeshimoth, and from the South under the [c]springs of [2]Pisgah. **4** They conquered also the coast of Og king of Bashan of the [3]remnant of the giants, which dwelt at Ashtaroth, and at Edrei, **5** And reigned in mount Hermon, and in Salcah, and in all Bashan, unto the border of the Geshurites, and the Maachathites, and half Gilead: even the border of Sihon king of Heshbon. **6** Moses the servant of the Lord, and the children of Israel smote them: [4]Moses also the servant of the Lord gave their land for a possession unto the Reubenites, and unto the Gadites, and to half the tribe of Manasseh. **7** These also are the kings of the country, which Joshua and the children of Israel smote on this side Jordan, Westward from Baal Gad in the valley of Lebanon, even unto the mount [d]Halak that goeth up to Seir, and Joshua gave it unto the tribes of Israel for a possession, according to their portions. **8** In the mountains, and in the valleys, and in the plains, and in the [e]hillsides, and in the wilderness, and in the South, where were the Hittites, the Amorites, and the Canaanites, the Perizzites, the Hivites, and the Jebusites. **9** [5]The King of Jericho was one: the [6]king of Ai, which is beside Bethel, one: **10** The king of Jerusalem, one: the king of Hebron, one: **11** [7]The king of Jarmuth, one: the king of Lachish, one: **12** The king of Eglon, one: the [8]king of Gezer, one: **13** The [9]king of Debir, one: the king of Geder, one: **14** The king of Hormah, one: the king of Arad, one: **15** The [10]king of Libnah, one: the king of Adullam, one: **16** The [11]king of Makkedah, one: the king of Bethel, one: **17** The king of Tappuah, one: the king of Hepher, one: **18** The king of Aphek, one: the king of Lasharon, one: **19** The king of Madon, one: the [12]king of Hazor, one: **20** The king of Shimron Meron, one: the king of Achshaph, one: **21** The king of Taanach, one: the king of Megiddo, one: **22** The king of Kedesh, one: the king of Jokneam [f]of Carmel,

---

j. Josh. 10:28 Or, every person, Josh. 6:21.
k. Josh. 10:30 Or, persons.
l. Josh. 10:40 Some read, Ashedoth, which signifieth the descents of the hills.
m. Josh. 10:42 In one battle.
n. Josh. 10:43 Where the ark was, there to give thanks for their victories.

JOSH. 10
1. Josh. 6:16,21
2. Josh. 8:3,28,29
3. Isa. 28:21
4. Deut. 21:23 / Josh. 8:29

JOSH. 11
a. Josh. 11:1 The more that God's power appeareth, the more the wicked rage against it.
b. Josh. 11:2 Which the Evangelists call the lake of Gennesaret, or Tiberias.
c. Josh. 11:3 Which was mount Sion, as Deut. 4:48.
d. Josh. 11:6 That neither they should serve to the use of war, nor the Israelites should put their trust in them.
e. Josh. 11:8 Which signifieth hot waters, or according to some, brine pits.
f. Josh. 11:11 Both men, women and children.
g. Josh. 11:13 Which were strong by situation and not hurt by war.
h. Josh. 11:14 All mankind.
i. Josh. 11:16 That is, Samaria.
j. Josh. 11:17 So called, because it was bare and without trees.
k. Josh. 11:17 Or, the valley of Gad.
l. Josh. 11:20 That is, to give them over to themselves: and therefore they could not but rebel against God and seek their own destruction.
m. Josh. 11:22 Out of the which came Goliath, 1 Sam. 17:4.

JOSH. 11
1. Num. 33:52 / Deut. 7:2
2. Exod. 34:11
3. Deut. 7:2
4. Josh. 9:3
5. Num. 26:53,55

JOSH. 12
a. Josh. 12:1 From Gilgal where Josh. camped.
b. Josh. 12:3 Or, wilderness.
c. Josh. 12:3 Or, hillsides.
d. Josh. 12:7 Read Josh. 11:17.
e. Josh. 12:8 Or, in Ashdoth.
f. Josh. 12:22 Or, near unto Carmel.

JOSH. 12
1. Num. 21:24 / Deut. 3:6
2. Deut. 3:17 / Deut. 4:49
3. Deut. 3:11 / Josh. 13:12
4. Num. 32:29 / Deut. 3:12 / Josh. 13:8
5. Josh. 6:2
6. Josh. 8:26
7. Josh. 10:13
8. Josh. 10:33
9. Josh. 10:39
10. Josh. 10:29,30
11. Josh. 10:23
12. Josh. 11:19
13. Gen. 14:1

one: **23** The king of Dor, in the country of Dor, one: the king of the [13]nations
of Gilgal, one: **24** The king of Tirzah, one All the kings were thirty and one.

13

3 The borders and coasts of the land of Canaan. 8 The possession of the Reubenites, Gadites, and of the half tribe of Manasseh. 14 The Lord is the inheritance of Levi. 22 Balaam was slain.

1 Now when Joshua was old, and [a]stricken in years, the Lord said unto him,
Thou art old and [b]grown in age, and there remaineth exceeding much land to be
[c]possessed: **2** This is the land that remaineth, all the [d]regions of the Philistines,
and all Geshuri. **3** From [e]Nilus which is [f]in Egypt, even unto the borders of
Ekron Northward: this is counted of the Canaanites, even five Lordships of the
Philistines, the Gazites, and the Ashdodites, the Ashkelonites, the Gittites, and
the Ekronites, and the Avites: **4** From the South, all the land of the Canaanites,
and the [g]cave that is beside the Sidonians, unto Aphek, and to the borders of the
Amorites: **5** And the land of the Gebalites, and all Lebanon toward the Sun ri-
sing from [h]Baal Gad under mount Hermon, until one come to Hamath. **6** All
the inhabitants of the mountains from Lebanon unto [i]Misrephoth, and all the Si-
donians, I will cast them out from before the children of Israel: only divide thou it
by lot unto the Israelites, to inherit, as I have commanded thee. **7** Now therefore
divide this land to inherit, unto the nine tribes, and to the half tribe of Manas-
seh. **8** For with half thereof the Reubenites and the Gadites have received their
inheritance, [1]which Moses gave them beyond Jordan Eastward, even as Moses the
servant of the Lord had given them. **9** From Aroer that is on the brink of the
river Arnon, and from the city that is in the midst of the [j]river, and all the plain of
Medeba unto Dibon, **10** And all the cities of Sihon king of the Amorites, which
reigned in Heshbon, unto the borders of the children of Ammon, **11** And Gi-
lead, and the borders of the Geshurites and of the Maachathites, and all mount
Hermon, with all Bashan unto Salcah: **12** All the kingdom of Og in Bashan,
which reigned in Ashtaroth and in Edrei: (who remained of [2]the rest of the gian-
ts) for these did Moses smite, and cast them out: **13** But the children of Israel
[k]expelled not the Geshurites nor the Maachathites: but the Geshurites and the
Maachathites dwell among the Israelites even unto this day. **14** Only unto the
tribe of Levi he gave none inheritance, but the sacrifices of the Lord God of Israel
are [l]his inheritance, as he said unto him. **15** Moses then gave unto the tribe of
the children of Reuben inheritance, according to their families. **16** And their co-
ast was from Aroer, that is on the brink of the river Arnon, and from the city that
is in the midst of the river, and all the plain which is by Medeba: **17** Heshbon
with all the cities thereof, that are in the plain: Dibon and [m]Bamoth Baal, and
Beth Baal Meon: **18** And Jahaza, and Kedemoth, and Mephaath: **19** Kirja-
thaim also, and Sibmah, and Zereth Shahar in the mount of [n]Emek: **20** And
Beth Peor, and [3]Ashdoth Pisgah, and Beth Jeshimoth: **21** And all the cities of
the plain, and all the kingdom of Sihon king of the Amorites, which reigned in
Heshbon, whom Moses [4]smote with the Princes of Midian, Evi and Rekem, and
Zur, and Hur, and Reba, the dukes of Sihon, dwelling in the country. **22** And
[o]Balaam the son of Beor the soothsayer did the children of Israel slay with the
sword, among them that were slain. **23** And the border of the children of Reu-
ben was Jordan with the coasts This was the inheritance of the children of Reuben
according to their families, with the cities and their villages. **24** Also Moses gave
inheritance unto the tribe of Gad, even unto the children of Gad according to their
families. **25** And their coasts were Jazer, and all the cities of Gilead, and half the
land of the children of Ammon unto Aroer, which is before Rabbah: **26** And
from Heshbon unto Ramath, Mizpah, and Betonim: and from Mahanaim unto
the borders of Debir: **27** And in the valley of Beth Haram, and Beth Nimrah,
and Succoth, and Zaphon, the rest of the kingdom of Sihon king of Heshbon unto
Jordan and the borders even unto the sea coast of Chinnereth, [p]beyond Jordan
Eastward. **28** This is the inheritance of the children of Gad, after their families,
with the cities and their villages. **29** Also Moses gave inheritance unto the half
tribe of Manasseh: and this belonged to the half tribe of the children of Manasseh
according to their families. **30** And their border was from Mahanaim, even all
Bashan, to wit, all the kingdom of Og king of Bashan, and all the towns of Jair
which are in Bashan, threescore cities, **31** And half Gilead, and Ashtaroth, and
Edrei, cities of the kingdom of Og in Bashan, [5]were given unto the [q]children of
Machir the son of Manasseh to half of the children of Machir after their fami-
lies. **32** These are the heritages, which Moses did distribute in the plain of Moab
beyond Jordan toward Jericho Eastward. **33** [6]But unto the tribe of Levi Moses
gave none inheritance: for the Lord God of Israel is their inheritance, [7]as he said
unto them.

14

1 The land of Canaan was divided among the nine tribes and the half. 6 Caleb requireth the heritage that was promised him. 13 Hebron was given him.

1 These also are the places which the children of Israel inherited in the land
of Canaan, [1]which Eleazar the Priest, and Joshua the son of Nun and the chief fa-
thers of the tribes of the children of Israel, distributed to them, **2** [2]By the lot of
their inheritance, as the Lord had commanded by the hand of Moses, to give to
the nine tribes, and the half tribe. **3** For Moses had given inheritance unto [a]two
tribes and an half tribe, beyond Jordan: but unto the Levites he gave none inheri-
tance among them. **4** For the children of Joseph were [b]two tribes, Manasseh and
Ephraim, therefore they gave no part unto the Levites in the land, save cities to
dwell in, with the suburbs of the same for their beasts and their substance. **5** [3]As
the Lord had commanded Moses, so the children of Israel did when they divided
the land. **6** Then the children of Judah came unto Joshua in Gilgal: and Ca-
leb the son of Jephunneh the Kenizzite said unto him, Thou knowest what the
Lord said unto Moses the man of God, concerning [c]thee and me in Kadesh Bar-
nea. **7** Forty years old was I, when Moses the servant of the Lord sent me from
Kadesh Barnea to espy the land, and I brought him word again, as I thought in
mine heart. **8** But my [d]brethren that went up with me, discouraged the heart of
the people: yet I followed still the Lord my God. **9** Wherefore Moses swore the
same day, saying, Certainly the land whereon thy feet have trodden, shall be thine
inheritance, and thy children's forever, because thou hast followed constantly the
Lord my God. **10** Therefore behold now, the Lord hath kept me alive, as he pro-
mised: this is the forty and fifth year since the Lord spake this thing unto Moses,
while the children of Israel wandered in the wilderness: and now lo, I am this day
four score and five years old: **11** And yet am as strong at this time, as I was when
Moses sent me: as strong as I was then, so strong am I now, either for war, or [e]for
government. **12** Now therefore give me this mountain whereof the Lord spake
in that day (for thou heardest in that day, how the [f]Anakim were there, and the
cities great and walled) [g]if so be the Lord will be with me that I may drive them
out, as the Lord said. **13** Then Joshua blessed him, and gave unto Caleb the son
of Jephunneh, Hebron for an inheritance. **14** [4]Hebron therefore became the
inheritance of Caleb the son of Jephunneh the Kenizzite, unto this day: because he
followed constantly the Lord God of Israel. **15** And the name of [5]Hebron was
before time, Kirjath Arba: which Arba was a [h]great man among the Anakim: thus
the land ceased from war.

15

1 The lot of the children of Judah, and the names of the cities and villages of the same. 13 Caleb's portion. 18 The request of Achsah.

1 This then was the lot of the tribe of the children of Judah by their fami-
lies: even [1]to the border of Edom and the wilderness of [2]Zin, Southward on the
South coast. **2** And their South border was the salt Sea coast, from the [a]point
that looketh Southward. **3** And it went out on the South side toward Maaleh
Akrabbim, and went along to Zin, and ascended up on the South side unto Ka-
desh Barnea, and went along to Hezron, and went up to Adar, and set a compass
to Karkaa. **4** From thence went it along to Azmon, and reached unto the river
of Egypt, and the end of that coast was on the West side: this shall be your South
coast. **5** Also the East border shall be the salt Sea, unto the [b]end of Jordan: and
the border on the North quarter from the point of the Sea, and from the end of
Jordan. **6** And this border goeth up to Beth Hoglah, and goeth along by the
North side of Beth Arabah: so the border from thence goeth up to the [c]stone of
Bohan the son of Reuben. **7** Again this border goeth up to Debir from the val-
ley of Achor, and Northward, turning toward Gilgal, that lieth before the going
unto Adummim, which is on the South side of the river: also this border goeth
up to the waters of [d]En Shemesh, and endeth at [3]En Rogel. **8** Then this border

---

JOSH. 13

- **a.** Josh. 13:1 Being almost an hundred and ten years old.
- **b.** Josh. 13:1 Hebrew, commen into years.
- **c.** Josh. 13:1 After that the enemies are overcome.
- **d.** Josh. 13:2 Or, borders.
- **e.** Josh. 13:3 Hebrew, Sihor.
- **f.** Josh. 13:3 Hebrew, upon the face of Egypt.
- **g.** Josh. 13:4 Or, Mearah.
- **h.** Josh. 13:5 Or, the plain of Gad.
- **i.** Josh. 13:6 Read Josh. 11:8.
- **j.** Josh. 13:9 Or, valley.
- **k.** Josh. 13:13 Because they destroyed not all as God had commanded, they that remained were snares and pricks to hurt them, Num. 33:35; Josh. 23:13; Judg. 2:3.
- **l.** Josh. 13:14 Levi shall live by the sacrifices, Num. 11:23.
- **m.** Josh. 13:17 Or, high places of Baal.
- **n.** Josh. 13:19 Or, the valley.
- **o.** Josh. 13:22 So that both they which obeyed wicked counsel and the wicked counselor perished by the just judgment of God.
- **p.** Josh. 13:27 That is, in the land of Moab.
- **q.** Josh. 13:31 Meaning, his nephews and posterity.

JOSH. 13

1. Num. 32:33 / Deut. 3:13 / Josh. 22:4
2. Deut. 3:11 / Josh. 22:4
3. Deut. 3:17
4. Num. 31:8
5. Num. 32:39
6. Josh. 18:7
7. Num. 18:20

JOSH. 14

- **a.** Josh. 14:3 As Reuben and Gad and half the tribe of Manasseh, Num. 32:33.
- **b.** Josh. 14:4 So though Levi lacked, yet were there still twelve tribes by this means.
- **c.** Josh. 14:6 Which was, that they two only should enter into the land, Num. 14:24.
- **d.** Josh. 14:8 Which were the ten other spies.
- **e.** Josh. 14:11 Hebrew, to go out and come in.
- **f.** Josh. 14:12 Or, giants.
- **g.** Josh. 14:12 This he spake of modesty, and not of doubting.
- **h.** Josh. 14:15 Either for his power or person.

JOSH. 14

1. Num. 34:17
2. Num. 26:55 / Num. 33:54
3. Num. 35:2 / Josh. 21:2,3
4. Josh. 21:11
5. Josh. 15:13

JOSH. 15

- **a.** Josh. 15:2 The Hebrew word signifieth tongue, whereby is meant either the arm of the Sea that cometh into the land, or a rock, or cape that goeth into the Sea.
- **b.** Josh. 15:5 Meaning the mouth of the river where it runneth into the salt Sea.
- **c.** Josh. 15:6 Which was a mark to part their countries.
- **d.** Josh. 15:7 Or, the fountain of the sun.

goeth up to the valley of the son of Hinnom; on the South side of the Jebusites: the same is Jerusalem Also this border goeth up to the top of the mountain that lieth before the valley of Hinnom Westward, which is by the end of the valley of [e]giants Northward. **9** So this border compasseth from the top of the mountain unto the fountain of the water of Nephtoah, and goeth out to the cities of mount Ephron: and this border draweth to Baalah which is [f]Kirjath Jearim. **10** Then this border compasseth from Baalah Westward unto mount Seir, and goeth along unto the side of mount Jearim, which is Chesalon on the North side: it cometh down to Beth Shemesh, and goeth to Timnah. **11** Also this border goeth out unto the side of Ekron Northward: and this border draweth to Shicron, and goeth along to mount Baalah, and stretcheth unto Jabneel: and the ends of this coast are unto the [g]Sea. **12** And the West border is to the great sea: so this border shall be the bounds of the children of Judah round about, according to their families. **13** And unto Caleb the son of Jephunneh did Joshua give a part among the children of Judah, as the Lord commanded him, even [4]Kirjath Arba of the father of Anak which is in Hebron. **14** And Caleb [h]drove thence three sons of Anak, Sheshai, and Ahiman, and Talmai, the sons of Anak. **15** And he went up thence to the inhabitants of Debir: and the name of Debir beforetime was Kirjath Sepher. **16** Then Caleb said, He that smiteth Kirjath Sepher, and taketh it, even to him will I give Achsah my daughter to wife. **17** And Othniel the son of Kenaz, the [i]brother of Caleb took it: and he gave him Achsah his daughter to wife. **18** And as she went in to him, she moved him, to ask of her father a field: [j]and she lighted off her ass, and Caleb said unto her, What wilt thou? **19** Then she answered, [k]Give me a blessing: for thou hast given me the South country: [l]give me also springs of water And he gave her the springs above, and the springs beneath. **20** This shall be the inheritance of the tribe of the children of Judah according to their families. **21** And the utmost cities of the tribe of the children of Judah, toward the coasts of Edom Southward were Kabzeel, and Eder, and Jagur, **22** And Kinah, and Dimonah, and Adadah, **23** And Kedesh, and Hazor, and Ithnan, **24** Ziph, and Telem, and Bealoth, **25** And Hazor, Hadattah, and Kerioth, Hezron (which is Hazor.) **26** Amam, and Shema, and Moladah, **27** And Hazar, Gaddah, and Heshmon, and Beth Pelet, **28** And Hazar Shual, and Beersheba, and Bizjothjah, **29** Baalah, and Ijim, and Ezem, **30** And Eltolad, and Chesil, and [m]Hormah, **31** And Ziklag, and Madmannah, and Sansannah, **32** And Lebaoth, and Shilhim, and Ain, and Rimmon: all these cities are twenty-nine with their villages. **33** In the low country were Eshtaol, and Zorah, and Ashnah. **34** And Zanoah, and En Gannim, Tappuah, and Enam, **35** Jarmuth, and Adullam, Socoh, and Azekah, **36** And Sharaim, and Adithaim, and Gederah, and Gederothaim: fourteen cities with their villages. **37** Zenan, and Hadashah, and Migdal Gad, **38** And Dilean, and Mizpah, and Joktheel, **39** Lachish, and Bozkath, and Eglon, **40** And Cabbon, and Lahmas, and Kithlish, **41** And Gederoth, Beth Dagon, and Naamah, and Makkedah: sixteen cities with their villages. **42** Libnah, and Ether, and Ashan, **43** And Jiphtah, and Ashnah, and Nezib, **44** And Keilah, and Achzib, and Mareshah: nine cities with their villages. **45** Ekron with her [n]towns and her villages, **46** From Ekron, even unto the Sea, all that lieth about Ashdod with their villages. **47** Ashdod with her towns and her villages: Gaza with her towns and her villages unto the [o]river of Egypt, and the great Sea was their coast. **48** And in the mountains were Shamir, and Jattir, and Sochoh, **49** And Dannah, and [p]Kirjath Sannah (which is Debir.) **50** And Anab, and Eshtemoh, and Anim, **51** And Goshen, and Holon, and Giloh: eleven cities with their villages. **52** Arab, and Dumah, and Eshean, **53** And Janum, and Beth Tappuah, and Aphekah, **54** And Humtah, and [5]Kirjath Arba, (which is Hebron) and Zior: nine cities with their villages, **55** Maon, Carmel, and Ziph, and Juttah, **56** And Jezreel, and Jokdeam, and Zanoah, **57** Kain, Gibeah, and Timnah: ten cities with their villages. **58** Halhul, Beth Zur, and Gedor, **59** And Maarath, and Beth Anoth, and Eltekon: six cities with their villages. **60** Kirjath Baal, which is Kirjath Jearim, and Rabbah: two cities with their villages. **61** In the wilderness were Beth Arabah, Middin, and Secacah, **62** And Nibshan, and the [q]city of salt, and En Gedi: five cities with their villages. **63** Nevertheless, the Jebusites that were the inhabitants of Jerusalem, could not the children of Judah cast [r]out, but the Jebusites dwell with the children of Judah at Jerusalem unto this day.

16

1 The lot or part of Ephraim. 10 The Canaanites dwelled among them.

1 And the lot fell to the [a]children of Joseph from Jordan by Jericho unto the water of Jericho Eastward, and to the wilderness that goeth up from Jericho by the mount Bethel: **2** And goeth out from Bethel to [1]Luz, and runneth along unto the borders of Archi Ataroth, **3** And goeth down Westward to the coast of Japhlet, unto the coast of Beth Horon the nether: and to Gezer, and the ends [b]thereof are at the Sea. **4** So the children of Joseph; Manasseh and Ephraim [c]took their inheritance. **5** Also the borders of the children of Ephraim according to their families, even the borders of their inheritance on the East side were Ataroth Addar, unto Beth Horon the upper. **6** And this border goeth out to the Sea unto Michmethath on the North side, and this border returneth Eastward unto Taanath Shiloh, and passeth it on the East side unto Janohah, **7** And goeth down from Janohah unto Ataroth, and Naarah, and cometh to Jericho, [d]and goeth out at Jordan. **8** And this border goeth from Tappuah Westward unto the river Kanah, and the ends thereof are at the Sea: this is the inheritance of the tribe of the children of Ephraim by their families. **9** And the [e]separate cities for the children of Ephraim were among the inheritance of the children of Manasseh: all the cities with their villages. **10** And they cast not out the Canaanite that dwelt in Gezer, but the Canaanite dwelt among the Ephraimites unto this day, and served under tribute.

17

1 The portion of the half tribe of Manasseh. 3 The daughters of Zelophehad. 13 The Canaanites are become tributaries. 14 Manasseh and Ephraim require a greater portion of heritage.

1 This was also the lot of the tribe of Manasseh: for he was the firstborn of Joseph, to wit, of Machir the [1]firstborn of Manasseh, and the father of Gilead: now because he was a man of war, he had Gilead and Bashan. **2** And also [2]of the [a]rest of the sons of Manasseh by their families, even of the sons of Abiezer, and of the sons of Helek, and of the sons of Asriel, and of the sons of Shechem, and of the sons of Hepher, and of the sons of Shemida: these were the males of Manasseh, the son of Joseph according to their families. **3** [3]But Zelophehad the son of Hepher, the son of Gilead, the son of Machir, the son of Manasseh, had no sons, but daughters: and these are the names of his daughters, Mahlah, and Noah, Hoglah, Milcah and Tirzah: **4** Which came before Eleazar the Priest, and before Joshua the son of Nun, and before the princes, saying, The Lord commanded Moses to give us an inheritance among our [b]brethren: therefore according to the commandment of the Lord, he gave them an inheritance among the brethren of their father. **5** And there fell ten portions to [c]Manasseh, beside the land of Gilead and Bashan, which is on the other side of Jordan, **6** Because the daughters of Manasseh did inherit among his sons: and Manasseh's other sons had the land of Gilead. **7** So the borders of Manasseh were from Asher to Michmethath that lieth before Shechem, and this border goeth on the right hand, even to the inhabitants of En Tappuah. **8** The land of Tappuah belonged to Manasseh, but [d]Tappuah beside the border of Manasseh belongeth to the sons of Ephraim. **9** Also this border goeth down unto the [e]river Kanah Southward to the river: these cities of Ephraim are among the cities of Manasseh: and the border of Manasseh is on the North side of the river, and the ends of it are at the [f]Sea, **10** The South pertaineth to Ephraim, and the North to Manasseh, and the sea is his border: and they met together in [g]Asher Northward, and in Issachar Eastward. **11** And Manasseh had in Issachar and in Asher, Beth Shean, and her towns, and Ibleam, and her towns, and the inhabitants of Dor with the towns thereof, and the inhabitants of En Dor with the towns thereof, and the inhabitants of Taanach with her towns, and the inhabitants of Megiddo with the towns of the same, even three countries. **12** Yet the children of Manasseh [h]could not destroy those cities, but the Canaanites dwelled still in that land. **13** Nevertheless, when the children of Israel were strong, they put the Canaanites under tribute, but cast them not out wholly. **14** Then the children of Joseph spake unto Joshua, saying, Why hast thou given me but one lot, and one portion to inherit, seeing I am a great people, forasmuch as the Lord hath [i]blessed me hitherto? **15** Joshua then answered them, If thou be much people, get thee up to the woods, and cut trees for thyself there in the land of the Perizzites, and of the giants, [j]if mount Ephraim be too narrow for thee. **16** Then the children of Joseph said, The mountain will not be enough for us: and all the Canaanites that dwell in the low country have chariots of iron, as well they in Beth Shean, and in

---

e. Josh. 15:8 Hebrew, Rephaim.
f. Josh. 15:9 Or, the city of wood.
g. Josh. 15:11 Meaning, toward Syria.
h. Josh. 15:14 This was done after the death of Josh., Judg. 1:10, 20.
i. Josh. 15:17 Or, cousins.
j. Josh. 15:18 Because her husband tarried too long.
k. Josh. 15:19 Or, grant me this petition.
l. Josh. 15:19 Because her country was barren, she desired of her father a field that had springs, Judg. 1:14, 15.
m. Josh. 15:30 Which before was called Zephath, Judg. 1:17.
n. Josh. 15:45 Hebrew, daughters.
o. Josh. 15:47 Meaning, Nilus, as Josh. 13:3.
p. Josh. 15:49 Which is also called Kirjath Sepher, verse 15.
q. Josh. 15:62 Of this city the salt sea hath his name.
r. Josh. 15:63 That is, utterly, though they slew the most part, and burnt their city, Judg. 1:8.

JOSH. 15

1. Num. 34:3
2. Num. 33:36
3. 1 Kings 2:9
4. Josh. 14:15
5. Josh. 14:15

JOSH. 16

a. Josh. 16:1 That is, to Ephraim and his children: for Manasseh's portion followeth.
b. Josh. 16:3 Of their inheritance.
c. Josh. 16:4 Severally, first Ephraim, and then Manasseh.
d. Josh. 16:7 For so far the coasts reach.
e. Josh. 16:9 Because Ephraim's tribe was far greater than Manasseh, therefore he had more cities.

JOSH. 16

1. Judg. 1:26

JOSH. 17

a. Josh. 17:2 For the other half tribe had their portion beyond Jordan.
b. Josh. 17:4 Among them of our tribe.
c. Josh. 17:5 In the land of Canaan: five to the males: and other five to the daughters of Zelophehad.
d. Josh. 17:8 Meaning, the city itself.
e. Josh. 17:9 Or, the brook of reeds.
f. Josh. 17:9 That is, toward the main sea.
g. Josh. 17:10 In the tribe of Asher, and tribe of Issachar.
h. Josh. 17:12 For at the first they lacked courage, and after agreed with them on condition, contrary to God's commandment.
i. Josh. 17:14 According to my father Jacob's prophecy, Gen. 48:19.
j. Josh. 17:15 If this mount be not large enough, why dost not thou get more by destroying God's enemies, as he hath commanded?

the towns of the same, as they in the valley of Jezreel. **17** And Joshua spake unto
the house of Joseph, to Ephraim and to Manasseh, saying, Thou art a great people,
and hast great power, and shalt not have one lot. **18** Therefore the mountain
shall be thine: for it is a wood, and thou shalt cut it down: and the ends of it shall
be thine, [k]and thou shalt cast out the Canaanites, though they have iron chariots,
and though they be strong.

18

1 The Tabernacle set in Shiloh. 4 Certain are sent to divide the land to the other seven tribes. 11 The lot of the children of Benjamin.

1 And the whole Congregation of the children of Israel came together at Shi-
loh: for they set up the [a]Tabernacle of the Congregation there, after the land was
subject unto them. **2** Now there remained among the children of Israel seven
tribes, to whom [b]they had not divided their inheritance. **3** Therefore Joshua said
unto the children of Israel, how long are you so slack to enter and possess the land
which the Lord God of your fathers hath given you? **4** Give from among you
for every tribe three men, that I may send them, and that they may rise and walk
through the land, and distribute it according to [c]their inheritance, and return to
me. **5** And that they may divide it unto them into seven parts, (Judah shall abi-
de in his coast at the South, and the house of Joseph shall [d]stand in their coasts
at the North.) **6** Ye shall describe the land therefore into seven parts, and shall
bring them hither to me, and I will cast lots for you here before the [e]Lord our
God. **7** But the Levites shall have no part among you: for the [f]Priesthood of the
Lord is their inheritance: also Gad and Reuben and half the tribe of Manasseh have
received their inheritance beyond Jordan Eastward, which Moses the servant of the
Lord gave them. **8** Then the men arose, and went their way, and Joshua charged
them that went to describe the land, saying, Depart, and go through the land, and
[g]describe it, and return to me, that I may here cast lots for you before the Lord in
Shiloh. **9** So the men departed, and passed through the land, and described it
by cities into seven parts in a book, and returned to Joshua into the camp at Shi-
loh. **10** Then Joshua [h]cast lots for them in Shiloh before the Lord, and there Jo-
shua divided the land unto the children of Israel, according to their portions. **11**
And the lot of the tribe of the children of Benjamin came forth according to their
families, and the cost of their lot lay [i]between the children of Judah, and the chil-
dren of Joseph. **12** And their coast on the North side was from Jordan, and
the border went up to the side of Jericho on the North part, and went up throu-
gh the mountains Westward, and the ends thereof are in the wilderness of Beth
Aven: **13** And this border goeth along from thence to Luz, even to the South side
of Luz (the same is [j]Bethel) and this border descendeth to Ataroth Addar, near the
mount that lieth on the South side of Beth Horon the nether. **14** So the border
turneth, and compasseth the corner of the Sea Southward, from the mount that
lieth before Beth Horon Southward: and the ends thereof are at Kirjath Baal (which
is Kirjath Jearim) a city of the children of Judah: this is the West quarter. **15** And
the South quarter is from the end of Kirjath Jearim, and this border goeth out
[k]Westward, and cometh to the fountain of waters of Nephtoah. **16** And this
border descendeth at the end of the mountain, that lieth before the valley of Ben
Hinnom, which is in the valley of the [l]giants Northward, and descendeth into the
valley of Hinnom by the side of [m]Jebus Southward, and goeth down to En Ro-
gel, **17** And compasseth from the North, and goeth forth to [n]En Shemesh, and
stretcheth to Geliloth, which is toward the going up unto Adummim, and goeth
down to the [1]stone of Bohan the son of Reuben. **18** So it goeth along to the
side over against the plain Northward, and goeth down into the plain. **19** After,
this border goeth along to the side of Beth Hoglah Northward: and the ends the-
reof, that is, of the border, reach to the point of the salt Sea Northward, and to the
[o]end of Jordan Southward: this is the South coast. **20** Also Jordan is the border
of it on the East side: this is the inheritance of the children of Benjamin by the
coasts thereof round about, according to their families. **21** Now the cities of
the tribe of the children of Benjamin, according to their families, are Jericho, and
Beth Hoglah, and the valley of Keziz, **22** And Beth Arabah, and Zemaraim, and
Bethel, **23** And Avim, and Parah, and Ophrah, **24** And Chephar, Haammoni,
and Ophni, and Gaba: twelve cities with their villages: **25** Gibeon, and Ramah,
and Beeroth, **26** And Mizpah, and Chephirah, and Mozah, **27** And Rekem,
and Irpeel, and Taralah, **28** And Zelah, Eleph, and Jebus, (which is [p]Jerusalem)
Gibeath, and Kirjath: fourteen cities with their villages: this is the inheritance of
the children of Benjamin, according to their families.

19

1 The portion of Simeon, 10 Of Zebulun, 17 Of Issachar, 24 Of Asher, 32 Of Naphtali, 40 Of Dan. 49 The possession of Joshua.

1 And the second lot came out to Simeon, even for the tribe of the children
of Simeon, according to their families: and their inheritance was in the [a]midst of
the inheritance of the children of Judah. **2** Now they had in their inheritan-
ce Beersheba, and Sheba, and Moladah, **3** And Hazar Shual, and Balah, and
Ezem, **4** And Eltolad, and Bethul, and Hormah, **5** And Ziklag, and Beth Mar-
caboth, and Hazar Susah, **6** And Beth Lebaoth, and Sharuhen: thirteen cities
with their villages. **7** Ain, Rimmon, and Ether, and Ashan: four cities with their
villages. **8** And all the villages that were round about these cities, unto Baalath
Beer, and [b]Ramah, Southward: this is the inheritance of the tribe of the children
of Simeon, according to their families. **9** Out of the portion of the children of
Judah came the inheritance of the children of Simeon: for the part of the children
of Judah was too [c]much for them: therefore the children of Simeon had their inhe-
ritance within their inheritance. **10** Also the third lot arose for the children of
Zebulun, according to their families: and the coasts of their inheritance came to
Sarid, **11** And their border goeth up [d]Westward, even to Maralah, and reacheth
to Dabbasheth, and meeteth with the river that lieth before Jokneam, **12** And
turneth from Sarid Eastward toward the Sun rising unto the border of Chisloth
Tabor, and goeth out to Daberath, and ascendeth to Japhia, **13** And from then-
ce goeth along Eastward toward the Sun rising to Gath Hepher, to Eth Kazin, and
goeth forth to Rimmon, and turneth to Neah. **14** And this border compasseth it
on the North side to Hannathon, and the ends thereof are in the valley of Jiphthah
El, **15** And Kattath, and Nahallal, and Shimron, and Idalah, and [e]Bethlehem:
twelve cities with their villages. **16** This is the inheritance of the children of
Zebulun, according to their families, that is, these cities and their villages. **17**
The fourth lot came out to Issachar, even for the children of Issachar, according
to their families. **18** And their coast was Jezreel, and Chesulloth, and Shu-
nem, **19** And Haphraim, and Shion, and Anaharath, **20** And Rabbith, and
Kishion, and Abez, **21** And Remeth, and [f]En Gannim, and En Haddah, and
Beth Pazzez. **22** And this coast reacheth to Tabor, and Shahazimah, and Beth
Shemesh, and the ends of their coast reach to Jordan: sixteen cities with their villa-
ges. **23** This is the inheritance of the tribe of the children of Issachar according
to their families: that is, the cities and their villages. **24** Also the fifth lot came
out for the tribe of the children of Asher according to their families. **25** And
their coast was Helkath, and Hali, and Beten, and Achshaph, **26** And Alam-
melech, and Amad, and Mishal, and came to Carmel Westward, and to Shihor
Libnath, **27** And turneth toward the Sun rising to Beth Dagon, and cometh to
[g]Zebulun, and to the valley of Jiphthah El, toward the North side of Beth Emek,
and Neiel, and goeth out on the left side of Cabul, **28** And to Ebron, and Rehob,
and Hammon, and Kanah, unto great Sidon. **29** Then the coast turneth to Ra-
mah and to the strong city of [h]Zor, and this border turneth to Hosah, and the ends
thereof are at the Sea from Hebel to Achzib, **30** Ummah also and Aphek, and
Rehob: two and twenty cities with their villages. **31** This is the inheritance of the
tribe of the children of Asher, according to their families: that is, these cities and
their villages. **32** The sixth lot came out to the children of Naphtali, even to the
children of Naphtali according to their families. **33** And their coast was from
[i]Heleph, and from Allon in Zaanannim, and Adami Nekeb, and Jabneel, even to
Lakkum, and the ends thereof are at Jordan. **34** So this coast turneth Westward
to Aznoth Tabor, and goeth out from thence to Hukkok, and reacheth to Zebulun
on the South side, and goeth to Asher on the West side, and to Judah [j]by Jordan
toward the sun rising. **35** And the strong cities are Ziddim, Zer, and Hammath,
Rakkath, and [k]Chinnereth, **36** And Adamah, and Ramah, and Hazor, **37** And
Kedesh, and Edrei, and En Hazor, **38** And Iron, and Migdal El, Horem, and
Beth Anath, and Beth Shemesh: nineteen cities with their villages. **39** This is
the inheritance of the tribe of the children of Naphtali according to their fami-
lies: that is, the cities and their villages. **40** The seventh lot came out for the
tribe of the children of Dan, according to their families. **41** And the coast of
their inheritance was Zorah, and Eshtaol, and Ir Shemesh, **42** And Shaalabbin,

---

k. Josh. 17:18 So that thou shalt enlarge thy portion thereby.

JOSH. 17

1. Gen. 41:51 / Gen. 46:20 / Gen. 50:23 / Num. 32:39
2. Num. 26:29
3. Num. 26:33 / Num. 27:1 / Num. 36:2,11

JOSH. 18

a. Josh. 18:1 For they had now removed it from Gilgal, and set it up in Shiloh.
b. Josh. 18:2 As Eleazar, Josh., and the heads of the tribes had done to Judah, Ephraim, and half of Manasseh.
c. Josh. 18:4 That is, into seven portions, to every tribe one.
d. Josh. 18:5 For these had their inheritance already appointed.
e. Josh. 18:6 Before the Ark of the Lord.
f. Josh. 18:7 That is, the sacrifices and offerings, Josh. 13:14.
g. Josh. 18:8 By writing the names of every country and city.
h. Josh. 18:10 That everyone should be content with God's appointment.
i. Josh. 18:11 Their inheritance bordered upon Judah and Joseph.
j. Josh. 18:13 Which was in the tribe of Ephraim: another Bethel was in the tribe of Benjamin.
k. Josh. 18:15 Or, to the sea.
l. Josh. 18:16 Or, Rephaim.
m. Josh. 18:16 Or, Jerusalem.
n. Josh. 18:17 Which is in the tribe of Ephraim.
o. Josh. 18:19 To the very strait, where the river runneth into the salt sea.
p. Josh. 18:28 Which was not wholly in the tribe of Benjamin, but part of it was also in the tribe of Judah.

JOSH. 18

1. Josh. 15:6

JOSH. 19

a. Josh. 19:1 According to Jacob's prophecy, that he should be scattered among the other tribes, Gen. 49:7.
b. Josh. 19:8 Or, Ramath Negeb.
c. Josh. 19:9 But this large portion was given them by God's providence to declare their increase in time to come.
d. Josh. 19:11 Meaning, toward the great Sea.
e. Josh. 19:15 There was another Bethlehem in the tribe of Judah.
f. Josh. 19:21 There was another city of this name in the tribe of Judah: for under divers tribes certain cities had all one name, and were distinct by the tribe only.
g. Josh. 19:27 Joineth to the tribe of Zebulun, which lay more Eastward.
h. Josh. 19:29 Which was Tyre, a strong city in the sea.
i. Josh. 19:33 These cities were in the country of Zaanannim.
j. Josh. 19:34 Or, even unto Jordan.
k. Josh. 19:35 Of the which the lake of Gennesaret had his name.

and Aijalon, and Jethlah, 43 And Elon, and Timnah, and Ekron, 44 And El-
tekeh, and Gibbethon, and Baalath, 45 And Jehud, and Bene Berak, and Gath
Rimmon, 46 And Me Jarkon, and Rakkon, with the border that lieth before [l]Ja-
pho. 47 But the coast of the children of Dan fell out too little for them: therefore
the children of Dan went up to [m]fight against Leshem, and took it, and smote it
with the edge of the sword, and possessed it, and dwelt therein, and called Leshem,
[1]Dan after the name of Dan their father. 48 This is the inheritance of the tribe
of the children of Dan according to their families: that is, these cities and their vil-
lages. 49 When they had made an end of dividing the land by the coasts thereof,
then the children of Israel gave an inheritance unto Joshua the son of Nun among
them. 50 According to the word of the Lord they gave him the city which he
asked, even [2]Timnath Serah in mount Ephraim: and he built the city and dwelt
therein. 51 [3]These are the heritages which Eleazar the Priest, and Joshua the son
of Nun, and the chief fathers of the tribes of the children of Israel divided by lot in
Shiloh before the Lord at the door of the Tabernacle of the Congregation: so they
made an end of dividing the country.

20

2 The Lord commandeth Joshua to appoint cities of refuge. 3 The use thereof, 7 and their names.

1 The Lord also spake unto Joshua, saying, 2 Speak to the children of Israel,
and say, [1]Appoint you cities of refuge, whereof I spake unto you by the hand of
Moses, 3 That the slayer that killeth any person [a]by ignorance, and unwittingly,
may flee thither, and they shall be your refuge from the avenger of blood. 4 And
he that doth flee unto one of those cities, shall stand at the entering of the gate
of the city, and shall show his cause [b]to the Elders of the city: and they shall re-
ceive him into the city unto them, and give him a place, that he may dwell with
them. 5 And if the [c]avenger of blood pursue after him, they shall not deliver the
slayer into his hand, because he smote his neighbor ignorantly, neither hated he
him beforetime: 6 But he shall dwell in that city until he stand before the Con-
gregation in [d]judgment, [2]or until the death of the high Priest that shall be in those
days: then shall the slayer return, and come unto his own city, and unto his own
house, even unto the city from whence he fled. 7 Then they appointed Kedesh
in [e]Galilee in mount Naphtali, and Shechem in mount Ephraim, and Kirjath Arba,
(which is Hebron) in the mountain of Judah. 8 And on the other side Jordan
toward Jericho Eastward, they appointed [3]Bezer in the wilderness upon the plain,
out of the tribe of Reuben, and Ramoth in Gilead, out of the tribe of Gad, and Go-
lan in Bashan, out of the [f]tribe of Manasseh. 9 These were the cities appointed
for all the children of Israel, and for the stranger that sojourned among them, that
whosoever killed any person ignorantly, might flee thither, and not die by the hand
of the avenger of blood, until he stood before the [g]Congregation.

21

3 The cities given to the Levites, 41 in number eight and forty. 44 The Lord according to his promise gave the children of Israel rest.

1 Then came the [a]principal fathers of the Levites unto Eleazar the Priest, and
unto Joshua the son of Nun, and unto the chief fathers of the tribes of the children
of Israel, 2 And spake unto them at Shiloh in the land of Canaan, saying, [1]The
Lord commanded [b]by the hand of Moses, to give us cities to dwell in, with the
suburbs thereof for our cattle. 3 So the children of Israel gave unto the Levites,
out of their inheritance at the commandment of the Lord these cities with their
suburbs. 4 And the lot came out for the families of the [c]Kohathites: and the chil-
dren of Aaron the Priest, which were of the Levites, had by lot, out of the tribe of
Judah, and out of the tribe of Simeon, and out of the tribe of Benjamin [d]thirteen
cities. 5 And the rest of the children of Kohath had by lot out of the families of
the tribe of Ephraim, and out of the tribe of Dan, and out of the half tribe of Ma-
nasseh, ten cities. 6 Also the children of Gershon had by lot out of the families of
the tribe of Issachar, and out of the tribe of Asher, and out of the tribe of Naphtali,
and out of the half tribe of Manasseh in Bashan, thirteen cities. 7 The children
of Merari according to their families had out of the tribe of Reuben, and out of the
tribe of Gad, and out of the tribe of Zebulun, twelve cities. 8 So the children of
Israel gave by lot unto the Levites these cities with their suburbs, as the Lord had
commanded by the hand of Moses. 9 And they gave out of the tribe of the chil-
dren of Judah, and out of the tribe of the children of Simeon, these cities which are
here named. 10 And they were the children of [e]Aaron being of the families of
the Kohathites, and of the sons of Levi, (for theirs was the first lot.) 11 So they
gave them Kirjath-arba of the father of Anak (which is Hebron) in the mountain of
Judah, with the suburbs of the same round about it. 12 (But the land of the city,
and the villages thereof, gave they to [2]Caleb the son of Jephunneh to be his posses-
sion.) 13 Thus they gave to the [f]children of Aaron the Priest, a city of refuge for
the slayer, even Hebron with her suburbs, and Libnah with her suburbs, 14 And
Jattir with her suburbs, and Eshtemoa, and her suburbs, 15 And Holon with
her suburbs, and Debir with her suburbs, 16 And Ain with her suburbs, and
Juttah with her suburbs, Beth Shemesh with her suburbs: nine cities out of tho-
se two tribes. 17 And out of the tribe of Benjamin they gave Gibeon with her
[g]suburbs, Geba with her suburbs, 18 Anathoth with her suburbs, and Almon
with her suburbs: four cities. 19 All the cities of the children of Aaron Priests,
were thirteen cities with their suburbs. 20 But to the families of the children
of Kohath of the Levites, [h]which were the rest of the children of Kohath (for the
cities of their lot were out of the tribe of Ephraim.) 21 They gave them the city
of refuge for the slayer, [i]Shechem with her suburbs in mount Ephraim, and Gezer
with her suburbs, 22 And Kibzaim with her suburbs, and Beth Horon with her
suburbs: four cities. 23 And out of the tribe of Dan, Eltekeh with her suburbs,
Gibbethon with her suburbs, 24 Aijalon with her suburbs, Gath Rimmon with
her suburbs: four cities. 25 And out of the [j]half tribe of Manasseh, Tanach with
her suburbs, and Gath Rimmon with her suburbs: two cities. 26 All the cities
for the other families of the children of Kohath were ten with their suburbs. 27
Also unto the children of Gershon of the families of the Levites, they gave out of
the half tribe of Manasseh, the city of refuge for the slayer, [k]Golan in Bashan with
her suburbs, and Be Eshterah with her suburbs: two cities. 28 And out of the
tribe of Issachar, Kishon with her suburbs, Daberath with her suburbs, 29 Jar-
muth with her suburbs, En Gannim with her suburbs: four cities. 30 And out of
the tribe of Asher, Mishal with her suburbs, Abdon with her suburbs, 31 Helka-
th with her suburbs, and Rehob with her suburbs: four cities. 32 And out of
the tribe of Naphtali, the city of refuge for the slayer, Kedesh in [l]Galilee with her
suburbs, and Hammoth Dor with her suburbs, and Kartan with her suburbs: three
cities. 33 All the cities of the Gershonites according to their families, were thirte-
en cities with their suburbs. 34 Also unto the families of the children of Merari
the [m]rest of the Levites, they gave out of the tribe of Zebulun, Jokneam with her
suburbs, and Kartah with her suburbs, 35 Dimnah with her suburbs, Nahalal
with her suburbs: four cities. 36 And out of the tribe of Reuben, [n]Bezer with her
suburbs, and Jahaz with her suburbs, 37 Kedemoth with her suburbs, and Me-
phaath with her suburbs: four cities. 38 And out of the tribe of Gad they gave for
a city of refuge for the slayer, Ramoth in Gilead with her suburbs, and Mahanaim
with her suburbs, 39 Heshbon with her suburbs, and Jazer with her suburbs:
four cities in all. 40 So all the cities of the children of Merari according to their
families (which were the rest of the families of the Levites) were by their lot, twelve
cities. 41 And all the cities of the Levites [o]within the possession of the children
of Israel, were eight and forty with their suburbs. 42 These cities lay every one
severally with their suburbs round about them: so were all these cities. 43 So the
Lord gave unto Israel all the land, which he had sworn to give unto their fathers:
and they possessed it, and dwelt therein. 44 Also the Lord gave them rest round
about according to all that he had sworn unto their fathers: and there stood not a
man of all their enemies before them: for the Lord delivered all their enemies into
their hand. 45 [3]There failed nothing of all the good things, which the Lord had
said unto the house of Israel, but all came to pass.

22

1 Reuben, Gad, and the half tribe of Manasseh are sent again to their possessions. 10 They build an altar for a memorial. 15 The Israelites reprove them. 21 Their answer for defense of the same.

1 Then [a]Joshua called the Reubenites, and the Gadites, and the half tribe of
Manasseh, 2 And said unto them, Ye have kept all that Moses the servant of
the Lord [b]commanded you, and have obeyed my voice in all that I commanded

---

l. Josh. 19:46 Called Joppa.
m. Josh. 19:47 According as Jacob had prophesied, Gen. 49:17.

JOSH. 19
1. Judg. 18:29
2. Josh. 24:30
3. Num. 34:17

JOSH. 20
a. Josh. 20:3 At unawares, and bearing him no grudge.
b. Josh. 20:4 Hebrew, in the ears of the Elders.
c. Josh. 20:5 That is, the nearest kinsman of him that is slain.
d. Josh. 20:6 Till his cause were proved.
e. Josh. 20:7 Or, Galilee.
f. Josh. 20:8 Out of the half tribe of Manasseh beyond Jordan.
g. Josh. 20:9 Before the Judges.

JOSH. 20
1. Exod. 21:13 / Num. 35:6,11,14 / Deut. 19:2
2. Num. 35:15
3. Deut. 4:43 / 1 Chron. 6:78

JOSH. 21
a. Josh. 21:1 Or, the chief of the fathers.
b. Josh. 21:2 By Moses, by whose ministry God showed his power.
c. Josh. 21:4 He meaneth them that were Priests: for some were but Levites.
d. Josh. 21:4 Every tribe gave more or fewer cities according as their inheritance was great or little, Num. 35:8.
e. Josh. 21:10 For Aaron came of Kohath, and therefore the Priests' office remained in that family.
f. Josh. 21:13 That is, the Priest of the family of the Kohathites, of whom Aaron was chief.
g. Josh. 21:17 The suburbs were a thousand cubits from the wall of the cities round about, Num. 35:4.
h. Josh. 21:20 That were not Priests.
i. Josh. 21:21 Hebron and Shechem were the two cities of refuge under the Kohathites.
j. Josh. 21:25 Which dwelt in Canaan.
k. Josh. 21:27 Golan and Kadesh were the cities of refuge under the Gershonites.
l. Josh. 21:32 Or, Galilee.
m. Josh. 21:34 They are here called the rest, because they are last numbered, and Merari was the younger brother, Gen. 46:11.
n. Josh. 21:36 Bezer and Ramoth were the cities of refuge under the Merarites and beyond Jordan, Josh. 20:8.
o. Josh. 21:41 Thus according to Jacob's prophecy they were scattered throughout the country, which God used to this end, that his people might be instructed in the true religion by them.

JOSH. 21
1. Num. 35:2
2. Josh. 14:14 / 1 Chron. 6:56
3. Josh. 23:14,15

JOSH. 22
a. Josh. 22:1 After that the Israelites enjoyed the land of Canaan.
b. Josh. 22:2 Which was to go armed before their brethren, Num. 32:29.

you: **3** You have not forsaken your brethren this long season unto this day, but
have diligently kept the commandment of the Lord your God. **4** And now the
Lord hath given rest unto your brethren, as he promised them: therefore now re-
turn ye, and go to your tents, to the land of your possession, which Moses the
servant of the Lord hath [1]given you beyond Jordan. **5** But take diligent heed,
to do the commandment and Law, which Moses the servant of the Lord com-
manded you: that is, [2]that ye [c]love the Lord your God, and walk in all his ways,
and keep his commandments, and cleave unto him, and serve him with all your
heart, and with all your soul. **6** So Joshua [d]blessed them, and sent them away,
and they went unto their tents. **7** Now unto one half of the tribe of Manasseh
Moses had given a possession in Bashan: and unto the other half thereof gave Jo-
shua among their brethren on this side Jordan Westward: therefore when Joshua
sent them away unto their tents, and blessed them, **8** Thus he spake unto them,
saying, Return with much riches unto your tents, and with a great multitude of
cattle, with silver and with gold, with brass and with iron, and with great abun-
dance of raiment: divide the spoil of your enemies with your [e]brethren. **9** So
the children of Reuben, and the children of Gad, and half the tribe of Manasseh
returned, and departed from the children of Israel from Shiloh (which is in the
land of Canaan) to go unto the country of Gilead to the land of their possession,
which they had obtained according to the word of the Lord by the hand of Mo-
ses. **10** And when they came unto the [f]borders of Jordan (which are in the land
of Canaan) then the children of Reuben, and the children of Gad, and the half
tribe of Manasseh, built [g]there an altar by Jordan, a great altar to see too. **11**
When the children of Israel heard say, Behold, the children of Reuben, and the
children of Gad, and the half tribe of Manasseh have built an altar in the forefront
of the land of Canaan, upon the borders of Jordan at the passage of the children
of Israel: **12** When the children of Israel heard it, then the whole Congregation
of the children of Israel gathered them together at Shiloh, to go up [h]to war against
them. **13** Then the children of Israel sent unto the children of Reuben, and to
the children of Gad, and to the half tribe of Manasseh into the land of Gilead,
Phinehas the son of Eleazar the Priest, **14** And with him ten princes, of every
chief house a prince, according to all the tribes of Israel: for every one was chief of
their father's household among the [i]thousands of Israel. **15** So they went unto
the children of Reuben, and to the children of Gad, and to the half tribe of Ma-
nasseh, unto the land of Gilead, and spake with them, saying, **16** Thus saith [j]the
whole Congregation of the Lord, What transgression is this that ye have transgres-
sed against the God of Israel, to turn away this day from the Lord, in that ye have
built you an altar for to rebel this day against the Lord? **17** Have we too little
for the wickedness of [3]Peor, whereof we are not [k]cleansed unto this day, though
a plague came upon the Congregation of the Lord? **18** Ye also are turned away
this day from the Lord: and seeing ye rebel today against the Lord, even tomorrow
he will be wroth with all the Congregation of Israel. **19** Notwithstanding, if the
land of your possession be [l]unclean, come ye over unto the land of the possession
of the Lord, wherein the Lord's Tabernacle dwelleth, and take possession among
us: but [m]rebel not against the Lord, nor rebel not against us in building you an
altar, beside the altar of the Lord our God. **20** Did not Achan the son of Zerah
trespass grievously in the execrable thing, and wrath fell on [4]all the Congregation
of Israel? and this man alone [n]perished not in his wickedness. **21** Then the chil-
dren of Reuben, and the children of Gad, and half the tribe of Manasseh answe-
red, and said unto the heads over the thousands of Israel, **22** The Lord God of
gods, the Lord God of gods, he knoweth, and Israel himself shall know: if by re-
bellion, or by transgression against the Lord we have done it, save thou us not this
day. **23** If we have built us an altar to return away from the Lord, either to offer
thereon burnt offering, or meat offering, or to offer peace offerings thereon, let the
Lord [o]himself require it: **24** And if we have not rather done it for fear of this
thing, saying, In time to come your children might say unto our children, What
have ye to do with the Lord God of Israel? **25** For the Lord hath made Jordan a
border between us and you, ye children of Reuben and of Gad: therefore ye have
no part in the Lord: so shall your children make our children [p]cease from fearing
the Lord. **26** Therefore we said, We will now go about to make us an altar, not
for burnt offering, nor for sacrifice, **27** But it shall be a [5]witness between us and
you, and between our generations after us, to execute the service of the Lord before
him, in our burnt offerings, and in our sacrifices, and in our peace offerings, and
that your children should not say to our children in time to come, Ye have no part
in the Lord. **28** Therefore said we, If so be that they should so say to us, or to
our [q]generations in time to come, then will we answer, Behold the fashion of the
altar of the Lord, which our fathers made, not for burnt offering, nor for sacrifi-
ce, but it is a witness between us and you. **29** God forbid, that we should rebel
against the Lord, and turn this day away from the Lord, to build an altar for burnt
offering, or for meat offering, or for sacrifice, save the altar of the Lord our God
that is before his Tabernacle. **30** And when Phinehas the Priest, and the prin-
ces of the Congregation and heads over the thousands of Israel, which were with
him, heard the words that the children of Reuben, and children of Gad, and the
children of Manasseh spake, [r]they were well content. **31** And Phinehas the son
of Eleazar the Priest said unto the children of Reuben, and to the children of Gad,
and to the children of Manasseh, This day we perceive, that the Lord is [s]among
us, because ye have not done this trespass against the Lord: now ye have [t]delivered
the children of Israel out of the hand of the Lord. **32** Then Phinehas the son
of Eleazar the Priest with the princes, returned from the children of Reuben, and
from the children of Gad, out of the land of Gilead, unto the land of Canaan, to
the children of Israel, and brought them answer. **33** And the saying pleased the
children of Israel: and the children of Israel [u]blessed God, and [v]minded not to go
against them in battle for to destroy the land, wherein the children of Reuben and
Gad dwelt. **34** Then the children of Reuben, and the children of Gad called the
altar [w]Ed: for it shall be a witness between us, that the Lord is God.

23

2 Joshua exhorteth the people, that they join not themselves to the Gentiles, 7 that they name not their idols. 14 The promise if they fear God, 15 and threatenings, if they forsake him.

1 And a long season after that the Lord had given rest unto Israel from all
their enemies round about, and Joshua was old, and [a]stricken in age, **2** Then
Joshua called all Israel, and their Elders, and their Heads, and their Judges, and
their officers, and said unto them, I am old, and stricken in age. **3** Also ye have
seen all that the Lord your God hath done unto all these nations [b]before you, how
the Lord your God himself hath fought for you. **4** Behold, I have [c]divided unto
you by lot these nations that remain, to be an inheritance according to your tribes,
from Jordan, with all the nations that I have destroyed, even unto the great Sea
[d]Westward. **5** And the Lord your God shall expel [e]them before you, and cast
them out of your sight, and ye shall possess their land, as the Lord your God hath
said unto you. **6** Be ye therefore of a valiant courage to observe and do all that is
written in the book of the Law of Moses, [1]that ye turn not there from to the right
hand nor to the left, **7** Neither company with these nations: that is, with them
that are [f]left with you, neither [2]make mention of the name of their gods, [g]nor cause
to swear by them, neither serve them, nor bow unto them: **8** But stick fast unto
the Lord your God, as ye have done unto this day. **9** For the Lord hath cast out
before you great nations and mighty, and no man hath stood before your face hi-
therto. **10** [3]One man of you shall chase a thousand: for the Lord your God he
fighteth for you, as he hath promised you. **11** Take good heed therefore unto
[h]yourselves, that ye love the Lord your God. **12** Else, if ye go back, and clea-
ve unto the rest of these nations: that is, of them that remain with you, and shall
[i]make marriages with them, and [j]go unto them, and they to you, **13** Know ye
for certain, that the Lord your God will cast out no more of these nations from
before you: [4]but they shall be a snare and destruction unto you, and a whip on
your sides, and thorns in your [k]eyes, until ye perish out of this good land, which
the Lord your God hath given you. **14** And behold, this day do I [l]enter into the
way of all the world, and ye know in all your [m]hearts and in all your souls, that
[5]nothing hath failed of all the good things which the Lord your God promised you,
but all are come to pass unto you: nothing hath failed thereof. **15** Therefore as
all [n]good things are come upon you, which the Lord your God promised you, so
shall the Lord bring upon you every [o]evil thing, until he have destroyed you out
of this good land, which the Lord your God hath given you. **16** When ye shall

---

c. Josh. 22:5 He showeth wherein consisteth the fulfilling of the Law.
d. Josh. 22:6 He commanded them to God, and prayed for them.
e. Josh. 22:8 Which remained at home and went not to the war, Num. 31:27; 1 Sam. 30:24.
f. Josh. 22:10 Hebrew, Geliloth, which country also was called Canaan, because the Amorites dwelling there were called Canaanites.
g. Josh. 22:10 That is, beyond Jordan: for sometimes the whole country on both sides of Jordan is meant by Canaan.
h. Josh. 22:12 Such now was their zeal, that they would rather lose their lives, than suffer the true religion to be changed or corrupted.
i. Josh. 22:14 Or, multitude.
j. Josh. 22:16 Not only of the princes, but also of the common people.
k. Josh. 22:17 Meaning, God is not fully pacified, forasmuch as no punishment can be sufficient for such wickedness and idolatry.
l. Josh. 22:19 In your judgment.
m. Josh. 22:19 To use any other service than God hath appointed, is to rebel against God, 1 Sam. 15:23.
n. Josh. 22:20 Signifying, that if many suffered for one man's fault, for the fault of many, all should suffer.
o. Josh. 22:23 Let him punish us.
p. Josh. 22:25 Or, to turn back from the true God.
q. Josh. 22:28 They signify a wonderful care that they bare toward their posterity, that they might live in the true service of God.
r. Josh. 22:30 Hebrew, it was good in their eyes.
s. Josh. 22:31 By preserving and governing us.
t. Josh. 22:31 Whom if ye had offended; he would have punished with you.
u. Josh. 22:33 Or, praised.
v. Josh. 22:33 Hebrew, said.
w. Josh. 22:34 Or, witness, as verse 27.

JOSH. 22
1. Num. 32:35 / Josh. 13:8
2. Deut. 10:12
3. Num. 25:4
4. Josh. 7:1,5
5. Gen. 31:48 / Josh. 22:34

JOSH. 23
a. Josh. 23:1 Hebrew, commen into years.
b. Josh. 23:3 Your eyes bearing witness.
c. Josh. 23:4 Or, overthrown those nations.
d. Josh. 23:4 Hebrew, at the sunset.
e. Josh. 23:5 Which yet remain and are not overcome, as Josh. 13:2.
f. Josh. 23:7 And not yet subdued.
g. Josh. 23:7 Let not the Judges admit an oath which any shall swear by their idols.
h. Josh. 23:11 Hebrew, souls.
i. Josh. 23:12 Or, be of their affinity.
j. Josh. 23:12 Or, have conversation with them.
k. Josh. 23:13 Meaning, they shall be a continual grief unto you, and so the cause of your destruction.
l. Josh. 23:14 I die according to the course of nature.
m. Josh. 23:14 Most certainly.
n. Josh. 23:15 Or, promises.
o. Josh. 23:15 Or, threatenings, as Josh. 24:20.

[p]transgress the Covenant of the Lord your God, which he commanded you, and shall go and serve other gods, and bow yourselves to them, then shall the wrath of the Lord wax hot against you, and ye shall perish quickly out of the good land which he hath given you.

24

2 Joshua rehearseth God's benefits, 14 and exhorteth the people to fear God. 25 The league renewed between God and the people. 29 Joshua dieth. 32 The bones of Joseph are buried. 33 Eleazar dieth.

1 And Joshua assembled again all the [a]tribes of Israel to Shechem, and called the Elders of Israel, and their heads, and their Judges, and their officers, and they presented themselves before [b]God. **2** Then Joshua said unto all the people, Thus saith the Lord God of Israel, [1]Your fathers dwelt beyond the [c]flood in old time, even Terah the father of Abraham, and the father of Nachor, and served other gods. **3** And I took your father Abraham from beyond the flood, and brought him through all the land of Canaan, and multiplied his seed, and [2]gave him Isaac. **4** And I gave unto Isaac, [3]Jacob and [4]Esau: and I gave unto Esau mount Seir, to possess it: but [5]Jacob and his children went down into Egypt. **5** [6]I sent Moses also and Aaron, and I plagued Egypt: and when I had so done among them, I brought you out. **6** So I [7]brought your fathers out of Egypt, and ye came unto the Sea, and the Egyptians pursued after your fathers with chariots and horsemen unto [8]the red Sea. **7** Then they cried unto the Lord, and he put [d]a darkness between you and the Egyptians, and brought the Sea upon them, and covered them: so your eyes have seen what I have done in Egypt: also ye dwelt in the wilderness a [e]long season. **8** After, I brought you into the land of the Amorites, which dwelt beyond Jordan, [9]and they fought with you: but I gave them into your hand, and ye possessed their country, and I destroyed them out of your sight. **9** [10]Also Balak the son of Zippor king of Moab, arose and warred against Israel, and sent to Balaam the son of Beor for to curse you, **10** But I would not hear Balaam: therefore he blessed you, and I delivered you out of his hand. **11** And ye went over Jordan, and came unto Jericho, and the [f]men of Jericho fought against you, the Amorites, and the Perizzites, and the Canaanites, and the Hittites, and the Girgashites, the Hivites, and the Jebusites, and I delivered them into your hand. **12** And I sent [11]hornets before you, which cast them out before you, even the two kings of the Amorites, and not with thy sword, nor with thy bow. **13** And I have given you a land, wherein ye did not labor, and cities which ye built not, and ye dwell in them, and eat of the vineyards and olive trees, which ye planted not. **14** Now therefore [g]fear the Lord, and serve him in uprightness and in truth, and put away the gods, which your fathers served beyond the flood, and in Egypt, and serve ye the Lord. **15** And [h]if it seem evil unto you to serve the Lord, choose you this day whom ye will serve, whether the gods which your fathers served (that were beyond the flood) or the gods of the Amorites, in whose land ye dwell: [i]but I and mine house will serve the Lord. **16** Then the people answered and said, God forbid, that we should forsake the Lord, to serve other gods. **17** For the Lord our God, he brought us and our fathers out of the land of Egypt, from the house of bondage, and he did those great miracles in our sight, and preserved us in all the way that we went, and among all the people through whom we came. **18** And the Lord did cast out before us all the people, even the Amorites which dwelt in the land: therefore will we also serve the Lord, [j]for he is our God. **19** And Joshua said unto the people, Ye cannot serve the Lord: for he is an holy God: he is a jealous God: he will not pardon your iniquity nor your sins. **20** If ye forsake the Lord and serve strange gods, [12]then he will return and bring evil upon you, and consume you, after that he hath done you good. **21** And the people said unto Joshua, Nay, but we will serve the Lord. **22** And Joshua said unto the people, Ye are witnesses [k]against yourselves, that ye have chosen you the Lord, to serve him: and they said, We are witnesses. **23** Then put away now, said he, the strange [l]gods which are among you, and bow your hearts unto the Lord God of Israel. **24** And the people said unto Joshua, The Lord our God will we serve, and his voice will we obey. **25** So Joshua [m]made a covenant with the people the same day, and gave them an ordinance and law in Shechem. **26** And Joshua wrote these words in the book of the Law of God and took a great stone, and pitched it there under an [n]oak that was in the Sanctuary of the Lord. **27** And Joshua said unto all the people, Behold, this stone shall be a witness unto us: for it [o]hath heard all the words of the Lord which he spake with us: it shall be therefore a witness against you, lest you deny your God. **28** Then Joshua let the people depart, every man unto his inheritance. **29** And after these things, Joshua the son of Nun, the servant of the Lord died, being an hundred and ten years old. **30** And they buried him in the border of his inheritance in [13]Timnath Serah, which is in mount Ephraim, on the North side of mount Gaash. **31** And Israel [p]served the Lord all the days of Joshua, and all the days of the Elders that overlived Joshua, and which had known all the works of the Lord that he had done for Israel. **32** And the [14]bones of Joseph, which the children of Israel brought out of Egypt, buried they in Shechem in a parcel of ground, which Jacob bought of [15]the sons of Hamor the father of Shechem, for an hundred pieces of silver, and the children of Joseph had them in their inheritance. **33** Also Eleazar the son of Aaron died, whom they buried in [q]the hill of Phinehas his son, which was given him in mount Ephraim.

---

p. Josh. 23:16 He showeth that no evil can come unto man, except he offend God by disobedience.

JOSH. 23

1. Deut. 5:32 / Deut. 28:14
2. Ps. 16:4
3. Lev. 26:8 / Deut. 32:30
4. Exod. 23:33 / Num. 33:55 / Deut. 7:16
5. Josh. 21:45

JOSH. 24

a. Josh. 24:1 That is, the nine tribes and the half.
b. Josh. 24:1 Before the Ark which was brought to Shechem, when they went to bury Joseph's bones.
c. Josh. 24:2 Euphrates in Mesopotamia, Gen. 11:26.
d. Josh. 24:7 Or, a cloud.
e. Josh. 24:7 Even forty years.
f. Josh. 24:11 Because it was the chief city, under it he containeth all the country: else they of the city fought not.
g. Josh. 24:14 This is the true use of God's benefits, to learn thereby to fear and serve him with an upright conscience.
h. Josh. 24:15 Hebrew, if it be evil in your sight.
i. Josh. 24:15 This teacheth us that if all the world would go from God, yet every one of us particularly is bound to cleave unto him.
j. Josh. 24:18 How much more are we bound to serve God in Christ, by whom we have received the redemption of our souls?
k. Josh. 24:22 If you do the contrary, your own mouths shall condemn you.
l. Josh. 24:23 Out of your hearts and otherwise.
m. Josh. 24:25 By joining God and the people together: also he repeated the promises and threatenings out of the Law.
n. Josh. 24:26 Or, elm.
o. Josh. 24:27 Rather than man's dissimulation should not be punished, the dumb creatures shall cry for vengeance.
p. Josh. 24:31 Such are the people commonly as their rulers are.
q. Josh. 24:33 Hebrew, Gibeath Phinehas.

JOSH. 24

1. Gen. 11:31
2. Gen. 21:2
3. Gen. 25:26
4. Gen. 36:8
5. Gen. 46:6
6. Exod. 3:10
7. Exod. 12:37
8. Exod. 14:9
9. Num. 21:29
10. Num. 22:5 / Deut. 23:4
11. Exod. 23:28 / Deut. 7:20 / Josh. 11:20
12. Josh. 23:15
13. Gen. 19:50 / Judg. 2:9
14. Gen. 50:15 / Exod. 13:19
15. Gen. 33:19

THE BOOK OF JUDGES

1 *After Joshua was dead, Judah was constituted captain. 6 Adoni-Bezek is taken. 14 The request of Achsah. 16 The children of Keni. 23 The Canaanites are made tributaries, but not destroyed.*

1 After that Joshua was dead, the children of Israel [a]asked the Lord, saying, [b]Who shall go up for us against the Canaanites to fight first against them? **2** And the Lord said, Judah shall go up: behold, I have given the land into his hand. **3** And Judah said unto Simeon his [c]brother, Come up with me into my lot, that we may fight against the Canaanites: and I likewise will go with thee into thy lot: so Simeon went with him. **4** Then Judah went up, and the Lord delivered the Canaanites and the Perizzites into their hands, and they slew of them in Bezek ten thousand men. **5** And they found [d]Adoni-Bezek in Bezek: and they fought against him, and slew the Canaanites, and the Perizzites. **6** But Adoni-Bezek fled, and they pursued after him, and caught him, and [e]cut off the thumbs of his hands and of his feet. **7** And Adoni-Bezek said, Seventy Kings having the thumbs of their hands and of their feet cut off, gathered bread under my table: as I have done, so God hath rewarded me, so they brought him to Jerusalem, and there he died. **8** (Now the children of Judah had fought against Jerusalem, and hath taken it and smitten it with the edge of the sword, and had set the [f]city on fire.) **9** Afterward also the children of Judah went down to fight against the Canaanites, that dwelt in the mountain, and toward the South, and in the low country. **10** And Judah went against the Canaanites that dwelt in Hebron, which Hebron beforetime was called [1]Kirjath Arba: and they slew [g]Sheshai, and Ahiman, and Talmai. **11** And from thence he went to the inhabitants of Debir, and the name of Debir in old time was Kirjath Sepher. **12** And Caleb said, He that smiteth Kirjath Sepher, and taketh it, even to him will I give Achsah my daughter to wife. **13** And Othniel the son of Kenaz Caleb's younger brother took it, to whom he gave Achsah his daughter to wife. **14** And when she came to him, she moved him to ask of her father a field, [h]and she lighted off her ass, and Caleb said unto her, What wilt thou? **15** And she answered him, Give me a blessing: for thou hast given me a South country, give me also Springs of water: and Caleb gave her the springs above, and the springs beneath. **16** And the children of [i]Keni Moses' father-in-law went up out of the city of the palm trees with the children of Judah, into the wilderness of Judah, that lieth in the South of Arad, and went and dwelt among the people. **17** But Judah went with Simeon his brother, and they slew the Canaanites that inhabited Zephath, and utterly destroyed it, and called the name of the city [2]Hormah. **18** Also Judah took [j]Gaza with the coasts thereof, and Ashkelon with the coasts thereof, and Ekron with the coasts thereof. **19** And the Lord was with Judah, and he possessed the mountains: for he could not drive out the inhabitants of the valleys, because they had chariots of iron. **20** And they gave Hebron unto Caleb, as [3]Moses had said, and he expelled thence the three sons of Anak. **21** But the children of Benjamin did not cast out the Jebusites, that [k]inhabited Jerusalem: therefore the Jebusites dwell with the children of Benjamin in Jerusalem unto this day. **22** They also that were of the house of Joseph, went up to Bethel, and the Lord was with them, **23** And the house of Joseph caused to view Bethel (and the name of the city beforetime was [4]Luz.) **24** And the spies saw a man come out of the city, and they said unto him, Show us, we pray thee, the way into the city, [5]and we will show thee mercy. **25** And when he had showed them the way into the city, they smote the city with the edge of the sword, but they let the man and all his household depart. **26** Then the man went into the land of the Hittites, and built a city, and called the name thereof Luz, which is the name thereof unto this day. **27** [6]Neither did Manasseh destroy Beth Shean with her towns, nor Taanach with her towns, nor the inhabitants of Dor with her towns, nor the inhabitants of Ibleam with her towns, neither the inhabitants of Megiddo with her towns: [l]but the Canaanites dwelled still in that land. **28** Nevertheless when Israel was strong, they put the Canaanites to tribute, and expelled them not wholly. **29** [7]Likewise Ephraim expelled not the Canaanites that dwelt in Gezer, but the Canaanites dwelt in Gezer among them. **30** Neither did [m]Zebulun expel the inhabitants of Kitron, nor the inhabitants of Nahalol, but the Canaanites dwelt among them, and became tributaries. **31** Neither did Asher cast out the inhabitants of Acco, nor the inhabitants of Sidon, nor of Ahlab, nor of Achzib, nor of Helbah, nor of Aphik, nor of Rehob, **32** But the Asherites dwelt among the Canaanites the inhabitants of the land: for they did not drive them [n]out. **33** Neither did Naphtali drive out the inhabitants of Beth Shemesh, nor the inhabitants of Beth Anath, but dwelt among the Canaanites the inhabitants of the land: nevertheless the inhabitants of Beth Shemesh, and of Beth Anath became tributaries unto them. **34** And the Amorites [o]drove the children of Dan into the mountain: so that they suffered them not to come down to the valley. **35** And the Amorites [p]dwelt still in mount Heres in Aijalon, and in Shaalbim, and when the [q]hand of Joseph's family prevailed, they became tributaries: **36** And the coast of the Amorites was from Maaleh-Akrabbim, even from [r]Sela and upward.

2 *1 The Angel rebuketh the people, because they had made peace with the Canaanites. 11 The Israelites fell to idolatry after Joshua's death. 14 They are delivered into the enemies' hands: 16 God delivereth them by Judges. 21 Why God suffered idolaters to remain among them.*

1 And an [a]Angel of the Lord came up from Gilgal to Bochim, and said, I made you to go up out of Egypt, and have brought you unto the land which I had sworn unto your fathers, and said, I will never break my covenant with you. **2** [1]Ye also shall make no covenant with the inhabitants of this land, [2]but shall break down their altars: but ye have not obeyed my voice. Why have ye done this? **3** Wherefore, I said also, I will not cast them out before you, but they shall be [3]as thorns unto your sides, and their gods shall be your [b]destruction. **4** And when the Angel of the Lord spake these words unto all the children of Israel, the people lifted up their voice, and wept. **5** Therefore they called the name of that place, [c]Bochim, and offered sacrifices there unto the Lord. **6** Now when Joshua had [d]sent the people away, the children of Israel went every man into his inheritance, to possess the land. **7** And the people had served the Lord all the days of Joshua, and all the days of the Elders that outlived Joshua, which had seen all the great [e]works of the Lord that he did for Israel. **8** But Joshua the son of Nun the servant of the Lord died, when he was an hundred and ten years old: **9** And they buried him in the coasts of his inheritance, in [f]Timnath Heres in mount Ephraim, on the North side of mount Gaash. **10** And so all that generation was gathered unto their fathers, and another generation arose after them, which neither knew the Lord, nor yet the works which he had done for Israel. **11** Then the children of Israel did wickedly in the sight of the Lord, and served [g]Baal, **12** And forsook the Lord God of their fathers, which brought them out of the land of Egypt and followed other gods, even the gods of the people that were round about them, and bowed unto them, and provoked the Lord to anger. **13** So they forsook the Lord, and served [4]Baal, and [h]Ashtoreth. **14** And the wrath of the Lord was hot against Israel, and he delivered them into the hands of spoilers, that spoiled them, and he [5]sold them into the hands of their enemies round about them, so that they could no longer stand before their enemies. **15** [i]Whithersoever they

---

JUDG. 1

- **a.** Judg. 1:1 By the judgment of Urim, read Exod. 28:30; Num. 27:21; 1 Sam. 28:6.
- **b.** Judg. 1:1 Who shall be our captain?
- **c.** Judg. 1:3 For the tribe of Simeon had their inheritance within the tribe of Judah, Josh. 19:1.
- **d.** Judg. 1:5 Or, the lord of Bezek.
- **e.** Judg. 1:6 This was God's just judgment, as the tyrant himself confesseth, that as he had done, so did he receive, Lev. 24:19,20.
- **f.** Judg. 1:8 Which was afterward built again, and possessed by the Jebusites, 2 Sam. 5:6.
- **g.** Judg. 1:10 These three were giants, and the children of Anak.
- **h.** Judg. 1:14 Read Josh. 15:18.
- **i.** Judg. 1:16 This was one of the names of Moses' father-in-law, read Num. 10:29.
- **j.** Judg. 1:18 These cities and others were afterward possessed of the Philistines, 1 Sam. 6:17.
- **k.** Judg. 1:21 For after that the tribe of Judah had burnt it, they built it again.
- **l.** Judg. 1:27 Wherefore God permitted the Canaanites to dwell still in the land, read Judg. 3:5.
- **m.** Judg. 1:30 That is, the tribe of Zebulun as is also to be understood of the rest.
- **n.** Judg. 1:32 But made them pay tribute as the others did.
- **o.** Judg. 1:34 Or, afflicted them.
- **p.** Judg. 1:35 Or, would dwell.
- **q.** Judg. 1:35 Meaning, when he was stronger than they.
- **r.** Judg. 1:36 Which was a city in Arabia, or as some read, from the rock.

JUDG. 1

1. Judg. 15:14
2. Num. 21:3
3. Num. 14:24 / Josh. 14:13 / Josh. 15:14
4. Gen. 28:19
5. Josh. 2:14
6. Josh. 17:11
7. Josh. 16:10

JUDG. 2

- **a.** Judg. 2:1 That is, messenger, or prophet, as some think, Phinehas.
- **b.** Judg. 2:3 Or, snare.
- **c.** Judg. 2:5 Or, weeping.
- **d.** Judg. 2:6 After that he had divided to every man his portion by lot, Josh. 24:28.
- **e.** Judg. 2:7 Meaning, the wonders and miracles.
- **f.** Judg. 2:9 Here, by turning the letters backward is Sereh, as Josh. 24:30.
- **g.** Judg. 2:11 That is, all manner of idols.
- **h.** Judg. 2:13 These were Idols, which had the form of an ewe or sheep among the Sidonians.
- **i.** Judg. 2:15 In all their enterprises.
- **j.** Judg. 2:15 The vengeance.

went out, the [j]hand of the Lord was sore against them, as the Lord had said, and as the Lord had sworn unto them: so he punished them sore. **16** Notwithstanding, the Lord raised up [k]Judges, which [l]delivered them out of the hands of their oppressors. **17** But yet they would not obey their Judges for they went a whoring after other gods, and worshipped them, and turned quickly out of the [m]way, wherein their fathers walked, obeying the commandments of the Lord: they did not so. **18** And when the Lord had raised them up Judges, the Lord was with the Judge, and delivered them out of the hand of their enemies all the days of the Judge (for the Lord [n]had compassion of their groanings, [o]because of them that oppressed them and tormented them.) **19** Yet [6]when the Judge was dead, they returned, and [p]did worse than their fathers, in following other gods to serve them and worship them: they ceased not from their own inventions, nor from their rebellious way. **20** Wherefore the wrath of the Lord was kindled against Israel, and he said, Because this people hath transgressed my covenant which I commanded their fathers, and hath not obeyed my voice, **21** Therefore will I no more cast out before them any of the [q]nations, which Joshua left when he died, **22** That through them I may [r]prove Israel, whether they will keep the way of the Lord, to walk therein, as their fathers kept it, or not. **23** So the Lord left those nations, and drove them not out immediately, neither delivered them into the hand of Joshua.

3

1 The Canaanites were left to try Israel. 9 Othniel delivereth Israel. 21 Ehud killeth King Eglon. 31 Shamgar killeth the Philistines.

1 These now are the nations which the Lord left, that he might prove Israel by them (even as many of Israel as had not known all the [a]wars of Canaan, **2** Only to make the generations of the children of Israel to know, and to teach them war, which doubtless their predecessors knew [b]not.) **3** Five princes of the Philistines, and all the Canaanites, and the Sidonians, and the Hivites that dwelt in mount Lebanon, from mount Baal Hermon until one come to Hamath. **4** And these remained to prove Israel by them, to wit, whether they would obey the commandments of the Lord, which he commanded their fathers by the hand of Moses. **5** And the children of Israel dwelt among the Canaanites, the Hittites, and the Amorites, and the Perizzites, and the Hivites, and the Jebusites, **6** And they took [c]their daughters to be their wives, and gave their daughters to their sons, and served their gods. **7** So the children of Israel did wickedly in the sight of the Lord, and forgot the Lord their God, and served Baal, and [d]Asherah. **8** Therefore the wrath of the Lord was kindled against Israel, and he sold them into the hand of Cushan-Rishathaim King of [e]Aram-naharaim, and the children of Israel served Cushan-Rishathaim eight years. **9** And when the children of Israel cried unto the Lord, the Lord stirred up a Savior to the children of Israel, and he saved them, even Othniel the son of Kenaz, Caleb's younger brother. **10** And the [f]Spirit of the Lord came upon him, and he judged Israel, and went out to war: and the Lord delivered Cushan-Rishathaim king of [g]Aram into his hand, and his hand prevailed against Cushan-Rishathaim. **11** So the land had rest [h]forty years, and Othniel the son of Kenaz died. **12** Then the children of Israel again committed wickedness in the sight of the Lord: and the Lord [i]strengthened Eglon king of Moab against Israel, because they had committed wickedness before the Lord. **13** And he gathered unto him the children of Ammon, and Amalek, and went and smote Israel, and they possessed the city of palm trees. **14** So the children of Israel served Eglon king of Moab eighteen years. **15** But when the children of Israel cried unto the Lord, the Lord stirred them up a savior, Ehud the son of Gera the son of [j]Jemini, a man [k]lame of his right hand: and the children of Israel sent a present by him unto Eglon king of Moab. **16** And Ehud [l]made him a dagger with two edges of a cubit length, and he did gird it under his raiment upon his right thigh, **17** And he presented the gift unto Eglon king of Moab (and Eglon was a very fat man.) **18** And when he had now presented the present, he sent away the people that bare the present, **19** But he turned again from the [m]quarries, that were by Gilgal, and said, I have a secret errand unto thee, O King. Who said, Keep [n]silence: and all that stood about him went out from him. **20** Then Ehud came unto him, (and he sat alone in a summer parlor, which he had) and Ehud said, I have a message unto thee from God. Then he arose out of his throne. **21** And Ehud put forth his left hand, and took the dagger from his right thigh, and thrust it into his belly, **22** So that the haft went in after the blade, and the fat closed about the blade, so that he could not draw the dagger out of his belly, but the dirt came out. **23** Then Ehud got him out into the [o]porch, and shut the doors of the parlor upon him, and locked them. **24** And when he was gone out, his servants came: who seeing that the doors of the parlor were locked, they said, Surely [p]he doeth his easement in his summer chamber. **25** And they tarried till they were ashamed: and seeing he opened not the doors of the parlor, they took the key, and opened them, and behold, their lord was fallen dead on the earth. **26** So Ehud escaped (while they tarried) and was past the quarries, and escaped unto Seirah, **27** And when he came home, he [q]blew a trumpet in mount Ephraim, and the children of Israel went down with him from the mountain, and he went before them. **28** Then said he unto them, Follow me: for the Lord hath delivered your enemies, even Moab into your hand. So they went down after him, and took the passages of Jordan toward Moab, and suffered not a man to pass over. **29** And they slew of the Moabites the same time about ten thousand men, all [r]fed men, and all were warriors, and there escaped not a man. **30** So Moab was [s]subdued that day, under the hand of Israel: and the [t]land had rest fourscore years. **31** And after him was Shamgar the son of Anath, which slew of the Philistines six hundred men with an ox [u]goad, and he also delivered Israel.

4

1 Israel sin and are given into the hands of Jabin. 4 Deborah judgeth Israel, and exhorteth Barak to deliver the people. 15 Sisera fleeth,. 17 and is killed by Jael.

1 And the children of Israel [a]began again to do wickedly in the sight of the Lord when Ehud was dead. **2** And the Lord sold them into the hand of [b]Jabin King of Canaan, that reigned in Hazor, whose chief captain was called Sisera, which dwelt in [c]Harosheth of the Gentiles. **3** Then the children of Israel cried unto the Lord: (for he had nine hundred chariots of iron, and twenty years he had vexed the children of Israel very sore.) **4** And at that time Deborah a Prophetess the wife of Lapidoth [d]judged Israel. **5** And this Deborah dwelt under a palm tree, between Ramah and Bethel in mount Ephraim, and the children of Israel came up to her for judgment. **6** Then she sent and called Barak the son of Abinoam out of Kedesh of Naphtali, and said unto him, Hath not the Lord God of Israel [e]commanded, saying, Go, and draw toward mount Tabor, and take with thee ten thousand men of the children of Naphtali, and of the children of Zebulun? **7** And I will draw unto thee to the [f,1]river Kishon, Sisera, the captain of Jabin's army with his chariots, and his multitude, and will deliver him into thine hand. **8** And Barak said unto her, [g]If thou wilt go with me, I will go: but if thou wilt not go with me, I will not go. **9** Then she answered, I will surely go with thee, but this journey that thou takest, shall not be for thine honor: for the Lord shall sell Sisera into the hand of a woman. And Deborah arose and went with Barak to Kedesh. **10** And Barak called Zebulun and Naphtali to Kedesh, and [h]he went up on his feet with ten thousand men, and Deborah went up with him. **11** (Now Heber the Kenite, which was of the [i]children of [2]Hobab the father-in-law of Moses, was departed from the [j]Kenites, and pitched his tent [k]until the plain of Zaanaim, which is by Kedesh.) **12** Then they showed Sisera, that Barak the son of Abinoam was gone up to mount Tabor. **13** And Sisera called for all his chariots, even nine hundred chariots of iron, and all the people that were with him from Harosheth of the Gentiles, unto the river Kishon. **14** Then Deborah said unto Barak, [l]Up: for this is the day that the Lord hath delivered Sisera into thine hand. Is not the Lord gone out before thee? So Barak went down from mount Tabor, and ten thousand men after him. **15** And the Lord destroyed Sisera and all his chariots, and all his host with the edge of the sword before Barak, so that Sisera lighted down off his chariot, and fled away on his feet. **16** But [3]Barak pursued after the chariots, and after the host unto Harosheth of the Gentiles: and all the host of Sisera fell upon the edge of the sword: there was not a man left. **17** Howbeit Sisera fled away on his feet to the tent of Jael the wife of [m]Heber the Kenite: (for peace was between Jabin the king of Hazor, and between the house of Heber the Kenite.) **18** And Jael went out to meet Sisera, and said unto him, Turn in, my

---

k. Judg. 2:16 Or, magistrates.
l. Judg. 2:16 Hebrew, saved.
m. Judg. 2:17 Meaning, from the true religion.
n. Judg. 2:18 Hebrew, repented.
o. Judg. 2:18 Seeing their cruelty.
p. Judg. 2:19 Hebrew, corrupt themselves.
q. Judg. 2:21 As the Hivites, Jebusites, Amorites, etc.
r. Judg. 2:22 So that both outward enemies and false prophets are but a trial to prove our faith, Deut. 13:3 and Judg. 3:1.

JUDG. 2

1. Deut. 7:2
2. Deut. 22:3
3. Josh. 23:13
4. Judg. 10:6
5. Ps. 44:12 / Isa. 50:1
6. Judg. 3:12

JUDG. 3

a. Judg. 3:1 Which were achieved by the hand of God, and not by the power of man.
b. Judg. 3:2 For they trusted in God, and he fought for them.
c. Judg. 3:6 Contrary to God's commandment, Deut. 3:7.
d. Judg. 3:7 Trees or woods erected for idolatry.
e. Judg. 3:8 Or, Mesopotamia.
f. Judg. 3:10 He was stirred up by the Spirit of the Lord.
g. Judg. 3:10 Or, Syria.
h. Judg. 3:11 That is, 32 under Joshua, and eight under Othniel.
i. Judg. 3:12 So that the enemies of God's people have no power over them, but by God's appointment.
j. Judg. 3:15 Or, Benjamin.
k. Judg. 3:15 Or, left handed.
l. Judg. 3:16 Or, caused a dagger to be made.
m. Judg. 3:19 Or, as some read from the places of idols.
n. Judg. 3:19 Till all be departed.
o. Judg. 3:23 Or, hall.
p. Judg. 3:24 Hebrew, he covereth his feet.
q. Judg. 3:27 Or, caused the trumpet to be blown, Num. 20:2,3.
r. Judg. 3:29 Or, strong, and big bodied.
s. Judg. 3:30 Hebrew, humbled.
t. Judg. 3:30 Meaning, the Israelites.
u. Judg. 3:31 So that it is not the number, nor the means that God regardeth, when he will get the victory.

JUDG. 4

a. Judg. 4:1 Hebrew, added, or continued to do evil.
b. Judg. 4:2 There was another Jabin, whom Joshua killed and burnt his city Hazor, Josh. 11:13.
c. Judg. 4:2 That is in a wood, or strong place.
d. Judg. 4:4 By the spirit of prophecy, resolving of controversies and declaring the will of God.
e. Judg. 4:6 And revealed unto me by the spirit of prophecy.
f. Judg. 4:7 Or, valley.
g. Judg. 4:8 Fearing his own weakness and his enemy's power, he desireth the prophetess to go with him to assure him of God's will from time to time.
h. Judg. 4:10 Or, he led after him 10,000 men.
i. Judg. 4:11 Or, posterity.
j. Judg. 4:11 Hebrew, from Cain.
k. Judg. 4:11 Meaning, that he possessed a great part of that country.
l. Judg. 4:14 She still encourageth him to this enterprise by assuring him of God's favor and aid.
m. Judg. 4:17 Whose ancestors were strangers, but worshipped the true God, and therefore were joined with Israel.
n. Judg. 4:18 Or, blanket.
o. Judg. 4:20 To wit, Sisera.

lord, turn into me: fear not. And when he had turned in unto her into her tent,
she covered him with a [n]mantel. **19** And he said unto her, Give me, I pray thee,
a little water to drink: for I am thirsty. And she opened a [4]bottle of milk, and gave
him drink, and covered him. **20** Again he said unto her, Stand in the door of
the tent, and when any man doth come and inquire of thee, saying, Is [o]any man
there? thou shalt say, Nay. **21** Then Jael Heber's wife took a [p]nail of the tent, and
took an hammer in her hand, and went softly unto him, and smote the nail into
his temples, and fastened it into the ground, (for he was fast asleep and weary)
and so he died. **22** And behold, as Barak pursued after Sisera, Jael came out to
meet him, and said unto him, Come, and I will show thee the man, whom thou
seekest: and when he came into her tent, behold, Sisera lay [q]dead, and the nail in
his temples. **23** So God brought down Jabin the king of Canaan that day before
the children of Israel. **24** And the hand of the children of Israel [r]prospered, and
prevailed against Jabin the king of Canaan, until they had destroyed Jabin king of
Canaan.

5

1 The song and thanksgiving of Deborah and Barak, after the victory.

1 Then sang Deborah, and Barak the son of Abinoam the same day,
saying, **2** Praise ye the Lord for the avenging of Israel, and for the [a]people that
offered themselves willingly. **3** Hear, ye kings, hearken ye princes: I, even I will
sing unto the Lord: I will sing praise unto the Lord God of Israel. **4** Lord, [1]when
thou wentest out of Seir, when thou departedst out of the field of [2]Edom, the
earth trembled, and the heavens rained, the clouds also dropped water. **5** [3]The
mountains melted before the Lord, [4]as did that Sinai before the Lord God of Isra-
el. **6** In the days of [5]Shamgar the son of Anath, in the days of [6]Jael, the highways
were [b]unoccupied, and the travelers walked through byways. **7** The towns were
not inhabited: they decayed, I say, in Israel, until I Deborah came up, which rose
up a [c]mother in Israel. **8** They chose new gods: then was war in the gates. Was
there a [d]shield or spear seen among forty thousand of Israel? **9** Mine heart is set
on the governors of Israel, and on them that are willing among the people: prai-
se ye the Lord. **10** Speak ye that ride on [e]white asses, ye that dwell [f]by Middin,
and that walk by the way. **11** For the noise of the archers appraised among the
[g]drawers of water: there shall they rehearse the righteousness of the Lord, his ri-
ghteousness of his towns in Israel: then did the people of the Lord go down to
the gates. **12** Up Deborah, up, arise, and sing a song: arise Barak, and lead [h]thy
captivity captive, thou son of Abinoam. **13** For they that remain, have domi-
nion over the mighty of the people: the Lord hath given me dominion over the
strong. **14** Of Ephraim [i]their root arose against Amalek: and after thee Benjamin
shall fight against thy people, O Amalek, of Machir came rulers, and of Zebulun,
they that handle the pen of the [j]writer. **15** And the princes of Issachar were with
Deborah, and [k]Issachar, and also Barak: he was set on his feet in the valley: for the
divisions of Reuben were great [l]thoughts of heart. **16** Why abodest thou among
the sheepfolds, to hear the bleatings of the flocks? for the divisions of Reuben
were great thoughts of heart. **17** [m]Gilead abode beyond Jordan: and why doth
Dan remain in ships? Asher sat on the seashore, and tarried in his [n]decayed pla-
ces. **18** But the people of Zebulun and Naphtali have jeopardized their lives unto
the death in the high places of the field. **19** The Kings came and fought: then
fought the Kings of Canaan in Taanach by the waters of Megiddo: they received
no gain of [o]money. **20** They fought from heaven, even the stars in their courses
fought against Sisera. **21** The River Kishon [p]swept them away, that ancient ri-
ver the river Kishon. O my soul, thou hast marched valiantly. **22** Then were the
horse hoofs broken with the oft beating together of their mighty men. **23** Curse
ye [q]Meroz: (said the Angel of the Lord) curse the inhabitants thereof, because they
came not to help the Lord, to help the Lord against the mighty. **24** Jael the wife
of Heber the Kenite shall be blessed above other women: blessed shall she be above
women dwelling in tents. **25** He asked water, and she gave him milk: she brou-
ght forth [r]butter in a lordly dish. **26** She put her hand to the nail, and her right
hand to the workman's hammer: with the hammer smote she Sisera: she smote off
his head, after she had wounded and pierced his temples. **27** He bowed him
down at her feet, he fell down, and lay still: at her feet he bowed him down, and
fell: and when he had sunk down, he lay there [s]dead. **28** The mother of Sisera
looked out at a window, and cried through the lattice, Why is his chariot so long a
coming? why tarry the [t]wheels of his chariots? **29** Her wise ladies answered her,
Yea. [u]She answered herself with her own words, **30** Have they not gotten, and
they divide the spoil? every man hath a maid or two. Sisera hath a prey of diverse
colored garments, a prey of sundry colors made of needle work: of diverse colors of
needle work on both sides, [v]for the chief of the spoil. **31** So let all thine enemies
perish, O Lord: but they that love him, shall be as the [w]Sun when he riseth in his
might, and the land had rest forty years.

6

1 Israel is oppressed of the Midianites for their wickedness. 14 Gideon is sent to be their deliverer. 37 He asketh a sign.

1 Afterward the children of Israel committed wickedness in the sight of the
Lord, and the Lord gave them into the hands of Midian seven years. **2** And the
hand of Midian prevailed against Israel, [a]and because of the Midianites the children
of Israel made them dens in the mountains, and caves, and strongholds. **3** When
Israel had sown, then came up the Midianites, the Amalekites, and they of the
[b]East, and came upon them, **4** And camped by them, and destroyed the fruit
of the earth, even till thou come unto [c]Gaza, and left no food for Israel, neither
sheep, nor ox, nor ass. **5** For they went up, and their cattle, and came with their
tents as grasshoppers in multitude: so that they and their camels were without
number: and they came into the land to destroy it. **6** So was Israel exceedingly
impoverished by the Midianites: therefore the [d]children of Israel cried unto the
Lord. **7** And when the children of Israel cried unto the Lord because of the Mi-
dianites, **8** The Lord sent unto the children of Israel a Prophet, who said unto
them, Thus saith the Lord God of Israel, I have brought you up from Egypt, and
have brought you out of the house of bondage, **9** And I have delivered you out of
the hand of the Egyptians, and out of the hand of all that oppressed you, and have
cast them out before you, and given you their land. **10** And I said unto you, I
am the Lord your God: [1]fear not the gods of the Amorites in whose land you dwell:
but ye have not obeyed my voice. **11** And the Angel of the Lord came, and sat
under the oak which was in Ophrah, that pertained unto Joash the father of the
Abiezrites, and his son Gideon threshed wheat by the winepress, [e]to hide it from
the Midianites. **12** Then the Angel of the Lord appeared unto him, and said
unto him, The Lord is with thee, thou valiant man. **13** To whom Gideon answe-
red, [f]Ah my Lord, if the Lord be with us, why then is all this come upon us? and
where be all his miracles which our fathers told us of, and said, Did not the Lord
bring us out of Egypt? but now the Lord hath forsaken us, and delivered us into
the hand of the Midianites. **14** And the [g]Lord looked upon him, and said, Go in
this thy [h]might, and thou shalt save Israel out of the hands of the Midianites: have
not I sent thee? **15** And he answered him, Ah my Lord, whereby shall I save Isra-
el? behold, my [i]father is poor in Manasseh, and I am the least in my father's hou-
se. **16** Then the Lord said unto him, I will therefore be with thee, and thou shalt
smite the Midianites, as one man. **17** And he answered him, I pray thee, if I have
found favor in thy sight, then show me [j]a sign, that thou talkest with me. **18** De-
part not hence, I pray thee, until I come unto thee, and bring mine offering, and
lay it before thee. And he said, I will tarry until thou come again. **19** Then Gide-
on went in, and made ready a kid, and unleavened bread of an [k]Ephah of flour, and
put the flesh in a basket, and put the broth in a pot, and brought it out unto him
under the oak, and presented it. **20** And the Angel of God said unto him, Take
the flesh and the unleavened bread, and lay them upon this stone, and pour out
the broth: and he did so. **21** Then the Angel of the Lord put forth the end of the
staff that he held in his hand, and touched the flesh and the unleavened bread: and
there arose up fire [l]out of the stone, and consumed the flesh and the unleavened
bread, so the Angel of the Lord departed out of his sight. **22** And when Gideon
perceived that it was an Angel of the Lord, Gideon then said, Alas, my Lord God:
[2]for because I have seen an Angel of the Lord face to face, I shall die. **23** And the
Lord said unto him, Peace be unto thee: fear not, thou shalt not die. **24** Then

---

p. Judg. 4:21 That is, the pin or stake, whereby it was fastened to the ground.
q. Judg. 4:22 So he saw that a woman had the honor, as Deborah prophesied.
r. Judg. 4:24 Hebrew, went and was strong.

JUDG. 4
1. Ps. 83:9,10
2. Num. 10:29
3. Ps. 38:10
4. Judg. 5:25

JUDG. 5
a. Judg. 5:2 To wit, the two tribes of Zebulun and Naphtali.
b. Judg. 5:6 For fear of the enemies.
c. Judg. 5:7 Miraculously stirred up of God to pity them and deliver them.
d. Judg. 5:8 They had no heart to resist their enemies.
e. Judg. 5:10 Ye governors.
f. Judg. 5:10 As in danger of your enemies.
g. Judg. 5:11 For now you may draw water without fear of your enemies.
h. Judg. 5:12 To wit, them that kept thy people in captivity.
i. Judg. 5:14 Joshua first fought against Amalek, and Saul destroyed him.
j. Judg. 5:14 Even the learned did help to fight.
k. Judg. 5:15 Even the whole tribe.
l. Judg. 5:15 They marveled, that they came not over Jordan to help them.
m. Judg. 5:17 She reproveth all them that came not to help their brethren in their necessity.
n. Judg. 5:17 Either by beating of the sea, or by mining.
o. Judg. 5:19 They won nothing, but lost all.
p. Judg. 5:21 As a besom doeth the filth of the house.
q. Judg. 5:23 It was a city near to Tabor, where they fought.
r. Judg. 5:25 Some read churned milk in a great cup.
s. Judg. 5:27 Hebrew, destroyed.
t. Judg. 5:28 Or, feet.
u. Judg. 5:29 That is, she comforted herself.
v. Judg. 5:30 Because he was chief of the army.
w. Judg. 5:31 Shall grow daily more and more in God's favor.

JUDG. 5
1. Deut. 4:11
2. Deut. 2:1
3. Ps. 97:5
4. Exod. 19:18
5. Judg. 3:31
6. Judg. 4:18

JUDG. 6
a. Judg. 6:2 For fear of the Midianites, they fled into the dens of the mountains.
b. Judg. 6:3 Or, of Kedem.
c. Judg. 6:4 Even almost the whole country.
d. Judg. 6:6 This is the end of God's punishments, to call his to repentance, that they may seek for help of him.
e. Judg. 6:11 Or, to prepare his flight.
f. Judg. 6:13 This came not of distrust, but of weakness of faith, which is in the most perfect: for no man in this life can have a perfect faith: yet the children of God have a true faith, whereby they be justified.
g. Judg. 6:14 That is, Christ appearing in visible form.
h. Judg. 6:14 Which I have given thee.
i. Judg. 6:15 Or, family.
j. Judg. 6:17 So that we see how the flesh is enemy unto God's vocation, which cannot be persuaded without signs.
k. Judg. 6:19 Of Ephah, read Exod. 16:37.
l. Judg. 6:21 By the power of God only, as in the sacrifice of Elijah, 1 Kings 18:38.

Gideon made an altar there unto the Lord, and called it [m]Jehovah Shalom: unto this day it is in Ophrah, of the father of the Abiezrites. **25** And the same night the Lord said unto him, Take thy father's young bullock, and another bullock [n]of seven years old, and destroy the altar of Baal that thy father hath, and cut down the grove that is by it, **26** And build an altar unto the Lord thy God upon the top of this rock, in a plain place: and take the second bullock, and offer a burnt offering with the wood of the [o]grove, which thou shalt cut down. **27** Then Gideon took ten men of his servants, and did as the Lord bade him: but because he feared to do it by day for his father's household and the men of the city, he did it by night. **28** And when the men of the city arose early in the morning, behold, the altar of Baal was broken, and the grove cut down that was by it, and the [p]second bullock offered upon the altar that was made. **29** Therefore they said one to another, Who hath done this thing? and when they inquired and asked, they said, Gideon the son of Joash hath done this thing. **30** Then the men of the city said unto Joash, Bring out thy son, that he may die: for he hath destroyed the altar of Baal, and hath also cut down the grove that was by it. **31** And Joash said unto all that stood by him, Will ye plead Baal's cause? or will ye save him? [q]he that will contend for him, let him die or the morning. If he be God, let him plead for himself against him that hath cast down his altar. **32** And in that day was Gideon called Jerubbaal, that is, Let Baal plead for himself because he hath broken down his altar. **33** Then all the Midianites and the Amalekites, and they of the East, were gathered together, and went and pitched in the valley of Jezreel. **34** But the Spirit of the Lord [r]came upon Gideon [3]and he blew a trumpet, and [s]Abiezer was joined with him. **35** And he sent messengers throughout all Manasseh, which was also joined with him, and he sent messengers unto Asher, and to Zebulun and to Naphtali, and they came up to meet them. **36** Then Gideon said unto God, [t]If thou wilt save Israel by mine hand, as thou hast said, **37** Behold, I will put a fleece of wool in the threshing place: if the dew come on the fleece only and it be dry upon all the earth, then shall I be sure, that thou wilt save Israel by mine hand, as thou hast said. **38** And so it was: for he rose up early on the morrow, and thrust the fleece together, and wringed the dew out of the fleece, and filled a bowl of water. **39** Again, Gideon said unto God, Be not angry with me, that [4]I may speak once more: let me prove once again, I pray thee, with the fleece: let it now be dry only upon the fleece, and let dew be upon all the ground. **40** And God did so the same night: for it was [u]dry upon the fleece only, and there was dew on all the ground.

7

The Lord commandeth Gideon to send away a great part of his company. 22 The Midianites are discomfitted by a wondrous sort. 25 Oreb and Zeeb are slain.

1 Then [1]Jerubbaal (who is Gideon) rose up early, and all the people that were with him, and pitched beside [a]the well of Harod, so that the host of the Midianites was on the North side of them, in the valley by the hill of [b]Moreh. **2** And the Lord said unto Gideon, The people that are with thee, are too many for me to give the Midianites into their hands, lest Israel make their vaunt [c]against me, and say, Mine hand hath saved me. **3** Now therefore proclaim in the audience of the people, and say, [2]Who so is timorous or fearful, let him return, and depart early from mount Gilead. And there returned of the people which were at mount Gilead, two and twenty thousand: so ten thousand remained. **4** And the Lord said unto Gideon, The people are yet too many: bring them down unto the water, and I will [d]try them for thee there: and of whom I say unto thee, This man shall go with thee, the same shall go with thee: and of whomsoever I say unto thee, This man shall not go with thee, the same shall not go. **5** So he brought down the people unto the water. And the Lord said unto Gideon, As many as lap the water with their tongues, as a dog lappeth, them put by themselves, and everyone that shall bow down his knees to drink, [e]put apart. **6** And the number of them that lapped by putting their hands to their mouths, were three hundred men: but all the remnant of the people kneeled down upon their knees to drink water. **7** Then the Lord said unto Gideon, By these three hundred men that lapped, will I save you, and deliver the Midianites into thine hand: and let all the other [f]people go every man unto his place. **8** So the people took victuals [g]with them, and their trumpets: and he sent all the rest of Israel, every man unto his tent, and [h]retained the three hundred men: and the host of Midian was beneath him in a valley. **9** And the same night the Lord said unto him, Arise, [i]get thee down unto the host: for I have delivered it into thine hand. **10** But if thou fear to go down, then go thou, and Purah thy servant down to the host, **11** And thou shalt hearken what they say, and so shall thine hands be strong to go down unto the host. Then went he down and Purah his servant unto the outside of the soldiers that were in the host. **12** And the Midianites, and the Amalekites and all [3]they of the East, lay in the valley like grasshoppers in multitude, and their camels were without number, as the sand which is by the seaside for multitude. **13** And when Gideon was come, behold, a man told a dream unto his neighbor, and said, Behold, I dreamed a dream and lo, a [j]cake of barley bread tumbled from above into the host of Midian, and came into a tent, and smote it that it fell, and overturned it, that the tent fell down. **14** And his fellow answered, and said, This is nothing else save the sword of Gideon the son of Joash a man of Israel: for into his hand hath God delivered Midian and all the host. **15** When Gideon heard the dream told, and the interpretation of the same, he [k]worshipped, and returned unto the host of Israel, and said, Up: for the Lord hath delivered into your hand the host of Midian. **16** And he divided the three hundred men into three bands, and gave every man a trumpet in his hand with empty pitchers, and [l]lamps [m]within the pitchers. **17** And he said unto them, Look on me, and do likewise, when I come to the side of the host: even as I do, so do you. **18** When I blow with a trumpet and all that are with me, blow ye with trumpets also on every side of the host, and say, [n]For the Lord, and for Gideon. **19** So Gideon and the hundred men that were with him, came unto the outside of the host, in the beginning of the middle watch, and they raised up the watchmen, and they blew with their trumpets, and brake the pitchers that were in their hands. **20** And the three companies blew with trumpets and brake the pitchers, and held the lamps in their left hands, and the trumpets in their right hands to blow withal: and they cried, The [o]sword of the Lord and of Gideon. **21** And they stood, every man in his place round about the host: and all the host [p]ran, and cried, and fled. **22** And the three hundred blew with trumpets, and [4]the Lord set every man's sword upon his [q]neighbor, and upon all the host: so the host fled to Beth Hashittah in Zererah, and to the border of Abel Meholah, unto Tabbath. **23** Then the men of Israel being gathered together out of Naphtali, and out of Asher, and out of all Manasseh, pursued after the Midianites. **24** And Gideon sent messengers unto all mount Ephraim, saying, Come down against the Midianites, and take before them the [r]waters unto Beth Barah and Jordan. Then all the men of Ephraim gathered together and took the waters unto Beth Barah, and Jordan. **25** And they took two [5]princes of the Midianites, Oreb and Zeeb, and slew Oreb upon the rock Oreb, and slew Zeeb at [s]the winepress of Zeeb, and pursued the Midianites, and brought the heads of Oreb and Zeeb to Gideon beyond Jordan.

8

1 Ephraim murmureth against Gideon, who appeaseth them. 4 He passeth the Jordan. 16 He revengeth himself on them of Succoth and Penuel. 27 He maketh an Ephod which was the cause of idolatry. 30 Of Gideon's sons and of his death.

1 Then the men of Ephraim said unto him, [a]Why hast thou served us thus that thou calledst us not, when thou wentest to fight with the Midianites? and they chide with him sharply. **2** To whom he said, What have I now done, in comparison of [b]you? is not the [c]gleaning of grapes of Ephraim better, than the vintage of Abiezer? **3** God hath delivered into your hands the princes of Midian, Oreb and Zeeb: and what was I able to do in comparison of you? and when he had thus spoken, then their spirits abated toward him. **4** And Gideon came to Jordan to pass over, he, and the three hundred men that were with him, weary, yet pursuing them. **5** And he said unto the men of Succoth, Give, I pray you, [d]morsels of bread unto the people [e]that follow me (for they be weary) that I may follow after Zebah and Zalmunna Kings of Midian. **6** And the princes of Succoth said, Are the [f]hands of Zebah and Zalmunna now in thine hands, that we should give

---

- **m.** Judg. 6:24 Or, the Lord of peace.
- **n.** Judg. 6:25 That is, as the Chaldea text writeth, fed seven years.
- **o.** Judg. 6:26 Which grew about Baal's altar.
- **p.** Judg. 6:28 Meaning, the fat bull, which was kept to be offered unto Baal.
- **q.** Judg. 6:31 Thus we ought to justify them that are zealous of God's cause, though all the multitude be against us.
- **r.** Judg. 6:34 Hebrew, clad Gideon.
- **s.** Judg. 6:34 The family of Abiezer, whereof he was.
- **t.** Judg. 6:36 This request proceeded not of infidelity, but that he might be confirmed in his vocation.
- **u.** Judg. 6:40 Whereby he was assured that it was a miracle of God.

JUDG. 6

1. 2 Kings 17:35,38 / Jer. 10:2
2. Ex. 33:20 / Judg. 13:22
3. Num. 10:3 / Judg. 3:27
4. Gen. 18:32

JUDG. 7

- **a.** Judg. 7:1 Hebrew, En-harod.
- **b.** Judg. 7:1 Hebrew, Hammoreh.
- **c.** Judg. 7:2 God will not that any creature deprive him of his glory.
- **d.** Judg. 7:4 I will give thee a proof to know them that shall go with thee.
- **e.** Judg. 7:5 Let them depart as unmeet for this enterprise.
- **f.** Judg. 7:7 That is, the one and thirty thousand, and 700. See verses 3 and 6.
- **g.** Judg. 7:8 Hebrew, in their hands.
- **h.** Judg. 7:8 Or, encouraged.
- **i.** Judg. 7:9 Thus the Lord by divers means doth strengthen him, that he faint not in so great an enterprise.
- **j.** Judg. 7:13 Some read, a trembling noise of barley bread: meaning, that one of no reputation should make their great army to tremble.
- **k.** Judg. 7:15 Or, gave God thanks, as it is in the Chaldea text.
- **l.** Judg. 7:16 Or, firebrands.
- **m.** Judg. 7:16 These weak means God used to signify that the whole victory came of him.
- **n.** Judg. 7:18 That is, the victory shall be the Lord's and Gideon's his servant.
- **o.** Judg. 7:20 Shall destroy the enemies.
- **p.** Judg. 7:21 Or, broke their array.
- **q.** Judg. 7:22 The Lord caused the Midianites to kill one another.
- **r.** Judg. 7:24 Meaning, the passages or the fords, that they should not escape.
- **s.** Judg. 7:25 These places had their names of the acts that were done there.

JUDG. 7

1. Judg. 8:35
2. Deut. 20:8
3. Judg. 6:33
4. Isa. 9:4
5. Ps. 83:11 / Isa. 10:26

JUDG. 8

- **a.** Judg. 8:1 They began to cavil, because he had the glory of the victory.
- **b.** Judg. 8:2 Which have slain two princes, Oreb and Zeeb.
- **c.** Judg. 8:2 This last act of the whole tribe is more famous, than the whole enterprise of one man of one family.
- **d.** Judg. 8:5 Or, some small portion.
- **e.** Judg. 8:5 Hebrew, that are at my feet.

bread unto thine army? **7** Gideon then said, Therefore when the Lord hath delivered Zebah and Zalmunna into mine hand, I will [g]tear your flesh with thorns of the wilderness and with briers. **8** And he went up thence to Penuel, and spake unto them likewise, and the men of Penuel answered him, as the men of Succoth answered. **9** And he said also unto the men of Penuel, When I come again [h]in peace, I will break down this tower. **10** Now Zebah and Zalmunna were [i]in Karkor, and their hosts with them, about fifteen thousand, all that were left of all the hosts of them of the East: for there was slain an hundred and twenty thousand men, that drew swords. **11** And Gideon went through them that dwelt in [j]Tabernacles on the East side of Nobah and Jogbehah, and smote the host: for the host was careless. **12** And when Zebah and Zalmunna fled, he followed after them, and took the two kings of Midian, Zebah and Zalmunna, and discomfited all the host. **13** So Gideon the son of Joash returned from battle, [k]the sun being yet high, **14** And took a servant of the men of Succoth, and inquired of him: and he [l]wrote to him the princes of Succoth and the Elders thereof, even seventy and seven men. **15** And he came unto the men of Succoth, and said, Behold Zebah, and Zalmunna, by whom ye upbraided me, saying, Are the hands of Zebah, and Zalmunna already in thine hands, that we should give bread unto thy weary men? **16** Then he took the Elders of the city, and thorns of the wilderness and briers, and [m]did tear the men of Succoth with them. **17** Also he brake down the tower of [1]Penuel, and slew the men of the city. **18** Then said he unto Zebah and Zalmunna, What manner of men were they, whom ye slew at Tabor? And they answered, [n]As thou art, so were they, every one was like the children of a king. **19** And he said, They were my brethren, even my [o]mother's children: as the Lord liveth, if ye had saved their lives, I would not slay you. **20** Then he said unto Jether his firstborn son, Up, and slay them: but the boy drew not his sword: for he feared, because he was yet young. **21** Then Zebah and Zalmunna said, Rise thou and fall upon us: for [p]as the man is, so is his strength. And Gideon arose and slew Zebah and Zalmunna, and took away the [q]ornaments, that were on their camels' necks. **22** Then the men of Israel said unto Gideon, Reign thou over us, both thou, and thy son and thy [r]son's son: for thou hast delivered us out of the hand of Midian. **23** And Gideon said unto them, I will not reign over you, neither shall my child reign over you, but the Lord shall reign over you. **24** Again Gideon said unto them, [s]I would desire a request of you, that you would give me every man the earrings of his prey (for they had golden earrings because they were Ishmaelites.) **25** And they answered, We will give them. And they spread a garment, and did cast therein every man the earrings of his prey. **26** And the weight of the golden earrings that he required, was a thousand and seven hundred shekels of gold, beside collars [t]and jewels, and purple raiment that was on the kings of Midian, and beside the chains that were about the camels' necks. **27** And Gideon made an [u]Ephod thereof, and put it in Ophrah his city: and all Israel went a whoring there after it, which was the destruction of Gideon and his house. **28** Thus was Midian brought low before the children of Israel, so that they lifted up their heads no more: and the country was in quietness forty years in the days of Gideon. **29** Then Jerubbaal the son of Joash went, and dwelt in his own house. **30** And Gideon had seventy sons [v]begotten of his body: for he had many wives. **31** And his concubine that was in Shechem, bare him a son also, whose name he called Abimelech. **32** So Gideon the son of Joash died in a good age, and was buried in the sepulcher of Joash his father in Ophrah, of the [w]father of the Abiezrites. **33** But when Gideon was dead, the children of Israel turned away, and went a whoring after Baal, and made [x]Baal-Berith their god. **34** And the children of Israel remembered not the Lord their God, which had delivered them out of the hands of all their enemies on every side. **35** Neither [y]showed they mercy on the house of Jerubbaal, or Gideon, according to all the goodness which he had showed unto Israel.

9

1 Abimelech usurpeth the kingdom, and putteth his brethren to death. 7 Jotham proposeth a parable. 23 Hatred between Abimelech and the Shechemites. 26 Gaal conspireth against him, and is overcome. 53 Abimelech is wounded to death by a woman.

1 Then Abimelech the son of Jerubbaal went to Shechem unto his [a]mother's brethren, and communed with them, and with all the family, and house of his mother's father, saying, **2** Say, I pray you, in the audience of all the men of Shechem, Whether is better for you, that all the sons of Jerubbaal, which are seventy persons, reign over you, either that one reign over you? Remember also, that I am your [b]bone, and your flesh. **3** Then his mother's brethren spake of him in the audience of all the men of Shechem, all these words: and their hearts were moved to follow Abimelech: for said they, He is our brother. **4** And they gave him seventy pieces of silver out of the house of Baal-Berith, wherewith Abimelech hired [c]vain and light fellows which followed him. **5** And he went unto his father's house at Ophrah, and [d]slew his brethren, the sons of Jerubbaal, about seventy persons upon one stone: yet Jotham the youngest son of Jerubbaal was left: for he hid himself. **6** And all the men of Shechem gathered together with all the house of [e]Millo, and came and made Abimelech King in the plain, where the stone was erected in Shechem. **7** And when they told it to Jotham, he went and stood in the top of mount Gerizim, and lifted up his voice, and cried, and said unto them, Hearken unto me, you men of Shechem, that God may hearken unto you. **8** [f]The trees went forth to anoint a King over them, and said unto the Olive tree, Reign thou over us. **9** But the Olive tree said unto them, Should I leave my fatness, wherewith by me they honor God and man, and go to advance me above the trees? **10** Then the trees said to the fig tree, Come thou, and be king over us. **11** But the fig tree answered them, Should I forsake my sweetness, and my good fruit, and go to advance me above the trees? **12** Then said the trees unto the vine, Come thou, and be king over us. **13** But the vine said unto them, Should I leave my wine, whereby I cheer God and man, and go to advance me above the trees? **14** Then said all the trees unto the [g]bramble, Come thou, and reign over us. **15** And the bramble said unto the trees, If ye will indeed anoint me king over you, come, and put your trust under my shadow: and if not, the [h]fire shall come out of the bramble, and consume the Cedars of Lebanon. **16** Now therefore, if ye do truly and incorruptly to make Abimelech King, and if ye have dealt well with Jerubbaal and with his house, and have done unto him according to the deserving of his hands, **17** (For my father fought for you, and [i]adventured his life, and delivered you out of the hands of Midian. **18** And ye are risen up against my father's house this day, and have slain his children, about seventy persons upon one stone, and have made Abimelech, the son of his maidservant, king over the men of Shechem, because he is your brother.) **19** If ye then have dealt truly and purely with Jerubbaal, and with his house this day, then [j]rejoice ye with Abimelech, and let him rejoice with you. **20** But if not, let a fire come out from Abimelech, and consume the men of Shechem and the house of Millo: also let a fire come forth from the men of Shechem, and from the house of Millo, and consume Abimelech. **21** And Jotham ran away, and fled, and went to Beer, and dwelt there for fear of Abimelech his brother. **22** So Abimelech reigned three years over Israel. **23** But God [k]sent an evil spirit between Abimelech, and the men of Shechem: and the men of Shechem brake their promise to Abimelech, **24** That the cruelty toward the seventy sons of Jerubbaal and their blood might come and be laid upon Abimelech their brother, which had slain them, and upon the men of Shechem, which had aided him to kill his brethren. **25** So the men of Shechem set men in wait for him in the tops of the mountains: who robbed all that passed that way by them: and it was told Abimelech. **26** Then Gaal the son of Ebed came with his brethren, and they went to Shechem: and the men of Shechem put their confidence in him. **27** Therefore they [l]went out into the field, and gathered in their grapes, and trode them, and made merry, and went into the house of their gods, and did eat and drink, and cursed Abimelech. **28** Then Gaal the son of Ebed said, Who is Abimelech? and who is Shechem, that we should serve him? Is he not the son of Jerubbaal? and Zebul is his officer? Serve rather the men of Hamor the father of Shechem: for why should we serve him? **29** Now would God this people were under mine hand: then would I put away Abimelech. And he said to [m]Abimelech, Increase thine army, and come out. **30** And when Zebul the ruler of the city heard the words of Gaal the son of Ebed, his wrath was kindled. **31** Therefore he sent messengers unto Abimelech [n]privily, saying, Behold, Gaal the son of Ebed and his brethren be come to Shechem, and behold, they fortify the city against thee. **32** Now therefore arise by night, thou and the people that is with thee, and

---

f. Judg. 8:6 Because thou hast overcome an handful, thinkest thou to have overcome the whole?
g. Judg. 8:7 Hebrew, beat in pieces.
h. Judg. 8:9 Having gotten the victory.
i. Judg. 8:10 A city Eastward beyond Jordan.
j. Judg. 8:11 He went by the wilderness where the Arabians dwelt in tents.
k. Judg. 8:13 Some read, before the Sun rose up.
l. Judg. 8:14 Or, described.
m. Judg. 8:16 Hebrew, break in pieces, as one thresheth corn.
n. Judg. 8:18 Or, they were like unto thee.
o. Judg. 8:19 We came all out of one belly: therefore I will be revenged.
p. Judg. 8:21 Meaning, that they would be rid out of their pain at once, or else to have a valiant man to put them to death.
q. Judg. 8:21 Or, collars.
r. Judg. 8:22 That is, thy posterity.
s. Judg. 8:24 His intent was to show himself thankful for this victory by restoring of religion, which because it was not according as God had commanded, turned to their destruction.
t. Judg. 8:26 Or, sweet balls.
u. Judg. 8:27 That is, such things as pertained to the use of the Tabernacle. See more of Ephod, Exod. 28:4,6; 1 Sam. 2:18 and 2 Sam. 6:14 and Judg. 17:5.
v. Judg. 8:30 Hebrew, which came out of his thigh.
w. Judg. 8:32 Which city belonged to the family of the Abiezrites.
x. Judg. 8:33 That is, Baal, to whom they had bound themselves by covenant.
y. Judg. 8:35 They were unmindful of God and unkind toward him, by whom they had received so great a benefit.

JUDG. 8

1. 1 Kings 12:25

JUDG. 9

a. Judg. 9:1 To practice with his kinsfolk for the attaining of the kingdom.
b. Judg. 9:2 Of your kindred by my mother's side.
c. Judg. 9:4 Or, idle fellows and vagabonds.
d. Judg. 9:5 Thus tyrants to establish their usurped power, spare not the innocent blood, 2 Kings 10:7; 2 Chron. 21:4.
e. Judg. 9:6 Which was as the town house, or common hall, which he calleth the tower of Shechem, verse 49.
f. Judg. 9:8 By this parable he declareth that those that are not ambitious, are most worthy of honor, and that the ambitious abuse their honor both to their own destruction and others.
g. Judg. 9:14 Or, thistle, or brier.
h. Judg. 9:15 Abimelech shall destroy the nobles of Shechem.
i. Judg. 9:17 Hebrew, he cast his life far from him.
j. Judg. 9:19 That he is your king, and you his subjects.
k. Judg. 9:23 Because the people consented with the king in shedding innocent blood, therefore God destroyeth both one and the other.
l. Judg. 9:27 Before they were afraid of Abimelech's power, and durst not go out of the city.
m. Judg. 9:29 Braggingly, as though he had been present, or to his captain Zebul.
n. Judg. 9:31 Hebrew, craftily.

lie in wait in the field. **33** And rise early in the morning as soon as the sun is up, and assault the city: and when he and the people that is with him, shall come out against thee, do to him [o]what thou canst. **34** So Abimelech rose up, and all the people that were with him by night: and they lay in wait against Shechem in four bands. **35** Then Gaal the son of Ebed went out, and stood in the entering of the gate of the city: and Abimelech rose up, and the folk that were with him, from lying in wait. **36** And when Gaal saw the people, he said to Zebul, Behold, there come people down from the tops of the mountains: and Zebul said unto him, The [p]shadow of the mountains seem men unto thee. **37** And Gaal spake again, and said, See, there come folk down [q]by the middle of the land, and another band cometh by the way of the plain of [r]Meonenim. **38** Then said Zebul unto him, Where is now thy mouth that said, Who is Abimelech, that we should serve him? Is not this the people that thou hast despised? Go out now, I pray thee and fight with them. **39** And Gaal [s]went out before the men of Shechem, and fought with Abimelech. **40** But Abimelech pursued him, and he fled before him, and many were overthrown and wounded even unto the entering of the gate. **41** And Abimelech dwelt at Arumah: and Zebul thrust out Gaal and his brethren that they should not dwell in Shechem. **42** And on the morrow, the people went out into the field: which was told Abimelech. **43** And he took the [t]people, and divided them into three bands, and laid wait in the fields, and looked, and behold, the people were come out of the city, and he rose up against them, and smote them. **44** And Abimelech, and the bands that were with him, rushed forward, and stood in the entering of the gate of the city: and the two other bands ran upon all the people that were in the field, and slew them. **45** And when Abimelech had fought against the city all that day, he took the city, and slew the people that was therein, and destroyed the city, and sowed [u]salt in it. **46** And when all the men of the tower of Shechem heard it, they entered into an hold of the house of the god [v]Berith. **47** And it was told Abimelech, that all the men of the tower of Shechem were gathered together. **48** And Abimelech got him up to mount Zalmon, he and all the people that were with him: and Abimelech took axes with him, and cut down boughs of trees, and took them, and bare them on his shoulder, and said unto the folk that were with him, What ye have seen me do, make haste, and do like me. **49** Then all the people also cut down every man his bough, and followed Abimelech, and put them to the hold, and set the hold on fire with them so all the men of the tower of Shechem [w]died also, about a thousand men and women. **50** Then went Abimelech to Thebez, and besieged Thebez, and took it. **51** But there was a strong tower within the city, and thither fled all the men and women, and all the chiefs of the city, and shut it to them, and went up to the top of the tower. **52** And Abimelech came unto the tower, and fought against it, and went hard unto the door of the tower to set it on fire. **53** But a certain woman [1]cast a piece of a millstone upon Abimelech's head, and brake his brainpan. **54** Then Abimelech called hastily his page that bore his harness, and said unto him, Draw thy sword and slay me, that men say not of me, A woman slew him. And his page [x]thrust him through, and he died. **55** And when the men of Israel saw that Abimelech was dead, they departed every man unto his own place. **56** Thus God rendered the wickedness of Abimelech, which he did unto his father in slaying his seventy brethren. **57** Also all the wickedness of the men of Shechem did God bring upon their heads. So upon them came the [y]curse of Jotham the son of Jerubbaal.

10

2 Tola dieth. 5 Jair also dieth. 7 The Israelites are punished for their sins. 10 They cry unto God, 16 and he hath pity on them.

1 After Abimelech, there arose to defend Israel, Tola, the son of Puah, the son of [a]Dodo, a man of Issachar, which dwelt in Shamir in mount Ephraim. **2** And he [b]judged Israel three and twenty years, and died, and was buried in Shamir. **3** And after him arose Jair a Gileadite, and judged Israel two and twenty years. **4** And he had thirty sons that [c]rode on thirty asscolts, and they had thirty cities, which are called [d]Havoth Jair unto this day, and are in the land of Gilead. **5** And Jair died, and was buried in Camon. **6** [1]And the children of Israel wrought wickedness again in the sight of the Lord, and served Baal and [2]Ashtoreth, and the gods of [e]Aram, and the gods of Sidon, and the gods of Moab, and the gods of the children of Ammon, and the gods of the Philistines, and forsook the Lord and served not him. **7** Therefore the wrath of the Lord was kindled against Israel, and he [f]sold them into the hands of the Philistines, and into the hands of the children of Ammon: **8** Who from that year vexed and oppressed the children of Israel eighteen years, [g]even all the children of Israel that were beyond Jordan, in the land of the Amorites, which is in Gilead. **9** Moreover, the children of Ammon went over Jordan to fight against Judah and against Benjamin, and against the house of Ephraim: so that Israel was sore tormented. **10** Then the children of Israel [h]cried unto the Lord, saying, We have sinned against thee, even because we have forsaken our own God, and have served Baal. **11** And the Lord [i]said unto the children of Israel, Did not I deliver you from the Egyptians and from the Amorites, from the children of Ammon, and from the Philistines? **12** The Sidonians also, and the Amalekites, and the Maonites did oppress you, and ye cried to me, and I saved you out of their hands. **13** Yet ye [3]have forsaken me, and served other gods: Wherefore I will deliver you no more. **14** Go, and cry unto the gods which ye have chosen: let them save you in the time of your tribulation. **15** And the children of Israel said unto the Lord, We have sinned: do thou unto us whatsoever please thee: only we pray thee to deliver us [j]this day. **16** Then they put away the strange gods from among them, and [k]served the Lord: and [l]his soul was grieved for the misery of Israel. **17** Then the children of Ammon gathered themselves together, and pitched in Gilead: and the children of Israel assembled themselves, and pitched in Mizpah. **18** And the people and princes of Gilead said one to another, Whosoever will begin the battle against the children of Ammon, the same shall be [4]head over all the inhabitants of Gilead.

11

2 Jephthah being chased away by his brethren, was after made captain over Israel. 30 He maketh a rash vow. 32 He vanquisheth the Ammonites, 39 and sacrificeth his daughter according to his vow.

1 Then Gilead begat Jephthah, and Jephthah the Gileadite was [a]a valiant man, but the son of an [b]harlot. **2** And Gilead's wife bare him sons, and when the woman's children were come to age, they thrust out Jephthah, and said unto him, Thou shalt not inherit in our father's house: for thou art the son of a [c]strange woman. **3** Then Jephthah fled from his brethren, and dwelt in the land of [d]Tob: and there gathered idle fellows to Jephthah, and [e]went out with him. **4** And in process of time, the children of Ammon made war with Israel. **5** And when the children of Ammon fought with Israel, the [f]Elders of Gilead went to fetch Jephthah out of the land of Tob. **6** And they said unto Jephthah, Come and be our captain, that we may fight [g]with the children of Ammon. **7** Jephthah then answered the Elders of Gilead, Did not ye hate me, and [h]expel me out of my father's house? how then come you unto me now in time of your tribulation? **8** Then the Elders of Gilead said unto Jephthah, Therefore we turn again to thee now, that thou mayest go with us, and fight against the children of Ammon, and be our head over all the inhabitants of Gilead. **9** And Jephthah said unto the Elders of Gilead, If ye bring me home again to fight against the children of Ammon, if the Lord give them before me, shall I be your head? **10** And the Elders of Gilead said unto Jephthah, The Lord [i]be witness between us, if we do not according to thy words. **11** Then Jephthah went with the Elders of Gilead, and the people made him head and captain over them: and Jephthah rehearsed all his words before the Lord in Mizpah. **12** Then Jephthah sent messengers unto the king of the children of Ammon, saying, What hast thou to do with me, that thou art come against me, to fight in my land? **13** And the king of the children of Ammon answered unto the messengers of Jephthah, [1]Because Israel took my land, when they came up from Egypt, from Arnon unto Jabbok, and unto Jordan: now therefore restore those lands [j]quietly. **14** Yet Jephthah sent messengers again unto the king of the children of Ammon, **15** And said unto him, Thus saith Jephthah, [2]Israel took not the land of Moab, nor the land of the children of Ammon. **16** But when Israel came up from Egypt, and walked through the wilderness unto the red sea, then they came to Kadesh. **17** [3]And Israel sent messengers unto the king of Edom, saying, Let me, I pray thee, go through thy land: but the king of Edom would not consent: and also they sent unto the king of Moab, but he would not: therefore Israel abode in Kadesh. **18** Then they went through the wilderness, and compassed the land of Edom, and the land of Moab, and came by the Eastside of the land of Moab, and pitched on the other side of Arnon, [4]and came not within

---

o. Judg. 9:33 Hebrew, what thine hand can find.
p. Judg. 9:36 Thou art afraid of a shadow.
q. Judg. 9:37 Hebrew, by the navel.
r. Judg. 9:37 Or, charmers.
s. Judg. 9:39 As their captain.
t. Judg. 9:43 Which were in his company.
u. Judg. 9:45 That it should be unfruitful, and never serve to any use.
v. Judg. 9:46 That is, of Baal-Berith, as Judg. 8:33.
w. Judg. 9:49 Meaning, that all were destroyed as well they in the tower, as the other.
x. Judg. 9:54 Thus God by such miserable death taketh vengeance on tyrants even in this life.
y. Judg. 9:57 For making a tyrant their king.

JUDG. 9
1. 2 Sam. 12:21

JUDG. 10
a. Judg. 10:1 Or, his uncle.
b. Judg. 10:2 Or, governed.
c. Judg. 10:4 Signifying, they were men of authority.
d. Judg. 10:4 Or, the towns of Jair, as Deut. 3:14.
e. Judg. 10:6 Or, Syrian.
f. Judg. 10:7 Or, delivered.
g. Judg. 10:8 As the Reubenites, Gadites, and half the tribe of Manasseh.
h. Judg. 10:10 They prayed to the Lord, and confessed their sins.
i. Judg. 10:11 By stirring them up some prophets, as Judg. 6:8.
j. Judg. 10:15 That is, from this present danger.
k. Judg. 10:16 This is true repentance, to put away the evil, and to serve God aright.
l. Judg. 10:16 Or, he pitied.

JUDG. 10
1. Judg. 2:11 / Judg. 3:7 / Judg. 4:1 / Judg. 6:1 / Judg. 13:1
2. Judg. 2:13
3. Deut. 32:15 / Jer. 2:13
4. Judg. 11:6

JUDG. 11
a. Judg. 11:1 Hebrew, a man of mighty force.
b. Judg. 11:1 Or, victualler.
c. Judg. 11:2 That is, of an harlot as verse 1.
d. Judg. 11:3 Where the governor of the country was called Tob.
e. Judg. 11:3 Joined with him, as some think, against his brethren.
f. Judg. 11:5 Or, ambassadors, sent for that purpose.
g. Judg. 11:6 Men oft times are constrained to desire help of them, whom before they have refused.
h. Judg. 11:7 Oft times those things which men reject, God chooseth to do great enterprises by.
i. Judg. 11:10 Hebrew, be the bearer.
j. Judg. 11:13 Hebrew, in peace.

the coast of Moab: for Arnon was the border of Moab. **19** Also Israel [5]sent mes-
sengers unto Sihon, king of the Amorites, the king of Heshbon, and Israel said
unto him, Let us pass, we pray thee, by thy land unto our [k]place. **20** But Sihon
[l]consented not to Israel, that he should go through his coast: but Sihon gathered
all his people together, and pitched in Jahaz, and fought with Israel. **21** And the
Lord God of Israel gave Sihon, and all his folk into the hands of Israel, and they
smote them: so Israel possessed all the land of the Amorites, the inhabitants of that
country: **22** And they possessed [6]all the coast of the Amorites, from Arnon unto
Jabbok, and from the wilderness even unto Jordan. **23** Now therefore the Lord
God of Israel hath cast out the Amorites before his people Israel, and shouldest
thou possess it? **24** Wouldest not thou possess that which Chemosh thy god
giveth thee to possess? So whomsoever the [m]Lord our God driveth out before us,
them will we possess. **25** [7]And art thou now far better than Balak the son of Zip-
por king of Moab? did he not strive with Israel and fight against them, **26** When
Israel dwelt in Heshbon and in her towns, and in Aroer and in her towns, and in
all the cities that are by the coasts of Arnon, three hundred years? why did ye not
then recover [n]them in that space? **27** Wherefore I have not offended thee: but
thou doest me wrong to war against me. The Lord the Judge [o]be judge this day
between the children of Israel, and the children of Ammon. **28** Howbeit the
king of the children of Ammon hearkened not unto the words of Jephthah, whi-
ch he had sent him. **29** Then the [p]Spirit of the Lord came upon Jephthah, and
he passed over to Gilead, and to Manasseh, and came to Mizpah in Gilead, and
from Mizpah in Gilead he went unto the children of Ammon. **30** And Jephthah
[q]vowed a vow unto the Lord, and said, If thou shalt deliver the children of Am-
mon into mine hands, **31** Then that thing that cometh out of the doors of mine
house to meet me, when I come home in peace from the children of Ammon,
shall be the Lord's, and I will offer it for a burnt offering. **32** And so Jephthah
went unto the children of Ammon to fight against them, and the Lord delivered
them into his hands. **33** And he smote them from Aroer even till thou come to
Minnith, twenty cities, and so forth to [r]Abel of the vineyards, with an exceeding
great slaughter. Thus the children of Ammon were humbled before the children
of Israel. **34** Now when Jephthah came to Mizpah unto his house, behold, his
daughter came out to meet him with [s]timbrels and dances, which was his only
child: he had none other son, nor daughter. **35** And when he saw her, he [t]rent
his clothes, and said, Alas my daughter, thou hast brought me low, and art of
them that trouble me: for I have opened my mouth unto the Lord, and cannot go
back. **36** And she said unto him, My father, if thou hast opened thy mouth unto
the Lord, do with me as thou hast promised, seeing that the Lord hath avenged
thee of thine enemies the children of Ammon. **37** Also she said unto her father,
Do thus much for me: suffer me two months, that I may go to the mountains, and
[u]bewail my virginity, I and my fellows. **38** And he said, Go: and he sent her away
two months: so she went with her companions, and lamented her virginity upon
the mountains. **39** And after the end of two months, she turned again unto her
father, who did with her according to his vow which he had vowed, and she had
known no man. And it was a custom in Israel: **40** The daughters of Israel went
year by year to lament the daughter of Jephthah the Gileadite, four days in a year.

12

6 Jephthah killeth two and forty thousand Ephraimites, 8 After Jephthah succeedeth Ibzan, 11 Elon, 13 and Abdon.

1 And the men of Ephraim gathered themselves together, and went [a]Nor-
thward, and said unto Jephthah, Wherefore wentest thou to fight against the chil-
dren of Ammon, and didst not call [b]us to go with thee? we will therefore burn
thine house upon thee with fire. **2** And Jephthah said unto them, I and my pe-
ople were at great strife with the children of Ammon, and when I called you, ye
delivered me not out of their hands. **3** So when I saw that ye delivered me not,
[c]I put my life in mine hands, and went upon the children of Ammon: so the Lord
delivered them into mine hands. Wherefore then are ye come upon me now to
fight against me? **4** Then Jephthah gathered all the men of Gilead, and fought
with Ephraim: and the men of Gilead smote Ephraim, because they said, Ye Gilea-
dites are runagates of Ephraim [d]among the Ephraimites, and among the Manassi-
tes. **5** Also the Gileadites took the passages of Jordan before the Ephraimites, and
when the Ephraimites that were escaped, said, Let me pass, then the men of Gilead
said unto him, Art thou an Ephraimite? If he said, Nay, **6** Then said they unto
him, Say now [e]Shibboleth: and he said Sibboleth: for he could not so pronounce:
then they took him, and slew him at the passages of Jordan: and there fell at that
time of the Ephraimites two and forty thousand. **7** And Jephthah judged Israel
six years: then died Jephthah the Gileadite, and was buried in one of the cities of
Gilead. **8** After him [f]Ibzan of Bethlehem judged Israel, **9** Who had thirty sons
and thirty daughters, which he sent out, and took in thirty daughters from abro-
ad for his sons: and he judged Israel seven years. **10** Then Ibzan died, and was
buried at Bethlehem. **11** And after him judged Israel Elon, a Zebulunite, and
he judged Israel ten years. **12** Then Elon the Zebulunite died, and was buried
in Aijalon in the country of Zebulun. **13** And after him Abdon the son of Hil-
lel the Pirathonite judged Israel. **14** And he had forty sons and thirty [g]nephews
that rode on seventy [h]asscolts: and he judged Israel eight years. **15** Then died
Abdon the son of Hillel the Pirathonite, and was buried in Pirathon, in the land of
Ephraim, in the mount of the Amalekites.

13

1 Israel for their wickedness is oppressed of the Philistines. 3 The Angel appeareth to Manoah's wife, 16 The Angel commandeth him to sacrifice unto the Lord. 24 The birth of Samson.

1 But the children of Israel continued to commit [1]wickedness in the sight of
the Lord, and the Lord delivered them into the hands of the Philistines forty ye-
ars. **2** Then there was a man in Zorah of the family of the Danites named Mano-
ah, whose wife was [a]barren, and bare not. **3** And the Angel of the Lord appeared
unto the woman, and said unto her, Behold now, thou art barren, and bearest not:
but thou shalt conceive, and bear a son. **4** And now therefore beware [2]that thou
drink no wine, nor strong drink, neither eat any unclean thing. **5** For lo, thou
shalt conceive and bear a son, and no razor shall [3]come on his head: for the child
shall be a [b]Nazirite unto God from his birth: and he shall begin to save Israel out of
the hands of the Philistines. **6** Then the wife came and told her husband, saying,
A man of God came unto me, and the fashion of him was like the fashion of the
Angel of God exceedingly [c]fearful, but I asked him not whence he was, neither told
he me his name, **7** But he said unto me, Behold, thou shalt conceive and bear a
son, and now thou shalt drink no wine nor strong drink, neither eat any unclean
thing, for the child shall be a Nazirite to God from his birth to the day of his dea-
th. **8** Then Manoah [d]prayed to the Lord, and said, I pray thee, my Lord, let the
man of God, whom thou sentest, come again now unto us, and teach us what we
shall do unto the child when he is born. **9** And God heard the voice of Manoah,
and the Angel of God came again unto the wife, as she sat in the field, but Manoah
her husband was not with her. **10** And the wife made haste and ran, and showed
her husband, and said unto him, Behold, the man hath appeared unto me, that
came unto me [e]today. **11** And Manoah arose and went after his wife, and came
to the [f]man, and said unto him, Art thou the man that spakest unto the woman?
and he said, Yea. **12** Then Manoah said, Now let thy saying come to pass: but
how shall we order the child and do unto him? **13** And the Angel of the Lord
said unto Manoah, The woman must beware of all that I said unto her. **14** She
may eat of nothing that cometh of the vine tree: she shall not drink wine nor
strong drink, nor eat any [g]unclean thing: let her observe all that I have comman-
ded her. **15** Manoah then said unto the Angel of the Lord, I pray thee, let us
retain thee, until we have made ready a kid for thee. **16** And the Angel of the
Lord said unto Manoah, Though thou make me abide, I will not eat of thy bread,
and if thou wilt make a burnt offering, offer it unto the [h]Lord: for Manoah knew
not that it was an Angel of the Lord. **17** Again Manoah said unto the Angel of
the Lord, What is thy name, that when thy saying is come to pass, we may honor
thee? **18** And the Angel of the Lord said unto him, Why askest thou thus after
my name, which is [i]secret? **19** Then Manoah took a kid with a meat offering,
and offered it upon a stone unto the Lord: and the Angel did [j]wondrously, while
Manoah and his wife looked on. **20** For when the flame came up toward heaven
from the altar, the Angel of the Lord ascended up in the flame of the altar, and Ma-
noah and his wife beheld it, and fell on their faces unto the ground. **21** (So the
Angel of the Lord did no more appear unto Manoah and his wife.) Then Manoah

---

k. Judg. 11:19 Or, country.
l. Judg. 11:20 He trusted them not to go through his country.
m. Judg. 11:24 For we ought more to believe and obey God, than thou thine idols.
n. Judg. 11:26 Meaning, their towns.
o. Judg. 11:27 To punish the offender.
p. Judg. 11:29 That is, the spirit of strength and zeal.
q. Judg. 11:30 As the Apostle commendeth Jephthah for his worthy enterprise in delivering the people, Heb. 11:32, so by his rash vow and wicked performance of the same, his victory was defaced: and here we see that the sins of the godly do not utterly extinguish their faith.
r. Judg. 11:33 Or, the plain.
s. Judg. 11:34 According to the manner after the victory.
t. Judg. 11:35 Being overcome with blind zeal, and not considering whether the vow was lawful or no.
u. Judg. 11:37 For it was counted as a shame in Israel, to die without children, and therefore they rejoiced to be married.

JUDG. 11
1. Num. 21:13
2. Deut. 2:9
3. Num. 20:14,20
4. Num. 21:13 / Num. 22:14
5. Deut. 2:26
6. Deut. 2:36
7. Num. 22:2 / Deut. 23:4 / Josh. 24:9

JUDG. 12
a. Judg. 12:1 After they had passed Jordan.
b. Judg. 12:1 Thus ambition envieth God's work in others as they did also against Gideon, Judg. 8:1.
c. Judg. 12:3 That is, I ventured my life, and when man's help failed, I put my trust only in God.
d. Judg. 12:4 Ye ran from us, and chose Gilead, and now in respect of us, ye are nothing.
e. Judg. 12:6 Which signifieth the fall of waters, or an ear of corn.
f. Judg. 12:8 Some think that this was Boaz the husband of Ruth.
g. Judg. 12:14 Hebrew, sons' sons.
h. Judg. 12:14 Or, horse colts.

JUDG. 13
a. Judg. 13:2 Signifying, that their deliverance came only of God, and not by man's power.
b. Judg. 13:5 Meaning, he should be separate from the world, and dedicated to God.
c. Judg. 13:6 If flesh be not able to abide the sight of an Angel, how much less the presence of God?
d. Judg. 13:8 He showeth himself ready to obey God's will, and therefore desireth to know farther.
e. Judg. 13:10 It seemth that the Angel appeared unto her twice in one day.
f. Judg. 13:11 He calleth him man, because he so seemed, but he was Christ the eternal word, which at his time appointed became man.
g. Judg. 13:14 Anything forbidden by the Law.
h. Judg. 13:16 Showing, that he sought not his own honor but God's, whose messenger he was.
i. Judg. 13:18 Or, marvelous.
j. Judg. 13:19 God sent fire from heaven to consume their sacrifice, to confirm their faith in his promise.

knew that it was an Angel of the Lord. **22** And Manoah said unto his wife, [4]We shall surely die, because we have seen God. **23** But his wife said unto him, If the Lord would kill us, he would not have received a [k]burnt offering, and a meat offering of our hands, neither would he have showed us all these things, nor would now have told us any such. **24** And the wife bore a son, and called his name Samson: and the child grew, and the Lord blessed him. **25** And the Spirit of the Lord began to [l]strengthen him in the host of Dan, between Zorah and Eshtaol.

14

2 Samson desireth to have a wife of the Philistines. 6 He killeth a lion. 12 He propoundeth a riddle. 19 He killeth thirty. 20 His wife forsaketh him, and taketh another.

1 Now Samson went down to Timnah, and saw a woman in Timnah of the daughters of the Philistines, **2** And he came up and told his father and his mother and said, I have seen a woman in Timnah of the daughters of the Philistines: now therefore [a]give me her to wife. **3** Then his father and his mother said unto him, Is there [b]never a wife among the daughters of thy brethren, and among all my people, that thou must go to take a wife of the uncircumcised Philistines? And Samson said unto his father, Give me her, for she pleaseth me well. **4** But his father and his mother knew not that it came of the Lord, that he should seek an occasion against the [c]Philistines: for at that time the Philistines reigned over Israel. **5** Then went Samson, and his father and his mother down to Timnah, and came to the vineyards of Timnah: and behold, a young lion roared upon him. **6** And the Spirit of the Lord [d]came upon him, and he tare him, as one should have rent a kid, and had nothing in his hand, neither told he his father nor his mother what he had done. **7** And he went down, and talked with the woman which was beautiful in the eyes of Samson. **8** And within a few days, when he returned [e]to receive her, he went aside to see the carcass of the lion: and behold, there was a swarm of bees, and honey in the body of the lion. **9** And he took thereof in his hands, and went eating, and came to his father and to his mother, and gave unto them, and they did eat: but he told not them, that he had taken the honey out of the body of the lion. **10** So his father went down unto the woman, and Samson made there a [f]feast: for so used the young men to do. **11** And when [g]they saw him, they brought thirty companions to be with him. **12** Then Samson said unto them, I will now put forth a riddle unto you: and if you can declare it me within seven days of the feast, and find it out, I will give you thirty sheets, and thirty [h]change of garments. **13** But if you cannot declare it me, then shall ye give me thirty sheets and thirty change of garments. And they answered him, Put forth thy riddle, that we may hear it. **14** And he said unto them, Out of the eater came meat, and out of the strong came sweetness: and they could not in three days expound the riddle. **15** And when the seventh day was [i]come, they said unto Samson's wife, Entice thine husband that he may declare us the riddle, lest we burn thee and thy father's house with fire. Have ye called us [j]to possess us? is it not so? **16** And Samson's wife wept before him, and said, Surely thou hatest me, and lovest me not: for thou hast put forth a riddle unto the [k]children of my people, and hast not told it me. And he said unto her, Behold, I have not told it my father nor my mother, and shall I tell it thee? **17** Then Samson's wife wept before him [l]seven days, while their feast lasted, and when the seventh day came, he told her, because she was importunate upon him: so she told the riddle to the children of her people. **18** And the men of the city said unto him the seventh day before the sun went down, What is sweeter than honey? and what is stronger than a Lion? Then said he unto them, [m]If ye had not plowed with my heifer, ye had not found out my riddle. **19** And the Spirit of the Lord came upon him, and he went down [n]to Ashkelon, and slew thirty men of them and spoiled them, and gave change of garments unto them, which expounded the riddle: and his wrath was kindled, and he went up to his father's house. **20** Then Samson's wife was given to his companion, whom he had used as his friend.

15

4 Samson tieth firebrands to the foxes' tails. 6 The Philistines burnt his father-in-law and his wife. 15 With the jawbone of an ass he killeth a thousand men. 19 Out of a great tooth in the jaw God gave him water.

1 But within a while after, in the time of wheat harvest, Samson visited his wife with a kid, saying, I will [a]go in to my wife into the chamber: but her father would not suffer him to go in. **2** And her father said, I thought that thou hadst hated her: therefore gave I her to thy companion. Is not her younger sister fairer than she? take her, I pray thee, instead of the other. **3** Then Samson said unto them, Now am I more [b]blameless than the Philistines: therefore will I do them displeasure. **4** And Samson went out, and took three hundred foxes, and took firebrands, and turned them tail to tail, and put a firebrand in the midst between two tails. **5** And when he had set the brands on fire, he sent them out into the standing corn of the Philistines, and burnt up both the [c]ricks and the standing corn, with the vineyards and olives. **6** Then the Philistines said, Who hath done this? And they answered, Samson the son-in-law of the [d]Timnite, because he had taken his wife, and given her to his companion. Then the Philistines came up and [e]burnt her and her father with fire. **7** And Samson said unto them, Though ye have done this, yet will I be avenged of you, and then I will cease. **8** So he smote them [f]hip and thigh with a mighty plague: then he went and dwelt in the top of the rock Etam. **9** Then the Philistines came up, and pitched in Judah, and [g]were spread abroad in Lehi. **10** And the men of Judah said, Why are ye come up unto us? And they answered, To [h]bind Samson are we come up, and to do to him as he hath done to us. **11** Then three thousand men of Judah went to the top of the rock Etam, and said to Samson, Knowest thou not that the Philistines are rulers over us? [i]Wherefore then hast thou done thus unto us? And he answered them, As they did unto me, so have I done unto them. **12** Again they said unto him, We are come to bind thee, and to deliver thee into the hand of the Philistines. And Samson said unto them, Swear unto me, that ye will not fall upon me yourselves. **13** And they answered him, saying, No, but we will bind thee and [j]deliver thee unto their hand, but we will not kill thee. And they bound him with two new cords, and brought him from the rock. **14** When he came to Lehi, the Philistines shouted against him, and the Spirit of the Lord came upon him, and the cords that were upon his arms, became as flax that was burnt with fire: for the bands loosed from his hands. **15** And he found a [k]new jawbone of an ass, and put forth his hands, and caught it, and slew a thousand men therewith. **16** Then Samson said, With the jaw of an ass are heaps upon heaps: with the jaw of an ass have I slain a thousand men. **17** And when he had left speaking, he cast away the jawbone out of his hand, and called that place, [l]Ramath Lehi. **18** And he was sore athirst, and [m]called on the Lord, and said, Thou hast given this great deliverance into the hand of thy servant: and now shall I die for thirst, and fall into the hand of the uncircumcised? **19** Then God brake the cheek tooth, that was in the jaw, and water came there out: and when he had drunk, his spirit came again, and he was revived: wherefore the name thereof is called, [n]En Hakkore, which is in Lehi unto this day. **20** And he judged Israel in the days of the Philistines twenty years.

16

3 Samson carrieth away the gates of Gaza. 18 He was deceived by Delilah. 30 He pulleth down the house upon the Philistines, and dieth with them.

1 Then went Samson to [a]Gaza, and saw there [b]an harlot, [c]and went in unto her. **2** And it was told to the Gazites, Samson is come hither. And they went about, and laid wait for him all night in the gate of the city, and were quiet all the night, saying, Abide [d]till the morning early, and we shall kill him. **3** And Samson slept till midnight, and arose at midnight, and took the doors of the gates of the city and the two posts, and lifted them away with the bars, and put them upon his shoulders, and carried them up to the top of the mountain that is before Hebron. **4** And after this he loved a woman by the [e]river of Sorek, whose name was Delilah: **5** Unto whom came the princes of the Philistines, and said unto her, Entice him, and see wherein his great strength lieth, and by what means we may overcome him, that we may bind him, and punish him, and every one of us shall give thee eleven hundred [f]shekels of silver. **6** And Delilah said to Samson, Tell me, I pray thee, wherein thy great strength lieth, and wherewith thou mightest be bound, to do thee hurt. **7** Samson then answered unto her, If they bind me with seven [g]green cords, that were never dried, then shall I be weak, and be as another man. **8** And the princes of the Philistines brought her seven green cords that

---

k. Judg. 13:23 These graces that we have received of God, and his accepting of our obedience, are sure tokens of his love toward us, so that nothing can hurt us.
l. Judg. 13:25 Or, to come upon him at divers times.

JUDG. 13

1. Judg. 2:11 / Judg. 3:7 / Judg. 4:1 / Judg. 6:1 / Judg. 10:6
2. Num. 6:2,3
3. 1 Sam. 1:11
4. Exod. 33:20 / Judg. 6:22

JUDG. 14

a. Judg. 14:2 Hebrew, take her for me to wife.
b. Judg. 14:3 Though his parents did justly reprove him, yet it appeareth that this was the secret work of the Lord, verse 4.
c. Judg. 14:4 To fight against them for the deliverance of Israel.
d. Judg. 14:6 Whereby he had strength and boldness.
e. Judg. 14:8 Or, to take her to his wife.
f. Judg. 14:10 Meaning, when he was married.
g. Judg. 14:11 That is, her parents or friends.
h. Judg. 14:12 To wear at feasts, or solemn days.
i. Judg. 14:15 Or, drew near: for it was the fourth day.
j. Judg. 14:15 Or, to impoverish us.
k. Judg. 14:16 Unto them which are of my nation.
l. Judg. 14:17 Or, to the seventh day beginning at the fourth.
m. Judg. 14:18 If ye had not used the help of my wife.
n. Judg. 14:19 Which was one of the five chief cities of the Philistines.

JUDG. 15

a. Judg. 15:1 That is, I will use her as my wife.
b. Judg. 15:3 For through his father-in-law's occasion, he was moved again to take vengeance of the Philistines.
c. Judg. 15:5 Or, that which was reaped and gathered.
d. Judg. 15:6 Or, the citizen of Timnath.
e. Judg. 15:6 So the wicked punish not vice for love of justice, but for fear of danger, which else might come to them.
f. Judg. 15:8 Or, horsemen and footmen.
g. Judg. 15:9 Or, camped.
h. Judg. 15:10 And so being our prisoner to punish him.
i. Judg. 15:11 Such was their gross ignorance, that they judged God's great benefits to be a plague unto them.
j. Judg. 15:13 Thus they had rather betray their brother, than use the means that God had given for their deliverance.
k. Judg. 15:15 That is, of an ass lately slain.
l. Judg. 15:17 Or, the lifting up of the jaw.
m. Judg. 15:18 Whereby appeareth that he did these things in faith, and so with a true zeal to glorify God, and deliver his country.
n. Judg. 15:19 Or, the fountain of him that prayed.

JUDG. 16

a. Judg. 16:1 One of the five chief cities of the Philistines.
b. Judg. 16:1 Or, victualler.
c. Judg. 16:1 That is, he lodged with her.
d. Judg. 16:2 Or, to the light of the morning.
e. Judg. 16:4 Or, plain.
f. Judg. 16:5 Of the value of a shekel, read Gen. 23:15.
g. Judg. 16:7 Or, new withes.
h. Judg. 16:9 Certain Philistines in a secret chamber.

were not dry, and she bound him therewith. **9** (And she had [h]men lying in wait with her in the chamber) Then she said unto him, The Philistines be upon thee, Samson. And he brake the cords, as a thread of tow is broken, when [i]it feeleth fire: so his strength was not known. **10** After Delilah said unto Samson, See, thou hast mocked me, and told me lies. I pray thee now, [j]tell me wherewith thou mightest be bound. **11** Then he answered her, If they bind me with new ropes that never were occupied, then shall I be weak, and be as another man. **12** Delilah therefore took new ropes, and bound him therewith, and said unto him, The Philistines be upon thee, Samson: (and men lay in wait in the chamber) and he brake them from his arms, as a thread. **13** Afterward Delilah said to Samson, Hitherto thou hast beguiled me, and told me lies: tell me how thou mightest be bound. [k]And he said unto her, If thou plattedst seven locks of mine head with the threads of the woof. **14** And she fastened it with a pin, and said unto him, The Philistines be upon thee, Samson. And he awoke out of his sleep, and went away with the [l]pin of the web, and the woof. **15** Again she said unto him, How canst thou say, [m]I love thee, when thine heart is not with me? thou hast mocked me these three times, and hast not told me wherein thy great strength lieth. **16** And because she was importunate upon him with her words continually, and vexed him, his soul was pained unto the death. **17** Therefore he told her all his [n]heart, and said unto her, There never came razor upon mine head: for I am a Nazirite unto God from my mother's womb: therefore if I be shaven, my strength will go from me, and I shall be weak and be like all other men. **18** And when Delilah saw that he had told her all his heart, she sent, and called for the Princes of the Philistines, saying, Come up once again: for he hath showed me all his heart. Then the Princes of the Philistines came up unto her, and brought the money in their hands. **19** And she made him sleep upon her knees, and she called a man, and made him to shave off the seven locks of his head, and she began to vex him, and his strength was gone [o]from him. **20** Then she said, The Philistines be upon thee, Samson. And he awoke out of his sleep, and thought, I will go out now as at other times, and shake myself, but he knew not that the Lord was departed from him. **21** Therefore the Philistines took him, and put out his eyes, and brought him down to Gaza, and bound him with fetters: and he did grind in the prison house. **22** And the hair of his head began to [p]grow again after that it was shaven. **23** Then the Princes of the Philistines gathered them together for to offer a great sacrifice unto Dagon their god, and to rejoice: for they said, Our god hath delivered Samson our enemy into our hands. **24** Also when the people saw him, they praised their god: for they said, Our god hath delivered into our hands our enemy and destroyer of our country, which hath slain many of us. **25** And when their hearts were merry, they said, Call Samson, that he may make us pastime: So they called Samson out of the prison house, and he [q]was a laughing stock unto them, and they set him between the pillars. **26** Then Samson said unto the servant that led him by the hand, Lead me, that I may touch the pillars that the house standeth upon, and that I may lean to them. **27** (Now the house was full of men and women, and there were all the princes of the Philistines: also upon the roof were about three thousand men and women, that beheld while Samson [r]played) **28** Then Samson called unto the Lord, and said, O Lord God, I pray thee, think upon me: O God, I beseech thee, strengthen me at this time only, that I may be [s]at once [t]avenged of the Philistines for my two eyes. **29** And Samson laid hold on the two middle pillars whereupon the house stood, and on which it was borne up: on the one with his right hand, and on the other with his left. **30** Then said Samson, [u]Let me lose my life with the Philistines: and he bowed him with all his might, and the house fell upon the princes, and upon all the people that were therein: so the dead which he slew at his death, were more than they which he had slain in his life. **31** Then his brethren, and all the house of his father came down and took him, and brought him up and buried him between Zorah and Eshtaol, in the sepulcher of Manoah his father: now he had judged Israel twenty years.

17

3 Micah's mother according to her vow, made her son two idols. 5 He made his son a Priest for his idols, 10 and after he hired a Levite.

1 There [a]was a man of mount Ephraim, whose name was Micah, **2** And he said unto his mother, The eleven hundred shekels of silver that were taken from thee, for the which thou cursedst, and spakedst it, even in mine hearing, behold, the silver is with me, I took it. Then his mother said, Blessed be my son of the Lord. **3** And when he had restored the eleven hundred shekels of silver to his mother, his mother said, I had dedicate the silver to the Lord of mine hand for my son, to make [b]a graven and molten image. Now therefore I will give it thee again. **4** And when he had restored the money unto his mother, his mother took two hundred shekels of silver, and gave them to the founder, which made thereof a graven and molten image, and it was in the house of Micah. **5** And this man Micah had an house of gods, and made an [c,1]Ephod, and [d,2]Teraphim, and [e]consecrated one of his sons, who was his Priest. **6** [3]In those days there was no [f]King in Israel, but every man did that which was good in his own eyes. **7** There was also a young man out of Bethlehem Judah, [g]of the family of Judah: who was a Levite, and sojourned there. **8** And the man departed out of the city, even out of Bethlehem Judah, to dwell where he could find a place: and as he journeyed, he came to mount Ephraim to the house of Micah. **9** And Micah said unto him, Whence comest thou? And the Levite answered him, [h]I come from Bethlehem Judah, and go to dwell where I may find a place. **10** Then Micah said unto him, Dwell with me, and be unto me a father and a Priest, and I will give thee ten shekels of silver by year, and a suit of apparel, and thy meat and drink. So the Levite went in. **11** And the Levite was [i]content to dwell with the man, and the young man was unto him as one of his own sons. **12** And Micah consecrated the Levite, and the young man was his Priest, and was in the house of Micah. **13** Then said Micah, Now I know that the Lord will be [j]good unto me, seeing I have a Levite to my Priest.

18

2 The children of Dan send men to search the land. 11 Then come the six hundred and take the gods, and the Priest of Micah away. 27 They destroy Laish, 28 They build it again. 30 And set up Idolatry.

1 In those days there was no [a]king in Israel, and at the same time the tribe of Dan sought them an inheritance to dwell in: for unto that time all their inheritance had not fallen unto them among the tribes of Israel. **2** Therefore the children of Dan sent of their family, five men out of their coasts, even men expert in war, out of Zorah and Eshtaol, to view the land and search it out, and said unto them, [b]Go, and search out the land. Then they came to mount Ephraim to the house of Micah and lodged there. **3** When they were in the house of Micah, they knew the [c]voice of the young man the Levite: and being turned in thither, they said unto him, Who brought thee hither? or what makest thou in this place? and what hast thou to do here? **4** And he answered them, Thus and thus dealeth Micah with me, and hath hired me, and I am his Priest. **5** Again they said unto him, Ask counsel now of God, that we may know whether the way which we go, shall be prosperous. **6** And the Priest said unto them, [d]Go in peace: for the Lord guideth your way which ye go. **7** Then the five men departed, and came to Laish, and saw the people that were therein, which dwelt careless, after the manner of the Sidonians, quiet and sure, because no man [e]made any trouble in the land, or usurped any dominion: also they were far from the Sidonians, and had no business with other men. **8** So they came again unto their brethren to Zorah and Eshtaol: and their brethren said unto them, What have ye done? **9** And they answered, Arise, that we may go up against them: for we have seen the land, and surely it is very good, and [f]do ye sit still? be not slothful to go and enter to possess the land: **10** (If ye will go, ye shall come unto a careless people, and the country is large) for God hath given it into your hand. It is a place which doth lack nothing that is in the world. **11** Then there departed thence of the family of the Danites, from Zorah and from Eshtaol, six hundred men appointed with instruments of war. **12** And they went up, and pitched in Kirjath Jearim in Judah: wherefore they called that place [g]Mahaneh Dan unto this day: and it is behind Kirjath Jearim. **13** And they went thence unto mount Ephraim, and came to the house of Micah. **14** Then answered the five men that went to spy out the country of

---

i. Judg. 16:9 When fire cometh near it.
j. Judg. 16:10 Though her falsehood tended to make him lose his life, yet his affection so blinded him, that he could not beware.
k. Judg. 16:13 It is impossible if we give place to our wicked affections, but at length we shall be destroyed.
l. Judg. 16:14 Or, beam.
m. Judg. 16:15 For this Samson used to say, I love thee.
n. Judg. 16:17 Thus his immoderate affections toward a wicked woman caused him to lose God's excellent gifts, and become slave unto them whom he should have ruled.
o. Judg. 16:19 Not for the loss of his hair, but for the contempt of the ordinance of God, which was the cause that God departed from him.
p. Judg. 16:22 Yet had he not his strength again, till he had called upon God, and reconciled himself.
q. Judg. 16:25 Thus by God's just judgments they are made slaves to infidels which neglect their vocation in defending the faithful.
r. Judg. 16:27 Or, was mocked.
s. Judg. 16:28 Hebrew, take one vengeance.
t. Judg. 16:28 According to my vocation which is to execute God's judgments upon the wicked.
u. Judg. 16:30 He speaketh not this of despair, but humbling himself for neglecting his office and the offence thereby given.

JUDG. 17

a. Judg. 17:1 Some think this history was in the time of Othniel, or as Josephus writeth, immediately after Joshua.
b. Judg. 17:3 Contrary to the commandment of God and true religion practiced under Joshua, they forsook the Lord and fell to idolatry.
c. Judg. 17:5 He would serve both God and Idols.
d. Judg. 17:5 By Teraphim some understand certain idols, having the likeness of a man, but others understand thereby all manner of things and instruments belonging unto those, who sought for any answer at God's hands, as Judg. 18:5,6.
e. Judg. 17:5 Hebrew, filled the hand of one.
f. Judg. 17:6 For where there is no Magistrate fearing God, there can be no true religion or order.
g. Judg. 17:7 Which Bethlehem was in the tribe of Judah.
h. Judg. 17:9 For in those days the service of God was corrupt in all estates, and the Levites were not looked unto.
i. Judg. 17:11 Not considering that he forsook the true worshipping of God for to maintain his own belly.
j. Judg. 17:13 Thus the idolaters persuade themselves of God's favor, when indeed he doth detest them.

JUDH. 17

1. Judg. 8:27
2. Gen. 31:19 / Hos. 3:4
3. Judg. 21:25

JUDG. 18

a. Judg. 18:1 Meaning, no ordinary Magistrate to punish vice according to God's word.
b. Judg. 18:2 For the portion which Joshua gave them, was not sufficient for all their tribe.
c. Judg. 18:3 They knew him by his speech that he was a stranger there.
d. Judg. 18:6 Thus God granteth the idolaters sometime their requests to their destruction that delight in errors.
e. Judg. 18:7 Hebrew, made them ashamed.
f. Judg. 18:9 Lose ye this good occasion through your slothfulness?
g. Judg. 18:12 Or, the tents of Dan.

Laish, and said unto their brethren, [h]Know ye not, that there is in these houses an Ephod, and Teraphim, and a graven and a molten image? Now therefore consider what ye have to do. **15** And they turned thitherward and came to the house of the young man the Levite, even unto the house of Micah, and saluted him peaceably. **16** And the six hundred men appointed with their weapons of war, which were of the children of Dan, stood by the entering of the gate. **17** Then the five men that went to spy out the land, went in thither, and took the [i]graven image and the Ephod, and the Teraphim, and the molten image: and the Priest stood in the entering of the gate with the six hundred men that were appointed with weapons of war. **18** And the other went into Micah's house, and fet the graven image, the Ephod and the Teraphim, and the molten image. Then said the Priest unto them, What do ye? **19** And they answered him, Hold thy peace: lay thine hand upon thy mouth, and come with us to be our father and Priest. Whether is it better that thou shouldest be a Priest unto the house of one man, or that thou shouldest be a Priest unto a tribe and to a family in Israel? **20** And the Priest's heart was glad, and he took the Ephod, and the Teraphim, and the graven image, and went among the [j]people. **21** And they turned and departed, and put the children, and the cattle, and the substance [k]before them. **22** When they were far off from the house of Micah, the men that were in the houses near to Micah's house, gathered together, and pursued after the children of Dan, **23** And cried unto the children of Dan: who turned their faces, and said unto Micah, What aileth thee that thou makest an outcry? **24** And he said, Ye have taken away my [l]gods, which I made, and the Priest, and go your ways: and what have I more? how then say ye unto me, What aileth thee? **25** And the children of Dan said unto him, Let not thy voice be heard among us, lest [m]angry fellows run upon thee, and thou lose thy life with the lives of thine household. **26** So the children of Dan went their ways: and when Micah saw that they were too strong for him, he turned and went back unto his house. **27** And they took the [n]things which Micah had made, and the Priest which he had, and came unto Laish, unto a quiet people, and without mistrust, and smote them with the edge of the sword, and burnt the city with fire: **28** And there was none to [o]help, because [p]Laish was far from Sidon, and they had no business with other men: also it was in the valley that lieth by Beth Rehob. After, they built the city, and dwelt therein, **29** [1]And called the name of the city Dan, after the name of Dan their father, which was born unto Israel: howbeit the name of the city was Laish at the beginning. **30** Then the children of Dan set them up the [q]graven image: and Jonathan the son of Gershom, the son of Manasseh, and his sons were the Priests in the tribe of the Danites, until the day of the [r]captivity of the land. **31** So they set them up the graven image, which Micah had made, all the while the house of God was in Shiloh.

19

1 A Levite's wife being an harlot forsook her husband, and he took her again. 25 At Gibeah she was most villainously abused to the death. 29 The Levite cutteth her in pieces, and sendeth her to the twelve tribes.

1 Also in those days, when there was no king in Israel, a certain Levite dwelt on the side of mount Ephraim, and took to wife a [1]concubine out of Bethlehem Judah, **2** And his concubine played the whore [a]there, and went away from him unto her father's house to Bethlehem Judah, and there continued the space of four months. **3** And her husband arose and went after her, to speak [b]friendly unto her, and to bring her again: he had also his servant with him, and a couple of asses: and she brought him unto her father's house, and when the young woman's father saw him, he rejoiced [c]of his coming. **4** And his father-in-law, the young woman's father received him: and he abode with him three days: so they did eat and drink, and lodged there. **5** And when the fourth day came, they arose early in the morning, and [d]he prepared to depart: then the young woman's father said unto his son-in-law, [e]Comfort thine heart with a morsel of bread, and then go your way. **6** So they sat down and did eat and drink, both of them together. And the [f]young woman's father said unto the man, Be content, I pray thee, and tarry all night, and let thine heart be merry. **7** And when the man rose up to depart, his father-in-law [g]was earnest: therefore he returned, and lodged there. **8** And he arose up early the fifth day to depart, and the young woman's father said, [h]Comfort thine heart, I pray thee: and they tarried until after midday, and they both did eat. **9** Afterward when the man arose to depart with his concubine and his servant, his father-in-law, the young woman's father said unto him, Behold now, the day [i]draweth toward even: I pray you, tarry all night: behold, the [j]sun goeth to rest: lodge here, that thine heart may be merry, and tomorrow get you early upon your way, and go to the [k]tent. **10** But the man would not tarry, but arose, and departed, and came over against Jebus, (which is Jerusalem) and his two asses laden, and his concubine were with him. **11** When they were near Jebus, the day [l]was sore spent, and the servant said unto his master, Come, I pray thee, and let us turn unto this city of the Jebusites, and lodge all night there. **12** And his master answered him, [m]We will not turn into the city of strangers that are not of the children of Israel, but we will go forth to Gibeah. **13** And he said unto his servant, Come, and let us draw near to one of these places, that we may lodge in Gibeah or in Ramah. **14** So they went forward upon their way, and the Sun went down upon them near to Gibeah, which is in Benjamin. **15** Then they turned thither to go in and lodge in Gibeah: and when he came, he sat him down in a street of the city: for there was no man that [n]took them into his house to lodging. **16** And behold, there came an old man from his work out of the field at even, and the man was of mount Ephraim, but dwelt in Gibeah: and the men of the place were the children of [o]Jemini. **17** And when he had lifted up his eyes, he saw a [p]wayfaring man in the streets of the city: then this old man said, Whither goest thou, and whence camest thou? **18** And he answered him, We came from Bethlehem Judah, unto the side of mount Ephraim: from thence am I: and I went to Bethlehem Judah, and go now to the [q]house of the Lord: and no man receiveth me to house, **19** Although we have straw and provender for our asses, and also bread and wine for me and thine handmaid, and for the boy that is with thy servant: we lack nothing. **20** And the old man said, [r]Peace be with thee: as for all that thou lackest, shalt thou find with me: only abide not in the street all night. **21** So he brought him into his house, and gave fodder unto the asses: and they washed their feet, and did eat and drink. **22** And as they were making their hearts merry, behold, the men of the city, [s]wicked men beset the house round about, and [t]smote at the door, and spake to this old man the master of the house, saying, Bring forth the man that came into thine house that we may know him. **23** And [2]this man the master of the house went out unto them, and said unto them, Nay my brethren, do not so wickedly, I pray you, seeing that this man is come into mine house, do not this villainy. **24** Behold, here is my daughter, a virgin, and his concubine: them will I bring out now, [u]and humble them, and do with them what seemeth you good: but to this man do not this villainy. **25** But the men would not hearken to him: therefore the man took his concubine, and brought her out unto them: and they knew her and abused her all the night unto the morning and when the day began to spring, they let her go. **26** So the woman came in the dawning of the day, and [v]fell down at the door of the man's house where her lord was, till the light day. **27** And her [w]lord arose in the morning, and opened the doors of the house, and went out to go his way, and behold, the woman his concubine was [x]dead at the door of the house, and her hands lay upon the threshold. **28** And he said unto her, up, and let us go: but she answered not. Then he took her up upon the ass, and the man rose up, and went unto his [y]place. **29** And when he was come to his house, he took a knife and laid hand on his concubine, and divided her in pieces with her bones into twelve parts, and sent her through all quarters of Israel. **30** And all that saw it, said, There was no [z]such thing done or seen since the time that the children of Israel came up from the land of Egypt unto this day: consider the matter, consult and give sentence.

20

1 The Israelites assemble at Mizpah, to whom the Levite declareth his wrong. 13 They sent for them that aid the villain. 45 The Israelites are twice overcome, 46 And at length get the victory.

1 Then [1]all the children of Israel went out, and the Congregation was gathered together as [a]one man, from Dan to Beersheba, with the land of Gilead, unto the [b]Lord in Mizpah. **2** And the [c]chief of all the people, and all the tribes of Israel assembled in the Congregation of the people of God four hundred thousand

---

h. Judg. 18:14 Because they before had had good success, they would that their brethren should be encouraged by hearing the same tidings.
i. Judg. 18:17 So superstition blinded them that they thought God's power was in these idols, and that they should have good success by them, though by violence and robbery they did take them away.
j. Judg. 18:20 With the six hundred men.
k. Judg. 18:21 Suspecting them that did pursue them.
l. Judg. 18:24 This declareth what opinion the idolaters have of their idols.
m. Judg. 18:25 Hebrew, who have their heart bitter.
n. Judg. 18:27 Meaning, the idols, as verse 18.
o. Judg. 18:28 Or, deliver them.
p. Judg. 18:28 Which after was called Cesarea Philippi.
q. Judg. 18:30 Thus instead of giving glory to God, they attributed the victory to their idols, and honored them therefore.
r. Judg. 18:30 That is, till the Ark was taken, 1 Sam. 5:1.

JUDG. 18
1. Josh. 19:47

JUDG. 19
a. Judg. 19:2 Hebrew, besides him, to wit, with others.
b. Judg. 19:3 Hebrew, to her heart.
c. Judg. 19:3 Or, at his meeting.
d. Judg. 19:5 Hebrew, rose up.
e. Judg. 19:5 Or, strengthen.
f. Judg. 19:6 That is, his concubine's father.
g. Judg. 19:7 Or, compelled him.
h. Judg. 19:8 Meaning, that he should refresh himself with meat, as verse 5.
i. Judg. 19:9 Hebrew, is weak.
j. Judg. 19:9 Or, the day lodgeth.
k. Judg. 19:9 To wit, to the town or city where he dwelt.
l. Judg. 19:11 Or, went down.
m. Judg. 19:12 Though in these days there were most horrible corruptions, yet very necessity could not compel them, to have to do with them that professed not the true God.
n. Judg. 19:15 Or gathered them.
o. Judg. 19:16 That is, of the tribe of Benjamin.
p. Judg. 19:17 Or, a man walking.
q. Judg. 19:18 To Shiloh of Mizpah where the Ark was.
r. Judg. 19:20 Or, be of good comfort.
s. Judg. 19:22 Hebrew, men of Belial, that is, given to all wickedness.
t. Judg. 19:22 To the intent they might break it.
u. Judg. 19:24 That is, abuse them, as Gen. 19:8.
v. Judg. 19:26 She fell down dead, as verse 27.
w. Judg. 19:27 Or, husband.
x. Judg. 19:27 Or, fallen.
y. Judg. 19:28 Meaning, home unto mount Ephraim.
z. Judg. 19:30 For this was like the sin of Sodom for the which God rained down fire and brimstone from heaven.

JUDG. 19
1. Judg. 17:6 / Judg. 18:1 / Gen. 25:6 **2.** Gen. 19:6

JUDG. 20
a. Judg. 20:1 That is, all with one consent.
b. Judg. 20:1 To ask counsel.
c. Judg. 20:2 Hebrew, corners.
d. Judg. 20:2 Meaning, men able to handle their weapons.
e. Judg. 20:3 To the Levite.

footmen that [d]drew sword. **3** (Now the children of Benjamin heard that the children of Israel were gone up to Mizpah) Then, the children of Israel [e]said, How is this wickedness committed? **4** And the same Levite, the woman's husband that was slain, answered and said, I came unto Gibeah that is in Benjamin with my concubine to lodge, **5** And the [f]men of Gibeah arose against me, and beset the house round about upon me by night, thinking to have slain me, and have forced my concubine that she is dead. **6** Then I took my concubine, and cut her in pieces, and sent [g]her throughout all the country of the inheritance of Israel: for they have committed abomination and villainy in Israel. **7** Behold, ye are all children of Israel, give your advice, and counsel herein. **8** Then all the people arose as one man, saying, There shall not a man of us go to his tent, neither any turn into his [h]house. **9** But now this is that thing which we will do to Gibeah: we will go up by lot against it. **10** And we will take ten men of the hundred throughout all the tribes of Israel, and an hundred of the thousand, and a thousand of ten thousand to bring [i]victual for the people, that they may do (when they come to Gibeah of Benjamin) according to all the villainy, that it hath done in Israel. **11** So all the men of Israel were gathered against the city, knit together as one man. **12** And the tribes of Israel sent men through all the [j]tribe of Benjamin, saying, What wickedness is this that is committed among you? **13** Now therefore deliver us those wicked men which are in Gibeah, that we may put them to death, and put away evil from Israel: but the children of Benjamin [k]would not obey the voice of their brethren the children of Israel. **14** But the children of Benjamin gathered themselves together out of the cities unto Gibeah, to come out and fight against the children of Israel. **15** And the children of Benjamin were numbered at that time, out of the cities, six and twenty thousand men that drew sword, beside the inhabitants of Gibeah, which were numbered seven hundred chosen men. **16** Of all this people were seven hundred chosen men, being [2]left handed: all these could sling stones at an hair breadth, and not fail. **17** Also the men of Israel beside Benjamin, were numbered four hundred thousand men that drew sword, even all men of war. **18** And the children of Israel arose, and went up [l]to the house of God, and asked of God, saying, Which of us shall go up first to fight against the children of Benjamin? and the Lord said, Judah shall be first. **19** Then the children of Israel arose up early and camped against Gibeah. **20** And the men of Israel went out to battle against Benjamin, and the men of Israel put themselves in array to fight against them beside Gibeah. **21** And the children of Benjamin came out of Gibeah, and slew down to the ground of the Israelites that day [m]two and twenty thousand men. **22** And the people, the men of Israel plucked up their hearts, and set their battle again in array in the place where they put them in array the first day. **23** (For the children of Israel had gone up and wept before the Lord unto the evening, and had asked of the Lord, saying, Shall I go again to battle against the children of Benjamin my brethren? and the Lord said, Go up against them.) **24** Then the children of Israel came near against the children of Benjamin the second day. **25** Also the second day Benjamin came forth to meet them out of Gibeah, and slew down to the ground of the children of Israel again eighteen thousand men: [n]all they could handle the sword. **26** Then all the children of Israel went up, and all the people came also unto the house of God, and wept, and sat there before the Lord, and fasted that day unto the evening, and offered burnt offerings and peace offerings before the Lord. **27** And the children of Israel asked the Lord (for [o]there was the Ark of the Covenant of God in those days, **28** And Phinehas the son of Eleazar, the son of Aaron [p]stood before it at that time) saying, Shall I yet go anymore to battle against the children of Benjamin my brethren, or shall I cease? And the Lord said, Go up: for tomorrow I will deliver them into your hand. **29** And Israel set men to lie in wait roundabout Gibeah. **30** And the children of Israel went up against the children of Benjamin the third day, and put themselves in array against Gibeah, as at other times. **31** Then the children of Benjamin coming out against the people, were [q]drawn from the city: and they began to smite of the people and kill as at other times, even by the ways in the field (whereof one goeth up to the house of God, and the other to Gibeah) upon a thirty men of Israel. **32** (For the children of Benjamin said, They are fallen before us, as at the first. But the children of Israel said, Let us flee and pluck them away from the city unto the [r]highways.) **33** And all the men of Israel rose up out of their place, and put themselves in array at Baal Tamar: and the men that lay in wait of the Israelites came forth of their place, even out of the meadows of Geba, **34** And they came over against Gibeah, ten thousand chosen men of all Israel, and the battle was sore: for they knew not that the [s]evil was near them. **35** And the Lord smote Benjamin before Israel, and the children of Israel destroyed of the Benjamites the same day five and twenty thousand and an hundred men: all they could handle the sword. **36** So the children of Benjamin saw that they were stricken down: for the men of Israel [t]gave place to the Benjamites, because they trusted to the men that lay in wait, which they had laid beside Gibeah. **37** And they that lay in wait hasted, and brake forth toward Gibeah, and the ambushment [u]drew themselves along, and smote all the city with the edge of the sword. **38** Also the men of Israel had appointed a certain time with the ambushments, that they should make a great flame and smoke arise up out of the city. **39** And when the men of Israel retired in the battle, Benjamin began to [v]smite and kill of the men of Israel about thirty persons: for they said, Surely they are stricken down before us, as in the first battle. **40** But when the flame began to rise out of the city as a pillar of smoke, the Benjamites looked back, and behold, the flame of the city began to ascend up to heaven. **41** Then the men of Israel turned [w]again, and the men of Benjamin were astonished: for they saw that evil was near unto them. **42** Therefore they fled before the men of Israel unto the way of the wilderness, but the battle overtook them: also they which came out of the cities, slew them [x]among them. **43** Thus they compassed the Benjamites about, and [y]chased them at ease, and overran them, even over against Gibeah on the East side. **44** And there were slain of Benjamin eighteen thousand men, which were all men of war. **45** And they turned and fled to the wilderness unto the rock of Rimmon: and the Israelites [z]gleaned of them by the way five thousand men, and pursued after them unto Gidom, and slew two thousand men of them, **46** So that all that were slain that day of Benjamin, were aafive and twenty thousand men that drew sword, which were all men of war. **47** [3]But six hundred men turned and fled to the wilderness unto the rock of Rimmon, and abode in the rock of Rimmon four months. **48** Then the men of Israel turned unto the children of Benjamin, and smote them with the edge of the sword, from the men of the city unto the beasts, and all that came to hand: also they set on fire all the abcities that they could come by.

21

1 The Israelites swear that they will not marry their daughters to the Benjamites. 10 They slay them of Jabeth Gilead, and give their virgins to the Benjamites. 21 The Benjamites take the daughters of Shiloh.

1 Moreover, the men of Israel [a]sware in Mizpah, saying, None of us shall give his daughter unto the Benjamites to wife. **2** And the people came unto the house of God and abode there till even before God, and lifted up their voices, and wept with great lamentation, **3** And said, O Lord God of Israel, why is this come to pass in Israel, that this day one tribe of Israel should want? **4** And on the morrow the people rose up and made there an [b]altar, and offered burnt offerings and peace offerings. **5** Then the children of Israel said, Who is he among all the tribes of Israel, that came not up with the Congregation unto the Lord? for they had made a great oath concerning him that came not up to the Lord to Mizpah, saying, Let him die the death. **6** And the children of Israel [c]were sorry for Benjamin their brother, and said, There is one tribe cut off from Israel this day. **7** How shall we do for wives to them that remain, seeing we have sworn by the Lord, that we will not give them of our daughters to wives? **8** Also they said, is there any of the tribes of Israel that [d]came not up to Mizpah to the Lord? and behold, there came none of Jabesh Gilead unto the host, and to the Congregation. **9** For when the people were viewed, behold, none of the inhabitants of Jabesh Gilead were there. **10** Therefore the Congregation sent thither twelve thousand men of the [e]most valiant, and commanded them, saying, Go and smite the inhabitants of Jabesh Gilead with the edge of the sword, both women and children. **11** [1]And this is it that ye shall do: ye shall utterly destroy all the males, and all the women that have lain by men. **12** And they found among the inhabitants of Jabesh Gilead four hundred maids, virgins that had known no man by lying with any male: and they brought them unto the host to Shiloh, which is in the land of Canaan. **13** Then the whole Congregation [f]sent and spake with the children of Benjamin that were in the rock of Rimmon, and called [g]peaceably unto them: **14** And Benjamin came again at that time, and they gave them wives which they had saved alive of the women of Jabesh Gilead: but they had not [h]so

---

f. Judg. 20:5 Or, chief, or lord.
g. Judg. 20:6 That is, her pieces, to every tribe a piece, Judg. 19:29.
h. Judg. 20:8 Before we have revenged this wickedness.
i. Judg. 20:10 These only should have the charge to provide for vittles for the rest.
j. Judg. 20:12 That is, every family of the tribe.
k. Judg. 20:13 Because they would not suffer the wicked to be punished, they declared themselves to maintain them in their evil, and therefore were all justly punished.
l. Judg. 20:18 That is, to the Ark, which was in Shiloh some think in Mizpah, as verse 1.
m. Judg. 20:21 This God permitted, because the Israelites partly in their strength, and partly God would by this means punish their sins.
n. Judg. 20:25 All they drawing the sword.
o. Judg. 20:27 To wit, in Shiloh.
p. Judg. 20:28 Or, served in the Priest's office at those days: for the Jews write, that he lived three hundred years.
q. Judg. 20:31 By the policy of the children of Israel.
r. Judg. 20:32 Meaning, crossways or paths to divers places.
s. Judg. 20:34 They knew not that God's judgment was at hand to destroy them.
t. Judg. 20:36 Retired to draw them after.
u. Judg. 20:37 Or, made a long sound with a trumpet.
v. Judg. 20:39 For they were waxen hardy by the two former victories.
w. Judg. 20:41 And withstood their enemies.
x. Judg. 20:42 For they were compassed in on every side.
y. Judg. 20:43 Or, drove them from their rest.
z. Judg. 20:45 They slew them by one and one, as they were scattered abroad.
aa. Judg. 20:46 Besides eleven hundred that had been slain in the former battles.
ab. Judg. 20:48 If they belonged to the Benjamites.

JUDG. 20
1. Hos. 10:9
2. Judg. 3:15
3. Judg. 21:13

JUDG. 21
a. Judg. 21:1 This oath came of rashness, and not of judgment: for after they brake it, in showing secretly the means to marry with certain of their daughters.
b. Judg. 21:4 According to their custom, when they would consult with the Lord.
c. Judg. 21:6 Or, repented that they had destroyed their brethren, as appeareth verse 15.
d. Judg. 21:8 Condemning them to be favors of vice, which would not put their hand to punish it.
e. Judg. 21:10 Hebrew, children of strength.
f. Judg. 21:13 To wit, about four months after the discomfiture, Judg. 20:47.
g. Judg. 21:13 Or, friendly.
h. Judg. 21:14 For there lacked two hundred.

enough for them. 15 And the people were sorry for Benjamin, because the Lord
had made a breach in the tribes of Israel. 16 Therefore the Elders of the Congre-
gation said, How shall we do for wives to the remnant? for the women of Benjamin
are destroyed. 17 And they said, There must be [i]an inheritance for them that be
escaped of Benjamin, that a tribe be not destroyed out of Israel. 18 Howbeit we
may not give them wives of our daughters: for the children of Israel had sworn,
saying, Cursed be he that giveth a wife to Benjamin. 19 Therefore they said,
Behold, there is a feast of the Lord every year in Shiloh, in a place, which is on the
[j]North side of Bethel, and on the East side of the way that goeth up from Bethel
to Shechem, and on the South of Lebonah. 20 Therefore they commanded the
children of Benjamin, saying, Go, and lie in wait in the vineyards. 21 And when
ye see that the daughters of Shiloh come out to dance in dances, then come ye out
of the vineyards, and catch you every man a wife of the daughters of Shiloh, and go
into the land of Benjamin. 22 And [k]when their fathers or their brethren come
unto us to complain, we will say unto them, Have pity on them for our sakes,
because we reserved not to each man his wife in the war, and because ye have not
given unto them hitherto, ye have sinned. 23 And the children of Benjamin did
so, and took wives of them that danced according to their [l]number: which they
took, and went away, and returned to their inheritance, and repaired the cities and
dwelt in them. 24 So the children of Israel departed thence at that time, every
man to his tribe, and to his family, and went out from thence every man to his
inheritance. 25 [2]In those days there was no king in Israel, but every man did that
which was good in his eyes.

i. Judg. 21:17 Benjamin must be reserved to have the twelfth portion in the inheritance of Jacob.
j. Judg. 21:19 He describeth the place where the maids used yearly to dance as the manner then was, and to sing Psalms and songs of God's works among them.
k. Judg. 21:22 Though they thought hereby to persuade men that they kept their oath, yet before God it was broken.
l. Judg. 21:23 Meaning, two hundred.

JUDG. 21

1. Num. 31:17
2. Judg. 17:6 / Judg. 13:1 / Judg. 19:1

THE BOOK OF RUTH

1

1 Elimelech goeth with his wife and children into the land of Moab. 3 He and his sons die. 19 Naomi and Ruth come to Bethlehem.

1 In the time that the Judges [a]ruled, there was a dearth in the [b]land, and a
man of Bethlehem [c]Judah went for to sojourn in the country of Moab, he, and his
wife, and his two sons. 2 And the name of the man was Elimelech, and the name
of his wife, Naomi, and the names of his two sons, Mahlon, and Chilion, Ephra-
thites of Bethlehem Judah: and when they came into the land of Moab, they con-
tinued there. 3 Then Elimelech the husband of Naomi died, and she remained
with her two sons, 4 Which took them wives of the [d]Moabites: the one's name
was Orpah, and the name of the other Ruth: and they dwelled there about ten ye-
ars. 5 And Mahlon and Chilion dieth also both twain: so the woman was left,
destitute of her two sons, and of her husband. 6 Then she arose with her dau-
ghters-in-law, and returned from the country of Moab: for she had heard say in the
country of Moab, that the Lord had [e]visited his people, and given them bread. 7
Wherefore she departed out of the place where she was, and her two daughters-
in-law with her, and they went on their way to return unto the land of Judah. 8
Then Naomi said unto her two daughters-in-law, Go, return each of you unto her
own mother's house: the Lord show favor unto you, as ye have done with the dead,
and with me. 9 The Lord grant you, that you may find [f]rest, either of you in
the house of her husband. And when she kissed them, they lift up their voice and
wept. 10 And they said unto her, Surely we will return with thee unto thy peo-
ple. 11 But Naomi said, Turn again my daughters: for what cause will ye go with
me? are there any more sons in my womb, that they may be your husbands? 12
Turn again my daughters: go your way: for I am too old to have an husband. If I
should say, I have hope, and if I had an husband this night: yea, and if I had borne
sons, 13 Would ye tarry for them, till they were of age? would ye be deferred
for them from taking of husbands? nay my daughters: for it grieveth me [g]much
for your sakes that the hand of the Lord is gone out against me. 14 Then they
lift up their voice and wept again, and Orpah [h]kissed her mother-in-law, but Ruth
abode still with her. 15 And Naomi said, Behold, thy sister-in-law is gone back
unto her people, and unto her gods: [i]return thou after thy sister-in-law. 16 And
Ruth answered, Entreat me not to leave thee, nor to depart from thee: for whither
thou goest, I will go: and where thou dwellest, I will dwell: thy people shall be my
people, and thy God my God. 17 Where thou diest, will I die, and there will
I be buried. The Lord do so to me and more also, if ought but death depart thee
and me. 18 When she saw that she was steadfastly minded to go with her, she
left speaking unto her. 19 So they went both until they came to Bethlehem: and
when they were come to Bethlehem, it was [j]noised of them through all the city, and
they said, Is not this Naomi? 20 And she answered them, Call me not [k]Naomi,
but call me [l]Mara: for the Almighty hath given me much bitterness. 21 I went
out full, and the Lord hath caused me to return empty: why call ye me Naomi,
seeing the Lord hath humbled me, and the Almighty hath brought me unto adver-
sity? 22 So Naomi returned and Ruth the Moabitess her daughter-in-law with
her, when she came out of the country of Moab: and they came to Bethlehem in
the beginning of [m]barley harvest.

2

2 Ruth gathered corn in the fields of Boaz. 8 The gentleness of Boaz toward her.

1 Then Naomi's husband had a kinsman, one of great [a]power of the family of
Elimelech, and his name was Boaz. 2 And Ruth the Moabitess said unto Naomi,
I pray thee, let me go to the field, and [b]gather ears of corn after him, in whose sight
I find favor. And she said unto her, Go my daughter. 3 And she went, and came
and gleaned in the field after the reapers, and it came to pass, that she met with the
portion of the field of Boaz, who was of the family of Elimelech. 4 And behold,
Boaz came from Bethlehem, and said unto the reapers, The Lord be with you: and
they answered him, The Lord bless thee. 5 Then said Boaz unto his servant that
was appointed over the reapers, Whose maid is this? 6 And the servant that was
appointed over the reapers, answered, and said, It is the Moabitish maid, that came
with Naomi out of the country of Moab: 7 And she said unto us, I pray you, let
me glean and gather after the reapers [c]among the sheaves: so she came, and hath
continued from that time in the morning unto now, save that she tarried a little in
the house. 8 Then said Boaz unto Ruth, Hearest thou, my daughter? go to none
other field to gather, neither go from hence: but abide here by my maidens. 9
[d]Let thine eyes be on the field that they do reap, and go thou after the maidens.

RUTH 1

a. Ruth 1:1 Hebrew, judged.
b. Ruth 1:1 In the land of Canaan.
c. Ruth 1:1 In the tribe of Judah, which was also called Bethlehem Ephrathah, because there was another city so called in the tribe of Zebulun.
d. Ruth 1:4 By this wonderful providence of God Ruth became one of God's household, of whom Christ came.
e. Ruth 1:6 By sending them plenty again.
f. Ruth 1:9 Hereby it appeareth that Naomi by dwelling among idolaters, was waxen cold in the true zeal of God, which rather hath respect to the ease of the body, than to the comfort of the soul.
g. Ruth 1:13 Or, more than you.
h. Ruth 1:14 When she took leave and departed.
i. Ruth 1:15 No persuasions can prevail to turn them back from God, whom he hath chosen to be his.
j. Ruth 1:19 Whereby appeareth that she was of a great family of good reputation.
k. Ruth 1:20 Or, beautiful.
l. Ruth 1:20 Or, bitter.
m. Ruth 1:22 Which was in the month Nisan, that containeth part of March and part of April.

RUTH 2

a. Ruth 2:1 Both for virtue, authority, and riches.
b. Ruth 2:2 This her humility declareth her great affection toward her mother-in-law, forasmuch as she spareth no painful diligence to get both their livings.
c. Ruth 2:7 Or, certain handfuls.
d. Ruth 2:9 That is, take heed in what field they do reap.

Have I not charged the servants, that they touch thee not? Moreover when thou art
athirst, go unto the vessels, and drink of that which the servants hath drawn. **10**
Then she fell on her face, and bowed herself to the ground, and said unto him,
How have I found favor in thine eyes, that thou shouldest know me, seeing I am a
[e]stranger? **11** And Boaz answered and said unto her, All is told and showed me
that thou hast done unto thy mother-in-law, since the death of thine husband, and
how thou hast left thy father and thy mother, and the land where thou wast born,
and art come unto a people which thou knewest not in time past. **12** The Lord
recompense thy work, and a full reward be given thee of the Lord God of Israel,
under whose [f]wings thou art come to trust. **13** Then she said, Let me find favor
in thy sight, my lord: for thou hast comforted me, and spoken comfortably unto
thy maid, though I be not like to one of thy maids. **14** And Boaz said unto her,
At the meal time come thou hither, and eat of the bread, and dip thy morsel in
the vinegar. And she sat beside the reapers, and he reached her parched corn: and
she did eat, and was sufficed, and [g]left thereof. **15** And when she arose to glean,
Boaz commanded his servants, saying, Let her gather among the sheaves, and do
not rebuke her. **16** Also let fall some of the sheaves for her, and let it lie, that
she may gather it up, and rebuke her not. **17** So she gleaned in the field until
evening, and she threshed that she had gathered, and it was about an [1]Ephah of
barley. **18** And she took it up, and went into the city, and her mother-in-law
saw what she had gathered: Also she [h]took forth, and gave to her that which she
had reserved, when she was sufficed. **19** Then her mother-in-law said unto her,
Where hast thou gleaned today? and where wroughtest thou? blessed be he, that
knew thee. And she showed her mother-in-law, with whom she had wrought, and
said, The man's name with whom I wrought today, is Boaz. **20** And Naomi said
unto her daughter-in-law, Blessed be he of the Lord: for he ceaseth not to do good
to the living and to the [i]dead. Again Naomi said unto her, The man is near unto us,
and of our affinity. **21** And Ruth the Moabitess said, He said also certainly unto
me, Thou shalt be with my servants, until they have ended all mine harvest. **22**
And Naomi answered unto Ruth her daughter-in-law, It is best, my daughter, that
thou go out with his maids, that they [j]meet thee not in another field. **23** Then
she kept her by the maids of Boaz, to gather unto the end of barley harvest, and of
wheat harvest, and [k]dwelt with her mother-in-law.

3

1 Naomi giveth Ruth counsel. 8 She sleepeth at Boaz's feet. 12 He acknowledgeth himself to be her kinsman.

1 Afterward Naomi her mother-in-law said unto her, My daughter, shall
not I seek [a]rest for thee, that thou mayest prosper? **2** Now also is not Boaz our
kinsman, with whose maids thou wast? Behold, he winnoweth barley tonight in
the [b]floor. **3** Wash thyself therefore, and anoint thee, and put thy raiment upon
thee, and get thee down to the floor: let not the [c]man know of thee, until he have
left eating and drinking. **4** And when he shall sleep, mark the place where he
layeth him down, and go, and uncover the place of his feet, and lay thee down,
and he shall tell thee what thou shalt do. **5** And she answered her, All that thou
biddest me, I will do. **6** So she went down unto the floor, and did according to
all that her mother-in-law bade her. **7** And when Boaz had eaten and drunken,
and [d]cheered his heart, he went to lie down at the end of the heap of corn, and she
came softly, and uncovered the place of his feet, and lay down. **8** And at mid-
night the man was afraid [e]and caught hold: and lo, a woman lay at his feet. **9**
Then he said, Who art thou? And she answered, I am Ruth thine handmaid: spre-
ad therefore the wing of thy garment over thine handmaid: for thou art the kin-
sman. **10** Then he said, Blessed be thou of the Lord, my daughter: thou hast
[f]showed more goodness in the latter end, than at the beginning, inasmuch as thou
followedst not young men, were they poor or rich. **11** And now, my daughter,
fear not: I will do to thee all that thou requirest: for all the city of my people doth
know that thou art a virtuous woman. **12** And now, it is true that I am thy kin-
sman, howbeit there is a kinsman nearer than I. **13** Tarry tonight, and when
morning is come, if he [g]will do the duty of a kinsman unto thee, well, let him do
the kinsman's duty: but if he will not do the kinsman's part, then will I do the duty
of a kinsman, as the Lord liveth: sleep until the morning. **14** And she lay at his
feet until the morning: and she arose before one could know another: for he said,
Let no man know, that a woman came into the floor. **15** Also he said, Bring the
[h]sheet that thou hast upon thee, and hold it. And when she held it, he measured
six measures of barley, and laid them on her, and she went into the city. **16** And
when she came to her mother-in-law, she said, [i]Who art thou, my daughter? And
she told her all that the man had done to her, **17** And said, These six measu-
res of barley gave he me: for he said to me, Thou shalt not come empty unto thy
mother-in-law. **18** Then said she, My daughter, sit still, until thou know how
the thing will fall: for the man will not be in rest, until he hath finished the matter
this same day.

4

1 Boaz speaketh to Ruth's next kinsman touching her marriage. 7 The ancient custom in Israel. 10 Boaz marrieth Ruth, of whom he begetteth Obed. 18 The generation of Perez.

1 Then went Boaz up to the [a]gate, and sat there, and behold, the kinsman,
of whom Boaz had spoken, came by: and he said, [b]Ho, such one, come, sit down
here. And he turned, and sat down. **2** Then he took ten men of the Elders of
the city, and said, Sit ye down here. And they sat down. **3** And he said unto the
kinsman, Naomi, that is come again out of the country of Moab, will sell a parcel
of land, which was our brother Elimelech's. **4** And I thought to advertise thee,
saying, Buy it before the [c]assistants, and before the Elders of my people. If thou
wilt redeem it, redeem it: but if thou wilt not redeem it, tell me: for I know that
there is none [d]besides thee to redeem it, and I am after thee. Then he answered, I
will redeem it. **5** Then said Boaz, What day thou buyest the field of the hand of
Naomi, thou must also buy it of Ruth the Moabitess the wife of the dead, to stir
up the name of the dead, upon his [e]inheritance. **6** And the kinsman answered, I
cannot redeem it, lest I destroy mine own inheritance: redeem my right to thee, for
I can not redeem it. **7** Now this was the manner beforetime in Israel, concerning
redeeming and changing for to stablish all things: a man did pluck off his shoe,
and gave it his neighbor: and this was a sure [f]witness in Israel. **8** Therefore the
kinsman said to Boaz, Buy it for thee: and he drew off his shoe. **9** And Boaz said
unto the Elders and unto all the people, Ye are witnesses this day, that I have bou-
ght all that was Elimelech's, and all that was Chilion's and Mahlon's, of the hand of
Naomi. **10** And moreover, Ruth the Moabitess the wife of Mahlon, have I bou-
ght to be my wife, to stir up the name of the dead upon his inheritance, and that
the name of the dead be not put out from among his brethren, and from the gate of
his [g]place: ye are witnesses this day. **11** And all the people that were in the gate,
and the Elders said, We are witnesses: the Lord make the wife that cometh into thi-
ne house, like Rachel and like Leah, which twain did build the house of Israel: and
that thou mayest do worthily in [h]Ephrathah, and be famous in Bethlehem. **12**
And that thine house be like the house of Perez ([1]whom Tamar bare unto Judah)
of the seed which the Lord shall give thee of this young woman. **13** So Boaz
took Ruth, and she was his wife: and when he went in unto her, the Lord gave that
she conceived, and bare a son. **14** And the women said unto Naomi, Blessed be
the Lord, which hath not left thee this day without a kinsman, and [i]his name shall
be continued in Israel. **15** And this shall bring thy life again, and cherish thine
old age: for thy daughter-in-law which loveth thee, hath borne unto him, and she
is better to thee than [j]seven sons. **16** And Naomi took the child, and laid it in
her lap, and became nurse unto it. **17** And the women her neighbors gave it a
name, saying, There is a child born to Naomi, and called the name thereof Obed:
the same was the father of Jesse, the father of David. **18** These now are the ge-
nerations of [k,2]Perez: Perez begat Hezron, **19** And Hezron begat Ram, and Ram
begat Amminadab, **20** And Amminadab begat Nahshon, and Nahshon begat
Salmon, **21** And Salmon begat Boaz, and Boaz begat Obed, **22** And Obed
begat Jesse, and Jesse begat David.

---

e. Ruth 2:10 Even of the Moabites, which are enemies to God's people.
f. Ruth 2:12 Signifying, that she shall never want anything, if she put her trust in God, and live under his protection.
g. Ruth 2:14 Which she brought home to her mother-in-law.
h. Ruth 2:18 To wit, of her bag, as is in the Chaldea text.
i. Ruth 2:20 To my husband and children, when they were alive, and now to us.
j. Ruth 2:22 Or, fall upon thee.
k. Ruth 2:23 Or, returned to her mother-in-law.

RUTH 2

1. Exod. 16:36

RUTH 3

a. Ruth 3:1 Meaning, that she would provide her of an husband, with whom she might live quietly.
b. Ruth 3:2 Or, in the barn.
c. Ruth 3:3 Boaz, nor yet any other.
d. Ruth 3:7 That is, had refreshed himself among his servants.
e. Ruth 3:8 Or, turned himself from one side to another.
f. Ruth 3:10 Thou showest thyself from time to time more virtuous.
g. Ruth 3:13 If he will take thee to be his wife by the title of affinity, according to God's law, Deut. 25 :5.
h. Ruth 3:15 Or, mantle.
i. Ruth 3:16 Perceiving by her coming home, that he had not taken her to his wife, she was astonied.

RUTH 4

a. Ruth 4:1 Which was the place of judgment.
b. Ruth 4:1 The Hebrews here use two words which have no proper signification, but serve to note a certain person, as we say, Ho sirrah, or ho such a one.
c. Ruth 4:4 Or, inhabitants.
d. Ruth 4:4 For thou art the next of the kin.
e. Ruth 4:5 That his inheritance might bear his name that is dead.
f. Ruth 4:7 That he had resigned his right, Deut. 25 :9.
g. Ruth 4:10 Or, of the city where he remained.
h. Ruth 4:11 Ephrathah and Bethlehem are both one.
i. Ruth 4:14 He shall leave continual posterity.
j. Ruth 4:15 Meaning, many sons.
k. Ruth 4:18 This genealogy is brought in, to prove that David by succession came of the house of Judah.

RUTH 4

1. Gen. 38:29
2. 1Chron. 2:4 / Matt. 1:3

THE FIRST BOOK OF
SAMUEL

1

1 The genealogy of Elkanah father of Samuel. 2 His two wives. 5 Hannah was barren, and prayed to the Lord. 15 Her answer to Eli. 20 Samuel is born. 24 She doth dedicate him to the Lord.

1 There was a man of one of the two [a]Ramathaim Zophim, of mount
Ephraim, whose name was Elkanah the son of Jeroham, the son of Elihu, the son
of Tohu, the son of Zuph, an Ephraimite. **2** And he had two wives: the name of
one was Hannah, and the name of the other Peninnah: and Peninnah had children,
but Hannah had no children. **3** [1]And this man went up out of his city every year,
to worship and to sacrifice unto the Lord of hosts in [b]Shiloh, where were the two
sons of Eli, Hophni, and Phinehas, Priests of the Lord. **4** And on a day, when
Elkanah sacrificed, he gave to Peninnah his wife and to all her sons and daughters
portions, **5** But unto Hannah he gave a worthy [c]portion: for he loved Hannah,
and the Lord had made her barren. **6** And her adversary vexed her sore, fora-
smuch as she upbraided her, because the Lord had made her barren. **7** (And so
did he year by year) and as oft as she went up to the house of the Lord, thus she
vexed her, that she wept and did not eat. **8** Then said Elkanah her husband to
her, Hannah, why weepest thou? and why eatest thou not? and why is thine heart
troubled? am not I better to thee than ten [d]sons? **9** So Hannah rose up after that
they had eaten and drunk in Shiloh (and Eli the Priest sat upon a stool by one of
the posts of the [e]Temple of the Lord) **10** And she was troubled in her mind, and
prayed unto the Lord, and wept sore: **11** Also she vowed a vow, and said, O Lord
of hosts, if thou wilt look on the trouble of thine handmaid, and remember me,
and not forget thine handmaid, but give unto thine handmaid a man-child, then I
will give him unto the Lord all the days of his life, [2]and there shall no razor come
upon his head. **12** And as she continued praying before the Lord, Eli marked
her mouth. **13** For Hannah spake in her heart: her lips did move only, but her
voice was not heard: therefore Eli thought she had been drunken. **14** And Eli
said unto her, How long wilt thou be drunken? Put away thy [f]drunkenness from
thee. **15** Then Hannah answered and said, Nay my lord, but I am a woman
[g]troubled in spirit: I have drunk neither wine nor strong drink, but have [3]poured
out my soul before the Lord. **16** Count not thine handmaid [h]for a wicked wo-
man: for of the abundance of my complaint and my grief have I spoken hither-
to. **17** Then Eli answered, and said, Go in peace, and the God of Israel grant thy
petition that thou hast asked of him. **18** She said again, Let thine handmaid find
[i]grace in thy sight: so the woman went her way, and did eat, and looked no more
sad. **19** Then they rose up early, and worshipped before the Lord, and returned,
and came to their house to Ramah. Now Elkanah knew Hannah his wife, and the
Lord [j]remembered her. **20** For in process of time Hannah conceived and bare
a son, and she called his name Samuel, Because, said she, I have asked him of the
Lord. **21** So the man [k]Elkanah and all his house, went up to offer unto the Lord
the yearly sacrifice and his vow: **22** But Hannah went not up: for she said unto
her husband, I will tarry until the child be weaned, then I will bring him that he
may appear before the Lord, and there abide forever. **23** And Elkanah her hu-
sband said unto her, Do what seemeth thee best: tarry until thou hast weaned him:
only the Lord accomplish his [l]word. So the woman abode, and gave her son suck
until she weaned him. **24** And when she had weaned him, she took him with her
with three bullocks and an Ephah of flour and a bottle of wine, and brought him
unto the house of the Lord in Shiloh, and the child was [m]young. **25** And they
slew a bullock, and brought the child to Eli. **26** And she said, Oh my Lord, as
thy [n]soul liveth, my lord, I am the woman that stood with thee here praying unto
the Lord. **27** I prayed for this child, and the Lord hath given me my desire whi-
ch I asked of him. **28** Therefore also I have [o]given him unto the Lord: as long
as he liveth he shall be given unto the Lord: and he [p]worshipped the Lord there.

2

1 The song of Hannah. 12 The sons of Eli, wicked. 13 The new custom of the Priests. 18 Samuel ministereth before the Lord. 20 Eli blesseth Elkanah and his wife. 23 Eli reproveth his sons. 27 God sendeth a Prophet to Eli. 31 Eli is menaced for not chastising his children.

1 And Hannah [a]prayed, and said, Mine heart rejoiceth in the Lord, mine
[b]horn is exalted in the Lord: my mouth is [c]enlarged over mine enemies, because
I rejoice in thy salvation. **2** There is none holy as the Lord: yea, there is none
besides thee, and there is no god like our God. **3** Speak [d]no more presumptuo-
usly: let not arrogancy come out of your mouth: for the Lord is a God of know-
ledge, and by him enterprises are established. **4** The bow and the mighty men
are broken, and the weak have girded themselves with strength. **5** They that
were full, are hired forth for [e]bread, and the hungry are no more hired, so that
the barren hath borne [f]seven: and she that had many children is feeble. **6** [1]The
Lord killeth and maketh alive: bringeth down to the grave and raiseth up. **7** The
Lord maketh poor and maketh rich: bringeth low, and exalteth. **8** [2]He raiseth
up the poor out of the dust, and lifteth up the beggar from the dunghill, to set
them among [g]princes, and to make them inherit the seat of glory: for the pillars
of the earth are the [h]Lord's, and he hath set the world upon them. **9** He will
keep the feet of his Saints, and the wicked shall keep silence in darkness: for in his
own might shall no man be strong. **10** The Lord's adversaries shall be destroyed,
and out of heaven shall he [3]thunder upon them: the Lord shall judge the ends of
the world, and shall give power unto his [i]King, and exalt the horn of his Anoin-
ted. **11** And Elkanah went to Ramah to his house, and the child did minister
unto the [j]Lord before Eli the Priest. **12** Now the sons of Eli were wicked men,
and [k]knew not the Lord. **13** For the Priests' custom toward the people was this:
when any man offered sacrifice, the Priest's [l]boy came, while the flesh was seething,
and a fleshhook with three teeth in his hand, **14** And thrust it into the kettle,
or into the caldron, or into the pan, or into the pot: [m]all that the fleshhook brou-
ght up, the Priest took for himself: thus they did unto all the Israelites, that came
thither to Shiloh. **15** Yea, before they burnt the [n]fat, the Priest's boy came and
said unto the man that offered, Give me flesh to roast for the Priest: for he will not
have sodden flesh of thee, but raw. **16** And if any man said unto him, Let them
burn the fat according to the [o]custom, then take as much as thine heart [p]desireth:
then he would answer, No, but thou shalt give it now: and if thou wilt not, I will
take it by force. **17** Therefore the sin of the young men was very great before
the Lord: for men [q]abhorred the offering of the Lord. **18** Now Samuel being
a young child ministered before the Lord, girded with a linen [4]Ephod. **19** And
his mother made him a little coat, and brought it to him from year to year, when
she came up with her husband, to offer the yearly sacrifice. **20** And Eli blessed
Elkanah and his wife, and said, The Lord give thee seed of this woman, for [r]the
petition that she asked of the Lord: and they departed unto their place. **21** And
the Lord visited Hannah, so that she conceived, and bare three sons, and two
daughters. And the child Samuel grew before the Lord. **22** So Eli was very old,
and heard all that his sons did unto all Israel, and how they lay with the women
that [s]assembled at the door of the Tabernacle of the Congregation. **23** And he
said unto them, Why do ye such things? for of all this people I hear evil reports of

---

1-SAM. 1

a. 1-Sam. 1:1 There were two Ramatus, so that in this city in mount Ephraim were Zophim, that is, the learned men and Prophets.
b. 1-Sam. 1:3 For the Ark was there at that time.
c. 1-Sam. 1:5 Some read, a portion with an hearty cheer.
d. 1-Sam. 1:8 Let this suffice thee, that I love thee no less, than if thou hadst many children.
e. 1-Sam. 1:9 That is of the house where the Ark was.
f. 1-Sam. 1:14 Hebrew, thy wine.
g. 1-Sam. 1:15 Hebrew, of an hard spirit.
h. 1-Sam. 1:16 Hebrew, for a daughter of Belial.
i. 1-Sam. 1:18 That is, pray unto the Lord for me.
j. 1-Sam. 1:19 According to her petition.
k. 1-Sam. 1:21 This Elkanah was a Levite, 1 Chron. 6:27, and as some write once a year they accustomed to appear before the Lord with their families.
l. 1-Sam. 1:23 Because her prayer took effect, therefore it was called the Lord's promise.
m. 1-Sam. 1:24 Hebrew, a child.
n. 1-Sam. 1:26 That is, most certainly.
o. 1-Sam. 1:28 Hebrew, lent.
p. 1-Sam. 1:28 Meaning, Eli gave thanks to God for her.

1-SAM. 1:

1. Deut. 16:16 **3.** Ps. 42:5
2. Num. 6:5 / Judg. 13:5

1-SAM. 2

a. 1-Sam. 2:1 After that she had obtained a son by prayer, she gave thanks.
b. 1-Sam. 2:1 I have recovered strength and glory by the benefit of the Lord.
c. 1-Sam. 2:1 I can answer them that reprove my barrenness.
d. 1-Sam. 2:3 In that ye condemn my barrenness, ye show your pride against God.
e. 1-Sam. 2:5 They sell their labors for necessary food.
f. 1-Sam. 2:5 Or, many.
g. 1-Sam. 2:8 He prefereth to honor, and putteth down according to his own will, though man's judgment be contrary.
h. 1-Sam. 2:8 Therefore he may dispose all things according to his will.
i. 1-Sam. 2:10 She grounded her prayer on Jesus Christ which was to come.
j. 1-Sam. 2:11 In all that Eli commanded him.
k. 1-Sam. 2:12 That is, they neglected his ordinance.
l. 1-Sam. 2:13 Or, son.
m. 1-Sam. 2:14 Transgressing the order appointed in the Law, Lev. 7:31, for their belly's sake.
n. 1-Sam. 2:15 Which was commanded first to have been offered to God.
o. 1-Sam. 2:16 Or, Law.
p. 1-Sam. 2:16 Not passing for their own profit, so that God might be served aright.
q. 1-Sam. 2:17 Seeing the horrible abuse thereof.
r. 1-Sam. 2:20 Or, for the thing that she hath lent to the Lord: to wit, Samuel.
s. 1-Sam. 2:22 Which was (as the Hebrews write) after their travail, when they came to be purified, read Exod. 38:8; Lev. 12:6.

you. **24** Do no more, my sons: for it is no good report that I hear, which is, that ye make the Lord's people to [t]trespass. **25** If one man sin against another, the Judge shall judge it: but if a man sin against the Lord, who will plead for him? Notwithstanding they obeyed not the voice of their father, because the Lord [u]would slay them. **26** (Now the child Samuel profited, and grew, and was in favor both with the Lord and also with men.) **27** And there came a man of God unto Eli, and said unto him, Thus saith the Lord, Did not I plainly appear unto the house of thy [v]father, when they were in Egypt in Pharaoh's house? **28** And I chose him out of all the tribes of Israel to be my Priest, to offer upon my altar, and to burn incense, and to wear an Ephod before me, and [5]I gave unto the house of thy father all the offerings made by fire of the children of Israel. **29** Wherefore have you [w]kicked against my sacrifice and mine offering, which I commanded in my Tabernacle, and honorest thy children above me, to make yourselves fat of the firstfruits of all the offerings of Israel my people? **30** Wherefore the Lord God of Israel saith, I said, that thine house, and the house of thy father should walk before me forever: but now the Lord saith, [x]It shall not be so: for them that honor me, I will honor, and they that despise me, shall be despised. **31** Behold, the days come, that I will cut off thine [y]arm, and the arm of thy fathers house, that there shall not be an old man in thine house. **32** And thou [z]shalt see thine enemy in the habitation of the Lord in all things wherewith God shall bless Israel, and there shall not be an old man in thine house forever. **33** Nevertheless, I will not destroy every one of thine from mine altar, to make thine eyes to fail, and to make thine heart sorrowful: and all the multitude of thine house shall [aa]die when they be men. **34** And this shall be a sign unto thee, that shall come upon thy two sons Hophni and Phinehas: in one day they shall die both. **35** And I will stir me up a [ab]faithful Priest, that shall do according to mine heart, and according to my mind: and I will build him a sure house, and he shall walk before mine Anointed forever. **36** And all that are left in thine house, shall come and [ac]bow down to him for a piece of silver and a morsel of bread, and shall say, Appoint me, I pray thee, to one of the Priest's offices, that I may eat a morsel of bread.

3

1 There was no manifest vision in the time of Eli. 4 The Lord calleth Samuel three times, 11 And showeth what shall come upon Eli and his house. 18 The same declareth Samuel to Eli.

1 Now the child Samuel ministered unto the Lord [a]before Eli: and the word of the Lord was [b]precious in those days: for there was no manifest vision. **2** And at that time, as Eli lay in his [c]place, his eyes began to wax dim that he could not see. **3** And yer the [d]light of God went out, Samuel slept in the temple of the Lord, where the Ark of God was. **4** Then the Lord [e]called Samuel: and he said, Here I am. **5** And he ran unto Eli, and said, Here am I, for thou calledst me. But he said, I called thee not: go again and sleep. And he went and slept. **6** And the Lord called once again, Samuel. And Samuel arose, and went to Eli, and said, I am here: for thou didst call me. And he answered, I called thee not my son: go again and sleep. **7** Thus did Samuel, before he knew [f]the Lord, and before the word of the Lord was revealed unto him. **8** And the Lord called Samuel again the third time: and he arose, and went to Eli, and said, I am here: for thou hast called me. Then Eli [g]perceived that the Lord had called the child. **9** Therefore Eli said unto Samuel, Go and sleep: and if he call thee, then say, Speak Lord, for thy servant heareth. So Samuel went, and slept in his place. **10** And the Lord came, and stood, and called as at other times, Samuel, Samuel. Then Samuel answered, Speak, for thy servant heareth. **11** Then the Lord said unto Samuel, Behold, I will do a thing in Israel, whereof whosoever shall hear, his two [1]ears shall [h]tingle. **12** In that day I will raise up against Eli all things which I have spoken concerning his house: when I begin, I will also make an end. **13** And I have told him that I will judge his house forever, for the iniquity which he knoweth, because his sons ran into a slander, and he stayed them not. **14** Now therefore I have sworn unto the house of Eli, that the wickedness of Eli's house shall not be purged with sacrifice nor offering [i]forever. **15** Afterward Samuel slept until the morning, and opened the doors of the house of the Lord, and Samuel feared to show Eli the vision. **16** Then Eli called Samuel, and said, Samuel my son. And he answered, Here I am. **17** Then he said, What is it, that the Lord said unto thee? I pray thee hide it not from me. God [j]do so to thee, and more also, if thou hide anything from me, of all that he said unto thee. **18** So Samuel told him every whit, and hid nothing from him. Then he said, It is the Lord: let him do what seemeth him good. **19** And Samuel grew, and the Lord was with him, and let none of his words [k]fall to the ground. **20** And all Israel from Dan to Beersheba knew [l]that faithful Samuel was the Lord's Prophet. **21** And the Lord appeared again in Shiloh: for the Lord revealed himself to Samuel in Shiloh by [m]his word.

4

1 Israel is overcome by the Philistines. 4 They do set the Ark, wherefore the Philistines do fear. 10 The Ark of the Lord is taken. 11 Eli and his children die. 19 The death of the wife of Phinehas the son of Eli.

1 And Samuel spake unto all Israel: [a]and Israel went out against the Philistines to battle, and pitched beside [b]Ebenezer: and the Philistines pitched in Aphek. **2** And the Philistines put themselves in array against Israel: and when they joined the battle, Israel was smitten down before the Philistines: who slew of the army in the field about four thousand men. **3** So when the people were come into the camp, the Elders of Israel said, [c]Wherefore hath the Lord smitten us this day before the Philistines? let us bring the Ark of the covenant of the Lord out of Shiloh unto us, that when it cometh among us, it may save us out of the hand of our enemies. **4** Then the people sent to Shiloh, and brought from thence the Ark of the covenant of the Lord of hosts, who [d]dwelleth between the Cherubims: and there were the two sons of Eli, Hophni and Phinehas, with the Ark of the covenant of God. **5** And when the Ark of the covenant of the Lord came into the host, all Israel shouted a mighty shout, so that the earth rang again. **6** And when the Philistines heard the noise of the shout, they said, What meaneth the sound of this mighty shout in the host of the Hebrews? and they understood, that the Ark of the Lord was come into the host. **7** And the Philistines were afraid, and said, God is come in the host: therefore said they, [e]Woe unto us: for it hath not been so heretofore. **8** Woe unto us, who shall deliver us out of the hand of these mighty Gods? these are the Gods that smote the Egyptians with all the plagues in the [f]wilderness. **9** Be strong and play the men, O Philistines, that ye be not servants unto the Hebrews, [1]as they have served you: be valiant therefore, and fight. **10** And the Philistines fought, and Israel was smitten down, and fled every man into his tent: and there was an exceeding great slaughter, for there fell of Israel [g]thirty thousand footmen. **11** And the Ark of God was taken, and the two sons of Eli, Hophni and Phinehas died. **12** And there ran a man of Benjamin out of the army, and came to Shiloh the same day with his clothes [h]rent, and earth upon his head. **13** And when he came, lo, Eli sat upon a seat by the wayside, waiting: for his heart [i]feared for the Ark of God: and when the man came into the city to tell it, all the city cried out. **14** And when Eli heard the noise of the crying, he said, What meaneth this noise of the tumult? and the man came in hastily, and told Eli. **15** (Now Eli was fourscore and eighteen years old, and [2]his eyes were dim that he could not see.) **16** And the man said unto Eli, I came from the army, and I fled this day out of the host: and he said, What thing is done, my son? **17** Then the messenger answered, and said, Israel is fled before the Philistines, and there hath been also a great slaughter among the people: and moreover thy two sons, Hophni and Phinehas [j]are dead, and the Ark of God is taken. **18** And when he had made mention of the Ark of God, Eli fell from his seat backward by the side of the gate, and his neck was broken, and he died: for he was an old man and heavy: and he had [k]judged Israel forty years. **19** And his daughter-in-law, Phinehas' wife, was with child, near [l]her travail: and when she heard the report that the Ark of God was taken, and that her father-in-law and her husband were dead, she [m]bowed herself, and travailed: for her pains came upon her. **20** And about

---

t. 1-Sam. 2:24 Because they contemn their duty to God, verse 17.
u. 1-Sam. 2:25 So that to obey good admonitions is God's mercy, and to disobey them is his just judgment for sin.
v. 1-Sam. 2:27 To wit, Aaron.
w. 1-Sam. 2:29 Why have you contemned my sacrifices, and as it were trod them under foot?
x. 1-Sam. 2:30 God's promises are only effectual to such as he giveth constancy unto, to fear and obey him.
y. 1-Sam. 2:31 Thy power and authority.
z. 1-Sam. 2:32 Thy posterity shall see the glory of the chief Priest translated to another, whom they shall envy, 1 Kings 2:27.
aa. 1-Sam. 2:33 Or, when they come to man's age.
ab. 1-Sam. 2:35 Meaning Zadok, who succeeded Abiathar, and was the figure of Christ.
ac. 1-Sam. 2:36 That is, shall be inferior unto him.

1-SAM. 2:
1. Deut. 32:39
2. Ps. 113:7
3. 1 Sam. 7:10
4. Exod. 28:4
5. Lev. 10:14

1-SAM. 3
a. 1-Sam. 3:1 The Chaldea text readeth, while Eli lived.
b. 1-Sam. 3:1 Because there were very few Prophets to declare it.
c. 1-Sam. 3:2 In the Court next to the Tabernacle.
d. 1-Sam. 3:3 That is, the lamps which burnt in the night.
e. 1-Sam. 3:4 Josephus writeth that Samuel was 12 years old, when the Lord appeared to him.
f. 1-Sam. 3:7 By vision.
g. 1-Sam. 3:8 Such was the corruption of those times that the chief Priest was become dull and negligent to understand the Lord's appearing.
h. 1-Sam. 3:11 God declareth what sudden fear shall come upon men, when they shall hear that the Ark is taken, and also see Eli's house destroyed.
i. 1-Sam. 3:14 Meaning that his posterity should never enjoy the chief Priest's office.
j. 1-Sam. 3:17 God punish thee after this and that sort, except thou tell me truth, Ruth 1:17.
k. 1-Sam. 3:19 The Lord accomplished whatsoever he had said.
l. 1-Sam. 3:20 Or, that Samuel was the faithful Prophet of the Lord.
m. 1-Sam. 3:21 Hebrew, by the word of the Lord.

1-SAM. 3
1. 2 Kings 21:12

1-SAM. 4
a. 1-Sam. 4:1 From the departure of the Israelites out of Egypt, unto the time of Samuel, are about 397 years.
b. 1-Sam. 4:1 Or, stone of help, 1 Sam. 7:12.
c. 1-Sam. 4:3 For it may seem that this war was undertaken by Samuel's commandment.
d. 1-Sam. 4:4 For he used to appear to the Israelites between the cherubim over the Ark of the covenant, Exod. 25:17.
e. 1-Sam. 4:7 Before we fought against men, and now God is come to fight against us.
f. 1-Sam. 4:8 For in the red sea in the wilderness the Egyptians were destroyed, which was the last of all his plagues.
g. 1-Sam. 4:10 David alluding to this place, Ps. 78:63, saith they were consumed with fire: meaning they were suddenly destroyed.
h. 1-Sam. 4:12 In token of sorrow and mourning.
i. 1-Sam. 4:13 Lest it should be taken of the enemies.
j. 1-Sam. 4:17 According as God had afore said.
k. 1-Sam. 4:18 Or, governed.
l. 1-Sam. 4:19 Or, to cry out.
m. 1-Sam. 4:19 And settled her body toward her travail.

the time of her death, the women that stood about her, said unto her, Fear not: for
thou hast borne a son: but she answered not, nor regarded it. 21 And she named
the child [n]Ichabod, saying, The glory is departed from Israel, because the Ark of
God was taken, and because of her father-in-law and her husband. 22 She said
again, [o]The glory is departed from Israel: for the Ark of God is taken.

5

2 The Philistines bring the Ark into the house of Dagon, which idol fell down before it. 6 The men of Ashdod are plagued. 8 The Ark is carried into Gath, and after to Ekron.

1 Then the Philistines took the Ark of God and carried it from Ebenezer unto
[a]Ashdod, 2 Even the Philistines took the Ark of God, and brought it into the
house of Dagon, and set it by [b]Dagon. 3 And when they of Ashdod rose the
next day in the morning, behold, Dagon was fallen upon his face on the ground
before the Ark of the Lord, and they took up Dagon, and set him in his place
again. 4 Also they rose up early in the morning the next day, and behold, Dagon
was fallen upon his face on the ground before the Ark of the Lord, and the head
of Dagon and the two palms of his hands were cut off upon the threshold: only
the stump of Dagon was left to him. 5 Therefore the Priests of Dagon, and all
that come into Dagon's house, [c]tread not on the threshold of Dagon in Ashdod,
unto this day. 6 But the hand of the Lord was heavy upon them of Ashdod, and
destroyed them, and smote them with the [1]emerods, both Ashdod, and the coa-
sts thereof. 7 And when the men of Ashdod saw this, they said, Let not the Ark
of the God of Israel abide with us: for his hand is sore upon us and upon Dagon
our god. 8 They sent therefore, and gathered all the princes of the Philistines
unto them, and said, [d]What shall we do with the Ark of the God of Israel? And
they answered, Let the Ark of the God of Israel be carried about unto Gath: and
they carried the Ark of the God of Israel about. 9 And when they had carried it
about, the hand of the Lord was against the city with a very great destruction, and
he smote the men of the city both small and great, and they had emerods in their
secret parts. 10 Therefore they sent the Ark of God to Ekron: and as soon as the
Ark of God came to Ekron, the Ekronites cried out, saying, They have brought the
Ark of the God of Israel to us to slay us and our people. 11 Therefore they sent,
and gathered together all the princes of the Philistines, and said, Send [e]away the
Ark of the God of Israel, and let it return to his own place, that it slay us not and
our people: for there was a destruction and death throughout all the city, and the
hand of God was very sore there. 12 And the men that died not, were smitten
with the emerods: and the cry of the city went up to heaven.

6

1 The time that the Ark was with the Philistines, which they sent again with a gift. 12 It cometh to Beth Shemesh. 17 The Philistines offer golden emerods. 19 The men of Beth Shemesh are stricken for looking into the Ark.

1 So the Ark of the Lord was in the country of the Philistines [a]seven mon-
ths. 2 And the Philistines called the Priests and the Soothsayers, saying, What
shall we do with the Ark of the Lord? tell us wherewith we shall send it home
again. 3 And they said, If you send away the Ark of the God of Israel, send it not
away empty, but give unto it [b]a sin offering: then shall ye be healed, and it shall be
known to you, why his hand departeth not from you. 4 Then said they, What
shall be the sin offering, which we shall give unto it? And they answered, Five gol-
den emerods, and five golden mice, according to the number of the princes of the
Philistines: for one plague was on you all, and on your princes. 5 Wherefore ye
shall make the similitudes of your emerods, and the similitudes of your mice that
destroy the land: so ye shall give glory unto the God of Israel, that he may take his
hand from you, and from your [c]gods, and from your land. 6 Wherefore then
should ye harden your hearts, as the Egyptians and Pharaoh hardened their hearts,
when he wrought wonderfully among them, [1]did they not let them go, and they
departed? 7 Now therefore make a new cart, and take two milch kine, on whom
there hath come no yoke: and tie the kine to the cart, and bring the calves home
from them. 8 Then take the Ark of the Lord, and set it upon the cart, and put
the [d]jewels of gold which ye give it for a sin offering in a coffer by the side thereof,
and send it away, that it may go. 9 And take heed, if it go up by the way of his
own coast to Beth Shemesh, it is [e]he that did us this great evil: but if not, we shall
know then, that it is not his hand that smote us, but it was a [f]chance that happened
us. 10 And the men did so: for they took two kine that gave milk, and tied them
to the cart, and shut the calves at home. 11 So they set the Ark of the Lord upon
the cart, and the coffer with the mice of gold, and with the similitudes of their
emerods. 12 And the kine went the straight way to Beth Shemesh, and kept
one path, and lowed as they went, and turned neither to the right hand nor to the
left: also the princes of the Philistines went after [g]them unto the borders of Beth
Shemesh. 13 Now they of Beth Shemesh were reaping their wheat harvest in the
valley, and they lift up their eyes, and spied the Ark, and rejoiced when they saw
it. 14 And the cart came into the field of Joshua a Beth Shemite, and stood still
there. There was also a great stone, and [h]they clave the wood of the cart, and offe-
red the kine for a burnt offering unto the Lord. 15 And the Levites took down
the Ark of the Lord, and the coffer that was with it, wherein the jewels of gold were,
and put them on the great stone, and the men of Beth Shemesh offered burnt offe-
ring, and sacrificed sacrifices that same day unto the Lord. 16 And when the five
princes of the Philistines had seen it, they returned to Ekron the same day. 17 So
these are the golden emerods, which the Philistines gave for a sin offering to the
Lord: for [i]Ashdod one, for Gaza one, for Askelon one, for Gath one, and for Ekron
one, 18 And golden mice, according to the number of all the cities of the Phili-
stines, belonging to the five princes, both of walled towns, and of towns unwalled
unto the great stone of [j]Abel, whereon they set the Ark of the Lord: which stone re-
maineth unto this day in the field of Joshua the Beth Shemite. 19 And he smote
of the men of Beth Shemesh, because they [k]had looked in the Ark of the Lord: he
slew even among the people fifty thousand men and threescore and ten men: and
the people lamented, because the Lord had slain the people with so great a slau-
ghter. 20 Wherefore the men of Beth Shemesh said, Who is able to stand before
this holy Lord God? and to whom shall he go from us? 21 And they sent mes-
sengers to the inhabitants of Kirjath Jearim, saying, The Philistines have brought
again the Ark of the Lord: come ye down, and take it up to you.

7

1 The Ark is brought to Kiriath Jearim. 3 Samuel exhorteth the people to forsake their sins, and turn to the Lord. 10 The Philistines fight against Israel, and are overcome. 16 Samuel judgeth Israel.

1 Then the men of [a]Kirjath Jearim came, and took up the Ark of the Lord,
and brought it into the house of Abinadab in the hill: and they sanctified Elea-
zar his son, to keep the Ark of the Lord. 2 (For while the Ark abode in Kirja-
th Jearim, the time was long, for it was twenty years) and all the house of Israel
lamented [b]after the Lord. 3 Then Samuel spake unto all the house of Israel,
saying, If ye be come again unto the Lord with all your heart, [1]put away the
strange gods from among you, and [2]Ashtoreth, and direct your hearts unto the
Lord, and serve him [3]only, and he shall deliver you out of the hand of the Phi-
listines. 4 Then the children of Israel did put away [4]Baal and Ashtoreth, and
served the Lord only. 5 And Samuel said, Gather all Israel to [c]Mizpah, and I
will pray for you unto the Lord. 6 And they gathered together to Mizpah, and
[d]drew water, and poured it out before the Lord, and fasted the same day, and said
there, We have sinned against the Lord. And Samuel judged the children of Israel
in Mizpah. 7 When the Philistines heard that the children of Israel were gathe-
red together to Mizpah, the Princes of the Philistines went up against Israel: and
when the children of Israel heard that, they were afraid of the Philistines. 8 And
the children of Israel said to Samuel, Cease not to [e]cry unto the Lord our God for
us, that he may save us out of the hand of the Philistines. 9 Then Samuel took
a sucking lamb, and offered it all together for a burnt offering unto the Lord, and
Samuel cried unto the Lord for Israel, and the Lord heard him. 10 And as Sa-
muel offered the burnt offering, the Philistines came to fight against Israel: but the
Lord [f]thundered with a great thunder that day upon the Philistines, and scatte-
red them: so they were slain before Israel. 11 And the men of Israel went from
Mizpah, and pursued the Philistines, and smote them until they came under Beth
Car. 12 Then Samuel took a stone, and pitched it between Mizpah and [g]Shen,

---

n. 1-Sam. 4:21 Or, No glory, or where is the glory?
o. 1-Sam. 4:22 She uttered her great sorrow by repeating her words.

1-SAM. 4
1. Judg. 13:1
2. 1 Sam. 3:2

1-SAM. 5
a. 1-Sam. 5:1 Which was one of the five principal cities of the Philistines.
b. 1-Sam. 5:2 Which was their chief idol, and as some write, from the navel downward was like a fish, and upward like a man.
c. 1-Sam. 5:5 Thus instead of acknowledging the true God by this miracle, they fall to a further superstition.
d. 1-Sam. 5:8 Though they had felt God's power, and were afraid thereof, yet they would further try him, which thing God turned to their destruction and his glory.
e. 1-Sam. 5:11 The wicked when they feel the hand of God, grudge and reject him, where the godly humble themselves, and cry for mercy.

1-SAM. 5
1. Ps. 78:66

1-SAM. 6
a. 1-Sam. 6:1 They thought by continuance of time the plague would have ceased, and so would have kept the Ark still.
b. 1-Sam. 6:3 The idolaters confess there is a true God, who justifieth sin justly.
c. 1-Sam. 6:5 This is God's judgment upon the idolaters, that knowing the true God, they worship him not aright.
d. 1-Sam. 6:8 Meaning, the golden emerods and the golden mice.
e. 1-Sam. 6:9 The God of Israel.
f. 1-Sam. 6:9 The wicked attribute almost all things to fortune and chance, whereas indeed there is nothing done without God's providence and decree.
g. 1-Sam. 6:12 For the trial of the matter.
h. 1-Sam. 6:14 To wit, the men of Beth Shemesh, which was Israelites.
i. 1-Sam. 6:17 These were the five principal cities of the Philistines, which were not all conquered unto the time of David.
j. 1-Sam. 6:18 Or, the plaint, or lamentation.
k. 1-Sam. 6:19 For it was not lawful to any either to touch or to see it, save only to Aaron and his sons, Num. 4:15, 20.

1-SAM. 6:
1. Exod. 12:31

1-SAM. 7
a. 1-Sam. 7:1 A city in the tribe of Judah, called also Kirjath Baal, Josh. 15:60.
b. 1-Sam. 7:2 Lamented for their sins, and followed the Lord.
c. 1-Sam. 7:5 For Shiloh was now desolate, because the Philistines had taken thence the Ark.
d. 1-Sam. 7:6 The Chaldea text hath, that they drew water out of their heart: that is, wept abundantly for their sins.
e. 1-Sam. 7:8 Signifying, that in the prayers of the godly, there ought to be a vehement zeal.
f. 1-Sam. 7:10 According to the prophecy of Hannah Samuel's mother, 1 Sam. 2:10.
g. 1-Sam. 7:12 Which was a great rock over against Mizpah.
h. 1-Sam. 7:14 Meaning, the Philistines.

and called the name thereof Ebenezer, and he said, Hitherto hath the Lord helped
us. **13** So the Philistines were brought under, and they came no more again into
the coasts of Israel: and the hand of the Lord was against the Philistines all the days
of Samuel. **14** Also the cities which the Philistines had taken from Israel, were
restored to Israel, from Ekron even to Gath: and Israel delivered the coasts of the
same out of the hands of the Philistines: and there was peace between Israel and the
[h]Amorites. **15** And Samuel judged Israel all the days of his life, **16** And went
about year by year to Bethel, and Gilgal, and Mizpah, and judged Israel in all those
places. **17** Afterward he returned to Ramah: for there was his house, and there
he judged Israel: also he built an [i]altar there unto the Lord.

8

1 Samuel maketh his sons Judges over Israel, who follow not his steps. 5 The Israelites ask a King. 11 Samuel declareth in what state they should be under the King. 19 Notwithstanding, they ask one still, and the Lord willeth Samuel to grant unto them.

1 When Samuel was now become old, he [a]made his sons Judges over Isra-
el, **2** (And the name of his eldest son was [b]Joel, and the name of the second Abi-
jah) even Judges in Beersheba. **3** And his sons walked not in his ways, but turned
aside after lucre, and [1]took rewards, and perverted the judgment. **4** Wherefore
all the Elders of Israel gathered them together, and came to Samuel unto [c]Ra-
mah, **5** And said unto him, Behold, thou art old, and thy sons walk not in thy
ways: [2]make us now a King to judge us like all nations. **6** But the thing [d]disple-
ased Samuel, when they said, Give us a King to judge us: and Samuel prayed unto
the Lord. **7** And the Lord said unto Samuel, Hear the voice of the people in all
that they shall say unto thee: for they have not cast thee away, but they have cast me
away, that I should not reign over them. **8** As they have ever done since I brou-
ght them out of Egypt even unto this day, (and have forsaken me, and served other
gods) even so do they unto thee. **9** Now therefore hearken unto their voice: how-
beit, yet [e]testify unto them, and show them the manner of the king that shall reign
over them. **10** So Samuel told all the words of the Lord unto the people that
asked a king of him. **11** And he said, This shall be the [f]manner of the king that
shall reign over you: he will take your sons, and appoint them to his chariots, and
to be his horsemen, and some shall run before his chariot. **12** Also he will make
them his captains over thousands, and captains over fifties, and to ear his ground,
and to reap his harvest, and to make instruments of war, and the things that serve
for his chariots. **13** He will also take your daughters and make them Apotheca-
ries, and Cooks, and Bakers. **14** And he will take your fields, and your vineyards,
and your best Olive trees, and give them to his servants. **15** And he will take the
tenth of your seed, and of your vineyards, and give it to his [g]Eunuchs, and to his
servants. **16** And he will take your menservants, and your maidservants, and the
chief of your young men, and your asses, and put them to his work. **17** He will
take the tenth of your sheep, and ye shall be his servants. **18** And ye shall cry out
at that day, because of your king, whom ye have chosen you, and the Lord will not
[h]hear you at that day. **19** But the people would not hear the voice of Samuel,
but did say, Nay, but there shall be a king over us. **20** And we also will be like
all other nations, and our king shall judge us, and go out before us and fight our
battles. **21** Therefore when Samuel heard all the words of the people, he rehe-
arsed them in the ears of the Lord. **22** And the Lord said to Samuel, [i]Hearken
unto their voice, and make them a king. And Samuel said unto the men of Israel,
Go every man unto his city.

9

3 Saul seeking his father's asses, by the counsel of his servant goeth to Samuel. 9 The Prophets called Seers. 15 The Lord revealeth to Samuel Saul's coming, commanding him to anoint him king. 22 Samuel bringeth Saul to the feast.

1 There was now a man of Benjamin, [a]mighty in power, named [1]Kish, the
son of Abiel, the son of Zeror, the son of Bechorath, the son of Aphiah, the son of
a man of Benjamin. **2** And he had a son called Saul, a [b]goodly young man and
a fair: so that among the children of Israel there was none goodlier than he: from
the shoulders upward, he was higher than any of the people. **3** And the asses of
Kish, Saul's father were lost: therefore Kish said to Saul his son, Take now one of
the servants with thee, and arise, go and [c]seek the asses. **4** So he passed through
mount Ephraim, and went through the land of Shalisha, but they found them not.
Then they went through the land of Shaalim, and there they were not: he went also
through the land of Benjamin, but they found them not. **5** When they came to
the land of [d]Zuph, Saul said unto his servant that was with him, Come and let us
return, lest my father leave the care of asses, and take thought for us. **6** And he
said unto him, Behold now, in this city is a man of God, and he is an honorable
man: all that he saith cometh to pass: let us now go thither, if so be that he can
show us what way we may go. **7** Then said Saul to his servant, Well then, let
us go: but what shall we bring unto the man? For the [e]bread is spent in our ves-
sels, and there is no present to bring to the man of God: what have we? **8** And
the servant answered Saul again, and said, Behold, I have found about me the
fourth part of a [f]shekel of silver: that will I give the man of God, to tell us our
way. **9** (Beforetime in Israel when a man went to seek an answer of God, thus he
spake, Come, and let us go to the [g]Seer: for he that is called now a Prophet, was
in the old time called a Seer) **10** Then said Saul to his servant, Well said, come,
let us go: so they went into the city where the man of God was. **11** And as they
were going up the highway to the city, they found maids that came out to draw
water, and said unto them, Is there here a Seer? **12** And they answered them,
and said, Yea, lo, he is before you: make haste now, for he came this day to the city:
for there is an [h]offering of the people this day in the high place. **13** When ye
shall come into the city, ye shall find him straightway ere he come up to the high
place to eat, for the people will not eat until he come, because he will [i]bless the
sacrifice; and then eat they that be bidden to the feast: now therefore go up, for
even now shall ye find him. **14** Then they went up into the city, and when they
were come into the midst of the city, Samuel came out against them, to go up to
the high place. **15** [2]But the Lord had revealed to Samuel [j]secretly (a day before
Saul came) saying, **16** Tomorrow about this time I will send thee a man out of
the land of Benjamin, him shalt thou anoint to be governor over my people Israel,
that he may [k]save my people out of the hands of the Philistines; for I have looked
upon my people, and their cry is come unto me. **17** When Samuel therefore
saw Saul, the Lord answered him, See, this is the man whom I spake to thee of, he
shall rule my people. **18** Then went Saul to Samuel in the midst of the gate, and
said, Tell me, I pray thee, where the Seer's house is. **19** And Samuel answered
Saul, and said, I am the Seer; go up before me unto the high place; for ye shall eat
with me today, and tomorrow I will let thee go, and will tell thee all that is in thine
[l]heart. **20** And as for thine asses that were lost three days ago, care not for them:
for they are found: and [m]on whom is set all the desire of Israel? is it not upon thee,
and on all thy father's house? **21** But Saul answered, and said, Am not I the son
of Benjamin of the smallest tribe of Israel? and my family is the least of all the fa-
milies of the tribe of Benjamin. Wherefore then speakest thou so to me? **22** And
Samuel took Saul and his servant, and brought them into the [n]chamber, and made
them sit in the chiefest place among them that were bidden: which were about thir-
ty persons. **23** And Samuel said unto the cook, Bring forth the portion which
I gave thee, and whereof I said unto thee, Keep it with thee. **24** And the cook
took up the shoulder, and that which was [o]upon it, and set it before Saul. And Sa-
muel said, Behold, that which is left, set it before thee, and eat: for hitherto hath
it been kept for thee, saying, Also I [p]have called the people. So Saul did eat with
Samuel that day. **25** And when they were come down from the high place into
the city, he communed with Saul upon the top of the house. **26** And when they
arose early about the spring of the day, Samuel called Saul to the [q]top of the house,
saying, Up, that I may send thee away. And Saul arose, and they went out, both he,
and Samuel. **27** And when they were come down to the end of the city, Samuel
said to Saul, Bid the servant go before us, (and he went) but stand thou still now,
that I may show thee [r]the word of God.

---

i. 1-Sam. 7:17 Which was not contrary to the Law: for as yet a certain place was not appointed.

1-SAM. 7

1. Josh. 24:15,23
2. Judg. 2:13
3. Deut. 6:4 / Matt. 4:19
4. Judg. 1:12,13

1-SAM. 8

a. 1-Sam. 8:1 Because he was not able to bear the charge.
b. 1-Sam. 8:2 Who was also called Vasheni, 1 Chron. 6:28.
c. 1-Sam. 8:4 For there his house was, 1 Sam. 7:17.
d. 1-Sam. 8:6 Because they were not content with the order that God had appointed, but would be governed as were the Gentiles.
e. 1-Sam. 8:9 To prove if they will forsake their wicked purpose.
f. 1-Sam. 8:11 Not that kings have this authority by their office, but that such as reign in God's wrath should usurp this over their brethren, contrary to the law, Deut. 17:20.
g. 1-Sam. 8:15 Or, chief officers.
h. 1-Sam. 8:18 Because ye repent not for your sins, but because ye smart for your afflictions, whereinto ye cast yourselves willingly.
i. 1-Sam. 8:22 Or, grant their request.

1-SAM. 8:

1. Deut. 16:19
2. Hos. 13:10 / Acts 13:21

1-SAM. 9

a. 1-Sam. 9:1 That is, both valiant and rich.
b. 1-Sam. 9:2 So that it might seem that God approved their request in appointing out such a person.
c. 1-Sam. 9:3 All these circumstances were means to serve unto God's providence, whereby Saul (though not approved of God) was made king.
d. 1-Sam. 9:5 Where was Ramathaim Zophim, the city of Samuel.
e. 1-Sam. 9:7 Or, vittles.
f. 1-Sam. 9:8 Which is about five pence, read Gen. 23:15.
g. 1-Sam. 9:9 So called because he foresaw things to come.
h. 1-Sam. 9:12 That is, a feast after the offering, which should be kept in an high place of the city appointed for that use.
i. 1-Sam. 9:13 That is, give thanks and distribute the meat according to their custom.
j. 1-Sam. 9:15 Hebrew, in his ear.
k. 1-Sam. 9:16 Notwithstanding their wickedness, yet God was ever mindful of his inheritance.
l. 1-Sam. 9:19 Meaning, all that thou desirest to know.
m. 1-Sam. 9:20 Whom doth Israel desire to be their King, but thee?
n. 1-Sam. 9:22 Where the feast was.
o. 1-Sam. 9:24 That is, the shoulder with the breast, which the Priest had for his family in all peace offerings, Lev. 10:14.
p. 1-Sam. 9:24 That both by the assembling of the people, and by the meat prepared for thee, thou mightest understand that I knew of thy coming.
q. 1-Sam. 9:26 To speak with him secretly: for the houses were flat above.
r. 1-Sam. 9:27 God's commandment as concerning thee.

1-SAM. 9

1. 1 Sam. 14:15 / 1 Chron. 8:33
2. 1 Sam. 15:1 / Acts 13:21

10

1 Saul is anointed King by Samuel. 9 God changeth Saul's heart, and he prophesieth. 17 Samuel assembleth the people, and showeth them their sins. 21 Saul is chosen King by lot. 25 Samuel writeth the King's office.

1 Then Samuel took a vial of [a]oil, and poured it upon his head, and kissed him, and said, Hath not the Lord anointed thee to be governor over his inheritance? **2** When thou shalt depart from me this day, thou shalt find two men by [1]Rachel's sepulcher in the border of Benjamin, even at Zelzah, and they will say unto thee, The [b]asses which thou wentest to seek, are found, and lo, thy father hath left the care of the asses, and sorroweth for you, saying, What shall I do for my son? **3** Then shalt thou go forth from thence, and shalt come to the [c]plain of Tabor, and there shall meet thee three men going up to God to Bethel, one carrying three kids, and another carrying three loaves of bread, and another carrying a bottle of wine: **4** And they will ask thee [d]if all be well, and will give thee the two loaves of bread, which thou shalt receive of their hands. **5** After that shalt thou come to the [e]hill of God, where is the garrisons of the Philistines: and when thou art come thither to the city, thou shalt meet a company of Prophets coming down from the high place with a vial, and a timbrel, and a pipe, and an harp before them, and they shall prophesy. **6** Then the Spirit of the Lord will come upon thee, and thou shalt prophesy with them, and shalt be turned into another man. **7** Therefore when these signs shall come unto thee, do as occasion shall serve: for God is with thee. **8** And thou shalt go down before me to Gilgal: and I also will come down unto thee to offer burnt offerings, and to sacrifice sacrifices of peace. [2]Tarry for me seven days, till I come to thee, and show thee what thou shalt do. **9** And when he had turned his [f]back to go from Samuel, God gave him another [g]heart; and all those tokens came to pass that same day. **10** And when they came thither to the hill, behold, the company of Prophets met him, and the Spirit of God came upon him, and he [h]prophesied among them. **11** Therefore all the people that knew him before, when they saw that he prophesied among the Prophets, said each to other, What is come unto the son of Kish? [3]is Saul also among the Prophets? **12** And one of the same place answered, and said, But who is their [i]father? Therefore it was a proverb, Is Saul also among the [j]Prophets? **13** And when he had made an end of Prophesying, he came to the high place. **14** And Saul's uncle said unto him, and to his servant, Whither went ye? And he said, To seek the asses: and when we saw that they were nowhere, we came to Samuel. **15** And Saul's uncle said, Tell me, I pray thee, what Samuel said unto you. **16** Then Saul said to his uncle, He told us plainly that the asses were found: but concerning the kingdom whereof Samuel spake, told he him not. **17** And Samuel [k]assembled the people unto the Lord in Mizpah, **18** And he said unto the children of Israel, Thus saith the Lord God of Israel, I have brought Israel out of Egypt, and delivered you out of the hand of the Egyptians, and out of the hands of all kingdoms that troubled you. **19** But ye have this day cast away your God, who only delivereth you out of all your adversities and tribulations: and ye said unto him, No, but appoint a king over us. Now therefore stand ye before the Lord according to your tribes, and according to your thousands. **20** And when Samuel had gathered together all the tribes of Israel, the tribe of Benjamin was [l]taken. **21** Afterward he assembled the tribe of Benjamin, according to their families, and the family of Matri was taken. So Saul the son of Kish was taken, and when they sought him, he could not be found. **22** Therefore they asked the Lord again, if that man should yet come thither. And the Lord answered, Behold, he hath [m]hid himself among the stuff. **23** And they ran, and brought him thence: and when he stood among the people, he was higher than any of the people from the shoulders upward. **24** And Samuel said to all the people, See ye not him, whom the Lord hath chosen, that there is none like him among all the people? and all the people shouted and said, [n]God save the King. **25** Then Samuel told the people [o]the duty of the kingdom, and wrote it in a book, and laid it up before the Lord, and Samuel sent all the people away every man to his house. **26** Saul also went home to Gibeah, and there followed him a band of men, whose heart God had touched. **27** But the wicked men said, How shall he save us? So they despised him, and brought him no presents: but he [p]held his tongue.

11

1 Nahash the Ammonite warreth against Jabesh Gilead, who asketh help of the Israelites. 6 Saul promiseth help. 11 The Ammonites are slain. 14 The kingdom is renewed.

1 Then Nahash the Ammonite [a]came up, and besieged Jabesh Gilead: and all the men of Jabesh said unto Nahash, Make a covenant with us, and we will be thy servants. **2** And Nahash the Ammonite answered them, On this condition will I make a covenant with you, that I may thrust out all your [b]right eyes, and bring that shame upon all Israel. **3** To whom the Elders of Jabesh said, Give us seven days respite, that we may send messengers unto all the coasts of Israel: and then if no man deliver us, we will come out to thee. **4** Then came the messengers to Gibeah of Saul, and told these tidings in the ears of the people: and all the people lift up their voices and wept. **5** And behold, Saul came following the cattle out of the field, and Saul said, What aileth this people, that they weep? And they told him the tidings of the men of Jabesh. **6** Then the Spirit of God [c]came upon Saul, when he heard those tidings, and he was exceeding angry, **7** And took a yoke of oxen, and hewed them in pieces, and sent them throughout all the coasts of Israel by the hands of messengers, saying, Whosoever cometh not forth after Saul, and after [d]Samuel, so shall his oxen be served. And the fear of the Lord fell on the people, and they came out [e]with one consent. **8** And when he numbered them in Bezek, the children of Israel were three hundred thousand men, and the men of Judah thirty thousand. **9** Then [f]they said unto the messengers that came, So say unto the men of Jabesh Gilead, Tomorrow by then the Sun be hot, ye shall have help. And the messengers came and showed it to the men of Jabesh, which were glad. **10** Therefore the men of Jabesh said, Tomorrow we will come out unto [g]you, and ye shall do with us all that pleaseth you. **11** And when the morrow was come, Saul put the people in three bands, and they came in upon the host in the morning watch, and slew the Ammonites until the heat of the day: and they that remained, were scattered, so that two of them were not left together. **12** Then the people said unto Samuel, [h]Who is he that said, Shall Saul reign over us? bring those men that we may slay them. **13** But Saul said, There shall no man [i]die this day: for today the Lord hath saved Israel. **14** Then said Samuel unto the people, Come, that we may go to Gilgal, and renew the kingdom there. **15** So all the people went to Gilgal, and made Saul King there before the Lord in Gilgal: and there they offered [j]peace offerings before the Lord: and there Saul and all the men of Israel rejoiced exceedingly.

12

1 Samuel declaring to the people his integrity, reproveth their ingratitude. 19 God by miracle causeth the people to confess their sin. 20 Samuel exhorteth the people to follow the Lord.

1 Samuel then said unto all Israel, Behold, I have [a]hearkened unto your voice in all that ye said unto me, and have appointed a King over you. **2** Now therefore behold, your King walketh [b]before you, and I am old and gray headed, and behold, my sons are with you: and I have walked before you from my childhood unto this day. **3** Behold, here I am: bear record of me before the Lord and before his anointed. [c]Whose ox have I taken? or whose ass have I taken? or whom have I done wrong to? or whom have I hurt? or of whose hand have I received any bribe, to blind mine eyes therewith, and I will restore it you? **4** Then they said, Thou hast done us no wrong, nor hast hurt us, neither hast thou taken ought of any man's hand. **5** And he said unto them, The Lord is witness against you, and his [d]Anointed is witness this day, that ye have found nought in mine hands. And they answered, He is witness. **6** Then Samuel said unto the people, It is the Lord that [e]made Moses and Aaron, and that brought your fathers out of the land of Egypt. **7** Now therefore stand still, that I may reason with you before the Lord according to all the [f]righteousness of the Lord, which he showed to you and to your fathers. **8** [1]After that Jacob was come into Egypt, and your fathers cried unto the Lord, then the Lord [2]sent Moses and Aaron which brought your fathers out of Egypt, and made them dwell in this place. **9** [3]And when they forgot the Lord their God, he sold them into the hand of Sisera [g]captain of the host of Hazor, and into the hand of the Philistines, and into the hand of the king of Moab, and they fought against them. **10** And they cried unto the Lord, and said, We

---

1-SAM. 10

- **a.** 1-Sam. 10:1 In the Law this anointing signified the gifts of the holy Ghost, which were necessary for them that should rule.
- **b.** 1-Sam. 10:2 Samuel confirmeth him by these signs, that God hath appointed him king.
- **c.** 1-Sam. 10:3 Or, oaks.
- **d.** 1-Sam. 10:4 Hebrew, of peace.
- **e.** 1-Sam. 10:5 Which was an high place in the city Kirjath Jearim, where the Ark was, 1 Sam. 7:2.
- **f.** 1-Sam. 10:9 Hebrew, shoulder.
- **g.** 1-Sam. 10:9 He gave him such virtues as were meet for a King.
- **h.** 1-Sam. 10:10 Or, sang praises.
- **i.** 1-Sam. 10:12 Meaning, that prophecy cometh not by succession, but is given to whom it pleaseth God.
- **j.** 1-Sam. 10:12 Noting thereby him that from low degree cometh suddenly to honor.
- **k.** 1-Sam. 10:17 Both to declare unto them their fault in asking a King, and also to show God's sentence therein.
- **l.** 1-Sam. 10:20 That is, by casting of lot.
- **m.** 1-Sam. 10:22 As though he were unworthy and unwilling.
- **n.** 1-Sam. 10:24 Hebrew, let the king live.
- **o.** 1-Sam. 10:25 As it is written in Deut. 17:15, etc.
- **p.** 1-Sam. 10:27 Both to avoid sedition, and also to win them by patience.

1-SAM. 10

1. Gen. 35:20
2. 1 Sam. 13:8
3. 1 Sam. 19:24

1-SAM. 11

- **a.** 1-Sam. 11:1 After that Saul was chosen king: for fear of whom they asked a king, as 1 Sam. 12:12.
- **b.** 1-Sam. 11:2 This declareth that the more near the tyrants are to their destruction, the more cruel they are.
- **c.** 1-Sam. 11:6 God gave him the spirit of strength and courage to go against this tyrant.
- **d.** 1-Sam. 11:7 He addeth Samuel because Saul was not yet approved of all.
- **e.** 1-Sam. 11:7 Hebrew, as one man.
- **f.** 1-Sam. 11:9 Meaning, Saul and Samuel.
- **g.** 1-Sam. 11:10 That is, to the Ammonites, dissembling that they had hope of aid.
- **h.** 1-Sam. 11:12 By this victory the Lord won the hearts of the people to Saul.
- **i.** 1-Sam. 11:13 By showing mercy he thought to overcome their malice.
- **j.** 1-Sam. 11:15 In sign of thanksgiving for the victory.

1-SAM. 12

- **a.** 1-Sam. 12:1 I have granted your petition.
- **b.** 1-Sam. 12:2 To govern you in peace and war.
- **c.** 1-Sam. 12:3 God would that this confession should be a pattern for all them that have any charge or office.
- **d.** 1-Sam. 12:5 Your King, who is anointed by the commandment of the Lord.
- **e.** 1-Sam. 12:6 Or, exalted.
- **f.** 1-Sam. 12:7 Or, benefits.
- **g.** 1-Sam. 12:9 Captain of Jabin's host, King of Hazor.

have sinned, because we have forsaken the Lord, and have served Baal and Ashtoreth. Now therefore deliver us out of the hands of our enemies, and we will serve thee. **11** Therefore the Lord sent Jerubbaal [h]and Bedan and [4]Jephthah, and [5]Samuel, and delivered you out of the hands of your enemies on every side, and ye dwelled safe. **12** Notwithstanding when you saw, that Nahash the king of the children of Ammon came against you, ye said unto me, [i]No, but a king shall reign over us: when yet the Lord your God was your King. **13** Now therefore behold the King whom ye have chosen, and whom ye have desired: lo therefore, the Lord hath set a King over you. **14** If ye will fear the Lord and serve him, and hear his voice, and not disobey the word of the Lord, both ye, and the king that reigneth over you, shall [j]follow the Lord your God. **15** But if ye will not obey the voice of the Lord, but disobey the Lord's mouth, then shall the hand of the Lord be upon you, and on your [k]fathers. **16** Now also stand and see this great thing which the Lord will do before your eyes. **17** Is it not now wheat harvest? I will call unto the Lord, and he shall send thunder and rain, that ye may perceive and see, how that your wickedness is [l]great, which ye have done in the sight of the Lord in asking you a king. **18** Then Samuel called unto the Lord, and the Lord sent thunder and rain the same day: and all the people feared the Lord and Samuel exceedingly. **19** And all the people said unto Samuel, Pray for thy servants unto the Lord thy God, that we die not: for we have sinned in asking us a King, beside [m]all our other sins. **20** And Samuel said unto the people, Fear not, (ye have indeed done all this wickedness, [n]yet depart not from following the Lord, but serve the Lord with all your heart, **21** Neither turn ye back: for that should be after vain things which cannot profit you, nor deliver you, for they are but vanity.) **22** For the Lord will not forsake his people for his great Name's sake: because it hath pleased the Lord to make you [o]his people. **23** Moreover God forbid, that I should sin against the Lord, and cease praying for you, but I will show you the good and right way. **24** Therefore fear you the Lord, and serve him in the truth with all your [p]hearts, and consider how great things he hath done for you. **25** But if ye do wickedly, ye shall perish, both ye and your King.

13

3 The Philistines are smitten of Saul and Jonathan. 13 Saul being disobedient to God's commandment, is showed of Samuel that he shall not reign. 19 The great slavery, wherein the Philistines kept the Israelites.

1 Saul now had been King [a]one year, and he reigned [b]two years over Israel. **2** Then Saul chose him three thousand of Israel: and two thousand were with Saul in Michmash, and in mount Bethel, and a thousand were with Jonathan in Gibeah of Benjamin: and the rest of the people he sent every one to his tent. **3** And Jonathan smote the garrison of the Phi-listines, that was in the [c]hill: and it came to the Phi-listines' ears: and Saul blew the [d]trumpet throughout all the land, saying, Hear, O ye Hebrews. **4** And all Israel heard say, Saul hath destroyed a garrison of the Philistines: wherefore Israel was had in abomination with the Philistines: and the people gathered together after Saul to Gilgal. **5** The Philistines also gathered themselves together to fight with Israel, thirty thousand chariots, and six thousand horsemen: for the people was like the sand which is by the seaside in multitude, and came up, and pitched in Michmash Eastward from [e]Beth Aven. **6** And when the men of Israel saw that they were in a strait (for the people were in distress) the people hid themselves in caves, and in holds, and in rocks, and in towers, and in pits. **7** And some of the Hebrews went over Jordan unto the land of [f]Gad and Gilead: and Saul was yet in Gilgal, and all the people for fear followed him. **8** And he tarried seven days, according unto the time that Samuel had appointed: but Samuel came not to Gilgal, therefore the people were [g]scattered from him. **9** And Saul said, Bring a burnt offering to me and peace offerings: and he offered a burnt offering. **10** And as soon as he had made an end of offering the burnt offering, behold, Samuel came: and Saul went forth to meet him, to [h]salute him. **11** And Samuel said, What hast thou done? Then Saul said, Because I saw that the people was [i]scattered from me, and that thou camest not within the days appointed, and that the Philistines gathered themselves together to Michmash, **12** Therefore said I, the Philistines will come down now upon me to Gilgal, and I have not made supplication unto the Lord. I was bold therefore and offered a burnt offering. **13** And Samuel said to Saul, Thou hast done foolishly: thou hast not kept the commandment of the Lord thy [j]God, which he commanded thee: for the Lord had now stablished thy kingdom upon Israel forever. **14** But now thy kingdom shall not continue: the Lord hath sought him a [k]man after his own heart, and the Lord hath commanded him to be governor over his people, because thou hast not kept that which the Lord had commanded thee. **15** And Samuel arose, and got him up from Gilgal in [l]Gibeah of Benjamin: and Saul numbered the people that were found with him, about six hundred men. **16** And Saul and Jonathan his son, and the people that were found with them, had their abiding in Gibeah of Benjamin: but the Philistines pitched in Michmash. **17** And there came out of the host of the Philistines [m]three bands to destroy, one band turned unto the way of Ophrah unto the land of Shual, **18** And another band turned toward the way to Beth Horon, and the [n]third band turned toward the way of the coast that looketh toward the valley of Zeboim, toward the wilderness. **19** Then there was no smith found throughout all the land of Israel: for the Philistines said, Lest the Hebrews make them swords or spears. **20** Wherefore, all the Israelites went down to the Philistines, to sharpen every man his share, his mattock, and his axe, and his weeding hook. **21** Yet they had a file for the shares, and for the mattocks, and for the pick forks, and for the axes, and for to sharpen the goads. **22** So when the day of battle was come, there was neither [o]sword nor spear found in the hands of any of the people that were with Saul and with Jonathan: but only with Saul and Jonathan his son was there found. **23** And the garrison of the Philistines came out to the passage of Michmash.

14

14 Jonathan and his armor bearer put the Philistines to flight. 24 Saul bindeth the people by an oath, not to eat till evening. 32 The people eat with the blood. 38 Saul would put Jonathan to death. 45 The people deliver him.

1 Then on a day Jonathan the son of Saul said unto the young man that bare his armor, [a]Come and let us go over toward the Philistines garrison, that is yonder on the other side, but he told not his father. **2** And Saul tarried in the border of Gibeah under a pomegranate tree, which was in Migron, and the people that were with him, were about six hundred men. **3** And Ahijah the son of Ahitub, [1]Ichabod's brother, the son of Phinehas, the son of Eli, was the Lord's Priest in Shiloh, and wore an Ephod: and the people knew not that Jonathan was gone. **4** Now in the way whereby Jonathan sought to go over to the Philistines garrison, there was a [b]sharp rock on the one side, and a sharp rock on the other side: the name of the one was called Bozez, and the name of the other Seneh. **5** The one rock stretched from the North toward Michmash, and the other was from the South toward Gibeah. **6** And Jonathan said to the young man that bare his armor, Come, and let us go over unto the garrison of these [c]uncircumcised: it may be that the Lord will work with us: for it is [d]not hard to the Lord [2]to save with many, or with few. **7** And he that bare his armor, said unto him, Do all that is in thine heart: go where it pleaseth thee: behold, [e]I am with thee as thine heart desireth. **8** Then said Jonathan, Behold, we go over unto those men, and will show ourselves unto them. **9** [f]If they say on this wise to us, Tarry until we come to you, then we will stand still in our place, and not go up to them. **10** But if they say, Come up unto us, then we will go up: for the Lord hath delivered them into our hand: and this shall be a sign unto us. **11** So they both showed themselves unto the garrison of the Philistines: and the Philistines said, See, the Hebrews come out of the [g]holes wherein they had hid themselves. **12** And the men of the garrison answered Jonathan and his armor bearer, and said, Come up to us: for we will show you a thing. Then Jonathan said unto his armor bearer, Come up after me: for the Lord hath delivered them into the hand of Israel. **13** So Jonathan went up upon [h]his hands and upon his feet, and his armor bearer after him: and some fell before Jonathan, and his armor bearer slew others after him. **14** So the [i]first slaughter which Jonathan and his armor bearer made, was about twenty men, as it were within half an acre of land which two oxen plow. **15** And there was a fear in the host, and in the field, and among all the people: the garrison also, and they that went out to spoil, were afraid themselves: and the earth [j]trembled: for it was stricken with fear by God. **16** Then the watchmen of Saul in Gibeah of Benjamin

---

h. 1-Sam. 12:11 That is, Samson, Judg. 13:25.
i. 1-Sam. 12:12 Leaving God to seek the help of man, 1 Sam. 8:5.
j. 1-Sam. 12:14 Ye shall be preserved as they that follow the Lord's will.
k. 1-Sam. 12:15 Meaning, the governors.
l. 1-Sam. 12:17 In that ye have forsaken him, who hath all power in his hand, for a mortal man.
m. 1-Sam. 12:19 Not only at other times, but now chiefly.
n. 1-Sam. 12:20 He showeth that there is no sin so great, but it shall be forgiven, if the sinner turn again to God.
o. 1-Sam. 12:22 Of his free mercy, and not of your merits, and therefore he will not forsake you.
p. 1-Sam. 12:24 Unfeignedly, and without hypocrisy.

1-SAM. 12

1. Gen. 46:5,6
2. Exod. 4:16
3. Judg. 4:2
4. Judg. 11:1
5. 1 Sam. 4:1

1-SAM. 13

a. 1-Sam. 13:1 While these things were done.
b. 1-Sam. 13:1 Before he took upon him the state of a King.
c. 1-Sam. 13:3 Of Kirjath Jearim, where the Ark was, 1 Sam. 10:5.
d. 1-Sam. 13:3 That everyone should prepare themselves to war.
e. 1-Sam. 13:5 Which was also called Bethel, in the tribe of Benjamin.
f. 1-Sam. 13:7 Where the two tribes and the half remained.
g. 1-Sam. 13:8 Thinking that the absence of the Prophet was a sign, that they should lose the victory.
h. 1-Sam. 13:10 Hebrew, bless him.
i. 1-Sam. 13:11 Though these causes seem sufficient in man's judgment: yet because they had not the word of God, they turned to his destruction.
j. 1-Sam. 13:13 Who willed thee to obey him, and rest upon the words spoken by his Prophet.
k. 1-Sam. 13:14 That is, David.
l. 1-Sam. 13:15 And went to his city Ramah.
m. 1-Sam. 13:17 Or, the destroyer: to wit, the captains came out with three bands.
n. 1-Sam. 13:18 So that to man's judgment these three armies would have overrun the whole country.
o. 1-Sam. 13:22 To declare that the victory only came of God, and not by their force.

1-SAM.14

a. 1-Sam. 14:1 By this example God would declare to Israel that the victory did not consist in multitude or armor, but only came of his grace.
b. 1-Sam. 14:4 Or, like a tooth.
c. 1-Sam. 14:6 To wit, the Philistines.
d. 1-Sam. 14:6 Or, none can let the Lord.
e. 1-Sam. 14:7 I will follow thee whithersoever thou goest.
f. 1-Sam. 14:9 This he spake by the spirit of prophecy, forasmuch hereby God gave him assurance of the victory.
g. 1-Sam. 14:11 Thus they spake contemptuously and by derision.
h. 1-Sam. 14:13 That is, he crept up, or went up with all haste.
i. 1-Sam. 14:14 The second was when they slew one another, and the third when the Israelites chased them.
j. 1-Sam. 14:15 In that the insensible creatures tremble for fear of God's judgment, it declareth how terrible his vengeance shall be against his enemies.

saw: and behold, the multitude was discomfited, and smitten as they went. **17** Therefore said Saul unto the people that were with him, Search now, and see, who is gone from us. And when they had numbered, behold, Jonathan and his armor bearer were not there. **18** And Saul said unto Ahijah, Bring hither the Ark of God (for the Ark of God was at that time with the children of Israel) **19** And while Saul talked unto the Priest, the noise that was in the host of the Philistines, spread farther abroad, and increased: therefore Saul said unto the Priest, [k]Withdraw thine hand. **20** And Saul was assembled with all the people that were with him, and they came to the battle: and behold, [3]every man's sword was against his fellow, and there was a very great discomfiture. **21** Moreover, the Hebrews that were with the Philistines beforetime, and were come with them into all parts of the host, even they also turned to be with the [l]Israelites that were with Saul and Jonathan. **22** Also all the men of Israel which had hid themselves in mount Ephraim, when they heard that the Philistines were fled, they followed after them in the battle. **23** And so the Lord saved Israel that day: and the battle continued unto Beth Aven. **24** And at that time the men of Israel were pressed with hunger: for Saul charged the people with an oath, saying, [m]Cursed be the man that eateth [n]food till night, that I may be avenged of mine enemies: so none of the people tasted any sustenance. **25** And all they of the land came to a wood, where honey lay upon the ground. **26** And the people came into the wood, and behold, the honey dropped, and no man moved his hand to his mouth: for the people feared the [o]oath. **27** But Jonathan heard not when his father charged the people with the oath: wherefore he put forth the end of the rod that was in his hand, and dipped it in an honey comb, and put his hand to his mouth, and his [p]eyes received sight. **28** Then answered one of the people, and said, Thy father made the people to swear, saying, Cursed be the man that eateth sustenance this day: and the people were [q]faint. **29** Then said Jonathan, My father hath [r]troubled the land: see now how mine eyes are made clear, because I have tasted a little of this honey: **30** How much more, if the people had eaten today of the spoil of their enemies which they found? for had there not been now a greater slaughter among the Philistines? **31** And they smote the Philistines that day, from Michmash to Aijalon: and the people were exceeding faint. **32** So the people turned to the spoil, and took sheep, and oxen, and calves and slew them on the ground, and the people did eat them [4]with the blood. **33** Then men told Saul, saying, Behold, the people sin against the Lord, in that they eat with the blood. And he said, Ye have trespassed: [s]roll a great stone unto me this day. **34** Again Saul said, Go abroad among the people, and bid them bring me every man his ox, and every man his sheep, and slay them here, and eat, and sin not against the Lord in eating with the blood. And the people brought every man his ox in his hand that night, and slew them there. **35** Then Saul made an altar unto the Lord, and that [t]was the first altar that he made unto the Lord. **36** And Saul said, Let us go down after the Philistines by night, and spoil them until the morning shine, and let us not leave a man of them. And they said, Do whatsoever thou thinkest best. Then said the Priest, Let us [u]draw near hither unto God. **37** So Saul asked of God, saying, Shall I go down after the Philistines? wilt thou deliver them into the hands of Israel? But he answered him not at that time. **38** And Saul said, [5]All [v]ye chief of the people, come ye hither, and know, and see by whom this sin is done this day. **39** For as the Lord liveth, which saveth Israel, though it be done by Jonathan my son, he shall die the death. But none of all the people answered him. **40** Then he said unto all Israel, Be ye on one side, and I and Jonathan my son will be on the other side. And the people said unto Saul, Do what thou thinkest best. **41** Then Saul said unto the Lord God of Israel, Give [w]a perfect lot. And Jonathan and Saul were taken, but the people escaped. **42** And Saul said, Cast lot between me and Jonathan my son. And Jonathan was taken. **43** Then Saul said to Jonathan, Tell me what thou hast done. And Jonathan told him, and said, I tasted a little honey with the end of the rod, that was in mine hand, and lo, I must die. **44** Again Saul answered, God do so and more also, unless thou die the death, Jonathan. **45** And the people said unto Saul, [x]Shall Jonathan die, who hath so mightily delivered Israel? God forbid. As the Lord liveth, there shall not one hair of his head fall to the ground: for he hath wrought with God this day. So the people delivered Jonathan that he died not. **46** Then Saul came up from the Philistines: and the Philistines went to their own place. **47** So Saul held the kingdom over Israel, and fought against all his enemies on every side, against Moab, and against the children of Ammon, and against Edom, and against the Kings of Zobah, and against the Philistines: and whithersoever he went, he [y]handled them as wicked men. **48** He gathered also an host and smote [z]Amalek, and delivered Israel out of the hands of them that spoiled them. **49** Now the sons of Saul were Jonathan, [aa]and Jishui, and Malchishua: and the names of his two daughters, the elder was called Merab, and the younger was named [ab]Michal. **50** And the name of Saul's wife was Ahinoam the daughter of Ahimaaz: and the name of his chief captain was [ac]Abner the son of Ner, Saul's uncle. **51** And Kish was Saul's father: and Ner the father of Abner was the son of Abiel. **52** And there was sore war against the Philistines all the days of Saul: and [ad]whomsoever Saul saw to be a strong man, and meet for the war, he took him unto him.

15

3 Saul is commanded to slay Amalek. 9 He spareth Agag, and the best things. 19 Samuel reproveth him. 28 Saul is rejected of the Lord, and his Kingdom given to another. 33 Samuel heweth Agag in pieces.

1 Afterward Samuel said unto Saul, [1]The Lord sent me to anoint thee King over his people, over Israel: now therefore [a]obey the voice of the words of the Lord. **2** Thus saith the Lord of hosts, I remember what Amalek did to Israel, [2]how they laid wait for them in the way, as they came up from Egypt. **3** Now therefore go, and smite Amalek, and destroy ye all that pertaineth unto them, and have no compassion on them, but [b]slay both man and woman, both infant and suckling, both ox, and sheep, both camel, and ass. **4** And Saul assembled the people, and [c]numbered them in Telaim, two hundred thousand footmen, and ten thousand men of Judah. **5** And Saul came to a city of Amalek, and [d]set watch at the river. **6** And Saul said unto the [e]Kenites, Go, depart, and get you down from among the Amalekites, lest I destroy you with them: for ye showed [f]mercy to all the children of Israel, when they came up from Egypt: and the Kenites departed from among the Amalekites. **7** So Saul smote the Amalekites from Havilah, as thou comest to Shur, that is before Egypt, **8** And took Agag the King of the Amalekites alive, and destroyed all the people with the edge of the sword. **9** But Saul and the people spared Agag, and the better sheep, and the oxen, and the fat beasts, and the lambs, and all that was good, and they would not destroy them; but everything that was vile and nought worth, that they destroyed. **10** Then came the word of the Lord unto Samuel, saying, **11** It [g]repenteth me that I have made Saul King; for he is turned from me, and hath not performed my commandments. And Samuel was moved, and cried unto the Lord all night. **12** And when Samuel arose early to meet Saul in the morning, one told Samuel, saying, Saul is gone to Carmel; and behold, he hath made him there a place, from whence he returned, and departed, and is gone down to Gilgal. **13** Then Samuel came to Saul, and Saul said unto him. Blessed be thou of the Lord, I have fulfilled the [h]commandment of the Lord. **14** But Samuel said, What meaneth then the bleating of the sheep in mine ears, and the lowing of the oxen which I hear? **15** And Saul answered, They have brought them from the Amalekites; for the people spared the best of the sheep, and of the oxen, to sacrifice them unto the Lord thy God, and the remnant have we destroyed. **16** Again Samuel said to Saul, Let me tell thee what the Lord hath said to me this night. And he said unto him, Say on. **17** Then Samuel said, When thou wast [i]little in thine own sight, wast thou not made the head of the tribes of Israel? for the Lord anointed thee King over Israel. **18** And the Lord sent thee on a journey, and said, Go, and destroy those sinners the Amalekites, and fight against them, until thou destroy them. **19** Now wherefore hast thou not obeyed the voice of the Lord, but hast turned to the prey, and hast done wickedly in the sight of the Lord? **20** And Saul said unto Samuel, Yea, [j]I have obeyed the voice of the Lord, and have gone the way which the Lord sent me, and have brought Agag the king of Amalek, and have destroyed the Amalekites. **21** But the people took of the spoil, sheep, and oxen, and the chiefest of the things which should have been destroyed, to offer unto the Lord thy God in Gilgal. **22** And Samuel said, Hath the Lord as great pleasure in burnt offerings and sacrifices, as when the voice of the Lord is obeyed? behold, [3]to obey is better than sacrifice, and to hearken is

---

k. 1-Sam. 14:19 Let the Ephod alone: for I have no leisure now to ask counsel of God, Num. 27:21.
l. 1-Sam. 14:21 Though before for fear of the Philistines they declared themselves as enemies to their brethren.
m. 1-Sam. 14:24 Such was his hypocrisy and arrogancy, that he thought to attribute to his policy that which God had given by the hand of Jonathan.
n. 1-Sam. 14:24 Hebrew, bread.
o. 1-Sam. 14:26 That is, the punishment, if they break their oath.
p. 1-Sam. 14:27 Which were dim before for weariness and hunger.
q. 1-Sam. 14:28 Or, weary.
r. 1-Sam. 14:29 By making this cruel law.
s. 1-Sam. 14:33 That the blood of the beast that shall be slain, may be pressed out upon it.
t. 1-Sam. 14:35 Or, of that stone began he to build an altar.
u. 1-Sam. 14:36 To ask counsel of him.
v. 1-Sam. 14:38 Hebrew, corners.
w. 1-Sam. 14:41 Cause the lot to fall on him that hath broken the oath: but he doth not consider his presumption in commanding the same oath.
x. 1-Sam. 14:45 The people thought it their duty to rescue him, who of ignorance had but broken a rash law, and by whom they had received so great a benefit.
y. 1-Sam. 14:47 Or, overcame them.
z. 1-Sam. 14:48 As the Lord had commanded, Deut. 25:17.
aa. 1-Sam. 14:49 Called also Abinadab, 1 Sam. 31:2.
ab. 1-Sam. 14:49 Which was the Wife of David, 1 Sam. 18:27.
ac. 1-Sam. 14:50 Whom Joab the captain of David slew, 2 Sam. 3:27.
ad. 1-Sam. 14:52 As Samuel had forewarned, 1 Sam. 8:11.

1-SAM. 14

1. 1 Sam. 4:21
2. 2 Chron. 14:11
3. Judg. 7:21,22 / 1 Chron. 20:23
4. Lev. 7:26 / Lev. 19:26 / Deut. 12:16
5. Judg. 20:2

1-SAM. 15

a. 1-Sam. 15:1 Because he hath preferred thee to this honor, thou art bound to obey him.
b. 1-Sam. 15:3 That this might be an example of God's vengeance against them that deal cruelly with his people.
c. 1-Sam. 15:4 Or, knew their number by the lambs which they brought.
d. 1-Sam. 15:5 Or, fought in the valley.
e. 1-Sam. 15:6 Which were the posterity of Jethro Moses' father-in-law.
f. 1-Sam. 15:6 For Jethro came to visit them, and gave them good counsel, Exod. 18:19.
g. 1-Sam. 15:11 God in his eternal counsel never changeth nor repenteth, as verse 29, though he seemeth to us to repent when anything goeth contrary to his temporal election.
h. 1-Sam. 15:13 This is the nature of hypocrites to be impudent against the truth, to condemn others, and justify themselves.
i. 1-Sam. 15:17 Meaning, of base condition, as 1 Sam. 9:21.
j. 1-Sam. 15:20 He standeth most impudently in his own defense both against God and his own conscience.
k. 1-Sam. 15:23 God hateth nothing more than the disobedience of his Commandment, though the intent seems never so good to man.
l. 1-Sam. 15:25 This was not true repentance, but dissimulation, fearing the loss of his kingdom.
m. 1-Sam. 15:28 That is, to David.

better than the fat of rams. **23** For [k]rebellion is as the sin of witchcraft, and transgression is wickedness and idolatry. Because thou hast cast away the word of the Lord, therefore he hath cast away thee from being king. **24** Then Saul said unto Samuel, I have sinned: for I have transgressed the Commandment of the Lord, and thy words, because I feared the people, and obeyed their voice. **25** Now therefore I pray thee, take away my [l]sin, and turn again with me, that I may worship the Lord. **26** But Samuel said unto Saul, I will not return with thee: for thou hast cast away the word of the Lord, and the Lord hath cast away thee, that thou shalt not be King over Israel. **27** And as Samuel turned himself to go away, he caught the lap of his coat, and it rent. **28** Then Samuel said unto him, The Lord hath rent the kingdom of Israel from thee this day, and hath given it to thy [m]neighbor, that is better than thou. **29** For indeed the [n]strength of Israel will not lie nor repent: for he is not a man that he should repent. **30** Then he said, I have sinned: but honor me, I pray thee, before the Elders of my people, and before Israel, and turn again with me, that I may worship the Lord thy God. **31** So Samuel turned again, and followed Saul: and Saul worshipped the Lord. **32** Then said Samuel, Bring ye hither to me Agag the king of the Amalekites: and Agag came unto him [o]pleasantly, and Agag said, Truly the [p]bitterness of death is passed. **33** And Samuel said, [4]As thy sword hath made women childless, so shall thy mother be childless among other women. And Samuel hewed Agag in pieces before the Lord in Gilgal. **34** So Samuel departed to [q]Ramah, and Saul went up to his house to Gibeah of Saul. **35** And Samuel came no more to [r]see Saul until the day of his death: but Samuel mourned for Saul, and the Lord [s]repented that he made Saul King over Israel.

16

1 Samuel is reproved of God, and is sent to anoint David. 7 God regardeth the heart. 13 The Spirit of the Lord cometh upon David. 14 The wicked Spirit is sent upon Saul. 19 Saul sendeth for David.

1 The Lord then said unto Samuel, How long wilt thou mourn for Saul, [a]seeing I have cast him away from reigning over Israel? fill thine horn with oil and come, I will send thee to Jesse the Bethlehemite: for I have provided me a King among his sons. **2** And Samuel said, How can I go? for if Saul shall hear it, he will kill me. Then the Lord answered, Take an heifer [b]with thee, and say, I am come [c]to do sacrifice to the Lord. **3** And call Jesse to the sacrifice, and I will show thee what thou shalt do, and thou shalt anoint unto me him whom I name unto thee. **4** So Samuel did that the Lord bade him, and came to Bethlehem, and the elders of the town were [d]astonished at his coming, and said, Comest thou peaceably? **5** And he answered, Yea: I am come to do sacrifice unto the Lord: sanctify yourselves, and come with me to the sacrifice. And he sanctified Jesse and his sons, and called them to the sacrifice. **6** And when they were come, he looked on Eliab, and said, Surely the Lord's [e]Anointed is before him. **7** But the Lord said unto Samuel, Look not on his countenance, nor on the height of his stature, because I have refused him: for God seeth not as man seeth: for man looketh on the outward appearance, but the Lord beholdeth the [1]heart. **8** Then Jesse called Abinadab, and made him come before Samuel. And he said, Neither hath the Lord chosen this. **9** Then Jesse made Shammah come. And he said, Neither yet hath the Lord chosen him. **10** Again Jesse made his seven sons to come before Samuel, and Samuel said unto Jesse, The Lord hath chosen none of these. **11** Finally, Samuel said unto Jesse, [f]Are there no more children but these? And he said, There remaineth yet a little one behind, that keepeth the sheep. Then Samuel said unto Jesse, [2]Send and fet him: for we will not sit down, till he be come hither. **12** And he sent, and brought him in: and he was ruddy, and of a good countenance, and comely visage. And the Lord said, Arise, and anoint him: for this is he. **13** Then Samuel took the horn of oil, and anointed him in the midst of his brethren. And the [3]Spirit of the Lord [g]came upon David, from that day forward: then Samuel rose up, and went to Ramah. **14** But the Spirit of the Lord departed from Saul, and an [h]evil spirit sent of the Lord, vexed him. **15** And Saul's servants said unto him, Behold now, the evil spirit of God vexeth thee. **16** Let our Lord therefore command thy servants that are before thee, to seek a man that is a cunning player upon the harp: that when the evil spirit of God cometh upon thee, he may play with his hand, and thou mayest be eased. **17** Saul then said unto his servants, Provide me a man, I pray you, that can play well, and bring him to me. **18** Then answered one of his servants, and said, Behold, I have seen a [i]son of Jesse, a Bethlehemite, that can play, and is strong, valiant, and a man of war, and wise in matters, and a comely person, and the Lord is with him. **19** Wherefore Saul sent messengers unto Jesse, and said, Send me David thy son, which is with the sheep. **20** And Jesse took an ass laden with bread and a flagon of wine and a kid, and sent them by the hand of David his son unto Saul. **21** And David came to Saul, and [j]stood before him: and he loved him very well, and he was his armor bearer. **22** And Saul sent to Jesse, saying, Let David now remain with me: for he hath found favor in my sight. **23** And so when the evil spirit of God came upon Saul, David took an harp and played with his hand, and Saul was [k]refreshed and was eased: for the evil spirit departed from him.

17

1 The Philistines make war against Israel. 10 Goliath defieth Israel. 17 David is sent to his brethren. 34 The strength and boldness of David. 47 The Lord saveth not by sword nor spear. 50 David killeth Goliath, and the Philistines flee.

1 Now the Philistines gathered their armies to battle, and came together to Sochoh which is in Judah, and pitched between Sochoh and Azekah, [a]in the coast of Dammim. **2** And Saul, and the men of Israel assembled and pitched in the valley [b]of Elah, and put themselves in battle array to meet the Philistines. **3** And the Philistines stood on a mountain on the one side, and Israel stood on a mountain on the other side: so a valley was between them. **4** Then came a man between them [c]both out of the tents of the Philistines, named Goliath of Gath: his height was six cubits and an hand breadth, **5** And had an helmet of brass upon his head, and a [d]brigandine upon him: and the weight of his brigandine was five thousand [e]shekels of brass. **6** And he had [f]boots of brass upon his legs, and a shield of brass upon his shoulders. **7** And the shaft of his spear was like a weaver's beam: and his spear head weighed six hundred shekels of iron: and one bearing a shield went before him. **8** And he stood, and cried against the host of Israel, and said unto them, Why are ye come to set your battle in array? am not I a Philistine, and you servants to Saul? choose you a man for you, and let him come down to me. **9** If he be able to fight with me, and [g]kill me, then will we be your servants: but if I overcome him, and kill him, then shall ye be our servants, and serve us. **10** Also the Philistine said, I defy the host of Israel this day: give me a man, that we may fight [h]together. **11** When Saul and all Israel heard those words of the Philistine, they were discouraged, and greatly afraid. **12** Now this David was the [1]son of an Ephrathite of Bethlehem Judah, named Jesse, which had eight sons: and [i]this man was taken for an old man in the days of Saul. **13** And the three eldest sons of Jesse went and followed Saul to the battle: and the names of his three sons that went to battle were Eliab the eldest, and the next Abinadab, and the third Shammah. **14** So David was the least: and the three eldest went after Saul. **15** David also [j]went, but he returned from Saul to feed his father's sheep in Bethlehem. **16** And the Philistine drew near in the morning, and evening, and continued forty days. **17** And Jesse said unto David his son, [k]Take now for thy brethren an Ephah of this parched corn, and these ten cakes, and run to the host to thy brethren. **18** Also carry these ten fresh cheeses unto the captain, and look how thy brethren fare, and receive their [l]pledge. **19** (Then Saul and they, and all the men of Israel were in the valley of Elah, fighting with the Philistines.) **20** So David rose up early in the morning, and left the sheep with a keeper, and took and went as Jesse had commanded him, and came within the compass of the host: and the host went out in array, and shouted in the battle. **21** For Israel and the Philistines had put themselves in array, army against army. **22** And David left the things which he bare, under the hands of the keeper of the [m]carriage, and ran into the host, and came, and asked his brethren [n]how they did. **23** And as he talked with them, behold, the man that was between the two armies, came up, (whose name was Goliath the Philistine of Gath) out of the [o]army of the Philistines, and spake [p]such words, and David heard them. **24** And all the men of Israel when they saw the man, ran away from him, and were sore afraid. **25** For every man

---

n. 1-Sam. 15:29 Meaning, God, who maintaineth and prefereth his.
o. 1-Sam. 15:32 Or, in bonds.
p. 1-Sam. 15:32 He suspected nothing less than death, or as some write, he passed not for death.
q. 1-Sam. 15:34 Where his house was.
r. 1-Sam. 15:35 Though Saul came where Samuel was, 1 Sam. 19:22.
s. 1-Sam. 15:35 As verse 11.

1-SAM. 15

1. 1 Sam. 9:16
2. Exod. 17:14 / Num. 24:20
3. Hos. 6:6,7 / Matt. 9:13 / Matt. 12:7
4. Exod. 17:11 / Num. 14:45

1-SAM. 16

a. 1-Sam. 16:1 Signifying, that we ought not to show ourselves more pitiful than God, nor to lament them whom he casteth out.
b. 1-Sam. 16:2 Hebrew, in thine hand.
c. 1-Sam. 16:2 That is, to make a peace offering, which might be done though the Ark was not there.
d. 1-Sam. 16:4 Fearing, lest some grievous crime had been committed, because the Prophet was not wont to come thither.
e. 1-Sam. 16:6 Thinking that Eliab had been appointed of God to be made King.
f. 1-Sam. 16:11 Hebrew, are the children ended?
g. 1-Sam. 16:13 Or, prospered.
h. 1-Sam. 16:14 The wicked spirits are at God's commandment to execute his will against the wicked.
i. 1-Sam. 16:18 Though David was now anointed King by the Prophet, yet God would exercise him in sundry sorts before he had the use of his kingdom.
j. 1-Sam. 16:21 Or, served him.
k. 1-Sam. 16:23 God would that Saul should receive this benefit as at David's hand: that his condemnation might be the more evident, for his cruel hate toward him.

1-SAM. 16

1. 1 Chron. 28:9 / Jer. 11:20 / Jer. 17:10 / Jer. 20:12 / Ps. 7:10
2. 2 Sam. 7:8 / Ps. 78:71 / Ps. 89:21
3. Acts 7:46 / Acts 13:22

1-SAM.17

a. 1-Sam. 17:1 Or, in Ephes Dammim.
b. 1-Sam. 17:2 Or, of the oak.
c. 1-Sam. 17:4 Between the two camps.
d. 1-Sam. 17:5 Or, coat of plate.
e. 1-Sam. 17:5 That is, 156 pounds 4 ounces after half an ounce the shekel: and 600 shekels weight amounteth to 18 pounds 3 quarters.
f. 1-Sam. 17:6 Or, greaves.
g. 1-Sam. 17:9 Hebrew, smite me.
h. 1-Sam. 17:10 Or, hand to hand.
i. 1-Sam. 17:12 Or, he was counted among them that bare office.
j. 1-Sam. 17:15 To serve Saul, as 1 Sam. 16:19.
k. 1-Sam. 17:17 Though Jesse meant one thing, yet God's providence directed David to another end.
l. 1-Sam. 17:18 If they have laid anything to gage for their necessity, redeem it out.
m. 1-Sam. 17:22 Hebrew, vessels.
n. 1-Sam. 17:22 Hebrew, of peace.
o. 1-Sam. 17:23 Or, valley.

of Israel said, Saw ye not this man that cometh up? even to revile Israel is he come up: and to him that killeth him, will the King give great riches, and will give him his [2]daughter, yea, and make his father's house [q]free in Israel. **26** Then David spake to the men that stood with him, and said, What shall be done to the man that killeth this Philistine, and taketh away the [r]shame from Israel? for who is this uncircumcised Philistine, that he should revile the host of the living God? **27** And the people answered him after this manner, saying, Thus shall it be done to the man that killeth him. **28** And Eliab his eldest brother heard when he spake unto the men, and Eliab was very angry with David, and said, Why camest thou down hither? and with whom hast thou left those few sheep in the wilderness? I know thy pride and the malice of thine heart, that thou art come down to see the battle. **29** Then David said, What have I now done? Is there not a [s]cause? **30** And he departed from him into the presence of another, and spake of the same manner, and the people answered him according to the former words. **31** And they that heard the words which David spake, rehearsed them before Saul, which caused him to be brought. **32** So David said to Saul, Let no man's heart fail him, because of him: thy servant will go, and fight with this Philistine. **33** And Saul said to David, Thou art not [t]able to go against this Philistine to fight with him: for thou art a boy, and he is a man of war from his youth. **34** And David answered unto Saul, Thy servant kept his father's sheep, and there came a [u]lion, and likewise a bear, and took a sheep out of the flock, **35** And I went out after him and smote him, and took it out of his mouth: and when he arose against me, I caught him by the beard, and smote him, and slew him. **36** So thy servant slew both the lion, and the bear: therefore this uncircumcised Philistine shall be as one of them, seeing he hath railed on the host of the living God. **37** Moreover David said, The Lord that delivered me out of the paw of the lion, and out of the paw of the bear, he will deliver me out of the hand of this Philistine. Then Saul said unto David, [v]Go, and the Lord be with thee. **38** And Saul put his raiment upon David, and put an helmet of brass upon his head, and put a brigandine upon him. **39** Then girded David his sword upon his raiment, and [w]began to go: for he never proved it: and David said unto Saul, I can not go with these: for I am not accustomed. Wherefore David put them off him. **40** Then took he his [x]staff in his hand, and chose him five smooth stones out of a brook, and put them in his shepherd's bag or scrip, and his sling was in his hand, and he drew near to the Philistine. **41** And the Philistine came and drew near unto David, and the man that bare the shield went before him. **42** Now when the Philistine looked about and saw David, he disdained him: for he was but young, ruddy, and of a comely face. **43** And the Philistine said unto David, Am I a dog, that thou comest to me with staves? And the Philistine [y]cursed David by his gods. **44** And the Philistine said to David, Come to me, and I will give thy flesh unto the fowls of the heaven, and to the beasts of the field. **45** Then said David to the Philistine, Thou comest to me with a sword, and with a spear, and with a shield, but I come to thee in the Name of the Lord of hosts, the God of the host of Israel, whom thou hast railed upon. **46** This [z]day shall the Lord close thee in mine hand, and I shall smite thee, and take thine head from thee, and I will give the carcasses of the host of the Philistines this day unto the fowls of the heaven, and to the beasts of the earth, that all the world may know that Israel hath a God, **47** And that all this assembly may know, that the Lord saveth not with sword nor with spear, (for the battle is the Lord's) and he will give you into our hands. **48** And when the Philistine arose to come and draw near unto David, David [aa]hasted and ran to fight against the Philistine. **49** And David put his hand in his bag, and took out a stone, and slang it, and smote the Philistine in his forehead, that the stone sticked in his forehead, and he fell groveling to the earth. **50** So David overcame the Philistine with a sling and with a stone, and smote the Philistine, and slew him, when David had no sword in his hand. **51** Then David ran, and stood upon the Philistine, and took his sword and drew it out of his sheath, and slew him, and cut off his head therewith. So when the Philistines saw that their champion was dead, they fled. **52** And the men of Israel and Judah arose, and shouted, and followed after the Philistines, until they came to the [ab]valley, and unto the gates of Ekron: and the Philistines fell down wounded by the way of Shaaraim, even to Gath and to Ekron. **53** And the children of Israel returned from pursuing the Philistines, and spoiled their tents. **54** And David took the head of the Philistine, and brought it to Jerusalem, and put his armor in his [ac]tent. **55** When Saul saw David go forth against the Philistine, he said unto Abner the captain of his host, Abner, [ad]whose son is this young man? and Abner answered, As thy soul liveth, O king, I cannot tell. **56** Then the King said, Inquire thou whose son this young man is. **57** And when David was returned from the slaughter of the Philistine, then Abner took him and brought him before Saul with the head of the Philistine in his hand. **58** And Saul said to him, Whose son art thou, thou young man? And David answered, I am the son of thy servant Jesse the Bethlehemite.

18

1 The amity of Jonathan and David. 8 Saul envieth David for the praise that the women gave him. 11 Saul would have slain David. 17 He promiseth him Merab to wife, but giveth him Michal. 27 David delivereth to Saul two hundred foreskins of the Philistines. 29 Saul feareth David, seeing that the Lord is with him.

1 And when he had made an end of speaking unto Saul, the [a]soul of Jonathan was knit with the soul of David, and Jonathan loved him, as his own soul. **2** And Saul took him that day, and would not let him return to his father's house. **3** Then Jonathan and David made a covenant: for he loved him as his own soul. **4** And Jonathan put off the robe that was upon him, and gave it David, and his garments, even to his sword, and to his bow, and to his girdle. **5** And David went out whithersoever Saul sent him, and behaved himself [b]wisely: so that Saul set him over the men of war, and he was accepted in the sight of all the people, and also in the sight of Saul's servants. **6** When they came again, and David returned from the slaughter of the [c]Philistine, the women came out of all cities of Israel singing and dancing to meet king Saul, with timbrels, with instruments of joy, and with rebecks. **7** And the women [d]sang by course in their play, and said, [1]Saul hath slain his thousand, and David his ten thousand. **8** Therefore Saul was exceedingly wroth, and the saying displeased him, and he said, They have ascribed unto David ten thousand, and to me they have ascribed but a thousand, and what can he have more save the kingdom? **9** Wherefore Saul [e]had an eye on David from that day forward. **10** And on the morrow, the evil spirit of God came upon Saul, and he [f]prophesied in the midst of the house: and David played with his hand like as at other times, and there was a spear in Saul's hand. **11** And Saul took the spear, and said, I will smite David through to the wall. But David avoided twice out of his presence. **12** And Saul was afraid of David, because the Lord was with him, and was departed from Saul. **13** Therefore Saul put him from him, and made him a captain over a thousand, and he went [g]out and in before the people. **14** And David behaved himself wisely in all his ways: for the Lord was with him. **15** Wherefore when Saul saw that he was very wise, he was afraid of him. **16** For all Israel and Judah loved David, because he went out and in before them. **17** Then Saul said to David, Behold mine eldest daughter Merab, her I will give thee to wife: only be a valiant son unto me, and [h]fight the Lord's battles: for Saul thought, Mine hand shall not be upon him, but the hand of the Philistines shall be upon him. **18** And David answered Saul, What am I? and what is my life, or the family of my father in Israel, that I should be son-in-law to the King? **19** Howbeit when Merab Saul's daughter should have been given to David, [i]she was given unto Adriel a Meholathite to wife. **20** Then Michal Saul's daughter loved David: and they showed Saul, and the thing pleased him. **21** Therefore Saul said, I will give him her, that she may be a [j]snare to him, and that the hand of the Philistines may be against him. Wherefore Saul said to David, Thou shalt this day be my son-in-law in the one of the twain. **22** And Saul commanded his servants, Speak with David secretly, and say, Behold, the king hath a favor to thee, and all his servants love thee: be now therefore the King's son-in-law. **23** And Saul's servants spake these words in the ears of David. And David said, [k]Seemeth it to you a light thing to be a king's son-in-law, seeing that I am a poor man and of small reputation? **24** And then Saul's servants brought him word again, saying, Such words spake David. **25** And Saul said, This wise shall ye say to David, The king desireth no dowry, but an hundred foreskins of the Philistines, to be avenged of the King's enemies: for Saul thought to make David fall into the hands of the Philistines. **26** And when his servants told David these words, it pleased David well, to be the [l]King's son-in-law: and the days were not expired. **27** Afterward David arose with his men, and went and slew of the Philistines two hundred men: and David brought their foreskins, and [m]they gave them wholly to the King that he might be the King's son-in-law: therefore Saul gave him Michal his daughter to wife. **28** Then Saul saw, and understood that the Lord was with David, and that

---

p. 1-Sam. 17:23 As are above rehearsed, verses 8 and 9.
q. 1-Sam. 17:25 From taxes and payments.
r. 1-Sam. 17:26 This dishonor that he doeth to Israel.
s. 1-Sam. 17:29 For his father's sending was a just occasion, and also he felt himself inwardly moved by God's Spirit.
t. 1-Sam. 17:33 Here Satan proveth David's faith, by the infidelity of Saul.
u. 1-Sam. 17:34 David by the experience that he hath had in time past of God's help, nothing doubteth to overcome this danger, seeing he was zealous for God's honor.
v. 1-Sam. 17:37 For by these examples he saw that the power of God was with him.
w. 1-Sam. 17:39 Or, assayed.
x. 1-Sam. 17:40 To the intent that by these weak means, God might only be known to be the author of this victory.
y. 1-Sam. 17:43 He sware by his gods that he would destroy him.
z. 1-Sam. 17:46 David being assured both of his cause and of his calling, prophesieth of the destruction of the Philistines.
aa. 1-Sam. 17:48 Being moved with a fervent zeal to be revenged upon this blasphemer of God's name.
ab. 1-Sam. 17:52 Or, Gath the city.
ac. 1-Sam. 17:54 Or house at Bethlehem.
ad. 1-Sam. 17:55 That is, of what family and tribe is he? or else he had forgotten David, albeit he had received so great a benefit by him.

1-SAM.17

1. 1 Sam. 16:1 **2.** Josh. 15:19

1-SAM. 18

a. 1-Sam. 18:1 His affection was fully bent toward him.
b. 1-Sam. 18:5 That is, he prospered in all his doings.
c. 1-Sam. 18:6 To wit, Goliath.
d. 1-Sam. 18:7 Hebrew, answered, playing.
e. 1-Sam. 18:9 Because he bare him envy and hatred.
f. 1-Sam. 18:10 That is, spake as a man beside himself: for so the people abused this word, when they could not understand.
g. 1-Sam. 18:13 Meaning, he was captain over the people.
h. 1-Sam. 18:17 Fight against them that war against God's people.
i. 1-Sam. 18:19 By whom he had five sons which David put to death at the request of the Gibeonites, 2 Sam. 21:8.
j. 1-Sam. 18:21 So his hypocrisy appeareth: for under pretence of favor he sought his destruction.
k. 1-Sam. 18:23 Meaning, that he was not able to endow his wife with riches.
l. 1-Sam. 18:26 Because he thought himself able to compass the King's request.
m. 1-Sam. 18:27 Meaning, David and his soldiers.
n. 1-Sam. 18:29 To be deprived of his kingdom.
o. 1-Sam. 18:30 That is, David had better success against the Philistines than Saul's men.

Michal the daughter of Saul loved him. **29** Then Saul was more and more afraid [n]of David, and Saul became always David's enemy. **30** And when the Princes of the Philistines went forth, at their going forth [o]David behaved himself more wisely than all the servants of Saul, so that his name was much set by.

19 *2 Jonathan declareth to David the wicked purpose of Saul. 11 Michal his wife saveth him. 18 David cometh to Samuel. 23 The Spirit of prophecy cometh on Saul.*

1 Then Saul spake to Jonathan his son, and to all his servants, that they should [a]kill David: but Jonathan Saul's son had a great favor to David. **2** And Jonathan told David, saying, Saul my father goeth about to slay thee: now therefore, I pray thee, take heed unto thyself unto the morning, and abide in a secret place, and hide thyself. **3** And I will go out and stand by my father in the field where thou [b]art, and will commune with my father of thee, and I will see what he saith, and will tell thee. **4** And Jonathan spake good of David unto Saul his father, and said unto him, Let not the king sin against his servant, against David: for he hath not sinned against thee, but his works have been to thee very good. **5** For he [c]did [1]put his life in danger, and slew the Philistine, and the Lord wrought a great salvation for all Israel: thou sawest it, and thou rejoicedst: wherefore then wilt thou sin against innocent blood, and slay David without a cause? **6** Then Saul hearkened unto the voice of Jonathan, and Saul [d]swore, As the Lord liveth, he shall not die. **7** So Jonathan called David, and Jonathan showed him all those words, and Jonathan brought David to Saul, and he was in his presence as in times past. **8** Again the war began, and David went out and fought with the Philistines, and slew them with a great slaughter, and they fled from him. **9** And the evil spirit of the Lord was upon Saul, as he sat in his house having his spear in his hand, and David [e]played with his hand. **10** And Saul intended to smite David to the wall with the spear: but he turned aside out of Saul's presence, and he smote the spear against the wall: but David fled, and escaped the same night. **11** Saul also sent messengers unto David's house, to watch him, and to slay him in the morning: and Michal David's wife told it him, saying, If thou save not thyself this night, tomorrow thou shalt be slain. **12** So Michal [f]let David down through a window: and he went, and fled, and escaped. **13** Then Michal took an image, and laid it in the bed, and put a pillow stuffed with goat's hair under the head of it, and covered it with a cloth. **14** And when Saul sent messengers to take David, she said, He is sick. **15** And Saul sent the messengers again to see David, saying, Bring him to me in the [g]bed, that I may slay him. **16** And when the messengers were come in, behold, an image was in the bed with a pillow of goat's hair under the head of it. **17** And Saul said unto Michal, Why hast thou mocked me so, and sent away mine enemy, that he is escaped? And Michal answered Saul, He said unto me, Let me go, or else I will kill thee. **18** So David fled, and escaped, and came to Samuel to Ramah, and told him all that Saul had done to him: and he and Samuel went and dwelt in [h]Naioth. **19** But one told Saul, saying, Behold, David is at Naioth in Ramah. **20** And Saul sent messengers to take David, and when they saw a company of Prophets prophesying, and Samuel standing [i]as appointed over them, the Spirit of God fell upon the messengers of Saul, and they also [j]prophesied. **21** And when it was told Saul, he sent other messengers, and they prophesied likewise: again Saul sent the third messengers, and they prophesied also. **22** Then went he himself to Ramah, and came to a great well that is in Sechu, and he asked, and said, Where are Samuel and David? And one said, Behold, they be at Naioth in Ramah. **23** And he [k]went thither, even to Naioth in Ramah, and the Spirit of God came upon him also, and he went prophesying until he came to Naioth in Ramah. **24** And he stripped off his [l]clothes, and he prophesied also before Samuel, and fell [m]down naked all that day and all that night: therefore they say, [2]Is Saul also among the Prophets?

20 *2 Jonathan comforteth David. 3 They renew their league. 33 Saul would have killed Jonathan. 38 Jonathan advertiseth David by three arrows, of his father's fury.*

1 And David [a]fled from Naioth in Ramah, and came and said before Jonathan, What have I done? and what is mine iniquity? and what sin have I committed before thy father, that he seeketh my life? **2** And he said unto him, God forbid, thou shalt not die: behold, my father will do nothing great nor small, but he will [b]show it me: and why should my father hide this thing from me? he will not do it. **3** And David swore again and said, Thy father knoweth that I have found grace in thine eyes: therefore he thinketh, Jonathan shall not know it, lest he be sorry: but indeed, as the Lord liveth, and as thy soul liveth, there is but a [c]step between me and death. **4** Then said Jonathan unto David, Whatsoever thy soul [d]requireth, that I will do unto thee. **5** And David said unto Jonathan, Behold, tomorrow is the [e]first day of the month, and I should sit with the king at meat: but let me go, that I may hide myself in the fields unto the third day at even. **6** If thy father make mention of me, then say, David asked leave of me, that he might go to Bethlehem to his own city: for there is a [f]yearly sacrifice for all that family. **7** And if he say thus, It is well, thy servant shall have peace: but if he be angry, be sure that wickedness is concluded of him. **8** So shalt thou show mercy unto thy servant: [1]for thou hast joined thy servant into a covenant of the Lord with thee, and if there be in me iniquity, slay thou me? for why shouldest thou bring me to thy father? **9** And Jonathan answered, God keep that from thee: for if I knew that wickedness were [g]concluded of my father to come upon thee, would not I tell it thee? **10** Then said David to Jonathan, Who [h]shall tell me? how shall I know, if thy father answer thee cruelly? **11** And Jonathan said to David, Come and let us go out into the field: and they twain went out into the field. **12** Then Jonathan said to David, O Lord God of Israel, when I have groped my father's mind tomorrow at this time, or within this three days, and if it be well with David, and I then send not unto thee, and show it thee, **13** The Lord [i]do so and much more unto Jonathan: but if my father have mind to do thee evil, I will show thee also, and send thee away, that thou mayest go in peace: and the Lord be with thee as he hath been with my father. **14** Likewise I require not whiles I live: for I doubt not but thou wilt show me the mercy of the Lord, [j]that I die not. **15** But I require that thou cut not off thy mercy from mine house forever: no, not when the Lord hath destroyed the enemies of David, every one from the earth. **16** So Jonathan made a bond with the house of David, saying, Let the Lord require it at the hands of David's enemies. **17** And again Jonathan swore unto David, because he loved him (for he loved him as his own soul,) **18** Then said Jonathan to him, Tomorrow is the first day of the month: and thou shalt be [k]looked for, for thy place shall be empty. **19** Therefore thou shalt hide thyself three days, then thou shalt go down quickly and come to the place where thou didst hide thyself, when this matter was in hand, and shalt remain by the stone [l]Ezel. **20** And I will shoot three arrows on the side thereof, as though I shot at a mark. **21** And after I will send a boy, saying, Go, seek the arrows. If I say unto the boy, See, the arrows are on this side thee, bring them, and come thou: for it is [m]well with thee, and no hurt, as the Lord liveth. **22** But if I say thus unto the boy, Behold, the arrows are beyond thee, go thy way: for the [n]Lord hath sent thee away. **23** As touching the thing which thou and I have spoken of, behold, the Lord be between thee and me forever. **24** So David hid himself in the field: and when the first day of the month came, the king sat to eat meat. **25** And the king sat, as at other times upon his seat, even upon his seat by the wall: and Jonathan arose, and Abner sat by Saul's side, but David's place was empty. **26** And Saul said nothing that day: for he thought, Something hath befallen him, though he were [o]clean, or else because he was not purified. **27** But on the morrow which was the second day of the month, David's place was empty again: and Saul said unto Jonathan his son, Wherefore cometh not [p]the son of Jesse to meat, neither yesterday nor today? **28** And Jonathan answered unto Saul, David required of me, that he might go to Bethlehem. **29** For he said, Let me go, I pray thee: for our family offereth [q]a sacrifice in the city, and my brother hath sent for me: therefore now, if I have found favor in thine eyes, let me go, I pray thee, and see my [r]brethren: this is the cause that he cometh not unto the king's table. **30** Then was Saul angry with Jonathan, and said unto him, Thou [s]son of the wicked rebellious woman, do not I know, that thou hast chosen the son of Jesse to thy confusion, and to the confusion and shame of thy mother? **31** For as long as the son of Jesse liveth upon the earth, thou shalt not be established, nor thy kingdom: wherefore now send and fet him unto me,

---

1-SAM. 18

1. 1 Sam. 21:11 / 1 Sam. 29:5

1-SAM. 19

a. 1-Sam. 19:1 Before Saul sought David's life secretly, but now his hypocrisy bursteth to open cruelty.
b. 1-Sam. 19:3 That I may give thee warning what to do.
c. 1-Sam. 19:5 Hebrew, he put his soul in his hand.
d. 1-Sam. 19:6 Whatsoever he pretended outwardly, yet his heart was full of malice.
e. 1-Sam. 19:9 He played on his harp to mitigate the rage of the evil spirit, as 1 Sam. 16:23.
f. 1-Sam. 19:12 Thus God moved both the son and daughter of this tyrant to favor David against their father.
g. 1-Sam. 19:15 Behold, how the tyrants to accomplish their rage, neither regard oath nor friendship, God nor man.
h. 1-Sam. 19:18 Naioth was a school where the word of God was studieth, near to Ramah.
i. 1-Sam. 19:20 Being their chief instructor.
j. 1-Sam. 19:20 Changed their minds and praised God.
k. 1-Sam. 19:23 With a mind to persecute them.
l. 1-Sam. 19:24 His kingly apparel.
m. 1-Sam. 19:24 He humbled himself as others did.

1-SAM. 19

1. Judg. 12:3 / 1 Sam. 28:21 / Ps. 119:109 **2.** 1 Sam. 10:11

1-SAM. 20

a. 1-Sam. 20:1 For Saul was stayed, and prophesied a day and a night by God's providence, that David might have time to escape.
b. 1-Sam. 20:2 Hebrew, reveal it in mine ear.
c. 1-Sam. 20:3 I am in great danger of death.
d. 1-Sam. 20:4 Hebrew, saith.
e. 1-Sam. 20:5 At what time there should be a solemn sacrifice, Num. 28:11, to the which they added peace offerings and feasts.
f. 1-Sam. 20:6 Read 1 Sam. 1:21.
g. 1-Sam. 20:9 That he were fully determined.
h. 1-Sam. 20:10 If thy father do favor me.
i. 1-Sam. 20:13 The Lord punish me most grievously.
j. 1-Sam. 20:14 I know that if thou werest now preferred to the Kingdom, thou wouldest not destroy me, but show thyself friendly to my posterity.
k. 1-Sam. 20:18 Or, mentioned.
l. 1-Sam. 20:19 Hebrew, of the way, because it served as a sign to show the way to them that passed by.
m. 1-Sam. 20:21 Hebrew, peace.
n. 1-Sam. 20:22 The Lord is the author of thy departure.
o. 1-Sam. 20:26 Yet he might have some business to let him.
p. 1-Sam. 20:27 Thus he speaketh contemptuously of David.
q. 1-Sam. 20:29 That is, a peace offering.
r. 1-Sam. 20:29 Meaning, all his kinsfolk.
s. 1-Sam. 20:30 Thou art ever contrary unto me as thy mother is.

for he [t]shall surely die. **32** And Jonathan answered unto Saul his father, and said unto him, Wherefore shall he [u]die? what hath he done? **33** And Saul cast a spear at him to hit him, whereby Jonathan knew, that it was determined of his father to slay David. **34** So Jonathan arose from the table in a great anger, and did eat no meat the second day of the month: for he was sorry for David, and because his father had reviled him. **35** On the next morning therefore Jonathan went out into the field, [v]at the time appointed with David, and a little boy with him. **36** And he said unto his boy, Run now, seek the arrows which I shoot, and as the boy ran, he shot an arrow beyond him. **37** And when the boy was come to the place where the arrow was that Jonathan had shot, Jonathan cried after the boy, and said, Is not the arrow beyond thee? **38** And Jonathan cried after the boy, [w]Make speed, haste and stand not still: and Jonathan's boy gathered up the arrows, and came to his master, **39** But the boy knew nothing: only Jonathan and David knew the matter. **40** Then Jonathan gave his [x]bow and arrows unto the boy that was with him, and said unto him, Go, carry them into the city. **41** As soon as the boy was gone, David arose out of a place that was toward the [y]South, and fell on his face to the ground, and bowed himself three times: and they kissed one another, and wept both twain, till David exceeded. **42** Therefore Jonathan said to David, Go in peace: that which we have [z]sworn both of us in the name of the Lord, saying, The Lord be between me and thee, and between my seed and between thy seed, let it stand forever. **43** And he arose and departed, and Jonathan went into the city.

21

1 David fleeth to Nob to Ahimelech the Priest. 6 He getteth of him the showbread to satisfy his hunger. 7 Doeg Saul's servant was present. 10 David fleeth to King Achish, 13 and there feigneth himself mad.

1 Then came David to [a]Nob, to Ahimelech the Priest, and Ahimelech was astonied at the meeting of David, and said unto him, Why art thou alone, and no man with thee? **2** And David said to Ahimelech the Priest, The [b]King hath commanded me a certain thing, and hath said unto me, Let no man know whereabout I send thee, and what I have commanded thee: and I have appointed my servants to such and such places. **3** Now therefore if thou hast ought under thine hand, give me five cakes of bread, or what cometh to hand. **4** And the Priest answered David, and said, There is no common bread under mine hand, but here is [1]hallowed bread, if the young men have kept themselves, at least from [c]women. **5** David then answered the Priest, and said unto him, Certainly women have been separate from us these two or three days since I came out: and the [d]vessels of the young men were holy, though the way were profane, and how much more then shall every one [e]be sanctified this day in the vessel? **6** So the Priest gave him hallowed bread: for there was no bread there, save the showbread that was taken from before the Lord, to put hot bread there, the day that it was taken away. **7** (And there was the same day one of the servants of Saul [f]abiding before the Lord, named Doeg the Edomite, the [g]chiefest of Saul's herdmen.) **8** And David said unto Ahimelech, Is there not here under thine hand a spear or a sword? for I have neither brought my sword nor mine harness with me, because the king's business required haste. **9** And the Priest said, The sword of Goliath the Philistine, whom thou slewest in the [2]valley of Elah, behold, it is wrapped in a cloth behind the [h]Ephod: if thou wilt take that to thee, take it: for there is none other save that here: And David said, There is none to that, give it me. **10** And David arose and fled the same day from the [i]presence of Saul, and went to Achish the king of Gath. **11** And the servants of Achish said unto him, Is not this David the [3]King of the land? did they not sing unto him in dances, saying, [4]Saul hath slain his thousand, and David his ten thousand? **12** And David [j]considered these words, and was sore afraid of Achish the king of Gath. **13** And he changed his behavior before them, and feigned himself mad in their hands, and [k]scrabbled on the doors of the gate, and let his spittle fall down upon his beard. **14** Then said Achish unto his servants, Lo, ye see the man is beside himself, wherefore have ye brought him to me? **15** Have I need of mad men, that ye have brought this fellow to play the mad man in my presence? [l]shall he come into mine house?

22

1 David hideth himself in a cave. 2 Many that were in trouble came unto him. 9 Doeg accuseth Ahimelech. 18 Saul causeth the Priests to be slain. 20 Abiathar escapeth.

1 David therefore departed thence, and saved himself in the cave [a]of Adullam: and when his brethren and all his father's house heard it, they went down thither to him. **2** And there gathered unto him all men that were in trouble, and all men that were in debt, and all those that were vexed in mind, and he was their [b]prince, and there were with him about four hundred men. **3** And David went thence to Mizpah in [c]Moab, and said unto the King of Moab, I pray thee, let my father and my mother come and abide with you, till I know what God will do for me. **4** And he [d]brought them before the King of Moab, and they dwelt with him all the while that David was in [e]the hold. **5** And the Prophet Gad said unto David, Abide not in the hold, but depart and go into the land of Judah. Then David departed and came into the forest of Hereth. **6** And Saul heard that David was [f]discovered, and the men that were with him, and Saul remained in Gibeah under a tree in Ramah, having his spear in his hand, and all his servants stood about him. **7** And Saul said unto his servants that stood about him, Hear now, the sons [g]of Benjamin, will the son of Jesse give every one of you fields and vineyards: will he make you all captains over thousands, and captains over hundreds: **8** That all ye have conspired against me, and there is none that telleth me that my son hath made a covenant with the son of Jesse? and there is none of you that is sorry for me, or showeth me, that my [h]son hath stirred up my servant to lie in wait against me, as appeareth this day? **9** Then answered Doeg the Edomite, (who was appointed over the servants of Saul) and said, I saw the son of Jesse, when he came to Nob, to Ahimelech the son of Ahitub, **10** Who asked counsel of the Lord for him, and gave him victuals, and he gave him also the sword of Goliath the Philistine. **11** Then the King sent to call Ahimelech the Priest the son of Ahitub, and all his father's house, to wit, [i]the Priests that were in Nob: and they came all to the King. **12** And Saul said, Hear now thou son of Ahitub. And he answered, Here I am, my lord. **13** Then Saul said unto him, Why have ye conspired against me, thou and the son of Jesse, in that thou hast given him victual, and a sword, and hast asked counsel of God for him, that he should rise against me, and lie in wait as appeareth this day? **14** And Ahimelech answered the King, and said, Who is so faithful among all thy servants as David, being also the king's son-in-law, and goeth at thy commandment, and is honorable in thine house? **15** [j]Have I this day first begun to ask counsel of God for him? be it far from me, let not the king impute anything unto his servant, nor to all the house of my father: for thy servant knew nothing of all this, less nor more. **16** Then the King said, Thou shalt surely die, Ahimelech, thou, and all thy father's house. **17** And the King said unto the [k]sergeants that stood about him, Turn, and slay the Priests of the Lord, because their hand also is with David, and because they knew when he fled, and showed it not unto me. But the servants of the King [l]would not move their hands to fall upon the Priests of the Lord. **18** Then the King said to Doeg, Turn thou and fall upon the Priests. And Doeg the Edomite turned, and ran upon the Priests, and slew that same day fourscore and five persons, that did wear a linen Ephod. **19** Also Nob the city of the Priests smote he with the edge of the sword, both man and woman, both child and suckling, both ox and ass, and sheep with the edge of the sword. **20** But one of the sons of Ahimelech the son of Ahitub (whose name was Abiathar) [m]escaped and fled after David. **21** And Abiathar showed David, that Saul had slain the Lord's Priests. **22** And David said unto Abiathar, I knew it the same day, when Doeg the Edomite was there, that he would tell Saul. I am the cause of the death of all the persons of thy father's house. **23** Abide thou with me, and fear not: for [n]he that seeketh my life, shall seek thy life also: for with me thou shalt be in safeguard.

---

t. 1-Sam. 20:31 Hebrew, son of death.
u. 1-Sam. 20:32 For it were too great tyranny to put one to death and not to show the cause why.
v. 1-Sam. 20:35 For this was the third day, as it was agreed upon, verse 5.
w. 1-Sam. 20:38 By these words he admonished David what he ought to do.
x. 1-Sam. 20:40 Hebrew, instruments.
y. 1-Sam. 20:41 It seemeth that he had shot on the North side of the stone, lest the boy should have espied David.
z. 1-Sam. 20:42 Which oath he calleth in the eighth verse, the covenant of the Lord.

1-SAM. 20
1. 1 Sam. 18:3 / 1 Sam. 23:18

1-SAM. 21
a. 1-Sam. 21:1 Where the ark then was to ask counsel of the Lord.
b. 1-Sam. 21:2 These infirmities that we see in the Saints of God, teach us that none hath his justice in himself, but receiveth it of God's mercy.
c. 1-Sam. 21:4 If they have not accompanied with their wives.
d. 1-Sam. 21:5 That is, their bodies.
e. 1-Sam. 21:5 Shall be more careful to keep his vessel holy, when he shall have eaten of this holy food?
f. 1-Sam. 21:7 Tarrying to worship before the Ark.
g. 1-Sam. 21:7 Or, master of them that kept Saul's castle.
h. 1-Sam. 21:9 Behind that place, where the high Priest's garment lay.
i. 1-Sam. 21:10 That is, out of Saul's dominion.
j. 1-Sam. 21:12 Hebrew, put these words in his heart.
k. 1-Sam. 21:13 By making marks and toys.
l. 1-Sam. 21:15 Is he meet to be in a king's house?

1-SAM. 21
1. Exod. 25:30 / Lev. 24:5 / Matt. 12:3,4
2. 1 Sam. 17:2
3. 1 Sam. 17:9
4. 1 Sam. 18:7 / 1 Sam. 29:5

1-SAM. 22
a. 1-Sam. 22:1 Which was in the tribe of Judah, and near to Bethlehem.
b. 1-Sam. 22:2 Or, captain.
c. 1-Sam. 22:3 For there was another so called in Judah.
d. 1-Sam. 22:4 For he feared the rage of Saul against his house.
e. 1-Sam. 22:4 That is, in Mizpah, which was a stronghold.
f. 1-Sam. 22:6 That a great brute went on him.
g. 1-Sam. 22:7 Ye that are of my tribe and lineage.
h. 1-Sam. 22:8 Hereby he would persuade them that this conspiracy was most horrible, where the son conspired against the father, and the servant against his master.
i. 1-Sam. 22:11 Which were the remnant of the house of Eli, whose house God threatened to punish.
j. 1-Sam. 22:15 Have I not at other times also, when he had great affairs, consulted with the Lord for him?
k. 1-Sam. 22:17 Or, footmen.
l. 1-Sam. 22:17 For they knew that they ought not to obey the wicked commandment of the king in slaying the innocents.
m. 1-Sam. 22:20 This was God's providence, who according to his promise preserved some of the house of Eli, 1 Sam. 2:33.
n. 1-Sam. 22:23 Or, he that taketh thy life, shall take mine also.

1-SAM. 23
a. 1-Sam. 23:1 Which was a city in the tribe of Judah, Josh. 15:44.
b. 1-Sam. 23:3 That is, in the midst of Judah, much more when we come to the borders against our enemies.

23

5 David chaseth the Philistines from Keilah. 13 David departeth from Keilah, and remaineth in the wilderness of Ziph. 16 Jonathan comforteth David. 28 Saul's enterprise is broken in pursuing David.

1 Then they told David, saying, Behold, the Philistines fight against [a]Keilah, and spoil the barns. **2** Therefore David asked counsel of the Lord, saying, Shall I go and smite these Philistines? And the Lord answered David, Go and smite the Philistines, and save Keilah. **3** And David's men said unto him, See, we be afraid here in [b]Judah, how much more if we come to Keilah against the host of the Philistines? **4** Then David asked counsel of the Lord again. And the Lord answered him, and said, Arise, go down to Keilah: for I will deliver the Philistines into thine hand. **5** So David and his men went to Keilah, and fought with the Philistines, and brought away their cattle, and smote them with a great slaughter: thus David saved the inhabitants of Keilah. **6** (And when Abiathar the son of Ahimelech [l]fled to David to Keilah, he brought an [c]Ephod [d]with him.) **7** And it was told Saul that David was come to Keilah, and Saul said, God hath delivered him into mine hand: for he is shut in, seeing he is come into a city that hath gates and bars. **8** Then Saul called all the people together to war for to go down to Keilah, and to besiege David and his men. **9** And David having knowledge that Saul imagined mischief against him, said to Abiathar the Priest, [e]Bring the Ephod. **10** Then said David, O Lord God of Israel, thy servant hath heard, that Saul is about to come to Keilah to destroy the city for my sake. **11** Will the lords of Keilah deliver me up into his hand? and will Saul come down, as thy servant hath heard? O Lord God of Israel, I beseech thee, tell thy servant. And the Lord said, He will come down. **12** Then said David, Will the [f]lords of Keilah deliver me up, and the men that are with me, into the hand of Saul? And the Lord said, They will deliver thee up. **13** Then David and his men, which were about six hundred, arose and departed out of Keilah, and went [g]whither they could. And it was told Saul, that David was fled from Keilah, and he left off his journey. **14** And David abode in the wilderness in the [h]holds, and remained in a mountain in the wilderness of Ziph. And Saul sought him every day, but God [i]delivered him not into his hand. **15** And David saw that Saul was come out for to seek his life: and David was in the wilderness of Ziph in the wood. **16** And Jonathan Saul's son arose and went to David into the wood, and comforted [j]him in God, **17** And said unto him, Fear not: for the hand of Saul my father shall not find thee, and thou shalt be [k]king over Israel, and I shall be next unto thee: and also Saul my father knoweth it. **18** So they twain made a covenant before the Lord: and David did remain in the wood: but Jonathan went to his house. **19** Then came up the Ziphites to Saul to Gibeah, saying, Doth not David hide himself by us in holds, in the wood in the hill of Hachilah, which is on the right side [l]of Jeshimon? **20** Now therefore, O king, come down according to all that thine heart can desire, and our part shall be to deliver him into the King's hands. **21** Then Saul said, [m]Be ye blessed of the Lord: for ye have had compassion on me. **22** Go, I pray you, and prepare ye yet better: know and see his place where he [n]haunteth, and who hath seen him there: for it is said to me, He is subtle, and crafty. **23** See therefore and know all the secret places where he hideth himself, and come ye again to me with the certainty, and I will go with you: and if he be in the [o]land, I will search him out throughout all the thousands of Judah. **24** Then they arose and went to Ziph before Saul, but David and his men were in the wilderness of Maon, in the plain on the right hand of Jeshimon. **25** Saul also and his men went to seek him, and they told David: wherefore he came down unto a rock, and abode in the wilderness of [p]Maon. And when Saul heard that, he followed after David in the wilderness of Maon. **26** And Saul and his men went on the one side of the mountain: and David and his men on the other side of the mountain: and David made haste to get from the presence of Saul: for Saul and his men compassed David and his men round about, to take them. **27** But there came a [q]messenger to Saul, saying, Haste thee, and come: for the Philistines have invaded the land. **28** Wherefore Saul returned from pursuing David, and went against the Philistines. Therefore they called that place, [r]Sela Hammahlekoth.

24

1 David hid in a cave spareth Saul. 10 He showeth to Saul his innocency. 18 Saul acknowledgeth his fault. 22 He causeth David to swear unto him to be favorable to his.

1 And David went thence, and dwelt in [a]holds at En Gedi. **2** When Saul was turned from the Philistines, they told him, saying, Behold, David is in the wilderness of [b]En Gedi. **3** Then Saul took three thousand chosen men out of all Israel, and went to seek David and his men upon the rocks among the wild goats. **4** And he came to the sheepcotes by the way where there was a cave, and Saul went in [c]to do his easement: and David and his men sat in the [d]inward parts of the cave. **5** And the men of David said unto him, See, the day is [e]come, whereof the Lord said unto thee, Behold, I will deliver thine enemy into thine hand, and thou shalt do to him as it shall seem good to thee. Then David arose and cut off the lap of Saul's garment privily. **6** And afterward David [f]was touched in his heart, because he had cut off the lap which was on Saul's garment. **7** And he said unto his men, The Lord keep me from doing that thing unto my master the Lord's anointed, to lay mine hand upon him: for he is the Anointed of the Lord. **8** So David overcame his servants with these words, and suffered them not to arise against Saul: for Saul rose up out of the cave and went away. **9** David also arose afterward, and went out of the cave, and cried after Saul, saying, O my lord the King. And when Saul looked behind him, David inclined his face to the earth, and bowed himself. **10** And David said to Saul, [g]Wherefore givest thou an ear to men's words, that say, Behold, David seeketh evil against thee? **11** Behold, this day thine eyes have seen, that the Lord had delivered thee this day into mine hand in the cave, and some bade me kill thee, but I had compassion on thee, and said, I will not lay mine hand on my master: for he is the Lord's Anointed. **12** Moreover my father, behold: behold, I say, the lap of thy garment in mine hand: for when I cut off the lap of thy garment, I killed thee not. Understand and see, that there is neither evil nor wickedness in me, neither have I sinned against thee, yet thou huntest after my soul, to take it. **13** The Lord be judge between thee and me, and the Lord avenge me of thee, and let not mine hand be upon thee. **14** According as the [h]old proverb saith, Wickedness proceedeth from the wicked, but mine hand be not upon thee. **15** After whom is the king of Israel come out? after whom dost thou pursue? after a dead dog, and after a flea? **16** The Lord therefore be judge, and judge between thee and me, and see, and plead my cause, and [i]deliver me out of thine hand. **17** When David had made an end of speaking these words to Saul, Saul said, [j]Is this thy voice, my son David? and Saul lift up his voice, and wept, **18** And said to David, Thou art more righteous than I: for thou hast rendered me good, and I have rendered thee evil. **19** And thou hast showed this day, that thou hast dealt well with me: forasmuch as when the Lord had closed me in thine hands, thou killedst me not. **20** For who shall find his enemy, and let him depart [k]free? wherefore the Lord render thee good for that thou hast done unto me this day. **21** For now behold, I [l]know that thou shalt be king, and that the kingdom of Israel shall be stablished in thine hand. **22** Swear now therefore unto me by the Lord, that thou wilt not destroy my seed after me, and that thou wilt not abolish my name out of my father's house. **23** So David swore unto Saul, and Saul went home: but David and his men went up unto the hold.

25

1 Samuel dieth. 3 Nabal and Abigail. 38 The Lord killeth Nabal. 43 Abigail and Ahinoam David's wives. 44 Michal is given to Palti.

1 Then [l]Samuel died, and all Israel assembled, and mourned for him, and buried him in his [a]own house at Ramah. And David arose and went down to the wilderness of Paran. **2** Now in [b]Maon was a man, who had his possession in Carmel, and the man was exceeding mighty, and had three thousand sheep, and a thousand goats, and he was shearing his sheep in Carmel. **3** The name also of the man was Nabal, and the name of his wife Abigail, and she was a woman of singular wisdom, and beautiful, but the man was churlish, and evil conditioned, and was of the family of Caleb. **4** And David heard in the wilderness, that Nabal did shear his sheep. **5** Therefore David sent ten young men, and David said unto the young men, Go up to Carmel, and go to Nabal, and ask him in my name [c]how

---

c. 1-Sam. 23:6 By God's providence the Ephod was preserved and kept with David the true king.
d. 1-Sam. 23:6 Hebrew, in his hand.
e. 1-Sam. 23:9 To consult with the Lord by Urim and Thummim.
f. 1-Sam. 23:12 Or, governors.
g. 1-Sam. 23:13 Or, to and fro, as having no certain place to go.
h. 1-Sam. 23:14 Or, strong places.
i. 1-Sam. 23:14 No power nor policy can prevail against God's children, but when he appointeth the time.
j. 1-Sam. 23:16 Hebrew, his hand.
k. 1-Sam. 23:17 Jonathan assureth David, that God will accomplish his promise, and that his father striveth against his own conscience.
l. 1-Sam. 23:19 Or, of the wilderness.
m. 1-Sam. 23:21 The Lord recompense this friendship.
n. 1-Sam. 23:22 Hebrew, where his foot hath been.
o. 1-Sam. 23:23 In your country of Ziph, which is in Judah.
p. 1-Sam. 23:25 Which was also in the tribe of Judah, Josh. 15:55.
q. 1-Sam. 23:27 Thus the Lord can pull back the bridle of the tyrants and deliver his out of the lion's mouth.
r. 1-Sam. 23:28 That is, stone of division, because there they divided themselves one from another.

1-SAM. 23
l. 1 Sam. 22:20

1-SAM. 24
a. 1-Sam. 24:1 That is, in strong places, which were defensed by nature.
b. 1-Sam. 24:2 A city of Judah, Josh. 15:62.
c. 1-Sam. 24:4 Hebrew, to cover his feet.
d. 1-Sam. 24:4 Hebrew, in the sides.
e. 1-Sam. 24:5 Here we see how ready we are to hasten God's promise, if the occasion serve never so little.
f. 1-Sam. 24:6 For seeing it was his own private cause, he repented that he had touched his enemy.
g. 1-Sam. 24:10 Contrary to the false report of them that said, David was Saul's enemy, he proveth himself to be his friend.
h. 1-Sam. 24:14 Or, the proverb of an ancient man.
i. 1-Sam. 24:16 Hebrew, judge.
j. 1-Sam. 24:17 Though he was a most cruel enemy to David, yet by his great gentleness his conscience compelled him to yield.
k. 1-Sam. 24:20 Hebrew, a good way.
l. 1-Sam. 24:21 Though this tyrant saw and confessed the favor of God toward David, yet he ceaseth not to persecute him against his own conscience.

1-SAM. 25
a. 1-Sam. 25:1 That is, among his own kindred.
b. 1-Sam. 25:2 Maon and Carmel were cities in the tribe of Judah. Carmel the mountain was in Galilee.
c. 1-Sam. 25:5 Hebrew, of peace.
d. 1-Sam. 25:6 Some read, so mayest thou live in prosperity the next year, both thou, etc.

he doeth. **6** And thus shall ye say [d,e]for salutation, Both thou, and thine house,
and all that thou hast, be in peace, wealth and prosperity. **7** Behold, I have he-
ard, that thou hast shearers: now thy shepherds were with us, and we did them no
hurt, neither did they miss anything all the while they were in Carmel. **8** Ask
thy servants, and they will show thee. Wherefore let these young men find favor in
thine eyes: (for we come in a good season) give, I pray thee, whatsoever [f]cometh to
thine hand unto thy servants, and to thy son David. **9** And when David's young
men came, they told Nabal all those words in the name of David, and held their
peace. **10** Then Nabal answered David's servants, and said, Who is David? and
who is the [g]son of Jesse? there be many servants nowadays, that break away every
man from his master. **11** Shall I then take my bread, and my water, and my flesh
that I have killed for my shearers, and give it unto men, whom I know not when-
ce they be? **12** So David's servants turned their way, and went again, and came
and told him all those things. **13** And David said unto his men, Gird every man
his sword about him. And they girded every man his sword: David also girded
his sword. And about four hundred men went up after David, and two hundred
abode by the [h]carriage. **14** Now one of the servants told Abigail Nabal's wife,
saying, Behold, David sent messengers out of the wilderness to salute our master,
and he [i]railed on them. **15** Notwithstanding, the men were very good [j]unto us,
and we had no displeasure, neither missed we anything as long as we were conver-
sant with them, when we were in the fields. **16** They were as a wall unto us both
by night and by day, all the while we were with them keeping sheep. **17** Now
therefore take heed, and see what thou shalt do: for evil [k]will surely come upon
our master, and upon all his family: for he is so wicked, that a man cannot spe-
ak to him. **18** Then Abigail made haste, and took two hundred [l]cakes, and two
bottles of wine, and five sheep ready dressed, and five measures of parched corn,
and an hundred [m]frails of raisins, and two hundred of figs, and laid them on as-
ses. **19** Then she said unto her servants, Go ye before me: behold, I will come
after you: yet she told not her [n]husband Nabal. **20** And as she rode on her ass,
she came down by a secret place of the mountain, and behold, David and his men
came down against her, and she met them. **21** And David said, Indeed I have
kept all in vain that this fellow had in the wilderness, so that nothing was missed
of all that pertained unto him: for he hath requited me evil for good. **22** So and
more also do God unto the enemies of David: for surely I will not leave of all that
he hath by the dawning of the day, any that [o]pisseth against the wall. **23** And
when Abigail saw David, she hasted and lighted off her ass, and fell before David
on her face, and bowed herself to the ground, **24** And fell at his feet, and said,
Oh, my lord, I have committed the iniquity, and I pray thee, let thine handmaid
speak [p]to thee, and hear thou the words of thine handmaid. **25** Let not my lord,
I pray thee, regard this wicked man, Nabal: for as his name is, so is he: [q]Nabal is
his name, and folly is with him: but I thine handmaid saw not the young men of
my lord whom thou sentest. **26** Now therefore my lord, as the Lord liveth, and
as thy soul liveth (the Lord, I say, that hath withholden thee from coming to shed
blood, and that thine [r]hand should not save thee) so now thine enemies shall be
as Nabal, and they that intend to do my lord evil. **27** And now this [s]blessing
which thine handmaid hath brought unto my lord, let it be given unto the young
men, that [t]follow my lord. **28** I pray thee, forgive the trespass of thine hand-
maid: for the Lord will make my lord a [u]sure house, because my lord fighteth the
battles of the Lord, and none evil hath been found in thee [v]in all thy life. **29** Yet
[w]a man hath risen up to persecute thee, and to seek thy soul, but the soul of my
lord shall be bound in the [x]bundle of life with the Lord thy God: and the soul of
thine enemies shall God cast out, as out of the middle of a sling. **30** And when
the Lord shall have done to my lord all the good that he hath promised thee, and
shall have made thee ruler over Israel, **31** Then shall it be no grief unto thee, nor
offence of mind unto my lord, that he hath not shed blood causeless, nor that my
lord hath [y]not preserved himself: and when the Lord shall have dealt well with my
lord, remember thine handmaid. **32** Then David said to Abigail, Blessed be the
Lord God of Israel, which sent thee this day to meet me. **33** And blessed be thy
counsel, and blessed be thou, which hast kept me this day from coming to shed
blood, [z]and that mine hand hath not saved me. **34** For indeed, as the Lord God
of Israel liveth, [aa]who hath kept me back from hurting thee, except thou hadst
hasted and met me, surely there had not been left unto Nabal by the dawning of
the day, any that pisseth against the wall. **35** Then David received of her hand
that which she had brought him, and said to her, Go up in peace to thine house:
behold, I have heard thy voice, and have [ab]granted thy petition. **36** So Abigail
came to Nabal, and behold, he made a feast in his house, like the feast of a king,
and Nabal's heart was merry within him, for he was very drunken: wherefore she
told him [ac]nothing, neither less nor more, until the morning arose. **37** Then
in the morning, when the wine was gone out of Nabal, his wife told him those
words, and his heart died within him, and he was like [ad]a stone. **38** And about
ten days after, the Lord smote Nabal, that he died. **39** Now when David heard
that Nabal was dead, he said, Blessed be the Lord, that hath [ae]judged the cause of
my rebuke of the hand of Nabal, and hath kept his servant from evil: for the Lord
hath recompensed the wickedness of Nabal upon his own head. Also David sent
to commune with Abigail, to [af]take her to his wife. **40** And when the servants
of David were come to Abigail to Carmel, they spake unto her, saying, David sent
us to thee, to take thee to his wife. **41** And she arose, and bowed herself on her
face to the earth, and said, Behold, let thine handmaid be a servant to wash the feet
of the servants of my lord. **42** And Abigail hasted, and arose, and rode upon an
ass, and her five maids [ag]followed her, and she went after the messengers of David,
and was his wife. **43** David also took Ahinoam of [2]Jezreel, and they were both
his wives. **44** Now Saul had given [3]Michal his daughter, David's wife, to Palti the
son of Laish, which was of [ah]Gallim.

26

1 David was discovered unto Saul by the Ziphites. 12 David taketh away Saul's spear, and a pot of water that stood at his head. 21 Saul confesseth his sin.

1 Again the Ziphites came unto Saul to Gibeah, saying, [1]Doth not David
hide himself [a]in the hill of Hachilah before [b]Jeshimon? **2** Then Saul arose, and
went down to the wilderness of Ziph, having three thousand [c]chosen men of Isra-
el with him, for to seek David in the wilderness of Ziph. **3** And Saul pitched
in the hill of Hachilah, which is before Jeshimon by the wayside. Now David
abode in the wilderness, and he saw that Saul came after him into the wilder-
ness. **4** (For David had sent out spies, and understood that Saul was come [d]in
very deed.) **5** Then David arose, and came to the place where Saul had pitched,
and when David beheld the place where Saul lay, and [2]Abner the son of Ner which
was his chief captain, (for Saul lay in the fort, and the people pitched round about
him.) **6** Then spake David, and said to Ahimelech the [e]Hittite, and to Abishai
the son of Zeruiah, brother to [f]Joab, saying, Who will go down with me to Saul
to the host? Then Abishai said, I will go down with thee. **7** So David and Abi-
shai came down to the people by night: and behold, Saul lay sleeping within the
fort, and his spear did stick in the ground at his [g]head: and Abner and the peo-
ple lay round about him. **8** Then said Abishai to David, God hath closed thine
enemy into thine hand this day: now therefore, I pray thee, let me smite him once
with a spear to the earth, and I will not smite him [h]again. **9** And David said to
Abishai, Destroy him not: for who can lay his hand [i]on the Lord's anointed, and
be guiltless? **10** Moreover David said, As the Lord liveth, either the Lord shall
smite him, or his day shall come to die, or he shall descend into battle, and peri-
sh. **11** The Lord keep me from laying mine hand upon the Lord's anointed: but,
I pray thee, take now the spear that is at his head, and the pot of water, and let us
go hence. **12** So David took the spear and the pot of water from Saul's head, and
they got them away, and no man saw it, nor marked it, neither did any awake, but
they were all asleep: for [j]the Lord had sent a dead sleep upon them. **13** Then Da-
vid went unto the other side, and stood on the top of an hill a far off, a great space
being between them. **14** And David cried to the people, and to Abner the son
of Ner, saying, [k]Hearest thou not, Abner? Then Abner answered, and said, Who
art thou that cryest to the King? **15** And David said to Abner, Art not thou a
[l]man? and who is like thee in Israel? wherefore then hast thou not kept thy Lord
the King? for there came one of the folk in to destroy the king thy lord. **16** This
is not well done of thee: as the Lord liveth, ye are [m]worthy to die, because ye have
not kept your master the Lord's anointed: and now see where the King's spear is,

---

e. 1-Sam. 25:6 Hebrew, for life.
f. 1-Sam. 25:8 Whatsoever thou hast ready for us.
g. 1-Sam. 25:10 Thus the covetous wretches instead of relieving the necessity of God's children, used to revile their persons and condemn their cause.
h. 1-Sam. 25:13 Hebrew, vessel.
i. 1-Sam. 25:14 Hebrew, drove them away.
j. 1-Sam. 25:15 When we kept our sheep in the wilderness of Paran.
k. 1-Sam. 25:17 Hebrew, is accomplished.
l. 1-Sam. 25:18 Hebrew, bread.
m. 1-Sam. 25:18 Or, clusters.
n. 1-Sam. 25:19 Because she knew his crooked nature, that he would rather have perished, than consented to her enterprise.
o. 1-Sam. 25:22 Meaning by this proverb, that he would destroy both small and great.
p. 1-Sam. 25:24 Hebrew, in thine ears.
q. 1-Sam. 25:25 Or, fool.
r. 1-Sam. 25:26 That is, that thou shouldest not be revenged of thine enemy.
s. 1-Sam. 25:27 Or, present.
t. 1-Sam. 25:27 Hebrew, walk at the feet.
u. 1-Sam. 25:28 Confirm his Kingdom to his posterity.
v. 1-Sam. 25:28 Hebrew, from thy days.
w. 1-Sam. 25:29 To wit, Saul.
x. 1-Sam. 25:29 God shall preserve thee long in his service, and destroy thine enemies.
y. 1-Sam. 25:31 That he hath not avenged himself, which things would have tormented his conscience.
z. 1-Sam. 25:33 Read verse 26.
aa. 1-Sam. 25:34 He attributeth it to the Lord's mercy, and not to himself that he was stayed.
ab. 1-Sam. 25:35 Hebrew, received thy face.
ac. 1-Sam. 25:36 For he had no reason either to consider, or to give thanks for this great benefit of deliverance.
ad. 1-Sam. 25:37 For fear of the great danger.
ae. 1-Sam. 25:39 Or, revenged.
af. 1-Sam. 25:39 For he had experience of her great godliness, wisdom and humility.
ag. 1-Sam. 25:42 Hebrew, went at her feet.
ah. 1-Sam. 25:44 Which was a place bordering on the country of the Moabites.

1-SAM. 25
1. 1 Sam. 28:3
2. Josh. 15:56
3. 2 Sam. 3:14,15

1-SAM. 26
a. 1-Sam. 26:1 Or, in Gibeah.
b. 1-Sam. 26:1 Or, the wilderness.
c. 1-Sam. 26:2 That is, of the most skillful and valiant soldiers.
d. 1-Sam. 26:4 Or, to a certain place.
e. 1-Sam. 26:6 Who was a stranger, and not an Israelite.
f. 1-Sam. 26:6 Who afterward was David's chief captain.
g. 1-Sam. 26:7 Or, bolster.
h. 1-Sam. 26:8 Meaning, he would make him sure at one stroke.
i. 1-Sam. 26:9 To wit, in his own private cause: for Jehu slew two Kings at God's appointment, 2 Kings 9:24.
j. 1-Sam. 26:12 Hebrew, the heavy sleep of the Lord was fallen upon them.
k. 1-Sam. 26:14 Hebrew, Answerest.
l. 1-Sam. 26:15 Esteemed most valiant and meet to save the King?
m. 1-Sam. 26:16 Hebrew, sons of death.

and the pot of water that was at his head. **17** And Saul knew David's voice, and said, Is this thy voice, [n]my son David? And David said, It is my voice, my lord, O King. **18** And he said, Wherefore doth my lord thus persecute his servant? for what have I done? or what evil is in mine hand? **19** Now therefore, I beseech thee, let my Lord the King hear the words of his servant. If the Lord have stirred thee up against me, [o]let him smell the savor of a sacrifice: but if the children of men have done it, cursed be they before the Lord: for they have cast me out this day from abiding in the inheritance of the Lord, saying, Go, serve [p]other gods. **20** Now therefore, let not my blood fall to the earth before the face of the Lord: for the King of Israel is come out to seek a flea, as one would hunt a partridge in the mountains. **21** Then said Saul, I have sinned: Come again, my son David: for I will do thee no more harm, because my soul was [q]precious in thine eyes this day: behold, I have done foolishly, and have erred exceedingly. **22** Then David answered, and said, Behold the King's spear, let one of the young men come over and fet it. **23** And let the Lord reward every man according to his [r]righteousness and faithfulness: for the Lord had delivered thee into mine hands this day, but I would not lay mine hand upon the Lord's anointed. **24** And behold, like as thy life was much set by this day in mine eyes: so let my life be set by in the eyes of the Lord, that he may deliver me out of all tribulation. **25** Then Saul said to David, Blessed art thou, my son David: for thou shalt do great things, and also prevail. So David went his way, and Saul returned to his [s]place.

27

2 David fleeth to Achish King of Gath, who giveth him Ziklag. 8 David destroyeth certain of the Philistines. 10 Achish is deceived by David.

1 And David said in his heart, I shall now [a]perish one day by the hand of Saul: is it not better for me that I save myself in the land of the Philistines, and that Saul may have no hope of me to seek me anymore in all the coasts of Israel, and so escape out of his hand? **2** David therefore arose, and he, and the six hundred men that were with him, went unto Achish the son of Maoch king of Gath. **3** And David [b]dwelt with Achish at Gath, he, and his men, every man with his household, David with his two wives, Ahinoam the Jezreelite, and Abigail Nabal's wife the Carmelite. **4** And it was told Saul that David was fled to Gath: so he sought no more for him. **5** And David said unto Achish, If I have now found grace in thine eyes, [c]let them give me a place in some other city of the country, that I may dwell there: for why should thy servant dwell in the head city of the kingdom with thee? **6** Then Achish gave him Ziklag that same day: therefore Ziklag pertaineth unto the kings of Judah unto this day. **7** And [d]the time that David dwelt in the country of the Philistines, was four months and certain days. **8** Then David and his men went up, and invaded the [e]Geshurites, and the Girzites, and the Amalekites: for they inhabited the land from the beginning, from the way, as thou goest to Shur, even unto the land of Egypt. **9** And David smote the land, and left neither man nor woman alive, and took sheep, and oxen, and asses, and camels, and apparel, and returned and came to Achish. **10** And Achish said, [f]Where have ye been a roving this day? And David answered, Against the South of Judah, and against the South of the [g]Jerahmeelites, and against the South of the Kenites. **11** And David saved neither man nor woman alive, to bring them to Gath, saying, Lest they should tell on us, and say, So did David, and so will be his manner all the while that he dwelleth in the country of the Philistines. **12** And Achish believed David, saying, [h]He hath made his people of Israel utterly to abhor him: therefore he shall be my servant forever.

28

1 David hath the chief charge promised about Achish. 8 Saul consulteth with a witch, and she causeth him to speak with Samuel, 18 Who declareth his ruin.

1 Now at that time the Philistines assembled their bands and army to fight with Israel: therefore Achish said to David, [a]Be sure, thou shalt go out with me to the battle, thou, and thy men. **2** And David said to Achish, Surely thou shalt know what thy servant can do. And Achish said to David, Surely I will make thee keeper of mine head forever. **3** ([1]Samuel was then dead, and all Israel had lamented him, and buried him in Ramah his own city: and Saul had [b]put away the sorcerers, and the Soothsayers out of the land.) **4** Then the Philistines assembled themselves, and came and pitched in Shunem: and Saul assembled all Israel, and they pitched in Gilboa. **5** And when Saul saw the host of the Philistines, he was afraid, and his heart was sore astonied. **6** Therefore Saul asked counsel of the Lord, and the Lord answered him not, neither by dreams, nor by [c]Urim, nor yet by Prophets. **7** Then said Saul unto his servants, Seek me a woman that hath a familiar spirit, that I may go to her, and ask of her. And his servants said to him, Behold, there is a woman at En Dor that hath a familiar spirit. **8** Then Saul [d]changed himself, and put on other raiment, and he went, and two men with him, and they came to the woman by night: and he said, I pray thee, conjecture unto me by the familiar spirit, and bring me him up whom I shall name unto thee. **9** And the woman said unto him, Behold, thou knowest what Saul hath done, how he hath destroyed the sorcerers, and the soothsayers out of the land: wherefore then seekest thou to take me in a snare to cause me to die? **10** And Saul swore to her by the Lord, saying, As the Lord liveth, no [e]harm shall come to thee for this thing. **11** Then said the woman, Whom shall I bring up unto thee? And he answered, Bring me up [f]Samuel. **12** And when the woman saw Samuel, she cried with a loud voice, and the woman spake to Saul, saying, Why hast thou deceived me? for thou art Saul. **13** And the king said unto her, Be not afraid: for what sawest thou? And the woman said unto Saul, I saw [g]gods ascending up out of the earth. **14** Then he said unto her, What fashion is he of? And she answered, An old man cometh up lapped in a mantel: and Saul knew that it was [h]Samuel, and he inclined his face to the ground, and bowed himself. **15** And Samuel said to Saul, Why hast thou disquieted me, to bring me up? Then Saul answered, I am in great distress: for the Philistines make war against me, and God is departed from me, and answereth me no more, neither [i]by Prophets, neither by dreams: therefore I have called thee, that thou mayest tell me, what I shall do. **16** Then said Samuel, Wherefore then dost thou ask of me, seeing, the Lord is gone from thee, and is thine enemy? **17** Even the Lord hath done to [j]him, as he spake [2]by mine [k]hand: for the Lord will rent the kingdom out of thine hand, and give it thy neighbor David. **18** Because thou obeyedst not the voice of the Lord, nor executedst his fierce wrath upon the Amalekites, therefore hath the Lord done this unto thee this day. **19** Moreover the Lord will deliver Israel with thee into the hands of the Philistines: [l]and tomorrow shalt thou and thy sons be with me, and the Lord shall give the host of Israel into the hands of the Philistines. **20** Then Saul fell straightway all along on the earth, and was sore [m]afraid because of the words of Samuel, so that there was no strength in him: for he had eaten no bread all the day nor all the night. **21** Then the woman came unto Saul, and saw that he was sore troubled, and said unto him, See, thine handmaid hath obeyed thy voice, and I [n]have put my soul in mine hand, and have obeyed thy words which thou saidest unto me. **22** Now therefore, I pray thee, hearken thou also unto the voice of thine handmaid, and let me set a morsel of bread before thee, that thou mayest eat and get thee strength, and go on thy journey. **23** But he refused and said, I will not eat: but his servants and the woman together compelled him, and he obeyed their voice: so he arose from the earth, and sat on the bed. **24** Now the woman had a fat calf in the house, and she hasted, and killed it, and took flour, and kneaded it, and baked of it [o]unleavened bread. **25** Then she brought them before Saul, and before his servants: and when they had eaten, they stood up, and went away the same night.

29

4 The princes of the Philistines cause David to be sent back from the battle against Israel, because they distrusted him.

1 So the Philistines were gathered together with all their armies in Aphek: and the Israelites pitched [a]by the fountain, which is in Jezreel. **2** And the [b]princes of the Philistines went forth by [c]hundreds and thousands, but David and his men came behind with Achish. **3** Then said the Princes of the Philistines, What do these Hebrews here? And Achish said unto the princes of the Philistines, Is not this

---

- **n.** 1-Sam. 26:17 Hereby it appeareth, that the hypocrite persecuted David against his own conscience, and contrary to his promise.
- **o.** 1-Sam. 26:19 Let his anger toward us be pacified by a sacrifice.
- **p.** 1-Sam. 26:19 As much as lay in them, they compelled him to idolatry because they forced him to flee to the idolaters.
- **q.** 1-Sam. 26:21 Because thou savedst my life this day.
- **r.** 1-Sam. 26:23 Thus he protesteth his innocency toward Saul, not defending his justice in the sight of God, in whose presence none is righteous, Ps 14:3 and 130:3.
- **s.** 1-Sam. 26:25 To Gibeah of Benjamin.

1-SAM. 26

- **1.** 1 Sam. 23:19
- **2.** 1 Sam. 14:50 / 1 Sam. 17:55

1-SAM. 27

- **a.** 1-Sam. 27:1 David distrusteth God's protection, and therefore fleeth unto the idolaters, who were enemies to God's people.
- **b.** 1-Sam. 27:3 Thus God by his providence changeth the enemy's hearts, and maketh them to favor his in their necessity.
- **c.** 1-Sam. 27:5 Let thine officers appoint me a place.
- **d.** 1-Sam. 27:7 Hebrew, the number of the days.
- **e.** 1-Sam. 27:8 These were the wicked Canaanites, whom God had appointed to be destroyed.
- **f.** 1-Sam. 27:10 Or, against whom.
- **g.** 1-Sam. 27:10 Which were a family of the tribe of Judah, 1 Chron. 2:9.
- **h.** 1-Sam. 27:12 Or, he doth surely abhor his people.

1-SAM.28

- **a.** 1-Sam. 28:1 Albeit it was a great grief to David to fight against the people of God, yet such was his infirmity, he durst not deny him.
- **b.** 1-Sam. 28:3 According to the commandment of God, Exod. 22:18 and Deut. 18:10, 11.
- **c.** 1-Sam. 28:6 Meaning, the high Priest, Exod. 28:30.
- **d.** 1-Sam. 28:8 He seeketh not to God in his misery, but is let by Satan to unlawful means, which in his conscience he condemneth.
- **e.** 1-Sam. 28:10 Or, punishment.
- **f.** 1-Sam. 28:11 He speaketh according to his gross ignorance, not considering the state of the Saints after this life, and how Satan hath no power over them.
- **g.** 1-Sam. 28:13 Or, an excellent person.
- **h.** 1-Sam. 28:14 To his imagination, albeit it was Satan, who to blind his eyes took upon him the form of Samuel, as he can do of an Angel of light.
- **i.** 1-Sam. 28:15 Hebrew, by the hand of Prophets.
- **j.** 1-Sam. 28:17 That is, to David.
- **k.** 1-Sam. 28:17 Or, ministry.
- **l.** 1-Sam. 28:19 Ye shall be dead, 1 Sam. 31:6.
- **m.** 1-Sam. 28:20 The wicked when they hear God's judgments, tremble and despair, but cannot seek for mercy by repentance.
- **n.** 1-Sam. 28:21 I have ventured my life.
- **o.** 1-Sam. 28:24 Because it required haste.

1-SAM.28

- **1.** 1 Sam. 25:1
- **2.** 1 Sam. 15:28

1-SAM. 29

- **a.** 1-Sam. 29:1 Or, in Ain.
- **b.** 1-Sam. 29:2 Or, captains.
- **c.** 1-Sam. 29:2 According to their bands, or ensigns.

David the servant of Saul the King of Israel, who hath been with me these days,
[d]or these years, and I have found nothing in him, since he [e]dwelt with me unto this
day? **4** But the princes of the Philistines were wroth with him, and the princes of
the Philistines said unto him, [1]Send this fellow back, that he may go again to his
place which thou hast appointed him, and let him not go down with us to battle,
lest that in the battle he be an adversary to us: for wherewith should he obtain the
favor of his master? should it not be with the [f]heads of these men? **5** Is not this
David, of whom they sang in dances, saying, [2]Saul slew his thousand, and David
his ten thousand? **6** Then Achish called David, and said unto him, As the Lord
liveth, thou hast been upright and good in my sight, when thou [g]wentest out and
in with me in the host, neither have I found evil with thee, since thou camest to me
unto this day, but [h]the princes do not favor thee. **7** Wherefore now return, and
go in peace, that thou displease not the princes of the Philistines. **8** And David
said unto Achish, But what have I done? and what hast thou found in thy servant
as long as I have been with thee unto this day, that I may [i]not go and fight against
the enemies of my Lord the King? **9** Achish then answered and said to David, I
know thou pleasest me as an Angel of God: but the princes of the Philistines have
said, Let him not go up with us to battle. **10** Wherefore now rise up early in the
morning with thy [j]master's servants that are come with thee: and when ye be up
early, as soon as ye have light, depart. **11** So David and his men rose up early to
depart in the morning, and to return into the land of the Philistines: and the Phi-
listines went up to Jezreel.

30

1 The Amalekites burn Ziklag. 5 David's two wives are taken prisoners. 6 The people would stone him. 8 He asketh counsel of the Lord, and pursuing his enemies recovereth the prey. 24 He divideth it equally, 26 And sendeth part to his friends.

1 But when David and his men were come to Ziklag [a]the third day, the Ama-
lekites had invaded upon the South, even unto Ziklag, and had [b]smitten Ziklag,
and burnt it with fire, **2** And had taken the women that were therein, priso-
ners, both small and great, and slew not a man, but carried them away, and went
their ways. **3** So David and his men came to the city, and behold, it was burnt
with fire, and their [c]wives and their sons, and their daughters were taken priso-
ners. **4** Then David and the people that were with him, lift up their voices and
wept, until they could weep no more. **5** David's two wives were taken prisoners
also, Ahinoam the Jezreelite, and Abigail the wife of Nabal the Carmelite. **6** And
David was in great sorrow: for the people [d]intended to stone him, because the he-
arts of all the people were vexed every man for his sons and for his daughters: but
David comforted himself in the Lord his God. **7** And David said to Abiathar the
Priest Ahimelech's son, I pray thee, bring me the Ephod. And Abiathar brought the
Ephod to David. **8** Then David asked counsel of the Lord, saying, Shall I follow
after this company? shall I overtake them? And he answered him, Follow: for thou
shalt surely overtake them, and [e]recover all. **9** So David and the six hundred
men that were with him, went, and came to the river Besor, where a part of them
abode: **10** But David and four hundred men followed (for two hundred abode
behind, being too weary to go over the river Besor.) **11** And they found an Egyp-
tian in the field, and brought him to David, and gave him [f]bread, and he did eat,
and they gave him water to drink. **12** Also they gave him a few figs, and two clu-
sters of raisins: and when he had eaten, his spirit came again to him: for he had ea-
ten no bread, nor drunk any water in three days, and three nights. **13** And David
said unto him, To whom belongest thou? and whence art thou? And he said, I am
a young man of Egypt, and servant to an Amalekite: and my master left me three
days ago because I fell sick. **14** We roved upon the South of Chereth, and upon
the coast belonging to Judah, and upon the South of Caleb, and we burnt Ziklag
with fire. **15** And David said unto him, Canst thou bring me to this company?
And he said, [g]Swear unto me by God, that thou will neither kill me, nor deliver
me into the hands of my master, and I will bring thee to this company. **16** And
when he had brought him thither, behold, they lay scattered abroad upon all the
earth, [h]eating and drinking, and dancing, because of all the great prey that they
had taken out of the land of the Philistines, and out of the land of Judah. **17** And
David smote them from the twilight even unto the evening [i]of the next morrow,
so that there escaped not a man of them, save four hundred young men, which
rode upon camels, and fled. **18** And David recovered all that the Amalekites had
taken: also David rescued his two wives. **19** And they lacked nothing, small or
great, son or daughter, or of the spoil of all that they had taken away: David reco-
vered them all. **20** David also took all the sheep, and the oxen, and they drove
them before his cattle, and said, This is David's [j]prey. **21** And David came to
the two hundred men that were too weary for to follow David: whom they had
made also to abide at the river Besor: and they came to meet David, and to meet
the people that were with him: so when David came near to the people, he salu-
ted them. **22** Then answered all the evil and wicked of the men that went with
David, and said, Because they went not with us, therefore will we give them none
of the prey that we have recovered, save to every man his [k]wife and his children:
therefore let them carry them away and depart. **23** Then said David, Ye shall not
do so, my brethren, with that which the Lord hath given us, who hath preserved
us, and delivered the company that came against us, into our hands. **24** For who
will obey you in this matter? but as his part is that goeth down to the battle, so
shall his part be, that tarrieth by the stuff: they shall part alike. **25** [l]So from that
day forward he made it a statute and a law in Israel, until this day. **26** When
David therefore came to Ziklag, he sent of the prey unto the Elders of Judah and
to his friends, saying, See there is a blessing for you of the spoil of the enemies of
the Lord. **27** He sent to them of Bethel, and to them of South Ramoth, and to
them of Jattir, **28** And to them of Aroer, and to them of Siphmoth, and to them
of Eshtemoa, **29** And to them of Rachal, and to them of the cities of the Jerah-
meelites, and to them of the cities of the Kenites, **30** And to them of Hormah,
and to them of Chorashan, and to them of Athach, **31** And to them of Hebron,
and [m]to all the places where David and his men had haunted.

31

4 Saul killeth himself. 6 His children are slain in the battle. 12 The men of Jabesh took down his body, which was hanged on the wall.

1 Now [1]the Philistines fought against Israel, and the men of Israel fled away
from the Philistines, and they fell down [a]wounded in mount Gilboa. **2** And the
Philistines pressed sore upon Saul and his sons, and slew Jonathan, and Abinadab,
and Malchishua Saul's sons. **3** And when the battle went sore against Saul, the
archers and bowmen [b]hit him, and he was sore [c]wounded of the archers. **4** Then
said Saul unto his armor bearer, [d]Draw out thy sword, and thrust me through the-
rewith, lest the uncircumcised come and thrust me through and mock me: but his
armor bearer would not, for he was sore afraid. Therefore Saul took a sword and
fell upon it. **5** And when his armor bearer saw that Saul was dead, he fell likewi-
se upon his sword, and died with him. **6** So Saul died, and his three sons, and
his armor bearer, and all his men that same day together. **7** And when the men
of Israel that were on the other side of the [e]valley, and they of the other side [f]Jor-
dan saw that the men of Israel were put to flight, and that Saul and his sons were
dead, then they left the cities, and ran away: and the Philistines came and dwelt in
them. **8** And on the morrow when the Philistines were come to spoil them that
were slain, they found Saul and his three sons lying in mount Gilboa, **9** And they
cut off his head, and stripped him out of his armor, and sent into the land of the
Philistines on every side, that they should [g]publish it in the temple of their idols,
and among the people. **10** And they laid up his armor in the house of Ashtoreth,
but they hanged up his body on the wall of Beth Shan. **11** When the inhabitan-
ts of [h]Jabesh Gilead heard what the Philistines had done to Saul, **12** Then they
arose (as many as were strong men) and went all night, and took the body of Saul,
and the bodies of his sons, from the wall of Beth Shan, and came to Jabesh, and
[2]burnt them there, **13** And took their bones and buried them under a tree at Ja-
besh, [3]and [i]fasted seven days.

---

d. 1-Sam. 29:3 Meaning, a long time, that is, four months and certain days, 1 Sam. 27:7.
e. 1-Sam. 29:3 Hebrew, fell, as Gen. 25:18.
f. 1-Sam. 29:4 Would not Saul receive him to favor, if he would betray us?
g. 1-Sam. 29:6 That is, wast conversant with me.
h. 1-Sam. 29:6 Hebrew, thou art not good in the eye of the princes.
i. 1-Sam. 29:8 This dissimulation cannot be excused: for it grieved him to go against the people of God.
j. 1-Sam. 29:10 With them that fled unto thee from Saul.

1-SAM. 29

1. 1 Chron. 12:19
2. 1 Sam. 18:7 / 1 Sam. 21:11

1-SAM. 30

a. 1-Sam. 30:1 After that he departed from Achish.
b. 1-Sam. 30:1 That is, destroyed the city.
c. 1-Sam. 30:3 For these only remained in the city, when the men were gone to war.
d. 1-Sam. 30:6 Thus we see that in troubles and adversity we do not consider God's providence, but like raging beasts forget both our own duty, and contemn God's appointment over us.
e. 1-Sam. 30:8 Though God seem to leave us for a time, yet if we trust in him, we shall be sure to find comfort.
f. 1-Sam. 30:11 God by his providence both provided for the necessity of this poor stranger, and made him a guide to David to accomplish his enterprise.
g. 1-Sam. 30:15 For oaths were in all ages had in most reverence, even among the heathen.
h. 1-Sam. 30:16 The wicked in their pomp and pleasures consider not the judgment of God, which is then at hand to smite them.
i. 1-Sam. 30:17 Some read, and unto the morrow of the two evenings: that is, three days.
j. 1-Sam. 30:20 Which the Amalekites had taken of others, and David from them, besides the goods of Ziklag.
k. 1-Sam. 30:22 Under these are comprehended the cattle and goods, which appertained to every man.
l. 1-Sam. 30:25 Some refer these words to David, that he alleged an old custom and law, as if it were written, it is both now, and hath been ever.
m. 1-Sam. 30:31 Showing himself mindful of their benefits towards him.

1-SAM. 31

a. 1-Sam. 31:1 Or, slain.
b. 1-Sam. 31:3 Hebrew, found him.
c. 1-Sam. 31:3 Or, afraid.
d. 1-Sam. 31:4 So we see that his cruel life hath a desperate end: as is commonly seen in them that persecute the children of God.
e. 1-Sam. 31:7 Near to Gilboa.
f. 1-Sam. 31:7 The Tribes of Reuben and Gad, and half the tribe of Manasseh.
g. 1-Sam. 31:9 In token of victory and triumph.
h. 1-Sam. 31:11 Whom he had delivered from their enemies, 1 Sam. 11:11.
i. 1-Sam. 31:13 According to the custom of mourners.

1-SAM. 31

1. 1 Chron. 10:1
2. Jer. 34:5
3. 2 Sam. 2:4

THE SECOND BOOK OF SAMUEL

1

4 It was told David of Saul's death. 15 He causeth him to be slain that brought the tidings. 19 He lamenteth the death of Saul and Jonathan.

1 After the death of Saul, when David was returned from the [1]slaughter of the Amalekites, and had been two days in Ziklag, **2** Behold, a man came the third day out of the host from Saul with [a]his clothes rent, and earth upon his head: and when he came to David, he fell to the earth, and did obeisance. **3** Then David said unto him, Whence comest thou? And he said unto him, Out of the host of Israel I am escaped. **4** And David said unto him, What is done? I pray thee, tell me. Then he said, that the people is fled from the battle, and many of the people are overthrown, and dead, and also Saul and Jonathan his son are dead. **5** And David said unto the young man that told it him, How knowest thou that Saul and Jonathan his son be dead? **6** Then the young man that told him, answered, [b]As I came to mount Gilboa, behold, Saul leaned upon his spear, and lo, the chariots and [c]horsemen followed hard after him. **7** And when he looked back, he saw me, and called me. And I answered, Here am I. **8** And he said unto me, Who art thou? And I answered him, I am an [d]Amalekite. **9** Then said he unto me, I pray thee,[e]come upon me, and slay me: for anguish is come upon me, because my [f]life is yet whole in me. **10** So [g]I came upon him, and slew him, and because I was sure that he could not live, after that he had fallen, I took the crown that was upon his head, and the bracelet that was on his arm, and brought them hither unto my lord. **11** Then David took hold on his clothes, [2]and rent them, and likewise all the men that were with him. **12** And they mourned and wept, and fasted until even, for Saul and for Jonathan his son, and for the people of the Lord, and for the house of Israel, because they were slain with the sword. **13** [h]Afterward David said unto the young man that told it him, Whence art thou? And he answered, I am the son of a stranger an Amalekite. **14** And David said unto him, [3]How wast thou not afraid, to put forth thine hand to destroy the Anointed of the Lord? **15** Then David called one of his young men, and said, Go near, and fall upon him. And he smote him that he died. **16** Then said David unto him, [i]Thy blood be upon thine own head: for thine own mouth hath testified against thee, saying, I have slain the Lord's Anointed. **17** Then David mourned with this lamentation over Saul, and over Jonathan his son, **18** (Also he bade them teach the children of Judah to [j]shoot, as it is written in the book of [k,4]Jasher.) **19** O noble Israel, [l]he is slain upon thy high places: how are the mighty overthrown! **20** [5]Tell it not in Gath, nor publish it in the streets of Ashkelon, lest the daughters of the Philistines rejoice, lest the daughters of the uncircumcised triumph. **21** Ye mountains of Gilboa, upon you be neither dew nor rain, nor [m]be there fields of offerings: for there the shield of the mighty is cast down, the shield of Saul, as though he had not been anointed with oil. **22** The bow of Jonathan never turned back, neither did the sword of Saul return empty from the blood of the slain, and from the fat of the mighty. **23** Saul and Jonathan were lovely and pleasant in their lives, and in their deaths they were not [n]divided: they were swifter than eagles, they were stronger than lions. **24** Ye daughters of Israel, weep for Saul, which clothed you in scarlet, [o]with pleasures, and hanged ornaments of gold upon your apparel. **25** How were the mighty slain in the midst of the battle! O Jonathan, thou wast slain in thine high places. **26** Woe is me for thee, my brother Jonathan: very kind hast thou been unto me: thy love to me was wonderful, passing the love of [p]women: how are the mighty overthrown, and the weapons of war destroyed!

2

1 David is anointed King in Hebron. 9 Abner maketh Ishbosheth King over Israel. 15 The battle of the servants of David and Ishbosheth. 32 The burial of Asahel.

1 After this, David [a]asked counsel of the Lord, saying, Shall I go up into any of the cities of Judah? And the Lord said unto him, Go up. And David said, Whither shall I go? He then answered, Unto [b]Hebron. **2** So David went up thither, and his two wives also, Ahinoam the Jezreelitess, and Abigail Nabal's wife the Carmelite. **3** And David brought up the men that were with [c]him, every man with his household, and they dwelt in the cities of Hebron. **4** Then the men of Judah came, and there they anointed David King over the house of Judah. And they told David, saying, [1]that the men of Jabesh Gilead buried Saul. **5** And David sent messengers unto the men of Jabesh Gilead, and said unto them, Blessed are ye of the Lord, that ye have showed such kindness unto your lord Saul, that you have buried him. **6** Therefore now the Lord show mercy and [d]truth unto you: and I will recompense you this benefit, because ye have done this thing. **7** Therefore now let your hands be strong, and be you valiant: albeit your master Saul be dead, yet nevertheless the house of Judah hath anointed me [e]King over them. **8** But Abner the son of Ner that was captain of Saul's host, took Ishbosheth the son of Saul, and brought him to Mahanaim, **9** And made him King over Gilead, and over the Ashurites, and over Jezreel, and over Ephraim, and over Benjamin, and over [f]all Israel. **10** Ishbosheth Saul's son was forty years old when he began to reign over Israel, and reigned two years: but the house of Judah followed David. **11** (And the time which David reigned in Hebron over the house of Judah, was seven years and six [g]months.) **12** And Abner the son of Ner, and the servants of Ishbosheth the son of Saul went out of Mahanaim to Gibeon. **13** And Joab the son of Zeruiah, and the servants of David went out and met one another by the pool of Gibeon: and they sat down, the one on the one side of the pool, and the other on the other side of the pool. **14** Then Abner said to Joab, Let the young men now arise, and [h]play before us. And Joab said, Let them arise. **15** Then there arose and went over twelve of Benjamin by number, which pertained to Ishbosheth the son of Saul, and twelve of the servants of David. **16** And every one caught his [i]fellow by the head, and thrust his sword in his fellow's side, so they fell down together: wherefore the place was called [j]Helkath Hazzurim, which is in Gibeon. **17** And the battle was exceedingly sore that same day: for Abner and the men of Israel [k]fell before the servants of David. **18** And there were three sons of Zeruiah there, Joab, and Abishai, and Asahel. And Asahel was as light on foot as a wild roe. **19** And Asahel followed after Abner, and in going he turned neither to the right hand nor to the left from Abner. **20** Then Abner looked behind him, and said, Art thou Asahel? And he answered, Yea. **21** Then Abner said, Turn thee either to the right hand or to the left, and take one of the young men, and take thee his [l]weapons: and Asahel would not depart from him. **22** And Abner said to Asahel, Depart from me: [m]wherefore should I smite thee to the ground? how then should I be able to hold up my face to Joab thy brother? **23** And when he would not depart, Abner with the hinder end of the spear smote him under the [n]fifth rib, that the spear came out behind him: and he fell down there, and died in his place. And as many as came to the place where Asahel fell down, and died, stood still. **24** Joab also and Abishai pursued after Abner: and the sun went down when they were come to the hill Ammah, that lieth before Giah by the way of the wilderness of Gibeon. **25** And the children of Benjamin gathered themselves together after Abner, and were on an heap, and stood on the top of an hill. **26** Then Abner called to Joab, and said, Shall the [o]sword devour forever? knowest thou not, that it will be bitterness in the latter end? how long then shall it be, or thou bid the people return from following their brethren? **27** And Joab said, As God liveth, if thou hadst

---

2-SAM. 1

- **a.** 2 Sam. 1:2 Seeming to lament the overthrow of the people of Israel.
- **b.** 2 Sam. 1:6 As I fled in the chase.
- **c.** 2 Sam. 1:6 Or, captains.
- **d.** 2 Sam. 1:8 He was an Amalekite born, but renounced his country, and joined with the Israelites.
- **e.** 2 Sam. 1:9 Hebrew, stand upon.
- **f.** 2 Sam. 1:9 I am sorry, because I am yet alive.
- **g.** 2 Sam. 1:10 Hebrew, I stood upon him.
- **h.** 2 Sam. 1:13 After the lamentation, he examined him again.
- **i.** 2 Sam. 1:16 Thou art justly punished for thy fault.
- **j.** 2 Sam. 1:18 That they might be able to match their enemies the Philistines in that art.
- **k.** 2 Sam. 1:18 Or, righteous.
- **l.** 2 Sam. 1:19 Meaning, Saul.
- **m.** 2 Sam. 1:21 Let their fertile fields be barren, and bring forth no fruit to offer to the Lord.
- **n.** 2 Sam. 1:23 They died both together in Gilboa.
- **o.** 2 Sam. 1:24 As rich garments and costly jewels.
- **p.** 2 Sam. 1:26 Either toward their husbands, or their children.

2-SAM. 1

- **1.** 1 Sam. 30:17
- **2.** 2 Sam. 3:31 / 2 Sam. 13:31
- **3.** Ps. 105:15
- **4.** Josh. 10:13
- **5.** Mic. 1:10

2-SAM. 2

- **a.** 2 Sam. 2:1 By the means of the high Priest, as 1 Sam. 23:2 and 2 Sam. 5:19.
- **b.** 2 Sam. 2:1 Which city was also called Kirjath Arba, Josh. 14:15.
- **c.** 2 Sam. 2:3 In the time of his persecution.
- **d.** 2 Sam. 2:6 According to his promise, which is to recompense them that are merciful.
- **e.** 2 Sam. 2:7 So that you shall not want a Captain and a defender.
- **f.** 2 Sam. 2:9 Over the eleven tribes.
- **g.** 2 Sam. 2:11 After this time was expired, he reigned over all the country 33 years, 2 Sam. 5:5.
- **h.** 2 Sam. 2:14 Let us see how they can handle their Weapons.
- **i.** 2 Sam. 2:16 Meaning, his adversary.
- **j.** 2 Sam. 2:16 Or, the field of strong men.
- **k.** 2 Sam. 2:17 After that these four and twenty were slain.
- **l.** 2 Sam. 2:21 Or, spoil.
- **m.** 2 Sam. 2:22 Why dost thou provoke me to kill thee?
- **n.** 2 Sam. 2:23 Some read, in those parts, whereas the lively parts lie: as the heart, the lungs, the liver, the milt, and the gall.
- **o.** 2 Sam. 2:26 Shall we not make an end of murdering?

not [p]spoken, surely even in the morning the people had departed every one back from his brother. **28** So Joab blew a trumpet, and all the people stood still, and pursued after Israel no more, neither fought they anymore. **29** And Abner and his men walked all that night through the [q]plain, and went over Jordan, and past through all Bithron till they came [r]to Mahanaim. **30** Joab also returned back from Abner: and when he had gathered all the people together, there lacked of David's servants nineteen men, and Asahel. **31** But the servants of David had smitten of Benjamin, and of Abner's men, so that three [s]hundred and threescore men died. **32** And they took up Asahel, and buried him in the sepulcher of his father, which was in Bethlehem: and Joab and his men went all night, and when they came to Hebron, the day arose.

3

1 Long war between the houses of Saul and David. 2 The children of David in Hebron. 12 Abner turneth to David. 27 Joab killeth him.

1 There was then [a]long war between the house of Saul and the house of David: but David waxed stronger, and the house of Saul waxed weaker. **2** And unto David were children born in Hebron: and his eldest son was Amnon of Ahinoam the Jezreelitess, **3** And his second, was [b]Chileab of Abigail the wife of Nabal the Carmelite: and the third, Absalom the son of Maacah the daughter of Talmai the king of Geshur, **4** And the fourth, Adonijah the son of Haggith: and the fifth, Shephatiah the son of Abital: **5** And the sixth, Ithream by Eglah David's wife: these were born to David in [c]Hebron. **6** Now while there was war between the house of Saul and the house of David, Abner made all his power for the house of Saul. **7** And Saul had a concubine named Rizpah, the daughter of Aiah. And Ishbosheth said to Abner, Wherefore hast thou gone in to my father's concubine? **8** Then was Abner very wroth for the words of Ishbosheth, and said, Am I a [d]dog's head, which against Judah do show mercy this day unto the house of Saul thy father, to his brethren, and to his neighbors, and have not delivered thee into the hand of David, that thou chargest me this day with a fault concerning this woman? **9** [e]So do God to Abner, and more also, except, as the Lord hath sworn to David, even so I do to him, **10** To remove the kingdom from the house of Saul, that the throne of David may be established over Israel, and over Judah, even from Dan to Beersheba. **11** And he durst no more answer to Abner: for he feared him. **12** Then Abner sent messengers to David [f]on his behalf, saying, Whose is the land? who should also say, Make covenant with me, and behold, mine hand shall be with thee, to bring all Israel unto thee. **13** Who said, Well, I will make a covenant with thee: but one thing I require of thee, that is, that thou see not my face, except thou bring Michal Saul's daughter when thou comest to see me. **14** Then David sent messengers to Ishbosheth Saul's son, saying, Deliver me my wife Michal, which I married for [1]an hundred foreskins of the Philistines. **15** And Ishbosheth sent, and took her from her husband [2]Paltiel the son of Laish. **16** And her husband went with her, and came weeping behind her, unto Bahurim: then said Abner unto him, Go, and return. So he returned. **17** And Abner had [g]communication with the Elders of Israel, saying, Ye fought for David in times past, that he might be your King. **18** Now then do it: for the Lord hath spoken of David, saying, By the hand of my servant David I will save my people Israel out of the hands of the Philistines, and out of the hands of all their enemies. **19** Also Abner spake [h]to Benjamin, and afterward Abner went to speak with David in Hebron, concerning all that Israel was content with, and the whole [i]house of Benjamin. **20** So Abner came to David to Hebron, having twenty men with him, and David made a feast unto Abner, and to the men that were with him. **21** Then Abner said unto David, I will rise up, and go gather all Israel unto my lord the King, that they may make a covenant with thee, and that thou mayest reign over all that thine heart desireth. Then David let Abner depart, who went [j]in peace. **22** And behold, the servants of David and Joab came [k]from the camp, and brought a great prey with them (but Abner was not with David in Hebron: for he had sent him away, and he departed in peace.) **23** When Joab, and all the host that was with him were come, men told Joab, saying, Abner the son of Ner came to the King, and he hath sent him away, and he is gone in peace. **24** Then Joab came to the King, and said, [l]What hast thou done? behold, Abner came unto thee, why hast thou sent him away, and he is departed? **25** Thou knowest Abner the son of Ner: for he came to deceive thee, and to know thy outgoing and ingoing, and to know all that thou doest. **26** And when Joab was gone out from David, he sent messengers after Abner, which brought him again from the well of Sirah unknowing to David. **27** And when Abner was come again to Hebron, [3]Joab took him aside in the gate to speak with him [m]peaceably, and smote him under the fifth rib, that he died, for the blood of [4]Asahel his brother. **28** And when afterward it came to David's ear, he said, I and my Kingdom are [n]guiltless before the Lord forever, concerning the blood of Abner the son of Ner. **29** Let the blood fall on the head of Joab, and on all his father's house, that the house of Joab be never without some that have running issues, or leper, or that leaneth on a staff, or that doeth fall on the sword, or that lacketh bread. **30** (So Joab and [o]Abishai his brother slew Abner, because he had slain their brother Asahel at Gibeon in battle.) **31** And David said to Joab, and to all the people that were with him, Rent your clothes, and put on sackcloth, and mourn [p]before Abner: and King David himself followed the bier. **32** And when they had buried Abner in Hebron, the King lift up his voice, and wept beside the sepulcher of Abner, and all the people wept. **33** And the King lamented over Abner, and said, Died Abner [q]as a fool dieth? **34** Thine hands were not bound, nor thy feet tied in fetters of brass: but as a man falleth before wicked men, so didst thou fall. And all the people wept again for him. **35** Afterward all the people came to cause David eat [r]meat while it was yet day, but David swore, saying, So do God to me and more also, if I taste bread, or ought else till the sun be down. **36** And all the people knew it, and it [s]pleased them: as whatsoever the King did, pleased all the people. **37** For all the people and all Israel understood that day, how that it was not the King's deed that Abner the son of Ner was slain. **38** And the King said unto his servants, Know ye not, that there is a prince and a great man fallen this day in Israel? **39** And I am this day weak and newly anointed King: and these men the sons of Zeruiah be too [t]hard for me: the Lord reward the doer of evil according to his wickedness.

4

5 Baanah and Rechab slay Ishbosheth the son of Saul. 12 David commandeth them to be slain.

1 And when Saul's [a]son heard that Abner was dead in Hebron, then his hands were [b]feeble, and all Israel was afraid, **2** And Saul's son had two men that were captains of bands: the one called Baanah, and the other called Rechab, the sons of Rimmon a Beerothite of the children of Benjamin: (for [c]Beeroth was reckoned to Benjamin, **3** Because the Beerothites fled to [d]Gittaim, and sojourned there, unto this day.) **4** And Jonathan Saul's son had a son that was lame on his feet: he was five years old when the tidings came of Saul and Jonathan out of Israel: then his nurse took him, and fled away. And as she made haste to flee, the child fell, and began to halt, and his name was Mephibosheth. **5** And the sons of Rimmon the Beerothite, Rechab and Baanah went and came in the heat of the day to the house of Ishbosheth (who slept on a bed at noon.) **6** And behold, Rechab and Baanah his brother came into the midst of the house, as they [e]would have wheat, and they [f]smote him under the fifth rib, and fled. **7** For when they came into the house, he slept on his bed in his bed chamber, and they smote him, and slew him, and beheaded him, and took his head, and got them away through the [g]plain all the night. **8** And they brought the head of Ishbosheth unto David to Hebron, and said to the king, Behold the head of Ishbosheth Saul's son thine enemy, who sought after thy life: and the Lord hath avenged my Lord the King this day of Saul, and of his seed. **9** Then David answered Rechab and Baanah his brother, the sons of Rimmon the Beerothite, and said unto them, As the Lord liveth, who hath delivered my soul out of all adversity, **10** When one [1]told me, and said that Saul was dead, (thinking to have brought good tidings) I took him and slew him in Ziklag, who thought that I would have given him a reward for his tidings: **11** How [h]much more when wicked men have slain a righteous person in his own house, and upon his bed? shall I not now therefore require his blood at your hand, and take you from the earth? **12** Then David commanded his young men, and they slew

---

p. 2 Sam. 2:27 If thou hadst not provoked them to battle, as verse 14.
q. 2 Sam. 2:29 Or, wilderness.
r. 2 Sam. 2:29 Or, to the tents.
s. 2 Sam. 2:31 Thus God would confirm David in his kingdom by the destruction of his adversaries.

2-SAM. 2
1. 1 Sam. 31:13

2-SAM. 3
a. 2 Sam. 3:1 That is, without intermission enduring two years, which was the whole reign of Ishbosheth.
b. 2 Sam. 3:3 Who is called also Daniel, 1 Chron. 3:1.
c. 2 Sam. 3:5 Within seven years and six months.
d. 2 Sam. 3:8 Dost thou esteem me no more than a dog, for all my service done to thy father's house?
e. 2 Sam. 3:9 We see how the wicked cannot abide to be admonished of their faults, but seek their displeasure, which go about to bring them from their wickedness.
f. 2 Sam. 3:12 Or, secretly.
g. 2 Sam. 3:17 Rather for malice that he bare toward Ishbosheth, than for love he bare to David.
h. 2 Sam. 3:19 Hebrew, in the ears of Benjamin.
i. 2 Sam. 3:19 Who challenged the Kingdom, because of their father Saul.
j. 2 Sam. 3:21 Or, without harm.
k. 2 Sam. 3:22 From war against the Philistines.
l. 2 Sam. 3:24 Here appeareth the malicious mind of Joab, who would have had the King to slay Abner for his private grudge.
m. 2 Sam. 3:27 Or, secretly.
n. 2 Sam. 3:28 The Lord knoweth that I did not consent to his death.
o. 2 Sam. 3:30 Abishai is said to slay him with Joab, because he consented to the murder.
p. 2 Sam. 3:31 Meaning before the corpse.
q. 2 Sam. 3:33 He declareth that Abner died not as a wretch or vile person, but as a valiant man might do, being traitorously deceived by the wicked.
r. 2 Sam. 3:35 According to their custom, which was to banquet at burials.
s. 2 Sam. 3:36 It is expedient sometimes not only to conceive inward sorrow, but also that it may appear to others, to the intent that they may be satisfied.
t. 2 Sam. 3:39 Or, cruel.

2-SAM. 3
1. 1 Sam. 18:25,27
2. 1 Sam. 25:44
3. 1 Kings 2:5
4. 2 Sam. 2:23

2-SAM. 4
a. 2 Sam. 4:1 That is, Ishbosheth.
b. 2 Sam. 4:1 Meaning, that he was discouraged.
c. 2 Sam. 4:2 This city Beeroth was in the tribe of Benjamin, Josh. 18:25.
d. 2 Sam. 4:3 After the death of Saul, for fear of the Philistines.
e. 2 Sam. 4:6 They disguised themselves as merchants, which came to buy wheat.
f. 2 Sam. 4:6 There is nothing so vile and dangerous, which the wicked will not enterprise in hope of lucre and favor.
g. 2 Sam. 4:7 Or, wilderness.
h. 2 Sam. 4:11 Forasmuch as neither the example of him that slew Saul, nor duty to their master, nor the innocency of the person, nor reverence of the place, nor time did move them, they deserved most grievous punishment.

2-SAM. 4
1. 2 Sam. 1:15
2. 2 Sam. 3:32

them, and cut off their hands and their feet, and hanged them up over the pool in Hebron: but they took the head of Ishbosheth, and buried it in the sepulcher of [2]Abner in Hebron.

5

3 David is made King over all Israel. 7 He taketh the fort of Zion. 19 He asketh counsel of the Lord. 23 And overcometh the Philistines twice.

1 Then [1]came all the tribes of Israel to David unto Hebron, and said thus, Behold, we are thy [a]bones and thy flesh. **2** And in time past when Saul was our King, thou leddest Israel in and out: and the Lord hath said to thee, [2]Thou shalt feed my people Israel, and thou shalt be a captain over Israel. **3** So all the Elders of Israel came to the king to Hebron: and King David made a covenant with them in Hebron [b]before the Lord, and they anointed David King over Israel. **4** David was thirty years old when he began to reign: and he reigned forty years. **5** In Hebron he reigned over Judah [3]seven years, and six months: and in Jerusalem he reigned thirty and three years over all Israel and Judah. **6** The King also and his men went to Jerusalem unto the Jebusites, the inhabitants of the land: who spake unto David, saying, Except thou take away the [c]blind and the lame, thou shalt not come in hither: thinking that David could not come thither: **7** But David took the fort of Zion: this is the city of David. **8** Now David had said the same day, Whosoever smiteth the Jebusites, and getteth up to the gutters and smiteth the lame and blind, which David's soul hateth, I will prefer him: [4]therefore they said, The blind and the lame shall not [d]come into that house. **9** So David dwelt in that fort, and called it the city of David, and David built round about it, from [e]Millo, and inward. **10** And David prospered and grew: for the Lord God of hosts was with him. **11** Hiram also king of [f]Tyre sent messengers to David, and cedar trees, and carpenters, and masons for walls: and they built David an house. **12** Then David knew that the Lord had established him King over Israel, and that he had exalted his kingdom for his people Israel's sake. **13** And David took him more [5]concubines and wives out of Jerusalem, after he was come from Hebron, and more sons and daughters were born to David. **14** [6]And these be the names of the sons, that were born unto him in Jerusalem, Shammua, and Shobab, and Nathan, and Solomon, **15** And Ibhar, and Elishua, and Nepheg, and Japhia, **16** And Elishama, and Eliada, and Eliphelet. **17** [7]But when the Philistines heard that they had anointed David king over Israel, all the Philistines came up to seek David: and when David heard, he went down to a fort. **18** But the Philistines came, and spread themselves in the valley of Rephaim. **19** Then David [g]asked counsel of the Lord, saying, Shall I go up to the Philistines? wilt thou deliver them into mine hands? And the Lord answered David, Go up: for I will doubtless deliver the Philistines into thine hands. **20** [8]Then David came to Baal Perazim, and smote them there, and said, The Lord hath divided mine enemies asunder before me, as waters be divided asunder: therefore he called the name of that place, [h]Baal Perazim. **21** And there they left their images, and David and his men [9]burnt them. **22** Again the Philistines came up, and spread themselves in the valley of [i]Rephaim. **23** And when David asked counsel of the Lord, he answered, Thou shalt not go up, but turn about behind them, and come upon them over against the mulberry trees. **24** And when thou hearest the noise of one going in the tops of the mulberry trees, then remove: for then shall the Lord go out before thee to smite the host of the Philistines. **25** Then David did so as the Lord had commanded him, and smote the Philistines from Geba, until thou come to [j]Gezer.

6

3 The Ark is brought forth of the house of Abinadab. 7 Uzzah is stricken, and dieth. 14 David danceth before it, 16 and is therefore despised of his wife Michal.

1 Again David gathered together all the [a]chosen men of Israel, even thirty thousand **2** [1]And David arose, and went with all the people that were with him from [b]Baale of Judah, to bring up from thence the Ark of God, whose Name is called by the Name of the Lord of hosts, that dwelleth upon it between the Cherubims. **3** And they put the Ark of God upon a new cart, and brought it out of the house of Abinadab, that was in [c]Gibeah. And Uzzah and Ahio the sons of Abinadab did drive the new cart. **4** And when they brought the Ark of God out of the house of [2]Abinadab, that was at Gibeah, Ahio went before the Ark. **5** And David and all the house of Israel [d]played before the Lord on all instruments made of fir, and on harps, and on Psalteries, and on timbrels, and on cornets, and on cymbals. **6** [3]And when they came to Nachon's threshing floor, Uzzah put his hand to the Ark of God, and held it: for the oxen did shake it. **7** And the Lord was very wroth with Uzzah, and God [e]smote him in the same place for his fault, and there he died by the Ark of God. **8** And David was displeased because the Lord had [f]smitten Uzzah: and he called the name of the place [g]Perez Uzzah until this day. **9** Therefore David that day feared the Lord, and said, How shall the Ark of the Lord come to me? **10** So David would not bring the Ark of the Lord unto him into the city of David, but David carried it into the house of Obed-Edom [h]a Gittite. **11** And the Ark of the Lord continued in the house of Obed-Edom the Gittite, three months, and the Lord blessed Obed-Edom, and all his household. **12** And one told King David, saying, [4]The Lord hath blessed the house of Obed-Edom, and all that he hath, because of the Ark of God: therefore David went and [i]brought the Ark of God from the house of Obed-Edom, into the city of David with gladness. **13** And when they that bare the Ark of the Lord had gone six paces, he offered an ox, and a fat beast. **14** And David danced before the Lord with all his might, and was girded with a linen [j]Ephod. **15** So David and all the house of Israel brought the Ark of the Lord with shouting, and sound of trumpet. **16** And as the Ark of the Lord came into the city of David, Michal Saul's daughter looked through a window, and saw King David leap, and dance before the Lord, and she [k]despised him in her heart. **17** And when they had brought in the Ark of the Lord, they set it in his place, in the midst of the Tabernacle that David had pitched for it: then David offered burnt offerings, and peace offerings before the Lord. **18** And as soon as David had made an end of offering burnt offerings and peace offerings, he [5]blessed the people in the Name of the Lord of hosts, **19** And gave among all the people, even among the whole multitude of Israel, as well to the women as men, to every one a cake of bread, and a piece of flesh, and a bottle of wine: so all the people departed every one to his house. **20** Then David returned to [l]bless his house, and Michal the daughter of Saul came out to meet David, and said, O how glorious was the King of Israel this day, which was uncovered today in the eyes of the maidens of his servants, as a [m]fool uncovereth himself! **21** Then David said unto Michal, [n]It was before the Lord, which chose me rather than thy father, and all his house, and commanded me to be ruler over the people of the Lord, even over Israel: and therefore will I play before the Lord, **22** And will yet be more vile than thus, and will be low in mine own sight, and of the very same maidservants, which thou hast spoken of, shall I be had in honor. **23** Therefore Michal the daughter of Saul had [o]no child unto the day of her death.

7

2 David would build God an house, but is forbidden by the Prophet Nathan. 8 God putteth David in mind of his benefits. 12 He promiseth continuance of his kingdom and posterity.

1 Afterward [1]when the King sat in his house, and the Lord had given him rest round about from all his enemies, **2** The King said unto Nathan the Prophet, Behold, now I dwell in an house of cedar trees, and the Ark of God remaineth within the [a]curtains. **3** Then Nathan said unto the king, Go, and do all that is in thine heart: for the Lord is with thee. **4** And the same night the word of the Lord came unto Nathan, saying, **5** Go and tell my servant David, Thus saith the Lord, [b]Shalt thou build me an house for my dwelling? **6** For I have dwelt in no house since the time that I brought the children of Israel out of Egypt unto this day, but have walked in a tent and Tabernacle. **7** In all the places wherein I have walked with all the children of Israel, spake I one [c]word with any of the tribes of Israel when I commanded the Judges to feed my people Israel? or said I, Why build ye not me an house of cedar trees? **8** Now therefore so say unto my servant David, Thus saith the Lord of hosts, [2]I took thee from the sheepcote following the sheep,

---

2-SAM. 5

- **a.** 2 Sam. 5:1 We are of thy kindred, and most near joined unto thee.
- **b.** 2 Sam. 5:3 That is, taking the Lord to witness: for the Ark was as yet in Abinadab's house.
- **c.** 2 Sam. 5:6 The children of God called idols blind and lame guides: therefore the Jebusites meant that they should prove that their gods were neither blind nor lame.
- **d.** 2 Sam. 5:8 The idols should enter no more into that place.
- **e.** 2 Sam. 5:9 He built from the town house round about to his own house, 1 Chron. 11:8.
- **f.** 2 Sam. 5:11 Hebrew, Zor.
- **g.** 2 Sam. 5:19 By Abiathar the Priest.
- **h.** 2 Sam. 5:20 Or, the plain of divisions.
- **i.** 2 Sam. 5:22 Meaning, the valley of giants, which David called Baal Perazim, because of his victory.
- **j.** 2 Sam. 5:25 Which was in the tribe of Benjamin, but the Philistines did possess it.

2-SAM. 5

1. 1 Chron. 11:1
2. Ps. 78:71
3. 2 Sam. 2:11
4. 2 Chron. 11:6
5. 1 Chron. 3:9
6. 1 Chron. 3:5
7. 1 Chron. 14:8 / 1 Chron. 11:16
8. Isa. 28:20
9. 1 Chron. 14:12

2-SAM. 6

- **a.** 2 Sam. 6:1 Or, chief.
- **b.** 2 Sam. 6:2 This was a city in Judah called also Kirjath Jearim, Josh. 15:9.
- **c.** 2 Sam. 6:3 Which was an high place of the city of Baal.
- **d.** 2 Sam. 6:5 Praised God, and sang Psalms.
- **e.** 2 Sam. 6:7 Here we see what danger it is to follow good intentions, or to do anything in God's service without his express word.
- **f.** 2 Sam. 6:8 Hebrew, made a breach.
- **g.** 2 Sam. 6:8 Or, the division of Uzzah.
- **h.** 2 Sam. 6:10 Who was a Levite, and had dwelt in Gittaim, 1 Chron. 15:25.
- **i.** 2 Sam. 6:12 Meaning, he caused the Levites to bear it, according to the Law.
- **j.** 2 Sam. 6:14 With a garment like to the Priest's garment.
- **k.** 2 Sam. 6:16 The worldlings are not able to comprehend the emotions that move the children of God to praise God by all manner of means.
- **l.** 2 Sam. 6:20 That is, to pray for his house, as he had done for the people.
- **m.** 2 Sam. 6:20 Or, vain man.
- **n.** 2 Sam. 6:21 It was for no worldly affection, but only for that zeal that I bare to God's glory.
- **o.** 2 Sam. 6:23 Which was a punishment because she mocked the servant of God.

2-SAM. 6

1. 1 Chron. 13:5,6
2. 1 Sam. 7:1
3. 1 Chron. 13:10
4. 1 Chron. 15:25
5. 1 Chron. 16:2

2-SAM. 7

- **a.** 2 Sam. 7:2 Within the Tabernacle covered with skins, Exod. 26:7.
- **b.** 2 Sam. 7:5 Meaning, he should not: yet Nathan speaking according to man's judgment and not by the spirit of prophecy, permitted him.
- **c.** 2 Sam. 7:7 As concerning building of an house: meaning, that without God's express word, nothing ought to be attempted.

that thou mightest be ruler over my people, over Israel. **9** And I was with thee
wheresoever thou hast walked, and have destroyed all thine enemies out of thy si-
ght, and have made thee a [d]great name, like unto the name of the great men that
are in the earth. **10** (Also I will appoint a place for my people Israel, and will
plant it, that they may dwell in a place of their own, and move [e]no more, neither
shall wicked people trouble them anymore as beforetime, **11** And since the time
that I set Judges over my people of Israel) and I will give thee rest from all thine
enemies: also the Lord telleth thee, that he will make thee an house. **12** [3]And
when thy days be fulfilled, thou shalt sleep with thy fathers, and I will set up thy
seed after thee, which shall proceed out of thy body, and will establish his king-
dom. **13** [4]He shall build an house for my Name, and I will establish the throne
of his kingdom forever. **14** [5]I will be his father, and he shall be my son: and if
he [6]sin, I will chasten him with the [f]rod of men, and with the plagues of the chil-
dren of men. **15** But my mercy shall not depart away from him, as I took it from
Saul whom I have put away before thee. **16** And thine house shall be established
and thy kingdom forever before thee, even thy throne shall be [g]established fore-
ver. **17** According to all these words, and according to all this vision, Nathan
spake thus unto David. **18** Then King David went in, and sat before the Lord,
and said, Who am I, O Lord God, and what is mine house, that thou hast brou-
ght me hitherto? **19** And this was yet a small thing in thy sight, O Lord God,
therefore thou hast spoken also of thy servant's house for a great while: but [h]doth
this appertain to [i]man, O Lord God? **20** And what can David say more unto
thee? for thou, Lord God, knowest thy servant. **21** For thy word's sake, and
according to thine own heart hast thou done all these great things, to make them
known unto thy servant. **22** Wherefore thou art great, O Lord God: for there is
none like thee, neither is there any God besides thee, according to all that we have
heard with our ears. **23** [7]And what one people in the earth is like thy people,
like Israel? whose God went and redeemed them to himself, that they might be
his people, and that he might make him a name, and do for [j]you great things, and
terrible for [k]thy land, O Lord, even for thy people, whom thou redeemedst to thee
out of Egypt, from the [l]nations, and their gods? **24** For thou hast [m]ordained to
thyself thy people Israel to be thy people forever: and thou Lord art become their
God. **25** Now therefore, O Lord God, confirm forever the word that thou hast
spoken concerning thy servant and his house, and do as thou hast said. **26** And
let thy Name be magnified forever by them that shall say, The Lord of hosts is
the God over Israel, and let the [n]house of thy servant David be established before
thee. **27** For thou, O Lord of hosts, God of Israel, hast revealed unto thy servant,
saying, I will build thee an house: therefore hath thy servant [o]been bold to pray this
prayer unto thee. **28** Therefore now, O Lord God, (for thou art God, and thy
words be true, and thou hast told this goodness unto thy servant.) **29** Therefore
now let it please thee to bless the house of thy servant, that it may continue forever
before thee: for thou, O Lord God, hast [p]spoken it: and let the house of thy servant
be blessed forever with thy blessing.

8

1 David overcometh the Philistines, and other strange nations, and maketh them tributaries to Israel.

1 After [1]this now, David smote the Philistines and subdued them, and David
took [a]the bridle of bondage out of the [b]hand of the Philistines. **2** And he smote
Moab, and measured them with a cord, and cast them down to the ground: he me-
asured them with [c]two cords to put them to death, and with one full cord to keep
them alive: so became the Moabites David's servants, and brought gifts. **3** David
smote also Hadadezer the son of Rehob king of Zobah, as he went to [d]recover his
border at the river [e]Euphrates. **4** And David took of them a thousand and seven
hundred horsemen, and twenty thousand footmen, and David [f]destroyed all the
chariots, but he reserved an hundred chariots of them. **5** Then came the [g]Ara-
mites of [h]Dammesek to succor Hadadezer king of Zobah, but David slew of the
Aramites two and twenty thousand men. **6** And David put a garrison in [i]Aram
of Dammesek: and the Aramites became servants to David, [j]and brought gifts.
And the Lord saved David wheresoever he went. **7** And David took the shields
of gold that belonged to the servants of Hadadezer, and brought them to [k]Jerusa-
lem. **8** And out of Betah, and Berothai (cities of Hadadezer) king David brou-
ght exceedingly much brass. **9** Then Toi king of [l]Hamath heard how David had
smitten all the host of Hadadezer, **10** Therefore Toi sent Joram his son unto king
David, [m]to salute him, and to [n],[o]rejoice with him, because he had fought against
Hadadezer, and beaten him (for Hadadezer had war with Toi) who [p]brought with
him vessels of silver, and vessels of gold, and vessels of brass. **11** And king Da-
vid dedicated them unto the Lord with the silver and gold that he had dedicated
of all the nations, which he had subdued: **12** Of [q]Aram, and of Moab, and of
the children of Ammon, and of the Philistines, and of Amalek, and of the spoil of
Hadadezer the son of Rehob king of Zobah. **13** So David got a name after that
he returned, and had slain of the Aramites in the [r]valley of salt eighteen thousand
men. **14** And he put a garrison in Edom: throughout all Edom put he soldiers,
and all they of Edom became David's servants: and the Lord kept David [s]whither-
soever he went. **15** Thus David reigned over all Israel, and executed [t]judgment
and justice unto all his people. **16** And Joab the son of Zeruiah was over the
host, and Jehoshaphat the son of Ahilud was [u]Recorder. **17** And Zadok the son
of Ahitub, and Ahimelech the son of Abiathar were the Priests, and Seraiah the
Scribe. **18** And Benaiah the son of Jehoiada [v]and the [w]Cherethites and the Pe-
lethites, and David's sons were chief rulers.

9

9 David restoreth all the lands of Saul's to Mephibosheth the son of Jonathan. 10 He appointeth Ziba to see to the profit of his lands.

1 And David said, Is there yet any man left of the house of Saul, that I may
show him mercy for [a]Jonathan's sake? **2** And there was of the household of Saul a
servant whose name was Ziba, and when they had called him unto David, the king
said unto him, Art thou Ziba? And he said, I thy servant am he. **3** Then the King
said, Remaineth there yet none of the house of Saul, on whom I may show the
[b]mercy of God? Ziba then answered the King, Jonathan hath yet a son [1]lame of his
feet. **4** Then the King said unto him, Where is he? And Ziba said unto the king,
Behold, he is in the house of Machir the son of Ammiel of Lo Debar. **5** Then
king David sent, and took him out of the house of Machir the son of [c]Ammiel of
Lo Debar. **6** Now when Mephibosheth the son of Jonathan the son of Saul was
come unto David, he fell on his face, and did reverence. And David said, Mephi-
bosheth? And he answered, Behold thy servant. **7** Then David said unto him,
Fear not: for I will surely show thee kindness for Jonathan thy father's sake, and will
restore thee all the [d]fields of Saul thy father, and thou shalt eat bread at my table
continually. **8** And he bowed himself, and said, What is thy servant, that thou
shouldest look upon such a [e]dead dog as I am? **9** Then the king called Ziba Saul's
servant, and said unto him, I have given unto thy master's [f]son all that pertained to
Saul and to all his house. **10** Thou therefore and [g]thy sons and thy servants shall
till the land for him, and bring in that thy master's son may have food to eat. And
Mephibosheth thy master's son shall eat bread always at my table (now Ziba had fi-
fteen sons, and twenty servants.) **11** Then said Ziba unto the king, According to
all that my lord the king hath commanded his servant, so shall thy servant do, [h]that
Mephibosheth may eat at my table, as one of the king's sons. **12** Mephibosheth
also had a young son named Micha, and all that dwelled in the house of Ziba, were
servants unto Mephibosheth. **13** And Mephibosheth dwelt in Jerusalem: for he
did eat continually at the king's table, and was lame on both his feet.

10

4 The messengers of David are villainously entreated of the king of Ammon. 7 Joab is sent against the Ammonites.

1 After this, the [1]King of the children of Ammon died, and Hanun his son rei-
gned in his stead. **2** Then said David, I will show kindness unto Hanun the son

---

d. 2 Sam. 7:9 I have made thee famous through all the world.
e. 2 Sam. 7:10 He promiseth them quietness, if they will walk in his fear and obedience.
f. 2 Sam. 7:14 That is, gently, as fathers used to chastise their children.
g. 2 Sam. 7:16 This was begun in Solomon, as a figure, but accomplished in Christ.
h. 2 Sam. 7:19 Hebrew, is this the law of man?
i. 2 Sam. 7:19 Cometh not this rather of thy free mercy, than of any worthiness that can be in man?
j. 2 Sam. 7:23 O Israel.
k. 2 Sam. 7:23 And inheritance, which is Israel.
l. 2 Sam. 7:23 From the Egyptians and their idols.
m. 2 Sam. 7:24 He showeth that God's free election is the only cause, why the Israelites were chosen to be his people.
n. 2 Sam. 7:26 This prayer is most effectual, when we chiefly seek God's glory, and the accomplishment of his promise.
o. 2 Sam. 7:27 Hebrew, found his heart disposed.
p. 2 Sam. 7:29 Therefore I firmly believe it shall come to pass.

2-SAM. 7
1. 1 Chron. 17:2
2. 1 Sam. 16:12 / Ps. 78:70
3. 1 Kings 8:20
4. 1 Kings 5:5 / 1 Kings 6:12 / 1 Chron. 22:10
5. Heb. 1:5
6. Ps. 89:31,32
7. Deut. 4:7

2-SAM. 8
a. 2 Sam. 8:1 Or, Metheg Ammah.
b. 2 Sam. 8:1 So that they paid no more tribute.
c. 2 Sam. 8:2 He slew two parts as it pleased him, and reserved the third.
d. 2 Sam. 8:3 Or, enlarge.
e. 2 Sam. 8:3 Hebrew, Perath.
f. 2 Sam. 8:4 Or, bought the horses of the chariots.
g. 2 Sam. 8:5 Or, the Syrians.
h. 2 Sam. 8:5 Or, of Damascus, that is, which dwelt near Damascus.
i. 2 Sam. 8:6 In that part of Syria, where Damascus was.
j. 2 Sam. 8:6 They paid yearly tribute.
k. 2 Sam. 8:7 For the use of the Temple.
l. 2 Sam. 8:9 Or, Antiochia.
m. 2 Sam. 8:10 Hebrew, to ask peace.
n. 2 Sam. 8:10 Hebrew, bless him.
o. 2 Sam. 8:10 For seeing David victorious, he was glad to entreat of peace.
p. 2 Sam. 8:10 Hebrew, in his hand.
q. 2 Sam. 8:12 Or, Syria, or Cœlosyria.
r. 2 Sam. 8:13 Or, in Gemelah.
s. 2 Sam. 8:14 Or, in all his enterprises.
t. 2 Sam. 8:15 He gave judgment in controversies, and was merciful toward the people.
u. 2 Sam. 8:16 Or, writer of Chronicles.
v. 2 Sam. 8:18 Or, was over the Cherethites.
w. 2 Sam. 8:18 The Cherethites and Pelethites were as the king's guard, and had charge of his person.

2-SAM. 8
1. 1 Chron. 18:1 / Ps. 60:2

2-SAM. 9
a. 2 Sam. 9:1 Because of mine oath and promise made to Jonathan, 1 Sam. 10:15.
b. 2 Sam. 9:3 Such mercy as shall be acceptable to God.
c. 2 Sam. 9:5 Who was also called Eliam the father of Bathsheba David's wife.
d. 2 Sam. 9:7 Or, lands.
e. 2 Sam. 9:8 Meaning, a despised person.
f. 2 Sam. 9:9 Or, nephew.
g. 2 Sam. 9:10 Be ye provident overseers and governors of his lands, that they may be profitable.
h. 2 Sam. 9:11 That Mephibosheth may have all things at commandment, as becometh a king's son.

2-SAM. 9
1. 2 Sam. 4:4

of Nahash, as his father [a]showed kindness unto me. And David sent his servants to
comfort him for his father. So David's servants came into the land of the children
of Ammon. **3** And the princes of the children of Ammon said unto Hanun their
lord, [b]Thinkest thou that David doth honor thy father, that he hath sent comfor-
ters to thee? hath not David rather sent his servants unto thee, [c]to search the city,
and to spy it out, and to overthrow it? **4** Wherefore Hanun took David's servan-
ts, and shaved off the half of their beard, and cut off their garments in the middle,
even to their buttocks, and sent them away. **5** When it was told unto David, he
sent to meet them (for the men were exceedingly ashamed) and the king said, Tarry
at Jericho, until your beards be grown, then return. **6** And when the children of
Ammon saw that they [d]stank in the sight of David, the children of Ammon sent
and hired the [e]Aramites of the house of Rehob, and the Aramites of Zoba, twenty
thousand footmen, and of king Maacah a thousand men, and of Ish-Tob twelve
thousand men. **7** And when David heard of it, he sent Joab, and all the host of
the strong men. **8** And the children of Ammon came out and put their army in
array at the entering in of the gate: and the Aramites of [f]Zoba, and of Rehob, and
of Ish-Tob, and of Maacah were by themselves in the field. **9** When Joab saw
that the front of the battle was against him before and behind, he chose of all the
choice of Israel, and put them in array against the Aramites. **10** And the rest of
the people, he delivered into the hand of Abishai his brother, that he might put
them in array against the children of Ammon. **11** And he said, If the Aramites
be stronger than I, thou shalt help me, and if the children of Ammon be too strong
for thee, I will come and succor thee. **12** Be strong and let us be valiant for [g]our
people, and for the cities of our God, and let the Lord do that which is good in
his eyes. **13** Then Joab, and the people that was with him, joined in battle with
the Aramites, who fled before him. **14** And when the children of Ammon saw
that the Aramites fled, they fled also before Abishai, and entered into the city. So
Joab returned from the children of Ammon, and came to Jerusalem. **15** And
when the Aramites saw that they were smitten before Israel, they gathered them to-
gether. **16** And [h]Hadarezer sent, and brought out the Aramites that were beyond
the [i]River: and they came to Helam, and Shobach the captain of the host of Ha-
dadezer went before them. **17** When it was showed David, then he gathered [j]all
Israel together, and passed over Jordan, and came to Helam: and the Aramites set
themselves in array against David, and fought with him: **18** And the Aramites
fled before Israel: and David destroyed [k]seven hundred chariots of the Aramites,
and forty thousand horsemen, and smote Shobach the captain of his host, who
died there. **19** And when all the kings, that were servants to Hadadezer, saw that
they fell before Israel, they made peace with Israel, and served them. and the Ara-
mites feared to help the children of Ammon anymore.

11

1 The city Rabbah is besieged. 4 David committeth adultery. 17 Uriah is slain. 27 David marrieth Bathsheba.

1 And when the year was [a]expired in the time when kings go forth to battle,
David sent [1]Joab, and his servants with him, and all Israel, who destroyed the chil-
dren of Ammon, and besieged Rabbah: but David remained in Jerusalem. **2** And
when it was evening-tide, David arose out of his [b]bed, and walked upon the roof
of the king's palace: and from the roof he saw a woman washing herself: and the
woman was very beautiful to look upon. **3** And David sent and inquired what
woman it was: and one said, Is not this Bathsheba the daughter of Eliam, wife to
Uriah the [c]Hittite? **4** Then David sent messengers, and took her away: and she
came unto him and he lay with her: (now she was [2]purified from her uncleanness)
and she returned unto her house. **5** And the woman conceived: therefore she
sent and [d]told David, and said, I am with child. **6** Then David sent to Joab,
saying, Send me Uriah the Hittite. And Joab sent Uriah to David. **7** And when
Uriah came unto him, David demanded him how Joab did, and how the people
fared, and how the war prospered. **8** Afterward David said to Uriah, [e]Go down
to thine house, and wash thy feet. So Uriah departed out of the king's palace, and
the king sent a present after him. **9** But Uriah slept at the door of the king's pa-
lace with all the servants of his lord, and went not down to his house. **10** Then
they told David, saying, Uriah went not down to his house: and David said unto
Uriah, Comest thou not from thy journey? why didst thou not go down to thine
house? **11** Then Uriah answered David, [f]The Ark and Israel, and Judah dwell
in tents: and my lord Joab and the servants of my lord abide in the open fields:
shall I then go into mine house to eat and drink, and lie with my wife? by thy
life, and by the life of thy soul, I will not do this thing. **12** Then David said
unto Uriah, Tarry yet this day, and tomorrow I will send thee away. So Uriah abo-
de in Jerusalem that day, and the morrow. **13** Then David called him, and he
did eat and drink before him, and he made him [g]drunk: and at even he went out
to lie on his couch with the servants of his lord, but went not down to his hou-
se. **14** And on the morrow David wrote a letter to Joab, and sent it by the hand
of Uriah. **15** And he wrote [h]thus in the letter, [i]Put ye Uriah in the forefront of
the strength of the battle, and recule ye back from him, that he may be smitten,
and die. **16** So when Joab besieged the city, he assigned Uriah unto a place, whe-
re he knew that strong men were. **17** And the men of the city came out, and fou-
ght with Joab: and there fell of the people of the servants of David, and Uriah the
Hittite also died. **18** Then Joab sent and told David all the things concerning the
war. **19** And he charged the messenger, saying, When thou hast made an end of
telling all the matters of the war unto the King, **20** [j]And if the king's anger arise,
so that he say unto thee, Wherefore approached ye unto the city to fight? knew ye
not that they would hurl from the wall? **21** Who smote Abimelech son of [k]Je-
rubbesheth? did not a woman cast a piece of a millstone upon him from the wall,
and he died in Thebez? why went you nigh the wall? Then say thou, Thy servant
Uriah the Hittite is also dead. **22** So the messenger went, and came and showed
David all that Joab had sent him for. **23** And the messenger said unto David,
Certainly the men prevailed against us, and came out unto us into the field, but we
[l]pursued them unto the entering of the gate. **24** But the shooters shot from the
wall against thy servants, and some of the king's servants be dead: and thy servant
Uriah the Hittite is also dead. **25** Then David said unto the messenger, [m]Thus
shalt thou say unto Joab, Let not this thing trouble thee: for the sword devoureth
[n]one as well as another: make thy battle more strong against the city, and destroy
it, and encourage thou him. **26** And when the wife of Uriah heard that her hu-
sband Uriah was dead, she mourned for her husband. **27** So when the mourning
was past, David sent and took her into his house, and she became his wife, and bare
him a son: but the thing that David had done, [o]displeased the Lord.

12

1 David reproved by Nathan, confesseth his sin. 18 The child conceived in adultery, dieth. 24 Solomon is born. 30 Rabbah is taken. 31 The citizens are grievously punished.

1 Then the Lord sent [a]Nathan unto David, who came to him, and said unto
him, There were two men in one city, the one rich, and the other poor. **2** The
rich man had exceedingly many sheep and oxen: **3** But the poor had none at all,
save one little sheep which he had bought and nourished up: and it grew up with
him, and with his children also, and did eat of his own morsels, and drank of his
own cup, and slept in his bosom, and was unto him as his daughter. **4** Now there
came a [b]stranger unto the rich man, who [c]refused to take of his own sheep, and of
his own oxen to dress for the stranger that was come unto him, but took the poor
man's sheep, and dressed it for the man that was come to him. **5** Then [d]David
was exceedingly wroth with the man, and said to Nathan, As the Lord liveth, the
man that hath done this thing, [e]shall surely die, **6** And he shall restore the lamb
[1]fourfold, because he did this thing, and had no pity thereof. **7** Then Nathan
said to David, Thou art the man. Thus saith the Lord God of Israel, I [2]anointed
thee King over Israel, and delivered thee out of the hand of Saul. **8** And gave
thee thy lord's [f]house, and thy lord's [g]wives into thy bosom, and gave thee the
house of Israel, and of Judah, and would moreover (if that had been too little)

2-SAM. 10

- **a.** 2 Sam. 10:2 The children of God are not unmindful of a benefit received.
- **b.** 2 Sam. 10:3 Hebrew, in thine eyes doth David.
- **c.** 2 Sam. 10:3 Their arrogant malice would not suffer them to see the simplicity of David's heart: therefore their counsel turned to the destruction of their country.
- **d.** 2 Sam. 10:6 That they had deserved David's displeasure, for the injury done to his ambassadors.
- **e.** 2 Sam. 10:6 Or, Syrians.
- **f.** 2 Sam. 10:8 These were divers parts of the country of Syria, whereby appeareth that the Syrians served where they might have entertainment, as now the Sweitzers do.
- **g.** 2 Sam. 10:12 Here is declared wherefore war ought to be undertaken: of the defense of true religion and God's people.
- **h.** 2 Sam. 10:16 Or, Hadarezer.
- **i.** 2 Sam. 10:16 Or, Euphrates.
- **j.** 2 Sam. 10:17 Meaning, the greatest part.
- **k.** 2 Sam. 10:18 Which were the chiefest and most principal: for in all he destroyed 7000, as 1 Chron. 19:18, or the soldiers which were in 700 chariots.

2-SAM. 10

- **1.** 1 Chron. 19:2

2-SAM. 11

- **a.** 2 Sam. 11:1 The year following about the spring time.
- **b.** 2 Sam. 11:2 Whereupon he used to rest at afternoon, as was read of Ishbosheth, 2 Sam. 4:7
- **c.** 2 Sam. 11:3 Who was not an Israelite born, but converted to the true religion.
- **d.** 2 Sam. 11:5 Fearing lest she should be stoned according to the Law.
- **e.** 2 Sam. 11:8 David thought that if Uriah lay with his wife, his fault might be cloaked.
- **f.** 2 Sam. 11:11 Hereby God would touch David's conscience, that seeing the fidelity and religion of his servant, he would declare himself so forgetful of God, and injurious to his servant.
- **g.** 2 Sam. 11:13 He made him drink more liberally than he was wont to do, thinking hereby he would have lain by his wife.
- **h.** 2 Sam. 11:15 Hebrew, saying.
- **i.** 2 Sam. 11:15 Except God continually uphold us with his mighty spirit, the most perfect fall headlong into all vice and abomination.
- **j.** 2 Sam. 11:20 Or, thou shalt do this, if.
- **k.** 2 Sam. 11:21 Meaning, Gideon, Judg. 9:52, 53.
- **l.** 2 Sam. 11:23 Hebrew, were against them.
- **m.** 2 Sam. 11:25 He dissembleth with the messenger, to the intent that neither his cruel commandment, nor Joab's wicked obedience might be espied.
- **n.** 2 Sam. 11:25 Hebrew, so and so.
- **o.** 2 Sam. 11:27 Hebrew, was evil in the eyes of the Lord.

2-SAM. 11

- **1.** 1 Chron. 20:1
- **2.** Lev. 15:1,9 / Lev. 18:19

2-SAM. 12

- **a.** 2 Sam. 12:1 Because David lay now drowned in sin, the loving mercy of God, which suffereth not his to perish, waketh his conscience by this similitude, and bringeth him to repentance.
- **b.** 2 Sam. 12:4 Or, wayfaring man.
- **c.** 2 Sam. 12:4 Or, spared.
- **d.** 2 Sam. 12:5 Hebrew, the anger of David was kindled.
- **e.** 2 Sam. 12:5 Hebrew, is the child of death.
- **f.** 2 Sam. 12:8 For David succeeded Saul in his kingdom.
- **g.** 2 Sam. 12:8 The Jews understand this of Eglah and Michal, or of Rizpah and Michal.

have given thee [h]such and such things. **9** Wherefore hast thou despised the commandment of the Lord, to do evil in his sight? thou hast killed Uriah the Hittite with the sword, and hast taken his wife to be thy wife, and hast slain him with the sword of the [i]children of Ammon. **10** Now therefore the sword shall never depart from thine house, because thou hast despised me, and taken the wife of Uriah the Hittite to be thy wife. **11** Thus said the Lord, Behold, I will raise up evil against thee out of thine own house, and will [3]take thy wives before thine eyes, and give them unto thy neighbor, and he shall lie with thy wives in the sight of his [j]sin. **12** For thou diddest it secretly: but I will do this thing before all Israel, and before the sun. **13** Then David said unto Nathan, I have sinned against the Lord. And Nathan said unto David, The Lord also hath [k]put away thy sin, thou shalt not die. **14** Howbeit, because by this deed thou hast caused the enemies of the Lord to [l]blaspheme, the child that is born unto thee, shall surely die. **15** So Nathan departed unto his house: and the Lord struck the child that Uriah's wife bare unto David, and it was sick. **16** David therefore besought God for the child, and fasted and [m]went in, and lay all night upon the earth. **17** Then the Elders of his house arose to come unto him, and to cause him to rise from the ground: but he would not, neither did he eat [n]meat with them. **18** So on the seventh day the child died: and the servants of David feared to tell him that the child was dead: for they said, Behold, while the child was alive, we spake unto him, and he would not hearken unto our voice: how then shall we say unto him, The child is dead, [o]to vex him more? **19** But when David saw that his servants whispered, David perceived that the child was dead: therefore David said unto his servants, Is the child dead? And they said, He is dead. **20** Then David [p]arose from the earth, and washed and anointed himself, and changed his apparel, and came into the house of the Lord, and worshipped, and afterward came to his own house, and bade that they should set bread before him, and he did eat. **21** Then [q]said his servants unto him, What thing is this that thou hast done? thou didst fast and weep for the child while it was alive, but when the child was dead, thou didst rise up, and eat meat, **22** And he said, While the child was yet alive, I fasted, and wept: for I said, Who can tell whether God will have mercy on me, that the child may live? **23** But now being dead, wherefore should I now fast? [r]Can I bring him again anymore? I shall go to him, but he shall not return to me. **24** And David comforted Bathsheba his wife, and went in unto her, and lay with her, [4]and she bare a son, and [s]he called his name Solomon: also the Lord loved him. **25** For the Lord had sent [t]by Nathan the [u]Prophet: therefore [v,5]he called his name Jedidiah, because the Lord loved him. **26** Then Joab fought against Rabbah of the children of Ammon, and took the [w]city of the Kingdom. **27** Therefore Joab sent messengers to David, saying, I have fought against Rabbah, and have taken the city of [x]waters. **28** Now therefore, gather the rest of the people together, and besiege the city, that thou mayest take it, lest [y]the victory be attributed to me. **29** So David gathered all the people together, and went against Rabbah, and besieged it, and took it. **30** [6]And he took their king's crown from his head, (which weighed a [z]talent of gold, with precious stones) and it was set on David's head: and he brought away the spoil of the city in exceedingly great abundance. **31** And he carried away the people that was therein, and put them under [aa]saws, and under iron harrows, and under axes of iron, and cast them into the tile-kiln: even thus did he with all the cities of the children of Ammon. Then David and all the people returned unto Jerusalem.

13

14 Amnon David's son defileth his sister Tamar. 20 Tamar is comforted by her brother Absalom. 29 Absalom therefore killeth Amnon.

1 Now after this, so it was, that Absalom the son of David having a fair sister, whose name was [a]Tamar, Amnon the son of David loved her. **2** And Amnon was so sore vexed, that he fell sick for his sister Tamar: for she was a [b]virgin, and it seemed hard to Amnon to do anything to her. **3** But Amnon had a friend called Jonadab, the son of Shimeah David's brother: and Jonadab was a very subtle man, **4** Who said unto him, Why art thou the king's son, so lean from day to day? wilt thou not tell me? Then Amnon answered him, I love Tamar my brother Absalom's sister. **5** And Jonadab said unto him, [c]Lie down on thy bed, and make thyself sick: and when thy father shall come to see thee, say unto him, I pray thee let my sister Tamar come, and give me meat, and let her dress meat in my sight, that I may see it, and eat it of her hand. **6** So Amnon lay down, and made himself sick: and when the king came to see him, Amnon said unto the king, I pray thee, let Tamar my sister come, and make me a couple of [d]cakes in my sight, that I may receive meat at her hand. **7** Then David sent home to Tamar, saying, Go now to thy brother Amnon's house, and dress him meat. **8** So Tamar went to her brother Amnon's house, and he lay down: and she took [e]flour, and knead it, and made cakes in his sight, and did bake the cakes. **9** And she took a pan, and [f]poured them out before him, but he would not eat. Then Amnon said, Cause ye every man to go out from [g]me: so every man went out from him. **10** Then Amnon said unto Tamar, Bring the meat into the chamber, that I may eat of thine hand. And Tamar took the cakes which she had made, and brought them into the chamber to Amnon her brother. **11** And when she had set them before him to eat, he took her, and said unto her, Come, lie with me, my sister. **12** But she answered him, Nay, my brother, do not force me: for no such thing [1]ought to be done in Israel: commit not this folly. **13** And I, [h]whither shall I cause my shame to go? and thou shalt be as one of [i]the fools in Israel: now therefore, I pray thee speak to the king, for he will not deny me unto thee. **14** Howbeit he would not hearken unto her voice, but being stronger than she, forced her, and lay with her. **15** Then Amnon hated her exceedingly, so that the hatred wherewith he hated her, was greater than the love wherewith he had loved her: and Amnon said unto her, Up, get thee hence. **16** And she answered him, [j]There is no cause: this evil (to put me away) is greater than the other that thou didst unto me: but he would not hear her, **17** But called his [k]servant that served him, and said, Put this woman now out from me, and lock the door after her. **18** (And she had a garment of [l]diverse colors upon her: for with such garments were the King's daughters that were virgins, appareled) Then his servant brought her out, and locked the door after her. **19** And Tamar put ashes on her head, and rent the garment of diverse colors which was on her, and laid her hand on her head, and went her way crying. **20** And Absalom her brother said unto her, Hath Amnon thy brother been with thee? Now yet be [m]still, my sister: he is thy brother: let not this thing grieve thine heart. So Tamar remained desolate in her brother Absalom's house. **21** But when King David heard all these things, he was very wroth. **22** And Absalom said unto his brother Amnon neither good nor bad: for Absalom hated Amnon, because he had forced his sister Tamar. **23** And after the time of two years, Absalom had sheepshearers in [n]Baal Hazor, which is beside Ephraim, and [o]Absalom called all the king's sons. **24** And Absalom came to the King, and said, Behold now, thy servant hath sheepshearers: I pray thee, that the king with his servants would go with thy servant. **25** But the King answered Absalom, Nay my son, I pray thee, let us not go all, lest we be chargeable unto thee. Yet Absalom lay sore upon him: howbeit he would not go, but [p]thanked him. **26** Then said Absalom, But, I pray thee, shall not my brother [q]Amnon go with us? And the king answered him, Why should he go with thee? **27** But Absalom was instant upon him, and he sent Amnon with him, and all the king's children. **28** Now had Absalom commanded his servants, saying, Mark now when Amnon's heart is merry with wine, and when I say unto you, Smite Amnon, kill him, fear not, for have not [r]I commanded you? be bold therefore, and play the men. **29** And the servants of Absalom did unto Amnon, as Absalom had commanded: and all the king's sons arose, and every man got him up upon his mule, and fled. **30** And while they were in the way, tidings came to David, saying, Absalom hath slain all the King's sons, and there is not one of them left. **31** Then the king arose, and tore his garments, and lay on the [s]ground, and all his servants stood by with their clothes rent. **32** And Jonadab the son of Shimeah David's brother answered and said, Let not my lord suppose that they have slain all the young men the King's sons: for Amnon only is dead, [t]because Absalom had reported so, since he forced his sister Tamar. **33** Now therefore let not my lord the King [u]take the thing so grievously;

---

h. 2 Sam. 12:8 That is, greater things than these: for God's love and benefits increase toward his, if by their ingratitude they stay him not.
i. 2 Sam. 12:9 Thou hast most cruelly given him into the hands of God's enemies.
j. 2 Sam. 12:11 Meaning, openly, as at noon-days.
k. 2 Sam. 12:13 For the Lord seeketh but that the sinner would turn to him.
l. 2 Sam. 12:14 In saying, that the Lord hath appointed a wicked man to reign over his people.
m. 2 Sam. 12:16 To wit, to his privy chamber.
n. 2 Sam. 12:17 Thinking by his instant prayer that God would have restored his child, but God hath otherwise determined.
o. 2 Sam. 12:18 Hebrew, and he will do himself evil.
p. 2 Sam. 12:20 Showing that our lamentations ought not to be excessive, but moderate: and that we must praise God in all his doings.
q. 2 Sam. 12:21 As they which considered not that God granteth many things to the sobs and tears of the faithful.
r. 2 Sam. 12:23 By this consideration he appeased his sorrow.
s. 2 Sam. 12:24 To wit, the Lord, 1 Chron. 22:9.
t. 2 Sam. 12:25 Hebrew, by the hand of.
u. 2 Sam. 12:25 To call him Solomon.
v. 2 Sam. 12:25 Meaning, David.
w. 2 Sam. 12:26 Or the chief city.
x. 2 Sam. 12:27 That is, the chief city and where all the conduits are, is as good as taken.
y. 2 Sam. 12:28 Hebrew, my name be called upon it.
z. 2 Sam. 12:30 That is: threescore pounds after the weight of the common talent.
aa. 2 Sam. 12:31 Signifying that as they were malicious enemies of God, so he put them to cruel death.

2-SAM. 12

1. Exod. 22:1
2. 1 Sam. 16:13
3. Deut. 28:30 / 2 Sam. 16:22
4. Matt. 1:6
5. 1 Chron. 22:9
6. 1 Chron. 20:2

2-SAM. 13

a. 2 Sam. 13:1 Tamar was Absalom's sister both by father and mother, and Amnon's only by father.
b. 2 Sam. 13:2 And therefore kept in her father's house, as virgins were accustomed.
c. 2 Sam. 13:5 Here we see that there is no enterprise so wicked that can lack counsel to further it.
d. 2 Sam. 13:6 Meaning, some delicate and dainty meat.
e. 2 Sam. 13:8 Or, past.
f. 2 Sam. 13:9 That is, she served them on a dish.
g. 2 Sam. 13:9 For the wicked are ashamed to do that before men, which they are not afraid to commit in the sight of God.
h. 2 Sam. 13:13 Or, how shall I put away my shame?
i. 2 Sam. 13:13 As a lewd and wicked person.
j. 2 Sam. 13:16 Or, for this cause.
k. 2 Sam. 13:17 Or, boy.
l. 2 Sam. 13:18 For that which was of divers colors or pieces, in those days was had in great estimation, Gen. 37:3; Judg. 5:30.
m. 2 Sam. 13:20 For though he conceived sudden vengeance in his heart, yet he dissembled it till occasion served, and comforted his sister.
n. 2 Sam. 13:23 Or, in the plain of Hazor.
o. 2 Sam. 13:23 To wit, to a banquet, thinking thereby to fulfill his wicked purpose.
p. 2 Sam. 13:25 Hebrew, blessed.
q. 2 Sam. 13:26 Pretending to the king that Amnon was most dear unto him.
r. 2 Sam. 13:28 Such is the pride of the wicked masters, that in all their wicked commandments they think to be obeyed.
s. 2 Sam. 13:31 Lamenting, as he that felt the wrath of God upon his house, 2 Sam. 12:10.
t. 2 Sam. 13:32 Hebrew, because it was put in Absalom's mouth.

to think that all the King's sons are dead: [v]for Amnon only is dead. **34** Then Absalom fled: and the young man that kept the watch, lift up his eyes, and looked, and behold, there came much people by the way of the hill side [w]behind him. **35** And Jonadab said unto the king, Behold, the king's sons come: as thy servant said, [x]so it is. **36** And as soon as he had left speaking, behold, the king's sons came, and lift up their voices, and wept: and the king also and all his servants wept exceedingly sore. **37** But Absalom fled away, and went to [y]Talmai the son of Ammihud king of Geshur: and David mourned for his son every day. **38** So Absalom fled, and went to Geshur, and was there three years. **39** And king David [z]desired to go forth unto Absalom, because he was pacified concerning Amnon, seeing he was dead.

14

2 Absalom is reconciled to his father by the subtlety of Joab. 24 Absalom may not see the King's face. 25 The beauty of Absalom. 30 He causeth Joab's corn to be burnt, and is brought to his father's presence.

1 Then Joab the son of Zeruiah perceived, that the king's [a]heart was toward Absalom, **2** And Joab sent to Tekoa, and brought thence a [b]subtle woman, and said unto her, I pray thee, feign thyself to mourn, and now put on mourning apparel, and [c]anoint not thyself with oil: but be as a woman that had now long time mourned for the dead. **3** And come to the king, and speak on this manner unto him, (for Joab [d]taught her what she should say). **4** Then the woman of Tekoa spake unto the king, and fell down on her face to the ground, and did obeisance, and said, [e]Help, O King. **5** Then the king said unto her, What aileth thee? And she answered, I am indeed a [f]widow, and mine husband is dead: **6** And thine handmaid had two [g]sons, and they two strove together in the field, (and there was none to part them) so the one smote the other, and slew him. **7** And behold the whole family is risen against thine handmaid, and they said, Deliver him that smote his brother, that we may kill him for the [h]soul of his brother whom he slew, that we may destroy the heir also: so they shall quench my sparkle which is left, and shall not leave to mine husband neither name nor posterity upon the earth. **8** And the king said unto the woman, Go to thine house, and I will give a charge for thee. **9** Then the woman of Tekoa said unto the King, My lord, O King, this [i]trespass be on me, and on my father's house, and the King and his throne be [j]guiltless. **10** And the King said, Bring him to me that speaketh against thee, and he shall touch thee no more. **11** Then said she, I pray thee, let the king [k]remember the Lord thy God, that thou wouldest not suffer many revengers of blood to destroy, lest they slay my son. And he answered, As the Lord liveth, there shall not one hair of thy son fall to the earth. **12** Then the woman said, I pray thee, let thine handmaid speak a word to my lord the King. And he said, Say on. **13** Then the woman said, Wherefore then hast thou [l]thought such a thing against the people of God? or why doth the King, as one which is faulty, speak this thing, that he will not bring again his banished? **14** For we must needs die, and we are as water spilt on the ground, which cannot be gathered up again: neither doth God [m]spare any person, yet doth he appoint [n]means, not to cast out from him, him that is expelled. **15** Now therefore, that I am come to speak of this thing unto my lord the King, the cause is that the people [o]have made me afraid: therefore thine handmaid said, Now will I speak unto the King: it may be that the king will perform the request of his handmaid. **16** For the king will hear, to deliver his handmaid out of the hand of the man that would destroy me, and also my son from the inheritance of God. **17** Therefore thine handmaid said, The word of my lord the king shall now be [p]comfortable: for my lord the King is even as an [q]Angel of God in hearing of good and bad: therefore the Lord thy God be with thee. **18** Then the king answered, and said unto the woman, Hide not from me, I pray thee, the thing that I shall ask thee. And the woman said, Let my lord the king now speak. **19** And the king said, Is not [r]the hand of Joab with thee in all this? Then the woman answered, and said, As thy soul liveth, my lord the King, I will not turn to the right hand nor to the left, from ought that my lord the king hath spoken: for even thy servant Joab bade me, and he put all these words in the mouth of thine handmaid. **20** For to the intent that I [s]should change the form of speech, thy servant Joab hath done this thing: but [t]my lord is wise according to the wisdom of an Angel of God, to understand all things that are in the earth. **21** And the king said unto Joab, Behold now, I have [u]done this thing: go then, and bring the young man Absalom again. **22** And Joab fell to the ground on his face, and bowed himself and [v]thanked the King. Then Joab said, This day thy servant knoweth, that I have found grace in thy sight, my lord the king, in that the king hath fulfilled the request of his servant. **23** And Joab arose, and went to Geshur, and brought Absalom to Jerusalem. **24** And the King said, Let him [w]turn to his own house, and not see my face. So Absalom turned to his own house, and saw not the king's face. **25** Now in all Israel there was none to be so much praised for beauty as Absalom: from the sole of his foot even to the top of his head there was no blemish in him. **26** And when he polled his head, (for at every year's end he polled it: because it was too heavy for him, therefore he polled it) he weighed the hair of his head at two hundred [x]shekels by the king's weight. **27** And Absalom had three sons, and one daughter named Tamar, which was a fair woman to look upon. **28** So Absalom dwelt the space of two years in Jerusalem, and saw not the king's face. **29** Therefore Absalom sent for Joab to send him to the King, but he would not come to him: and when he sent again, he would not come. **30** Therefore he said unto his servants, Behold, Joab hath a [y]field by my place, and hath barley therein: go, and set it [z]on fire: and Absalom's servants set the field on fire. **31** Then Joab arose, and came to Absalom unto his house, and said unto him, Wherefore have thy servants burnt my field with fire? **32** And Absalom answered Joab, Behold, I sent for thee, saying, Come thou hither, and I will send thee to the king for to say, Wherefore am I come from Geshur? It had been better for me to have been there still: now therefore let me see the king's face: and [aa]if there be any trespass in me, let him kill me. **33** Then Joab came to the king, and told him: and he called for Absalom, who came to the king, and bowed himself to the ground on his face before the king, and the king kissed Absalom.

15

2 The practices of Absalom to aspire to the kingdom. 14 David and his flee. 31 David's prayer. 34 Hushai is sent to Absalom to discover his counsel.

1 After this, Absalom [a]prepared him chariots, and horses, and fifty men to [b]run before him. **2** And Absalom rose up early, and stood hard by the entering in of the gate: and every man that had any [c]matter, and came to the king for judgment, him did Absalom call unto him, and said, Of what city art thou? And he answered, Thy servant is of one of the [d]tribes of Israel. **3** Then Absalom said unto him, See, thy matters are good and righteous, but there is no man deputed of the king to hear thee. **4** Absalom said moreover, [e]Oh that I were made Judge in the land, that every man which hath any matter of controversy, might come to me, that I might do him justice. **5** And when any man came near to him, and did him obeisance, he put forth his hand, and took him, and kissed him. **6** And on this manner did Absalom to all Israel, that came to the King for judgment: so Absalom [f]stole the hearts of the men of Israel. **7** And after [g]forty years, Absalom said unto the King, I pray thee, let me go to Hebron, and render my vow which I have vowed unto the Lord. **8** For thy servant vowed a vow when I remained at Geshur, in Aram, saying, If the Lord shall bring me again indeed to Jerusalem, I will [h]serve the Lord. **9** And the King said unto him, Go in peace. So he arose, and went to Hebron. **10** Then Absalom sent spies throughout all the tribes of Israel, saying, When ye hear the sound of the trumpet, ye shall say, Absalom reigneth in Hebron. **11** And with Absalom went two hundred men out of Jerusalem, that were [i]called: and they went in their simplicity, knowing nothing. **12** Also Absalom sent for Ahithophel the Gilonite David's counselor, from his city Giloh, while he offered sacrifices: and the treason was great: for the people [j]increased still with Absalom. **13** Then came a messenger to David, saying, The hearts of the men of Israel are turned after Absalom. **14** Then David said unto all his servants that were with him at Jerusalem, Up, and let us flee: for we shall not escape from [k]Absalom: make speed to depart, lest he come suddenly and take us, and bring

---

u. 2 Sam. 13:33 Or, take it to heart.
v. 2 Sam. 13:33 Or, but.
w. 2 Sam. 13:34 Or, one after another.
x. 2 Sam. 13:35 That only Amnon is dead.
y. 2 Sam. 13:37 For Maacah his mother was the daughter of this Talmai, 2 Sam. 3:3.
z. 2 Sam. 13:39 Or, ceased.

2-SAM. 13
1. Lev. 18:9

2-SAM. 14
a. 2 Sam. 14:1 That the king favored him.
b. 2 Sam. 14:2 Or, wife.
c. 2 Sam. 14:2 In token of mourning: for they used anointing to seem cheerful.
d. 2 Sam. 14:3 Hebrew, put words in her mouth.
e. 2 Sam. 14:4 Hebrew, Save.
f. 2 Sam. 14:5 Hebrew, a widow woman.
g. 2 Sam. 14:6 Under this parable she describeth the death of Amnon by Absalom.
h. 2 Sam. 14:7 Because he hath slain his brother he ought to be slain according to the Law, Gen. 9:6; Exod. 21:12.
i. 2 Sam. 14:9 As touching the breach of the Law which punisheth blood, let me bear the blame.
j. 2 Sam. 14:9 Or, innocent.
k. 2 Sam. 14:11 Swear that they shall not revenge the blood, which are many in number.
l. 2 Sam. 14:13 Why dost thou give contrary sentence in thy son Absalom?
m. 2 Sam. 14:14 Or, accept.
n. 2 Sam. 14:14 God hath provided ways (as sanctuaries) to save them oft times, whom man judgeth worthy death.
o. 2 Sam. 14:15 For I thought they would kill this mine heir.
p. 2 Sam. 14:17 Hebrew, rest.
q. 2 Sam. 14:17 Is of great wisdom to discern right from wrong.
r. 2 Sam. 14:19 Hast not thou done this by the counsel of Joab.
s. 2 Sam. 14:20 By speaking further in a parable then plainly.
t. 2 Sam. 14:20 Or, none can hide ought from the King.
u. 2 Sam. 14:21 I have granted thy request.
v. 2 Sam. 14:22 Hebrew, blessed.
w. 2 Sam. 14:24 Covering hereby his affection, and showing some part of justice to please the people.
x. 2 Sam. 14:26 Which weighed 6 pounds 4 ounces after half an ounce the shekel.
y. 2 Sam. 14:30 Or, possession.
z. 2 Sam. 14:30 The wicked are impatient in their affections, and spare no unlawful means to compass them.
aa. 2 Sam. 14:32 If I have offended by revenging my sister's dishonor: thus the wicked justify themselves in their evil.

2-SAM. 15
a. 2 Sam. 15:1 Hebrew, made him.
b. 2 Sam. 15:1 Which were as a guard to set forth his estate.
c. 2 Sam. 15:2 Or, controversy.
d. 2 Sam. 15:2 That is, noting of what city or place he was.
e. 2 Sam. 15:4 Thus by slander, flattery and fair promises the wicked seek preferment.
f. 2 Sam. 15:6 By enticing them from his father to himself.
g. 2 Sam. 15:7 Counting from the time that the Israelites had asked a King of Samuel.
h. 2 Sam. 15:8 By offering a peace offering, which was lawful to do in any place.
i. 2 Sam. 15:11 And bid to his feast in Hebron.
j. 2 Sam. 15:12 Hebrew, went and increased.
k. 2 Sam. 15:14 Whose heart he saw that Satan had so possessed, that he would leave no mischief unattempted.

evil upon us, and smite the city with the edge of the sword. **15** And the king's servants said unto him, Behold, thy servants are ready to do according to all that my lord the king shall [l]appoint. **16** So the king departed and all his household [m]after him, and the king left ten concubines to keep the house. **17** And the king went forth and all the people after him, and tarried in a [n]place [o]far off. **18** And all his servants went about him, and all the [p]Cherethites and all the Pelethites, and all the Gittites, even six hundred men which were come after him from Gath, went before the king. **19** Then said the King to [q]Ittai the Gittite, Wherefore comest thou also with us? Return and abide with the King, for thou art a stranger, depart thou therefore to thy place. **20** Thou camest yesterday, and should I cause thee to wander today and go with us? I will go whither I can: therefore return thou, and carry again thy [r]brethren: mercy and [s]truth be with thee. **21** And Ittai answered the King, and said, As the Lord liveth, and as my lord the king liveth, in what place my lord the king shall be, whether in death or life, even there surely will thy servant be. **22** Then David said to Ittai, Come, and go forward. And Ittai the Gittite went, and all his men, and all the children that were with him. **23** And all the country wept with a loud voice, and [t]all the people went forward, but the King passed over the brook Kidron: and all the people went over toward the way of the wilderness. **24** And lo, Zadok also was there, and all the Levites with him, [u]bearing the Ark of the covenant of God: and they set down the Ark of God: and Abiathar went [v]up until the people were all come out of the city. **25** Then the King said unto Zadok, Carry the Ark of God again into the city: if I shall find favor in the eyes of the Lord, he will bring me again, and show me both it, and the [w]Tabernacle thereof. **26** But if he thus say, I have no delight in thee, behold, [x]here am I, let him do to me as seemeth good in his eyes. **27** The King said again unto Zadok the Priest, Art not thou a [1]Seer? return into the city in peace, and your two sons with you: to wit, Ahimaaz thy son, and Jonathan the son of Abiathar. **28** Behold, I will tarry in the fields of the wilderness, until there come some word from you to be told me. **29** Zadok therefore and Abiathar carried the Ark of God again to Jerusalem, and they tarried there. **30** And David went up the mount of olives, and wept as he went up, and had his head [y]covered, and went barefooted: and all the people that was with him, had every man his head covered, and as they went up, they wept. **31** Then one told David, saying, Ahithophel is one of them that have conspired with Absalom: and David said, O Lord, I pray thee, turn the [z]counsel of Ahithophel into foolishness. **32** Then David came to the top of the mount where he worshipped God: and behold, Hushai the Archite came against him with his coat torn, and having earth upon his head. **33** Unto whom David said, If thou go with me, thou shalt be a burthen unto me. **34** But if thou return to the city, and say unto Absalom, I will be thy [aa]servant, O King (as I have been in time past thy father's servant, so will I now be thy servant) then thou mayest bring me the counsel of Ahithophel to nought. **35** And hast thou not there with thee Zadok and Abiathar the Priests? therefore whatsoever thou shalt hear out of the King's house, thou shalt show to Zadok and Abiathar the Priests. **36** Behold, there are with them their two sons: Ahimaaz Zadok's son, and Jonathan Abiathar's son: by them also shall ye send me everything that ye can hear. **37** So Hushai David's friend went into the city: and Absalom came into Jerusalem.

16

1 The infidelity of Ziba. 5 Shimei curseth David. 16 Hushai cometh to Absalom. 21 The counsel of Ahithophel for the concubines.

1 When David was a little past the [a]top of the hill, behold, Ziba the servant of Mephibosheth met him with a couple of asses saddled, and upon them two hundred cakes of bread, and an hundred bunches of raisins, and an hundred of [b]dried figs, and a bottle of wine. **2** And the King said unto Ziba, What meanest thou by these? And Ziba said, They be [c]asses for the king's household to ride on, and bread, and dried figs for the young men to eat, and wine, that the faint may drink in the wilderness. **3** And the King said, But where is thy master's son? Then Ziba answered the King, Behold, he remaineth in Jerusalem: for he said, This day shall the house of Israel restore me the kingdom of my father. **4** Then said the King to Ziba, Behold, thine are all that pertained unto Mephibosheth. And Ziba said, [d]I beseech thee, let me find grace in thy sight, my lord, O King. **5** And when King David came to [e]Bahurim, behold, thence came out a man of the family of the house of Saul, named Shimei, the son of Gera: and he came out and cursed. **6** And he cast stones at David, and at all the servants of King David: and all the people, and all the men of war were on his [f]right hand, and on his left. **7** And thus said Shimei when he cursed, Come forth, come forth thou [g]murderer, and [h]wicked man. **8** The Lord hath brought upon thee all the [i]blood of the house of Saul, in whose stead thou hast reigned: and the Lord hath delivered thy kingdom into the hand of Absalom thy son: and behold, thou art taken in thy wickedness, because thou art a murderer. **9** Then said Abishai the son of Zeruiah unto the King, Why doth [1]this dead dog curse my lord the King: let me go, I pray thee, and take away his head. **10** But the King said, What have I to do with you, ye sons of Zeruiah? for he curseth, even because the Lord hath [j]bidden him curse David: who dare then say, Wherefore hast thou done so? **11** And David said to Abishai, and to all his servants, Behold, my son which came out of mine own bowels, seeketh my life: then how much more now may this son of Benjamin? Suffer him to curse: for the Lord hath bidden him. **12** It may be that the Lord will look on [k]mine affliction, and [l]do me good for his cursing this day. **13** And as David and his men went by the way, Shimei went by the side of the mountain over against him, and cursed as he went, and threw stones against him, and cast dust. **14** Then came the King and all the people that were with him weary, and refreshed themselves [m]there. **15** And Absalom, and all the people the men of Israel, came to Jerusalem, and Ahithophel with him. **16** And when Hushai the Archite, David's friend, was come unto Absalom, Hushai said unto Absalom, [n]God save the King, God save the King. **17** Then Absalom said to Hushai, Is this thy kindness to thy [o]friend? Why wentest thou not with thy friend? **18** Hushai then answered unto Absalom, Nay, but whom the Lord, and this people, and all the men of Israel choose, his will I be, and with them will I dwell. **19** And [p]moreover, unto whom shall I do service? not to his son? as I served before thy father, so will I before thee. **20** Then spake Absalom to Ahithophel, Give counsel what we shall do. **21** And [q]Ahithophel said unto Absalom, Go in to thy father's concubines, which he hath left to keep the house: and when all Israel shall hear that thou art abhorred of thy father, the hands of all that are with thee, shall be strong. **22** So they spread Absalom a tent upon the top of the house, and Absalom went in to his father's concubines in the sight of all Israel. **23** And the counsel of Ahithophel which he counseled in those days, was like as one had asked [r]counsel at the oracle of God: so was all the counsel of Ahithophel both with David and with Absalom.

17

7 Ahithophel's counsel is overthrown by Hushai. 14 The Lord had so ordained. 19 The Priest's sons are hidden in the well. 22 David goeth over Jordan. 23 Ahithophel hangeth himself. 27 They bring victuals to David.

1 Moreover, Ahithophel said to Absalom, [a]Let me choose out now twelve thousand men, and I will up and follow after David this night, **2** And I will come upon him: for he is weary, and weak handled: so I will fear him, and all the people that are with him shall flee, and I will smite the king only, **3** And I will bring again all the people unto thee, and when all shall return, ([b]the man whom thou seekest being slain) all the people shall be in peace. **4** And the saying [c]pleased Absalom well, and all the Elders of Israel. **5** Then said Absalom, Call now Hushai the Archite also, and let us hear likewise [d]what he saith. **6** So when Hushai came to Absalom, Absalom spake unto him, saying, Ahithophel hath [e]spoken thus: shall we do after his saying, or no? tell thou. **7** Hushai then answered unto Absalom, The counsel that Ahithophel hath given, is not [f]good at this time. **8** For, said Hushai, thou knowest thy father, and his men, that they be strong men, and are chafed in mind as a bear robbed of her whelps in the field: also thy father is a valiant warrior, and will not [g]lodge with the people. **9** Behold, he is hid now in some cave, or in some place: and though some of them be overthrown at the first, yet the people shall hear, and say, The people that follow Absalom, [h]be overthrown. **10** Then he also that is valiant, whose heart is as the heart of a lion, shall [i]shrink and faint:

---

l. 2 Sam. 15:15 Hebrew, choose.
m. 2 Sam. 15:16 Hebrew, at his feet.
n. 2 Sam. 15:17 Or, house.
o. 2 Sam. 15:17 To wit, from Jerusalem.
p. 2 Sam. 15:18 These were as the king's guard, or as some write, his counselors.
q. 2 Sam. 15:19 Who as some write was the king's son of Gath.
r. 2 Sam. 15:20 Meaning, them of his family.
s. 2 Sam. 15:20 God require thee thy friendship and fidelity.
t. 2 Sam. 15:23 To wit, the six hundred men.
u. 2 Sam. 15:24 Which was the charge, of the Kohathites, Num. 4:4.
v. 2 Sam. 15:24 To stand by the Ark.
w. 2 Sam. 15:25 Or, his tabernacle.
x. 2 Sam. 15:26 The faithful in all their afflictions show themselves obedient to God's will.
y. 2 Sam. 15:30 With ashes and dust in sign of sorrow.
z. 2 Sam. 15:31 The counsel of the crafty worldlings doth more harm than the open force of the enemy.
aa. 2 Sam. 15:34 Though Hushai dissembled here at the King's request, yet may we not use this example to excuse our dissimulation.

2-SAM. 15
1. 1 Sam. 9:9

2-SAM. 16
a. 2 Sam. 16:1 Which was the hill of olives, 2 Sam. 15:30.
b. 2 Sam. 16:1 Or, fig cakes.
c. 2 Sam. 16:2 Commonly there are no viler traitors than they, which under pretence of friendship accuse others.
d. 2 Sam. 16:4 Hebrew, I worship.
e. 2 Sam. 16:5 Which was a city in the tribe of Benjamin.
f. 2 Sam. 16:6 That is, round about him.
g. 2 Sam. 16:7 Hebrew, man of blood.
h. 2 Sam. 16:7 Hebrew, man of Belial.
i. 2 Sam. 16:8 Reproaching him, as though by his means Ishbosheth and Abner were slain.
j. 2 Sam. 16:10 David felt that this was the judgment of God for his sin, and therefore humbleth himself to his rod.
k. 2 Sam. 16:12 Or, my tears.
l. 2 Sam. 16:12 Meaning, that the Lord will send comfort to his, when they are oppressed.
m. 2 Sam. 16:14 To wit, at Bahurim.
n. 2 Sam. 16:16 Hebrew, let the king live.
o. 2 Sam. 16:17 Meaning, David.
p. 2 Sam. 16:19 Hebrew, the second time.
q. 2 Sam. 16:21 Suspecting the change of the Kingdom, and so his own overthrow, he giveth such counsel as might most hinder his father's reconciliation: and also declare to the people that Absalom was in highest authority.
r. 2 Sam. 16:23 It was so esteemed for the success thereof.

2-SAM. 16
1. 1 Sam. 24:14 / 2 Sam. 3:8

2-SAM. 17
a. 2 Sam. 17:1 The wicked are so greedy to execute their malice, that they leave none occasion, that may further the same.
b. 2 Sam. 17:3 Meaning, David.
c. 2 Sam. 17:4 Hebrew, was right in the eyes of Absalom.
d. 2 Sam. 17:5 Hebrew, what is in his mouth.
e. 2 Sam. 17:6 Or, given such counsel.
f. 2 Sam. 17:7 Hushai showeth himself faithful to David, in that he reproveth this wicked counsel and purpose.
g. 2 Sam. 17:8 Or, tarry all night.
h. 2 Sam. 17:9 Hebrew, have a breach of ruin.
i. 2 Sam. 17:10 Hebrew, melt.
j. 2 Sam. 17:12 Or, we will camp against him.

for all Israel knoweth that thy father is valiant, and they which be with him, stout men. **11** Therefore my counsel is, that all Israel be gathered unto thee, from Dan even to Beersheba as the sand of the Sea in number, and that thou go to battle in thine own person. **12** So shall we come upon him in some place, where we shall find him, and [j]we will upon him as the dew falleth on the ground: and of all the men that are with him, we will not leave him one. **13** Moreover, if he be gotten into a city, then shall all the men of Israel bring ropes to that city, and we will draw it into the river, until there be not one small stone found there. **14** Then Absalom and all the men of Israel said, The counsel of Hushai the Archite, is better, than the counsel of Ahithophel: for the Lord had [k]determined to destroy the [l]good counsel of Ahithophel, that the Lord might [m]bring evil upon Absalom. **15** Then said Hushai unto Zadok and to Abiathar the Priests, Of this and that manner did Ahithophel and the Elders of Israel counsel Absalom: and thus and thus have I counseled. **16** Now therefore send quickly, and show David, saying, Tarry not this night in the fields of the wilderness, but rather get thee [n]over, lest the king be devoured, and all the people that are with him. **17** Now Jonathan and Ahimaaz abode by [o]En Rogel: (for they might not be seen to come into the city) and a maid went, and [p]told them, and they went and showed king David. **18** Nevertheless, a young man saw them, and told it to Absalom. Therefore they both departed quickly, and came to a man's house in Bahurim, who had a well in his court, into the which they went down. **19** And [q]the wife took and spread a covering over the well's mouth, and spread ground corn thereon, that the thing should not be known. **20** And when Absalom's servants came to the wife into the house, they said, Where is Ahimaaz and Jonathan? And the woman answered them, They be gone over the [r]brook of water. And when they had sought them, and could not find them, they returned to Jerusalem. **21** And as soon as they were departed, the other came out of the well, and went and told king David, and said unto him, Up, and get you quickly over the water: for [s]such counsel hath Ahithophel given against you. **22** Then David arose, and all the people that were with him, and they went over Jordan [t]until the dawning of the day, so that there lacked not one of them, that was not come over Jordan. **23** Now when Ahithophel saw that his counsel was not followed, he saddled his ass, and arose, and he went home unto his city, and put his household in order, and [u]hanged himself, and died, and was buried in his father's grave. **24** Then David came to Mahanaim. And Absalom passed over Jordan, he, and all the men of Israel with him. **25** And Absalom made Amasa captain of the host in the stead of Joab: which Amasa was a man's son named Jithra, an Israelite, that went in to Abigail the daughter of [v]Nahash, sister to Zeruiah Joab's mother. **26** So Israel and Absalom pitched in the land of Gilead. **27** And when David was come to Mahanaim, Shobi the son of Nahash out of Rabbah of the children of Ammon, and Machir the son of Ammiel out of Lo Debar, and Barzillai the Gileadite out of Rogelim, **28** [w]Brought beds, and basins, and earthen vessels, and wheat, and barley, and flour, and parched corn, and beans, and lentils, and parched corn. **29** And they brought honey, and butter, and sheep, and cheese of kine for David, and for the people that were with him, to eat: for they said, The people is hungry, and weary, and thirsty in the wilderness.

18

2 David divideth his army into three parts. 9 Absalom is hanged, slain, and cast into a pit. 33 David lamenteth the death of Absalom.

1 Then David [a]numbered the people that were with him, and set over them captains of thousands, and captains of hundreds. **2** And David sent forth the third part of the people under the hand of Joab, and the third part under the hand of Abishai Joab's brother, the son of Zeruiah: and the other third part under the hand of Ittai the Gittite. And the King said unto the people, I will go with you myself also. **3** But the people answered, Thou shalt not go forth: for if we flee away, they will not regard us, neither will they pass for us, though half of us were slain: but thou art [b]now worth ten thousand of us: therefore now it is better that thou succor us out of the city. **4** Then the king said unto them, What seemeth you best, that I will do. So the king stood by the gate side, and all the people came out by hundreds and by thousands. **5** And the king commanded Joab and Abishai, and Ittai, saying, Entreat the young man Absalom gently for my sake. And all the people heard when the King gave all the Captains charge concerning Absalom. **6** So the people went out into the field to meet Israel, and the battle was in the [c]wood of Ephraim: **7** Where the people of Israel were slain before the servants of David: so there was a great slaughter that day, even of twenty thousand. **8** For the battle was scattered over all the country: and the wood devoured much more people that day than did the sword. **9** Now Absalom met the servants of David, and Absalom rode upon a mule, and the mule came under a great thick oak: and his head caught hold of the oak, and he was taken up [d]between the heaven and the earth: and the mule that was under him went away. **10** And one that saw it, told Joab, saying, Behold, I saw Absalom hanged in an oak. **11** Then Joab said unto the man that told him, And hast thou indeed seen? why then didst thou not there smite him to the ground, and I would have given thee ten [1]shekels of silver, and a girdle? **12** Then the man said unto Joab, Though I should [e]receive a thousand shekels of silver in mine hand, yet would I not lay mine hand upon the King's son: for in our hearing the King charged thee, and Abishai, and Ittai, saying, Beware, lest any touch the young man Absalom. **13** If I had done it, it had been [f]the danger of my life: for nothing can be hid from the King: yea, thou thyself wouldest have been against me. **14** Then said Joab, I will not thus tarry with thee. And he took three darts in his hand, and thrust them [g]through Absalom, while he was yet alive in the midst of the oak. **15** And ten servants that bare Joab's armor, compassed about and smote Absalom, and slew him. **16** Then Joab [h]blew the trumpet, and the people returned from pursuing after Israel: for Joab held back the people. **17** And they took Absalom, and cast him into a great [i]pit in the wood, and laid a mighty great heap of stones upon him: and all Israel fled every one to his tent. **18** Now Absalom in his life time had taken and reared him up a pillar, which is in the [2]King's dale: for he said, I have no [j]son to keep my name in remembrance: and he called the pillar after his own name, and it is called unto this day, Absalom's place. **19** Then said Ahimaaz the son of Zadok, I pray thee, let me run and bear the King tidings that the Lord hath [k]delivered him out of the hand of his enemies. **20** And Joab said unto him, Thou [l]shalt not be the messenger today, but thou shalt bear tidings another time, but today thou shalt bear none: for the King's son is dead. **21** Then said Joab to Cushi, Go, tell the King, what thou hast seen. And Cushi bowed himself unto Joab, and ran. **22** Then said Ahimaaz the son of Zadok again to Joab, What, I pray thee, if I also run after Cushi? And Joab said, Wherefore now wilt thou run my son, seeing that thou hast no tidings to bring? **23** Yet what if I run? Then he said unto him, Run. So Ahimaaz ran by the way of the plain, and overwent Cushi. **24** Now David sat between the two [m]gates. And the watchman went to the top of the gate upon the wall, and lift up his eyes, and saw, and behold, a man came running alone. **25** And the watchman cried, and told the king. And the King said, If he be alone, [n]he bringeth tidings. And he came apace, and drew near. **26** And the watchman saw another man running, and the watchman called unto the potter, and said, Behold, another man runneth alone. And the King said, He also bringeth tidings. **27** And the watchman said, [o]Me thinketh the running of the foremost is like the running of Ahimaaz the son of Zadok. Then the King said, He is a [p]good man, and cometh with good tidings. **28** And Ahimaaz called, and said unto the King, Peace be with thee: and he fell down to the earth upon his face before the King, and said, Blessed be the Lord thy God, who hath [q]shut up the men that lift up their hands against my Lord the King. **29** And the King said, Is the young man Absalom safe? And Ahimaaz answered, When Joab sent the King's [r]servant, and me thy servant, I saw a great tumult, but I knew not what. **30** And the King said unto him, Turn aside, and stand here: so he turned aside and stood still. **31** And behold, Cushi came, and Cushi said, [s]Tidings, my lord the King: for the Lord hath delivered thee this day out of the hand of all that rose against thee. **32** Then the King said unto Cushi, Is the young man Absalom safe? And Cushi answered, The enemies of my lord the King, and all that rise against thee to do thee hurt, be as that young man is. **33** And the King was [t]moved, and went up to the chamber over the gate, and wept: and as he went, thus he said, O my son Absalom, my son, my son Absalom: would God I had died for thee, O Absalom, my son, my son.

---

k. 2 Sam. 17:14 Or, commanded.
l. 2 Sam. 17:14 That counsel which seemed good at the first to Absalom, verse 4.
m. 2 Sam. 17:14 For by the counsel of Hushai, he went to the battle, where he was destroyed.
n. 2 Sam. 17:16 That is, over Jordan.
o. 2 Sam. 17:17 Or, the well of Rogel.
p. 2 Sam. 17:17 Meaning, the message from their fathers.
q. 2 Sam. 17:19 Thus God sendeth succor to his, in their greatest dangers.
r. 2 Sam. 17:20 The Chaldea text readeth: Now they have passed the Jordan.
s. 2 Sam. 17:21 To wit, to pursue thee with all haste.
t. 2 Sam. 17:22 They traveled all night, and by morning had all their company passed over.
u. 2 Sam. 17:23 God's just vengeance even in this life is poured on them which are enemies, traitors, or persecutors of his Church.
v. 2 Sam. 17:25 Who was also called Jesse David's Father.
w. 2 Sam. 17:28 God showeth himself most liberal to his, when they seem to be utterly destitute.

2-SAM. 18

a. 2 Sam. 18:1 For certain of the Reubenites, Gadites, and of the half tribe, could not bear the insolence of the son against the father, and therefore joined with David.
b. 2 Sam. 18:3 Signifying, that a good governor ought to be so dear unto his people, that they will rather lose their lives, than that ought should come unto him.
c. 2 Sam. 18:6 So called, because the Ephraimites (as some say) fed their cattle beyond Jordan in this wood.
d. 2 Sam. 18:9 This is a terrible example of God's vengeance against them that are rebels or disobedient to their parents.
e. 2 Sam. 18:12 Hebrew, weigh upon mine hand.
f. 2 Sam. 18:13 Hebrew, a lie against my soul.
g. 2 Sam. 18:14 Hebrew, in the heart of Absalom.
h. 2 Sam. 18:16 For he had pity of the people, which was seduced by Absalom's flattery.
i. 2 Sam. 18:17 Thus God turned his vain glory to shame.
j. 2 Sam. 18:18 It seemed that God had punished him in taking away his children, 2 Sam. 14:27.
k. 2 Sam. 18:19 Hebrew, judged.
l. 2 Sam. 18:20 For Joab bare a good affection to Ahimaaz, and doubted how David would take the report of Absalom's death.
m. 2 Sam. 18:24 He sat in the gate of the city of Mahanaim.
n. 2 Sam. 18:25 Hebrew, tidings are in his mouth.
o. 2 Sam. 18:27 Hebrew, I see the running.
p. 2 Sam. 18:27 He had experience of his fidelity, 2 Sam. 17:21.
q. 2 Sam. 18:28 Or, delivered up.
r. 2 Sam. 18:29 To wit, Cushi, who was an Ethiopian.
s. 2 Sam. 18:31 Hebrew, tidings is brought.
t. 2 Sam. 18:33 Because he considereth both the judgment of God against his sin, and could not otherwise hide his fatherly affection toward his son.

2-SAM. 18

1. Gen. 23:15
2. Gen. 14:17

19 *7 Joab encourageth the king. 8 David is restored. 23 Shimei is pardoned. 24 Mephibosheth meeteth the king. 39 Barzillai departeth. 41 Israel striveth with Judah.*

1 And it was told Joab, Behold, the King weepeth and mourneth for Absalom. **2** Therefore the [a]victory of that day was turned into mourning to all the people: for the people heard say that day, The King sorroweth for his son. **3** And the people went that day into the city [b]secretly, as people confounded hide themselves when they flee in battle. **4** So the King [c]hid his face, and the king cried with a loud voice, My son Absalom, Absalom my son, my son. **5** Then Joab came into the [d]house to the King, and said, Thou hast shamed this day the faces of all thy servants, which this day have saved thy life, and the lives of thy sons, and of thy daughters, and the lives of thy wives, and the lives of thy concubines, **6** In that thou lovest thine enemies, and hatest thy friends: for thou hast declared this day, that thou regardest neither thy [e]princes, nor servants: therefore this day I perceive, that if Absalom had lived, and we all had died this day, that then it would have [f]pleased thee well. **7** Now therefore up, come out, and speak [g]comfortably unto thy servants: for I swear by the Lord, except thou come out, there will not tarry one man with thee this night: and that will be worse unto thee, than all the evil that fell on thee from thy youth hitherto. **8** Then the king arose, and sat in the [h]gate: and they told unto all the people, saying, Behold, the king doth sit in the gate: and all the people came before the king: for Israel had fled every man to his tent. **9** Then all the people were at [i]strife throughout all the tribes of Israel, saying, The King saved us out of the hand of our enemies, and he delivered us out of the hand of the Philistines, and now he is fled out of the land for Absalom. **10** And Absalom, whom we anointed over us, is dead in battle: therefore why are ye so slow to bring the king again? **11** But King David sent to Zadok and to Abiathar the [j]Priests, saying, Speak unto the Elders of Judah, and say, Why are ye behind to bring the King again to his house (for the saying of all Israel is come unto the King, even to his house.) **12** Ye are my brethren: my bones and my flesh are ye: Wherefore then are ye the last that bring the King again? **13** Also say ye to Amasa, Art thou not my bone and my flesh? God do so to me, and more also, if thou be not captain of the host to me forever in the [k]room of Joab. **14** So he bowed the hearts of all the men of Judah, as of one man: therefore they sent to the King, saying, Return thou with all thy servants. **15** So the king returned, and came to Jordan. And Judah came to Gilgal, for to go to meet the king, and to conduct him over Jordan. **16** And [l]Shimei the son of Gera, the son of Benjamin, which was of Bahurim, hasted and came down with the men of Judah to meet king David, **17** And a thousand men of Benjamin with him, and [1]Ziba the servant of the house of Saul, and his fifteen sons and twenty servants with him: and they went over Jordan before the king. **18** And there went over a boat to carry over the king's household, and to do him pleasure. Then Shimei the son of Gera fell before the king, when he was come over Jordan, **19** And said unto the king, Let not my lord impute [2]wickedness unto me, nor remember the thing that thy servant did [m]wickedly when my lord the King departed out of Jerusalem, that the king should take it to his heart. **20** For thy servant doth know, that I have done amiss: therefore behold, I am the first this day of all the house of [n]Joseph, that am come to go down to meet my lord the king. **21** But Abishai the son of Zeruiah answered, and said, Shall not Shimei die for this, because he cursed the Lord's anointed? **22** And David said, What have I to do with you, ye sons of Zeruiah, that this day ye should be adversaries unto me? shall there any man die this day in Israel? for do not I know that I am this day king over Israel? **23** Therefore the king said unto Shimei, Thou shalt not [o]die, and the king swore unto him. **24** And Mephibosheth the son of Saul came down to meet the king, and had neither washed his feet, nor dressed his beard, nor washed his clothes from the time the king departed, until he returned in peace. **25** And when [p]he was come to Jerusalem, and met the king, the king said unto him, Wherefore wentest not thou with me, Mephibosheth? **26** And he answered, My lord the King, my servant deceived me: for thy servant said, I would have mine ass saddled to ride thereon, for to go with the king, because thy servant is lame. **27** And he hath [3]accused thy servant unto my lord the king: but my lord the king is as an [q]angel of God: do therefore thy pleasure. **28** For all my father's house were [r]but dead men before my lord the king, yet didst thou set thy servant among them that did eat at thine own table: what right therefore have I yet to cry anymore unto the king? **29** And the king said unto him, Why speakest thou anymore of thy matters? I have said, Thou, and Ziba, divide the [s]lands. **30** And Mephibosheth said unto the king, Yea, let him take all, seeing my lord the king is come home in peace. **31** Then Barzillai the Gileadite came down from Rogelim, and went over Jordan with the king, to conduct him over Jordan. **32** Now Barzillai was a very aged man, even fourscore years old, and he had provided the king of sustenance, while he lay at Mahanaim: for he was a man of very great substance. **33** And the king said unto Barzillai, Come over with me, and I will feed thee with me in Jerusalem. **34** And Barzillai said unto the king, [t]How long have I to live, that I should go up with the king to Jerusalem? **35** I am this day fourscore years old: and can I discern between good or evil? Hath thy servant any taste in that I eat, or in that I drink? Can I hear anymore the voice of singing men and women? wherefore then should thy servant be anymore a [u]burthen unto my lord the king? **36** Thy servant will go a little way over Jordan with the king, and why will the king recompense it me with such a reward? **37** I pray thee, let thy servant turn back again, that I may die in mine own city, and be buried in the grave of my father and of my mother: but behold thy servant [v]Chimham, let him go with my lord the King, and do to him what shall please thee. **38** And the king answered, Chimham shall go with me, and I will do to him that thou shalt be content with: and whatsoever thou shalt [w]require of me, that will I do for thee. **39** So all the people went over Jordan: and the king passed over: and the king kissed Barzillai, and [x]blessed him, and he returned unto his own place. **40** Then the King went to [y]Gilgal, and Chimham went with him, and all the people of Judah conducted the king, and also half the people of [z]Israel. **41** And behold, all the men of Israel came to the king, and said unto the king, Why have our brethren the men of Judah stolen thee away, and have brought the king and his household, and all David's men with him over [aa]Jordan? **42** And all the men of Judah answered the men of Israel, Because the king is near of kin to us: and wherefore now be ye angry for this matter? have we eaten of the king's cost, or have we taken any bribes? **43** And the men of Israel answered the men of Judah, and said, We have ten parts in the king, and have also more right to David than ye: Why then did ye despise us [ab]that our advise should not be first had in restoring our king? And the words of the men of Judah were fiercer than the words of the men of Israel.

20 *1 Sheba raiseth Israel against David. 10 Joab killeth Amasa traitorously. 22 The head of Sheba is delivered to Joab. 23 David's chief officers.*

1 Then there was come [a]thither a wicked man (named Sheba the son of Bichri, a man of Benjamin) and he blew the trumpet, and said, We have no part in [b]David, neither have we inheritance in the son [c]of Ishai: every man to his tents, O Israel. **2** So every man of Israel went from David and followed Sheba the son of Bichri: but the men of Judah clave fast unto their King, from [d]Jordan even to Jerusalem. **3** When David then came to his house to Jerusalem, the king took the ten women his [1]concubines, that he had left behind him to keep the house, and put them in ward, and fed them, but lay no more with them: but they were enclosed unto the day of their death, living in widowhood. **4** Then said the King to [e]Amasa, Assemble me the men of Judah within three days, and be thou here present. **5** So Amasa went to assemble Judah, but he tarried longer than the time which he had appointed him. **6** Then David said to Abishai, Now shall Sheba the son of Bichri do us more harm than did Absalom: take thou therefore thy [f]lord's servants and follow after him, lest he get him walled cities, and escape us. **7** And there went out after him Joab's men, and the [2]Cherethites and the Pelethites, and all the mighty men: and they departed out of Jerusalem, to follow after Sheba the son of Bichri. **8** When they were at the great stone, which is in Gibeon, Amasa went before them, and Joab's [g]garment, that he had put on, was girded unto him, and upon it was a sword girded, which hanged on his loins in the sheath, and as he went, it used to fall out. **9** And Joab said to Amasa, Art thou in [h]health, my brother? and Joab took Amasa by the beard with the right hand to kiss him. **10** But Amasa took no heed to the sword that was in Joab's hand: for

---

2-SAM. 19

a. 2 Sam. 19:2 Hebrew, salvation, or deliverance.
b. 2 Sam. 19:3 Or, by stealth.
c. 2 Sam. 19:4 As they do that mourn.
d. 2 Sam. 19:5 At Mahanaim.
e. 2 Sam. 19:6 Or, captains.
f. 2 Sam. 19:6 Hebrew, been right in thine eyes.
g. 2 Sam. 19:7 Hebrew, to the heart of thy servant.
h. 2 Sam. 19:8 Where the most resort of the people haunted.
i. 2 Sam. 19:9 Everyone blamed another and strove who should first bring him home.
j. 2 Sam. 19:11 That they should reprove the negligence of the Elders, seeing the people were so forward.
k. 2 Sam. 19:13 By this policy David thought that by winning of the captain, he should have the hearts of all the people.
l. 2 Sam. 19:16 Who had before reviled him, 2 Sam. 16:13.
m. 2 Sam. 19:19 For in his adversity he was his most cruel enemy, and now in his prosperity, seeketh by flattery to creep into favor.
n. 2 Sam. 19:20 By Joseph he meaneth Ephraim, Manasseh and Benjamin (whereof he was) because these three were under one standard, Num. 2:18.
o. 2 Sam. 19:23 By my hands, or during my life, as read 1 Kings 2:8, 9.
p. 2 Sam. 19:25 When Mephibosheth being at Jerusalem had met the King.
q. 2 Sam. 19:27 Able for his wisdom to judge in all matters.
r. 2 Sam. 19:28 Worthy to die for Saul's cruelty toward thee.
s. 2 Sam. 19:29 David did evil in taking his lands from him before he knew the cause, but much worse, that knowing the truth, he did not restore them.
t. 2 Sam. 19:34 Hebrew, how many days are the years of my life?
u. 2 Sam. 19:35 He thought it not meet to receive benefits of him to whom he was not able to do service again.
v. 2 Sam. 19:37 My son.
w. 2 Sam. 19:38 Or, choose.
x. 2 Sam. 19:39 Or, bade him farewell.
y. 2 Sam. 19:40 Where the tribe of Judah tarried to receive him.
z. 2 Sam. 19:40 Which had taken part with the King.
aa. 2 Sam. 19:41 Toward Jerusalem.
ab. 2 Sam. 19:43 Or, have not we first spoken to bring home the King? verse 11.

2-SAM. 19

1. 2 Sam. 16:2
2. 2 Sam. 16:15
3. 2 Sam. 16:3

2-SAM. 20

a. 2 Sam. 20:1 Where the ten tribes contended against Judah.
b. 2 Sam. 20:1 As they of Judah say.
c. 2 Sam. 20:1 He thought by speaking contemptuously of the king, to stir the people rather to sedition, or else by causing Israel to depart, thought that they of Judah would have less esteemed him.
d. 2 Sam. 20:2 From Gilgal, which was near Jordan.
e. 2 Sam. 20:4 Who was his chief captain in Joab's room, 2 Sam. 19:13.
f. 2 Sam. 20:6 Either them which had been under Joab or David's men.
g. 2 Sam. 20:8 Which was his coat, that he used to wear in the wars.
h. 2 Sam. 20:9 Hebrew, peace.

therewith he smote him in the fifth rib, and shed out his bowels to the ground,
and [i]smote him not the second time: so he died: then Joab and Abishai his brother
followed after Sheba the son of Bichri. **11** And one of Joab's men [j]stood by him,
and said, He that favoreth Joab, and he that is of David's part, let him go after
Joab. **12** And Amasa wallowed in blood in the midst of the way: and when the
man saw that all the people stood still, he removed Amasa out of the way into the
field, and cast a cloth upon him, because he saw that everyone that came by him,
stood still. **13** When he was removed out of the way, every man went after Joab,
to follow after Sheba the son of Bichri. **14** And he went through all the tribes of
Israel unto Abel, and [k]Beth Maachah and all places of Berim: and they gathered
together, and went also after him. **15** So they came, and besieged him in Abel,
near to Beth Maachah, and they cast up a mount against the city, and the people
thereof stood on the rampart, and all the people that was with Joab, [l]destroyed and
cast down the wall. **16** Then cried a wise woman out of the city, Hear, hear, I
pray you, say unto Joab, Come thou hither, that I may speak with thee. **17** And
when he came near unto her, the woman said, Art thou Joab? And he answered,
Yea. And she said to him, Hear the words of thine handmaid. And he answered,
I do hear. **18** Then she spake thus, [m]They spake in the old time, saying, They
should ask of Abel: and so they have continued. **19** I am [n]one of them that
are peaceable, and faithful in Israel: and thou goest about to destroy a city, and a
mother in Israel: why wilt thou devour the inheritance of the Lord? **20** And Joab
answered, and said, God forbid, God forbid it me, that I should devour, or destroy
it. **21** The [o]matter is not so, but a man of mount Ephraim (Sheba the son of Bi-
chri by name) hath lift up his hand against the king, even against David: deliver us
him only, and I will depart from the city. And the woman said unto Joab, Behold,
his head shall be thrown to thee over the wall. **22** Then the woman went unto all
the people with her wisdom, and they cut off the head of Sheba the son of Bichri,
and cast it to Joab: then he blew the trumpet, and [p]they retired from the city, every
man to his tent: and Joab returned to Jerusalem unto the King. **23** [3]Then Joab
was over all the host of Israel, and Benaiah the son of Jehoiada over the Cherethites,
and over the Pelethites, **24** And Adoram over the tribute, and Jehoshaphat the
son of Ahilud the Recorder, **25** And Sheva was Scribe, and Zadok and Abiathar
the Priests **26** And also Ira the Jairite was [q]chief about David.

21

1 Three dear years. 9 The vengeance of the sins of Saul lighteth on his seven sons, which are hanged. 15 Four great battles, which David had against the Philistines.

1 Then there was a famine in the days of David, three years [a]together: and
David [b]asked counsel of the Lord, and the Lord answered, It is for Saul, and for
his bloody house, because he slew the [c]Gibeonites. **2** Then the King called the
Gibeonites, and said unto them, (Now the Gibeonites were not of the children
of Israel, but a [1]remnant of the Amorites, unto whom the children of Israel had
sworn: but Saul sought to slay them for his zeal toward the children of Israel and
Judah) **3** And David said unto the Gibeonites, [d]What shall I do for you, and
wherewith shall I make the atonement, that ye may bless the inheritance of the
Lord? **4** The Gibeonites then answered him, We will have no silver nor gold of
Saul nor of his house, neither for us shalt thou kill [e]any man in Israel. And he said,
What ye shall say that will I do for you. **5** Then they answered the king, The man
that consumed us, and that imagined evil against us, so that we are destroyed from
remaining in any coast of Israel, **6** Let seven men of his [f]sons be delivered unto
us, and we will hang them up [g]unto the Lord in Gibeah of Saul, the Lord's chosen,
And the king said, I will give them. **7** But the king had compassion on Mephi-
bosheth the son of Jonathan the son of Saul, because of the [2]Lord's oath, that was
between them, even between David and Jonathan the son of Saul. **8** But the king
took the two sons of Rizpah the daughter of Aiah, whom she bare unto Saul, even
Armoni and Mephibosheth, and the five sons of [h]Michal, the daughter of Saul,
whom she bare to Adriel the son of Barzillai the Meholathite. **9** And he delive-
red them unto the hands of the Gibeonites, which hanged them in the mountain
before the Lord: so they [i]died all seven together: and they were slain in the time of
harvest: in the [j]first days, and in the beginning of barley harvest. **10** Then Rizpah
the daughter of Aiah took [k]sackcloth and hanged it up for her upon the rock, from
the beginning of harvest, until [l]water dropped upon them from the heaven, and
suffered neither the birds of the air to [m]light on them by day, nor beasts of the field
by night. **11** And it was told David, what Rizpah the daughter of Aiah the con-
cubine of Saul had done. **12** And David went and took the bones of Saul, and
the bones of Jonathan his son from the citizens of Jabesh Gilead, which had stolen
them from the street of Beth Shan, where the Philistines had [3]hanged them, when
the Philistines had slain Saul in Gilboa. **13** So he brought thence the bones of
Saul, and the bones of Jonathan his son, and they gathered the bones of them that
were hanged. **14** And the bones of Saul and of Jonathan his son buried they in
the country of Benjamin in Zelah, in the grave of Kish his father: and when they
had performed all that the King had commanded, God was then [n]appeased with
the land. **15** Again the Philistines hath war with Israel: and David went down,
and his servants with him, and they fought against the Philistines, and David fain-
ted. **16** Then Ishbi-Benob which was of the sons of [o]Haraphah (the head of
whose spear weighed three hundred [p]shekels of brass) even he being girded with
a new sword, thought to have slain David. **17** But Abishai the son of Zeruiah
succored him, and smote the Philistine, and killed him. Then David's men swore
unto him, saying, Thou shalt go no more out with us to battle, lest thou quench
the [q]light of Israel. **18** And after this also there was a battle with the Philistines
at [r]Gob, then Sibbechai the Hushathite slew Saph, which was one of the sons of
Haraphah. **19** And there was yet another battle in Gob with the Philistines,
where Elhanan the son of Jaare-Oregim, a Bethlehemite slew [s]Goliath the Gittite:
the staff of whose spear was like a weaver's beam. **20** Afterward there was also a
battle in Gath, where was a man of a great stature, and had on every hand six fin-
gers, and on every foot six toes, four and twenty in number: who was also the son
of Haraphah. **21** And when he reviled Israel, Jonathan the son of [4]Shimea the
brother of David slew him. **22** These four were born to Haraphah in Gath, and
died by the hand of David, and by the hands of his servants.

22

2 David after his victories praiseth God. 8 The anger of God toward the wicked. 44 He prophesieth of the rejection of the Jews, and vocation of the Gentiles.

1 And David spake the words of this [a]song unto the Lord, what time the
Lord had delivered him out of the hands of all his enemies, and out of the hand of
Saul. **2** And he said, [1]The Lord is my [b]rock and my fortress, and he that delive-
reth me. **3** God is my [c]strength, in him will I trust: my shield, and the horn of
my salvation, my high tower and my refuge: my Savior, thou hast saved me from
violence. **4** I will call on the Lord, who is worthy to be praised: so shall I be safe
from mine enemies. **5** For the [d]pangs of death have compassed me: the floods
of ungodliness have made me afraid. **6** The sorrows of the grave compassed me
about: the snares of death overtook me. **7** But in my tribulation did I call upon
the Lord, and cry to my God, and he did hear my voice out of his Temple, and
my cry did enter into his ears. **8** Then the earth trembled and quaked: the foun-
dations of the heavens moved and shook, because he was angry. **9** [e]Smoke went
out at his nostrils, and consuming [f]fire out of his mouth: coals were kindled there-
at. **10** He [g]bowed the heavens also, and came down, and darkness was under his
feet. **11** And he rode upon [h]Cherub and did fly, and he was seen upon the wings
of the wind. **12** And he made darkness a Tabernacle round about him, even the
gatherings of waters, and the clouds of the air. **13** At the brightness of his presen-
ce [i]the coals of fire were kindled. **14** The Lord thundered from heaven, and the
most High gave his voice. **15** He shot arrows also, and scattered them: to wit, li-
ghtning, and destroyed them. **16** The [j]channels also of the sea appeared, even the
foundations of the world were discovered by the rebuking of the Lord, and at the
blast of the breath of his nostrils. **17** He sent from above, and took me: he drew
me out of many waters. **18** He delivered me from my strong enemy, and from

---

i. 2 Sam. 20:10 Hebrew, doubled not his stroke.
j. 2 Sam. 20:11 He stood by Amasa at Joab's appointment.
k. 2 Sam. 20:14 Unto the city Abel, which was near to Beth Maachah.
l. 2 Sam. 20:15 That is, he went about to overthrow it.
m. 2 Sam. 20:18 She showeth that the old custom was not to destroy a city before peace was offered, Deut. 20:10, 11.
n. 2 Sam. 20:19 She speaketh in the name of the city.
o. 2 Sam. 20:21 Hearing his fault told him, he gave place to reason, and required only him that was author of the treason.
p. 2 Sam. 20:22 Hebrew, they were scattered.
q. 2 Sam. 20:26 Either in dignity or familiarity.

2-SAM. 20
1. 2 Sam. 16:22
2. 2 Sam. 8:18
3. 2 Sam. 8:16

2-SAM. 21
a. 2 Sam. 21:1 Hebrew, year after year.
b. 2 Sam. 21:1 Hebrew, sought the face of the Lord.
c. 2 Sam. 21:1 Thinking to gratify the people, because these were not of the seed of Abraham.
d. 2 Sam. 21:3 Wherewith may your wrath be appeased, that you may pray to God to remove this plague from his people.
e. 2 Sam. 21:4 Save only of Saul's stock.
f. 2 Sam. 21:6 Of Saul's kinsmen.
g. 2 Sam. 21:6 To pacify the Lord.
h. 2 Sam. 21:8 Here Michal is named for Merab, Adriel's wife, as appeareth, 1 Sam. 18:19, for Michal was the wife of Paltiel, 1 Sam. 25:44, and never had child, 2 Sam. 6:23.
i. 2 Sam. 21:9 Hebrew, fell.
j. 2 Sam. 21:9 Which was in the month Abib or Nisan, which contained part of March and part of April.
k. 2 Sam. 21:10 To make her a tent wherein she prayed to God to turn away his wrath.
l. 2 Sam. 21:10 Because drought was the cause of this famine, God by sending of rain showed that he was pacified.
m. 2 Sam. 21:10 Or, rest.
n. 2 Sam. 21:14 For where the magistrate suffereth faults unpunished, there the plague of God lieth upon the land.
o. 2 Sam. 21:16 That is, of the race of giants.
p. 2 Sam. 21:16 Which amount to nine pounds three quarters.
q. 2 Sam. 21:17 For the glory and wealth of the country standeth in the preservation of the godly magistrate.
r. 2 Sam. 21:18 Called Gezer, and Saph is called Sippai, 1 Chron. 20:4.
s. 2 Sam. 21:19 That is, Lahmi the brother of Goliath, whom David slew, 1 Chron. 20:5.

2-SAM. 21
1. Josh. 9:3,16,17
2. 1 Sam. 18:3 / 1 Sam. 20:8,42
3. 1 Sam. 31:10
4. 1 Sam. 16:9

2-SAM. 22
a. 2 Sam. 22:1 In token of the wonderful benefits that he received of God.
b. 2 Sam. 22:2 By the diversity of these comfortable means, he showeth how his faith was strengthened in all tentations.
c. 2 Sam. 22:3 Or, rock.
d. 2 Sam. 22:5 As David (who was the figure of Christ) was by God's power delivered from all dangers: so Christ and his Church shall overcome most grievous dangers, tyranny and death.
e. 2 Sam. 22:9 That is, clouds, and vapors.
f. 2 Sam. 22:9 Lightning and thundering.
g. 2 Sam. 22:10 So it seemeth when the air is dark.
h. 2 Sam. 22:11 To fly in a moment through the world.
i. 2 Sam. 22:13 By this description of a tempest he declareth the power of God against his enemies.
j. 2 Sam. 22:16 He alludeth to the miracle of the red Sea.

them that hated me: for they were too strong for me. **19** They [k]prevented me in the day of my calamity, but the Lord was my stay, **20** And brought me forth into a large place: he delivered me, because he favored me. **21** The Lord rewarded me according to my [l]righteousness: according to the pureness of mine hands he recompensed me. **22** For I kept the ways of the Lord, and did not [m]wickedly against my God. **23** For all his laws were before me, and his statutes: I did not depart therefrom. **24** I was upright also toward him, and have kept me from my wickedness. **25** Therefore the Lord did reward me according to my righteousness, according to my pureness before his eyes. **26** With the godly thou wilt show thyself godly: with the upright man thou wilt show thyself upright. **27** With the pure thou wilt show thyself pure, and with the [n]froward thou wilt show thyself froward. **28** Thus thou wilt save the poor people: but thine eyes are upon the haughty, to humble them. **29** Surely thou art my light, O Lord: and the Lord will lighten my darkness. **30** For by thee have I broken through an host, and by my God have I leaped over a wall. **31** The way of God is [o]uncorrupt: the word of the Lord is tried in the fire: he is a shield to all that trust in him. **32** For who is God besides the Lord? and who is mighty, save our God? **33** God is my strength in battle, and maketh my way upright. **34** He maketh my feet like [p]hinds feet, and hath set me upon mine high places. **35** He teacheth mine hands to fight, so that a bowl [q]of brass is broken with mine arms. **36** Thou hast also given me the shield of thy salvation, and thy loving kindness hath caused me to increase. **37** Thou hast enlarged my steps under me, and mine heels have not slid. **38** I have pursued mine enemies, and destroyed them, and have not turned again until I had consumed them. **39** Yea, I have consumed them and thrust them through, and they shall not arise, but shall fall under my feet. **40** For thou hast [r]girded me with power to battle, and them that rose against me, hast thou subdued under me. **41** And thou hast given me the necks of mine enemies, that I might destroy them that hate me. **42** They looked about, but there was none to save them, even unto the [s]Lord, but he answered them not. **43** Then did I beat them as small as the dust of the earth: I did tread them flat as the clay of the street, and did spread them abroad. **44** Thou hast also delivered me from the contentions of my [t]people: thou hast preserved me to be the head over nations: the people which I knew not, do serve me. **45** Strangers [u]shall be in subjection to me: as soon as they hear, they shall obey me. **46** Strangers shall shrink away, and fear in their privy chambers. **47** Let the Lord live, [v]and blessed be my strength: and God, even the force of my salvation be exalted. **48** It is God that giveth me power to revenge me, and subdue the people under me, **49** And rescueth me from mine enemies: (thou also hast lift me up from them that rose against me, thou hast delivered me from the cruel man. **50** Therefore I will praise thee, O Lord, among the [2]nations, and will sing unto thy Name.) **51** He is the tower of salvation for his King, and showeth mercy to his anointed, even to David, and to his seed [3]forever.

23

1 The last words of David. 6 The wicked shall be plucked up as thorns. 8 The names and facts of his mighty men. 15 He desired water, and would not drink it.

1 These also be the [a]last words of David, David the son of Jesse saith, even the man who was set up on high, the anointed of the God of Jacob, and the sweet singer of Israel saith, **2** The Spirit of the Lord spake by me, and his word was in my [b]tongue. **3** The God of Israel spake to me, the strength of Israel said, Thou shalt bear rule over men, being just, and ruling in the fear of God. **4** Even as the morning light when the sun riseth, the morning, I say, without clouds, so shall mine house be, and not as the [c]grass of the earth is by the bright rain. **5** For so shall not mine house be with God: for he hath made with me an everlasting covenant, perfect in all points, and sure: therefore all mine health and whole desire is, that he will not make it [d]grow so. **6** But the wicked shall be every one as thorns thrust away, because they cannot be taken with hands. **7** But the man that shall touch them, must be defenced with iron, or with the shaft of a spear: and they shall be burnt with fire in the same place. **8** These be the names of the mighty men whom David hath: He that sat in the seat of [e]wisdom, being chief of the princes, was Adino of Ezni, he slew eight hundred at one time. **9** And after him was [1]Eleazar the son of Dodo, the son of Ahohi, one of the three worthies with David, when they [f]defied the Philistines gathered there to battle, when the men of Israel were [g]gone up. **10** He arose and smote the Philistines, until his hand was weary, and his [h]hand clave unto the sword: and the Lord gave great victory the same day, and the people returned after him only to spoil. **11** After him was [2]Shammah the son of Agee the Hararite: for the Philistines assembled at a town, where was a piece of a field full of lentils, and the people fled from the Philistines. **12** But he stood in the midst of the field, and defended it, and slew the Philistines: so the Lord gave [i]great victory. **13** Afterward three of the thirty captains went down, and came to David in the harvest time unto the cave of Adullam, and the host of the Philistines pitched in the valley of [j]Rephaim. **14** And David was then in an hold, and the garrison of the Philistines was then in Bethlehem. **15** And David [k]longed, and said, Oh, that one would give me to drink of the water of the well of Bethlehem which is by the gate. **16** Then the three mighty brake into the host of the Philistines, and drew water out of the well of Bethlehem that was by the gate, and took and brought it to David, who would not drink thereof, but [l]poured it for an offering unto the Lord, **17** And said, O Lord, be it far from me, that I should do this. Is not this the blood of the men that went in jeopardy of their lives? therefore he would not drink it. These things did these three mighty men. **18** [3]And Abishai the brother of Joab, the son of Zeruiah, was chief among the three, and he lifted up his spear against three hundred, [m]and slew them, and he had the name among the three. **19** For he was most excellent of the three, and was their captain, but he attained not unto the first three. **20** And Benaiah the son of Jehoiada the son of [n]a valiant man, which had done many acts, and was of Kabzeel, slew two strong men of Moab: he went down also, and slew a lion in the midst of a pit in the time of snow. **21** And he slew an Egyptian a [o]man of great stature, and the Egyptian had a [p]spear in his hand: but he went down to him with a staff, and plucked the spear out of the Egyptian's hand, and slew him with his own spear. **22** These things did Benaiah the son of Jehoiada, and had the name among the three worthies. **23** He was honorable among [q]thirty, but he attained not to the first three: and David made him of his counsel. **24** [4]Asahel the brother of Joab was one of the thirty: Elhanan the son of Dodo of Bethlehem: **25** Shammoth the Harorite: Elika the Harodite: **26** Helez the [r,5]Paltite: Ira the son of Ikkesh the Tekoite: **27** Abiezer the Anathothite: [s]Mebunnai the Hushathite: **28** Zalmon an Ahohite: Maharai the Netophathite: **29** Heleb the son of Baanah a Netophathite: Ittai the son of Ribai of Gibeah of the children of Benjamin: **30** Benaiah the Pirathonite: Hiddai of the river of Gaash: **31** Abi-Albon the Arbathite: Azmaveth the Barhumite: **32** Eliahba the Shaalbonite: of the sons of Jashen, Jonathan: **33** Shammah the Hararite: Ahiam the son of Sharar the Hararite: **34** Eliphelet the son of Ahasbai, the son of Maachathi: Eliam the son of Ahithophel the Gilonite: **35** Hezrai the Carmelite: Paarai the Arbite: **36** Igal the son of Nathan of Zobah: Bani the Gadite: **37** Zelek the Ammonite: Naharai the Beerothite, the armor-bearer of Joab the son of Zeruiah: **38** Ira the Ithrite: Gareb the Ithrite: **39** Uriah the Hittite, [t]thirty and seven in all.

24

1 David causeth the people to be numbered. 10 He repenteth,and chooseth to fall into God's hands. 15 Seventy thousand perish with the pestilence.

1 And the wrath of the Lord was [a]again kindled against Israel, and [b]he moved David against them, in that he said, Go, number Israel and Judah. **2** For the King said to Joab the captain of the host, which was with him, Go speedily now through all the tribes of Israel, from Dan even to Beersheba, and number ye the people, that I may know the [c]number of the people. **3** And Joab said unto the King, The Lord thy God increase the people an hundredfold more than they be, and that the eyes of my lord the King may see it: but why doth my lord the King desire this thing? **4** Notwithstanding the King's word prevailed against Joab and against the captains of the host: therefore Joab and the captains of the host went

---

k. 2 Sam. 22:19 I was so beset, that all means seemed to fail.
l. 2 Sam. 22:21 Toward Saul and mine enemies.
m. 2 Sam. 22:22 I attempted nothing without his commandment.
n. 2 Sam. 22:27 Their wickedness is cause that thou seemest to forget thy wonted mercy.
o. 2 Sam. 22:31 The manner that God useth to succor his, never faileth.
p. 2 Sam. 22:34 He useth extraordinary means to make me win most strongholds.
q. 2 Sam. 22:35 Or, steel.
r. 2 Sam. 22:40 He acknowledgeth that God was the author of his victories, who gave him strength.
s. 2 Sam. 22:42 The wicked in their necessity are compelled to flee to God, but it is too late.
t. 2 Sam. 22:44 Meaning, of the Jews, who conspired against me.
u. 2 Sam. 22:45 Not willingly obeying me, but dissemblingly.
v. 2 Sam. 22:47 Let him show his power, that he is the governor of all the world.

2-SAM. 22
1. Ps. 18:2
2. Rom. 15:9
3. 2 Sam. 7:13

2-SAM. 23
a. 2 Sam. 23:1 Which he spake after that he had made the Psalms.
b. 2 Sam. 23:2 Meaning, he spake nothing but by the motion of God's Spirit.
c. 2 Sam. 23:4 Which groweth quickly, and fadeth soon.
d. 2 Sam. 23:5 But that my kingdom may continue forever according to his promise.
e. 2 Sam. 23:8 As one of the King's counsel.
f. 2 Sam. 23:9 Or, assailed with danger of their lives.
g. 2 Sam. 23:9 Meaning, fled from the battle.
h. 2 Sam. 23:10 By a cramp which came of weariness and striving.
i. 2 Sam. 23:12 Which hath neither respect to many nor few, when he will show his power.
j. 2 Sam. 23:13 Or, giants.
k. 2 Sam. 23:15 Being overcome with weariness and thirst.
l. 2 Sam. 23:16 Bridling his affection, and also desiring God not to be offended for that rash enterprise.
m. 2 Sam. 23:18 Hebrew, slain.
n. 2 Sam. 23:20 Or, Jesse
o. 2 Sam. 23:21 Or, a comely man.
p. 2 Sam. 23:21 Which was as big as a weaver's beam, 1 Chron. 11:23.
q. 2 Sam. 23:23 He was more valiant than the thirty that follow, and not so valiant as the six before.
r. 2 Sam. 23:26 Or, Pelonite.
s. 2 Sam. 23:27 Divers of these had two names, appeareth 1 Chron. 11, and also many more are there mentioned.
t. 2 Sam. 23:39 These came to David, and helped to restore him to his Kingdom.

2-SAM. 23
1. 1 Chron. 11:12
2. 1 Chron. 11:27
3. 1 Chron. 11:20
4. 2 Sam. 2:18
5. 1 Chron. 11:27

2-SAM. 24
a. 2 Sam. 24:1 Before they were plagued with famine, 2 Sam. 21:1.
b. 2 Sam. 24:1 The Lord permitted Satan, as 1 Chron. 21:2.
c. 2 Sam. 24:2 Because he did this to try his power, and so to trust therein, it offended God, else it was lawful to number the people, Exod. 30:12; Num. 1:2.

out from the presence of the King to number the people of Israel. 5 And they
passed over Jordan, and pitched in Aroer at the right side of the city that is in the
midst of the [d]valley of Gad, and toward Jazer. 6 Then they came to Gilead, and
to [e]Tahtim Hodshi, so they came to Dan Jaan, and so about to Sidon, 7 And
came to the fortress of [f]Tyre and to all the cities of the Hivites and of the Canaa-
nites, and went toward the South of Judah, even to Beersheba. 8 So when they
had gone about all the land, they returned to Jerusalem at the end of nine mon-
ths and twenty days. 9 And Joab delivered the number and sum of the people
unto the King: and there were in Israel [g]eight hundred thousand strong men that
drew swords, and the men of Judah were [h]five hundred thousand men. 10 Then
David's heart smote him, after that he had numbered the people: and David said
unto the Lord, I have sinned exceedingly, in that I have done: therefore now, Lord,
I beseech thee, take away the trespass of thy servant: for I have done very fooli-
shly. 11 And when David was up in the morning, the word of the Lord came
unto the Prophet Gad David's [i]Seer, saying, 12 Go, and say unto David, Thus
saith the Lord, I offer thee three things, choose thee which of them I shall do unto
thee. 13 So Gad came to David, and showed him, and said unto him, Wilt thou
that [j]seven years famine come upon thee in thy land, or wilt thou flee three mon-
ths before thine enemies, they following thee, or that there be three days pestilence
in my land? now advise thee, and see, what answer I shall give to him that sent
me. 14 And David said unto Gad, I am in a wonderful strait: let us fall now into
the hand of the Lord, (for his mercies are great) and let me not fall into the hand of
man. 15 So the Lord sent a pestilence in Israel from the morning even unto the
time appointed: and there died of the people from [k]Dan even to Beersheba seventy
thousand men. 16 And when the Angel stretched out his hand upon Jerusalem
to destroy it, the Lord [1]repented of the evil, and said to the Angel, that destroyed
the people, It is sufficient, [l]hold now thine hand. And the Angel of the Lord was by
the threshing place of Araunah the Jebusite. 17 And David spake unto the Lord
(when he saw the Angel that smote the people) and said, Behold, I have sinned,
yea, I have done wickedly, but these sheep, what have they [m]done? let thine hand,
I pray, thee, be against me and against my father's house. 18 So Gad came the
same day to David, and said unto him, Go up, rear an altar unto the Lord in the
threshing floor of Araunah the Jebusite. 19 And David (according to the saying
of Gad) went up, as the Lord had commanded. 20 And Araunah looked, and
saw the king and his servants coming toward him, and Araunah went out, and
bowed himself before the King on his face to the ground. 21 And [n]Araunah said,
Wherefore is my lord the king come to his servant? Then David answered, to buy
the threshing floor of thee for to build an altar unto the Lord, that the plague may
cease from the people. 22 Then Araunah said unto David, Let my lord the King
take and offer what seemeth him good in his eyes: behold the oxen for the burnt
offering, and chariots, and the instruments of the oxen for wood. 23 (All these
things did Araunah [o]as a king give unto the king: and Araunah said unto the king,
The Lord thy God be favorable unto thee.) 24 Then the king said unto Araunah,
Not so, but I will buy it of thee at a price, and will not offer burnt offering unto the
Lord my God of that which doth cost me nothing. So David bought the threshing
floor, and the oxen for [p]fifty shekels of silver. 25 And David built there an altar
unto the Lord, and offered burnt offerings and peace offerings, and the Lord was
appeased toward the land, and the plague ceased from Israel.

---

d. 2 Sam. 24:5 Or, river.
e. 2 Sam. 24:6 Or, to the nether land newly inhabited.
f. 2 Sam. 24:7 Or, Zor.
g. 2 Sam. 24:9 According to Joab's count: for in all there were eleven hundred thousand, 1 Chron. 21:5.
h. 2 Sam. 24:9 Concluding under them the Benjamites: for else they had but four hundred and seventy thousand, 1 Chron. 21:5.
i. 2 Sam. 24:11 Whom God had appointed for David and his time.
j. 2 Sam. 24:13 For three years of famine were past for the Gibeonites' matter: this was the fourth year to the which should have been added other three years more, 1 Chron. 21:12.
k. 2 Sam. 24:15 From the one side of the country to the other.
l. 2 Sam. 24:16 The Lord spared this place, because he had chosen it to build his Temple there.
m. 2 Sam. 24:17 David saw not the just cause why God plagued the people, and therefore he offereth himself to God's corrections as the only cause of this evil.
n. 2 Sam. 24:21 Called also Ornan, 1 Chron. 21:20.
o. 2 Sam. 24:23 That is, abundantly: for as some write, he was King of Jerusalem before David won the tower.
p. 2 Sam. 24:24 Some write that every tribe gave 50 which makes 600, or that afterward he bought as much as came to 550 shekels, 1 Chron. 21:25.

2-SAM. 24
1. 1 Sam. 15:11

THE FIRST BOOK OF THE
KINGS

1

3 Abishag keepeth David in his extreme age. 5 Adonijah usurpeth the kingdom. 30 Solomon is anointed king, 50 Adonijah fleeth to the altar.

1 Now when King David was [a]old, and stricken in years, they covered him
with clothes, but no [b]heat came unto him. 2 Wherefore his servants said unto
him, Let there be sought for my lord the king a young virgin, and let her [c]stand
before the king, and cherish him: and let her lie in thy bosom, that my lord the
King may get heat. 3 So they sought for a fair young maid throughout all the
coasts of Israel, and found one Abishag [d]a Shunammite, and brought her to the
king. 4 And the maid was exceedingly fair, and cherished the king, and mini-
stered to him, but the king knew her not. 5 Then Adonijah the son of Haggith,
exalted himself, saying, I will be king. And he got him chariots and horsemen, and
[e]fifty men to run before him. 6 And his father would not displease him from his
[f]childhood, to say, Why hast thou done so? And he was a very goodly man, and his
mother bare him next after Absalom. 7 And he [g]took counsel of Joab the son of
Zeruiah, and of Abiathar the Priest: and they [h]helped forward Adonijah. 8 But
Zadok the Priest, and Benaiah the son of Jehoiada, and Nathan the Prophet, and
Shimei, and Rei, and the men of might, which were with David, were not with
Adonijah. 9 Then Adonijah sacrificed sheep and oxen, and fat cattle by the stone
of Zoheleth, which is by [i]En Rogel, and called all his brethren the king's sons, and
all the men of Judah the king's servants. 10 But Nathan the Prophet, and Bena-
iah, and [j]the mighty men, and Solomon his brother he called not. 11 Where-
fore Nathan spake unto Bathsheba the mother of Solomon, saying, Hast thou not
heard that Adonijah the son of [1]Haggith doth reign, and David our lord knoweth
it not? 12 Now therefore come, and I will now give thee counsel, how to save
thine own [k]life, and the life of thy son Solomon. 13 Go, and get thee in unto
King David, and say unto him, Didst not thou, my lord, O King, swear unto
thine handmaid, saying, Assuredly, Solomon thy son shall reign after me, and he
shall sit upon my throne? why is then Adonijah King? 14 Behold, while thou
yet talkest there with the King, I also will come in after thee, and [l]confirm thy
words. 15 So Bathsheba went in unto the King into the chamber, and the king
was very old, and Abishag the Shunammite ministered unto the King. 16 And
Bathsheba bowed and made obeisance unto the king. And the king said, What is
thy matter? 17 And she answered him, My lord, thou swearest by the Lord thy
God unto thine handmaid, saying, Assuredly Solomon thy son shall reign after
me, and he shall sit upon my throne. 18 And behold, now is Adonijah king,
and now my lord, O King, thou knowest [m]it not. 19 And he hath offered many
oxen, and fat cattle, and sheep, and hath called all the sons of the King, and Abia-
thar the Priest, and Joab the Captain of the host: but Solomon thy servant hath
he not bidden. 20 And thou, my lord, O King, knowest that the eyes of all
Israel are on thee, that thou shouldest tell them, who should sit on the throne of
my lord the King after him. 21 For else when my lord the King shall sleep with
his fathers, I and my son Solomon shall be [n]reputed [o]vile. 22 And lo, while she
yet talked with the king, Nathan also the Prophet came in. 23 And they told
the King, saying, Behold, Nathan the Prophet. And when he was come in to the
King, he made obeisance before the king upon his face [p]to the ground. 24 And
Nathan said, My lord, O king, hast thou said, Adonijah shall reign after me, and
he shall sit upon my throne? 25 For he is gone down this day, and hath slain
many oxen, and fat cattle, and sheep, and hath called all the king's sons, and the
captains of the host, and Abiathar the Priest: and behold, they eat and drink befo-
re him, and say, [q]God save king Adonijah. 26 But me thy servant, and Zadok
the Priest, and Benaiah the son of Jehoiada, and thy servant Solomon hath he not
called. 27 Is this thing done by my lord the king, and thou hast not showed
it unto thy [r]servant, who should sit on the throne of my lord the king after him?
28 Then king David answered, and said, Call me Bathsheba. And she came into
the king's presence, and stood before the King. 29 And the King sware, saying,
As the Lord liveth, who hath redeemed my soul out of all adversity, 30 That as
I [s]sware unto thee by the Lord God of Israel, saying, Assuredly Solomon thy son
shall reign after me, and he shall sit upon my throne in my place, so will I certainly
do this day. 31 Then Bathsheba bowed her face to the earth, and did reverence
unto the king, and said, God save my lord king David forever. 32 And king Da-
vid said, Call me Zadok the Priest, and Nathan the Prophet, and Benaiah the son
of Jehoiada. And they came before the King. 33 Then the king said unto them,
Take with you the [t]servants of your lord, and cause Solomon my son to ride upon
mine own mule, and carry him down to Gihon. 34 And let Zadok the Priest
and Nathan the Prophet anoint him there king over Israel, and blow ye the trum-
pet, and say, God save King Solomon. 35 Then come up after him, that he may
come and sit upon my throne: and he shall be King in my stead: for I have [u]ap-
pointed him to be prince over Israel, and over Judah. 36 Then Benaiah the son
of Jehoiada answered the king, and said, So be it, and the Lord God of my lord the
king [v]ratify it. 37 As the Lord hath been with my lord the king, so be he with
Solomon, and exalt his throne above the throne of my lord king David. 38 So
Zadok the Priest, and Nathan the Prophet, and Benaiah the son of Jehoiada, and
the Cherethites, and the Pelethites went down and caused Solomon to ride upon
king David's mule, and brought him to Gihon. 39 And Zadok the Priest took
an horn of [w]oil out of the Tabernacle, and anointed Solomon: and they blew the
trumpet, and all the people said, God save king Solomon. 40 And all the people
came up after him, and the people piped with pipes, and rejoiced with great joy, so
that the earth [x]rang with the sound of them. 41 And Adonijah and all the gue-
sts that were with him, heard it: (and they had made an end of eating) and when
Joab heard the sound of the trumpet, he said, What meaneth this noise and uproar
in the city? 42 And as he yet spake, behold, Jonathan the son of Abiathar the
Priest came: and Adonijah said, Come in: for thou art a [y]worthy man, and bringest
[z]good tidings. 43 And Jonathan answered, and said to Adonijah, Verily our lord
king David hath made Solomon king. 44 And the king hath sent with him Za-
dok the Priest, and Nathan the Prophet, and Benaiah the son of Jehoiada, and the
Cherethites, and the Pelethites, and they have caused him to ride upon the king's
mule. 45 And Zadok the Priest, and Nathan the Prophet have anointed him
king in Gihon: and they are gone up from thence with joy, and the city is moved:
this is the noise that ye have heard. 46 And Solomon also sitteth on the throne
of the kingdom. 47 And moreover the king's servants came [aa]to bless our lord
king David, saying, God make the name of Solomon more famous than thy name,
and exalt his throne above thy throne: therefore the king worshipped upon the
[ab]bed. 48 And thus said the king also, Blessed be the Lord God of Israel, who
hath made one to sit on my throne this day, even in my sight. 49 Then all the
guests that were with Adonijah, were afraid, and rose up, and went every man his
way. 50 And Adonijah fearing the presence of Solomon, arose and went, and
took hold on the horns of the [ac]altar. 51 And one told Solomon, saying, Behold,
Adonijah doth fear king Solomon: for lo, he hath caught hold on the horns of the
altar, saying, Let King Solomon swear unto me this day, that he will not slay his
servant with the sword. 52 Then Solomon said, If he will show himself a worthy
man, there shall not an hair of him fall to the earth, but if wickedness be found in
him, he shall die. 53 Then king Solomon sent, and they brought him from the
altar, and he came and did obeisance unto King Solomon. And Solomon said unto
him, Go to thine house.

1-KINGS 1

a. 1 Kings 1:1 He was about 70 years old, 2 Sam. 5:4.
b. 1 Kings 1:1 For his natural heat was worn away with travails.
c. 1 Kings 1:2 Or, serve him.
d. 1 Kings 1:3 Which city was in the tribe of Issachar, as Josh. 19:18.
e. 1 Kings 1:5 Read 2 Sam. 15:1.
f. 1 Kings 1:6 Hebrew, days.
g. 1 Kings 1:7 Hebrew, his words were with Joab.
h. 1 Kings 1:7 They took his part and followed him.
i. 1 Kings 1:9 Or, the fountains.
j. 1 Kings 1:10 As the Cherethites and Pelethites.
k. 1 Kings 1:12 For Adonijah will destroy thee and thy son, if he reigns.
l. 1 Kings 1:14 By declaring such things, as may further the same.
m. 1 Kings 1:18 The king being worn with age, could not attend to the affairs of the realm, and also Adonijah had many flatterers which kept it from the king.
n. 1 Kings 1:21 And so put to the death as wicked transgressors.
o. 1 Kings 1:21 Hebrew, sinners.
p. 1 Kings 1:23 Acknowledging him to be the true and worthy King appointed of God, as the figure of his Christ.
q. 1 Kings 1:25 Hebrew, let the king Adonijah live.
r. 1 Kings 1:27 Meaning, that he ought in such affairs enterprise nothing except he had consulted with the Lord.
s. 1 Kings 1:30 Moved by the Spirit of God so to do, because he foresaw that Solomon should be the figure of Christ.
t. 1 Kings 1:33 Meaning, the king's servants and such as were of his guard.
u. 1 Kings 1:35 Hebrew, commanded.
v. 1 Kings 1:36 Hebrew, say so.
w. 1 Kings 1:39 Wherewith they accustomed to anoint the Priests and the holy instruments, Exod. 30:23.
x. 1 Kings 1:40 Hebrew, brake.
y. 1 Kings 1:42 Hebrew, a man of power.
z. 1 Kings 1:42 He praised Jonathan, thinking to have heard comfortable news but God wrought things contrary to his expectation, and so did beat down his pride.
aa. 1 Kings 1:47 To salute him, and to pray and praise God for him.
ab. 1 Kings 1:47 He gave God thanks for the good success.
ac. 1 Kings 1:50 Which David his father had built in the floor of Araunah, 2 Sam. 24:25.

1-KINGS 1

1. 2 Sam. 3:4

2

1 David exhorteth Solomon, and giveth charge concerning Joab, Barzillai, and Shimei. 10 The death of David. 17 Adonijah asketh Abishag to wife. 25 He is slain. 35 Zadok was placed in Abiathar's room.

1 Then the days of David drew near that he should die, and he charged Solomon his son, saying, **2** I go the [a]way of all the earth: be strong therefore, and show thyself a man, **3** And take heed to the [b]charge of the Lord thy God, to walk in his ways, and keep his statutes, and his commandments, and his judgments, and his testimonies, as it is written in the Law of Moses, that thou mayest [c,1]prosper in all that thou doest, and in everything whereunto thou turnest thee, **4** That the Lord may confirm his word which he spake unto me, saying, If thy sons take heed to their way, that they walk before me in [d]truth, with all their hearts, and with all their souls, [e,2]thou shalt not (said he) want one of thy posterity upon the throne of Israel. **5** Thou knowest also what Joab the son of Zeruiah did to me, and what he did to the two captains to the hosts of Israel, unto [3]Abner the son of Ner, and unto [4]Amasa the son of Jether, whom he slew, and [f]shed blood of battle in peace, and [g]put the blood of war upon his girdle that was about his loins, and in his shoes that were on his feet. **6** Do therefore according to thy wisdom, and let thou not his hoar head go down to the grave in peace. **7** But show kindness unto the sons of [5]Barzillai the Gileadite, and let them be among them that eat at thy table: [h]for so they came to me when I fled from Absalom thy brother. **8** And behold, with thee [6]is Shimei the son of Gera, the son of Benjamin, of Bahurim, which cursed me with an horrible curse in the day when I went to Mahanaim: but he came down to meet me at Jordan, and I sware to him by the Lord, saying, [7]I will not slay thee with the sword. **9** But thou shalt not count him innocent: for thou art a wise man, and knowest what thou oughtest to do unto him: therefore thou shalt cause his hoar head to go down to the grave with [i]blood. **10** So [8]David slept with his fathers, and was buried in the city of David. **11** And the days which David [9]reigned upon Israel, were forty years: seven years reigned he in Hebron, and thirty and three years reigned he in Jerusalem. **12** [10]Then sat Solomon upon the throne of David his father, and his kingdom was established mightily. **13** And Adonijah the son of Haggith came to Bathsheba the mother of Solomon: and she said, [j]Comest thou peaceably? and he said, Yea. **14** He said moreover, I have a suit unto thee. And she said, Say on. **15** Then he said, Thou knowest that the kingdom was mine, and that all Israel set [k]their faces on me, that I should reign: howbeit the kingdom is turned away, and is my brother's: for it came to him by the Lord. **16** Now therefore I ask thee one request, [l]refuse me not. And she said unto him, Say on. **17** And he said, Speak, I pray thee, unto Solomon the King, (for he will not say thee nay) that he give me Abishag the Shunammite to wife. **18** And Bathsheba said, Well, I will speak for thee unto the King. **19** Bathsheba therefore went unto King Solomon, to speak unto him for Adonijah: and the king rose to meet her, and [m]bowed himself unto her, and sat down on his throne: and he caused a seat to be set for the king's mother, and she sat at his right hand. **20** Then she said, I desire a small request of thee, say me not nay. Then the King said unto her, Ask on, my mother: for I will not say thee nay. **21** She said then, Let Abishag the Shunammite be given to Adonijah thy brother to wife. **22** But king Solomon answered and said unto his mother, And why dost thou ask Abishag the Shunammite for Adonijah? ask for him the [n]kingdom also: for he is mine elder brother, and hath for him both Abiathar the Priest, and Joab the son of Zeruiah. **23** Then King Solomon sware by the Lord, saying, God do so to me and more also, if Adonijah hath not spoken this word against his own life. **24** Now therefore as the Lord liveth, who hath established me, and set me on the throne of David my father, who hath also made me an house, as he [11]promised, Adonijah shall surely die this day. **25** And King Solomon sent by the hand of Benaiah the son of Jehoiada, and he [o]smote him that he died. **26** Then the King said unto Abiathar the Priest, Go to Anathoth unto thine own [p]fields: for thou art [q]worthy of death: but I will not this day kill thee, because thou [r]barest the Ark of the Lord God before David my father, and because thou hast suffered in all, wherein my father hath been afflicted. **27** So Solomon cast out Abiathar from being Priest unto the Lord, that he might [12]fulfill the words of the Lord, which he spake against the house of Eli in Shiloh. **28** Then tidings came to Joab: (for Joab had [s]turned after Adonijah, but he turned not after Absalom) and Joab fled unto the Tabernacle of the Lord, and caught hold on the horns of the altar. **29** And it was told king Solomon, that Joab was fled unto the Tabernacle of the Lord, and behold, he is by the [t]altar. Then Solomon sent Benaiah the son of Jehoiada, saying, Go, fall upon him. **30** And Benaiah came to the Tabernacle of the Lord, and said unto him, Thus saith the King, Come out. And he said, Nay, but I will die here. Then Benaiah brought the king word again, saying, Thus said Joab, and thus he answered me. **31** And the king said unto him, Do as he hath said, and [u]smite him, and bury him, that thou mayest take away the blood, which Joab shed causeless, from me, and from the house of my father. **32** And the Lord shall bring his blood upon his own head, for he smote two men more righteous and better than he, and slew them with the sword, and my father David knew not: to wit, [13]Abner the son of Ner, captain of the host of Israel, and [14]Amasa the son of Jether captain of the host of Judah. **33** Their blood shall therefore return upon the [v]head of Joab, and on the head of his seed forever: but upon David, and upon his seed, and upon his house and upon his throne shall there be peace forever from the Lord. **34** So Benaiah the son of Jehoiada went up, and smote him and slew him, and he was buried in his own house in the wilderness. **35** And the King put Benaiah the son of Jehoiada in his room over the host: and the king set Zadok the [w]Priest in the room of Abiathar. **36** Afterward the king sent, and called Shimei and said unto him, Build thee an house in Jerusalem, and dwell there, and depart not thence any whither. **37** For that day that thou goest out, and passest over the river of Kidron, know assuredly, that thou shalt die the death: thy blood shall be upon thine own head. **38** And Shimei said unto the king, The thing is good: as my lord the king hath said, so will thy servant do. So Shimei dwelt in Jerusalem many days. **39** And after three years two of the [x]servants of Shimei fled away unto Achish son of Maachah king of Gath: and they told Shimei, saying, Behold, thy servants be in Gath. **40** And Shimei arose, and saddled his ass, and went to Gath to Achish, to seek his servants: and [y]Shimei went, and brought his servants from Gath. **41** And it was told Solomon, that Shimei had gone from Jerusalem to Gath, and was come again. **42** And the King sent and called Shimei, and said unto him, Did I not make thee to swear by the Lord, and protested unto thee, saying, That day that thou goest out, and walkest any whither, know assuredly that thou shalt die the death? And thou saidest unto me, The thing is good, that I have heard. **43** Why then hast thou not kept the oath of the Lord, and the commandment wherewith I charged thee? **44** The King said also to Shimei, [z]Thou knowest all the wickedness whereunto thine heart is privy, that thou didst to David my father: the Lord therefore shall bring thy wickedness upon thine own head. **45** And let king Solomon be blessed, and the throne of David established before the Lord forever. **46** So the king commanded Benaiah the son of Jehoiada: who went out and smote him that he died. And the [15]kingdom was [aa]established in the hand of Solomon.

3

1 Solomon taketh Pharaoh's daughter to wife. 5 The Lord appeareth to him, and giveth him wisdom. 17 The pleading of the two harlots, and Solomon's sentence therein.

1 Solomon [1]then made affinity with Pharaoh king of Egypt, and took Pharaoh's daughter, and brought her into the [a]city of David, until he had made an end of building his own house, and the house of the Lord, and the wall of Jerusalem round about. **2** Only the people sacrificed in the [b]high places, because there was no house built unto the Name of the Lord, until those days. **3** And Solomon loved the Lord, walking in the ordinances of David his [c]father: only he sacrificed and offered incense in the high places. **4** And the King went to [d]Gibeon to sacrifice there, for that was the chief high place: a thousand burnt offerings did Solomon offer upon that altar. **5** In Gibeon the Lord appeared to Solomon in a dream by night: and God said, Ask what I shall give thee. **6** And Solomon said, Thou hast showed unto thy servant David my father great mercy, [e]when he walked before thee in truth, and in righteousness, and in uprightness of heart with thee: and thou hast [f]kept for him this great mercy, and hast given him a son, to sit on his throne,

---

1-KINGS 2

- **a.** 1 Kings 2:2 I am ready to die as all men must.
- **b.** 1 Kings 2:3 He showeth how hard a thing it is to govern, and that none can do it well except he obey God.
- **c.** 1 Kings 2:3 Or, do wisely.
- **d.** 1 Kings 2:4 And without hypocrisy.
- **e.** 1 Kings 2:4 Hebrew, a man shall not be cut off to thee from off the throne.
- **f.** 1 Kings 2:5 He shed his blood in time of peace, as if there had been war.
- **g.** 1 Kings 2:5 He put the bloody sword into his sheath.
- **h.** 1 Kings 2:7 That is, they dealt mercifully with me.
- **i.** 1 Kings 2:9 Let him be punished with death, see 1 Kings 2:46.
- **j.** 1 Kings 2:13 For she feared lest he would work treason against the king.
- **k.** 1 Kings 2:15 In sign of their favor and consent.
- **l.** 1 Kings 2:16 Hebrew, cause not my face to turn away.
- **m.** 1 Kings 2:19 In token of reverence, and that others by his example might have her in greater honor.
- **n.** 1 Kings 2:22 Meaning, that if he should have granted Abishag, which was so dear to his father, he would afterward have aspired to the kingdom.
- **o.** 1 Kings 2:25 Or, fell upon him.
- **p.** 1 Kings 2:26 Or, possessions.
- **q.** 1 Kings 2:26 Hebrew, man of death.
- **r.** 1 Kings 2:26 When he fled before Absalom, 2 Sam. 15:24.
- **s.** 1 Kings 2:28 He took Adonijah's part when he would have usurped the kingdom, 1 Kings 1:7.
- **t.** 1 Kings 2:29 Thinking to be saved by the holiness of the place.
- **u.** 1 Kings 2:31 For it was lawful to take the willful murderer from the altar, Exod. 21:14.
- **v.** 1 Kings 2:33 Joab shall be justly punished for the blood that he hath cruelly shed.
- **w.** 1 Kings 2:35 And so took the office of the high Priest from the house of Eli, and restored it to the house of Phinehas.
- **x.** 1 Kings 2:39 Thus God appointeth the ways and means to bring his just judgments upon the wicked.
- **y.** 1 Kings 2:40 His covetous mind moved him rather to venture his life, than to lose his worldly profit, which he had by his servants.
- **z.** 1 Kings 2:44 For though thou wouldest deny, yet thine own conscience would accuse thee for reviling and doing wrong to my father, 2 Sam 16:5.
- **aa.** 1 Kings 2:46 Because all his enemies were destroyed.

1-KINGS 2

1. Deut. 29:9 / Josh. 1:7
2. 2 Sam. 7:12
3. 2 Sam. 3:27
4. 2 Sam. 29:10
5. 2 Sam. 19:31
6. 2 Sam. 16:5
7. 2 Sam. 19:23
8. Acts 2:29 / Acts 13:36
9. 2 Sam. 5:4 / 1 Chron. 29:26,27
10. 1 Chron. 29:25
11. 2 Sam. 7:12,13
12. 1 Sam. 2:31,35
13. 2 Sam. 3:27
14. 2 Sam. 20:7
15. 2 Chron. 1:1

1-KINGS 3

- **a.** 1 Kings 3:1 Which was Bethlehem.
- **b.** 1 Kings 3:2 Where altars were appointed before the temple was built, to offer unto the Lord.
- **c.** 1 Kings 3:3 For his father had commanded him to obey the Lord and walk in his ways, 1 Kings 2:3.
- **d.** 1 Kings 3:4 For there the Tabernacle was, 2 Chron. 1:3.
- **e.** 1 Kings 3:6 Or, as he walked.
- **f.** 1 Kings 3:6 Thou hast performed thy promise.

as appeareth this day. **7** And now, O Lord my God, thou hast made thy servant king instead of David my father: and I am but a young child, and know not how to [g]go out and in. **8** And thy servant is in the midst of thy people, which thou hast chosen, even a great people, which cannot be told nor numbered for multitude. **9** [2]Give therefore unto thy servant an [h]understanding heart, to judge thy people: that I may discern between good and bad: for who is able to judge this thy [i]mighty people? **10** And this pleased the Lord well, that Solomon had desired this thing. **11** And God said unto him, Because thou hast asked this thing, and hast not asked for thyself long life, neither hast asked riches for thyself, nor hast asked the life of thine [j]enemies, but hast asked for thyself understanding to hear judgment, **12** Behold, I have done according to thy words: lo, I have given thee a wise and understanding heart, so that there hath been none like thee before thee, neither after thee shall arise the like unto thee. **13** And I have also [3]given thee that, which thou hast not asked, both riches and honor, so that among the Kings there [k]shall be none like unto thee all thy days. **14** And if thou wilt walk in my ways, to keep mine ordinances and my commandments, [4]as thy father David did walk, I will prolong thy days. **15** And when Solomon awoke, behold it was [l]a dream, and he came to Jerusalem, and stood before the Ark of the covenant of the Lord, and offered burnt offerings, and made peace offerings, and made a feast to all his servants. **16** Then came two [m]harlots unto the king, and [n]stood before him. **17** And the one woman said, Oh my lord, I and this woman dwell in one house, and I was delivered of a child with her in the house. **18** And the third day after that I was delivered, this woman was delivered also, and we were in the house together: no stranger was with us in the house save we twain. **19** And this woman's son died in the night: for she overlay him. **20** And she rose at midnight, and [o]took my son from my side, while thine handmaid slept, and laid him in her bosom, and laid her dead son in my bosom. **21** And when I arose in the morning to give my son suck, behold, he was dead: and when I had well considered him in the morning, behold, it was not my son, whom I had borne. **22** Then the other woman said, Nay, but my son liveth, and thy son is dead. Again she said, No, but thy son is dead, and mine alive: thus they spake before the king. **23** Then said the king, She saith, This that liveth is my son, and the dead is thy son: and the other saith, Nay, but the dead is thy son, and the living is my son. **24** Then the King said, [p]Bring me a sword: and they brought out a sword before the king. **25** And the king said, Divide ye the living child in twain, and give the one half to the one, and the other half to the other. **26** Then spake the woman, whose the living child was, unto the king, for her compassion was kindled toward her son, and she said, Oh my lord, give her the living child and [q]slay him not: but the other said, Let it be neither mine nor thine, but divide it. **27** Then the king answered, and said, Give her the living child, and slay him not: this is his mother. **28** And all Israel heard the judgment which the king had judged, and they feared the king: for they saw that the wisdom of God was in him to do justice.

4

2 The princes and rulers under Solomon. 22 The purveyance for his victuals. 26 The number of his horses. 32 His books and writings.

1 And king Solomon was king over all Israel. **2** And these were [a]his princes, [b]Azariah the son of Zadok the Priest, **3** Elihoreph and Ahijah the sons of Shisha, Scribes, Jehoshaphat the son of Ahilud, the Recorder, **4** And Benaiah the son of Jehoiada was over the host, and Zadok and [c]Abiathar, Priests, **5** And Azariah the son of Nathan was over the officers, and Zabud the son of Nathan, Priest, was the king's friend, **6** And Ahishar was over the household, and [1]Adoniram the son of Abda was over the tribute. **7** And Solomon had twelve officers over all Israel, which provided victuals for the king and his household: each man had a month in the year to provide victuals. **8** And these are their names: the son of Hur in mount Ephraim: **9** The son of Deker in Makaz, and in Shaalbim and Beth Shemesh, and [d]Elon and Beth Hanan: **10** The son of Hesed in Arubboth, to whom pertained Sochoh, and all the land of Hepher: **11** The son of Abinadab in all the region of Dor, which had Taphath the daughter of Solomon to wife. **12** Baana the son of Ahilud in Taanach, and Megiddo, and in all Beth Shean, which is by Zaretan beneath Jezreel, from Beth Shean [e]to Abel Meholah, even till beyond over against Jokneam: **13** The son of Geber in Ramoth Gilead, and his were the towns of [f]Jair, the son of Manasseh, which are in Gilead, and under him was the region of Argob, which is in Bashan: threescore great cities with walls and bars of brass. **14** Ahinadab the son of Iddo had to Mahanaim: **15** Ahimaaz in Naphtali, and he took Basemath the daughter of Solomon to wife: **16** Baanah the son of Hushai in Asher and in Aloth: **17** Jehoshaphat the son of Paruah in [g]Issachar: **18** Shimei the son of Elah in Benjamin: **19** Geber the son of Uri in the country of Gilead, the land of Sihon king of the Amorites, and of Og king of Bashan, and was officer alone in the land. **20** Judah and Israel were many, as the sand of the sea in number, [h]eating, drinking, and making merry. **21** And Solomon reigned over all kingdoms, from the [i]River unto the land of the Philistines, and unto the border of Egypt, and they brought presents, and served Solomon all the days of his life. **22** And Solomon's victuals for one day were thirty [j]measures of fine flour, and threescore measures of meal: **23** Ten fat oxen, and twenty oxen of the pastures, and an hundred sheep, besides harts, and bucks, and bugles, and fat fowl. **24** For he ruled in all the region on the other side of the River, from Tiphsah even unto [k]Gaza, over all the [l]kings on the other side the River: and he had peace round about him on every side. **25** And Judah and Israel dwelt without fear every man under his vine, and under his fig tree, from [m]Dan, even to Beersheba, all the days of Solomon. **26** And Solomon had [2]forty thousand stalls of horses for his chariots, and twelve thousand horsemen. **27** And these officers provided victual for king Solomon, and for all that came to king Solomon's table, every man his month, and they suffered to lack nothing. **28** Barley also and straw for the horses and mules, brought they unto the place where the officers were, every man according to his charge. **29** And God gave Solomon wisdom and understanding exceeding much, and [n]a large heart, even as the sand that is on the seashore, **30** And Solomon's wisdom excelled the wisdom of all the children of the [o]East, and all the wisdom of Egypt. **31** For he was wiser than any man: yea, than were Ethan the Ezrahite, than Heman, than Chalcol, than Darda the sons of Mahol: and he was famous throughout all nations round about. **32** And Solomon spake three thousand [p]proverbs: and his songs were a thousand and five. **33** And he spake of trees, from the cedar tree that is in Lebanon, even unto the [q]hyssop that springeth out of the wall: he spake also of beasts, and of fowls, and of creeping things, and of fishes. **34** And there came of all people to hear the wisdom of Solomon, from all kings of the earth, which had heard of his wisdom.

5

1 Hiram sendeth to Solomon, and Solomon to him, purposing to build the house of God. 6 He prepareth the stuff for the building. 13 The number of the workmen.

1 And Hiram king of [a]Tyre sent his servants unto Solomon, (for he had heard that they had anointed him king in the room of his father) because Hiram had ever loved David. **2** [1]And Solomon sent him to Hiram, saying, **3** Thou knowest that David my father could not build an house unto the name of the Lord his God, for the wars which were about him on every side, until the Lord had put [b]them under the soles of his feet. **4** But now the Lord my God hath given me [c]rest on every side, so that there is neither adversary, nor evil to resist. **5** And behold, I purpose to build an house unto the Name of the Lord my God, [2]as the Lord spake unto David my father, saying, Thy son, whom I will set upon thy throne for thee, he shall build an house unto my Name. **6** Now therefore command, that they hew me cedar trees out of Lebanon, and my servants shall be with thy servants, and unto thee will I give the [d]hire for thy servants, according to all that thou shalt appoint: for thou knowest that there are none among us, that can hew timber like unto the Sidonians. **7** And when [e]Hiram heard the words of Solomon, he rejoiced greatly, and said, Blessed be the Lord this day, which hath given unto David a wise son over this mighty people. **8** And Hiram sent to Solomon, saying, I have considered the things, for the which thou sentest unto me, and will accomplish all thy desire, concerning the cedar trees and fir trees. **9** My servants shall bring them down from Lebanon to the sea: and I will convey them by sea [f]in rafts unto the place that thou shalt show me, and will cause them to be discharged there, and thou shalt receive them: now thou shalt do me a pleasure to minister

---

g. 1 Kings 3:7 That is, to behave himself in executing this charge of ruling.
h. 1 Kings 3:9 Or, obedient.
i. 1 Kings 3:9 Which are so many in number.
j. 1 Kings 3:11 That is, that thine enemy should die.
k. 1 Kings 3:13 Or, hath been none.
l. 1 Kings 3:15 He knew that God had appeared unto him in a dream.
m. 1 Kings 3:16 Or, victuallers.
n. 1 Kings 3:16 By this example it appeareth that God kept his promise with Solomon in granting him wisdom.
o. 1 Kings 3:20 She stole the quick child away, because she might both avoid the shame and punishment.
p. 1 Kings 3:24 Except God give Judges understanding, the impudency of the trespasser shall overthrow the just cause of the innocent.
q. 1 Kings 3:26 Her motherly affection herein appeareth that she had rather endure the rigor of the Law, than see her child cruelly slain.

1-KINGS 3
1. 1 Kings 7:8 **2.** 2 Chron. 1:10 **3.** Matt. 6:33 **4.** 1 Kings 35:5

1-KINGS 4
a. 1 Kings 4:2 That is, his chief officers.
b. 1 Kings 4:2 He was the son of Ahimaaz and Zadok's nephew.
c. 1 Kings 4:4 Not Abiathar whom Solomon had put from his office, 1 Kings 2:27, but another of that Name.
d. 1 Kings 4:9 Or, Elon in Beth Aven.
e. 1 Kings 4:12 Or, to the plain.
f. 1 Kings 4:13 Which towns bare Jair's name, because he took them of the Canaanites, Num. 32:41.
g. 1 Kings 4:17 Solomon observed not the division that Joshua made, but divided it as might best serve for his purpose.
h. 1 Kings 4:20 They lived in all peace and security.
i. 1 Kings 4:21 Which is Euphrates.
j. 1 Kings 4:22 Hebrew, Kors.
k. 1 Kings 4:24 Or, Gaza.
l. 1 Kings 4:24 For they were all tributaries unto him.
m. 1 Kings 4:25 Throughout all Israel.
n. 1 Kings 4:29 Meaning, great understanding and able to comprehend all things.
o. 1 Kings 4:30 To wit, the Philosophers and Astronomers, which were judged most wise.
p. 1 Kings 4:32 Which for the most part are thought to have perished in the captivity of Babylon.
q. 1 Kings 4:33 From the highest to the lowest.

1-KINGS 4
1. 1 Kings 5:14 **2.** 2 Chron. 9:23

1-KINGS 5
a. 1 Kings 5:1 Or, Zor.
b. 1 Kings 5:3 Or, his enemies.
c. 1 Kings 5:4 He declareth that he was bound to set forth God's glory, forasmuch as the Lord had sent him rest and peace.
d. 1 Kings 5:6 This was his equity, that he would not receive a benefit without some recompense.
e. 1 Kings 5:7 In Hiram is prefigured the vocation of the Gentiles, who should help to build the Spiritual Temple.
f. 1 Kings 5:9 Or, floats.
g. 1 Kings 5:9 While my servants are occupied about thy business.
h. 1 Kings 5:11 Hebrew, Kors.

food for [g]my family. **10** So Hiram gave Solomon cedar trees and fir trees, even
his full desire. **11** And Solomon gave Hiram twenty thousand [h]measures of
wheat for food to his household, and twenty measures of [i]beaten oil. Thus much
gave Solomon to Hiram year by year. **12** And the Lord gave Solomon wisdom
as he [3]promised him. And there was peace between Hiram and Solomon, and they
[j]two made a covenant. **13** And King Solomon raised a sum out of all Israel, and
the sum was thirty thousand men: **14** Whom he sent to Lebanon, ten thousand
a month by course: they were a month in Lebanon, and two months at home.
And [4]Adoniram was over the sum. **15** And Solomon had seventy thousand that
bare burdens, and fourscore thousand masons in the mountain, **16** Besides the
[k]princes, whom Solomon appointed over the work, even three thousand and three
hundred, which ruled the people that wrought in the work. **17** And the King
commanded them, and they brought great stones and costly stones to make the
foundations of the house, even hewed stones. **18** And Solomon's workmen, and
the workmen of Hiram, and the [l]masons hewed and prepared timber and stones
for the building of the house.

6

1 The building of the Temple and the form thereof. 12 The promise of the Lord to Solomon.

1 And [1]in the four hundred and fourscore year (after the children of Israel
were come out of the land of Egypt) and in the fourth year of the reign of Solomon
over Israel, in the month [a]Ziv, (which is the second month) he built the [b]house
of the Lord. **2** And the house which king Solomon built for the Lord, was thre-
escore cubits long, and twenty broad, and thirty cubits high. **3** And the [c]porch
before the Temple of the house was twenty cubits long according to the breadth of
the house, and ten cubits broad before the house. **4** And in the house he made
windows, [d]broad without, and narrow within. **5** And by the wall of the house
he made [e]galleries round about, even by the walls of the house round about the
Temple and [f]the oracle, and made chambers round about. **6** And the nethermost
gallery was five cubits broad, and the middlemost six cubits broad, and the third
seven cubits broad: for he made [g]rests round about without the house, that the
beams should not be fastened in the walls of the house. **7** And when the hou-
se was built, it was built of stone perfect, before it was brought, so that there was
neither hammer, nor axe, nor any tool of iron heard in the house, while it was in
building. **8** The door of the middle [h]chamber was in the right side of the house,
and men went up with winding stairs into the middlemost, and out of the middle-
most into the third. **9** So he built the [i]house and finished it, and ceiled the hou-
se, being vaulted with ceiling of cedar trees. **10** And he built the galleries upon
all the wall of the house of five cubits height, and they were joined to the house
with beams of cedar. **11** And the word of the Lord came to Solomon, saying,
12 Concerning this house which thou buildest, if thou wilt walk in mine ordinan-
ces, and execute my judgments, and keep all my commandments, to walk in them,
then will I perform unto thee my promise, [2]which I promised to David thy father.
13 And I will [j]dwell among the children of Israel, and will not forsake my people
Israel. **14** So Solomon built the house and finished it, **15** And built the walls
of the house within, with boards of Cedar tree from the pavement of the house
unto [k]the walls of the ceiling, and within he covered them with wood, and covered
the floor of the house with planks of fir. **16** And he built twenty cubits in the
sides of the house with boards of Cedar, from the floor to the walls, and he prepa-
red a place within it for the oracle, even the most holy place. **17** But the [l]house,
that is, the Temple before it, was forty cubits long. **18** And the Cedar of the
house within was carved with [m]knops, and graven with flowers: all was Cedar, so
that no stone was seen. **19** Also he prepared the place of the oracle in the midst
of the [n]house within, to set the Ark of the covenant of the Lord there. **20** And
the place of the oracle within was twenty cubits long, and twenty cubits broad, and
twenty cubits high: and he covered it with pure gold, and covered the altar with
Cedar. **21** So Solomon covered the house within with pure gold, and he [o]shut
the place of the oracle with chains of gold, and covered it with gold. **22** And
he overlaid all the house with gold, until all the house was made perfect. Also he
covered the [p]whole altar, that was before the oracle, with gold. **23** And within
the oracle he made two Cherubims of [q]Olive tree, ten cubits high. **24** The wing
also of the one Cherub was five cubits, and the wing of the other Cherub was five
cubits: from the uttermost part of one of his wings unto the uttermost part of the
other of his wings, were ten cubits. **25** Also the other Cherub was of ten cubi-
ts: both the Cherubims were of one measure and one size. **26** For the height of
the one Cherub was ten cubits, and so was the other Cherub. **27** And he put
the Cherubims within the inner house, [3]and the Cherubims stretched out their
wings, so that the wing of the one touched the one wall, and the wing of the other
Cherub touched the other wall: and their other wings touched one another in the
midst of the house. **28** And he [r]overlaid the Cherubims with gold. **29** And
he carved all the walls of the house round about with graven figures of Cherubims
and of Palm trees, and graven flowers within and without. **30** And the floor of
the house he covered with gold within and without. **31** And in the entering of
the oracle he made two doors of Olive trees: and the upper post and side posts were
five square. **32** The two doors also were of Olive tree, and he graved them with
graving of Cherubims, and Palm trees, and graven flowers, and covered them with
gold, and laid [s]thin gold upon the Cherubims and upon the Palm trees. **33** And
so made he for the door of the Temple, posts of Olive trees foursquare. **34** But
the two doors were of fir tree, the two sides of the one door were [t]round, and the
two sides of the other door were round. **35** And he graved Cherubims, and
Palm trees, and carved flowers, and covered the carved work with gold finely wrou-
ght. **36** And he built the [u]court within with three rows of hewed stone, and one
row of beams of Cedar. **37** In the fourth year was the foundation of the house
of the Lord laid in the month of Ziv: **38** And in the eleventh year in the month
of [v]Bul, (which is the eighth month) he finished the house with all the furniture
thereof, and in every point: so was he seven years in building it.

7

1 The building of the house of Solomon. 15 The excellent workmanship of Hiram in the pieces which he made for the Temple.

1 But Solomon was building his own house [1]thirteen years, and [a]finished all
his house. **2** He built also an house [b]called the forest of Lebanon, an hundred
cubits long, and fifty cubits broad, and thirty cubits high, upon four rows of Ce-
dar pillars: and Cedar beams were laid upon the pillars. **3** And it was covered
above with cedar upon the beams, that lay on the forty and five pillars, fifteen in
a row. **4** And the windows were in three rows, and window was [c]against win-
dow in three ranks. **5** And all the doors, and the side posts with the windows
were foursquare, and window was over against window in three ranks. **6** And he
made a porch of pillars fifty cubits long, and thirty cubits broad, and the porch
was before [d]them, even before them were thirty pillars. **7** Then he made a por-
ch [e]for the throne, where he judged, even a porch of judgment, and it was ceiled
with cedar from pavement to pavement. **8** And in his house where he dwelt was
another hall more inward than the porch which was of the same work. Also So-
lomon made an house for Pharaoh's daughter ([2]whom he had taken to wife) like
unto this porch. **9** All these were [f]of costly stones, hewed by measure, and sawed
with saws within and without, from the foundation unto [g]the stones of an [h]hand
breadth, and on the outside to the great court. **10** And the foundation was of
costly stones, and great stones, even of stones of ten cubits, and stones of eight
cubits. **11** [i]Above also were costly stones squared by rule, and boards of cedar.
12 And the great court round about was with three rows of hewed stones, and a
row of cedar beams: [j]so was it to the inner court of the house of the Lord, and to
the porch of the house. **13** Then King Solomon sent, and fet one Hiram out
of [k]Tyre. **14** He was a widow's son of the tribe of Naphtali, his father being a
man of Tyre, and wrought in brass: [l]he was full of wisdom, and understanding,
and knowledge to work all manner of work in brass: who came to King Solomon,

---

i. 1 Kings 5:11 Or, pure.
j. 1 Kings 5:12 As touching the furniture of wood and vittles.
k. 1 Kings 5:16 Or, masters of the work.
l. 1 Kings 5:18 The Hebrew word is Giblim, which some say were excellent masons.

1-KINGS 5

1. 2 Chron. 2:3
2. 2 Sam. 7:13 / 2 Chron. 22:10
3. 1 Kings 3:12
4. 1 Kings 4:6

1-KINGS 6

a. 1 Kings 6:1 Which month containeth part of April and part of May.
b. 1 Kings 6:1 Whereby is meant the Temple and the Oracle.
c. 1 Kings 6:3 Or the court where the people prayed, which was before the place where the altar of burnt offerings stood.
d. 1 Kings 6:4 Or, to open and to shut.
e. 1 Kings 6:5 Or, lofts.
f. 1 Kings 6:5 Whence God spake between the Cherubims, called also the most holy place.
g. 1 Kings 6:6 Which were certain stones coming out of the wall, as stays for the beams to rest upon.
h. 1 Kings 6:8 Or, Gallery.
i. 1 Kings 6:9 In Exodus it is called the Tabernacle: and the Temple is here called the Sanctuary, and the Oracle the most holy place.
j. 1 Kings 6:13 According as he promised unto Moses, Exod. 25:22.
k. 1 Kings 6:15 Meaning, unto the roof which was also ceiled.
l. 1 Kings 6:17 For when he spake of the house in the first verse, he meant both the Oracle, and the Temple.
m. 1 Kings 6:18 Or, wild cucumbers.
n. 1 Kings 6:19 That is, in the most inward place of the house.
o. 1 Kings 6:21 Hebrew, he drew through chains of gold before.
p. 1 Kings 6:22 Meaning, the altar of incense, Exod. 30:1.
q. 1 Kings 6:23 Or, Pine tree
r. 1 Kings 6:28 For the others which Moses made of beaten gold, were taken away with the other jewels by their enemies, whom God permitted divers times to overcome them for their great sins.
s. 1 Kings 6:32 So that the fashion of the carved work might still appear.
t. 1 Kings 6:34 Or, folding.
u. 1 Kings 6:36 Where the Priests were, and was thus called in respect of the great court, which is called in Acts 3:11, the porch of Solomon, where the people used to pray.
v. 1 Kings 6:38 Which containeth part of October and part of November.

1-KINGS 6

1. 2 Chron. 3:1
2. 2 Sam. 7:13
3. Exod. 25:20

1-KINGS 7

a. 1 Kings 7:1 After he had built the Temple.
b. 1 Kings 7:2 For the beauty of the place, and great abundance of cedar trees that went to the building thereof, it was compared to mount Lebanon in Syria: this house he used in summer for pleasure and recreation.
c. 1 Kings 7:4 There were as many, and like proportion on the one side as the other, and at every end even three in a row one above another.
d. 1 Kings 7:6 Before the pillars of the house.
e. 1 Kings 7:7 For his house which was at Jerusalem.
f. 1 Kings 7:9 Or, precious.
g. 1 Kings 7:9 Which were rests and stays for the beams to lie upon.
h. 1 Kings 7:9 Or, span.
i. 1 Kings 7:11 From the foundation upward.
j. 1 Kings 7:12 As the Lord's house was built, so was this: only the great court of Solomon's house was uncovered.
k. 1 Kings 7:13 Or, Zor.
l. 1 Kings 7:14 Thus when God will have his glory set forth, he raiseth up men, and giveth them excellent gifts for the accomplishment of the same, Exod. 31:2,3.

and wrought all his work. **15** For he cast two pillars of brass: the height of a pillar was eighteen cubits, and a thread of twelve cubits did compass [m]either of the pillars. **16** And he made two [n]chapiters of molten brass to set on the tops of the pillars: the height of one of the chapiters was five cubits, and the height of the other chapiter was five cubits. **17** He made grates like network and [o]wreathen work like chains for the chapiters that were on the top of the pillars, even seven for the one chapiter, and seven for the other chapiter. **18** So he made the pillars and two rows of pomegranates round about in the one grate to cover the chapiters that were upon the top. And thus did he for the other chapiter. **19** And the chapiters that were on the top of the pillars were after [p]lily work in the porch, four cubits. **20** And the chapiters upon the two pillars had also above, [q]over against the belly [r]within the network pomegranates: for two hundred pomegranates were in the two ranks about upon [s]either of the chapiters. **21** And he set up the pillars in the [t]porch of the Temple. And when he had set up the right pillar, he called the name thereof [u]Jachin: and when he had set up the left pillar, he called the name thereof [v]Boaz. **22** And upon the top of the pillars was work of lilies: so was the workmanship of the pillars finished. **23** And he made a molten [w]sea of ten cubits wide from brim to brim, round in compass, and five cubits high, and a line of thirty cubits did compass it about. **24** And under the brim of it were knops like wild cucumbers compassing it round about, ten in one cubit, compassing the sea [3]round about: and the two rows of knops were cast, when it was molten. **25** It stood on twelve bulls, three looking toward the North, and three toward the West, and three toward the South, and three toward the East: and the sea stood above upon them, and all their hinder parts were inward. **26** It was [x]an handbreadth thick, and the brim thereof was like the work of the brim of a cup with flowers of lilies: it contained two thousand [y]baths. **27** And he made ten bases of brass, one base was four cubits long, and four cubits broad, and three cubits high. **28** And the work of the bases was on this manner, They had borders, and the borders were between the ledges: **29** And on the borders that were between the ledges, were lions, bulls and Cherubims: and upon the ledges there was a base above: and beneath the lions and bulls, were additions made of thin work. **30** And every base had four brazen wheels, and plates of brass: and the four corners had [z]undersetters: under the caldron were undersetters molten at the side of every addition. **31** And the [aa]mouth of it was within the chapiter and above to measure by the cubit: for the mouth thereof was round, made like a base, and it was a cubit and half a cubit: and also upon the mouth thereof were graven works, whose borders were foursquare, and not round. **32** And under the borders were four wheels and the axletrees of the wheels joined to the base: and the height of a wheel was a cubit, and half a cubit. **33** And the fashion of the wheels was like the fashion of a chariot wheel, their axletrees, and their naves and their [ab]felloes, and their spokes were all molten. **34** And four undersetters were upon the four corners of one base: and the undersetters thereof were of the base itself. **35** And in the top of the base was a round [ac]compass of half a cubit high round about: and upon the top of the base the ledges thereof, and the borders thereof were of the same. **36** And upon the tables of the ledges thereof, and on the borders thereof he did grave Cherubims, lions and palm trees, on the side of every one, and additions round about. **37** Thus made he the ten bases, They had all one casting, one measure, and one size. **38** Then made he [ad]ten cauldrons of brass, one cauldron contained forty baths, and every cauldron was four cubits, one cauldron was upon one base throughout the ten bases. **39** And he set the bases, five on the right side of the house, and five on the left side of the house. And he set the sea on the right side of the [ae]house Eastward toward the South. **40** And Hiram made cauldrons, and besoms, and basins, and Hiram finished all the work that he made to King Solomon for the house of the Lord: **41** To wit, two pillars and two bowls of the chapiters that were on the top of the two pillars, and two grates to cover the two bowls of the chapiters which were upon the top of the pillars, **42** And four hundred pomegranates for the two grates, even two rows of pomegranates for every grate to cover the two bowls of the chapiters, that were upon the pillars, **43** And the ten bases, and ten cauldrons upon the bases, **44** And the sea, and twelve bulls under that sea, **45** And pots, and besoms, and basins: and all these vessels, which [af]Hiram made to king Solomon for the house of the Lord, were of shining brass. **46** In the plain of Jordan did the King cast them in [ag]clay between Succoth and Zaretan. **47** And Solomon left to weigh all the vessels, because of the exceeding abundance, neither could the weight of the brass be counted. **48** So Solomon made all the vessels that pertained unto the house of the Lord, the [ah]golden altar, and the golden table, whereon the showbread was, **49** And the candlesticks, five at the right side, and five at the left, before the oracle of pure gold, and the flowers, and the lamps, and the snuffers of gold, **50** And the bowls, [ai]and the hooks, and the basins, and the spoons, and the ashpans of pure gold, and hinges of gold for the doors of the house within, even for the most holy place, and for the doors of the house, to wit, of the Temple. **51** So was finished all the work that king Solomon made for the house of the Lord, and Solomon brought in the things which [4]David his father had dedicated: the silver and the gold and the vessels, and laid them among the treasures of the house of the Lord.

8

4 The Ark is borne into the Temple. 10 A cloud filleth the Temple. 14 The king blesseth the people.

1 Then King Solomon assembled [1]the Elders of Israel, even all the heads of the tribes, the chief fathers of the children of Israel unto [a]him in Jerusalem, for to [b]bring up the Ark of the covenant of the Lord from the city of David, which is Zion. **2** And all the men of Israel assembled unto King Solomon at the feast in the month of [c]Ethanim, which is the seventh month. **3** And all the Elders of Israel came, and the Priests took the Ark. **4** They bare the Ark of the Lord, and they bare the Tabernacle of the Congregation, and all the holy vessels that were in the Tabernacle: those did the Priests and Levites bring up. **5** And King Solomon and all the Congregation of Israel that were assembled unto him, were with him before the Ark, offering sheep and beeves, which could not be told, nor numbered for multitude. **6** So the [d]Priests brought the Ark of the Covenant of the Lord unto his place, into the oracle of the house into the most holy place, even under the wings of the Cherubims. **7** For the Cherubims stretched out their wings over the place of the Ark, and the Cherubims covered the Ark, and the bars thereof above. **8** And they [e]drew out the bars, that the ends of the bars might appear out of the Sanctuary before the oracle, but they were not seen without: and there they are unto this day. **9** Nothing was in the Ark [f]save the two tables of stone which Moses had put there at Horeb, where the Lord made a covenant with the children of Israel, when he brought them out of the land of Egypt. **10** And when the Priests were come out of the Sanctuary, the [2]cloud filled the house of the Lord, **11** So that the Priests could not stand to minister, because of the cloud: for the glory of the Lord had filled the house of the Lord. **12** Then spake Solomon, The Lord [3]said, that he would dwell in the dark cloud. **13** I have built thee an house to dwell in, an habitation for thee to abide in for [g]ever. **14** And the King turned his face and blessed all the Congregation of Israel: for all the Congregation of Israel stood there. **15** And he said, Blessed be the Lord God of Israel, who spake with his mouth unto David my father, and hath with his hand fulfilled it, saying, **16** Since the day that I brought my people Israel out of Egypt, I chose no city of all the tribes of Israel, to build an house that my Name might be there: but I have chosen [4]David to be over my people Israel. **17** And it was in the heart of David my father, to build an house to the Name of the Lord God of Israel. **18** And the Lord said unto David my father, Whereas it was in thine heart to build an house unto my Name, thou didst well, that thou wast so minded: **19** Nevertheless thou shalt not build the house, but thy son that shall come out of thy loins, he shall build the house unto my Name. **20** And the Lord hath [h]made good his word that he spake: and I am risen up in the room of David my father, and sit on the throne of Israel, as the Lord promised, and have built the house for the Name of the Lord God of Israel. **21** And I have prepared therein a place for the Ark, wherein is the [i]covenant of the Lord which he made with our fathers, when he brought them out of the land of Egypt. **22** Then Solomon stood before [5]the altar of the Lord in the sight of all the Congregation of Israel, and stretched out his hands toward heaven, **23** And said, O Lord God of Israel, there is no God like thee in heaven above, or in the earth beneath, thou that keepest covenant and mercy with thy servants that walk before thee, with [j]all their heart, **24** Thou that hast kept with thy servant David my father, that thou hast promised him: for thou spakest with thy mouth, and hast fulfilled it with thine hand, as appeareth this day.

---

m. 1 Kings 7:15 Hebrew, the second.
n. 1 Kings 7:16 Or, pommels.
o. 1 Kings 7:17 Or, cords like chains.
p. 1 Kings 7:19 As was seen commonly wrought in costly porches.
q. 1 Kings 7:20 Or, round about the midst.
r. 1 Kings 7:20 Or, bound.
s. 1 Kings 7:20 Hebrew, the second.
t. 1 Kings 7:21 Which was in the inner court between the Temple and the oracle.
u. 1 Kings 7:21 That is, he will stablish, to wit, his promise toward this house.
v. 1 Kings 7:21 That is, in strength: meaning the power thereof shall continue.
w. 1 Kings 7:23 So called for the hugeness of the vessel.
x. 1 Kings 7:26 Or, a span.
y. 1 Kings 7:26 Bath and Ephah seem to be both one measure, Ezek. 45:11, every bath contained about ten pottles.
z. 1 Kings 7:30 Hebrew, shoulders.
aa. 1 Kings 7:31 The mouth of the great base or frame entered into the chapiter, or pillar that bare up the cauldron.
ab. 1 Kings 7:33 Or, rings.
ac. 1 Kings 7:35 Which was called the pillar, chapiter, or small base, wherein the cauldron stood.
ad. 1 Kings 7:38 To keep waters for the use of the sacrifices.
ae. 1 Kings 7:39 To wit, of the Temple or Sanctuary.
af. 1 Kings 7:45 By this name also Hiram the king of Tyre was called.
ag. 1 Kings 7:46 Or, thick earth.
ah. 1 Kings 7:48 This was done according to the form that the Lord prescribed unto Moses in Exodus.
ai. 1 Kings 7:50 Some take this for some instrument of music.

1-KINGS 7

1. 1 Kings 9:10
2. 1 Kings 3:1
3. 2 Chron. 4:3
4. 2 Chron. 5:1

1-KINGS 8

a. 1 Kings 8:1 Hebrew, Solomon.
b. 1 Kings 8:1 For David brought it from Obed-edom, and placed it in the Tabernacle which he had made for it, 2 Sam. 6:17.
c. 1 Kings 8:2 Containing part of September and part of October in the which month they held three solemn feasts, Num. 29:1.
d. 1 Kings 8:6 That is, the Kohathites, Num. 4:5.
e. 1 Kings 8:8 They drew them only out so far as they might be seen: for they might not pull them altogether out, Exod. 25:15.
f. 1 Kings 8:9 For it is like that the enemies when they had the Ark in their hands, took away the rod of Aaron and the pot with Manna.
g. 1 Kings 8:13 He spake according to the tenor of God's promise which was conditionally that they should serve him aright.
h. 1 Kings 8:20 Hebrew, confirmed.
i. 1 Kings 8:21 The two Tables wherein the articles of the covenant were written.
j. 1 Kings 8:23 Unfainedly and without all hypocrisy.

25 Therefore, now Lord God of Israel, keep with thy servant David my father that
thou hast promised him, saying, [6]Thou shalt not want a man in my sight to sit
upon the throne of Israel: so that thy children take heed to their way, that they walk
before me, as thou hast walked in my sight. **26** And now, O God of Israel, I pray
thee, let thy word be verified, which thou spakest unto thy servant David my fa-
ther. **27** [k]Is it true indeed that God will dwell on the earth? behold, the heavens,
and the heavens of heavens are not able to contain thee: how much more unable is
this house that I have built? **28** But have thou respect unto the prayer of thy
servant, and to his supplication, O Lord my God, to hear the cry and prayer which
thy servant prayeth before thee this day: **29** That thine eyes may be open toward
this house, night and day, even toward the place whereof thou hast said, [7]My
Name shall be there: that thou mayest hearken unto the prayer which thy servant
prayeth in this place. **30** Hear thou therefore the supplication of thy servant,
and of thy people Israel which pray in this place, and hear thou [l]in the place of thi-
ne habitation, even in heaven, and when thou hearest, have mercy. **31** When a
man shall trespass against his neighbor, and [m]he lay upon him an oath to cause him
to swear, and [n]the swearer shall come before thine altar into this house, **32** Then
hear thou in heaven, and [o]do and judge thy servants, that thou condemn the wi-
cked to bring his way upon his head, and justify the righteous, to give him accor-
ding to his righteousness. **33** When thy people Israel shall be overthrown before
the enemy, because they have sinned against thee, and turn again to thee, and
[p]confess thy Name, and pray and make supplication unto thee in this house,
34 Then hear thou in heaven, and be merciful unto the sin of thy people Israel,
and bring them again unto the land, which thou gavest unto their fathers.
35 When heaven shall be [q]shut up, and there shall be no rain because they have
sinned against thee, and shall pray in this place, and confess thy Name, and turn
from their sin, when thou dost afflict them, **36** Then hear thou in heaven, and
pardon the sin of thy servants and of thy people Israel (when thou hast taught them
the good way wherein they may walk) and give rain upon the land that thou hast
given thy people to inherit. **37** When there shall be famine in the land, when
there shall be pestilence, when there shall be blasting, mildew, grasshopper or ca-
terpillar, when their enemies shall besiege them in the [r]cities of their land, or any
plague, or any sickness, **38** Then what prayer, and supplication soever shall be
made of any man or of all thy people Israel, when everyone shall know the plague
in his own [s]heart, and stretch forth his hands in this house, **39** Hear thou then
in heaven, in thy dwelling place, and be merciful, and do, and give every man ac-
cording to all his ways, as thou knowest his heart, (for thou only knowest the hearts
of all the children of men) **40** That they may fear thee as long as they live in the
land, which thou gavest unto our fathers. **41** Moreover as touching the [t]stranger
that is not of thy people Israel, who shall come out of a far country for thy Name's
sake, **42** (When they shall hear of thy great Name, and of thy mighty hand, and
of thy stretched out arm) and shall come and pray in this house, **43** Hear thou
in heaven thy dwelling place, and do according to all that the stranger calleth for
unto thee: that all the people of the earth may know thy Name, and fear thee, as
do thy people Israel: and that they may know that thy [u]Name is called upon in this
house which I have built. **44** When thy people shall go out to battle against their
enemy by the way that thou shalt send them, and shall pray unto the Lord [8]toward
the way of the city which thou hast chosen, and toward the house that I have built
for thy Name, **45** Hear thou then in heaven their prayer and their supplication,
and [v]judge their cause. **46** If they sin against thee, ([9]for there is no man that
sinneth not) and thou be angry with them, and deliver them unto the enemies, so
that they carry them away prisoners unto the land of the enemies, either far or near,
47 Yet [w]if they turn again unto their heart in the land (to the which they be carried
away captives) and return and pray unto thee [x]in the land of them that carried
them away captives, saying, We have sinned, we have transgressed, and done wi-
ckedly, **48** If they turn again unto thee with all their heart, and with all their
soul in the land of their enemies, which led them away captives, and pray unto thee
toward [y]the way of their land, which thou gavest unto their fathers, and toward the
city which thou hast chosen, and the house which I have built for thy Name,
49 Then hear thou their prayer and their supplication in heaven thy dwelling pla-
ce, and [z]judge their cause, **50** And be merciful unto thy people that have sinned
against thee, and unto all their iniquities (wherein they have transgressed against
thee) and cause that they which led them away captives, may [aa]have pity and com-
passion on them. **51** For they be thy people, and thine inheritance, which thou
broughtest out of Egypt from the midst of the iron furnace. **52** Let thine eyes
be open unto the prayer of thy servant, and unto the prayer of thy people Israel, to
hearken unto them, in all that they call for unto thee. **53** For thou didst separate
them to thee from among all people of the earth for an inheritance, as thou saidest
by the hand of Moses thy servant, when thou broughtest our [10]fathers out of
Egypt, O Lord God. **54** And when Solomon had made an end of praying all this
[ab]prayer and supplication unto the Lord, he rose from before the altar of the Lord,
from kneeling on his knees, and stretching of his hands to heaven, **55** And stood
and blessed all the Congregation of Israel, with a loud voice, saying, **56** Blessed
be the Lord that hath given rest unto his people Israel, according to all that he pro-
mised: there hath not failed one word of all his good promise which he promised
by the hand of Moses his servant. **57** The Lord our God be with us, as he was
with our fathers, that he forsake us not, neither leave us, **58** That he may [ac]bow
our hearts unto him, that we may walk in all his ways, and keep his commandmen-
ts, and his statutes, and his laws, which he commanded our fathers. **59** And
these my words, which I have prayed before the Lord, be near unto the Lord our
God day and night, that he defend the cause of his servant, and the cause of his
people Israel [ad]always as the matter requireth, **60** That all the people of the earth
may know, that the Lord is God, and none other. **61** Let your heart therefore be
perfect with the Lord our God, to walk in his statutes, and to keep his command-
ments, as this day. **62** [11]Then the king and all Israel with him offered sacrifice
before the Lord. **63** And Solomon offered a sacrifice of peace offerings which he
offered unto the Lord, to wit, two and twenty thousand beeves, and an hundred
and twenty thousand sheep: so the King and all the children of Israel dedicated the
[ae]house of the Lord. **64** The same day did the King hallow the middle of the
court, that was before the house of the Lord: for there he made burnt offerings, and
the meat offerings, and the fat of the peace offerings, because the [12]brazen altar that
was before the Lord, was too little to receive the burnt offerings, and the meat of-
ferings, and the fat of the peace offerings. **65** And Solomon made at that time a
feast and all Israel with him, a very great Congregation, even from the entering in
of [af]Hamath unto the river of Egypt, before the Lord our God, [ag]seven days and
seven days, even fourteen days. **66** And the eighth day he sent the people away:
and they [ah]thanked the King, and went unto their tents joyous, and with glad he-
art, because of all the goodness that the Lord had done for David his servant, and
for Israel his people.

9

2 The Lord appeareth the second time to Solomon. 11 Solomon giveth cities to Hiram. 20 The Canaanites become tributaries. 28 He sendeth forth a navy for gold.

1 When [1]Solomon had finished the building of the house of the Lord, and
the King's palace, and all that Solomon desired and minded to do, **2** Then the
Lord appeared unto Solomon the second time, as he [2]appeared unto him at Gi-
beon. **3** And the Lord said unto him, I have heard thy prayer and thy supplica-
tion, that thou hast made before me: I have hallowed this house (which thou hast
built) to [3]put my Name there forever, and mine eyes, and my heart shall be there
perpetually. **4** And [a]if thou wilt walk before me (as David thy father walked in
pureness of heart and in righteousness) to do according to all that I have com-
manded thee, and keep my statutes, and my judgments, **5** Then will I stablish
the throne of thy kingdom upon Israel forever, as I promised to David thy father,
saying, Thou shalt not want a man upon the throne of Israel. **6** But if ye and
your children turn away from me, and will [b]not keep my Commandments, and
my statutes (which I have set before you) but go and serve other gods, and wor-
ship them, **7** Then will I cut off Israel from the land, which I have given them,
and the house which I have hallowed [5]for my Name, will I cast out of my sight,
and Israel shall be a [c]proverb, and a common talk among all people. **8** Even this
high house shall be so: everyone that passeth by it, shall be astonied, and shall hiss,
and they shall say, [6]Why hath the Lord done thus unto this land and to this hou-
se? **9** And they shall answer, Because they forsook the Lord their God, which
brought their fathers out of the land of Egypt, and have taken hold upon other

---

k. 1 Kings 8:27 He is ravished with the admiration of God's mercies, who being incomprehensible and Lord over all will become familiar with men.
l. 1 Kings 8:30 Or, from.
m. 1 Kings 8:31 To wit, the judge or neighbor.
n. 1 Kings 8:31 Hebrew, the oath.
o. 1 Kings 8:32 That is, make it known.
p. 1 Kings 8:33 Acknowledge thy just judgment, and praise thee.
q. 1 Kings 8:35 So that there be a drought to destroy the fruit of the land.
r. 1 Kings 8:37 Hebrew, in the land of their gates.
s. 1 Kings 8:38 For such are most meet to receive God's mercies.
t. 1 Kings 8:41 He meaneth such as should be turned from their idolatry to serve the true God.
u. 1 Kings 8:43 That this is the true religion wherewith thou wilt be worshipped.
v. 1 Kings 8:45 Or, maintain their right.
w. 1 Kings 8:47 Or, if they repent.
x. 1 Kings 8:47 Though the Temple was the chief place of prayer, yet he secludeth not them, that being let with necessity call upon him in other places.
y. 1 Kings 8:48 As Daniel did, Dan. 6:10.
z. 1 Kings 8:49 Or, avenge their wrong.
aa. 1 Kings 8:50 He understood by faith, that God of enemies would make friends unto them that did convert unto him.
ab. 1 Kings 8:54 Solomon is a figure of Christ, who continually is the Mediator between God and his Church.
ac. 1 Kings 8:58 He concludeth that man of himself is enemy unto God, and that all obedience to his Law proceedeth of his mere mercy.
ad. 1 Kings 8:59 Hebrew, the thing of a day in his day.
ae. 1 Kings 8:63 Before the oracle where the Ark was.
af. 1 Kings 8:65 That is, from North to South: meaning all the country.
ag. 1 Kings 8:65 Seven days for the dedication, and seven for the feast.
ah. 1 Kings 8:66 Hebrew, blessed.

1-KINGS 8
1. 1 Chron. 5:3
2. Exod. 40:34
3. 2 Chron. 6:1
4. 2 Sam. 7:8
5. 2 Chron. 6:13
6. 1 Kings 2:4
7. Deut. 12:11
8. Dan. 6:10
9. 2 Chron. 6:36 / Eccl. 7:22 / 1 John 1:8,10
10. Exod. 19:6
11. 2 Chron. 7:4
12. 2 Chron. 7:7

1-KINGS 9
a. 1 Kings 9:4 If thou walk in my fear, and withdraw thyself from the common manner of men, which follow their sensuality.
b. 1 Kings 9:6 God declareth that disobedience against him, is the cause of his displeasure, and so of all misery.
c. 1 Kings 9:7 The world shall make of you a mocking stock for the vile contempt and abusing of God's most liberal benefits.

gods, and have worshipped them, and served them, therefore hath the Lord brou-
ght upon them all this evil. **10** [7]And at the end of twenty years, when Solomon
had built the two houses, the house of the Lord, and the King's palace, **11** (For
the which Hiram the king of [d]Tyre had brought to Solomon timber of Cedar and
fir trees, and gold, and whatsoever he desired) then king Solomon gave to Hiram
twenty cities in the land of [e]Galilee. **12** And Hiram came out from Tyre to see
the cities which Solomon had given him, and they pleased him not. **13** There-
fore he said, What cities are these which thou hast given me, my brother? And he
called them the land of [f]Cabul unto this day. **14** And Hiram had sent the King
[g]sixscore [h]talents of gold. **15** And this is the cause of the tribute, why King Solo-
mon raised tribute, to wit, to build the house of the Lord, and his own house, and
[i]Millo, and the wall of Jerusalem, and Hazor, and Megiddo, and Gezer. **16** Pha-
raoh king of Egypt had come up, and taken Gezer, and burnt it with fire, and slew
the Canaanites that dwelt in the city, and gave it for a present unto his daughter
Solomon's wife. **17** (Therefore Solomon built Gezer and Beth Horon the nether,
18 And Baalath, and Tadmor in the wilderness of the land, **19** And all the cities
[j]of store, that Solomon had, even cities for chariots, and cities for horsemen, and
all that Solomon desired and would build in Jerusalem, and in Lebanon, and in
all the land of his dominion) **20** All the people that were [k]left of the Amorites,
Hittites, Perizzites, Hivites, and Jebusites, which were not of the children of Israel
21 To wit, their children that were left after them in the land whom the children
of Israel were not able to destroy, those did Solomon make tributaries unto this
day **22** But of the children of Israel did Solomon [8]make no bondmen: but they
were men of war and his servants, and his princes, and his captains, and rulers of
his chariots and his horsemen. **23** These were the princes of the officers, that
were over Solomon's work: even [l]five hundred and fifty, and they ruled the people
that wrought in the work. **24** And Pharaoh's daughter came up from the city of
David unto the house which Solomon had built for her: then did he build Millo.
25 And thrice a year did Solomon offer burnt offerings and peace offerings upon
the altar which he built unto the Lord: and he burnt incense upon the altar that
was before the Lord, when he had finished the house. **26** Also king Solomon
made a navy of ships in Ezion Geber, which is beside Elath, and the brink of the
red sea, in the land of Edom. **27** And Hiram sent with the navy, his servants,
that were mariners, and had knowledge of the sea, with the servants of Solomon.
28 And they came to Ophir, and fet from thence [m]four hundred and twenty talen-
ts of gold, and brought it to king Solomon.

10

1 The Queen of Sheba cometh to hear the wisdom of Solomon. 18 His royal throne. 23 His power and magnificence.

1 And the [1]Queen of [a]Sheba hearing the fame of Solomon (concerning the
Name of the Lord) came to prove him with hard questions. **2** And she came
to Jerusalem with a very great train, and camels that bare sweet odors, and gold
exceeding much, and precious stones: and she came to Solomon, and commu-
ned with him of all that was in her heart. **3** And Solomon declared unto her
all her questions: nothing was hid from the king, which he expounded not unto
her. **4** Then the Queen of Sheba saw all Solomon's wisdom, and the house that
he had built, **5** And the [b]meat of his table, and the sitting of his servants, and
the order of his ministers, and their apparel, and his drinking vessels, and his bur-
nt offerings, that he offered in the house of the Lord, and [c]she was greatly asto-
nied. **6** And she said unto the King, It was a true word that I heard in mine own
land of thy sayings, and of thy wisdom. **7** Howbeit I believed not this report, till
I came, and had seen it with mine eyes: but lo, the one half was not told me: for
thou hast more wisdom and prosperity, than I have heard by report. **8** Happy
are thy men, happy are these thy servants, which stand ever before thee, and hear
thy [d]wisdom. **9** Blessed be the Lord thy God, which [e]loved thee, to set thee on
the throne of Israel, because the Lord loved Israel forever, and made thee king to
do [f]equity and righteousness. **10** And she gave the king sixscore talents of gold,
and of sweet odors exceeding much, and precious stones. There came no more such
abundance of sweet odors, as the queen of Sheba gave to king Solomon. **11** The
navy also of Hiram (that carried gold from Ophir) brought likewise great plenty
of [2]Almuggim trees from Ophir, and precious stones. **12** And the king made
of the Almuggim trees pillars for the house of the Lord, and for the king's palace,
and made harps and psalteries for singers. There came no more such Almuggim
trees, nor were any more seen unto this day. **13** And King Solomon gave unto
the Queen of Sheba, whatsoever she would ask, besides that, which Solomon gave
her of his [g]kingly liberality: so she returned and went to her own country, both she
and her servants. **14** Also the weight of gold, that came to Solomon in one year,
was six hundred threescore and six [3]talents of gold, **15** Besides that he had of
merchant men and of the merchandises of them that sold spices, and of all the kin-
gs of Arabia, and of the princes of the [h]country. **16** And King Solomon made
two hundred targets of beaten gold, six hundred shekels of gold went to a target:
17 And three hundred shields of beaten gold, three pounds of gold went to one
shield: and the King put them in the [4]house of the wood of Lebanon. **18** Then
the King made a great throne of ivory, and covered it with the best gold. **19** And
the throne had six steps, and the top of the throne was round behind, and there
were [i]stays on either side on the place of the throne, and two lions standing by the
stays. **20** And there stood twelve lions on the six steps on either side: there was
not the like made in any kingdom. **21** And all King Solomon's drinking ves-
sels were of gold, and all the vessels of the house of the wood of Lebanon were of
pure gold, none were of silver: for it was nothing esteemed in the days of Solomon
22 For the King had on the sea the navy of Tarshish with the navy of Hiram: once
in three years came the navy of [j]Tarshish, and brought gold and silver, ivory, and
apes and peacocks. **23** So King Solomon exceeded all the kings of the earth
both in riches and in wisdom. **24** And all the world sought to see Solomon, to
hear his wisdom, which God had put in his heart, **25** And they brought every
man his present, vessels of silver, and vessels of gold, and raiment, and armor, and
sweet odors, horses and mules, from year to year. **26** Then Solomon gathered
together [5]chariots and horsemen: and he had a thousand and four hundred cha-
riots, and twelve thousand horsemen, whom he placed in the chariot cities, and
with the King at Jerusalem. **27** And the King [k]gave silver in Jerusalem as stones,
and gave cedars as the wild fig trees that grow abundantly in the plain. **28** Also
Solomon had horses brought out of Egypt, and fine linen: [l]the king's merchants
received the linen for a price. **29** There came up and went out of Egypt some
chariot worth six hundred shekels of silver: that is, one horse, an hundred and fifty.
And thus they brought horses to all the Kings of the Hittites and to the Kings of
Aram by their [m]means.

11

3 Solomon hath a thousand wives and concubines, which bring him to idolatry. 14 His God raiseth up adversaries against him. 43 He dieth.

1 But King Solomon loved [1]many [a]outlandish women: both the daughter
of Pharaoh, and the women of Moab, Ammon, Edom, Sidon, and Heth, **2** Of
the nations, whereof the Lord had said unto the children of Israel, [2]Go not ye in
to them, nor let them come in to you: for surely they will turn your hearts after
their gods, to them, I say, did Solomon join in love. **3** And he had seven hun-
dred wives, that were [b]princesses, and three hundred [c]concubines, and his wives
turned away his heart. **4** For when Solomon was old, his wives turned his heart
after other gods, so that his heart was not [d]perfect with the Lord his God as was
the heart of David his father. **5** For Solomon followed [3]Ashtoreth the god of
the Sidonians, and [e]Milcom the abomination of the Ammonites. **6** So Solomon
wrought wickedness in the sight of the Lord, but continued not to follow the Lord,
as did David his father. **7** Then did Solomon build an high place for Chemosh,
the [f]abomination of Moab, in the mountain that is over against Jerusalem, and
unto Molech the abomination of the children of Ammon. **8** And so did he for
all his outlandish wives, which burnt incense and offered unto their gods. **9** The-
refore the Lord was angry with Solomon, because he had turned his heart from the
Lord God of Israel, [4]which had appeared unto him twice, **10** And had given
him a [5]charge concerning this thing, that he should not follow other gods: but he
kept not that, which the Lord had commanded him. **11** Wherefore the Lord
said unto Solomon, Forasmuch as [g]this is done of thee, and thou hast not kept
my Covenant, and my statutes (which I commanded thee) [6]I will surely rent thy

---

d. 1 Kings 9:11 Or, Zor.
e. 1 Kings 9:11 Or, Galilee.
f. 1 Kings 9:13 Or, dirty, or barren.
g. 1 Kings 9:14 For his tribute toward the building.
h. 1 Kings 9:14 The common talent was about threescore pounds weight.
i. 1 Kings 9:15 Millo was as the town house or place of assembly which was open above.
j. 1 Kings 9:19 Cities for his munitions of war.
k. 1 Kings 9:20 These were as bondmen and paid what was required, either labor or money.
l. 1 Kings 9:23 The overseers of Solomon's works, were divided into three parts: the first contained 3300, the second 300, and the third 250, which were Israelites: so here are contained the two last parts, which make 550, see 2 Chron. 8:10.
m. 1 Kings 9:28 In 2 Chron. 8:18, is made mention of thirty more, which seem to have been employed for their charges.

1-KINGS 9

1. 2 Chron. 7:11
2. 1 Kings 3:5
3. 1 Kings 8:29 / Deut. 12:21
4. 2 Sam. 7:12 / 1 Chron. 22:10
5. Jer. 7:14
6. Deut. 29:24 / Jer. 22:8
7. 2 Chron. 8:1
8. Lev. 25:59

1-KINGS 10

a. 1 Kings 10:1 Josephus saith, that she was Queen of Ethiopia, and that Sheba was the name of the chief city of Meroe, which is an island of Nile.
b. 1 Kings 10:5 That is, the whole order, and trade of his house.
c. 1 Kings 10:5 Hebrew, there was no more spirit in her.
d. 1 Kings 10:8 But much more happy are they, which hear the wisdom of God revealed in his word.
e. 1 Kings 10:9 It is a chief sign of God's favor, when godly and wise rulers sit in the throne of justice.
f. 1 Kings 10:9 This is the cause, why Kings are appointed.
g. 1 Kings 10:13 Hebrew, by the hand of the King.
h. 1 Kings 10:15 To wit, of Arabia, which for the great abundance of all things was called Happy.
i. 1 Kings 10:19 As the chair bows, or places to lean upon.
j. 1 Kings 10:22 By Tarshish is meant Cilicia, which was abundant in variety of precious things.
k. 1 Kings 10:27 Or, he made silver as plenteous as stones.
l. 1 Kings 10:28 Or, for the company of the King's merchants did receive a number at a price.
m. 1 Kings 10:29 Hebrew, hands.

1-KINGS 10

1. 2 Chron. 9:1 / Matt. 12:42 / Luke 11:31
2. 2 Chron. 9:10
3. Exod. 25:39
4. 1 Kings 7:2
5. 2 Chron. 1:14

1-KINGS 11

a. 1 Kings 11:1 Which were idolaters.
b. 1 Kings 11:3 Or, Queens.
c. 1 Kings 11:3 To whom appertained no dowry.
d. 1 Kings 11:4 He served not God with a pure heart.
e. 1 Kings 11:5 Who was also called Molech, verse 7, read 2 Kings 23:10.
f. 1 Kings 11:7 Thus the Scripture termeth whatsoever man doth reverence and serve as God.
g. 1 Kings 11:11 That thou hast forsaken me and worshipped idols.

kingdom from thee, and will give it to thy servant. **12** Notwithstanding in thy days I will not do it, because of David thy father, but I will rent it out of the hand of thy son: **13** Howbeit I will not rent all the kingdom, but will give one [h]tribe to thy son, because of David my servant, and because of Jerusalem which I have chosen. **14** Then the Lord stirred up an adversary unto Solomon, even Hadad the Edomite, of the king's [i]seed, which was in Edom. **15** [7]For when David was in Edom, and Joab the captain of the host had smitten all the males in Edom, and was gone up to bury the [j]slain, **16** (For six months did Joab remain there and all Israel, till he had destroyed all the males in Edom.) **17** Then this Hadad [k]fled, and certain other Edomites of his father's servants with him, to go into Egypt, Hadad being yet a little child. **18** And they arose out of Midian, and came to Paran, and took men with them out of Paran, and came to Egypt unto Pharaoh king of Egypt, which gave him an house, and appointed him vittles and gave him land. **19** So Hadad [l]found great favor in the sight of Pharaoh, and he gave him to wife the sister of his own wife, even the sister of Tahpenes the Queen. **20** And the sister of Tahpenes bare him Genubath his son, whom Tahpenes weaned in Pharaoh's house: and Genubath was in Pharaoh's house among the sons of Pharaoh. **21** And when Hadad heard in Egypt that David slept with his fathers, and that Joab the captain of the host was dead, Hadad said to Pharaoh, Let me depart, that I may go to mine own country. **22** But Pharaoh said unto him, What hast thou lacked with me, that thou wouldest thus go to thine own country? And he answered, Nothing, but in any wise let me go. **23** [8]And God stirred him up another adversary, Rezon the son of Eliadah, which [m]fled from his lord Hadadezer king of Zobah. **24** And he gathered men unto him, and had been captain over the company, when David slew them. And they went to Damascus, and dwelt there, [n]and they made him king in Damascus. **25** Therefore was he an adversary to Israel all the days of Solomon: besides the evil that Hadad did, he also abhorred Israel, and reigned over Aram **26** [9]And Jeroboam the son of Nebat an Ephraimite of Zereda Solomon's servant (whose mother was called Zeruah a widow) lifted up his hand against the king. **27** And this was the cause that he lifted up his hand against the king, When Solomon built Millo, he repaired the broken places of the city of David his father. **28** And this man Jeroboam was a man of strength and courage, and Solomon seeing that the young man was meet for the work, he made him [o]overseer of all the labor of the house of Joseph. **29** And at that time, when Jeroboam went out of Jerusalem, the Prophet Ahijah the Shilonite found him in the way, having a new garment on him, and they two were alone in the field. **30** Then Ahijah caught the new garment that was on him, and [p]rent it in twelve pieces, **31** And said to Jeroboam, Take unto thee ten pieces: for thus saith the Lord God of Israel, Behold, I will rent the kingdom out of the hands of Solomon, and will give ten tribes to thee. **32** But he shall have one tribe for my servant David's sake, and for Jerusalem the city, which I have chosen out of all the tribes of Israel, **33** Because they have forsaken me, and have worshipped Ashtoreth the god of the Sidonians, and Chemosh the god of the Moabites, and Milcom the god of the Ammonites, and have not walked in my ways (to [q]do right in mine eyes, and my statutes, and my laws) as did David his father. **34** But I will not take the whole kingdom out of his hand: for I will make him prince all his life long for David my servant's sake, whom I have chosen, and who kept my commandments and my statutes. **35** [10]But I will take the kingdom out of his son's hand, and will give it unto thee, even the ten tribes. **36** And unto his son will I give one tribe, that David my servant may have a [r]light always before me in Jerusalem the city, which I have chosen me to put my Name there. **37** And I will take thee, and thou shalt reign [s]even as thine heart desireth, and shalt be king over Israel. **38** And if thou hearken unto all that I command thee, and wilt walk in my ways, and do right in my sight, to keep my statutes and my commandments as David my servant did, then will I be with thee, and build thee a sure house, as I built unto David, and will give Israel unto thee. **39** And I will [t]for this afflict the seed of David, [u]but not forever. **40** Solomon sought therefore to kill Jeroboam, and Jeroboam arose, and fled into Egypt unto Shishak king of Egypt, and was in Egypt until the death of Solomon. **41** And the rest of the words of Solomon, and all that he did, and his wisdom, are they not written in the [v]book of the acts of Solomon? **42** The time that Solomon reigned in Jerusalem over all Israel, was [11]forty years. **43** And Solomon slept with his fathers: and was buried in the city of David his father: and Rehoboam his son reigned in his stead.

12

1 Rehoboam succeedeth Solomon. 8 He refuseth the counsel of the Ancient. 20 Jeroboam reigneth over Israel. 21 God commandeth Rehoboam not to fight. 28 Jeroboam maketh golden calves.

1 And [1]Rehoboam went to Shechem: for all Israel were come to Shechem, to make him king. **2** And when Jeroboam the son of Nebat heard of it (who was yet in Egypt, [2]whither Jeroboam had fled from king Solomon, and [a]dwelt in Egypt.) **3** Then they sent and called him: and Jeroboam and all the Congregation of Israel came and spake unto Rehoboam, saying, **4** Thy father made our [3]yoke grievous: now therefore make thou the grievous servitude of thy father, and his sore yoke which he put upon us, [b]lighter, and we will serve thee. **5** And he said unto them, Depart yet for three days, then come again to me. And the people departed. **6** And king Rehoboam took counsel with the old men that [c]had stood before Solomon his father, while he yet lived, and said, What counsel give ye, that I may make an answer to this people? **7** And they spake unto him, saying, If thou be a [d]servant unto this people this day, and serve them, and answer them, and speak kind words to them, they will be thy servants forever. **8** But he forsook the counsel that the old men had given him, and asked counsel of the young men that had been brought up with him, and waited on him. **9** And he said unto them, [e]What counsel give ye, that we may answer this people, which have spoken to me, saying, Make the yoke, which thy father hath put upon us, lighter? **10** Then the young men that were brought up with him, spake unto him, saying, Thus shalt thou say unto this people, that have spoken unto thee, and said, Thy father hath made our yoke heavy, but make thou it lighter unto us: even thus shalt thou say unto them, My [f]least part shall be [g]bigger than my father's loins. **11** Now whereas my father did burden you with a grievous yoke, I will yet make your yoke heavier: my father hath chastised you with rods, but I will correct you with [h]scourges. **12** Then Jeroboam and all the people came to Rehoboam the third day, as the king had [i]appointed, saying, Come to me again the third day. **13** And the king answered the people sharply, and left the old men's counsel that they gave him, **14** And spake to them after the counsel of the young men, saying, My father made your yoke grievous, and I will make your yoke more grievous: my father hath chastised you with rods, but I will correct you with scourges. **15** And the king hearkened not unto the people: for it was the [j]ordinance of the Lord, that he might perform his saying, which the Lord had spoken by [4]Ahijah the Shilonite unto Jeroboam the son of Nebat. **16** So when all Israel saw that the king regarded them not, the people answered the king thus, saying, What portion have we in [k]David? we have none inheritance in the son of Jesse. To your tents, O Israel: now see to thine own house, David. So Israel departed unto their tents. **17** Howbeit over the children of Israel, which dwelt in the cities of Judah, did Rehoboam reign still. **18** Now the king Rehoboam sent Adoram the receiver of the tribute, and all Israel stoned him to death: then the king Rehoboam [l]made speed to get him up to his chariot, to flee to Jerusalem. **19** And Israel rebelled against the house [m]of David unto this day. **20** And when all Israel had heard that Jeroboam was come again, they sent and called him to the assembly, and made him king over all Israel: none followed the house of David, but the tribe of Judah [5]only. **21** And when Rehoboam was come to Jerusalem, he [n]gathered all the house of Judah with the tribe of Benjamin, an hundred and fourscore thousand of chosen men (which were good warriors) to fight against the house of Israel, and to bring the kingdom again to Rehoboam the son of Solomon. **22** [6]But the word of God came unto Shemaiah the [o]man of God, saying, **23** Speak unto Rehoboam the son of Solomon king of Judah, and unto all the house of Judah and Benjamin, and the remnant of the people, saying, **24** Thus saith the [p]Lord, Ye shall not go up, nor fight against your brethren the children of Israel: return every man to his house: for this thing is done by me. They obeyed therefore the word of the Lord, and returned, and departed according to the word of the Lord. **25** Then Jeroboam built Shechem in mount Ephraim,

---

h. 1 Kings 11:13 Because the tribes of Judah and Benjamin had their possessions mixed, they are here taken as one tribe.
i. 1 Kings 11:14 Of the king of Edom's stock.
j. 1 Kings 11:15 Of the Edomites.
k. 1 Kings 11:17 Thus God reserved this idolater to be a scourge to punish his people's sins.
l. 1 Kings 11:19 God brought him to honor, that his power might be more able to compass his enterprises against Solomon's house.
m. 1 Kings 11:23 When David had discomfited Hadadezer and his army.
n. 1 Kings 11:24 To wit, the men whom he had gathered unto him.
o. 1 Kings 11:28 He was overseer of Solomon's works, for the tribe of Ephraim and Manasseh.
p. 1 Kings 11:30 By these visible signs the Prophets would more deeply print their message into their hearts to whom they were sent.
q. 1 Kings 11:33 Or, to do that, that pleaseth me.
r. 1 Kings 11:36 He hath respect unto the Messiah, which should be the bright star that should shine through all the world.
s. 1 Kings 11:37 Hebrew, in all that thy soul.
t. 1 Kings 11:39 For this idolatry that Solomon hath committed.
u. 1 Kings 11:39 For the whole spiritual kingdom was restored in Messiah.
v. 1 Kings 11:41 Which book as is thought, was lost in their captivity.

1-KINGS 11

1. Deut. 17:17
2. Exod. 34:16
3. Judg. 2:15
4. 1 Kings 3:5 / 1 Kings 9:2
5. 1 Kings 6:12
6. 1 Kings 2:15
7. 2 Sam. 8:14
8. 2 Sam. 8:3
9. 2 Chron. 13:6
10. 1 Kings 12:15
11. 2 Chron. 9:30

1-KINGS 12

a. 1 Kings 12:2 Or, return from Egypt.
b. 1 Kings 12:4 Oppress us not with so great charges, which we are not able to sustain.
c. 1 Kings 12:6 Or, had been of his ancient counselors.
d. 1 Kings 12:7 They showed him that there was no way to win the people's hearts, but to grant them their just petition.
e. 1 Kings 12:9 There is nothing harder for them that are in authority, than to bridle their affections, and to follow good counsel.
f. 1 Kings 12:10 Or, little finger.
g. 1 Kings 12:10 I am much more able to keep you in subjection than my father was.
h. 1 Kings 12:11 Or, scorpions.
i. 1 Kings 12:12 The people declare their obedience in this that they would attempt nothing before the king had given them just occasion.
j. 1 Kings 12:15 Or, the Lord was the cause.
k. 1 Kings 12:16 Though their cause were good, yet it is most hard for the people to bridle their affections, as these vile words declare.
l. 1 Kings 12:18 Hebrew, strengthened himself.
m. 1 Kings 12:19 By the just judgment of God for Solomon's sins.
n. 1 Kings 12:21 For as yet he perceived not that the Lord had so appointed it.
o. 1 Kings 12:22 That is, the Prophet.
p. 1 Kings 12:24 Who of his just judgment will punish the trespasser, and of his mercy spare the innocent people.

and dwelt therein, and went from thence, and built Penuel. **26** And Jeroboam thought in his heart, Now shall the kingdom return to the house of David. **27** If this people go up and do sacrifice in the house of the Lord [q]at Jerusalem, then shall the hearts of this people turn again unto their lord, even to Rehoboam king of Judah: so shall they kill me, and go again to Rehoboam king of Judah. **28** Whereupon the king took counsel, and made two calves of gold, and said unto them, [r]It is too much for you to go up to Jerusalem: Behold, O Israel, thy gods which brought thee up out of the land of Egypt. **29** And he set the one in Bethel, and the other set he in Dan. **30** And this thing turned to sin: for the people went (because of the one) even to Dan. **31** Also he made an [s]house of high places, and made priests of the lowest of the people, which were not of the sons of Levi. **32** And Jeroboam made a feast the [t]fifteenth day of the eighth month, like unto the feast that is in Judah, and offered on the altar. So did he in Bethel and offered unto the calves that he had made: and he placed in Bethel the Priests of the high places, which he had made. **33** And he offered upon the altar, which he had made in Bethel, the fifteenth day of the eighth month, (even in the month which he had forged of his own heart) and made a solemn feast unto the children of Israel, and he went up to the altar, to burn incense.

13

1 Jeroboam is reprehended of the Prophet. 4 His hand drieth up. 13 The Prophet is seduced, 24 and is killed of a lion. 33 The obstinacy of Jeroboam.

1 And behold, there came [a]a man of God out of Judah (by the commandment of the Lord) unto [b]Bethel, and Jeroboam stood by the altar to offer incense. **2** And he cried against the altar by the commandment of the Lord, and said, O altar, altar, thus saith the Lord, Behold, a child shall be born unto the house of David, [1]Josiah by name, and upon thee shall he sacrifice the priests of the high places that burn incense upon thee, and they shall burn men's bones upon thee. **3** And he gave a sign the same time, saying, This is the [c]sign, that the Lord hath spoken, Behold, the altar shall rent, and the ashes that are upon it, shall [d]fall out. **4** And when the king had heard the saying of the man of God, which he had cried against the altar in Bethel, Jeroboam stretched out his hand for the altar, saying, [e]Lay hold on him: but his hand which he put forth against him, dried up, and he could not pull it in again to him. **5** The altar also clave asunder, and the ashes fell out from the altar, according to the sign, which the man of God had given by the [f]commandment of the Lord. **6** Then the king answered and said unto the man of God, [g]I beseech thee, pray unto the Lord thy God, and make intercession for me, that mine hand may be restored unto me. And the man of God besought the Lord, and the King's hand was restored, and became as it was afore. **7** Then the King said unto the man of God, Come home with me, that thou mayest [h]dine, and I will give thee a reward. **8** But the man of God said unto the King, If thou wouldest give me half thine house, I would not go with thee, neither would I eat bread nor drink water in this place. **9** For so [i]was it charged me by the word of the Lord, saying, [j]Eat no bread nor drink water, nor turn again by the same way that thou camest. **10** So he went another way, and returned not by the way that he came to Bethel. **11** And an old Prophet dwelt in Bethel, and his sons came and told him all the works, that the man of God had done that day in Bethel, and the words which he had spoken unto the king, told they their father. **12** And their father said unto them, What way went he? and his sons [k]showed him what way the man of God went, which came from Judah. **13** And he said unto his sons, Saddle me the ass. Who saddled him the ass, and he rode thereon, **14** And went after the man of God, and found him sitting under an oak: and he said unto him, Art thou the man of God, that camest from Judah? And he said, [l]Yea. **15** Then he said unto him, [m]Come home with me, and eat bread. **16** But he answered, I may not return with thee, nor go in with thee, neither will I eat bread nor drink water with thee in this place. **17** For it was charged me by the word of the Lord, saying, Thou shalt eat no bread, nor drink water there, nor turn again to go by the way that thou wentest. **18** And he said unto him, I am a Prophet also as thou art, and an [n]Angel spake unto me by the word of the Lord, saying, Bring him again with thee into thine house, that he may eat bread and drink water: but he lied unto him. **19** So he went again with him, and did eat bread in his house, and drank water. **20** And as they sat at the table, the word of the Lord came unto the Prophet, that brought him again. **21** And he cried unto the man of God that came from Judah, saying, Thus saith the Lord, [o]Because thou hast disobeyed the mouth of the Lord, and hast not kept the commandment which the Lord thy God commanded thee, **22** But camest back again, and hast eaten bread and drunk water in the place (whereof he did say unto thee, Thou shalt eat no bread nor drink any water) thy carcass shall not come unto the sepulcher of thy fathers. **23** And when he had eaten bread and drunk, he saddled him the ass, to wit, to the Prophet whom he had brought again, **24** And when he was gone, [p]a lion met him by the way, and slew him, and his body was cast in the way, and the ass stood thereby: the Lion stood by the corpse also. **25** And behold, men that passed by, saw the carcass cast in the way, and the Lion standing by the corpse: and they came and told it in the town where the old Prophet dwelt. **26** And when the Prophet that brought him back again from the way, heard thereof, he said, It is the man of God, who hath been disobedient unto the Commandment of the Lord: therefore the Lord hath delivered him unto the Lion, which hath rent him and slain him, according to the word of the Lord, which he spake unto him. **27** And he spake to his sons, saying, Saddle me the ass. And they saddled him. **28** And he went and found his body cast in the way, and the ass and the Lion stood by the corpse: and the lion had [q]not eaten the body, nor torn the ass. **29** And the Prophet took up the body of the man of God, and laid it upon the ass, and brought it again, and the old Prophet came to the city, to lament and bury him. **30** And he laid his body in his [r]own grave, and they lamented over him, saying, Alas, my brother. **31** And when he had buried him, he spake to his sons, saying, When I am dead, bury ye me also in the sepulcher, wherein the man of God is buried: lay my bones beside his bones. **32** For that thing which he cried by the word of the Lord against the altar that is in Bethel, and against all the houses of the high places, which are in the cities of Samaria, shall surely come to pass. **33** Howbeit after this Jeroboam [s]converted not from his wicked way, but turned again, and made of the lowest of the people priests of the high places. Who would, might [t]consecrate himself and be of the priests of the high places. **34** And this thing turned to sin unto the house of Jeroboam, even to root it out, and destroy it from the face of the earth.

14

2 Jeroboam sendeth his wife disguised to Ahijah the Prophet, who declareth unto him the destruction of his house. 25 Judah is punished by Shishak.

1 At that time Abijah the son of Jeroboam fell sick. **2** And Jeroboam said unto his wife, Up, I pray thee, [a]and disguise thyself that they know not that thou art the wife of Jeroboam, and go to Shiloh: for there is Ahijah the Prophet, which told me [1]that I should be king over this people, **3** And take [b]with [c]thee, ten loaves and [d]cracknels, and a bottle of honey, and go to him: he shall tell thee what shall become of the young man. **4** And Jeroboam's wife did so, and arose, and went to Shiloh, and came to the house of Ahijah: but Ahijah could not see, for his [e]sight was decayed for his age. **5** Then the Lord said unto Ahijah, Behold, the wife of Jeroboam cometh to ask a thing of thee for her son, for he is sick: thus and thus shalt thou say unto her: for when she cometh in, she shall feign herself to be [f]another. **6** Therefore when Ahijah heard the sound of her feet as she came in at the door, he said, Come in thou [g]wife of Jeroboam: why feignest thou thus thyself to be another? I am sent to thee with heavy tidings. **7** Go tell Jeroboam, Thus saith the Lord God of Israel, Forasmuch as I have exalted [h]thee from among the people, and have made thee prince over my people Israel, **8** And have rent the kingdom away from the house of David, and have given it thee, and thou hast not been as my servant David, which kept my Commandments, and followed me with all his heart, and did only that which was right in mine eyes, **9** But hast done evil above all that were before thee (for thou hast gone and made thee other gods, and [i]molten images, to provoke me, and hast cast me behind thy back.)

---

q. 1 Kings 12:27 He feared lest his people should have by this means been enticed to rebel against him.
r. 1 Kings 12:28 So crafty are carnal persuasions of princes, when they will make a religion to serve to their appetite.
s. 1 Kings 12:31 That is, a temple, where altars were built for idolatry.
t. 1 Kings 12:32 Because he would the more bind the people's devotion to his idolatry, he made a new holy day, besides those that the Lord had appointed in the Law.

1-KINGS 12

1. 2 Chron. 10:1
2. 1 Kings 11:40
3. 1 Kings 4:7
4. 1 Kings 11:11
5. 1 Kings 11:13
6. 2 Chron. 11:2

1-KINGS 13

a. 1 Kings 13:1 That is, a Prophet.
b. 1 Kings 13:1 Not that that was called Luz in Benjamin, but another of that name.
c. 1 Kings 13:3 By this sign ye shall know that the Lord hath sent me.
d. 1 Kings 13:3 Or, be poured out.
e. 1 Kings 13:4 The wicked rage against the Prophets of God, when they declare them God's judgments.
f. 1 Kings 13:5 Hebrew, mouth.
g. 1 Kings 13:6 Though the wicked humble themselves for a time when they feel God's judgment, yet after they return to their old malice, and declare that they are but vile hypocrites.
h. 1 Kings 13:7 Or, take sustenance.
i. 1 Kings 13:9 Or, he charged me: to wit, an Angel.
j. 1 Kings 13:9 Seeing he had the express word of God, he ought not to have declined therefrom neither for the persuasion of man nor Angel.
k. 1 Kings 13:12 Hebrew, looked.
l. 1 Kings 13:14 Hebrew, I am.
m. 1 Kings 13:15 This he did of a simple mind, thinking it his duty to declare friendship to a Prophet.
n. 1 Kings 13:18 His fault is here double: first in that he suffereth not the Prophet to obey God's express commandment: and next, that he feigneth to have a revelation to the contrary.
o. 1 Kings 13:21 God would reprove his folly by him, who was the occasion to bring him into error.
p. 1 Kings 13:24 By this fearful example, God setteth forth how dangerous a thing it is for men to behave themselves coldly, or deceitfully in their charge whereunto God hath called them.
q. 1 Kings 13:28 To declare that this was only the judgment of God: for if the Lion had done it for hunger, he would also have devoured the body.
r. 1 Kings 13:30 Which he had prepared for himself.
s. 1 Kings 13:33 So the wicked profit not by God's threatenings, but go backward, and become worse and worse, 2 Tim. 3:13.
t. 1 Kings 13:33 Hebrew, fill his hand.

1-KINGS 13

1. 2 Kings 23:17

1-KINGS 14

a. 1 Kings 14:2 His own conscience bare him witness, that the Prophet of God would not satisfy his affections, which was a wicked man.
b. 1 Kings 14:3 Hebrew, in thine hand.
c. 1 Kings 14:3 According to the custom when they went to ask counsel of Prophets, 1 Sam. 9:7.
d. 1 Kings 14:3 Or, wafers.
e. 1 Kings 14:4 Hebrew, eyes stood.
f. 1 Kings 14:5 Then the wife of Jeroboam.
g. 1 Kings 14:6 For God ofttimes discloseth unto his the craft and subtlety of the wicked.
h. 1 Kings 14:7 Which wast but a servant.

10 Therefore behold, I will bring evil upon the house of Jeroboam, and will cut
off from Jeroboam him that [j,2]pisseth against the wall, as well him that [k]is shut up,
as him that is left in Israel, and will sweep away the remnant of the house of Je-
roboam, as a man sweepeth away dung till it be all gone. **11** The dogs shall eat
him of Jeroboam's stock that dieth in the city, and the fowls of the air shall eat him
that dieth in the field: [l]for the Lord hath said it. **12** Up therefore and get thee to
thine house: for when thy feet enter into the city, the child shall die. **13** And all
Israel shall mourn for him, and bury him: for he only of Jeroboam shall come to
the grave, because in him there is found [m]some goodness toward the Lord God of
Israel in the house of Jeroboam. **14** Moreover, the Lord shall stir him up a King
over Israel which shall destroy the house of Jeroboam in that day: [n]what? yea, even
now. **15** For the Lord shall smite Israel, as when a reed is shaken in the water,
and he shall weed Israel out of this good land, which he gave to their fathers, and
shall scatter them beyond the [o]River, because they have made them groves, pro-
voking the Lord to anger. **16** And he shall give Israel up, because of the sins of
Jeroboam, who did sin, and [p]made Israel to sin. **17** And Jeroboam's wife aro-
se, and departed, and came to Tirzah, and when she came to the threshold of the
house, the young man died. **18** And they buried him, and all Israel lamented
him, according to the word of the Lord which he spake by the hand of his servant
Ahijah the Prophet. **19** And the rest of Jeroboam's acts, how he warred, and how
he reigned, behold, they are written in the book of the Chronicles of the Kings of
Israel. **20** And the days which Jeroboam reigned, were two and twenty years:
and he [q]slept with his fathers, and Nadab his son reigned in his stead. **21** Also
Rehoboam the son of Solomon reigned in Judah. Rehoboam was one and forty
years old, when he began to reign, and reigned seventeen [r]years in Jerusalem, the
city which the Lord did choose out of all the tribes of Israel, to put his name the-
re: and his mother's name was Naamah an Ammonite. **22** And Judah wrought
wickedness in the sight of the Lord: and they provoked him more with their sins,
which they had committed, [s]than all that which their fathers had done. **23** For
they also made them high places, and images, and groves on every high hill, and
under every green tree. **24** There were also Sodomites in the [t]land, they did ac-
cording to all the abominations of the nations, which the Lord hast cast out before
the children of Israel. **25** And in the fifth year of King Rehoboam, Shishak king
of Egypt came up against Jerusalem, **26** And took the treasures of the house of
the Lord, and the treasures of the King's house, and took away all: so he carried
away all the shields of gold [3]which Solomon had made. **27** And king Reho-
boam made for them brazen shields, and committed them unto the hands of the
chief of the guard, which waited at the door of the king's house. **28** And when
the King went into the house of the Lord, the guard bare them, and brought them
again into the guard chamber. **29** And the rest of the acts of Rehoboam, and
all that he did, are they not written in [u]the book of the Chronicles of the kings of
Judah? **30** And there was war between Rehoboam and Jeroboam [v]continually.
31 And Rehoboam slept with his fathers, and was buried with his fathers in the
city of David: his mother's name was Naamah an [w]Ammonite: and Abijam his son
reigned in his stead.

15

1 Abijam reigneth over Judah. 9 Asa succeedeth in his room. 16 The battle between Asa and Baasha. 24 Jehoshaphat succeedeth Asa. 25 Nadab succeedeth Jeroboam. 28 Baasha killeth Nadab.

1 And in the eighteenth year of King [1]Jeroboam the son of Nebat, reigned
Abijam over Judah. **2** Three years reigned he in Jerusalem, and his mother's name
was Maachah the daughter of [a]Abishalom. **3** And he walked in all the sins of his
father, which he had done before him: and his heart was not perfect with the Lord
his God, as the heart of David his father. **4** But for David's sake did the Lord his
God give him a [b]light in Jerusalem, and set up his son after him, and established
Jerusalem, **5** Because David did that which was right in the sight of the Lord,
and turned from nothing that he commanded him all the days of his life, [2]save
only in the matter of Uriah the Hittite. **6** And there was war between Rehobo-
am and Jeroboam as long as he lived. **7** The rest also of the acts of Abijam, and
all that he did, are they not written in the [3]book of the Chronicles of the kings of
Judah? there was also war between Abijam and Jeroboam. **8** And Abijam slept
with his fathers, and they buried him in the city of David: and Asa his son reigned
in his stead. **9** [4]And in the twenty years of Jeroboam King of Israel, reigned Asa
over Judah. **10** He reigned in Jerusalem one and forty years, and his [c]mother's
name was Maachah, the daughter of Abishalom. **11** And Asa did right in the
eyes of the Lord, as did David his father. **12** And he took away the Sodomites
out of the land, and put away all the idols that his fathers had made. **13** And
he [d]put down [5]Maachah his mother also from her estate, because she had made an
idol in a grove: and Asa destroyed her idols, and burnt them by the brook Kidron.
14 But they put not down the high places. Nevertheless Asa's heart was [e]upright
with the Lord all his days. **15** Also he brought in the holy vessels of his father,
and the things that he had dedicated unto the house of the Lord, silver and gold,
and vessels. **16** And there was war between Asa and Baasha king of Israel all their
days. **17** Then Baasha King of Israel went up against Judah, and built [f]Ramah,
so that he would let none go out or in to Asa king of Judah. **18** Then Asa took
all the silver and the gold that was left in the treasures of the house of the Lord, and
the treasures of the king's house, and delivered them into the hands of his servants,
and king Asa sent them to [6]Ben-Hadad the son of Tabrimmon, the son of Hezion
king of [g]Aram that dwelt at Damascus, saying, **19** There is a covenant between
me and thee, and between my father and thy father: Behold, I have sent unto thee
a present of silver and gold: come, break thy covenant with Baasha King of Israel,
that he may [h]depart from me. **20** So Ben-Hadad hearkened unto king Asa, and
sent the captains of the hosts, which he had, against the cities of Israel, and smote
Ijon, and Dan, and Abel Beth Maachah, and all Chinneroth, with all the land of
Naphtali. **21** And when Baasha heard thereof, he left building of Ramah, and
dwelt in Tirzah. **22** Then king Asa [i]assembled all Judah [j]none excepted, and
they took the stones of Ramah, and the timber thereof, wherewith Baasha had bu-
ilt, and king Asa built with them Geba of Benjamin and Mizpah. **23** And the
rest of all the acts of Asa, and all his might, and all that he did, and the cities which
he built, are they not written in the book of the Chronicles of the Kings of Judah?
but in his old age he was diseased in his [k]feet. **24** And Asa slept with his fathers,
and was buried with his fathers in the city of David his [l]father. And Jehoshaphat
his son reigned in his stead. **25** And Nadab the son of Jeroboam began to reign
over Israel the second year of Asa king of Judah, and reigned over Israel two years.
26 And he did evil in the sight of the Lord, walking in the way of his father, and
in his sin wherewith he made Israel to sin. **27** And Baasha the son of Ahijah of
the house of Issachar conspired against him, and Baasha slew him at Gibbethon,
which belonged to the Philistines: for Nadab and all Israel laid siege to Gibbethon.
28 Even in the third year of Asa king of Judah did Baasha slay him, and reigned
in his stead. **29** And when he was king, he [m]smote all the house of Jeroboam,
he left none alive to Jeroboam, until he had destroyed him, according to the [7]word
of the Lord which he spake by his servant Ahijah the Shilonite, **30** Because of
the sins of Jeroboam which he committed, and wherewith he made Israel to sin, by
his [n]provocation, wherewith he provoked the Lord God of Israel. **31** And the
residue of the acts of Nadab, and all that he did, are they not written in the book
of the Chronicles of the kings of Israel? **32** And there was war between Asa and
Baasha king of Israel, all their days. **33** In the third year of Asa king of Judah,
began Baasha the son of Ahijah to reign over all Israel in [o]Tirzah, and reigned four
and twenty years. **34** And he did evil in the sight of the Lord, walking in the way
of Jeroboam, and in his sin, wherewith he made Israel to sin.

16

1 Of Baasha, 6 Elah, 9 Zimri, 16 Omri. 31 Ahab marrieth Jezebel. 34 Jericho is built again.

1 Then the word of the Lord came to Jehu the son of Hanani against Baasha,
saying, **2** [a]Forasmuch as I exalted thee out of the dust, and made thee captain
over my people Israel, and thou hast walked in the way of Jeroboam, and hast
made my people Israel to sin, to provoke me with their sins, **3** Behold, I will take
away the posterity of Baasha, and the posterity of his house, and will make [b]thine

---

i. 1 Kings 14:9 To wit, two calves.
j. 1 Kings 14:10 Every male even to the dogs, 1 Sam. 25:22.
k. 1 Kings 14:10 As well him that is in the stronghold, as him that is abroad.
l. 1 Kings 14:11 They shall lack the honor of burial in token of God's malediction.
m. 1 Kings 14:13 In the midst of the wicked, God hath some on whom he doth bestow his mercies.
n. 1 Kings 14:14 The Lord will begin to destroy it out of hand.
o. 1 Kings 14:15 Meaning, Euphrates.
p. 1 Kings 14:16 The people shall not be excused when they do evil at the commandment of their governors.
q. 1 Kings 14:20 The Lord smote him that he died, 2 Chron. 13:20.
r. 1 Kings 14:21 And died before Jeroboam about four years.
s. 1 Kings 14:22 Or, besides all that their fathers had done by their sins.
t. 1 Kings 14:24 Where idolatry reigneth, all horrible vices are committed, till at length God's just judgment destroy them utterly.
u. 1 Kings 14:29 Which books were called the books of Shemaiah and Iddo the Prophets, 2 Chron. 12:15.
v. 1 Kings 14:30 That is, all the days of Rehoboam's life.
w. 1 Kings 14:31 Whose idolatry Rehoboam her son followed.

1-KINGS 14

1. 1 Kings 11:31
2. 1 Kings 21:21 / 2 Kings 9:8
3. 1 Kings 10:16

1-KINGS 15

a. 1 Kings 15:2 Some think that this was Absalom Solomon's son.
b. 1 Kings 15:4 Meaning, a son to reign over Judah.
c. 1 Kings 15:10 That is, his grandmother, as David is oft times called father of them, whose grandfather he was.
d. 1 Kings 15:13 Neither kindred nor authority ought to be regarded, when they blaspheme God, and become idolaters, but must be punished.
e. 1 Kings 15:14 For in that that he suffered them to worship God in other places, than he had appointed, it came of ignorance, and not of malice.
f. 1 Kings 15:17 Of the same purpose that Jeroboam did, because the people should not go up to Jerusalem, lest they should follow Asa.
g. 1 Kings 15:18 Or, Syria.
h. 1 Kings 15:19 And vex me no longer.
i. 1 Kings 15:22 Or, make a proclamation.
j. 1 Kings 15:22 Hebrew, none innocent.
k. 1 Kings 15:23 He had the gout and put his trust rather in Physicians than in the Lord, 2 Chron. 16:12.
l. 1 Kings 15:24 His great-grandfather.
m. 1 Kings 15:29 So God stirred up one tyrant to punish the wickedness of another.
n. 1 Kings 15:30 By causing the people to commit idolatry with his calves, and so provoking God to anger.
o. 1 Kings 15:33 Which was the place where the kings of Israel remained.

1-KINGS 15

1. 2 Chron. 11:12
2. 2 Sam. 11:4 / 2 Sam. 12:9
3. 2 Chron. 13:3
4. 2 Chron. 14:1
5. 2 Chron. 15:16
6. 2 Chron. 16:2
7. 1 Kings 14:10

1-KINGS 16

a. 1 Kings 16:2 Thus spake Jehu to Baasha in the Name of the Lord.

house like the [1]house of Jeroboam, the son of Nebat. **4** [2]He that dieth of Baasha's stock in the city, him shall the dogs eat: and that man of him which dieth in the fields, shall the fowls of the air eat. **5** And the rest of the acts of Baasha, and what he did, and his [c]power, are they not written in the book of the [3]Chronicles of the kings of Israel? **6** So Baasha slept with his fathers, and was buried in Tirzah, and Elah his son reigned in his stead. **7** And also [d]by the hand of Jehu the son of Hanani the Prophet, came the word of the Lord to Baasha, and to his house, that he should be like the house of Jeroboam, even for all the wickedness that he did in the sight of the Lord, in provoking him with the work of his hands, and because he killed [e]him. **8** In the six and twenty years of Asa king of Judah, began Elah the son of Baasha to reign over Israel in Tirzah, and reigned two years. **9** And his servant Zimri, captain of half his chariots, conspired against him, as he was in Tirzah [f]drinking, till he was drunken in the house of Arza steward of his house in Tirzah. **10** And Zimri came and smote him, and killed him in the seven and twenty years of Asa king of Judah, and reigned in his stead. **11** And when he was king, and sat on his throne, he slew all the house of Baasha, not leaving thereof one to piss against a wall, neither of his kinsfolks, nor of his friends. **12** So did Zimri destroy all the house of Baasha, according to the word of the Lord which he spake against Baasha by the hand of Jehu the [g]Prophet, **13** For all the sins of Baasha, and sins of Elah his son, which they sinned, and made Israel to sin, and provoked the Lord God of Israel with their vanities. **14** And the rest of the acts of Elah, and all that he did, are they not written in the book of the Chronicles of the kings of Israel? **15** In the seven and twenty years of Asa king of Judah did Zimri reign seven days in Tirzah, and the people was then in camp [h]against Gibbethon, which belonged to the Philistines. **16** And the people of the host heard say, Zimri hath conspired, and hath also slain the king. Wherefore all Israel made Omri the captain of the host, king over Israel that same day, even in the host. **17** Then Omri went up from Gibbethon, and all Israel with him, and they besieged [i]Tirzah. **18** And when Zimri saw, that the city was taken, he went into the palace of the king's house, and [j]burnt himself, and the king's house with fire, and so died, **19** For his sins which he sinned, in doing that which is evil in the sight of the Lord, in walking in the way of Jeroboam, and in his sins which he did, causing Israel to sin. **20** And the rest of the acts of Zimri, and his treason that he wrought, are they not written in the book of the Chronicles of the kings of Israel? **21** Then were the people of Israel divided into two parts: for [k]half the people followed Tibni the son of Ginath to make him king, and the other half followed Omri. **22** But the people that followed Omri, prevailed against the people that followed Tibni the son of Ginath: so Tibni died, and Omri reigned. **23** In the one and thirty years of Asa king of Judah began Omri to reign over Israel, and reigned twelve years. Six years reigned he in Tirzah. **24** And he bought the mountain [l]Samaria of one Shemer for two talents of silver, and built in the mountain, and called the name of the city, which he built, after the name of Shemer lord of the mountain, Samaria. **25** But Omri did evil in the eyes of the Lord, and did [m]worse than all that were before him. **26** For he walked in all the way of Jeroboam the son of Nebat, and in his sins wherewith he made Israel to sin in provoking the Lord God of Israel with their vanities. **27** And the rest of the acts of Omri, that he did, and his strength that he showed, are they not written in the book of the Chronicles of the Kings of Israel? **28** And Omri slept with his fathers, and was buried in [n]Samaria: and Ahab his son reigned in his stead. **29** Now Ahab the son of Omri began to reign over Israel, in the eight and thirty years of Asa king of Judah, and Ahab the son of Omri reigned over Israel in Samaria two and twenty years. **30** And Ahab the son of Omri did worse in the sight of the Lord than all that were before him. **31** For was it a light thing for him to walk in the sins of Jeroboam the son of Nebat, except he took Jezebel also the daughter of Ethbaal king of the Sidonians [o]to wife, and went and served Baal, and worshipped him? **32** Also he reared up an altar to Baal in the house of Baal, which he had built in Samaria. **33** And Ahab made a grove, and Ahab proceeded, and did provoke the Lord God of Israel more than all the kings of Israel that were before him. **34** In his days did Hiel the Bethelite build [p]Jericho: he laid the foundation thereof in Abiram his eldest son, and set up the gates thereof in his youngest son Segub, according to the word of the Lord which he spake [q]by Joshua the son of Nun.

17

1 Elijah forewarneth of the famine to come. 4 He is fed of Ravens. 9 He is sent to Zarephath, where he restoreth his hostess's son to life.

1 And Elijah the Tishbite one of the inhabitants of Gilead said unto Ahab, [1]As the Lord God of Israel liveth, before whom I [a]stand, there shall be neither dew nor rain these years, but [b]according to my word. **2** And the word of the Lord came unto him, saying, **3** Go hence, and turn thee Eastward, and hide thyself in the [c]river Cherith, that is over against Jordan, **4** And thou shalt drink of the river: and I have commanded the [d]ravens to feed thee there. **5** So he went and did according unto the word of the Lord: for he went, and remained by the river Cherith that is over against Jordan **6** And the ravens brought him bread and flesh in the morning, and bread and flesh in the evening, and he drank of the river. **7** And after a while the river dried up, because there fell no rain upon the earth. **8** And the [e]word of the Lord came unto him, saying, **9** [2]Up, and get thee to Zarephath, which is in Sidon, and remain there: behold, I have commanded a widow there to sustain thee. **10** So he arose and went to Zarephath: and when he came to the gate of the city, behold, the widow was there [f]gathering sticks: and he called her, and said, Bring me, I pray thee, a little water in a vessel, that I may drink. **11** And as she was going to fetch it, he called to her, and said, Bring me, I pray thee, a morsel of bread in thine hand. **12** And she said, As the Lord thy God liveth, I have not a cake, but even an handful of meal in a barrel, and a little oil in a cruse: and behold, I am gathering [g]a few sticks for to go in, and dress it for me and my son, that we may eat it, and [h]die. **13** And Elijah said unto her, Fear not, come do as thou hast said, but make me thereof a little cake first of all, and bring it unto me, and afterward make for thee and thy son. **14** For thus saith the Lord God of Israel, [i]The meal in the barrel shall not be wasted, neither shall the oil in the cruse be diminished, unto the time that the Lord send rain upon the earth. **15** So she went, and did as Elijah said, and she did eat: so did he and her house [j]for a certain time. **16** The barrel of the meal wasted not, nor the oil was spent out of the cruse, according to the word of the Lord, which he spake by the hand of Elijah. **17** And after these things, the son of the wife of the house fell sick, and his sickness was so sore, [k]that there was no [l]breath left in him. **18** And she said unto Elijah, What have I to do with thee, O thou man of God? art thou come unto me to call my sin to remembrance, and to slay my son? **19** And he said unto her, Give me thy son: and he took him out of her bosom, and carried him up into a chamber, where he abode, and laid him upon his own bed. **20** Then he called unto the Lord, and said, O Lord my God, hast thou [m]punished also this widow, with whom I sojourn, by killing her son? **21** And he stretched himself upon the child three times, and called unto the Lord, and said, O Lord my God, I pray thee, let this child's soul come into him again. **22** Then the Lord heard the voice of Elijah, and the soul of the child came into him again, and he revived. **23** And Elijah took the child, and brought him down out of the chamber into the house, and delivered him unto his mother, and Elijah said, Behold, thy son liveth. **24** And the woman said unto Elijah, Now [n]I know that thou art a man of God, and that the word of the Lord in thy mouth is true.

18

1 Elijah is sent to Ahab. 13 Obadiah hideth an hundred Prophets. 40 Elijah killeth all Baal's prophets. 45 He obtaineth rain.

1 After many days, the word of the Lord came to Elijah, in the [a]third year, saying, Go, show thyself unto Ahab, and I will send rain upon the earth. **2** And Elijah went to show himself unto Ahab, and there was a great famine in Samaria. **3** And Ahab called Obadiah the governor of his house: (and Obadiah [b]feared God greatly: **4** For when Jezebel destroyed the Prophets of the Lord, Obadiah took an hundred Prophets, and hid them by fifty in a cave, and he fed them with bread and water.) **5** And Ahab said unto Obadiah, Go into the land, unto all the fountains of water, and unto all the rivers, if so be that we may find grass to save the horses and the mules alive, lest we deprive the land of the beasts. **6** And so they divided the land between them to walk through it. Ahab went one way by himself, and Obadiah went another way by himself. **7** And as Obadiah was in the way, behold, Elijah [c]met him: and he knew him, and fell on his face, and said, Art not

---

b. 1 Kings 16:3 Meaning, the house of Baasha.
c. 1 Kings 16:5 Or, valiantness.
d. 1 Kings 16:7 That is, the Prophet did his message.
e. 1 Kings 16:7 Meaning, Nadab Jeroboam's son.
f. 1 Kings 16:9 The Chaldea text hath thus, Drinking till he was drunken in the Temple of Arza the idol by his house in Tirzah.
g. 1 Kings 16:12 Both Hanani his father and he were Prophets.
h. 1 Kings 16:15 The siege had continued from the time of Nadab Jeroboam's son.
i. 1 Kings 16:17 Where Zimri kept himself in hold.
j. 1 Kings 16:18 Hebrew, burnt the King's house upon him.
k. 1 Kings 16:21 That is, the people which were not at the siege of Gibbethon: for there they had chosen Omri.
l. 1 Kings 16:24 Or, Shomeron.
m. 1 Kings 16:25 For such is the nature of idolatry, that the superstition thereof doth daily increase, and the older it is the more abominable it is before God and his Church.
n. 1 Kings 16:28 He was the first king that was buried in Samaria, after that the kings house was burnt in Tirzah.
o. 1 Kings 16:31 By whose means he fell to all wicked and strange idolatry, and cruel persecution.
p. 1 Kings 16:34 Read Josh. 6:26.
q. 1 Kings 16:34 Hebrew, by the hand of Joshua.

1-KINGS 16

1. 1 Kings 15:29
2. 1 Kings 14:11
3. 1 Chron. 16:1

1-KINGS 17

a. 1 Kings 17:1 That is, whom I serve.
b. 1 Kings 17:1 But as I shall declare it by God's revelation.
c. 1 Kings 17:3 Or, brook.
d. 1 Kings 17:4 To strengthen his faith against persecution, God promiseth to feed him miraculously.
e. 1 Kings 17:8 As the troubles of the Saints of God are many, so his mercy is ever at hand to deliver them.
f. 1 Kings 17:10 All this was to strengthen the faith of Elijah, to the intent that he should look upon nothing worldly, but only trust on God's providence.
g. 1 Kings 17:12 Hebrew, two.
h. 1 Kings 17:12 For there is no hope of any more sustenance.
i. 1 Kings 17:14 God receiveth no benefit for the use of his, but he promiseth a most ample recompense for the same.
j. 1 Kings 17:15 That is, till he had rain and food on the earth.
k. 1 Kings 17:17 Or, that he died.
l. 1 Kings 17:17 God would try whether she had learned by his merciful providence to make him her only stay and comfort.
m. 1 Kings 17:20 He was afraid lest God's name should have been blasphemed and his ministers contemned, except he should have continued his mercies as he had begun them, specially while he there remained.
n. 1 Kings 17:24 So hard a thing it is to depend on God, except we be confirmed by miracles.

1-KINGS 17

1. James 5:16,17
2. Luke 4:25,26

1-KINGS 18

a. 1 Kings 18:1 After that he departed from the river Cherith.
b. 1 Kings 18:3 God had begun to work his fear in his heart, but had not yet brought him to that knowledge, which is also requisite of the godly: that is, to profess his Name openly.
c. 1 Kings 18:7 God pitieth oft times the wicked for the godly's sake, and causeth Elijah to meet with Obadiah, that the benefit might be known to be granted for God's children's sake.

thou my lord Elijah? **8** And he answered him, Yea, go tell thy lord, Behold, Elijah is here. **9** And he said, What have I sinned, that thou wouldest deliver thy servant into the hand of Ahab, to slay me? **10** As the Lord thy God liveth, there is no nation or kingdom, whither my lord hath not sent to seek thee: and when they said, He is not here, he took an oath of the kingdom and nation, if they had not found thee. **11** And now thou sayest, Go, tell thy lord, Behold, Elijah is here. **12** And when I am gone from thee, the Spirit of the Lord shall carry thee into some place that I do not know: so when I come and tell Ahab, if he cannot find thee, then will he kill me: But I thy servant [d]fear the Lord from my youth. **13** Was it not told my lord, what I did when Jezebel slew the Prophets of the Lord, how I hid an hundred men of the Lord's Prophets by fifties in a cave, and fed them with bread and water? **14** And now thou sayest, Go, tell thy lord, Behold, Elijah is here, that he may slay me. **15** And Elijah said, As the Lord of hosts liveth, before whom I stand, I will surely show [e]myself unto him this day. **16** So Obadiah went to meet Ahab, and told him. And Ahab went to meet Elijah. **17** And when Ahab saw Elijah, Ahab said unto him, Art thou he that troubleth Israel? **18** And he answered, I have not troubled Israel, but [f]thou and thy father's house, in that ye have forsaken the commandments of the Lord, and thou hast followed Baal. **19** Now therefore send, and gather to me all Israel unto mount Carmel, and the prophets of Baal four hundred and fifty, and the prophets of the groves four hundred, which eat at Jezebel's table. **20** So Ahab sent unto all the children of Israel, and gathered the prophets together unto mount Carmel. **21** And Elijah came unto all the people, and said, How long [g]halt ye between two opinions? If the Lord be God, follow him, but if Baal be he, then go after him. And the people answered him not a word. **22** Then said Elijah unto the people, I only remain a Prophet of the Lord: but Baal's prophets are four hundred and fifty men. **23** Let them therefore give us two bullocks, and let them choose the one, and cut him in pieces, and lay him on the wood, but put no fire under, and I will prepare the other bullock, and lay him on the wood, and will put no fire under. **24** Then call ye on the name of your god, and I will call on the Name of the Lord: and then the God that answereth [h]by fire, let him be God. And all the people answered, and said, It is well spoken. **25** And Elijah said unto the prophets of Baal, Choose you a bullock, and prepare him first, (for ye are many) and call on the name of your gods, but put no fire under. **26** So they took the one bullock that was given them, and they prepared it, and called on the name of Baal from morning to noon, saying, O Baal, hear us: but there was no voice, nor any to answer: and they [i]leapt upon the altar that was made. **27** And at noon Elijah mocked them, and said, Cry aloud: for he is a [j]god: either he talketh or pursueth his enemies, or is in his journey, or it may be that he sleepeth, and must be [k]awaked. **28** And they cried loud, and cut themselves as their manner was, with knives and lancers, till the blood gushed out upon them. **29** And when midday was passed, and they had prophesied until the offering of the evening sacrifice, there was neither voice, nor one to answer, nor any that regarded. **30** And Elijah said unto all the people, Come to me. And all the people came to him. And he repaired the altar of the Lord that was broken down. **31** And Elijah took twelve stones, according to the number of the tribes of the sons of Jacob, (unto whom the word of the Lord came, saying, [1]Israel shall be thy name) **32** And with the stones he built an altar in the Name of the Lord: and he made a ditch round about the altar, as great as would contain two [l]measures of seed. **33** And he put the wood in order, and hewed the bullock in pieces, and laid him in the wood: **34** And said, Fill four barrels with water, and pour it upon the burnt offering and on the wood. Again he said, Do so again. And they did so the second time. And he said, Do it the third time. And they did it the third time. **35** And the water ran round about the altar: and he [m]filled the ditch with water also. **36** And when they should offer the evening sacrifice, Elijah the Prophet came and said, Lord God of Abraham, Isaac, and of Israel, let it be known this day, that thou art the God of Israel, and that I am thy servant, and that I have done all these things at thy commandment. **37** Hear me, O Lord, hear me, and let this people know that thou art the Lord God, and that thou hast turned their heart again [n]at the last. **38** Then the fire of the Lord fell, and consumed the burnt offering, and the wood, and the stones, and the dust, and licked up the water that was in the ditch. **39** And when all the people saw it, they fell on their faces, and said, The Lord is God, the Lord is God. **40** And Elijah said unto them, Take the prophets of Baal, let not [o]a man of them escape: and they took them, and Elijah brought them to the brook Kishon, and slew them there. **41** And Elijah said unto Ahab, Get thee up, eat and drink, for there is a sound of much rain. **42** So Ahab went up to eat and to drink, and Elijah went up to the top of Carmel: and he crouched unto the earth, and put his face between his knees, **43** And said to his servant, Go up now, and look toward the way of the Sea. And he went up, and looked, and said, There is nothing. Again he said, Go again [p]seven times. **44** And at the seventh time he said, Behold, there ariseth a little cloud out of the Sea like a man's hand. Then he said, Up, and say unto Ahab, Make ready the chariot, and get thee down, that the rain stay thee not. **45** And [q]in the meanwhile the heaven was black with clouds and wind, and there was a great rain. Then Ahab went up, and came to Jezreel, **46** And the hand of the Lord was on Elijah, and he girded up his loins, and ran [r]before Ahab till he came to Jezreel.

19

5 Elijah fleeing from Jezebel, is nourished by the Angel of God. 15 He is commanded to anoint Hazael, Jehu, and Elisha.

1 Now Ahab told Jezebel all that Elijah had done, and how he had slain all the [a]prophets with the sword. **2** Then Jezebel sent a messenger unto Elijah, saying, [b]The gods do so to me and more also, if I make not thy life like one of their lives by tomorrow this time. **3** When he saw that, he arose, and went [c]for his life, and came to Beersheba, which is in Judah, and left his servant there. **4** But he went a day's journey into the wilderness, and came and sat down under a Juniper tree, and desired that he might die, and said, It is now enough: O Lord, [d]take my soul, for I am no better than my fathers. **5** And as he lay and slept under the Juniper tree, behold now, an Angel touched him, and said unto him, Up, and eat. **6** And when he looked about, behold, there was a cake baken on the coals, and a pot of water at his head: so he did eat and drink, and returned and slept. **7** And the Angel of the Lord came again the second time, and touched him, and said, Up, and eat: for [e]thou hast a great journey. **8** Then he arose, and did eat and drink, and walked in the strength of that meat forty days and forty nights, unto Horeb the mount of God. **9** And there he entered into a cave, and lodged there: and behold, the Lord spake to him, and said unto him, What doest thou here, Elijah? **10** And he answered, I have [f]been very jealous for the Lord God of hosts: for the children of Israel have forsaken thy covenant, broken down thine altars, and slain thy Prophets with the sword, [1]and I only am left, and they seek my life to take it away. **11** And he said, Come out, and stand upon the mount before the Lord. And behold, the Lord went by, and a mighty strong wind rent the mountains, and brake the rocks before the Lord: but the Lord was [g]not in the wind: and after the wind came an earthquake: but the Lord was not in the earthquake: **12** And after the earthquake came fire: but the Lord was not in the fire: and after the fire came a still and soft voice. **13** And when Elijah heard it, he covered his face with his mantle, and went out, and stood in the entering of the cave: and behold, there came a voice unto him, and said, What doest thou here, Elijah? **14** And he answered, I have been very jealous for the Lord God of hosts, [h]because the children of Israel have forsaken thy covenant, cast down thine altars, and slain thy Prophets with the sword, and I only am left, and they seek my life to take it away. **15** And the Lord said unto him, Go, return by the wilderness unto Damascus, and when thou comest there, anoint Hazael king over [i]Aram. **16** And Jehu the son of Nimshi shalt thou anoint King over Israel: and Elisha the son of Shaphat of Abel Meholah shalt thou anoint to be Prophet in thy room. **17** And [2]him that escapeth from the sword of Hazael, shall Jehu slay: and him that escapeth from the sword of Jehu, shall Elisha slay. **18** Yet will [3]I leave seven thousand in Israel: even [j]all the knees that have not bowed unto Baal, and every mouth that hath not kissed him. **19** So he departed thence, and found Elisha the son of Shaphat, who was plowing with twelve yoke of oxen before him, and was with the twelfth: and Elijah went towards him, and cast his mantel upon him. **20** And he left the oxen, and ran after Elijah, and said, [k]Let me, I pray thee, kiss my father and my mother, and then I will follow thee. Who answered him, Go, return: for what have I done to thee? **21** And when he went back again from him, he took a couple

---

d. 1 Kings 18:12 I am none of the wicked persecutors that thou shouldest procure unto me such displeasure, but serve God, and favor his children.
e. 1 Kings 18:15 By my presence I will declare that thou hast told him the truth.
f. 1 Kings 18:18 The true ministers of God ought not only not to suffer the truth to be unjustly slandered, but to reprove boldly the wicked slanderers without respect of person.
g. 1 Kings 18:21 Be constant in religion, and make it not as a thing indifferent, whether ye follow God or Baal, or whether ye serve God wholly or in part, Zeph. 1:5.
h. 1 Kings 18:24 By sending down fire from heaven to burn the sacrifice.
i. 1 Kings 18:26 As men ravished with some strange spirit.
j. 1 Kings 18:27 You esteem him as God.
k. 1 Kings 18:27 He mocketh their beastly madness, which think that by any instance or suit, the dead and vile idols can help their worshippers in their necessity.
l. 1 Kings 18:32 Hebrew, seahs, which some think contain about three pottles and a third part a piece.
m. 1 Kings 18:35 Hereby he declared the excellent power of God, who contrary to nature could make the fire burn even in the water, to the intent they should have none occasion to doubt that he is the only God.
n. 1 Kings 18:37 Though God suffer his to run in blindness and error for a time, yet at the length he calleth them home to him by some notorious sign and work.
o. 1 Kings 18:40 He commanded them that as they were truly persuaded to confess the only God: so they would serve him with all their power, and destroy the idolaters his enemies.
p. 1 Kings 18:43 As God's spirit moved him to pray, so was he strengthened by the same, that he did not faint, but continued still till he had obtained.
q. 1 Kings 18:45 Or, here and there.
r. 1 Kings 18:46 He was so strengthened with God's spirit, that he ran faster than the chariot was able to run.

1-KINGS 18
1. Gen. 32:28 / 2 Kings 17:34

1-KINGS 19
a. 1 Kings 19:1 To wit, of Baal.
b. 1 Kings 19:2 Though the wicked rage against God's children, yet he holdeth them back that they cannot execute their malice.
c. 1 Kings 19:3 Or, whither his mind led him.
d. 1 Kings 19:4 So hard a thing it is to bridle our impatience in affliction, that the Saints could not overcome the same.
e. 1 Kings 19:7 He declareth that except God had nourished him miraculously, it had not been possible for him to have gone this journey.
f. 1 Kings 19:10 He complaineth that the more zealous that he showed himself to maintain God's glory, the more cruelly was he persecuted.
g. 1 Kings 19:11 For the nature of man is not able to come near unto God, if he should appear in his strength and full majesty, and therefore of his mercy he submitteth himself to our capacity.
h. 1 Kings 19:14 We ought not to depend on the multitude in maintaining God's glory, but because our duty so requireth, we ought to do it.
i. 1 Kings 19:15 Or, Syria.
j. 1 Kings 19:18 He declareth that wicked dissemblers and idolaters are not his.

of oxen, and slew them, and sod their flesh with the [l]instruments of the oxen, and gave unto the people, and they did eat: then he arose and went after Elijah, and ministered unto him.

20

1 Samaria is besieged. 13 The Lord promiseth the victory to Ahab by a Prophet. 31 The King of Israel made peace with Ben-Hadad, and is reproved therefore by the Prophet.

1 Then Ben-Hadad the king of [a]Aram assembled all his army, and two and thirty [b]kings with him, with horses, and chariots, and went up and besieged [c]Samaria, and fought against it. **2** And he sent messengers to Ahab king of Israel, into the city, **3** And said unto him, Thus saith Ben-Hadad, Thy silver and thy gold is mine: also thy women, and thy fair children are mine. **4** And the king of Israel answered, and said, My lord king, according to thy saying, [d]I am thine, and all that I have. **5** And when the messengers came again, they said, Thus commandeth Ben-Hadad, and saith, When I shall send unto thee, and command, thou shalt deliver me thy silver and thy gold, and thy women, and thy children, **6** [e]Or else I will send my servants unto thee by tomorrow this time, and they shall search thine house, and the houses of thy servants: and whatsoever is pleasant in thine eyes, they shall take it in their hands, and bring it away. **7** Then the King of Israel sent for all the Elders of the land, and said, Take heed, I pray you, and see how he seeketh mischief: for he sent unto me for my wives, and for my children, and for my silver, and for my gold, and I denied him not. **8** And all the Elders, and all the people said to him, Hearken [f]not unto him, nor consent. **9** Wherefore he said unto the messengers of Ben-Hadad, Tell my lord the king, All that thou didst send for to thy servant at the first time, that I will do, but this thing I may not do. And the messengers departed, and brought him an answer. **10** And Ben-Hadad sent unto him, and said, The gods do so to me and more also, if the [g]dust of Samaria be enough to all the people that follow me, for every man an handful. **11** And the king of Israel answered, and said, Tell him, Let not him that girdeth his harness, boast himself, as he that [h]putteth it off. **12** And when he heard that tidings, as he was with the kings drinking in the pavilions, he said unto the servants, [i]Bring forth your engines. And they set them against the city. **13** And behold, there came a Prophet unto Ahab king of Israel, saying, Thus saith the Lord, Hast thou seen all this great multitude? behold, I will deliver it into thine hand this day, that thou mayest know, [j]that I am the Lord. **14** And Ahab said, By whom? and he said, Thus saith the Lord, By the servants of the princes of the provinces. He said again, Who shall order the battle? and he answered, Thou. **15** Then he numbered the servants of the princes of the provinces, and they were two hundred, two and thirty: and after them he numbered the whole people of all the children of Israel, even seven thousand. **16** And they went out at noon: but Ben-Hadad did drink till he was drunken in the tents, both he and the kings: for two and thirty kings helped him. **17** So the [k]servants of the princes of the provinces went out first: and Ben-Hadad sent out, and they showed him, saying, There are men come out of Samaria. **18** And he said, Whether they be come out for peace, take them alive: or whether they be come out to fight, take them yet alive. **19** So they came out of the city, to wit, the servants of the princes of the provinces, and the host which followed them. **20** And they slew everyone his [l]enemy: and the [m]Aramites fled, and Israel pursued them: but Ben-Hadad the king of Aram escaped on an horse with his [n]horsemen. **21** And the king of Israel went out, and smote the horses and chariots, and with a great slaughter slew the Aramites. **22** (For there had come a Prophet to the king of Israel, and had said unto him, Go, be of good courage, and consider, and take heed what thou doest: for when the year is gone about, the king of Aram will come up against thee.) **23** Then the servants of the king of Aram said unto him, Their [o]gods are gods of the mountains, and therefore they overcame us: but let us fight against them in the plain, and doubtless we shall overcome them. **24** And this do, Take the kings away, everyone out of his place, and place captains for them. **25** And number thyself an army, like the army that thou hast lost, with such horses, and such chariots, and we will fight against them in the plain, and doubtless we shall overcome them: and he hearkened unto their voice, and did so. **26** And after the year was gone about, Ben-Hadad numbered the Aramites, and went up to Aphek to fight against Israel. **27** And the children of Israel were numbered, and were all [p]assembled, and went against them, and the children of Israel pitched before them like two little flocks of kids: but the Aramites filled the country. **28** And there came a man of God, and spake unto the king of Israel, saying, Thus saith the Lord, Because the Aramites have said, The Lord is the God of the mountains, and not God of the valleys, therefore will I deliver all this great multitude into thine hand, and ye shall know that [q]I am the Lord. **29** And they pitched one over against the other seven days, and in the seventh day the battle was joined: and the children of Israel slew of the Aramites an hundred thousand footmen in one day. **30** But the rest fled to Aphek into the city: and there fell a wall upon seven and twenty thousand men that were left: and Ben-Hadad fled into the city, and came into [r]a secret chamber. **31** And his servants said unto him, Behold now, we have heard say that the Kings of the house of Israel are merciful Kings: we pray thee, let us put sackcloth about our [s]loins, and ropes about our heads, and go out to the King of Israel: it may be that he will save thy life. **32** Then they girded sackcloth about their loins, and put ropes about their heads, and came to the King of Israel, and said, Thy servant Ben-Hadad saith, I pray thee, let me live: and he said, Is he yet alive? he is my brother. **33** Now the men took diligent heed, [t]if they could catch anything of him, and made haste, and said, Thy brother [u]Ben-Hadad. And he said, Go, bring him. So Ben-Hadad came out unto him, and he caused him to come up into the chariot. **34** And Ben-Hadad said unto him, The cities which my father took from thy father, I will restore, and thou shalt make streets for thee in [v]Damascus, as my father did in Samaria. Then said Ahab, I will let thee go with this covenant. So he made a covenant with him, and let him go. **35** Then a certain man of the [w]children of the Prophets said unto his neighbor by the commandment of the Lord, [x]Smite me, I pray thee. But the man refused to smite him. **36** Then said he unto him, Because thou hast not obeyed the voice of the Lord, behold, as soon as thou art departed from me, a lion shall [y]slay thee. So when he was departed from him, a lion found him, and slew him. **37** Then he found another man, and said, Smite me, I pray thee. And the man smote him, and in smiting wounded him. **38** So the Prophet departed, and waited for the King by the way, and disguised himself with ashes upon his face. **39** And when the King came by, he cried unto the King, and said, [z]Thy servant went into the midst of the battle, and behold, there went away a man, whom another man brought unto me, and said, Keep this man: if he be lost, and want, thy life shall go for his life, or else thou shalt pay a talent of silver. **40** And as thy servant had here and there to do, he was gone: And the King of Israel said unto him, So shall thy judgment be: thou hast given sentence. **41** And he hasted, and took the ashes away from his face: and the King of Israel knew him that he was of the Prophets: **42** And he said unto him, Thus saith the Lord, [1]Because thou hast let go out of thine hands a man whom I appointed to die, thy life shall go for his life, and thy people for his people. **43** And the King of Israel went to his house heavy and in displeasure, and came to [aa]Samaria.

21

8 Jezebel commandeth to kill Naboth, for the vineyard that he refused to sell to Ahab. 19 Elijah reproveth Ahab, and he repenteth.

1 After [a]these things, Naboth the Jezreelite had a vineyard in Jezreel, hard by the palace of Ahab king of Samaria. **2** And Ahab spake unto Naboth, saying, [b]Give me thy vineyard, that I may make me a garden of herbs thereof, because it is nearby mine house: and I will give thee for it a better vineyard than it is: or if it please thee, I will give thee the worth of it in money. **3** And Naboth said to Ahab, The Lord keep me from giving the inheritance of my father unto thee. **4** Then Ahab came into his house heavy and in displeasure, because of the word which Naboth the Jezreelite had spoken unto him. For he had said, I will not give thee the inheritance of my fathers, and he lay [c]upon his bed, and turned his face and would eat no bread. **5** Then Jezebel his wife came unto him, and said unto him, Why is thy spirit so sad that thou eatest no bread? **6** And he said unto her, Because I spake unto Naboth the Jezreelite, and said unto him, Give me thy vineyard for

---

k. 1 Kings 19:20 Though this natural affection is not to be contemned, yet it ought not to move us when God calleth us to serve him.
l. 1 Kings 19:21 He would not stay till wood was brought, so great was his desire to follow his vocation.

1-KINGS 19
1. Rom. 11:13
2. 2 Kings 9:1,3
3. Rom. 11:4

1-KINGS 20
a. 1 Kings 20:1 Or, Syria
b. 1 Kings 20:1 That is, governors and rulers of provinces.
c. 1 Kings 20:1 Or, Shomeron.
d. 1 Kings 20:4 I am content to obey and pay tribute.
e. 1 Kings 20:6 He would not accept his answer except he did out of hand deliver whatsoever he should ask, for he sought an occasion how to make war against him.
f. 1 Kings 20:8 They thought it their duties rather to venture their lives, than to grant to that thing which was not lawful, only to satisfy the lust of a tyrant.
g. 1 Kings 20:10 Much less shall there be found any prey that is worth anything, when they shall be so many.
h. 1 Kings 20:11 Boast not before the victory be gotten.
i. 1 Kings 20:12 Or, put yourselves in order.
j. 1 Kings 20:13 Before God went about with signs and miracles to pull Ahab from his impiety, and now again with wonderful victories.
k. 1 Kings 20:17 That is, young men trained in the service of princes.
l. 1 Kings 20:20 Hebrew, man.
m. 1 Kings 20:20 Or, Syrians.
n. 1 Kings 20:20 Which them that were appointed for the preservation of his person.
o. 1 Kings 20:23 Thus the wicked blaspheme God in their fury, whom notwithstanding he suffereth not unpunished.
p. 1 Kings 20:27 All they, which were in the battle of the former year, verse 15.
q. 1 Kings 20:28 Who am of like power in the valley, as I am on the hills, and can as well destroy a multitude with few as with many.
r. 1 Kings 20:30 Hebrew, from chamber, to chamber.
s. 1 Kings 20:31 In sign of submission, and that we have deserved death, if he will punish us with rigor.
t. 1 Kings 20:33 Or, and caught it of him.
u. 1 Kings 20:33 He is alive.
v. 1 Kings 20:34 Thou shalt appoint in my chief city what thou wilt, and I will obey thee.
w. 1 Kings 20:35 Or, of the disciples.
x. 1 Kings 20:35 By this external sign he would more lively touch the king's heart.
y. 1 Kings 20:36 Because thou hast transgressed the commandment of the Lord.
z. 1 Kings 20:39 By this parable he maketh Ahab condemn himself, who made a covenant with God's enemy, and let him escape, whom God had appointed to be slain.
aa. 1 Kings 20:43 Or, Shomeron.

1-KINGS 20
1. 1 Kings 22:38

1-KINGS 21
a. 1 Kings 21:1 Or, at this time.
b. 1 Kings 21:2 Though Ahab's tyranny be condemned by the holy Spirit, yet he was not so rigorous that he would take from another man his right without full recompense.
c. 1 Kings 21:4 Thus the wicked consider not what is just and lawful, but fret inwardly, when they cannot have their inordinate appetites satisfied.

money, or if it please thee, I will give thee another vineyard for it: but he answered,
I will not give thee my vineyard. 7 Then Jezebel his wife said unto him, [d]Dost
thou now govern the kingdom of Israel? Up, eat bread, and [e]be of good cheer, I will
give thee the vineyard of Naboth the Jezreelite. 8 So she wrote letters in Ahab's
name, and sealed them with his seal, and sent the letters unto the Elders, and to the
nobles that were in his city dwelling with Naboth. 9 And she wrote in the letters,
saying, Proclaim a [f]fast, and set Naboth among the chief of the people, 10 And
set two wicked men before him, and let them witness against him, saying, Thou
didst blaspheme God and the king: then carry him out, and stone him that he may
die. 11 And the [g]men of the city, even the Elders and governors which dwelt
in his city, did as Jezebel had sent unto them: as it was written in the letters, whi-
ch she had sent unto them. 12 They proclaimed a fast, and set Naboth among
the chief of the people, 13 And there came two wicked men, and sat before
him: and the wicked men witnessed against Naboth in the presence of the people
saying, Naboth did [h]blaspheme God and the King. Then they carried him away
out of the city, and stoned him with stones, that he died. 14 Then they sent to
Jezebel, saying, Naboth is stoned and is dead. 15 And when Jezebel heard that
Naboth was stoned and was dead, Jezebel said to Ahab, [i]Up, and take possession
of the vineyard of Naboth the Jezreelite, which he refused to give thee for money:
for Naboth is not alive, but is dead. 16 And when Ahab heard that Naboth was
dead, he rose to go down to the vineyard of Naboth the Jezreelite, to take posses-
sion of it. 17 And the word of the Lord came unto Elijah the Tishbite, saying,
18 Arise, go down to meet Ahab King of Israel, which is in Samaria: lo, he is in the
vineyard of Naboth, whither he is gone down to take possession of it. 19 The-
refore shalt thou say unto him, Thus saith the Lord, [j]Hast thou killed, and also
gotten possession? And thou shalt speak unto him, saying, Thus saith the Lord, [k]In
the place where dogs licked the blood of Naboth, shall dogs lick even thy blood
also. 20 And Ahab said to Elijah, Hast thou found me, O mine enemy? And he
answered, I have found thee: for thou hast sold thyself to work wickedness in the
sight of the Lord. 21 [1]Behold, I will bring evil upon thee, and will take away
thy posterity, and will cut off from Ahab him that [2]pisseth against the wall, as well
him that is [3]shut up, as him that is left in Israel, 22 And I will make thine house
like the house of [4]Jeroboam the son of Nebat, and like the house of [5]Baasha the
son of Ahijah, for the provocation wherewith thou hast provoked and made Israel
to sin. 23 And also of Jezebel spake the Lord, saying, [6]The dogs shall eat Jezebel,
[l]by the wall of Jezreel. 24 The dogs shall eat him of Ahab's stock, that dieth in
the city: and him that dieth in the fields, shall the fowls of the air eat. 25 (But
there was none like Ahab, who did [m]sell himself to work wickedness, in the sight
of the Lord, whom Jezebel his wife provoked. 26 For he did exceeding abomi-
nably in following idols, according to all that the Amorites did, whom the Lord
cast out before the children of Israel.) 27 Now when Ahab heard those words,
he rent his clothes, and put sackcloth upon [n]him, and fasted, and lay in sackcloth,
and went [o]softly. 28 And the word of the Lord came to Elijah the Tishbite,
saying, 29 Seest thou how Ahab is humbled before me? because he submitteth
himself before me, I will not bring that evil in his days, but in his [p]sons' days will
I bring evil upon his house.

22

2 Jehoshaphat and Ahab fight against the King of Syria. 15 Micaiah showeth the king what shall be the success of their enterprise. 24 Zedekiah the false prophet smiteth him. 34 Ahab is slain. 40 Ahaziah his son succeedeth. 41 The reign of Jehoshaphat, 50 and Jehoram his son.

1 And [1]they continued [a]three years without war between Aram and Isra-
el. 2 And in the third year did Jehoshaphat the king of Judah [b]come down to
the king of Israel. 3 (Then the king of Israel said unto his servants, Know ye not
that [c]Ramoth Gilead was ours? and we stay, and take it not out of the hand of the
King of Aram?) 4 And he said unto Jehoshaphat, Wilt thou go with me to batt-
le against Ramoth Gilead? And Jehoshaphat said unto the king of Israel, [d]I am
as thou art, my people as thy people, and mine horses as thine horses. 5 Then
Jehoshaphat said unto the King of Israel, [e]Ask counsel, I pray thee, of the Lord
today. 6 Then the king of Israel gathered the [f]prophets upon a four hundred
men, and said unto them, Shall I go against Ramoth Gilead to battle, or shall I let
it alone? And they said, Go up, for the Lord shall deliver it into the hands of the
King. 7 And Jehoshaphat said, Is there here never a Prophet of the [g]Lord more,
that we might inquire of him? 8 And the king of Israel said unto Jehoshaphat,
There is yet one man (Micaiah the son of Imlah) by whom we may ask counsel of
the Lord, but [h]I hate him: for he doth not prophesy good unto me, but evil. And
Jehoshaphat said, Let not the king say so. 9 Then the king of Israel called an [i]Eu-
nuch, and said, Call quickly Micaiah the son of Imlah. 10 And the king of Israel
and Jehoshaphat the king of Judah sat either of them on his throne in their [j]appa-
rel in the void place at the entering in of the gate of Samaria, and all the prophets
prophesied before them. 11 And Zedekiah the son of Chenaanah made him
[k]horns of iron, and said, Thus saith the Lord, With these shalt thou push the Ara-
mites, until thou hast consumed them. 12 And all the prophets prophesied so,
saying, Go up to Ramoth Gilead, and prosper: for the Lord shall deliver it into the
king's hand. 13 And the messenger that was gone to call Micaiah, spake unto
him, saying, Behold now, the words of the prophets declare good unto the king
with [l,m]one accord, let thy word therefore, I pray thee, be like the word of one of
them, and speak thou good. 14 And Micaiah said, As the Lord liveth, whatso-
ever the Lord saith unto me, that will I speak. 15 So he came to the King, and
the king said unto him, Micaiah, shall we go against Ramoth Gilead to battle, or
shall we leave off? And he answered him, [n]Go up, and prosper: and the Lord shall
deliver it into the hand of the king. 16 And the king said unto him, How oft
shall I charge thee that thou tell me nothing but that which is true in the Name
of the Lord? 17 Then he said, I saw all Israel scattered upon the mountains, as
sheep that had no shepherd. And the Lord said, [o]These have no master, let every
man return unto his house in peace. 18 (And the king of Israel said unto Jeho-
shaphat, Did I not tell thee that he would prophesy no good unto me, but evil?)
19 Again he said, Hear thou therefore the word of the Lord. I saw the Lord sit
on his throne, and all the [p]host of heaven stood about him on his right hand and
on his left hand. 20 And the Lord said, Who shall [q]entice Ahab that he may
go and fall at Ramoth Gilead? And one said on this manner, and another said on
that manner. 21 Then there came forth a spirit, and [r]stood before the Lord, and
said, I will entice him. And the Lord said unto him, Wherewith? 22 And he
said, I will go out, and be a [s]false spirit in the mouth of all his prophets. Then he
said, Thou shalt entice him, and shalt also prevail: go forth, and do so. 23 Now
therefore behold, the Lord hath put a lying spirit in the mouth of all these thy
prophets, and the Lord hath appointed evil against thee. 24 Then Zedekiah the
son of Chenaanah came near, and smote Micaiah on the cheek, and said, [t,2]When
went the spirit of the Lord from me, to speak unto thee? 25 And Micaiah said,
Behold, thou shalt see in that day, when thou shalt go from chamber to chamber
to hide thee. 26 And the king of Israel said, Take Micaiah and carry him unto
Amon the governor of the city, and unto Joash the king's son, 27 And say, Thus
saith the King, Put this man in the prison house, and feed him with [u]bread of affli-
ction, and with water of affliction, until I return in peace. 28 And Micaiah said,
If thou return in peace, the Lord hath not spoken by me. And he said, [v]Hearken all
ye people. 29 So the king of Israel and Jehoshaphat the king of Judah went up
to Ramoth Gilead. 30 And the king of Israel said to Jehoshaphat, I will change
mine apparel, and will enter into the battle, but put thou on thine apparel. And
the king of Israel changed himself, and went into the battle. 31 And the king
of Aram commanded his two and thirty captains over his chariots, saying, Fight
neither with small nor great, save only against the king of Israel. 32 And when

---

d. 1 Kings 21:7 As though she said, Thou knowest not what it is to reign. Command and entreat not.
e. 1 Kings 21:7 Hebrew, let thine heart be merry.
f. 1 Kings 21:9 For then they used to inquire of men's faults: for none could fast truly that were notorious sinners.
g. 1 Kings 21:11 Thus the worldlings contrary to God's commandment, who willeth not to consent to the shedding of innocent blood, obey rather the wicked commandments of princes than the just laws of God.
h. 1 Kings 21:13 Hebrew, bless.
i. 1 Kings 21:15 This example of monstrous cruelty the holy Ghost leaveth to us, to the intent that we should abhor all tyranny, and specially in them whom nature and kind should move to be pitiful and inclined to mercy.
j. 1 Kings 21:19 Dost thou think to have any advantage by murdering of an innocent?
k. 1 Kings 21:19 This was fulfilled in Jehoram his son, as 2 Kings 9:25, 26.
l. 1 Kings 21:23 Or, fortress, or possession.
m. 1 Kings 21:25 By the wicked counsel of his wife he became a vile idolater, and cruel murderer, as one that gave himself wholly to serve sin.
n. 1 Kings 21:27 Hebrew, his flesh.
o. 1 Kings 21:27 In token of mourning, or as some read, barefooted.
p. 1 Kings 21:29 Meaning, in Jehoram's time, 2 Kings 9:26.

1-KINGS 21

1. 1 Kings 14:10 / 2 Kings 9:8
2. 1 Sam. 15:22
3. 1 Kings 14:10
4. 1 Kings 15:29
5. 1 Kings 16:3
6. 2 Kings 9:33,36

1-KINGS 22

a. 1 Kings 22:1 Ben-Hadad the king of Syria, and Ahab made a peace which endureth three years.
b. 1 Kings 22:2 To see and visit him.
c. 1 Kings 22:3 The kings of Syria kept Ramoth before this league was made by Ben-Hadad: therefore he thought not himself bound thereby to restore it.
d. 1 Kings 22:4 I am ready to join and go with thee, and all mine is at thy commandment.
e. 1 Kings 22:5 He seemed that he would not go to the war, except God reproved it, yet when Micaiah counseled the contrary, he would not obey.
f. 1 Kings 22:6 Meaning, the false prophets, which were flatterers and served for lucre, whom Jezebel had assembled and kept after the death of those whom Elijah slew.
g. 1 Kings 22:7 Jehoshaphat did not acknowledge the false prophets to be God's ministers, but did contemn them.
h. 1 Kings 22:8 Whereby we see that the wicked cannot abide to hear the truth, but hate the Prophets of God and molest them.
i. 1 Kings 22:9 Read Gen. 37:36.
j. 1 Kings 22:10 In their kingly apparel.
k. 1 Kings 22:11 The true Prophets of God were accustomed to use signs for the confirmation of their doctrine, Isa. 20:2; Jer. 7:2. Wherein the false Prophets did imitate them, thinking thereby to make their doctrine more commendable.
l. 1 Kings 22:13 Hebrew, mouth.
m. 1 Kings 22:13 This is the common argument of the wicked, who think that none should speak against a thing, if the greater part approve it, be they never so ungodly.
n. 1 Kings 22:15 He speaketh this in derision, because the king attributed so much to the false prophets, meaning, that by experience he should try that they were but flatterers.
o. 1 Kings 22:17 It is better they return home than to be punished and scattered, because they take war in hand without God's counsel and approbation.
p. 1 Kings 22:19 Meaning, his Angels.
q. 1 Kings 22:20 Or, persuade and deceive.
r. 1 Kings 22:21 Here we see that though the devil be ever ready to bring us to destruction, yet he hath no further power than God giveth him.
s. 1 Kings 22:22 I will cause all his prophets to tell lies.
t. 1 Kings 22:24 Thus the wicked would seem that none were in the favor of God, but they, and that God hath given his graces to none so much as to them.
u. 1 Kings 22:27 Let him be pined away with hunger, and be fed with a small portion of bread and water.
v. 1 Kings 22:28 That when ye shall see these things come to pass, ye may give God the glory, and know that I am his true Prophet.

the captains of the chariots saw Jehoshaphat, they said, Surely it is the king of Israel: and they turned to fight against him: and Jehoshaphat [w]cried. **33** And when the captains of the chariots saw that he was not the king of Israel, they turned back from him. **34** Then a certain man drew a bow [x]mightily, and smote the king of Israel between the joints [y]of his brigandine. Wherefore he said unto his chariot man, Turn thine hand, and carry me out of the host: for I am [z]hurt. **35** And the battle increased that day, and the [aa]king stood still in his chariot against the Aramites, and died at even: and the blood ran out of the wound into the midst of the chariot. **36** And there were a proclamation throughout the [ab]host about the going down of the Sun, saying, Every man to his city, and every man to his own country. **37** So the king died, and was brought to Samaria, and they buried the king in Samaria. **38** And one washed the chariot in the pool of Samaria, and the dogs licked up his blood (and [ac]they washed his armor) according [3]unto the word of the Lord which he spake. **39** Concerning the rest of the acts of Ahab, and all that he did, and the ivory house which he built, and all the cities that he built, are they not written in the book of the Chronicles of the kings of Israel? **40** So Ahab slept with his fathers, and Ahaziah his son reigned in his stead. **41** [4]And Jehoshaphat the son of Asa began to reign upon Judah in the fourth year of Ahab king of Israel. **42** Jehoshaphat was five and thirty years old when he began to reign, and reigned five and twenty years in Jerusalem. And his mother's name was Azubah the daughter of Shilhi. **43** And he walked in all the ways of Asa his father, and declined not there from, but did that which was right in the eyes of the Lord. Nevertheless, [ad]the high places were not taken away: for the people offered still, and burnt incense in the high places. **44** And Jehoshaphat made peace with the king of Israel. **45** Concerning the rest of the acts of Jehoshaphat, and his worthy deeds that he did, and his battles which he fought, are they not written in the book of the Chronicles of the kings of Judah? **46** And the Sodomites, which remained in the days of his father Asa, he put clean out of the land. **47** There was then no King in Edom: the [ae]deputy was king. **48** Jehoshaphat made ships of [af]Tarshish to sail to [ag]Ophir for gold, but they went not, for the ships were broken at Ezion Geber. **49** Then said Ahaziah the son of Ahab unto Jehoshaphat, Let my servants go with thy servants in the ships, But Jehoshaphat would not. **50** And Jehoshaphat did sleep with his fathers, and was buried with his fathers in the city of David his father, and Jehoram his son reigned in his stead. **51** Ahaziah the son of Ahab began to reign over Israel in Samaria, the seventeenth year of Jehoshaphat king of Judah, and reigned two years over Israel. **52** But he did evil in the sight of the Lord, and walked in the way of his father, and in the way of his mother, and in the way of Jeroboam the son of Nebat, which made Israel to sin. **53** For he served Baal, and worshipped him, and provoked the Lord God of Israel unto wrath, [ah]according unto all that his father had done.

---

w. 1 Kings 22:32 That is, to the Lord for help.
x. 1 Kings 22:34 Or, in his simplicity, and ignorantly.
y. 1 Kings 22:34 Hebrew, and between the brigandine.
z. 1 Kings 22:34 Hebrew, sick.
aa. 1 Kings 22:35 To wit, Ahab, king of Israel.
ab. 1 Kings 22:36 Of the Israelites.
ac. 1 Kings 22:38 Or, the harlots washed it.
ad. 1 Kings 22:43 Meaning, that he was led with an error, thinking that they might still sacrifice to the Lord in those places, as well as they did before the Temple was built.
ae. 1 Kings 22:47 In the time of this king, Idumea was subject to Judah, and was governed by whom they of Judah appointed.
af. 1 Kings 22:48 By Tarshish the Scripture meaneth Cilicia and all the sea called Mediterranean.
ag. 1 Kings 22:48 Josephus writeth that Ophir is in India, where the Egyptians and Arabians traffic for gold.
ah. 1 Kings 22:53 Or, in all points as his father did.

1-KINGS 22
1. 2 Chron. 18:1,2
2. 2 Chron. 18:23
3. 1 Kings 31:19
4. 2 Chron. 20:31

THE SECOND BOOK OF THE
KINGS

---

1 *2 Ahaziah by a fall falleth sick, and consulteth with Baal-Zebub. 3 He is reproved by Elijah. 10 The captains over fifty were sent to Elijah, whereof two were burnt with fire from heaven by his prayer. 17 Ahaziah dieth, and Jehoram his brother succeedeth him.*

1 Then Moab rebelled against Israel after the death of Ahab: **2** And [a]Ahaziah fell through the lattice window in his upper chamber which was in Samaria: so he was sick: then he sent messengers, to whom he said, Go, and inquire of [b]Baal-Zebub the god of Ekron, if I shall recover of this my disease. **3** Then the Angel of the Lord said to Elijah the Tishbite, Arise, and go up to meet the messengers of the king of Samaria, and say unto them, [c]Is it not because there is no God in Israel, that ye go to inquire of Baal-Zebub the god of Ekron? **4** Wherefore thus saith the Lord, Thou shalt not come down from the bed on which thou art gone up, but shalt die the death. So Elijah departed. **5** And the messengers returned unto him, to whom he said, Why are ye now returned? **6** And they answered him, There came a man and met us, and said unto us, Go, and return unto the king which sent you, and say unto him, Thus saith the Lord, [d]Is it not because there is no God in Israel, that thou sendest to inquire of Baal-Zebub the God of Ekron? Therefore thou shalt not come down from the bed, on which thou art gone up, but shalt die the death. **7** And he said unto them, What manner of man was he which came and met you, and told you these words? **8** And they said unto him, He was an [e]hairy man, and girded with a girdle of leather about his loins. Then said he, It is Elijah the Tishbite. **9** Therefore the King sent unto him a captain over fifty with his fifty men, who went up unto him: for behold, he sat on the top [f]of a mountain, and he said unto him, O man of God, the king hath commanded that thou come down. **10** But Elijah answered, and said to the captain over the fifty, If that I be a man of God, let fire come down from the heaven, and devour thee and thy fifty. [g]So fire came down from the heaven and devoured him and his fifty. **11** Again also he sent unto him another captain over fifty with his fifty. Who spake, and said unto him, [h]O man of God, thus the King commandeth, Come down quickly. **12** But Elijah answered, and said unto them, [i]If I be a man of God, let fire come down from the heaven and devour thee and thy fifty. So fire came down from the heaven, and devoured him and his fifty. **13** Yet again he sent the third captain over fifty with his fifty. And the third captain over fifty went up, and came, and fell on his knees before Elijah, and besought him, and said unto him, O man of God, I pray thee, let my [j]life and the life of these thy fifty servants be [k]precious in thy sight. **14** Behold, there came fire down from the heaven, and devoured the two former captains over fifty with their fifties: therefore let my life now be precious in thy sight. **15** And the Angel of the Lord said unto Elijah, Go down with him, be [l]not afraid of his presence. So he arose, and went down with him unto the king. **16** And he said unto him, Thus saith the Lord, Because thou hast sent messengers to inquire of Baal-Zebub the god of Ekron, (was it not because there was no God in Israel to inquire of his word?) therefore thou shalt not come down off the bed, on which thou art gone up, but shalt die the death. **17** So he died

---

2-KINGS 1
a. 2 Kings 1:2 So that he was punished for his idolatry after two sorts: for the Moabites which were wont to pay him tribute, rebelled, and he fell down at a grate which was upon his house to give light beneath.
b. 2 Kings 1:2 The Philistines which dwelt at Ekron, worshipped this idol, which figureth the god of flies, thinking that he could preserve them from the biting of flies: or else he was so called, because flies were engendered in great abundance of the blood of the sacrifices that were offered to that idol.
c. 2 Kings 1:3 He showeth that idolaters have not the true God, for else they would seek to none but to him alone.
d. 2 Kings 1:6 Ignorance is the mother of error and idolatry.
e. 2 Kings 1:8 Some think that this is meant of his garments, which were rough and made of hair.
f. 2 Kings 1:9 To wit, Carmel.
g. 2 Kings 1:10 He declareth what power God's word hath in the mouth of his servants, when they threaten God's judgments against the wicked.
h. 2 Kings 1:11 He spake this in mockery, and therefore provoked God's wrath so much the more.
i. 2 Kings 1:12 Meaning, that God would show by effect whether he was a true Prophet or not.
j. 2 Kings 1:13 Which humble myself before God and his servant.
k. 2 Kings 1:13 That is, spare my life, and let me not die as the other two.
l. 2 Kings 1:15 Thus the Lord giveth boldness to his, that they fear not the threatenings of tyrants, which otherwise of themselves are afraid to do God's message.
m. 2 Kings 1:17 Jehoshaphat going to battle against the Syrians, made his son Jehoram king in the 17th year of his reign: and

according to the word of the Lord which Elijah had spoken. And Jehoram began to reign in his stead in the second year of [m]Jehoram the son of Jehoshaphat king of Judah, because he had no son. **18** Concerning the rest of the acts of Ahaziah, that he did, are they not written in the book of the Chronicles of the kings of Israel?

2

1 Elijah divided the waters with his cloak. 11 He is taken up into heaven. 13 Elisha taketh his cloak and divideth Jordan. 20 The bitter and venomous waters are healed. 23 The children that mock Elisha, are rent in pieces with bears.

1 And when the Lord would take up Elijah into heaven by a whirlwind, Elijah went with Elisha from [a]Gilgal. **2** Then Elijah said to Elisha, Tarry here, I pray thee: for the Lord hath sent me to Bethel. But Elisha said, As the Lord liveth, and as thy soul liveth, I will not leave thee. So they came down to Bethel. **3** And the [b]children of the Prophets that were at Bethel, came out to Elisha, and said unto him, Knowest thou that the Lord will take thy master from [c]thine head this day? And he said, Yea, I [d]know it: hold ye your peace. **4** Again Elijah said unto him, Elisha, tarry here, I pray thee: for the Lord hath sent me to Jericho. But he said, As the Lord liveth, and as thy soul liveth, I will not leave thee. So they came to Jericho. **5** And the children of the Prophets that were at [e]Jericho, came to Elisha, and said unto him, Knowest thou, that the Lord will take thy master from thine head this day? And he said, Yea, I know it: hold ye your peace. **6** Moreover Elijah said unto him, Tarry, I pray thee, here: for the Lord hath sent me to Jordan. But he said, As the Lord liveth, and as thy soul liveth, I will not leave thee. So they went both together. **7** And fifty men of the sons of the Prophets went and stood on the other side a far off, and they two stood by Jordan. **8** Then Elijah took his cloak, and wrapped it together, and smote the [f]waters, and they were divided hither and thither, and they twain went over on the dry land. **9** Now when they were passed over, Elijah said unto Elisha, Ask what I shall do for thee before I be taken from thee. And Elisha said, I pray thee, let thy Spirit [g]be double upon me. **10** And he said, Thou hast asked an hard thing: yet if thou see me when I am taken from thee, thou shalt have it so: and if not, it shall not be. **11** And as they went walking and talking, behold, there appeared a chariot of fire, and horses of fire, and did separate them twain. So Elijah went up by a whirlwind into [h]heaven. **12** And Elisha saw it, and he cried, My father, my father, the chariot of Israel, and the horsemen thereof: and he saw him no more: and he took his own clothes, and rent them in two pieces. **13** He took up also the cloak of Elijah, that fell from him, and returned, and stood by the bank of Jordan. **14** After, he took the cloak of Elijah, that fell from him, and smote the waters, and said, Where is the Lord God of Elijah? And so he also, after he had stricken the waters, so that they were divided this way and that way, went over, even Elisha. **15** And when the children of the Prophets, which were at Jericho, saw him on the other side, they said, [i]The Spirit of Elijah doeth rest on Elisha: and they came to meet him, and fell to the ground before him, **16** And said unto him, Behold now, there be with thy servants fifty strong men: let them go, we pray thee, and seek thy [j]master, if so be the Spirit of the Lord hath taken him up, and cast him upon some mountain, or into some valley. But he said, [k]Ye shall not send. **17** Yet they were instant upon him, till he was ashamed: wherefore he said, Send. So they sent fifty men, which sought three days, but found him not. **18** Therefore they returned to him, (for he tarried at Jericho) and he said unto them, Did not I say unto you, Go not? **19** And the men of the city said unto Elisha, Behold, we pray thee: the situation of this city is pleasant, as thou, my lord, seest, but the water is naught, and the ground [l]barren. **20** Then he said, Bring me a new cruse, and put salt therein. And they brought it to him. **21** And he went unto the spring of the waters, and cast there [m]the salt, and said, Thus saith the Lord, I have healed this water: death shall no more come thereof, neither barrenness to the ground. **22** So the waters were healed unto this day, according to the word of Elisha which he had spoken. **23** And he went up from thence unto Bethel. And as he was going up the way, little children came out of the city, and mocked him, and said unto him, Come up, thou bald head, come up, thou bald head. **24** And he turned back, and looked on them, and [n]cursed them in the name of the Lord. And two bears came out of the forest, and tore in pieces two and forty children of them. **25** So he went from thence to mount Carmel, and from thence he returned to Samaria.

3

1 The reign of Jehoram. 6 He and Jehoshaphat go to war against Moab which rebelled. 13 Elisha reproveth him, 17 and giveth their hosts water. 24 The Moabites are overcome. 27 Their King sacrificeth his son.

1 Now Jehoram the son of Ahab began to reign over Israel in Samaria, the [a]eighteenth year of Jehoshaphat King of Judah, and reigned twelve years. **2** And he wrought evil in the sight of the Lord, but not like his father nor like his mother: for he took away the image of Baal that his father had made. **3** Nevertheless, he cleaved unto the [b]sins of Jeroboam, the son of Nebat, which made Israel to sin, and departed not therefrom. **4** Then [c]Mesha king of Moab had store of sheep, and rendered unto the king of Israel an hundred thousand rams with the wool. **5** But when Ahab was dead, the king of Moab rebelled against the king of Israel. **6** Therefore King Jehoram went out of Samaria the same season, and numbered all Israel, **7** And went, and sent to Jehoshaphat king of Judah, saying, The king of Moab hath rebelled against me: wilt thou go with me to battle against Moab? And he answered, I will go up: for [d]I am, as thou art, my people, as thy people, and mine horses, as thine horses. **8** Then said he, What way shall we go up? And he answered, The way of the wilderness of Edom. **9** So went the king of Israel and the king of Judah, and the [e]king of Edom, and when they had compassed the way seven days, they had no water for the host, nor for the cattle that [f]followed them. **10** Therefore the king of Israel said, Alas, that the Lord hath called these three kings, to give them into the hand of Moab. **11** But Jehoshaphat said, Is there not here a Prophet of the Lord, that we may inquire of the Lord by him? And one of the king of Israel's servants answered, and said, Here is Elisha the son of Shaphat, which [g]poured water on the hands of Elijah. **12** Then Jehoshaphat said, [h]The word of the Lord is with him. Therefore the king of Israel, and Jehoshaphat, and the king of Edom went down to him. **13** And Elisha said unto the king of Israel, [i]What have I to do with thee? get thee to the Prophets of thy father, and to the Prophets of thy mother. And the king of Israel said unto him, [j]Nay: for the Lord hath called these three kings, to give them into the hand of Moab. **14** Then Elisha said, As the Lord of hosts liveth, in whose sight I stand, if it were not, that I regard the presence of Jehoshaphat the king of Judah, I would [k]not have looked toward thee, nor seen thee. **15** But now bring me a minstrel. And when the minstrel [l]played, the hand of the Lord came upon him. **16** And he said, Thus saith the Lord, Make this valley full of ditches. **17** For thus saith the Lord, Ye shall neither see wind nor see rain, yet the valley shall be filled with water, that ye may drink, both ye and your cattle, and your beasts. **18** But this is a [m]small thing in the sight of the Lord: for he will give Moab into your hand. **19** And ye shall smite every strong town, and every chief city, and shall fell every fair tree, and shall stop all the fountains of water, and [n]mar every good field with stones. **20** And in the morning when the meat offering was offered, behold, there came water by the way of Edom: and the country was filled with water. **21** And when all the Moabites heard that the kings were come up to fight against them, they gathered all that was able [o]to put on harness, and upward, and stood in their border. **22** And they rose early in the morning, when the Sun arose upon the water, and the Moabites saw the water over against them, as red as blood. **23** And they said, [p]This is blood: the kings are surely slain, and one hath smitten another: now therefore Moab, to the spoil. **24** And when they came to the host of Israel, the Israelites arose up, and smote the Moabites, so that they fled before them, but they [q]invaded them, and smote Moab. **25** And they destroyed the cities: and on all the good field every

---

in the 18th year which was the second year of his son, Jehoram the son of Ahab reigned in Israel: and in the fifth year of this Jehoram Jehoshaphat died, and the kingdom of Judah was confirmed to his son.

2-KINGS 2

- **a.** 2 Kings 2:1 Which was that place where the children of Israel were circumcised after they came over Jordan, and had been forty years in the wilderness, as Josh. 5:9.
- **b.** 2 Kings 2:3 So called, because they are begotten as it were anew by the heavenly doctrine.
- **c.** 2 Kings 2:3 That is, from being anymore thine head: for to be as the head, is to be the master, as to be at the feet, is to be a scholar.
- **d.** 2 Kings 2:3 For the Lord had revealed it unto him.
- **e.** 2 Kings 2:5 Not only at Bethel, but at Jericho and other places were there Prophets, which had scholars, whom they instructed and brought up in the true fear of God.
- **f.** 2 Kings 2:8 To wit, of Jordan.
- **g.** 2 Kings 2:9 Let thy Spirit have double force in me, because of these dangerous times: or let me have twice so much as the rest of the Prophets: or thy spirit being divided into three parts, let me have two.
- **h.** 2 Kings 2:11 Thus God hath left a testimony in all ages (both before the Law, in the Law, and in the time of the Gospel) of our resurrection.
- **i.** 2 Kings 2:15 The Spirit of prophecy is given to him, as it was to Elijah.
- **j.** 2 Kings 2:16 Meaning, Elijah: for they thought his body had been cast in some mountain.
- **k.** 2 Kings 2:16 Because the fact was extraordinary, they doubted where he was become, but Elisha was assured that he was taken up to God.
- **l.** 2 Kings 2:19 Or, killeth the inhabitants.
- **m.** 2 Kings 2:21 Thus God gave him power, even contrary to nature, to make that water profitable for man's use, which before was hurtful.
- **n.** 2 Kings 2:24 Perceiving their malicious heart against the Lord and his word, he desireth God to take vengeance of that injury done unto him.

2-KINGS 3

- **a.** 2 Kings 3:1 Read the annotation in the first chapter and seventh verse.
- **b.** 2 Kings 3:3 He sacrificed to the golden calves that Jeroboam had made.
- **c.** 2 Kings 3:4 This was done after that David had made the Moabites tributaries to his successors.
- **d.** 2 Kings 3:7 Read 1 Kings 22:4.
- **e.** 2 Kings 3:9 Meaning, the viceroy, or lieutenant of the king of Judah, read 1 Kings 22:47.
- **f.** 2 Kings 3:9 Hebrew, that were at their feet.
- **g.** 2 Kings 3:11 That is, who was his servant.
- **h.** 2 Kings 3:12 He is able to instruct us what is God's will in this point.
- **i.** 2 Kings 3:13 He knew that this wicked king would have but used his counsel to serve his turn, and therefore, he disdained to answer him.
- **j.** 2 Kings 3:13 The wicked esteem not the servants of God, but when they are driven by every necessity and fear of the present danger.
- **k.** 2 Kings 3:14 God suffereth his word to be declared to the wicked, because of the godly that are among them.
- **l.** 2 Kings 3:15 He sang songs to God's glory, and so stirred up the Prophet's heart to prophesy.
- **m.** 2 Kings 3:18 He will not only miraculously give you waters, but your enemies also into your hand.
- **n.** 2 Kings 3:19 Though God bestow his benefits for a time upon the enemies, yet he hath his seasons, when he will take them away to the intent they might see his vengeance which is prepared against them.
- **o.** 2 Kings 3:21 Hebrew, to gird himself with a girdle.
- **p.** 2 Kings 3:23 The sudden joy of the wicked is but a preparation to their destruction, which is at hand.
- **q.** 2 Kings 3:24 Meaning, they followed them into the towns.

man cast his stone, and filled them and they stopped all the fountains of water, and felled all the good trees: only in [r]Kir Haraseth left they the stones thereof: howbeit they went about it with slings, and smote it. **26** And when the King of Moab saw that the battle was too sore for him, he took with him seven hundred men that drew the sword, to break through unto the king of Edom: but they could not. **27** Then he took his eldest son, that should have reigned in his stead, and [s]offered him for a burnt offering upon the wall: so that Israel was sore grieved, and they departed from him, and returned to their country.

4

4 God increaseth the oil to the poor widow by Elisha. 12 He obtaineth for the Shunammite a son at God's hand. 18 Who dying, 32 he raiseth him up again. 40 He maketh sweet the pottage, 42 and multiplied the loaves.

1 And one of the wives of the sons [a]of the Prophets cried unto Elisha, saying, Thy servant mine husband is dead, and thou knowest, that thy servant did [b]fear the Lord: and the creditor is come to take my two sons to be his [c]bondmen. **2** Then Elisha said unto her, What shall I do for thee? tell me, what hast thou at home? And she said, Thine handmaid hath nothing at home, save a [d]pitcher of oil. **3** And he said, Go and borrow thee vessels abroad of all thy neighbors, empty vessels, and spare not. **4** And when thou art come in, thou shalt shut the door upon thee and upon thy sons, and pour out into [e]all those vessels, and set aside those that are full. **5** So she departed from him, and shut the door upon her, and upon her sons. And they brought to her, and she poured out. **6** And when the vessels were full, she said unto her son, Bring me yet a vessel. And he said unto her, There is no more vessels. And the oil [f]ceased. **7** Then she came and told the man of God. And he said, Go and sell the oil, and pay them that thou art in debt unto, and live thou and thy children of the [g]rest. **8** And on a time Elisha came to Shunem, and there a woman of great estimation constrained him to eat bread: and as he passed by, he turned in thither to eat bread. **9** And she said unto her husband, Behold, I know now, that this is an holy man of God that passeth by us continually. **10** Let us make [h]him a little chamber, I pray thee, with walls, and let us set him there a bed, and a table, and a stool, and a candlestick, that he may turn in thither when he cometh to us. **11** And on a day, he came thither and turned into the chamber, and lay therein, **12** And said to Gehazi his servant, Call this Shunammite: and when he called her, she stood before him. **13** Then he said unto him, Say unto her now, Behold, thou hast had all this great care for us, [i]what shall we do for thee? Is there anything to be spoken for thee to the king or to the captain of the host? And she answered, I [j]dwell among mine own people. **14** Again he said, What is then to be done for her? Then Gehazi answered, Indeed she hath [k]no son, and her husband is old. **15** Then said he, Call her. And he called her, and she stood in the door. **16** And he said, [1]At this time appointed, according to the time of life, thou shalt embrace a son. And she said, Oh my Lord, thou man of God, do not lie unto thine handmaid. **17** So the woman conceived, and bore a son at that same season, according to the time of life, that Elisha had said unto her. **18** And when the child was grown, it fell on a day, that he went out to his father, and to the reapers. **19** And he said to his father, [l]Mine head, mine head. Who said to his servant, Bear him to his mother. **20** And he took him and brought him to his mother, and he sat on her knees till noon, and died. **21** Then she went up, and laid him on the bed of the man of God, and shut the door upon him and went out. **22** Then she called to her husband, and said, Send with me, I pray thee, one of the young men and one of the asses: for I will haste to the man of God, and come again. **23** And he said, Wherefore wilt thou go to him today? it is neither [m]new moon nor Sabbath day. And she answered, [n]All shall be well. **24** Then she saddled an ass, and said to her servant, Drive, and go forward: stay not for me to get up, except I bid thee. **25** So she went, and came unto the man of God to mount Carmel. And when the man of God saw her [o]over against him, he said to Gehazi his servant, Behold, the Shunammite. **26** Run now, I say, to meet her, and say unto her, Art thou in health? is thine husband in health? and is the child in health? And she answered, We are in health. **27** And when she came to the man of God unto the mountain, she [p]caught him by his feet: and Gehazi went to her, to thrust her away: but the man of God said, Let her alone: for her soul is [q]vexed within her, and the Lord hath hid it from me, and hath not told it me. **28** Then she said, Did I desire a son of my lord? did I not say, Deceive me not? **29** Then he said to Gehazi, Gird thy loins, and take my staff in thine hand, and go thy way: [r]if thou meet any, salute him not: and if any salute thee, answer him not: and lay my staff upon the face of the child. **30** And the mother of the child said, As the Lord liveth, and as thy soul liveth, I will not leave thee. Therefore he arose, and followed her. **31** But Gehazi was gone before them, and had laid the staff upon the face of the child, but he neither spake nor heard: wherefore he returned to meet him, and told him, saying, The child is not waken. **32** Then came Elisha into the house, and behold, the child was dead, and laid upon his bed. **33** He went in therefore, and shut the door upon them twain, and prayed unto the Lord. **34** After he went up, and [s]lay upon the child, and put his mouth on his mouth, and his eyes upon his eyes, and his hands upon his hands, and stretched himself upon him, and the flesh of the child waxed warm. **35** And he went from him, and walked up and down in the house, and went up and spread himself upon him: then the child sneezed [t]seven times, and opened his eyes. **36** Then he called Gehazi, and said, Call this Shunammite. So he called her, which came in unto him. And he said unto her, Take thy son. **37** And she came, and fell at his feet, and bowed herself to the ground, and took up her son, and went out. **38** Afterward Elisha returned to Gilgal, and a famine was in the [u]land, and the children of the Prophets dwelt with him. And he said unto his servant, Set on the great pot, and seethe pottage for the children of the Prophets. **39** And one went out into the field, to gather herbs, and found as it were a wild vine, and gathered thereof [v]wild gourds his garment full, and came and shred them into the pot of pottage: for they knew it not. **40** So they poured out for the men to eat: and when they did eat of the pottage, they cried out, and said, O thou man of God, [w]death is in the pot: and they could not eat thereof. **41** Then he said, Bring meal. And he cast it into the pot, and said, Pour out for the people, that they may eat: and there was none evil in the pot. **42** Then came a man from Baal Shalisha, and brought the man of God bread of the firstfruits, even twenty loaves of barley, and full ears of corn in the husk. And he said, Give unto the people, that they may eat. **43** And his servant answered, How should I set this before an hundred men? He said again, Give it unto the people, that they may eat: for thus saith the Lord, They [x]shall eat, and there shall remain. **44** So he set it before them, and they did eat, and left over, according to the word of the Lord.

5

1 Naaman the Syrian is healed of his leprosy. 16 Elisha refuseth his gifts. 27 Gehazi is stricken with leprosy, because he took money and raiment of Naaman.

1 Now was there one Naaman captain of the host of the King of Aram, a great man, and honorable in the sight of his lord, because that by him the Lord had [a]delivered the Aramites. He also was a mighty man and valiant, but a leper. **2** And the Aramites had gone out by bands, and had taken a little maid of the land of Israel, and she [b]served Naaman's wife. **3** And she said unto her mistress, Would God my lord were with the [c]Prophet that is in Samaria, he would soon deliver him of his leprosy. **4** And [d]he went in, and told his lord, saying, Thus and thus saith the maid that is of the land of Israel. **5** And the king of Aram said, Go thy way thither, and I will send a letter unto the King of Israel. And he departed, and [e]took [f]with him ten talents of silver, and six thousand pieces of gold, and ten changes of raiments, **6** And brought the letter to the king of Israel to this effect, Now when this letter is come unto thee, understand, that I have sent thee Naaman my servant, that thou mayest heal him of his leprosy. **7** And when the king of Israel had read the letter, he rent his clothes, and said, Am I God to kill and to give life that he doth send to me, that I should heal a man from his leprosy? wherefore consider, I pray you, and see how he seeketh a quarrel against me. **8** But when Elisha the man of God had heard that the King of Israel had rent his clothes, he

---

r. 2 Kings 3:25 Which was one of the principle cities of the Moabites, wherein they left nothing but the walls.
s. 2 Kings 3:27 Some refer it to the king of Edom's son, whom they say he had taken in that skirmish: but rather it seemed to be his own son, whom he offered to his gods to pacify them: which barbarous cruelty moved the Israelites' hearts of pity to depart.

2-KINGS 4

a. 2 Kings 4:1 Read 2 Kings 2:3.
b. 2 Kings 4:1 And therefore fell not into debt by unthriftiness or prodigality, but by the hand of the Lord.
c. 2 Kings 4:1 Because I am poor and not able to pay.
d. 2 Kings 4:2 Thus God suffereth his many times to be brought to extreme necessity, before he succor them, that afterward they may the more praise his mercy.
e. 2 Kings 4:4 The Prophet declareth hereby unto her, that God never faileth to provide for his servants, their wives and children, if they trust in him.
f. 2 Kings 4:6 To augment and increase in the vessels.
g. 2 Kings 4:7 God here did not only provide for his servant, that his debts should be paid and so kept his doctrine and profession without slander, but also for his wife and children.
h. 2 Kings 4:10 Which should be separate from the rest of the house, that he might more commodiously give himself to study and prayers.
i. 2 Kings 4:13 Thus the servants of God are not unthankful for the benefits they receive.
j. 2 Kings 4:13 I am content with that that God hath sent me, and can want nothing that one can do for another.
k. 2 Kings 4:14 Which then was a reproach, and therefore he would that his master should pray to God for her that she might be fruitful.
l. 2 Kings 4:19 His head ached sore, and therefore he cried thus.
m. 2 Kings 4:23 For at such times the people were wont to resort to the Prophets for doctrine and consolation.
n. 2 Kings 4:23 Hebrew, peace.
o. 2 Kings 4:25 Or, far off.
p. 2 Kings 4:27 In token of humility and joy that she had met with him.
q. 2 Kings 4:27 Hebrew, her soul is in bitterness.
r. 2 Kings 4:29 Make such speed that nothing may let thee in the way, Luke 10:4.
s. 2 Kings 4:34 The like did Elijah to the widow's son at Zarephath, 1 Kings 17:21 and St. Paul, Acts 20:10, signifying the care that ought to be in them, that bear the word of God, and are distributors of the spiritual life.
t. 2 Kings 4:35 Meaning, oftentimes.
u. 2 Kings 4:38 That is, in the land of Israel.
v. 2 Kings 4:39 Which the Apothecaries call colloquintida, and is most vehement and dangerous in purging.
w. 2 Kings 4:40 They feared that they were poisoned, because of the bitterness.
x. 2 Kings 4:43 It is not the quantity of bread that satisfieth, but the blessing that God giveth.

2-KINGS 4

1. Gen. 18:10

2-KINGS 5

a. 2 Kings 5:1 Here appeareth that among the infidels God hath his, and also that the infidels have them in estimation which do good to their country.
b. 2 Kings 5:2 Hebrew, she was before.
c. 2 Kings 5:3 Meaning, Elisha.
d. 2 Kings 5:4 That is, Naaman told it to the king of Syria.
e. 2 Kings 5:5 To give this as a present to the Prophet.
f. 2 Kings 5:5 Hebrew, in his hand.
g. 2 Kings 5:8 The Prophet rebuketh the king because he did not consider that God was true in his promise, and therefore would not leave his Church destitute of a Prophet, whose

sent unto the King, saying, [g]Wherefore hast thou rent thy clothes? Let him come now to me, and he shall know that there is a Prophet in Israel. **9** Then Naaman came with his horses, and with his chariots, and stood at the door of the house of Elisha. **10** And Elisha sent a messenger unto him, saying, Go and wash thee in Jordan seven times, and thy flesh shall come again to thee, and thou shalt be cleansed. **11** But Naaman was [h]wroth and went away, and said, Behold, I thought with myself, He will surely come out, and stand, and call on the Name of the Lord his God, and put his hand on the place, and heal the leprosy. **12** Are not Abanah and Pharpar, rivers of Damascus, better than all the waters of Israel? may I not wash me in them, and be cleansed? so he turned, and departed in displeasure. **13** But his servants came, and spake unto him, and said, [i]Father, if the Prophet had commanded thee a great thing, wouldest thou not have done it? how much rather then, when he saith to thee, Wash, and be clean? **14** Then went he down, and [1]washed himself seven times in Jordan, according to the saying of the man of God: and his flesh came again, like unto the flesh of a little child, and he was clean. **15** And he turned again to the man of God, he, and all his company, and came and stood before him, and said, Behold now, I know that there is no God in all the world but in Israel: now therefore, I pray thee, take a [j]reward of thy servant. **16** But he said, As the Lord liveth (before whom I stand) I will not receive it. And he would have constrained him to receive it, [k]but he refused. **17** Moreover Naaman said, Shall there not be given to thy servant two mules' load of this earth? for thy servant will henceforth offer neither burnt sacrifice nor offering unto any other god, save unto the Lord. **18** Herein the Lord be [l]merciful unto thy servant, that when my master goeth into the house of Rimmon, to worship there, and leaneth on mine hand, and I bow myself in the house of Rimmon: when I do bow down, I say, in the house of Rimmon, the Lord be merciful unto thy servant in this point. **19** Unto whom he said, [m]Go in peace. So he departed from him about half a day's journey of ground. **20** And Gehazi the servant of Elisha the man of God said, Behold, my master hath spared this Aramite Naaman, receiving not those things at his hand that he brought: As the Lord liveth, I will run after him, and take somewhat of him. **21** So Gehazi followed speedily after Naaman. And when Naaman saw him running after him, [n]he lighted down from the chariot to meet him, and said, Is all well? **22** And he answered, All is well: my master hath set me, saying, Behold, there be come to me, even now from mount Ephraim two young men of the children of the Prophets: give them, I pray thee, a talent of silver, and two changes of garments. **23** And Naaman said, Yea, take two talents: and he compelled him, and bound two talents of silver in two bags, with two changes of garments, and gave them unto two of his servants, that they might bear them before him. **24** And when he came to the [o]tower, he took them out of their hands, and laid them in the house, and sent away the men: and [p]they departed. **25** Then he went in, and stood before his master. And Elisha said unto him, Whence comest thou, Gehazi? And he said, Thy servant went no whither. **26** But he said unto him, [q]Went not mine heart with thee, when the man turned again from his chariot to meet thee? Is this a time to take money, and to receive garments, [r]and olives, and vineyards, and sheep, and oxen, and menservants, and maidservants? **27** The leprosy therefore of Naaman shall cleave unto thee, and to thy [s]seed forever. And he went out from his presence a leper white as snow.

6

6 Elisha maketh iron to swim above the water. 8 He discloseth the king of Syria's counsel to the king of Israel, 13 who sending certain to take him, were kept fast in Samaria. 24 Samaria is besieged, and endureth extreme famine.

1 And the children of the Prophets said unto Elisha, Behold, we pray thee, the place where we dwell with thee, is too little for us. **2** Let us now go to Jordan, that we may take thence every man a [a]beam, and make us a place to dwell in. And he answered, Go. **3** And one said, Vouchsafe, I pray thee, to go with thy servants. And he answered, I will go. **4** So he went with them, and when they came to Jordan, they cut down wood. **5** And as one was felling of a tree, the [b]iron fell into the water: then he cried, and said, Alas master, it was but borrowed. **6** And the man of God said, Where fell it? And he showed him the place. Then he cut down a piece of wood, and cast in thither, and he caused the iron to [c]swim. **7** Then he said, Take it up to thee. And he stretched out his hand, and took it. **8** Then the king of Aram warred against Israel, and took counsel with his servants, and said, In [d]such and such a place shall be my camp. **9** Therefore the man of God sent unto the king of Israel, saying, Beware thou go not over to such a place: for there the Aramites are come down. **10** So the king of Israel sent to the place which the man of God told him, and warned him of, and [e]saved himself from thence, not once, nor twice. **11** And the heart of the king of Aram was troubled for this thing: therefore he called his servants, and said unto them, Will ye not show me, which of us bewrayeth our counsel to the king of Israel? **12** Then one of his servants said, None, my lord, O king, but Elisha the Prophet that is in Israel, telleth the king of Israel, even the words that thou speakest in thy [f]privy chamber. **13** And he said, Go, and espy where he is, that I may send and fetch him. And one told him, saying, Behold, he is in Dothan. **14** So he sent thither horses, and chariots, and a [g]mighty host: and they came by night, and compassed the city. **15** And when the servant of the man of God arose early to go out, behold, an host compassed the city with horses and chariots. Then his servant said unto him, Alas master, how shall we do? **16** And he answered, [h]Fear not: [1]for they that be with us, are more than they that be with them. **17** Then Elisha prayed, and said, Lord, I beseech thee, open his eyes, [i]that he may see. And the Lord opened the eyes of the servant, and he looked, and behold, the mountain was full of horses and chariots of fire round about Elisha. **18** So [j]they came down to him, but Elisha prayed unto the Lord, and said, Smite this people, I pray thee, with blindness. And he smote them with blindness, according to the word of Elisha. **19** And Elisha said unto them, This is not the way, neither is this the city: follow me, and I will lead you to the man whom ye seek. But he led [k]them to Samaria. **20** And when they were come to Samaria, Elisha said, Lord, open their eyes that they may see. And the Lord opened their eyes, and they saw, and behold, they were in the midst of Samaria. **21** And the king of Israel said unto Elisha when he saw them, [l]My father, shall I smite them, shall I smite them? **22** And he answered, Thou shalt not smite them: doest thou not smite them that thou hast taken with thy sword, and with thy bow? but set bread and water before them, that they may eat and drink and go to their master. **23** And he made great preparation for them: and when they had eaten and drunken, he sent them away: and they went to their master. So the bands of Aram came [m]no more into the land of Israel. **24** But afterward Ben-Hadad king of Aram gathered all his host, and went up and besieged Samaria. **25** So there was a great famine in Samaria: for lo, they besieged it until an asses head was at four score pieces of silver, and the fourth part of a cab of dove's [n]dung at five pieces of silver. **26** And as the king of Israel was going upon the wall, there cried a woman unto him, saying, Help, my lord, O King. **27** And he said, Seeing the Lord doth not succor thee, how should I help thee with the [o]barn, or with the wine press? **28** Also the king said unto her, What aileth thee? And she answered, This woman said unto me, Give thy son that we may eat him today, and we will eat my son tomorrow, **29** [2]So we sod my son, and did eat him: and I said to her the day after, Give thy son, that we may eat him, but she hath hid her son. **30** And when the king had heard the words of the woman, he rent his clothes, (and as he went upon the wall, the people looked, and behold, he had sackcloth [p]within [q]upon his flesh) **31** And he said, God do so to me and more also, if the head of Elisha the son of Shaphat shall stand on him this day. **32** (Now Elisha sat in his house, and the Elders sat with him.) And the King sent a man before him: but before the messenger came to him, he said to the Elders, See ye not how this [r]murderer's son hath sent to take away mine head? take heed when the messenger cometh, and shut the door, and handle him roughly at the door: is not the sound of his master's feet behind him? **33** While he yet talked with them, behold, the messenger came down unto him, and said, Behold, this evil cometh of the Lord: [s]should I attend on the Lord any longer?

---

prayers he would hear, and to whom others should have recourse for comfort.

h. 2 Kings 5:11 Man's reason murmureth, when it considereth only the signs and outward things, and hath not regard to the word of God, which is there contained.

i. 2 Kings 5:13 This declareth that servants ought to reverence and love their masters as children their fathers, and likewise masters toward their servants, must be affectioned as toward their children.

j. 2 Kings 5:15 Hebrew, blessing.

k. 2 Kings 5:16 So the Lord commandeth that they that receive freely, should give also freely.

l. 2 Kings 5:18 He feeleth his conscience wounded in being present at idol's service, and therefore desireth God to forgive him, lest others by his example might fall to idolatry: for as for his own part he confesseth that he will never serve any but the true God.

m. 2 Kings 5:19 The Prophet did not approve his act, but after the common manner of speech he biddeth him farewell.

n. 2 Kings 5:21 Declaring thereby, what honor and affection he bare to the Prophet his master.

o. 2 Kings 5:24 Or, fortress, or secret place.

p. 2 Kings 5:24 Naaman's servants.

q. 2 Kings 5:26 Was I not present with thee in spirit?

r. 2 Kings 5:26 That is, money to buy possessions with: meaning, that it is detestable in the servants of God to have covetous minds.

s. 2 Kings 5:27 To be an example to all such, as by whose covetousness God's word might be slandered.

2-KINGS 5

1. Luke 4:27

2-KINGS 6

a. 2 Kings 6:2 Or a piece of wood fit to build with.

b. 2 Kings 6:5 Or, the axe head.

c. 2 Kings 6:6 God wrought this miraculously to confirm the authority of Elisha, to whom he had given such abundance of his Spirit.

d. 2 Kings 6:8 Meaning, that he would lie in ambush, and take the Israelites at unawares.

e. 2 Kings 6:10 The wicked conspire nothing so craftily, but God can reveal it to his servants, and cause their counsel to be disclosed.

f. 2 Kings 6:12 There is nothing so secret that thou canst go about, but he knoweth it, and discovereth it unto his King.

g. 2 Kings 6:14 Though it had been nothing in man's judgment to have taken Elisha, yet the wicked ever doubt, and think they are never able to prepare power enough, though it be but against one or a few.

h. 2 Kings 6:16 For he was assured of God's help, and that millions of Angels camped about the godly to deliver them.

i. 2 Kings 6:17 That he may behold how thou hast prepared an army to rescue us.

j. 2 Kings 6:18 Meaning, the Syrians his enemies, which came down, thinking themselves sure of him.

k. 2 Kings 6:19 Thus he did being led by the Spirit of God, and not because he sought his own revengeance, but only to set forth the glory of God.

l. 2 Kings 6:21 The wicked use reverent and grave words toward the servants of God, when they think to have any commodity by them, though in their heart they cannot abide them.

m. 2 Kings 6:23 For this gentle entreaty and the miracle wrought by the Prophet, did more prevail for common quietness, than if they had been overcome in battle: for they returned no more at that time to fight against Israel, or in that King's days.

n. 2 Kings 6:25 The Hebrews write, that they burned it in the siege for lack of wood.

o. 2 Kings 6:27 Meaning, any kind of vittle, as corn and wine, etc.

p. 2 Kings 6:30 Or, under his clothes.

q. 2 Kings 6:30 Thus hypocrites when they feel God's judgments, think to please him with outward ceremonies, whom in prosperity they will not know.

r. 2 Kings 6:32 Meaning, Jehoram Ahab's son, who killed the Prophets, and caused Naboth to be stoned.

s. 2 Kings 6:33 So the wicked fall into a rage and desperation, if they find not sudden remedy against their afflictions.

2-KINGS 6

1. 1 Chron. 32:7 **2.** Deut. 28:53-57

7 *1 Elisha prophesieth plenty of vittles, and other things to Samaria. 6 The Syrians run away and have no man following them. 17 The prince that would not believe the word of Elisha, is trodden to death.*

1 Then Elisha said, Hear ye the word of the Lord: thus saith the Lord, [a]To-
morrow this time a measure of fine flour shall be sold for a shekel, and two measu-
res of barley for a shekel in the gate of Samaria. **2** Then a prince, on whose hand
the king [b]leaned, answered the man of God, and said, Though the Lord would
make [c]windows in the heaven, could this thing come to pass? And he said, Behold,
thou shalt see it with thine eyes, but thou shalt not [d]eat thereof. **3** Now there
were four leprous men at the [e]entering in of the gate: and they said one to another,
Why sit we here until we die? **4** If we say, We will enter into the city, the famine
is in the city, and we shall die there: and if we sit here, we die also. Now therefore
come, and let us fall into the camp of the Aramites: if they save our lives, we shall
live: and if they kill us, we are but dead. **5** So they rose up in the twilight, to go
to the camp of the Aramites: and when they were come to the utmost part of the
camp of the Aramites, lo, there was no man there. **6** For the Lord had caused
the camp of the Aramites to hear a [f]noise of chariots and a noise of horses, and a
noise of a great army, so that they said one to another, Behold, the King of Israel
hath hired against us the kings of the Hittites, and the kings of the Egyptians to
come upon us. **7** Wherefore they arose, and fled in the twilight, and left their
tents and their horses, and their asses, even the camp as it was, and [g]fled for their
lives. **8** And when these lepers came to the utmost part of the camp, they ente-
red into one tent, and did eat and drink, and carried thence silver and gold, and
raiment, and went and hid it: after, they returned, and entered into another tent,
and carried thence also, and went and hid it. **9** Then said one to another, We
do not well: this day is a day of good tidings, and we hold our peace. If we tarry
till daylight, some [h]mischief will come upon us. Now therefore, come, let us go,
and tell the king's household. **10** So they came and called unto the porters of
the city, and told them, saying, We came to the camp of the Aramites, and lo, the-
re was no man there, neither voice of man, but horses tied and asses tied: and the
tents are as they were. **11** And the porters cried and declared to the king's house
within. **12** Then the King arose in the night, and said unto his servants, [i]I will
show you now, what the Aramites have done unto us. They know that we are fa-
mished, therefore they are gone out of the camp to hide themselves in the field,
saying, When they come out of the city, we shall catch them alive, and get into
the city. **13** And one of his servants answered, and said, Let me take now five
of the horses that remain, and are left in the city, (behold, they are even as all the
[j]multitude of Israel that are left therein: behold, I say, they are as the multitude of
the Israelites that are consumed) and we will send to see. **14** So they took [k]two
chariots of horses, and the king sent after the host of the Aramites, saying, Go and
see. **15** And they went after them unto Jordan, and lo, all the way was full of
clothes and vessels which the Aramites had cast from them in their haste: and the
messengers returned, and told the king. **16** Then the people went out and spoi-
led the camp of the Aramites: so a measure of fine flour was at a shekel, and two
measures of barley at a shekel [l]according to the word of the Lord. **17** And the
king gave the prince (on whose hand he leaned) the charge of the gate, and the pe-
ople [m]trode upon him in the gate, and he died, as the man of God had said, which
spake it, when the king came down to him. **18** And it came to pass, as the man
of God had spoken to the King, saying, Two measures of barley at a shekel, and a
measure of fine flour shall be at a shekel, tomorrow about this time in the gate of
Samaria. **19** But the prince had answered the man of God, and said, Though the
Lord would make windows in the heaven, could it come so to pass? And he said,
Behold, thou shalt see it with thine eyes, but thou shalt not eat thereof. **20** And
so it came unto him: for the people trode upon him in the gate, and he died.

8 *1 Elisha prophesieth unto the Shunammite the dearth of seven years. 12 He prophesieth to Hazael, that he shall be king of Syria. 15 He reigneth after Ben-Hadad. 16 Jehoram reigneth over Judah. 20 Edom falleth from Judah. 25 Ahaziah succeedeth Jehoram.*

1 Then spake Elisha unto the woman, [1]whose son he had restored to life,
saying, Up, and go, thou, and thine house, and sojourn where thou [a]canst sojourn:
for the Lord hath called for a famine, and it cometh also upon the land seven ye-
ars. **2** And the woman arose, and did after the saying of the man of God, and
went both she and her household, and sojourned in the land of the Philistines
seven years. **3** And at the seven year's end, the woman returned out of the land
of the Philistines, and went out [b]to call upon the king for her house and for her
land. **4** And the King talked with Gehazi the servant of the man of God, saying,
Tell me, I pray thee, all the great acts, that Elisha hath done. **5** And as he told
[c]the king, how he had restored one dead to life, behold, the woman, whose son he
had raised to life, called upon the king for her house and for her land. Then Gehazi
said, My lord, O King, this is the woman, and this is her son, whom Elisha restored
to life. **6** And when the king asked the woman, she told him: so the King appoin-
ted her an Eunuch, saying, Restore thou all that are hers, and all the [d]fruits of her
land since the day she left the land, even until this time. **7** Then Elisha came to
Damascus, and Ben-Hadad the king of Aram was sick: and one told him, saying,
The man of God is come hither. **8** And the king said unto Hazael, Take a present
in thine hand, and go meet the man of God, that thou mayest inquire of the Lord
by him, saying, Shall I recover of this disease? **9** So Hazael went to meet him, and
took the present in his hand, and of every [e]good thing of Damascus, even the bur-
den of forty camels, and came and stood before him, and said, Thy son Ben-Hadad
king of Aram hath sent me to thee, saying, Shall I recover of this disease? **10** And
Elisha said to him, Go, and say unto him, Thou shalt [f]recover: howbeit the Lord
hath showed me, that he shall surely die. **11** And he looked upon him steadfa-
stly, till Hazael was ashamed, and the man of God wept. **12** And Hazael said,
Why weepeth my lord? And he answered, because I know the evil that thou shalt
do unto the children of Israel: for their strong cities shalt thou set on fire, and their
young men shalt thou slay with the sword, and shalt dash their infants against the
stones, and rent in pieces their women with child. **13** Then Hazael said, What?
is thy servant [g]a dog, that I should do this great thing? And Elisha answered, The
Lord hath showed me, that thou shalt be King of Aram. **14** So he departed from
Elisha, and came to his master, who said to him, What said Elisha to thee? And he
answered, He told me that thou shouldest recover. **15** And on the morrow he
took a thick cloth and dipped in it water, and [h]spread it on his face, and he died:
and Hazael reigned in his stead. **16** [2]Now in the fifth year of Joram the son of
Ahab king of Israel, and of Jehoshaphat King of Judah, [i]Jehoram the son of Jeho-
shaphat king of Judah began [j]to reign. **17** He was two and thirty years old, when
he began to reign: and he reigned eight years in Jerusalem. **18** And he walked in
the ways of the Kings of Israel, as did the house of Ahab: for the [k]daughter of Ahab
was his wife, and he did evil in the sight of the Lord. **19** Yet the Lord would not
destroy Judah, for David his servant's sake, [3]as he had promised him to give him
a light, and to his children forever. **20** In those days Edom [l]rebelled from under
the hand of Judah, and made a King over themselves. **21** Therefore Joram went
to Zair, and all his chariots with him, and he arose by night, and smote the Edo-
mites which were about him, with the captains of the chariots, and the people fled
into their tents. **22** So Edom rebelled from under the hand of Judah unto this
day: then [m]Libnah rebelled at that same time. **23** Concerning the rest of the acts
of Joram and all that he did, are they not written in the book of the Chronicles of
the kings of Judah? **24** And Joram slept with his fathers, and was buried with his
fathers in the city of David. And [4]Ahaziah his son reigned in his stead. **25** In the
twelfth year of Joram the son of Ahab King of Israel, did Ahaziah the son of Jeho-
ram king of Judah begin to reign. **26** [n]Two and twenty years old was Ahaziah
when he began to reign, and he reigned one year in Jerusalem, and his mother's
name was Athaliah the daughter of Omri king of Israel. **27** And he walked in
the way of the house of Ahab, and did evil in the sight of the Lord, like the house
of Ahab: for he was the son in law of the house of Ahab. **28** And he went with
Joram the son of Ahab to war against Hazael king of Aram in [o]Ramoth Gilead, and
the Aramites smote Joram. **29** And king Joram returned to be healed in [p]Jezre-
el of the wounds which the Aramites had given him at Ramah, when he fought

---

2-KINGS 7

a. 2 Kings 7:1 The godly are ever assured of God's help in their necessities, but the times and hours are only revealed by God's Spirit.
b. 2 Kings 7:2 To whom the king gave the charge and oversight of things, as verse 17.
c. 2 Kings 7:2 He mocked at the Prophet's words, saying, that if God rained down corn from heaven, yet this could not come to pass.
d. 2 Kings 7:2 Thy infidelity shall be punished herein when thou shalt see this miracle, and yet not be partaker thereof.
e. 2 Kings 7:3 For it was commanded in the law that they should dwell apart, and not among their brethren, Lev. 13:46.
f. 2 Kings 7:6 Thus God needeth no great preparation to destroy the wicked, though they be never so many: for he can scatter them with a small noise, or shaking of a leaf.
g. 2 Kings 7:7 The wicked need no greater enemy than their own conscience to pursue them.
h. 2 Kings 7:9 Or, we shall be punished for our faults.
i. 2 Kings 7:12 He mistrusted the Prophet's words, and therefore could believe nothing, as they which are more politic than godly ever cast more perils than needeth.
j. 2 Kings 7:13 There are no more left, but they, or the rest are consumed with the famine, as the rest of the people.
k. 2 Kings 7:14 Or, two horses of the chariot, which were accustomed to draw in the chariot.
l. 2 Kings 7:16 Which he spake by the mouth of Elisha, verse 1.
m. 2 Kings 7:17 As the people preased out of the gate to run to the Syrian's tents, where they had heard was meat, and great spoil left.

2-KINGS 8

a. 2 Kings 8:1 Where thou canst find a commodious place to dwell, where as is plenty.
b. 2 Kings 8:3 That is, to complain on them which had taken her possessions while she was absent.
c. 2 Kings 8:5 God's wonderful providence appeareth in this, that he caused the King to be desirous to hear of him, whom before he contemned, and also hereby prepared an entrance to the poor widow's suit.
d. 2 Kings 8:6 The King caused that to be justly restored, which was wrongfully holden from her.
e. 2 Kings 8:9 Of all the chiefest and precious things of the country.
f. 2 Kings 8:10 Meaning, that he should recover of this disease: but he knew that this messenger Hazael should slay him to obtain the kingdom.
g. 2 Kings 8:13 That I should be without all humanity and pity.
h. 2 Kings 8:15 Under pretence to refresh or ease him, he stifled him with his cloth.
i. 2 Kings 8:16 Read 2 Kings 1:17.
j. 2 Kings 8:16 He was confirmed in his kingdom after his father's death.
k. 2 Kings 8:18 The holy Ghost showeth hereby what danger it is to join with infidels.
l. 2 Kings 8:20 Which had been subject from David's time, until this time of Jehoram.
m. 2 Kings 8:22 This was a city in Judah given to the Levites, Josh. 21:13, and after turned from King Jehoram, because of his idolatry.
n. 2 Kings 8:26 Which is to be understood, that he was made king when his father reigned, but after his father's death he was confirmed king when he was forty-two years old, as 2 Chron. 22:2.
o. 2 Kings 8:28 Which was a city in the tribe of Gad beyond Jordan.
p. 2 Kings 8:29 This is a city belonging to the tribe of Issachar.

against Hazael king of Aram. And Ahaziah the son of Jehoram king of Judah went down to see Joram the son of Ahab in Jezreel, because he was sick.

9

6 Jehu is made king of Israel. 24 And killeth Jehoram the king thereof, 27 And Ahaziah, otherwise called Jehoahaz, the king of Judah. 33 And causeth Jezebel to be cast down out of a window, and the dogs did eat her.

1 Then Elisha the Prophet called one of the children of the Prophets, and said unto him, [a,1]Gird thy loins, and take this box of oil in thine hand, and get thee to Ramoth Gilead. **2** And when thou comest thither, look where is Jehu the son of Jehoshaphat, the son of Nimshi, and go, and make him arise up from among his brethren, and lead him [b]to a secret chamber. **3** Then take the box of oil and pour it on his head, and say, Thus saith the Lord, I have anointed thee for king over Israel: then open the door, and flee without any tarrying. **4** So the servant of the Prophet got him to Ramoth Gilead. **5** And when he came in, behold, the captains of the army were sitting. And he said, I have a message to thee, O captain. And Jehu said, Unto which of all us? And he answered, To thee, O captain. **6** And he arose, and went into the house, and he poured the oil on his head and said unto him, Thus saith the Lord God of Israel, I have [c]anointed thee for king over the people of the Lord, even over Israel. **7** And thou shalt smite the house of Ahab thy master, that I may avenge the blood of my servants the Prophets, and the blood of all the servants of the Lord [2]of the hand of Jezebel. **8** For the whole house of Ahab shall be destroyed: and [3]I will cut off from Ahab, him that maketh water against the wall, as well him that is shut up, as him that is left in Israel. **9** And I will make the house of Ahab, like the house [4]of Jeroboam the son of Nebat, and like the house [5]of Baasha the son of Ahijah. **10** And the dogs shall eat Jezebel in the field of Jezreel, and there shall be none to bury her. And he opened the door, and fled. **11** Then Jehu came out to the [d]servants of his lord. And one said unto him, Is all well? wherefore came this [e]mad fellow to thee? And he said unto them, Ye know the man, and what his talk was. **12** And they said, It is false, tell us it now. Then he said, Thus and thus spake he to me, saying, Thus saith the Lord, I have anointed thee for King over Israel. **13** Then they made haste, and took every man his garment, and put it under him on the top of the stairs, and blew the trumpet, saying, Jehu is King. **14** So Jehu the son of Jehoshaphat the son of Nimshi conspired against Joram: (Now Joram kept Ramoth Gilead, he and all Israel, because of Hazael king of Aram. **15** And [6]king Joram returned to be healed in Jezreel of the wounds, which the Aramites had given him, when he fought with Hazael king of Aram) and Jehu said, If it be your minds, let no man depart and escape out of the city, to go and tell in Jezreel. **16** So Jehu got up into a chariot, and went to Jezreel: for Joram lay there, and [f]Ahaziah king of Judah was come down to see Joram. **17** And the watchman that stood in the tower in Jezreel spied the company of Jehu as he came, and said, I see a company. And Jehoram said, Take a horseman and send to meet them, that he may say, Is it peace? **18** So there went one on horseback to meet him, and said, Thus saith the King, Is it peace? And Jehu said, What hast thou to do with peace? [g]turn behind me. And the watchman told, saying, The messenger came to them, but he cometh not again. **19** Then he sent out another on horseback, which came to them, and said, Thus saith the king, Is it peace? And Jehu answered, What hast thou to do with peace? turn behind me. **20** And the watchman told, saying, He came to them also, but cometh not again, and the marching is like the marching of Jehu the son of Nimshi: for he marcheth [h]furiously. **21** Then Jehoram said, Make ready: and his chariot was made ready. And Jehoram king of Israel, and Ahaziah king of Judah went out either of them in his chariot against Jehu, and met him in the field of Naboth the Jezreelite. **22** And when Jehoram saw Jehu, he said, Is it peace, Jehu? And he answered, What [i]peace? whiles the whoredomes of thy mother Jezebel, and her witchcrafts are yet in great number? **23** Then Jehoram turned his hand, and fled, and said to Ahaziah, O Ahaziah, there is treason. **24** But Jehu took a bow in his hand, and smote Jehoram between the shoulders, that the arrow went through his heart: and he fell down in his chariot. **25** Then said Jehu to Bidkar a captain, Take, and cast him in some place of the field of Naboth the Jezreelite: for I remember that when I and thou rode together after Ahab his father, the Lord [j]laid this burden upon him. **26** [7]Surely I have seen yesterday the blood of Naboth, and the blood of his [k]sons, said the Lord, and I will render it thee in this field, saith the Lord: now therefore take and cast him in the field according to the word of the Lord. **27** But when Ahaziah the king of Judah saw this, he fled by the way of the garden house: And Jehu pursued after him, and said, Smite him also in the chariot: and they smote him in the going up to Gur, which is by Ibleam. And he fled to [l]Megiddo, and there died. **28** And his servants carried him in a chariot to Jerusalem, and buried him in his sepulcher with his fathers in the city of David. **29** And in the [m]eleventh year of Joram the son of Ahab, began Ahaziah to reign over Judah. **30** And when Jehu was come to Jezreel, Jezebel heard of it, and painted her face, and tired her head, and [n]looked out at a window. **31** And as Jehu entered at the gate, she said, Had [o]Zimri peace, which slew his master? **32** And he lift up his eyes to the window, and said, Who is on my side, who? Then two or three of her [p]Eunuchs looked unto him. **33** And he said, Cast her down: and they cast her down, [q]and he sprinkled of her blood upon the wall, and upon the horses, and he trode her under foot. **34** And when he was come in, he did eat and drink, and said, Visit now yonder cursed woman, and bury her: for she is a [r]King's daughter. **35** And they went to bury her, but they found no more of her, than the skull and the feet, and the palms of her hands. **36** Wherefore they came again and told him. And he said, This is the word of the Lord, which he spake [s]by his servant Elijah the Tishbite, saying, [8]In the field of Jezreel shall the dogs eat the flesh of Jezebel. **37** And the carcass of Jezebel shall be as dung upon the ground in the field of Jezreel, so that none shall say, [t]This is Jezebel.

10

6 Jehu causeth the seventy sons of Ahab to be slain, 14 And after that forty and two of Ahaziah's brethren. 25 He killeth also all the Priests of Baal. 35 After his death his son reigneth in his stead.

1 Ahab had now seventy [a]sons in Samaria. And Jehu wrote letters, and sent to Samaria unto the rulers of Jezreel, and to the Elders, and to the bringers up of Ahab's children, to this effect, **2** Now when this letter cometh to you, (for ye have with you your master's sons, ye have with you both chariots and horses, and a defensed city, and armor) **3** Consider therefore which of your master's sons is best and most meet, and [b]set him on his father's throne, and fight for your master's house. **4** But they were exceedingly afraid, and said, Behold two kings could not stand before him, how shall we then stand? **5** And he that was governor of Ahab's house, and he that ruled the city, and the Elders, and the bringers up of the children sent to Jehu, saying, We are thy servants, and will do all that thou shalt bid us: we will make no king: do what seemeth good to thee. **6** Then he wrote another letter to them, saying, If ye be mine, and will obey my voice, [c]take the heads of the men that are your master's sons, and come to me to Jezreel by tomorrow this time. (Now the king's sons, even seventy persons were with the great men of the city, which brought them up) **7** And when the letter came to them, they took the King's sons, and slew the seventy persons, and laid their heads in baskets, and sent them unto him to Jezreel. **8** Then there came a messenger and told him, saying, They have brought the heads of the King's sons. And he said, Let them lay them on two heaps at the entering in of the gate until the morning. **9** And when it was day he went out, and stood and said to all the people, Ye be [d]righteous: behold, I conspired against my master, and slew him: but who slew all these? **10** Know now that there shall fall unto the earth nothing of the word of the Lord, which the Lord spake concerning the house of Ahab: for the Lord hath brought to pass the things that he spake [e]by his servant [1]Elijah. **11** So Jehu slew all that remained of the house of Ahab in Jezreel, and all that were great with him, and his familiars, and his [f]priests, so that he let none of his remain. **12** And he arose, and departed, and came to Samaria. And as Jehu was in the way by an house where

---

2-KINGS 8

1. 2 Kings 4:35
2. 2 Chron. 21:4
3. 2 Sam. 7:13
4. 1 Chron. 22:1

2-KINGS 9

a. 2 Kings 9:1 Prepare thyself to go diligently about thy business: for in those countries they used long garments which they tucked up, when they went about earnest business.
b. 2 Kings 9:2 Hebrew, from chamber to chamber.
c. 2 Kings 9:6 This anointing was for Kings, Priests and Prophets, which were all figures of Messiah, in whom these three offices were accomplished.
d. 2 Kings 9:11 That is, the rest of the army, whom he called before, his brethren, verse 2.
e. 2 Kings 9:11 In this estimation the world hath the ministers of God: notwithstanding forasmuch as the world hath ever slandered the children of God (yea they called the Son of God a deceiver, and said he had the devil) therefore they ought not to be discouraged.
f. 2 Kings 9:16 God had thus ordained, as is read, 2 Chron. 22:7, that this wicked and idolatrous King, who was more ready to gratify wicked Joram, than to obey the will of God, should perish with him, by whose means he thought to have been stronger.
g. 2 Kings 9:18 Or, follow me.
h. 2 Kings 9:20 As one that went earnestly about his enterprise.
i. 2 Kings 9:22 Meaning, that forasmuch as God is their enemy because of their sins that he will ever stir up some to revenge his cause.
j. 2 Kings 9:25 Or, spake this prophecy against him.
k. 2 Kings 9:26 By this place it is evident, that Jezebel caused both Naboth and his sons to be put to death, that Ahab might enjoy his vineyard more quietly: for else his children might have claimed possession.
l. 2 Kings 9:27 After that he was wounded in Samaria, he fled to Megiddo, which was a city of Judah.
m. 2 Kings 9:29 That is, eleven whole years: for 2 Kings 8:25, before, when he said that he began to reign the twelfth year of Joram, he taketh part of the year for the whole.
n. 2 Kings 9:30 Being of an harsh and cruel nature she would still retain her princely state and dignity.
o. 2 Kings 9:31 As though she would say, Can any traitor, or any that riseth against his superior, have good success? read 1 Kings 16:10.
p. 2 Kings 9:32 Or, chief servants.
q. 2 Kings 9:33 This he did by the motion of the Spirit of God, that her blood should be shed, that had shed the blood of innocents, to be a spectacle and example of God's judgments to all tyrants.
r. 2 Kings 9:34 To wit, of the king of Sidon, 1 Kings 16:31.
s. 2 Kings 9:36 Hebrew, by the hand of.
t. 2 Kings 9:37 Thus God's judgments appear even in this world against them that suppress his word and persecute his servants.

2-KINGS 9

1. 1 Kings 19:16,17
2. 1 Kings 21:15,25
3. 1 Kings 14:10; 1 Kings 21:21
4. 1 Kings 14:10; 1 Kings 21:22
5. 1 Kings 16:3-11
6. 2 Kings 8:29
7. 1 Kings 21:29
8. 1 Kings 21:23

2-KINGS 10

a. 2 Kings 10:1 The Scripture useth to call them sons, which are either children or nephews.
b. 2 Kings 10:3 He wrote this, to prove them whether they would take his part or no.
c. 2 Kings 10:6 God as a just judge punisheth the wicked children of wicked parents unto the third and fourth generation.
d. 2 Kings 10:9 Ye cannot justly condemn me for the king's death, seeing ye have done the like to his posterity: for the Lord commanded me, and moved you to execute this his judgment.
e. 2 Kings 10:10 Hebrew, by the hand of.
f. 2 Kings 10:11 Meaning, which were the idolatrous priests.

the shepherds did shear, **13** He met with the brethren of Ahaziah king of Judah,
and said, Who are ye? And they answered, We are the brethren of Ahaziah, and go
down to salute the children of the King and the children of the Queen. **14** And
he said, Take them alive. And they took them alive, and slew them at the well be-
side the house where the sheep are shorn, even two and forty men, and he [g]left
not one of them. **15** And when he was departed thence, he met with Jehonadab
the son of Rechab coming to meet him, and he [h,i]blessed him, and said to him, Is
thine heart upright, as mine heart is toward thine? And Jehonadab answered, Yea,
doubtless. Then give me thine hand. And when he had given him his hand, he
took him up to him into the chariot. **16** And he said, Come with me, and see
the zeal that I have for the Lord: so they made him ride in his chariot. **17** And
when he came to Samaria, he slew all that remained unto Ahab in Samaria, till
he had destroyed him, according to the word of the Lord, which he spake to Eli-
jah. **18** Then Jehu assembled all the people, and said unto them, Ahab served
[j]Baal a little, but Jehu shall serve him much more. **19** Now therefore call unto
me all ye prophets of Baal, all his servants, and all his priests, and let not a man
be lacking: for I have a great sacrifice for Baal: whosoever is lacking, he shall not
live. But Jehu did it by a subtlety to destroy the servants of Baal. **20** And Jehu
said, [k]Proclaim a solemn assembly for Baal. And they proclaimed it. **21** So Jehu
sent unto all Israel, and all the servants of Baal came, and there was not a man left
that came not. And they came into the house of Baal, and the house of Baal was
full from end to end. **22** Then he said unto him that had the charge of the ve-
stry, Bring forth vestments for all the servants of Baal. And he brought them out
vestments. **23** And when Jehu went, and Jehonadab the son of Rechab into the
house of Baal, he said unto the servants of Baal, Search diligently, and look, lest
there be here with you any of the [l]servants of the Lord, but the servants of Baal
only. **24** And when they went in to make sacrifice and burnt offering, Jehu ap-
pointed four score men without, and said, If any of the men whom I have brought
into your hands, escape, [m]his soul shall be for his soul. **25** And when he had
made an end of the burnt offering, Jehu said to the guard, and to the captains,
Go in, slay them, let not a man come out. And they smote them with the edge
of the sword. And the guard, and the captains cast them out, and went unto the
[n]city, where was the temple of Baal. **26** And they brought out the images of the
temple of Baal, and burnt them. **27** And they destroyed the image of Baal, and
threw down the house of Baal, and made a jakes of it unto this day. **28** So Jehu
destroyed Baal out of Israel. **29** But from the sins of Jeroboam the son of Nebat
which made Israel to sin, Jehu departed not from them, neither from the golden
calves that were in Bethel and that were in Dan. **30** And the Lord said unto Jehu,
Because thou hast diligently executed that which was right in mine eyes, and hast
done unto the house of Ahab according to all things that were in mine heart, there-
fore shall thy [o]sons unto the fourth generation sit on the throne of Israel. **31** But
Jehu regarded not to walk in the law of the Lord God of Israel with all his heart:
for he departed not from the sins of Jeroboam, which made Israel to sin. **32** In
those days the Lord began to [p]loathe Israel, and Hazael smote them in all the coa-
sts of Israel, **33** From Jordan Eastward, even all the land of Gilead, the Gadites,
and the Reubenites, and them that were of Manasseh, from Aroer (which is by the
river Arnon) and Gilead and Bashan. **34** Concerning the rest of the acts of Jehu,
and all that he did, and all his valiant deeds, are they not written in the book of the
Chronicles of the kings of Israel? **35** And Jehu slept with his fathers, and they
buried him in Samaria, and Jehoahaz his son reigned in his stead. **36** And the
time that Jehu reigned over Israel in Samaria is eight and twenty years.

11

1 Athaliah putteth to death all the King's sons, except Joash the son of Ahaziah. 4 Joash is appointed King. 15 Jehoiada causeth Athaliah to be slain. 17 He maketh a covenant between God and the people. 18 Baal and his priests are destroyed.

1 Then [1]Athaliah the mother of Ahaziah when she saw that her son was dead,
she arose, and destroyed all the [a]King's seed. **2** But Jehosheba the daughter of
king Joram, and sister to Ahaziah [b]took Joash the son of Ahaziah, and stole him
from among the King's sons that should be slain, both him and his nurse, kee-
ping them in [c]the bedchamber, and they hid him from Athaliah, so that he was
not slain. **3** And he was with her hid in the house of the Lord six years, and
Athaliah did reign over the land. **4** [2]And the seventh year [d]Jehoiada sent and
took the captains over hundreds, with other captains and them of the guard, and
caused them to come unto him into the house of the Lord, and made a covenant
with them, and took an oath of them in the house of the Lord, and showed them
the King's son. **5** And he commanded them, saying, This is it that ye must do,
The third part of [e]you, that cometh on the Sabbath, shall [f]ward toward the King's
house: **6** And another third part in the gate of [g]Sur: and another third part in
the gate behind them of the guard: and ye shall keep watch [h]in the house of Mas-
sah. **7** And two parts of you, that is, all that [i]go out on the Sabbath day, shall
keep the watch of the house of the Lord about the king. **8** And ye shall compass
the King round about, every man with his weapon in his hand, and whosoever
cometh within the ranges, let him be slain: be you with the King, as he goeth out
and in. **9** And the captains of the hundreds did according to all that Jehoiada
the Priest commanded, and they took every man of his men that entered into
their charge on the Sabbath, with them that went out of it on the [j]Sabbath, and
came to Jehoiada the Priest. **10** And the [k]Priest gave to the captains of hundreds
the spears and the shields that were King David's, and were in the house of the
Lord. **11** And the guard stood, every man with his weapon in his hand, from the
right side of the house to the left side, about the altar and about the house, round
about the King. **12** Then he brought out [l]the king's son, and put the crown upon
him, and gave him [m]the Testimony, and they made him king: also they anointed
him, and clapped their hands, and said, God save the King. **13** And when Atha-
liah heard the noise of the running of the people, she came into the people in the
house of the Lord. **14** And when she looked, behold, the King stood by a [n]pillar,
as the manner was, and the princes and the trumpeters by the King, and all the pe-
ople of the land rejoiced, and blew with trumpets. Then Athaliah rent her clothes,
and cried, Treason, treason. **15** But Jehoiada the Priest commanded the captains
of the hundreds that had the rule of the host, and said unto them, Have her [o]forth
of the ranges, and he that [p]followeth her, let him die by the sword: for the Priest
had said, Let her not be slain in the house of the Lord. **16** Then they laid hands
on her, and she went by the way, by the which the horses go to the house of the
King, and there was she slain. **17** And Jehoiada made a covenant between the
Lord, [q]and the King and the people, that they should be the Lord's people: likewi-
se between the [r]King and the people. **18** Then all the people of the land went
into the house of Baal, and destroyed it with his altars, and his images brake they
down courageously, and slew Mattan the Priest of Baal before the [s]altars: and the
[t]Priest set a guard over the house of the Lord. **19** Then he took the captains of
hundreds, and the other captains, and the guard, and all the people of the land:
and they brought the King from the house of the Lord, and came by the way of the
gate of the guard to the King's house: and he sat him down on the throne of the
kings. **20** And all the people of the land rejoiced, and the city was in quiet: [u]for
they had slain Athaliah with the sword beside the king's house. **21** Seven years
old was Jehoash when he began to reign.

12

6 Jehoash maketh provision for the repairing of the Temple. 16 He slayeth the king of Syria by a present from coming against Jerusalem. 20 He is killed by two of his servants.

1 In [1]the seventh year of Jehu Jehoash began to reign, and reigned forty years
in Jerusalem, and his mother's name was Zibiah of Beersheba. **2** And Jehoash
did that which was good in the sight of the Lord all his time that [a]Jehoiada the
Priest taught him. **3** But [b]the high places were not taken away: for the people
offered yet and burnt incense in the high places. **4** And Jehoash said to the Pries-
sts, All the silver of dedicated things that be brought to the house of the Lord,
that is, the money of them that are under the [c]count, the money that every man

---

g. 2 Kings 10:14 Thus God's vengeance is upon them that have any part or familiarity with the wicked.
h. 2 Kings 10:15 For he feared God, and lamented the wickedness of those times: therefore Jehu was glad to join with him: of Rechab read Jer. 35:2.
i. 2 Kings 10:15 Or, praised God for him.
j. 2 Kings 10:18 Here Baal is taken for Ashtoreth the idol of the Sidonians, which Jezebel caused to be worshipped, as it is also so used, 1 Kings 16 and 22:53.
k. 2 Kings 10:20 Hebrew, sanctify.
l. 2 Kings 10:23 Thus God would have his servants preserved, and idolaters destroyed, as in his law he giveth express commandment, Deut. 13.
m. 2 Kings 10:24 Or, he shall die for him.
n. 2 Kings 10:25 Which city was near to Samaria.
o. 2 Kings 10:30 Thus God approveth and rewardeth his zeal, in executing God's judgment, albeit his wickedness was afterward punished.
p. 2 Kings 10:32 Or, to cut them off.

2-KINGS 10
1. 1 Kings 21:29

2-KINGS 11
a. 2 Kings 11:1 Meaning, all the posterity of Jehoshaphat, to whom the kingdom appertained: thus God used the cruelty of this woman to destroy the whole family of Ahab.
b. 2 Kings 11:2 The Lord promised to maintain the family of David, and not to quench the light thereof, therefore he moved the heart of Jehosheba to preserve him.
c. 2 Kings 11:2 Where the Priests did lie.
d. 2 Kings 11:4 The chief priest, Jehosheba's husband.
e. 2 Kings 11:5 Of the Levites, which had charge of the keeping of the Temple, and kept watch by course.
f. 2 Kings 11:5 That none should come upon them, while they were crowning the king.
g. 2 Kings 11:6 Called the East gate of the Temple, 2 Chron. 23:5.
h. 2 Kings 11:6 Or, that none break his order.
i. 2 Kings 11:7 Whose charge is ended.
j. 2 Kings 11:9 Read verses 5 and 7.
k. 2 Kings 11:10 To wit, Jehoiada.
l. 2 Kings 11:12 That is, Joash, which had been kept secret six years.
m. 2 Kings 11:12 Meaning, the Law of God, which is his chief charge, and whereby only his throne is established.
n. 2 Kings 11:14 Where the king's place was in the Temple.
o. 2 Kings 11:15 Or, out of the Temple.
p. 2 Kings 11:15 To take her part.
q. 2 Kings 11:17 That both the King and the people should maintain the true worship of God and destroy all idolatry.
r. 2 Kings 11:17 That he should govern and they obey in the fear of God.
s. 2 Kings 11:18 Even in the place where he had blasphemed God, and thought to have been helped by his idol, there God poured his vengeance upon him.
t. 2 Kings 11:18 To wit, Jehoiada.
u. 2 Kings 11:20 Which by her cruelty and persecution had vexed the whole land before.

2-KINGS 11
1. 2 Chron. 22:10 **2.** 2 Chron. 13:13

2-KINGS 12
a. 2 Kings 12:2 So long as rulers give ear to the true ministers of God, they prosper.
b. 2 Kings 12:3 So hard a thing it is for them, that are in authority, to be brought to the perfect obedience of God.
c. 2 Kings 12:4 That is, the money of redemption, Exod. 30:12, also the money which the Priest valued the vows at, Lev. 27:2, and their free liberality.

is set at, and all the money that one offereth willingly, and bringeth into the house of the Lord, **5** Let the Priests take it to them, every man of his acquaintance: and they shall repair the [d]broken places of the house, wheresoever any decay is found. **6** Yet in the three and twentieth year of King Jehoash the Priests had not mended that which was decayed in the Temple. **7** Then King Jehoash called for Jehoiada the Priest, and the other Priests, and said unto them, Why repair ye not the ruins of the Temple? now therefore [e]receive no more money of your acquaintance, except ye deliver it to repair the ruins of the Temple. **8** So the Priests consented to receive no more money of the people, neither to repair the decayed places of the Temple. **9** Then Jehoiada the Priest took a chest and bored an hole in the lid of it, and set it beside the altar, on the [f]right side, as every man cometh into the Temple of the Lord. And the Priests that kept the [g]door, put therein all the money that was brought into the house of the Lord. **10** And when they saw there was much money in the chest, the king's Secretary came up and the high Priest, and put it up after that they had told the money that was found in the house of the Lord, **11** And they gave the money made ready into the hands of them, [h]that undertook the work, and that had the oversight of the house of the Lord: and they paid it out to the carpenters and builders that wrought upon the house of the Lord, **12** And to the masons and hewers of stone, and to buy timber and hewed stone, to repair that was decayed in the house of the Lord, and for all that which was laid out for the reparation of the Temple. **13** Howbeit there was [i]not made for the house of the Lord bowls of silver, instruments of music, basins, trumpets, nor any vessels of gold, or vessels of silver of the money that was brought into the house of the Lord. **14** But they gave it to the workmen, which repaired therewith the house of the Lord. **15** Moreover, they reckoned not with the men, into whose hands they delivered that money to be bestowed on workmen: for they dealt faithfully. **16** The money of the trespass offering, and the money of the sin offerings was not brought into the house of the Lord: for it was the Priests'. **17** Then came up Hazael king of Aram, and fought against Gath, and took it, and Hazael set his face to go up to Jerusalem. **18** And [j]Jehoash king of Judah took all the hallowed things that Jehoshaphat, and Jehoram, and Ahaziah, his fathers, kings of Judah had dedicated, and that he himself had dedicated, and all the gold that was found in the treasures of the house of the Lord, and in the king's house, and sent it to Hazael king of Aram, and he departed from Jerusalem. **19** Concerning the rest of the acts of Joash and all that he did, are they not written in the book of the Chronicles of the kings of Judah? **20** And his servants arose and wrought treason, and [k]slew Joash in the house of [l]Millo, when he came down to Silla. **21** Even [m]Jozachar the son of Shimeath, and Jehozabad the son of Shomer his servants smote him and he died, and they buried him with his fathers in the city of David. And Amaziah his son reigned in his stead.

13

3 Jehoahaz the son of Jehu is delivered into the hands of the Syrians. 4 He prayeth unto God, and is delivered. 9 Joash his son reigneth in his stead. 20 Elisha dieth. 24 Hazael dieth.

1 In the three and twentieth year of Joash the son of Ahaziah king of Judah, Jehoahaz the son of Jehu began to reign over Israel in Samaria, and he reigned seventeen years. **2** And he did evil in the sight of the Lord, and followed the sins of Jeroboam the son of Nebat, which made Israel to [a]sin, and departed not therefrom. **3** And the Lord was angry with Israel, and delivered them into the hand of Hazael king of Aram, and into the hand of Ben-Hadad the son of Hazael, all [b]his days. **4** And Jehoahaz besought the Lord, and the Lord heard him: for he saw the trouble of Israel, wherewith the king of Aram troubled them. **5** (And the Lord gave Israel a [c]deliverer, so that they came out from under the subjection of the Aramites. And the children of Israel [d]dwelt in their tents as [e]beforetime. **6** Nevertheless, they departed not from the sins of the house of Jeroboam which made Israel sin, but walked in them, even the [f]grove also remained still in Samaria) **7** For he had left of the people to Jehoahaz but fifty horsemen, and ten chariots, and ten thousand footmen, because the king [g]of Aram had destroyed them, and made them like dust beaten to powder. **8** Concerning the rest of the acts of Jehoahaz and all that he did, and his valiant deeds, are they not written in the book of the Chronicles of the kings of Israel? **9** And Jehoahaz slept with his fathers, and they buried him in Samaria, and Joash his son reigned in his stead. **10** In the seven and thirtieth year of Joash king [h]of Judah began Jehoash the son of Jehoahaz to reign over Israel in Samaria, and reigned sixteen years. **11** And did evil in the sight of the Lord: for he departed not from all the sins of Jeroboam the son of Nebat that made Israel to sin, but he walked therein. **12** Concerning the rest of the acts of Joash, and all that he did, and his valiant deeds, and how he fought against Amaziah king of Judah, are they not written in the book of the Chronicles of the kings of Israel? **13** And Joash slept with his fathers, and Jeroboam sat upon his seat: and Joash was buried in Samaria among the kings of Israel. **14** When Elisha fell sick of his sickness whereof he died, Joash the king of Israel came down unto him, and wept upon his face, and said, [i]O my father, my father, the chariot of Israel, and the horsemen of the same. **15** Then Elisha said unto him, Take a bow and arrows. And he took unto him bow and arrows. **16** And he said to the king of Israel, Put thine hand upon the bow. And he put his hand upon it. And Elisha put his hands upon the king's hands, **17** And said, Open the window [j]Eastward. And when he had opened it, Elisha said, Shoot. And he shot. And he said, Behold, the arrow of the Lord's deliverance, and the arrow of deliverance against Aram: for thou shalt smite the Aramites in Aphek, till thou hast consumed them. **18** Again he said, Take the arrows. And he took them. And he said unto the king of Israel, Smite the ground. And he smote thrice, and ceased. **19** Then the man of God was [k]angry with him, and said, Thou shouldest have smitten five or six times, so thou shouldest have smitten Aram, till thou hadst consumed it, where now thou shalt smite Aram but thrice. **20** So Elisha died, and they buried him. And certain bands of the Moabites came into the land that year. **21** And as they were burying a man: behold, they saw the soldiers: therefore they cast the man into the sepulcher of Elisha. And when the man was down, and touched the bones of Elisha, he [l]revived and stood upon his feet. **22** But Hazael king of Aram vexed Israel all the days of Jehoahaz. **23** Therefore the Lord had mercy on them and pitied them, and had respect unto them, because of his covenant with Abraham, Isaac, and Jacob, and would not destroy them, neither cast he them from him as [m]yet. **24** So Hazael the King of Aram died: and Ben-Hadad his son reigned in his stead. **25** Therefore Jehoash the son of Jehoahaz returned, and took out of the hand of Ben-Hadad the son of Hazael the cities which he had taken away by war out of the hand of Jehoahaz his father: for three times did Joash beat him, and restored the cities unto Israel.

14

2 Amaziah the king of Judah putteth to death them that slew his father, 7 and after smiteth Edom. 15 Joash dieth, and Jeroboam his son succeedeth him. 29 And after him reigneth Zechariah.

1 The second year of Joash son of Jehoahaz king of Israel, reigned [1]Amaziah the son of Joash king of Judah. **2** He was five and twenty years old when he began to reign, and reigned nine and twenty years in Jerusalem, and his mother's name was Jehoaddan of Jerusalem. **3** And he did [a]uprightly in the sight of the Lord, yet not like David his father, but did according to all that Joash his father had done. **4** Notwithstanding the high places were not taken away: for as yet the people did sacrifice, and burnt incense in the high places. **5** And when the kingdom was confirmed in his hand, he slew his servants which had [2]killed the king his father. **6** But the children of those that did slay him, he [b]slew not, according unto that which is written in the book of the Law of Moses, wherein the Lord commanded, saying, [3]The fathers shall not be put to death for the children, nor the children put to death for the fathers: but every man shall be put to death for his own sin. **7** He slew also of [c]Edom in the valley of salt, ten thousand, and took [d]the city of Sela by war, and called the name thereof Joktheel unto this

---

d. 2 Kings 12:5 For the Temple which was built an hundred fifty and five years before, had many things decayed in it, both by the negligence of the King's predecessors, and also by the wickedness of the idolaters.
e. 2 Kings 12:7 He taketh from them the ordering of the money, because of their negligence.
f. 2 Kings 12:9 That is, on the South side.
g. 2 Kings 12:9 Or, vessel.
h. 2 Kings 12:11 For the King had appointed others which were meet for that purpose, 2 Kings 22:5.
i. 2 Kings 12:13 For these men had only the charge of the reparation of the Temple, and the rest of the money was brought to the king, who caused these afterward to be made, 2 Chron. 24:14.
j. 2 Kings 12:18 After the death of Jehoiada, Joash fell to idolatry: therefore God rejected him, and stirreth up his enemy against him, whom he pacified with the treasures of the Temple: for God would not be served with those gifts, seeing the king's heart was wicked.
k. 2 Kings 12:20 Because he had put Zechariah the son of Jehoiada to death, 2 Chron. 24:25.
l. 2 Kings 12:20 Read 2 Sam. 3:9.
m. 2 Kings 12:21 Or, Jozahar.

2-KINGS 12
1. 2 Chron. 24:1

2-KINGS 13
a. 2 Kings 13:2 By worshipping the calves which Jeroboam did erect in Israel.
b. 2 Kings 13:3 While Jehoahaz lived.
c. 2 Kings 13:5 To wit, Joash the son of Jehoahaz.
d. 2 Kings 13:5 Safely and without danger.
e. 2 Kings 13:5 Hebrew, as yesterday and before yesterday.
f. 2 Kings 13:6 Wherein they did commit their idolatry, and which the Lord had commanded to be destroyed, Deut. 16:21.
g. 2 Kings 13:7 That is, Hazael and Ben-Hadad his son, as verse 3. Read of Hazael, 2 Kings 8:12.
h. 2 Kings 13:10 His chief purpose is to describe the kingdom of Judah, and how God performed his promise made to the house of David: but by the way he showeth how Israel was afflicted and punished for their great idolatry, who though they had now degenerated, yet God both by sending them sundry Prophets and divers punishments, did call them unto him again.
i. 2 Kings 13:14 Thus they used to call the Prophets and servants of God, by whom God blesseth his people, as 2 Kings 2:12, meaning that by their prayers they did more prosper their country than by force of arms.
j. 2 Kings 13:17 That is, toward Syria: so that he did not only prophesy with words, but also confirmed him by these signs that he should have the victory.
k. 2 Kings 13:19 Because he seemed content to have victory against the enemies of God for twice or thrice, and had not a zeal to overcome them continually, and to destroy them utterly.
l. 2 Kings 13:21 By this miracle God confirmed the authority of Elisha, whose doctrine in his life they contemned, that at this sight they might return and embrace the same doctrine.
m. 2 Kings 13:23 That is, until their sins were come to a full measure, and there was no more hope of amendment.

2-KINGS 14
a. 2 Kings 14:3 In the beginning of his reign he seemed to have an outward show of godliness, but afterward he became an idolater and worshipped the idols of the Idumeans.
b. 2 Kings 14:6 Because they neither consented nor were partakers with their fathers in that act.
c. 2 Kings 14:7 For the Idumeans, whom David had brought to subjection, did rebel in the time of Jehoram son of Jehoshaphat.
d. 2 Kings 14:7 Or, the tower, or rock, 2 Chron. 25:32.

day. **8** Then Amaziah sent messengers to Jehoash the son of Jehoahaz, son of Jehu king of Israel, saying, Come, [e]let us see one another in the face. **9** Then Jehoash the king of Israel sent to Amaziah king of Judah, saying, The thistle that is in Lebanon, sent to the [f]Cedar that is in Lebanon, saying, Give thy daughter to my son to wife: and the wild beast that was in Lebanon, went and trode down the thistle. **10** Because thou hast smitten Edom, thine heart hath made thee proud: [g]brag of glory, and tarry at home. Why doest thou provoke to thine hurt, that thou shouldest fall, and Judah with thee? **11** But Amaziah would not hear: therefore Jehoash king of Israel went up: and he and Amaziah king of Judah saw one another in the face at Beth Shemesh which is in Judah. **12** And Judah was put to the worse before Israel, and they fled every man to their tents. **13** But Jehoash king of Israel took Amaziah king of Judah, the son of Jehoash the son of Ahaziah at Beth Shemesh, and [h]came to Jerusalem, and brake down the wall of Jerusalem from the gate of Ephraim to the corner gate, four hundred cubits. **14** And he took all the gold and silver, and all the vessels that were found in the house of the Lord, and in the treasures of the king's house, and the children that were in [i]hostage, and returned to Samaria. **15** Concerning the rest of the acts of Jehoash which he did, and his valiant deeds, and how he fought with Amaziah king of Judah, are they not written in the book of the Chronicles of the kings of Israel? **16** And Jehoash slept with his fathers, and was buried at Samaria among the kings of Israel: and Jeroboam his son reigned in his stead. **17** And Amaziah the son of Joash king of Judah, lived after the death of Jehoash son of Jehoahaz king of Israel, fifteen years. **18** Concerning the rest of the acts of Amaziah, are they not written in the book of the Chronicles of the kings of Judah? **19** But they [4]wrought treason against him in Jerusalem, and he fled to [j]Lachish, but they sent after him to Lachish, and slew him there. **20** And they brought him on horses, and he was buried at Jerusalem with his fathers in the city of David. **21** Then all the people of Judah took [k]Azariah which was sixteen years old, and made him king for his father Amaziah. **22** He built [l]Elath, and restored it to Judah, after that the king slept with his fathers. **23** In the fifteenth year of Amaziah the son of Joash king of Judah, was Jeroboam the son of Joash made king over Israel in Samaria, and reigned one and forty years. **24** And he did evil in the sight of the Lord: for he departed not from all the [m]sins of Jeroboam the son of Nebat, which made Israel to sin. **25** He restored the coast of Israel, from the entering of Hamath, unto the sea of the wilderness, according to the word of the Lord God of Israel, which he spake [n]by his servant Jonah the son of Amittai the Prophet, which was of Gath Hepher. **26** For the Lord saw the exceedingly bitter affliction of Israel, so that there was none [o]shut up, nor any left, neither yet any that could help Israel. **27** Yet the Lord [p]had not decreed to put out the name of Israel from under the heaven: therefore he preserved them by the hand of Jeroboam the son of Joash. **28** Concerning the rest of the acts of Jeroboam, and all that he did, and his valiant deeds, and how he fought, and how he restored Damascus, and [q]Hamath to Judah in Israel, are they not written in the book of the Chronicles of the kings of Israel? **29** So Jeroboam slept with his fathers, even with the kings of Israel, and Zechariah his son reigned in his stead.

15

1 Azariah the King of Judah becometh a leper. 5 Of Jotham, 10 Shallum, 14 Menahem, 23 Pekahiah, 30 Uzziah, 32 Jotham, 38 and Ahaz.

1 In the [a]seven and twentieth year of Jeroboam king of Israel, began Azariah son of Amaziah king of Judah to reign. **2** Sixteen years old was he, when he was made king, and he reigned two and fifty years in Jerusalem: and his mother's name was Jecholiah of Jerusalem. **3** And he did [b]uprightly in the sight of the Lord, according to all that his father Amaziah did. **4** But the high places were not put away: for the people yet offered, and burned incense in the high places. **5** And the Lord [c]smote the king, and he was a leper unto the day of his death, and dwelt in an house apart, and Jotham the king's son governed the house, and [d]judged the people of the land. **6** Concerning the rest of the acts of Azariah, and all that he did, are they not written in the book of the Chronicles of the Kings of Judah? **7** So Azariah slept with his fathers, and they buried him with his fathers in the city of David, and Jotham his son reigned in his stead. **8** In the eight and thirtieth year of Azariah King of Judah, did Zechariah the son of Jeroboam reign over Israel in Samaria six [e]months, **9** And did evil in the sight of the Lord, as did his fathers: for he departed not from the sins of Jeroboam the son of Nebat, which made Israel to sin. **10** And Shallum the son of Jabesh conspired against him, and smote him, in the sight of the people, and [f]killed him, and reigned in his stead. **11** Concerning the rest of the acts of Zechariah, behold, they are written in the book of the Chronicles of the Kings of Israel. **12** This was the [1]word of the Lord, which he spake unto Jehu, saying, Thy sons shall sit on the throne of Israel unto the fourth generation after thee. And it came to pass. **13** Shallum the son of Jabesh began to reign in the nine and thirtieth year of Uzziah King of Judah: and he reigned the space of a month in Samaria. **14** For Menahem the son of Gadi went up from Tirzah, and came to Samaria, and smote Shallum the son of Jabesh in Samaria, and slew him, and reigned in his stead. **15** Concerning the rest of the acts of Shallum, and the treason which he wrought, behold, they are written in the book of the Chronicles of the Kings of Israel. **16** Then Menahem destroyed [g]Tiphsah, and all that were therein, and the coasts thereof from Tirzah, because they opened not to him, and he smote it, and ripped up all their women with child. **17** The nine and thirtieth year of Azariah King of Judah, began Menahem the son of Gadi to reign over Israel, and reigned ten years in Samaria. **18** And he did evil in the sight of the Lord, and departed not all his days from the sin of Jeroboam the son of Nebat, which made Israel to sin. **19** Then Pul the king of Assyria came against the [h]land: and Menahem gave Pul a thousand [i]talents of silver, that his hand might be with him, and establish the kingdom in his hand. **20** And Menahem exacted the money in Israel that all men of substance should give the king of Assyria fifty shekels of silver a piece: so the king of Assyria returned, and tarried not there in the land. **21** Concerning the rest of the acts of Menahem, and all that he did, are they not written in the book of the Chronicles of the kings of Israel? **22** And Menahem slept with his fathers, and Pekahiah his son did reign in his stead. **23** In the fiftieth year of Azariah king of Judah, began Pekahiah the son of Menahem to reign over Israel in Samaria, and reigned two years. **24** And he did evil in the sight of the Lord: for he departed not from the sins of Jeroboam the son of Nebat which made Israel to sin. **25** And Pekah the son of Remaliah, his captain conspired against him, and smote him in Samaria in the place of the king's palace with [j]Argob and Arieh, and with him fifty men of the Gileadites: so he killed him, and reigned in his stead. **26** Concerning the rest of the acts of Pekahiah, and all that he did, behold, they are written in the book of the Chronicles of the kings of Israel. **27** In the two and fiftieth year of Azariah King of Judah, began Pekah the son of Remaliah to reign over Israel in Samaria, and reigned twenty years. **28** And he did evil in the sight of the Lord: for he departed not from the sins of Jeroboam the son of Nebat that made Israel to sin. **29** In the days of Pekah king of Israel [k]came Tiglath-Pileser king of Assyria, and took Ijon, and Abel Beth Maachah, and Janoah, and Kedesh, and Hazor, and Gilead, and Galilee, and all the land of Naphtali, and carried them away to Assyria. **30** And Hoshea the son of Elah wrought treason against Pekah the son of Remaliah, and smote him, and slew him, and reigned in his stead in the twentieth year of Jotham the son of Uzziah. **31** Concerning the rest of the acts of Pekah, and all that he did, behold, they are written in the book of the Chronicles of the kings of Israel. **32** [2]In the second year of Pekah the son of Remaliah King of Israel, began Jotham son of [l]Uzziah King of Judah to reign. **33** Five and twenty years old was he, when he began to reign, and he reigned sixteen years in Jerusalem: and his mother's name was Jerusha the daughter of Zadok. **34** And he did uprightly in the sight of the Lord: he did according [m]to all that his father Uzziah had done. **35** But the high places were not put away: for the people yet offered and burnt incense in the high places: he built the highest gate of the house of the Lord. **36** Concerning the rest of the acts of Jotham, and all that he did, are they not written in the book of the Chronicles of the Kings of Judah? **37** In [n]those days the Lord began to send against Judah, Rezin the king of Aram, and [o]Pekah the son of Remaliah. **38** And Jotham slept with his fathers, and was buried with his fathers in the city of David his father, and Ahaz his son reigned in his stead.

---

e. 2 Kings 14:8 Let us fight hand to hand, and try it by battle, and not destroy one another's cities.
f. 2 Kings 14:9 By this parable Jehoash compareth himself to a cedar tree, because of his great kingdom over ten tribes, and Amaziah to a thistle, because he ruled but over two tribes, and the wild beasts are Jehoash's soldiers, that spoiled the cities of Judah.
g. 2 Kings 14:10 Brag of the victory, so that thou tarry at home, and envy me not.
h. 2 Kings 14:13 Or, brought him.
i. 2 Kings 14:14 That is, which the Israelites had given to them of Judah for an assurance of peace.
j. 2 Kings 14:19 Which city Rehoboam built in Judah for a fortress, 2 Chron. 11:9.
k. 2 Kings 14:21 Who is also called Uzziah, 2 Chron. 26:1.
l. 2 Kings 14:22 Which is also called Elanon or Eloth.
m. 2 Kings 14:24 Because this idolatry was so vile and almost incredible, that men should forsake the living God, to worship calves, the work of man's hands, therefore the Scripture doth ofttimes repeat it in the reproach of all idolaters.
n. 2 Kings 14:25 Hebrew, by the hand of.
o. 2 Kings 14:26 Read 1 Kings 14:10.
p. 2 Kings 14:27 Hebrew, had not spoken.
q. 2 Kings 14:28 Which was also called Antioch of Syria, or Riblah.

2-KINGS 14

1. 2 Chron. 25:1
2. 2 Kings 12:20
3. Deut. 24:16; Ezek. 18:20
4. 2 Chron. 25:27

2-KINGS 15

a. 2 Kings 15:1 Hebrew, in the twentieth year and seventh year.
b. 2 Kings 15:3 So long as he gave ear to Zechariah the Prophet.
c. 2 Kings 15:5 His father and grandfather were slain by their subjects and servants, and he because he would usurp the Priest's office contrary to God's ordinance was smitten immediately by the hand of God with the leprosy, 2 Chron. 26:21.
d. 2 Kings 15:5 As viceroy, or deputy to his father.
e. 2 Kings 15:8 He was the fourth in descent from Jehu, who reigned according to God's promise, but in him God began to execute his wrath against the house of Jehu.
f. 2 Kings 15:10 Zechariah was the last in Israel, that had the kingdom by succession, save only Pekahiah the son of Menahem, who reigned but two years.
g. 2 Kings 15:16 Which was a city of Israel that would not receive him to be king.
h. 2 Kings 15:19 That is, of Israel.
i. 2 Kings 15:19 Instead of seeking help of God, he went about by money to purchase the favor of this king being an infidel, and therefore God forsook him, and Pul soon afterward brake promise, destroyed his country, and led his people away captive.
j. 2 Kings 15:25 Which were of the same conspiracy.
k. 2 Kings 15:29 For God stirred up Pul and Tiglath-Pileser against Israel for their sins, 1 Chron. 5:26.
l. 2 Kings 15:32 Or, Azariah.
m. 2 Kings 15:34 He showeth that his uprightness was not such, but that he had many and great faults.
n. 2 Kings 15:37 After the death of Jotham.
o. 2 Kings 15:37 Which slew of Judah in one day sixscore thousand fighting men, 2 Chron. 28:6, because they had forsaken the true God.

2-KINGS 15

1. 2 Kings 10:30
2. 2 Chron. 28:6

16

3 Ahaz King of Judah consecrateth his son in fire. 5 Jerusalem is besieged. 9 Damascus is taken, and Rezin slain. 11 Idolatry. 19 The death of Ahaz. 20 Hezekiah succeedeth him.

1 The seventeenth year of Pekah the son of Remaliah, [a]Ahaz the son of Jotham King of Judah began to reign. **2** Twenty years old was Ahaz, when he began to reign, and he reigned sixteen years in Jerusalem, and did not uprightly in the sight of the Lord his God, like David his father: **3** But walked in the way of the kings of Israel, yea, and made his son to [b]go through the fire, after the abominations of the heathen, whom the Lord had cast out before the children of Israel. **4** Also he offered and burnt incense in the high places, and on the hills, and under every green tree. **5** [1]Then Rezin King of Aram and Pekah son of Remaliah king of Israel came up to Jerusalem, to fight: and they besieged Ahaz, but could not overcome [c]him. **6** At the same time Rezin king of Aram restored [d]Elath to Aram, and drove the Jews from Elath: so the Aramites came to Elath, and dwelt there unto this day. **7** Then Ahaz sent [e]messengers to Tiglath-Pileser king of Assyria, saying, I am thy servant and thy son: come up, and deliver me out of the hand of the king of Aram, and out of the hand of the king of Israel which rise up against me. **8** And Ahaz took the silver and the gold that was found in the [f]house of the Lord, and in the treasures of the king's house, and sent a present unto the king of Assyria. **9** And the king of Assyria consented unto him: and the king of Assyria went up against Damascus. and when he had taken it, he carried the people away to Kir, and slew Rezin. **10** And king Ahaz went unto Damascus to meet Tiglath-Pileser king of Assyria: and when king Ahaz saw the altar that was at Damascus, he sent to Urijah the Priest the pattern of the altar, and the fashion of it, and all the workmanship thereof. **11** And Urijah the Priest made an altar [g]in all points like to that which King Ahaz had sent from Damascus, so did Urijah the Priest against king Ahaz came from Damascus. **12** So when the king was come from Damascus, the king saw the altar: and the king drew near to the altar, and offered [h]thereon. **13** And he burnt his burnt offering, and his meat offering, and poured his drink offering, and sprinkled the blood of his peace offerings besides the altar. **14** And set it by the brazen altar which was before the Lord, and brought it in further before the house between the altar and the house of the Lord, and set it on the [i]North side of the altar. **15** And king Ahaz commanded Urijah the Priest, and said, Upon the great altar set on fire in the morning the burnt offering, and in the even the meat offering, and the king's burnt offering and his meat offering, with the burnt offering of all the people of the land, and their meat offering, and their drink offerings: and pour thereby all the blood of the burnt offering, and all the blood of the sacrifice, and the [j]brazen altar shall be for me to inquire of God. **16** And Urijah the Priest did according to all that King Ahaz had commanded. **17** And King Ahaz brake the borders of the bases, and took the caldrons from off them, and took down the sea from the brazen oxen that were under it, and put it upon a pavement of stones. **18** And the [k]veil for the Sabbath (that they had made in the house) and the king's entry without turned he to the house of the Lord, [l]because of the king of Assyria. **19** Concerning the rest of the acts of Ahaz, which he did, are they not written in the book of the Chronicles of the Kings of Judah? **20** And Ahaz slept with his fathers, and was buried with his fathers in the city of David, and Hezekiah his son reigned in his stead.

17

3 Hoshea King of Israel is taken, 4 And he and all his realm brought to the Assyrians, 18 for their idolatry. 25 Lions destroy the Assyrians that dwelt in Samaria. 29 Every one worshippeth the god of his nation, 35 Contrary to the commandment of God.

1 In the twelfth year of Ahaz king of Judah began Hoshea the son of Elah to reign in Samaria over Israel, and reigned nine years. **2** And he did evil in the sight of the Lord, [a]but not as the kings of Israel, that were before him. **3** And Shalmaneser king of Assyria came up against him, and Hoshea became his servant, and gave him presents. **4** And the king of Assyria found treason in Hoshea: for he had sent messengers to So king of Egypt, and brought no present unto the king of Assyria, [b]as he had done yearly: therefore the king of Assyria shut him up, and put him in prison. **5** Then the king of Assyria came up throughout all the land, and went against Samaria, and besieged it three years. **6** [1]In the ninth year of Hoshea, the king of Assyria took Samaria, and carried Israel away unto Assyria, and put them in Halah, and in Habor by the river of Gozan, and in the cities of the [c]Medes. **7** For when the children of Israel [d]sinned against the Lord their God, which had brought them out of the land of Egypt, from under the hand of Pharaoh king of Egypt, and feared other gods, **8** And walked according to the fashions of the Heathen, whom the Lord had cast out before the children of Israel, and after the manners of the kings of Israel, which they used, **9** And the children of Israel had done secretly things that were not upright before the Lord their God, and throughout all their cities had built high places, both from the tower [e]of the watch, to the defensed city, **10** And had made them images and groves upon every high hill, and under every green tree, **11** And there burnt incense in all the high places, as did the heathen, whom the Lord had taken away before them, and wrought wicked things to anger the Lord, **12** And served idols: whereof the Lord had said unto them, [2]Ye shall do no such thing, **13** Notwithstanding the Lord testified to Israel, and to Judah [f]by all the Prophets, and by all the Seers, saying, [3]Turn from your evil ways, and keep my commandments, and my statutes, according to all the Law, which I commanded your fathers, and which I sent to you by my servants the Prophets. **14** Nevertheless they would not obey, [4]but hardened their necks, like to the necks of their [g]fathers, that did not believe in the Lord their God. **15** And they refused his statutes and his covenant, that he made with their fathers, and his testimonies (wherewith he witnessed unto them) and they followed vanity, and became vain, and followed the heathen that were round about them: concerning whom the Lord had charged them, that they should not do like them. **16** Finally they left all the commandments of the Lord their God, and made them molten images, [5]even two calves, and made a grove, and worshipped all the [h]host of heaven, and served Baal. **17** And they made their sons and their daughters [i]pass through the fire, and used witchcraft and enchantments, yea, [j]sold themselves to do evil in the sight of the Lord, to anger him. **18** Therefore the Lord was exceedingly wroth with Israel, and put them out of his sight, and none was left but the tribe of Judah [k]only. **19** Yet Judah kept not the commandments of the Lord their God, but walked according to the fashion of Israel, which they used. **20** Therefore the Lord cast off all the seed of Israel, and afflicted them, and delivered them into the hands of spoilers, until he had cast them out of his [l]sight. **21** [m]For he cut off Israel from the house of David, and they made Jeroboam the son of Nebat King: and Jeroboam drew Israel away from following the Lord, and made them sin a great sin. **22** For the children of Israel walked in all the sins of Jeroboam, which he did, and departed not therefrom, **23** Until the Lord put Israel away out of his sight, as he had said [n]by all his servants the [6]Prophets, and carried Israel away out of their land to Assyria unto this day. **24** And the king of Assyria brought folk from Babylon, and from [o]Cuthah, and from Ava, and from Hamath, and from Sepharvaim, and placed them in the cities of Samaria instead of the children of Israel: so they possessed Samaria, and dwelt in the cities thereof. **25** And at the beginning of their dwelling there, they [p]feared not the Lord: therefore the Lord sent lions among them, which slew them. **26** Wherefore they spake to the king of Assyria, saying, The nations which thou hast removed and placed in the cities of Samaria, know not the manner of the God of the land: therefore he hath sent Lions among them, and behold, they slay them, because they know not the manner of the God of the land. **27** Then the king of Assyria commanded, saying, Carry thither one of the Priests whom ye brought thence, and let him go and dwell there, and teach them the manner of the God [q]of the country. **28** So one of the Priests, which they had carried from Samaria, came and dwelt in Bethel, and taught them

---

2-KINGS 16

- **a.** 2 Kings 16:1 This was a wicked son of a godly father, as of him again came godly Hezekiah, and of him wicked Manasseh, save that God in the end showed him mercy. Thus we see how uncertain it is to depend on the dignity of our fathers.
- **b.** 2 Kings 16:3 That is, offered him to Molech, or made him to pass between two fires, as the manner of the Gentiles was, Lev. 18:21; Deut. 18:10.
- **c.** 2 Kings 16:5 For the Lord preserved the city and his people for his promise sake made to David.
- **d.** 2 Kings 16:6 Which city Azariah had taken from the Aramites and fortified it, 2 Kings 14:22.
- **e.** 2 Kings 16:7 Contrary to the admonition of the Prophet Isaiah, Isa. 7:4.
- **f.** 2 Kings 16:8 Thus he spared not to spoil the Temple of God, to have succor of men and would not once lift his heart toward God to desire his help, nor yet hear his Prophet's counsel.
- **g.** 2 Kings 16:11 We see that there is no prince so wicked, be he shall find flatterers and false ministers to serve his turn.
- **h.** 2 Kings 16:12 Either offerings for peace or prosperity, or thanksgiving, as Lev. 3:1, or else meaning the morning and evening offering, Exod. 29:38, Num. 28:3, and thus he contemned the means and the altar which God had commanded by Solomon, to serve God after his own fantasy.
- **i.** 2 Kings 16:14 That is, at the right hand, as men went into to Temple.
- **j.** 2 Kings 16:15 Here he establisheth by commandment his own wicked proceedings, and doth abolish the commandment and ordinance of God.
- **k.** 2 Kings 16:18 Or, tent, wherein they lay on the Sabbath, which had served their week in the Temple, and so departed home.
- **l.** 2 Kings 16:18 Either to flatter the King of Assyria, when he should thus see him change the ordinance of God, or else that the Temple might be a refuge for him if the King should suddenly assail his house.

2-KINGS 16

1. Isa. 7:1

2-KINGS 17

- **a.** 2 Kings 17:2 Though he invented no new idolatry, or impiety as others did, yet he sought for help at the Egyptians, which God had forbidden.
- **b.** 2 Kings 17:4 For he had paid tribute for the space of eight years.
- **c.** 2 Kings 17:6 For at this time the Medes and Persians were subject to the Assyrians.
- **d.** 2 Kings 17:7 He setteth forth at length the cause of this great plague and perpetual captivity, to admonish all people, and nations to cleave to the Lord God, and only worship him for fear of like judgment.
- **e.** 2 Kings 17:9 Meaning, throughout all their borders.
- **f.** 2 Kings 17:13 Hebrew, by the hand of.
- **g.** 2 Kings 17:14 So that to allege the authority of our fathers or great antiquity, except we can prove that they were godly, is but to declare that we are the children of the wicked.
- **h.** 2 Kings 17:16 That is, the sun, the moon, and stars, Deut. 4:19.
- **i.** 2 Kings 17:17 Read 2 Kings 16:3.
- **j.** 2 Kings 17:17 Read of this phrase, 1 Kings 21:20, 25.
- **k.** 2 Kings 17:18 No whole tribe was left but Judah, and they of Benjamin and Levi, which remained, were counted with Judah.
- **l.** 2 Kings 17:20 Out of the land where he showed the greatest tokens of his presence and favor.
- **m.** 2 Kings 17:21 That is, God cut off the ten tribes, 1 Kings 12:16, 20.
- **n.** 2 Kings 17:23 Hebrew, by the hand of.
- **o.** 2 Kings 17:24 Of these peoples came the Samaritans, whereof mention is so much made in the Gospel, and with whom the Jews would have nothing to do, John 4:9.
- **p.** 2 Kings 17:25 That is, they served him not: therefore, lest they should blaspheme him, as though there were no God, because he chastised the Israelites, he showeth his mighty power among them by this strange punishment.
- **q.** 2 Kings 17:27 That is, how to worship him: thus the wicked rather than to lose their commodities will change to all religions.

how they should fear the Lord. **29** Howbeit, every nation made their gods, and put them in the houses of the high places, which the Samaritans had made, every nation in their cities wherein they dwelt. **30** For the men of Babylon made [r]Succoth Benoth: and the men of Cuth made Nergal, and the men of Hamath made Ashima, **31** And the Avites made Nibhaz, and Tartak: and the Sepharvites burnt their children in the fire to Adrammelech, and Anammelech the gods of Sepharvaim. **32** Thus they feared the Lord, and appointed out Priests out of themselves for the high places, who prepared for them sacrifices in the houses of the high places. **33** [7]They [s]feared the Lord, but served their gods after the manner of the nations whom they carried thence. **34** Unto this day they do after the old manner: they neither fear God, neither do after [t]their ordinances, nor after their customs, nor after the Law, nor after the commandment, which the Lord commanded the children of Jacob [8]whom he named Israel, **35** And with whom the Lord had made a covenant, and charged them, saying, [9]Fear none other gods, nor bow yourselves to them, nor serve them, nor sacrifice to them: **36** But fear the Lord which brought you out of the land of Egypt with great power, and a stretched out arm: him fear ye, and worship him and sacrifice to him. **37** Also keep ye diligently the statutes and the ordinances and the law, and the commandment, which he wrote for you, that ye do them continually, and fear not other gods. **38** And forget not the covenant that I have made with you, neither fear ye other gods. **39** But fear the Lord your God, and he will deliver you out of the hands of all your enemies. **40** Howbeit they obeyed not, but did after their old custom. **41** So these [u]nations feared the Lord, and served their images also: so did their children, and their children's children: as did their fathers, so do they unto this day.

18

4 Hezekiah king of Judah putteth down the brazen serpent, and destroyeth the idols, 7 and prospereth. 11 Israel is carried away captive. 30 The blasphemy of Sennacherib.

1 Now in the third year of Hoshea, son of Elah king of Israel, [1]Hezekiah the son of Ahaz king of Judah began to reign. **2** He was five and twenty years old when he began to reign, and reigned nine and twenty years in Jerusalem. His mother's name also was Abi the daughter of Zechariah, **3** And he did [a]uprightly in the sight of the Lord, according to all that David his father had done. **4** He took away the high places, and brake the images, and cut down the groves, and brake in pieces the [2]brazen serpent that Moses had made: for unto those days the children of Israel did burn incense to it, and he called it [b]Nehushtan. **5** He trusted in the Lord God of Israel: so that after him was none like him among all the kings of Judah, neither were there any such before him. **6** For he clave to the Lord and departed not from him, but kept his commandments, which the Lord had commanded Moses. **7** So the Lord was with him, and he prospered in all things which he took in hand, also he rebelled against the king of Assyria, and served him not. **8** He smote the Philistines unto Gaza, and the coasts thereof, [c]from the watchtower unto the defensed city. **9** [3]And in the fourth year of King Hezekiah, (which was the seventh year of Hoshea son of Elah king of Israel) Shalmaneser king of Assyria came up against Samaria, and besieged it. **10** And after three years they took it, even in the sixth year of Hezekiah: that is, [4]the ninth year of Hoshea king of Israel was Samaria taken. **11** Then the king of Assyria did carry away Israel unto Assyria, and put them in Halah and in Habor, by the river of Gozan, and in the cities of the Medes, **12** Because they would not obey the voice of the Lord their God, but transgressed his covenant: that is, all that Moses the servant of the Lord had commanded, and would neither obey nor do them. **13** [5]Moreover, in the fourteenth year of king Hezekiah, Sennacherib king of Assyria came up against all the strong cities of Judah, and took them. **14** Then Hezekiah king of Judah sent unto the king of Assyria to Lachish, saying, [d]I have offended: depart from me, and what thou layest upon me, I will bear it. And the king of Assyria appointed unto Hezekiah king of Judah three hundred talents of silver, and thirty talents of gold. **15** Therefore Hezekiah gave all the silver that was found in the house of the Lord, and in the treasures of the king's house. **16** At the same season did Hezekiah pull off the plates of the doors of the Temple of the Lord, and the pillars (which the said Hezekiah king of Judah had covered over) and gave them to the king of Assyria. **17** And the king of Assyria sent [e]Tartan, and Rabsaris, and Rabshakeh from Lachish to king Hezekiah with a great host against Jerusalem. And they went up, and came to Jerusalem, and when they were come up, they stood by the conduit of the upper pool, which is by the path of the fuller's field, **18** And called to the king. Then came out to them Eliakim the son of Hilkiah, which was steward of the house, and Shebna the chancellor, and Joah the son of Asaph the [f]recorder. **19** And Rabshakeh said unto them, Tell ye Hezekiah, I pray you, Thus saith the great king, even the great king of Assyria, What confidence is this wherein thou trustest? **20** Thou thinkest, Surely I have [g]eloquence, [h]but counsel and strength are for the war. On whom then doest thou trust, that thou rebellest against me? **21** Lo, thou trustest now in this broken staff of reed, to wit, on [i]Egypt, on which if a man lean, it will go into his hand, and pierce it: so is Pharaoh king of Egypt unto all that trust on him. **22** But if ye say unto me, We trust in the Lord our God, is not that he whose high places, and whose altars Hezekiah hath [j]taken away, and hath said to Judah and Jerusalem, Ye shall worship before this altar in Jerusalem? **23** Now therefore give [k]hostages to my lord the king of Assyria, and I will give thee two thousand horses, if thou be able to set riders upon them. **24** For how canst thou despise any captain of the least of my master's servants, and put thy trust on Egypt for chariots and horsemen? **25** Am I now come up without the [l]Lord to this place, to destroy it? the Lord said to me, Go up against this land, and destroy it. **26** Then Eliakim the son of Hilkiah, and Shebna, and Joah said unto Rabshakeh, Speak I pray thee, to thy servants in the [m]Aramites' language, for we understand it, and talk not with us in the Jews' tongue, in the audience of the people that are on the wall. **27** But Rabshakeh said unto them, Hath my master sent me to thy master and to thee to speak these words, and not to the men which sit on the wall, that they may eat their own dung, and drink [n]their own piss with you? **28** So Rabshakeh stood, and spake, saying, Hear the words of the great king, of the king of Assyria. **29** Thus saith the king, Let not Hezekiah deceive you: for he shall not be able to deliver you [o]out of mine hand. **30** Neither let Hezekiah make you to trust in the Lord, saying, The Lord will surely deliver us, and this city shall not be given over into the hand of the king of Assyria. **31** Hearken not unto Hezekiah: for thus saith the king of Assyria, Make [p]appointment with me, and come out to me, that every man may eat of his own vine, and every man of his own fig tree, and drink every man of the water of his own well, **32** Till [q]I come, and bring you to a land like your own land, even a land of wheat and wine, a land of bread and vineyards, a land of olive's oil, and honey, that ye may live and not die: and obey not Hezekiah, for he deceiveth you, saying, The Lord will deliver us. **33** Hath any of the gods of the nations delivered his land out of the hand of the king of Assyria? **34** Where is the god of Hamath, and of Arpad? where is the god of Sepharvaim, Hena and Ivah? how have they delivered Samaria out of mine hand? **35** Who are they among all the gods of the nations, that have delivered their land out of mine hand, that the [r]Lord should deliver Jerusalem out of mine hand? **36** But the people held their peace, and answered not him a word: for the king's commandment was, saying, Answer ye him not. **37** Then Eliakim the son of Hilkiah which was steward of the house, and Shebna the chancellor, and Joah the son of Asaph the recorder came to Hezekiah with their clothes rent, and told him the words of Rabshakeh.

19

6 God promiseth by Isaiah victory to Hezekiah. 35 The Angel of the Lord killeth an hundred and fourscore and five thousand men of the Assyrians. 37 Sennacherib is killed of his own sons.

1 And [1]when King Hezekiah heard it, he rent his clothes and put on sackcloth, and came into the house of the Lord, **2** And sent Eliakim which was the steward of the house, and Shebna the chancellor, and the Elders of the Priests clothed in sackcloth [a]to Isaiah, the Prophet the son of Amoz. **3** And they said unto him, Thus saith Hezekiah, This day is a day of tribulation and of rebuke,

---

r. 2 Kings 17:30 Meaning that every country served that idol, which was most esteemed in that place whence they came.
s. 2 Kings 17:33 That is, they had a certain knowledge of God, and feared him because of the punishment, but they continued still idolaters as do the Papist, which worship both God and idols: but this is not to fear God, as appeareth verse 34.
t. 2 Kings 17:34 He meaneth this by the Israelites to whom God had given his commandments.
u. 2 Kings 17:41 That is, these strangers which were sent into Samaria by the Assyrians.

2-KINGS 17

1. 2 Kings 18:10
2. Deut. 4:19
3. Jer. 18:11; Jer. 25:5; Jer. 35:15
4. Deut. 31:27
5. Exod. 32:8; 1 Kings 12:28
6. Jer. 25:9
7. Ezek. 20:39; Zeph. 1:5
8. Gen. 32:28; 1 Kings 18:34
9. Judg. 6:10; Jer. 10:2

2-KINGS 18

a. 2 Kings 18:3 Although they of Judah were given to idolatry and impiety, as they of Israel were, yet God for his promise sake was merciful unto the throne of David, and yet by his judgment toward the other, provoked to repentance.
b. 2 Kings 18:4 That is, a piece of Brass: thus he calleth the serpent by contempt, which notwithstanding was set up by the word of God, and miracles were wrought by it: yet when it was abused to idolatry this good king destroyed it, not thinking it worthy to be called a serpent, but a piece of brass.
c. 2 Kings 18:8 Read 2 Kings 17:9.
d. 2 Kings 18:14 As his zeal was before praised, so his weakness is here set forth, that none should glory in himself.
e. 2 Kings 18:17 After certain years, when Hezekiah ceased to send the tribute appointed by the king of the Assyrians, he sent his captains and army against him.
f. 2 Kings 18:18 Or, writer of Chronicles, or secretary.
g. 2 Kings 18:20 Hebrew, talk of the lips.
h. 2 Kings 18:20 Thou thinkest that words will serve to persuade thy people, or to move my master.
i. 2 Kings 18:21 Egypt shall not only not be able to succor thee, but shall be an hurt unto thee.
j. 2 Kings 18:22 Thus the idolaters think that God's religion is destroyed, when superstition and idolatry are reformed.
k. 2 Kings 18:23 Meaning, that it was best for him to yield to the king of Assyria, because his power was so small that he had not men to furnish two thousand horses.
l. 2 Kings 18:25 The wicked always in their prosperity flatter themselves, that God doth favor them. Thus he speaketh to fear Hezekiah that by resisting him he should resist God.
m. 2 Kings 18:26 Or, Syrians.
n. 2 Kings 18:27 Hebrew, the water of their feet.
o. 2 Kings 18:29 Or, by his hand.
p. 2 Kings 18:31 Hebrew, blessing: meaning the conditions of peace.
q. 2 Kings 18:32 He maketh himself so sure, that he will not grant them truce, except they render themselves to him to be led away captives.
r. 2 Kings 18:35 This is an execrable blasphemy against the true God, to make him equal with the idols of other nations: therefore God did most sharply punish it.

2-KINGS 18

1. 2 Chron. 28:27; 2 Chron. 29:1
2. Num. 21:8,9
3. 2 Kings 17:3
4. 2 Kings 17:6
5. 2 Chron. 32:1; Isa. 36:1

2-KINGS 19

a. 2 Kings 19:2 To hear some new prophecy, and to have comfort of him.

and blasphemy: for the children are come to [b]the birth, and there is no strength
to bring forth. 4 If so be the Lord thy God hath heard all the words of Rabsha-
keh, whom the king of Assyria his master hath sent to rail on the living God, and
to reproach him with words which the Lord thy God hath heard, then lift thou
up thy prayer for the [c]remnant that are left. 5 So the servants of king Hezekiah
came to Isaiah. 6 And Isaiah said unto them, So shall ye say to your master, Thus
saith the Lord, Be not afraid of the words which thou hast heard, wherewith the
servants of the king of Assyria have blasphemed me. 7 Behold, I will send a blast
[d]upon him, and he shall hear a noise, and return to his own land: and I will cause
him to fall by the sword in his own land. 8 So Rabshakeh returned, and found
the king of Assyria fighting against Libnah: for he had heard that he was departed
from Lachish. 9 [e]He heard also men say of Tirhakah king of [f]Ethiopia, [g]Behold,
he is come out to fight against thee: he therefore departed and sent other messen-
gers unto Hezekiah, saying, 10 Thus shall ye speak to Hezekiah king of Judah,
and say, Let not thy [h]God deceive thee in whom thou trustest, saying, Jerusalem
shall not be delivered into the hand of the king of Assyria. 11 Behold, thou hast
heard what the kings of Assyria have done to all lands, how they have destroyed
them: and shalt thou be delivered? 12 Have the gods of the heathen delivered
them which my fathers have destroyed? as Gozan, and Haran, and Rezeph, and
the children of Eden, which were in Telassar? 13 Where is the king of Hama-
th, and the king of Arpad, and the king of the city of Shepharvaim, Hena and
Ivah? 14 So Hezekiah received the letter of the hand of the messengers, and read
it: and Hezekiah went up into the house of the Lord, and Hezekiah spread it before
the [i]Lord. 15 And Hezekiah [j]prayed before the Lord, and said, O Lord God of
Israel, which dwellest between the Cherubims, thou art very God alone over all the
kingdoms of the earth: thou hast made the heaven and the earth. 16 Lord [k]bow
down thine ear, and hear: Lord open thine eyes and behold, and hear the words of
Sennacherib, who hath sent to blaspheme the [l]living God. 17 Truth it is, Lord,
that the kings of Assyria have destroyed the nations and their lands, 18 And
have set fire on their gods: for they were no gods, but the work of man's hands,
even wood and stone: therefore they destroyed them. 19 Now therefore, O Lord
our God, I beseech thee, save thou us out of his hand, that all the [m]kingdoms of
the earth may know, that thou O Lord, art only God. 20 Then Isaiah the son of
Amoz sent to Hezekiah, saying, Thus saith the Lord God of Israel, I have heard that
which thou hast prayed me, concerning Sennacherib king of Assyria. 21 This is
the word that the Lord hath spoken against him, O [n]Virgin daughter of Zion, he
hath despised thee, and laughed thee to scorn: O daughter of Jerusalem, he hath
shaken his head at thee. 22 Whom hast thou railed on? and whom hast thou bla-
sphemed? and against whom hast thou exalted thy voice, and lifted up thine eyes
on high? even [o]against the holy One of Israel. 23 By thy messengers thou hast
railed on the Lord, and said, By the multitude of my chariots I am come up to the
top of the mountains, by the sides of Lebanon, and will cut down the high cedars
thereof, and the fair fir trees thereof, and I will go into the [p]lodging of his borders,
and into the forest of his [q]Carmel. 24 I have dug and drunk the waters of others,
and with the plant of my feet have I dried all the [r]floods closed in. 25 Hast thou
not heard, how I have of old time made it, and have formed it long ago? [s]and
should I now bring it, that it should be destroyed, and laid on ruinous heaps, as
cities defensed? 26 Whose [t]inhabitants have small power, and are afraid, and
confounded: they are like the grass of the field, and green herb, or grass on the
house tops, or as corn blasted before it be grown. 27 I know thy dwelling, yea,
thy going out and thy coming in, and thy fury against me. 28 And because thou
ragest against me, and thy tumult is come up to mine ears, I will put mine [u]hook in
thy nostrils, and my bridle in thy lips, and will bring thee back again the same way
thou camest. 29 And this shall be a [v]sign unto thee, O Hezekiah, Thou shalt eat
this year such things as grow of themselves, and the next year such as grow without
sowing, and the third year sow ye and reap, and plant vineyards, and eat the fruits
thereof. 30 And the remnant that is escaped of the house of Judah, shall again
take [w]root downward, and bear fruit upward. 31 For out of Jerusalem shall go
a remnant, and some that shall escape out of mount Zion: the [x]zeal of the Lord
of hosts shall do this. 32 Wherefore thus saith the Lord, concerning the king of
Assyria, He shall not enter into this city, nor shoot an arrow there, nor come be-
fore it with shield, nor cast a mount against it: 33 But he shall return the way
he came, and shall not come into this city, saith the Lord. 34 For I will defend
this city to save it for mine own sake, and for David my servant's sake. 35 [2]And
the same night the Angel of the Lord went out and smote in the camp of Assyria
an hundred four score and five thousand: so when they rose early in the morning,
behold, they were all dead corpses. 36 So Sennacherib king of Assyria departed,
and went his way, and returned and dwelt in Nineveh. 37 And as he was in the
Temple worshipping Nisroch his god, Adrammelech and Sharezer his sons [y]slew
him with the sword: and they escaped into the land of Ararat, and Esarhaddon his
son reigned in his stead.

20

1 Hezekiah is sick, and receiveth the sign of his health, 12 He receiveth rewards of Berodach, 13 Showeth his treasures, and is reprehended of Isaiah. 21 He dieth, and Manasseh his son reigneth in his stead.

1 About that time [1]was Hezekiah sick unto death: and the Prophet Isaiah
the son of Amoz came to him, and said unto him, Thus saith the Lord, Put thine
house in an order: for thou shalt die, and not live. 2 Then he turned his face to
the [a]wall, and prayed to the Lord, saying, 3 I beseech thee, O lord, remember
now, how I have walked before thee in truth and with a [b]perfect heart, and have
done that which is good in thy sight: and Hezekiah [c]wept sore. 4 And afore Isa-
iah was gone out into the middle of the court, the word of the Lord came to him,
saying, 5 Turn again, and tell Hezekiah the captain of my people, Thus saith
the Lord God of David thy father, I have heard thy [d]prayer, and seen thy tears:
behold, I have healed thee, and the third day thou shalt go up to the [e]house of the
Lord, 6 And I will add unto thy days fifteen years, and will deliver thee and this
city out of the hand of the king of Assyria, and will defend this city for mine own
sake, and for David my servant's sake. 7 Then Isaiah said, Take a [f]lump of dry
figs. And they took it, and laid it on the boil, and he recovered. 8 For Hezekiah
had said unto Isaiah, What shall be the sign that the Lord will heal me, and that I
shall go up into the house of the Lord the third day? 9 And Isaiah answered, This
sign shalt thou have of the Lord, that the Lord will do that he hath spoken, Wilt
thou that the shadow go forward ten degrees, or go back ten degrees? 10 And
Hezekiah answered, It is a light thing for the shadow to pass forward ten degrees:
not so then, but let the shadow [g]go back ten degrees. 11 And Isaiah the Prophet
called unto the Lord, and he brought again the shadow ten degrees back by the
degrees whereby it had gone down in the [h]dial of Ahaz. 12 [2]The same season
Berodach-Baladan the son of Baladan king of Babylon sent letters and a [i]present
to Hezekiah: for he had heard how that Hezekiah was sick. 13 And Hezekiah
heard them, and showed them all his treasure house, to wit, the silver, and the
gold, and the spices, and the precious ointment, and all the house of his armor,
and all that was found in his treasures: there was nothing in his house, and in all
his [j]realm, that Hezekiah showed them not. 14 Then Isaiah the Prophet came
unto King Hezekiah, and said unto him, What said these men? and from whence
came they to thee? And Hezekiah said, They be come from a far country, even from
Babylon. 15 Then said he, What have they seen in thine house? And Hezekiah
answered, All that is in mine house have they seen: there is nothing among my tre-
asures, that I have not showed them. 16 And Isaiah said unto Hezekiah, Hear
the word of the Lord. 17 Behold, the days come, that all that is in thine house,
and whatsoever thy fathers have laid up in store unto this day, [3]shall be carried into
Babylon: Nothing shall be left, saith the Lord. 18 And of thy sons, that shall pro-
ceed out of thee, and which thou shalt beget, shall they take away, and they shall
be eunuchs in the palace of the king of Babylon. 19 Then Hezekiah said unto

---

b. 2 Kings 19:3 The dangers are so great, that we can neither avenge this blasphemy, nor help ourselves no more than a woman in her travail.
c. 2 Kings 19:4 Meaning, for Jerusalem which only remained of all the cities of Judah.
d. 2 Kings 19:7 The Lord can with one blast blow away all the strength of man, and turn it into dust.
e. 2 Kings 19:9 That is, Sennacherib.
f. 2 Kings 19:9 Or, black Moors.
g. 2 Kings 19:9 For the Kings of Ethiopia and Egypt joined together against the King of Assyria because of his oppression of other countries.
h. 2 Kings 19:10 The more near that the wicked are to their destruction, the more they blaspheme.
i. 2 Kings 19:14 Before the Ark of the covenant.
j. 2 Kings 19:15 He showeth what is the true refuge and succor in all dangers, to wit, to flee to the Lord by earnest prayer.
k. 2 Kings 19:16 Show by effect that thou wilt not suffer thy Name to be blasphemed.
l. 2 Kings 19:16 By this title he discerneth God from all idols and false gods.
m. 2 Kings 19:19 He showeth for what end the faithful desire of God to be delivered: to wit, that he may be glorified by their deliverance.
n. 2 Kings 19:21 Because as yet Jerusalem had not been taken by the enemy, therefore he calleth her virgin.
o. 2 Kings 19:22 God counteth that injury done to him, and will revenge it, which is done to any of his Saints.
p. 2 Kings 19:23 Meaning, Jerusalem, which Isaiah calleth the height of his borders, to wit, of Judah, Isa. 37:24.
q. 2 Kings 19:23 Or, pleasant country.
r. 2 Kings 19:24 Or, the waters of cities besieged.
s. 2 Kings 19:25 He declareth that forasmuch as he is the author and beginning of his Church, he will never suffer it utterly to be destroyed, as other cities and kingdoms.
t. 2 Kings 19:26 Thus he describeth the wicked, which for a time flourish, and afterward fade and decay like flowers.
u. 2 Kings 19:28 I will bridle thy rage, and turn thee to and fro as pleaseth me.
v. 2 Kings 19:29 God did not only promise him the victory, but giveth him a sign to confirm his faith.
w. 2 Kings 19:30 The Lord will multiply in great number, that small remnant of Judah that is escaped.
x. 2 Kings 19:31 The love, that God beareth toward his Church shall overcome the counsels and enterprises of men.
y. 2 Kings 19:37 This was the just judgment of God for his blasphemy, that he should be slain before that idol, whom he preferred to the living God, and by them, by whom ought by nature to have been defended.

2-KINGS 19
1. Isa. 37:1
2. Isa. 37:36

2-KINGS 20
a. 2 Kings 20:2 That his mind might not be troubled.
b. 2 Kings 20:3 Meaning, without all hypocrisy.
c. 2 Kings 20:3 Not so much for his own death, as for fear that idolatry should be restored, which he had destroyed, and so God's Name be dishonored.
d. 2 Kings 20:5 Because of his unfained repentance and prayer, God turned away his wrath.
e. 2 Kings 20:5 To give thanks for thy deliverance.
f. 2 Kings 20:7 He declareth that albeit God can heal without other medicines, yet he showeth that he will not have these inferior means contemned.
g. 2 Kings 20:10 Let the sun go so many degrees back, that the hours may be so many the fewer in the king's dial.
h. 2 Kings 20:11 Which dial was set the top of the stairs that Ahaz had made.
i. 2 Kings 20:12 Moved with the favor that God showed to Hezekiah, and also because he had declared himself enemy to Sennacherib his enemy which was now destroyed.
j. 2 Kings 20:13 Being moved with ambition and vain glory, and also because he seemed to rejoice in the friendship of him that was God's enemy and an infidel.

Isaiah, The word of the Lord, which thou hast [k]spoken, is good: for said he, Shall
it not be good if [l]peace and truth be in my days? **20** Concerning the rest of the
acts of Hezekiah, and all his valiant deeds, and how he made a pool and a conduit,
and brought water into the city, are they not written in the book of the Chronicles
of the kings of Judah? **21** And Hezekiah slept with his fathers: and Manasseh his
son reigned in his stead.

21

3 King Manasseh restoreth idolatry, 16 And useth great cruelty. 18 He dieth and Amon his son succeedeth, 23 Who is killed of his own servants. 26 After him reigneth Josiah.

1 Manasseh [1]was twelve years old when he began to reign, and reigned fifty
and five years in Jerusalem: his mother's name also was Hephzibah. **2** And he
did evil in the sight of the Lord after the abomination of the heathen, whom the
[2]Lord had cast out before the children of Israel. **3** For he went back and built the
high places, [3]which Hezekiah his father had destroyed: and he erected up altars for
Baal, and made a grove, as did Ahab king of Israel, and worshipped all the host of
heaven and served them. **4** [4]Also he built altars in the house of the Lord, of the
which the Lord said, [5]In Jerusalem will I put my Name. **5** And he built altars
for all the host of the heaven in the two courts of the house of the Lord. **6** And
he caused his sons [a]to pass through the fire, and gave himself to witchcraft and
sorcery, and he used them that had familiar spirits and were soothsayers, and did
much evil in the sight of the Lord to anger him. **7** And he set the image of the
grove, that he had made in the house, whereof the Lord had said to David and to
Solomon his son, [6]In this house and in Jerusalem, which I have chosen out of all
the tribes of Israel, will I put my Name forever. **8** Neither will I make the feet of
Israel move anymore out of the land, which I gave their fathers: so that they will
[b]observe and do all that I have commanded them, and according to all the Law
that my servant Moses commanded them. **9** Yet they obeyed not, but Manas-
seh led them out of the way, to do more wickedly than did the heathen people,
whom the Lord destroyed before the children of Israel. **10** Therefore the Lord
spake by his servants the Prophets, saying, **11** [7]Because that Manasseh king of
Judah hath done such abominations, and hath wrought more wickedly than all
that the Amorites (which were before him) did, and hath made Judah sin also with
his idols. **12** Therefore thus saith the Lord God of Israel, Behold, I will bring an
evil upon Jerusalem and Judah, that who so heareth of it, both his [8]ears shall [c]tin-
gle. **13** And I will stretch over Jerusalem the line [d]of Samaria, and the plummet
of the house of Ahab: and I will wipe Jerusalem, as a man wipeth a dish, which
he wipeth, and turneth it upside down. **14** And I will forsake the [e]remnant of
mine inheritance, and deliver them into the hand of their enemies, and they shall
be robbed and spoiled of all their adversaries, **15** Because they have done evil in
my sight, and have provoked me to anger, since the time their fathers came out of
Egypt until this day. **16** Moreover, Manasseh shed [f]innocent blood exceedingly
much, till he replenished Jerusalem from corner to corner, beside his sin wherewi-
th he made Judah to sin, and to do evil in the sight of the Lord. **17** Concerning
the rest of the acts of Manasseh, and all that he did, and his sin that he sinned, are
they not written in the book of the Chronicles of the kings of Judah? **18** And
Manasseh slept with his fathers, and was buried in the garden of his own house,
even in the garden of Uzza: and Amon his son reigned in his stead. **19** [9]Amon
was two and twenty years old, when he began to reign, and he reigned two years
in Jerusalem: his mother's name also was Meshullemeth the daughter of Haruz
of Jotbah. **20** And he did evil in the sight of the Lord, as his father Manasseh
did. **21** For he walked in all the way that his father walked in, and served the
idols that his father served, and worshipped them. **22** And he forsook the Lord
God of his fathers, and walked not in the [g]way of the Lord. **23** And the servants
of Amon conspired against him, and slew the King in his own house. **24** And
the people of the land slew all them that had conspired against King Amon, and
the people made Josiah his son King in his stead. **25** Concerning the rest of the
acts of Amon, which he did, are they not written in the book of the Chronicles of
the Kings of Judah? **26** And [h]they buried him in his sepulcher in the garden of
Uzza: and Josiah his son reigned in his stead.

22

4 Josiah repaireth the Temple. 8 Hilkiah findeth the book of the Law, and causeth it to be presented to Josiah. 12 Who sendeth to Huldah the Prophetess to inquire the Lord's will.

1 Josiah was [1]eight years old when he began to reign, and he reigned one
and thirty years in Jerusalem. His mother's name also was Jedidah the daughter of
Adaiah of Bozkath. **2** And he did uprightly in the sight of the Lord, and [a]walked
in all the ways of David his father, and bowed neither to the right hand, nor to
the left. **3** And in the eighteenth year of King Josiah, the king sent Shaphan the
son of Azaliah the son of Meshullam the chancellor, to the house of the Lord,
saying, **4** Go up to Hilkiah the high Priest, that he may [b]sum the silver which is
brought into the house of the Lord, which the keepers of the [c,d]door have gathe-
red of the people. **5** And let [e]them deliver it into the hand of them that do the
work, and have the oversight of the house of the Lord, let them give it to them that
work in the house of the Lord, to repair the decayed places of the house: **6** To
wit, unto the artificers and carpenters, and masons, and to buy timber, and hewed
stone to repair the house. **7** Howbeit, let no reckoning be made with them of the
money, that is delivered into their hand: for they deal [f]faithfully. **8** And Hilkiah
the high Priest said unto Shaphan the chancellor, I have found the [g]book of the
Law in the house of the Lord: and Hilkiah gave the book to Shaphan, and he read
it. **9** So Shaphan the chancellor came to the king, and brought him word again,
and said, Thy servants have [h]gathered the money that was found in the house, and
have delivered it unto the hands of them that do the work, and have the oversi-
ght of the house of the Lord. **10** Also Shaphan the chancellor showed the king,
saying, Hilkiah the Priest hath delivered me a book. And Shaphan read it before
the King. **11** And when the king had heard the words of the book of the Law,
he rent his clothes. **12** Therefore the king commanded Hilkiah the Priest, and
Ahikam the son of Shaphan, and Achbor the son of Michaiah, and Shaphan the
chancellor, and Asahiah the king's servant, saying, **13** Go ye and [i]inquire of the
Lord for me and for the people, and for all Judah concerning the words of this
book that is found: for great is the wrath of the Lord that is kindled against us,
because our fathers have not obeyed the words of this book, to do according unto
all that which is written therein for us. **14** So Hilkiah the Priest, and Ahikam,
and Achbor, and Shaphan, and Asahiah went unto Huldah the Prophetess the wife
of Shallum, the son of Tikvah, the son of Harhas keeper of the wardrobe: (and
she dwelt in Jerusalem in the [j]college) and they communed with her. **15** And
she answered them, Thus saith the Lord God of Israel, Tell the man that sent you
to me, **16** Thus saith the Lord, Behold, I will bring evil upon this place, and on
the inhabitants thereof, even all the words of the book which the king of Judah
hath read, **17** Because they have forsaken me, and have burnt incense unto other
gods, to anger me with all the [k]works of their hands: my wrath also shall be kindled
against this place, and shall not be quenched: **18** But to the king of Judah, who
sent you to inquire of the Lord, so shall ye say unto him, Thus saith the Lord God
of Israel, The words that thou hast heard, shall come to pass. **19** But because
thine heart did [l]melt, and thou hast humbled thyself before the Lord when thou
heardest what I spake against this place, and against the inhabitants of the same, to
wit, that it should be destroyed and accursed, and hast rent thy clothes, and wept
before me, I have also heard it, saith the Lord. **20** Behold therefore, I will gather
thee to thy fathers, and thou shalt be put in thy grave in [m]peace, and thine eyes
shall not see all the evil which I will bring upon this place. Thus they brought the
king word again.

---

k. 2 Kings 20:19 He acknowledgeth Isaiah to be the true Prophet of God, and therefore humbleth himself to his word.

l. 2 Kings 20:19 Seeing that God hath showeth me this favor to grant me quietness during my life: for he was afraid lest the enemies should have had occasion to rejoice, if the Church had decayed in his time, because he had restored religion.

2-KINGS 20

1. 2 Chron. 32:24; Isa. 38:1
2. Isa. 39:1
3. 2 Kings 24:13; 2 Kings 25:13; Jer. 27:19

2-KINGS 21

a. 2 Kings 21:6 Read 2 Kings 16:3.

b. 2 Kings 21:8 Therefore seeing they obeyed not the commandment of God, they were justly cast forth of that land, which they had but on condition.

c. 2 Kings 21:12 Meaning, that whosoever shall hear of this great plague, shall be astonished.

d. 2 Kings 21:13 As I have destroyed Samaria and the house of Ahab, so will I destroy Judah.

e. 2 Kings 21:14 Meaning, Judah and Benjamin, which were only left of the rest of the tribes.

f. 2 Kings 21:16 The Hebrews write that he slew Isaiah the Prophet, who was his father-in-law.

g. 2 Kings 21:22 That is, according to his commandments.

h. 2 Kings 21:26 Or, he buried him, to wit, Josiah his son.

2-KINGS 21

1. 2 Chron. 33:1
2. Deut. 18:9
3. 2 Kings 18:4
4. Jer. 32:34
5. 2 Sam. 7:13
6. 1 Kings 8:19; 1 Kings 9:3; 2 Kings 23:27
7. Jer. 15:4
8. 1 Sam. 3:11
9. 2 Chron. 33:20,21

2-KINGS 22

a. 2 Kings 22:2 His zeal was prophesied of, and his name mentioned by Iddo the Prophet, more than three hundred years before, 1 Kings 13:2, and being but eight years old, he sought the God of his father David, 2 Chron. 34:3.

b. 2 Kings 22:4 Or, coin, as verse 9.

c. 2 Kings 22:4 Or, vessel.

d. 2 Kings 22:4 Certain of the Priests were appointed to this office, as 2 Kings 12:9.

e. 2 Kings 22:5 From the time of Joash for the space of 244 years, the Temple remained without reparation through the negligence of the priests, this declareth, that they that have a charge and execute it not, ought to have it taken from them.

f. 2 Kings 22:7 So God provided him of faithful servants, seeing he went about so zealously to set forth the work of God.

g. 2 Kings 22:8 This was the copy that Moses left them, as appeareth, 2 Chron. 34:14, which either by the negligence of the Priests had been lost, or else by the wickedness of idolatrous kings had been abolished.

h. 2 Kings 22:9 Hebrew, melted.

i. 2 Kings 22:13 Meaning, to some Prophet whom God revealeth the knowledge of things unto, as Jer. 21:8, though at other times they inquired the Lord by Urim and Thummim.

j. 2 Kings 22:14 Or the house of doctrine, which was near to the Temple, and where the learned assembled to entreat the Scriptures, and the doctrine of the Prophets.

k. 2 Kings 22:17 The works of man's hand here signify all that man inventeth beside the word of God, which are abominable in God's service.

l. 2 Kings 22:19 Meaning, that he did repent, as they that do not repent, are said to harden their heart, Ps. 95:8.

m. 2 Kings 22:20 Whereupon we may gather that the anger of God is ready against the wicked, when God taketh his servants out of this world.

2-KINGS 22

1. 2 Chron. 34:1

23

2 Josiah readeth the Law before the people. 3 He maketh a covenant with the Lord. 4 He putteth down the idols, after he had killed their Priests. 22 He keepeth Passover. 24 He destroyeth the conjurers. 29 He was killed in Megiddo. 30 And his son Jehoahaz reigneth in his stead. 33 After he was taken, his son Jehoiakim was made King.

1 Then [1]the King [a]sent, and there gathered unto him all the Elders of Judah and of Jerusalem. **2** And the king went up into the house of the Lord, with all the men of Judah, and all the inhabitants of Jerusalem with him, and the Priests and Prophets, and all the people both small and great: and he read in their ears all the words of the book of the covenant, which was found in the house of the Lord. **3** And the king stood by [b]the pillar, and made a [c]covenant before the Lord, that they should walk after the Lord, and keep his commandments, and his testimonies, and his statutes, with all their heart, and with all their soul, that they might accomplish the words of this covenant written in this book. And all the people stood to the covenant. **4** Then the king commanded Hilkiah the high [d]Priest, and the Priests of the second order, and the keepers of the door, to bring out of the temple of the Lord all the vessels that were made for Baal, and for the grove, and for all the host of heaven, and he burnt them without Jerusalem in the fields of Kidron, and carried [e]the powder of them into Bethel. **5** And he put down the [f]Chemarims, whom the kings of Judah had founded to burn incense in the high places, and in the cities of Judah and about Jerusalem, and also them that burnt incense unto Baal, to the sun and to the moon, and to the planets, and to all the host of heaven. **6** And he brought out the [g]grove from the Temple of the Lord, without Jerusalem unto the valley of Kidron, and burnt it in the valley Kidron, and stamped it to powder, and cast the dust thereof upon the [h]graves of the children of the people. **7** And he brake down the houses of the Sodomites, that were in the house of the Lord, where the women wove hangings for the grove. **8** Also he brought all the priests out of the cities of Judah, and defiled the high places where the Priests had burnt incense, even from Geba to Beersheba, and destroyed the high places of the gates, that were in the entering in of the gate of Joshua the governor of the city, which was at the left hand of the gate of the city. **9** Nevertheless the Priests of the high places [i]came not up to the altar of the Lord in Jerusalem, save only they did eat of the unleavened bread among their brethren. **10** He defiled also [j]Topheth, which was in the valley of the children of Hinnom, that no man should make his son or his daughter pass through the fire to Molech. **11** He put down also the [k]horses that the Kings of Judah had given to the sun at the entering in of the house of the Lord, by the chamber of Nethan-Melech the eunuch, which was ruler of the suburbs, and burnt the chariots of the sun with fire. **12** And the altars that were on the top of the chamber of Ahaz, which the kings of Judah had made, and the altars which Manasseh had made in the two courts of the house of the Lord did the king break down, and hasted thence, and cast the dust of them in the [l]brook Kidron. **13** Moreover the King defiled the high places that were before Jerusalem, and on the right hand of the [m]mount of corruption (which [2]Solomon the king of Israel had built for Ashtoreth the idol of the Sidonians, and for Chemosh the idol of the Moabites, and for Milcom the abomination of the children of Ammon) **14** And he brake the images in pieces, and cut down the groves, and filled their places with the bones of men. **15** Furthermore [n]the altar that was at Bethel, and the high place made by Jeroboam the son of Nebat, which made Israel to sin, both this altar and also the high place, brake he down, and burnt the high place, and stamped it to powder and burnt the grove. **16** And as Josiah turned himself, he spied the graves that were in the mount, and sent and took the bones out of the graves, and burnt them upon the altar and polluted it, according to the word of the Lord, that the [o]man of God proclaimed, which cried the same words. **17** Then he said, What title is that which I see? And the men of the city said unto him, It is the sepulcher of the man of God, which came from Judah, and told these things that thou hast done to the altar of Bethel. **18** Then said he, Let him alone: let none remove his bones. So his bones were saved with the bones of the [p]Prophet that came from Samaria. **19** Josiah also took away all the houses of the high places, which were in the cities of Samaria, which the kings of Israel had made to anger the Lord, and did to them according to all the facts that he had done in Bethel. **20** And he sacrificed all the Priests of the high places that were there upon the altars, and burnt men's bones upon them, and returned to Jerusalem. **21** Then the king commanded all the people, saying, [3]Keep the Passover unto the Lord your God, [4]as it is written in the book of this covenant. **22** And there was no Passover holden [q]like that from the days of the Judges that judged Israel, nor in all the days of the kings of Israel, and of the kings of Judah. **23** And in the eighteenth year of King Josiah was this Passover celebrated to the Lord in Jerusalem. **24** Josiah also took away them that had familiar spirits, and the soothsayers, and the images, and the idols, and all the abominations that were espied in the land of Judah and in Jerusalem, to perform the words of the [5]Law, which were written in the book that Hilkiah the Priest found in the house of the Lord. **25** Like unto him was there no king before him, that turned to the Lord with all his heart, and with all his soul, and with all his might according to all the Law of Moses, neither after him arose there any like him. **26** Notwithstanding the Lord turned not from the [r]fierceness of his great wrath wherewith he was angry against Judah, because of all the provocations wherewith Manasseh had provoked him. **27** Therefore the Lord said, I will put Judah also out of my sight, as I have put away Israel, and will cast off this city Jerusalem, which I have chosen, and the house whereof I said, [6]My name shall be there. **28** Concerning the rest of the acts of Josiah, and all that he did, are they not written in the book of the Chronicles of the kings of Judah? **29** [7]In his days Pharaoh Necho king of Egypt [s]went up against the king of Assyria to the river Perath. And king Josiah went against him, whom when Pharaoh saw, he slew him at Megiddo. **30** Then his servants carried him dead from Megiddo, and brought him to Jerusalem, and buried him in his own sepulcher. And the people of the land took Jehoahaz the son of Josiah, and anointed him, and made him king in his father's stead. **31** [8]Jehoahaz was three and twenty years old when he began to reign, and reigned three months in Jerusalem. His mother's name also was Hamutal the daughter of Jeremiah of Libnah. **32** And he did evil in the sight of the Lord, according to all that his [t]fathers had done. **33** And Pharaoh Necho put him in bonds [u]at Riblah in the land of Hamath [v]while he reigned in Jerusalem, and put the land to a tribute of an hundred talents of silver, and a talent of gold. **34** And Pharaoh Necho made Eliakim the son of Josiah king instead of Josiah his father, and turned his name to Jehoiakim, and took Jehoahaz away, which when he came to Egypt, died there. **35** And Jehoiakim gave the silver and the gold to Pharaoh, and taxed the land to give the money, according to the commandment of Pharaoh: he levied of every man of the people of the land, according to his value, silver and gold to give unto Pharaoh Necho. **36** Jehoiakim was five and twenty years old, when he began to reign, and he reigned eleven years in Jerusalem. His mother's name also was Zebudah the daughter of Pedaiah of Rumah. **37** And he did evil in the sight of the Lord, according to all that his fathers had done.

24

1 Jehoiakim made subject to Nebuchadnezzar, rebelleth. 3 The cause of his ruin and all Judah's. 6 Jehoiachin reigneth. 15 He, and his people are carried unto Babylon. 17 Zedekiah is made king.

1 In his [a]days came Nebuchadnezzar king of Babylon up, and Jehoiakim became his servant three years: afterward he turned, and rebelled against him. **2** And the Lord sent against him bands of the Chaldeans, and bands of the Aramites, and bands of the Moabites, and bands of the Ammonites, and he sent them against Judah to destroy it, [1]according to the word of the Lord, which he spake by his servants the Prophets. **3** Surely by the [b]commandment of the Lord came this upon Judah, that he might put them out of his sight for the sins of Manasseh, according to all that he did, **4** And for the innocent blood that he shed, (for he filled Jerusalem with innocent blood) therefore the Lord would not pardon it. **5** Concerning

---

2-KINGS 23

- **a.** 2 Kings 23:1 Because he saw the great plagues of God that were threatened, he knew no more speedy way to avoid them, than to turn to God by repentance which cannot come but of faith, and faith by hearing of the word of God.
- **b.** 2 Kings 23:3 Where the king had his place, 2 Kings 11:14.
- **c.** 2 Kings 23:3 As Joshua did, Josh. 24:22, 25.
- **d.** 2 Kings 23:4 Meaning, them which were next in dignity to the high Priest.
- **e.** 2 Kings 23:4 In contempt of that altar, which Jeroboam had there built to sacrifice to his calves.
- **f.** 2 Kings 23:5 Meaning, the priests of Baal, which were called Chemarims, either because they wore black garments, or else were smoked with burning incense to idols.
- **g.** 2 Kings 23:6 He removed the grove which idolaters for devotion had planted near unto the Temple, contrary to the commandment of the Lord, Deut. 16:21, or as some read, the similitude of a grove which was hung in the Temple.
- **h.** 2 Kings 23:6 Both in contempt of the idols and reproach of them which had worshipped them in their lives.
- **i.** 2 Kings 23:9 Because that those that had forsaken the Lord to serve idols, were not meet to minister in the service of the Lord for the instruction of others.
- **j.** 2 Kings 23:10 Which was a valley near to Jerusalem, and signifieth a taboret, because they smote on the taboret while their children were burning, that their cry should not be heard, Lev. 18:21, where after Josiah commanded carrions to be cast in contempt thereof.
- **k.** 2 Kings 23:11 The idolatrous kings had dedicated horses and chariots to the sun, either to carry the image thereof about as the heathen did, or else to sacrifice them as a sacrifice most agreeable.
- **l.** 2 Kings 23:12 Or, valley.
- **m.** 2 Kings 23:13 That was the mount of olives, so called because it was full of idols.
- **n.** 2 Kings 23:15 Which Jeroboam had built in Israel, 1 Kings 12:28, 29.
- **o.** 2 Kings 23:16 According to the prophecy of Iddo, 1 Kings 13:2.
- **p.** 2 Kings 23:18 Meaning, the Prophet which came after him, and caused him to eat contrary to the commandment of the Lord, which were both two buried in one grave, 1 Kings 13:31.
- **q.** 2 Kings 23:22 For the multitude and zeal of the people with the great preparation.
- **r.** 2 Kings 23:26 Because of the wicked heart of the people, which would not turn unto him by repentance.
- **s.** 2 Kings 23:29 Because he passed through his country, he feared lest he would have done him harm, and therefore would have stayed him, yet he consulted not with the Lord, and therefore was slain.
- **t.** 2 Kings 23:32 Meaning, the wicked kings before.
- **u.** 2 Kings 23:33 Which was Antioch in Syria, called also Hamath.
- **v.** 2 Kings 23:33 Or, that he should not reign.

2-KINGS 23

1. 2 Chron. 34:30
2. 1 Kings 11:7
3. 2 Chron. 35:1
4. Exod. 12:3; Deut. 16:2
5. Lev. 20:27; Deut. 18:11
6. 1 Kings 8:29; 1 Kings 9:3; 2 Kings 2:7
7. 2 Chron. 35:20
8. 2 Chron. 36:1,2

2-KINGS 24

- **a.** 2 Kings 24:1 In the end of the third year of his reign, and in the beginning of the fourth, Dan. 1:1.
- **b.** 2 Kings 24:3 Though God used these wicked tyrants to execute his just judgments, yet they are not to be excused, because they proceeded of ambition and malice.

the rest of the acts of Jehoiakim, and all that he did, are they not written in the book of the Chronicles of the kings of Judah? **6** So Jehoiakim [c]slept with his fathers, and Jehoiachin his son reigned in his stead. **7** And the king of Egypt came no more out of his land: for the king of Babylon had taken from the river of Egypt, unto the river [d]Perath, all that pertained to the king of Egypt. **8** Jehoiachin was eighteen years old, when he began to reign, and reigned in Jerusalem three months. His mother's name also was Nehushta, the daughter of Elnathan of Jerusalem. **9** And he did evil in the sight of the Lord, according to all that his father had done. **10** [2]In that time came the servants of Nebuchadnezzar king of Babylon up against Jerusalem: so the city was besieged. **11** And Nebuchadnezzar king of Babylon came against the city, and his servants did besiege it. **12** Then Jehoiachin the king of Judah [e]came out against the king of Babylon, he, and his mother and his servants, and his princes, and his eunuchs: and the king of Babylon took him in the eighth year [f]of his reign. **13** [2]And he carried out thence all the treasures of the house of the Lord, and the treasures of the king's house, and brake all the vessels of gold which Solomon king of Israel had made in the Temple of the Lord, as the Lord had said. **14** And he carried away all Jerusalem, and all the princes, and all the strong men of war, even ten thousand into captivity, and all the workmen, and cunning men: so none remained saving the poor people of the land. **15** [4]And he carried away Jehoiachin into Babylon, and the king's mother, and the king's wives, and his eunuchs, and the mighty of the land, carried he away into captivity from Jerusalem to Babylon, **16** And all the men of war, even seven thousand, and carpenters, and locksmiths a thousand: all that were strong and apt for war, did the king of Babylon bring to Babylon captives. **17** [5]And the king of Babylon made Mattaniah his uncle king in his stead, and changed his name to Zedekiah. **18** Zedekiah was one and twenty years old, when he began to reign, and he reigned eleven years in Jerusalem. His mother's name also was Hamutal the daughter of Jeremiah of Libnah. **19** And he did evil in the sight of the Lord, according to all that Jehoiakim had done. **20** Therefore certainly the wrath of the Lord was against Jerusalem and Judah, until he cast them out of his [g]sight. And Zedekiah rebelled against the king of Babylon.

25

1 Jerusalem is besieged of Nebuchadnezzar, and taken. 7 The sons of Zedekiah are slain before his eyes, and after are his own eyes put out. 11 Judah is brought to Babylon. 25 Gedaliah is slain. 27 Jehoiachin is exalted.

1 [1]And in the [a]ninth year of his reign, the [b]tenth month, and tenth day of the month Nebuchadnezzar king of Babylon came, he, and all his host against Jerusalem, and pitched against it, and they built [c]forts against it round about it. **2** So the city was besieged unto the eleventh year of King Zedekiah. **3** And the ninth day of the month the famine was [d]sore in the city, so that there was no bread for the people of the land. **4** Then the city was broken up, and all the men of war fled by night, by the way of the [e]gate, which is between two walls that was by the king's garden: now the Chaldeans were by the city round about: and the king went by the way of the wilderness. **5** But the army of the Chaldeans pursued after the king, and took him in the deserts of Jericho, and all his host was scattered from him. **6** Then they took the king, and carried him up to the king of Babylon to Riblah, where they [f]gave judgment upon him. **7** And they slew the sons of Zedekiah before his eyes, and put out the eyes of Zedekiah, and bound him in chains, and carried him to Babylon. **8** And in the fifth month, and [g]seventh day of the month, which was the nineteenth year of king Nebuchadnezzar king of Babylon, came Nebuzaradan [h]chief steward and servant of the king of Babylon, to Jerusalem, **9** And burnt the house of the Lord, and the king's house, and all the houses of Jerusalem, and all the great houses burnt he with fire. **10** And all the army of the Chaldeans that were with the chief steward, brake down the walls of Jerusalem round about. **11** And the rest of the people that were left in the city, and those that were fled and [i]fallen to the king of Babylon, with the remnant of the multitude, did Nebuzaradan chief steward carry away captive. **12** But the chief steward left of the poor of the land to dress the vines, and to till the land. **13** [2]Also the pillars of brass that were in the house of the Lord, and the bases, and the brazen Sea that was in the house of the Lord, did the Chaldeans break, and carried the brass of them to Babylon. **14** The pots [j]also and the besoms, and the instruments of music, and the incense dishes, and all the vessels of brass that they ministered in, took they away. **15** And the ash pans, and the basins, and all that was of gold, and that was of silver, took the chief steward away, **16** With the two pillars, one Sea and the bases, which Solomon had made for the house of the Lord: the brass of all these vessels was without weight. **17** [3]The height of the one pillar was eighteen cubits, and the chapiter thereon was brass, and the height of the chapiter was with network three cubits, and pomegranates upon the chapiter round about, all of brass: and likewise was the second pillar with the network. **18** And the chief steward took Seraiah the chief Priest, and Zephaniah the [k]second Priest, and the three keepers of the door. **19** And out of the city he took an Eunuch that had the oversight of the men of war, and [l]five men of them that were in the King's presence, which were found in the city, and Sopher captain of the host, who mustered the people of the land, and threescore men of the people of the land, that were found in the city. **20** And Nebuzaradan the chief steward took them, and brought them to the king of Babylon to Riblah. **21** And the king of Babylon smote them, and slew them at Riblah in the land of Hamath. So Judah was carried away captive out of his own land. **22** [4]Howbeit, there remained people in the land of Judah, whom Nebuchadnezzar king of Babylon left, and made Gedaliah the son of Ahikam the son of Shaphan ruler over them. **23** Then when all the captains of the host and their men heard, that the king of Babylon had made Gedaliah governor, they came to Gedaliah to Mizpah, to wit, Ishmael the son of Nethaniah, and Johanan the son of Careah, and Seraiah the son of Tanhumeth the Netophathite, and Jaazaniah the son of Maachathi, they and their men. **24** And Gedaliah [m]sware to them, and to their men, and said unto them, Fear not to be the servants of the Chaldeans: dwell in the land, and serve the king of Babylon, and ye shall be well. **25** [5]But in the seventh month Ishmael the son of Nethaniah the son of Elishama, of the king's seed, came, and ten men with him, and smote Gedaliah, and he died, and so did he the Jews, and the Chaldeans that were with him at Mizpah. **26** Then all the people both small and great, and the captains of the army arose, and came to [n]Egypt: for they were afraid of the Chaldeans. **27** Notwithstanding in the seven and thirtieth year after [o]Jehoiachin King of Judah was carried away, in the twelfth month and the seven and twentieth day of the month, Evil-Merodach king of Babylon in the year that he began to reign, did lift up the head of Jehoiachin king of Judah out of the prison, **28** And spake kindly to him, and set his throne above the throne of the kings that were with him in Babylon, **29** And changed his prison garments: and he did continually eat bread before him, all the days of his life. **30** And his [p]portion was a continual portion given him by the king, every day a certain, all the days of his life.

---

c. 2 Kings 24:6 Not that he was buried with his fathers, but he died in the way, as they led him prisoner toward Babylon, read Jer. 22:19.
d. 2 Kings 24:7 Or, Euphrates.
e. 2 Kings 24:12 That is, yielded himself unto him by the counsel of Jeremiah.
f. 2 Kings 24:12 In the reign of the king of Babylon.
g. 2 Kings 24:20 Out of Jerusalem and Judah into Babylon.

2-KINGS 24
1. 2 Kings 20:17; 2 Kings 23:27
2. Dan. 1:1
3. 2 Kings 20:17; Isa. 39:6
4. 2 Chron. 36:10; Esther 2:6
5. Jer. 37:1; Jer. 52:1

2-KINGS 25
a. 2 Kings 25:1 That is, of Zedekiah.
b. 2 Kings 25:1 Which the Hebrews call Tebet, and it containeth part of December, and part of January.
c. 2 Kings 25:1 Or, a mount.
d. 2 Kings 25:3 Insomuch that the mothers did eat their children, Lam. 4:10.
e. 2 Kings 25:4 Which was a postern door, or some secret gate to issue out at.
f. 2 Kings 25:6 Or, condemned him for his perjury and treason, 2 Chron. 36:13.
g. 2 Kings 25:8 Jeremiah writeth, Jer. 52:12, the tenth day, because the fire continued from the seventh day to the tenth.
h. 2 Kings 25:8 Or, captain of the guard.
i. 2 Kings 25:11 While the siege endured.
j. 2 Kings 25:14 Of these read Exod. 27:3.
k. 2 Kings 25:18 That is, one appointed to succeed in the high Priest's room, if he were sick or else otherwise letted.
l. 2 Kings 25:19 Jeremiah maketh mention of seven, but here he speaketh of them that were the chiefest.
m. 2 Kings 25:24 That is, he did exhort them in the Name of the Lord, according to Jeremiah's counsel, to submit themselves to Nebuchadnezzar, seeing it was the revealed will of the Lord.
n. 2 Kings 25:26 Contrary to Jeremiah's counsel, Jer. 40–43.
o. 2 Kings 25:27 Thus long was he, his wife and his children in Babylon, whom Nebuchadnezzar's son, after his father's death preferred to honor: thus by God's providence the seed of David was preserved even unto Christ.
p. 2 Kings 25:30 Meaning, that he had an ordinary in the court.

2-KINGS 25
1. Jer. 39:1; Jer. 52:4
2. 2 Kings 20:17; Jer. 27:19,20
3. 1 Kings 7:15; Jer. 52:21; 1 Chron. 3:15
4. Jer. 40:5,6
5. Jer. 41:1

THE FIRST BOOK OF THE [a]CHRONICLES, OR [b]PARALIPOMENON

1

1 The genealogy of Adam and Noah until Abraham. 27 And from Abraham to Esau. 35 His children. 43 Kings and Dukes came of him.

1 Adam, [c]Seth, Enosh, 2 Cainan, Mahalalel, Jared, 3 Enoch, Methuse-
lah, Lamech, 4 Noah, [d]Shem, Ham, and Japheth. 5 [1]The sons of Japheth were
Gomer, and Magog, and Madai, and Javan, and Tubal, and Meshech, and Ti-
ras. 6 And the sons of Gomer, Ashkenaz, and [e]Diphath and Togarmah. 7 Also
the sons of Javan, Elishah and Tarshishah, Kittim, and [f]Dodanim. 8 The sons
of Ham were Cush, and Mizraim, Put and Canaan. 9 And the sons of Cush,
Seba, and Havilah, and Sabta, and Raama, and Sabtecha. Also the sons of Raama
were Sheba and Dedan. 10 And Cush begat [g,2]Nimrod, who began to be mi-
ghty in the earth. 11 And Mizraim begat Ludim and Anamim, Lehabim, and
Naphtuhim: 12 Pathrusim also, and Casluhim, of whom came the Philistines,
and Caphtorim. 13 Also Canaan begat Sidon his firstborn, and Heth, 14 And
the Jebusite, and the Amorite, and the Girgashite, 15 And the Hivite, and the
Arkite, and the Sinite, 16 And the Arvadite, and the Zemarite, and the Hama-
thite. 17 [3]The sons of Shem were Elam and Asshur, and Arphaxad, and Lud,
and [h]Aram, and Uz, and Hul, and Gether, and Meshech. 18 Also Arphaxad be-
gat Shelah, and Shelah begat [i]Eber. 19 Unto Eber also were born two sons: the
name of the one was Peleg: for in his days was the earth divided, and his brother's
name was Joktan. 20 Then Joktan begat Almodad and Sheleph, and Hazarma-
veth and Jerah, 21 And Hadoram, and Uzal and Diklah, 22 And Ebal, and
Abimael, and Sheba, 23 And Ophir, and Havilah, and Jobab: all these were the
sons of Joktan. 24 [j]Shem, [k]Arphaxad, Shelah, 25 Eber, Peleg, Reu, 26 Se-
rug, Nahor, Terah, 27 [4]Abram, which is Abraham. 28 The sons of Abraham
were Isaac, and Ishmael. 29 These are their generations. [5]The eldest son of Ish-
mael was Nebajoth, and Kedar, and Adbeel, and Mibsam, 30 Mishma, and Du-
mah, Massa, [l]Hadad, and Tema, 31 Jetur, Naphish and Kedemah: these are the
sons of Ishmael. 32 And Keturah Abraham's [m]concubine bare sons, Zimran, and
Jokshan, and Medan, and Midian, and Ishbak, and Shuah: and the sons of Jok-
shan, Sheba, and Dedan. 33 And the sons of Midian were Ephah, and Epher,
and Hanoch and Abida, and Eldaah: [6]All these are the sons of Keturah. 34 And
[7]Abraham begat Isaac: the sons of Isaac, Esau and Israel. 35 The sons of Esau
were [n,8]Eliphaz, Reuel, and Jeush, and Jaalam, and Korah. 36 The sons of Eli-
phaz, Teman, and Omar, [o]Zephi, and Gatam, Kenaz, and [p]Timna, and Ama-
lek. 37 The sons of Reuel, Nahath, Zerah, Shammah and Mizzah. 38 And
the sons of [q]Seir, Lotan, and Shobal, and Zibeon, and Anah, and Dishon, and
Ezer, and Dishan. 39 And the sons of Lotan, Hori, and Homam, and Tim-
na Lotan's sister. 40 The sons of Shobal were Alian, and Manahath, and Ebal,
Shephi, and Onam. And the sons of Zibeon, Ajah and Anah. 41 The son of
Anah was Dishon. And the sons of Dishon, Hamran, and Eshban, and Ithran, and
Cheran. 42 The sons of Ezer were Bilhan, and Zaavan, and Jaakan. The sons of
Dishan were Uz, and Aran. 43 And these were the [r]Kings that reigned in the
land of Edom, before a King reigned over the children of Israel, to wit, Bela the
son of Beor, and the name of his city was Dinhabah. 44 Then Bela died, and
Jobab the son of Zerah of [s]Bozrah reigned in his stead. 45 And when Jobab was
dead, Husham of the land of the Temanites reigned in his stead. 46 And when
Husham was dead, Hadad the son of Bedad, which smote Midian in the field of
Moab, reigned in his stead, and the name of his city was Avith. 47 So Hadad
died, and Samlah of Masrekah reigned in his stead. 48 And Samlah died, and
Saul of Rehoboth by the river reigned in his stead. 49 And when Saul was dead,
Baal-Hanan the son of Achbor reigned in his stead. 50 And Baal-Hanan died,
and Hadad reigned in his stead, and the name of his city was [t]Pai, and his wi-
fe's name Mehetabel the daughter of Matred the daughter of Mezahab. 51 Ha-
dad died also, and there were dukes in Edom, duke Timnah, duke [u]Aliah, duke
Jetheth, 52 Duke Aholibamah, duke Elah, duke Pinon, 53 Duke Kenaz, duke
Teman, duke Mibzar, 54 Duke Magdiel, duke Iram: these were the dukes of
Edom.

2

3 The genealogy of Judah unto Jesse the father of David.

1 These are the sons of Israel, [1]Reuben, Simeon, Levi, and Judah,
Issachar, and Zebulun, 2 Dan, Joseph, and Benjamin, Naphtali, Gad, and
Asher. 3 [2]The sons of [a]Judah, Er, and Onan, and Shelah. These three were born
to him of the daughter of Shua the Canaanite: but Er the eldest son of Judah was
evil in the sight of the Lord, and he slew him. 4 [3]And Tamar his daughter-in-law
bare him Perez, and Zerah: so all the sons of Judah were five. 5 [4]The sons of Pe-
rez, Hezron, and Hamul. 6 The sons also of Zerah were [b]Zimri, and [c]Ethan, and
Heman, and Calcol, and Dara, which were five in all. 7 And the son of Carmi,
[d,5]Achar that troubled Israel, transgressing in the thing excommunicate. 8 The
son also of Ethan, Azariah. 9 And the sons of Hezron that were born unto him,
Jerahmeel, and [e]Ram and Chelubai. 10 And Ram begat Amminadab, and Am-
minadab begat Nahshon [f]prince of the children of Judah, 11 And Nahshon be-
gat Salma, and Salma begat Boaz, 12 And Boaz begat Obed, and Obed begat
[g]Ishai, 13 [6]And Jesse begat his eldest son Eliab, and Abinadab the second, and
[h]Shimea the third, 14 Nethanel the fourth, Raddai the fifth, 15 Ozem the
sixth, and David the seventh. 16 Whose sisters were Zeruiah and Abigail. And
the sons of Zeruiah, Abishai, and Joab, and Asahel. 17 And Abigail bare Ama-
sa: and the father of Amasa was Jether an Ishmaelite. 18 And [i]Caleb the son of
Hezron begat Jerioth of Azubah his wife, and her sons are these, Jesher, and Sho-
bab, and Ardon. 19 And when Azubah was dead, Caleb took unto him Ephrath,
which bare him Hur. 20 [7]And Hur begat Uri, and Uri begat Bezalel. 21 And
afterward came Hezron to the daughter of Machir the father of [j]Gilead, and took
her when he was threescore years old, and she bare him Segub. 22 And Segub
begat Jair, which had three and twenty cities in the land of Gilead. 23 And Ge-
shur with Aram took the towns of Jair [k]from them, and Kenath and the towns
thereof, even threescore cities. All these were the sons of Machir the father of
Gilead. 24 And after that Hezron was dead at [l]Caleb Ephrathah, then Abijah
Hezron's wife bare him also Ashhur the [m]father of Tekoa. 25 And the sons of
Jerahmeel the eldest son of Hezron were Ram the eldest, then Bunah, and Oren
and Ozem and Ahijah. 26 Also Jerahmeel had another wife named Atarah,
which was the mother of Onam. 27 And the sons of Ram the eldest son of

---

1-CHRON 1

- **a.** TITLE - Hebrew, words of days.
- **b.** TITLE - Or, things omitted, to wit, in the books of the kings.
- **c.** 1 Chron. 1:1 Meaning, that Seth was Adam's son, and Enosh Seth's son.
- **d.** 1 Chron. 1:4 It had been sufficient to have named Shem of whom came Abraham and David, but because the world was restored by these three, mention is also made of Ham and Japheth.
- **e.** 1 Chron. 1:6 Or, Riphath.
- **f.** 1 Chron. 1:7 Or, Rodanim.
- **g.** 1 Chron. 1:10 Who did first lift up himself above others.
- **h.** 1 Chron. 1:17 Of whom came the Syrians, and therefore they are called Aramites throughout all the Scripture.
- **i.** 1 Chron. 1:18 Of him came the Hebrews, which were afterward called Israelites of Israel, which was Jacob: and Jews of Judah because of the excellency of that tribe.
- **j.** 1 Chron. 1:24 He repeateth Shem again because he would come to the stock of Abraham.
- **k.** 1 Chron. 1:24 Who came of Shem, and of him Shelah.
- **l.** 1 Chron. 1:30 Or, Hadar.
- **m.** 1 Chron. 1:32 Read Gen. 25:4.
- **n.** 1 Chron. 1:35 These were born of three divers mothers, read Gen. 36:4.
- **o.** 1 Chron. 1:36 Or, Zepho.
- **p.** 1 Chron. 1:36 Which was Eliphaz's concubine, read Gen. 36:12.
- **q.** 1 Chron. 1:38 He is also called Seir the Horite, which inhabited mount Seir, Gen. 36:20.
- **r.** 1 Chron. 1:43 He maketh mention of the Kings that came of Esau according to God's promise made to Abraham concerning him, that kings should come of him. These eight kings reigned one after another in Idumea unto the time of David, who conquered their country.
- **s.** 1 Chron. 1:44 Which was the principal city of the Edomites.
- **t.** 1 Chron. 1:50 Or, Pau.
- **u.** 1 Chron. 1:51 Or, Aluah.

1-CHRON 1

1. Gen. 10:2
2. Gen. 10:8
3. Gen. 10:22 / Gen. 11:10
4. Gen. 11:20 / Gen. 17:6 / Gen. 21:2
5. Gen. 25:13
6. Gen. 25:4
7. Gen. 21:2
8. Gen. 36:9

1-CHRON 2

- **a.** 1 Chron. 2:3 Though Judah was not Jacob's eldest son, yet he first beginneth at him, because he would come to the genealogy of David, of whom came Christ.
- **b.** 1 Chron. 2:6 Or, Zabdi.
- **c.** 1 Chron. 2:6 Of these read 1 Kings 4:31.
- **d.** 1 Chron. 2:7 Or, Achan.
- **e.** 1 Chron. 2:9 Whom Saint Matthew calleth Aram, Matt. 1:3.
- **f.** 1 Chron. 2:10 That is, chief of the family.
- **g.** 1 Chron. 2:12 Or, Jesse.
- **h.** 1 Chron. 2:13 Or, Shammah.
- **i.** 1 Chron. 2:18 Who was called Chelubai the son of Hezron, verse 9.
- **j.** 1 Chron. 2:21 Who was prince of mount Gilead, read Num. 32:40.
- **k.** 1 Chron. 2:23 That is, the Geshurites and Syrians took the towns from Jair's children.
- **l.** 1 Chron. 2:24 Which was a town named of the husband and wife, called also Bethlehem Ephrathah.
- **m.** 1 Chron. 2:24 Meaning, the chief and prince.

Jerahmeel were Maaz, and Jamin and Eker. **28** And the sons of Onam were Shammai and Jada. And the sons of Shammai, Nadab and Abishur. **29** And the name of the wife of Abishur was called Abihail, and she bare him Ahban and Molid. **30** The sons also of Nadab were Seled and Appaim: but Seled died without children. **31** And the son of Appaim was Ishi, and the son of Ishi, Sheshan, and the son of Sheshan, [n]Ahlai. **32** And the sons of Jada the brother of Shammai were Jether and Jonathan: but Jether died without children. **33** And the sons of Jonathan were Peleth and Zaza. These were the sons of Jerahmeel. **34** And Sheshan had no sons, but daughters. And Sheshan had a servant that was an Egyptian named Jarha. **35** And Sheshan gave his daughter to Jarha his servant to wife, and she bare him Attai. **36** And Attai begat Nathan, and Nathan begat Zabad, **37** And Zabad begat Ephlal, and Ephlal begat Obed, **38** And Obed begat Jehu, and Jehu begat Azariah, **39** And Azariah begat Helez, and Helez begat Eleasah, **40** And Eleasah begat Sismai, and Sismai begat Shallum, **41** And Shallum begat Jekamiah, and Jekamiah begat Elishama. **42** Also the sons of Caleb the brother of Jerahmeel, were Mesha his eldest son, which was the [o]father of Ziph: and the sons of Mareshah the father of Hebron. **43** And the sons of Hebron were Korah and Tappuah, and Rekem and Shema. **44** And Shema begat Raham the father of Jorkoam: and Rekem begat Shammai. **45** The son also of Shammai was Maon: and Maon was the father of Beth Zur. **46** And Ephah a [p]concubine of Caleb bare Haran and Moza, and Gazez: Haran also begat Gazez. **47** The sons of Jahdai were Regem, and Jotham, and Geshan, and Pelet, and Ephah, and Shaaph. **48** Caleb's concubine Maachah bare Sheber and Tirhanah. **49** She bare also Shaaph the father of Madmannah, and Sheva the father of Machbenah, and the father of Gibea. [8]And Achsah was Caleb's daughter. **50** These were the sons of Caleb the son of Hur the eldest son of Ephrathah, Shobal the father of Kirjath Jearim. **51** Salma the father of Bethlehem, and Hareph the father of Beth Gader. **52** And Shobal the father of Kirjath Jearim had sons, and he [q]was the overseer of half Manuhoth. **53** And the families of Kirjath Jearim were the Ithrites, and the Puthites, and the Shumathites, and the Mishraites: of them came the Zorathites, and the Eshtaolites. **54** The sons of Salma of Bethlehem, and the Netophathites, the [r]crowns of the house of Joab, and [s]half the Manahethites and the Zorites. **55** And the families of the [t]Scribes dwelling at Jabez, the Tirathites, the Shimeathites, the Suchathites, which are the [u]Kenites, that came of Hammath the father of the house of Rechab.

3

1 The genealogy of David, and his posterity unto the sons of Josiah.

1 These also were the sons of [a]David, which were born unto him in Hebron: the eldest Amnon of Ahinoam, the Jezreelitess: the second [b]Daniel of Abigail the Carmelitess: **2** The third Absalom the son of Maacah daughter of Talmai King of Geshur: the fourth Adonijah the son of Haggith: **3** The fifth Shephatiah of Abital, the sixth Ithream by Eglah his wife. **4** These six were born unto him in Hebron: and there he reigned seven years and six months: and in Jerusalem he reigned three and thirty years. **5** And these four were born unto him in Jerusalem, Shimea, and Shobab, and Nathan, and Solomon of [c]Bathshua the daughter of Ammiel: **6** Ibhar also, and [d]Elishama, and Eliphelet, **7** And Nogah, and Nepheg, and Japhia, **8** And Elishama, and Eliada, and Eliphelet, nine in number. **9** These are all the sons of David, besides the sons of the concubines, and Tamar their sister. **10** And Solomon's son was Rehoboam, whose son was Abijah, and Asa his son, and Jehoshaphat his son, **11** And Joram his son, and Ahaziah his son, and Joash his son, **12** And Amaziah his son, and Azariah his son, and Jotham his son, **13** And Ahaz his son, and Hezekiah his son, and Manasseh his son, **14** And Amon his son, and Josiah his son. **15** And of the sons of Josiah, the [e]eldest was [f]Johanan, the second Jehoiakim, the third Zedekiah, and the fourth Shallum. **16** And the sons of Jehoiakim were Jeconiah his son, and Zedekiah his son. **17** And the sons of Jeconiah, Assir and Shealtiel his son: **18** Malchiram also and Pedaiah, and Shenazzar, Jecamiah, Hoshama, and Nedabiah. **19** And the sons of Pedaiah were [g]Zerubbabel, and Shimei: and the sons of Zerubbabel were Meshullam, and Hananiah, and Shelomith their sister, **20** And Hashubah, and Ohel, and Berechiah, and Hasadiah, and Jushab-Hesed, five in number. **21** And the sons of Hananiah were Pelatiah, and Jeshaiah, the sons of Rephaiah, the sons of Arnan, the sons of Obadiah, the sons of Shechaniah. **22** And the son of Shechaniah was Shemaiah: and the sons of Shemaiah were Hattush and Igal, and Bariah, and Neariah, and Shaphat, [h]six. **23** And the sons of Neariah were Elioenai, and Hezekiah, and Azrikam, three. **24** And the sons of Elioenai were Hodaviah, and Eliashib, and Pelaiah, and Akkub, and Johanan, and Delaiah, and Anani, seven.

4

1 The genealogy of the sons of Judah. 5 Of Asher, 9 Of Jabez and his prayer, 11 Of Chelub, 24 And Simeon: their habitations. 38 And conquests.

1 The [a]sons of Judah were [1]Perez, Hezron, and Carmi, and Hur, and Shobal. **2** And Reaiah the son of Shobal begat Jahath, and Jahath begat Ahumai, and Lahad: these are the families of the Zorathites. **3** And these were of the father of Etam, Jezreel, and Ishma and Idbash: and the name of their sister was Hazelelponi. **4** And Penuel was the father of Gedor, and Ezer the father of Hushah: these are the sons of Hur the [b]eldest son of Ephrathah, the father of Bethlehem. **5** But Ashhur the father of Tekoa had two wives, Helah, and Naarah. **6** And Naarah bare him Ahuzzam, and Hepher, and Temeni and Haahashtari: these were the sons of Naarah. **7** And the sons of Helah were Zereth, Zohar and Ethnan. **8** Also Koz begat Anub, and Zobebah, and the families of Aharhel the son of Harum. **9** But Jabez was more honorable than his brethren: and his mother called his name [c]Jabez, saying, Because I bare him in sorrow. **10** And Jabez called on the God of Israel, saying, If thou wilt bless me in deed, and enlarge my coasts, and [d]if thine hand be with me, and thou wilt cause me to be delivered from evil, that I be not hurt. And God granted the thing that he asked. **11** And Chelub the brother of Shuhah begat Mehir, which was the father of Eshton. **12** And Eshton begat Beth-Rapha, and Paseah, and Tehinnah the father of the city of Ir-Nahash: these are the men of Rechah. **13** And the sons of Kenaz were Othniel, and Seraiah, and the son of Othniel, Hathath. **14** And Meonothai begat Ophrah. And Seraiah begat Joab the [e]father of the valley of craftsmen: for they were craftsmen. **15** And the sons of Caleb the son of [f]Jephunneh were Iru, Elah, and Naam. And the son of Elah was Kenaz. **16** And the sons of Jehallelel were Ziph, and Ziphah, Tiria, and Asarel. **17** And the sons of Ezrah were Jether and Mered, and Epher, and Jalon, and he begat Miriam, and Shammai, and Ishbah the father of Eshtemoa. **18** Also his [g]wife Jehudijah bare Jered the father of Gedor, and Heber the father of Sochoh, and Jekuthiel the father of Zanoah: and these are the sons of Bithiah the daughter of Pharaoh [h]which Mered took. **19** And the sons of the wife of Hodiah, the sister of Naham the father of Keilah were the Garmites, and Eshtemoa the Maachathite. **20** And the sons of Shimon were Amnon and Rinnah, Ben-Hanan and Tilon. And the sons of Ishi were Zoheth, and Ben-Zoheth. **21** [2]The sons of Shelah, the son of Judah were Er the father of Lecah, and Laadah the father of Mareshah, and the families of the households of them that wrought fine linen in the house of Ashbea. **22** And Jokim, and the men of Chozeba and Joash, and Saraph, which had the dominion in Moab, and [i]Jashubi-Lehem. These also are ancient things. **23** These were porters, and dwelt among plants and hedges: [j]there they dwelt with the king for his work. **24** [3]The sons of Simeon were Nemuel, and Jamin, Jarib, Zerah, and [k]Shaul. **25** Whose son was Shallum, and his son Mibsam, and his son Mishma. **26** And the sons of Mishma, Hamuel was his son, Zacchur his son, and Shimei his son. **27** And Shimei had sixteen sons, and six daughters, but his brethren had not many children, neither was all their family like to the children of Judah in multitude. **28** And they dwelt at [l]Beersheba, and at Moladah, and at Hazar Shual, **29** And at Bilhah, and at Ezem, and at Tolad, **30** And at Bethuel, and at Hormah, and at Ziklag, **31** And at Beth Marcaboth, and at Hazar Susim, at Beth Biri, and at Shaaraim: these were their cities unto the reign of [m]David. **32** And their towns were Etam, and Ain, Rimmon, and Tochen, and Ashan, five cities. **33** And all their towns that were round about these cities unto Baal, these are their habitations and the declaration of their genealogy, **34** And Meshobab, and Jamlech,

---

n. 1 Chron. 2:31 Who died while his father was alive, and therefore it is said, verse 34, that Sheshan had no sons.
o. 1 Chron. 2:42 That is, the chief governor or prince of the Ziphims, because the prince ought to have a fatherly care and affection toward his people.
p. 1 Chron. 2:46 This difference was between the wife and the concubine, that the wife was taken with certain solemnities of marriage, and her children did inherit: the concubine had no solemnities in marriage, neither did her children inherit, but had a portion of goods or money given them.
q. 1 Chron. 2:52 Or, he that saw the half, because the prince ought to oversee his subjects.
r. 1 Chron. 2:54 Meaning, the chief and principle.
s. 1 Chron. 2:54 Or, the Zorites, the half of the Manahethites.
t. 1 Chron. 2:55 Which were men learned and expert in the law.
u. 1 Chron. 2:55 Read Num. 10:29; Judg. 1:16.

1-CHRON 2

1. Gen. 29:32 / Gen. 30:5 / Gen. 35:28
2. Gen. 38:3 / Gen. 46:12 / 1 Chron. 4:1
3. Gen. 38:29 / Matt. 1:3
4. Ruth 4:18
5. Josh. 7:1
6. 1 Sam. 16:19 / 1 Sam. 17:12
7. Exod. 31:2
8. Josh. 15:17

1-CHRON 3

a. 1 Chron. 3:1 He returneth to the genealogy of David, to show that Christ came of his stock.
b. 1 Chron. 3:1 Which 2 Sam. 3:3, is called Chileab, born of her that was Nabal's wife the Carmelite.
c. 1 Chron. 3:5 Called also Bathsheba the daughter of Eliam: for they gave them divers names.
d. 1 Chron. 3:6 Elishama, or Elishua, 2 Sam. 5:15, and Eliphelet died, and David named those sons, which were next born, by the same names: in the book of Kings his children are mentioned which were alive, and here both they that were alive and dead.
e. 1 Chron. 3:15 So called because he was preferred to the dignity royal before his brother Jehoiakim which was the elder.
f. 1 Chron. 3:15 Or, Jehoahaz, 2 Kings 23:30.
g. 1 Chron. 3:19 St. Matthew saith that Zerubbabel was son of Shealtiel, meaning, that he was his nephew according to the Hebrew speech: for he was Pedaiah's son.
h. 1 Chron. 3:22 So that Shemaiah was Shechaniah's natural son, and the other five his nephews, and in all were six.

1-CHRON 4

a. 1 Chron. 4:1 Meaning, they came of Judah, as nephews and kinsmen: for only Perez was his natural son.
b. 1 Chron. 4:4 The firstborn of his mother, and not the eldest son of his father.
c. 1 Chron. 4:9 Otherwise called Othniel, Judg. 1:13.
d. 1 Chron. 4:10 It is to be understood, that then he would accomplish his vow which he made.
e. 1 Chron. 4:14 The Lord of that valley where the artificers did work.
f. 1 Chron. 4:15 Called also Esron.
g. 1 Chron. 4:18 Or, she bare, meaning, the second wife of Ezra.
h. 1 Chron. 4:18 Or, of whom he had Mered.
i. 1 Chron. 4:22 Or, of the inhabitants of Lehem.
j. 1 Chron. 4:23 They were king David's gardeners, and served him in his works.
k. 1 Chron. 4:24 His son Ohad is here omitted.
l. 1 Chron. 4:28 These cities belonged of Judah, Josh. 19:2, and were given to the tribe of Simeon.
m. 1 Chron. 4:31 Then David restored them to the tribe of Judah.

and Joshah the son of Amaziah, **35** And Joel and Jehu the son of Joshibiah, the
son of Seraiah, the son of Asiel, **36** And Elioenai, and Jaakobah, and Jeshoha-
iah, and Asaiah, and Adiel, and Jesimiel, and Benaiah, **37** And Ziza the son of
Shiphi, the son of Allon, the son of Jedaiah, the son of Shimri, the son of Shema-
iah. **38** These were famous Princes in their families, and increased greatly their
father's houses. **39** And they [n]went to the entering in of Gedor, even unto the
East side of the valley, to seek pasture for their sheep. **40** And they found fat pa-
sture and good, and a wide land both quiet and fruitful: for they of Ham had dwelt
there before. **41** And these described by name, came in the days of Hezekiah
king of Judah, and smote their tents, and the inhabitants that were found there,
and destroyed them utterly unto this day, and dwelt in their room, because there
was pasture there for their sheep. **42** And besides these, five hundred men of the
sons of Simeon went to mount Seir, and Pelatiah, and Neariah, and Rephaiah, and
Uzziel the sons of Ishi were their captains. **43** And they smote the rest of Amalek
that had [o]escaped, and they dwelt there unto this day.

5

1 The birthright taken from Reuben and given to the sons of Joseph. 3 The genealogy of Reuben, 11 and Gad, 23 and of the half tribe of Manasseh.

1 The sons also of Reuben the eldest son of Israel (for he was the eldest, [1]but
had defiled his father's bed, therefore his birthright was given unto the [a]sons of
Joseph the son of Israel, so that the genealogy is not reckoned after his birthri-
ght. **2** For Judah prevailed above his brethren, and of him came [b]the prince,
but the birthright was Joseph's) **3** [2]The sons of Reuben the eldest son of Isra-
el, were Hanoch and Pallu, Hezron and Carmi. **4** The sons of Joel, Shemaiah
his son, Gog his son, and Shimei his son, **5** Micah his son, Reaiah his son, and
Baal his son, **6** Beerah his son: whom Tiglath-Pileser king of Assyria [c]carried
away, he was a prince of the Reubenites. **7** And when his brethren in their fa-
milies reckoned the genealogy of their generations, Jeiel and Zechariah were the
chief, **8** And Bela the son of Azaz, the son of Shema, the son of Joel, which dwelt
in [d]Aroer even unto Nebo and Baal Meon. **9** Also Eastward he inhabited unto
the entering in of the wilderness from the river [e]Perath: for they had much cattle
in the land of Gilead. **10** And in the days of Saul they warred with the [f]Hagri-
tes, which fell by their hands: and they dwelt in their tents in all the East parts
of Gilead. **11** And the children of Gad dwelt over against them in the land of
Bashan, unto Salcah. **12** Joel was the chiefest, and Shapham the second, but Ja-
anai and Shaphat were in Bashan. **13** And their brethren of the house of their
fathers were Michael, and Meshullam, and Sheba, and Jorai, and Jachan, and Zia
and Eber, seven. **14** These are the children of Abihail, the son of Huri, the son
of Jaroah, the son of Gilead, the son of Michael, the son of Jeshishai, the son of
Jahdo, the son of Buz. **15** Ahi the son of Abdiel, the son of Guni was chief of
the household of their fathers. **16** And they dwelt in Gilead in [g]Bashan, and
in the towns thereof, and in all the suburbs of Sharon by their borders. **17** All
these were reckoned by genealogies in the days of Jotham King of Judah, and in
the days of Jeroboam king of Israel. **18** The sons of Reuben and of Gad, and of
half the tribe of Manasseh of those that were valiant men, able to bear shield and
sword, and to draw a bow exercised in war, were four and forty thousand, seven
hundred and threescore, that went out to the war. **19** And they made war with
the Hagrites, with [h]Jetur, and Naphish, and Nodab. **20** And they were [i]helped
against them, and the Hagrites were delivered into their hand, and all that were
with them: for they cried to God in the battle, and he heard them, because they
trusted in him. **21** And they led away their cattle, even their camels fifty thou-
sand, and two hundred and fifty thousand sheep, and two thousand asses, and of
[j]persons an hundred thousand. **22** For many fell down wounded, because the
war was of God. And they dwelt in their steads until the [k]captivity. **23** And the
children of the half tribe of Manasseh dwelt in the land, from Bashan unto [l]Baal
Hermon, and Senir, and unto mount Hermon: for they increased. **24** And these
were the heads of the households of their fathers, even Epher and Ishi, and Eliel
and Azriel, and Jeremiah, and Hodaviah, and Jahdiel, strong men, valiant and fa-
mous, heads of the households of their fathers. **25** But they transgressed against
the God of their fathers, and went a whoring after the gods of the people of the
land, whom God had destroyed before them. **26** And the God of Israel [m]stirred
up the spirit of Pul king of Assyria, and the spirit of Tiglath-Pileser king of Assyria,
and he carried them away: even the Reubenites, and the Gadites, and the half tri-
be of Manasseh, and brought them unto [3]Halah and Habor, and Hara, and to the
river Gozan, unto this day.

6

1 The genealogy of the sons of Levi. 31 Their order in the ministry of the Tabernacle. 49 Aaron and his sons Priests. 54, 57 Their inhabitations.

1 The sons of Levi were Gershon, Kohath, and Merari. **2** [1]And the sons
of Kohath, Amram, Izhar, and Hebron, and Uzziel. **3** And the children of
Amram, Aaron, and Moses and Miriam. And the sons of Aaron, [2]Nadab, and
Abihu, and [3]Eleazar, and Ithamar. **4** Eleazar begat Phinehas, Phinehas begat
Abishua, **5** And Abishua begat Bukki, and Bukki begat Uzzi, **6** And Uzzi be-
gat Zerahiah, and Zerahiah begat Meraioth. **7** Meraioth begat Amariah, and
Amariah begat Ahitub, **8** And Ahitub begat [a]Zadok, and Zadok begat Ahima-
az, **9** And Ahimaaz begat Azariah, and Azariah begat Johanan, **10** And Joha-
nan begat Azariah (it was he that was [b]Priest in the house that Solomon built in Je-
rusalem.) **11** And Azariah begat Amariah, and Amariah begat Ahitub, **12** And
Ahitub begat Zadok, and Zadok begat Shallum, **13** And Shallum begat Hilkiah,
and Hilkiah begat Azariah, **14** And Azariah begat Seraiah, and Seraiah begat
Jehozadak, **15** And [c]Jehozadak departed when the Lord carried away into capti-
vity Judah and Jerusalem by the hand of Nebuchadnezzar. **16** The sons of Levi
were Gershon, Kohath and Merari. **17** And these be the names of the sons of
Gershon, Libni, and Shimei. **18** And the sons of Kohath were Amram, and Izhar,
and Hebron and Uzziel. **19** The sons of Merari, Mahli and Mushi: and these are
the families of Levi concerning their fathers. **20** Of Gershon, Libni his son, Jaha-
th his son, Zimmah his son, **21** Joah his son, Iddo his son, Zerah his son, Jeathe-
rai his son. **22** The sons of Kohath, [d]Amminadab his son, [4]Korah his son, Assir
his son, **23** Elkanah his son, and Ebiasaph his son, and Assir his son, **24** Taha-
th his son, Uriel his son, Uzziah his son, and Shaul his son, **25** And the sons
of Elkanah, Amasai, and Ahimoth. **26** Elkanah, the sons of Elkanah, Zophai
his son, and Nahath his son, **27** Eliab his son, Jeroham his son, Elkanah his
son, **28** And the sons of Samuel, the eldest [e]Vasheni, then Abijah. **29** The sons
of Merari were Mahli, Libni his son, Shimei his son, Uzzah his son, **30** Shimea
his son, Haggiah his son, Asaiah his son. **31** And these be they whom David set
for to sing in the house of the Lord, after that the Ark had [f]rest. **32** And they
ministered before the Tabernacle, even the Tabernacle of the Congregation with
[g]singing, until Solomon had built the house of the Lord in Jerusalem: then they
continued in their office, according to their custom. **33** And these ministered
with their children: of the sons of Kohath, Heman a singer, the son of Joel, the son
of Samuel, **34** The son of Elkanah, the son of Jeroham, the son of Eliel, the son
of Toah, **35** The son of Zuph, the son of Elkanah, the son of Mahath, the son
of Amasai, **36** The son of Elkanah, the son of Joel, the son of Azariah, the son
of Zephaniah, **37** The son of Tahath, the [h]son of Assir, the son of Ebiasaph, the
son of Korah, **38** The son of Izhar, the son of Kohath, the son of Levi, the son
of Israel, **39** And his [i]brother [j]Asaph stood on his right hand: and Asaph was
the son of Berachiah, the son of Shimea, **40** The son of Michael, the son of Ba-
aseiah, the son of Malchijah, **41** The son of Ethni, the son of Zerah, the son of
Adaiah, **42** The son of Ethan, the son of Zimmah, the son of Shimei, **43** The
son of Jahath, the son of Gershon, the son of Levi. **44** And their brethren the
sons of Merari were on the left hand, even Ethan the son of Kishi, the son of Abdi,
the son of Malluch, **45** The son of Hashabiah, the son of Amaziah, the son of
Hilkiah, **46** The son of Amzi, the son of Bani, the son of Shamer, **47** The son
of Mahli, the son of Mushi, the son of Merari, the son of Levi. **48** And their
[k]brethren the Levites were [l]appointed unto all the service of the Tabernacle of the
house of God, **49** But Aaron and his sons burnt incense upon the altar of burnt
offering, and on the altar of incense, for all that was to do in the most holy pla-
ce, and to make an atonement for Israel according to all that Moses the servant
of God had commanded. **50** These are also the sons of Aaron, Eleazar his son,
Phinehas his son, Abishua his son, **51** Bukki his son, Uzzi his son, Zerahiah his

---

n. 1 Chron. 4:39 For the tribe of Simeon was so great in number, that in the time of Hezekiah they sought new dwellings unto Gedor, which is in the tribe of Dan.
o. 1 Chron. 4:43 And were not slain by Saul and David.

1-CHRON 4

1. Gen. 38:29 / Gen. 46:12 / 1 Chron. 2:4
2. Gen. 38:1,3,8
3. Gen. 46:10 / Exod. 6:15

1-CHRON 5

a. 1 Chron. 5:1 Because they were made two tribes, they had a double portion.
b. 1 Chron. 5:2 That is, he was the chiefest of all the tribes according to Jacob's prophecy, Gen. 49:8, and because Christ should come of him.
c. 1 Chron. 5:6 To wit, in the time of Uzziah King of Israel, 2 Kings 15:23.
d. 1 Chron. 5:8 These places were beyond Jordan toward the East in the land given to the Reubenites.
e. 1 Chron. 5:9 Or, Euphrates.
f. 1 Chron. 5:10 The Ishmaelites that came of Hagar Abraham's concubine.
g. 1 Chron. 5:16 Both the whole country and one peculiar city were called Bashan.
h. 1 Chron. 5:19 These twain were the sons of Ishmael, Gen. 25:15.
i. 1 Chron. 5:20 To wit, by the Lord that gave them the victory.
j. 1 Chron. 5:21 Hebrew, souls of men.
k. 1 Chron. 5:22 Meaning, the captivity of the ten tribes under Tiglath Pileser.
l. 1 Chron. 5:23 Otherwise called Baal Gad.
m. 1 Chron. 5:26 Thus God stirred up the wicked, and used them as instruments to execute his just judgment against sinners, although they were led with malice and ambition.

1-CHRON 5

1. Gen. 35:22 / Gen. 49:4
2. Gen. 46:9 / Exod. 6:14 / Num. 26:5
3. 2 Kings 18:11

1-CHRON 6

a. 1 Chron. 6:8 Which was high priest after that Abiathar was deposed, according to the prophecy of Eli the Priest, 1 Sam. 2:31, 35.
b. 1 Chron. 6:10 And did valiantly resist king Uzziah, who would have usurped the Priest's office, 2 Chron. 26:17, 18.
c. 1 Chron. 6:15 That is, he was led into captivity with his father Seraiah the high Priest, 2 Kings 25:18.
d. 1 Chron. 6:22 Who seemeth to be called Izhar, Exod. 6:21.
e. 1 Chron. 6:28 Who is also called Joel, 1 Sam. 8:2 and 1 Chron. 6:33.
f. 1 Chron. 6:31 After it was brought to that place where the Temple should be built and was no more carried to and fro.
g. 1 Chron. 6:32 Read Exod. 27:21.
h. 1 Chron. 6:37 Or, nephews.
i. 1 Chron. 6:39 Or, cousin.
j. 1 Chron. 6:39 Meaning, the cousin of Heman, verse 33.
k. 1 Chron. 6:48 The Levites are called the singers brethen because they came of the same stock.
l. 1 Chron. 6:48 Read Num. 4:4.

son, 52 Meraioth his son, Amariah his son, Ahitub his son, 53 Zadok his son, and Ahimaaz his son. 54 And these are the [m]dwelling places of them throughout their towns and coasts, even of the sons of Aaron for the family of the Kohathites, for the [n]lot was theirs. 55 So they gave them [o]Hebron in the land of Judah and the suburbs thereof round about it. 56 But the field of the city, and the villages thereof they gave to Caleb the son of Jephunneh. 57 And to the sons of Aaron they gave the cities of Judah for [p]refuge, even Hebron and Libnah with their suburbs, and Jattir, and Eshtemoa with their suburbs, 58 And [q]Hilen with her suburbs, and Debir with her suburbs, 59 And Ashan and her suburbs, and Beth Shemesh and her suburbs: 60 And of the tribe of Benjamin, Geba and her suburbs, and [r]Alemeth with her suburbs, and Anathoth with her suburbs: all their cities were thirteen cities by their families. 61 And unto the sons of [s]Kohath the remnant of the family of the tribe, even of the half tribe of the half of Manasseh, by lot ten cities. 62 And to the sons of Gershon according to their families out of the tribe of Issachar, and out of the tribe of Asher, and out of the tribe of Naphtali, and out of the tribe of Manasseh in Bashan, thirteen cities. 63 Unto the sons of Merari according to their families out of the tribe of Reuben, and out of the tribe of Gad, and out of the tribe of Zebulun, by lot twelve cities. 64 Thus the children of Israel gave to the Levites cities with their suburbs. 65 And they gave by lot out of the tribe of the children of Judah, and out of the tribe of the children of Simeon, and out of the tribe of the children of Benjamin, these cities, which they called by their names. 66 And they of the families of the sons of Kohath, had cities and their coasts out of the tribe of Ephraim. 67 [5]And they gave unto them cities of refuge, Shechem in mount Ephraim, and her suburbs, and Gezer and her suburbs, 68 Jokmeam also and her suburbs, and Beth Horon with her suburbs, 69 And Aijalon and her suburbs, and Gath Rimmon and her suburbs. 70 And out of the half tribe of Manasseh, [t]Aner and her suburbs, and [u]Bileam and her suburbs, for the families of the remnant of the sons of Kohath. 71 Unto the sons of [v]Gershon out of the family of the half tribe of Manasseh, Golan in Bashan, and her suburbs, and [w]Ashtaroth with her suburbs. 72 And out of the tribe of Issachar, [x]Kedesh and her suburbs, Daberath and her suburbs, 73 [y]Ramoth also and her suburbs, and [z]Anem with her suburbs. 74 And out of the tribe of Asher, Mashal and her suburbs, and Abdon and her suburbs, 75 And [aa]Hukok and her suburbs, and Rehob and her suburbs, 76 And out of the tribe of Naphtali, Kedesh in Galilee and her suburbs, and [ab]Hammon and her suburbs, and [ac]Kirjathaim and her suburbs. 77 Unto the rest of the children of Merari were given out of the tribe of Zebulun [ad]Rimmon and her suburbs, [ae]Tabor and her suburbs, 78 And on the other side Jordan by Jericho, even on the Eastside of Jordan, out of the tribe of Reuben, [6]Bezer in the wilderness with her suburbs, and Jahzah with her suburbs, 79 And Kedemoth with her suburbs, and Mephaath with her suburbs. 80 And out of the tribe of Gad Ramoth in Gilead with her suburbs, and Mahanaim with her suburbs, 81 And Heshbon with her suburbs, and Jazer with her suburbs.

7

1 The genealogy of Issachar, Benjamin, 13 Naph-tali, 14 Manasseh, 20 Ephraim, 30 and Asher.

1 And the sons of Issachar were Tola and [a]Puah, [b]Jashub, and Shimron, four, 2 And the sons of Tola, Uzzi, and Rephaiah and Jeriel, and Jahmai, and Jibsam, and Shemuel, heads in the households of their fathers. Of Tola were valiant men of war in their generations, [c]whose number was in the days of David two and twenty thousand, and six hundred. 3 And the son of Uzzi was Izrahiah, and the sons of Izrahiah, Michael, and Obadiah, and Joel, and Ishiah, [d]five men all princes. 4 And with them in their generations after the household of their fathers were bands of men of war for battle six and thirty thousand: for they had many wives and children. 5 And their [e]brethren among all the families of Issachar were valiant men of war, reckoned in all by their genealogies fourscore and seven thousand. 6 The sons of Benjamin were Bela, and Becher, and [f]Jediael, [g]three. 7 And the sons of Bela, Ezbon, and Uzzi, and Uzziel, and Jerimoth, and Iri five heads of the households of their fathers, valiant men of war, and were reckoned by their genealogies, two and twenty thousand and thirty and four. 8 And the sons of Becher, Zemirah, and Joash, and Eliezer, and Elioenai, and Omri, and Jerimoth, and Abijah, and Anathoth, and Alemeth: all these were the sons of Becher. 9 And they were numbered by their genealogies according to their generations, and the chief of the houses of their fathers, valiant men of war, twenty thousand and two hundred. 10 And the son of Jediael was Bilhan, and the sons of Bilhan, Jeush, and Benjamin, and Ehud, and Chenaanah, and Zethan, and Tharshish, and Ahishahar. 11 All these were the sons of Jediael, chief of the fathers, valiant men of war seventeen thousand and two hundred, marching in battle array to the war. 12 And Shuppim, and Huppim were the sons of [h]Ir, but Hushim was the son [i]of [j]another. 13 The sons of Naphtali, Jahziel, and Guni, and Jezer, and [k]Shallum [l]of the sons of Bilhah. 14 The son of Manasseh was Asriel whom she bare unto him, but his concubine of Aram bare Machir the [1]father of Gilead. 15 And Machir took to wife the sister of Huppim and Shuppim, and the name of their sister was Maachah. And the name of the second son was Zelophehad, and Zelophehad had had daughters. 16 And Maachah the wife of Machir bare a son, and called his name [m]Peresh, and the name of his brother was Sheresh: and his sons were Ulam and Rakem. 17 And the son of Ulam was Bedan. These were the sons of Gilead the son of Machir, the son of Manasseh. 18 And [n]his sister Hammoleketh bare Ishhod, and Abiezer, and Mahlah. 19 And the sons of Shemida were Ahian, and Shechem, and Likhi, and Aniam. 20 The sons also of Ephraim were Shuthelah, and Bered his son, and Tahath his son, and his son Eladah, and Tahath his son, 21 And Zabad his son, and Shuthelah his son, and Ezer, and Elead: and the men of [o]Gath that were born in the land, slew them, because they came down to take away their cattle. 22 Therefore Ephraim their father mourned many days, and his [p]brethren came to comfort him. 23 And when he went in to his wife, she conceived, and bare him a son, and he called his name Beriah, because affliction was in his house. 24 And his [q]daughter was Sheerah, which built Beth Horon the nether, and the upper, and Uzzen Sheerah. 25 And Rephah was his [r]son, and Resheph, and Telah his son, and Tahan his son, 26 Laadan his son, Ammihud his son, Elishama his son, 27 Nun his son, Joshua his son. 28 And their possessions and their habitations were Bethel, and the villages thereof, and Eastward Naaran, and Westward Gezer with the villages thereof, Shechem also and the villages thereof, unto [s]Ayyah, and the villages thereof, 29 And by the places of the children of Manasseh, Beth Shean and her villages, Taanach and her villages, Megiddo and her villages, Dor and her villages. In those dwelt the children of Joseph the son of Israel. 30 [2]The sons of Asher were Imnah, and Ishvah, and Ishvi, and Beriah, and Serah their sister. 31 And the sons of Beriah, Heber, and Malchiel, which is the father of Birzaith. 32 And Heber begat Japhlet, and Shomer, and Hotham, and Shua their sister. 33 And the sons of Japhlet were Pasach, and [t]Bimhal, and Ashvath: these were the children of Japhlet. 34 And the sons of Shemer, Ahi, and Rohgah, Jehubbah, and Aram. 35 And the sons of his brother Helem were Zophah and Imna, and Shelesh, and Amal. 36 The sons of Zophah, Suah, and Harnepher, and Shual, and Beri, and Imrah, 37 Bezer and Hod, and Shamma, and Shilshah, and Jithran, and Beera. 38 And the sons of Jether, Jephunneh, and Pispah and Ara. 39 And the sons of Ulla, Arah, and Haniel, and Rizia. 40 All these were the children of Asher, the heads of their father's houses, noble men, valiant men of war and chief princes, and they were reckoned by their genealogies for war and for battle to the number of six and twenty thousand men.

8

1 The sons of Benjamin. 33 And race of Saul.

1 Benjamin also [a]begat Bela his eldest son, Ashbel the second, and Aharah the third, 2 Nohah the fourth, and Rapha the fifth. 3 And the sons of Bela were Addar, and Gera, and Abihud, 4 And Abishua, and Naaman, and Ahoah, 5 And Gera, and Shephuphan, and Huram. 6 And these are the sons of Ehud: these were the chief fathers of those that inhabited Geba: and [b]they were carried away captives to Manahath, 7 And Naaman, and Ahijah, and Gera, he carried them away captives: and [c]he begat Uzza, and Ahihud. 8 And Shaharaim

---

m. 1 Chron. 6:54 Or, cities which were given to the Levites.
n. 1 Chron. 6:54 They were first appointed, and prepared for.
o. 1 Chron. 6:55 Which was also called Kirjath Arba, Gen. 23:2; Josh. 21:11.
p. 1 Chron. 6:57 That he that had killed a man might flee thereunto for succor till his cause were tried, Deut. 19:2.
q. 1 Chron. 6:58 Which Joshua calleth Holon, Josh. 15:51 and 21:15.
r. 1 Chron. 6:60 Or, Almon, Josh. 21:18.
s. 1 Chron. 6:61 That is, they gave a portion to the Kohathites, which were the remnant of the tribe of Levi, out of the half tribe of Manasseh and out of Ephraim, verse 66.
t. 1 Chron. 6:70 Or, Tanach, Josh. 21:25.
u. 1 Chron. 6:70 Or, Gath Rimmon.
v. 1 Chron. 6:71 Who in the first verse is called also Gershon.
w. 1 Chron. 6:71 Or, Be Eshterah, Josh. 21:27.
x. 1 Chron. 6:72 Or, Kishion, Josh. 21:28.
y. 1 Chron. 6:73 Or, Jarmuth, Josh. 21:29.
z. 1 Chron. 6:73 Or, En Gannim, Josh. 21:29.
aa. 1 Chron. 6:75 Or, Helkath, Josh. 21:31.
ab. 1 Chron. 6:76 Or, Hammoth Dor, Josh. 21:32.
ac. 1 Chron. 6:76 Or, Kartan, Josh. 21:32.
ad. 1 Chron. 6:77 Or, Jokneam.
ae. 1 Chron. 6:77 Or, Kartah, Josh. 21:34.

1-CHRON 6
1. Gen. 46:11 / Exod. 6:16 / 1 Chron. 23:12
2. Lev. 10:1
3. Num. 20:29
4. Num. 16:1
5. Josh 21:21
6. Josh. 20:8 / Josh. 21:36

1-CHRON 7
a. 1 Chron. 7:1 Or, Punah.
b. 1 Chron. 7:1 Who also is called Job, Gen. 46:13.
c. 1 Chron. 7:2 That is, their number was found thus great when David numbered the people, 2 Sam. 24:1.
d. 1 Chron. 7:3 Meaning, the four sons, and the father.
e. 1 Chron. 7:5 Or, kinsmen.
f. 1 Chron. 7:6 Called also Ashbel, Gen. 46:21; Num. 26:38.
g. 1 Chron. 7:6 Which were the chief: for else there were seven in all as appeareth, Gen. 46:21.
h. 1 Chron. 7:12 Or, Iri.
i. 1 Chron. 7:12 Meaning, that he was not the son of Benjamin but of Dan, Gen. 46:23.
j. 1 Chron. 7:12 Or, of Aher.
k. 1 Chron. 7:13 Or Shillem, Gen. 46:24.
l. 1 Chron. 7:13 These came of Dan, and Naphtali, which were the sons of Bilhah, Gen. 46:23, 24, 25.
m. 1 Chron. 7:16 Or, Jeezer, Num. 26:30.
n. 1 Chron. 7:18 Meaning, the sister of Gilead.
o. 1 Chron. 7:21 Which was one of the five principal cities of the Philistines, slew the Ephraimites.
p. 1 Chron. 7:22 Or, kinsfolk.
q. 1 Chron. 7:24 Or, neice.
r. 1 Chron. 7:25 To wit, of Ephraim.
s. 1 Chron. 7:28 Or, Adaiah.
t. 1 Chron. 7:33 Or, Kimbal.

1-CHRON 7
1. Num. 26:29,31 / Josh. 17:1
2. Gen. 45:17

1-CHRON 8
a. 1 Chron. 8:1 He continueth in the description of the tribe of Benjamin, because his purpose is to set forth the genealogy of Saul.
b. 1 Chron. 8:6 Meaning, the inhabitants of the city of Geba.
c. 1 Chron. 8:7 To wit, Ehud.
d. 1 Chron. 8:8 After he had put away his two wives.

begat certain in the country of Moab, after he had sent [d]away Hushim and Baara his wives. 9 He begat, I say, of Hodesh his wife, Jobab and Zibia, and Mesha and Malcam, 10 And Jeuz and Sachiah and Mirmah: these were his sons, and chief fathers. 11 And of Hushim he begat Abitub and Elpaal. 12 And the sons of Elpaal were Eber, and Misham and Shemed (which built Ono and Lod, and the villages thereof.) 13 And Beriah and Shema (which were the chief fathers among the inhabitants of Aijalon: they drave away the inhabitants of Gath.) 14 And Ahio, Shashak, and Jeremoth, 15 And Zebadiah, and Arad, and Eder, 16 And Michael, and Ispah, and Joha, the sons of Beriah, 17 And Zebadiah, and Meshullam, and Hizki, and Heber, 18 And Ishmerai, and Jizliah, and Jobab, the sons of Elpaal, 19 Jakim also, and Zichri, and Zabdi, 20 And Elienai, and Zillethai, and Eliel, 21 And [e]Adaiah, and Beraiah, and Shimrath the sons of Shimei, 22 And Ishpan, and Eber, and Eliel, 23 And Abdon, and Zichri, and Hanan, 24 And Hananiah, and Elam, and Antothijah, 25 Iphdeiah and Penuel the sons of Shashak, 26 And Shamsherai, and Shehariah, and Athaliah, 27 And Jaareshiah, and Elijah, and Zichri, the sons of Jeroham. 28 These were the chief [f]fathers according to their generations, even princes, which dwelt in Jerusalem. 29 And at [1]Gibeon dwelt the father of Gibeon, and the name of his wife was Maacah. 30 And his eldest son was Abdon, then Zur, and Kish, and Baal, and Nadab, 31 And Gedor, and Ahio, and Zecher, 32 And Mikloth begat Shimeah: these also dwelt with their brethren in Jerusalem, even by their brethren. 33 And [g]Ner begat Kish, and Kish begat Saul, and Saul begat Jonathan, and Malchishua, and Abinadab, and [h]Esh-Baal. 34 And the son of Jonathan was [i]Merib-Baal, and Merib-Baal begat Micah. 35 And the sons of Micah were Pithon, and Melech, and Tarea, and Ahaz, 36 And Ahaz begat Jehoaddah, and Jehoaddah begat Alemeth, and Azmaveth, and Zimri, and Zimri begat Moza, 37 And Moza begat Binea, whose son was Raphah, and his son Eleasah, and his son Azel. 38 And Azel had six sons, whose names are these: Azrikam, Bocheru, and Ishmael, and Sheariah, and Obadiah, and Hanan: all these were the sons of Azel. 39 And the sons of Eshek his brother were Ulam his eldest son, Jeush the second, and Eliphelet the third. 40 And the sons of Ulam were valiant men of war which shot with the bow, and had many sons and nephews, an hundred and fifty: all these were of the sons of Benjamin.

9

1 All Israel and Judah numbered. 10 Of the Priests and Levites, 11, 18 And of their offices.

1 Thus all Israel were numbered by their genealogies: and behold, they are written in the book of the Kings of Israel and of Judah, and they were [a]carried away to Babel for their transgression. 2 And the chief inhabitants that dwelt in their own possessions, and in their own cities, even Israel, the Priests, the Levites, and the [b]Nethinim. 3 And in Jerusalem dwelt of the children of Judah, and of the children of Benjamin, and of the children of Ephraim, and Manasseh. 4 Uthai the son of Ammihud the son of Omri, the son of Imri, the son of Bani, of the children of Perez, the son of Judah. 5 And of Shiloni, Asaiah the eldest, and his sons. 6 And the sons of Zerah, Jeuel, and their brethren six hundred and ninety. 7 And of the sons of Benjamin, Sallu, the son of Meshullam, the son of Hodaviah, the son of Hassenuah. 8 And Ibneiah the son of Jeroham, and Elah the son of Uzzi, the son of Michri, and Meshullam the son of Shephatiah, the son of Reuel the son of Ibnijah. 9 And their brethren according to their generations nine hundred, fifty and six: all these men were [c]chief fathers in the households of their fathers. 10 And of the Priests, Jedaiah, and Jehoiarib, and Jachin, 11 And Azariah the son of Hilkiah, the son of Meshullam, the son of Zadok, the son of Meraioth, the son of Ahitub the [d]chief of the house of God, 12 And Adaiah the son of Jeroham, the son of Pashur, the son of Malchijah, and Maasai the son of Adiel, the son of Jahzerah, the son of Meshullam, the son of Meshillemith, the son of Immer. 13 And their brethren the chief of the households of their fathers, a thousand seven hundred and threescore valiant men, for the [e]work of the service of the house of God. 14 And of the Levites, Shemaiah the son of Hasshub, the son of Azrikam, the son of Hashabiah, of the sons of Merari, 15 And Bakbakkar, Heresh and Galal, and Mattaniah the son of Micah, the son of Zichri, the son of Asaph, 16 And Obadiah the son of Shemaiah, the son of Galal, the son of Jeduthun, and Berechiah the son of Asa, the son of Elkanah, that dwelt in the villages of the Netophathites. 17 And the porters were Shallum, and Akkub, and Talmon, and Ahiman, and their brethren: Shallum was the chief. 18 For they were porters to this time by companies of the children of Levi unto the [f]King's gate Eastward. 19 And Shallum the son of Kore the son of Ebiasaph the son of Korah, and his brethren the Korahites (of the house of their father) were over the work, and office to keep the gates of the [g]Tabernacle: so their families were over the host of the Lord keeping the entry. 20 And Phinehas the son of Eleazar was their guide, and the Lord was with him. 21 Zechariah the son of Meshelemiah was the porter of the door of the Tabernacle of the Congregation. 22 All these were chosen for porters of the gates, two hundred and twelve, which were numbered according to their genealogies by their towns. David established these, and Samuel the Seer [h]in their perpetual office. 23 So they and their children had the oversight of the gates of the house of the Lord, even of the house of the Tabernacle by wards. 24 The porters were in four quarters Eastward, Westward, Northward and Southward. 25 And their brethren, which were in their towns, came at [i]seven days from time to time with them. 26 For these four chief porters were in perpetual office, and were of the Levites, and had charge of the [j]chambers, and of the treasures in the house of God. 27 And they lay round about the house of God, because the charge was theirs, and they caused it to be opened every morning. 28 And certain of them had the rule of the ministering vessels: for they brought them in by tally, and brought them out by tally. 29 Some of them also were appointed over the instruments, and over all the vessels of the Sanctuary, and of the [k]flour, and the wine, and the oil, and the incense, and the sweet odors. 30 And certain of the sons of the Priests made ointments of sweet odors. 31 And Mattithiah one of the Levites which was the eldest son of Shallum the Korahite, had the charge of the things that were made in the frying pan. 32 And other of their brethren the sons of Kohath had the oversight of the [1]showbread to prepare it every Sabbath. 33 And these are the singers, the chief fathers of the Levites, which dwelt in the chambers, [l]and had none other charge: for they had to do in that business day and night. 34 These were the chief fathers of the Levites according to their generations, and the principal which dwelt at Jerusalem. 35 [2]And in Gibeon dwelt [m]the father of Gibeon, Jeiel, and the name of his wife was Maachah. 36 And his eldest son was Abdon, then Zur, and Kish, and Baal, and Ner, and Nadab, 37 And Gedor, and Ahio, and Zechariah, and Mikloth. 38 And Mikloth begat Shimeam: they also dwelt with their brethren at Jerusalem, even by their brethren. 39 And [3]Ner begat Kish, and Kish begat Saul, and Saul begat Jonathan, and Malchishua, and Abinadab and Esh-Baal. 40 And the son of Jonathan was Merib-Baal, and Merib-Baal begat Micah. 41 And the sons of Micah were Pithon, and Melech and Tahrea. 42 And Ahaz begat [n]Jarah, and Jarah begat Alemeth, and Azmaveth, and Zimri, and Zimri begat Moza. 43 And Moza begat Binea, whose son was Rephaiah, and his son was Eleasah, and his son Azel. 44 And Azel had six sons, whose names are these, Azrikam, Bocheru, and Ismael, and Sheariah, and Obadiah, and Hanan: these are the sons of Azel.

10

1 The battle of Saul against the Philistines, 4 In which he dieth, 6 And his sons also. 13 The cause of Saul's death.

1 Then [1]the Philistines fought against Israel, and the men of Israel fled before the Philistines, and fell down slain in mount Gilboa. 2 And the Philistines pursued after Saul and after his sons, and the Philistines smote Jonathan, and Abinadab, and Malchishua the sons of Saul. 3 And the battle was sore against Saul, and the archers [a]hit him, and he was wounded of the archers. 4 Then said Saul to his armor-bearer, Draw out thy sword, and thrust me through therewith, lest these uncircumcised come and mock at me: but his armor-bearer would not, for he was sore afraid: therefore Saul took the sword, and fell upon it. 5 And when his armor-bearer saw that Saul was dead, he fell likewise upon the sword, and died. 6 So Saul died, and his three sons, and all his house, they died together. 7 And when all the men of Israel that were in the valley, saw how they fled, and that Saul and his sons were dead, they forsook their cities and fled away, and the Philistines came and dwelt in them. 8 And on the morrow when the Philistines came to spoil them that were slain, they found Saul and his sons [b]lying in mount Gilboa. 9 And when they had stripped him, they took his head and his armor, and sent them into the land of the Philistines round about, to publish it unto their idols, and to the people. 10 And they laid up his armor in the house of their god, and set up his head in the house of [c]Dagon. 11 When all they of Jabesh Gilead heard all that the Philistines had done to Saul, 12 Then they arose

---

e. 1 Chron. 8:21 Or, Araiah.
f. 1 Chron. 8:28 The chief of the tribe of Benjamin, that dwelt in Jerusalem.
g. 1 Chron. 8:33 Who in 1 Sam. 9:1 is called Abiel.
h. 1 Chron. 8:33 He is also named Ishbosheth, 2 Sam. 2:8.
i. 1 Chron. 8:34 He is likewise called Mephibosheth, 2 Sam. 9:6.

1-CHRON 8
1. 1 Chron. 9:35

1-CHRON 9
a. 1 Chron. 9:1 Hitherto he hath described their genealogies before they went into captivity, and now he describeth their history after their return.
b. 1 Chron. 9:2 Meaning, the Gibeonites, which served in the Temple, read Josh. 9:13.
c. 1 Chron. 9:9 Or, chief of the families.
d. 1 Chron. 9:11 That is, he was the high Priest.
e. 1 Chron. 9:13 To serve in the Temple, every one according to his office.
f. 1 Chron. 9:18 So called because the king came into the Temple thereby, and not the common people.
g. 1 Chron. 9:19 Their charge was that none should enter into those places, which were only appointed for the Priests to minister in.
h. 1 Chron. 9:22 Or, for their fidelity.
i. 1 Chron. 9:25 They served weekly, as Ezek. 4:10.
j. 1 Chron. 9:26 Or, opening of the doors.
k. 1 Chron. 9:29 Whereof the meat offering was made, Lev. 1:8.
l. 1 Chron. 9:33 But were continually occupied in singing praises to God.
m. 1 Chron. 9:35 Or, Abi Gibeon.
n. 1 Chron. 9:42 Who was also called Jehoaddah, 1 Chron. 8:36.

1-CHRON 9
1. Exod. 25:30
2. 1 Chron. 8:29
3. 1 Sam. 14:51 / 1 Chron. 8:33

1-CHRON 10
a. 1 Chron. 10:3 Hebrew, found.
b. 1 Chron. 10:8 Hebrew, fallen.
c. 1 Chron. 10:10 Which was the idol of the Philistines, and from the belly downward had the form of a fish, and upward of a man.

(all the valiant men) and took the body of Saul, and the bodies of his sons, and brought them to Jabesh, and buried the bones of them under an oak in Jabesh, and fasted seven days. **13** So Saul died for his transgression that he committed against the Lord, [2]even against the word of the Lord which he kept not, and in that he sought and asked counsel of a [d,3]familiar spirit, **14** And asked not of the Lord: therefore he slew him, and turned the kingdom unto David the son of Jesse.

11

3 After the death of Saul, David is anointed in Hebron. 5 The Jebusites rebel against David, from whom he taketh the tower of Zion. 6 Joab is made captain. 10 His valiant men.

1 Then [1]all Israel [a]gathered themselves to David unto Hebron, saying, Behold, we are thy bones and thy flesh. **2** And in time past, even when Saul was king, thou leddest Israel out and in: and the Lord thy God said unto thee, Thou shalt feed my people Israel, and thou shalt be captain over my people Israel. **3** So came all the Elders of Israel to the King to Hebron, and David made a covenant with them in Hebron before the Lord. And they anointed David king over Israel, [2]according to the word of the Lord, by the hand of Samuel. **4** And David and all Israel went to Jerusalem: which is Jebus, where were the Jebusites, the inhabitants of the land. **5** And the inhabitants of Jebus said to David, Thou shalt not come in hither. Nevertheless David took the tower of Zion, which is the city of David. **6** And David said, [3]Whosoever smiteth the Jebusites first, shall be the chief and captain. So Joab the son of Zeruiah went first up, and was captain. **7** And David dwelt in the tower: therefore they called it the city of David. **8** [4]And he built the city on every side, from Millo even round about: and Joab repaired the rest of the city. **9** And David prospered and grew: for the Lord of hosts was with him. **10** [5]These also are the chief of the valiant men that were with David, and joined their force with him in his kingdom with all Israel, to make him king over Israel, according to the word of the Lord. **11** And this is the number of the valiant men whom David had, Jashobeam the son of Hachmoni, the [b]chief among thirty: he lift up his spear against three hundred, whom he slew at one time. **12** And after him was Eleazar the son of [c]Dodo the Ahohite, which was one of the three valiant men. **13** He was with David at Pasdammim, and there the Philistines were gathered together to battle: and there was a parcel of ground full of barley, and the people fled before the Philistines. **14** And they stood in the midst of the field, [d]and saved it, and slew the Philistines: so the Lord gave a great victory. **15** And three of the [e]thirty captains went to a rock to David, into the cave of Adullam. And the army of the Philistines camped in the valley of Rephaim. **16** And when David was in the hold, the Philistines garrison was at Bethlehem. **17** And David longed, and said, [6]Oh, that one would give me to drink of the water of the well of Bethlehem that is at the gate. **18** Then these three brake through the host of the Philistines, and drew water out of the well of Bethlehem that was by the gate, and took it, and brought it to David: but David would not drink of it, but poured it for an oblation to the Lord, **19** And said, Let not my God suffer me to do this: should I drink the [f]blood of these men's lives? for they have brought it with the jeopardy of their lives: therefore he would not drink it: these things did these three mighty men. **20** And Abishai the brother of Joab, he was chief of the three, and he lift up his spear against three hundred, and slew them, and had the name among the three. **21** Among the three he was more honorable than the two, and he was their captain: [7]but he attained not unto the first three. **22** Benaiah the son of Jehoiada (the son of a valiant man) which had done many acts, and was of Kabzeel, he slew two [g]strong men of Moab, he went down also and slew a Lion in the midst of a pit in time of snow. **23** And he slew an Egyptian, a man of great stature, even five cubits long, and in the Egyptian's hand was a spear like a weaver's beam: and he went down to him with a staff, and plucked the spear out of the Egyptian's hand, and slew him with his own spear. **24** These things did Benaiah the son of Jehoiada, and had the name among the three worthies. **25** Behold, he was honorable among thirty, but he attained not unto the [h]first three. [8]And David made him of his counsel. **26** These also were valiant men of war, Asahel the brother of Joab, Elhanan the son of Dodo of Bethlehem, **27** [i]Shammoth the Harorite, Helez the Pelonite, **28** Ira the son of Ikkesh the Tekoite, Abiezer the Anathothite, **29** [j]Sibbechai the Hushathite, Ilai the Ahohite, **30** Maharai the Netophathite, Heled the son of Baanah the Netophathite, **31** Ithai the son of Ribai of Gibeah of the children of Benjamin, Benaiah the Pirathonite, **32** Hurai of the rivers of Gaash, Abiel the Arbathite, **33** Azmaveth the Baharumite, Eliahba the Shaalbonite, **34** The sons of Hashem the Gizonite, Jonathan the son of Shageh the Harite, **35** Ahiam the son of Sacar the Hararite, Eliphal the son of Ur, **36** Hepher the Mecherathite, Ahijah the Pelonite, **37** Hezro the Carmelite, Naarai the son of Ezbai, **38** Joel the brother of Nathan, Mibhar the son of Hagri, **39** Zelek the Ammonite, Naharai the Berothite, the armor bearer of Joab the son of Zeruiah, **40** Ira the Ithrite, Gareb the Ithrite, **41** Uriah the Hittite, Zabad the son of Ahlai, **42** Adina the son of Shiza the Reubenite, a captain of the Reubenites, and thirty with him. **43** Hanan the son of Maachah, and Joshaphat the Mithnite, **44** Uzzia the Ashterathite, Shama and Jeiel the sons of Hotham the Aroerite, **45** Jediael the son of Shimri, and Joha his brother the Tizite, **46** Eliel the Mahavite, and Jeribai and Joshaviah the sons of Elnaam, and Ithmah the Moabite, **47** Eliel and Obed, and Jaasiel the Mezobaite.

12

3 Who they were that went with David when he fled from Saul. 14 Their valiantness. 23 They that came unto him unto Hebron out of every tribe to make him King.

1 These also are they that came to David to [a]Ziklag, while he was yet kept close, because of Saul the son of Kish: and they were among the valiant and helpers of the battle. **2** They were weaponed with bows, and could use the right and the left hand with stones, and with arrows and with bows, and were of Saul's [b]brethren, even of Benjamin. **3** The chief were Ahiezer, and Joash the sons of Shemaah a Gibeathite, and Jeziel, and Pelet the sons of Azmaveth, Berachah and Jehu the Anathothite, **4** And Ishmaiah the Gibeonite, a valiant man among thirty, and above the thirty, and Jeremiah, and Jahaziel, and Johanan, and Jozabad the Gederathite, **5** Eluzai, and Jerimoth, and Bealiah, and Shemariah, and Shephatiah the Haruphite, **6** Elkanah, and Jisshiah, and Azarel, and Joezer, Jashobeam of Korah, **7** And Joelah, and Zebadiah the sons of Jeroham of [c]Gedor, **8** And of the Gadites there separated themselves some unto David into the hold of the wilderness, valiant men of war, and men of arms, and apt for battle, which could handle [d]spear and shield, and their faces were like the faces of [e]lions, and were like the roes in the mountains in swiftness, **9** Ezer the chief, Obadiah the second, Eliab the third, **10** [f]Mishmannah the fourth, Jeremiah the fifth, **11** Attai the sixth, Eliel the seventh, **12** Johanan the eight, Elzabad the ninth, **13** Jeremiah the tenth, Machbanai the eleventh. **14** These were the sons of Gad, captains of the host: one of the least could resist an hundred, and the greatest a thousand. **15** These are they that went over Jordan in the [g]first month, when he had filled over all his banks, and put to flight all them of the valley, toward the East and the West. **16** And there came of the children of Benjamin, and Judah to the hold unto David, **17** And David went out to meet them, and answered and said unto them, If ye be come peaceably unto me to help me, mine heart shall be knit unto you: but if you come to betray me to mine adversaries, seeing there is no wickedness in mine hands, the God of our fathers behold it, and rebuke it. **18** And the [h]spirit came upon Amasai, which was the chief of thirty, and he said, Thine are we, David, and with thee, O son of Jesse. Peace, peace be unto thee, and peace be unto thine helpers: for thy God helpeth thee. Then David received them, and made them captains of the garrison. **19** And of Manasseh, some fell to David, when he came with the Philistines against Saul to battle, but they [i]helped them not: for the Princes of the Philistines [1]by advisement sent him away, saying, He will fall to his master Saul [j]for our heads. **20** As he went to Ziklag, there fell to him of Manasseh, Adnah, and Jozabad, and Jediael, and Michael, and Jozabad, and Elihu, and Zillethai, heads of the thousands that were of Manasseh. **21** And they helped David against [k]that band: for they were all valiant men, and were captains in the host. **22** For at that time day by day, there came to David to help him, until it was a great host, like the host of [l]God. **23** And these are the numbers of the captains that were armed to battle, and came to David to Hebron to turn the kingdom of Saul to him, according to the word of the Lord. **24** The children of Judah that bare shield and [m]spear, were six thousand and eight hundred armed to the war. **25** Of the children of Simeon valiant men of war, seven thousand and an hundred. **26** Of the children of Levi four thousand and six hundred. **27** And

---

d. 1 Chron. 10:13 Or, witch, and sorceress.

1-CHRON 10
1. 1 Sam. 31:1
2. 1 Sam. 15:23
3. 1 Sam. 28:8

1-CHRON 11
a. 1 Chron. 11:1 This was after the death of Ishbosheth Saul's son, when David had reigned over Judah seven years and six months in Hebron, 2 Sam. 5:5.
b. 1 Chron. 11:11 Meaning, the most excellent and best esteemed for his valiantness: some read, the chief of the princes.
c. 1 Chron. 11:12 Or, his uncle.
d. 1 Chron. 11:14 This act is referred to Shammah, 2 Sam. 23:11, which seemeth was the chiefest of these.
e. 1 Chron. 11:15 That is, Eleazar and his two companions.
f. 1 Chron. 11:19 That is, this water, for the which they ventured their blood.
g. 1 Chron. 11:22 Or, lions.
h. 1 Chron. 11:25 Meaning, those three which brought the water to David.
i. 1 Chron. 11:27 Called also Shammah, 2 Sam. 23:25.
j. 1 Chron. 11:29 He is also called Mebunnai, 2 Sam. 23:27.

1-CHRON 11
1. 2 Sam. 5:1
2. 2 Sam. 16:13
3. 2 Sam. 5:8
4. 2 Sam. 5:9
5. 2 Sam. 23:8
6. 2 Sam. 23:15
7. 2 Sam. 23:19
8. 2 Sam. 23:23

1-CHRON 12
a. 1 Chron. 12:1 To take his part against Saul, who persecuted him.
b. 1 Chron. 12:2 That is, of the tribe of Benjamin, whereof Saul was, and wherein were excellent throwers with slings, Judg. 20:16.
c. 1 Chron. 12:7 Or, Gedua.
d. 1 Chron. 12:8 Or, buckler.
e. 1 Chron. 12:8 Meaning, fierce and terrible.
f. 1 Chron. 12:10 Or, Mashmannah.
g. 1 Chron. 12:15 Which the Hebrews called Nisan, or Abib, containing half March, and half April, when Jordan was wont to overflow his banks, read Josh. 3:15.
h. 1 Chron. 12:18 The spirit of boldness and courage moved him to speak thus.
i. 1 Chron. 12:19 They came only to help David, and not to succor the Philistines, which were enemies to their country.
j. 1 Chron. 12:19 Or, on the jeopardy of our heads.
k. 1 Chron. 12:21 To wit, of the Amalekites which had burned the city Ziklag, 1 Sam. 30:1,9.
l. 1 Chron. 12:22 Meaning, mighty or strong: for the Hebrews say a thing is of God, when it is excellent.
m. 1 Chron. 12:24 Or, buckler.

Jehoiada was the chief of them of [n]Aaron: and with him three thousand and seven hundred. **28** And Zadok a young man very valiant, and of his father's household came two and twenty captains. **29** And of the children of Benjamin the brethren of Saul three thousand: for a great part of them unto that time [o]kept the ward of the house of Saul. **30** And of the children of Ephraim twenty thousand, and eight hundred valiant men and famous men in the household of their fathers. **31** And of the half tribe of Manasseh eighteen thousand, which were appointed by name to come and make David King. **32** And of the children of Issachar which were men that had understanding of the [p]times, to know what Israel ought to do: the heads of them were two hundred, and all their brethren were at their commandment. **33** Of Zebulun that went out to battle, expert in war, and in all instruments of war, fifty thousand [q]which could set the battle in array: they were not of a [r]double heart. **34** And of Naphtali thousand captains, and with them with shield and spear seven and thirty thousand. **35** And of Dan expert in battle, eight and twenty thousand and six hundred. **36** And of Asher that went out to the battle and were trained in the wars, forty thousand. **37** And of the other side of Jordan of the Reubenites, and of the Gadites, and of the half tribe of Manasseh with all instruments of war to fight with, an hundred and twenty thousand. **38** [s]All these men of war [t]that could lead an army, came with [u]upright heart to Hebron to make David king over all Israel: and all the rest of Israel was of one accord to make David King. **39** And there they were with David three days, eating and drinking: for their [v]brethren had prepared for them. **40** Moreover, they that were near them until Issachar, and Zebulun, and Naphtali brought bread upon asses, and on camels, and on mules, and on oxen, even meat, flour, figs, and raisins, and wine and oil, and beeves and sheep abundantly: for there was joy in Israel.

13

6 The Ark is brought again from Kirjath Jearim to Jerusalem. 10 Uzza dieth because he toucheth it.

1 And David counseled with the captains of thousands and of hundreds, and with all the governors. **2** And David said to all the Congregation of Israel, If it seem good to you, and that it proceedeth of the Lord our God, we will send to and fro unto our brethren, that are left in all the land of Israel (for with them are the Priests and the Levites in the cities and their suburbs) that they may assemble themselves unto us. **3** And we will bring again the [a]Ark of our God to us: for we sought not unto it in the days of Saul. **4** And all the Congregation answered, Let us do so: for the thing seemed good in the eyes of all the people. **5** [1]So David gathered all Israel together from [b]Shihor in Egypt, even unto the entering of Hamath, to bring the Ark of God from [c]Kirjath Jearim. **6** And David went up and all Israel to [d]Baalah in Kirjath Jearim, that was in Judah, to bring up from thence the Ark of God the Lord that dwelleth between the Cherubims, where his Name is called on. **7** And they carried the Ark of God in a new cart out of the house of Abinadab: and Uzza and Ahio [e]guided the cart. **8** And David and all Israel played before [f]God with all their might, both with songs and with harps, and with viols, and with timbrels, and with cymbals, and with trumpets. **9** And when they came unto the threshingfloor of [g]Chidon, Uzza put forth his hand to hold the Ark, for the oxen did shake it. **10** But the wrath of the Lord was kindled against Uzza, and he smote him, because he laid his hand upon the Ark: so he died there [h]before God. **11** And David was angry, because the Lord had made a breach in Uzza, and he called the name of that place, Perez Uzza unto this day. **12** And David feared God that day, saying, How shall I bring in to me the Ark of God? **13** Therefore David brought not the Ark to him into the city of David, but caused it to turn into the house of [i]Obed-Edom the Gittite. **14** So the Ark of God remained in the house of Obed-Edom, even in his house three months: and the Lord blessed the house of Obed-Edom, and all that he had.

14

1 Hiram sendeth wood and workmen to David. 4 The names of his children. 8, 14 By the counsel of God he goeth against the Philistines, and overcometh them. 15 God fighteth for him.

1 Then [1]sent Hiram the King of [a]Tyre messengers to David, and Cedar trees, with masons and carpenters to build him an house. **2** Therefore David knew that the Lord had confirmed him King over Israel, and that his kingdom was lift up on high, because of his [b]people Israel. **3** Also David took more wives at Jerusalem, and David begat more sons and daughters. **4** And these are the names of the children which he had at Jerusalem, Shammua, and Shobab, Nathan, and Solomon, **5** And Ibhar, and Elishua, and [c]Elpelet, **6** And Nogah, and Nepheg, and Japhia, **7** And Elishama, and [d]Beeliada, and Eliphelet. **8** But when the Philistines heard that David was anointed King over Israel, all the Philistines came up to seek David. And when David heard, he went out against them. **9** And the Philistines came, and spread themselves in the valley of Rephaim. **10** Then David asked counsel at God, saying, Shall I go up against the Philistines, and wilt thou deliver them into mine hand? And the Lord said unto him, Go up: for I will deliver them into thine hand. **11** So they came up to Baal Perazim, and David smote them there: and David said, God hath divided mine enemies with mine hand, as waters are divided: therefore they called the name of that place, [e]Baal Perazim. **12** And there they had left their gods: and David said, Let them even be burnt with fire. **13** Again the Philistines came and spread themselves in the valley. **14** And when David asked again counsel at God, God said to him, Thou shalt not go up after them, but turn away from them, that thou mayest come upon them over against the mulberry trees. **15** And when thou hearest the noise of one going in the tops of the mulberry trees, then go out to battle: for God is gone forth before thee, to smite the host of the Philistines. **16** So David did as God had commanded him: and they smote the host of the Philistines from Gibeon even to Gezer. **17** And the fame of David went out into all lands: and the Lord brought the fear of him upon all nations.

15

1 David prepareth an house for the Ark. 4 The number and order of the Levites. 16 The singers are chosen out among them. 25 They bring again the Ark with joy. 29 David dancing before it is despised of his wife Michal.

1 And David made him houses in the [a]city of David, and prepared a place for the Ark of God, and pitched for it a tent. **2** Then David said, [1]None ought to carry the Ark of God, but the Levites: for the Lord hath chosen them to bear the Ark of the Lord, and to minister unto him forever. **3** And David gathered all Israel together to Jerusalem to bring up the [b]Ark of the Lord unto his place, which he had ordained for it. **4** And David assembled the sons of Aaron, and the Levites. **5** Of the sons of Kohath, Uriel the chief, and his [c]brethren six score. **6** Of the sons of Merari, Asaiah the chief, and his brethren two hundred and twenty. **7** Of the sons of Gershom, Joel the chief, and his brethren an hundred and thirty. **8** Of the sons of [d]Elizaphan, Shemaiah the chief, and his brethren two hundred. **9** Of the sons of [e]Hebron, Eliel the chief, and his brethren fourscore. **10** Of the sons of Uzziel, Amminadab the chief, and his brethren an hundred and twelve. **11** And David called Zadok and Abiathar the Priests, and of the Levites, Uriel, Asaiah and Joel, Shemaiah and Eliel, and Amminadab. **12** And he said unto them, Ye are the chief fathers of the Levites: [f]sanctify yourselves, and your brethren, and bring up the Ark of the Lord God of Israel unto the place that I have prepared for it. **13** [2]For because ye were not there at the first, the Lord our God made a breach among us: for we sought him not after due [g]order. **14** So the Priests and the Levites sanctified themselves to bring up the Ark of the Lord God of Israel. **15** And the sons of the Levites bare the Ark of God upon their shoulders with the bars as Moses had commanded, [3]according to the word of the Lord, **16** And David spake to the chief of the Levites, that they should appoint certain of their brethren to sing with [h]instruments of music, with viols and harps, and cymbals, that they might make a sound, and lift up their voice

---

n. 1 Chron. 12:27 Of the Levites which came by descent of Aaron.
o. 1 Chron. 12:29 That is, the greatest number took Saul's part.
p. 1 Chron. 12:32 Men of good experience, which knew at all times what was to be done.
q. 1 Chron. 12:33 Or, set themseves in array.
r. 1 Chron. 12:33 Hebrew, heart and heart.
s. 1 Chron. 12:38 So that his whole host were three hundred twenty and two thousand, two hundred twenty and two.
t. 1 Chron. 12:38 Or, fight in their array.
u. 1 Chron. 12:38 Or, with a good courage.
v. 1 Chron. 12:39 The rest of the Israelites.

1-CHRON 12
1. 1 Sam. 29:4

1-CHRON 13
a. 1 Chron. 13:3 His first care was to restore religion, which had in Saul's days been corrupted and neglected.
b. 1 Chron. 13:5 Or, Nile.
c. 1 Chron. 13:5 That is, from Gibea, where the inhabitants of Kirjath Jearim had placed it in the house of Abinadab, 2 Sam. 6:3.
d. 1 Chron. 13:6 Or, Baal, read 2 Sam. 6:2.
e. 1 Chron. 13:7 The sons of Abinadab.
f. 1 Chron. 13:8 That is, before the Ark, where God showed himself: so that the sign is taken for the thing signified, which is common to all sacraments both in the old and new Testament.
g. 1 Chron. 13:9 Called also Nachon, 2 Sam. 6:6.
h. 1 Chron. 13:10 Before the Ark for usurping that which did not appertain to his vocation: for this charge was given to the Priests, Num. 4:15, so that here all good intentions are condemned, except they be commanded by the word of God.
i. 1 Chron. 13:13 Who was a Levite, and called Gittite, because he had dwelt at Gath.

1-CHRON 13
1. 2 Sam. 6:2

1-CHRON 14
a. 1 Chron. 14:1 Hebrew, Zor.
b. 1 Chron. 14:2 Because of God's promise made to the people of Israel.
c. 1 Chron. 14:5 Elpelet and Nogah are not mentioned, 2 Sam. 5:14, so there are but eleven, and here thirteen.
d. 1 Chron. 14:7 Or, Eliada.
e. 1 Chron. 14:11 That is, the valley of divisions, because the enemies were dispersed there like waters.

1-CHRON 14
1. 2 Sam. 5:11

1-CHRON 15
a. 1 Chron. 15:1 That was in the place of the city, called Zion, 2 Sam. 5:7, 9.
b. 1 Chron. 15:3 From the house of Obed-Edom, 2 Sam. 6:10, 12.
c. 1 Chron. 15:5 Or, kinsmen.
d. 1 Chron. 15:8 Who was the son of Uzziel, the fourth son of Kohath, Exod. 6:18, 22; Num. 3:30.
e. 1 Chron. 15:9 The third son of Kohath, Exod. 6:18.
f. 1 Chron. 15:12 Prepare yourselves and be pure, abstain from all things whereby ye might be polluted, and so not able to come to the Tabernacle.
g. 1 Chron. 15:13 According as he hath appointed in the law.
h. 1 Chron. 15:16 These instruments and other ceremonies, which they observed, were instructions of their infancy, which continued to the coming of Christ.
i. 1 Chron. 15:18 Which were inferior in dignity.

with joy. 17 So the Levites appointed Heman the son of Joel, and of his brethren
Asaph the son of Berechiah, and of the sons of Merari their brethren, Ethan the
son of Kushaiah, 18 And with them their brethren in the [i]second degree, Zecha-
riah, Ben, and Jaaziel, and Shemiramoth, and Jehiel, and Unni, Eliab, and Benaiah,
and Maaseiah, and Mattithiah, and Elipheleh, and Mikneiah, and Obed-Edom,
and Jeiel the porters. 19 So Heman, Asaph, and Ethan, were singers to make a
sound with cymbals of brass, 20 And Zechariah, and Aziel, and Shemiramoth,
and Jehiel, and Unni, and Eliab, and Maaseiah, and Benaiah with viols on [j]A-
lamoth, 21 And Mattithiah, and Elipheleh, and Mikneiah, and Obed-Edom,
and Jeiel, and Azaziah, with harps upon [k]Sheminith Jenazzeah. 22 But Che-
naniah the chief of the Levites had the [l]charge bearing the burden in the charge,
for he was able to instruct. 23 And Berechiah and Elkanah were porters for the
Ark. 24 And Shebaniah, and Joshaphat and Nethanel and Amasai, and Zecha-
riah, and Benaiah, and Eliezer the Priests did blow with trumpets before the Ark of
God, and Obed-Edom and Jehiah were porters [m]for the Ark. 25 [4]So David and
the Elders of Israel and the captains of thousands went to bring up the Ark of the
Covenant of the Lord from the house of Obed-Edom with joy. 26 And because
that God [n]helped the Levites that bare the Ark of the covenant of the Lord, they
offered [o]seven bullocks and seven rams. 27 And David had on him a linen gar-
ment, as all the Levites that bare the Ark, and the singers, and Chenaniah that had
the chief charge of the singers: and upon David was a linen [p]Ephod. 28 Thus
all Israel brought up the Ark of the Lord's covenant with shouting, and sound of
cornet, and with trumpets, and with cymbals, making a sound with viols and with
harps. 29 And when the Ark of the [q]covenant of the Lord came into the city of
David, Michal the daughter of Saul looked out at a window, and saw king David
dancing and playing, and [5]she despised him in her heart.

16

1 The Ark being placed, they offer sacrifices. 4 David ordaineth Asaph and his brethren to minister before the Lord. 8 He appointeth a notable Psalm to be sung in praise of the Lord.

1 So [1]they brought in the Ark of God, and set it in the midst of the Tabernacle
that David had pitched for it, and they offered burnt offerings and peace offerings
before God. 2 And when David had made an end of offering the burnt offering
and the peace offerings, he [a]blessed the people in the Name of the Lord. 3 And
he dealt to every one of Israel both man and woman, to every one a cake of bre-
ad, and a piece of flesh, and a bottle of wine. 4 And he appointed certain of the
Levites to minister before the Ark of the Lord, and to [b]rehearse and to thank and
praise the Lord God of Israel: 5 Asaph the chief, and next to him Zechariah,
Jeiel, and Shemiramoth, and Jehiel, and Mattithiah, and Eliab, and Benaiah, and
Obed-Edom, even Jeiel with instruments, viols, and harps, and Asaph to make a
sound with cymbals, 6 And Benaiah and Jahaziel Priests, with trumpets conti-
nually before the Ark of the covenant of God. 7 Then at that time David did
[c]appoint at the beginning to give thanks to the Lord by the hand of Asaph and his
brethren. 8 [2]Praise the Lord and call upon his Name: declare his [d]works among
the people. 9 Sing unto him, sing praise unto him, and talk of all his [e]wonderful
works. 10 Rejoice in his holy Name: let the hearts of them that seek the Lord,
rejoice. 11 Seek the Lord and his strength: seek his face continually. 12 Re-
member his marvelous works that he hath done, his wonders, and the [f]judgmen-
ts of his mouth, 13 O seed of Israel his servant, O the children of Jacob his
[g]chosen. 14 He is the Lord our God: his judgments are throughout all the ear-
th. 15 Remember his Covenant forever, and the word, which he commanded to
a thousand generations: 16 [3]Which he made with Abraham, and his oath to Isa-
ac: 17 And hath confirmed it to Jacob for a Law, and to Israel for an everlasting
Covenant, 18 Saying, To thee will I give the land of Canaan, the [h]lot of your
inheritance. 19 When ye were [i]few in number, yea, a very few, and strangers
therein, 20 And walked about from nation to nation, and from one kingdom to
another people, 21 He suffered no man to do them wrong, but rebuked [j]Kings
for their sakes, saying, 22 Touch not mine [k]anointed, and do my [l]Prophets no
harm. 23 [4]Sing unto the Lord all the earth: declare his salvation from day to
day. 24 Declare his glory among the nations, and his wonderful works among all
people. 25 For the Lord is great and much to be praised, and he is to be feared
above all gods. 26 For all the gods of the people are [m]idols, but the Lord made
the heavens. 27 Praise and glory are before him: power and beauty are in his pla-
ce. 28 Give unto the Lord, ye families of the people: give unto the Lord glory
and power. 29 Give unto the Lord the glory of his Name: bring an offering and
come before him, and worship the Lord in the glorious Sanctuary. 30 [n]Tremble
ye before him all the earth, surely the world shall be, and not move. 31 Let the
[o]heavens rejoice, and let the earth be glad, and let them say among the nations,
The Lord reigneth. 32 Let the sea roar, and all that therein is: let the field be
joyful and all that is in it. 33 Let the trees of the wood then rejoice at the pre-
sence of the Lord: for he cometh to [p]judge the earth. 34 Praise the Lord, for he
is good, for his mercy endureth forever. 35 And say ye, Save us, O God, our
salvation, and gather us, and deliver us from the heathen, that we may praise thi-
ne holy Name, and [q]glory in thy praise. 36 Blessed be the Lord God of Israel
forever and ever: and let all people say, [r]So be it, and praise the Lord. 37 Then
he left there before the Ark of the Lord's Covenant Asaph and his brethren to mi-
nister continually before the Ark, that which was to be done every day: 38 And
Obed-Edom and his brethren, threescore and eight: and Obed-Edom the son of
Jeduthun, and Hosah were porters. 39 And Zadok the Priest and his brethren
the Priests were before the Tabernacle of the Lord, in the high place that was at
Gibeon, 40 To offer burnt offerings unto the Lord, upon the burnt offering al-
tar continually, in the morning and in the evening, even according unto all that is
written in the Law of the Lord, which he commanded Israel. 41 And with [s]them
were Heman, and Jeduthun, and the rest that were chosen (which were appointed
by names) to praise the Lord, because his mercy endureth forever. 42 Even with
them were Heman and Jeduthun, to make a sound with the cornets and with the
cymbals, with excellent instruments of music: and the sons of Jeduthun were at the
gate. 43 And all the people departed, every man to his house: and David retur-
ned to [t]bless his house.

17

3 David is forbidden to build an house unto the Lord. 12 Christ is promised under the figure of Solomon. 18 David giveth thanks, 23 and prayeth unto God.

1 Now [1]afterward when David dwelt in his house, he said to Nathan the
Prophet, Behold, I dwell in an house of [a]cedar trees, but the Ark of the Lord's Co-
venant remaineth under [b]curtains. 2 Then Nathan said to David, Do [c]all that
is in thine heart: for God is with thee. 3 And the same [d]night even the word of
God came to Nathan, saying, 4 Go, and tell David my servant, Thus saith the
Lord, Thou shalt not build me an house to dwell in: 5 For I have dwelt in no
house since the day that I brought out the children of Israel unto this day, but I
have been from tent to [e]tent, and from habitation to habitation. 6 Wherefore I
have [f]walked with all Israel, spake I one word to any of the Judges of Israel (whom
I commanded to feed my people) saying, Why have ye not built me an house of ce-
dar trees? 7 Now therefore thus shalt thou say unto my servant David, Thus saith
the Lord of hosts, I took thee from the sheepcote [g]and from following the sheep,
that thou shouldest be a prince over my people Israel. 8 And I have been with
thee whithersoever thou hast walked, and have destroyed all thine enemies out of
thy sight, and have [h]made thee a name, like the name of the great men that are in

---

j. 1 Chron. 15:20 This was an instrument of music, or a certain tune, whereunto they accustomed to sing Psalms.
k. 1 Chron. 15:21 Which was the eighth tune, over the which he that was most excellent had charge.
l. 1 Chron. 15:22 To wit, to appoint Psalms, and songs to them that sung.
m. 1 Chron. 15:24 With Berechiah and Elkanah, verse 23.
n. 1 Chron. 15:26 That is, gave them strength to execute their office.
o. 1 Chron. 15:26 Besides the bullock and the fat beast which David offered at every sixth pace, 2 Sam. 6:13.
p. 1 Chron. 15:27 Read 2 Sam. 6:14.
q. 1 Chron. 15:29 It was so called because it put the Israelites in remembrance of the Lord's covenant made with them.

1-CHRON 15
1. Num. 4:2,20
2. 1 Chron. 13:10
3. Exod. 25:14,15
4. 2 Sam. 6:12
5. 2 Sam. 6:16

1-CHRON 16
a. 1 Chron. 16:2 He called upon the Name of God, desiring him to prosper the people, and give good success to their beginnings.
b. 1 Chron. 16:4 To wit, God's benefits toward his people.
c. 1 Chron. 16:7 David gave them this Psalm to praise the Lord, signifying, that in all our enterprises the Name of God ought to be praised and called upon.
d. 1 Chron. 16:8 Whereof this is the chiefest, that he hath chosen himself a Church to call upon his Name.
e. 1 Chron. 16:9 Who of his wonderful providence hath chosen a few of the stock of Abraham to be his children.
f. 1 Chron. 16:12 In overcoming Pharaoh, which judgments were declared by God's mouth to Moses.
g. 1 Chron. 16:13 Meaning hereby that the promise of adoption only appertaineth to the Church.
h. 1 Chron. 16:18 Hebrew, cord, whereby parcels of land were measured.
i. 1 Chron. 16:19 Meaning, from the time that Abraham entered, unto the time that Jacob went into Egypt for famine.
j. 1 Chron. 16:21 As Pharaoh and Abimelech.
k. 1 Chron. 16:22 Mine elect people and them whom I have sanctified.
l. 1 Chron. 16:22 To whom God declared his word, and they declared it to their posterity.
m. 1 Chron. 16:26 His strong faith appeareth herein, though all the world would follow idols, yet he would cleave to the living God.
n. 1 Chron. 16:30 Humble yourselves under the mighty hand of God.
o. 1 Chron. 16:31 He exhorteth the dumb creatures to rejoice with him in considering the greatness of the grace of God.
p. 1 Chron. 16:33 To restore all things to their estate.
q. 1 Chron. 16:35 He esteemeth this to be the chiefest felicity of man.
r. 1 Chron. 16:36 He willeth all the people both in heart and mouth to consent to these praises.
s. 1 Chron. 16:41 With Zadok and the rest of the Priests.
t. 1 Chron. 16:43 Declaring that after our duty to God we are chiefly bound to our own house, for the which as for all other things we ought to pray unto God, and instruct our families to praise his Name.

1-CHRON 16
1. 2 Sam. 6:17
2. Ps. 105:1 / Isa. 12:4
3. Gen. 22:16, 17,28 / Luke 1:73 / Heb. 6:17
4. Ps. 95:1

1-CHRON 17
a. 1 Chron. 17:1 Well built and fair.
b. 1 Chron. 17:1 That is, in tents covered with skin.
c. 1 Chron. 17:2 As yet God had not revealed to the Prophet what he purposed concerning David: therefore seeing God favored David, he spake what he thought.
d. 1 Chron. 17:3 After that Nathan had spoken to David.
e. 1 Chron. 17:5 That is, in a tent which removed to and fro.
f. 1 Chron. 17:6 Meaning, wheresoever his Ark went, which was a sign of his presence.
g. 1 Chron. 17:7 Of a shepherd of sheep I made thee a shepherd of men: so that thou camest not to this dignity through thine own merits, but by my pure grace.
h. 1 Chron. 17:8 Or, gotten thee fame.
i. 1 Chron. 17:9 Make them sure that they shall not remove.
j. 1 Chron. 17:9 Hebrew, sons of iniquity.
k. 1 Chron. 17:9 Or, consume.
l. 1 Chron. 17:10 Will give thee great posterity.

the earth. 9 (Also I will appoint a place for my people Israel, and will [i]plant it,
that they may dwell in their place, and move no more: neither shall the [j]wicked pe-
ople [k]vex them anymore, as at the beginning, 10 And since the time that I com-
manded judges over my people Israel) And I will subdue all thine enemies: there-
fore I say unto thee, that the Lord will [l]build thee an house. 11 And when thy
days shall be fulfilled to go with thy fathers, then will I raise up thy seed after thee,
which shall be of thy sons, and will establish his kingdom. 12 He shall build me
an house, and I will establish his throne [m]forever. 13 I will be his father, and he
shall be my son, and I will not take my mercy away from him, as I took it from
him that was before [n]thee. 14 But I will establish him in mine house, and in my
kingdom forever, and his throne shall be established forever, 15 According to all
these words, and according to all this vision. So Nathan spake to David. 16 And
David the king [o]went in and [p]sat before the Lord, and said, Who am I, O Lord
God, and what is mine house, that thou hast brought me [q]hitherto? 17 Yet thou
esteeming this a small thing, O God, hast also spoken concerning the house of thy
servant for a great while, and hast regarded me according to the estate of a man
of [r]high degree, O Lord God. 18 What can David desire more of thee for the
honor of thy servant? for thou knowest thy servant. 19 O Lord, for thy servant's
sake, even according to thine [s]heart hast thou done all this great thing to declare
all magnificence. 20 Lord, there is none like thee, neither is there any God be-
sides thee according to all that we have heard with our ears. 21 Moreover what
one nation in the earth is like thy people Israel, whose God went to redeem them
to be his people, and to make thyself a Name, and to do great and terrible thin-
gs by casting out Nations from before thy people, whom thou hast delivered out
of Egypt? 22 For thou hast ordained thy people Israel to be thine own people
forever, and thou Lord art become their God. 23 Therefore now Lord, let the
thing that thou hast spoken concerning thy servant, and concerning his house,
be confirmed forever, and do as thou hast said, 24 And let thy Name be stable
and magnified forever, that it may be said, The Lord of hosts, God of Israel, is
the God of [t]Israel, and let the house of David thy servant be established before
thee. 25 For thou, O my God, hast [u]revealed unto the ear of thy servant, that
thou wilt build him an house: therefore thy servant hath [v]been bold to pray before
thee. 26 Therefore now Lord (for thou art [w]God, and hast spoken this goodness
unto thy servant.) 27 Now therefore it hath pleased thee to bless the house of
thy servant, that it may be before thee forever: for thou, O Lord, hast blessed it,
and it shall be blessed forever.

18

1 The battle of David against the Philistines, 2 And against Moab, 3 Zobah, 5 Aram, 12 And Edom.

1 And after this, David smote the Philistines, and subdued them, and took
[a]Gath, and the villages thereof out of the hand of the Philistines. 2 And he smo-
te Moab, and the Moabites became David's servants, and [b]brought gifts. 3 And
David smote [c]Hadadezer King of Zobah unto Hamath, as he went to establish his
border by the river [d]Perath. 4 And David took from him a thousand chariots,
and seven thousand horsemen, and twenty thousand footmen, and [1]destroyed all
the chariots, but he reserved of them an hundred chariots. 5 Then came the
Aramites of Damascus to succor Hadadezer king of Zobah, but David slew of the
Aramites two and twenty thousand. 6 And David put a garrison in Aram of [e]Da-
mascus, and the Aramites became David's servants, and brought gifts: and the Lord
[f]preserved David wheresoever he went. 7 And David took the shields of gold
that were of the servants of Hadadezer, and brought them to Jerusalem. 8 And
from [g]Tibhath, and from Chun (cities of Hadadezer) brought David exceeding
much brass, wherewith Solomon made the brazen [2]Sea, and the pillars and the
vessels of brass. 9 Then Tou King of Hamath heard how David had smitten
all the host of Hadadezer king of Zobah: 10 Therefore he sent [h]Hadoram his
son to king David, to salute him, and to rejoice with him, because he had fought
against Hadadezer, and beaten him (for Tou had war with Hadadezer) who brou-
ght all vessels of gold and silver and brass. 11 And king David did dedicate them
unto the Lord, with the silver and gold that he brought from all the nations, from
[i]Edom, and from Moab, and from the children of Ammon, and from the Philisti-
nes, and from Amalek. 12 And Abishai the son of Zeruiah smote of Edom in
the salt valley [j]eighteen thousand, 13 And he put a garrison in Edom, and all
the Edomites became David's servants: and the Lord preserved David wheresoever
he went. 14 So David reigned over all Israel, and executed judgment and justice
to all his people. 15 And Joab the son of Zeruiah was over the host, and Jeho-
shaphat the son of Ahilud Recorder, 16 And Zadok the son of Ahitub, and Abi-
melech the son of Abiathar were the Priests, and [k]Shavsha the Scribe, 17 [3]And
Benaiah the son of Jehoiada was over the [l]Cherethites and the Pelethites: and the
sons of David were chief about the King.

19

4 Hanun King of the children of Ammon doeth great injuries to the servants of David. 6 He prepareth an army against David, 15 and is overcome.

1 After this also [1]Nahash the king of the children of Ammon died, and his
son reigned in his stead. 2 And David said, I will show kindness unto Hanun
the son of Nahash, because his [a]father showed kindness unto me. And David sent
messengers to comfort him for his father. So the servants of David came into the
land of the children of Ammon to Hanun, to comfort him. 3 And the princes of
the children of Ammon said to Hanun, Thinkest thou that David doth honor thy
father, that he hath sent comforters unto thee? Are not his servants come to thee
to [b]search, to seek and to spy out the land? 4 Wherefore Hanun took David's
servants, and [c]shaved them, and cut off their [d]garments by the half unto the but-
tocks, and sent them away. 5 And there went certain and told David concerning
the men: and he sent to meet them (for the men were exceedingly ashamed) and
the King said, Tarry at Jericho, until your beards be grown: then return. 6 When
the children of Ammon saw that they [e]stank in the sight of David, then sent Ha-
nun and the children of Ammon a thousand talents of silver, to hire them cha-
riots and horsemen out of Aram Naharaim, and out [2]of Aram Maacah, and out
of [f]Zobah. 7 And they hired them two and thirty thousand chariots, and the
king of Maacah and his people, which came and pitched before [g]Medeba: and the
children of Ammon gathered themselves together from their cities, and came to
the battle. 8 And when David heard it, he sent Joab and all the host of the va-
liant men. 9 And the children of Ammon came out, and set their battle in array
at the gate of the city. And the kings that were come, were by themselves in the
field. 10 When Joab saw that the front of the battle was against him before and
behind, then he chose out of all the choice of Israel, and set himself in array to
meet the Aramites. 11 And the rest of the people he delivered unto the hand of
Abishai his brother, and they put themselves in array against the children of Am-
mon. 12 And he said, If Aram be too strong for me, then thou shalt succor me:
and if the children of Ammon prevail against thee, then I will succor thee. 13 Be
strong, and let us show ourselves valiant for our [h]people, and for the cities of our
God, and let the Lord do that which is good in his own sight. 14 So Joab and
the people that was with him, came near before the Aramites unto the battle, and
they fled before him. 15 And when the children of Ammon saw that the Ara-
mites fled, they fled also before Abishai his brother, and entered into the city: so
Joab came to Jerusalem. 16 And when the Aramites saw that they were discom-
fited before Israel, they sent messengers, and caused the Aramites to come forth
that were beyond the [i]river: and Shophach the captain of the host of Hadadezer
went before them. 17 And when it was showed David, he gathered all Isra-
el, and went over Jordan, and came unto them, and put himself in array against
them: And when David had put himself in battle array to meet the Aramites, they
fought with him. 18 But the Aramites fled before Israel, and David destroyed

---

m. 1 Chron. 17:12 That is, unto the coming of Christ: for then these figures should cease.
n. 1 Chron. 17:13 Which was Saul.
o. 1 Chron. 17:16 He went into the tent where the Ark was, showing what we ought to do when we receive any benefits of the Lord.
p. 1 Chron. 17:16 Or, remained.
q. 1 Chron. 17:16 Meaning to this kingly estate.
r. 1 Chron. 17:17 Thou hast promised a kingdom that shall continue to me and my posterity, and that Christ shall proceed of me.
s. 1 Chron. 17:19 Freely and according to the purpose of thy will, without any deserving.
t. 1 Chron. 17:24 That is, he showeth himself in deed to be their God, by delivering them from dangers, and preserving them.
u. 1 Chron. 17:25 Thou hast declared unto me by Nathan the Prophet.
v. 1 Chron. 17:25 Hebrew, hath found.
w. 1 Chron. 17:26 And canst not break promise.

1-CHRON 17
1. 2 Sam. 7:2

1-CHRON 18
a. 1 Chron. 18:1 Which in 2 Sam. 8:1, is called the bridle of bondage, because it was a strong town, and kept the country round about in subjection.
b. 1 Chron. 18:2 Or, paid tribute.
c. 1 Chron. 18:3 Or, Hadadezer.
d. 1 Chron. 18:3 Or, Euphrates.
e. 1 Chron. 18:6 Or, Darmesek.
f. 1 Chron. 18:6 That is, in all things that he enterprised.
g. 1 Chron. 18:8 Which in 2 Sam. 8:8, are called Betah and Berothai.
h. 1 Chron. 18:10 Called also Joram, 2 Sam. 8:10.
i. 1 Chron. 18:11 Because the Edomites and the Syrians joined their power together, it is said, 2 Sam. 8:12, that the Aramites were spoiled.
j. 1 Chron. 18:12 Which is understood that Joab slew twelve thousand, as is in the title of the threescore Psalm and Abishai the rest.
k. 1 Chron. 18:16 Or, Seraiah.
l. 1 Chron. 18:17 Read 2 Sam. 8:18.

1-CHRON 18
1. 2 Sam. 8:4
2. 1 Kings 7:23 / Jer. 52:20
3. 2 Sam. 8:17,18

1-CHRON 19
a. 1 Chron. 19:2 Because Nahash received David and his company, when Saul persecuted him he would now show pleasure to his son for the same.
b. 1 Chron. 19:3 Thus the malicious ever interpret the purpose of the godly in the worst sense.
c. 1 Chron. 19:4 They shaved off the half of their beards, 2 Sam. 10:4.
d. 1 Chron. 19:4 To put them to shame and villainy, whereas the ambassadors ought to have been honored: and because the Jews used to wear side garments and beards, they thus disfigured them, to make them odious to others.
e. 1 Chron. 19:6 Or, had made themselves to be abhorred of David.
f. 1 Chron. 19:6 Which were five in all.
g. 1 Chron. 19:7 Which was a city of the tribe of Reuben beyond Jordan.
h. 1 Chron. 19:13 He declareth that where the cause is evil, the courage cannot be valiant, and that in good causes men ought to be courageous, and commit the success to God.
i. 1 Chron. 19:16 That is, Euphrates.
j. 1 Chron. 19:18 For this place, read 2 Sam. 10:18.

1-CHRON 19
1. 2 Sam. 10:1
2. 2 Sam. 10:6,8

of the Aramites [j]seven thousand chariots, and forty thousand footmen, and killed Shophach the captain of the host. **19** And when the servants of Hadadezer saw that they fell before Israel, they made peace with David, and served him. And the Aramites would no more succor the children of Ammon.

20

1 Rabbah destroyed. 3 The Ammonites tormented. 4 The Philistines are thrice overcome with their giants.

1 And [1]when the year was expired, in the time that kings go out a warfare, Joab carried out the strength of the army, and destroyed the country of the children of Ammon, and came and besieged [a]Rabbah (but David tarried at Jerusalem) and Joab smote Rabbah, and destroyed it. **2** [2]Then David took the crown of their king from off his head, and found it the weight of a [b]talent of gold with precious stones in it: and it was set on David's head, and he brought away the spoil of the city exceeding much. **3** And he carried away the people that were in it, and cut them with saws, and with harrows of iron, and with axes: even thus did David with all the cities of the children of Ammon. Then David and all the people came again to Jerusalem. **4** [3]And after this also there arose war at [c]Gezer with the Philistines: then Sibbechai the Hushathite slew [d]Sippai of the children of [e]Haraphah, and they were subdued. **5** And there was yet another battle with the Philistines: and Elhanan the son of Jair slew [f]Lahmi the brother of Goliath the Gittite, whose spear staff was like a weaver's beam. **6** And yet again there was a battle at Gath, where was a man of a great stature, and his fingers were by [g]sixes, even four and twenty, and was also the son of Haraphah. **7** And when he reviled Israel, Jonathan the son of Shimea David's brother did slay him. **8** These were born unto Haraphah at Gath, and fell by the hand of David, and by the hands of his servants.

21

1 David causeth the people to be numbered, 14 and there dieth seventy thousand men of the pestilence.

1 And [a]Satan stood up against Israel, and provoked David to number Israel.

2 Therefore David said to Joab, and to the rulers of the people, Go, and number Israel from [b]Beersheba even to Dan, and bring it to me, that I may know the number of them. **3** And Joab answered, The Lord increased his people an hundred times so many as they be, O my lord the king: are they not all my lord's servants? wherefore doeth my lord require this thing? why should he be a cause of [c]trespass to Israel? **4** Nevertheless, the king's word prevailed against Joab. And Joab departed and went through all Israel, and returned to Jerusalem. **5** And Joab gave the number and sum of the people unto David: and all Israel were [d]eleven hundred thousand men that drew sword: and Judah was [e]four hundred and seventy thousand men that drew sword. **6** But the Levites and Benjamin counted he not among them: for the King's word was abominable to Joab. **7** And God was displeased with this thing: therefore he smote Israel. **8** Then David said unto God, I have sinned greatly, because I have done this thing: but now, I beseech thee, remove the iniquity of thy servant: for I have done very foolishly. **9** And the Lord spake unto Gad David's [f]Seer, saying, **10** Go and tell David, saying, Thus saith the Lord, I offer thee three things: choose thee one of them, that I may do it unto thee. **11** So Gad came to David, and said unto him, Thus saith the Lord, Take to thee, **12** Either three years famine, or three months to be destroyed before thine adversaries, and the sword of thine enemies [g]to take thee, or else the sword of the Lord and pestilence in the land three days, that the Angel of the Lord may destroy throughout all the coasts of Israel: now therefore advise thee, what word I shall bring again to him that sent me. **13** And David said unto Gad, I am in a wonderful strait, let me now fall into the hand of the Lord: for his mercies are exceedingly great, and let me not fall into the hand of man. **14** So the Lord sent a pestilence in Israel, and there fell of Israel seventy thousand men. **15** And God sent the Angel into Jerusalem to destroy it. And [h]as he was destroying, the Lord beheld, and [i]repented of the evil, and said to the Angel that destroyed, It is now enough, let thine hand cease. Then the Angel of the Lord stood by the threshing floor of [j]Ornan the Jebusite. **16** And David lifted up his eyes, and saw the Angel of the Lord stand between the earth and the heaven, with his sword drawn in his hand and stretched out toward Jerusalem. Then David and the Elders of Israel which were clothed in sack, fell upon their faces. **17** And David said unto God, Is it not I that commanded to number the people? It is even I that have sinned and have committed evil, but these sheep, what have they done? O Lord my God, I beseech thee, let thine hand be on me and on my father's house, and not on [k]thy people for their destruction. **18** Then the Angel of the Lord commanded Gad to say to David, that David should go up, and set up an altar unto the Lord in the threshing floor of Ornan the Jebusite. **19** So David went up according to the saying of Gad, which he had spoken in the Name of the Lord. **20** And Ornan turned about and saw the Angel, and his four sons that were with him, [l]hid themselves, and Ornan threshed wheat. **21** And as David came to Ornan, Ornan looked and saw David, and went out of the threshing floor, and bowed himself to David with his face to the ground. **22** And David said to Ornan, Give me the place of thy threshing floor, that I may build an [m]altar therein unto the Lord: give it me for sufficient money, that the plague may be stayed from the people. **23** Then Ornan said unto David, Take it to thee, and let my lord the king do that which seemeth him good: lo, I give thee bullocks for burnt offerings, and threshing instruments for wood, and wheat for meat offering, I give it all. **24** And King David said to Ornan, Not so: but I will buy it for sufficient [n]money: for I will not take that which is thine for the Lord, nor offer burnt offerings without cost. **25** So David gave to Ornan for that place [o]six hundred shekels of gold by weight. **26** And David built there an altar unto the Lord, and offered burnt offerings, and peace offerings, and called upon the Lord, and he [p]answered him by fire from heaven upon the altar of burnt offering. **27** And when the Lord had spoken to the Angel, he put up his sword again into his sheath. **28** At that time when David saw that the Lord had heard him in the threshing floor of Ornan the Jebusite, then he sacrificed there. **29** (But the Tabernacle of the Lord which Moses had made in the wilderness, and the altar of burnt offering were at that season in the high place at Gibeon. **30** And David could not go before it to ask counsel at God: for he was afraid of the sword of the Angel of the Lord.)

22

2 David prepareth things necessary for the building of the Temple. 6 He commandeth his son Solomon to build the Temple of the Lord, which thing he himself was forbidden to do. 9 Under the figure of Solomon Christ is promised.

1 And David said, This is the [a]house of the Lord God, and this is the altar for the burnt offering of Israel. **2** And David commanded to gather together the [b]strangers that were in the land of Israel, and he set masons to hew and polish stones to build the house of God. **3** David also prepared [c]much iron for the nails of the doors and of the gates, and for the joinings, and abundance of brass passing weight, **4** And cedar trees without number: for the Sidonians and they of Tyre brought much cedar wood to David. **5** And David said, Solomon my son is young and tender, and we must build an house for the Lord, magnifical, excellent and of great fame and dignity throughout all countries: I will therefore now prepare for him. So David prepared very much before his death. **6** Then he called Solomon his son, and charged him to build an house for the Lord God of Israel. **7** And David said to Solomon, [1]My son, I purposed with myself to build an house to the Name of the Lord my God, **8** But the word of the Lord came to me, saying, [d,2]Thou hast shed much blood, and hast made great battles: thou shalt not build an house unto my name: for thou hast shed much blood upon the earth in my sight. **9** Behold, a son is born to thee, which shall be a man of rest, for I will give him rest from all his enemies round about: therefore his name is Solomon: and I will send peace and quietness upon Israel in his days. **10** [3]He shall build an house for my Name, and he shall be my son, and I will be his father, and I will establish the throne of his kingdom upon Israel forever. **11** Now therefore

---

1-CHRON 20

a. 1 Chron. 20:1 Which was the chief city of the Ammonites.
b. 1 Chron. 20:2 Which mounteth about the value of seven thousand and seventy crowns, which is about threescore pound weight.
c. 1 Chron. 20:4 Or, Gob, 2 Sam. 21:18.
d. 1 Chron. 20:4 Or, Saph.
e. 1 Chron. 20:4 Or, Raphaim, or the giants.
f. 1 Chron. 20:5 Read 2 Sam. 21:19.
g. 1 Chron. 20:6 Meaning, that he had six apiece on hands and feet.

1-CHRON 20

1. 2 Sam. 11:1
2. 2 Sam. 12:29,30
3. 2 Sam. 21:18

1-CHRON 21

a. 1 Chron. 21:1 He tempted David, in setting before his eyes his excellency and glory, his power and victories, read 2 Sam. 24:1.
b. 1 Chron. 21:2 That is, from South to North.
c. 1 Chron. 21:3 It was a thing indifferent and usual to number the people, but because he did it of an ambitious mind, as though his strength stood in his people, God punished him.
d. 1 Chron. 21:5 Joab partly for grief, and partly through negligence, gathered not the whole sum as it is here declared.
e. 1 Chron. 21:5 In Samuel is mention of thirty thousand more, which was either by joining to them some of the Benjamites which were mixed with Judah, or as the Hebrews write, here the chief and princes are left out.
f. 1 Chron. 21:9 Or, Prophet.
g. 1 Chron. 21:12 Or, smite thee.
h. 1 Chron. 21:15 Read 2 Sam. 24:16.
i. 1 Chron. 21:15 When God draweth back his plagues, he seemeth to repent, read Gen. 6:6.
j. 1 Chron. 21:15 Or, Araunah.
k. 1 Chron. 21:17 Thus he both showeth a true repentance and a fatherly care toward his people, which desireth God to spare them, and to punish him and his.
l. 1 Chron. 21:20 If man hide himself at the sight of an Angel which is a creature, how much as a sinner able to appear before the face of God?
m. 1 Chron. 21:22 Thus he did by the commandment of God, as verse 18, for else it had been abominable, except he had either God's word, or revelation.
n. 1 Chron. 21:24 That is, as much as it is worth: for having enough of his own, and yet to have taken of another man's goods to offer unto the Lord, it had been theft and not acceptable to God.
o. 1 Chron. 21:25 Read 2 Sam. 24:24.
p. 1 Chron. 21:26 God declared that he heard his request, in that he sent down fire from heaven, for else they might use no fire in sacrifice, but of that which was reserved still upon the altar, Lev. 6:13, and came down from heaven, Lev. 9:24, as appeared by the punishment of Nadab and Abihu, Lev. 10:1.

1-CHRON 22

a. 1 Chron. 22:1 That is, the place wherein he will be worshipped.
b. 1 Chron. 22:2 Meaning, cunning men of other nations which dwelt among the Jews.
c. 1 Chron. 22:3 To wit, which weighed fifty shekels of gold, 2 Chron. 3:9.
d. 1 Chron. 22:8 This declareth how greatly God detesteth the shedding of blood, seeing David for this cause is stayed to build the Temple of the Lord, albeit he enterprised no war, but by God's commandment and against his enemies.
e. 1 Chron. 22:11 He showeth that there can be no prosperity, but when the Lord is with us.
f. 1 Chron. 22:12 These are only the means whereby Kings govern their subjects aright, and whereby the Realms do prosper and flourish.

my son, the Lord shall be with thee, and thou shalt [e]prosper, and thou shalt build
an house to the Lord thy God, as he hath spoken of thee. **12** Only the Lord give
thee [f]wisdom and understanding, and give thee charge over Israel, even to keep
the Law of the Lord thy God. **13** Then thou shalt prosper, if thou take heed to
observe the statutes and the judgments which the Lord commanded Moses for
Israel: be strong and of good courage: fear not, neither be afraid. **14** For behold,
according to my [g]poverty have I prepared for the house of the Lord an hundred
thousand talents of gold, and a thousand thousand talents of silver, and of brass
and of iron passing weight: for there was abundance. I have also prepared timber
and stone, and thou mayest provide more thereto. **15** Moreover thou hast wor-
kmen with thee enough, [h]hewers of stone, and workmen of timber, and all men
expert in every work. **16** Of gold, of silver, and of brass, and of iron there is no
number: [i]Up therefore, and be doing, and the Lord will be with thee. **17** David
also commanded all the princes of Israel to help Solomon his son, saying, **18** Is
not the Lord your God with you, and hath given you rest on every side? for he hath
given the [j]inhabitants of the land into mine hand, and the land is subdued before
the Lord, and before his people. **19** Now set [k]your hearts and your souls to seek
the Lord your God, and arise, and build the Sanctuary of the Lord God, to bring
the Ark of the covenant of the Lord, and the holy vessels of God into the house
built for the Name of the Lord.

23

1 David being old, ordaineth Solomon King. 3 He causeth the Levites to be numbered, 4 and assigneth them to their offices. 13 Aaron and his sons are for the high Priest. 14 The sons of Moses.

1 So when David was old and full of days, [1]he made Solomon his son King
over Israel. **2** And he gathered together all the princes of Israel with the Priests
and the Levites. **3** And the Levites were numbered from the age of thirty years
and above, and their number according to their sum was eight and thirty thousand
men. **4** Of these four and twenty thousand were set to [a]advance the work of the
house of the Lord, and six thousand were overseers and judges. **5** And four thou-
sand were porters, and four thousand praised the Lord with instruments which
[b]he made to praise the Lord. **6** [2]So David divided offices unto them, to wit, to
the sons of Levi, to [3]Gershon, Kohath, and Merari. **7** Of the Gershonites were
[c]Laadan and Shimei. **8** The sons of Laadan, the chief was Jehiel, and Zetham
and Joel, three. **9** The Sons of Shimei, Shelomith, and Haziel, and Haran, three:
these were the chief fathers of Laadan. **10** Also the sons of Shimei were Jahath,
Zina, Jeush, and Beriah: these four were the sons of Shimei. **11** And Jahath was
the chief, and [d]Zizah the second, but Jeush and Beriah had not many sons: there-
fore they were in the families of their father, counted but as one. **12** The sons of
Kohath were Amram, Izhar, Hebron and Uzziel, four. **13** [4]The sons of Amram,
Aaron and Moses: and Aaron was separated to [e]sanctify the most holy place, he
and his sons forever to burn incense before the Lord, to minister to him, and to
bless in his Name forever. **14** Moses also the man of God and his children were
named with the [f]tribe of Levi. **15** The sons of Moses were Gershon, and Elie-
zer. **16** Of the sons of [5]Gershon was Shebuel the chief. **17** And the son of Elie-
zer was Rehabiah the [g]chief: for Eliezer had none other sons: but the sons of Reha-
biah were very many. **18** The son of Izhar was Shelomith the chief. **19** The
sons of Hebron were Jeriah the first, Amariah the second, Jahaziel the third, and
Jekameam the fourth. **20** The sons of Uzziel were Michah the first, and Jesshiah
the second. **21** The sons of Merari were Mahli and Mushi. The sons of Mahli,
Eleazar and Kish. **22** And Eleazar died, and had no sons, but daughters, and
their [h]brethren the sons of Kish took them. **23** The sons of Mushi were Mahli,
and Eder, and Jeremoth, three. **24** These were the sons of Levi according to the
house of their fathers, even the chief fathers according to their offices, according
to the number of names, and their sum that did the work for the service of the
house of the Lord from the age of [i]twenty years and above. **25** For David said,
The Lord God of Israel hath given rest unto his people, that they may dwell in Je-
rusalem forever. **26** And also the Levites shall no more bear the Tabernacle and
all the vessels for the service thereof. **27** Therefore according to the last words of
David, the Levites were numbered from twenty years and above, **28** And their
office was under the hand of the sons of Aaron, for the service of the house of the
Lord in the courts, and chambers, and in the [j]purifying of all holy things, and in
the work of the service of the house of God, **29** Both for the showbread, and for
the fine flour, for the meat offering, and for the unleavened cakes, and for the fri-
ed things, and for that which was roasted, and for all measures and size, **30** And
for to stand every morning, to give thanks and praise to the Lord, and likewise at
even, **31** And to offer all burnt offerings unto the Lord in the Sabbaths, in the
months, and at the appointed times, according to the number and according to
their custom, continually before the Lord, **32** And that they should keep the
charge of the Tabernacle of the Congregation, and the charge of the holy place,
and the charge of the sons of Aaron their brethren in the service of the house of
the Lord.

24

3 David assigneth offices to the sons of Aaron.

1 These are also the [1]divisions of the sons of Aaron: The sons of
Aaron were Nadab, and Abihu, Eleazar, and Ithamar. **2** But Nadab and Abihu
died [a]before their father, and had no children: therefore Eleazar and Ithamar execu-
ted the Priest's office. **3** And David distributed them, even Zadok of the [b]sons of
Eleazar, and Ahimelech of the sons of Ithamar according to their offices in their mi-
nistration. **4** And there were found more of the sons of Eleazar by the [c]number
of men, than of the sons of Ithamar, and they divided them, to wit, among the sons
of Eleazar, sixteen heads, according to the household of their fathers, and among
the sons of Ithamar, according to the household of their fathers, eight. **5** Thus
they distributed them by lot the one from the other, and so the rulers of the San-
ctuary and the rulers of the house of God were of the sons of Eleazar, and of the
sons of Ithamar. **6** And Shemaiah the son of Nethanel the Scribe of the Levites,
wrote them before the king and the princes, and Zadok the Priest, and Ahimelech
the son of Abiathar, and before the chief fathers of the Priests and of the Levites,
one family being reserved for Eleazar, and another reserved for Ithamar. **7** And
the first [d]lot fell to Jehoiarib, and the second to Jedaiah, **8** The third to Harim,
the fourth to Seorim, **9** The fifth to Malchijah, the sixth to Mijamin, **10** The
seventh to Hakkoz, the eight to [e]Abijah, **11** The ninth to Jeshua, the tenth to
Shecaniah, **12** The eleventh to Eliashib, the twelfth to Jakim, **13** The thirte-
enth to Huppah, the fourteenth to Jeshebeab, **14** The fifteenth to Bilgah, the
sixteenth to Immer, **15** The seventeenth to Hezir, the eighteenth to Happiz-
zez, **16** The nineteenth to Pethahiah, the twentieth to Jehezekel, **17** The one
and twenty to Jachin, the two and twenty to Gamul, **18** The three and twen-
ty to Delaiah, the four and twenty to Maaziah. **19** These were their orders ac-
cording to their offices, when they entered into the house of the Lord according
to their custom under [f]the hand of Aaron their father, as the Lord God of Israel
had commanded him. **20** And of the sons of Levi that remained of the sons of
Amram, was Shubael, of the sons of Shubael, Jehdeiah, **21** Of Rehabiah, even
of the sons of Rehabiah, the first Isshiah, **22** Of Izhari, Shelomoth, of the sons
of Shelomoth, Jahath, **23** And his sons, Jeriah the first, Amariah the second, Ja-
haziel the third, and Jekameam the fourth, **24** The son of Uzziel was Michah,
the son of Michah was Shamir, **25** The brother of Michah was Isshiah, the son
of Isshiah, Zechariah, **26** The sons of Merari, were Mahli and Mushi, the son of
Jaaziah was Beno, **27** The sons of Merari, of Jaaziah were Beno, and Shoham,
and Zaccur and Ibri. **28** Of Mahli came Eleazar, which had no sons. **29** Of
Kish: the son of Kish was Jerahmeel, **30** And the sons of [g]Mushi were Mahli,
and Eder, and Jerimoth: these were sons of the Levites after the household of their
fathers. **31** And these also cast [h]lots with their brethren the sons of Aaron before
King David, and Zadok and Ahimelech and the chief fathers of the Priests, and of
the Levites, even the chief of the families against their younger brethren.

25

The singers are appointed with their places and lots.

1 So David and the captains of the army [a]separated for the mi-
nistry the sons of Asaph, and Heman, and Jeduthun, who should sing prophe-
sies with harps, with viols, and with cymbals, and their number was even of the

---

g. 1 Chron. 22:14 For David was poor in respect of Solomon.
h. 1 Chron. 22:15 Or, masons and carpenters.
i. 1 Chron. 22:16 That is, go about it quickly.
j. 1 Chron. 22:18 The nations round about.
k. 1 Chron. 22:19 For else he knew that God would plague them, and not prosper their labor, except they sought with all their hearts to set forth his glory.

1-CHRON 22
1. 2 Sam. 7:13
2. 1 Chron. 28:3
3. 2 Sam. 7:13 / 1 Kings 5:5

1-CHRON 23
a. 1 Chron. 23:4 Or, to have care over.
b. 1 Chron. 23:5 Hebrew, I made, meaning David.
c. 1 Chron. 23:7 Or, Libni, 1 Chron. 6:17.
d. 1 Chron. 23:11 Or, Zina.
e. 1 Chron. 23:13 That is, to serve in the most holy place, and to consecrate the holy things.
f. 1 Chron. 23:14 They were but of the order of the Levites, and not of the Priests as Aaron's sons.
g. 1 Chron. 23:17 The Scripture useth to call chief or the first-born, although he be alone and there be none born after, Matt. 1:25.
h. 1 Chron. 23:22 Meaning, their cousins.
i. 1 Chron. 23:24 David did choose the Levites twice, first at the age of thirty, as verse 3 and again afterward at 20, as the necessity of the office did require: at the beginning they had no charge in the Temple, before they were five and twenty years old, and had none after fifty, Num. 4:3.
j. 1 Chron. 23:28 In washing and cleansing all the holy vessels.

1-CHRON 23
1. 1 Kings 1:30
2. 1 Chron. 6:1
3. Exod. 6:17
4. Exod. 2:2 / Exod. 6:20 / Heb. 5:4,5
5. Exod. 2:22 / Exod. 18:3

1-CHRON 24
a. 1 Chron. 24:2 While their father yet lived.
b. 1 Chron. 24:3 Or, cousins.
c. 1 Chron. 24:4 Hebrew, heads.
d. 1 Chron. 24:7 This lot was ordained to take away all occasion of envy or grudging of one against another.
e. 1 Chron. 24:10 Zacharias the father of John the Baptist was of this course or lot of Abija, Luke 1:5.
f. 1 Chron. 24:19 By the dignity that God gave to Aaron.
g. 1 Chron. 24:30 Which was the second son of Merari.
h. 1 Chron. 24:31 That is, every one had that dignity, which fell unto him by lot.

1-CHRON 24
1. Lev. 10:4,6 / Num. 3:4 / Num. 26:60

1-CHRON 25
a. 1 Chron. 25:1 The singers were divided into 24 courses, so that every course or order contained twelve, and in all there were 288, as verse 7.
b. 1 Chron. 25:2 Hebrew, hands.
c. 1 Chron. 25:3 Whereof one is not here numbered.
d. 1 Chron. 25:3 Meaning, Psalms and songs to praise God.

men for the office of their ministry, to wit, **2** Of the sons of Asaph, Zaccur, and Joseph, and Nethaniah, and Asharelah the sons of Asaph were under the hand of Asaph, which sang prophecies by the [b]commission of the King. **3** Of Jeduthun, the sons of Jeduthun, Gedaliah, and Zeri, and Jeshaiah, Hashabiah and Mattithiah, [c]six, under the hands of their father: Jeduthun sang [d]prophecies with an harp, for to give thanks and to praise the Lord. **4** Of Heman, the sons of Heman, Bukkiah, Mattaniah, Uzziel, Shebuel, and Jerimoth, Hananiah, Hanani, Eliathah, Giddalti, and Romamti-Ezer, Joshbekashah, Mallothi, Hothir, and Mahazioth. **5** All these were the sons of Heman, the King's [e]Seer in the words of God to lift up the [f]horn: and God gave to Heman fourteen sons and three daughters. **6** All these were under the [g]hand of their father singing in the house of the Lord with cymbals, viols and harps, for the service of the house of God, and Asaph, and Jeduthun, and Heman were at the King's [h]commandment. **7** So was their number with their brethren that were instructed in the songs of the Lord, even of all that were cunning, two hundred fourscore and eight. **8** And they cast lots, [i]charge against charge, as well [j]small as great, the cunning man as the scholar. **9** And the first lot fell to [k]Joseph, which was of Asaph, the second, to Gedaliah, who with his brethren and his sons were twelve. **10** The third, to Zaccur, he, his sons and his brethren were twelve. **11** The fourth, to [l]Jizri, he, his sons and his brethren twelve. **12** The fifth, to Nethaniah, he, his sons and his brethren twelve. **13** The sixth, to Bukkiah, he, his sons and his brethren twelve. **14** The seventh, to Jesharelah, he, his sons and his brethren twelve. **15** The eighth to Jeshaiah, he, his sons and his brethren twelve. **16** The ninth to Mattaniah, he, his sons and his brethren twelve. **17** The tenth to Shimei, he, his sons and his brethren twelve. **18** The eleventh to Azarel, he, his sons and his brethren twelve. **19** The twelfth to Hashabiah, he, his sons and his brethren twelve. **20** The thirteenth to Shubael, he, his sons and his brethren twelve. **21** The fourteenth to Mattithiah, he, his sons and his brethren twelve. **22** The fifteenth to Jeremoth, he, his sons and his brethren twelve. **23** The sixteenth to Hananiah, he, his sons and his brethren twelve. **24** The seventeenth to Joshbekashah, he, his sons and his brethren twelve. **25** The eighteenth to Hanani, he, his sons and his brethren twelve. **26** The nineteenth to Mallothi, he, his sons and his brethren twelve. **27** The twentieth to Eliathah, he, his sons and his brethren twelve. **28** The one and twentieth to Hothir, he, his sons and his brethren twelve. **29** The two and twentieth to Giddalti, he, his sons and his brethren twelve. **30** The three and twentieth to Mahazioth, he, his sons and his brethren twelve. **31** The four and twentieth to Romamti-Ezer, he, his sons and his brethren twelve.

26

1 The porters of the Temple are ordained, every man to the gate, which he should keep, 20 and over the treasure.

1 Concerning the [a]divisions of the porters, of the Korahites, Meshelemiah the son of Kore of the sons of [b]Asaph. **2** And the sons of Meshelemiah, Zechariah the eldest, Jediael the second, Zebadiah the third, Jathniel the fourth, **3** Elam the fifth, Jehohanan the sixth, and Eliehoenai the seventh. **4** And the sons of Obed-Edom, Shemaiah the eldest, Jehozabad the second, Joah the third, and Sacar the fourth, and Nethanel the fifth, **5** Ammiel the sixth, Issachar the seventh, Peulthai the eight: for God had [c]blessed him. **6** And to Shemaiah his son were sons born that [d]ruled in the house of their father, for they were men of might. **7** The sons of Shemaiah were Othni, and Rephael, and Obed, Elzabad, and his brethren, strong men: Elihu also, and Semachiah. **8** All these were of the [e]sons of Obed-Edom, they and their sons and their brethren mighty and [f]strong to serve, even threescore and two of Obed-Edom. **9** And of Meshelemiah sons and brethren, eighteen mighty men. **10** And of Hosah of the sons of Merari, the sons were Shimri the chief, and (though he was not the eldest, yet his father made him the chief) **11** Hilkiah the second, Tebaliah the third, and Zechariah the fourth: all the [g]sons and the brethren of Hosah were thirteen. **12** Of these were the [h]divisions of the porters, of the chief men, having the charge [i]against their brethren, to serve in the house of the Lord. **13** And they cast lots both small and great, for the house of their fathers, for every gate. **14** And the lot on the East side fell to [j]Shelemiah: then they cast lots for Zechariah his son a [k]wise counselor, and his lot came out Northward: **15** To Obed-Edom Southward, and to his sons the house of [l]Asuppim: **16** To Shuppim and to Hosah Westward with the gate [m]of Shallecheth by the paved street that goeth upward, ward over against ward. **17** Eastward were six Levites, and Northward four a day, and Southward four a day, and toward Asuppim [n]two and two. **18** In [o]Parbar toward the West were four by the paved street, and two in Parbar. **19** These are the divisions of the porters of the sons of Korah, and of the sons of Merari. **20** And of the Levites. Ahijah was over the treasures of the house of God, and over the treasures of the dedicate things. **21** Of the sons of Laadan the sons of the Gershonites descending of Laadan, the chief fathers of Laadan were Gershon and Jehieli. **22** The sons of Jehieli were Zetham and Joel his brother, appointed over the treasures of the house of the Lord. **23** Of the [p]Amramites, of the Izharites, of the Hebronites, and of the Uzzielites. **24** And Shebuel the son of Gershom, the son of Moses, a ruler over the treasures. **25** And of his [q]brethren which came of Eliezer, was Rehabiah his son, and Jeshaiah his son, and Joram his son, and Zichri his son, and Shelomith his son. **26** Which Shelomith and his brethren were over all the treasures of the dedicate things, which David the king, and the chief fathers, the captains over thousands, and hundreds, and the captains of the army had [r]dedicated. **27** (For of the battles and of the spoils they did dedicate to maintain the house of the Lord.) **28** And all that Samuel the Seer had dedicated, and Saul the son of Kish, and Abner the son of Ner, and Joab the son of Zeruiah, and whosoever had dedicated anything, it was under the hand of Shelomith, and his brethren. **29** Of the Izharites was Chenaniah and his sons, for the business [s]without over Israel, for officers and for Judges. **30** Of the Hebronites, Hashabiah and his brethren, men of activity, a thousand and seven hundred were officers for Israel beyond Jordan Westward in all the business of the Lord, and for the service of [t]the King. **31** Among the Hebronites was Jerijah the chiefest, even the Hebronites by his generations according to the families. And in the fortieth year of the reign of David they were sought for: and there were found among them men of activity at Jazer in Gilead. **32** And his [u]brethren men of activity, two thousand and seven hundred chief fathers, whom King David made rulers over the Reubenites, and the Gadites, and the half tribe of Manasseh, for every matter pertaining to [v]God, and for the king's business.

27

Of the princes and rulers that ministered unto the King.

1 The children of Israel also after their number, even the chief fathers and captains of thousands and of hundreds, and their officers that served the king by divers [a]courses, [b]which came in and went out, month by month throughout all the months of the year: in every course were four and twenty thousand. **2** Over the first course for the first month was Jashobeam the son of Zabdiel: and in his course were four and twenty thousand. **3** Of the sons of Perez was the chief over all the princes of the armies for the first month. **4** And over the course of the second month was Dodai an Ahohite, and this was his course, and Mikloth was [c]a captain, and in his course were four and twenty thousand. **5** The captain of the third host for the third month was Benaiah the son of Jehoiada the chief Priest: and in his course were four and twenty thousand. **6** This Benaiah was mighty among [/]thirty and above the thirty, and in his course was Ammizabad his son. **7** The fourth for the fourth month was Asahel the brother of Joab, and Zebadiah his son after him: and in his course were four and twenty thousand. **8** The fifth for the fifth month was prince Shamhuth the Izrahite: and in his course four and twenty thousand. **9** The sixth for the sixth month was Ira the son of Ikkesh the Tekoite: and in his course four and twenty thousand. **10** The seventh for the seventh month was Helez the Pelonite, of the sons of Ephraim: and in his course four and twenty thousand. **11** The eight for the eight month was Sibbechai the Hushathite of the Zarhites: and in his course four and twenty thousand. **12** The ninth for the ninth month was Abiezer the Anathothite of the sons of [d]Jemini: and in his course four and twenty thousand. **13** The tenth for the tenth month was Maharai the Netophathite of the Zarhites: and in his course four and twenty thousand. **14** The eleventh for the eleventh month was Benaiah the Pirathonite of the sons of Ephraim: and in his course four and twenty thousand. **15** The twelfth for the twelfth month was Heldai the Netophathite, of Othniel: and in his course four and twenty thousand. **16** Moreover [e]the rulers over the tribes of Israel were these: over the Reubenites was ruler, Eliezer the son of Zichri: over the Simeonites, Shephatiah the son of Maachah: **17** Over the Levites, Hashabiah the son of Kemuel: over them of Aaron, and Zadok: **18** Over Judah, Elihu of the brethren of David: over Issachar,

---

e. 1 Chron. 25:5 Or, Prophet.
f. 1 Chron. 25:5 Or, power, meaning of the king.
g. 1 Chron. 25:6 Or, government.
h. 1 Chron. 25:6 Hebrew, hand.
i. 1 Chron. 25:8 Who should be in every company and course.
j. 1 Chron. 25:8 Without respect to age or cunning.
k. 1 Chron. 25:9 So that he served in the first turn, and the rest everyone as his turn followed orderly.
l. 1 Chron. 25:11 Or, the Zerites.

1-CHRON 26

a. 1 Chron. 26:1 Or, courses, or turns.
b. 1 Chron. 26:1 This Asaph was not the notable musician, but another of that name called also Ebiasaph, 1 Chron. 6:23, 37 and 9:19 and also Jasaph.
c. 1 Chron. 26:5 In giving him many children.
d. 1 Chron. 26:6 Or, like their father's house, meaning, worthy men, and valiant.
e. 1 Chron. 26:8 Or, nephews.
f. 1 Chron. 26:8 And meet to serve the office of the portership.
g. 1 Chron. 26:11 Or, cousins.
h. 1 Chron. 26:12 Or, courses.
i. 1 Chron. 26:12 According to their turns as well the one as the other.
j. 1 Chron. 26:14 Or, Meshelemiah.
k. 1 Chron. 26:14 One expert and meet to keep that gate.
l. 1 Chron. 26:15 This was an house, where they used to resort to consult of things concerning the Temple, as a convocation house.
m. 1 Chron. 26:16 Whereat they used to cast out the filth of the city.
n. 1 Chron. 26:17 Meaning two one day, and two another.
o. 1 Chron. 26:18 Which was an house wherein they kept the instruments of the Temple.
p. 1 Chron. 26:23 These also had charge over the treasures.
q. 1 Chron. 26:25 Or, cousins.
r. 1 Chron. 26:26 According as the Lord commanded, Num. 31:28.
s. 1 Chron. 26:29 Meaning, of things that were out of the city.
t. 1 Chron. 26:30 That is, for the king's house.
u. 1 Chron. 26:32 To wit, the cousins of Jerijah.
v. 1 Chron. 26:32 Both in spiritual and temporal things.

1-CHRON 27

a. 1 Chron. 27:1 Hebrew, divisions, or bands.
b. 1 Chron. 27:1 Which executed their charge and office, which is meant by coming in, and going out.
c. 1 Chron. 27:4 That is, Dodai's lieutenant.
d. 1 Chron. 27:12 Or, Benjamin.
e. 1 Chron. 27:16 Meaning, besides these twelve captains.
f. 1 Chron. 27:21 Which is beyond Jordan, in respect of Judah: also one captain was over the Reubenites and the Gadites.
g. 1 Chron. 27:24 And the commandment of the King was abominable to Joab, 1 Chron. 21:6.

Omri the son of Michael: **19** Over Zebulun, Ishmaiah the son of Obadiah: over Naphtali, Jerimoth the son of Azriel: **20** Over the sons of Ephraim, Hoshea the son of Azaziah: over the half tribe of Manasseh, Joel the son of Pedaiah: **21** Over the [f]other half of Manasseh in Gilead, Iddo the son of Zechariah: over Benjamin, Jaasiel the son of Abner: **22** Over Dan, Azarel the son of Jeroham. These are the princes of the tribes of Israel. **23** But David took not the number of them from twenty years old and under, because the Lord had said that he would increase Israel like unto the stars of the heavens. **24** And [2]Joab the son of Zeruiah began to number: but he finished it not, [g]because there came wrath for it against Israel: neither was the number put into the [h]Chronicles of king David. **25** And over the king's treasures was Azmaveth the son of Adiel: and over the treasures in the fields, in the cities and in the villages, and in the towers was Jehonathan the son of Uzziah: **26** And over the workmen in the field that tilleth the ground, was Ezri the son of Chelub: **27** And over them that dressed the vines, was Shimei the Ramathite: and over that which appertained to the vines, and over the store of the wine was Zabdi the Shiphmite: **28** And over the olive trees and mulberry trees that were in the valleys, was Baal-Hanan the Gederite: and over the store of the oil was Joash: **29** And over the oxen that fed in Sharon, was Shitrai the Sharonite: and over the oxen in the valleys was Shaphat the son of Adlai: **30** And over the camels was Obil the Ishmaelite: and over the asses was Jehdeiah the Meronothite: **31** And over the sheep was Jaziz the Hagrite: all these were the rulers of the substance that was king David's. **32** And Jehonathan David's uncle a man of counsel and understanding (for he was a [i]scribe) and Jehiel the son of Hachmoni were with the King's [j]sons. **33** And Ahithophel was the king's counselor, and Hushai the Archite the king's friend. **34** And [k]after Ahithophel was Jehoiada the son of Benaiah and Abiathar: and captain of the King's army was Joab.

28

3 Because David was forbidden to build the Temple, he willeth Solomon and the people to perform it. 8 Exhorting him to fear the Lord.

1 Now David assembled all the princes of Israel: the princes of the tribes, and the captains of the bands that served the King, and the captains of thousands, and the captains of hundreds, and the rulers of all the substance and possession of the king, and of his sons, with the [a]eunuchs, and the mighty, and all the men of power, unto Jerusalem. **2** And King David stood up upon his feet, and said, Hear ye me, my brethren and my people: I purposed to have built an house of [b]rest for the Ark of the covenant of the Lord, and for a [1]footstool of our God, and have made ready for the building, **3** But God said unto me, [2]Thou shalt not build an house for my Name, because thou hast been a man of war, and hast shed blood. **4** Yet as the Lord God of Israel chose me before all the house of my father, to be King over Israel forever (for in Judah would he choose a prince, and of the house of [c]Judah is the house of my father, and among the sons of my father he delighted in me to make me king over all Israel) **5** So of all my sons (for the Lord hath given me many sons) he hath even chosen Solomon my son to sit upon the throne of the kingdom of the Lord over Israel. **6** And he said unto me, Solomon thy son, he shall build mine house and my courts: for I have chosen him to be my son, and I will be his father. **7** I will establish therefore his kingdom forever, if he endeavor himself to do my commandments, and my judgments, as [d]this day. **8** Now therefore in the sight of all Israel the congregation of the Lord, and in the audience of our God, keep and seek for all the commandments of the Lord your God, that ye may possess this [e]good land, and leave it for an inheritance for your children after you [f]forever. **9** And thou, Solomon my son, know thou the God of thy father, and serve him with a perfect heart, and with a willing mind: [3]For the Lord searcheth all hearts, and understandeth all the imaginations of thoughts: if thou seek him, he will be found of thee, but if thou forsake him, he will cast thee off forever. **10** Take heed now, for the Lord hath chosen thee to build [g]the house of the Sanctuary: be strong therefore and [h]do it. **11** Then David gave to Solomon his son the pattern of the porch and of the houses thereof, and of the closets thereof, and of the galleries thereof, and of the chambers thereof that are within, and of the house of the mercy seat, **12** And the pattern of all that [i]he had in his mind for the courts of the house of the Lord, and for all the chambers round about, for the treasures of the house of God, and for the treasures of the dedicate things, **13** And for the courses of the Priests, and of the Levites, and for all the work for the service of the house of the Lord, and for all the vessels of the ministry of the house of the Lord. **14** He gave of gold by weight, for the vessels of gold, for all the vessels of all manner of service, and all the vessels of silver by weight, for all manner vessels of all manner of service. **15** The weight also of gold for the [j]candlesticks, and gold for their lamps, with the weight for every candlestick, and for the lamps thereof, and for the candlesticks of silver by the weight of the candlestick, and the lamps thereof according to the use of every candlestick, **16** And the weight of the gold for the tables of showbread, for every table, and silver for the tables of silver, **17** And pure gold for the fleshhooks, and the bowls, and [k]plates, and for basins, gold in weight for every basin, and for silver basins, by weight for every basin, **18** And for the altar of incense, pure gold by weight, and gold for the pattern of [l]the chariot of the Cherubs that spread themselves, and covered the Ark of the covenant of the Lord: **19** All, said he, by writing sent to me [m]by the hand of the Lord, which made me understand all the workmanship of the pattern. **20** And David said to Solomon his son, Be strong and of a valiant courage, and do it: fear not, nor be afraid: for the Lord God, even my God is with thee: he will not leave thee, nor forsake thee, till thou hast finished all the work for the service of the house of the Lord. **21** Behold also, the companies of the Priests and the Levites for all the service of the house of God, even they shall be with thee for the whole work, [n]with every free heart that is skillful in any manner of service. The princes also and all the people will be [o]wholly at thy commandment.

29

2 The offering of David and of the princes for the building of the Temple. 10 David giveth thanks to the Lord. 20 He exhorteth the people to do the same. 22 Solomon is created king. 28 David dieth, and Solomon his son reigneth in his stead.

1 Moreover, David the King said unto all the Congregation, God hath chosen Solomon mine only son, young and tender, and the work is great: for this house is not for man, but for the [a]Lord God. **2** Now I have prepared with all my power for the house of my God, gold for vessels of gold, and silver for them of silver, and brass for things of brass, iron for things of iron, and wood for things of wood, and onyx stones, and stones to be set, and carbuncle stones, and of divers colors, and all precious stones, and marble stones in abundance. **3** Moreover, because I have [b]delight in the house of my God, I have of mine own gold and silver, which I have given to the house of my God, beside all that I have prepared for the house of the Sanctuary, **4** Even [c]three thousand talents of gold of the gold of Ophir, and seven thousand talents of fined silver to overlay the walls of the houses. **5** The gold for the things of gold, and the silver for things of silver, and for all the work by the hands of artificers: and who is [d]willing [e]to fill his hand today unto the Lord? **6** So the princes of the families, and the princes of the tribes of Israel, and the captains of thousands and of hundreds, with the rulers of the king's work, offered willingly, **7** And they gave for the service of the house of God, five thousand talents of gold, and ten thousand pieces, and ten thousand talents of silver, and eighteen thousand talents of brass, and one hundred thousand talents of iron. **8** And they with whom precious stones were [f]found, gave them to the treasure of the house of the Lord, by the hand of Jehiel the Gershonite. **9** And the people rejoiced when they offered willingly: for they offered willingly unto the Lord, with a [g]perfect heart. And David the king also [1]rejoiced with great joy. **10** Therefore David blessed the Lord before all the Congregation, and David said, Blessed be thou, O Lord God of [h]Israel our father, forever and ever. **11** Thine, O Lord, is greatness and power, and glory and victory, and praise: for all that is in heaven and in earth is thine: thine is the kingdom, O Lord, and thou excellest as head over all. **12** Both riches and honor come of thee, and thou reignest over all, and in thine hand is power and strength, and in thine hand it is to make great, and to

---

h. 1 Chron. 27:24 The Hebrews make both these books of Chronicles but one, and at this verse make the midst of the book as touching the number of verses.
i. 1 Chron. 27:32 That is, a man learned in the word of God.
j. 1 Chron. 27:32 To be their schoolmasters and teachers.
k. 1 Chron. 27:34 After that Ahithophel had hanged himself, 2 Sam. 17:23, Jehoiada was made counselor.

1-CHRON 27

1. 2 Sam. 23:20 / 2 Sam. 22:23
2. 1 Chron. 21:7

1-CHRON 28

a. 1 Chron. 28:1 Or, chief servants, Gen. 37:36.
b. 1 Chron. 28:2 Where the Ark should remain, and remove no more to and fro.
c. 1 Chron. 28:4 According to the prophecy of Jacob, Gen. 49:8.
d. 1 Chron. 28:7 If he continue to keep my law and depart not therefrom, as he doeth hitherto.
e. 1 Chron. 28:8 To wit, of Canaan.
f. 1 Chron. 28:8 He declareth that nothing can separate them from the commodity of this land, both for themselves and their posterity, but their sins and iniquity.
g. 1 Chron. 28:10 Meaning, for his Ark.
h. 1 Chron. 28:10 Put it in execution.
i. 1 Chron. 28:12 Hebrew, that were in his spirit with him.
j. 1 Chron. 28:15 That is, the ten candlesticks, 1 Kings 7:49.
k. 1 Chron. 28:17 Or, coverings.
l. 1 Chron. 28:18 Meaning, of the mercy seat which covered the Ark, which was called the chariot, because the Lord declared himself there.
m. 1 Chron. 28:19 For all this was left in writing in the book of the Law, Exod. 25:40, which book the king was bound to put in execution, Deut. 17:19.
n. 1 Chron. 28:21 That is, everyone will be ready to help thee with those gifts that God hath given him.
o. 1 Chron. 28:21 Hebrew, at all thy words.

1-CHRON 28

1. Ps. 96:5
2. 2 Sam. 7:5,13 / 1 Chron. 22:8
3. 1 Sam. 16:7 / Ps. 7:9 / Jer. 11:20 / Jer. 17:10 / Jer. 20:12

1-CHRON 29

a. 1 Chron. 29:1 And therefore is taught to be excellent in all points.
b. 1 Chron. 29:3 His great zeal toward the furtherance of the Temple made him to spare no expenses, but to bestow his own peculiar treasure.
c. 1 Chron. 29:4 He showeth what he had of his own store for the Lord's house.
d. 1 Chron. 29:5 He was not only liberal himself, but provoked others to set forth the works of God.
e. 1 Chron. 29:5 Or, to offer.
f. 1 Chron. 29:8 Meaning, them that had any.
g. 1 Chron. 29:9 That is, with a good courage and without hypocrisy.
h. 1 Chron. 29:10 Which didst reveal thyself to our father Jacob.
i. 1 Chron. 29:14 We gave thee nothing of our own, but that which we have received of thee: for whether the gifts be corporal or spiritual, we receive them all of God, and therefore must give him the glory.
j. 1 Chron. 29:15 And therefore have this land but lent to us for a time.
k. 1 Chron. 29:15 Hebrew, waiting for them to return.

give strength unto all. **13** Now therefore, our God, we thank thee, and praise
thy glorious Name. **14** But who am I, and what is my people, that we should be
able to offer willingly after this sort? for all things [i]come of thee: and of thine own
hand we have given thee. **15** For we are [j]strangers before thee, and sojourners
like all our fathers: our days are like the shadow upon the earth, and there is none
[k]abiding. **16** O Lord our God, all this abundance that we have prepared to build
thee an house for thine holy Name, is of thine hand, and all is thine. **17** I know
also my God, that thou [2]triest the heart, and hast pleasure in righteousness: I have
offered willingly in the uprightness of mine heart all these things: now also have I
seen thy people which are found here, to offer unto thee willingly with joy. **18** O
Lord God of Abraham, Isaac, and Israel our fathers, keep this forever in the [l]pur-
pose, and the thoughts of the heart of thy people, and prepare their hearts unto
thee. **19** And give unto Solomon my son a perfect heart to keep thy command-
ments, thy testimonies, and thy statutes, and to do all things, and to build the hou-
se which I have prepared. **20** And David said to all the congregation, Now bless
the Lord your God. And all the Congregation blessed the Lord God of their fathers,
and bowed down their heads, and worshipped the Lord and the [m]king. **21** And
they offered sacrifices unto the Lord, and on the morrow after that day, they offered
burnt offerings unto the Lord, even a thousand young bullocks, a thousand rams,
and a thousand sheep, with their [n]drink offerings, and sacrifices in abundance for
all Israel. **22** And they did eat and drink before the Lord the same day with great
joy, and they made Solomon the son of David king the second time, and anoin-
ted him prince before the Lord, and Zadok for the high Priest. **23** So Solomon
sat on the [o]throne of the Lord, as king instead of David his father, and prospered:
and all Israel obeyed him. **24** And all the princes and men of power, and all the
sons of king David [p]submitted themselves under king Solomon. **25** And the
Lord magnified Solomon in dignity, in the sight of all Israel, and gave him so glo-
rious a kingdom, as no king had before him in Israel. **26** [3]Thus David the son
of Jesse reigned over all Israel. **27** And the space that he reigned over Israel, was
forty years: seven years reigned he in Hebron, and three and thirty years reigned
he in Jerusalem: **28** And he died in a good age, full of days, riches and honor,
and Solomon his son reigned in his stead. **29** Concerning the acts of David the

l. 1 Chron. 29:18 Continue them in his good mind, that they may serve thee willingly.
m. 1 Chron. 29:20 That is, did reverence the king.
n. 1 Chron. 29:21 Meaning, all kind of liquor which they mingled with their sacrifices, as wine, oil, etc.
o. 1 Chron. 29:23 This declareth that the Kings of Judah were figures of Christ, who was the true anointed, and to whom God gave the chief government of all things.
p. 1 Chron. 29:24 Hebrew, gave the hand.
q. 1 Chron. 29:29 The books of Nathan and Gad are thought to have been lost in the captivity.
r. 1 Chron. 29:30 Meaning, the troubles and griefs.

1-CHRON 29
1. Ps. 122:1
2. 1 Sam. 16:7 / 1 Chron. 28:9
3. 1 Kings 2:11

THE SECOND BOOK OF THE CHRONICLES

1

6 The offering of Solomon at Gibeon. 8 He prayeth unto God to give him wisdom: 11 Which he giveth him, and more. 14 The number of his chariots and horsemen, 15 and of his riches.

1 Then Solomon the son of David was [a]confirmed in his kingdom: and the
Lord his God was with him, and magnified him highly. **2** And Solomon [b]spake
unto all Israel, to the captains of thousands, and of hundreds, and to the judges,
and to all the governors in all Israel, even the chief fathers. **3** So Solomon and all
the Congregation with him went to the high place that was at [c]Gibeon: for there
was the Tabernacle [d]of the Congregation of God which Moses the servant of the
Lord had made in the wilderness. **4** But the Ark of God had David brought up
from Kirjath Jearim, when David had made preparation for it: for he had pitched
a tent for it in Jerusalem. **5** Moreover, the [e]brazen altar [1]that Bezalel the son of
Uri, the son of Hur had made, did he set before the Tabernacle of the Lord: and
Solomon and the Congregation sought it. **6** And Solomon offered there before
the Lord upon the brazen altar that was in the Tabernacle of the Congregation:
[2]even a thousand burnt offerings offered he upon it. **7** The same night did God
appear unto Solomon, and said unto him, Ask what I shall give thee. **8** And
Solomon said unto God, Thou hast showed great mercy unto David my father,
and hast made me to reign in his stead. **9** Now therefore, O Lord God, let thy
promise unto David my father be [f]true: for thou hast made me King over a great
people, like to the dust of the earth. **10** Give me now wisdom and knowledge,
that I may [g]go out and go in before this people: for who can judge this thy great
people? **11** And God said to Solomon, Because this was in thine heart, and thou
hast not asked riches, treasures nor honor, nor the [h]lives of thine enemies, neither
yet hast asked long life, but hast asked for thee wisdom and knowledge, that thou
mightest judge my people, over whom I have made thee King, **12** Wisdom and
knowledge is granted unto thee, and I will give thee riches and treasures and ho-
nor, so that there hath not been the like among the kings which were before thee,
neither after thee shall there be the like. **13** Then Solomon came from the high
place that was at Gibeon, to Jerusalem from before the Tabernacle of the Congre-
gation, and reigned over Israel. **14** [3]And Solomon gathered the chariots and
horsemen: and he had a thousand and four hundred chariots, and twelve thousand
horsemen, whom he placed in the [i]chariot cities, and with the King at Jerusa-
lem. **15** And the king gave gold and silver at Jerusalem as [j]stone, and gave cedar
trees as the wild fig trees, that are abundantly in the plain. **16** Also Solomon had
horses brought out of Egypt, and [4]fine linen: [k]the King's merchants received the
fine linen for a price. **17** They came up also and brought out of Egypt some cha-
riot, worth six hundred shekels of silver, that is an horse for an hundred and fifty:
and thus they brought horses to all the kings of the Hittites, and to the kings of
Aram by their [l]means.

2

2 The number of Solomon's workmen to build the Temple. 3 Solomon sendeth to Huram the King of Tyre for wood and workmen.

1 Then Solomon determined to build an house for the Name of the Lord, and
an [a]house for his kingdom. **2** And Solomon told out seventy thousand that bare
burdens, and fourscore thousand men to hew stones in the mountain, and three
thousand and [b]six hundred to oversee them. **3** And Solomon sent to [c]Huram
the king of Tyre, saying, As thou hast done to David my father, and didst [1]send
him cedar trees to build him an house to dwell in so do to me. **4** Behold, I bu-
ild an house unto the Name of the Lord my God, to sanctify it unto him, and
to burn sweet incense before him, and for the continual showbread, and for the
burnt offerings of the morning and evening, on the Sabbath days, and in the new
months, and in the solemn feasts of the Lord our God: this is a perpetual thing
for Israel. **5** And the house which I build, is great: for great is our God above all
gods. **6** Who is he then that can be able to build him an house, when the heaven
and the heaven of heavens can not contain him? who am I then that I should build
him an house? but I do it to burn [d]incense before him. **7** Send me now there-
fore a cunning man that can work in gold, in silver, and in brass, and in iron, and

2-CHRON. 1
a. 2 Chron. 1:1 Or, stablished, and strong, read 1 Kings 2:46.
b. 2 Chron. 1:2 That is, he proclaimed a solemn sacrifice, and commanded that all should be at the same.
c. 2 Chron. 1:3 Read 1 Kings 3:4.
d. 2 Chron. 1:3 So called, because that God thereby showed certain signs to the congregation of his presence.
e. 2 Chron. 1:5 Which was for the burnt offerings, Exod. 27:1.
f. 2 Chron. 1:9 Perform thy promise made to my father concerning me.
g. 2 Chron. 1:10 That I may govern this people, read 1 Chron. 27:1 and 1 Kings 3:7.
h. 2 Chron. 1:11 That is, to be revenged on thine enemies.
i. 2 Chron. 1:14 Which were cities appointed to keep and maintain the chariots.
j. 2 Chron. 1:15 He caused so great plenty, that it was no more esteemed than stones.
k. 2 Chron. 1:16 Read 1 Kings. 10:28.
l. 2 Chron. 1:17 Hebrew, hands.

2-CHRON. 1
1. Exod. 38:1,2
2. 2 Kings 3:4
3. 1 Kings 10:26
4. Isa. 19:9 / Ezek. 27:7

2-CHRON. 2
a. 2 Chron. 2:1 Or, Palace.
b. 2 Chron. 2:2 Which is to be understood of all sorts of officers and overseers: for else the chief officers were but 3300, as in 1 Kings 5:16.
c. 2 Chron. 2:3 Or, Hiram.

king, first and last, behold they are written in the book of Samuel the Seer, and in
the book of [q]Nathan the Prophet, and in the book of Gad the Seer, **30** With all
his reign and his power, and [r]times that went over him, and over Israel, and over
all the kingdoms of the earth.

in purple, and in [e]crimson and blue silk, and that can grave in graven work with the cunning men that are with me in Judah and in Jerusalem, whom David my father hath prepared. **8** Send me also cedar trees, fir trees and [f,g]Algummim trees from Lebanon: for I know that thy servants can skill to hew timber in Lebanon: and behold, my servants shall be with thine, **9** That they may prepare me timber in abundance: for the house which I do build, is great and wonderful. **10** And behold, I will give to thy servants the cutters and the hewers of timber twenty thousand [h]measures of beaten wheat, and twenty thousand measures of barley, and twenty thousand baths of wine, and twenty [i]thousand baths of oil. **11** Then Huram king of Tyre answered in writing which he sent to Solomon, Because the Lord hath loved his people, he hath made thee King over them. **12** Huram said moreover, Blessed be the Lord God of Israel, which made the heaven and the earth, and that hath given unto David the King a [j]wise son, that hath discretion, prudence and understanding to build an house for the Lord, and a palace for his kingdom. **13** Now therefore I have sent a wise man, and of understanding of my father Huram's, **14** The son of a woman, of the [k]daughters of Dan: and his father was a man of Tyre, and he can skill to work in gold, in silver, in brass, in iron, in stone, and in timber, in purple, in blue silk, and in fine linen, and in crimson, and can grave in all graven works, and broider in all broidered work that shall be given him, with thy cunning men, and with the cunning men of my lord David thy father. **15** Now therefore the wheat and the barley, the oil and the wine, which my lord hath spoken of, let him send unto his servants. **16** And we will cut wood in Lebanon as much as thou shalt need, and will bring it to thee in [l]rafts by the sea to [m]Japho, so thou mayest carry them to Jerusalem. **17** And Solomon numbered all the strangers that were in the land of Israel, after the numbering that his father David had numbered them: and they were found an hundred and three and fifty thousand, and six hundred. **18** And he set seventy thousand of them to the burden, and fourscore thousand to hew stones in the mountain, and three thousand and six hundred overseers to cause the people to work.

3

1 The Temple of the Lord, and the porch are built, with other things thereto belonging.

1 So [1]Solomon began to build the house of the Lord in Jerusalem, in mount [a]Moriah which had been declared unto David his father, in the place that David prepared in the threshing floor of [2]Ornan the Jebusite. **2** And he began to build in the second month and the second day, in the fourth year of his reign. **3** And these are the measures whereon Solomon grounded to build the house of God: the length of cubits after the first [b]measure was threescore cubits, and the breadth twenty cubits: **4** And the porch that was before the length in the front [c]of the breadth was twenty cubits, and the height was an [d]hundred and twenty, and he overlaid it within with pure gold. **5** And the greater house he ceiled with fir tree which he overlaid with good gold, and graved thereon palm trees and chains. **6** And he overlaid the house with precious stones for beauty: and the gold was gold of [e]Parvaim. **7** The house, I say, the beams, posts, and walls thereof and the doors thereof overlaid he with gold, and graved Cherubims upon the walls. **8** He made also the house of the most holy place: the length thereof was in the front of the breadth of the house, twenty cubits, and the breadth thereof twenty cubits: and he overlaid it with the best gold, of six hundred talents. **9** And the weight of the nails was fifty shekels of gold, and he overlaid the chambers with gold. **10** And in the house of the most holy place he made two Cherubims wrought like children, and overlaid them with gold. **11** [3]And the wings of the Cherubims were twenty cubits long: the one wing was five cubits, reaching to the wall of the house, and the other wing five cubits, reaching to the wing of the other Cherub. **12** Likewise the wing of the other Cherub was five cubits, reaching to the wall of the house, and the other wing five cubits, joining to the wing of the other Cherub. **13** The wings of these Cherubims were spread abroad twenty cubits, they stood on their feet, and their faces were toward the house. **14** He made also the [f]veil of blue silk and purple, and crimson, and fine linen, and wrought Cherubims thereon. **15** And he made before the house two pillars [g]of five and thirty cubits high: and the chapiter that was upon the top of each of them, was five cubits. **16** He made also chains for the Oracle, and put them on the heads of the pillars, and made an [h]hundred pomegranates, and put them among the chains. **17** And he set up the pillars before the Temple, one on the right hand, and the other on the left, and called that on the right hand Jachin, and that on the left hand Boaz.

4

1 The altar of brass. 2 The molten sea. 6 The caldrons. 7 The candlesticks, etc.

1 And he made an altar of brass twenty cubits long, and twenty cubits broad, and ten cubits high. **2** And he made a molten [a]Sea of ten cubits from brim to brim, round in compass, and five cubits high: and a line of thirty cubits did compass it about. **3** And under [b]it was the fashion of oxen, which did compass it round about, [c]ten in a cubit compassing the Sea about: two rows of oxen were cast when it was molten. **4** It stood upon twelve oxen: three looked toward the North, and three looked toward the West, and three looked toward the South, and three looked toward the East, and the Sea stood above upon them, and all their hinder parts were inward. **5** And the thickness thereof was an hand breadth, and the brim thereof was like the work of the brim of a cup, with flowers of [d]lilies: it contained [e]three thousand baths. **6** He made also ten caldrons, and put five on the right hand, and five on the left, to wash in them, and to cleanse in them that which appertained to the burnt offerings: but the Sea was for the Priests to wash in. **7** And he made ten candlesticks of gold (according to [f]their form) and put them in the Temple, five on the right hand, and five on the left. **8** And he made ten tables, and put them in the Temple, five on the right hand, and five on the left: and he made an hundred basins of gold. **9** And he made the [g]court of the Priests, and the great court and doors for the court, and overlaid the doors thereof with brass. **10** And he set the Sea on the right side Eastward toward the South. **11** And Huram made [h]pots and besoms and basins, and Huram finished the work that he should make for King Solomon for the house of God, **12** To wit, two pillars, and the bowls and the chapiters on the top of the two pillars, and two grates to cover the two bowls of the chapiters which were upon the top of the pillars: **13** And four hundred pomegranates for the two grates, two rows of pomegranates for every grate to cover the two bowls of the chapiters, that were upon the pillars. **14** He made also bases, and made caldrons upon the bases: **15** And a Sea, and twelve bulls under it: **16** Pots also and besoms, and flesh hooks, and all these vessels made Huram [i]his father to King Solomon for the house of the Lord of shining brass. **17** In the plain of Jordan did the King cast them in clay between Succoth and Zeredathah. **18** And Solomon made all these vessels in great abundance: for the weight of brass could not be reckoned. **19** And Solomon made all the vessels that were for the house of God: the golden altar also and the tables, whereon the [j]showbread stood. **20** Moreover, the candlesticks with their lamps, to burn them after the manner before the Oracle, of pure gold. **21** And the flowers and the lamps, and the snuffers of gold, which was fine gold. **22** And the [k]hooks, and the basins, and the spoons, and the ash pans of pure gold: the entry also of the house and doors thereof within, even of the most holy place: and the doors of the house, to wit, of the Temple were [l]of gold.

5

1 The things dedicated by David are put in the Temple. 2 The Ark is brought into the Tmple. 10 What was within it. 12 They sing praise to the Lord.

1 So [1]was all the work finished that Solomon made for the house of the Lord, and Solomon brought in the things that David his father had dedicated, with the silver and the gold, and all the vessels, and put them among the treasures of the house of God. **2** Then Solomon assembled the Elders of Israel, and all the

---

d. 2 Chron. 2:6 That is, to do the service which he hath commanded, signifying that none is able to honor and serve God in that perfection as his majesty deserveth.
e. 2 Chron. 2:7 Or, scarlet.
f. 2 Chron. 2:8 Some take it for Brasil, or the wood called Ebenum, others for coral.
g. 2 Chron. 2:8 Or, Almuggim.
h. 2 Chron. 2:10 Hebrew, Corins.
i. 2 Chron. 2:10 Of Bath read 1 Kings 7:26, it is called also Ephah, but Ephah is to measure dry things, as Bath is a measure for liquors.
j. 2 Chron. 2:12 The very heavens confessed that it was a singular gift of God, when he gave to any nation a King that was wise and of understanding, albeit it appeareth that this Hiram had the true knowledge of God.
k. 2 Chron. 2:14 It is also written that she was of the tribe of Naphtali, 1 Kings 7:14, which may be understood that by reason of the confusion of tribes, which then began to be, they married in divers tribes, so that by her father she might be of Dan, and by her mother of Naphtali.
l. 2 Chron. 2:16 Or, ships.
m. 2 Chron. 2:16 Or, Joppa.

2-CHRON. 2
1. 2 Sam. 5:11

2-CHRON. 3
a. 2 Chron. 3:1 Which is the mountain where Abraham thought to have sacrificed his son, Gen. 22:2.
b. 2 Chron. 3:3 According to the whole length of the Temple, comprehending the most holy place with the rest.
c. 2 Chron. 3:4 It contained as much as did the breadth of the Temple, 1 Kings 6:3.
d. 2 Chron. 3:4 From the foundation to the top: for in the book of the kings mention is made from the foundation to the first stage.
e. 2 Chron. 3:6 Some think it is that place which is called Peru.
f. 2 Chron. 3:14 Which separated the Temple from the most holy place.
g. 2 Chron. 3:15 Every one was eighteen cubits long, but the half cubit could not be seen, for it was hid in the roundness of the chapiter, and therefore he giveth to every one but 17 and an half.
h. 2 Chron. 3:16 For every pillar an hundred, read 1 Kings 7:20.

2-CHRON. 3
1. 1 Kings 6:1
2. 2 Sam. 24:16,21
3. 1 Kings 6:14

2-CHRON. 4
a. 2 Chron. 4:2 A great vessel of brass, so called, because of the great quantity of water, which it contained, 1 Kings 7:24.
b. 2 Chron. 4:3 Meaning, under the brim of the vessel, as 1 Kings 7:24.
c. 2 Chron. 4:3 In the length of every cubit were ten heads or knops which in all are 300.
d. 2 Chron. 4:5 Or, flower delices.
e. 2 Chron. 4:5 In 1 Kings 7:26, mention is only made of two thousand, but the less number was taken there, and here according as the measures proved afterward, is declared.
f. 2 Chron. 4:7 Even as they should be made.
g. 2 Chron. 4:9 Called also the porch of Solomon, Act 3:11. It is also taken for the Temple where Christ preached, Matt. 21:23.
h. 2 Chron. 4:11 Or, cauldrons.
i. 2 Chron. 4:16 Whom Solomon reverenced for the gifts that God had given him, as a father: he had the same name also that Huram the king of Tyre had, his mother was a Jewess, and his father a Tyrian. Some read for his father, the author of this work.
j. 2 Chron. 4:19 In Hebrew, the bread of the faces, because they were set before the Ark, where the Lord showed his presence.
k. 2 Chron. 4:22 Or, instruments of music.
l. 2 Chron. 4:22 That is, covered with plates of gold.

heads of the tribes, the chief fathers of the children of Israel unto Jerusalem, to
bring up the Ark of the covenant of the Lord from the [a]city of David, which is
Zion. **3** And all the men of Israel assembled unto the king at the [b]feast: it was
in the seventh [c]month. **4** And all the Elders of Israel came, and the Levites took
up the Ark. **5** And they carried up the Ark, and the Tabernacle of the Congrega-
tion: and all the holy vessels that were in the Tabernacle, those did the Priests and
Levites bring up. **6** And king Solomon and all the Congregation of Israel that
were assembled unto him, were before the Ark, offering sheep and bullocks, which
could not be told nor numbered for multitude. **7** So the Priests brought the Ark
of the covenant of the Lord unto his place, into the Oracle of the house, into the
most Holy place, even under the wings of the Cherubims. **8** For the Cherubims
stretched out their wings over the place of the Ark, and the Cherubims covered the
Ark and the bars thereof above. **9** And they drew out the bars, that the ends of
the bars might be seen out of the Ark before the Oracle, but they were not seen
[d]without: and there they are unto this day. **10** Nothing was in the Ark, save [e]the
two Tables, which Moses gave at Horeb, where the Lord made a covenant with the
children of Israel when they came out of Egypt. **11** And when the Priests were
come out of the Sanctuary (for all the Priests that were present, were [f]sanctified and
did not wait by course. **12** And the Levites the singers of all sorts, as of Asaph,
of Heman, of Jeduthun, and of their sons and of their brethren, being clad in fine
linen, stood with cymbals, and with viols, and harps at the East end of the Altar,
and with them an hundred and twenty Priests blowing with trumpets. **13** And
they were [g]as one, blowing trumpets, and singing, and made one sound to be he-
ard in praising and thanking the Lord, and when they lifted up their voice with
trumpets, and with cymbals, and with instruments of music, and when they prai-
sed the Lord, singing, [h]For he is good, because his mercy lasteth forever) then the
house, even the house of the Lord was filled with a cloud, **14** So that the Priests
could not stand to minister, because of the cloud: for the glory of the Lord had
filled the house of God.

6

3 Solomon blesseth the people. 4 He praiseth the Lord. 14 He prayeth unto God for those that shall pray in the Temple.

1 Then [1]Solomon [a]said, The Lord hath said that he would dwell in the dark
cloud: **2** And I have built thee an house to dwell in, an habitation for thee to
dwell in forever. **3** And the King turned his face, and blessed all the Congregation
of Israel (for all the Congregation of Israel stood there.) **4** And he said, Blessed be
the Lord God of Israel, who spake with his mouth unto David my father, and hath
with his [b]hand fulfilled it, saying, **5** Since the day that I brought my people out
of the land of Egypt, I chose no city of all the tribes of Israel to build an [c]house,
that my Name might be there, neither chose I any man to be a ruler over my people
Israel: **6** But I have chosen Jerusalem, that my Name might be there, and have
chosen David to be over my people Israel. **7** [2]And it was in the heart of David
my father to build an house unto the Name of the Lord God of Israel. **8** But the
Lord said to David my father, Whereas it was in thine heart to build an house unto
my Name, thou diddest well, that [d]thou wast so minded. **9** Notwithstanding,
thou shalt not build the house, but thy son, which shall come out of thy loins, he
shall build an house unto my Name. **10** And the Lord hath performed his word
that he spake: and I am risen up in the room of David my father, and am set on
the throne of Israel as the Lord promised, and have built an house to the Name of
the Lord God of Israel. **11** And I have set the Ark there, wherein is the [e]covenant
of the Lord, that he made with the children of Israel. **12** And the [f]king stood
before the altar of the Lord, in the presence of all the Congregation of Israel, and
stretched out his hands, **13** (For Solomon had made a brazen scaffold, and set it
in the midst of the court, of five cubits long, and five cubits broad, and three cubits
of height, and upon it he stood, and kneeled down upon his knees before all the
Congregation of Israel, and [g]stretched out his hands toward heaven.) **14** And
said, O Lord God of Israel, there is no God like thee in heaven nor in earth, whi-
ch keepest covenant and mercy unto thy servants, that walk before thee with all
their heart. **15** Thou that hast kept with thy servant David my father, that thou
hast promised him: for thou spakest with thy mouth, and hast fulfilled it with
thine [h]hand, as appeareth this day. **16** Therefore now, Lord God of Israel, keep
with thy servant David my father, that thou hast promised him, saying, Thou
[i]shalt not want a man in my sight, that shall sit upon the throne of Israel, so that
thy sons take heed to their ways to walk in my Law, as thou hast walked before
me. **17** And now, O Lord God of Israel, let thy word be verified, which thou
spakest unto thy servant David. **18** (Is it true indeed that God will dwell with
man on earth? behold, the [3]heavens, and the heavens of heavens are not able to
contain thee: how much more unable is this house which I have built?) **19** But
have thou respect to the prayer of thy servant, and to his supplication, O Lord my
God, to hear the cry and prayer which thy servant prayeth before thee, **20** That
thine [j]eyes may be open toward this house day and night, even toward the place,
whereof thou hast said, that thou wouldest put thy Name there, that thou mayest
hearken unto the prayer, which thy servant prayeth in this place. **21** Hear thou
therefore the supplication of thy servant, and of thy people Israel, which they pray
in this place: and hear thou in the place of thine habitation, even in heaven, and
when thou hearest, be merciful. **22** [4]When a man shall sin against his [k]neighbor,
and he lay upon him an oath to cause him to swear, and the [l]swearer shall come
before thine altar in this house, **23** Then hear thou in heaven, and do, and judge
thy servants, in recompensing the wicked to bring his way [m]upon his head, and
in justifying the righteous, to give him according to his righteousness. **24** And
when thy people Israel shall be overthrown before the enemy, because they have
sinned against thee, and turn again, and [n]confess thy Name, and pray, and make
supplication before thee in this house, **25** Then hear thou in heaven, and be
merciful unto the sin of thy people Israel, and bring them again unto the land
which thou gavest to them and to their fathers. **26** When heaven shall be shut
up, and there shall be no rain, because they have sinned against thee, and shall
pray in this place and confess thy Name, and [o]turn from their sin, when thou dost
afflict them, **27** Then hear thou in heaven, and pardon the sin of thy servants,
and of thy people Israel (when thou hast taught them the good way wherein they
may walk) and give rain upon thy land, which thou hast given unto thy people for
an inheritance. **28** [5]When there shall be famine in the land, when there shall
be pestilence, blasting, or mildew, when there shall be grasshopper, or caterpillar,
when their enemy shall besiege them [p]in the cities of their land, or any plague or
any sickness, **29** Then what prayer and supplication soever shall be made of any
man, or of all thy people Israel, when every one shall know his own plague, and his
own disease, and shall stretch forth his hands toward this house, **30** Hear thou
then in heaven, thy dwelling place, and be merciful, and give every man according
unto all his ways, as thou dost know his [q]heart (for thou only knowest the hearts
of the children of men) **31** That they may fear thee, and walk in thy ways, as
long as they live in the land which thou gavest unto our fathers. **32** Moreover,
as touching the stranger which is not of thy people Israel, who shall come out of
a far country for thy great Name's sake, and thy mighty hand, and thy stretched
out arm: when they shall come and [r]pray in this house, **33** Hear thou in heaven,
thy dwelling place, and do according to all that the stranger calleth for unto thee,
that all the people of the earth may know thy Name, and fear thee like thy people
Israel, and that they may know that thy Name is called upon in this house which
I have built. **34** When thy people shall go out to battle against their enemies,
by the way that [s]thou shalt send them, and they pray to thee, [t]in the way toward
this city, which thou hast chosen, even toward the house which I have built to thy
Name, **35** Then hear thou in heaven their prayer and their supplication, and ju-
dge their cause. **36** If they sin against thee ([6]for there is no man that sinneth not)
and thou be angry with them, and deliver them unto the enemies, and they take
them and carry them away captive unto a land far or near, **37** If they [u]turn again
to their heart in the land whither they be carried in captives, and turn and pray
unto thee in the land of their captivity, saying, We have sinned, we have transgres-
sed and have done wickedly, **38** If they turn again to thee with all their heart,
and with all their soul in the land of their captivity, whither they have carried them
captives, and pray toward their land, which thou gavest unto their fathers, and
toward the city which thou hast chosen, and toward the house which I have built
for thy Name, **39** Then hear thou in heaven, in the place of thine habitation,
their prayer and their supplication, and [v]judge their cause, and be merciful unto

---

2-CHRON. 5

- **a.** 2 Chron. 5:2 Read 2 Sam. 6:12.
- **b.** 2 Chron. 5:3 When the things were dedicated and brought into the Temple.
- **c.** 2 Chron. 5:3 Called in Hebrew Ethanim, containing part of September and part of October, 1 Kings 8:2, which moveth the Jews called the first month, because they say, that the world was created in that month, and after they came from Egypt, they began at March: but because this opinion is uncertain, we make March ever the first, as best writers do.
- **d.** 2 Chron. 5:9 Or, without the Oracle.
- **e.** 2 Chron. 5:10 For Aaron's rod and Manna were taken thence before it was brought to this place.
- **f.** 2 Chron. 5:11 Were prepared to serve the Lord.
- **g.** 2 Chron. 5:13 They agreed all in one tune.
- **h.** 2 Chron. 5:13 This was the effect of their songs, Ps. 118:1 and 136:1.

2-CHRON. 5

1. 1 Kings 7:51 / 1 Kings 8:1

2-CHRON. 6

- **a.** 2 Chron. 6:1 After that he had served the glory of the Lord in the cloud.
- **b.** 2 Chron. 6:4 Or, power.
- **c.** 2 Chron. 6:5 Or, Temple.
- **d.** 2 Chron. 6:8 Hebrew, that it was in thine heart.
- **e.** 2 Chron. 6:11 Meaning, the two Tables, wherein is contained the effect of the covenant that God made with our fathers.
- **f.** 2 Chron. 6:12 On a scaffold that was made for that purpose, that he praying for the whole people might be heard of all, as 1 Kings 8:22.
- **g.** 2 Chron. 6:13 Both to give thanks for the great benefits of God bestowed upon him, and also to pray for the perseverance and prosperity of his people.
- **h.** 2 Chron. 6:15 Or, in effect, or by thy power.
- **i.** 2 Chron. 6:16 Hebrew, a man shall not be cut off.
- **j.** 2 Chron. 6:20 That thou mayest declare in effect that thou hast a continual care over this place.
- **k.** 2 Chron. 6:22 By retaining anything from him, or by denying that which he hath left him to keep, or do him any wrong.
- **l.** 2 Chron. 6:22 Hebrew, oath.
- **m.** 2 Chron. 6:23 Meaning, to give him that which he hath deserved.
- **n.** 2 Chron. 6:24 Or, praise.
- **o.** 2 Chron. 6:26 Or, toward this place.
- **p.** 2 Chron. 6:28 Hebrew, in the land of their gates.
- **q.** 2 Chron. 6:30 He declareth that the prayers of hypocrites cannot be heard, nor of any but of them which pray unto God with an unfeigned faith and in true repentance.
- **r.** 2 Chron. 6:32 He showeth that before God there is no deception of person, but all people that feareth him and worketh righteousness, are accepted, Acts 10:35.
- **s.** 2 Chron. 6:34 Meaning, that none ought to enterprise any war, but at the Lord's commandment, that is, which is lawful by his word.
- **t.** 2 Chron. 6:34 Or, according to the manner of this city.
- **u.** 2 Chron. 6:37 Or, repent.
- **v.** 2 Chron. 6:39 Or, maintain their right.

thy people, which have sinned against thee. **40** Now my God, I beseech thee,
let thine eyes be open, and thine ears attent unto the prayer that is made in this
place. **41** [7]Now therefore arise, O Lord God, to come into thy [w]rest, thou, and
the Ark of thy strength: O Lord God, let thy Priests be clothed with [x]salvation, and
let thy Saints rejoice in goodness. **42** O Lord God, refuse not the face of [y]thine
anointed: remember the mercies promised to David thy servant.

7

1 The fire consumeth the sacrifice. 2 The glory of the Lord filleth the Temple. 12 He heareth his prayer, 17 and promised to exalt him and his throne.

1 And when Solomon had made an end of praying, [a]fire came down from
heaven, and consumed the burnt offering and the sacrifices: and the glory of the
Lord filled the house, **2** So that the Priests could not enter into the house of the
Lord, because the glory of the Lord had filled the Lord's house. **3** And when all
the children of Israel saw the fire, and the glory of the Lord come down upon the
house, they bowed themselves with their faces to the earth upon the pavement,
and worshipped and praised the Lord, saying, For he is good, because his mercy
lasteth forever. **4** [1]Then the King and all the people offered sacrifices before the
Lord. **5** And king Solomon offered a sacrifice of two and twenty thousand bul-
locks, and an hundred and twenty thousand sheep. So the king and all the people
dedicated the house of God. **6** And the Priests waited on their offices, and the
Levites with the instruments of music of the Lord, which king David had made
to praise the Lord, because his mercy lasteth forever: when David praised God [b]by
them, the Priests also blew trumpets over against them: and all they of Israel stood
by. **7** Moreover, Solomon hallowed the middle of the court that was before the
house of the Lord: for there he had prepared burnt offerings, and the fat of the
peace offerings, because the brazen altar which Solomon had made, was not able
to receive the burnt offering, and the meat offering, and the fat. **8** And Solo-
mon made [c]a feast at that time of seven days, and all Israel with him, a very great
Congregation, from the entering in of Hamath, unto the river of Egypt. **9** And
in the eight day they [d]made a solemn assembly: for they had made the dedication
of the altar seven days, and the feast seven days. **10** And the [e]three and twen-
tieth day of the seventh month, he sent the people away into their tents, joyous
and with glad heart, because of the goodness that the Lord had done for David
and for Solomon, and for Israel his people. **11** [2]So Solomon finished the house
of the Lord, and the king's house, and all that came into Solomon's heart to make
in the house of the Lord: and he prospered in his house. **12** And the Lord [3]ap-
peared to Solomon by night, and said to him, I have heard thy prayer, and have
chosen this place for myself to be an house of sacrifice. **13** If I shut the heaven
that there be no rain, or if I command the grasshopper to devour the land, or if I
send pestilence among my people, **14** If my people, among whom my Name is
called upon, do humble themselves, and pray and seek my presence, and turn from
their wicked ways, then will I hear in heaven and be merciful to their sin, and will
[f]heal their land: **15** Then mine eyes shall be open and mine ears attent unto the
prayer made in this place. **16** For I have now chosen and sanctified this house,
that my Name may be there forever: and mine eyes and mine heart shall be there
perpetually. **17** And if thou wilt walk before me, as David thy father walked, to
do according unto all that I have commanded thee, and shalt observe my statutes
and my judgments, **18** Then will I establish the throne of thy kingdom, accor-
ding as I made the covenant with David thy father, saying, [4]Thou shalt not want
a man to be ruler in Israel. **19** But if ye turn away, and forsake my statutes and
my commandments which I have set before you, and shall go and serve other gods,
and worship them, **20** Then will I pluck them up out of my land, which I have
given them, and this house which I have [g]sanctified for my Name, will I cast out
of my sight, and will make it to be a proverb and a common talk among all peo-
ple. **21** And this house which is most high, shall be an astonishment to everyone
that passeth by it, so that he shall say, Why hath the Lord done thus to this land,
and to this house? **22** And they shall answer, Because they forsook the Lord God
of their fathers, which brought them out of the land of Egypt, and have taken hold
on other gods, and have worshipped them, and served them, therefore hath he
brought all this evil upon them.

8

2 The cities that Solomon built. 7 People that were made tribute unto him. 12 His sacrifices. 17 He sendeth to Ophir.

1 And [1]after [a]twenty years when Solomon had built the house of the Lord,
and his own house, **2** Then Solomon built the cities that Huram [b]gave to So-
lomon, and caused the children of Israel to dwell there. **3** And Solomon went
to Hamath Zobah, and overcame it. **4** And he built Tadmor in the wilderness,
and repaired all [c]the cities of store which he built in Hamath. **5** And he built
[d]Beth Horon the upper, and Beth Horon the nether, cities defensed with walls,
gates and bars: **6** Also Baalath, and all the cities of store that Solomon had, and
all the chariot cities, and the cities of the horsemen, and every pleasant place that
Solomon had a mind to build in Jerusalem, and in [e]Lebanon, and throughout all
the land of his dominion. **7** And all the people that were left to the Hittites, and
the Amorites, and Perizzites, and the Hivites, and the Jebusites, which were not of
Israel, **8** But of their children which were left after them in the land, whom the
children of Israel had not consumed, even them did Solomon make [f]tributaries un-
til this day. **9** But of the children of Israel did Solomon make no servants for his
work: for they were men of war, and his chief princes, and the captains of his cha-
riots and of his horsemen. **10** So these were the chief, of the officers which Solo-
mon had, even [g]two hundred and fifty that bare rule over the people. **11** Then
Solomon brought up the daughter of Pharaoh out of the city of David, into the
house that he had built for her: for he said, My wife shall not dwell in the house
of David king of Israel: for it is holy, because that the Ark of the Lord came unto
it. **12** Then Solomon offered burnt offerings unto the Lord, on the [2]altar of the
Lord, which he had built before the porch, **13** To [3]offer according to the com-
mandment of Moses [h]every day, in the Sabbaths, and in the new moons, and in the
solemn feasts, [i]three times in the year, that is, in the feast of the Unleavened bread,
and in the feast of the Weeks, and in the feast of the Tabernacles. **14** And he set
the courses of the Priests to their offices according to the order of David his father,
and the Levites in their watches, for to praise and minister before the Priests every
day, and the porters by their [4]courses, at every gate: for so was the commandment
of David the man of God. **15** And they declined not from the commandment of
the king, concerning the Priests and the Levites, touching all things, and touching
the treasures. **16** Now Solomon had made provision for all the [j]work from the
day of the foundation of the house of the Lord, until it was finished: so the house
of the Lord was perfect. **17** Then went Solomon to Ezion Geber, and to Eloth by
the [k]Sea side in the land of Edom. **18** And Huram sent him by the hands of his
servants, ships and servants that had knowledge of the sea: and they went with the
servants of Solomon to Ophir, and brought thence [l]four hundred and fifty talents
of gold, and brought them to King Solomon.

9

1, 9 The Queen of Sheba cometh to see Solomon, and bringeth gifts. 13 His yearly revenues. 30 The time of his reign. 31 His death.

1 And [1]when the Queen of Sheba heard of the fame of Solomon, she came
to [a]prove Solomon with hard questions at Jerusalem, with a very great train, and
camels that bare sweet odors and much gold, and precious stones: and when she
came to Solomon, she communed with him of all that was in her heart. **2** And
Solomon declared her all her questions, and there was [b]nothing hid from Solo-
mon, which he declared not unto her. **3** Then the Queen of Sheba saw the wi-
sdom of Solomon, and the house that he had built, **4** And the meat of his table,
and the sitting of his servants, and the order of his waiters, and their apparel, and
his butlers, and their apparel, and his [c]burnt offerings which he offered in the
house of the Lord, and she was greatly [d]astonied. **5** And she said to the King,
It was a true word which I heard in mine own land of thy [e]sayings, and of thy

---

w. 2 Chron. 6:41 That is, into thy Temple.
x. 2 Chron. 6:41 Let them be preserved by thy power, and made virtuous and holy.
y. 2 Chron. 6:42 Hear my prayer which am thine anointed king.

2-CHRON. 6

1. 1 Kings 8:12
2. 2 Sam. 7:5
3. 1 Kings 8:27
4. 1 Kings 8:31
5. 2 Chron. 20:9
6. 1 Kings 8:46 / 1 John 1:8
7. Ps. 132:8

2-CHRON. 7

a. 2 Chron. 7:1 Hereby God declared that he was pleased with Solomon's prayer.
b. 2 Chron. 7:6 Hebrew, by their hands.
c. 2 Chron. 7:8 The feast of the Tabernacles which was kept in the seventh month.
d. 2 Chron. 7:9 They assembled to hear the word of God, after that they had remained seven days in the booths or Tabernacles.
e. 2 Chron. 7:10 They had leave to depart the two and twentieth day, 1 Kings 8:66, but they went not away till the next day.
f. 2 Chron. 7:14 I will cause the pestilence to cease and destroy the beasts that hurt the fruits of the earth, and send rain in due season.
g. 2 Chron. 7:20 Which thing declareth that God had more respect to their salvation, than to the advancement of his own glory: and whereas men abuse those things which God hath appointed to set forth his praise, he doth withdraw his graces thence.

2-CHRON. 7

1. 1 Kings 8:62,63
2. 1 Kings 9:1
3. Num. 12:6
4. 2 Chron. 6:16

2-CHRON. 8

a. 2 Chron. 8:1 Signifying that he was twenty years in building them.
b. 2 Chron. 8:2 That is, which Hiram gave again to Solomon because they pleased him not: and therefore called them Cabul, that is, dirt or filth, 1 Kings 9:13.
c. 2 Chron. 8:4 Meaning, of Munitions and treasures for the war.
d. 2 Chron. 8:5 That is, he repaired and fortified them: for they were built long before by Sheerah a noble woman of the tribe of Ephraim, 1 Chron. 6:68 and 7:24.
e. 2 Chron. 8:6 Read 1 Kings 7:2
f. 2 Chron. 8:8 Hebrew, to come up to tribute.
g. 2 Chron. 8:10 For in all there were 3300 but here he meaneth of them that had the principal charge, read 1 Kings 9:23.
h. 2 Chron. 8:13 Or, after the manner of every day.
i. 2 Chron. 8:13 Read Lev. 23.
j. 2 Chron. 8:16 Both for the matter and also for the workmanship.
k. 2 Chron. 8:17 Meaning, the red Sea.
l. 2 Chron. 8:18 Which sum is thought to mount to three million and six hundred thousand crowns, for here is mention made of thirty more than are spoken of, 1 Kings 9:28.

2-CHRON. 8

1. 1 Kings 9:10
2. 2 Chron. 4:1
3. Exod. 29:39
4. 1 Chron. 24:1

2-CHRON. 9

a. 2 Chron. 9:1 To know whether his wisdom were so great as the report was.
b. 2 Chron. 9:2 There was no question so hard that he did not resolve.
c. 2 Chron. 9:4 Or, galleries whereby he went up.
d. 2 Chron. 9:4 Hebrew, there was no spirit in her.

wisdom: 6 Howbeit, I believed not their report, until I came, and mine eyes had
seen it: and behold, the one half of thy great wisdom was not told me: for thou
exceedest the fame that I heard. 7 Happy are thy men, and happy are these thy
servants, which stand before thee always, and hear thy wisdom. 8 Blessed be the
Lord thy God, which loved thee, to set thee on his [f]throne as king, in the stead of
the Lord thy God: because thy God loveth Israel, to establish it forever, therefore
hath he made thee king over them, to execute judgments and justice. 9 Then she
gave the King sixscore talents of gold, and of sweet odors exceedingly much, and
precious stones: neither was there such sweet odors since, as the Queen of Sheba
gave unto King Solomon. 10 And the servants also of Huram, and the servan-
ts of Solomon which brought gold from Ophir, brought [g]Algummim wood and
precious stones. 11 And the King made of the Algummim wood [h]stairs in the
house of the Lord, and in the king's house, and harps and viols for singers: and
there was no such seen before in the land of Judah. 12 And King Solomon gave
to the Queen of Sheba every pleasant thing that she asked, [i]besides for that whi-
ch she had brought unto the king: so she returned and went to her own country,
both she, and her servants. 13 Also the weight of gold that came to Solomon
in one year, was six hundred threescore and six talents of gold, 14 Besides that
which chapmen and merchants brought: and all the Kings of Arabia, and the prin-
ces of the country brought gold and silver to Solomon. 15 And King Solomon
made two hundred targets of beaten gold, and [j]six hundred shekels of beaten gold
went to one target. 16 And three hundred shields of beaten gold: three hun-
dred [k]shekels of gold went to one shield, and the king put them in the house of
the wood of Lebanon. 17 And the king made a great throne of ivory, and over-
laid it with pure gold. 18 And the throne had six steps, with a footstool of gold
[l]fastened to the throne, and stays on either side on the place of the seats, and two
lions standing by the [m]stays. 19 And twelve lions stood there on the six steps on
either side: there was not the like made in any kingdom. 20 And all King So-
lomon's drinking vessels were of gold, and all the vessels of the house of the wood
of Lebanon were of pure gold: for silver was nothing esteemed in the days of So-
lomon. 21 For the king's ships went to Tarshish with the servants of Huram,
every three years once came the ships of [n]Tarshish, and brought gold, and silver,
ivory, and apes, and peacocks. 22 So king Solomon excelled all the kings of the
earth in riches and wisdom. 23 And all the Kings of the earth sought the presen-
ce of Solomon, to hear his wisdom that God had put in his heart. 24 And they
brought every man his present, vessels of silver, and vessels of gold, and raiment,
armor, and sweet odors, horses, and mules, from year to year. 25 And Solomon
had [o]four thousand stalls of horses, and chariots, and twelve thousand horsemen,
whom he bestowed in the chariot cities, and with the king at Jerusalem. 26 And
he reigned over all the kings from the [p]River even unto the land of the Philistines,
and to the border of Egypt. 27 And the king gave silver in Jerusalem, [q]as stones,
and gave cedar trees as the wild fig trees, that are abundant in the plain. 28 And
they brought unto Solomon horses out of Egypt, and out of all lands. 29 Con-
cerning the rest of the acts of Solomon first and last, are they not written in the
book of Nathan the Prophet, and in the prophecy of Ahijah the Shilonite, and in
the visions of [r]Iddo the Seer [s]against Jeroboam the son of Nebat? 30 And Solo-
mon reigned in Jerusalem over all Israel forty years. 31 And Solomon [2]slept with
his fathers, and they buried him in the city of David his father: and Rehoboam his
son reigned in his stead.

10

4, 14 The rigor of Rehoboam. 13 He followeth lewd counsel. 16 The people rebel.

1 Then [1]Rehoboam [a]went to Shechem: for to Shechem came all Israel to make
him king. 2 And when Jeroboam the son of Nebat heard it (which was in Egypt,
whither he had fled from the presence of Solomon the king) he returned out of
Egypt. 3 And they sent and called him: so came Jeroboam and all Israel, and
communed with Rehoboam, saying, 4 Thy father [b]made our yoke grievous: now
therefore make thou the grievous servitude of thy father, and his sore yoke that he
put upon us, lighter, and we will serve thee. 5 And he said to them, Depart yet
three days, then come again unto me. And the people departed. 6 And King
Rehoboam took counsel with the old men that had stood before Solomon his fa-
ther, while he yet lived, saying, What counsel give ye that I may answer this peo-
ple? 7 And they spake unto him, saying, If thou be kind to this people, and plea-
se them, and speak loving words to them, they will be thy servants forever. 8 But
he left the counsel of the ancient men that they had given him, and took counsel
of the young men that were brought up with him, and [c]waited on him. 9 And
he said unto them, What counsel give ye, that we may answer this people, which
have spoken to me, saying, Make the yoke which thy father did put upon us, li-
ghter? 10 And the young men that were brought up with him, spake unto him,
saying, Thus shalt thou answer the people that spake to thee, saying, Thy father
made our yoke heavy, but make thou it lighter for us: thus shalt thou say unto
them, My [d]least part shall be bigger than my father's loins. 11 Now whereas my
father did burden you with a grievous yoke, I will yet increase your yoke: my fa-
ther hath chastised you with rods, but I will correct you with [e]scourges. 12 Then
Jeroboam and all the people came to Rehoboam the third day, as the king had
appointed, saying, Come again to me the third day. 13 And the king answered
them sharply: and king Rehoboam left the counsel of the ancient men, 14 And
spake to them after the counsel of the young men, saying, My father made your
yoke grievous, but I will increase it: my father chastised you with rods, but I will
correct you with scourges. 15 So the king hearkened not unto the people: for it
was the [f]ordinance of God, that the Lord might perform his saying, which he had
spoken [g]by Ahijah the Shilonite to Jeroboam the son of Nebat. 16 So when all
Israel saw that the king would not hear them, the people answered the king, saying,
[2]What portion have we in David? for we have none inheritance in the son of Jesse.
O Israel, every man to your tents: now see to thine own house, David. So all Isra-
el departed to their tents. 17 Howbeit Rehoboam reigned over the children of
Israel, that dwelt in the cities of Judah. 18 Then King Rehoboam sent Hadoram
that was [h]over the tribute, and the children of Israel stoned him with stones, that
he died: then King Rehoboam [i]made speed to get him up to his chariot, to flee
to Jerusalem. 19 And Israel rebelled against the house of David unto this day.

11

4 Rehoboam is forbidden to fight against Jeroboam. 5 Cities which he built. 21 He hath eighteen wives, and threescore concubines, and by them eight and twenty sons, and threescore daughters.

1 And [1]when Rehoboam was come to Jerusalem, he gathered of the house
of Judah and [a]Benjamin ninescore thousand chosen men of war to fight against
[b]Israel, and to bring the kingdom again to Rehoboam. 2 But the word of the
Lord came to Shemaiah the man of God, saying, 3 Speak unto Rehoboam the
son of Solomon King of Judah, and to all Israel that are in Judah and Benjamin,
saying, 4 Thus saith the Lord, Ye shall not go up, nor fight against your brethren:
return every man to his house: for this thing is done of me. They obeyed there-
fore the word of the Lord, and returned from going against Jeroboam. 5 And
Rehoboam dwelt in Jerusalem, and [c]built strong cities in Judah. 6 He bu-
ilt also Bethlehem, and Etam, and Tekoa, 7 And Beth Zur, and Sochoh, and
Adullam, 8 And Gath, and Mareshah, and Ziph, 9 And Adoraim, and Lachish,
and Azekah, 10 And Zorah, and Aijalon, and Hebron, which were in Judah
and Benjamin strong cities. 11 And he [d]repaired the strongholds and put cap-
tains in them, and store of vittles, and oil and wine. 12 And in all cities he put
shields and spears and made them exceedingly strong: so Judah and Benjamin
were his. 13 And the Priests and the Levites that were in all Israel, [e]resorted
unto him out of all their coasts. 14 For the Levites left their suburbs and their
possessions, and came to Judah and to Jerusalem: [2]for Jeroboam and his sons had
cast them out from ministering in the Priests' office unto the Lord. 15 [3]And
he ordained him Priests for the high places, and for the [f]devils and for the calves
which he had made. 16 And after the Levites there came to Jerusalem of all the
tribes of Israel, such as set their [g]hearts to seek the Lord God of Israel, to offer unto
the Lord God of their fathers. 17 So they strengthened the kingdom of Judah,
and made Rehoboam the son of Solomon mighty, three years long: for three years

---

e. 2 Chron. 9:5 Or, acts.
f. 2 Chron. 9:8 Meaning, that the Israelites were God's peculiar people, and that Kings are the lieutenants of God, which ought to grant unto him the superiority, and minister justice to all.
g. 2 Chron. 9:10 Read 2 Chron. 2:8 and 1 Kings 10:11.
h. 2 Chron. 9:11 Or pillars: meaning, the garnishing, and trimming of the stairs or pillars.
i. 2 Chron. 9:12 That is, which the King gave her for recompense of the treasure which she brought.
j. 2 Chron. 9:15 Which sum mounteth to 2400 crowns of the sun, Budeus De Asse.
k. 2 Chron. 9:16 Or, pounds called mina, whereof every one seemed to make an hundred shekels.
l. 2 Chron. 9:18 That is, the steps and the footstool were fastened to the throne.
m. 2 Chron. 9:18 Upon the pommels or knops.
n. 2 Chron. 9:21 Which country of the best writers is thought to be Cilicia, read 1 Kings 10:22.
o. 2 Chron. 9:25 That is, ten horses in every stable, which in all amounts to forty thousand , as 1 Kings 4:26.
p. 2 Chron. 9:26 Or, Euphrates.
q. 2 Chron. 9:27 The abundance of these temporal treasures in Solomon's kingdom is a figure of the Spiritual treasures, which the elect shall enjoy in the heavens under the true Solomon, Christ.
r. 2 Chron. 9:29 Or, Iddo.
s. 2 Chron. 9:29 That is, which prophesied against him.

2-CHRON. 9

1. 1 Kings 10:1 / Matt. 12:42 / Luke 11:3
2. 1 Kings 11:41,42

2-CHRON. 10

a. 2 Chron. 10:1 After the death of Solomon.
b. 2 Chron. 10:4 That is, handled us rudely, it seemeth that God hardened their hearts, so that they thus murmured without cause: which declareth also the inconstancy of the people.
c. 2 Chron. 10:8 Or, that stood by him, that is, which were of his counsel and secrets.
d. 2 Chron. 10:10 Or, little finger, meaning that he was of far greater power, than was his father.
e. 2 Chron. 10:11 Or, scorpions.
f. 2 Chron. 10:15 God's will imposeth such a necessity to the second causes, that nothing can be done but according to the same, and yet man's will worketh as of itself, so that it cannot be excused in doing that it is God's ordinance.
g. 2 Chron. 10:15 Hebrew, by the hand of.
h. 2 Chron. 10:18 Or, receiver.
i. 2 Chron. 10:18 Hebrew, strengthened himself.

2-CHRON. 10

1. 1 Kings 12:1
2. 1 Kings 12:16

2-CHRON. 11

a. 2 Chron. 11:1 That is, the half tribe of Benjamin: for the other half was gone after Jeroboam.
b. 2 Chron. 11:1 Meaning the ten tribes which rebelled.
c. 2 Chron. 11:5 Or, repaired them and made them strong to be more able to resist Jeroboam.
d. 2 Chron. 11:11 Or, strengthened.
e. 2 Chron. 11:13 Hebrew, stood.
f. 2 Chron. 11:15 Meaning, idols, read Isa. 44:15.
g. 2 Chron. 11:16 Which were zealous of true religion, and feared God.
h. 2 Chron. 11:17 So long as they feared God, and set forth his word, they prospered.

they [h]walked in the way of David and Solomon. **18** And Rehoboam took him Mahalath the daughter of Jerimoth the son of David to wife, and Abihail the daughter of Eliah the son of Jesse, **19** Which bare him sons Jeush, and Shamariah, and Zaham. **20** And after her he took Maachah the daughter of Absalom which bare him Abijah, and Attai, and Ziza, and Shelomith. **21** And Rehoboam loved Maachah the daughter of Absalom above all his wives and his concubines: for he took eighteen wives and threescore concubines, and begat eight and twenty sons, and threescore daughters. **22** And Rehoboam made [i]Abijah the son of Maachah the chief ruler among his brethren: for he thought to make him King. **23** And he taught him: and dispersed all his sons throughout all the countries of Judah and Benjamin unto every strong city: and he gave them abundance of vittles, and [j]desired many wives.

12

1 Rehoboam forsaketh the Lord, and is punished by Shishak. 5 Shemaiah reproveth him. 6 He humbleth himself. 7 God sendeth him succor. 9 Shishak taketh his treasures. 13 His reign and death. 16 Abijah his son succeedeth him.

1 And when [a]Rehoboam had established the kingdom and made it strong, he forsook the Law of the Lord, and [b]all Israel with him. **2** Therefore in the fifth year of king Rehoboam, Shishak the king of Egypt came up against Jerusalem (because they had transgressed against the Lord) **3** With twelve hundred chariots, and threescore thousand horsemen, and the people were without number, that came with him from Egypt, even the Lubim, [c]Sukkiim, and the [d]Ethiopians. **4** And he took the strong cities which were of Judah, and came unto Jerusalem. **5** Then came Shemaiah the Prophet to Rehoboam, and to the princes of Judah that were gathered together in Jerusalem, because of Shishak, and said unto them, Thus saith the Lord, Ye have forsaken me, [e]therefore have I also left you in the hands of Shishak. **6** Then the princes of Israel, and the King humbled themselves, and said, The Lord is [f]just. **7** And when the Lord saw that they humbled themselves, the word of the Lord came to Shemaiah, saying, They have humbled themselves, therefore I will not destroy them, but I will send them deliverance shortly, and my wrath shall not [g]be poured out upon Jerusalem by the hand of Shishak. **8** Nevertheless they shall be his servants: so shall they know my [h]service, and the service of the kingdoms of the earth. **9** Then Shishak king of Egypt came up against Jerusalem, and took the treasures of the house of the Lord, and the treasures of the King's house: he took even all, and he carried away the shields of gold, [1]which Solomon had made. **10** In stead whereof King Rehoboam made shields of brass, and committed them to the hands of the chief of the guard, that waited at the door of the king's house. **11** And when the king entered into the house of the Lord, the guard came and bare them and brought them again unto the guard chamber. **12** And because he [i]humbled himself, the wrath of the Lord turned from him, that he would not destroy all together. And also in Judah the things prospered. **13** [2]So King Rehoboam was strong in Jerusalem and reigned: for Rehoboam was one and forty years old, when he began to reign, and reigned [j]seventeen years in Jerusalem, the city which the Lord had chosen out of all the tribes of Israel to put his Name there. And his mother's name was Naamah an Ammonitess. **14** And he did evil: for he prepared not his heart to seek the Lord. **15** The acts also of Rehoboam, first and last, are they not written in the [k]book of Shemaiah the Prophet, and Iddo the Seer, in rehearsing the genealogy? and there was war always between Rehoboam and Jeroboam. **16** And Rehoboam slept with his fathers, and was buried in the city of David, and [l]Abijah his son reigned in his stead.

13

1 Abijah maketh war against Jeroboam. 4 He showeth the occasion. 12 He trusteth in the Lord and overcometh Jeroboam. 21 Of his wives and children.

1 In the eighteenth year of King Jeroboam, began Abijah to reign over [a]Judah. **2** He reigned three years in Jerusalem: (his mother's name also was [b]Michaiah the daughter of [c]Uriel of Gibeah) and there was war between Abijah and Jeroboam. **3** And Abijah set the battle in array with the army of valiant men of war, even four hundred thousand chosen men. Jeroboam also set the battle in array against him with eight hundred thousand chosen men which were strong and valiant. **4** And Abijah stood up upon mount [d]Zemaraim, which is in mount Ephraim, and said, O Jeroboam, and all Israel, hear you me, **5** Ought you not to know that the Lord God of Israel hath given the kingdom over Israel to [e]David forever, even to him and to his sons by a covenant [f]of salt? **6** And Jeroboam the son of Nebat the servant of Solomon the son of David is risen up, and hath [1]rebelled against his lord: **7** And there are gathered to him [g]vain men and [h]wicked, and made themselves strong against Rehoboam the son of Solomon: for Rehoboam was [i]but a child and [j,2]tender hearted, and could not resist them. **8** Now therefore ye think that ye be able to resist against the kingdom of the Lord, which is in the hands of the sons of David, and ye be a great multitude, and the golden calves are with you which Jeroboam made you for gods. **9** [3]Have ye not driven away the Priests of the Lord the sons of Aaron and the Levites, and have made you Priests like the people of other countries? whosoever cometh to [k]consecrate with a [l]young bullock and seven rams, the same may be a Priest of them that are no gods. **10** But we belong unto the Lord our God, and have not forsaken him, and the Priests the sons of Aaron minister unto the Lord, and the Levites in their office. **11** And they burn unto the Lord every [m]morning and every evening burnt offerings and sweet incense, and the bread is set in order upon the pure table, and the candlestick of gold with the lamps thereof, to burn every evening: for we keep the watch of the Lord our God: but ye have forsaken him. **12** And behold, this God is [n]with us as a captain, and his Priests with the sounding trumpets to cry an alarm against you. O ye children of Israel, fight not against the Lord God of your fathers: for ye shall not prosper. **13** But Jeroboam caused an ambushment [o]to compass, and come behind them, when they were before Judah, and the ambushment behind them. **14** Then Judah looked, and behold, the battle was before and behind them, and they cried unto the Lord, and the Priests blew with the trumpets, **15** And the men of Judah gave a shout: and even as the men of Judah shouted, God [p]smote Jeroboam and also Israel before Abijah and Judah. **16** And the children of Israel fled before Judah, and God delivered them into their hand. **17** And Abijah and his people slew a great slaughter of them, so that there fell down wounded of Israel five hundred thousand chosen men. **18** So the children of Israel were brought under at that time: and the children of Judah prevailed, [q]because they stayed upon the Lord God of their fathers. **19** And Abijah pursued after Jeroboam, and took cities from him, even Bethel and the [r]villages thereof, and Jeshanah with her villages, and Ephron with her villages. **20** And Jeroboam recovered no strength again in the days of Abijah, but the Lord plagued him, and he died. **21** So Abijah waxed mighty, and married fourteen wives, and begat two and twenty sons, and sixteen daughters. **22** The rest of the acts of Abijah, and his manners and his sayings, are written in the story of the Prophet Iddo.

14

3 Asa destroyeth idolatry, and commandeth his people to serve the true God. 11 He prayed unto God when he should go to fight. 12 He obtaineth the victory.

1 So [1]Abijah slept with his fathers, and they buried him in the city of David, and Asa his son reigned in his stead: in whose days the land was quiet ten years. **2** And Asa did that was good and right in the eyes of the Lord his God. **3** For he took away the altars of the strange gods, and the high places, and brake down the images, and cut down the [a]groves, **4** And commanded Judah to seek the Lord God of their fathers, and to do according to the Law and the Commandment. **5** And he took away out of all the cities of Judah the high places, and

---

i. 2 Chron. 11:22 Called also Abijam, who reigned three years, 1 Kings 15:2.
j. 2 Chron. 11:23 He gave himself to have many wives.

2-CHRON. 11

1. 1 Kings 12:20,21
2. 2 Chron. 13:5
3. 1 Kings 12:31

2-CHRON. 12

a. 2 Chron. 12:1 Or, when the Lord had established Rehoboam's kingdom.
b. 2 Chron. 12:1 For such is the inconstancy of the people, that for the most part they follow the vices of their governors.
c. 2 Chron. 12:3 Which were a people of Africa called the Troglodytes because they dwelled in holes.
d. 2 Chron. 12:3 Or, black Moores.
e. 2 Chron. 12:5 Signifying, that no calamity can come unto us except we forsake God, and that he never leaveth us till we have cast him off.
f. 2 Chron. 12:6 And therefore doth justly punish you for your sins.
g. 2 Chron. 12:7 Hebrew, drop down.
h. 2 Chron. 12:8 He showeth that God's punishments are not to destroy his utterly, but to chastise them, to bring them to the knowledge of themselves, and to know how much better it is to serve God than tyrants.
i. 2 Chron. 12:12 Which declareth that God seeketh not the death of a sinner, but his conversion, Ezek. 18:32 and 23:11.
j. 2 Chron. 12:13 That is, twelve years after that he had been overcome by Shishak, verse 2.
k. 2 Chron. 12:15 Hebrew, sayings.
l. 2 Chron. 12:16 Or, Abijam.

2-CHRON. 12

1. 2 Chron. 9:15,16
2. 1 Kings 14:21

2-CHRON. 13

a. 2 Chron. 13:1 He meaneth Judah and Benjamin.
b. 2 Chron. 13:2 Or, Maachah, 1 Kings 15:2.
c. 2 Chron. 13:2 Called also Abishalom, for Abishalom was her grandfather, 1 Kings 15:2.
d. 2 Chron. 13:4 Which was one of the tops of mount Ephraim.
e. 2 Chron. 13:5 And therefore whosoever doth usurp it or take it from that stock, transgresseth the ordinance of the Lord. Thus like an hypocrite he allegeth the word of God for his advantage.
f. 2 Chron. 13:5 That is, perpetual because that thing which is salted, is preserved from corruption: he meaneth also that it was made solemnly, and confirmed by offering of sacrifices, where as they used salt according as was ordained, Num. 18:19.
g. 2 Chron. 13:7 This word in the Chaldean tongue is Raca, which our Savior useth, Matt. 5:22.
h. 2 Chron. 13:7 Hebrew, children of Belial.
i. 2 Chron. 13:7 Meaning, in heart and courage.
j. 2 Chron. 13:7 Or, faint hearted.
k. 2 Chron. 13:9 Hebrew, fill his hand.
l. 2 Chron. 13:9 He showeth the nature of idolaters which take no trial of the vocation, life and doctrine of their ministers, but think the most vilest and greatest beasts sufficient to serve their turn.
m. 2 Chron. 13:11 As it was appointed in the Law, Exod. 29:39.
n. 2 Chron. 13:12 Because their cause was good and approved by the Lord, they doubted not of the success and victory.
o. 2 Chron. 13:13 Contemning the good counsel which came of the Spirit of God, he thought to have overcome by deceit.
p. 2 Chron. 13:15 Or, gave him the overthrow.
q. 2 Chron. 13:18 He showeth that the stay of all kingdoms, and assurance of victories depend upon our trust and confidence in the Lord.
r. 2 Chron. 13:19 Hebrew, daughters.

2-CHRON. 13

1. 1 Kings 11:26
2. Lev. 26:36
3. 1 Kings 12:31 / 2 Chron. 11:14

2-CHRON. 14

a. 2 Chron. 14:3 Which were planted contrary to the Law, Deut. 16:21.

the images: therefore the Kingdom was [b]quiet before him. **6** He built also strong cities in Judah, because the land was in rest, and he had no war in those years: for the Lord had given him rest. **7** Therefore he said to Judah, Let us build these cities, and make walls about, and towers, gates, and bars, while the land is [c]before us: because we have sought the Lord our God, we have sought him, and he hath given us rest on every side: so they built and prospered. **8** And Asa had an army of Judah, that bare shields and spears, three hundred thousand, and of Benjamin that bare shields and drew bows, two hundred and fourscore thousand: all these were valiant men. **9** And there came out against him Zerah [d]of Ethiopia with an host of ten hundred thousand, and three hundred chariots, and came unto [e]Mareshah. **10** Then Asa went out before him, and they set the battle in array in the valley of Zephathah, beside Mareshah. **11** And Asa cried unto the Lord his God, and said, Lord, [2]it is nothing with thee to help [f]with many, or with no power: help us, O Lord our God: for we rest on thee, and in thy Name are we come against this multitude: O Lord, thou art our God: [g]let not man prevail against thee. **12** So the Lord smote the Ethiopians before Asa and before Judah, and the Ethiopians fled. **13** And Asa and the people that was with him, pursued them unto Gerar. And the Ethiopians' host was overthrown, so that there was no life in them: for they were destroyed before the Lord and before his host: and they carried away a mighty great spoil. **14** And they smote all the cities round about Gerar: for the [h]fear of the Lord came upon them, and they spoiled all the cities, for there was exceeding much spoil in them. **15** Yea, and they smote the tents of cattle, and carried away plenty of sheep and camels, and returned to Jerusalem.

15

2 The exhortation of Azariah. 8 Asa purgeth his country of idolatry. 11 He sacrificeth with the people. 14 They swear together to serve the Lord. 16 He deposeth his mother for her idolatry.

1 Then the Spirit of God came upon [a]Azariah the son of Obed. **2** And he went out to meet Asa, and said unto him, O Asa, and all Judah and Benjamin, hear ye me, The Lord is with you, while ye be with him: and if ye seek him, he will be found of you, but if ye forsake him, he will forsake you. **3** Now for a long season Israel hath been without the [b]true God, and without Priest to teach, and without Law. **4** But whosoever returned in his affliction to the Lord God of Israel, and sought him, he [c]was found of him. **5** And in that time there was no peace to him, that did go out and go in: but great troubles were to all the inhabitants of the earth. **6** For nation was destroyed of nation, and city of city: for God troubled them with all adversity. **7** Be ye strong therefore, and let not your hands be weak: for your [d]work shall have a reward. **8** And when Asa heard these words, and the prophecy of Obed the Prophet, he was encouraged, and took away the abominations out of all the land of Judah and Benjamin, and out of the cities which he had taken of mount Ephraim, and he renewed the altar of the Lord, that was before the porch of the Lord. **9** And he gathered all Judah and Benjamin, and the strangers with them out of Ephraim, and Manasseh, and out of Simeon: for there fell many to him out of Israel, when they saw that the Lord his God was with him. **10** So they assembled to Jerusalem in the [e]third month, in the fifteenth year of the reign of Asa. **11** And they offered unto the Lord the same time of the [f]spoil which they had brought, even seven hundred bullocks, and seven thousand sheep. **12** And they made a covenant to seek the Lord God of their fathers, with all their heart, and with all their soul. **13** And [g]whosoever will not seek the Lord God of Israel, shall be slain, whether he were small or great, man or woman. **14** And they sware unto the Lord with a loud voice, and with shouting, and with trumpets, and with cornets. **15** And all Judah rejoiced at the oath: for they had sworn unto the Lord with all their heart, and sought him with a whole desire, and he was [h]found of them. And the Lord gave them rest round about. **16** And King Asa deposed [1]Maachah his [i]mother from her regency, because she had made an idol in a grove: and Asa brake down her idol, and stamped it, and burnt it at the brook Kidron. **17** But the high places were not [j]taken away out of [k]Israel: yet the heart of Asa was [l]perfect all his days. **18** Also he brought into the house of God the things that his father had dedicated, and that he had dedicated, silver, and gold, and vessels. **19** And there was no war unto the five and thirtieth year of the reign of Asa.

16

2 Asa for fear of Baasha king of Israel, maketh a covenant with Ben-Hadad king of Aram. 7 He is reproved by the Prophet. 10 Whom he putteth in prison. 12 He putteth his trust in the Physicians. 13 His death.

1 In the six and thirtieth year of the reign of Asa came [a,1]Baasha king of Israel up against Judah, and built [b]Ramah, to let none pass out or go in to Asa king of Judah. **2** Then Asa brought out silver and gold out of the treasures of the house of the Lord, and of the king's house, and sent to Ben-Hadad king of Aram that dwelt at [c]Damascus, saying, **3** There is a covenant between me and thee, and between my father and thy father: behold, I have sent thee silver and gold: come, [d]break thy league with Baasha king of Israel, that he may depart from me. **4** And Ben-Hadad hearkened unto King Asa, and sent the captains of the army which he had, against the cities of Israel. And they smote Ijon, and Dan, and Abel Maim, and all the store cities of Naphtali. **5** And when Baasha heard it, he left building of Ramah, and let his work cease. **6** Then Asa the king took all Judah, and carried away the stones of Ramah and the timber thereof, wherewith Baasha did build, and he built therewith Geba and Mizpah. **7** And at that same time Hanani the [e]Seer came to Asa king of Judah, and said unto him, Because thou hast rested upon the king of Aram, and not rested in the Lord thy God, therefore is the host of the king of Aram escaped out of thine hand. **8** [2]The Ethiopians and the Lubim, were they not a great host with chariots and horsemen, exceedingly many? yet because thou didst rest upon the Lord, he delivered them into thine hand. **9** For the eyes of the Lord behold all the earth, to show himself strong with them that are of perfect heart toward him: thou hast then done foolishly in this: therefore from henceforth thou shalt have wars. **10** Then Asa was wroth with the Seer, and put him into a [f]prison: for he was [g]displeased with him, because of this thing. And Asa oppressed certain of the people at the same time. **11** And behold, the acts of Asa first and last, lo, they are written in the book of the Kings of Judah and Israel. **12** And Asa in the nine and thirtieth year of his reign was [h,3]diseased in his feet, and his disease was [i,j]extreme: yet he sought not the Lord in his disease, but to the [k]Physicians. **13** So Asa slept with his fathers, and died in the one and fortieth year of his reign. **14** And they buried him in one of his sepulchers, which he had made for himself in the city of David, and laid him in the bed, which they had filled with sweet odors and divers kinds of spices made by the art of the Apothecary: and they burnt odors for him with an exceeding great fire.

17

5 Jehoshaphat trusting in the Lord, prospereth in riches and honor. 6 He abolisheth idolatry, 7 and causeth the people to be taught. 11 He receiveth tribute of strangers. 13 His munitions, and men of war.

1 And Jehoshaphat his son reigned in his stead, and prevailed against Israel. **2** And he put garrisons in all the strong cities of Judah, and set bands in the land of Judah and in the cities of Ephraim, which Asa his father had taken. **3** And the Lord was with Jehoshaphat, because he walked in the [a]first ways of his father David, and sought not [b]Baalim, **4** But sought the Lord God of his father, and walked in his commandment, and not after the [c]trade of Israel. **5** Therefore the

---

b. 2 Chron. 14:5 He showeth that the rest and quietness of kingdoms standeth in abolishing idolatry, and advancing true religion.
c. 2 Chron. 14:7 While we have the full government thereof.
d. 2 Chron. 14:9 The king of Ethiopia, or Egypt.
e. 2 Chron. 14:9 Which was a city in Judah, Josh. 15:44, where Michaiah the Prophet was born.
f. 2 Chron. 14:11 Or, against many, without power.
g. 2 Chron. 14:11 Thus the children of God neither trust in their own power or policy, neither fear the strength and subtlety of their enemies, but consider the cause and see whether their enterprises tend to God's glory, and thereupon assure themselves of the victory by him, which is only Almighty, and can turn all flesh into dust with the breath of his mouth.
h. 2 Chron. 14:14 The Lord had stricken them with fear.

2-CHRON. 14
1. 1 Kings 15:8
2. 1 Sam. 14:6

2-CHRON. 15
a. 2 Chron. 15:1 Who was called Obed, as his father was, verse 8.
b. 2 Chron. 15:3 For the space of twelve years under Rehoboam, and three years under Abijah, religion was neglected, and idolatry planted.
c. 2 Chron. 15:4 He showeth, that notwithstanding the wickedness of tyrants and their rage, yet God hath his, whom he heareth in their tribulation, as he delivered his from Zerah king of the Ethiopians, 2 Chron. 14:9, 12, and out of all other dangers, when they called upon the Lord.
d. 2 Chron. 15:7 Your confidence and trust in God shall not be frustrated.
e. 2 Chron. 15:10 Called Sivan, containing part of May, and part of June.
f. 2 Chron. 15:11 Which they had taken of the Ethiopians.
g. 2 Chron. 15:13 These were the words of their covenant, which commanded all idolaters to be put to death, according to the Law of God, Deut. 13:5, 9, 15.
h. 2 Chron. 15:15 So long as they served him aright, so long did he preserve and prosper them.
i. 2 Chron. 15:16 Or grandmother: and herein he showed that he lacked zeal, for she ought to have died both by the covenant, as verse 13, and by the Law of God: but he gave place to foolish pity and would also seem after a sort to satisfy the Law.
j. 2 Chron. 15:17 Which partly came through lack of zeal in him, partly through the negligence of his officers, and partly by the superstition of the people, that all were not taken away.
k. 2 Chron. 15:17 Because that God was called the God of Israel, by reason of his promise to Jacob: therefore Israel is sometimes taken for Judah, because Judah was his chief people.
l. 2 Chron. 15:17 In respect of his predecessors.

2-CHRON. 15
1. 1 Kings 15:13

2-CHRON. 16
a. 2 Chron. 16:1 Who reigned after Nadab the son of Jeroboam.
b. 2 Chron. 16:1 He fortified it with walls and ditches: it was a city in Benjamin near to Gibeon.
c. 2 Chron. 16:2 Or, Darmesek.
d. 2 Chron. 16:3 He thought to repulse his adversary by an unlawful means, that is, by seeking help of infidels, as they that seek the Turks' amity, thinking thereby to make themselves more strong.
e. 2 Chron. 16:7 Or, Prophet.
f. 2 Chron. 16:10 Hebrew, prison house.
g. 2 Chron. 16:10 Thus instead of turning to God by repentance, he disdained the admonition of the Prophet, and punished him, as the wicked do when they be told of their faults.
h. 2 Chron. 16:12 Or, gouty, or swollen.
i. 2 Chron. 16:12 Or, to the top of his head.
j. 2 Chron. 16:12 God plagued his rebellion, and hereby declareth that it is nothing to begin well, except we so continue to the end, that is, zealous of God's glory, and put our whole trust in him.
k. 2 Chron. 16:12 He showeth that it is in vain to seek to the Physicians, except we first seek to God to purge our sins, which are the chief cause of all our diseases, and after use the help of the Physician, as a means by whom God worketh.

2-CHRON. 16
1. 1 Kings 15:17
2. 2 Chron. 14:9
3. 1 Kings 15:23

2-CHRON. 17
a. 2 Chron. 17:3 That is, his virtues: meaning before he had committed with Bathsheba, and against Uriah.
b. 2 Chron. 17:3 Sought not help at strange Gods.
c. 2 Chron. 17:4 Hebrew, work.

Lord established the kingdom in his hand, and all Judah brought presents to Jehoshaphat, so that he had of riches and honor in abundance. **6** And he [d]lifted up his heart unto the ways of the Lord, and he took away moreover the high places and the groves out of Judah. **7** And in the third year of his reign he sent his princes, Ben-Hail, and Obadiah, and Zechariah, and Nethanel, and Michaiah, that they should [e]teach in the cities of Judah, **8** And with them Levites, Shemaiah, and Nethaniah, and Zebadiah, and Asahel, and Shemiramoth, and Jehonathan, and Adonijah, and Tobijah, and Tobadonijah, Levites, and with them Elishama and Jehoram, Priests. **9** And they taught in Judah, and had the book of the Law of the Lord with them, and went about throughout all the cities of Judah, and taught the people. **10** And the fear of the Lord fell upon all the kingdoms of the lands that were round about Judah, and they [f]fought not against Jehoshaphat. **11** Also some of the Philistines brought Jehoshaphat gifts and tribute silver, and the Arabians brought him flocks, seven thousand and seven hundred rams, and seven thousand and seven hundred he goats. **12** So Jehoshaphat prospered and grew up on high, and he built in Judah palaces and cities of store. **13** And he had great works in the cities of Judah, and men of war, and valiant men in Jerusalem. **14** And these are the numbers of them after the house of their fathers, In Judah were captains of thousands, Adnah the captain, and [g]with him of valiant men three hundred thousand. **15** And [h]at his hand Jehohanan a captain, and with him two hundred and fourscore thousand. **16** And at his hand Amasiah the son of Zichri, [i]which willingly offered himself unto the Lord, and with him two hundred thousand valiant men. **17** And of Benjamin, Eliada a valiant man, and with him armed men with bow and shield, two hundred thousand. **18** And at his hand Jehozabad, and with him an hundred and fourscore thousand armed to the war. **19** These [j]waited on the king, besides those which the king put in the strong cities throughout all Judah.

18

1 Jehoshaphat maketh affinity with Ahab. 10 Four hundred Prophets counsel Ahab to go to war. 16 Michaiah is against them. 23 Zedekiah smiteth him. 25 The king putteth him in prison. 29 The effect of his prophecy.

1 And [1]Jehoshaphat had riches and honor in abundance, but he was joined in [a]affinity with Ahab. **2** And after certain [b]years he went down to Ahab to Samaria: and Ahab slew sheep and oxen for him in great number, and for the people that he had with him, and enticed him to go up unto [c]Ramoth Gilead. **3** And Ahab king of Israel said unto Jehoshaphat king of Judah, Wilt thou go with me to Ramoth Gilead? And he answered him, I am as thou art, and my people as thy people, and we will join with thee in the war. **4** And Jehoshaphat said unto the king of Israel, Ask counsel, I pray thee, at the [d]word of the Lord this day. **5** Therefore the King of Israel gathered of [e]Prophets four hundred men, and said unto them, Shall we go to Ramoth Gilead to battle, or shall I cease? And they said, Go up: for God shall deliver it into the king's hand. **6** But Jehoshaphat said, Is there here never a Prophet more of the Lord that we might inquire of him? **7** And the king of Israel said unto Jehoshaphat, There is yet one man by whom we may ask counsel of the Lord: but I [f]hate him: for he doth not prophesy good unto me, but always evil: it is Michaiah the son of Imla. Then Jehoshaphat said, Let not the king say [g]so. **8** And the king of Israel called an eunuch, and said, Call quickly Michaiah the son of Imla. **9** And the king of Israel, and Jehoshaphat King of Judah sat either of them on his throne clothed in their [h]apparel: they sat even in the threshing floor at the entering in of the gate of Samaria: and all the Prophets prophesied before them. **10** And Zedekiah the son of Chenaanah made him [i]horns of iron, and said, Thus saith the Lord, With these shalt thou push the Aramites until thou hast consumed them. **11** And all the Prophets prophesied so, saying, Go up in Ramoth Gilead, and prosper: for the Lord shall deliver it unto the hand of the king. **12** And the messenger that went to call Michaiah, spake to him, saying, Behold, the words of the Prophets declare good to the king with one [j]accord: let thy word therefore, I pray thee, be like one of theirs, and speak thou good. **13** And Michaiah said, As the Lord liveth, whatsoever my God saith, that will I speak. **14** So he came to the king, and the King said unto him, Michaiah, shall we go to Ramoth Gilead to battle, or shall I leave off? And he said, [k]Go ye up, and prosper, and they shall be delivered into your hand. **15** And the King said to him, How oft shall I charge thee, that thou tell me nothing but the truth in the Name of the Lord? **16** Then he said, I saw all Israel scattered in the mountains, as sheep that have no shepherd: and the Lord said, [l]These have no master: let them return every man to his house in peace. **17** And the King of Israel said to Jehoshaphat, Did I not tell thee, that he would not prophesy good unto me, but evil? **18** Again he said, Therefore hear ye the word of the Lord: I saw the Lord sit upon his throne, and all the [m]host of heaven standing at his right hand, and at his left. **19** And the Lord said, Who shall [n]persuade Ahab King of Israel, that he may go up, and fall at Ramoth Gilead? And one spake and said thus, and another said that. **20** Then there came forth a spirit and stood before the Lord, and said, I will persuade him. And the Lord said unto him, Wherein? **21** And he said, I will go out, and be a false spirit in the mouth of all his Prophets. And [o]he said, Thou shalt persuade, and shalt also prevail: go forth and do so. **22** Now therefore behold, the Lord hath put a [p]false spirit in the mouth of these thy Prophets, and the Lord hath determined evil against thee. **23** Then Zedekiah the son of Chenaanah came near, and smote Michaiah upon the [q]cheek, and said, By what way went the Spirit of the Lord from me, to speak with thee? **24** And Michaiah said, Behold, thou shalt see that day when thou shalt go from chamber to chamber to hide thee. **25** And the King of Israel said, Take ye Michaiah, and carry him to Amon the governor of the city, and to Joash the king's son, **26** And say, Thus saith the king, Put this man in the prison house, and feed him with bread of [r]affliction and with water of affliction, until I return in peace. **27** And Michaiah said, If thou return in peace, the Lord hath not spoken by me. And [s]he said, Hear, all ye people. **28** So the King of Israel and Jehoshaphat the King of Judah went up to Ramoth Gilead. **29** And the King of Israel said unto Jehoshaphat, I will [t]change myself, and enter into the battle: but put thou on thine apparel. So the king of Israel changed himself, and they went into the battle. **30** And the king of Aram had commanded the captains of the chariots that were with him, saying, Fight you not with small nor great, but against the king of Israel only. **31** And when the captains of the chariots saw Jehoshaphat, they said, It is the king of Israel: and they compassed about him to fight. But Jehoshaphat [u]cried, and the Lord helped him and moved them to depart from him. **32** For when the captains of the chariots saw that he was not the King of Israel, they turned back from him. **33** Then a certain man drew a bow [v]mightily, and smote the King of Israel between the joints [w]of his brigandine: Therefore he said to his chariotman, Turn thine hand, and carry me out of the host: for I am hurt. **34** And the battle increased that day: and the king of Israel [x]stood still in his chariot against the Aramites until even, and died at the time of the sun going down.

19

4 After Jehoshaphat was rebuked by the Prophet, he called again the people to the honoring of the Lord. 5 He appointed Judges and minsters, 9 and exhorteth them to fear God.

1 And Jehoshaphat the king of Judah returned [a]safe to his house in Jerusalem. **2** And Jehu the son of Hanani the Seer went out to meet him, and said to King Jehoshaphat, [b]Wouldest thou help the wicked, and love them that hate the Lord? therefore for this thing the wrath [c]of the Lord is upon thee. **3** Nevertheless good things are found in thee, because thou hast taken away the groves out of the land, and hast prepared thine heart to seek God. **4** So Jehoshaphat dwelt at Jerusalem, and returned and went [d]through the people from Beersheba to mount Ephraim, and brought them again unto the Lord God of their fathers. **5** And he set judges in the land throughout all the strong cities of Judah, city by city, **6** And said to the judges, Take heed what ye do: for ye execute not the judgments of man, but of the Lord, and he will be [e]with you in the cause and

---

d. 2 Chron. 17:6 He gave himself wholly to serve the Lord.
e. 2 Chron. 17:7 He knew it was in vain to profess religion, except such were appointed which could instruct the people in the same, and had authority to put away all idolatry.
f. 2 Chron. 17:10 Thus God prospereth all such that with a pure heart seek his glory, and keepeth their enemies in fear, that they cannot be able to execute their rage against them.
g. 2 Chron. 17:14 Hebrew, in his hand.
h. 2 Chron. 17:15 Or, next to him.
i. 2 Chron. 17:16 Meaning, which was a Nazirite, Num. 6.
j. 2 Chron. 17:19 That is, they were as his ordinary guard.

2-CHRON. 18

a. 2 Chron. 18:1 For Joram Jehoshaphat's son married Ahab's daughter.
b. 2 Chron. 18:2 That is, the third year, 1 Kings 22:2.
c. 2 Chron. 18:2 To recover it out of the hands of the Syrians.
d. 2 Chron. 18:4 Hear the advice of some Prophet, to know whether it be God's will.
e. 2 Chron. 18:5 Which were the prophets of Baal, signifying that the wicked esteem none but flatterers, and such as will bear with their inordinate affections.
f. 2 Chron. 18:7 Yet the true ministers of God ought not to cease to do their duty, though the wicked magistrates cannot abide them to speak the truth.
g. 2 Chron. 18:7 Meaning, that he ought not to refuse to hear any that was of God.
h. 2 Chron. 18:9 That is, in their majesty and royal apparel.
i. 2 Chron. 18:10 Read 1 Kings 22:11.
j. 2 Chron. 18:12 Thinking, that whereas four hundred prophets had agreed in one thing, that he being but one man and in least estimation, durst not gainsay it.
k. 2 Chron. 18:14 He spake this by derision of the false prophets, as the King well perceived.
l. 2 Chron. 18:16 He prophesieth of how the people should be dispersed and Ahab slain.
m. 2 Chron. 18:18 Meaning, his Angels.
n. 2 Chron. 18:19 Or, deceive.
o. 2 Chron. 18:21 That is, the Lord.
p. 2 Chron. 18:22 To them that will not believe the truth, God sendeth strong delusion that they should believe lies, 2 Thess. 2:10.
q. 2 Chron. 18:23 By this cruelty, his ambition and hypocrisy was discovered: thus the hypocrites boast of the Spirit which they have not, and declare their malice against them in whom the true Spirit is.
r. 2 Chron. 18:26 Keep him straitly in prison, and let him feel hunger and thirst.
s. 2 Chron. 18:27 Or, Micaiah.
t. 2 Chron. 18:29 Thus the wicked think by their own subtlety to escape God's judgments which he threateneth by his word.
u. 2 Chron. 18:31 He cried to the Lord by acknowledging his fault in going with this wicked king to war against the word of the Lord by his Prophet, and also by desiring mercy for the same.
v. 2 Chron. 18:33 Hebrew, in his simplicity, or ignorantly.
w. 2 Chron. 18:33 Or, between the habergeon.
x. 2 Chron. 18:34 He dissembled his hurt that his soldiers might fight more courageously.

2-CHRON. 18

1. 1 Kings 22:3

2-CHRON. 19

a. 2 Chron. 19:1 Hebrew, in peace.
b. 2 Chron. 19:2 He declareth that the wrath and judgment of God is over all such that support the wicked, and rather show not in deed that they are enemies to all such as hate the Lord.
c. 2 Chron. 19:2 Hebrew, wrath from the Lord.
d. 2 Chron. 19:4 He visited all his country, and brought his people from idolatry to the knowledge of the true God.
e. 2 Chron. 19:6 Both to preserve you, if you do justly, or to punish you, if you do the contrary.

judgment. **7** Wherefore now let the fear of the Lord be upon you: take heed, and do it: for there is no [f]iniquity with the Lord our God, neither [1]respect of persons, nor receiving of reward. **8** Moreover in Jerusalem did Jehoshaphat set of the Levites, and of the Priests and of the chief of the families of Israel, for the judgment and cause of the Lord: and they [g]returned to Jerusalem. **9** And he charged them, saying, Thus shall ye do in the fear of the Lord faithfully and with a perfect heart. **10** And in every cause that shall come to you of your brethren that dwell in your cities, between [h]blood and blood, between law and precept, statutes and judgments, ye shall judge them and admonish them that they trespass not against the Lord, that [i]wrath come not upon you and upon your brethren. This shall ye do and trespass not. **11** And behold, Amariah the Priest shall be the chief over you in all matters of the Lord, and Zebadiah the son of Ishmael, a ruler of the house of Judah, shall be for all the [j]King's affairs, and the Levites shall be officers [k]before you. Be of courage, and do it, and the Lord shall be with the [l]good.

20

3 Jehoshaphat and the people pray unto the Lord. 22 The marvelous victory that the Lord gave him against his enemies. 30 His reign and acts.

1 After this also came the children of Moab and the children of Ammon, and with them of the [a]Ammonites against Jehoshaphat to battle. **2** Then there came that told Jehoshaphat, saying, There cometh a great multitude against thee from beyond the [b]Sea, out of Aram: and behold, they be in Hazazon Tamar, which is En Gedi. **3** And Jehoshaphat feared, and set himself [c]to seek the Lord, and proclaimed a fast throughout all Judah. **4** And Judah gathered themselves together to ask counsel of the Lord: they came even out of all the cities of Judah to inquire of the Lord. **5** And Jehoshaphat stood in the Congregation of Judah and Jerusalem in the house of the Lord before the new court, **6** And said, O Lord God of our fathers, art not thou God in heaven? and reignest not thou on all the kingdoms of the heathen? and in thine hand is power and might, and none is able to withstand thee. **7** Didst not thou our God cast out the inhabitants of this land before thy people Israel, and [d]gavest it to the seed of Abraham thy friend forever? **8** And they dwelt therein, and have built thee a Sanctuary therein for thy Name, saying, **9** [1]If evil come upon us, as the [e]sword of judgment, or pestilence, or famine, we will stand before this house and in thy presence (for thy name [f]is in this house) and will cry unto thee in our tribulation, and thou wilt hear and help. **10** And now, behold, the children of [2]Ammon and Moab, and mount Seir, by whom thou wouldest not let Israel go, when they came out of the land of Egypt: but they turned aside from them, and destroyed them not: **11** Behold, I say, they reward us, in coming to cast us out of thine inheritance, which thou hast caused us to inherit: **12** O our God, wilt thou not judge them? for there is no strength in us to stand before this great multitude that cometh against us, neither do we know what to do: but our eyes [g]are toward thee. **13** And all Judah stood [h]before the Lord with their young ones, their wives, and their children. **14** And Jahaziel the son of Zechariah, the son of Benaiah, the son of Jeiel, the son of Mattaniah, a Levite of the sons of Asaph, was there, upon whom came [i]the Spirit of the Lord, in the midst of the Congregation. **15** And he said, Hearken ye all Judah, and ye inhabitants of Jerusalem, and thou, King Jehoshaphat: thus saith the Lord unto you, Fear you not, neither be afraid for this great multitude: for the [j]battle is not yours, but God's. **16** Tomorrow go ye down against them: behold, they come up by the cleft of Ziz, and ye shall find them at the end of the brook before the wilderness of Jeruel. **17** Ye shall not need to fight in this battle: [3]stand still, move not, and behold the [k]salvation of the Lord towards you: O Judah, and Jerusalem, fear ye not, neither be afraid: tomorrow go out against them, and the Lord will be with you. **18** Then Jehoshaphat [l]bowed down with his face to the earth, and all Judah and the inhabitants of Jerusalem fell down before the Lord, worshipping the Lord. **19** And the Levites of the children of the Kohathites, and of the children of the Korahites stood up to praise the Lord God of Israel with a loud voice on high. **20** And when they arose early in the morning, they went forth to the wilderness of Tekoa: and as they departed, Jehoshaphat stood and said, Hear ye me, O Judah, and ye inhabitants of Jerusalem: put your trust in the Lord your God, and ye shall be assured: believe his [m]Prophets, and ye shall prosper. **21** And when he had consulted with the people, and appointed singers unto the Lord, and them that should praise him that is in the beautiful Sanctuary, in going forth before the men of arms, and saying, [n]Praise ye the Lord, for his mercy lasteth forever. **22** And when they began to shout, and to praise, the Lord laid ambushments against the children of Ammon, Moab, and [o]mount Seir, which were come against Judah, and they slew one another. **23** For the children of Ammon and Moab rose against the inhabitants of mount Seir, to slay and to destroy them: and when they had made an end of the inhabitants of Seir, every one helped to [p]destroy another. **24** And when Judah came toward Mizpah in the wilderness, they looked unto the multitude: and behold, the carcasses were fallen to the earth, and none escaped. **25** And when Jehoshaphat and his people came to take away the spoil of them, they found among them in abundance both of substance and also of bodies laden with precious jewels, which they took for themselves, till they could carry no more: they were three days in gathering of the spoil: for it was much. **26** And in the fourth day they [q]assembled themselves in the valley of Berachah: for there they blessed the Lord: therefore they called the name of that place, The valley of Berachah unto this day. **27** Then every man of Judah and Jerusalem returned with Jehoshaphat their head to go again to Jerusalem with joy: for the Lord had made them to rejoice over their enemies. **28** And they came to Jerusalem with viols, and with harps, and with trumpets, even unto the house of the Lord. **29** And the [r]fear of God was upon all the kingdoms of the earth, when they had heard that the Lord had fought against the enemies of Israel. **30** So the kingdom of Jehoshaphat was quiet, and his God gave him rest on every side. **31** And [4]Jehoshaphat reigned over Judah, and was five and thirty years old, when he began to reign: and reigned five and twenty years in Jerusalem, and his mother's name was Azubah the daughter of Shilhi. **32** And he walked in the way of [s]Asa his father, and departed not there from, doing that which was right in the sight of the Lord. **33** Howbeit the high places were [t]not taken away: for the people had not yet prepared their hearts unto the God of their fathers. **34** Concerning the rest of the acts of Jehoshaphat first and last, behold, they are written in the book of Jehu the son of Hanani, which [5]is mentioned in the book of the kings of Israel. **35** Yet after this did Jehoshaphat king of Judah join himself with Ahaziah king of Israel, who was given to do evil. **36** And he joined with him, to [6]make ships to go to Tarshish: and they made the ships in Ezion Geber. **37** Then Eliezer the son of Dodavah of Mareshah prophesied against Jehoshaphat, saying, Because thou hast [u]joined thyself with Ahaziah, the Lord hath broken thy works: and the ships were broken, that they were not able to go to Tarshish.

21

1 Jehoshaphat died. 3 Jehoram succeedeth him, 4 which killeth his brethren. 6 He was brought to idolatry, 11 and succeedeth the people. 16 He is oppressed of the Philistines. 18 His miserable end.

1 Jehoshaphat then slept with his fathers, and was buried with his fathers in the city of David: and Jehoram his son reigned in his stead. **2** And he had brethren the sons of Jehoshaphat, Azariah, and Jehiel, and Zechariah, and Azariah, and Michael, and Shephatiah. All these were the sons of Jehoshaphat king of [a]Israel. **3** And their father gave them great gifts of silver and of gold, and of precious things, with strong cities in Judah, but the kingdom gave he to Jehoram: for he was the eldest. **4** [1]And Jehoram rose up upon the kingdom of his father,

---

f. 2 Chron. 19:7 He will declare by the sharpness of the punishment, that he hateth all iniquity.
g. 2 Chron. 19:8 The Priests and Levites, which should judge matters according to the word of the Lord.
h. 2 Chron. 19:10 That is, to try whether the murder was done at unawares, or else on set purpose, Num. 35:11; Deut. 4:41.
i. 2 Chron. 19:10 Meaning, that God would punish them most sharply, if they would not execute justice aright.
j. 2 Chron. 19:11 Shall be chief overseer of the public's affairs of the Realm.
k. 2 Chron. 19:11 They shall have the handling of inferior causes.
l. 2 Chron. 19:11 God will assist them that do justice.

2-CHRON. 19
1. Deut. 10:17 / Job 34:19 / Acts 10:34 / Rom. 2:11 / Gal. 2:6 / Eph. 6:9 / Col. 3:25 / 1 Pet. 1:17

2-CHRON. 20
a. 2 Chron. 20:1 That is, which counterfeited the Ammonites in language and apparel. The Hebrews think that they were the Amalekites, but as may appear by the tenth verse they were the Idumeans of mount Seir.
b. 2 Chron. 20:2 Called the dead Sea, where God destroyed the five cities for sin.
c. 2 Chron. 20:3 This declareth what the fear of the godly is, which is as the prick to stir them to prayer, and to depend on the Lord, whereas it moveth the wicked either to seek after worldly means and policies, or else to fall into despair.
d. 2 Chron. 20:7 He groundeth his prayer upon God's power, whereby he is able to help, and also on his mercy, which he will continue toward his, forasmuch as he hath once chosen them and began to show his graces toward them.
e. 2 Chron. 20:9 Meaning war which cometh by God's just judgments for our sins.
f. 2 Chron. 20:9 That is, it is here called upon, and thou declarest thy presence and favor.
g. 2 Chron. 20:12 We only put our trust in thee, and wait for our deliverance from heaven.
h. 2 Chron. 20:13 That is, before the Ark of the Covenant.
i. 2 Chron. 20:14 Which was moved by the Spirit of God to prophesy.
j. 2 Chron. 20:15 They fight against God and not against you, therefore he will fight for you.
k. 2 Chron. 20:17 Or, deliverance.
l. 2 Chron. 20:18 Declaring his faith and obedience to the word of the Lord, and giving thanks for the deliverance promised.
m. 2 Chron. 20:20 Give credit to their words and doctrine.
n. 2 Chron. 20:21 This was a Psalm of thanksgiving which they used commonly to sing when they praised the Lord for his benefits, and was made by David, Ps. 136.
o. 2 Chron. 20:22 Meaning, the Idumeans which dwelt in mount Seir.
p. 2 Chron. 20:23 Thus the Lord according to Jehoshaphat's prayer declared his power, when he delivered his by causing their enemies to kill one another.
q. 2 Chron. 20:26 To give thanks to the Lord for the victory: and therefore the valley was called Berachah, that is, blessing or thanksgiving, which was also called the Valley of Jehoshaphat, Joel 3:2,12, because the Lord judged the enemies according to Jehoshaphat's prayer.
r. 2 Chron. 20:29 He declareth hereby, that the works of God bring ever comfort or deliverance to his, and fear or destruction to his enemies.
s. 2 Chron. 20:32 Meaning, in his virtues, and those ways wherein he followed God.
t. 2 Chron. 20:33 If the great care and diligence of this good king was not able utterly to abolish all superstition of this people, but that they would still retain theirs, how much less are they able to reform evil, which either have little zeal, or not such as he had: though here he was not to be excused?
u. 2 Chron. 20:37 Thus God would not have his to join in society with idolaters and wicked men.

2-CHRON. 20
1. 1 Kings 8:37 / 2 Chron. 6:28
2. Deut. 2:9 / Neh. 13:1
3. Exod. 14:13,14
4. 1 Kings 22:42
5. 1 Kings 16:1
6. 1 Kings 2:48,49

2-CHRON. 21
a. 2 Chron. 21:2 Read 2 Chron. 15:17, how by Israel he meant Judah.
b. 2 Chron. 21:4 Because the wicked live ever in fear, and also are ambitious, they become cruel, and spare not to murder

and made himself strong, and [b]slew all his brethren with the sword, and also of the princes of [c]Israel. **5** Jehoram was two and thirty years old, when he began to reign, and he reigned eight years in Jerusalem. **6** And he walked in the way of the kings of Israel, as the house of Ahab had done: for he had the daughter of Ahab to [d]wife, and he wrought evil in the eyes of the Lord. **7** Howbeit the Lord would not destroy the house of David, because of the [2]covenant that he had made with David, and because he had promised to give a light to him, and to his sons forever. **8** In his days Edom rebelled from under the hand of Judah, and made a king over them. **9** And Jehoram went forth with his princes, and all his chariots with him: and he rose up by night, and smote Edom, which had compassed him in, and the captains of the chariots. **10** But Edom rebelled from under the hand of Judah unto this day. Then did [e]Libnah rebel at the same time from under his hand, because he had forsaken the Lord God of his fathers. **11** Moreover he made high places in the mountains of Judah, and caused the inhabitants of Jerusalem to commit [f]fornication, and compelled Judah thereto. **12** And there came a writing to him from [g]Elijah the Prophet, saying, Thus saith the Lord God of David thy father, Because thou hast not walked in the ways of Jehoshaphat thy father, nor in the ways of Asa king of Judah, **13** But hast walked in the way of the kings of Israel, and hast made Judah and the inhabitants of Jerusalem to go a whoring, as the house of Ahab went a whoring, and hast also slain thy brethren of thy father's house, which were better than thou. **14** Behold, with a great plague will the Lord smite thy people, and thy children, and thy wives, and all thy substance, **15** And thou shalt be in great diseases in the disease of thy bowels, until [h]thy bowels fall out for the disease, day by day. **16** So the Lord stirred up against Jehoram the spirit of the Philistines, and the Arabians that were beside the [i]Ethiopians. **17** And they came up into Judah, and brake into it, and carried away all the substance that was found in the king's house, and his sons also, and his wives, so that there was not a son left him, save [j]Jehoahaz the youngest of his sons. **18** And after all this, the Lord smote him in his bowels with an incurable disease. **19** And in process of time, even after the end of two years, his guts fell out with his disease: so he died of sore diseases: and his people made no burning for him like the burning of his fathers. **20** When he began to reign, he was two and thirty years old, and reigned in Jerusalem eight years, [k]and lived without being desired: yet they buried him in the city of David, but not among the sepulchers of the Kings.

22

Ahaziah reigneth after Jehoram. 9 Jehu king of Israel killeth Ahaziah. 10 Athaliah putteth to death all the King's lineage. 11 Joash escapeth.

1 And [1]the inhabitants of Jerusalem made Ahaziah his youngest son King in his stead: for the army that came with [a]the Arabians to the camp, had slain all the eldest: therefore Ahaziah the son of Jehoram king of Judah reigned. **2** Two and [b]forty years old was Ahaziah when he began to reign, and he reigned [c]one year in Jerusalem. And his mother's name was Athaliah the daughter [d]of Omri. **3** He walked also in the ways of the house of Ahab: for his mother counseled him to do wickedly. **4** Wherefore he did evil in the sight of the Lord, like the house of Ahab: for they were his [e]counselors after the death of his father, to his destruction. **5** And he walked after their counsel, and went with Jehoram the son of Ahab king of Israel to fight against Hazael king of Aram at Ramoth Gilead: and the Aramites smote Joram. **6** And he returned to be healed in Jezreel, because of the wounds wherewith they had wounded him at Ramah, when he fought with Hazael king of Aram. Now Azariah the son of Jehoram king of Judah went down to see Jehoram the son of Ahab at Jezreel, because he was diseased. **7** And the destruction of Ahaziah [f]came of God, in that he went to Joram: for when he was come, he went forth with Jehoram against Jehu the son of Nimshi, [2]whom the Lord had anointed to destroy the house of Ahab. **8** Therefore when Jehu [g]executed judgment upon the house of Ahab, and found the princes of Judah and the sons of the brethren of Ahaziah that waited on Ahaziah, he slew them also. **9** And he sought Ahaziah, and they caught him where he was hid in Samaria, and brought him to Jehu, and slew him and buried him, because said they, he is the son of [h]Jehoshaphat, which sought the Lord with all his heart. So the house of Ahaziah was not able to retain the kingdom. **10** [3]Therefore when Athaliah the mother of Ahaziah saw that her son was dead, she arose and [i]destroyed all the king's seed of the house of Judah. **11** But Jehoshabeath the daughter of the king, took Joash the son of Ahaziah, and stole him from among the king's sons, that should be slain, and put him and his nurse in the bed chamber: so Jehoshabeath the daughter of king Jehoram the wife of Jehoiada the Priest (for she was the sister of Ahaziah) hid him from Athaliah: so she slew him not. **12** And he was with them hid in the [j]house of God six years, while Athaliah reigned over the [k]land.

23

Joash the son of Ahaziah is made king. 15 Athaliah is put to death. 17 The temple of Baal is destroyed. 16 Jehoiada appointeth ministers in the Temple.

1 And [a,1]in the seventh year Jehoiada waxed bold, and took the captains of hundreds, to wit, Azariah the son of Jeroham, and Ishmael the son of Jehohanan, and Azariah the son of Obed, and Maaseiah the son of Adaiah, and Elishaphat the son of Zichri in covenant with him. **2** And they went about in Judah, and gathered the Levites out of all the cities of Judah, and the [b]chief fathers of Israel: and they came to Jerusalem. **3** And all the congregation made a covenant with the King in the house of God: and he said unto them, Behold, the King's son must reign, [2]as the Lord hath said of the sons of David. **4** This is it that ye shall do, The third part of you that come on the Sabbath of the Priests, and the Levites, shall be porters of the doors. **5** And another third part toward the King's house, and another third part at the [3]gate of the [c]foundation, and all the people shall be in the courts of the house of the Lord. **6** But let none come into the house of the Lord, save the Priests, and the Levites that minister, they shall go in, for they are holy: but all the people shall keep the watch of the Lord. **7** And the Levites shall compass the King round about, and every man with his weapon in his hand, and he that entereth [d]into the house, shall be slain, and be you with the king, when he cometh in, and when he goeth out. **8** So the Levites and all Judah did according to all things that Jehoiada the Priest had commanded, and took every man his men that came on the Sabbath, with them that [e]went out on the Sabbath: for Jehoiada the Priest did not discharge the courses. **9** And Jehoiada the Priest delivered to the captains of hundreds spears, and shields, and bucklers which had been King David's, and were in the house of God. **10** And he caused all the people to stand (every man with his weapon in his hand) from the right side of the house, to the left side of the house by the altar and by the [f]house round about the king. **11** Then they brought out the king's son, and put upon him the crown and gave him the [g]testimony, and made him King. And Jehoiada and his sons anointed him, and said, God save the king. **12** But when Athaliah heard the noise of the people running and praising the King, she came to the people into the house of the Lord. **13** And when she [h]looked, behold, the king stood by his pillar at the entering in, and the princes and the trumpets by the King, and all the people of the land rejoiced, and blew the trumpets, and the singers were with instruments of music, and they that could sing praise: then Athaliah rent her clothes, and said, [i]Treason, treason. **14** Then Jehoiada the Priest brought out the captains of hundreds that were governors of the host, and said unto them, Have her forth of the ranges, and he that [j]followeth her, let him die by the sword: for the Priest had said, Slay her not in the house of the Lord. **15** So they laid hands on her: and when she was come to the entering of the horse gate by the king's house, they slew her there. **16** And Jehoiada made a [k]covenant between him and all the people, and the king, that they would

---

them, whom by nature they ought most to cherish and defend.

c. 2 Chron. 21:4 Meaning, of Judah and Benjamin.
d. 2 Chron. 21:6 So that we see how it cannot be that we should join with the wicked, and serve God.
e. 2 Chron. 21:10 Read 2 Kings 8:22.
f. 2 Chron. 21:11 Meaning, idolatry because that the idolater breaketh promise with God, as doth the adulteress to her husband.
g. 2 Chron. 21:12 Some think that this was Elisha, so called because he had the Spirit in abundance, as had Elijah.
h. 2 Chron. 21:15 We see this example daily practiced upon them that fall away from God, and become idolaters and murderers of their brethren.
i. 2 Chron. 21:16 There were other Arabians in Africa Southward toward Egypt.
j. 2 Chron. 21:17 Called also Ahaziah, as 2 Chron. 22:1, or Azariah, verse 6 following.
k. 2 Chron. 21:20 That is, as some write, he was not regarded, but deposed for his wickedness, and idolatry: so that his son reigned 22 years (his father yet living) without honor, and after his father's death he was confirmed to reign still, as 2 Chron. 22:2.

2-CHRON. 22

a. 2 Chron. 22:1 Meaning, the Philistines.
b. 2 Chron. 22:2 Read 2 Chron. 21:20.
c. 2 Chron. 22:2 That is, after the death of his father.
d. 2 Chron. 22:2 She was Ahab's daughter, who was the son of Omri.
e. 2 Chron. 22:4 He showeth that it must needs follow that the rulers are such as their counselors be, and that there cannot be a good King, that suffereth wicked counselors.
f. 2 Chron. 22:7 Hereby we see how nothing can come to any but by God's providence and as he hath appointed, and therefore he causeth all means to serve to his will.
g. 2 Chron. 22:8 Or, took vengeance.
h. 2 Chron. 22:9 This was the just plague of God, because he joined himself with God's enemies: yet God to declare the worthiness of Jehoshaphat his grandfather, moved them to give him the honor of burial.
i. 2 Chron. 22:10 To the intent that there should be none to make title to the crown, and so she might usurp the government.
j. 2 Chron. 22:12 Meaning, in the chamber, where the Priests and Levites slept, which kept their courses weekly in the Temple.
k. 2 Chron. 22:12 To wit, of Judah.

2-CHRON. 23

a. 2 Chron. 23:1 Of the reign of Athaliah, or after the death of Ahaziah.
b. 2 Chron. 23:2 Meaning of Judah and Benjamin: read why they are called Israel, 2 Chron. 15:17.
c. 2 Chron. 23:5 Which was the chief gate of the Temple toward the East.
d. 2 Chron. 23:7 Meaning, to make any tumult, or to hinder their enterprise.
e. 2 Chron. 23:8 Which had finished their course on the Sabbath, and so the other part entered to keep their turn.
f. 2 Chron. 23:10 Meaning, the most holy place where the Ark stood.
g. 2 Chron. 23:11 That is, the book of the Law, or as some read, they put upon him his royal apparel.
h. 2 Chron. 23:13 Or, saw the king standing.
i. 2 Chron. 23:13 Declaring her vile impudence, which having unjustly and by murder usurped the crown, would still have defeated the true possessor, and therefore called true obedience treason.
j. 2 Chron. 23:14 To join with her party, and to maintain her authority.
k. 2 Chron. 23:16 That they would only serve him and renounce all idolatry.

2-CHRON. 21

1. 2 Kings 8:16
2. 2 Sam. 7:12,16 / 1 Kings 2:4 / 1 Kings 9:5 / 2 Kings 8:19 / 2 Chron. 6:16

2-CHRON. 22

1. 2 Kings 8:24
2. 2 Kings 9:7
3. 2 Kings 11:1

be the Lord's people. **17** And all the people went to the house of Baal, and [l]de-
stroyed, and brake his altars and his images, and slew [m]Mattan the priest of Baal
before the altars. **18** And Jehoiada appointed officers for the house of the Lord,
under the [n]hands of the Priests and Levites, whom David had distributed for the
house of the Lord, to offer burnt offerings unto the Lord, [4]as it is written in the
Law of Moses, with rejoicing and singing by the appointment of David. **19** And
he set porters by the gates of the house of the Lord, that none that was unclean
in anything, should enter in. **20** And he took the captains of hundreds, and the
noble men, and the governors of the people, and all the people of the land, and he
caused the king to come down out of the house of the Lord, and they went throu-
gh the [o]high gate of the king's house, and set the king upon the throne of the kin-
gdom. **21** Then all the people of the land rejoiced, and the city was quiet [p]after
that they had slain Athaliah with the sword.

24

Joash repaireth the house of the Lord. 17 After the death of Jehoiada he falleth to idolatry. 21 He stoneth to death Zechariah the Prophet. 25 Joash is killed of his own servants. 27 After him reigneth Amaziah.

1 Joash [1]was seven years old when he began to reign, and he reigned forty ye-
ars in Jerusalem: and his mother's name was Zibiah of Beersheba. **2** And Joash
did uprightly in the sight of the Lord all the days of [a]Jehoiada the Priest. **3** And
Jehoiada [b]took him two wives, and he begat sons and daughters. **4** And afterward
it came into Joash's mind to renew the house of the Lord. **5** And he assembled
the Priests and the Levites, and said to them, Go out unto the cities of Judah, and
gather of all [c]Israel money to repair the house of your God, from year to year, and
haste the thing, but the Levites hasted not. **6** Therefore the king called Jehoiada
the [d]chief, and said unto him, Why hast thou not required of the Levites to bring
in out of Judah and Jerusalem [2]the tax of Moses the servant of the Lord, and of the
Congregation of Israel, for the Tabernacle of the testimony? **7** For [e]wicked Atha-
liah, and her children brake up the house of God: and all the things that were dedi-
cated for the house of the Lord, did they bestow upon Baal. **8** Therefore the king
commanded, [3]and they made a chest, and set it at the gate of the house of the Lord
without. **9** And they made proclamation through Judah and Jerusalem, to bring
unto the Lord [4]the tax of Moses the servant of God, laid upon Israel in the wilder-
ness. **10** And all the princes and all the people rejoiced, and brought in, and cast
into the chest, until they had finished. **11** And when it was time, [f]they brought
the chest unto the King's officer by the hand of the Levites: and when they saw
that there was much silver, then the King's Scribe (and one appointed by the high
Priest) came and emptied the chest, and took it, and carried it to his place again:
thus they did day by day, and gathered silver in abundance. **12** And the King
and [g]Jehoiada gave it to such as did the labor and work in the house of the Lord,
and hired masons and carpenters to repair the house of the Lord: they gave it also
to workers of iron and brass, to repair the house of the Lord. **13** So the workmen
wrought, and the work [h]amended through their hands: and they restored the hou-
se of God to his state, and strengthened it. **14** And when they had finished it,
they brought the rest of the silver before the king and Jehoiada, and he made there-
of [i]vessels for the house of the Lord, even vessels to minister, both mortars and in-
cense cups, and vessels of gold, and of silver: and they offered burnt offerings in the
house of the Lord continually all the days of Jehoiada. **15** But Jehoiada waxed
old and was full of days, and died. An hundred and thirty years old was he when
he died. **16** And they buried him in the city of David with the [j]kings, because he
had done good in Israel, and toward God and his house. **17** And after the dea-
th of Jehoiada, came the [k]princes of Judah, and did reverence to the king, and the
king hearkened unto them. **18** And they left the house of the Lord God of their
fathers, and served groves and idols: and wrath came upon Judah and Jerusalem,
because of this their trespass. **19** And God sent Prophets among them, to bring
them again unto the Lord: and they [l]made protestation among them, but they
would not hear. **20** And the Spirit of God came upon Zechariah the son of Jeho-
iada the Priest, which stood [m]above the people, and said unto them, Thus saith
God, Why transgress ye the commandments of the Lord? surely ye shall not pro-
sper: because ye have forsaken the Lord, he also hath forsaken you. **21** Then they
conspired against him, and stoned him with stones at the [n]commandment of the
king, in the court of the house of the Lord. **22** Thus Joash the king remembe-
red not the kindness which Jehoiada his father had done to him, but slew his son.
And when he died, he said, The Lord [o]look upon it and require it. **23** And when
the year was out, the host of Aram came up against him, and they came against
Judah and Jerusalem, and destroyed all the princes of the people from among the
people, and sent all the spoil of them unto the king of Damascus. **24** Though
the army of Aram came with a small company of men, yet the Lord delivered a
very great army into their hand, because they had forsaken the Lord God of their
fathers: and they [p]gave sentence against Joash. **25** And when they were departed
from him, (for they left him in great diseases) his own servants conspired against
him for the blood of the [q]children of Jehoiada the Priest, and slew him on his bed,
and he died, and they buried him in the city of David: but they buried him not in
the sepulchers of the kings. **26** And these are they that conspired against him,
Zabad the son of Shimrath an Ammonitess, and Jehozabad the son of Shimrith a
Moabitess. **27** But [r]his sons, and the sum of the tax gathered by him, and the
[s]foundation of the house of God, behold, they are written in the story of the book
of the Kings. And Amaziah his son reigned in his stead.

25

Amaziah putteth him to death which slew his father. 10 He sendeth back them of Israel. 11 He overcometh the Edomites. 14 He falleth to idolatry. 17 And Joash king of Israel overcometh Amaziah. 27 He is slain by a conspiracy.

1 Amaziah was five and twenty years old when he began to reign, and he rei-
gned nine and twenty years in [1]Jerusalem, and his mother's name was Jehoaddan of
Jerusalem. **2** And he did [a]uprightly in the eyes of the Lord, but not with a perfect
heart. **3** And when the kingdom was established unto him, he slew his servants,
that had slain the king his father. **4** But he slew not their children, but did as
it is written in the Law, and in the book of Moses, where the Lord commanded,
saying, [2]The fathers shall not die for the [b]children, neither shall the children die for
the fathers, but every man shall die for his own sin. **5** And Amaziah assembled
Judah, and made them captains over thousands, and captains over hundreds, ac-
cording to the houses of their fathers, throughout all Judah and Benjamin: and he
numbered them from [c]twenty years old and above, and found among them three
hundred thousand chosen men, to go forth to the war, and to handle spear and
shield. **6** He hired also an hundred thousand valiant men [d]out of Israel for an
hundred talents of silver. **7** But a man of God came to him, saying, O king, let
not the army of Israel go with thee: for the Lord is not [e]with Israel, neither with
all the house of Ephraim. **8** If [f]not, go thou on, do it, make thyself strong to the
battle, but God shall make thee fall before the enemy: for God hath power to help,
and to cast down. **9** And Amaziah said to the man of GOD, What shall we do
then for the hundred talents, which I have given to the host of Israel? Then the man
of God answered, The Lord is able to [g]give thee more than this. **10** So Amaziah
separated them, to wit, the army that was come to him out of Ephraim, to return
to their place: wherefore their wrath was kindled greatly against Judah, and they
returned to their places with great anger. **11** Then Amaziah was encouraged, and
led forth his people, and went to the salt valley, and smote of the children of [h]Seir,
ten thousand. **12** And other ten thousand did the children of Judah take alive,

---

l. 2 Chron. 23:17 According to their covenant made to the Lord.
m. 2 Chron. 23:17 As the Lord commanded in his Law both for the person and also the city, Deut. 13:9 and 15.
n. 2 Chron. 23:18 Or, charge.
o. 2 Chron. 23:20 Which was the principal gate, that the King might be seen of all the people.
p. 2 Chron. 23:21 For where a tyrant and an idolater reigneth, there can be no quietness for the plagues of God are ever among such people.

2-CHRON. 23
1. 2 Kings 11:4
2. 2 Sam. 7:12,16 / 1 Kings 2:4 / 2 Chron. 21:7
3. 2 Kings 11:6
4. Num. 28:3

2-CHRON. 24
a. 2 Chron. 24:2 Who was a faithful counselor, and governed him by the word of God.
b. 2 Chron. 24:3 Or, gave him two wives.
c. 2 Chron. 24:5 He meaneth not the ten tribes, but only the two tribes of Judah and Benjamin.
d. 2 Chron. 24:6 For he was the high Priest.
e. 2 Chron. 24:7 The Scriptures doth term her thus, because she was a cruel murderer, and a blasphemous idolatress.
f. 2 Chron. 24:11 Such as were faithful men, whom the king had appointed for that matter.
g. 2 Chron. 24:12 Signifying that this thing was done by advice and counsel, and not by any one man's affection.
h. 2 Chron. 24:13 Hebrew, a medicine was upon the work, meaning it was repaired.
i. 2 Chron. 24:14 For the wicked kings his predecessors, and Athaliah had destroyed the vessels of the Temple, or turned them to the use of their idols.
j. 2 Chron. 24:16 Signifying that they could not honor him too much, who had so excellently served in the work of the Lord, and in the affairs of the commonwealth.
k. 2 Chron. 24:17 Which were flatterers, and knew now that the king was destitute of him who did watch over him as a father, and therefore brought him to most vile idolatry.
l. 2 Chron. 24:19 They took heaven and earth and all creatures to witness, that except they returned to the Lord, he would most grievously punish their infidelity and rebellion, Neh. 9:26.
m. 2 Chron. 24:20 In a place above the people, to the intent that he might be heard.
n. 2 Chron. 24:21 There is no rage so cruel and beastly as of them whose hearts God hath hardened, and which delight more in superstition and idolatry than in the true service of God and pure simplicity of his word.
o. 2 Chron. 24:22 Revenge my death and require my blood at your hands: or he speaketh this by prophecy, because he knew that God would do it. This Zechariah is also called the son of Berechiah, Matt. 23:35, because his progenitors were Iddo, Berechiah, Jehoiada, etc.
p. 2 Chron. 24:24 That is, reproved and checked him, and handled him rigorously.
q. 2 Chron. 24:25 Meaning, Zechariah, which was one of Jehoiada's sons, and a Prophet of the Lord.
r. 2 Chron. 24:27 That is, concerning his sons, etc.
s. 2 Chron. 24:27 That is, the reparation.

2-CHRON. 24
1. 2 Kings 12:1
2. Exod. 30:13
3. 2 Kings 12:9
4. Exod. 30:13

2-CHRON. 25
a. 2 Chron. 25:2 Meaning, in respect of his predecessors albeit he had his imperfections.
b. 2 Chron. 25:4 That is, for that fault wherefore the child is punished, except he be culpable of the same.
c. 2 Chron. 25:5 So many as were able men to bear weapons and go to the war.
d. 2 Chron. 25:6 That is, out of the ten tribes, which had separated themselves before, both from God and their true king.
e. 2 Chron. 25:7 And therefore to think to have help of them, whom the Lord favoreth not, is to cast off the help of the Lord.
f. 2 Chron. 25:8 If thou wilt not give credit to my words.
g. 2 Chron. 25:9 He showeth that if we depend only upon God, we shall not need to be troubled with these worldly respects, for he will give at all times that which shall be necessary, if we obey his word.
h. 2 Chron. 25:11 For the Idumeans whom David had brought to subjection, rebelled under Jehoram Jehoshaphat's son.

and carried them to the top of a [i]rock, and cast them down from the top of the rock, and they all burst to pieces. **13** But the men of the [j]army, which Amaziah sent away, that they should not go with his people to battle, fell upon the cities of Judah from Samaria unto Beth Horon, and smote three thousand of them, and took much spoil. **14** Now after that Amaziah was come from the slaughter of the Edomites, he brought the gods of the children of Seir, and set them up to be his gods, and [k]worshipped them, and burned incense unto them. **15** Wherefore the Lord was wroth with Amaziah, and sent unto him a Prophet, which said unto him, Why hast thou sought the gods of the people, which were not able to [l]deliver their own people out of thine hand? **16** And as he talked with him, [m]he said unto him, Have they made thee the King's counselor? cease thou: why should they [n]smite thee? And the Prophet ceased, but said, I know that God hath determined to destroy thee, because thou hast done this, and hast not obeyed my counsel. **17** Then Amaziah King of Judah took counsel, and sent to Joash the son of Jehoahaz, the son of Jehu king of Israel, saying, Come, [o]let us see one another in the face. **18** But Joash king of Israel sent to Amaziah king of Judah, saying, The thistle that is in Lebanon, sent to the cedar that is in Lebanon, saying, [3]Give thy daughter to my son to wife: and the wild beast that was in Lebanon went and trode down the thistle. **19** Thou thinkest: lo, thou hast smitten Edom, and thine heart lifteth thee up to brag: abide now at home: why dost thou provoke to thine hurt, that thou shouldest fall, and Judah with thee? **20** But Amaziah would not hear: for [p]it was of God, that he might deliver them into his hand, because they had sought the gods of Edom. **21** So Joash the king of Israel went up: and he and Amaziah king of Judah saw one another in the face at Bethshemesh, which is in Judah. **22** And Judah was put to the worse before Israel, and they fled every man to his tents. **23** But Joash the king of Israel took Amaziah king of Judah, the son of Joash, the son of Jehoahaz, in Bethshemesh, and brought him to Jerusalem, and brake down the wall of Jerusalem, from the gate of Ephraim unto the corner gate, four hundred cubits. **24** And he took all the gold and the silver, and all the vessels that were found in the house of God with [q]Obed Edom, and in the treasures of the king's house, and the children that were in hostage, and returned to Samaria. **25** And Amaziah the son of Joash king of Judah lived after the death of Joash son of Jehoahaz king of Israel, fifteen years. **26** Concerning the rest of the acts of Amaziah first and last, are they not written in the book of the kings of Judah and Israel? **27** Now after the time that Amaziah did turn away from the Lord, [4]they wrought treason against him in Jerusalem: and when he was fled to Lachish, they sent to Lachish after him, and slew him there. **28** And they brought him upon horses, and buried him with his fathers in the city of Judah.

26

1, 5 Uzziah obeying the Lord, prospereth in his enterprises. 16 He waxeth proud and usurpeth the Priests' office. 19 The Lord plagueth him. 20 The Priests drive him out of the Temple, and exclude him out of the Lord's house. 23 His burial, and his successor.

1 Then all the [1]people of Judah took [a]Uzziah which was sixteen years old, and made him king in the stead of his father Amaziah. **2** He built [b]Eloth, and restored it to Judah, after that the king slept with his fathers. **3** [2]Sixteen years old was Uzziah, when he began to reign, and he reigned two and fifty years in Jerusalem, and his mother's name was Jecholiah of Jerusalem. **4** And he did uprightly in the sight of the Lord, according to all that his father Amaziah did. **5** And he sought God in the days of [c]Zechariah (which understood the visions of God) and when as [d]he sought the Lord, God made him to prosper. **6** For he went forth and fought against the Philistines and brake down the wall of Gath, and the wall of Jabneh, and the wall of Ashdod, and built cities in Ashdod, and among the Philistines. **7** And God helped him against the Philistines, and against the Arabians that dwelt in Gur Baal and Hammeunim. **8** And the Ammonites gave [e]gifts to Uzziah, and his name spread to the entering in of Egypt: for he did most valiantly. **9** Moreover Uzziah built towers in Jerusalem at the corner gate, and at the valley gate, and at the [f,3]turning, and made them strong. **10** And he built towers in the wilderness, and dug many [g]cisterns: for he had much cattle both in the valleys and plains, plowmen, and dressers of vines in the mountains, and in [h]Carmel: for he loved husbandry. **11** Uzziah also had an host of fighting men that went out to war by bands, according to the count of their number under the hand of Jeiel the Scribe, and Maaseiah the ruler, and under the hand of Hananiah, one of the King's captains. **12** The whole [i]number of the chief of the families of the valiant men were two thousand and six hundred. **13** And under their hand was the army for war, three hundred and seven thousand, and five hundred that fought valiantly to help the King against the enemy. **14** And Uzziah prepared them throughout all the host, shields, and spears, and helmets, and brigandines, and bows, and stones to sling. **15** He made also very [j]artificial engines in Jerusalem, to be upon the towers and upon the corners, to shoot arrows and great stones: and his name spread far abroad, because God did help him marvelously till he was mighty. **16** But when he was strong, his heart [k]was lifted up to his destruction: for he transgressed against the Lord his God, and went into the Temple of the Lord to burn incense upon the altar of incense. **17** And Azariah the Priest went in after him, and with him fourscore Priests of the Lord, valiant men. **18** And they withstood Uzziah the King, and said unto him, [4]It pertaineth not to thee, Uzziah, to burn incense unto the Lord, but to the Priests the sons of Aaron, that are consecrated for to offer incense: [l]go forth of the Sanctuary: for thou hast transgressed, and thou shalt have none honor of the Lord God. **19** Then Uzziah was wroth, and had incense in his hand to burn it: and while he was wroth with the Priests, the leprosy rose up in his forehead before the Priests in the house of the Lord beside the incense altar. **20** And when Azariah the chief Priest with all the Priests looked upon him, behold, he was leprous in his forehead, and they caused him hastily to depart thence: and he was even compelled to go out, because the Lord had smitten him. **21** [5]And Uzziah the King was a leper unto the day of his death, and dwelt as a leper in an [m]house apart, because he was cut off from the house of the Lord: and Jotham his son ruled over the King's house, and judged the people of the land. **22** Concerning the rest of the acts of Uzziah, first and last, did Isaiah the Prophet the son of Amoz write. **23** So Uzziah slept with his fathers, and they buried him with his fathers in the field of the burial, which pertained to the Kings: for they said, He [n]is a leper. And Jotham his son reigned in his stead.

27

1 Jotham reigned, and overcometh the Ammonites. 8 His reign and death. 9 Ahaz his son reigneth in his stead.

1 Jotham [1]was five and twenty years old when he began to reign, and reigned sixteen years in Jerusalem, and his mother's name was Jerushah the daughter of Zadok. **2** And he did uprightly in the sight of the Lord, according to all that his father Uzziah did, save that he entered not into the [a]Temple of the Lord, and the people did yet [b]corrupt their ways. **3** He built the high [c]gate of the house of the Lord, and he built very much on the wall of the castle. **4** Moreover he built cities in the mountains of Judah, and in the forests he built palaces and towers. **5** And he fought with the kings of the children of Ammon, and prevailed against them. And the children of Ammon gave him the same year an hundred talents of silver, and ten thousand [d]measures of wheat, and ten thousand of barley: this did the children of Ammon give him [e]both in the second year and the third. **6** So Jotham became mighty, [f]because he directed his way before the Lord his God. **7** Concerning the rest of the acts of Jotham and all his wars and his ways, lo, they are written in the book of the Kings of Israel, and Judah. **8** He was five and twenty years old, when he began to reign, and reigned sixteen years in Jerusalem. **9** And Jotham slept with his fathers, and they buried him in the city of David: and Ahaz his son reigned in his stead.

---

i. 2 Chron. 25:12 In 2 Kings 14:7, this rock is called the city Sela.
j. 2 Chron. 25:13 That is, the hundred thousand of Israel.
k. 2 Chron. 25:14 Thus where he should have given the praise to God for his benefits and great victory, he fell from God, and did most vilely dishonor him.
l. 2 Chron. 25:15 He proveth that whatsoever cannot save himself nor his worshippers, is no God but an idol.
m. 2 Chron. 25:16 Meaning, the King.
n. 2 Chron. 25:16 So hard it is, for the carnal man to be admonished of his fault, that he contemneth, mocketh, and threateneth him that warneth him: yea, imprisoneth him and putteth him to death, 2 Chron. 16:10 and 18:26 and 24:21.
o. 2 Chron. 25:17 That is, let us try the matter hand to hand: for he was offended, that the army of the Israelites, whom he had in wages, and dismissed by the counsel of the Prophet, had destroyed certain of the cities of Judah.
p. 2 Chron. 25:20 Thus God oft times plagueth by those means wherein men most trust, to teach them to have their recourse only to him, and to show his judgments, moveth their hearts to follow that which shall be their destruction.
q. 2 Chron. 25:24 Meaning, the successors of Obed Edom: for the house bare the name of the chief father.

2-CHRON. 25
1. 2 Kings 14:2
2. Deut. 24:16 / 2 Kings 14:6 / Jer. 31:30 / Ezek. 18:10
3. 2 Kings 14:9
4. 2 Kings 14:19

2-CHRON. 26
a. 2 Chron. 26:1 Called also Azariah.
b. 2 Chron. 26:2 He fortified it and made it strong: this city was also called Elath and Elanon near to the red Sea.
c. 2 Chron. 26:5 This was not that Zechariah that was the son of Jehoiada, but some other Prophet of that name.
d. 2 Chron. 26:5 For God never forsakes any that seeketh unto him, and therefore man is the cause of his own destruction.
e. 2 Chron. 26:8 That is, they paid tribute in sign of subjection.
f. 2 Chron. 26:9 Whereas the wall or tower turneth.
g. 2 Chron. 26:10 Or, pits.
h. 2 Chron. 26:10 That is, in mount Carmel, or as the word signifieth in the fruitful field: it is also taken for a green ear of corn, when it is full, as Lev. 2:14.
i. 2 Chron. 26:12 Of the chief officers of the king's house, or of the captains and sergeants for war.
j. 2 Chron. 26:15 Hebrew, engines by the invention of an inventive man.
k. 2 Chron. 26:16 Thus prosperity causeth men to trust in themselves, and by forgetting him which is the author thereof, procure their own perdition.
l. 2 Chron. 26:18 Though his zeal seemed to be good and also his intention, yet because they were not governed by the word of God, he did wickedly, and was therefore both justly resisted and also punished.
m. 2 Chron. 26:21 According to the commandment of the Lord, Lev. 13:46.
n. 2 Chron. 26:23 And therefore was buried apart in the same field, but not in the same sepulchers with his predecessors.

2-CHRON. 26
1. 2 Kings 14:21
2. 1 Kings 15:2
3. Neh. 3:19,24
4. Num. 18:7
5. 2 Kings 15:5

2-CHRON. 27
a. 2 Chron. 27:2 To wit, to offer incense against the word of God, which thing is spoken in the commendation of Jotham.
b. 2 Chron. 27:2 They were not clean purged from idolatry.
c. 2 Chron. 27:3 Which was sixscore cubits high, and was for the height called Ophel: it was at the East gate, and mention is made of it, 2 Chron. 3:4.
d. 2 Chron. 27:5 Hebrew, Corim.
e. 2 Chron. 27:5 Or, yearly.
f. 2 Chron. 27:6 He showeth that all prosperity cometh of God, who never faileth when we put our trust in him.

2-CHRON. 27
1. 2 Kings 15:33

28

1 Ahaz an idolater is given into the hands of the Syrians and the king of Israel. 9 The Prophet reproveth the Israelites' cruelty. 18 Judah is molested with enemies. 23 Ahaz increaseth his idolatry. 26 His death and successor.

1 Ahaz [1]was twenty years old when he began to reign, and reigned sixteen years in Jerusalem, and did not uprightly in the sight of the Lord, like David his [a]father. **2** But [b]he walked in the ways of the kings of Israel, and made even molten images for [c]Baalim. **3** Moreover he burnt incense in the valley of Ben-hinnom, and [d]burnt his sons with fire, after the abominations of the heathen whom the Lord had cast out before the children of Israel. **4** He sacrificed also and burnt incense in the high places, and on hills, and under every green tree. **5** Wherefore the Lord his God delivered him into the hand of the king of the Aramites, and they smote him, and took of his [e]many prisoners, and brought them to Damascus: and he was also delivered into the hand of the king of Israel, which smote him with a great slaughter. **6** For [f]Pekah the son of Remaliah slew in Judah sixscore thousand in one day, all [g]valiant men, because they had forsaken the Lord God of their fathers. **7** And Zichri a [h]mighty man of Ephraim slew Maaseiah the king's son, and Azrikam the governor of the house, and Elkanah the second after the king. **8** And the children of Israel took prisoners of their brethren, [i]two hundred thousand of women, sons and daughters, and carried away much spoil of them, and brought the spoil to Samaria. **9** But there was a Prophet of the Lord, (whose name was Oded) and he went out before the host that came to Samaria, and said unto them, Behold, [j]because the Lord God of your fathers is wroth with Judah, he hath delivered them into your hand, and ye have slain them in a rage, that reacheth up to heaven. **10** And now ye purpose to keep under the children of Judah and Jerusalem, as servants and handmaids unto you, but are not you such that [k]sins are with you before the Lord your God? **11** Now therefore hear me, and deliver the captives again, which ye have taken prisoners of your brethren: for the fierce wrath of the Lord is toward you. **12** Wherefore certain of the chiefs of the children of [l]Ephraim, Azariah the son of Johanan, Berechiah the son of Meshillemoth, and Jehizkiah the son of Shallum, and Amasa the son of Hadlai, stood up against them that came from the war, **13** And said unto them, Bring not in the captives hither: for this shall be [m]a sin upon us against the Lord: ye intended to add more to our sins and to our trespass, though our trespass be great, and the fierce wrath of God is against Israel. **14** So the army left the captives and the spoil before the princes and all the Congregation. **15** And the men that were [n]named by name, rose up and took the prisoners, and with the spoil clothed all that were naked among them, and arrayed them, and shod them, and gave them meat, and gave them drink, and [o]anointed them, and carried all that were feeble of them upon asses, and brought them to Jericho the city of Palm trees to their [p]brethren: so they returned to Samaria. **16** At that time did King Ahaz send unto the [q]kings of Assyria to help him. **17** (For the Edomites came moreover, and slew of Judah, and carried away captives. **18** The Philistines also invaded the cities in the low country, and toward the South of Judah, and took Beth Shemesh, and Aijalon, and Gederoth and Sochoh, with the villages thereof, and Timnah, with her villages, and Gimzo, with her villages, and they dwelt there. **19** For the Lord had humbled Judah, because of Ahaz king of [r]Israel: for he had brought vengeance upon Judah, and had grievously transgressed against the Lord.) **20** And Tilgath-Pilneser king of Assyria came unto him, who troubled him and did not strengthen him. **21** For Ahaz [s]took a portion [2]out of the house of the Lord and out of the king's house and of the princes', and gave unto the king of Assyria: yet it helped him not. **22** And in the time of his tribulation did he yet trespass more against the Lord, (this is king Ahaz) **23** For he sacrificed unto the gods of Damascus, which [t]plagued him, and he said, Because the gods of the kings of Aram helped them, I will sacrifice unto them, and they will [u]help me: yet they were his ruin, and of all [v]Israel. **24** And Ahaz gathered the vessels of the house of God, and brake the vessels of the house of God, and shut up the doors of the house of the Lord, and made him altars in every corner of Jerusalem. **25** And in every city of Judah he made high places, to burn incense unto other gods, and provoked to anger the Lord God of his fathers. **26** Concerning the rest of his acts, and all his ways first and last, behold, they are written in the book of the Kings of Judah, and Israel. **27** And Ahaz slept with his fathers, and they buried him in the city [w]of Jerusalem, but brought him not unto the [x]sepulchers of the Kings of Israel: and Hezekiah his son reigned in his stead.

29

3, 5 Hezekiah repaireth the Temple, and advertiseth the Levites of the corruption of religion. 12 The levites prepare the Temple. 20 The king and his princes sacrifice in the Temple. 25 The Levites sing praises. 31 The oblation of the people.

1 Hezekiah [1]began to reign, when he was five and twenty years old, and reigned nine and twenty years in Jerusalem: and his mother's name was [a]Abijah the daughter of Zechariah. **2** And he did uprightly in the sight of the Lord, according to all that David his father had done. **3** He opened the [b]doors of the house of the Lord in the [c]first year, and in the first month of his reign, and repaired them. **4** And he brought in the Priests and the Levites, and gathered them into the East street, **5** And said unto them, Hear me, ye Levites: sanctify now yourselves, and sanctify the house of the Lord God of your fathers, and carry forth [d]the filthiness out of the Sanctuary. **6** For our fathers have trespassed and done evil in the eyes of the Lord our God, and have forsaken him, and turned away their faces from the Tabernacle of the Lord, and turned their backs. **7** They have also shut the doors of the porch, and quenched the lamps, and have neither burnt incense, nor offered burnt offerings in the Sanctuary unto the God of Israel. **8** [e]Wherefore the wrath of the Lord hath been on Judah and Jerusalem, and he hath made them a [f]scattering, a desolation, and an hissing, as ye see with your eyes. **9** For lo, our fathers are fallen by the sword, and our sons, and our daughters, and our wives are in captivity for the same cause. **10** Now [g]I purpose to make a covenant with the Lord God of Israel, that he may [h]turn away his fierce wrath from us. **11** Now my sons, be not deceived: for the Lord hath [2]chosen you to stand before him, to serve him, and to be his ministers, and to burn incense. **12** Then the Levites arose, Mahath the son of Amasai, and Joel the son of Azariah of the sons of the Kohathites: and of the sons of Merari, Kish the son of Abdi, and Azariah the son of Jehallelel: and of the Gershonites, Joah the son of Zimmah, and Eden the son of Joah: **13** And of the sons of Elizaphan, Shimri, and Jeiel: and of the sons of Asaph, Zechariah, and Mattaniah: **14** And of the sons of Heman, Jehiel, and Shimei: and of the sons of Jeduthun, Shemaiah and Uzziel. **15** And they gathered their brethren, and sanctified themselves and came according to the commandment of the king, and [i]by the words of the Lord, for to cleanse the house of the Lord. **16** And the Priests went into the inner parts of the house of the Lord, to [j]cleanse it and brought out all the uncleanness that they found in the Temple of the Lord, into the court of the house of the Lord: and the Levites took it, to carry it out unto the brook Kidron. **17** They began the first day of the [k]first month to sanctify it, and the eight day of the month came they to the porch of the Lord: so they sanctified the house of the Lord in eight days, and in the sixteenth day of the first month, they made an end. **18** Then they went in to Hezekiah the king and said, We have cleansed all the house of the Lord, and the altar of burnt offering, with all the vessels thereof, and the [l]showbread table, with all the vessels thereof: **19** And all the vessels which King Ahaz had cast aside when he reigned, and transgressed, have we prepared and sanctified: and behold, they are before the altar of the Lord. **20** And Hezekiah the king [m]rose early, and gathered the princes of the city, and went up to the house of the Lord. **21** And they brought seven bullocks, and seven rams, and seven lambs, and seven he goats for a [3]sin offering for the kingdom, and for the sanctuary, and for Judah. And he commanded the Priests the sons of Aaron, to offer them on the altar of the Lord. **22** So they slew the bullocks, and the Priests received the blood, and [n]sprinkled it upon the altar: they slew also the rams, and sprinkled the blood upon the altar, and they slew the

---

2-CHRON. 28

- **a.** 2 Chron. 28:1 Or, predecessor.
- **b.** 2 Chron. 28:2 He was an idolater like them.
- **c.** 2 Chron. 28:2 As the idolaters have certain chief idols, who are as patrons (as were these Baalim) so have they others which are inferior and do represent the great idols.
- **d.** 2 Chron. 28:3 Or, made them pass through the fire, as 2 Chron. 33:6; Lev. 13:21.
- **e.** 2 Chron. 28:5 Hebrew, a great captivity.
- **f.** 2 Chron. 28:6 Who was king of Israel.
- **g.** 2 Chron. 28:6 Hebrew, sons of strength.
- **h.** 2 Chron. 28:7 Or, tyrant.
- **i.** 2 Chron. 28:8 Thus by the just judgment of God, Israel destroyed Judah.
- **j.** 2 Chron. 28:9 For they thought they had overcome them by their own valiantness, and did not consider that God had delivered them into their hands, because Judah had offended him.
- **k.** 2 Chron. 28:10 May not God as well punish you for your sins as he hath done these men for theirs, seeing yours are greater?
- **l.** 2 Chron. 28:12 Which tribe was now greatest, and had most authority.
- **m.** 2 Chron. 28:13 God will not suffer this sin, which we commit against him, to be unpunished.
- **n.** 2 Chron. 28:15 Whose name were rehearsed before, verse 12.
- **o.** 2 Chron. 28:15 Either for their wounds or weariness.
- **p.** 2 Chron. 28:15 To them of the tribe of Judah.
- **q.** 2 Chron. 28:16 To Tiglath-Pileser and those kings that were under his dominion, 2 Kings 16:7.
- **r.** 2 Chron. 28:19 He meaneth Judah, because Ahaz forsook the Lord and sought help of the infidels. Read of Israel taken for Judah, 2 Chron. 15:17.
- **s.** 2 Chron. 28:21 Hebrew, divided.
- **t.** 2 Chron. 28:23 As he falsely supposed.
- **u.** 2 Chron. 28:23 Thus the wicked measure God's favor by prosperity and adversity: for if idolaters prosper, they make their idols gods, not considering that God punisheth them oft times whom he loveth, and giveth his enemies good success for a time, whom afterward he will destroy.
- **v.** 2 Chron. 28:23 Or, Judah and Benjamin.
- **w.** 2 Chron. 28:27 Or, in Jerusalem.
- **x.** 2 Chron. 28:27 They buried him not in the city of David, where were the sepulchers of the kings.

2-CHRON. 28

1. 2 Kings 16:2
2. 2 Kings 16:8

2-CHRON. 29

- **a.** 2 Chron. 29:1 Or, Abi.
- **b.** 2 Chron. 29:3 Which Ahaz had shut up, 2 Chron. 28:24.
- **c.** 2 Chron. 29:3 This is a notable example for all princes, first to establish the pure religion of God, and to procure that the Lord may be honored and served aright.
- **d.** 2 Chron. 29:5 Meaning, all the idols, altars, groves and whatsoever was occupied in their service, and wherewith the Temple was polluted.
- **e.** 2 Chron. 29:8 He showeth that the contempt of religion is the cause of all God's plagues.
- **f.** 2 Chron. 29:8 Or, a nodding of the head and mockery.
- **g.** 2 Chron. 29:10 Hebrew, it is in mine heart.
- **h.** 2 Chron. 29:10 He proveth by the judgments of God upon those that have contemned his word, that there is no way to avoid his plagues, but by conforming themselves to his will.
- **i.** 2 Chron. 29:15 Or, concerning the things of the Lord.
- **j.** 2 Chron. 29:16 From the pollutions and filth that Ahaz had brought in.
- **k.** 2 Chron. 29:17 Which contained part of March and part of April.
- **l.** 2 Chron. 29:18 Or, table where the bread was set in order.
- **m.** 2 Chron. 29:20 By this manner of speech the Hebrews mean a certain diligence and speed to do a thing: and when there is no delay.
- **n.** 2 Chron. 29:22 For without sprinkling of blood nothing could be sanctified, Heb. 9:21; Exod. 24:8.

lambs, and they sprinkled the blood upon the altar. **23** Then they brought the he goats for the sin offering before the king and the Congregation, [o]and they laid their hands upon them. **24** And the Priests slew them, and with the blood of them they cleansed the altar to reconcile all Israel: for the king had commanded for all Israel the burnt offering, and the sin offering. **25** He appointed also the Levites in the house of the Lord with cymbals, with viols, and with harps, [4]according to the commandment of David, and Gad the King's Seer, and Nathan the Prophet: for the [p]commandment was by the hand of the Lord, and by the hand of his Prophets. **26** And the Levites stood with the instruments of David, and the priests with the trumpets. **27** And Hezekiah commanded to offer the burnt offering upon the altar: and when the burnt offering began, the song of the [q]Lord began with the trumpets, and the instruments [r]of David king of Israel. **28** And all the congregation worshipped, singing a song, and they blew the trumpets: all this continued until the burnt offering was finished. **29** And when they had made an end of offering, the king and all that were present with him, bowed themselves, and worshipped. **30** Then Hezekiah the king and the princes commanded the Levites to praise the Lord with the [s]words of David, and of Asaph the Seer. So they praised with joy, and they bowed themselves, and worshipped. **31** And Hezekiah spake, and said, Now ye have [t]consecrated yourselves to the Lord: come near and bring the sacrifices and offerings of praise into the house of the Lord. And the Congregation brought sacrifices and offerings of praises, and every man that was willing in heart offered burnt offerings. **32** And the number of the burnt offerings, which the Congregation brought, was seventy bullocks, an hundred rams, and two hundred lambs: all these were for a burnt offering to the Lord: **33** And for [u]sanctification six hundred bullocks, and three thousand sheep. **34** But the Priests were too few, and were not able to flay all the burnt offerings: therefore their brethren the Levites did help them, till they had ended the work, and until other Priests were sanctified: for the Levites were [v]more upright in heart to sanctify themselves than the Priests. **35** And also the burnt offerings were many, with the [5]fat of the peace offerings and the drink offerings for the burnt offering: so the service of the house of the Lord was set in order. **36** Then Hezekiah rejoiced, and all the people, that God had made the people so [w]ready: for the thing was done suddenly.

30

1, 13 The keeping of the Passover by the king's commandment. 6 He exhorteth Israel to turn to the Lord. 18 He prayeth for the people. 24 His oblation and the princes'. 27 The Levites bless the people.

1 And Hezekiah sent to all Israel and Judah, and also wrote letters to [a]Ephraim and Manasseh, that they should come to the house of the Lord at Jerusalem, to keep the Passover unto the Lord God of Israel. **2** And the king and his princes and all the Congregation had taken counsel in Jerusalem to keep the Passover in the [b]second month. **3** For they could not keep it at this time, because there were not Priests enough sanctified, neither was the people gathered to Jerusalem. **4** And the thing pleased the king, and all the Congregation. **5** And they decreed to make proclamation throughout all Israel from [c]Beersheba even to Dan, that they should come to keep the Passover unto the Lord God of Israel at Jerusalem: for they had not done it of a great time, [d]as it was written. **6** So the posts went with letters by the commission of the King, and his princes, throughout all Israel and Judah, and with the commandment of the King, saying, Ye children of Israel, turn again unto the Lord God of Abraham, Isaac, and Israel, and [e]he will return to the remnant that are escaped of you, out of the hands of the kings of Assyria. **7** And be not ye like your fathers, and like your brethren, which trespassed against the Lord God of their fathers: and therefore he made them desolate, as ye see. **8** Be not ye now stiff-necked like your fathers, but [f]give the hand to the Lord, and come into his Sanctuary, which he hath sanctified forever, and serve the Lord your God, and the fierceness of his wrath shall turn away from you. **9** For if ye return unto the Lord, your brethren and your children shall find mercy before them that led them captives, and they shall [g]return unto this land: for the Lord your God is gracious and merciful, and will not turn away his face from you, if ye convert unto him. **10** So the posts went from city to city through the land of Ephraim and Manasseh, even unto Zebulun: but they [h]laughed them to scorn and mocked them. **11** Nevertheless, divers of Asher, and Manasseh, and of Zebulun, submitted themselves, and came to Jerusalem. **12** And the hand of God was in Judah, so that he gave them one [i]heart to do the commandment of the king, and of the rulers, according to the word of the Lord. **13** And there assembled to Jerusalem much people, to keep the feast of the unleavened bread in the second month, a very great assembly. **14** And they arose, and took away the [j]altars that were in Jerusalem, and all those for incense took they away, and cast them into the brook Kidron. **15** Afterward they slew the Passover the fourteenth day of the second month: and the Priests and Levites were [k]ashamed, and sanctified themselves, and brought the burnt offerings into the house of the Lord. **16** And they stood in their place after their manner, according to the Law of Moses the man of God: and the Priests sprinkled the [l]blood returned of the hands of the Levites. **17** Because there were many in the Congregation that were not sanctified, therefore the Levites had the charge of the killing of the Passover for all that were not clean, to sanctify it to the Lord. **18** For a multitude of the people, even a multitude of Ephraim, and Manasseh, Issachar and Zebulun had not cleansed themselves, yet did eat the Passover, but not as it was written: wherefore Hezekiah prayed for them, saying, The [m]good Lord be merciful toward him, **19** That prepareth his whole heart to seek the Lord God, the God of his fathers, though he be not cleansed, according to the purification of the Sanctuary. **20** And the Lord heard Hezekiah, and [n]healed the people. **21** And the children of Israel that were present at Jerusalem, kept the feast of the unleavened bread seven days with great joy, and the Levites, and the priests praised the Lord day by day, singing with loud instruments unto the Lord. **22** And Hezekiah [o]spake comfortably unto all the Levites that had good knowledge to sing unto the Lord: and they did eat in that feast seven days, and offered peace offerings, and praised the Lord God of their fathers. **23** And the whole assembly took counsel to keep it another seven days. So they kept it seven days with joy. **24** For Hezekiah king of Judah had given to the Congregation a [p]thousand bullocks, and seven thousand sheep. And the princes had given to the Congregation a thousand bullocks, and ten thousand sheep: and many Priests were sanctified. **25** And all the Congregation of Judah rejoiced with the Priests and the Levites, and all the Congregation that came out of Israel, and the strangers that came out of the land of Israel, and that dwelt in Judah. **26** So there was great joy in Jerusalem: for since the time of Solomon the son of David king of Israel there was not the like thing in Jerusalem. **27** Then the Priests and the Levites arose, and [q]blessed the people, and their voice was heard, and their prayer came up unto heaven, to his holy habitation.

31

1 The people destroy idolatry. 2 Hezekiah appointeth Priests and Levites, 4 And provideth for their livings. 13 He ordaineth overseers to distribute to every one his portion.

1 And when all these things were finished, all Israel, that were found in the cities of Judah, went out and [a]brake the images, and cut down the groves, and brake down the high places, and the altars throughout all Judah and Benjamin, in Ephraim also and Manasseh, until they had made an end: afterward all the [b]children of Israel returned every man to his possession, into their own cities. **2** And Hezekiah appointed the courses of the Priests and Levites by their turns, every man according to his office, both Priests and Levites for the burnt offering and peace offerings, to minister and to give thanks, and to praise in the gates of the [c]tents of the Lord. **3** (And the king's portion was of his own substance for the burnt

---

o. 2 Chron. 29:23 That is, the King and the Elders, as Lev. 4:15, for they that offered a sin offering, must lay their hands upon it, to signify that they had deserved that death, and also that they did consecrate it to God to be thereby sanctified, Exod. 29:10.
p. 2 Chron. 29:25 This thing was not appointed of man, but it was the commandment of God.
q. 2 Chron. 29:27 The Psalm which David had appointed to be sung for thanksgiving.
r. 2 Chron. 29:27 Which David had appointed to praise the Lord with.
s. 2 Chron. 29:30 With that Psalm whereof mention is made, 1 Chron. 16:7.
t. 2 Chron. 29:31 Hebrew, filled your hands.
u. 2 Chron. 29:33 That is, for the holy offerings.
v. 2 Chron. 29:34 Meaning, were more zealous to set forward the religion.
w. 2 Chron. 29:36 He showeth that religion cannot proceed except God touch the heart of the people.

2-CHRON. 29

1. 2 Kings 18:1
2. Num. 18:6
3. Lev. 4:14
4. 1 Chron. 16:4
5. Lev. 3:2,3

2-CHRON. 30

a. 2 Chron. 30:1 Meaning, all Israel, whom Tiglath-Pileser had not taken away into the captivity, 2 Kings 15:29.
b. 2 Chron. 30:2 Though they ought to have done it in the first month, as Exod. 12:18; Num. 9:3, yet if any were not clean, or else had a long journey, they might defer it unto the second month, as Num. 9:10, 11.
c. 2 Chron. 30:5 From one end of the land to the other, North and South.
d. 2 Chron. 30:5 In such sort and perfection as God had appointed.
e. 2 Chron. 30:6 He will have compassion on them, and preserve them.
f. 2 Chron. 30:8 Submit yourselves to the Lord, and rebel no more.
g. 2 Chron. 30:9 God will not only preserve you, but through your repentance restore your brethren, which for their sins he gave into the hands of the enemies.
h. 2 Chron. 30:10 Though the wicked mock at the servants of God, by whom he calleth them to repentance, as Gen. 19:14, yet the word ceaseth not to fructify in the hearts of God's elect.
i. 2 Chron. 30:12 He showeth the cause why some obey and some mock at God's calling, to wit, because his Spirit is with the one sort, and moveth their heart, and the others are left to themselves.
j. 2 Chron. 30:14 Which declareth that we must put away those things wherewith God is offended, before we can serve him aright.
k. 2 Chron. 30:15 Seeing their own negligence (who should have been most prompt) and the readiness of the people, 2 Chron. 29:36.
l. 2 Chron. 30:16 To wit, of the lamb of the Passover.
m. 2 Chron. 30:18 He knew that faith and sincerity of heart was more agreeable to God, than the observation of the ceremonies, and therefore he prayed unto God to pardon this fault unto the people which did not offend of malice but of ignorance.
n. 2 Chron. 30:20 That is, did accept them as purified.
o. 2 Chron. 30:22 Hebrew, spake to the heart.
p. 2 Chron. 30:24 This great liberality declareth how kings, princes, and all they to whom God hath given wherewith, ought to be most ready to bestow it in setting forth of God's glory.
q. 2 Chron. 30:27 According to that which is written, Num. 6:23, when they should dismiss the people.

2-CHRON. 31

a. 2 Chron. 31:1 According to the commandment of the Lord, Deut. 7:25; Josh. 7:1.
b. 2 Chron. 31:1 That is, all they which came to the Passover.
c. 2 Chron. 31:2 That is, in the Temple, where they assembled as in a tent.

offerings, even for the burnt offerings of the morning and of the evening, and the burnt offerings for the Sabbaths, and for the new moons and for the solemn feasts, [1]as it is written in the Law of the Lord) **4** He commanded also the people that dwelt in Jerusalem, to give a [d]part to the Priests, and Levites, that they might be [e]encouraged in the law of the Lord. **5** And when the commandment was [f]spread, the children of Israel brought abundance of firstfruits, of corn, wine, and oil, and honey, and of all the increase of the field, and the tithes of all things brought they abundantly. **6** And the children of Israel and Judah that dwelt in the cities of Judah, they also brought the tithes of bullocks and sheep, and the holy tithes [g]which were consecrated unto the Lord their God, and laid them on [h]many heaps. **7** In the third month they began to lay the foundation of the heaps, and finished them in the seventh month. **8** And when Hezekiah and the princes came, and saw the heaps, they [i]blessed the Lord and his people Israel. **9** And Hezekiah questioned with the Priests and the Levites concerning the heaps. **10** And Azariah the chief Priest of the house of Zadok answered him, and said, Since the people began to bring the offerings into the house of the Lord, we have [j]eaten, and have been satisfied, and there is left in abundance: for the Lord hath blessed his people, and this abundance that is left. **11** And Hezekiah commanded to prepare chambers in the house of the Lord: and they prepared them, **12** And carried in the firstfruits, and the tithes, and the dedicated things faithfully: and over them was Conaniah the Levite the chief, and Shimei his brother the second. **13** And Jehiel, and Azaziah and Nahath, and Asahel, and Jerimoth, and Jozabad, and Eliel, and Ismachiah, and Mahath, and Benaiah were overseers [k]by the appointment of Conaniah, and Shimei his brother, and by the commandment of Hezekiah the King, and of Azariah the chief of the house of God. **14** And Kore the son of Imnah the Levite, porter toward the East, was over the things that were willingly offered unto God, to distribute the oblations of the Lord, and the holy things that were consecrated. **15** And at his hand were Eden, and Miniamin, and Jeshua, and Shemaiah, Amariah, and Shechaniah, in the cities of the Priests, to distribute with fidelity to their brethren by courses, both to the great and small, **16** Their daily portion: beside their generation, being males [l]from three years old and above, even to all that entered into the house of the Lord to their office in their charge, according to their courses: **17** Both to the generation of the Priests after the house of their fathers, and to the Levites from twenty years old and above, according to their charge in their courses: **18** And to the generation of all their children, their wives, and their sons, and their daughters throughout all the Congregation: for by their [m]fidelity are they partakers of the holy things. **19** Also to the sons of Aaron, the Priests, which were in the fields and suburbs of their cities, in every city the men that were appointed by names, should give portions to all the males of the Priests, and to all the generation of the Levites. **20** And thus did Hezekiah throughout all Judah, and did well, and uprightly, and truly before the Lord his God. **21** And in all the works that he began for the service of the house of God, both in the Law and in the commandments, to seek his God, he did it with all his heart, and prospered.

32

1 Sennacherib invadeth Judah. 3 Hezekiah prepareth for the war. 7 He exhorteth the people to put their trust in the Lord. 9 Sennacherib blasphemeth God. 20 Hezekiah prayeth. 21 The Angel destroyeth the Assyrians and the king is slain. 25 Hezekiah is not thankful toward the Lord. 33 His death.

1 After these things faithfully described, [1]Sennacherib king of Assyria came and entered into Judah, and besieged the strong cities, and thought to [a]win them for himself. **2** When Hezekiah saw that Sennacherib was come, and that his [b]purpose was to fight against Jerusalem, **3** Then he took counsel with his princes and his nobles, to stop the water of the fountains without the city: and they did help him. **4** So many of the people assembled themselves, and stopped all the fountains, and the river that ran through the midst of the country, saying, Why should the kings of Assyria come, and find much water? **5** And [c]he took courage, and built all the broken wall, and made up the towers, and another wall without, and repaired [d]Millo in the [e]city of David, and made many [f]darts and shields. **6** And he set captains of war over the people, and assembled them to him in the broad place of the gate of the city, and [g]spake comfortably unto them, saying, **7** Be strong and courageous: fear not, neither be afraid for the king of Assyria, neither for all the multitude that is with him: [2]for there be more with us, then is with him. **8** With him is an [h]arm of flesh, but with us is the [i]Lord our God for to help us, and to fight our battles. Then the people were confirmed by the words of Hezekiah king of Judah. **9** [3]After this, did Sennacherib king of Assyria send his servants to Jerusalem (while he was [j]against Lachish, and all his dominion with him) unto Hezekiah king of Judah, and unto all Judah that were at Jerusalem, saying, **10** Thus saith Sennacherib the king of Assyria, Wherein do ye trust, that ye will remain in Jerusalem, during the siege? **11** Doth not Hezekiah entice you to give over yourselves unto death by famine and by thirst, saying, The Lord our God shall deliver us out of the hand of the king of Assyria? **12** Hath not the same Hezekiah taken away his high places, and his [k]altars, and commanded Judah, and Jerusalem, saying, Ye shall worship before one altar, and burn incense upon it? **13** Know ye not what I and my fathers have done unto all the people of other countries? were the gods of the nations of other lands able to deliver their land out of mine hand? **14** Who is he of all the [l]gods of those nations (that my fathers have destroyed) that could deliver his people out of mine hand, that your God should be able to deliver you out of mine hand? **15** Now therefore let not Hezekiah deceive you, nor seduce you after this sort, neither believe ye him: for none of all the gods of any nation or kingdom was able to deliver his people out of [m]mine hand, and out of the hand of my fathers: how much less shall your gods deliver you out of mine hand? **16** And his servants spake yet more against the Lord God, and against his [n]servant Hezekiah. **17** He wrote also letters, blaspheming the Lord God of Israel, and speaking against him, saying, As the gods of the nations of other countries could not deliver their people out of mine hand, so shall not the God of Hezekiah deliver his people out of mine hand. **18** Then they [o]cried with a loud voice in the Jews speech unto the people of Jerusalem that were on the wall, to fear them and to astonish them, that they might take the city. **19** Thus they spake against the God of Jerusalem, as against the gods of the people of the earth, even the [p]works of man's hands, **20** But Hezekiah the King, and the Prophet Isaiah the son of Amoz [q]prayed against this and cried to heaven. **21** And the Lord sent an Angel, which destroyed all the valiant men, and the princes and [r]captains of the host of the king of Assyria: so he returned [s]with shame to his own land. And when he was come into the house of his god, they that came forth of his [t]own bowels, slew him there with the sword. **22** So the Lord saved Hezekiah and the inhabitants of Jerusalem from the hand of Sennacherib king of Assyria, and from the hand of all others, and [u]maintained them on every side. **23** And many brought offerings unto the Lord to Jerusalem, and presents to Hezekiah king of Judah, so that he was [v]magnified in the sight of all nations from thenceforth. **24** [4]In those days Hezekiah was sick unto the death, and prayed unto the Lord, who spake unto him, and gave him [w]a sign. **25** But Hezekiah did not render according to the reward bestowed upon him: for his heart [x]was lifted up, and wrath came upon him, and upon Judah and Jerusalem. **26** Notwithstanding Hezekiah humbled himself (after that his heart was lifted up) he and the inhabitants of Jerusalem, and the wrath of the Lord came not upon them in the days of Hezekiah. **27** Hezekiah also had exceeding much riches and honor, and he got him treasures of silver, and of gold, and of precious stones, and of sweet odors, and of shields, and of all pleasant vessels: **28** And of store houses for the increase of wheat and wine and oil, and stalls for all beasts, and [y]rows for the [z]stables. **29** And he made him cities, and had possession of sheep and oxen in abundance: for God had given him substance exceeding much. **30** This same Hezekiah also stopped the upper water springs of [aa]Gihon, and led them straight underneath toward the city of David Westward: so Hezekiah

---

d. 2 Chron. 31:4 The tithes and first fruits for the maintenance of the Priests and Levites.
e. 2 Chron. 31:4 That their minds might not be entangled with provision of worldly things, but that they might wholly and cheerfully serve the Lord.
f. 2 Chron. 31:5 Or, published.
g. 2 Chron. 31:6 Which they had dedicated to the Lord by a vow.
h. 2 Chron. 31:6 For the relief of the Priests, Levites, widows, pupils, fatherless, strangers, and such as were in necessity.
i. 2 Chron. 31:8 They praised the Lord and prayed for all prosperity to his people.
j. 2 Chron. 31:10 He showeth that this plenteous liberality is expedient for the maintenance of the ministers, and that God therefore prospereth his people, and increaseth by his blessing that which is given.
k. 2 Chron. 31:13 Hebrew, by the hand.
l. 2 Chron. 31:16 Who had also a portion and allowance in this distribution.
m. 2 Chron. 31:18 Meaning, that either by the faithful distributions of the officers, everyone had their part in the things that were offered, or else that their wives and children were relieved, because the Levites were faithful in their office, and so depended on them.

2-CHRON. 31
1. Num. 28:3,9

2-CHRON. 32
a. 2 Chron. 32:1 Hebrew, break them up.
b. 2 Chron. 32:2 Hebrew, face.
c. 2 Chron. 32:5 Hebrew, he was strengthened.
d. 2 Chron. 32:5 He made a double wall.
e. 2 Chron. 32:5 Read 2 Sam. 5:9.
f. 2 Chron. 32:5 Some read, swords or daggers.
g. 2 Chron. 32:6 Hebrew, he spake to their heart.
h. 2 Chron. 32:8 That is, the power of man.
i. 2 Chron. 32:8 This declareth that Hezekiah did ever put his trust in God, and yet made himself strong and used lawful means, lest he should seem to tempt God.
j. 2 Chron. 32:9 While he besieged Lachish.
k. 2 Chron. 32:12 Thus the wicked put no difference between true religion and false, God and idols: for Hezekiah only destroyed idolatry, and placed true religion. Thus the Papists slander the servants of God: for when they destroy idolatry, they say that they abolish religion.
l. 2 Chron. 32:14 This is his blasphemy, that he will compare the living God to vile idols.
m. 2 Chron. 32:15 When man hath prosperity, he swelleth in pride, and thinketh himself able to resist and overcome even God himself.
n. 2 Chron. 32:16 Herein we see that when the wicked speak evil of the servants of God, they care not to blaspheme God himself: for if they feared God, they would love his servants.
o. 2 Chron. 32:18 Their words are written, 2 Kings 18:19.
p. 2 Chron. 32:19 Which were invented, made and authorized by man.
q. 2 Chron. 32:20 This showeth what is the best refuge in all troubles and dangers.
r. 2 Chron. 32:21 To the number of an hundred fourscore and five thousand, as 2 Kings 19:35, 36.
s. 2 Chron. 32:21 Hebrew, with shame of face.
t. 2 Chron. 32:21 Meaning, Adrammelech and Sharezer his sons.
u. 2 Chron. 32:22 Or, governed.
v. 2 Chron. 32:23 Thus after trouble God sendeth comfort to all them that patiently wait on him, and constantly put their trust in his mercies.
w. 2 Chron. 32:24 To confirm his faith in God's promise, who declared to him by his Prophet that his life should be prolonged fifteen years.
x. 2 Chron. 32:25 He was lifted up with the pride of his victory and treasures, and showeth them for an ostentation to the ambassadors of Babylon.
y. 2 Chron. 32:28 Or, ranges and partitions.
z. 2 Chron. 32:28 Or, racks.
aa. 2 Chron. 32:30 Which also was called Shiloah [Siloam], whereof mention is made, Isa. 8:6; John 9:7.
ab. 2 Chron. 32:31 Here we see the cause, why the faithful are tempted, which is to try whether they have faith or no, and that they may feel the presence of God, who suffereth them

prospered in all his works. **31** But because of the ambassadors of the princes of Babel, which sent unto him to inquire of the wonder that was done in the land, God left him to [ab]try him, and to know all that was in his heart. **32** Concerning the rest of the acts of Hezekiah, and his goodness, behold, they are written in the vision of Isaiah the Prophet the son of Amoz, in the book of the kings of Judah and Israel. **33** So Hezekiah slept with his fathers, and they buried him in the highest sepulcher of the sons of David: and all Judah and the inhabitants of Jerusalem did him honor at his death, and Manasseh his son reigned in his stead.

33

Manasseh an idolater. 9 He causeth Judah to err. 11 He is led away prisoner into Babylon. 12 He prayeth to the Lord, and is delivered. 14 He abolisheth idolatry, 16 and setteth up true religion. 20 He dieth, and Amon his son succeedeth. 24 Whom his own servants slay.

1 Manasseh was twelve years old, [1]when he began to reign, and he reigned five and fifty years in Jerusalem: **2** And he did evil in the sight of the Lord, like the abominations of the heathen, [2]whom the Lord had cast out before the children of Israel. **3** For he went back and built the high places, [3]which Hezekiah his father had broken down: [4]and he set up altars for Baal, and made groves and worshipped all the host of the heaven, and served them. **4** Also he built altars in the house of the Lord, whereof the Lord had said, [5]In Jerusalem shall my Name be forever. **5** And he built altars for all the host of the heaven in the two courts of the house of the Lord. **6** And he caused his sons to [a]pass through the fire in the valley of Ben-hinnom: he gave himself to witchcraft and to charming, and to sorcery, and he used them that had familiar spirits, and soothsayers: he did very much evil in the sight of the Lord to anger him. **7** He put also the carved image, which he had made, in the house of God: whereof God had said to David and to Solomon his son, [6]In this house and in Jerusalem, which I have chosen before all the tribes of Israel, will I put my Name forever. **8** Neither will I [7]make the foot of Israel to remove anymore out of the land which I have appointed for your fathers, so that they take heed, and do all that I have commanded them, according to the Law and statutes and judgments by the [b]hand of Moses. **9** So Manasseh made Judah and the inhabitants of Jerusalem to err, and to do worse than the heathen, whom the Lord had destroyed before the children of Israel. **10** And the Lord spake to [c]Manasseh and to his people, but they would not regard. **11** Wherefore the Lord brought upon them the captains of the host of the king of Assyria, which took Manasseh and put him in fetters, and bound him in chains, and carried him to Babel. **12** And when he was in tribulation, he prayed to the Lord his God, and humbled himself greatly before the God of his fathers, **13** And prayed unto him: and God was [d]entreated of him, and heard his prayer, and brought him again to Jerusalem into his kingdom: then Manasseh knew that the Lord was God. **14** Now after this he built a wall without the city of David, on the West side of [e]Gihon in the valley, even at the entry of the fish gate, and compassed about [f]Ophel, and raised it very high, and put captains of war in all the strong cities of Judah. **15** And he took away the strange gods and the image out of the house of the Lord, and all the altars that he had built in the mount of the house of the Lord, and in Jerusalem, and cast them out of the city. **16** Also he prepared the [g]altar of the Lord, and sacrificed thereon peace offerings, and of thanks, and commanded Judah to serve the Lord God of Israel. **17** Nevertheless the people did sacrifice still in the high places, but unto the [h]Lord their God. **18** Concerning the rest of the acts of Manasseh, and his [i]prayer unto his God, and the words of the Seers, that spake to him in the Name of the Lord God of Israel, behold, they are written in the book of the Kings of Israel. **19** And his prayer and how God was entreated of him, and all his sin, and his trespass, and the places wherein he built high places, and set groves and images (before he was humbled) behold, they are written in the book of the [j]Seers. **20** So Manasseh slept with his fathers, and they buried him in his own [k]house: and Amon his son reigned in his stead. **21** ¶Amon was two and twenty years old, when he began to reign, and reigned two years in Jerusalem. **22** But he did evil in the sight of the Lord, as did Manasseh his father: for Amon sacrificed to all the images, which Manasseh his father had made, and served them. **23** And he humbled not himself before the Lord, as Manasseh his father had humbled himself: but this Amon trespassed more and more. **24** And his servants [8]conspired against him, and slew him in his own house. **25** But the people of the land slew all them that had conspired against King Amon: and the people of the land made Josiah his son King in his stead.

34

1 Josiah destroyeth the idols. 8 And restoreth the Temple. 14 The book of the Law is found. 21 He sendeth to Huldah the Prophetess for counsel. 27 God heareth his prayer. 31 He maketh a covenant with God.

1 Josiah [1]was eight years old when he began to reign, and he reigned in Jerusalem one and thirty years. **2** And he did uprightly in the sight of the Lord, and walked in the ways of [a]David his father, and bowed neither to the right hand nor to the left. **3** And in the eighth year of his reign (when he was yet a [b]child) he began to seek after the God of David his father: and in the twelfth year he began to purge Judah, and Jerusalem from the high places, and the groves, and the carved images, and molten images. **4** And they brake down [c]in his sight the altars of Baal, and he caused to cut down the images that were on high upon them: he brake also the groves, and the carved images and the molten images, and stamped them to powder, and strowed it upon the graves of them that had sacrificed unto them. **5** Also he burnt the [d]bones of the Priests upon their altars, and purged Judah and Jerusalem. **6** And in the cities of Manasseh, and Ephraim, and Simeon, even unto Naphtali, with their mauls they brake all round about. **7** And when he had [e]destroyed the altars, and the groves, and had broken and stamped to powder the images, and had cut down all the idols throughout all the land of Israel, he returned to Jerusalem. **8** [2]Then in the eighteenth year of his reign, when he had purged the land and the temple, he sent Shaphan the son of Azaliah and Maaseiah the governor of the city, and Joah the son of Joahaz the Recorder to repair the house of the Lord his God. **9** And when they came to Hilkiah the high Priest, they delivered the money that was brought into the house of God, which the Levites that kept the door, had gathered at the hand of Manasseh, and Ephraim, and of all the residue of Israel, and of all Judah and Benjamin, and [f]of the inhabitants of Jerusalem. **10** And they put it in the hands of [g]them that should do the work, and had the oversight in the house of the Lord: and they gave it to the workmen that wrought in the house of the Lord to repair and amend the house. **11** Even to the workmen and to the builders gave they it to buy hewed stone and timber for couples, and for beams of the [h]houses, which the kings of Judah had destroyed. **12** And the men did the work [i]faithfully, and the overseers of them were Jahath and Obadiah the Levites, of the children of Merari, and Zechariah, and Meshullam, of the children of the Kohathites to set it forward: and of the Levites all that could skill of instruments of music. **13** And they were over the bearers of burdens, and them that set forward all the workmen in every work: and of the Levites were scribes, and officers and porters. **14** And when they brought out the money that was brought into the house of the Lord, Hilkiah the Priest found the [j]book of the Law of the Lord given by the hand of Moses. **15** Therefore Hilkiah answered and said to Shaphan the chancellor, I have found the book of the Law in the house of the Lord: and Hilkiah gave the book to Shaphan. **16** And Shaphan carried the book to [k]the King, and brought the King word again, saying, All that is committed to the hand of thy servants, that do they. **17** For they have gathered the money that was found in the house of the Lord, and have delivered it into the hands of the overseers, and to the hands of the workmen. **18** Also Shaphan the chancellor declared to the King, saying, Hilkiah the Priest hath given me a book, and Shaphan read it before the King. **19** And when the King had heard the words of the Law, he [l]tare his clothes, **20** And the King commanded Hilkiah and Ahikam the son of Shaphan, and Abdon the son of Micah, and Shaphan the chancellor, and Asaiah the king's servant, saying, **21** Go and inquire of the Lord for me, and for the rest in Israel and Judah, concerning the words of this book that is found: for great is the wrath of the Lord that is fallen upon us, because our [m]fathers have not kept the word of the Lord, to do after all that is written in this book. **22** Then Hilkiah and they that the king had appointed went to Huldah the prophetess the

---

not to be overcome by tentations, but in their weakness ministereth strength.

2-CHRON. 32

1. 2 Kings 18:13 / Isa. 30:1
2. 2 Kings 6:16
3. 2 Kings 18:17
4. 2 Kings 20:1 / Isa. 38:1

2-CHRON. 33

a. 2 Chron. 33:6 Read 2 Kings 16:3.
b. 2 Chron. 33:8 By the charge given to Moses.
c. 2 Chron. 33:10 Meaning by his Prophets, but their hearts were not touched to believe and repent, without the which the preaching of the word taketh no place.
d. 2 Chron. 33:13 Thus affliction giveth understanding: for he that hated God in his prosperity, now in his misery he seeketh unto him.
e. 2 Chron. 33:14 Read 2 Chron. 32:30.
f. 2 Chron. 33:14 Read 2 Chron. 27:3.
g. 2 Chron. 33:16 Which Solomon had caused to be made.
h. 2 Chron. 33:17 Thus by ignorance they were deceived, thinking it nothing to keep the altars, so that they worshipped God: but it is idolatry to worship God any otherwise than he hath appointed.
i. 2 Chron. 33:18 Which albeit that it is not contained in the Hebrew, yet because it is here mentioned and is written in the Greek, we have placed it in the end of this book.
j. 2 Chron. 33:19 Or, Hozai.
k. 2 Chron. 33:20 Because he had so horribly offended against the Lord, they did not bury him in the sepulchers of the Kings, but in the garden of the King's house.

2-CHRON. 33

1. 2 Kings 21:5
2. Deut. 18:9
3. 2 Kings 18:4
4. Jer. 32:34 / 2 Kings 17:10
5. 2 Kings 11:4
6. 1 Kings 8:39 / 1 Kings 9:3 / 1 Kings 21:7 / 1 Kings 23:17
7. 2 Sam. 7:10
8. 2 Kings 21:23

2-CHRON. 34

a. 2 Chron. 34:2 He followed David in all points that he followed the Lord.
b. 2 Chron. 34:3 When he was but sixteen years old he showed himself zealous of God's glory, and at twenty years old he abolished idolatry, and restored the true religion.
c. 2 Chron. 34:4 Which showeth that he would see the reformation with his own eyes.
d. 2 Chron. 34:5 Read 2 Kings 23:16.
e. 2 Chron. 34:7 This great zeal of this godly King the holy Ghost setteth forth as an example and pattern to other kings and rulers, to teach them what God requireth of them.
f. 2 Chron. 34:9 Or, they returned to Jerusalem.
g. 2 Chron. 34:10 Meaning Shaphan, etc.
h. 2 Chron. 34:11 For there were many portions and pieces annexed to the Temple.
i. 2 Chron. 34:12 Meaning, that they were in such credit for their fidelity, that they made none accounts of that which they received, 2 Kings 22:7, 9.
j. 2 Chron. 34:14 Read 2 Kings 22:8.
k. 2 Chron. 34:16 For the king was commanded to have continually a copy of this book, and to read therein day and night, Deut. 17:18.
l. 2 Chron. 34:19 For sorrow that the word of God had been so long suppressed and the people kept in ignorance, considering also the curses contained therein against the transgressors.
m. 2 Chron. 34:21 Thus the godly do not only lament their own sins, but also that their fathers and predecessors have offended God.

wife of Shallum, the son of [n]Tokhath, the son of [o]Hasrah keeper of the [p]wardrobe (and she dwelt in Jerusalem within the [q]college) and they communed hereof with her. **23** And she answered them, Thus saith the Lord God of Israel, Tell ye [r]the man that sent you to me, **24** Thus saith the Lord, Behold, I will bring evil upon this place, and upon the inhabitants thereof, even all the curses, that are written in the book which they have read before the King of Judah: **25** Because they have forsaken me, and burnt incense unto other gods, to anger me with all the works of their [s]hands, therefore shall my wrath fall upon this place, and shall not be quenched. **26** But to the king of Judah, who sent you to inquire of the Lord, so shall ye say unto him, Thus saith the Lord God of Israel, The words which thou hast heard, shall come to pass. **27** But because thine heart did [t]melt, and thou didst humble thyself before God, when thou heardest his words against this place, and against the inhabitants thereof, and humbledst thyself before me, and tearest thy clothes, and weptest before me, I have also heard it, saith the Lord. **28** Behold, I will gather thee to thy fathers, and thou shalt be put in thy grave in peace, and thine eyes shall not see all the evil, which I will bring upon this [u]place and upon the inhabitants of the same. Thus they brought the King word again. **29** Then the King sent and gathered all the Elders of Judah and Jerusalem. **30** And the King went up into the house of the Lord, and all the men of Judah, and the inhabitants of Jerusalem, and the Priests and the Levites, and all the people from the greatest to the [v]smallest, and he read in their ears all the words of the book of the Covenant that was found in the house of the Lord. **31** And the King stood by his pillar, and made a covenant before the Lord, to walk after the Lord, and to keep his commandments, and his testimonies, and his statutes with all his heart, and with all his soul, and that he would accomplish the words of the Covenant written in the same book. **32** And he caused all that were found in Jerusalem, and Benjamin to stand to it: and the inhabitants of Jerusalem did according to the Covenant of God, even the God of their fathers. **33** So Josiah took away all the abominations out of all the countries that pertained to the children of Israel, and compelled all [w]that were found in Israel, to serve the Lord their God: so all his days they turned not back from the Lord God of their fathers.

35

1 Josiah keepeth the Passover. 2 He setteth forth God's service. 20 He fighteth against the king of Egypt, and dieth. 24 The people bewail him.

1 Moreover, [1]Josiah kept a Passover unto the Lord in Jerusalem, and they slew the [a]Passover in the fourteenth day of the first month. **2** And he appointed the Priests to their charges, and encouraged them to the service of the house of the Lord, **3** And he said unto the Levites that [b]taught all Israel and were sanctified unto the Lord, Put the holy Ark in the house which Solomon the son of David King of Israel did build: it shall be no more a [c]burden upon your shoulders: serve now the Lord your God, and his people Israel, **4** And prepare yourselves by the houses of your fathers according to your courses, [2]as David the king of Israel hath written, and according to the writing of Solomon his son, **5** And stand in the Sanctuary according to the division of the families of your brethren [d]the children of the people, and after the division of the family of the Levites: **6** So kill the Passover, and sanctify yourselves, and [e]prepare your brethren that they may do according to the word of the Lord by the hand of Moses. **7** Josiah also gave to the [f]people sheep, lambs and kids, all for the Passover, even to all that were present, to the number of thirty thousand, and three thousand bullocks: these were of the king's substance. **8** And his princes offered willingly unto the people, to the Priests and to the Levites: Hilkiah, and Zechariah, and Jehiel, rulers of the house of God gave unto the Priests for the Passover, even two thousand and six hundred sheep, and three hundred bullocks. **9** [g]Conaniah also and Shemaiah and Nethanel his brethren, and Hashabiah and Jeiel, and Jozabad, chief of the Levites gave unto the Levites for the Passover, five thousand sheep, and five hundred bullocks. **10** Thus the service was prepared, and the Priests stood in their places, also the Levites in their orders, according to the king's commandment: **11** And [3]they slew the Passover, and the Priests [h]sprinkled the blood with their hands, and the Levites flayed them. **12** And they took away from the [i]burnt offering to give it according to the divisions of the families of the children of the people, to offer unto the Lord, as it is written in the book of Moses, and so of the bullocks. **13** And they roasted the Passover with fire, according to the custom, but the sanctified things they sod in pots, pans, and cauldrons, and distributed them quickly to all the people. **14** Afterward also they prepared for themselves and for the Priests: for the Priests the sons of Aaron were occupied in offering of burnt offerings, and the fat until night: therefore the Levites prepared for themselves, and for the Priests the sons of Aaron. **15** And the singers the sons of Asaph stood in their standing [4]according to the commandment of David, and Asaph, and Heman, and Jeduthun the king's [j]Seer: and the porters at every gate, who might not depart from their service: therefore their brethren the Levites prepared for them. **16** So all the service of the Lord was prepared the same day to keep the Passover, and to offer burnt offerings upon the altar of the Lord, according to the commandment of King Josiah. **17** And the children of Israel that were present, kept the Passover the same time, and the feast of the unleavened bread seven days. **18** And there was no Passover kept like that in Israel, from the days of Samuel the Prophet: neither did all the kings of Israel keep such a Passover as Josiah kept, and the Priests and the Levites, and all Judah, and Israel that were [k]present, and the inhabitants of Jerusalem. **19** This Passover was kept in [l]the eighteenth year of the reign of Josiah. **20** [5]After all this, when Josiah had prepared the Temple Necho king of Egypt came up to fight against [m]Carchemish by [n]Perath and Josiah went out against him. **21** But he sent messengers to him, saying, What have I to do with thee, thou king of Judah? I come not against thee this day, but against the house [o]of mine enemy, and God commanded me to make haste: leave off to come against God, which is with me, lest he destroy thee. **22** But Josiah would not turn his face from him, but [p]changed his apparel to fight with him, and hearkened not unto the words of Necho, which were of the mouth of God, but came to fight in the valley of Megiddo. **23** And the shooters shot at king Josiah: then the king said to his servants, Carry me away, for I am very sick. **24** So his servants took him out of that chariot, and put him in the second chariot which he had, and when they had brought him to Jerusalem, he died, and was buried in the sepulchers of his fathers: and all Judah and Jerusalem [q]mourned for Josiah. **25** And Jeremiah lamented Josiah, and all singing men and singing women mourned for Josiah in their lamentations to this day, and made the same for an ordinance unto Israel: and behold, they be written in the [r]Lamentations. **26** Concerning the rest of the acts of Josiah, and his goodness, doing as it was written in the Law of the Lord, **27** And his deeds first and last, behold, they are written in the book of the Kings of Israel, and Judah.

36

After Josiah reigneth Jehoahaz. 4 After Jehoahaz, Jehoiakim. 8 After him Jehoiachin. 11 After him Zedekiah. 14, 17 In whose time all the people were carried away to Babel for contemning the Admonition of the Prophets, 22 and were restored again the seventieth year after by king Cyrus.

1 Then [1]the people of the land took Jehoahaz the son of Josiah, and made him King in his father's stead in Jerusalem. **2** Jehoahaz was three and twenty years old when he began to reign, and he reigned three [a]months in Jerusalem. **3** And the king of Egypt took him away at Jerusalem, and condemned the land in an [b]hundred talents of silver, and a talent of gold. **4** And the king of Egypt made Eliakim his brother king over Judah and Jerusalem, and turned his name to Jehoiakim:

---

n. 2 Chron. 34:22 Or, Tiknah.
o. 2 Chron. 34:22 Or, Harhas.
p. 2 Chron. 34:22 Meaning, either of the Priest's apparel, or of the King's.
q. 2 Chron. 34:22 Read hereof, 2 Kings 22:15.
r. 2 Chron. 34:23 That is, to the King.
s. 2 Chron. 34:25 This she speaketh in contempt of the idolaters, who contrary to reason and nature make that a god, which they have made and framed with their own hands.
t. 2 Chron. 34:27 This declareth what is the end of God's threatenings, to call his to repentance, and to assure the unrepentant of their destruction.
u. 2 Chron. 34:28 It may appear that very few were touched with true repentance, seeing that God spared them for a time only for the king's sake.
v. 2 Chron. 34:30 Forasmuch as neither young nor old could be exempted from the curses contained therein, if they did transgress, he knew it pertained to all, and was his duty to see it read to all sorts, that everyone might learn to avoid those punishments by serving God aright.
w. 2 Chron. 34:33 Because he had charge over all, and must answer for everyone that perished: he thought it his duty to see that all should make profession to receive the word of God.

2-CHRON. 34
1. 2 Kings 22:1
2. 2 Kings 33:5

2-CHRON. 35
a. 2 Chron. 35:1 The Scripture useth in sundry places to call the lamb the Passover, which was but the sign of the Passover, because in all sacraments the signs have the names of the things which are signified.
b. 2 Chron. 35:3 So that the Levite's charge was not only to minister in the Temple, but also to instruct the people in the word of God.
c. 2 Chron. 35:3 As it was before the Temple was built: therefore your office only is now to teach the people, and to praise God.
d. 2 Chron. 35:5 Or, the people.
e. 2 Chron. 35:6 Exhort everyone to examine themselves, that they be not unmeet to eat of the Passover.
f. 2 Chron. 35:7 Hebrew, sons of the people.
g. 2 Chron. 35:9 So that everyone and of all sorts gave of that they had, a liberal portion to the service of God.
h. 2 Chron. 35:11 Meaning, of the Lamb, which was called the Passover: for only the Priests might sprinkle, and in necessity the Levites might kill the sacrifice.
i. 2 Chron. 35:12 They reserved for the people that which was not expedient to be offered, that every man might offer peace offerings, and so have his portion.
j. 2 Chron. 35:15 Meaning hereby his Prophet, because he appointed the Psalms and prophecies which were to be sung.
k. 2 Chron. 35:18 Hebrew, found.
l. 2 Chron. 35:19 Which was in his six and twentieth year of his age.
m. 2 Chron. 35:20 Which was a city of the Assyrians, and Josiah fearing lest he passing through Judah, would have taken his kingdom, made war against him, and consulted not with the Lord.
n. 2 Chron. 35:20 Or, Euphrates.
o. 2 Chron. 35:21 Hebrew, of my battle.
p. 2 Chron. 35:22 That is, armed himself, or disguised himself, because he might not be known.
q. 2 Chron. 35:24 The people so much lamented the loss of this good king, that after when there was any great lamentation this was spoken of as a proverb, read Zech. 12:11.
r. 2 Chron. 35:25 Which some think Jeremiah made, wherein he lamenteth the state of the Church after this king's death.

2-CHRON. 35
1. 2 Kings 23:21
2. 1 Chron. 13:24-26
3. Exod. 12:8
4. 1 Chron. 25:1
5. 2 Kings 23:29

2-CHRON. 36
a. 2 Chron. 36:2 For three months after the death of Josiah, came Necho to Jerusalem, and so the plagues began, which Huldah and the Prophetess forewarned should come upon Jerusalem.
b. 2 Chron. 36:3 To pay this as a yearly tribute.

and Necho took Jehoahaz his brother, and carried him to Egypt. **5** Jehoiakim
was five and twenty years old when he began to reign, and he reigned eleven ye-
ars in Jerusalem, and did [c]evil in the sight of the Lord his God. **6** Against him
came up Nebuchadnezzar king of Babel, and bound him with chains to carry
him to Babel. **7** Nebuchadnezzar also [2]carried of the vessels of the house of the
Lord to Babel, and put them in his temple at Babel. **8** Concerning the rest of
the acts of Jehoiakim, and his abominations which he did, and [d]that which was
found upon him, behold, they are written in the book of the kings of Israel and
Judah, and Jehoiachin his son reigned in his stead. **9** Jehoiachin was [e]eight years
old when he began to reign, and he reigned three months and ten days in Jerusa-
lem, and did evil in the sight of the Lord. **10** And when the year was out, king
Nebuchadnezzar sent and brought him to Babel, with the precious vessels of the
house of the Lord, and he made Zedekiah his [f]brother king over Judah and Jeru-
salem. **11** Zedekiah was one and twenty years old when he began to reign, and
reigned eleven years in Jerusalem. **12** [3]And he did evil in the sight of the Lord
his God, and humbled not himself before Jeremiah the Prophet at the command-
ment of the Lord. **13** But he rebelled moreover against Nebuchadnezzar, which
had caused him to swear by God: and he hardened his neck and made his heart
obstinate, that he might not return to the Lord God of Israel. **14** All the chief
of the Priests also and of the people trespassed wonderfully, according to all the
abominations of the heathen, and polluted the houses of the Lord which he had
sanctified in Jerusalem. **15** Therefore the Lord God of their fathers sent to them
[g]by his messengers, [h]rising early and sending: for he had compassion on his people,
and on his habitation. **16** But they mocked the messengers of God, and despised
his words, and misused his Prophets, until the wrath of the Lord arose against his
people, and till there was no [i]remedy. **17** For he brought upon them the king
of the Chaldeans, who slew their young men with the sword [j]in the house of their
Sanctuary, and spared neither young man nor virgin, ancient, nor aged. God [k]ga-
ve all into his hand, **18** And all the vessels of the house of God great and small,
and the treasures of the house of the Lord, and the treasures of the king, and of his
princes: all these carried he to Babel. **19** And they burnt the house of God, and
brake down the wall of Jerusalem, and burnt all the palaces thereof with fire, and
all the precious vessels thereof, to destroy all. **20** And they that were left by the
sword, carried he away to Babel, and they were servants to him, and to his sons,
until the kingdom of the [l]Persians had rule, **21** To fulfill the word of the Lord
by the [m]mouth of Jeremiah, until the land had her fill of her Sabbaths: for all the
days that she lay desolate, she kept Sabbath, to fulfill seventy years. **22** [4]But in
the [n]first year of Cyrus king of Persia (when the word of the Lord, spoken by the
mouth of Jeremiah, was finished) the Lord stirred up the spirit of Cyrus king of
Persia, and he made a proclamation through all his kingdom, and also by writing,
saying, **23** Thus saith Cyrus king of Persia, All the kingdoms of the earth hath
the Lord God of heaven given me, and hath [o]commanded me to build him an hou-
se in Jerusalem, that is in Judah. Who is among you of all his people, with whom
the Lord his God is? let him go up.

---

c. 2 Chron. 36:5 Because he and the people turned not to God by his first plague, he brought a new upon him, and at length rooted them out.
d. 2 Chron. 36:8 He meaneth superstitious marks which were found upon his body, when he was dead, which thing declared how deeply idolatry was rooted in his heart, seeing he bare the marks in his flesh.
e. 2 Chron. 36:9 That is, he began his reign at eight years old, and reigned ten years when his father was alive, and after his father's death, which was the eighteenth year of his age, he reigned alone three months and ten days.
f. 2 Chron. 36:10 Or, uncle.
g. 2 Chron. 36:15 Hebrew, by the hand of his.
h. 2 Chron. 36:15 By this phrase the Scripture meaneth, oftentimes, and diligently, as Jer. 11:7 and 25:3 and 26:5 and 32:33.
i. 2 Chron. 36:16 Till God could no longer suffer their sins, but must needs punish them.
j. 2 Chron. 36:17 Whither they fled, thinking to have been saved for the holiness thereof.
k. 2 Chron. 36:17 Which is not because God approveth him, which yet is the minister of his justice, but because God would by his just judgment punish this people: for this king was led with ambition and vain glory, whereunto were joined fury and cruelty: therefore his work was condemnable, notwithstanding it was just and holy on God's part, who used this wicked instrument to declare his justice.
l. 2 Chron. 36:20 When Cyrus King of Persia had made the Babylonians subject.
m. 2 Chron. 36:21 Who threatened the vengeance of God and seventy years captivity, which he calleth the Sabbaths or rest of the land, Jer. 25:11.
n. 2 Chron. 36:22 In the first year that he reigned over the Chaldeans, Ezra 1:1.
o. 2 Chron. 36:23 God had so forewarned by his Prophet above an hundred years before Cyrus was born, Isa. 44:28, that Jerusalem and the Temple should be built again by Cyrus his anointed: so called, because God used his service for a time to deliver his Church.

2-CHRON. 36
1. 2 Kings 23:30
2. 2 Kings 24:13
3. 1 Kings 24:17,19 / Jer. 52:2
4. Jer. 25:13 / Jer. 29:10

EZRA

1

1 Cyrus sendeth again the people that was in captivity, 8 and restoreth them their holy vessels.

1 Now [1]in [a]the first year of Cyrus King of Persia (that the word of the LORD,
spoken by the [b]mouth of Jeremiah, might be accomplished) the Lord stirred up
the [c]spirit of Cyrus King of Persia, and he made a proclamation through all his
kingdom, and also by writing, saying, **2** Thus saith Cyrus King of Persia, The
Lord God of heaven hath given me [d]all the kingdoms of the earth, and he hath
commanded me to build him an house in Jerusalem, which is in Judah. **3** Who
is he among you of all his people with whom his God is? let him go up to Jeru-
salem which is in Judah, and build the house of the Lord God of Israel: he is the
God, which is in Jerusalem. **4** And everyone that remaineth in any place (where
he sojourneth) [e]let the men of his place relieve him with silver and with gold, and
with substance, and with cattle, [f]and with a willing offering, for the house of God
that is in Jerusalem. **5** Then the chief fathers of Judah and Benjamin, and the
Priests and the Levites rose up, with all them whose spirit God had raised to go
up, to build the house of the Lord which is in Jerusalem. **6** And all [g]they that
were about them, strengthened their hands with vessels of silver, with gold, with
substance and with cattle, and with precious things, besides all that was willingly
offered. **7** Also the king Cyrus brought forth the vessels of the house of the Lord,
[2]which Nebuchadnezzar had taken out of Jerusalem, and had put them in the hou-
se of his god. **8** Even them did Cyrus king of Persia bring forth by the hand of
Mithredath the treasurer, and counted them unto [h]Sheshbazzar the Prince of Ju-
dah. **9** And this is the number of them, thirty basins of gold, a thousand basins
of silver, nine and twenty [i]knives, **10** Thirty bowls of gold, and of silver bowls of
the second sort, four hundred and ten, and of other vessels, a thousand. **11** All
the vessels of gold and silver were five thousand and four hundred. Sheshbazzar
brought up all [j]with them of the captivity that came up from Babel to Jerusalem.

2

The number of them that returned from the captivity.

1 These [1]also are the sons [a]of the province that went up out of the
captivity (whom Nebuchadnezzar king of Babel had carried away unto Babel) and
returned to Jerusalem, and to Judah, everyone unto his city, **2** Which came up
with [b]Zerubbabel, to wit, Jeshua, Nehemiah, Seraiah, Reelaiah, [c]Mordecai, Bil-
shan, Mispar, Bigvai, Rehum, Baanah. The number of the men [d]of the people

---

EZRA 1
a. Ezra 1:1 After that he and Darius had won Babylon.
b. Ezra 1:1 Who promised them deliverance after that seventy years were past, Jer. 25:12.
c. Ezra 1:1 That is, moved him, and gave him heart.
d. Ezra 1:2 For he was chief Monarch, and had many nations under his dominion, which this heathen king confesseth to have received of the living God.
e. Ezra 1:4 If any through poverty were not able to return, the king's commission was that he should be furnished with necessaries.
f. Ezra 1:4 Which they themselves should send toward the reparation of the Temple.
g. Ezra 1:6 The Babylonians and Chaldeans gave them these presents: thus rather than the children of God should want for their necessities, he would stir up the heart of the very infidels to help them.
h. Ezra 1:8 So the Chaldeans called Zerubbabel who was the chief governor, so that the preeminence still remained in the house of David.
i. Ezra 1:9 Which served to kill the beasts that were offered in sacrifice.
j. Ezra 1:11 With the Jews that had been kept captives in Babylon.

EZRA 1
1. 2 Chron. 3:22 / Jer. 25:12 / Jer. 29:10
2. 2Kings 25:13 / 2 Chron. 36:7 / Jer. 27:19,20 / Dan. 1:2

EZRA 2
a. Ezra 2:1 Meaning, Judea, which was a province, that is, a country which was in subjection.
b. Ezra 2:2 Zerubbabel was chief captain, and Jeshua the high Priest: but Nehemiah a man of great authority went not now, but came after 64 years.
c. Ezra 2:2 This was not that Mordecai which was Esther's kinsman.
d. Ezra 2:2 Meaning, of the common people.

of Israel was, **3** The sons of Parosh, two thousand, an hundred seventy and two: **4** The sons of Shephatiah, three hundred, seventy and two: **5** The sons of Arah, seven hundred, and seventy and five: **6** The sons of [e]Pahath-Moab, of the sons of Jeshua, and Joab, two thousand, eight hundred and twelve: **7** The sons of Elam, a thousand, two hundred and four and fifty: **8** The sons of Zattu, nine hundred and five and forty: **9** The sons of Zaccai, seven hundred and threescore: **10** The sons of Bani, six hundred and two and forty: **11** The sons of Bebai, six hundred, and three and twenty: **12** The sons of Azgad, a thousand, two hundred and two and twenty: **13** The sons of Adonikam, six hundred, three score and six: **14** The sons of Bigvai, two thousand, and six and fifty: **15** The sons of Adin, four hundred and four and fifty: **16** The sons of Ater of [f]Hezekiah, ninety and eight: **17** The sons of Bezai, three hundred and three and twenty: **18** The sons of Jorah, an hundred and twelve: **19** The sons of Hashum, two hundred and three and twenty: **20** The sons of Gibbar, ninety and five: **21** [g]The sons of Bethlehem, an hundred and three and twenty: **22** The men of Netophah, six and fifty: **23** The men of Anothoth, an hundred and eight and twenty: **24** The sons of Azmaveth, two and forty: **25** The sons of Kirjath Arim, of Chephirah, and Beeroth, seven hundred and three and forty: **26** The sons of Ramah and Geba, six hundred and one and twenty: **27** The men of Michmas, an hundred and two and twenty: **28** The sons of Bethel, and Ai, two hundred and three and twenty: **29** The sons of Nebo, two and fifty: **30** The sons of Magbish, an hundred and six and fifty: **31** The sons of the other Elam, a thousand, and two hundred and four and fifty: **32** The sons of Harim, three hundred and twenty: **33** The sons of Lod, Hadid, and Ono, seven hundred and five and twenty: **34** The sons of Jericho, three hundred and five and forty: **35** The sons of Senaah, three thousand six hundred and thirty: **36** The [h]Priests: of the sons of Jedaiah of the house of Jeshua, nine hundred seventy and three: **37** The sons of Immer, a thousand and two and fifty: **38** The sons of Pashur, a thousand, two hundred and seven and forty: **39** The sons of Harim, a thousand and seventeen. **40** The Levites: the sons of Jeshua, and Kadmiel of the sons of Hodaviah, seventy and four. **41** The Singers: the sons of Asaph, an hundred and eight and twenty. **42** The sons of the porters: the sons of Shallum, the sons of Ater, the sons of Talmon, the sons of Akkub, the sons of Hatita, the sons of Shobai: all were an hundred and nine and thirty. **43** The [i]Nethinim: the sons of Ziha, the sons of Hasupha, the sons of Tabbaoth, **44** The sons of Keros, the sons of Siaha, the sons of Padon, **45** The sons of Lebanah, the sons of Hagabah, the sons of Akkub, **46** The sons of Hagab, the sons of Shamlai, the sons of Hanan, **47** The sons of Giddel, the sons of Gahar, the sons of Reaiah, **48** The sons of Rezin, the sons of Nekoda, the sons of Gazzam, **49** The sons of Uzza, the sons of Paseah, the sons of Besai, **50** The sons of Asnah, the sons of Meunim, the sons of Nephusim, **51** The sons of Bakbuk, the sons of Hakupha, the sons of Harhur, **52** The sons of Bazluth, the sons of Mehida, the sons of Harsha, **53** The sons of Barkos, the sons of Sisera, the sons of Thamah, **54** The sons of Neziah, the sons of Hatipha, **55** The sons of Solomon's [j]servants: the sons of Sotai, the sons of Sophereth, the sons of Peruda, **56** The sons of Jaala, the sons of Darkon, the sons of Giddel, **57** The sons of Shephatiah, the sons of Hattil, the sons of Pochereth Hazzebaim, the sons of Ami. **58** All the Nethinim, and the sons of Solomon's servants were three hundred ninety and two. **59** And these went up from Tel Melah, and from Tel Harsha, Cherub, Addan, and Immer, but they could not discern their father's house and their seed, whether they were of Israel. **60** The sons of Delaiah, the sons of Tobiah, the sons of Nekoda, six hundred and two and fifty. **61** And of the sons of the Priests, the sons of Habaiah, the sons of Koz, the sons of [k]Barzillai: which took of the daughters of Barzillai the Gileadite to wife, and was called after their name. **62** These sought their writing of the genealogies, but they were not found: therefore were they put from the Priesthood. **63** And [l]Tirshatha said unto them, that they should not eat of the most holy thing, till there rose up a Priest with [m]Urim and Thummim. **64** The whole Congregation together was two and forty thousand, three hundred and threescore, **65** Beside their servants and their maids: of whom were seven thousand, three hundred and seven and thirty: and among them were two hundred singing men and singing women. **66** Their horses were seven hundred, and six and thirty: their mules, two hundred, and five and forty: **67** Their camels four hundred, and five and thirty: their asses, six thousand, seven hundred and twenty. **68** And certain of the chief fathers, when they came to the house of the Lord, which was in Jerusalem, they offered willingly for the house of God, to set it up upon his foundation. **69** They gave after their ability unto the treasure of the work, even one and threescore thousand [n]drams of gold, and five thousand [o]pieces of silver, and an hundred Priests' garments. **70** So the Priests and the Levites, and a certain of the people, and the singers, and the porters, and the Nethinim dwelt in their cities, and all Israel in their cities.

3

2 They build the Altar of God. 6 They offer to the Lord. 7 They prepare for the Temple, 11 And sing unto the Lord.

1 And when the [a]seventh month was come, and the children of Israel were in their cities, the people assembled themselves as one man unto Jerusalem. **2** Then stood up Jeshua the son of Jozadak, and his brethren the Priests, and Zerubbabel the [b]son of Shealtiel, and his brethren, and built the Altar of the God of Israel to offer burnt offerings thereon, as it is written in the Law of Moses the man of God, **3** And they set the Altar upon [c]his bases (for fear was among them, because of the people of those countries) therefore they offered burnt offerings thereon unto the Lord, even burnt offerings in the morning, and at even. **4** They kept also the feast of the Tabernacles, as it is written, and they burnt offering [1]daily, by number according to the custom day by day, **5** And afterward [d]the continual burnt offering, both in the new months and in all the feast days that were consecrated unto the Lord, and in all the oblations willingly offered unto the Lord. **6** From the first day of the seventh month began they to offer burnt offerings unto the Lord: but the foundation of the Temple of the Lord was not laid. **7** They gave money also unto the masons, and to the workmen, and meat and drink, and oil unto them of Zidon and of Tyre, to bring them cedar wood from Lebanon to the sea unto [e]Japho, according to the grant that they had of Cyrus king of Persia. **8** And in the second year of their coming unto the house of God in Jerusalem, in the [f]second month began Zerubbabel the son of Shealtiel, and Jeshua the son of Jozadak, and the remnant of their brethren the Priests, and the Levites, and all they that were come out of the captivity unto Jerusalem, and appointed the Levites from twenty years old and above, to set forward the work of the house of the Lord. **9** And Jeshua [g]stood with his sons, and his brethren, and Kadmiel with his sons, and the sons of Judah together, to set forward the workmen in the house of God, and the sons of Henadad with their sons, and their brethren the Levites. **10** And when the builders laid the foundation of the Temple of the Lord, they appointed the Priests in their apparel with trumpets, and the Levites the sons of Asaph with cymbals, to praise the Lord, [2]after the ordinance of David king of Israel. **11** Thus they sang when they gave praise, and when they gave thanks unto the Lord, For he is good, for his mercy endureth forever toward Israel. And all the people shouted with a great shout, when they praised the Lord, because the foundation of the house of the Lord was laid. **12** Many also of the Priests and the Levites and the chief of the fathers, ancient men which had seen the first house, (when the foundation of this house was laid before their eyes) [h]wept with a loud voice, and many shouted aloud for joy, **13** So that the people could not discern the sound of the shout for joy, from the noise of the weeping of the people: for the people shouted with a loud cry, and the noise was heard far off.

4

2 The building of the Temple is hindered, and how, 11 Letters to Artaxerxes, and the answer.

1 But [a]the adversaries of Judah and Benjamin heard, that the children of the captivity built the Temple unto the Lord God of Israel. **2** And they came to Zerubbabel, and to the chief fathers, and said unto them, We will build with you: for we seek the Lord your God as ye do, and we have sacrificed unto him since the time of Esarhaddon king of Assyria, which brought us up hither. **3** Then Zerubbabel, and Jeshua, and the rest of the chief fathers of Israel said unto them, It is not for you, but for us to build the house unto our God: [b]for we ourselves

---

e. Ezra 2:6 Or, of the Duke of Moab.

f. Ezra 2:16 Which were of the posterity of Hezekiah.

g. Ezra 2:21 That is, inhabitants, for so this word (some) signifieth when it is joined with the names of places.

h. Ezra 2:36 Before he hath declared the two tribes of Judah and Benjamin, and now cometh to the tribe of Levi, and beginneth at the Priests.

i. Ezra 2:43 So called, because they were given to the Temple, to cut wood and bear water for the use of the sacrifices, and came of the Gibeonites, which were appointed to this use by Joshua, Josh. 9:23.

j. Ezra 2:55 Which came of them that Solomon had appointed for the work of the Temple.

k. Ezra 2:61 Of him is made mention, 2 Sam. 17:27 and 19:31, and because the Priest's office was had in contempt, these would have changed their estate by their name, and so by God's just judgment lost both the estimation of the world and the dignity of their office.

l. Ezra 2:63 This is a Chaldean name, and signifieth him that hath authority over others.

m. Ezra 2:63 Read Exod. 28:30.

n. Ezra 2:69 Which mount to of our money, 24,826 pounds, 13 shillings and 4 pence, esteeming the French crown at 6 shillings and 4 pence for the dram is the eighth part of an ounce, and the ounce the eighth part of a mark.

o. Ezra 2:69 Which are called, mina, and contain a piece two marks: so 50,000 minas make 55,000 franks, which mount to of our money 69,666 pounds, 13 shillings 4 pence so that the whole sum was 94,493 pounds, 6 shillings, 8 pence.

EZRA 2

1. Neh. 7:6

EZRA 3

a. Ezra 3:1 Called Tishri which answereth to part of September and part of October.

b. Ezra 3:2 Meaning, nephew: for he was the son of Pedaiah, read 1 Chron. 3:19.

c. Ezra 3:3 In the place where Solomon had placed it.

d. Ezra 3:5 That is, after the feast of Tabernacles.

e. Ezra 3:7 Or, Joppa.

f. Ezra 3:8 Which month contained part of April and part of May: for in the mean season they had provided for things necessary for the work.

g. Ezra 3:9 They gave them exhortations, and encouraged every man forward in the work.

h. Ezra 3:12 Because they saw that it was nothing so glorious as that Temple, which Solomon had built, notwithstanding Aggeus comforteth them, and prophesieth that it shall be more beautiful than the first: meaning the spiritual Temple, which are the members of Christ's body.

EZRA 3

1. Exod. 23:16

2. 1 Chron. 16:7,8

EZRA 4

a. Ezra 4:1 Meaning, the inhabitants of Samaria, whom the king of Assyria had placed in the stead of the ten tribes, 2 Kings 17:24 and 19:37. These professed God, but worshipped idols also, and therefore were the greatest enemies to the true servants of God.

b. Ezra 4:3 For they perceived what their pretence was, to wit, to erect idolatry instead of true religion.

together will build it unto the Lord God of Israel, as king Cyrus the king of Per-
sia hath commanded us. **4** Wherefore the people of the land [c]discouraged the
people of Judah, and troubled them in building. **5** And they [d]hired counselors
against them, to hinder their devise all the days of Cyrus king of Persia, even un-
til the reign of Darius king of Persia. **6** And in the reign of [e]Ahasuerus (in the
beginning of his reign) wrote they an accusation against the inhabitants of Judah
and Jerusalem. **7** And in the days of [f]Artachshashta, Mithredath, Tabeel, and the
rest of their companions wrote when it was peace, unto Artaxerxes king of Persia,
and the writing of the letter was the Aramites writing, and the thing declared was
in the language of the Aramites. **8** Rehum the [g]chancellor, and Shimshai the
scribe wrote a letter against Jerusalem to Artaxerxes the king, in this sort. **9** Then
wrote Rehum the chancellor, and Shimshai the scribe, and their companions [h]Di-
nai, and Apharsathcai, Tarpelai, Persia, Archevai, Bablai, Shushanchai, Dehave,
Elamai, **10** And the rest of the people whom the great and noble [i]Osnapper
brought over, and set in the cities of Samaria, and other that are beyond the [j]Ri-
ver and [k]Cheeneth. **11** This is the copy of the letter that they sent unto King
Artaxerxes, THY SERVANTS the men beyond the River and Cheeneth, salute
thee. **12** Be it known unto the King that the Jews, which came up from thee
to us, are come unto Jerusalem (a city rebellious and wicked) and build, and lay
the foundations of the walls, and have joined the foundations. **13** Be it known
now unto the king, that if this city be built, and the foundations of the walls laid,
they will not give toll, tribute, nor [l]custom: so shalt thou hinder the king's tribu-
te. **14** Now therefore because [m]we have been brought up in the King's palace,
it was not meet for us to see the King's dishonor: for this cause have we sent and
certified the King, **15** That one may search in the book of the Chronicles of thy
fathers, and thou shalt find in the book of the Chronicles, and perceive that this
city is rebellious and noisome unto kings and provinces, and that they have moved
sedition of old time, for the which cause this city was destroyed. **16** We certify
the king therefore, that if this city be built, and the foundation of the walls laid, by
this means the portion beyond the River shall not be thine. **17** The King sent an
answer unto Rehum the chancellor, and Shimshai the scribe, and to the rest of their
companions that dwelt in Samaria, and unto the other beyond the River, [n]Shelam
and [o]Cheeth. **18** The letter which ye sent unto us, hath been openly read before
me, **19** And I have commanded and they have searched, and found, that this city
of old time hath made insurrection against kings, and hath rebelled, and rebellion
hath been committed therein. **20** There have been mighty kings also over Jeru-
salem, which have ruled over all beyond the River, and toll, tribute and custom was
given unto them. **21** Make ye now a decree that those men may cease, and that
the city be not built, till I have given another commandment. **22** Take heed now
that ye fail not to do this: why should damage grow to hurt the king? **23** When
the copy of king Artaxerxes's letter was read before Rehum and Shimshai the scri-
be, and their companions, they went up in all the haste to Jerusalem unto the Jews,
and caused them to cease by force and power. **24** Then [p]ceased the work of the
house of God, which was in Jerusalem, and did stay unto the second year of Da-
rius king of Persia.

5

1 Haggai and Zechariah do prophesy. 3 The work of the Temple goeth forward contrary to the mind of Tattenai. 6 His letters to Darius.

1 Then [a,1]Haggai a Prophet, and Zechariah the son of Iddo a Prophet prophe-
sied unto the Jews that were in Judah, and Jerusalem, in the Name of the God
of Israel, even unto them. **2** Then Zerubbabel the son of Shealtiel, and Jeshua
the son of Jozadak arose, and began to build the house of God at Jerusalem, and
with them were the Prophets of God, which [b]helped them. **3** At the same time
came to them Tattenai which was captain beyond the River, and Shethar-Boznai,
and their companions, and said thus unto them, Who hath given you command-
ment to build this house, and to lay the foundations of these walls? **4** [c]Then
said we unto them after this manner, What are the names of the men that build
this building? **5** But the [d]eye of their God was upon the Elders of the Jews, that
they could not cause them to cease, till the matter came to Darius: and then they
answered by letters thereunto. **6** The copy of the letter, that Tattenai captain
beyond the River, and Shethar-Boznai and his companions, Persians, (which were
beyond the river) sent unto King Darius. **7** They sent a letter unto him, wherein
it was written thus, UNTO DARIUS the king, all peace. **8** Be it known unto
the king, that we went into the province of Judea, to the house of the great God,
which is built with [e]great stones, and beams are laid in the walls, and this work is
wrought speedily, and prospereth in their hands. **9** Then asked we those Elders,
and said unto them thus, Who hath given you commandment to build this house,
and to lay the foundation of these walls? **10** We asked their names also that we
might certify thee, and that we might write the names of the men that were their
rulers. **11** But they answered us thus, and said, We are the servants of the God
of heaven and earth, and build the house that was built of old and many years ago,
which a [f]great king of Israel [2]built, and founded it. **12** But after that our fathers
had provoked the God of heaven unto wrath, [3]he gave them over into the hand
of Nebuchadnezzar king of Babel the Chaldean, and he destroyed this house, and
carried the people away captive unto Babel. **13** But in the [g]first year of Cyrus
king of Babel, King Cyrus made a decree to build this house of God. **14** And
the vessels of gold and silver of the house of God, which Nebuchadnezzar took out
of the Temple, that was in Jerusalem, and brought them into the Temple of Babel,
those did Cyrus the king take out of the Temple of Babel, and they gave them unto
one [h]Sheshbazzar by his name, whom he had made captain. **15** And he said
unto him, Take these vessels and go thy way, and put them in the Temple that is
in Jerusalem, and let the house of God be built in his place. **16** Then came the
same Sheshbazzar and laid the foundation of the house of God, which is in Jeru-
salem, and since that time even until now, hath it been in building, yet is it not
finished. **17** Now therefore if it please the king, let there be search made in the
house of the king's [i]treasures, which is there in Babel, whether a decree hath been
made by king Cyrus, to build this house of God in Jerusalem, and let the King send
his mind concerning this.

6

At the commandment of Darius king of Persia, after the Temple was built and dedicated, the children of Israel keep the feast of unleavened bread.

1 Then king Darius gave commandment, and they made search in the [a]library
of the treasures, which were there laid up in Babel. **2** And there was found in a
[b]coffer (in the palace that was in the province of the Medes) a volume, and the-
rein was it thus written, as a memorial, **3** IN THE FIRST year of King Cyrus,
King Cyrus made a decree for the house of God in Jerusalem, Let the house be
built, even the place where they offered sacrifices, and let the walls thereof be joi-
ned together: let the height thereof be threescore cubits, and the breadth thereof
threescore cubits, **4** Three [c]orders of [d]great stones, and one order of timber, and
let the expenses be given of the king's house. **5** And also let them render the
vessels of the house of God (of gold and silver, which Nebuchadnezzar took out
of the Temple, which was in Jerusalem, and brought unto Babel) and let [e]him go
unto the Temple that is in Jerusalem to his place, and put them in the house of
God. **6** Therefore Tattenai captain beyond the river, and Shethar-Boznai, (and
their companions Apharsecai, which are beyond the River) be ye far [f]from then-
ce. **7** Suffer ye the work of this house of God, that the captain of the Jews and
the Elders of the Jews may build this house of God in his place. **8** For I have
given a commandment what ye shall do to the Elders of these Jews, for the buil-
ding of this house of God, that of the revenues of the King, which is of the tribute
beyond the River, there be incontinently expenses given unto these men that they
[g]cease not. **9** And that which they shall have need of, let it be given unto them
day by day, whether it be young bullocks, or rams, or lambs for the burnt offerings
of the God of heaven, wheat, salt, wine, and oil, according to the appointment of
the Priests that are in Jerusalem, that there be no fault, **10** That they may have
to offer sweet odors unto the God of heaven, and pray for the king's life, and for
his sons. **11** And I have made a decree, that whosoever shall alter this sentence,
the wood shall be pulled down from his house, and shall be set up, and he shall
be hanged thereon, and his house shall be made a dunghill for this. **12** And the
God that hath caused his Name [h]to dwell there, destroy all kings and people that
put to their hand to alter and to destroy this house of God, which is in Jerusalem. I
Darius have made a decree, let it be done with speed. **13** Then Tattenai the Cap-
tain beyond the River, and Shethar-Boznai and their companions, according to
that which Darius had sent, so they did speedily. **14** So the elders of the Jews bu-
ilt, and they prospered by the prophesying of [i]Haggai the Prophet, and Zechariah

---

c. Ezra 4:4 Hebrew, made their hands weak.
d. Ezra 4:5 They bribed the governors under the king to hinder their work: Thus they that halt, cannot abide that God should be purely served.
e. Ezra 4:6 He was also called Artaxerxes, which is a Persian name, some think it was Cambises Cyrus' son, or Darius, as verse 5.
f. Ezra 4:7 Called Artaxerxes, which signifieth in the Persian tongue, an excellent warrior.
g. Ezra 4:8 Or, counselor.
h. Ezra 4:9 These were certain people which the Assyrians placed in Samaria instead of the ten tribes.
i. Ezra 4:10 Some think it was Sennacherib, but rather Shalmaneser.
j. Ezra 4:10 To wit, Euphrates: and he meaneth in respect of Babel that they dwelt beyond it.
k. Ezra 4:10 Which were a certain people that envied the Jews.
l. Ezra 4:13 Meaning, the gifts that are wont to be given to kings when they pass by any country.
m. Ezra 4:14 Hebrew, in the Chaldea, we have eaten the salt of the palace.
n. Ezra 4:17 Some read for Shalom, salutation or greeting.
o. Ezra 4:17 Called also Cheeneth, as verse 11.
p. Ezra 4:24 Not altogether for the Prophets exhorted them to continue, but they used less diligence because of the troubles.

EZRA 5

a. Ezra 5:1 Or, Haggeni.
b. Ezra 5:2 Which encouraged them to go forward, and accused them that they were more careful to build their own houses, than zealous to build the Temple of God.
c. Ezra 5:4 That is, the enemies asked this, as verse 10.
d. Ezra 5:5 His favor and the spirit of strength.
e. Ezra 5:8 Or, masonry.
f. Ezra 5:11 To wit, Solomon.
g. Ezra 5:13 Read Ezra 1:1, 2.
h. Ezra 5:14 Read Ezra 1:8.
i. Ezra 5:17 Meaning, in the library, or places where lay the register or records of times.

EZRA 5

1. Hag. 1:1
2. 1Kings 6:2 / 2Chron. 24:12
3. 2Kings 24:12 / 2Kings 25:9

EZRA 6

a. Ezra 6:1 Hebrew, house of books.
b. Ezra 6:2 Wherein were the acts of the kings of the Medes and Persians.
c. Ezra 6:4 Or, rows, or courses.
d. Ezra 6:4 Or, Marble.
e. Ezra 6:5 Meaning, Zerubbabel to whom he giveth charge.
f. Ezra 6:6 Meddle not with them neither hinder them.
g. Ezra 6:8 For lack of money.
h. Ezra 6:12 Who hath appointed that place to have his Name called upon there.

the son of Iddo, and they built and finished it, by the appointment of the God of
Israel, and by the commandment of Cyrus and Darius, and Artaxerxes king of Per-
sia. **15** And this house was finished the third day of the month [j]Adar, which was
[k]the sixth year of the reign of King Darius. **16** And the children of Israel, the
Priests, and the Levites, and the residue of the children of the captivity kept the de-
dication of this house of God with joy, **17** And offered at the dedication of this
house of God an hundred bullocks, two hundred rams, four hundred lambs, and
twelve goats, for the sin of all Israel, according to the number of the tribes of Isra-
el. **18** And they set the Priests in their order, and the Levites in their courses over
the service of God in Jerusalem, as it is written in the [1]book of Moses. **19** And
the children of the captivity kept the Passover on the fourteenth day of the first
month. **20** (For the Priests and the Levites were purified altogether) and they kil-
led the Passover for all the children of the captivity, and for their brethren the Prie-
sts, and for themselves. **21** So the children of Israel which were come again out
of captivity, and all such as had [l]separated themselves unto them, from the filthi-
ness of the Heathen of the land to seek the Lord God of Israel, did eat, **22** And
they kept the feast of unleavened bread seven days with joy: for the Lord had made
them glad, and turned the heart of the king of [m]Assyria unto them, to [n]encourage
them in the work of the house of God, even the God of Israel.

7

13 By the commandment of the king, Ezra and his companions come to Jerusalem. 27 He giveth thanks to God.

1 Now after these things, in the reign of [a]Artaxerxes king of Persia, was Ezra
the son of Seraiah, the son of Azariah, the son of Hilkiah, **2** The son of Shal-
lum, the son of Zadok, the son of Ahitub, **3** The son of Amariah, the son of
Azariah, the son of Meraioth, **4** The son of Zerahiah, the son of Uzzi, the son
of Bukki, **5** The son of Abishua, the son of Phinehas, the son of Eleazar, the son
of [b]Aaron, the chief Priest. **6** This Ezra came up from Babel, and was a [c]Scribe,
prompt in the Law of Moses, which the Lord God of Israel had given, and the
king gave him all his request according to the hand of the Lord his God, which
was upon him. **7** And there went up certain of the children of Israel, and of the
Priests, and the Levites, and the singers, and the porters, and the Nethinim unto
Jerusalem, in the seventh year of king Artaxerxes. **8** And he came to Jerusalem
in the [d]fifth month, which was in the seventh year [e]of the king. **9** For upon the
first day of the first month began he to go up from Babel, and on the first day of
the fifth month came he to Jerusalem according to the good hand of his God that
was upon him. **10** For Ezra had prepared his heart to seek the Law of the Lord,
and to do it, and to teach the precepts and judgments in Israel. **11** And this is the
copy of the letter that king Artaxerxes gave unto Ezra the Priest and Scribe, even
a writer of the words of the commandments of the Lord, and of his statutes over
Israel. **12** ARTAXERXES king of kings, to Ezra the Priest and perfect Scribe of
the Law of the God of heaven, and to [f]Cheeneth. **13** I have given command-
ment, that everyone that is willing in my kingdom of the people of Israel, and of
the Priests, and Levites, [g]to go to Jerusalem with thee, shall go. **14** Therefore art
thou sent of the king and his seven counselors, to [h]enquire in Judah and Jerusalem,
according to the Law of thy God, which is in [i]thine hand, **15** And to carry the
silver and the gold, which the king and his counselors willingly offer unto the God
of Israel (whose habitation is in Jerusalem) **16** And all the silver and gold that
thou canst find in all the province of Babel, with the free offering of the people,
and that which the Priests offer willingly to the house of their God which is in Je-
rusalem, **17** That thou mayest buy speedily with this silver, bullocks, rams, lam-
bs, with their meat offerings, and their drink offerings: and thou shalt offer them
upon the Altar of the house of your God, which is in Jerusalem. **18** And whatso-
ever it pleaseth thee and thy brethren to do with the rest of the silver and gold, do
ye it according to the will of your [j]God. **19** And the vessels that are given thee
for the service of the house of thy God, those deliver thou before God in Jerusa-
lem. **20** And the residue that shall be needful for the house of thy God, which
shall be meet for thee to bestow, thou shalt bestow it out of the King's treasure
house, **21** And I king Artaxerxes have given commandment to all the treasurers
which are beyond [k]the River, that whatsoever Ezra the Priest and Scribe of the Law
of the God of heaven shall require of you, that it be done incontinently, **22** Unto
an hundred talents of silver, unto an hundred [l]measures of wheat, and unto an
hundred [m]baths of wine, and unto an hundred baths of oil, and salt without wri-
ting. **23** Whatsoever is by the commandment of the God of heaven, let it be
done speedily for the house of the God of heaven: for why should he be wroth [n]a-
gainst the realm of the King and his children? **24** And we certify you, that upon
any of the Priests, Levites, singers, porters, Nethinim, or Ministers in this house
of God, there shall no governor lay upon them toll, tribute nor custom. **25** And
thou Ezra (after the wisdom of thy God, that is in thine hand) [o]set judges and ar-
biters, which may judge all the people that is beyond the River, even all that know
the law of thy God, and teach ye them that know it not. **26** And whosoever will
not do the Law of thy God, and the king's law, let him have judgment without de-
lay, whether it be unto death, or to banishment, or to confiscation of goods, or to
imprisonment. **27** [p]Blessed be the Lord God of our fathers, which so hath put
in the king's heart, to beautify the house of the Lord that is in Jerusalem, **28** And
hath inclined mercy toward me, before the king and his counselors, and before all
the king's mighty Princes: and I was comforted by the hand of the Lord my God
which was upon me, and I gathered the chief of Israel to go up with me.

8

1 The number of them that returned to Jerusalem with Ezra. 21 He causeth them to fast. 24 He admonisheth the Priests of their duty. 31 What they did when they came to Jerusalem.

1 These are now the chief fathers of them, and the genealogy of them that
came up with me from Babel, in the reign of king [a]Artaxerxes. **2** Of the sons
of Phinehas, Gershom: of the sons of Ithamar, Daniel: of the sons of David, Hat-
tush: **3** Of the sons of Shechaniah, of the sons of Pharosh, Zechariah, and with
him the count of the males, an hundred and fifty. **4** Of the sons of [b]Pahath-Mo-
ab, Elihoenai, the son of Zerahiah, and with him two hundred males. **5** Of
the sons of Shechaniah, the son of Jahaziel, and with him three hundred ma-
les. **6** And of the sons of Adin, Ebed the son of Jonathan, and with him fifty
males. **7** And of the sons of Elam, Jeshaiah the son of Athaliah, and with him
seventy males. **8** And of the sons of Shephatiah, Zebadiah the son of Michael,
and with him fourscore males. **9** Of the sons of Joab, Obadiah the son of Jehiel,
and with him two hundred and eighteen males. **10** And of the sons of Shelomi-
th the son of Josiphiah, and with him an hundred and threescore males. **11** And
of the sons of Bebai, Zechariah the son of Bebai, and with him eight and twenty
males. **12** And of the sons of Azgad, Johanan the son of Hakkatan, and with
him an hundred and ten males. **13** And of the sons of Adonikam, that were
the [c]last, whose names are these: Eliphelet, Jehiel and Shemaiah, and with them
threescore males. **14** And of the sons of Bigvai, Uthai, and Zabbud, and with
them seventy males. **15** And I gathered them to the [d]river that goeth toward
Ahava, and there abode we three days: then I viewed the people, and the Priests,
and found there none of the sons of Levi. **16** Therefore sent I to Eliezer, to Ariel,
to Shemeiah, and to Elnathan, and to Jarib, and to Elnathan, and to Nathan, and
to Zechariah, and to Meshullam the chief, and to Joiarib, and to Elnathan men
of understanding, **17** And I gave them commandment, to Iddo the [e]chiefest at
the place of Casiphia, and I [f]told them the words that they should speak to Iddo,
and to his brethren the Nethinim at the place of Casiphia, that they should cause
the ministers of the house of our God to come unto us. **18** So by the good hand
of our God, which was upon us, they brought us a man of understanding of the
sons of Mahli the son of Levi the son of Israel, and Sherebiah with his sons and his
brethren, even eighteen. **19** Also Hashabiah, and with him Jeshaiah of the sons
of Merari, with his brethren, and their sons twenty. **20** And of the [g]Nethinim,
whom David had set, and the Princes for the service of the Levites, two hundred
and twenty of the Nethinim, which all were named by name. **21** And there at
the river, by Ahava, I proclaimed a fast, that we might humble [h]ourselves before
our God, and seek of him a right way for us, and for our children, and for all our
substance. **22** For I was [i]ashamed to require of the king an army and horsemen,
to help us against the enemy in the way, because we had spoken to the king, saying,
The hand of our God is upon all them that seek him in goodness, but his power

---

i. Ezra 6:14 Whom God stirs up to assure them that he would give their work good success.
j. Ezra 6:15 This is the twelfth month and containeth part of February and part of March.
k. Ezra 6:15 And the two and fortieth year after their first return.
l. Ezra 6:21 Which were of the heathen, and forsaked their idolatry to worship the true God.
m. Ezra 6:22 Meaning, Darius who was king of the Medes, Persians, and Assyrians.
n. Ezra 6:22 Hebrew, to strengthen their hands.

EZRA 6

1. Num. 3:6 / Num. 8:9

EZRA 7

a. Ezra 7:1 The Hebrews write, that divers of the kings of Persia were called by this name, as Pharaoh was a common name to the kings of Egypt, and Caesar to the Emperors Roman.
b. Ezra 7:5 Ezra deduceth his kindred, till he cometh to Aaron, to prove that he came of him.
c. Ezra 7:6 He showeth here what a Scribe is, who had charge to write the Law and to expound it, whom Mark calleth a Scribe, Mark 12:28, Matthew and Luke called him a Lawyer or doctor of the Law, Matt. 22:35; Luke 10:25.
d. Ezra 7:8 That contained part of July, and part of August.
e. Ezra 7:8 Of king Darius.
f. Ezra 7:12 Some take this for the name of a people, some for time or continuance, meaning that the king wished him long life.
g. Ezra 7:13 Which remained as yet in Babylon and had not returned with Zerubbabel.
h. Ezra 7:14 To examine who lived according to the Law.
i. Ezra 7:14 Whereof thou art expert.
j. Ezra 7:18 As ye know best may serve to God's glory.
k. Ezra 7:21 Which was the river Euphrates, and they were beyond it in respect of Babylon.
l. Ezra 7:22 Hebrew, Corim.
m. Ezra 7:22 Read 1 Kings 7:26; 2 Chron. 2:10.
n. Ezra 7:23 This declareth that the fear of God's judgments causeth him to use this liberality, and not the love that he bare to God's glory: or affection to his people.
o. Ezra 7:25 He gave Ezra full authority to restore all things according to the word of God, and to punish them that resisted, and would not obey.
p. Ezra 7:27 Thus Ezra gave God thanks for that he gave him so good success in his affairs by reason of the king.

EZRA 8

a. Ezra 8:1 Read Ezra 7.
b. Ezra 8:4 Or, captains of Moab.
c. Ezra 8:13 That came to go with Ezra.
d. Ezra 8:15 To that place of Euphrates, where Ahava the river entereth into it.
e. Ezra 8:17 He was the chiefest that taught there the Law of God unto the Levites.
f. Ezra 8:17 Hebrew, put words in their mouth.
g. Ezra 8:20 Read Ezra 2:43.
h. Ezra 8:21 He showeth that the end of fasting, is to humble the body to the spirit, which must proceed of the heart lively touched, or else it is but hypocrisy.
i. Ezra 8:22 He thought it better to commit himself to the protection of God, than by seeking these ordinary means to give occasion to others to think that he did doubt of God's power.

and his wrath is against all them that forsake him. **23** So we fasted, and besou-
ght our God for this: and he was entreated of us. **24** Then I separated twelve of
the chief of the Priests, Sherebiah, and Hashabiah, and ten of their brethren with
them, **25** And weighed them the silver and the gold and the vessels, even the
offering of the house of our God, which the king and his counselors and his Prin-
ces, and all Israel that were present had offered. **26** And I weighed unto their
hand six hundred and fifty [j]talents of silver, and in silver vessel an hundred talents,
and in gold, an hundred talents, **27** And twenty basins of gold, of a thousand
[k]drams, and two vessels of shining brass very good, and precious as gold. **28** And
I said unto them, Ye are consecrated unto the Lord, and the vessels are consecra-
ted, and the gold and the silver are freely offered unto the Lord God of your fa-
thers. **29** Watch ye, and keep them until ye weigh them before the chief Priests
and the Levites, and the chief fathers of Israel in Jerusalem in the chambers of the
house of the Lord. **30** So the Priests and the Levites received the weight of the
silver, and of the gold, and of the vessels to bring them to Jerusalem, unto the hou-
se of our God. **31** Then we departed from the river of Ahavah on the twelfth
day of the first month, to go unto Jerusalem, and the hand of our God was upon
us, and delivered us from the hand of the enemy, and of such as laid [l]wait by the
way. **32** And we came to Jerusalem, and abode there three days. **33** And on
the fourth day was the silver weighed, and the gold, and the vessel, in the house
of our God, by the hand of Meremoth the son of Uriah the Priest, and with him
was Eleazar the son of Phinehas, and with them was Jozabad the son of Jeshua,
and Noadiah the son of Binnui the [m]Levites, **34** By number and by weight of
every one, and all the weight was written at the same time. **35** Also the children
of the captivity, which were come out of captivity, offered burnt offerings unto the
God of Israel, twelve bullocks for all Israel, ninety and six rams, seventy and seven
lambs, and twelve he goats for sin: all was a burnt offering of the Lord. **36** And
they delivered the King's commission unto the King's officers, and to the captains
beyond the river: and they promoted the people, and the house of God.

9

1 Ezra complaineth on the people that had turned themselves from God, and married with the Gentiles. 5 He prayeth unto God.

1 When as these things were done, the rulers came to me, saying, The peo-
ple of Israel, and the Priests, and the Levites are not [a]separated from the people of
the lands (as touching their abominations) to wit, of the Canaanites, the Hittites,
the Perizzites, the Jebusites, the Ammonites, the Moabites, the Egyptians, and the
Amorites. **2** For they have taken their daughters to themselves, and to their sons,
and they have mixed the holy seed with the people of the lands, and the hand of
the [b]Princes and rulers have been chief in this trespass. **3** But when I heard this
saying, I rent my clothes and my garment, and plucked off the hair of mine head,
and of my beard, and sat down [c]astonied. **4** And there assembled unto me all
that feared the words of the God of Israel, because of the transgression of them of
the captivity. And I sat down astonied until the [1]evening sacrifice. **5** And at the
evening sacrifice I rose up from mine heaviness, and when I had rent my clothes
and my garment, I fell upon my knees, and spread out mine hands unto the Lord
my God, **6** And said, O my God, I am confounded and ashamed to lift up mine
eyes unto thee my God: for our iniquities are increased over [d]our head, and our tre-
spass is grown up unto the [e]heaven. **7** From the days of our fathers have we been
in a great trespass unto this day, and for our iniquities have we, our kings, and our
Priests been delivered into the hand of the kings of the lands, unto the sword, into
captivity, into a spoil, and into confusion of face, as appeareth this day. **8** And
now for a little space grace hath been showed from the Lord our God, in causing
a remnant to escape, and in giving us a [f]nail in his holy place, that our God may
light our eyes, and give us a little reviving in our servitude. **9** For though we were
bondmen, yet our God hath not forsaken us in our bondage, but hath inclined
mercy unto us in the sight of the kings of Persia, to give us life, and to erect the
house of our God, and to redress the desolate places thereof, and to give us a wall in
Judah and in Jerusalem. **10** And now, our God, what shall we say after this? for
we have forsaken thy commandments, **11** Which thou hast commanded by thy
servants the Prophets, saying, [2]The land whereunto ye go to possess it, is an uncle-
an land, because of the filthiness of the people of the lands, which by their abomi-
nations, and by their uncleanness have filled it from corner to corner. **12** Now
therefore shall ye not give your daughters unto their sons, neither shall ye take their
daughters unto your sons, nor seek their [3]peace nor wealth forever, that ye may be
strong and eat the goodness of the land, and leave it for an inheritance to your sons
forever. **13** And after all that is come upon us for our evil deeds, and for our gre-
at trespasses, (seeing that thou our God hast stayed us from being beneath [g]for our
iniquities, and hast given us such deliverance.) **14** Should we return to break thy
commandments, and join in affinity with the people of such abominations? woul-
dest not thou be angry toward us till thou hadst consumed us, so that there should
be no remnant nor any escaping? **15** O Lord God of Israel, thou art just, for we
have been [h]reserved to escape, as appeareth this day: behold, we are before thee in
our trespass: therefore we cannot stand before thee because of it.

10

1 The people repent and turn, and put away their strange wives.

1 While Ezra prayed thus, and [a]confessed himself weeping, and
falling down before the house of God, there assembled unto him of Israel a very
great Congregation of men and women and children: for the people wept with a
great lamentation. **2** Then Shechaniah the son of Jehiel one of the sons of Elam
answered, and said to Ezra, We have trespassed against our God, and have taken
strange wives of the people of the land, yet now there is [b]hope in Israel concerning
this. **3** Now therefore let us make a covenant with our God, to put away [c]all the
wives (and such as are born of them) according to the counsel of the Lord, and of
those that fear the commandments of our God, and let it be done according to the
Law. **4** Arise: for the matter [d]belongeth unto thee: we also will be with thee: be
of comfort and do it. **5** Then arose Ezra, and caused the chief Priests, the Levites,
and all Israel, to swear that they would do according to this word. So they swa-
re. **6** And Ezra rose up from before the house of God, and went into the cham-
ber of Johanan the son of Eliashib: he went even thither, but he did eat neither
bread nor drunk water: for he mourned, because of the transgression of them of
the captivity. **7** And they caused a proclamation to go throughout Judah and Je-
rusalem, unto [e]all them of the captivity, that they should assemble themselves unto
Jerusalem. **8** And whosoever would not come within three days according to the
counsel of the Princes and Elders, all his substance should be [f]forfeit, and he should
be separate from the Congregation of them of the captivity. **9** Then all the men
of Judah and Benjamin assembled themselves unto Jerusalem within three days,
which was the twentieth day of the [g]ninth month, and all the people sat in the
street of the house of God, trembling for this matter, and for the [h]rain. **10** And
Ezra the Priest stood up, and said unto them, Ye have transgressed, and have taken
strange wives, to [i]increase the trespass of Israel. **11** Now therefore [j]give praise
unto the Lord God of your fathers, and do his will, and separate yourselves from
the people of the land, and from the strange wives. **12** And all the Congrega-
tion answered, and said with a loud voice, So will we do according to thy words
unto us. **13** But the people are many, and it is a rainy weather, and we are not
able to stand without, neither is it the work of one day or two: for we are many
that have offended in this thing. **14** Let our rulers stand therefore [k]before all the
Congregation, and let all them which have taken strange wives in our cities, come
at the time appointed, and with them the Elders of every city and the judges the-
reof, till the fierce wrath of our God for this matter turn away from us. **15** Then
were appointed Jonathan the son of Asahel, and Jahaziah the son of Tikvah over
this matter, and Meshullam and Shabbethai the Levites helped them. **16** And
they of the captivity did so, and [l]departed, even Ezra the Priest, and the men
that were chief fathers to the family of their fathers by name, and sat down in
the first day of the tenth month to examine the matter. **17** And until the first
day of the first month they were finishing the business with all the men that had
taken strange wives. **18** And of the sons of the Priests there were men found,
that had taken strange wives, to wit, of the sons of Jeshua, the son of Jozadak, and
of his brethren, Maaseiah, Eliezer, and Jarib, and Gedaliah. **19** And they gave
[m]their hands, that they would put away their wives, and they that had trespassed
gave a ram for their trespass. **20** And of the sons of Immer, Honani, and Zeba-
diah. **21** And of the sons of Harim, Maaseiah, and Elijah, and Shemaiah, and
Jehiel, and Uzziah. **22** And of the sons of Pashur, Elioenai, Maaseiah, Ishmael,
Nethanel, Jozabad, and Elasah. **23** And of the Levites, Jozabad and Shimei, and
Kelaiah, (which is Kelita) Pethahiah, Judah and Eliezer. **24** And of the singers,

---

j. Ezra 8:26 Read 1 Kings 9:14.
k. Ezra 8:27 Read Ezra 2:29.
l. Ezra 8:31 This declared that their journey was full of danger, and yet God delivered them according to their prayer.
m. Ezra 8:33 This was a token of a good conscience and of his integrity, that he would have witnesses of his fidelity.

EZRA 9

a. Ezra 9:1 From the time they came home under Zerubbabel until the coming of Ezra, they had degenerated contrary to the Law of God, and married where it was not lawful, Deut. 7:3.
b. Ezra 9:2 That is, the governors are the chief beginners hereof.
c. Ezra 9:3 As one doubting whether God would continue his benefits towards us, or else destroy this which he had begun.
d. Ezra 9:6 That is, we are drowned in sin.
e. Ezra 9:6 They so exceed that they cannot grow greater.
f. Ezra 9:8 In giving us a resting place. It is a similitude taken of them that remain still in a place, which smite nails to hang things upon, Isa. 22:23.
g. Ezra 9:13 Hast not utterly cast us down and destroyed us for our sins, Deut. 28:13.
h. Ezra 9:15 He showeth that God is just in punishing his people, and yet merciful in reserving a residue in whom he showeth favor.

EZRA 9

1. Exod. 29:39 / Num. 28:3,4
2. Exod. 23:32 / Exod. 34:12, 15-16 / Deut. 7:13
3. Deut. 23:6

EZRA 10

a. Ezra 10:1 He confessed his sins, and the sins of the people.
b. Ezra 10:2 Meaning, that God would receive them to mercy.
c. Ezra 10:3 Which are strangers and married contrary to the Law of God.
d. Ezra 10:4 Because God hath given thee authority and learning to persuade the people herein, and to command them.
e. Ezra 10:7 Hebrew, the sons of the captivity.
f. Ezra 10:8 Or, condemned.
g. Ezra 10:9 Which contained part of November and part of December.
h. Ezra 10:9 For the season was given to rain and so the weather was more sharp and cold, and also their conscience touched them.
i. Ezra 10:10 Ye have laid one sin upon another.
j. Ezra 10:11 Read Josh. 7:19.
k. Ezra 10:14 Let them be appointed to examine this matter.
l. Ezra 10:16 They went to the chief cities to sit on this matter which was three months in finishing.
m. Ezra 10:19 As a token that they would keep promise and do it.

Eliashib. And of the porters, Shallum, and Telem, and Uri. 25 And of [n]Israel: of
the sons of Parosh, Ramiah, and Jeziah, and Malchiah, and Mijamin, and Eleazar,
and Malchijah, and Benaiah. 26 And of the sons of Elam, Mattaniah, Zechariah,
and Jehiel, and Abdi, and Jeremoth, and Eliah. 27 And of the sons of Zattu,
Elioenai, Eliashib, Mattaniah, and Jerimoth, and Zabad, and Aziza. 28 And of
the sons of Bebai, Jehohanan, Hananiah, Zabbai, Athlai. 29 And of the sons of
Bani, Meshullam, Malluch, and Adaiah, Jashub, and Sheal, Jeremoth. 30 And of
the sons of [o]Pahath-Moab, Adna, and Chelal, Benaiah, Maaseiah, Mattaniah, Be-
zaleel, and Binnui, and Manasseh. 31 And of the sons of Harim, Eliezer, Ishijah,
Malchiah, Shemaiah, Shimeon, 32 Benjamin, Malluch, Shamariah. 33 Of the
sons of Hashum, Mattenai, Mattattah, Zabad, Eliphelet, Jeremai, Manasseh, Shi-
mei. 34 Of the sons of Bani, Maadai, Amram, and Uel, 35 Banaiah, Bedeiah,
Chelluh, 36 Vaniah, Meremoth, Eliashib, 37 Mattaniah, Mattenai, and Jaa-
sai, 38 And Bani, and Binnui, Shimei, 39 And Shelemiah, and Nathan, and
Adaiah, 40 Machnadebai, Shashai, Sharai, 41 Azarel, and Shelemiah, Shema-
riah, 42 Shallum, Amariah, Joseph. 43 Of the sons of Nebo, Jeiel, Mattithiah,
Zabad, Zebina, Jadai, and Joel, Benaiah. 44 All these had taken strange wives:
and among them were women that had [p]children.

- **n.** Ezra 10:25 Meaning, of the common people: for before he spake of the Priests and Levites.
- **o.** Ezra 10:30 Or, the captain of Moab.
- **p.** Ezra 10:44 Which also were made illegitimate because the marriage was unlawful.

NEHEMIAH

1

4 Nehemiah bewaileth the calamity of Jerusalem. 5 He confesseth the sins of the people, and praiseth God for them.

1 The words of Nehemiah the son of Hachaliah. In the month [a]Chislev, in
the twentieth year, as I was in the palace of Shushan, 2 Came Hanani, one of
my [b]brethren, he and the men of Judah, and I asked them concerning the Jews
that were delivered, which were of the residue of the captivity, and concerning
Jerusalem. 3 And they said unto me, The residue that are left of the captivity
there in the [c]province, are in great affliction and in reproach, and the wall of Jeru-
salem is broken down, and the gates thereof are burnt with fire. 4 And when I
heard these words, I sat down and wept, and mourned certain days, and I fasted
and prayed before the God of heaven, 5 And said, [1]O Lord God of heaven, the
great and terrible God, that keepeth covenant and mercy for them that love him,
and observe his commandments, 6 I pray thee let thine ears be attent, and thine
eyes open, to hear the prayer of thy servant, which I pray before thee daily, day and
night for the children of Israel thy servants, and confess the sins of the children
of Israel, which we have sinned against thee, both I and my father's house have
sinned: 7 We have [d]grievously sinned against thee, and have not kept the com-
mandments, nor the statutes, nor the judgments, which thou commandedst thy
servant Moses. 8 I beseech thee, remember the word that thou commandedst thy
servant Moses, saying, Ye will transgress, and [2]I will scatter you abroad among the
people. 9 But if ye return unto me, and keep my commandments, and do them,
[3]though your scattering were to the uttermost part of the heaven, yet will I gather
you from thence, and will bring you unto the place that I have chosen to place my
Name there. 10 Now these are thy servants and thy people whom thou hast re-
deemed by thy great power, and by thy mighty hand. 11 O Lord, I beseech thee,
let thine ear now hearken to the prayer of thy servant, and to the prayer of thy ser-
vants, who desire to [e]fear thy Name, and I pray thee, cause thy servant to prosper
this day, and give him favor in the presence of [f]this man: for I was the king's butler.

2

1 After Nehemiah had obtained letters of Artaxerxes, 11 he came to Jerusalem, 17 and built the walls.

1 Now in the month [a]Nisan in the twentieth year of king [b]Artaxerxes, the
wine stood before him, and I took up the wine, and gave it unto the king. Now I
was not before time sad in his presence. 2 And the king said unto me, Why is
thy countenance sad, seeing thou art not sick? this is nothing, but sorrow of heart.
Then was I sore afraid, 3 And I said to the King, God save the king forever: why
should not my countenance be sad, when the city and house of the sepulchers of
my fathers lieth waste, and the gates thereof are devoured with fire? 4 And the
king said unto me, For what thing doest thou require? Then I prayed [c]to the God
of heaven, 5 And said unto the king, If it please the king, and if thy servant have
found favor in thy sight, I desire that thou wouldest send me to Judah unto the
city of the sepulchers of my fathers, that I may build it. 6 And the King said
unto me, (the Queen also sitting by him:) How long shall thy journey be? and
when wilt thou come again? So it pleased the king, and he sent me, and I set him
a time. 7 After I said unto the King, If it please the King, let them give me let-
ters to the captains beyond the [d]River, that they may convey me over, till I come
into Judah, 8 And letters unto Asaph the keeper of the king's [e]park, that he may
give me timber to build the gates of the palace (which appertained to the house)
and for the walls of the city, and for the house that I shall enter into. And the king
gave me according to [f]the good hand of my God upon me. 9 Then came I to the
captains beyond the River, and gave them the king's letters. And the king had sent
captains of the army and horsemen with me. 10 But [g]Sanballat the Horonite,
and Tobiah a servant an Ammonite heard it, and it grieved them sore, that there
was come a man which sought the wealth of the children of Israel. 11 So I came
to Jerusalem, and was there three days. 12 And I rose in the night, I, and a few
men with me: for I told no man, what God had put in mine heart to do at Jerusa-
lem, and there was not a beast with me, save the beast whereon I rode. 13 And I
went out by night by the gate of the valley, and came before the dragon well, and to
the dung port, and viewed the walls of Jerusalem, how they were broken down, and
the ports thereof devoured with the fire. 14 Then I went forth unto the gate of
the [h]fountain, and to the king's fish pool, and there was no room for the beast that
was under me to pass. 15 Then went I up in the night by the brook, and viewed
the wall, and turned back, and coming back, I entered by the gate of the valley, and
returned. 16 And the rulers knew not whither I was gone, nor what I did, nei-
ther did I as yet tell it unto the Jews, nor to the Priests, nor to the noble men, nor

NEHEMIAH 1

- **a.** Neh. 1:1 Which containeth part of November and part of December, and was their ninth month.
- **b.** Neh. 1:2 A Jew as I was.
- **c.** Neh. 1:3 Meaning, in Judea.
- **d.** Neh. 1:7 Hebrew, corrupted.
- **e.** Neh. 1:11 That is, to worship thee.
- **f.** Neh. 1:11 To wit, the king Artaxerxes.

NEHEMIAH 1

- **1.** Dan. 9:4
- **2.** Deut. 29:21,28
- **3.** Deut. 30:4

NEHEMIAH 2

- **a.** Neh. 2:1 Which was the first month of the year, and containeth part of March and part of April.
- **b.** Neh. 2:1 Who is also called Darius, read Ezra 7:1, and was the son of Hystaspis.
- **c.** Neh. 2:4 I desired God in mine heart to prosper mine enterprise.
- **d.** Neh. 2:7 Or, Euphrates.
- **e.** Neh. 2:8 Or, Paradise.
- **f.** Neh. 2:8 As God moved me to ask, and as he gave me good success therein.
- **g.** Neh. 2:10 These were great enemies to the Jews, and labored always both by force and subtlety to overcome them, and Tobiah, because his wife was a Jewess, had advertisement ever of their affairs, and so wrought them great trouble.
- **h.** Neh. 2:14 Or, conduit.
- **i.** Neh. 2:17 That is, contemned of other nations, as though God had forsaken us.
- **j.** Neh. 2:18 They were encouraged, and gave themselves to do well, and to travel in this worthy enterprise.
- **k.** Neh. 2:19 These were three chief governors under the king of Persia beyond Euphrates.
- **l.** Neh. 2:19 Thus the wicked when they will burden the children of God, ever lay treason unto their charge, both because it maketh them most odious to the world, and also stirreth the hatred of princes most against them.
- **m.** Neh. 2:20 Neither are ye of the number of the children of God (to whom he hath appointed this city only) neither did any of your predecessors ever fear God.

NEHEMIAH 3

- **a.** Neh. 3:1 In Hebrew, they sanctified it, that is, they finished it, and so dedicated it to the Lord by prayer, in desiring him to maintain it.
- **b.** Neh. 3:5 The rich and mighty would not obey them which were appointed officers in this work, neither would they help thereunto.
- **c.** Neh. 3:7 Unto the place where the Duke was wont to sit in judgment, who governed the country in their absence.
- **d.** Neh. 3:8 Or, Zorephim.
- **e.** Neh. 3:8 Or, of the Apothecaries.
- **f.** Neh. 3:11 Or, measure.
- **g.** Neh. 3:15 Or, Shoa.
- **h.** Neh. 3:19 Where the weapons and armor of the city lay.

to the rulers, nor to the rest that labored in the work. **17** Afterward I said unto them, Ye see the misery that we are in, how Jerusalem lieth waste, and the gates thereof are burnt with fire: come, and let us build the wall of Jerusalem, that we be no more [i]a reproach. **18** Then I told them of the hand of my God, (which was good over me) and also of the king's words that he had spoken unto me. And they said, Let us rise, and build. So they [j]strengthened their hand to good. **19** But when Sanballat the Horonite, and Tobiah the servant an Ammonite, and [k]Geshem the Arabian heard it, they mocked us, and despised us, and said, What a thing is this that ye do? Will ye [l]rebel against the king? **20** Then answered I them, and said to them, The God of heaven, he will prosper us, and we his servants will rise up and build: but as for you, ye have no portion nor right, nor [m]memorial in Jerusalem.

3

The number of them that built the walls.

1 Then arose Eliashib the high Priest with his brethren the Priests, and they built the sheep gate: they [a]repaired it, and set up the doors thereof: even unto the tower of Meah repaired they it, and unto the tower of Hananel. **2** And next unto him built the men of Jericho, and beside him Zaccur the son of Imri. **3** But the fish port did the sons of Senaah build, which also laid the beams thereof, and set on the doors thereof, the locks thereof, and the bars thereof. **4** And next unto them fortified Meremoth, the son of Urijah, the son of Koz: and next unto them fortified Meshullam, the son of Berechiah, the son of Meshezabel: and next unto them fortified Zadok, the son of Baana: **5** And next unto them fortified the Tekoites: but the great men of them [b]put not their necks to the works of their lords. **6** And the gate of the [1]old fish pool fortified Jehoiada the son of Paseah, and Meshullam the son of Besodeiah: they laid the beams thereof, and set on the doors thereof, and the locks thereof, and the bars thereof. **7** Next unto them also fortified Melatiah the Gibeonite, and Jadon the Meronothite, men of Gibeon, and of Mizpah, unto the [c]throne of the Duke, which was beyond the River. **8** Next unto him fortified Uzziel the son of Harhaiah [d]of the goldsmiths: next unto him also fortified Hananiah the son [e]of Harakkahim, and they repaired Jerusalem unto the broad wall. **9** Also next unto them fortified Rephaiah, the son of Hur, the ruler of the half part of Jerusalem. **10** And next unto him fortified Jedaiah the son of Harumaph, even over against his house: and next unto him fortified Hattush the son of Hashabniah. **11** Malchijah the son of Harim, and Hashub the son of Pahath-Moab fortified the second [f]portion, and the tower of the furnaces. **12** Next unto him also fortified Shallum the son of Hallohesh, the ruler of the half part of Jerusalem, he and his daughters. **13** The valley gate fortified Hanun, and the inhabitants of Zanoah: they built it, and set on the doors thereof, the locks thereof, and the bars thereof, even a thousand cubits on the wall unto the dung port. **14** But the dung port fortified Malchijah the son of Rechab, the ruler of the fourth part of Beth Haccarem: he built it, and set on the doors thereof, the locks thereof, and the bars thereof. **15** But the gate of the fountain fortified Shallun the son of Col-Hozeh, the ruler of the fourth part of Mizpah: he built it, and covered it, and set on the doors thereof, the locks thereof, and the bars thereof, and the wall unto the fish pool of [g]Shelah by the king's garden, and unto the steps that go down from the city of David. **16** After him fortified Nehemiah the son of Azbuk, the ruler of the half part of Beth Zur until the other side over against the sepulchers of David and to the fish pool that was repaired, and unto the house of the mighty. **17** After him fortified the Levites, Rehum the son of Bani, and the next unto him fortified Hashabiah the ruler of the half part of Keilah in his quarter. **18** After him fortified their brethren: Bavai, the son of Henadad the ruler of the half part of Keilah: **19** And next unto him fortified Ezer, the son of Jeshua the ruler of Mizpah, the other portion over against the going up to the [h]corner of the armor. **20** After him was earnest Baruch the son of Zabbai, and fortified another portion from the corner unto the door of the house of Eliashib the high Priest. **21** After him fortified Meremoth the son of Urijah, the son of Koz, another portion from the door of the house of Eliashib, even as long as the house of Eliashib extended. **22** After him also fortified the Priests, the men of [i]the plain. **23** After them fortified Benjamin, and Hasshub over against their house: after him fortified Azariah the son of Maaseiah, the son of Ananiah, by his house. **24** After him fortified Binnui, the son of Henadad another portion, from the house of Azariah unto the turning and unto the corner. **25** Palal, the son of Uzai, from over against the corner, and the high tower, that lieth out from the King's house, which is beside the court of the prison. After him Pedaiah the son of Parosh. **26** And the [j]Nethinim they dwelt in the fortress unto the place over against the water gate Eastward, and to the tower that lieth out. **27** After him fortified the Tekoites another portion over against the great tower that lieth out even unto the wall of the fortress. **28** From above the horse gate forth fortified the Priests, every one over against his house. **29** After them fortified Zadok the son of Immer over against his house: and after him fortified Shemaiah the son of Shechaniah the keeper of the East gate. **30** After him fortified Hananiah the son of Shelemiah, and Hanun the son of Zalaph, the [k]sixth, another portion: after him fortified Meshullam, the son of Berechiah, over against his chamber. **31** After him fortified Malchijah the goldsmith's son, until the house of the Nethinim, and of the Merchants over against the gate [l]Miphkad, and to the chamber in the corner. **32** And between the chamber of the corner unto the sheep gate fortified the goldsmiths and the merchants.

4

7 The building of Jerusalem is hindered, 15 but God breaketh their enterprise. 17 The Jews build with one hand, and hold their weapons in the other.

1 But when Sanballat heard that we built the wall, then was he wroth and sore grieved, and mocked the Jews, **2** And said before his [a]brethren and the army of Samaria, thus he said, What do these [b]weak Jews? will they fortify themselves? will they sacrifice? will they finish it in a day? will they make the stones whole again out of the heaps of dust, seeing they are burnt? **3** And Tobiah the Ammonite was beside him, and said, Although they build, yet if a fox go up, he shall even break down their stony wall. **4** [c]Hear, O our God (for we are despised) and turn their shame upon their own head, and give them unto a prey [d]in the land of their captivity, **5** And cover not their [e]iniquity, neither let their sin be put out in thy presence: for they have provoked us before the builders. **6** So we built the wall, and all the wall was joined unto the [f]half thereof, and the heart of the people was to work. **7** But when Sanballat, and Tobiah, and the Arabians, and the Ammonites, and the Ashdodims heard that the walls of Jerusalem were repaired, (for the breaches began to be stopped) then they were very wroth, **8** And conspired all together to come and to fight against Jerusalem, and to [g]hinder them. **9** Then we prayed unto our God, and set watchmen by them, day and night, because of them. **10** And Judah said, The strength of the bearers is weakened, and there is much earth, so that we are not able to build the wall. **11** Also our adversaries had said, They shall not know, neither see, till we come into the midst of them, and slay them, and cause the work to cease. **12** But when the Jews (which dwelt beside them) came, they told us [h]ten times, [i]From all places, whence ye shall return, they will be upon us. **13** Therefore set I in the lower places behind the wall upon the tops of the stones, and placed the people by their families, with their swords, their spears, and their bows. **14** Then I beheld, and rose up, and said unto the princes, and to the rulers, and to the rest of the people, Be not afraid of them: [j]remember the great Lord, and fearful, and fight for your brethren, your sons, and your daughters, your wives, and your houses. **15** And when our enemies heard that it was known unto us, then God brought their counsel to nought, and we turned all again to the wall, every one unto his work. **16** And from that day half of the young men did the labor, and the other half part of them held the spears, and shields, and bows, and habergeons: and the Rulers stood [k]behind all the house of Judah. **17** They that built on the wall, and they that bare burdens, and they that laded, did the work with one hand, and with the other held the sword. **18** For every one of the builders had his sword girded on his loins, and so built: and he that blew the trumpet, was beside me. **19** Then said I unto the Princes, and to the rulers, and to the rest of the people, The work is great and large, and we are separated upon the wall, one far from another. **20** In what place therefore ye hear the sound of the trumpet, [l]resort ye thither unto us: our God shall fight for us. **21** So we labored in the work, and half of them held the spears, from the appearing of the morning, till the stars came forth. **22** And at the same time said I unto the people, Let everyone with his servant lodge within Jerusalem, that they may be a watch for us in the night, and labor in the day. **23** So neither I, nor my brethren, nor my servants, nor the men of the ward (which followed me) none of us did put off our clothes, save everyone put them off [m]for washing.

---

i. Neh. 3:22 Which dwelt in the plain country by Jordan and Jericho.
j. Neh. 3:26 Read Ezra 2:43.
k. Neh. 3:30 Meaning the sixth of his sons.
l. Neh. 3:31 Which was the place of judgment or execution.

NEHEMIAH 3

1. Isa. 22:11

NEHEMIAH 4

a. Neh. 4:2 Of his companions that dwelt in Samaria.
b. Neh. 4:2 Thus the wicked that consider not that God's power is ever in a readiness for the defense of his, mock them as though they were weak and feeble.
c. Neh. 4:4 This is the remedy that the children of God have against the derision and threatenings of their enemies, to flee to God by prayer.
d. Neh. 4:4 Let them be spoiled and led away captive.
e. Neh. 4:5 Let the plagues declare to the world that they set themselves against thee and against thy Church: that he prayeth only having respect to God's glory and not for any private affection, or grudge.
f. Neh. 4:6 Or, half height.
g. Neh. 4:8 Hebrew, make to stay, meaning the people.
h. Neh. 4:12 That is, oftentimes.
i. Neh. 4:12 They which brought the tidings, said thus, When you leave your work, and go either to eat or to rest, your enemies will assail you.
j. Neh. 4:14 Who is ever at hand to deliver his out of danger: and therefore seeing they should fight for the maintenance of God's glory, and for the preservation of their own lives and of theirs, he encourageth them to play the valiant men.
k. Neh. 4:16 To oversee them and to encourage them to their work.
l. Neh. 4:20 Meaning, to resist their enemies, if need required.
m. Neh. 4:23 That is, when they purified themselves, or else when they washed their clothes.

5

1 The people are oppressed and in necessity. 6 Nehemiah remedieth it. 14 He took not the portion of others that had ruled before, lest he should grieve the people.

1 Now there was a great cry of the people, and of their wives [a]against their brethren the Jews. **2** For there were that said, We, our sons and our daughters are many, therefore we take up [b]corn, that we may eat and live. **3** And there were that said, We must gage our lands, and our vineyards, and our houses, and take up corn for the famine. **4** There were also that said, We have borrowed money for the king's [c]tribute upon our lands and our vineyards. **5** And now our flesh is as [d]the flesh of our brethren, and our sons as their sons: and lo, we bring into subjection our sons and our daughters, as servants, and there be of our daughters now in subjection, and there is no power [e]in our hands: for other men have our lands and our vineyards. **6** Then was I very angry when I heard their cry and these words. **7** And I thought in my mind, and I rebuked the princes, and the rulers, and said unto them, You lay [f]burdens every one upon his brethren: and I set a great [g]assembly against them, **8** And I said unto them, We (according to our ability) have redeemed our brethren the Jews, which were sold unto the heathen: and will you sell your brethren again, or shall they be [h]sold unto us? Then held they their peace, and could not answer. **9** [i]I said also, That which ye do, is not good. Ought ye not to walk in the fear of our God, for the [j]reproach of the heathen our enemies? **10** For even I, my brethren, and my servants do lend them money and corn: I pray you, let us leave off this [k]burden. **11** Restore, I pray you, unto them this day their lands, their vineyards, their olives, and their houses, and remit the hundredth part of the silver and of the corn, of the wine, and of the oil [l]that ye exact of them. **12** Then said they, We will restore it, and will not require it of them: we will do as thou hast said. Then I called the Priests and caused them to swear, that they should do according to this promise. **13** So I shook my lap, and said, So let God shake out every man that will not perform this promise, from his house, and from his labor: even thus let him be shaken out and emptied. And all the Congregation said, Amen, and praised the Lord: and the people did according to this promise. **14** And from the time that the King gave me charge to be governor in the land of Judah, from the twentieth year, even unto the two and thirtieth year of King Artaxerxes, that is, twelve years, I, and my brethren have not eaten the [m]bread of the governor. **15** For the former governors that were before me, had been chargeable unto the people, and had taken of them bread and wine, besides forty shekels of silver: yea, and their servants bare rule over the people: but so did not I, because of the fear of God. **16** But rather I fortified a portion in the work of this wall, and we bought no land, and all my servants came thither together unto the work. **17** Moreover there were at my table an hundred and fifty of the Jews, and rulers, which came unto us from among the heathen that are about us. **18** And there was prepared daily an ox, and six chosen sheep, and birds were prepared for me, and [n]within ten days wine for all [o]in abundance. Yet for all this I required not the bread of the governor: for the bondage was grievous unto this people. **19** Remember me, O my God, in goodness, according to all that I have done for this people.

6

8 Nehemiah answereth with great wisdom and zeal to his adversary. 11 He is not discouraged by the false Prophets.

1 And when Sanballat, and Tobiah, and Geshem the Arabian, and the rest of our enemies heard that I had built the wall, and that there were no more [a]breaches therein (though at that time I had not set up the doors upon the gates) **2** Then sent Sanballat and Geshem unto me, saying, come thou that we may meet together in the villages in the plain of Ono: and they thought to do me evil. **3** Therefore I sent messengers unto them, saying, I have a great work to do, and I cannot come down: [b]why should the work cease, while I leave it and come down to you? **4** Yet they sent unto me four times after this sort. And I answered them after the same manner. **5** Then sent Sanballat his servant after this sort unto me the fifth time, with an open letter in his hand, **6** Wherein was written, It is reported among the heathen, and [c]Gashmu hath said it, that thou and the Jews think to rebel, for the which cause thou buildest the wall, and thou wilt be their king according to these [d]words. **7** Thou hast also ordained [e]the Prophets to preach of thee at Jerusalem, saying, There is a King in Judah: and now according to these words it shall come to the King's ears: come now therefore, and let us take counsel together. **8** Then I sent unto him, saying, It is not done according to these words that thou sayest: for thou feignest them of thine own heart. **9** For all they afraid us, saying, Their hands shall be weakened from the work, and it shall not be done: now therefore [f]encourage thou me. **10** And I came to the house of Shemaiah the son of Delaiah the son of Mehetabel, and he was [g]shut up, and he said, Let us come together into the house of God in the midst of the Temple, and shut the doors of the Temple: for they will come to slay thee: yea, in the night will they come to kill thee. **11** Then I said, [h]Should such a man as I, flee? Who is he, being as I am, that would go into the Temple to live? I will not go in. **12** And lo, I perceived that God had not sent him, but that he pronounced this prophecy against me: for Tobiah and Sanballat had hired him. **13** Therefore was he hired, that I might be afraid, and do thus, and sin, and that they might have an evil report, that they might reproach me. **14** My God, remember thou Tobiah, and Sanballat according unto these their works, and Noadiah the [i]Prophetess also, and the rest of the prophets that would have put me in fear. **15** Notwithstanding the wall was finished on the five and twentieth day of [j]Elul, in two and [k]fifty days. **16** And when all our enemies heard thereof, even all the heathen that were about us, they were afraid, and their courage failed them: for they knew that this work was wrought by our God. **17** And in these days were there many of the princes of Judah, whose [l]letters went unto Tobiah, and those of Tobiah came unto them. **18** For there were many in Judah, that were sworn unto him: for he was the son in law of Shechaniah, the son of Arah: and his son Jehohanan had the daughter of Meshullam, the son of Berechiah. **19** Yea, they spake in his praise before me, and told him my words, and Tobiah sent letters to put me in fear.

7

1 After the wall once built, is the watch appointed. 6 They that returned from the captivity are numbered.

1 Now when the wall was built, and I had set up the doors, and the porters, and the singers and the Levites were appointed, **2** Then I commanded my brother Hanani and Hananiah, the prince of the palace in Jerusalem (for he was doubtless a faithful man, and feared God above many) **3** And I said unto them, Let not the gates of Jerusalem be opened, until the heat of the sun: and while [a]they stand by, let them shut the doors, and [b]make them fast: and I appointed wards of the inhabitants of Jerusalem, everyone in his ward, and everyone over against his house. **4** Now the city was large and great, but the people were few therein, and the houses were not built. **5** And my God put into mine heart, and I gathered the princes, and the rulers, and the people, to count their genealogies: and I found a book of the genealogy of them, [f]which came up at the first, and found written therein, **6** These are the [c]sons of the province that came up from the captivity that was carried away (whom Nebuchadnezzar king of Babel had carried away) and they returned to Jerusalem and to Judah, every one unto his city. **7** They which came with Zerubbabel, Jeshua, Nehemiah, [d]Azariah, Raamiah, Nahamani, Mordecai, Bilshan, Mispereth, Bigvai, Nehum, Baanah. This is the number of the men of the people of Israel. **8** The sons of Parosh, two thousand an hundred seventy and two. **9** The sons of Shephatiah, three hundred seventy and two. **10** The sons of Arah, six hundred fifty and two. **11** The sons of [e]Pahath-Moab of the sons of Jeshua and Joab, two thousand eight hundred and eighteen. **12** The sons of Elam, a thousand two hundred fifty and four. **13** The sons of Zattu, eight hundred and five and forty. **14** The sons of Zaccai, seven hundred and threescore. **15** The sons of Binnui, six hundred and eight and forty. **16** The sons of Bebai, six hundred and eight and twenty. **17** The sons of Azgad, two thousand three hundred and two and twenty. **18** The sons of Adonikam, six hundred

---

NEHEMIAH 5

- **a.** Neh. 5:1 Against the rich which oppressed them.
- **b.** Neh. 5:2 This is the complaint of the people, showing to what extremity they were brought unto.
- **c.** Neh. 5:4 To pay our tribute to the king of the Persians, which was exacted yearly of us.
- **d.** Neh. 5:5 By nature the rich is no better than the poor.
- **e.** Neh. 5:5 We are not able to redeem them, but for poverty are constrained to hire them to others.
- **f.** Neh. 5:7 You press them with usury, and seek how to bring all things into your hands.
- **g.** Neh. 5:7 Both because they should be moved with pity, seeing how many were by them oppressed, and also hear the judgment of others, which should be as it were witnesses of their dealings toward their brethren.
- **h.** Neh. 5:8 Seeing God hath once delivered them from the bondage of the heathen, shall we make them our slaves?
- **i.** Neh. 5:9 Meaning, Neh..
- **j.** Neh. 5:9 Who by this occasion will blaspheme the Name of God, seeing that our acts are no better than theirs.
- **k.** Neh. 5:10 Or, usury.
- **l.** Neh. 5:11 Which ye take of them for the loan.
- **m.** Neh. 5:14 I received not that portion and diet, which the governors that were before me exacted, wherein he declareth that he rather sought the wealth of the people than his own commodity.
- **n.** Neh. 5:18 Or, once in ten days.
- **o.** Neh. 5:18 Whereas at other times they had by measure, at this time they had most liberally.

NEHEMIAH 6

- **a.** Neh. 6:1 That is, that they were joined together, as Neh. 4:6.
- **b.** Neh. 6:3 Meaning, that if he should obey their request, the work which God had appointed, should cease: showing hereby that we should not commit ourselves to the hands of the wicked.
- **c.** Neh. 6:6 Or, Geshem.
- **d.** Neh. 6:6 As the same goeth.
- **e.** Neh. 6:7 Thou hast bribed and set up false prophets, to make thyself king, and so to defraud the king of Persia of that subjection which you owe unto him.
- **f.** Neh. 6:9 Hebrew, strengthen thou mine hand.
- **g.** Neh. 6:10 As though he would be secret, to the intent that he might pray unto God with greater liberty, and receive some revelation, which in him was but hypocrisy.
- **h.** Neh. 6:11 He doubted not but God was able to preserve him, and knew that if he had obeyed this counsel he should have discouraged all the people: thus God giveth power to his to resist false prophecies, though they seem to have never so great probability.
- **i.** Neh. 6:14 Very grief caused him to pray against such, which under the pretence of being the ministers of God, were adversaries to his glory, and went about to overthrow his Church, declaring also hereby that where there is one true minister of God, the devil hath a great sort of hirelings.
- **j.** Neh. 6:15 Which was the sixth month and contained part of August, and part of September.
- **k.** Neh. 6:15 After that I had sent Sanballat his answer.
- **l.** Neh. 6:17 Thus the Church of God hath evermore enemies within itself, which are more dangerous than the outward and professed enemy.

NEHEMIAH 7

- **a.** Neh. 7:3 To wit, they that are mentioned, verse 2.
- **b.** Neh. 7:3 Hebrew, hold them, meaning, till the bars were put in.
- **c.** Neh. 7:6 That is, the inhabitants of Judah.
- **d.** Neh. 7:7 Azariah in Ezra is called Seraiah, and Raamiah, Reelaiah, Ezra 2:2.
- **e.** Neh. 7:11 Or, the captain of Moab.

threescore and seven. **19** The sons of Bigvai, two thousand threescore and seven. **20** The sons of Adin, six hundred and five and fifty. **21** The sons of Ater of Hezekiah, ninety and eight. **22** The sons of Hashum, three hundred and eight and twenty. **23** The sons of Bezai, three hundred and four and twenty. **24** The sons of Hariph, an hundred and twelve. **25** The [f]sons of Gibeon, ninety and five. **26** The men of Bethlehem and Netophah, an hundred fourscore and eight. **27** The men of Anathoth, an hundred and eight and twenty. **28** The men of Beth Azmaveth, two and forty. **29** The men of Kirjath Jearim, Chephirah, and Beeroth, seven hundred and three and forty. **30** The men of Ramah and Geba, six hundred and one and twenty. **31** The men of Michmas, an hundred and two and twenty. **32** The men of Bethel and Ai, an hundred and three and twenty. **33** The men [g]of the other Nebo, two and fifty. **34** The sons of the other Elam, a thousand two hundred and four and fifty. **35** The sons of Harim, three hundred and twenty. **36** The sons of Jericho, three hundred and five and forty. **37** The sons of Lod, Hadid and Ono, seven hundred and one and twenty. **38** The sons of Senaah, three thousand nine hundred and thirty. **39** The Priests: the sons of Jedaiah of the house of Jeshua, nine hundred seventy and three. **40** The sons of Immer, a thousand and two and fifty. **41** The sons of Pashur, a thousand two hundred and seven and forty. **42** The sons of Harim, a thousand and seventeen. **43** The Levites: the sons of Jeshua of Kadmiel, and of the sons of [h]Hodevah, seventy and four. **44** The singers: the children of Asaph, an hundred and eight and forty. **45** The porters: the sons of Shallum, the sons of Ater, the sons of Talmon, the sons of Akkub, the sons of Hatita, the sons of Shobai, an hundred and eight and thirty. **46** The [i]Nethinim: the sons of Ziha, the sons of Hasupha, the sons of Tabbaoth, **47** The sons of Keros, the sons of Sia, the sons of Padon, **48** The sons of Lebana, the sons of Hagaba, the sons of Shalmai, **49** The sons of Hanan, the sons of Giddel, the sons of Gahar, **50** The sons of Reaiah, the sons of Rezin, the sons of Nekoda, **51** The sons of Gazzam, the sons of Uzza, the sons of Paseah, **52** The sons of Besai, the sons of Meunim, the sons of Nephishesim, **53** The sons of Bakbuk, the sons of Hakupha, the sons of Harhur, **54** The sons of Bazlith, the sons of Mehida, the sons of Harsha, **55** The sons of Barkos, the sons of Sisera, the sons of Tamah, **56** The sons of Neziah, the sons of Hatipha, **57** The sons of Solomon's servants, the sons of Sotai, the sons of Sophereth, the sons of Perida, **58** The sons of Jaala, the sons of Darkon, the sons of Giddel, **59** The sons of Shephatiah, the sons of Hattil, the sons of Pochereth of Zebaim, the sons of Amon. **60** All the Nethinim, and the sons of Solomon's servants were three hundred, ninety and two. **61** And these came up from Tel Melah, Tel Harsha, Cherub, Addon, and Immer: but they could not show their father's house, nor their seed, or if they were of Israel. **62** The sons of Delaiah: the sons of Tobiah, the sons of Nekoda, six hundred and two and forty. **63** And of the Priests: the sons of Habaiah, the sons of Koz, the sons of Barzillai, which took one of the daughters of Barzillai the Gileadite to wife, and was named after their name. **64** These sought their writing of the genealogies, but it was not found: therefore they were put from the Priesthood. **65** And [j]the Tirshatha said unto them, that they should not eat of the most holy, till there rose up a Priest with [2]Urim and Thummim. **66** All the Congregation together was two and forty thousand, three hundred and threescore, **67** Besides their servants and their maids, which were seven thousand, three hundred and seven and thirty: and they had two hundred and five and forty singing men and singing women. **68** Their horses were seven hundred and six and thirty, and their mules two hundred and five and forty. **69** The camels four hundred and five and thirty, and six thousand seven hundred and twenty asses. **70** And certain of the chief fathers gave unto the work. The Tirshatha gave to the treasure, a thousand [k]drams of gold, fifty basins, five hundred and thirty Priest's garments. **71** And some of the chief fathers gave unto the treasure of the work, twenty thousand drams of gold, and two thousand and two hundred [l]pieces of silver. **72** And the rest of the people gave twenty thousand drams of gold, and two thousand pieces of silver, and threescore and seven Priest's garments. **73** And the Priests, and the Levites, and the porters and the singers, and the rest of the people and the Nethinim, and all Israel dwelt in their cities: and when the [m]seventh month came, the children of Israel were in their cities.

8

2 Ezra gathereth together the people, and readeth to them the Law. 12 They rejoice in Israel for the knowledge of the word of God. 15 They keep the feast of Tabernacles or booths.

1 And all the people assembled themselves [a]together, in the street that was before the water gate, and they spake unto Ezra the [b]Scribe, that he would bring the book of the Law of Moses, which the Lord had commanded to Israel. **2** And Ezra the Priest brought the Law before the Congregation both of men and women, and of all [c]that could hear and understand it, in the first day of the seventh month, **3** And he read therein in the street that was before the water gate (from the morning until [d]the midday) before men and women, and them that understood it, and the ears of all the people hearkened unto the book of the Law. **4** And Ezra the Scribe stood upon a pulpit of wood which he had made for the preaching, and beside him stood Mattithiah, and Shema, and Anaiah, and Urijah, and Hilkiah, and Maaseiah on his right hand, and on his left hand Pedaiah, and Mishael, and Malchijah, and Hashum, and Hashbadana, Zechariah, and Meshullam. **5** And Ezra opened the book before all the people: for he was [e]above all the people: and when he opened it, all the people stood up. **6** And Ezra praised the Lord the great God, and all the people answered, Amen, Amen, with lifting up their hands: and they bowed themselves, and worshipped the Lord with their faces toward the ground. **7** Also Jeshua, and Bani, and Sherebiah, Jamin, Akkub, Shabbethai, Hodijah, Maaseiah, Kelita, Azariah, Jozabad, Hanan, Pelaiah, and the Levites caused the people to understand the Law, and the people stood in their place. **8** And they read in the book of the Law of God distinctly, and gave the sense, and caused them to understand the reading. **9** Then Nehemiah (which is Tirshatha) and Ezra the Priest and Scribe, and the Levites that instructed the people, said unto all the people, This day is holy unto the Lord your God: mourn not, neither weep: for all the people [f]wept, when they heard the words of the Law. **10** He said also unto them, Go and eat of the fat, and drink the sweet, and send part unto them, for whom none is [g]prepared: for this day is holy unto our Lord: be ye not sorry therefore: for the [h]joy of the Lord is your strength. **11** And the Levites made silence throughout all the people, saying, Hold your peace: for the day is holy, be not sad therefore. **12** Then all the people went to eat and to drink, and to send away part, and to make great joy, because they had understood the words that they had taught them. **13** And on the second day the chief fathers of all the people, the Priests and the Levites were gathered unto Ezra the Scribe, that he also might instruct them in the words of the Law. **14** And they found written in the Law, (that the Lord had commanded Moses) that the children of Israel should dwell in [1]booths in the feast of the seventh month, **15** And that they should cause it to be declared and proclaimed in all their cities, and in Jerusalem, saying, Go forth unto the mount, and bring olive branches, and pine branches, and branches of [i]myrtle, and palm branches, and branches of thick trees, to make booths, as it is written. **16** So the people went forth and brought them, and made them booths, every one upon the [j]roof of his house, and in their courts, and in the courts of the house of God, and in the street by the water gate, and in the street of the gate of Ephraim. **17** And all the Congregation of them that were come again out of the captivity, made booths, and sat under the booths: for since the [k]time of Jeshua the son of Nun unto this day, had not the children of Israel done so, and there was very great joy. **18** And he read in the book of the Law of God every day, from the first day unto the last day. And they kept the feast seven days, and on the eighth day a solemn assembly, according unto the manner.

9

The people repent, and forsake their strange wives. 5 The Levites exhort them to praise God, 6 Declaring his wonders, 26 And their ingratitude, 30 And God's great mercies toward them.

1 In the four and twentieth day of this [a]month the children of Israel were assembled with fasting, and with sackcloth, and earth upon them. **2** (And they that were of the seed of Israel were separated from all the [b]strangers) and they stood and confessed their sins and the iniquities of their fathers. **3** And they stood up in their place and read in the book of the Law of the Lord their God four times on the day, and they [c]confessed and worshipped the Lord their God four times. **4** Then stood up upon the stairs of the Levites, Jeshua, and Bani, Kadmiel, Shebaniah, Bunni, Sherebiah, Bani, and Chenani, and cried with a loud voice unto the Lord their God. **5** And the Levites said, even Jeshua and Kadmiel, Bani, Hashabniah, Sherebiah, Hodijah, Shebaniah and Pethahiah, Stand up and praise the Lord your God forever and ever, and let them praise thy glorious Name, O God, which excelleth above all thanksgiving and praise. **6** Thou art Lord alone: thou hast made heaven, and the heaven of all heavens, with all their host, the earth, and all things that are therein, the seas, and all that are in them and thou

---

f. Neh. 7:25 That is, the inhabitants of Gibeon.
g. Neh. 7:33 For there were two cities of this name.
h. Neh. 7:43 Or, Hodaiah.
i. Neh. 7:46 Read Ezra 2:43.
j. Neh. 7:65 Meaning, Neh.: for Tirshatha in the Chaldean tongue signifieth a butler.
k. Neh. 7:70 Read Ezra 2:69.
l. Neh. 7:71 Or, minas.
m. Neh. 7:73 Which containeth part of September and part of October.

NEHEMIAH 7

1. Ezra 2:2
2. Exod. 28:30

NEHEMIAH 8

a. Neh. 8:1 Hebrew, as one man.
b. Neh. 8:1 Read Ezra 7:6.
c. Neh. 8:2 Which had age and discretion to understand.
d. Neh. 8:3 This declareth the great zeal, that the people had to hear the word of God.
e. Neh. 8:5 To the intent that his voice might be the better heard.
f. Neh. 8:9 In considering their offences against the Law. Therefore the Levites do not reprove them for mourning, but assure them of God's mercies forasmuch as they are repentant.
g. Neh. 8:10 That is, remember the poor.
h. Neh. 8:10 Rejoice in the Lord, and he will give you strength.
i. Neh. 8:15 Or, goodly branches, as Lev. 3:40.
j. Neh. 8:16 For their houses were made flat above, read Deut. 22:8.
k. Neh. 8:17 Which was almost a thousand years.

NEHEMIAH 8

1. Lev. 23:34

NEHEMIAH 9

a. Neh. 9:1 Meaning, the seventh.
b. Neh. 9:2 Hebrew, strange children.
c. Neh. 9:3 They made confession of their sins, and used prayers.

preservest them all and the host of the heaven worshippeth thee. **7** Thou art, O Lord, the God, that hast chosen Abram, and broughtest him out of [1]Ur in Chaldeans, and [2]madest his name Abraham, **8** And foundest his heart faithful before thee, and [3]madest a Covenant with him, to give unto his seed the land of the Canaanites, Hittites, Amorites, and Perizzites, and Jebusites, and Girgashites, and hast performed thy words, because thou art just. **9** [4]Thou hast also considered the affliction of our fathers in Egypt, and heard their cry by the red Sea, **10** And showed tokens and wonders upon Pharaoh, and on all his servants, and on all the people of his land: for thou knewest that they dealt proudly against them: therefore thou madest thee a Name, as appeareth this day. **11** [5]For thou didst break up the Sea before them, and they went through the midst of the sea on dry land: and those that pursued them, hast thou cast into the bottoms as a stone, in the mighty waters: **12** And [6]leddest them in the day with a pillar of a cloud, and in the night with a pillar of fire to give them light in the way that they went. **13** [7]Thou camest down also upon mount Sinai, and spakest unto them from heaven, and gavest them right judgments, and true laws, ordinances and good Commandments, **14** And declaredst unto them thine holy Sabbath, and commandedst them precepts, and ordinances, and laws, by the hand of Moses thy servant: **15** [8]And gavest them bread from heaven for their hunger, and [9]broughtest forth water for them out of the rock for their thirst: and [10]promisedst them that they should go in, and take possession of the land: for the which thou hadst lifted up thine hand for to give them. **16** But they and our fathers behaved themselves proudly and hardened their neck, so that they hearkened not unto thy Commandments, **17** But refused to obey, and would not remember thy marvelous works that thou hadst done for them, but hardened their necks, and had in their heads to return to their bondage by their rebellion: but thou, O God of mercies, gracious and full of compassion, of long-suffering, and of great mercy, yet forsookest them not. **18** Moreover, when they made them a molten calf (and said, This is thy God that brought thee up out of the land of Egypt) and committed great blasphemies, **19** Yet thou for thy great mercies forsookest them not in the wilderness: [11]the pillar of the cloud departed not from them by day to lead them the way, neither the pillar of fire by night, to show them light, and the way whereby they should go. **20** Thou gavest also thy good Spirit to instruct them, and withheldest not thy Manna from their mouth, and gavest them water for their thirst. **21** Thou didst also feed them forty years in the wilderness: they lacked nothing: [12]their clothes waxed not old, and their feet [d]swelled not. **22** And thou gavest them kingdoms and people, and [e]scatteredst them into corners: so they possessed [13]the land of Sihon, and the land of the king of Heshbon, and the land of Og king of Bashan. **23** And thou didst multiply their children like the stars of the heaven, and broughtest them into the land, whereof thou hadst spoken unto their fathers, that they should go, and possess it. **24** So the children went in, and possessed the land, and thou subduedst before them the inhabitants of the land, even the Canaanites, and gavest them into their hands, with their kings and the people of the land, that they might do with them what they would. **25** And they took their strong cities and the fat land, and possessed houses full of all goods, cisterns dug out, vineyards and olives, and trees for food in abundance, and they did eat, and were filled, and became fat, and lived in pleasure through thy great goodness. **26** Yet they were disobedient, and rebelled against thee, and cast thy Law behind their backs, and slew thy Prophets (which [f]protested among them to turn them unto thee) and committed great blasphemies. **27** Therefore thou deliveredst them into the hand of their enemies that vexed them: yet in the time of their affliction, when they cried unto thee, thou heardest them from the heaven, and through thy great mercies thou gavest them saviors, who saved them out of the hand of their adversaries. **28** But when they had [g]rest, they returned to do evil before thee: therefore leftest thou them in the hand of their enemies, so that they had the dominion over them, yet when they converted and cried unto thee, thou heardest them from heaven, and deliveredst them according to thy great mercies many times, **29** And protestedst among them, that thou mightest bring them again unto thy Law: but they behaved themselves proudly, and hearkened not unto thy commandments, but sinned against thy judgments ([14]which a man should do and live in them) and [h]pulled away the shoulder, and were stiff-necked, and would not [i]hear. **30** Yet thou [j]didst forbear them many years, and protestedst among them by thy Spirit, even by the hand of thy Prophets, but they would not hear: therefore gavest thou them into the hand of the people of the lands. **31** Yet for thy great mercies thou hast not consumed them, neither forsaken them: for thou art a gracious and merciful God. **32** Now therefore our God, [15]thou great God, mighty and terrible, that keepest covenant and [16]mercy, let not all the affliction that hath come unto us, seem a little before thee, that is, to our Kings, to our Princes, and to our Priests, and to our Prophets, and to our fathers, and to all thy people since the time of the [k]kings of Assyria unto this day. **33** Surely thou art just in all that is come upon us: for thou hast [l]dealt truly, but we have done wickedly. **34** And our kings and our princes, our priests and our fathers have not done thy Law, nor regarded thy commandments, nor thy protestations, wherewith thou hast [m]protested among them. **35** And they have not served thee in their kingdom, and in thy great goodness that thou showedst unto them, and in the large and fat land which thou didst set before them, and have not converted from their evil works. **36** Behold, we are servants this day, and the land that thou gavest unto our fathers, to eat the [n]fruit thereof, and the goodness thereof, behold, we are servants therein. **37** And it yieldeth much fruit unto the kings whom thou hast set over us, because of our sins: and they have dominion over our bodies, and over our cattle at their pleasure, and we are in great affliction. **38** Now because of all this we make [o]a sure covenant, and write it, and our princes, our Levites, and our Priests seal unto it.

10

1 The names of them that sealed the covenant between God and the people.

1 Now they that sealed, were Nehemiah the [a]Tirshatha the son of Hachaliah, and Zidkijah, **2** Seraiah, Azariah, Jeremiah, **3** Pashur, Amariah, Malchijah, **4** Hattush, Shebaniah, Malluch, **5** Harim, Meremoth, Obadiah, **6** Daniel, Ginnethon, Baruch, **7** Meshullam, Abijah, Mijamin, **8** Maaziah, Bilgai, Shemaiah: these are [b]the Priests. **9** And the Levites: Jeshua the son of Azaniah, Binnui, of the sons of Henadad, Kadmiel. **10** And their brethren, Shebaniah, Hodijah, Kelita, Pelaiah, Hanun, **11** Micha, Rehob, Hashabiah, **12** Zaccur, Sherebiah, Shebaniah, **13** Hodijah, Bani, Beninu. **14** The chief of the people were Parosh, [c]Pahath-Moab, Elam, Zattu, Bani, **15** Bunni, Azgad, Bebai, **16** Adonijah, Bigvai, Adin, **17** Ater, Hezekiah, Azzur, **18** Hodijah, Hashum, Bezai, **19** Hariph, Anathoth, Nebai, **20** Magpiash, Meshullam, Hezir, **21** Meshezabeel, Zadok, Jaddua, **22** Pelatiah, Hanan, Anaiah, **23** Hoshea, Hananiah, Hashub, **24** Hallohesh, Pileha, Shobek, **25** Rehum, Hashabnah, Maaseiah, **26** And Ahijah, Hanan, Anan, **27** Malluch, Harim, Baanah. **28** And the rest of the people, the Priests, the Levites, the porters, the singers, the [d]Nethinim, and all that were [e]separated from the people of the lands unto the Law of God, their wives, their sons and their daughters, all that could understand. **29** The chief of them [f]received it for their brethren, and they came to the [g]curse and to the oath to walk in God's Law, which was given by Moses the servant of God, to observe and do all the commandments of the Lord our God, and his judgments and his statutes: **30** And that we would not give our daughters to the people of the land, neither take their daughters for our sons. **31** And if the people of the land brought ware on the Sabbath, or any vittles to sell, [h]that we would not take it of them on the Sabbath, and on the holy days: [1]and that we would let the seventh year be free, and the debts of every [i]person. **32** And we made statutes for ourselves to give by the year, the third part of a shekel for the service of the house of our God, **33** For the [j]showbread, and for the daily offering, and for the daily burnt offering, the Sabbaths, the new moons, for the solemn feasts, and for the things that were sanctified, and for the sin offerings, to make an atonement for Israel, and for all the work of the house of our God. **34** We cast also lots for the offering of the wood, even the Priests, the Levites, and the people, to bring it into the house of our God, [k]by the house of our fathers, yearly at the times appointed, to burn it upon the Altar of the Lord our God,

---

d. Neh. 9:21 Though the way was tedious and long.
e. Neh. 9:22 Meaning, the heathen whom he drove out.
f. Neh. 9:26 Taking heaven and earth to witness, that God would destroy them, except they returned, as 2 Chron. 24:19.
g. Neh. 9:28 He declareth how God's mercies ever contended with the wickedness of the people, who ever in their prosperity forgat God.
h. Neh. 9:29 Which is a similitude taken of oxen that shrink at the yoke or burden, as Zech. 7:11.
i. Neh. 9:29 When thou didst admonish them by thy Prophets.
j. Neh. 9:30 Hebrew, thou didst prolong upon them many years.
k. Neh. 9:32 By whom we were led away into captivity, and have been appointed to be slain, as Esther 3:13.
l. Neh. 9:33 He confesseth that all these things came to them justly for their sins, but he appealeth from God's justice to his mercies.
m. Neh. 9:34 That thou wouldest destroy them, except they would return to thee, as verse 26.
n. Neh. 9:36 That is, to be the Lord's therof.
o. Neh. 9:38 Thus by affliction they promise to keep God's commandments, whereunto they could not be brought by God's great benefits.

NEHEMIAH 9

1. Gen. 11:31
2. Gen. 17:5
3. Gen. 15:18
4. Exod. 2:76 / Exod. 14:16
5. Exod. 14:10
6. Exod. 13:10
7. Exod. 19:18,20 / Exod. 20:1
8. Exod. 16:18
9. Exod. 17:6
10. Deut. 1:8
11. Exod. 13:22 / Num. 14:14 / 1Cor. 10:1
12. Deut. 8:4
13. Num. 21:26
14. Lev. 18:5 / Ezek. 20:11 / Rom. 10:5 / Gal. 3:12
15. Exod. 34:6,7
16. Ps. 143:1,2

NEHEMIAH 10

a. Neh. 10:1 Or, butler.
b. Neh. 10:8 Which subscribed to keep the promise.
c. Neh. 10:14 Or, captain of Moab.
d. Neh. 10:28 Read Ezra 2:43.
e. Neh. 10:28 Which being idolaters forsook their wickedness, and gave themselves to serve God.
f. Neh. 10:29 They made the oath in the name of the whole multitude.
g. Neh. 10:29 Whereunto they gave themselves if they brake the Law, as Deut. 28:15.
h. Neh. 10:31 Which notwithstanding they brake soon after, as Neh. 13:15.
i. Neh. 10:31 Hebrew, hand.
j. Neh. 10:33 This declareth wherefore they gave this third part of the shekel, which was besides the half shekel that they were bound to pay, Exod. 30:13.
k. Neh. 10:34 Or, into the house of.
l. Neh. 10:36 By this rehearsal is meant that there was no part nor ceremony in the Law, whereunto they did not bind themselves by covenant.
m. Neh. 10:37 Wheresoever we labored, or travailed, there the tithes were due unto the Lord both by the Law, and according to the oath and covenant that we made.
n. Neh. 10:39 We will not leave it destitute of that that shall be necessary for it.

NEHEMIAH 10

1. Lev. 25:4 / Deut. 15:1
2. Num. 18:26

NEHEMIAH 11

a. Neh. 11:1 Because their enemies dwelt round about them, they provided that it might be replenished with men, and used this policy, because there were few that offered themselves willingly.
b. Neh. 11:4 Which came of Perez the son of Judah.
c. Neh. 11:5 Or, of a Shilonite.

as it is written in the Law, **35** And to bring the firstfruits of our land, and the first of all the fruits of all trees, year by year, into the house of the Lord, **36** And the firstborn of our sons, and of our cattle, as it is [l]written in the Law, and the firstborn of our bullocks, and of our sheep, to bring it into the house of our God, unto the Priests that minister in the house of our God, **37** And that we should bring the firstfruit of our dough, and our offerings, and the fruit of every tree, of wine and of oil, unto the Priests, to the chambers of the house of our God: and the tithes of our land unto the Levites, that the Levites might have the tithes in all the cities of our [m]travail. **38** And the Priest, the son of Aaron shall be with the Levites, when the Levites take tithes, and the Levites shall [2]bring up the tenth part of the tithes unto the house of our God, unto the chambers of the treasure house. **39** For the children of Israel, and the children of Levi shall bring up the offering of the corn, of the wine, and of the oil, unto the chambers: and there shall be the vessels of the Sanctuary, and the Priests that minister, and the porters, and the singers, and [n]we will not forsake the house of our God.

11

1 Who dwelled in Jerusalem after it was built, 20 and who in the cities of Judah.

1 And the rulers of the people dwelt in Jerusalem: the other people also cast lots, [a]to bring one out of ten to dwell in Jerusalem the holy city, and nine parts to be in the cities. **2** And the people thanked all the men that were willing to dwell in Jerusalem. **3** These now are the chief of the province, that dwelt in Jerusalem, but in the cities of Judah, everyone dwelt in his own possession in their cities of Israel, the Priests and the Levites, and the Nethinim, and the sons of Solomon's servants. **4** And in Jerusalem dwelt certain of the children of Judah, and of the children of Benjamin: Of the sons of Judah, Athaiah, the son of Uziah, the son of Zechariah, the son of Amariah, the son of Shephatiah, the son of Mahalalel, of the sons of [b]Perez, **5** And Maaseiah the son of Baruch, the son of Col-Hozeh, the son of Hazaiah, the son of Adaiah, the son of Joiarib, the son of Zechariah, the son of [c]Shiloni. **6** All the sons of Perez that dwelt at Jerusalem, were four hundred threescore and eight valiant men. **7** These also are the sons of Benjamin, Sallu, the son of Meshullam, the son of Joed, the son of Pedaiah, the son of Kolaiah, the son of Maaseiah, the son of Ithiel, the son of Jeshaiah. **8** And after him Gabbai, Sallai, nine hundred and twenty and eight. **9** And Joel the son of Zichri was governor over them: and Judah the son of Senuah was the second over the city: **10** Of the Priests, Jedaiah, the son of Joiarib, Jachin. **11** Seraiah, the son of Hilkiah, the son of Meshullam, the son of Zadok, the son of Meraioth, the son of Ahitub, [d]was chief of the house of God. **12** And their brethren [e]that did the work in the Temple, were eight hundred, twenty and two: and Adaiah, the son of Jeroham, the son of Pelaliah, the son of Amzi, the son of Zechariah, the son of Pashur, the son of Malchijah: **13** And his brethren, chief of the fathers, two hundred and two and forty: and Amashsai the son of Azarel, the son of Ahazai, the son of Meshilemoth, the son of Immer: **14** And their brethren valiant men, an hundred and eight and twenty: and their overseer was Zabdiel the son [f]of Haggedolim. **15** And of the Levites, Shemaiah, the son of Hashub, the son of Azrikam, the son of Hashabiah, the son of Bunni. **16** And Shabbethai, and Jozabad of the chief of the Levites were over the works of the house of God without. **17** And Mattaniah, the son of Micha, the son of Zabdi, the son of Asaph was the chief to [g]begin the thanksgiving and prayer: and Bakbukiah the second of his brethren, and Abda, the son of Shammua, the son of Galal, the son of Jeduthun. **18** All the Levites in the holy city were two hundred fourscore and four. **19** And the porters Akkub, Talmon, and their brethren that kept the [h]gates, were an hundred twenty and two. **20** And the [i]residue of Israel, of the Priests, and of the Levites dwelt in all the cities of Judah, everyone in his inheritance. **21** And the Nethinim dwelt in the [j]fortress, and Ziha, and Gispa was over the Nethinim. **22** And the overseer of the Levites in Jerusalem was Uzzi the son of Bani, the son of Hashabiah, the son of Mattaniah, the son of Micha: of the sons of Asaph singers were over the work of the house of God. **23** For it was the king's commandment concerning them, that faithful provision should be for the singers every day. **24** And Pethahiah the son of Meshezabel, of the sons of Zerah, the son of Judah [k]was at the king's hand in all matters concerning the people. **25** And in the villages in their lands, some of the children of Judah dwelt in Kirjath Arba, and in the villages thereof, and in Dibon, and in the villages thereof, and in Jekabzeel, and in the villages thereof, **26** And in Jeshua, and in Moladah, and in Beth Pelet, **27** And in Hazar Shual, and in Beersheba, and in the villages thereof, **28** And in Ziklag, and in Mekonah, and in the villages thereof, **29** And in En Rimmon, and in Zorah, and in Jarmuth, **30** Zanoah, Adullam, and in their villages, in Lachish, and in the fields thereof, at Azekah, and in the villages thereof: and they dwelt from Beersheba, unto the valley of Hinnom. **31** And the sons of Benjamin from Geba, in Michmash, and Aija, and Bethel, and in the villages thereof, **32** And Anathoth, Nob, Ananiah, **33** Hazor, Ramah, Gittaim, **34** Hadid, Zeboim, Neballat, **35** Lod and Ono, in the carpenters valley. **36** And of the Levites were divisions in Judah and in Benjamin.

12

1 The Priests and Levites which came with Zerubbabel unto Jerusalem, are numbered, 27 and the wall is dedicated.

1 These also are the Priests and the Levites that [a]went up with Zerubbabel, the son of Shealtiel, and Jeshua: to wit, Seraiah, Jeremiah, Ezra, **2** Amariah, Malluch, Hattush, **3** Shecaniah, Rehum, Meremoth, **4** Iddo, Ginnethoi, Abijah, **5** Mijamin, Maadiah, Bilgah, **6** Shemaiah, and Joiarib, Jedaiah, **7** Sallu, Amok, Hilkiah, Jedaiah: these were the [b]chief of the Priests, and of their brethren in the days of Jeshua. **8** And the Levites, Jeshua, Binnui, Kadmiel, Sherebiah, Judah, Mattaniah [c]were over the thanksgivings, he, and his brethren. **9** And Bakbukiah and Unni, and their brethren were about them in the [d]watches. **10** And Jeshua begat Joiakim: Joiakim also begat Eliashib, and Eliashib begat Joiada. **11** And Joiada begat Jonathan, and Jonathan begat Jaddua, **12** And in the days of Joiakim were these the chief fathers of the Priests: under [e]Seraiah was Meraiah, under Jeremiah, Hananiah, **13** Under Ezra, Meshullam, under Amariah, Jehohanan, **14** Under Melichu, Jonathan, under Shebaniah, Joseph, **15** Under Harim, Adna, under Maraioth, Helkai, **16** Under Iddo, Zechariah, under Ginnethon, Meshullam, **17** Under [f]Abijah, Zichri, under Minjamin, and under Moadiah, Piltai, **18** Under Bilgah, Shammua, under Shemaiah, Jehonathan, **19** Under Joiarib, Mattenai, under Jedaiah, Uzzi, **20** Under Sallai, Kallai, under Amok, Eber, **21** Under Hilkiah, Hashabiah, under Jedaiah, Nethanel. **22** In the days of Eliashib, Joiada, and Johanan and Jaddua were the chief fathers of the Levites written, and the Priests in the reign of Darius the Persian. **23** The sons of Levi, the chief fathers were written in the book of the Chronicles even unto the days of Johanan the son of Eliashib. **24** And the chief of the Levites were Hashabiah, Sherebiah, and Jeshua the son of Kadmiel, and their brethren about them to give praise and thanks, according to the ordinances of David the man of God, ward over [g]against ward. **25** Mattaniah and Bakbukiah, Obadiah, Meshullam, Talmon and Akkub were porters keeping the ward at the thresholds of the gates. **26** These were in the days of Joiakim the son of Jeshua, the son of Jozadak, and in the days of Nehemiah the captain, and of Ezra the Priest and Scribe. **27** And in the dedication of the wall at Jerusalem, they sought the Levites out of all their places to bring them to Jerusalem to keep the dedication and gladness, both with thanksgivings and with songs, cymbals, viols, and with harps. **28** Then the [h]singers gathered themselves together both from the plain country about Jerusalem, and from the villages of [i]Netophathi, **29** And from the house of Gilgal, and out of the countries of Geba, and Azmaveth: for the singers had built them villages round about Jerusalem. **30** And the Priests and Levites were purified, and cleansed the people, and the gates, and the wall. **31** And [j]I brought up the princes of Judah upon the wall, and appointed two great companies to give thanks, and the one went on the right hand of the wall toward the dung gate. **32** And after them went Hoshaiah, and half of the princes of Judah, **33** And Azariah, Ezra and Meshullam, **34** Judah, Benjamin, and Shemaiah, and Jeremiah, **35** And of the Priest's sons with trumpets, Zechariah, the son of Jonathan, the son of Shemaiah, the son of Mattaniah, the son of Michaiah, the son of Zaccur, the son of Asaph. **36** And [k]his brethren, Shemaiah, and Azarel, Milalai, Gilalai, Maai, Nethanel, and Judah, Hanani, with the musical instruments of David the man of God: and Ezra the Scribe went before them. **37** And to the gate of the fountain, even over against them went they up by the [l]stairs of the city of David, at the going up of the wall beyond the house of David, even unto the water gate Eastward. **38** And the second company of them that gave thanks, went on the other side, and I after them, and the half of the people was upon the wall, and upon the tower of the furnaces even unto the broad wall. **39** And upon the gate of Ephraim, and upon the old gate, and upon the fish gate, and the tower of Hananel, and the tower of Meah, even unto the sheep gate: and they stood in the gate of the ward. **40** So stood the two companies (of them that gave thanks) in the house of God, and I and the half of the rulers with me. **41** The Priests also, Eliakim, Maaseiah, Minjamin, Michaiah, Elioenai, Zechariah, Hananiah, with trumpets, **42** And Maaseiah, and Shemaiah, and Eleazar, and Uzzi, and Jehohanan, and Malchijah, and Elam, and Ezer: and the singers [m]sang loud, having Jezrahiah which was the overseer. **43** And the same day they offered great sacrifices and rejoiced: for God had given them great joy, so that both the women, and the children were joyful: and the joy of Jerusalem was heard far off. **44** Also

---

d. Neh. 11:11 That is, was the high Priest.
e. Neh. 11:12 That served and ministered in the Temple.
f. Neh. 11:14 Or, of one of the great men.
g. Neh. 11:17 That is, he began the Psalm, and was the chanter.
h. Neh. 11:19 Meaning, of the Temple.
i. Neh. 11:20 Of them, which dwelt not in Jerusalem.
j. Neh. 11:21 Or, Ophel.
k. Neh. 11:24 Was chief about the king for all his affairs.

NEHEMIAH 12

a. Neh. 12:1 From Babylon to Jerusalem.
b. Neh. 12:7 Next in dignity to the high Priests, and which were of the stock of Aaron.
c. Neh. 12:8 Had charge of them that sang the Psalms.
d. Neh. 12:9 They kept the wards and watches according to their turns, as 2 Chron. 23:6.
e. Neh. 12:12 That is, next to Seraiah, or rather of the order, which was called after the name of Seraiah.
f. Neh. 12:17 Whereof was Zacharias, John Baptist's father.
g. Neh. 12:24 That is, one after another, and every one in his course.
h. Neh. 12:28 Hebrew, the sons of the singers.
i. Neh. 12:28 Which were a certain family, and had their possessions in the fields, 1 Chron. 2:54.
j. Neh. 12:31 Meaning, Neh..
k. Neh. 12:36 That is, the brethren of Zaccur.
l. Neh. 12:37 Which was the going up to the mount Zion, which is called the city of David.
m. Neh. 12:42 Hebrew, caused to hear.
n. Neh. 12:44 Which were chambers appointed by Hezekiah to put in the tithes, and such things, 2 Chron. 31:11 and now were repaired again for the same use.
o. Neh. 12:47 That is, the tenth part of the tithes.

at the same time were men appointed [n]over the chambers of the store for the offerings, (for the firstfruits, and for the tithes) to gather into them out of the fields of the cities, the portions of the Law for the Priests, and the Levites, for Judah rejoiced for the Priests and for the Levites, that served. **45** And both the singers and the Levites kept the ward of their God, and the ward of the purification according to the commandment of David, and Solomon his son. **46** [1]For in the days of David and Asaph, of old were chief singers, and songs of praise and thanksgiving unto God. **47** And in the days of Zerubbabel, and in the days of Nehemiah did all Israel give portions unto the singers and porters, every day his portion, and they gave the holy things unto the Levites, and the Levites [o]gave the holy things unto the sons of Aaron.

13

1 The Law is read. 3 They separate from them all strangers. 15 Nehemiah reproveth them that break the Sabbath. 30 An ordinance to serve God.

1 And on that day they did read in the book of Moses, in the audience of the people, and it was found written therein, that the Ammonite, and the Moabite [1]should not enter into the Congregation of God, **2** Because they met not the children of Israel with bread and with water, [2]but hired Balaam against them, that he should curse them: and our God turned the curse into a blessing. **3** Now when they had heard the Law, they separated from Israel [a]all those that were mixed. **4** And before [b]this had the Priest Eliashib the oversight of the chamber of the house of our God, being [c]kinsman to Tobiah: **5** And he had made him a great chamber, and there had they aforetime laid the offerings, the incense, and the vessels, and the tithes of corn, of wine, and of oil (appointed for the Levites, and the singers, and the porters) and the offerings of the Priests. **6** But in all this time was not I in Jerusalem: for in the two and thirtieth year of [d]Artachshashta King of Babel, came I unto the King, and [e]after certain days I obtained of the King. **7** And when I was come to Jerusalem, I understood [f]the evil that Eliashib had done for Tobiah, in that he had made him a chamber in the court of the house of God, **8** And it grieved me sore: therefore I cast forth all the vessels of the house of Tobiah out of the chamber. **9** And I commanded them to cleanse the chambers: and thither brought I again the vessels of the house of God with the meat offering and the incense. **10** And I perceived that the portions of the Levites had not been given, and that everyone was fled to his land, even the Levites and singers that executed the work. **11** Then reproved I the rulers and said, Why is the house of God forsaken? And I assembled them, and set them in their place. **12** Then brought all Judah the tithes of corn and of wine, and of oil unto the treasures. **13** And I made treasurers over the treasures, Shelemiah the Priest, and Zadok the scribe, and of the Levites, Pedaiah, and under their hand Hanan the son of Zaccur the son of Mattaniah: for they were counted faithful, and their office was to distribute unto their brethren. **14** Remember me, O my God, herein, and wipe not out my [g]kindness that I have showed on the house of my God, and on the offices thereof. **15** In those days saw I in Judah them, that trod wine presses on the Sabbath, and that brought in sheaves, and which laded asses also with wine, grapes, and figs, and all burdens, and brought them into Jerusalem upon the Sabbath day: and [h]I protested to them in the day that they sold vittles. **16** There dwelt men of Tyre also therein, which brought fish and all wares, and sold on the Sabbath unto the children of Judah even in Jerusalem. **17** Then reproved I the rulers of Judah, and said unto them, What evil thing is this that ye do, and break the Sabbath day? **18** Did not your fathers [i]thus, and our God brought all this plague upon us, and upon this city? yet ye increase the wrath upon Israel, in breaking the Sabbath. **19** And when the gates of Jerusalem began to be [j]dark before the Sabbath, I commanded to shut the gates, and charged, that they should not be opened till after the Sabbath, and some of my servants set I at the gates, that there should no burden be brought in on the Sabbath day. **20** So the chapmen and merchants of all merchandise remained once or twice all night without Jerusalem. **21** And I protested among them, and said unto them, Why tarry ye all night about the wall? If ye do it once again, I will lay hands upon you. From that time came they no more on the Sabbath. **22** And I said unto the Levites, that they should cleanse themselves, and that they should come and [k]keep the gates, to sanctify the Sabbath day. Remember me, O my God, concerning this, and pardon me according to thy great mercy. **23** In those days also I saw Jews that married wives of [l]Ashdod, of Ammon, and of Moab. **24** And their children spake half in the speech of Ashdod, and could not speak in the Jews' language, and according to the language of the one people, and of the other people. **25** Then I reproved them, and [m]cursed them, and smote certain of them, and pulled off their hair, and took an oath of them by God, Ye shall not give your daughters unto their sons, neither shall ye take of their daughters unto your sons nor for yourselves. **26** [3]Did not Solomon the king of Israel sin by these things? yet among many nations was there no King like him: for he was [4]beloved of his God, and God had made him King over Israel: [5]yet strange women caused him to sin. **27** Shall we then obey unto you, to do all this great evil, and to transgress against our God, even to marry strange wives? **28** And one of the sons of Joiada the son of Eliashib the high Priest was the son-in-law of Sanballat the Horonite: but I chased him from me. **29** Remember them, O my God, that [n]defile the Priesthood, and the covenant of the Priesthood, and of the Levites. **30** Then cleansed I them from all strangers, and appointed the wards of the Priests and of the Levites, every one in his office, **31** And for the offering of the wood at times appointed, and for the firstfruits. Remember me, O my God, [o]in goodness.

NEHEMIAH 12

1. 1 Chron. 15:16

NEHEMIAH 13

a. Neh. 13:3 That is, all such which had joined in unlawful marriage, and also those with whom God had forbidden them to have society.
b. Neh. 13:4 That the separation was made.
c. Neh. 13:4 He was joined in affinity with Tobiah the Ammonite and enemy of the Jews.
d. Neh. 13:6 Called also Darius, Ezra 7:1.
e. Neh. 13:6 Or, at the year's end.
f. Neh. 13:7 Thus we see to what inconveniences the people fall into, when they are destitute of one that hath the fear of God, seeing that their chief governor was but a while absent, and yet they fell into such great absurdities: as appeareth also, Exod. 32:1.
g. Neh. 13:14 He protesteth that he did his duty with a good conscience, yet he doth not justify himself in therein, but desireth God to favor him and to be merciful unto him for his own goodness sake, as verse 22 and 31.
h. Neh. 13:15 I declared unto them, that God would not suffer such transgressors of his Law to be unpunished.
i. Neh. 13:18 Was not this a great cause, why God plagued us in times past: meaning, that if they transgressed now in the same again, their plague should be greater.
j. Neh. 13:19 About the time that the Sun went down: for the Sabbath lasted from the Sun going down of the one day, to the Sun setting of the other.
k. Neh. 13:22 Meaning, of the Temple, that none that was unclean, should enter.
l. Neh. 13:23 Which was a city of the Philistines, and they had married wives thereof, and so had corrupted their speech and Religion.
m. Neh. 13:25 That is, I did excommunicate them, and drive them out of the congregation.
n. Neh. 13:29 Punish them according to their fault and evil example, which they have given to the rest of thy people contrary to their vocation.
o. Neh. 13:31 That is, to show mercy unto me.

NEHEMIAH 13

1. Deut. 23:3 / Num. 22:5,6
2. 2 Kings 3:7,12
3. 2 Sam. 12:24,25
4. 1 Kings 11:1,4

ESTHER

1

3 King Ahasuerus maketh a royal feast. 12 Whereunto the Queen Vashti will not come. 19 For which cause she is divorced. 20 The King's decree touching the pre-eminence of man.

1 In the days of [a]Ahasuerus (this is Ahasuerus that reigned from India even unto Ethiopia, over an [b]hundred, and seven and twenty provinces.) **2** In those days when the king Ahasuerus [c]sat on his throne, which was in the palace of [1]Shushan, **3** In the third year of his reign, he made a feast unto all his princes and his servants, even the power of Persia and Media, and to the captains and governors of the provinces which were before him, **4** That he might show the riches and glory of his kingdom, and the honor of his great majesty many days, even an hundred and fourscore days. **5** And when these days were expired, the king made a feast to all the people that were found in the palace of Shushan, both unto great and small, seven days, in the court of the garden of the king's palace, **6** Under an hanging of white, green, and blue cloths, fastened with cords of fine linen and purple, in silver rings, and pillars of marble: the [d]beds were of gold and of silver upon a pavement of porphyry, and marble and alabaster, and blue color. **7** And they gave them drink in vessels of gold, and changed vessel after vessel, and royal wine in abundance, according to the [e]power of the king. **8** And the drinking was by an order, none might [f]compel: for so the king had appointed unto all the officers of his house, that they should do according to every man's pleasure. **9** The Queen Vashti made a feast also for the women in the royal house of King Ahasuerus. **10** Upon the [g]seventh day when the King was merry with wine, he commanded Mehuman, Biztha, Harbona, Bigtha, and Abagtha, Zethar, and Carcas, the seven eunuchs, (that served in the presence of king Ahasuerus) **11** To bring Queen Vashti before the king with the crown royal, that he might show the people and the princes her beauty: for she was fair to look upon. **12** But the Queen Vashti refused to come at the king's word, [h]which he had given in charge to the eunuchs: therefore the King was very angry, and his wrath kindled in him. **13** Then the King said to the wise men, [i]that knew the times (for so was the King's manner towards all that knew the law and the judgment: **14** And the next unto him was Carshena, Shethar, Admatha, Tarshish, Meres, Marsena, and Memucan the seven Princes of Persia, and Media, which saw the [j]King's face, and sat the first in the kingdom.) **15** What shall we do unto the Queen Vashti according to the law, because she did not according to the word of the King Ahasuerus by the commission of the eunuchs? **16** Then Memucan answered before the king and the Princes, The Queen Vashti hath not only done [k]evil against the King, but against all the Princes, and against all the people that are in all the provinces of King Ahasuerus. **17** For the [l]act of the Queen shall come abroad unto all women, so that they shall despise their husbands in their own eyes, and shall say, The King Ahasuerus commanded Vashti the Queen to be brought in before him, but she came not. **18** So shall the [m]Princesses of Persia and Media this day say unto all the King's Princes, when they hear of the act of the Queen: thus shall there be much despitefulness and wrath. **19** If it please the King, let a royal decree proceed from him, and let it be written among the statutes of Persia and Media, (and let it not be transgressed) that Vashti come [n]no more before king Ahasuerus: and let the king give her royal estate unto her companion that is better than she. **20** And when the decree of the King which shall be made, shall be published throughout all his kingdom (though it be [o]great) all the women shall give their husbands honor, both great and small. **21** And this saying pleased the King and the Princes, and the King did according to the word of Memucan. **22** For he sent letters into all the provinces of the King, into every province according to the writing thereof, and to every people after their language, that every man should [p]bear rule in his own house, and that he should publish it in the language of that same people.

2

2 After the Queen is put away, certain young maids are brought to the king. 17 Esther pleaseth the King, and is made Queen. 22 Mordecai discloseth unto the king those that would betray him.

1 After these things, when the wrath of King Ahasuerus was appeased, he [a]remembered Vashti, and what she had done, and what was decreed [b]against her. **2** And the King's servants that ministered unto him, said, Let them seek for the King beautiful young virgins, **3** And let the King appoint officers through all the provinces of his Kingdom, and let them gather all the beautiful young virgins unto the palace of Shushan, into the house of the women, under the hand of Hegai the King's eunuch, [c]keeper of the women, to give them their things [d]for purification. **4** And the maid that shall please the King, let her reign in the stead of Vashti. And this pleased the king, and he did so. **5** In the city of Shushan there was a certain Jew, whose name was Mordecai, the son of Jair, the son of Shimei, the son of Kish a man of Benjamin, **6** Which had been carried away from Jerusalem [1]with the captivity that was carried away with Jeconiah King of Judah (whom Nebuchadnezzar king of Babel had carried away.) **7** And he nourished Hadassah, that is, Esther, his uncle's daughter: for she had neither father nor mother, and the maid was fair and beautiful to look on: and after the death of her father, and her mother, Mordecai took her for his own daughter. **8** And when the king's commandment, and his decree was published, and many maids were brought together to the palace of Shushan, under the hand of Hegai, Esther was brought also unto the King's house under the hand of Hegai the keeper of the women. **9** And the maid pleased him, and she found favor in his sight, therefore he caused her things for purification to be given her speedily, and her [e]state, and seven comely maids to be given her out of the King's house, and he gave change to her and to her maids of the best in the house of the women. **10** But Esther showed not her people and her kindred: for Mordecai had charged her that she should not tell it. **11** And Mordecai walked [f]every day before the court of the women's house, to know if Esther did well, and what should be done with her. **12** And when the course of every maid came, to go in to King Ahasuerus, after that she had been twelve months according to the manner of the women (for so were the days of their purifications accomplished, six months with oil of myrrh, and six months with sweet odors and in the purifying of the women: **13** And thus went the maids unto the King) whatsoever she required, was [g]given her to go with her out of the women's house unto the king's house. **14** In the evening she went, and on the morrow she returned into the second house of the women under the hand of Shaashgaz the King's eunuch, which kept the concubines: she came in to the King no more, except she pleased the King, and that she were called by name. **15** Now when the course of Esther the daughter of Abihail the uncle of Mordecai (which had taken her as his own daughter) came, that she should go in to the king, she desired nothing, but what [h]Hege the king's eunuch the keeper of the women [i]said: and Esther found favor in the sight of all them that looked upon her. **16** So Esther was taken unto king Ahasuerus into his house royal in the tenth month, which is the [j]month Tebeth, in the seventh year of his reign. **17** And the King loved Esther above all the women, and she found grace and favor in his sight more than all the virgins: so that he set the crown of the kingdom upon her head, and made her Queen instead of Vashti. **18** Then the king made a great feast unto all his princes, and his servants, which was [k]the feast of Esther, and gave rest [l]unto the

---

ESTHER 1

a. Esther 1:1 Called also Darius, who was now the sovereign Monarch and had the government of the Medes, Persians, and Chaldeans, some think he was Darius Hystaspis' son called also Artaxerxes.
b. Esther 1:1 Dan. 6:1, maketh mention but of sixscore, leaving out the number that is unprecise as the Scripture in divers places useth.
c. Esther 1:2 That is, had rest and quietness.
d. Esther 1:6 Which they used in those countries instead of tables.
e. Esther 1:7 As was beseeming for so magnificent a king.
f. Esther 1:8 None might be compelled to drink more than it pleased him.
g. Esther 1:10 Which was the last day of the feast that the king made for the people, as verse 5.
h. Esther 1:12 Hebrew, which was in the hand of the eunuchs.
i. Esther 1:13 That had experience of things as they had learned by diligent marking in continuance of time.
j. Esther 1:14 Which were his chief counselors, that might have always access to him.
k. Esther 1:16 By her disobedience she hath given an example to all women to do the like to their husbands.
l. Esther 1:17 That is, her disobedience.
m. Esther 1:18 Meaning, that they would take first occasion thereof to do the like, and that the rest of women would by continuance do the same.
n. Esther 1:19 Let her be divorced, and another made Queen.
o. Esther 1:20 For he had under him an hundred twenty and seven countries.
p. Esther 1:22 That is, that the wife should be subject to the husband and at his commandment.

ESTHER 1

1. Neh 1:1

ESTHER 2

a. Esther 2:1 That is, he called the matter again into communication.
b. Esther 2:1 By the seven wise men of his counsel.
c. Esther 2:3 The abuse of these countries was so great, that they invented many means to serve the lusts of Princes, and therefore as they ordained wicked laws, that the king might have whose daughters he would, so they had divers houses appointed, as one for them while they were virgins, another when they were concubines and for the Queens another.
d. Esther 2:3 Read what this purification was, verse 12.
e. Esther 2:9 Hebrew, portions.
f. Esther 2:11 For though she was taken away by a cruel law, yet he ceased not to have a fatherly care over her, and therefore did resort ofttimes to hear of her.
g. Esther 2:13 What apparel she asked of the eunuch, that was he bound to give her.
h. Esther 2:15 Or, Hegai.
i. Esther 2:15 Wherein her modesty appeared, because she sought not apparel to commend her beauty, but stood to the Eunuch's appointment.
j. Esther 2:16 Which contained part of December and part of January.
k. Esther 2:18 That is, made for her sake.
l. Esther 2:18 He released their tribute.
m. Esther 2:18 That is, great and magnificent.

provinces, and gifts, according to the [m]power of a king. 19 And when the vir-
gins were gathered the [n]second time, then Mordecai sat in the king's gate. 20
Esther had not yet showed her kindred nor her people, as Mordecai had charged
her: for Esther did after the word of Mordecai, as when she was nourished with
him. 21 In those days when Mordecai sat in the king's gate, two of the king's
eunuchs, Bigthan and Teresh, which kept the door, were wroth, and sought to lay
[o]hand on the King Ahasuerus. 22 And the thing was known to Mordecai, and
he told it unto Queen Esther, and Esther certified the king thereof in Mordecai's
name: and when inquisition was made, it was found so: therefore they were both
hanged on a tree: and it was written in the book of the [p]Chronicles before the king.

3

1 Haman, after he was exalted, obtained of the King, that all the Jews should be put to death, because Mordecai had not done him worship as others had.

1 After these things did king Ahasuerus promote Haman the son of Hamme-
datha the Agagite, and exalted him, and set his seat above all the princes that were
with him. 2 And all the king's servants that were at the king's gate, bowed their
knees, and reverenced Haman: for the king had so commanded concerning him:
but Mordecai [a]bowed not the knee, neither did reverence. 3 Then the king's ser-
vants which were at the king's gate, said unto Mordecai, Why transgressest thou
the king's commandment? 4 And albeit they spake daily unto him, yet he would
not hear them: therefore they [b]told Haman, that they might see how Mordecai's
matters would stand: for he had told them, that he was a Jew. 5 And when Ha-
man saw that Mordecai bowed not the knee unto him, nor did reverence unto him,
then Haman was full of wrath. 6 Now he [c]thought it too little to lay hands only
on Mordecai: and because they had showed him the people of Mordecai, Haman
sought to destroy all the Jews that were throughout the whole kingdom of Aha-
suerus, even the people of Mordecai. 7 In the first month (that is the month
[d]Nisan) in the twelfth year of king Ahasuerus, they cast Pur (that is a lot) [e]before
Haman, from day to day, and from month to month unto the twelfth month, that
is the month [f]Adar. 8 Then Haman said unto king Ahasuerus, There is a people
scattered, and dispersed among the people in all the provinces of thy kingdom,
and their laws are divers from all people, and they do not observe the [g]King's laws:
therefore it is not the king's profit to suffer them. 9 If it please the king, let it
be written that they may be destroyed, and I will [h]pay ten thousand talents of sil-
ver by the hands of them that have the charge of this business to bring it into the
king's treasury. 10 Then the king took his ring from his hand, and gave it unto
Haman the son of Hammedatha the Agagite the Jews' adversary. 11 And the
king said unto Haman, Let the silver be thine, and the people to do with them as
it pleaseth thee. 12 Then were the king's [i]Scribes called on the thirteenth day of
the first month, and there was written (according to all that Haman commanded)
unto the king's officers, and to the captains that were over every province, and to
the rulers of every people, and to every province, according to the writing thereof,
and to every people according to their language: in the name of king Ahasuerus was
it written, and sealed with the king's ring. 13 And the letters were sent [j]by posts
into all the king's provinces, to root out, to kill and to destroy all the Jews, both
young and old, children and women, in one day upon the thirteenth day of the
twelfth month (which is the month Adar) and to spoil them as a prey. 14 The
contents of the writing was, that there should be given a commandment in all pro-
vinces, and published unto all people, that they should be ready against the same
day. 15 And the posts compelled by the King's commandment went forth, and
the commandment was given in the palace at Shushan: and the king and Haman
sat drinking, but the [k]city of Shushan was in perplexity.

4

5 Mordecai giveth the Queen knowledge of the cruel decree of the king against the Jews. 16 She willeth that they pray for her.

1 Now when Mordecai perceived all that was done, Mordecai rent his clothes,
and put on sackcloth, and ashes, and went out into the midst of the city, and cried
with a great cry, and a bitter. 2 And he came even before the King's [a]gate, but
he might not enter within the king's gate, being clothed with sackcloth. 3 And
in every province and place, whither the king's charge and his commission came,
there was great sorrow among the Jews, and fasting, and weeping, and mourning,
and [b]many lay in sackcloth and in ashes. 4 Then Esther's maids and her Eunu-
chs came and told it her: therefore the queen was very heavy, and she sent raiment
to clothe Mordecai, and to take away his sackcloth from him, but he received it
not. 5 Then called Esther Hathach one of the King's eunuchs, whom he [c]had
appointed to serve her, and gave him a commandment unto Mordecai, to know
what it was, and why it was. 6 So Hathach went forth to Mordecai unto the
street of the city, which was before the king's gate. 7 And Mordecai told him
of all that which had come unto him, and of the [d]sum of the silver that Haman
had promised to pay unto the King's treasures, because of the Jews, for to destroy
them. 8 Also he gave him the [e]copy of the writing and commission that was gi-
ven at Shushan, to destroy them, that he might show it unto Esther and declare it
unto her, and to charge her that she should go in to the king, and make petition
and supplication before him for her people. 9 So when Hathach came, he told
Esther the words of Mordecai. 10 Then Esther said unto Hathach, and com-
manded him to say unto Mordecai, 11 All the king's servants and the people of
the King's provinces do know, That whosoever, man or woman, that cometh to the
king into the inner court, which is not called, there is a law of his, that he shall die,
except him to whom the king holdeth out the golden rod, that he may live. Now I
have not been called to come unto the king these thirty days. 12 And they cer-
tified Mordecai of Esther's words. 13 And Mordecai said, that they should an-
swer Esther thus, Think not with thyself that thou shalt escape in the king's house,
more than all the Jews. 14 For if thou holdest thy peace at this time, [f]comfort
and deliverance [g]shall appear to the Jews out of another place, but thou and thy fa-
ther's house shall perish: and who knoweth whether thou art come to the kingdom
for [h]such a time? 15 Then Esther commanded to answer Mordecai, 16 Go,
and assemble all the Jews that are found in Shushan, and fast ye for me, and eat
not, nor drink in three days, day nor night. I also and my maids will fast likewise,
and so will I go in to the King, which is not according to the law: and if I perish, [i]I
perish. 17 So Mordecai went his way, and did according to all that Esther had
commanded him.

5

1 Esther entereth to the King, and biddeth him and Haman to a feast. 14 Haman prepareth a gallows for Mordecai.

1 And on the third [a]day Esther put on her royal apparel, and stood in the
court of the King's palace within, over against the King's house: and the King sat
upon his royal throne in the king's palace over against the gate of the house. 2
And when the King saw Esther the Queen standing in the court, she found favor in
his sight: and the King [b]held out the golden scepter that was in his hand: so Esther
drew near, and touched the top of the scepter. 3 Then said the King unto her,
What wilt thou, Queen Esther? and what is thy request? it shall be even [c]given thee
to the half of the kingdom. 4 Then said Esther, If it please the king, let the King
and Haman come this day unto the banquet, that I have prepared for him. 5
And the king said, Cause Haman to make haste, that he may do as Esther hath
said. So the king and Haman came to the banquet that Esther had prepared. 6
And the king said unto Esther at the banquet of [d]wine, What is thy petition, that
it may be given thee? and what is thy request? it shall even be performed unto the
half of the kingdom. 7 Then answered Esther, and said, My petition, and my re-
quest is, 8 If I have found favor in the sight of the king, and if it please the king
to give me my petition, and to perform my request, let the king and Haman come
to the banquet that I shall prepare for them, and I will do tomorrow according to
the king's [e]saying. 9 Then went Haman forth the same day joyful, and with a
glad heart. But when Haman saw Mordecai in the king's gate, that he stood not
up, nor moved for him, then was Haman full of indignation at Mordecai. 10
Nevertheless, Haman refrained himself: and when he came home, he sent, and cal-
led for his friends, and Zeresh his wife. 11 And Haman told them of the glory
of his riches, and the multitude of his children, and all the things wherein the king

---

n. Esther 2:19 That is, at the marriage of Esther, which was the second marriage of the king.
o. Esther 2:21 Meaning, to kill him.
p. Esther 2:22 In the Chronicles of the Medes and Persians, as Esther 10:2.

ESTHER 2
1. 2 Kings 14:15

ESTHER 3
a. Esther 3:2 The Persians' manner was to kneel down and reverence their kings, and such as he appointed in chief authority, which Mordecai would not do to this ambitious and proud man.
b. Esther 3:4 Thus we see that there is none so wicked, but they have their flatterers to accuse the godly.
c. Esther 3:6 Hebrew, despised in his eyes.
d. Esther 3:7 Which answereth to part of March and part of April.
e. Esther 3:7 To know what month and day should be good to enterprise this thing, that it might have good success: but God disappointed their lots, and expectation.
f. Esther 3:7 Containing part of February and part of March.
g. Esther 3:8 These be the two arguments which commonly the worldlings and the wicked use toward princes against the godly, that is, the contempt of their laws, and diminishing of their profit: without respect how God is either pleased or displeased.
h. Esther 3:9 Hebrew, weigh.
i. Esther 3:12 Or, secretaries.
j. Esther 3:13 Hebrew, the hands of posts.
k. Esther 3:15 To wit, the Jews that were in Shushan.

ESTHER 4
a. Esther 4:2 Because he would advertise Esther of this cruel proclamation.
b. Esther 4:3 Hebrew, sackcloth and ashes were spread for many.
c. Esther 4:5 Hebrew, had caused to stand before her.
d. Esther 4:7 Hebrew, declaration.
e. Esther 4:8 Or, contents.
f. Esther 4:14 Hebrew, breathing.
g. Esther 4:14 Thus Mordecai spake in the confidence of that faith which all God's children ought to have: which is, that God will deliver them, though all worldly means fail.
h. Esther 4:14 For to deliver God's Church out of these present dangers.
i. Esther 4:16 I will put my life in danger and refer the success to God, seeing it is for his glory and the deliverance of his Church.

ESTHER 5
a. Esther 5:1 To wit, after that the Jews had begun to fast.
b. Esther 5:2 Which was a sign that her coming was agreeable unto him, as Esther 4:11.
c. Esther 5:3 Meaning hereby, that whatsoever she asked should be granted, as Mark 6:23.
d. Esther 5:6 Because they used to drink excessively in their banquets, they called the banquet by the name of that which was most in use or esteemed.
e. Esther 5:8 I will declare what thing I demand.
f. Esther 5:11 Thus the wicked when they are promoted, instead of acknowledging their charge and humbling themselves, wax ambitious, disdainful, and cruel.

had [f]promoted him, and how that he had set him above the princes and servants of
the king. **12** Haman said moreover, Yea, Esther the queen did let no man come
in with the king to the banquet that she had prepared, save me: and tomorrow am
I bidden unto her also with the king. **13** But all this doth nothing avail me, as
long as I see Mordecai the Jew sitting at the king's gate. **14** Then said Zeresh his
wife and all his friends unto him, Let them make a tree of fifty [g]cubits high, and
tomorrow speak thou unto the king, that Mordecai may be hanged thereon: then
shalt thou go joyfully with the king unto the banquet. And the thing pleased Ha-
man, and he caused to make the tree.

6

*2 The king turneth over the Chronicles, and findeth the fidelity of Morde-
cai, 10 and commandeth Haman to cause Mordecai to be had in honor.*

1 The same night [a]the king slept not, and he commanded to bring the book
of the Records, and the Chronicles: and they were read before the king. **2** Then
it was found written that Mordecai [1]had told of Bigthana and Teresh, two of the
king's eunuchs keepers of the door, who sought to lay hands on the King Ahasue-
rus. **3** Then the king said, What honor and dignity hath been given to Mordecai
[b]for this? And the king's servants that ministered unto him, said, There is nothing
done for him. **4** And the king said, Who is in the court? (Now Haman was come
into the inner court of the king's house, that he might speak unto the king to [c]hang
Mordecai on the tree that he had prepared for him.) **5** And the king's servants
said unto him, Behold, Haman standeth in the court. And the king said, Let him
come in. **6** And when Haman came in, the king said unto him, What shall be
done unto the man whom the king will honor? Then Haman thought in his heart,
To whom would the king do honor more than to me? **7** And Haman answered
the king, The man whom the king would honor, **8** Let them bring for him royal
apparel, which the king useth to wear, and the [d]horse that the king rideth upon,
and that the crown royal may be set upon his head. **9** And let the raiment and
the horse be delivered by the hand of one of the king's most noble princes, and let
them apparel the man (whom the king will honor) and cause him to ride upon
the horse through the street of the city, and proclaim before him, Thus shall it be
done unto the man whom the king will honor. **10** Then the king said to Ha-
man, Make haste, take the raiment and the horse, as thou hast said, and do so unto
Mordecai the Jew, that sitteth at the king's gate: let nothing fail of all that thou hast
spoken. **11** So Haman took the raiment and the horse, and arrayed Mordecai,
and brought him on horseback through the street of the city, and proclaimed be-
fore him, Thus shall it be done to the man whom the king will honor. **12** And
Mordecai came again to the king's gate, but Haman hasted home mourning and
his head covered. **13** And Haman told Zeresh his wife, and all his friends, all
that had befallen him. Then said his wise men, and Zeresh his wife unto him, If
Mordecai be of the seed of the Jews, before whom thou hast begun to fall, thou
shalt not prevail against him, [e]but shalt surely fall before him. **14** And while
they were yet talking with him, came the king's eunuchs and hasted to bring Ha-
man unto the banquet that Esther had prepared.

7

*3 The queen biddeth the king and Haman again, and prayeth for herself and
her people. 6 She accuseth Haman, and he is hanged on the gallows which
he had prepared for Mordecai.*

1 So the king and Haman came to banquet with the queen Esther. **2** And
the king said again unto Esther on the second day at the banquet of [a]wine, What
is thy petition, Queen Esther, that it may be given thee? and what is thy request? It
shall be even performed unto the half of the kingdom. **3** And Esther the queen
answered, and said, If I have found favor in thy sight, O king, and if it please the
king, let my life be given me at my petition, and my people at my request. **4** For
we are sold, I, and my people, to be destroyed, to be slain, and to perish: but if we
were sold for servants, and for handmaids, I would have held my tongue, althou-
gh the adversary could not [b]recompense the king's loss. **5** Then king Ahasuerus
answered, and said unto the queen Esther, Who is he? and where is he that [c]pre-
sumeth to do thus? **6** And Esther said, The adversary and enemy is this wicked
Haman. Then Haman was afraid before the king and the queen. **7** And the king
arose from the banquet of wine in his wrath, and went into the palace garden: but
Haman stood up to make request for his life to the queen Esther: for he saw that
there was a [d]mischief prepared for him of the king. **8** And when the king came
again out of the palace garden, into the house where they drank wine, Haman was
[e]fallen upon the bed whereon Esther sat: therefore the King said, Will he force the
Queen also before me in the house? As the word went out of the King's mouth,
they [f]covered Haman's face. **9** And Harbonah one of the eunuchs, said in the
presence of the King, Behold, there standeth yet the tree in Haman's house fifty cu-
bits high, which Haman had prepared for Mordecai, that spake [g]good for the king.
Then the King said, Hang him thereon. **10** So they hanged Haman on the tree,
that he had prepared for Mordecai: then was the King's wrath pacified.

8

*1 After the death of Haman was Mordecai exalted. 14 Comfortable letters
are sent unto the Jews.*

1 The same day did King Ahasuerus give the house of Haman the adversary of
the Jews, unto the Queen Esther. And Mordecai [a]came before the King: for Esther
told what he was [b]unto her. **2** And the King took off his ring, which he had ta-
ken from Haman, and gave it unto Mordecai: and Esther set Mordecai over the
house of Haman. **3** And Esther spake yet more before the King, and fell down at
his feet weeping, and besought him that he would put away the [c]wickedness of Ha-
man the Agagite, and his device that he had imagined against the Jews. **4** And
the King held out the golden [d]scepter toward Esther. Then arose Esther, and stood
before the King, **5** And said, If it please the King, and if I have found favor in his
sight, and the thing be acceptable before the King, and I please him, let it be writ-
ten, that the letters of the device of Haman the son of Hammedatha the Agagite
may be called again, which he wrote to destroy the Jews, that are in all the King's
provinces. **6** For how can I suffer and see the evil, that shall come unto my peo-
ple? Or how can I suffer and see the destruction of my kindred? **7** And the king
Ahasuerus said unto the Queen Esther, and to Mordecai the Jew, Behold, I have
given Esther the house of Haman, whom they have hanged upon the tree, because
he [e]laid hand upon the Jews. **8** Write ye also for the Jews, as it liketh you in the
King's name, and seal it with the King's ring, (for the writings written in the King's
name, and sealed with the king's ring, may [f]no man revoke.) **9** Then were the
King's Scribes called at the same time, even in the third month, that is the month
[g]Sivan, on the three and twentieth day thereof: and it was written, according to all
as Mordecai commanded, unto the Jews and to the princes, and captains and rulers
of the provinces, which were from India even unto Ethiopia, an hundred and seven
and twenty provinces, unto every province according to the [h]writing thereof, and
to every people after their speech, and to the Jews, according to their writing, and
according to their language. **10** And he wrote in the King Ahasuerus's name,
and sealed it with the King's ring, and he sent letters by posts on horseback and
that rode on beasts of price, as dromedaries, and [i]colts of mares. **11** Wherein
the King granted the Jews (in what cities soever they were) to gather themselves
together, and to stand for [j]their life, and to root out, to slay and to destroy all the
power of the people and of the province that vexed them, both children and wo-
men, and to spoil their goods: **12** Upon one day in all the provinces of King
Ahasuerus, even in the thirteenth day of the twelfth month, which is the month
[k]Adar. **13** The copy of the writing was, how there should be a commandment
given in all and every province, published among all the people, and that the Jews
should be ready against that day, to [l]avenge themselves on their enemies. **14** So
the posts rode upon beasts of price, and dromedaries, and went forth with speed,
to execute the King's commandment, and the decree was given at Shushan the pa-
lace. **15** And Mordecai went out from the King in royal apparel of blue, and
white, and with a great crown of gold, and with a garment of fine linen and purple,
and the city of Shushan rejoiced and was glad. **16** And unto the Jews was come
light and [m]joy and gladness, and honor. **17** Also in all and every province, and
in all and every city and place, where the King's commandment and his decree
came, there was joy and gladness to the Jews, a feast and good day, and many of the
people of the land [n]became Jews: for the fear of the Jews fell upon them.

---

g. Esther 5:14 Meaning, the highest that could be found.

ESTHER 6

a. Esther 6:1 Hebrew, the king's sleep departed.
b. Esther 6:3 For he thought it unworthy his estate to receive a benefit, and not reward it.
c. Esther 6:4 Thus while the wicked imagine the destruction of others, they themselves fall into the same pit.
d. Esther 6:8 Meaning hereby that the king should make him next unto himself, as Joseph hereby was known to be next to Pharaoh, Gen. 41:41.
e. Esther 6:13 Thus God sometimes putteth in the mouth of the very wicked, to speak that thing which he hath decreed shall come to pass.

ESTHER 6

1. Esther 2:22

ESTHER 7

a. Esther 7:2 Read Esther 5:6.
b. Esther 7:4 Haman could not so much profit the king by this his malice, as he should hinder him by the loss of the Jews, and the tribute which he hath of them.
c. Esther 7:5 Hebrew, filleth his heart.
d. Esther 7:7 His conscience did accuse him that as he had conspired the death of innocents, so the vengeance of God might fall upon him for the same.
e. Esther 7:8 He fell down at the bed's feet or couch, whereupon she sat, and made request for his life.
f. Esther 7:8 This was the manner of the Persians, when one was out of the King's favor.
g. Esther 7:9 Which discovered the conspiracy against the king, Esther 2:21, 22.

ESTHER 8

a. Esther 8:1 That is, was received into the king's favor and presence.
b. Esther 8:1 That he was her uncle, and had brought her up.
c. Esther 8:3 Meaning, that he should abolish the wicked decrees, which he had made for the destruction of the Jews.
d. Esther 8:4 Read Esther 5:2.
e. Esther 8:7 Or, went about to slay the Jews.
f. Esther 8:8 This was the law of the Medes and Persians, as Dan. 6:15, notwithstanding the king revoked the former decree granted to Haman, for Esther's sake.
g. Esther 8:9 Which containeth part of May and part of June.
h. Esther 8:9 That is, in such letters and language, as was usual in every province.
i. Esther 8:10 Or, mules.
j. Esther 8:11 That is, to defend themselves against all that would assail them.
k. Esther 8:12 Which hath part of February and part of March.
l. Esther 8:13 The king gave them liberty to kill all that did oppress them.
m. Esther 8:16 He showeth by these words that follow, what this light was.
n. Esther 8:17 Conformed themselves to the Jew's religion.

9 *1 At the commandment of the King, the Jews put their adversaries to death. 14 The ten sons of Haman are hanged. 17 The Jews keep a feast in remembrance of their deliverance.*

1 So in the twelfth month, which is the month Adar, upon the thirteenth day of the same, when the King's commandment and his decree drew near to be put in execution, in the day that the enemies of the Jews hoped to have power over them (but it [a]turned contrary: for the Jews had rule over them that hated them.) **2** The Jews gathered themselves together into their cities throughout all the provinces of the King Ahasuerus, to lay hand on such as sought their hurt, and no man could withstand them: for the fear of them fell upon all people. **3** And all the rulers of the provinces, and the princes and the captains, and the officers of the King [b]exalted the Jews: for the fear of Mordecai fell upon them. **4** For Mordecai was great in the King's house, and the report of him went through all the provinces: for this man Mordecai waxed greater and greater. **5** Thus the Jews smote all their [c]enemies with strokes of the sword and slaughter, and destruction, and did what they would unto those that hated them. **6** And at Shushan the palace slew the Jews and destroyed [d]five hundred men, **7** And Parshandatha, and Dalphon, and Aspatha, **8** And Poratha, and Adalia, and Aridatha, **9** And Parmashta, and Arisai, and Aridai, and Vajezatha, **10** The ten sons of Haman, the son of Hammedatha, the adversary of the Jews slew they: but they laid not their hands [e]on the spoil. **11** On the same day came the number of those that were slain, unto the palace of Shushan before the King. **12** And the King said unto the Queen Esther, The Jews have slain in Shushan the palace, and destroyed five hundred men, and the ten sons of Haman: what have they done in the rest of the King's provinces? and what is thy petition, that it may be given thee? or what is thy request moreover, that it may be performed? **13** Then said Esther, If it please the King, let it be granted also tomorrow to the Jews that are in Shushan, to do according [f]unto this day's decree, that they may hang upon the tree Haman's ten sons. **14** And the King charged to do so, and the decree was given at Shushan, and they hanged Haman's ten sons. **15** So the Jews that were in Shushan, assembled themselves upon the fourteenth day of the month Adar, and slew three hundred men in Shushan, but on the spoil they laid not their hand. **16** And the rest of the Jews that were in the King's provinces assembled themselves, and stood for [g]their lives, and had rest from their enemies, and slew of them that [h]hated them, seventy and five thousand: but they laid not their hand on the spoil. **17** This they did on the [i]thirteenth day of the month Adar, and rested the fourteenth day thereof, and kept it a day of feasting and joy. **18** But the Jews that were in Shushan assembled themselves on the thirteenth day, and on the fourteenth thereof, and they rested on the fifteenth of the same, and kept it a day of feasting and joy. **19** Therefore the Jews of the villages that dwelt in the unwalled towns, [j]kept the fourteenth day of the month Adar with joy and feasting, even a joyful day, and everyone sent presents unto his neighbor. **20** And Mordecai wrote [k]these words, and sent letters unto all the Jews that were through all the provinces of the King Ahasuerus, both near and far, **21** Enjoining them that they should keep the fourteenth day of the month Adar, and the fifteenth day of the same, every year. **22** According to the days wherein the Jews rested from their enemies, and the month which was turned unto them from sorrow to joy, and from mourning into a joyful day, to keep them the days of feasting and joy, and to [l]send presents every man to his neighbor, and gifts to the poor. **23** And the Jews promised to do as they had begun, and as Mordecai had written unto them, **24** Because Haman the son of Hammedatha the Agagite all the Jews' adversary had imagined against the Jews to destroy them, and had [m]cast Pur (that is a lot) to consume and destroy them. **25** And when [n]she came before the king, he commanded by letters, Let this wicked [o]device (which he imagined against the Jews) turn upon his own head, and let them hang him and his sons on the tree. **26** Therefore they called these days Purim, by the name of Pur, and because of all the words of this letter, and of that which they had seen besides this, and of that which had come unto them. **27** The Jews also ordained, and promised for them and for their seed, and for all that joined unto them, that they would not [p]fail to observe those two [q]days every year, according to their writing, and according unto their season, **28** And that these days should be remembered, and kept throughout every generation and every family, and every province, and every city: even these days of Purim should not fail among the Jews, and the memorial of them should not perish from their seed. **29** And the Queen Esther the daughter of Abihail and Mordecai the Jew wrote with all [r]authority (to confirm this letter of Purim the second time.) **30** And he sent letters unto all the Jews to the hundred and seven and twenty provinces of the kingdom of Ahasuerus, with [s]words of peace and truth, **31** To confirm these days of Purim according to their seasons, as Mordecai the Jew and Esther the Queen had appointed them, and as they had promised for [t]themselves and for their seed with [u]fasting and prayer. **32** And the decree of Esther confirmed these words of Purim, and was written in the book.

10 *1 The estimation and authority of Mordecai.*

1 And the King Ahasuerus laid a tribute upon the land, and upon the isles of the sea. **2** And all the acts of his power, and of his might, and the declaration of the dignity of Mordecai, wherewith the King magnified him, are they not written in the book of the Chronicles of the Kings of Media and Persia? **3** For Mordecai the Jew was the second unto king Ahasuerus, and great among the Jews, and [a]accepted among the multitude of his brethren, who procured the wealth of his people, and spake peaceably to all his seed.

ESTHER 9

a. Esther 9:1 This was by God's great providence, who turneth the joy of the wicked into sorrow, and the tears of the godly into gladness.
b. Esther 9:3 Did them honor, and showed them friendship.
c. Esther 9:5 Which had conspired their death by the permission of the wicked Haman.
d. Esther 9:6 Besides those three hundred, that they slew the second day, as verse 15.
e. Esther 9:10 Whereby they declared that this was God's just judgment upon the enemies of his Church, forasmuch as they sought not their own gain, but to execute his vengeance.
f. Esther 9:13 This she requireth not for desire of vengeance, but with zeal to see God's judgments executed against his enemies.
g. Esther 9:16 Read Esther 8:11.
h. Esther 9:16 Meaning, that they laid hands on none that were not this enemies of God.
i. Esther 9:17 Meaning, in all places saving in Shushan.
j. Esther 9:19 As the Jews do even to this day, calling it in the Persian language Purim, that is, the day of lots.
k. Esther 9:20 The Jews gather hereof that Mordecai wrote this story: but it seemeth that he wrote but only these letters and decrees that follow.
l. Esther 9:22 He setteth before our eyes the use of this feast, which was for the remembrance of God's deliverance, the maintenance of mutual friendship and relief of the poor.
m. Esther 9:24 Read Esther 3.
n. Esther 9:25 That is, Esther.
o. Esther 9:25 These are the words of the king's commandment to disannul Haman's wicked enterprise.
p. Esther 9:27 Or, transgress.
q. Esther 9:27 Meaning, the fourteenth and fifteenth day of the month of Adar.
r. Esther 9:29 Or, strength, or efficacy.
s. Esther 9:30 Which were letters declaring unto them quietness, and assurance and putting them out of doubt and fear.
t. Esther 9:31 Hebrew, souls.
u. Esther 9:31 That they would observe this feast with fasting and earnest prayer, which in Hebrew is signified by this word (they cry).

ESTHER 10

a. Esther 10:3 These three points are here set forth as commendable and necessary for him that is in authority, to have the favor of the people, to procure their wealth, and to be gentle and loving toward them.

JOB

1

1 The holiness, riches, and care of Job for his children. 10 Satan hath permission to tempt him. 13 He tempteth him by taking away his substance, and his children. 20 His faith and patience.

1 There was a man in the land of [a]Uz called Job, and this man [b]was an upright and just man, [c]one that feared God, and eschewed evil. **2** And he had seven sons, and three daughters. **3** His [d]substance also was seven thousand sheep, and three thousand camels, and five hundred yoke of oxen, and five hundred she asses, and his family was very great, so that this man was the greatest of all the [e]men of [f]the East. **4** And his sons went and banqueted in their houses, every one his day, and sent, and called their three sisters to eat and to drink with them. **5** And when the days of their banqueting were gone about, Job sent, and [g]sanctified them, and rose up early in the morning, and [h]offered burnt offerings according to the number of them all. For Job thought, It may be that my sons have sinned, and [i]blasphemed God in their hearts, thus did Job [j]every day. **6** Now on a day when the [k]children of God came and stood [l]before the Lord, Satan [m]came also among them. **7** Then the Lord said unto Satan, Whence [n]comest thou? And Satan answered the Lord, saying, [o]From compassing the earth to and fro, and from walking in it. **8** And the Lord said unto Satan, Hast thou not considered my servant Job, how none is like him in the earth? an upright and just man, one that feareth God, and escheweth evil? **9** Then Satan answered the Lord, and said, Doth Job fear God for [p]nought? **10** Hast thou not made [q]an hedge about him and about his house, and about all that he hath on every side? thou hast blessed the work of his hands, and his substance is increased in the land. **11** But stretch out now thine hand and [r]touch all that he hath, to see if he will not blaspheme thee [s]to thy face. **12** Then the Lord said unto Satan, Lo, all that he hath is in [t]thine hand: only upon himself shalt thou not stretch out thine hand. So Satan departed from the [u]presence of the Lord. **13** And on a day, when his sons and his daughters were eating and drinking wine in their eldest brother's house, **14** There came a messenger unto Job, and said, The oxen were plowing, and the asses feeding in their places, **15** And the [v]Sabeans came violently, and took them: yea, they have slain the servants with the edge of the sword: but I only am escaped alone to tell thee. **16** And while he was yet speaking, another came, and said, The [w]fire of God is fallen from the heaven, and hath burnt up the sheep and the servants, and devoured them: but I only am escaped alone to tell thee. **17** And while he was yet speaking, another came, and said, The Chaldeans set on three bands, and fell upon the camels, and have taken them, and have slain the servants with the edge of the sword: but I only am escaped alone to tell thee. **18** And while he was yet speaking, came another, and said, Thy [x]sons, and thy daughters were eating, and drinking wine in their eldest brother's house, **19** And behold, there came a great wind from beyond the wilderness, and smote the four corners of the house, which fell upon the children, and they are dead, and I only am escaped alone to tell thee. **20** Then Job arose, and [y]rent his garment, and shaved his head, and fell down upon the ground, and worshipped, **21** And said, [1]Naked came I out of my mother's womb, and naked shall I return [z]thither: the Lord hath given, and the Lord hath taken it: [aa]blessed be the Name of the Lord. **22** In all this did not Job sin, nor charge God [ab]foolishly.

2

6 Satan hath permission to afflict Job. 9 His wife tempteth him to forsake God. 11 His three friends visit him.

1 And on a day the [a]children of God came and stood before the Lord, and [b]Satan came also among them, and stood before the Lord. **2** Then the Lord said unto Satan, Whence comest thou? And Satan answered the Lord, and said, From compassing the earth to and fro, and from walking in it. **3** And the Lord said unto Satan, Hast thou not considered my servant Job, how none is like him in the earth? [1]an upright and just man, one that feareth God, and escheweth evil? for yet he continueth in his uprightness, [c]although thou movedst me against him, to destroy [d]him without cause. **4** And Satan answered the Lord, and said, [e]Skin for skin, and all that ever a man hath, will he give for his life. **5** But stretch now out thine hand, and touch his [f]bones and his flesh, to see if he will not blaspheme thee to thy face. **6** Then the Lord said unto Satan, Lo, he is in thine hand, but save [g]his life. **7** So Satan departed from the presence of the Lord, and smote Job with sore [h]boils, from the sole of his foot unto his crown. **8** And he took a [i]potsherd to scrape him, and he sat down among the ashes. **9** Then said his [j]wife unto him, Dost thou [k]continue yet in thine uprightness? [l]Blaspheme God, and die. **10** But he said unto her, Thou speakest like a foolish woman: what? shall we receive good at the hand of God, and not [m]receive evil? In all this did not Job sin with his [n]lips. **11** Now when Job's three [o]friends heard of all this evil that was come upon him, they came every one from his own place, to wit, Eliphaz the Temanite, and Bildad the Shuhite, and Zophar the Naamathite: for they were agreed together to come to lament with him, and to comfort him. **12** So when they lifted up their eyes afar off, they knew him not: therefore they lifted up their voices and wept, and every one of them rent his garment and sprinkled [p]dust upon their heads toward

---

JOB 1

a. Job 1:1 That is, of the country of Idumea, as Lam. 4:21, or bordering thereupon: for the land was called by the name of Uz, the son of Dishan the son of Seir, Gen. 36:28.

b. Job 1:1 Forasmuch as he was a Gentile, and not a Jew, and yet is pronounced upright, and without hypocrisy, it declareth that among the heathen God hath his.

c. Job 1:1 Hereby is declared, what is meant by an upright and just man.

d. Job 1:3 His children and riches are declared, to commend his virtue in his prosperity and his patience, and constancy, when God had taken them from him.

e. Job 1:3 Hebrew, children.

f. Job 1:3 Meaning, the Arabians, Chaldeans, Idumeans, etc.

g. Job 1:5 That is, commanded them to be sanctified: meaning, that they should consider the faults that they had committed, and reconcile themselves for the same.

h. Job 1:5 That is, he offered for every one of his children an offering of reconciliation, which declared his religion toward God, and the care that he had toward his children.

i. Job 1:5 In Hebrew it is, and blessed God, which is sometimes taken for blaspheming and cursing, as here and 1 Kings 21:10, 13, etc.

j. Job 1:5 While the feast lasted.

k. Job 1:6 Meaning, the Angels, which are called the sons of God, because they are willing to execute his will.

l. Job 1:6 Because our infirmity cannot comprehend God in his majesty, he is set forth unto us as a King, that our capacity may be able to understand that which is spoken of him.

m. Job 1:6 This declareth, that although Satan be adversary to God, yet he is compelled to obey him, and do him all homage, without whose permission and appointment he can do nothing.

n. Job 1:7 This question is asked for our infirmity: for God knew whence he came.

o. Job 1:7 Herein is described the nature of Satan, which is ever ranging for his prey, 1 Pet. 5:8.

p. Job 1:9 He feareth thee not for thine own sake, but for the commodity that he received by thee.

q. Job 1:10 Meaning, the grace of God, which served Job as a rampart against all tentations.

r. Job 1:11 This signifieth, that Satan is not able to touch us, but it is God that must do it.

s. Job 1:11 Satan noteth the vice whereunto men are commonly subject, that is, to hide their rebellion, and to be content with God in the time of prosperity, which view is disclosed in the time of their adversity.

t. Job 1:12 God giveth not Satan power over man to gratify him, but to declare that he hath no power over man, but that which God giveth him.

u. Job 1:12 That is, went to execute that which God had permitted him to do: for else he can never go out of God's presence.

v. Job 1:15 That is, the Arabians.

w. Job 1:16 Which thing was also done by the craft of Satan, to tempt Job the more grievously, forasmuch as he might see, that not only men were his enemies, but that God made war against him.

x. Job 1:18 This last plague declareth, that when one plague is past which seemeth hard to be borne, God can send us another far more grievous, to try his, and teach them obedience.

y. Job 1:20 Which came not of impatience, but declareth that the children of God are not insensible like blocks, but that in their patience they feel affliction and grief of mind: yet they keep a mean herein, and rebel not against God, as the wicked do.

z. Job 1:21 That is, into the belly of the earth, which is the mother of all.

aa. Job 1:21 Hereby he confesseth that God is just, and good, although his hand be sore upon him.

ab. Job 1:22 But declared that God did all things according to justice and equity.

JOB 1

1. Eccl. 5:14 / 1 Tim. 6:7

JOB 2

a. Job 2:1 That is, the Angels, as Job 1:6.

b. Job 2:1 Read Job 1:6.

c. Job 2:3 He proveth Job's integrity by this that he ceased not to fear God when his plagues were grievously upon him.

d. Job 2:3 That is, when thou hadst nought against him, or when thou wast not able to bring thy purpose to pass.

e. Job 2:4 Hereby he meant, that a man's own skin is dearer unto him than another man's.

f. Job 2:5 Meaning, his own person.

g. Job 2:6 Thus Satan can go no further in punishing, than God hath limited him.

h. Job 2:7 This sore was most vehement, wherewith also God plagued the Egyptians, Exod. 9:9, and threateneth to punish the rebellious people, Deut. 28:27, so that this tentation was most grievous: for if Job had measured God's favor by the vehemency of his disease, he might have thought that God had cast him off.

i. Job 2:8 As destitute of all other help and means, and wonderfully afflicted with the sorrow of his disease.

j. Job 2:9 Satan useth the same instrument against Job, as he did against Adam.

k. Job 2:9 Meaning, what gainest thou to serve God, seeing he thus plagueth thee, as though he were thine enemy? This is the most grievous temptation of the faithful, when their faith is assailed, and when Satan goeth about to persuade them that they trust in God in vain.

l. Job 2:9 For death was appointed to the blasphemer, and so she meant that he should soon be rid out of his pain.

m. Job 2:10 That is, to be patient in adversity, as we rejoice when he sendeth prosperity, and so to acknowledge him to be both merciful and just.

n. Job 2:10 He so bridled his affections, that his tongue through impatience did not murmur against God.

o. Job 2:11 Which were men of authority, wise and learned, and as the Septuagint writes, Kings, and came to comfort him, but when they saw how he was visited, they conceived an evil opinion of him, as though he had been but an hypocrite, and so justly plagued of God for his sins.

p. Job 2:12 This was also a ceremony, which they used in those countries, as the renting of their clothes in sign of sorrow, etc.

the heaven. **13** So they sat by him upon the ground seven days, and seven nights, and none spake a word unto him: for they saw that the grief was very [q]great.

3

1 Job complaineth, and curseth the day of his birth. 11 He desireth to die, as though death were the end of all man's misery.

1 Afterward [a]Job opened his mouth, and [b]cursed his day. **2** And Job cried out, and said, **3** Let the day [c]perish wherein I was born, and the night when it was said, There is a man child conceived. **4** Let that day be darkness, let not God [d]regard it from above, neither let the light shine upon it, **5** But let darkness and the [e]shadow of death stain it: let the cloud remain upon it, and let them make it fearful as a bitter day. **6** Let darkness possess that night, let it not be joined unto the days of the year, nor let it come into the count of the months. **7** Yea, desolate be that night, and let no joy be in it. **8** Let them that curse the day, (being [f]ready to renew their mourning) curse it. **9** Let the stars of that twilight be dim through darkness of it: let it look for light, but have none: neither let it [g]see [h]the dawning of the day, **10** Because it shut not up the doors of my mother's womb, nor hid sorrow from mine eyes. **11** [i]Why died I not in the birth? or why died I not, when I came out of the womb? **12** Why did the knees prevent me? and why did I suck the breasts? **13** For so should I now have [j]lain and been quiet, I should have slept then, and been at rest, **14** With the kings and counselors of the earth, which have built themselves [k]desolate places: **15** Or with the princes that had gold, and have filled their houses with silver. **16** Or why was I not hid, as an untimely birth, either as infants, which have not seen the light? **17** The wicked [l]have there ceased from their tyranny, and there they that labored valiantly, are at rest. **18** The [m]prisoners rest together, and hear not the voice of the oppressor. **19** There are small and great, and the servant is free from his master. **20** Wherefore is the light given to him that is in misery? and [n]life unto them that have heavy hearts? **21** Which long for death, and if it come not, they would even search it more than treasures: **22** Which joy for gladness, and rejoice, when they can find the grave. **23** Why is the light given to the man whose way is [o]hid, and whom God hath hedged in? **24** For my sighing cometh before I eat, and my roarings are poured out like the water. **25** For the thing I [p]feared, is come upon me, and the thing that I was afraid of, is come unto me. **26** I had no peace, neither had I quietness, neither had I rest, [q]yet trouble is come.

4

5 Job is reprehended of impatience, 7 and injustice, 17 and of the presumption of his own righteousness.

1 Then Eliphaz the Temanite, answered and said, **2** If we assay to commune with thee, wilt thou be grieved? but [a]who can withhold himself from speaking? **3** Behold, thou hast taught many, and [b]hast strengthened the weary hands. **4** Thy words have confirmed him that was falling, and thou hast strengthened the weak knees. **5** But now it is come upon thee, and thou art grieved: it toucheth thee, and thou art troubled. **6** Is not this thy [c]fear, thy confidence, thy patience, and uprightness of thy ways? **7** Remember, I pray thee: who ever perished, being an [d]innocent? or where were the upright destroyed? **8** As I have seen, they that [e]plow iniquity, and sow wickedness, reap the same. **9** With the [f]blast of God they perish, and with the breath of his nostrils are they consumed. **10** The roaring of the [g]Lion, and the voice of the Lioness, and the teeth of the Lion's whelps are broken. **11** The Lion perisheth for lack of prey, and the Lion's whelps are scattered abroad. **12** But a thing was brought to me [h]secretly, and mine ear hath received a little thereof. **13** In the thoughts of the visions of the night, when sleep falleth on men, **14** Fear came upon me, and dread which made all my bones [i]to tremble. **15** And the wind passed before me, and made the hairs of my flesh to stand up. **16** Then stood one, and I knew not his face: an image was before mine eyes, and in [j]silence heard I a voice, saying, **17** Shall man be more [k]just than God? or shall a man be more pure than his Maker? **18** Behold, he found no steadfastness in his servants, and laid folly upon his [l]Angels. **19** How much more in them that dwell in houses of [m]clay, whose foundation is in the dust, which shall be destroyed before the moth? **20** They be destroyed from the [n]morning unto the evening: they perish forever, [o]without regard. **21** Doth not their dignity go away with them? do they not die, and that without [p]wisdom?

5

1, 2 Eliphaz showeth the difference between the children of God and the wicked. 3 The fall of the wicked. 9 God's power who destroyeth the wicked, and delivereth his.

1 Call now, if any will [a]answer thee, and to which of the Saints wilt thou turn? **2** Doubtless [b]anger killeth the foolish, and envy slayeth the idiot. **3** I have seen the [c]foolish well rooted, and suddenly I [d]cursed his habitation, saying, **4** His [e]children shall be far from salvation, and they shall be destroyed in the [f]gate, and none shall deliver them. **5** The hungry shall eat up his harvest: yea, they shall take it from among the [g]thorns, and the thirsty shall drink up their substance. **6** For misery cometh not forth of the dust, [h]neither doeth affliction spring out of the earth. **7** But man is born unto [i]travail, as the sparks fly upward. **8** But I would inquire at [j]God, and turn my talk unto God: **9** Which [k]doeth great things, and unsearchable, and marvelous things without number. **10** He [l]giveth rain upon the earth, and poureth water upon the streets, **11** And setteth up on high them that be low, that the sorrowful may be exalted to salvation. **12** He scattereth the devices of the crafty: so that their hands cannot accomplish that which they do enterprise. **13** [l]He taketh the wise in their craftiness, and the counsel of the wicked is made foolish. **14** They meet with [m]darkness in the daytime, and [n]grope at noonday, as in the night. **15** But he saveth the [o]poor from the sword, from their [p]mouth, and from the hand of the violent man, **16** So that the poor

---

q. Job 2:13 And therefore thought that he would not have hearkened unto their counsel.

JOB 2

1. Ezek. 14:14 / Job 1:1

JOB 3

a. Job 3:1 The seven days ended, Job 2:13.
b. Job 3:1 Here Job beginneth to feel his great imperfection in this battle between the spirit and the flesh, Rom. 7:18, and after a manner yieldeth, yet in the end he getteth victory, though he was in the mean time greatly wounded.
c. Job 3:3 Men ought not to be weary of their life, and curse it, because of the infirmities that it is subject unto, but because they are given to sin and rebellion against God.
d. Job 3:4 Let it be put out of the number of days, and let it not have the light of the Sun to separate it from the night.
e. Job 3:5 That is, most obscure darkness, which maketh them afraid of death that are in it.
f. Job 3:8 Which curse the day of their birth, let them lay that curse upon this night.
g. Job 3:9 Let it be always night, and never see day.
h. Job 3:9 Hebrew, The eyelids of the morning.
i. Job 3:11 This, and that which followeth, declareth, that when man giveth place to his passions, he is not able to stay nor keep measure, but runneth headlong into all evil, except God call him back.
j. Job 3:13 The vehemency of his afflictions made him to utter these words, as though death were the end of all miseries, and as if there were no life after this, which he speaketh not as though it were so, but the infirmities of his flesh caused him to burst out in this error of the wicked.
k. Job 3:14 He noteth the ambition of them, which for their pleasure as it were change the order of nature, and build in most barren places, because they would hereby make their names immortal.
l. Job 3:17 That is, by death the cruelty of the tyrants hath ceased.
m. Job 3:18 All they that sustain any kind of calamity and misery in this world: which he speaketh after the judgment of the flesh.
n. Job 3:20 He showeth that the benefits of God are not comfortable, expect the heart be joyful, and the conscience quieted.
o. Job 3:23 That seeth not how to come out of his miseries, because he dependeth not on God's providence.
p. Job 3:25 In my prosperity I looked ever for a fall, as is come now to pass.
q. Job 3:26 The fear of troubles that should ensue, caused my prosperity to seem to me as nothing, and yet I am not exempted from trouble.

JOB 4

a. Job 4:2 Seeing this thine impatience.
b. Job 4:3 Thou hast comforted others in their afflictions, and canst not now comfort thyself.
c. Job 4:6 This he concludeth that Job was but an hypocrite, and had no true fear nor trust in God.
d. Job 4:7 He concludeth that Job was reproved, seeing that God handled him so extremely, which is the argument that the carnal men make against the children of God.
e. Job 4:8 They that do evil, cannot but receive evil.
f. Job 4:9 He showeth that God needeth no great preparation to destroy his enemies: for he can do it with the blast of his mouth.
g. Job 4:10 Though men according to their office do not punish tyrants (whom for their cruelty he compareth to lions, and their children to their whelps) yet God both is able, and his justice will punish them.
h. Job 4:12 A thing that I knew not before, was declared unto me by vision, that is, that whosoever thinketh himself just, shall be found a sinner, when he cometh before God.
i. Job 4:14 In these visions which God showeth to his creatures, there is ever a certain fear joined, that the authority thereof might be had in greater reverence.
j. Job 4:16 When all things were quiet, or when the fear was somewhat assuaged, as God appeared to Elijah, 1 Kings 19:12.
k. Job 4:17 He proveth that if God did punish the innocent, the creature should be more just than the Creator, which were a blasphemy.
l. Job 4:18 If God find imperfection in his Angels, when they are not maintained by his power, how much more shall he lay folly to man's charge when he would justify himself against God?
m. Job 4:19 That is, in this mortal body, subject to corruption, as 2 Cor. 5:1.
n. Job 4:20 They see death continually before their eyes, and daily approaching toward them.
o. Job 4:20 No man for all this doth consider it.
p. Job 4:21 That is, before that any of them were so wise, as to think on death.

JOB 5

a. Job 5:1 He willeth Job to consider the example of all them that have lived or do live godly, whether any of them be like unto him in raging against God as he doth.
b. Job 5:2 Murmuring against God in afflictions increaseth the pain, and uttered man's folly.
c. Job 5:3 That is, the sinner that hath not the fear of God.
d. Job 5:3 I was not moved with his prosperity, but knew that God had cursed him and his.
e. Job 5:4 Though God sometimes suffer the fathers to pass in this world, yet his judgments will light upon their wicked children.
f. Job 5:4 By public judgment they shall be condemned, and none shall pity them.
g. Job 5:5 Though there be but two or three ears left in the hedges, yet these shall be taken from him.
h. Job 5:6 That is, the earth is not the cause of barrenness and man's misery, but his own sin.
i. Job 5:7 Which declareth that sin is ever in our corrupt nature: for before sin it was not subject to pain and affliction.
j. Job 5:8 If I suffered as thou doest, I would seek unto God.
k. Job 5:9 He counselleth Job to humble himself unto God to whom all creatures are subject and whose works declare that man is inexcusable except he glorify God in all his works.
l. Job 5:10 He showeth by particular examples, what the works of God are.
m. Job 5:14 In things plain and evident they show themselves fools instead of wise men.
n. Job 5:14 This declareth that God punisheth the worldly wise, as he threatened, Deut. 28:29.
o. Job 5:15 That is, he that humbleth himself before God.
p. Job 5:15 He compareth the slander of the wicked to sharp swords.
q. Job 5:16 If the wicked be compelled at God's works to stop their mouths, much more they that profess God.

hath his hope, but iniquity shall [q]stop her mouth. **17** Behold, blessed is the man whom God correcteth: therefore refuse not thou the chastising of the Almighty. **18** For he maketh the wound, and bindeth it up: he smiteth, and his hands make whole. **19** He shall deliver thee in [r]six troubles, and in the seventh the evil shall not touch thee. **20** In famine he shall deliver thee from death: and in battle from the power of the sword. **21** Thou shalt be hid from the scourge of the tongue, and thou shalt not be afraid of destruction when it cometh. **22** But thou shalt [s]laugh at destruction and dearth, and shalt not be afraid of the beast of the earth. **23** For the stones of the field [t]shall be in league with thee, and the beasts of the field shall be at peace with thee. **24** And thou shalt know, that peace shall be in thy tabernacle, and thou shalt visit thine habitation, and shalt not [u]sin. **25** Thou shalt perceive also that thy seed shall be great, and thy posterity as the grass of the earth. **26** Thou shalt go to thy grave in [v]a full age, as a rick of corn cometh in due season into the barn. **27** Lo, [w]thus have we inquired of it, and so it is: hear this and know it for thyself.

6

1 Job answereth, that his pain is more grievous than his fault. 8 He wisheth death. 14 He complaineth of his friends.

1 But Job answered and said, **2** Oh that my grief were well weighed, and my miseries were laid together in the [a]balance! **3** For it would be now heavier than the sand of the sea: therefore my words are [b]swallowed up. **4** For the arrows of the Almighty are in me, the venom whereof doth drink up my spirit, and the terrors of God [c]fight against me. **5** Doth the [d]wild ass bray when he hath grass? or loweth the ox when he hath fodder? **6** That which is [e]unsavory, shall it be eaten without salt? or is there any taste in the white of an egg? **7** Such things as my soul refused to touch, as were sorrows, are my meat. **8** Oh that I might have my [f]desire, and that God would grant me the thing that I long for! **9** That is, that God would destroy me: that he would let his hand go, and cut me off. **10** Then should I yet have comfort, (though I burn with sorrow, let him not spare) [g]because I have not denied the words of the Holy one. **11** What power have I that I should endure? or what is mine [h]end, if I should prolong my life? **12** Is my strength the strength of stones? or is my flesh of brass? **13** Is it not so, that there is in me no [i]help? and that [j]strength is taken from me? **14** He that is in misery, ought to be comforted of his neighbor: but men have forsaken the fear of the Almighty. **15** My brethren have deceived me as a [k]brook, and as the rising of the rivers they pass away. **16** Which are blackish with ice, and wherein the snow is hid. **17** But in time they are dried up with heat and are consumed: and when it is hot they fail out of their places, **18** Or they depart from their way and course, yea, they vanish and perish. **19** They that go to Tema, [l]considered them, and they that go to Sheba, waited for them. **20** But they were confounded: when they hoped, they came thither, and were ashamed. **21** Surely now are ye like [m]unto it: ye have seen my fearful plague, and are afraid. **22** Was it because I said, Bring unto me? or give a reward to me of your [n]substance? **23** And deliver me from the enemy's hand, or ransom me out of the hand of tyrants? **24** Teach me, and I will [o]hold my tongue: and cause me to understand, wherein I have erred. **25** How [p]steadfast are the words of righteousness? and what can any of you justly reprove? **26** Do ye imagine to reprove [q]words, that the talk of the afflicted should be as the wind? **27** Ye make your wrath to fall upon the fatherless, and dig a pit for your friend. **28** Now therefore be content to [r]look upon me: for I will not lie before your face. **29** Turn, I pray you, let there be none iniquity: return, I say, and ye shall see yet my righteousness in that behalf. Is there iniquity in my tongue? doth not my mouth feel sorrows?

7

1 Job showeth the shortness and misery of man's life.

1 Is there not an appointed time to man upon earth? and are not his days as the days of an [a]hireling? **2** As a servant longeth for the shadow, and as an hireling looketh for the end of his work, **3** So have I had as an inheritance the [b]months of vanity, and painful nights have been appointed unto me. **4** If I laid me down, I said, When shall I arise? and measuring the evening, I am even full with tossing to and fro unto the dawning of the day. **5** My flesh is [c]clothed with worms and filthiness of the dust: my skin is rent, and become horrible. **6** My days are swifter than [d]a weaver's shuttle, and they are spent without hope. **7** Remember that my life is but a wind, and that mine eye shall not return to see pleasure. **8** The eye that hath seen me, shall see me no more: thine eyes are upon me, and I shall be no longer. **9** [e]As the cloud vanisheth and goeth away, so he that goeth down to the grave, shall [f]come up no more. **10** He shall return no more to his house, neither shall his place know him anymore. **11** Therefore I will not [g]spare my mouth, but will speak in the trouble of my spirit, and muse in the bitterness of my mind. **12** Am I a sea [h]or a whalefish, that thou keepest me in ward? **13** When I say, My couch shall relieve me, and my bed shall bring comfort in my meditation, **14** Then fearest thou me [i]with dreams, and astonishest me with visions. **15** Therefore my soul [j]chooseth rather to be strangled and to die, than to be in my bones. **16** I abhor it: I shall not live always: [k]spare me then, for my days are but vanity. **17** What is man, that thou [l]dost magnify him, and that thou settest thine heart upon him? **18** And dost visit him every morning, and triest him every moment? **19** How long will it be ere thou depart from me? thou wilt not let me alone while I may swallow my spittle. **20** I have [m]sinned, what shall I do unto thee? O thou preserver of men, why hast thou set me as a mark against thee, so that I am a burden unto myself? **21** And why dost thou not pardon my trespass? and take away mine iniquity? for now shall I sleep in the dust, and if thou seek me in the morning, I shall [n]not be found.

8

1 Bildad showeth that Job is a sinner, because that God punisheth the wicked, and preserveth the good.

1 Then answered Bildad the Shuhite, and said, **2** How long wilt thou talk of these things? and how long shall the words of thy mouth [a]be as a mighty wind? **3** Doth God pervert judgment? or doth the Almighty subvert justice? **4** If thy sons have sinned against him, and he hath sent them into the place of their [b]iniquity, **5** Yet if thou [c]wilt early seek unto God, and pray to the Almighty, **6** If thou be pure and upright, then surely he will awake up unto thee, and he will make the habitation of thy righteousness prosperous. **7** And

---

r. Job 5:19 He will send trouble after trouble that his children may not for one time, but continually trust in him: but they shall have a comfortable issue, even in the greatest and the last, which is here called the seventh.
s. Job 5:22 Whereas the wicked lament in their troubles, thou shalt have occasion to rejoice.
t. Job 5:23 When we are in God's favor, all creatures shall serve us.
u. Job 5:24 God shall so bless thee, that thou shalt have occasion to rejoice in all things, and not to be offended.
v. Job 5:26 Though the children of God have not always this promise performed, yet God doth recompense it otherwise to their advantage.
w. Job 5:27 We have learned these points by experience, that God punisheth not the innocent, that man cannot compare in justice with him, that the hypocrites shall not long prosper, and that the affliction which man sustaineth, cometh for his own sin.

JOB 5
1. 1 Cor. 3:19

JOB 6
a. Job 6:2 To know whether I complain without just cause.
b. Job 6:3 My grief is so great that I lack words to express it.
c. Job 6:4 Which declareth that he was not only afflicted in body, but wounded in conscience, which is the greatest battle that the faithful can have.
d. Job 6:5 Think you that I cry without cause, seeing the brute beasts do not complain when they have what they would.
e. Job 6:6 Can a man's taste delight in that, that hath no savor? meaning, that none take pleasure in affliction, seeing they cannot do away with things that are unsavory to the mouth.
f. Job 6:8 Herein he sinneth double, both in wishing through impatience to die, and also in desiring of God a thing which was not agreeable to his will.
g. Job 6:10 That is, let me die at once, before I come to distrust in God's promise through my impatience.
h. Job 6:11 He fearest lest he should be brought to inconveniences, if his sorrows should continue.
i. Job 6:13 Have I not sought to help myself as much as was possible?
j. Job 6:13 Or, wisdom, or law.
k. Job 6:15 He compareth those friends which comfort us not in misery, to a brook, which in summer, when we need water, is dry, in winter is hard frozen, and in the time of rain, when we have no need, overfloweth with water.
l. Job 6:19 They that pass thereby to go into the hot countries of Arabia, think to find water there to quench their thirst, but they are deceived.
m. Job 6:21 That is, like to this brook which deceiveth them that think to have water there in their need, as I looked for consolation at your hands.
n. Job 6:22 He toucheth the worldlings, which for necessity will give part of their goods, and much more these men, which would not give him comfortable words.
o. Job 6:24 Show me wherein I have erred, and I will confess my fault.
p. Job 6:25 He that hath a good conscience doth not shrink at the sharp words or reasonings of others, except they be able to persuade him by reason.
q. Job 6:26 Do you cavil at my words because I should be thought to speak foolishly, which am now in misery?
r. Job 6:28 Consider whether I speak as one that is driven to this impatience through very sorrow, or as an hypocrite as you condemn me.

JOB 7
a. Job 7:1 Hath not an hired servant some rest and ease? then in this my continual torment I am worse than an hireling.
b. Job 7:3 My sorrow hath continued from month to month, and I have looked for hope in vain.
c. Job 7:5 This signifieth that his disease was rare and most horrible.
d. Job 7:6 Thus he speaketh in respect of the brevity of man's life, which passeth without hope of returning: in consideration whereof he desireth God to have compassion on him.
e. Job 7:9 If thou behold me in thine anger, I shall not be able to stand in thy presence.
f. Job 7:9 Shall no more enjoy this mortal life.
g. Job 7:11 Seeing I can by none other means comfort myself, I will declare my grief by words, and thus he speaketh as one overcome with grief of mind.
h. Job 7:12 Am not I a poor wretch? what needest thou then to lay so much pain on me?
i. Job 7:14 So that I can have no rest, night nor day.
j. Job 7:15 He speaketh as one overcome with sorrow, and not of judgment, or of the examination of his faith.
k. Job 7:16 Seeing my term of life is so short, let me have some rest and ease.
l. Job 7:17 Seeing that man of himself is so vile, why dost thou give him that honor to contend against him? Job useth all kinds of persuasion with God, that he might stay his hand.
m. Job 7:20 After all tentations faith bursteth forth and leadeth Job to repentance: yet it was not in such perfection, that he could bridle himself from reasoning with God, because that he still tried his faith.
n. Job 7:21 That is, I shall be dead.

JOB 8
a. Job 8:2 He declareth that their words which would diminish anything from the justice of God, is but as a puff of wind that vanisheth away.
b. Job 8:4 That is, hath rewarded them according to their iniquity: meaning, that Job ought to be warned by the example of his children, that he offend not God.
c. Job 8:5 That is, if thou turn betime while God calleth thee to repentance.

though thy beginning [d]be small, yet thy latter end shall greatly increase. **8** [e]Inquire therefore, I pray thee, of the former age, and prepare thyself to search of their fathers. **9** (For we are but [f]of yesterday, and are ignorant: for our days upon earth are but a shadow) **10** Shall not they teach thee and tell thee, and utter the words of their heart? **11** Can a rush [g]grow without mire? or can the grass grow without water? **12** Though it were in green and not cut down, yet shall it wither before any other herb. **13** So are the paths of all that forget God, and the hypocrite's hope shall perish. **14** His confidence also shall be cut off, and his trust shall be as the house of a [h]spider. **15** He shall lean upon his house, but it shall not stand: he shall hold him fast by it, yet shall it not endure. **16** The [i]tree is green before the Sun, and the branches spread over the garden thereof. **17** The roots thereof are wrapped about the fountain, and are folded about the house of stones. **18** If any pluck it from his place, and it [j]deny, saying, I have not seen thee, **19** Behold, it will rejoice [k]by this means, that it may grow in another mold. **20** Behold, God will not cast away an upright man, neither will he take the wicked by the hand, **21** Till he have filled thy mouth with [l]laughter, and thy lips with joy. **22** They that hate thee, shall be clothed with shame, and the dwelling of the wicked shall not remain.

9

2 Job declareth the mighty power of God, and that man's righteousness is nothing.

1 Then Job answered, and said, **2** I know verily that it is so: for how should man compared unto God, be [a]justified? **3** If he would dispute with him, he could not answer him one thing of [b]thousand. **4** He is wise in heart, and mighty in strength: who hath been fierce against him, and hath prospered? **5** He removeth the mountains, and they feel not when he overthroweth them in his wrath. **6** He [c]removeth the earth out of her place, that the pillars thereof do shake. **7** He commandeth the Sun, and it riseth not: he closeth up the stars, as under a signet. **8** He himself alone spreadeth out the heavens, and walketh upon the height of the Sea. **9** He maketh the stars [d]Arcturus, Orion, and Pleiades, and the climates of the South. **10** He doeth great things, and unsearchable: yea, marvelous things without number. **11** Lo, when he goeth [e]by me, I see him not: and when he passeth by, I perceive him not: **12** Behold, when he taketh a prey, [f]who can make him to restore it? who shall say unto him, What doest thou? **13** God [g]will not withdraw his anger, and the most mighty helpers [h]do stoop under him. **14** How much less shall I answer him? or how should I find out [i]my words with him? **15** For though I were just, yet could I [j]not answer, but I would make supplication to my Judge. **16** If I [k]cry, and he answer me, yet would I not believe, that he heard my voice. **17** For he destroyeth me with a tempest, and woundeth me [l]without cause. **18** He will not suffer me to take my breath, but filleth me with bitterness. **19** If we speak of strength, behold, he is [m]strong: if we speak of judgment, who shall bring me in to plead? **20** If I should justify myself, mine own mouth shall condemn me: [n]if I would be perfect, he shall judge me wicked. **21** Though I were perfect, yet I know not my soul: therefore abhor I my life. **22** This is one point: therefore I said, He destroyeth the [o]perfect and the wicked. **23** If the scourge should suddenly [p]slay, should God [q]laugh at the punishment of the innocent? **24** The earth is given into the hand of the wicked: [r]he covereth the faces of the judges thereof: if not, where [s]is he? or who is he? **25** My days have been more swift than a post: they have fled, and have seen no good thing. **26** They are passed as with the most swift ships, and as the Eagle that flieth to the prey. **27** If [t]I say, I will forget my complaint, I will cease from my wrath, and comfort me, **28** Then I am afraid of all my sorrows, knowing that thou wilt not judge me innocent. **29** If I be wicked, why [u]labor I thus in vain? **30** If I wash [v]myself with snow water, and purge mine hands most clean, **31** Yet shalt thou plunge me in the pit, and mine own [w]clothes shall make me filthy. **32** For he is not a man as I am, that I should answer him, if we come together to judgment. **33** Neither is there any umpire [x]that might lay his hand upon us both. **34** Let him take his rod away from me, and let not his fear astonish me: **35** Then will I speak, and fear him not: [y]but because I am not so, I hold me still.

10

1 Job is weary of his life, and setteth out his fragility before God. 20 He desireth him to stay his hand. 22 A description of death.

1 My soul is cut off [a]though I live: I will leave my [b]complaint upon myself, and will speak in the bitterness of my soul. **2** I will say unto God, [c]Condemn me not: show me, wherefore thou contendest with me. **3** Thinkest thou it [d]good to oppress me, and to cast off the [e]labor of thine hands, and to favor the [f]counsel of the wicked? **4** Hast thou [g]carnal eyes? or dost thou see as man seeth? **5** Are thy days as man's [h]days? or thy years as the time of man, **6** That thou inquirest of mine iniquity, and searchest out my sin? **7** Thou knowest that I cannot do [i]wickedly: for none can deliver me out of thine hand. **8** Thine [j]hands have made me, and fashioned me wholly round about, and wilt thou destroy me? **9** Remember, I pray thee, that thou hast made me as [k]the clay, and wilt thou bring me into dust again? **10** Hast thou not poured me out as milk? and turned me to curds like cheese? **11** Thou hast clothed me with skin and flesh, and joined me together with bones and sinews. **12** Thou hast given me life, and [l]grace: and the [m]visitation hath preserved my spirit. **13** Though thou hast hid these things in thine heart, yet I know [n]that it is so with thee. **14** If I have sinned, then thou wilt straightly look unto me, and wilt not hold me guiltless of mine iniquity. **15** If I have done wickedly, woe unto me: if I have done righteously, I will not [o]lift up mine head, being full of confusion, because I see mine affliction. **16** But let it increase: hunt thou me as a lion: return and show thyself [p]marvelous upon me. **17** Thou renewest thy plagues against me, and thou increasest thy wrath against me: [q]changes and armies of sorrows are against me. **18** Wherefore then hast thou brought me out of the womb? Oh that I had perished, and that none eye had seen me! **19** And that I were as I had not been, but brought from the womb to the grave! **20** Are not my days few? let him [r]cease, and leave off from me, that I may take a little comfort, **21** Before I go and shall not [s]return, even

---

d. Job 8:7 Though the beginnings be not so pleasant as thou wouldest desire, yet in the end thou shalt have sufficient occasion to content thyself.
e. Job 8:8 He willeth Job to examine all antiquity, and he shall find it true which he here saith.
f. Job 8:9 Meaning, that it is not enough to have the experience of ourselves, but to be confirmed by the examples of them that went before us.
g. Job 8:11 As a rush cannot grow without moistness, so cannot the hypocrite, because he hath not faith, which is moistened with God's Spirit.
h. Job 8:14 Which is today, and tomorrow swept away.
i. Job 8:16 He compareth the just to a tree, which although it be removed out of one place unto another, yet flourisheth: so the affliction of the godly turneth to their profit.
j. Job 8:18 That is, so that there remain nothing there to prove whether the tree had grown there or no.
k. Job 8:19 To be planted in another place, where it may grow at pleasure.
l. Job 8:21 If thou be godly, he will give thee occasion to rejoice, and if not, thine affliction shall increase.

JOB 9

a. Job 9:2 Job here answereth to that point of Eliphaz and Bildad's oration, touching the justice of God, and his innocency, confessing God to be infinite in justice, and man to be nothing in respect.
b. Job 9:3 Of a thousand things, which God could lay to his charge, man cannot answer him one.
c. Job 9:6 He declareth what is the infirmity of man, by the mighty and incomprehensible power that is in God, showing what he could do if he would set forth his power.
d. Job 9:9 These are the names of certain stars whereby he meaneth that all stars both known and unknown are at his appointment.
e. Job 9:11 I am not able to comprehend his works, which are common and daily before my eyes, much less in those things, which are hid and secret.
f. Job 9:12 He showeth that when God doth execute his power, he doeth it justly, forasmuch as none can control him.
g. Job 9:13 God will not be appeased for ought that man can say for himself for his justification.
h. Job 9:13 That is, all the reasons that men can lay to approve their cause.
i. Job 9:14 How should I be able to answer him by eloquence? whereby he noteth his friends, that albeit they were eloquent in talk, yet they felt not in heart, that which they spake.
j. Job 9:15 Meaning, in his own opinion, signifying, that man will sometimes flatter himself to be righteous, which before God is abomination.
k. Job 9:16 While I am in my pangs, I cannot but burst forth into many inconveniences, although I know still that God is just.
l. Job 9:17 I am not able to feel my sins so great, as I feel the weight of his plagues; and this he speaketh to condemn his dullness, and to justify God.
m. Job 9:19 After he hath accused his own weakness, he continueth to justify God and his power.
n. Job 9:20 If I would stand in mine own defense, yet God hath just cause to condemn me, if he examine mine heart and conscience.
o. Job 9:22 If God punish according to his justice, he will destroy as well them, that are counted perfect as them that are wicked.
p. Job 9:23 To wit, the wicked.
q. Job 9:23 This is spoken according to our apprehension, as though he would say, If God destroy but the wicked, as Job 5:3, why should he suffer the innocent to be so long tormented by them?
r. Job 9:24 That they cannot see to do justice.
s. Job 9:24 That can show the contrary?
t. Job 9:27 I think not to fall into these afflictions, but my sorrows bring me to these manifold infirmities, and my conscience condemneth me.
u. Job 9:29 Why doth not God destroy me at once? thus he speaketh according to the infirmity of the flesh.
v. Job 9:30 Though I seem never so pure in mine own eyes, yet all is but corruption before God.
w. Job 9:31 Whatsoever I would use to cover my filthiness with, shall disclose me so much more.
x. Job 9:33 Which might make an accord between God and me, speaking of impatience, and yet confessing God to be just in punishing him.
y. Job 9:35 Signifying that God's judgments keep him in awe.

JOB 10

a. Job 10:1 I am more like to a dead man, than to one that liveth.
b. Job 10:1 I will make an ample declaration of my torments, accusing myself and not God.
c. Job 10:2 He would not that God should proceed against him by his secret justice, but by the ordinary means that he punisheth others.
d. Job 10:3 Is it agreeable to thy justice to do me wrong?
e. Job 10:3 Wilt thou be without compassion?
f. Job 10:3 Wilt thou gratify the wicked and condemn me?
g. Job 10:4 Doest thou this of ignorance?
h. Job 10:5 Art thou inconstant and changeable, as the times, today a friend, tomorrow an enemy?
i. Job 10:7 By affliction thou keepest me as in a prison, and restrainest me from doing evil, neither can any set me at liberty.
j. Job 10:8 In these eight verses following he describeth the mercy of God, in the wonderful creation of man: and thereon groundeth that God should not show himself rigorous against him.
k. Job 10:9 As brittle as a pot of clay.
l. Job 10:12 That is, reason and understanding, and many other gifts, whereby man excelleth all earthly creatures.
m. Job 10:12 That is, thy fatherly care and providence whereby thou preservest me, and without the which I should perish straightway.
n. Job 10:13 Though I be not fully able to comprehend these things, yet I must needs confess that it is so.
o. Job 10:15 I will always walk in fear and humility, knowing that none is just before thee.
p. Job 10:16 Job being sore assaulted in this battle between the flesh and the spirit, bursteth out into these affections, wishing rather short days than long pain.
q. Job 10:17 That is, diversity of diseases and in great abundance: showing that God hath infinite means to punish man.
r. Job 10:20 He wisheth that God would leave off his affliction, considering his great misery and the brevity of his life.
s. Job 10:21 He speaketh thus in the person of a sinner, that is overcome with passions and with the feeling of God's judgments, and therefore cannot apprehend in that state the mercies of God, and comfort of the resurrection.

to the land of darkness and shadow of death: **22** Into a land, I say, dark as darkness itself, and into the shadow of death, where is none [t]order, but the light is there as darkness.

11

1 Job is unjustly reprehended of Zophar. 7 God is incomprehensible. 14 He is merciful to the repentant. 18 Their assurance that live godly.

1 Then answered Zophar the Naamathite, and said, **2** Should not the multitude of words be answered? or should a great [a]talker be justified? **3** Should men hold their peace at thy lies? and when thou mockest others, shall none make thee ashamed? **4** For thou hast said, [b]My doctrine is pure, and I am clean in thine eyes. **5** But, oh that God would speak and open his lips against thee! **6** That he might show thee the [c]secrets of wisdom how thou hast deserved double, according to right: know therefore that God hath forgotten thee for thine iniquity. **7** Canst thou by searching find out God? canst thou find out the Almighty to his perfection? **8** The heavens are high, what canst thou do? [d]it is deeper than the hell, how canst thou know it? **9** The measure thereof is longer than the earth, and it is broader than the Sea. **10** If he cut off and [e]shut up, or gather together, who can turn him back? **11** For he knoweth vain men, and seeth iniquity, and him that understandeth nothing. **12** Yet vain man would be wise, though man newborn is like a wild [f]ass colt. **13** If thou [g]prepare thine heart, and stretch out thine hands toward him: **14** If iniquity be in thine [h]hand, put it far away, and let no wickedness dwell in thy Tabernacle. **15** Then truly shalt thou lift up thy [i]face without spot, and shalt be stable, and shalt not fear. **16** But thou shalt forget thy misery, and remember it as waters that are past. **17** Thine age also shall appear more clear than the noon day: thou shalt shine and be as the morning. **18** And thou shalt be bold, because there is hope: and thou shalt dig pits, and shalt lie down safely. **19** [1]For when thou takest thy rest, none shall make thee afraid: yea, many shall make suit unto thee. **20** But the eyes [j]of the wicked shall fail, and their refuge shall perish, and their hope shall be sorrow of mind.

12

2 Job accuseth his friends of ignorance. 7 He declareth the might, and power of God. 17 And how he changeth the course of things.

1 Then Job answered, and said, **2** Indeed because that ye are the people only, [a]wisdom must die with you. **3** But I have understanding as well as you, and am not inferior unto you: yea, who knoweth not such things? **4** [1]I am [b]as one mocked of his neighbor, who calleth upon God, and he [c]heareth him: the just and the upright is laughed to scorn. **5** [d]He that is ready to fall, is as a lamp despised in the opinion of the rich. **6** The tabernacles of robbers do prosper, and they are in safety, that provoke God, [e]whom God hath enriched with his hand. **7** Ask now the beasts, [f]and they shall teach thee, and the fowls of the heaven, and they shall tell thee: **8** Or speak to the earth, and it shall show thee: or the fishes of the sea, and they shall declare unto thee. **9** Who is ignorant of all these, but that the hand of the Lord hath made these? **10** In whose hand is the soul of every living thing, and the breath of all [g]mankind. **11** Doth not the ears [h]discern the words, and the mouth taste meat for itself? **12** Among the [i]ancient is wisdom, and in the length of days is understanding. **13** With him is wisdom and strength: he hath counsel and understanding. **14** Behold, he will break down, and it cannot be built: he shutteth a man up, and he cannot be loosed. **15** Behold, he withholdeth the waters, and they dry up: but when he sendeth them out, they destroy the earth. **16** With him is strength and wisdom: he that is deceived, and that [j]deceiveth, are his. **17** He causeth the counselors to go as spoiled, and maketh the judges fools. **18** [k]He looseth [l]the collar of kings, and girdeth their loins with a girdle. **19** He leadeth away the princes as a prey, and overthroweth the mighty. **20** He taketh away the speech from the [m]faithful counselors, and taketh away the judgment of the ancient. **21** He poureth contempt upon princes, and maketh the strength of the mighty weak. **22** He discovereth the deep places from their darkness, and bringeth forth the shadow of death to light. **23** He [n]increaseth the people, and destroyeth them: he enlargeth the nations, and bringeth them in again. **24** He taketh away the hearts of them that are the chief over the people of the earth, and maketh them to wander in the wilderness out of the way. **25** They grope in the dark without light: and he maketh them to stagger like a drunken man.

13

3 Job compareth his knowledge with the experience of his friends. 16 The penitent shall be saved, and the hypocrite condemned, 20 He prayeth unto God, that he would not handle him rigorously.

1 Lo, mine eye hath seen all this: mine ear hath heard, and understood it. **2** I know also as much as you know: I am not inferior unto you. **3** But I will speak to the Almighty, and I desire [a]to dispute with God. **4** For indeed ye forge lies, and all you are [b]physicians of no value. **5** Oh, that you would hold your tongue, that it might be imputed to you for wisdom! **6** Now hear my disputation, and give ear to the arguments of my lips. **7** Will ye speak [c]wickedly for God's defense, and talk deceitfully for his cause? **8** Will ye accept his person? or will ye contend for God? **9** Is it well that he should seek of you? will you make a lie for him, as one lieth for a man? **10** He will surely reprove you, if ye do secretly accept any person. **11** Shall not his excellency make you afraid? and his fear fall upon you? **12** Your [d]memories may be compared unto ashes, and your bodies unto bodies of clay. **13** Hold your tongues in my presence, that I may speak, and let come upon what will. **14** Wherefore do I [e]take my flesh in my teeth, and put my soul in my hand? **15** Lo, though he slay me, yet will I trust in him, and I will reprove my ways in his sight. **16** He shall be my salvation also: for the [f]hypocrite shall not come before him. **17** Hear diligently my words, and mark my talk. **18** Behold now: if I prepare me to judgment, I know that I shall be [g]justified. **19** Who is he that will plead [h]with me? for if I now hold my tongue, I [i]die. **20** But do not these two things unto me: then will I not hide myself from thee. **21** [j]Withdraw thine hand from me, and let not thy fear make me afraid. **22** Then call thou, and I will answer: or let me speak, and answer thou me. **23** How many are [k]mine iniquities and sins, show me my rebellion and my sin. **24** Wherefore hidest thou thy face, and takest me for thine enemy? **25** Wilt thou break a leaf driven to and fro? and wilt thou pursue the dry stubble? **26** For thou writest bitter things against me, and makest me to possess the [l]iniquities of my youth. **27** Thou puttest my feet also in the [m]stocks, and lookest narrowly unto all my paths, and makest the print thereof in the [n]heels of my feet. **28** Such a one consumeth like a rotten thing, and as a garment that is moth-eaten.

---

t. Job 10:22 No distinction between light and darkness, but where all is very darkness itself.

JOB 11

a. Job 11:2 Should he persuade by his great talk, that he is just?
b. Job 11:4 He chargeth Job with this, that he should say, that the thing which he spake was true, and that he was without sin in the sight of God.
c. Job 11:6 Which is not to stand in justifying of thyself: he signifieth that man will never be overcome, while he reasoneth with another, and therefore God must break off the controversy, and stop man's mouth.
d. Job 11:8 That is, this perfection of God, and if man be not able to comprehend the height of the heaven, the depth of hell, the length of the earth, the breadth of the Sea, which are but creatures: how can he attain to the perfection of the Creator?
e. Job 11:10 If God should turn the state of things, and establish a new order in nature, who could control him?
f. Job 11:12 That is, without understanding: so that whatsoever gifts he hath afterward, come of God, and not of nature.
g. Job 11:13 If thou repent, pray unto him.
h. Job 11:14 Renounce thine own evil works, and see that they offend not God, over whom thou hast charge.
i. Job 11:15 He declareth what quietness of conscience and success in all things such shall have, which turn to God by true repentance.
j. Job 11:20 He showeth that contrary things shall come unto them that do not repent.

JOB 11

1. Lev. 26:5,6

JOB 12

a. Job 12:2 Because you feel not that which you speak, you think the whole standeth in words, and so flatter yourselves as though none knew anything, or could know but you.
b. Job 12:4 He reproveth these his friends of two faults: the one that they thought they had better knowledge than indeed they had: and the other, that instead of true consolation, they did deride and despise their friend in his adversity.
c. Job 12:4 The which neighbor being a mocker and a wicked man, thinketh that no man is in God's favor but he, because he hath all things that he desireth.
d. Job 12:5 As the rich esteem not a light, or torch that goeth out, so is he despised that falleth from prosperity to adversity.
e. Job 12:6 Hebrew, to whom God hath brought in with his hand.
f. Job 12:7 He declareth to them that did dispute against him, that their wisdom is common to all, and such as the very brute beasts do daily teach.
g. Job 12:10 Or, flesh.
h. Job 12:11 He exhorteth them to be wise in judging, and as well to know the right use why God hath given them ears, as he hath done a mouth.
i. Job 12:12 Though men by age, and continuance of time attain to wisdom, yet it is not comparable to God's wisdom, nor able to comprehend his judgments, wherein he answereth to that which was alleged, Job 8:8.
j. Job 12:16 He showeth that there is nothing done in this world without God's will and ordinance, for else he should not be Almighty.
k. Job 12:18 He taketh wisdom from them.
l. Job 12:18 He abateth the honor of princes, and bringeth them into the subjection of others.
m. Job 12:20 He causeth that their words have no credit, which is when he will punish sin.
n. Job 12:23 In this discourse of God's wonderful works, Job showeth that whatsoever is done in this world both in the order and change of things, is by God's will and appointment: wherein he declareth that he thinketh well of God, and is as able to set forth his power in words as they that reasoned against, were.

JOB 12

1. Prov. 14:2

JOB 13

a. Job 13:3 For although he knew that God had a justice, which was manifest in his ordinary working and another in his secret counsel, yet he would utter his affection to God, because he was not able to understand the cause why he did thus punish him.
b. Job 13:4 You do not well apply your medicine to the disease.
c. Job 13:7 He condemneth their zeal, which had not knowledge, neither regarded they to comfort him, but always grated on God's justice, as though it was not evidently seen in Job, except they had undertaken the probation thereof.
d. Job 13:12 Your fame shall come to nothing.
e. Job 13:14 Is not this a manifest sign of mine affliction, and that I do not complain without cause, seeing that I am thus tormented as though I should tear mine own flesh, and put my life in danger?
f. Job 13:16 Whereby he declareth that he is not an hypocrite as they charged him.
g. Job 13:18 That is, cleared and not cast off for my sins, as you reason.
h. Job 13:19 To prove that God doth thus punish me for my sins.
i. Job 13:19 If I defend not my cause, every man will condemn me.
j. Job 13:21 He showeth what these two things are.
k. Job 13:23 His pangs thus move him to reason with God, not denying but that he had sinned: but he desired to understand what were his great sins that had deserved such rigor, wherein he offended that he would know a cause of God why he did punish him.
l. Job 13:26 Thou punishest me now for the faults that I committed in my youth.
m. Job 13:27 Thou makest me thy prisoner, and dost so press me that I cannot stir hand nor foot.

14

1 Job describeth the shortness and misery of the life of man. 14 Hope sustaineth the godly. 21 The condition of man's life.

1 Man [a]that is born of woman, is of short continuance and full of trouble. **2** He shooteth forth as a flower, and is cut down: he vanisheth also as a [1]shadow, and continueth not. **3** And yet thou openest thine eyes upon such [b]one, and causest me to enter into judgment with thee. **4** [1]Who can bring a clean thing out of filthiness? there is not one. **5** Are not his days determined? the number of his months are with thee: thou hast appointed his bound, which he cannot pass. **6** Turn from him that he may cease until his desired day, [c]as an hireling. **7** For there is hope of a tree, if it be cut down, that it will yet sprout, and the branches thereof will not cease. **8** Though the root of it wax old in the earth, and the stock thereof be dead in the ground, **9** Yet by the scent of water it will bud, and bring forth boughs like a plant. **10** [d]But man is sick, and dieth, and man perisheth, and where is he? **11** As the waters pass from the sea, and as the flood decayeth and drieth up, **12** So man sleepeth and riseth not: for he shall not wake again, nor be raised from his sleep till the heaven be no more. **13** Oh that thou wouldest hide me in the grave, and keep me secret, until thy [e]wrath were past, and wouldest give me term, and [f]remember me! **14** If a man die, shall he live again? All the days of mine appointed time will I wait, till [g]my changing shall come. **15** Thou shalt call me, and I will [h]answer thee: thou lovest the work of thine own hands. **16** But now thou numberest my steps, and doest not delay my sins. **17** Mine iniquity is sealed up, as in a [i]bag, and thou addest unto my wickedness. **18** And surely as the mountain that falleth, cometh to nought, and the [j]rock that is removed from his place: **19** As the water breaketh the stones, when thou overflowest the things which grow in the dust of the earth: so thou destroyest the hope of man. **20** Thou prevailest always against him, so that he passeth away: he changeth his face when thou castest him away. **21** And he knoweth not if his sons shall be honorable, neither shall he understand concerning them, whether they shall be of low degree, **22** But while his [k]flesh is upon him, he shall be sorrowful, and while his soul is in him, it shall mourn.

15

1 Eliphaz reprehendeth Job, because he ascribeth wisdom and pureness to himself. 16 He describeth the curse that falleth on the wicked, reckoning Job to be one of the number.

1 Then answered Eliphaz the Temanite, and said, **2** Shall a wise man speak words of the [a]wind? and fill his belly [b]with the East wind? **3** Shall he dispute with words not comely? or with talk that is not profitable? **4** Surely thou hast cast off [c]fear, and restrainest prayer before God: **5** For thy mouth declareth thine iniquity, seeing thou hast chosen the [d]tongue of the crafty. **6** Thine own mouth condemneth thee, and not I, and thy lips testify against thee. **7** Art thou the [e]first man that was born? and wast thou made before the hills? **8** Hast thou heard the secret counsel of God, and dost thou restrain wisdom [f]to thee? **9** What knowest thou that we know not? and understandest that is not in us? **10** With us are both ancient and very aged men, far older than thy father. **11** Seem the consolations of God [g]small unto thee? is this thing strange unto thee? **12** Why doth thine heart [h]take thee away, and what do thine eyes mean, **13** That thou answerest to God [i]at thy pleasure, and bringest such words out of thy mouth? **14** What is man, that he should be clean? and he that is born of woman, that he should [j]be just? **15** Behold, he found no steadfastness in his Saints: yea, the heavens are not clean in his sight. **16** How much more is man abominable, and filthy, which [k]drinketh iniquity like water? **17** I will tell thee: hear me, and I will declare that which I have seen: **18** Which wise men have told, as they have heard of their fathers, and have not kept it secret: **19** To whom alone the land was [l]given, and no stranger passed through them. **20** The wicked man is continually as one that travaileth of child, and the number [m]of years is hid from the tyrant. **21** A sound of fear is in his ears, and in his prosperity the destroyer shall come upon him. **22** He believeth not to return out of [n]darkness: for he seeth the sword before him. **23** He wandereth [o]to and fro for bread where he may: he knoweth that the day of darkness is prepared at hand. **24** Affliction and [p]anguish shall make him afraid: they shall prevail against him as a king ready to the battle. **25** For he hath stretched out his hand against God, and made himself strong against the Almighty. **26** Therefore God shall run upon him, even upon his neck, and against the most thick part of his shield. **27** Because he hath covered his face with [q]his fatness, and hath collops in his flank. **28** Though he dwell [r]in desolate cities, and in houses which no man inhabiteth, but are become heaps, **29** He shall not be rich, neither shall his substance continue, neither shall he prolong the [s]perfection thereof in the earth. **30** He shall never depart out of darkness: the flame shall dry up his branches, and he shall go away with the breath of his mouth. **31** He [t]believeth not that he erreth in vanity: therefore vanity shall be his change. **32** His branch shall not be green, but shall be cut off before his day. **33** God shall destroy him as the vine her sour [u]grape, and shall cast him off, as the olive doth her flower. **34** For the congregation of the hypocrite shall be desolate, and fire shall devour the houses of [v]bribes. **35** For they [w]conceive mischief and bring forth vanity, and their belly hath prepared deceit.

16

1 Job moved by the importunacy of his friends, 7 Counteth in what extremity he is. 19 And taketh God to witness of his innocence.

1 But Job answered and said, **2** I have oftentimes heard such things: miserable comforters are ye all. **3** Shall there be none end of words of [a]wind? or what maketh thee bold so to [b]answer? **4** I could also speak as ye do: (but would God your [c]soul were in my soul's stead) I could keep you company in speaking, and could [d]shake mine head at you, **5** But I would strengthen you [e]with my mouth, and the comfort of my lips should assuage your sorrow. **6** Though I speak, my sorrow [f]cannot be assuaged: though I cease, what release have I? **7** But now [g]he maketh me weary: O God, thou hast made all my [h]congregation desolate, **8** And hast made me full of [i]wrinkles which is a witness thereof, and my leanness riseth up in me, testifying the same in my face. **9** [j]His wrath hath torn me, and he hateth me, and gnasheth upon me with his teeth: mine enemy hath sharpened his eyes against me. **10** They have opened their mouths upon me, and smitten me on the [k]cheek in reproach: they gathered themselves together against me. **11** God hath delivered me to the unjust, and hath made me to turn out of the way by the [l]hands of the wicked. **12** I was in wealth, but he hath brought me to nought: he hath taken me by the neck and beaten me, and set me as a mark for himself. **13** His [m]archers compass me round about: he cutteth my reins, and doth not spare, and poureth my gall [n]upon the ground. **14** He hath broken me with one breaking

---

n. Job 13:27 Hebrew, roots.

JOB 14

a. Job 14:1 Taking occasion of his adversary's words, he describeth the state of man's life from his birth to his death.
b. Job 14:3 His meaning is, that seeing that man is so frail a creature, God should not handle him so extremely, wherein Job showeth the wickedness of the flesh, when it is not subject to the Spirit.
c. Job 14:6 Until the time that thou hast appointed for him to die, which he desireth as the hireling waiteth for the end of his labor to receive his wages.
d. Job 14:10 He speaketh not here as though he had not hope of the immortality, but as a man in extreme pain, when reason is overcome by affections and torments.
e. Job 14:13 Hereby he declareth that the fear of God's judgment was the cause why he desired to die.
f. Job 14:13 That is, release my pains and take me to mercy.
g. Job 14:14 Meaning, unto the day of the resurrection when he should be changed, and renewed.
h. Job 14:15 Though I be afflicted in this life, yet in the resurrection I shall feel thy mercies and answer when thou callest me.
i. Job 14:17 Thou layest them all together, and sufferest none of my sins unpunished.
j. Job 14:18 He murmureth through the impatience of the flesh against God, as though he used as great severity against him as against the hard rocks, or waters that overflow, so that hereby all the occasion of his hope is taken away.
k. Job 14:22 Yet while he shall be in pain, and misery.

JOB 14

1. Job. 8:9 / Ps. 144:4
2. ps. 51:5,7
3. Prov. 5:21

JOB 15

a. Job 15:2 That is, vain words, and without consolation?
b. Job 15:2 Meaning, with matters that are of none importance, which are forgotten as soon as they are uttered, as the East wind drieth up the moisture as soon as it falleth.
c. Job 15:4 He chargeth Job as though his talk caused men to cast off the fear of God, and prayer.
d. Job 15:5 Thou speakest as do the mockers and contemners of God.
e. Job 15:7 That is, the most ancient, and so by reason the most wise?
f. Job 15:8 Art thou only wise?
g. Job 15:11 He accuseth Job's pride and ingratitude, that will not be comforted by God, nor by their counsel.
h. Job 15:12 Why dost thou stand in thine own conceit?
i. Job 15:13 Hebrew, in thy spirit.
j. Job 15:14 His purpose is to prove that Job as an unjust man, and an hypocrite is punished for his sins, like as he did before, Job 4:8.
k. Job 15:16 Which hath a desire to sin, as he that is thirsty to drink.
l. Job 15:19 Who by their wisdom so governed, that no stranger invaded them, and so the land seemed to be given to them alone.
m. Job 15:20 The cruel man is ever in danger of death, and is never quiet in conscience.
n. Job 15:22 Out of that misery whereunto he once falleth.
o. Job 15:23 God doth not only impoverish the wicked oft times, but even in their prosperity he punisheth them with a greediness evermore to gather: which is as a beggary.
p. Job 15:24 He showeth what weapons God useth against the wicked, which lift up themselves against him, to wit, terror of conscience, and outward afflictions.
q. Job 15:27 That is, he was so puffed up with great prosperity and abundance of all things, that he forgat God: noting, that Job in his felicity had not the true fear of God.
r. Job 15:28 Though he build and repair ruinous places to get him fame, yet God shall bring all to naught, and turn his great prosperity into extreme misery.
s. Job 15:29 Meaning, that his sumptuous buildings should never come to perfection.
t. Job 15:31 He standeth so in his own conceit, that he will give no place to good counsel, therefore his own pride shall bring him to destruction.
u. Job 15:33 As one that gathereth grapes before they be ripe.
v. Job 15:34 Which were built or maintained by powling and bribery.
w. Job 15:35 And therefore all their vain devises shall turn to their own destruction.

JOB 16

a. Job 16:3 Which serve for vain ostentation and for no true comfort.
b. Job 16:3 For Eliphaz did reply against Job's answer.
c. Job 16:4 I would you felt that which I do.
d. Job 16:4 That is, mock at your misery, as you do at mine.
e. Job 16:5 If this were in my power, yet would I comfort you, and not do as ye do to me.
f. Job 16:6 If they would say, Why dost thou not then comfort thyself? he answereth, that the judgments of God are more heavy than he is able to assuage either by words or silence.
g. Job 16:7 Meaning, God.
h. Job 16:7 That is, destroyed most of my family.
i. Job 16:8 In token of sorrow and grief.
j. Job 16:9 That is, God by his wrath: and in this diversity of words and high style, he expresseth how grievous the hand of God was upon him.
k. Job 16:10 That is, hath handled me most contemptuously: for so smiting on the cheek signified, 1 Kings 22:24; Mark 14:65.
l. Job 16:11 They have led me whither they would.
m. Job 16:13 His manifold afflictions.
n. Job 16:13 I am wounded to the heart.
o. Job 16:15 Meaning, his glory was brought low.
p. Job 16:17 Signifying, that he is not able to comprehend the cause of this his grievous punishment.

upon another, and runneth upon me like a giant. **15** I have sowed a sackcloth
upon my skin, and have abased mine [o]horn unto the dust. **16** My face is withe-
red with weeping, and the shadow of death is upon mine eyes, **17** Though there
be no wickedness in [p]mine hands, and my prayer [q]be pure. **18** O earth, cover
not thou my [r]blood, and let my crying find no place. **19** For lo, now my [s]wit-
ness is in the heaven, and my record is on high. **20** My friends [t]speak eloquently
against me: but mine eye poureth out tears unto God. **21** Oh that a man might
[u]plead with God, as man with his neighbor! **22** For the years accounted come,
and I shall go the way, whence I shall not return.

17

1 Job sayeth that he consumeth away, and yet doth patiently abide it. 10 He exhorteth his friends to repentance, 13 showing that he looketh out for death.

1 My breath is corrupt: my days are cut off, and the grave is ready for
me. **2** There are none but [a]mockers with me, and mine eye continueth in [b]their
bitterness. **3** [c]Lay down now, and put me in surety for thee: who is he, that [d]will
touch mine hand? **4** For thou hast hid their heart from [e]understanding: there-
fore shalt thou not set them up on high. **5** [f]For the eyes of his children shall fail,
that speaketh flattery to his friends. **6** He hath also made me a [g]byword of the
people, and I am as a tabret [h]before them. **7** Mine eye therefore is dim for grief,
and all my strength is like a shadow. **8** The righteous shall be astonied at [i]this,
and the innocent shall be moved against the hypocrite. **9** But the righteous will
hold his [j]way, and he whose hands are pure, shall increase his strength. **10** All
[k]you therefore turn you, and come now, and I shall not find one wise among
you. **11** My days are past, mine enterprises are broken, and the thoughts of mine
heart **12** Have changed the [l]night for the day, and the light that approached,
for darkness. **13** Though I hope, [m]yet the grave shall be mine house, and I shall
make my bed in the dark. **14** I shall say to corruption, Thou art my [n]father, and
to the worm, Thou art my mother and my sister. **15** Where is then now mine
hope? or who shall consider the thing that I hoped for? **16** [o]They shall go down
into the bottom of the pit: surely it shall lie together in the dust.

18

1 Bildad rehearseth the pains of the unfaithful and wicked.

1 Then answered Bildad the Shuhite, and said, **2** When will
[a]ye make an end of your words? [b]cause us to understand, and then we will spe-
ak. **3** Wherefore are we counted as beasts, and are vile in your sight? **4** Thou
art [c]as one that teareth his soul in his anger. Shall the [d]earth be forsaken for thy
sake? or the rock removed out of his place? **5** Yea, the light of the wicked shall be
[e]quenched, and the spark of his fire shall not shine. **6** The light shall be dark in
his dwelling, and his candle shall be put out with him. **7** The steps of his strength
shall be restrained, and his own counsel shall cast him down. **8** For he is taken
in the net by his feet, and he [f]walketh upon the snares. **9** The grenne shall take
him by the heel, and the chief shall come upon him. **10** A snare is laid for him in
the ground, and a trap for him in the way. **11** Fearfulness shall make him afraid
on every side, and shall drive him to his feet. **12** His strength shall be [g]famine:
and destruction shall be ready at his side. **13** It shall devour the inner parts of his
skin, and the [h]firstborn of death shall devour his strength. **14** His hope shall be
rooted out of his dwelling, and shall cause him to go to the [i]king of fear. **15** Fear
shall dwell in his house (because it is not [j]his) [k]and brimstone shall be scattered
upon his habitation. **16** His roots shall be dried up beneath, and above shall his
branch be cut down. **17** His remembrance shall perish from the earth, and he
shall have no name in the street. **18** They shall drive him out of the [l]light unto
darkness, and chase him out of the world. **19** He shall neither have son nor ne-
phew among his people, nor any posterity in his dwellings. **20** The posterity
shall be astonied at his [m]day, and fear shall come upon the ancient. **21** Surely
such are the habitations of the wicked, and this is the place of him that knoweth
not God.

19

2 Job reproveth his friends, 8 and reciteth his miseries and grievous pains. 25 He assureth himself of the general resurrection.

1 But Job answered, and said, **2** How long will ye vex my soul, and torment
me with words? **3** Ye have now [a]ten times reproached me, and are not ashamed:
ye are impudent toward me. **4** And though I had indeed erred, mine error [b]re-
maineth with me. **5** But indeed if ye will advance yourselves against me, and
rebuke me for my reproach, **6** Know now, that God hath [c]overthrown me, and
hath compassed me with his net. **7** Behold, I cry out of violence, but I have none
answer: I cry, but there is no judgment. **8** He hath hedged up my way that I can-
not [d]pass, and he hath set darkness in my paths. **9** He hath spoiled me of mine
honor, and taken the [e]crown away from mine head. **10** He hath destroyed me on
every side, and I am gone: and he hath removed mine hope like [f]a tree. **11** And
he hath kindled his wrath against me, and counteth me as one of his ene-
mies. **12** His [g]armies came together, and made their way upon me, and camped
about my tabernacle. **13** He hath removed my brethren far from me, and also
mine acquaintance were strangers unto me. **14** My neighbors have forsaken me,
and my familiars have forgotten me. **15** [h]They that dwell in mine house, and my
maids took me for a stranger: for I was a stranger in their sight. **16** I called my
servant, but he would not answer, though I prayed him with my mouth. **17** My
breath was strange unto my wife, though I prayed her for the children's sake of
mine [i]own body. **18** The wicked also despised me, and when I rose, they spake
against me. **19** All my secret friends abhorred me, and they whom I loved, are
turned against me. **20** My bone [j]cleaveth to my skin and to my flesh, and I have
escaped with the [k]skin of my teeth. **21** Have pity upon me: have [l]pity upon me,
(O ye my friends) for the hand of God hath touched me. **22** Why do ye persecu-
te me, as [m]God? and are not satisfied with my [n]flesh? **23** Oh that my words were
now written! oh that they were written even in a book, **24** And graven with [o]an
iron pen in lead, or in stone forever! **25** For I am sure that my [p]Redeemer liveth,
and he shall stand the last on the earth. **26** And though after my skin worms
destroy this body, yet shall I see God [q]in my flesh. **27** Whom I myself shall see,
and mine eyes shall behold, and none other for me, though my reins are consumed
within me. **28** But ye said, Why is he persecuted? And there was a [r]deep matter
in me. **29** Be ye afraid of the sword: for the sword will be [s]avenged of wicked-
ness, that ye may know that there is a judgment.

---

q. Job 16:17 That is, unfeigned, and without hypocrisy.
r. Job 16:18 Let my sin be known if I be such a sinner as mine adversaries accuse me, and let me find no favor.
s. Job 16:19 Though man condemn me, yet God is witness of my cause.
t. Job 16:20 Use painted words instead of true consolation.
u. Job 16:21 Thus by his great torments he is carried away, and breaketh out into passions, and speaketh unadvisedly, as though God should entreat man more gently, seeing he hath but a short time here to live.

JOB 17

a. Job 17:2 Instead of comfort, being now at death's door, he had but them that mocked at him, and discouraged him.
b. Job 17:2 I see still that they seek but to vex me.
c. Job 17:3 He reasoneth with God as a man beside himself, to the intent that his cause might be brought to light.
d. Job 17:3 And answers for thee?
e. Job 17:4 That these mine afflictions are thy just judgments, though man know not the cause.
f. Job 17:5 He that flattereth a man, and only judgeth him happy in his prosperity, shall not himself only but in his posterity be punished.
g. Job 17:6 God hath made all the world to speak of me, because of mine afflictions.
h. Job 17:6 That is, as a continual sound in their ears.
i. Job 17:8 To wit, when they see the godly punished: but in the end they shalt come to understanding, and know what shall be the reward of the hypocrite.
j. Job 17:9 That is, will not be discouraged, considering that the godly are punished as well as the wicked.
k. Job 17:10 Job speaketh to them three that came to comfort him.
l. Job 17:12 That is, have brought me sorrow instead of comfort.
m. Job 17:13 Though I should hope to come from adversity to prosperity, as your discourse pretendeth.
n. Job 17:14 I have no more hope in father, mother, sister, or any worldly thing: for the dust and worms shall be to me instead of them.
o. Job 17:16 All worldly hope and prosperity fail which you say, are only signs of God's favor: but seeing that these things perish, I set mine hope in God and in the life everlasting.

JOB 18

a. Job 18:2 Which count yourselves just, as Job 12:4.
b. Job 18:2 Whom you take to be but beasts, as Job 12:7.
c. Job 18:4 That is, like a madman.
d. Job 18:4 Shall God change the order of nature for thy sake, by dealing with thee otherwise than he doth with all men?
e. Job 18:5 When the wicked is in his prosperity, then God changeth his state: and this is his ordinary working for their sins.
f. Job 18:8 Meaning, that the wicked are in continual danger.
g. Job 18:12 That which should nourish him shall be consumed by famine.
h. Job 18:13 That is, some strong and violent death shall consume his strength: or as the Hebrew word signifieth, his members or parts.
i. Job 18:14 That is, with most great fear.
j. Job 18:15 Meaning, not truly come by.
k. Job 18:15 Though all the world would favor him, yet God would destroy him and his.
l. Job 18:18 He shall fall from prosperity to adversity.
m. Job 18:20 When they shall see what came unto him.

JOB 19

a. Job 19:3 That is, many times, as Neh. 4:12.
b. Job 19:4 That is, I myself shall be punished for it, or you have not yet confuted it.
c. Job 19:6 He bursteth out again into his passions, and declareth still that his affliction cometh of God, though he be not able to feel the cause in himself.
d. Job 19:8 Meaning, out of his afflictions.
e. Job 19:9 Meaning, his children, and whatsoever was dear unto him in this world.
f. Job 19:10 Which is plucked up, and hath no more hope to grow.
g. Job 19:12 His manifold afflictions.
h. Job 19:15 Mine household servants: by all these losses Job showeth that touching the flesh he had great occasion to be moved.
i. Job 19:17 Which were hers and mine.
j. Job 19:20 Besides these great losses and most cruel unkindness, he was touched in his own person, as followeth.
k. Job 19:20 All my flesh was consumed.
l. Job 19:21 Seeing I have these just causes to complain, condemn me not as an hypocrite, specially ye which should comfort me.
m. Job 19:22 Is it not enough that God doth punish me, except you by reproaches increase my sorrow?
n. Job 19:22 To see my body punished, except ye trouble my mind?
o. Job 19:24 He protesteth that notwithstanding his sore passions his religion is perfect: and that he is not a blasphemer as they judged him.
p. Job 19:25 I do not so justify myself before the world, but I know that I shall come before the great Judge, who shall be my deliverer and Savior.
q. Job 19:26 Herein Job declareth plainly that he had a full hope, that both the soul and body should enjoy the presence of God in the last resurrection.
r. Job 19:28 Though his friends thought that he was but persecuted of God for his sins, yet he declareth that there was a deeper consideration, to wit, the trial of his faith and patience, and so to be an example for others.
s. Job 19:29 God will be revenged of this hasty judgment, whereby you condemned me.

20

1 Zophar showeth, that the wicked and the covetous shall have a short end, 22 though for a time they flourish.

1 Then answered Zophar the Naamathite, and said, 2 Doubtless my thou-
ghts cause me to answer, and therefore I make haste. 3 I have heard [a]the cor-
rection of my reproach: therefore the spirit of mine understanding causeth me to
answer. 4 Knowest thou not this of old? and since God placed man upon the
earth, 5 That the rejoicing of the wicked is short, and that the joy of the hypo-
crites is but a moment? 6 Though [b]his excellency mount up to the heaven, and
his head reach unto the clouds, 7 Yet shall he perish forever like his dung, and
they which have seen him, shall say, Where is he? 8 He shall flee away as a dre-
am, and they shall not find him, and shall pass away as a vision of the night. 9 So
that the eye which had seen him, shall do so no more, and his place shall see him
no more. 10 His children shall [c]flatter the poor, and his hands shall [d]restore his
substance. 11 His bones are full of the sin of his youth, and [e]it shall lie down
with him in the dust. 12 When wickedness was [f]sweet in his mouth, and he hid
it under his tongue, 13 And favored it, and would not forsake it, but kept it
close in his mouth, 14 Then his meat in his bowels was turned: the gall of Asps
was in the midst of him. 15 He hath devoured substance, and he shall vomit it:
for God shall draw it out of his belly. 16 He shall suck the [g]gall of Asps, and the
viper's tongue shall slay him. 17 He shall not see the [h]rivers, nor the floods and
streams of honey and butter. 18 He shall restore the labor, and shall devour no
more: even according to the substance shall be his exchange, [i]and he shall enjoy
it no more. 19 For he hath undone many: he hath forsaken the poor, and hath
spoiled houses which he built not. 20 Surely he shall feel no quietness in his
body, neither shall he reserve of that which he desired. 21 There shall none of his
[j]meat be left: therefore none shall hope for his goods. 22 When he shall be filled
with his abundance, he shall be in pain, and the hand [k]of all the wicked shall assail
him. 23 He shall be about to fill his belly, but God shall send upon him his fierce
wrath, [l]and shall cause to rain upon him, even upon his meat. 24 He shall flee
from the iron weapons, and the bow of steel shall strike him through. 25 The
arrow is drawn out, and cometh forth of the [m]body, and shineth of his gall, so fear
cometh upon him. 26 [n]All darkness shall be hid in his secret places: the fire that
is not [o]blown shall devour him, and that which remaineth in his tabernacle shall
be destroyed. 27 The heaven shall declare his wickedness, and the earth shall rise
up against him. 28 The [p]increase of his house shall go away: it shall flow away in
the day of his wrath. 29 This is the portion of the wicked man from [q]God, and
the heritage that he shall have of God, for his [r]words.

21

7 Job declareth how the prosperity of the wicked maketh them proud. 15 Insomuch that they blaspheme God. 16 Their destruction is at hand. 23 None ought to be judged wicked for affliction, neither good for prosperity.

1 But Job answered, and said, 2 Hear diligently my words, and this [a]shall
be instead of your consolations. 3 Suffer me that I may speak, and when I have
spoken, mock on. 4 Do I direct my talk to man? If it [b]were so, how should not
my spirit be troubled? 5 Mark me, and be abashed, and lay your hand upon your
[c]mouth. 6 Even when I remember, I am afraid, and fear taketh hold on my fle-
sh. 7 Wherefore do the wicked [d]live, and wax old, and grow in wealth? 8 Their
seed is established in their sight with them, and their generation before their
eyes. 9 Their houses are peaceable without fear, and the rod of God is not upon
them. 10 Their bullock gendereth, and faileth not: their cow calveth, and ca-
steth not her calf. 11 They send forth their children [e]like sheep, and their sons
dance. 12 They take the tambourine and harp, and rejoice in the sound of the
organs. 13 They spend their days in wealth, and suddenly [f]they go down to the
grave. 14 They say also unto God, Depart from us: for we desire not the [g]know-
ledge of thy ways. 15 Who is the Almighty, that we should serve him? and what
profit should we have, if we should pray unto him? 16 Lo, their wealth is not in
their [h]hand: therefore let the counsel of the wicked [i]be far from me. 17 How oft
shall the candle of the wicked be put out and their destruction come upon them?
he will divide their lives in his wrath. 18 They shall be as stubble before the
wind, and as chaff that the storm carrieth away. 19 God will lay up the sorrow of
the father for his children: when he rewardeth him, he shall know it. 20 [j]His eyes
shall see his destruction, and he shall drink of the wrath of the Almighty. 21 For
what pleasure hath he in his house after him, when the number of his months
is cut off? 22 Shall any teach [k]God knowledge, who judgeth the highest thin-
gs? 23 One [l]dieth in his full strength, being in all ease and prosperity. 24 His
breasts are full of milk, and his bones run full of marrow. 25 And another
[m]dieth in the bitterness of his soul, and never eateth with pleasure. 26 They
shall sleep both in [n]the dust, and the worms shall cover them. 27 Behold, I
know your thoughts, and the enterprises wherewith ye do me wrong. 28 For ye
say, Where is the prince's [o]house? and where is the tabernacle of the wicked's dwel-
ling? 29 May ye [p]not ask them that go by the way? and ye cannot deny their
signs. 30 But the wicked is kept unto the day of [q]destruction, and they shall be
brought forth to the day of wrath. 31 Who shall declare his way [r]to his face? and
who shall reward him for that he hath done? 32 Yet shall he be brought to the
grave, and remain in the heap. 33 The [s]slimy valley shall be sweet unto him, and
every man shall draw after him, as before him there were innumerable. 34 How
then comfort [t]ye me in vain, seeing in your answer there remain but lies?

22

2 Eliphaz affirmeth that Job is punished for his sins. 6 He accuseth him of unmercifulness. 13 And that he denied God's providence. 21 He exhorteth to repentance.

1 Then Eliphaz the Temanite answered, and said, 2 May a man be [a]profi-
table unto God, as he that is wise may be profitable to himself? 3 Is it anything
unto the Almighty, that thou art righteous? or is it profitable to him, that thou
makest thy ways upright? 4 Is it for fear [b]of thee that he will accuse thee? or go
with thee into judgment? 5 Is not thy wickedness great, and thine iniquities in-
numerable? 6 For thou hast taken the [c]pledge from thy brother for nought, and
spoiled the clothes of the naked. 7 To such as were weary, thou hast not given
water to drink, and hast withdrawn bread from the hungry. 8 But the mighty
man [d]had the earth, and he that was in authority, dwelt in it. 9 Thou hast cast
out widows empty, and the arms of the [e]fatherless were broken. 10 Therefore
snares are round about thee, and fear shall suddenly trouble thee. 11 Or dark-
ness that thou shouldest not see, and [f]abundance of waters shall cover thee. 12 Is
not God on [g]high in the heaven? and behold the height of the [h]stars how high
they are. 13 But thou sayest, How should God [i]know? can he judge through the

---

JOB 20

- **a.** Job 20:3 He declareth that two things moved him to speak: to wit, because Job seemed to touch him, and because he thought he had knowledge sufficient to confute him.
- **b.** Job 20:6 His purpose is to prove Job to be a wicked man, and an hypocrite, because God punished him, and changed his prosperity into adversity.
- **c.** Job 20:10 Whereas the father through ambition and tyranny oppressed the poor, the children through poverty and misery, shall seek favor at the poor.
- **d.** Job 20:10 So that the thing which he hath taken away by violence shall be restored again by force.
- **e.** Job 20:11 Meaning, that he shall carry nothing away with him but his sin.
- **f.** Job 20:12 As poison that is sweet in the mouth, bringeth destruction when it cometh into the body: so all vice at the first is pleasant, but afterward God turneth it to destruction.
- **g.** Job 20:16 He compareth evil gotten goods to the venom of Asps, which serpent is most dangerous: noting that Job's great riches were not truly come by and therefore God did plague him justly for the same.
- **h.** Job 20:17 Though God give to all other abundance of his blessings, yet he shall have no part thereof.
- **i.** Job 20:18 That is, these raveners and spoilers of the poor shall enjoy their theft but for a time: for after, God will take it from them, and cause them to make restitution, so that it is but an exchange.
- **j.** Job 20:21 He shall leave nothing to his posterity.
- **k.** Job 20:22 The wicked shall never be in rest: for one wicked man shall seek to destroy another.
- **l.** Job 20:23 Some read, upon his flesh, alluding to Job, whose flesh was smitten with a scab.
- **m.** Job 20:25 Some read, of the quiver.
- **n.** Job 20:26 All fear and sorrow shall light upon him, when he thinketh to escape.
- **o.** Job 20:26 That is, fire from heaven, or the fire of God's wrath.
- **p.** Job 20:28 Meaning, the children of the wicked shall flow away like rivers, and be dispersed in divers places.
- **q.** Job 20:29 Thus God will plague the wicked.
- **r.** Job 20:29 Against God, thinking to excuse himself, and to escape God's hand.

JOB 21

- **a.** Job 21:2 Your diligent marking of my words shall be to me a great consolation.
- **b.** Job 21:4 As though he would say, I do not talk with man but with God, who will not answer me, and therefore my mind must needs be troubled.
- **c.** Job 21:5 He chargeth them as though they were not able to comprehend this his feeling of God's judgment, and exhorteth them therefore to silence.
- **d.** Job 21:7 Job proveth against his adversaries that God punisheth not straightways the wicked, but oft times giveth them long life, and prosperity: so that we must not judge God just or unjust by the things that appear to our eyes.
- **e.** Job 21:11 They have store of children, lusty and healthful, and in these points he answereth to that which Zophar alleged before.
- **f.** Job 21:13 Not being tormented with long sickness.
- **g.** Job 21:14 They desire nothing more than to be exempt from all subjection that they should bear to God: thus Job showeth his adversaries, that if they reason only by that which is seen by common experience, the wicked that hate God, are better dealt withal, than they that love him.
- **h.** Job 21:16 It is not their own, but God only lendeth it unto them.
- **i.** Job 21:16 God keep me from their prosperity.
- **j.** Job 21:20 When God recompenseth his wickedness, he shall know that his prosperity was but vanity.
- **k.** Job 21:22 Who sendeth to the wicked prosperity, and punisheth the godly.
- **l.** Job 21:23 Meaning, the wicked.
- **m.** Job 21:25 To wit, the godly.
- **n.** Job 21:26 As concerning their bodies: and this he speaketh according to the common judgment.
- **o.** Job 21:28 Thus they called Job's house in derision, concluding that it was destroyed because he was wicked.
- **p.** Job 21:29 Which through long travailing have experience and tokens thereof, to wit, that the wicked do prosper, and the godly live in affliction.
- **q.** Job 21:30 Though the wicked flourish here, yet God will punish him in the last day.
- **r.** Job 21:31 Though men do flatter him, and none dare reprove him in this world, yet death is a token that he will bring him to an account.
- **s.** Job 21:33 He shall be glad to lie in a slimy pit, which before could not be content with a royal palace.
- **t.** Job 21:34 Saying, that the just in this world have prosperity, and the wicked adversity.

JOB 22

- **a.** Job 22:2 Though man were just, yet God could have no profit of this his justice: and therefore when he punished him, he hath no regard to his justice, but to his sin.
- **b.** Job 22:4 Lest thou shouldest reprove or hurt him?
- **c.** Job 22:6 Thou hast been cruel and without charity, and wouldest do nothing for the poor, but for thine own advantage.
- **d.** Job 22:8 When thou wast in power and authority, thou didst not justice but wrong.
- **e.** Job 22:9 Thou hast not only not showed pity, but oppressed them.
- **f.** Job 22:11 That is, manifold afflictions.
- **g.** Job 22:12 He accuseth Job of impiety and contempt of God, as though he would say, If thou pass not for men, yet consider the height of God's majesty.
- **h.** Job 22:12 That so much the more by that excellent work thou mayest fear God, and reverence him.
- **i.** Job 22:13 He reproveth Job, as though he denied God's providence and that he could not see the things that were done in this world.

dark cloud? **14** The clouds hide him that he cannot see, and he walketh in the
circle of heaven. **15** Hast thou marked the way of the world, [j]wherein wicked
men have walked? **16** Which were [k]cut down before the time, whose founda-
tion was as a river that overflowed: **17** Which said unto God, Depart from us,
and asked what the Almighty could do for them. **18** Yet he [l]filled their houses
with good things: but let the counsel of the wicked be far from me. **19** The ri-
ghteous shall see them, and shall rejoice, [m]and the innocent shall laugh them to
scorn. **20** Surely [n]our substance is hid: but the fire hath devoured the remnant
of [o]them. **21** Therefore acquaint thyself, I pray thee, [p]with him, and make peace:
thereby thou shalt have prosperity. **22** Receive, I pray thee, the law of his mouth,
and lay up his words in thine heart. **23** If thou return to the Almighty, thou shalt
[q]be built up, and thou shalt put iniquity far from thy tabernacle. **24** Thou shalt
lay up gold for [r]dust, and the gold of Ophir, as the flints of the rivers. **25** Yea,
the Almighty shall be thy defense, and thou shalt have plenty of silver. **26** And
thou shalt then delight in the Almighty, and lift up thy face unto God. **27** Thou
shalt make thy prayer unto him, and he shall hear thee, and thou shalt render thy
vows. **28** Thou shalt also decree a thing, and he shall establish it unto thee, and
the [s]light shall shine upon thy ways. **29** [t]When others are cast down, then shalt
thou say, I am lifted up: and God shall save the humble person. **30** The innocent
shall deliver the [u]island, and it shall be preserved by the pureness of thine hands.

23

Job affirmeth that he both knoweth and feareth the power and sentence of the Judge, 10 And that he is not punished only for his sins.

1 But Job answered, and said, **2** Though my talk be this day in [a]bitterness,
and my plague greater than my groaning, **3** Would God yet I knew how to find
him, I would enter unto his place. **4** I would plead the cause before him, and
fill my mouth with arguments. **5** I would know the words, that he would an-
swer me, and would understand what he would say unto me. **6** Would he [b]plead
against me with his great power? No, but he would [c]put strength in me. **7** [d]The-
re the righteous might reason with him, so I should be delivered forever from my
Judge. **8** [e]Behold, if I go to the East, he is not there: if to the West, yet I cannot
perceive him: **9** If to the North where he worketh, yet I cannot see him: he will
hide himself in the South, and I cannot behold him. **10** But he knoweth my
[f]way, and trieth me, and I shall come forth like gold. **11** My foot hath followed
his steps: his way have I kept, and have not declined: **12** Neither have I departed
from the commandment of his lips, and I have [g]esteemed the words of his mouth
more than mine appointed food. **13** Yet he is in one mind, and who can [h]turn
him? yea, he doeth what his mind desireth. **14** For he will perform that which
is decreed of me, and [i]many such things are with him. **15** Therefore I am trou-
bled at his presence, and in considering it, I am afraid of him. **16** For [j]God hath
softened mine heart, and the Almighty hath troubled me. **17** For I am not cut
off in [k]darkness, but he hath hid the darkness from my face.

24

2 Job describeth the wickedness of men, and showeth what curse belongeth to the wicked. 12 How all things are governed by God's providence. 17 And the destruction of the wicked.

1 How should not the times [a]be hid from the Almighty, seeing that they whi-
ch know him, see not his [b]days? **2** Some remove the landmarks, that rob the
flocks and feed thereof. **3** They lead away the ass of the fatherless, and take the
widow's ox to pledge. **4** They make the poor to turn out of the way, so that the
poor of the earth hide themselves [c]together. **5** Behold, others as wild asses in the
wilderness, go forth to their business, and [d]rise early for a prey: the wilderness [e]gi-
veth him and his children food. **6** They reap [f]his provision in the field, but they
gather the late [g]vintage of the wicked. **7** They cause the naked to lodge without
garment, and without covering in the cold. **8** They are wet with the showers
of the mountains, [h]and they embrace the rock for want of a covering. **9** They
pluck the fatherless [i]from the breast, and take the pledge of [j]the poor. **10** They
cause him to go naked without clothing, and take the gleaning from the hun-
gry. **11** They that make oil [k]between their walls, and tread their winepresses,
suffer thirst. **12** Men [l]cry out of the city, and the souls of the slain [m]cry out:
yet God [n]doth not charge them with folly. **13** These are they that abhor the [o]li-
ght: they know not the ways thereof, nor continue in the paths thereof. **14** The
murderer riseth early, and killeth the poor and the needy: and in the night he is
as a thief. **15** The eye also of the [p]adulterer waiteth for the twilight, and saith,
None eye shall see me, and disguiseth his face. **16** They dig through houses
in the dark, which they marked for themselves in the day: they know not the li-
ght. **17** But the morning is even to them as the shadow of death: if one know
them, they are in the terrors of the shadow of death. **18** He is swift upon the
[q]waters: their [r]portion shall be cursed in the earth: he will not behold the way of
the vineyards. **19** As the dry ground and heat consume the snow waters, so shall
the grave [s]the sinners. **20** [t]The pitiful man shall forget him: the worm shall feel
his sweetness: he shall be no more remembered, and the wicked shall be broken
like a tree. **21** He [u]doth evil entreat the barren that doth not bear, neither doeth
he good to the widow. **22** He draweth also the [v]mighty by his power, and when
he riseth up, none is sure of life. **23** Though men give him assurance to be in
safety, yet his eyes are upon their ways. **24** They are exalted for a little, but they
are gone, and are brought low as all others: they are destroyed, and cut off as the
top of an ear of corn. **25** But if it be not [w]so, where is he? or who will prove me
a liar, and make my words of no value?

25

Bildad proveth that no man is clean nor without sin before God.

1 Then answered Bildad the Shuhite, and said, **2** [a]Power and
fear is with him, that maketh peace in his places. **3** Is there any number in his
armies? [b]and upon whom shall not his light arise? **4** And how may a man [c]be
justified with God? or how can he be clean that is born of woman? **5** Behold, he
will give no light to the Moon, [d]and the Stars are unclean in his sight. **6** How
much more man, a worm, even the son of man, which is but a worm?

---

j. Job 22:15 How God hath punished them from the beginning?
k. Job 22:16 He proveth God's providence by the punishment of the wicked, whom he taketh away before they can bring their wicked purposes to pass.
l. Job 22:18 He answereth to that which Job had said, Job 21:7, that the wicked have prosperity in this world: desiring that he might not be partaker of the like.
m. Job 22:19 The just rejoice at the destruction of the wicked for two causes: first, because God showeth himself judge of the world and by this means continueth his honor and glory: secondly, because God showeth that he hath care over his in that he punished their enemies.
n. Job 22:20 That is, the state and preservation of the godly, is hid under God's wings.
o. Job 22:20 Meaning, of the wicked.
p. Job 22:21 He exhorteth Job to repentance, and to return to God.
q. Job 22:23 God will restore unto thee all thy substance.
r. Job 22:24 Which shall be in abundance like dust.
s. Job 22:28 That is, the favor of God.
t. Job 22:29 God will deliver his when the wicked are destroyed round about them, as in the flood and in Sodom.
u. Job 22:30 God will deliver a whole country from peril, even for the just man's sake.

JOB 22

1. Job. 35:7

JOB 23

a. Job 23:2 He showeth the just cause of his complaining, and as touching that Eliphaz had exhorteth him to return to God, Job 22:21, he declareth that he desireth nothing more, but it seemed that God would not be found of him.
b. Job 23:6 Using his absolute power, and saying, because I am God, I may do what I will.
c. Job 23:6 Of his mercy he would give me power to answer him.
d. Job 23:7 When he of his mercy hath given strength to maintain their cause.
e. Job 23:8 Meaning, that if he consider God's justice, he is not able to comprehend his judgments on what side or what part soever he turneth himself.
f. Job 23:10 God hath this preeminence about me, that he knoweth my way: to wit, that I am innocent, and I am not able to judge of his works: he showeth also his confidence, that God doth use him for his profit.
g. Job 23:12 His word is more precious unto me, than the meat wherewith the body is sustained.
h. Job 23:13 Job confesseth that at this present he felt not God's favor, and yet was assured that he had appointed him to a good end.
i. Job 23:14 In many points man is not able to attain to God's judgments.
j. Job 23:16 That I should not be without fear.
k. Job 23:17 He showeth the cause of his fear, which is, that he being in trouble seeth none end, neither yet knoweth the cause.

JOB 24

a. Job 24:1 Thus Job speaketh in his passions, and after the judgment of the flesh: that is, that he seeth not the things that are done at times, neither yet hath a peculiar care over all, because he punisheth not the wicked, nor revengeth the godly.
b. Job 24:1 When he punisheth the wicked, and rewardeth the good.
c. Job 24:4 And for cruelty and oppression dare not show their faces.
d. Job 24:5 That is, spareth diligence.
e. Job 24:5 He and his live by robbing and murdering.
f. Job 24:6 Meaning, the poor man's.
g. Job 24:6 Signifying, that one wicked man will not spoil another, but for necessity.
h. Job 24:8 The poor are driven by the wicked into the rocks and holes where they cannot lie dry for the rain.
i. Job 24:9 That is, they so powle and pill the poor widow, that she cannot have to sustain herself that she may be able to give her child suck.
j. Job 24:9 That is, his garment, wherewith he should be covered or clad.
k. Job 24:11 In such places which are appointed for that purpose: meaning, that those that labor for the wicked, are pined for hunger.
l. Job 24:12 For the great oppression and extortion.
m. Job 24:12 Cry out and call for vengeance.
n. Job 24:12 God doth not condemn the wicked, but seemeth to pass over it by his long silence.
o. Job 24:13 That is, God's word, because they are reproved thereby.
p. Job 24:15 By these particular vices and the licence thereunto, he would prove that God punished not the wicked, and rewardeth the just.
q. Job 24:18 He fleeth to the waters for his succor.
r. Job 24:18 They think that all the world is bent against them, and dare not go by the high way.
s. Job 24:19 As the dry ground is never full with waters, so will they never cease sinning till they come to the grave.
t. Job 24:20 Though God suffer the wicked for a time, yet their end shall be most vile destruction, and in this point Job commiteth to himself, and showeth his confidence.
u. Job 24:21 He showeth why the wicked shall not be lamented, because he did not pity others.
v. Job 24:22 He declareth that after that the wicked have destroyed the weakest, they will do like to the stranger, and therefore are justly punished by God's judgments.
w. Job 24:25 That is, that contrary to your reasoning no man can give perfect reasons of God's judgments, let me be reproved.

JOB 25

a. Job 25:2 His purpose is to prove that albeit God try and afflict the just, yet soon after he sendeth prosperity, and because he did not so to Job he concludeth that he is wicked.
b. Job 25:3 Who can hide him from his presence?
c. Job 25:4 That is, be just in respect of God?
d. Job 25:5 If God show his power, the Moon and Stars cannot have that light which is given them, much less can man have any excellency, but of God.

26 *Job showeth that man cannot help God, and proveth it by his miracles.*

1 But Job answered, and said, **2** [a]Whom helpest thou? him that
hath no power? savest thou the arm that hath no strength? **3** Whom counselest
thou? him that hath no wisdom? [b]thou showest right well as the thing is. **4** To
whom dost thou declare these words? or whose spirit [c]cometh out of thee? **5** The
[d]dead things are formed under the waters, and near unto them. **6** The grave is
[e]naked before him, and there is no covering for [f]destruction. **7** He stretcheth out
the [g]North over the empty place, and hangeth the earth upon nothing. **8** He
bindeth the waters in his clouds, and the cloud is not broken under them. **9** He
holdeth back the face of his throne, and spreadeth his cloud upon it. **10** He hath
set bounds [h]about the waters, until the [i]day and night come to an end. **11** The
[j]pillars of heaven tremble and quake at his reproof. **12** The sea is calm by his
power, and by his understanding he smiteth the pride thereof. **13** His Spirit hath
garnished the heavens, and his hand hath formed the crooked [k]serpent. **14** Lo,
these are part of his ways: but [l]how little a portion hear we of him? and who can
understand his fearful power?

27 *3 The constancy and perfectness of Job. 13 The reward of the wicked and of the tyrants.*

1 Moreover Job proceeded and continued his parable, saying, **2** The living
God hath taken away my [a]judgment: for the Almighty hath put my soul in bit-
terness. **3** Yet so long as my breath is in me, and the Spirit of God in my no-
strils, **4** [b]My lips surely shall speak no wickedness, and my tongue shall utter
no deceit. **5** God forbid, that I should [c]justify you: until I die, I will never take
away mine [d]innocency from myself. **6** I will keep my righteousness, and will
not forsake it: mine heart shall not reprove me of my [e]days. **7** Mine enemy
shall be as the wicked, and he that riseth against me, as the unrighteous. **8** For
what [f]hope hath the hypocrite when he hath heaped up riches, if God take away
his soul? **9** Will God hear his cry, when trouble cometh upon him? **10** Will
he set his delight on the Almighty? will he call upon God at all times? **11** I will
teach you what is in the hand of [g]God, and I will not conceal that which is with
the Almighty. **12** Behold, all ye yourselves [h]have seen it: why then do you thus
vanish [i]vanity? **13** This is the [j]portion of a wicked man with God, and the he-
ritage of tyrants, which they shall receive of the Almighty. **14** If his children
be in great number, the sword shall destroy them, and his posterity shall not be
satisfied with bread. **15** His remnant shall be buried in death, and his widows
[k]shall not weep. **16** Though he should heap up silver as the dust, and prepare
raiment as the clay, **17** He may prepare it, but the just shall put it on, and the
innocent shall divide the silver. **18** He buildeth his house as the [l]moth, and as a
lodge that the watchman maketh. **19** When the rich man sleepeth, [m]he shall not
be gathered to his fathers: they opened their eyes, and he was gone. **20** Terrors
shall take him as waters, and a tempest shall carry him away by night. **21** The
East wind shall take him away, and he shall depart: and it shall hurl him out of
his place. **22** And God shall cast upon him and not spare, though he would fain
flee out of his hand. **23** Every man shall clap their hands at him, and hiss at him
out of their place.

28 *Job showeth that the wisdom of God is unsearchable.*

1 The silver surely hath his vein, [a]and the gold his palace, where
they take it. **2** Iron is taken out of the dust, and brass is molten out of the sto-
ne. **3** God putteth an end to darkness, [b]and he trieth the perfection of all things:
he setteth a bond of darkness, and of the shadow of death. **4** The flood breaketh
out against the [c]inhabitant, and the waters [d]forgotten of the foot, being higher
than man, are gone away. **5** Out of the same earth cometh [e]bread, and under it,
as it were fire is turned up. **6** The stones thereof are a place [f]of Sapphires, and the
dust of it is gold. **7** There is a path which no fowl hath known, neither hath the
kite's eye seen it. **8** The Lion's whelps have not walked it, nor the Lion passed the-
reby. **9** He putteth his hand upon the [g]rocks, and overthroweth the mountains
by the roots. **10** He breaketh rivers in the roots, and his eye seeth every precious
thing. **11** He bindeth the floods, that they do not overflow, and the thing that is
hid, bringeth he to light. **12** But where is wisdom found? [h]and where is the place
of understanding? **13** Man knoweth not [i]the price thereof: for it is not found in
the land of the living. **14** The depth saith, It is not in me: the Sea also saith, It
is not with me. **15** [j]Gold shall not be given for it, neither shall silver be weighed
for the price thereof. **16** It shall not be valued with the wedge of gold of Ophir,
nor with the precious onyx, nor the sapphire. **17** The gold nor the crystal shall
be equal unto it, nor the exchange shall be for plate of fine gold. **18** No mention
shall be made of coral, nor of the [k]gabish: for wisdom is more precious than pear-
ls. **19** The Topaz of Ethiopia shall not be equal unto it, neither shall it be valued
with the wedge of pure gold. **20** Whence then cometh wisdom? and where is the
place of understanding, **21** Seeing it is hid from the eyes of all the living, and is
hid from the [l]fowls of the heaven? **22** Destruction and death say, We have heard
the fame thereof with our ears. **23** But God understandeth the [m]way thereof,
and he knoweth the place thereof. **24** For he beholdeth the ends of the world,
and seeth all that is under heaven, **25** To make the weight of the winds and to
weigh the waters by measure. **26** When he made a decree for the rain, and a way
for the lightning of the thunders, **27** Then did he see it, and counted it: he pre-
pared it, and also considered it. **28** And unto man he said, Behold, [1]the [n]fear of
the Lord is wisdom, and to depart from evil is understanding.

29 *1 Job complaineth of the prosperity of the time past. 7, 21 His authority. 22 Justice and equity.*

1 So Job proceeded, and continued his parable, saying, **2** Oh that I were as
[a]in times past, when God preserved me! **3** When his [b]light shined upon mine
head: and when by his light I walked through the [c]darkness, **4** As I was in the
days of my youth: when [d]God's providence was upon my tabernacle: **5** When the
Almighty was yet with me, and my children round about me: **6** when I washed
my paths [e]with butter, and when the rock poured me out rivers of oil: **7** When
I went out to the gate, even to the judgment seat, and when I caused them to pre-
pare my seat in the street. **8** The young men saw me, and [f]hid themselves, and
the aged arose, and stood up. **9** The princes stayed talk, and laid their hand on
their [g]mouth. **10** The voice of princes was hid, and their tongue cleaved to the
roof of their mouth. **11** And when the [h]ear heard me, it blessed me, and when
the eye saw me, it gave witness to [i]me. **12** For I delivered the [j]poor that cried,
and the fatherless, and him that had none to help him. **13** [k]The blessing of him

---

JOB 26

- **a.** Job 26:2 Thou concludest nothing: for neither thou helpest me, which am destitute of all help, neither yet speakest sufficiently on God's behalf, who hath no need of thy defense.
- **b.** Job 26:3 But thou dost not apply it to the purpose.
- **c.** Job 26:4 That is, moveth thee to speak this?
- **d.** Job 26:5 Job beginneth to declare the force of God's power and providence in the mines and metals in the deep places of the earth.
- **e.** Job 26:6 There is nothing hid in the bottom of the earth but he seeth it.
- **f.** Job 26:6 Meaning, the grave wherein things putrify.
- **g.** Job 26:7 He causeth the whole heaven to turn about the North pole.
- **h.** Job 26:10 That is, he hid the heavens which are called his throne.
- **i.** Job 26:10 So long as this world endureth.
- **j.** Job 26:11 Not that heaven hath pillars to uphold it, but he speaketh by a similitude, as though he would say, The heaven itself is not able to abide his reproach.
- **k.** Job 26:13 Which is a figure of stars fashioned like a serpent, because of the crookedness.
- **l.** Job 26:14 If these few things, which we see daily with our eyes, declare his great power and providence, how much more would they appear, if we were to comprehend all his works?

JOB 27

- **a.** Job 27:2 He hath so sore afflicted me, that men cannot judge of mine uprightness: for they judge only by outward signs.
- **b.** Job 27:4 However men judge of me, yet will I not speak contrary to that which I have said, and so do wickedly in betraying the truth.
- **c.** Job 27:5 Which condemns me as a wicked man, because the hand of God is upon me.
- **d.** Job 27:5 I will not confess that God doth thus punish me for my sins.
- **e.** Job 27:6 Of my life past.
- **f.** Job 27:8 What advantage hath the dissembler to gain never so much, seeing he shall lose his own soul?
- **g.** Job 27:11 That is, what God reserveth to himself, and whereof he giveth not the knowledge to all.
- **h.** Job 27:12 That is, these secret judgments of God, and yet do not understand them.
- **i.** Job 27:12 Why maintain you then this error?
- **j.** Job 27:13 Thus will God order the wicked, and punish him even unto his posterity.
- **k.** Job 27:15 None shall lament him.
- **l.** Job 27:18 Which breedeth in another man's possession or garment, but is soon shaken out.
- **m.** Job 27:19 He meaneth, that the wicked tyrants shall not have a quiet death, nor be buried honorably.

JOB 28

- **a.** Job 28:1 His purpose is to declare that man may attain in this world to divers secrets of nature, but man is never able to comprehend the wisdom of God.
- **b.** Job 28:3 There is nothing but it is compassed within certain limits, and hath an end, but God's wisdom.
- **c.** Job 28:4 Meaning, him that dwelleth thereby.
- **d.** Job 28:4 Which a man cannot wade through.
- **e.** Job 28:5 That is, come, and underneath is brimstone or coal, which easily conceiveth fire.
- **f.** Job 28:6 He alludeth to the mines and secrets of nature, which are under the earth, whereinto neither fowls nor beasts can enter.
- **g.** Job 28:9 After that he hath declared the wisdom of God in the secrets of nature he describeth his power.
- **h.** Job 28:12 Though God's power and wisdom may be understood in earthly things, yet his heavenly wisdom cannot be attained unto.
- **i.** Job 28:13 It is too high a thing for man to attain unto in this world.
- **j.** Job 28:15 It can neither be bought for gold nor precious stones, but is only the gift of God.
- **k.** Job 28:18 Which is thought to be a kind of precious stone.
- **l.** Job 28:21 Meaning, that there is no natural means whereby man might attain to the heavenly wisdom: which he meaneth by the souls that fly high.
- **m.** Job 28:23 He maketh God only the author of this wisdom, and the giver thereof.
- **n.** Job 28:28 He declareth that man hath so much of this heavenly wisdom, as he showeth by fearing God, and departing from evil.

JOB 28

1. Prov. 1:7

JOB 29

- **a.** Job 29:2 Hebrew, month before.
- **b.** Job 29:3 When I felt his favor.
- **c.** Job 29:3 I was free from affliction.
- **d.** Job 29:4 That is, seemed by evident tokens to be more present with me.
- **e.** Job 29:6 By these similitudes he declareth the great prosperity that he was in, so that he had none occasion to be such a sinner as they accused him.
- **f.** Job 29:8 Being ashamed of their lightness and afraid of my gravity.
- **g.** Job 29:9 Acknowledging my wisdom.
- **h.** Job 29:11 All that heard me, praised me.
- **i.** Job 29:11 Testifying, that I did good justice.

that was ready to perish, came upon me, and I caused the widow's heart to rejoi-
ce. **14** I put [l]on justice, and it covered me: my judgment was as a robe, and a
crown. **15** I was the eyes to the blind, and I was the feet to the lame. **16** I was
a father unto the poor, and when I knew not the cause, I sought it out diligent-
ly. **17** I brake also the jaws of the unrighteous man, and plucked the prey out of
his teeth. **18** Then I said, I shall die in my [m]nest, and I shall multiply my days as
the sand. **19** For my root is [n]spread out by the water, and the dew shall lie upon
my branch. **20** My glory shall renew toward me, and my bow shall be restored
in mine hand. **21** Unto me men gave ear, and waited, and held their tongue at
my counsel. **22** After my words they replied not, and my talk [o]dropped upon
them. **23** And they waited for me, as for the rain, and they opened their mouth
[p]as for the latter rain. **24** If I [q]laughed on them, they believed it not: neither did
they cause the light of my countenance [r]to fall. **25** I appointed out [s]their way,
and did sit as chief, and dwelt as a King in the army, and like him that comforteth
the mourners.

30

1 Job complaineth that he is contemned of the most contemptible, 11, 21 because of his adversity and affliction. 23 Death is the house of all flesh.

1 But now they that are younger than I, [a]mock me: yea, they whose fathers
I have refused to set with the [b]dogs of my flocks. **2** For whereto should the
strength of their hands have served me, seeing age [c]perished in them? **3** For po-
verty and famine they were solitary, fleeing into the wilderness, which is dark,
desolate and waste. **4** They cut up [d]nettles by the bushes, and the juniper ro-
ots was their meat. **5** They were [e]chased forth from among men: they shouted
at them, as at a thief. **6** Therefore they dwelt in the clefts of rivers, in the holes
of the earth and rocks. **7** They roared among the bushes, and under the thistles
they gathered themselves. **8** They were the children of fools, and the children
of villains, which were more vile than the earth. **9** And now am I their [f]song,
and I am their talk. **10** They abhor me, and flee far from me, and spare not
to spit in my face. **11** Because that God hath loosed my [g]cord and humbled
me, [h]they have loosed the bridle before me. **12** The youth rise up at my right
hand: they have pushed my feet, and have trode on me as on the [i]paths of their
destruction. **13** They have destroyed my paths: they took pleasure at my cala-
mity, they had no [j]help. **14** They came as a great breach of waters, and [k]under
this calamity they come on heaps. **15** Fear is turned upon me: and they pursue
my soul as the wind, and mine health passeth away as a cloud. **16** Therefore my
soul is now [l]poured out upon me, and the days of affliction have taken hold on
me. **17** [m]It pierceth my bones in the night, and my sinews take no rest. **18** For
the great vehemency is my garments changed, which compasseth me about, as the
collar of my coat. **19** [n]He hath cast me into the mire, and I am become like
ashes and dust. **20** When I cry unto thee, thou dost not hear me, neither re-
gardest me, when I stand up. **21** Thou turnest thyself [o]cruelly against me, and
art enemy unto me with the strength of thine hand. **22** Thou takest me up and
causest me to ride upon the [p]wind, and makest my [q]strength to fail. **23** Surely
I know that thou wilt bring me to death, and to the house appointed for all the
living. **24** Doubtless none can stretch his hand [r]unto the grave, though they cry
in his destruction. **25** Did not I weep with him that was in trouble? was not my
soul in heaviness for the poor? **26** Yet when I looked for good, [s]evil came unto
me: and when I waited for light, there came darkness. **27** My bowels did boil
without rest: for the days of affliction are come upon me. **28** I went mourning
[t]without sun: I stood up in the Congregation [u]and cried. **29** I am a brother to
the [v]Dragons, and a companion to the Ostriches. **30** My skin is black upon me,
and my bones are burnt with [w]heat. **31** Therefore mine harp is turned to mour-
ning, and mine organs into the voice of them that weep.

31

1 Job reciteth the innocence of his living and number of his virtues, which declareth what ought to be the life of the faithful.

1 I made a covenant with mine [a]eyes: why then should I think on [b]a
maid? **2** For what portion should I have of God from above? and what inhe-
ritance of the almighty from on high? **3** Is not destruction to the wicked, and
strange punishment to [c]the workers of iniquity? **4** Doth not he behold my ways,
and tell all my steps? **5** If I have walked in vanity, or if my foot hath made haste
to deceit? **6** Let God weigh me in the just balance, and he shall know my [d]upri-
ghtness. **7** If my step hath turned out of the way, or mine heart hath [e]walked
after mine eye, or if any blot hath cleaved to mine hands, **8** Let me sow, and let
another [f]eat: yea, let my plants be rooted out. **9** If mine heart hath been deceived
by a woman, or if I have laid wait at the door of my neighbor, **10** Let my wife
[g]grind unto another man, and let other men bow down upon her. **11** For this
is a wickedness, and iniquity to be condemned. **12** Yea, this is a fire that shall
devour [h]to destruction, and which shall root out all my increase. **13** If I did con-
temn the judgment of my servant, and of my maid, when they [i]did contend with
me, **14** What then shall I do when [j]God standeth up? and when he shall visit me,
what shall I answer? **15** He that hath made me in the womb, hath he not made
[k]him? hath not he alone fashioned us in the womb? **16** If I restrained the poor
of their desire, or have caused the eyes of the widow [l]to fail, **17** Or have eaten
my morsels alone, and the fatherless hath not eaten thereof, **18** (For from my
youth hath he grown up with me [m]as with a father, and from my mother's womb
have I been a guide unto her.) **19** If I have seen any perish for want of clothing,
or any poor without covering, **20** If his loins have not blessed me, because he
was warmed with the fleece of my sheep, **21** If I have lifted [n]up mine hand
against the fatherless, when I saw that I might help him in the gate, **22** Let mine
[o]arm fall from my shoulder, and mine arm be broken from the bone. **23** For
God's punishment was [p]fearful unto me, and I could not be delivered from his
Highness. **24** If I made gold mine hope, or have said to the wedge of gold,
Thou art my confidence, **25** If I rejoiced because my substance was great, or
because mine hand had gotten much, **26** If I did behold the [q]sun, when it shi-
ned, or the moon walking in her brightness, **27** If mine heart did flatter me in
secret, or if my mouth did kiss mine [r]hand, **28** (This also had been an iniquity
to be condemned: for I had denied the God [s]above.) **29** If I rejoiced at his de-
struction that hated me, or was moved to joy when evil came upon him, **30** Nei-
ther have I suffered my mouth to sin, by wishing a curse unto his soul. **31** Did
not the men of my [t]Tabernacle say, Who shall give us of his flesh? we cannot be
satisfied. **32** The stranger did not lodge in the street, but I opened my doors
unto him, that went by the way. **33** If I have hid [u]my sins, as Adam, concealing
mine iniquity in my bosom, **34** Though I could have made afraid a great mul-
titude, yet the most contemptible of the families did [v]fear me: so I kept [w]silence,
and went not out of the door. **35** Oh that I had some to hear me! behold my
[x]sign that the Almighty will witness for me: though mine adversary should write
a book against me, **36** Would not I take it upon my shoulder, and bind it as a

---

j. Job 29:12 Because his adversaries did so much charge him with wickedness, he is compelled to render account of his life.
k. Job 29:13 That is, I did succor him that was in distress, and so he had cause to praise me.
l. Job 29:14 I delighted to do justice, as others did to wear costly apparel.
m. Job 29:18 That is, at home in my bed without all trouble and unquietness.
n. Job 29:19 My felicity doth increase.
o. Job 29:22 That is, was pleasant unto them.
p. Job 29:23 As the dry ground thirsteth for the rain.
q. Job 29:24 That is, they thought it not to be a rest, or they thought not that I would condescend unto them.
r. Job 29:24 They were afraid to offend me and cause me to be angry.
s. Job 29:25 I had them at commandment.

JOB 30

a. Job 30:1 That is, mine estate is changed, and whereas before the ancient men were glad to do me reverence, the young men now contemn me.
b. Job 30:1 Meaning to be my shepherds, or to keep my dogs.
c. Job 30:2 That is, their fathers died for famine before they came to age.
d. Job 30:4 Or, mallows.
e. Job 30:5 Job showeth that these that mocked him in his affliction, were like to their fathers, wicked and lewd fellows, such as he here describeth.
f. Job 30:9 They make songs of me, and mock at my misery.
g. Job 30:11 God hath taken from me the force, credit, and authority wherewith I kept them in subjection.
h. Job 30:11 He said that the young men when they saw him, hid themselves, as Job 29:8, and now in his misery they were impudent and licentious.
i. Job 30:12 That is, they sought by all means how they might destroy me.
j. Job 30:13 They need none to help them.
k. Job 30:14 By my calamity they took an occasion against me.
l. Job 30:16 My life faileth me, and I am as half dead.
m. Job 30:17 Meaning, sorrow.
n. Job 30:19 That is, God hath brought me into contempt.
o. Job 30:21 He speaketh not thus to accuse God, but to declare the vehemency of his affliction, whereby he was carried beside himself.
p. Job 30:22 He compareth his afflictions to a tempest or whirlwind.
q. Job 30:22 Or, wisdom, or law.
r. Job 30:24 None can deliver me thence, though they lament at my death.
s. Job 30:26 Instead of comforting they mocked at me.
t. Job 30:28 Not delighting in any worldly thing, no not so much as in the use of the Sun.
u. Job 30:28 Lamenting them that were in affliction, and moving others to pity them.
v. Job 30:29 I am like the wild beasts that desire most solitary places.
w. Job 30:30 With the heat of affliction.

JOB 31

a. Job 31:1 I kept my eyes from all wanton looks.
b. Job 31:1 Would not God then have punished me?
c. Job 31:3 Job declareth that the fear of God was a bridle to stay him from all wickedness.
d. Job 31:6 He showeth wherein his uprightness standeth, that is, inasmuch as he was blameless before men, and sinned not against the second Table.
e. Job 31:7 That is, hath accomplished the lust of mine eyes.
f. Job 31:8 According to the curse of the law, Deut. 28:33.
g. Job 31:10 Let her be made a slave.
h. Job 31:12 He showeth that albeit man neglect the punishment of adultery, yet the wrath of God will never cease till such be destroyed.
i. Job 31:13 When they thought themselves evil entreated by me.
j. Job 31:14 If I had oppressed others, how should I have escaped God's judgment.
k. Job 31:15 He was moved to show pity unto servants, because they were God's creatures as he was.
l. Job 31:16 By long waiting for her request.
m. Job 31:18 He nourished the fatherless, and maintained the widow's cause.
n. Job 31:21 To oppress him and to do him injury.
o. Job 31:22 Let me rot in pieces.
p. Job 31:23 I refrained not from sinning for fear of men, but because I feared God.
q. Job 31:26 If I was proud of my worldly prosperity and felicity, which is meant by the shining of the sun, and brightness of the moon.
r. Job 31:27 If mine own doings delighted me.
s. Job 31:28 By putting confidence in anything but in him alone.
t. Job 31:31 My servants moved me to be revenged of mine enemy, yet did I never wish him hurt.
u. Job 31:33 And not confessed it freely: whereby it is evident that he justified himself before men, and not before God.
v. Job 31:34 That is, I reverenced the most weak and contemned, and was afraid to offend them.
w. Job 31:34 I suffered them to speak evil of me, and went not out of my house to revenge it.
x. Job 31:35 This is a sufficient token of my righteousness, that God is my witness and will justify my cause.

[y]crown unto me? 37 I will tell him the number of my goings, and go unto him
as to a [z]prince. 38 If my land [aa]cry against me, or the furrows thereof complain
together, 39 If I have eaten the fruits thereof without silver: or if I have grieved
[ab]the souls of the masters thereof, 40 Let thistles grow instead of wheat, and
cockle in the stead of barley. THE [ac]WORDS OF JOB ARE ENDED.

32

2 Elihu reproveth them of folly. 8 Age maketh not a man wise, but the spirit of God.

1 So these three men ceased to answer Job, because he [a]esteemed himself
just. 2 Then the wrath of Elihu the son of Barachel the [b]Buzite, of the family
of [c]Ram, was kindled: his wrath, I say, was kindled against Job, because he justi-
fied himself [d]more than God. 3 Also his anger was kindled against his three
friends, because they could not find an answer, and yet condemned Job. 4 (Now
Elihu had waited till Job had spoken: for [e]they were more ancient in years than
he.) 5 So when Elihu saw, that there was none answer in the mouth of the three
men, his wrath was kindled. 6 Therefore Elihu the son of Barachel, the Buzite
answered and said, I am young in years, and ye are ancient: therefore I doubted,
and was afraid to show you mine opinion. 7 For I said, The days [f]shall spe-
ak, and the multitude of years shall teach wisdom. 8 Surely there is a spirit in
man, [g]but the inspiration of the Almighty giveth understanding. 9 Great men
are not always wise, neither do the aged always understand judgment. 10 The-
refore I say, Hear me and I will show also mine opinion. 11 Behold, I did wait
upon your words, and hearkened unto your knowledge, while you sought out [h]rea-
sons. 12 Yea, when I had considered you, lo, there was none of you that reproved
Job, nor answered his words: 13 Lest ye should say, We have [i]found wisdom: for
God hath cast him down, and no man. 14 Yet hath [j]he not directed his words to
me, neither will I answer [k]him by your words. 15 Then they fearing, answered
no more, but left off their talk. 16 When I had waited (for they spake not, but
stood still and answered no more) 17 Then answered I in my turn, and I showed
mine opinion. 18 For I am full of [l]matter, and the spirit within me compelleth
me. 19 Behold, my belly is as the wine, which hath no vent, and like the new
bottles that burst. 20 Therefore will I speak, that I may take breath: I will open
my lips, and will answer. 21 I will not now accept the person of man, [m]neither
will I give titles to man. 22 For I may not give [n]titles, lest my Maker should take
me away suddenly.

33

5 Elihu accuseth Job of ignorance. 14 He showeth that God hath divers means to instruct man and to draw him from sin. 19, 29 He afflicteth man and suddenly delivereth him. 26 Man being delivered giveth thanks to God.

1 Wherefore, Job, I pray thee, hear my talk, and hearken unto all my
words. 2 Behold now, I have opened my mouth: my tongue hath spoken in
my mouth. 3 My words are in the uprightness of mine heart, and my lips shall
speak pure knowledge. 4 The [a]Spirit of God hath made me, and the breath of
the Almighty hath given me life. 5 If thou canst give me answer, prepare thyself
and stand before me. 6 Behold, I am according to thy wish in [b]God's stead: I
am also formed of the clay. 7 Behold, my terror shall not fear thee, neither shall
mine hand [c]be heavy upon thee. 8 Doubtless thou hast spoken in mine ears, and
I have heard the voice of thy words. 9 I am [d]clean, without sin: I am innocent
and there is none iniquity in me. 10 Lo, he hath found occasions against me,
and counted me for his enemy. 11 He hath put my feet in the stocks, and lo-
oketh narrowly unto all my paths. 12 Behold, in this hast thou not done right: I
will answer thee, that God is greater than man. 13 Why dost thou strive against
him? for he doth not [e]give account of all his matters. 14 For God speaketh [f]on-
ce or twice, and one seeth it not. 15 In dreams and [g]visions of the night, when
sleep falleth upon men, and they sleep upon their beds, 16 Then he openeth the
ears of men, even by their corrections, which he [h]had sealed, 17 That he might
cause man to turn away from his enterprise, and that he might hide the [i]pride of
man, 18 And keep back his soul from the pit, and that his life should not pass
by the sword. 19 He is also stricken with sorrow upon his bed, and the grief of
his bones is sore, 20 So that his [j]life causeth him to abhor bread, and his soul
dainty meat. 21 His flesh faileth that it cannot be seen, and his bones which
were not seen, clatter. 22 So his soul draweth to the grave, and his life [k]to the
buriers. 23 If there be a [l]messenger with him, or an interpreter, one of a thou-
sand [m]to declare unto man his righteousness, 24 Then will he have [n]mercy upon
him, and will say, [o]Deliver him, that he go not down into the pit: for I have re-
ceived a reconciliation. 25 Then shall his flesh be [p]as fresh as a child's, and shall
return as in the days of his youth. 26 He shall pray unto God, and he will be
favorable unto him, and he shall see his face with joy: for he will render unto man
his [q]righteousness. 27 He looketh upon men, and if one say, I have sinned, and
[r]perverted righteousness, and it did not profit [s]me, 28 [t]He will deliver his soul
from going into the pit, and his life shall see the light. 29 Lo, all these things will
God work [u]twice or thrice with a man, 30 That he may turn back his soul from
the pit, to be illuminated in the light of the living. 31 Mark well, O Job, and
hear me: keep silence and I will speak. 32 If there be [v]matter, answer me, and
speak: for I desire to [w]justify thee. 33 If thou hast not, hear me: hold thy tongue,
and I will teach thee wisdom.

34

5 Elihu chargeth Job, that he called himself righteous. 12 He showeth that God is just in his judgments. 24 God destroyeth the mighty. 30 By him the hypocrite reigneth.

1 Moreover Elihu answered and said, 2 Hear my words, ye [a]wise men, and
hearken unto me ye that have knowledge. 3 For the ear trieth the words, as the
mouth tasteth meat. 4 Let us seek [b]judgment among us, and let us know among
ourselves what is good. 5 For Job hath said, I am righteous, and God hath taken
[c]away my judgment. 6 Should I lie in my [d]right? my wound of the arrow is [e]grie-
vous without my sin. 7 What man is like Job, that drinketh [f]scornfulness like
water? 8 Which goeth in the [g]company of them that work iniquity, and walketh
with wicked men? 9 For he hath said, It [h]profiteth a man nothing that he should
[i]walk with God. 10 Therefore hearken unto me, ye men of wisdom, God forbid
that wickedness should be in God, and iniquity in the Almighty. 11 For he will
render unto man according to his work, and cause everyone to find according to
his way. 12 And certainly God will not do wickedly, neither will the Almighty
pervert judgment. 13 Whom [j]hath he appointed over the earth besides himself?
or who hath placed the whole world? 14 If [j]he set his heart upon man, and ga-
ther unto himself his spirit [k]and his breath, 15 All flesh shall perish together, and
man shall return unto dust. 16 And if thou hast understanding, hear this, and
hearken to the voice of my words. 17 Shall he that hateth judgment, [l]govern?

---

y. Job 31:36 Should not this book of his accusations be a praise and commendation to me?
z. Job 31:37 I will make him account of all my life, without fear.
aa. Job 31:38 As though I had withheld their wages that labored in it.
ab. Job 31:39 Meaning, that he was no briber nor extortioner.
ac. Job 31:40 That is, the talk which he had with his three friends.

JOB 32

a. Job 32:1 Hebrew, was just in his own eyes.
b. Job 32:2 Which came of Buz, the son of Nahor, Abraham's brother.
c. Job 32:2 Or, as the Chaldean paraphrase readeth, Abram.
d. Job 32:2 By making himself innocent, and by charging God of rigor.
e. Job 32:4 That is, the three mentioned before.
f. Job 32:7 Meaning, the ancient, which have experience.
g. Job 32:8 It is a special gift of God that man hath understanding, and cometh neither of nature nor by age.
h. Job 32:11 To prove that Job's affliction came for his sins.
i. Job 32:13 And flatter yourselves, as though you had overcome him.
j. Job 32:14 To wit, Job.
k. Job 32:14 He useth almost the like arguments, but without taunting and reproaches.
l. Job 32:18 I have conceived in my mind great store of reasons.
m. Job 32:21 I will neither have regard to riches, credit, nor authority, but will speak the very truth.
n. Job 32:22 The Hebrew word signifieth, to change the name, as to call a fool a wise man: meaning, that he would not cloak the truth to flatter men.

JOB 33

a. Job 33:4 I confess the power of God, and am one of his, therefore thou oughtest to hear me.
b. Job 33:6 Because Job had wished to dispute his cause with God, Job 16:21, so that he might do it without fear, Elihu saith, he will reason in God's stead, whom he needeth not to fear, because he is a man made of the same matter that he is.
c. Job 33:7 I will not handle thee so roughly as these others have done.
d. Job 33:9 He repeateth Job's words, whereby he protested his innocence in divers places, but specially in Job 13, 16 and 30.
e. Job 33:13 The cause of his judgments is not always declared to man.
f. Job 33:14 Though God by sundry examples of his judgments speak unto man, yet the reason thereof is not known: yea and though God should speak, yet is he not understood.
g. Job 33:15 God saith he, speaketh commonly, either by visions to teach us the cause of his judgments, or else by afflictions, or by his messenger.
h. Job 33:16 That is, determined to send upon them.
i. Job 33:17 He showeth for what end God sendeth afflictions: to beat down man's pride, and to turn from evil.
j. Job 33:20 That is, his painful and miserable life.
k. Job 33:22 To them that shall bury him.
l. Job 33:23 A man sent of God to declare his will.
m. Job 33:23 A singular man, and as one chosen out of a thousand, which is able to declare the great mercies of God unto sinners: and wherein man's righteousness standeth, which is through the justice of Jesus Christ and faith therein.
n. Job 33:24 He showeth that it is a sure token of God's mercy toward sinners, when he causeth his word to be preached unto them.
o. Job 33:24 That is, the minister shall by the preaching of the word pronounce unto him the forgiveness of his sins.
p. Job 33:25 He shall feel God's favor and rejoice: declaring hereby wherein standeth the true joy of the faithful, and that God will restore him to health of body, which is a token of his blessing.
q. Job 33:26 God will forgive his sins, and accept him as just.
r. Job 33:27 That is, done wickedly.
s. Job 33:27 But my sins hath been the cause of God's wrath toward me.
t. Job 33:28 God will forgive the penitent sinner.
u. Job 33:29 Meaning, oftentimes, even as oft as a sinner doth repent.
v. Job 33:32 If thou doubt of anything, or see occasion to speak against it.
w. Job 33:32 That is, to show thee, wherein man's justification consisteth.

JOB 34

a. Job 34:2 Which are esteemed wise of the world.
b. Job 34:4 Let us examine the matter uprightly.
c. Job 34:5 That is, hath afflicted me without measure.
d. Job 34:6 Should I say, I am wicked, being an innocent?
e. Job 34:6 I am sorer punished, than my sin deserveth.
f. Job 34:7 Which is compelled to receive thy reproach and scorns of many for his foolish words.
g. Job 34:8 Meaning, that Job was like to the wicked, because he seemed not to glorify God and submit himself to his judgments.
h. Job 34:9 He wresteth Job's words who said that God's children are ofttimes punished in this world, and the wicked go free.
i. Job 34:9 That is, live godly, as Gen. 5:22.
j. Job 34:14 To destroy him.
k. Job 34:14 The breath of life which he gave man.
l. Job 34:17 If God were not just, how could he govern the world?

and wilt thou judge him wicked that is most just? **18** Wilt thou say unto a king, Thou art [m]wicked? or to princes, Ye are ungodly? **19** How much less to him that accepteth not the persons of princes, and regardeth not the rich, more than the poor? for they be all the work of his hands. **20** They shall die suddenly, [n]and the people shall be troubled at midnight, [o]and they shall pass forth and take away the mighty without hand. **21** For his eyes are upon the ways of man, and he seeth all his goings. **22** There is no darkness nor shadow of death, that the workers of iniquity might be hid therein. **23** For he will not lay on man so much, that he should [p]enter into judgment with God. **24** He shall break the mighty without [q]seeking, and shall set up others in their stead. **25** Therefore shall he declare their [r]works: he shall turn the [s]night, and they shall be destroyed. **26** He striketh them as wicked men in the places of the [t]seers, **27** Because they have turned back from him, and would not consider all his ways: **28** So that they have caused the voice of the poor to [u]come unto him, and he hath heard the cry of the afflicted. **29** And when he giveth quietness, who can make trouble? and when he hideth his face, who can behold him, whether it be upon nations, or upon a man only? **30** Because the [v]hypocrite doth reign, and because the people are snared. **31** Surely it appertaineth unto God [w]to say, I have pardoned, I will not destroy. **32** [x]But if I see not, teach thou me: if I have done wickedly, I will do no more. **33** Will he perform the thing through [y]thee? for thou hast reproved [z]it, because that thou hast chosen, and not I: now speak what thou knowest. **34** Let men of understanding tell me, and let a wise man hearken unto me. **35** Job hath not spoken of knowledge, neither were his words according to wisdom. **36** I desire that Job may be [aa]tried, unto the end, touching the answers for wicked men. **37** For he abaddeth rebellion unto his sin, he clappeth his hands among us, and multiplieth his words against God.

35

6 Neither doth godliness profit, or ungodliness hurt God, but man. 13 The wicked cry unto God and are not heard.

1 Elihu spake moreover, and said, **2** Thinkest thou this right, that thou hast said, I am [a]more righteous than God? **3** For thou hast said, What profiteth it thee, and what availeth it me, to purge me from my sin? **4** Therefore will I answer thee, and thy [b]companions with thee. **5** Look unto the heaven, and see and behold the [c]clouds which are higher than thou. **6** If thou sinnest, what doest thou [d]against him, yea, when thy sins be many, what doest thou unto him? **7** If thou be righteous, what givest thou unto him? or what receiveth he at thine hand? **8** Thy wickedness may hurt a man as thou art: and thy righteousness may profit the son of man. **9** They cause many that are oppressed, [e]to cry, which cry out for the violence of the mighty. **10** But none saith, Where is God that made me, which giveth songs in the night? **11** Which teacheth us more than the beasts of the earth, and giveth us more wisdom than the fowls of the heaven. **12** Then they cry because of the violence of the wicked, [f]but he answereth not. **13** Surely God will not hear vanity, neither will the Almighty regard it. **14** Although thou sayest to God, Thou wilt not regard it, [g]yet judgment is before him: trust thou in him. **15** But now because his anger hath not visited, nor called to count the evil with great extremity, **16** Therefore Job [h]openeth his mouth in vain, and multiplieth words without knowledge.

36

1 Elihu showeth the power of God. 6 And his justice. 9 And wherefore he punisheth. 13 The property of the wicked.

1 Elihu also proceeded and said, **2** Suffer me a little and I will instruct thee: for I have yet to speak on God's behalf. **3** I will fetch [a]my knowledge afar off, and will attribute righteousness unto my maker. **4** For truly my words shall not be false, and he that is [b]perfect in knowledge, speaketh with thee. **5** Behold, the mighty God casteth away none that is [c]mighty and valiant of courage. **6** He [d]maintaineth not the wicked, but he giveth judgment to the afflicted. **7** He withdraweth not his eyes from the righteous, but they are with [e]kings in the throne, where he placeth them forever: thus they are exalted. **8** And if they be bound in fetters and tied with the cords of affliction, **9** Then will he show them their [f]work and their sins, because they have been proud. **10** He openeth also their ear to discipline, and commandeth them that they return from iniquity. **11** [1]If they obey and serve him, they shall end their days in prosperity, and their years in pleasures: **12** But if they will not obey, they shall pass by the sword and perish [g]without knowledge. **13** But the hypocrites [h]of heart increase the wrath: for they [i]call not when he bindeth them. **14** Their soul dieth in [j]youth, and their life among the whoremongers. **15** He delivereth the poor in his afflictions, and openeth their ear in trouble. **16** Even so would he have taken thee out of the straight place into a broad place, and not shut up beneath: and [k]that which resteth upon thy table had been full of fat. **17** But thou art full of the [l]judgment of the wicked, though judgment and equity maintain all things. **18** [m]For God's wrath is, lest he should take thee away in thine abundance: for no multitude of gifts can deliver thee. **19** Will he regard thy riches? he regardeth not gold, nor all them that excel in strength. **20** [n]Be not careful in the night, how he destroyeth the people out of their place. **21** Take thou heed: look not to [o]iniquity: for thou hast chosen it rather than affliction. **22** Behold, God exalteth by his power: what teacher is like him? **23** Who hath appointed to him his way? or who can say, Thou hast done wickedly? **24** Remember that thou magnify his work, which men behold. **25** All men see it, and men behold it [p]afar off. **26** Behold, God is excellent, [q]and we know him not, neither can the number of his years be searched out. **27** When he restraineth the drops of water, the rain [r]poureth down by the vapor thereof, **28** Which rain the clouds do drop and let fall abundantly upon man. **29** Who can know the divisions of the clouds, and the thunders of his [s]Tabernacle? **30** Behold, he spreadeth his light upon [t]it, and covereth the [u]bottom of the sea. **31** For thereby he judgeth [v]the people, and giveth meat abundantly. **32** He covereth the light with the clouds, and commanded them to go [w]against it. **33** [x]His companion showeth him therefore, and there is anger in rising up.

37

1 Elihu proveth that the unsearchable wisdom of God is manifest by his works. 4 As by the thunders. 6 The snow. 9 The whirlwind. 11 And the rain.

1 At this also mine heart is [a]astonied, and is moved out of his place. **2** Hear the [b]sound of his voice, and the noise that goeth out of his mouth. **3** He directeth it under the whole heaven, and his light unto the ends of the world. **4** After it

---

m. Job 34:18 If man of nature fear to speak evil of such as have power, then much more ought they to be afraid to speak evil of God.
n. Job 34:20 When they look not for it.
o. Job 34:20 The messengers of visitation that God shall send.
p. Job 34:23 God doth not afflict man above measure, so that he should have occasion to contend with him.
q. Job 34:24 For all his creatures are at hand to serve him, so that he needeth not to seek for any other army.
r. Job 34:25 Make them manifest that they are wicked.
s. Job 34:25 Declare the things that were hid.
t. Job 34:26 Meaning, openly in the sight of all men.
u. Job 34:28 By their cruelty and extortion.
v. Job 34:30 When tyrants sit in the throne of justice which under pretence of executing justice are but hypocrites and oppress the people, it is a sign that God hath drawn back his countenance of favor from that place.
w. Job 34:31 Only it belongeth to God to moderate his corrections, and not unto man.
x. Job 34:32 Thus Elihu speaketh in the person of God, as it were mocking Job, because he would be wiser than God.
y. Job 34:33 Will God use thy counsel in doing his works?
z. Job 34:33 Thus he speaketh in the person of God, as though Job should choose and refuse affliction at his pleasure.
aa. Job 34:36 That he may speak as much as he can, that we may answer him and all the wicked that shall use such arguments.
ab. Job 34:37 He standeth stubbornly in the maintenance of his cause.

JOB 34
1. Job. 26:23

JOB 35
a. Job 35:2 Job never spake these words: but because he maintained his innocence, it seemed as though he would say, that God tormented him without just cause.
b. Job 35:4 Such as are in the like error.
c. Job 35:5 If thou canst not control the clouds, wilt thou presume to instruct God?
d. Job 35:6 Neither doth thy sin hurt God, nor thy justice profit him: for he will be glorified without thee.
e. Job 35:9 The wicked may hurt man and cause him to cry, who if he sought to God which sendeth comfort should be delivered.
f. Job 35:12 Because they pray not in faith, as feeling God's mercies.
g. Job 35:14 God is just, howsoever thou judgest of him.
h. Job 35:16 For if he did punish thee as thou deservest, thou shouldest not be able to open thy mouth.

JOB 36
a. Job 36:3 He showeth that when we speak of God, we must lift up our spirits more high, than our natural sense is able to reach.
b. Job 36:4 Thou shalt perceive that I am a faithful instructor, and that I speak to thee in the name of God.
c. Job 36:5 Strong and constant, and of understanding: for these are the gifts of God, and he loveth them in man: but forasmuch as God punished now Job, it is a sign that these are not in him.
d. Job 36:6 Therefore he will not preserve the wicked: but to the humble and afflicted heart he will show grace.
e. Job 36:7 He preferreth the godly to honor.
f. Job 36:9 He will move their hearts to feel their sins that they may come to him by repentance as he did Manasseh.
g. Job 36:12 That is, in their folly or obstination, and so shall be cause of their own destruction.
h. Job 36:13 Which are maliciously bent against God, and flatter themselves in their vices.
i. Job 36:13 When they are in affliction, they seek not to God for succor, as Asa in 2 Chron. 16:12; Rev.16:11.
j. Job 36:14 They die of some vile death, and that before they come to age.
k. Job 36:16 If thou hadst been obedient to God, he would have brought thee to liberty and wealth.
l. Job 36:17 Thou art altogether after the manner of the wicked: for thou dost murmur against the justice of God.
m. Job 36:18 God doth punish thee, lest thou shouldest forget God in thy wealth and so perish.
n. Job 36:20 Be not thou curious in seeking the cause of God's judgments, when he destroyeth any.
o. Job 36:21 And so murmur against God through impatience.
p. Job 36:25 The works of God are so manifest, that a man may see them afar off, and know God by the same.
q. Job 36:26 Our infirmity hindereth us so, that we cannot attain to the perfect knowledge of God.
r. Job 36:27 That is, the rain cometh of those drops of water, which he keepeth in the clouds.
s. Job 36:29 Meaning, of the clouds, which he calleth the Tabernacle of God.
t. Job 36:30 Upon the cloud.
u. Job 36:30 That men cannot come to the knowledge of the springs thereof.
v. Job 36:31 He showeth that the rain hath double use: the one that it declareth God's judgments, when it doth overflow any places, and the other that it maketh the land fruitful.
w. Job 36:32 That is, one cloud to dash against another.
x. Job 36:33 The cold vapor showeth him: that is, the cloud of the hot exhalation, which being taken in the cold cloud mounteth up toward the place where the fire is, and so anger is engendered: that is, noise, and thunderclaps.

JOB 36
1. Isa. 1:19

JOB 37
a. Job 37:1 At the marvelling of the thunder and lightnings: whereby he declareth that the faithful are lively touched with the majesty of God, when they behold his works.
b. Job 37:2 That is, the thunder, whereby he speaketh to men to waken their dullness, and to bring them to the consideration of his works.

a noise soundeth: he thundereth with the voice of his majesty, and he will not stay [c]them when his voice is heard. 5 God thundereth marvelously with his voice: he worketh great things, which we know not. 6 For he saith to the snow, Be thou upon the earth [d]likewise to the small rain and to the great rain of his power. 7 With the force thereof he [e]shutteth up every man, that all men may know his work. 8 Then the beasts go into the den, and remain in their places. 9 The whirlwind cometh out of the South, and the cold from the [f]North wind. 10 At the breath of God the frost is given, and the breadth of the waters [g]is made narrow. 11 He maketh also the clouds to [h]labor, to water the earth, and scattereth the cloud of [i]his light. 12 And it is turned about by his government, that they may do whatsoever he commandeth them upon the whole world: 13 Whether it be for [j]punishment, or for his land, or of mercy, he causeth it to come. 14 Hearken unto this, O Job: stand and consider the wondrous works of God. 15 Didst thou know when God disposed them? and caused the [k]light of his cloud to shine? 16 Hast thou known the [l]variety of the cloud, and the wondrous works of him that is perfect in knowledge? 17 Or how thy clothes are [m]warm, when he maketh the earth quiet through the South wind? 18 Hast thou stretched out the heavens, which are strong, and as a molten [n]glass? 19 Tell us what we shall say unto him: for we cannot dispose our matter because of [o]darkness. 20 Shall it be [p]told him when I speak? or shall man speak when he shall be [q]destroyed? 21 And now men see not the light, [r]which shineth in the clouds, but the wind passeth and cleanseth them. 22 The [s]brightness cometh out of the North: the praise thereof is to God, which is terrible. 23 It is the Almighty: we cannot find him out: he is excellent in power and judgment, and abundant in justice: he [t]afflicteth not. 24 Let men therefore fear him: for he will not regard any that are wise in their own conceit.

38

1 God speaketh to Job, and declareth the weakness of man in the consideration of his creatures, by whose excellency the power, justice, and providence of the Creator is known.

1 Then answered the Lord unto Job out of the [a]whirlwind, and said, 2 Who is this that [b]darkeneth the counsel by words without knowledge? 3 Gird up now thy loins like a man: I [c]will demand of thee, and declare thou unto me. 4 Where wast thou when I [d]laid the foundations of the earth? declare, if thou hast understanding. 5 Who hath laid the measures thereof, if thou knowest, or who hath stretched the line over it: 6 Whereupon are the foundations thereof set: or who laid the cornerstone thereof: 7 When the stars of the morning [e]praised me together, and all the [f]children of God rejoiced: 8 Or who hath shut up the Sea with doors, when it issued and came forth as out of the womb: 9 When I made the clouds as a covering thereof, and darkness as the [g]swaddling bands thereof: 10 When I establisheth my commandment upon it, and set bars and doors, 11 And said, hitherto shalt thou come, but no further, and here shall it [h]stay thy proud waves. 12 Hast thou commanded the [i]morning since thy days? hast thou caused the morning to know his place? 13 That it might take hold of the corners of the earth, and that the wicked might be [j]shaken out of it? 14 It is turned as clay to fashion, [k]and all stand up as a garment. 15 And from the wicked their light shall be taken away, and the high arm shall be broken. 16 Hast thou entered into the bottoms of the sea? or hast thou walked to seek out the [l]depth? 17 Have the gates of death been opened unto thee? or hast thou seen the gates of the shadow of death? 18 Hast thou perceived the breadth of the earth? tell if thou knowest all this. 19 Where is the way where light dwelleth? and where is the place of darkness, 20 That thou [m]shouldest receive it in the bounds thereof, and that thou shouldest know the paths to the house thereof? 21 Knewest thou it, because thou wast then born? and because the number of thy days is great? 22 Hast thou entered into the treasures of the snow? or hast thou seen the treasures of the hail, 23 Which I have hid [n]against the time of trouble, against the day of war and battle? 24 By what way is the light parted, which scattereth the East wind upon the earth? 25 Who hath divided the spouts for the rain? or the way for the lightning of the thunders, 26 To cause it to rain on the earth where no man is, and in the wilderness where there is no man? 27 To fulfill the wild and waste place, and to cause the bud of the herb to spring forth? 28 Who is the father of the rain? or who hath begotten the drops of the dew? 29 Out of whose womb came the ice? who hath engendered the frost of the heaven? 30 The waters are hid [o]as with a stone: and the face of the depth is frozen. 31 Canst thou restrain the sweet influences of [p]the Pleiades, or loose the bands of [q]Orion? 32 Canst thou bring forth [r]Mazzaroth in their time? canst thou also guide [s]Arcturus with his sons? 33 Knowest thou the course of heaven, or canst thou set the [t]rule thereof in the earth? 34 Canst thou lift up thy voice to the clouds, that the abundance of water may cover thee? 35 Canst thou send the lightnings that they may walk, and say unto thee, Lo, here we are? 36 Who hath put wisdom in the [u]reins? or who hath given the heart understanding? 37 Who can number clouds by wisdom? or who can cause to cease the [v]bottles of heaven, 38 When the earth groweth into hardness, [w]and the clots are fast together?

39

The bounty and providence of God, which extendeth even to the young ravens, giveth man full occasion to put his confidence in God. 37 Job confesseth and humbleth himself.

1 Wilt [a]thou hunt the prey for the lion? or fill the appetite of the lion's whelps, 2 When they crouch in their places, and remain in the covert to lie in wait? 3 Who prepareth for the raven his meat, when his birds [b]cry unto God, wandering for lack of meat? 4 Knowest thou the time when the wild goats bring forth young? or dost thou mark when the [c]hinds do calve? 5 Canst thou number the months that they [d]fulfill? or knowest thou the time when they bring forth? 6 They bow themselves: they [e]bruise their young and cast out their sorrows. 7 Yet their young wax fat, and grow up with corn: they go forth and return not unto them. 8 Who hath set the wild ass at liberty? or who hath loosed the bonds of the wild ass? 9 It is I which have made the wilderness his house, and the [f]salt places his dwellings. 10 He derideth the multitude of the city: he heareth not the cry of the driver. 11 He seeketh out the mountain for his pasture, and searcheth after every green thing. 12 Will the unicorn [g]serve thee? or will he tarry by thy crib? 13 Canst thou bind the unicorn with his band to labor in the furrow? or will he plow the valleys after thee? 14 Wilt thou trust in him, because his strength is great, and cast off thy labor unto him? 15 Wilt thou believe him, that he will bring home thy seed, and gather it unto thy barn? 16 Hast thou given the pleasant wings unto the peacocks? or wings and feathers unto the ostrich? 17 Which leaveth his eggs in the earth, and maketh them [h]hot in the dust, 18 And forgetteth that the foot might scatter them, or that the wild beast might break them. 19 He showeth himself cruel unto his young ones, as they were not his, and is without fear, as if he travailed [i]in vain. 20 For God had deprived him of [j]wisdom, and hath given him no part of understanding. 21 When

---

c.
d. Job 37:4 Meaning, the rains and thunders.
e. Job 37:6 So that neither small rain, nor great, snow nor anything else cometh without God's appointment.
f. Job 37:7 By rains and thunders God causeth men to keep themselves within their houses.
g. Job 37:9 In Hebrew it is called the scattering wind, because it driveth away the clouds and purgeth the air.
h. Job 37:10 That is, is frozen up and dried.
i. Job 37:11 Gather the vapors and move to and fro to water the earth.
j. Job 37:11 That is, the cloud that hath lightning in it.
k. Job 37:13 Rain, cold, heat, tempests and such like are sent of God, either to punish man, or to profit the earth, or to declare his favor toward man, as Job 36:31.
l. Job 37:15 That is, the lightning to break forth in the clouds?
m. Job 37:16 Which is sometimes changed into rain, or snow, hail, or such like.
n. Job 37:17 Why thy clothes should keep thee warm when the South wind bloweth, rather than when any other wind bloweth?
o. Job 37:18 For their clearness.
p. Job 37:19 That is, our ignorance: signifying that Job was so presumptuous, that he would control the works of God.
q. Job 37:20 Hath God need that any should tell him when man murmureth against him?
r. Job 37:20 If God would destroy a man, should he repine?
s. Job 37:21 The cloud stoppeth the shining of the sun, that man cannot see it till the wind have chased away the cloud: and if man be not able to attain to the knowledge of these things, how much less of God's judgments?
t. Job 37:22 In Hebrew, gold, meaning, fair weather and clear as gold.
u. Job 37:23 Meaning, without cause.

JOB 38

a. Job 38:1 That his words might have greater majesty, and that Job might know with whom he had to do.
b. Job 38:2 Which by seeking out the secret counsel of God by man's reason, maketh it more obscure, and showeth his own folly.
c. Job 38:3 Because he had wished to dispute with God, Job 23:3, God reasoneth with him, to declare his rashness.
d. Job 38:4 Seeing he could not judge of those things which were done so long before he was born, he was not able to comprehend all God's works: much less the secret causes of his judgments.
e. Job 38:7 The stars and dumb creatures are said to praise God, because his power, wisdom and goodness is manifest and known therein.
f. Job 38:7 Meaning, the Angels.
g. Job 38:9 As though the great sea were but as a little babe in the hands of God to turn to and fro.
h. Job 38:11 That is, God's decree and commandment, as verse 10.
i. Job 38:12 To wit, to rise, since thou wast born?
j. Job 38:13 Who having in the night been given to wickedness, cannot abide the light, but hide themselves.
k. Job 38:14 The earth which seemed in the night to have no form, by the rising of the sun, is as it were created anew, and all things therein clad with new beauty.
l. Job 38:16 If thou art not able to seek out the depth of the sea, how much less art thou able to comprehend the counsel of God?
m. Job 38:20 That thou mightest appoint it highway and limits.
n. Job 38:23 To punish mine enemies with them, Exod. 9:18; Josh. 10:11.
o. Job 38:30 The ice covereth it, as though it were paved with stone.
p. Job 38:31 Which stars arise when the sun is in Taurus, which is the springtime, and bring flowers.
q. Job 38:31 Which star bringeth in winter.
r. Job 38:32 Certain stars so called: some think they were the twelve signs.
s. Job 38:32 The North star with those that are about him.
t. Job 38:33 Canst thou cause the heavenly bodies to have any power over the earthly bodies?
u. Job 38:36 In the secret parts of man.
v. Job 38:37 That is, the clouds wherein the water is contained as in bottles.
w. Job 38:38 For when God doth not open these bottles, the earth cometh to this inconvenience.

JOB 39

a. Job 39:1 After he had declared God's works in the heavens, he showeth his marvelous providence in earth, even toward the brute beasts.
b. Job 39:3 Read Ps. 147:9.
c. Job 39:4 He chiefly maketh mention of wild goats and hinds, because they bring forth their young with most difficulty.
d. Job 39:5 That is, how long they go with young?
e. Job 39:6 They bring forth with great difficulty.
f. Job 39:9 That is, the barren ground where no good fruits grow.
g. Job 39:12 Is it possible to make the unicorn tame? signifying that if man cannot rule a creature, that it is much more impossible that he should appoint the wisdom of God, whereby he governeth all the world.
h. Job 39:17 They write that the ostrich covereth her eggs in the sand, and because the country is hot and the sun still keepeth them warm, they are hatched.
i. Job 39:19 If he should take care of them.

[k]time is, he mounteth on high: he mocketh the horse and his rider. **22** Hast
thou given the horse strength, or covered his neck with [l]neighing? **23** Hast thou
made him afraid as the grasshopper? his strong neighing is fearful. **24** He [m]dig-
geth in the valley, and rejoiceth in his strength: he goeth forth to meet the harnes-
sed man. **25** He mocketh at fear, and is not afraid, and turneth not back from
the sword, **26** Though the quiver rattle against him, the glittering spear and the
shield. **27** He [n]swalloweth the ground for fierceness and rage, and he believeth
not that it is the noise of the trumpet. **28** He saith among the trumpets, Ha,
ha: he smelleth the battle afar off, and the noise of the captains, and the shou-
ting. **29** Shall the hawk fly by thy wisdom, stretching out his wings even toward
the [o]South? **30** Doth the eagle mount up at thy commandment, or make his
nest on high? **31** She abideth and remaineth in the rock, even upon the top of
the rock, and the tower, **32** From thence she spieth for meat, and her eyes behold
afar off. **33** His young ones also suck up blood: and where the slain are, there is
she. **34** Moreover the Lord spake unto Job, and said, **35** Is this [p]to learn, to
strive with the Almighty? he that reproveth God, let him answer to it. **36** Then
Job answered the Lord, saying, **37** Behold, I am [q]vile: what shall I answer thee?
I will lay mine hand upon my mouth. **38** Once have I spoken, but I will answer
no more, yea twice, but I will proceed no further.

40

2 How weak man's power is, being compared to the work of God: 10 Whose power appeareth in the creation, and governing of the great beasts.

1 Again the Lord answered Job out of [1]the whirlwind, and said, **2** Gird
up now thy loins like a man: I will demand of thee, and declare thou unto
me. **3** Wilt thou disannul [a]my judgment? or wilt thou condemn me, that thou
mayest be justified? **4** Or hast thou an arm like God? or dost thou thunder with
a voice like him? **5** Deck thyself now with [b]majesty and excellency, and array
thyself with beauty and glory. **6** Cast abroad the indignation of thy wrath, and
behold everyone that is proud, and abase him. **7** Look on everyone that is arro-
gant, and bring him low: and destroy the wicked in their place. **8** Hide them in
the dust together, and bind [c]their faces in a secret place. **9** Then will I confess
unto thee also, that thy right hand can [d]save thee. **10** Behold now [e]Behemoth
(whom I made [f]with thee) which eateth [g]grass as an ox. **11** Behold now, his
strength is in his loins, and his force is in the navel of his belly. **12** When he
taketh pleasure, his tail is like a cedar: the sinews of his stones are wrapped to-
gether. **13** His bones are like staves of brass, and his small bones like staves of
iron. **14** [h]He is the chief of the ways of God: [i]he that made him, will make his
sword to approach unto him. **15** Surely the mountains bring him forth grass,
where all the beasts of the field play. **16** Lieth he under the trees in the covert of
the reed and fens? **17** Can the trees cover him with their shadow? or can the wil-
lows of the river compass him about? **18** Behold, he spoileth the river, [j]and ha-
steth not: he trusteth that he can draw up Jordan into his mouth. **19** He taketh it
with his eyes, and thrusteth his nose through whatsoever meeteth him. **20** Canst
thou draw out [k]Leviathan with an hook, and with a line which thou shalt cast
down unto his tongue? **21** Canst thou cast an hook into his nose? canst thou
[l]pierce his jaws with an angle? **22** Will he make many prayers unto thee? and
speak thee fair? **23** Will he make a covenant with thee? and wilt thou take [m]him
as a servant forever? **24** Wilt thou play with him as with a bird? or wilt thou bind
him for thy maids? **25** Shall the companions banquet with him? shall they divide
him among the merchants? **26** Canst thou fill the basket with his skin? or the
fishpanier with his head? **27** Lay thine hand upon him: remember [n]the battle,
and do no more so. **28** Behold, [o]his hope is in vain: for shall not one perish even
at the sight of him?

41

1 By the greatness of this monster Leviathan, God showeth his greatness and his power, which nothing can resist.

1 None is so fierce that dare stir him up. Who is he then that can [a]stand
before me? **2** Who hath prevented me that I should [b]make an end? All under
heaven is mine. **3** I will not keep silence concerning [c]his parts, nor his power,
nor his comely proportion. **4** Who can discover the face [d]of his garment? or
who shall come to him with a double [e]bridle? **5** Who shall [f]open the doors of
his face? his teeth are fearful round about. **6** The majesty of his scales is like
strong shields, and are sure sealed. **7** One is set to another, that no wind can
come between them. **8** One is joined to another: they stick together, that they
cannot be sundered. **9** His sneezings [g]make the light to shine, and his eyes are
like the eyelids of the morning. **10** Out of his mouth go lamps, and sparks of
fire leap out. **11** Out of his nostrils cometh out smoke, as out of a boiling pot
or caldron. **12** His breath maketh the coals burn: for a flame goeth out of his
mouth. **13** In his neck remaineth strength, and [h]labor is rejected before his
face. **14** The members of his body are joined: they are strong in themselves,
and cannot be moved. **15** His heart is as strong as a stone, and as hard as the
nether millstone. **16** The mighty are afraid of his majesty, and for fear they faint
in themselves. **17** When the sword doth touch him, he will not rise up, nor for
the spear, dart nor habergeon. **18** He esteemeth iron as straw, and brass as rotten
wood. **19** The archer cannot make him flee: the stones of the sling are turneth
into stubble unto him. **20** The darts are counted as straw: and he laugheth at
the shaking of the spear. **21** Sharp stones [i]are under him, and he spreadeth sharp
things upon the mire. **22** He maketh the depth to [j]boil like a pot, and maketh
the Sea like a pot of ointment. **23** He maketh a path to [k]shine after him, one
would think the depth as an hoar head. **24** In the earth there is none like him:
he is made without fear. **25** He beholdeth [l]all high things: he is a King over all
the children of pride.

42

6 The repentance of Job. 9 He prayeth for his friends. 12 His goods are restored double unto him. 13 His children, age and death.

1 Then Job answered the Lord, and said, **2** I know that thou canst do all
things, and that there is no [a]thought hid from thee. **3** Who is he that hideth
counsel without [b]knowledge? therefore have I spoken that I understood not, even
things too wonderful for me, [c]and which I knew not. **4** Hear, I beseech thee, and
I will speak: I will demand of thee, [d]and declare thou unto me. **5** I have [e]heard of
thee by the hearing of the ear, but now mine eye seeth thee. **6** Therefore I abhor
myself, and repent in dust and ashes. **7** Now after that the Lord had spoken
these words unto Job, the Lord also said unto Eliphaz the Temanite, My wrath is
kindled against thee and against thy two friends: for ye have not spoken of me the
thing that is [f]right, like my servant [g]Job. **8** Therefore take unto you now seven
bullocks, and seven rams, and go to my servant Job, and offer up for yourselves a
burnt offering, and my servant Job shall [h]pray for you: for I will accept him, lest
I should put you to shame, because ye have not spoken of me the thing which is
right, like my servant Job. **9** So Eliphaz the Temanite, and Bildad the Shuhite,
and Zophar the Naamathite, went, and did according as the Lord had said unto
them, and the Lord accepted Job. **10** Then the Lord turned the [i]captivity of Job,
when he prayed for his friends: also the Lord gave Job twice so much as he had
before. **11** Then came unto him all his [j]brethren, and all his sisters, and all they
that had been of his acquaintance before, and did eat bread with him in his house,
and had compassion on him, and comforted him for all the evil that the Lord had
brought upon him, and every man gave him a [k]piece of money, and everyone an

---

j. Job 39:20 That is, to have a care and natural affection toward his young.
k. Job 39:21 When the young ostrich is grown up, he outrunneth the horse.
l. Job 39:22 That is, given him courage? which is meant by neighing and shaking his mane: for with his breath he covereth his neck.
m. Job 39:24 He beateth with his hoof.
n. Job 39:27 He so rideth the ground that it seemeth nothing under him.
o. Job 39:29 That is, when cold cometh, to fly into the warm countries.
p. Job 39:35 Is this the way for a man that will learn, to strive with God? which thing he reproveth in Job.
q. Job 39:37 Whereby he showeth that he repented, and desired pardon for his faults.

JOB 40

a. Job 40:3 Signifying that they that justify themselves, condemn God as unjust.
b. Job 40:5 Meaning, that these were proper unto God, and belonged to no man.
c. Job 40:8 Cause them to die if thou canst.
d. Job 40:9 Proving hereby that whosoever attributeth to himself power and ability to save himself, maketh himself God.
e. Job 40:10 This beast is thought to be the elephant, or some other, which is unknown.
f. Job 40:10 Whom I made as well as thee.
g. Job 40:10 This commendeth the providence of God toward man: for if he were given to devour as a lion, nothing were able to resist him, or content him.
h. Job 40:14 He is one of the chiefest works of God among the beasts.
i. Job 40:14 Though man dare not come near him, yet God can kill him.
j. Job 40:18 He drinketh at leisure, and feareth nobody.
k. Job 40:20 Meaning, the whale.
l. Job 40:21 Because he feareth lest thou shouldest take him.
m. Job 40:23 To do thy business, and be at thy commandment?
n. Job 40:27 If thou once consider the danger, thou wilt not meddle with him.
o. Job 40:28 To wit, that trusteth to take him.

JOB 40

1. Job. 38:1

JOB 41

a. Job 41:1 If none dare stand against a whale, which is but a creature, who is able to compare with God the Creator?
b. Job 41:2 Who hath taught me to accomplish my work?
c. Job 41:3 The parts and members of the whale?
d. Job 41:4 That is, who dare pull off his skin?
e. Job 41:4 Who dare put a bridle in his mouth?
f. Job 41:5 Who dare look in his mouth?
g. Job 41:9 That is, casteth out flames of fire.
h. Job 41:13 Nothing is painful or hard unto him.
i. Job 41:21 His skin is so hard that he lieth with a great ease on the stones as in the mire.
j. Job 41:22 Either he maketh the sea to seem as it boiled by his wallowing, or else he spouteth water in such abundance as it would seem that the sea boiled.
k. Job 41:23 That is, a white froth and shining stream before him.
l. Job 41:25 He despiseth all other beasts and monsters, and is the proudest of all others.

JOB 42

a. Job 42:2 No thought so secret, but thou dost see it, nor anything that thou thinkest, but thou canst bring it to pass.
b. Job 42:3 Is there any but I? for this God laid to his charge, Job 38:2.
c. Job 42:3 I confess herein mine ignorance, and that I spake I wist not what.
d. Job 42:4 He showeth that he will be God's scholar to learn of him.
e. Job 42:5 I knew thee only before by hearsay: but now thou hast caused me to feel what thou art to me, that I may resign myself over unto thee.
f. Job 42:7 You took in hand an evil cause, in that you condemned him by his outward afflictions, and not comforted him with my mercies.
g. Job 42:7 Who had a good cause, but handled it evil.
h. Job 42:8 When you have reconciled yourselves to him for the faults that you have committed against him, he shall pray for you, and I will hear him.
i. Job 42:10 He delivered him out of the affliction wherein he was.
j. Job 42:11 That is, all his kindred, read Job 19:13.

earring of gold. **12** So the Lord blessed the last days of Job more than the first: for he had [l]fourteen thousand sheep, and six thousand camels, and a thousand yoke of oxen, and a thousand she asses. **13** He had also seven sons, and three daughters. **14** And he called the name of one [m]Jemimah, and the name of the second [n]Keziah, and the name of the third [o]Keren-Happuch. **15** In all the land were no women found so fair as the daughters of Job, and their father gave them inheritance among their brethren. **16** And after this lived Job an hundred and forty years, and saw his sons, and his son's sons, even four generations. **17** So Job died, being old, and full of days.

---

k. Job 42:11 Or, lamb, or money so marked.
l. Job 42:12 God made him twice so rich in cattle as he was afore, and gave him as many children as he had taken from him.
m. Job 42:14 That is, of long life, or beautiful as the day.
n. Job 42:14 As pleasant as cassia or sweet spice.
o. Job 42:14 That is, the horn of beauty.

THE

[a]PSALMS OF DAVID

1

Whether it was Esdras, or any other that gathered the Psalms into a book, it seemeth he did set this Psalm first in manner of a preface, to exhort all godly men to study and meditate the heavenly wisdom. For the effect hereof is, 1 That they be blessed which give themselves wholly all their life to the holy Scriptures; 4 and that the wicked contemners of God, though they seem for a while happy, yet at length shall come to miserable destruction.

1 Blessed is the man that doth not walk in the [b]counsel of the wicked, nor stand in the way of sinners, nor sit in the seat of the scornful. **2** But his delight is in the [1]law of the Lord, and in his [c]law doth he meditate day and night. **3** For he shall be like a [2]tree planted by the rivers of waters, that will bring forth her fruits in due season: whose leaf shall not fade: so [d]whatsoever he shall do, shall prosper. **4** [e]The wicked are not so, but as the chaff, which the wind driveth away. **5** Therefore the wicked shall not stand in the [f]judgment, nor sinners in the assembly of the righteous. **6** For the Lord [g]knoweth the way of the righteous, and the way of the wicked shall perish.

2

The Prophet David rejoiceth, that notwithstanding his enemies' rage, yet God will continue his kingdom forever, and advance it even to the end of the world, 10 and therefore exhorteth kings and rulers, that they would humbly submit themselves under God's yoke, because it is in vain to resist God. Herein is figured Christ's kingdom.

1 Why do the [a]heathen [1]rage, and the people murmur in vain. **2** The kings of the earth band themselves, and the Princes are assembled together against the Lord, and against his [b]Christ. **3** [c]Let us break their bands, and cast their cords from us. **4** [2]But he that dwelleth in the heaven shall laugh: the Lord shall have them in derision. **5** [d]Then shall he speak unto them in his wrath, and vex them in his sore displeasure, saying, **6** Even I have set my King upon Zion mine holy mountain. **7** I will declare the [e]decree: that is, the Lord hath said unto me, [3]Thou art my son; this [f]day have I begotten thee. **8** Ask of me, and I shall give thee the heathen for thine inheritance, and the [g]ends of the earth for thy possession. **9** [4]Thou shalt crush them with a scepter of iron, and break them in pieces like a potter's vessel. **10** [h]Be wise now therefore, ye kings: be learned ye judges of the earth. **11** Serve the Lord in fear, and rejoice in trembling. **12** [i]Kiss the Son, lest he be angry, and ye [j]perish in the way, when his wrath shall suddenly burn. Blessed are all that trust in him.

3

David driven forth of his kingdom, was greatly tormented in mind for his sins against God: 4 And therefore calleth upon God, and waxeth bold through his promises, against the great railings and terrors of his enemies, yea against death itself, which he saw present before his eyes. 7 Finally, he rejoiceth for the good success that God gave him and all the Church.

A Psalm of David, when he fled from his son Absalom. **1** Lord, how are mine adversaries [a]increased? how many rise against me? **2** Many say to my soul, There is no help for him in God. [b]Selah. **3** But thou Lord art a buckler for me, my glory, and the lifter up of mine head. **4** I did call unto the Lord with my voice, and he heard me out of his holy mountain. Selah. **5** I laid me down and slept, and rose up again: for the Lord sustained me. **6** I will not be afraid for [c]ten thousand of the people, that should beset me round about. **7** O Lord, arise: help me, my God: for thou hast smitten all mine enemies upon the cheekbone: thou hast broken the teeth of the wicked. **8** [d]Salvation belongeth unto the Lord, and thy blessing is upon thy people. Selah.

4

When Saul persecuted him, he called upon God, trusting most assuredly in his promise, and therefore boldly reproveth his enemies, who willfully resisted his dominion, 7 and finally preferreth the favor of God before all worldly treasures.

[a]To him that excelleth on Neginoth. A Psalm of David. **1** Hear me when I call, [b]O God of my righteousness: thou hast set me at liberty, when I was in [c]distress: have mercy upon me, and hearken unto my prayer. **2** O ye [d]sons of men, how long will ye turn my glory into shame, [e]loving vanity, and seeking lies? Selah. **3** For be ye sure that the Lord hath chosen to himself [f]a godly man, the Lord will hear when I call unto him. **4** [g]Tremble and sin not: examine your own heart upon your bed, and be [h]still. Selah. **5** [i]Offer the sacrifices of righteousness,

---

PSALM 1

a. TITLE - Or, praises, according to the Hebrews: and were chiefly instituted to praise and give thanks to God for his benefits. They are called the Psalms or Songs of David, because the most part were made by him.
b. Psalm 1:1 When a man hath given once place to evil counsel, or to his own concupiscence, he beginneth to forget himself in his sin, and so falleth into contempt of God, which contempt is called the seat of the scorners.
c. Psalm 1:2 In the holy Scriptures.
d. Psalm 1:3 God's children are so moistened ever with his grace, that whatsoever cometh unto them, tendeth unto their salvation.
e. Psalm 1:4 Though the wicked seem to bear the swinge in this world, yet the Lord driveth them down that they shall not rise nor stand in the company of the righteous.
f. Psalm 1:5 But tremble when they feel God's wrath.
g. Psalm 1:6 Doth approve and prosper, like as not to know, is to reprove and reject.

PSALM 1

1. Deut. 6:6 - Josh. 1:8 - Prov. 6:10
2. Jer. 17:8

PSALM 2

a. Psalm 2:1 The conspiracy of the Gentiles, the murmuring of the Jews, and power of kings cannot prevail against Christ.
b. Psalm 2:2 Or, anointed.
c. Psalm 2:3 Thus the wicked say, that they will cast off the yoke of God, and of his Christ.
d. Psalm 2:5 God's plagues will declare that in resisting his Christ, they fought against him.
e. Psalm 2:7 To show that my vocation to the kingdom, is of God.
f. Psalm 2:7 That is to say, as touching man's knowledge, because it was the first time that David appeared to be elected of God. So is it applied to Christ in his first coming and manifestation to the world.
g. Psalm 2:8 Not only the Jews, but the Gentiles also.
h. Psalm 2:10 He exhorteth all rulers to repent in time.
i. Psalm 2:12 In sign of homage.
j. Psalm 2:12 When the wicked shall say, Peace and rest, seeming yet to be but in the mind way of their purposes, then shall destruction suddenly come, 1 Thess. 5:3.

PSALM 2

1. Acts 4:25
2. Prov. 1:26
3. Acts 13:23,33 - Heb.1:5
4. Rev. 2:27

PSALM 3

a. Psalm 3:1 This was a token of his stable faith, that for all his troubles he had his recourse to God.
b. Psalm 3:2 Selah here signifieth a lifting up of the voice, to cause us to consider the sentence, as a thing of great importance.
c. Psalm 3:6 When he considered the truth of God's promise, and tried the same, his faith increased marvelously.
d. Psalm 3:8 Be the dangers never so great or many, yet God hath ever means to deliver his.

PSALM 4

a. Psalm 4:1 Among them that were appointed to sing the Psalms, and to play on the instruments, one was appointed chief to set the tune, and to begin: who had the charge, because he was most excellent, and he began this Psalm on the instrument calleth Neginoth, or in a tune so called.
b. Psalm 4:1 Thou that art the defender of my just cause.
c. Psalm 4:1 Both of mind and body.
d. Psalm 4:2 Ye that think yourselves noble in this world.
e. Psalm 4:2 Though your enterprises please your never so much, yet God will bring them to nought.
f. Psalm 4:3 A king that walketh in his vocation.
g. Psalm 4:4 For fear of God's judgment.

and trust in the Lord. **6** Many say, Who will show us any [j]good? but Lord, lift up
the light of thy countenance upon us. **7** Thou hast given me more joy of heart,
than they have had, when their wheat and their wine did abound. **8** I will lay
me down, and also sleep in peace: for thou, [k]Lord, only makest me dwell in safety.

5

David oppressed with the cruelty of his enemies, and fearing greater dangers, calleth to God for succor, showing how requisite it is that God should punish the malice of his adversaries. 7 After, being assured of prosperous success, he conceiveth comfort, 12 concluding, that when God shall deliver him, others also shall be partakers of the same mercies.

To him that excelleth upon [a]Nehiloth. A Psalm of David. **1** Hear my
words, O Lord: understand my [b]meditation. **2** Hearken unto the voice of
my cry, my king and my God: for unto thee do I pray. **3** Hear my voice in
the morning, O Lord: for in the morning will I direct me unto thee, and I will
[c]wait. **4** For thou art not a God that loveth [d]wickedness, neither shall evil dwell
with thee. **5** [e]The foolish shall not stand in thy sight: for thou hatest all them that
work iniquity. **6** Thou shalt destroy them that speak lies: the Lord will abhor the
bloody man and deceitful. **7** But I [f]will come into thine house in the multitude of
thy mercy: and in thy fear will I worship toward thine holy Temple. **8** Lead me,
O Lord, in thy righteousness, [g]because of mine enemies: make thy way plain before
my face. **9** For no constancy is in their mouth: within they are very corruption:
their [1]throat is an open sepulcher, and they flatter with their tongue. **10** Destroy
them, O God, [h]let them [i]fall from their counsels: cast them out for the multitude
of their iniquities, because they have rebelled against thee. **11** And [j]let all them
that trust in thee, rejoice and triumph forever, and cover thou them: and let them
that love thy name, rejoice in thee. **12** For thou Lord, wilt [k]bless the righteous,
and with favor [l]wilt compass him, as with a shield.

6

When David by his sins had provoked God's wrath, and now felt not only his hand against him, but also conceived the horrors of death everlasting, he desireth forgiveness. 6 Bewailing that if God took him away in his indignation, he should lack occasion to praise him as he was wont to do while he was among men. 9 Then suddenly feeling God's mercy, he sharply rebuketh his enemies which rejoiced in his affliction.

**To him that excelleth on Neginoth, upon the eight tune. A Psalm of Da-
vid.** **1** O Lord, [1,a]rebuke me not in thine anger, neither chastise me in thy wra-
th. **2** Have mercy upon me, O Lord, for I am weak: O Lord heal me, for my
[b]bones are vexed. **3** [c]My soul is also sore troubled: but Lord, how long wilt thou
delay? **4** Return, O Lord: deliver my soul: save me for thy mercy's sake. **5** For
in [d]death there is no remembrance of thee: in the grave who shall praise thee? **6** I
fainted in my mourning: I cause my bed every night to swim, and water my cou-
ch with my tears. **7** [e]Mine eye is dimmed for despite, and sunk in because of all
mine enemies. **8** [f]Away from me all ye workers of iniquity: for the Lord hath he-
ard the voice of my weeping. **9** The Lord hath heard my petition: the Lord will
receive my prayer. **10** All mine enemies shall be confounded and sore vexed: they
shall be turned back, and put to shame [g]suddenly.

7

Being falsely accused by Cush one of Saul's kinsmen, he calleth to God to be his defender, 3 to whom he commendeth his innocence, 9 first showing that his conscience did not accuse him of any evil toward Saul. 10 Next that it touched God's glory to award sentence against the wicked. 12 And so entering into the consideration of God's mercies and promise, he waxeth bold, and derideth the vain enterprises of his enemies, 15 threatening that that shall fall on their own neck which they have purposed for others.

**[a]Shiggaion of David, which he sang unto the Lord, concerning the [b]words
of [1]Cush the son of Benjamin.** **1** O Lord my God, in thee I put my trust: save
me from all that persecute me, and deliver me, **2** Lest [c]he devour my soul like
a lion, and tear it in pieces, while there is none to help. **3** O Lord my God, if
I have done [d]this thing, if there be any wickedness in mine hands, **4** [e]If I have
rewarded evil unto him that had peace with me, (yea I have delivered him that
vexed me without cause.) **5** Then let the enemies persecute my soul, and take it:
yea, let him tread my life down upon the earth, and lay mine [f]honor in the dust.
Selah. **6** Arise, O Lord, in thy wrath, and lift up thyself against the rage of mine
enemies, and awake for me according to the [g]judgment that thou hast appoin-
ted. **7** So shall the congregation of the people compass thee about: for their sakes
therefore [h]return on high. **8** The Lord shall judge the people: judge thou me, O
Lord, according to my [i]righteousness, and according to mine innocency that is in
me. **9** Oh let the malice of the wicked come to an end: but guide thou the just:
for the righteous God trieth the [j]hearts and reins. **10** My defense is in God,
who preserveth the upright in heart. **11** God judgeth the righteous, and him
that contemneth God, [k]every day. **12** Except [l]he turn, he hath whet his sword:
he hath bent his bow, and made it ready. **13** He hath also prepared him deadly
weapons: he will ordain his arrows for them that persecute me. **14** [2]Behold, he
shall travail with wickedness: for he hath conceived mischief, but he shall bring
forth a lie. **15** He hath made a pit, and dug it, and is fallen into the pit that he
made. **16** His mischief shall return upon his own head, and his cruelty shall fall
upon his own pate. **17** I will praise the Lord according to his [m]righteousness,
and will sing praise to the Name of the Lord most high.

8

1 The Prophet considering the excellent liberality and Fatherly providence of God toward man, whom he made as it were a god over all his works, doth not only give great thanks, but is astonished with the admiration of the same, as one nothing able to compass such great mercies.

To him that excelleth on [a]Gittith. A Psalm of David. **1** O Lord our Lord,
how [b]excellent is thy Name in all the world! which hast set thy glory above the
heavens. **2** Out of the mouth [c]of babes and sucklings hast thou [d]ordained stren-
gth, because of thine enemies, that thou mightest [e]still the enemy and the aven-
ger. **3** When I behold thine heavens, even the works of thy fingers, the moon and
the stars, which thou hast ordained, **4** What is [f]man, say I, that thou art mindful
of him? and the son of man that thou visitest him? **5** For thou hast made him a
little lower than [g]God, and crowned him with glory and worship. **6** Thou hast
made him to have dominion in the works of thine hands, thou hast put all things
under his feet: **7** All [h]sheep and oxen: yea, and the beasts of the field: **8** The
fowls of the air, and the fish of the sea, and that which passeth through the paths of
the seas. **9** O Lord our Lord, how excellent is thy Name in all the world!

---

h. Psalm 4:4 Cease your rage.
i. Psalm 4:5 Serve God purely, and not with outward ceremonies.
j. Psalm 4:6 The multitude seek worldly wealth, but David setteth his felicity in God's favor.
k. Psalm 4:8 This word in Hebrew may be referred to God, as it is here translated, or to David, signifying that he should dwell as joyful alone, as if he had many about him, because the Lord is with him.

PSALM 5

a. Psalm 5:1 Or, a musical instrument or tune.
b. Psalm 5:1 That is, my vehement prayer, and secret complaint and sighings.
c. Psalm 5:3 With patience and trust till I be heard.
d. Psalm 5:4 Seeing that God of nature hateth wickedness, he must needs punish the wicked, and save the godly.
e. Psalm 5:5 Which run most ragingly after their carnal affections.
f. Psalm 5:7 In the deepest of his tentations he putteth his full confidence in God.
g. Psalm 5:8 Because thou art just, therefore lead me out of the dangers of mine enemies.
h. Psalm 5:10 Or, cause them to err.
i. Psalm 5:10 Let their devices come to nought.
j. Psalm 5:11 Thy favor toward me shall confirm the faith of all others.
k. Psalm 5:12 Or, give good success.
l. Psalm 5:12 So that he shall be safe from all dangers.

PSALM 5

1. Rom. 3:!3

PSALM 6

a. Psalm 6:1 Though I deserve destruction, yet let thy mercy pity my frailty.
b. Psalm 6:2 For my whole strength is abated.
c. Psalm 6:3 His conscience is also touched with the fear of God's judgment.
d. Psalm 6:5 He lamenteth that occasion should be taken from him to praise God in the congregation.
e. Psalm 6:7 Or, mine eye is eaten as it were with worms.
f. Psalm 6:8 God sendeth comfort and boldness, in affliction, that we may triumph over our enemies.
g. Psalm 6:10 When the wicked think that the godly shall perish, God delivereth them suddenly, and destroyeth their enemies.

PSALM 6

1. Jer. 10:24

PSALM 7

a. Psalm 7:1 Or, kind of tune.
b. Psalm 7:1 Or, accusation.
c. Psalm 7:2 He desireth God to deliver him from the rage of cruel Saul.
d. Psalm 7:3 Wherewith Cush chargeth me.
e. Psalm 7:4 If I reverenced not Saul for affinities sake and preserved his life, 1 Sam. 26:8,9.
f. Psalm 7:5 Let me not only die, but be dishonored forever.
g. Psalm 7:6 In promising me the kingdom.
h. Psalm 7:7 Not only for mine, but for thy Church's sake, declare thy power.
i. Psalm 7:8 As touching my behavior toward Saul and mine enemies.
j. Psalm 7:9 Though they pretend a just cause against me: yet God shall judge their hypocrisy.
k. Psalm 7:11 He doth continually call the wicked to repentance by some signs of his judgments.
l. Psalm 7:12 Except Saul turn his mind, I die: for he hath both men and weapons to destroy me. Thus considering his great danger, he magnifieth God's grace.
m. Psalm 7:17 In keeping faithfully his promise with me.

PSALM 7

1. 2 Sam. 16:7
2. Isa. 59:4 - Job 15:35

PSALM 8

a. Psalm 8:1 Or, kind of instrument, or tune.
b. Psalm 8:1 Or, noble, or marvelous.
c. Psalm 8:2 Though the wicked would hide God's praises, yet the very babes are sufficient witnesses of the same.
d. Psalm 8:2 Or, established.
e. Psalm 8:2 Or, confound.
f. Psalm 8:4 It had been sufficient, for him to have set forth his glory by the heavens, though he had not come so low as to man, which is but dust.
g. Psalm 8:5 Touching his first creation.
h. Psalm 8:7 By the temporal gifts of man's creation, he is led to consider the benefits which he hath by his regeneration through Christ.

9 *1 After he had given thanks to God for the sundry victories that he had sent him against his enemies, and also proved by manifold experience, how ready God was at hand in all his troubles. 14 He being now likewise in danger of new enemies, desireth God to help him according to his wont, 17 and to destroy the malicious arrogance of his adversaries.*

To him that excelleth upon [a]Muth Labben. A Psalm of David. **1** I will praise the Lord with my [b]whole heart: I will speak of all thy marvelous works. **2** I will be glad, and rejoice in thee: I will sing praise to thy Name, O most High. **3** For that mine enemies are turned back: they shall fall and perish at thy presence. **4** For [c]thou hast maintained my right and my cause: thou art set in the throne, and judgest right. **5** Thou hast rebuked the heathen: thou hast destroyed the wicked: thou hast put out their name forever and ever. **6** [d]O enemy, destructions are come to a perpetual end, and thou hast destroyed the cities: their memorial is perished with them. **7** But the Lord [e]shall sit forever: he hath prepared his throne for judgment. **8** For he shall judge the world in righteousness, and shall judge the people with equity. **9** The Lord also will be a refuge for the [f]poor, a refuge in due time, even in affliction. **10** And they that know thy Name, will trust in thee: for thou, Lord, hast not failed them that seek thee. **11** Sing praises to the Lord, which dwelleth in Zion: show the people his works. **12** For [g]when he maketh inquisition for blood, he remembereth it, and forgetteth not the complaint of the poor. **13** Have mercy upon me, O Lord: consider my trouble which I suffer of them that hate me, thou that liftest me up from the gates of death, **14** That I may show all thy praises within the [h]gates of the daughter of Zion, and rejoice in thy salvation. **15** The heathen are [i]sunken down in the pit that they made: in the net that they hid, is their foot taken. **16** [j]The Lord is known by executing judgment: the wicked is snared in the work of his own hands, [k]Higgaion. Selah. **17** The wicked shall turn into hell, and all nations that forget God. **18** For the poor shall not be always forgotten: the hope [l]of the afflicted shall not perish forever. **19** Up Lord: let not man prevail: let the heathen be judged in thy sight. **20** Put them in fear, O Lord, that the heathen may know that they are but [m]men. Selah.

10 *1 He complaineth of the fraud, rapine, tyranny, and all kinds of wrong, which worldly men use, assigning the cause thereof, that wicked men, being as it were drunken with worldly prosperity, and therefore setting apart all fear and reverence towards God, think they may do all things without controlling. 15 Therefore he calleth upon God to send some remedy against these desperate evils, 16 and at length comforteth himself with hope of deliverance.*

1 Why standest thou far off, O Lord, and hidest thee in [a]due time, even in affliction? **2** The wicked with pride doth persecute the poor; let them be taken in the crafts that they have imagined. **3** For the wicked hath [b]made boast of his own heart's desire, and the covetous blesseth himself, he contemneth the Lord. **4** The wicked is so proud, that he seeketh not for God: he thinketh always, There is no God. **5** His ways always prosper: thy judgments are high above his sight; therefore [c]defieth he all his enemies. **6** He saith in his heart, I shall [d]never be moved, [e]nor be in danger. **7** His mouth is full of cursing, and deceit, and fraud; under his tongue is mischief and iniquity. **8** [f]He lieth in wait in the villages; in the secret places doth he murder the innocent; his eyes are bent against the poor. **9** He lieth in wait secretly, even as a lion in his den; he lieth in wait to spoil the poor; he doth spoil the poor, when he draweth him into his net. **10** He croucheth and boweth; therefore heaps of the [g]poor do fall by his might. **11** He hath said in his heart, God hath forgotten, he hideth away his face, and will never see. **12** [h]Arise, O Lord God, lift up thine hand; forget not the poor. **13** Wherefore doth the wicked contemn God? he saith in his heart, Thou wilt not [i]regard. **14** Yet thou hast seen it; for thou beholdest mischief and wrong; that thou mayest [j]take it into thine hands; the poor committeth himself unto thee; for thou art the helper of the fatherless. **15** Break thou the arm of the wicked and malicious; search his wickedness, and thou shalt find [k]none. **16** The Lord is King forever and ever; the [l]heathen are destroyed forth of his land. **17** Lord, thou hast heard the desire of the poor; thou preparest their heart; thou bendest thine ear to them, **18** [m]To judge the fatherless and poor, that earthly man [n]cause to fear no more.

11 *1 This Psalm containeth two parts. In the first David showeth how hard assaults of temptations he sustained, and in how great anguish of mind he was, when Saul did persecute him. 4 Then next he rejoiceth that God sent him succor in his necessity, declaring his justice as well in governing the good, and the wicked men, as the whole world.*

To him that excelleth. A Psalm of David. **1** In the Lord put I my trust; how say ye then to my soul, [a]Flee to your mountain as a bird? **2** For lo, the wicked bend their bow, and make ready their arrows upon the string, that they may secretly shoot at them which are upright in heart. **3** For the [b]foundations are cast down, what hath the [c]righteous done? **4** The Lord is in his holy palace; the Lord's throne is in the heaven; his eyes [d]will consider; his eyelids will try the children of men. **5** The Lord will try the righteous; but the wicked, and him that loveth iniquity, doth his soul hate. **6** Upon the wicked he shall rain snares, [e]fire, and brimstone, and stormy tempest; this is the [f]portion of their cup. **7** For the righteous Lord loveth righteousness: his countenance doth behold the just.

12 *1 The Prophet lamenting the miserable estate of the people, and the decay of all good order, desireth God speedily to send succor to his children. 7 Then comforting himself, and others with the assurance of God's help, he commendeth the constant verity that God observeth in keeping his promises.*

To him that excelleth upon the eight tune. A Psalm of David. **1** Help Lord, for there is not [a]a godly man left: for the faithful are failed from among the children of men. **2** They speak deceitfully every one with his neighbor, [b]flattering with their lips, and speak with a double heart. **3** The Lord cut off all flattering lips, and the tongue that speaketh proud things: **4** Which have said, [c]With our tongue will we prevail; our lips are our own; who is Lord over us? **5** [d]Now for the oppression of the needy, and for the sighs of the poor, I will up, saith the Lord, and will [e]set at liberty him, whom the wicked hath snared. **6** The words of the Lord are pure words, as the silver, tried in a furnace of earth, fined sevenfold. **7** Thou wilt keep [f]them, O Lord; thou wilt preserve him from this generation forever. **8** The wicked walk on every side; when they are exalted, [g]it is a shame for the sons of men.

13 *1 David as it were overcome with sundry and new afflictions, fleeth to God as his only refuge, 3 and so at the length being encouraged through God's promises, he conceiveth most sure confidence against the extreme horrors of death.*

To him that excelleth. A Psalm of David. **1** How long wilt thou forget me, O Lord, [a]forever? how long wilt thou hide thy face from me? **2** How long shall I take [b]counsel within myself having weariness daily in mine heart? how long shall mine enemy be exalted above me? **3** Behold, and hear me, O Lord my God: lighten mine eyes, that I sleep not in death. **4** Lest mine enemy say, I have

---

PSALM 9

- **a.** Psalm 9:1 Or, kind of instrument, or tune, or for the death of Labben or Goliath.
- **b.** Psalm 9:1 God is not praised, except the whole glory be given to him alone.
- **c.** Psalm 9:4 Howsoever the enemy seems for a time to prevail, yet God preserveth the just.
- **d.** Psalm 9:6 A derision of the enemy, that mindeth nothing but destruction: but the Lord will deliver his, and bring him into judgment.
- **e.** Psalm 9:7 Or, reign as Judge.
- **f.** Psalm 9:9 Our miseries are means to cause us to feel God's present care over us.
- **g.** Psalm 9:12 Though God revengeth not suddenly the wrong done to his, yet he suffereth not the wicked unpunished.
- **h.** Psalm 9:14 In the open assembly of the Church.
- **i.** Psalm 9:15 For God overthroweth the wicked in their enterprises.
- **j.** Psalm 9:16 The mercy of God toward his Saints must be declared, and the fall of the wicked must always be considered.
- **k.** Psalm 9:16 Or, this is worthy to be noted.
- **l.** Psalm 9:18 God promiseth not to help us before we have felt the cross.
- **m.** Psalm 9:20 Which they cannot learn without the fear of thy judgment.

PSALM 10

- **a.** Psalm 10:1 So soon as we enter into affliction, we think God should help us, but that is not always his due time.
- **b.** Psalm 10:3 The wicked man rejoiceth in his own lust, he boasteth when he hath that he would: he braggeth of his wit and wealth, and blesseth himself, and thus blasphemeth the Lord.
- **c.** Psalm 10:5 Or, snuffeth at.
- **d.** Psalm 10:6 Or, not be moved, because he was never in evil.
- **e.** Psalm 10:6 The evil shall not touch me, Isa. 28:15, or else he speaketh thus because he never felt evil.
- **f.** Psalm 10:8 He showeth that the wicked have many means to hide their cruelty, and therefore ought more to be feared.
- **g.** Psalm 10:10 By the hypocrisy of them that have authority, the poor are devoured.
- **h.** Psalm 10:12 He calleth to God for help, because wickedness is so far overgrown, that God must now help or never.
- **i.** Psalm 10:13 Therefore thou must needs punish this their blasphemy.
- **j.** Psalm 10:14 To judge between the right and the wrong.
- **k.** Psalm 10:15 For thou hast utterly destroyed him.
- **l.** Psalm 10:16 The hypocrites or such as live not after God's Law, shall be destroyed.
- **m.** Psalm 10:18 God helpeth when man's help ceaseth.
- **n.** Psalm 10:18 Or, destroy no more man upon the earth.

PSALM 11

- **a.** Psalm 11:1 This is the wicked counsel of his enemies to him and his companions to drive him from the hope of God's promise.
- **b.** Psalm 11:3 All hope of succor is taken away.
- **c.** Psalm 11:3 Yet am I innocent and my cause good.
- **d.** Psalm 11:4 Though all things in earth be out of order, yet God will execute judgment from heaven.
- **e.** Psalm 11:6 As in the destruction of Sodom and Gomorrah.
- **f.** Psalm 11:6 Which they shall drink even to the dregs, Ezek. 23:34.

PSALM 12

- **a.** Psalm 12:1 Which dare defend the truth and show mercy to the oppressed.
- **b.** Psalm 12:2 He meaneth the flatterers of the court which hurt him more with their tongues, than with their weapons.
- **c.** Psalm 12:4 They think themselves able to persuade whatsoever they take in hand.
- **d.** Psalm 12:5 The Lord is moved with the complaints of his, and delivereth in the end from all dangers.
- **e.** Psalm 12:5 Because the Lord's word and promise is true and unchangeable, he will perform it and preserve the poor from this wicked generation.
- **f.** Psalm 12:7 That is, thine though he were but one man.
- **g.** Psalm 12:8 For they suppress the godly and maintain the wicked.

PSALM 13

- **a.** Psalm 13:1 He declareth that his afflictions lasted a long time, and that his faith fainted not.
- **b.** Psalm 13:2 Changing my purposes as the sick man doth his place.
- **c.** Psalm 13:4 Which might turn to God's dishonor: if he did not defend his.
- **d.** Psalm 13:5 The mercy of God is the cause of our salvation.
- **e.** Psalm 13:5 Both by the benefits past, and by others to come.

[c]prevailed against him: and they that afflict me, rejoice, when I slide. **5** But I trust in thy [d]mercy: mine heart shall rejoice in thy salvation; I will sing to the Lord, because he hath [e]dealt lovingly with me.

14

1 He describeth the perverse nature of men, which were so grown to licentiousness, that God was brought to utter contempt. 7 For the which thing, although he was greatly grieved, yet being persuaded that God would send some present remedy, he comforteth himself and others.

To him that excelleth. A Psalm of David. **1** The [1]fool hath said in his heart, [a]There is no God: they have [b]corrupted, and done an abominable work: there is none that doeth good. **2** The Lord looked down from heaven upon the children of men, to see if there were any that would understand, and seek God. **3** [c]All are gone out of the way: they are all corrupt: there is none that doeth good, no not one. **4** Do not all the workers of iniquity know that they eat up my people, as they eat bread? they call not upon the Lord. **5** [d]There they shall be taken with fear, because God is in the generation of the just. **6** You have made [e]a mock at the counsel of the poor, because the Lord is his trust. **7** Oh give salvation unto [f]Israel out of Zion: when the Lord turneth the captivity of his people, then Jacob shall rejoice, and Israel shall be glad. Note that of Psalm **14** :**5** -**7** , which are put into the common translation, and may seem unto some to be left out in this, are not in the same Psalm in the Hebrew text, but rather are put in more fully to express the manners of the wicked, and are gathered out of Psalms **5** , **10** , **36** , **14 0**; Isa. **59** , and are alleged by S. Paul, and placed together in Romans **3** .

15

1 This Psalm teacheth on what condition God did choose the Jews for his peculiar people; and wherefore he placed his Temple among them, which was to the intent that they by living uprightly and godly, might witness that they were his special and holy people.

A Psalm of David. **1** Lord, who shall dwell in thy Tabernacle? who shall rest in thine holy Mountain? **2** He that [a]walketh uprightly and worketh righteousness, and speaketh the truth in his heart. **3** He that slandereth not with his tongue, nor doeth evil to his neighbor, nor receiveth a false report against his neighbor. **4** [b]In whose eyes a vile person is contemned, but he honoreth them that fear the Lord: he that sweareth to his own hindrance and changeth not. **5** He that [c]giveth not his money unto usury, nor taketh reward against the innocent: he that doeth these things, [d]shall never be moved.

16

1 David prayeth to God for succor not for his works, but for his faith's sake. 4 Protesting that he hateth all idolatry, taking God only for his comfort and felicity. 8 Who suffereth his to lack nothing.

[a]Michtam of David. **1** Preserve me, O GOD: for in thee do I [b]trust. **2** O my soul, thou hast said unto the Lord, Thou art my Lord: my [c]well doing extendeth not to thee, **3** But to the Saints that are in the earth, and to the excellent: all my delight is in them. **4** The [d]sorrows of them, that offer to another god, shall be multiplied: [e]their offerings of blood will I not offer, neither make [1]mention of their names with my lips. **5** The Lord is the portion of mine inheritance and of my cup: thou shalt maintain my lot. **6** The [f]lines are fallen unto me in pleasant places: yea, I have a fair heritage. **7** I will praise the Lord, who hath given me counsel: my [g]reins also teach me in the nights. **8** I have set the Lord always before me: for he is at my right hand: therefore I [h]shall not slide. **9** Wherefore [i]mine heart is glad, and my tongue rejoiceth: my flesh also doth rest in hope. **10** For thou [j]wilt not leave my soul in the grave: neither wilt thou suffer thine holy One to see corruption. **11** Thou wilt show me the path of life: in thy [k]presence is the fullness of joy: and at thy right hand there are pleasures forevermore.

17

1 Here he complaineth to God of the cruel pride and arrogance of Saul, and the rest of his enemies, who thus raged without any cause given on his part. 6 Therefore he desireth God to revenge his innocence and deliver him.

The prayer of David. **1** Hear [a]the right, O Lord, consider my cry: hearken unto my prayer of lips unfeigned. **2** Let my [b]sentence come forth from thy presence, and let thine eyes behold equity. **3** Thou hast [c]proved and visited mine heart in the night: thou hast tried me, and foundest nothing: for I was purposed that my [d]mouth should not offend. **4** Concerning the works of men, by the [e]words of thy lips I kept me from the paths of the cruel man. **5** Stay my steps in thy paths, that my feet do not slide. **6** I have called upon thee: [f]surely thou wilt hear me, O God: incline thine ear to me, and hearken unto my words. **7** Show thy marvelous mercies: thou that art the Savior of them that trust in thee, from such as [g]resist thy right hand. **8** Keep me as the apple of the eye: hide me under the shadow of thy wings, **9** From the wicked that oppress me, from mine enemies, which compass me round about for [h]my soul. **10** They are enclosed in their own [i]fat, and they have spoken proudly with their mouth. **11** They have compassed us now in our steps: they have set their eyes to bring down to the ground: **12** Like as a lion that is greedy of prey, and as it were a Lion's whelp lurking in secret places. **13** Up Lord, [j]disappoint him: cast him down: deliver my soul from the wicked [k]with thy sword, **14** From men by thine [l]hand, O Lord, from men [m]of the world, who have their [n]portion in this life, whose bellies thou fillest with thine hid treasure: their children have enough, and leave the rest of their substance for their children. **15** But I will behold thy face [o]in righteousness, and when I [p]wake, I shall be satisfied with thine image.

18

1 This Psalm is the first beginning of his gratulation, and thanksgiving in the entering into his kingdom, wherein he extolleth and praiseth most highly the marvelous mercies and grace of God, who hath thus preserved and defended him. 32 Also he setteth forth the image of Christ's kingdom, that the faithful may be assured that Christ shall always conquer and overcome by the unspeakable power of his Father, though all the whole world should strive there against.

To him that excelleth. A Psalm of David the servant of the Lord, which spake unto the Lord the words of this song (in the day that the Lord delivered him from the hand of all his enemies, and from the hand of Saul) and said, **1** I will love thee dearly, O Lord my strength. **2** [1,a]The Lord is my rock, and my fortress, and he that delivereth me, my God and my strength: in him will I trust, my shield, the horn also of my salvation, and my refuge. **3** I will call upon the Lord, which is worthy to be [b]praised: so shall I be safe from mine enemies. **4** [c]The sorrows of death compassed me, and the floods of wickedness made me afraid. **5** The [d]sorrows of the grave have compassed me about: the snares of death overtook me. **6** But in my trouble did I call upon the Lord, and cried unto my God: he heard my voice out of his Temple, and my cry did come before him, even into his ears. **7** [e]Then the earth trembled and quaked: the foundations also of the mountains moved and shook, because he was angry. **8** Smoke went out at his nostrils, and a [f]consuming fire out of his mouth: coals were kindled thereat. **9** He bowed the heavens also and came down, and [g]darkness was under his feet. **10** And he rode upon [h]Cherub, and did fly, and he came flying upon the wings of the wind. **11** He made darkness his [i]secret place, and his pavilion round about him, even darkness of waters, and clouds of the air. **12** At the brightness of his presence his clouds passed, hailstones and coals of fire. **13** The Lord also

---

PSALM 14

- **a.** Psalm 14:1 He showeth that the cause of all wickedness is to forget God.
- **b.** Psalm 14:1 There is nothing but disorder and wickedness among them.
- **c.** Psalm 14:3 David here maketh comparison between the faithful and the reprobate, but S. Paul speaketh the same of all men naturally, Rom. 3:10.
- **d.** Psalm 14:5 Where they think themselves most sure.
- **e.** Psalm 14:6 You mock them that put their trust in God.
- **f.** Psalm 14:7 He prayeth for the whole Church whom he is assured God will deliver: for none but he only can do it.

PSALM 15

- **a.** Psalm 15:2 First God requireth uprightness of life, next doing well to others, and thirdly, truth and simplicity in our words.
- **b.** Psalm 15:4 He that flattereth not the ungodly in their wickedness.
- **c.** Psalm 15:5 To the hindrance of his neighbor.
- **d.** Psalm 15:5 That is, shall not be cast forth of the Church as hypocrites.

PSALM 16

- **a.** Psalm 16:1 Or, a certain tune.
- **b.** Psalm 16:1 He showeth that we cannot call upon God except we trust in him.
- **c.** Psalm 16:2 Though we can not enrich God, yet we must bestow God's gifts to the use of his children.
- **d.** Psalm 16:4 As grief of conscience and miserable destruction.
- **e.** Psalm 16:4 He would neither by outward profession nor in heart, nor in mouth consent to their idolatries.
- **f.** Psalm 16:6 Wherewith my portion is measured.
- **g.** Psalm 16:7 God teacheth me continually by secret inspiration.
- **h.** Psalm 16:8 The faithful are sure to persevere to the end.
- **i.** Psalm 16:9 That is, I rejoice both in body and in soul.
- **j.** Psalm 16:10 This is chiefly meant of Christ, by whose resurrection all his members have immortality.
- **k.** Psalm 16:11 Where God favoreth, there is perfect felicity.

PSALM 16

- **1.** Exod. 23:23

PSALM 17

- **a.** Psalm 17:1 My righteous cause.
- **b.** Psalm 17:2 The vengeance that thou shalt show against mine enemies.
- **c.** Psalm 17:3 When thy Spirit examined my conscience.
- **d.** Psalm 17:3 I was innocent toward mine enemy both in deed and thought.
- **e.** Psalm 17:4 Though the wicked provoked me to do evil for evil, yet thy word kept me back.
- **f.** Psalm 17:6 He was assured that God would not refuse his request.
- **g.** Psalm 17:7 For all rebel against thee, which trouble thy Church.
- **h.** Psalm 17:9 For their cruelty cannot be satisfied but with my death.
- **i.** Psalm 17:10 They are puffed up with pride, as the stomach that is choked with fat.
- **j.** Psalm 17:13 Stop his rage.
- **k.** Psalm 17:13 Or, which is thy sword.
- **l.** Psalm 17:14 By thine heavenly power.
- **m.** Psalm 17:14 Or, whose tyranny hath too long endured.
- **n.** Psalm 17:14 And feel not the smart that God's children oft times do.
- **o.** Psalm 17:15 This is the full felicity, comforting against all assaults, to have the face of God and favorable countenance opened unto us.
- **p.** Psalm 17:15 And am delivered out of my great troubles.

PSALM 18

- **a.** Psalm 18:2 He useth this diversity of names, to show that as the wicked have many means to hurt, so God hath many ways to help.
- **b.** Psalm 18:3 For none can obtain their requests of God, that join not his glory with their petition.
- **c.** Psalm 18:4 He speaketh of the dangers and malice of his enemies from the which God had delivered him.
- **d.** Psalm 18:5 Or, cords, or, cables
- **e.** Psalm 18:7 A description of the wrath of God against his enemies, after he had heard his prayers.
- **f.** Psalm 18:8 He showeth how horrible God's judgments shall be to the wicked.
- **g.** Psalm 18:9 Darkness signifieth the wrath of God as the clear light signifieth God's favor.
- **h.** Psalm 18:10 This is described at large, Ps. 104.

thundered in the heaven, and the Highest gave [j]his voice, hailstones and coals of fire. **14** Then he sent out [k]his arrows and scattered them, and he increased lightnings and destroyed them. **15** And the channels of waters were seen, and the [l]foundations of the world were discovered at thy rebuking, O Lord, at the blasting of the breath of thy nostrils. **16** He hath sent down from above and taken me: he hath drawn me out of many [m]waters. **17** He hath delivered me from my [n]strong enemy, and from them which hate me: for they were [o]too strong for me. **18** They prevented me in the day of my calamity: but the Lord was my stay. **19** He brought me forth also into a large place: [p]he delivered me because he favored me. **20** The Lord rewarded me according to my [q]righteousness: according to the pureness of mine hand he recompensed me: **21** Because I kept the ways of the Lord, and did not wickedly against my God. **22** For all his laws were before me, and I did not cast away his [r]commandments from me. **23** I was upright also with him, and have kept me from my [s]wickedness. **24** Therefore the Lord rewarded me according to my righteousness, and according to the pureness of mine hands in his sight. **25** With the [t]godly thou wilt show thyself godly: with the upright man thou wilt show thyself upright. **26** With the pure thou wilt show thyself pure, and with the froward thou wilt show thyself froward. **27** Thus thou wilt save the poor people, and wilt [u]cast down to proud looks. **28** Surely thou wilt light my candle: the Lord my God will lighten my darkness. **29** For by thee I have [v]broken through an host, and by my God I have leaped over a wall. **30** The way of God is uncorrupt: the [w]word of the Lord is tried in the fire: he is a shield to all that trust in him. **31** For who is God besides the Lord? and who is mighty save our God? **32** God girdeth me with strength, and maketh my [x]way upright. **33** He maketh my feet like hind's feet, and setteth me upon mine [y]high places. **34** He teacheth mine hands to fight: so that a bow of [z]brass is broken with mine arms. **35** Thou hast also given me the [aa]shield of thy salvation, and thy right hand hath stayed me, and thy [ab]lovingkindness hath caused me to increase. **36** Thou hast enlarged my steps under me, and my heels have not slid. **37** [ac]I have pursued mine enemies, and taken them, and have not turned again till I had consumed them. **38** I have wounded them, that they were not able to rise, they are fallen under my feet. **39** For thou hast girded me with strength to battle: them that rose against me, thou hast subdued under me. **40** And thou hast [ad]given me the necks of mine enemies, that I might destroy them that hate me. **41** They [ae]cried, but there was none to save them, even unto the Lord, but he answered them not. **42** Then I did beat them small as the dust before the wind: I did tread them flat as the clay in the streets. **43** Thou hast delivered me from the contentions of the people: thou hast made me the head of the [af]heathen, a people, whom I have not [ag]known, shall serve me. **44** As soon as they hear they shall obey me: the strangers shall [ah]be in subjection to me. **45** Strangers shall [ai]shrink away, and fear in their pure chambers. **46** Let the Lord live, and blessed be my strength, and the God of my salvation be exalted. **47** It is God that giveth me power to avenge me, and subdued the people under me. **48** O my deliverer from mine enemies, even thou hast set me up from those that rose against me; thou hast delivered me from the [aj]cruel man. **49** Therefore [ak]I will praise thee, O Lord, among the nations, and will sing unto thy Name. **50** Great deliverances giveth he unto his king, and showeth mercy to his anointed, even to David, and to his [al]seed forever.

19

1 To the intent he might move the faithful to deeper consideration of God's glory, he setteth before their eyes the most exquisite workmanship of the heavens, with their proportion, and ornaments. 8 And afterward calleth them to the Law, wherein God hath revealed himself more familiarly to his chosen people. The which peculiar grace by commending the Law, he setteth forth more at large.

To him that excelleth. A Psalm of David. **1** The [1,a]heavens declare the glory of God, and the firmament showeth the work of his hands. **2** [b]Day unto day uttereth the same, and night unto night teacheth knowledge. **3** There is no speech nor [c]language, where their voice is not heard. **4** Their [d]line is gone forth through all the earth, and their words into the ends of the world: in them hath he set a tabernacle for the Sun. **5** Which cometh forth as a bridegroom out of his [e]chamber, and rejoiceth like a mighty man to run his race. **6** His going out is from the end of the heaven, and his compass is unto the ends of the same, and none is hid from the heat thereof. **7** The [f]Law of the Lord is perfect, converting the soul: the testimony of the Lord is sure, and giveth wisdom unto the simple. **8** The statutes of the Lord are right, and rejoice the heart, the commandment of the Lord is pure, and giveth light unto the eyes. **9** The fear of the Lord is clean, and endureth forever: the judgments of the Lord are [g]truth: they are righteous [h]altogether, **10** And more to be [i]desired than gold, yea, than much fine gold: sweeter also than honey, and the honeycomb. **11** Moreover by them is thy servant made circumspect, and in keeping of them there is great [j]reward. **12** Who can understand his [k]faults? cleanse me from secret faults. **13** Keep thy servant also from [l]presumptuous sins: let them not reign over me: [m]so shall I be upright, and made clean from much wickedness. **14** Let the words of my mouth, and the [n]meditation of mine heart be acceptable in thy sight, O Lord my strength, and my redeemer.

20

A prayer of the people unto God, that it would please him to hear their king and receive his sacrifice, which he offered before he went to battle against the Ammonites.

To him that excelleth. A Psalm of David.

1 The [a]Lord hear thee in the day of trouble: the [b]Name of the God of Jacob defend thee: **2** Send thee help from the Sanctuary, and strengthen thee out of Zion. **3** Let him remember all thine offerings, and [c]turn thy burnt offerings into ashes. Selah. **4** And grant thee according to thine heart, and fulfill all thy purpose: **5** That we may rejoice in thy [d]salvation, and set up the banner in the Name of our God, when the Lord shall perform all thy petitions. **6** Now [e]know I that the Lord will help his anointed, and will hear him from his [f]Sanctuary, by the mighty help of his right hand. **7** Some trust in chariots, and some in horses: but we will remember the Name of the Lord our God. **8** [g]They are brought down and fallen, but we are risen, and stand upright. **9** Save Lord: [h]Let the King hear us in the day that we call.

---

i. Psalm 18:11 As a king angry with the people, will not show himself unto them.
j. Psalm 18:13 Thundered, lightninged and hailed.
k. Psalm 18:14 His lightnings.
l. Psalm 18:15 That is, the deep bottoms were seen when the red sea was divided.
m. Psalm 18:16 Out of sundry and great dangers.
n. Psalm 18:17 To wit, Saul.
o. Psalm 18:17 Therefore God sent me succor.
p. Psalm 18:19 The cause of God's deliverance is his only favor and love to us.
q. Psalm 18:20 David was sure of his righteous cause, and good behavior toward Saul and his enemies, and therefore was assured of God's favor and deliverance.
r. Psalm 18:22 For all his dangers he exercised himself in the Law of God.
s. Psalm 18:23 I neither gave place to their wicked tentations, nor to mine own affections.
t. Psalm 18:25 Here he speaketh of God according to our capacity, who showeth mercy to his and punisheth the wicked, as is said also, Lev. 26:21, 24.
u. Psalm 18:27 When their sin is come to the full measure.
v. Psalm 18:29 He attributeth it to God that he both got the victory in the field, and also destroyed the cities of his enemies.
w. Psalm 18:30 Be the dangers never so many or great, yet God's promise must take effect.
x. Psalm 18:32 He giveth good success to all mine enterprises.
y. Psalm 18:33 As towers and forts, which he took out of the hands of God's enemies.
z. Psalm 18:34 Or, steel.
aa. Psalm 18:35 To defend me from dangers.
ab. Psalm 18:35 He attributed the beginning, continuance and increase in well doing only to God's favor.
ac. Psalm 18:37 David declareth that he did nothing besides his vocation, but was stirred up by God's Spirit to execute his judgments.
ad. Psalm 18:40 Thou hast given them into mine hands to be slain.
ae. Psalm 18:41 They that reject the cry of the afflicted, God will also reject them, when they cry for help: for either pain or fear cause those hypocrites to cry.
af. Psalm 18:43 Which dwell round about me.
ag. Psalm 18:43 The kingdom of Christ is in David's kingdom prefigured, who by the preaching of his word bringeth all to his subjection.
ah. Psalm 18:44 Or, lie: signifying a subjection constrained and not voluntary.
ai. Psalm 18:45 Fear shall cause them to be afraid and come forth of their secret holes and holds to seek pardon.
aj. Psalm 18:48 That is, Saul, who of malice persecuted him.
ak. Psalm 18:49 This prophecy appertaineth to the kingdom of Christ and vocation of the Gentiles, as Rom. 15:9.
al. Psalm 18:50 This did not properly appertain to Solomon, but to Jesus Christ.

PSALM 18

1. 2 Sam. 22:2

PSALM 19

a. Psalm 19:1 He reproacheth unto man his ingratitude, seeing the heavens, which are dumb creatures, set forth God's glory.
b. Psalm 19:2 The continual success of the day and the night is sufficient to declare God's power and goodness.
c. Psalm 19:3 The heavens are a Schoolmaster to all nations, be they never so barbarous.
d. Psalm 19:4 The heavens are as a line of great capital letters to show unto us God's glory.
e. Psalm 19:5 Or veil. The manner was that the bride and bridegroom should stand under a veil together, and after come forth with great solemnity, and rejoicing of the assembly.
f. Psalm 19:7 Though the creatures cannot serve, yet this ought to be sufficient to lead us unto him.
g. Psalm 19:9 So that all man's inventions and intentions are lies.
h. Psalm 19:9 Everyone without exception.
i. Psalm 19:10 Except God's word be esteemed above all worldly things, it is contemned.
j. Psalm 19:11 For God accepteth our endeavor, though it be far imperfect.
k. Psalm 19:12 Then there is no reward of duty, but of grace: for where sin is, there death is the reward.
l. Psalm 19:13 Which are done purposely and of malice.
m. Psalm 19:13 If thou suppress my wicked affections by thine holy spirit.
n. Psalm 19:14 That I may obey thee in thought, word and deed.

PSALM 19

1. Rom. 1:20

PSALM 20

a. Psalm 20:1 Hereby kings are also admonished to call to God in their affairs.
b. Psalm 20:1 The virtue, power and grace of God.
c. Psalm 20:3 In token that they are acceptable unto him.
d. Psalm 20:5 Granted to the King in whose wealth our felicity standeth.
e. Psalm 20:6 The Church feeleth that God had heard their petition.
f. Psalm 20:6 As by the visible Sanctuary God's familiarity appeared toward his people, so by the heavenly is meant his power and majesty.
g. Psalm 20:8 The worldlings that put not their only trust in God.
h. Psalm 20:9 Let the king be able to deliver us by thy strength, when we seek unto him for succor.

21

*1 David in the person of the people praiseth God for the victory, attribu-
ting it to God, and not to the strength of man. Wherein the holy Ghost
directeth the faithful to Christ, who is the perfection of this kingdom.*

To him that excelleth. A Psalm of David. 1 The King shall [a]rejoice in thy
strength, O Lord: yea how greatly shall he rejoice in thy salvation? 2 Thou hast
given him his heart's desire, and hast not denied him the request of his lips. Se-
lah. 3 For thou [b]didst prevent him with liberal blessings, and didst set a crown
of pure gold upon his head. 4 [c]He asked life of thee, and thou gavest him a long
life forever and ever. 5 His glory is great in thy salvation: dignity and honor hast
thou laid upon him. 6 For thou hast set him as [d]blessings forever: thou hast
made him glad with the joy of thy countenance. 7 Because the king trusteth
in the Lord, and in the mercy of the most high, he shall not slide. 8 [e]Thine
hand shall find out all thine enemies, and thy right hand shall find out them that
hate thee. 9 Thou shalt make them like a fiery oven in time of thine anger: the
Lord shall destroy them in his [f]wrath, and the fire shall devour them. 10 Their
fruit shalt thou destroy from the earth, and their seed from the children of
men. 11 For they [g]intended evil against thee, and imagined mischief, but they
shall not prevail. 12 Therefore shalt thou put them [h]apart, and the strings of thy
bow shalt thou make ready against their faces. 13 [i]Be thou exalted, O Lord, in
thy strength: so will we sing and praise thy power.

22

*1 David complained because he was brought into such extremities that he
was past all hope, but after he had rehearsed the sorrows and griefs, whe-
rewith he was vexed. 10 He recovereth himself from the bottomless pit of tentations,
and groweth in hope. And here under his own person he setteth forth the figure of
Christ, whom he did foresee by the spirit of prophecy, that he should marvelously, and
strangely be rejected, and abased, before his Father should raise and exalt him again.*

To him that excelleth upon [a]Aijeleth Hashahar. A Psalm of David. 1 My
[b]God, my God, why hast thou forsaken me, and art so far from mine health, and
from the words of my [c]roaring? 2 O my God, I cry by day, but thou hearest not:
and by night, but [d]have no audience. 3 But thou art holy, and dost inhabit the
[e]praises of Israel. 4 Our fathers trusted in thee: they trusted, and thou didst de-
liver them. 5 They called upon thee, and were delivered: they trusted in thee,
and were not confounded. 6 But I am a [f]worm, and not a man: a shame of men,
and the contempt of the people. 7 All they that see me, have me in derision:
they make a mow and nod the head, saying, 8 [1,g]He trusted in the Lord, let
him deliver him: let him save him, seeing he loveth him. 9 But thou didst draw
me out of the [h]womb: thou gavest me hope, even at my mother's breasts. 10 I
was cast upon thee, even from the [i]womb: thou art my God from my mother's
belly. 11 Be not far from me, because trouble is near: for there is none to help
me. 12 Many young bulls have compassed me: mighty [j]bulls of Bashan have clo-
sed me about. 13 They gape upon me with their mouths, as a ramping and roa-
ring lion. 14 I am like [k]water poured out, and all my bones are out of joint: mine
heart is like wax: it is molten in the midst of my bowels. 15 My strength is dried
up like a potsherd, and my tongue cleaveth to my jaws, and thou [l]hast brought me
into the dust of death. 16 For dogs have compassed me, and the assembly of the
wicked have enclosed me: they [m]pierced mine hands and my feet. 17 I may tell
all my bones, yet they behold, and look upon me. 18 They part my garments
among them, and cast lots upon my vesture. 19 But be not thou far off, O
Lord, my strength: hasten to help me. 20 Deliver my soul from the sword: my
[n]desolate soul from the power of the dog. 21 [o]Save me from the lion's mouth,
and answer me in saving me from the horns of the unicorns. 22 [2]I will declare
thy Name unto my brethren: in the midst of the Congregation will I praise thee,
saying, 23 [p]Praise the Lord, ye that fear him: magnify ye him, all the seed of Ja-
cob, and fear ye him all the seed of Israel. 24 For he hath not despised nor abhor-
red the affliction of the [q]poor: neither hath he hid his face from him, but when he
called unto him, he heard. 25 My praise shall be of thee in the great Congrega-
tion: my [r]vows will I perform before them that fear him. 26 [s]The poor shall eat
and be satisfied: they that seek after the Lord, shall praise him: your heart shall live
forever. 27 All the ends of the world shall remember themselves and turn to the
Lord, and all the kindreds of the nations shall worship before thee. 28 For the
kingdom is the Lord's, and he ruleth among the nations. 29 All they that be fat
[t]in the earth shall eat and worship: all they that go down into the dust, shall bow
before him, [u]even he that cannot quicken his own soul. 30 [v]Their seed shall ser-
ve him: it shall be counted unto the Lord for a generation. 31 They shall come
and shall declare his righteousness unto a people that shall be born, because he
hath [w]done it.

23

*1 Because the Prophet had proved the great mercies of God at divers times,
and in sundry manners, he gathereth a certain assurance, fully persuading
himself that God will continue the very same goodness towards him forever.*

A Psalm of David. 1 The Lord is my [1]shepherd, [a]I shall not want. 2 He
maketh me to rest in green pasture, and leadeth me by the still waters. 3 He
[b]restoreth my soul, and leadeth me in the [c]paths of righteousness for his Name's
sake. 4 Yea, though I should walk through the valley of the [d]shadow of dea-
th, I will fear no evil; for thou art with me: thy rod and thy staff, they comfort
me. 5 Thou dost prepare a [e]table before me in the sight of mine adversaries: thou
dost [f]anoint mine head with oil, and my cup runneth over. 6 Doubtless kindness
and mercy shall follow me all the days of my life, and I shall remain a long season
in the [g]house of the Lord.

24

*1 Albeit the Lord God hath made, and governeth all the world, yet toward
his chosen people, his gracious goodness doth most abundantly appear, in
that among them he will have his dwelling place. Which thought it was appointed
among the children of Abraham, yet only they do enter aright into this Sanctuary,
which are the true worshippers of God, purged from the sinful filth of this world. 7
Finally he magnifieth God's grace for the building of the Temple, to the end he might
stir up all the faithful to the true service of God.*

A Psalm of David. 1 The earth [1]is the Lord's, and all that therein is; the
world and they that dwell therein. 2 For he hath founded it upon the [a]seas;
and established it upon the floods. 3 Who shall ascend into the mountain of
the Lord? and who shall stand in his holy place? 4 Even he that hath innocent
hands, and a pure heart; which hath not lifted up his mind unto vanity, nor sworn
deceitfully. 5 He shall receive a blessing from the Lord, and righteousness from
the God of his salvation. 6 This is the [b]generation of them that seek him, of
them that seek thy face, this is Jacob. Selah. 7 [c]Lift up your heads ye gates, and

---

PSALM 21

- **a.** Psalm 21:1 When he shall overcome his enemies, and so be assured of his vocation.
- **b.** Psalm 21:3 Thou declarest thy liberal favor toward him before he prayed.
- **c.** Psalm 21:4 David did not only obtain life, but also assurance that his posterity should reign forever.
- **d.** Psalm 21:6 Thou hast made him thy blessings to others, and a perpetual example of thy favor forever.
- **e.** Psalm 21:8 Here he describeth the power of Christ's kingdom against the enemies thereof.
- **f.** Psalm 21:9 This teacheth us patiently to endure the cross till God destroy the adversary.
- **g.** Psalm 21:11 They laid as it were their nets to make God's power to give place to their wicked enterprises.
- **h.** Psalm 21:12 As a mark to shoot at.
- **i.** Psalm 21:13 Maintain thy Church against thine adversaries, that we may have ample occasion to praise thy Name.

PSALM 22

- **a.** Psalm 22:1 Or, the hind of the morning: and this was the name of some common song.
- **b.** Psalm 22:1 Here appeareth that horrible conflict, which he sustained between faith and desperation.
- **c.** Psalm 22:1 Being tormented with extreme anguish.
- **d.** Psalm 22:2 Or, I cease not.
- **e.** Psalm 22:3 He meaneth the place of praising, even the Tabernacle: or else it is so called, because he gave the people continually occasion to praise him.
- **f.** Psalm 22:6 And seeming most miserable of all creatures, which was meant of Christ. And herein appeareth the unspeakable love of God toward man, that he would thus abase his Son for our sakes.
- **g.** Psalm 22:8 Hebrew, rolled upon God.
- **h.** Psalm 22:9 Even from my birth thou hast given me occasion to trust in thee.
- **i.** Psalm 22:10 For except God's providence preserve the infants, they should perish a thousand times in the mother's womb.
- **j.** Psalm 22:12 He meaneth, that his enemies were so fat, proud, and cruel, that they were rather beasts than men.
- **k.** Psalm 22:14 Before he spake of the cruelty of his enemies, and now he declareth the inward griefs of the mind, so that Christ was tormented both in soul and body.
- **l.** Psalm 22:15 Thou had suffered me to be without all hope of life.
- **m.** Psalm 22:16 Thus David complaineth as though he were nailed by his enemies both hands and feet: but this was accomplished in Christ.
- **n.** Psalm 22:20 My life that is solitary, left alone and forsaken of all, Ps. 35:17 and 25:16.
- **o.** Psalm 22:21 Christ is delivered with a more mighty deliverance by overcoming death, than if he had not tasted death at all.
- **p.** Psalm 22:23 He promiseth to exhort the Church that they by his example might praise the Lord.
- **q.** Psalm 22:24 The poor afflicted are comforted by this example of David, or Christ.
- **r.** Psalm 22:25 Which were sacrifices of thanksgiving, which they offered by God's commandment, when they were delivered out of any great danger.
- **s.** Psalm 22:26 He doth allude still to the sacrifice.
- **t.** Psalm 22:29 Though the poor be first named, as verse 26, yet the wealthy are not separated from the grace of Christ's kingdom.
- **u.** Psalm 22:29 In whom there is no hope that he shall recover life: so neither poor nor rich, quick nor dead shall be rejected from his kingdom.
- **v.** Psalm 22:30 Meaning, the prosperity, which the Lord keepeth as a seed to the Church to continue his praise among men.
- **w.** Psalm 22:31 That is, God hath fulfilled his promise.

PSALM 22

1. Matt. 27:43

PSALM 23

- **a.** Psalm 23:1 He hath care over me and ministereth unto me all things.
- **b.** Psalm 23:3 He comforteth or refresheth me.
- **c.** Psalm 23:3 Plain, or straight ways.
- **d.** Psalm 23:4 Though he were in danger of death, as the sheep that wandereth in the dark valley without his shepherd.
- **e.** Psalm 23:5 Albeit his enemies sought to destroy him, yet God delivereth him, and dealeth most liberally with him in despite of them.
- **f.** Psalm 23:5 As was the manner of great feasts.
- **g.** Psalm 23:6 He setteth not his felicity in the pleasures of this world, but in the fear and service of God.

PSALM 23

1. Isa. 40:11 - Jer. 23:5 - Ezek. 34:23 - John. 10:11 - 1Pet. 2:25

PSALM 24

- **a.** Psalm 24:2 He noteth two things: the one, that the earth to man's judgment seemeth above the waters: and next, that God miraculously preserveth the earth, that it is not drowned with the waters, which naturally are above it.
- **b.** Psalm 24:6 Though circumcision separate the carnal seed of Jacob, from the Gentiles, yet he that seeketh God, is the true Jacob and the very Israelite.

be ye lifted up ye everlasting doors, and the King of glory shall come in. **8** Who is this King of glory? the Lord, strong and mighty, even the Lord mighty in battle. **9** Lift up your heads, ye gates, and lift up yourselves ye everlasting doors, and the King of glory shall come in. **10** Who is this King of glory? the Lord of hosts, he is the King of glory. Selah.

25

1 The Prophet touched with the consideration of his sins, and also grieved with the cruel malice of his enemies, 6 Prayeth to God most fervently to have his sins forgiven. 7 Especially such as he had committed in his youth. He beginneth every verse according to the Hebrew letters, two or three except.

A Psalm of David. **1** Unto thee, [a]O Lord, lift I up my soul. **2** My God, I [b]trust in thee; let me not be confounded: let not mine enemies rejoice over me. **3** [1]So all that hope in thee, shall not be ashamed; but let them be confounded, that transgress without cause. **4** [c]Show me thy ways, O Lord, and teach me thy paths. **5** Lead me forth in thy truth, and teach me: for thou art the God of my salvation: in thee do I trust [d]all the day. **6** Remember, O Lord, thy tender mercies, and thy lovingkindness: for they have been forever. **7** Remember not the [e]sins of my youth, nor my rebellions, but according to thy kindness remember thou me, even for thy goodness sake, O Lord. **8** Gracious and righteous is the Lord: therefore will he [f]teach sinners in the way. **9** Them that be meek, will he [g]guide in judgment, and teach the humble his way. **10** All the paths of the Lord are mercy and truth unto such as keep his covenant and his testimonies: **11** For thy [h]Name's sake, O Lord, be merciful unto mine iniquity, for it is great. **12** What [i]man is he that feareth the Lord? him will he teach the way that he shall [j]choose. **13** His soul shall dwell at [k]ease, and his seed shall inherit the land. **14** The [l]secret of the Lord is revealed to them that fear him: and his Covenant to give them understanding. **15** Mine eyes are ever toward the Lord: for he will bring my feet out of the net. **16** Turn thy face unto me, and have mercy upon me: for I am desolate and poor. **17** The sorrows of mine heart [m]are enlarged: draw me out of my troubles. **18** Look upon mine affliction and my travail, and forgive all my sins. **19** Behold mine [n]enemies, for they are many, and they hate me with cruel hatred. **20** Keep my soul and deliver me: let me not be confounded: for I trust in thee. **21** Let [o]mine uprightness and equity preserve me; for mine hope is in thee. **22** Deliver Israel, O God, out of all his troubles.

26

1 David oppressed with many injuries, finding no help in the world, calleth for aid from God: and assured of his integrity towards Saul, desireth God to be his judge, and to defend his innocence. 6 Finally he maketh mention of his sacrifice, which he will offer for his deliverance, and desireth to be in the company of the faithful in the Congregation of God, whence he was banished by Saul, promising integrity of life, and open praises and thanksgiving.

A Psalm of David. **1** Judge me, [a]O Lord, for I have walked in mine innocency: my trust hath been also in the Lord: therefore shall I not slide. **2** Prove me, O Lord, and try me: examine my [b]reins, and mine heart. **3** For thy [c]lovingkindness is before mine eyes: therefore have I walked in thy truth. **4** I have not [d]haunted with vain persons, neither kept company with the dissemblers. **5** I have hated the assembly of the evil, and have not companied with the wicked. **6** I will [e]wash mine hands in innocency, O Lord, and compass thine altar, **7** That I may declare with the voice of thanksgiving, and set forth all thy wondrous works. **8** O Lord, I have loved the habitation of thine house, and the place where thine honor dwelleth. **9** [f]Gather not my soul with the sinners, nor my life with the bloody men: **10** In whose hand is [g]wickedness, and their right hand is full of bribes. **11** But I will walk in mine innocency: redeem me therefore, and be merciful unto me. **12** My foot standeth in [h]uprightness: I will praise thee, O Lord, in the Congregations.

27

1 David maketh this Psalm being delivered from great perils, as appeareth by the praises and thanksgiving annexed: 6 Wherein we may see the constant faith of David against the assaults of all his enemies. 7 And also the end wherefore he desireth to live and to be delivered, only to worship God in his Congregation.

A Psalm of David. **1** The Lord is my [a]light and my salvation, whom shall I fear? the Lord is the strength of my life, of whom shall I be afraid? **2** When the wicked, even mine enemies and my foes came upon me to eat up my flesh, they stumbled and fell. **3** Though an host pitched against me, mine heart should not be afraid: though war be raised against me, I will trust in [b]this. **4** [c]One thing have I desired of the Lord, that I will require, even that I may dwell in the house of the Lord all the days of my life, to behold the beauty of the Lord, and to visit his Temple. **5** For in the time of trouble he shall hide me in his Tabernacle: in the secret place of his pavilion shall he hide me, and set me up upon a rock. **6** [d]And now shall he lift up mine head above mine enemies round about me: therefore will I offer in his Tabernacle sacrifices of joy: I will sing and praise the Lord. **7** Hearken unto my voice, O Lord, when I cry: have mercy also upon me and hear me. **8** When thou saidest, [e]Seek ye my face, mine heart answered unto thee, O Lord, I will seek thy face. **9** Hide not therefore thy face from me, nor cast thy servant away in displeasure: thou hast been my succor, leave me not, neither forsake me, O God of my salvation. **10** [f]Though my father and my mother should forsake me, yet the Lord will gather me up. **11** Teach me thy way, O Lord, and lead me in a right path, because of mine enemies. **12** Give me not unto the [g]lust of mine adversaries: for there are false witnesses risen up against me, and such as speak cruelly. **13** I should have fainted, except I had believed to see the goodness of the Lord [h]in the land of the living. **14** [i]Hope in the Lord: be strong, and he shall comfort thine heart, and trust in the Lord.

28

1 Being in great fear and heaviness of heart to see God dishonored by the wicked, he desireth to be rid of them. 4 And crieth for vengeance against them: and at length assureth himself, that God hath heard his prayer, 9 Unto whose tuition he commendeth all the faithful.

A Psalm of David. **1** Unto thee, O Lord, do I cry: O my strength, be not deaf toward me, lest if thou answer me not, I be like [a]them that go down into the pit. **2** Hear the voice of my petitions, when I cry unto thee, when I hold up my hands toward thine [b]holy Oracle. **3** [c]Draw me not away with the wicked, and with the workers of iniquity: which speak friendly to their neighbors, when malice is in their hearts. **4** [d]Reward them according to their deeds, and according to the wickedness of their inventions: recompense them after the work of their hands: render them their reward. **5** For they reward not the works of the Lord, nor the operation of his hands: therefore [e]break them down, and build them not up. **6** [f]Praised be the Lord, for he hath heard the voice of my petitions. **7** The Lord is my strength and my shield: mine heart trusted in him, and I was helped: therefore mine heart shall rejoice, and with my song will I praise him. **8** The

---

c. Psalm 24:7 David desireth the building up of the Temple, wherein the glory of God should appear, and under the figure of this Temple, he also prayeth for the spiritual Temple, which is eternal, because of the promise which was made to the Temple, as it is written, Ps. 132:14.

PSALM 24

1. Deut. 10:14 - Job 18:14 - 1Cor. 10:26

PSALM 25

a. Psalm 25:1 I put not my trust in any worldly thing.
b. Psalm 25:2 That thou wilt take away mine enemies, which are thy rods.
c. Psalm 25:4 Retain me in the faith of thy promise, that I swerve not on any side.
d. Psalm 25:5 Constantly, and against all tentations.
e. Psalm 25:7 He confesseth that his manifold sins were the cause that his enemies did thus persecute him, desiring that the cause of the evil may be taken away, to the intent that the effect may cease.
f. Psalm 25:8 That is, call them to repentance.
g. Psalm 25:9 He will govern and comfort them that are truly humbled for their sins.
h. Psalm 25:11 And for none other respect.
i. Psalm 25:12 Meaning, the number is very small.
j. Psalm 25:12 He will direct such with his spirit to follow the right way.
k. Psalm 25:13 He shall prosper both in spiritual and corporal things.
l. Psalm 25:14 His counsel contained in his word, whereby he declareth that he is the protector of the faithful.
m. Psalm 25:17 My grief is increased because of mine enemies' cruelty.
n. Psalm 25:19 The greater that his afflictions were and the more that his enemies increased, the more near felt he God's help.
o. Psalm 25:21 Forasmuch as I have behaved myself uprightly toward mine enemies, let them know that thou art the defender of my just cause.

PSALM 25

1. Isa. 28:26 - Rom. 10:11

PSALM 26

a. Psalm 26:1 He fleeth to God to be the Judge of his just cause; seeing there is no equity among men.
b. Psalm 26:2 My very affections and inward motions of the heart.
c. Psalm 26:3 He showeth what stayed him, that he did not recompense evil for evil.
d. Psalm 26:4 He declareth that they cannot walk in simplicity before God, that delight in the company of the ungodly.
e. Psalm 26:6 I will serve thee with a pure affection, and with the godly that sacrifice unto thee.
f. Psalm 26:9 Destroy me not in the overthrow of the wicked.
g. Psalm 26:10 Whose cruel hands do execute the malicious devices of their hearts.
h. Psalm 26:12 I am preserved from mine enemies by the power of God, and therefore will praise him openly.

PSALM 27

a. Psalm 27:1 Because he was assured of good success in all his dangers, and that his salvation was surely laid up in God, he feared not the tyranny of his enemies.
b. Psalm 27:3 That God will deliver me and give my faith the victory.
c. Psalm 27:4 The loss of country, wife, and all worldly commodities grieve me not in respect of this one thing, that I may not praise thy Name in the midst of the congregation.
d. Psalm 27:6 David assured himself by the Spirit of prophecy that he should overcome his enemies, and serve God in his Tabernacle.
e. Psalm 27:8 He groundeth upon God's promise, and showeth that he is most willing to obey his commandment.
f. Psalm 27:10 He magnifieth God's love toward his, which far passeth the most tender love of parents towards their children.
g. Psalm 27:12 But either pacify their wrath, or bridle their rage.
h. Psalm 27:13 In this present life before I die, as Isa. 38:11.
i. Psalm 27:14 He exhorteth himself to depend on the Lord, seeing he never failed in his promises.

PSALM 28

a. Psalm 28:1 He counteth himself as a dead man, till God show his favor toward him, and grant him his petition.
b. Psalm 28:2 He used this outward means to help the weakness of his faith: for in that place was the Ark, and there God promised to show the tokens of his favor.
c. Psalm 28:3 Destroy not the good with the bad.
d. Psalm 28:4 He thus prayeth in respect to God's glory and not for his own cause, being assured that God would punish the persecutors of his Church.
e. Psalm 28:5 Let them be utterly destroyed, as Mal. 1:4.
f. Psalm 28:6 Because he felt the assurance of God's help in his heart, his mouth was opened to sing his praises.
g. Psalm 28:8 Meaning, his soldiers, who were as means, by whom God declared his power.

Lord is [g]their strength, and he is the strength of the deliverances of his anoin-
ted. **9** Save thy people, and bless thine inheritance: feed them also, and exalt
them forever.

29

1 The Prophet exhorteth the princes and rulers of the world (which for the most part think there is no God.) 3 At the least to fear him for the thunders and tempests, for fear whereof all creatures tremble. 11 And though thereby God threateneth sinners, yet he is always merciful to his, and moveth them thereby to praise his Name.

A Psalm of David. **1** Give unto the Lord, ye [a]sons of the mighty, give unto
the Lord glory and strength. **2** Give unto the Lord glory due unto his Name:
worship the Lord in the glorious Sanctuary. **3** The [b]voice of the Lord is upon
the waters: the God of glory maketh it to thunder: the Lord is upon the great wa-
ters. **4** The voice of the Lord is mighty: the voice of the Lord is glorious. **5** The
[c]voice of the Lord breaketh the cedars: yea, the Lord breaketh the cedars of Leba-
non. **6** He maketh them also to leap like a calf: Lebanon also and [d]Shirion like
a young unicorn. **7** The voice of the Lord divideth the [e]flames of fire. **8** The
voice of the Lord maketh the wilderness to tremble: the Lord maketh the wilder-
ness of [f]Kadesh to tremble. **9** The voice of the Lord maketh the hinds to [g]calve,
and [h]discovereth the forests: therefore in his [i]Temple doth every man speak of his
glory. **10** The Lord sitteth upon the [j]floods, and the Lord doth remain King fo-
rever. **11** The Lord shall give strength unto his people: the Lord shall bless his
people with peace.

30

1 When David was delivered, from great danger, he rendered thanks to God, exhorting others to do the like, and to learn by his example, that God is rather merciful than severe and rigorous towards his children. 7 And also that the fall from prosperity to adversity is sudden. 8 This done, he returneth to prayer, promising to praise God forever.

[1]A Psalm or song of the [2]dedication of the [a]house of David. **1** I will
magnify thee, O Lord: [b]thou hast exalted me, and hast not made my foes to
rejoice over me. **2** O Lord my God, I cried unto thee, and thou hast [c]restored
me. **3** O Lord, thou hast brought up my [d]soul out of the grave: thou hast revi-
ved me from them that go down into the pit. **4** Sing praises unto the Lord, ye
[e]his Saints, and give thanks [f]before the remembrance of his Holiness. **5** [3]For he
endureth but a while in his anger: but in his favor is life: weeping may abide at
evening, but joy cometh in the morning. **6** And in my [g]prosperity I said, I shall
never be moved. **7** For thou Lord of thy goodness hadst made my [h]mountain to
stand strong: but thou didst hide thy face, and I [i]was troubled. **8** Then cried I
unto thee, O Lord, and prayed to my Lord. **9** What profit is there in my blood,
when I go down to the pit! shall the [j]dust give thanks unto thee? or shall it decla-
re thy truth? **10** Hear, O Lord, and have mercy upon me: Lord, be thou mine
helper. **11** Thou hast turned my mourning into joy: thou hast loosed my sack,
and girded me with gladness. **12** Therefore shall my [k]tongue praise thee and not
cease: O Lord my God, I will give thanks unto thee forever.

31

1 David delivered from some great danger, first rehearseth what meditation he had by the power of faith, when death was before his eyes, his enemy being ready to take him. 15 Then he affirmeth that the favor of God is always ready to those that fear him. 20 Finally he exhorteth all the faithful to trust in God and to love him, because he preserveth and strengtheneth them, as they may see by his example.

To him that excelleth. A Psalm of David. **1** In [1]thee, O Lord, have I put
my trust: let me never be confounded: deliver me in thy [a]righteousness. **2** Bow
down thine ear to me: make haste to deliver me: be unto me a strong rock, and an
house of defense to save me. **3** For thou art my rock and my fortress: therefore for
thy Name's sake direct me and guide me. **4** Draw me out of the [b]net, that they
have laid privily for me: for thou art my strength. **5** Into thine [c]hand I commend
my spirit: for thou hast redeemed me, O Lord God of truth. **6** I have hated them
that give themselves to deceitful vanities: for I [d]trust in the Lord. **7** I will be glad
and rejoice in thy mercy: for thou hast seen my trouble: thou hast known my soul
in adversities, **8** And thou hast not shut me up in the hand of the enemy, but
hast set my feet at [e]large. **9** Have mercy upon me, O Lord: for I am in trouble:
mine [f]eye, my soul and my belly are consumed with grief. **10** For my life is wa-
sted with heaviness, and my years with mourning: my strength faileth for my pain,
and my bones are consumed. **11** I was a [g]reproach among all mine enemies, but
specially among my neighbors: and a fear to mine acquaintance, [h]who seeing me
in the street, fled from me. **12** I am forgotten as a dead man out of mind: I am
like a broken vessel. **13** For I have heard the railing of [i]great men: fear was on
every side, while they conspired together against me, and consulted to take my
life. **14** But I trusted in thee, O Lord: I said, [j]Thou art my God. **15** My [k]times
are in thine hand: deliver me from the hand of mine enemies, and from them that
persecute me. **16** Make thy face to shine upon thy servant: and save me through
thy mercy. **17** Let me not be confounded, O Lord: for I have called upon thee:
let the wicked be put to confusion, and to [l]silence in the grave. **18** Let the lying
lips be made dumb, which cruelly, proudly, and spitefully speak against the righte-
ous. **19** How great is thy goodness, which thou [m]hast laid up for them that fear
thee! and done to them that trust in thee, even before the sons of men! **20** Thou
dost hide them [n,o]privily in thy presence from the pride of men: thou keepest them
secretly in thy Tabernacle from the strife of tongues. **21** Blessed be the Lord: for
he hath showed his marvelous kindness toward me in a [p]strong city. **22** Though
I said in mine [q]haste, I am cast out of thy sight, yet thou heardest the voice of my
prayer, when I cried unto thee. **23** Love ye the Lord all his [r]Saints: for the Lord
preserveth the faithful, and rewardeth abundantly the proud doer. **24** All ye that
trust in the Lord, be [s]strong, and he shall establish your heart.

32

1 David punished with grievous sickness for his sins, counteth them blessed to whom God doth not impute their transgressions. 5 And after that he had confessed his sins, and obtained pardon, 6 he exhorteth the wicked men to live godly, 11 and the good to rejoice.

A Psalm of David to give [a]instruction. **1** Blessed is he whose wickedness is
[b]forgiven, and whose sin is covered. **2** Blessed is the man, unto whom the Lord
imputeth not iniquity, and in whose spirit there is no guile. **3** When I held my
[c]tongue, my bones consumed, or when I [d]roared all the day, **4** (For thine hand
is heavy upon me day and night: and my moisture is turned into the drought of
Summer. Selah.) **5** Then I [e]acknowledged my sin unto thee, neither hid I mine

---

PSALM 29

- **a.** Psalm 29:1 He exhorteth the proud tyrants to humble themselves under God's hand, and not to be inferior to brute beasts and dumb creatures.
- **b.** Psalm 29:3 The thunder claps that are heard out of the clouds, ought to make the wicked to tremble for fear of God's anger.
- **c.** Psalm 29:5 That is, the thunderbolt breaketh the most strong trees, and shall men think their power to be able to resist God?
- **d.** Psalm 29:6 Called also Hermon.
- **e.** Psalm 29:7 It causeth the lightnings to shoot and glide.
- **f.** Psalm 29:8 In places most desolate, whereas seemeth there is no presence of God.
- **g.** Psalm 29:9 For fear maketh them to cast their calves.
- **h.** Psalm 29:9 Maketh the trees bare, or pierceth the most secret places.
- **i.** Psalm 29:9 Though the wicked are nothing moved with these lights, yet the faithful praise God.
- **j.** Psalm 29:10 To moderate the rage of the tempest and waters, that they destroy not all.

PSALM 30

- **a.** Psalm 30:1 After that Absalom had polluted it with most filthy fornication.
- **b.** Psalm 30:1 He condemneth them of great ingratitude, which do not praise God for his benefits.
- **c.** Psalm 30:2 Restored from the rebellion of Absalom.
- **d.** Psalm 30:3 Meaning, that he escaped death most narrowly.
- **e.** Psalm 30:4 The word signifieth them that have received mercy, and show mercy liberally unto others.
- **f.** Psalm 30:4 Before his Tabernacle.
- **g.** Psalm 30:6 I put too much confidence in my quiet state, as Jer. 31:18; 2 Chron. 32:24, 25.
- **h.** Psalm 30:7 I thought thou hadst established me in Zion most surely.
- **i.** Psalm 30:7 After that thou hast withdrawn thine help, I felt my misery.
- **j.** Psalm 30:9 David meaneth that the dead are not profitable to the Congregation of the Lord here in the earth: therefore he would live to praise his Name, which is the end of man's creation.
- **k.** Psalm 30:12 Because thou hast preserved me that my tongue should praise thee, I will not be unmindful of my duty.

PSALM 30

- **1.** 1 Sam. 7:2
- **2.** Deut. 20:5
- **3.** Ps. 145:8
- **4.** Isa. 54:8
- **5.** 2Cor. 4:17

PSALM 31

- **a.** Psalm 31:1 For then God declareth himself just, when he preserveth his according as he hath promised.
- **b.** Psalm 31:4 Preserve me from the crafty counsels and subtle practice of mine enemies.
- **c.** Psalm 31:5 He desireth God not only to take care for him in this life, but that his soul may be saved after this life.
- **d.** Psalm 31:6 This affection ought to be in all God's children, to hate whatsoever thing is not grounded upon a sure trust in God, as deceitful and vain.
- **e.** Psalm 31:8 Largeness signifieth comfort, as straightness, sorrow and peril.
- **f.** Psalm 31:9 Meaning, that his sorrow and torment had continued a great while.
- **g.** Psalm 31:11 Mine enemies had drawn all men to their part against me, even my chief friends.
- **h.** Psalm 31:11 They were afraid to show me any token of friendship.
- **i.** Psalm 31:13 They that were in authority, condemned me as a wicked doer.
- **j.** Psalm 31:14 I had this testimony of conscience, that thou wouldest defend mine innocence.
- **k.** Psalm 31:15 Whatsoever changes come, thou governest them by thy providence.
- **l.** Psalm 31:17 Let death destroy them to the intent that they may hurt no more.
- **m.** Psalm 31:19 The treasures of God's mercy are always laid up in store for his children, albeit at all times they do not enjoy them.
- **n.** Psalm 31:20 Hebrew, in the secret of thy face.
- **o.** Psalm 31:20 That is, in a place where they shall have thy comfort, and be hid safely from the enemies' pride.
- **p.** Psalm 31:21 Meaning, there was no city so strong to preserve him, as the defense of God's favor.
- **q.** Psalm 31:22 And so by my rashness and infidelity deserved to have been forsaken.
- **r.** Psalm 31:23 Or, ye that feel his mercies.
- **s.** Psalm 31:24 Be constant in your vocation, and God will confirm you with heavenly strength.

PSALM 31

- **1.** Ps. 71:1

PSALM 32

- **a.** Psalm 32:1 Concerning the free remission of sins, which is the chiefest point of our faith.
- **b.** Psalm 32:1 To be justified by faith, is to have our sins freely remitted, and to be reputed just, Rom. 4:6.
- **c.** Psalm 32:3 Between hope and despair.
- **d.** Psalm 32:3 Neither by silence nor crying found I ease, signifying that before the sinner be reconciled to God, he feeleth a perpetual torment.

iniquity: for I thought, I will confess against myself my wickedness unto the Lord, and thou forgavest the punishment of my sin. Selah. **6** Therefore shall everyone that is godly, make his prayer unto thee in a [f]time, when thou mayest be found: surely in the flood of great waters [g]they shall not come near him. **7** Thou art my secret place: thou preservest me from trouble: thou compassest me about with joyful deliverance. Selah. **8** I will [h]instruct thee, and teach thee in the way that thou shalt go, and I will guide thee with mine eye. **9** Be ye not like an horse, or like a mule which understand not: whose [i]mouths thou dost bind with bit and bridle, lest they come near thee. **10** Many sorrows shall come to the wicked: but he that trusteth in the Lord, mercy shall compass him. **11** Be glad ye righteous, and [j]rejoice in the Lord, and be joyful all ye, that are upright in heart.

33

1 He exhorteth good men to praise God, for that he hath not only created all things, and by his providence governeth the same, but also is faithful in his promises, 10 he understandeth man's heart, and scattereth the counsel of the wicked, 16 so that no man can be preserved by any creature or man's strength: by they, that put their confidence in his mercy, shall be preserved from all adversities.

1 Rejoice in the Lord, O ye righteous: for it [a]becometh upright men to be thankful. **2** Praise the Lord with harp: sing unto him with viol and [b]instrument of ten strings. **3** Sing unto him a new song: sing cheerfully with a loud voice. **4** For the [c]word of the Lord is righteous, and all his [d]works are faithful. **5** He [e]loveth righteousness and judgment: the earth is full of the goodness of the Lord. **6** By the word of the Lord were the heavens made, and all the host of them by the breath of his mouth. **7** He [f]gathereth the waters of the sea together as upon an heap, and layeth up the depths in his treasures. **8** Let all the earth fear the Lord: let all them that dwell in the world, fear him. **9** For he spake, and it was done: he commanded, and it [g]stood. **10** The Lord breaketh the [h]counsel of the heathen, and bringeth to nought the devices of the people. **11** The counsel of the Lord shall stand forever, and the thoughts of his heart throughout all ages. **12** Blessed is that nation, whose [i]God is the Lord: even the people that he hath chosen for his inheritance. **13** The Lord [j]looketh down from heaven, and beholdeth all the children of men. **14** From the habitation of his dwelling, he beholdeth all them that dwell in the earth. **15** He [k]fashioneth their hearts every one, and understandeth all their works. **16** The [l]King is not saved by the multitude of an host, neither is the mighty man delivered by great strength. **17** A horse is a vain help, and shall not deliver any by his great strength. **18** Behold, [m]the eye of the Lord is upon them that fear him, and upon them that trust in his mercy, **19** To deliver their souls from death, and to preserve them in famine. **20** [n]Our soul waiteth for the Lord: for he is our help and our shield. **21** Surely our heart shall rejoice in him, because we trusted in his holy Name. **22** Let thy mercy, O Lord, be upon us, as we trusted in thee.

34

1 After David had escaped Achish, according as it is written in 1 Sam. 2:11, whom in this title he calleth Abimelech (which was a general name to all the Kings of the Philistines) he praiseth God for his deliverance, 3 provoking all others by his example to trust in God, to fear and serve him, 7 who defendeth the godly with his Angels, 16 and utterly destroyeth the wicked in their sins.

A Psalm of David, when he changeth his behavior before Abimelech, who drave him away, and he departed. **1** I will [a]always give thanks unto the Lord: his praise shall be in my mouth continually. **2** My soul shall glory in the Lord: the [b]humble shall hear it and be glad. **3** Praise ye the Lord with me, and let us magnify his Name together. **4** I sought the Lord, and he heard me: yea, he delivered me out of all my [c]fear. **5** They [d]shall look unto him, and run to him: and their faces shall not be ashamed, saying, **6** This poor man cried, and the Lord heard him, and saved him out of all his troubles. **7** The [e]Angel of the Lord pitched round about them, that fear him, and delivereth them. **8** Taste ye and see, how gracious the Lord is: blessed is the man that trusteth in him. **9** Fear the Lord ye his Saints: for nothing wanteth to them that fear him. **10** The [f]lions do lack and suffer hunger, but they which seek the Lord, shall [g]want nothing that is good. **11** Come children, hearken unto me: I will teach you the [h]fear of the Lord. **12** [1]What man is he that desireth life, and loveth long days for to [i]see good? **13** Keep thy tongue from evil, and thy lips, that they speak no guile. **14** Eschew evil and do good: seek peace and follow after it. **15** The eyes of the Lord are upon the righteous, and his ears are open unto their cry. **16** But the [j]face of the Lord is against them that do evil, to cut off their remembrance from the earth. **17** The righteous cry, and the Lord heareth them, and delivereth them out of all their troubles. **18** The Lord is near unto them that are of a [k]contrite heart, and will save such as be afflicted in spirit. **19** Great are the troubles of the righteous: but the Lord delivereth him out of them all. **20** [l]He keepeth all his bones: not one of them is broken. **21** But malice shall slay the [m]wicked: and they that hate the righteous, shall perish. **22** The Lord [n]redeemeth the souls of his servants: and none that trust in him, shall perish.

35

1 So long as Saul was enemy to David, all that had any authority under him, to flatter their king (as is the course of the world) did also most cruelly persecute David: against whom he prayeth God to plead and to avenge his cause, 8 that they may be taken in their nets and snares, which they laid for him, that his innocency may be declared, 27 and that the innocent, which taketh part with him, may rejoice and praise the Name of the Lord, that thus delivereth his servant. 28 And so he promiseth to speak forth the justice of the Lord, and to magnify his Name all the days of his life.

A Psalm of David. **1** Plead thou my [a]cause, O Lord, with them that strive with me: fight thou against them that fight against me. **2** [b]Lay hand upon the shield and buckler, and stand up for my help. **3** Bring out also the spear, and stop the way against them that persecute me, say unto my [c]soul, I am thy salvation. **4** Let them be confounded and put to shame, that seek after my soul: let them be turned back, and brought to confusion, that imagine mine hurt. **5** Let them be as chaff before the wind, and let the Angel of the Lord [d]scatter them. **6** Let their way be dark and slippery: and let the Angel of the Lord persecute them. **7** For [e]without cause they have hid the pit and their net for me: without cause have they dug a pit for my soul. **8** Let destruction come upon [f]him at unawares, and let his net, that he hath laid privily, take him: let him fall into [g]the same destruction. **9** Then my soul shall be joyful in the Lord: it shall rejoice in his salvation. **10** All my [h]bones shall say, Lord, who is like unto thee, which deliverest the poor from him, that is too strong for him! yea, the poor and him that is in misery, from him that spoileth him! **11** [i]Cruel witnesses did rise up: they asked of me things that I knew not. **12** They rewarded me evil for good, to [j]have spoiled my soul. **13** Yet I, when they were sick, I was clothed with a sack: I humbled my soul with fasting: and [k]my prayer was turned upon my

---

- **e.** Psalm 32:5 He showeth that as God's mercy is the only cause of forgiveness of sins, so the means thereof are repentance and confession which proceed of faith.
- **f.** Psalm 32:6 When necessity causeth him to seek to thee for help, Isa. 55:6.
- **g.** Psalm 32:6 To wit, the waters and great dangers.
- **h.** Psalm 32:8 David promiseth to make the rest of God's children partakers of the benefits which he felt, and that he will diligently look and take care to direct them in the way of salvation.
- **i.** Psalm 32:9 If men can rule brute beasts, think they that God will not bridle and tame their rage?
- **j.** Psalm 32:11 He showeth that peace and joy of conscience in the holy Ghost, is the fruit of faith.

PSALM 33

- **a.** Psalm 33:1 It is the duty of the godly to set forth the praises of God for his mercy and power showed toward them.
- **b.** Psalm 33:2 To sing on instruments, was a part of the ceremonial service of the Temple, which doth no more appertain unto us, than the sacrifices, censings, and lights.
- **c.** Psalm 33:4 That is, counsel or commandment in governing the world.
- **d.** Psalm 33:4 That is, the effect and execution.
- **e.** Psalm 33:5 Howsoever the world judgeth of God's works, yet he doeth all things according to justice and mercy.
- **f.** Psalm 33:7 By the creation of the heavens and beautiful ornament with the gathering also of the waters, he setteth forth the power of God, that all creatures might fear him.
- **g.** Psalm 33:9 Or, was created.
- **h.** Psalm 33:10 No counsel can prevail against God, but he defeateth it, and it shall have evil success.
- **i.** Psalm 33:12 He showeth that all our felicity standeth in this, that the Lord is our God.
- **j.** Psalm 33:13 He proveth, that all things are governed by God's providence and not by fortune.
- **k.** Psalm 33:15 Therefore he knoweth their wicked enterprises.
- **l.** Psalm 33:16 If kings and the mighty of the world cannot be saved by worldly means, but only by God's providence, what have others to trust in, that have not like means?
- **m.** Psalm 33:18 God showeth that toward his of his mercy, which man by no means is able to compass.
- **n.** Psalm 33:20 Thus he speaketh in the name of the whole Church, which only depend on God's providence.

PSALM 34

- **a.** Psalm 34:1 He promised never to become unmindful of God's great benefit for his deliverance.
- **b.** Psalm 34:2 They that are beaten down with the experience of their own evils.
- **c.** Psalm 34:4 Which I conceived for the danger wherein I was.
- **d.** Psalm 34:5 They shall be bold to flee to thee for succor, when they shall see thy mercies toward me.
- **e.** Psalm 34:7 Though God's power be sufficient to govern us, yet for man's infirmity he appointeth his Angels to watch over us.
- **f.** Psalm 34:10 The godly by their patient obedience profit more than they which ravine and spoil.
- **g.** Psalm 34:10 If they abide the last trial.
- **h.** Psalm 34:11 That is, the true religion and worship of God.
- **i.** Psalm 34:12 Seeing all men naturally desire felicity, he wondereth why they cast themselves willingly into misery.
- **j.** Psalm 34:16 The anger of God doth not only destroy the wicked, but also abolisheth their name forever.
- **k.** Psalm 34:18 When they seem to be swallowed up with afflictions, then God is at hand to deliver them.
- **l.** Psalm 34:20 And as Christ saith, all the hairs of his head.
- **m.** Psalm 34:21 Their wicked enterprises shall turn to their own destruction.
- **n.** Psalm 34:22 For when they seem to be overcome with great dangers and death itself, then God showeth himself their redeemer.

PSALM 34

- **1.** 1 Pet. 3:10

PSALM 35

- **a.** Psalm 35:1 He desireth God to undertake his cause against them that did persecute him and slander him.
- **b.** Psalm 35:2 Albeit God can with his breath destroy all his enemies, yet the holy Ghost attributeth unto him these outward weapons to assure us of his present power.
- **c.** Psalm 35:3 Assure me against these tentations, that thou art the author of my salvation.
- **d.** Psalm 35:5 Smite them with the spirit of giddiness that their enterprises may be foolish, and they received just reward.
- **e.** Psalm 35:7 Showing that we may not call God to be a revenger, but only for his glory, and when our cause is just.
- **f.** Psalm 35:8 When he promiseth to himself peace.
- **g.** Psalm 35:8 Which he prepared against the children of God.
- **h.** Psalm 35:10 He attributeth his deliverance only to God, praising him therefore both in soul and body.
- **i.** Psalm 35:11 That would not suffer me to purge myself.
- **j.** Psalm 35:12 To have taken from me all comfort and brought me into despair.
- **k.** Psalm 35:13 I prayed for them with inward affection, as I would have done for myself: or, I declared mine affection with bowing down mine head.

bosom. 14 I behaved myself as to my friend, or as to my brother: I humbled
myself, mourning as one that bewaileth his mother. 15 But in mine [l]adversity
they rejoiced, and gathered themselves together: the abjects assembled themselves
against me, and I knew not: they tare [m]me, and ceased not, 16 With the false
scoffers at [n]banquets, gnashing their teeth against me. 17 Lord, how long wilt
thou behold this? deliver my soul from their tumult, even my desolate soul from
the lions. 18 So will I give thee thanks in a great Congregation: I will prai-
se thee among much people. 19 Let not them that are mine enemies unjustly
rejoice over me, neither let them [o]wink with the eye, that hate me without a cau-
se. 20 For they speak not as friends: but they imagine deceitful words against the
[p]quiet of the land. 21 And they gaped on me with their mouths, saying, Aha,
aha, [q]our eye hath seen. 22 Thou hast seen it, O Lord: keep not silence: be not
far from me, O Lord. 23 Arise and wake to my judgment, even to my cause, my
God, and my Lord. 24 Judge me, O Lord my God, according to thy [r]righte-
ousness, and let them not rejoice over me. 25 Let them not say in their hearts,
[s]O our soul rejoice: neither let them say, We have devoured him. 26 Let them
be confounded, and put to shame [t]together, that rejoice at mine hurt: let them be
clothed [u]with confusion and shame, that lift up themselves against me. 27 But
let them be joyful and glad, [v]that love my righteousness: yea, let them say always,
Let the Lord be magnified, which loveth the [w]prosperity of his servant. 28 And
my tongue shall utter thy righteousness, and thy praise every day.

36

*1 The Prophet grievously vexed by the wicked, doth complain of their
malicious wickedness. 6 Then he turneth to consider the unspeakable
goodness of God toward all creatures. 9 But specially towards his children, that by
the faith thereof he may be comforted and assured of his deliverance by this ordinary
course of God's work. 12 Who in the end destroyeth the wicked, and saveth the just.*

To him that excelleth. A Psalm of David, the servant of the Lord. 1 Wi-
ckedness saith to the wicked man, [a]even in mine heart, that there is no fear of God
before his eyes. 2 For he [b]flattereth himself in his own eyes, while his iniquity
is found worthy to be hated. 3 The words of his mouth are iniquity and [c]de-
ceit: he hath left off to understand and to do good. 4 He [d]imagineth mischief
upon his bed: he setteth himself upon a way, that is not good, and doth not abhor
evil. 5 Thy [e]mercy, O Lord, reacheth unto the heavens, and thy faithfulness unto
the clouds. 6 Thy righteousness is like the [f]mighty mountains: thy judgments are
like a great [g]deep: thou Lord, dost save man and beast. 7 How excellent is thy
mercy, O God! therefore the children of men trust under the shadow of thy win-
gs. 8 They shall be [h]satisfied with the fatness of thine house, and thou shalt give
them drink out of the river of thy pleasures. 9 For with thee is the well of life,
and in thy light shall we see light. 10 Extend thy loving-kindness unto them that
[i]know thee, and thy righteousness unto them that are upright in heart. 11 Let
not the [j]foot of pride come against me, and let not the hand of the wicked men
move me. 12 [k]There they are fallen that work iniquity: they are cast down, and
shall not be able to rise.

37

*1 This Psalm containeth exhortation and consolation for the weak, that
are grieved at the prosperity of the wicked, and the affliction of the go-
dly. 7 For how prosperously soever the wicked do live for the time, he doth affirm
their felicity to be vain and transitory, because they are not in the favor of God, but in
the end they are destroyed as his enemies. 11 And how miserably that the righteous
seemeth to live in the world, yet his end is peace, and he is in the favor of God, he is
delivered from the wicked, and preserved.*

A Psalm of David. 1 Fret not [a]thyself because of the wicked men, neither be
envious for the evildoers. 2 For they shall soon be [b]cut down like grass, and shall
wither as the green herb. 3 [c]Trust thou in the Lord and do good: dwell in the
land, and thou shalt be fed assuredly: 4 And delight thyself in the Lord, and he
shall give thee thine heart's desire. 5 [d]Commit thy way unto the Lord, and trust
in him, and he shall bring it to pass. 6 And he shall bring forth thy righteousness
as the light, and thy [e]judgment as the noon day. 7 Wait patiently upon the Lord,
and hope in him: fret not thyself for him [f]which prospereth in his way, nor for the
man that bringeth his enterprises to pass. 8 Cease from anger, and leave off wra-
th: fret not thyself [g]also to do evil. 9 For evildoers shall be cut off, and they that
wait upon the Lord, they shall inherit the land. 10 [h]Therefore yet a little while
and the wicked shall not appear, and thou shalt look after his place, and he shall
not be found. 11 But [l]meek men shall possess the earth, and shall have their de-
light in the multitude of peace. 12 [i]The wicked practiceth against the just, and
gnasheth his teeth against him. 13 But the Lord shall laugh him to scorn: for he
seeth that his day is coming. 14 The wicked have drawn their sword and have
bent their bow, to cast down the poor and needy, and to slay such as be of upright
conversation. 15 But their sword shall enter into their own heart, and their bows
shall be broken. 16 [j]A small thing unto the just man is better than great riches
to the wicked and mighty. 17 For the arms of the wicked shall be broken: but
the Lord upholdeth the just men. 18 The Lord [k]knoweth the days of upright
men, and their inheritance shall be perpetual. 19 They shall not be confounded
in the perilous time, and in the days of famine they shall have [l]enough. 20 But
the wicked shall perish, and the enemies of the Lord shall be consumed as the [m]fat
of lambs: even with the smoke shall they consume away. 21 The wicked bor-
roweth and payeth not again: but the righteous is merciful and [n]giveth. 22 For
such as be blessed of God shall inherit the land, and they that be cursed of him,
shall be cut off. 23 [o]The paths of man are directed by the Lord: for he loveth
his way. 24 Though he [p]fall, he shall not be cast off, for the Lord putteth under
his hand. 25 I have been young, and am old: yet I saw never the righteous for-
saken, nor his [q]seed begging bread. 26 But he is ever merciful and lendeth, and
his seed enjoyeth the blessing. 27 Flee from evil and do good, and dwell fore-
ver. 28 For the Lord loveth judgment, and forsaketh not his Saints: they shall be
preserved forevermore: but the seed of the wicked shall be cut off. 29 The righte-
ous men shall inherit the land, and dwell therein [r]forever. 30 The [s]mouth of the
righteous will speak of wisdom, and his tongue will talk of judgment. 31 For the
Law of his God is in his heart, and his steps shall not slide. 32 The wicked wa-
tched the righteous, and seeketh to slay him. 33 But the Lord will not leave him
in his hand, nor condemn him, when he is [t]judged. 34 Wait thou on the Lord,
and keep his way, and he shall exalt thee, that thou shalt inherit the land: when the
wicked men shall perish, thou shalt see. 35 I have seen the wicked strong, and
spreading himself like a green bay tree. 36 Yet he [u]passed away, and lo, he was
gone, and I sought him, but he could not be found. 37 [v]Mark the upright man,
and behold the just: for the end of that man is peace. 38 But their transgressors

---

l. Psalm 35:15 When they saw me ready to slip, and as one that halted for infirmity.
m. Psalm 35:15 With their railing words.
n. Psalm 35:16 The word signifieth cakes: meaning that the proud courtiers at their dainty feasts scoff, rail, and conspire his death.
o. Psalm 35:19 In token of contempt and mocking.
p. Psalm 35:20 Or, clefts of the earth: meaning, himself and others in their misery.
q. Psalm 35:21 They rejoiced as though they had now seen David overthrown.
r. Psalm 35:24 It is the justice of God to give to the oppressors affliction and torment, and to the oppressed aid and relief, 2 Thess. 1:6.
s. Psalm 35:25 Because we have that which we sought for, seeing he is destroyed.
t. Psalm 35:26 That is, at once, were they never so many or mighty.
u. Psalm 35:26 This prayer shall always be verified against them that persecute the faithful.
v. Psalm 35:27 That at least favor my right, though they be not able to help me.
w. Psalm 35:27 He exhorteth the Church to praise God for the deliverance of his servants, and for the destruction of his adversaries.

PSALM 36

a. Psalm 36:1 I see evidently by his deeds, that sin pusheth forward the reprobate from wickedness to wickedness, albeit he go about to cover his impiety.
b. Psalm 36:2 Though all others detest his vile sin, yet he himself seeth it not.
c. Psalm 36:3 The reprobate mock at wholesome doctrine, and put not difference between good and evil.
d. Psalm 36:4 By describing at large the nature of the reprobate, he admonisheth the godly to beware of these vices.
e. Psalm 36:5 Though wickedness seemeth to overflow all the world, yet by thine heavenly providence thou governest heaven and earth.
f. Psalm 36:6 Hebrew, the mountains of God: for whatsoever is excellent, is thus called.
g. Psalm 36:6 The depth of thy providence governeth all things, and disposeth them, albeit the wicked seem to overwhelm the world.
h. Psalm 36:8 Only God's children have enough of all things both concerning this life and the life to come.
i. Psalm 36:10 He showeth who are God's children, to wit, they that know him, and lead their lives uprightly.
j. Psalm 36:11 Let not the proud advance himself against me, neither the power of the wicked drive me away.
k. Psalm 36:12 That is, in their pride wherein they flatter themselves.

PSALM 37

a. Psalm 37:1 He admonisheth us neither to vex ourselves for the prosperous estate of the wicked, neither to desire to be like them to make our state the better.
b. Psalm 37:2 For God's judgment cutteth down their state in a moment.
c. Psalm 37:3 To trust in God, and do according to his will, are sure tokens that his providence will never fail us.
d. Psalm 37:5 Be not led by thine own wisdom, but obey God, and he will finish his work in thee.
e. Psalm 37:6 As the hope of the daylight causeth us not to be offended with the darkness of the night: so ought we patiently to trust that God will clear our cause and restore us to our right.
f. Psalm 37:7 When God suffereth the wicked to prosper, it seemeth to the flesh that he favoreth their doings, Job 21:7 etc.
g. Psalm 37:8 Meaning, except he moderate his affections, he shall be led to do as they do.
h. Psalm 37:10 He correcteth the impatience of our nature, which cannot abide till the fullness of God's time be come.
i. Psalm 37:12 The godly are assured that the power and craft of the wicked shall not prevail against them, but fall on their own necks, and therefore ought patiently to abide God's time, and in the meanwhile bewail their sins, and offer up their tears, is a sacrifice of their obedience.
j. Psalm 37:16 For they are daily fed as with Manna from heaven, and have sufficient, when the wicked have never enough, but ever hunger.
k. Psalm 37:18 God knoweth what dangers hang over his, and by what means to deliver them.
l. Psalm 37:19 For God will give them contented minds: and that which shall be necessary.
m. Psalm 37:20 They shall vanish away suddenly, for they are fed for the day of slaughter.
n. Psalm 37:21 God so furnisheth him with his blessings, that he is able to help others.
o. Psalm 37:23 God prospereth the faithful, because they walk in his ways with an upright conscience.
p. Psalm 37:24 When God doth exercise his faith with divers tentations.
q. Psalm 37:25 Though the just man die, yet God's blessings are extended to his posterity, and though God suffer some just man to lack temporal benefits, yet he recompenseth him with spiritual treasures.
r. Psalm 37:29 They shall continually be preserved under God's wings, and have at least inward rest.
s. Psalm 37:30 These three points are required of the faithful, that their talk be godly, that God's law be in their heart, and that their life be upright.
t. Psalm 37:33 For though it be sometime so expedient both for God's glory and their salvation, yet he will approve their cause, and revenge their wrong.
u. Psalm 37:36 So that the prosperity of the wicked is but as a cloud, which vanisheth away in a moment.

shall be destroyed together, and the end of the wicked shall be cut off. **39** But the [w]salvation of the righteous men shall be of the Lord: he shall be their strength in the time of trouble. **40** For the Lord shall help them, and deliver them: he shall deliver them from the wicked, and shall save them, because they trust in him.

38

1 David lying sick of some grievous disease, acknowledgeth himself to be chastised of the Lord for his sins, and therefore prayeth God to turn away his wrath. 5 He uttereth the greatness of his grief by many words and circumstances, as wounded with the arrows of God's ire, forsaken of his friends, evil intreated of his enemies. 22 But in the end with firm confidence he commendeth his cause to God, and hopeth for speedy help at his hand.

A Psalm of David for [a]remembrance. **1** O Lord, rebuke me not in thine [b]anger, neither chastise me in thy wrath. **2** For thine [c]arrows have light upon me, and thine hand lieth upon me. **3** There is nothing sound in my flesh, because of thine anger: neither is there rest in my bones, because of my [d]sin. **4** For mine [e]iniquities are gone over mine head, and as a weighty burden they are too heavy for me. **5** My wounds are putrefied, and corrupt because of [f]my foolishness. **6** I am bowed, and crooked very sore: I go [g]mourning all the day. **7** For my reins are full of burning, and there is nothing sound in my flesh. **8** I am weakened and sore broken: I [h]roar for the very grief of mine heart. **9** Lord, I pour my whole desire before thee, and my sighing is not hid from thee. **10** Mine heart [i]panteth: my strength faileth me, and the light of mine eyes, even [j]they are not mine own. **11** My lovers and my friends stand aside from my plague, and my [k]kinsmen stand afar off. **12** They also that seek after my life, lay snares, and they that go about to do me evil, talk wicked things and imagine deceit continually. **13** But I as a [l]deaf man heard not, and am as a dumb man, which openeth not his mouth. **14** Thus am I as a man, that heareth not, and in whose mouth are no reproofs. **15** For on thee, O Lord, do I wait: thou wilt hear me, my Lord, my God. **16** For I said, Hear me, lest they rejoice over me: for [m]when my foot slippeth, they extol themselves against me. **17** Surely I am ready to [n]halt, and my sorrow is ever before me. **18** When I declare my pain, and am sorry for my sin, **19** Then mine [o]enemies are alive, and are mighty, and they that hate me wrongfully are many. **20** They also, that reward evil for good, are mine adversaries, because I follow [p]goodness. **21** Forsake me not, O Lord, be not thou far from me, my God. **22** Haste thee, to help me, O my Lord, my [q]salvation.

39

1 David uttereth with what great grief and bitterness of mind he was driven to these outrageous complaints of his infirmities. 2 For he confesseth that when he had determined silence, that he brast forth yet into words, that he would not, through the greatness of his grief. 4 Then he rehearseth certain requests which taste of the infirmity of man. 8 And mixeth with them many prayers: but all do show a mind wonderfully trembled, that it may plainly appear how he did strive mightily against death and desperation.

To the excellent Musician [a]Jeduthun. A Psalm of David. **1** I thought, [b]I will take heed to my ways, that I sin not with my tongue: I will keep my mouth bridled, while the wicked is in my sight. **2** I was dumb and spake nothing: I kept silence even from good, [c]and my sorrow was more stirred. **3** Mine heart was hot within me, and while I was musing, the fire kindled, and I [d]spake with my tongue, saying, **4** Lord, let me know mine end, and the measure of my days, what it is: let me know how long I have to live. **5** Behold, thou hast made my days as an hand breadth, and mine age as nothing in respect of thee: surely every man in his best state is altogether [e]vanity. Selah. **6** Doubtless man walketh in a shadow, and disquieteth himself in vain: he heapeth up riches, and cannot tell who shall gather them. **7** And now Lord, what wait I for? mine hope is even in thee. **8** Deliver me from all my transgressions, and make me not a rebuke unto the [f]foolish. **9** I should have been dumb, and not have opened my mouth, because [g]thou didst it. **10** Take thy plague away from me: for I am consumed by the stroke of thine hand. **11** When thou with rebukes dost chastise man for iniquity, thou as a moth [h]makest his [i]beauty to consume: surely every man is vanity. Selah. **12** Hear my prayer, O Lord, and hearken unto my cry: keep not silence at my tears, for I am a stranger with thee, and a sojourner as all my fathers. **13** Stay thine anger from me, that I may recover my strength, [j]before I go hence and be not.

40

1 David delivered from great danger doth magnify and praise the grace of God for his deliverance, and commendeth his providence toward all mankind. 5 Then doth he promise to give himself wholly to God's service, and so declareth how God is truly worshipped. 14 Afterwards he giveth thanks and praiseth God, and having complained of his enemies, with good courage he calleth for aid and succor.

To him that excelleth. A Psalm of David. **1** I waited [a]patiently for the Lord, and he inclined unto me, and heard my cry. **2** He brought me also out of the [b]horrible pit, out of the miry clay, and set my feet upon the rock, and ordered my goings. **3** And he hath put in my mouth [c]a new song of praise unto our God: many shall see it and fear, and shall trust in the Lord. **4** Blessed is the man that maketh the Lord his trust, and regardeth [d]not the proud, nor such as turn aside to lies. **5** [e]O Lord my God, thou hast made thy wonderful works so many, that none can count in order to thee thy thoughts toward us: I would declare and speak of them, but they are more than I am able to express. **6** Sacrifice and offering thou didst not desire: (for [f]mine ears hast thou prepared) burnt offering and sin offering hast thou not required. **7** [g]Then said I, Lo, I come: for in the roll of the book it is written of me. **8** I desired to do thy good will, O my God: yea, thy Law is within mine heart. **9** I have declared thy righteousness in the [h]great congregation: lo, I will not refrain my lips: O Lord, thou knowest. **10** I have not hid thy righteousness within mine heart, but I have declared thy [i]truth and thy salvation: I have not concealed thy mercy, and thy truth from the great Congregation. **11** Withdraw not thou thy tender mercy from me, O Lord, let thy mercy and thy truth always preserve me. **12** For innumerable troubles have compassed me: my sins have taken such hold upon me, that I am not able to look up: yea, they are more in number than the hairs of mine head: therefore mine heart hath [j]failed me. **13** Let it please thee, O Lord, to deliver me: make haste, O Lord, to help me. **14** Let them be [k]confounded and put to shame together, that seek my soul to destroy it: let them be driven backward and put to rebuke that desire mine hurt. **15** Let them be [l]destroyed for a reward of their shame, which say unto me, Aha, aha. **16** Let all them that seek thee, rejoice and be glad in thee, and let them that love thy salvation, say always, [m]The Lord be praised. **17** Though I be poor and needy, the Lord thinketh on me: thou art mine helper and my deliverer: my God, make no tarrying.

---

v. Psalm 37:37 He exhorteth the faithful to mark diligently the examples both of God's mercies, and also of his judgments.
w. Psalm 37:39 He showeth that the patient hope of the godly is never in vain, but in the end hath good success, though for a time God prove them by sundry tentations.

PSALM 37
1. Matt. 5:5

PSALM 38
a. Psalm 38:1 To put himself and others in mind of God's chastisement for sin.
b. Psalm 38:1 He desireth not to be exempted from God's rod, but that he would so moderate his hand, that he might be able to bear it.
c. Psalm 38:2 Thy sickness, wherewith thou hast visited me.
d. Psalm 38:3 David acknowledgeth God to be just in his punishments, because his sins had deserved much more.
e. Psalm 38:4 He confesseth his sins, God's justice, and maketh prayer his refuge.
f. Psalm 38:5 That rather gave place to mine own lusts, than to the will of God.
g. Psalm 38:6 Or, black as one that is disfigured and consumed with sickness.
h. Psalm 38:8 This example warneth us never to despair, be the torment never so great: but always to cry unto God with sure trust for deliverance.
i. Psalm 38:10 Hebrew, runneth about, or, is tossed to and fro, meaning, that he was destitute of all help and counsel.
j. Psalm 38:10 My sight faileth me for very sorrow.
k. Psalm 38:11 Partly for fear and partly for pride, they denied all duty and friendship.
l. Psalm 38:13 For I can have no audience before men, and therefore patiently wait for the help of God.
m. Psalm 38:16 That is, if they see that thou succor me not in time, they will mock and triumph, as though thou hadst forsaken me.
n. Psalm 38:17 I am without hope to recover my strength.
o. Psalm 38:19 In my greatest misery they most rejoice.
p. Psalm 38:20 He had rather have the hatred of all the world, than to fail in any part of his duty to Godward.
q. Psalm 38:22 Which are the author of my salvation: and this declareth that he prayed with sure hope of deliverance.

PSALM 39
a. Psalm 39:1 This was one of the chief singers, 1 Chron. 16:41.
b. Psalm 39:1 Albeit he had appointed with himself patiently to have tarried God's leisure, yet the vehemency of his pain caused him to break his purpose.
c. Psalm 39:2 Though when the wicked ruled, he thought to have kept silence, yet his zeal caused him to change his mind.
d. Psalm 39:3 He confesseth that he grudged against God, considering the greatness of his sorrows, and the shortness of his life.
e. Psalm 39:5 Yet David offended in that that he reasoned with God as though that he were too severe toward his weak creature.
f. Psalm 39:8 Make me not a mocking stock to the wicked, or wrap me not up with the wicked, when they are put to shame.
g. Psalm 39:9 Seeing my troubles came of thy providence, I ought to have endured them patiently.
h. Psalm 39:11 Though thine open plagues light not evermore upon them, yet thy secret curse continually fretteth them.
i. Psalm 39:11 The word signifieth all that he desireth, as health, force, strength, beauty, and in whatsoever he hath delight, so that the rod of God taketh away all that is desired in this world.
j. Psalm 39:13 For his sorrow caused him to think that God would destroy him utterly: whereby we see how hard it is for the very Saints to keep a measure in their words, when death and despair assail them.

PSALM 40
a. Psalm 40:1 Though God deferred his help, yet he patiently abode till he was heard.
b. Psalm 40:2 He hath delivered me from most great dangers.
c. Psalm 40:3 That is, a special occasion to praise him: for God's benefits are so many occasions for us to praise his Name.
d. Psalm 40:4 To follow their example, which he must needs do that trusteth not only in the Lord.
e. Psalm 40:5 David goeth from one kind of God's favor to the contemplation of his providence over all, and confesseth that his counsels towards us are far above our capacities: we cannot so much as tell them in order.
f. Psalm 40:6 Thou hast opened mine ears to understand the spiritual meaning of the sacrifices: and here David esteemeth the ceremonies of the law nothing in respect of the spiritual service.
g. Psalm 40:7 When thou hadst opened mine ears and heart, I was ready to obey thee, being assured that I was written in the book of thine elect for this end.
h. Psalm 40:9 In the Church assembled in the Sanctuary.
i. Psalm 40:10 David here numbereth 3 degrees of our salvation: God's mercy, whereby he pitieth us: his righteousness, which signifieth his continual protection: and his truth, whereby appeareth his constant favor, so that hereof proceedeth our salvation.
j. Psalm 40:12 As touching the judgment of the flesh, I was utterly destitute of all counsel, yet faith inwardly moved mine heart to pray.
k. Psalm 40:14 He desireth that God's mercy may contend for him against the rage of his enemies.
l. Psalm 40:15 Let the same shame and confusion light upon them, which they intended to have brought upon me.

41

1 David being grievously afflicted, blesseth them that pity his case, 9 and complaineth of the treason of his own friends and familiars, as came to pass in Judas, John 13:18. After he feeling the great mercies of God gently chastising him, and not suffering his enemies to triumph against him, 13 giveth most hearty thanks to God.

To him that excelleth. A Psalm of David. **1** Blessed is he that [a]judgeth
wisely of the poor: the Lord shall deliver him in the time of trouble. **2** The Lord
will keep him and preserve him alive, he shall be blessed upon the earth: and thou
wilt not deliver him unto the will of his enemies. **3** The Lord will strengthen him
upon the [b]bed of sorrow: thou hast turned all his [c]bed in his sickness. **4** The-
refore I said, Lord have mercy upon me: heal my soul, for I have sinned against
thee. **5** Mine enemies [d]speak evil of me, saying, When shall he die, and his name
perish? **6** And if he come to see me, he speaketh [e]lies, but his heart heapeth ini-
quity within him, and when he cometh forth, he telleth it. **7** All they that hate me
whisper together against me: even against me do they imagine mine hurt. **8** [f]A
mischief is light upon him, and he that lieth, shall no more rise. **9** Yea, my [g]fa-
miliar friend, whom I trusted, which did eat of my bread, [h]hath lifted up the heel
against me. **10** Therefore, O Lord, have mercy upon me, and raise me up: so
shall I reward them. **11** By this I know that thou favorest me, because mine
enemy doth not triumph against me. **12** And as for me thou upholdest me [i]in
mine integrity, and dost set me before thy [j]face forever. **13** Blessed be the Lord
God of Israel world without end. [k]So be it, even so be it.

42

1 The Prophet grievously complaineth, that being letted by his persecutors, he could not be present in the congregation of God's people, protesting that although he was separated in body from them, yet his heart was thitherward affectioned. 7 And least of all he showed that he was not so far overcome with these sorrows and thoughts, 8 but that he continually put his confidence in the Lord.

**To him that excelleth. A Psalm to give instruction, [a]committed to the sons
of Korah.** **1** As the Hart brayeth for the rivers of water, so [b]panted my soul after
thee, O God. **2** My soul thirsteth for God, even for the living God: when shall I
come and appear before the presence of God? **3** [c]Mine tears have been my meat
day and night, while they daily say unto me, Where is thy God? **4** When I re-
membered [d]these things, I poured out my very heart, because I had gone with the
multitude, and led them into the house of God with the voice of singing, and prai-
se, as a multitude that keepeth a feast. **5** Why art thou cast down, my soul, and
unquiet within me? [e]wait on God: for I will yet give him thanks for the help of his
presence. **6** My God, my soul is cast down within me, [f]because I remembered
thee, from the land of Jordan, and Hermon, and from the mount Mizar. **7** One
[g]deep calleth another deep by the noise of thy waterspouts: all thy waves and thy
floods are gone over me. **8** The Lord [h]will grant his loving-kindness in the day,
and in the night shall I sing of him, even a prayer unto the God of my life. **9** I
will say unto God, which is my rock, Why hast thou forgotten me? why go I mour-
ning, when the enemy oppresseth me? **10** My [i]bones are cut asunder, while mine
enemies reproach me, saying daily unto me, Where is thy God? **11** [j]Why art
thou cast down, my soul? and why art thou disquieted within me? wait on God:
for I will yet give him thanks: he is my present help and my God.

43

1 He prayeth to be delivered from them that conspire against him, that he might joyfully praise God in his holy congregation.

1 Judge [a]me, O God, and defend my cause against the unmerciful [b]people:
deliver me from the deceitful and wicked man. **2** For thou art the God of my
strength: why hast thou put me away? why go I so mourning, when the enemy op-
pressed me? **3** Send thy [c]light and thy truth: let them lead me: let them bring me
unto thine holy Mountain, and to thy Tabernacles. **4** Then [d]will I go unto the
altar of God, even unto the God of my joy and gladness: and upon the harp will I
give thanks unto thee, O God my God. **5** Why art thou cast down, my soul? and
why art thou disquieted within me: [e]wait on God: for I will yet give him thanks, he
is my present help and my God.

44

1 The faithful remember the great mercy of God toward his people. 9 After they complain, because they feel it no more. 17 Also they allege the covenant made with Abraham, for the keeping whereof they show what grievous things they suffered. 23 Finally, they pray unto God not to contemn their affliction, seeing the same redoundeth to the contempt of his honor.

**To him that excelleth. A Psalm to give instruction, committed to the sons
of Korah.** **1** We have heard with our [a]ears, O God: our fathers have told us the
works that thou hast done in their days, in the old time: **2** How thou hast driven
out the [b]heathen with thine hand, and planted [c]them: how thou hast destroyed the
[d]people, and caused [e]them to grow. **3** For they inherited not the land by their
own sword, neither did their own arm save them: but thy right hand, and thine
arm, and the light of thy countenance, because thou didst [f]favor them. **4** Thou
art my king, O God: send help unto [g]Jacob. **5** [h]Through thee have we thrust
back our adversaries: by thy Name have we trodden down them that rose up against
us. **6** For I do not trust in my bow, neither can my sword save me. **7** But
thou hast saved us from our adversaries, and hast put them to confusion that hate
us. **8** Therefore will we praise God continually, and will confess thy Name fore-
ver. Selah. **9** But now thou art far off, and puttest us to [i]confusion, and goest not
forth with our armies. **10** Thou makest us to turn back from the adversary, and
they which hate us, spoil [j]for themselves. **11** *1*Thou givest us [k]as sheep to be ea-
ten, and dost scatter us among the nations. **12** Thou sellest thy people [l]without
gain, and dost not increase their price. **13** Thou makest us a reproach to our
neighbors, a jest and laughing stock to them that are round about us. **14** Thou
makest us a proverb among the nations, and a nodding of the head among the
people. **15** My [m]confusion is daily before me, and the shame of my face hath
covered me, **16** For the voice of the slanderer and rebuker, for the enemy and
[n]avenger. **17** All this is come upon us, yet do we not [o]forget thee, neither deal
we falsely concerning thy covenant. **18** Our heart is not turned back: neither our
steps gone out of thy paths, **19** Albeit thou hast smitten us down into the place
of [p]dragons, and covered us with the shadow of death. **20** If we have forgotten
the Name of our God, and held up our hands to a [q]strange god, **21** Shall not

---

m. Psalm 40:16 As the faithful always praise God for his benefits, so the wicked mocked God's children in their afflictions.

PSALM 41

a. Psalm 41:1 Not condemning him as accursed whom God doth visit, knowing that there are divers causes why God layeth his hand upon us, yea and afterward he restoreth us.
b. Psalm 41:3 When for sorrow and grief of mind he calleth himself upon his bed.
c. Psalm 41:3 Thou hast restored him in his sick bed and sent him comfort.
d. Psalm 41:5 That is, curse me and cannot have their cruel hate quenched, but with my shameful death.
e. Psalm 41:6 For pretending to comfort me, he conspireth my death in his heart, and braggeth thereof.
f. Psalm 41:8 The enemies thought by his sharp punishments that God was become his mortal enemy.
g. Psalm 41:9 Hebrew, the man of my peace.
h. Psalm 41:9 As David felt this falsehood, and as it was chiefly accomplished in Christ, John 13:18, so shall his members continually prove the same.
i. Psalm 41:12 Meaning, either in prosperity of life, or in the true fear of God against all tentations.
j. Psalm 41:12 Showing me evident signs of thy fatherly providence.
k. Psalm 41:13 By this repetition he stirreth up the faithful to praise God.

PSALM 42

a. Psalm 42:1 As a treasure to be kept of them, which were of the number of the Levites.
b. Psalm 42:1 By these similitudes of thirst and panting, he showeth his fervent desire to serve God in his Temple.
c. Psalm 42:3 As others take pleasure in eating and drinking, so he was altogether given to weeping.
d. Psalm 42:4 That is, how I led the people to serve thee in thy Tabernacle, and now seeing my contrary estate, I die for sorrow.
e. Psalm 42:5 Though he sustained grievous assaults of the flesh to cast him into despair, yet his faith grounded on God's accustomed mercies getteth the victory.
f. Psalm 42:6 That is, when I remember thee in this land of my banishment among the mountains.
g. Psalm 42:7 Afflictions came so thick upon me, that I felt my self as overwhelmed: whereby he showeth there is no end of our misery till God be pacified and send remedy.
h. Psalm 42:8 He assureth himself of God's help in time to come.
i. Psalm 42:10 That is, I am most grievously tormented.
j. Psalm 42:11 This repetition doth declare that David did not overcome at once, to teach us to be constant, forasmuch as God will certainly deliver his.

PSALM 43

a. Psalm 43:1 He desireth God to undertake his cause against the enemies but chiefly that he would restore him to the Tabernacle.
b. Psalm 43:1 That is, the cruel company of mine enemies.
c. Psalm 43:3 To wit, thy favor, which appeareth by the performance of thy promises.
d. Psalm 43:4 He promiseth to offer a solemn sacrifice of thanksgiving in token of his great deliverance.
e. Psalm 43:5 Whereby he admonisheth the faithful not to relent, but constantly to wait on the Lord, though their troubles be long and great.

PSALM 44

a. Psalm 44:1 This psalm seemeth to have been made by some excellent Prophet for the use of the people, when the Church was in extreme misery, either at their return from Babylon, or under Antiochus, or in such like affliction.
b. Psalm 44:2 That is, the Canaanites.
c. Psalm 44:2 To wit, our fathers.
d. Psalm 44:2 Of Canaan.
e. Psalm 44:2 That is, our fathers.
f. Psalm 44:3 God's free mercy and love is the only fountain and beginning of the Church, Deut. 4:37.
g. Psalm 44:4 Because thou art our king, therefore deliver thy people from their misery.
h. Psalm 44:5 Because they and their forefathers made both one Church, they apply that to themselves which before they did attribute to their fathers.
i. Psalm 44:9 As they confessed before that their strength came of God, so now they acknowledge that this affliction came by his just judgment.
j. Psalm 44:10 Or, at their pleasure.
k. Psalm 44:11 Knowing God to be author of this calamity, they murmur not, but seek remedy at his hands, who wounded them.
l. Psalm 44:12 As slaves which are sold for a low price, neither lookest thou for him that offereth most, but takest the first chapman.
m. Psalm 44:15 I dare not lift up my head for shame.
n. Psalm 44:16 Meaning, the proud and cruel tyrant.
o. Psalm 44:17 They boast not of their virtues, but declare that they rest upon God in the midst of their afflictions: who punished not now their sins, but by hard afflictions called them to the consideration of the heavenly joys.
p. Psalm 44:19 Or, whales: meaning, the bottomless seas of tentations: here we see the power of faith, which can be overcome by no perils.
q. Psalm 44:20 They show that they honored God aright, because they trusted in him alone.

God [r]search this out? for he knoweth the secrets of the heart. **22** Surely for thy sake [s]are we slain continually, and are counted as sheep for the slaughter. **23** Up, why sleepest thou, O Lord? awake, be not far off forever. **24** Wherefore hidest thou thy face? and forgettest our misery and our affliction? **25** For our soul is [t]beaten down unto the dust: our belly cleaveth to the ground. **26** Rise up for our succor, and redeem us for thy [u]mercy's sake.

45

1 The majesty of Solomon, his honor, strength, beauty, riches, and power are praised, and also his marriage with the Egyptian being an heathen woman, is blessed. 10 If that she can renounce her people and the love of her country, and gave herself wholly to her husband. Under the which figure, the wonderful majesty and increase of the kingdom of Christ and his Church his spouse, now taken of the Gentiles, is described.

To him that excelleth on [a]Shoshannim, a song of [b]love to give instruction, committed to the sons of Korah. **1** Mine heart will utter forth a good matter: I will entreat in my works of the king: my tongue is as the pen of a swift writer. **2** Thou art [c]fairer than the children of men: grace is poured in thy lips, because God hath blessed thee forever. **3** Gird thy sword upon thy thigh, O most mighty, to wit, thy worship and thy glory: **4** And prosper with thy glory: [d]ride upon the word of truth and of meekness and of righteousness: so thy right hand shall teach thee terrible things. **5** Thine arrows are sharp to pierce the heart of the King's enemies: therefore the people shall fall under thee. **6** Thy [e]throne, O God, is forever and ever: the scepter of thy kingdom, is a scepter of righteousness. **7** Thou lovest righteousness, and hatest wickedness, because God, even thy God, hath [f]anointed thee with the oil of gladness above thy fellows. **8** All thy garments smell of myrrh and aloes, and cassia, when thou comest out of the ivory palaces [g]where they have made thee glad. **9** King's daughters were among thine honorable wives: upon thy right hand did stand the [h]Queen in a vesture of gold of Ophir. **10** [i]Hearken, O daughter, and consider, and incline thine ear: forget also thine own people and thy father's house. **11** So shall the King have pleasure in thy beauty: for he is thy Lord, and reverence thou him. **12** And the [j]daughter of [k]Tyre with the rich of the people, shall do homage before thy face with presents. **13** The King's daughter is all glorious [l]within: her clothing is of broidered gold. **14** She shall be brought unto the King in raiment of needlework: the virgins that follow after her, and her companions shall be brought unto thee. **15** With joy and gladness shall they be brought, and shall enter into the king's palace. **16** Instead of thy fathers shall thy [m]children be: thou shalt make them princes [n]through all the earth. **17** I will make thy [o]Name to be remembered through all generations: therefore shall the people give thanks unto thee, world without end.

46

1 A song of triumph or thanksgiving for the deliverance of Jerusalem, after Sennacherib with his army was driven away, or some other like sudden and marvelous deliverance by the mighty hand of God. 8 Whereby the Prophet commending this great benefit, doth exhort the faithful to give themselves wholly into the hand of God, doubting nothing but that under his protection they shall be safe against all the assaults of their enemies, because this is his delight to assuage the rage of the wicked, when they are most busy against the just.

To him that excelleth upon [a]Alamoth, a song committed to the sons of Korah. **1** God is our [b]hope and strength, and help in [c]troubles, ready to be found. **2** Therefore will not we [d]fear, though the earth be moved, and though the mountains fall into the midst of the sea, **3** Though the waters thereof [e]rage and be troubled, and the mountains shake at the surges of the same. Selah. **4** Yet there is a [f]River, whose stream shall make glad the City of God: even the Sanctuary of the Tabernacles of the most High. **5** God is in the midst of it: therefore shall it not be moved: God shall help it [g]very early. **6** When the nations raged, and the kingdoms were moved, God [h]thundered, and the earth melted. **7** The Lord of hosts is [i]with us; the God of Jacob is our refuge. Selah. **8** Come and behold the works of the Lord, [j]what desolations he hath made in the earth. **9** He maketh wars to cease unto the ends of the world, he breaketh the bow, and cutteth the spear, and burneth the chariots with fire. **10** Be [k]still and know that I am God, I will be exalted among the heathen, and I will be exalted in the earth. **11** The Lord of hosts is with us; the God of Jacob is our refuge. Selah.

47

1 The Prophet exhorteth all people to the worship of the true and everlasting God, commending the mercy of God toward the posterity of Jacob. 9 And after prophesieth of the kingdom of Christ in the time of the Gospel.

To him that excelleth. A Psalm committed to the sons of Korah. **1** All people [a]clap your hands; sing loud unto God with a joyful voice. **2** For the Lord is high, and terrible; a great King over all the earth. **3** He hath [b]subdued the people under us, and the nations under our feet. **4** He hath chosen [c]our inheritance for us: even the glory of Jacob whom he loved. Selah. **5** God is gone up with triumph, even the Lord with the [d]sound of the trumpet. **6** Sing praises to God, sing praises: sing praises unto our King, sing praises. **7** For God is the king of all the earth: sing praises everyone that hath [e]understanding. **8** God reigneth over the heathen: God sitteth upon his holy Throne. **9** The princes of the people are gathered unto the people of the God of Abraham: for the shields of the world belong to God: he [f]is greatly to be exalted.

48

1 A notable deliverance of Jerusalem from the hands of many kings is mentioned, for the which thanks are given to God, and the state of that city is praised, that hath God so presently at all times ready to defend them. This Psalm seemeth to be made in the time of Ahaz, Jehoshaphat, Asa, or Hezekiah: for in their times chiefly was the city by foreign princes assaulted.

[a]A song or Psalm committed to the sons of Korah. **1** Great is the Lord, and greatly to be praised in the [b]City of our God, even upon his holy Mountain. **2** Mount Zion, lying Northward, is fair in situation: it is the [c]joy of the whole earth, and the City of the great king. **3** In the palaces thereof God is known for a [d]refuge. **4** For lo, the kings were [e]gathered, and went together. **5** When they saw [f]it, they marveled: they were astonied, and suddenly driven back. **6** Fear came there upon them, and sorrow, as upon a woman in travail. **7** As with an East wind thou breakest the ships [g]of Tarshish, so were they destroyed. **8** As we have [h]heard, so have we seen in the City of the Lord of hosts, in the city of our God: God will establish it forever. Selah. **9** We wait for thy loving-kindness, O God, in the midst of thy Temple. **10** O God, according to thy Name, so is

---

- **r.** Psalm 44:21 They take God to witness that they were upright to himward.
- **s.** Psalm 44:22 The faithful make this their comfort, that the wicked punish them not for their sins, but for God's cause, Matt. 5:10; 1 Pet. 4:14.
- **t.** Psalm 44:25 There is no hope of recovery, except thou put to thine hand and raise us up.
- **u.** Psalm 44:26 Which is the only sufficient ransom to deliver both body and soul from all kinds of slavery and misery.

PSALM 44

- **1.** Rom. 8:36

PSALM 45

- **a.** Psalm 45:1 This was a certain tune or an instrument.
- **b.** Psalm 45:1 Of that perfect love that ought to be between the husband and the wife.
- **c.** Psalm 45:2 Solomon's beauty and eloquence to win favor with his people, and his power to overcome his enemies, is here described.
- **d.** Psalm 45:4 He alludeth to them that ride in chariots in their triumphs, showing that the quiet state of a kingdom standeth in truth, meekness and justice, not in worldly pomp and vanity.
- **e.** Psalm 45:6 Under this figure of this kingdom of justice is set forth the everlasting kingdom of Christ.
- **f.** Psalm 45:7 Hath established thy kingdom as the figure of Christ, which is the peace and joy of the Church.
- **g.** Psalm 45:8 In the which palace the people made thee joyful to see them give thanks and rejoice for thee.
- **h.** Psalm 45:9 Though he had many Kings' daughters among his wives, yet he loved Pharaoh's daughter best.
- **i.** Psalm 45:10 Under the figure of Pharaoh's daughter, he showeth that the Church must cast off all carnal affections to obey Christ only.
- **j.** Psalm 45:12 He signifieth that divers of them that be rich shall be benefactors to the Church, albeit they give not perfect obedience to the Gospel.
- **k.** Psalm 45:12 Or, Zor.
- **l.** Psalm 45:13 There is nothing feigned, nor hypocritical, but she is glorious both within and without: and howbeit the Church hath not at all times this outward glory, the fault is to be imputed only to their own ingratitude.
- **m.** Psalm 45:16 They shall have greater graces than their fathers.
- **n.** Psalm 45:16 He signifieth the great compass of Christ's kingdom, which shall be sufficient to enrich all his members.
- **o.** Psalm 45:17 This only must be referred to Christ and not to Solomon.

PSALM 46

- **a.** Psalm 46:1 Which was either a musical instrument or a solemn tune, unto the which this Psalm was sung.
- **b.** Psalm 46:1 Or, protection.
- **c.** Psalm 46:1 In all manner of troubles God showeth his speedy mercy and power in defending his.
- **d.** Psalm 46:2 That is, we will not be overcome with fear.
- **e.** Psalm 46:3 Though the afflictions rage never so much, yet the rivers of God's mercies bring sufficient comfort to his.
- **f.** Psalm 46:4 The river of Shiloah, which passed through Jerusalem: meaning, though the defense seem never so small, yet if God have appointed it, it is sufficient.
- **g.** Psalm 46:5 Always when need requireth.
- **h.** Psalm 46:6 Hebrew, gave his voice.
- **i.** Psalm 46:7 They are assured that God can and will defend his Church from all dangers and enemies.
- **j.** Psalm 46:8 To wit, how oft he hath destroyed his enemies, and delivered his people.
- **k.** Psalm 46:10 He warneth them that persecute the Church, to cease their cruelty: for else they shall feel that God is too strong for them against whom they fight.

PSALM 47

- **a.** Psalm 47:1 Here is figured Christ, unto whom all his should give willing obedience, and who would show himself terrible to the wicked.
- **b.** Psalm 47:3 He hath made the Jews, who were the keepers of the Law and Prophets, schoolmasters to the Gentiles, that they should with gladness obey them.
- **c.** Psalm 47:4 God hath chosen us above all other nations, to enjoy a most glorious inheritance.
- **d.** Psalm 47:5 He doth allude unto the trumpets, that were blown at solemn feasts: but he doth further signify the triumph of Christ and his glorious ascension into the heavens.
- **e.** Psalm 47:7 He requireth that understanding be joined with singing, lest the Name of God be profaned with vain crying.
- **f.** Psalm 47:9 He praiseth God's highness, for that he joineth the great princes of the world (whom he calleth shields) to the fellowship of his Church.

PSALM 48

- **a.** Psalm 48:1 Some put this difference between a song and Psalm, saying that it is called a song, when there is no instrument, but the voice: and the Psalm, the contrary. The song of the Psalm is when the instruments begin, and the voice followeth. The Psalm of the song the contrary.
- **b.** Psalm 48:1 Albeit God shows his wonders through all the world, yet he will be chiefly praised in his Church.
- **c.** Psalm 48:2 Because the word of salvation came thence to all them that should believe.
- **d.** Psalm 48:3 Except God were the defense thereof, neither situation nor munition could prevail.
- **e.** Psalm 48:4 They conspired and went against God's people.
- **f.** Psalm 48:5 The enemies were afraid at the sight of the City.
- **g.** Psalm 48:7 That is, of Cilicia, or of the sea called Mediterranean.
- **h.** Psalm 48:8 To wit, of our fathers: so have we proved: or God hath performed his promise.

thy praise unto the [i]world's end: thy right hand is full of righteousness. **11** Let [j]mount Zion rejoice, and the daughters of Judah be glad, because of thy judgments. **12** [k]Compass about Zion, and go round about it, and tell the towers thereof. **13** Mark well the wall thereof: behold her towers, that ye may tell your posterity. **14** For this God is our God forever and ever, he shall be our guide unto the death.

49

1 The holy Ghost calleth all men to the consideration of man's life, 7 showing them not to be most blessed that are most wealthy, and therefore not to be feared: but contrariwise he lifteth up our minds to consider how all things are ruled by God's providence: 14 Who as he judgeth these worldly misers to everlasting torments, 15 so doth he preserve his, and will reward them in the day of the resurrection, 1 Thess. 1:6.

To him that excelleth. A Psalm committed to the sons of Korah. **1** Hear [a]this all ye people: give ear, all ye that dwell in the world, **2** As well low as high, both rich and poor. **3** My mouth shall speak of wisdom, and the meditation of mine heart is of knowledge. **4** I will incline mine ear to a parable, and utter my grave matter upon the harp. **5** Wherefore should I [b]fear in the evil days, when iniquity shall compass me about, as at mine heels? **6** They trust in their [c]goods, and boast themselves in the multitude of their riches. **7** Yet a man can by no means redeem his brother: he cannot give his ransom to God, **8** (So [d]precious is the redemption of their souls, [e]and the continuance forever) **9** That he may live still forever, and not see the grave. **10** For he seeth that wise men [f]die: and also that the ignorant and foolish perish, and leave their riches for [g]others. **11** Yet they think their houses and their habitations shall continue forever, even from generation to generation, and [h]call their lands by their names. **12** But man shall not continue in honor; he is like the [i]beasts that die. **13** This their way uttereth their foolishness; yet their posterity [j]delight in their talk. Selah. **14** [k]Like sheep they lie in grave; [l]death devoureth them; and the righteous shall have domination over them in the [m]morning; for their beauty shall consume, when they shall go from their house to grave. **15** But God shall deliver my soul from the power of the grave; [n]for he will receive me. Selah. **16** Be not thou afraid when one is made rich, and when the glory of his house is increased. **17** [1]For he shall take nothing away, when he dieth, neither shall his pomp descend after him. **18** For while he lived, [o]he rejoiced himself; and [p]men will praise thee, when thou makest much of thyself. **19** [q,r]He shall enter into the generation of his fathers, [s]and they shall not live forever. **20** Man is in honor; and [t]understandeth not; he is like to beasts that perish.

50

1 Because the Church is always full of hypocrites, 8 which do imagine that God will be worshipped with outward ceremonies only without the heart: and especially the Jews were of this opinion, because of their figures and ceremonies of the Law, thinking that their sacrifices were sufficient. 21 Therefore the Prophet doth reprove this gross error, and pronounceth the Name of God to be blasphemed where holiness is set in ceremonies. 23 For he declareth the worship of God to be spiritual, whereof are two principal parts, invocation and thanksgiving.

A Psalm of [a]Asaph. **1** The God of gods, even the Lord hath spoken and called the [b]earth from the rising up of the Sun, unto the going down thereof. **2** Out of Zion, which is the [c]perfection of beauty, hath God shined. **3** Our God shall come, and shall not keep silence: [d]a fire shall devour before him, and a mighty tempest shall be moved round about him. **4** He shall call the heaven above, and [e]the earth to judge his people. **5** Gather my [f]Saints together unto me, those that make a covenant with me with [g]sacrifice. **6** And the heavens shall declare his righteousness: for God is Judge himself. Selah. **7** Hear, O my people and I will speak: hear, O Israel, and I will testify unto thee: for I am God, even thy God. **8** I will not [h]reprove thee for thy sacrifices, or thy burnt offerings, that have not been continually before me. **9** I will take no bullock out of thine house, nor goats out of thy folds. **10** [i]For all the beasts of the forest are mine, and the beasts on a thousand mountains. **11** I know all the fowls on the mountains, and the wild beasts of the field are mine. **12** If I be hungry, I will not tell thee: for the world is mine and all that therein is. **13** [j]Will I eat the flesh of bulls? or drink the blood of goats? **14** Offer unto God praise, and [k]pay thy vows unto the most High, **15** And call upon me in the day of trouble: so will I deliver thee, and thou shalt glorify me. **16** But unto the wicked said God, [l]What hast thou to do to declare mine ordinances, that thou shouldest take my covenant in thy mouth, **17** Seeing thou hatest [m]to be reformed, and hast cast my words behind thee? **18** For when thou seest a thief, [n]thou runnest with him, and thou art partaker with the adulterers. **19** Thou givest thy mouth to evil, and with thy tongue thou forgest deceit. **20** Thou [o]sittest, and speakest against thy brother, and slanderest thy mother's son. **21** These things hast thou done, and I held my tongue: therefore thou thoughtest that I was like thee: but I will reprove thee, and [p]set them in order before thee. **22** Oh consider this ye that forget God, lest I tear you in pieces, and there be none that can deliver you. **23** He that offereth [q]praise, shall glorify me: and to him that [r]disposeth his way aright, will I [s]show the salvation of God.

51

When David was rebuked by the Prophet Nathan for his great offenses, he did not only acknowledge the same to God, with protestation of his natural corruption and iniquity, but also left a memorial thereof to his posterity. 7 Therefore first he desireth God to forgive his sins, 10 And to renew in him his holy Spirit. 13 With promise that he will not be unmindful of those great graces. 18 Finally, fearing lest God would punish the whole Church for his fault, he requireth that he would rather increase his graces toward the same.

To him that excelleth. A Psalm of David, when the Prophet Nathan [a]came unto him, after he had gone in to Bathsheba. **1** Have mercy upon me, O God, [b]according to thy loving-kindness: according to the multitude of thy compassions put away mine iniquities. **2** Wash me [c]thoroughly from mine iniquity, and cleanse me from mine sin. **3** For I [d]know mine iniquities, and my sin is ever before me. **4** Against thee, against thee only have I sinned, and done evil in thy sight, that thou mayest be just when thou [e]speakest, and pure when thou judgest. **5** Behold, I was born in iniquity, and in sin hath my mother conceived me. **6** Behold, thou [f]lovest truth in the inward affections: therefore hast thou taught me wisdom in the secret of mine heart. **7** Purge me with [1]hyssop, and I shall be clean: wash me, and I shall be whiter than snow. **8** Make me to hear [g]joy

---

i. Psalm 48:10 In all places where thy Name shall be heard of, men shall praise thee, when they hear of thy marvelous works.
j. Psalm 48:11 Let Jerusalem and the cities of Judea rejoice, for thy just judgments against thine enemies.
k. Psalm 48:12 For in this outward defense and strength God's blessings did also appear: but the chief is to be referred to God's favor and secret defense, who never leaveth his.

PSALM 49

a. Psalm 49:1 He will entreat how God governeth the world by his providence, which cannot be perceived by the judgment of the flesh.
b. Psalm 49:5 Though wickedness reign, and enemies rage, seeing God will execute his judgments against the wicked in time convenient.
c. Psalm 49:6 To trust in riches is mere madness, seeing they can neither restore life, nor prolong it.
d. Psalm 49:8 That is, so rare or not to be found, as prophecy was precious in the days of Eli, 1 Sam. 3:1.
e. Psalm 49:8 Meaning, it is impossible to live forever: also that life and death are only in God's hands.
f. Psalm 49:10 In that that death maketh no difference between the persons.
g. Psalm 49:10 That is, not to their children, but to strangers. Yet the wicked profit not by these examples, but still dream an immortality in earth.
h. Psalm 49:11 Or, labor that their name may be famous in earth.
i. Psalm 49:12 As touching the death of the body.
j. Psalm 49:13 They speak and do the same thing that their fathers did.
k. Psalm 49:14 As sheep are gathered into the fold, so shall they be brought to the grave.
l. Psalm 49:14 Because they have no part of life everlasting.
m. Psalm 49:14 Christ's coming is as the morning, when the elect shall reign with Christ their head over the wicked.
n. Psalm 49:15 Or, because he hath received me.
o. Psalm 49:18 Hebrew, he blessed his soul.
p. Psalm 49:18 The flatterers praise them that live in delight and pleasures.
q. Psalm 49:19 Or, his soul.
r. Psalm 49:19 And not pass the term appointed for life.
s. Psalm 49:19 Both they and their fathers shall live here but a while, and at length die forever.
t. Psalm 49:20 He condemneth man's ingratitude, who having received excellent gifts of God, abuseth them like a beast to his own condemnation.

PSALM 49

1. Job 27:19 **2.** 1 Tim. 6:7

PSALM 50

a. Psalm 50:1 Who was either the author, or a chief singer, to whom it was committed.
b. Psalm 50:1 To plead against his dissembling people before heaven and earth.
c. Psalm 50:2 Because God had chosen it to have his Name there called upon, and also his image shined there, in the doctrine of the Law.
d. Psalm 50:3 As when God gave his Law in mount Sinai, he appeared terrible with thunder and tempest, so will he appear terrible to take account for the keeping thereof.
e. Psalm 50:4 As witnesses against the hypocrites.
f. Psalm 50:5 God in respect of his elect calleth the whole body holy, Saints, and his people.
g. Psalm 50:5 Which should know that Sacrifices are sealed of the covenant between God and his people, and not set religion therein.
h. Psalm 50:8 For I pass not for sacrifices, except the true use be there, which is to confirm your faith in my promises.
i. Psalm 50:10 Though he did delight in sacrifice, yet had he no need of man's help thereunto.
j. Psalm 50:13 Though man's life for the infirmity thereof hath need of food, yet God whose life quickeneth all the world, hath no need of such means.
k. Psalm 50:14 Show thyself mindful of God's benefits by thanksgiving.
l. Psalm 50:16 Why dost thou feign to be of my people, and talkest of my covenant, seeing thou art but an hypocrite?
m. Psalm 50:17 And to live according to my word.
n. Psalm 50:18 He showeth what are the fruits of them that contemn God's word.
o. Psalm 50:20 He noteth the cruelty of hypocrites, which spare not in their talk or judgment their own mother's sons.
p. Psalm 50:21 I will write all thy wicked deeds in a roll, and make thee to read and acknowledge them, whither thou wilt or no.
q. Psalm 50:23 Under the which is contained faith and invocation.
r. Psalm 50:23 As God hath appointed.
s. Psalm 50:23 That is, declare myself to be his Savior.

PSALM 51

a. Psalm 51:1 To reprove him because he had committed so horrible sins, and lain in the same without repentance more than a whole year.
b. Psalm 51:1 As his sins were manifold and great, so he requireth that God would give him the feeling of his excellent and abundant mercies.
c. Psalm 51:2 My sins strike so fast in me, that I have need of some singular kind of washing.
d. Psalm 51:3 My conscience accuseth me so, that I can have no rest till I be reconciled.
e. Psalm 51:4 When thou givest sentence against sinners, they must needs confess thee to be just, and themselves sinners.
f. Psalm 51:6 He confesseth that God who loveth pureness of heart, may justly destroy man, who of nature is a sinner much more him, whom he had instructed in his heavenly wisdom.
g. Psalm 51:8 He meaneth God's comfortable mercies toward repentant sinners.
h. Psalm 51:8 By the bones he understandeth all strength of soul and body, which by cares and mourning are consumed.

and gladness, that the [h]bones, which thou hast broken, may rejoice. **9** Hide thy face from my sins, and put away all mine iniquities. **10** [i]Create in me a clean heart, O God, and renew a right spirit within me. **11** Cast me not away from thy presence, and take not thine holy Spirit from me. **12** Restore to me the joy of thy salvation, and establish me with thy [j]free Spirit. **13** Then shall I teach thy [k]ways unto the wicked, and sinners shall be converted unto thee. **14** Deliver me from [l]blood, O God, which art the God of my salvation, and my tongue shall sing joyfully of thy righteousness. **15** [m]Open thou my lips, O Lord, and my mouth shall show forth thy praise. **16** For thou desirest no sacrifice, though I would give it: thou delightest not in burnt offering. **17** The sacrifices of God are a [n]contrite spirit: a contrite and a broken heart, O God, thou wilt not despise. **18** Be favorable unto [o]Zion for thy good pleasure: build the walls of Jerusalem. **19** Then shalt thou accept the sacrifices of [p]righteousness, even the burnt offering and oblation: then shall they offer calves upon thine altar.

52

1 David describeth the arrogant tyranny of his adversary Doeg: who by false surmises cause Ahimelech with the rest of the Priests to be slain. 5 David prophesieth his destruction, 6 and encourageth the faithful to put their confidence in God, whose judgments are most sharp against his adversaries. 9 And finally, he rendereth thanks to God for his deliverance. In this Psalm is timely set forth the kingdom of Antichrist.

To him that excelleth. A Psalm of David to give instruction. When Doeg the Edomite came and showed Saul, and said to him, David is come to the house of Ahimelech. **1** Why boastest thou thyself in thy wickedness, O [a]man of power? the loving-kindness of God endureth daily. **2** Thy tongue imagineth [b]mischief, and is like a sharp razor, that cutteth deceitfully. **3** Thou dost love evil more than good, and lies more than to speak the [c]truth. Selah. **4** Thou lovest all words that may destroy: O deceitful tongue! **5** So shall God [d]destroy thee forever: he shall take thee and pluck thee out of thy tabernacle, and [e]root thee out of the land of the living. Selah. **6** The [f]righteous also shall see it, [g]and fear, and shall laugh at him, saying, **7** Behold the man that took not God for his strength, but trusteth unto the multitude of his riches, and put his strength [h]in his malice. **8** But I shall be like a [i]green olive tree in the house of God: for I trusted in the mercy of God forever and ever. **9** I will always praise thee, for that thou hast done [j]this, and I will [k]hope in thy name, because it is good before thy Saints.

53

1 He describeth the crooked nature. 4 The cruelty, 5 And punishment of the wicked, when they look not for it, 6 And desireth the deliverance of the godly, that they may rejoice together.

To him that excelleth on [a]Mahalath. A Psalm of David to give instruction. **1** The fool hath said in his heart, There is [b]no God, they have corrupted and done abominable wickedness, there is none that doeth good. **2** God looked down from heaven upon the children of men, to see if there were any that would understand and [c]seek God. **3** [1]Everyone is gone back: they are altogether corrupt: there is none that doeth good, no not one. **4** Do not the [d]workers of iniquity know that they eat up my people as they eat bread? they call not upon God. **5** There they were afraid for fear, where no [e]fear was: for God hath scattered the [f]bones of him that besieged thee: thou hast put them to confusion, because God hath cast them off. **6** Oh give salvation unto Israel out of Zion: when God turneth the captivity of his people, then Jacob shall rejoice, and Israel shall be glad.

54

1 David brought into great danger by reason of the Ziphites, 5 Calleth upon the Name of God to destroy his enemies, 6 Promising sacrifices and free offerings for so great deliverance.

To him that excelleth on Neginoth. A Psalm of David, to give instruction. When the Ziphims came and said unto Saul, [1]Is not David hid among us?

1 Save me, O God, [a]by thy Name, and by thy power judge me. **2** O God, hear my prayer: hearken unto the words of my mouth. **3** For [b]strangers are risen up against me, and [c]tyrants seek my soul: they have not set God before them. Selah. **4** Behold, God is mine helper: the Lord is with [d]them that uphold my soul. **5** He shall reward evil unto mine enemies: Oh cut them off in thy [e]truth! **6** Then I will sacrifice [f]freely unto thee: I will praise thy Name, O Lord, because it is good. **7** For he hath delivered me out of all trouble, and mine eye hath [g]seen my desire upon mine enemies.

55

1 David being in great heaviness and distress, complaineth of the cruelty of Saul, 13 and of the falsehood of his familiar acquaintance, 17 Uttering the most ardent affections to move the Lord to pity him. 22 After, being assured of deliverance, he setteth forth the grace of God, as though he had already obtained his request.

To him that excelleth on Neginoth. A Psalm of David to give instruction. **1** Hear [a]my prayer, O God, and hide not thyself from my supplication. **2** Hearken unto me, and answer me: I mourn in my prayer, and make a noise, **3** For the [b]voice of the enemy, and for the vexation of the wicked, because [c]they have brought iniquity upon me, and furiously hate me. **4** Mine heart trembleth within me, and the terrors of death are fallen upon me. **5** Fear and trembling are come upon me, and an horrible fear hath [d]covered me. **6** And I said, Oh that I had wings like a dove: then would I [e]fly away and rest. **7** Behold I would take my flight far off, and lodge in the wilderness. Selah. **8** He would make haste for my deliverance [f]from the stormy wind and tempest. **9** Destroy, O Lord, and [g]divide their tongues: for I have seen cruelty and strife in the city. **10** Day and night they go about it upon the walls thereof, both [h]iniquity and mischief are in the midst of it. **11** Wickedness is in the midst thereof: deceit and guile depart not from her streets. **12** Surely mine [i]enemy did not defame me, for I could have borne it: neither did mine adversary exalt himself against me: for I would have hid me from him. **13** But it was thou, O man, even my [j]companion, my guide, and my familiar: **14** Which delighted in consulting together, and went into the house of God as companions. **15** Let death seize upon them: let them [k]go down quick into the grave: for wickedness is in their dwellings even in the midst of them. **16** But I will call unto God, and the Lord will save me. **17** Evening and morning, and at noon will I pray [l]and make a noise, and he will hear my voice. **18** He hath delivered my soul in peace from the battle that was against me: for [m]many were with me. **19** God shall hear and afflict them, even he that reigneth of old, Selah: because they [n]have no changes, therefore they fear not God. **20** He [o]laid his hand upon such as be at peace with

---

i. Psalm 51:10 He confesseth that when God's Spirit is cold in us, to have it again revived, is as a new creation.
j. Psalm 51:12 Which may assure me that I am drawn out of the slavery of sin.
k. Psalm 51:13 He promiseth to endeavor that others by his example may turn to God.
l. Psalm 51:14 From the murder of Uriah, and the others that were slain with him, 2 Sam. 11:17.
m. Psalm 51:15 By giving me occasion to praise thee, when thou shalt forgive my sins.
n. Psalm 51:17 Which is a wounding of the heart, proceeding of faith, which seeketh unto God for mercy.
o. Psalm 51:18 He prayeth for the whole Church, because through his sin it was in danger of God's judgment.
p. Psalm 51:19 That is, just and lawful, applied to the right end, which is the exercise of faith and repentance.

PSALM 51
1. Lev. 14:6

PSALM 52
a. Psalm 52:1 O Doeg, which hast credit with the tyrant Saul, and hast power to murder the Saints of God.
b. Psalm 52:2 Thy malice moveth thee by crafty flatteries and lies to accuse and destroy the innocents.
c. Psalm 52:3 Hebrew, righteousness.
d. Psalm 52:5 Though God forbear for a time, yet at length he will recompense thy falsehood.
e. Psalm 52:5 Albeit thou seem to be never so sure settled.
f. Psalm 52:6 For the eyes of the reprobate are shut up at God's judgments.
g. Psalm 52:6 With joyful reverence, seeing that he taketh their part against the wicked.
h. Psalm 52:7 Or, in his substance.
i. Psalm 52:8 He rejoiceth to have a place among the servants of God, that he may grow in the knowledge of godliness.
j. Psalm 52:9 Executed his vengeance.
k. Psalm 52:9 Or, wait upon thy grace and promise.

PSALM 53
a. Psalm 53:1 Which was an instrument or kind of note.
b. Psalm 53:1 Whereas no regard is had of honesty or dishonesty, of virtue nor of vice, there the Prophet pronounceth that the people have no God.
c. Psalm 53:2 Whereby he condemneth all knowledge and understanding, that tendeth not to seek God.
d. Psalm 53:4 David pronounceth God's vengeance against cruel governors, who having charge to defend and preserve God's people, do most cruelly devour them.
e. Psalm 53:5 When they thought there was none occasion to fear, the sudden vengeance of God lighted upon them.
f. Psalm 53:5 Be the enemy's power never so great, nor the danger so fearful, yet God delivereth his in due time.

PSALM 53
1. Rom. 3:10

PSALM 54
a. Psalm 54:1 He declareth that when all means do fail, God will deliver even as it were by miracle, them that call unto him with an upright conscience.
b. Psalm 54:3 To wit, the Ziphims.
c. Psalm 54:3 Saul and his army, which were like cruel beasts, and could not be satisfied but by his death.
d. Psalm 54:4 Be they never so few, as he was with Jonathan.
e. Psalm 54:5 According to thy faithful promise for my defense.
f. Psalm 54:6 For hypocrites serve God for fear or upon conditions.
g. Psalm 54:7 We may lawfully rejoice for God's judgments against the wicked, if our affections be pure.

PSALM 54
1. 1 Sam. 13:19

PSALM 55
a. Psalm 55:1 The earnestness of his prayer declareth the vehemency of his grief insomuch as he is compelled to burst out into cries.
b. Psalm 55:3 For the threatnings of Saul and his adherents.
c. Psalm 55:3 They have defamed me as a wicked person, or they have imagined my destruction.
d. Psalm 55:5 There was no part of him, that was not astonished with extreme fear.
e. Psalm 55:6 Fear had driven him to so great distress, that he wished to be hid in some wilderness, and to be banished from that kingdom which God had promised that he should enjoy.
f. Psalm 55:8 From the cruel rage and tyranny of Saul.
g. Psalm 55:9 As in the confusion of Babylon when the wicked conspired against God.
h. Psalm 55:10 All laws and good orders are broken, and only vice and dissolation reigneth under Saul.
i. Psalm 55:12 If mine open enemy had sought mine hurt, I could the better have avoided him.
j. Psalm 55:13 Which was not only joined to me in friendship and counsel in worldly matters, but also in religion.
k. Psalm 55:15 As Korah, Dathan and Abiram.
l. Psalm 55:17 Which signifieth a fervent mind and sure trust to obtain his portion, which thing made him earnest at all times in prayer.
m. Psalm 55:18 Even the Angels of God fought on my side against mine enemies, 2 Kings 6:16.
n. Psalm 55:19 But their prosperous estate still continueth.

him, and he brake his covenant. **21** The words of his mouth were softer than
butter, yet war was in his heart, his words were more gentle than oil, yet they were
swords. **22** Cast thy [p]burden upon the Lord, and he shall nourish thee: he will
not suffer the righteous to fall [q]forever. **23** And thou, O God, shalt bring them
down into the pit of corruption: the bloody, and deceitful men shall not live [r]half
their days: but I will trust in thee.

56

1 David being brought to Achish the king of Gath, 1 Sam. 21:12, complaineth of his enemies, demandeth succor, 3 Putteth his trust in God and in his promises, 12 And promiseth to perform his vows which he had taken upon him, whereof this was the effect, to praise God in his Church.

To him that excelleth. A Psalm of David on Michtam, concerning the [a]dumb
dove in a far country, when the Philistines took him in Gath. **1** Be merciful unto
me, O God, for [b]man would swallow me up: he fighteth continually and vexeth
me. **2** Mine enemies would daily swallow me up: for many fight against me,
O thou most High. **3** When I was afraid, I trusted in thee. **4** I will rejoice in
God, because of his [c]word, I trust in God, and will not fear what flesh can do unto
me. **5** Mine own [d]words grieve me daily: all their thoughts are against me to do
me hurt. **6** [e]They gather together, and keep themselves close: they mark my steps,
because they wait for my soul. **7** [f]They think they shall escape by iniquity: O
God, cast these people down in thine anger. **8** Thou hast counted my wanderin-
gs; put my [g]tears into thy bottle; are they not in thy register? **9** When I cry, then
mine enemies shall turn back; this I know, for God is with me. **10** I will rejoice
in God because of his word; in the Lord will I rejoice because of his word. **11** In
God do I trust; I will not be afraid what man can do unto me. **12** [h]Thy vows
are upon me, O God, I will render praises unto thee. **13** For thou hast delivered
my soul from death, and also my feet from falling, that I may [i]walk before God in
the [j]light of the living.

57

1 David being in the desert of Ziph, where the inhabitants did betray him, and at length in the same cave with Saul, 2 Calleth most earnestly unto God, with full confidence that he will perform his promise, and take his cause in hand. 5 Also that he will show his glory in the heavens and the earth against his cruel enemies. 9 Therefore doth he render laud and praise.

**To him that excelleth. [a]Destroy not. A Psalm of David on Michtam.
[1]When he fled from Saul in the cave.** **1** Have mercy upon me, O God, have
mercy upon me; for my soul trusteth in thee, and in the shadow of thy wings will
I [b]trust, till these [c]afflictions overpass. **2** I will call unto the most high God,
even the God, that [d]performeth his promise toward me. **3** He will send from
[e]heaven, and save me from the reproof of him that would swallow me. Selah.
God will send his mercy, and his truth. **4** My soul is among lions; I lie among
the children of men, that are set on fire; whose teeth are [f]spears and arrows, and
their tongue a sharp sword. **5** [g]Exalt thyself, O God, above the heaven, and let
thy glory be upon all the earth. **6** They have laid a net for my steps; [h]my soul is
pressed down, they have dug a pit before me, and are fallen into the midst of it.
Selah. **7** Mine heart is [i]prepared, O God, mine heart is prepared; I will sing and
give praise. **8** [j]Awake my tongue, awake viol and harp: I will awake early. **9** I
will praise thee, O Lord, among the people, and I will sing unto thee among the
nations. **10** For thy mercy is great unto the heavens, and thy truth unto the
[k]clouds. **11** Exalt thyself, O God, above the heavens, and let thy glory be upon
all the earth.

58

1 He describeth the malice of his enemies, the flatterers of Saul, who both secretly and openly sought his destruction, from whom he appealeth to God's judgment, 10 Showing that the just shall rejoice, when they see the punishment of the wicked to the glory of God.

To him that excelleth. Destroy not. A Psalm of David on Michtam. **1** Is it
true? O [a]congregation, speak ye justly? O sons of men judge ye uprightly? **2** Yea,
rather ye imagine mischief in your heart: [b]your hands execute cruelty upon the
earth. **3** The wicked [c]are strangers from the womb: even from the belly have
they erred, and speak lies. **4** Their poison is even like the poison of a serpent;
like the deaf [d]adder that stoppeth his ear. **5** Which heareth not the voice of the
enchanter, though he be most expert in charming. **6** Break their [e]teeth, O God,
in their mouths: break the jaws of the young lions, O Lord. **7** Let them [f]melt
like the waters, let them pass away; when he shooteth his arrows, let them be as
broken. **8** Let them consume like a snail that melteth, and like the untimely
fruit of a woman, that hath not seen the sun. **9** [g]As raw flesh before your pots
feel the fire of thorns: so let them carry them away as with a whirlwind in his wra-
th. **10** The righteous shall [h]rejoice when he seeth the vengeance; he shall wash
his feet in the [i]blood of the wicked. **11** And men shall say, [j]Verily there is fruit
for the righteous; doubtless there is a God that judgeth in the earth.

59

1 David being in great danger of Saul, who sent to slay him in his bed, prayeth unto God, 3 Declaring his innocency, and their fury, 5 Desiring God to destroy all those that sin of malicious wickedness. 11 Whom though he keep alive for a time to exercise his people, yet in the end he will consume them in his wrath, 13 That he may be known to be the God of Jacob to the end of the world. 16 For this he singeth praises to God assured of his mercies.

**To him that excelleth. Destroy not. A Psalm of David, on [a]Michtam.
[1]When Saul sent and they did watch the house to kill him.** **1** O my God, [b]de-
liver me from mine enemies; defend me from them that rise up against me. **2** De-
liver me from the wicked doers, and save me from the bloody men. **3** For lo, they
have laid wait for my soul; the mighty men are gathered against me, not for mine
[c]offense, nor for my sin, O Lord. **4** They run and prepare themselves without a
fault on my part: arise therefore to assist me, and behold. **5** Even thou, O Lord
God of hosts, O God of Israel, awake to visit all the heathen, and be not [d]merciful
unto all that transgress maliciously. Selah. **6** They go to and fro in the evening:
they bark like [e]dogs, and go about the city. **7** Behold, they [f]brag in their talk, and
swords are in their lips: for who, say they, doth hear? **8** But thou, O Lord, shalt
have them in derision, and thou shalt laugh at all the heathen. **9** [g]He is strong:
but I will wait upon thee: for God is my defense. **10** My merciful God will
[h]prevent me: God will let me see my desire upon mine enemies. **11** Slay them
[i]not, lest my people forget it: but scatter them abroad by thy power, and put them
down, O Lord, our shield, **12** For the sin of their mouth, and the words of their

---

o. Psalm 55:20 I did not provoke him, but was as at peace with him, yet he made war against me.
p. Psalm 55:22 Or, gift, to wit, which thou wouldest that God should give thee.
q. Psalm 55:22 Though for their bettering and trial, he suffer them to slip for a time.
r. Psalm 55:23 Though they sometimes live longer, yet their life is cursed of God, unquiet, and worse than any death.

PSALM 56

a. Psalm 56:1 Being chased by the fury of his enemies into a strange country, he was a dumb dove not seeking revengeance.
b. Psalm 56:1 He showeth that it is either now time or never, that God help him, for all the world is against him and ready to devour him.
c. Psalm 56:4 He stayeth his conscience upon God's promise, though he see not present help.
d. Psalm 56:5 All my counsels have evil success, and turn to mine own sorrow.
e. Psalm 56:6 As all the world against one man, and cannot be satiate, except they have my life.
f. Psalm 56:7 They think not only to escape punishment, but the more wicked they are, the more impudent they wax.
g. Psalm 56:8 If God keep the tears of his Saints in store, much more will he remember their blood, to avenge it: and though tyrants burn the bones, yet can they not blot the tears and blood out of God's register.
h. Psalm 56:12 Having received that which I required, I am bound to pay my vows of thanksgiving, as I promised.
i. Psalm 56:13 As mindful of his great mercies, and giving him thanks for the same.
j. Psalm 56:13 That is, in this life and light of the sun.

PSALM 57

a. Psalm 57:1 This was either the beginning of a certain song, or the words which David uttered when he stayed his affection.
b. Psalm 57:1 Or, dwell most safely.
c. Psalm 57:1 He compareth the afflictions which God layeth upon his children, to a storm that cometh and goeth.
d. Psalm 57:2 Who leaveth not his works begun imperfect.
e. Psalm 57:3 He would rather deliver me by a miracle, than that I should be overcome.
f. Psalm 57:4 He meaneth their calumnies and false reports.
g. Psalm 57:5 Suffer me not to be destroyed to the contempt of thy Name.
h. Psalm 57:6 For very fear seeing the great dangers on all sides.
i. Psalm 57:7 That is, wholly bent to give thee praise for my deliverance.
j. Psalm 57:8 He showeth that both his heart shall praise God, and his tongue shall confess him, and also he will use other means to provoke himself forward to the same.
k. Psalm 57:10 Thy mercies do not only appertain to the Jews, but also to the Gentiles.

PSALM 57

1. 1 Sam. 24:4

PSALM 58

a. Psalm 58:1 Ye counselors of Saul, who under pretence of consulting for the common wealth, conspire my death being an innocent.
b. Psalm 58:2 Ye are not ashamed to execute that cruelty publicly, which ye have imagined in your hearts.
c. Psalm 58:3 That is, enemies to the people of God even from their birth.
d. Psalm 58:4 They pass in malice and subtlety the crafty serpent which could preserve himself by stopping his ear from the enchanter.
e. Psalm 58:6 Take away all occasions and means whereby they hurt.
f. Psalm 58:7 Considering God's divine power, he showeth that God in a moment can destroy their force whereof they brag.
g. Psalm 58:9 As flesh is taken raw out of the pot before the water seethe: so he desireth God to destroy their enterprises before they bring them to pass.
h. Psalm 58:10 With a pure affection.
i. Psalm 58:10 Their punishment and slaughter shall be so great.
j. Psalm 58:11 Seeing God governeth all by his providence, he must needs put difference between the godly and the wicked.

PSALM 59

a. Psalm 59:1 Read Ps. 16.
b. Psalm 59:1 Though his enemies were even at hand to destroy him, yet he assureth himself that God had ways now in hand to deliver him.
c. Psalm 59:3 For I am innocent to themwards, and have not offended them.
d. Psalm 59:5 Seeing it appertaineth to God's judgments to punish the wicked, he desiresth God to execute his vengeance on the reprobate, who maliciously persecute his Church.
e. Psalm 59:6 He compareth their cruelty to hungry dogs, showing that they are never weary in doing evil.
f. Psalm 59:7 They boast openly in their wicked devices, and every word is as a sword: for they neither fear God nor are ashamed of men.
g. Psalm 59:9 Though Saul have never so great power, yet I know that thou dost bridle him: therefore will I patiently hope on thee.
h. Psalm 59:10 He will not fail to succor me when need requireth.
i. Psalm 59:11 Altogether, but by little and little, that the people seeing oftentimes thy judgments, may be mindful of thee.
j. Psalm 59:12 That in their misery and shame they may be as glasses and examples of God's vengeance.

lips: and let them be [j]taken in their pride, even for their perjury and lies, that they speak. **13** [k]Consume them in thy wrath: consume them that they be no more: and let them know that God ruleth in Jacob, even unto the ends of the world. Selah. **14** And in the evening they [l]shall go to and fro, and bark like dogs, and go about the city. **15** They shall run here and there for meat, and surely they shall not be satisfied, though they tarry all night. **16** But I will sing of thy [m]power, and will praise thy mercy in the morning: for thou hast been my defense and refuge in the day of my trouble. **17** Unto thee, O my [n]Strength will I sing: for God is my defense, and my merciful God.

60

1 David being now king over Judah, and having had many victories, showeth by evident signs that God elected him King, assuring the people that God will prosper them, if they approve the same. 14 After, he prayeth unto God to finish that that he hath begun.

To him that excelleth upon [a]Shushan Eduth, or Michtam. A Psalm of David to teach. [1]When he fought against [b]Aram Naharaim, and against Aram [c]Zobah, when Joab returned and slew twelve thousand Edomites in the salt valley. **1** O God, thou hast cast us out, thou hast [d]scattered us, thou hast been angry, turn again unto us. **2** Thou hast made the land to tremble, and hast made it to [e]gape: heal the breaches thereof, for it is shaken. **3** Thou hast [f]showed thy people heavy things: thou hast made us to drink the wine of giddiness. **4** But now thou hast given [g]a banner to them that fear thee, that it may be displayed because of thy truth. Selah. **5** That thy beloved may be delivered, help with thy right hand and hear me. **6** God hath spoken in his [h]holiness: therefore I will rejoice: I shall divide Shechem, and measure the valley of Succoth. **7** Gilead shall be mine, and Manasseh shall be mine: Ephraim also shall be the [i]strength of mine head: [j]Judah is my lawgiver. **8** Moab shall be my [k]washpot: over Edom will I cast out my shoe: [l]Philistia show thyself joyful for me. **9** Who will lead me into the [m]strong city? who will bring me unto Edom? **10** Wilt not thou, O God, which hadst cast us off, and didst not go forth, O God, with our armies? **11** Give us help against trouble: for vain is the help of man. **12** Through God we shall do valiantly; for he shall tread down our enemies.

61

1 Whether that he were in danger of the Ammonites, or being pursued of Absalom, here he crieth to be heard and delivered, 7 And confirmed in his kingdom. 8 He promiseth perpetual praises.

To him that excelleth on Neginoth. A Psalm of David. **1** Hear my cry, O God: give ear unto my prayer. **2** From [a]the ends of the earth will I cry unto thee: when mine heart is oppressed, bring me upon the rock that is [b]higher than I. **3** For thou hast been my hope, and a strong tower against the enemy. **4** I will dwell in thy Tabernacle forever, and my trust shall be under the covering of thy wings. Selah. **5** For thou, O God, [c]hast heard my desires; thou hast given an heritage unto those that fear thy Name. **6** Thou shalt give the King a [d]long life; his years shall be as many ages. **7** He shall dwell before God forever; prepare [e]mercy and faithfulness, that they may preserve him. **8** So will I always sing praise unto thy Name, in performing daily my vows.

62

This Psalm partly containeth meditation, whereby David encourageth himself to trust in God against the assaults of temptations. And because our minds are easily drawn from God by the allurements of the world, he sharply reproveth this vanity, to the intent he might cleave fast to the Lord.

To the excellent Musician [1]Jeduthun. A Psalm of David. **1** Yet [a]my soul keepeth silence unto God; of him cometh my salvation. **2** [b]Yet he is my strength and my salvation, and my defense; therefore I shall not much be moved. **3** How long will ye imagine mischief against a [c]man? ye shall be all slain; ye shall be as a bowed wall, or as a [d]wall shaken. **4** Yet they consult to cast him down from his dignity; their delight is in lies: they bless with their mouths, but curse with their hearts. Selah. **5** [e]Yet my soul, keep thou silence unto God: for mine hope is in him. **6** Yet is he my strength and my salvation, and my defense: therefore I shall not be moved. **7** In God is my salvation and my [f]glory, the rock of my strength; in God is my trust. **8** Trust in him always, ye people; [g]pour out your hearts before him, for God is our hope. Selah. **9** Yet the children of men are vanity, the chief men are liars: to lay them upon a balance they are altogether lighter than vanity. **10** Trust not in oppression nor in robbery: [h]be not vain: if riches increase, set not your heart thereon. **11** God spake [i]once or twice, I have heard it, that power belongeth unto God, **12** And to thee, O Lord, mercy: for thou [j]rewardest everyone according to his work.

63

1 David after he had been in great danger by Saul in the desert of Ziph, made this Psalm. 3 Wherein he giveth thanks to God for his wonderful deliverance, in whose mercies he trusted, even in the midst of his miseries. 9 Prophesying the destruction of God's enemies: 11 And contrariwise happiness to all them that trust in the Lord.

A Psalm of David, when he was in the [a]wilderness of Judah. **1** O God, thou art my God, early will I seek thee: my soul [b]thirsteth for thee: my flesh longeth greatly after thee in a barren and dry land without water: **2** Thus [c]I behold thee as in the Sanctuary, when I behold thy power and thy glory. **3** For thy loving-kindness is better than life: therefore my lips shall praise thee. **4** Thus will I magnify thee all my life, and lift up mine hands in thy Name. **5** My soul shall be satisfied, as with [d]marrow and fatness, and my mouth shall praise thee with joyful lips, **6** When I remember thee on my bed, and when I think upon thee in the night watches. **7** Because thou hast been mine helper, therefore under the shadow of thy wings will I rejoice. **8** My soul [e]cleaveth unto thee: for thy right hand upholdeth me. **9** Therefore they that seek my soul to destroy it, they shall go into the lowest parts of the earth. **10** [f]They shall cast him down with the edge of the sword, and they shall be a portion for foxes. **11** But the king shall rejoice in God, and all that [g]swear by him shall rejoice in him: for the mouth of them that speak lies, shall be stopped.

64

1 David prayeth against the fury and false reports of his enemies. 7 He declareth their punishment and destruction. 10 To the comfort of the just and the glory of God.

To him that excelleth. A Psalm of David. **1** Hear my [a]voice, O God, in my prayer: preserve my life from fear of the enemy. **2** Hide me from the [b]conspiracy

---

k. Psalm 59:13 When thy time shall come, and when they have sufficiently served for an example of thy vengeance unto others.
l. Psalm 59:14 He mocketh at their vain enterprises, being assured that they shall not bring their purpose to pass.
m. Psalm 59:16 Which didst use the policy of a weak woman to confound the enemy's strength, as 1 Sam. 19:12.
n. Psalm 59:17 Confessing himself to be void of all virtue and strength, he attributeth the whole to God.

PSALM 59
1. 1 Sam. 19:11

PSALM 60
a. Psalm 60:1 These were certain songs after the note whereof this Psalm was sung.
b. Psalm 60:1 Or, Syria, called Mesopotamia.
c. Psalm 60:1 Called also Sophene, which standeth by Euphrates.
d. Psalm 60:1 For when Saul was not able to resist the enemy, the people fled hither and thither: for they could not be safe in their own houses.
e. Psalm 60:2 As cleft with an earthquake.
f. Psalm 60:3 Thou hast handled thy people sharply, in taking from them sense and judgment, in that they aided Saul the wicked King, and pursued him to whom God had given the just title of the realm.
g. Psalm 60:4 In making me king, thou hast performed thy promise, which seemed to have lost the force.
h. Psalm 60:6 It is so certain as if it were spoken by an oracle, that I shall possess those places which Saul hath left to his children.
i. Psalm 60:7 For it was strong and well peopled.
j. Psalm 60:7 David meaneth, that in this tribe his kingdom shall be established, Gen. 49:10.
k. Psalm 60:8 In most vile subjection.
l. Psalm 60:8 For thou wilt dissemble, and feign as though thou werest glad.
m. Psalm 60:9 He was assured that God would give him the strong cities of his enemies, wherein they thought themselves sure.

PSALM 60
1. 2 Sam. 8:1 - 2 Sam. 10:1 - 1 Chron. 18:13

PSALM 61
a. Psalm 61:2 From the place where I was banished, being driven out of the city and Temple by my son Absalom.
b. Psalm 61:2 Unto the which without thy help I cannot attain.
c. Psalm 61:5 There is nothing that doth more strengthen our faith, than the remembrance of God's succor in times past.
d. Psalm 61:6 This chiefly is referred to Christ, who liveth eternally not only in himself, but also in his members.
e. Psalm 61:7 For the stability of my kingdom standeth in thy mercy and truth.

PSALM 62
a. Psalm 62:1 Though Satan tempted him to murmur against God, yet he bridled his affections, and resting upon God's promise.
b. Psalm 62:2 It appeareth by the oft repetition of this word, that the Prophet abode manifold tentations, but by resting on God, and by patience he overcame them all.
c. Psalm 62:3 He meaneth himself, being the man whom God had appointed to the kingdom.
d. Psalm 62:3 Though, ye seem to be in honor, yet God will suddenly destroy you.
e. Psalm 62:5 David was greatly moved with these troubles, therefore he stirreth up himself to trust in God.
f. Psalm 62:7 These vehement and often repetitions were necessary to strengthen his faith against the horrible assault of Satan.
g. Psalm 62:8 He admonisheth us of our wicked nature, which rather hide our sorrow and bite on the bridle, than utter our grief to God to obtain remedy.
h. Psalm 62:10 Give yourselves wholly to God by putting away all things that are contrary to his Law.
i. Psalm 62:11 He hath plainly borne witness of his power, so that none needeth to doubt thereof.
j. Psalm 62:12 So that the wicked shall feel thy power, and the godly thy mercy.

PSALM 62
1. 1 Chron. 16:41

PSALM 63
a. Psalm 63:1 To wit, of Ziph, 1 Sam. 23:14.
b. Psalm 63:1 Though he was both hungry and in great distress, yet he made God his sufficiency and above all meat and drink.
c. Psalm 63:2 In this misery I exercise myself in the contemplation of thy power and glory, as if I were in the Sanctuary.
d. Psalm 63:5 The remembrance of thy favor is more sweet unto me than all the pleasures and dainties of the world.
e. Psalm 63:8 He assureth himself by the Spirit of God to have the gift of constancy.
f. Psalm 63:10 He prophecieth of the destruction of Saul and them that take his part, whose bodies shall not be buried, but be devoured with wild beasts.
g. Psalm 63:11 All that swear by God aright or profess him, shall rejoice in this worthy king.

PSALM 64
a. Psalm 64:1 In that he calleth to God with his voice, it is a sign that his prayer was vehement, and that his life was in a danger.

of the wicked, and from the [c]rage of the works of iniquity. **3** Which have whet their tongue like a sword, and shot for their arrows [d]bitter words: **4** To shoot at the upright in secret: they shoot at him suddenly and [e]fear not. **5** They [f]encourage themselves in a wicked purpose: they commune together to lay snares privily, and say, Who shall see them? **6** They have sought out iniquities, and have accomplished that which they sought out, even everyone [g]his secret thoughts, and the depth of his heart. **7** But God will shoot an arrow at them suddenly: their strokes shall be at once. **8** They shall cause their own tongue to fall upon them: and whosoever shall see them, shall [h]flee away. **9** And all men shall see it, and declare the work of God, and they shall understand, what he hath wrought. **10** But the righteous [i]shall be glad in the Lord, and trust in him: and all that are upright of heart, shall rejoice.

65

1 A praise and thanksgiving unto God by the faithful, who are signified by Zion, 4 For the choosing, preservation, and governance of them, 9 And for the plentiful blessings poured forth upon all the earth, but especially toward his Church.

To him that excelleth. A Psalm or song of David. **1** O God, [a]praise waiteth for thee in Zion, and unto thee shall the vow be performed. **2** Because thou hearest the prayer, unto thee shall all [b]flesh come. **3** Wicked deeds [c]have prevailed against me: but thou wilt be merciful unto our transgressions. **4** Blessed is he, whom thou choosest and causest to come to thee: he shall dwell in thy courts, and we shall be satisfied with the pleasures of thine House, even of thine holy Temple. **5** O God of our salvation, thou wilt [d]answer us with fearful signs in thy righteousness, O thou the hope of all the ends of the earth, and of them that are far off in the [e]Sea. **6** He establisheth the mountains by his power: and is girded about with strength. **7** He appeaseth the [f]noise of the seas, and the noise of the waves thereof, and the tumults of the people. **8** They also that dwell in the uttermost parts of the earth, shall be afraid of thy signs; thou shalt make [g]the East and the West to rejoice. **9** Thou [h]visitest the earth, and waterest it; thou makest it very rich: the [i]river of God is full of water, thou preparest them corn; for so thou appointest [j]it. **10** Thou [k]waterest abundantly the furrows thereof; thou causest the rain to descend into the valleys thereof; thou makest it soft with showers, and blessest the bud thereof. **11** Thou crownest the year with thy goodness, and thy steps drop fatness. **12** They drop upon the pastures of the wilderness: and the hills shall be compassed with gladness. **13** The pastures are clad with sheep; the valleys also shall be covered with corn; therefore they shout for joy, [l]and sing.

66

1 He provoketh all men to praise the Lord and to consider his works. 6 He setteth forth the power of God to affray the rebels. 10 And showeth how God hath delivered Israel from great bondage and afflictions. 13 He promiseth to give sacrifice, 16 And provoketh all men to hear what God hath done for him, and to praise his Name.

To him that excelleth. A song or Psalm. **1** Rejoice in God, [a]all ye inhabitants of the earth. **2** Sing forth the glory of his Name: make his praise glorious. **3** Say unto God, How terrible art thou in thy works! through the greatness of thy power shall thine enemies be [b]in subjection unto thee. **4** All the world shall worship thee, and sing unto thee, even sing of thy Name. Selah. **5** [c]Come and behold the works of God: he is terrible in his doings toward [d]the sons of men. **6** He hath turned the sea into dry land: they passed through the river on foot: there did we rejoice in him. **7** He ruleth the world with his power: his eyes behold the nations: the rebellious shall not [e]exalt themselves. Selah. **8** Praise our God, ye people, and make the voice of his praise to be heard. **9** Which [f]holdeth our souls in life, and suffereth not our feet to slip. **10** For thou, O God, hast proved us, thou hast tried us as silver is tried. **11** Thou hast brought us unto the [g]snare, and laid a strait chain upon our loins. **12** Thou hast caused men to ride over our heads: we went into fire and into water, but thou broughtest us out into a wealthy place. **13** I will go into thine [h]House with burnt offerings, and will pay thee my vows, **14** Which my lips have promised, and my mouth hath spoken in mine affliction. **15** I will offer unto thee the burnt offerings of fat rams with incense: I will prepare bullocks and goats. Selah. **16** [i]Come and hearken, all ye that fear God, and I will tell you what he hath done to my soul. **17** I called unto him with my mouth, and he was exalted with my tongue. **18** [j]If I regard wickedness in mine heart, the Lord will not hear me. **19** But God hath heard me, and considered the voice of my prayer. **20** Praised be God, which hath not put back my prayer, nor his mercy from me.

67

1 A prayer of the Church to obtain the favor of God and to be lightened with his countenance. 2 To the end that his way and judgment may be known throughout the earth. 7 And finally is declared the kingdom of God, which should be universally erected at the coming of Christ.

To him that excelleth on Neginoth. A Psalm or song. **1** God be merciful unto us, and bless us, and [a]cause his face to shine among us. (Selah.) **2** That [b]they may know thy way upon earth, and thy saving health among all nations. **3** Let the people praise thee, O God: let all the people praise thee. **4** [c]Let the people be glad and rejoice: for thou shalt judge the people righteously, and govern the nations upon the earth. Selah. **5** Let the people praise thee, O God: let all the people praise thee. **6** Then shall [d]the earth bring forth her increase, and God, even our God shall bless us. **7** God shall bless us, and all the ends of the earth [e]shall fear him.

68

1 In this Psalm David setteth forth as in a glass the wonderful mercies of God toward his people: 5 Who by all means and most strange sorts declared himself to them. 15 And therefore God's Church by reason of his promises, graces, and victories, doth excel without comparison all worldly things. 34 He exhorteth therefore all men to praise God forever.

To him that excelleth. A Psalm or song of David. **1** God [a]will arise, and his enemies shall be scattered: they also that hate him, shall flee before him. **2** As the smoke vanisheth, so shalt thou drive them away: and as wax melteth before the fire, so shall the wicked perish at the presence of God. **3** [b]But the righteous shall be glad, and rejoice before God: yea, they shall leap for joy. **4** Sing unto God, and sing praises unto his name: exalt him that rideth upon the heavens, in his Name [c]Jah, and rejoice before him. **5** He is a Father of the fatherless, and a Judge of the widows, even God in his holy habitation. **6** God [d]maketh the solitary to dwell in families, and delivereth them that were prisoners in stocks: but the rebellious shall dwell in a [e]dry land. **7** [f]O God, when thou wentest forth before thy people: when thou wentest through the wilderness, (Selah.) **8** The earth shook, and the heavens dropped at the presence of this God: even Sinai was moved at

---

b. Psalm 64:2 That is, from their secret malice.
c. Psalm 64:2 To wit, their outward violence.
d. Psalm 64:3 False reports and slanders.
e. Psalm 64:4 To be without fear of God, and reverence of man, is a sign of reprobation.
f. Psalm 64:5 The more that the wicked see God's children in misery, the more bold and impudent are they in oppressing them.
g. Psalm 64:6 There is no way so secret and subtle to do hurt, which they invented not for his destruction.
h. Psalm 64:8 To see God's heavy judgments against them, and how he hath caught them in their own snares.
i. Psalm 64:10 When they shall consider that he will be favorable to them as he was to his servant David.

PSALM 65

a. Psalm 65:1 Thou givest daily new occasion to thy Church to praise thee.
b. Psalm 65:2 Not only the Jews but also the Gentiles in the kingdom of Christ.
c. Psalm 65:3 He imputeth it to his sins and to the sins of the people, that God who was accustomed to assist them withdraweth his succor from them.
d. Psalm 65:5 Thou wilt declare thyself to be the preserver of thy Church in destroying thine enemies, as thou didst in the red Sea.
e. Psalm 65:5 As of all barbarous nations and far off.
f. Psalm 65:7 He showeth that there is no part nor creature in the world which is not governed by God's power and providence.
g. Psalm 65:8 Hebrew, the going forth of the morning and of the evening.
h. Psalm 65:9 To wit, with rain.
i. Psalm 65:9 That is, Shiloh or the rain.
j. Psalm 65:9 Thou hast appointed the earth to bring forth food to man's use.
k. Psalm 65:10 By this description he showeth that all the order of nature is a testimony of God's love toward us, who causeth all creatures to serve our necessity.
l. Psalm 65:13 That is, the dumb creatures shall not only rejoice for a time for God's benefits, but shall continually sing.

PSALM 66

a. Psalm 66:1 He prophecieth that all nations shall come to the knowledge of God, who then was only known in Judea.
b. Psalm 66:3 As the faithful shall obey God willingly, so the infidels for fear shall dissemble themselves to be subject.
c. Psalm 66:5 He toucheth the slothful dullness of man, who is cold in the consideration of God's works.
d. Psalm 66:5 His providence is wonderful in maintaining their estate.
e. Psalm 66:7 He proveth that God will extend his grace also to the Gentiles, because he punisheth among them such as will not obey his calling.
f. Psalm 66:9 He signifieth some special benefit, that God had showed to his Church of the Jews, in delivering them from some great danger: whereof or of the like he promiseth that the Gentiles shall be partakers.
g. Psalm 66:11 The condition of the Church is here described, which is to be led by God's providence into troubles to be subject under tyrants, and to enter into manifold dangers.
h. Psalm 66:13 The duty of the faithful is here described, which are never unmindful to render God praise for his benefits.
i. Psalm 66:16 It is not enough to have received God's benefits and to be mindful thereof, but also we are bound to make others to profit thereby and praise God.
j. Psalm 66:18 If I delight in wickedness, God will not hear me, but if I confess it, he will receive me.

PSALM 67

a. Psalm 67:1 That is, move our hearts with his holy Spirit, that we may feel his favor towards us.
b. Psalm 67:2 That both Jews and Gentiles may know God's covenant made with them.
c. Psalm 67:4 By these oft repetitions he showeth that the people can never rejoice sufficiently and give thanks for the great benefits that they shall receive under the kingdom of Christ.
d. Psalm 67:6 He showeth that where God favoreth, there shall be abundance of all other things.
e. Psalm 67:7 When they feel his great benefits both spiritual and corporal toward them.

PSALM 68

a. Psalm 68:1 The Prophet showeth that albeit God suffereth the wicked tyrants to oppress his Church for a time, yet at length he will be revenged of them.
b. Psalm 68:3 He showeth that when God declareth his power against the wicked, that it is for the commodity and salvation of his Church, which praise him therefore.
c. Psalm 68:4 Yah and Jehovah are the names of God, which do signify his essence and majesty incomprehensible, so that hereby is declared that all idols are but vanity, and that the God of Israel is the only true God.
d. Psalm 68:6 He giveth children to them that be childless, and increaseth their families.
e. Psalm 68:6 Which is barren of God's blessings, which before they had abused.
f. Psalm 68:7 He teacheth that God's favor peculiarly belongeth to his Church, as appeareth by their wonderful deliverance out of Egypt.

the presence of God, even the God of Israel. **9** Thou, O God, sentest a gracious rain upon thine inheritance, and thou didst refresh it when it was weary. **10** Thy Congregation dwelled therein: for thou, O God, hast of thy [g]goodness prepared it for the poor. **11** The Lord gave matter to the [h]women to tell of the great army. **12** Kings of the armies did flee: they did flee, and [i]she that remained in the house, divided the spoil. **13** Though ye have lain among [j]pots, yet shall ye be as the wings of a dove that is covered with silver, and whose feathers are like yellow gold. **14** When the Almighty scattered kings [k]in it, it was white as the snow in Zalmon. **15** [l]The mountain of God is like the mountain of Bashan: it is an high mountain, as mount Bashan. **16** [m]Why leap ye, ye high mountains? as for this Mountain, God delighteth to dwell in it: yea, the Lord will dwell in it forever. **17** The chariots of God are twenty thousand thousand Angels, and the Lord is among them, as in the Sanctuary of Sinai. **18** Thou art gone up on high: thou hast [n]led captivity captive, and received gifts for men: yea, even the rebellious hast thou led, that the Lord God might dwell there. **19** Praised be the Lord, even the God of our salvation, which ladeth us daily with benefits. Selah. **20** This is our God, even the God that saveth us: and to the Lord God belong the [o]issues of death. **21** Surely God will wound the head of his enemies, and the hairy pate of him that walketh in his sins. **22** The Lord hath said, I will bring my people again from [p]Bashan: I will bring them again from the depths of the Sea: **23** That thy foot may be dipped in blood, and the tongue of thy dogs in the blood of the enemies, even in [q]it. **24** They have seen, O God, thy [r]goings, the goings of my God, and my king, which art in the Sanctuary. **25** The [s]singers went before, the players of instruments after: in the midst were the maids playing with timbrels. **26** Praise ye God in the assemblies, and the Lord, ye that are of the fountain [t]of Israel. **27** There was [u]little Benjamin with their [v]ruler, and the Princes of Judah with their assembly, the princes of Zebulun, and the princes of Naphtali. **28** Thy GOD hath appointed thy strength: establish, O God, that which thou first wrought in us, **29** [w]Out of thy Temple upon Jerusalem, and kings shall bring presents unto thee. **30** Destroy the company of the spearmen, and multitude of the mighty bulls with the calves of the people, that [x]tread under feet pieces of silver: scatter the people that delight in war. **31** Then shall the princes come out [y]of Egypt: Ethiopia shall haste to stretch her hands unto God. **32** Sing unto God, O ye kingdoms of the earth: sing praise unto the Lord, (Selah) **33** To him that rideth upon the most high heavens, which were from the beginning: behold, he will send out by his [z]voice a mighty sound. **34** Ascribe the power to God: for his majesty is upon Israel, and his strength is in the clouds. **35** O God, thou art [aa]terrible out of thine holy [ab]places: the God of Israel is he that giveth strength and power unto the people: praised be God.

69

1 The complaints, prayers, fervent zeal and great anguish of David is set forth as a figure of Christ and all his members. 21 The malicious cruelty of the enemies. 22 And their punishment also. 26 Where Judas and such traitors are accursed. 30 He gathereth courage in his affliction, and offereth praises unto God, 32 Which are more acceptable than all sacrifices: whereof all the afflicted may take comfort. 35 Finally, he doth provoke all creatures to praises, prophesying of the kingdom of Christ, and the preservation of the Church, where all the faithful, 27 And their seed shall dwell forever.

To him that excelleth upon [a]Shoshannim. A Psalm of David. **1** Save me, O God: for the [b]waters are entered even to my soul. **2** I stick fast in the deep mire, where no [c]stay is: I am come into deep waters, and the streams run over me. **3** I am weary of crying: my throat is dry: mine [d]eyes fail, while I wait for my God. **4** They that hate me without a cause, are more than the hairs of mine head: they that would destroy me, and are mine enemies [e]falsely, are mighty, so that I restored that which I [f]took not. **5** O God, thou knowest my [g]foolishness, and my faults are not hid from thee. **6** Let not them that trust in thee, O Lord God of hosts, be ashamed for [h]me: let not those that seek thee, be confounded through me, O God of Israel. **7** For thy sake have I suffered reproof: shame hath covered my face. **8** I am become a stranger unto my brethren, even an alien unto my mother's sons. **9** [i]For the zeal of thine house hath eaten me, and the rebukes of them that rebuked thee, are fallen upon me. **10** I [j]wept and my soul fasted, but that was to my reproof. **11** I put on a sack also: and I became a proverb unto them. **12** They that [k]sat in the gate, spake of me, and the drunkards sang of me. **13** But Lord, I make my prayer unto thee in an [l]acceptable time, even in the multitude of thy mercy: O God, hear me in the truth of thy salvation. **14** Deliver me out of the mire, that I sink not: let me be delivered from them that hate me, and out of the [m]deep waters. **15** Let not the water flood drown me, neither let the deep swallow me up: and let not the pit shut her mouth upon me. **16** Hear me, O Lord, for thy loving-kindness is good: turn unto me according to the multitude of thy tender mercies. **17** And [n]hide not thy face from thy servant, for I am in trouble; make haste and hear me. **18** Draw near unto my soul and redeem it: deliver me because of mine enemies. **19** Thou hast known my reproof and my shame, and my dishonor: all mine [o]adversaries are before thee. **20** Rebuke hath broken mine heart, and I am full of heaviness, and [p]I looked for some to have pity on me, but there was none: and for comforters, but I found none. **21** For they gave me gall in my meat, and in my thirst they gave me vinegar to drink. **22** Let their [q]table be a snare before them, and their prosperity their ruin. **23** Let their eyes be blinded that they see not: and make their [r]loins always to tremble. **24** Pour out thine anger upon them, and let thy wrathful displeasure take them. **25** Let their [s]habitation be void, and let none dwell in their tents. **26** For they persecute him, whom thou hast smitten: and they add unto the sorrow of them, whom thou hast wounded. **27** Lay [t]iniquity upon their iniquity, and let them not come into thy righteousness. **28** Let them be put out of the [u]book of life, neither let them be written with the righteous. **29** When I am poor and in heaviness, thine help, O God, shall exalt me. **30** I will praise the Name of God with a song, and magnify him with thanksgiving. **31** This also shall please the Lord better than a [v]young bullock that hath horns and hoofs. **32** The humble shall see this, and they that seek God shall be glad, and your heart shall live. **33** For the Lord heareth the poor, and despiseth not his [w]prisoners. **34** Let heaven and earth praise him: the seas and all that moveth in them. **35** For God will save Zion, and build the cities of Judah, that men may

---

g. Psalm 68:10 God blessed the land of Canaan, because he had chosen that place for his Church.
h. Psalm 68:11 The fashion then was that women sang songs after the victory, as Miriam, Deborah, Judith, and others.
i. Psalm 68:12 The prey was so great, that not only the soldiers, but women also had part thereof.
j. Psalm 68:13 Though God suffer his Church for a time to lie in black darkness, yet he will restore it, and make it most shining and white.
k. Psalm 68:14 In the land of Canaan, where his Church was.
l. Psalm 68:15 Zion the Church of God, doth excel all worldly things, not in pomp and outward show, but by the inward grace of God, which there remaineth, because of his dwelling there.
m. Psalm 68:16 Why boast ye of your strength and beauty against this Mountain of God?
n. Psalm 68:18 As God overcame the enemies of his Church, took them prisoners, and made them tributaries: so Christ, which is God manifested in the flesh, subdued Satan and sin under us, and gave unto his Church most liberal gifts of his Spirit, Eph. 4:8.
o. Psalm 68:20 In most extreme dangers God hath infinite ways to deliver his.
p. Psalm 68:22 As he delivered his Church once from Og of Bashan, and other tyrants, and from the danger of the red Sea, so will he still do as oft as necessity requireth.
q. Psalm 68:23 That is, in the blood of that great slaughter, where dogs shall lap blood.
r. Psalm 68:24 That is, how thou which art chief King goest out with thy people to war, and givest them the victory.
s. Psalm 68:25 He describeth the order of the people, when they went to the Temple to give thanks for the victory.
t. Psalm 68:26 Which come of the Patriarch Jacob.
u. Psalm 68:27 Benjamin is called little, because he was the youngest son of Jacob.
v. Psalm 68:27 Who was some chief ruler of the tribe.
w. Psalm 68:29 Declare out of thine holy palace thy power for the defense of thy Church Jerusalem.
x. Psalm 68:30 He desireth that the pride of the mighty may be destroyed, which accustomed to garnish their shoes with silver, and therefore for their glittering pomp thought themselves above all men.
y. Psalm 68:31 He prophecieth that the Gentiles shall come to the true knowledge and worship of God.
z. Psalm 68:33 By his terrible thunders he will make himself to be known the God of all the world.
aa. Psalm 68:35 In showing fearful judgments against thine enemies for the salvation of thy people.
ab. Psalm 68:35 He alludeth to the Tabernacle which was divided in three parts.

PSALM 69

a. Psalm 69:1 Of Shoshannim, read Ps. 45.
b. Psalm 69:1 David signifieth by the waters, in what great dangers he was, out of the which God did deliver him.
c. Psalm 69:2 No firmity of stableness to settle my feet.
d. Psalm 69:3 Though his senses failed him, yet his faith was constant and encouraged him still to pray.
e. Psalm 69:4 Condemning me guiltless.
f. Psalm 69:4 They judged me poor innocent as a thief, and gave my goods to others, as though I had stolen them.
g. Psalm 69:5 Though I be guilty to theeward, yet am I innocent toward them.
h. Psalm 69:6 Let not mine evil entreaty of the enemies be an occasion, that the faithful fall from thee.
i. Psalm 69:9 When I saw thine enemies pretend thy Name only in mouth, and in their life deny the same, thine holy Spirit, thrust me forward, to reprove them and defend thy glory.
j. Psalm 69:10 My zeal moved me to lament and pray for my salvation.
k. Psalm 69:12 The more he sought to win them to God, the more they were against him both poor and rich.
l. Psalm 69:13 Knowing that albeit I suffer now trouble, yet thou hast a time wherein thou hast appointed my deliverance.
m. Psalm 69:14 He showeth a lively faith, in that that he assureth himself, that God is favorable to him, when he seemeth to be angry: and at hand when he seemeth to be far off.
n. Psalm 69:17 Not that he feared that God would not hear him, but that care made him to think that God deferred long.
o. Psalm 69:19 Thou seest that I am beset as a sheep among many wolves.
p. Psalm 69:20 He showeth that it is in vain to put our trust in men in our great necessities, but that our comfort only dependeth of God: for man rather increaseth our sorrows, than diminisheth them, John 19:29.
q. Psalm 69:22 He desireth God to execute his judgments against the reprobate, which cannot by any means be turned, Rom. 11:9.
r. Psalm 69:23 Take both judgment and power from them, Acts 1:20.
s. Psalm 69:25 Punish not only them, but their posterity, which shall be like unto them.
t. Psalm 69:27 By their continuance and increasing in their sins, let it be known that they be of the reprobate.
u. Psalm 69:28 They which seemed by their profession to have been written in thy book, yet by their fruits prove the contrary, let them be known as reprobate.
v. Psalm 69:31 There is no sacrifice, which God more esteemeth, than thanksgiving for his benefits.
w. Psalm 69:33 For as he delivered his servant David, so will he do all that are in distress, and call upon him.
x. Psalm 69:36 Under the temporal promise of the land of Canaan, he comprehendeth the promise of life everlasting to the faithful and their posterity.

PSALM 70

a. Psalm 70:1 Which might put him in remembrance of his deliverance.
b. Psalm 70:1 He teacheth us to be earnest in prayer, though God seem to stay: for at his time he will hear us.
c. Psalm 70:2 He was assured that the more they raged, the nearer they were to destruction, and he the nearer to his deliverance.
d. Psalm 70:3 Hereby we are taught not to mock at others in their misery, lest the same fall on our own necks.

dwell there and have it in possession. **36** The [x]seed also of his servants shall inherit it: and they that love his name shall dwell therein.

70

1 He prayeth to be right speedily delivered. 2 He desireth the shame of his enemies, 4 And the joyful comfort of all those that seek the Lord.

To him that excelleth. A Psalm of David, to put [a]in remembrance. **1** O [1]God, [b]haste thee to deliver me: make haste to help me, O Lord. **2** Let them be [c]confounded and put to shame, that seek my soul: let them be turned backward and put to rebuke, that desire mine hurt. **3** Let them be turned back for a reward of their [d]shame, which say, Aha, aha. **4** But let all those that seek thee, be joyful and glad in thee, and let all that love thy salvation, say always, God be praised. **5** Now I am [e]poor and needy: O God, make haste to me: thou art my helper, and my deliverer: O Lord, make no tarrying.

71

He prayeth in faith, established by the word of promise, 5 And confirmed by the work of God from his youth. 10 He complaineth of the cruelty of his enemies, 17 And desireth God to continue his graces toward him, 22 Promising to be mindful and thankful for the same.

1 In [1,a]thee, O Lord, I trust: let me never be ashamed. **2** Rescue me and deliver me in thy [b]righteousness: incline thine ear unto me and save me. **3** Be thou my strong rock, whereunto I may always resort: thou [c]hast given commandment to save me: for thou art my rock, and my fortress. **4** Deliver me, O my God, out of the hand [d]of the wicked: out of the hand of the evil and cruel man. **5** For thou art mine hope, O Lord God, even my [e]trust from my youth. **6** Upon thee have I been stayed from the womb: thou art he that took me out of my mother's bowels: my praise shall be always of thee. **7** I am become as it were a [f]monster unto many: but thou art my sure trust. **8** Let my mouth be filled with thy praise, and with thy glory every day. **9** Cast me not off in the time of [g]age: forsake me not when my strength faileth. **10** For mine enemies speak of me, and they that lay wait for my soul, take their counsel together, **11** Saying, [h]God hath forsaken him: pursue and take him, for there is none to deliver him. **12** Go not far from me, O God: [i]my God haste thee to help me. **13** Let them be confounded and consumed that are against my soul: let them be covered with reproof and confusion, that seek mine hurt. **14** But I will wait continually, and will praise thee more and more. **15** My mouth shall daily rehearse thy righteousness, and thy salvation: [j]for I know not the number. **16** I will [k]go forward in the strength of the Lord God, and will make mention of thy righteousness, even of thine only. **17** O God, thou hast taught me from my youth even until now: therefore will I tell of thy wondrous works, **18** [l]Yea even unto mine old age and gray head, O God: forsake me not, until I have declared thine arm unto this generation, and thy power to all them that shall come. **19** And thy [m]righteousness, O God, I will exalt on high: for thou hast done great things: [n]O God, who is like unto thee! **20** Which hast showed me great troubles and [o]adversities, but thou wilt return and revive me, and wilt come again, and take me up from the depth of the earth. **21** Thou wilt increase mine honor, and return and comfort me. **22** Therefore will I praise thee for thy [p]faithfulness, O God, upon instrument and viol: unto thee will I sing upon the harp, O Holy one of Israel. **23** My lips will rejoice when I sing unto thee, and my [q]soul which thou hast delivered. **24** My tongue also shall talk of thy righteousness daily: for they are confounded and brought unto shame, that seek mine hurt.

72

1 He prayeth for the prosperous estate of the kingdom of Solomon, who was the figure of Christ, 4 under whom shall be righteousness, peace, and felicity. 10 Unto whom all Kings and nations shall do homage, 17 Whose name and power shall endure forever, and in whom all nations shall be blessed.

A Psalm [a]of Solomon. **1** Give thy [b]judgments to the King, O God, and thy righteousness to the King's [c]son. **2** Then shall he judge thy people in righteousness, and thy poor with equity. **3** The [d]mountains, and the hills shall bring peace to the people by justice. **4** He shall [e]judge the poor of the people: he shall save the children of the needy, and shall subdue the oppressor. **5** They shall [f]fear thee as long as the sun and moon endureth, from generation to generation. **6** He shall come [g]down like the rain upon the mown grass, and as the showers that water the earth. **7** In his days shall the righteous flourish, and abundance of peace shall be so long as the moon endureth. **8** His dominion shall be also from [h]sea to sea, and from the river unto the ends of the land. **9** They that dwell in the wilderness, shall kneel before him, and his enemies shall lick the dust. **10** The kings of [i]Tarshish and of the isles shall bring presents: the kings [j]of Sheba and Seba shall bring gifts. **11** Yea, all kings shall worship him: all nations shall serve him. **12** For he shall deliver the poor when he crieth: the needy also, and him that hath no helper. **13** He shall be merciful to the poor and needy, and shall preserve the souls of the poor. **14** He shall redeem their souls from deceit and violence, and [k]dear shall their blood be in his sight. **15** Yea, he shall live, and unto him shall they give of the [l]gold of Sheba: they shall also pray for him continually, and daily bless him. **16** An handful of corn shall be sown in the earth, even in the top of the mountains, and the [m]fruit thereof shalt shake like the trees of Lebanon: and the children shall flourish out of the city like the grass of the earth. **17** His name shall be forever: his name shall endure as long as the Sun: all nations shall bless [n]him, and be blessed in him. **18** Blessed be the Lord God, even the God of Israel which only doeth [o]wondrous things. **19** And blessed be his glorious Name forever: and let all the earth be filled with his glory. So be it, even so be it. **20** Here end the [p]prayers of David the son of Jesse.

73

1 The Prophet teacheth by his example that neither the worldly prosperity of the ungodly, 14 nor yet the affliction of the good ought to discourage God's children: but rather ought to move us to consider our Father's providence, and to cause us to reverence God's judgments, 19 forasmuch as the wicked vanish away, 24 and the godly enter into life everlasting, 28 in hope whereof he resigneth himself into God's hands.

A Psalm committed to Asaph. **1** Yet [a]God is good to Israel: even to the pure in heart. **2** As for me, my feet were almost gone: my steps had well near slipped. **3** For I fretted at the foolish, when I saw the prosperity of the wicked. **4** For there are [b]no bands in their death, but they are lusty and strong. **5** They are not in trouble as other men, neither are they plagued with other men. **6** [c]Therefore pride is as a chain unto them, and cruelty covereth them as a garment. **7** Their eyes stand out for fatness: [d]they have more than heart can wish. **8** They are licentious, and speak wickedly of their oppression: they talk presumptuously. **9** They [e]set their mouth against heaven, and their tongue

---

e. Psalm 70:5 Because he had felt God's help before, he groundeth on experience, and boldly seeketh unto him for succor.

PSALM 70

1. Ps. 40:13

PSALM 71

a. Psalm 71:1 He prayeth to God with full assurance of faith, that he will deliver him from his adversaries.
b. Psalm 71:2 By declaring thyself true of promise.
c. Psalm 71:3 Thou hast infinite means, and all creatures are at thy commandment: therefore show some sign, whereby I shall be delivered.
d. Psalm 71:4 That is, from Absalom, Ahithophel and that conspiracy.
e. Psalm 71:5 He strengtheneth his faith by the experience of God's benefits, who did not only preserve him in his mother's belly, but took him thence, and ever since hath preserved him.
f. Psalm 71:7 All the world wondereth at me because of my miseries: as well they in authority as the common people, yet being assured of thy favor, I remained steadfast.
g. Psalm 71:9 Thou that didst help me in my youth, when I had more strength, help me now so much the more in mine old age and weakness.
h. Psalm 71:11 Thus the wicked both blaspheme God, and triumph against his Saints, as though he had forsaken them, if he suffer them to fall into their hands.
i. Psalm 71:12 In calling him his God, he putteth back the false reports of the adversaries, that said, God had forsaken him.
j. Psalm 71:15 Because thy benefits toward me are innumerable, I cannot but continually meditate and rehearse them.
k. Psalm 71:16 I will remain steadfast, being upholden with the power of God.
l. Psalm 71:18 He desireth that as he hath begun, he would so continue his benefits, that his liberality may have perfect praise.
m. Psalm 71:19 Thy just performance of thy promise.
n. Psalm 71:19 His faith breaketh through all tentations, and by this exclamation he praiseth the power of God.
o. Psalm 71:20 As he confesseth that God is the only author of his deliverance: so he acknowledgeth that these evils were sent unto him by God's providence.
p. Psalm 71:22 He confesseth that his long tarriance was well recompensed, when God performed his promise.
q. Psalm 71:23 For there is no true praising of God, except it come from the heart: and therefore he promiseth to delight in nothing, but wherein God be glorified.

PSALM 71

1. Ps. 31:1

PSALM 72

a. Psalm 72:1 Composed by David as touching the reign of his son Solomon.
b. Psalm 72:1 Endue the king with the Spirit of wisdom and justice, that he reign not as do the worldly tyrants.
c. Psalm 72:1 To wit, to his posterity.
d. Psalm 72:3 When justice reigneth, even the places most barren shall be enriched with thy blessings.
e. Psalm 72:4 He showeth wherefore the sword is committed to Kings: to wit, to defend the innocent, and suppress the wicked.
f. Psalm 72:5 The people shall embrace thy true religion, when thou givest a King that ruleth according to thy word.
g. Psalm 72:6 As this is true in all godly kings, so it is chiefly verified in Christ, who with his heavenly dew, maketh his Church ever to flourish.
h. Psalm 72:8 That is, from the red sea to the sea called Syriacum, and from Euphrates forward, meaning, that Christ's Kingdom should be large and universal.
i. Psalm 72:10 Of Cilicia, and of all other countries, beyond the sea, which he meaneth by the isles.
j. Psalm 72:10 That is, of Arabia that rich country, whereof Sheba was a part bordering upon Ethiopia.
k. Psalm 72:14 Though tyrants pass not to shed blood, yet this godly king shall preserve his subjects from all kind of wrong.
l. Psalm 72:15 God will both prosper his life, and also make the people most willing to obey him.
m. Psalm 72:16 Under such a king shall be most great plenty, both of fruit and also of the increase of mankind.
n. Psalm 72:17 They shall pray to God for his continuance, and know that God doth prosper them for his sake.
o. Psalm 72:18 He confesseth that except God miraculously preserve his people, that neither the king nor the kingdom can continue.
p. Psalm 72:20 Concerning his son Solomon.

PSALM 73

a. Psalm 73:1 As it were between hope and despair he bursteth forth into this affection, being assured that God would continue his favor toward such as were godly indeed, and not hypocrites.
b. Psalm 73:4 The wicked in this life live at pleasure and are not drawn to death like prisoners: that is, by sickness which is death's messenger.
c. Psalm 73:6 They glory in their pride as some do in their chains, and in cruelty, as some do in apparel.
d. Psalm 73:7 Hebrew, they pass the desires of the heart.
e. Psalm 73:9 They blaspheme God, and fear not his power and rail upon men, because they esteem themselves above all others.

walketh through the earth. **10** Therefore his [f]people turn hither: for waters of a full cup are wrung out to them. **11** And they [g]say, How doth God know it? or is there knowledge in the most High? **12** Lo these are the wicked, yet prosper they always, and increase in riches. **13** Certainly I have cleansed mine heart in vain, and washed mine hands in innocency. **14** For daily have I been punished, and chastened every morning. **15** If I say, [h]I will judge thus, behold the generation of thy children, I have trespassed. **16** Then thought I to know this, but it was too painful for me, **17** Until I went into the [i]Sanctuary of God: then understood I their end. **18** Surely thou hast set them in slippery places, and castest them down into desolation. **19** How suddenly are they destroyed, perished and [j]horribly consumed, **20** As a dream when one awaketh! O Lord, when [k]thou raisest us up, thou shalt make their image despised. **21** Certainly mine heart was vexed, and I was pricked in my reins. **22** So foolish was I and ignorant: I was a [l]beast before thee. **23** Yet I was always [m]with thee: thou hast holden me by my right hand. **24** Thou wilt guide me by thy counsel, and afterward receive me to glory. **25** Whom have I in [n]heaven but thee? and I have desired none in the earth with thee. **26** My flesh faileth and mine heart also: but God is the strength of mine heart, and my [o]portion forever. **27** For lo, that they withdraw themselves from thee, shall perish: thou destroyest all them that [p]go a whoring from thee. **28** As for me, it is good for me [q]to draw near to God: therefore I have put my trust in the Lord God, that I may declare all thy works.

74

1 The faithful complain of the destruction of the Church and true religion, 2 Under the Name of Zion, and the Temple destroyed: 11 and trusting in the might and free mercies of God, 20 by his covenant, 21 they require help and succor for the glory of God's holy Name, for the salvation of his poor afflicted servants, 23 and the confusion of his proud enemies.

A Psalm to give instruction, committed to Asaph. **1** O God, [a]why hast thou put us away forever? why is thy wrath kindled against the sheep of thy pasture? **2** Think upon the congregation, which thou hast possessed of old, and on the [b]rod of thine inheritance, which thou hast redeemed, and on this mount Zion, wherein thou hast dwelt. **3** Lift up thy [c]strokes, that thou mayest forever destroy every enemy that doeth evil to the Sanctuary. **4** Thine adversaries roar in the midst of thy congregation, and [d]set up their banners for signs. **5** He that [e]lifted the axes upon the thick trees, was renowned as one that brought a thing to perfection: **6** But now they break down the carved work thereof with axes and hammers. **7** They have cast thy Sanctuary into the fire, and razed it to the ground, and have defiled the dwelling place of thy Name. **8** They said in their [f]hearts, Let us destroy them altogether: they have burnt all the Synagogues of God in the land. **9** We see not our signs: there is not one Prophet more, nor any with us that knoweth [g]how long. **10** O God, how long shall the adversary reproach thee? shall the enemy blaspheme thy Name forever? **11** Why withdrawest thou thine hand, even thy right hand? draw it out of thy bosom, and [h]consume them. **12** Even God is my king of old, working salvation [i]in the midst of the earth. **13** Thou didst divide the sea by thy power: thou brakest the heads of the [j]dragons in the waters. **14** Thou brakest the head of [k]Leviathan in pieces, and gavest him to be [l]meat for the people in wilderness. **15** Thou brakest up the fountain and river: thou driest up mighty rivers. **16** The [m]day is thine, and the night is thine: thou hast prepared the light and the sun. **17** Thou hast set all the borders of the earth: thou hast made Summer and Winter. **18** Remember this, that the enemy hath reproached the Lord, and the foolish people hath blasphemed thy Name. **19** Give not the soul of thy [n]turtle dove unto the beast, and forget not the Congregation of thy poor forever. **20** Consider thy covenant: for [o]the dark places of the earth are full of the habitations of the cruel. **21** O let not the oppressed return ashamed, but let the poor and needy praise thy Name. **22** Arise, O God: maintain thy [p]own cause: remember thy daily reproach by the foolish man. **23** Forget not the voice of thine enemies: for the tumult of them that rise against thee, [q]ascendeth continually.

75

1 The faithful do praise the Name of the Lord, 2 Which shall come to judge at the time appointed: 8 When the wicked shall be put to confusion, and drink of the cup of his wrath. 10 Their pride shall be abated, and the righteous shall be exalted to honor.

To him that excelleth. [a]Destroy not. A Psalm, or song committed to Asaph. **1** We will praise thee, O God, we will praise thee, for thy Name is near: therefore [b]they will declare thy wondrous works. **2** [c]When I shall take a convenient time, I will judge righteously. **3** The earth and all the inhabitants thereof are dissolved: but I will establish the pillars [d]of it. Selah. **4** I said unto the foolish, Be not so foolish, and to the wicked, Lift not up the horn. **5** Lift not up your [e]horn on high, neither speak with a stiff neck. **6** For to come to preferment is neither from the East, nor from the West, nor from the South, **7** But God is the judge: he maketh low, and he maketh high. **8** For in the hand of the Lord is a [f]cup, and the wine is red: it is full mixed, and he poureth out of the same: surely all the wicked of the earth shall wring out and drink the dregs thereof. **9** But I will declare forever, and sing praises unto the God of Jacob. **10** All the horns of the wicked also will I break: but the horns of the [g]righteous shall be exalted.

76

1 This Psalm setteth forth the power of God, and care for the defense of his people in Jerusalem, in the destruction of the army of Sennacherib: 11 and exhorteth the faithful to be thankful for the same.

To him that excelleth on Neginoth. A Psalm, or song committed to Asaph. **1** God is [a]known in Judah: his Name is great in Israel. **2** For in [b]Salem is his Tabernacle, and his dwelling in Zion. **3** There brake he the arrows of the bow, the shield, and the sword, and the battle. Selah. **4** Thou art more bright and puissant, than [c]the mountains of prey. **5** The stouthearted are spoiled: they have slept their sleep, and all the men of strength have not [d]found their hands. **6** At thy rebuke, O God of Jacob, both the chariot and horse are cast asleep. **7** Thou, even thou art to be feared; and who shall stand in thy [e]sight, when thou art angry! **8** Thou didst cause thy judgment to be heard from heaven; therefore the earth feared, and was still, **9** When thou, O God, arose to judgment, to [f]help all the meek of the earth. Selah. **10** Surely the [g]rage of man shall turn to thy praise; the remnant of the rage shalt thou restrain. **11** Vow and perform unto the Lord your God, all ye that be [h]round about him; let them bring presents unto him that ought to be feared. **12** He shall [i]cut off the spirit of princes; he is terrible to the kings of the earth.

---

f. Psalm 73:10 Not only the reprobate, but also the people of God oftentimes fall back, seeing the prosperous estate of the wicked, and are overwhelmed with sorrows, thinking that God considereth not aright the estate of the godly.
g. Psalm 73:11 Thus the flesh moveth even the godly to dispute with God touching their poor estate, and the prosperity of the wicked.
h. Psalm 73:15 If I give place to this wicked thought, I offend against thy providence, seeing thou disposeth all things most wisely and preservest thy children in their greatest dangers.
i. Psalm 73:17 Until I entered into thy school and learned by thy word and holy Spirit, that thou orderest all things most wisely and justly.
j. Psalm 73:19 By thy fearful judgment.
k. Psalm 73:20 When thou openest our eyes to consider thy heavenly felicity, we contemn all their vain pomp.
l. Psalm 73:22 For the more that man goeth about by his own reason to seek out God's judgments, the more doth he declare himself a beast.
m. Psalm 73:23 By faith I was assured that thy providence did watch always over me, to preserve me.
n. Psalm 73:25 He sought neither help nor comfort of any save of God only.
o. Psalm 73:26 He teacheth us to deny ourselves, to have God our whole sufficiency, and only contentment.
p. Psalm 73:27 That is, forsake thee to seek others.
q. Psalm 73:28 Though all the world shrink from God, yet he promiseth to trust in him and to magnify his works.

PSALM 74

a. Psalm 74:1 The Church of God being oppressed by the tyranny, either of the Babylonians or of Antiochus, prayeth to God by whose hand this yoke was laid upon them for their sins.
b. Psalm 74:2 Which inheritance thou hast measured out for thyself as with a line or rod.
c. Psalm 74:3 Or, feet.
d. Psalm 74:4 They have destroyed thy true religion, and spread their banners in sign of defiance.
e. Psalm 74:5 He commendeth the temple for the costly matter, the excellent workmanship, and beauty thereof, which notwithstanding the enemies did destroy.
f. Psalm 74:8 They encouraged one another to cruelty, that not only God's people might be destroyed, but also his religion utterly in all places suppressed.
g. Psalm 74:9 They lament that they have no Prophet among them to show them how long their misery should endure.
h. Psalm 74:11 They join their deliverance with God's glory and power, knowing that the punishment of the enemy should be their deliverance.
i. Psalm 74:12 Meaning, in the sight of all the world.
j. Psalm 74:13 To wit, Pharaoh's army.
k. Psalm 74:14 Which was a great monster of the sea, or whale, meaning, Pharaoh.
l. Psalm 74:14 His destruction did rejoice them as meat refresheth the body.
m. Psalm 74:16 Seeing that God by his providence governeth and disposeth all things, he gathereth that he will take care chiefly for his children.
n. Psalm 74:19 He meaneth the Church of God, which is exposed as a prey to the wicked.
o. Psalm 74:20 That is, all places where thy word shineth not, there reigneth tyranny and ambition.
p. Psalm 74:22 He showeth that God cannot suffer his Church to be oppressed, except he loose his own right.
q. Psalm 74:23 Or, increaseth more and more.

PSALM 75

a. Psalm 75:1 Read Ps. 57:1.
b. Psalm 75:1 He declareth how the faithful shall ever have just occasion to praise God, forasmuch as in their need they shall feel his power at hand to help them.
c. Psalm 75:2 When I see my time (saith God) to help your miseries, I will come and set all things in good order.
d. Psalm 75:3 Though all things be brought to ruin, yet I can restore and preserve them.
e. Psalm 75:5 The Prophet warneth the wicked that they would not set themselves against God's people, seeing that God at his time destroyeth them that rule wickedly.
f. Psalm 75:8 God's wrath is compared to a cup of strong and delicate wine, wherewith the wicked are made so drunk, that by drinking till they come to the very dregs they are utterly destroyed.
g. Psalm 75:10 The godly shall better prosper by their innocent simplicity, than the wicked shall by all their craft and subtlety.

PSALM 76

a. Psalm 76:1 He declareth that God's power is evidently seen in preserving his people and destroying his enemies.
b. Psalm 76:2 Which afterward was called Jerusalem.
c. Psalm 76:4 He compareth the kingdoms full of extortion and rapine to the mountains that are full of ravening beasts.
d. Psalm 76:5 God hath taken their spirits and strength from them as though their hands were cut off.
e. Psalm 76:7 God with a look is able to destroy all the power and activity of the enemies, were they never so many, or mighty.
f. Psalm 76:9 To revenge the wrongs done to thy Church.
g. Psalm 76:10 For the end shall show that the enemy was able to bring nothing to pass: also thou shalt bridle their rage that they shall not compass their purpose.
h. Psalm 76:11 To wit, the Levites, that dwell about the Tabernacle, or the people among whom he doth dwell.
i. Psalm 76:12 The Hebrew word signifieth to vintage, or gather grapes: meaning, that he shall make the counsels and enterprises of wicked tyrants foolish and vain.

77

1 The Prophet in the Name of the Church rehearseth the greatness of his affliction, and his grievous temptations, 6 Whereby he was driven to this end to consider his former conversation, 11 and the continual course of God's works in the preservation of his servants, and so he confirmeth his faith against these temptations.

For the excellent Musician [1]Jeduthun. A Psalm committed to Asaph. **1** My [a]voice came to God, when I cried: my voice came to God; and he heard me. **2** In the day of my trouble I sought the Lord: [b]my sore ran and ceased not in the night: my soul refused comfort. **3** I did think upon God, and was [c]troubled: I prayed, and my spirit was full of anguish. Selah. **4** Thou keepest mine eyes [d]waking: I was astonied, and could not speak. **5** Then I considered the days of old: and the years of ancient time. **6** I called to remembrance my [e]song in the night: I communed with mine own heart, and my spirit searched [f]diligently. **7** Will the Lord absent himself forever? and will he show no more favor? **8** Is his [g]mercy clean gone forever? doth his promise fail forevermore? **9** Hath God forgotten to be merciful? hath he shut up his tender mercies in displeasure? Selah. **10** And I said, This is my [h]death: yet I remembered the years of the right hand of the most High. **11** I remembered the works of the Lord: certainly I remembered thy wonders of old. **12** I did also meditate all thy works, and did devise of thine acts, saying, **13** Thy way, O God, is [i]in the Sanctuary: who is so great a [j]God, as our God! **14** Thou art the God that doest wonders; thou hast declared thy power among the people. **15** Thou hast redeemed thy people with thine arm, even the sons of Jacob and Joseph. Selah. **16** The [k]waters saw thee, O God: the waters saw thee, and were afraid: yea, the depths trembled. **17** The clouds poured out water: the heavens gave a [l]sound: yea, thine arrows went abroad. **18** The voice of thy thunder was round about; the lightnings lightened the world: the earth trembled and shook. **19** Thy way is in the sea, and thy paths in the great waters, and thy footsteps are not [m]known. **20** Thou didst lead thy people like sheep by the hand of Moses and Aaron.

78

1 He showeth how God of his mercy chose his Church of the posterity of Abraham, 8 Reproaching the stubborn rebellion of their fathers, that the children might not only understand. 11 That God of his free mercy made his Covenant with their ancestors, 17 But also seeing them so malicious and perverse, might be ashamed, and so turn wholly to God. In this Psalm the holy Ghost hath comprehended, as it were, the sum of all God's benefits, to the intent the ignorant and gross people might see in few words the effect of the whole histories of the Bible.

A Psalm to give [a]instruction, committed to Asaph. **1** Hear my [b]doctrine, O my people: incline your ears unto the words of my mouth. **2** I will open my mouth in a parable: I will declare high sentences of old. **3** Which we have heard and known, and our [c]fathers have told us. **4** We will not hide them from their children, but to the generation to come we will show the praise of the Lord, his power also, and his wonderful works that he hath done: **5** How he established a [d]testimony in Jacob, and ordained a Law in Israel, which he commanded our fathers, that they should teach their children: **6** That the [e]posterity might know it, and the children, which should be born, should stand up, and declare it to their children. **7** That they might [f]set their hope on God, and not forget the works of God, but keep his commandments: **8** And not to be as their [g]fathers, a disobedient and rebellious generation: a generation that set not their heart aright, and whose spirit was not faithful unto God. **9** The children of [h]Ephraim being armed and shooting with the bow, turned back in the day of battle. **10** They kept not the Covenant of God, but refused to walk in his Law, **11** And forgate his acts, and his wonderful works that he had showed them. **12** He did marvelous things in the sight of their [i]fathers in the land of Egypt; even in the field of Zoan. **13** [1]He divided the Sea, and led them through: he made also the waters to stand as an heap. **14** [2]In the daytime also he led them with a cloud, and all the night with a light of fire. **15** [3]He clave the rocks in the wilderness, and gave them drink as of the great depths. **16** [4]He brought floods also out of the stony rock, so that he made the waters to descend like the rivers. **17** Yet they [j]sinned still against him, and provoked the Highest in the wilderness, **18** And tempted God in their hearts in [k]requiring meat for their lust. **19** [5]They spake against God also, saying, Can God [l]prepare a table in the wilderness? **20** [6]Behold, he smote the rock, that the water gushed out, and the streams overflowed: can he give bread also? or prepare flesh for his people? **21** Therefore the Lord heard, and was angry, and the [7]fire was kindled in Jacob, and also wrath came upon Israel, **22** Because they believed not in God, and [m]trusted not in his help. **23** Yet he had commanded the [n]clouds above, and had opened the doors of heaven, **24** And had rained down Manna upon them for to eat, and had given them of the wheat of heaven. **25** [8]Man did eat the bread of Angels: he sent them meat enough. **26** He caused the [o]East wind to pass in the heaven: and through his power he brought in the South wind. **27** He rained flesh also upon them as dust, and feathered fowl as the sand of the sea. **28** And he made it fall in the midst of their camp, even round about their habitations. **29** So they did eat, and were well filled: for he gave them their desire. **30** They were not turned from their [p]lusts, but the meat was yet in their mouths, **31** When the wrath of God came even upon them, and slew [q]the strongest of them, and smote down the chosen men of Israel. **32** For all this they [r]sinned still, and believed not his wondrous works. **33** Therefore their days did he consume in vanity, and their years hastily. **34** And when he [s]slew them, they sought him, and they returned, and sought God early. **35** And they remembered that God was their strength, and the most high God their redeemer. **36** But they flattered him with their mouth, and dissembled with him with their tongue. **37** For their [t]heart was not upright with him: neither were they faithful in his covenant. **38** Yet he being merciful, [u]forgave their iniquity, and destroyed them not, but oft times called back his anger, and did not stir up all his wrath. **39** For he remembered that they were flesh: yea, a wind that passeth and cometh not again. **40** How oft did they provoke him in the wilderness? and grieve him in the desert? **41** Yea, they [v]returned and tempted God, and [w]limited the Holy one of Israel. **42** They [x]remembered not his hand, nor the day when he delivered them from the enemy, **43** Nor him that set his signs in Egypt, and his wonders in the field of Zoan, **44** And turned their rivers into blood, and their floods, that they could not drink. **45** He sent [y]a swarm of flies among them, which devoured them, and frogs, which destroyed them. **46** He [z]gave also their fruits unto the caterpillar, and their labor unto the grasshopper. **47** He destroyed their vines with hail, and their wild fig trees with the hailstone. **48** He gave their cattle also to the hail, and their flocks to the thunderbolts. **49** He cast upon them the fierceness of his anger, indignation and wrath, and vexation by the sending out of aaevil angels. **50** He made a way to his anger: he spared not their soul from death, but gave their life to the pestilence, **51** And smote all

---

PSALM 77

- **a.** Psalm 77:1 The Prophet teacheth us by his example to flee unto God for help in our necessities.
- **b.** Psalm 77:2 Or, mine hand was stretched out.
- **c.** Psalm 77:3 He showeth that we must patiently abide, although God deliver us not out of our troubles at the first cry.
- **d.** Psalm 77:4 Meaning, that his sorrows were as watchmen that kept his eyes from sleeping.
- **e.** Psalm 77:6 Of thanksgiving, which I was accustomed to sing in my prosperity.
- **f.** Psalm 77:6 Both the causes why I was chastened, and when my sorrows should have an end.
- **g.** Psalm 77:8 As if he should say, It is impossible: whereby he exhorteth himself to patience.
- **h.** Psalm 77:10 Though I first doubted of my life, yet considering that God had his years, that is, change of times, and was accustomed also to lift up them, whom he hath beaten, I took heart again.
- **i.** Psalm 77:13 That is in heaven, whereunto we must ascend by faith, if we will know the ways of God.
- **j.** Psalm 77:13 He condemneth all that worship anything save the only true God, whose glory appeareth through the world.
- **k.** Psalm 77:16 He declareth wherein the power of God was declared when he delivered the Israelites through the red sea.
- **l.** Psalm 77:17 That is, thundered and lightninged.
- **m.** Psalm 77:19 For when thou hadst brought over thy people, the water returned to her course, and the enemies that thought to have followed them, could not pass through, Exod. 14:28, 29.

PSALM 77

1. Ps. 39 - Ps. 62 - 1 Chron. 16:41

PSALM 78

- **a.** Psalm 78:1 Read Ps. 32.
- **b.** Psalm 78:1 The Prophet under the name of a teacher calleth the people his, and the doctrine his, as Paul calleth the Gospel his, whereof he was but the preacher, as Rom. 2:16 and 16:25.
- **c.** Psalm 78:3 Which were the people of God.
- **d.** Psalm 78:5 By the testimony, and law, he meaneth the law written, which they were commanded to teach their children, Deut. 6:7.
- **e.** Psalm 78:6 He showeth wherein the children should be like their fathers: that is, in maintaining God's pure Religion.
- **f.** Psalm 78:7 He showeth wherein the use of this doctrine standeth: in faith, in the meditation of God's benefits, and in obedience.
- **g.** Psalm 78:8 Though these fathers were the seed of Abraham and the chosen people, yet he showeth by their rebellion, provocation, falsehood, and hypocrisy, that the children ought not to follow their examples.
- **h.** Psalm 78:9 By Ephraim he meaneth also the rest of the tribes, because they were most in number: whose punishment declareth that they were unfaithful to God, and by their multitude and authority had corrupt all others.
- **i.** Psalm 78:12 He proveth that not only the posterity but also their forefathers were wicked and rebellious to God.
- **j.** Psalm 78:17 Their wicked malice could be overcome by no benefits, which were great and many.
- **k.** Psalm 78:18 Then to require more than is necessary, and to separate God's power from his will, is to tempt God.
- **l.** Psalm 78:19 Thus when we give place to sin, we are moved to doubt of God's power, except he will always be ready to serve our lust.
- **m.** Psalm 78:22 That is, in his fatherly providence, whereby he careth for his, and provideth sufficiently.
- **n.** Psalm 78:23 So that they had that, which was necessary and sufficient: but their lust made them to covet that which they knew God had denied them.
- **o.** Psalm 78:26 God used the means of the wind to teach them that all elements were at his commandment, and that no distance or place could let his working.
- **p.** Psalm 78:30 Such is the nature of concupiscence, that the more it hath, the more it lusteth.
- **q.** Psalm 78:31 Though others were not spared, yet chiefly they suffered, which trusted in their strength against God.
- **r.** Psalm 78:32 Thus sin by continuance maketh man insensible, so that by no plagues they can be amended.
- **s.** Psalm 78:34 Such was their hypocrisy, that they sought unto God for fear of punishment, though in their heart they loved him not.
- **t.** Psalm 78:37 Whatsoever cometh not from the pure fountain of the heart, is hypocrisy.
- **u.** Psalm 78:38 Because he would ever have some remnant of a Church to praise his Name in earth, he suffered not their sins to overcome his mercy.
- **v.** Psalm 78:41 That is, they tempted him oft times.
- **w.** Psalm 78:41 As they all do that measure the power of God by their capacity.
- **x.** Psalm 78:42 The forgetfulness of God's benefits is the root of rebellion and all vice.
- **y.** Psalm 78:45 This word signifieth a confused mixture of flies and venomous worms. Some take it for all sorts of serpents: some for all wild beasts.
- **z.** Psalm 78:46 He repeateth not here all the miracles that God did in Egypt, but certain which might be sufficient to convince the people of malice and ingratitude.
- **aa.** Psalm 78:49 So called either of the effect, that is, of punishing the wicked: or else because they were wicked spirits, whom God permitted to vex men.
- **ab.** Psalm 78:51 The firstborn are so called, as Gen. 49:3.

the firstborn in Egypt, even the abbeginning of their strength in the tabernacles of acHam. **52** But he made his people to go out like sheep, and led them in the wilderness like a flock. **53** Yea, he carried them out safely, and they adfeared not, and the Sea covered their enemies. **54** And he brought them unto the borders of his aeSanctuary: even to this Mountain which his right hand purchased. **55** [9]He cast out the heathen also before them, and caused them to fall to the lot of his inheritance, and made the tribes of Israel to dwell in their tabernacles. **56** Yet they tempted, and provoked the most high God, and kept not his testimonies, **57** But turned back, and dealt affalsely like their fathers: they turned like a deceitful bow. **58** And they agprovoked him to anger with their high places, and moved him to wrath with their graven images. **59** God heard this and was wroth, and greatly abhorred Israel, **60** So that he ahforsook the habitation of Shiloh, even the Tabernacle where he dwelt among men, **61** And delivered his aipower into captivity, and his beauty into the enemy's hand. **62** And he gave up his people to the sword, and was angry with his inheritance. **63** The fire ajdevoured their chosen men, and their maids were not akpraised. **64** Their Priests fell by the sword, and their alwidows lamented not. **65** But the Lord awaked as one out of sleep, and as a strong man that after his amwine crieth out, **66** And smote his enemies in the hinder parts, and put them to a perpetual shame. **67** Yet he refused the tabernacle of anJoseph, and chose not the tribe of Ephraim: **68** But chose the tribe of Judah, and mount Zion which he loved. **69** And he aobuilt his Sanctuary as an high palace, like the earth, which he established forever. **70** He chose David also his servant, and took him from the sheepfolds. **71** Even from behind the ewes with young, brought he him to feed his people in Jacob, and his inheritance in Israel. **72** So aphe fed them according to the simplicity of his heart, and guided them by the discretion of his hands.

79

1 The Israelites complain to God for the great calamity and oppression that they suffered by God's enemies, 8 and confessing their sins, flee to God's mercies with full hope of deliverance, 10 Because their calamities were joined with the contempt of his Name, 13 for the which they promise to be thankful.

A Psalm committed to Asaph. **1** O God, [a]the heathen are come into thine inheritance: thine holy Temple have they defiled, and made Jerusalem heaps of stones. **2** The [b]dead bodies of thy servants have they given to be meat unto fowls of the heaven, and the flesh of thy saints unto the beasts of the earth. **3** Their blood have they shed like waters, round about Jerusalem, and there was none to [c]bury them. **4** We are a reproach to our [d]neighbors, even a scorn and derision unto them that are round about us. **5** Lord, how long wilt thou be angry, forever? shall thy jealousy [e]burn like fire? **6** [1]Pour out thy wrath upon the heathen that have not known thee, and upon the kingdoms that have not called upon thy Name. **7** For they have devoured Jacob, and made his dwelling place desolate. **8** Remember not against us the [f]former iniquities, but [g]make haste, and let thy tender mercies prevent us: for we are in great misery. **9** Help us, O God of our [h]salvation, for the glory of thy Name, and deliver us, and be merciful unto our sins for thy Name's sake. **10** Wherefore should the heathen say, Where is their God? let them be known among the heathen in our sight by the vengeance of the blood of thy servants that is shed. **11** Let the sighing of the [i]prisoners come before thee: according to thy mighty arm preserve [j]the children of death, **12** And render to our neighbors sevenfold into their bosom their reproach, wherewith they have reproached thee, O Lord. **13** So we thy people, and sheep of thy pasture shall praise thee forever: and from generation to generation [k]we will set forth thy praise.

80

1 A lamentable prayer to God to help the miseries of his Church, 8 Desiring him to consider their first estate, when his favor shined toward them, to the intent that he might finish that work which he had begun.

To him that excelleth on Shoshannim Eduth, A Psalm committed to Asaph. **1** Hear, [a]O thou shepherd of Israel, thou that leadest Joseph like sheep: show thy brightness, thou that sittest between the [b]Cherubims. **2** Before Ephraim and Benjamin and Manasseh stir up thy strength, and come to help us. **3** [c]Turn us again, O God, and cause thy face to shine that we may be saved. **4** O Lord God of hosts, how long wilt thou be [d]angry against the prayer of thy people? **5** Thou hast fed them with the bread of tears, and given them tears to drink with great measure. **6** Thou hast made us a [e]strife unto our neighbors, and our enemies laugh at us among themselves. **7** [f]Turn us again, O God of hosts: cause thy face to shine, and we shall be saved. **8** Thou hast brought a [g]vine out of Egypt: thou hast cast out the heathen, and planted it. **9** Thou madest room for it, and didst cause it to take root, and it filled the land. **10** The mountains were covered with the shadow of it, and the boughs thereof were like the [h]goodly cedars. **11** She stretched out her branches unto the Sea, and her boughs unto the [i]river. **12** Why hast thou then broken down her hedges, so that all they, which pass by the way, have plucked her? **13** The wild [j]boar out of the wood hath destroyed it, and the wild beasts of the field have eaten it up. **14** Return, we beseech thee, O God of hosts: look down [k]from heaven and behold, and visit this vine, **15** And the vineyard, that thy right hand hath planted, and the young vine, which thou madest [l]strong for thyself. **16** It is burnt with fire, and cut down: and they perish at the [m]rebuke of thy countenance. **17** Let thine hand be upon the [n]man of thy right hand, and upon the son of man, whom thou madest strong for thine own self. **18** So will not we go back from thee, [o]revive thou us, and we shall call upon thy Name. **19** Turn us again, O Lord God of hosts: cause thy face to shine, and we shall be saved.

81

1 An exhortation to praise God both in heart and voice for his benefits, 8 and to worship him only. 11 God condemneth their ingratitude, 12 and showeth what great benefit they have lost through their own malice.

To him that excelleth upon [a]Gittith. A Psalm committeth to Asaph. **1** Sing [b]joyfully unto God our strength: sing loud unto the God of Jacob. **2** Take the song and bring forth the timbrel, the pleasant harp with the viol. **3** Blow the trumpet in the [c]new moon, even in the time appointed at our feast day. **4** For this is a statute for Israel, and a Law of the God of Jacob. **5** He set this in [d]Joseph for a testimony, when he came out of the land of Egypt, where I heard a language, that

---

ac. Psalm 78:51 That is, Egypt: for it was called Mizraim, or Egypt of Mizraim that was the son of Ham.
ad. Psalm 78:53 That is, they had none occasion to fear, forasmuch as God destroyed their enemies, and delivered them safely.
ae. Psalm 78:54 Meaning, Canaan, which God had consecrated to himself, and appointed to his people.
af. Psalm 78:57 Nothing more displeaseth God in the children, than when they continue in that wickedness, which their fathers had begun.
ag. Psalm 78:58 By serving God otherwise than he had appointed.
ah. Psalm 78:60 For their ingratitude he suffered the Philistines to take the Ark, which was the sign of his presence, from among them.
ai. Psalm 78:61 The Ark is called his power and beauty, because thereby he defended his people, and beautifully appeared unto them.
aj. Psalm 78:63 They were suddenly destroyed, 1 Sam. 4:10.
ak. Psalm 78:63 They had no marriage songs: that is, they were not married.
al. Psalm 78:64 Either they were slain before, or taken prisoners of their enemies, and so were forbidden.
am. Psalm 78:65 Because they were drunken in their sins, they judged God's patience to be a slumbering, as though he were drunken, therefore he answering their beastly judgment, saith, he will awake and take sudden vengeance.
an. Psalm 78:67 Showing that he spared not altogether the Israelites, though he punished their enemies.
ao. Psalm 78:69 By building the Temple, and established the kingdom, he declareth that the signs of his favor were among them.
ap. Psalm 78:72 He showeth wherein a king's charge standeth: to wit, to provide faithfully for his people, to guide them by counsel, and defend them by power.

PSALM 78

1. Exod. 14:21
2. Exod. 14:24
3. Exod. 17:6 - Num. 20:12 - Ps. 105:41
4. 1 Cor. 10:4
5. Num. 11:1
6. Exod. 17:6 - Num. 20:11 - Ps. 105:41 - 1Cor. 10:4
7. Num. 11:1
8. John 6:31 - 1 Cor. 10:3
9. Josh. 11:6 - Josh. 13:6

PSALM 79

a. Psalm 79:1 The people cry unto God against the barbarous tyranny of the Babylonians, who spoiled God's inheritance, polluted his Temple, destroyed his religion, and murdered his people.
b. Psalm 79:2 The Prophet showeth to what extremities God suffereth sometime his Church to fall, to exercise their faith, before he set his hand to deliver them.
c. Psalm 79:3 Their friends and kinsfolks durst not bury them for fear of the enemies.
d. Psalm 79:4 Whereof some came of Abraham but were degenerate: and others were open enemies to thy religion, but they both laughed at our miseries.
e. Psalm 79:5 Wilt thou utterly consume us for our sins, before thou takest us to mercy?
f. Psalm 79:8 Which we and our fathers have committed.
g. Psalm 79:8 And stay not till we have recompensed for our sins.
h. Psalm 79:9 Seeing we have none other Savior, neither can we help ourselves, and also by our salvation thy Name shall be praised: therefore, O Lord, help us.
i. Psalm 79:11 Who though in respect of God they were justly punished for their sins: yet in consideration of their cause were unjustly murdered.
j. Psalm 79:11 Which were captives among their enemies, and could look for nothing but death.
k. Psalm 79:13 We ought to desire no benefit of God, but on this condition to praise his name, Isa. 43:21.

PSALM 79

1. Jer. 10:25

PSALM 80

a. Psalm 80:1 This Psalm was made as a prayer for to desire God to be merciful to the ten tribes.
b. Psalm 80:1 Move their hearts, that they may return to worship God aright: that is, in the place where thou hast appointed.
c. Psalm 80:3 Join thy whole people, and all thy tribes together again.
d. Psalm 80:4 The faithful fear God's anger, when they perceive that their prayers are not forthwith heard.
e. Psalm 80:6 Our neighbors have continual strife and war against us.
f. Psalm 80:7 Because that repentance only cometh of God, they most instantly and ofttimes call to God for it as a means whereby they shall be saved.
g. Psalm 80:8 Seeing that of thy mercy thou hast made us a most dear possession to thee, and we through our sins are made open for wild beasts to devour us, declare again thy love, and finish the work that thou hast begun.
h. Psalm 80:10 Hebrew, cedars of God.
i. Psalm 80:11 To wit, Euphrates.
j. Psalm 80:13 That is, as well they that hate our religion, as they that hate our persons.
k. Psalm 80:14 They gave not place to tentation, knowing that albeit there were no help in earth, yet God was able to succor them from heaven.
l. Psalm 80:15 So that no power can prevail against it, and which as a young bud thou raisest up again as out of the burnt ashes.
m. Psalm 80:16 Only when thou art angry and not of the sword of the enemy.
n. Psalm 80:17 That is, upon this vine or people, whom thou hast planted with thy right hand, that they should be as one man or one body
o. Psalm 80:18 For none can call upon God but such as are raised up as it were from death to life, and regenerate by the holy Spirit.

[e]I understood not. **6** I have withdrawn his shoulder from the burden, and his hands have left the [f]pots. **7** Thou calledst in affliction, and I delivered thee, and [g]answered thee in the secret of the thunder: I proved thee at the waters of [h]Meribah. Selah. **8** [i]Hear, O my people, and I will protest unto thee: O Israel, if thou wilt hearken unto me, **9** And wilt have no strange god in thee, neither worship any strange god, **10** (For I am the Lord thy God, which brought thee out of the land of Egypt:) [j]open thy mouth wide, and I will fill it. **11** But my people would not hear my voice, and Israel would none of me, **12** So I gave them up unto the hardness of their heart, and they have walked in their own counsels. **13** [k]Oh that my people had hearkened unto me, and Israel had walked in my ways! **14** I would soon have humbled their enemies, and turned mine hand [l]against their adversaries. **15** The haters of the Lord should have been subject unto him, and their time [m]should have endured forever. **16** And God would have fed them with the [n]fat of wheat, and with honey out of the rock would I have sufficed thee.

82

1 The Prophet declaring God to be present among the Judges and Magistrates, 2 Reproveth their partiality. 3 And exhorteth them to do justice. 5 But seeing none amendment, 8 He desireth God to undertake the matter and execute justice himself.

A Psalm committeth to Aspah. **1** God standeth in the assembly of [a]gods: he judgeth among gods. **2** How long will ye judge unjustly, and accept the persons of the [b]wicked? Selah. **3** Do right to the poor and fatherless: do justice to the poor and needy. **4** Deliver the poor and [c]needy: save them from the hand of the wicked. **5** They know not and understand nothing: they walk in darkness, albeit all the [d]foundations of the earth be moved. **6** I have said, Ye are gods, and ye all are children of the most High. **7** [e]But ye shall die as a man, and ye princes shall fall like others. **8** O God, arise, therefore judge thou the earth: for thou shalt inherit [f]all nations.

83

1 The people of Israel pray unto the Lord to deliver them from their enemies both at home and far off, which imagined nothing but their destruction. 9 And they desire that all such wicked people may according as God was accustomed, be stricken with the stormy tempest of God's wrath, 18 That they may know that the Lord is most high upon the earth.

A song or Psalm committed to Asaph. **1** Keep [a]not thou silence, O God: be not still, and cease not, O God. **2** For lo, thine [b]enemies make a tumult, and they that hate thee, have lifted up the head. **3** They have taken crafty counsel against thy people, and have consulted against thy [c]secret ones. **4** They have said, Come and let us [d]cut them off from being a nation: and let the name of Israel be no more in remembrance. **5** For they have consulted together in [e]heart, and have made a league [f]against thee: **6** The tabernacles of Edom, and the Ishmaelites, Moab and the Hagarites: **7** Gebal and Ammon, and Amalek, the Philistines, with the inhabitants of [g]Tyre. **8** Assyria also is joined with them: they have been an arm to the children [h]of Lot. Selah. **9** Do thou to them as unto the [i]Midianites: as to Sisera and as to Jabin at the river of Kishon. **10** They perished at En Dor, and were [j]dung for the earth. **11** Make them, even their princes, like [1]Oreb and like Zeeb: yea, all their princes like Zebah and like Zalmunna, **12** Which have said, Let us take for our possession the [k]habitations of God. **13** O my God, make them like unto a [l]wheel, and as the stubble before the wind. **14** As the fire burneth the forest, and as the flame setteth the mountains on fire: **15** So persecute them with thy tempest, and make them afraid with thy storm. **16** Fill their faces with shame, that they may [m]seek thy Name, O Lord. **17** Let them be confounded and troubled forever: yea, let them be put to shame, and perish, **18** That they may [n]know that thou, which art calleth Jehovah, art alone, even the most High over all the earth.

84

1 David driven forth of his country, 2 Desireth most ardently to come again to the tabernacle of the Lord and the assembly of the Saints to praise God, 4 pronouncing them blessed that may so do. 6 Then he praiseth the courage of the people, that pass through the wilderness to assemble themselves in Zion. 10 Finally, with praise of this matter and confidence of God's goodness, he endeth the Psalm.

To him that excelleth upon Gittith. A Psalm committed to the sons of Korah. **1** O [a]Lord of hosts, how amiable are thy Tabernacles? **2** My soul longeth, yea, and fainted for the [b]courts of the Lord: for my heart and my flesh rejoice in the living God. **3** Yea, the sparrow hath found her an house, and the swallow a nest for her, where she may lay her young: even by thine [c]altars, O Lord of hosts, my king and my God. **4** Blessed are they that dwell in thine house, they will ever praise thee. Selah. **5** Blessed is the man whose [d]strength is in thee, and in whose heart are thy ways. **6** They going through the valley of [e]Baca, make wells therein: the rain also covereth the pools. **7** They go from [f]strength to strength, till every one appear before God in Zion. **8** O Lord God of hosts, hear my prayer, hearken, O God of Jacob. Selah. **9** Behold, O God, our shield, and look upon the face of thine [g]Anointed. **10** For [h]a day in thy courts is better than a thousand other where: I had rather be a doorkeeper in the house of my God, than to dwell in the tabernacles of wickedness. **11** For the Lord God is the sun and shield unto us: the Lord will give grace and glory, and no [i]good thing will he withhold from them that walk uprightly. **12** O Lord of hosts, blessed is the man that trusteth in thee.

85

1 Because God withdrew not his rods from his Church after their return from Babylon, first they put him in mind of their deliverance, to the intent that he should not leave the work of his grace imperfect. 5 Next they complain of their long affliction. 8 And thirdly, they rejoice in hope of felicity promised. 9 For their deliverance was a figure of Christ's kingdom, under the which should be perfect felicity.

To him that excelleth. A Psalm committed to the sons of Korah. **1** Lord, thou hast been [a]favorable unto thy land: thou hast brought again the captivity of Jacob. **2** Thou hast forgiven the iniquity of thy people, and [b]covered all their sins. Selah. **3** Thou hast withdrawn all thine anger, and hast turned back from the [c]fierceness of thy wrath. **4** Turn us, O God of our salvation, and release thine

---

PSALM 81

a. Psalm 81:1 An instrument of music brought from Geth.
b. Psalm 81:1 It seemeth that this Psalm was appointed for solemn feasts and assemblies of the people to whom for a time these ceremonies were ordained, but now under the Gospel are abolished.
c. Psalm 81:3 Under this feast he comprehendeth all other solemn days.
d. Psalm 81:5 That is, in Israel: for Joseph's family was counted the chief before that Judah was preferred.
e. Psalm 81:5 God speaketh in the person of the people because he was their leader.
f. Psalm 81:6 If they were never able to give sufficient thanks to God for this deliverance from corporal bondage, how much more are we indebted to him for our spiritual deliverance from the tyranny of Satan and sin?
g. Psalm 81:7 By a strange and wonderful fashion.
h. Psalm 81:7 Or, contention, Exod. 17:7.
i. Psalm 81:8 He condemneth all assemblies, where the people are not attentive to hear God's voice, and to give obedience to the same.
j. Psalm 81:10 God accuseth their incredulity, because they opened not their mouths to receive God's benefits in such abundance as he poureth them out.
k. Psalm 81:13 God by his word calleth all, but his secret election appointeth who shall hear with fruit.
l. Psalm 81:14 If their sins had not letted.
m. Psalm 81:15 If the Israelites had not broken covenant with God, he would have given them victory against their enemies.
n. Psalm 81:16 That is, with most fine wheat and abundance of honey.

PSALM 82

a. Psalm 82:1 The Prophet showeth that if princes and judges do not their duty, God whose authority is above them, will take vengeance on them.
b. Psalm 82:2 For thieves and murderers find favor in judgment, when the cause of the godly cannot be heard.
c. Psalm 82:4 Not only when they cry for help, but when their cause requireth aid and support.
d. Psalm 82:5 That is, all things are out of order either by their tyranny or careless negligence.
e. Psalm 82:7 No title of honor shall excuse you, but you shall be subject to God's judgment, and render account as well as other men.
f. Psalm 82:8 Therefore no tyrant shall pluck thy right and authority from thee.

PSALM 83

a. Psalm 83:1 This Psalm seemeth to have been composed as a form of prayer against the dangers that the Church was in, in the days of Jehoshaphat.
b. Psalm 83:2 He calleth them God's enemies, which are enemies to his Church.
c. Psalm 83:3 The elect of God are his secret ones: for he hideth them in the secret of his tabernacle, and preserveth them from all dangers.
d. Psalm 83:4 They were not content to take the Church as prisoner: but sought utterly to destroy it.
e. Psalm 83:5 By all secret means.
f. Psalm 83:5 They thought to have subverted thy counsel wherein the perpetuity of the Church was established.
g. Psalm 83:7 Or, Zor.
h. Psalm 83:8 The wickedness of the Ammonites and Moabites is described in that they provoked these other nations to fight against the Israelites their brethren.
i. Psalm 83:9 By these examples they were confirmed, that God would not suffer his people to be utterly destroyed, Judg. 7:21 and 4:15.
j. Psalm 83:10 Trodden under feet as mire.
k. Psalm 83:12 That is, Judea: for where his Church is, there dwelleth he among them.
l. Psalm 83:13 Because the reprobate could by no means be amended, he prayeth that they may utterly be destroyed, be unstable, and led with all winds.
m. Psalm 83:16 That is, be compelled by thy plagues to confess thy power.
n. Psalm 83:18 Though they believe not, yet they may prove by experience, that it is in vain to resist against thy counsel in establishing thy Church.

PSALM 83

1. Judg. 7:25 - Judg. 8:21

PSALM 84

a. Psalm 84:1 David complaineth that he cannot have access to the Church of God to make profession of his faith, and to profit in religion.
b. Psalm 84:2 For none but the Priests could enter into the Sanctuary, and the rest of the people into the courts.
c. Psalm 84:3 So that the poor birds have more liberty than I.
d. Psalm 84:5 Who trusteth nothing in himself, but in thee only, and learneth of thee to rule his life.
e. Psalm 84:6 That is of mulberry trees, which was a barren place: so that they which passed through, must dig pits for water: signifying, that no lets can hinder them that are fully bent to come to Christ's Church, neither yet that God will ever fail them.
f. Psalm 84:7 They are never weary but increase in strength and courage till they come to God's house.
g. Psalm 84:9 That is, for Christ's sake, whose figure I represent.
h. Psalm 84:10 He would wish to live but one day rather in God's Church, than a thousand among the worldlings.
i. Psalm 84:11 But will from time to time increase his blessings toward his more and more.

PSALM 85

a. Psalm 85:1 They confess that God's free mercy was the cause of their deliverance, because he loved the land which he had chosen.
b. Psalm 85:2 Thou hast buried them that they shall not come into judgment.
c. Psalm 85:3 Not only in withdrawing thy rod, but in forgiving of sins, and in touching our hearts to confess them.

anger toward us. **5** Wilt thou be angry with us [d]forever? and wilt thou prolong thy wrath from one generation to another? **6** Wilt thou not turn again and quicken us, that thy people may rejoice in thee? **7** Show us thy mercy, O Lord, and grant us thy [e]salvation. **8** I will hearken what the Lord God will say: for he will speak [f]peace unto his people, and to his Saints, that they turn not again to folly. **9** Surely his salvation is near to them that fear him, that glory may dwell in our land. **10** Mercy and truth shall meet, righteousness and peace shall kiss one another. **11** [g]Truth shall bud out of the earth, and righteousness shall look down from heaven. **12** Yea, the Lord shall give good things, and our land shall give her increase. **13** [h]Righteousness shall go before him, and shall set her steps in the way.

86

1 David sore afflicted and forsaken of all, prayeth fervently for deliverance: sometimes rehearsing his miseries, 5 Sometimes the mercies received. 11 Desiring also to be instructed of the Lord, that he may fear him, and glorify his Name. 14 He complaineth also of his adversaries, and requireth to be delivered from them.

A prayer of David. **1** Incline [a]thine ear, O Lord, and hear me: for I am poor and needy. **2** Preserve thou my soul, for I am [b]merciful: my God, save thou thy servant, that trusteth in thee. **3** Be merciful unto me, O Lord: for I [c]cry upon thee continually. **4** Rejoice the soul of thy servant: for unto thee, O Lord, do I lift up my soul. **5** For thou, Lord, art good and [d]merciful, and of great kindness unto all them that call upon thee. **6** Give ear, Lord, unto my prayer, and [e]hearken to the voice of my supplication. **7** In the day of my trouble I will call upon thee: for thou hearest me. **8** Among the gods there is none like thee, O Lord, and there is none [f]that can do like thy works. **9** All nations whom thou hast made, shall come and [g]worship before thee, O Lord, and shall glorify thy Name. **10** For thou art great and doest wondrous things: thou art God alone. **11** [h]Teach me thy way, O Lord, and I will walk in thy truth: knit mine heart unto thee, that I may fear thy Name. **12** I will praise thee, O Lord my God, with all mine heart: yea, I will glorify thy Name forever. **13** For great is thy mercy toward me, and thou hast delivered my soul from [i]the lowest grave. **14** O God, the proud are risen against me, and the assemblies of violent men have [j]sought my soul, and have not set thee before them. **15** But thou, O Lord, art a pitiful God and merciful, slow to anger, and great in kindness and truth. **16** Turn unto me, and have mercy upon me: give thy strength unto thy servant, and save the [k]son of thine handmaid. **17** Show a token of thy goodness toward me, that they which hate me, may see it, and be ashamed, because thou, O Lord, hast helped me and comforted me.

87

1 The holy Ghost promiseth, that the condition of the Church which was in misery after the captivity of Babylon, should be restored to great excellency. 4 So that there should be nothing more comfortable, than to be numbered among the members thereof.

A Psalm or song committed to the sons of Korah. **1** God laid his [a]foundations among the holy mountains. **2** The Lord loveth the gates of Zion above all the habitations of Jacob. **3** [b]Glorious things are spoken of thee, O city of God. Selah. **4** I will make mention of [c]Rahab and Babel among them that know me: behold Palestine and Tyre with Ethiopia, [d]There is he born. **5** And of Zion it shall be said, [e]Many are born in her: and he, even the most High shall stablish her. **6** The Lord shall count, when he [f]writeth the people, He was born there. Selah. **7** As well the singers as the players on instruments shall praise thee: all my [g]springs are in thee.

88

1 A grievous complaint of the faithful, sore afflicted by sickness, persecutions and adversity, 7 Being as it were left of God without any consolation. 13 Yet he calleth on God by faith, and striveth against desperation. 18 Complaining himself to be forsaken of all earthly help.

A song or Psalm of [1]Heman the Ezrahite to give instruction, committed to the sons of Korah for him that excelleth upon Mahalath [a]Leannoth. **1** O Lord God of my salvation, I cry day and night [b]before thee. **2** Let my prayer enter into thy presence: incline thine ear unto my cry. **3** For my soul is filled with evils, and my life draweth near to the grave. **4** I am counted among them that go down unto the pit, and am as a man without strength, **5** [c]Free among the dead, like the slain laying in the grave, when thou rememberest no more, and they are cut off from thy [d]hand. **6** Thou hast laid me in the lowest pit, in darkness, and in the deep. **7** Thine indignation lieth upon me, and thou hast vexed me with all thy [e]waves. Selah. **8** Thou hast put away mine [f]acquaintance far from me, and made me to be abhorred of them: [g]I am shut up, and cannot get forth. **9** [h]Mine eye is sorrowful through mine affliction: Lord, I call daily upon thee: I stretch out mine hands unto thee. **10** Wilt thou show [i]a miracle to the dead? or shall the dead rise and praise thee? Selah. **11** Shall thy loving kindness be declared in the grave? or thy faithfulness in destruction? **12** Shall thy wondrous works be known in the dark? and thy righteousness in the land [j]of oblivion? **13** But unto thee, have I cried, O Lord, and early shall my prayer come before thee. **14** Lord, why dost thou reject my soul, and hidest thy face from me? **15** I am afflicted and at the point of death: [k]from my youth I suffer thy terrors, doubting of my life. **16** Thine indignations go over me, and thy fear hath cut me off. **17** They came round about me daily like water, and compassed me together. **18** My lovers and friends hast thou put away from me, and mine acquaintance [l]hid themselves.

89

1 With many words doth the Prophet praise the goodness of God, 23 For his testament and covenant, that he had made between him and his elect by Jesus Christ the son of David. 38 Then doth he complain of the great ruin, and desolation of the kingdom of David, so that to the outward appearance the promise was broken. 46 Finally, he prayeth to be delivered from his afflictions, making mention of the shortness of man's life, and confirming himself by God's promise.

A Psalm to give instruction, of Ethan the Ezrahite. **1** I will [a]sing the mercies of the Lord forever: with my mouth will I declare thy truth from generation to generation. **2** For I [b]said, Mercy shall be set up forever: thy truth shalt thou [c]stablish in the very heavens. **3** [d]I have made a covenant with my chosen: I have sworn to David my servant, **4** Thy seed will I stablish forever, and set up thy throne from generation to generation. Selah. **5** O Lord, even the [e]heavens shall praise thy wondrous work: yea, thy truth in the [f]Congregation

---

d. Psalm 85:5 As in times past they had felt God's mercies, so now being oppressed by the long continuance of evils, they pray unto God that according to his nature he would be merciful unto them.
e. Psalm 85:7 He confesseth that our salvation cometh only of God's mercy.
f. Psalm 85:8 He will send all prosperity to his Church, when he hath sufficiently corrected them, also by his punishments the faithful shall learn to beware that they return not like offences.
g. Psalm 85:11 Though for a time God thus exerciseth them with his rods, yet under the kingdom of Christ they should have peace and joy.
h. Psalm 85:13 Justice shall then flourish, and have free course and passage in every place.

PSALM 86

a. Psalm 86:1 David persecuted of Saul, thus prayed, leaving the same to the Church as a monument, how to seek redress against their miseries.
b. Psalm 86:2 I am not enemy to them, but pity them though they be cruel toward me.
c. Psalm 86:3 Which was a sure token that he believed that God would deliver him.
d. Psalm 86:5 He doth confess that God is good to all, but only merciful to poor sinners.
e. Psalm 86:6 By crying and calling continually, he showeth how we may not be weary, though God grant not forthwith our request, but that we must earnestly and often call upon him.
f. Psalm 86:8 He condemneth all idols, forasmuch as they can do no works to declare that they are gods.
g. Psalm 86:9 This proveth that David prayed in the Name of Christ the Messiah, of whose kingdom he doth here prophesy.
h. Psalm 86:11 He confesseth himself ignorant till God hath taught him, and his heart variable and separate from God, till God join it to him, and confirm it in his obedience.
i. Psalm 86:13 That is, from most great danger of death: out of the which none but only the almighty hand of God could deliver him.
j. Psalm 86:14 He showeth that there can be no moderation nor equity, where proud tyrants reign, and that the lack of God's fear is as a privilege to all vice and cruelty.
k. Psalm 86:16 He boasteth not of his own virtues, but confesseth that God of his free goodness hath ever been merciful unto him, and given him power against his enemies, as to one of his own household.

PSALM 87

a. Psalm 87:1 God did choose that place among the hills, to establish Jerusalem and his Temple.
b. Psalm 87:3 Though thy glorious estate does not yet appear, yet wait with patience, and God will accomplish his promise.
c. Psalm 87:4 That is, Egypt and these other countries shall come to the knowledge of God.
d. Psalm 87:4 It shall be said of him that is regenerate and come to the Church, that he is as one that was born in the Church.
e. Psalm 87:5 Out of all quarters they shall come to the Church, and be counted as citizens.
f. Psalm 87:6 When he calleth by his word them into the Church, whom he had elected and written in the book.
g. Psalm 87:7 The Prophet setteth his whole affections and comfort in the Church.

PSALM 88

a. Psalm 88:1 That is, to humble. It was the beginning of a song, by the tune whereof this Psalm was sung.
b. Psalm 88:1 Though many cry in their sorrows, yet they cry not earnestly to God for remedy, as he did whom he confessed to be the author of his salvation.
c. Psalm 88:5 For he that is dead, is free from all cares and business of this life: and thus he saith, because he was unprofitable for all matters concerning man's life, and as it were cut off from this world.
d. Psalm 88:5 That is, from thy providence and care, which is meant according to the judgment of the flesh.
e. Psalm 88:7 The storms of thy wrath have overwhelmed me.
f. Psalm 88:8 He attributeth the loss and displeasure of his friends to God's providence, whereby he partly punisheth and partly trieth his.
g. Psalm 88:8 I see none end of my sorrows.
h. Psalm 88:9 Mine eyes and face declare my sorrows.
i. Psalm 88:10 He showeth that the time is more convenient for God to help, when men call unto him in their dangers, than to tarry till they be dead, and then raise them up again.
j. Psalm 88:12 That is, in the grave, where only the body lieth without all sense and remembrance.
k. Psalm 88:15 I am ever in great dangers and sorrows, as though my life should utterly be cut off every moment.
l. Psalm 88:18 Hebrew, were in darkness.

PSALM 88

1. 1 Kings 4:31 - Ps. 53

PSALM 89

a. Psalm 89:1 Though the horrible confusion of things might cause them to despair of God's favor, yet the manifold examples of his mercies cause them to trust in God, though to man's judgment they saw none occasion.
b. Psalm 89:2 As he that surely believed in heart.
c. Psalm 89:2 As thine invisible heaven is not subject to any alteration and change: so shall the truth of thy promise be unchangeable.
d. Psalm 89:3 The Prophet showeth what was the promise of God, whereon he grounded his faith.
e. Psalm 89:5 The Angels shall praise thy power and faithfulness in delivering thy Church.
f. Psalm 89:5 That is, in the heavens.
g. Psalm 89:6 Meaning, the Angels.

of the Saints. 6 For who is equal to the Lord in the heaven? and who is like the
Lord among the [g]sons of the gods? 7 God is very terrible in the assembly of
the [h]Saints, and to be reverenced above all that are about him. 8 O Lord God
of hosts, who is like unto thee, which art a mighty Lord, and thy truth is about
thee? 9 [i]Thou rulest the raging of the Sea: when the waves thereof arise, thou
stillest them. 10 Thou hast beaten down Rahab as a man slain: thou hast scat-
tered thine enemies with thy mighty arm. 11 The heavens are thine, the ear-
th also is thine: thou hast laid the foundation of the world, and all that therein
is. 12 Thou hast created the North and the South: [j]Tabor and Hermon shall
rejoice in thy Name. 13 Thou hast a mighty arm: strong is thy hand, and high is
thy right hand. 14 [k]Righteousness and equity are the stablishment of thy thro-
ne: mercy and truth go before thy face. 15 Blessed is the people that can [l]rejoice
in thee: they shall walk in the light of thy [m]countenance, O Lord. 16 They shall
rejoice continually in thy Name, and in thy righteousness shall they exalt them-
selves. 17 For thou art the [n]glory of their strength, and by thy favor our horns
shall be exalted. 18 For our [o]shield appertaineth to the Lord, and our King to
the Holy one of Israel. 19 Thou spakest then in a vision unto [p]thine Holy one,
and saidest, I have laid help upon one that is [q]mighty: I have exalted one chosen
out of the people. 20 I have found David my servant: with mine holy oil have I
anointed him. 21 Therefore mine hand shall be established with him, and mine
arm shall strengthen him. 22 The enemy shall not oppress him, neither shall
the wicked hurt him. 23 But I will [r]destroy his foes before his face, and plague
them that hate him. 24 My truth also and my [s]mercy shall be with him, and in
my Name shall his [t]horn be exalted. 25 I will set his hand also in the sea, and
his right hand in the [u]floods. 26 He shall cry unto me, Thou art my [v]Father,
my God, and the rock of my salvation. 27 Also I will make him my firstborn,
higher than the kings of the earth. 28 My mercy will I keep for him for ever-
more, and my Covenant shall stand fast with him. 29 His seed also will I make
to endure [w]forever, and his throne as the days of heaven. 30 But if his children
forsake my Law, and walk not in my judgments: 31 [1]If they break my statutes,
and keep not my commandments: 32 Then will I visit their transgression with
the rod, and their iniquity with strokes. 33 [x]Yet my loving kindness will I not
take from him, neither will I falsify my truth. 34 My Covenant will I not break,
nor [y]alter the thing that is gone out of my lips. 35 I have sworn once by mine
holiness, [z]that I will not fail David, saying, 36 His seed shall endure forever, and
his throne shall be as the sun before me. 37 He shall be established for evermore
as the moon, and as a faithful aawitness in the heaven. Selah. 38 But thou hast
rejected and abhorred, thou hast been angry with thine anointed. 39 Thou hast
abbroken the Covenant of thy servant, and profaned his accrown, casting it on
the ground. 40 Thou hast broken down all his walls: thou hast laid his fortres-
ses in ruin. 41 All that go by the way, spoil him: he is a rebuke unto his neigh-
bors. 42 Thou hast set up the right hand of his enemies, and made all his adver-
saries to rejoice. 43 Thou hast also turned the edge of his sword, and hast not
made him to stand in the battle. 44 Thou hast caused his dignity to decay, and
cast his throne to the ground. 45 The days of his adyouth hast thou shortened,
and covered him with shame. Selah. 46 aeLord, how long wilt thou hide thy-
self, forever? shall thy wrath burn like fire? 47 Remember afof what time I am:
wherefore shouldest thou create in vain all the children of men? 48 What man
liveth, and shall not see death? shall he deliver his soul from the hand of the grave?
Selah. 49 Lord, where are thy former mercies, which thou swarest unto David
in thy truth? 50 Remember, O Lord, the rebuke of thy servants, which I bear
in my agbosom of all the mighty people. 51 For ahthine enemies have repro-
ched thee, O Lord, because they have reproached the aifootsteps of thine Anoin-
ted. 52 Praised be the Lord for evermore. So be it, even so be it.

90

1 Moses in his prayer setteth before us the eternal favor of God toward his, 3 who are neither admonished by the brevity of their life, 7 nor by his plagues to be thankful, 12 therefore Moses prayeth God to turn their hearts, and continue his mercies toward them and their posterity forever.

A prayer of Moses, [a]the man of God. 1 Lord, thou hast been our [b]habi-
tation from generation to generation. 2 Before the [c]mountains were made, and
before thou hadst formed the earth, and the world, even from everlasting to ever-
lasting thou art our God. 3 Thou [d]turnest man to destruction: again thou sayest,
Return ye sons of Adam. 4 [e]For a thousand years in thy sight are as yesterday
when it is past, and as a watch in the night. 5 Thou hast [f]overflowed them, they
are as a sleep, in the morning he groweth like the grass: 6 In the morning it flou-
risheth and groweth, but in the evening it is cut down and withereth. 7 For we
are [g]consumed by thine anger, and by thy wrath are we troubled. 8 Thou hast
set our iniquities before thee, and our secret sins in the light of thy countenan-
ce. 9 For all our days are past in thine anger: we have [h]spent our years as a thou-
ght. 10 The time of our life is threescore years and ten, and if they be of strength,
[i]fourscore years: yet their strength is but labor and sorrow: for it is cut off quickly,
and we flee away. 11 [j]Who knoweth the power of thy wrath? for according to thy
fear is thine anger. 12 Teach us so to number our days, that we may apply our
hearts unto [k]wisdom. 13 Return (O Lord, [l]how long?) and be [m]pacified toward
thy servants. 14 Fill us with thy mercy in the morning: so shall we rejoice and be
glad all our days? 15 Comfort us according to the days that thou hast afflicted
us, and according to the years that we have seen evil. 16 [n]Let thy work be seen
toward thy servants, and thy glory upon their [o]children. 17 And let the [p]beauty
of the Lord our God be upon us, and [q]direct thou the work of our hands upon us,
even direct the work of our hands.

91

1 Here is described in what assurance he liveth, that putteth his whole trust in God, and commiteth himself wholly to his protection in all temptations. 14 A promise of God to those that love him, know him, and trust in him to deliver them, and give them immortal glory.

1 Who so dwelleth in the [a]secret of the most High, shall abide in the shadow
of the Almighty. 2 [b]I will say unto the Lord, O my hope, and my fortress: he is
my God, in him will I trust. 3 Surely I will deliver thee from the [c]snare of the
hunter, and from the noisome pestilence. 4 He will cover thee under his wings,
and thou shalt be sure under his feathers: his [d]truth shall be thy shield and buck-
ler. 5 [e]Thou shalt not be afraid of the fear of the night: nor of the arrow that

---

h. Psalm 89:7 If the Angels tremble before God's majesty and infinite justice, what earthly creature by oppressing the Church, dare set himself against God?
i. Psalm 89:9 For as he delivered the Church by the red Sea, and by destroying Rahab, that is, the Egyptians: so will he eftsoons deliver it, when the dangers be great.
j. Psalm 89:12 Tabor is a mountain Westward from Jerusalem, and Hermon Eastward: so the Prophet signifieth that all parts and places of the world shall obey God's power for the deliverance of his Church.
k. Psalm 89:14 For hereby he judgeth the world, and showeth himself a merciful Father, and faithful protector unto his.
l. Psalm 89:15 Feeling in their conscience that God is their Father.
m. Psalm 89:15 They shall be preserved by thy Fatherly providence.
n. Psalm 89:17 In that they are preserved and continue, they ought to give the praise and glory only to thee.
o. Psalm 89:18 In that that our King hath power to defend us, it is the gift of God.
p. Psalm 89:19 To Samuel and to others, to assure that David was thy chosen one.
q. Psalm 89:19 Whom I have both chosen and given him strength to execute his office, as verse 21.
r. Psalm 89:23 Though there shall be evermore enemies against God's kingdom, yet he promiseth to overcome them.
s. Psalm 89:24 I will mercifully perform my promises to him, notwithstanding his infirmities and offences.
t. Psalm 89:24 His power, glory and estate.
u. Psalm 89:25 He shall enjoy the land round about.
v. Psalm 89:26 His excellent dignity shall appear herein, that he shall be named the son of God, and the firstborn wherein he is a figure of Christ.
w. Psalm 89:29 Though for the sins of the people the state of this kingdom decayed: yet God reserved still a root, till he had accomplished this promise in Christ.
x. Psalm 89:33 Though the faithful answer not in all points to their profession, yet God will not break his Covenant with them.
y. Psalm 89:34 For God in promising hath respect to his mercy, and not to man's power in performing.
z. Psalm 89:35 Hebrew, If I lie unto David, which is a manner of oath.
aa. Psalm 89:37 As long as the Sun and Moon endure, they shall be witnesses to me of this promise.
ab. Psalm 89:39 Because of the horrible confusion of things, the Prophet complaineth to God, as though he saw not the performance of his promise. And thus discharging his cares on God, he resisteth doubt and impatience.
ac. Psalm 89:39 By this he meaneth the horrible dissipation and renting of the kingdom, which was under Jeroboam: or else by the Spirit of prophecy Ethan speaketh of those great miseries, which came soon afterward to pass at the captivity of Babylon.
ad. Psalm 89:45 He showeth that the kingdom fell before it came to perfection, or was ripe.
ae. Psalm 89:46 The Prophet in joining prayer with his complaint, showeth that his faith never failed.
af. Psalm 89:47 Seeing man's life is short, and thou hast created man to bestow thy benefits upon him, except thou haste to help, death will prevent thee.
ag. Psalm 89:50 He meaneth that God's enemies did not only slander him behind his back: but also mocked him to his face, and as it were cast their injuries in his bosom.
ah. Psalm 89:51 So he calleth them that persecute the Church.
ai. Psalm 89:51 They laugh at us which patiently wait for the coming of thy Christ.

PSALM 89
1. 2 Sam. 7:14

PSALM 90
a. Psalm 90:1 Thus the Scripture useth to call the Prophets.
b. Psalm 90:1 Thou hast been as an house and defense unto us in all our troubles and travels now this four hundred years.
c. Psalm 90:2 Thou hast chosen us to be thy people before the foundations of the world were laid.
d. Psalm 90:3 Moses by lamenting the frailty and shortness of man's life moveth God to pity.
e. Psalm 90:4 Though man thinks his life long, which is indeed most short, yea though it were a thousand years: yet in God's sight it is as nothing, and as the watch that lasteth but three hours.
f. Psalm 90:5 Thou takest them away suddenly as with a flood.
g. Psalm 90:7 Thou callest us by thy rods to consider the shortness of our life, and for our sins thou abridgest our days.
h. Psalm 90:9 Our days are not only short, but miserable, forasmuch as our sins daily provoke thy wrath.
i. Psalm 90:10 Meaning, according to the common state of life.
j. Psalm 90:11 If man's life for the brevity be miserable, much more if thy wrath lie upon it, as they which fear thee, only know.
k. Psalm 90:12 Which is, by considering the shortness of our life, and by meditating the heavenly joys.
l. Psalm 90:13 Meaning, wilt thou be angry?
m. Psalm 90:13 Or, take comfort in thy servants.
n. Psalm 90:16 Even thy mercy, which is the chiefest work.
o. Psalm 90:16 As God's promises appertained as well to their posterity, as to them, so Moses prayeth for the posterity.
p. Psalm 90:17 Meaning, that is was obscured, when he ceaseth to do good to his Church.
q. Psalm 90:17 For except thou guide us with thine holy Spirit, our enterprises can have no good success.

PSALM 91
a. Psalm 91:1 He that maketh God his defense and trust, shall perceive his protection to be a most sure safeguard.
b. Psalm 91:2 Being assured of this protection, he prayeth unto the Lord.
c. Psalm 91:3 That is, God's help is most ready for us, whether Satan assail us secretly, which he calleth a snare: or openly, which is here meant by the pestilence.
d. Psalm 91:4 That is, his faithful keeping of promise to help thee in thy necessity.
e. Psalm 91:5 The care that God hath over his, is most sufficient to defend them from all dangers.

flieth by day: **6** Nor of the pestilence that walketh in the darkness: nor of the plague that destroyeth at noon day. **7** A thousand shall fall at thy side, and ten thousand at thy right hand, but it shall not come near thee. **8** Doubtless with thine [f]eyes shalt thou behold and see the reward of the wicked. **9** For thou hast said, The Lord is mine hope: thou hast set the most High for thy refuge. **10** There shall none evil come unto thee, neither shall any plague come near thy tabernacle. **11** [g]For he shall give his Angels charge over thee to keep thee in all thy ways. **12** They shall bear thee in their hands, that thou hurt not thy foot against a stone. **13** Thou shalt walk upon the lion and asp: the [h]young lion, and the dragon shalt thou tread under feet. **14** [i]Because he hath loved me, therefore will I deliver him: I will exalt him because he hath known my Name. **15** He shall call upon me, and I will hear him: I will be with him in trouble: I will deliver him, and glorify him. **16** With [j]long life will I satisfy him, and show him my salvation.

92

1 This Psalm was made to be sung on the Sabbath, to stir up the people to acknowledge God, and to praise him in his works: the Prophet rejoiceth therein. 6 But the wicked is not able to consider, that the ungodly, when he is most flourishing, shall most speedily perish. 12 In the end is described the felicity of the just, planted in the house of God to praise the Lord.

A Psalm or song for the [a]Sabbath day. **1** It is a good thing to praise the Lord, and to sing unto thy Name, O most High, **2** To declare thy loving kindness in the [b]morning, and thy truth in the night, **3** Upon an [c]instrument of ten strings, and upon the viol, with the song upon the harp. **4** For thou Lord, hast made me glad by thy [d]works, and I will rejoice in the works of thine hands. **5** O Lord, how glorious are thy works! and thy thoughts are very deep. **6** An [e]unwise man knoweth it not, and a fool doth not understand this, **7** (When the wicked grow as the grass, and all the workers of wickedness do flourish) that they shall be destroyed forever. **8** But thou, O Lord, art [f]most High forevermore. **9** For lo, thine enemies, O Lord: for lo, thine enemies shall perish: all the workers of iniquity shall be destroyed. **10** [g]But thou shalt exalt mine horn, like the unicorns, and I shall be anointed with fresh oil. **11** Mine eye also shall see my desire against mine enemies: and mine ears shall hear my wish against the wicked, that rise up against me. **12** The righteous shall [h]flourish like a palm tree, and shall grow like a cedar in Lebanon. **13** Such as be planted in the house of the Lord, shall flourish in the courts of our God. **14** They shall still bring forth fruit in their [i]age: they shall be fat and flourishing, **15** To declare that the Lord my rock is righteous, and that none iniquity is in him.

93

1 He praiseth the power of God in the creation of the world, and beateth down all people which lift them up against his majesty, 5 and provoked to consider his promises.

1 The Lord [a]reigneth, and is clothed with majesty: the Lord is clothed, and girded with power, the world also shall be established, that it cannot be moved. **2** Thy [b]throne is established of old: thou art from everlasting. **3** [c]The floods have lifted up, O Lord: the floods have lifted up their voice: the floods lift up their waves. **4** The waves of the sea are marvelous through the noise of many waters, yet the Lord on high is more mighty. **5** Thy [d]testimonies are very sure: holiness becometh thine House, O Lord, forever.

94

1 He prayeth unto God against the violence and arrogance of tyrants, 10 warning them of God's judgments. 12 Then doth he comfort the afflicted by the good issue of their afflictions, as he felt in himself, and did set in others, and by the ruin of the wicked, 23 whom the Lord will destroy.

1 O Lord God [a]the avenger, O God the avenger, show thyself [b]clearly. **2** Exalt thyself, O Judge of the world, and render a reward to the proud. **3** Lord, how long shall the wicked, how long shall the wicked [c]triumph? **4** They prate and speak fiercely: all the workers of iniquity vaunt themselves. **5** They [d]smite down thy people, O Lord, and trouble thine heritage. **6** They slay the widow and the stranger, and murder the fatherless. **7** [e]Yet they say, The Lord shall not see: neither will the God of Jacob regard it. **8** Understand, ye unwise among the people: and ye fools, when will ye be wise? **9** He that [f]planted the ear, shall he not hear? or he that formed the eye, shall he not see? **10** Or he that chastiseth the [g]nations, shall he not correct? he that teacheth man knowledge, shall he not know? **11** The Lord knoweth the thoughts of man, that they are vanity. **12** Blessed is the man whom thou [h]chastisest, O Lord, and teachest him in thy Law, **13** That thou mayest give him rest from the days of evil, while the pit is dug for the wicked. **14** Surely the Lord will not fail his people, neither will he forsake his inheritance. **15** For [i]judgment shall return to justice, and all the upright in heart shall follow after it. **16** Who will rise up with me against the wicked? or who will take my part against the workers of iniquity? **17** If the Lord had not [j]helped me, my soul had almost dwelt in silence. **18** When I said, [k]My foot slideth, thy mercy, O Lord, stayed me. **19** In the multitude of my [l]thoughts in mine heart, thy comforts have rejoiced my soul. **20** Hath the throne of iniquity [m]fellowship with thee, which forgeth wrong for a Law? **21** They gather them together against the soul of the righteous, and condemn the innocent blood. **22** But the Lord is my refuge, and my God is the rock of mine hope. **23** And he will recompense them their wickedness, and [n]destroy them in their own malice, yea, the Lord our God shall destroy them.

95

1 An earnest exhortation to praise God, 4 for the government of the world and the election of the Church. 8 An admonition not to follow the rebellion of the old fathers, that tempted God in the wilderness. 11 For the which they might not enter into the land of promise.

1 Come, let us rejoice unto the Lord: let us sing [a]aloud unto the rock of our salvation. **2** Let us come before his face with praise: let us sing loud unto him with Psalms. **3** For the Lord is a great God, and a great King above all [b]gods, **4** In whose hand are the deep places of the earth, and the [c]heights of the mountains are his, **5** To whom the Sea belongeth, for he made it, and his hands formed the dry land. **6** Come, let us [d]worship and fall down, and kneel before the Lord our maker. **7** For he is our God, and we are the people of his pasture, and the sheep of his [e]hand: today, if ye will hear his voice, **8** [f]Harden not your heart, as in [g]Meribah, and as in the day of [h]Massah in the wilderness, **9** When your fathers [i]tempted me, proved me, though they had seen my work. **10** Forty years have I contended with this generation, and said, They are a people that [i]err in heart, for they have not known my ways. **11** Wherefore I sware in my wrath, saying, Surely they shall not enter into [j]my rest.

---

f. Psalm 91:8 The godly shall have some experience of God's judgments against the wicked even in this life, but fully they shall see it at that day when all things shall be revealed.
g. Psalm 91:11 God hath not appointed every man one Angel, but many to be ministers of his providence to keep his, and defend them in their vocation, which is the way to walk in without tempting God.
h. Psalm 91:13 Thou shalt not only be preserved from all evil, but overcome it whether it be secret or open.
i. Psalm 91:14 To assure the faithful of God's protection, he bringeth in God to confirm the same.
j. Psalm 91:16 For he is contented with that life that God giveth: for by death the shortness of this life is recompensed with immortality.

PSALM 92
a. Psalm 92:1 Which teacheth that the use of the Sabbath standeth in praising God, and not only in ceasing from work.
b. Psalm 92:2 For God's mercy and fidelity in his promises toward his, bind them to praise him continually both day and night.
c. Psalm 92:3 These instruments were then permitted, but at Christ's coming abolished.
d. Psalm 92:4 He showeth what is the use of the Sabbath day: to wit, to meditate God's works.
e. Psalm 92:6 That is, the wicked consider not God's works, nor his judgments against them, and therefore most justly perish.
f. Psalm 92:8 Thy judgments are most constant against the wicked and pass our reach.
g. Psalm 92:10 Thou wilt strengthen them with all power, and bless them with all felicity.
h. Psalm 92:12 Though the faithful seem to wither and be cut down by the wicked, yet they shall grow again and flourish in the Church of God as the cedars do in mount Lebanon.
i. Psalm 92:14 The children of God shall have a power above nature, and their age shall bring forth most fresh fruits.

PSALM 93
a. Psalm 93:1 As God by his power and wisdom hath made and governeth the world: so must the same be our defense against all enemies and dangers.
b. Psalm 93:2 Wherein thou sittest and governest the world.
c. Psalm 93:3 God's power appeareth in ruling the furious waters.
d. Psalm 93:5 Besides God's power and wisdom in creating and governing, his great mercy also appeareth in that he hath given his people his word and covenant.

PSALM 94
a. Psalm 94:1 Whose office it is to take vengeance on the wicked.
b. Psalm 94:1 Show by effect that thou art Judge of the world to punish the wicked.
c. Psalm 94:3 That is, brag of their cruelty and oppression: or esteem themselves above all others.
d. Psalm 94:5 Seeing the Church was then so sore oppressed, it ought not to seem strange to us, if we see it so now, and therefore we must call to God, to take our cause in hand.
e. Psalm 94:7 He showeth that they are desperate in malice, forasmuch as they feared not God, but gave themselves wholly to do wickedly.
f. Psalm 94:9 He showeth that it is impossible, but God should hear, see, and understand their wickedness.
g. Psalm 94:10 If God punish whole nations for their sins, it is mere folly for any one man, or else a few to think that God will spare them.
h. Psalm 94:12 God hath care over his, and chastised them for their wealth, that they should not perish forever with the wicked.
i. Psalm 94:15 God will restore the state and government of things to their right use, and then the Godly shall follow him cheerfully.
j. Psalm 94:17 He complaineth of them which would not help him to resist the enemies: yet was assured that God's help would not fail.
k. Psalm 94:18 When I thought there was no way but death.
l. Psalm 94:19 In my trouble and distress I ever found thy present help.
m. Psalm 94:20 Though the wicked judges pretend justice in oppressing the Church, yet they have not that authority of God.
n. Psalm 94:23 It is a great token of God's judgment when the purpose of the wicked is broken, but most, when they are destroyed in their own malice.

PSALM 95
a. Psalm 95:1 He showeth that God's service standeth not in dead ceremonies, but chiefly in the sacrifice of praise and thanksgiving.
b. Psalm 95:3 Even the Angels (who in respect of men are thought as gods) are nothing in his sight, much less the idols, which man's brain inventeth.
c. Psalm 95:4 All things are governed by his providence.
d. Psalm 95:6 By these three words he signifieth one thing: meaning that they must wholly give themselves to serve God.
e. Psalm 95:7 That is, the flock, whom he governeth with his own hand. He showeth wherein they are God's flock, that is, if they hear his voice.
f. Psalm 95:8 By the contemning of God's word.
g. Psalm 95:8 Or, in strife: whereof the place was so called.
h. Psalm 95:8 Or, tentation, read Exod. 17:7.
i. Psalm 95:10 They were without judgment and reason.
j. Psalm 95:11 That is, into the land of Canaan, where he promised them rest.

96

1 An exhortation both to the Jews and Gentiles to praise God for his mercy. And this specially ought to be referred to the kingdom of Christ.

1 Sing [a]unto the Lord a new song: sing unto the Lord all the earth. **2** Sing unto the Lord, and praise his Name: declare his salvation from day to day. **3** Declare his glory among all nations, and his wonders among all people. **4** For the Lord is [b]great and much to be praised: he is to be feared above all gods. **5** For all the gods of the people are [c]idols: but the Lord [d]made the heavens. **6** [e]Strength and glory are before him: power and beauty are in his Sanctuary. **7** Give unto the Lord, ye families of the people: give unto the Lord glory and [f]power. **8** Give unto the Lord the glory of his Name: bring [g]an offering, and enter into his courts. **9** Worship the Lord in the glorious Sanctuary: tremble before him all the earth. **10** Say among the [h]Nations, The Lord reigneth: Surely the world shall be stable, and not move, and he shall judge the people [i]in righteousness. **11** Let the heavens rejoice, and let the earth be glad: let the sea roar, and all that therein is. **12** Let the field be joyful, and all that is in it: let all the [j]trees of the wood then rejoice, **13** Before the Lord: for he cometh, for he cometh to judge the earth: he will judge the world with righteousness, and the people in his truth.

97

1 The Prophet exhorteth all to rejoice for the coming of the kingdom of Christ, 7 dreadful to the rebels and idolaters, 8 and joyful to the just, whom he exhorteth to innocency, 12 to rejoicing and thanksgiving.

1 The [a]Lord reigneth: let the earth rejoice: let the [b]multitude of the Isles be glad. **2** [c]Clouds and darkness are round about him: righteousness and judgment are the foundation of his throne. **3** There shall go a fire before him, and burn up his enemies round about. **4** His lightnings gave light unto the world: the earth saw it and was [d]afraid. **5** The mountains melted like wax at the presence of the Lord, at the presence of the Lord of the whole earth. **6** The heavens declare his righteousness, and all the people see his glory. **7** [e]Confounded be all they that serve graven images, and that glory in idols: worship him [f]all ye gods. **8** Zion heard of it, and was glad: and the [g]daughters of Judah rejoiced, because of thy judgments, O Lord. **9** For thou, Lord, art most High above all the earth: thou art much exalted above all gods. **10** Ye that [h]love the Lord, hate evil: he preserveth the souls of his Saints: he will deliver them from the hand of the wicked. **11** [i]Light is sown for the righteous, and joy for the upright in heart. **12** Rejoice ye righteous in the Lord, and give thanks for his holy [j]remembrance.

98

1 An earnest exhortation to all creatures to praise the Lord for his power, mercy and fidelity in his promise by Christ, 10 by whom he hath communicated his salvation to all nations.

A Psalm. **1** Sing [a]unto the Lord a new song: for he hath done marvelous things: [1]his right hand, and his holy [b]arm have gotten him the victory. **2** The Lord declared his [c]salvation: his righteousness hath he revealed in the sight of the nations. **3** He hath [d]remembered his mercy and his truth toward the house of Israel: all the ends of the earth have seen the salvation of our God. **4** All the earth, sing ye loud unto the Lord: cry out and rejoice, and sing praises. **5** Sing praise to the Lord upon the harp, even upon the harp with a singing voice. **6** With [e]shalms and sound of trumpets sing loud before the Lord the king. **7** Let the sea roar, and all that therein is, the world, and they that dwell therein. **8** Let the floods clap their hands, and let the mountains rejoice together, **9** Before the Lord: for he is come to judge the earth: with righteousness shall he judge the world: and the people with equity.

99

1 He commendeth the power, equity, and excellency of the kingdom of God by Christ over the Jews and Gentiles, 5 And provoketh them to magnify the same, and to serve the Lord, 6 following the example of the ancient fathers, Moses, Aaron, Samuel, who calling upon God, were heard in their prayers.

1 The Lord reigneth, let the [a]people tremble: he sitteth between the [1]Cherubims, let the earth be moved. **2** The Lord is great in Zion, and he is high above all the people. **3** They shall [b]praise thy great and fearful Name (for it is holy.) **4** And the King's power, that loveth judgment: for thou hast prepared equity: thou hast executed judgment and justice in Jacob. **5** Exalt the Lord our God, and fall down before his [c]footstool: for he is holy. **6** Moses and Aaron were among his Priests, [d]and Samuel among such as call upon his Name: these called upon the Lord, and he heard them. **7** He spake unto them in the cloudy pillar: they kept his testimonies, and the Law that he gave them. **8** Thou heardest them, O Lord our God: thou wast a favorable God unto them, though thou didst take vengeance for [e]their inventions. **9** Exalt the Lord our God and fall down before his holy Mountain: for the Lord our God is holy.

100

1 He exhorteth all to serve the Lord, 3 who hath chosen us, and preserved us, 4 and to enter into his assemblies to praise his Name.

A Psalm of praise. **1** Sing [a]ye loud unto the Lord, all the earth. **2** Serve the Lord with gladness; come before him with joyfulness. **3** Know ye that even the Lord is God; he hath [b]made us, and not we ourselves: we are his people, and the sheep of his pasture. **4** [c]Enter into his gates with praise, and into his courts with rejoicing: praise him and bless his Name. **5** For the Lord is good: his mercy is [d]everlasting, and his truth is from generation to generation.

101

1 David describeth what government he will observe in his house and kingdom. 5 He will punish and correct, by rooting forth the wicked, 6 and cherishing the godly persons.

A Psalm of David. **1** I will [a]sing mercy and judgment: unto thee, O Lord, will I sing. **2** I will do wisely in the perfect way, [b]till thou comest to me, I will walk in the uprightness of mine heart in the midst of my house. **3** I will set no wicked thing before mine eyes: I hate [c]the work of them that fall away: it shall not cleave unto me. **4** A froward heart shall depart from me; I will know none evil. **5** Him that privily [d]slandereth his neighbor, will I destroy: him that hath a proud look and high heart, I cannot suffer. **6** Mine eyes shall be unto the [e]faithful of the land, that they may dwell with me: he that walketh in a perfect way, he shall serve me. **7** There shall no deceitful person dwell within my house: he that telleth lies, shall not remain in my sight. **8** [f]Betimes will I destroy all the wicked of the land that I may cut off all the workers of iniquity from the City of the Lord.

PSALM 95

1. Exod. 17:1

PSALM 96

a. Psalm 96:1 The Prophet showeth that the time shall come, that all nations shall have occasion to praise the Lord for the revealing of his Gospel.
b. Psalm 96:4 Seeing he will reveal himself to all nations contrary to their own expectation, they ought all to worship him contrary to their own imaginations, and only as he hath appointed.
c. Psalm 96:5 Or, vanities.
d. Psalm 96:5 Then the idols, or whatsoever made not the heavens, are not God.
e. Psalm 96:6 God cannot be known, but by his strength and glory, the signs whereof appear in his Sanctuary.
f. Psalm 96:7 As by experience ye see that it is only due unto him.
g. Psalm 96:8 By offering up yourselves wholly unto God, declare that you worship him only.
h. Psalm 96:10 He prophecieth that the Gentiles shall be partakers with the Jews of God's promise.
i. Psalm 96:10 He shall regenerate them anew with his Spirit, and restore them to the image of God.
j. Psalm 96:12 If the insensible creatures shall have cause to rejoice, when God appeareth, much more we, from whom he hath taken malediction and sin.

PSALM 97

a. Psalm 97:1 He showeth that where God reigneth, there is all felicity, and spiritual joy.
b. Psalm 97:1 For the Gospel shall not be only preached in Judea, but through all isles and countries.
c. Psalm 97:2 He is thus described to keep his enemies in fear, which commonly contemn God's power.
d. Psalm 97:4 This fear bringeth not the wicked to true obedience, but maketh them to run away from God.
e. Psalm 97:7 He signifieth that God's judgments are in a readiness to destroy the idolaters.
f. Psalm 97:7 Let all that which is esteemed in the world fall down before him.
g. Psalm 97:8 The Jews shall have occasion to rejoice, that the Gentiles are made partakers with them of God's favor.
h. Psalm 97:10 He requireth two things of his children: the one that they detest vice, the other, that they put their trust in God for their deliverance.
i. Psalm 97:11 Though God's deliverance appear not suddenly, yet it is sown and laid up in store for them.
j. Psalm 97:12 Be mindful of his benefits and only trust in his defense.

PSALM 98

a. Psalm 98:1 That is, some song newly made in token of their wonderful deliverance by Christ.
b. Psalm 98:1 He preserveth his Church miraculously.
c. Psalm 98:2 For the deliverance of his Church.
d. Psalm 98:3 God was moved by none other means to gather his Church of the Jews and Gentiles, but because he would perform his promise.
e. Psalm 98:6 By this repetition and earnest exhortation to give praises with instruments, and also of the dumb creatures, he signifieth that the world is never able to praise God sufficiently for their deliverance.

PSALM 98

1. Isa. 59:16

PSALM 99

a. Psalm 99:1 When God delivereth his Church, all the enemies shall have cause to tremble.
b. Psalm 99:3 Though the wicked rage against God, but the godly shall praise his Name and mighty power.
c. Psalm 99:5 That is, before his Temple or Ark, where he promised to hear when they worshipped him, as now he promiseth his spiritual presence, whersoever his Church is assembled.
d. Psalm 99:6 Under these three he comprehendeth the whole people of Israel, with whom God made his promise.
e. Psalm 99:8 For the more liberally that God dealeth with his people, the more doth he punish them that abuse his benefits.

PSALM 99

1. Exod. 25:22

PSALM 100

a. Psalm 100:1 He prophecieth that God's benefit in calling the Gentiles shall be so great, that they shall have wonderful occasion to praise his mercy and rejoice.
b. Psalm 100:3 He chiefly meaneth, touching the spiritual regeneration, whereby we are his sheep and people.
c. Psalm 100:4 He showeth that God will not be worshipped, but by that means which he hath appointed.
d. Psalm 100:5 He declareth that we ought never to be weary in praising him, seeing his mercies towards us last forever.

PSALM 101

a. Psalm 101:1 David considereth what manner of King he would be, when God should place him in the throne, promising openly, that he would be merciful and just.
b. Psalm 101:2 Though as yet thou deferrest to place me in the Kingly dignity, yet will I give myself to wisdom and uprightness being a private man.
c. Psalm 101:3 He showeth that Magistrates do not their duties, except they be enemies to all vice.

102

1 It seemeth that this prayer was appointeth to the faithful to pray in the captivity of Babylon. 16 A consolation for the building of the Church: 18 whereof followeth the praise of God to be published unto all posterity. 22 The conversion of the Gentiles, 28 and the stability of the Church.

A prayer [a]of the afflicted, when he shall be in distress, and pour forth his meditation before the Lord. **1** O Lord hear my prayer, and let my [b]cry come unto thee. **2** Hide not thy face from me in the time of my trouble: incline thine ears unto me, when I call, make haste to hear me. **3** For my days are [c]consumed like smoke, and my bones are burnt like an hearth. **4** Mine heart is smitten, and withered like grass, because I forgat [d]to eat my bread. **5** For the voice of my groaning, my bones do cleave to my skin. **6** I am like a [e]pelican of the wilderness: I am like an owl of the deserts. **7** I watch, and am as a sparrow alone upon the house top. **8** Mine enemies revile me daily, and they that rage against me, have [f]sworn against me. **9** Surely I have [g]eaten ashes as bread, and mingled my drink with weeping, **10** Because of thine [h]indignation and thy wrath: for thou hast heaved me up, and cast me down. **11** My days are like a shadow that fadeth, and I am withered like grass. **12** But thou, O Lord, dost [i]remain forever, and thy remembrance from generation to generation. **13** Thou wilt arise and have mercy upon Zion: for the time to have mercy thereon, for the [j]appointed time is come. **14** For thy servants delight in the [k]stones thereof, and have pity on the dust thereof. **15** Then the heathen shall fear the Name of the Lord, and all the kings of the earth thy glory, **16** When the Lord shall build up Zion, and shall appear [l]in his glory, **17** And shall turn unto the prayer of the desolate, and not despise their prayer. **18** This shall be written for the generation to come: and the people which shall be [m]created, shall praise the Lord. **19** For he hath looked down from the height of his Sanctuary: out of the heaven did the Lord behold the earth, **20** That he might hear the mourning of the prisoner, and deliver the [n]children of death. **21** That they may declare the Name of the Lord in Zion, and his praise in Jerusalem, **22** When the people shall be gathered [o]together, and the kingdoms to serve the Lord. **23** He [p]abated my strength in the way, and shortened my days. **24** And I said, O my God, take me not away in the midst of my days: thy years endure from generation to generation. **25** Thou hast aforetime laid the foundation of the earth, and the heavens are the work of thine hands. **26** [q]They shall perish, but thou shalt endure: even they all shall wax old as doth a garment: as a vesture shalt thou change them, and they shall be changed. **27** But thou art the same, and thy years shall not fail. **28** The children of thy servants shall continue, and their seed shall stand [r]fast in thy sight.

103

1 He provoketh all to praise the Lord, which hath pardoned his sins, delivered him from destruction and given him sufficient of all good things. 10 Then he addeth the tender mercies of God, which he showeth like a most tender Father toward his children. 14 The frailty of man's life. 20 An exhortation to man and Angels to praise the Lord.

A Psalm of David. **1** My soul, [a]praise thou the Lord, and all that is within me, praise his holy Name. **2** My soul, praise thou the Lord, and forget not all his benefits. **3** Which [b]forgiveth all thine iniquity, and healeth all thine infirmities. **4** Which redeemeth thy life from the [c]grave; and crowneth thee with mercy and compassions. **5** Which satisfieth thy mouth with good things: and thy [d]youth is renewed like the eagle's. **6** The Lord executeth righteousness and judgment to all that are oppressed. **7** He made his ways known unto [e]Moses, and his works unto the children of Israel. **8** The Lord is full of compassion and mercy, slow to anger and of great kindness. **9** He will not always [f]chide, neither keep his anger forever. **10** He hath not [g]dealt with us after our sins, nor rewarded us according to our iniquities. **11** For as high as the heaven is above the earth, so great is his mercy toward them that fear him. **12** As far as [h]the East is from the West: so far hath he removed our sins from us. **13** As a father hath compassion on his children, so hath the Lord compassion on them that fear him. **14** For he knoweth whereof we be made: he remembereth that we are but dust. **15** The days of [i]man are as grass: as a flower of the field, so flourisheth he. **16** For the wind goeth over it, and it is gone, and the place thereof shall know it no more. **17** But the loving kindness of the Lord endureth forever and ever upon them that fear him, and his [j]righteousness upon children's children, **18** Unto them that keep his [k]covenant, and think upon his commandments to do them. **19** The Lord hath prepared his throne in heaven, and his kingdom ruleth over all. **20** Praise the Lord, ye [l]his Angels, that excel in strength, that do his commandment in obeying the voice of his word. **21** Praise the Lord all ye his hosts, ye his servants that do his pleasure. **22** Praise the Lord all ye his works, in all places of his dominion: my soul, praise thou the Lord.

104

1 An excellent Psalm to praise God for the creation of the world, and the governance of the same by his marvelous providence. 35 Wherein the Prophet prayeth against the wicked, who are occasions that God diminisheth his blessings.

1 My soul, praise thou the Lord: O Lord my God, thou art exceeding great, thou art [a]clothed with glory and honor. **2** Which covereth himself with light, as with a garment, and spreadeth the heavens like a curtain. **3** Which layeth the beams of his chambers in the waters, and maketh the clouds his chariot, and walketh upon the wings of the wind. **4** Which [b]maketh the spirits his messengers, and a flaming fire his ministers. **5** He set the earth upon her foundations, so that it shall never move. **6** Thou coverest it with the [c]deep as with a garment: the [d]waters would stand above the mountains. **7** But at thy rebuke they flee: at the voice of thy thunder they haste away. **8** And the mountains ascend, and the valleys descend to the place which thou hast established for them. **9** But thou hast set them a bound which they shall not pass: they shall not return to cover the earth. **10** He sendeth the springs into the valleys, which run between the mountains. **11** They shall give drink to all the [e]beasts of the field, and the wild asses shall quench their thirst. **12** By these [f]springs shall the fowls of the heaven dwell, and sing among the branches. **13** He watereth the mountains from his [g]chambers, and the earth is filled with the fruit of thy works. **14** He causeth grass to grow for the cattle, and herb for the use of [h]man, that he may bring forth bread out of the earth, **15** And wine that maketh glad the heart of man, and oil to make his face to shine, and bread that strengtheneth man's heart. **16** The high trees are satisfied, even the cedars of Lebanon, which he hath planted, **17** That the birds may make their nests there: the stork dwelleth in the fir trees. **18** The high mountains are for the [i]goats: the rocks are a refuge for the

---

d. Psalm 101:5 In promising to punish these vices, which are most pernicious in them that are about Kings, he declareth that he will punish all.
e. Psalm 101:6 He showeth what is the true use of the sword: to punish the wicked, and to maintain the good.
f. Psalm 101:8 Magistrates must immediately punish vice, lest it grow to further inconvenience: and if heathen magistrates are bound to do this, how much more they that have the charge of the Church of God?

PSALM 102

a. Psalm 102:1 Whereby is signified, that albeit we be in never so great miseries, yet there is ever place left for prayer.
b. Psalm 102:1 He declareth that in our prayer we must lively feel that, which we desire, and steadfastly believe to obtain.
c. Psalm 102:3 These excessive kinds of speech show how much the affliction of the Church ought to wound the hearts of the godly.
d. Psalm 102:4 My sorrows were so great, that I passed not for mine ordinary food.
e. Psalm 102:6 Ever mourning and solitary, casting out fearful cries.
f. Psalm 102:8 Have conspired my death.
g. Psalm 102:9 I have not risen out of my mourning to take my refection.
h. Psalm 102:10 He showeth that the afflictions did not only thus move him, but chiefly the feeling of God's displeasure.
i. Psalm 102:12 Howsoever we be frail, yet thy promise is sure, and the remembrance thereof shall confirm us forever.
j. Psalm 102:13 That is, the seventy years which by the Prophet Jeremiah thou didst appoint, Jer. 29:12.
k. Psalm 102:14 The more that the Church is in misery and desolation, the more ought the faithful to love and pity it.
l. Psalm 102:16 That is, when he shall have drawn his church out of the darkness of death.
m. Psalm 102:18 The deliverance of the Church is a most excellent benefit, and therefore he compareth it to a new creation: for in their banishment the body of the Church seemed to have been dead, which by deliverance was as it were created anew.
n. Psalm 102:20 Who now in their banishment could look for nothing but death.
o. Psalm 102:22 He showeth that God's Name is never more praised, than when religion flourisheth and the church increaseth: which thing is chiefly accomplished under the kingdom of Christ.
p. Psalm 102:23 The Church laments that they see not the time of Christ, which was promised, but have but few years and short days.
q. Psalm 102:26 If heaven and earth perish, much more man shall perish: but the Church by reason of God's promise endureth forever.
r. Psalm 102:28 Seeing thou hast chosen thy Church out of the world, and joined it to thee, it cannot but continue forever: for thou art everlasting.

PSALM 103

a. Psalm 103:1 He wakeneth his dullness to praise God, showing that both understanding and affections, mind and heart are too little to set forth his praise.
b. Psalm 103:3 That is, the beginning and chiefest of all benefits, remission of sin.
c. Psalm 103:4 For before that we have remission of our sins, we are as dead men in the grave.
d. Psalm 103:5 As the eagle, when her beak overgroweth, sucketh blood, and so is renewed in strength, even so God miraculously giveth strength to his Church above all man's expectation.
e. Psalm 103:7 As to his chief minister, and next to his people.
f. Psalm 103:9 He showeth first his severe judgment, but so soon as the sinner is humbled, he received him to mercy.
g. Psalm 103:10 Who have proved by continual experience, that his mercy hath ever prevailed against our offences.
h. Psalm 103:12 As great as the world is, so full is it of signs of God's mercies toward his faithful, when he hath removed their sins.
i. Psalm 103:15 He declareth that man hath nothing in himself to move God to mercy, but only the confession of his infirmity and misery.
j. Psalm 103:17 His just and faithful keeping of his promise.
k. Psalm 103:18 To whom he giveth grace to fear him, and to obey his word.
l. Psalm 103:20 In that that we, which naturally are slow to praise God, exhort the Angels, who willingly do it, we stir up ourselves to consider our duty, and awake out of our sluggishness.

PSALM 104

a. Psalm 104:1 The Prophet showeth that we need not to enter into the heavens to seek God, forasmuch as all the order of nature, with the propriety, and placing of the elements, are most lively mirrors to see his majesty in.
b. Psalm 104:4 As the Prophet here showeth that all visible powers are ready to serve God: so the Apostle to the Hebrews 1:7, beholdeth in this glass how the very Angels also, are obedient to his commandment.
c. Psalm 104:6 Thou makest the sea to be an ornament unto the earth.
d. Psalm 104:6 If by thy power thou didst not bridle the rage of the waters, it were not possible, but the whole world should be destroyed.
e. Psalm 104:11 If God provide for the very beasts, much more will he extend his provident care to man.
f. Psalm 104:12 There is no part of the world so barren, where most evident signs of God's blessings appear not.
g. Psalm 104:13 From the clouds.
h. Psalm 104:14 He describeth God's provident care over man, who doth not only provide necessary things for him, as herbs and other meat: but also things to rejoice and comfort him as wine and oil, or ointments.

conies. 19 He appointed [j]the moon for certain seasons: [k]the sun knoweth his going down. 20 Thou makest darkness, and it is night, wherein all the beasts of the forest creep forth. 21 The lions roar after their prey, and seek their meat [l]at God. 22 When the sun riseth, they retire, and couch in their dens. 23 [m]Then goeth man forth to his work, and to his labor until the evening. 24 O Lord, how [n]manifold are thy works! in wisdom hast thou made them all: the earth is full of thy riches. 25 So is the sea great and wide: for therein are things creeping innumerable, both small beasts and great. 26 There go the ships, yea that [o]Leviathan, whom thou hast made to play therein. 27 [p]All these wait upon thee, that thou mayest give them food in due season. 28 Thou givest it to them, and they gather it, thou openest thy hand, and they are filled with good things. 29 But if thou [q]hide thy face, they are troubled: if thou take away their breath, they die and return to their dust: 30 Again if thou [r]send forth thy spirit, they are created, and thou renewest the face of the earth. 31 Glory be to the Lord forever: let the Lord rejoice in his works. 32 He looketh on the earth and it trembleth: he toucheth the mountains, and they [s]smoke. 33 I will sing unto the Lord all my life: I will praise my God, while I live. 34 Let my words be acceptable unto him: I will rejoice in the Lord. 35 Let the sinners be [t]consumed out of the earth, and the wicked till there be no more: O my soul, praise thou the Lord. Praise ye the Lord.

105

1 He praiseth the singular grace of God, who hath of all the people of the world chosen a peculiar people to himself, and having chosen them, never ceaseth to do them good, even for his promise's sake.

1 Praise the Lord, and call upon his Name: [a]declare his works among the people. 2 Sing unto him, sing praise unto him, and talk of all his wondrous works. 3 Rejoice in his holy Name, let the heart of them that seek the Lord, rejoice. 4 Seek the Lord and his [b]strength: seek his face continually. 5 Remember his [c]marvelous works that he hath done, his wonders, and the [d]judgments of his mouth, 6 Ye seed of Abraham his servant, ye children of Jacob, which are his elect. 7 He is the Lord our God: his judgments are through all the earth. 8 He hath always remembered his covenant, and promise, that he made to a thousand generations, 9 Even that which he [e]made with Abraham, and his oath unto Isaac: 10 And since hath confirmed it to Jacob for a law, and to Israel for an everlasting covenant, 11 Saying, [f]Unto thee will I give the land of Canaan, the lot of your inheritance. 12 Albeit they were few in number, yea very few, and strangers in the land, 13 And walked about from nation to nation, from one kingdom to another people, 14 Yet suffered he no man to do them wrong, but reproved [g]Kings for their sakes, saying, 15 Touch not mine [h]anointed, and do my [i]Prophets no harm. 16 Moreover, he called a famine upon the land, and utterly brake the [j]staff of bread. 17 But he sent a man before them: Joseph was sold for a slave. 18 They held his feet in the stocks, and he was laid in irons, 19 Until [k]his appointed time came, and the counsel of the Lord had tried him. 20 The King sent and loosed him: even the Ruler of the people delivered him. 21 He made him lord of his house, and ruler of all his substance, 22 That he should bind his [l]princes unto his will, and teach his Ancients wisdom. 23 Then Israel came to Egypt, and Jacob was a stranger in the land of Ham. 24 And he increased his people exceedingly, and made them stronger than their oppressors. 25 [m]He turned their heart to hate his people, and to deal craftily with his servants. 26 Then sent he Moses his servant, and Aaron whom he had chosen. 27 They showed among them the message of his signs, and wonders in the land of Ham. 28 He sent darkness, and made it dark: and they were not [n]disobedient unto his commission. 29 [1]He turned their waters into blood, and slew their fish. 30 [2]Their land brought forth frogs, even in their King's chambers. 31 He [o]spake, and there came swarms of flies and lice in all their quarters. 32 He gave them [p]hail for rain, and flames of fire in their land. 33 He smote their vines also and their fig trees, and brake down the trees in their coasts. 34 [q]He spake and the grasshoppers came, and caterpillars innumerable, 35 And did eat up all the grass in their land, and devoured the fruit of their ground. 36 [3]He smote also all the firstborn in their land, even the beginning of all their strength. 37 He brought them forth also with silver and gold, and there was [r]none feeble among their tribes. 38 Egypt was [s]glad at their departing: for the fear of them had fallen upon them. 39 He spread a cloud to be a covering, and fire to give light in the night. 40 They [t]asked, and he brought quails, and he filled them with the bread of heaven. 41 He opened the rock, and the water flowed out, and ran in the dry places like a river. 42 For he remembered his holy [u]promise to Abraham his servant, 43 And he brought forth his people with [v]joy, and his chosen with gladness, 44 And gave them the lands of the heathen, and they took the labors of the people in possession, 45 That they might [w]keep his statutes, and observe his Laws. Praise ye the Lord.

106

1 The people dispersed under Antiochus, do magnify the goodness of God among the just and repentant: 4 Desiring to be brought again into the land by God's merciful visitation. 8 And after the manifold marvels of God wrought in their deliverance forth of Egypt, And the great ingratitude of the people rehearsed. 47 They do pray and desire to be gathered from among the heathen, to the intent that they may praise the Name of the God of Israel.

Praise ye the Lord. 1 Praise [a]ye the Lord because he is good, for his mercy endureth forever. 2 Who can express the noble acts of the Lord, or show forth all his praise? 3 Blessed are they that [b]keep judgment, and do righteousness at all times. 4 Remember me, O Lord, with the [c]favor of thy people: visit me with thy salvation, 5 That I may see the felicity of thy chosen, and rejoice in the joy of thy people, and glory with thine inheritance. 6 We have [d]sinned with our fathers: we have committed iniquity, and done wickedly. 7 Our fathers understood not thy wonders in Egypt, neither remembered they the multitude of thy mercies, but rebelled at the Sea, even at the red sea. 8 Nevertheless he [e]saved them for his Name's sake, that he might make his power to be known. 9 And he rebuked the red sea, and it was dried up, and he led them in the deep, as in the wilderness. 10 And he saved them from the adversary's hand, and delivered them from the hand of the enemy. 11 [1]And the waters covered their oppressors: not one of them was left. 12 Then [f]believed they his words, and sang praise unto him. 13 But incontinently they forgat his works, they waited not for his [g]counsel, 14 But lusted with concupiscence in the wilderness, and tempted God in the desert. 15 Then he gave them their desire: but he sent [h]leanness into their soul. 16 They envied Moses also in the tents, and Aaron the holy one of the Lord. 17 Therefore the earth opened and [i]swallowed up Dathan, and covered the company of Abiram. 18 And the fire was kindled in their assembly:

- **i.** Psalm 104:18 Or, does, roes, and such like.
- **j.** Psalm 104:19 As to separate the night from the day, and to note days, months and years.
- **k.** Psalm 104:19 That is, by his course, either far or near, it noteth summer, winter and other seasons.
- **l.** Psalm 104:21 That is, they only find meat according to God's providence, who careth even for the brute beasts.
- **m.** Psalm 104:23 To wit, when the day springeth: for the light is as it were a shield to defend man against the tyranny and fierceness of beasts.
- **n.** Psalm 104:24 He confesseth that no tongue is able to express God's works, nor mind to comprehend them.
- **o.** Psalm 104:26 Or, whale.
- **p.** Psalm 104:27 God is a most nourishing Father, who provideth for all creatures their daily foods.
- **q.** Psalm 104:29 As by thy presence all things have life: so if thou withdraw thy blessings, they all perish.
- **r.** Psalm 104:30 As the death of creatures showeth that we are nothing of ourselves: so their generation declareth that we receive all things of our Creator.
- **s.** Psalm 104:32 God's merciful face giveth strength unto the earth, but his severe countenance burneth the mountains.
- **t.** Psalm 104:35 Who infect the world, and so cause God that he cannot rejoice in his works.

PSALM 105

- **a.** Psalm 105:1 Forasmuch as the Israelites were exempted from the common condemnation of the world, and were elected to be God's people, the Prophet willeth them to show themselves mindful by thanksgiving.
- **b.** Psalm 105:4 By the strength and face he meaneth the Ark where God declared his power and his presence.
- **c.** Psalm 105:5 Which he hath wrought in the deliverance of his people.
- **d.** Psalm 105:5 Because his power was thereby as lively declared, as if he should have declared it by mouth.
- **e.** Psalm 105:9 The promise which God made to Abraham to be his God, and the God of his seed after him, he renewed and repeated it again to his seed after him.
- **f.** Psalm 105:11 He showeth that they should not enjoy the land of Canaan by any other means, but by reason of his covenant made with their fathers.
- **g.** Psalm 105:14 That is, the king of Egypt and the king of Gerar, Gen. 12:17 and 20:3.
- **h.** Psalm 105:15 Those whom I have sanctified to be my people.
- **i.** Psalm 105:15 Meaning, the old fathers, to whom God showed himself plainly, and who were setters forth of his word.
- **j.** Psalm 105:16 Either by sending scarcity, or by taking away the strength and nourishment thereof.
- **k.** Psalm 105:19 So long he suffered adversity as God had appointed, and till he had tried sufficiently his patience.
- **l.** Psalm 105:22 That the very princes of the countries should be at Joseph's commandment, and learn wisdom at him.
- **m.** Psalm 105:25 So it is in God, either to move the hearts of the wicked to love or to hate God's children.
- **n.** Psalm 105:28 Meaning, Moses and Aaron.
- **o.** Psalm 105:31 So that this vermin came not by fortune, but as God had appointed, and his prophet Moses spake.
- **p.** Psalm 105:32 It was strange to see rain in Egypt, much more it was fearful to see hail.
- **q.** Psalm 105:34 He showeth that all creatures are armed against man when God is his enemy, as at his commandment the grasshoppers destroyed the land.
- **r.** Psalm 105:37 When their enemies felt God's plagues his children by his providence were exempted.
- **s.** Psalm 105:38 For God's plagues caused them rather to depart with the Israelites, than with their lives.
- **t.** Psalm 105:40 Not for necessity, but for satisfying of their lust.
- **u.** Psalm 105:42 Which he confirmeth to the posterity, in whom after a sort the dead live and enjoy the promises.
- **v.** Psalm 105:43 When the Egyptians lamented and were destroyed.
- **w.** Psalm 105:45 This is the end, why God preserveth his Church, because they should worship, and call upon him in this world.

PSALM 105

- **1.** Exod. 7:20
- **2.** Exod. 8:6
- **3.** Exod. 12:29

PSALM 106

- **a.** Psalm 106:1 The Prophet exhorteth the people to praise God for his benefits past, that thereby their minds may be strengthened against all present troubles and despair.
- **b.** Psalm 106:3 He showeth that it is not enough to praise God with the mouth, except the whole heart agree thereunto, and all our life be thereunto framed.
- **c.** Psalm 106:4 Let the good will that thou bearest to thy people, extend unto me, that thereby I may be received into the number of thine.
- **d.** Psalm 106:6 By earnest confession as well of their own, as of their fathers' sins, they show that they had hope that God according to his promise would pity them.
- **e.** Psalm 106:8 The inestimable goodness of God appeareth in this, that he would change the order of nature, rather than his people should not be delivered, although they were wicked.
- **f.** Psalm 106:12 The wonderful works of God caused them to believe for a time, and to praise him.
- **g.** Psalm 106:13 They would prevent his wisdom and providence.
- **h.** Psalm 106:15 The abundance that God gave them, profited not, but made them pine away, because God cursed it.
- **i.** Psalm 106:17 By the greatness of the punishment the heinous offence may be considered: for they that rise against God's ministers, rebel against him.

the flame burnt up the wicked. **19** They made a calf in Horeb, and worshipped the molten image. **20** Thus they turned their [j]glory into the similitude of a bullock, that eateth grass. **21** They forgat God their Savior, which had done great things in Egypt, **22** Wondrous works in the land of Ham, and fearful things by the red sea. **23** Therefore he minded to destroy them, had [k]not Moses his chosen stood in the breach before him to turn away his wrath, lest he should destroy them. **24** Also they contemned [l]that pleasant land, and believed not his word, **25** But murmured in their tents, and hearkened not unto the voice of the Lord. **26** Therefore [m]he lifted up his hand against them, to destroy them in the wilderness, **27** And to destroy their seed among the nations, and to scatter them throughout the countries. **28** They joined themselves also unto [n]Baal of Peor, and did eat the offerings of the [o]dead. **29** Thus they [p]provoked him unto anger with their own inventions, and the plague brake in upon them. **30** But [q]Phinehas stood up, and executed judgment, and the plague was stayed. **31** [2]And it was [r]imputed unto him for righteousness from generation to generation forever. **32** They angered him also at the waters of [3]Meribah, so that [s]Moses was punished for their sakes, **33** Because they vexed his Spirit, so that he spake unadvisedly with his lips. **34** Neither destroyed they the people, as the Lord had commanded them, **35** But were mingled among the heathen, and learned their works, **36** And served their idols, which were their ruin. **37** Yea, they offered their [t]sons, and their daughters unto devils, **38** And shed innocent blood, even the blood of their sons, and of their daughters whom they offered unto the idols of Canaan, and the land was defiled with blood. **39** Thus were they stained with their own works, and went [u]a whoring with their own inventions. **40** Therefore was the wrath of the Lord kindled against his people, and he abhorred his own inheritance. **41** And he gave them into the hand of the heathen: and they that hated them were lords over them. **42** Their enemies also oppressed them, and they were humbled under their hand. **43** Many [v]a time did he deliver them, but they provoked him by their counsels: therefore they were brought down by their iniquity. **44** Yet he saw when they were in affliction, and he heard their cry. **45** And he remembered his covenant toward them, and [w]repented according to the multitude of his mercies, **46** And gave them favor in the sight of all them that led them captives. **47** Save us, O Lord our God, and [x]gather us from among the heathen, that we may praise thine holy Name, and glory in thy praise. **48** Blessed be the Lord God of Israel forever and ever, and let all the people say, So be it. Praise ye the Lord.

107

1 The Prophet exhorteth all those that are redeemed by the Lord and gathered unto him, to give thanks, 9 for this merciful providence of God governing all things at his good pleasures, 20 sending good and evil, prosperity and adversity to bring men unto him. 42 Therefore as the righteous thereat rejoice, so shall the wicked have their mouth stopped.

1 Praise [a]the Lord, because he is good: for his mercy endureth forever. **2** Let them, [b]which have been redeemed of the Lord, show how he hath delivered them from the hand of the oppressor, **3** And gathered them out of the lands, from the East and from the West, from the North and from the [c]South. **4** When they wandered in the desert and wilderness out of the way, and found no city to dwell in, **5** [d]Both hungry and thirsty, their soul fainted in them. **6** Then they cried unto the Lord in their trouble, and he delivered them from their distress, **7** And led them forth by the right way, that they might go to a city of habitation. **8** Let them therefore confess before the Lord his loving kindness, and his wonderful works before the sons of men. **9** For he satisfied the thirsty soul, and filled the hungry soul with goodness. **10** They that dwell in darkness and in the shadow of death, being bound in misery and iron, **11** Because they [e]rebelled against the words of the Lord, and despised the counsel of the most High, **12** When he humbled their heart with heaviness, then they fell down, and there was no helper. **13** Then they [f]cried unto the Lord in their trouble, and he delivered them from their distress. **14** He brought them out of darkness, and out of the shadow of death, and brake their bands asunder. **15** Let them therefore confess before the Lord his loving-kindness, and his wonderful works before the sons of men. **16** For he hath broken the [g]gates of brass, and burst the bars of iron asunder, **17** [h]Fools by reason of their transgression, and because of their iniquities are afflicted. **18** Their soul abhorreth all meat, and they are brought to death's door. **19** Then they cry unto the Lord in their trouble, and he delivereth them from their distress. **20** [i]He sendeth his word and healeth them, and delivereth them from their [j]graves. **21** Let them therefore confess before the Lord his loving kindness, and his wonderful works before the sons of men, **22** And let them offer sacrifices of [k]praise, and declare his works with rejoicing. **23** They that go down to the [l]sea in ships, and occupy by the great waters, **24** They see the works of the Lord, and his wonders in the deep. **25** For he commandeth and raiseth the stormy wind, and it lifteth up the waves thereof. **26** They mount up to the heaven, and descend to the deep, so that their soul [m]melteth for trouble. **27** They are tossed to and fro, and stagger like a drunken man, and all their [n]cunning is gone. **28** Then they cry unto the Lord in their trouble, and he bringeth them out of their distress. **29** He turneth the storm to calm, so that the waves thereof are still. **30** When they are [o]quieted, they are glad, and he bringeth them unto the haven, where they would be. **31** Let them therefore confess before the Lord his loving kindness, and his wonderful works before the sons of men. **32** And let them exalt him in the [p]congregation of the people, and praise him in the assembly of the Elders. **33** He turneth the floods to a wilderness, and the springs of waters into dryness, **34** And a fruitful land into [q]barrenness, for the wickedness of them that dwell therein. **35** Again he [r]turneth the wilderness into pools of water, and the dry land into water springs. **36** And there he placeth the hungry, and they build a city to dwell in, **37** And sow the fields, and plant vineyards, which bring forth fruitful [s]increase. **38** For he blesseth them, and they multiply exceedingly, and he diminisheth not their cattle. **39** [t]Again men are diminished, and brought low by oppression, evil and sorrow. **40** He poureth [u]contempt upon princes, and causeth them to err in desert places out of the way. **41** Yet he raiseth up the poor out of misery, and maketh him families like a flock of sheep. **42** The [v]righteous shall see it, and rejoice, and all iniquity shall stop her mouth. **43** Who is wise that he may observe these things? for they shall understand the loving kindness of the Lord.

108

This Psalm is composed of two other Psalms before the seven and fiftieth and the sixtieth. The matter here contained is, 1 That David giveth himself with heart and voice to praise the Lord, 7 and assureth himself of the promise of God concerning his kingdom over Israel, and his power against other nations: 11 Who though he seem to forsake us for a time, yet he alone will in the end cast down our enemies.

---

j. Psalm 106:20 He showeth that all idolaters renounce God to be their glory, when instead of him they worship any creature, much more wood, stone, metal, or calves.
k. Psalm 106:23 If Moses by his intercession had not obtained God's favor against their rebellions.
l. Psalm 106:24 That is, Canaan, which was as it were an earnest penny of the heavenly inheritance.
m. Psalm 106:26 That is, he sware. Sometimes also it meaneth, to punish.
n. Psalm 106:28 Which was the idol of the Moabites.
o. Psalm 106:28 Sacrifices offered to the dead idols.
p. Psalm 106:29 Signifying that whatsoever man inventeth of himself to serve God by, is detestable, and provoketh his anger.
q. Psalm 106:30 When all others neglected God's glory, he in his zeal killed the adulterers and prevented God's wrath.
r. Psalm 106:31 This act declared his lively faith, and for his faith's sake was accepted.
s. Psalm 106:32 If so notable a Prophet of God escape not punishment, though others provoked him to sin, how much more shall they be subject to God's judgment, which cause God's children to sin?
t. Psalm 106:37 He showeth how monstrous a thing idolatry is, which can win us to things abhorring to nature, whereas God's word cannot obtain most small things.
u. Psalm 106:39 Then true chastity is to cleave wholly and only unto God.
v. Psalm 106:43 The prophet showeth that neither by menaces, nor promises we can come to God, except we be altogether newly reformed, and that his mercy overcover and hide our malice.
w. Psalm 106:45 Not that God is changeable in himself, but that then he seemeth to us to repent when he altereth his punishment, and forgiveth us.
x. Psalm 106:47 Gather thy Church, which is dispersed, and give us constancy under the cross, that with one consent we may all praise thee.

PSALM 106
1. Exod. 14:27
2. Num. 25:12
3. Num. 20:13 - Ps. 95:8

PSALM 107
a. Psalm 107:1 This notable sentence was in the beginning used as the foot or tenor of the song, which was oftentimes repeated.
b. Psalm 107:2 As this was true in the Jews, so there is none of God's elect, that feel not his help in their necessity.
c. Psalm 107:3 Or, from the sea: meaning the red sea, which is on the South part of the land.
d. Psalm 107:5 He showeth that there is none affliction so grievous, out of the which God will not deliver his, and also exhorteth them that are delivered to be mindful of so great a benefit.
e. Psalm 107:11 Then the true way to obey God, is to follow his express commandment: also hereby all are exhorted to descend into themselves, forasmuch as none are punished but for their sins.
f. Psalm 107:13 He showeth that the cause why God doth punish us extremely, is because we can be brought unto him by none other means.
g. Psalm 107:16 When there seemeth to man's judgment no recovery, but all things are brought to despair, then God chiefly showeth his mighty power.
h. Psalm 107:17 They that have no fear of God, by his sharp rods are brought to call upon him, and so find mercy.
i. Psalm 107:20 By healing them he declareth his good will toward them.
j. Psalm 107:20 Meaning, their diseases, which had almost brought them to the grave and corruption.
k. Psalm 107:22 Praise and confession of God's benefits are the true sacrifices of the godly.
l. Psalm 107:23 He showeth by the sea what care God hath over man, for in that that he delivereth them from the great danger of the sea, he delivereth them, as it were from a thousand deaths.
m. Psalm 107:26 Their fear and danger is so great.
n. Psalm 107:27 When their art and means fail them, they are compelled to confess that only God's providence doth preserve them.
o. Psalm 107:30 Though before every drop seemed to fight one against another, yet at his commandment they are as still, as though they were frozen.
p. Psalm 107:32 This great benefit ought not only to be considered particularly, but magnified in all places and assemblies.
q. Psalm 107:34 Or, saltness.
r. Psalm 107:35 For the love that he beareth to his Church, he changeth the order of nature for their commodity.
s. Psalm 107:37 Continual increase and yearly.
t. Psalm 107:39 As God by his providence doth exalt men, so doth he also humble them by afflictions to know themselves.
u. Psalm 107:40 For their wickedness and tyranny he causeth the people and subjects to contemn them.
v. Psalm 107:42 They, whose faith is lightened by God's spirit, shall rejoice to see God's judgments against the wicked and ungodly.

PSALM 108
a. Psalm 108:1 This earnest affection declareth that he is free from hypocrisy, and that sluggishness stayeth him not.
b. Psalm 108:1 Or, my glory, because it chiefly setteth forth the glory of God.

A song or Psalm of David. 1 O God, mine heart is [a]prepared, so is [b]my
tongue: I will sing and give praise. 2 Awake viol and harp, I will awake ear-
ly. 3 I will praise thee, O Lord, among the [c]people, and I will sing unto thee
among the nations. 4 For thy mercy is great above the heavens, and thy truth
unto the clouds. 5 [d]Exalt thyself, O God, above the heavens, and let thy glory
be upon all the earth, 6 That thy beloved may be delivered: [e]help with thy right
hand and hear me. 7 God hath spoken in his [f]holiness: therefore I will rejoice, I
shall divide Shechem and measure the valley of Succoth. 8 Gilead shall be mine,
and Manasseh shall be mine: Ephraim also shall be the strength of mine head: Ju-
dah is my lawgiver. 9 [1]Moab shall be my washpot: over Edom will I cast out my
shoe: upon Palestine will I triumph. 10 Who will lead me into the strong city?
who will bring me unto Edom? 11 [g]Wilt not thou, O God, which hadst forsa-
ken us, and didst not go forth, O God, with our armies? 12 Give us help against
trouble: for vain is the help of man. 13 Through God we shall do valiantly: for
he shall tread down our enemies.

109

1 David being falsely accused by flatterers unto Saul, prayeth God to help him, and to destroy his enemies. 8 And under them he speaketh of Judas the traitor unto Jesus Christ, and of all the like enemies of the children of God: 27 And desireth so to be delivered, that his enemies may know the work to be of God. 30 Then doth he promise to give praise unto God.

To him that excelleth. A Psalm of David. 1 Hold not thy tongue, O
God of my [a]praise. 2 For the mouth of the wicked, and the mouth full of de-
ceit are opened upon me: they have spoken to me with a lying tongue. 3 They
compassed me about also with words of hatred, and fought against me without
a cause. 4 For my friendship they were my adversaries, [b]but I gave myself to
prayer. 5 And they have rewarded me evil for good, and hatred for my friend-
ship. 6 [c]Set thou the wicked over him, and let the adversary stand at his right
hand. 7 When he shall be judged, let him be condemned, and let his [d]prayer be
turned into sin. 8 Let his days be few, and let another take his [e]charge. 9 Let
his children be fatherless, and his wife a widow. 10 Let his children be vaga-
bonds, and beg and seek bread, coming out of their places destroyed. 11 Let [f]the
extortioner catch all that he hath, and let the strangers spoil his labor. 12 Let
there be none to extend mercy unto him: neither let there be any to show mercy
upon his fatherless children. 13 Let his posterity be destroyed, and in the gene-
ration following, let their name be put out. 14 [g]Let the iniquity of his fathers
be had in remembrance with the Lord: and let not the sin of his mother be done
away. 15 But let them always be before the Lord, that he may cut off their me-
morial from the earth. 16 Because [h]he remembered not to show mercy, but per-
secuted the afflicted and poor man, and the sorrowful hearted to slay him. 17 As
he loved cursing, [i]so shall it come unto him, and as he loved not blessing, so shall
it be far from him. 18 As he clothed himself with cursing like a raiment, so shall
it come into his bowels like water, and like oil into his bones. 19 Let it be unto
him as a garment to cover him, and for a girdle, wherewith he shall be always gir-
ded. 20 Let this be the reward of mine adversary [j]from the Lord, and of them
that speak evil against my soul. 21 But thou, O Lord my God, deal with me
according unto thy [k]Name: deliver me, (for thy mercy is good) 22 Because I
am poor and needy, and mine heart is wounded within me. 23 I depart like the
shadow that declineth, and am shaken off as the [l]grasshopper. 24 My knees are
weak through fasting, and my flesh [m]hath lost all fatness. 25 I became also a re-
buke unto them: they that looked upon me, shaked their heads. 26 Help me, O
Lord my God: [n]save me according to thy mercy. 27 And they shall know that
this is thine hand, and that thou, Lord, hast done it. 28 Though [o]they curse,
yet thou wilt bless: they shall arise and be confounded, but thy servant shall rejoi-
ce. 29 Let mine adversaries be clothed with shame, and let them cover them-
selves with their confusion as with a cloak. 30 I will give thanks unto the Lord
greatly with my [p]mouth, and praise him among the multitude. 31 For he will
stand at the right hand of the poor, to save him from them that would [q]condemn
his soul.

110

1 David prophesieth of the power and everlasting kingdom given to Christ, 4 and of his Priesthood, which should put an end to the Priesthood of Levi.

A Psalm of David. 1 The [a]Lord said unto my Lord, Sit thou at my right
hand, until I make thine enemies thy footstool. 2 The Lord shall send the rod
of thy power out of [b]Zion: be thou ruler in the midst of thine enemies. 3 Thy
people shall come willingly at the time of assembling [c]thine army in holy beauty:
the youth of thy womb shall be as the morning dew. 4 The Lord sware, and will
not repent, Thou art a Priest forever, after the order of [d]Melchizedek. 5 The Lord
that is at thy right hand, shall wound kings in the day of his wrath. 6 He shall
be judge among the heathen: he shall fill all with dead bodies, and smite the [e]head
over great countries. 7 He shall [f]drink of the brook in the way: therefore shall
he lift up his head.

111

1 He giveth thanks to the Lord for his merciful works toward his Church, 10 and declareth wherein true wisdom and right knowledge consisteth.

Praise ye the Lord. 1 I will [a]praise the Lord with my whole heart in the
assembly and the congregation of the just. 2 The works of the Lord are [b]great,
and ought to be sought out of all them that love them. 3 His work is beautiful
and glorious, and his righteousness endureth forever. 4 He hath made his won-
derful works to be had in remembrance: the Lord is merciful and full of compas-
sion. 5 He hath given [c]a [d]portion unto them that fear him: he will ever be min-
dful of his covenant. 6 He hath showed to his people the power of his works,
in giving unto them the heritage of the heathen. 7 The [e]works of his hands are
truth and judgment: all his statutes are true. 8 They are established forever and
ever, and are done in truth and equity. 9 He sent redemption unto his people:
he hath commanded his covenant forever: holy and fearful is his Name. 10 [f]The
beginning of wisdom is the fear of the Lord: all they that observe [g]them, have good
understanding: his praise endureth forever.

112

1 He praiseth the felicity of them that fear God, 10 and condemneth the cursed state of the contemners of God.

Praise ye the Lord. 1 Blessed is the man that [a]feareth the Lord, and deli-
ghteth greatly in his commandments. 2 His seed shall be mighty upon earth: the
generation of the righteous shall be blessed. 3 [b]Riches and treasures shall be in

---

c. Psalm 108:3 He prophecieth of the calling of the Gentiles: for except they were called, they could not hear the goodness of God.
d. Psalm 108:5 Let all the world see thy judgments in that that thou art God over all, and so confess that thou art glorious.
e. Psalm 108:6 When God by his benefits maketh us partakers of his mercies, he admonisheth us to be earnest in prayer, to desire him to continue and finish his graces.
f. Psalm 108:7 As he hath spoken to Samuel concerning me, so will he show himself constant, and holy in his promise, so that these nations following shall be subject unto me.
g. Psalm 108:11 From the sixth verse of this Psalm unto the last, read the exposition of Ps. 60:5.

PSALM 108

1. Ps. 60:8

PSALM 109

a. Psalm 109:1 Though all the world condemn me, yet thou wilt approve mine innocence, and that is a sufficient praise to me.
b. Psalm 109:4 To declare that I had no other refuge, but thee, in whom my conscience was at rest.
c. Psalm 109:6 Whether it were Doeg, or Saul, or some familiar friend that had betrayed him, he prayeth not of private affection, but moved by God's Spirit, that God would take vengeance upon him.
d. Psalm 109:7 As to the elect all things turn to their profit: so to the reprobate, even those things that are good, turn to their damnation.
e. Psalm 109:8 This was chiefly accomplished in Judas, Acts 1:20.
f. Psalm 109:11 He declareth that the curse of God lieth upon the extortioners, who thinking to enrich their children by their unlawfull gotten goods, are by God's just judgment deprived of all.
g. Psalm 109:14 Thus punisheth the Lord to the third and fourth generation the wickedness of the parents in their wicked children.
h. Psalm 109:16 He showeth that God accustometh to plague them after a strange sort that show themselves cruel toward others.
i. Psalm 109:17 Thus giveth the Lord to every man the thing wherein he delighteth, that the reprobate cannot accuse God of wrong, when they are given up to their lusts and reprobate minds.
j. Psalm 109:20 For being destitute of man's help, he fully trusted in the Lord, that he would deliver him.
k. Psalm 109:21 As thou art named merciful, gracious and long suffering, so show thyself in effect.
l. Psalm 109:23 Meaning, that he hath no stay nor assurance in this world.
m. Psalm 109:24 For hunger, that came of sorrow, he was lean, and his natural moisture failed him.
n. Psalm 109:26 The more grievously Satan assailed him, the more earnest and instant was he in prayer.
o. Psalm 109:28 They shall gain nothing by cursing me.
p. Psalm 109:30 Not only in confessing it secretly in myself, but also in declaring it before all the congregation.
q. Psalm 109:31 Hereby he showeth that he had not to do with them that were of little power, but with the judges and princes of the world.

PSALM 110

a. Psalm 110:1 Jesus Christ in Matt. 22:44, giveth the interpretation hereof, and showeth that this cannot properly be applied unto David but to himself.
b. Psalm 110:2 And thence it shalt stretch through all the world: and this power chiefly standeth in the preaching of his word.
c. Psalm 110:3 By the word thy people shall be assembled into thy Church whose increase shall be so abundant and wonderous as the drops of the water.
d. Psalm 110:4 As Melchizedek the figure of Christ was both a King and Priest, so this effect cannot be accomplished on any king save only Christ, Heb. 7:26.
e. Psalm 110:6 No power shall be able to resist him.
f. Psalm 110:7 Under this similitude of a captain that is so greedy to destroy his enemies, that he will not scarce drink by the way, he showeth how God will destroy his enemies.

PSALM 111

a. Psalm 111:1 The Prophet declareth that he will praise God both privately and openly, and that from the heart, as he that consecrateth himself wholly and only unto God.
b. Psalm 111:2 He showeth that God's works are a sufficient cause wherefore we should praise him, but chiefly his benefits toward his Church.
c. Psalm 111:5 God hath given to his people all that was necessary for them, and will do still even for his covenant's sake, and in this sense the Hebrew word is taken, Prov. 30:8 and 31:15.
d. Psalm 111:5 Or, prey, and food.
e. Psalm 111:7 As God promised to take the care of his Church: so in effect doth he declare himself just and true in the government of the same.
f. Psalm 111:10 They only are wise, that fear God, and none have understanding, but they that obey the word.
g. Psalm 111:10 To wit, his commandments, as verse 7.

PSALM 112

a. Psalm 112:1 He meaneth that reverent fear, which is in the children of God, which causeth them to delight only in the word of God.

his house, and his righteousness endureth forever. **4** Unto the [c]righteous ariseth light in darkness: he is merciful and full of compassion and righteous. **5** A good man is merciful, and [d]lendeth, and will measure his affairs by judgment. **6** Surely he shall never be moved: but the righteous shall be had in everlasting remembrance. **7** He will not be afraid of evil tidings: for his heart is fixed, and believeth in the Lord. **8** His heart is established: therefore he will not fear, until he see his desire upon his enemies. **9** He hath [e]distributed and given to the poor: his righteousness remaineth forever: his [f]horn shall be exalted with glory. **10** The wicked shall see it, and be angry: he shall gnash with his teeth, and [g]consume away: the desire of the wicked shall perish.

113

1 An exhortation to praise the Lord for his providence 7 in that that contrary to the course of nature he worketh in his Church.

Praise ye the Lord. **1** Praise, O ye servants of the Lord, [a]praise the Name of the Lord. **2** Blessed be the Name of the Lord from henceforth and forever. **3** The Lord's Name is praised from the rising of the sun, unto the going down of the same. **4** The Lord is high above all [b]nations, and his glory above the heavens. **5** Who is like unto the Lord our God, that hath his dwelling on high. **6** Who abaseth himself to behold things in the heavens and in the earth! **7** He raiseth the needy out of the dust, and lifteth up the [c]poor out of the dung, **8** That he may set him with the princes, even with the princes of his people. **9** He maketh the barren woman to dwell with a family, and a joyful mother of children. Praise ye the Lord.

114

1 How the Israelites were delivered forth of Egypt, and of the wonderful miracles that God wrought at that time. Which put us in remembrance of God's great mercy toward his Church, who when the course of nature faileth, preserveth his miraculously.

1 When [1]Israel went out of Egypt, and the house of Jacob from the [a]barbarous people, **2** Judah was his [b]sanctification, and Israel his dominion. **3** The sea saw it, and fled: Jordan was turned back. **4** The [c]mountains leaped like rams, and the hills as lambs! **5** What ailed thee, O sea, that thou fleddest? O Jordan, why wast thou turned back? **6** Ye mountains why leaped ye like rams, and ye hills as lambs? **7** The [d]earth trembled at the presence of the Lord, at the presence of the God of Jacob, **8** Which [e]turneth the rock into waterpools, and the flint into a fountain of water.

115

1 A prayer of the faithful oppressed by idolatrous tyrants, against whom they desire that God would succor them, 9 trusting most constantly that God will preserve them in this their need, seeing, that he hath adopted and received them into his favor. 13 Promising finally that they will not be unmindful of so great a benefit if it would please God to hear their prayer, and deliver them by his omnipotent power.

1 Not [a]unto us, O Lord, not unto us, but unto thy Name give the glory for thy loving mercy, and for thy truth's sake. **2** Wherefore shall the heathen say, [b]Where is now their God? **3** But our God is in heaven: he doeth whatsoever he [c]will. **4** Their idols are [d]silver and gold, even the work of men's hands. **5** They have a mouth, and speak not: they have eyes, and see not. **6** They have ears, and hear not: they have noses and smell not. **7** They have [e]hands, and touch not: they have feet, and walk not: neither make they a sound with their throat. **8** They that make them are [f]like unto them: so are all that trust in them. **9** O Israel, trust thou in the Lord: for he is their help, and their shield. **10** [g]O house of Aaron trust ye in the Lord, for he is their help, and their shield. **11** Ye that fear the Lord, trust in the Lord: for he is their helper, and their shield. **12** The Lord hath been mindful of us, he will bless, he [h]will bless the house of Israel, he will bless the house of Aaron. **13** He will bless them that fear the Lord, both small and great. **14** The Lord will increase his graces toward you, even toward you, and toward your children. **15** Ye are blessed of the Lord, which [i]made the heaven and the earth. **16** The [j]heavens, even the heavens are the Lord's: but he hath given the earth to the sons of men. **17** The dead praise not the Lord, neither any that [k]go down into the place of silence. **18** But we will praise the Lord from henceforth and forever. Praise ye the Lord.

116

1 David being in great danger of Saul in the desert of M…, perceiving the great and inestimable love of God toward him, magnifieth such great mercies, 13 and protesteth that he will be thankful for the same.

1 I [a]love the Lord, because he hath heard my voice and my prayers. **2** For he hath inclined his ear unto me, when I did call upon him [b]in my days. **3** When the snares of death compassed me, and the griefs of the grave caught me: When I found trouble and sorrow. **4** Then I called upon the Name of the Lord, saying, I beseech thee, O Lord, deliver my soul. **5** The Lord is [c]merciful and righteous, and our God is full of compassion. **6** The Lord preserveth the simple: I was in misery, and he saved me. **7** Return unto thy rest, O [d]my soul: for the Lord hath been beneficial unto thee, **8** Because thou hast delivered my soul from death, mine eyes from tears, and my feet from falling. **9** I shall [e]walk before the Lord in the land of the living. **10** [f]I believed, therefore did I speak: for I was sore troubled. **11** I said in my [g]fear, All men are liars. **12** What shall I render unto the Lord for all his benefits toward me? **13** I will [h]take the cup of salvation, and call upon the Name of the Lord. **14** I will pay my vows unto the Lord, even now in the presence of all his people. **15** Precious in the sight of the Lord is the [i]death of his Saints. **16** Behold, Lord: for I am thy servant, I am thy servant, and the son of thine handmaid: thou hast broken my bonds. **17** I will offer to thee a sacrifice of praise, and will call upon the Name of the Lord. **18** I will pay my [j]vows unto the Lord, even now in the presence of all his people, **19** In the courts of the Lord's house, even in the midst of thee, O Jerusalem. Praise ye the Lord.

117

1 He exhorteth the Gentiles to praise God, because he hath accomplished as well to them as to the Jews, the promise of life everlasting by Jesus Christ.

1 All [1]nations, praise ye the Lord: all ye people, praise him. **2** For his loving kindness is great toward us, and the [a]truth of the Lord endureth forever. Praise ye the Lord.

---

b. Psalm 112:3 The godly shall have abundance, and contentment, because their heart is satisfied in God only.
c. Psalm 112:4 The faithful in all their adversities, know that all shall go well with them, for God will be merciful and just.
d. Psalm 112:5 He showeth what is the fruit of mercy to lend freely; and not for gain; and so to measure his doings that he may be able to help where need requireth, and not to bestow all on himself.
e. Psalm 112:9 The godly pinch not niggardly, but distribute liberally, as the necessity of the poor requireth, and as his power is able.
f. Psalm 112:9 His power and prosperous estate.
g. Psalm 112:10 The blessings of God upon his children shall cause the wicked to die for envy.

PSALM 113

a. Psalm 113:1 By this oft repetition he stirreth up our cold dullness to praise God, seeing his works are so wonderful, and that we are created for the same cause.
b. Psalm 113:4 If God's glory shine through all the world, and therefore of all ought to be praised, what great condemnation were it to his people, among whom chiefly it shineth, if they should not earnestly extol his Name?
c. Psalm 113:7 By preferring the poor to high honor and giving the barren children, he showeth that God worketh not only in his Church by ordinary means, but also by miracles.

PSALM 114

a. Psalm 114:1 That is, from them that were of a strange language.
b. Psalm 114:2 The whole people were witnesses of his holy majesty, in adopting them, and of his mighty power in delivering them.
c. Psalm 114:4 Seeing that these dead creatures felt God's power, and after a sort saw it, much more his people ought to consider it, and glorify him for the same.
d. Psalm 114:7 Ought then his people to be insensible when they see his power and majesty?
e. Psalm 114:8 That is, caused miraculously water to come out of the rock in most abundance, Exod. 17:6.

PSALM 114

1. Exod. 13:5

PSALM 115

a. Psalm 115:1 Because God promised to deliver them, not for their sakes, but for his Name, Isa. 48:11, therefore they ground their prayer upon this promise.
b. Psalm 115:2 When the wicked see that God accomplisheth not his promise as they imagine, they think there is no God.
c. Psalm 115:3 No impediments can let his work, but he useth even the impediments to serve his will.
d. Psalm 115:4 Seeing that neither the matter nor the form can commend their idols, it followeth that there is nothing why they should be esteemed.
e. Psalm 115:7 He showeth what great vanity it is to ask help of them, which not only have no help in them, but lack sense and reason.
f. Psalm 115:8 As much without sense, as blocks and stones.
g. Psalm 115:10 For they were appointed by God as instructors and teachers of faith and religion for others to follow.
h. Psalm 115:12 That is, he will continue his graces toward his people.
i. Psalm 115:15 And therefore doth still govern and continue all things therein.
j. Psalm 115:16 And they declare enough his sufficiency, so that the world serveth him nothing, but to show his fatherly care toward men.
k. Psalm 115:17 Though the dead set forth God's glory, yet he meaneth here, that they praise him not in his Church and Congregation.

PSALM 116

a. Psalm 116:1 He granteth that no pleasure is so great as to feel God's help in our necessity, neither that anything more stirreth up our love toward him.
b. Psalm 116:2 That is in convenient time to seek help, which was when he was in distress.
c. Psalm 116:5 He showeth forth the fruit of his love in calling upon him, confessing him to be just and merciful, and to help them that are destitute of aid and counsel.
d. Psalm 116:7 Which was unquieted before, now rest upon the Lord, for he hath been beneficial towards thee.
e. Psalm 116:9 The Lord will preserve me, and save my life.
f. Psalm 116:10 I felt all these things, and therefore was moved by faith to confess them, 2 Cor. 4:13.
g. Psalm 116:11 In my great distress I thought God would not regard man, which is but lies and vanity, yet I overcame this tentation, and felt the contrary.
h. Psalm 116:13 In the Law they used to make a banquet when they gave solemn thanks to God, and to take the cup and drink in sign of thanksgiving.
i. Psalm 116:15 I perceive that God hath a care over his, so that he both disposeth their death, and taketh an account.
j. Psalm 116:18 I will thank him for his benefits, for that is a just payment, to confess that we owe all to God.

PSALM 117

a. Psalm 117:2 That is, the most certain and continual testimonies of his Fatherly graces.

PSALM 117

1. Rom. 15:11

118

1 David rejected of Saul and of the people at the time appointed obtained the kingdom. 4 For the which he biddeth all them, that fear the Lord, to be thankful. And under his person in all this was Christ lively set forth, who should be of his people rejected.

1 Praise [a]ye the Lord, because he is good: for his mercy endureth fore-
ver. **2** Let Israel now say, That his mercy endureth forever. **3** Let the house of
Aaron now say, That his mercy endureth forever. **4** Let them that fear the Lord,
now say, That his mercy endureth forever. **5** I called upon the Lord in [b]trouble,
and the Lord heard me, and set me at large. **6** The Lord is with me: therefore I
will not fear what [c]man can do unto me. **7** The Lord is with me among them
that help me: therefore shall I see my desire upon mine enemies. **8** It is better
to trust in the Lord, than to have confidence [d]in man. **9** It is better to trust in
the Lord, than to have confidence in princes. **10** All nations have compassed
me: but in the Name of the Lord shall I destroy them. **11** They have compas-
sed me, yea, they have compassed me: but in the Name of the Lord I shall destroy
them. **12** They came about me like bees, but they were quenched as a fire of
thorns: for in the Name of the Lord I shall destroy them. **13** [e]Thou hast thrust
sore at me, that I might fall: but the Lord hath helped me. **14** The Lord is my
strength and [f]song: for he hath been my deliverance. **15** The [g]voice of joy and
deliverance shall be in the tabernacles of the righteous, saying, The right hand of
the Lord hath done valiantly. **16** [h]The right hand of the Lord is exalted: the right
hand of the Lord hath done valiantly. **17** I shall not die, but live, and declare the
works of the Lord. **18** The Lord had chastened me sore, but he hath not deli-
vered me to death. **19** Open ye unto me the [i]gates of righteousness, that I may
go into them, and praise the Lord. **20** This is the gate of the Lord: the righteous
shall enter into it. **21** I will praise thee: for thou hast heard me, and hast been my
deliverance. **22** [1]The stone, which the builders [j]refused, is the head of the cor-
ner. **23** This was the Lord's doing, and it is marvelous in our eyes, **24** This is
the [k]day, which the Lord hath made: let us rejoice and be glad in it. **25** [l]O Lord,
I pray thee, save now: O Lord, I pray thee now give prosperity. **26** Blessed be
he, that cometh in the Name of the Lord: [m]we have blessed you out of the house
of the Lord. **27** The Lord is mighty, and hath given us [n]light: bind the sacrifice
with cords unto the horns of the altar. **28** Thou art my God, and I will praise
thee, even my God: therefore I will exalt thee. **29** Praise ye the Lord, because he
is good: for his mercy endureth forever.

119

1 The Prophet exhorteth the children of God to frame their lives according to his holy word. 123 Also he showeth wherein the true service of God standeth, that is, when we serve him according to his word, and not after our own fantasies.

ALEPH: **1** Blessed are [a]those that are upright in their way, and walk in
the Law of the Lord. **2** Blessed are they that keep his testimonies, and seek
him with their whole heart. **3** Surely they work [b]none iniquity, but walk in his
ways. **4** Thou hast commanded to keep thy precepts diligently. **5** [c]Oh that my
ways were directed to keep thy statutes! **6** Then should I not be confounded,
when I have respect unto all thy commandments. **7** I will praise thee with an
upright [d]heart, when I shall learn the [e]judgments of thy righteousness. **8** I will
keep thy statutes: forsake me not [f]overlong.

BETH: **9** Wherewith shall a [g]young man redress his way? in taking heed
thereto according to thy word. **10** With my whole heart have I sought thee:
let me not wander from thy commandments. **11** I have [h]hid thy promise in
mine heart, that I might not sin against thee. **12** Blessed art thou, O Lord: te-
ach me thy statutes. **13** With my lips have I declared all the judgments of thy
mouth. **14** I have had as great [i]delight in the way of thy testimonies, as in all
riches. **15** I will meditate in thy precepts, and consider thy ways. **16** I will de-
light in thy statutes, and I will not forget thy word.

GIMEL: **17** Be beneficial unto thy servant, that I may [j]live and keep thy
word. **18** Open mine eyes, that I may see the wonders of thy Law. **19** I am
a [k]stranger upon earth: hide not thy commandments from me. **20** Mine heart
breaketh for the desire to thy judgments always. **21** Thou [l]hast destroyed the
proud: cursed are they that do err from thy commandments. **22** Remove from
me shame and contempt: for I have kept thy testimonies. **23** [m]Princes also did
sit, and speak against me: but thy servant did meditate in thy statutes. **24** Also
thy testimonies are my delight, and my counselors.

DALETH: **25** My soul cleaveth to the [n]dust: quicken me according to thy
word. **26** I have [o]declared my ways, and thou heardest me: teach me thy statu-
tes. **27** Make me to understand the way of thy precepts, and I will meditate in
thy wondrous works. **28** My soul melteth for heaviness: raise me up according
to thy [p]word. **29** Take from me the [q]way of lying, and grant me graciously thy
Law. **30** I have chosen the way of truth, and thy judgments have I laid before
me. **31** I have cleaved to thy testimonies, O Lord: confound me not. **32** I will
run the way of thy commandments, when thou [r]shalt enlarge mine heart.

HE: **33** Teach [s]me, O Lord, the way of thy statutes, and I will keep it unto
the end. **34** Give me understanding and I will keep thy Law, yea, I will keep it
with my whole [t]heart. **35** Direct me in the path of thy commandments: for the-
rein is my delight. **36** Incline mine heart unto thy testimonies: and not to [u]cove-
tousness. **37** Turn away mine [v]eyes from regarding vanity, and quicken me in thy
way. **38** Stablish thy promise to thy servant, because he feareth thee. **39** Take
away [w]my rebuke that I fear: for thy judgments are good. **40** Behold, I desire thy
commandments: [x]quicken me in thy righteousness.

VAU: **41** And let thy loving [y]kindness come unto me, O Lord, and thy sal-
vation according to thy promise. **42** So shall I [z]make answer unto my blasphe-
mers: for I trust in thy word. **43** And take not the word of truth utterly out of
my mouth: for I wait for thy judgments. **44** So shall I always keep thy Law fore-
ver and ever. **45** And I will [aa]walk at liberty: for I seek thy precepts. **46** I will
speak also of thy testimonies before [ab]Kings, and will not be ashamed. **47** And
my delight shall be in thy Commandments, which I have loved. **48** Mine hands
also will I lift up unto thy Commandments, which I have loved, and I will medi-
tate in thy statutes.

PSALM 118

a. Psalm 118:1 Because God by creating David King, showed his mercy toward his afflicted Church, the Prophet doth not only himself thank God, but exhorteth all the people to do the same.
b. Psalm 118:5 We are here taught that the more that troubles oppress us, the more ought we to be instant in prayer.
c. Psalm 118:6 Being exalted to this estate, he assured himself to have man ever to be his enemy. Yet he doubted not, but God would maintain him, because he had placed him.
d. Psalm 118:8 He showeth that he had trusted in vain if he had put his confidence in man, to have been preferred to the kingdom and therefore he put his trust in God and obtained.
e. Psalm 118:13 He noteth Saul his chief enemy.
f. Psalm 118:14 In that he was delivered, it came not of himself, nor of the power of man, but only of God's favor, therefore he will praise him.
g. Psalm 118:15 He promiseth both to render graces himself, and to cause others to do the same, because that in his person the Church was restored.
h. Psalm 118:16 So that all, that are both far and near, may see his mighty power.
i. Psalm 118:19 He willeth the doors of the Tabernacle to be opened, that he may declare his thankful mind.
j. Psalm 118:22 Though Saul and the chief powers refused me to be King, yet God hath preferred me above them all.
k. Psalm 118:24 Wherein God hath showeth chiefly his mercy, by appointing me king and delivering his Church.
l. Psalm 118:25 The people pray for the prosperity of David's kingdom, who was the figure of Christ.
m. Psalm 118:26 Which are the Priests, and have the charge thereof, as Num. 6:23.
n. Psalm 118:27 Because he hath restored us from darkness to light, we will offer sacrifices and praises unto him.

PSALM 118

1. Isa. 28:16 - Matt. 21:42 - Acts 4:11 - Rom. 9:33 - 1 Pet. 26:7

PSALM 119

a. Psalm 119:1 Here they are not called blessed, which think themselves wise in their own judgment, nor which imagine to themselves a certain holiness, but they whose conversation is without hypocrisy.
b. Psalm 119:3 For they are ruled by God's Spirit and embrace no doctrine but his.
c. Psalm 119:5 David acknowledgeth his imperfection, desiring God to reform it, that his life may be conformable to God's word.
d. Psalm 119:7 For true religion standeth in serving God without hypocrisy.
e. Psalm 119:7 That is, thy precepts, which contain perfect righteousness.
f. Psalm 119:8 He refuseth not to be tried by tentations, but he feareth to faint, if God succor not his infirmity in time.
g. Psalm 119:9 Because youth is most given to licentiousness, he chiefly warneth them to frame their lives betimes to God's word.
h. Psalm 119:11 If God's word be graven in our hearts, we shall be more able to resist the assaults of Satan: and therefore the Prophet desireth God to instruct him daily more and more therein.
i. Psalm 119:14 The Prophet not boast of his virtues, but setteth forth an example for others to follow God's word, and leave worldly vanities.
j. Psalm 119:17 He showeth that we ought not to desire to live but to serve God, and that we cannot serve him aright except he open our eyes and minds.
k. Psalm 119:19 Seeing man's life in this world is but a passage, what should become of him, if thy word were not his guide?
l. Psalm 119:21 In all ages thou hast plagued all such which maliciously and contemptuously depart from thy truth.
m. Psalm 119:23 When the powers of the world gave false sentence against me, thy word was a guide and counselor to teach me what to do, and to comfort me.
n. Psalm 119:25 That is, it is almost brought to the grave, and without thy word I cannot live.
o. Psalm 119:26 I have confessed mine offences, and now depend wholly on thee.
p. Psalm 119:28 If God did not maintain us by his word, our life would drop away like water.
q. Psalm 119:29 Instruct me in thy word, whereby my mind may be purged from vanity, and taught to obey thy will.
r. Psalm 119:32 By this he showeth that we can neither choose good, cleave to God's word, nor turn forward in his way, except he make our hearts large to receive grace, and willing to obey.
s. Psalm 119:33 He showeth that he cannot follow on to the end, except God teach him ofttimes, and lead him forward.
t. Psalm 119:34 Not only in outward conversation, but also with inward affection.
u. Psalm 119:36 Hereby meaning all other vices, because that covetousness is the root of all evil.
v. Psalm 119:37 Meaning, all his senses.
w. Psalm 119:39 Let me not fall to thy dishonor, but let mine heart still delight in thy gracious word.
x. Psalm 119:40 Give me strength to continue in thy word even to the end.
y. Psalm 119:41 He showeth that God's mercy and love is the first cause of our salvation.
z. Psalm 119:42 By trusting in God's word he assureth himself to be able to confute the slanders of his adversaries.
aa. Psalm 119:45 They that simply walk after God's word, have no lets to entangle them, whereas they that do contrary, are ever in nets and snares.
ab. Psalm 119:46 He showeth that the children of God ought not to suffer their father's glory to be obscured by the vain pomp of princes.

ZAIN: 49 Remember [ac]the promise made to thy servant, wherein thou hast caused me to trust. **50** It is my comfort in my trouble; for thy promise hath quickened me. **51** The [ad]proud have had me exceedingly in derision: yet have I not declined from thy Law. **52** I remembered thy [ae]judgments of old, O Lord, and have been comforted. **53** [af]Fear is come upon me for the wicked, that forsake thy Law. **54** Thy statutes have been my songs in the house of my [ag]pilgrimage. **55** I have remembered thy Name, O Lord, in the [ah]night, and have kept thy Law. **56** [ai]This I had because I kept thy precepts.

CHETH: 57 O Lord, that art my [aj]portion, I have determined to keep thy words. **58** I made my supplication in thy presence with my whole heart: be merciful unto me according to thy promise. **59** I have considered my [ak]ways, and turned my feet into thy testimonies. **60** I made haste and delayed not to keep thy commandments. **61** The bands of the wicked have [al]robbed me: but I have not forgotten thy Law. **62** At midnight will I rise to give thanks unto thee, because of thy righteous judgments. **63** I am [am]companion of all them that fear thee, and keep thy precepts. **64** The earth, O Lord, is full of thy mercy: [an]teach me thy statutes.

TETH: 65 O Lord, thou hast dealt [ao]graciously with thy servant, according unto thy word. **66** Teach me good judgment and knowledge: for I have believed thy commandments. **67** Before I was [ap]afflicted, I went astray: but now I keep thy word. **68** Thou art good and gracious: teach me thy statutes. **69** The proud have imagined a lie against me: but I will keep thy precepts with my whole heart. **70** [aq]Their heart is fat as grease, but my delight is in thy Law. **71** It is [ar]good for me that I have been afflicted, that I may learn thy statutes. **72** The Law of thy mouth is better unto me, than thousands of gold and silver.

JOD: 73 Thine hands have [as]made me and fashioned me: give me understanding therefore, that I may learn thy commandments. **74** So they that [at]fear thee, seeing me, shall rejoice, because I have trusted in thy word. **75** I know, O Lord, that thy judgments are right, and that thou hast afflicted me [au]justly. **76** I pray thee that thy mercy may comfort me, according to thy promise unto thy servant. **77** Let thy tender mercies come unto me, that I may [av]live: for thy Law is my delight. **78** Let the proud be ashamed: for they have dealt wickedly and falsely with me: but I meditate in thy precepts. **79** Let such as fear thee [aw]turn unto me, and they that [ax]know thy testimonies. **80** Let mine heart be upright in thy statutes, that I be not ashamed.

CAPH: 81 My soul [ay]fainted for thy salvation: yet I wait for thy word. **82** Mine eyes fail for thy promise, saying, When wilt thou comfort me? **83** For I am like a [az]bottle in the smoke; yet do I not forget thy statutes. **84** How many are the [ba]days of thy servant? When wilt thou execute judgment on them that persecute me? **85** The proud have [bb]dug pits for me, which is not after thy Law. **86** All thy commandments are true: they persecute me falsely: [bc]help me. **87** They had almost consumed [bd]me upon the earth: but I forsook not thy precepts. **88** Quicken me according to thy loving kindness: so shall I keep the testimony of thy mouth.

LAMED: 89 O Lord, thy word endureth forever in [be]heaven. **90** Thy truth is from generation to generation: thou hast laid the foundation of the earth, and it abideth. **91** They [bf]continue even to this day by thine ordinances: for all are thy servants. **92** Except thy law had been my delight, I should now have perished in mine affliction. **93** I will never forget thy precepts: for by them thou hast quickened me. **94** I am [bg]thine, save me: for I have sought thy precepts. **95** The wicked have waited for me to destroy me: but I will consider thy testimonies. **96** I [bh]have seen an end of all perfection: but thy commandment is exceeding large.

MEM: 97 Oh how love I thy law! it is my meditation [bi]continually. **98** By thy commandments thou hast made me wiser than mine enemies: for they are ever with me. **99** I have had more [bj]understanding than all my teachers: for thy testimonies are my meditation. **100** I understood more than the ancient, because I kept thy precepts. **101** I have refrained my feet from every evil way, that I might keep thy word. **102** I have not declined from thy judgments: for [bk]thou didst teach me. **103** How sweet are thy promises unto my mouth! yea, more than honey unto my mouth. **104** By thy precepts I have gotten understanding: therefore I hate all the ways of falsehood.

NUN: 105 Thy word is a [bl]lantern unto my feet, and a light unto my paths. **106** I have [bm]sworn and will perform it, that I will keep thy righteous judgments. **107** I am very sore afflicted: O Lord, quicken me according to thy word. **108** O Lord, I beseech thee, accept the [bn]free offering of my mouth, and teach me thy judgments. **109** My [bo]soul is continually in mine hand: yet do I not forget thy law. **110** The wicked have laid a snare for me: but I swerved not from thy precepts. **111** Thy testimonies have I taken as an [bp]heritage forever: for they are the joy of mine heart. **112** I have applied mine heart to fulfill thy statutes always, even unto the end.

SAMECH: 113 I hate [bq]vain inventions: but thy Law do I love. **114** Thou art my refuge and shield, and I trust in thy word. **115** [br]Away from me, ye wicked: for I will keep the commandments of my God. **116** Stablish me according to thy promise, that I may live, and disappoint me not of mine hope. **117** [bs]Stay thou me, and I shall be safe, and I will delight continually in thy statutes. **118** Thou hast trodden down all them that depart from thy statutes: for their [bt]deceit is vain. **119** Thou hast taken away all the wicked of the earth like [bu]dross: therefore I love thy testimonies. **120** My flesh [bv]trembleth for fear of thee, and I am afraid of thy judgments.

AIN: 121 I have executed judgment and justice: leave me not to mine oppressor. **122** [bw]Answer for thy servant in that which is good, and let not the proud oppress me. **123** Mine eyes have failed in waiting for thy salvation, and for thy just promise. **124** Deal with thy [bx]servant according to thy mercy, and teach me thy statutes. **125** I am thy servant: grant me therefore understanding, that I may know thy testimonies. **126** It is [by]time for thee, Lord, to work: for they have destroyed thy Law. **127** Therefore love I thy commandments above gold, yea, above most fine gold. **128** Therefore I esteem all thy precepts most just, and hate all false [bz]ways.

---

ac. Psalm 119:49 Though he feel God's hand still to lie upon him, yet he resteth on his promise, and comforteth himself therein.
ad. Psalm 119:51 Meaning, the wicked, which contemn God's word, and tread his Religion under foot.
ae. Psalm 119:52 That is, the examples, whereby thou declarest thyself to be judge of the world.
af. Psalm 119:53 That is, a vehement zeal to thy glory and indignation against the wicked.
ag. Psalm 119:54 In the course of this life and sorrowful exit.
ah. Psalm 119:55 Even when others sleep.
ai. Psalm 119:56 That is, all these benefits.
aj. Psalm 119:57 I am persuaded that to keep thy Law is an heritage and great gain for me.
ak. Psalm 119:59 He showeth that none can embrace the word of God, except he consider his own imperfections and ways.
al. Psalm 119:61 They have gone about to draw me into their company.
am. Psalm 119:63 Not only in mutual consent, but also with aid and succor.
an. Psalm 119:64 For the knowledge of God's word is a singular token of his favor.
ao. Psalm 119:65 Having proved by experience that God was true in his promise, he desireth that he would increase in him knowledge and judgment.
ap. Psalm 119:67 So Jeremiah saith, that before the Lord touched him, he was like a calf untamed: so that the use of God's rod is to call us home to God.
aq. Psalm 119:70 Their heart is indurated and hardened, puffed up with prosperity and vain estimation of themselves.
ar. Psalm 119:71 He confesseth that before that he was chastened, he was rebellious, as man by nature is.
as. Psalm 119:73 Because God leaveth not his work that he hath begun, he desireth a new grace: that is, that he would continue his mercies.
at. Psalm 119:74 When God showeth his grace toward any, he testifieth to others, that he faileth not them that trust in him.
au. Psalm 119:75 Hebrew, in truth.
av. Psalm 119:77 He declareth, that when he felt not God's mercies, he was as dead.
aw. Psalm 119:79 That is, be comforted by mine example.
ax. Psalm 119:79 He showeth that there can be no true fear of God without the knowledge of his word.
ay. Psalm 119:81 Though my strength fail me, yet my soul groaneth and sigheth, resting still in thy word.
az. Psalm 119:83 Like a skin bottle or bladder that is parched in the smoke.
ba. Psalm 119:84 How long wilt thou afflict thy servant.
bb. Psalm 119:85 They have not only oppressed me violently, but also craftily conspired against me.
bc. Psalm 119:86 He assureth himself, that God will deliver his, and destroy such as unjustly persecute them.
bd. Psalm 119:87 Finding no help in earth, he lifteth up his eyes to heaven.
be. Psalm 119:89 Because none should esteem God's word according to the changes of things in this world, he showeth that it abideth in heaven, and therefore is immutable.
bf. Psalm 119:91 Seeing the earth and all creatures remain in that estate wherein thou hast created them, much more thy truth remaineth constant and unchangeable.
bg. Psalm 119:94 He proveth by effect that he is God's child, because he seeketh to understand his word.
bh. Psalm 119:96 There is nothing so perfect in earth, but it hath an end, only God's word lasteth forever.
bi. Psalm 119:97 He showeth that we cannot love God's word, except we exercise ourselves therein and practice it.
bj. Psalm 119:99 Whosoever doth submit himself only to God's word, shall not only be safe against the practices of his enemies, but also learn more wisdom than they that profess it, and are men of experience.
bk. Psalm 119:102 So then of ourselves we can do nothing: but when God doth inwardly instruct us with his spirit, we feel his graces sweeter than honey.
bl. Psalm 119:105 Of ourselves we are but darkness and cannot see except we be lightened with God's Word.
bm. Psalm 119:106 So all the faithful ought to bind themselves to God by a solemn oath and promises, to stir up their zeal to embrace God's word.
bn. Psalm 119:108 That is, my prayers and thanksgiving which sacrifice Hosea calleth the calves of the lips, Hos. 14:3.
bo. Psalm 119:109 That is, I am in continual danger of my life.
bp. Psalm 119:111 I esteemed no worldly things, but made thy word mine inheritance.
bq. Psalm 119:113 Whosoever will embrace God's word aright, must abhor all fantasies and imaginations both of himself and others.
br. Psalm 119:115 And hinder me not to keep the Law of the Lord.
bs. Psalm 119:117 He desireth God's continual assistance, lest he should faint in this race, which he had begun.
bt. Psalm 119:118 The crafty practices of them that contemn thy Law, shall be brought to naught.
bu. Psalm 119:119 Which infected thy people, as dross doth the metal.
bv. Psalm 119:120 Thy judgments do not only teach me obedience, but cause me to fear, considering mine own weakness, which fear causeth repentance.
bw. Psalm 119:122 Put thyself between mine enemies and me, as if thou were my pledge.
bx. Psalm 119:124 He boasteth not that he is God's servant, but hereby putteth God in mind that as he made him his by his grace, so he would continue his favor toward him.
by. Psalm 119:126 The Prophet showeth that when the wicked have brought all things to confusion, and God's word to utter contempt, then it is God's time to help and send remedy.
bz. Psalm 119:128 That is, whatsoever dissenteth from the purity of thy word.
ca. Psalm 119:129 Containing high and secret mysteries, so that I am moved with admiration and reverence.

PE: 129 Thy testimonies are [ca]wonderful: therefore doth my soul keep them. 130 The entrance into thy [cb]words showeth light, and giveth understanding to the simple. 131 I opened my mouth, and [cc]panted, because I loved thy commandments. 132 Look upon me and be merciful unto me, as thou usest to do unto those that love thy Name. 133 Direct my steps in thy word, and let none iniquity have dominion over me. 134 Deliver me from the oppression of men, and I will keep thy precepts. 135 Show the light of thy countenance upon thy servant, and teach me thy statute. 136 Mine eyes gush [cd]out with rivers of water, because they keep not thy Law.

TZADDI: 137 Righteous art thou, O Lord, and just are thy judgments. 138 Thou hast commanded [ce]justice by thy testimonies and truth especially. 139 [1]My zeal hath even consumed me: because mine enemies have forgotten thy words. 140 Thy word is proved [cf]most pure, and thy servant loveth it. 141 I am [cg]small and despised: yet do I not forget thy precepts. 142 Thy righteousness is an everlasting righteousness, and thy Law is truth. 143 Trouble and anguish are come upon me: yet are the commandments my delight. 144 The righteousness of thy testimonies is everlasting: grant me understanding, and I shall [ch]live.

KOPH: 145 I have [ci]cried with my whole heart: hear me, O Lord, and I will keep thy statutes. 146 I called upon thee: save me, and I will keep thy testimonies. 147 I prevented the morning light, and cried: for I waited on thy word. 148 Mine eyes [cj]prevent the night watches, to meditate in thy word. 149 Hear my voice according to thy loving kindness: O Lord, quicken me according to thy [ck]judgment. 150 They draw near that follow after [cl]malice, and are far from thy Law. 151 Thou art near, O Lord: for all thy commandments are true. 152 I have known long since [cm]by thy testimonies, that thou hast established them forever.

RESH: 153 Behold mine affliction, and deliver me: for I have not forgotten thy law. 154 Plead my cause, and deliver me: quicken me according unto thy [cn]word. 155 Salvation is far from the wicked, because they seek not thy statutes. 156 Great art thy tender mercies, O Lord: quicken me according to thy [co]judgments. 157 My persecutors and mine oppressors are many: yet do I not swerve from thy testimonies. 158 I saw the transgressors and was [cp]grieved, because they kept not thy word. 159 Consider, O Lord, how I [cq]love thy precepts: quicken me according to thy loving kindness. 160 The [cr]beginning of thy word is truth, and all the judgments of thy righteousness endure forever.

SCHIN: 161 Princes have [cs]persecuted me without cause: but mine heart stood in awe of thy words. 162 I rejoice at thy word, as one that findeth a great spoil. 163 I hate falsehood and abhor it, but thy Law do I love. 164 [ct]Seven times a day do I praise thee, because of thy righteous judgments. 165 They that [cu]love thy law, shall have great prosperity, and they shall have none hurt. 166 Lord, I have [cv]trusted in thy salvation, and have done thy commandments. 167 My soul hath kept thy testimonies: for I love them exceedingly. 168 I have kept thy precepts and thy testimonies: [cw]for all my ways are before thee.

TAU: 169 Let my complaint come before thee, O Lord, and give me understanding [cx]according unto thy word. 170 Let my supplication come before thee, and deliver me according to thy promise. 171 My lips shall [cy]speak praise, when thou hast [cz]taught me thy statutes. 172 My tongue shall entreat of thy word: for all thy commandments are righteous. 173 Let thine hand help me: for I have chosen thy precepts. 174 I have longed for thy salvation, O Lord, and thy Law is my delight. 175 Let my soul live, and it shall praise thee, and thy [da]judgments shall help me. 176 I have [db]gone astray like a lost sheep: seek thy servant, for I do not forget thy commandments.

120

1 The prayer of David being vexed by the false reports of Saul's flatterers. 5 And therefore he lamenteth his long abode among those infidels, 7 Who were given to all kinds of wickedness and contention.

A song of [a]degrees. 1 I called unto the Lord in my [b]trouble, and he heard me. 2 Deliver my soul, O Lord, from lying lips, and from a deceitful tongue. 3 What doth thy [c]deceitful tongue bring unto thee? or what doth it avail thee? 4 It is as the [d]sharp arrows of a mighty man, and as the coals of Juniper. 5 Woe is to me that I remain in [e]Meshech, and dwell in the tents of [f]Kedar. 6 My soul hath too long dwelt with him that hateth peace. 7 I seek [g]peace, and when I speak thereof, they are bent to war.

121

1 This Psalm teacheth that the faithful ought only to look for help at God, 7 who only doth maintain, preserve and prosper his Church.

A song of degrees. 1 I will lift up mine eyes [a]unto the mountains, from whence my help shall come. 2 Mine help cometh from the Lord, which hath made the [b]heaven and the earth. 3 He will not suffer thy foot to slip: for he that keepeth thee, will not [c]slumber. 4 Behold, he that keepeth Israel, will neither slumber nor sleep. 5 The Lord is thy keeper: the Lord is thy shadow at thy right hand. 6 The sun shall not [d]smite thee by day, nor the moon by night. 7 The Lord shall preserve thee from all evil: he shall keep thy soul. 8 The Lord shall preserve thy [e]going out, and thy coming in from henceforth and forever.

122

1 David rejoiceth in the name of the faithful, that God hath accomplished his promise and placed his Ark in Zion. 5 For the which he giveth thanks, 8 And prayeth for the prosperity of the Church.

A song of degrees, or Psalm of David. 1 I [1,a]rejoiced when they said to me, We will go into the house of the Lord. 2 Our [b]feet shall stand in thy gates, O Jerusalem. 3 Jerusalem is built as a city, that is [c]compact together in itself: 4 Whereunto [d]the Tribes, even the Tribes of the Lord go up according to the testimony to Israel, to praise the Name of the Lord. 5 For there are thrones set for judgment, even the thrones of the house of [e]David. 6 Pray for the peace of Jerusalem: let them prosper that love thee. 7 Peace be within thy [f]walls, and prosperity within thy palaces. 8 For my [g]brethren and neighbors' sakes, I will wish thee now prosperity. 9 Because of the House of the Lord our God, I will procure thy wealth.

---

cb. Psalm 119:130 The simple idiots that submit themselves to God, have their eyes opened and their minds illuminated, so soon as they begin to read God's word.
cc. Psalm 119:131 My zeal toward thy word was so great.
cd. Psalm 119:136 He showeth what ought to be the zeal of God's children, when they see his word contemned.
ce. Psalm 119:138 We cannot confess God to be righteous, except we live uprightly and truly, as he hath commanded.
cf. Psalm 119:140 Gold hath need to be fined, but thy word is perfection itself.
cg. Psalm 119:141 This is the true trial, to praise God in adversity.
ch. Psalm 119:144 So that the life of man without the knowledge of God, is death.
ci. Psalm 119:145 He showeth that all his affections and whole heart were bent to Godward for to have help in his dangers.
cj. Psalm 119:148 He was more earnest in the study of God's word, than they that kept the watch were in their charge.
ck. Psalm 119:149 Or, custom.
cl. Psalm 119:150 He showeth the nature of the wicked to be to persecute against their conscience.
cm. Psalm 119:152 His faith is grounded upon God's word, that he would ever be at hand when his children be oppressed.
cn. Psalm 119:154 For without God's promise there is no hope of deliverance.
co. Psalm 119:156 According to thy promise made in the law, which because the wicked lack, they can have no hope of salvation.
cp. Psalm 119:158 My zeal consumed me when I saw their malice and contempt of thy glory.
cq. Psalm 119:159 It is a sure sign of our adoption, when we love the Law of God.
cr. Psalm 119:160 Since thou first promised it, even to the end all thy sayings are true.
cs. Psalm 119:161 The threatenings and persecutions of princes could not cause me to shrink to confess thee whom I more fear than men.
ct. Psalm 119:164 That is, often and sundry times.
cu. Psalm 119:165 For their conscience assureth them that they please thee, whereas they that love not thee, have the contrary.
cv. Psalm 119:166 He showeth that we must first have faith before we can work and please God.
cw. Psalm 119:168 I had no respect of men, but set thee always before mine eyes, as the judge of my doings.
cx. Psalm 119:169 As thou hast promised to be the schoolmaster unto all them that depend upon thee.
cy. Psalm 119:171 The word signifieth to pour forth continually.
cz. Psalm 119:171 All his prayer and desire is to profit in the word of God.
da. Psalm 119:175 That is, thy provident care over me, and wherewith thou wilt judge mine enemies.
db. Psalm 119:176 Being chased to and fro by mine enemies, and having no place to rest in.

PSALM 119
1. Ps. 69:9 - John 2:17

PSALM 120
a. Psalm 120:1 That is, of lifting up the tune and rising in singing.
b. Psalm 120:1 Albeit the children of God ought to rejoice when they suffer for righteous sake, yet it is a great grief to the flesh to hear evil for well doing.
c. Psalm 120:3 He assured himself that God would turn their craft to their own destruction.
d. Psalm 120:4 He showeth that there is nothing so sharp to pierce, nor so hot to set on fire, as a slanderous tongue.
e. Psalm 120:5 These were people of Arabia, which came of Japheth, Gen. 10:2.
f. Psalm 120:5 That is, of the Ishmaelites.
g. Psalm 120:7 He declareth what he meaneth by Meshech, and Kedar, to wit, the Israelites which had degenerate from their godly fathers, and hated and contended against the faithful.

PSALM 121
a. Psalm 121:1 Or, about the mountains: meaning, that there is nothing so high in this world, wherein he can trust, but only in God.
b. Psalm 121:2 He accuseth man's ingratitude, which cannot depend on God's power.
c. Psalm 121:3 He showeth that God's providence not only watcheth over his Church in general: but also over every member thereof.
d. Psalm 121:6 Neither heat nor cold, nor any incommodity shall be able to destroy God's Church, albeit for a time they may molest it.
e. Psalm 121:8 Whatsoever thou dost enterprise, shall have good success.

PSALM 122
a. Psalm 122:1 He rejoiceth that God had appointed a place, where the Ark should still remain.
b. Psalm 122:2 Which were wont to wander to and fro, as the Ark removed.
c. Psalm 122:3 By the artificial joining and beauty of the houses, he meaneth the concord and love that was between the citizens.
d. Psalm 122:4 All the tribes according to God's covenant shall come and pray there.
e. Psalm 122:5 In whose house God placed the throne of justice, and made it a figure of Christ's kingdom.
f. Psalm 122:7 The favor of God prosper thee both within and without.
g. Psalm 122:8 Not only for mine own sake, but for all the faithful.

PSALM 122
1. 1Chron. 29:9

123

A prayer of the faithful, which were afflicted either in Babylon or under Antiochus, by the wicked worldlings and contemners of God.

A song of degrees. **1** I lift up mine eyes to thee, that dwellest in the heavens. **2** Behold, as the eyes of [a]servants look unto the hand of their masters, and as the eyes of a maiden unto the hand of her mistress: so our eyes wait upon the Lord our God, until he have mercy upon us. **3** Have mercy unto us, O Lord, have mercy upon us: for we have [b]suffered too much contempt. **4** Our soul is filled too full of the mocking of the wealthy, and of the despitefulness of the proud.

124

The people of God, escaping a great peril, do acknowledge themselves to be delivered, not by their own force, but by the power of God. 4 They declare the greatness of the peril. 6 And praise the Name of God.

A song of degrees, or Psalm of David. **1** If the Lord had not been [a]on our side, (may Israel now say) **2** If the Lord had not been on our side, when men rose up against us, **3** They had then swallowed us up [b]quick, when their wrath was kindled against us. **4** Then the [c]waters had drowned us, and the stream had gone over our soul: **5** Then had the swelling waters gone over our soul. **6** Praised be the Lord, which hath not given us as a prey unto their teeth. **7** Our soul is escaped, even as a bird out of the [d]snare of the fowlers: the snare is broken, and we are delivered. **8** Our help is in the Name of the Lord, which hath made heaven and earth.

125

1 He describeth the assurance of the faithful in their afflictions. 4 And desireth their wealth, 5 And the destruction of the wicked.

A song of degrees. **1** They that trust in the Lord, shall be as mount Zion, which cannot [a]be removed, but remaineth forever. **2** As the mountains are about Jerusalem: so is the Lord about his people from henceforth and forever. **3** For the [b]rod of the wicked shall not rest on the lot of the righteous, lest the righteous put forth their hand unto wickedness. **4** Do well, O Lord, unto those that be good and true in their hearts. **5** [c]But these that turn aside by their crooked ways, them shall the Lord lead with the workers of iniquity: but peace shall be upon Israel.

126

1 This Psalm was made after the return of the people from Babylon, and showeth that the means of their deliverance was wonderful after the seventy years of captivity forspoken by Jeremiah, in Jer. 25:12 and 29:10.

A song of degrees, or Psalm of David. **1** When the Lord brought again the captivity of Zion, we were like them that [a]dream. **2** Then was our mouth [b]filled with laughter, and our tongue with joy: then said they among the [c]heathen, The Lord hath done great things for them. **3** The Lord hath done great things for us, whereof we rejoice. **4** O Lord, bring again our captivity, as the [d]rivers in the South. **5** They that sow in tears, shall reap in joy. **6** They went weeping, and carried [e]precious seed: but they shall return with joy, and bring their sheaves.

127

1 He showeth that the whole estate of the world, both domestical and political, standeth by God's mere providence and blessing, 3 And that to have children well nurtured, is an especial grace and gift of God.

A song of degrees, or Psalm of Solomon. **1** Except the Lord [a]build the house, they labor in vain that build it: except the Lord keep the [b]city, the keeper watcheth in vain. **2** It is in vain for [c]you to rise early, and to lie down late, and eat the bread [d]of sorrow: but he will surely give [e]rest to his beloved. **3** Behold, children are the inheritance of the Lord, and the fruit of the womb his reward. **4** As are the arrows in the hand of the strong man; so are the [f]children of youth. **5** Blessed is the man that hath his quiver full of them: for they [g]shall not be ashamed, when they speak with their enemies in the gate.

128

He showeth that blessedness appertaineth not to all universally, but to them only that fear the Lord, and walk in his ways.

A song of degrees. **1** Blessed is everyone that feareth the Lord, and walketh in his [a]ways. **2** When thou eatest the labors of thine [b]hands, thou shalt be blessed, and it shall be well with thee. **3** Thy wife shall be as the fruitful vine on the sides of thine house, and thy [c]children like the olive plants round about thy table. **4** Lo, surely thus shall the man be blessed, that feareth the Lord. **5** The Lord out of Zion shall [d]bless thee, and thou shalt see the wealth of [e]Jerusalem all the days of thy life. **6** Yea, thou shalt see thy children's children, and peace upon Israel.

129

1 He admonisheth the Church to rejoice though it be afflicted. 4 For by the righteous Lord it shall be delivered. 6 And the enemies for all their glorious show, shall suddenly be destroyed.

A song of degrees. **1** They have oftentimes afflicted me from my youth (may [a]Israel now say) **2** They have oftentimes afflicted me from my youth: but they could not prevail against me. **3** The plowers plowed upon my back, and made long furrows. **4** But the [b]righteous Lord hath cut the cords of the wicked. **5** They that hate Zion, shall be all ashamed and turned backward. **6** [c]They shall be as the grass on the house tops, which withereth afore it cometh forth. **7** Whereof the mower filleth not his hand, neither the gleaner his lap: **8** [d]Neither they which go by, say, The blessing of the Lord be upon you, or, We bless you in the Name of the Lord.

130

The people of God from their bottomless miseries do cry unto God, and are heard. 3 They confess their sins, and flee unto God's mercies.

A song of degrees. **1** Out of the [a]deep places have I called unto thee, O Lord. **2** Lord, hear my voice: let thine ears attend to the voice of my prayers. **3** If thou, O Lord, straightly markest iniquities, O Lord, [b]who shall stand? **4** But mercy is with thee, that thou [c]mayest be feared. **5** I have waited on the Lord: my soul hath waited, and I have trusted in his word. **6** My soul waiteth on the Lord more than the morning watch watcheth for the morning. **7** Let Israel wait on the Lord: for with the Lord is [d]mercy, and with him is great redemption. **8** And he shall redeem Israel from all his iniquities.

PSALM 123

- **a.** Psalm 123:2 He compareth the condition of the godly, to servants that are destitute of all help, assuring that when all other helps fail, God is ever at hand and like himself.
- **b.** Psalm 123:3 He declareth that when the faithful are so full, that they can no more endure the oppressions and scornings of the wicked, there is always help above, if with hungry desires they call for it.

PSALM 124

- **a.** Psalm 124:1 He showeth that God was ready to help at need, and that there was none other way to be saved, but by his only means.
- **b.** Psalm 124:3 So unable were we to resist.
- **c.** Psalm 124:4 He useth most proper similitudes to express the great danger that the Church was in, and out of the which God miraculously delivered them.
- **d.** Psalm 124:7 For the wicked did not only furiously rage against the faithful, but craftily imagined to destroy them.

PSALM 125

- **a.** Psalm 125:1 Though the world be subject to mutations, yet the people of God shall stand sure, and be defended by God's providence.
- **b.** Psalm 125:3 Though God suffer his to be under the cross, lest they should embrace wickedness, yet this cross shall not so rest upon them, that it should drive them from hope.
- **c.** Psalm 125:5 He desireth God to purge his Church from hypocrites, and such as have no zeal of the truth.

PSALM 126

- **a.** Psalm 126:1 Their deliverance was as a thing incredible, and therefore took away all excuse of ingratitude.
- **b.** Psalm 126:2 He showeth how the godly ought to rejoice when God gathereth his Church or delivereth it.
- **c.** Psalm 126:2 If the infidels confess God's wonderful work, the faithful can never show themselves sufficiently thankful.
- **d.** Psalm 126:4 It is no more impossible to God to deliver his people, than to cause the rivers to run in the wilderness and barren places.
- **e.** Psalm 126:6 That is, seed which was scarce and dear: meaning, that they which trusted in God's promise to return, had their desire.

PSALM 127

- **a.** Psalm 127:1 That is, govern and dispose all things pertaining to the family.
- **b.** Psalm 127:1 The public estate of the commonwealth.
- **c.** Psalm 127:2 Which watch and ward, and are also magistrates, and rulers of the city.
- **d.** Psalm 127:2 Either that which is gotten by hard labor, or eaten with grief of mind.
- **e.** Psalm 127:2 Not exempting them from labor, but making their labors comfortable, and as it were a rest.
- **f.** Psalm 127:4 That is, endued with strength and virtues from God: for these are signs of God's blessings, and not the number.
- **g.** Psalm 127:5 Such children shall be able to stop their adversaries' mouths, when their godly life is maliciously accused before Judges.

PSALM 128

- **a.** Psalm 128:1 God approveth not our life, except it be reformed according to his word.
- **b.** Psalm 128:2 The world esteemeth them happy, which live in wealth and idleness: but the holy Ghost approveth them best that live of the mean profit of their labors.
- **c.** Psalm 128:3 Because God's favor appeareth in none outward thing, more than in increase of children, he promiseth to enrich the faithful with this gift.
- **d.** Psalm 128:5 Because of the spiritual blessing which God hath made to his Church, these temporal things shall be granted.
- **e.** Psalm 128:5 For except God blessed his Church publicly, this private blessing were nothing.

PSALM 129

- **a.** Psalm 129:1 The Church now afflicted ought to remember how her condition hath ever been such from the beginning to be molested most grievously by the wicked: yet in time it hath ever been delivered.
- **b.** Psalm 129:4 Because God is righteous, he cannot but plague his adversary, and deliver his, as oxen out of the plough.
- **c.** Psalm 129:6 The enemies that lift themselves most high, and as it were approach near to the Sun, are consumed with the heat of God's wrath, because they are not grounded in godly humility.
- **d.** Psalm 129:8 That is, the wicked shall perish, and none shall pass for them.

PSALM 130

- **a.** Psalm 130:1 Being in great distress and sorrow.
- **b.** Psalm 130:3 He declareth that we cannot be just before God but by forgiveness of sins.
- **c.** Psalm 130:4 Because of nature thou art merciful: therefore the faithful reverence thee.
- **d.** Psalm 130:7 He showeth to whom the mercy of God doth appertain: to Israel, that is, to the Church and not to the reprobate.

PSALM 131

- **a.** Psalm 131:1 He setteth forth his great humility, as an example to all rulers and governors.
- **b.** Psalm 131:1 Which pass the measure and limits of his vocation.
- **c.** Psalm 131:2 He was void of ambition and wicked desires.

131

1 David charged with ambition and greedy desire to reign, protesteth his humility and modesty before God, and teacheth all men what they should do.

A song of degrees, or Psalm of David. **1** Lord, [a]mine heart is not haughty, neither are mine eyes lofty, neither have I walked in great [b]matters and hid from me. **2** Surely I have behaved myself, like one weaned from his mother, and kept silence: I am in myself as one that is [c]weaned. **3** Let Israel wait on the Lord from henceforth and forever.

132

1 The faithful grounding on God's promise made unto David, desire that he would establish the same, both as touching his posterity, and the building of the Temple, to pray there as was forspoken, Deut. 12:5.

A song of degrees. **1** Lord, remember David with all his [a]affliction, **2** Who sware unto the Lord, and vowed unto the mighty God, of Jacob, saying, **3** I [b]will not enter into the Tabernacle of mine house, nor come upon my pallet or bed, **4** Nor suffer mine eyes to sleep, nor mine eyelids to slumber, **5** Until I find out a place for the [c]Lord, an habitation for the mighty God of Jacob. **6** Lo, we heard of it in [d]Ephrathah, and found it in the fields of the forest. **7** We will enter into his Tabernacles, and worship before his footstool. **8** Arise, O Lord, to come into thy [e]rest, thou, and the Ark of thy strength. **9** Let thy Priests be clothed with [f]righteousness, and let thy Saints rejoice. **10** For thy [g]servant David's sake refuse not the face of thine Anointed. **11** The Lord hath sworn in truth unto David, and he will not shrink from it, saying, Of the fruit of thy body will I set upon thy throne. **12** If thy sons keep my Covenant, and my testimonies, that I shall teach them, their sons also shall sit upon thy throne [h]forever. **13** For the Lord hath chosen Zion, and loved to dwell in it, saying, **14** This is my rest forever: here will I dwell, for I have a [i]delight therein. **15** I will surely bless her vittles, and will satisfy her poor with bread, **16** And will clothe her Priests with [j]salvation, and her Saints shall shout for joy. **17** There will I make the [k]horn of David to bud: for I have ordained a light for mine Anointed. **18** His enemies will I clothe with shame, but on him his crown shall flourish.

133

1 This Psalm containeth the commendation of brotherly amity among the servants of God.

A song of degrees, or Psalm of David. **1** Behold, how good and how comely a thing it is, brethren to dwell even [a]together. **2** It is like to the precious [b]ointment upon the head, that runneth down upon the beard, even unto Aaron's beard, which went down on the border of his garments, **3** And as the dew of [c]Hermon which falleth upon the mountains of Zion: for [d]there the Lord appointed the blessing and life forever.

134

1 He exhorteth the Levites watching in the Temple, to praise the Lord.

A song of degrees. **1** Behold, praise ye the Lord, all ye [a]servants of the Lord, ye that by night stand in the house of the Lord. **2** Lift up your [b]hands to the Sanctuary, and praise the Lord. **3** The Lord that [c]hath made heaven and earth, bless thee out of Zion.

135

1 He exhorteth all the faithful, of what estate soever they be, to praise God for his marvelous works. 12 And specially for his graces toward his people, wherein he hath declared his Majesty, 15 To the confusion of all idolaters and their idols.

Praise ye the Lord. **1** Praise, the Name of the Lord; ye servants of the Lord, praise him. **2** Ye that [a]stand in the House of the Lord, and in the [b]courts of the House of our God, **3** Praise ye the Lord: for the Lord is good: sing praises unto his Name: for it is a comely thing. **4** For the Lord hath [c]chosen Jacob to himself, and Israel for his chief treasure. **5** For I know that the Lord is great, and that our Lord is above all gods. **6** Whatsoever pleased the Lord, that [d]did he in heaven and in earth, in the sea, and in all the depths. **7** He bringeth up the clouds from the ends of the earth, and maketh the [1]lightnings with the rain: he draweth forth the wind out of his treasures. **8** [2]He smote the firstborn of Egypt both of man and beast. **9** He hath sent tokens and wonders into the midst of thee, O Egypt, upon Pharaoh, and upon all his servants. **10** [3]He smote many nations, and slew mighty Kings: **11** As Sihon King of the Amorites, and Og king of Bashan, and all the kingdoms of Canaan: **12** And [e]gave their land for an inheritance, even an inheritance unto Israel his people. **13** Thy Name, O Lord, endureth forever: O Lord, thy remembrance is from generation to generation. **14** For the Lord will [f]judge his people, and be pacified toward his servants. **15** The [g]idols of the heathen are silver and gold, even the work of men's hands. **16** They have a mouth, and speak not: they have eyes and see not. **17** They have ears and hear not, neither is there any breath in their mouth. **18** They that make them, are like unto them: so are all that trust in them. **19** Praise the Lord, ye house of Israel: praise the Lord, ye house of Aaron. **20** Praise the Lord, ye house of Levi; ye that fear the Lord, praise the Lord. **21** Praised be the Lord out of Zion, which dwelleth in Jerusalem. Praise ye the Lord.

136

1 A most earnest exhortation to give thanks unto God for the creation and governance of all things, which standeth in confessing that he giveth us all of his mere liberality.

1 Praise ye the Lord, because he is good: for his [a]mercy endureth forever. **2** Praise ye the God of gods: for his mercy endureth forever: **3** Praise ye the Lord of lords: for his mercy endureth forever: **4** Which only doeth great wonders; for his mercy endureth forever: **5** Which by his wisdom made the heavens: for his mercy endureth forever: **6** Which hath stretched out the earth upon the waters: for his [b]mercy endureth forever: **7** Which made great lights: for his mercy endureth forever: **8** As the Sun to rule the day; for his mercy endureth forever: **9** The Moon and the stars to govern the night: for his mercy endureth forever: **10** Which smote Egypt with their firstborn, (for his mercy endureth forever) **11** And [c]brought out Israel from among them; for his mercy endureth forever: **12** With a mighty hand and [d]stretched out arm; for his mercy endureth forever: **13** Which divideth the Sea into two parts; for his mercy endureth forever: **14** And made Israel to pass through the midst of it; for his mercy endureth forever: **15** And overthrew Pharaoh and his host in the red Sea; for his mercy endureth forever: **16** Which led his people through the [e]wilderness; for his mercy endureth forever: **17** Which smote great Kings: for his mercy endureth forever: **18** And slew [f]mighty Kings: for his mercy endureth forever: **19** As Sihon King of the Amorites: for his mercy endureth forever: **20** And Og the king of

---

PSALM 132

a. Psalm 132:1 That is, with how great difficulty he came to the kingdom, and with how great zeal and care he went about to build thy Temple.
b. Psalm 132:3 Because the chief charge of the king was to set forth God's glory, he showeth that he could take no rest, neither would go about any worldly thing, were it never so necessary, before he had executed his office.
c. Psalm 132:5 That is, the Ark, which was a sign of God's presence.
d. Psalm 132:6 The common bruit was that the Ark should remain in Ephrathah, that is, in Bethlehem a plentiful place: but after we perceived that thou wouldest place it in Jerusalem, which was barren as a forest, and compassed about only with hills.
e. Psalm 132:8 That is, Jerusalem, because that afterward his Ark should remove to none other place.
f. Psalm 132:9 Let the effect of thy grace both appear in the Priests and in the people.
g. Psalm 132:10 As thou first madest promise to David, so continue it to his posterity, that whatsoever they shall ask for their people, it may be granted.
h. Psalm 132:12 Because this cannot be accomplished but in Christ, it followeth, that the promise was spiritual.
i. Psalm 132:14 Meaning, for his own sake, and not for the plentifulness of the place: for he promiseth to bless it, declaring before that it was barren.
j. Psalm 132:16 That is, with my protection, whereby they shall be safe.
k. Psalm 132:17 Though his force for a time seemed to be broken, yet he promiseth to restore it.

PSALM 133

a. Psalm 133:1 Because the greatest part were against David, though some favored him, yet when he was established king at length, they joined all together like brethren: and therefore he showeth by these similitudes the commodity of brotherly love.
b. Psalm 133:2 The ointment was a figure of the graces which come from Christ the head upon his Church.
c. Psalm 133:3 By Hermon and Zion he meaneth the plentiful country about Jerusalem.
d. Psalm 133:3 Where there is such concord.

PSALM 134

a. Psalm 134:1 Ye that are Levites and chiefly appointed to this office.
b. Psalm 134:2 For their charge was not only to keep the Temple, but to pray there, and to give God thanks.
c. Psalm 134:3 And therefore hath all power, bless thee with his Fatherly love declared in Zion. Thus the Levites used to praise the Lord, and bless the people.

PSALM 135

a. Psalm 135:2 Ye Levites that are in his Sanctuary.
b. Psalm 135:2 Meaning, the people: for the people and Levites had their courts, which were places of the Temple separate.
c. Psalm 135:4 That is, hath freely loved the posterity of Abraham.
d. Psalm 135:6 He joined God's power with his will, to the intent that we should not separate them, and hereby he willeth God's people to depend on his power which he confirmeth by examples.
e. Psalm 135:12 He showeth what fruit the godly conceive of God's power, whereby they see how he destroyeth his enemies, and delivereth his people.
f. Psalm 135:14 That is, govern and defend his people.
g. Psalm 135:15 By showing what punishment God appointeth for the heathen idolaters, he warneth his people to beware the like offenses, seeing that idols have neither power nor life, and that their deliverance came not by idols, but by the mighty power of God, read Ps. 115:4.

PSALM 135

1. Jer. 10:13
2. Exod. 12:29
3. Num. 21:24,34

PSALM 136

a. Psalm 136:1 By this repetition he showeth that the least of God's benefits bind us to thanksgiving: but chiefly his mercy, which is principally declared towards his Church.
b. Psalm 136:6 This was a common kind of thanksgiving, which the whole people used, when they had received any benefit of God, as 2 Chron. 7:6 and 20:21, meaning, that God was not only merciful to their fathers, but also continued the same to their posterity.
c. Psalm 136:11 God's merciful providence toward man appeareth in all his creatures, but chiefly in that that he delivered his Church from the thraldom of their enemies.
d. Psalm 136:12 In doing such a work as was never done before, nor that any other could do.
e. Psalm 136:16 Where for the space of forty years he showed infinite and most strange wonders.
f. Psalm 136:18 Declaring thereby that no power nor authority was so dear unto him, as the love of his Church.
g. Psalm 136:23 In our greatest affliction and slavery, when we looked for nothing less than to have had any succor.
h. Psalm 136:25 Seeing that God provideth even for the beasts, much more hath he care over his.

Bashan: for his mercy endureth forever: **21** And gave their land for an heritage; for his mercy endureth forever: **22** Even an heritage unto Israel his servant; for his mercy endureth forever: **23** Which remembered us in our [g]base estate; for his mercy endureth forever: **24** And hath rescued us from our oppressors; for his mercy endureth forever: **25** Which giveth food to all [h]flesh; for his mercy endureth forever: **26** [i]Praise ye the God of heaven; for his mercy endureth forever.

137

1 The people of God in their banishment seeing God's true Religion decay, lived in great anguish and sorrow of heart: the which grief the Chaldeans did so little pity, 3 That they rather increased the same daily with taunts, reproaches and blasphemies against God. 7 Wherefore the Israelites desire God, first to punish the Edomites, who provoked the Babylonians against them, 8 And moved by the Spirit of God, prophesy the destruction of Babylon, where they were handled so tyrannously.

1 By the rivers of Babel we [a]sat, and there we wept, when we remembered Zion. **2** We hanged our harps upon the willows in the midst [b]thereof. **3** Then they that led us captive, [c]required of us songs and mirth, when we had hanged up our harps, saying, Sing us one of the songs of Zion. **4** How shall we sing, said we, a song of the Lord in a strange land? **5** [d]If I forget thee, O Jerusalem, let my right hand forget to play. **6** If I do not remember thee, let my tongue cleave to the roof of my mouth: yea, if I prefer not Jerusalem to my [e]chief joy. **7** Remember the children of [f]Edom, O Lord, in the [g]day of Jerusalem, which said, Raze it, raze it to the foundation thereof. **8** O daughter of Babel, worthy to be destroyed, blessed shall he be that rewardeth thee, as thou hast served us. **9** [h]Blessed shall he be that taketh and dasheth thy children against the stones.

138

1 David with great courage praiseth the goodness of God toward him, the which is so great, 4 That it is known to foreign princes, who shall praise the Lord together with him. 6 And he is assured to have the like comfort of God in the time following, as he had heretofore.

A Psalm of David. **1** I will praise thee with my whole heart: even before the [a]gods will I praise thee. **2** I will worship toward thine holy [b]Temple and praise thy Name, because of thy loving-kindness and for thy truth: for thou hast magnified thy Name above all things by thy word. **3** When I called, then thou heardest me, and hast [c]increased strength in my soul. **4** All the [d]kings of the earth shall praise thee, O Lord: for they have heard the words of thy mouth. **5** And they shall sing of the ways of the Lord, because the glory of the Lord is great. **6** For the Lord is high, yet he beholdeth the lowly, but the proud he knoweth [e]afar off. **7** Though I walk in the midst of trouble, yet wilt thou revive me: thou wilt stretch forth thine hand upon the wrath of mine enemies, and thy right hand shall save me. **8** The Lord will [f]perform his work toward me: O Lord, thy mercy endureth forever: forsake not the works of thine hands.

139

1 David cleanseth his heart from all hypocrisy, showeth that there is nothing so hid, which God seeth not. 13 Which he confirmeth by the creation of man. 14 After declaring his zeal and fear of God, he professeth to be enemy to all them that contemn God.

To him that excelleth. A Psalm of David. **1** O Lord, thou hast tried me, and known me. **2** Thou knowest my [a]sitting and my rising: thou understandest my thought afar off. **3** Thou [b]compassest my paths, and my lying down, and art accustomed to all my ways. **4** For there is not a word in my [c]tongue, but lo, thou knowest it wholly, O Lord. **5** Thou holdest me strait behind and before, and layest thine [d]hand upon me. **6** Thy knowledge is too wonderful for me: it is so high that I cannot attain unto it. **7** Whither shall I go from thy [e]Spirit? or whither shall I flee from thy presence? **8** If I ascend into heaven, thou art there: if I lie down in hell, thou art there. **9** Let me take the wings of the morning, and dwell in the uttermost parts of the sea: **10** Yet thither shall thine hand [f]lead me, and thy right hand hold me. **11** If I say, Yet the darkness shall hide me, even the night shall be [g]light about me. **12** Yea, the darkness hideth not from thee: but the night shineth as the day: the darkness and light are both alike. **13** For thou hast [h]possessed my reins: thou hast covered me in my mother's womb. **14** I will praise thee, for I am [i]fearfully and wondrously made: marvelous are thy works, and my soul knoweth it well. **15** My bones are not hid from thee, though I was made in a secret place, and fashioned [j]beneath in the earth. **16** Thine eyes did see me, when I was without form: [k]for in thy book were all things written, which in continuance were fashioned, when there was none of them before. **17** How [l]dear therefore are thy thoughts unto me, O God! how great is the sum of them! **18** If I should count them, they are more than the sand: when I awake, [m]I am still with thee. **19** Oh that thou wouldest slay, O God, the wicked and bloody men, to whom I say, Depart ye from me: **20** Which speak wickedly of thee, and being thine enemies are lifted up in vain. **21** Do not I [n]hate them, O Lord, that hate thee? and do not I earnestly contend with those that rise up against thee? **22** I hate them with an unfeigned hatred, as they were mine utter enemies. **23** Try me, O God, and know mine heart: prove me and know my thoughts, **24** And consider if there be any [o]way of wickedness in me, and lead me in the [p]way forever.

140

1 David complaineth of the cruelty, falsehood and injuries of his enemies. 8 Against the which he prayeth unto the Lord, and assureth himself of his help and succor. 12 Wherefore he provoketh the just to praise the Lord, and to assure themselves of his tuition.

To him that excelleth. A Psalm of David. **1** Deliver me, O Lord, from the evil man: preserve me from the [a]cruel man: **2** Which imagine evil things in their [b]heart, and make war continually. **3** They have sharpened their tongues like a serpent: [c]adders' poison is under their lips. Selah. **4** Keep [d]me, O Lord, from the hands of the wicked; preserve me from the cruel man, which purposeth to cause my steps to slide. **5** The proud have laid a snare for me, and spread a net with cords in my pathway, and set gins for me. Selah. **6** Therefore I said unto the Lord, Thou art my God: hear, O Lord, the voice of my prayers. **7** O Lord God the strength of my salvation, thou [e]hast covered my head in the day of battle. **8** Let not the wicked have his desire, O Lord; [f]perform not his wicked thought, lest they be proud. Selah. **9** As for [g]the chief of them that compass me about, let the mischief of their own lips come upon them. **10** Let coals fall upon them: let [h]him cast them into the fire, and into the deep pits that they rise not. **11** For the backbiter shall not be established upon the earth, evil shall [i]hunt the cruel man to destruction. **12** I know that the Lord will avenge the afflicted, and judge the poor. **13** Surely the righteous shall praise thy Name, and the just shall [j]dwell in thy presence.

---

i. Psalm 136:26 Seeing that all ages have had most plain testimonies of God's benefits.

PSALM 137

a. Psalm 137:1 That is, we abode a long time, and albeit that the country was pleasant, yet could not stay our tears, nor turn us from the true service of our God.
b. Psalm 137:2 To wit, of that country.
c. Psalm 137:3 The Babylonians speak thus in mocking us, as though by our silence we should signify that we hoped no more in God.
d. Psalm 137:5 Albeit the faithful are touched with their particular griefs, yet the common sorrow of the Church is most grievous unto them, and is such as they cannot but remember and lament.
e. Psalm 137:6 The decay of God's religion in their country was so grievous, that no joy could make them glad, except it were restored.
f. Psalm 137:7 According as Ezekiel 25:13 and Jer. 49:7, prophesied: and Obadiah, verse 10, showeth that the Edomites which came of Esau, conspired with the Babylonians against their brethren and kinsfolk.
g. Psalm 137:7 When thou didst visit Jerusalem.
h. Psalm 137:9 He alludeth to Isaiah's prophecy, Isa. 13:16, promising good success to Cyrus and Darius, whom ambition moved to fight against Babylon, but God used them as his rods to punish his enemies.

PSALM 138

a. Psalm 138:1 Even in the presence of Angels and of them that have authority among men.
b. Psalm 138:2 Both the Temple and ceremonial service at Christ's coming were abolished: so that now God will be worshipped only in spirit and truth, John 4:23.
c. Psalm 138:3 Thou hast strengthened me against mine outward and inward enemies.
d. Psalm 138:4 All the world shall confess that thou hast wonderfully preserved me, and performed thy promise.
e. Psalm 138:6 Distance of place cannot hinder God to show mercy to his, and to judge the wicked though they think that he is far off.
f. Psalm 138:8 Though mine enemies rage never so much, yet the Lord, which hath begun his work in me, will continue his grace to the end.

PSALM 139

a. Psalm 139:2 He confesseth that neither our actions, thoughts, or any part of our life can be hid from God, though he seem to be far off.
b. Psalm 139:3 So that they are evidently known to thee.
c. Psalm 139:4 Thou knowest my meaning before I speak.
d. Psalm 139:5 Thou so guidest me with thine hand, that I can turn no way, but where thou appointest me.
e. Psalm 139:7 From thy power and knowledge?
f. Psalm 139:10 Thy power doth so fast hold me, that I can escape by no means from thee.
g. Psalm 139:11 Though darkness be an hindrance to man's sight, yet it serveth thine eyes as well as the light.
h. Psalm 139:13 Thou hast made me in all parts, and therefore must needs know me.
i. Psalm 139:14 Considering thy wonderful work in forming me, I cannot but praise thee and fear thy mighty power.
j. Psalm 139:15 That is, in my mother's womb: which he compareth to the inward parts of the earth.
k. Psalm 139:16 Seeing that thou didst know me before I was composed of either flesh or bone, much more now must thou know me when thou hast fashioned me.
l. Psalm 139:17 How ought we to esteem the excellent declaration of thy wisdom in the creation of man?
m. Psalm 139:18 I continually see new occasions to meditate in thy wisdom, and to praise thee.
n. Psalm 139:21 He teacheth us boldly to contemn all the hatred of the wicked, and friendship of the world, when they would let us to serve God sincerely.
o. Psalm 139:24 Or any heinous way or rebellious: meaning, that though he were subject to sin, yet he was not given to wickedness, and to provoke God by rebellion.
p. Psalm 139:24 That is, continue thy favor towards me to the end.

PSALM 140

a. Psalm 140:1 Which persecuteth me of malice and without cause.
b. Psalm 140:2 That is, by their false cavillations and lies they kindle the hatred of the wicked against me.
c. Psalm 140:3 He showeth what weapons the wicked use, when power and force fail them.
d. Psalm 140:4 He declareth what is the remedy of the godly, when they are oppressed by the worldlings.
e. Psalm 140:7 He calleth to God with lively faith, being assured of his mercies, because he had before time proved, that God helped him ever in his dangers.
f. Psalm 140:8 For it is in God's hand to overthrow the counsels and enterprises of the wicked.
g. Psalm 140:9 It seemeth that he alludeth to Saul.
h. Psalm 140:10 To wit, God: for David saw that they were reprobate, and that there was no hope of repentance in them.
i. Psalm 140:11 God's plagues shall light upon him in such sort, that he shall not escape.
j. Psalm 140:13 That is, shall be defended and preserved by thy fatherly providence and care.

141

1 David being grievously persecuted under Saul, only fleeth unto God to have succor. 3 Desiring him to bridle his affections, that he may patiently abide till God take vengeance of his enemies.

A Psalm of David. **1** O Lord, I [a]call upon thee: haste thee unto me: hear my voice, when I cry unto thee. **2** Let my prayer be directed in thy sight as incense, and the [b]lifting up of mine hands as an evening sacrifice. **3** Set a watch, O Lord, before my mouth, and keep the [c]door of my lips. **4** Incline not mine heart to evil, that I should commit wicked works with them that work iniquity: and let me not eat of their [d]delicates. **5** Let the righteous smite me: for that is a benefit: and let [e]him reprove me, and it shall be a precious oil that shall not break mine head: for within a while I shall even [f]pray in their miseries. **6** When their judges shall be cast down in stony places, they shall [g]hear my words, for they are sweet. **7** Our bones lie scattered at the [h]grave's mouth, as he that heweth wood or diggeth in the earth. **8** But mine eyes look unto thee, O Lord God: in thee is my trust: leave not my soul destitute. **9** Keep me from the snare, which they have laid for me, and from the gins of the workers of iniquity. **10** Let the wicked fall into [i]his nets [j]together, while I escape.

142

The Prophet neither astonied with fear, nor carried away with anger, nor forced by desperation, would kill Saul: but with a quiet mind directed his earnest prayer to God, who did preserve him.

A Psalm of David, to give instruction, and a prayer when he was in the cave. **1** I cried unto the Lord with my voice: with my voice I [a]prayed unto the Lord. **2** I poured out my meditation before him, and declared mine affection in his presence. **3** Though my spirit [b]was in perplexity in me, yet thou knewest my path: in the way wherein I walked, have they privily laid a snare for me. **4** I looked upon my right hand, and beheld, but there was none that would know me: all refuge failed me, and [c]none cared for my soul. **5** Then cried I unto thee, O Lord, and said, Thou art mine [d]hope, and my portion in the land of the living. **6** Hearken unto my cry, for I am brought very low: deliver me from my persecutors, for they are too strong for me. **7** Bring my soul out of [e]prison, that I may praise thy Name: then shall the righteous [f]come about me, when thou art beneficial unto me.

143

1 An earnest prayer for remission of sins, acknowledging that the enemies did thus cruelly persecute him by God's just judgment. 8 He desireth to be restored to grace, 10 To be governeth by his holy Spirit, that he may spend the remnant of his life in the true fear and service of God.

A Psalm of David. **1** Hear my prayer, O Lord, and hearken unto my supplication: answer me in thy [a]truth, and in thy [b]righteousness. **2** (And enter not into judgment with thy servant: for in thy [c]sight shall none that liveth, be justified.) **3** For the enemy hath persecuted my soul: he hath smitten my life down to the earth: he hath laid me in the darkness, as they that have been dead [d]long ago: **4** And my spirit was in perplexity in me, and mine [e]heart within me was amazed. **5** Yet do I remember the time [f]past: I meditate in all thy works, yea, I do meditate in the works of thine hands. **6** I stretch forth mine hands unto thee: my soul desireth after thee, as the thirsty land. Selah. **7** Hear me speedily, O Lord, for my spirit faileth: hide not thy face from me, else I shall be like unto them that go down into the pit. **8** Let me hear thy loving-kindness in the [g]morning, for in thee is my trust; [h]show me the way, that I should walk in, for I lift up my soul unto thee. **9** Deliver me, O Lord, from mine enemies: for [i]I hid me with thee. **10** [j]Teach me to [k]do thy will, for thou art my God: let thy good Spirit lead me unto the land of righteousness. **11** Quicken me, O Lord, for thy Name's sake, and for thy righteousness bring my soul out of trouble. **12** And for thy mercy [l]slay mine enemies, and destroy all them that oppress my soul: for I am thy [m]servant.

144

He praiseth the Lord with great affection and humility for his kingdom restored, and for his victories obtained. 5 Demanding help, and the destruction of the wicked, 9 Promising to acknowledge the same with songs of praises, 15 And declareth wherein the felicity of any people consisteth.

A Psalm of David. **1** Blessed be the Lord my strength, which [a]teacheth mine hands to fight, and my fingers to battle. **2** He is my goodness and my fortress, my tower and [b]my deliverer, my shield and in him I trust, [c]which subdueth my people under me. **3** Lord, what is man that thou [d]regardest him! or the son of man that thou thinkest upon him? **4** Man is like to vanity; his days are like a shadow that vanisheth. **5** [e]Bow thine heavens, O Lord, and come down; touch the mountains, and they shall smoke. **6** [f]Cast forth the lightning and scatter them; shoot out thine arrows and consume them. **7** Send thine hand from above: deliver me, and take me out of the great [g]waters, and from the hand of strangers, **8** Whose mouth talketh vanity, and their right hand is a right hand [h]of falsehood. **9** I will sing a [i]new song unto thee, O God, and sing unto thee upon a viol, and an instrument of ten strings. **10** It is he that giveth deliverance unto kings, and rescueth David his [j]servant from the hurtful sword. **11** Rescue me, and deliver me from the hand of strangers, whose mouth talketh vanity, and their right hand is a right hand of falsehood: **12** [k]That our sons may be as the plants growing up in their youth, and our daughters as the corner stones, graven after the similitude of a palace: **13** That our [l]corners may be full and abounding with divers sorts, and that our sheep may bring forth thousands and ten thousand in our streets. **14** That our [m]oxen may be strong to labor; that there be none invasion, nor going out, nor no crying in our streets. **15** Blessed are the people, that be [n]so, yea blessed are the people whose God is the Lord.

145

This Psalm was composed when the kingdom of David flourished. 1 Wherein he describeth the wonderful providence of God, as well in governing man, as in preserving all the rest of his creatures. 17 He praiseth God for his justice and mercy. 18 But specially for his loving-kindness toward those that call upon him, that fear him, and love him: 21 For the which he promiseth to praise him forever.

A Psalm of David of praise. **1** O my God and King, [a]I will extol thee, and will bless thy Name forever and ever. **2** I will bless thee daily, and praise thy Name forever and ever. **3** [b]Great is the Lord, and most worthy to be praised, and

---

PSALM 141

a. Psalm 141:1 He showeth that there is none other refuge in our necessities, but only to flee unto God for comfort of soul.

b. Psalm 141:2 He meaneth his earnest zeal and gesture, which he used in prayer: alluding of the sacrifices which were by God's commandment offered in the old Law.

c. Psalm 141:3 He desireth God to keep his thoughts and ways either from thinking or executing vengeance.

d. Psalm 141:4 Let not their prosperity allure me to be wicked as they are.

e. Psalm 141:5 He could abide all corrections, that came of a loving heart.

f. Psalm 141:5 By patience I shall see the wicked so sharply handled, that I shall for pity pray for them.

g. Psalm 141:6 The people which followeth their wicked rulers in persecuting the Prophet, shall repent and turn to God, when they see their wicked rulers punished.

h. Psalm 141:7 Here appeareth that David was miraculously delivered out of many deaths, as 2 Cor. 1:9, 10.

i. Psalm 141:10 Into God's nets, whereby he catcheth the wicked in their own malice.

j. Psalm 141:10 So that none of them escape.

PSALM 142

a. Psalm 142:1 David's patience and instant prayer to God condemneth their wicked rage, which in their troubles either despair and murmur against God, or else seek to others than to God, to have redress in their miseries.

b. Psalm 142:3 Hebrew, was folden or wrapped in me: meaning, as a thing that could have no issue.

c. Psalm 142:4 Or, sought for myself.

d. Psalm 142:5 Though all means failed him, yet he knew that God would never forsake him.

e. Psalm 142:7 For he was on all sides beset with his enemies, as though he had been in a most straight prison.

f. Psalm 142:7 Either to rejoice at my wonderful deliverance, or to set a crown upon mine head.

PSALM 143

a. Psalm 143:1 That is, as thou hast promised to be faithful in thy promise to all that trust in thee.

b. Psalm 143:1 That is, according to thy free goodness, whereby thou defendest thine.

c. Psalm 143:2 He know that his afflictions were God's messengers to call him to repentance for his sins, though toward his enemies he was innocent, and that in God's sight all men are sinners.

d. Psalm 143:3 He acknowledgeth that God is the only and true physician and heal him: and that he is able to raise him to life, though he were dead long ago, and turned to ashes.

e. Psalm 143:4 So that only by faith and by the grace of God's Spirit was he upheld.

f. Psalm 143:5 To wit, thy great benefits of old, and the manifold examples of thy favor towards thine.

g. Psalm 143:8 That is, speedily and in due season.

h. Psalm 143:8 Let thine holy Spirit counsel me how to come forth of these great cares and troubles.

i. Psalm 143:9 I hid myself under the shadow of thy wings that I might be defended by thy power.

j. Psalm 143:10 He confesseth that both the knowledge and obedience of God's will cometh by the Spirit of God, who teacheth us by his word, giveth understanding by his Spirit, and frameth our hearts by his grace to obey him.

k. Psalm 143:10 That is, justly and aright: for so soon as we decline from God's will, we fall into error.

l. Psalm 143:12 Which shall be a sign of thy Fatherly kindness toward me.

m. Psalm 143:12 Resigning myself wholly unto thee, and trusting in thy protection.

PSALM 144

a. Psalm 144:1 Who of a poor shepherd hath made me a valiant warrior and mighty conqueror.

b. Psalm 144:2 Hebrew, my deliverer unto me: for the Prophet cannot satisfy himself with any words.

c. Psalm 144:2 He confesseth that neither by his own authority, power or policy his kingdom was quiet, but by the secret grace of God.

d. Psalm 144:3 To give unto God just praise, is to confess ourselves to be unworthy of so excellent benefits, and that he bestoweth them upon us of his free mercy.

e. Psalm 144:5 He desireth God to continue his graces, and to send help for the present necessity.

f. Psalm 144:6 By these manner of speeches he showeth that all the lets in the world cannot hinder God's power, which he apprehended by faith.

g. Psalm 144:7 That is, deliver me from the tumults of them that should be my people, but are corrupt in their judgment and enterprises, as though they were strangers.

h. Psalm 144:8 For though they shake hands, yet they keep not promise.

i. Psalm 144:9 That is, a rare and excellent song, as thy great benefits deserve.

j. Psalm 144:10 Though wicked kings be called God's servants, as Cyrus, Isa. 45:1, forasmuch as he useth them to execute his judgments: yet David because of God's promise, and they that rule godly, are properly so called, because they serve not their own affections, but set forth God's glory.

k. Psalm 144:12 He desireth God to continue his benefits toward his people, counting the procreation of children and their good education among the chiefest of God's benefits.

l. Psalm 144:13 That the very corners of our houses may be full of store for the great abundance of thy blessings.

m. Psalm 144:14 He attributeth not only the great commodities, but even the least also to God's favor.

n. Psalm 144:15 And if God give not to all his children all these blessings, yet he recompenseth them with better things.

PSALM 145

a. Psalm 145:1 He showeth what sacrifices are pleasant and acceptable unto God, even praise and thanksgiving, and seeing that God still continueth his benefits towards us, we ought never to be weary in praising him for the same.

his greatness is incomprehensible. **4** Generation shall praise thy works unto [c]ge-
neration, and declare thy power. **5** I will meditate of the beauty of thy glorious
majesty, and thy wonderful works. **6** And they shall speak of the power of thy
[d]dreadful acts, and I will declare thy greatness. **7** They shall break out into the
mention of thy great goodness, and shall sing aloud of thy righteousness. **8** [1]The
Lord is gracious, and [e]merciful, slow to anger, and of great mercy. **9** The Lord is
good to all, and his mercies are over all his works. **10** All thy works praise thee,
O Lord, and thy Saints bless thee. **11** [f]They show the glory of thy kingdom, and
speak of thy power, **12** To cause his [g]power to be known to the sons of men, and
the glorious renown of his kingdom. **13** Thy [2]kingdom is an everlasting king-
dom, and thy dominion endureth throughout all ages. **14** The Lord upholdeth
all that [h]fall, and lifteth up all that are ready to fall. **15** The eyes of [i]all wait upon
thee, and thou givest them their meat in due season. **16** Thou openest thine
hand, and fillest all things living of thy good pleasure. **17** The Lord is [j]righteous
in all his ways, and holy in all his works. **18** The Lord is near unto all that call
upon him, yea, to all that call upon him in [k]truth. **19** He will fulfill the [l]desi-
re of them that fear him; he will also hear their cry, and will save them. **20** The
Lord preserveth all them that love him; but he will destroy the wicked. **21** My
mouth shall speak the praise of the Lord, and all [m]flesh shall bless his holy Name
forever and ever.

146

1 David declareth his great zeal that he hath to praise God. 3 And teacheth, not to trust in man, but only in God Almighty, 7 Which delivereth the afflicted, 9 Defendeth the strangers, comforteth the fatherless, and the widows, 10 And reigneth forever.

Praise ye the Lord. **1** Praise thou the Lord, O my [a]soul. **2** I will prai-
se the Lord during my life; as long as I have any being, I will sing unto my
God. **3** Put not your trust in [b]Princes, nor in the son of man, for there is no help
in him. **4** His breath departeth, and he returneth to his earth; then his [c]thoughts
perish. **5** Blessed is he that hath the God of Jacob for his help, whose hope is in
the Lord his God, **6** Which made [d]heaven and earth, the sea, and all that therein
is; which keepeth his fidelity forever, **7** Which executeth justice [e]for the oppres-
sed, which giveth bread to the hungry; the Lord looseth the prisoners. **8** The
Lord giveth sight to the blind: the Lord raiseth up the crooked: the Lord [f]loveth the
righteous. **9** The Lord keepeth the [g]strangers: he relieveth the fatherless and wi-
dow: but he overthroweth the way of the wicked. **10** The Lord shall [h]reign fore-
ver: O Zion, thy God endureth from generation to generation. Praise ye the Lord.

147

1 The Prophet praiseth the bounty, wisdom, power, justice, and providence of God upon all his creatures. 2 But specially upon his Church, which he gathereth together after their dispersion, 19 Declaring his word and judgment so unto them, as he hath done to none other people.

1 Praise ye the Lord, for it is good to sing unto our God: for it is a [a]pleasant
thing, and praise is comely. **2** The Lord doth build up [b]Jerusalem, and gather
together the dispersed of Israel. **3** He healeth those that are [c]broken in heart,
and bindeth up their sores. **4** He [d]counteth the number of the stars, and cal-
leth them all by their names. **5** Great is our Lord, and great is his power: his
wisdom is infinite. **6** The Lord relieveth the meek, and abaseth the wicked to
the [e]ground. **7** Sing unto the Lord with praise: sing upon the harp unto our
God, **8** Which [f]covereth the heaven with clouds, and prepareth rain for the ear-
th, and maketh the grass to grow upon the mountains: **9** Which giveth to bea-
sts their food, and to the young ravens that [g]cry. **10** He hath no pleasure in the
[h]strength of an horse, neither delighteth he in the legs of man. **11** But the Lord
delighteth in them that fear him, and attend upon his mercy. **12** Praise the Lord,
O Jerusalem: praise thy God, O Zion. **13** For he hath made the bars of the gates
[i]strong, and hath blessed thy children within thee. **14** He setteth peace in thy
borders, and satisfieth thee with the [j]flour of wheat. **15** He sendeth forth his
[k]commandment upon earth, and his word runneth very [l]swiftly. **16** He giveth
snow like wool, and scattereth the hoary frost like ashes. **17** He casteth forth his
ice like morsels: who can abide the cold thereof? **18** He sendeth his word and
melteth them: he causeth his wind to blow, and the waters flow. **19** He showeth
his [m]word unto Jacob, his statutes and his judgments unto Israel. **20** He hath
not dealt so with every nation, neither have they [n]known his judgments. Praise ye
the Lord.

148

1 He provoketh all creatures to praise the Lord in heaven and earth, and all places. 14 Specially his Church, for the power that he hath given to the same, after that he had chosen them and joined them unto him.

Praise ye the Lord. **1** Praise ye the Lord from the heaven: praise ye
him in the high places. **2** Praise ye him, all ye [a]his Angels: praise him, all his
army. **3** Praise ye him, [b]sun and moon: praise ye him all bright stars. **4** Praise
ye him [c]heavens of heavens, and [d]waters, that be above the heavens. **5** Let them
praise the Name of the Lord: for he commanded, and they were created. **6** And
he hath established them forever and ever: he hath made an ordinance, which shall
not pass. **7** Praise ye the Lord from the earth, ye [e]dragons and all depths: **8** [f]Fi-
re and hail, snow and vapors, stormy wind, which execute his word. **9** Moun-
tains and all hills, fruitful trees, and all cedars: **10** Beasts and all cattle, creeping
things and feathered fowls: **11** [g]Kings of the earth and all people, princes and
all judges of the world: **12** Young men and maidens, also old men and chil-
dren: **13** Let them praise the Name of the Lord: for his Name only is to be exal-
ted, and his praise above the earth and the heavens. **14** For he hath exalted the
[h]horn of his people, which is a praise for all his Saints, even for the [i]children of
Israel, a people that is near unto him. Praise ye the Lord.

---

b. Psalm 145:3 Hereby he declareth that all power is subject unto God, and that no worldly promotion ought to obscure God's glory.
c. Psalm 145:4 Forasmuch as the end man's creation, and of his preservation in this life is to praise God, therefore he requireth that not only we ourselves do this, but cause all others to do the same.
d. Psalm 145:6 Of thy terrible judgments against the wicked.
e. Psalm 145:8 He describeth after what sort God showeth himself to all his creatures, though our sins have provoked his vengeance against all: to wit, merciful, not only in pardoning the sins of his elect, but in doing good even to the reprobate, albeit they cannot feel the sweet comfort of the same.
f. Psalm 145:11 The Praise of thy glory appeareth in all thy creatures: and though the wicked would obscure the same by their silence, yet the faithful are ever mindful of the same.
g. Psalm 145:12 He showeth that all things are out of order; but only where God reigneth.
h. Psalm 145:14 Who being in misery and affliction would faint and fall away, if God did not uphold them, and therefore they ought to reverence him that reigneth in heaven, and suffer themselves to be governed by him.
i. Psalm 145:15 To wit, as well of man, as of beast.
j. Psalm 145:17 He praiseth God, not only because he is beneficial to all his creatures, but also in that he justly punisheth the wicked, and mercifully examineth his by the cross, giving them strength and delivering them.
k. Psalm 145:18 Which only appertaineth to the faithful: and this virtue is contrary to infidelity, doubting, impatience and murmuring.
l. Psalm 145:19 For they will ask or wish for nothing, but according to his will, 1 John 5:14.
m. Psalm 145:21 That is, all men shall be bound to praise him.

PSALM 145

1. Exod. 34:6 **2.** Luke 1:33 - Dan. 7:14

PSALM 146

a. Psalm 146:1 He stirreth up himself and all his affections to praise God.
b. Psalm 146:3 That God may have the whole praise: wherein he forbiddeth all vain confidence, showing that of nature we are more inclined to put our trust in creatures, than in God the Creator.
c. Psalm 146:4 As their vain opinions, whereby they flattered themselves and so imagined wicked enterprises.
d. Psalm 146:6 He encourageth the godly to trust only in the Lord, both for that his power is able to deliver them from all danger, and from his promise sake, his will is most ready to do it.
e. Psalm 146:7 Whose faith and patience for a while he trieth, but at length he punisheth the adversaries, that he may be known to be judge of the world.
f. Psalm 146:8 Though he visit them by affliction, hunger, imprisonment and such like, yet his fatherly love and pity never faileth them, yea, rather to his these are signs of his love.
g. Psalm 146:9 Meaning, all them that are destitute of worldly means and succor.
h. Psalm 146:10 He assureth the Church that God reigneth forever for the preservation of the same.

PSALM 147

a. Psalm 147:1 He showeth wherein we ought to exercise ourselves continually, and to take our pastime: to wit, in praising God.
b. Psalm 147:2 Because the Lord is the founder of the Church, it cannot be destroyed, though the members thereof be dispersed, and seem as it were for a time to be cut off.
c. Psalm 147:3 With affliction, or sorrow for sin.
d. Psalm 147:4 Though it seem to man incredible, that God should assemble his Church, being so dispersed, yet nothing can be too hard to him that can number and name all the stars.
e. Psalm 147:6 For the more high that the wicked climb the greater is their fall in the end.
f. Psalm 147:8 He showeth by the examples of God's mighty power, goodness, and wisdom, that he can never want most just occasion to praise God.
g. Psalm 147:9 For their crying is as it were a confession of their need, which cannot be relieved, but by God only, then if God show himself mindful of the most contemptible souls, can he suffer them to die with famine, whom he hath assured of life everlasting?
h. Psalm 147:10 Though to use lawful means is both profitable and pleaseth God, yet to put our trust in them, is to defraud God of his honor.
i. Psalm 147:13 He doth not only furnish his Church with all things necessary, but preserveth also the same, and maketh it strong against all outward force.
j. Psalm 147:14 Hebrew, fat.
k. Psalm 147:15 His secret working in all creatures is as a commandment to keep them in order, and to give them moving and force.
l. Psalm 147:15 For immediately and without resisting all things obey him.
m. Psalm 147:19 As before he called God's secret working in all his creatures his word: so he meaneth here by his word the doctrine of life everlasting, which he hath left to his Church as a most precious treasure.
n. Psalm 147:20 The cause of this difference is God's free mercy, which hath elected his in his Son Christ Jesus to salvation: and his just judgment, whereby he hath appointed the reprobate to eternal damnation.

PSALM 148

a. Psalm 148:2 Because they are members of the same body, he setteth them before our eyes, which are most willing hereunto, and by their prompt obedience teach us to do our duty.
b. Psalm 148:3 In that God's glory shineth in these insensible creatures, this their beauty is as a continual praising of God.
c. Psalm 148:4 Not that there are divers heavens, but because of the spheres and of the situation of the fixed stars and planets, he comprehendeth by this word the whole heaven.
d. Psalm 148:4 That is, the rain which is in the middle region of the air, which he here comprehendeth under the name of the heavens.
e. Psalm 148:7 Meaning, the great and monstrous fishes, as whales and such like.
f. Psalm 148:8 Which come not by chance or fortune, but by God's appointed ordinance.
g. Psalm 148:11 For the greater gifts that any hath received, and the more high that one is preferred, the more bound is he to praise God for the same: but neither high nor low condition or degree can be exempted from this duty.
h. Psalm 148:14 That is, the dignity, power and glory of his Church.
i. Psalm 148:14 By reason of his covenant made with Abraham.

149

1 An exhortation to the Church to praise the Lord for his victory and conquest, that he giveth his Saints against all man's power.

Praise ye the Lord. 1 Sing ye unto the Lord [a]a new song: let his praise be
heard in the Congregation of Saints. 2 Let Israel rejoice in him that [b]made him,
and let the children of Zion rejoice in their [c]King. 3 Let them praise his Name
with the flute: let them sing praises unto him with the timbrel and harp. 4 For
the Lord hath pleasure in his people: he will make the meek glorious by deli-
verance. 5 Let the Saints be joyful with glory: let them sing loud upon their
[d]beds. 6 Let the high Acts of God be in their mouth, and a two edged sword in
their hands, 7 [e]To execute vengeance upon the heathen, and corrections among
the people: 8 To bind [f]their kings in chains, and their nobles with fetters of
iron, 9 That they may execute upon them the judgment that is [g]written: this
honor shall be to all his Saints. Praise ye the Lord.

150

1 An exhortation to praise the Lord without cease by all manner of ways for all his mighty and wonderful works.

Praise ye the Lord. 1 Praise ye God in his [a]Sanctuary: praise ye him in the
[b]firmament of his power. 2 Praise ye him in his mighty Acts: praise ye him ac-
cording to his excellent greatness. 3 Praise ye him in the sound of the [c]trumpet:
praise ye him upon the viol and the harp. 4 Praise ye him with timbrel and flute:
praise ye him with virginals and organs. 5 Praise ye him with sounding cymbals:
praise ye him with high sounding cymbals. 6 Let everything that hath [d]breath
praise the Lord. Praise ye the Lord.

PSALM 149

a. Psalm 149:1 For his rare and manifold benefits bestowed on his Church.
b. Psalm 149:2 In that they were preferred before all other nations, it was as a new creation, and therefore, Ps. 95:7, they were called the sheep of God's hands.
c. Psalm 149:2 For God as he is the creator of the soul and body, so wills he that both … serve him and that his people be continually subject to him, as to their most lawful king.
d. Psalm 149:5 He alludeth to that continual rest and quietness which they should have if they would suffer God to rule them.
e. Psalm 149:7 This is chiefly accomplished in the kingdom of Christ when God's people for just causes execute God's judgments against his enemies: and it giveth no liberty to any to revenge their private injuries.
f. Psalm 149:8 Not only the people, but the kings that were their enemies should be destroyed.
g. Psalm 149:9 Hereby God bindeth the hands and minds of all his to enterprise no farther than he appointeth.

PSALM 150

a. Psalm 150:1 That is, in the heaven.
b. Psalm 150:1 For his wonderful power appeareth in the firmament, which in Hebrew is called a stretching out, or spreading abroad, wherein the mighty work of God shineth.
c. Psalm 150:3 Exhorting the people only to rejoice in praising God, he maketh mention of those instruments which by God's commandment were appointed in the old Law, but under Christ the use thereof is abolished in the Church.
d. Psalm 150:6 He showeth that all the order of nature is bound to this duty, and much more God's children, who ought never to cease to praise him, till they be gathered into that kingdom, which he hath prepared for his, where they shall sing everlasting praise.

THE [a]PROVERBS OF SOLOMON

1

2 The power and use of the word of God. 7 Of the fear of God and knowledge of his word. 10 We may not consent to the enticings of sinners. 20 Wisdom complaineth that she is contemned. 24 The punishment of them that contemn her.

1 The Parables of Solomon the son of David king of Israel, 2 To know wi-
sdom, [b]and instruction, to understand the words [c]of knowledge, 3 To receive
[d]instruction to do wisely, by [e]justice and judgment and equity, 4 To give unto
the [f]simple sharpness of wit, and to the child knowledge and discretion. 5 And
wise man shall hear and increase in learning, and a man of [g]understanding shall
attain unto wise counsels, 6 To understand a parable, and the interpretation, the
words of the wise, and their dark sayings. 7 [1]The fear of the Lord is the beginning
of knowledge: but fools despise wisdom and instruction. 8 My son, hear thy [h]fa-
ther's instruction, and forsake not thy [i]mother's teaching. 9 For they shall be [j]a
comely ornament unto thine head, and as chains for thy neck. 10 My son, [k]if
sinners do entice thee, consent thou not. 11 If they say, Come with us, we will
lay wait for [l]blood, and lie privily for the innocent without a cause: 12 We will
swallow them up alive like a [m]grave, even whole, as those that go down into the
pit: 13 We shall find all precious riches, and fill our houses with spoil: 14 Cast
in thy lot among us, we will all have one [n]purse: 15 My son, walk not thou in
the way with them: refrain thy foot from their [o]path. 16 For their feet run to
evil, and make haste to shed blood. 17 Certainly as without cause the net is
spread before the eyes of all that hath wing: 18 So they lay wait for blood, and
lie privily for [p]their lives. 19 Such are the ways of everyone that is greedy of
gain: he would take away [q]the life of the owners thereof. 20 [r]Wisdom crieth
without: she uttereth her voice in the [s]streets. 21 She calleth in the high street,
among the prease in the enterings of the gates, and uttereth her words in the city,
saying, 22 O ye [t]foolish, how long will ye love foolishness? and the scornful take
their pleasure in scorning? and the fools hate knowledge? 23 (Turn you at my
correction: lo, I will pour out my mind unto you, and make you understand my
words.) 24 Because I have called, and ye refused: I have stretched out mine hand,
and none would regard. 25 But ye have despised all my counsel, and would none
of my correction, 26 I will also [u]laugh at your destruction, and mock when
your fear cometh. 27 When [v]your fear cometh like sudden desolation, and your
destruction shall come like a whirlwind: when affliction and anguish shall come
upon you, 28 Then shall they call upon me, but I will not answer: they shall seek
me early, but they shall not [w]find me, 29 Because they hated knowledge, and
did not choose the fear of the Lord. 30 They would none of my counsel, but

---

PROVERBS 1

a. Prov. 1:1 This word Proverb, or Parable, signifieth a grave and notable sentence, worthy to be kept in memory: and is sometimes taken in the evil part for a mock or scoff.
b. Prov. 1:2 That is, what we ought to know and follow, and what we ought to refuse.
c. Prov. 1:2 Meaning, the word of God wherein is the only true knowledge.
d. Prov. 1:3 To learn to submit ourselves to the correction of those that are wise.
e. Prov. 1:3 By living justly and rendering to every man that which appertaineth unto him.
f. Prov. 1:4 To such as have no discretion to rule themselves.
g. Prov. 1:5 As he showeth that these parables containing the effect of religion as touching manners and doctrine, do appertain to the simple people: so doth he declare that the same is also necessary for them that are wise and learned.
h. Prov. 1:8 He speaketh this in the Name of God, which is the universal Father of all creatures, or in the name of the pastor of the Church, who is as a father.
i. Prov. 1:8 That is, of the Church, wherein the faithful are begotten by the incorruptible seed of God's word.
j. Prov. 1:9 Hebrew, increase of grace.
k. Prov. 1:10 To wit, the wicked which have not the fear of God.
l. Prov. 1:11 He speaketh not only of the shedding of blood with hand, but of all crafty practices which tend to the detriment of our neighbor.
m. Prov. 1:12 As the grave is never satiated, so the avarice of the wicked and their cruelty hath none end.
n. Prov. 1:14 He showeth whereby the wicked are allured to join together, because they have every one part of the spoil of the innocent.
o. Prov. 1:15 That is, have nothing at all to do with them.
p. Prov. 1:18 He showeth that there is no cause to move these wicked to spoil the innocent, but their avarice and cruelty.
q. Prov. 1:19 Whereby he concludeth, that the covetous man is a murderer.
r. Prov. 1:20 This wisdom is the eternal word of God.
s. Prov. 1:20 So that none can pretend ignorance.
t. Prov. 1:22 Wisdom reproveth three kinds of men: the foolish or simple which err of ignorance, and the mockers that cannot suffer to be taught, and the fools which are drowned in worldly lusts and hate the knowledge of godliness.
u. Prov. 1:26 This is spoken according to our capacity, signifying that the wicked, which mock and jest at God's word, shall have the just reward of their mocking.
v. Prov. 1:27 That is, your destruction, which thing you feared.
w. Prov. 1:28 Because they sought not with an affection to God, but for ease of their own grief.
x. Prov. 1:30 Showing that without faith and obedience, we can not call upon God aright.
y. Prov. 1:31 They shall feel what commodity their wicked life shall give them.
z. Prov. 1:32 That is, the prosperity and sensuality wherein they delight.

PROVERBS 1

1. Ps. 111:10 - Eccl. 1:16

[x]despised all my correction. **31** Therefore shall they eat of the [y]fruit of their own
way, and be filled with their own devices. **32** For [z]ease slayeth the foolish, and
the prosperity of fools destroyeth them. **33** But he that obeyeth me, shall dwell
safely, and be quiet from fear of evil.

2

1 Wisdom exhorteth to obey her. 5 She teacheth the fear of God. 6 She is given of God. 10 She preserveth from wickedness.

1 My son, if thou wilt receive my words, and [a]hide my commandments wi-
thin thee, **2** And cause thine ears to hearken unto wisdom, and incline [b]thine
heart to understanding, **3** (For if thou callest after knowledge, [c]and cryest for
understanding: **4** If thou seekest her as silver, and searchest for her as for [d]treasu-
res, **5** Then shalt thou understand the fear of the Lord, and find the [e]knowledge
of God. **6** For the Lord giveth wisdom, out of his mouth cometh knowledge
and understanding. **7** He [f]preserveth the state of the righteous, he is a shield to
them that walk uprightly, **8** That they may keep the ways of judgment: and he
preserveth the way of his Saints). **9** Then shalt thou understand righteousness
and judgment, and equity, and every good path. **10** When wisdom entereth
into thine heart, and knowledge delighteth thy soul, **11** Then shall [g]counsel pre-
serve thee, and understanding shall keep thee, **12** And deliver thee from the
evil way, and from the man that speaketh froward things, **13** And from them
that leave the [h]ways of righteousness to walk in the ways of darkness: **14** Which
rejoice in doing evil, and delight [i]in the frowardness of the wicked, **15** Who-
se ways are crooked, and they are lewd in their paths. **16** And it shall deliver
thee from the strange [j]woman, even from the stranger which flattereth with her
words. **17** Which forsaketh the [k]guide of her youth, and forgetteth the [l]cove-
nant of her God. **18** Surely her [m]house tendeth to death, and her paths unto
[n]the dead. **19** All they that go unto her, return not again, neither take they hold
of the ways of life. **20** Therefore walk thou in the way of good men, and keep the
ways of the righteous. **21** For the just shall dwell in the [o]land, and the upright
men shall remain in it. **22** But the wicked shall be cut off from the earth, and the
transgressor shall be rooted out of it.

3

1 The words of God giveth life. 5 Trust in God. 7 Fear him. 9 Honor him. 11 Suffer his correction: 21 To them that follow the word of God, all things shall succeed well.

1 My son, forget not thou my Law, but let thine heart [1]keep my command-
ments. **2** For they shall increase the length of thy [a]days and the years of life, and
thy prosperity. **3** Let not [b]mercy and truth forsake thee: bind them on thy [c]neck,
and write them upon the table of thine [d]heart. **4** So shalt thou find favor and
good understanding in the sight of God and man. **5** Trust in the Lord with all
thine heart, and lean not unto thine own wisdom. **6** In all thy ways acknowledge
him, and he shall direct thy ways. **7** Be not wise in thine own eyes: but fear the
Lord, and depart from evil. **8** So health shall be unto thy [e]navel, and marrow
unto thy bones. **9** [f]Honor the Lord with thy riches, and with the first fruits of all
thine increase. **10** So shall thy barns be filled with abundance, and thy presses
shall [g]burst with new wine. **11** My son, refuse not the chastening of the Lord,
neither be grieved with his correction. **12** [2]For the Lord correcteth him, whom
he loveth, even as the father doth the child, in whom he delighteth. **13** Blessed is
the man that findeth wisdom, and the man that getteth understanding. **14** For
the merchandise thereof is better than the merchandise of silver, and the gain the-
reof is better than gold. **15** It is more precious than pearls: and all things that
thou canst desire, are not to be compared unto her. **16** Length of days is in her
right hand, [h]and in her right hand riches and glory. **17** Her ways are ways of
pleasure, and all her paths prosperity. **18** She is a tree [i]of life to them that lay
hold on her, and blessed is he that retaineth her. **19** The Lord by wisdom hath
laid the [j]foundation of the earth, and hath stablished the heavens through under-
standing. **20** By his knowledge the depths are broken up, and the clouds drop
down the dew. **21** My son, let not these things depart from thine eyes, but ob-
serve wisdom and counsel. **22** So they shall be life to thy soul, and grace unto
thy [k]neck. **23** Then shalt thou walk safely by the way: and thy foot shall not
stumble. **24** If thou sleepest, thou shalt not be afraid: and when thou sleepest,
thy sleep shall be sweet. **25** [l]Thou shalt not fear for any sudden fear, neither for
destruction of the wicked, when it cometh. **26** For the Lord shall be for thine
assurance, and shall preserve thy foot from taking. **27** Withhold not the good
from [m]the owners thereof, though there be power in thine hand to do it. **28** Say
not unto thy neighbor, Go and come again, and tomorrow will I give thee, if thou
now have it. **29** Intend none hurt against thy neighbor, seeing he doth dwell
[n]without fear by thee. **30** Strive not with a man causeless, when he hath done
thee no harm. **31** Be not [o]envious for the wicked man, neither choose any of
his ways, **32** For the froward is abomination unto the Lord: but his [p]secret is
with the righteous. **33** The curse of the Lord is in the house of the wicked: but
he blesseth the habitation of the righteous. **34** With the scornful [q]he scorneth,
but he giveth grace unto the humble. **35** The wise shall inherit glory: but fools
dishonor, though they be exalted.

4

1 Wisdom and her fruits ought to be searched. 14 The way of the wicked must be refused. 20 By the word of God the heart, eyes, and course of life must be guided.

1 Hear, O ye children, the instruction of a [a]father, and give ear to le-
arn understanding. **2** For I do give you a good doctrine: therefore forsake ye
not my law. **3** For I was my father's son, tender and dear in the sight of my
mother, **4** When he [b]taught me, and said unto me, Let thine heart hold fast my
words: keep my commandments, and thou shalt live. **5** Get wisdom: get under-
standing: forget not, neither decline from the words of my mouth. **6** Forsake her
not, and she shall keep thee: love her and she shall preserve thee. **7** [c]Wisdom is
the beginning: get wisdom therefore: and above all thy possession get understan-
ding. **8** Exalt her, and she shall exalt thee: she shall bring thee to honor, if thou
embrace her. **9** She shall give a comely ornament unto thine head, yea, she shall
give thee a crown of glory. **10** Hear, my son: and receive my words, and the
years of thy life shall be many. **11** I have [d]taught thee in the way of wisdom,
and led thee in the paths of righteousness. **12** When thou goest, thy gait shall
not be [e]strait, and when thou runnest, thou shalt not fall. **13** Take hold of in-
struction, and leave not: keep her, for she is thy life. **14** Enter not into the way
of the wicked, and walk not in the way of evil men. **15** Avoid it, and go not by
it: turn from it, and pass by. **16** For they cannot [f]sleep, except they have done
evil, and their sleep departeth except they cause some to fall. **17** For they eat
the bread of [g]wickedness, and drink the wine of violence. **18** But the way of
the righteous shineth as the light, that [h]shineth more and more unto the perfect
day. **19** The way of the wicked is as the darkness: they know not wherein they
shall fall. **20** My son, hearken unto my words, incline thine ear unto my sayin-
gs. **21** Let them not depart from thine eyes, but keep them in the midst of thine
heart. **22** For they are life unto those that find them: and health unto all their
[i]flesh. **23** Keep thine heart with all diligence: for thereout cometh [j]life. **24** Put

---

PROVERBS 2

- **a.** Prov. 2:1 That is, keep them in thine heart.
- **b.** Prov. 2:2 If thou give thyself to the true knowledge of God without hypocrisy.
- **c.** Prov. 2:3 Meaning, that we must seek the knowledge of God with care and diligence.
- **d.** Prov. 2:4 Showing that no labor must be spared.
- **e.** Prov. 2:5 This (saith he) is the true wisdom, to know and fear God.
- **f.** Prov. 2:7 Or, hideth the salvation.
- **g.** Prov. 2:11 The word of God shall teach thee, and counsel thee how to govern thyself.
- **h.** Prov. 2:13 That is, the word of God, which is the only light, to follow their own fantasies which are darkness.
- **i.** Prov. 2:14 When they see any given to evil as they are.
- **j.** Prov. 2:16 Meaning, that wisdom which is the word of God, shall preserve us from all vices: naming this vice of whoredom whereunto man is most prone.
- **k.** Prov. 2:17 That is, her husband, which is her head and guide to govern her, from whom she ought not to depart, but remain in his subjection.
- **l.** Prov. 2:17 Which is the promise made in marriage.
- **m.** Prov. 2:18 Her acquaintance with her familiars, and them that haunt her.
- **n.** Prov. 2:18 To them that are dead in body and soul.
- **o.** Prov. 2:21 They shall enjoy the temporal and spiritual promises of God, as the wicked shall be void of them.

PROVERBS 3

- **a.** Prov. 3:2 Long life is the blessing of God which he giveth to his, so far forth as it is expedient for them.
- **b.** Prov. 3:3 By mercy and truth he meaneth the commandments of the first and second table: or else the mercy and faithfulness that we ought to use toward our neighbors.
- **c.** Prov. 3:3 Keep them as a most precious jewel.
- **d.** Prov. 3:3 Have them ever in remembrance.
- **e.** Prov. 3:8 By this part he comprehendeth the whole body, as by health he meaneth all the benefits promised in the Law both corporal and spiritual.
- **f.** Prov. 3:9 As was commanded in the Law, Exod. 23:19; Deut. 26:2, and by this they acknowledged that God was the giver of all things, and that they were ready to bestow all at his commandment.
- **g.** Prov. 3:10 For the faithful distributor God giveth in greater abundance.
- **h.** Prov. 3:16 Meaning, that he that seeketh wisdom, that is, suffereth himself to be governeth by the Word of God, shall have all prosperity both corporal and spiritual.
- **i.** Prov. 3:18 Which bringeth forth such fruit that they that eat thereof have life: and he alludeth to the tree of life in paradise.
- **j.** Prov. 3:19 Hereby he showeth that this wisdom, whereof he speaketh, is everlasting, because it was before all creatures, and that all things even the whole world were made by it.
- **k.** Prov. 3:22 Or, throat, read Prov. 1:9.
- **l.** Prov. 3:25 For when God destroyeth the wicked, he will save his as he did Lot in Sodom.
- **m.** Prov. 3:27 Not only from them to whom the possession belongeth, but also thou shalt not keep it from them which have need of the use thereof.
- **n.** Prov. 3:29 That is, putteth his trust in thee.
- **o.** Prov. 3:31 Desire not to be like unto him.
- **p.** Prov. 3:32 That is, his covenant and fatherly affection which is hid and secret from the world.
- **q.** Prov. 3:34 He will show by his plagues, that their scorns shall turn to their own destruction, as Prov. 1:26.

PROVERBS 3

1. Deut. 8:1 - Deut. 30:16 **2.** Heb. 12:5 - Rev. 3:19

PROVERBS 4

- **a.** Prov. 4:1 He speaketh this in the person of a Preacher and Minister, which is as a father unto the people, read Prov. 2:8.
- **b.** Prov. 4:4 Meaning, David his father.
- **c.** Prov. 4:7 He showeth that we must first begin at God's word, if so be we will that other things prosper with us, contrary to the judgment of the world, which make it their last study, or else care not for it at all.
- **d.** Prov. 4:11 Solomon declareth what care his father had to bring him up in the true fear of God: for this was David's protestation.
- **e.** Prov. 4:12 Thou shalt walk at liberty without offence.
- **f.** Prov. 4:16 Meaning, that to do evil is more proper and natural to the wicked than to sleep, eat or drink.
- **g.** Prov. 4:17 Gotten by wicked means and cruel oppression.
- **h.** Prov. 4:18 Signifying, that the godly increase daily in knowledge and perfection, till they come to full perfection, which is when they shall be joined to their head in the heavens.
- **i.** Prov. 4:22 That is, they shall have health of body: under the which all other blessings promised in the law are contained.
- **j.** Prov. 4:23 For as the heart is either pure or corrupt, so is the whole course of man's life.
- **k.** Prov. 4:26 Keep a measure in all thy doings.

PROVERBS 5

- **a.** Prov. 5:1 Or, understanding.

away from thee a froward mouth, and put wicked lips far from thee. **25** Let thine
eyes behold the right, and let thine eyelids direct thy way before thee. **26** [k]Pon-
der the path of thy feet, and let all thy ways be ordered aright. **27** Turn not to
the right hand, nor to the left, but remove thy foot from evil.

5

3 Whoredom is forbidden, 9 And prodigality. 15 He willeth a man to live on his labors and to help others, 18 To love his wife. 22 The wicked taken in their own wickedness.

1 My son, hearken unto my wisdom, and incline thine ear unto my [a]k-
nowledge, **2** That thou mayest regard counsel, and thy lips observe knowled-
ge. **3** For the lips [b]of a strange woman drop as an honeycomb, and her mouth
is more soft than [c]oil. **4** But the end of her is bitter as wormwood, and sharp as
a two-edged sword. **5** Her [d]feet go down to death, and her steps take hold on
hell. **6** She weigheth not the way of life: [e]her paths are moveable: thou canst
not know them. **7** Hear ye me now therefore, O children, and depart not from
the words of my mouth. **8** Keep thy way far from her, and come not near the
door of her house, **9** Lest thou give thine [f]honor unto others, and thy years to
the cruel: **10** Lest the stranger should be filled with thy strength, and thy [g]la-
bors be in the house of a stranger, **11** And thou mourn at thine end, (when
thou hast consumed thy flesh and thy body) **12** And say, How have I hated in-
struction, and mine heart despised correction! **13** And have not obeyed the voice
of them that taught me, nor inclined mine ear to them that instructed me! **14** I
was almost brought into all evil in the midst of the Congregation and [h]assem-
bly. **15** Drink the water of [i]thy cistern, and of the rivers out of the midst of
thine own well. **16** Let thy fountains flow forth, and the rivers of waters in
the streets. **17** But let them be thine, even [j]thine only, and not the strangers
with thee. **18** Let thy [k]fountain be blessed, and rejoice with the wife of thy
[l]youth. **19** Let her be as the loving hind and pleasant roe: let her breasts sati-
sfy thee at all times, and delight in her love continually. **20** For why shouldest
thou [m]delight, my son, in a strange woman, or embrace the bosom of a stran-
ger? **21** For the ways of man are before the [n]eyes of the Lord, and he pondereth
all his paths. **22** His own iniquities shall take the wicked himself, and he shall be
holden with the cords of his own sin. **23** He shall [o]die for fault of instruction,
and shall go astray through his great folly.

6

1 Instruction for sureties. 6 The slothful and sluggish is stirred to work. 12 He describeth the nature of the wicked. 16 The things that God hateth. 20 To observe the word of God. 24 To flee adultery.

1 My son, if thou be surety for thy neighbor, and hast stricken hands with the
stranger, **2** Thou art [a]snared with the words of thy mouth: thou art even taken
with the words of thine own mouth. **3** Do this now, my Son, and deliver thy-
self: seeing thou art come into the hand of thy neighbor, go, and humble thyself,
and solicit thy friends. **4** Give no sleep to thine eyes, nor slumber to thine eye-
lids. **5** Deliver thyself as a Doe from the hand of the hunter, and as a bird from
the hand of the fowler. **6** Go to [b]the pismire, O sluggard: behold her ways, and
be wise. **7** For she having no guide, governor, nor ruler, **8** Prepareth her meat
in the summer, and gathereth her food in harvest. **9** How long wilt thou sleep,
O sluggard? when wilt thou arise out of the sleep? **10** [l]Yet a little sleep, a little
slumber, [c]a little folding of the hands to sleep. **11** Therefore thy poverty cometh
as one that [d]traveleth by the way, and thy necessity like [e]an armed man. **12** The
unthrifty man [f]and the wicked man walketh with a froward mouth. **13** He ma-
keth a sign with his eyes: he [g]signifieth with his feet: he [h]instructeth with his fin-
gers. **14** Lewd things are in his heart: he imagineth evil at all times, and raiseth
up contentions. **15** Therefore shall his destruction come speedily: he shall be de-
stroyed suddenly without recovery. **16** These six things doth the Lord hate: yea,
his soul abhorreth seven: **17** The haughty eyes, a lying tongue, and the hands
that shed innocent blood, **18** An heart that imagineth wicked enterprises, [i]feet
that be swift in running to mischief, **19** A false witness that speaketh lies, and
him that raiseth up contentions among [j]brethren. **20** My son, keep thy father's
commandment, and forsake not thy mother's instruction. **21** Bind them always
upon thine [k]heart, and tie them about thy neck. **22** It shall lead thee when thou
walkest: it shall watch for thee when thou sleepest, and when thou wakest, it shall
talk with thee. **23** For the [l]commandment is a lantern, and instruction a light:
and [m]corrections for instruction are the way of life, **24** To keep thee from the wi-
cked woman, and from the flattery of the tongue of a strange woman. **25** Desire
not her beauty in thine heart, neither let her take thee with her [n]eye lids. **26** For
because of the whorish woman, a man is brought to a morsel of bread, and a wo-
man will hunt for the precious life of a man. **27** [o]Can a man take fire in his bo-
som, and his clothes not be burnt? **28** Or can a man go upon coals, and his feet
not be burnt? **29** So he that goeth into his neighbor's wife, shall not be inno-
cent, whosoever toucheth her. **30** Men do not [p]despise a thief, when he stealeth
to satisfy his [q]soul, because he is hungry. **31** But if he be found, he shall restore
sevenfold, or he shall give all the substance of his house. **32** But he that commi-
teth adultery with a woman, he [r]is destitute of understanding: he that doeth it, de-
stroyeth his own soul. **33** He shall find [s]a wound and dishonor, and his reproach
shall never be put away. **34** For jealousy is the rage of a man: therefore he will
not [t]spare in the day of vengeance. **35** He cannot bear the sight of any ransom:
neither will he consent, though thou augment the gifts.

7

1 An exhortation to wisdom and to the word of God. 5 Which will preserve us from the harlot, 6 Whose manners are described.

1 My son keep my words, and hide my commandments with thee. **2** Keep
my commandments, and thou shalt live, and mine instruction, as the [a]apple of
thine eyes. **3** Bind them upon thy fingers, and write them upon the table of
thine heart. **4** Say unto wisdom, Thou art my sister, and call understanding thy
kinswoman, **5** That they may keep thee from the strange woman, even from the
strange that is smooth in her words. **6** [b]As I was in the window of mine hou-
se, I looked through my window, **7** And I saw among the fools, and conside-
red among the children a young man destitute of understanding, **8** Who passed
through the street by her corner, and went toward her house, **9** In the twilight in
the evening, when the night began to be [c]black and dark. **10** And behold, there
met him a woman with an harlot's [d]behavior, and [e]subtle in heart. **11** (She [f]is
babbling and loud, whose feet cannot abide in her house. **12** Now she is wi-
thout, now in the streets, and lieth in wait at every corner) **13** So she caught him
and kissed him, and [g]with an impudent face said unto him, **14** I have [h]peace
offerings: this [i]day have I paid my vows. **15** Therefore came I forth to meet thee,
that I might seek thy face: and I have found thee. **16** I have decked my bed with
ornaments, [j]carpets and laces of Egypt. **17** I have perfumed my bed with myrrh,
aloes, and cinnamon. **18** Come, let us take our fill of love until the morning:
let us take our pleasure in dalliance. **19** For mine husband is not at home: he
is gone a journey far off. **20** He hath taken [k]with him a bag of silver, and will

---

b. Prov. 5:3 That is, an harlot which giveth herself to another than to her husband.
c. Prov. 5:3 By oil and honey he meaneth flattering and crafty enticements.
d. Prov. 5:5 All her doings lead to destruction.
e. Prov. 5:6 She hath ever new means to allure to wickedness.
f. Prov. 5:9 That is, thy strength and goods to her that will have no pity upon thee: as is read of Samson, and the prodigal son.
g. Prov. 5:10 The goods gotten by thy travel.
h. Prov. 5:14 Although I was faithfully instructed in the truth, yet had I almost fallen to utter shame and destruction notwithstanding my good bringing up in the assembly of the godly.
i. Prov. 5:15 He teacheth us sobriety, exhorting us to live of our own labors and to be beneficial to the godly that want.
j. Prov. 5:17 Distribute them not to the wicked and infidels, but reserve them for thyself, thy family and them that are of the household of faith.
k. Prov. 5:18 Thy children which shall come of thee in great abundance, showing that God blesseth marriage, and curseth whoredom.
l. Prov. 5:18 Which thou didst marry in thy youth.
m. Prov. 5:20 Or, go astray with a stranger?
n. Prov. 5:21 He declareth that except man do join to his wife both in heart and in outward conversation, that he shall not escape the judgments of God.
o. Prov. 5:23 Because he will not give ear to God's word and be admonished.

PROVERBS 6

a. Prov. 6:2 He forbiddeth us not to become surety one for another, according to the rule of charity, but that we consider for whom and after what sort, so that the creditor may not be defrauded.
b. Prov. 6:6 If the word of God cannot instruct thee, yet learn at the little pismire to labor for thyself and not to burden others.
c. Prov. 6:10 He expresseth lively the nature of the sluggards, which though they sleep never so long, yet have never enough, but ever seek occasions thereunto.
d. Prov. 6:11 That is, suddenly, and when thou lookest not for it.
e. Prov. 6:11 It shall come in such sort, as thou are not able to resist it.
f. Prov. 6:12 He showeth to what inconvenience the idle persons and sluggards come, by calling them unthrifty, or the men of Belial, and slanderous.
g. Prov. 6:13 Hebrew, speaketh.
h. Prov. 6:13 Thus all his gesture tendeth to wickedness.
i. Prov. 6:18 Meaning, the raging affections, which carry a man away in such sort that he cannot tell what he doeth.
j. Prov. 6:19 Or, neighbors.
k. Prov. 6:21 Read Prov. 3:3.
l. Prov. 6:23 By the commandment, he meaneth the word of God: and by the instruction, the preaching and declaration of the same, which is committed to the Church.
m. Prov. 6:23 And reprehensions when the word is preached bring us to life.
n. Prov. 6:25 With her wanton looks and gesture.
o. Prov. 6:27 Meaning, that she will never cease till she have brought thee to beggary, and then seek thy destruction.
p. Prov. 6:30 He reproveth not theft, but showeth that it is not so abominable as whoredom, forasmuch as theft might be redeemed: but adultery was a perpetual infamy, and death by the law of God.
q. Prov. 6:30 Meaning, for very necessity.
r. Prov. 6:32 Hebrew, faileth in heart.
s. Prov. 6:33 That is, death appointed by the Law.
t. Prov. 6:34 He showeth that man by nature seeketh his death, that hath abused his wife, and so concludeth, that neither God's Law nor the law of nature admitteth any ransom for the adultery.

PROVERBS 6

1. Prov. 24:33

PROVERBS 7

a. Prov. 7:2 By this diversity of words, he meaneth that nothing ought to be so dear unto us as the word of God, nor that we look on anything more nor mind anything so much.
b. Prov. 7:6 Solomon useth this parable to declare their folly, that suffer themselves to be abused by harlots.
c. Prov. 7:9 He showeth that there was almost none so impudent, but they were afraid to be seen, and also their own consciences did accuse them which caused them to seek the night to cover their filthiness.
d. Prov. 7:10 Or, garment.
e. Prov. 7:10 Or, hid.
f. Prov. 7:11 He describeth certain conditions, which are peculiar to harlots.
g. Prov. 7:13 Hebrew, she strengthened her face.
h. Prov. 7:14 Because that in peace offerings a portion returned to them that offered, she showeth him that she hath meat at home to make good cheer with: or else she would use some cloak of holiness till she had gotten him in her snares.
i. Prov. 7:14 Which declareth that harlots outwardly will seem holy and religious: both because they may the better deceive others, and also thinking by observing of ceremonies and offerings to make satisfaction for their sins.
j. Prov. 7:16 Or, carved work.
k. Prov. 7:20 Hebrew, in his hand.

come home at the day appointed. **21** Thus with her great craft she caused him
to yield, and with her flattering lips she enticed him. **22** And he followed her
straightway, as an [l]ox that goeth to the slaughter, and [m]as a fool to the stocks for
correction, **23** Till a dart strike through his liver, as a bird hasteth to the snare,
not knowing that [n]he is in danger. **24** Hear me now therefore, O children, and
hearken to the words of my mouth. **25** Let not thine heart decline to her ways:
wander thou not in her paths. **26** For she hath caused many to fall down woun-
ded, and the [o]strong men are all slain by her. **27** Her house is the way [1]unto the
grave, which goeth down to the chambers of death.

8

*1 Wisdom declareth her excellency, 11 riches, 15 power, 22 eterni-
ty. 32 She exhorteth all to love and follow her.*

1 Doth [1]not [a]wisdom cry? and understanding utter her voice? **2** She stan-
deth in the top of the high places, by the way in the place of the paths. **3** She
crieth besides [b]the gates before the city at the entry of the doors, **4** O men, I
call unto you, and utter my voice to the children of men. **5** O ye foolish men,
understand wisdom, and ye, O fools, be wise in heart. **6** Give ear, for I will
speak of excellent things, and the opening of my lips shall teach things that be ri-
ght. **7** For my mouth shall speak the truth, and my lips abhor wickedness. **8** All
the words of my mouth are righteous: there is no lewdness, nor frowardness in
them. **9** They are all [c]plain to them that will understand, and straight to them
that would find knowledge. **10** Receive mine instruction, and not silver, and
knowledge rather than fine gold. **11** For wisdom is better than precious sto-
nes: and all pleasures are not to be compared unto her. **12** I wisdom dwell with
[d]prudence, and I find forth knowledge and counsels. **13** The fear of the Lord is
to hate [e]evil, as pride, and arrogancy, and the evil way: and a mouth that speaketh
lewd things I do hate. **14** I have counsel and wisdom: I am understanding, and
I have strength. **15** By me [f]kings reign, and princes decree justice. **16** By me
princes rule, and the nobles, and all the judges of the earth. **17** I love them that
love me: and they that seek me [g]early shall find me. **18** Riches and honor are
with me: [h]even durable riches and righteousness. **19** My fruit is better than gold,
even than fine gold, and my revenues better than fine silver. **20** I cause to walk
in the way of righteousness, and in the midst of the paths of [i]judgment, **21** That
I may cause them that love me, to inherit substance, and I will fill their treasu-
res. **22** The Lord hath possessed me in the beginning of his way: I was [j]before his
works of old. **23** [k]I was set up from everlasting, from the beginning, and before
the earth. **24** When there were no depths, was I begotten, when there were no
fountains abounding with water. **25** Before the mountains were settled: and be-
fore the hills, was I begotten. **26** He had not yet made the earth, nor the open
places, nor the height of the dust in the world. **27** When he prepared the hea-
vens, I was there, when he set the compass upon the deep: **28** When he establi-
shed the clouds above: when he confirmed the fountains of the deep: **29** When
he gave his decree to the sea, that the waters should not pass his commandment,
when he appointed the foundations of the earth. **30** Then was I with him [l]as a
nourisher, and I was daily his delight, rejoicing always before him, **31** And took
my [m]solace in the compass of [n]his earth: and my delight is with the children of
men. **32** Therefore now hearken, O children, unto me: for blessed are they that
keep my ways. **33** Hear instruction, and be ye wise, and refuse it not: blessed
is the man that heareth me, watching daily at my gates, and giving attendance at
the posts of my doors. **34** For he that findeth me, findeth life, and shall obtain
favor of the Lord. **35** But he that sinneth against me, hurteth his own soul: and
all that hate me, love death.

9

*2 Wisdom calleth all to her feast. 7 The scorner will not be corrected. 10
The fear of God. 13 The conditions of the harlot.*

1 Wisdom hath built her [a]house, and hewn out her [b]seven pillars. **2** She
hath killed her victuals, drawn her wine, and [c]prepared her table. **3** She hath sent
forth her [d]maidens, and crieth upon the highest places of the city, saying, **4** Who
so is [e]simple, let him come hither, and to him that is destitute of wisdom, she
saith, **5** Come, and eat of my [f]meat, and drink of the wine that I have
drawn. **6** Forsake your way, ye foolish, and ye shall live: and walk in the way of
understanding. **7** He that reproveth a scorner, purchaseth to himself shame: and
he that rebuketh the wicked, getteth himself a [g]blot. **8** Rebuke not a [h]scorner,
lest he hate thee: but rebuke a wise man, and he will love thee. **9** Give admoni-
tion to the wise, and he will be the wiser: teach a righteous man, and he will in-
crease in learning. **10** The beginning of wisdom is the fear of the Lord, and the
knowledge of holy things, is [i]understanding. **11** For thy days shall be multiplied
by me, and the years of thy life shall be augmented. **12** If thou be wise, thou
shalt be wise for [j]thyself, and if thou be a scorner, thou alone shalt suffer. **13** A
[k]foolish woman is troublesome; she is ignorant and knoweth nothing. **14** But
she sitteth at the door of her house on a seat in the high places of the city, **15** To
call them that pass by the way, that go right on their way, saying, **16** Who so
is simple let him come hither, and to him that is destitute of wisdom, she saith
also, **17** Stolen waters are sweet, and hid bread is pleasant. **18** But he knoweth
not, that the dead are there, and that her guests are in the depth of hell.

10

*In this Chapter, and all that follow, unto the thirtieth, the wise man exhor-
teth by divers sentences, which he calleth Parables, to follow virtue, and flee
vice: and also showeth what profit cometh of wisdom, and what hindrance proceedeth
of foolishness.*

THE PARABLE OF SOLOMON. 1 A wise [1]son maketh a glad father:
but a foolish son is an heaviness to his mother. **2** The treasures of [a]wickedness
profit nothing: but righteousness delivereth from death. **3** The Lord will [b]not
famish the soul of the righteous: but he casteth away the substance of the wi-
cked. **4** A [c]slothful hand maketh poor: but the hand of the diligent maketh
rich. **5** He that gathereth in summer, is the son of wisdom: but he that sleepeth
in harvest, is the son of confusion. **6** Blessings are upon the head of the righte-
ous: but iniquity shall cover the mouth of [d]the wicked. **7** The memorial of the
just shall be blessed: but the name of the wicked shall [e]rot. **8** The wise in he-
art will receive commandments: but the foolish in [f]talk shall be beaten. **9** He
that walketh uprightly, walketh [g]boldly: but he that perverteth his ways, shall be
known. **10** He that [h]winketh with the eye, worketh sorrow, and he that is [i]fo-
olish in talk, shall be beaten. **11** The mouth of a righteous man is a wellspring
of life: but iniquity covereth the mouth of the wicked. **12** Hatred stirreth up
contentions: [2]but love covereth all trespasses. **13** In the lips of him that hath

---

l. Prov. 7:22 Which thinking he goeth to the pasture, goeth willingly to his own destruction.
m. Prov. 7:22 Which goeth cheerfully, not knowing that he shall be chastised.
n. Prov. 7:23 Hebrew, It is for his life.
o. Prov. 7:26 Neither wit nor strength can deliver them that fall into the hands of the harlot.

PROVERBS 7
1. Prov. 2:18

PROVERBS 8
a. Prov. 8:1 Solomon declareth that man is cause of his own perdition, and that he can pretend no ignorance, forasmuch as God calleth to all men by his word, and by his works to follow virtue, and to flee from vice.
b. Prov. 8:3 Where the people did most resort, and which was the place of justice.
c. Prov. 8:9 Meaning, that the word of God is easy unto all that have a desire unto it, and which are not blinded by the prince of this world.
d. Prov. 8:12 That is, except a man have wisdom, which is the true knowledge of God, he can neither be prudent nor good counselor.
e. Prov. 8:13 So that he that doth not hate evil, feareth not God.
f. Prov. 8:15 Whereby he declareth that honors, dignity or riches come not of man's wisdom or industry, but by the providence of God.
g. Prov. 8:17 That is, study the word of God diligently, and with a desire to profit.
h. Prov. 8:18 Signifying that he chiefly meaneth the spiritual treasures and heavenly riches.
i. Prov. 8:20 For there can be no true justice or judgment, which is not rejected by this wisdom.
j. Prov. 8:22 He declareth hereby the divinity and eternity of this wisdom, which he magnifieth and praiseth through this book: meaning thereby the eternal son of God Jesus Christ our Savior, whom Saint John calleth that word that was in the beginning, John 1:1.
k. Prov. 8:23 He declareth the eternity of the Son of God, which is meant by this word, wisdom, who was before all time, and ever present with the father.
l. Prov. 8:30 Some read, a chief worker: signifying that this wisdom, even Christ Jesus, was equal with God his father, and created, preserveth and still worketh with him, as John 5:17.
m. Prov. 8:31 Whereby is declared that the work of the creation was no pain, but a solace unto the wisdom of God.
n. Prov. 8:31 By earth he meaneth man, which is the work of God in whom wisdom took pleasure: insomuch as for man's sake the divine wisdom took man's nature, and dwelt among us, and filled us with unspeakable treasures: and this is that solace and pastime whereof is here spoken.

PROVERBS 8
1. Prov. 1:20

PROVERBS 9
a. Prov. 9:1 Christ hath prepared him a Church.
b. Prov. 9:1 That is, many chief stays and principal parts of his Church, as were the Patriarchs, Prophets, Apostles, Pastors, and Doctors.
c. Prov. 9:2 He compareth wisdom with great princes that keep open house for all that come.
d. Prov. 9:3 Meaning, true preachers, which are not infected with man's wisdom.
e. Prov. 9:4 He that knoweth his own ignorance, and is void of malice.
f. Prov. 9:5 By the meat and drink, is meant the word of God, and the ministration of the Sacraments, whereby God nourisheth his servants in his house, which is the Church.
g. Prov. 9:7 For the wicked will contemn him and labor to defame him.
h. Prov. 9:8 Meaning them that are incorrigible, which Christ calleth dogs and swine: or he speaketh this in comparison, not that the wicked should not be rebuked, but he showeth their malice, and the small hope of profit.
i. Prov. 9:10 He showeth what true understanding is, to know the will of God in his word which is meant by holy things.
j. Prov. 9:12 Thou shalt have the chief profit and commodity thereof.
k. Prov. 9:13 By the foolish woman, some understand the wicked preachers, who counterfeit the word of God: as appeareth verse 16, which were the words of the true preachers, as verse 4, but their doctrine is but as stolen waters: meaning, that they are but men's traditions, which are more pleasant to the flesh than the word of God, and therefore they themselves boast thereof.

PROVERBS 10
a. Prov. 10:2 That is, wickedly gotten.
b. Prov. 10:3 Though he suffer the just to want for a time, yet he will send him comfort in due season.
c. Prov. 10:4 Or, deceitful.
d. Prov. 10:6 When their wickedness shall be discovered, they shall be as dumb, and not know what to say.
e. Prov. 10:7 Shall be vile and abhorred both of God and man, contrary to their own expectation, which think to make their name immortal.
f. Prov. 10:8 Hebrew, lips.
g. Prov. 10:9 Or, surely.
h. Prov. 10:10 That beareth a fair countenance, and imagineth mischief in his heart, as Prov. 6:13.
i. Prov. 10:10 For the corruption of his heart is known by his talk.
j. Prov. 10:13 That is, God will find him out to punish him.
k. Prov. 10:15 And so maketh him bold to do evil, whereas poverty bridleth the poor from many evil things.
l. Prov. 10:21 For they speak truth, and edify many by exhortations, admonition, and counsel.

understanding, wisdom is found, and [j]a rod shall be for the back of him that is de-
stitute of wisdom. 14 Wise men lay up knowledge: but the mouth of the fool is
a present destruction. 15 The rich man's goods are his [k]strong city: but the fear
of the needy is their poverty. 16 The labor of the righteous tendeth to life: but
the revenues of the wicked to sin. 17 He that regardeth instruction is in the way
of life: but he that refuseth correction, goeth out of the way. 18 He that dissem-
bleth hatred with lying lips, and he that inventeth slander, is a fool. 19 In many
words there cannot want iniquity: but he that refraineth his lips, is wise: 20 The
tongue of the just man is as fined silver: but the heart of the wicked is little wor-
th. 21 The lips of the righteous do [l]feed many: but fools shall die for want of
wisdom. 22 The blessing of the Lord, it maketh rich, and he doth add [m]no sor-
rows with it. 23 It is a pastime to a fool to do wickedly: but wisdom is under-
standing to a man. 24 That which the wicked feareth, shall come upon him: but
God will grant the desire of the righteous. 25 As the whirlwind passeth, so is the
wicked no more: but the righteous is as an everlasting foundation. 26 As vine-
gar is to the teeth, and as smoke to the eyes, so is the slothful to them that [n]send
him. 27 The fear of the Lord increaseth the days: but the years of the wicked
[o]shall be diminished. 28 The patient abiding of the righteous shall be gladness:
but the hope of the wicked shall perish. 29 The way of the Lord is strength to the
upright man: but fear shall be for the workers of iniquity. 30 The righteous shall
[p]never be removed: but the wicked shall not dwell in the land. 31 The mouth
of the just shall be fruitful in wisdom: but the tongue of the froward shall be cut
out. 32 The lips of the righteous know what is acceptable: but the mouth of the
wicked speaketh froward things.

11 *Chapter 11*

1 False [a]balances are an abomination unto the Lord: but a perfect
[b]weight pleaseth him. 2 When pride cometh, then cometh [c]shame: but with the
lowly is wisdom. 3 The uprightness of the just shall guide them: but the frowar-
dness of the transgressors shall destroy them. 4 [1]Riches avail not in the day of
wrath: but righteousness delivereth from death. 5 The righteousness of the upri-
ght shall direct his way: but the wicked shall fall in his own wickedness. 6 The
righteousness of the just shall deliver them: but the transgressors shall be taken
in their own wickedness. 7 When a wicked man dieth, his hope perisheth, and
the hope of the unjust shall perish. 8 The righteous escapeth out of trouble,
and the wicked shall come in his [d]stead. 9 An [e]hypocrite with his mouth hur-
teth his neighbor: but the righteous shall be delivered by knowledge. 10 In the
prosperity of the righteous the city [f]rejoiceth: and when the wicked perish, there
is joy. 11 By the [g]blessing of the righteous the city is exalted: but it is subverted
by the mouth of the wicked. 12 He that despiseth his neighbor, is destitute of
wisdom: but a man of understanding will [h]keep silence. 13 He that goeth about
as a slanderer, discovereth a secret: but he that is of a faithful heart, concealeth a
matter. 14 Where no counsel is, the people fall: but where many [i]counselors are,
there is health. 15 He shall be sore vexed, that is surety for a [j]stranger, and he
that hateth suretiship, is sure. 16 A [k]gracious woman attaineth honor, and the
strong men attain riches. 17 He that is merciful, [l]rewardeth his own soul: but he
that troubleth his own [m]flesh, is cruel. 18 The wicked worketh a deceitful work:
but he that soweth righteousness, shall receive a sure reward. 19 As righteou-
sness leadeth to life: so he that followeth evil, seeketh his own death. 20 They
that are of a froward heart, are abomination to the Lord: but they that are upright
in their way, are his delight. 21 [n]Though hand join in hand, the wicked shall not
be unpunished: but the seed of the righteous shall escape. 22 As a jewel of gold
in a swine's snout: so is a fair woman which [o]lacketh discretion. 23 The desire of
the righteous is only good: but the hope of the wicked [p]is indignation. 24 There
is that scattereth, [q]and is more increased: but he that spareth more [r]than is right,
surely cometh to poverty. 25 The [s]liberal person shall have plenty: and he that
watereth, shall also have rain. 26 He that withdraweth the corn, the people will
curse him: but blessing shall be upon the head of him that [t]selleth corn. 27 He
that seeketh good things getteth favor: but he that seeketh evil, it shall come to
him. 28 He that trusteth in his riches, shall fall: but the righteous shall flourish
as a leaf. 29 He that troubleth his own [u]house, shall inherit the wind, and the
fool shall be [v]servant to the wise in heart. 30 The fruit of the righteous is as a
tree of life, and he that [w]winneth souls is wise. 31 Behold, the righteous shall be
[x]recompensed in the earth: how much more the wicked and the sinner?

12 *Chapter 12*

1 He that loveth instruction, loveth knowledge: but he that hateth
correction, is a fool. 2 A good man getteth favor of the Lord: but the man of wi-
cked imaginations will he condemn. 3 A man cannot be established by wicked-
ness: but the [a]root of the righteous shall not be moved. 4 A [b]virtuous woman is
the crown of her husband: but she that maketh him ashamed, is as corruption in
his bones. 5 The thoughts of the just are right: but the counsels of the wicked are
deceitful. 6 The talking of the wicked is to lie in wait for blood: but the mouth
of the righteous will [c]deliver them. 7 God overthroweth the wicked, and they
are not: but the house of the righteous shall stand. 8 A man shall be commended
for his wisdom: but the froward of heart shall be despised. 9 He that is despi-
sed, [d]and is his own servant, is better than he that boasteth himself, and lacketh
bread. 10 A righteous man [e]regardeth the life of his beast: but the mercies of
the wicked are cruel. 11 [1]He that tilleth his land, shall be satisfied with bread:
but he that followeth the idle, is destitute of [f]understanding. 12 The wicked de-
sireth the [g]net of evils: but the [h]root of the righteous giveth fruit. 13 The evil
man is snared by the wickedness of his lips, but the just shall come out of adversi-
ty. 14 A man shall be satiate with good things by the fruit of his mouth, and the
recompense of a man's hands shall God give unto him. 15 The way of a fool is
[i]right in his own eyes: but he that heareth in counsel, is wise. 16 A fool in a day
shall be known by his anger: but he [j]that covereth shame, is wise. 17 He that spe-
aketh truth, will show righteousness: but a false witness useth deceit. 18 [2]There
is that speaketh words like the prickings of [k]a sword: but the tongue of wise men
is health. 19 The lip of truth shall be stable forever: but a lying tongue varieth
incontinently. 20 Deceit is in the heart of them that imagine evil: but to the
counselors of peace shall be joy. 21 There shall none iniquity come to the just:
but the wicked are full of evil. 22 The lying lips are an abomination to the Lord:
but they that deal truly are his delight. 23 A wise man concealeth knowledge:
but the heart of the fools publisheth foolishness. 24 [3]The hand of the diligent
shall bear rule: but the idle shall be under tribute. 25 Heaviness in the heart of
man doth bring it down: but a [l]good word rejoice it. 26 The righteous [m]is more
excellent than his neighbor: but the way of the wicked will deceive them. 27 The
deceitful man roasteth not that he [n]took in hunting: but the riches of the diligent
man are precious. 28 Life is in the way of righteousness, and in that pathway
there is no death.

---

m. Prov. 10:22 Meaning, that all worldly things bring care, and sorrow, whereas they that feel the blessings of God, have none.
n. Prov. 10:26 He is but a trouble and grief to him about any business.
o. Prov. 10:27 The time of their prosperity shall be short because of their great fall, though they seem to live long.
p. Prov. 10:30 They enjoy in this life by faith and hope, their everlasting life.

PROVERBS 10
1. Prov. 15:20
2. 1 Cor. 13:4 - 1 Pet. 4:8

PROVERBS 11
a. Prov. 11:1 Under this word he condemneth all false weights, measures and deceit.
b. Prov. 11:1 Hebrew, stone.
c. Prov. 11:2 When man so getteth himself, and thinketh to be exalted above his vocation, then God bringeth him to confusion.
d. Prov. 11:8 That is, shall enter into trouble.
e. Prov. 11:9 A dissembler that pretendeth friendship, but is a privy enemy.
f. Prov. 11:10 The country is blessed, where there are godly men, and they ought to rejoice when the wicked are taken away.
g. Prov. 11:11 Or, prosperity.
h. Prov. 11:12 Will not make light report of others.
i. Prov. 11:14 Where God giveth store of men of wisdom and counsel: whose conversation he knoweth not.
j. Prov. 11:15 He that doeth not without judgment and consideration of the circumstances, puts himself in danger, as Prov. 6:1.
k. Prov. 11:16 Or, modest.
l. Prov. 11:17 Is both good to himself and to others.
m. Prov. 11:17 Or, neighbor.
n. Prov. 11:21 Though they make never so many friends, or think themselves never so sure, yet they shall not escape.
o. Prov. 11:22 Or, of uncomely behavior.
p. Prov. 11:23 They can look for nothing but God's vengeance.
q. Prov. 11:24 Meaning them that give liberally, whom God blesseth.
r. Prov. 11:24 That is, the niggard.
s. Prov. 11:25 Or, generous.
t. Prov. 11:26 That provideth for the use of them that are in necessity.
u. Prov. 11:29 The covetous men that spare their riches to the hindrance of their families, shall be deprived thereof miserably.
v. Prov. 11:29 For though the wicked be rich, yet are they but slaves to the godly, which are the true possessors of the gifts of God.
w. Prov. 11:30 That is, bringeth them to the knowledge of God.
x. Prov. 11:31 Shall be punished as he deserveth, 1 Pet. 4:18.

PROVERBS 11
1. Ezek. 7:19

PROVERBS 12
a. Prov. 12:3 They are so grounded in the favor of God, that their root shall prosper continually.
b. Prov. 12:4 Hebrew, strong, or painful.
c. Prov. 12:6 As their conscience is upright, so shall they be able to speak for themselves against their accusers.
d. Prov. 12:9 The poor man that is contemned and yet liveth of his own travail.
e. Prov. 12:10 Is merciful, even to the very beast that doeth him service.
f. Prov. 12:11 Or, defense.
g. Prov. 12:12 Continually imagineth means how to do harm to others.
h. Prov. 12:12 Meaning, their heart within, which is upright, and doeth good to all.
i. Prov. 12:15 He standeth in his own conceit, and condemneth all others in respect of himself.
j. Prov. 12:16 Which bridleth his affections.
k. Prov. 12:18 Which seek nothing more than to provoke others to anger.
l. Prov. 12:25 That is, words of comfort, or, a cheerful mind which is declared by his words, rejoiceth a man, as a covetous mind killeth him.
m. Prov. 12:26 That is, more liberal in giving.
n. Prov. 12:27 Although he get much by unlawful means, yet will he not spend it upon himself.

PROVERBS 12
1. Prov. 28:19
2. Prov. 14:5
3. Prov. 10:4

13 *Chapter 13*

1 A wise son will obey the instruction of his father: but a scorner
will hear no rebuke. **2** A man shall eat good things by the fruit [a]of his mouth:
but the soul of the trespasser shall suffer violence. **3** He that keepeth his mouth,
keepeth his life: but he that openeth his lips, destruction shall be to him. **4** The
sluggard [b]lusteth, but his soul hath nought: but the soul of the diligent shall have
plenty. **5** A righteous man hateth lying words: but the wicked causeth slander
and shame. **6** Righteousness preserveth the upright of [c]life: but wickedness over-
throweth the sinner. **7** There is that maketh himself rich, and hath nothing, and
that maketh himself poor, having great riches. **8** A man will give his riches for
the ransom of his life: but the poor [d]cannot hear the reproach. **9** The light of the
righteous rejoiceth: but the candle of the wicked shall be put out. **10** Only by
pride [e]doth man make contention: but with the well-advised is wisdom. **11** The
[f]riches of vanity shall diminish: but he that gathereth with [g]the hand, shall increa-
se them. **12** The hope that is deferred, is the fainting of the heart, but when the
desire cometh, it is as a tree of life. **13** He that despiseth [h]the word, he shall be
destroyed, but he that feareth the commandment, he shall be rewarded. **14** The
instruction of a wise man is as the wellspring of life, to turn away from the snares
of death. **15** Good understanding maketh acceptable: but the way of the disobe-
dient is hated. **16** Every wise man will work by knowledge: but a fool will spread
abroad folly. **17** [1]A wicked messenger falleth [i]into evil: but a faithful ambassa-
dor is preservation. **18** Poverty and shame is to him that refuseth instruction:
but he that regardeth correction, shall be honored. **19** A desire accomplished,
delighteth the soul: but it is an abomination to fools to depart from evil. **20** He
that walketh with the wise shall be wise: but a companion of fools shall be [j]affli-
cted. **21** Affliction followeth sinners: but unto the righteous, God will recom-
pense good. **22** The good man shall give inheritance unto his children's children:
and the [k]riches of the sinner is laid up for the just. **23** Much food is in the field
of the [l]poor, but the field is destroyed without discretion. **24** [2]He that spareth
his rod, hateth his son: but he that loveth him chasteneth him betime. **25** The
righteous eateth to the contentation of his mind: but the belly of the wicked shall
want.

14 *Chapter 14*

1 A wise woman [a]buildeth her house: but the foolish destroyeth
it with her own hands. **2** [1]He that walketh in his [b]righteousness, feareth the
Lord: but he that is lewd in his ways, despiseth him. **3** In the mouth of the fo-
olish is the [c]rod of pride: but the lips of the wise preserve them. **4** Where none
[d]oxen are, there the crib is empty: but much increase cometh by the strength of
the ox. **5** A faithful witness will not lie: but a false record will speak lies. **6** [e]A
scorner seeketh wisdom, and findeth it not: but knowledge is easy to him that will
understand. **7** Depart from the foolish man, when thou perceivest not in him
the lips of knowledge. **8** The wisdom of the prudent is to understand his way:
but the foolishness of the fools is deceit. **9** The fool maketh a mock of [f]sin: but
among the righteous there is favor. **10** The heart knoweth the [g]bitterness of his
soul, and the stranger shall not meddle with his joy. **11** The house of the wicked
shall be destroyed: but the tabernacle of the righteous shall flourish. **12** [2]There
is a way that seemeth right to a man: but the issues thereof are the ways of dea-
th. **13** Even in laughing the heart is sorrowful, [h]and the end of that mirth is he-
aviness. **14** The heart that declineth, [i]shall be satiated with his own ways: but a
good man shall depart from him. **15** The foolish will believe everything: but the
prudent will consider his steps. **16** A wise man feareth, and departeth from evil,
but a fool rageth, and is careless. **17** He that is hasty to anger, commiteth folly,
and a [j]busybody is hated. **18** The foolish do inherit folly: but the prudent are
crowned with knowledge. **19** The evil shall bow before the good, and the wicked
[k]at the gates of the righteous. **20** The poor is hated even of his own neighbor:
but the friends of the rich are many. **21** The sinner despiseth his neighbor: but
he that hath mercy on the poor, is blessed. **22** Do not they err that imagine evil?
but to them that think on good things, shall be mercy and truth. **23** In all labor
there is abundance: but the talk of the lips bringeth only want. **24** The crown of
the wise is their riches, and the folly of fools is foolishness. **25** A faithful witness
delivereth souls: but a deceiver speaketh lies. **26** In the fear of the Lord is an as-
sured strength, and his children shall have hope. **27** The fear of the Lord is as a
wellspring of life, to avoid the snares of death. **28** In the multitude of the [l]people
is the honor of a King, and for the want of people cometh the destruction of the
Prince. **29** He that is slow to wrath, is of great wisdom: but he that is of an hasty
mind, exalteth folly. **30** A sound heart is the life of the [m]flesh: but envy is the
rotting of the bones. **31** [3]He that oppresseth the poor, reproveth him that made
him: but he honoreth him, that hath mercy on the poor. **32** The wicked shall be
cast away for his malice: but the righteous hath hope in his death. **33** Wisdom
resteth in the heart of him that hath understanding, and is known [n]in the midst of
fools. **34** Justice exalteth a nation, [o]but sin is a shame to the people. **35** The
pleasure of a King is in a wise servant: but his wrath shall be toward him that is
lewd.

15 *Chapter 15*

1 [1]A soft answer putteth away wrath: but grievous words stir up
anger. **2** The tongue of the wise useth knowledge aright: but the mouth of fo-
ols [2]babbleth out foolishness. **3** The eyes of the Lord in every place behold the
evil and the good. **4** A wholesome tongue is as a tree of life: but the frowardness
thereof is the breaking of the mind. **5** A fool despiseth his father's instruction,
but he that regardeth correction, is prudent. **6** The house of the righteous hath
much treasure: but in the revenues of the wicked is [a]trouble. **7** The lips of the
wise do spread abroad knowledge: but the heart of the foolish doth not so. **8** The
[b]sacrifice of the wicked is abomination unto the Lord: but the prayer of the righte-
ous is acceptable unto him. **9** The way of the wicked is an abomination unto the
Lord: but he loveth him that followeth righteousness. **10** Instruction is evil to
him that [c]forsaketh the way, and he that hateth correction, shall die. **11** [d]Hell
and destruction are before the Lord, how much more the hearts of the sons of
men? **12** A scorner loveth not him that rebuketh him, neither will he go unto
the wise. **13** [3]A joyful heart maketh a cheerful countenance: but by the sorrow
of the heart the mind is heavy. **14** The heart of him that hath understanding,
seeketh knowledge: but the mouth of the fool is fed with foolishness. **15** All the
days of the afflicted are evil; but a good [e]conscience is a continual feast. **16** [4]Bet-
ter is a little with the fear of the Lord, than great treasure and trouble therewi-
th. **17** Better is a dinner of green herbs where love is, than a stalled ox and
hatred therewith. **18** [5]An angry man stirreth up strife: but he that is slow to
wrath, appeaseth strife. **19** The way of a slothful man is as an hedge of [f]thorns:
but the way of the righteous is plain. **20** [6]A wise son rejoiceth the father: but a
foolish man despiseth his mother. **21** Foolishness is joy to him that is destitute
of understanding: but a man of understanding walketh uprightly. **22** Without
counsel, thoughts come to nought: but [g]in the multitude of counselors there is
steadfastness. **23** A joy cometh to a man by the answer of his mouth: and how
good is a word [h]in due season? **24** The way of life is on high to the prudent, to
avoid from hell beneath. **25** The Lord will destroy the house of the proud men:
but he will stablish the borders of the widow. **26** The thoughts of the wicked are
abomination to the Lord: but the pure have [i]pleasant words. **27** He that is gree-
dy of gain, troubleth his own house: but he that beareth gifts, shall live. **28** The
heart of the righteous studieth to answer: but the wicked man's mouth babbleth
evil things. **29** The Lord is far off from the wicked: but he heareth the prayer
of the righteous. **30** The light of the eyes rejoiceth the heart, and a good name

---

PROVERBS 13

- **a.** Prov. 13:2 If he use his tongue to God's glory, and the profit of his neighbor, God shall bless him.
- **b.** Prov. 13:4 He ever desireth, but taketh no pains to get anything.
- **c.** Prov. 13:6 Hebrew, way.
- **d.** Prov. 13:8 For his poverty, he is not able to escape the threatenings, which the cruel oppressors use against him.
- **e.** Prov. 13:10 When as every man contendeth to have the preeminence, and will not give place to another.
- **f.** Prov. 13:11 That is, goods evil gotten.
- **g.** Prov. 13:11 That is, with his own labor.
- **h.** Prov. 13:13 Meaning, the word of God, whereby he is admonished of his duty.
- **i.** Prov. 13:17 Bringeth many inconveniences both to himself and to others.
- **j.** Prov. 13:20 As he is partaker of their wickedness, and beareth with their vices, so shall he be punished alike as they are.
- **k.** Prov. 13:22 Read Job 27:16, 17.
- **l.** Prov. 13:23 God blesseth the labor of the poor, and consumeth their goods which are negligent, because they think they have enough.

PROVERBS 13

1. Prov. 25:13
2. Prov. 23:13

PROVERBS 14

- **a.** Prov. 14:1 That is, taketh pain to profit her family, and to do that which concerneth her duty in her house.
- **b.** Prov. 14:2 That is, in uprightness of heart, and without hypocrisy.
- **c.** Prov. 14:3 His proud tongue shall cause him to be punished.
- **d.** Prov. 14:4 By the ox is meant labor, and by the crib the barn: meaning, without labor there is no profit.
- **e.** Prov. 14:6 For the maintenance of his own ambition, and not for God's glory, as Simon Magus.
- **f.** Prov. 14:9 Doth not know the grievousness thereof, nor God's judgments against the same.
- **g.** Prov. 14:10 As a man's conscience is witness of his own grief, so another cannot feel the joy and comfort which a man feeleth in himself.
- **h.** Prov. 14:13 He showeth the allurement unto sin, seemeth sweet, but the end thereof is destruction.
- **i.** Prov. 14:14 He that forsaketh God shall be punished, and made weary of his sins, wherein he delighted.
- **j.** Prov. 14:17 Hebrew, the man of imaginations.
- **k.** Prov. 14:19 If this come not daily to pass, we must consider that it is because of our sins, which let God's working.
- **l.** Prov. 14:28 That is, the strength of a king standeth in many people.
- **m.** Prov. 14:30 Or, body.
- **n.** Prov. 14:33 Forasmuch as they are convicted thereby and put to silence.
- **o.** Prov. 14:34 Or, and the mercy of the people is a sacrifice for sin.

PROVERBS 14

1. Job. 12:4
2. Prov. 16:25
3. Prov. 17:5

PROVERBS 15

- **a.** Prov. 15:6 For though they have much, yet it is full of trouble and care.
- **b.** Prov. 15:8 That thing is abominable before God, which the wicked think to be most excellent, and whereby they think most to be accepted.
- **c.** Prov. 15:10 He that swerveth from the word of God, cannot abide to be admonished.
- **d.** Prov. 15:11 There is nothing so deep or secret that can be hid from the eyes of God, much less man's thoughts.
- **e.** Prov. 15:15 Hebrew, heart.
- **f.** Prov. 15:19 That is, he ever findeth some let or stay, and dare not go forward.
- **g.** Prov. 15:22 Read Prov. 11:14.
- **h.** Prov. 15:23 If we will that our talk be comfortable, we must wait for time and season.
- **i.** Prov. 15:26 That is, wholesome and profitable to the hearers.
- **j.** Prov. 15:31 That suffereth himself to be admonished by God's word, which bringeth life: and so amendeth.

maketh the bones fat. **31** The ear that hearkeneth to the [j]correction of life, shall lodge among the wise. **32** He that refuseth instruction, despiseth his own soul: but he that obeyeth correction, getteth understanding. **33** The fear of the Lord is the instruction of wisdom: and before honor goeth [k]humility.

16

Chapter 16

1 The [a]preparations of the heart are in man: but the answer of the tongue is of the Lord. **2** All the ways of a man are [b]clean in his own eyes: but the Lord pondereth the spirits. **3** [c]Commit thy works unto the Lord, and thy thoughts shall be directed. **4** The Lord hath made all things for his own sake: yea, even the wicked for the day of [d]evil. **5** All that are proud in heart, are an abomination to the Lord: though [1]hand join in hand, he shall not be unpunished. **6** By [e]mercy and truth iniquity shall be forgiven, and by the fear of the Lord they depart from evil. **7** When the ways of a man please the Lord, he will make also his enemies at peace with him. **8** [2]Better is a little with righteousness, than great revenues without equity. **9** The heart of [f]man purposeth his way: but the Lord doth direct his steps. **10** A divine sentence shall be in the lips of the king: his mouth shall not transgress in judgment. **11** [3]A true weight and balance are of the Lord: and the weights of the bag are his [g]work. **12** It is an abomination to kings to commit wickedness: for the throne is stablished [h]by justice. **13** Righteous lips are the delight of kings, and the king loveth him that speaketh right things. **14** The wrath of a king is as [i]messengers of death: but a wise man will pacify it. **15** In the light of the king's countenance is life: and his favor is [j]as a cloud of the latter rain. **16** [4]How much better is it to get wisdom than gold? and to get understanding, is more to be desired than silver. **17** The path of the righteous is to decline from evil, and he keepeth his soul that keepeth his way. **18** Pride goeth before destruction, and an high mind before the fall. **19** Better it is to be of humble mind with the lowly, than to divide the spoils with the proud. **20** He that is wise in his business, shall find good: and [5]he that trusteth in the Lord, he is blessed. **21** The wise in heart shall be called prudent and [k]the sweetness of the lips shall increase doctrine. **22** Understanding is a wellspring of life unto them that have it: and the [l]instruction of fools is folly. **23** The heart of the wise guideth his mouth wisely, and addeth doctrine to his lips. **24** Fair words are as an honey comb, sweetness to the soul, and health to the bones. **25** [6]There is a way that seemeth right unto man, but the issue thereof are the ways of death. **26** The person that travaileth, travaileth for himself: for his mouth [m]craveth it of him. **27** A wicked man diggeth up evil, and in his lips is like [n]burning fire. **28** A froward person soweth strife: and a taleteller maketh division among princes. **29** A wicked man deceiveth his neighbor, and leadeth him into the way that is not good. **30** [o]He shutteth his eyes to devise wickedness: he moveth his lips, and bringeth evil to pass. **31** Age is a crown of glory, when it is found in the way of [p]righteousness. **32** He that is slow unto anger, is better than the mighty man: and he that ruleth his own mind, is better than he that winneth a city. **33** The lot is cast into the lap: but the whole disposition thereof is [q]of the Lord.

17

Chapter 17

1 Better is a dry morsel, if peace be with it, than an house full of [a]sacrifices with strife. **2** A discrete servant shall have rule over a lewd son, and he shall divide the [b]heritage among the brethren. **3** As is the fining pot for silver, and the furnace for gold, so the Lord trieth the hearts. **4** The wicked giveth heed to false lips, and a liar hearkeneth to the naughty tongue. **5** [1]He that mocketh the poor, reproacheth him that made him: and he that rejoiceth at destruction, shall not be unpunished. **6** Children's children are the crown of the elders: and the glory of the children are their fathers. **7** [c]High talk becometh not a fool, much less a lying talk a prince. **8** A reward is as a stone pleasant in the eyes of them that have it: it prospereth, whithersoever it [d]turneth. **9** He that covereth a transgression, seeketh love: but he that repeateth a matter, separateth the [e]prince. **10** A reproof entereth more into him that hath understanding, than an hundred stripes into a fool. **11** A seditious person seeketh only evil, and a cruel [f]messenger shall be sent against him. **12** It is better for a man to meet a bear robbed of her whelps, than [g]a fool in his folly. **13** [2]He that rewardeth evil for good, evil shall not depart from his house. **14** The beginning of strife is as one that openeth the waters: therefore, or the contention be meddled with, leave off. **15** [3]He that justifieth the wicked, and he that condemneth the just, even they both are abomination to the Lord. **16** Wherefore is there a [h]price in the hand of the fool to get wisdom, and he hath none heart? **17** A friend loveth at all times; and a [i]brother is born for adversity. **18** A man destitute of understanding, [j]toucheth the hand, and becometh surety for his neighbor. **19** He loveth transgression that loveth strife: and he that exalteth his [k]gate, seeketh destruction. **20** The froward heart findeth no good: and he that hath a naughty tongue, shall fall into evil. **21** He that begetteth a fool, getteth himself sorrow, and the father of a fool can have no joy. **22** [4]A joyful heart causeth good health: but a sorrowful mind drieth the bones. **23** A wicked man taketh a gift out of the [l]bosom to wrest the ways of judgment. **24** [5]Wisdom is in the face of him that hath understanding: but the eyes of a fool are in the [m]corners of the world. **25** A foolish son is a grief unto his father, and a [6]heaviness to her that bare him. **26** Surely it is not good to condemn the just, nor that the princes should smite such [n]for equity. **27** He that hath knowledge, spareth his words, and a man of understanding is of an excellent spirit. **28** Even a fool, (when he holdeth his peace) is counted wise, and he that stoppeth his lips, prudent.

18

Chapter 18

1 For the desire thereof he will [a]separate himself to seek it, and occupy himself in all wisdom. **2** A fool hath no delight in understanding: but that his heart may be [b]discovered. **3** When the wicked cometh, then cometh [c]contempt, and with the vile man reproach. **4** The words of a man's mouth are like deep [d]waters, and the wellspring of wisdom is like a flowing river. **5** It is not good to [e]accept the person of the wicked, to cause the righteous to fall in judgment. **6** A fool's lips come with strife, and his mouth calleth for stripes. **7** A fool's mouth is his own destruction, and his lips are a snare for his soul. **8** The words of a talebearer are as flatterings, and they go down into the [f]bowels of the belly. **9** He also that is slothful in his work, is even the brother of him that is a great waster. **10** The name of the Lord is a strong tower: the righteous runneth [g]unto it, and is exalted. **11** [1]The rich man's riches are his strong city: and as an high wall in his imagination. **12** [2]Before destruction the heart of a man is haughty, and before glory goeth lowliness. **13** He that answereth a matter before he hear it, it is folly and shame unto him. **14** The spirit of a man will sustain his infirmity: but [h]a wounded spirit, who can bear it? **15** A wise heart getteth knowledge, and the ear of the wise seeketh learning. **16** A man's gift [i]enlargeth him, and leadeth him before great men. **17** [j]He that is first in his own cause, is just:

---

k. Prov. 15:33 Meaning, that God exalteth none but them that are truly humbled.

PROVERBS 15

1. Prov. 25:15
2. Prov. 15:18
3. Prov. 17:22
4. Ps. 37:16
5. Prov. 29:22
6. Prov. 10:1

PROVERBS 16

a. Prov. 16:1 He derideth the presumption of man, who dare attribute to himself any thing, as to prepare his heart or such like, seeing that he is not able to speak a word, except God give it him.
b. Prov. 16:2 He showeth hereby that man flattereth himself in his doings, calling that virtue, which God termeth vice.
c. Prov. 16:3 Hebrew, role.
d. Prov. 16:4 So that the justice of God shall appear to his glory, even in the destruction of the wicked.
e. Prov. 16:6 Their upright and repenting life shall be a token that their sins are forgiven.
f. Prov. 16:9 He showeth the folly of man, which thinketh that his ways are in his own hand, and yet it is able to remove one foot except God give force.
g. Prov. 16:11 If they be true and just, they are God's work, and he delighteth therein, but otherwise if they be false, they are the work of the devil, and to their condemnation that use them.
h. Prov. 16:12 They are appointed by God to rule according to equity and justice.
i. Prov. 16:14 That is, he findeth out many means to execute his wrath.
j. Prov. 16:15 Which is most comfortable to the dry ground, Deut. 11:14.
k. Prov. 16:21 The sweet words of consolation, which come forth of a godly heart.
l. Prov. 16:22 Either that which the wicked teach others, or else it is folly to teach them that are malicious.
m. Prov. 16:26 Hebrew, boweth upon him.
n. Prov. 16:27 For he consumeth himself and others.
o. Prov. 16:30 With his whole endeavor he laboreth to bring his wickedness to pass.
p. Prov. 16:31 That is, when it is joined with virtue: or else the elder that the wicked are, the more they are to be abhorred.
q. Prov. 16:33 So that there is nothing that ought to be attributed to fortune: for all things are determined in the counsel of God which shall come to pass.

PROVERBS 16

1. Prov. 11:21
2. Prov. 15:16 / Ps. 37:16
3. Prov. 11:1
4. Prov. 8:10
5. Ps. 125:1
6. Prov. 14:12

PROVERBS 17

a. Prov. 17:1 For whereas were many sacrifices, there were many portions given to the people, wherewith they feasted.
b. Prov. 17:2 That is, shall be made governor over the children.
c. Prov. 17:7 Hebrew, the lip of excellency.
d. Prov. 17:8 The reward hath great force to gain the hearts of men.
e. Prov. 17:9 He that admonisheth the prince of his fault, maketh him his enemy.
f. Prov. 17:11 By the messenger is meant such means as God useth to punish the rebels.
g. Prov. 17:12 Whereby he meaneth the wicked in his rage, who hath no fear of God.
h. Prov. 17:16 What availeth it the wicked to be rich, seeing he setteth not his mind to wisdom?
i. Prov. 17:17 So that he is more than a friend, even a brother that helpeth in time of adversity.
j. Prov. 17:18 Read Prov. 6:1.
k. Prov. 17:19 Lifteth up himself above his degree.
l. Prov. 17:23 That is, secretly and out of the bosom of the rich.
m. Prov. 17:24 That is, wander to and fro, and seek not after wisdom.
n. Prov. 17:26 For their well doing.

PROVERBS 17

1. Prov. 14:31
2. Rom. 12:17 / 1 Thess. 5:15 /1 Pet. 3:9
3. Isa. 5:23 / Prov. 24:24
4. Prov. 15:13
5. Eccl. 2:14 / Eccl. 8:1

PROVERBS 18

a. Prov. 18:1 He that loveth wisdom, will separate himself from all impediments, and give himself wholly to seek it.
b. Prov. 18:2 That is, that he may talk licentiously of whatsoever cometh to mind.
c. Prov. 18:3 Meaning, such one as contemneth all others.
d. Prov. 18:4 Which can never be drawn empty, but bring ever profit.
e. Prov. 18:5 That is, to favor him and support him.
f. Prov. 18:8 They are soon believed, and enter most deeply.
g. Prov. 18:10 He showeth what is the refuge of the godly against all trouble.
h. Prov. 18:14 The mind can well bear the infirmity of the body, but when the spirit is wounded, it is a thing most hard to sustain.
i. Prov. 18:16 Getteth him liberty to speak, and favor of them that are most in estimation.

then cometh his neighbor and maketh inquiry of him. **18** The lot [k]causeth contentions to cease, and [l]maketh a partition among the mighty. **19** A brother offended is harder to win than a strong city, and their contentions are like the [m]bar of a palace. **20** With the fruit of a man's mouth shall his belly be satisfied, and with the increase of his lips shall he be filled. **21** Death and life are in the power of the tongue, and they that [n]love it, shall eat the fruit thereof. **22** He that findeth a [o]wife, findeth a good thing, and receiveth favor of the Lord. **23** The poor speaketh with prayers: but the rich answereth roughly. **24** A man that hath friends, ought to show himself friendly: for a friend is nearer [p]than a brother.

19 *Chapter 19*

1 Better [1]is the poor that walketh in his uprightness, than he that abuseth his lips, and is a fool. **2** For without knowledge the mind is not good, and he that hasteth with his feet, sinneth. **3** The foolishness of a man perverteth his way, and his heart fretteth against the Lord. **4** Riches gather many friends: but the poor is separated from his neighbor. **5** [2]A false witness shall not be unpunished: and he that speaketh lies, shall not escape. **6** Many reverence the face of the prince, and every man is friend to him that giveth gifts. **7** All the brethren of the poor do hate him: how much more will his friends depart far from him? though he be instant [a]with words, yet they will not. **8** He that possesseth understanding, [b]loveth his own soul, and keepeth wisdom to find goodness. **9** A false witness shall not be unpunished: and he that speaketh lies, shall perish. **10** [c]Pleasure is not comely for a fool, much less for a servant to have rule over princes. **11** The discretion of man deferreth his anger: and his glory is [d]to pass by an offence. **12** [3]The king's wrath is like the roaring of a lion: but his favor is like the dew upon the grass. **13** [4]A foolish son is the calamity of his father, [5]and the contentions of a wife are like a continual [e]dropping. **14** House and riches are the inheritance of the fathers: but a [6]prudent wife cometh of the Lord. **15** Slothfulness causeth to fall asleep, and a deceitful person shall be affamished. **16** He that keepeth the commandment, keepeth his own soul: but he that despiseth his ways, shall die. **17** He that hath mercy upon the poor, lendeth unto the Lord: and the Lord will recompense him that which he hath given. **18** Chasten thy son while there is hope, and let not thy soul spare for his murmuring. **19** A man of much anger shall suffer punishment, and though thou [f]deliver him, yet will his anger come again. **20** Hear counsel and receive instruction, that thou mayest be wise in thy latter end. **21** Many devices are in a [g]man's heart: but the counsel of the Lord shall stand. **22** That that is to be desired of a man, is his [h]goodness, and a poor man is better than a liar. **23** The fear of the Lord leadeth to life: and he that is filled therewith, shall continue, and shall not be visited with evil. **24** [7]The slothful hideth his hand in his bosom, and will not put it to his mouth again. **25** [8]Smite a scorner, and the [i]foolish will beware: and reprove the prudent, and he will understand knowledge. **26** He that destroyeth his father, or chaseth away his mother, is a lewd and shameful child. **27** My son, hear no more the instruction, that causeth to err from the words of knowledge. **28** A wicked witness mocketh at judgment, and the mouth of the wicked [j]swalloweth up iniquity. **29** But judgments are prepared for the scorners, and stripes for the back of the fools.

20 *Chapter 20*

1 Wine [a]is a mocker, and strong drink is raging: and whosoever is deceived thereby, is not wise. **2** [1]The fear of the King is like the roaring of a lion: he that provoketh him unto anger [b]sinneth against his own soul. **3** It is a man's honor to cease from strife: but every fool will be meddling. **4** The slothful will not plow, because of winter: therefore shall he beg in summer, but have nothing. **5** The counsel in the heart of [c]man is like deep waters: but a man that hath understanding, will draw it out. **6** Many men will boast every one of his own goodness: but who can find a faithful man? **7** He that walketh in his integrity, is just, and blessed shall his children be after him. **8** A king that sitteth in the throne of judgment, [d]chaseth away all evil with his eyes. **9** [2]Who can say, I have made mine heart clean, I am clean from my sin? **10** Divers [e]weights, and divers measures, both [f]these are even abomination unto the Lord. **11** A child also is known by his doings, whether his word be pure and right. **12** The Lord hath made both these, even the ear to hear, and the eye to see. **13** Love not sleep, lest thou come unto poverty: open thine eyes, and thou shalt be satisfied with bread. **14** It is naught, it is naught, saith the buyer: but when he is gone apart, he boasteth. **15** There is gold, and a multitude of precious stones: but the lips of knowledge are a precious jewel. **16** [3]Take his [g]garment, that is surety for a stranger, and a pledge of him for the stranger. **17** The bread of deceit is sweet to a man: but afterward his mouth shall be filled with gravel. **18** Establish thy thoughts by counsel; and by counsel make war. **19** He that goeth about as a slanderer, discovereth [4]secrets: therefore meddle not with him that flattereth with his lips. **20** [5]He that curseth his father or his mother, his light shall be put out in obscure darkness. **21** An heritage is hastily gotten at the beginning, but the end thereof shall not be blessed. **22** Say not thou, [6]I will recompense evil, but wait upon the Lord, and he shall save thee. **23** [7]Diverse weights are an abomination unto the Lord, and deceitful balances are not good. **24** [8]The steps of man are ruled by the Lord: how can a man then understand his own way? **25** It is a destruction for a man to [h]devour that which is sanctified, and after the vows to inquire. **26** A wise King scattereth the wicked, and causeth the [i]wheel to turn over them. **27** The [j]light of the Lord is the breath of man, and searcheth all the bowels of the belly. **28** [9]Mercy and truth preserve the king: for his throne shall be established with mercy. **29** The beauty of young men is their strength, and the glory of the aged is the gray head. **30** [k]The blueness of the wound serveth to purge the evil, and the stripes within the bowels of the belly.

21 *Chapter 21*

1 The [a]King's heart is in the hand of the Lord, as the rivers of waters: he turneth it whithersoever it pleaseth him. **2** Every [1]way of a man is right in his own eyes: but the Lord pondereth the hearts. **3** [2]To do justice and judgment is more acceptable to the Lord than sacrifice. **4** A haughty look, and a proud heart which is the [b,c]light of the wicked, is sin. **5** The thoughts of the diligent do surely bring abundance; but [d]whosoever is hasty, cometh surely to poverty. **6** [3]The gathering of treasures by a deceitful tongue, is vanity tossed to and fro of them that seek death. **7** The [e]robbery of the wicked shall destroy them; for they have refused to execute judgment. **8** The way of some is perverted and strange, but of the pure man, his work is right. **9** [4]It is better to dwell in a corner of the house top, than with a contentious woman in a [f]wide house. **10** The soul of the wicked wisheth evil, and his neighbor hath no favor in his eyes. **11** [g]When the scorner is punished, the foolish is wise, and when one instructeth the wise, he

---

j. Prov. 18:17 He that speaketh first, is best heard of the wicked judge, but when his adversary inquireth out the matter, it turneth to his shame.
k. Prov. 18:18 If a controversy cannot otherwise be decided, it is best to cast lots to know whose the thing shall be.
l. Prov. 18:18 Appeaseth their controversy, which are so stout that cannot otherwise be pacified.
m. Prov. 18:19 Which for the strength thereof will not bow nor yield.
n. Prov. 18:21 By the using of the tongue well or evil, cometh the fruit thereof either good or bad.
o. Prov. 18:22 He that is joined with a virtuous woman in marriage, is blessed of the Lord, as Prov. 19:14.
p. Prov. 18:24 That is, ofttimes such are found which are more ready to do pleasure, than he that is more bound by duty.

PROVERBS 18

1. Prov. 10:15
2. Prov. 16:18

PROVERBS 19

a. Prov. 19:7 To have comfort of them.
b. Prov. 19:8 He that is upright in judgment findeth favor of God.
c. Prov. 19:10 The free use of things are not to be permitted to him that cannot use them aright.
d. Prov. 19:11 That is, to cover it by charity, and to do therein as may most serve to God's glory.
e. Prov. 19:13 As rain that droppeth and rotteth the house.
f. Prov. 19:19 Though for a time he give place to counsel, yet soon after will he give place to his raging affections.
g. Prov. 19:21 Man's device shall not have success, except God govern it, whose purpose is unchangeable.
h. Prov. 19:22 That is, that he be honest: for the poor man that is honest, is to be esteemed above the rich which is not virtuous.
i. Prov. 19:25 That is, the simple and ignorant men learn, when they see the wicked punished.
j. Prov. 19:28 Taketh a pleasure and delight therein, as gluttons and drunkards in delicate meats and drinks.

PROVERBS 19

1. Prov. 28:6
2. Deut. 19:19 / Dan. 13:62
3. Prov. 20:2
4. Prov. 17:21
5. Prov. 21:9
6. Prov. 18:22
7. Prov. 26:15
8. Prov. 21:11

PROVERBS 20

a. Prov. 20:1 By wine here is meant him that is given to wine, and so by strong drink.
b. Prov. 20:2 Putteth his life in danger.
c. Prov. 20:5 It is hard to find out: for it is as deep waters, whose bottom cannot be found: yet the wise man will know a man either by his words or manners.
d. Prov. 20:8 Where righteous judgment is executed, there sin ceaseth, and vice dare not appear.
e. Prov. 20:10 Hebrew, stone and stone, ephah and ephah.
f. Prov. 20:10 Read Prov. 16:11.
g. Prov. 20:16 Teach him wit, that he cast not himself rashly into danger.
h. Prov. 20:25 That is, to apply it, or take it to his own use, which was appointed to God's, and then inquire how they may be exempted from the fault.
i. Prov. 20:26 Which was a kind of punishment then used.
j. Prov. 20:27 The word of God giveth life unto man, and causeth us to see and try the secret of our dark hearts, Heb. 4:12.
k. Prov. 20:30 Sharp punishment that pierceth even the inward parts, is profitable for the wicked, to bring them to amendment.

PROVERBS 20

1. Prov. 19:12
2. 1Kings 8:46 / 2Chron. 6:36 / Eccl. 7:22 1John 1:8
3. Prov. 27:13
4. Prov. 11:13
5. Exod. 21:17 /Lev. 20:9 / Matt. 15:4
6. Deut. 32:35 / Prov. 17:13 / Prov. 24:29 / Rom. 12:17 / 1 Thess. 5:15 / 1 Pet. 3:9
7. Prov. 11:1 / Prov. 20:10
8. Jer. 10:13
9. Prov. 19:14

PROVERBS 21

a. Prov. 21:1 Though Kings seem to have all things at commandment, yet are they not able to bring their own purposes to pass any otherwise than God hath appointed: much less are the inferiors able.
b. Prov. 21:4 Or, plowing.
c. Prov. 21:4 That is, the thing whereby he is guided or which he bringeth forth as the fruit of his work.
d. Prov. 21:5 He that goeth rashly about his business, and without counsel.
e. Prov. 21:7 He meaneth this chiefly of Judges, and Princes which leave that vocation, whereunto God hath called them, and powle their subjects to maintain their lusts.
f. Prov. 21:9 Or, in a great family.
g. Prov. 21:11 Read Prov. 19:25.

will receive knowledge. **12** The righteous [h]teacheth the house of the wicked;
but God overthroweth the wicked for their evil. **13** He that stoppeth his ear at
the crying of the poor, he shall also cry and not be heard. **14** A [i]gift in secret
pacifieth anger, and a gift in the bosom, great wrath. **15** It is joy to the just to
do judgment; but destruction shall be to the workers of iniquity. **16** A man
that wandereth out of the way of wisdom, shall remain in the congregation of the
dead. **17** He that loveth pastime, shall be a poor man; and he that loveth wine
and oil, shall not be rich. **18** The [j]wicked shall be a ransom for the just, and the
transgressor for the righteous. **19** It is better to dwell in the wilderness, than
with a contentious and angry woman. **20** In the house of the wise is a pleasant
treasure and [k]oil; but a foolish man devoureth it. **21** He that followeth after ri-
ghteousness and mercy, shall find life, righteousness and glory. **22** A [l]wise man
goeth up into the city of the mighty, and casteth down the strength of the confi-
dence thereof. **23** He that keepeth his mouth and his tongue, keepeth his soul
from afflictions. **24** Proud, haughty, and scornful is his name that worketh in his
arrogancy wrath. **25** The desire of the slothful [m]slayeth him; for his hands refuse
to work. **26** He coveteth evermore greedily: but the righteous giveth and spareth
not. **27** The [5]sacrifice of the wicked is an abomination: how much more when
he bringeth it with a wicked mind? **28** [6]A false witness shall perish: but he that
heareth, [n]speaketh continually. **29** A wicked man hardeneth his face: but the
just, he will direct his way. **30** There is no wisdom, neither understanding, nor
counsel against the Lord. **31** The horse is prepared against the day of battle: but
salvation is of the Lord.

22 *Chapter 22*

1 [1]A good name is to be chosen above great riches, and [a]loving fa-
vor is above silver and above gold. **2** [2]The rich and poor [b]meet together, the Lord
is the maker of them all. **3** [3]A prudent man [c]seeth the plague, and hideth him-
self: but the foolish go on still, and are punished. **4** The reward of humility, and
the fear of God is riches, and glory, and life. **5** Thorns and snares are in the way
of the froward: but he that regardeth his soul, will depart far from them. **6** Te-
ach a child [d]in the trade of his way, and when he is old he shall not depart from
it. **7** The rich ruleth the poor, and the borrower is servant to the man that len-
deth. **8** He that soweth iniquity, shall reap affliction, and the [e]rod of his anger
shall fail. **9** He that hath a good [f]eye, he shall be blessed: for he giveth of his bre-
ad unto the poor. **10** Cast out the scorner, and strife shall go out: so contention
and reproach shall cease. **11** He that loveth pureness of heart for the grace of his
lips, the [g]king shall be his friend. **12** The eyes of the Lord preserve [h]knowledge:
but he overthroweth the words of the transgressor. **13** The slothful man saith, [i]A
lion is without, I shall be slain in the street. **14** The mouth of strange women is
as a deep pit: he with whom the Lord is angry, [j]shall fall therein. **15** Foolishness
is bound [k]in the heart of a child: but the rod of correction shall drive it away from
him. **16** He that oppresseth the poor to increase himself, and giveth unto the
rich, shall surely come to poverty. **17** Incline thine ear, and hear the words of the
wise, and apply thine heart unto my knowledge. **18** For it shall be pleasant, if
thou keep them in thy belly, and if they be directed together in thy lips. **19** That
thy confidence may be in [l]the Lord, I have showed thee this day: thou therefore
take heed. **20** Have not I written unto thee [m]three times in counsels and know-
ledge, **21** That I might show thee the assurance of the words of truth, to answer
the words of truth to them that send to thee? **22** Rob not the poor, because he
is poor, neither oppress the afflicted [n]in judgment. **23** For the Lord [4]will defend
their cause, and spoil the soul of those that spoil them. **24** Make [o]no friendship
with an angry man, neither go with the furious man, **25** Lest thou learn his
ways, and receive destruction to thy soul. **26** Be not thou of them that [p]tough
the hand, nor among them that are surety for debts. **27** If thou hast nothing to
pay, why causest thou that he should take thy bed from under thee? **28** Thou
shalt not [5]remove the ancient bounds which thy fathers have made. **29** Thou
seest that a diligent man in his business standeth before Kings, and standeth not
before the base sort.

23 *Chapter 23*

1 When thou sittest to eat with a ruler, [a]consider diligently
what is before thee, **2** [b]And put thy knife to thy throat, if thou be a man gi-
ven to the appetite. **3** Be not desirous of his dainty meats: [c]for it is a deceivable
meat. **4** Travail not too much to be rich: but cease from thy [d]wisdom. **5** Wilt
thou cast thine eyes upon it, which is nothing? for riches taketh her to her wings,
as an Eagle, and flieth into the heaven. **6** Eat thou not the bread of him that
hath an [e]evil eye, neither desire his dainty meats. **7** For as though he thought
it in his heart: so will he say unto thee, Eat and drink: but his heart is not with
thee. **8** Thou shalt vomit thy [f]morsel that thou hast eaten, and thou shalt lose
thy sweet words. **9** Speak not in the ears of a fool: for he will despise the wi-
sdom of thy words. **10** [1]Remove not the ancient bounds, and enter not into
the fields of the fatherless. **11** For he that redeemeth them, is mighty: he will
[2]defend their cause against thee. **12** Apply thine heart to instruction, and thine
ears to the words of knowledge. **13** [3]Withhold not correction from the child:
if thou smite him with the rod, he shall not die. **14** Thou shalt smite him with
the rod, and shalt deliver his soul from [g]hell. **15** My son, if thine heart be wise,
mine heart shall rejoice, and I also, **16** And my reins shall rejoice, when thy lips
speak righteous things. **17** [4]Let not thine heart be envious against sinners: but
let it be in the fear of the Lord continually. **18** For surely there is an end, [h]and
thy hope shall not be cut off. **19** O thou my son, hear, and be wise, and guide
thine heart in the [i]way. **20** Keep not company with [j]drunkards, nor with [k]glut-
tons. **21** For the drunkard and the glutton shall be poor, and the sleeper shall
be clothed with rags. **22** Obey thy father that hath begotten thee, and despise
not thy mother when she is old. **23** Buy [l]the truth, but sell it not: likewise wi-
sdom, instruction, and understanding. **24** The father of the righteous shall great-
ly rejoice, and he that begetteth a wise child, shall have joy of him. **25** Thy father
and thy mother shall be glad, and she that bare thee shall rejoice. **26** My son,
give me [m]thine heart, and let thine eyes delight in my ways. **27** [5]For a whore is
as a deep ditch, and a strange woman is as a narrow pit. **28** [6]Also she lieth in wait
as for a prey, [n]and she increaseth the transgressors among men. **29** To whom is
woe? to whom is sorrow? to whom is strife? to whom is murmuring? to whom are
wounds without cause? and to whom is the redness of the eyes? **30** Even to them
that tarry long at the wine, to them that go, [o]and seek mixed wine. **31** Look not
thou upon the wine, when it is red, and when it showeth his color in the cup, or
goeth down pleasantly. **32** In the end thereof it will bite like a serpent, and hurt
like a cockatrice. **33** Thine [p]eyes shall look upon strange women, and thine heart
shall speak lewd things. **34** And thou shalt be as one that sleepeth in the midst
of the [q]sea, and as he that sleepeth in the top of the mast. **35** They have stricken
me, shalt thou say, but I was not sick: they have beaten me, but I knew not, when
I awoke: therefore will I [r]seek it yet still.

24 *Chapter 24*

1 [1]Be not thou envious against evil men, neither desire to be
with them. **2** For their heart imagineth destruction, and their lips speak mi-
schief. **3** Through wisdom is an house built, and with understanding it is establi-
shed. **4** And by knowledge shall the chambers be filled with all precious and

---

h. Prov. 21:12 Though the godly admonish them both by words and example of life, yet the wicked will not amend, till God destroy them.
i. Prov. 21:14 To do a pleasure to the angry man pacifieth him.
j. Prov. 21:18 God shall cause that to fall on their own heads, which they intended against the just by delivering the just, and putting the wicked in their places.
k. Prov. 21:20 Meaning, abundance of all things.
l. Prov. 21:22 Wisdom overcometh strength and confidence in worldly things.
m. Prov. 21:25 He thinketh to live by wishing and desiring all things, but will take no pain to get ought.
n. Prov. 21:28 He may boldly testify the truth that he hath heard.

PROVERBS 21

1. Prov. 16:2
2. Mic. 6:8
3. Prov. 13:11
4. Prov. 19:13 / Prov. 25:24
5. Prov. 15:8 / Isa. 1:13
6. Prov. 19:5

PROVERBS 22

a. Prov. 22:1 Which cometh by well doing.
b. Prov. 22:2 Live together, and have need the one of the other.
c. Prov. 22:3 That is, the punishment, which is prepared for the wicked, and fleeth not to God for succor.
d. Prov. 22:6 Bring him up virtuously, and he shall so continue.
e. Prov. 22:8 His authority, whereby he did oppress others, shall be taken from him.
f. Prov. 22:9 He that is merciful and liberal.
g. Prov. 22:11 He showeth that princes should use their familiarity, whose conscience is good, and their talk wise and godly.
h. Prov. 22:12 Favor them that love knowledge.
i. Prov. 22:13 He derideth them that invent vain excuses, because they would not do their duty.
j. Prov. 22:14 So God punisheth one sin by another, when he suffereth the wicked to fall into the acquaintance of an harlot.
k. Prov. 22:15 He is naturally given unto it.
l. Prov. 22:19 He showeth what the end of wisdom is: to wit, to direct us to the Lord.
m. Prov. 22:20 That is, sundry times.
n. Prov. 22:22 Hebrew, in the gates.
o. Prov. 22:24 Have not to do with him that is not able to rule his affections: for he would hurt thee by his evil conversation.
p. Prov. 22:26 Which rashly put themselves in danger for others, as Prov. 6:2.

PROVERBS 22

1. Eccl. 7:1
2. Prov. 29:13
3. Prov. 27:12
4. Prov. 23:11
5. Deut. 17:17 / Prov. 23:10

PROVERBS 23

a. Prov. 23:1 Eat with sobriety.
b. Prov. 23:2 Bridle thine appetite, as it were by force and violence.
c. Prov. 23:3 For oftimes the rich when they bid their inferiors to their tables, it is not for the love they bear them, but for their own secret purposes.
d. Prov. 23:4 Bestow not the gifts that God hath given thee, to get worldly riches.
e. Prov. 23:6 That is, covetous, as contrary a good eye is taken for liberal, as Prov. 22:9.
f. Prov. 23:8 He will not cease till he hath done thee some harm, and his flattering words shall come to no use.
g. Prov. 23:14 That is, from destruction.
h. Prov. 23:18 The prosperity of the wicked shall not continue.
i. Prov. 23:19 In the observation of God's commandments.
j. Prov. 23:20 Hebrew, wine-bibbers.
k. Prov. 23:20 Hebrew, devourers of flesh.
l. Prov. 23:23 Spare no cost for truth's sake, neither depart from it for any gain.
m. Prov. 23:26 Give thyself wholly to wisdom.
n. Prov. 23:28 She seduceth many and causeth them to offend God.
o. Prov. 23:30 Which by art make wine stronger and more pleasant.
p. Prov. 23:33 That is, drunkenness shall bring thee to whoredom.
q. Prov. 23:34 In such great danger shalt thou be.
r. Prov. 23:35 Though drunkenness make them more insensible than beasts, yet can they not refrain.

PROVERBS 23

1. Deut. 27:17 / Prov. 22:28
2. Prov. 12:13
3. Prov. 13:24 / Prov. 19:18
4. Ps. 37:1 / Prov. 24:1
5. Prov. 22:14
6. Prov. 7:12

pleasant riches. **5** A wise man is strong: for a man of understanding increaseth his strength. **6** [2]For with counsel thou shalt enterprise thy war, and in the multitude of them that can give counsel, is health. **7** Wisdom is high to a fool: therefore he cannot open his mouth in the [a]gate. **8** He that imagineth to do evil, men shall call him an author of wickedness. **9** The wicked thought of a fool is sin, and the scorner is an abomination unto men. **10** If thou be [b]faint in the day of adversity, thy strength is small. **11** Deliver them that are drawn [c]to death, and wilt thou not preserve them that are led to be slain? **12** If thou say, Behold, we knew not of it: he that pondereth the hearts, doth not he understand it? and he that keepeth thy soul, knoweth he it not? will he not also recompense every man according to his works? **13** My son, eat [d]honey, for it is good, and the honey comb, for it is sweet unto thy mouth. **14** So shall the knowledge of wisdom be unto thy soul if thou find it, and there shall be an [e]end, and thine hope shall not be cut off. **15** Lay no wait, O wicked man, against the house of the righteous, and spoil not his resting place. **16** For a just man [f]falleth seven times, and riseth again: but the wicked fall into mischief. **17** Be thou not glad when thine enemy falleth, and let not thine heart rejoice when he stumbleth, **18** Lest the Lord see it, and it displease him, and he turn his wrath [g]from him. **19** [3]Fret not thyself because of the malicious, neither be envious at the wicked. **20** For there shall be none end of plagues to the evil man, [4]the light of the wicked shall be put out. **21** My son, fear the Lord, and the King and meddle not with them that are seditious. **22** For their destruction shall rise suddenly, and who knoweth the ruin of them [h]both? **23** Also these things pertain to the wise, It is not good [i]to have respect of any person in judgment. **24** He that saith to the wicked, [5]Thou art righteous, him shall the people curse, and the multitude shall abhor him. **25** But to them that rebuke him, shall be pleasure, and upon them shall come the blessing of goodness. **26** They shall kiss the lips of him that answereth upright words. **27** Prepare thy work without, and make ready thy things in the field, [j]and after, build thine house. **28** Be not a witness against thy neighbor without cause: for wilt thou deceive with thy lips? **29** [6]Say not, I will do to him as he hath done to me, I [k]will recompense every man according to his work. **30** I passed by the field of the slothful, and by the vineyard of the man destitute of understanding. **31** And lo, it was all grown over with thorns, and nettles had covered the face thereof, and the stone wall thereof was broken down. **32** Then I beheld, and I considered it well: I looked upon it, and received [l]instruction. **33** Yet a little sleep, [m]a little slumber, a little folding of the hands to sleep. **34** So thy poverty cometh as one that traveleth by the way, and thy necessity like an armed man.

25 *Chapter 25*

1 These are also parables of Solomon, which the [a]men of Hezekiah King of Judah [b]copied out. **2** The glory of God is to [c]conceal a thing secret: but the [d]King's honor is to search out a thing. **3** The heavens in height, and the earth in deepness: and the [e]king's heart can no man search out. **4** Take the [f]dross from the silver, and there shall proceed a vessel for the finer. **5** Take [g]away the wicked from the King, and his throne shall be established in righteousness. **6** Boast not thyself before the King, and stand not in the place of great men. **7** [1]For it is better, that it be said unto thee, Come up hither, than thou to be put lower in the presence of the Prince whom thine eyes have seen. **8** Go not forth hastily to strife, lest thou know not what to do in the end thereof, when thy neighbor hath put thee to shame. **9** Debate thy matter with thy neighbor, and discover not the secret to another, **10** Lest he that heareth it, put thee to shame, and thine infamy do not [h]cease. **11** A word spoken in his place, is like apples of gold with pictures of silver. **12** He that reproveth the wise and the obedient ear, is as a golden earring, and an ornament of fine gold. **13** As the cold of the snow [i]in the time of harvest, so is a faithful messenger to them that send him: for he refresheth the soul of his masters. **14** A man that boasteth of false liberality, is like [j]clouds and wind without rain. **15** A Prince is pacified by staying of [k]anger, and a soft tongue breaketh the [l]bones. **16** If thou have found honey, eat that is [m]sufficient for thee, lest thou be overfull, and vomit it. **17** Withdraw thy foot from thy neighbor's house, lest he be weary of thee, and hate thee. **18** A man that beareth false witness against his neighbor, is like an hammer and a sword, and a sharp arrow. **19** Confidence in an unfaithful man in time of trouble, is like a broken tooth and a sliding foot. **20** He that taketh away the garment in the cold season, is like vinegar poured upon [n,o]nitre, or like him that singeth songs to an heavy heart. **21** [2]If he that hateth thee be hungry, give him bread to eat, and if he be thirsty, give him water to drink: **22** For thou shalt lay [p]coals upon his head, and the Lord shall recompense thee. **23** As the Northwind driveth away the rain, so doth an angry countenance the slandering tongue. **24** [3]It is better to dwell in a corner of the house top, than with a contentious woman in a wide house. **25** As are the cold waters to a weary soul, so is good news from a far country. **26** A righteous man falling down before the wicked, is like a troubled well and a corrupt spring. **27** It is not good to eat much honey: so to search their own glory, is not glory. **28** A man that refraineth not his appetite, is like a city which is [q]broken down and without walls.

26 *Chapter 26*

1 As the snow in the Summer, and as the rain in the Harvest are not meet, so is honor unseemly for a fool. **2** As the sparrow by flying, and the swallow by flying escape, so the curse that is causeless, shall not come. **3** Unto the horse belongeth a whip, to the ass a bridle, and a rod to the fool's back. **4** Answer not a fool [a]according to his foolishness, lest thou also be like him. **5** Answer a fool [b]according to his foolishness, lest he be wise in his own [c]conceit. **6** He that sendeth a message by the hand of a fool, is as he that cutteth off [d]the feet, [e]and drinketh iniquity. **7** As they that lift up the legs of the lame, so is a parable in a fool's mouth. **8** As the closing up of a precious stone in an heap of stones, so is he that giveth glory to a fool. **9** As a thorn standing [f]up in the hand of a drunkard, so is a parable in the mouth of fools. **10** [g]The Excellent that formed all things, both rewardeth the fool, and rewardeth the transgressors. **11** [1]As a dog turneth again to his own vomit, so a fool turneth to his foolishness. **12** Seest thou a man wise in his own conceit? [h]more hope is of a fool than of him. **13** The slothful man saith, [i]A lion is in the way: a lion is in the streets. **14** As the door turneth upon his hinges, so doth the slothful man upon his bed. **15** [2]The slothful hideth his hand in his bosom, and it grieveth him to put it again to his mouth. **16** The sluggard is wiser in his own conceit, than seven men that can render a reason. **17** He that passeth by and medleth with the strife that belongeth not unto him, is as one that taketh a dog by the ears. **18** As he that feigneth himself mad, casteth firebrands, arrows, and mortal things, **19** So dealeth the deceitful man with [j]his friend, and saith, Am not I in sport? **20** Without wood the fire is quenched, and without a talebearer strife ceaseth. **21** As the coal maketh burning coals, and wood a fire, so the contentious man is apt to kindle strife. **22** [3]The words of a talebearer are as flatterings, and they go down into the bowels of the belly. **23** As silver dross overlaid upon a potsherd, so are burning lips, and [k]an evil heart. **24** He that hateth, will counterfeit with his lips, but in his heart he layeth up deceit. **25** Though he speak favorably, believe him not: for there are [l]seven abominations in his heart. **26** Hatred may be covered by deceit: but the malice thereof shall be discovered in the [m]congregation. **27** [4]He that diggeth a pit shall fall therein, and he that rolleth a stone, it shall return unto him. **28** A false tongue hateth the afflicted, and a flattering mouth causeth ruin.

PROVERBS 24

- **a.** Prov. 24:7 In the place where wisdom should be showed.
- **b.** Prov. 24:10 Man hath no trial of his strength till he be in troubles.
- **c.** Prov. 24:11 None can be excused, if he help not the innocent when he is in danger.
- **d.** Prov. 24:13 As honey is sweet and pleasant to the taste, so wisdom is to the soul.
- **e.** Prov. 24:14 Or, reward.
- **f.** Prov. 24:16 He is subject to many perils, but God delivereth him.
- **g.** Prov. 24:18 To be avenged on thee.
- **h.** Prov. 24:22 Meaning, either of the wicked and seditious, as verse 19 and 21, or, of them that fear not God, nor obey their King.
- **i.** Prov. 24:23 Hebrew, to know the face.
- **j.** Prov. 24:27 Be sure of the means how to compass it, before thou take any enterprise in hand.
- **k.** Prov. 24:29 He showeth what is the nature of the wicked, to revenge wrong for wrong.
- **l.** Prov. 24:32 That I might learn by another man's fault.
- **m.** Prov. 24:33 Read Prov. 6:10.

PROVERBS 24

- **1.** Ps. 37:1 / Prov. 23:17
- **2.** Prov. 20:18
- **3.** Ps. 37:1 / Prov. 33:17
- **4.** Prov. 13:9
- **5.** Prov. 17:25 / Isa. 5:23
- **6.** Prov. 20:22

PROVERBS 25

- **a.** Prov. 25:1 Whom Hezekiah appointed for this purpose.
- **b.** Prov. 25:1 That is, gathered out of divers books of Solomon.
- **c.** Prov. 25:2 God doth not reveal the cause of his judgments to man.
- **d.** Prov. 25:2 Because the king ruleth by the revealed word of God, the cause of his doings must appear, and therefore he must use diligence in trying out of causes.
- **e.** Prov. 25:3 He showeth that it is too hard for man to attain to the reason of all the secret doings of the King, even when he is upright, and doeth his duty.
- **f.** Prov. 25:4 When vice is removed from a king, he is a meet vessel for the Lord's use.
- **g.** Prov. 25:5 It is not enough that he be pure himself: but that he put away others that be corrupted.
- **h.** Prov. 25:10 Lest whereas thou thinkest by this means to have an end of the matter, it put thee to further trouble.
- **i.** Prov. 25:13 In the time of great heat, when men desire cold.
- **j.** Prov. 25:14 Which have an outward appearance, and are nothing within.
- **k.** Prov. 25:15 By not ministering occasion to provoke him further.
- **l.** Prov. 25:15 That is, the heart that is bent to anger, as Prov. 15:1.
- **m.** Prov. 25:16 Use moderately the pleasures of this world.
- **n.** Prov. 25:20 Which melteth it, and consumeth it.
- **o.** Prov. 25:20 Or, alum.
- **p.** Prov. 25:22 Thou shalt, as it were by force, overcome him, insomuch that his own conscience shall move him to acknowledge the benefits, and his heart shall be inflamed.
- **q.** Prov. 25:28 And so is in extreme danger.

PROVERBS 25

- **1.** Luke 14:10
- **2.** Rom. 12:20
- **3.** Prov. 21:9

PROVERBS 26

- **a.** Prov. 26:4 Consent not unto him in his doings.
- **b.** Prov. 26:5 Reprove him as the matter requireth.
- **c.** Prov. 26:5 Hebrew, eyes.
- **d.** Prov. 26:6 To wit, of the messenger whom he sendeth.
- **e.** Prov. 26:6 That is, receiveth damage thereby.
- **f.** Prov. 26:9 Whereby he both hurteth himself and others.
- **g.** Prov. 26:10 Meaning, God.
- **h.** Prov. 26:12 For the fool will rather be counseled than he: also the fool sinneth of ignorance, and the other of malice.
- **i.** Prov. 26:13 Read Prov. 22:13.
- **j.** Prov. 26:19 Which dissembleth himself to be that he is not.
- **k.** Prov. 26:23 They will soon break out and utter themselves.
- **l.** Prov. 26:25 Meaning, many: he useth the number certain, for the uncertain.
- **m.** Prov. 26:26 In the assembly of the godly.

PROVERBS 26

- **1.** 2 Pet. 2:22
- **2.** Prov. 19:24
- **3.** Prov. 18:8
- **4.** Eccl. 10:8

27 *Chapter 27*

1 Boast not thyself of [a]tomorrow, for thou knowest not what a day may bring forth. **2** Let another man praise thee, and not thine own mouth: a stranger, and not thine own lips. **3** A stone is heavy, and the sand weighty: but a fool's wrath is heavier than them both. **4** Anger is cruel, and wrath is raging: but who can stand before [b]envy? **5** Open rebuke is better than secret love. **6** The wounds of a lover are faithful, and the kisses of an enemy are [c]pleasant. **7** [1]The person that is full, despiseth an honeycomb: but unto the hungry soul every bitter thing is sweet. **8** As a bird that wandereth from her nest, so is a man that wandereth from his own place. **9** As ointment and perfume rejoice the heart, so doth the sweetness of a man's friend by hearty counsel. **10** Thine own friend and thy father's friend forsake thou not: neither enter into thy brother's [d]house in the day of thy calamity: for better is a neighbor that is near, than a brother far off. **11** My son, be wise, and rejoice mine heart, that I may answer him that reproacheth me. **12** [e]A prudent man seeth the plague, and hideth himself: but the foolish go on still, and are punished. **13** [2]Take his garment that is surety for a stranger, and a pledge of him for the stranger. **14** He that [f]praiseth his friend with a loud voice, rising [g]early in the morning, it shall be counted to him as a curse. **15** [3]A continual dropping in the day of rain, and a contentious woman are alike. **16** He that hideth her, hideth the wind, and she is as the oil in his right hand that uttereth itself. **17** Iron sharpeneth iron, so doth [h]man sharpen the face of his friend. **18** He that keepeth the fig tree, shall eat the fruit thereof: so he that waiteth upon his master, shall come to honor. **19** As in water face answereth to face, [i]so the heart of man to man. **20** The grave and destruction can never be full, so the eyes of man can never be satisfied. **21** [4]As is the fining pot for silver, and the furnace for gold, so is every man according to his [j]dignity. **22** Though thou shouldest bray a fool in a mortar among wheat brayed with a pestle, yet will not his foolishness depart from him. **23** Be diligent to know the state of thy flock, and take heed to the herds. **24** For riches remain not always, nor the crown from generation to generation. **25** The hay discovereth itself, and the grass appeareth, and the herbs of the mountains are gathered. **26** The [k]lambs are for thy clothing, and the goats are the price of the field. **27** And let the milk of the goats be sufficient for thy food, for the food of thy family, and for the sustenance of thy maids.

28 *Chapter 28*

1 The wicked [a]flee when none pursueth: but the righteous are bold as a lion. **2** For the transgression of the land [b]there are many princes thereof: but by a man of understanding and knowledge a realm likewise endureth long. **3** A poor man, if he oppress the poor, is like a raging rain that leaveth no food. **4** They that forsake the Law, praise the wicked: but they that keep the Law, set themselves against them. **5** Wicked men understand not judgment: but they that seek the Lord, understand all things. **6** [1]Better is the poor that walketh in his uprightness, than he that perverteth his ways, though he be rich. **7** He that keepeth the Law, is a child of understanding: but he that feedeth the gluttons, shameth his father. **8** He that increaseth his riches by usury and interest, gathereth [c]them for him that will be merciful unto the poor. **9** He that turneth away his ear from hearing the Law, even his prayer shall be [d]abominable. **10** He that causeth the righteous to go astray by an evil way, shall fall into his own pit, and the upright shall inherit good things. **11** The rich man is wise in his own conceit: but the poor that hath understanding, can try [e]him. **12** [2]When righteous men rejoice, there is great glory: but when the wicked come up, the man [f]is tried. **13** He that hideth his sins, shall not prosper: but he that confesseth, and forsaketh them, shall have mercy. **14** Blessed is the man that [g]feareth always: but he that hardeneth his heart, shall fall into evil. **15** As a roaring lion, and an hungry bear, so is [h]a wicked ruler over the poor people. **16** A prince destitute of understanding is also a great oppressor: but he that hateth covetousness, shall prolong his days. **17** A man that doeth violence against the blood of a person, shall flee unto the grave, and they shall not [i]stay him. **18** He that walketh uprightly shall be saved: but he that is froward in his ways, shall once fall. **19** [3]He that tilleth his land, shall be satisfied with bread, but he that followeth the idle, shall be filled with poverty. **20** A faithful man shall abound in blessings, and [4]he that maketh haste to be rich, shall not be innocent. **21** To have respect of persons is not good: for that man will transgress for a piece of [j]bread. **22** A man with a wicked [k]eye hasteth to riches, and knoweth not that poverty shall come upon him. **23** He that rebuketh a man, shall find more favor at the length, than he that flattereth with his tongue. **24** He that robbeth his father and mother, and saith, It is no transgression, is the companion of a man that destroyeth. **25** He that is of a proud heart, stirreth up strife: but he that trusteth in the Lord, shall be [l]fat. **26** He that trusteth in his own heart, is a fool: but he that walketh in wisdom, shall be delivered. **27** He that giveth unto the poor, shall not lack: but he that hideth his eyes, shall have many curses. **28** [5]When the wicked rise up, men hide themselves: but when they perish, the righteous increase.

29 *Chapter 29*

1 A man that hardeneth his neck when he is rebuked, shall suddenly be destroyed, and cannot be cured. **2** [1]When the righteous [a]are in authority, the people rejoice: but when the wicked beareth rule, the people sigh. **3** A man that loveth wisdom rejoiceth his father: but [2]he that feedeth harlots wasteth his substance. **4** A king by judgment maintaineth the country: but a man receiving gifts, destroyeth it. **5** A man that flattereth his neighbor, [b]spreadeth a net for his steps. **6** In the transgression of an evil man is his [c]snare: but the righteous doth sing and rejoice. **7** The righteous knoweth the cause of the poor: but the wicked regardeth not knowledge. **8** Scornful men bring a city into a snare: but wise men turn away wrath. **9** If a wise man contend with [d]a foolish man, whether he be angry or laugh, there is no rest. **10** Bloody men hate him that is upright: but the just have care of his soul. **11** A fool poureth out all his mind: but a wise man keepeth it in till afterward. **12** Of a prince that hearkeneth to lies, all his servants are wicked. **13** [3]The poor and the usurer meet together, and the Lord lighteneth both their eyes. **14** A [4]King that judgeth the poor in truth, his throne shall be established forever. **15** The rod and correction give wisdom, but a child set at liberty, maketh his mother ashamed. **16** When the wicked are increased, transgression increaseth: but the righteous shall see their fall. **17** Correct thy son, and he will give thee rest, and will give pleasures to thy soul. **18** [e]Where there is no vision, the people decay: but he that keepeth the law is blessed. **19** A [f]servant will not be chastised with words: though he understand, yet he will not [g]answer. **20** Seest thou a man hasty in his matters? there is more hope of a fool, than of him. **21** He that delicately bringeth up his servant from youth, at length he will be even as his son. **22** [5]An angry man stirreth up strife, and a furious man aboundeth in transgression. **23** [6]The pride of a man shall bring him low: but the humble in spirit shall enjoy glory. **24** He that is partner with a thief, hateth his own soul: he heareth cursing and declareth it not. **25** The fear of man bringeth a [h]snare: but he that trusteth in the Lord shall be exalted. **26** Many do seek the face of the ruler: but every man's [i]judgment cometh from the Lord. **27** A wicked man is abomination to the just, and he that is upright in his way, is abomination to the wicked.

30 *2 To humble ourselves in consideration of God's works. 5 The word of God is perfect. 11 Of the wicked and hypocrites. 15 Of things that are never satiate. 18 Of others that are wonderful.*

THE WORDS OF [a]AGUR THE SON OF JAKEH. **1** The prophecy which the man spake unto Ithiel, even to [b]Ithiel, and Ucal. **2** Surely I am more [c]foolish than any man, and have not the understanding of a man in me. **3** For I have

---

PROVERBS 27

- **a.** Prov. 27:1 Delay not the time, but take occasion when it is offered.
- **b.** Prov. 27:4 For the envious are obstinate, and cannot be reconciled.
- **c.** Prov. 27:6 They are flattering, and seem friendful.
- **d.** Prov. 27:10 Trust not to any worldly help in the day of thy trouble.
- **e.** Prov. 27:12 Read Prov. 22:3.
- **f.** Prov. 27:14 Hebrew, blesseth.
- **g.** Prov. 27:14 Hastily and without cause.
- **h.** Prov. 27:17 One hasty man provoketh another to anger.
- **i.** Prov. 27:19 There is no difference between man and man by nature, but only the grace of God maketh the difference.
- **j.** Prov. 27:21 That is, he is either known to be ambitious, and glorious, or humble and modest.
- **k.** Prov. 27:26 This declareth the great goodness of God towards man, and the diligence that he requireth of him for the preservation of his gifts.

PROVERBS 27

1. Job. 6:6
2. Prov. 20:16
3. Prov. 29:13 / Prov. 21:9
4. Prov. 17:3

PROVERBS 28

- **a.** Prov. 28:1 Because their own conscience accuseth them.
- **b.** Prov. 28:2 The state of the commonweal is oftentimes changed.
- **c.** Prov. 28:8 For God will take away the wicked usurer, and give his goods to him that shall bestow them well.
- **d.** Prov. 28:9 Because it is not of faith which is grounded of God's word or Law, which the wicked contemn.
- **e.** Prov. 28:11 And judge that he is not wise.
- **f.** Prov. 28:12 He is known by his doings to be wicked.
- **g.** Prov. 28:14 Which standeth in awe of God, and is afraid to offend him.
- **h.** Prov. 28:15 For he can never be satisfied, but ever oppresseth and spoileth.
- **i.** Prov. 28:17 None shall be able to deliver him.
- **j.** Prov. 28:21 He will be abused for nothing.
- **k.** Prov. 28:22 Meaning, him that is covetous.
- **l.** Prov. 28:25 Shall have all things in abundance.

PROVERBS 28

1. Prov. 19:1
2. Prov. 29:2
3. Prov. 12:11
4. Prov. 13:11 / Prov. 20:21
5. Prov. 29:2

PROVERBS 29

- **a.** Prov. 29:2 Or, are increased.
- **b.** Prov. 29:5 He that giveth ear to the flatterer, is in danger as the bird is before the fowler.
- **c.** Prov. 29:6 He is ever ready to fall into the snare that he layeth for others.
- **d.** Prov. 29:9 He can hear no admonition in what sort soever it is spoken.
- **e.** Prov. 29:18 Where there are not faithful ministers of the word of God.
- **f.** Prov. 29:19 He that is of a servile and rebellious nature.
- **g.** Prov. 29:19 Or, regard.
- **h.** Prov. 29:25 He that feareth man more than God, falleth into a snare and is destroyed.
- **i.** Prov. 29:26 He needeth not to flatter the ruler: for what God hath appointed, that shall come to him.

PROVERBS 29

1. Prov. 28:12,28
2. Luke 15:13
3. Prov. 22:2
4. Prov. 20:28
5. Prov. 15:28
6. Job. 22:29

PROVERBS 30

- **a.** Prov. 30:1 Who was an excellent man in virtue and knowledge in the time of Solomon.

not learned wisdom, nor attained to the knowledge of holy things. **4** Who hath
ascended up to [d]heaven, and descended? Who hath gathered the wind in his fist?
Who hath bound the waters in a garment? Who hath established all the ends of the
world? What is his name, and what is his son's name, if thou canst tell? **5** [1]Every
word of God is pure: he is a shield to those that trust in him. **6** [2]Put nothing
unto his words, lest he reprove thee, and thou be found a liar. **7** Two [e]things
have I required of thee: deny me them not before I die. **8** Remove far from me
vanity and lies: give me not poverty, nor riches: feed me with food convenient
for me, **9** Lest I be full, and deny thee, and say, [f]Who is the Lord? or lest I be
poor and steal, and take the Name of my God in vain. **10** Accuse not a servant
unto his master, lest he curse thee, [g]when thou hast offended. **11** There is a ge-
neration that curseth their father, and doth not bless their mother. **12** There
is a generation that are pure in their own conceit, and yet are not washed from
their filthiness. **13** There is a generation whose eyes are haughty, and their eye
lids are lifted up. **14** There is a generation, whose teeth are as swords, and their
chaws as knives to eat up the afflicted out of the earth, and the poor from among
men. **15** The horseleech hath two [h]daughters which cry, Give, give. There be
three things that will not be satisfied: yea, four that say not, It is enough. **16** The
grave, and the barren womb, the earth, that cannot be satisfied with water, and the
fire that saith not, It is enough. **17** The eye that mocketh his father and despi-
seth the instruction of his mother, let the ravens [i]of the valley pick it out, and the
young eagles eat it. **18** There be three things hid from me: yea, four that I know
not: **19** The way of an eagle in the air, the way of a serpent upon a stone, the way
of a ship in the midst of the sea, and the way of a man with a maid. **20** Such is
the way also of an adulterous woman: she eateth and [j]wipeth her mouth, and saith,
I have not committed iniquity. **21** For three things the earth is moved: yea, for
four it cannot sustain itself. **22** For [k]a servant when he reigneth, and a fool when
he is filled with meat, **23** For the hateful woman, when she is married, and for a
handmaid that is [l]heir to her mistress. **24** These be four small things in the ear-
th, yet they are [m]wise, and full of wisdom. **25** The pismires a people not strong,
yet prepare they their meat in summer: **26** The conies a people not mighty, yet
make they their houses in the rock: **27** The grasshopper hath no king, yet go they
forth all by bands: **28** The spider taketh hold [n]with her hands, and is in king's
palaces. **29** There be three things that order well their going: yea, four are comely
in going: **30** A lion which is strong among beasts, and turneth not at the sight
of any: **31** A lusty greyhound, and a goat, and a king against whom there is no
rising up. **32** If thou hast been foolish in lifting thyself up, and if thou hast thou-
ght wickedly, lay thine hand [o]upon thy mouth. **33** When one churneth milk, he
bringeth forth butter: and he that wringeth his nose, causeth blood to come out, so
he that forceth wrath, bringeth forth strife.

31

2 He exhorteth to chastity and justice, 10 and showeth the conditions of a wise and worthy woman.

1 THE WORDS OF KING [a]LEMUEL: The [b]prophecy which his mother
taught him. **2** What my son! and what the son of [c]my womb! and what, O
son of my desires! **3** Give not thy strength unto women, [d]nor thy ways whi-
ch is to destroy kings. **4** It is not for kings, O Lemuel, it is not for kings to
drink wine, nor for princes [e]strong drink, **5** Lest he drink and forget the de-
cree, and change the judgment of all the children of affliction. **6** Give ye strong
drink unto him that is ready to perish, and wine unto them that have grief of he-
art. **7** Let him drink, that he may forget [f]his poverty, and remember his misery
no more. **8** Open thy mouth for the [g]dumb in the cause of all the children of
destruction. **9** Open thy mouth, judge righteously, and judge the afflicted, and
the poor. **10** Who shall find a virtuous woman? for her price is far above the pe-
arls. **11** The heart of her husband trusteth in her, and he shall have no need of
[h]spoil. **12** She will do him good, and not evil all the days of her life. **13** She
seeketh wool and flax, and laboreth cheerfully with her hands. **14** She is like the
ships of merchants: she bringeth her food from afar. **15** And she ariseth, while
it is yet night: and giveth [i]the portion to her household, and the [j]ordinary to her
maids. **16** She considereth a field, and [k]getteth it: and with the fruit of her hands
she planteth a vineyard. **17** She girdeth her loins with strength, and strengthe-
neth her arms. **18** She feeleth that her merchandise is good: her candle is not
put out by night. **19** She putteth her hands to the wheel, and her hands handle
the spindle. **20** She stretcheth out her hand to the poor, and putteth forth her
hands to the needy. **21** She feareth not the snow for her family: for all her family
is clothed with [l]scarlet. **22** She maketh herself carpets: fine linen and purple is
her garment. **23** Her husband is known in the [m]gates, when he sitteth with the
Elders of the land. **24** She maketh [n]sheets, and selleth them, and giveth girdles
unto the merchant. **25** [o]Strength and honor is her clothing, and in the latter day
she shall rejoice. **26** She openeth her mouth with wisdom, and the [p]law of grace
is in her tongue. **27** She overseeth the ways of her household, and eateth not the
bread of idleness. **28** Her children rise up, and [q]call her blessed: her husband
also shall praise her, saying, **29** Many daughters have done virtuously: but thou
surmountest them all. **30** Favor is deceitful, and beauty is vanity: but a woman
that feareth the Lord she shall be praised. **31** Give [r]her of the fruit of her hands,
and let her own works praise her in the [s]gates.

---

b. Prov. 30:1 Which were Agur's scholars or friends.
c. Prov. 30:2 Herein he declareth his great humility, which would not attribute any wisdom to himself, but all unto God.
d. Prov. 30:4 Meaning, to know the secrets of God, as though he would say, None.
e. Prov. 30:7 He maketh this request to God.
f. Prov. 30:9 Meaning, that they that put their trust in their riches, forget God, and that by too much wealth men have an occasion to the same.
g. Prov. 30:10 In accusing him without cause.
h. Prov. 30:15 The leech hath two forks in her tongue, which here he calleth her two daughters, whereby she sucketh the blood, and is never satiated: even so are the covetous extortioners insatiable.
i. Prov. 30:17 Which haunt in the valley for carrions.
j. Prov. 30:20 She hath her desires, and after counterfeiteth as though she were an honest woman.
k. Prov. 30:22 These commonly abuse the state whereunto they are called.
l. Prov. 30:23 Which is married to her master after the death of her mistress.
m. Prov. 30:24 They contain great doctrine and wisdom.
n. Prov. 30:28 If man be not able to compass these common things by his wisdom, we cannot attribute wisdom to man, but folly.
o. Prov. 30:32 Make a stay, and continue not in doing evil.

PROVERBS 30

1. Ps. 19:8 **2.** Deut. 4:2 / Deut. 12:32

PROVERBS 31

a. Prov. 31:1 That is, of Solomon, who was called Lemuel, that is, of God, because God had ordained him to be king over Israel.
b. Prov. 31:1 The doctrine which his mother Bathsheba taught him.
c. Prov. 31:2 By this often repetition of one thing, she declareth her motherly affection.
d. Prov. 31:3 Meaning, that women are the destruction of kings, if they haunt them.
e. Prov. 31:4 That is, the King must not give himself to wantonness, and neglect of his office, which is to execute judgment.
f. Prov. 31:7 For wine doth comfort the heart, as Ps. 104:15.
g. Prov. 31:8 Defend their cause that are not able to help themselves.
h. Prov. 31:11 He shall not need to use any unlawful means to gain his living.
i. Prov. 31:15 Or, meat, as Ps. 111:5
j. Prov. 31:15 She prepareth their meat betime.
k. Prov. 31:16 She purchaseth it with the gains of her travail.
l. Prov. 31:21 Or, with double.
m. Prov. 31:23 In the assemblies and places of judgment.
n. Prov. 31:24 Or, linen cloth.
o. Prov. 31:25 After that he had spoken of the apparel of the body, he now declareth the apparel of the spirit.
p. Prov. 31:26 Her tongue is as a book whereby one might learn many good things: for she delighteth to talk of the word of God.
q. Prov. 31:28 That is, do her reverence.
r. Prov. 31:31 Confess her diligent labors, and commend her therefore.
s. Prov. 31:31 Forasmuch as the most honorable are clad in the apparel that she made.

ECCLESIASTES

OR THE PREACHER

1 *2 All things in this world are full of vanity, and of none endurance. 13 All man's wisdom is but folly and grief.*

1 The words of the [a]Preacher, the son of David king in Jerusalem. **2** [b]Va-
nity of vanities, saith the Preacher: vanity of vanities, all is vanity. **3** What re-
maineth unto man in all his [c]travail, which he suffereth under the sun? **4** One
generation passeth, and another generation succeedeth: but the earth remaineth
[d]forever. **5** The sun riseth, and the sun goeth down, and draweth to his place
where he riseth. **6** The [e]wind goeth toward the South, and compasseth toward
the North: the wind goeth round about, and returneth by his circuits. **7** All the
rivers go into the sea, yet the sea is not full: for the rivers go unto the place [f]whence
they return, and go. **8** All things are full of labor: man cannot utter it: the eye is
not satisfied with seeing, nor the ear filled with hearing. **9** [g]What is it that hath
been? that that shall be: and what is it that hath been done? that which shall be
done: and there is no new thing under the sun. **10** Is there anything, whereof
one may say, Behold this, it is new? it hath been already in the old time that was
before us. **11** There is no memory of the former, neither shalt there be a remem-
brance of the latter that shall be, with them that shall come after. **12** [h]I the Prea-
cher have been king over Israel in Jerusalem: **13** And I have given mine heart to
search and find out wisdom by all things that are done under the heaven: (this sore
travail hath God given to the sons of men, [i]to humble them thereby.) **14** I have
considered all the works that are done under the sun, and behold, all is vanity, and
vexation of the spirit. **15** That which is [j]crooked, can none make straight: and
that which faileth, cannot be numbered. **16** I thought in mine heart, and said,
Behold, I am become great, and excel in wisdom all them that have been before me
in Jerusalem: and mine heart hath seen much wisdom and knowledge. **17** And
I gave mine heart to know wisdom and knowledge, [k]madness and foolishness: I
knew also that this is a vexation of the spirit. **18** For in the multitude of wisdom
is much [l]grief: and he that increaseth knowledge, increaseth sorrow.

2 *Pleasures, sumptuous buildings, riches and possessions are but vanity. 14 The wise and the fool have both one end touching the bodily death.*

1 I said in mine heart, Go to now, I will prove [a]thee with joy: therefore take
thou pleasure in pleasant things: and behold, this also is vanity. **2** I said of lau-
ghter, Thou art mad: and of joy, What is this that thou doest? **3** I sought in mine
heart [b]to give myself to wine, and to lead mine heart in [c]wisdom, and to take
hold of folly, till I might see where is that goodness of the children of men, which
they [d]enjoy under the Sun, the whole number of the days of their life. **4** I have
made my great works: I have built me houses: I have planted me vineyards. **5** I
have made me gardens and [e]orchards, and planted in them trees of all fruit. **6** I
have made me cisterns of water, to water therewith the woods that grow with tre-
es. **7** I have gotten servants and maids, and had children born in the [f]house: also
I had great Possession of beeves and sheep above all that were before me in Jeru-
salem. **8** I have gathered unto me also silver and gold, and the chief treasures of
Kings and provinces: I have provided me men singers, and women singers, and the
[g]delights of the sons of men, as a woman [h]taken captive, and women taken capti-
ves. **9** And I was great, and increased above all that were before me in Jerusalem:
also my wisdom [i]remained with me. **10** And whatsoever mine eyes desired, I
withheld it not from them: I withdrew not mine heart from any joy: for mine he-
art rejoiced in all my labor: and this was my [j]portion of all my travail. **11** Then
I looked on all my works that mine hands had wrought, and on the travail that I
had labored to do: and behold, all is vanity and vexation of the spirit: and there is
no profit under the Sun. **12** And I turned to behold [k]wisdom, and madness, and
folly: (for who is the man that [l]will come after the King in things, which men now
have done?) **13** Then I saw that there is profit in wisdom more than in folly: as
the light is more excellent than darkness. **14** [1]For the wise man's [m]eyes are in his
head, but the fool walketh in darkness: yet I know also that the same [n]condition
falleth to them all. **15** Then I thought in mine heart, It befalleth unto me, as it
befalleth to the fool. Why therefore do I then labor to be more wise? And I said
in mine heart, that this also is vanity. **16** For there shall be no remembrance of
the wise, nor of the fool [o]forever: for that that now is, in the days to come, shall
all be forgotten. And [p]how dieth the wise man, as doth the fool? **17** Therefore
I hated life: for the work that is wrought under the Sun is grievous unto me: for
all is vanity, and vexation of the spirit. **18** I hated also all my labor, wherein
I had travailed under the Sun, which I shall leave to the man that shall be after
me. **19** And who knoweth whether he shall be wise or foolish? yet shall he have
rule over all my labor, wherein I have travailed, and wherein I have showed myself
wise under the Sun. This is also vanity. **20** Therefore I went about to make mine
heart [q]abhor all the labor, wherein I had travailed under the Sun. **21** For there is
a man whose travail is in wisdom, and in knowledge, and in equity: yet to a man
that hath not travailed herein, shall he [r]give his portion: this also is vanity, and a
great grief. **22** For what hath man of all his travail and grief of his heart, wherein
he hath travailed under the Sun? **23** For all his days are sorrows, and his travail
grief: his heart also taketh not rest in the night: which also is vanity. **24** There is
no profit to man, but that he eat and drink, and [s]delight his soul with the profit of
his labor: I saw also this, that it was of the hand of God. **25** For who could eat,
and who could haste to [t]outward things more than I? **26** Surely to a man that is
good in his sight, God giveth wisdom, and knowledge, and joy: but to the sinner
he giveth pain to gather, and to heap to give to him that is good before God: this
also is vanity, and vexation of the spirit.

ECCLESIASTES 1

- **a.** Eccles. 1:1 Solomon is here called a preacher, or one that assembleth the people, because he teacheth the true knowledge of God, and how men ought to pass their life in this transitory world.
- **b.** Eccles. 1:2 He condemneth the opinions of all men that set felicity in any thing, but in God alone, seeing that in this world all things are as vanity and nothing.
- **c.** Eccles. 1:3 Solomon doth not condemn man's labor or diligence, but showeth that there is no full contentation in any thing under the heaven, nor in any creature, forasmuch as all things are transitory.
- **d.** Eccles. 1:4 One man dieth after another, and the earth remaineth longest, even to the last day, which yet is subject to corruption.
- **e.** Eccles. 1:6 By the sun, wind and rivers, he showeth that the greatest labor and longest hath an end, and therefore there can be no felicity in this world.
- **f.** Eccles. 1:7 The sea which compasseth all the earth, filleth the veins thereof, the which pour out springs and rivers into the sea again.
- **g.** Eccles. 1:9 He speaketh of times and seasons, and things done in them, which as they have been in times past, so come they to pass again.
- **h.** Eccles. 1:12 He proveth that if any could have attained to felicity in this world by labor, and study, he chiefly should have obtained it, because he had gifts and aids of God thereunto above all others.
- **i.** Eccles. 1:13 Man of nature hath a desire to know, and yet is not able to come to the perfection of knowledge, which is the punishment of sin, to humble man, and to teach him to depend only upon God.
- **j.** Eccles. 1:15 Man is not able by all his diligence to cause things to go otherwise than they do: neither can he number the faults that are committed, much less remedy them.
- **k.** Eccles. 1:17 That is, vain things, which served unto pleasure, wherein was no commodity, but grief and trouble of conscience.
- **l.** Eccles. 1:18 Wisdom and knowledge cannot be come by without great pain of body and mind: for when a man hath attained to the highest, yet is his mind never fully content: therefore in this world is no true felicity.

ECCLESIASTES 2

- **a.** Eccles. 2:1 Solomon maketh this discourse with himself, as though he would try whether there were contentation in ease and pleasures.
- **b.** Eccles. 2:3 Hebrew, draw my flesh to wine.
- **c.** Eccles. 2:3 Albeit I gave myself to pleasures, yet I thought to keep wisdom and the fear of God in mine heart, and govern mine affairs by the same.
- **d.** Eccles. 2:3 Hebrew, do.
- **e.** Eccles. 2:5 Hebrew, paradises.
- **f.** Eccles. 2:7 Meaning, of the servants or slaves, which he had bought: so the children born in their servitude, were the masters.
- **g.** Eccles. 2:8 That is, whatsoever men take pleasure in.
- **h.** Eccles. 2:8 Which were the most beautiful of them that were taken in war, as Judg. 5:30. Some understand by these words, no women, but instruments of music.
- **i.** Eccles. 2:9 For all this God did not take his gift of wisdom from me.
- **j.** Eccles. 2:10 This was the fruit of all my labor, a certain pleasure mixed with care, which he calleth vanity in the next verse.
- **k.** Eccles. 2:12 I bethought with myself whether it were better to follow wisdom, or mine own affections and pleasures, which he calleth madness.
- **l.** Eccles. 2:12 Or, compare with the King.
- **m.** Eccles. 2:14 He forseeth things, which the fool cannot for lack of wisdom.
- **n.** Eccles. 2:14 For both die and are forgotten as verse 16, or they both alike have prosperity or adversity.
- **o.** Eccles. 2:16 Meaning, in this world.
- **p.** Eccles. 2:16 He wondereth that men forget a wise man, being dead, as soon as they do a fool.
- **q.** Eccles. 2:20 That I might seek the true felicity which is in God.
- **r.** Eccles. 2:21 Among other griefs that was not the least, to leave that which he had gotten by great travail, to one that had taken no pain therefore, and whom he knew not whether he were a wise man or a fool.
- **s.** Eccles. 2:24 When man hath all labored, he can get no more than food and refreshing, yet he confesseth also that this cometh of God's blessing, as Eccl. 3:13.
- **t.** Eccles. 2:25 Meaning, to pleasures.

ECCLESIASTES 2

1. Prov. 17:24

3

1 All things have their time. 14 The works of God are perfect, and cause us to fear him. 17 God shall judge both the just and unjust.

1 To all things there is an [a]appointed time, and a time to every purpose under the heaven. **2** A time to be born, and a time to die: a time to plant, and a time to pluck up that which is planted. **3** A time to slay, and a time to heal: a time to break down, and a time to build. **4** A time to weep, and a time to laugh: a time to mourn, and a time to dance. **5** A time to cast away stones, and a time to gather stones: a time to embrace, and a time to be far from embracing. **6** A time to seek, and a time to lose: a time to keep, and a time to cast away. **7** A time to rent, and a time to sow: a time to keep silence, and a time to speak. **8** A time to love, and a time to hate: a time of war, and a time of peace. **9** What profit hath he that worketh of the thing wherein he travaileth? **10** I have seen the travail that God hath given to the sons of men, [b]to humble them thereby. **11** He hath made everything beautiful in his time: also he hath set the [c]world in their heart, yet cannot man find out the work that God hath wrought from the beginning even to the end. **12** I know that there is nothing good in them, but to rejoice, and to do good in his life. **13** And also that every man eateth and drinketh, and seeth the commodity of all his labor. This is the [d]gift of God. **14** I know that whatsoever God shall do, it shall be [e]forever: to it can no man add, and from it can none diminish: for God hath done it, that they should fear before him. **15** What is that that hath been? that is now: and that that shall be, hath now been: for God [f]requireth that which is past. **16** And moreover, I have seen under the Sun the place of judgment, where was wickedness, and the place of justice, where was iniquity. **17** I thought in mine heart, God will judge the just and the wicked: for time is [g]there for every purpose and for every work. **18** I considered in mine heart the state of the children of men, that God had [h]purged them: yet to see too, they are in themselves as beasts. **19** For the condition of the children of men, and the condition of beasts are even as one [i]condition unto them. As the one dieth, so dieth the other: for they have all one breath, and there is no excellency of man above the beast: for all is vanity. **20** All go to one place, and all was of the dust, and all shall return to the dust. **21** Who [j]knoweth whether the spirit of man ascend upward, and the spirit of the beast descend downward to the earth? **22** Therefore I see that there is nothing better than that a man should [k]rejoice in his affairs, because that is his portion. For who shall bring him to see what shall be after him?

4

2 The innocents are oppressed. 4 Man's labors are full of abuse and vanity. 9 Man's society is necessary. 13 A young man poor and wise, is to be preferred to an old King that is a fool.

1 So [a]I turned and considered all the oppressions that are wrought under the sun, and behold, the tears of the oppressed, and none comforteth them, and lo, the strength is of the hand of them that oppress them, and none comforteth them. **2** Wherefore I praised the [b]dead which now are dead, above the living, which are yet alive. **3** And I count him [c]better than them both, which hath not yet been: for he hath not seen the evil works which are wrought under the sun. **4** Also I beheld all travail, and all [d]perfection of works, that this is the envy of a man against his neighbor: this also is vanity and vexation of spirit. **5** The fool foldeth his hands, and [e]eateth up his own flesh. **6** Better is an handful with quietness, than two handfuls with labor and vexation of spirit. **7** Again I returned, and saw vanity under the sun. **8** There is one alone, and there is not a second, which hath neither son nor brother, yet is there none end of all his travail, neither can his eye be satisfied with riches: neither doth he think, For whom do I travail and defraud my soul of pleasures? this also is vanity, this is an evil travail. **9** [f]Two are better wages for their labor. **10** For if they fall, the one will lift up his fellow: but woe unto him that is alone: for he falleth, and there is not a second to lift him up. **11** Also if two sleep together, then shall they have heat: but to one how should there be heat? **12** And if one overcome him, two shall stand against him: and a threefold [g]cord is not easily broken. **13** Better is a poor and wise child, than an old and foolish King, which will no more be admonished. **14** For out of the [h]prison he cometh forth to reign: when as he that is [i]born in his kingdom, is made poor. **15** I beheld all the living, which walk under the Sun [j]with the second child, which shall stand up in his place. **16** There is none [k]end of all the people, nor of all that were before them, and they that come after, shall not rejoice in him: surely this is also vanity and vexation of spirit. **17** Take heed to thine [l]foot when thou enterest into the house of God, and be more near to hear than to give the sacrifice of [m]fools: for they know not that they do evil.

5

1 Not to speak lightly, chiefly in God's matters. 9 The covetous can never have enough. 11 The laborer's sleep is sweet. 14 Man when he dieth, taketh nothing with him. 18 To live joyfully, and with a contented mind, is the gift of God.

1 Be not [a]rash with thy mouth, nor let thine heart be hasty to utter a thing before God: for God is in the heavens, and thou art on the earth: therefore let thy words be [b]few. **2** For as a dream cometh by the multitude of business: so the voice of a fool is in the multitude of words. **3** [1]When thou hast vowed a vow to God, defer not to pay it: for he delighteth not in fools: pay therefore that thou hast [c]vowed. **4** It is better that thou shouldest not vow, than that thou shouldest vow and not pay it. **5** Suffer not thy mouth to make thy [d]flesh to sin: neither say before the [e]Angel, that this is ignorance: wherefore shall God be angry by thy voice, and destroy the work of thine hands? **6** For in the multitude of dreams, and vanities are also many words: but fear thou God. **7** If in a country thou seest the oppression of the poor, and the defrauding of judgment and justice, be not astonied at the matter: for he that is [f]higher than the highest, regardeth, and there be higher than they. **8** And the [g]abundance of the earth is over all: the king [h]also consisteth by the field that is tilled. **9** He that loveth silver, shall not be satisfied with silver, and he that loveth riches, shall be without the fruit thereof: this is also vanity. **10** When goods increase, they are increased that eat them: and what good cometh to the owners thereof, but the beholding thereof with their eyes? **11** The sleep of him that travaileth, is sweet, whether he eat little or much: but the [i]satiety of the rich will not suffer him to sleep. **12** There is an evil sickness that I have seen under the sun: to wit, riches [j]reserved to the owners thereof for their evil. **13** And these riches perish by evil travail, and he begetteth a son, and in his [k]hand is nothing. **14** [2]As he came forth of his mother's belly, he shall return naked to go as he came, and shall bear away nothing of his labor, which he hath caused to pass by his hand. **15** And this also is an evil sickness, that in all points as he came, so shall he go, and what profit hath he that he hath travailed for the [l]wind? **16** Also all his days he eateth in [m]darkness with much grief, and in his sorrow and anger. **17** Behold then, what I have seen good, that it is comely to [n]eat, and to drink, and to take pleasure in all his labor, wherein he travaileth under the sun, the whole number of the days of his life, which God giveth him: for this is his portion. **18** Also to every man to whom God hath given riches and treasures, and giveth him power to eat thereof, and to take his part, and to enjoy his labor:

ECCLESIASTES 3

- **a.** Eccles. 3:1 He speaketh of this diversity of time for two causes: first to declare that there is nothing in this world perpetual: next to teach us not to be grieved, if we have not all things at once according to our desires, neither enjoy them so long as we would wish.
- **b.** Eccles. 3:10 Read Eccl. 1:13.
- **c.** Eccles. 3:11 God hath given man a desire, and affection to seek out the things of this world, and to labor therein.
- **d.** Eccles. 3:13 Read Eccl. 2:24, and these places declare that we should do all things with sobriety and in the fear of God, forasmuch as he giveth not his gifts to the intent that they should be abused.
- **e.** Eccles. 3:14 That is, man shall never be able to let God's work, but as he hath determined, so it shall come to pass.
- **f.** Eccles. 3:15 God only causeth that, which is past, to return.
- **g.** Eccles. 3:17 Meaning, with God, howsoever man neglect his duty.
- **h.** Eccles. 3:18 And made them pure in their first creation.
- **i.** Eccles. 3:19 Man is not able by his reason and judgment to put difference between man and beast, as touching those things whereunto both are subject: for the eye cannot judge any otherwise of a man being dead, than of a beast, which is dead: yet by the word of God and faith we easily know the diversity, as verse 21.
- **j.** Eccles. 3:21 Meaning, that reason cannot comprehend that which faith believeth herein.
- **k.** Eccles. 3:22 By the often repetition of this sentence, as Eccl. 2:24; 3:12, 22; 5:17 and 8:15, he declareth that man by reason can comprehend nothing better in this life, than to use the gifts of God soberly and comfortably: for to know further, is a special gift of God revealed by his Spirit.

ECCLESIASTES 4

- **a.** Eccles. 4:1 He maketh here another discourse with himself concerning the tyranny of them that oppressed the poor.
- **b.** Eccles. 4:2 Because they are no more subject to these oppressions.
- **c.** Eccles. 4:3 He speaketh according to the judgment of the flesh, which cannot abide to feel or see troubles.
- **d.** Eccles. 4:4 The more perfect that the work is, the more it is envied of the wicked.
- **e.** Eccles. 4:5 For idleness he is compelled to destroy himself.
- **f.** Eccles. 4:9 Forasmuch as when man is alone, he can neither help himself nor others, he showeth that men ought to live in mutual society to the intent they may be profitable one to another, and that their things may increase.
- **g.** Eccles. 4:12 By this proverb he declareth how necessary it is, that men should live in society.
- **h.** Eccles. 4:14 That is, from a poor and base estate, or out of trouble and prison, as Joseph did, Gen. 41:14.
- **i.** Eccles. 4:14 Meaning, that is born a King.
- **j.** Eccles. 4:15 Which follow and flatter the King's son, or him that shall succeed, to enter into credit with them in hope of gain.
- **k.** Eccles. 4:16 They never cease by all means to creep into favor, but when they obtain not, their greedy desires, they think themselves abused, as others have been in time past, and so care no more for him.
- **l.** Eccles. 4:17 That is, with what affection thou comest to hear the word of God.
- **m.** Eccles. 4:17 Meaning, of the wicked, which think to please God with common uses, and have neither faith nor repentance.

ECCLESIASTES 5

- **a.** Eccles. 5:1 Either in vowing or in praying: meaning, that we should use all reverence to Godward.
- **b.** Eccles. 5:1 He heareth thee not for thy many words' sake, or often repetitions, but considereth thy faith and servant mind.
- **c.** Eccles. 5:3 He speaketh of vows, which are approved by God's word, and serve to his glory.
- **d.** Eccles. 5:5 Cause not thyself to sin by vowing rashly: as they do which make a vow to live unmarried, and such like.
- **e.** Eccles. 5:5 That is, before God's messenger, when he shall examine thy doing, as though thy ignorance should be a just excuse.
- **f.** Eccles. 5:7 Meaning, that God will redress these things, and therefore we must depend upon him.
- **g.** Eccles. 5:8 The earth is to be preferred above all things which appertain to this life.
- **h.** Eccles. 5:8 Kings and Princes cannot maintain their estate without tillage, which thing commendeth the excellency of tillage.
- **i.** Eccles. 5:11 That is, his great abundance of riches, or the surfeiting, which cometh by his great feeding.
- **j.** Eccles. 5:12 When covetous men heap up riches, which turn to their destruction.
- **k.** Eccles. 5:13 He doth not enjoy his father's riches.
- **l.** Eccles. 5:15 Meaning, in vain, and without profit.
- **m.** Eccles. 5:16 In affliction and grief of mind.
- **n.** Eccles. 5:17 Read Eccl. 3:22.
- **o.** Eccles. 5:19 He will take no great thought for the pains that he hath endured in time past.

ECCLESIASTES 5

1. Deut. 23:21
2. Job 1:21
3. 1 Tim. 6:7

this is the gifts of God. **19** Surely he will not much remember the days of his
[o]life, because God answereth to the joy of his heart.

6

The miserable estate of him to whom God hath given riches, and not the grace to use them.

1 There is an evil, which I saw under the sun, and it is much among
men: **2** A man to whom God hath given riches and treasures and honor, and
he wanteth nothing for his soul of all that he desireth: but [a]God giveth him not
power to eat thereof, but a strange man shall eat it up: this is vanity, and this is
an evil sickness. **3** If a man beget an hundred children and live many years, and
the days of his years be multiplied: and his soul be not [b]satisfied with good things,
and he be not [c]buried, I say that an untimely fruit is better than he. **4** For [d]he
cometh into vanity, and goeth into darkness: and his name shall be covered with
darkness. **5** Also he hath not seen the sun, nor known it: therefore this hath
more rest than the other. **6** And if he had lived a thousand years twice told, and
had seen no good, shall not all go to one place? **7** All the labor of man is for his
mouth: yet the [e]soul is not filled. **8** For what hath the wise man more than the
fool? what hath the poor that [f]knoweth how to walk before the living? **9** The
[g]sight of the eye is better than to walk in the lusts: this also is vanity, and vexation
of spirit. **10** What is that that hath been? the name thereof is now named: and
it is known that it is man: and he cannot strive with him that is [h]stronger than he.

7

Divers precepts to follow that which is good, and to avoid the contrary.

1 Surely there be many things that increase vanity, and what avai-
leth it a man? **2** For who knoweth what is [a]good for man in the life, and in the
number of the days of the life of his vanity, seeing he maketh them as a [1]shadow?
for who can show unto man what shall be after him under the sun? **3** [2]A good
name is better than a good ointment, and the day of [b]death, than the day that one
is born. **4** It is better to go to the house of [c]mourning, than to go to the hou-
se of feasting, because this is the end of all men: and the living shall lay it to his
heart. **5** Anger is better than laughter: for by a sad look the heart is made bet-
ter. **6** The heart of the wise is in the house of mourning: but the heart of fools is
in the house of mirth. **7** Better it is to hear the rebuke of a wise man, than that a
man should hear the song of fools. **8** For like the noise of the [d]thorns under the
pot, so is the laughter of the fool: this also is vanity. **9** Surely oppression maketh
a wise man [e]mad: and the reward destroyeth the heart. **10** The [f]end of a thing is
better than the beginning thereof, and the patient in spirit is better than the proud
in spirit. **11** Be not thou of an hasty spirit to be angry: for anger resteth in the
bosom of fools. **12** Say not thou, Why is it that the former days were better than
these? for thou dost not inquire [g]wisely of this thing. **13** Wisdom is good with
an [h]inheritance, and excellent to them that see the sun. **14** For man shall rest
in the shadow of wisdom, and in the shadow of silver: but the excellency of the
knowledge of wisdom giveth life to the possessors thereof. **15** Behold the work
of God; for who can make [3]straight that which he hath made crooked? **16** In
the day of wealth be of good comfort, and in the day of affliction [i]consider: God
also hath made this contrary to that, to the intent that man should find [j]nothing
after him. **17** I have seen all things in the days of my vanity: there is a just man
that perisheth in his [k]justice, and there is a wicked man that continueth long in
his malice. **18** Be not thou just [l]overmuch, neither make thyself overwise: whe-
refore shouldest thou be desolate? **19** Be not thou wicked [m]overmuch, neither
be thou foolish: wherefore shouldest thou perish not in thy time? **20** It is good
that thou lay hold on [n]this: but yet withdraw not thine hand from [o]that: for he
that feareth God shall come forth of them all. **21** Wisdom shall strengthen the
wise men more than ten mighty princes that are in the city. **22** [4]Surely there is
no man just in the earth that doeth good and sinneth not. **23** Give not thine
[p]heart also to all the words that men speak, lest thou do hear thy servant cursing
thee. **24** For oftentimes also thine heart knoweth that thou likewise hast [q]cur-
sed others. **25** All this have I proved by wisdom: I thought, I will be wise, but
it went far from me. **26** It is far off, what may [r]it be? and it is a profound de-
epness, who can find it? **27** I have compassed about, both I and mine heart to
know and to inquire and to search wisdom, and reason, and to know the wicke-
dness of folly, and the foolishness of madness, **28** And I find more bitter than
death the woman whose heart is as nets and snares, and her hands as bands: he
that is good before God, shall be delivered from her, but the sinner shall be taken
by her. **29** Behold, saith the Preacher, this have I found, seeking one by one to
[s]find the count: **30** And yet my soul seeketh, but I find it not. I have found one
man of a thousand: but a woman among them all have I not found. **31** Only
lo, this have I found, that God hath made man righteous: but they have sought
many [t]inventions.

8

2 To obey Princes and Magistrates. 17 The works of God pass man's knowledge.

1 Who is as the wise man? and who knoweth the interpretation of a thing?
the wisdom of a man doth make his face [a]to shine: and [b]the strength of his face
shall be changed. **2** I advertise thee to take heed to the [c]mouth of the king, and
to the word of the oath of God. **3** [d]Haste not to go forth of his sight: stand not
in an evil thing: for he will do whatsoever pleaseth him. **4** Where the word of
the King is, there is power, and who shall say unto him, What doest thou? **5** He
that keepeth the commandment, shall know none evil thing, and the heart of
the wise shall know the [e]time, and judgment. **6** For to every purpose there is
a time and judgment, because the [f]misery of man is great upon him. **7** For he
knoweth not that which shall be: for who can tell him when it shall be? **8** Man
is not Lord [g]over the spirit to retain the spirit: neither hath he power in the day
of death, nor deliverance in the battle, neither shall wickedness deliver the pos-
sessors thereof. **9** All this have I seen, and have given mine heart to every work
which is wrought under the sun, and I saw a time that man ruleth over man to
his own [h]hurt. **10** And likewise I saw the wicked buried, and [i]they returned,
and they that came from the holy [j]place, were yet forgotten in the city, where they
had done right: this also is vanity. **11** Because sentence against an evil work is
not [k]executed speedily, therefore the heart of the children of men is fully set in
them to do evil. **12** Though a sinner do evil an hundred times, and God pro-
longeth his days, yet I know that it shall be well with them that fear the Lord,
and do reverence before him. **13** But it shall not be well to the wicked, neither
shall he prolong his days: he shall be like a shadow, because he feareth not before
God. **14** There is a vanity, which is done upon the earth, that there be righteous
men to whom it cometh according to the [l]work of the wicked: and there be wicked
men to whom it cometh according to the work of the just: I thought also that this
is vanity. **15** And I praised joy, for there is no goodness to man under the sun,
save [m]to eat and to drink and to rejoice: for this is adjoined to his labor the days of
his life that God hath given him under the sun. **16** When I applied mine heart
to know wisdom, and to behold the business that is done on earth, that neither day
nor night the eyes of man take sleep, **17** Then I beheld the whole work of God,
that man cannot find out the work that is wrought under the sun: for the which
man laboreth to seek it, and cannot find it: yea, and though the wise man think to
know it, he cannot find it.

ECCLESIASTES 6

- **a.** Eccles. 6:2 He showeth that it is the plague of God when the rich man hath not a liberal heart to use his riches.
- **b.** Eccles. 6:3 If he can never have enough.
- **c.** Eccles. 6:3 As we see oftentimes that the covetous man either falleth into crimes that deserve death, or is murdered or drowned or hangeth himself, or such like, and so lacketh the honor of burial, which is the last office of humanity.
- **d.** Eccles. 6:4 Meaning, the untimely fruit whose life did neither profit or hurt any.
- **e.** Eccles. 6:7 His desire and affection.
- **f.** Eccles. 6:8 That knoweth to use his goods well in the judgment of men.
- **g.** Eccles. 6:9 To be content with that which God hath given, is better than to follow the desires that never can be satisfied.
- **h.** Eccles. 6:10 Meaning, God who will make him to feel that he is mortal.

ECCLESIASTES 7

- **a.** Eccles. 7:2 There is no state wherein man can live to have perfect quietness in this life.
- **b.** Eccles. 7:3 He speaketh thus after the judgment of the flesh, which thinketh death to be the end of all evils, or else, because that this corporal death is the entering into life everlasting.
- **c.** Eccles. 7:4 Where we may see the hand of God, and learn to examine our lives.
- **d.** Eccles. 7:8 Which crackle for a while and profit nothing.
- **e.** Eccles. 7:9 A man that is esteemed wise, when he falleth to oppression, becometh like a beast.
- **f.** Eccles. 7:10 He noteth their lightness which enterprise a thing and suddenly leave it off again.
- **g.** Eccles. 7:12 Murmur not against God when he sendeth adversities for man's sins.
- **h.** Eccles. 7:13 He answereth to them that esteem not wisdom except riches be joined therewith, showing that both are the gifts of God, but that wisdom is far more excellent, and may be without riches.
- **i.** Eccles. 7:16 Consider wherefore God doth send it and what may comfort thee.
- **j.** Eccles. 7:16 That man should be able to control nothing in his works.
- **k.** Eccles. 7:17 Meaning, that cruel tyrants put the godly to death and let the wicked go free.
- **l.** Eccles. 7:18 Boast not too much of thine own justice and wisdom.
- **m.** Eccles. 7:19 Tarry not long when thou art admonished to come out of the way of wickedness.
- **n.** Eccles. 7:20 To wit, on these admonitions that go before.
- **o.** Eccles. 7:20 Consider what desolation and destruction shall come, if thou do not obey them.
- **p.** Eccles. 7:23 Credit them not, neither care for them.
- **q.** Eccles. 7:24 Or, spoken evil of others.
- **r.** Eccles. 7:26 Meaning, wisdom.
- **s.** Eccles. 7:29 That is, to come to a conclusion.
- **t.** Eccles. 7:31 And so are cause of their own destruction.

ECCLESIASTES 7

1. Job 14:2 - Ps. 144:4
2. Prov. 22:1
3. Eccl. 1:15
4. 1 Kings 8:36 - 2 Chron. 6:36 - Prov. 20:9 - 1 John. 1:8

ECCLESIASTES 8

- **a.** Eccles. 8:1 That is, doth get him favor and prosperity.
- **b.** Eccles. 8:1 Whereas before he was proud and arrogant, he shall become humble and meek.
- **c.** Eccles. 8:2 That is, that thou obey the king and keep the oath that thou hast made for the same cause.
- **d.** Eccles. 8:3 Withdraw not thyself lightly from the obedience of thy prince.
- **e.** Eccles. 8:5 That is, when time is to obey, and how far he should obey.
- **f.** Eccles. 8:6 Man of himself is miserable, and therefore ought to do nothing to increase the same, but to work all things by wisdom and counsel.
- **g.** Eccles. 8:8 Man hath no power to save his own life, and therefore must not rashly cast himself into danger.
- **h.** Eccles. 8:9 As cometh ofttimes to tyrants and wicked rulers.
- **i.** Eccles. 8:10 That is, others as wicked as they.
- **j.** Eccles. 8:10 They that feared God and worshipped him according as he had appointed.
- **k.** Eccles. 8:11 Where justice is delayed, there sin reigneth.
- **l.** Eccles. 8:14 Which are punished as though they were wicked, as Eccl. 7:17.
- **m.** Eccles. 8:15 Read Eccl. 3:22.

9

1 By no outward thing can man know whom God loveth or hateth. 12 No man knoweth his end. 16 Wisdom excelleth strength.

1 I have surely given mine heart to all this, and to declare all this, that the just, and the wise, and their works are in the hand of God: and no man knoweth either love or [a]hatred of all that is before them. **2** All things come alike to all: and the same condition is to the just and to the wicked, to the good and to the pure, and to the polluted, and to him that sacrificeth, and to him that sacrificeth not: as is the good, so is the sinner, he that sweareth, as he that feareth an oath. **3** This is evil among all that is done under the sun, that there is one [b]condition to all, and also the heart of the sons of men is full of evil, and madness is in their hearts while they live, and after that, they go to the dead. **4** Surely whosoever is joined to all the living, there is hope: for it is better to a [c]living dog, than to a dead lion. **5** For the living know that they shall die, but the dead know nothing at all: neither have they anymore a reward: for their remembrance is forgotten. **6** Also their love and their hatred, and their envy is now perished, and they have no more portion forever, in all that is done under the sun. **7** Go, eat thy bread with joy, and drink thy wine with a cheerful heart: for God now [d]accepteth thy works. **8** At all times let thy garments be [e]white, and let not oil be lacking upon thine head. **9** [f,1]Rejoice with the wife whom thou hast loved all the days of the life of thy vanity, which God hath given thee under the sun all the days of thy vanity: for this is thy portion in the life, and in thy travail wherein thou laborest under the sun. **10** All that thine hand shall find to do, do it with all thy power: for there is neither work nor invention, nor knowledge, nor wisdom in the grave whither thou goest. **11** I returned, and I saw under the sun that the race is not to the swift, nor the battle to the strong, nor yet bread to the wise, nor also riches to men of understanding, neither yet favor to men of knowledge: but time and [g]chance cometh to them all. **12** For neither doth man know his [h]time, but as the fishes which are taken in an evil net, and as the birds that are caught in the snare: so are the children of men snared in the evil time, when it falleth upon them suddenly. **13** I have also seen this wisdom under the sun, and it is great unto me. **14** A little city and few men in it, and a great King came against it, and compassed it about, and built forts against it. **15** And there was found therein a poor and wise man, and he delivered the city by his wisdom, but none remembered this poor man. **16** Then said I, Better is wisdom than strength: yet the wisdom of the poor is despised, and his words are not heard. **17** The words of the wise are more heard in quietness, than the cry of him that ruleth among fools. **18** Better is wisdom than weapons of war: but one sinner destroyeth much good.

10

1 The difference of foolishness and wisdom. 11 A slanderer is like a serpent that cannot be charmed. 16 Of foolish kings and drunken princes, 17 And of good Kings and Princes.

1 Dead flies cause to stink, and putrefy the ointment of the apothecary: so doth a little folly him that is in estimation for wisdom, and for glory. **2** The heart of a [a]wise man is at his right hand: but the heart of a fool is at his left hand. **3** And also when the fool goeth by the way, his heart faileth, and he [b]telleth unto all that he is a fool. **4** If the [c]spirit of him that ruleth, rise up against thee, leave not thy place: for gentleness pacifieth great sins. **5** There is an evil that I have seen under the sun, as an [d]error that proceedeth from the face of him that ruleth. **6** Folly is set in great excellency, and the [e]rich sit in the low place. **7** I have seen servants on horses, and princes walking as servants on the ground. **8** [1]He that diggeth a pit, shall fall into it, and he that breaketh the hedge, a serpent shall bite him. **9** He that removeth stones, shall hurt himself thereby, and he that cutteth wood, shall be in danger thereby. **10** If the iron be blunt, and one hath not whet the edge, he must then put to more [f]strength: but the excellency to direct a thing is wisdom. **11** If the serpent bite, when he is not charmed: no better is a babbler. **12** The words of the mouth of a wise man have grace: but the lips of a fool devour himself. **13** The beginning of the words of his mouth is foolishness, and the latter end of his mouth is wicked madness. **14** For the fool multiplieth words, saying, Man knoweth not what shall be: and who can tell him what shall be after him? **15** The labor of the foolish doth weary him: for he knoweth not to go into the [g]city. **16** Woe to thee, O land, when thy king is a [h]child, and thy princes [i]eat in the morning. **17** Blessed art thou, O land, when thy King is the son [j]of nobles, and thy princes eat in time, for strength and not for drunkenness. **18** By slothfulness the roof of the house goeth to decay, and by the idleness of the hands the house droppeth through. **19** They prepare bread for laughter, and wine comforteth the living, but silver answereth to all. **20** Curse not the king, no not in thy thought, neither curse the rich in thy bed chamber: for the [k]fowl of the heaven shall carry the voice, and that which hath wings, shall declare the matter.

11

1 To be liberal to the poor. 4 Not to doubt of God's providence. 8 All worldly prosperity is but vanity. 9 God will judge all.

1 Cast thy bread upon the [a]waters: for after many days thou shalt find it. **2** Give a portion to seven, and also to eight: for thou knowest not what evil shall be upon the earth. **3** If the [b]clouds be full, they will pour forth rain upon the earth: and if the [c]tree do fall toward the South, or toward the North, in the place that the tree falleth, there it shall be. **4** He that observeth the [d]wind shall not sow, and he that regardeth the clouds, shall not reap. **5** As thou knowest not which is the way of the spirit, nor how the bones do grow in the womb of her that is with child: so thou knowest not the work of God that worketh all. **6** In the morning sow thy seed, and in the evening let not thine hand [e]rest: for thou knowest not whether shall prosper, this or [f]that, or whether both shall be a like good. **7** Surely the light is a pleasant thing: and it is a good thing to the eyes to see the sun. **8** Though a man live many years, and in them all he rejoice, yet he shall remember the days of [g]darkness, because they are many, all that cometh is vanity. **9** [h]Rejoice, O young man, in thy youth, and let thine heart cheer thee in the days of thy youth: and walk in the ways of thine heart, and in the sight of thine eyes: but know that for all these things, God will bring thee to judgment. **10** Therefore take away [i]grief out of thine heart, and cause evil [j]to depart from thy flesh: for childhood and youth are vanity.

12

1 To think on God in youth, and not to defer till age. 7 The soul returneth to God. 11 Wisdom is the gift of God, and consisteth in fearing him and keeping his commandments.

1 Remember now thy Creator in the days of thy youth, while the evil days come not, nor the years approach, wherein thou shalt say, I have no pleasure in them: **2** While the sun is not dark, nor the light, nor the moon, nor the stars, nor the [a]clouds return after the rain. **3** When the [b]keepers of the house shall tremble, and the [c]strong men shall bow themselves, and the [d]grinders shall cease, because they are few, and they wax dark that [e]look out by the windows: **4** And the [f]doors shall be shut without by the base sound of the [g]grinding, and he shall rise up at the voice of the [h]bird: and all the [i]daughters of singing shall be abased: **5** Also they

---

ECCLESIASTES 9

a. Eccles. 9:1 Meaning, what things he ought to choose or refuse: or man knoweth not by these outward things, that is, by prosperity or adversity, whom God doth favor or hate, for he sendeth them as well to the wicked as to the godly.
b. Eccles. 9:3 In outward things, as riches and poverty, sickness and health, there is no difference between the godly and the wicked: but the difference is that the godly are assured by faith of God's favor and assistance.
c. Eccles. 9:4 He noteth the Epicureans and carnal men, which made their belly their god, and had no pleasure, but in this life, wishing rather to be an abased and vile person in this life, than a man of authority, and so to die, which is meant by the dog and lion.
d. Eccles. 9:7 They flatter themselves to be in God's favor, because they have all things in abundance.
e. Eccles. 9:8 Rejoice, be merry, and spare for no cost, thus speak the wicked belly-gods.
f. Eccles. 9:9 Hebrew, regard the life.
g. Eccles. 9:11 Thus the worldlings say to prove that all things are lawful for them, and attribute that to chance and fortune, which is done by the providence of God.
h. Eccles. 9:12 That is, he doth not foresee what shall come.

ECCLESIASTES 9

1. Eccl. 5:18

ECCLESIASTES 10

a. Eccles. 10:2 So that he doeth all things well and justly, where as the fool doeth the contrary.
b. Eccles. 10:3 By his doings he betrayeth himself.
c. Eccles. 10:4 If thy superior be angry with thee, be thou discrete, and not moved.
d. Eccles. 10:5 Meaning, that it is an evil thing when they that are in authority, fail and do not their duty.
e. Eccles. 10:6 They that are rich in wisdom and virtue.
f. Eccles. 10:10 Without wisdom whatsoever a man taketh in hand, turneth to his own hurt.
g. Eccles. 10:15 The ignorance and beastliness of the wicked is such that they know not common things, and yet will they discuss high matters.
h. Eccles. 10:16 That is, without wisdom and counsel.
i. Eccles. 10:16 Are given to their lusts, and pleasures.
j. Eccles. 10:17 Meaning, when he is noble for virtue and wisdom, and with the gifts of God.
k. Eccles. 10:20 Thou canst not work evil so secretly, but it shall be known.

ECCLESIASTES 10

1. Ps. 7:15 - Prov. 26:27

ECCLESIASTES 11

a. Eccles. 11:1 That is, be liberal to the poor, and though it seem to be as a thing ventured on the sea, yet it shall bring thee profit.
b. Eccles. 11:3 As the clouds that are full, pour out rain, so the rich that have abundance, must distribute it liberally.
c. Eccles. 11:3 He exhorteth to be liberal while we live: for after, there is no power.
d. Eccles. 11:4 He that feareth inconveniences, when necessity requireth, shall never do his duty.
e. Eccles. 11:6 Be not weary of well doing.
f. Eccles. 11:6 That is, which of thy works are most agreeable to God.
g. Eccles. 11:8 That is, of affliction and trouble.
h. Eccles. 11:9 He derideth them that set their delight in worldly pleasures, as though God would not call count.
i. Eccles. 11:10 To wit, anger, and envy.
j. Eccles. 11:10 Meaning, carnal lusts, whereunto youth is given.

ECCLESIASTES 12

a. Eccles. 12:2 Before thou come to a continual misery: for when the clouds remain after the rain, man's grief is increased.
b. Eccles. 12:3 The hands, which keep the body.
c. Eccles. 12:3 The legs.
d. Eccles. 12:3 The teeth.
e. Eccles. 12:3 The eyes.
f. Eccles. 12:4 The lips, or mouth.
g. Eccles. 12:4 When the jaws, shall scarce open, and not be able to chew anymore.
h. Eccles. 12:4 He shall not be able to sleep.
i. Eccles. 12:4 That is, the wind pipes, or the ears shall be deaf and not able to hear singing.
j. Eccles. 12:5 To climb high because of their weakness, or they stoop down, as though they were afraid, lest anything should hit them.
k. Eccles. 12:5 They shall tremble as they go, as though they were afraid.
l. Eccles. 12:5 Their head shall be as white as the blossoms of an almond tree.
m. Eccles. 12:5 They shall be able to bear nothing.

shall be afraid of the [j]high thing, and fear shall be in the [k]way, and the almond
tree shall [l]flourish, and the [m]grasshopper shall be a burden, and concupiscence
shall be driven away: for man goeth to the house of his age, and the mourners
go about in the street. **6** While the [n]silver cord is not lengthened, nor the gol-
den [o]ewer broken, nor the [p]pitcher broken at the [q]well, nor the [r]wheel broken at
the [s]cistern, **7** And dust return to the earth as it was, and the [t]spirit return to
God that gave it. **8** Vanity of vanities, saith the Preacher, all is vanity. **9** And
the more wise the Preacher was, the more he taught the people knowledge, and
caused them to hear, and searched forth, and prepared many parables. **10** The
Preacher sought to find out pleasant words, and an upright writing, even the words
of truth. **11** The words of the wise are like goads, and like nails [u]fastened by the
masters of the assemblies, which are given by one [v]pastor. **12** And of other things
beside these, my son, take thou heed: for there is none end in making many [w]bo-
oks, and much reading is a weariness of the flesh. **13** Let us hear the end of all:
fear God and keep his commandments: for this is the whole duty of man. **14** For
God will bring every work unto judgment, with every secret thing, whether it be
good or evil.

n. Eccles. 12:6 Meaning, the marrow of the backbone and the sinews.
o. Eccles. 12:6 The little skin that covereth the brain, which is in color like gold.
p. Eccles. 12:6 That is, the veins.
q. Eccles. 12:6 Meaning, the liver.
r. Eccles. 12:6 Which is the head.
s. Eccles. 12:6 That is, the heart, out of which the head draweth the powers of life.
t. Eccles. 12:7 The soul incontinently goeth either to joy or torment, and sleepeth not as the wicked imagine.
u. Eccles. 12:11 Which are well applied by the ministers, whom he calleth masters.
v. Eccles. 12:11 That is, by God.
w. Eccles. 12:12 These things cannot be comprehended in books or learned by study, but God must instruct thine heart that thou mayest only know that wisdom is the true felicity, and the way thereunto is to fear God.

AN [a]EXCELLENT SONG WICH WAS SOLOMON'S

1

1 The familiar talk and mystical communication of the spiritual love between Jesus Christ and his Church. 5 The domestical enemies that persecute the Church.

1 Let [b]him kiss me with the kisses of his mouth: for thy love is better than
wine. **2** Because of the [c]savor of thy good ointments, thy name is as an ointment
poured out: therefore the [d]virgins love thee. **3** [e]Draw me: we will run after thee:
the King hath brought me into his [f]chambers: we will rejoice and be glad in thee:
we will remember thy love more than wine: the righteous do love thee. **4** I am
[g]black, O daughters of Jerusalem, but comely, as the tents of [h]Kedar, and as the
[i]curtains of Solomon. **5** Regard ye me not because I am [j]black: for the [k]sun hath
looked upon me. The [l]sons of my mother were angry against me: they made me the
keeper of the vines: but I [m]kept not mine own vine. **6** Show me, [n]O thou whom
my soul loveth, where thou feedest, where thou liest at noon: for why should I be
as she that turneth aside to the stocks of [o]thy companions? **7** [p]If thou know not,
O thou the fairest among women, get thee forth by the steps of the flock, and feed
thy kids by the tents of the shepherds. **8** I have compared thee, O my love, to
the troupe of horses in the [q]chariots of Pharaoh. **9** Thy cheeks are comely with
rows of stones, and thy neck with chains. **10** We will make thee borders of gold
with floods of silver. **11** [r]While the King was at his repast, my spikenard gave
the smell thereof. **12** My well-beloved is as a bundle of myrrh unto me: he shall
lie between my [s]breasts. **13** My well-beloved is as a cluster of camphire unto
me in the vines of En Gedi. **14** My love, behold, thou art [t]fair: behold, thou
art fair: thine eyes are like the doves. **15** My well-beloved, behold, thou art fair,
and pleasant: also our [u]bed is green. **16** The beams of our house are cedars, our
rafters are of fir.

2

3 The Church desireth to rest under the shadow of Christ. 8 She heareth his voice. 14 She is compared to the dove. 15 And the enemies to the foxes.

1 I am the rose of the field, and the lily of the valleys. **2** Like a lily among
the thorns, so is my [a]love among the daughters. **3** [b]Like the apple tree among
the trees of the forest, so is my well-beloved among the sons of men: under his sha-
dow had I delight, and sat down: and his fruit was sweet unto my mouth. **4** He
brought me into the wine cellar, and love was his banner over me. **5** Stay me
with flagons, and comfort me with apples: for I am sick of love. **6** His left hand
is under mine head, and his right hand doth embrace me. **7** [c]I charge you, O
daughters of Jerusalem, by the roes and by the hinds of the field, that ye stir not
up, nor waken my love, until she please. **8** [d]It is the voice of my well-beloved:
behold, he cometh leaping by the mountains, and skipping by the hills. **9** My
well-beloved is like a roe, or a young hart: lo, he [e]standeth behind our wall, looking
forth of the windows, showing himself through the [f]grates. **10** My well-beloved
spake and said unto me, Arise, my love, my fair one, and come thy way. **11** For
behold, [g]winter is past: the rain is changed, and is gone away. **12** The flowers
appear in the earth: the time of the singing of birds is come, and the voice of the
turtle is heard in our land. **13** The fig tree hath brought forth her young figs: and
the vines with their small grapes have cast a savor: arise my love, my fair one, and
come away. **14** My dove, that art in the [h]holes of the rock, in the secret places of
the stairs, show me thy sight, let me hear thy voice: for thy voice is sweet, and thy

SONG 1

a. TITLE - Hebrew, a song of songs: so called because it is the chiefest of those 1005, which Solomon made, as is mentioned, I Kings 4:32.
b. Song 1:1 This is spoken in the person of the Church, or of the faithful soul inflamed with the desire of Christ, whom she loveth.
c. Song 1:2 The feeling of thy great benefits.
d. Song 1:2 They that are pure in heart and conversation.
e. Song 1:3 The faithful confess that they cannot come to Christ, except they be drawn.
f. Song 1:3 Meaning, the secret joy that is not known to the world.
g. Song 1:4 The Church confesseth her spots and sin, but hath confidence in the favor of Christ.
h. Song 1:4 Kedar was Ishmael's son, of whom came the Arabians that dwelt in tents.
i. Song 1:4 Which within were all set with precious stones and Jewels.
j. Song 1:5 Consider not the Church by the outward appearance.
k. Song 1:5 The corruption of nature through sin and afflictions.
l. Song 1:5 Mine own brethren, which should have most favored me.
m. Song 1:5 She confesseth her own negligence.
n. Song 1:6 The spouse feeling her fault fleeth to her husband only for succor.
o. Song 1:6 Whom thou hast called to the dignity of pastors, and they set forth their own dreams instead of thy doctrine.
p. Song 1:7 Christ speaketh to his Church, bidding them that are ignorant, to go to the pastors to learn.
q. Song 1:8 For thy spiritual beauty and excellency there was no worldly treasure to be compared unto thee.
r. Song 1:11 The Church rejoiceth that she is admitted to the company of Christ.
s. Song 1:12 He shall be most dear unto me.
t. Song 1:14 Christ accepteth his Church, and commendeth her beauty.
u. Song 1:15 That is, the heart of the faithful, wherein Christ dwelleth by his Spirit.

SONG 2

a. Song 2:2 Thus Christ preferreth his Church above all other things.
b. Song 2:3 The spouse testifieth her great desire toward her husband, but her strength faileth her, and therefore she desireth to be comforted, and felt it.
c. Song 2:7 Christ chargeth them which have to do in the Church as it were by a solemn oath, that they trouble not the quietness thereof.
d. Song 2:8 This is spoken of Christ, who took upon his our nature to come to help his Church.
e. Song 2:9 Forasmuch as his divinity was hid under the cloak of our flesh.
f. Song 2:9 So that we cannot have full knowledge of him in this life.
g. Song 2:11 That is, sin and error is driven back by the coming of Christ, which is here described by the spring time, when all things flourish.
h. Song 2:14 Thou that art ashamed of thy sins, come and show thyself unto me.

sight comely. **15** Take us the foxes, the [i]little foxes, which destroy the vines: for our vines have small grapes. **16** My well-beloved is mine, and I am his: he feedeth among the lilies, **17** Until the daybreak, and the shadows flee away: return, my well-beloved, and be like a [j]roe, or a young hart upon the mountains of Bether.

3

1 The Church desireth to be joined inseparably to Christ her husband. 6 Her deliverance out of the wilderness.

1 In my bed by [a]night I sought him that my soul loved: I sought him, but I found him not. **2** I will rise therefore now, and go about in the city, by the streets, and by the open places, and will [b]seek him that my soul loveth: I sought him, but I found him not. **3** The [c]watchmen that went about the city, found me: to whom I said, Have you seen him whom my soul loveth? **4** When I had passed a little from them, then I found him whom my soul loved: I took hold on him, and left him not, till I had brought him unto my mother's house, into the chamber of her that conceived me. **5** [d]I charge you, O daughters of Jerusalem, by the roes and by the hinds of the field, that ye stir not up, nor waken my love until she please. **6** Who is she that cometh up out of the [e]wilderness like pillars of smoke perfumed with myrrh and incense, and with all the [f]spices of the merchant? **7** Behold his [g]bed, which is Solomon's: threescore strong men are round about it, of the valiant men of Israel. **8** They all handle the sword, and are expert in war, everyone hath his sword upon his thigh for the fear [h]by night. **9** King Solomon made himself a [i]palace of the trees of Lebanon. **10** He made the pillars thereof of silver, and the pavement thereof of gold, the hangings thereof of purple, whose midst was paved with the love of the daughters of Jerusalem. **11** Come forth, ye [j]daughters of Zion, and behold the King Solomon with the [k]crown, wherewith his mother crowned him in the day of his marriage, and in the day of the gladness of his heart.

4

1 The praises of the Church. 7 She is without blemish in his sight. 9 The love of Christ towards her.

1 Behold, thou art [a]fair, my love: behold, thou art fair: thine eyes are like the doves: among thy locks [l]thine hair is like the [b]flock of goats, which look down from the mountain of Gilead. **2** Thy teeth are like a flock of sheep in good order, which go up from the washing: which every one brings out twins, and none is barren among them. **3** Thy lips are like a thread of scarlet, and thy talk is comely: thy temples are within thy locks as a piece of a pomegranate. **4** Thy neck is as the tower of David built for defense: a thousand shields hang therein, and all the targets of the strong men. **5** Thy two [c]breasts are as two young roes that are twins, feeding among the lilies. **6** Until the day break, and the shadows fly away, I will go into the mountain of myrrh, and to the mountain of incense. **7** Thou art all fair my love, and there is no spot in thee. **8** [d]Come with me from Lebanon, my spouse, even with me from Lebanon, and look from the top of Amana, from the top of Senir, and Hermon, from the dens of the lions, and from the mountains of the leopards. **9** My [e]sister, my spouse, thou hast wounded mine heart: thou hast wounded mine heart with one of thine [f]eyes, and with a chain of thy neck. **10** My sister, my Spouse, how fair is thy love? how much better is thy love than wine? and the savor of thine ointments than all spices? **11** Thy [g]lips, my Spouse, drop as honeycombs: honey and milk are under thy tongue, and the savor of thy garment is as the savor of Lebanon. **12** My sister, my spouse is as a garden enclosed, as a spring shut up, and a fountain sealed up. **13** Thy plants are as an orchard of pomegranates with sweet fruits, as camphire, spikenard, **14** Even spikenard, and saffron: calamus, and cinnamon, with all the trees of incense, myrrh and aloes, with all the chief spices. **15** [h]O fountain of the gardens, O well of living waters, and the springs of Lebanon. **16** Arise, O [i]North, and come, O South, and blow on my garden, that the spices thereof may flow out: let my well-beloved come to his garden, and eat his pleasant fruit.

5

1 Christ calleth his Church to the participation of all his treasures. 2 She heareth his voice. 3 She confesseth her nakedness. 10 She praiseth Christ her husband.

1 I am come into my [a]garden, my sister, my spouse, I gathered my myrrh with my spice: I ate mine honeycomb with mine honey, I drank my wine with my milk: eat, O friends, drink, and make you merry, O well-beloved. **2** [b]I sleep, but mine heart waketh, it is the voice of my well-beloved that knocketh, saying, Open unto me, my sister, my love, my dove, my undefiled: for mine head is full of dew, and my locks with the drops of the [c]night. **3** I have put off my [d]coat, how shall I defile put it on? I have washed my feet, how shall I defile them? **4** My well-beloved put in his hand by the hole of the door, and [e]mine heart was affectioned toward him. **5** I rose up to open to my well-beloved, and mine hands did drop down myrrh, and my [f]fingers pure myrrh upon the handles of the bar. **6** I opened to my well-beloved: but my well-beloved was gone and past: mine heart was gone when he did speak: I sought him, but I could not find him: I called him, but he answered me not. **7** The [g]watchmen that were about the city, found me: they smote me, and wounded me: the watchmen of the walls took away my veil from me. **8** I charge you, [h]O daughters of Jerusalem, if you find my well-beloved, that you tell him that I am sick of love. **9** [i]O the fairest among women, what is thy well-beloved more than other well-beloved? what is thy well-beloved more than another lover, that thou dost so charge us? **10** My well-beloved is white and ruddy, the chiefest of ten thousand. **11** His [j]head is as fine gold, his locks curled, and black as a raven. **12** His eyes are like doves upon the rivers of waters, which are washed with milk, and remain by the full vessels. **13** His cheeks are as a bed of spices, and as sweet flowers, and his lips like lilies dropping down pure myrrh. **14** His hands as rings of gold set with the [k]chrysolite, his belly like white ivory covered with sapphires. **15** His legs are as pillars of marble set upon sockets of fine gold: his countenance as Lebanon, excellent as the cedars. **16** His mouth is as sweet things, and he is wholly delectable: this is my well-beloved, and this is my lover, O daughters of Jerusalem. **17** [l]O the fairest among women, whither is thy well-beloved gone? whither is thy well-beloved turned aside, that we may seek him with thee?

6

1 The Church assureth herself of the love of Christ. 3 The praises of the Church. 8 She is but one and undefiled.

1 My well-beloved is gone down into his [a]garden to the beds of spices, to feed in the gardens, and to gather lilies. **2** I am my well-beloved's, and my well-beloved is mine, who feedeth among the lilies. **3** Thou art beautiful, my love, as [b]Tirzah, comely as Jerusalem, terrible as an army with banners. **4** [c]Turn away thine eyes from me: for they overcome me: [l]thine hair is like a flock of goats, which look down from Gilead. **5** Thy teeth are like a flock of sheep, which go up from the washing, which every one bring out twins, and none is barren among them. **6** Thy temples are within thy locks as a piece of a pomegranate. **7** There are [d]threescore Queens, and fourscore concubines, and of the damsels without number. **8** But my dove is alone, and my undefiled, she is the only daughter of her mother, and she is dear to her that bare her: the daughters have seen her, and counted her blessed: even the Queens and the concubines, and they have praised her. **9** [e]Who is she that looketh forth as the morning, fair as the moon, pure as the sun, terrible as an army with banners! **10** I went down to the [f]garden of nuts,

---

- **i.** Song 2:15 Suppress the heretics while they are young, that is, when they begin to show their malice, and destroy the vine of the Lord.
- **j.** Song 2:17 The Church desireth Christ to be most ready to help her in all dangers.

SONG 3

- **a.** Song 3:1 The Church by night, that is, in troubles, seeketh to Christ, but is not incontinently heard.
- **b.** Song 3:2 Showing that although we be not heard at the first, yet we must still continue in prayer, till we feel comfort.
- **c.** Song 3:3 Which declareth that we must seek unto all of whom we hope to have any succor.
- **d.** Song 3:5 Read Song 2:7.
- **e.** Song 3:6 This is referred to the Church of Israel, which was led by the wilderness forty years.
- **f.** Song 3:6 Hebrew, powder.
- **g.** Song 3:7 By the bed is meant the Temple which Solomon made.
- **h.** Song 3:8 He alludeth to the watch which kept the Temple.
- **i.** Song 3:9 Or, chariot.
- **j.** Song 3:11 All ye that are of the number of the faithful.
- **k.** Song 3:11 Christ become man was crowned by the love of God with the glorious crown of his divinity.

SONG 4

- **a.** Song 4:1 Because Christ delighteth in his Church, he commendeth all that is in her.
- **b.** Song 4:1 He hath respect to the multitude of the faithful, which are many in number.
- **c.** Song 4:5 Wherein are knowledge and zeal two precious jewels.
- **d.** Song 4:8 Christ promiseth his Church to call his faithful from all the corners of the world.
- **e.** Song 4:9 Christ calleth his Church sister, in respect that he had taken the flesh of man.
- **f.** Song 4:9 In that he made his Church beautiful and rich, he loved his gifts in her.
- **g.** Song 4:11 Because of thy confession and thanksgiving.
- **h.** Song 4:15 The Church confesseth that all her glory and beauty cometh of Christ, who is the true fountain of all grace.
- **i.** Song 4:16 She desireth Christ to comfort her and to pour the graces of his Spirit upon her, which Spirit is meant by the North and South wind.

SONG 4

- **1.** Song 6:4

SONG 5

- **a.** Song 5:1 The garden signifieth the kingdom of Christ, where he prepareth the banquet for his elect.
- **b.** Song 5:2 The spouse saith that she is troubled with the cares of worldly things, which is meant by sleeping.
- **c.** Song 5:2 Declaring the long patience of the Lord toward sinners.
- **d.** Song 5:3 The spouse confesseth her nakedness, and that of herself she hath nothing, or seeing that she is once made clean, she promiseth not to defile herself again.
- **e.** Song 5:4 Hebrew, my bowels were moved towards him.
- **f.** Song 5:5 The spouse which should be anointed of Christ, shall not find him if she think to anoint him with her good works.
- **g.** Song 5:7 These are the false teachers, which wound the conscience with their traditions.
- **h.** Song 5:8 She asketh of them which are godly (forasmuch as the law and salvation should come out of Zion and Jerusalem) that they would direct her to Christ.
- **i.** Song 5:9 Thus say they of Jerusalem.
- **j.** Song 5:11 She describeth Christ to be of perfect beauty and comeliness.
- **k.** Song 5:14 Hebrew, Tarshish.
- **l.** Song 5:17 Hearing of the excellency of Christ, the faithful desire to know how to find him.

SONG 6

- **a.** Song 6:1 That is, is conversant here in earth among men.
- **b.** Song 6:3 Which was a fair and strong city, 1 Kings 14:17.
- **c.** Song 6:4 This declareth the exceeding love of Christ toward his Church.
- **d.** Song 6:7 Meaning, that the gifts are infinite which Christ giveth to his Church: or that his faithful are many in number
- **e.** Song 6:9 He showeth that the beginning of the Church was small, but that it grew up to a great multitude.

to see the fruits of the valley, to see if the vine budded, and if the pomegranates
flourished. **11** [g]I knew nothing, my soul set me [h]as the chariots of my noble pe-
ople. **12** Return, return, O [i]Shulamite, return: return that we may behold thee.
What shall you see in the Shulamite, but as the company of an army?

7

1 The beauty of the Church in all her members. 10 She is assured of Christ's love towards her.

1 How beautiful are thy [a]goings with shoes, O prince's daughter! the joints of
thy thighs are like jewels: the work of the hand of a cunning workman. **2** Thy
navel is as a round cup that wanteth not liquor: thy belly is as an heap of wheat
compassed about with lilies. **3** [b]Thy two breasts are as two young roes that are
twins. **4** Thy neck is like a tower of ivory; thine eyes are like the fish pools in
Heshbon by the gate of Bath Rabbim: thy nose is as the tower of Lebanon that
looketh toward Damascus. **5** Thine head upon thee is as scarlet, and the bush of
thine head like purple: the king is tied [c]in the [d]rafters. **6** How fair art thou, and
how pleasant art thou, O my love, in pleasures! **7** This thy stature is like a palm
tree, and thy breasts like clusters. **8** I said, I will go up into the palm tree, I will
take hold of her boughs: thy breasts shall now be like the clusters of the vine: and
the savor of thy nose like apples, **9** And the roof of thy mouth like good wine,
which goeth straight to my well-beloved, and causeth the lips of the ancient to
speak. **10** [e]I am my well-beloved's, and his desire is toward me. **11** Come my
well-beloved, let us go forth into the field: let us remain in the villages. **12** Let
us get up early to the vines, let us see if the [f]vine flourish, whither it hath budded
the small grape, or whither the pomegranates flourish: there will I give thee my
love. **13** The mandrakes have given a smell, and in our gates are all sweet things,
new and old: my well-beloved, I have kept them for thee.

8

2 The Church will be taught by Christ. 3 She is upheld by him. 6 The vehement love wherewith Christ loveth her. 11 She is the vine that bringeth forth fruit to the spiritual Solomon, which is Jesus Christ.

1 Oh [a]that thou werest as my brother that sucked the breasts of my mother:
I would find thee without, I would kiss thee, then they should not despise
[b]thee. **2** I will lead thee and bring thee into my mother's house: there thou shalt
teach me: and I will cause thee to drink spiced wine, and new wine of the pome-
granate. **3** [c]His left hand shall be under mine head, and his right hand shall
embrace me. **4** [d]I charge you, O daughters of Jerusalem, that you stir not up,
nor waken my love until she please. **5** (Who is this that cometh up out of the
wilderness, leaning upon her well-beloved?) I raised thee up under an apple tree:
there the mother conceived thee: there she conceived that bare thee. **6** [e]Set me
as a seal on thine heart, and as a signet upon thine arm: for love is strong as dea-
th: jealousy is cruel as the grave: the coals thereof are fiery coals, and a vehement
flame. **7** Much water cannot quench love, neither can the floods drown it: if a
man should give all the substance of his house for love, they would greatly contemn
it. **8** [f]We have a little sister, and she hath no breasts: what shall we do for our
sister when she shall be spoken for? **9** [g]If she be a wall, we will build upon her a
silver palace: and if she be a door, we will keep her in with boards of cedar. **10** [h]I
am a wall, and my breasts are as towers: then was I in his eyes as one that findeth
peace. **11** [i]Solomon had a vine in Baal Hamon: he gave the vineyard unto kee-
pers: everyone bringeth for the fruit thereof a thousand pieces of silver. **12** But
my vineyard which is mine, is before me: to thee, O Solomon, appertaineth a thou-
sand pieces of silver, and two hundred to them that keep the fruit thereof. **13** O
thou that dwellest in the [j]gardens, the companions hearken unto thy voice: cause
me to hear it. **14** O my well-beloved, [k]flee away and be like unto the roe, or to
the young hart upon the mountains of spices.

---

f. Song 6:10 He went down into the Synagogue to see what fruits came of the Law, and the Prophets.
g. Song 6:11 I found nothing but rebellion.
h. Song 6:11 Or, set me on the chariots of my willing people.
i. Song 6:12 O ye people of Jerusalem: for Jerusalem was called Salem which signifieth peace.

SONG 6

1. Song 4:1

SONG 7

a. Song 7:1 He describeth the comely beauty of the Church in every part, which is to be understood spiritually.
b. Song 7:3 Read Song 4:5.
c. Song 7:5 He delighteth to come near thee, and to be in thy company.
d. Song 7:5 Or, galleries.
e. Song 7:10 This the spouse speaketh.
f. Song 7:12 If the people that are called to Christ, bring forth any fruit.

SONG 8

a. Song 8:1 The Church called of the Gentiles, speaketh thus to the Church of Jerusalem.
b. Song 8:1 Or, me.
c. Song 8:3 Read Song 2:6.
d. Song 8:4 Read Song 3:5.
e. Song 8:6 The spouse desireth Christ to be joined in perpetual love with him.
f. Song 8:8 The Jewish Church speaketh this of the Church of the Gentiles.
g. Song 8:9 If she be sure and fast, she is meet for the husband to dwell in.
h. Song 8:10 The Church promiseth fidelity and constancy.
i. Song 8:11 This is the vineyard of the Lord hired out, Matt. 21:33.
j. Song 8:13 Christ dwelleth in his Church, whose voice the faithful hear.
k. Song 8:14 The Church desireth Christ that if he depart from them, yet that he would haste to help them in their troubles.

ISAIAH

1

2 Isaiah reproveth the Jews of their ingratitude and stubbornness, that neither for benefits nor punishments would amend. 11 He showed why their sacrifices are rejected, and wherein God's true service standeth. 24 He prophesieth of the destruction of Jerusalem, 25 and of the restitution thereof.

1 A [a]vision of Isaiah, the son of Amoz, which he saw [b]concerning Judah
and Jerusalem, in the days of [c]Uzziah, Jotham, Ahaz, and Hezekiah Kings of Ju-
dah. 2 Hear, O [d]heavens, and hearken, O earth: for the Lord hath said, I have
nourished and brought up [e]children, but they have rebelled against me. 3 The
[f]ox knoweth his owner, and the ass his master's crib: but Israel hath not known:
my people hath not understood. 4 Ah, sinful nation, a people laden with iniqui-
ty: a [g]seed of the wicked, corrupt children: they have forsaken the Lord: they have
provoked the [h]Holy one of Israel to anger: they are gone backward. 5 Wherefore
should ye be [i]smitten anymore? for ye fall away more and more: the whole [j]head
is sick, and the whole heart is heavy. 6 From the [k]sole of the foot unto the head,
there is nothing whole therein, but wounds and swelling, and sores full of corrup-
tion: they have not been wrapped, [l]nor bound up nor mollified with oil. 7 Your
land is waste: your cities are burnt with fire: strangers devour your land in your
presence, and it is desolate like the overthrow of [m]strangers. 8 And the daughter
of [n]Zion shall remain like a cottage in a vineyard, like a lodge in a garden of cu-
cumbers, and like a besieged city. 9 Except the Lord of hosts [o]had reserved unto
us even a small remnant, we should have been [p]as Sodom, and should have been
like unto Gomorrah. 10 Hear the word of the Lord, O [q]princes of Sodom: he-
arken unto the Law of our God, O people of Gomorrah. 11 What have I to do
with the multitude of your sacrifices, saith the Lord? I am full of the burnt offe-
rings of rams, and of the fat of fed beasts: and I [r]desire not the blood of bullocks,
nor of lambs, nor of goats. 12 When ye come to appear before me, who requi-
red this of your hands to tread in my courts? 13 Bring no more oblations, [s]in
vain: incense is an abomination unto me: I cannot suffer your new moons, nor
Sabbath, nor solemn days (it is iniquity) nor solemn assemblies. 14 My soul
hateth your [t]new moons and your appointed feasts: they are a burden unto me: I
am weary to bear them. 15 And when you shall stretch out your hands, I will
hide mine eyes from you: and though ye make many prayers, I will not hear: for
your hands are full [u]of blood. 16 [v]Wash you, make you clean, take away the
evil of your works from before mine eyes: cease to do evil. 17 Learn to [w]do
well: seek judgment, relieve the oppressed: judge the fatherless, and defend the
widow. 18 Come now, [x]and let us reason together, saith the Lord: though your
sins were as crimson, they shall be made [y]white as snow: though they were red
like scarlet, they shall be as wool, 19 If ye [z]consent and obey, ye shall eat the
good things of the land. 20 But if ye refuse and be rebellious, ye shall be devou-
red with the sword: for the mouth of the Lord hath spoken it. 21 How is the
[aa]faithful city become an harlot? it was full of judgment, and justice lodged the-
rein, but now [ab]they are murderers. 22 Thy [ac]silver is become dross: thy wine is
mixed with water. 23 Thy princes are rebellious, and companions of [ad]thieves:
every one loveth gifts, and followeth after rewards: they judge not the fatherless,
neither doth the widow's cause come before them. 24 Therefore saith the Lord
God of hosts, the [ae]Mighty one of Israel, Ah, I will [af]ease me of mine adversaries,
and avenge me of mine enemies. 25 Then I will turn mine hand upon thee, and
burn out thy dross, till it [ag]be pure, and take away all thy tin. 26 [ah]And I will
restore thy Judges as at the first, and thy counselors as at the beginning: afterward
shalt thou be called a city of righteousness, and a faithful city. 27 Zion shall be
redeemed in judgment, and they that return in her, in [ai]justice. 28 And the [aj]
destruction of the transgressors and of the sinners shall be together: and they that
forsake the Lord, shall be consumed. 29 For they shall be confounded for the
[ak]oaks, which ye have desired, and ye shall be ashamed of the gardens that ye have
chosen, 30 For ye shall be as an oak, whose leaf fadeth: and as a garden that hath
no water. 31 And the strong shall be as [al]tow, and the maker thereof as a spark:
and they shall both burn together, and none shall quench them.

2

2 The Church shall be restored by Christ, and the Gentiles called. 6 The punishment of the rebellious and obstinate.

1 The word that Isaiah the son of Amoz saw upon Judah and Jerusa-
lem, 2 [1]It [a]shall be in the last days, that the mountain of the House of the Lord
shall be prepared in the top of the mountains, and [b]shall be exalted above the hills,
and all nations shall [c]flow unto it. 3 And many people shall go, and say, Come,
and let us go up to [d]the mountain of the Lord, to the house of the God of Jacob;
and he will teach us his ways, and we will walk in his paths, [2]for the [e]Law shall go
forth of Zion, and the word of the Lord from [f]Jerusalem. 4 And [g]he shall judge
among the nations, and [h]rebuke many people: they shall [i]break their swords also

---

ISA 1

- **a.** Isa. 1:1 That is, a revelation or prophecy, which was one of the two means whereby God declared himself to his servants in old time, as Num. 12:6, and therefore the Prophets were called Seers, 1 Sam. 9:9.
- **b.** Isa. 1:1 Isaiah was chiefly sent to Judah and Jerusalem, but not only: for in this book are prophecies concerning other nations also.
- **c.** Isa. 1:1 Called also Azariah, 2 Kings 15:1, of these Kings, read 2 Kings 14–21, and 2 Chron. 25–33.
- **d.** Isa. 1:2 Because men were obstinate and insensible, he calleth to the dumb creatures, which were more prompt to obey God's word, as Deut. 32:1.
- **e.** Isa. 1:2 He declareth his great mercy toward the Jews forasmuch as he chose them above all other nations to be his people and children, as Deut. 10:15.
- **f.** Isa. 1:3 The most dull and brute beasts do more acknowledge their duty toward their masters, than my people do toward me, of whom they have received benefits without comparison.
- **g.** Isa. 1:4 They were not only wicked as were their fathers, but utterly corrupt, and by their evil example infected others.
- **h.** Isa. 1:4 That is, him that sanctifieth Israel.
- **i.** Isa. 1:5 What availeth it to seek to amend you by punishment, seeing the more I correct you, the more ye rebel?
- **j.** Isa. 1:5 By naming the chief parts of the body, he signifieth that there was no part of the whole body of the Jews free from his rods.
- **k.** Isa. 1:6 Every part of the body as well the least as the chiefest, was plagued.
- **l.** Isa. 1:6 Their plagues were so grievous, that they were incurable, and yet they would not repent.
- **m.** Isa. 1:7 Meaning, of them that dwell far off, which because they look for no advantage of that which remaineth destroy all before them.
- **n.** Isa. 1:8 That is, Jerusalem.
- **o.** Isa. 1:9 Because that he will ever have a Church to call upon his Name.
- **p.** Isa. 1:9 That is, all destroyed.
- **q.** Isa. 1:10 Ye that for your vices deserved all to be destroyed, as they of Sodom, save that God of his mercy reserved a little number, Lam. 3:22.
- **r.** Isa. 1:11 Although God commanded these sacrifices for a time, as aids and exercises of their faith: yet because the people had not faith nor repentance, God detesteth them, Ps. 50:13; Jer. 6:20; Amos 5:22; Mic. 6:7.
- **s.** Isa. 1:13 Without faith and repentance.
- **t.** Isa. 1:14 Your sacrifices offered in the new moons and feasts: he condemneth hereby hypocrites, which think to please God with ceremonies, and they themselves are void of faith and mercy.
- **u.** Isa. 1:15 He showeth that where men be given to avarice, deceit, cruelty and extortion, which is meant by blood, there God will show his anger, and not accept them, though they seem never so holy, as Isa. 59:3.
- **v.** Isa. 1:16 By this outward washing, he meaneth the spiritual: exhorting the Jews to repent and amend their lives.
- **w.** Isa. 1:17 This kind of reasoning by the second Table, the Scriptures use in many places against the hypocrites, who pretend most holiness and religion in word, but when the charity and love toward their brethren should appear, they declare that they have neither faith nor religion.
- **x.** Isa. 1:18 To know if I do accuse you without cause.
- **y.** Isa. 1:18 Lest sinners should pretend any rigor on God's part, he only willeth them to be pure in heart, and he will forgive all their sins, were they never so many or great.
- **z.** Isa. 1:19 He showeth that whatsoever adversity man endureth, it ought to be attributed to his own incredulity and disobedience.
- **aa.** Isa. 1:21 That is, Jerusalem, which had promised fidelity unto me, as a wife to her husband.
- **ab.** Isa. 1:21 Given to covetousness and extortion, which he signified before by blood, verse 15.
- **ac.** Isa. 1:22 Whatsoever was pure in thee before, is now corrupt, though thou have an outward show.
- **ad.** Isa. 1:23 That is, they maintain the wicked and the extortioners: and not only do not punish them, but are themselves such.
- **ae.** Isa. 1:24 When God will show himself merciful to his Church, he calleth himself, The Holy one of Israel, but when he hath to do with his enemies, he is called Mighty, as against whom no power is able to resist.
- **af.** Isa. 1:24 I will take vengeance of mine adversaries the Jews, and so satisfy my desire by punishing them. Which thing yet he doeth with a grief, because of his Covenant.
- **ag.** Isa. 1:25 Lest the faithful among them should be overcome with his threatening, he addeth this consolation.
- **ah.** Isa. 1:26 It is only the work of God to purify the heart of man, which thing he doeth because of his promise, made concerning the salvation of his Church.
- **ai.** Isa. 1:27 By justice is meant God's faithful promise, which is the cause of the deliverance of his Church.
- **aj.** Isa. 1:28 The wicked shall not be partakers of God's promise, Ps. 92:9.
- **ak.** Isa. 1:29 That is, the trees and pleasant places, where ye commit idolatry, which was forbidden, Deut. 16:22.
- **al.** Isa. 1:31 The false god, wherein ye put your confidence, shall be consumed as easily as a piece of tow.

ISA 2

- **a.** Isa. 2:2 The decree and ordinance of God, touching the restoration of the Church, which is chiefly meant of the time of Christ.
- **b.** Isa. 2:2 In an evident place to be seen and discerned.
- **c.** Isa. 2:2 When the kingdom of Christ shall be enlarged by the preaching of the doctrine. Here also is declared the zeal of the children of God, when they are called.
- **d.** Isa. 2:3 Alluding to mount Zion, where the visible Church then was.
- **e.** Isa. 2:3 Meaning, the whole doctrine of salvation.
- **f.** Isa. 2:3 This was accomplished, when the Gospel was first preached in Jerusalem, and from thence went through all the world.
- **g.** Isa. 2:4 The Lord, which is Christ, shall have all power given him.
- **h.** Isa. 2:4 That they may acknowledge their sins, and turn to him.
- **i.** Isa. 2:4 He showeth the fruit of the peace, which the Gospel should bring: to wit, that men should do good one to another, whereas before they were enemies.
- **j.** Isa. 2:4 He speaketh not against the use of weapons and lawful war, but showeth how the hearts of the godly shall be affected one toward another: Which peace and love doth begin and grow in this life, but shall be perfected when we are joined with our Head Christ Jesus.
- **k.** Isa. 2:5 Seeing the Gentiles will be so ready, make you haste, and show them the way to worship God.
- **l.** Isa. 2:6 The Prophet seeing the small hope that the Jews would convert, complaineth to God, as though he had utterly forsaken them for their sins.

into mattocks, and their spears into scythes: nation shall not lift up a sword against
nation, neither shall they learn [j]to fight anymore. **5** O house of Jacob, come ye,
and let us [k]walk in the Law of the Lord. **6** Surely thou [l]hast forsaken thy peo-
ple, the house of Jacob, because they are [m]full of the East manners, and are sorce-
rers as the Philistines, [n]and abound with strange children. **7** Their land also was
full of [o]silver and gold, and there was none end of their treasures: and their land
was full of horses, and their chariots were infinite. **8** Their land was also full of
idols; they worshipped the work of their own hands, which their own fingers have
made. **9** And a man bowed himself, and a man [p]humbled himself: therefore
[q]spare them not. **10** Enter into the rock, and hide thee in the dust from before
the fear of the Lord, and from the glory of his Majesty. **11** The high look of man
shall be humbled, and the loftiness of men shall be abased, and the Lord only shall
be exalted in [r]that day. **12** For the day of the Lord of hosts is upon all the proud
and haughty, and upon all that is exalted: and it shall be made low. **13** Even
upon all the cedars of Lebanon, that are high and exalted, and upon all the oaks
of Bashan, **14** And upon all the high [s]mountains, and upon all the hills that are
lifted up, **15** And upon every high tower, and upon every strong wall, **16** And
upon [t]all the ships of Tarshish, and upon all pleasant pictures. **17** And the hau-
ghtiness of men shall be brought low, and the loftiness of men shall be abased,
and the Lord shall only be exalted in that day. **18** And the idols will he utterly
destroy. **19** Then shall they go [3]into the holes of the rocks, and into the caves of
the earth from before the fear of the Lord, and from the glory of his majesty, when
he shall arise to destroy the earth. **20** At that day shall man cast away his silver
idols and his golden idols (which they had made themselves to worship them) [u]to
the moles, and to the backs, **21** To go into the holes of the rocks, and into the
tops of the ragged rocks from before the fear of the Lord, and from the glory of
his majesty, when he shall rise to destroy the earth. **22** Cease you from the man,
whose [v]breath is in his nostrils: for wherein is he to be esteemed?

3

1 For the sin of the people, God will take away the wise men, and give them foolish princes. 14 The covetousness of the governors. 26 The pride of the women.

1 For lo, the Lord God of hosts will take away from Jerusalem and from Ju-
dah the stay [a]and the strength: even all the stay of bread, and all the stay of wa-
ter, **2** The strong man, and the man of war, [b]the judge, and the Prophet, the pru-
dent and the aged, **3** The captain of fifty, and the honorable, and the counselor,
and the cunning artificer, and [c]eloquent man. **4** And I will appoint [d]children
to be their princes, and babes shall rule over them. **5** The people shall be [e]op-
pressed one of another, and every one by his neighbor: the children shall presume
against the ancient, and the vile against the honorable. **6** When everyone shall
[f]take hold of his brother of the house of his father, and say, Thou hast clothing,
thou shalt be our prince, and let this fall be under thine hand: **7** In that day he
shall [g]swear, saying, I cannot be an helper: for there is no bread in mine house, nor
clothing: therefore make me no prince of the people. **8** Doubtless Jerusalem is
fallen, and Judah is fallen down, because their tongue and works are against the
Lord, to provoke the eyes of his glory. **9** The [h]trial of their countenance testifieth
against them, yea, they declare their sins, as Sodom, they hide them not. Woe be
unto their souls: for they have rewarded evil unto themselves. **10** [i]Say ye, Surely
it shall be well with the just: for they shall eat the fruit of their works. **11** Woe
be to the wicked, it shall be evil with him: for the reward of his hands shall be gi-
ven him. **12** [j]Children are extortioners of my people, and women have rule over
them: O my people, they that lead thee, cause thee to err, and destroy the way of
thy paths. **13** The Lord standeth up to plead, yea, he standeth to judge the peo-
ple. **14** The Lord shall enter into judgment with the [k]Ancients of his people and
the princes thereof: for ye have eaten up the vineyard: the spoil of the poor is in
your houses. **15** What have ye to do that ye beat my people to pieces, [l]and grind
the faces of the poor, saith the Lord, even the Lord of hosts? **16** The Lord also
saith, [m]Because the daughters of Zion are haughty, and walk with [n]stretched out
necks, and with [o]wandering eyes, walking and [p]mincing as they go, and making
a [q]tinkling with their feet, **17** Therefore shall the Lord make the heads of the
daughters of Zion bald, and the Lord shall discover their secret parts. **18** In that
day shall the Lord take away the ornament of the slippers, and the cauls, and the
round tyres, **19** The sweet balls, and the bracelets, and the bonnets, **20** The
tyres of the head, and the slops, and the headbands, and the tablets, and the earrin-
gs, **21** The rings and the mufflers, **22** The costly apparel and the veils, and the
wimples, and the crisping pins, **23** And the glasses and the fine linen, and the
hoods and the [r]lawns. **24** And instead of sweet savor, there shall be stink, and
instead of girdle, a rent, and instead of dressing of the hair, baldness, and instead of
a stomacher, a girding of sackcloth, and burning instead of beauty. **25** Thy men
shall fall by the [s]sword, and thy strength in the battle. **26** Then shall her gates
mourn and lament, and she being desolate, shall sit upon the ground.

4

1 The small remnant of men after the destruction of Jerusalem. 2 The graces of God upon them that remain.

1 And in that day shall [a]seven women take hold of one man, saying, We will
eat our own bread, and we will wear our own garments: only [b]let us be called by
thy name, and take away our [c]reproach. **2** In that day shall the [d]bud of the Lord
be beautiful and glorious, and the fruit of the earth shall be excellent and pleasant
for them that are escaped of Israel. **3** Then he that shall be left in Zion, and he
that shall remain in Jerusalem, shall be called holy, and every one shall be [e]written
among the living in Jerusalem, **4** When the Lord shall wash the filthiness of the
daughters of Zion, and purge the [f]blood of Jerusalem out of the midst thereof by
the spirit of [g]judgment, and by the spirit of burning. **5** And the Lord shall create
upon every place of mount Zion, and upon the assemblies thereof, [h]a cloud and
smoke by day, and the shining of a flaming fire by night: for upon all the [i]glory
shall be a defense. **6** And a covering shall be for a shadow in the day for the heat,
and a place of refuge and a covert for the storm [j]and for the rain.

5

1 Under the similitude of the vine, he describeth the state of the people. 8 Of their avarice. 11 Their drunkenness. 13 Of their captivity.

1 Now will [a]I sing to my [b]beloved a song of my beloved to his vineyard, [1]My
beloved had a [c]vineyard in a very fruitful hill. **2** And he hedged it, and gathered
out the stones of it, and he planted it with the best plants, [d]and he built a tower

---

m. Isa. 2:6 Full of the corruptions that reigned chiefly in the East parts.
n. Isa. 2:6 They altogether gave themselves to the fashions of other nations.
o. Isa. 2:7 The Prophet first condemned their superstition and idolatry: next their covetousness, and thirdly their vain trust in worldly means.
p. Isa. 2:9 He noteth the nature of the idolaters, which are never satisfied in their superstitions.
q. Isa. 2:9 Thus the Prophet spake, being inflamed with the zeal of God's glory, and that he might fear them with God's judgment.
r. Isa. 2:11 Meaning, as soon as God shall begin to execute his judgments.
s. Isa. 2:14 By high trees and mountains are meant them that are proud and lofty, and think themselves most strong in this world.
t. Isa. 2:16 He condemneth their vain confidence, which they had in strongholds, and in their rich merchandise, which brought in vain pleasures, wherewith men's minds became effeminate.
u. Isa. 2:20 They shall cast them into most vile and filthy places, when they perceive that they are not able to help them.
v. Isa. 2:22 Cast off your vain confidence of man, whose life is so frail, that if his nose be stopped, he is dead, and consider that you have to do with God.

ISA 2
1. Mic. 4:1
2. Mic. 4:2
3. Hos. 10:8 / Luke 23:30 / Rev. 6:16 / Rev. 9:6

ISA 3
a. Isa. 3:1 Because they trusted in their abundance and prosperity, he showeth that they should be taken from them.
b. Isa. 3:2 The temporal governor and the minister.
c. Isa. 3:3 By these he meaneth that God would take away everything that was in any estimation, and wherein they had any occasion to vaunt themselves.
d. Isa. 3:4 Not only in age: but in wit, manners, knowledge and strength.
e. Isa. 3:5 For lack of good regiment and order.
f. Isa. 3:6 He showeth that this plague shall be so horrible, that contrary to the common manner of men, which by nature are ambitious, none shall be found able or willing to be their governor.
g. Isa. 3:7 Fear shall rather cause him to forswear himself, than to take such a dangerous charge upon him.
h. Isa. 3:9 When God shall examine their deeds whereupon they now set an impudent face, he shall find the mark of their impiety in their forehead.
i. Isa. 3:10 Be ye that are godly, assured that God will defend you in the midst of these troubles.
j. Isa. 3:12 Because the wicked people were more addicted to their princes, than to the commandments of God, he showeth that he would give them such princes, by whom they should have no help, but that should be manifest tokens of his wrath, because they should be fools and effeminate.
k. Isa. 3:14 Meaning, that the rulers and governors had destroyed his Church, and not preserved it, according to their duty.
l. Isa. 3:15 That is, ye show all cruelty against them.
m. Isa. 3:16 He meaneth the people because of the arrogancy and pride of their women, which gave themselves to all wantonness and dissolution.
n. Isa. 3:16 Which declared their pride.
o. Isa. 3:16 As a sign, that they were not chaste.
p. Isa. 3:16 Which showed their wantonness.
q. Isa. 3:16 They delighted then in slippers that did creak, or had little plates sewed upon them, which tinkled as they went.
r. Isa. 3:23 In rehearsing all these things particularly, he showeth the lightness and vanity of such as cannot be content with comely apparel according to their degree.
s. Isa. 3:25 Meaning, that God will not only punish the women, but their husbands which have suffered this dissoluteness, and also the commonweal, which hath not remedied it.

ISA 4
a. Isa. 4:1 When God shall execute this vengeance, there shall not be one man found to be the head to many women, and they contrary to womanly shamefacedness, shall seek unto men, and offer themselves to any condition.
b. Isa. 4:1 Be thou our husband, and let us be called thy wives.
c. Isa. 4:1 For so they thought it to be without an head and husband.
d. Isa. 4:2 He comforteth the Church in this desolation, which shall spring up like a bud, signifying that God's graces should be as plentiful toward the faithful, as though they sprang out of the earth, as Isa. 45:8. Some by the bud of the Lord mean Christ.
e. Isa. 4:3 He alludeth to the book of life, whereof read Exod. 32:32, meaning, God's secret counsel, wherein his elect are predestinate to life everlasting.
f. Isa. 4:4 That is, the cruelty, extortion, avarice, and all wickedness.
g. Isa. 4:4 When things shall be redressed that were amiss.
h. Isa. 4:5 He alludeth to the pillar of the cloud, Exod. 13:21, meaning, that God's favor and protection should appear in every place.
i. Isa. 4:5 The faithful are called the glory of God, because his image and tokens of his grace shine in them.
j. Isa. 4:6 God promiseth to be the defense of his Church against all troubles and dangers.

ISA 5
a. Isa. 5:1 The Prophet by this song doth set before the people's eyes their ingratitude, and God's mercy.
b. Isa. 5:1 That is, to God.
c. Isa. 5:1 Meaning, that he had planted his Church in a place most plentiful and abundant.
d. Isa. 5:2 He spared no diligence nor cost.
e. Isa. 5:2 In the seventh verse he declareth what they were.

in the midst thereof, and made a winepress therein, then he looked that it should bring forth grapes: but it brought forth [e]wild grapes. **3** Now therefore, O inhabitants of Jerusalem and men of Judah, judge, I pray you, [f]between me and my vineyard. **4** What could I have done anymore to my vineyard that I have not done unto it? why have I looked that it should bring forth grapes, and it bringeth forth wild grapes? **5** And now I will tell you what I will do to my vineyard: I [g]will take away the hedge thereof, and it shall be eaten up: I will break the wall thereof, and it shall be trodden down: **6** And I will lay it waste: it shall not be cut, nor dug, but briers and thorns shall grow up: I will also command the clouds that they rain no rain upon it. **7** Surely the vineyard of the Lord of hosts is the house of Israel, and the men of Judah are his pleasant plant, and he looked for [h]judgment, but behold oppression: for righteousness, but behold [i]a crying. **8** Woe unto them that join house to house, and lay field to field, till there be no [j]place, that ye may be placed by yourselves in the midst of the earth. **9** This is in mine [k]ears, saith the Lord of hosts. Surely many houses shall be desolate, even great and fair without inhabitant. **10** For ten acres of vines shall yield one [l]bath, and the seed of an [m]homer shall yield an [n]ephah. **11** Woe unto them, that [o]rise up early to follow drunkenness, and to them that continue until [p]night, till the wine do inflame them, **12** And the harp and viol, timbrel and pipe, and wine are in their feasts: but they regard not the [q]work of the Lord, neither consider the work of his hands. **13** Therefore my people [r]is gone into captivity, because they had [s]no knowledge, and the glory thereof are men famished, and the multitude thereof is dried up with thirst. **14** Therefore [t]hell hath enlarged itself, and hath opened his mouth without measure, and their glory, and their multitude, and their pomp, and he that rejoiceth among them, shall descend into it. **15** And man shall be brought down, and man shall be humbled, even the eyes of the proud shall be humbled. **16** And the Lord of hosts shall be exalted in judgment, and the holy God shall be sanctified in justice. **17** Then shall [u]the lambs feed after their manner, and the strangers shall eat the desolate places of the fat. **18** Woe unto them that draw iniquity with [v]cords of vanity, and sin, as with cart ropes: **19** Which say, [w]Let him make speed: let him hasten his work, that we may see it: and let the counsel of the Holy One of Israel draw near and come, that we may know it. **20** Woe unto them that speak good of evil, [x]and evil of good, which put darkness for light, and light for darkness, that put bitter for sweet, and sweet for sour. **21** Woe unto them that are [y]wise in their own eyes, and prudent in their own sight. **22** Woe unto them that are [z]mighty to drink wine, and unto them that are strong to pour in strong drink: **23** Which justify the wicked for a reward, and take away the righteousness of the righteous from him. **24** Therefore as the flame of fire devoureth the stubble, and as the chaff is consumed of the flame: so their [aa]root shall be a rottenness, and their bud shall rise up like dust, because they have cast off the Law of the Lord of hosts, and contemned the word of the Holy one of Israel. **25** Therefore is the wrath of the Lord kindled against his people, and he hath stretched out his [ab]hand upon them, and hath smitten them that the mountains did tremble: and their carcasses were torn in the midst of the streets, and for all this his wrath was not turned away, but his hand was stretched out still. **26** And he will lift up a sign [ac]unto the nations afar, and will hiss unto them from the end of the earth: and behold, they shall come hastily with speed. **27** None shall [ad]faint nor fall among them: none shall slumber nor sleep, neither shall the girdle of his loins be loosed, nor [ae]the latchet of his shoes be broken. **28** Whose arrows shall be sharp, and all his bows bent: his horse hoofs shall be thought like flint, and his wheels like whirlwind. **29** His roaring shall be like a lion, and he shall roar like lion's whelps: they shall [af]roar, and lay hold of the prey: they shall take it away, and none shall deliver it. **30** And in that day they shall roar upon them, as the roaring of the sea: and if [ag]they look unto the earth, behold darkness and sorrow, and the light shall be darkened in their [ah]sky.

6

1 Isaiah showeth his vocation by the vision of the divine majesty. 9 He showeth the obstinacy of the people. 11 The destruction of the land. 13 The remnant reserved.

1 In the year of the death of king Uzziah, [a]I saw also the Lord sitting upon an [b]high throne, and lifted up, and the lower [c]parts thereof filled the Temple. **2** The [d]Seraphims stood upon it, every one had six wings: with twain he covered his [e]face, and with twain he covered his [f]feet, and with twain he did [g]fly. **3** And one cried to another, and said, [h]Holy, holy, holy is the Lord of hosts: the whole [i]world is full of his glory. **4** And the lintels of the door cheeks [j]moved at the voice of him that cried, and the house was filled with smoke. **5** Then I said, [k]Woe is me: for I am undone, because I am a man of polluted lips, and I dwell in the midst of a people of polluted lips: for mine eyes have seen the King, and Lord of hosts. **6** Then flew one of the Seraphims unto me with an hot coal in his hand, which he had taken from the [l]altar with the tongs: **7** And he touched my mouth, and said, Lo, this hath touched thy lips, and thine iniquity shall be taken away, and thy [m]sin shall be purged. **8** Also I heard the voice of the Lord, saying, Whom shall I send? and who shall go for us? Then I said, Here am I, send me. **9** And he said, Go, and say unto this people, [n]Ye shall hear indeed, but ye shall not understand: ye shall plainly see, and not perceive. **10** Make the heart of this people fat, make their ears heavy, and shut their eyes, lest they see with their eyes, and hear with their ears, and understand with their heart, and convert, and he heal them. **11** Then said I, Lord, [o]how long? And he answered, Until the cities be wasted without inhabitant, and the houses without man, and the land be utterly desolate, **12** And the Lord have removed men far away, and there be a great desolation in the midst of the land. **13** But yet in it shall be [p]a tenth, and shall return, and shall be eaten up as an elm [q]or an oak, which have a substance in them, when they cast their leaves: so the holy seed shall be the substance thereof.

7

1 Jerusalem is besieged. 4 Isaiah comforteth the king. 14 Christ is promised.

1 And in the days of [1]Ahaz, the son of Jotham, the son of Uzziah king of Judah, Rezin the king of [a]Aram [b]came up, and Pekah the son of Remaliah king of Israel, to Jerusalem to fight against it, but he could not overcome it. **2** And it was told the house of [c]David, saying, Aram is joined with [d]Ephraim: therefore his

---

f. Isa. 5:3 He maketh them judges in their own cause, forasmuch as it was evident that they were the cause of their own ruin.
g. Isa. 5:5 I will take no more care for it: meaning, that he would take from them his word and ministers, and all other comforts, and send them contrary plagues.
h. Isa. 5:7 Judgment and righteousness are true fruits of the fear of God, and therefore in the cruel oppression there is no religion.
i. Isa. 5:7 Of them that are oppressed.
j. Isa. 5:8 To wit, for the poor to dwell in.
k. Isa. 5:9 I have heard the complaint and cry of the poor.
l. Isa. 5:10 Which containeth about ten pottels: so that every acre should but yield one pottel.
m. Isa. 5:10 Which containeth an hundred pottels.
n. Isa. 5:10 An Ephah containeth ten pottels and is in dry things as much as Bath is in liquors.
o. Isa. 5:11 That spare no pain nor diligence to follow their lusts.
p. Isa. 5:11 Which are never weary of their rioting and excessive pleasures, but use all means to provoke to the same.
q. Isa. 5:12 They regard not the provident care of God over them, nor for what end he hath created them.
r. Isa. 5:13 That is, shall certainly go: for so the Prophets use to speak, as though the thing which shall come to pass, were done already.
s. Isa. 5:13 Because they would not obey the word of God.
t. Isa. 5:14 Meaning, the grave shall swallow up them that shall die for hunger and thirst, and yet for all this great destruction it shall ever be satiate.
u. Isa. 5:17 God comforteth the poor lambs of his Church, which had been strangers in other countries, promising that they should dwell in these places again, whereof they had been deprived by the fat and cruel tyrants.
v. Isa. 5:18 Which use all allurements, occasions, and excuses to harden their conscience in sin.
w. Isa. 5:19 He showeth what are the words of the wicked, when they are menaced with God's judgments, 2 Pet. 3:4.
x. Isa. 5:20 Which are not ashamed of sin, nor care for honesty, but are grown to a desperate impiety.
y. Isa. 5:21 Which are contemners of all doctrine and admonition.
z. Isa. 5:22 Which are never weary, but show their strength, and brag in gluttony and drunkenness.
aa. Isa. 5:24 Both they and their posterity, so that nothing shall be left.
ab. Isa. 5:25 He showeth that God had so sore punished this people, that the dumb creatures, if they had been so plagued, would have been more sensible, and therefore his plagues must continue, till they begin to feel them.
ac. Isa. 5:26 He will make the Babylonians to come against them at his beck, and to fight under his standard.
ad. Isa. 5:27 They shall be prompt and lusty to execute God's vengeance.
ae. Isa. 5:27 The enemy shall have none impediment.
af. Isa. 5:29 Whereby is declared the cruelty of the enemy.
ag. Isa. 5:30 The Jews shall find no succor.
ah. Isa. 5:30 In the land of Judah.

ISA 5

1. Jer. 2:21 / Matt. 21:33

ISA 6

a. Isa. 6:1 God showeth not himself to man in his majesty, but according as man's capacity is able to comprehend him, that is, by visible signs, as John Baptist saw the holy Ghost in the form of a dove.
b. Isa. 6:1 As a Judge ready to give sentence.
c. Isa. 6:1 Of his garment, or of his throne.
d. Isa. 6:2 They were Angels, so called, because they were of a fiery color, to signify that they burnt in the love of God, or were light as fire to execute his will.
e. Isa. 6:2 Signifying, that they were not able to endure the brightness of God's glory.
f. Isa. 6:2 Whereby was declared that man was not able to see the brightness of God in them.
g. Isa. 6:2 Which thing declareth the prompt obedience of the Angels to execute God's commandment.
h. Isa. 6:3 This oft repetition signifieth, that the Holy Angels cannot satisfy themselves in praising God, to teach us that in all our lives we should give ourselves to the continual praise of God.
i. Isa. 6:3 His glory doth not only appear in the heavens, but through all the world, and therefore all creatures are bound, to praise him.
j. Isa. 6:4 Which things were to confirm the Prophet, that it was not the voice of man: and by the smoke was signified the blindness that should come upon the Jews.
k. Isa. 6:5 He speaketh this for two causes: the one because he that was a mortal creature, and therefore had more need to glorify God than the Angels, did it not: and the other because the more near that man approacheth to God, the more doth he know his own sin and corruption.
l. Isa. 6:6 Of the burnt offerings, where the fire never went out.
m. Isa. 6:7 This declareth that man cannot render due obedience to God, till he have purged us.
n. Isa. 6:9 Whereby is declared that for the malice of man God will not immediately take away his word, but he will cause it to be preached to their condemnation, when as they will not learn thereby to obey his will, and be saved: hereby he exhorteth the ministers to do their duty, and answereth to the wicked murmurers, that through their own malice their heart is hardened, Matt. 13:14; Acts 28:26; Rom. 11:8.
o. Isa. 6:11 As he was moved with the zeal of God's glory, so was he touched with a charitable affection toward the people.
p. Isa. 6:13 Meaning, the tenth part: or as some write, it was revealed to Isa. for the confirmation of his prophecy, that ten Kings should come before their captivity, as were from Uzziah to Zedekiah.
q. Isa. 6:13 For the fewness they shall seem to be eaten up: yet they shall after flourish as a tree, which in winter loseth leaves, and seemeth to be dead, yet in Summer is fresh and green.

ISA 7

a. Isa. 7:1 Or, Syria.
b. Isa. 7:1 To wit, the second time: for in the first battle Ahaz was overcome.
c. Isa. 7:2 Meaning, the King's house.
d. Isa. 7:2 That is, Israel, because that tribe was the greatest, Gen. 48:19.
e. Isa. 7:2 For fear.

heart was [e]moved, and the heart of his people, as the trees of the forest are moved by the wind. **3** Then said the Lord unto Isaiah, Go forth now to meet Ahaz (thou and [f]Shear-Jashub thy son) at the end of the conduit of the upper pool, in the path of the fuller's field, **4** And say unto him, Take heed, and be still: fear not, neither be fainthearted for the two tails of these smoking [g]firebrands, for the furious wrath of Rezin and of Aram, and of Remaliah's son, **5** Because Aram hath taken wicked counsel against thee, and Ephraim and Remaliah's son, saying, **6** Let us go up against Judah, and let us waken them up, and make a breach therein for us, and set a king in the midst thereof, even the son of [h]Tabel. **7** Thus saith the Lord God, It shall not stand, neither shall it be. **8** For the head of Aram is Damascus, and the head of Damascus is Rezin: and within five and [i]threescore years, Ephraim shall be destroyed from being a people. **9** And the head of Ephraim is Samaria, and the head of Samaria is Remaliah's son. If ye believe not, surely ye shall not be established. **10** And the Lord spake again unto Ahaz, saying, **11** Ask [j]a sign for thee of the Lord thy God: ask it either in the depth beneath, or in the height above. **12** But Ahaz said, I will not ask, neither will I [k]tempt the Lord. **13** Then he said, Hear you now, O house of David, is it a small thing for you to grieve [l]men, that ye will also grieve my God? **14** Therefore the Lord [m]himself will give you a sign. Behold, the virgin shall conceive and bear a son, and she shall call his name [n]Immanuel. **15** [o]Butter and honey shall he eat, till he have knowledge to refuse the evil, and to choose the good. **16** For afore the [p]child shall have knowledge to eschew the evil, and to choose the good, the land that thou abhorrest, shall be forsaken of both her kings. **17** The Lord shall bring upon thee, and upon thy people, and upon thy Father's house (the days that are not come from the day that [q]Ephraim departed from Judah) even the King of [r]Assyria. **18** And in that day shall the Lord hiss for the [s]fly that is at the uttermost parts of the floods of Egypt, and for the Bee which is in the land of Assyria, **19** And they shall come and shall light all in the desolate valleys, and in the holes of the rocks, and upon all thorny places, and upon all bushy [t]places. **20** In that day shall the Lord shave with a razor that is hired, even by them beyond the River, by the King of Assyria, the head and the hair of the [u]feet, and it shall consume the beard. **21** And in the same day shall a man [v]nourish a young cow, and two sheep. **22** And for the [w]abundance of milk, that they shall give, he shall eat butter: for butter and honey shall everyone eat, which is left within the land. **23** And at the same day every place, wherein shall be a thousand vines, shall be at a thousand pieces of silver: so it shall be for the briers and for the thorns. **24** With arrows and with [x]bow shall one come thither: because all the land shall be briers and thorns. **25** But on [y]all the mountains, which shall be dug with the mattock, there shall not come thither the fear of briers and thorns: but they shall be for the sending out of bullocks, and for the treading of sheep.

8

1 The captivity of Israel and Judah by the Assyrians. 6 The infidelity of the Jews. 9 The destruction of the Assyrians. 14 Christ the stone of stumbling to the wicked. 19 The word of God must be inquired at.

1 Moreover the Lord said unto me, Take thee a [a]great roll, and write it [b]with a man's pen, Make speed to the spoil: haste to the prey. **2** Then I took unto me [c]faithful witnesses to record, Uriah the Priest, and Zechariah the son of Jeberechiah. **3** After, I came unto the [d]Prophetess, which conceived, and bare a son. Then said the Lord to me, Call his name, [e]Maher-Shalal-Hash-Baz. **4** For before the [f]child shall have knowledge to cry, My father, and my mother, he shall take away the riches of Damascus, and the spoil of Samaria, before the [g]King of Assyria. **5** And the Lord spake yet again unto me, saying, **6** Because this people hath refused the waters of [h]Shiloah that run softly, and rejoice with Rezin, and the son of Remaliah, **7** Now therefore, behold, the Lord bringeth up upon them the waters of [i]the River mighty and great, even the King of Assyria with all his glory, and he shall come up upon all their rivers, and go over all their banks, **8** And shall break into Judah, and shall overflow, and pass through, and shall come up to the [j]neck, and the stretching out of his wings shall fill the breadth of thy land, O [k]Immanuel. **9** Gather together on heaps, O ye [l]people, and ye shall be broken in pieces, and hearken all ye of far countries: gird yourselves, and you shall be broken in pieces: gird yourselves, and you shall be broken in pieces. **10** Take counsel together, yet, it shall be brought to naught: pronounce a decree, yet shall it not stand: for God is with us. **11** For the Lord spake thus to me, in taking [m]of mine hand, and taught me, that I should not walk in the way of this people, saying, **12** Say ye not, A [n]confederacy, to all them to whom this people saith a confederacy, neither fear you [o]their fear, nor be afraid of them. **13** [p]Sanctify the Lord of hosts, and let him be your fear, and let him be your dread, **14** And he shall be as a [q]Sanctuary: but as a stumbling stone, and as a rock to fall upon, to both the houses of Israel, and as a snare and as a net to the inhabitants of Jerusalem. **15** And many among them shall stumble, and shall fall, and shall be broken, and shall be snared, and shall be taken, **16** [r]Bind up the testimony: seal up the Law among my disciples. **17** Therefore I will wait upon the Lord that hath hid his face from the house of Jacob, and I will look for him. **18** Behold, I and the [s]children whom the Lord hath given me, are as signs and as wonders in Israel, [t]by the Lord of hosts, which dwelleth in Mount Zion. **19** And when they shall say unto you, Inquire at them that have a spirit of divination, and at the soothsayers which whisper and murmur, [u]Should not a people inquire at their God? from the [v]living to the dead? **20** To the [w]Law, and to the testimony, if they speak not according to this word: it is because there is no [x]light in them. **21** Then he that is afflicted and famished, shall go to and fro in [y]it: and when he shall be hungry, he shall even fret himself, [z]and curse his king and his gods, and shall look upward. **22** And when he shall look to the earth, behold trouble, and [aa]darkness, vexation, and anguish, and he is driven to darkness.

9

1 The vocation of the Gentiles. 6 A prophecy of Christ. 14 The destruction of the ten tribes for their pride and contempt of God.

1 Yet [a]the darkness shall not be according to the affliction, [b]that it had when at the first he touched lightly the land of Zebulun and the land of Naphtali, nor afterward when he was more grievous by the way of the sea beyond Jordan in Galilee of [c]the Gentiles. **2** The people that [d]walked in darkness, have seen a great [e]light: they that dwelled in the land of the shadow of death, upon them hath the [f]light shined. **3** Thou hast [g]multiplied the nation, and not increased their joy:

---

f. Isa. 7:3 That is to say, the rest shall return, which name Isa. gave his son, to signify that the rest of the people should return out of their captivity.
g. Isa. 7:4 Which have but a little smoke and shall quickly be quenched.
h. Isa. 7:6 Which was an Israelite, and as seemeth, enemy to the house of David.
i. Isa. 7:8 Counting from the five and twentieth year of the reign of Uzziah, at what time Amos prophesied this thing, and now Isa. confirmeth that the Israelites should be led into perpetual captivity, which thing came to pass within 20 years after that Isa. did this message.
j. Isa. 7:11 For the confirmation of this thing that thine enemies shall be destroyed and thou preserved.
k. Isa. 7:12 Not to believe God's word without a sign, is to tempt God, but to refuse a sign when God offereth it for the aid and help of our infirmity, is to rebel against him.
l. Isa. 7:13 You think you have to do with men, when ye contemn God's messengers: but it is God against whom you bend yourselves.
m. Isa. 7:14 Forasmuch as thou art unworthy, the Lord for his own promise sake will give a sign, which shall be that Christ the Savior of his Church, and the effect of all signs and miracles shall be revealed.
n. Isa. 7:14 Or, God with us, which name can agree to none, but to him that is both God and man.
o. Isa. 7:15 Meaning, that Christ is not only God, but man also, because he shall be nourished as other men until the age of discretion.
p. Isa. 7:16 Not meaning Christ, but any child: for before a child can come to the years of discretion, the kings of Samaria and Syria shall be destroyed.
q. Isa. 7:17 Since the time that the twelve Tribes rebelled under Rehoboam.
r. Isa. 7:17 In whom thou hast put thy trust.
s. Isa. 7:18 Meaning, the Egyptians: for by reason the country is hot and moist, it is full of flies, as Assyria is full of bees.
t. Isa. 7:19 Signifying, that no place shall be free from them.
u. Isa. 7:20 That is, that which is from the belly downward: meaning, that he would destroy both great and small.
v. Isa. 7:21 He that before had a great number of cattle, shall be content with one cow and two sheep.
w. Isa. 7:22 The number of men shall be so small, that a few beasts shall be able to nourish all abundantly.
x. Isa. 7:24 As they that go to seek wild beasts among the bushes.
y. Isa. 7:25 The mountains contrary to their wont, shall be tilled by such as shall flee to them for succor.

ISA 7

1. 2 Kings 16:5

ISA 8

a. Isa. 8:1 That thou mayest write in great letters, to the intent it may be more easily read.
b. Isa. 8:1 Meaning, after the common fashion, because all men might read it.
c. Isa. 8:2 Because the thing was of great importance, he took these two witnesses, which were of credit with the people, when he set this up upon the door of the Temple, albeit Uriah was a flattering hypocrite, 2 Kings 16:11.
d. Isa. 8:3 Meaning, to his wife, and this was done in a vision.
e. Isa. 8:3 Or, make speed to the spoil: haste to the prey.
f. Isa. 8:4 Before any child be able to speak.
g. Isa. 8:4 That is, the army of Assyria.
h. Isa. 8:6 Which was a fountain at the foot of mount Zion, out of the which ran a small river through the city: meaning, that they of Judah, distrusting their own power, which was small, desired such power and riches as they saw in Syria and Israel.
i. Isa. 8:7 That is, the Assyrians which dwell beyond Euphrates.
j. Isa. 8:8 It shall be ready to drown them.
k. Isa. 8:8 He speaketh this to Messiah, or Christ, in whom the faithful were comforted, and who would not suffer his Church to be destroyed utterly.
l. Isa. 8:9 To wit, ye that are enemies to the Church, as the Assyrians, Egyptians, Syrians, etc.
m. Isa. 8:11 To encourage me that I should not shrink for the infidelity of this people, and so neglect mine office.
n. Isa. 8:12 Consent not ye that are godly, to the league and friendship that this people seek with strangers and idolaters.
o. Isa. 8:12 Meaning, that they should not fear the thing that they feared, which have no hope in God.
p. Isa. 8:13 In putting your trust only in him, in calling upon him in adversity, patiently looking for his help, and fearing to do anything contrary to his will.
q. Isa. 8:14 He will defend you which are his elect, and reject all the rest, which is meant of Christ, against whom the Jews should stumble and fall, Luke 2:34; Rom. 9:33; 1 Pet. 2:7, 8.
r. Isa. 8:16 Though all forsake me, yet ye that are mine, keep my word sure sealed in your hearts.
s. Isa. 8:18 Meaning, them that were willing to hear and obey the word of God, whom the world hated, as though they were monsters and not worthy to live.
t. Isa. 8:18 This was a consolation in their troubles, knowing that nothing could come unto them, but by the will of the Lord.
u. Isa. 8:19 Answer the wicked thus, Should not God's people seek succor only at him?
v. Isa. 8:19 This is, will they refuse to be taught of the Prophet, who is the mouth of God, and seek help at the dead, which is the illusion of Satan?
w. Isa. 8:20 Seek remedy in the word of God, where his will is declared.
x. Isa. 8:20 They have no knowledge, but are blind leaders of the blind.
y. Isa. 8:21 That is, in Judah, where they should have had rest, if they had not thus grievously offended God.
z. Isa. 8:21 In whom afore they put their trust.
aa. Isa. 8:22 They shall think that heaven and earth and all creatures are bent against them to trouble them.

ISA 9

a. Isa. 9:1 He comforteth the Church again after these great threatenings, promising to restore them to great glory in Messiah.
b. Isa. 9:1 Wherewith Israel was punished, first by Tiglath-pileser, which was a light scourge in respect of that which they

they have rejoiced before thee according to the joy in harvest, and as men rejoice when they divide a spoil. **4** For the [h]yoke of their burden, and the staff of their shoulder, and the rod of their oppressor hast thou broken, as in the day of Midian. **5** Surely every battle of the warrior is with noise, and with tumbling of garments in blood: but this shall be [i]with burning, and devouring of fire. **6** For unto us a child is born, and unto us a Son is given: and the government is upon his shoulder, and he shall call his name, Wonderful, Counselor, The mighty God, The everlasting [j]Father, The prince of peace. **7** The increase of his government and peace shall have none end: he shall sit upon the throne of David, and upon his kingdom, to order it, and to stablish it with judgment, and with justice, from henceforth, even forever: [k]the zeal of the Lord of hosts will perform this. **8** The Lord hath sent a word into Jacob, and it lighted upon [l]Israel. **9** And all the people shall know, even Ephraim, and the inhabitant of Samaria, that say in the pride and presumption of their heart, **10** The [m]bricks are fallen, but we will build it with hewn stones: the wild fig trees are cut down, but we will change them into cedars. **11** Nevertheless, the Lord will raise up the adversaries of [n]Rezin against him, and join his enemies together. **12** Aram before and the Philistines behind, and they shall devour Israel with open mouth: yet for all this his wrath is not turned away, but his hand is stretched out still. **13** For the people turneth not unto him that smiteth them, neither do they seek the Lord of hosts. **14** Therefore will the Lord cut off from Israel head and tail, branch and rush in one day. **15** The ancient and the honorable man, he is the head: and the prophet that teacheth lies, he is the tail. **16** For the leaders of the people cause them to err: and they that are led by them are devoured. **17** Therefore shall the Lord have no pleasure in their young men, neither will he have compassion of their fatherless and of their widows: for everyone is an hypocrite and wicked, and every mouth speaketh folly: yet for all this his wrath is not turned away, but his hand is stretched out still. **18** For wickedness [o]burneth as a fire: it devoureth the briers and the thorns, and will kindle in the thick places of the forest: and they shall mount up like the lifting up of smoke. **19** By the wrath of the Lord of hosts shall the land be darkened, and the people shall be as the meat of the fire: no man shall [p]spare his brother. **20** And he shall snatch at the right hand, and be hungry: and he shall eat on the left hand, and shall not be satisfied: everyone shall eat the [q]flesh of his own arm. **21** Manasseh Ephraim: and Ephraim Manasseh, and they both shall be against Judah: yet for all this his wrath is not turned away, but his hand is stretched out still.

10

1 Of wicked lawmakers. 5 God will punish his people by the Assyrians and after destroy them. 21 The remnant of Israel shall be saved.

1 Woe unto them that decree wicked decrees, and [a]write grievous things,

2 To keep back the poor from judgment, and to take away the judgment of the poor of my people, that widows may be their prey, and that they may spoil the fatherless. **3** What will ye do now in the day of visitation, and of destruction, which shall come from [b]far? to whom will ye flee for help and where will ye leave your [c]glory? **4** [d]Without me everyone shall fall among them that are bound, and they shall fall down among the slain: yet for all this his wrath is not turned away, but his hand is stretched out still. **5** O [e]Assyria, the rod of my wrath: and the staff in their hands is mine indignation. **6** I will send [f]him to a dissembling nation, and I will give him a charge against the people of my wrath to take the spoil and to take the prey, and to tread them under feet like the mire in the street. **7** But he thinketh not so, neither doth his heart esteem it so: but he imagineth to destroy and to cut off not a few nations. **8** For he saith, Are not my princes altogether Kings? **9** Is not Calno as [g]Carchemish? Is not Hamath like Arpad? Is not Samaria as Damascus? **10** Like as mine hand hath found the kingdoms of the idols, seeing their idols were above Jerusalem, and above Samaria: **11** Shall not I, as I have done to Samaria, and to the idols thereof, so do to Jerusalem, and to the idols thereof? **12** But when the Lord hath accomplished [h]all his work upon mount Zion and Jerusalem, I will visit the fruit of the proud heart [i]of the king of Assyria, and his glorious and proud looks, **13** Because he said, By the power of mine own hand have I done it, and by my wisdom, because I am wise: therefore I have removed the borders of the people, and have spoiled their treasures, and have pulled down the inhabitants like a valiant man. **14** And mine hand hath found as a nest the riches of the people, and as one that gathereth eggs that are left, so have I gathered all the earth: and there was none to move the wing or to open the mouth, or to whisper. **15** Shall the [j]axe boast itself against him that heweth therewith? or shall the saw exalt itself against him that moveth it? as if the rod should lift up itself against him that taketh it up, or the staff should exalt itself as it were no wood. **16** Therefore shall the Lord God of hosts send among his fat men leanness, and under his glory he shall kindle a burning, like the burning of fire. **17** And the light of Israel shall be as a [k]fire, and the Holy one thereof as a flame, and it shall burn, and devour [l]his thorns and his briers in one day: **18** And shall consume the glory of his forest, and of his fruitful fields both soul [m]and flesh: and he shall be as the [n]fainting of a standard bearer. **19** And the rest of the trees of his forest shall be few, that a child may tell them. **20** And at that day shall the remnant of Israel and such as are escaped of the house of Jacob, stay no more upon him that smote them, but shall [o]stay upon the Lord, the Holy one of Israel in truth. **21** The remnant shall return, even the remnant of Jacob unto the mighty God. **22** For though thy people, O Israel, be as the sand of the sea, yet shall the remnant of them return. The consumption [p]decreed shall overflow with righteousness. **23** For the Lord God of hosts shall make the consumption even [q]determined, in the midst of all the land. **24** Therefore thus saith the Lord God of hosts, O my people, that dwellest in Zion, be not afraid of Assyria: he shall smite thee with a rod, and shall lift up his staff against thee after the manner of [r]Egypt. **25** But yet a very little time, and the wrath shall be consumed, and mine anger in their destruction. **26** And the Lord of hosts shall raise up a scourge for him, according to the plague of [s]Midian in the rock Oreb: and as his staff was upon the [t]Sea, so he will lift it up after the manner of Egypt. **27** And at that day shall his burden be taken away from off thy shoulder, and his yoke from off thy neck: and the yoke shall be destroyed because of [u]the anointing. **28** He is come to [v]Aiath: he is passed into Migron: at Michmash shall he lay up his armor. **29** They have gone over the ford: they lodged in the lodging at Geba: Ramah is afraid: Gibeah of Saul is fled away. **30** Lift up thy voice, O daughter Gallim, cause Laish to hear, O poor Anathoth. **31** Madmenah is removed: the inhabitants of Gebim have gathered themselves together. **32** Yet there is a time that he will stay at Nob: he shall lift up his hand toward the mount of the daughter Zion, the hill of Jerusalem. **33** Behold, the Lord God of hosts shall cut off the [w]bough with fear, and they of high stature shall be cut off, and the high shall be humbled. **34** And he shall cut away the thick places of the forest with iron, and Lebanon shall have a mighty fall.

11

1 Christ born of the root of Jesse. 2 His virtues and kingdom. 6 The fruits of the Gospel. 10 The calling of the Gentiles.

---

suffered afterward by Shalmaneser, who carried the Israelites away captives.

c. Isa. 9:1 Whereas the Jews and Gentiles dwelt together by reason of those twenty cites, which Solomon gave to Hiram.

d. Isa. 9:2 Which were captivity in Babylon: and the Prophet speaketh of that thing which should come to pass threescore years after, as though it were now done.

e. Isa. 9:2 Meaning, the comfort of their deliverance.

f. Isa. 9:2 This captivity and deliverance were figures of our captivity by sin, and of our deliverance by Christ through the preaching of the Gospel, Matt. 4:15, 16.

g. Isa. 9:3 Their number was greater when they went into captivity, than when they returned, but their joy was greater at their return, Hag. 2:9.

h. Isa. 9:4 Thou gavest them perfect joy by delivering them, and by destroying the tyrants, that had kept them in cruel bondage, as thou didst deliver them by Gideon from the Midianites, Judg. 7:21.

i. Isa. 9:5 He speaketh of the deliverance of his Church, which he hath delivered miraculously from his enemies, but especially by the coming of Christ, of whom he prophesieth in the next verse.

j. Isa. 9:6 The author of eternity, and by whom the Church and every member thereof shall be preserved forever, and have immortal life.

k. Isa. 9:7 His singular love and care for his elect.

l. Isa. 9:8 This is another prophecy against them of Samaria, which were mockers and contemners of God's promises and menaces.

m. Isa. 9:10 We were but weak, when the enemy overcame us, but we will make ourselves so strong, that we will neither care for our enemies, nor fear God's threatenings.

n. Isa. 9:11 Rezin king of Syria, who was in league with Israel, was slain by the Assyrians, after whose death Aram, that is, the Syrians were against Israel, which on the other side were assailed by the Philistines.

o. Isa. 9:18 Wickedness as a bellows kindleth the fire of God's wrath, which consumeth all his obstinate enemies.

p. Isa. 9:19 Though there were no foreign enemy, yet they shall destroy one another.

q. Isa. 9:20 Their greediness shall be insatiable, so that one brother shall eat up another, as though he should eat his own flesh.

ISA 10

a. Isa. 10:1 Which write and pronounce a wicked sentence to oppress the poor: meaning, that the wicked magistrates, which were the chief cause of mischief, should be first punished.

b. Isa. 10:3 To wit, from Assyria.

c. Isa. 10:3 Your riches and authority, that they may be safe, and that ye may receive them again.

d. Isa. 10:4 Because they have forsaken me, some shall go into captivity, and the rest shall be slain.

e. Isa. 10:5 God calleth for the Assyrians to be the executioners of his vengeance.

f. Isa. 10:6 That is, the Assyrians against the Jews, which are but hypocrites: and in the sixth and seventh verse is declared the difference of the work of God, and of the wicked in one very thing and act: for God's intention is to chastise them for their amendment, and the Assyrians' purpose is to destroy them to enrich themselves: thus in respect of God's justice, it is God's work, but in respect of their own malice, it is the work of the devil.

g. Isa. 10:9 Seeing that I have overcome as well one city as another, so that none could resist, shall Jerusalem be able to escape mine hands?

h. Isa. 10:12 When he hath sufficiently chastised his people (for he beginneth at his own house) then will he burn the rods.

i. Isa. 10:12 Meaning of Sennacherib.

j. Isa. 10:15 Here we see that no creature is able to do anything, but as God appointeth him, and that they are all but his instruments to do his work, though the intentions be divers, as verse 6.

k. Isa. 10:17 Meaning, that God is a light to comfort his people, and a fire to burn his enemies.

l. Isa. 10:17 That is, the Assyrians.

m. Isa. 10:18 To wit, body and soul utterly.

n. Isa. 10:18 When the battle is lost and the standard taken.

o. Isa. 10:20 This is the end of God's plagues toward his, to bring them to him, and to forsake all trust in others.

p. Isa. 10:22 This small number which seemed to be consumed, and yet according to God's decree is saved, shall be sufficient to fill all the world with righteousness.

q. Isa. 10:23 God will destroy this land as he hath determined, and after save a small portion.

r. Isa. 10:24 As the Egyptians did punish thee.

s. Isa. 10:26 Read Isa. 9:4.

t. Isa. 10:26 When the Israelites passed through by the lifting up of Moses' rod, and the enemies were drowned, Exod. 14:28.

u. Isa. 10:27 Because of the promise made to that kingdom, whereby Christ's kingdom was prefigured.

v. Isa. 10:28 He describeth by what way the Assyrians should come against Jerusalem, to confirm the faithful, when it should come to pass, that as their plague was come, so should they be delivered.

w. Isa. 10:33 Fear and destruction shall come upon Judah for the princes and the people shall be all led away captives.

ISA 11

a. Isa. 11:1 Because the captivity of Babylon was a figure of the spiritual captivity under sin, he showeth that our true

1 But there shall come a [a]rod forth of the stock of Jesse, and a grass shall grow out of his roots. **2** And the Spirit of the Lord shall rest upon him: the Spirit of wisdom and understanding, the Spirit of counsel and strength, the Spirit of knowledge, and of the fear of the Lord, **3** And shall make him prudent in the fear of the Lord: for he shall not judge after the sight of his eyes, neither reprove by the hearing of his ears. **4** But with righteousness shall he judge the poor, and with equity shall he reprove for the meek of the earth: and he shall [b]smite the earth with the rod of his mouth, and with the breath of his lips shall he slay the wicked. **5** And justice shall be the girdle of his loins, and faithfulness the girdle of his reins. **6** The [c]wolf also shall dwell with the lamb, and the leopard shall lie with the kid, and the calf, and the lion, and the fat beast together, and a little child shall lead them. **7** And the cow and the bear shall feed: their young ones shall lie together: and the lion shall eat straw like the bullock. **8** And the sucking child shall play upon the hole of the asp, and the weaned child shall put his hand upon the cockatrice hole. **9** Then shall none hurt nor destroy in all the mountain of mine holiness: for the earth shall be full of the knowledge of the Lord, as [d]the waters that cover the sea. **10** And in that day the root of Jesse, which shall stand up for a sign unto the [e]people, the nations shall seek unto it, and his [f]rest shall be glorious. **11** And in the same day shall the Lord stretch out his hand [g]again the second time, to possess the remnant of his people, (which shall be left) of Assyria, and of Egypt, and of Pathros, and of Ethiopia, and of Elam, and of Shinar, and of Hamath, and of the isles of the sea. **12** And he shall set up a sign to the nations, and assemble the dispersed of Israel, and gather the scattered of Judah from the four corners of the world. **13** The hatred also of Ephraim shall depart, and the adversaries of Judah shall be cut off: Ephraim shall not envy [h]Judah, neither shall Judah vex Ephraim: **14** But they shall flee upon the shoulders of the Philistines toward the West: they shall spoil them of the East together: Edom and Moab shall be the stretching out of their hands, and the children of Ammon in their obedience. **15** The Lord also shall utterly destroy the [i]tongue of the Egyptian's sea, and with his mighty wind shall lift up his hand [j]over the river, and shall smite him in his seven streams, and cause men to walk therein with shoes. **16** And there shall be a path to the remnant of his people which are left of Assyria, like as it was unto Israel in the day that he came up out of the land of Egypt.

12

A thanksgiving of the faithful for the mercies of God.

1 And thou [a]shalt say in that day, O Lord, I will praise thee: though thou wast angry with me, thy wrath is turned away, and thou comfortest me. **2** Behold, God is my [b]salvation: I will trust, and will not fear: for the Lord God is [1]my strength and song: he is also become my salvation. **3** Therefore with joy shall ye [c]draw waters out of the wells of salvation. **4** And ye shall say in that day, [2]Praise the Lord: call upon his Name: declare his works among the people: make mention of them, for his Name is exalted. **5** Sing unto the Lord, for he hath done excellent things: this is known in all the world. **6** Cry out, and shout, [d]O inhabitant of Zion: for great is the Holy one of Israel in the midst of thee.

13

The Medes and Persians shall destroy Babylon.

1 The [a]burden of Babel, which Isaiah the son of Amoz did see. **2** Lift up a standard upon the high mountain: lift up the voice unto them: wag the [b]hand, that they may go into the gates of the nobles. **3** I have commanded them, that I have [c]sanctified: and I have called the mighty to my wrath, and them that rejoice in my [d]glory. **4** The noise of a multitude is in the mountains like a great people: a tumultuous voice of the kingdoms of the nations gathered together: the Lord of hosts numbereth the host of the battle. **5** They come from a far country, from the end of the heaven: even the Lord with the [e]weapons of his wrath to destroy the whole land. **6** Howl [f]you, for the day of the Lord is at hand: it shall come as a destroyer from the Almighty. **7** Therefore shall all hands be weakened, and all men's hearts shall melt. **8** And they shall be afraid: anguish and sorrow shall take them, and they shall have pain, as a woman that travaileth: everyone shall be amazed at his neighbor, and their faces shall be like [g]flames of fire. **9** Behold, the day of the Lord cometh, cruel, with wrath and fierce anger to lay the land waste: and he shall destroy the sinners out of it. **10** For the [h]stars of heaven and the planets thereof shall not give their light: the sun shall be darkened in his going forth, and the moon shall not cause her light to shine. **11** And I will visit the wickedness upon the [i]world, and their iniquity upon the wicked, and I will cause the arrogancy of the [j]proud to cease, and will cast down the pride of tyrants. **12** I will make a [k]man more precious than fine gold, even a man above the wedge of gold of Ophir. **13** Therefore I will shake the heaven, and the earth shall remove out of her place in the wrath of the Lord of hosts, and in the day of his fierce anger. **14** And [l]it shall be as a chased Doe, and as a sheep that no man taketh up; every man shall turn to his own people, and flee each one to his own land. **15** Everyone that is found, shall be stricken through: and whosoever joineth himself, shall fall by the sword. **16** [1]Their [m]children also shall be broken in pieces before their eyes: their houses shall be spoiled; and their wives ravished. **17** Behold, I will stir up the Medes against them, which shall not regard silver, nor be desirous of gold. **18** With bows also shall they destroy the children, and shall have no compassion upon the fruit of the womb, and their eyes shall not spare the children. **19** And Babel the glory of kingdoms, the beauty and pride of the Chaldeans, shall be as the destruction of God [2]in Sodom and Gomorrah. **20** It shall not be inhabited forever, neither shall it be dwelled in from generation to generation: neither shall the [n]Arabian pitch his tents there, neither shall their shepherds make their folds there. **21** But [o]Zijm shall lodge there, and their houses shall be full of Ohim: Ostriches shall dwell there, and the Satyrs shall dance there. **22** And Iim shall cry in their palaces, and dragons in their pleasant palaces: and the time thereof is ready to come, and the days thereof shall not be prolonged.

14

1 The return of the people from captivity. 4 The derision of the King of Babylon. 11 The death of the king. 29 The destruction of the Philistines.

1 For [a]the Lord will have compassion of Jacob, and will yet choose Israel, and cause them to rest in their own land: and the stranger [b]shall join himself unto them, and they shall cleave to the house of Jacob. **2** And the people shall receive them and bring them to their own place, and the house of Israel shall possess them in the land of the Lord, for [c]servants and handmaids: and they shall take them prisoners, whose captives they were, and have rule over their oppressors. **3** And in that day when the Lord shall give thee rest from thy sorrow, and from thy fear, and from the sore bondage, wherein thou didst serve, **4** Then shalt thou take up this proverb against the King of Babel, and say, How hath the oppressor ceased? and the gold thirsty Babel rested? **5** The Lord hath broken the rod of the wicked,

---

deliverance must come by Christ: for as David came out of Jesse a man without dignity, so Christ should come of a poor carpenter's house as out of a dead stock, Isa. 53:2.

b. Isa. 11:4 All these properties can agree to none, but only unto Christ: for it is he that toucheth the hearts of the faithful, and mortifieth their concupiscences: and to the wicked he is the savor of death, and to them that shall perish: so that all the world shall be smitten with his rod, which is his word.

c. Isa. 11:6 Men because of their wicked affections are named by the names of beasts, wherein the like affections reign: but Christ by his Spirit shall reform them, and work in them such mutual charity, that they shall be like lambs, favoring and loving one another, and cast off all their cruel affections, Isa. 65:25.

d. Isa. 11:9 It shall be in as great abundance as the waters in the sea.

e. Isa. 11:10 He prophesieth of the calling of the Gentiles.

f. Isa. 11:10 That is, the Church, which he also calleth his rest, Ps. 132:14.

g. Isa. 11:11 For God first delivered his people out of Egypt, and now promiseth to deliver them out of their enemies' hands as from the Parthians, Persians, Chaldeans, and them of Antiochia, among whom they were dispersed: and this is chiefly meant of Christ, who calleth his people being dispersed through all the world.

h. Isa. 11:13 Here he describeth the consent that shall be in his Church, and their victory against their enemies.

i. Isa. 11:15 Meaning, a corner of the sea, that entereth into the land, and hath the form of a tongue.

j. Isa. 11:15 To wit, Nile, the great river of Egypt, which entereth into the sea with seven streams.

ISA 12

a. Isa. 12:1 He showeth how the Church shall praise God, when they are delivered from their captivity.

b. Isa. 12:2 Our salvation standeth only in God, who giveth us an assured confidence, constancy, and occasion, to praise him for the same.

c. Isa. 12:3 The graces of God shall be so abundant, that ye may receive them in as great plenty, as waters out of a fountain that is full.

d. Isa. 12:6 Ye that are of the Church.

ISA 12

1. Exod. 15:2 / Ps. 118:14 **2.** 1Chron. 16:8

ISA 13

a. Isa. 13:1 That is, the great calamity, which was prophesied to come on Babel, as a most grievous burden, which they were not able to bear. In these twelve chapters following, he speaketh of the plagues wherewith God would smite the strange nations (whom they knew) to declare that God chastised the Israelites as his children, and these others as his enemies: and also if that God spare not these that are ignorant, that they must not think strange, if he punish them which have knowledge of his Law, and keep it not.

b. Isa. 13:2 To wit, the Medes and Persians.

c. Isa. 13:3 That is, prepared and appointed to execute my judgments.

d. Isa. 13:3 Which willingly go about to the work whereunto I appoint them, but how the wicked do this, read Isa. 10:6.

e. Isa. 13:5 The army of the Medes and the Persians against Babylon.

f. Isa. 13:6 Ye Babylonians.

g. Isa. 13:8 The Babylonians' anger and grief shall be so much, that their faces shall burn as fire.

h. Isa. 13:10 They that are overcome shall think that all the powers of heaven and earth are against them, Ezek. 32:7; Joel 3:15; Matt. 24:29.

i. Isa. 13:11 He compareth Babylon to the whole world, because they so esteemed themselves by reason of their great empire.

j. Isa. 13:11 He noteth the principal vice, whereunto they are most given, as are all that abound in wealth.

k. Isa. 13:12 He noteth the great slaughter that shall be, seeing the enemy shall neither for gold, or silver spare a man's life, as verse 17.

l. Isa. 13:14 Meaning, the power of Babylon with their hired soldiers.

m. Isa. 13:16 This was not accomplished when Cyrus took Babylon, but after the death of Alexander the great.

n. Isa. 13:20 Who useth to go from country to country to find pasture for their beasts, but there shall they find none.

o. Isa. 13:21 Which were either wild beasts, or fowls, or wicked spirits, whereby Satan deluded man, as by the fairies, goblins, and such like fantasies.

ISA 13

1. Ps. 137:9 **2.** Gen. 19:24 / Jer. 50:40

ISA 14

a. Isa. 14:1 He showeth why God will haste to destroy his enemies, to wit, because he will deliver his Church.

b. Isa. 14:1 Meaning, that the Gentiles shalt be joined with the Church, and worship God.

c. Isa. 14:2 Signifying, that the Jews should be superiors to the Gentiles, and that they should be brought under the service of Christ by the preaching of the Apostles, whereby all are brought to the subjection of Christ, 2 Cor. 10:5.

and the scepter of the rulers: **6** Which smote the people in anger with a continual plague, and ruled the nations in wrath: if any were persecuted, he did [d]not let. **7** The whole world is at [e]rest and is quiet: they sing for joy. **8** Also the fir trees rejoiced of thee, and the cedars of Lebanon, saying, Since thou art laid down, no hewer came up against us. **9** Hell beneath is moved for thee to [f]meet thee at thy coming, raising up the dead for thee, even all the princes of the earth, and hath raised from their thrones all the Kings of the nations. **10** All they shall cry and say unto thee, Art thou become weak also as we? art thou become like unto us? **11** Thy pomp is brought down to the grave, and the sound of the viols: the worm [g]is spread under thee, and the worms cover thee. **12** How art thou fallen from heaven, O [h]Lucifer, son of the morning? and cut down to the ground, which didst cast lots upon the nations? **13** Yet thou saidest in thine heart, I will ascend into heaven, and exalt my throne above beside the stars of God: I will sit also upon the mount of the congregation in the sides of the [i]North. **14** I will ascend above the height of the clouds, and I will be like the most high. **15** But thou shalt be brought down to the grave, to the side of the pit. **16** They that see thee, shall [j]look upon thee and consider thee, saying, Is this the man that made the earth to tremble, and that did shake the kingdoms? **17** He made the world as a wilderness, and destroyed the cities thereof, and opened not [k]the house of his prisoners. **18** All the kings of the nations, even they all sleep in glory, everyone in his own house. **19** But thou art [l]cast out of thy grave like an abominable branch: like the raiment of those that are slain, and thrust through with a sword, which go down to the stones of the pit, as a carcass trodden under feet. **20** Thou shalt not be joined with them in the grave, because thou hast destroyed thine own land, and slain thy people: the seed of the wicked shall not be renowned forever. **21** [m]Prepare a slaughter for his children, for the iniquity of their fathers: let them not rise up nor possess the land, nor fill the face of the world with enemies. **22** For I will rise up against them (saith the Lord of hosts) and will cut off from Babel the name and the remnant, and the son, and the nephew, saith the Lord: **23** And I will make it a possession to the [n]hedgehog, and pools of water, and I will sweep it with the besom of destruction, saith the Lord of hosts. **24** The Lord of hosts hath sworn, saying, Surely like as I have purposed, so shall it come to pass, and as I have consulted, it shall stand: **25** [o]That I will break to pieces Assyria in my land, and upon my mountains will I tread him under foot, so that his yoke shall depart from [p]them, and his burden shall be taken from off their shoulder. **26** This is the counsel that is consulted upon the whole world, and this is the hand stretched out over all the nations, **27** Because the Lord of hosts hath determined, and who shall disannul it? and his hand is stretched out, and who shall turn it away? **28** In the year that king Ahaz died, was this [q]burden. **29** Rejoice not, (thou whole [r]Philistia) because the rod of him that did beat thee is broken: for out of the serpent's root shall come forth a cockatrice, and the fruit thereof shall be a fiery flying serpent. **30** For the [s]first born of the poor shall be fed, and the needy shall lie down in safety: and I will kill thy root with famine, and [t]it shall slay thy remnant. **31** Howl, O gate, cry, O city: thou whole land of Philistia art dissolved, for there shall come from the [u]North a smoke, and none shall be [v]alone, at his time appointed. **32** What shall then one answer the [w]messengers of the Gentiles? that the Lord hath stablished [x]Zion, and the poor of his people shall trust in it.

15

A prophecy against Moab.

1 The [a]burden of Moab. Surely [b]Ar of Moab was destroyed, and brought to silence in a night: surely Kir of Moab was destroyed, and brought to silence in a night. **2** [c]He shall go up to the Temple, and to Dibon to the high places to weep: for [d]Nebo and for Medeba shall Moab howl: upon all [e]their heads shall be baldness, and every beard shaven. **3** In their streets shall they be girded with sackcloth: on the tops of their houses, and in their streets everyone shall howl, and come down with weeping. **4** And Heshbon shall cry, and Elealeh: their voice shall be heard unto Jahaz: therefore the warriors of Moab shall shout: the soul of everyone shall lament in himself. **5** Mine [f]heart shall cry for Moab: his fugitives shall flee unto Zoar, [g]an heifer of three years old: for they shall go up with weeping by the mounting up of Luhith: and by the way of Horonaim they [h]shall raise up a cry of destruction. **6** For the waters of Nimrim shall be dried up: therefore the grass is withered, the herbs consumed, and there was no green herb. **7** Therefore what every man hath left, and their substance shall they bear to the [i]brook of the willows. **8** For the cry went round about the borders of Moab, and the howling thereof unto Eglaim, and the skriking thereof unto Beer Elim, **9** Because the waters of Dimon shall be full [j]of blood: for I will bring more upon Dimon, even lions [k]upon him that escapeth of Moab, and to the remnant of the land.

16

The causes wherefore the Moabites are destroyed.

1 Send [a]ye a lamb to the ruler of the world from the rock of the wilderness, unto the mountain of the daughter Zion. **2** For it shall be as a bird that [b]flieth, and a nest forsaken: the daughters of Moab shall be at the fords of Arnon. **3** Gather a counsel, execute judgment, [c]make thy shadow as the night in the midday: hide them that are chased out: bewray not him that is fled. **4** Let my banished dwell with thee: Moab, be thou their covert from the face of the destroyer: for the extortioner [d]shall end: the destroyer shall be consumed, and the oppressor shall cease out of the land. **5** And in mercy shall the throne be prepared, [e]and he shall sit upon it in steadfastness, in the tabernacle of David, judging, and seeking judgment, and hasting justice. **6** We have heard of the pride of Moab (he is very proud) even his pride, and his arrogancy, and his indignation, but his [f]lies shall not be so. **7** Therefore shall Moab howl unto Moab, everyone shall howl: for the foundations of Kir Hareseth shall ye mourn, yet they shall be [g]stricken. **8** For the vineyards of Heshbon are cut down, and the vine of Sibmah: [h]the lords of the heathen have broken the principal vines thereof: they are come unto [i]Jazer: they wandered in the wilderness: her goodly branches stretched out themselves, and went over the sea. **9** Therefore will [j]I weep with the weeping of Jazer, and of the vine of Sibmah, O Heshbon: and Elealeh, I will make thee drunk with my tears, because upon thy summer fruits, and upon thy harvest [k]a shouting is fallen. **10** And gladness is taken away, and joy out of the plentiful field: and in the vineyards shall be no singing nor shouting for joy: the treader shall not tread wine in the wine presses: I have caused the rejoicing to cease. **11** Wherefore, my [l]bowels shall sound like an harp for Moab, and mine inward parts for Kir Heres. **12** And when it shall appear that Moab shall be weary of his high places, then shall he come to his [m]temple to pray, but he shall not prevail. **13** This is the word that the Lord hath spoken against Moab since that time. **14** And now the Lord hath spoken, saying, [n]In three years as the years of an [o]hireling, and the glory of Moab shall be contemned in all the great multitude, and the remnant shall be very small and feeble.

---

d. Isa. 14:6 That is, he suffered all violence and injuries to be done.
e. Isa. 14:7 Meaning, that when tyrants reign, there can be no rest nor quietness, and also how detestable a thing tyranny is, seeing the insensible creatures have occasion to rejoice at their destruction.
f. Isa. 14:9 As though they feared, lest thou shouldest trouble the dead, as thou didst the living: and here he derideth the proud tyranny of the wicked, which know not that all creatures wish their destruction, that they may rejoice.
g. Isa. 14:11 Instead of thy costly carpets and coverings.
h. Isa. 14:12 Thou that thoughtest thyself most glorious, and as it were placed in the heaven: for the morning star that goeth before the sun, is called Lucifer, to whom Nebuchadnezzar is compared.
i. Isa. 14:13 Meaning, Jerusalem, whereof the Temple was of the North side, Ps. 48:2, whereby he meaneth that tyrants fight against God, when they persecute his Church, and would set themselves in his place.
j. Isa. 14:16 In marveling at thee.
k. Isa. 14:17 To set them at liberty: noting his cruelty.
l. Isa. 14:19 Thou wast not buried in the sepulchre of thy fathers, thy tyranny was so abhorred.
m. Isa. 14:21 He called to the Medes and Persians, and all those that should execute God's vengeance.
n. Isa. 14:23 Or, tortoise.
o. Isa. 14:25 As I have begun to destroy the Assyrians in Sennacherib: so will I continue, and destroy them wholly, when I shall deliver you from Babylon.
p. Isa. 14:25 From the Jews.
q. Isa. 14:28 Read Isa. 13:1.
r. Isa. 14:29 He willeth the Philistines not to rejoice because the Jews are diminished in their power, for their strength shall be greater than ever it was.
s. Isa. 14:30 The Israelites, which were brought to most extreme misery.
t. Isa. 14:30 To wit, my people.
u. Isa. 14:31 That is, from the Jews or Assyrians: for they were brought to most extreme misery.
v. Isa. 14:31 But they shall be all ready, and join together.
w. Isa. 14:32 Which shall come to inquire of the state of the Church.
x. Isa. 14:32 They shall answer that the Lord doth defend his Church, and them that join themselves thereunto.

ISA 15

a. Isa. 15:1 Read Isa. 13:1.
b. Isa. 15:1 The chief city, whereby the whole country was meant.
c. Isa. 15:2 The Moabites shall flee to their idols for succor, but it shall be too late.
d. Isa. 15:2 Which were cites of Moab.
e. Isa. 15:2 For as in the west parts the people used to let their hair grow long, when they mourned, so in the East part they cut it off.
f. Isa. 15:5 The Prophet speaketh this in the person of the Moabites: or as one that felt the great judgment of God that God should come upon them.
g. Isa. 15:5 Meaning, that it was a city that ever lived in pleasure, and never felt sorrow.
h. Isa. 15:5 He describeth the miserable dissipation and flight of the Moabites.
i. Isa. 15:7 To hide themselves, and their goods there.
j. Isa. 15:9 Of them that are slain.
k. Isa. 15:9 So that by no means they should escape the hand of God: thus will God punish the enemies of his Church.

ISA 16

a. Isa. 16:1 That is, offer a sacrifice, whereby he derideth their long delay, which would not repent when the Lord called them, showing them that it is now too late, seeing the vengeance of God is upon them.
b. Isa. 16:2 There is no remedy, but you must flee.
c. Isa. 16:3 He showeth what Moab should have done, when Israel their neighbor was in affliction, to whom because they would give no shadow nor comfort, they are now left comfortless.
d. Isa. 16:4 The Assyrians shall oppress the Israelites, but for a while.
e. Isa. 16:5 Meaning, Christ.
f. Isa. 16:6 Their vain confidence, and proud brags shall deceive them, Jer. 48:2.
g. Isa. 16:7 For all your mourning, yet the city shall be destroyed, even unto the foundation.
h. Isa. 16:8 That is, the Assyrians and other enemies.
i. Isa. 16:8 Meaning, that the country of Moab was now destroyed, and all the precious things thereof were carried into the borders, yea into other countries, and over the sea.
j. Isa. 16:9 He showeth that their plague was so great, that it would have moved any man to lament with them, as Ps. 141:5.
k. Isa. 16:9 The enemies are come upon thee, and shout for joy, when they carry thy commodities from thee, as Jer. 48:33.
l. Isa. 16:11 For very sorrow and compassion.
m. Isa. 16:12 They shall use all means to seek help of their idols, and all in vain: for Chemosh their great god shall not be able to help them.

17

1 A prophecy of the destruction of Damascus and Ephraim, 7 calamity moveth to repentance.

1 The [a]burden of [b]Damascus. Behold, Damascus is taken away from being a city, for it shall be a ruinous heap. **2** The cities of [c]Aroer shall be forsaken: they shall be for the flocks: for they shall lie there, and none shall make them afraid. **3** The munition also shall cease from [d]Ephraim, and the kingdom from Damascus, and the remnant of Aram shall be as the [e]glory of the children of Israel, saith the Lord of hosts. **4** And in that day the glory of [f]Jacob shall be made clean. **5** And it shall be as when the harvest man gathereth [g]the corn, and reapeth the ears with his arm, and he shall be as he that gathereth the ears in the valley of [h]Rephaim. **6** Yet a gathering of grapes shall [i]be left in it: as the shaking of an olive tree, two or three berries are in the top of the upmost boughs, and four or five in the high branches of the fruit thereof, saith the Lord God of Israel. **7** At that day shall a man look to his [j]maker, and his eyes shall look to the holy one of Israel. **8** And he shall not look to the altars, the works of his own hands, neither shall he look to those things which his own fingers have made, as groves and images. **9** In that day shall the cities of their strength be as the forsaking of boughs and branches, which [k]they did forsake, because of the children of Israel, and there shall be desolation. **10** Because thou hast forgotten the God of thy salvation, and hast not remembered the God of thy strength, therefore shalt thou set pleasant plants, and shalt graft strange [l]vine branches. **11** In the day shalt thou make thy plant to grow, and in the morning shalt thou make thy seed to flourish: but the harvest shall be gone in the day [m]of possession, and there shall be desperate sorrow. **12** [n]Ah, the multitude of many people, they shall make a sound like the noise of the sea: for the noise of the people shall make a sound like the noise of mighty waters. **13** The people shall make a sound like the noise of many waters: but God shall [o]rebuke them, and they shall flee far off, and shall be chased as the chaff of the mountains before the wind, and as a rolling thing before the whirlwind. **14** And lo, in the evening there is [p]trouble: but afore the morning it is gone. This is the portion of them that spoil us, and the lot of them that rob us.

18

1 Of the enemies of the Church. 7 And of the vocation of the Gentiles.

1 Oh, the [a]land shadowing with wings, which is beyond the rivers of Ethiopia, **2** Sending ambassadors by the sea, even in vessels of [b]reeds upon the waters, saying, [c]Go, ye swift messengers, to a nation that is scattered abroad, and spoiled, unto a terrible [d]people from their beginning even hitherto: a nation by little and little even trodden under foot: whose land the [e]floods have spoiled. **3** All ye the inhabitants of the world, and dwellers in the earth, shall see when [f]he setteth up a sign in the mountains, and when he bloweth the trumpet, ye shall hear. **4** For so the Lord said unto me, I will [g]rest and behold in my tabernacle, as [h]the heat drying up the rain, and as a cloud of dew in the heat of harvest. **5** For afore the harvest, when the flour is finished, and the fruit is ripening in the flour, then he shall cut down the branches with hooks, and shall take away, and cut off the boughs: **6** They shall be left together unto the fowls of the mountains, and to the [i]beasts of the earth: for the fowl shall summer upon it, and every beast of the earth shall winter upon it. **7** At that time shall a [j]present be brought unto the Lord of hosts (a people that is scattered abroad, and spoiled, and of a terrible people from their beginning hitherto, a nation by little and little even trodden under foot, whose land the rivers have spoiled) to the place of the name of the Lord of hosts, even the mount Zion.

19

1 The destruction of the Egyptians by the Assyrians. 18 Of their conversion to the Lord.

1 The [a]burden of Egypt. Behold, the Lord [b]rideth upon a swift cloud, and shall come into Egypt, and the idols of Egypt shall be moved at his presence, and the heart of Egypt shall melt in the midst of her. **2** And I will set the Egyptians against the Egyptians: so everyone shall [c]fight against his brother, and everyone against his neighbor, city against city, and kingdom against kingdom. **3** And the [d]spirit of Egypt shall fail in the midst of her, and I will destroy their counsel, and they shall seek at the idols, and at the sorcerers, and at them that have spirits of divination, and at the soothsayers. **4** And I will deliver the Egyptians into the hand of the cruel lords, and a mighty king shall rule over them, saith the Lord God of hosts. **5** Then the waters of the sea shall [e]fail, and the river shall be dried up, and wasted. **6** And the [f]rivers shall go far away: the rivers of defense shall be emptied and dried up: the reeds and flags shall be cut down. **7** The grass in the river, and at the [g]head of the rivers, and all that groweth by the river shall wither, and be driven away, and be no more. **8** The fishers also shall [h]mourn, and all they that cast angle into the river, shall lament, and they that spread their net upon the waters, shall be weakened. **9** Moreover, they that work in flax of divers sorts, shall be confounded, and they that weave nets. **10** For their nets shall be broken, and all they that make ponds shall be heavy in heart. **11** Surely the princes of [i]Zoan are fools: the counsel of the wise counselors of Pharaoh, is become foolish: how say ye unto Pharaoh, I [j]am the son of the wise? I am the son of the ancient kings? **12** Where are now the wise men, that they may tell thee, or may know what the Lord of hosts hath determined against Egypt? **13** The princes of Zoan are become fools: the princes of [k]Noph are deceived, they have deceived Egypt, even the [l]corners of the tribes thereof. **14** The Lord hath mingled among them the spirits [m]of errors: and they have caused Egypt to err in every work thereof, as a drunken man erreth in his vomit. **15** Neither shall there be any work in Egypt, which the head may [n]do, nor the tail, the branch nor the rush. **16** In that day shall Egypt be like unto women: for it shall be afraid and fear because of the moving of the hand of the Lord of hosts, which he shaketh over it. **17** And the land of Judah shall be a fear [o]unto Egypt: everyone that maketh mention of it, shall be afraid thereat, because of the counsel of the Lord of hosts, which he hath determined upon it. **18** In that day shall five cities in the land of Egypt [p]speak the language of Canaan, and shall [q]swear by the Lord of hosts: one shall be called the city of [r]destruction. **19** In that day shall the altar of the Lord be in the midst of the

---

n. Isa. 16:14 He appointed a certain time to punish the enemies in.
o. Isa. 16:14 Who will observe justly the time for the which he is hired, and serve no longer, but will ever long for it.

ISA 17

a. Isa. 17:1 Read Isa. 13:1.
b. Isa. 17:1 The chief city of Syria.
c. Isa. 17:2 It was a country of Syria by the river Arnon.
d. Isa. 17:3 It seemeth that the Prophet would comfort the Church in declaring the destruction of these two kings of Syria and Israel, when as they had conspired the overthrow of Judah.
e. Isa. 17:3 The ten tribes gloried in their multitude and alliance with other nations: therefore he saith that they shall be brought down, and the Syrians also.
f. Isa. 17:4 Meaning, of the ten tribes, which boasted themselves of their nobility, prosperity, strength and multitude.
g. Isa. 17:5 As the abundance of corn doth not fear the harvest men that should cut it down: no more shall the multitude of Israel make the enemies to shrink, whom God shall appoint to destroy them.
h. Isa. 17:5 Which valley was plentiful and fertile.
i. Isa. 17:6 Because God would have his covenant stable, he promiseth to reserve some of this people, and to bring them to repentance.
j. Isa. 17:7 He showeth that God's corrections ever bring forth some fruit, and cause his to turn from their sins, and to humble themselves to him.
k. Isa. 17:9 As the Canaanites left their cities when God did place the Israelites there, so the cities of Israel shall no more be able to defend their inhabitants than bushes, when God shall send the enemy to plague them.
l. Isa. 17:10 Which are excellent, and brought out of other countries.
m. Isa. 17:11 As the Lord threateneth the wicked in his Law, Lev. 26:16.
n. Isa. 17:12 The Prophet lamenteth, considering the horrible plague that was prepared against Israel by the Assyrians, which were infinite in number, and gathered of many nations.
o. Isa. 17:13 He addeth this for the consolation of the faithful which were in Israel.
p. Isa. 17:14 He compareth the enemies the Assyrians to a tempest, which riseth overnight, and in the morning is gone.

ISA 18

a. Isa. 18:1 He meaneth that part of Ethiopia, which lieth toward the sea, which was so full of ships that the sails (which he compareth to wings) seemed to shadow the sea.
b. Isa. 18:2 Which in those countries were great, insomuch as they made ships of them for swiftness.
c. Isa. 18:2 This may be taken, that they sent others to comfort the Jews, and to promise them help against their enemies, and so the Lord did threaten to take away their strength, that the Jews should not trust therein: or that they did solicit the Egyptians, and promised them aid to go against Judah.
d. Isa. 18:2 To wit, the Jews, who because of God's plague, made all other nations afraid of the like, as God threatened, Deut. 28:37.
e. Isa. 18:2 Meaning, the Assyrians, as Isa. 8:7.
f. Isa. 18:3 When the Lord prepared to fight against the Ethiopians.
g. Isa. 18:4 I will stay a while from punishing the wicked.
h. Isa. 18:4 Which two seasons are most profitable for the ripening of fruits, whereby he meaneth, that he will seem to favor them, and give them abundance for a time, but he will suddenly cut them off.
i. Isa. 18:6 Not only men shall contemn them, but the brute beasts.
j. Isa. 18:7 Meaning, that God will pity his Church, and receive that little remnant as an offering unto himself.

ISA 19

a. Isa. 19:1 Read Isa. 13:7.
b. Isa. 19:1 Because the Egyptians trusted in the defense of their country, in the multitude of their idols, and in the valiantness of their men, the Lord showeth that he will come over all their munitions in a swift cloud, and that their idols shall tremble at his coming and that men's hearts shall faint.
c. Isa. 19:2 As he caused the Ammonites, Moabites and Idumeans to kill one another, when they came to destroy the Church of God, 2 Chron. 20:22; Isa. 49:26.
d. Isa. 19:3 Meaning, their policy and wisdom.
e. Isa. 19:5 He showeth that the sea and Nile their great river, whereby they thought themselves most sure, should not be able to defend them from his anger, but that he would send the Assyrians among them, that should keep them under as slaves.
f. Isa. 19:6 For the Nile ran into the sea by seven streams, as though they were so many rivers.
g. Isa. 19:7 The Hebrew word is mouth, whereby they mean the spring out of the which the water gusheth as out of a mouth.
h. Isa. 19:8 The Scriptures used to describe the destruction of a country by taking away of the commodities thereof, as by vines, flesh, fish, and such other things, whereby countries are enriched.
i. Isa. 19:11 Called also Tanis, a famous city upon the Nile.
j. Isa. 19:11 He noteth the flatterers of Pharaoh: who persuaded the king that he was wise and noble, and that his house was most ancient, and so he flattered himself, saying, I am wise.
k. Isa. 19:13 Or, Memphis, others Alexandria, and now called the great Cairo.
l. Isa. 19:13 The principal upholders thereof are the chiefest cause of their destruction.
m. Isa. 19:14 For the spirit of wisdom he hath made them drunken and giddy with the spirit of error.
n. Isa. 19:15 Neither the great nor the small, the strong nor the weak.
o. Isa. 19:17 Considering that through their occasion the Jews made not God their defense: but put their trust in them, and were therefore now punished, they shall fear lest the like light upon them.
p. Isa. 19:18 Shall make one confession of faith with the people of God: by the speech of Canaan, meaning the language wherein God was then served.
q. Isa. 19:18 Shall renounce their superstitions and protest to serve God aright.
r. Isa. 19:18 Meaning, of six cities, five should serve God, and the sixth remain in their wickedness: and so of the sixth part there should be but one lost.

land of Egypt, and [s]a pillar by the border thereof unto the Lord. **20** And it shall be for a sign and for a witness unto the Lord of hosts in the land of Egypt: for they shall cry unto the Lord, because of the oppressors, and he shall send them [t]a Savior, and a great man, and shall deliver them. **21** And the Lord shall be known of the Egyptians, and the Egyptians shall know the Lord in that day, and do [u]sacrifice and oblation, and shall vow vows unto the Lord, and perform them. **22** So the Lord shall smite Egypt, he shall smite and heal it: for he shall return unto the Lord, and he shall be entreated of them and shall heal them. **23** In that day shall there be a path from [v]Egypt to Assyria, and Assyria shall come into Egypt, and Egypt into Assyria: so the Egyptians shall worship with Assyria. **24** In that day shall Israel be the third with Egypt and Assyria: even a blessing in the midst of the land. **25** For the Lord of hosts shall bless it, saying, Blessed be my people Egypt and Assyria, the work of mine hands, and Israel mine inheritance.

20

2 The three years captivity of Egypt and Ethiopia described by the three years going naked of Isaiah.

1 In the year that [a]Tartan came to [b]Ashdod, (when [c]Sargon king of Assyria sent him) and had fought against Ashdod, and taken it, **2** At the same time spake the Lord by the hand of Isaiah the son of Amoz, saying, Go, and loose the [d]sackcloth from thy loins, and put off thy shoe from thy foot. And he did so, walking naked and barefoot. **3** And the Lord said, Like as my servant Isaiah hath walked naked and barefoot three years as a sign and wonder upon Egypt, and Ethiopia, **4** So shall the king of Assyria take away the captivity of Egypt, and the captivity of Ethiopia, both young men and old men, naked and barefoot, with their buttocks uncovered, to the shame of Egypt. **5** And they shall fear, and be ashamed of [e]Ethiopia their expectation, and of Egypt their [f]glory. **6** Then shall the inhabitants of this [g]isle say in that day, Behold, such is our expectation, whither we fled for help to be delivered from the king of Assyria, and how shall we be delivered?

21

1 Of the destruction of Babylon by the Persians and Medes. 11 The ruin of Idumea, 13 and of Arabia.

1 The burden of the [a]desert sea. As the whirlwinds in the South used to pass from the wilderness, so shall it [b]come from the horrible land. **2** A grievous vision was showed unto me, The [c]Transgressor against a transgressor, and the destroyer against a destroyer. Go up [d]Elam, besiege Media: I have caused all the mourning [e]thereof to cease. **3** Therefore are my [f]loins filled with sorrow: sorrows have taken me as the sorrows of a woman that travaileth: I was bowed down when I heard it, and I was amazed when I saw it. **4** Mine heart failed: fearfulness troubled me: the night [g]of my pleasures hath he turned into fear unto me. **5** Prepare thou the table: watch in the watch tower: eat, drink: [h]arise, ye princes, anoint the shield: **6** For thus hath the [i]Lord said unto me, Go, set a watchman, to tell what he seeth. **7** And he saw a chariot with two horsemen: [j]a chariot of an ass, and a chariot of a camel: and he hearkened and took diligent heed. **8** And he cried, A [k]lion: my Lord, I stand continually upon the watch tower in the daytime, and I am set in my watch every night: **9** And behold, this man's chariot cometh with two horsemen. And [l]he answered and said, [1]Babel is fallen: it is fallen, and all the images of her gods hath he broken unto the ground. **10** O [m]my threshing, and the [n]corn of my floor. That which I have heard of the Lord of hosts the God of Israel, have I showed unto you. **11** The burden of [o]Dumah, he calleth unto me out of [p]Seir, Watchman, what was in the night? Watchman, what was in the night? **12** The watchman said, The [q]morning cometh, and also the night. If ye will as he, inquire: return and come. **13** The burden against Arabia. In [r]the forest of Arabia shall ye tarry all night, even in the ways of Dedanites. **14** O inhabitants of the land of Tema, bring forth [s]water to meet the thirsty, and prevent him that fleeth with his bread. **15** For they flee from the drawn swords, even from the drawn sword, and from the bent bow, and from the grievousness of war. **16** For thus hath the Lord said unto me, Yet a year [t]according to the years of an [u]hireling, and all the glory of Kedar shall fail. **17** And the residue of the number of the strong archers of the sons of [v]Kedar shall be few: for the Lord God of Israel hath spoken it.

22

1 He prophesieth of the destruction of Jerusalem by Nebuchadnezzar. 15 A threatening against Shebna. 20 To whose office Eliakim is preferred.

1 The burden of the [a]valley of vision. What [b]aileth thee now that thou art wholly gone up unto the house tops? **2** Thou that art full of [c]noise, a city full of brute, a joyous city, thy slain men shall not be slain [d]with sword, nor die in battle. **3** All thy princes shall flee together from the bow: they shall be [e]bound: all that shall be found in thee, shall be bound together, which have fled from [f]far. **4** Therefore said I, Turn away from me, I will weep [g]bitterly: labor not to comfort me for the destruction of the daughter of my people. **5** For it is a day of trouble, and of ruin, and of perplexity by the Lord God of hosts in the valley of vision, breaking down the city: and a [h]crying unto the mountains. **6** And Elam [i]bare the quiver in a man's chariot with horsemen, and Kir uncovered the shield. **7** And thy chief valleys were full of chariots, and the horsemen set themselves in array against the gate. **8** And he discovered the [j]covering of Judah: and thou didst look in that day to the armor of the house of the forest. **9** And ye have seen [k]the breaches of the city of David: for they were many, and ye gathered the waters of the lower pool. **10** And ye numbered the houses [l]of Jerusalem, and the houses have ye broken down to fortify the wall, **11** And have also made a ditch between the two walls, for the [m]waters of the old pool, and have not looked unto the maker [n]thereof, neither had respect unto him that formed it of old. **12** And in that day did the Lord God of hosts call unto weeping and mourning, and to baldness and girding with sackcloth. **13** And behold, joy and gladness, slaying oxen and killing sheep, eating flesh, and drinking wine, [o]eating and drinking, for tomorrow we shall die. **14** And it was declared in the ears of the Lord of hosts. Surely this iniquity shall not be purged from you, till ye die, saith the Lord God of hosts. **15** Thus saith the Lord God of hosts, Go, get thee to that [p]treasurer, to Shebna, the steward of the house, and say, **16** What hast thou to do here? and whom hast thou [q]here? that thou shouldest here hew thee out a sepulcher, as he

---

s. Isa. 19:19 There shall be evident signs and tokens, that God's religion is there: which manner of speech is taken of the Patriarchs and ancient times, when God hath not as yet appointed the place, and full manner how he would be worshipped.
t. Isa. 19:20 This declareth that this prophecy should be accomplished in the time of Christ.
u. Isa. 19:21 By these ceremonies he comprehendeth the spiritual service under Christ.
v. Isa. 19:23 By these two nations, which were then chief enemies of the Church, he showeth that the Gentiles and the Jews should be joined together in one faith and religion, and should be all one fold under Christ their shepherd.

ISA 20

a. Isa. 20:1 Who was captain of Sennacherib, 2 Kings 18:17.
b. Isa. 20:1 A city of the Philistines.
c. Isa. 20:1 The Hebrews write that Sennacherib was so called.
d. Isa. 20:2 Which signifieth that the Prophet did lament the misery that he saw prepared, before the three years that he went naked and barefooted.
e. Isa. 20:5 In whose aid they trusted.
f. Isa. 20:5 Of whom they boasted and gloried.
g. Isa. 20:6 Meaning, Judea, which was compassed about with their enemies, as an isle with waters.

ISA 21

a. Isa. 21:1 On the seaside between Judea and Chaldea was a wilderness, whereby he meaneth Chaldea.
b. Isa. 21:1 That is, the ruin of Babylon by the Medes and Persians.
c. Isa. 21:2 The Assyrians and Chaldeans, which had destroyed other nations, shall be overcome of the Medes and Persians: and this he prophesied an hundred years before it came to pass.
d. Isa. 21:2 By Elam he meaneth the Persians.
e. Isa. 21:2 Because they shall find no succor, they shall mourn no more, or, I have caused them to cease mourning, whom Babylon had afflicted.
f. Isa. 21:3 This the Prophet speaketh in the person of the Babylonians.
g. Isa. 21:4 He prophesieth the death of Belshazzar, as Dan. 5:30, who in the midst of his pleasures was destroyed.
h. Isa. 21:5 While they are eating and drinking, they shall be commanded to run to their weapons.
i. Isa. 21:6 To wit, in a vision by the spirit of prophecy.
j. Isa. 21:7 Meaning, chariots of men of war, and others that carried the baggage.
k. Isa. 21:8 Meaning, Darius, which overcame Babylon.
l. Isa. 21:9 The watchman whom Isa. set up, told him who came toward Babylon, and the Angel declared that it should be destroyed: all this was done in a vision.
m. Isa. 21:10 Meaning, Babylon.
n. Isa. 21:10 Hebrew, son.
o. Isa. 21:11 Which was a city of the Ishmaelites, and was so named of Dumah, Gen. 25:14.
p. Isa. 21:11 A mountain of the Idumeans.
q. Isa. 21:12 He describeth the unquietness of the people of Dumah, who were night and day in fear of their enemies, and ever ran to and fro to inquire news.
r. Isa. 21:13 For fear, the Arabians shall flee into the woods, and he appointeth what way they shall take.
s. Isa. 21:14 Signifying, that for fear they shall not tarry to eat nor drink.
t. Isa. 21:16 He appointeth them respite for one year only, and then they should be destroyed.
u. Isa. 21:16 Read Isa. 16:14.
v. Isa. 21:17 Which was the name of a people of Arabia: and by the horrible destruction of all these nations, he teacheth the Jews that there is no place for refuge or to escape God's wrath, but only to remain in his Church, and to live in his fear.

ISA 21

1. Jer. 5:18 / Rev. 14:8

ISA 22

a. Isa. 22:1 Meaning, Judea, which was compassed about with mountains, and was called the valley of visions, because of the Prophets, which were always there, whom they named Seers.
b. Isa. 22:1 He speaketh to Jerusalem, whose inhabitants were fled up to the housetops for fear of their enemies.
c. Isa. 22:2 Which was wont to be full of people and joy.
d. Isa. 22:2 But for hunger.
e. Isa. 22:3 And led into captivity.
f. Isa. 22:3 Which have fled from other places to Jerusalem for succor.
g. Isa. 22:4 He showeth what is the duty of the godly, when God's plagues hang over the Church, and especially of the ministers, Jer. 9:1.
h. Isa. 22:5 That is, the shout of the enemies whom God had appointed to destroy the city.
i. Isa. 22:6 He putteth them in mind how God delivered them once from Sennacherib, who brought the Persians and Cyrenians with him, that they might by returning to God avoid that great plague which they should else suffer by Nebuchadnezzar.
j. Isa. 22:8 The secret place where the armor was: to wit, in the house of the forest, 1 Kings 7:2.
k. Isa. 22:9 Ye forfeited the ruinous places which were neglected in times of peace: meaning, the whole City, and the City of David, which was within the compass of the other.
l. Isa. 22:10 Either to pull down such as might hurt, or else to know what men they were able to make.
m. Isa. 22:11 To provide if need should be of water.
n. Isa. 22:11 To God that made Jerusalem: that is, they trusted more in these worldly means, than in God.
o. Isa. 22:13 Instead of repentance ye were joyful and made great cheer, contemning the admonitions of the Prophets, saying, Let us eat and drink for our Prophets say, that we shall die tomorrow.
p. Isa. 22:15 Because the Hebrew word doth also signify one that doth nourish and cherish, there are of the learned that think that this wicked man did nourish secret friendship with the Assyrians and Egyptians to betray the Church, and to provide for himself against all dangers: in the mean season he packed craftily, and got of the best offices into his hand under Hezekiah, ever aspiring to the highest.
q. Isa. 22:16 Meaning, that he was a stranger, and came up of nothing.
r. Isa. 22:16 Whereas he thought to make his name immortal by his famous sepulcher, he died most miserably among the Assyrians.

that heweth out his sepulcher in a high place, or that graveth an habitation [r]for himself in a rock? **17** Behold, the Lord will carry thee away with a great captivity, and will surely cover thee. **18** He will surely roll and turn thee like a ball in a large country: there shalt thou die, and there the chariots of thy glory shall be the [s]shame of thy lord's house. **19** And I will drive thee from thy station, and out of thy dwelling will he destroy thee. **20** And in that day will I [t]call my servant Eliakim the son of Hilkiah, **21** And with thy garments will I clothe him, and with thy girdle will I strengthen him: thy power also will I commit into his hand, and he shall be a father of the inhabitants of Jerusalem, and of the house of Judah. **22** And the [u]key of the house of David will I lay upon his shoulder: so he shall open, and no man shall shut: and he shall shut, and no man shall open. **23** And I will fasten him as a [v]nail in a sure place, and he shall be for the throne of glory to his father's house. **24** And they shall hang upon him all the glory of his father's house, even of the nephews and posterity [w]all small vessels, from the vessels of the cups, even to all the instruments of music. **25** In that day saith the Lord of hosts, shall the [x]nail that is fastened in the sure place, depart and shall be broken and fall, and the burden that was upon it, shall be cut off: for the Lord hath spoken it.

23

1 A Prophecy against Tyre. 17 A promise that it shall be restored.

1 The [a]burden of Tyre. Howl ye ships of [b]Tarshish: for [c]it is destroyed, so that there is none house: none shall come from the land of [d]Kittim: it is [e]revealed unto them. **2** Be still, ye that dwell in the isles: the merchants of Sidon, and such as pass over the sea, have [f]replenished thee. **3** The [g]seed of Nile growing by the abundance of waters, and the harvest of the river was her revenues, and she was a mart of the nations. **4** Be ashamed, thou Sidon: for the [h]sea hath spoken, even the strength of the sea, saying, I have not [i]travailed, nor brought forth children, neither nourished young men, nor brought up virgins. **5** When the fame cometh to the Egyptians, they shall be [j]sorry, concerning the rumor of Tyre. **6** Go you over to [k]Tarshish: howl, ye that dwell in the isles. **7** Is not this that your glorious city? her antiquity is of ancient days: her own feet shall lead her afar off to be a sojourner. **8** Who hath decreed this against Tyre (that [l]crowneth men) whose merchants are princes? whose chapmen are the nobles of the world? **9** The Lord of hosts hath decreed this, to stain the pride of all glory, and to bring to contempt all them that be glorious in the earth. **10** Pass through thy land like a flood to the [m]daughter of Tarshish: there is no more strength. **11** He stretched out his hand upon the sea: he shook the kingdoms: the Lord hath given a commandment concerning the place of merchandise, to destroy the power thereof. **12** And he said, Thou shalt no more rejoice when thou art oppressed: [n]O virgin [o]daughter of Sidon: rise up, go out unto Kittim: yet there thou shalt have no rest. **13** Behold the land of the Chaldeans: this was no people: [p]Assyria founded it by the inhabitants of the wilderness: they set up the towers thereof: they raised the palaces thereof, and he [q]brought it to ruin. **14** Howl ye ships of Tarshish, for your [r]strength is destroyed. **15** And in that day shall Tyre be forgotten seventy years (according to the years of one King) at the end of [s]seventy years shall Tyre [t]sing as an harlot. **16** Take an harp and go about the city (thou harlot that hast been forgotten) [u]make sweet melody, sing more songs that thou mayest be remembered. **17** And at the end of seventy years shall the Lord visit Tyre, and she shall return to her [v]wages, and shall commit fornication with all the kingdoms of the earth, that are in the world. **18** Yet her occupying and her wages shall be [w]holy unto the Lord: it shall not be laid up nor kept in store, but her merchandise shall be for them that dwell before the Lord, to eat sufficiently, and to have durable clothing.

24

1 A prophecy of the curse of God for the sins of the people. 13 A remnant reserved shall praise the Lord.

1 Behold, the Lord maketh the [a]earth empty, and he maketh it waste: he turneth it upside down, and scattereth abroad the inhabitants thereof. **2** And there shall be like people, like [b]Priest, and like servant, like master, like maid, like mistress, like buyer, like seller, like lender, like borrower, like giver, like taker to usury. **3** The earth shall be clean emptied, and utterly spoiled: for the Lord hath spoken this word. **4** The earth lamenteth and fadeth away, the world is feebled and decayed: the proud people of the earth are weakened. **5** The earth [c]also deceiveth, because of the inhabitants thereof: for they transgressed the laws: they changed the ordinances, and brake the everlasting Covenant. **6** Therefore hath the [d]curse devoured the earth, and the inhabitants thereof are desolate. Wherefore the inhabitants of the land are [e]burned up, and few men are left. **7** The wine faileth, the vine hath no might: all that were of merry heart, do mourn. **8** The mirth of tabrets ceaseth: the noise of them that rejoice, endeth: the joy of the harp ceaseth. **9** They shall not drink wine with mirth: strong drink shall be bitter to them that drink it. **10** The city of [f]vanity is broken down: every house is shut up, that no man may come in. **11** There is a crying for wine in the streets: all joy is darkened: the [g]mirth of the world is gone away. **12** In the cities is left desolation, and the gate is smitten with destruction. **13** Surely thus shall it be in the midst of the earth, among the people, [h]as the shaking of an olive tree, and as the grapes when the vintage is ended. **14** They shall lift up their voice: they shall shout for the magnificence of the Lord: they shall rejoice from [i]the sea. **15** Wherefore praise ye the Lord in the valleys, even the Name of the Lord God of Israel, in the isles of the sea. **16** From the uttermost part of the earth we have heard praises, even glory to the [j]just, and I said, [k]My leanness, my leanness, woe is me: the transgressors have offended: yea, the transgressors have grievously offended. **17** Fear, and the pit, and the snare are upon thee, O inhabitant of the earth. **18** And he that fleeth from the noise of the fear, shall fall into the pit: and he that cometh up out of the pit, shall be taken in the snare: for the [l]windows from on high are open, and the foundations of the earth do shake. **19** The earth is utterly broken down: the earth is clean dissolved: the earth is moved exceedingly. **20** The earth shall reel to and fro like a drunken man, and shall be removed like a tent, and the iniquity thereof shall be heavy upon it: so that it shall fall, and rise no more. **21** And in that day shall the Lord [m]visit the host above that is on high, even the kings of the world that are upon the earth. **22** And they shall be gathered together as the prisoners in the pit: and they shall be shut up in the prison, and after many days shall they be [n]visited. **23** [o]Then the moon shall be abashed, and the sun ashamed, when the Lord of hosts shall reign in mount Zion and in Jerusalem: and glory shall be before his ancient men.

---

s. Isa. 22:18 Signifying that whatsoever dignity the wicked attain unto, at length it will turn to the shame of those princes, by whom they are preferred.
t. Isa. 22:20 To be steward again, out of the which office he had been put, by the craft of Shebna.
u. Isa. 22:22 I will commit unto him the full charge and government of the king's house.
v. Isa. 22:23 I will establish him, and confirm him in his office: of this phrase, read Ezra 9:9.
w. Isa. 22:24 Meaning that both small and great that shall come of Eliakim, shall have praise and glory by his faithful officer.
x. Isa. 22:25 He meaneth Shebna, who in man's judgment should never have fallen.

ISA 23

a. Isa. 23:1 Read Isa. 13:1.
b. Isa. 23:1 Ye of Cilicia that come thither for merchandise.
c. Isa. 23:1 Tyre is destroyed by Nebuchadnezzar.
d. Isa. 23:1 By Kittim they meant all the isles and countries Westward from Palestine.
e. Isa. 23:1 All men know of this destruction.
f. Isa. 23:2 Have haunteth thee, and enriched thee.
g. Isa. 23:3 Meaning, the corn of Egypt, which was fed by the overflowing of the Nile.
h. Isa. 23:4 That is, Tyre, which was the chief part of the sea.
i. Isa. 23:4 I have no people left in me, and am as a barren woman that never had children.
j. Isa. 23:5 Because these two countries were joined in league together.
k. Isa. 23:6 Tyre willeth other merchants to go to Cilicia, and to come no more there.
l. Isa. 23:8 Who maketh her merchants like princes.
m. Isa. 23:10 Thy strength will no more serve thee: therefore flee to other countries for succor.
n. Isa. 23:12 For Tyre was never touched nor afflicted before.
o. Isa. 23:12 Because Tyre was built by them of Sidon.
p. Isa. 23:13 The Chaldeans which dwelt in tents in the wilderness, were gathered by the Assyrians into cities.
q. Isa. 23:13 The people of the Chaldeans destroyed the Assyrians: whereby the Prophet meaneth, that seeing the Chaldeans were able to overcome the Assyrians which were so great a nation, much more shall these two nations of Chaldea and Assyria be able to overthrow Tyre.
r. Isa. 23:14 That is, Tyre by whom ye are enriched.
s. Isa. 23:15 Tyre shall lie destroyed seventy years which he calleth the reign of one King, or a man's age.
t. Isa. 23:15 Shall use all craft and subtlety to entice men again unto her.
u. Isa. 23:16 She shall labor by all means to recover her first credit: as an harlot when she is long forgotten, seeketh by all means to entertain her lovers.
v. Isa. 23:17 Though she have been chastised of the Lord, yet she shall return to her old wicked practices, and for gain shall give herself to all men's lusts like an harlot.
w. Isa. 23:18 He showeth that God yet by the preaching of the Gospel will call Tyre to repentance, and turn her heart from avarice and filthy gain, unto the true worshipping of God, and liberality toward his Saints.

ISA 24

a. Isa. 24:1 This prophecy is as a conclusion of that which hath been threatened to the Jews, and other nations from chap. 13, and therefore by the earth he meaneth those lands which were before named.
b. Isa. 24:2 Because this was a name of dignity, it was also applied to them, which were not of Aaron's family, and so signifieth also a man of dignity, as 2 Sam. 8:18 and 20:25; 1 Chron. 18:17, and by these words the Prophet signifieth an horrible confusion, where there shall be neither religion, order, nor policy, Hos. 4:9.
c. Isa. 24:5 That is, rendereth not her fruit for the sin of the people, whom the earth deceived of their nourishment, because they deceived God of his honor.
d. Isa. 24:6 Written in the Law, as Lev. 26:14; Deut. 28:16, thus the Prophets used to apply particularly the menaces and promises, which are general in the Law.
e. Isa. 24:6 With heat and drought, or else that they were consumed with the fire of God's wrath.
f. Isa. 24:10 Which as it was without order, so now should it be brought to desolation and confusion: and this was not only meant of Jerusalem, but of all the other wicked cities.
g. Isa. 24:11 Because they did not use God's benefits aright, their pleasures should fail, and they fall to mourning.
h. Isa. 24:13 He comforteth the faithful, declaring that in this great desolation the Lord will assemble his Church which shall praise his Name, as Isa. 10:22.
i. Isa. 24:14 From the utmost coasts of the world, where the Gospel shall be preached, as verse 16.
j. Isa. 24:16 Meaning, to God, who will publish his Gospel through all the world.
k. Isa. 24:16 I am consumed with care, considering the affliction of the Church, both by foreign enemies and domestic. Some read, my secret, my secret: that is, it was revealed to the Prophet, that the good should be preserved, and the wicked destroyed.
l. Isa. 24:18 Meaning, that God's wrath and vengeance should be over and under them: so that they should not escape no more than they did at Noah's flood.
m. Isa. 24:21 There is no power so high or mighty, but God will visit him with his rods.
n. Isa. 24:22 Not with his rods, as verse 21, but shall be comforted.
o. Isa. 24:23 When God shall restore his Church, the glory thereof shall so shine, and his ministers (which are called his ancient men) that the sun and the moon shall be dark in comparison thereof.

25

A thanksgiving to God in that that he showeth himself judge of the world, by punishing the wicked, and maintaining the godly.

1 O Lord, thou [a]art my God: I will exalt thee, I will praise thy Name: for thou hast done wonderful things, according to the counsels of old, with a stable truth. 2 For thou hast made of a [b]city an heap, of a strong city, a ruin: even the place [c]of strangers of a city, it shall never be built. 3 Therefore shall the [d]mighty people give glory unto thee: the city of the strong nations shall fear thee. 4 For thou hast been a strength unto the poor, even a strength to the needy in his trouble, a refuge against the tempest, a shadow against the heat: for the blast [e]of the mighty is like a storm against the wall. 5 Thou shalt bring down the noise of the strangers, [f]as the heat in a dry place; he will bring down the song of the mighty, as [g]the heat in the shadow of a cloud. 6 And in this [h]mountain shall the Lord of hosts make unto all people a feast of fat things, even a feast of fined wines, and of fat things full of marrow, of wines fined and purified. 7 And he will destroy in this mountain [i]the covering that covereth all people, and the veil that is spread upon all nations. 8 He will destroy death forever: and the Lord God will [j]wipe away the tears from all faces, and the rebuke of his people will he take away out of all the earth: for the Lord hath spoken it. 9 And in that day shall men say, Lo, this is our God: we have waited for him, and he will save us. This is the Lord, we have waited for him, we will rejoice and be joyful in salvation. 10 For in this mountain shall the hand of the Lord rest, and [k]Moab shall be threshed under him even as straw is threshed in [l]Madmenah. 11 And he shall stretch out his hand in the midst of them (as he that swimmeth stretcheth them out to swim) and with the strength of his hands shall he bring down their pride. 12 The defense also of the height of thy walls shall he bring down and lay low, and cast them to the ground, even unto the dust.

26

A song of the faithful, wherein is declared, in what consisteth the salvation of the Church, and wherein they ought to trust.

1 In that day shall [a]this song be sung in the land of Judah, We have a strong city: [b]salvation shall God set for walls and bulwarks. 2 [c]Open ye the gates that the righteous nation, which keepeth the truth, may enter in. 3 By an assured [d]purpose wilt thou preserve perfect peace, because they trusted in thee. 4 Trust in the Lord forever: for in the Lord God is strength forevermore. 5 For he will bring down them that dwell on high: [e]the high city he will abase: even unto the ground will he cast it down, and bring it unto dust. 6 The foot shall tread it down, even the feet of the [f]poor, and the steps of the needy. 7 The way of the just is righteousness: thou wilt make equal the righteous path of the just. 8 Also we, O Lord, have waited for thee in the way of thy [g]judgments: the desire of our soul is to thy Name, and to the remembrance of thee. 9 With my soul have I desired thee in the night, and with my spirit within me will I seek thee in the morning: for seeing thy judgments are in the earth, the inhabitants of the world shall learn [h]righteousness. 10 Let mercy [i]be showed to the wicked, yet he will not learn righteousness: in the land of uprightness will he do wickedly, and will not behold the majesty of the Lord. 11 O Lord, they will not behold thine high hand: but they shall see it, and be confounded with [j]the zeal of the people, and the fire of thine [k]enemies shall devour them. 12 Lord unto us thou wilt ordain peace: for thou also hast wrought all our works for us. 13 O Lord our God, other [l]lords beside thee, have ruled us, but we will remember thee only, and thy Name. 14 The [m]dead shall not live, neither shall the dead arise, because thou hast visited and scattered them, and destroyed all their memory. 15 Thou hast increased [n]the nation, O Lord: thou hast increased the nation: thou art made glorious, thou hast enlarged all the coasts of the earth. 16 Lord, in trouble have they [o]visited thee: they poured out a prayer when thy chastening was upon them. 17 Like as a woman with child, that draweth near to the travail, is in sorrow, and crieth in her pains, so have we been in thy [p]sight, O Lord. 18 We have conceived, we have born in pain, as though we should have brought forth [q]wind: there was no help in the earth, neither did the inhabitants of [r]the world fall. 19 [s]Thy dead men shall live: even with my body shall they rise. Awake and sing, ye that dwell in dust: for thy [t]dew is as the dew of herbs, and the earth shall cast out the dead. 20 Come, my people: [u]enter thou into thy chambers, and shut thy doors after thee: hide thyself for a very little while, until the indignation pass over. 21 For lo, the Lord cometh out of his place, to visit the iniquity of the inhabitants of the earth upon them: and the earth shall disclose her [v]blood, and shall no more hide her slain.

27

A prophecy against the kingdom of Satan. 2 And of the joy of the Church for their deliverance.

1 In that [a]day the Lord with his sore and great and mighty [b]sword shall visit Leviathan, that piercing serpent, even Leviathan, that crooked serpent, and he shall slay the dragon that is in the sea. 2 In that day sing of the vineyard [c]of red wine. 3 I the Lord do keep it: I will water it every moment: lest any assail it, I will keep it night and day. 4 Anger [d]is not in me: who would set the briers and the thorns against me in battle? I would go through them, I would burn them together. 5 Or will he [e]feel my strength, that he may make peace with me, and be at one with me? 6 [f]Hereafter Jacob shall take root: Israel shall flourish and grow: and the world shall be filled with fruit. 7 Hath he smitten [g]him, as he smote those that smote him? or is he slain according to the slaughter of them that were slain by him? 8 In [h]measure in the branches thereof wilt thou contend with it, when he bloweth with his rough wind in the day of the East wind. 9 By this therefore shall the iniquity of Jacob be purged, and this is all the [i]fruit, the taking away of his sin: when he shall make all the stones of the altars, as chalk stones broken in pieces, that the groves and images may not stand up. 10 Yet the [j]defensed city shall be desolate, and the habitation shall be forsaken, and left like a wilderness. There shall the calf feed, and there shall he lie and consume the branches thereof. 11 When the boughs of it are dry, they shall be broken: the [k]women come and set them on fire: for it is a people of none understanding: therefore he that made them shall not have compassion of them, and he that formed them, shall have no mercy on them. 12 And in that day shall the Lord thresh from the channel of the [l]river unto the river of Egypt, and ye shall be gathered, one by one, O children of Israel. 13 In that day also shall the great trumpet be [m]blown, and they shall come, which perished in the land of Assyria, and they that were chased into the land of Egypt, and they shall worship the Lord in the holy Mount at Jerusalem.

ISA 25

- **a.** Isa. 25:1 Thus the Prophet giveth thanks to God because he will bring under subjection these nations by his corrections, and make them of his Church, which before were his enemies.
- **b.** Isa. 25:2 Not only of Jerusalem, but also of these other cities which have been thine enemies.
- **c.** Isa. 25:2 That is, a place whereas all vagabonds may live without danger, and as it were at ease, as in a palace.
- **d.** Isa. 25:3 The arrogant and proud, which before would not know thee, shall by thy corrections fear and glorify thee.
- **e.** Isa. 25:4 The rage of the wicked is furious, till God break the force thereof.
- **f.** Isa. 25:5 Meaning, that as the heat is abated by the rain, so shall God bring down the rage of the wicked.
- **g.** Isa. 25:5 As a cloud shadoweth from the heat of the sun, so shall God assuage the rejoicing of the wicked against the godly.
- **h.** Isa. 25:6 To wit, in Zion, whereby he meaneth his Church, which should under Christ be assembled of the Jews and the Gentiles, and is here described under the figure of a costly banquet, as Matt. 22:2.
- **i.** Isa. 25:7 Meaning, that ignorance and blindness, whereby we are kept back from Christ.
- **j.** Isa. 25:8 He will take away all occasions of sorrow and fill his with perfect joy, Rev. 7:17 and 21:4.
- **k.** Isa. 25:10 By Moab are meant all the enemies of his Church.
- **l.** Isa. 25:10 There were two cities of this name: one in Judah, 1 Chron. 2:49, and another in the land of Moab, Jer. 48:2, which seemeth to have been a plentiful place of corn, Isa. 10:31.

ISA 26

- **a.** Isa. 26:1 This song was made to comfort the faithful when their captivity should come, assuring them also of their deliverance, for the which they should sing this song.
- **b.** Isa. 26:1 God's protection and defense shall be sufficient for us.
- **c.** Isa. 26:2 He assureth the godly to return after the captivity to Jerusalem.
- **d.** Isa. 26:3 Thou hast decreed so, and thy purpose cannot be changed.
- **e.** Isa. 26:5 There is no power so high that can let God, when he will deliver his.
- **f.** Isa. 26:6 God will set the poor afflicted over the power of the wicked.
- **g.** Isa. 26:8 We have constantly aboade in the adversities wherewith thou had afflicted us.
- **h.** Isa. 26:9 Meaning, that by afflictions men shall learn to fear God.
- **i.** Isa. 26:10 The wicked though God show them evident signs of his grace, shall be never the better.
- **j.** Isa. 26:11 Through envy and indignation against thy people.
- **k.** Isa. 26:11 The fire and vengeance, wherewith thou dost destroy thine enemies.
- **l.** Isa. 26:13 The Babylonians, which have not governed according to thy word.
- **m.** Isa. 26:14 Meaning, that the reprobate, even in this life shall have the beginning of everlasting death.
- **n.** Isa. 26:15 To wit, the company of the faithful by the calling of the Gentiles.
- **o.** Isa. 26:16 That is, the faithful by the rods were moved to pray unto thee for deliverance.
- **p.** Isa. 26:17 To wit, in extreme sorrow.
- **q.** Isa. 26:18 Our sorrows had none end, neither did we enjoy the comfort that we looked for.
- **r.** Isa. 26:18 The wicked and men without religion were not destroyed.
- **s.** Isa. 26:19 He comforteth the faithful in their afflictions, showing them that even in death they shall have life: and that they should most certainly rise to glory, the contrary should come to the wicked, as verse 14.
- **t.** Isa. 26:19 As herbs dead in winter flourisheth again by the rain in the springtime: so they that lie in the dust, shall rise up to joy, when they feel the dew of God's grace.
- **u.** Isa. 26:20 He exhorteth the faithful to be patient in their afflictions, and to wait upon God's work.
- **v.** Isa. 26:21 The earth shall vomit and cast out the innocent blood, which it hath drunk, that it may cry for vengeance against the wicked.

ISA 27

- **a.** Isa. 27:1 At the time appointed.
- **b.** Isa. 27:1 That is, by his mighty power, and by his word. He prophesieth here of the destruction of Satan and his kingdom under the name of Leviathan, Assyria, and Egypt.
- **c.** Isa. 27:2 Meaning, of the best wine, which this vineyard, that is, the Church should bring forth, as most agreeable to the Lord.
- **d.** Isa. 27:4 Therefore he will destroy the kingdom of Satan, because he loveth his Church for his own mercy's sake, and cannot be angry with it, but wisheth that he may pour his anger upon the wicked infidels, whom he meaneth by briers and thorns.
- **e.** Isa. 27:5 He marveleth that Israel will not come by gentleness, except God make them to feel his rods, and so bring them unto him.
- **f.** Isa. 27:6 Though I afflict and diminish my people for a time, yet shall the root spring again and bring forth in great abundance.
- **g.** Isa. 27:7 He showeth that God punisheth his in mercy, and his enemies in justice.
- **h.** Isa. 27:8 That is, thou wilt not destroy the root of thy Church, though the branches thereof seem to perish by the sharp wind of affliction.
- **i.** Isa. 27:9 He showeth that there is no true repentance, nor full reconciliation to God, till the heart be purged from all idolatry, and the monuments thereof be destroyed.
- **j.** Isa. 27:10 Notwithstanding his favor that he will show them after, yet Jerusalem shall be destroyed, and grass for cattle shall grow in it.
- **k.** Isa. 27:11 God shall not have need of mighty enemies: for the very women shall do it to their great shame.
- **l.** Isa. 27:12 He shall destroy all from Euphrates to the Nile: for some fled toward Egypt, thinking to have escaped.

28

Against the pride and drunkenness of Israel. 9 The untowardness of them that should learn the word of God. 24 God doeth all things in time and place.

1 Woe to the [a]crown of pride, the drunkards of Ephraim: for his glorious beauty shall be a fading flower, which is upon the head of the [b]valley of them that be fat, and are overcome with wine. **2** Behold, the Lord hath a mighty and [c]strong host like a tempest of hail, and a whirlwind that overthroweth, like a tempest of mighty waters that overflow, which throw to the ground mightily. **3** They shall be trodden under foot, even the crown and the pride of the drunkards of Ephraim. **4** For his glorious beauty shall be a fading flower, which is upon the head of the valley of them that be fat, and as [d]the hasty fruit afore Summer, which when he hath looketh upon it, seeth it, while it is in his hand, he eateth it. **5** In that day shall the Lord of hosts be for a crown of glory, and for a diadem of beauty unto the [e]residue of his people: **6** And for a spirit of judgment to him that sitteth in judgment, and for [f]strength unto them that turn away the battle to the gate. **7** But [g]they have erred because of wine, and are out of the way by strong drink: the Priest and the prophet have erred by strong drink: they are swallowed up with wine: they have gone astray through strong drink: they fail in vision: they stumble in judgment. **8** For all their tables are full of filthy vomiting: no place is clean. **9** [h]Whom shall he teach knowledge? and whom shall he make to understand the things that he heareth? them that are weaned from the milk, and drawn from the breasts. **10** For [i]precept must be upon precept, precept upon precept, line unto line, line unto line, there a little, and there a little. **11** For with a stammering [j]tongue, and with a strange language shall he speak unto this people. **12** Unto whom [k]he said, [l]This is the rest: [m]give rest unto him that is weary, and this is the refreshing, but they would not hear. **13** Therefore shall the word of the [n]Lord be unto them precept upon precept, precept upon precept, line unto line, line unto line, there a little and there a little: that they may go and fall backward, and be broken, and be snared, and be taken. **14** Wherefore hear the word of the Lord, ye scornful men, that rule this people, which is at Jerusalem. **15** Because ye have said, We have made a [o]covenant with death, and with hell are we at agreement: though a scourge run over, and pass through, it shall not come at us: for we have made [p]falsehood our refuge, and under vanity are we hid, **16** Therefore thus saith the Lord God, Behold, I will lay in Zion a stone, a [q]tried stone, a precious cornerstone, a sure foundation. He that believeth, [r]shall not make haste. **17** Judgment also will I lay to the rule, and [s]righteousness to the balance, and the [t]hail shall sweep away the vain confidence, and the waters shall overflow [u]the secret place. **18** And your covenant with death shall be disannulled, and your agreement with hell shall not stand: when a scourge shall run over and pass through, then shall ye be trodden down by it. **19** When it passeth over, it shall take you away: for it shall pass through every morning in the day and in the night, and there shall be only [v]fear, to make you to understand the hearing. **20** For the bed is [w]strait, that it cannot suffice, and the covering narrow, that one cannot wrap himself. **21** For the Lord shall stand as in mount [x]Perazim: he shall be wroth as in the valley [y]of Gibeon, that he may do his work, his strange work, and bring to pass his act, his strange act. **22** Now therefore be no mockers, lest your bonds increase: for I have heard of the Lord of hosts a consumption, even determined upon the whole earth. **23** Hearken ye, and hear my voice: hearken ye, and hear my speech. **24** Doth the plowman plow all the day, to sow? doth he open, and break the clots of his ground? **25** When he hath made it [z]plain, will he not then sow the fitches, and sow cumin, and cast in wheat by measure, and the appointed barley and rye in their place? **26** For his God doth instruct him to have discretion, and doth teach him. **27** For fitches shall not be threshed with a threshing instrument, neither shall a cartwheel be turned about upon the cumin: but the fitches are beaten out with a staff, and cumin with a rod. **28** Bread corn when it is threshed, he doth not always thresh it, neither doth the wheel of his cart still make a noise, neither will he break it with the teeth thereof. **29** This also cometh from the Lord of hosts, which is wonderful in counsel, and excellent in works.

29

1 A prophecy against Jerusalem. 13 The vengeance of God on them that follow the traditions of men.

1 Ah [a]altar, altar of the city that David dwelt in: add year unto year: [b]let them kill lambs. **2** But I will bring the altar into distress, and there shall be heaviness and sorrow, and it shall be unto me like [c]an altar. **3** And I will besiege thee as a circle, and fight against thee on a mount, and will cast up ramparts against thee. **4** So shalt thou be humbled, and shalt speak out of the [d]ground, and thy speech shall be as out of the dust: thy voice also shall be out of the ground like him that hath a spirit of divination, and thy talking shall whisper out of the dust. **5** Moreover, multitude of thy [e]strangers shall be like small dust, and the multitude of strong men shall be as chaff that passeth away: and it shall be in a moment, even suddenly. **6** Thou shalt be visited of the Lord of hosts with thunder, and shaking, and a great noise, a whirlwind, and a tempest, and a flame of a devouring fire. **7** And the [f]multitude of all the nations that fight against the altar, shall be as a dream or vision by night: even all they that make the war against it, and strongholds against it, and lay siege unto it. **8** And it shall be like as an hungry man dreameth, and behold, [g]he eateth: and when he awaketh, his soul is empty: or like as a thirsty man dreameth, and lo, he is drinking, and when he awaketh, behold, he is faint, and his soul longeth: so shall the multitude of all nations be that fight against mount Zion. **9** [h]Stay yourselves and wonder: they are blind, and make you blind: they are drunken, but not with wine: they stagger, but not by strong drink. **10** For the Lord hath covered you with a spirit of slumber, and hath shut up your eyes: the Prophet, and your chief Seers hath he covered. **11** And the vision of them all is become unto you, as the words of a book that is sealed up, which they deliver to one that can read, saying, Read this, I pray thee. Then shall he say, I [i]cannot; for it is sealed. **12** And the book is given unto him that cannot read, saying, Read this, I pray thee. And he shall say, I cannot read. **13** Therefore the Lord said, Because this people [j]come near unto me with their mouth, and honor me with their lips, but have removed their heart far from me, and their [k]fear toward me was taught by the precept of men, **14** Therefore behold, I will again do a marvelous work in this people, even a marvelous work, and a wonder: for the wisdom of their wise men shall [l]perish, and the understanding of their prudent men shall be hid. **15** Woe unto them that [m]seek deep to hide their counsel from the Lord: for their works are in darkness, and they say, Who seeth us? and who knoweth us? **16** Your turning of devices shall it not be esteemed [n]as the potter's clay? for shall the work say of him that made it, He made

---

m. Isa. 27:13 In the time of Cyrus, by whom they should be delivered: but this was chiefly accomplished under Christ.

ISA 28

a. Isa. 28:1 Meaning, the proud kingdom of the Israelites, which were drunken with worldly prosperity.
b. Isa. 28:1 Because the Israelites for the most part dwelt in plentiful valleys, he meaneth hereby the valley of them that had abundance of worldly prosperity, and were as it were crowned therewith as with garlands.
c. Isa. 28:2 He seemeth to mean the Assyrians, by whom the ten tribes were carried away.
d. Isa. 28:4 Which is not of long continuance, but is soon ripe and first eaten.
e. Isa. 28:5 Signifying, that the faithful, which put not their trust in any worldly prosperity, but made God their glory, shall be preserved.
f. Isa. 28:6 He will give counsel to the governor, and strength to the captain, to drive the enemies in at their own gates.
g. Isa. 28:7 Meaning, the hypocrites which were among them, and were altogether corrupt in life and doctrine, which is here meant by drunkenness and vomiting.
h. Isa. 28:9 For there was none that was able to understand any good doctrine: but were foolish and as unmeet as young babes.
i. Isa. 28:10 They must have one thing ofttimes told.
j. Isa. 28:11 Let one teach what he can, yet they shall no more understand him, than if he spake in a strange language.
k. Isa. 28:12 That is, the Prophet, whom God should send.
l. Isa. 28:12 This is the doctrine, whereupon ye ought to stay and rest.
m. Isa. 28:12 Show to them that are weary and have need of rest, what is the true rest.
n. Isa. 28:13 Because they will not receive the word of God, when it is offered, it cometh of their own malice, if after their hearts be so hardened, that they care not for it, as before, Isa. 6:9.
o. Isa. 28:15 They thought they had shifts to avoid God's judgments, and that they could escape though all others perished.
p. Isa. 28:15 Though the prophets condemned their idols and vain trust of falsehood and vanity, yet the wicked thought in themselves that they would trust in these things.
q. Isa. 28:16 That is, Christ, by whom all the building must be tried and upheld, Ps. 118:22; Matt. 21:42; Acts 4:11; Rom. 9:33; 1 Pet. 2:6.
r. Isa. 28:16 He shall be quiet, and seek none other remedies, but be content with Christ.
s. Isa. 28:17 In the restitution of his Church, judgment and justice shall reign.
t. Isa. 28:17 God's corrections and afflictions.
u. Isa. 28:17 Affliction shall discover their vain confidence, which they kept secret to themselves.
v. Isa. 28:19 Terror and destruction shall make you to learn that, which exhortations and gentleness could not bring you unto.
w. Isa. 28:20 Your affliction shall be so sore, that you are not able to endure it.
x. Isa. 28:21 When David overcame the Philistines, 2 Sam. 5:20; 1 Chron. 14:11.
y. Isa. 28:21 Where Joshua discomfited five kings of the Amorites, Josh. 10:12.
z. Isa. 28:25 As the plowman hath his appointed time, and divers instruments for his labor, so hath the Lord for his vengeance: for he punisheth some at one time, and some at another, some after one sort, and some after another, so that his chosen seed is beaten and tried, but not broken, as are the wicked.

ISA 29

a. Isa. 29:1 The Hebrew word Ariel signifieth the Lion of God, and signifieth the Altar, because the altar seemed to devour the sacrifice that was offered to God, as Ezek. 43:16.
b. Isa. 29:1 Your vain confidence in your sacrifices shall not last long.
c. Isa. 29:2 Your city shall be full of blood, as an altar whereon they sacrifice.
d. Isa. 29:4 Thy speech shall be no more so lofty, but abased and low as the very charmers, which are in low places, and whisper, so that their voice can scarce be heard.
e. Isa. 29:5 Thine hired soldiers in whom thou trustest, shall be destroyed as dust or chaff in a whirlwind.
f. Isa. 29:7 The enemies that I will bring to destroy thee, and that which thou makest thy vain trust, shall come at unawares, even as a dream in the night. Some read, as if this were a comfort to the Church for the destruction of their enemies.
g. Isa. 29:8 That is, he thinketh that he eateth.
h. Isa. 29:9 Muse hereon as long as ye list, yet shall ye find nothing but occasion to be astonied: for your Prophets are blind, and therefore cannot direct you.
i. Isa. 29:11 Meaning, that it is all alike, either to read, or not to read, except God open the heart to understand.
j. Isa. 29:13 Because they are hypocrites and not sincere in heart, as Matt. 15:8.
k. Isa. 29:13 That is, their religion was learned by man's doctrine, and not by my word.
l. Isa. 29:14 Meaning, that where as God is not worshipped according to his word, both magistrates and ministers are but fools and without understanding.
m. Isa. 29:15 This is spoken of them which in heart despised God's word, and mocked at the admonitions, but outwardly bare a good face.
n. Isa. 29:16 For all your craft saith the Lord, you cannot be able to escape mine hands no more than the clay, that is in the potter's hands, hath power to deliver itself.

me not? or the thing formed, say of him that fashioned it, He had none understanding? **17** Is it not yet but a little while, and Lebanon shall be [o]turned into Carmel? and Carmel shall be counted as a forest? **18** And in that day shall the deaf hear the words of the book, and the eyes of the blind shall see out of obscurity, and out of darkness. **19** The meek in the Lord shall receive joy again, and the poor men shall rejoice in the Holy one of Israel. **20** For the cruel man shall cease, and the scornful shall be consumed: and all that hasted to iniquity, shall be cut off: **21** Which made a man to sin in the [p]word, and took him in a snare: which reproved them in the gate, and made the just to fall without cause. **22** Therefore thus saith the Lord unto the house of Jacob, even he that redeemed Abraham: Jacob shall not now be confounded, neither now shall his face be pale. **23** But when he seeth his children, the work of mine hands, in the midst of him, they shall sanctify my Name, and sanctify the Holy one of Jacob, and shall fear the God of Israel. **24** Then they that erred in spirit, [q]shall have understanding, and they that murmured, shall learn doctrine.

30

1 He reproveth the Jews, which in their adversity used their own counsels, 2 and sought help of the Egyptians, 10 despising the Prophets. 16 Therefore he showeth what destruction shall come upon them, 18 but offereth mercy to the repentant.

1 Woe to the [a]rebellious children, saith the Lord, that take counsel, but not of me, and [b]cover with a covering, but not by my spirit, that they may lay sin upon sin: **2** Which walk forth to go down into Egypt (and have not asked at my mouth) to strengthen themselves with the strength of Pharaoh, and trust in the shadow of Egypt. **3** But the strength of Pharaoh shall be your shame, and the trust in the shadow of Egypt your confusion. **4** For his [c]princes were at Zoan, and his ambassadors came unto Hanes. **5** They shall be all ashamed of the people that cannot profit them, nor help, nor do them good, but shall be a shame and also a reproach. **6** The [d]burden of the beasts of the South, in a land of trouble and anguish, from whence shall come the young and old lion, the viper and fiery flying serpent against them that shall bear their riches upon the shoulders of the colts, and their treasures upon the bunches of the camels, to a people that cannot profit. **7** For the Egyptians are vanity, and they shall help in vain. Therefore have I cried unto [e]her, Their strength [f]is to sit still. **8** Now go, and write [g]it before them in a table, and note it in a book, that it may be for the [h]last day forever and ever: **9** That it is a rebellious people, lying children, and children that would not [i]hear the Law of the Lord. **10** Which say unto the Seers, See not: and to the Prophets, Prophesy not unto us right things: but speak flattering things unto us: prophesy [j]errors. **11** Depart out of the way: go aside out of the path: cause the Holy one of Israel to cease from us. **12** Therefore thus saith the Holy one of Israel, Because you have cast off this word, and trust in [k]violence, and wickedness, and stay thereupon, **13** Therefore this iniquity shall be unto you as a breach that falleth, or a swelling in an high wall, whose breaking cometh suddenly in a moment. **14** And the breaking thereof is like the breaking of a potter's pot, which is broken without pity, and in the breaking thereof is not found [l]a shard to take fire out of the hearth, or to take water out of the pit. **15** For thus said the [m]Lord God, the Holy one of Israel, In rest and quietness shall ye be saved: in quietness and in confidence shall be your strength, but ye would not. **16** For ye have said, No, but we will flee away upon [n]horses. Therefore shall ye flee. We will ride upon the swiftest. Therefore shall your persecutors be swifter. **17** A thousand as one shall flee at the rebuke of one: at the rebuke of five shall ye flee, till ye be left as a ship mast upon the [o]top of a mountain, and as a beacon upon an hill. **18** Yet therefore will the Lord wait, that he may have [p]mercy upon you, and therefore will he be exalted, that he may have compassion upon you: for the Lord is the God of [q]judgment. Blessed are all they that wait for him. **19** Surely a people shall dwell in Zion, and in Jerusalem: thou shalt weep no more: he will certainly have mercy upon thee at the voice of thy cry: when he heareth thee, he will answer thee. **20** And when the Lord hath given you the bread of adversity, and the water of affliction, thy rain shall be no more kept back, but thine eyes shall see thy [r]rain. **21** And thine ears shall hear a word behind thee, saying, This is the way, [s]walk ye in it, when thou turnest to the right hand, and when thou turnest to the left. **22** And ye shall [t]pollute the covering of the images of silver, and the rich ornament of thine images of gold, and cast them away as a menstruous cloth, and thou shalt say unto it, [u]Get thee hence. **23** Then shall he give rain unto thy seed, when thou shalt sow the ground, and bread of the increase of the earth, and it shall be fat and as oil: in that day shall thy cattle be fed in large pastures. **24** The oxen also and the young asses, that till the ground, shall eat clean provender, which is winnowed with the shovel and with the fan. **25** And upon every high [v]mountain, and upon every high hill shall there be rivers, and streams of waters, in the day of the great slaughter, when the towers shall fall. **26** Moreover, the light of the Moon shall be as the light of the [w]Sun, and the light of the Sun shall be sevenfold, and like the light of seven days in the day that the Lord shall bind up the breach of his people, and heal the stroke of their wound. **27** Behold, [x]the Name of the Lord cometh from far, his face is burning, and the burden thereof is heavy: his lips are full of indignation, and his tongue is as a devouring fire. **28** And his spirit is as a river that overfloweth up to the neck: it divideth asunder, to fan the nations with the fan of [y]vanity, and there shall be a bridle to cause them to err in the jaws of the people. **29** But there shall be a song unto you as in the [z]night, when a solemn feast is kept; and gladness of heart, as he that cometh with a pipe to go unto the mount of the Lord, to the Mighty one of Israel. **30** And the Lord shall cause his glorious voice to be heard, and shall declare the lighting down of his arm with the anger of his countenance, and flame of a devouring fire, with scattering and tempest, and hailstones. **31** For with the voice of the Lord shall Assyria be destroyed, which smote with the [aa]rod. **32** And in every place that the staff shall pass, it shall [ab]cleave fast, which the Lord shall lay upon him with [ac]tabrets and beards and with battles, and lifting up of hands shall he fight [ad]against it. **33** For [ae]Tophet is prepared of old; it is even prepared for the [af]King; he hath made it [ag]deep and large: the burning thereof is fire and much wood; the breath of the Lord, like a river of brimstone, doth kindle it.

31

1 He curseth them that forsake God, and seek for the help of men.

1 Woe unto them that [a]go down into Egypt for help, and stay upon horses, and trust in chariots, because they are many, and in horsemen, because they be very strong; but they look not unto the Holy one of Israel, nor [b]seek unto the Lord. **2** But he yet is [c]wisest; therefore he will bring evil, and not turn back his word, but he will arise against the house of the wicked, and against the help of them that work vanity. **3** Now the Egyptians are men and not God, and their horses flesh, and not spirit; and when the Lord shall stretch out his hand, the [d]helper shall fall, and he that is helped shall fall, and they shall altogether fail. **4** For this hath the Lord spoken unto me, As the lion or lion's whelp roareth

---

o. Isa. 29:17 Shall there not be a change of all things? And Carmel that is a plentiful place in respect of that it shall be then, may be taken as a forest, as Isa. 32:15, and thus he speaketh to comfort the faithful.
p. Isa. 29:21 They that went about to find fault with the Prophet's words, and would not abide admonitions, but would entangle them and bring them into danger.
q. Isa. 29:24 Signifying, that except God give understanding, and knowledge, man cannot but still err and murmur against him.

ISA 30

a. Isa. 30:1 Who contrary to their promise take not me for their protector, and contrary to my commandment seek help at strangers.
b. Isa. 30:1 They seek shifts to cloak their doings, and not godly means.
c. Isa. 30:4 The chief of Israel went into Egypt in embassy to seek help, and abode at these cities.
d. Isa. 30:6 That is, a heavy sentence or prophecy against the beasts that carried their treasures into Egypt, by the wilderness, which was south from Judah, signifying that if the beasts should not be spared, the men should be punished much more grievously.
e. Isa. 30:7 To wit, to Jerusalem.
f. Isa. 30:7 And not to come to and fro to seek help.
g. Isa. 30:8 That is, this prophecy.
h. Isa. 30:8 That it may be a witness against them for all posterity.
i. Isa. 30:9 He showeth what was the cause of their destruction, and bringeth also all misery to man: to wit, because they would not hear the word of God, but delighted to be flattered, and led in error.
j. Isa. 30:10 Threaten us not by the word of God, neither be so rigorous, nor talk unto us in the Name of the Lord, as Jer. 11:21.
k. Isa. 30:12 Meaning, in their stubbornness against God and the admonitions of his Prophets.
l. Isa. 30:14 Signifying, that the destruction of the wicked shall be without recovery.
m. Isa. 30:15 Ofttimes by his Prophets he put you in remembrance of this, that you should only depend on him.
n. Isa. 30:16 We will trust to escape by our horses.
o. Isa. 30:17 Whereas all the trees are cut down save two or three to make masts.
p. Isa. 30:18 He commendeth the great mercies of God, who with patience waiteth to call sinners to repentance.
q. Isa. 30:18 Not only in punishing, but in using moderation in the same, as Jer. 10:24 and 30:11.
r. Isa. 30:20 Or, instructor.
s. Isa. 30:21 God shall direct all thy ways, and appoint thee how to go either hither or thither.
t. Isa. 30:22 Ye shall cast away your idols, which you have made of gold, and silver, with all that belongeth unto them, as a most filthy thing, and polluted.
u. Isa. 30:22 Showing, that there can be no true repentance, except both in heart and deed we show ourselves enemies to idolatry.
v. Isa. 30:25 By these divers manners of speech he showeth that the felicity of the Church shall be so great, that none is able sufficiently to express it.
w. Isa. 30:26 When the Church shall be restored, the glory thereof shall pass seven times the brightness of the Sun: for by the Sun and Moon, which are two excellent creatures, he showeth what shall be the glory of the children of God in the kingdom of Christ.
x. Isa. 30:27 This threatening is against the Assyrians the chief enemies of the people of God.
y. Isa. 30:28 To drive thee to nothing: and thus God consumeth the wicked by that means, whereby he cleanseth his.
z. Isa. 30:29 Ye shall rejoice at the destruction of your enemies, as they that sung for joy of the solemn feast, which began in the evening.
aa. Isa. 30:31 God's plague.
ab. Isa. 30:32 It shall destroy.
ac. Isa. 30:32 With joy and assurance of the victory.
ad. Isa. 30:32 Against Babel: meaning the Assyrians and Babylonians.
ae. Isa. 30:33 Here it is taken for hell, where the wicked are tormented, read 2 Kings 23:10.
af. Isa. 30:33 So that their estate or degree cannot exempt the wicked.
ag. Isa. 30:33 By these figurative speeches he declareth the condition of the wicked after this life.

ISA 31

a. Isa. 31:1 There were two special causes, why the Israelites should not join amity with the Egyptians: first, because the Lord had commanded them never to return thither, Deut. 17:16 and 28:68, lest they should forget the benefit of their redemption: and secondly, lest they should be corrupted with the superstition and idolatry of the Egyptians, and so forsake God, Jer. 2:18.
b. Isa. 31:1 Meaning, that they forsake the Lord, that put their trust in worldly things: for they cannot trust in both.
c. Isa. 31:2 And knoweth their crafty enterprises, and will bring all to naught.
d. Isa. 31:3 Meaning, both the Egyptians and the Israelites.
e. Isa. 31:4 He showeth the Jews, that if they would put their trust in him, he is so able, that none can resist his power:

upon his prey, against whom if a multitude of shepherds be called, he will not be
afraid at their voice, neither will humble himself at their noise: so shall the Lord of
hosts come [e]down to fight for mount Zion, and for the hill thereof. **5** As birds
that fly, so shall the Lord of hosts defend Jerusalem by defending and delivering,
by passing through and preserving it. **6** O ye children of Israel, turn again, in
as much as ye are [f]sunken deep in rebellion. **7** For in that day every man shall
[g]cast out his idols of silver, and his idols of gold, which your hands have made you,
even a sin. **8** [h]Then shall Assyria fall by the sword, not of man, neither shall the
sword of man devour him, and he shall flee from the sword, and his young men
shall faint. **9** And he shall go for fear to his [i]tower, and his princes shall be afraid
of the standard, saith the Lord, whose [j]fire is in Zion, and his furnace in Jerusalem.

32

The conditions of good rulers and officers describeth by the government of Hezekiah, who was the figure of Christ.

1 Behold, [a]a King shall reign in justice, and the princes shall [b]rule in judg-
ment. **2** And that man shall be as an hiding place from the wind, and as a refu-
ge for the tempest, as rivers of water in a dry place, and as the shadow of a great
rock in [c]a weary land. **3** The eyes of [d]the seeing shall not be shut, and the ears
of them that hear, shall hearken. **4** And the heart of the foolish shall understand
knowledge, and the tongue of the stutters shall be ready to speak distinctly. **5** A
[e]niggard shall no more be called liberal, nor the churl rich. **6** But the niggard
will speak of niggardness, and his heart will work iniquity, and do wickedly, and
speak falsely against the Lord, to make empty the hungry soul, and to cause the
drink of the thirsty to fail. **7** For the weapons of the churl are wicked: he devi-
seth wicked counsels to undo the poor with lying words, and to speak against the
poor in judgment. **8** But the liberal man will devise of liberal things, and he
will continue his liberality. **9** Rise up ye women that are at ease: hear my voi-
ce, ye [f]careless daughters, hearken to my words. **10** Ye women that are careless,
shall be in fear [g]above a year in days, [h]for the vintage shall fail, and the gathe-
rings shall come no more. **11** Ye women that are at ease, be astonied; fear, O
ye careless women: put off the clothes; make bare, and gird sackcloth upon the
loins. **12** Men shall lament for the [i]teats, even for the pleasant fields, and for the
fruitful vine. **13** Upon the land of my people shall grow thorns and briers: yea,
upon all the houses of joy in the city of rejoicing, **14** Because the palace shall
be forsaken, and the [j]noise of the city shall be left: the tower and fortress shall be
dens forever, and the delight of wild asses, and a pasture for flocks, **15** Until the
[k]Spirit be poured upon us from above, and the wilderness become a fruitful field,
and the [l]plenteous field be counted as a forest. **16** And judgment shall dwell
in the desert, and justice shall remain in the fruitful field. **17** And the work of
justice shall be peace, even the work of justice and quietness, and assurance fore-
ver. **18** And my people shall dwell in the tabernacle of peace, and in sure dwel-
lings, and in safe resting places. **19** When it haileth, it shall fall on the forest, and
the [m]city shall be in the low place. **20** Blessed are ye [n]that sow upon all waters,
and [o]drive thither the feet of the ox and the ass.

33

1 The destruction of them by whom God hath punished his Church.

1 Woe to thee that [a]spoilest, and wast not spoiled: and doest wi-
ckedly, and they did not wickedly against thee: when thou shalt [b]cease to spoil,
thou shalt be spoiled: when thou shalt make an end of doing wickedly, [c]they shall
do wickedly against thee. **2** [d]O Lord, have mercy upon us, we have waited for
thee: be thou, which wast [e]their arm in the morning, our help also in time of trou-
ble. **3** At the noise of the tumult, the [f]people fled: at thine [g]exalting the nations
were scattered. **4** And your spoil shall be gathered like the gathering of [h]cater-
pillars: and [i]he shall go against him like the leaping of grasshoppers. **5** The Lord
is exalted: for he dwelleth on high: he hath filled Zion with judgment and justi-
ce. **6** And there shall be stability of [j]the times, strength, salvation, wisdom, and
knowledge: for the fear of the Lord shall be his treasure. **7** Behold, [k]their messen-
gers shall cry without, and the [l]ambassadors of peace shall weep bitterly. **8** The
[m]paths are waste: the wayfaring man ceaseth: he hath broken the covenant: he hath
contemned the cities: he regardeth no man. **9** The earth mourneth and fainteth:
Lebanon is ashamed, and hewn down: [n]Sharon is like a wilderness, and Bashan is
shaken and Carmel. **10** Now will I [o]arise, saith the Lord: now will I be exalted,
now will I lift up myself. **11** [p]Ye shall conceive chaff, and bring forth stubble:
the fire of your breath shall devour you. **12** And the people shall be as the bur-
ning of lime: and as the thorns cut up, shall they be burnt in the fire. **13** Hear, ye
that are [q]far off, what I have done, and ye that are near, know my power. **14** The
[r]sinners in Zion are afraid: a fear is come upon the hypocrites: who among us shall
dwell with the devouring fire? who among us shall dwell with the everlasting bur-
nings? **15** He that walketh in justice, and speaketh righteous things, refusing
gain of oppression, shaking his hands from taking of gifts, stopping his ears from
hearing of blood, and shutting his eyes from seeing evil, **16** He shall dwell on
[s]high: his defense shall be the munitions of rocks: bread shall be given him, and
his waters shall be sure. **17** Thine eyes shall [t]see the King in his glory: they shall
behold the [u]land far off. **18** Thine heart [v]shall meditate fear, Where is the scribe?
where is the receiver? where is he that counted the towers? **19** Thou shalt not see
a fierce people, a people of a dark speech, that thou canst not perceive, and of a
stammering tongue that thou canst not understand. **20** Look upon Zion the city
of our solemn feasts: thine eyes shall see Jerusalem a quiet habitation, a tabernacle
that cannot be removed: and the stakes thereof can never be taken away, neither
shall any of the cords thereof be broken. **21** For surely there the mighty Lord
will be unto us, as a place [w]of floods, and broad rivers, whereby shall pass no ship
with oars, neither shall great ship pass thereby. **22** For the Lord is our Judge, the
Lord is our lawgiver: the Lord is our King, he will save us. **23** Thy [x]cords are lo-
osed: they could not well strengthen their mast, neither could they spread the sail:
then shall the [y]prey be divided for a great spoil: yea, the lame shall take away the
prey. **24** And none inhabitant shall say, I am sick: the people that dwell therein,
shall have their iniquity forgiven.

---

and so careful over them, as a bird over her young, which ever flieth about them for their defense: which similitude the scripture useth in divers places, as Deut. 32:11; Matt. 23:37.

f. Isa. 31:6 He toucheth their conscience, that they might earnestly feel their grievous sins, and so truly repent, forasmuch as now they are almost drowned and past recovery.

g. Isa. 31:7 By these fruits your repentance shall be known, as Isa. 2:20.

h. Isa. 31:8 When your repentance appeareth.

i. Isa. 31:9 This was accomplished soon after when Sennacherib's army was discomfited, and he fled to his castle in Nineveh for succor.

j. Isa. 31:9 To destroy his enemies.

ISA 32

a. Isa. 32:1 This prophecy is of Hezekiah, who was a figure of Christ, and therefore it ought chiefly to be referred to him.

b. Isa. 32:1 By judgment and justice is meant an upright government, both in policy, and religion.

c. Isa. 32:2 Where men are weary with traveling for lack of water.

d. Isa. 32:3 He promiseth to give the true light, which is the pure doctrine of God's word, and understanding, and zeal of the same, are contrary to the threatenings against the wicked, Isa. 6:9 and 29:10.

e. Isa. 32:5 Vice shall no more be called virtue, nor virtue esteemed by power and riches.

f. Isa. 32:9 He prophesieth of such calamity to come, that they will not spare the women and children, and therefore willeth them to take heed and provide.

g. Isa. 32:10 Meaning, that the affliction should continue long, and when one year were past, yet they should look for new plagues.

h. Isa. 32:10 God will take from you the means and occasions, which made you to contemn him: to wit, abundance of worldly goods.

i. Isa. 32:12 By the teats he meaneth the plentiful fields, whereby men are nourished as children with the teat: or, the mothers for sorrow and heaviness shall lack milk.

j. Isa. 32:14 Or, multitude.

k. Isa. 32:15 That is, when the Church shall be restored: thus the Prophets, after they have denounced God's judgments against the wicked, used to comfort the godly, lest they should faint.

l. Isa. 32:15 The field which is now fruitful, shall be but as a barren forest in comparison of that it shall be then, as Isa. 29:17, which shall be fulfilled in Christ's time, for then they that were before as the barren wilderness, being regenerate shall be fruitful, and they that had some beginning of godliness, shall bring forth fruits in such abundance, that their former life shall seem but as a wilderness where no fruits were.

m. Isa. 32:19 They shall not need to build it in high places for fear of the enemy: for God will defend it, and turn away the storms from hurting of their commodities.

n. Isa. 32:20 That is, upon fat ground and well watered, which bringeth forth in abundance, or in places which before were covered with waters, and now made dry for your uses.

o. Isa. 32:20 The fields shall be so rank, that they shall send out their cattle to eat up the first crop, which abundance shall be signs of God's love and favor toward them.

ISA 33

a. Isa. 33:1 Meaning, the enemies of the Church, as were the Chaldeans and Assyrians, but chiefly of Sennacherib, but not only.

b. Isa. 33:1 When thine appointed time shall come that God shall take away thy power: and that which thou hast wrongfully gotten, shall be given to others, as Amos 5:11.

c. Isa. 33:1 The Chaldeans shall do like to the Assyrians, as the Assyrians did to Israel, and the Medes and Persians shall do the same to the Chaldeans.

d. Isa. 33:2 He declareth hereby what is the chief refuge of the faithful, when troubles come, to pray, and seek help of God.

e. Isa. 33:2 Which helped our fathers so soon as they called upon thee.

f. Isa. 33:3 That is, the Assyrians fled before the army of the Chaldeans, or the Chaldeans for fear of the Medes and Persians.

g. Isa. 33:3 When thou, O Lord, didst lift up thine arm to punish thine enemies.

h. Isa. 33:4 Ye that as caterpillars destroyed with your number the whole world, shall have no strength to resist your enemies the Chaldeans: but shall be gathered on an heap and destroyed.

i. Isa. 33:4 Meaning, the Medes and Persians against the Chaldeans.

j. Isa. 33:6 That is, in the days of Hezekiah.

k. Isa. 33:7 Sent from Sennacherib.

l. Isa. 33:7 Whom they of Jerusalem sent to entreat of peace.

m. Isa. 33:8 These are the words of the ambassadors, when they returned from Sennacherib.

n. Isa. 33:9 Which was a plentiful country, meaning, that Sennacherib would destroy all.

o. Isa. 33:10 To help and deliver my Church.

p. Isa. 33:11 This is spoken against the enemies, who thought all was their own: but he showeth that their enterprise shall be in vain, and that the fire which they had kindled for others, should consume them.

q. Isa. 33:13 His vengeance shall be so great, that all the world shall talk thereof.

r. Isa. 33:14 Which do not believe the words of the Prophet, and the assurance of their deliverance.

s. Isa. 33:16 Meaning, that God will be a sure defense to all them that live according to his word.

t. Isa. 33:17 They shall see Hezekiah delivered from his enemies, and restored to honor and glory.

u. Isa. 33:17 They shall be no more shut in as they were of Sennacherib, but go where it pleaseth them.

v. Isa. 33:18 Before that this liberty cometh thou shalt think that thou art in great danger: for the enemy shall so sharply assail you, that one shall cry, where is the clerk that writeth the names of them that are taxed? another, Where is the receiver? another shall cry for him that valueth the rich houses, but God will deliver you from this fear.

w. Isa. 33:21 Let us be content with this small river of Shiloah and not desire the great streams and rivers, whereby the enemies may bring in ships and destroy us.

x. Isa. 33:23 He derideth the Assyrians and enemies of the Church, declaring their destruction as they that perish by shipwreck.

y. Isa. 33:23 He comforteth the Church, and showeth that they shall be enriched with all benefits both of body and soul.

34

1 He showeth that God punisheth the wicked for the love that he beareth toward his Church.

1 Come near, ye [a]nations and hear, and hearken, ye people: let the earth hear and all that is therein, the world and all that proceedeth thereof. **2** For the indignation of the Lord is upon all nations, and his wrath upon all their armies: he hath [b]destroyed them and delivered them to the slaughter. **3** And their slain shall be cast out, and their stink shall come up out of their bodies, and the mountains shall be melted with their blood. **4** And all the host of heaven [c]shall be dissolved, and the heavens shall be folded like a book: and all their hosts shall fall as the leaf falleth from the vine, and as it falleth from the fig tree. **5** For my sword shall be [d]drunken in the heaven: behold, it shall come down upon Edom, even upon the people of [e]my curse to judgment. **6** The sword of the Lord is filled with blood: it is made fat with the fat and with the blood of the [f]lambs and the goats, with the fat of the kidneys of the rams: for the Lord hath a sacrifice in [g]Bozrah, and a great slaughter in the land of Edom. **7** And the [h]unicorn shall come down with them, and the heifers with the bulls, and their land shall be drunken with blood, and their dust made fat with fatness. **8** For it is the day of the Lord's vengeance, and the year of recompense for the judgment of Zion. **9** And the rivers thereof shall be turned into pitch, and the dust thereof into [i]brimstone, and the land thereof shall be burning pitch. **10** It shall not be quenched night nor day: the smoke thereof shall go up evermore: it shall be desolate from generation to generation; none shall pass through it forever. **11** But the pelican [j]and the hedgehog shall possess it, and the great owl, and the raven shall dwell in it, and he shall stretch out upon it the line of [k]vanity, and the stones of emptiness. **12** [l]The nobles thereof shall call to the kingdom, and there shall be none, and all the princes thereof shall be as nothing. **13** And it shall bring forth thorns in the palaces thereof, nettles, and thistles in the strongholds thereof, and it shall be an habitation for dragons, and a court for ostriches. **14** There shall [m]meet also Ziim and Iim, and the Satyr shall cry to his fellow, and the screech owl shall rest there, and shall find for herself a quiet dwelling. **15** There [n]shall the owl make her nest, and lay and hatch, and gather them under her shadow: there shall the vultures also be gathered, every one with her make. **16** Seek in the [o]book of the Lord, and read: none of [p]these shall fail, none shall want her make: for [q]his mouth hath commanded, and his very spirit hath gathered them. **17** And he hath cast the [r]lot for them, and his hand hath divided unto them by line: they shall possess it forever: from generation to generation shall they dwell in it.

35

1 The great joy of them that believe in Christ. 3 Their office which preach the Gospel. 8 The fruits that follow thereof.

1 The [a]desert and the wilderness shall rejoice, and the waste ground shall be glad and flourish as the rose. **2** It shall flourish abundantly, and shall greatly rejoice also and joy: the glory of Lebanon shall be given unto it: the beauty of [b]Carmel, and of Sharon, they shall [c]see the glory of the Lord, and the excellency of our God. **3** [d]Strengthen the weak hands, and comfort the feeble knees. **4** Say unto them that are fearful, Be you strong, fear not: behold, your God cometh with [e]vengeance: even God with a recompense, he will come and save you. **5** Then shall the eyes of the [f]blind be lightened, and the ears of the deaf be opened. **6** Then shall the lame man leap as an hart, and the dumb man's tongue shall sing: for in the [g]wilderness shall waters break out, and rivers in the desert. **7** And the dry ground shall be as a pool, and the thirsty as springs of water: in the habitation of dragons, where they lay, shall be a place for reeds and rushes. **8** And there shall be a path and a way, and the way shall be called [h]holy: the polluted shall not pass by it: for [i]he shall be with them, and walk in the way, and the fools shall not err. **9** There shall be [j]no lion, nor noisome beasts shall ascend by it, neither shall they be found there, that the redeemed may walk. **10** Therefore the [k]redeemed of the Lord shall return and come to Zion with praise: and everlasting joy shall be upon their heads: they shall obtain joy and gladness, and sorrow and mourning shall flee away.

36

1 Sennacherib sendeth Rabshakeh to besiege Jerusalem. 15 His blasphemies against God.

1 Now [a]in the [b]fourteenth year of King Hezekiah, Sennacherib King of Assyria came up against all the strong cities of Judah, and took them. **2** And the King of Assyria sent Rabshakeh from Lachish toward Jerusalem unto king Hezekiah, with a great host, and he stood by the conduit of the upper pool in the path of the fuller's field. **3** Then came forth unto him Eliakim the son of Hilkiah the [c]steward of the house, and Shebna [d]the chancellor, and Joah the son of Asaph the recorder. **4** And [e]Rabshakeh said unto them, Tell you Hezekiah, I pray you, Thus saith the great king, the King of Assyria, What confidence is this, wherein thou trustest? **5** I say, [f]Surely I have eloquence, but counsel and strength are for the war: on whom then dost thou trust, that thou rebellest against me? **6** Lo, thou trustest in this broken staff of reed, on Egypt, whereupon if a man lean, it will go into his hand, and pierce it: so is [g]Pharaoh King of Egypt unto all that trust in him. **7** But if thou say unto me, We trust in the Lord our God, is not that he, whose high places and whose altars Hezekiah took down, and said to Judah and to Jerusalem, Ye shall worship before this altar? **8** Now therefore give hostages to my Lord the king of Assyria, and I will give thee two thousand horses, if thou be able on thy part to set riders upon them. **9** For how canst thou [h]despise any captain of the [i]least of my lord's servants? and put thy trust on Egypt for chariots and for horsemen? **10** And am I now come up without the Lord to this land to destroy it? The Lord said unto me, [j]Go up against this land and destroy it. **11** Then said Eliakim, and Shebna and Joah unto Rabshakeh, [k]Speak, I pray thee, to thy servants in the Aramite's language (for we understand it) and talk not with us in the Jews' tongue, in the audience of the people that are on the wall. **12** Then said Rabshakeh, Hath my master sent me to thy master, and to thee, to speak these words, and not to the men that sit on the wall? that they may eat their own thing, and drink their own [l]piss with you? **13** So Rabshakeh stood, and cried with a loud voice in the Jews' language, and said, Hear the words of the great King, of the King of Assyria. **14** Thus saith the king, Let not Hezekiah deceive you: for he shall not be able to deliver you. **15** Neither let Hezekiah make you to trust in the Lord, saying, The Lord will surely deliver us: this city shall not be given over into the hand of the king of Assyria. **16** Hearken not to Hezekiah: for thus saith the king of Assyria, Make [m]appointment with me, and come out to me, that every man may eat of his own vine, and every man of his own fig tree, and drink every man the water of his own well, **17** Till I come and bring you to a land like your own land, even a land of wheat and wine, a land of bread and vineyards, **18** Lest Hezekiah deceive you, saying, The Lord will deliver us. Hath any of the gods of the nations delivered his land out of the hand of the king of Assyria? **19** Where is the god of [n]Hamath, and of Arpad? where is the god of Sepharvaim? or how have they delivered Samaria out of my hand? **20** Who is he among all the gods of these

---

ISA 34

- **a.** Isa. 34:1 He prophesieth of the destruction of the Edomites and other nations which were enemies to the Church.
- **b.** Isa. 34:2 God hath determined in his counsel, and hath given sentence for their destruction.
- **c.** Isa. 34:4 He speaketh this in respect of man's judgment, who in great fear and horrible troubles, thinketh that heaven and earth perisheth.
- **d.** Isa. 34:5 I have determined in my secret counsel, and in the heavens to destroy them till my sword be weary with shedding of blood.
- **e.** Isa. 34:5 They had an opinion of holiness, because they came of the Patriarch Isaac, but in effect were accursed of God, and enemies unto his Church, as the Papists are.
- **f.** Isa. 34:6 That is, both of young and old, poor and rich of his enemies.
- **g.** Isa. 34:6 That famous city shall be consumed as a sacrifice burnt to ashes.
- **h.** Isa. 34:7 The mighty and rich shall be as well destroyed as the inferiors.
- **i.** Isa. 34:9 He alludeth to the destruction of Sodom and Gomorrah, Gen. 19:24.
- **j.** Isa. 34:11 Read Isa. 13:21 and Zeph. 2:14.
- **k.** Isa. 34:11 In vain shall any man go about to build it again.
- **l.** Isa. 34:12 Meaning, here shall be neither order nor policy, nor state of commonweal.
- **m.** Isa. 34:14 Read Isa. 13:21.
- **n.** Isa. 34:15 Signifying, that Edom should be an horrible desolation and barren wilderness.
- **o.** Isa. 34:16 That is, in the Law where such curses are threatened against the wicked.
- **p.** Isa. 34:16 To wit, beasts and souls.
- **q.** Isa. 34:16 That is, the mouth of the Lord.
- **r.** Isa. 34:17 He hath given the beasts and fowls Edom for an inheritance.

ISA 35

- **a.** Isa. 35:1 He prophesieth of the full restoration of the Church both of the Jews and Gentiles under Christ, which shall be fully accomplished at the last day: albeit as yet it is compared to a desert and wilderness.
- **b.** Isa. 35:2 The Church which was before compared to a barren wilderness shall by Christ be made most plenteous and beautiful.
- **c.** Isa. 35:2 He showeth that the presence of God is the cause that the Church doth bring forth fruit and flourish.
- **d.** Isa. 35:3 He willeth all to encourage one another, and specially the ministers to exhort and strengthen the weak, that they may patiently abide the coming of God, which is at hand.
- **e.** Isa. 35:4 To destroy your enemies.
- **f.** Isa. 35:5 When the knowledge of Christ is revealed.
- **g.** Isa. 35:6 They that were barren and destitute of the graces of God, shall have them given by Christ.
- **h.** Isa. 35:8 It shall be for the Saints of God and not for the wicked.
- **i.** Isa. 35:8 God shall lead and guide them, alluding to the bringing forth of Egypt.
- **j.** Isa. 35:9 As he threateneth to the wicked to be destroyed hereby, Isa. 30:6.
- **k.** Isa. 35:10 Whom the Lord shall deliver from the captivity of Babylon.

ISA 36

- **a.** Isa. 36:1 This history is rehearsed because it is as a seal and confirmation of the doctrine afore, both for the threatenings and promises: to wit, that God would suffer his Church to be afflicted, but at length would send deliverance.
- **b.** Isa. 36:1 When he had abolished superstition, and idolatry, and restored religion, yet God would exercise his Church to try their faith and patience.
- **c.** Isa. 36:3 For he was now restored to his office, as Isa. had prophesied, Isa. 22:20.
- **d.** Isa. 36:3 This declareth that there were few godly to be found in the king's house, when he was driven to send this wicked man in such a weighty matter.
- **e.** Isa. 36:4 Sennacherib's chief captain.
- **f.** Isa. 36:5 He speaketh this in the person of Hezekiah, falsely charging him that he put his trust in his wit and eloquence, whereas his only confidence was in the Lord.
- **g.** Isa. 36:6 Satan labored to pull the godly King from one vain confidence to another: to wit, from trust in the Egyptians, whose power was weak and would deceive them, to yield himself to the Assyrians, and so not to hope for any help of God.
- **h.** Isa. 36:9 Or, turn back.
- **i.** Isa. 36:9 He reproacheth to Hezekiah his small power, which is not able to resist one of Sennacherib's least captains.
- **j.** Isa. 36:10 Thus the wicked to deceive us, will pretend the Name of the Lord: but we must try the spirits, whether they be of God or no.
- **k.** Isa. 36:11 They were afraid, lest by his words, he should have stirred up the people against the King, and also pretended to grow to some appointment with him.
- **l.** Isa. 36:12 Hebrew, the water of their feet.
- **m.** Isa. 36:16 The Hebrew word signifieth blessing, whereby this wicked captain would have persuaded the people, that their condition should be better under Sennacherib than under Hezekiah.
- **n.** Isa. 36:19 That is, of Antioch in Syria, of the which these two other cities also were: whereby we see how every town had his peculiar idol, and how the wicked make God an idol because

lands, that hath delivered their country out of mine hand, that the Lord should deliver Jerusalem out of mine hand? **21** Then they [o]kept silence, and answered him not a word: for the king's commandment was, saying, Answer him not. **22** Then came Eliakim the son of Hilkiah the steward of the house, and Shebna the chancellor, and Joah the son of Asaph the recorder, unto Hezekiah with rent clothes, and told him the words of Rabshakeh.

37

2 Hezekiah asketh counsel of Isaiah, who promiseth him the victory. 10 The blasphemy of Sennacherib. 16 Hezekiah's prayer. 36 The army of Sennacherib is slain of the Angel. 38 And he himself of his own sons.

1 And [1]when the King Hezekiah heard it, he [a]rent his clothes, and put on sackcloth and came into the house of the Lord. **2** And he sent Eliakim the steward of the house, and Shebna the chancellor, with the Elders of the Priests, clothed in sackcloth unto [b]Isaiah the Prophet the son of Amoz. **3** And he said unto him, Thus saith Hezekiah, This day is a day of tribulation and of rebuke and blasphemy: for the children are come to the [c]birth, and there is no strength to bring forth. **4** If so be the Lord thy God hath [d]heard the words of Rabshakeh, whom the King of Assyria his master hath sent to rail on the living God, and to reproach him with words, which the Lord thy God hath heard, then [e]lift thou up thy prayer for the remnant that are left. **5** So the servants of the King Hezekiah came to Isaiah. **6** And Isaiah said unto them, Thus say unto your master, Thus saith the Lord, Be not afraid of the words that thou hast heard, wherewith the servants of the King of Assyria have blasphemed me. **7** Behold, I will send a blast upon him, and he shall hear a [f]noise, and return to his own land, and I will cause him to fall by the sword in his own land. **8** So Rabshakeh returned, and found the King of Assyria fighting against [g]Libnah: for he had heard that he was departed from Lachish. **9** He heard also men say of Tirhakah, King of Ethiopia, Behold, he is come out to fight against thee: and when he heard it, he sent other messengers to Hezekiah, saying, **10** Thus shall ye speak to Hezekiah King of Judah, saying, Let not thy God [h]deceive thee, in whom thou trustest, saying, Jerusalem shall not be given into the hand of the King of Assyria. **11** Behold, thou hast heard what the Kings of Assyria have done to all lands in destroying them, and shalt thou be delivered? **12** Have the gods of the nations delivered them, which my fathers have destroyed? as [i]Gozan, and [j]Haran, and Rezeph, and the children of Eden, which were at Telassar? **13** Where is the king of Hamath, and the King of Arpad, and the King of the city of Sepharvaim, Hena, and Ivah? **14** So Hezekiah received the letter of the hand of the messengers, and read it, and he went up into the house of the Lord, and Hezekiah spread it before the Lord. **15** And Hezekiah prayed unto the Lord, saying, **16** O Lord of hosts, God of Israel, which [k]dwellest between the Cherubims, thou art very God alone over all the kingdoms of the earth: thou hast made the heaven and the earth. **17** Incline thine ear, O Lord, and hear: open thine eyes, O Lord, and see, and hear all the words of Sennacherib, who hath sent to blaspheme the living God. **18** Truth it is, O Lord, that the Kings of Assyria have destroyed all lands and [l]their country, **19** And have cast their gods in the fire: for they were no gods, but the work of men's hands, even wood or stone: therefore they destroyed them. **20** Now therefore, O Lord our God, save thou us out of his hand, that [m]all the kingdoms of the earth may know, that thou only art the Lord. **21** Then Isaiah the son of Amoz sent unto Hezekiah, saying, Thus saith the Lord God of Israel, Because thou hast prayed unto me, concerning Sennacherib king of Assyria, **22** This is the word that the Lord hath spoken against him, The [n]virgin, the daughter of Zion, hath despised thee, and laughed thee to scorn: the daughter of Jerusalem hath shaken her head at thee. **23** Whom hast thou railed on and blasphemed? and against whom hast thou exalted thy voice, and lifted up thine eyes on high? even against the [o]holy One of Israel. **24** By thy servants hast thou railed on the Lord, and said, By the multitude of my chariots I am come up to the top of the mountains to the sides of Lebanon, and will cut down the high cedars thereof, and the fair fir trees thereof, and I will go up to the heights of his top, and to the forest of his fruitful places. **25** I have dug, [p]and drunk the waters, and with the plant of my feet have I dried all the rivers closed in. **26** Hast thou not heard how I have of old time made it, [q]and have formed it long ago? and should I now bring it, that it should be destroyed, and laid on ruinous heaps, as cities defensed? **27** Whose inhabitants have [r]small power, and are afraid and confounded: they are like the grass of the field and green herb, or grass on the house tops, or corn blasted [s]afore it be grown. **28** But I know thy dwelling, and thy [t]going out, and thy coming in, and thy fury against me. **29** Because thou ragest against me, and thy tumult is come unto mine ears, therefore will I put mine [u]hook in thy nostrils, and my bridle in thy lips, and will bring thee back again the same way thou [v]camest. **30** And this shall be a [w]sign unto thee, O Hezekiah, Thou shalt eat this year such as groweth of itself: and the [x]second year such things as grow without sowing: and in the third year, sow ye and reap, and plant vineyards, and eat the fruit thereof. **31** And [y]the remnant that is escaped of the house of Judah, shall again take root downward and bear fruit upward. **32** For out of Jerusalem shall go a remnant, and they that escape out of mount Zion: the zeal of the Lord of hosts shall do this. **33** Therefore thus saith the Lord concerning the King of Assyria, He shall not enter into this city, nor shoot an arrow there, nor come before it with shield, nor cast a mount against it. **34** By the same way that he came, he shall return, and not come into this city, saith the Lord. **35** For I will defend this city to save it, for mine own sake, and for my servant [z]David's sake. **36** [2]Then the Angel of the Lord went out, and smote in the camp of Assyria, an hundred fourscore, and five thousand: so when they arose early in the morning, behold, they were all dead corpses. **37** So Sennacherib king of Assyria departed, and went away and returned and dwelt at [aa]Nineveh. **38** And as he was in the Temple worshipping of Nisroch his god, Adrammelech and Sharezer his sons slew him with the sword, and they escaped into the land of [ab]Ararat: and [ac]Esarhaddon his son reigned in his stead.

38

1 Hezekiah is sick. 5 He is restored to health by the Lord, and liveth fifteen years after. 10 He giveth thanks for his benefit.

1 About [1]that [a]time was Hezekiah sick unto the death, and the Prophet Isaiah son of Amoz came unto him, and said unto him, Thus saith the Lord, Put thine house in an order, for thou shalt die, and not live. **2** Then Hezekiah [b]turned his face to the wall, and prayed to the Lord, **3** And said, I beseech thee, Lord, remember now how I have walked before thee in truth, and with a perfect heart, and have done that which is good in thy sight: and Hezekiah wept sore. **4** Then came the word of the Lord to Isaiah, saying, **5** Go, and say unto Hezekiah, Thus saith the Lord God of David thy father, I have heard thy prayer, and seen thy tears: behold, I will add unto thy days fifteen years. **6** And I will deliver thee [c]out of the hand of the king of Assyria, and this city: for I will defend this city. **7** And

---

they do not understand that God maketh them his scourge, and punisheth cities for sin.

o. Isa. 36:21 Not that they did not show by evident signs that they did detest his blasphemy: for they had now rent their clothes, but they knew it was in vain to use long reasoning with this infidel, whose rage they should have so much more provoked.

ISA 37

a. Isa. 37:1 In sign of grief and repentance.
b. Isa. 37:2 To have comfort of him by the word of God, that his faith might be confirmed and so his prayer be more earnest: teaching hereby that in all dangers these two are the only remedies, to seek unto God and his ministers.
c. Isa. 37:3 We are in as great sorrow as a woman that travaileth of child, and cannot be delivered.
d. Isa. 37:4 That is, will declare by effect that he hath heard it: for when God deferreth to punish, it seemeth to the flesh, that he knoweth not the sin, or heareth not the cause.
e. Isa. 37:4 Declaring that the minister's office doth not only stand in comforting by the word, but also in praying for the people.
f. Isa. 37:7 Of the Egyptians and Ethiopians, that shall come and fight against him.
g. Isa. 37:8 Which was a city toward Egypt, thinking thereby to have stayed the force of his enemies.
h. Isa. 37:10 Thus God would have him to utter a most horrible blasphemy before his destruction: as to call the author of all truth, a deceiver: some gather hereby that Shebna had disclosed unto Sennacherib the answer that Isa. sent to the king.
i. Isa. 37:12 Which was a city of the Medes.
j. Isa. 37:12 Called also Charre a city in Mesopotamia, whence Abraham came after his father's death.
k. Isa. 37:16 He groundeth his prayer on God's promise, who promised to hear them from between the Cherubims.
l. Isa. 37:18 Meaning, the ten tribes.
m. Isa. 37:20 He declareth for what cause he prayed, that they might be delivered: to wit, that God might be glorified thereby through all the world.
n. Isa. 37:22 Whom God had chosen to himself as a chaste virgin, and over whom he had care to preserve her from the lusts of the tyrant, as a father would have over his daughter.
o. Isa. 37:23 Declaring hereby that they that are enemies to God's Church, fight against him whose quarrel his Church only maintaineth.
p. Isa. 37:25 He boasteth of his policy, in that that he can find means to nourish his army: and of his power in that that his army is so great, that it is able to dry up whole rivers, and to destroy the waters which the Jews had closed in.
q. Isa. 37:26 Signifying, that God made not his Church to destroy it, but to preserve it: and therefore he saith that he formed it of old, even in his eternal counsel which cannot be changed.
r. Isa. 37:27 Hebrew, are short in hand.
s. Isa. 37:27 He showeth that the state and power of most flourishing cities endureth but a moment in respect of the Church, which shall remain forever, because God is the maintainer thereof.
t. Isa. 37:28 Meaning, his counsels and enterprises.
u. Isa. 37:29 Because Sennacherib showed himself, as a devouring fish and furious beast, he useth these similitudes, to teach how he will take him and guide him.
v. Isa. 37:29 Thou shalt lose thy labor.
w. Isa. 37:30 God giveth signs after two sorts: some go before the thing, as the signs that Moses wrought in Egypt, which were for the confirmation of their faith, and some go after the thing, as the sacrifice, which they were commanded to make three days after their departure: and these latter are to keep the benefits of God in our remembrance: of the which sort this here is.
x. Isa. 37:30 He promiseth that for two years the ground of itself should feed them.
y. Isa. 37:31 They whom God hath delivered out of the hands of the Assyrians, shall prosper: and this properly belongeth to the Church.
z. Isa. 37:35 For my promise sake made to David.
aa. Isa. 37:37 Which was the chiefest city of the Assyrians.
ab. Isa. 37:38 Or, Armenia.
ac. Isa. 37:38 Who was also called Sardanapalus, in whose days ten years after Sennacherib's death the Chaldeans overcame the Assyrians by Merodach their king.

ISA 37

1. 2 Kings. 19:1
2. 2 Kings 19:35 / 2 Chron. 32:21

ISA 38

a. Isa. 38:1 Soon after that the Assyrians were slain: so that God will have the exercise of his children continually, that they may learn only to depend upon God and aspire to the heavens.
b. Isa. 38:2 For his heart was touched with fear of God's judgment, seeing he had appointed him to die so quickly after his deliverance from so great calamity, as one unworthy to remain in that estate, and also foreseeing the great change that should come in the Church, forasmuch as he left no son to reign after him: for as yet Manasseh was not born, and when he reigned, we see what a tyrant he was.
c. Isa. 38:6 He doth not only promise to prolong his life, but to give him rest and quietness from the Assyrians, who might have renewed their army to revenge their former discomfiture.
d. Isa. 38:7 For Hezekiah had asked for the confirmation of his faith, a sign, as verse 22, and 2 Kings 20:8, whereunto he was moved by the singular motion of God's spirit.

[d]this sign shalt thou have of the Lord, that the Lord will do this thing that he hath spoken, **8** Behold, I will bring again the shadow of the degrees (whereby it is gone down in the dial of Ahaz by the [e]sun) ten degrees backward: so the sun returned by ten degrees, by the which degrees it was gone down. **9** [f]The writing of Hezekiah king of Judah, when he had been sick, and was recovered of his sickness. **10** I said in the [g]cutting off of my days, I shall go to the gates of the grave: I am deprived of the residue of my years. **11** I said, [h]I shall not see the Lord, even the Lord in the land of the living: I shall see man no more among the inhabitants of the world. **12** Mine habitation is departed, and is removed from me, like a shepherd's tent: I [i]have cut off like a weaver my life: he will cut me off from the height: from day [j]to night, thou wilt make an end of me. **13** I reckoned [k]to the morning: but he brake all my bones like a lion, from day to night wilt thou make an end of me. **14** Like a crane or a swallow, so did I [l]chatter: I did mourn as a dove: mine eyes were lifted up on high: O Lord, [m]it hath oppressed me, comfort me. **15** What shall I say, [n]for he hath said it to me, and he hath done it: I shall walk [o]weakly all my years in the bitterness of my soul. **16** O Lord, [p]to them that overlive them, and to all that are in them, the life of my spirit shall be known, that thou causest me to [q]sleep and hast given life to me. **17** Behold, for [r]felicity I had bitter grief, but it was thy pleasure to deliver my soul from the pit of corruption: for thou hast cast all my [s]sins behind thy back. **18** For [t]the grave cannot confess thee: death cannot praise thee: they that go down into the pit, cannot hope for thy truth. **19** But the living, the living, he shall confess thee, as I do this day: the father to the [u]children shall declare thy truth. **20** The Lord was ready to save me: therefore we will sing my song, all the days of [v]our life in the house of the Lord. **21** Then said Isaiah, Take a lump of dry figs and [w]lay it upon the boil, and he shall recover. **22** Also Hezekiah [x]had said, What is the sign, that I shall go up into the house of the Lord?

39

Hezekiah is reproved because he showed his treasures unto the ambassadors of Babylon.

1 At [1]the same time, [a]Merodach Baladan, the son of Baladan, King of Babel, sent [b]letters, and a present to Hezekiah: for he had heard that he had been sick, and was recovered. **2** And Hezekiah was [c]glad of them, and showed them the house of the treasures, the silver, and the gold, and the spices, and the precious ointment, and all the house of his armor, and all that was found in his treasures; there was nothing in his house, nor in all his kingdom that Hezekiah showed them not. **3** Then came Isaiah the Prophet unto King Hezekiah, and said unto him, What said these men? and from whence came they to thee? And Hezekiah said, They are come from a far country unto me, from Babel. **4** Then said he, What have [d]they seen in thine house? And Hezekiah answered, All that is in mine house have they seen; there is nothing among my treasures, that I have not showed them. **5** And Isaiah said to Hezekiah, Hear the word of the Lord of hosts, **6** Behold, the days come, that all that is in thine house, and which thy fathers have laid up in store until this day, shall be [e]carried to Babel: nothing shall be left, saith the Lord. **7** And of thy sons, that shall proceed out of thee, and which thou shalt beget, shall they take away, and they shall be [f]eunuchs in the palace of the King of Babel. **8** [g]Then said Hezekiah to Isaiah, The word of the Lord is good, which thou hast spoken: and he said, Yet let there be peace, and truth in my days.

40

2 Remission of sins by Christ. 3 The coming of John Baptist. 18 The Prophet reproveth the Idolaters, and them that trust not in the Lord.

1 Comfort [a]ye, comfort ye my people, will your God say. **2** Speak comfortably to Jerusalem, and cry unto her, that her [b]warfare is accomplished, that her iniquity is pardoned; for she hath received of the Lord's hand [c]double for all her sins. **3** A [d]voice crieth in the [e]wilderness, [f]Prepare ye the way of the Lord: make straight in the desert a path for our God. **4** Every valley shall be exalted, and every [g]mountain and hill shall be made low; and the crooked shall be straight, and the rough places plain. **5** And the glory of the Lord shall be revealed, and all [h]flesh shall see it together: for the mouth of the Lord hath spoken it. **6** A [i]voice said, Cry. And he said, What shall I cry? All flesh is grass, and all the [j]grace thereof is as the flowers of the field. **7** The grass withereth, the flower fadeth, because the [k]Spirit of the Lord bloweth upon it: surely the people is grass. **8** The grass withereth, the flower fadeth: but the [l]word of our God shall stand forever. **9** O Zion, that bringest good tidings, get thee up into the high [m]mountain: O Jerusalem, that bringest good tidings, lift up thy voice with strength: lift it up, be not afraid: say unto the cities of Judah, Behold [n]your God. **10** Behold, the Lord God will come with power, and [o]his arm shall rule for him: behold, his reward is with him, and his work before him. **11** He shall feed his flock like a shepherd: he shall gather the lambs with his arm, and carry them in his bosom, and shall guide them with [p]young. **12** Who hath measured the waters in his [q]fist? and counted heaven with the span, and comprehended the dust of the earth in a measure? and weighed the mountains in a weight, and the hills in a balance? **13** Who hath instructed the spirit of the Lord? or was [r]his counselor, or taught him? **14** Of whom took the counsel, and who instructed him and taught him in the way of judgment? or taught him knowledge, and showed unto him the way of understanding? **15** Behold, the nations are as a drop of a bucket, and are counted as the dust of the balance: behold, he taketh away the isles as a little dust. **16** And Lebanon is not sufficient for fire, nor the beasts thereof sufficient for a burnt offering. **17** All nations before him are as [s]nothing, and they are counted to him, less than nothing, and vanity. **18** To whom then [t]will ye liken God? or what similitude will ye set up unto him? **19** The workman melteth an image, or the goldsmith beateth it out in gold, or the goldsmith maketh silver plates. **20** Doth not [u]the poor choose out a tree that will not rot, for an oblation? he seeketh also unto him a cunning workman, to prepare an image that shall not be moved. **21** Know ye nothing? have ye not heard [v]it? hath it not been told you from the beginning? have ye not understood it by the [w]foundation of the earth? **22** He sitteth upon the circle of the earth, and the inhabitants thereof are as grasshoppers, he stretcheth out the heavens as a curtain, and spreadeth them out, as a tent to dwell in. **23** He bringeth the

---

e. Isa. 38:8 Read 2 Kings 20:10.
f. Isa. 38:9 He left this song of his lamentation and thanksgiving to all posterity, as a monument of his own infirmity and thankful heart for God's benefits, as David did, Ps. 51.
g. Isa. 38:10 At what time it was told me, that I should die.
h. Isa. 38:11 I shall no more praise the Lord here in this Temple among the faithful: thus God suffereth his dearest children to want his consolation for a time, that his grace afterward may the more appear when they feel their own weakness.
i. Isa. 38:12 By my sin I have provoked God to take my life from me.
j. Isa. 38:12 That is, in one day, or shortly.
k. Isa. 38:13 Over night I thought that I should live till morning, but my pangs in the night persuaded me the contrary: he showeth the horror that the faithful have when they apprehend God's judgment against their sin.
l. Isa. 38:14 I was so oppressed with sorrow, that I was not able to utter my words, but only to groan and sigh.
m. Isa. 38:14 To wit, sorrow and grief both of the body and mind.
n. Isa. 38:15 God hath declared by his Prophet that I shall die and therefore I will yield unto him.
o. Isa. 38:15 I shall have no release, but continual sorrows while I live.
p. Isa. 38:16 They that shall overlive the men that are now alive, and all they that are in these years shall acknowledge this benefit.
q. Isa. 38:16 That after that thou hadst condemned me to death thou restoredst me to life.
r. Isa. 38:17 Whereas I thought to have lived in rest and ease being delivered from mine enemy, I had grief upon grief.
s. Isa. 38:17 He esteemeth more the remission of his sins, and God's favor than a thousand lives.
t. Isa. 38:18 Forasmuch as God hath placed man in this world to glorify him, the godly take it as a sign of his wrath, when their days were shortened, either because that they seemed unworthy for their sins to live longer in his service, or for their zeal to God's glory, seeing that there are so few in earth that do regard it, as Ps. 6:5; 115:17.
u. Isa. 38:19 All posterity shall acknowledge, and the fathers according to their duty toward their children shall instruct them in thy graces, and mercies toward me.
v. Isa. 38:20 He showeth what is the use of the Congregation and Church, to wit, to give the Lord thanks for his benefits.
w. Isa. 38:21 Read 2 Kings 20:7.
x. Isa. 38:22 As verse 7.

ISA 38
1. 2Kings 20:1 / 2 Chron. 32:4

ISA 39
a. Isa. 39:1 This was the first king of Babylon, which overcame the Assyrians in the tenth year of his reign.
b. Isa. 39:1 Partly moved with the greatness of the miracle, partly because he showed himself enemy to his enemies, but chiefly because he would join with them whom God favored, and have their help, if occasion served.
c. Isa. 39:2 Read 2 Kings 20:13 and 2 Chron. 32:25, 31.
d. Isa. 39:4 He asketh him of the particulars, to make him understand the craft of the wicked, which he before being overcome with their flattery and blinded with ambition, could not see.
e. Isa. 39:6 By the grievousness of the punishment is declared how greatly God detested ambition and vain glory.
f. Isa. 39:7 That is, officers and servants.
g. Isa. 39:8 Read 2 Kings 20:19.

ISA 39
1. 2 Kings 20:12

ISA 40
a. Isa. 40:1 This is a consolation for the Church, assuring them, that they shall be never destitute of Prophets whereby he exhorteth the true ministers of God that then were, and those also that should come after him, to comfort the poor afflicted, and to assure them of their deliverance both of body and soul.
b. Isa. 40:2 The time of her affliction.
c. Isa. 40:2 Meaning, sufficient, as Isa. 61:7, and full correction, or double grace, whereas she deserved double punishment.
d. Isa. 40:3 To wit, of the Prophets.
e. Isa. 40:3 That is, in Babylon and other places, where they were kept in captivity, and misery.
f. Isa. 40:3 Meaning Cyrus and Darius which should deliver God's people out of captivity, and make them a ready way to Jerusalem: and this was fully accomplished, when John the Baptist brought tidings of Jesus Christ's coming, who was the true deliverer of his Church from sin and Satan, Matt. 3:3.
g. Isa. 40:4 Whatsoever may let or hinder this deliverance, shall be removed.
h. Isa. 40:5 This miracle shall be so great, that it shall be known through all the world.
i. Isa. 40:6 The voice of God which spake to the Prophet Isa..
j. Isa. 40:6 Meaning, all man's wisdom and natural powers, James 1:10; 1 Pet. 1:24.
k. Isa. 40:7 The spirit of God shall discover the vanity in all that seem to have any excellency of themselves.
l. Isa. 40:8 Though considering the frailty of man's nature many of the Jews should perish, and so not be partakers of this deliverance, yet God's promise should be fulfilled, and they that remained, should feel the fruit thereof.
m. Isa. 40:9 To publish this benefit through all the world.
n. Isa. 40:9 He showeth at one word the perfection of all man's felicity, which is to have God's presence.
o. Isa. 40:10 His power shall be sufficient without help of any other, and shall have all means in himself to bring his will to pass.
p. Isa. 40:11 He shall show his care and favor over them that are weak and tender.
q. Isa. 40:12 Declaring that as God only hath all power, so doth he use the same for the defense and maintenance of his Church.
r. Isa. 40:13 He showeth God's infinite wisdom for the same.
s. Isa. 40:17 He speaketh all this to the intent that they should neither fear man nor put their trust in any, save only in God.
t. Isa. 40:18 Hereby he armeth them against the idolatry, wherewith they should be tempted in Babylon.
u. Isa. 40:20 He showeth the rage of the idolaters, seeing that the poor that have not to suffice their own necessities, will defraud themselves to serve their idols.
v. Isa. 40:21 Have ye not the word of God, which plainly condemneth idolatry?
w. Isa. 40:21 Can you not learn by the visible creatures whom God hath made to observe your use, that you should not serve them nor worship them?

princes to nothing, and maketh the judges of the earth, as vanity, **24** As though
they were not planted, as though they were not sown, as though their stock took
no root in the earth: for he did even [x]blow upon them, and they withered, and the
whirlwind will take them away as stubble. **25** To whom now will ye liken me,
that I should be like him, saith the Holy one? **26** Lift up your eyes on high, and
behold who hath created these things, and bringeth [y]out their armies by number,
and calleth them all by names: by the greatness of his power and mighty strength
nothing faileth. **27** Why sayest thou, O Jacob, and speakest O Israel, [z]My way
is hid from the Lord, and my judgment is passed over of my God? **28** Knowest
thou not? or hast thou not heard, that the everlasting God, the Lord hath created
the [aa]ends of the earth? he neither fainteth, nor is weary: there is no searching of
his [ab]understanding. **29** But he giveth strength unto him that fainteth, and unto
him that hath no strength, he increaseth power. **30** [ac]Even the young men shall
faint, and be weary, and the young men shall stumble and fall. **31** But they that
wait upon the Lord, shall renew their strength: they shall lift up the wings, as the
eagles: they shall run, and not be weary, and they shall walk and not faint.

41

2 God's mercy in choosing his people. 6 Their idolatry. 27 Deliverance promised to Zion.

1 Keep [a]silence before me, O islands, and let the people [b]renew their stren-
gth: let them come near, and let them speak: let us come together into judg-
ment. **2** Who raised up [c]justice from the East, and called him to his foot? and
gave the nations before him, and subdued the kings? he gave them as dust to his
sword, and as scattered stubble unto his bow. **3** He pursued them, and passed
safely by the way that he had not gone with his feet. **4** Who hath wrought and
done it? he that calleth the [d]generations from the beginning. I the Lord am the
[e]first, and with the last I am the same. **5** The isles saw it, and did [f]fear, and the
ends of the earth were abashed, drew near, and [g]came. **6** Every man helped his
neighbor, and said to his brother, [h]Be strong. **7** So the workman comforted the
founder, and he that smote with the hammer, him that smote by course, saying, It
is ready for the soldering, and he fastened it with nails that it should not be mo-
ved. **8** But thou, Israel, art my [i]servant, and thou Jacob, whom I have chosen, the
seed of Abraham my friend. **9** For I have taken thee from the ends of the earth,
and called thee before the chief thereof, and said unto thee, Thou art my servant: I
have chosen thee, and not cast thee away. **10** Fear thou not, for I am with thee:
be not afraid, for I am thy God: I will strengthen thee, and help thee, and will su-
stain thee with the [j]right hand of my justice. **11** Behold, all they that provoke
thee, shall be ashamed, and confounded: they shall be as nothing, and they that
strive with thee shall perish. **12** Thou shalt seek them and shalt not [k]find them:
to wit, the men of thy strife, for they shall be as nothing, and the men that war
against thee, as a thing of nought. **13** For I the Lord thy God will hold thy ri-
ght hand, saying unto thee, Fear not, I will help thee. **14** Fear not thou [l]worm,
Jacob, and ye men of Israel: I will help thee, saith the Lord, and thy redeemer the
holy One of Israel. **15** Behold, I will make thee a roller, and a new threshing
instrument having teeth: thou shalt thresh the [m]mountains, and bring them to
powder, and shalt make the hills as chaff. **16** Thou shalt fan them, and the wind
shall carry them away, and the whirlwind shall scatter them: and thou shalt rejoice
in the Lord, and shalt glory in the holy One of Israel. **17** When [n]the poor and
the needy seek water, and there is none (their tongue faileth for thirst: I the Lord
will hear them: I the God of Israel will not forsake them:) **18** I will open rivers in
the tops of the hills, and fountains in the midst of the valleys: I will make the wil-
derness as a pool of water, and the waste [o]land as springs of water. **19** I will set in
the wilderness the cedar, the Shittah, and the myrrhe tree, and the pine tree, and I
will set in the wilderness the fir tree, the elm and the box tree together. **20** The-
refore let them see and know, and let them consider and understand together that
the hand of the Lord hath done this, and the holy One of Israel [p]hath created
it. **21** [q]Stand to your cause, saith the Lord: bring forth your strong reasons saith
the King of Jacob. **22** Let them bring them forth, and let them tell us what shall
come, let them show the former things what they be, that we may consider them,
and know the latter end of them: either declare us things for to come. **23** Show
the things that are to come hereafter, that we may know that ye are gods: yea, do
good or do evil, that we may declare it, and behold it together. **24** Behold, ye are
of no value, and your making is of naught: man hath [r]chosen an abomination by
them. **25** I have raised up from the [s]North, and he shall come: from the East sun
shall he [t]call upon my name, and shall come upon [u]princes as upon clay, and as the
potter treadeth mire under the foot. **26** Who hath declared from the beginning,
that we may know? or before time, that we may say, He is righteous? Surely there
is none that showeth: surely there is none that declareth: surely there is none that
heareth [v]your words. **27** I am the first, that saith to Zion, Behold, behold [w]them:
and I will give to Jerusalem [x]one that shall bring good tidings. **28** But when [y]I
beheld, there was none: and when I inquired of them, there was no counselor, and
when I demanded of them, they answered not a word. **29** Behold, they are all
vanity: their work is of nothing, their images are wind and confusion.

42

1 The obedience and humility of Christ. 6 Why he was sent into the world. 11 The vocation of the Gentiles.

1 Behold, [a]my servant: [b]I will stay upon him: mine elect, in whom my soul
[c]delighteth: I have put my Spirit upon him: he shall bring forth [d]judgment to the
Gentiles. **2** He shall not [e]cry, nor lift up, nor cause his voice to be heard in the
street. **3** A [f]bruised reed shall he not break, and the smoking [g]flax shall he not
quench: he shall bring forth judgment in [h]truth. **4** He shall not fail nor be di-
scouraged till he have [i]set judgment in the earth: and the [j]isles shall wait for his
Law. **5** Thus saith God the Lord (he that created the heavens and spread them
abroad: he that stretched forth the earth, and the buds thereof: he that giveth
breath unto the people upon it, and spirit to them that walk therein) **6** I the
Lord have called thee in [k]righteousness, and will hold [l]thine hand, and I will keep
thee, and give thee for a [m]covenant of the people, and for a light of the Genti-
les, **7** That thou mayest open the eyes of the blind, and bring out the prisoners
from the prison: and them that sit in darkness, out of the prison house. **8** I am
the Lord, this is my Name, and my [n]glory will I not give to another, neither my
praise to graven images. **9** Behold, the former things are [o]come to pass, and new
things do I declare: before they come forth, I tell you of them. **10** Sing unto
the Lord a new song, and his praise from the end of the earth: ye that go down to
the sea, and all that is therein, the isles and the inhabitants thereof. **11** Let the

---

x. Isa. 40:24 So that his power appeareth in every place wheresoever we turn our eyes.
y. Isa. 40:26 Who hath set in order the infinite number of the stars.
z. Isa. 40:27 He rebuketh the Jews, because they did not rest on the providence of God, but thought that he had forsaken them in their troubles.
aa. Isa. 40:28 And therefore all power is in his hand to deliver when his time cometh.
ab. Isa. 40:28 Showing that men must patiently abide, and not curiously seek out the cause of God's delay in our afflictions.
ac. Isa. 40:30 They that trust in their own virtue, and do not acknowledge that all cometh of God.

ISA 41

a. Isa. 41:1 God as though he pleaded his cause with all nations, requireth silence, that he may be heard in his right.
b. Isa. 41:1 That is, gather all their power and supports.
c. Isa. 41:2 Who called Abraham (who was the pattern of God's justice in delivering his Church) from the idolatry of the Chaldeans to go to and fro at his commandment, and placed him in the land of Canaan.
d. Isa. 41:4 Who hath created man and maintained his succession.
e. Isa. 41:4 Though the world set up never so many gods, yet they diminish nothing of my glory: for I am all one, unchangeable, which have ever been, and shall be forever.
f. Isa. 41:5 Considering mine excellent works among my people.
g. Isa. 41:5 They assembled themselves and conspired against me to maintain their idolatry.
h. Isa. 41:6 He noteth the obstinacy of the idolaters to maintain their superstitions.
i. Isa. 41:8 And therefore oughtest not to pollute thyself with the superstition of the Gentiles.
j. Isa. 41:10 That is, by the force of promise, in the performance whereof I will show myself faithful and just.
k. Isa. 41:12 Because they shall be destroyed.
l. Isa. 41:14 Thus he calleth them because they were contemned of all the world, and that they considering their own poor estate, should seek unto him for help.
m. Isa. 41:15 I will make thee able to destroy all thine enemies, be they never so mighty: and this chiefly is referred to the kingdom of Christ.
n. Isa. 41:17 That is, they that shall be afflicted in the captivity of Babylon.
o. Isa. 41:18 God will rather change the order of nature than they should want anything, that cry to him by true faith in their miseries: declaring to them hereby that they shall lack nothing by the way, when they return from Babylon.
p. Isa. 41:20 That is, hath appointed and determined that it shall come so to pass.
q. Isa. 41:21 He biddeth the idolaters to prove their religion, and to bring forth their idols, that they may be tried whether they know all things, and can do all things: which if they cannot do, he concludeth that they are no gods, but vile idols.
r. Isa. 41:24 So that a man cannot make an idol, but he must do that which God detesteth and abhorreth: for he chooseth his own devices and forsaketh the Lord's.
s. Isa. 41:25 Meaning, the Chaldeans.
t. Isa. 41:25 That is, Cyrus, who shall do all things in my name and by my direction: whereby he meaneth that both their captivity and deliverance shall be ordered by God's providence and appointment.
u. Isa. 41:25 Both of the Chaldeans and others.
v. Isa. 41:26 Meaning, that none of the Gentile gods can work any of these things.
w. Isa. 41:27 That is, the Israelites which return from the captivity.
x. Isa. 41:27 To wit, a continual succession of Prophets and ministers.
y. Isa. 41:28 When I looked whether the idols could do these things, I found that they had neither wisdom nor power to do anything: therefore he concludeth that all are wicked, that trust in such vanities.

ISA 42

a. Isa. 42:1 That is, Christ, who in respect of his manhood is called here servant. The Prophets used to make mention of Christ after that they have declared any great promise, because he is the foundation whereupon all the promises are made and ratified.
b. Isa. 42:1 For I have committed all my power to him, as to a most faithful steward: Some read, I will establish him: to wit, in his office by giving him the fullness of my Spirit.
c. Isa. 42:1 He only is acceptable to me, and they that come unto me by him: for there is no other means of reconciliation, Matt. 12:18; Eph. 4:1.
d. Isa. 42:1 He shall declare himself governor over the Gentiles, and call them by his word, and rule them by his Spirit.
e. Isa. 42:2 His coming shall not be with pomp and noise, as earthly princes.
f. Isa. 42:3 He will not hurt the weak and feeble, but support and comfort them.
g. Isa. 42:3 Meaning, the wick of a lamp, or candle which is almost out, but he will cherish it and snuff it, that it may shine brighter.
h. Isa. 42:3 Although he favor the weak, yet will he not spare the wicked, but will judge them according to truth and equity.
i. Isa. 42:4 Till he have set all things in good order.
j. Isa. 42:4 The Gentiles shall be desirous to receive his doctrine.
k. Isa. 42:6 Meaning, unto a lawful and just vocation.
l. Isa. 42:6 To assist and guide thee.
m. Isa. 42:6 As him, by whom the promise made to all nations in Abraham shall be fulfilled.
n. Isa. 42:8 I will not suffer my glory to be diminished: which I should do if I were not faithful in performing the same, and the idolaters thereby would extol their idols above me.
o. Isa. 42:9 As in time past I have been true in my promises, so will I be in time to come.

wilderness and the cities thereof lift up their voice, the towns that [p]Kedar doth inhabit: let the inhabitants of the rocks sing: let them shout from the top of the mountains. **12** Let them give glory unto the Lord, and declare his praise in the islands. **13** The Lord shall go forth as a [q]giant; he shall stir up his courage like a man of war: he shall shout and cry, and shall prevail against his enemies. **14** I have a long time held my peace: I have been still and refrained myself; now will I cry like a [r]travailing woman: I will destroy and devour at once. **15** I will make waste mountains, and hills, and dry up all their herbs, and I will make the floods islands, and I will dry up the pools. **16** And I will bring the [s]blind by a way, that they knew not, and lead them by paths that they have not known: I will make darkness light before them, and crooked things straight. These things will I do unto them, and not forsake them. **17** They shall be turned back: they shall be greatly ashamed, that trust in graven images, and say to the molten images, Ye are our gods. **18** Hear, ye deaf: and ye blind, regard, that ye may see. **19** Who is blind but my [t]servant? or deaf as my [u]messenger, that I sent? who is blind as the [v]perfect, and blind as the Lord's servant? **20** Seeing many things, but thou keepest them not? opening the ears, but he heareth not? **21** The Lord is willing for his righteousness sake, that he may magnify the Law and exalt it. **22** But this people is [w]robbed and spoiled, and shall be all snared in dungeons, and they shall be hid in prison houses; they shall be for prey, and none shall deliver: a spoil, and none shall say, [x]Restore. **23** Who among you shall hearken to this, and take heed, and hear for [y]afterwards? **24** Who gave Jacob for a spoil, and Israel to the robbers? Did not the Lord, because we have sinned against him? for they would not walk in his ways, neither be obedient unto his Law. **25** Therefore he hath poured upon him his fierce wrath, and the strength of battle; and it set him on fire round about, and he knew not, and it burned him up, yet he considered not.

43

1 The Lord comforteth his people. He promiseth deliverance to the Jews. 11 There is no God but one alone.

1 But now thus saith the Lord, [a]that created thee, O Jacob: and he that formed thee, O Israel, [b]Fear not: for I have redeemed thee: I have called thee by thy name, thou art mine. **2** When thou passest through the [c]waters, I will be with thee, and through the floods, that they do not overflow thee. When thou walkest through the very fire, thou shalt not be burnt, neither shall the flame kindle upon thee. **3** For I am the Lord thy God, the holy one of Israel, thy Savior: I gave [d]Egypt for thy ransom, Ethiopia, and Seba for thee. **4** Because thou wast precious in my sight, and thou wast honorable, and I loved thee, therefore will I give [e]man for thee, and people for thy sake. **5** Fear not, for I am with thee: I will bring thy seed from the [f]East, and gather thee from the West. **6** I will say to the North, Give: and to the South, Keep not back: bring my sons from far, and my daughters from the ends of the earth. **7** Everyone shall be called by my [g]Name: for I created him for my glory, formed him and made him. **8** I will bring forth the blind people, and they shall have eyes, and the deaf, and they shall have ears. **9** Let all the nations be gathered [h]together, and let the people be assembled: who among them can declare this, and show us former things? let them bring forth their [i]witnesses, that they may be justified: but let them [j]hear, and say, It is truth. **10** You [k]are my witnesses, saith the Lord, and my [l]servant, whom I have chosen: therefore ye shall know and believe me, and ye shall understand that I am: before me there was no God formed, neither shall there be after me. **11** I, even I am the Lord, and beside me there is no Savior. **12** I have declared, and I have saved, and I have showed, when there was no strange god among you: therefore you are my witnesses, saith the Lord, that I am God. **13** Yea, before the day was, I am, and there is none that can deliver out of mine hand: I will do it, and who shall let it? **14** Thus saith the Lord your redeemer, the holy one of Israel, For your sake I have sent to Babel, and [m]brought it down: they are all fugitives, and the Chaldeans cry in [n]the ships. **15** I am the Lord your holy one, the creator of Israel, your King. **16** Thus saith the Lord which maketh a way in [o]the Sea, and a path in the mighty [p]waters. **17** When he [q]bringeth out the [r]chariot and horse, the army and the power lie together, and shall not rise, they are extinct, and quenched as tow. **18** Remember ye not the former things, neither regard the things of old. **19** Behold, I do a new thing: now shall it come forth: shall you not know it? I will even make a way in the [s]desert, and floods in the wilderness. **20** The wild [t]beasts shall honor me, the dragons and the ostriches, because I gave water in the desert, and floods in the wilderness to give drink to my people, even to mine elect. **21** This people have I formed for myself: they shall show forth my praise. **22** And thou hast not [u]called upon me, O Jacob, but thou hast [v]wearied me, O Israel. **23** Thou [w]hast not brought me the sheep of thy burnt offerings, neither hast thou honored me with thy sacrifices. I have not caused thee to serve with an offering, nor wearied thee with incense. **24** Thou broughtest me no sweet [x]savor with money, neither hast thou made me drunk with the fat of thy sacrifices, but thou hast made me to [y]serve with thy sins, and wearied me with thine iniquities. **25** I, even I am he that putteth away thine iniquities for mine own sake, and will not remember thy sins. **26** Put me in [z]remembrance: let us be judged together: count thou that thou mayest be justified. **27** Thy [aa]first father hath sinned, and thy [ab]teachers have transgressed against me. **28** Therefore I have [ac]profaned the rulers of the Sanctuary, and have made Jacob a curse, and Israel a reproach.

44

1 The Lord promiseth comfort, and that he will assemble his Church of divers nations. 9 The vanity of Idols. 17 The beastliness of idolaters.

1 Yet now hear, O Jacob my servant, and Israel whom I have chosen. **2** Thus saith the Lord, that made thee, and formed [a]thee from the womb: he will help thee. Fear not, O Jacob, my servant, and thou righteous [b]whom I have chosen. **3** For I will pour water upon the [c]thirsty, and floods upon the dry ground: I will pour my spirit upon thy seed, and my blessing upon thy buds. **4** And they [d]shall grow as among the grass, and as the willows by the rivers of waters. **5** One shall say, I am the Lord's: another [e]shall be called by the name of Jacob: and another shall subscribe with his hand unto the Lord, and name himself by the name of Israel. **6** Thus saith the Lord the King of Israel and his redeemer, the Lord of hosts, [f]I am the first, and I am the last, and without me is there no God. **7** And who is like me, that shall [g]call and shall declare it, and set [h]it in order before me, since I appointed the [i]ancient people? and what is at hand, and what things are to come? let [j]them show

---

p. Isa. 42:11 Meaning, the Arabians, under whom he comprehendeth all the people of the East.
q. Isa. 42:13 He showeth the zeal of the Lord, and his power in the conservation of his Church.
r. Isa. 42:14 I will haste to execute my vengeance, which I have so long deferred as a woman that desireth to be delivered, when she is in travail.
s. Isa. 42:16 That is, my poor people, which are in perplexity and care.
t. Isa. 42:19 To wit, Israel, which should have most light because of my Law.
u. Isa. 42:19 The Priest to whom my word is committed, which should not only hear it himself, but cause others to hear it.
v. Isa. 42:19 As the Priests and Prophets that should be lights to others?
w. Isa. 42:22 Because they will not acknowledge this benefit of the Lord, who is ready to deliver them, he suffereth them to be spoiled of their enemies through their own fault and incredulity.
x. Isa. 42:22 There shall be none to succor them, or to will the enemy to restore that which he hath spoiled.
y. Isa. 42:23 Meaning, God's wrath.

ISA 43

a. Isa. 43:1 After these threatenings he promiseth deliverance to his Church, because he hath regenerated them, adopted them, and called them.
b. Isa. 43:1 When thou seest dangers and conspiracies on all sides, remember this benefit and the love of thy God, and it shall encourage thee.
c. Isa. 43:2 By water and fire he meaneth all kind of troubles and perils.
d. Isa. 43:3 I turned Sennacherib's power against these countries, and made them to suffer that affliction which thou shouldest have done, and so were as the payment of thy ransom, Isa. 37:9.
e. Isa. 43:4 I will not spare any man, rather than thou shouldest perish, for God more esteemeth one of his faithful than all the wicked in the world.
f. Isa. 43:5 He prophesieth of their deliverance from the captivity of Babylon, and so of the calling of the universal Church, alluding to that which is written, Deut. 30:3.
g. Isa. 43:7 Meaning, that he could not be unmindful of them, except he would neglect his own Name and glory.
h. Isa. 43:9 Signifying, that no power can resist him in doing this miraculous work, nor all their idols are able to do the like, as Isa. 41:22.
i. Isa. 43:9 To prove that the things which are spoken of them, are true.
j. Isa. 43:9 Showing, that the malice of the wicked hindereth them in the knowledge of the truth, because they will not hear when God speaketh by his word.
k. Isa. 43:10 The Prophets and people to whom I have given my Law.
l. Isa. 43:10 Meaning specially Christ, and by him all the faithful.
m. Isa. 43:14 By Darius and Cyrus.
n. Isa. 43:14 They shall cry when they would escape by my water, seeing that the course of Euphrates is turned another way by the enemy.
o. Isa. 43:16 When he delivered Israel from Pharaoh, Exod. 14:22.
p. Isa. 43:16 When the Israelites passed through Jordan, Josh. 3:17.
q. Isa. 43:17 When he delivered his people out of Egypt.
r. Isa. 43:17 Pharaoh and his mighty army.
s. Isa. 43:19 Meaning, that their deliverance out of Babylon should be more famous than that from Egypt was, Jer. 23:7; Hag. 2:10; 2 Cor. 5:17; Rev. 21:5, 7.
t. Isa. 43:20 They shall have such abundance of all things as they return home, even in the dry and barren places, that the very beasts shall feel my benefits, and shall acknowledge them: much more men ought to be thankful for the same.
u. Isa. 43:22 Thou hast not worshipped me as thou oughtest to have done.
v. Isa. 43:22 Because thou hast not willingly received that which I did command thee, thou didst grieve me. Whereby he showeth that his mercies were the only cause of their deliverance, forasmuch as they had deserved the contrary.
w. Isa. 43:23 Meaning, in true faith and obedience.
x. Isa. 43:24 Either for the composition of the sweet ointment, Exod. 30:34, or for the sweet incense, Exod. 30:7.
y. Isa. 43:24 Thou hast made me to bear an heavy burden by thy sins.
z. Isa. 43:26 If I forget anything that may make for thy justification, put me in remembrance and speak for thyself.
aa. Isa. 43:27 Thine ancestors.
ab. Isa. 43:27 Thy Priests and thy Prophets.
ac. Isa. 43:28 That is, rejected, abhorred, and destroyed them in the wilderness and at other times.

ISA 44

a. Isa. 44:2 He treated and chose thee from the beginning of his own mercy, and before thou couldest merit anything.
b. Isa. 44:2 Whom God accepteth as righteous: or which haddest occasion thereunto because of the Law, and of thine holy vocation.
c. Isa. 44:3 Because man of himself is as the dry and barren land, he promiseth to moisten him with the waters of his holy Spirit, Joel 2:28; John 7:38; Acts 2:17.
d. Isa. 44:4 That is, thy children and posterity shall increase wonderfully after their deliverance from Babylon.
e. Isa. 44:5 By this diversity of speech he meaneth one thing, that is, that the people shall be holy, and receive the true religion of God, as Ps. 87:5.
f. Isa. 44:6 I am always like myself, that is, merciful toward my Church, and most able to maintain it, as Isa. 41:4 and 48:12; Rev. 1:17 and 22:13.
g. Isa. 44:7 And appoint them that shall deliver the Church.
h. Isa. 44:7 That is, declare unto me how I ought to proceed herein.
i. Isa. 44:7 God calleth the Israelites ancient, because he preferred them to all others in his eternal election.
j. Isa. 44:7 Meaning, their idols.

unto them. **8** Fear ye not, neither be afraid: have not I told thee of old, and have declared it? [k]you are even my witnesses, whether there be a God beside me, and that there is no God that I know not. **9** All they that make an image, are vanity, and [l]their delectable things shall nothing profit: and they are their own witnesses, [m]that they see not nor know: therefore they shall be confounded. **10** Who hath made a [n]god, or molten an image, that is [o]profitable for nothing? **11** Behold, all that are of the [p]fellowship thereof, shall be confounded: for the workmen themselves are men: let them all be gathered together, and [q]stand up, yet they shall fear, and be confounded together. **12** The smith taketh an instrument, and worketh in the coals, and fashioneth it with hammers, and worketh it with the strength of his arms, yea, he is [r]an hungered, and his strength faileth, he drinketh no water, and is faint. **13** The carpenter stretcheth forth a line, he fashioneth it with a red thread, he planeth it, and he portrayeth it with the compass, and maketh it after the figure of a man, and according to the beauty of a man, that it may remain in [s]an house. **14** He will hew him down cedars, and take the pine tree and the oak, and taketh courage among the trees of the forest; he planteth a fir tree, and the rain doth nourish it. **15** And man burneth thereof; for he will take thereof, and [t]warm himself: he also kindleth it, and baketh bread, yet he maketh a god, and worshippeth it; he maketh it an idol, and boweth unto it. **16** He burneth the half thereof even in the fire, and upon the half thereof he [u]eateth flesh; he roasteth the roast, and is satisfied; also he warmeth himself and saith, Aha, I am warm, I have been at the fire. **17** And the residue thereof he maketh a god, even his idol; he boweth unto it, and worshippeth and prayeth unto it, and saith, Deliver me; for thou art my god. **18** They have not known, nor understood: [v]for God hath shut their eyes that they cannot see, and their heart, that they cannot understand. **19** And none [w]considereth in his heart, neither is there knowledge nor understanding to say, I have burnt half of it, even in the fire, and have baked bread also upon the coals thereof: I have roasted flesh, and eaten it, and shall I make the residue thereof an abomination? shall I bow to the stock of a tree? **20** He feedeth [x]of ashes: a seduced heart hath deceived him, that he cannot deliver his soul, nor say, Is there not a lie in my right hand? **21** [y]Remember these (O Jacob and Israel) for thou art my servant: I have formed thee; thou art my servant: O Israel forget me not. **22** I have put away thy transgressions like a cloud, and thy sins as a mist; turn unto me, for I have redeemed thee. **23** [z]Rejoice ye heavens; for the Lord hath done it; shout, ye lower parts of the earth; burst forth into praises, ye mountains, O forest and every tree therein: for the Lord hath redeemed Jacob, and will be glorified in Israel. **24** Thus saith the Lord thy redeemer, and he that formed thee from the womb, I am the Lord that made all things, that spread out the heavens alone, and stretched out the earth by myself. **25** I destroy the [aa]tokens of the soothsayers, and make them that conjecture, fools, and turn the wise men backward, and make their knowledge foolishness. **26** He confirmeth the word of his [ab]servant, and performeth the counsel of his messengers, saying to Jerusalem, Thou shalt be inhabited: and to the cities of Judah, Ye shall be built up, and I will repair the decayed places thereof. **27** He saith to the [ac]deep, Be dry, and I will dry up thy floods. **28** He saith to [ad]Cyrus, Thou art my shepherd, and he shall perform all my desire: saying also to Jerusalem, Thou shalt be built, and to the Temple, Thy foundation shall be surely laid.

45

1 The deliverance of the people by Cyrus. 9 God is just in all his works. 20 The calling of the Gentiles.

1 Thus saith the Lord unto [a]Cyrus his [b]anointed, whose right hand I have holden to [c]subdue nations before him: therefore will I weaken the loins of kings, and open the doors before him, and the gates shall not be shut. **2** I will go before thee, and make the [d]crooked straight: I will break the brazen doors, and burst the iron bars. **3** And I will give thee the treasures of darkness, and the things hid in secret places, that thou mayest [e]know that I am the Lord which call thee by thy name, even the God of Israel. **4** For Jacob my servant's [f]sake, and Israel mine elect, I will even call thee by thy name, and name thee, though thou hast not known me. **5** I am the Lord, and there is none other; there is no God besides me: I [g]girded thee, though thou hast not known me. **6** That they may know from the rising of the sun, and from the West, that there is none besides me. I am the Lord, and there is none other. **7** I form the [h]light, and create darkness: I make peace, and create evil: I the Lord do all these things. **8** Ye heavens send the dew from above, and let the clouds drop down [i]righteousness: let the earth open, and let salvation and justice grow forth: let it bring them forth together: I the Lord have [j]created him. **9** [k]Woe be unto him that striveth with his maker, the potsherd with the potsherds of the earth: shall the clay say to him that fashioneth it, What makest thou? or thy work, [l]It hath none hands? **10** Woe unto him that saith to his father, What hast thou begotten? or to his mother, What hast thou brought forth? **11** Thus saith the Lord, the only one of Israel, and his maker, Ask me [m]of things to come concerning my sons, and concerning the works of mine hands: commend you me. **12** I have made the earth, and created man upon it: I, whose hands have spread out the heavens, I have even commanded all their [n]army. **13** I have raised [o]him up in righteousness, and I will direct all his ways: he shall build my city, and he shall let go my captives, not for [p]price nor reward, saith the Lord of hosts. **14** Thus saith the Lord, The labor [q]of Egypt, and the merchandise of Ethiopia, and of the Sabeans, men of stature shall come unto thee, and they shall be [r]thine: they shall follow thee, and shall go in chains: they shall fall down before thee, and make supplication unto thee, saying, Surely God is in thee, and there is none other God besides. **15** Verily, thou O God [s]hidest thyself, O God, the Savior of Israel. **16** All they shall be ashamed and also confounded: they shall go to confusion together, that are the makers of images. **17** But Israel shall be saved in the Lord, with an everlasting salvation: ye shall not be ashamed nor confounded world without end. **18** For this saith the Lord (that created heaven, God himself that formed the earth, and made it: he that prepared it, he created it not in vain: he formed it to be [t]inhabited) I am the Lord, and there is none other. **19** I have not spoken in secret, neither [u]in a place of darkness in the earth: I said not in vain unto the seed of Jacob, Seek you me: I the Lord do speak righteousness, and declare righteous things. **20** Assemble yourselves, and come: draw near together, [v]ye abject of the Gentiles: they have no knowledge, that set up the wood of their idol, and pray unto a god, that cannot save them. **21** Tell ye and bring them, and let them take counsel together, who hath declared this from the beginning, or hath told it of old? Have not I the Lord? and there is none other God beside me, a just God, and a Savior: there is none beside me. **22** Look unto me, and

---

k. Isa. 44:8 Read Isa. 43:10.
l. Isa. 44:9 Whatsoever they bestow upon their idols, to make them to seem glorious.
m. Isa. 44:9 That is, the idolaters seeing their idols blind, most needs be witnesses of their own blindness, and feeling that they are not able to help them, must confess that they have no power.
n. Isa. 44:10 Meaning, that whatsoever is made by the hand of man, if he be esteemed as God, is most detestable.
o. Isa. 44:10 Whereby appeareth their blasphemy, which call images the books of the laity, seeing that they are not only here called unprofitable, but Isa 41:24 abominable, and Jeremiah calleth them the work of errors, Jer. 10:15; Habakkuk, a lying teacher, Hab. 2:18.
p. Isa. 44:11 That is, which by any way consent either to the making or worshipping.
q. Isa. 44:11 Signifying, that the multitude shall not then save the idolaters, when God will take vengeance, although they excuse themselves thereby among men.
r. Isa. 44:12 He describeth the raging affection of the idolaters, which forget their own necessities to set forth their devotion toward their idols.
s. Isa. 44:13 To place it in some Temple.
t. Isa. 44:15 He setteth forth the obstinacy and malice of the idolaters, which though they see by daily experience that their idols are no better than the rest of the matter whereof they are made, yet they refuse the one part, and make a god of the other, as the Papists make their cake god, and the rest of their idols.
u. Isa. 44:16 That is, he either maketh a table or trenchers.
v. Isa. 44:18 The Prophet giveth here an answer to all them that wonder how it is possible that any should be so blind to commit such abomination, saying, that God hath blinded their eyes, and hardened their hearts.
w. Isa. 44:19 Hebrew, turneth.
x. Isa. 44:20 He is abused as one that would eat ashes, thinking to satisfy his hunger.
y. Isa. 44:21 Showing that man's heart is most inclined to idolatry, and therefore he warneth his people by these examples, that they should not cleave to any but to the living God, when they should be among the idolaters.
z. Isa. 44:23 He showeth that the work of the Lord toward his people shall be so great, that the insensible creatures shall be moved therewith.
aa. Isa. 44:25 He armeth them against the soothsayers of Babylon, which would have borne them in hand, that they knew by the stars, that God would not deliver them, and that Babylon should stand.
ab. Isa. 44:26 Of Isa. and the rest of his Prophets, which did assure the Church of God's favor and deliverance.
ac. Isa. 44:27 He showeth that God's work should be no less notable in this their deliverance, than when he brought them out of Egypt, through the sea.
ad. Isa. 44:28 To assure them of their deliverance, he nameth the person by whom it should be, more than an hundred years before he was born.

ISA 45

a. Isa. 45:1 To assure the Jews of their deliverance against the great tentations that they should abide, he nameth the person and the means.
b. Isa. 45:1 Because Cyrus should execute the office of a deliverer, God called him his anointed for a time, but after another sort than he called David.
c. Isa. 45:1 To guide him in the deliverance of my people.
d. Isa. 45:2 I will take away all impediments and lets.
e. Isa. 45:3 Not that Cyrus did know God to worship him aright, but he had a certain particular knowledge as profane men may have of his power, and so was compelled to deliver God's people.
f. Isa. 45:4 Not for any thing that is in thee, or for thy worthiness.
g. Isa. 45:5 I have given thee strength, power and authority.
h. Isa. 45:7 I send peace and war, prosperity and adversity, as Amos 3:6.
i. Isa. 45:8 He comforteth the Jews, as if he would say, Though when ye look to the heavens and earth for succor, ye see nothing now but signs of God's wrath, yet will cause them to bring forth most certain tokens of your deliverance, and of the performance of my promise: which is meant by righteousness.
j. Isa. 45:8 I have appointed Cyrus to this use and purpose.
k. Isa. 45:9 Hereby he bridleth their impatience, which in adversity and trouble murmur against God, and will not tarry his pleasure: willing that man should match with his like, and not contend against God.
l. Isa. 45:9 That is, it is not perfectly made.
m. Isa. 45:11 Instead of murmuring, humble yourselves, and ask what ye will for the consolation of my children, and you shall be sure of it, as ye are of these things which are at your commandment. Some read it with an interrogation, and make it the application of the similitude.
n. Isa. 45:12 That is, the stars.
o. Isa. 45:13 To wit, Cyrus, that I may show by him the faithfulness of my promise in delivering my people.
p. Isa. 45:13 Meaning, freely and without ransom, or any grievous condition.
q. Isa. 45:14 These people were tributaries to the Persians, and so king Artaxerxes gave this money toward the building of the Temple, Ezra 7:27.
r. Isa. 45:14 Whereas to fore they were thine enemies, they shall now honor thee, and thou shalt rule them: which was accomplished in the time of Christ.
s. Isa. 45:15 Hereby he exhorteth the Jews to patience, though their deliverance be deferred for a time: showing that they should not repent their long patience, but the wicked and idolaters shall be destroyed.
t. Isa. 45:18 To wit, of men, but chiefly of his Church.
u. Isa. 45:19 As do the false gods, which give uncertain answers.
v. Isa. 45:20 All ye idolaters which though you seem to have never so much worldly dignity, yet in God's sight you are vile and abject.
w. Isa. 45:22 He calleth the idolaters to repentance, willing them to look unto him with the eye of faith.

ye shall be saved: all [w]the ends of the earth shall be saved: for I am God, and there is none other. **23** I have sworn by myself: the word is gone out of my mouth in [x]righteousness, and shall not return, That every [y]knee shall bow unto me, and every tongue shall swear by me. **24** Surely [z]he shall say, In the Lord have I righteousness and strength: he shall come unto him, and all that [aa]provoke him shall be ashamed. **25** The whole seed of Israel shall be justified, and glory in the Lord.

46

1 The destruction of Babylon and of their idols. 3 He calleth the Jews to the consideration of his works.

1 Bel is bowed down: [a]Nebo is fallen: their idols were upon their [b]beasts, and upon the cattle: they which did bear you, were laden with a weary burden. **2** [c]They are bowed down, and fallen together, for they could not rid them of the burden, and their [d]soul is gone into captivity. **3** Hear ye me, O house of Jacob, and all that remain of the house of Israel, which are [e]born of me from the womb, and brought up of me from the birth. **4** Therefore unto [f]old age, I the same, even I will bear you until the hoary hairs: I have made you: I will also bear you, and I will carry you, and I will deliver you. **5** To whom will ye make me like, or make me equal, or [g]compare me that I should be like him? **6** They draw gold out of the bag, and weigh silver in the balance, and hire a goldsmith to make a god of it, and they bow down and worship it. **7** They bear it upon the shoulders: they carry him and set him in his place: so doth he stand, and cannot remove from his place. Though one cry unto him, yet can he not answer, nor deliver him out of his tribulation. **8** Remember this, and be ashamed: bring it again to [h]mind, O you transgressors. **9** Remember the former things of old: for I am God, and there is none other God, and there is nothing like me, **10** Which declare the last thing from the beginning, and from of old: the things that were not done, saying, My counsel shall stand, and I will do whatsoever I will. **11** I call a [i]bird from the East, and the man of my [j]counsel from far: as I have spoken, so will I bring it to pass: I have purposed it, and I will do it. **12** Hear me ye stubborn hearted, that are far from [k]justice. **13** I bring [l]near my justice: it shall not be far off, and my salvation shall not tarry: for I will give salvation in Zion, and my glory unto Israel.

47

The destruction of Babylon, and the causes wherefore.

1 Come down and sit in the dust: O [a]virgin, daughter Babel, sit on the ground: there is no [b]throne, O daughter of the Chaldeans; for thou shalt no more be called, Tender and delicate. **2** Take the millstones, and [c]grind meal; loose thy locks: [d]make bare the feet: uncover the leg, and pass through the floods. **3** Thy filthiness shall be discovered, and thy shame shall be seen: I will take vengeance, and I will not meet thee as a [e]man. **4** [f]Our redeemer, the Lord of hosts is his Name, the holy One of Israel. **5** [g]Sit still, and get thee into darkness, O daughter of the Chaldeans; for thou shalt no more be called, The lady of kingdoms. **6** I was wroth with my people: I have polluted mine inheritance, and given them into thine hand, thou didst show them no [h]mercy, but thou didst lay thy very heavy yoke upon the ancient. **7** And thou saidest, I shall be a lady forever, so that thou didst not set thy mind to these things, neither didst thou remember the latter end thereof. **8** Therefore now hear, thou that art given to pleasures, and dwellest careless, She saith in her heart, I am and none else: I shall not sit as a widow, neither shall know the loss of children. **9** But these two things shall come to thee suddenly on one day, the loss of children and widowhood; they shall come upon thee in their [i]perfection, for the multitude of thy divinations, and for the great abundance of thine enchanters. **10** For thou hast trusted in thy wickedness; thou hast said, None seeth me. Thy [j]wisdom and thy knowledge, they have caused thee to rebel, and thou hast said in thine heart, I am, and none else. **11** Therefore shall evil come upon thee, and thou shalt not know the morning thereof; destruction shall fall upon thee, which thou shalt not be able to put away: destruction shall come upon thee suddenly, or thou beware. **12** Stand now among thine enchanters, and in the multitude of thy soothsayers (with whom thou hast [k]wearied thyself from thy youth) if so be thou mayest have profit, or if so be thou mayest have strength. **13** Thou art wearied in the multitude of thy counsels: let now the astrologers, the stargazers, and prognosticators stand up, and save thee from these things that shall come upon thee. **14** Behold, they shall be as stubble: the fire shall burn them; they shall not deliver their own lives from the power of the flame: there shall be no coals [l]to warm at, nor light to sit by. **15** Thus shall they serve thee, with whom thou hast wearied thee, even thy merchants from thy youth; every one shall wander to his own [m]quarters: none shall save thee.

48

1 The hypocrisy of the Jews is reproved. 12 The Lord alone will be worshipped. 20 Of their deliverance out of Babylon.

1 Hear ye this, O house of Jacob, which are [a]called by the name of Israel, and are come out of [b]the waters of Judah: which swear by the name of the Lord, and make mention of the God of Israel, but not in truth nor in righteousness. **2** For they are called of the holy city, and stay themselves [c]upon the God of Israel, whose Name is the Lord of hosts. **3** I have declared the former things of old, and they went out of my mouth, and I showed [d]them: I did them suddenly and they came to pass. **4** Because I knew that [e]thou art obstinate, and thy neck is an iron sinew, and thy brow brass, **5** Therefore I have declared it to thee of old: before it came to pass, I showed [f]it thee, lest thou shouldest say, Mine idol hath done them, and my carved image, and my molten image hath commanded them. **6** Thou hast heard, behold all this, and will not ye [g]declare it? I have showed thee new things, even now, and hid things, which thou knewest not. **7** They are created now, and not of old, and even before this thou heardest them not, lest thou shouldest say, Behold, I [h]knew them. **8** Yet thou heardest them not, neither didst know them, neither yet was thine ear opened of old; for I knew that thou wouldest grievously transgress: therefore have I called thee a transgressor from the [i]womb. **9** For my Name's sake will I defer my wrath, and for my praise, will I refrain it from thee, [j]that I cut thee not off. **10** Behold, I have fined thee, but [k]not as silver: I have [l]chosen thee in the furnace of affliction. **11** For mine own sake, for mine own sake will I do it; for how should my Name [m]be polluted? [n]surely I will not give my glory unto another. **12** Hear me, O Jacob and Israel, my called, [o]I am, I am the first, and I am the last. **13** Surely mine hand hath laid the foundation of the earth, and my right hand hath spanned the heavens: when I call them, [p]they stand up together. **14** All you, assemble yourselves, and hear: which among them hath declared these things? The Lord hath loved [q]him, he will do his will in Babel, and his arm shall be against the Chaldeans. **15** I, even I have spoken it, and I have called him, I have brought him, and his way shall prosper. **16** Come near unto me: hear ye this: I have not spoken it in secret from the [r]beginning: from the time that the thing was, I was there, and now the Lord God and his Spirit hath [s]sent

---

x. Isa. 45:23 That is, that the thing which I have promised shall be faithfully performed.
y. Isa. 45:23 The knowledge of God and the true worshipping shall be through all the world, Rom. 14:11; Phil. 2:10, whereby he signifieth that we must not only serve God in heart, but declare the same also by outward profession.
z. Isa. 45:24 Meaning, the faithful shall feel and confess this.
aa. Isa. 45:24 All the contemners of God.

ISA 46

a. Isa. 46:1 These were the chief idols of Babylon.
b. Isa. 46:1 Because they were of gold and silver, the Medes and Persians carried them away.
c. Isa. 46:2 The beasts that carried the idols, fell down under their burden.
d. Isa. 46:2 He derideth the idols, which had neither soul nor sense.
e. Isa. 46:3 He showeth the difference between the idols and the true God: for they must be carried of others, but God himself carrieth his, as Deut. 32:11.
f. Isa. 46:4 Seeing I have begotten you, I will nourish and preserve you forever.
g. Isa. 46:5 The people of God, setting their own calamity, and the flourishing estate of the Babylonians, should be tempted to think that their God was not so mighty as the idols of their enemies: therefore he describeth the original of all the idols to make them to be abhorred of all men: showing that the most that can be spoken in their commendation, is but to prove them vile.
h. Isa. 46:8 Become wise, meaning, that all idolaters are without wit or sense, like mad men.
i. Isa. 46:11 That is, Cyrus, which shall come as swift as a bride, and fight against Babylon.
j. Isa. 46:11 Him by whom I have appointed to execute that which I have determined.
k. Isa. 46:12 Which by your incredulity would let the performance of my promise.
l. Isa. 46:13 He showeth that man's incredulity cannot abolish the promise of God, Rom. 3:3.

ISA 47

a. Isa. 47:1 Which hast lived in wealth and wantonness, and hast not yet been overcome by any enemy.
b. Isa. 47:1 Thy government shall be taken from thee.
c. Isa. 47:2 Thou shalt be brought to most vile servitude: for to turn the mill was the office of slaves.
d. Isa. 47:2 The things wherein she setteth her greatest pride, shall be made vile, even from the head to the foot.
e. Isa. 47:3 I will use no humanity nor pity toward thee.
f. Isa. 47:4 The Israelites shall confess that the Lord doeth this for his Church's sake.
g. Isa. 47:5 For very shame, and hide thyself.
h. Isa. 47:6 They abused God's judgments, thinking that he punished the Israelites, because he would utterly cast them off, and therefore instead of pitying their misery, thou didst increase it.
i. Isa. 47:9 So that thy punishment shall be so great, as is possible to be imagined.
j. Isa. 47:10 Thou didst think that thine own wisdom and policy would have saved thee.
k. Isa. 47:12 He derideth their vain confidence, that put their trust in anything but in God, condemning also such vain sciences, which serve to no use, but to delude the people, and to bring them from depending only on God.
l. Isa. 47:14 They shall utterly perish, and no part of them remain.
m. Isa. 47:15 They shall flee everyone to that place, which he thought by his speculations to be most sure: but that shall deceive them.

ISA 48

a. Isa. 48:1 He detecteth their hypocrisy which vaunteth themselves to be Israelites, and were not so indeed.
b. Isa. 48:1 Meaning, the fountain and stock.
c. Isa. 48:2 They make a show, as though they would have none other God.
d. Isa. 48:3 He showeth that they could not accuse him in anything, forasmuch as he had performed whatsoever he had promised.
e. Isa. 48:4 I have done for thee more than I promised, that thy stubbornness and impudence might have been overcome.
f. Isa. 48:5 How thou shouldest be delivered out of Babylon.
g. Isa. 48:6 Will ye not acknowledge this my benefit, and declare it unto others?
h. Isa. 48:7 Showing that man's arrogance is the cause why God doth not declare all things at once, lest they should attribute this knowledge to their own wisdom.
i. Isa. 48:8 From the time that I brought thee out of Egypt: for that deliverance was as the birth of the Church.
j. Isa. 48:9 As it was my free mercy that I did choose thee: so it is my free mercy that must save thee.
k. Isa. 48:10 For I had respect to thy weakness and infirmity: for in silver there is some pureness, but in us there is nothing but dross.
l. Isa. 48:10 I took thee out of the furnace where thou shouldest have been consumed.
m. Isa. 48:11 God joineth the salvation of his with his own honor: so that they cannot perish, but his glory should be diminished, as Deut. 32:27.
n. Isa. 48:11 Read Isa. 42:8.
o. Isa. 48:12 Read Isa. 41:4.
p. Isa. 48:13 To obey me, and to do whatsoever I command them.
q. Isa. 48:14 Meaning, Cyrus, whom he had chosen to destroy Babylon.

me. **17** Thus saith the Lord thy redeemer, the Holy one of Israel, I am the Lord thy God, which teach thee [t]to profit, and lead thee by the way that thou shouldest go. **18** Oh, that thou hadst hearkened to my commandments! then had thy prosperity been as the flood, and thy righteousness as the waves of the sea. **19** Thy seed also had been as the sand, and the fruit of thy body like the gravel thereof: his [u]name should not have been cut off nor destroyed before me. **20** [v]Go ye out of Babel: flee ye from the Chaldeans with a voice of joy: tell and declare this: show it forth to the end of the earth: say ye, The Lord hath redeemed his servant Jacob. **21** And they [w]were not thirsty: he led them through the wilderness: he caused the waters to flow out of the rock for them: for he clave the rock and the water gushed out. **22** There is no [x]peace, saith the Lord, unto the wicked.

49

1 The Lord God exhorteth all nations to believe his promises. 6 Christ is the salvation of all that believe, and will deliver them from the tyranny of their enemies.

1 Hear ye me, O isles, and hearken, ye people from far. The Lord hath called [a]me from [b]the womb, and made mention of my name from my mother's belly. **2** And he hath made my mouth like a sharp [c]sword: under the shadow of his hand hath he [d]hid me, and made me a chosen shaft, and hid me in his quiver, **3** And said unto me, Thou art my servant [e]Israel, for I will be glorious in thee. **4** And I said, I have [f]labored in vain: I have spent my strength in vain and for nothing; but my judgment is with the Lord, and my work with my God. **5** And now saith the Lord that formed me from the womb to be his servant, that I may bring Jacob again to him (though Israel be not gathered, [g]yet shall I be glorious in the eyes of the Lord; and my God shall be my strength.) **6** And he said, It is a small thing that thou shouldest be my servant to raise up the tribes of Jacob, and to restore the desolations of Israel: I will also give [h]thee for a light of the Gentiles, that thou mayest be my salvation unto the end of the world. **7** Thus saith the Lord the redeemer of Israel, and his holy One, to him that is despised in soul, to a nation that is abhorred, to a [i]servant of rulers, Kings shall see, and [j]arise, and princes shall worship, because of the Lord, that is faithful: and the holy One of Israel, which hath chosen thee. **8** Thus saith the Lord, [k]In an acceptable time have I heard thee, and in a day of salvation have I helped thee: and I will preserve thee, and will give [l]thee for a covenant of the people, that thou mayest raise up the [m]earth, and obtain the inheritance of the desolate heritages: **9** That thou mayest say to the [n]prisoners, Go forth; and to them that are in darkness, Show yourselves; they shall feed in the ways, and their [o]pastures shall be in all the tops of the hills. **10** They shall not be hungry, neither shall they be thirsty, neither shall the heat smite them, nor the sun, for he that hath compassion [p]on them, shall lead them; even to the springs of water shall he drive them. **11** And I will make all my mountains, as a way, and my paths shall be exalted. **12** Behold, these shall come from far: and lo, these from the North and from the West, and these from the land of [q]Sinim. **13** Rejoice, O [r]heavens; and be joyful, O earth; burst forth into praise, O mountains; for God hath comforted his people, and will have mercy upon his afflicted. **14** But Zion said, The Lord hath [s]forsaken me, and my Lord hath forgotten me. **15** Can a woman forget her child, and not have compassion on the son of her womb? though they should forget, yet will I not forget thee. **16** Behold, I have graven thee upon the palm of mine [t]hands: thy [u]walls are ever in my sight. **17** Thy builders make [v]haste: thy destroyers and they that made thee waste, are departed from thee. **18** Lift up thine eyes round about and behold: all these gather themselves together and come to thee: as I live, saith the Lord, thou shalt surely [w]put them all upon thee as a garment, and gird thyself with them like a bride. **19** For thy desolations, and thy waste places, and thy land destroyed, shall surely be now narrow for them that shall dwell in it, and they that dwell devour thee, shall be far away. **20** The children of thy barrenness shall say again in thine ears, The place is strait for me: give place to me that I may dwell. **21** Then shalt thou say in thine heart, Who hath begotten me these, seeing I am barren and desolate, a captive and a wanderer to and fro? and who hath nourished them? behold, I was left alone: whence are these? **22** Thus saith the Lord God, Behold, I will lift up mine hand to the [x]Gentiles, and set up my standard to the people, and they shall bring thy sons in their arms: and thy daughters shall be carried upon their shoulders. **23** And Kings [y]shall be thy nursing fathers, and Queens shall be thy nurses: they shall worship thee with their faces toward the earth, and lick up the [z]dust of thy feet: and thou shalt know that I am the Lord: for they shall not be ashamed that wait for me. **24** Shall the prey be [aa]taken from the mighty? or the just captivity delivered? **25** But thus saith the Lord, [ab]Even the captivity of the mighty shall be taken away: and the prey of the tyrant shall be delivered: for I will contend with him that contendeth with thee, and I will save thy children, **26** And will feed them that spoil thee, with [ac]their own flesh, and they shall be drunken with their own blood, as with sweet wine; and all flesh shall know that I the Lord am thy Savior and thy Redeemer, the mighty one of Jacob.

50

1 The Jews forsaken for a time. 2 Yet the power of God is not diminished. 5 Christ's obedience and victory.

1 Thus saith the Lord, Where is that [a]bill of your mother's divorcement, [b]whom I have cast off? or who is the creditor [c]to whom I sold you? Behold, for your iniquities are ye sold, and because of your transgressions is your mother forsaken. **2** [d]Wherefore came I, and there was no man? I called, and none answered: is mine hand so [e]shortened, that it cannot help? or have I no power to deliver? Behold, at my rebuke I dry up the sea: I make the floods desert; their fish rotteth for want of water, and dieth for thirst. **3** I clothe the heavens with darkness, and make a [f]sack their covering. **4** The Lord God hath given [g]me a tongue of the learned, that I should know to minister a word in time to him that is [h]weary; he will raise me up in the morning, in the morning he will waken mine ear to hear, [i]as the learned. **5** The Lord God hath opened mine ear, and I was not rebellious, neither turned I back. **6** I gave my back unto the [j]smiters, and my cheeks to the nippers: I hid not my face from shame and spitting. **7** For the Lord God will help me, therefore shall I not be confounded: therefore have I set my face like a flint, and I know that I shall not be ashamed. **8** He is near that justifieth me: who will contend with me? Let us stand together? who is mine adversary? let him come near to me. **9** Behold, the Lord God will help me: who is he that can condemn me? lo, they shall wax old as a garment: the moth shall eat them up. **10** [k]Who is among you that feareth the Lord? let him hear the voice of his servant: he that walketh in darkness and hath no light, let him trust in the Name of the Lord, and stay upon

---

r. Isa. 48:16 Since the time that I declared myself to your fathers.
s. Isa. 48:16 Thus the Prophet speaketh for himself, and to assure them of these things.
t. Isa. 48:17 What things shall do thee good.
u. Isa. 48:19 That is, the prosperous estate of Israel.
v. Isa. 48:20 After that he had forewarned them of their captivity, and of the cause thereof, he showeth them the great joy that shall come of their deliverance.
w. Isa. 48:21 He showeth that it shall be as easy to deliver them, as he did their fathers out of Egypt.
x. Isa. 48:22 Thus he speaketh that the wicked hypocrites should not abuse God's promise, in whom was neither faith nor repentance, as Isa. 57:21.

ISA 49

a. Isa. 49:1 This is spoken in the person of Christ, to assure the faithful that these promises should come to pass: for they were all made in him, and in him should be performed.
b. Isa. 49:1 This is meant of the time that Christ should be manifested to the world, as Ps. 2:7.
c. Isa. 49:2 By the sword and shaft, he signifieth the virtue and efficacy of Christ's doctrine.
d. Isa. 49:2 God hath taken me to his protection and defense: this chiefly is meant of Christ, and may also be applied to the ministers of his word.
e. Isa. 49:3 By Israel is meant Christ, and all the body of the faithful, as the members, and their head.
f. Isa. 49:4 Thus Christ in his members complaineth, that his labor and preaching take none effect, yet he is contented that his doings are approved of God.
g. Isa. 49:5 Though the Jews refuse my doctrine, yet God will approve my ministry.
h. Isa. 49:6 To declare my Gospel, to the Gentiles, Isa. 42:6; Acts 13:47; Luke 2:32.
i. Isa. 49:7 Meaning, the Jews, whom tyrants kept in bondage.
j. Isa. 49:7 The benefit of their deliverance shall be so great, that great and small shall acknowledge it, and reverence God for it.
k. Isa. 49:8 Thus he speaketh of his Church when he would show his mercy toward it, 2 Cor. 6:2.
l. Isa. 49:8 Meaning, Christ alone.
m. Isa. 49:8 Signifying, that before Christ renew the earth by his word, there is nothing but confusion and disorder.
n. Isa. 49:9 To them that are in the prison of sin and death.
o. Isa. 49:9 Being in Christ's protection, they shall be safe against all dangers, and free from the fear of the enemies.
p. Isa. 49:10 Meaning, that there should be nothing in their way from Babylon that should hinder or hurt them: but this is accomplished spiritually.
q. Isa. 49:12 Meaning, the South country, so that Christ shall deliver his from all the parts of the world.
r. Isa. 49:13 Read Isa. 44:23.
s. Isa. 49:14 He objecteth what the faithful might say in their long affliction, and answereth thereunto to comfort them, with a most proper similitude, and full of consolation.
t. Isa. 49:16 Because I would not forget thee.
u. Isa. 49:16 Meaning, the good order of policy, and discipline.
v. Isa. 49:17 I have continual care to build thee up again, and to destroy thine enemies.
w. Isa. 49:18 He showeth what are the ornaments of the Church: to have many children, which are assembled by the word of God, and governed by his Spirit.
x. Isa. 49:22 He showeth that Christ will not only gather this great number of the Jews, but also of the Gentiles.
y. Isa. 49:23 Meaning, that Kings shall be converted to the Gospel, and bestow their power and authority for the preservation of the Church.
z. Isa. 49:23 Being joined with the Church, they shall humble themselves to Christ their head, and give him all honor.
aa. Isa. 49:24 He maketh this as an objection, as though the Chaldeans were strong, and had them in just possession.
ab. Isa. 49:25 This is the answer to their objection, that none is stronger than the Lord, neither hath a more just title unto them.
ac. Isa. 49:26 I will cause them to destroy one another, as Judg. 7:22; 2 Chron. 20:22; Isa. 19:2.

ISA 50

a. Isa. 50:1 Meaning, that he hath not forsaken her, but through her own occasion, as Hos. 2:2.
b. Isa. 50:1 Which should declare that I have cut her off: meaning, that they could show none.
c. Isa. 50:1 Signifying, that he sold them not for any debt or poverty, but that they sold themselves to sins to buy their own lusts and pleasures.
d. Isa. 50:2 He came by his Prophets and ministers, but they would not believe their doctrine and convert.
e. Isa. 50:2 Am I not able to help you, as I have helped your fathers of old, when I dried up the red Sea, and killed the fish in the rivers, and also afterward in Jordan?
f. Isa. 50:3 As I did in Egypt in token of my displeasure, Exod. 10:21.
g. Isa. 50:4 The Prophet doth represent here the person and charge of them that are justly called to the ministry of God's word.
h. Isa. 50:4 To him that is oppressed by affliction and misery.
i. Isa. 50:4 As they that are taught, and made meet by him.
j. Isa. 50:6 I did not shrink from God for any persecution or calamity. Whereby he showeth that the true ministers of God can look for none other recompense of the wicked, but after this sort, and also what is their comfort.
k. Isa. 50:10 Showing that it is a rare thing that any should obey aright God's true ministers, though they labor to bring them from hell to heaven.
l. Isa. 50:11 You have sought consolation by your own devices, and have refused the light, and consolation which God hath offered: therefore ye shall remain in sorrow, and not be comforted.

his God. **11** Behold, all you kindle [l]a fire, and are compassed about with sparks: walk in the light of your fire, and in the sparks that ye have kindled. This shall ye have of mine hand: ye shall lie down in sorrow.

51

1 To trust in God alone by Abraham's example. 7 Not to fear men. 17 The great affliction of Jerusalem, 22 and her deliverance.

1 Hear me [a]ye that follow after righteousness, and ye that seek the Lord: look unto the [b]rock, whence you are hewn, and to the hole of the pit, whence ye are dug. **2** Consider Abraham your father, and Sarah that bare you: for I called him alone, and blessed him and increased him. **3** Surely the Lord shall comfort Zion: he shall comfort all her desolations, and he shall make her desert [c]like Eden, and her wilderness like the garden of the Lord: joy and gladness shall be found therein: praise, and the voice of singing. **4** Hearken ye unto me my people, and give ear unto me, O my people: for a [d]Law shall proceed from me, and I will bring forth my judgment for the light of the people. **5** My [e]righteousness is near: my salvation goeth forth, and mine [f]arm shall judge the people: the isles shall wait for me, and shall trust unto mine arm. **6** Lift up your eyes to the heavens, and look upon the earth beneath: for the [g]heavens shall vanish away like smoke, and the earth shall wax old like a garment, and they that dwell therein, shall perish in like manner: but my salvation shall be forever, and my righteousness shall not be abolished. **7** Hearken unto me ye that know righteousness, the people in whose heart is my Law. Fear ye not the reproach of men, neither be ye afraid of their rebukes. **8** For the moth shall eat them up like a garment, and the worm shall eat them like wood: but my righteousness shall be forever, and my salvation from generation to generation. **9** Rise up, Rise up, and put on strength, O arm of the Lord: rise up as [h]in the old time in the generations of the world. Art not thou the same, that hath cut [i]Rahab, and wounded the [j]dragon? **10** Art not thou the same, which hath dried the Sea, even the waters of the great deep, making the depth of the sea a way for the redeemed to pass over? **11** Therefore the redeemed of the Lord shall [k]return, and come with joy unto Zion, and everlasting joy shall be upon their head: they shall obtain joy and gladness: and sorrow and mourning shall flee away. **12** I, even I am he that comfort you. Who art thou that thou shouldest fear a mortal man, and the son of man, which shall be made as grass? **13** And forgettest the Lord thy maker, that hath spread out the heavens, and laid the foundations of the earth? and hast feared continually all the day, because of the rage of the oppressor, which is ready to destroy? Where is now the rage of the oppressor? **14** The captive [l]hasteneth to be loosed, and that he should not die in the pit, nor that his bread should fail. **15** And I am the Lord thy God that divided the sea, when his waves roared: the Lord of hosts is his Name. **16** And I have put my words in thy [m]mouth, and have defended thee in the shadow of mine hand, that I may plant the [n]heavens, and lay the foundation of the earth, and say unto Zion, Thou art my people. **17** Awake, awake, and stand up, O Jerusalem, which hast drunk at the hand of the Lord the [o]cup of his wrath: thou hast drunken the dregs of the cup of trembling, and wrung them out. **18** There is none to guide her among all her sons, whom she hath brought forth: there is none that taketh her by the hand of all the sons that she hath brought up. **19** These two [p]things are come unto thee: who will lament thee? desolation and destruction and famine, and the sword: by whom shall I comfort thee? **20** Thy sons have fainted, and lie at the head of all the streets as a wild bull in a net, and are full of the wrath of the Lord, and rebuke of thy God. **21** Therefore hear now this, thou miserable and drunken, but [q]not with wine. **22** Thus saith thy Lord God, even God that pleadeth the cause of his people, Behold, I have taken out of thine hand the cup of trembling, even the dregs of the cup of my wrath: thou shalt drink it no more. **23** But I will put it into their hand that spoil thee, which have said to thy soul, Bow down that we may go over, and thou hast laid thy body as the ground, and as the streets to them that went over.

52

1 A consolation to the people of God. 7 Of the messengers thereof.

1 Arise, arise: put on thy strength, O Zion: put on the garments of thy beauty, O Jerusalem, the holy City: for henceforth there shall no [a]more come into thee the uncircumcised and the unclean. **2** Shake thyself from the [b]dust, arise, and sit down, O Jerusalem: loose the bands of thy neck, O thou captive daughter Zion. **3** For thus saith the Lord, Ye were sold for [c]naught; therefore shall ye be redeemed without money. **4** For thus saith the Lord God, My people went [d]down afore time into Egypt to sojourn there, and Assyria [e]oppressed them without cause. **5** Now therefore what have I here, saith the Lord, that my people is taken away for naught, and they that rule over them, make them to howl, saith the Lord? and my Name all the day continually is [f]blasphemed? **6** Therefore my people shall know my name: therefore they shall know in that day, that I am he that do speak: behold, it is I. **7** How [g]beautiful upon the mountains are the feet of him, that declareth and publisheth peace! that declareth good tidings, and publisheth salvation, saying unto Zion, Thy God reigneth! **8** [h]The voice of thy watchmen shall be heard: they shall lift up their voice, and shout together: for they shall see eye to eye, when the Lord shall bring again Zion. **9** O ye desolate places of Jerusalem, be glad and rejoice together, for the Lord hath comforted his people: he hath redeemed Jerusalem. **10** The Lord hath made [i]bare his holy arm in the sight of all the Gentiles, and all the ends of the earth shall see the salvation of our God. **11** [j]Depart, depart ye: go ye out from thence, and touch no unclean thing, go out of the midst of her, be ye clean, that [k]bear the vessels of the Lord. **12** For ye shall not go out [l]with haste, nor depart by fleeing away: but the Lord will go before you, and the God of Israel will gather you together. **13** Behold, my [m]servant shall prosper: he shall be exalted and extolled, and be very high. **14** As many were astonied at thee (his visage was so [n]deformed of men, and his form of the sons of men) so [o]shall he sprinkle many nations: the Kings shall shut their [p]mouths at him: for that which had not been told them, shall they see, and that which they had not heard shall they [q]understand.

53

1 Of Christ and his kingdom, whose word few will believe. 6 All men are sinners. 11 Christ is our righteousness, 12 and is dead for our sins.

1 Who [a]will believe our report? and to whom is the [b]arm of the Lord revealed? **2** But he shall grow up before him as a branch, and as a [c]root out of a dry [d]ground; he hath neither form nor beauty: when we shall see him, there shall be no form that we should desire him. **3** He is despised and rejected of men: he is a man full of sorrows, and hath experience of [e]infirmities: we hid as it were our faces from him: he was despised, and we esteemed him not. **4** Surely, he hath born our infirmities, and carried [f]our sorrows, yet we did judge him as [g]plagued and smitten of God, and humbled. **5** But he was wounded for our transgressions: he was broken for our iniquities: the [h]chastisement of our peace was upon him, and with his stripes are we healed. **6** All we like sheep have gone astray: we have turned every one to his own way, and the Lord hath laid upon him the [i]iniquity of us all. **7** He was oppressed, and he was afflicted, yet did he not [j]open his

---

ISA 51

- **a.** Isa. 51:1 He comforteth the Church, that they should not be discouraged for their small number.
- **b.** Isa. 51:1 That is, to Abraham, of whom ye were begotten, and to Sarah, of whom we were born.
- **c.** Isa. 51:3 As plentiful as Paradise, Gen. 2:8.
- **d.** Isa. 51:4 I will rule and govern my Church by my word and doctrine.
- **e.** Isa. 51:5 The time that I will accomplish my promise.
- **f.** Isa. 51:5 My power and strength.
- **g.** Isa. 51:6 He forewarneth them of the horrible changes and mutations of all things, and how he will preserve his church in the midst of all these dangers.
- **h.** Isa. 51:9 He putteth them in remembrance of his great benefit for their deliverance out of Egypt, that thereby they might learn to trust in him constantly.
- **i.** Isa. 51:9 Meaning, Egypt, Ps. 87:4.
- **j.** Isa. 51:9 To wit, Pharaoh, Ezek. 29:3.
- **k.** Isa. 51:11 From Babylon.
- **l.** Isa. 51:14 He comforteth them by the short time of their banishment: for in seventy years they were restored, and the greatest empire of the world destroyed.
- **m.** Isa. 51:16 Meaning, of Isa., and of all true ministers, who are defended by his protection.
- **n.** Isa. 51:16 That all things may be restored in heaven and earth, Eph. 1:10.
- **o.** Isa. 51:17 Thou hast been justly punished and sufficiently as Isa. 40:2, and this punishment in the elect is by measure, and according as God giveth grace to bear it: but in the reprobate it is the just vengeance of God to drive them to an insensibleness and madness, as Jer. 25:15, 16.
- **p.** Isa. 51:19 Whereof the one is outward, as of the things that come to the body, as war, and famine, and the other is inward, and appertaineth to the mind: that is, to be without comfort: therefore he saith, How shalt thou be comforted?
- **q.** Isa. 51:21 But with trouble and fear.

ISA 52

- **a.** Isa. 52:1 No wicked tyrant, which shall subvert God's true religion, and oppress the conscience.
- **b.** Isa. 52:2 Put off the garments of sorrow and heaviness, and put on the apparel of joy and gladness.
- **c.** Isa. 52:3 The Babylonians paid nothing to me for you: therefore I will take you again without ransom.
- **d.** Isa. 52:4 When Jacob went thither in time of famine.
- **e.** Isa. 52:4 The Egyptians might pretend some cause to oppress my people because they went thither, and remained among them, but the Assyrians have no title to excuse their tyranny by, and therefore will I punish them more than I did the Egyptians.
- **f.** Isa. 52:5 To wit, by the wicked, which think that I have no power to deliver them.
- **g.** Isa. 52:7 Signifying, that the joy and good tidings of their deliverance should make their affliction in the mean time more easy: but this is chiefly meant of the spiritual joy, as Nah. 1:15; Rom. 10:15.
- **h.** Isa. 52:8 The Prophets which are thy watchmen shall publish this thy deliverance: this was begun under Zerubbabel, Ezra, and Nehemiah, but was accomplished under Christ.
- **i.** Isa. 52:10 As ready to smite his enemies, and to deliver his people.
- **j.** Isa. 52:11 He warneth the faithful not to pollute themselves with the superstitions of the Babylonians, as Isa. 48:20; 2 Cor. 6:17.
- **k.** Isa. 52:11 For the time is at hand that the Priests and Levites chiefly (and so by them all the people, which shall be as the Levites in this office) shall carry home vessels of the Temple which Nebuchadnezzar had taken away.
- **l.** Isa. 52:12 As your fathers did out of Egypt.
- **m.** Isa. 52:13 Meaning, Christ, by whom our spiritual deliverance should be wrought, whereof this was a figure.
- **n.** Isa. 52:14 In the corrupt judgment of man, Christ in his person was not esteemed.
- **o.** Isa. 52:14 He shall spread his word through many nations.
- **p.** Isa. 52:14 In sign of reverence, and as being astonished at his excellency.
- **q.** Isa. 52:14 By the preaching of the Gospel.

ISA 53

- **a.** Isa. 53:1 The Prophet showeth that very few shall receive this their preaching of Christ, and of their deliverance by him, John 12:38; Rom. 10:16.
- **b.** Isa. 53:1 Meaning, that none can believe, but whose hearts God toucheth with the virtue of his holy Spirit.
- **c.** Isa. 53:2 The beginning of Christ's kingdom shall be small and contemptible in the sight of man, but it shall grow wonderfully, and flourish before God.
- **d.** Isa. 53:2 Read Isa. 11:1.
- **e.** Isa. 53:3 Which was by God's singular providence for the comfort of sinners, Heb. 4:15.
- **f.** Isa. 53:4 That is, the punishment due to our sins: for the which he hath both suffered and made satisfaction, Matt. 8:17; 1 Pet. 2:24.
- **g.** Isa. 53:4 We judgeth evil, thinking that he was punished for his own sins, and not for ours.
- **h.** Isa. 53:5 He was chastised for our reconciliation, 1 Cor. 15:3.
- **i.** Isa. 53:6 Meaning, the punishment of our iniquity, and not the fault itself.

mouth: he is brought as a sheep to the slaughter, and as a sheep before her shearer is dumb, so he opened not his mouth. **8** He was taken out from [k]prison, and from judgment: [l]and who shall declare his age? for he was cut out of the land of the living: for the transgression of my people was he plagued. **9** [m]And he made his grave with the wicked, and with the rich in his death, though he had done no wickedness, neither was any deceit in his mouth. **10** Yet the Lord would break him and make him subject to infirmities: when [n]he shall make his soul an offering for sin, he shall see his seed and shall prolong his days, and the will of the Lord shall prosper in his hand. **11** He shall see of the [o]travail of his soul, and shall be satisfied; by his knowledge shall my [p]righteous servant justify many: for he shall bear their iniquities. **12** Therefore will I give him a portion with the great, and he shall divide the spoil with the strong, because [q]he hath poured out his soul unto death; and he was counted with the transgressors, and he bare the sin [r]of many, and prayed for the trespassers.

54

1 More of the Gentiles shall believe the Gospel than of the Jews. 7 God leaveth his for a time, to whom afterward he showeth mercy.

1 Rejoice, O [a]barren that didst not bear: break forth into joy and rejoice, thou that didst not travail with child; for the [b]desolate hath more children than the married wife, saith the Lord. **2** [c]Enlarge the place of thy tents, and let them spread out the curtains of thine habitations: spare not: stretch out thy cords, and make fast thy stakes. **3** For thou shalt increase on the right hand and on the left, and thy seed shall possess the Gentiles, and dwell in the desolate cities. **4** Fear not: for thou shalt not be ashamed, neither shalt thou be confounded: for thou shalt not be put to shame: yea, thou shalt forget the shame of thy [d]youth, and shalt not remember the reproach of thy [e]widowhood anymore. **5** For he that [f]made thee, is thine husband, (whose name is the Lord of hosts) and thy redeemer the holy One of Israel, shall be called the God of the whole [g]world. **6** For the Lord hath called thee, being as a woman forsaken, and afflicted in spirit, and as a [h]young wife when thou wast refused, saith thy God. **7** For a little while have I forsaken thee, but with great compassion will I gather thee. **8** For a moment in mine anger, I hid my face from thee for a little season, but with everlasting mercy have I had compassion on thee, saith the Lord thy redeemer. **9** For this is unto me as the [i]waters of Noah; for as I have sworn that the waters of Noah should no more go over the earth, so have I sworn that I would not be angry with thee, nor rebuke thee. **10** For the mountains shall remove, and the hills shall fall down; but my mercy shall not depart from thee, neither shall the covenant of my peace fall away, saith the Lord, that hath compassion on thee. **11** O thou afflicted and tossed with tempest, that hast no comfort, behold, I will lay thy stones with the [j]carbuncle, and lay thy foundation with sapphires, **12** And I will make thy windows of [k]emeralds, and thy gates shining stones, and all thy borders of pleasant stones. **13** And all thy children shall be [l]taught of the Lord, and much peace shall be to thy children. **14** In [m]righteousness shalt thou be established, and be far from oppression; for thou shalt not fear it: and from fear; for it shall not come near thee. **15** Behold, the enemies shall gather himself, but without [n]me: whosoever shall gather himself in thee, [o]against thee, shall fall. **16** Behold, I have created the [p]smith that bloweth the coals in the fire, and him that bringeth forth an instrument for his work, and I have created the destroyer to destroy. **17** But all the weapons that are made against thee, shall not prosper: and every tongue that shall rise against thee in judgment, thou shalt condemn. This is the heritage of the Lord's servants, and their righteousness is of me, saith the Lord.

55

1 An exhortation to come to Christ. 8 God's counsels are not as man's. 12 The joy of the faithful.

1 Ho, everyone that [a]thirsteth, come ye to the waters, and ye that have [b]no silver, come, buy and eat: come, I say, buy [c]wine and milk without silver and without money. **2** Wherefore do ye lay out silver, and not for bread? [d]and your labor without being satisfied? hearken diligently unto me, and eat that which is good, and let your soul delight in [e]fatness. **3** Incline your ears, and come unto me: hear, and your soul shall live, and I will make an everlasting covenant with you, even the [f]sure mercies of David. **4** Behold, I gave [g]him for a witness to the people, for a prince and a master unto the people. **5** Behold, thou shalt call a nation that thou knowest not, [h]and a nation that knew not thee, shall run unto thee because of the Lord thy God, and the Holy one of Israel: for he hath glorified thee. **6** Seek ye the Lord while he may be [i]found: call ye upon him while he is near. **7** Let the wicked [j]forsake his ways, and the unrighteous his own imaginations, and return unto the Lord, and he will have mercy upon him; and to our God, for he is very ready to forgive. **8** For my [k]thoughts are not your thoughts, neither are your ways my ways, saith the Lord. **9** For as the heavens are higher than the earth, so are my ways higher than your ways, and my thoughts above your thoughts. **10** Surely as the rain cometh down, and the snow from heaven, and returneth not thither but watereth the earth, and maketh it to bring forth and bud, that it may give seed to the sower, and bread unto him that eateth, **11** So shall my [l]word be, that goeth out of my mouth: it shall not return unto me void, but it shall accomplish that which I will, and it shall prosper in the thing whereto I sent it. **12** Therefore ye shall go out with joy, and be led forth with peace; the [m]mountains and the hills shall break forth before you into joy, and all the trees of the field shall clap their hands. **13** For thorns there shall grow fir trees; for nettles shall grow the myrrh tree, and it shall be to the Lord [n]for a name, and for an everlasting [o]sign that shall not be taken away.

56

1 An exhortation to judgment and justice. 10 Against shepherds that devour their flock.

1 Thus saith the Lord, [a]Keep judgment and do justice, for my salvation is at hand to come, and my [b]righteousness to be revealed. **2** Blessed is the man that doeth this, and the son of man which layeth hold on it; he that keepeth the [c]Sabbath, and polluteth it not, and keepeth his hand from doing any evil. **3** And let not the son of the strangers, which [d]is joined to the Lord, speak and say, The Lord hath surely separated me from his people; neither let the Eunuch say, Behold, I am a dry tree. **4** For thus saith the Lord unto the Eunuchs that keep my Sabbaths, and choose the thing that pleaseth me, and take hold of my covenant, **5** Even unto them will I give in mine [e]House and within my walls, a place, and a [f]name better than of the sons and of the daughters; I will give them an everlasting name,

---

j. Isa. 53:7 But willingly and patiently obeyed his father's appointment, Matt. 26:63; Acts 8:32.
k. Isa. 53:8 From the cross and grave, after that he was condemned.
l. Isa. 53:8 Though he died for sin, yet after his resurrection he shall live forever and this his death is to restore life to his members, Rom. 6:9.
m. Isa. 53:9 God the Father delivered him into the hands of the wicked, and to the powers of the world to do with him what they would.
n. Isa. 53:10 Christ by offering up himself shall give life to his Church, and so cause them to live with him forever.
o. Isa. 53:11 That is, the fruit and effect of his labor, which is the salvation of his Church.
p. Isa. 53:11 Christ shall justify by faith through his word, whereas Moses could not justify by the law.
q. Isa. 53:12 Because he humbled himself, therefore he shall be extolled to glory, Phil. 2:7-12.
r. Isa. 53:12 That is, of all that believe in him.

ISA 54

a. Isa. 54:1 After that he hath declared the death of Christ, he speaketh to the Church, because it should feel the fruit of the same, and calleth her barren, because that in the captivity she was a widow without hope to have any children.
b. Isa. 54:1 The Church in this her affliction and captivity shall bring forth more children, than when she was at liberty: or this may be spoken by admiration, considering the great number that should come of her. Her deliverance under Cyrus was as her childhood, and therefore this was accomplished, when she came to her age, which was under the Gospel.
c. Isa. 54:2 Signifying, that for the great number of children that God should give her, she should seem to lack room to lodge them.
d. Isa. 54:4 The afflictions which thou suffered at the beginning.
e. Isa. 54:4 When as thou wast refused for thy sins, Isa. 50:1.
f. Isa. 54:5 That did regenerate thee by his holy Spirit.
g. Isa. 54:5 His glory shall shine through the whole World, which seemed before to be shut up in Judea.
h. Isa. 54:6 As a wife which wast forsaken in thy youth.
i. Isa. 54:9 As sure as the promise that I made to Noah, that the waters should no more overflow the earth.
j. Isa. 54:11 Hereby he declareth the excellent estate of the Church under Christ.
k. Isa. 54:12 Or, jasper, or pearl.
l. Isa. 54:13 By the hearing of his word and inward moving of his Spirit.
m. Isa. 54:14 In stability and sureness, so that it shall stand forever.
n. Isa. 54:15 And therefore shall not prevail.
o. Isa. 54:15 Meaning, the domestical enemies of the Church, as are the hypocrites.
p. Isa. 54:16 Signifying hereby, that man can do nothing, but so far as God giveth power: for seeing that all are his creatures, he must needs govern and guide them.

ISA 55

a. Isa. 55:1 Christ by proposing his graces and gifts to his Church, exempteth the hypocrites which are full with their imagined works, and the Epicureans, which are full with their worldly lusts, and so thirst not after these waters.
b. Isa. 55:1 Signifying, that God's benefits cannot be bought for money.
c. Isa. 55:1 By waters, wine, milk and bread, he meaneth all things necessary to the spiritual life, as these are necessary to this corporal life.
d. Isa. 55:2 He reproveth their ingratitude, which refuse those things that God offereth willingly, and in the meantime spare neither cost nor labor to obtain those which are nothing profitable.
e. Isa. 55:2 You shall be fed abundantly.
f. Isa. 55:3 The same covenant which through my mercy I ratified and confirmed to David, that it should be eternal, 2 Sam. 7:13; Acts 13:34.
g. Isa. 55:4 Meaning Christ, of whom David was a figure.
h. Isa. 55:5 To wit, the Gentiles, which before thou didst not receive to be thy people.
i. Isa. 55:6 When he offereth himself by the preaching of his word.
j. Isa. 55:7 Hereby he showeth that repentance must be joined with faith, and how we cannot call upon God aright, except the fruits of our faith appear.
k. Isa. 55:8 Although you are not soon reconciled one to another and judge me by yourselves, yet I am most easy to be reconciled, yea, I offer my mercies to you.
l. Isa. 55:11 If these small things have their effect, as daily experience showeth, much more shall my promise which I have made and confirmed, bring to pass the things which I have spoken for your deliverance.
m. Isa. 55:12 Read Isa. 44:23 and 49:13.
n. Isa. 55:13 To set forth his glory.
o. Isa. 55:13 Of God's deliverance, and that he will never forsake his Church.

ISA 56

a. Isa. 56:1 God showeth what he requireth of them after that he hath delivered them: to wit, the works of charity whereby true faith is declared.
b. Isa. 56:1 Which I will declare toward you, and pour into your hearts by my Spirit.
c. Isa. 56:2 Under the Sabbath he comprehendeth the whole service of God and true religion.
d. Isa. 56:3 Let none think himself unmeet to receive the graces of the Lord: for the Lord will take away all impediments, and will forsake none which will keep his true religion, and believe in him.
e. Isa. 56:5 Meaning, in his Church.
f. Isa. 56:5 They shall be called after my people, and be of the same religion: yea, under Christ the dignity of the faithful shall be greater than the Jews were at that time.

that shall not be put out. **6** Also the strangers that cleave unto the Lord, to serve him, and to love the Name of the Lord, and to be his servants; everyone that keepeth the Sabbath, and polluteth it not, and embraceth my covenant, **7** Them will I bring also to mine holy mountain, and make them joyful in mine House of prayer; their burnt [g]offerings and their sacrifices shall be accepted upon mine altar: for mine house shall be called an house of prayer for [h]all people. **8** The Lord God saith, which gathereth the scattered of Israel, Yet will I gather to them those that are to be gathered to them. **9** All ye [i]beasts of the field, come to devour, even all ye beasts of the forest. **10** Their [j]watchmen are all blind: they have no knowledge: they are all dumb dogs: they cannot bark: they lie and sleep, and delight in sleeping. **11** And these greedy dogs can never have enough: and these shepherds cannot understand: for they all look to their own way, everyone for his advantage, and for his own purpose. **12** Come, I will bring wine, and we will fill ourselves with strong drink, and [k]tomorrow shall be as this day, and much more abundant.

57

1 God taketh away the good, that he should not see the horrible plagues to come. 3 Of the wicked idolaters, 9 and their vain confidence.

1 The righteous perisheth, and no man considereth it in heart, and merciful men are taken away, and no man understandeth that the righteous is taken away [a]from the evil to come. **2** [b]Peace shall come: they shall rest in their beds, everyone that walketh before him. **3** But you [c]witches' children, come hither, the seed of the adulterer and of the whore. **4** On whom have ye jested? upon whom have ye gaped and thrust out your tongue? are not ye rebellious children, and a false seed? **5** Inflamed with idols under every green tree? and sacrificing the [d]children in the valleys under the tops of the rocks? **6** Thy portion is in the smooth stones [e]of the river: they, they are thy lot: even to them hast thou poured a drink offering: thou hast offered a sacrifice. Should I delight in [f]these? **7** Thou hast made thy [g]bed upon a very high mountain: thou wentest up thither, even thither wentest thou to offer sacrifice. **8** Behind the [h]doors also and posts hast thou set up thy remembrance: for thou hast discovered thyself to another, than me, and wentest up, and didst [i]enlarge thy bed, and make a covenant between thee and them, and lovedst their bed in every place where thou sawest it. **9** Thou wentest [j]to the kings with oil, and didst increase thine ointments, and send thy messengers far off, and didst humble thyself unto hell. **10** Thou weariedst thyself in thy manifold journeys, yet saidest thou not, [k]There is no hope: thou [l]hast found life by thine hand, therefore thou wast not grieved. **11** And whom didst thou reverence or fear, seeing thou hast [m]lied unto me, and hast not remembered me, neither set thy mind thereon? is it not because I hold my peace, and that of long [n]time? therefore thou fearest not me. **12** I will declare thy righteousness [o]and thy works, and they shall not profit thee. **13** When thou cryest, let them that thou hast gathered together, deliver thee: but the wind [p]shall take them all away: vanity shall pull them away: but he that trusteth in me shall inherit the land, and shall possess mine holy Mountain. **14** [q]And he shall say, Cast up, cast up: prepare the way: take up the stumbling blocks out of the way of my people. **15** For thus saith he that is high and excellent, he that inhabiteth the eternity, whose Name is the Holy one, I dwell in the high and holy place: with him also that is of a contrite and humble spirit to revive the spirit of the humble, and to give life to them that are of a contrite heart. **16** For I will not contend forever: neither will I be always wroth, [r]for the spirit should fail before me: and I have made the breath. **17** For his [s]wicked covetousness I am angry with him, and have smitten him: I hid me, and was angry, yet he went away, and turned after the way of his own heart. **18** I have seen his ways, and will [t]heal him: I will lead him also, and restore comfort unto him, and to those that lament him. **19** I create the [u]fruit of the lips, to be peace: peace unto them that are [v]far off, and to them that are near, saith the Lord: for I will heal him. **20** But the wicked are like the raging sea, that [w]cannot rest, whose waters cast up mire and dirt. **21** There is no peace, saith my God, to the wicked.

58

1 The office of God's ministers. 2 The works of the hypocrites. 6 The fast of the faithful. 13 Of the true Sabbath.

1 Cry [a]aloud, spare not: lift up thy voice like a trumpet, and show my people their transgression, and to the house of Jacob their sins. **2** Yet they [b]seek me daily, and will know my ways, even as a nation that did righteously, and had not forsaken the statutes of their God: they ask of me the ordinances of justice: they will draw near unto God, saying, **3** [c]Wherefore have we fasted, and thou seest it not? we have punished ourselves, and thou regardest it not. Behold, in the day of your fast you will seek [d]your will, and require all your debts. **4** Behold, ye fast to strife and debate, and to smite with the fist of wickedness: ye shall not fast as ye do today, to make your voice to be [e]heard above. **5** Is it such a fast that I have chosen, that a man should afflict his soul for a day, and to bow down his head, as a bull rush, and to lie down in sackcloth and ashes? wilt thou call this a fasting, or an acceptable day to the Lord? **6** Is not this the fasting that I have chosen? to loose the bands of wickedness, to take off the heavy burdens, and to let the oppressed go free, and that ye break every [f]yoke? **7** Is it not to deal thy bread to the hungry, and that thou bring the poor that wander, unto thine house? when thou seest the naked, that thou cover him, and hide not thyself from [g]thine own flesh? **8** Then shall thy [h]light break forth as the morning, and thine health shall grow speedily: thy [i]righteousness shall go before thee, and the glory of the Lord shall embrace thee. **9** Then shalt thou call, and the Lord shall answer: thou shalt cry, and he shall say, Here I am: if thou take away from the midst of thee the yoke, the putting forth of the [j]finger, and wicked speaking: **10** If thou [k]pour out thy soul to the hungry, and refresh the troubled soul: then shall thy light spring out in the [l]darkness, and thy darkness shall be as the noon day. **11** And the Lord shall guide thee continually, and satisfy thy soul in drought, and make fat thy bones, and thou shalt be like a watered garden, and like a spring of water, whose waters fail not. **12** And they shall be of thee, that shall build the old [m]waste places: thou shalt raise up the foundations for many generations, and thou shalt be called the repairer of the breach, and the restorer of the paths to dwell in. **13** If thou [n]turn away thy foot from the Sabbath, from doing thy will on mine Holy day, and call the Sabbath a delight to consecrate it, as glorious to the Lord, and shalt honor him, not doing thine own ways, nor seeking thine own will, nor speaking a vain word, **14** Then shalt thou delight in the Lord, and I will cause thee to mount upon the high places of the earth, and feed thee with the heritage of Jacob thy father: for the mouth of the Lord hath spoken it.

---

g. Isa. 56:7 Hereby he meaneth the spiritual service of God, to whom the faithful offer continual thanksgiving, yea themselves and all that they have, as a lively and acceptable sacrifice.
h. Isa. 56:7 Not only for the Jews, but for all others, Matt. 21:13.
i. Isa. 56:9 Meaning, the enemies of the Church, as the Babylonians, Assyrians, etc., thus he speaketh to fear the hypocrites and to assure the faithful that when this cometh, they may know it was told them before.
j. Isa. 56:10 He showeth that this affliction shall come through the fault of the governors, prophets, and pastors, whose ignorance, negligence, avarice and obstinacy provoked God's wrath against them.
k. Isa. 56:12 We are well yet, and tomorrow shall be better: therefore let us not fear the plagues before they come: thus the wicked contemned the admonitions and exhortations which were made them in the Name of God.

ISA 57

a. Isa. 57:1 From the plague that is at hand, and also because God will punish the wicked.
b. Isa. 57:2 The soul of the righteous shall be in joy, and their body shall rest in the grave unto the time of the resurrection, because they walked before the Lord.
c. Isa. 57:3 He threateneth the wicked hypocrites, who under the pretence of the name of God's people, derided God's word and his promises: boasting openly that they were the children of Abraham, but because they were not faithful and obedient as Abraham was, he calleth them bastards, and the children of sorcerers, which forsook God, and fled to wicked means for succor.
d. Isa. 57:5 Read Lev. 18:21; 2 Kings 23:10.
e. Isa. 57:6 Meaning, every place was polluted with their idolatry: or every fair stone that they found, they made an idol of it.
f. Isa. 57:6 In the sacrifices which you offering before these idols, thought you did serve God.
g. Isa. 57:7 To wit, thine altars in an open place, like an impudent harlot, that careth not for the sight of her husband.
h. Isa. 57:8 Instead of setting up the word of God in the open places on the posts and doors to have it in remembrance, Deut. 6:9 and 27:1, thou hast set up signs and marks of thine idolatry in every place.
i. Isa. 57:8 That is, didst increase thine idolatry more and more.
j. Isa. 57:9 Thou didst seek the favor of the Assyrians by gifts and presents to help thee against the Egyptians: and when they failed thou soughtest to the Babylonians, and more and more didst torment thyself.
k. Isa. 57:10 Although thou sawest all thy labors to be in vain, yet wouldest thou never acknowledge thy fault, and leave off.
l. Isa. 57:10 He derideth their unprofitable diligence, which thought to have made all sure, and yet were deceived.
m. Isa. 57:11 Broken promise with me.
n. Isa. 57:11 Meaning, that the wicked abuse God's lenity, and grow to further wickedness.
o. Isa. 57:12 That is, thy naughtiness, idolatries, and impieties which the wicked call God's service: thus he derideth their obstinacy.
p. Isa. 57:13 Meaning, the Assyrians and others, whose help they looked for.
q. Isa. 57:14 God shall say to Darius and Cyrus.
r. Isa. 57:16 I will not use my power against frail man, whose life is but a blast.
s. Isa. 57:17 That is, for the vices and faults of the people, which is meant here by covetousness.
t. Isa. 57:18 Though they were obstinate, yet I did not withdraw my mercy from them.
u. Isa. 57:19 That is, I frame the speech and words of my messengers which shall bring peace.
v. Isa. 57:19 As well to him that is in captivity as to him that remaineth at home.
w. Isa. 57:20 Their evil conscience doth ever torment them, and therefore they can never have rest, read Isa. 48:22.

ISA 58

a. Isa. 58:1 The Lord thus speaketh to the Prophet, willing him to use all diligence and severity to rebuke the hypocrites.
b. Isa. 58:2 They will seem to worship me and have outward holiness.
c. Isa. 58:3 He setteth forth the malice and disdain of the hypocrites, which grudge against God, if their works be not accepted.
d. Isa. 58:3 Thus he convinceth the hypocrites by the second table, and by their duty toward their neighbor, that they have neither faith nor religion.
e. Isa. 58:4 So long as you use contention and oppression, your fasting and prayers shall not be heard.
f. Isa. 58:6 That you leave off all your extortions.
g. Isa. 58:7 For in him thou seest thyself as in a glass.
h. Isa. 58:8 That is, the prosperous estate wherewith God will bless thee.
i. Isa. 58:8 The Testimony of thy goodness shall appear before God and man.
j. Isa. 58:9 Whereby is meant all manner of injury.
k. Isa. 58:10 That is, have compassion on their miseries.
l. Isa. 58:10 Thine adversity shall be turned into prosperity.
m. Isa. 58:12 Signifying, that of the Jews should come such as should build again the ruins of Jerusalem and Judea: but chiefly this is meant of the spiritual Jerusalem, whose builders were the Apostles.
n. Isa. 58:13 If thou refrain thyself from thy wicked works.

59

1 The wicked perish through their own iniquities. 12 The confession of sins. 16 God alone will preserve his Church though all men fail.

1 Behold, [1]the Lord's hand is not shortened, that it cannot save: neither is
his ear heavy, that it cannot hear. **2** But [2]your iniquities have separated betwe-
en you and your God, and your sins have hid his face from you, that he will not
hear. **3** For your hands are defiled with [a]blood, and your fingers with iniquity:
your lips have spoken lies, and your tongue hath murmured iniquity. **4** No man
calleth for justice: no man [b]contendeth for truth: they trust in vanity, and spe-
ak vain things: they conceive mischief, and [c]bring forth iniquity. **5** They hatch
cockatrice [d]eggs, and weave the spider's [e]web: he that eateth of their eggs, died, and
that which is trode upon, breaketh out into a serpent. **6** Their webs shall be no
garment, neither shall they cover themselves with their labors: for their works are
works of iniquities, and the work of cruelty is in their hands. **7** Their feet turn
to evil, and they make haste to shed innocent blood: their thoughts are wicked
thoughts: desolation and destruction is in their paths. **8** The way of peace they
know not, and there is none equity in their goings: they have made them crooked
paths: whosoever goeth therein, shall not know peace. **9** Therefore is [f]judgment
far from us, neither doth [g]justice come near unto us: we wait for light, but lo, it
is darkness: for brightness, but we walk in darkness. **10** We grope for the wall
like the [h]blind, and we grope as one without eyes: we stumble at the noon day as
in the twilight: we are in solitary places, as dead men. **11** We roar all like [i]bears,
and mourn like doves: we look for equity, but there is none: for health, but it is far
from us. **12** For our trespasses are many before thee, and our [j]sins testify against
us: for our trespasses are with us, and we know our iniquities **13** In trespassing
and lying against the Lord, and we have departed away from our God, and have
spoken of cruelty and rebellion, conceiving and uttering out of the heart [k]false
matters. **14** Therefore [l]judgment is turned backward, and justice standeth far off:
for truth is fallen in the street, and equity cannot enter. **15** Yea, truth faileth, and
he that refraineth from evil, maketh himself [m]a prey: and when the Lord saw it, it
displeased him, that there was no judgment. **16** And when he saw that there was
no man, he wondered that none would offer himself. [n]Therefore his arm did [o]save
it, and his righteousness itself did sustain it. **17** For he put on righteousness, as
an habergeon, and an [p]helmet of salvation upon his head, and he put on the gar-
ments of vengeance for clothing, and was clad with zeal as a cloak. **18** As to make
recompense, as to requite the fury of the adversaries with a recompense to his ene-
mies: he will fully repair the [q]islands. **19** So shall they fear the Name of the Lord
from the West, and his glory from the rising of the Sun; for the enemy shall [r]come
like a flood; but the Spirit of the Lord shall chase him away. **20** And the Redee-
mer shall come unto Zion, and unto [s]them that turn from iniquity in Jacob, saith
the Lord. **21** And I will make this my Covenant with them, saith the Lord, My
Spirit that is upon thee, and my words, which I have put in thy mouth, [t]shall not
depart out of thy mouth, nor out of the mouth of thy seed, nor out of the mouth
of the seed of thy seed, saith the Lord, from henceforth even forever.

60

3 The Gentiles shall come to the knowledge of the Gospel. 8 They shall come to the Church in abundance. 16 They shall have abundance though they suffer for a time.

1 Arise, O Jerusalem; be bright, for thy [a]light is come, and the glory of the
Lord is risen upon thee. **2** For behold, darkness shall cover the [b]earth, and gross
darkness the people; but the Lord shall arise upon thee, and his glory shall be seen
upon thee. **3** And the Gentiles shall walk in [c]thy light, and Kings at the bright-
ness of thy rising up. **4** Lift up thine eyes round about, and behold: all [d]these are
gathered, and come to thee: thy sons shall come from far, and thy daughters shall
be nourished at thy side. **5** Then thou shalt see and shine: thine heart shall be
astonied [e]and enlarged, because the multitude of the sea shall be converted unto
thee, and the riches of the Gentiles shall come unto thee. **6** The [f]multitude of
camels shall cover thee: and the dromedaries of Midian and of Ephah: all they of
Sheba shall come: they shall bring gold and incense, and show forth the praises of
the Lord. **7** All the sheep of [g]Kedar shall be gathered unto thee: the rams of Ne-
bajoth shall serve thee: they shall come up to be accepted upon mine [h]altar: and I
will beautify the house of my glory. **8** Who are these [i]that fly like a cloud, and
as the doves to their windows? **9** Surely the isles shall wait for me, and the ships
[j]of Tarshish, as at the beginning, that they may bring thy sons from far, and their
silver and their gold with them unto the Name of the Lord thy God, and to the
Holy one of Israel, because he hath glorified thee. **10** And the sons of strangers
shall build up thy walls, and their [k]Kings shall minister unto thee: for in my wra-
th I smote thee, but in my mercy I had compassion on thee. **11** Therefore thy
gates shall be open continually: neither day nor night shall they be shut, that men
may bring unto thee the riches of the Gentiles, and that their kings may be brou-
ght. **12** For the nation and the [l]kingdom, that will not serve thee, shall perish:
and those nations shall be utterly destroyed. **13** The [m]glory of Lebanon shall
come unto thee, the fir tree, the elm and the box tree together to beautify the place
of my Sanctuary: for I will glorify the place of my [n]feet. **14** The sons also of them
that afflicted thee, shall come and bow unto thee: and all they that despised thee,
shall fall [o]down at the soles of thy feet: and they shall call thee; The city of the Lord,
Zion of the Holy one of Israel. **15** Whereas thou hast been forsaken and hated,
so that no man went by thee, I will make thee an eternal glory, and a joy from gene-
ration to generation. **16** Thou shalt also suck the milk of the Gentiles, and shalt
suck the [p]breasts of Kings: and thou shalt know, that I the Lord am thy Savior, and
thy Redeemer, the mighty one of Jacob. **17** For brass will I bring gold, and for
iron will I bring silver, and for wood brass, and for stones iron. I will also make thy
government [q]peace, and thine exactors righteousness. **18** Violence shall no more
be heard of in thy land, neither desolation, nor destruction within thy borders: but
thou shalt [r]call salvation, thy walls, and praise, thy gates. **19** Thou shalt have no
more Sun to shine by day, neither shall the brightness of the [s]Moon shine unto
thee: for the Lord shall be thine everlasting light, and thy God, thy glory. **20** Thy
Sun shall never go down, neither shall thy Moon be hid: for the Lord shall be thine
everlasting light, and the days of thy sorrow shall be ended. **21** Thy people also
shall be all righteous: they shall possess the land forever, the [t]grass of my planting
shall be the work of mine hands, that I may be glorified. **22** A little one shall
become as a [u]thousand, and a small one as a strong nation: I the Lord will hasten
it in due time.

61

1 He prophesieth that Christ shall be anointed, and sent to preach. 10 The joy of the faithful.

1 The [1]Spirit of the Lord God is [a]upon me, therefore hath the Lord anoin-
ted me: he hath sent me to preach good tidings unto the poor, to bind up the
[b]broken hearted, to preach liberty to the [c]captives, and to them that are bound,
the opening of the prison, **2** To preach the [d]acceptable year of the Lord, and the

---

ISA 59

- **a.** Isa. 59:3 Read Isa. 1:15.
- **b.** Isa. 59:4 All men wink at the injuries and oppressions, and none go about to remedy them.
- **c.** Isa. 59:4 According to their wicked devices, they hurt their neighbors.
- **d.** Isa. 59:5 Whatsoever cometh from them is poison, and bringeth death.
- **e.** Isa. 59:5 They are profitable to no purpose.
- **f.** Isa. 59:9 That is, God's vengeance to punish our enemies.
- **g.** Isa. 59:9 God's protection to defend us.
- **h.** Isa. 59:10 We are altogether destitute of counsel, and can find no end of our miseries.
- **i.** Isa. 59:11 We express our sorrows by outward signs, some more, some less.
- **j.** Isa. 59:12 This confession is general to the Church to obtain remission of sins, and the Prophets did not exempt themselves from the same.
- **k.** Isa. 59:13 To wit, against our neighbors.
- **l.** Isa. 59:14 There is neither justice nor uprightness among men.
- **m.** Isa. 59:15 The wicked will destroy him.
- **n.** Isa. 59:16 Meaning, to do justice, and to remedy the things that were so far out of order.
- **o.** Isa. 59:16 That is, his Church or his arm did help itself, and did not seek aid of any other.
- **p.** Isa. 59:17 Signifying, that God hath all means at hand to deliver his Church and to punish their enemies.
- **q.** Isa. 59:18 To wit, your enemies, which dwell in divers places, and beyond the sea.
- **r.** Isa. 59:19 He showeth that there shall be great affliction in the Church, but God will ever deliver his.
- **s.** Isa. 59:20 Whereby he declareth that the true deliverance from sin and Satan belongeth to none, but to the children of God, whom he justifieth.
- **t.** Isa. 59:21 Because the doctrine is made profitable by the virtue of the Spirit, he joineth the one with the other, and promiseth to give them both to his Church forever.

ISA 59

1. Num. 11:23 / Isa. 50:2 **2.** Jer. 5:25

ISA 60

- **a.** Isa. 60:1 The time of thy prosperity and felicity: whereas speaking of Babylon, he commanded her to go down, Isa. 47:1.
- **b.** Isa. 60:2 Signifying, that all men are in darkness till God give them the light of his Spirit, and that this light shineth to none, but to those that are in his Church.
- **c.** Isa. 60:3 Meaning, that Judea should be as the morning star, and that the Gentiles should receive light of her.
- **d.** Isa. 60:4 An infinite number from all countries, as Isa. 49:18.
- **e.** Isa. 60:5 For joy, as the heart is drawn in for sorrow.
- **f.** Isa. 60:6 Meaning, that everyone shall honor the Lord with what wherewith he is able: signifying, that it is no true serving of God, except we offer ourselves to serve his glory, and all that we have.
- **g.** Isa. 60:7 That is, the Arabians, that have great abundance of cattle.
- **h.** Isa. 60:7 Because the Altar was a figure of Christ, Heb. 13:10, he showeth that nothing can be acceptable to him, which is not offered to him by this Altar, who was both the offering and the altar itself.
- **i.** Isa. 60:8 Showing what great number shall come to the Church, and with what great diligence and zeal.
- **j.** Isa. 60:9 The Gentiles that are now enemies, shall become friends and setters forth of the Church.
- **k.** Isa. 60:10 Meaning, Cyrus and his successors, but chiefly this is accomplished in them that serve Christ, being converted by his Gospel.
- **l.** Isa. 60:12 He showeth that God hath given all power and authority here in earth for the use of his Church, and that they which will not serve and profit the same, shall be destroyed.
- **m.** Isa. 60:13 There is nothing so excellent which shall not serve the necessity of the Church.
- **n.** Isa. 60:13 Signifying, that God's Majesty is not included in the Temple, which is but the place for his feet, that we may learn to rise us to the heavens.
- **o.** Isa. 60:14 To worship their head Christ, by obeying his doctrine.
- **p.** Isa. 60:16 Both high and low shall be ready to help and succor thee.
- **q.** Isa. 60:17 Thy governors shall love thee, and seek thy wealth and prosperity.
- **r.** Isa. 60:18 Meaning, not a temporal felicity, but a spiritual, which is fulfilled in Christ's kingdom.
- **s.** Isa. 60:19 Signifying, that all worldly means shall cease, and that Christ shall be all in all, as Rev. 21:23 and 22:5.
- **t.** Isa. 60:21 The children of the Church.
- **u.** Isa. 60:22 Meaning, that the Church should be miraculously multiplied.

ISA 61

- **a.** Isa. 61:1 Thus appertaineth to all the Prophets and ministers of God, but chiefly to Christ, of whose abundant graces everyone receiveth according as it pleaseth him to distribute.
- **b.** Isa. 61:1 To them that are lively touched with the feeling of their sins.
- **c.** Isa. 61:1 Which are in the bondage of sin.

day of [e]vengeance of our God, to comfort all that mourn, **3** To appoint unto them that mourn in Zion, and to give unto them beauty for [f]ashes, the oil of joy for mourning, the garment of gladness for the spirit of heaviness, that they might be called [g]trees of righteousness, the planting of the Lord, that he might be glorified. **4** And they shall build the old waste places, and raise up the former desolations, and they shall repair the cities that were desolate and waste through many [h]generations. **5** And the strangers shall [i]stand and feed your sheep, and the sons of the strangers shall be your plowmen, and dressers of your vines. **6** But ye shall be named the [j]Priests of the Lord, and men shall say unto you, The ministers of our God: Ye shall eat the [k]riches of the Gentiles, and shall be exalted with their glory. **7** For your shame you shall receive [l]double, and for confusion, [m]they shall rejoice in [n]their portion: for in their land they shall possess the [o]double: everlasting joy shall be unto them. **8** For I the Lord love judgment, and hate [p]robbery for burnt offering, and I will direct their work in truth, and I will make an everlasting covenant with them. **9** And [q]their seed shall be known among the Gentiles, and their buds among the people. All that see them, shall know them, that they are the seed which the Lord hath blessed. **10** [r]I will greatly rejoice in the Lord, and my soul shall be joyful in my God: for he hath clothed me with the garments of salvation, and covered me with the robe of righteousness: he hath decked me like a bridegroom, and as a bride attireth herself with her jewels. **11** For as the earth bringeth forth her bud, and as the garden causeth to grow that which is sown in it: so the Lord God will cause righteousness to grow, and praise before all the heathen.

62

1 The great desire that the Prophets have had for Christ's coming. 6 The diligence of the Pastors to preach.

1 For Zion's sake I will not [a]hold my tongue, and for Jerusalem's sake I will not rest, until the righteousness thereof break forth as the [b]light, and salvation thereof as a burning lamp. **2** And the Gentiles shall see thy righteousness, and all Kings thy glory: and thou shalt be called by [c]a new name, which the mouth of the Lord shall name. **3** Thou shalt also be a [d]crown of glory in the hand of the Lord, and a royal diadem in the hand of thy God. **4** It shall no more be said unto thee, [e]Forsaken, neither shall it be said anymore to thy land, Desolate, but thou shalt be called [f]Hephzibah, and thy land [g]Beulah: for the Lord delighteth in thee, and thy land shalt have an [h]husband. **5** For as a young man marrieth a virgin, so shall thy sons [i]marry thee: and as a bridegroom is glad of the bride, so shall thy God rejoice over thee. **6** I have set [j]watchmen upon thy walls, O Jerusalem, which all the day and all the night continual shall not cease: [k]ye that are mindful of the Lord, keep not silence, **7** And give him no rest, till he repair, and until he set up Jerusalem the [l]praise of the world. **8** The Lord hath sworn by his right hand and by his strong arm, Surely I will no more give thy corn to be meat for thine enemies, and surely the sons of the strangers shall not drink thy wine, for the which thou hast labored. **9** But they that have gathered it, shall eat it, and praise the Lord, and the gatherers thereof shall drink it in the courts of my Sanctuary. **10** [m]Go through, go through the gates: prepare you the way for the people: cast up, cast up the way, and gather out the stones, and set up a standard for the people. **11** Behold, the Lord hath proclaimed unto the ends of the world, [n]tell the daughter Zion, Behold, thy Savior cometh: Behold, his wages is with him, and [o]his work is before him. **12** And they shall call them, The holy people, the redeemed of the Lord, and thou shalt be named, A [p]city sought out and not forsaken.

63

1 God shall destroy his enemies for his Church's sake. 7 God's benefits toward his Church.

1 Who is this that cometh [a]from Edom, with red garments from Bozrah? he is glorious in his apparel, and walketh in his great strength. [b]I speak in righteousness, and am mighty to save. **2** [c]Wherefore is thine apparel red, and thy garments like him that treadeth in the winepress? **3** I have trodden the winepress alone, and of all people there was none with me: for I will tread them in mine anger, and tread them under foot in my wrath, and their blood shall be sprinkled upon my garments, and I will stain all my raiment. **4** For the day of vengeance is in mine heart, and the [d]year of my redeemed is come. **5** And I looked, and there was none to help, and I wondered that there was none to uphold: therefore mine own [e]arm helped me, and my wrath itself sustained me. **6** Therefore I will tread down the people in my wrath, and make them [f]drunken in mine indignation, and will bring down their strength to the earth. **7** I will [g]remember the mercy of the Lord, and the praises of the Lord, according unto all that the Lord hath given us, and for the great goodness toward the house of Israel, which he hath given them according to his tender love, and according to his great mercies. **8** For he said, Surely they are my [h]people, children that will not lie: so he was their Savior. **9** In all their troubles he was [i]troubled, and the Angel [j]of his presence saved them: in his love and in his mercy he redeemed them, and he bare them and carried them always continually. **10** But they rebelled and vexed his holy Spirit: therefore was he turned to be their enemy, and he fought against them. **11** Then he [k]remembered the old time of Moses and his people, saying, Where is he that brought them up out of the sea with the [l]shepherd of his sheep? Where is he that put his holy Spirit within [m]him? **12** He led them by the right hand of Moses with his own glorious arm, dividing the water before them, to make himself an everlasting Name. **13** He led them through the deep, as an [n]horse in the wilderness, that they should not stumble. **14** As the beast goeth down into the valley, the Spirit of the Lord gave them rest: so didst thou lead thy people, to make thyself a glorious Name. **15** [o]Look down from heaven, and behold from the dwelling place of thine holiness, and of thy glory. Where is thy [p]zeal and thy strength, the multitude of thy mercies, and of thy compassion? they are restrained from [q]me. **16** Doubtless thou art our Father: though [r]Abraham be ignorant of us, and Israel know us not, yet thou, O Lord, art our Father, and our redeemer: thy Name is forever. **17** O Lord, why hast [s]thou made us to err from thy ways? and hardened our heart from thy fear? Return for thy [t]servant's sake, and for the tribes of thine inheritance. **18** The people of thine holiness have possessed it, but a little [u]while: for our adversaries have trodden down thy Sanctuary. **19** We have been as they, over whom thou never barest rule, and upon whom thy name was not called.

---

d. Isa. 61:2 The time when it pleased God to show his good favor to man, which S. Paul calleth the fullness of time, Gal. 4:4.
e. Isa. 61:2 For when God delivereth his Church, he punisheth his enemies.
f. Isa. 61:3 Which was the sign of mourning.
g. Isa. 61:3 Trees that bring forth good fruits, as Matt. 3:8.
h. Isa. 61:4 That is, for a long time.
i. Isa. 61:5 They shall be ready to serve you in all your necessities.
j. Isa. 61:6 This is accomplished in the time of Christ, by whom all the faithful are made Priests and Kings, 1 Pet. 2:9; Rev. 1:6 and 5:10.
k. Isa. 61:6 Read Isa. 6:11, 16.
l. Isa. 61:7 Abundant recompense, as this word is used, Isa. 40:2.
m. Isa. 61:7 That is, the Jews.
n. Isa. 61:7 To wit, of the Gentiles.
o. Isa. 61:7 Whereas the Gentiles had dominion over the Jews in times past, now they shall have double authority over them and possess twice so much.
p. Isa. 61:8 I will not receive their offerings which are extortioners, deceivers, hypocrites, or that deprive me of my glory.
q. Isa. 61:9 That is, of the Church.
r. Isa. 61:10 He showeth what shall be the affection, when they feel this their deliverance.

ISA 61
1. Luke 4:18

ISA 62
a. Isa. 62:1 The Prophet saith that he will never cease to declare unto the people the good tidings of their deliverance.
b. Isa. 62:1 Till they have full deliverance: and this the Prophet speaketh to encourage all other ministers to the setting forth of God's mercies toward his Church.
c. Isa. 62:2 Thou shalt have a more excellent fame than thou hast had hitherto.
d. Isa. 62:3 He shall esteem thee as dear and precious as a king doth his crown.
e. Isa. 62:4 Thou shalt no more be contemned as a woman forsaken of her husband.
f. Isa. 62:4 Or, my delight in her.
g. Isa. 62:4 Or, married.
h. Isa. 62:4 That it may be replenished with children.
i. Isa. 62:5 Forasmuch as they confess one faith and religion with thee, they are in the same bond of marriage with thee, and they are called the children of the Church, inasmuch as Christ maketh her plentiful to bring forth children unto him.
j. Isa. 62:6 Prophets, Pastors, and Ministers.
k. Isa. 62:6 He exhorteth the ministers never to cease to call upon God by prayer for the deliverance of his Church, and to teach others to do the same.
l. Isa. 62:7 For the restoration whereof all the world shall praise him.
m. Isa. 62:10 Signifying the great number that should come to the Church, and what means he would prepare for the restitution of the same, as Isa. 57:14.
n. Isa. 62:11 Ye Prophets and Ministers show the people of this their deliverance: which was chiefly meant of our salvation by Christ, Zech. 9:9; Matt. 21:5.
o. Isa. 62:11 He shall have all power to bring his purpose to pass, as Isa. 40:10.
p. Isa. 62:12 That is, one over whom God hath had a singular care to recover her when she was lost.

ISA 63
a. Isa. 63:1 This prophecy is against the Idumeans and enemies which persecuted the Church, on whom God will take vengeance, and is here set forth all bloody after he hath destroyed them in Bozrah, the chief city of the Idumeans: for these were their greatest enemies, and under the title of circumcision and the kindred of Abraham, claimed to themselves the chief religion, and hated the true worshippers, Ps. 137:7.
b. Isa. 63:1 God answereth them that asked this question, Who is this? etc. and saith, Ye see now performed in deed the vengeance which my Prophets threatened.
c. Isa. 63:2 Another question, to the which the Lord answereth.
d. Isa. 63:4 Showing that when God punisheth his enemies, it is for the profit and deliverance of his Church.
e. Isa. 63:5 God showeth that he hath no need of man's help for the deliverance of his, and though men refuse to do their duty through negligence and ingratitude, yet he himself will deliver his Church, and punish the enemies, read Isa. 59:16.
f. Isa. 63:6 I will so astonish them and make them so giddy, that they shall not know which way to go.
g. Isa. 63:7 The Prophet speaketh this to move the people to remember God's benefits in times past, that they may be confirmed in their troubles.
h. Isa. 63:8 For I did choose them to be mine, that they should be holy, and not deceive mine expectation.
i. Isa. 63:9 He bare their afflictions and griefs as though they had been his own.
j. Isa. 63:9 Which was a witness of God's presence, and this may be referred to Christ, to whom belongeth the office of Salvation.
k. Isa. 63:11 That is, the people of Israel, being afflicted, called to remembrance God's benefits, which he had bestowed upon their fathers in times past.
l. Isa. 63:11 Meaning, Moses.
m. Isa. 63:11 That is, in Moses that he might well govern the people: some refer this giving of the spirit to the people.
n. Isa. 63:13 Peaceably and gentle, as an horse is led to his pasture.
o. Isa. 63:15 Having declared God's benefits showed to their forefathers, he turned himself to God by prayer, desiring him to continue the same graces toward them.
p. Isa. 63:15 Thy great affection, which thou barest towards us.
q. Isa. 63:15 Meaning, from the whole body of the Church.
r. Isa. 63:16 Though Abraham would refuse us to be his children, yet thou wilt not refuse to be our father.
s. Isa. 63:17 By taking away the holy Spirit from us, by whom we were governed, and so for our ingratitude didst deliver us up to our own concupiscence, and didst punish sin by sin according to thy just judgment.
t. Isa. 63:17 Meaning, for the Covenant's sake made to Abraham, Isaac, and Jacob his servants.
u. Isa. 63:18 That is, in respect of the promise, which is perpetual: albeit they had now possessed the land of Canaan, a thousand and four hundred years: and thus they lament, to

64

1 The Prophet prayeth for the sins of the people. 6 Man's righteousness is like a filthy cloth.

1 Oh, that thou wouldest [a]break the heavens, and come down, and that the mountains might melt at thy presence! **2** As the melting fire burned, as the fire caused [b]the waters to boil, (that thou mightest declare thy Name to thine adversaries) the people did tremble at thy presence. **3** When thou didst terrible things, which we looked not for, thou camest down, and the mountains melted at thy presence. **4** For since the beginning of the world, they have not [c]heard nor understood with the ear, neither hath the eye seen another God beside thee, which doeth so to him that waiteth for him. **5** Thou didst meet him, [d]that rejoiced in thee, and did justly: they remembered thee in thy [e]ways: behold, thou art angry, for we have sinned: yet in [f]them is continuance, and we [g]shall be saved. **6** But we have all been as an unclean thing, and all our [h]righteousness is as filthy cloths, and we all do fade like a leaf, and our iniquities like the wind have taken us away. **7** And there is none that calleth upon thy Name, neither that stirreth up himself to take hold of thee: for thou hast hid thy face from us, and hast consumed us because of our iniquities. **8** But now, O Lord, thou art our Father: we are the [i]clay, and thou art our potter, and we all are the work of thine hands. **9** Be not angry, O Lord, [j]above measure, neither remember iniquity forever: Lo, we beseech thee, behold, we are all thy people. **10** [k]Thine holy cities lie waste: Zion is a wilderness, and Jerusalem a desert. **11** The house of our Sanctuary, and of our glory, [l]where our fathers praised thee, is burnt up with fire, and all our pleasant things are wasted. **12** Wilt thou hold thyself still [m]at these things, O Lord? wilt thou hold thy peace and afflict us above measure?

65

1 The vocation of the Gentiles, and the rejection of the Jews. 13 The joy of the elect, and the punishment of the wicked.

1 I have been sought of them that [a]asked not: I was found of them that sought me not: I said, Behold me, behold me, unto a nation that called not upon my Name. **2** I have [b]spread out mine hands all the day unto a rebellious people, which walked in a way that was not good, even after their own [c]imaginations. **3** A people that provoked me ever unto my face: that sacrificeth in [d]gardens, and burneth incense upon [e]bricks. **4** Which remain among the [f]graves, and lodge in the deserts, which eat [g]swine's flesh, and the broth of things polluted are in their vessels. **5** Which say, [h]Stand apart, come not near to me; for I am holier than thou; these are a smoke in my wrath, and a fire that [i]burneth all the day. **6** Behold, it is [j]written before me; I will not keep silence, but will render it and recompense it into their bosom. **7** Your iniquities, and the iniquities of your fathers, shall be [k]together (saith the Lord) which have burnt incense upon the mountains, and blasphemed me upon the hills; therefore will I measure their old work into their bosom. **8** Thus saith the Lord, As the wine is found in the cluster, and one saith, Destroy it not, for a [l]blessing is in it, so will I do for my servants' sakes, that I may not destroy them whole. **9** But I will bring a seed out of Jacob, and out of Judah that shall inherit my mountain; and mine elect shall inherit it, and my servants shall dwell there. **10** And [m]Sharon shall be a sheepfold, and the valley of Achor shall be a resting place for the cattle of my people, that have sought me. **11** But ye are they that have forsaken the Lord, and forgotten mine holy Mountain, and have prepared a table for the [n]multitude, and furnish the drink offerings unto the number. **12** Therefore will I [o]number you to the sword, and all you shall bow down to the slaughter, because I called, and ye did not answer; I [p]spake, and ye heard not, but did evil in my sight, and did choose that thing which I would not. **13** Therefore thus saith the Lord God, Behold, my servants shall [q]eat, and ye shall be hungry; behold, my servants shall drink, and ye shall be thirsty; behold, my servants shall rejoice, and ye shall be ashamed. **14** Behold, my servants shall sing for joy of heart, and ye shall cry for sorrow of heart, and shall howl for vexation of mind. **15** And ye shall leave your name as a curse unto my [r]chosen; for the Lord God shall slay you, and call his servants by [s]another name. **16** He that shall bless in the [t]earth, shall bless himself in the true God; and he that sweareth in the earth, shall swear by the true God; for the former [u]troubles are forgotten, and shall surely hide themselves from mine eyes. **17** For lo, I will create [v]new heavens and a new earth; and the former shall not be remembered nor come into mind. **18** But be you glad and rejoice forever in the things that I shall create; for behold, I will create Jerusalem, as a rejoicing, and her people as a joy. **19** And I will rejoice in Jerusalem, and joy in my people, and the voice of weeping shall be no more heard in her, nor the voice of crying. **20** There shall be no more there a child of years, nor an old man that hath [w]not filled his days: for he that shall be an hundred years old, shall die as a young man: but the sinner being [x]an hundred years old shall be accursed. **21** And they shall [y]build houses, and inhabit them, and they shall plant vineyards, and eat the fruit of them. **22** They shall not build, and another inhabit: they shall not plant, and another eat: for as the days of the tree are the days of my people, and mine elect shall enjoy in old age the work of their hands. **23** They shall not labor in vain, nor bring forth in fear: for they are the seed of the blessed of the Lord, and their buds with them. **24** Yea, before they call, I will answer, and whiles they speak, I will hear. **25** The [z]wolf and the lamb shall feed together, and the lion shall eat straw like the bullock: and to the serpent dust shall be his meat. They shall no more hurt nor destroy in all mine holy Mountain, saith the Lord.

66

1 God dwelleth not in Temples made with hands. 3 He despiseth sacrifices done without mercy and faith. 5 God comforteth them that are troubled for his sake. 19 The vocation of the Gentiles. 23 The perpetual Sabbath. 24 The punishment of the wicked is everlasting.

1 Thus saith the Lord, [1]The [a]heaven is my throne, and the earth is my footstool: where is that house that ye will build unto me? and where is that place of my rest? **2** For all these things hath mine hand made, [b]and all these things have been, saith the Lord: and to him will I look, even to him that is poor, and of [c]a contrite spirit, and trembleth at my words. **3** He that killeth a bullock, is as if he [d]slew a man: he that sacrificeth a sheep, as if he cut off a dog's neck: he that offereth an oblation, as if he offered swine's blood: he that remembereth incense, as if

---

move God rather to remember his Covenant, than to punish their sins.

ISA 64

- **a.** Isa. 64:1 The Prophet continueth his prayer, desiring God to declare his love toward his Church by miracles, and mighty power, as he did in mount Sinai.
- **b.** Isa. 64:2 Meaning, the rain, hail, fire, thunder, and lightnings.
- **c.** Isa. 64:4 S. Paul useth the same kind of admiration, 1 Cor. 2:9, marveling at God's great benefit showed to his Church, by the preaching of the Gospel.
- **d.** Isa. 64:5 Thou showedst favor toward our fathers, when they trusted in thee, and walked after thy Commandments.
- **e.** Isa. 64:5 They considered thy great mercies.
- **f.** Isa. 64:5 That is, in thy mercies, which he calleth the ways of the Lord.
- **g.** Isa. 64:5 Thou wilt have pity upon us.
- **h.** Isa. 64:6 We are justly punished and brought into captivity, because we have provoked thee to anger, and though we would excuse ourselves, yet our righteousness, and best virtues are before thee as vile cloths, or (as some read) like the menstruous clothes of a woman.
- **i.** Isa. 64:8 Albeit, O Lord, by thy just judgment thou mayest utterly destroy us as the potter may his pot, yet we appeal to thy mercies, whereby it hath pleased thee to adopt us to be thy children.
- **j.** Isa. 64:9 For so the flesh judgeth when God doth not immediately send succor.
- **k.** Isa. 64:10 Which were dedicated to thy service, and to call upon thy Name.
- **l.** Isa. 64:11 Wherein we rejoiced and worshipped thee.
- **m.** Isa. 64:12 That is, at the contempt of thine own glory? though our sins have deserved this, yet thou wilt not suffer thy glory thus to be diminished.

ISA 65

- **a.** Isa. 65:1 Meaning, the Gentiles which knew not God, should seek after him, when he had moved their heart with his holy Spirit, Rom. 10:20.
- **b.** Isa. 65:2 He showeth the cause of the rejection of the Jews, because they would not obey him for any admonition of his Prophets, by whom he called them continually and stretched out his hand to draw them.
- **c.** Isa. 65:2 He showeth that to delight in our own fantasies, is the declining from God and the beginning of all superstition and Idolatry.
- **d.** Isa. 65:3 Which were dedicated to idols.
- **e.** Isa. 65:3 Meaning, their altars, which he thus named by contempt.
- **f.** Isa. 65:4 To consult with spirits, and to conjure devils, which was forbidden, Deut.18:11.
- **g.** Isa. 65:4 Which was contrary to God's Commandment, Lev. 11:7; Deut. 14:8.
- **h.** Isa. 65:5 He showeth that hypocrisy is ever joined with pride and contempt of others.
- **i.** Isa. 65:5 Their punishment shall never have end.
- **j.** Isa. 65:6 So that the remembrance thereof cannot be forgotten.
- **k.** Isa. 65:7 Shall be both punished together: and this declareth how the children are punished for their fathers' faults, to wit, when the same faults or like are found in them.
- **l.** Isa. 65:8 That is, it is profitable: meaning, that God will not destroy the faithful branches of his vineyard, when he destroyeth the rotten stocks, that is, the hypocrites.
- **m.** Isa. 65:10 Which was a plentiful place in Judea to feed sheep, as Achor was for cattle.
- **n.** Isa. 65:11 By the multitude and number he meaneth their innumerable idols of whom they thought they could never have enough.
- **o.** Isa. 65:12 Seeing you cannot number your gods, I will number you with the sword.
- **p.** Isa. 65:12 By my Prophets, whom ye would not obey.
- **q.** Isa. 65:13 By these words, Eat and drink, he meaneth, the blessed life of the faithful, which have always consolation and full contentment of all things in their God, though sometimes they lack these corporal things.
- **r.** Isa. 65:15 Meaning, that he would call the Gentiles, who should abhor even the very name of the Jews for their infidelities' sake.
- **s.** Isa. 65:15 Than by the name of the Jews.
- **t.** Isa. 65:16 By blessing, and by swearing is meant the praising of God for his benefits, and the true worshipping of him, which shall not be only in Judea, but through all the world.
- **u.** Isa. 65:16 I will no more suffer my Church to be desolate as in times past.
- **v.** Isa. 65:17 I will so alter and change the state of my church, that it shall seem to dwell in a new world.
- **w.** Isa. 65:20 Meaning, in this wonderful restoration of the Church there should be no weakness of youth, nor infirmities of age, but all should be fresh and flourishing: and this is accomplished in the heavenly Jerusalem, when all sin shall cease, and the tears shall be wiped away.
- **x.** Isa. 65:20 Whereby he showeth that the infidels and unrepentant sinners have no part of this benediction.
- **y.** Isa. 65:21 He proposeth to the faithful the blessings which are contained in the Law, and so under temporal things comprehendeth the spiritual promises.
- **z.** Isa. 65:25 Read Isa. 11:6.

ISA 66

- **a.** Isa. 66:1 My majesty is so great, that it filleth both heaven and earth, and therefore cannot be included in a temple like an idol: condemning hereby their vain confidence, which trusted in the Temple and sacrifices.
- **b.** Isa. 66:2 Seeing that both the Temple and the things therein, with the sacrifices, were made and done by his appointment, he showeth that he hath no need thereof, and that he can be without them, Ps. 50:10.
- **c.** Isa. 66:2 To him that is humble and pure in heart, which receiveth my doctrine with reverence and fear.
- **d.** Isa. 66:3 Because the Jews thought themselves holy by offering of their sacrifices, and in the mean season had neither faith nor repentance, God showeth that he doth no less detest these ceremonies than he doth the sacrifices of the heathen, who offered men, dogs, and swine to their idols, which things were expressly forbidden in the Law.
- **e.** Isa. 66:4 I will discover their wickedness and hypocrisy, wherewith they think to blind mine eyes, to all the world.

he blessed an idol: yea, they have chosen their own ways, and their soul delighteth in their abominations. **4** Therefore will I [e]choose out their delusions, and I will bring their fear upon them, because I called and none would answer: I speak, and they would not hear: but they did evil in my sight, and chose the things which I would not. **5** Hear the word of the Lord, all ye that tremble at his [f]word, Your brethren that hated you, and cast you out for my Name's sake, said, Let the Lord be glorified: but he shall appear to your joy, and they shall be ashamed. **6** [g]A voice soundeth from the city, even a voice from the Temple, the voice of the Lord, that recompenseth his enemies fully. **7** Before [h]she travailed, she brought forth: and before her pain came, she was delivered of a man child. **8** Who hath heard such a thing? who hath seen such things? shall the earth be brought forth in one [i]day? or shall a nation be born at once? for as soon as Zion travailed, she brought forth her children. **9** Shall I [j]cause to travail, and not bring forth? shall I cause to bring forth, and shall be barren, saith thy God? **10** Rejoice ye with Jerusalem, and be glad with her, all ye that love her: rejoice for joy with her, all ye that mourn for her, **11** That ye may suck, [k]and be satisfied with the breasts of her consolation: that ye may milk out, and be delighted with the brightness of her glory. **12** For thus saith the Lord, behold, I will extend [l]peace over her like a flood, and the glory of the [m]Gentiles like a flowing stream: then shall ye suck, ye shall be [n]born upon her sides, and be joyful upon her knees. **13** As one whom his mother comforteth, so will I comfort you, and ye shall be comforted in Jerusalem. **14** And when ye see this, your hearts shall rejoice, and your [o]bones shall flourish like an herb: and the hand of the Lord shall be known among his servants, and his indignation against his enemies. **15** For behold, the Lord will come with fire, and his chariots like a whirlwind, that he may [p]recompense his anger with wrath, and his indignation with the flame of fire. **16** For the Lord will judge with fire, and with his sword all flesh, and the flame of the Lord shall be many. **17** They that sanctify [q]themselves, and purify themselves in the gardens behind one tree in the midst eating [r]swine's flesh, and such abomination, even the mouse, shall be consumed together, saith the Lord. **18** For I will visit their works, and their imaginations, for it shall come that I will gather all nations, and tongues, and they shall come, and see my [s]glory. **19** And I will set a [t]sign among them, and will send those that [u]escape of them unto the nations of [v]Tarshish, [w]Pul, and [x]Lud, and to them that draw the [y]bow, to [z]Tubal and [aa]Javan, isles afar off, that have not heard my fame, neither have seen my glory, and [ab]they shall declare my glory among the Gentiles. **20** And they shall bring all your [ac]brethren for an offering unto the Lord out of all nations, upon [ad]horses, and in chariots, and in horse litters, and upon mules, and swift beasts, to Jerusalem mine holy Mountain, saith the Lord, as the children of Israel offer in a clean vessel in the House of the Lord. **21** And I will take of them for [ae]Priests, and for Levites, saith the Lord. **22** For as the new [af]heavens, and the new earth, which I will make, shall remain before me, saith the Lord, so shall your seed and your name continue. **23** And from month to month, and from Sabbath to Sabbath shall all flesh come to worship before me, saith the Lord. **24** And they shall go forth, and look upon the [ag]carcasses of the men that have transgressed against me: for their [ah]worm shall not die, neither shall their fire be quenched, and they shall be an abhorring [ai]unto all flesh.

---

f. Isa. 66:5 He encourageth the faithful by promising to destroy their enemies, which pretended to be as brethren, but were hypocrites, and hated them that feared God.
g. Isa. 66:6 The enemies shall shortly hear a more terrible voice, even fire and slaughter, seeing they would not hear the gentle voice of the Prophets, which called them to repentance.
h. Isa. 66:7 Meaning, that the restoration of the Church should be so sudden and contrary to all men's opinions, as when a woman is delivered before she looked for it, and that without pain in travail.
i. Isa. 66:8 This shall pass the capacity of man to see such a multitude that shall come up at once, meaning, under the preaching of the Gospel, whereof they that came up out of Babylon were a sign.
j. Isa. 66:9 Declaring hereby, that as in his power and providence women travailed and delivered, so he giveth the power to bring forth the Church at his time appointed.
k. Isa. 66:11 That is, may rejoice for all the benefits that God bestoweth upon his Church.
l. Isa. 66:12 I will give her felicity and prosperity in great abundance.
m. Isa. 66:12 Read Isa. 60:16.
n. Isa. 66:12 Ye shall be cherished as her dearly beloved children.
o. Isa. 66:14 Ye shall have new strength and new beauty.
p. Isa. 66:15 This vengeance God began to execute at the destruction of Babylon, and hath ever continued it against the enemies of his Church, and will do till the last day, which shall be the accomplishment thereof.
q. Isa. 66:17 Meaning, the hypocrites.
r. Isa. 66:17 Whereby are meant them that did maliciously transgress the Law, by eating beasts forbidden, even to the mouse, which nature abhoreth.
s. Isa. 66:18 The Gentiles shall be partakers of that glory, which before I showed to the Jews.
t. Isa. 66:19 I will make these that I chose, that they perish not with the rest of the infidels: whereby he alludeth to the marking of the posts of his people, whom he preserved, Exod. 12:7.
u. Isa. 66:19 I will scatter the rest of the Jews, which escaped destruction, into divers nations.
v. Isa. 66:19 That is, Cilicia.
w. Isa. 66:19 Meaning Africa.
x. Isa. 66:19 To wit, Lydia, or Asia minor.
y. Isa. 66:19 Signifying the Parthians.
z. Isa. 66:19 Italy.
aa. Isa. 66:19 Greece.
ab. Isa. 66:19 Meaning, the Apostles, Disciples, and others, which he did first choose of the Jews to preach unto the Gentiles.
ac. Isa. 66:20 That is, the Gentiles, which by faith shall be made the children of Abraham as you are.
ad. Isa. 66:20 Whereby he meaneth that no necessary means shall want, when God shall call the Gentiles to the knowledge of the Gospel.
ae. Isa. 66:21 To wit, of the Gentiles, as he did Luke, Timothy, and Titus first, and others after to preach his word.
af. Isa. 66:22 Hereby he signifieth the kingdom of Christ wherein his Church shall be renewed, and whereas before there were appointed seasons to sacrifice, in this there shall be one continual Sabbath, so that all times and seasons shall be meet.
ag. Isa. 66:24 As he that declared the felicity that shall be within the Church for the comfort of the godly, so doth he show what horrible calamity shall come to the wicked, that are out of the Church.
ah. Isa. 66:24 Meaning, a continual torment of conscience, which shall ever gnaw them, and never suffer them to be at rest, Mark 9:44.
ai. Isa. 66:24 This is the just recompense for the wicked, which contemning God and his word, shall be by God's just judgment abhorred of all his creatures.

ISA 66

1. Acts 7:48,49

JEREMIAH

1

1 In what time Jeremiah prophesied. 6 He acknowledgeth his imperfection, and is strengthened of the Lord. 11 The Lord showeth him the destruction of Jerusalem. 17 He commandeth him to preach his word without fear.

1 The [a]words of Jeremiah the son of [b]Hilkiah one of the Priests that were at
[c]Anathoth in the land of Benjamin. **2** To whom the [d]word of the Lord came in
the days of Josiah the son of Amon King of Judah in the thirteenth year of his rei-
gn: **3** And also in the days of Jehoiakim the [e]son of Josiah king of Judah unto the
end of the eleventh year of Zedekiah, the son of Josiah king of Judah, even unto the
carrying away of Jerusalem captive in the fifth [f]month. **4** Then the word of the
Lord came unto me, saying, **5** Before I [g]formed thee in the womb, I knew thee,
and before thou camest out of the womb, I sanctified thee, and ordained thee to
be a Prophet unto the [h]nations. **6** Then said I, [i]Oh, Lord God, behold, I cannot
speak, for I am a child. **7** But the Lord said unto me, Say not, I am a child: for
thou shalt go to all that I shall send thee, and whatsoever I command thee, shalt
thou speak. **8** Be not afraid of their faces: for I am with thee to deliver thee, saith
the Lord. **9** Then the Lord stretched out his hand, and [j]touched my mouth, and
the Lord said unto me, Behold, I have put my words in thy mouth. **10** Behold,
this day have I set thee over the [k]nations, and over the kingdoms, to pluck up, and
to root out, and to destroy, and throw down, to build, and to plant. **11** After this
the word of the Lord came unto me, saying, Jeremiah, what seest thou? And I said,
I see a [l]rod of almond tree. **12** Then said the Lord unto me, Thou hast seen ari-
ght: for I will hasten my word to perform it. **13** Again the word of the Lord came
unto me the second time, saying, What seest thou? And I said, I see a seething [m]pot
looking out of the North. **14** Then said the Lord unto me, Out of the [n]North
shall a plague be spread upon all the inhabitants of the land. **15** For lo, I will call
all the families of the kingdoms of the North, saith the Lord, and they shall come,
and everyone shall set his throne in the entering of the gates of Jerusalem, and on
all the walls thereof round about, and in all the cities of Judah. **16** And I will
declare unto them my [o]judgments touching all the wickedness of them that have
forsaken me, and have burnt incense unto other gods, and worshipped the works
of their own hands. **17** Thou therefore truss up thy loins, and arise and speak
unto them all that I command thee: be not afraid of their faces, lest I [p]destroy thee
before them. **18** For I, behold, I this day have made thee a defenced city, and an
[q]iron pillar and walls of brass against the whole land, against the Kings of Judah,
and against the Princes thereof, against the Priests thereof, and against the people
of the land. **19** For they shall fight against thee, but they shall not prevail against
thee: for I am with thee to deliver thee, saith the Lord.

2

2 God rehearseth his benefits done unto the Jews. 8 Against the priests and false prophets. 12 The Jews are destroyed because they forsake God.

1 Moreover, the word of the Lord came unto me, saying, **2** Go and cry in
the ears of Jerusalem, saying, Thus saith the Lord, I remember thee, with the [a]kin-
dness of thy youth and the love of thy marriage, when thou wentest after me in the
wilderness [b]in a land that was not sown. **3** Israel was as a thing [c]hallowed unto
the Lord, and his firstfruits: all they [d]that eat it, shall offend: evil shall come upon
them, saith the Lord. **4** Hear ye the word of the Lord, O house of Jacob, and all
the families of the house of Israel. **5** Thus saith the Lord, What iniquity have your
fathers found in me, that they are gone [e]far from me, and have walked after vanity,
and are become [f]vain? **6** For they said not, Where is the Lord that brought us up
out of the land of Egypt, that led us through the wilderness, through a desert, and
waste land, through a dry land, and by [g]the shadow of death, by a land that no man
passed through, and where no man dwelt? **7** And I brought you into a plentiful
country, to eat the fruit thereof, and the commodities of the same: but when ye en-
tered, ye defiled [h]my land, and made mine heritage an abomination. **8** The prie-
sts said not, [i]Where is the Lord? and they that should minister the [j]Law, knew me
not: the [k]pastors also offended against me, and the prophets prophesied in [l]Baal,
and went after things that did not profit. **9** Wherefore I will yet [m]plead with you,
saith the Lord, and I will plead with your children's children. **10** For go ye to the
isles of [n]Chittim, and behold, and send unto [o]Kedar, and take diligent heed, and
see whether there be such things. **11** Hath any nation changed their gods, which
yet are no gods? but my people have changed their [p]glory, for that which doth not
[q]profit. **12** O ye [r]heavens, be astonied at this: be afraid and utterly confounded,
saith the Lord. **13** For my people have committed two evils: they have forsaken
me [s]the fountain of living waters, to dig them pits, even broken pits that can hold
no water. **14** Is Israel a [t]servant, or is he born in the house? why then is he spoi-
led? **15** The [u]Lions roared upon him and yelled, and they have made his land
waste: his cities are burnt without [v]an inhabitant. **16** Also the children of [w]Noph
and Tahapanes have [x]broken thine head. **17** Hast not thou procured this unto
thyself, because thou hast forsaken the Lord thy God, when he [y]led thee by the
way? **18** And what hast thou now to do in the way of [z]Egypt? to drink the water
of Nilus? or what makest thou in the way of Assyria? to drink the water of the [aa]Ri-
ver? **19** Thine own wickedness shall [ab]correct thee, and thy turnings back shall
reprove thee: know therefore and behold, that it is an evil thing, and bitter, that
thou hast forsaken the Lord thy God, and that my fear is not in thee, saith the Lord
God of hosts. **20** For of old time I have broken thy yoke, and burst thy bonds,

---

JER. 1

a. Jer. 1:1 That is, the sermons and prophecies.
b. Jer. 1:1 Which is thought to be he that found the book of the Law under king Josiah, 2 Kings 22:8.
c. Jer. 1:1 This was a city about three miles distant from Jerusalem, and belonged to the Priests, the sons of Aaron, Josh. 21:18.
d. Jer. 1:2 This is spoken to confirm his vocation and office, forasmuch as he did not presume of himself to preach and prophesy, but was called thereunto by God.
e. Jer. 1:3 Meaning, the nephew of Josiah: for Jehoahaz was his father, who reigned but three months, and therefore is not mentioned, no more is Jehoiakim that reigned no longer.
f. Jer. 1:3 Of the eleventh year of Zedekiah, who was also called Mattaniah, and at this time the Jews were carried away into Babylon by Nebuchadnezzar.
g. Jer. 1:5 The scripture useth this manner of speech, to declare that God hath appointed his minsters to their offices before they were born, as Isa. 49:1; Gal. 1:15.
h. Jer. 1:5 For Jer. did not only prophesy against the Jews, but also against the Egyptians, Babylonians, Moabites, and other nations.
i. Jer. 1:6 Considering the great judgments of God, which according to his threatening should come upon the world, he was moved with a certain compassion on the one side to pity them that should thus perish, and on the other side by the infirmity of man's nature, knowing how hard a thing it was to enterprise such a charge, as Isa. 6:11; Exod. 3:21 and 4:1.
j. Jer. 1:9 Which declareth that God maketh them meet, and assureth them, whom he calleth to set forth his glory: giving them all means necessary for the same, Exod. 4:12; Isa. 6:7.
k. Jer. 1:10 He showeth what is the authority of God's true ministers, which by his word have power to bear down whatsoever lifteth itself up against God: and to plant and assure the humble, and such as give themselves to the obedience of God's word, 2 Cor. 10:4, 5; Heb. 4:12, and these are the keys which Christ hath left to loose, and bind, Matt. 18:18.
l. Jer. 1:11 He joineth the sign with the word, for a more ample confirmation: signifying by the rod of the Almond tree, which first buddeth, the hasty coming of the Babylonians against the Jews.
m. Jer. 1:13 Signifying, that the Chaldeans and Assyrians should be as a pot to seethe the Jews which boiled in their pleasures and lust.
n. Jer. 1:14 Syria and Assyria were Northward in respect of Jerusalem, which were the Chaldeans' dominion.
o. Jer. 1:16 I will give them charge and power to execute my vengeance against the Idolaters which have forsaken me for their idols.
p. Jer. 1:17 Which declareth that God's vengeance is prepared against them, which dare not execute their duty faithfully, either for fear of man, or for any other cause, 1 Cor. 9:16.
q. Jer. 1:18 Signifying, on the one part, that the more that Satan and the world rage against God's Ministers, the more present will he be to help them, Josh. 1:5; Heb. 13:5, and on the other part, that they are utterly unmeet to serve God in his Church, which are afraid, and do not resist wickedness, whatsoever danger depend thereon, Isa. 50:7; Ezek. 3:8.

JER. 2

a. Jer. 2:2 According to that grace and favor which I showed thee from the beginning, when I did first choose thee to be my people, and married thee to myself, Ezek. 16:8.
b. Jer. 2:2 When I had delivered thee out of Egypt.
c. Jer. 2:3 Chosen above all others to serve the Lord only, and the first offered to the Lord of all other nations.
d. Jer. 2:3 Whosoever did challenge this people, or else did annoy them, was punished.
e. Jer. 2:5 That is, fallen to most vile idolatry.
f. Jer. 2:5 Altogether given to vanity, and are become blind and insensible as the idols that they serve.
g. Jer. 2:6 Where for lack of all things necessary for life, ye could look for nothing every hour but present death.
h. Jer. 2:7 By your idolatry and wicked manners, Ps. 78:58 and 106:38.
i. Jer. 2:8 They taught not the people to seek after God.
j. Jer. 2:8 As the Scribes, which should have expounded the Law to the people.
k. Jer. 2:8 Meaning, the Princes and Ministers: signifying, that all estates were corrupt.
l. Jer. 2:8 That is, spake vain things, and brought the people from the true worship of God to serve idols: for by Baal, which was the chief idol of the Moabites, are meant all idols.
m. Jer. 2:9 Signifying that he would not as he might, straightway condemn them, but showeth them by evident examples their great ingratitude that they might be ashamed and repent.
n. Jer. 2:10 Meaning, the Grecians and Italians.
o. Jer. 2:10 Unto Arabia.
p. Jer. 2:11 That is, God which is their glory, and who maketh them glorious above all other people, reproving the Jews that they were less diligent to serve the true God, than were the idolaters to honor their vanities.
q. Jer. 2:11 Meaning, the idols which were their destruction, Ps. 106:36.
r. Jer. 2:12 He showeth that the insensible creatures abhor this vile ingratitude, and as it were tremble for fear of God's great judgments against the same.
s. Jer. 2:13 Signifying, that when men forsake God's word, which is the fountain of life, they reject God himself, and so fall to their own inventions, and vain confidence, and procure to themselves destruction, Jonah 2:8; Zech. 10:2.
t. Jer. 2:14 Have I ordered them like servants and not like dearly beloved children? Exod. 4:22, therefore it is their fault only, if the enemy spoil them.
u. Jer. 2:15 The Babylonians, Chaldeans, and Assyrians.
v. Jer. 2:15 Not one shall be left to dwell there.
w. Jer. 2:16 That is, the Egyptians: for these were two great cities in Egypt.
x. Jer. 2:16 Have grievously vexed thee at sundry times.
y. Jer. 2:17 Showing that God would have still led them aright, if they would have followed him.
z. Jer. 2:18 To seek help of man, as though God were not able enough to defend thee, which is to drink of the puddles, and to leave the fountain, read Isa. 31:1.
aa. Jer. 2:18 To wit, Euphrates.
ab. Jer. 2:19 Meaning, that the wicked are insensible, till the punishment for their sin waken them as verse 26; Isa. 3:9.

and thou saidest, [ac]I will no more transgress, but like an harlot thou runnest about upon all high hills, and under all green trees. **21** Yet I had planted thee a noble vine, whose [ad]plants were all natural: how then art thou turned unto me into the plants of a strange vine? **22** Though thou wash thee with [ae]nitre, and take thee much soap, yet thine iniquity is marked before me, saith the Lord God. **23** How canst thou say, I am not polluted, neither have I [af]followed Baal? behold thy ways in the valley, and know what thou hast done: thou art like a swift [ag]dromedary, that runneth by his ways. **24** And as a wild [ah]ass used to the wilderness that snuffeth up the wind by occasion at her pleasure: who can turn her back? all they that seek her, will not weary themselves, but will find her in her [ai]month. **25** Keep thou thy feet from [aj]bareness, and thy throat from thirst: but thou saidest desperately, No, for I have loved strangers, and them will I follow. **26** As the [ak]thief is ashamed when he is found, so is the house of Israel ashamed, they, their kings, their princes and their priests, and their prophets, **27** Saying to a tree, Thou art my [al]father, and to a stone, Thou hast begotten me: for they have turned their back unto me, and not their face: but in the time of their trouble they will say, Arise, and help us. **28** But where are thy gods, that thou hast made thee? let them arise, if they can help thee in the time of thy trouble: for according [am]to the number of thy cities, are thy gods, O Judah. **29** Wherefore will [an]ye plead with me? ye all have rebelled against me, saith the Lord. **30** I have smitten your children in vain, they received no correction: your own [ao]sword hath devoured your Prophets like a destroying lion. **31** O generation, take heed to the word of the Lord: have I been as a [ap]wilderness unto Israel? or a land of darkness? Wherefore saith my people then, We are lords, [aq]we will come no more unto thee? **32** Can a maid forget her ornament, or a bride her attire? yet my people have forgotten me, days without number. **33** Why dost thou prepare thy way, to [ar]seek amity? even therefore will I teach thee, that thy ways are wickedness. **34** Also in thy [as]wings is found the blood of the souls of the poor innocents: I have not found it in holes, but upon all these places. **35** Yet thou sayest, Because I am guiltless, surely his wrath shall turn from me: behold, I will enter with thee into judgment, because thou sayest, I have not sinned. **36** Why runnest thou about so much to change thy ways? for thou shalt be confounded of Egypt, [at]as thou art confounded of Assyria. **37** For thou shalt go forth from thence, and thine hands upon [au]thine head, because the Lord hath rejected thy confidence, and thou shalt not prosper thereby.

3

God calleth his people unto repentance. 14 He promiseth the restitution of his Church. 20 He reproveth Judah and Israel, comparing them to a woman disobedient to her husband.

1 They [a]say, If a man put away his wife, and she go from him, and become another man's, shall he return again unto her? shall not this land [b]be polluted? but thou hast played the harlot with many [c]lovers: yet [d]turn again to me, saith the Lord. **2** Lift up thine eyes unto the high places, and behold, where thou hast not played the harlot: thou hast sat waiting for them in the ways, as the [e]Arabian in the wilderness: and thou hast polluted the land with thy whoredoms, and with thy malice. **3** Therefore the showers have been restrained, and the [f]latter rain came not, and thou haddest a [g]whore's forehead: thou wouldest not be ashamed. **4** Didst thou not still cry [h]unto me, Thou art my father, and the guide of my youth? **5** Will he keep his anger forever? will he reserve it to the end? thus hast thou spoken, but thou doest evil, even more and more. **6** The Lord said also unto me, in the days of Josiah the King, Hast thou seen what this rebel [i]Israel hath done? for she hath gone up upon every high mountain, and under every green tree, and there played the harlot. **7** And I said, when she had done all this, Turn thou unto me: but she returned not, as her rebellious sister Judah saw. **8** When I saw, how that by all occasions rebellious Israel had played the harlot, I cast [j]her away, and gave her a bill of divorcement: yet her rebellious sister Judah was not afraid, but she went also and played the harlot. **9** So that for the [k]lightness of her whoredom she hath even defiled the land: for she hath committed fornication with stones and stocks. **10** Nevertheless for all this, her rebellious sister Judah hath not returned unto me with [l]her whole heart, but feignedly, saith the Lord. **11** And the Lord said unto me, The rebellious Israel hath [m]justified herself more than the rebellious Judah. **12** Go and cry these words toward [n]the North, and say, Thou disobedient Israel, return, saith the Lord, and I will not let my wrath fall upon you: for I am merciful, saith the Lord, and I will not always keep mine anger. **13** But know thine iniquity: for thou hast rebelled against the Lord thy God, and hast [o]scattered thy ways to the strange gods under every green tree, but ye would not obey my voice, saith the Lord. **14** O ye disobedient children, turn again, saith the Lord, for I am your Lord, and I will take you one of a city, and two of a tribe, and will bring you to Zion, **15** And I will give you pastors according to mine heart, which shall feed you with knowledge and understanding. **16** Moreover, when ye be increased and multiplied in the land, in those days, saith the Lord, they shall say no more, The [p]Ark of the covenant of the Lord: for it shall come no more to mind, neither shall they remember it, neither shall they visit it, for that shall be no more done. **17** At that time they shall call Jerusalem, [q]The throne of the Lord, and all the nations shall be gathered unto it, even to the Name of the Lord in Jerusalem: and thence forth they shall follow no more the hardness of their wicked heart. **18** In those days the house of Judah shall walk with the house of Israel, and they shall come together out of the land of the [r]North, into the land that I have given for an inheritance unto your fathers. **19** But I said, How did I take thee for children, and give thee a pleasant land, even the glorious heritage of the armies of the heathen, and say, Thou shalt call me, saying, My father, and shall not turn from me? **20** But as a woman rebelleth against her [s]husband: so have ye rebelled against me, O house of Israel, saith the Lord. **21** [t]A voice was heard upon the high places, weeping, and supplications of the children of Israel: for they have perverted their way, and forgotten the Lord their God. **22** O ye disobedient children, return and I will heal your rebellions. [u]Behold, we come unto thee, for thou art the Lord our God. **23** Truly the hope of the hills is but vain, nor the multitude of mountains: but in the Lord our God is the health of Israel. **24** For confusion hath devoured our [v]father's labor, from our youth, their sheep and their bullocks, their sons and their daughters. **25** We lie down in our confusion, and our shame covereth us: [w]for we have sinned against the Lord our God, we and our fathers from our youth, even unto this day, and have not obeyed the voice of the Lord our God.

---

ac. Jer. 2:20 When I delivered thee out of Egypt, Exod. 19:8; Deut. 5:27; Josh. 24:16; Ezra 10:12; Heb. 8:6.

ad. Jer. 2:21 Hebrew, seed was all true.

ae. Jer. 2:22 Though thou use all the purifications and ceremonies of the law, thou canst not escape punishment, except thou turn to me by faith and repentance.

af. Jer. 2:23 Meaning, that hypocrites deny that they worship the idols, but that they honor God in them, and therefore they call their doings, God's service.

ag. Jer. 2:23 He compareth the idolaters to these beasts, because they never cease running to and fro: for both valleys and hills are full of their idolatry.

ah. Jer. 2:24 He compareth the idolaters to a wild ass: for she can never be tamed nor yet wearied: for as she runneth she can take her wind at every occasion.

ai. Jer. 2:24 That is, when she is with foal, and therefore the hunters wait their time: so though thou canst not be turned back now from thine idolatry, yet when thine iniquity shall be at the fall, God will meet with thee.

aj. Jer. 2:25 Hereby he warneth them that they should not go into strange countries to seek help: for they should but spend their labor, and hurt themselves, which is here meant by the bare foot and thirst, Isa. 57:10.

ak. Jer. 2:26 As a thief will not acknowledge his fault, till he be taken with the deed, and ready to be punished, so they will not confess their idolatry, till the plagues due to the same light upon them.

al. Jer. 2:27 Meaning, that idolaters spoil God of his honor: and whereas he hath taught to call him the father of all flesh, they attribute this title to their idols.

am. Jer. 2:28 Thou thoughtest that thy gods of blocks and stones could have helped thee, because they were many in number and present in every place: but now let us see whether either the multitude, or their presence can deliver thee from my plague, Jer. 11:13.

an. Jer. 2:29 As though I did you injury in punishing you, seeing that your faults are so evident.

ao. Jer. 2:30 That is, you have killed your Prophets, that exhorted you to repentance, as Zechariah, Isaiah, etc.

ap. Jer. 2:31 Have I not given them abundance of all things?

aq. Jer. 2:31 But will trust in our own power and policy.

ar. Jer. 2:33 With strangers.

as. Jer. 2:34 The Prophets and the faithful are slain in every corner of your country.

at. Jer. 2:36 For the Assyrians had taken away the ten tribes out of Israel, and destroyed Judah even unto Jerusalem: and the Egyptians slew Josiah, and vexed the Jews in sundry sorts.

au. Jer. 2:37 In sign of lamentation, as 2 Sam. 13:19.

JER. 3

a. Jer. 3:1 According as it is written, Deut. 24:4.

b. Jer. 3:1 If he take such one to wife again.

c. Jer. 3:1 That is, with idols, and with them whom thou hast put thy confidence in.

d. Jer. 3:1 And I will not cast thee off, but receive thee, according to my mercy.

e. Jer. 3:2 Which dwelleth in tents and waiteth for them that pass by to spoil them.

f. Jer. 3:3 As God threatened by his Law, Deut. 28:24.

g. Jer. 3:3 Thou wouldest never be ashamed of thine acts and repent: and this impudency is common to idolaters, which will not give off, though they be never so manifestly convicted.

h. Jer. 3:4 He showeth that the wicked in their miseries will cry unto God and use outward prayer as the godly do, but because they turn not from their evil, they are not heard, Isa. 58:3, 4.

i. Jer. 3:6 Meaning, the ten tribes.

j. Jer. 3:8 And gave her into the hands of the Assyrians.

k. Jer. 3:9 The Hebrew word may either signify lightness, and wantonness, or noise and brute.

l. Jer. 3:10 Judah feigned for a time that she did return, as under Josiah and other good kings, but she was never truly touched, or wholly reformed, as appeared when occasion was offered by any wicked prince.

m. Jer. 3:11 Israel hath not declared herself so wicked as Judah, which yet hath had more admonitions and examples to call her to repentance.

n. Jer. 3:12 Whereas the Israelites were now kept in captivity by the Assyrians, to whom he promiseth mercy, if they will repent.

o. Jer. 3:13 There was no way, which thou didst not haunt to seek after the idols, and to trot a pilgrimage.

p. Jer. 3:16 This is to be understood of the coming of Christ: for then they shall not seek the Lord by ceremonies, and all figures shall cease.

q. Jer. 3:17 Meaning, the Church, where the Lord will be present to the world's end, Matt. 28:20.

r. Jer. 3:18 Where they are now in captivity.

s. Jer. 3:20 The Hebrew word signifieth a friend or companion, and here may be taken for a husband, as it is used also, Hos. 3:1.

t. Jer. 3:21 Signifying, that God, whom they had forsaken, would bring their enemies unto them, who should lead them captive, and make them to cry and lament.

u. Jer. 3:22 This is spoken in the person of Israel to the shame of Judah, which stayed so long to turn unto God.

v. Jer. 3:24 For their idolatry God's vengeance hath light upon them and theirs.

w. Jer. 3:25 They justify not themselves, or say that they would follow their fathers, but condemn their wicked doings and desire forgiveness of the same, as Ezra 9:7; Ps. 106:6; Isa. 64:6.

4

1 True repentance. 4 He exhorteth to the circumcision of the heart. 5 The destruction of Judah is prophesied for the malice of their hearts. 19 The Prophet lamenteth it.

1 O Israel, if thou return, [a]return unto me, saith the Lord: and if thou put
away thine abominations out of my sight, then shalt thou not remove. **2** And
thou shalt [b]swear, The Lord liveth in truth, in judgment and in righteousness,
and the nations shall be blessed in him, and shall glory in him. **3** For thus sai-
th the Lord to the men of Judah, and to Jerusalem, **4** Break up [c]your fallow
ground, and sow not among the thorns: be circumcised to the Lord, and take
away the foreskins of your hearts, ye men of Judah, and inhabitants of Jerusalem,
lest my wrath come forth like fire, and burn, that none can quench it, because
of the wickedness of your inventions. **5** [d]Declare in Judah, and show forth in
Jerusalem, and say, Blow the trumpet in the land: cry, and gather together, and
say, Assemble yourselves, and let us go into strong cities. **6** Set up the standard
in Zion: [e]prepare to flee, and stay not: for I will bring a plague from the North,
and a great destruction. **7** The [f]lion is come up from his den, and the destroyer
of the Gentiles is departed, and gone forth of his place to lay thy land waste, and
thy cities shall be destroyed without an inhabitant. **8** Wherefore gird you with
sackcloth: lament, and howl, for the fierce wrath of the Lord is not turned back
from us. **9** And in that day, saith the Lord, the heart of the king shall perish,
and the heart of the princes and the Priests shall be astonished, and the [g]Prophets
shall wonder. **10** Then said I, Ah, Lord God, surely thou hast [h]deceived this
people, and Jerusalem, saying, Ye shall have peace, and the sword pierceth unto
the heart. **11** At that time shall it be said to this people and to Jerusalem, A dry
[i]wind in the high places of the wilderness cometh toward the daughter of my pe-
ople, but neither [j]to fan nor to cleanse. **12** A mighty wind shall come unto me
from those places, and now will I also give sentence upon them. **13** Behold, he
shall come up as the [k]clouds, and his chariots shall be as a tempest: his horses are
lighter than eagles. [l]Woe unto us, for we are destroyed. **14** O Jerusalem, wash
thine heart from wickedness, that thou mayest be saved: how long shall thy wicked
thoughts remain within thee? **15** For a voice declareth from [m]Dan, and publi-
sheth affliction from mount [n]Ephraim. **16** Make ye mention of the heathen,
and publish in Jerusalem, Behold, the scouts come from a far country, and cry out
against the cities of Judah. **17** They have compassed her about as the watchmen
of the [o]field, because it hath provoked me unto wrath, saith the Lord. **18** Thy
ways and thine inventions have procured thee these things, such is thy wickedness:
therefore it shall be bitter, therefore it shall pierce unto thine heart. **19** My belly,
my [p]belly, I am pained, even at the very heart: mine heart is troubled within me: I
cannot be still: for my soul hath heard the sound of the trumpet, and the alarm of
the battle. **20** Destruction upon destruction is cried, for the whole land is wa-
sted: suddenly are my [q]tents destroyed, and my curtains in a moment. **21** How
long shall I see the standard, and hear the sound of the trumpet? **22** For my
people is foolish, they have not known me: they are foolish children, and have
none understanding: [r]they are wise to do evil, but to do well they have no know-
ledge. **23** I have looked upon the earth, and lo, it was without form and [s]void:
and to the heavens, and they had no light. **24** I beheld the mountains: and lo,
they trembled, and all the hills shook. **25** I beheld, and lo, there was no man,
and all the birds of the heaven were departed. **26** I beheld, and lo, the fruitful
place was a wilderness, and all the cities thereof were broken down at the presence
of the Lord, and by his fierce wrath. **27** For thus hath the Lord said, The whole
land shall be desolate: yet will I [t]not make a full end. **28** Therefore shall the earth
mourn, and the heavens above shall be darkened, because I have pronounced it:
I have thought it, and will not repent, neither will I turn back from it. **29** The
whole city shall flee, for the noise of the horsemen and bowmen: they shall go into
thickets, and climb up upon the rocks: every city shall be forsaken, and not a man
dwell therein. **30** And when thou shalt be destroyed, what wilt thou do? Thou-
gh thou [u]clothest thyself with scarlet, though thou deckest thee with ornaments of
gold, though thou paintest thy face with colors, yet shalt thou trim thyself in vain:
for thy lovers will abhor thee and seek thy life. **31** For I have heard a noise as of
a woman travailing, or as one laboring of her first child, even the voice of the dau-
ghter Zion that sigheth and stretcheth out her hands: [v]woe is me now: for my soul
fainteth because of the murderers.

5

1 In Judah no righteous man is found, neither among the people nor the rulers. 15 Wherefore Judah is destroyed of the Chaldeans.

1 Run to and fro by the streets of Jerusalem, and behold now, and know, and
inquire in the open places thereof, if ye can find a man, or if there be any that exe-
cuteth judgment, and seeketh the truth, and I will spare [a]it. **2** For though they
say, The [b]Lord liveth, yet do they swear falsely. **3** O Lord, are not thine eyes upon
the [c]truth? thou hast [d]stricken them, but they have not sorrowed: thou hast consu-
med them, but they have refused to receive correction: they have made their faces
harder than a stone, and have refused to return. **4** Therefore I said, Surely they
are poor, they are foolish, for they know not the way of the Lord, nor the judgment
of their God. **5** I will get me unto the [e]great men, and will speak unto them: for
they have known the way of the Lord, and the judgment of their God: but these
have altogether broken the yoke, and burst the bonds. **6** Wherefore a [f]lion out of
the forest shall slay them, and a wolf of the wilderness shall destroy them: a leopard
shall watch over their cities: everyone that goeth out thence, shall be torn in pie-
ces, because their trespasses are many, and their rebellions are increased. **7** How
should I spare thee for this? thy children have forsaken me, and [g]sworn by them
that are no gods: though I fed them to the full, yet they committed adultery, and
assembled themselves by companies in the harlot's houses. **8** They rose up in the
morning like fed horses: for every man [ʼ]neighed after his neighbor's wife. **9** Shall
I not visit for these things, saith the Lord? shall not my soul be avenged on such
a nation as this? **10** [h]Climb up upon their walls, and destroy them, but make
not a full end: [i]take away their battlements, for they are not the Lord's. **11** For
the house of Israel, and the house of Judah have grievously trespassed against me,
saith the Lord. **12** They have [j]denied the Lord, and said, It is not he, neither
shall the plague come upon us, neither shall we see sword nor famine. **13** And
the Prophets shall be as [k]wind, and the word is [l]not in them: thus shall it come
unto them. **14** Wherefore thus saith the Lord God of hosts, Because ye speak
such words, behold, I will put my words into [m]thy mouth, like a fire, and this
people shall be as wood, and it shall devour them. **15** Lo, I will bring a nation
upon you [n]from far, O house of Israel, saith the Lord, which is a mighty nation,
and an ancient nation, a nation whose language thou knowest not, neither under-
standest what they say. **16** Whose quiver is as an [o]open sepulcher: they are all
very strong. **17** And they shall eat thine harvest and thy bread: they shall devour
thy sons and thy daughters: they shall eat up thy sheep and thy bullocks: they shall
eat thy vines and thy fig trees: they shall destroy with the sword thy fenced cities,
wherein thou didst trust. **18** Nevertheless, at those days, saith the Lord, I will
not make a full end of [p]you. **19** And when [2]ye shall say, Wherefore doth the
Lord our God do these things unto us? then shalt [q]thou answer them, Like as ye
have forsaken me and served strange gods in your land, so shall ye serve strangers
in a land that is not yours. **20** Declare this in the house of Jacob, and publish it

---

JER. 4

a. Jer. 4:1 That is, wholly, and without hypocrisy, Joel 2:12, not dissembling to turn and serve God as they do which serve him by halves, as Hos. 7:16.
b. Jer. 4:2 Thou shalt detest the name of idols, Ps. 16:4, and shalt with reverence swear by the living God, when thine oath may advance God's glory, and profit others: and here, by swearing he meaneth the true religion of God.
c. Jer. 4:4 He willeth them to pluck up the impiety and wicked affection and worldly respects out of their heart, that the true seed of God's word may be sown therein, Hos. 10:12, and this is the true circumcision of the heart, Deut. 10:16; Rom. 2:29; Col. 2:11.
d. Jer. 4:5 He warneth them of the great dangers that shall come upon them by the Chaldeans, except, they repent and turn to the Lord.
e. Jer. 4:6 He speaketh this to admonish them of the great danger when every man shall prepare to save himself, but it shall be too late, 2 Kings 25:4.
f. Jer. 4:7 Meaning, Nebuchadnezzar King of Babylon, 2 Kings 24:1.
g. Jer. 4:9 That is, the false prophets, which still prophesied peace and security.
h. Jer. 4:10 By the false prophets which promised peace and tranquility: and thus thou hast punished their rebellious stubbornness by causing them to hearken unto lies which would not believe thy truth, 1 Kings 22:23; Ezek. 14:9; 2 Thess. 2:11.
i. Jer. 4:11 The North wind whereby he meaneth Nebuchadnezzar.
j. Jer. 4:11 But to carry away both corn, and chaff.
k. Jer. 4:13 Meaning, that Nebuchadnezzar should come as suddenly, as a cloud that is carried with the wind.
l. Jer. 4:13 This is spoken in the person of all the people, who in their affliction should cry thus.
m. Jer. 4:15 Which was a city in the utmost border of Israel Northward toward Babylon.
n. Jer. 4:15 Which was in the mid-way between Dan and Jerusalem.
o. Jer. 4:17 Which keep the fruits so straightly, that nothing can come in nor out: so should the Babylonians compass Judah.
p. Jer. 4:19 He showeth that the true ministers are lively touched with the calamities of the Church, so that all the parts of their body feel the grief of their heart, albeit with zeal to God's glory they pronounce his judgments against the people.
q. Jer. 4:20 Meaning, the cities, which were as easily cast down as a tent.
r. Jer. 4:22 Their wisdom and policy tend to their own destruction and pulleth them from God.
s. Jer. 4:23 By these manner of speeches he showeth the horrible destruction that should come upon the land, and also condemneth the obstinacy of the people, who repent not at the fear of these terrible tidings, seeing that the insensible creatures are moved therewith, as if the order of nature should be changed, Isa. 13:10 and 24:23; Ezek. 32:7; Joel 2:31 and 3:15.
t. Jer. 4:27 But for his mercy's sake, he will reserve himself a residue to be his Church, and to praise him in earth, Isa. 1:9.
u. Jer. 4:30 Neither thy ceremonies nor rich gifts shall deliver thee.
v. Jer. 4:31 As the Prophets were moved to pity the destruction of their people, so they declared it to the people to move them to repentance, Isa. 22:4; Jer. 9:1.

JER. 5

a. Jer. 5:1 That is, the city.
b. Jer. 5:2 Though they pretend religion and holiness, yet all is but hypocrisy: for under this kind of swearing is contained the true religion.
c. Jer. 5:3 Dost not thou love uprightness and faithful dealing?
d. Jer. 5:3 Thou hast ofttimes punished them, but all is in vain, Isa. 9:13.
e. Jer. 5:5 He speaketh this to the reproach of them which should govern and teach others, and yet are farther out of the way than the simple people.
f. Jer. 5:6 Meaning, Nebuchadnezzar and his army.
g. Jer. 5:7 He showeth that to swear by anything than by God, is to forsake him.
h. Jer. 5:10 He commandeth the Babylonians and enemies to destroy them.
i. Jer. 5:10 Read Jer. 4:27.
j. Jer. 5:12 Because they gave no credit to the words of his Prophets, as Isa. 28:15.
k. Jer. 5:13 Their words shall be of none effect, but vain.
l. Jer. 5:13 They are not sent of the Lord, and therefore that which they threaten to us shall come upon them.
m. Jer. 5:14 Meaning, Jer..
n. Jer. 5:15 To wit, the Babylonians and Chaldeans.
o. Jer. 5:16 Who shall kill many with their arrows.
p. Jer. 5:18 Here the Lord declareth his unspeakable favor toward his Church, as Jer. 4:27.
q. Jer. 5:19 Meaning, the Prophet Jer.

in Judah, saying, **21** Hear now this, O foolish people, and [r]without understanding, which have [3]eyes and see not, which have ears and hear not. **22** Fear ye not me, saith the Lord? or will ye not be afraid at my presence, which have placed the sand for the [4]bounds of the sea by the perpetual decree that it cannot pass it, and though the waves thereof rage, yet can they not prevail, though they roar, yet can they not pass over it? **23** But this people hath an unfaithful and rebellious heart: they are departed and gone. **24** For they say not in their heart, Let us now fear the Lord our God, that giveth rain both early and late in due season: he reserveth unto us the appointed weeks of the harvest. **25** Yet your [s]iniquities have turned away these things, and your sins have hindered good things from you. **26** For among my people are found wicked persons, that lay wait as he that setteth snares: they have made a pit, to catch men. **27** As a cage is full of birds, so are their houses full of deceit: thereby they are become great and waxen rich. **28** They are waxen fat and shining: they do overpass the deeds of the wicked: [5]they execute no judgment, no not the judgment of the fatherless: yet they [t]prosper, though they execute no judgment for the poor. **29** Shall I not visit for these things, saith the Lord? or shall not my soul be avenged on such a nation as this? **30** An horrible and filthy thing is committed in the land. **31** The [u]prophets prophesy lies, and the priests [v]receive gifts in their hands, and my people delight therein. What will ye then do in the end thereof?

6

1 The coming of the Assyrians and Chaldeans. 16 He exhorteth the Jews to repentance.

1 O ye children of [a]Benjamin, prepare to flee out of the midst of Jerusalem, and blow the trumpet in [b]Tekoa: set up a standard upon [c]Beth-Haccerem: for a plague appeareth out of the North and great destruction. **2** I have compared the daughter of Zion to [d]a beautiful and dainty woman. **3** The Pastors with their flocks [e]shall come unto her: they shall pitch their tents round about by her, and everyone shall feed in his place. **4** [f]Prepare war against her: arise, and let us go up toward the South: woe unto us: for the day declineth, and the shadows of the evening are stretched out. **5** Arise, and let us go up by night, and destroy her palaces. **6** For thus hath the Lord of hosts said, Hew down wood, and cast a mount against Jerusalem: this city must be visited; all oppression is in the midst of it. **7** As the fountain casteth out her waters, so she casteth out her malice; [g]cruelty and spoil is continually heard in her before me, with sorrow and strokes. **8** Be thou instructed, O [h]Jerusalem, lest my soul depart from thee, lest I make thee desolate as a land that none inhabiteth. **9** Thus saith the Lord of hosts, They shall gather as a vine, the residue of Israel: turn [i]back thine hand as the grape gatherer into the baskets. **10** Unto whom shall I speak, and admonish that they may hear? behold, their ears are [j]uncircumcised, and they cannot hearken: behold, the word of the Lord is unto them as a reproach: they have no delight in it. **11** Therefore I am full of the wrath of the Lord: I am weary with holding it: [k]I will pour it out upon the [l]children in the street, and likewise upon the assembly of the young men: for the husband shall even be taken with the wife, and the aged with him that is full of days. **12** And their houses with their lands, and wives also shall be turned unto strangers: for I will stretch out mine hand upon the inhabitants of the land, saith the Lord. **13** For from the least of them, even unto the greatest of them, everyone is given unto covetousness, and from the Prophet even unto the Priest, they all deal falsely. **14** They have healed also the hurt of the daughter of my people with sweet words, saying, [m]Peace, peace, when there is no peace. **15** Were they ashamed when they had committed abomination? nay, they were not ashamed, no neither could they have any shame: therefore they shall fall among the [n]slain: when I shall visit them, they shall be cast down, saith the Lord. **16** Thus saith the Lord, Stand in the ways and behold, and ask for the [o]old way, which is the good way, and walk therein, and ye shall find rest for your souls: but they said, We will not walk therein. **17** Also I set [p]watchmen over you, which said, Take heed to the sound of the trumpet: but they said, We will not take heed. **18** Hear therefore, ye [q]Gentiles, and thou Congregation know, what is among them. **19** Hear, O earth, behold, I will cause a plague to come upon this people, even the fruit of their own imaginations: because they have not taken heed unto my words, nor to my Law, but cast it off. **20** To what purpose bringest thou me [r]incense from Sheba, and sweet calamus from a far country? Your burnt offerings are not pleasant, nor your sacrifices sweet unto me. **21** Therefore thus saith the Lord, Behold, I will lay stumbling blocks before this people, and the fathers and the sons together shall fall upon them: the neighbor and his friend shall perish. **22** Thus saith the Lord, Behold, a people cometh from the [s]North country, and a great nation shall arise from the sides of the earth. **23** With bow and shield shall they be weaponed: they are cruel and will have no compassion: their voice roareth like the sea, and they ride upon horses well appointed, like men of war against thee, O daughter Zion. **24** We have heard their fame, and our hands wax [t]feeble: sorrow is come upon us, as the sorrow of a woman in travail. **25** Go not forth into the field, nor walk by the way: for the sword of the enemy and fear is on every side. **26** O daughter of my people, gird thee with sackcloth, and wallow thyself in the ashes: make lamentation, and bitter mourning as for thine only son: for the destroyer shall suddenly come upon us. **27** I have set [u]thee for a defense and fortress among my people, that thou mayest know and try their ways. **28** They are all rebellious traitors, walking craftily; they are brass and iron, they all are destroyers, **29** The [v]bellows are burnt; the lead is consumed in the fire; the founder melteth in vain; for the wicked are not taken away. **30** They shall call them reprobate silver, because the Lord hath rejected them.

7

2 Jeremiah is commanded to show unto the people the words of God, which trusteth in the outward service of the Temple. 13 The evils that shall come to the Jews, for the despising of their Prophets. 21 Sacrifices doth not the Lord chiefly require of the Jews, but that they should obey his word.

1 The words that came to Jeremiah from the Lord, saying, **2** Stand in the gate of the Lord's house, and cry this word there, and say, Hear the word of the Lord, all ye of Judah that enter in at these gates to worship the Lord. **3** Thus saith the Lord of hosts, the God of Israel, [1]Amend your ways and your works, and I will let you dwell in this place. **4** Trust not in [a]lying words, saying, The Temple of the Lord, the Temple of the Lord; this is the Temple of the Lord. **5** For if you amend and redress your ways and your works; if you execute judgment between a man and neighbor, **6** And oppress not the stranger, the fatherless, and the widow, and shed no innocent blood in this place, neither walk after other gods to your destruction, **7** Then [b]will I let you dwell in this place in the land that I gave unto your fathers forever and ever. **8** Behold, you trust in lying words, that cannot profit. **9** Will you steal, murder, and commit adultery, and swear falsely, and burn incense unto Baal, and walk after other gods whom ye know not? **10** And come and stand before me in this House, whereupon my Name is called, and say, We are delivered, though we have done all these abominations? **11** Is this House become [c]a den of thieves, whereupon my Name is called before your eyes? Behold, even I see it, saith the Lord. **12** But go ye now unto my place which was in Shiloh, [d]where I set my Name at the beginning, and behold, what I did to it for the wickedness, of my people Israel. **13** Therefore now because ye have done all these works, saith the Lord, (and I [e]rose up early and spake unto you: but when I spake, ye would not hear me, neither when I called, would [f]ye

---

r. Jer. 5:21 Hebrew, without heart.
s. Jer. 5:25 If there be any stay, that we receive not God's blessings in abundance, we must consider that it is for our own iniquities, Isa. 59:1, 2.
t. Jer. 5:28 They feel not the plague of God for it.
u. Jer. 5:31 Meaning that there could be nothing but disorder, where the ministers were wicked persons and corrupt.
v. Jer. 5:31 Or, [bearest].

JER. 5
1. Ezek. 22:11
2. Jer. 16:10
3. Isa. 6:9 / Matt. 13:14 / Acts 28:27 / Rom. 11:8
4. Job. 26:10
5. Isa. 1:23 / Ezek. 7:9

JER. 6
a. Jer. 6:1 He speaketh to them chiefly because they should take heed by the example of their brethren, the other half of their tribe, which were now carried away prisoners.
b. Jer. 6:1 Which was a city in Judah, six miles from Bethlehem, 2 Chron. 11:6.
c. Jer. 6:1 Read Neh. 3:14.
d. Jer. 6:2 I have entreated her gently, and given her abundance of all things.
e. Jer. 6:3 She shall be so destroyed; that the sheep may be fed in her.
f. Jer. 6:4 He speaketh this in the person of the Babylonians, which complain that the time faileth them before they have brought their enterprises to pass.
g. Jer. 6:7 He showeth the cause why it should be destroyed, and how it cometh of themselves.
h. Jer. 6:8 He warneth them to amend by his correction, and turn to him by repentance.
i. Jer. 6:9 He exhorteth the Babylonians to be diligent to search out all and to leave none.
j. Jer. 6:10 They delight to hear vain things, and to shut up their ears to true doctrine.
k. Jer. 6:11 As the Lord had given him his word to be as a fire of his indignation to burn the wicked, Jer. 5:14, so he kindleth it now when he seeth that all remedies are past.
l. Jer. 6:11 None shall be spared.
m. Jer. 6:14 When the people began to fear God's judgments, the false prophets comforted them by flatterings, showing that God would send peace and not war.
n. Jer. 6:15 Hebrew, them that fall.
o. Jer. 6:16 Wherein the Patriarchs and Prophets walked, directed by the word of God: signifying that there is no true way, but that which God prescribeth.
p. Jer. 6:17 Prophets which should warn you of the dangers that were at hand.
q. Jer. 6:18 God taketh all the world to witness, and the insensible creatures, of the ingratitude of the Jews.
r. Jer. 6:20 Read Isa. 1:11 and Amos 5:21.
s. Jer. 6:22 From Babylon by Dan, which was North from Jerusalem.
t. Jer. 6:24 For fear of the enemy: he speaketh this in the person of the Jews.
u. Jer. 6:27 Meaning, Jer., whom God had appointed to try out the godly from the wicked, as a founder doth the pure metal from the dross.
v. Jer. 6:29 All the pain and labor that hath been taken with them, is lost.

JER. 7
a. Jer. 7:4 Believe not the false prophets, which say that for the Temple's sake, and the sacrifices there, the Lord will preserve you, and so nourish you in your sin, and vain confidence.
b. Jer. 7:7 God showeth on what condition he made his promise to this Temple: that they should be an holy people unto him, as he would be a faithful God to them.
c. Jer. 7:11 As thieves hid in holes and dens think themselves safe, so when you are in my Temple, you think to be covered with the holiness thereof, and that I cannot see your wickedness, Matt. 21:13.
d. Jer. 7:12 Because they depended so much on the Temple, which was for his promise, that he would be present and defend them where the Ark was, he sendeth them to God's judgments against Shiloh, where the Ark had remained about 300 years, and after was taken, the Priests slain, and the people miserably discomfited, 1 Sam. 4:11; Jer. 26:6.
e. Jer. 7:13 That is, I never ceased to warn you, as Isa. 65:2; Prov. 1:23.
f. Jer. 7:13 He showeth what is the only remedy to redress our faults: to suffer God to lead us into the way, and to obey his calling, Isa. 66:4.

answer.) **14** Therefore will I do unto this house, whereupon my Name is called, wherein also ye trust, even unto the place that I gave to you, and to your fathers, as I have done unto Shiloh. **15** And I will cast [g]you out of my sight, as I have cast out all your brethren, even the whole seed of Ephraim. **16** Therefore thou shalt not [h]pray for this people, neither lift up cry or prayer for them, neither entreat me, for I will not hear thee. **17** Seest thou not what they do in the cities of Judah, and in the streets of Jerusalem? **18** The children gather wood, and the fathers kindle the fire, and the women kneed the dough to make cakes to [i]the Queen of heaven, and to pour out drink offerings unto other gods, that they may provoke me unto anger. **19** Do they provoke me to anger, saith the Lord, and not themselves to the confusion of their own faces? **20** Therefore thus saith the Lord God, Behold, mine anger and my wrath shall be poured upon this place; upon man and upon beast, and upon the tree of the field, and upon the fruit of the ground, and it shall burn and not be quenched. **21** Thus saith the Lord of hosts, the God of Israel, Put your burnt offerings unto your sacrifices, and eat the flesh. **22** For [j]I spake not unto your fathers, nor commanded them, when I brought them out of the land of Egypt, concerning burnt offerings and sacrifices. **23** But this thing commanded I them, saying, Obey my voice, and I will be your God, and ye shall be my people: and walk ye in all the ways which I have commanded you, that it may be well unto you. **24** But they would not obey, nor incline their ear, but went after the counsels, and the stubbornness of their wicked heart, and went backward and not forward. **25** Since the day that your fathers came up out of the land of Egypt, unto [k]this day, I have even sent unto you all my servants the Prophets, [l]rising up early every day, and sending them. **26** Yet would they not hear me, nor incline their ear, but hardened their neck, and did worse than their fathers. **27** Therefore shalt thou speak all these words unto them, but they [m]will not hear thee: thou shalt also cry unto them, but they will not answer thee. **28** But thou shalt say unto them, This is a nation that heareth not the voice of the Lord their God, nor receiveth discipline: truth is perished, and is clean gone out of their mouth. **29** Cut off thine [n]hair, O Jerusalem, and cast it away, and take up a complaint on the high places: for the Lord hath rejected and forsaken the generation of his [o]wrath. **30** For the children of Judah have done evil in my sight, saith the Lord: they have set their abominations in the house, whereupon my Name is called to pollute it. **31** And they have built the high place of [p]Tophet, which is in the valley of Ben-Hinnom to burn their sons and their daughters in the fire, which I [q]commanded them not, neither came it in mine heart. **32** Therefore behold, the days come, saith the Lord, that it shall no more be called Tophet, nor the valley of Ben-Hinnom, but the valley of slaughter: for they shall bury in Tophet till there be no place. **33** And the carcasses of this people shall be meat for the fowls of the heaven, and for the beasts of the earth, and none shall fray them away. **34** [2]Then I will cause to cease from the cities of Judah, and from the streets of Jerusalem the voice of mirth, and the voice of gladness, the voice of the bridegroom, and the voice of the bride: for the land shall be desolate.

8

1 The destruction of the Jews. 4 The Lord moveth the people to amendment. 10 He reprehendeth the lying doctrine and the covetousness of the Prophets and Priests.

1 At that time, saith the Lord, they shall bring out the bones of the kings of Judah, and the bones of their Princes, and the bones of the Priests, and the bones of the Prophets, and the bones of the inhabitants of Jerusalem out of their [a]graves. **2** And they shall spread them before the sun, and the moon, and all the host of heaven, whom they have loved, and whom they have served, and whom they have followed, and whom they have sought, and whom they have worshipped: they shall not be gathered nor be buried, but shall be as dung upon the earth. **3** And death shall be desired [b]rather than life of all the residue that remaineth of this wicked family, which remain in all the places where I have scattered them, saith the Lord of hosts. **4** Thou shalt say unto them also, Thus saith the Lord, Shall they [c]fall, and not arise? shall he turn away and not turn again? **5** Wherefore is this people of Jerusalem turned back by a perpetual rebellion? they gave themselves to deceit, and would not return. **6** I hearkened and heard, but none spake aright: no man repented him of his wickedness, saying, What have I done? [d]everyone turned to their race, as the horse rusheth into the battle. **7** Even the stork in the air knoweth her appointed times, and the turtle, and the crane and the swallow observe the time of their coming, but my people knoweth not the [e]judgment of the Lord. **8** How do ye say, We are wise, and the Law of the Lord is with us? Lo, [f]certainly in vain made he it, the pen of the scribes is in vain. **9** The [g]wise men are ashamed: they are afraid and taken: lo, they have rejected the word of the Lord, and what wisdom is in them? **10** Therefore will I give their wives unto others, and their fields to them that shall possess them: [1]for everyone from the least even unto the greatest is given to covetousness, and from the Prophet even unto the Priest, everyone dealeth falsely. **11** For they have healed the hurt of the daughter of my people with sweet words, saying, [h]Peace, peace, when there is no peace. **12** Were they ashamed when they had committed abomination? nay, they were not ashamed, neither could they have any shame: therefore shall they fall among the slain: when I shall visit them, they shall be cast down, saith the Lord. **13** I will surely consume them, saith the Lord: there shall be no grapes on the vine, nor figs on the fig tree, and the leaf shall fade, and the things that I have given them shall depart from them. **14** Why do we stay? [i]assemble yourselves, and let us enter into the strong cities, and let us be quiet there: for the Lord our God hath put us to silence, and given us water with [j]gall to drink, because we have sinned against the Lord. **15** [2]We looked for peace, but no good came, and for a time of health, and behold troubles. **16** The neighing of his horses was heard from [k]Dan, the whole land trembled at the noise of the neighing of his strong horses: for they are come, and have devoured the land with all that is in it, the city, and those that dwell therein. **17** For behold, I will [l]send serpents, and cockatrices among you, which will not be charmed, and they shall sting you, saith the Lord. **18** I would have [m]comforted myself against sorrow, but mine heart is heavy in me. **19** Behold, the voice of the cry of the daughter of my people for fear of them of a far country, Is not the Lord in Zion? is not her king in her? Why [n]have they provoked me to anger with their graven images, and with the vanities of a strange god? **20** The [o]harvest is past, the Summer is ended, and we are not holpen. **21** I am [p]sore vexed for the hurt of the daughter of my people, I am heavy, and astonishment hath taken me. **22** Is there no balm [q]at Gilead? is there no Physician there? Why then is not the health of the daughter of my people recovered?

9

1 The complaint of the Prophet for the malice of the people. 24 In the knowledge of God ought we only to rejoice. 26 The uncircumcision of the heart.

1 Oh, that mine head were full of [a]water, and mine eyes a fountain of tears, that I might weep day and night for the slain of the daughter of my people. **2** Oh, that I had in the wilderness a [b]cottage of wayfaring men, that I might leave my people, and go from them: for they be all [c]adulterers, and an assembly of rebels. **3** And they bend their tongues like their bows for [d]lies: but they have no courage for the truth upon the earth, for they proceed from evil to worse, and they have not known me, saith the Lord. **4** Let everyone take heed of his neighbor, and trust you not in any [e]brother: for every brother will use deceit, and every

---

g. Jer. 7:15 I will send you into captivity as I have done Ephraim, that is, the ten tribes.
h. Jer. 7:16 To assure them that God had determined with himself to punish their wickedness, he showeth that the prayer of the godly can nothing avail them, whiles they remain in their obstinacy against God, and will not use the means that he useth to call them to repentance, Jer. 11:14 and 14:11.
i. Jer. 7:18 That is, they sacrifice to the Sun, Moon and Stars, which they called the queen of heaven, Jer. 44:17; 2 Kings 23:5.
j. Jer. 7:22 Showing that it was not his chief purpose and intent, that they should offer sacrifices: but that they should regard, wherefore they were ordained: to wit, to be joined to the word as seals and confirmations of remissions of sins in Christ: for without the word they were vain and unprofitable.
k. Jer. 7:25 Which was about fourteen hundred years.
l. Jer. 7:25 Read verse 13.
m. Jer. 7:27 Whereby he showeth that the pastors ought not to leave their flocks in their obstinacy, for the Lord will use the means of his servants to make the wicked more faulty and to prove his.
n. Jer. 7:29 In sign of mourning, as Job 1:20.
o. Jer. 7:29 Against whom he had just occasion to pour out his wrath, Mic. 1:6.
p. Jer. 7:31 Of Tophet, read 2 Kings 23:10.
q. Jer. 7:31 But commanded the contrary, as Lev. 18:21 and 20:3; Deut. 18:10.

JER. 7
1. Jer. 26:13 **2.** Ezek. 26:13

JER. 8
a. Jer. 8:1 The enemy for greediness of gain shall rifle your graves, and lay you before those idols, which in your life you worshipped, to see if they can help you.
b. Jer. 8:3 Because of the afflictions that they shall feel through God's judgments.
c. Jer. 8:4 Is there no hope that they will return?
d. Jer. 8:6 They are full of hypocrisy, and everyone followeth his own fantasy without any consideration.
e. Jer. 8:7 He accuseth them in that that they are more ignorant of God's judgments, than these birds are of their appointed seasons to discern the cold and heat, as Isa. 1:3.
f. Jer. 8:8 The Law doth not profit you, neither need it to have been written for ought that you have learned by it.
g. Jer. 8:9 They that seem wise, may be ashamed of their ignorance, for all wisdom consisteth in God's word.
h. Jer. 8:11 Read Jer. 6:14.
i. Jer. 8:14 He speaketh in the person of the people, who when the enemy cometh, will turn about to hide themselves, and acknowledge that it is God's hand.
j. Jer. 8:14 That is, hath brought us into extreme affliction, and thus they shall not attribute this plague to fortune, but to God's just judgment, Jer. 9:15 and 23:15.
k. Jer. 8:16 Read Jer. 4:15.
l. Jer. 8:17 God threateneth to send the Babylonians among them, who shall utterly destroy them in such sort, as by no means they shall escape.
m. Jer. 8:18 Read Jer. 4:19.
n. Jer. 8:19 Thus the Lord speaketh.
o. Jer. 8:20 The people wonder that they have so long time looked for succor in vain.
p. Jer. 8:21 The Prophet speaketh this.
q. Jer. 8:22 Meaning, that no man's help or means could save them: for in Gilead was precious balm, Jer. 46:11, or else deriding the vain confidence of the people, who looked for help at their Priests, who should have been the Physicians of their souls, and dwelt at Gilead, Hos. 6:8.

JER. 8
1. Isa. 56:11 / Jer. 5:31 / Jer. 6:13 **2.** Jer. 14:19

JER. 9
a. Jer. 9:1 The Prophet showeth the great compassion that he had toward this people, seeing that he could never sufficiently lament the destruction that he saw to hang over them, which is a special note to discern the true pastors from the hirelings, read Jer. 4:19.
b. Jer. 9:2 He showeth that this were more quietness and greater safety for him to dwell among the wild beasts than among this wicked people, save that God hath enjoined him this charge.
c. Jer. 9:2 Utterly turned from God.
d. Jer. 9:3 To belie and slander their neighbors.
e. Jer. 9:4 Meaning, that all were corrupt, and none could find an honest man.

friend will deal deceitfully, **5** And everyone will deceive his friend, and will not speak the truth: for they [f]have taught their tongue to speak lies, and take great pains to do wickedly. **6** Thine habitation is in the midst of deceivers: [g]because of their deceit they refuse to know me, saith the Lord. **7** Therefore thus saith the Lord of hosts, Behold, I will [h]melt them, and try them: for what should I else do for the daughter of my people? **8** Their tongue [1]is as an arrow shot out, and speaketh deceit: one speaketh peaceably to his neighbor with his mouth, but in his heart he layeth wait for him. **9** Shall I not visit them for these things, saith the Lord? or shall not my soul be avenged on such a nation as this? **10** Upon the [i]mountains will I take up a weeping and a lamentation, and upon the fair places of the wilderness a mourning, because they are burnt up, so that none can pass through them, neither can men hear the voice of the flock: both the fowl of the air, and the beast are fled away and gone. **11** And I will make Jerusalem an heap, and a den of dragons, and I will make the cities of Judah waste without an inhabitant. **12** Who is [j]wise to understand this? and to whom the mouth of the Lord hath spoken, even he shall declare it. Why doth the land perish, and is burnt up like a wilderness, that none passeth through? **13** And the Lord saith, because they have forsaken my Law, which I set before them, and have not obeyed my voice, neither walked thereafter, **14** But have walked after the stubbornness of their own heart, and after Baal, which [k]their fathers taught them. **15** Therefore thus saith the Lord of hosts, the God of Israel, Behold, I will feed this people with wormwood, and give them waters of gall [l]to drink: **16** I will scatter them also among the heathen, whom neither they nor their fathers have known, and I will send a sword after them, till I have consumed them. **17** Thus saith the Lord of hosts, Take heed, and call for [m]the mourning women, that they may come, and send for skillful women, that they may come, **18** And let them make haste, and let them take up a lamentation for us, that our eyes may cast out tears, and our eyelids gush out of water. **19** For a lamentable noise is heard out of Zion, How are we destroyed, and utterly confounded, for we have forsaken the land, and our dwellings [n]have cast us out. **20** Therefore hear the word of the Lord, O ye women, and let your ears regard the words of his mouth, and [o]teach your daughters to mourn, and everyone her neighbor to lament. **21** For death is come up into our [p]windows, and is entered into our palaces, to destroy the children without, and the young men in the streets. **22** Speak, Thus saith the Lord, The carcasses of men shall lie, even as the dung upon the field, and as the handful after the mower, and none shall gather them. **23** Thus saith the Lord, Let not the [q]wise man glory in his wisdom, nor the strong man glory in his strength, neither the rich man glory in his riches. **24** But let him that glorieth, glory in this, that he understandeth and knoweth me: for I am the Lord, which [r]show mercy, judgment, and righteousness in the earth: for in these things I delight, saith the Lord. **25** Behold, the days come saith the Lord, that I will visit all them which are [s]circumcised with the uncircumcised: **26** Egypt and Judah, and Edom, and the children of Ammon, and Moab, and all the utmost corners of them that dwell in the wilderness: for all these nations are uncircumcised, and all the house of Israel are uncircumcised in the heart.

10

The constellations of the stars are not to be feared. 5 The weakness of idols. 6 Of the power of God. 21 Their Pastors are become brute beasts.

1 Hear ye the word of the Lord that he speaketh unto you, O house of Israel. **2** Thus saith the Lord, Learn not the way of the heathen, and be not afraid for the [a]signs of heaven, though the heathen be afraid of such. **3** For the [b]customs of the people are vain: for one cutteth a tree out of the forest (which is the work of the hands of the carpenter) with the axe, **4** And another decketh it [c]with silver, and with gold: they fasten it with nails and hammers that it fall not. **5** The idols stand up as the palm tree, but speak not: they are borne because they cannot go: fear them not, for they cannot do evil, neither can they do good. **6** There is none like unto thee, O Lord: [d]thou art great, and thy Name is great in power. **7** Who would not fear thee, O king of nations? for to thee appertaineth the dominion: for among all the wise men of the Gentiles, and in all their kingdoms there is none like thee. **8** But altogether they dote, and are foolish: for the stock is a [e]doctrine of vanity. **9** Silver plates are brought from Tarshish, and gold [f]from Uphaz, for the work of the workman, and the hands of the founder: the blue silk, and the purple is their clothing: all these things are made by cunning men. **10** But the Lord is the God of truth: he is the living God, and an everlasting King: at his anger the earth shall tremble, and the nations cannot abide his wrath. **11** (Thus shall you say unto them, The gods [g]that have not made the heavens and the earth, shall perish from the earth, and from under these heavens.) **12** He hath made the earth by his power, and established the world by his wisdom, and hath stretched out the heaven by his discretion. **13** He giveth by his voice the multitude of waters in the heaven, and he causeth the clouds to ascend from the ends of the earth: he turneth lightnings to rain, and bringeth forth the wind out of his treasures. **14** Every man is a [h]beast by his own knowledge: every founder is confounded by the graven image: for his melting is but falsehood, and there is no breath therein. **15** They are vanity, and the work of errors: in the time of their visitation they shall perish. **16** The [i]portion of Jacob is not like them: for he is the maker of all things, and Israel is the rod of his inheritance: the Lord of hosts is his Name. **17** [j]Gather up thy wares out of the land, O thou that dwellest in the strong place. **18** For thus saith the Lord, Behold, at this time I will throw as with a sling the inhabitants of the land, and will trouble them, and they shall find it so. **19** Woe is me for my destruction, and my grievous plague: but I thought, Yet it [k]is my sorrow, and I will bear it. **20** [l]My Tabernacle is destroyed, and all my cords are broken: my children are gone from me, and are not: there is none to spread out my tent anymore, and to set up my curtains. **21** For the Pastors [m]are become beasts, and have not sought the Lord: therefore have they none understanding: and all the flocks of their pastures are scattered. **22** Behold, the noise of the bruit is come, and a great commotion out of the [n]North country, to make the cities of Judah desolate, and a den of dragons. **23** O Lord, I know that [o]the way of man is not in himself, neither is it in man to walk and to direct his steps. **24** O Lord, correct me, but with [p]judgment, not in thine anger, lest thou bring me to nothing. **25** Pour out [q]thy wrath upon the heathen that know thee not, and upon the families that call not on thy Name: for they have eaten up Jacob, and devoured him, and consumed him, and have made his habitation desolate.

---

f. Jer. 9:5 They have so practiced deceit, that they cannot forsake it.
g. Jer. 9:6 They had rather forsake God, than leave their wicked trade.
h. Jer. 9:7 With the fire of affliction.
i. Jer. 9:10 Signifying, that all the places about Jerusalem should be destroyed.
j. Jer. 9:12 Meaning, that they are all without sense and understanding, and that God hath taken his spirit from them.
k. Jer. 9:14 He showeth that the children cannot excuse themselves by their fathers: for both father and child if they be wicked shall perish.
l. Jer. 9:15 Read Jer. 8:14.
m. Jer. 9:17 Seeing you cannot lament your own sins, call for those foolish women, whom of a superstition you have to lament for the dead, that they by their feigned tears may provoke you to some sorrow.
n. Jer. 9:19 As though they were weary of us, because of our iniquities, Lev. 18:28 and 20:22.
o. Jer. 9:20 He derideth the superstition of the women which made an art of mourning, and taught to weep with feigned tears.
p. Jer. 9:21 Signifying, that there is no means to deliver the wicked from God's judgments: but when they think to be most sure, and most far off, then they are soonest taken.
q. Jer. 9:23 Forasmuch as none can save himself by his own labor, or any worldly means, he showeth that it is vain to put our trust therein, but that we trust in the Lord, and rejoice in him, who only can deliver us, 1 Cor. 1:31; 2 Cor. 10:17.
r. Jer. 9:24 These three points are necessary to know aright: his mercy, wherein consisteth our salvation, his judgment, which he executeth continually against the wicked, and his justice, whereby he defendeth and maintaineth the faithful.
s. Jer. 9:25 Meaning, both Jews and Gentiles, as in this next verse he showeth the cause, read Jer. 4:4.

JER. 9
1. Ps. 28:3 / Ps. 120:4

JER. 10
a. Jer. 10:2 God forbiddeth his people to give credit or fear the constellations and conjunctions of stars and planets which have no power of themselves, but are governed by him, and their secret motions and influences are not known to man and therefore there can be no certain judgment thereof, Deut. 18:9.
b. Jer. 10:3 Meaning, not only in the observation of the stars, but their laws and ceremonies whereby they confirm their idolatry, which is forbidden, Deut. 12:30.
c. Jer. 10:4 The Prophets use thus plainly and simply to set forth the vile absurdity of the idolaters, that men might learn to be ashamed of that whereunto their corrupt nature is most subject, read Isa. 44:12.
d. Jer. 10:6 He teacheth the people to lift up their eyes to God, who hath all power and therefore ought only to be feared: and herein he showeth them not only the evil that they ought to eschew: but the good which they ought to follow, Rev. 15:4.
e. Jer. 10:8 Because the people thought that to have images, was a means to serve God, and to bring them to the knowledge of him, he showeth that nothing more displeaseth God, nor bringeth man into greater errors and ignorance of God: and therefore he calleth them the doctrine of vanity, the work of errors, verse 15, and Hab. 2:18 calleth them the teachers of lies: contrary to that wicked opinion, that they are the books of the lay people.
f. Jer. 10:9 Whereas they found the best gold: showing, that they thought nothing too dear for their idols, some read Ophir, as 1 Kings 9:28.
g. Jer. 10:11 This declareth that all that hath been in this chapter spoken of idols, was to arm the Jews when they should be in Chaldea among the idolaters, and now with one sentence he instructeth them both how to protect their own religion against the idolaters, and how to answer them to their shame which should exhort them to idolatry, and therefore he writeth this sentence in the Chaldean's tongue for a memorial, whereas all the rest of his writing is Hebrew.
h. Jer. 10:14 The more that man thinketh to do anything well by his own wisdom, and not as God instructeth him, the more doth he prove himself to be a vile beast.
i. Jer. 10:16 By these words Portion and Rod, he signifieth their inheritance, meaning, that God should be all sufficient for them: and that their felicity consisted in him alone, and therefore they ought to renounce all other helps and succors as of idols, etc. Deut. 32:9; Ps. 16:5.
j. Jer. 10:17 The Prophet willeth the Jews to prepare themselves to this captivity, showing that it was now at hand that they should feel the things whereof he had told them.
k. Jer. 10:19 It is my just plague, and therefore I will take it patiently: whereby he teacheth the people how to behave themselves toward God.
l. Jer. 10:20 He showeth how Jerusalem shall lament.
m. Jer. 10:21 The governors and ministers.
n. Jer. 10:22 Read Jer. 4:15.
o. Jer. 10:23 He speaketh this because that Nebuchadnezzar purposed to have made war against the Moabites and Ammonites, but hearing of Zedekiah's rebellion, he turned his power to go against Jerusalem, Ezek. 21:21, therefore the Prophet saith, that this was the Lord's direction.
p. Jer. 10:24 Considering that God had revealed unto him the certitude of their captivity, Jer. 7:16, he only prayeth, that he would punish them with mercy, which Isaiah calleth in measure, Isa. 27:8, measuring his rods by their infirmity, 1 Cor. 10:13, for here by judgment is meant not only the punishment, but also the merciful moderation of the same, as Jer. 30:11.
q. Jer. 10:25 Forasmuch as God cannot only be known and glorified by his mercy, that he useth toward his Church, but also by his justice in punishing his enemies, he prayeth that this glory may fully appear both in the one and the other, Ps. 79:6.

11 *3 A curse of them that obey not the word of God's covenant. 10 The people of Judah following the steps of their fathers, worship strange gods. 15 The Lord forbiddeth Jeremiah to pray for them.*

1 The word that came to Jeremiah from the Lord, saying, **2** Hear ye the words of this covenant, and speak unto the men of Judah, and to the inhabitants of Jerusalem, **3** And say thou unto them, Thus saith the Lord God of Israel, [a]Cursed be the man that obeyeth not the words of this covenant, **4** Which I commanded unto your fathers, when I brought them out of the land of Egypt, from the iron furnace, saying, Obey my voice, and do according to all these things which I command you: so shall ye be my people, and I will be your God, **5** That I may confirm the oath, that I have sworn unto your fathers, to give them a land, which floweth with milk and honey, as appeareth this day. Then answered [b]I, and said, So be it, O Lord. **6** Then the Lord said unto me, Cry all these words in the cities of Judah, and in the streets of Jerusalem, saying, Hear ye the words of this covenant, and do them. **7** For I have protested unto your fathers, when I brought them up out of the land of Egypt unto this day, [c]rising early and protesting, saying, Obey my voice. **8** Nevertheless they would not obey, nor incline their ear: but everyone walked in the stubbornness of his [d]wicked heart: therefore I will bring upon them all the [e]words of this covenant which I commanded them to do, but they did it not. **9** And the Lord said unto me, A [f]conspiracy is found among the men of Judah, and among the inhabitants of Jerusalem. **10** They are turned back to the iniquities of their forefathers, which refused to hear my words: and they went after other gods to serve them: thus the house of Israel and the house of Judah have broken my covenant, which I made with their fathers. **11** Therefore thus saith the Lord, Behold, I will bring a plague upon them, which they shall not be able to escape, and though they cry unto me, [g]I will not hear them. **12** Then shall the cities of Judah, and the inhabitants of Jerusalem go, and cry unto the gods unto whom they offer incense, but they shall not be able to help them in time of their trouble. **13** [h]For according to the number of thy cities were thy gods, O Judah, and according to the number of the streets of Jerusalem have ye set up altars of confusion, even altars to burn incense unto Baal. **14** Therefore thou shalt not [i]pray for this people, neither lift up a cry or prayer for them: for when they cry unto me in their trouble, I will not hear them. **15** What should my [j]beloved tarry in mine house, seeing they have committed abomination with many, and the holy flesh [k]goeth away from thee: yet when thou doest evil, thou rejoicest. **16** The Lord called thy name, A green olive tree, fair, and of goodly fruit: but with [l]noise and great tumult he hath set fire upon it, and the branches of it are broken. **17** For the Lord of hosts that planted thee, hath pronounced a plague against thee, for the wickedness of the house of Israel, and of the house of Judah, which they have done against themselves to provoke me to anger in offering incense unto Baal, **18** And the Lord hath taught me, and I know it, even then thou showedst me [m]their practices. **19** But I was like a lamb, or a bullock, that is brought to the slaughter, and I knew not that they had devised thus against me, saying, Let us [n]destroy the tree with the fruit thereof, and cut him out of the land of the living, that his name may be no more in memory, **20** But O Lord of hosts, that judgest righteously, and triest the reins and the heart, let me see thy [o]vengeance on them: for unto thee have I opened my cause. **21** The Lord therefore speaketh thus of the men of [p]Anathoth, (that seek thy life, and say, [q]Prophesy not in the name of the Lord, that thou die not by our hands.) **22** Thus therefore saith the Lord of hosts, Behold, I will visit them: the young men shall die by the sword: their sons and their daughters shall die by famine, **23** And none of them shall remain: for I will bring a plague upon the men of Anathoth, even the year of their visitation.

12 *1 The Prophet marvelleth at the prosperity of the wicked, although he confess God to be righteous. 7 The Jews are forsaken of the Lord. 10 He speaketh against pastors and preachers, that seduce the people. 14 The Lord threateneth destruction unto the nations that troubled Judah.*

1 O Lord, if I dispute with thee, thou art [a]righteous: yet let me talk with thee of thy judgments: wherefore doth the way of the wicked [b]prosper? why are all they in wealth that rebelliously transgress? **2** Thou hast planted them, and they have taken root: they grow, and bring forth fruit, thou art near in their mouth, and far from their [c]reins. **3** But thou, Lord, knowest me: thou hast seen me, and tried mine heart toward thee: pull them out like sheep for the slaughter, and [d]prepare them for the day of slaughter. **4** How long shall the land mourn, and the herbs of every field wither, for the wickedness of them that dwell therein? the beasts are consumed, and the birds, because they said, [e]He will not see our last end. **5** If thou hast run with the [f]footmen, and they have wearied thee, then how canst thou match thyself with horses? and if thou thoughtest thyself safe in a peaceable land, what wilt thou do in the swelling of Jordan? **6** For even thy brethren and the house of thy father, even they have dealt unfaithfully with thee, and they have cried out altogether upon thee: but believe them not, though they speak fair to thee. **7** I have forsaken [g]mine house: I have left mine heritage: I have given the dearly beloved of my soul into the hands of her enemies. **8** Mine heritage is unto me, as a [h]lion in the forest: it crieth out against me, therefore have I hated it. **9** Shall mine heritage be unto me, as a bird [i]of divers colors? are not the birds about her, saying, Come, assemble all the beasts of the field, come to eat her? **10** Many pastors have destroyed my [j]vineyard, and trodden my portion under foot: of my pleasant portion they have made a desolate wilderness. **11** They have laid it waste, and it, being waste mourneth unto me, and the whole land lieth waste, because no man setteth his mind on [k]it. **12** The destroyers are come upon all the high places in the wilderness: for the sword of the Lord shall devour from the one end of the land, even to the other end of the land: no flesh shall have peace. **13** [l]They have sown wheat, and reaped thorns: they were [m]sick, and had no profit: and they were ashamed of [n]your fruits, because of the fierce wrath of the Lord. **14** Thus saith the Lord against all mine evil [o]neighbors, that touch the inheritance, which I have caused my people Israel to inherit, Behold, I will pluck them out of their land, and pluck out the house of Judah from among them. **15** And after that I have plucked them out, I [p]will return, and have compassion on them, and will bring again every man to his heritage, and every man to his land. **16** And if they will learn the [q]ways of my people, to swear by my Name, (The [r]Lord liveth, as they taught my people to swear by Baal) then shall they be built [s]in the midst of my people. **17** But if they will not obey, then will I utterly pluck up, and destroy that nation, saith the Lord.

13 *The destruction of the Jews is prefigured. 11 Why Israel was received to be the people of God, and why they were forsaken. 15 He exhorteth them to repentance.*

1 Thus saith the Lord unto me, Go, and buy thee a linen girdle, and put it upon thy loins, and put it not in water. **2** So I bought the girdle according to

---

JER. 11

a. Jer. 11:3 He calleth the Jews to the consideration of God's mercy, who freely chose them, made a covenant of eternal felicity with them, and how he ever performed it on his behalf, and how they ever showed themselves rebellious and ingrate toward him, and brake it on their part, and so are subject to the curse of the Law, Deut. 27:26.

b. Jer. 11:5 Thus he speaketh in the person of the people, which agreed to the covenant.

c. Jer. 11:7 Read Jer. 7:13.

d. Jer. 11:8 According to his own fantasy, and not as my word appointed him.

e. Jer. 11:8 Meaning, the menaces and curses contained in the Law, Lev. 26:14; Deut. 28:16.

f. Jer. 11:9 That is, a general consent to rebel against me.

g. Jer. 11:11 Because they will not pray with true faith and repentance, but for the smart and grief which they feel, Prov. 1:28.

h. Jer. 11:13 Read Jer. 2:28.

i. Jer. 11:14 Read Jer. 7:16 and 14:11.

j. Jer. 11:15 My people of Israel, whom I have hitherto so greatly loved.

k. Jer. 11:15 Meaning, that they offer not in the Temple to God, but on the altars of Baal and the idols, and so rejoiced in their wickedness.

l. Jer. 11:16 Of the Babylonians and Chaldeans.

m. Jer. 11:18 Which went about privily to conspire my death.

n. Jer. 11:19 Let us destroy the Prophet and his doctrine. Some read, Let us corrupt his meat with wood, meaning, poison.

o. Jer. 11:20 Thus he spake, not for hatred, but being moved with the Spirit of God, he desireth the advancement of God's glory, and the verifying of his word, which is by the destruction of his enemies.

p. Jer. 11:21 To wit, both the Priests and the rest of the people: for this town was the Priests, and they dwelt in it, read Jer. 1:1.

q. Jer. 11:21 Not that they could not abide to hear God named: (for herein they would show themselves most holy) but because they could not abide to be sharply reproved, and therefore desired to be flattered, Isa. 30:10, and to be maintained in their pleasures, Mic. 2:11, and not to hear vice condemned, Amos 7:12.

JER. 12

a. Jer. 12:1 The Prophet confesseth God to be just in all his doings, although man be not able to give a reason of all his acts.

b. Jer. 12:1 This question hath been always a great tentation to the godly, to see the wicked enemies of God in prosperity, and his dear children in adversity, as Job 21:7; Ps. 37:1 and 73:3; Hab. 1:3.

c. Jer. 12:2 They profess God in mouth, but deny him in heart, which is here meant by the reins, Isa. 29:13; Matt. 15:8.

d. Jer. 12:3 The Hebrew word is, Sanctify them, meaning, that God would be sanctified in the destruction of the wicked, to whom God for a while giveth prosperity, that afterward they should the more feel his heavy judgment when they lack their riches which were a sign of his mercy.

e. Jer. 12:4 Abusing God's lenity and his promises, they flattered themselves as though God would ever be merciful, and not utterly destroy them: therefore they hardened themselves in sin, till at length the beasts and insensible creatures felt the punishment of their stubborn rebellion against God.

f. Jer. 12:5 Some think that God reproveth Jer., in that that he would reason with him, saying, that if he were not able to march with men, that he were far unable to dispute with God. Others, by the footmen, mean them of Anathoth: and by the horsemen, them of Jerusalem, which should trouble the Prophet worse than his own countrymen did.

g. Jer. 12:7 God willeth the Prophet to denounce his judgments against Jerusalem, notwithstanding that they shall both by threatenings and flatteries, labor to put him to silence.

h. Jer. 12:8 Ever ramping and raging against me and my Prophets.

i. Jer. 12:9 Instead of bearing my livery, and wearing only my colors, they have change and diversity of colors of their idols and superstitions, therefore their enemies as thick as the fowls of the air shall come about them to destroy them.

j. Jer. 12:10 He prophecieth of the destruction of Jerusalem, by the captains of Nebuchadnezzar, whom he calleth pastors.

k. Jer. 12:11 Because no man regardeth my word, or the plagues that I have sent upon the land.

l. Jer. 12:13 To wit, the Prophets.

m. Jer. 12:13 They lamented the sins of the people.

n. Jer. 12:13 For instead of amendment, you grew worse and worse, as God's plagues testified.

o. Jer. 12:14 Meaning, the wicked enemies of his Church, which blasphemed his Name, and whom he would punish after that he hath delivered his people.

p. Jer. 12:15 After that I have punished the Gentiles, I will have mercy upon them.

q. Jer. 12:16 The true doctrine and manner to serve God.

r. Jer. 12:16 Read Jer. 4:2.

s. Jer. 12:16 They shall be of the number of the faithful, and have a place in my Church.

the commandment of the Lord, and put it upon my loins. 3 And the word of the Lord came unto me the second time, saying, 4 Take the girdle that thou hast bought, which is upon thy loins, and arise, go toward [a]Perath, and hide it there in the cleft of the rock. 5 So I went, and hid it by Perath, as the Lord had commanded me. 6 And after many days the Lord said unto me, Arise, go toward Perath, and take the girdle from thence, which I commanded thee to hide there. 7 Then went I to Perath, and dug, and took the girdle from the place where I had hid it, and behold, the girdle was corrupt, and was profitable for nothing. 8 Then the word of the Lord came unto me, saying, 9 Thus saith the Lord, After this manner will I destroy the pride of Judah, and the great pride of Jerusalem. 10 This wicked people have refused to hear my word, and walk after the stubbornness of their own heart, and walk after other gods to serve them, and to worship them: therefore they shall be as this girdle, which is profitable to nothing. 11 For as the girdle cleaveth to the loins of a man, so have I tied to me the whole house of Israel, and the whole house of Judah, saith the Lord, that they might be my people: that they might have a name, and praise, and glory, but they would not hear. 12 Therefore thou shalt say unto them this word, Thus saith the Lord God of Israel, Every [b]bottle shall be filled with wine, and they shall say unto thee, do we not know that every bottle shall be filled with wine? 13 Then shalt thou say unto them, Thus saith the Lord, Behold, I will fill all the inhabitants of this land, even the kings that sit upon the throne of David, and the Priests and the Prophets, and all the inhabitants of Jerusalem with drunkenness. 14 And I will [c]dash them one against another, even the fathers and the sons together, saith the Lord: I will not spare, I will not pity, nor have compassion, but destroy them. 15 Hear and give ear, be not proud: for the Lord hath spoken it. 16 Give glory to the Lord your God before he bring [d]darkness, and or ever your feet stumble in the dark mountains, and while you look for [e]light, he turn it into the shadow of death and make it as darkness. 17 But if ye will not hear this, my soul shall [f]weep in secret for your pride, and mine eye shall weep and drop down tears, because the Lord's flock is carried away captive. 18 Say unto the [g]King and to the Queen: Humble yourselves, sit down, for the crown of your glory shall come down from your heads. 19 The cities of [h]the South shall be shut up, and no man shall open them: all Judah shall be carried away captive: it shall be wholly carried away captive: 20 Lift up your eyes, and behold them that come from the North: where is the [i]flock that was given thee, even thy beautiful flock? 21 What wilt thou say when he shall visit thee? (for thou hast [j]taught them to be captains and as chief over thee) shall not sorrow take thee as a woman in travail? 22 And if thou say in thine heart, Wherefore come these things upon me? For the multitude of thine iniquities are thy skirts [k]discovered and thy heels made bare. 23 Can the black Moor change his skin? or the leopard his spots, then may ye also do good, that are accustomed to do evil? 24 Therefore will I scatter them, as the stubble that is taken away with the South wind. 25 This is thy portion, and the part of thy measures from me, saith the Lord, because thou hast forgotten me, and trusted in lies. 26 Therefore I have also discovered thy skirts upon thy face, [l]that thy shame may appear. 27 I have seen thine adulteries, and thy [m]neighings, the filthiness of thy whoredom on the hills in [n]the fields, and thine abominations. Woe] unto thee, O Jerusalem: wilt thou not be made clean? when shall it once be?

14

1 Of the death that should come. 7 The prayer of the people asking mercy of the Lord. 10 The unfaithful people are not heard. 12 Of prayer, fasting, and of false prophets that seduce the people.

1 The word of the Lord that came unto Jeremiah, concerning the [a,b]dearth. 2 Judah hath mourned, and the gates thereof are desolate, they have been [c]brought to heaviness unto the ground, and the cry of Jerusalem goeth up. 3 And their nobles have sent their inferiors to the water, who came to the wells, and found no water: they returned with their vessels empty: they were ashamed and confounded: and [d]covered their heads. 4 For the ground was destroyed, because there was no rain in the earth: the plowmen were ashamed, and covered their heads. 5 Yea, the hind also calved in the field, and forsook [e]it, because there was no grass. 6 And the wild asses did stand in the high places, and drew in their wind like [f]dragons: their eyes did fail, because there was no grass. 7 [g]O Lord, though our iniquities testify against us, deal with us according to thy Name: for our rebellions are many, we sinned against thee. 8 O thou hope of Israel, the savior thereof in the time of trouble, why art thou as a [h]stranger in the land, as one that passeth by, to tarry for a night? 9 Why art thou as a man astonied, and as [i]a strong man that cannot help? yet thou, O Lord, art in the midst of us, and thy name is called upon us: forsake us not. 10 Thus saith the Lord unto this people, Thus have they delighted to wander: they have not refrained their feet, therefore the Lord hath no delight in them: but he will now remember their iniquity, and visit their sins. 11 Then said the Lord unto me, [j]Thou shalt not pray to do this people good. 12 When they fast, I will not hear their cry, and when they offer burnt offering, and an oblation, I will not accept them: but I will consume them by the sword, and by the famine, and by the pestilence. 13 Then answered I, Ah Lord God, behold, the [k]prophets say unto them, Ye shall not see the sword, neither shall famine come upon you, but I will give you assured peace in this place. 14 Then the Lord said unto me, The prophets prophesy lies in my name: [1]I have not sent them, neither did I command them, neither spake I unto them, but they prophesy unto you a false vision, and divination, and vanity, and deceitfulness of their own heart. 15 Therefore thus saith the Lord, Concerning the prophets that prophesy in my Name, whom I have not sent, yet they say, Sword and famine shall not be in this land, by sword and famine shall those prophets be consumed. 16 And the people to whom these prophets do prophesy shall be cast out in the streets of Jerusalem, because of the famine, and the sword, and there shall be none to bury them: both they and their wives, and their sons, and their daughters: for I will pour their wickedness upon them. 17 Therefore thou shalt say this word unto them, Let mine eyes drop down [l]tears night and day without ceasing: for the virgin daughter of my people is destroyed with a great destruction, and with a sore grievous plague. 18 For if I go into the field, behold the slain with the sword: and if I enter into the city, behold them that are sick for hunger also: moreover, the Prophet also and the Priest go a wandering [m]into a land that they know not. 19 Hast thou utterly rejected [n]Judah, or hath thy soul abhorred Zion? why hast thou smitten us, that we cannot be healed? We looked for peace, and there is no good, and for the time of health, and behold trouble. 20 We [o]acknowledge, O Lord, our wickedness, and the iniquity of our fathers: for we have sinned against thee. 21 Do not abhor us: for thy Name's sake cast not down the throne of thy glory: remember and break not thy covenant with us. 22 Are there any among the [p]vanities of the Gentiles, that can give rain? or can the heavens give showers? Is it not thou, O Lord our God? therefore we will wait upon thee: for thou hast made all these things.

15

1 The Lord would hear no prayer for the Jews, 3 but threateneth to destroy them with four plagues.

1 Then said the Lord unto me, [a]Though Moses and Samuel stood before me, yet mine affection could not be toward this people: cast them out of my sight, and let them depart. 2 And if they say unto thee, Whither shall we depart? then tell them, Thus saith the Lord, [1]Such as are appointed to death, unto death: and such as are for the sword, to the sword: and such as are for the famine, to the famine: and such as are for the captivity, to the captivity. 3 And I will appoint over them four kinds, saith the Lord, the sword to slay, and the [b]dogs to tear in pieces, and

---

JER. 13

a. Jer. 13:4 Because this river Perath or Euphrates was far from Jerusalem, it is evident that this was a vision, whereby was signified that the Jews should pass over Euphrates to be captives in Babylon, and there for length of time should seem to be rotten, although they were joined to the Lord before as a girdle about a man.
b. Jer. 13:12 Every one of you shall be filled with spiritual drunkenness, and be without all knowledge to seek how to help yourselves.
c. Jer. 13:14 It shall be as easy for me to destroy the greatest and the strongest, as it is for a man to break earthen bottles.
d. Jer. 13:16 That is, affliction and misery by the Babylonians, Isa. 8:22.
e. Jer. 13:16 Meaning, for help and support of the Egyptians.
f. Jer. 13:17 You shall surely be led away captive, and I, according to mine affection towards you, shall weep and lament for your stubbornness.
g. Jer. 13:18 For Jehoiachin and his mother rendered themselves by Jer.'s counsel to the king of Babylon, 2 Kings 24:12.
h. Jer. 13:19 That is, of Judah, which lieth Southward from Babylon.
i. Jer. 13:20 He asketh the king, where his people is become.
j. Jer. 13:21 By seeking to strangers for help, thou hast made them skillful to fight against thee.
k. Jer. 13:22 The cloak of hypocrisy shall be pulled off, and thy shame seen.
l. Jer. 13:26 As thine iniquities have been manifest to all the world, so shall thy shame and punishment.
m. Jer. 13:27 He compareth idolaters to horses inflamed after mares.
n. Jer. 13:27 There is no place so high nor low, whereas the marks and signs of thine idolatry appear not.

JER. 14

a. Jer. 14:1 Which came for lack of rain, as verse 4.
b. Jer. 14:1 Or, restraint.
c. Jer. 14:2 The word signifieth to be made black, and so is here taken for extreme sorrow.
d. Jer. 14:3 To wit, with ashes in token of sorrow.
e. Jer. 14:5 Meaning, that the brute beasts for drought were compelled to forsake their young, contrary to nature, and to go seek water which they could not find.
f. Jer. 14:6 Which are so hot of nature, that they cannot be cooled with drinking of water, but still gape for the air to resisteth them.
g. Jer. 14:7 He showeth the only way to remedy to God's plagues, which is by unfeigned confession of our sins, and returning to him by repentance.
h. Jer. 14:8 That taketh no care for us.
i. Jer. 14:9 As one that hath strength to help, and yet is afraid to put to his hand.
j. Jer. 14:11 Read Jer. 7:16 and 11:14.
k. Jer. 14:13 He pitieth the people, and accuseth the false prophets, which deceived them: but the Lord answered, that both the prophets, which deceived, and the people, which suffered themselves to be seduced, shall perish, Jer. 23:15 and 27:8, 9 and 29:8.
l. Jer. 14:17 The false prophets promised peace and assurance, but Jer. calleth to tears, and repentance for their affliction, which is at hand, as Jer. 9:1; Lam. 1:16 and 2:18.
m. Jer. 14:18 Both high and low shall be led captives into Babylon.
n. Jer. 14:19 Though the Prophet knew that God had cast off the multitude, which were hypocrites, and bastard children, yet he was assured that for his promise sake he would have still a Church, for the which he prayeth.
o. Jer. 14:20 He teacheth the Church a form of prayer to humble themselves to God by true repentance, which is the only means to avoid this famine, which was the beginning of God's plagues.
p. Jer. 14:22 Meaning, their idols, read Jer. 10:15.

JER. 14

1. Jer. 23:21 / Jer. 27:10,15 / Jer. 29:9

JER. 15

a. Jer. 15:1 Meaning, that if there were any man living moved with so great zeal toward the people as were these two, yet that he would not grant this request, forasmuch as he had determined the contrary, Ezek. 14:14.
b. Jer. 15:3 The dogs, birds, and beasts should devour them that were slain.
c. Jer. 15:4 The word signifieth to run to and fro for fear, and unquietness of conscience, as did Cain.

the fowls of the heaven, and the beasts of the earth to devour, and to destroy. 4 I
will [c]scatter them also in all kingdoms of the earth, [d]because of Manasseh the son
of Hezekiah King of Judah for that which he did in Jerusalem. 5 Who shall then
have pity upon thee, O Jerusalem? or who shall be sorry for thee? or who shall go to
pray for thy peace? 6 Thou hast forsaken me, saith the Lord, and gone backward:
therefore will I stretch out mine hand against thee, and destroy thee: for I [e]am we-
ary with repenting. 7 And I will scatter them with the fan [f]in the gates of the
earth: I have wasted, and destroyed my people, yet they would not return from
their ways. 8 Their widows [g]are increased by me above the sand of the sea: I have
brought upon them, and against the [h]assembly of the young men, a destroyer at
noon day: I have caused him to fall upon them, and the city, suddenly and [i]spee-
dily. 9 She that hath borne [j]seven, hath been made weak: her heart hath failed:
the sun hath failed [k]her, while it was day, she hath been confounded, and ashamed,
and the residue of them will I deliver unto the sword before their enemies, saith
the Lord. 10 [l]Woe is me, my mother, that thou hast borne me, a contentious
man, and a man that striveth with the whole earth: I have neither [m]lent on usury,
nor men have lent unto me on usury: yet everyone doth curse me. 11 The Lord
said, [n]Surely thy remnant shall have wealth: surely I will cause thine enemy to en-
treat thee in the time of trouble, and in the time of affliction. 12 Shall the [o]iron
break the iron, and the brass that cometh from the North? 13 Thy substance
and thy treasures will I give to be spoiled without [p]gain, and that for all thy sins
even in all thy borders. 14 And I will make thee to go with thine enemies into
a land that thou knowest not, for a fire is kindled in mine anger, which shall burn
you. 15 O Lord, thou knowest, remember me, and visit me, and revenge me of
my [q]persecutors: take me not away in the continuance of thine anger: know that
for thy sake I have suffered rebuke. 16 Thy words were found by me, and I did
[r]eat them, and thy word was unto me the joy and rejoicing of mine heart: for thy
Name is called upon me, O Lord God of hosts. 17 I sat not in the assembly of
the mockers, neither did I rejoice, but sat alone [s]because of thy plague: for thou
hast filled me with indignation. 18 Why is mine heaviness continual? and my
plague desperate and cannot be healed, why art thou unto me [t]as a liar, and as wa-
ters that fail? 19 Therefore thus saith the Lord, If thou [u]return, then will I bring
thee again, and thou shalt stand before me: and if thou take away the [v]precious
from the vile, thou shalt be [w]according to my word: let them return [x]unto thee, but
return not thou unto them. 20 And I will make thee unto this people a strong
brazen wall, and they shall fight against thee, but they shall not [y]prevail against
thee: for I am with thee to save thee, and to deliver thee, saith the Lord. 21 And
I will deliver thee out of the hand of the wicked, and I will redeem thee out of the
hand of the tyrants.

16

2 The Lord forbidding Jeremiah to marry, showeth him what should be the afflictions upon Judah. 13 The captivity of Babylon. 15 Their deliverance. 19 The calling of the Gentiles.

1 The word of the Lord came also unto me, saying, 2 Thou shalt not take
[a]thee a wife, nor have sons nor daughters in this place. 3 For thus saith the Lord
concerning the sons, and concerning the daughters, that are born in this place, and
concerning their mothers that bear them, and concerning their fathers that beget
them in this land, 4 They shall die of deaths and diseases: they shall not be la-
mented, neither shall they be buried, but they shall be as dung upon the earth, and
they shall be consumed by the sword, and by famine, and their carcasses shall be
meat for the fowls of the heaven, and for the beasts of the earth. 5 For thus saith
the Lord, [b]Enter not into the house of mourning, neither go to lament, nor be mo-
ved for them: for I have taken my peace from this people, saith the Lord, even mer-
cy and compassion. 6 Both the great, and the small shall die in this land: they
shall not be buried, neither shall men lament for them, [c]nor cut themselves, nor
make themselves bald for them. 7 They shall not stretch out the hands for them
in the mourning to comfort them for the dead, neither shall they give them the
[d]cup of consolation to drink for their father or for their mother. 8 Thou shalt not
also go into the house of feasting, to sit with them to eat and to drink. 9 For thus
saith the Lord of hosts, the God of Israel, Behold, I will cause to cease out of this
place in your eyes, even in your days, the voice of mirth, and the voice of gladness,
the voice of the bridegroom, and the voice of the bride. 10 And when thou shalt
show this people all these words, and they shall say unto thee, [1]Wherefore hath
the Lord pronounced all this great plague against us? or what is [e]our iniquity? and
what is our sin that we have committed against the Lord our God? 11 Then shalt
thou say unto them, Because your fathers have forsaken me, saith the Lord, and
have walked after other gods, and have served them, and worshipped them, and
have forsaken me, and have not kept my Law, 12 ([2]And ye have done worse than
your fathers: for behold, you walk everyone after the stubbornness of his wicked
heart, and will not hear me.) 13 Therefore will I drive you out of this land into a
land that ye know not, neither you nor your fathers, and there ye shall serve other
gods day and night: for I will show you no grace. 14 [3]Behold therefore saith the
Lord, the days come that it shall no more be said, The Lord liveth, which brou-
ght up the children of Israel out of the land of Egypt, 15 But, The Lord liveth,
that brought up the children of Israel [f]from the land of the North, and from all
the lands where he had scattered them, and I will bring them again into their land
that I gave unto their fathers. 16 Behold, saith the Lord, I will send out many
[g]fishers, and they shall fish them, and after will I send out many hunters, and they
shall hunt them from every mountain, and from every hill, and out of the caves of
the rocks. 17 For mine eyes are upon all their ways: they are not hid from my
face, neither is their iniquity hid from mine eyes. 18 And first I will recompense
their iniquity and their sin double, because they have defiled my land, and have
filled mine inheritance with their filthy [h]carrions and their abominations. 19 O
Lord, thou art my [i]fortress, and my strength and my refuge in the day of affliction:
the Gentiles shall come unto thee from the ends of the world, and shall say, Surely
our fathers have inherited [j]lies, and vanity, wherein there was no profit. 20 Shall
a man make gods unto himself, and they are no gods? 21 Behold, therefore I will
this once [k]teach them: I will show them mine hand and my power, and they shall
know that my Name is the Lord.

17

1 The frowardness of the Jews. 5 Cursed be those that put their confidence in man. 9 Man's heart is wicked. 10 God is the searcher of the heart. 13 The living waters are forsaken. 21 The right keeping of the Sabbath commanded.

1 The sin of Judah is [a]written with a pen of iron, and with the point of a
diamond, and graven upon the [b]table of their heart, and upon the horns of your
[c]altars. 2 [d]They remember their altars as their children, with their groves by the
green trees upon the high hills. 3 [e]O my mountain in the field, I will give thy

---

d. Jer. 15:4 Not that the people was punished for the king's sin only, but for their own sins also, because they consented to his wickedness, 2 Kings 21:9.
e. Jer. 15:6 That is, I will not call back my plagues or spare thee any more.
f. Jer. 15:7 Meaning, the cities.
g. Jer. 15:8 Because I had slain their husbands.
h. Jer. 15:8 Or, mother.
i. Jer. 15:8 Or, fearfully.
j. Jer. 15:9 She that had many, lost all her children.
k. Jer. 15:9 She was destroyed in the midst of her prosperity.
l. Jer. 15:10 By these are the Prophet's words, complaining of the obstinacy of the people and that he was reserved to so wicked a time: wherein also he showeth what is the condition of God's ministers, to wit, to have all the world against them, though they give none occasion.
m. Jer. 15:10 Which is an occasion of contention and hatred.
n. Jer. 15:11 In this perplexity the Lord comforted me, and said that my last days should be quiet: and by the enemy he meaneth here, Nebuzaradan the captain of Nebuchadnezzar, who gave Jer. the choice either to remain in his country, or to go whither he would: or by the enemy he meaneth the Jews, which should afterward know Jer.'s fidelity, and therefore favor him.
o. Jer. 15:12 As for the people, though they seemed strong as iron, yet should they not be able to resist the hard iron of Babylon, but should be led captives.
p. Jer. 15:13 Or, ransom.
q. Jer. 15:15 He speaketh not this for desire of revengeance, but wishing that God would deliver his Church of them whom he knew to be hardened and incorrigible.
r. Jer. 15:16 I received them with a great joy, as he that is famished, eateth meat.
s. Jer. 15:17 I had nothing a do with the wicked contemners of thy word, but lamented bitterly for thy plagues: showing what the faithful should do when they see tokens of God's anger.
t. Jer. 15:18 And hast not assisted me according to the promise? wherein appeareth that in the Saints of God is imperfection of faith, which through impatience is ofttimes assailed, as Jer. 20:7.
u. Jer. 15:19 If thou forget these carnal considerations, and faithfully execute thy charge.
v. Jer. 15:19 That is, seek to win the good from the bad.
w. Jer. 15:19 To wit, as my mouth hath pronounced, Jer. 1:18, and as here followeth, verse 20.
x. Jer. 15:19 Conform not thyself to their wickedness, but let them follow thy godly example.
y. Jer. 15:20 I will learn thee with an invincible strength and constancy, so that all the powers of the world shall not overcome thee.

JER. 15
1. Zech. 11:9

JER. 16
a. Jer. 16:2 Meaning, that the affliction should be so horrible in Jerusalem, that wife and children should but increase his sorrow.
b. Jer. 16:5 Signifying, that the affliction should be so great, that one should not have leisure to comfort another.
c. Jer. 16:6 That is, should not rent their clothes in sign of mourning.
d. Jer. 16:7 For in these great extremities all consolation and comfort shall be in vain.
e. Jer. 16:10 Because the wicked are always rebellious, and dissemble their own sins, and murmur against God's judgments, as though he had no just cause to punish them, he showeth him what to answer.
f. Jer. 16:15 Signifying, the benefit of their deliverance out of Babylon should be so great, that it should abolish the remembrance of their deliverance from Egypt: but he hath here chiefly respect to the spiritual deliverance under Christ.
g. Jer. 16:16 By the fishers and hunters are meant the Babylonians and Chaldeans, who should destroy them in such sort, that if they escaped the one, the other should take them.
h. Jer. 16:18 That is, their sons and daughters, which they offered to Molech.
i. Jer. 16:19 He wondereth at the great mercy of God in this deliverance, which shall not only extend to the Jews, but also to the Gentiles.
j. Jer. 16:19 Our fathers were most vile idolaters, therefore it cometh only of God's mercy, that he performeth his promise, and hath not utterly cast us off.
k. Jer. 16:21 They shall once again feel my power and mercy for their deliverance, that they may learn to worship me.

JER. 16
1. Jer. 5:19
2. Jer. 7:26
3. Jer. 23:7

JER. 17
a. Jer. 17:1 The remembrance of their contempt of God cannot pass, albeit for a time he defer the punishment, for it shall be manifest to men and Angels.
b. Jer. 17:1 Instead of the Law of God, they have written idolatry and all abominations in their heart.
c. Jer. 17:1 Your sins appear in all the altars that you have erected to idols.
d. Jer. 17:2 Some read, So that their children remember their altars, that is, follow their fathers' wickedness.
e. Jer. 17:3 Zion that was my mountain, shall now be left as a waste field.

substance, and all thy treasures to be spoiled, for the sin of thy high places throughout all thy borders. **4** And thou shalt rest, [f]and in thee shall be a rest from thine heritage that I gave thee, and I will cause thee to serve thine enemies in the land, which thou knowest not: for ye have kindled a fire in mine anger, which shall burn forever. **5** Thus saith the Lord, [g]Cursed be the man that trusteth in man, and maketh flesh his arm, and withdraweth his heart from the Lord. **6** For he shall be like the heath in the wilderness, and shall not see when any good cometh, but shall inhabit the parched places in the wilderness, in a salt land, and not inhabited. **7** Blessed be the man that trusteth in the Lord, and whose hope the Lord is. **8** [h]For he shall be as a tree that is planted by the water, which spreadeth out her roots by the river, and shall not feel when the heat cometh, but her leaf shall be green, and shall not care for the year of drought, neither shall cease from yielding fruit. **9** [i]The heart is deceitful and wicked above all things, who can know it? **10** I the Lord search the heart, and try the reins, even to give every man according to his ways, and according to the fruit of his works. **11** [j]As the partridge gathereth the young, which she hath not brought forth: so he that getteth riches, and not by right, shall leave them in the midst of his days, and at his end shall be a fool. **12** As a glorious throne [k]exalted from the beginning, so is the place of our Sanctuary. **13** O Lord, the hope of Israel, that forsake thee, shall be confounded: they that depart from thee, shall be written [l]in the earth, because they have forsaken the Lord, the fountain of living waters. **14** Heal me, O Lord, and I shall be whole: [m]save me, and I shall be saved: for thou art my praise. **15** Behold, [n]they say unto me, Where is the word of the Lord? let it come now. **16** But [o]I have not thrust in myself for a pastor after thee, neither have I desired the day of misery, thou knowest that which came out of my lips was right before thee. **17** Be not [p]terrible unto me: thou art mine hope in the day of adversity. **18** Let them be confounded, that persecute me, but let not me be confounded: let them be afraid, but let not me be afraid: bring upon them the day of adversity, [q]and, destroy them with double destruction. **19** Thus hath the Lord said unto me, Go and stand in the [r]gate of the children of the people, whereby the Kings of Judah come in, and by the which they go out, and in all the gates of Jerusalem, **20** And say unto them, Hear the word of the Lord, ye kings of Judah, and all Judah, and all the inhabitants of Jerusalem, that enter in by these gates. **21** Thus saith the Lord, Take heed to your souls, and bear no burden in the [s]Sabbath day, nor bring it in by the gates of Jerusalem. **22** Neither carry forth burdens out of your houses in the Sabbath day: neither do ye any work, but sanctify the Sabbath, as I commanded your fathers. **23** But they obeyed not, neither inclined their ears, but made their necks stiff, and would not hear, nor receive correction. **24** Nevertheless, if ye will hear me, saith the Lord, and bear no burden through the gates of the city in the Sabbath day, but sanctify the Sabbath day, so that ye do no work therein, **25** Then shall the Kings and the Princes enter in at the gates of this city, and shall sit [1]upon the throne of David, and shall ride upon chariots and upon horses, both they and their princes, the men of Judah, and the inhabitants of Jerusalem: and this city shall remain forever. **26** And they shall come from the cities of Judah, and from about Jerusalem, and from the land of Benjamin, and from the plain, and from the mountains, and from the South, which shall bring burnt offerings, and sacrifices, and meat offerings, and incense, and shall bring sacrifice of praise into the house of the Lord. **27** But if ye will not hear me to sanctify the Sabbath day, and not to bear a burden, nor to go through the gates of Jerusalem in the Sabbath day, then will I kindle a fire in the gates thereof, and it shall devour the palaces of Jerusalem, and it shall not be quenched.

18

2 God showeth by the example of a potter, that it is in his power to destroy the despisers of his word. 18 The conspiracy of the Jews against Jeremiah. 19 His prayer against his adversaries.

1 The word which came to Jeremiah from the Lord, saying, **2** Arise, and go down into the potter's house, and there shall I show thee my words. **3** Then I went down to the potter's house, and behold, he wrought a work on the wheels. **4** And the vessel that he made [a]of clay, was broken in the hand of the potter, so he returned, and made it another vessel, as seemed good to the potter to make it. **5** Then the word of the Lord came unto me, saying, **6** O house of Israel, cannot I do with you as this potter, saith the Lord? behold, as the clay is in the potter's hand, so are you in mine hand, O house of Israel. **7** I will speak suddenly against a nation, or against a kingdom to pluck it up, and to root it out, and to destroy it. **8** But if this nation against whom I have pronounced turn from their wickedness, I will [b]repent of the plague that I thought to bring upon them. **9** And I will speak suddenly concerning a nation, and concerning a kingdom to build it and to plant it. **10** But if it do evil in my sight, and hear not my voice, I will repent of the good that I thought to do for them. **11** Speak thou now therefore unto the men of Judah, and to the inhabitants of Jerusalem, saying, Thus saith the Lord, Behold, I prepare a plague for you, and purpose a thing against you: return you therefore every one from his evil way, and make your ways and your works good. **12** But they said [c]desperately, Surely we will walk after our own imaginations, and do every man after the stubbornness of his wicked heart. **13** Therefore thus saith the Lord, Ask now among the heathen, who hath heard such things? the virgin of Israel hath done very filthily. **14** Will a man forsake the snow of Lebanon, which cometh from the rock of the field? [d]or shall the cold flowing waters, that come from another place, be forsaken? **15** Because my people hath forgotten me, and have burnt incense to vanity, and their prophets have caused them to stumble in their ways from the [e]ancient ways, to walk in the paths and way that is not trodden, **16** To make their land desolate, and a perpetual derision, so that everyone that passeth thereby, shall be astonished and wag his head, **17** I will scatter them with an East wind before the enemy: I will show them the back, and [f]not the face in the day of their destruction. **18** Then said they, Come, and let us imagine some device against Jeremiah: for the Law [g]shall not perish from the Priest, nor counsel from the wise, nor the word from the Prophet: come, and let us smite him with the [h]tongue, and let us not give heed to any of his words. **19** Hearken unto me, O Lord, and hear the voice of them that contend with me. **20** Shall evil be recompensed for good? for they have dug a pit for my soul: remember that I stood before thee, to speak good for them, and to turn away thy wrath from them. **21** Therefore, [i]deliver up their children to famine, and let them drop away by the force of the sword, let their wives be robbed of their children, and be widows: and let their husbands be put to death, and let their young men be slain by the sword in the battle. **22** Let the cry be heard from their houses, when thou shalt bring an host suddenly upon them: for they have dug a pit to take me, and hid snares for my feet. **23** Yet Lord thou knowest all their counsel against me tendeth to death: forgive not their iniquity, neither put out their sin from thy sight, but let them be overthrown before thee: deal thus with them in the time of thine anger.

19

He prophesieth the destruction of Jerusalem for the contempt and despising of the word of God.

1 Thus saith the Lord, Go, and buy an earthen bottle of a potter, and take of the ancients for the people, and of the ancients of the Priests, **2** And go forth

---

f. Jer. 17:4 Because thou wouldest not give the land rest, at such times, days, and years as I appointed, thou shalt hereafter be carried away, and it shall rest for lack of laborers.

g. Jer. 17:5 The Jews were given to worldly policies, and thought to make themselves strong by the friendship of the Egyptians, Isa. 31:3, and strangers, and in the mean season did not depend on God, and therefore he denounceth God's plagues against them, showing that they prefer corruptible man to God, which is immortal, Isa. 2:22; Jer. 48:6, 7.

h. Jer. 17:8 Read Ps. 1:3.

i. Jer. 17:9 Because the wicked have ever some excuse to defend their doings, he showeth that their own lewd imaginations deceive them, and bring them to these inconveniences: but God will examine their deeds by the malice of their hearts, 1 Sam. 16:7; 1 Chron. 28:9; Ps. 7:10; Jer. 11:20 and 20:12; Rev. 2:13.

j. Jer. 17:11 As the Partridge by calling gathered others which forsake her, when they see that she is not their dam: so the covetous man is forsaken of his riches, because he cometh by them falsely.

k. Jer. 17:12 Showing that the godly ought to glory in nothing, but in God, who doth exalt his, and hath left a sign of his favor in his Temple.

l. Jer. 17:13 Their names shall not be registered in the book of life.

m. Jer. 17:14 He desireth God to preserve him that he fall not into tentation, considering the great contempt of God's word, and the multitude that fall from God.

n. Jer. 17:15 The wicked say that my prophecy shall not come to pass, because thou deferrest the time of thy vengeance.

o. Jer. 17:16 I am assured of my vocation, and therefore know that the thing which thou speakest by me, shall come to pass, and that I speak not of any worldly affection.

p. Jer. 17:17 Howsoever the wicked deal rigorously with me, yet let me find comfort in thee.

q. Jer. 17:18 Read Jer. 11:20.

r. Jer. 17:19 Whereas thy doctrine may be best understood both of high and low.

s. Jer. 17:21 By naming the Sabbath day, he comprehendeth the thing that is thereby signified: for if they transgressed in the ceremony, they must needs be culpable of the rest, read Exod. 20:8, and by the breaking of this one commandment, he maketh them transgressors of the whole law, forasmuch as the first and second table are contained herein.

JER. 17

1. Jer. 22:4

JER. 18

a. Jer. 18:4 As the potter hath power over the clay to make what pot he will, or to break them, when he hath made them: so have I power over you to do with you as seemeth good to me, Isa. 45:9; Rom. 9:20, 21.

b. Jer. 18:8 When the Scripture attributeth repentance unto God, it is not that he doeth contrary to that which he hath ordained in his secret counsel: but when he threateneth, it is a calling to repentance, and when he giveth man grace to repent, the threatening (which ever containeth a condition in it) taketh no place: and this the scripture calleth repentance in God, because it so appeareth to man's judgment.

c. Jer. 18:12 As men that had no remorse, but were altogether bent to rebellion and to their own self-will.

d. Jer. 18:14 As no man that hath thirst refuseth fresh conduit waters which he hath at home, to go and seek waters abroad to quench his thirst: so they ought not to seek for help and succor at strangers, and leave God which was present with them.

e. Jer. 18:15 That is, the way of truth which God had taught by his law, read Jer. 6:16.

f. Jer. 18:17 I will show mine anger and not my favor toward them.

g. Jer. 18:18 This argument the wicked have ever used against the servants of God. The Church cannot err: we are the Church, and therefore whosoever speaketh against us, they ought to die, 1 Kings 22:24; Jer. 7:4 and 20:2; Mal. 2:4, and thus the false Church persecuteth the true Church, which standeth not in outward pomp, and in multitude, but is known by the graces of the holy Ghost.

h. Jer. 18:18 Let us slander him, and accuse him: for we shall be believed.

i. Jer. 18:21 Seeing the obstinate malice of the adversaries, which grew daily more and more, the Prophet being moved with God's Spirit, without any carnal affection prayeth for their destruction, because he knew that it should tend to God's glory, and profit of his Church.

unto the valley of Ben-Hinnom, which is by the entry of the [a]East gate: and thou
shalt preach there the words, that I shall tell thee, 3 And shalt say, Hear ye the
word of the Lord, O [b]Kings of Judah, and inhabitants of Jerusalem, Thus saith the
Lord of hosts, the God of Israel, Behold, I will bring a plague upon this place, the
which whosoever heareth, his ears shall [c]tingle. 4 Because they have forsaken
me, and profaned this place, and have burnt incense in it unto other gods, whom
neither they, nor their fathers have known, nor the Kings of Judah (they have filled
this place also with the blood of innocents, 5 And they have built the high places
of Baal, to burn their sons with fire for burnt offerings unto Baal, which I [d]com-
manded not, nor spake it, neither came it into my mind) 6 Therefore behold, the
days come, saith the Lord, that this place shall no more be called [e]Topheth, nor the
valley of Ben-Hinnom, but the valley of slaughter. 7 And I will bring the coun-
sel of Judah and Jerusalem to nought in this place, and I will cause them to fall by
the sword before their enemies, and by the hand of them that seek their lives: and
their carcasses will I give to be meat for the fowls of the heaven, and to the beasts of
the field. 8 [1]And I will make this city desolate, and an hissing, so that everyone
that passeth thereby, shall be astonished and hiss because of all the plagues there-
of. 9 [2]And I will feed them with the flesh of their sons, and with the flesh of their
daughters, and everyone shall eat the flesh of his friend in the siege and straitness,
wherewith their enemies that seek their lives, shall hold them strait. 10 Then
shalt thou break the bottle in the sight of the men that go with thee, 11 And
shalt say unto them, Thus saith the Lord of hosts, Even so will I break this people
and this city, as one breaketh a [f]potter's vessel, that cannot be made whole again,
and they shall bury them in Topheth till there be no place to bury. 12 Thus will
I do unto this place, saith the Lord, and to the inhabitants thereof, and I will make
this city like Topheth. 13 For the houses of Jerusalem, and the houses of the
Kings of Judah shall be defiled as the place of Topheth, because of all the [g]hou-
ses upon whose [h]roofs they have burnt incense unto all the host of heaven, and
have poured out drink offerings unto other gods. 14 Then came Jeremiah from
Topheth, where the Lord had sent him to prophesy, and he stood in the court of
the Lord's house, and said to all the people, 15 Thus saith the Lord of hosts, the
God of Israel, Behold, I will bring upon this city, and upon all her towns, all the
plagues that I have pronounced against it, because they have hardened their necks,
and would not hear my words.

20

Jeremiah is smitten and cast into prison for preaching of the word of God. 3 He prophesieth the captivity of Babylon. 7 He complaineth that he is a mocking stock for the word of God. 9 He is compelled by the spirit to preach the word.

1 When Pashhur, the son of Immer, the priest, which was appointed governor
in the house of the Lord, heard that Jeremiah prophesied these things, 2 Then
Pashhur smote Jeremiah the Prophet, and put him in the [a]stocks that were in
the high gate of Benjamin, which was by the house of the Lord. 3 And on the
morning, Pashhur brought Jeremiah out of the stocks. Then said Jeremiah unto
him, The Lord hath not called thy name Pashhur, but [b]Magor-Missabib. 4 For
thus saith the Lord, behold, I will make thee to be a terror to thyself, and to all
thy friends, and they shall fall by the sword of their enemies, and thine eyes shall
behold it, and I will give all Judah into the hand of the king of Babel, and he shall
carry them captive into Babel, and shall slay them with the sword. 5 Moreover,
I will deliver all the substance of this city, and all the labors thereof, and all the
precious things thereof, and all the treasures of the Kings of Judah will I give into
the hand of their enemies, which shall spoil them, and take them away and carry
them to Babel. 6 And thou Pashhur, and all that dwell in thine house, shall go
into captivity, and thou shalt come to Babel, and there thou shalt die, and shalt be
buried there, thou and all thy [c]friends, to whom thou hast prophesied lies. 7 O
Lord, thou hast deceived me, and I am [d]deceived: thou art stronger than I, and
hast [e]prevailed: I am in derision daily: everyone mocketh me. 8 For since I spa-
ke, I cried out of wrong, and proclaimed [f]desolation: therefore the word of the
Lord was made a reproach unto me, and in derision daily. 9 Then I said, I will
not make mention of him, nor speak anymore in his Name. But his word was in
mine heart as a burning fire shut up in my bones, and I was weary with forbearing,
and I could not stay. 10 For I had heard the railing of many, and fear on every
side. [g]Declare, said they, and we will declare it: all my familiars watched for mine
halting, saying, It may be that he is deceived: so we shall prevail against him, and
we shall execute our vengeance upon him. 11 [h]But the Lord is with me like a
mighty giant: therefore my persecutors shall be overthrown, and shall not prevail,
and shall be greatly confounded: for they have done unwisely, and their everlasting
shame shall never be forgotten. 12 [1]But, O Lord of hosts, that triest the righte-
ous, and seest the reins and the heart, let me see thy vengeance on them: for unto
thee have I opened my cause. 13 Sing unto the Lord, praise ye the Lord: for he
hath delivered the soul of the poor from the hand of the wicked. 14 [i]Cursed be
the day wherein I was born: and let not the day wherein my mother bare me, be
blessed. 15 Cursed be the man that showed my father, saying, A man child is
born unto thee, and comforted him. 16 And let that man be as the [j]cities, which
the Lord hath overturned and repented not: and let him hear the cry in the mor-
ning, and the shouting at noon tide, 17 Because he hath not slain me, even from
the womb, or that my mother might have been my grave, or her womb a perpetual
[k]conception. 18 How is it, that I came forth of the womb, to see labor and sor-
row, that my days should be consumed with shame?

21

He prophesieth that Zedekiah shall be taken, and the city burned.

1 The word which came unto Jeremiah from the Lord, when king
Zedekiah sent unto him Pashhur, the son of Melchiah, and Zephaniah, the son
of Maaseiah the Priest, saying, 2 [a]Inquire, I pray thee, of the Lord for us, (for
Nebuchadnezzar king of Babel maketh war against us) if so be that the Lord will
deal with us according to all his wondrous works, that he may return up from
us. 3 Then said Jeremiah, Thus shall you say to Zedekiah, 4 Thus saith the
Lord God of Israel, Behold, I will [b]turn back the weapons of war that are in your
hands, wherewith ye fight against the king of Babel, and against the Chaldeans,
which besiege you without the walls, and I will assemble them into the midst of
this city. 5 And I myself will fight against you with an outstretched hand, and
with a mighty arm, even in anger and in wrath, and in great indignation. 6 And
I will smite the inhabitants of this city, both man and beast: they shall die of a gre-
at pestilence. 7 And after this, saith the Lord, I will deliver Zedekiah the King
of Judah, and his servants, and the people, and such as are left in this city, from
the pestilence, from the sword, and from the famine, into the hand of Nebucha-
dnezzar king of Babel, and into the hand of their enemies, and into the hand of
those that seek their lives, and he shall smite them with the edge of the sword: he
shall not spare them, neither have pity nor compassion. 8 And unto this peo-
ple thou shalt say, Thus saith the Lord, Behold, I set before you the [c]way of life,
and the way of [d]death. 9 [1]He that abideth in this city, shall die by the sword,
and by the famine, and by the pestilence: but he that goeth out, and falleth to
the Chaldeans, that besiege you, he shall live, and his life shall be unto him for a
[e]prey. 10 For I have set my face against this city, for evil and not for good, saith
the Lord: it shall be given into the hand of the king of Babel, and he shall burn
it with fire. 11 And say unto the house of the King of Judah, Hear ye the word
of the Lord. 12 O house of David, Thus saith the Lord, [2]Execute judgment [f]in
the morning, and deliver the oppressed out of the hand of the oppressor, lest my
wrath go out like fire, and burn that none can quench it, because of the wickedness
of your works. 13 Behold, I come against thee, [g]O inhabitant of the valley, and
rock of the plain, saith the Lord, which say, Who shall come down against us? or
who shall enter into our habitations? 14 But I will visit you according to the fruit

---

JER. 19

a. Jer. 19:2 Or, gate of the sun.
b. Jer. 19:3 By Kings here and in other places are meant counselors and governors of the people: which he calleth the ancients, verse 1.
c. Jer. 19:3 Read of this phrase, 1 Sam. 3:11.
d. Jer. 19:5 Whereby is declared, that whatsoever is not commanded by God's word touching his service, is against his word.
e. Jer. 19:6 Read Jer. 7:31 and 2 Kings 23:10; Isa. 30:33.
f. Jer. 19:11 This visible sign was to confirm them touching the assurance of this plague, which the Lord threatened by his prophet.
g. Jer. 19:13 He noteth the great rage of the idolaters, which left no place free from their abominations, insomuch as they polluted their own houses therewith, as we see yet among the Papists.
h. Jer. 19:13 Read Deut. 22:8.

JER. 19

1. Jer. 18:16 / Jer. 49:13 / Jer. 50:13
2. Deut. 28:53 / Lam. 4:10

JER. 20

a. Jer. 20:2 Thus we see that the thing which neither the King, nor the princes, nor the people durst enterprise against the Prophet of God, this Priest as a chief instrument of Satan first attempted, read Jer. 18:18.
b. Jer. 20:3 Or, fear round about.
c. Jer. 20:6 Which have suffered themselves to be abused by thy false prophecies.
d. Jer. 20:7 Herein appeareth the impatience, which oftentimes overcometh the servants of God, when they see not their labors to profit, and also feel their own weakness, read Jer. 15:18.
e. Jer. 20:7 Thou didst thrust me forth to this work against my will.
f. Jer. 20:8 He showeth that he did his office in that he reproved the people of their vices, and threatened them with God's judgments: but because he was derided and persecuted for this, he was discouraged, and thought to have ceased to preach, save that God's Spirit did force him thereunto.
g. Jer. 20:10 Thus the enemies conferred together to know what they had heard him say, that they might accuse him thereof, read Isa. 29:21.
h. Jer. 20:11 Here he showeth how his faith did strive against tentation, and sought to the Lord for strength.
i. Jer. 20:14 How the children of God are overcome in this battle of the flesh and the Spirit, and into what inconveniences they fall till God raise them up again: read Job 3:1 and Jer. 15:10.
j. Jer. 20:16 Alluding to the destruction of Sodom and Gomorrah, Gen. 19:25.
k. Jer. 20:17 Meaning, that the fruit thereof might never come to profit.

JER. 20

1. 1 Sam. 16:7 / 1 Chron. 28:9 / Ps. 7:9 / Jer. 11:20 / Jer. 17:10

JER. 21

a. Jer. 21:2 Not that the King was touched with repentance of his sins, and so sought to God, as did Hezekiah, when he sent to Isaiah, 2 Kings 19:1; Isa. 37:2, but because the Prophet might pray unto God to take this present plague away, as Pharaoh sought unto Moses, Exod. 9:28.
b. Jer. 21:4 To wit, from your enemies to destroy yourselves.
c. Jer. 21:8 By yielding yourselves to Nebuchadnezzar.
d. Jer. 21:8 By resisting him.
e. Jer. 21:9 As a thing recovered from extreme danger, Jer. 37:2, 39:18 and 45:5.
f. Jer. 21:12 Be diligent to do justice.
g. Jer. 21:13 Meaning, Jerusalem which was built part on the hill, and part in the valley, and was compassed about with mountains.
h. Jer. 21:14 That is, in the houses thereof, which stood as thick as trees in the forest.

of your works, saith the Lord, and I will kindle a fire [h]in the forest thereof, and it shall devour round about it.

22

1 He exhorteth the King to judgment and righteousness. 9 Why Jerusalem is brought into captivity. 11 The death of Shallum the son of Josiah is prophesied.

1 Thus said the Lord, Go down to the house of the King of Judah, and speak there this thing, **2** And say, Hear the word of the Lord, O King of Judah, that sittest upon the throne of David, thou and thy servants, and thy people that enter in by these gates. **3** Thus saith the Lord, [1]Execute ye judgment and [a]righteousness, and deliver the oppressed from the hand of the oppressor, and vex not the stranger, the fatherless, nor the widow: do no violence, nor shed innocent blood in this place. **4** For if ye do this thing, then shall the kings sitting upon the throne of David enter in by the gates of this House, [2]and ride upon chariots and upon horses, both he and his servants and his people. **5** But if ye will not hear these words, I [b]swear by myself, saith the Lord, that this House shall be waste. **6** For thus hath the Lord spoken upon the king's house of Judah, Thou art [c]Gilead unto me, and the head of Lebanon, yet surely I will make thee a wilderness, and as cities not inhabited. **7** And I will [d]prepare destroyers against thee, everyone with his weapons, and they shall cut down thy chief [e]cedar trees, and cast them in the fire. **8** [f]And many nations shall pass by this city, and they shall say every man to his neighbor, Wherefore hath the Lord done thus unto this great city? **9** Then shall they answer, Because they have forsaken the covenant of the Lord their God, and worshipped other gods, and served them. **10** Weep not for the dead, and be not moved for them, but weep for him [g]that goeth out: for he shall return no more, nor see his native country. **11** For thus saith the Lord, As touching [h]Shallum the son of Josiah King of Judah, which reigned for Josiah his father, which went out of this place, he shall not return thither, **12** But he shall die in the place, whither they have led him captive, and shall see this land no more. **13** Woe unto him that buildeth his house by [i]unrighteousness, and his chambers without equity: he useth his neighbor without wages, and giveth him not for his work. **14** He saith, I will build me a wide house and large chambers: so he will make himself large windows, and ceiling with cedar, and paint them with vermilion. **15** Shalt thou reign, because thou closest thyself in cedar? did not thy [j]father eat and drink and prosper, when he executed judgment and justice? **16** When he judged the cause of the afflicted and the poor, he prospered: was not this because he knew me, saith the Lord? **17** But thine eyes and thine heart are but only for thy covetousness, and for to shed innocent blood, and for oppression, and for destruction, even to do this. **18** Therefore thus saith the Lord against Jehoiakim, the son of Josiah king of Judah, They shall not [k]lament him, saying, Ah, my brother, or ah sister: neither shall they mourn for him, saying, Ah, lord, or ah, his glory. **19** He shall be buried, as an ass [l]is buried, even drawn and cast forth without the gates of Jerusalem. **20** Go up to [m]Lebanon, and cry: shout in [n]Bashan, and cry by the passages: for all thy lovers are destroyed. **21** I spake unto thee when thou wast in prosperity: but thou saidest, I will not hear, this hath been thy manner from thy youth, that thou wouldest not obey my voice. **22** The wind shall feed all thy pastors, [o]and thy lovers shall go into captivity: and then shalt thou be ashamed and confounded of all thy wickedness. **23** Thou that dwellest in Lebanon, and makest thy nest in the [p]cedars, how beautiful shalt thou be when sorrows come upon thee, as the sorrow of a woman in travail? **24** As I live, saith the Lord, though [q]Coniah the son of Jehoiakim king of Judah, were the signet of my right hand, yet would I pluck thee thence. **25** And I will give thee into the hand of them that seek thy life, and into the hand of them, whose face thou fearest, even into the hand of Nebuchadnezzar king of Babel, and into the hand of the Chaldeans. **26** And I will cause them to carry thee away, and thy mother that bare thee into another country, where ye were not born, and there shall ye die. **27** But to the land, whereunto they desire to return, they shall not return thither. **28** Is not this man Coniah as a despised and broken idol? or as a vessel, wherein is no pleasure? wherefore are they carried away, he and his seed, and cast out into a land that they know not? **29** O [r]earth, earth, earth, hear the word of the Lord. **30** Thus saith the Lord, Write this [s]man destitute of children, a man that shall not prosper in his days: for there shall be no man of his seed that shall prosper and sit upon the throne of David, or bear rule anymore in Judah.

23

1 Against false pastors. 5 A prophecy of the great Pastor Jesus Christ.

1 Woe be unto [a]the pastors that destroy and scatter the [b]sheep of my pasture, saith the Lord. **2** Therefore thus saith the Lord God of Israel unto the pastors that [c]feed my people, Ye have scattered my flock, and thrust them out, and have not visited them: behold, I will visit you for the wickedness of your works, saith the Lord. **3** And I will gather the [d]remnant of my sheep out of all countries, whither I had driven them, and will bring them again to their folds, and they shall grow and increase: **4** And I will set up shepherds over them, which shall feed them: and they shall dread no more nor be afraid, neither shall any of them be lacking, saith the Lord. **5** Behold, the days come, saith the Lord, that I will raise unto David a righteous [e]branch, and a King shall reign and prosper, and shall execute judgment and justice in the earth. **6** In his days Judah shall be saved, and [1]Israel shall dwell safely, and this is the Name whereby they shall call him, [2]The Lord our righteousness. **7** Therefore behold, the days come, saith the Lord, that they shall no more say, The [f]Lord liveth, which brought up the children of Israel out of the land of Egypt. **8** But the Lord liveth, which brought up and led the seed of the house of Israel out of the North country, and from all countries where I had scattered them, and they shall dwell in their own land. **9** Mine heart breaketh within me, because of the [g]prophets, all my bones shake: I am like a drunken man (and like a man whom wine hath [h]overcome) for the presence of the Lord and for his holy words. **10** For the land is full of adulterers, and because of oaths the land mourneth, the pleasant places of the wilderness are dried up, and their [i]course is evil, and their force is not right. **11** For both the Prophet and the Priest [j]do wickedly: and their wickedness have I found in mine [k]House, saith the Lord. **12** Wherefore their way shall be unto them as slippery ways in the darkness: they shall be driven forth and fall therein: for I will bring a plague upon them, even the year of their visitation, saith the Lord. **13** And I have seen foolishness in the prophets of Samaria that prophesied in Baal, and caused my people Israel to err. **14** I have seen also in the prophets of Jerusalem [l]filthiness: they commit adultery and walk in lies: they strengthen also the hands of the wicked, that none can return from his wickedness: they are all [m]unto me as Sodom, and the inhabitants thereof as Gomorrah. **15** Therefore thus saith the Lord of hosts concerning the prophets, Behold, I will feed them with [n]wormwood, and make them drink the water of gall: for from the prophets of Jerusalem is [o]wickedness gone forth into all the land. **16** Thus saith the Lord of hosts, Hear not the words of the prophets that prophesy unto you, and teach you vanity: they speak the vision of their own [p]heart, and not out of the mouth of the Lord. **17** They say still unto them that despise me, The Lord hath said, Ye [q]shall have peace: and they say unto everyone that walketh after the stubbornness of his own heart, No evil shall come upon you. **18** For [r]who hath stood in the counsel of the Lord that he hath perceived,

---

JER. 21

1. Jer. 38:2 / Jer. 22:3

JER. 22

a. Jer. 22:3 This was his ordinary manner of preaching before the Kings, from Josiah unto Zedekiah, which was about forty years.
b. Jer. 22:5 Showing that there is none greater than he is, Heb. 6:13, and that he will most certainly perform his oath.
c. Jer. 22:6 He compareth Jerusalem to Gilead, which was beyond Jordan, and the beauty of Judea to Lebanon.
d. Jer. 22:7 The Hebrew word signifieth to sanctify, because the Lord doth dedicate to his use and purpose such as he prepareth to execute his work, Isa. 13:3; Jer. 6:4 and 12:3.
e. Jer. 22:7 Thy buildings made of Cedar trees.
f. Jer. 22:8 As they that wonder at a thing which they thought would never have come so to pass, Deut. 29:24; 1 Kings 9:8.
g. Jer. 22:10 Signifying, that they should lose their king: for Jehoiachin went forth to meet Nebuchadnezzar and yielded himself, and was carried into Babylon, 2 Kings 24:12.
h. Jer. 22:11 Whom some think to be Jehoiachin, and that Josiah was his grandfather: but as seemeth, this was Jehoiakim, as verse 18.
i. Jer. 22:13 By bribes, and extortion.
j. Jer. 22:15 Meaning, Josiah, who was not given to ambition and superfluity, but was content with mediocrity, and did only delight in setting forth God's glory, and to do justice to all.
k. Jer. 22:18 For everyone shall have enough to lament for himself.
l. Jer. 22:19 Not honorably among his fathers, but as carrions are cast in a hole, because their stink should not infect, read 2 Kings 24:9. Josephus Antiquities 10:8, writeth that the enemy slew him in the city and commanded him to be cast before the walls unburied, see Jer. 36:30.
m. Jer. 22:20 To call to the Assyrians for help.
n. Jer. 22:20 For this was the way out of India to Assyria, whereby is meant that all help should fail: for the Chaldeans have subdued both them and the Egyptians.
o. Jer. 22:22 Both thy governors and they that should help thee, shall vanish away as wind.
p. Jer. 22:23 Thou that art built of the fair Cedar trees of Lebanon.
q. Jer. 22:24 Who was called Jehoiachin, or Jeconiah, whom he calleth here Coniah in contempt, who thought his kingdom could never depart from him, because he came of the stock of David, and therefore for the promise sake could not be taken from his house: but he abused God's promise, and therefore was justly deprived of the kingdom.
r. Jer. 22:29 He showeth that all posterities shall be witnesses of his just plague, as though it were registered for perpetual memory.
s. Jer. 22:30 Not that he had no children (for after that he begat Shealtiel in the captivity, Matt. 1:12) but that none should reign after him as King.

JER. 22

1. Jer. 21:12 / Jer. 17:25

JER. 23

a. Jer. 23:1 Meaning, the princes, governors and false prophets, as Ezek. 34:2.
b. Jer. 23:1 For the which I have especial care, and have prepared good pastures for them.
c. Jer. 23:2 Whose charge is to feed the flock, but they eat the fruit thereof, Ezek. 34:3.
d. Jer. 23:3 Thus the Prophets ever used to mix the promises with the threatenings, lest the godly should be too much beaten down, and therefore he showeth how God will gather his Church after this dispersion.
e. Jer. 23:5 This prophecy is of the restitution of the Church in the time of Jesus Christ, who is the true branch, read Isa. 11:1 and 45:8; Jer. 35:15; Dan. 9:24.
f. Jer. 23:7 Read Jer. 16:14.
g. Jer. 23:9 Meaning, the false prophets which deceive the people: wherein appeareth his great love toward his nation, read Jer. 14:13.
h. Jer. 23:9 Hebrew, passed over or troubled.
i. Jer. 23:10 They run headlong to wickedness, and seek vain help.
j. Jer. 23:11 Or, are hypocrites.
k. Jer. 23:11 My Temple is full of their idolatry and superstitions.
l. Jer. 23:14 They which should have profited by my rods against Samaria, are become worse than they.
m. Jer. 23:14 Though to the world they seem holy fathers, yet I detest them as I did these abominable cities.
n. Jer. 23:15 Read Jer. 8:14.
o. Jer. 23:15 Or, hypocrisy.
p. Jer. 23:16 Which they have invented of their own brain.
q. Jer. 23:17 Read Jer. 6:14 and 8:11.
r. Jer. 23:18 Thus they did deride Jer., as though the word of God were not revealed unto him: so also spake Zedekiah to Micaiah, 1 Kings 22:24.

and heard his word? Who hath marked his word and heard it? **19** Behold, the tempest of the Lord goeth forth in his wrath, and a violent whirlwind shall fall down upon the head of the wicked. **20** The anger of the Lord shall not return until he have executed, and till he have performed the thoughts of his heart: in the latter days ye [s]shall understand it plainly. **21** [3]I have not sent these prophets, saith the Lord, yet they ran; I have not spoken to them, and yet they prophesied. **22** But if they had stood in my counsel, and [t]had declared my words to my people, then they should have turned them from their evil way, and from the wickedness of their inventions. **23** Am I a God at hand, saith the Lord, and not a God [u]far off? **24** Can any hide himself in secret places, that I shall not see him, saith the Lord? Do not I fill heaven and earth, saith the Lord? **25** I have heard what the prophets said, that prophesied lies in my Name, saying, I [v]have dreamed, I have dreamed. **26** How long? [w]Do the prophets delight to prophesy lies, even prophesying the deceit of their own heart? **27** Think they to cause [x]my people to forget my Name by their dreams, which they tell every man to his neighbor, as their forefathers have forgotten my Name for Baal? **28** The prophet that hath a dream, let him [y]tell a dream, and he that hath my word, let him speak my word faithfully: [z]what is the chaff to the wheat, saith the Lord? **29** Is not my word even like a fire, saith the Lord? and like an hammer, that breaketh the stone? **30** Therefore behold, I will come against the prophets, saith the Lord, that [aa]steal my word every one from his neighbor. **31** Behold, I will come against the prophets, saith the Lord, which have sweet tongues, and say, [ab]He saith. **32** Behold, I will come against them that prophesy false dreams, saith the Lord, and do tell them, and cause my people to err by their lies, and by their flatteries, and I sent them not, nor commanded them: therefore they bring no profit unto this people, saith the Lord. **33** And when this people, or the prophet, or a Priest shall ask thee, saying, What is the [ac]burden of the Lord? thou shalt then say unto them, What burden? I will even forsake you, saith the Lord. **34** And the prophet, or the priest, or the people that shall say, The [ad]burden of the Lord, I will even visit every such one, and his house. **35** Thus shall ye say every one to his neighbor, and every one to his brother, What hath the Lord answered? and what hath the Lord spoken? **36** And the burden of the Lord shall ye mention no more: for every man's [ae]word shall be his burden: for ye have perverted the words of the living God, the Lord of hosts our God. **37** Thus shalt thou say to the Prophet, What hath the Lord answered thee? and what hath the Lord spoken? **38** And if you say, The burden of the Lord, Then thus saith the Lord, Because ye say this word, The burden of the Lord, and I have sent unto you, saying, Ye shall not say, The burden of the Lord. **39** Therefore behold, I, even I will utterly [af]forget you, and I will forsake you, and the city that I gave you and your fathers, and cast you out of my presence, **40** And will bring [4]an everlasting reproach upon you, and a perpetual shame which shall never be forgotten.

24

The vision of the baskets of figs, 5 Signifieth that part of the people should be brought again out of captivity. 8 And that Zedekiah and the rest of the people should be carried away.

1 The Lord showed me, and behold, two [a]baskets of figs were set before the Temple of the Lord, after that Nebuchadnezzar king of Babel had carried away captive Jeconiah the son of Jehoiakim king of Judah, and the princes of Judah with the workmen, and cunning men of Jerusalem, and had brought them to Babel. **2** One basket had very good figs, even like the figs that are first ripe, and the other basket had very naughty figs, which could not be eaten, they were so evil. **3** Then said the Lord unto me, What seest thou, Jeremiah? And I said, Figs: the good figs very good, and the naughty very naughty, which cannot be eaten, they are so evil. **4** Again the word of the Lord came unto me, saying, **5** Thus saith the Lord the God of Israel, Like these good figs, so will I know them that are carried away captive of Judah to be good, whom I have sent out of this [b]place, into the land of the Chaldeans. **6** For I will set mine eyes upon them for good, and I will bring them again to this land, and I will build them and not destroy them, and I will plant them, and not root them out. **7** And I will give them [c]an heart to know me, that I am the Lord, and they shall be [1]my people, and I will be their God: for they shall return unto me with their whole heart. **8** [2]And as the naughty figs which cannot be eaten, they are so evil (surely thus saith the Lord) so will I give Zedekiah the King of Judah, and his princes, and the residue of Jerusalem, that remain in this land, and them that dwell [d]in the land of Egypt: **9** I will even give them for a terrible plague to all the kingdoms of the earth, and for a reproach and for a proverb, for a common talk, and for a curse, in all places where I shall cast them. **10** And I will send the sword, the famine, and the pestilence among them, till they be consumed out of the land, that I gave unto them, and to their fathers.

25

1 He prophesieth that they shall be in captivity seventy years. 12 And that after the seventy years the Babylonians should be destroyed. 15 The destruction of all nations is prophesied.

1 The word that came to Jeremiah, concerning all the people of Judah, in the [a]fourth year of Jehoiakim the son of Josiah king of Judah, that was in the first year of Nebuchadnezzar king of Babel: **2** The which Jeremiah the Prophet spake unto all the people of Judah, and to all the inhabitants of Jerusalem, saying, **3** From the thirteenth year of Josiah the son of Amon king of Judah, even unto [b]this day (that is the three and twentieth year) the word of the Lord hath come unto me, and I have spoken unto you [c]rising early and speaking, but ye would not hear. **4** And the Lord hath sent unto you all his servants the Prophets, rising early, and sending them, but ye would not hear, nor incline your ears, to obey. **5** They [d]said, Turn again now everyone from his evil way, and from the wickedness of your inventions, and ye shall dwell in the land that the Lord hath given unto you, and to your fathers forever and ever. **6** And go not after other gods to serve them and to worship them, and provoke me not to anger with the works of your hands, and I will not punish you. **7** Nevertheless, ye would not hear me, saith the Lord, but have provoked me to anger with the works of your hands to your own hurt. **8** Therefore thus saith the Lord of hosts, Because ye have not heard my words, **9** Behold, I will send and take to me all the [e]families of the North, saith the Lord, and Nebuchadnezzar the king of Babel my [f]servant, and will bring them against this land, and against the inhabitants thereof, and against all these nations [g]round about, and will destroy them, and make them an astonishment and an hissing, and a continual desolation. **10** [1]Moreover I will [h]take from them the voice of mirth and the voice of gladness, the voice of the bridegroom and the voice of the bride, the noise of the [i]millstones, and the light of the candle. **11** And this whole land shall be desolate, and an astonishment, and these nations shall serve the king of Babel seventy years. **12** And when the [j]seventy years are accomplished, I will visit [k]the king of Babel and that nation, saith the Lord, for their iniquities, even the land of the Chaldeans, and will make it a perpetual desolation. **13** And I will bring upon that land all my words which I have pronounced against it, even all that is written in this book, which Jeremiah hath prophesied against all nations. **14** For many nations, and great kings shall even [l]serve themselves of them: thus will I recompense them according to their deeds, and according to the works of their own hands. **15** For thus hath the Lord God of Israel spoken unto me, [m]Take the

---

s. Jer. 23:20 Both that God hath sent me, and that my words shall be true.
t. Jer. 23:22 He showeth the difference between the true Prophets and the false, between the hireling and the true minister.
u. Jer. 23:23 Do I not see your falsehood, however you cloak it, and wheresoever you commit it?
v. Jer. 23:25 I have a prophecy revealed unto me, as Num. 12:6.
w. Jer. 23:26 Hebrew, Is it in the heart of the Prophets?
x. Jer. 23:27 He showeth that Satan raiseth up false prophets to bring the people from God.
y. Jer. 23:28 Let the false prophet declare that it is his own fantasy, and not slander my word as though it were a cloak to cover his lies.
z. Jer. 23:28 Meaning, that it is not sufficient for God's ministers to abstain from lies, and to speak the word of God: but that there be judgment in alleging it, and that it may appear to be applied to the same purpose that it was spoken, Ezek. 3:27; 1 Cor. 2:13 and 4:2; 2 Tim. 2:25; 2 Pet. 4:10, 11.
aa. Jer. 23:30 Which set forth in my Name that which I have not commanded.
ab. Jer. 23:31 To wit, the Lord.
ac. Jer. 23:33 The Prophets called their threatenings God's burden, which the sinners were not able to sustain, therefore the wicked in deriding the word, would ask of the Prophets, what was the burden, as though they would say, You seek nothing else, but to lay burdens on our shoulders: and thus they rejected the word of God, as a grievous burden.
ad. Jer. 23:34 Because this word was brought to contempt and derision, he will teach them another manner of speech, and will cause this word burden to cease, and teach them to ask with reverence, What saith the Lord?
ae. Jer. 23:36 The thing which they mock and contemn, shall come upon them.
af. Jer. 23:39 Or, take you away.

JER. 23

1. Deut. 33:28
2. Jer. 33:16
3. Jer. 14:13,14 / Jer. 27:15 / Jer. 29:8,9
4. Jer. 20:11

JER. 24

a. Jer. 24:1 The good figs signified them that were gone into captivity, and so saved their life, as Jer. 21:8, and the naughty figs them that remained, which were yet subject to the sword, famine and pestilence.
b. Jer. 24:5 Whereby he approveth the yielding of Jeconiah and his company, because they obeyed the Prophet, who exhorted them thereunto.
c. Jer. 24:7 Which declareth that man of himself can know nothing, till God give the heart and understanding.
d. Jer. 24:8 Which fled thither for succor.

JER. 24

1. Jer. 31:33 / Heb. 8:10
2. Jer. 29:17

JER. 25

a. Jer. 25:1 That is, in the third year accomplished and in the beginning of the fourth: for though Nebuchadnezzar began to reign in the end of the third year of Jehoiakim's reign, yet that year is not here counted, because it was almost expired, Dan. 1:1.
b. Jer. 25:3 Which was the fifth year and the ninth month of Jehoiakim's reign.
c. Jer. 25:3 That is, I have spared no diligence or labor, Jer. 7:13.
d. Jer. 25:5 He showeth that the Prophets, wholly with one consent did labor to pull the people from those vices, which then reigned, to wit, from idolatry, and the vain confidence of men: for under these two all others were contained, 2 Kings 17:13; Jer. 18:11 and 35:15; Jonah 3:8.
e. Jer. 25:9 The Chaldeans and all their power.
f. Jer. 25:9 So the wicked and Satan himself are God's servants, because he maketh them to serve him by constraint, and turneth that which they do of malice, to his honor and glory.
g. Jer. 25:9 As the Philistines, Ammonites, Egyptians and others.
h. Jer. 25:10 Or, destroy.
i. Jer. 25:10 Meaning, that bread and all things that should serve unto their feasts, should be taken away.
j. Jer. 25:12 This revelation was for the confirmation of his prophecy, because he told them of the time that they should enter and remain in captivity, 2 Chron. 36:22; Ezra 1:1; Jer. 29:10; Dan. 9:2.
k. Jer. 25:12 For seeing the judgment began at his own house, the enemies must needs be punished most grievously, Ezek. 9:6, 1 Pet. 4:17.
l. Jer. 25:14 That is, of the Babylonians, as Jer. 27:7.
m. Jer. 25:15 Signifying, the extreme affliction, that God had appointed for everyone, as Ps. 75:8; Isa. 51:17, and this cup, which the wicked drink, is more bitter than that which he giveth to his children, for he measureth the one by mercy, and the other by justice.

cup of wine of this mine indignation at mine hand, and cause all the nations, to whom I send thee, to drink it. **16** And they shall drink, and be moved, and be mad, because of the sword that I will send among them. **17** Then took I the cup at the Lord's hand, and made all people to drink, unto whom the Lord had sent me: **18** Even Jerusalem, and the cities of Judah, and the kings thereof, and the princes thereof, to make them desolate, an astonishment, an hissing, and a curse, [n]as appeareth this day: **19** Pharaoh also, King of Egypt, and his servants, and his princes, and all his people: **20** And all sorts of people, and all the Kings of the land [o]of Uz: and all the kings of the land of the Philistines, and [p]Ashkelon, and Gaza, and Ekron, and the remnant of Ashdod: **21** [q]Edom, and Moab, and the Ammonites, **22** And all the Kings of Tyre, and all the kings of Sidon, and the kings of the [r]Isles, that are beyond the sea, **23** And [s]Dedan, and Tema, and Buz, and all that dwell in the uttermost corners, **24** And all the kings of Arabia, and all the kings of Arabia that dwell in the [t]desert, **25** And all the kings of Zimri, and all the kings of [u]Elam, and all the kings of the Medes, **26** And all the kings of the North, far and near one to another, and all the kingdoms of the world, which are upon the earth, and the king of [v]Sheshach shall drink after them. **27** Therefore say thou unto them, Thus saith the Lord of hosts, the God of Israel, Drink and be drunken, and spew and fall, and rise no more, because of the sword, which I will send among you. **28** But if they refuse to take the cup at thine hand to drink, then tell them, Thus saith the Lord of hosts, Ye shall certainly drink. **29** For lo, [w]I begin to plague the city, where my Name is called upon, and should you go free? Ye shall not go acquited: for I will call for a sword upon all the inhabitants of the earth, saith the Lord of hosts. **30** Therefore prophesy thou against them all these words, and say unto them, [2]The Lord shall roar from above, and thrust out his voice from his holy habitation: he shall roar upon his habitation, and cry aloud, as they that press the grapes, against all the inhabitants of the earth. **31** The sounds shall come to the ends of the earth: for the Lord hath a controversy with the nations, and will enter into judgment with all flesh, and he will give them that are wicked, to the sword, saith the Lord. **32** Thus saith the Lord of hosts, Behold, a plague shall go forth from nation to nation, and a [3]great whirlwind shall be raised up from the coasts of the earth. **33** And [x]the slain of the Lord shall be at that day, from one end of the earth, even unto the other end of the earth: they shall not be mourned, neither gathered nor buried, but shall be as the dung upon the ground. **34** Howl, [y]ye shepherds, and cry, and wallow yourselves in the ashes, ye principal of the flock: for your days of slaughter are accomplished, and of your dispersion, and ye shall fall like [z]precious vessels. **35** And the [aa]flight shall fail from the shepherds, and the escaping from the principal of the flock. **36** A voice of the cry of the shepherds, and an howling of the principal of the flock, shall be heard: for the Lord hath destroyed their pasture. **37** And the [ab]best pastures are destroyed because of the wrath and indignation of the Lord. **38** He hath forsaken his covert, as the lion: for their land is waste, because of the wrath of the oppressor, and because of the wrath of his indignation.

26

2 Jeremiah moveth the people to repentance. 7 He is taken of the false prophets and priests, and brought to judgment. 23 Urijah the Prophet is killed of Jehoiakim contrary to the will of God.

1 In the beginning of the reign of Jehoiakim the son of Josiah King of Judah, came this word from the Lord, saying, **2** Thus saith the Lord, Stand in the [a]court of the Lord's House, and speak unto all the cities of Judah, which come to worship in the Lord's House, all the words that I command thee to speak unto them: keep not [b]a word back, **3** If so be they will hearken, and turn every man from his evil way, that I may [c]repent me of the plague, which I have determined to bring upon them because of the wickedness of their works. **4** And thou shalt say unto them, Thus saith the Lord, If ye will not hear me to walk in my Laws, which I have set before you, **5** And to hear the words of my servants the Prophets, whom I sent unto you, both rising up early, and sending them, and will not obey them, **6** Then will I make this House like [d]Shiloh, and will make this city [e]a curse to all nations of the earth. **7** So the Priests, and the Prophets, and all the people heard Jeremiah speaking these words in the House of the Lord. **8** Now when Jeremiah had made an end of speaking all that the Lord had commanded him to speak unto all the people, then the Priests, and the Prophets, and all the people took him, and said, Thou shalt die the death. **9** Why hast thou prophesied in the name of the Lord, saying, [f]This House shall be like Shiloh, and this city shall be desolate without an inhabitant? and all the people were gathered against Jeremiah in the house of the Lord. **10** And when the Princes of Judah heard of these things, they came up from the king's house into the House of the Lord, and sat down in the entry of the [g]new gate of the Lord's House. **11** Then spake the Priests, and the Prophets unto the Princes, and to all the people, saying, [h]This man is worthy to die: for he hath prophesied against this city, as ye have heard with your ears. **12** Then spake Jeremiah unto all the Princes and to all the people, saying, The Lord hath [i]sent me to prophesy against this House and against this city all the things that ye have heard. **13** Therefore now amend your ways, and your works, and hear the voice of the Lord your God, that the Lord may repent him of the plague, that he hath pronounced against you. **14** As for me, behold, I am in your hands: do with me as ye think good and right: **15** But know ye for certain, that if ye put me to death, ye shall surely bring innocent blood upon yourselves, and upon this city, and upon the inhabitants thereof: for of a truth the Lord hath sent me unto you, to speak all these words in your ears. **16** Then said the Princes and all the people unto the Priests, and to the Prophets, This man is not worthy to die: for he hath spoken unto us in the Name of the Lord our God. **17** Then rose up certain of the Elders of the land, and spake to all the assembly of the people, saying, **18** Micah the Morashite [1]prophesied in the days of Hezekiah king of Judah, and spake to all the people of Judah, saying, Thus saith the Lord of hosts, Zion shall be plowed like a field, and Jerusalem shall be an heap, and the mountain of the [j]house shall be as the high places of the forest. **19** Did Hezekiah King of Judah, and all Judah put him to death? did he not fear the Lord, and prayed before the Lord, and the Lord repented him of the [k]plague, that he had pronounced against them? Thus might we procure great evil against our souls. **20** And there was also a man that prophesied in the Name of the Lord, one Urijah the son of Shemaiah, of Kirjath Jearim, who prophesied against this city, and against this land, according to all the words of Jeremiah. **21** Now when Jehoiakim the king with all his men of power, and all the princes heard his words, the King sought to slay him. But when Urijah heard it, he was afraid and fled, and went into Egypt. **22** Then Jehoiakim the king [l]sent men into Egypt, even Elnathan the son of Achbor, and certain with him into Egypt. **23** And they fetched Urijah out of Egypt, and brought him unto Jehoiakim the king, who slew him with the sword, and [m]cast his dead body into the graves of the children of the people. **24** But the hand of Ahikam [n]the son of Shaphan was with Jeremiah that they should not give him into the hand of the people to put him to death.

27

1 Jeremiah at the commandment of the Lord sendeth bonds to the King of Judah and to the other Kings that were near, whereby they are monished to be subjects unto Nebuchadnezzar. 9 He warneth the people, and the Kings and rulers that they believe not false Prophets.

1 In the beginning of the reign of [a]Jehoiakim the son of Josiah King of Judah came this word unto Jeremiah from the Lord, saying, **2** Thus saith the Lord to me, Make thee [b]bonds, and yokes, and put them upon thy neck, **3** And send

---

n. Jer. 25:18 For now it beginneth and shall so continue till it be accomplished.
o. Jer. 25:20 Read Job 1:1.
p. Jer. 25:20 Which were cities of the Philistines.
q. Jer. 25:21 Edom is here taken for the whole country, and Uz for a part thereof.
r. Jer. 25:22 As Greece, Italy and the rest of those countries.
s. Jer. 25:23 These were people of Arabia which came of Dedan the son of Abraham and Keturah.
t. Jer. 25:24 For there were two countries so named, the one called plentiful, and the other barren, or desert.
u. Jer. 25:25 Or, Persia.
v. Jer. 25:26 That is, of Babylon, as Jer. 51:41.
w. Jer. 25:29 That is, Jerusalem, read verse 12.
x. Jer. 25:33 They which are slain at the Lord's appointment.
y. Jer. 25:34 Ye that are chief rulers, and governors.
z. Jer. 25:34 Which are most easily broken.
aa. Jer. 25:35 It shall not help them to seek to flee.
ab. Jer. 25:37 Hebrew, peaceable.

JER. 25
1. Jer. 16:9
2. Joel. 3:16 / Amos 1:2
3. Jer. 30:23

JER. 26
a. Jer. 26:2 That is, in that place of the Temple whereunto the people resort out of all Judah to sacrifice.
b. Jer. 26:2 To the intent that they should pretend no ignorance, as Acts 20:27.
c. Jer. 26:3 Read Jer. 18:8
d. Jer. 26:6 Read Jer. 7:12.
e. Jer. 26:6 So that when they would curse any, they shall say, God do to thee as to Jerusalem.
f. Jer. 26:9 Because of God's promises to the Temple, Ps. 132:14, that he would forever remain there, the hypocrites thought this Temple could never perish, and therefore thought it blasphemy to speak against it, Matt. 26:61; Acts 6:13, not considering that this was meant of the Church, where God will remain forever.
g. Jer. 26:10 So called, because it was repaired by Jotham, 2 Kings 15:35.
h. Jer. 26:11 Hebrew, judgments of death belongeth to this man.
i. Jer. 26:12 He both showeth the cause of his doings plainly, and also threateneth them that they should nothing avail, though they should put him to death, but heap greater vengeance upon their heads.
j. Jer. 26:18 That is, of the House of the Lord, to wit, Zion, and these examples the godly alleged to deliver Jer. out of the Priests' hands, whose rage else would not have been satisfied but by his death.
k. Jer. 26:19 So that the city was not destroyed, but by miracle was delivered out of the hands of Sennacherib.
l. Jer. 26:22 Here is declared the fury of tyrants, who cannot abide to hear God's word declared, but persecute the ministers thereof, and yet in the end they prevail nothing but provoke God's judgments so much the more.
m. Jer. 26:23 As in the first Hezekiah's example is to be followed, so in this other Jehoiakim's act is to be abhorred: for God's plague did light on him, and his household.
n. Jer. 26:24 Which declareth that nothing could have appeased their fury, if God had not moved this noble man to stand valiantly in his defense.

JER. 26
1. Mic. 1:1 / Mic. 3:12

JER. 27
a. Jer. 27:1 As touching the disposition of these prophecies, they that gathered them into a book, did not altogether observe the order of times, but did set some afore, which should be after, and contrary wise, which if the reader mark well it shall avoid many doubts, and make the reading much more easy.
b. Jer. 27:2 By such signs the Prophets used sometimes to confirm their prophecies which notwithstanding they could not do of themselves, but in as much as they had a revelation for the same, Isa. 20:2, and therefore the false Prophets to get more credit, did use also such visible signs, but they had no revelation, 1 Kings 22:12.
c. Jer. 27:6 Read Jer. 25:9.
d. Jer. 27:7 Meaning, Evil-Merodach, and his son Belshazzar.
e. Jer. 27:7 They shall bring him and his kingdom in subjection, as Jer. 25:14.

them to the king of Edom, and to the king of Moab, and to the king of the Ammonites, and to the king of Tyre, and to the king of Sidon, by the hand of the messengers which come to Jerusalem unto Zedekiah the king of Judah, **4** And command them to say unto their masters, Thus saith the Lord of hosts the God of Israel, Thus shall ye say unto your masters, **5** I have made the earth, the man, and the beast that are upon the ground, by my great power, and by my outstretched arm, and have given it unto whom it pleased me. **6** But now I have given all these lands into the hand of Nebuchadnezzar the king of Babel my [c]servant, and the beasts of the field have I also given him to serve him. **7** And all nations shall serve him, and his [d]son, and his son's son until the very time of his land come also: then many nations and great kings shall [e]serve themselves of him. **8** And the nation and kingdom which will not serve the same Nebuchadnezzar king of Babel, and that will not put their neck under the yoke of the king of Babel, the same nation will I visit saith the Lord, with the sword, and with the famine, and with the pestilence, until I have wholly given them into his hands. **9** Therefore hear not your prophets nor your soothsayers, nor your dreamers, nor your enchanters, nor your sorcerers which say unto you thus, Ye shall not serve the king of Babel. **10** For they prophesy a lie unto you to cause you to go far from your land, and that I should cast you out, and you should perish. **11** But the nation that put their necks under the yoke of the king of Babel, and serve him, those will I let remain still in their own land, saith the Lord, and they shall occupy it, and dwell therein. **12** I spake also to Zedekiah king of Judah according to all these words, saying, Put your necks under the yoke of the king of Babel, and serve him and his people, that ye may live. **13** Why will ye die, thou, and thy people by the sword, by the famine, and by the pestilence, as the Lord hath spoken against the nation, that will not serve the king of Babel? **14** Therefore hear not the words of the prophets that speak unto you, saying, Ye shall not serve the king of Babel: for they prophesy a lie unto you. **15** For I have not [1]sent them, saith the Lord, yet they prophesy a lie in my Name, that I might cast you out, and that ye might perish, both you, and the Prophets that prophesy unto you. **16** Also I spake to the Priests, and to all this people, saying, Thus saith the Lord, Hear not the words of your prophets that prophesy unto you, saying, Behold, [2]the vessels of the house of the Lord shall now shortly be [f]brought again from Babel: for they prophesy a lie unto you. **17** Hear them not, but serve the king of Babel, that ye may live: wherefore should this city be desolate? **18** But if they be Prophets, and if the word of the Lord be with them, let them [g]entreat the Lord of hosts, that the vessels, which are left in the House of the Lord, and in the house of the king of Judah, and at Jerusalem, go not to Babel. **19** For thus saith the Lord of hosts, concerning the [3]pillars, and concerning the sea, and concerning the bases, and concerning the residue of the vessels that remain in this city, **20** Which Nebuchadnezzar King of Babel took not, when he carried [4]away captive Jeconiah the son of Jehoiakim king of Judah from Jerusalem to Babel, with all the nobles of Judah, and Jerusalem. **21** For thus saith the Lord of hosts the God of Israel, concerning the vessels that remain in the house of the Lord, and in the house of the king of Judah, and at Jerusalem, **22** They shall be brought to Babel, and there they shall be until the day that I visit [h]them, saith the Lord: then will I bring them up, and restore them unto this place.

28

1 The false prophecy of Hananiah. 12 Jeremiah reproveth Hananiah, and prophesieth.

1 And that same year in the beginning of the [a]reign of Zedekiah King of Judah, in the [b]fourth year, and in the fifth month, Hananiah the son of Azur the prophet, which was of [c]Gibeon, spake to me in the house of the Lord in the presence of the Priests, and of all the people, and said, **2** Thus speaketh the Lord of hosts, the God of Israel, saying, I have broken the yoke of the King of Babel. **3** [d]Within two years space I will bring into this place all the vessels of the Lord's House, that Nebuchadnezzar king of Babel took away from this place, and carried them into Babel. **4** And I will bring again to this place Jeconiah the son of Jehoiakim King of Judah, with all them that were carried away captive of Judah, and went into Babel, saith the Lord: for I will break the yoke of the king of Babel. **5** Then the Prophet Jeremiah said unto the [e]Prophet Hananiah in the presence of the Priests, and in the presence of all the people that stood in the House of the Lord. **6** Even the Prophet Jeremiah said, So be it: the [f]Lord so do, the Lord confirm thy words which thou hast prophesied, to restore the vessels of the Lord's house, and all that is carried captive from Babel, into this place. **7** But hear thou now this word that I will speak in thine ears, and in the ears of all the people. **8** The Prophets that have been before me, and before thee in time past, [g]prophesied against many countries, and against great kingdoms, of war, and of plagues, and of pestilence. **9** And the Prophet which prophesieth of peace, when the word of the Prophet shall come to pass, then shall the Prophet be known that the Lord hath truly sent him. **10** Then Hananiah the Prophet took the yoke from the Prophet Jeremiah's neck, and [h]brake it. **11** And Hananiah spake in the presence of all the people, saying, Thus saith the Lord, Even so will I break the yoke of Nebuchadnezzar king of Babel, from the neck of all nations within the space of two years: and the Prophet Jeremiah went his way. **12** Then the word of the Lord came unto Jeremiah the Prophet, (after that Hananiah the Prophet had broken the yoke from the neck of the Prophet Jeremiah) saying, **13** Go and tell Hananiah, saying, Thus saith the Lord, Thou hast broken the yokes of wood, but thou shalt make for them yokes of iron. **14** For thus saith the Lord of hosts the God of Israel, I have put a [i]yoke of iron upon the neck of all these nations, that they may serve Nebuchadnezzar King of Babel: for they shall serve him, and I have given him the [j]beasts of the field also. **15** Then said the Prophet Jeremiah, unto the Prophet Hananiah, Hear now Hananiah, the Lord hath not sent thee, but thou makest this people to trust in a lie. **16** Therefore thus saith the Lord, Behold, I will cast thee from of the earth: this year thou shalt die, because thou hast spoken rebelliously against the Lord. **17** So Hananiah the Prophet [k]died the same year in the seventh month.

29

1 Jeremiah writeth unto them that were in captivity in Babylon. 10 He prophesieth their return after seventy years. 16 He prophesieth the destruction of the King and of the people that remain in Jerusalem. 21 He threateneth the prophets that seduce the people. 25 The death of Shemaiah is prophesied.

1 Now these are the words of the [a]book that Jeremiah the Prophet sent from Jerusalem unto [b]the residue of the Elders, which were carried away captives, and to the Priests, and to the Prophets, and to all the people, whom Nebuchadnezzar had carried away captive from Jerusalem to Babel: **2** (After that Jeconiah the King, and the [c]Queen, and the eunuchs, the [1]princes of Judah, and of Jerusalem, and the workmen, and cunning men were departed from Jerusalem) **3** By the hand of Elasah the son of Shaphan and Gemariah the son of Hilkiah, (whom Zedekiah king of Judah [d]sent unto Babel to Nebuchadnezzar king of Babel) saying, **4** Thus hath the Lord of hosts the God of Israel spoken unto all that are carried away captives, whom I have [e]caused to be carried away captives from Jerusalem unto Babel: **5** Build you houses to dwell in, and plant you gardens, and eat the fruits of them. **6** Take you wives, and beget sons and daughters, and take wives for your sons, and give your daughters husbands, that they may bear sons and daughters, that ye may be increased there, and not diminished. **7** And seek the prosperity of the city, whither I have caused you to be carried away captives, and [f]pray unto the Lord for it: for in the peace thereof shall you have peace. **8** For thus saith the Lord of hosts the God of Israel, Let not your prophets, and your soothsayers that be among you, deceive you, neither give ear to your dreams, which you dream. **9** For they prophesy you a lie in my Name: I have not sent them, saith the Lord. **10** But thus saith the Lord, that after seventy years be accomplished at Babel, I will visit you, and perform my good promise toward you, and cause you to return to this place. **11** For I know the thoughts, that I have thought towards you, saith the Lord, even the thoughts of peace, and not of trouble, to give you an end, and your hope. **12** Then shall you cry unto me, and ye shall go and pray unto me, and I will hear you, **13** And ye shall seek me, and find me, because ye shall seek me with all [g]your heart. **14** And I will be found of you, saith the Lord,

---

f. Jer. 27:16 Which were taken when Jeconiah was led captive into Babel.
g. Jer. 27:18 For it was not only the Prophet's office to show the word of God, but also to pray for the sins of the people, Gen. 20:7, which these could not do because they had no express word: for God had pronounced the contrary.
h. Jer. 27:22 That is, for the space of seventy years till I have caused the Medes and Persians to overcome the Chaldeans.

JER. 27

1. Jer. 14:14 / Jer. 23:11 / Jer. 29.9
2. Jer. 28:3
3. 2 Kings 25:13
4. 2 Kings 24:12,15

JER. 28

a. Jer. 28:1 When Jer. began to bear these bonds and yokes.
b. Jer. 28:1 After that the land hast rested, as Lev. 25:2.
c. Jer. 28:1 This was a city in Benjamin belonging to the sons of Aaron, Josh. 21:17.
d. Jer. 28:3 Hebrew, two years of days.
e. Jer. 28:5 He was so esteemed though he was a false prophet.
f. Jer. 28:6 That is, I would wish the same for God's honor, and wealth of my people, but he hath appointed the contrary.
g. Jer. 28:8 Meaning, that the Prophets that did either denounce war or peace, were tried either true or false by the success of their prophecies, albeit God maketh to come to pass sometimes that which the false prophet speaketh to try the faith of his, Deut. 13:3.
h. Jer. 28:10 This declareth the impudence of the wicked hirelings, which have no zeal to the truth, but are led with ambition to get the favor of men, and therefore cannot abide any that might discredit them but burst forth into rages and contrary to their own conscience, pass not what lies they report or how wickedly they do, so that they may maintain their estimation.
i. Jer. 28:14 That is, a hard and cruel servitude.
j. Jer. 28:14 Signifying, that all should be his, as Dan. 2:38.
k. Jer. 28:17 Seeing this thing was evident in the eyes of the people, and yet they returned not to the Lord, it is manifest, that miracles cannot move us, neither the word itself, except God touch the heart.

JER. 29

a. Jer. 29:1 Or, letter.
b. Jer. 29:1 For some died in the way.
c. Jer. 29:2 Meaning, Jeconiah's mother.
d. Jer. 29:3 To entreat of some equal conditions.
e. Jer. 29:4 To wit, the Lord, whose work this was.
f. Jer. 29:7 The Prophet speaketh not this for the affection that he bare to the tyrant, but that they should pray for the common rest and quietness, that their troubles might not be increased, and that they might with more patience and less grief wait for the time of their deliverance, which God had appointed most certain: for else not only the Israelites, but all the world, yea, and the insensible creatures should rejoice when these tyrants should be destroyed, as Isa. 14:4.
g. Jer. 29:13 When your oppression shall be great, and your afflictions cause you to repent your disobedience, and also when the seventy years of your captivity shall be expired, 2 Chron. 36:22; Ezra 1:1; Jer. 25:12; Dan. 9:2.
h. Jer. 29:15 As Ahab, Zedekiah and Shemaiah.

and I will turn away your captivity, and I will gather you from all the nations, and from all the places, whither I have cast you, saith the Lord, and will bring you again unto the place, whence I caused you to be carried away captive. **15** Because ye have said, The Lord hath raised us up [h]Prophets in Babel. **16** Therefore thus saith the Lord of the King, that sitteth upon the throne of David, and of all the people that dwell in this city, your brethren that are not gone forth with you into captivity: **17** Even thus saith the Lord of hosts, Behold, I will send upon them the [i]sword, the famine, and the pestilence, and will make them like vile [j]figs, that cannot be eaten, they are so naughty. **18** And I will persecute them with the sword, with the famine, and with the pestilence: and I will make them a terror to all kingdoms of the earth, and [k]a curse, and astonishment, and an hissing and a reproach among all the nations whither I have cast them, **19** Because they have not heard my words saith the Lord, which I sent unto them by my servants the Prophets, [l]rising up early, and sending them, but ye would not hear, saith the Lord. **20** Hear ye therefore the word of the Lord, all ye of the captivity, whom I have sent from Jerusalem to Babel. **21** Thus saith the Lord of hosts, the God of Israel, of Ahab the son of Kolaiah, and of Zedekiah the son of Maaseiah, which prophesy lies unto you in my Name, Behold, I will deliver them into the hand of Nebuchadnezzar King of Babel, and he shall slay them before your eyes. **22** And all they of the captivity of Judah, that are in Babel, shall take up this curse against them, and say, The Lord make thee like Zedekiah, and like Ahab, whom the King of Babel burnt [m]in the fire, **23** Because they have committed [n]villainy in Israel, and have committed adultery with their neighbor's wives, and have spoken lying words in my Name, which I have not commanded them, even I know it, and testify it, saith the Lord. **24** Thou shalt also speak to Shemaiah the [o]Nehelamite, saying, **25** Thus speaketh the Lord of hosts, the God of Israel, saying, Because thou hast sent letters in thy name unto all the people, that are at Jerusalem, and to Zephaniah the son of Maaseiah the Priest, and to all the Priests, saying, **26** The Lord hath made thee Priest, for [p]Jehoiada the Priest, that ye should be officers in the House of the Lord, for every man that raveth and maketh himself a Prophet, to put him in prison and in the stocks. **27** Now therefore why hast not thou reproved Jeremiah of Anathoth, which prophesieth unto you? **28** For, for this cause he sent unto us in Babel, saying, This captivity is long: build houses to dwell in, and plant gardens, and eat the fruits of them. **29** And Zephaniah the Priest read this letter in the ears of Jeremiah the Prophet. **30** Then came the word of the Lord unto Jeremiah, saying, **31** Send to all them of the captivity, saying, Thus saith the Lord of Shemaiah the Nehelamite, Because that Shemaiah hath prophesied unto you, and I sent him not, and he caused you to trust in a lie, **32** Therefore thus saith the Lord, Behold, I will visit Shemaiah the Nehelamite, and his seed: he shall not have a man [q]to dwell among this people, neither shall he behold the good, that I will do for my people, saith the Lord, because he hath spoken rebelliously against the Lord.

30

1 The return of the people from Babylon. 16 He menaceth the enemies, 18 and comforteth the Church.

1 The word, that came to Jeremiah from the Lord, saying, **2** Thus speaketh the Lord God of Israel, saying, Write thee all the words that I have spoken unto thee, in [a]a book. **3** For lo, the days come, saith the Lord, that I will bring again the captivity of my people Israel and Judah, saith the Lord: for I will restore them unto the land, that I gave to their fathers, and they shall possess it. **4** Again, these are the words that the Lord spake concerning Israel, and concerning Judah. **5** For thus saith the Lord, We have heard a [b]terrible voice, of fear and not of peace. **6** Demand now and behold, if man travail with child: wherefore do I behold every man with his hands on his loins as a woman in travail, and all faces are turned into a paleness? **7** Alas, for this [c]day is great: none hath been like it: it is even the time of Jacob's trouble, yet shall he be delivered from it. **8** [d]For in that day, saith the Lord of hosts, I will break [e]his yoke from off thy neck, and break thy bonds, and strangers shall no more serve themselves [f]of him. **9** But they shall serve the Lord their God, and [g]David their King, whom I will raise up unto them. **10** Therefore fear not, O my servant Jacob, saith the Lord, neither be afraid, O Israel: for lo, I will deliver thee from a far country, and thy seed from the land of their captivity, and Jacob shall turn again, and shall be in rest and prosperity, and none shall make him afraid. **11** For I am with thee saith the Lord, to save thee: though I utterly destroy all the nations where I have scattered thee, yet will I not utterly destroy thee, but I will correct thee by judgment, and not utterly cut thee off. **12** For thus saith the Lord, Thy bruising is incurable, and thy wound is dolorous. **13** There is none to judge thy cause, or to lay a plaster: there are no medicines, nor help for thee. **14** All thy lovers have forgotten thee: they seek thee not: for I have stricken thee with the wound of an enemy, and with a sharp chastisement for the multitude of thine iniquities, because thy sins were increased. **15** Why cryest thou for thine affliction? thy sorrow is incurable, for the multitude of thine iniquities: because thy sins were increased, I have done these things unto thee. **16** [h]Therefore all they that devour thee, shall be devoured, and all thine enemies everyone shall go into captivity, and they that spoil thee, shall be spoiled, and all they that rob thee, will I give to be robbed. **17** For I will restore health unto thee, and I will heal thee of thy wounds, saith the Lord, because they called thee, The castaway, saying, This is Zion whom no man seeketh after. **18** Thus saith the Lord, Behold, I will bring again the captivity of Jacob's tents, and have compassion on his dwelling places, and the city shall be built upon her own heap, [i]and the palace shall remain after the manner thereof. **19** And out of them shall proceed [j]thanksgiving, and the voice of them that are joyous, and I will multiply them, and they shall not be few: I will also glorify them, and they shall not be diminished. **20** Their children also shall be as afore time, and their congregation shall be established before me: and I will visit all that vex them. **21** And their [k]noble ruler shall be of themselves, and their governor shall proceed from the midst of them, and I will cause him to draw near and approach unto me: for who is this that directeth his [l]heart to come unto me, saith the Lord? **22** And ye shall be my people, and I will be your God. **23** Behold, [m]the tempest of the Lord goeth forth with wrath: the whirlwind that hangeth over, shall light upon the head of the wicked. **24** The fierce wrath of the Lord shall not return, until he have done, and until he have performed the intents of his heart: in the [n]latter days ye shall understand it.

31

1 He rehearseth God's benefits after their return from Babylon. 13 And the spiritual joy of the faithful in the Church.

1 At the [a]same time, saith the Lord, will I be the God of all the families of Israel, and they shall be my people. **2** Thus saith the Lord, The people which [b]escaped the sword, found grace in the wilderness: [c]he walketh before Israel to cause him to rest. **3** The Lord hath appeared unto me [d]of old, say they: [e]Yea, I have loved thee with an everlasting love, therefore with mercy I have drawn thee. **4** Again I will build thee, and thou shalt be built, O virgin Israel: thou shalt still [f]be adorned with thy timbrels, and shalt go forth in the dance of them that be joyful. **5** Thou shalt yet plant vines upon the mountains of [g]Samaria, and the planters that plant them, [h]shall make them common. **6** For the days shall come, that the [i]watchmen upon the mount of Ephraim shall cry, Arise, and let us go up unto [j]Zion to the Lord our God. **7** For thus saith the Lord, Rejoice with gladness for Jacob, and shout for joy among the chief of the Gentiles: publish praise and say, O Lord, save thy people, the remnant of Israel. **8** [k]Behold, I will bring them from the North country, and gather them from the coasts of the world, with the blind and the lame among them, with the woman with child, and her that is delivered also: a great company shall return hither. **9** They shall come [l]weeping, and with mercy will I bring them again: I will lead them by the rivers of [m]water

---

i. Jer. 29:17 Whereby he assureth them, that there shall be no hope of returning before the time appointed.
j. Jer. 29:17 According to the comparison, Jer. 24:1, 2.
k. Jer. 29:18 Read Jer. 26:6.
l. Jer. 29:19 Read Jer. 7:13, 25:3 and 26:5.
m. Jer. 29:22 Because they gave the people hope of speedy returning.
n. Jer. 29:23 Which was adultery, and falsifying the word of God.
o. Jer. 29:24 Or, dreamer.
p. Jer. 29:26 Shemaiah the false prophet flattereth Zephaniah the chief Priest, as though God had given him the spirit and zeal of Jehoiada to punish whosoever trespassed against the word of God, of the which he would have made Jer. one, calling him a raver and a false prophet.
q. Jer. 29:32 He and his seeds shall be destroyed, so that none of them should see the benefit of this deliverance.

JER. 29
1. Jer. 24:1

JER. 30
a. Jer. 30:2 Because they should be assured and their posterity confirmed in the hope of this deliverance promised.
b. Jer. 30:5 He showeth that before that this deliverance shall come, the Chaldeans should be extremely afflicted by their enemies, and that they should be in such perplexity and sorrow as a woman in her travail, as Isa. 13:8.
c. Jer. 30:7 Meaning, that the time of their captivity should be grievous.
d. Jer. 30:8 When I shall visit Babylon.
e. Jer. 30:8 Of the King of Babylon.
f. Jer. 30:8 To wit, of Jacob.
g. Jer. 30:9 That is, Messiah which should come of the stock of David, according to the flesh and should be the true pastor, as Ezek. 34:23, who is set forth and his kingdom that should be everlasting in the person of David, Hos. 3:5.
h. Jer. 30:16 Herein is commended God's great mercy toward his, who doth not destroy them for their sins, but correct and chastise them till he have purged and pardoned them, and so burneth the rods by the which he did punish them, Isa. 33:1.
i. Jer. 30:18 Meaning, that the city and the Temple should be restored to their former estate.
j. Jer. 30:19 He showeth how the people shall with praise and thanksgiving acknowledge these benefits.
k. Jer. 30:21 Meaning, Zerubbabel, who was the figure of Christ, in whom this was accomplished.
l. Jer. 30:21 Signifying, that Christ doth willingly submit himself to the obedience of God his father.
m. Jer. 30:23 Lest the wicked hypocrites should flatter themselves with these promises, the Prophets showeth what shall be their portion.
n. Jer. 30:24 When this Messiah and deliverer is sent.

JER. 31
a. Jer. 31:1 When this noble governor shall come, meaning, Christ, not only Judah, and Israel, but the rest of the world shall be called.
b. Jer. 31:2 Which were delivered from the cruelty of Pharaoh.
c. Jer. 31:2 To wit, God.
d. Jer. 31:3 The people thus reason as though he were not so beneficial to them now, as he had been of old.
e. Jer. 31:3 Thus the Lord answereth that his love is not changeable.
f. Jer. 31:4 Thou shalt have still occasion to rejoice: which is meant by timbrels, and dancing, as their custom was after notable victories, Exod. 15:20; Judg. 5:2 and Jer. 18:34.
g. Jer. 31:5 Because the Israelites, which were the ten tribes never returned to Samaria, therefore this must be spiritually understood under the kingdom of Christ, which was the restoration of the true Israel.
h. Jer. 31:5 That is, shall eat the fruit thereof, as Lev. 19:23-25; Deut. 20:6.
i. Jer. 31:6 The Ministers of the word.
j. Jer. 31:6 They shall exhort all to the embracing of the Gospel, as Isa. 2:3.
k. Jer. 31:8 He showeth what shall be the concord and love of all under the Gospel, when none shall be refused for their infirmities: and everyone shall exhort one another to embrace it.
l. Jer. 31:9 That is, lamenting their sins, which had not given ear to the Prophets, and therefore it followeth that God received

in a straight way, wherein they shall not stumble: for I am a father to Israel, and Ephraim is [n]my firstborn. **10** Hear the word of the Lord, O ye Gentiles, and declare in the isles afar off, and say, He that scattered Israel, will gather him, and will keep him, as a shepherd doth his flock. **11** For the Lord hath redeemed Jacob, and ransomed him from the hand [o]of him, that was stronger than he. **12** Therefore they shall come, and rejoice in the height of Zion, and shall run to the bountifulness of the Lord, even for the [p]wheat and for the wine, and for the oil, and for the increase of sheep and bullocks: and their soul shall be as a watered garden, and they shall have no more sorrow. **13** Then shall the virgin rejoice in the [q]dance, and the young men and the old men together: for I will turn their mourning into joy, and will comfort them, and give them joy for their sorrows. **14** And I will replenish the soul of the Priests with [r]fatness, and my people shall be satisfied with my goodness, saith the Lord. **15** Thus saith the Lord, A voice was heard on high, a mourning, and bitter weeping. [s]Rachel weeping for her children, refused to be comforted for her children, because they were not. **16** Thus saith the Lord, Refrain the voice from weeping, and thine eyes from tears: for thy work shall be rewarded, saith the Lord, and they shall come again from the land of the enemy: **17** And there is hope in thine end, saith the Lord, that thy children shall come again to their own borders. **18** I have heard [t]Ephraim lamenting thus, Thou hast corrected me, and I was chastised as an [u]untamed calf: [v]convert thou me, and I shall be converted: for thou art the Lord my God. **19** Surely after that I was converted, I repented, and after that I was instructed, I smote upon my [w]thigh: I was ashamed, yea, even confounded, because I did bear the reproach of my youth. **20** Is Ephraim [x]my dear son or pleasant child? yet since I spake unto him, I still [y]remembered him: therefore my bowels are troubled for him. I will surely have compassion upon him, saith the Lord. **21** Set thee up [z]signs: make thee heaps: set thine heart toward the path and way, that thou hast walked: turn again, O virgin of Israel: turn again to these thy cities. **22** How long wilt thou go astray, O thou rebellious daughter? for the Lord hath created [aa]a new thing in the earth: A WOMAN shall compass a man. **23** Thus saith the Lord of hosts the God of Israel, Yet shall they say this thing in the land of Judah, and in the cities thereof, when I shall bring again their captivity, The Lord bless thee, O habitation of justice and holy mountain. **24** And Judah shall dwell in it, and all the cities thereof together, the husbandmen and they that go forth with the flock. **25** For I have satiated the weary soul, and I have replenished every sorrowful soul. **26** Therefore I awaked and beheld, and my sleep [ab]was sweet unto me. **27** Behold, the days come, saith the Lord, that I will sow the house of Israel, and the house of Judah [ac]with the seed of man, and with the seed of beast. **28** And like as I have watched upon them, to pluck up and to root out, and to throw down, and to destroy, and to plague them, so will I watch over them, to build and to plant them, saith the Lord. **29** In those days shall they say no more, The fathers have [ad]eaten a sour grape, and the children's teeth are set on edge. **30** But everyone shall die for his own iniquity, every man that eateth the sour grape, his teeth shall be set on edge. **31** Behold, the days come, saith the Lord, that I will make a [ae]new covenant with the house of Israel, and with the house of Judah, **32** Not according to the covenant that I made with their fathers, when I took them by the hand to bring them out of the land of Egypt, the which my covenant they [af]brake, although I was [ag]an husband unto them, saith the Lord. **33** But this shall be the covenant that I will make with the house of Israel, After [ah]those days, saith the Lord, I will put my law in their inward parts, and write it in their hearts, and will be their God, and they shall be my people. **34** And they shall [ai]teach no more every man his neighbor, and every man his brother, saying, Know the Lord: for they shall all know me from the least of them unto the greatest of them, saith the Lord: for I will forgive their iniquity, and will remember their sins no more. **35** Thus saith the Lord, which giveth [aj]the sun for a light to the day, and the courses of the moon and of the stars for a light to the night, which breaketh the sea, when the waves thereof roar: his Name is the Lord of hosts. **36** If these ordinances depart out of my sight, saith the Lord, then shall the seed of Israel cease from being a nation before me, forever. **37** Thus saith the Lord, If the heavens can be measured, [ak]or the foundations of the earth be searched out beneath, then will I cast off all the seed of Israel, for all that they have done, saith the Lord. **38** Behold, the days come, saith the Lord, that the [al]city shall be built to the Lord from the tower of Hananel, unto the gate of the corner. **39** And the line of the measure shall go forth [in] his presence upon the hill Gareb, and shall compass about to Goath. **40** And the whole valley of the dead bodies, and of the ashes, and all the fields unto the brook of Kidron, and unto the corner of the horsegate toward the East, shall be holy unto the Lord, neither shall it be plucked up nor destroyed anymore forever.

32

Jeremiah is cast into prison because he prophesied that the city should be taken of the king of Babylon. 7 He showeth that the people should come again to their own possession. 38 The people of God are his servants, and he is their Lord.

1 The word that came unto Jeremiah from the Lord, in the [a]tenth year of Zedekiah king of Judah, which was the eighteenth year of Nebuchadnezzar. **2** For then the king of Babel's host besieged Jerusalem: and Jeremiah the Prophet was shut up in the court of the prison, which was in the King of Judah's house. **3** For Zedekiah king of Judah had shut him up, saying, Wherefore dost thou prophesy, and say, Thus saith the Lord, *Behold, I will give this city into the hands of the King of Babel, and he shall take it? **4** And Zedekiah the king of Judah shall not escape out of the hand of the Chaldeans, but shall surely be delivered into the hands of the king of Babel, and shall speak with him mouth to mouth, and his eyes shall behold his face, **5** And he shall lead Zedekiah to Babel, and there shall he be, until [b]I visit him, saith the Lord: though ye fight with the Chaldeans, ye shall not prosper. **6** And Jeremiah said, The word of the Lord came unto me, saying, **7** Behold, Hanamel, the son of Shallum thine uncle, shall come unto thee and say, [c]Buy unto thee my field, that is in Anathoth: for the [d]title by kindred appertaineth unto thee [e]to buy it. **8** So Hanamel mine uncle's son came to me in the court of the prison, according to the word of the Lord, and said unto me, Buy my [f]field, I pray thee, that is in Anathoth, which is in the country of Benjamin: for the right of the possession is thine, and the purchase belongeth unto thee: buy it for thee. Then I knew that this was the word of the Lord. **9** And I bought the field of Hanamel, mine uncle's son, that was in Anathoth, and weighed him the silver, even seven [g]shekels, and ten pieces of silver. **10** And I wrote it in the book and signed it, and took witnesses, and weighed him the silver in the balances. **11** So I took the book of the possession, being sealed [h]according to the Law, and custom, with the book that was open, **12** And I gave the book of the possession unto Baruch the son of Neriah, the son of Mahseiah, in the sight of Hanamel mine uncle's son, and in the presence of the witnesses, written in the book of the possession, before all the Jews that sat in the court of the prison. **13** And I

---

them to mercy, Jer. 50:4. Some take it that they should weep for joy.

m. Jer. 31:9 Where they found no impediments, but abundance of all things.

n. Jer. 31:9 That is, my dearly beloved, as the first child is to the father.

o. Jer. 31:11 That is, from the Babylonians, and other enemies.

p. Jer. 31:12 By these temporal benefits he meaneth the spiritual graces, which are in the Church, and whereof there should be ever plenty, Isa. 58:11, 12.

q. Jer. 31:13 In the company of the faithful, which ever praise God for his benefits.

r. Jer. 31:14 Meaning, the spirit of wisdom, knowledge, and zeal.

s. Jer. 31:15 To declare the greatness of God's mercy in delivering the Jews, he showeth them that they were like to the Benjamites of Israelites, that is, utterly destroyed and carried away, insomuch, that if Rachel the mother of Benjamin could have risen again to seek for her children, she should have found none remaining.

t. Jer. 31:18 That is, the people that were led captive.

u. Jer. 31:18 Which was wanton and could not be subject to the yoke.

v. Jer. 31:18 He showeth how the faithful used to pray: that is, desire God to turn them forasmuch as they cannot turn of themselves.

w. Jer. 31:19 In sign of repentance and detestation of my sin.

x. Jer. 31:20 As though he would say: No, for by his iniquity he did what lay in him to cast me off.

y. Jer. 31:20 To wit, in pity him for my promise's sake.

z. Jer. 31:21 Mark by what way thou didst go into captivity, and thou shalt turn again by the same.

aa. Jer. 31:22 Because their deliverance from Babylon, was a figure of their deliverance from sin, he showeth how this should be procured, to wit, by Jesus Christ, whom a woman should conceive and bear in her womb. Which is a strange thing in earth, because he should be born of a virgin without man, or he meaneth that Jerusalem, which was like a barren woman in her captivity, should be fruitful as she, that is joined in marriage, and whom God blesseth with children.

ab. Jer. 31:26 Having understood this vision of the Messiah to come, in whom the two houses of Israel and Judah should be joined, I rejoiced.

ac. Jer. 31:27 I will multiply and enrich them with people and cattle.

ad. Jer. 31:29 The wicked used this proverb, when they did murmur against God's judgments pronounced by the Prophets, saying, That their fathers had committed the fault and that the children were punished, Ezek. 18:3.

ae. Jer. 31:31 Though the covenant of redemption made to the fathers, and this which was given after, seem divers, yet they are all one, and grounded on Jesus Christ, save that this is called new, because of the manifestation of Christ, and the abundant graces of the holy Ghost given to his Church under the Gospel.

af. Jer. 31:32 And so were the occasion of their own divorcement through their infidelity, Isa. 50:1.

ag. Jer. 31:32 Or, master.

ah. Jer. 31:33 In the time of Christ, my law shall instead of tables of stone be written in their hearts by mine holy Spirit, Heb. 8:10.

ai. Jer. 31:34 Under the kingdom of Christ there shall be none blinded with ignorance, but I will give them faith, and knowledge of God for remission of their sins and daily increase the same: so that it shall not seem to come so much by the preaching of my ministers, as by the instruction of my holy Spirit, Isa. 54:13, but the full accomplishing hereof is referred to the kingdom of Christ, when we shall be joined with our head.

aj. Jer. 31:35 If the sun, moon and stars cannot but give light according to mine ordinance, so long as this world lasteth, so shall my Church never fail, neither shall anything hinder it: and as sure as I will have a people, so certain is it, that I will leave them my word forever to govern them with.

ak. Jer. 31:37 The one and the other is impossible.

al. Jer. 31:38 As it was performed, Neh. 3:1. By this description he showeth that the city should be as ample, and beautiful as ever it was: but he alludeth to the spiritual Jerusalem, whose beauty should be incomparable.

JER. 32

a. Jer. 32:1 So that Jer. had now prophesied from the thirteenth year of Josiah unto the last year save one of Zedekiah's reign, which was almost forty years.

b. Jer. 32:5 Till I take Zedekiah away by death: for he shall not die by the sword, as Jer. 34:4.

c. Jer. 32:7 Whereby was meant that the people should return again out of captivity and enjoy their possessions and vineyards, as verses 15 and 44.

d. Jer. 32:7 Or, right to redeem it.

e. Jer. 32:7 Because he was next of the kindred, as Ruth 4:4.

f. Jer. 32:8 Of the possession of the Levites, read Lev. 25:32.

g. Jer. 32:9 Which mounteth to of our money about ten shillings six pence, if this shekel were the common shekel, read Gen. 23:15, for the shekel of the Temple was of double value, and ten pieces of silver were half a shekel: for twenty made the shekel.

h. Jer. 32:11 According to the custom the instrument or evidence was sealed up with the common seal, and a copy thereof remained, which contained the same in effect, but was not so authentical as the other, but was left open to be seen if anything should be called into doubt.

charged Baruch before them, saying, **14** Thus saith the Lord of hosts the God of
Israel, Take the writings, even this book of the possession, both that is sealed, and
this book that is open, and put them in an earthen [i]vessel, that they may continue
a long time. **15** For the Lord of hosts, the God of Israel saith thus, Houses and
fields, and vineyards shall be possessed again in this land. **16** Now when I had
delivered the book of the possession unto Baruch the son of Neriah, I prayed unto
the Lord, saying, **17** Ah Lord God, behold, thou hast made the heaven and the
earth by thy great power, and by thy stretched out arm, and there is nothing [j]hard
unto thee. **18** [2]Thou showest mercy unto thousands, and recompensest the ini-
quity of the fathers into the bosom of their [k]children after them: O God the great
and mighty, whose name is the Lord of hosts, **19** Great in counsel, and mighty
in work, (for thine eyes are open upon all the ways of the sons of men, to give to
everyone according to his ways, and according to the fruit of his works) **20** Whi-
ch hast set signs and wonders in the land of Egypt unto this day, and in Israel and
among all men, and hast made thee a Name, [l]as appeareth this day, **21** And hast
brought thy people Israel out of the land of Egypt with signs, and with wonders,
and with a strong hand, and a stretched out arm, and with great terror, **22** And
hast given them this land, which thou didst swear to their fathers to give them,
even a land that floweth with milk and honey, **23** And they came in, and pos-
sessed it, but they obeyed not thy voice, neither walked in thy Law: all that thou
commandedst them to do, they have not done: therefore thou hast caused this
whole plague to come upon them. **24** Behold, the [m]mounts, they are come into
the city to take it, and the city is given into the hand of the Chaldeans, that fight
against it by means of the sword, and of the famine, and of the pestilence, and what
thou hast spoken, is come to pass, and behold, thou seest it. **25** And thou hast
said unto me, O Lord God, Buy unto thee the field for silver, and take witnesses:
for the city shall be given into the hand of the Chaldeans. **26** Then came the
word of the Lord unto Jeremiah, saying, **27** Behold, I am the LORD GOD of
all [n]flesh: is there anything too hard for me? **28** Therefore thus saith the Lord,
Behold, I will give this city into the hand of the Chaldeans, and into the hand of
Nebuchadnezzar, king of Babel, and he shall take it. **29** And the Chaldeans shall
come and fight against this city, and set fire on this city, and burn it with the hou-
ses, upon whose roofs they have offered incense unto Baal, and poured drink offe-
rings unto other gods, to provoke me unto anger. **30** For the children of Israel,
and the children of Judah have surely done evil before me, from their [o]youth: for
the children of Israel have surely provoked me to anger with the works of their
hands, saith the Lord. **31** Therefore this city hath been unto me as a provoca-
tion of mine anger, and of my wrath, from the day that they built it, even unto
this day, that I should remove it out of my sight, **32** Because of all the evil of the
children of Israel, and of the children of Judah, which they have done to provoke
me to anger, even they, their Kings, their Princes, their Priests, and their Prophets,
and the men of Judah, and the inhabitants of Jerusalem. **33** And they have tur-
ned unto me the back and not the face: though I taught them, [p]rising up early,
and instructing them, yet they were not obedient to receive doctrine, **34** But
they set their abominations in the house (whereupon my Name was called) to
defile it. **35** And they built the high [q]places of Baal, which are in the valley of
[r]Ben-Hinnom, to cause their sons and their daughters to [s]pass through the fire
unto Molech, which I commanded them not, neither came it into my mind, that
they should do such abomination, to cause Judah to sin. **36** And now [t]therefo-
re, thus hath the Lord God of Israel spoken concerning this city, whereof ye say,
It shall be delivered into the hand of the king of Babel by the sword, and by the
famine, and by the pestilence. **37** [3]Behold, I will gather them out of all coun-
tries, wherein I have scattered them in mine anger, and in my wrath, and in great
indignation, and I will bring them again unto this place, and I will cause them to
dwell safely. **38** And they shall be [4]my people, and I will be their God. **39** And
I will give them [u]one heart and one way, that they may fear me forever for the we-
alth of them, and of their children after them. **40** And I will make an everlasting
[v]covenant with them, that I will never turn away from them to do them good, but
I will put my fear in their hearts, that they shall not depart from me. **41** Yea, I
will delight in them to do them good, and I will plant them in this land assuredly
with my whole heart, and with all my soul. **42** For thus saith the Lord, Like as
I have brought all this great plague upon this people, so will I bring upon them all
the good that I have promised them. **43** And the fields shall be possessed in this
land, whereof ye say, it is desolate without man or beast, and shall be given into
the hand of the Chaldeans. **44** Men shall buy [w]fields for silver, and make wri-
tings and seal them, and take witnesses in the land of Benjamin, and round about
Jerusalem, and in the cities of Judah, and in the cities of the mountains, and in the
cities of the plain, and in the cities of the South: for I will cause their captivity to
return, saith the Lord.

33

1 The Prophet is monished of the Lord to pray for the deliverance of the people which the Lord promised. 8 God forgiveth sins for his own glory. 15 Of the birth of Christ. 20 The kingdom of Christ in the Church shall never be ended.

1 Moreover the word of the Lord came unto Jeremiah the second time (whi-
le he was yet shut up in the [a]court of prison) saying, **2** Thus saith the Lord,
the [b]maker thereof, the Lord that formed it, and established it, the Lord is his
Name. **3** Call unto me, and I will answer thee, and show thee great and mighty
things, which thou knowest not. **4** For thus saith the Lord God of Israel, con-
cerning the houses of this city, and concerning the houses of the Kings of Judah,
which are destroyed by the [c]mounts, and by the sword, **5** They come to [d]fight
with the Chaldeans, but it is to fill themselves with the dead bodies of men, whom
I have slain in mine anger and in my wrath: for I have hid my [e]face from this
city, because of all their wickedness. **6** Behold, I [f]will give it health and amend-
ment: for I will cure them, and will reveal unto them the abundance of peace, and
truth. **7** And I will cause the captivity of Judah and the captivity of Israel to re-
turn, and will build them as at the first. **8** And I will [g]cleanse them from all their
iniquity, whereby they have sinned against me: yea, I will pardon all their iniqui-
ties, whereby they have sinned against me, and whereby they have rebelled against
me. **9** And it shall be to me a name, a [h]joy, a praise, and an honor before all the
nations of the earth, which shall hear all the good that I do unto them: and they
shall fear and tremble for all the goodness, and for all the wealth, that I show unto
this city. **10** Thus saith the Lord, Again there shall be heard in this place (which
ye say shall be desolate, without man, and without beast, even in the cities of Ju-
dah, and in the streets of Jerusalem, that are desolate without man, and without
inhabitant, and without beast) **11** The voice of joy and the voice of gladness, the
voice of the bridegroom, and the voice of the bride, the voice of them that shall say,
[i]Praise the Lord of hosts, because the Lord is good: for his mercy endureth forever,
and of them that offer the sacrifice of praise in the house of the Lord, for I will cau-
se to return the captivity of the land, as at the first, saith the Lord. **12** Thus saith
the Lord of hosts, Again in this place, which is desolate, without man, and without
beast, and in all the cities thereof there shall be dwelling for shepherds to rest their
flocks. **13** In the cities of the [j]mountains, in the cities in the plain, and in the
cities of the South, and in the land of Benjamin and about Jerusalem, and in the
cities of Judah shall the sheep pass again, under the hand of him that telleth them,
saith the Lord. **14** Behold, the days come, saith the Lord, that I will perform that
good thing, which I have promised unto the house of Israel, and to the house of
Judah. **15** In those days, and at that time will I cause [k]the Branch of righteou-
sness to grow up unto David, and he shall execute judgment and righteousness in
the land. **16** In those days shall Judah be saved, and Jerusalem shall dwell safely,
and he that shall call [l]her, is the Lord our [m]righteousness. **17** For thus saith the
Lord, David shall never want a man to sit upon the throne of the house of Isra-
el. **18** Neither shall the Priests and Levites want a man before me to offer [n]burnt
offerings, and to offer meat offerings, and to do sacrifice continually. **19** And the
word of the Lord came unto Jeremiah, saying, **20** Thus saith the Lord, If you can

---

i. Jer. 32:14 And so to hide them in the ground, that they might be preserved as a token of their deliverance.
j. Jer. 32:17 Or, hid.
k. Jer. 32:18 Because the wicked are subject to the curse of God, he showeth that their posterity which by nature are under this malediction, shall be punisheth both for their own wickedness, and that the iniquity of their fathers, which is likewise in them, shall be also revenged on their head.
l. Jer. 32:20 Meaning, that his miracles in delivering his people, should never be forgotten.
m. Jer. 32:24 The word signifieth anything that is cast up, as a mount or rampart, and is also used for engines of war, which were laid on an high place to shoot into a city before that guns were in use.
n. Jer. 32:27 That is, of every creature: who as they are his work, so doth he govern and guide them as pleaseth him, whereby he showeth that as he is the author of this their captivity for their sins, so will he for his mercies be their redeemer to restore them again to liberty.
o. Jer. 32:30 From the time that I brought them out of Egypt, and made them my people, and called them my firstborn.
p. Jer. 32:33 Read Prov. 1:24; Isa. 65:2; Jer. 7:13 and 13:3 and 26:5 and 29:19; and 2 Chron. 36:15; Jer. 35:14 and 44:4.
q. Jer. 32:35 That is, the altars which were made to offer sacrifices upon to their idols.
r. Jer. 32:35 Read Jer. 7:31; 2 Kings 21:4, 6.
s. Jer. 32:35 Read 2 Kings 16:3.
t. Jer. 32:36 Read Jer. 30:16.
u. Jer. 32:39 One consent and one religion, as Ezek. 11:19 and 36:27.
v. Jer. 32:40 Read Jer. 31, 32, 33.
w. Jer. 32:44 This is the declaration of that which was spoken verse 8.

JER. 32

1. Jer. 29:16,17 / Jer. 34:2
2. Exod. 34:7 / Deut. 5:9
3. Deut. 30:3
4. Jer. 30:22

JER. 33

a. Jer. 33:1 Which was in the king's house at Jerusalem, as Jer. 32:1, 2.
b. Jer. 33:2 To wit, of Jerusalem, who as he made it, so will he preserve it, read Isa. 37:26.
c. Jer. 33:4 Read Jer. 32:24.
d. Jer. 33:5 The Jews think to overcome the Chaldeans, but they seek their own destruction.
e. Jer. 33:5 He showeth that God's favor is cause of all prosperity, as his anger is of all adversity.
f. Jer. 33:6 In the midst of his threatenings God remembereth his, and comforteth them.
g. Jer. 33:8 Declaring that there is no deliverance nor joy, but whereas we feel remission of sins.
h. Jer. 33:9 Whereby he showeth that the Church wherein is remission of sins, is God's honor and glory, so that whosoever is enemy to it, laboreth to dishonor God.
i. Jer. 33:11 Which was a song appointed for the Levites to praise God by, 1 Chron. 16:8; Ps. 105:1; Isa. 12:4; Ps. 106:1; 107:1; 118:1; 136:1.
j. Jer. 33:13 Meaning, that all the country of Judah shall be inhabited again.
k. Jer. 33:15 That is, I will send the Messiah, which shall come of the house of David, of whom this prophecy is meant, as testify all the Jews, and that which is written, Jer. 23:5.
l. Jer. 33:16 To wit, Christ that shall call his Church.
m. Jer. 33:16 That is, Christ is our Lord God, our righteousness, sanctification, and redemption, 1 Cor. 1:30.
n. Jer. 33:18 That is chiefly meant of the spiritual sacrifice of thanksgiving, which is left to the Church in the time of Christ, who was the everlasting Priest, and the everlasting sacrifice figured by the sacrifices of the Law.
o. Jer. 33:20 Read Jer. 31:35.
p. Jer. 33:24 Meaning, the Chaldeans and other infidels which thought God had utterly cast off Judah and Israel or Benjamin, because he did correct them for a time for their amendment.

break my covenant of the [o]day, and my covenant of the night, that there should
not be day and night in their season, **21** Then may my covenant be broken with
David my servant, that he should not have a son to reign upon his throne, and
with the Levites, and Priests my ministers. **22** As the army of heaven cannot be
numbered, neither the sand of the sea measured: so will I multiply the seed of Da-
vid my servant, and the Levites, that minister unto me. **23** Moreover, the word
of the Lord came to Jeremiah, saying, **24** Considerest thou not what [p]this people
have spoken, saying, The two families, which the Lord hath chosen, he hath even
cast them off? thus they have despised my people, that they should be no more a
nation before them. **25** Thus saith the Lord, If my covenant be not with day and
night, and if I have not appointed the order of heaven and earth, **26** Then will
I cast away the seed of Jacob and David my servant, and not take of his seed to be
rulers over the seed of Abraham, Isaac, and Jacob: for I will cause their captivity to
return, and have compassion on them.

34

1 He threateneth that the city, and the King Zedekiah shall be given into the hands of the king of Babylon. 11 He rebuketh their cruelty toward their servants.

1 The word which came unto Jeremiah from the Lord (when [a]Nebuchadnez-
zar king of Babel, and all his host, and all the kingdoms of the earth, that were un-
der the power of his hand, and all people fought against Jerusalem, and against all
the cites thereof) saying, **2** Thus saith the Lord God of Israel, Go, and speak to
Zedekiah king of Judah, and tell him, Thus saith the Lord, behold, [1]I will give this
city into the hand of the king of Babel, and he shall burn it with fire, **3** And thou
shall not escape out of his hand, but shalt surely be taken, and delivered into his
hand, and thine eyes shall behold the face of the king of Babel, and he shall speak
with thee mouth to mouth, and thou shalt go to Babel. **4** Yet hear the word of
the Lord, O Zedekiah king of Judah, thus saith the Lord of thee, Thou shalt not
die by the sword, **5** But thou shalt die in [b]peace: and according to the burning
for thy fathers the former kings which were before thee, so shall they burn odors
for thee, and they shall lament thee, saying, Oh [c]Lord: for I have pronounced the
word, saith the Lord. **6** Then Jeremiah the Prophet spake all these words unto
Zedekiah king of Judah in Jerusalem, **7** (When the King of Babel's host fought
against Jerusalem, and against all the cities of Judah, that were left, even against
Lachish, and against Azekah: for these strong cities remained of the cities of Ju-
dah) **8** This is the word that came unto Jeremiah from the Lord, after that the
king Zedekiah had made a covenant with all the people, which were at Jerusalem,
[d]to proclaim liberty unto them, **9** That every man should let his [e]servant go
free, and every man his handmaid, which was an Hebrew or an Hebrewess, and
that none should serve himself of them, to wit, of a Jew his brother. **10** Now
when all the princes, and all the people which was agreed to the covenant, he-
ard that everyone should let his servant go free, and everyone his handmaid, and
that none should serve themselves of them anymore, they obeyed and let them
go. **11** But afterward they [f]repented and caused the servants and the handmaids,
whom they had let go free, to return, and held them in subjection as servants and
handmaids. **12** Therefore the word of the Lord came unto Jeremiah from the
Lord, saying, **13** Thus saith the Lord God of Israel, I made a covenant with your
fathers, when I brought them out of the land of Egypt, out of the house of [g]ser-
vants, saying, **14** [2]At the term of seven years, let ye go every man his brother an
Hebrew which hath been sold unto thee: and when he hath served thee six years,
thou shalt let him go free from thee: but your fathers obeyed me not, neither in-
clined their ears. **15** And ye were now turned, and had done right in my sight
in proclaiming liberty, every man to his neighbor, and ye had made a covenant be-
fore me in [h]the house, whereupon my Name is called. **16** But ye repented, and
polluted my Name: for ye have caused every man his servant, and every man his
handmaid, whom ye had set at liberty at their pleasure, to return, and hold them
in subjection to be unto you as servants and as handmaids. **17** Therefore thus
saith the Lord, Ye have not obeyed me, in proclaiming freedom every man to his
brother, and every man to his neighbor: behold, I proclaim a liberty for you, saith
the Lord, to [i]the sword, to the pestilence, and to the famine, and I will make you
a terror to all the kingdoms of the earth. **18** And I will give those men that have
broken my Covenant, and have not kept the words of the Covenant, which they
had made before me, when they [j]cut the calf in twain, and passed between the par-
ts thereof, **19** The princes of Judah, and the princes of Jerusalem, the Eunuchs,
and the Priests, and all the people of the land, which passed between the parts of
the calf, **20** I will even give them into the hand of their enemies, and into the
hands of them that seek their life: and their dead bodies shall be for meat unto the
fowls of the heaven, and to the beasts of the earth. **21** And Zedekiah king of Ju-
dah, and his princes will I give into the hand of their enemies, and into the hand of
them that seek their life, and into the hand of the king of Babel's host, which [k]are
gone up from you. **22** Behold, I will command, saith the Lord, and cause them
to return to this city, and they shall fight against it, and take it and burn it with fire:
and I will make the cities of Judah desolate without an inhabitant.

35

He purposeth the obedience of the Rechabites, and thereby confoundeth the pride of the Jews.

1 The word which came unto Jeremiah from the Lord, in the days [a]of Jehoia-
kim the son of Josiah king of Judah, saying, **2** Go unto the house of the [b]Recha-
bites, and speak unto them, and bring them into the house of the Lord into one of
the chambers, and give them wine to drink. **3** Then took I Jaazaniah, the son of
Jeremiah the son of Habazziniah, and his brethren, and all his sons, and the who-
le house of the Rechabites, **4** And I brought them into the house of the Lord,
into the chamber of the sons of Hanan the son of Igdaliah a man [c]of God, which
was by the chamber of the princes, which was above the chamber of Maaseiah the
son of Shallum, the keeper of the [d]treasure. **5** And I set before the sons of the
house of the Rechabites pots full of wine, and cups, and [e]said unto them, Drink
wine. **6** But they said, We will drink no wine: for [f]Jonadab the son of Rechab our
father commanded us, saying, [g]Ye shall drink no wine, neither you nor your sons
forever. **7** Neither shall ye build house, nor sow seed, nor plant vineyard, nor
have any, but all your days ye shall dwell in tents, that ye may live a long time in
the land where ye be strangers. **8** Thus have we obeyed the voice of Jonadab the
son of Rechab our father, in all that he hath charged us, and we drink no wine all
our days, neither we, our wives, our sons, nor our daughters. **9** Neither build we
houses for us to dwell in, neither have we vineyard, nor field, nor seed, **10** But
we have remained in tents, and have obeyed, and done according to [h]all that Jo-
nadab our father commanded us. **11** But when Nebuchadnezzar king of Babel
came up into the land, we said, Come, and let us go to Jerusalem, from the host of
the Chaldeans, and from the host of Aram: so we [i]dwell at Jerusalem. **12** Then
came the word of the Lord unto Jeremiah, saying, **13** Thus saith the Lord of
hosts, the God of Israel, Go, and tell the men of Judah, and the inhabitants of Je-
rusalem, Will [j]ye not receive doctrine to obey my words, saith the Lord? **14** The
commandment of Jonadab the son of Rechab that he commanded his sons, that
they should drink no wine, is surely kept: for unto this day they drink none, but
obey their father's commandment: notwithstanding I have spoken unto you, [k]ri-
sing early, and speaking, but ye would not obey me. **15** I have sent also unto you
all my servants the Prophets: rising up early, and sending them, saying, [1]Return
now every man from his evil way, and amend your works, and go not after other
gods to serve them, and ye shall dwell in the land which I have given unto you, and
to your fathers, but ye would not incline your ear, nor obey me. **16** Surely the
sons of Jonadab the son of Rechab, have kept the commandment of their father,
which he gave them, but this people hath not obeyed me. **17** [2]Therefore thus
saith the Lord of hosts, the God of Israel, Behold, I will bring upon Judah, and
upon all the inhabitants of Jerusalem, all the evil that I have pronounced against
them, because I have [l]spoken unto them, but they would not hear, and I have cal-
led unto them, but they would not answer. **18** And Jeremiah said to the house
of the Rechabites, Thus saith the Lord of hosts, the God of Israel, Because ye have
obeyed the commandment of Jonadab your father, and kept all his precepts, and
done according unto all that he hath commanded you, **19** Therefore thus saith
the Lord of hosts, the God of Israel, Jonadab the son of Rechab shall [m]not want a
man, to stand before me forever.

JER. 34

- **a.** Jer. 34:1 Who commonly of Jer. was called Nebuchadrezzar, and of others Nebuchadnezzar.
- **b.** Jer. 34:5 Not of any violent death.
- **c.** Jer. 34:5 The Jews shall lament for thee their lord and king.
- **d.** Jer. 34:8 When the enemy was at hand, and they saw themselves in danger, they would seem holy, and so began some kind of reformation: but soon after they uttered their hypocrisy.
- **e.** Jer. 34:9 According to the Law, Exod. 21:2; Deut. 15:12.
- **f.** Jer. 34:11 Hebrew, returneth.
- **g.** Jer. 34:13 Or, bondage.
- **h.** Jer. 34:15 Meaning, in the Temple, to declare that it was a most solemn and straight covenant, made in the Name of the Lord.
- **i.** Jer. 34:17 That is, I give the sword liberty to destroy you.
- **j.** Jer. 34:18 As touching this manner of solemn covenant which the ancients used by passing between the two parts of a beast, to signify that the transgressor of the same covenant should be so divided in pieces, read Gen. 15:10.
- **k.** Jer. 34:21 To fight against the Egyptians, as Jer. 37:11.

JER. 34

- **1.** 2Chron. 36:19 / Jer. 29:16,17 / Jer. 32:3
- **2.** Deut. 15:1,12

JER. 35

- **a.** Jer. 35:1 For the disposition and order of these prophecies, read Jer. 27:1.
- **b.** Jer. 35:2 They came of Hobab Moses' father-in-law, who was no Israelite, but after joined with them in the service of God.
- **c.** Jer. 35:4 That is, a Prophet.
- **d.** Jer. 35:4 Or, door.
- **e.** Jer. 35:5 The Prophet saith not. The Lord saith thus, for then they ought to have obeyed, but he tendeth to another end: that is, to declare their obedience to man, seeing the Jews would not obey God himself.
- **f.** Jer. 35:6 Whom Jehu the King of Israel favored for his zeal, 2 Kings 10:15.
- **g.** Jer. 35:6 Teaching them hereby to flee all occasion of intemperancy, ambition and avarice, and that they might know that they were strangers in the earth, and be ready to depart at all occasions.
- **h.** Jer. 35:10 Which was now for the space of three hundred years from Jehu to Jehoiakim.
- **i.** Jer. 35:11 Which declareth that they were not so bound to their vow, that it could not be broken for any necessity: for where they were commanded to dwell in tents, they dwell now at Jerusalem for fear of the wars.
- **j.** Jer. 35:13 Whom I have chosen to be my children, seeing these which were the children of an heathen man, obeyed the commandment of their father.
- **k.** Jer. 35:14 I have most diligently exhorted and warned you both by myself and my Prophet.
- **l.** Jer. 35:17 That is, by his Prophets and ministers, which showeth that it is as much, as though he should speak to us himself, when he sendeth his ministers to speak in his Name.
- **m.** Jer. 35:19 His posterity shall continue and be in my favor forever.

JER. 35

- **1.** Jer. 18:11 / Jer. 25:5

36

Baruch writeth as Jeremiah inditeth, the book of the curses against Judah and Israel. 9 He is sent with the book unto the people, and readeth it before them all. 14 He is called before the rulers, and readeth it before them also. 23 The king casteth it in the fire. 28 There is another written at the commandment of the Lord.

1 And in the fourth [a]year of Jehoiakim the son of Josiah king of Judah came this word unto Jeremiah from the Lord, saying, **2** Take thee a roll or book, and write therein all the words that I have spoken to thee against Israel, and against Judah, and against all the nations, from the day that I spake unto thee, even [b]from the days of Josiah unto this day. **3** It may be that the house of Judah will hear of all the evil, which I determined to do unto them, that they may return every man from his evil way, that I may forgive their iniquity and their sins. **4** Then Jeremiah called Baruch the son of Neriah, and Baruch wrote [c]at the mouth of Jeremiah all the words of the Lord, which he had spoken unto him, upon a roll or book. **5** And Jeremiah commanded Baruch, saying, I am [d]shut up, and cannot go into the House of the Lord. **6** Therefore go thou, and read the roll wherein thou hast written at my mouth the words of the Lord, in the audience of the people in the Lord's house upon the [e]fasting day: also thou shalt read them in the hearing of all Judah, that come out of their cities. **7** It may be that they will [f]pray before the Lord, and everyone return from his evil way, for great is the anger and the wrath that the Lord hath declared against this people. **8** So Baruch the son of Neriah did according unto all, that Jeremiah the Prophet commanded him, reading in the book the words of the Lord in the Lord's house. **9** And in the fifth [g]year of Jehoiakim the son of Josiah King of Judah, in the ninth month, they proclaimed a fast before the Lord to all the people in Jerusalem, and to all the people that came from the cities of Judah unto Jerusalem. **10** Then read Baruch in the book the words of Jeremiah in the house of the Lord, in the chamber of Gemariah the son of Shaphan the Secretary, in the higher court at the entry of the [h]new gate of the Lord's house in the hearing of all the people. **11** When Michaiah the son of Gemariah, the son of Shaphan had heard out of the book all the words of the Lord, **12** Then he went down to the King's house into the Chancellor's chamber, and lo, all the princes sat there, even Elishama the Chancellor, and Delaiah the son of Shemaiah, and Elnathan the son of Achbor, and Gemariah the son of Shaphan, and Zedekiah the son of Hananiah, and all the princes. **13** Then Michaiah declared unto them all the words that he had heard when Baruch read in the book in the audience of the people. **14** Therefore all the princes sent Jehudi the son of Nethaniah, the son of Shelemiah, the son of Cushi, unto Baruch, saying, Take in thine hand the roll, wherein thou hast read in the audience of the people, and come. So Baruch the son of Neriah took the roll in his hand, and came unto them. **15** And they said unto him, Sit down now, and read it, that we may hear. So Baruch read it in their audience. **16** Now when they had heard all the words, they were [i]afraid both one and other, and said unto Baruch, We will certify the King of all these words. **17** And they examined Baruch, saying, Tell us now, how didst thou write all these words at his mouth? **18** Then Baruch answered them, He pronounced all these words unto me with his mouth, and I wrote them with ink in the book. **19** Then said the princes unto Baruch, Go, [j]hide thee, thou and Jeremiah, and let no man know where ye be. **20** And they went in to the king to the court, but they laid up the roll in the chamber of Elishama the Chancellor, and told the King all the words, that he might hear. **21** So the King sent Jehudi to fetch the roll, and he took it out of Elishama the Chancellor's chamber, and Jehudi read it in the audience of the King, and in the audience of all the princes, which stood beside the King. **22** Now the King sat in the winter house, in the [k]ninth month, and there was a fire burning before him. **23** And when Jehudi had read three or four sides, he cut it with the penknife, and cast it into the fire that was on the hearth, until all the roll was consumed in the fire, that was on the hearth. **24** Yet they were not afraid, nor rent [l]their garments, neither the King, nor any of his servants that heard all these words. **25** Nevertheless, Elnathan, and Delaiah, and Gemariah had besought the King, that he would not burn the roll: but he would not hear them. **26** But the King commanded Jerahmeel the son of Hammelech, and Seraiah the son of Azriel, and Shelemiah the son of Abdeel, to take Baruch the Scribe, and Jeremiah the Prophet, but the Lord [m]hid them. **27** Then the word of the Lord came to Jeremiah (after that the King had burnt the roll and the words that Baruch wrote at the mouth of Jeremiah) saying, **28** Take thee again [n]another roll, and write in it all the former words that were in the first roll which Jehoiakim the King of Judah hath burnt, **29** And thou shalt say to Jehoiakim King of Judah, Thus saith the Lord, thou hast burnt this roll, saying, [o]Why hast thou written therein, saying, That the King of Babel shall certainly come and destroy this land, and shall take thence both man and beast? **30** Therefore thus saith the Lord of Jehoiakim King of Judah, He shall have [p]none to sit upon the throne of David, and his [q]dead body shall be cast out in the day to the heat, and in the night to the frost. **31** And I will visit him and his seed, and his servants for their iniquity, and I will bring upon them, and upon the inhabitants of Jerusalem, and upon the men of Judah all the evil that I have pronounced against them: but they would not hear. **32** Then took Jeremiah another roll, and gave it to Baruch the Scribe the son of Neriah, which wrote therein at the mouth of Jeremiah all the words of the book which Jehoiakim King of Judah had burnt in the fire, and there were added besides them many like words.

37

1 Zedekiah succeedeth Jeconiah. 3 He sendeth unto Jeremiah to pray for him. 12 Jeremiah going into the land of Benjamin is taken. 15 He is beaten and put in prison.

1 And [1]King Zedekiah the son of Josiah reigned for [a]Coniah the son of Jehoiakim, whom Nebuchadnezzar king of Babel [b]made king in the land of Judah. **2** But neither he, nor his servants, nor the people of the land would obey the words of the Lord which he spake by the [c]ministry of the Prophet Jeremiah. **3** And Zedekiah the king [d]sent Jehucal the son of Shelemiah, and Zephaniah the son of Maaseiah the Priest to the Prophet Jeremiah, saying, Pray now unto the Lord our God for us. **4** (Now Jeremiah went [e]in and out among the people: for they had not put him into the prison. **5** Then Pharaoh's host was [f]come out of Egypt: and when the Chaldeans that besieged Jerusalem, heard tidings of them, they [g]departed from Jerusalem.) **6** Then came the word of the Lord unto the Prophet Jeremiah, saying, **7** Thus saith the Lord God of Israel, Thus shall ye say to the King of Judah, that sent you unto me to inquire of me, Behold, Pharaoh's host, which is come forth to help you, shall return to Egypt into their own land. **8** And the Chaldeans shall come again, and fight against this city, and take it and burn it with fire. **9** Thus saith the Lord, [h]Deceive not yourselves, saying, The Chaldeans shall surely depart from us: for they shall not depart. **10** For though ye had smitten the whole host of the Chaldeans that fight against you, and there remained, but wounded men among them, yet should every man rise up in his tent, and burn this city with fire. **11** When the host of the Chaldeans was broken up from Jerusalem, because of Pharaoh's army, **12** Then Jeremiah went out of Jerusalem to go into the [i]land of Benjamin, separating himself thence from among the people. **13** And when he was in the [j]gate of Benjamin, there was a chief officer, whose name was Irijah, the son of Shelemiah, the son of Hananiah, and he took Jeremiah the Prophet, saying, Thou [k]fleest to the Chaldeans. **14** Then said Jeremiah, That is false, I flee not to the Chaldeans: but he would not hear him: so Irijah took Jeremiah, and brought him to the princes. **15** Wherefore the princes were angry with Jeremiah, and smote him, and laid him in prison in the house of Jehonathan the Scribe: for they had made that the [l]prison. **16** When Jeremiah was entered into the dungeon, and into the prisons, and had remained there a long time, **17** Then Zedekiah the king sent, and took him out, and the king asked him secretly, in his house, and said, Is there any word from the Lord? And Jeremiah said, Yea: for, said he, thou shalt be delivered into the hand of the king of Babel. **18** Moreover, Jeremiah said unto king Zedekiah, What have I offended against thee, or against thy servants, or against this people, that ye have put me in prison? **19** [2]Where are now your prophets, which prophesied unto you, saying, The king of Babel shall not come against you, nor against this land? **20** Therefore hear now, I pray thee, O my lord the King: let my prayer be [m]acceptable before thee, that thou cause me not to return to the house of Jehonathan the scribe, lest I die there. **21** Then Zedekiah the King commanded,

---

JER. 36

a. Jer. 36:1 Read Jer. 25:1.
b. Jer. 36:2 Which were twenty and three years, as Jer. 25:3, counting from the thirteenth year of Josiah's reign.
c. Jer. 36:4 As he did indite.
d. Jer. 36:5 Meaning, in prison, through the malice of the Priests.
e. Jer. 36:6 Which was proclaimed for fear of the Babylonians, as their custom was when they feared war, or any great plague of God.
f. Jer. 36:7 He showeth that fasting without prayer and repentance, availeth nothing, but is mere hypocrisy.
g. Jer. 36:9 The fast was then proclaimed, and Baruch read this rule, which was a little before that Jerusalem was first taken, and then Jehoiakim, and Daniel and his companions were led away captives.
h. Jer. 36:10 Which is the East gate of the Temple.
i. Jer. 36:16 The godly were afraid, seeing God so offended, and the wicked were astonied for the horror of the punishment.
j. Jer. 36:19 They that were godly among the princes gave this counsel, by whose means it is like that Jer. was delivered: for they knew the rage of the king and of the wicked to be such, that they could not escape without danger of their lives.
k. Jer. 36:22 Which contained part of November, and part of December.
l. Jer. 36:24 Showing that the wicked instead of repenting when they hear God's judgments, grow into further malice against him and his word.
m. Jer. 36:26 Thus we see the continual care, that God hath ever over his to preserve them from the rage of the wicked.
n. Jer. 36:28 Though the wicked think to have abolished the word of God, when they have burnt the book thereof: yet this declareth that God will not only raise it up again, but also increase it in greater abundance to their condemnation, as verse 32.
o. Jer. 36:29 These are Jehoiakim's words.
p. Jer. 36:30 Though Jehoiachin his son succeeded him, yet because he reigned but three months, it was esteemed as no reign.
q. Jer. 36:30 Read Jer. 22:19.

JER. 37

a. Jer. 37:1 Who was called Jehoiachin, or Jeconiah.
b. Jer. 37:1 And called him Zedekiah, whereas before his name was Mattaniah, 2 Kings 24:17.
c. Jer. 37:2 Hebrew, hand.
d. Jer. 37:3 Because he was afraid of the Chaldeans that came against him.
e. Jer. 37:4 That is, was out of prison, and at liberty.
f. Jer. 37:5 To help the Jews.
g. Jer. 37:5 Hebrew, went up.
h. Jer. 37:9 Or, lift not up your minds.
i. Jer. 37:12 As some think, to go to Anathoth his own town.
j. Jer. 37:13 By the which men went into the country of Benjamin.
k. Jer. 37:13 Hebrew, fallest.
l. Jer. 37:15 Because it was a vile and straight prison.
m. Jer. 37:20 Hebrew, fall.
n. Jer. 37:21 That is, so long as there was any bread in the city: thus God provideth for his, that he will cause their enemies to preserve them to that end whereunto he hath appointed them.

that they should put Jeremiah in the court of the prison, and that they should give him daily a piece of bread out of the baker's street until all the [n]bread in the city were eaten up. Thus Jeremiah remained in the court of the prison.

38

1 By the motion of the rulers Jeremiah is put into a dungeon. 14 At the request of Ebed-Melech the King commandeth Jeremiah to be brought forth of the dungeon. 17 Jeremiah showeth the King how he might escape death.

1 Then Shephatiah the son of Mattan, and Gedaliah the son of Pashhur, and Jucal the son of Shelemiah, and Pashhur the son of [a]Malchiah, heard the words that Jeremiah had spoken unto all the people, saying, **2** Thus saith the Lord, He that remaineth in this city, shall die by the sword, by the famine and by the pestilence: but he that goeth forth to the Chaldeans, shall live: for he shall have his life for [b]a prey, and shall live. **3** Thus saith the Lord, This city shall surely be given into the hand of the king of Babel's army, which shall take it. **4** Therefore the Princes said unto the king, We beseech you, let this man be put to death: for thus he [c]weakeneth the hands of the men of war [d]that remain in this city, and the hands of all the people, in speaking such words unto them: for this man seeketh not the wealth of this people, but the hurt. **5** Then Zedekiah the king said, Behold, he is in your hands, for the king can deny [e]you nothing. **6** Then took they Jeremiah, and cast him into the dungeon of Malchiah the son of Hammelech, that was in the court of the prison: and they let down Jeremiah with cords: and in the dungeon there was no water but mire: so Jeremiah stuck fast in the mire. **7** Now when Ebed-Melech ye [f]black Moor, one of the Eunuchs which was in the king's house, heard that they had put Jeremiah in the dungeon, (then the king sat in the [g]gate of Benjamin) **8** And Ebed-Melech went out of the king's house, and spake to the king, saying, **9** My lord the king, [h]these men have done evil in all that they have done to Jeremiah the Prophet, whom they have cast into the dungeon, and he dieth for hunger in the place where he is: for there is no more bread in the city. **10** Then the king commanded Ebed-Melech the black Moor, saying, Take from hence thirty men [i]with thee, and take Jeremiah the Prophet out of the dungeon before he die. **11** So Ebed-Melech took the men with him, and went to the house of the king under the treasury, and took there old rotten rags, and old worn clouts, and let them down by cords into the dungeon to Jeremiah. **12** And Ebed-Melech the black Moor said unto Jeremiah, Put now these old rotten rags and worn, under thine arm holes, between the cords. And Jeremiah did so. **13** So they drew up Jeremiah with cords, and took him up out of the dungeon, and Jeremiah remained in the [j]court of the prison. **14** Then Zedekiah the king sent, and took Jeremiah the Prophet unto him, into the third entry that is in the House of the Lord, and the king said unto Jeremiah, I will ask thee a thing: hide nothing from me. **15** Then Jeremiah said to Zedekiah, If I declare it unto thee, wilt thou not slay me? and if I give thee counsel, thou wilt not hear me. **16** So the King sware secretly unto Jeremiah, saying, As the Lord liveth, that made us these souls, I will not slay thee, nor give thee into the hands of those men that seek thy life. **17** Then said Jeremiah unto Zedekiah, Thus saith the Lord God of hosts the God of Israel, If thou wilt go forth unto the king of Babel's [k]princes, then thy soul shall live, and this city shall not be burnt up with fire, and thou shalt live, and thine house. **18** But if thou wilt not go forth to the king of Babel's princes, then shall this city be given into the hand of the Chaldeans, and they shall burn it with fire, and thou shalt not escape out of their hands. **19** And Zedekiah the king said unto Jeremiah, I am careful for the Jews that are fled unto the Chaldeans, lest they deliver me into their hands, and they [l]mock me. **20** But Jeremiah said, They shall not deliver thee: hearken unto the voice of the Lord, I beseech thee, which I speak unto thee: so shall it be well unto thee, and thy soul shall live. **21** But if thou wilt refuse to go forth, this is the word that the Lord hath showed me. **22** And behold, all the women that are [m]left in the king of Judah's house, shall be brought forth to the king of Babel's princes, and those women shall say, Thy friends have persuaded thee, and have prevailed against thee: thy feet are fastened in the mire, and they are turned back. **23** So they shall bring out all thy wives, and thy children to the Chaldeans, and thou shalt not escape out of their hands, but shalt be taken by the hand of the king of Babel: and this city shalt thou cause to be burnt with fire. **24** Then said Zedekiah unto Jeremiah, Let no man know of these words, and thou shalt not die. **25** But if the princes understand that I have talked with thee, and they come unto thee, and say unto thee, Declare unto us now, what thou hast said unto the king, hide it not from us, and we will not slay thee: also what the King said unto thee, **26** Then shalt thou say unto them, I humbly [n]besought the king that he would not cause me to return to Jonathan's house, to die there. **27** Then came all the princes unto Jeremiah and asked him, And he told them according to all these words that the king had commanded: so they left off speaking with him, for the matter was not perceived. **28** So Jeremiah abode still in the court of the prison until the day that Jerusalem was taken: and he was there when Jerusalem was taken.

39

2 Nebuchadnezzar beseigeth Jerusalem. 4 Zedekiah fleeing, is taken of the Chaldeans. 6 His sons are slain. 7 His eyes are thrust out. 11 Jeremiah is provided for. 26 Ebed-Melech is delivered from captivity.

1 In [1]the ninth year of Zedekiah King of Judah in the tenth month, came Nebuchadnezzar King of Babel and all his host against Jerusalem, and they besieged it. **2** And in the eleventh year of Zedekiah in the fourth month, the ninth day of the month, the city was broken [a]up. **3** And all the princes of the King of Babel came in, and sat in the middle gate, even Nergal-Sharezer, Samgar-Nebo, Sarsechim, Rabsaris, Nergal-Sharezer, Rabmag, with all the residue of the princes of the king of Babel. **4** And when Zedekiah the king of Judah saw them, and all the men of war, then they fled, and went out of the city by night, through the king's garden, and by the [b]gate between the two walls, and he went toward the wilderness. **5** But the Chaldean's host pursued after them, and overtook Zedekiah in the desert of Jericho: and when they had taken him, they brought him to Nebuchadnezzar king of Babel unto [c]Riblah in the land of Hamath, where he gave judgment upon him. **6** Then the king of Babel slew the sons of Zedekiah in Riblah before his eyes: also the king of Babel slew all the nobles of Judah. **7** Moreover he put out Zedekiah's eyes, and bound him in chains to carry him to Babel. **8** And the Chaldeans burnt the king's house, and the houses of the people with fire, and brake down the walls of Jerusalem. **9** Then Nebuzaradan the [d]chief steward carried away captive into Babel the remnant of the people that remained in the city, and those that were fled and fallen unto him, with the rest of the people that remained. **10** But Nebuzaradan the chief steward left the [e]poor that had nothing in the land of Judah, and gave them vineyards and fields at the same time. **11** Now Nebuchadnezzar king of Babel gave charge concerning Jeremiah [f]unto Nebuzaradan the chief steward, saying, **12** Take him, and [g]look well to him, and do him no harm, but do unto him [h]even as he shall say unto thee. **13** So Nebuzaradan the chief steward sent, and Nebushasban, Rabsaris, and Nergal-Sharezar, Rabmag, and all the King of Babel's princes: **14** Even they sent, and took Jeremiah out of the court of the prison, and committed him unto [i]Gedaliah the son of Ahikam the son of Shaphan, that he should carry him home: so he dwelt among the people. **15** Now the word of the Lord came unto Jeremiah, while he was shut up in the court of the prison, saying, **16** Go and speak to Ebed-Melech the black Moor, saying, Thus saith the Lord of hosts the God of Israel, Behold, I will bring my words upon this city for evil, and not for good, and they shall be accomplished in that day before thee. **17** But I will deliver thee in that day, saith the Lord, and thou shalt not be given into the hand of the men whom thou fearest. **18** For I will surely deliver thee, and thou shalt not fall by the sword, but thy life shall be for a prey unto thee, because thou [j]hast put thy trust in me, saith the Lord.

40

Jeremiah hath license to go whither he will. 6 He dwelleth with the people that remain with Gedaliah.

1 The word which came to Jeremiah from the Lord after that Nebuzaradan the chief steward had let him go from Ramah, when he had taken him being bound in chains among all that were carried away captive of Jerusalem and Judah, which were carried away captive unto Babel. **2** [a]And the chief steward took Jeremiah and said unto him, The Lord thy God hath pronounced this plague upon this place. **3** Now the Lord hath brought it, and done according as he hath said:

JER. 37

1. 2 Kings 24:17 / 2 Chron. 36:10 / Jer. 5:21
2. Jer. 28:4

JER. 38

a. Jer. 38:1 For Zedekiah had sent these to Jer., to inquire at the Lord for the state of the country now when Nebuchadnezzar came, as Jer. 21:1.
b. Jer. 38:2 Read Jer. 21:9 and 45:5.
c. Jer. 38:4 Or, discourageth.
d. Jer. 38:4 Thus we see how the wicked when they cannot abide to hear the truth of God's word, seek to put the ministers to death, as transgressors of policies.
e. Jer. 38:5 Wherein he grievously offended in that that not only he would not hear the truth spoken by the Prophet, but also gave him to the lusts of the wicked to be cruelly entreated.
f. Jer. 38:7 Hebrew, Cushite, or Ethiopian.
g. Jer. 38:7 To hear matters and give sentence.
h. Jer. 38:9 Hereby is declared that the Prophet found more favor at this stranger's hands, than he did by all them of his country, which was to their great condemnation.
i. Jer. 38:10 Hebrew, under thine hand.
j. Jer. 38:13 Where the king had set him before to be at more liberty, as Jer. 37:21.
k. Jer. 38:17 And yield thyself unto them.
l. Jer. 38:19 Which declareth that he more feared the reproach of men, than the threatenings of God.
m. Jer. 38:22 When Jeconiah and his mother, with others, were carried away, these women of the king's house were left: which shall be taken, saith the Prophet, and tell the king of Babel how Zedekiah hath been seduced by his familiar friends and false prophets, which have left him in the mire.
n. Jer. 38:26 Herein appeareth the infirmity of the Prophet, who did dissemble to save his life albeit it was not to the denial of his doctrine, or to the hurt of any.

JER. 39

a. Jer. 39:2 The gates and walls were broken down.
b. Jer. 39:4 Which was a postern door, read 2 Kings 25:4.
c. Jer. 39:5 Which is called Antioch in Syria.
d. Jer. 39:9 Or, captain of the guard.
e. Jer. 39:10 For the rich and the mighty which put their trust in their shifts and means, were by God's just judgments most rigorously handled.
f. Jer. 39:11 Hebrew, by the hand of.
g. Jer. 39:12 Hebrew, set thine eyes upon them.
h. Jer. 39:12 Thus God preserved his prophet by his means, whom he made the scourge to punish the king, and them that were his enemies.
i. Jer. 39:14 Whom the King of Babel had now appointed governor over the rest of the Jews that he left behind.
j. Jer. 39:18 Thus God recompensed his zeal and favor, which he showed to his Prophet in his troubles.

JER. 39

1. 2 Kings 25:15 / Jer. 52:4

JER. 40

a. Jer. 40:2 From this second verse unto Jer. 42:7, it seemeth to be as a parenthesis, and separated matter: and there this story beginneth again, and this vision is declared what it was.

because ye have [b]sinned against the Lord, and have not obeyed his voice, therefore this thing is come upon you. **4** And now behold, I loose thee this day from the chains which were on thine hands: if it please thee to come with me into Babel, come, and I will look well unto thee: but if it please thee not to come with me into Babel, [c]tarry still: behold, all the land is [d]before thee: whither it seemeth good, and convenient for thee to go, thither go. **5** For yet he was not returned: therefore he said, Return to Gedaliah the son of Ahikam, the son of Shaphan, whom the king of Babel hath made governor over all the cities of Judah, and dwell with him among the people, or go wheresoever it pleaseth thee to go. So the chief steward gave him vittles and a reward, and let him go. **6** Then went Jeremiah unto Gedaliah the son of Ahikam, to [e]Mizpah, and dwelt there with him among the people that were left in the land. **7** Now when all the captains of the host, [f]which were in the fields, even they and their men heard, that the king of Babel had made Gedaliah the son of Ahikam governor in the land, and that he had committed unto him men, and women, and children, and of the poor of the land, that were not carried away captive to Babel, **8** Then they came to Gedaliah to Mizpah, even [g]Ishmael the son of Nethaniah, and Johanan, and Jonathan the sons of Kareah, and Seraiah the son of Tanhumeth, and the sons of Ephai, the Netophathite, and Jezaniah the son of Maachathi, they and their men. **9** And Gedaliah the son of Ahikam, the son of Shaphan [1]sware unto them, and to their men, saying, Fear not to serve the Chaldeans: dwell in the land, and serve the king of Babel, and it shall be well with you: **10** As for me, Behold, I will dwell at Mizpah to [h]serve the Chaldeans, which will come unto us: but you, gather you wine, and summer fruits, and oil, and put them in your vessels, and dwell in your cities, that ye have [i]taken. **11** Likewise when all the Jews that were in [j]Moab, and among the Ammonites, and in Edom, and that were in all the countries, heard that the king of Babel had left a remnant of Judah, and that he had set over them Gedaliah the son of Ahikam the son of Shaphan, **12** Even all the Jews returned out of all places where they were driven, and came to the land of Judah to Gedaliah unto Mizpah, and gathered wine and summer fruits, very much. **13** Moreover Johanan the son of Kareah, and all the captains of the host, that were in the fields, came to Gedaliah to Mizpah, **14** And said unto him, Knowest thou not that [k]Baalis the King of the Ammonites hath sent Ishmael the son of Nethaniah to slay thee? But Gedaliah the son of Ahikam believed them not. **15** Then Johanan the son of Kareah spake to Gedaliah in Mizpah secretly, saying, Let me go, I pray thee, and I will slay Ishmael the son of Nethaniah, and no man shall know it. Wherefore should he kill thee, that all the Jews, which are gathered unto thee, should be scattered, and the remnant in Judah perish? **16** But Gedaliah the son of Ahikam said unto Johanan the son of Kareah, Thou shalt [l]not do this thing: for thou speakest falsely of Ishmael.

41

2 Ishmael killeth Gedaliah guilefully, and many others with him. 11 Johanan followeth after Ishmael.

1 But in the [a]seventh month came Ishmael the son of Nethaniah, the son of Elishama of the seed royal, and the princes of the [b]king, and ten men with him, unto Gedaliah the son of Ahikam to Mizpah, and there they did [c]eat bread together in Mizpah. **2** Then arose Ishmael the son of Nethaniah with these ten men that were with him, and smote Gedaliah the son of Ahikam the son of Shaphan with the sword, and slew him whom the king of Babel had made governor over the land. **3** Ishmael also slew all the Jews that were with Gedaliah at Mizpah, and all the Chaldeans that were found there, and the men of war. **4** Now the second day that he had slain Gedaliah, and no man knew it, **5** There came men from Shechem, from Shiloh, and from Samaria, even fourscore men having their beards shaven, and their clothes rent and cut, with [d]offerings and incense in their hands to offer in the house of the Lord. **6** And Ishmael the son of Nethaniah went forth from Mizpah to meet them, weeping, as he went: and when he met them, he said unto them, Come [e]to Gedaliah the son of Ahikam. **7** And when they came into the midst of the city, Ishmael the son of Nethaniah slew them, and cast them into the midst of the pit, he and the men that were with him. **8** But ten men were found among them, that said unto Ishmael, Slay us not: for we have treasures in the field, of wheat, and of barley, and of oil, and of honey: so he stayed, and slew them not among their brethren. **9** Now the pit] wherein Ishmael had cast the dead bodies of the men (whom he had slain because of Gedaliah) is it, which Asa the king had [f]made because of Baasha king of Israel, and Ishmael the son of Nethaniah filled it with them that were slain. **10** Then Ishmael carried away captive all the residue of the people that were in Mizpah, even the King's daughters, and all the people that remained in Mizpah, whom Nebuzaradan the chief steward had committed to Gedaliah the son of Ahikam, and Ishmael the son of Nethaniah carried them away captive, and departed to go over to the Ammonites. **11** But when Johanan the son of Kareah, and all the [g]captains of the host that were with him, heard of all the evil that Ishmael the son of Nethaniah had done, **12** Then they all took their men, and went to fight with Ishmael the son of Nethaniah, and found him by the great waters that are in Gibeon. **13** Now when all the people whom Ishmael carried away captive, saw Johanan the son of Kareah, and all the captains of the host, that were with him, they were glad. **14** So all the people that Ishmael had carried away captive from Mizpah, returned and came again, and went unto Johanan the son of Kareah. **15** But Ishmael the son of Nethaniah, escaped from Johanan with eight men, and went to the [h]Ammonites. **16** Then took Johanan the son of Kareah, and all the captains of the host that were with him, all the remnant of the people, whom Ishmael the son of Nethaniah had carried away captive from Mizpah, (after that he had slain Gedaliah the son of Ahikam) even the strong men of war, and the women, and the children, and the eunuchs, whom he had brought again from Gibeon. **17** And they departed and dwelt in Geruth [i]Chimham, which is by Bethlehem, to go and to enter into Egypt, **18** Because of the Chaldeans: for they feared them, because Ishmael the son of Nethaniah had slain Gedaliah the son of Ahikam, whom the king of Babel made governor in the land.

42

1 The captains ask counsel of Jeremiah what they ought to do. 7 He admonisheth the remnant of the people not to go into Egypt.

1 Then all the captains of the host, and Johanan the son of Kareah, and Jezaniah the son of Hoshaiah, and all the people from the least unto the most, came, **2** And said unto Jeremiah the Prophet, [a]Hear our prayer, we beseech thee, and pray for us unto the Lord thy God, even for all this remnant (for we are left, but a few of many, as thine eyes do behold) **3** That the Lord thy God may show us the way wherein we may walk, and the thing that we may [b]do. **4** Then Jeremiah the Prophet said unto them, I have heard you: behold, I will pray unto the Lord your God according to your words, and whatsoever thing the Lord shall answer you, I will declare it unto you: I will keep nothing back from you. **5** Then they said to Jeremiah, [c]The Lord be a witness of truth, and faith between us, if we do not even according to all things for the which the Lord thy God shall send thee to us. **6** Whether it be good or evil, we will obey the voice of the Lord God, to whom we send thee, that it may be well with us, when we obey the voice of the Lord our God. **7** [d]And so after ten days came the word of the Lord unto Jeremiah. **8** Then called he Johanan the son of Kareah, and all the captains of the host, which were with him, and all the people from the least to the most, **9** And said unto them, Thus saith the Lord God of Israel, unto whom ye sent me to present your prayers before him, **10** If ye will dwell in this land, then I will build you, and not destroy you, and I will plant you, and not root you out: for I [e]repent me of the evil that I have done unto you. **11** Fear not for the king of Babel, of whom ye are afraid: be not afraid of him, saith the Lord: for I am with you, to save you, and to deliver you [f]from his hand, **12** And I will grant you mercy that he may have compassion upon you, and he shall cause you to [g]dwell in your own land. **13** But if ye say, We will not dwell in this land, neither hear the voice of the Lord your God, **14** Saying, Nay, but we will go into the land of Egypt, where we shall see no war, nor hear the sound of the trumpet, nor have hunger of bread, and there will we dwell, **15** (And now therefore hear the word of the Lord, ye remnant of Judah: thus saith the Lord of hosts, the God of Israel, If ye set your faces to enter into Egypt, and go to dwell there,) **16** Then the sword that ye feared, [h]shall take you there in the land of Egypt, and the famine, for the which ye

---

b. Jer. 40:3 God moved this infidel to speak this to declare the great blindness and obstinacy of the Jews, which could not feel that which this heathen man confessed.
c. Jer. 40:4 Hebrew, cease.
d. Jer. 40:4 Or, at thy commandment.
e. Jer. 40:6 Which was a city of Judah.
f. Jer. 40:7 Which were scattered abroad for fear of the Chaldeans.
g. Jer. 40:8 Who was of the king's blood and after slew him, Jer. 41:2.
h. Jer. 40:10 Or, to receive them, or to entreat them for you.
i. Jer. 40:10 Or, chosen to dwell in.
j. Jer. 40:11 Which were fled also for fear of the Chaldeans.
k. Jer. 40:14 For under the color of entertaining of Ishmael, he sought only to make them destroy one another.
l. Jer. 40:16 Thus the godly, which think no harm to others, are soonest deceived, and never lack such as conspire their destruction.

JER. 40
1. 2 Kings 25:24

JER. 41
a. Jer. 41:1 The city was destroyed in the fourth month: and in the seventh month, which contained part of September, and part of October, was the governor Gedaliah slain.
b. Jer. 41:1 Meaning, Zedekiah.
c. Jer. 41:1 They did eat together as familiar friends.
d. Jer. 41:5 For they thought that the Temple had not been destroyed and therefore came up to the feast of Tabernacles: but hearing of the burning thereof in the way, they showed these signs of sorrow.
e. Jer. 41:6 For his death was kept secret, and he feigned that he lament for the destruction of Jerusalem, and the Temple: but after slew them when they seemed to favor Gedaliah.
f. Jer. 41:9 Asa fortified Mizpah for fear of the enemy, and cast ditches and trenches, 1 Kings 15:22.
g. Jer. 41:11 Which had been captains under Zedekiah.
h. Jer. 41:15 For Baalis the king of the Ammonites was the cause of this murder.
i. Jer. 41:17 Which place David of old had given to Chimham the son of Barzillai the Gileadite, 2 Sam. 19:38.

JER. 42
a. Jer. 42:2 Hebrew, Let our prayer fall before thee, as Jer. 36:7
b. Jer. 42:3 This declareth the nature of hypocrites, which would know of God's word what they should do, but will not follow it, but inasmuch as it agreeth with that thing, which they have purposed to do.
c. Jer. 42:5 There are none more ready to abuse the Name of God and take it in vain, than the hypocrites, which to color their falsehood use it without all reverence, and make it a means for them to deceive the simple and the godly.
d. Jer. 42:7 Here is declared the vision and the occasion thereof, whereof mention was made, Jer. 40:1.
e. Jer. 42:10 Read Jer. 18:8.
f. Jer. 42:11 Because all kings' hearts and ways are in his hands, he can turn them and dispose them as it pleaseth him, and therefore they need not to fear man, but only obey God, Prov. 21:1.
g. Jer. 42:12 Or, return.
h. Jer. 42:16 Thus God turneth the policy of the wicked to their own destruction: for they thought themselves sure in Egypt, and there Nebuchadnezzar destroyed them and the Egyptians, Jer. 46:25.

care, shall there hang upon you in Egypt, and there shall ye die. **17** And all the men that set their faces to enter into Egypt to dwell there, shall die by the sword, by the famine, and by the pestilence, and none of them shall remain, nor escape from the plague, that I will bring upon them. **18** For thus saith the Lord of hosts, the God of Israel, As mine anger and my wrath hath been poured forth upon the inhabitants of Jerusalem: so shall my wrath be poured forth upon you, when ye shall enter into Egypt, and ye shall be a detestation, and an astonishment, and a [i]curse, and a reproach, and ye shall see this place no more. **19** O ye remnant of Judah, the Lord hath said concerning you, Go not into Egypt: know certainly that I have admonished you this day. **20** Surely ye [j]dissembled in your hearts when ye sent me unto the Lord your God, saying, Pray for us unto the Lord our God, and declare unto us even according unto all that the Lord our God shall say, and we will do it. **21** Therefore I have this day declared it you, but you have not obeyed the voice of the Lord your God, nor anything for the which he hath sent me unto you. **22** Now therefore, know certainly that ye shall die by the sword, by the famine, and by the pestilence [k]in the place whither ye desire to go and dwell.

43

Johanan carrieth the remnant of the people into Egypt, contrary to the mind of Jeremiah. 8 Jeremiah prophesieth the destruction of Egypt.

1 Now when Jeremiah had made an end of speaking unto the whole people all the words of the Lord their God, for the which the Lord their God had sent him to them, even all these words, **2** Then spake [a]Azariah the son of Hoshaiah, and Johanan the son of Kareah, and all the [b]proud men, saying unto Jeremiah, [c]Thou speakest falsely: the Lord our God hath [d]not sent thee to say, Go not into Egypt to dwell there, **3** But Baruch the son of Neriah [e]provoketh thee against us, for to deliver us into the hand of the Chaldeans, that they might slay us, and carry us away captives into Babel. **4** So Johanan the son of Kareah, and all the captains of the host, and all the people obeyed not the voice of the Lord, to dwell in the land of Judah. **5** But Johanan the son of Kareah, and all the captains of the host took all the remnant of Judah that were returned from all [f]nations, whither they had been driven, to dwell in the land of Judah: **6** Even men and women, and children, and the king's daughters, and every person that Nebuzaradan the chief steward had left with Gedaliah the son of Ahikam, the son of Shaphan, and Jeremiah the [g]Prophet, and Baruch the son of Neriah. **7** So they came into the land of Egypt: for they obeyed not the voice of the Lord: thus came they to [h]Tahpanhes. **8** Then came the word of the Lord unto Jeremiah in Tahpanhes, saying, **9** Take great stones in thine hand, and [i]hide them in the clay in the brick kiln, which is at the entry of Pharaoh's house in Tahpanhes in the sight of the men of Judah, **10** And say unto them, Thus saith the Lord of hosts the God of Israel, Behold, I will send and bring Nebuchadnezzar the king of Babel [j]my servant, and will set his throne upon these stones that I have hid, and he shall spread his pavilion over them. **11** And when he shall come, he shall smite the land of Egypt: [k]such as are appointed for death, to death, and such as are for captivity, to captivity, and such as are for the sword, to the sword. **12** And I will kindle a fire in the houses of the gods of Egypt, and he shall burn them and carry them away captives, and he shall array himself with the land of Egypt, as a [l]shepherd putteth on his garment, and shall depart from thence in peace. **13** He shall break also the images of [m]Beth Shemesh, that is in the land of Egypt, and the houses of the gods of the Egyptians shall he burn with fire.

44

He reproveth the people for their idolatry. 15 They that set light by the threatening of the Lord, are chastened. 26 The destruction of Egypt, and of the Jews therein, is prophesied.

1 The word that came to Jeremiah concerning all the Jews, which dwell in the land of Egypt, and remained at Migdol and at [a]Tahpanhes, and at Noph, and in the country of Pathros, saying, **2** Thus saith the Lord of hosts the God of Israel, Ye have seen all the evil that I have brought upon Jerusalem, and upon all the cities of Judah: and behold, this day they are desolate and no man dwelleth therein, **3** Because of their wickedness which they have committed, to provoke me to anger in that they went to burn incense, and to serve other gods whom they knew not, neither they nor you, nor your fathers. **4** Howbeit I sent unto you all my servants the Prophets [b]rising early, and sending them, saying, Oh do not this abominable thing that I hate. **5** But they would not hear nor incline their ear to turn from their wickedness, and to burn no more incense unto other gods. **6** Wherefore [c]my wrath, and mine anger was poured forth, and was kindled in the cities of Judah, and in the streets of Jerusalem, and they are desolate, and wasted, as appeareth this day. **7** Therefore now thus saith the Lord of hosts the God of Israel, wherefore commit ye this great evil against your souls, to cut off from you man and woman, child and suckling out of Judah, and leave you none to remain? **8** In that ye provoke me unto wrath with the works of your hands, burning incense unto other gods in the land of Egypt, whither ye be gone to dwell: that ye might bring destruction unto yourselves, and that ye might be a curse and a reproach among all nations of the earth. **9** Have ye forgotten the wickedness of your fathers, and the wickedness of the [d]kings of Judah, and the wickedness of their wives, and your own wickedness, and the wickedness of your wives, which they have committed in the land of Judah, and in the streets of Jerusalem? **10** They are not [e]humbled unto this day, neither have they feared nor walked in my law nor in my statutes, that I set before you and before your fathers. **11** Therefore thus saith the Lord of hosts, the God of Israel, Behold, I will set my face against you [I]to evil, and to destroy all Judah, **12** And I will take the remnant of Judah that [f]have set their faces to go into the land of Egypt there to dwell, and they shall all be consumed and fall in the land of Egypt: they shall even be consumed by the sword and by the famine: they shall die from the least unto the most, by the sword, and by the famine and they shall be a detestation and an astonishment, and a [g]curse and a reproach. **13** For I will visit them that dwell in the land of Egypt, as I have visited Jerusalem, by the sword, by the famine, and by the pestilence, **14** So that none of the remnant of Judah, which are gone into the land of Egypt to dwell there shall escape or remain, that they should return into the land of Judah to the which they [h]have a desire to return to dwell there: for none shall return but [i]such as shall escape. **15** Then all the men which knew that their wives had burnt incense unto other gods, and all the women that stood by, a great multitude, even all the people that dwelt in the land of Egypt in Pathros, answered Jeremiah, saying, **16** The word that thou hast spoken unto us in the Name of the Lord, we will [j]not hear it of thee, **17** But we will do whatsoever thing goeth out of our own mouth, as to burn incense unto [k]the Queen of heaven, and to pour out drink offerings unto her, as we have done, both we and our fathers, our kings and our princes in the cities of Judah, and in the streets of Jerusalem: for then [l]had we [m]plenty of vittles and were well and [n]felt none evil. **18** But since we left off to burn incense to the Queen of heaven, and to pour out drink offerings unto her, we have had [o]scarceness of all things, and have been consumed by the sword and by the famine. **19** And when we burnt incense unto the Queen of heaven, and poured out drink offerings unto her, did we make her cakes [p]to make her glad, and pour out drink offerings unto her without [q]our husbands? **20** Then said Jeremiah unto all the people, to the men, and to the women, and to all the people which had given him that answer, saying, **21** Did not the Lord remember the incense, that ye burnt in the cities of Judah, and in the streets of Jerusalem, both you and your fathers, your kings, and your Princes, and the people of the land, and [r]hath he not considered it? **22** So that the Lord could no longer forbear, because of the wickedness of your inventions, and because of the abominations, which ye have committed: therefore is your land desolate, and an astonishment, and a curse, and without inhabitant, as appeareth this day. **23** Because you have burnt incense, and because ye have sinned against the Lord, and

---

i. Jer. 42:18 Read Jer. 26:6 and 24:12, showing that this should come upon them for their infidelity and stubbornness.
j. Jer. 42:20 For ye were fully minded to go into Egypt, whatsoever God spake to the contrary.
k. Jer. 42:22 To wit, in Egypt.

JER. 43

a. Jer. 43:2 Who was also called Jezaniah, Jer. 42:1.
b. Jer. 43:2 This declareth that pride is the cause of rebellion: and contempt of God's ministers.
c. Jer. 43:2 When the hypocrisy of the wicked is discovered, they burst forth into open rage: for they can abide nothing but flattery, read Isa. 30:10.
d. Jer. 43:2 He showeth what is the nature of the hypocrites: to wit, to feign that they would obey God and embrace his word, if they were assured that his messenger spake the truth: though indeed they be most far from all obedience.
e. Jer. 43:3 Thus the wicked do not only contemn and hurt the messengers of God, but slander, and speak wickedly of all them that support or favor the godly.
f. Jer. 43:5 As from the Moabites, Ammonites, and Edomites, Jer. 40:11.
g. Jer. 43:6 Whom these wicked lead away by force.
h. Jer. 43:7 A city in Egypt near to Nilus.
i. Jer. 43:9 Which signified that Nebuchadnezzar should come even to the gates of Pharaoh, where were his brick kilns for his buildings.
j. Jer. 43:10 Read Jer. 25:9.
k. Jer. 43:11 Everyone shall be slain by that means that God hath appointed, Jer. 15:2.
l. Jer. 43:12 Meaning, most easily and suddenly shall he carry the Egyptians away.
m. Jer. 43:13 Or, the house of the Sun.

JER. 44

a. Jer. 44:1 These were all famous and strange cities in Egypt, where the Jews that were fled, dwelt for their safety: but the Prophet declareth that there is no hold so strong that can preserve them from God's vengeance.
b. Jer. 44:4 Read Jer. 7:25; 25:3; 36:5; 29:19 and 32:33.
c. Jer. 44:6 He setteth before their eyes God's judgments against Judah and Jerusalem for their idolatry, that they might beware by their example, and not with the like wickedness provoke the Lord: for then they should be double punished.
d. Jer. 44:9 He showeth that we ought to keep in memory God's plagues from the beginning, that considering them, we might live in his fear, and know if he have not spared our fathers, yea, kings, princes, and rulers, and also whole countries, and nations for their sins, that we vile worms, cannot look to escape punishment for ours.
e. Jer. 44:10 Or, beaten down.
f. Jer. 44:12 Which have fully set their minds, and are gone thither on purpose. Whereby he excepteth the innocents, as Jer. and Baruch that were forced: therefore the Lord showeth that he will set his face against them: that is, purposely destroy them.
g. Jer. 44:12 Read Jer. 26:6 and 41:18.
h. Jer. 44:14 Hebrew, lift up their souls.
i. Jer. 44:14 Meaning, but a few.
j. Jer. 44:16 This declareth how dangerous a thing it is to decline once from God, and to follow our own fantasies: for Satan ever soliciteth such, and doth not leave them till he have brought them to extreme impudency and madness, even to justify their wickedness against God and his Prophets.
k. Jer. 44:17 Read Jer. 7:18, it seemeth that the Papists gathered of this place Salve Regina, and Regina caeli latare, calling the virgin Mary Queen of heaven, and so of the blessed virgin and mother of our Savior Christ, made an idol: for here the Prophet condemneth their idolatry.
l. Jer. 44:17 Hebrew, we were satiated with bread.
m. Jer. 44:17 This is still the argument of idolaters, which esteem religion by the belly, and instead of acknowledging God's works, who sendeth both plenty and dearth, health and sickness, they attribute it to their idols, and so dishonor God.
n. Jer. 44:17 Or, saw.
o. Jer. 44:18 Or, want.
p. Jer. 44:19 Or, to appease her.
q. Jer. 44:19 This teacheth us how great danger it is for the husbands to permit their wives anything whereof they be not assured by God's word: for thereby they take an occasion to justify their doings, and their husbands shall give an account thereof before God, read Isa. 3:25.
r. Jer. 44:21 Hebrew, is it not come up into his heart?

have not obeyed the voice of the Lord, nor walked in his law, nor in his statutes, nor in his testimonies, therefore this plague is come upon you, as appeareth this day. **24** Moreover Jeremiah said unto all the people and to all the women, Hear the word of the Lord, all Judah, that are in the land of Egypt. **25** Thus speaketh the Lord of hosts, the God of Israel, saying, Ye and your wives have both spoken with your mouths, and fulfilled with your [s]hand, saying, We will perform our vows that we have vowed to burn incense to the Queen of heaven, and to pour out drink offerings to her: ye will perform your vows, and do the things that ye have vowed. **26** Therefore hear the word of the Lord, all Judah that dwell in the land of Egypt, Behold, I have sworn by my great Name, saith the Lord, that my Name [t]shall no more be called upon by the mouth of any man of Judah, in all the land of Egypt, saying, The Lord God liveth. **27** Behold, I will watch over them for evil, and not for good, and all men of Judah that are in the land of Egypt, shall be consumed by the sword, and by the famine, until they be utterly destroyed. **28** Yet a small number that escape the sword, [u]shall return out of the land of Egypt into the land of Judah: and all the remnant of Judah that are gone into the land of Egypt to dwell there, shall know whose words shall stand, mine or theirs. **29** And this shall be a sign unto you, saith the Lord, when I visit you in this place, that ye may know that my words shall surely stand against you for evil. **30** Thus saith the Lord, Behold, I will [v]give Pharaoh Hophra King of Egypt into the hand of his enemies, and into the hand of them that seek his life: as I gave Zedekiah king of Judah into the hand of Nebuchadnezzar king of Babel his enemy, who also sought his life.

45

2 Jeremiah comforteth Baruch, assuring him that he should not perish in the destruction of Jerusalem.

1 The word that Jeremiah the Prophet spake unto [a]Baruch the son of Neriah, when he had written these [b]words in a book at the mouth of Jeremiah, in the fourth year of Jehoiakim, the son of Josiah king of Judah, saying, **2** Thus saith the Lord God of Israel unto thee, O Baruch, **3** Thou didst say, Woe is me now: for the Lord hath laid sorrow unto my sorrow: I [c]fainted in my mourning, and I can find no rest. **4** Thus shalt thou say unto him, The Lord saith thus, Behold, that which I have built, will I [d]destroy, and that which I have planted, will I pluck up, even this whole land. **5** And seekest [e]thou great things for thyself? seek them not: for behold, I will bring a plague upon all flesh, saith the Lord: but thy life will I give thee for [f]a prey in all places, whither thou goest.

46

He prophesieth the destruction of Egypt. 27 Deliverance is promised to Israel.

1 The words of the Lord, which came to Jeremiah the Prophet against the [a]Gentiles, **2** As against Egypt, against the army of [b]Pharaoh Necho king of Egypt, which was by the river Perath in Carchemish, which Nebuchadnezzar king of Babel smote in the fourth year of Jehoiakim the son of Josiah king of Judah. **3** [c]Make ready buckler and shield, and go forth to battle. **4** Make ready the horses, and let the horsemen get up, and stand up with your sallets, furbish the spears, and put on the brigandines. **5** [d]Wherefore have I seen them afraid, and driven back? for their mighty men are smitten, and are fled away, and look not back: for fear was round about, saith the Lord. **6** The swift shall not flee away, nor the strong man escape: they shall stumble, and [e]fall toward the North by the river Perath. **7** Who is this that cometh up as [f]a flood, whose waters are moved like the rivers? **8** Egypt riseth up like the flood, and his waters are moved like the rivers, and he saith, I will go up, and will cover the earth: I will destroy the city with them that dwell therein. **9** Come up ye horses, and rage ye chariots, and let the valiant men come forth, [g]the black Moors, and the Libyans that bear the shield, and the Lydians that handle and bend the bow. **10** For this is the day of the Lord God of hosts, and a day of vengeance, that he may avenge him of his enemies: for the sword shall devour, and it shall be satiate, and made drunk with their blood: for the Lord God of hosts hath [h]a sacrifice in the North country [i]by the river Perath. **11** Go up unto Gilead, [j]and take balm, [k]O virgin, the daughter of Egypt: in vain shalt thou use many [l]medicines: for thou shalt have no health. **12** The nations have heard of thy shame, and thy cry hath filled the land: for the strong hath stumbled against the strong, and they are fallen both together. **13** The word that the Lord spake to Jeremiah the Prophet, how Nebuchadnezzar king of Babel should come and smite the land of Egypt. **14** Publish in Egypt and declare in Migdol, and proclaim in Noph, and in Tahpanhes, and say, Stand still and prepare thee, for the sword shall devour round about thee. **15** Why are thy valiant men put back? they could not stand, because the Lord did drive them. **16** He made many to fall, and one fell upon another: and they said, Arise, let us go again to our [m]own people, and to the land of our nativity from the sword of the violent. **17** They did cry there, Pharaoh king of Egypt, and of a great multitude, [n]hath passed the time appointed. **18** As I live, saith the King, whose Name is the Lord of hosts, surely as Tabor is in the mountains, and as Carmel is in the sea: so shall [o]it come. **19** O thou daughter dwelling in Egypt, make thee gear to go into captivity: for Noph shall be waste and desolate, without an inhabitant. **20** Egypt is like a [p]fair calf, but destruction cometh: out of the North it cometh. **21** Also her hired men [q]are in the midst of her like fat calves: they are also turned back and fled away together: they could not stand, because the day of their destruction was come upon them, and the time of their visitation. **22** The voice thereof shall go forth like a [r]serpent: for they shall march with an army, and come against [s]her with axes, as hewers of wood. **23** They shall cut down [t]her forest, saith the Lord: for they cannot be counted, because they are more than the [u]grasshoppers, and are innumerable. **24** The daughter of Egypt shall be confounded: she shall be delivered into the hands of the people of the North. **25** Thus saith the Lord of hosts, the God of Israel, Behold, I will visit thy [v]common people of No and Pharaoh, and Egypt, with their gods and their kings, even Pharaoh, and all them that trust in him, **26** And I will deliver them into the hands of those that seek their lives, and into the hand of Nebuchadnezzar king of Babel, and into the hands of his servants, and afterward she shall dwell as [w]in the old time, saith the Lord. **27** [x]But fear not thou, O my servant Jacob, and be not thou afraid, O Israel: for behold, I will deliver thee from a far country, and thy seed from the land of their captivity, and Jacob shall return and be in rest, and prosperity, and none shall make him afraid. **28** Fear thou not, O Jacob my servant, saith the Lord, for I am with thee, and I will utterly destroy all the nations, whither I have driven thee: but I will not utterly destroy thee, but correct [y]thee by judgment, and not utterly cut thee off.

47

The word of the Lord against the Philistines.

1 The words of the Lord that came to Jeremiah the Prophet, against the Philistines, before that Pharaoh smote [a]Gaza. **2** Thus saith the Lord, Behold, waters rise up out of the [b]North, and shall be as a swelling flood, and shall overflow the land, and all that is therein, and the cities with them that dwell therein: then the men shall cry, and all the inhabitants of the land shall howl, **3** At the noise and stamping of the hoofs of his strong horses, at the noise of his chariots, and at the rumbling of his wheels: [c]the fathers shall not look back to their children, for feebleness of [d]hands, **4** Because of the day that cometh to destroy all the

---

- **s.** Jer. 44:25 You have committed double evil in making wicked vows, and in performing the same.
- **t.** Jer. 44:26 This declareth an horrible plague toward idolaters, seeing that God will not vouchsafe to have his Name mentioned by such as have polluted it.
- **u.** Jer. 44:28 We see therefore that God hath a perpetual care over his, wheresoever they are scattered: for though they be but two or three, yet he will deliver them when he destroyeth his enemies.
- **v.** Jer. 44:30 He showeth the means whereby they should be destroyed to assure them of the certainty of the plague, and yet they remain still in their obstinacy till they perish: for Josephus, lib. 10, de Antiq., cap. 11, writeth that five years after the taking of Jerusalem, Nebuchadnezzar the younger having overcome the Moabites and the Ammonites, went against Egypt, and slew the king, and so brought these Jews and others into Babylon.

JER. 44

- **1.** Amos. 9:4

JER. 45

- **a.** Jer. 45:1 Which was Jer.'s disciple, and wrote his prophecies under him.
- **b.** Jer. 45:1 Whereof read Jer. 36:9, 10.
- **c.** Jer. 45:3 Baruch moved with an inconsiderate zeal of Jer.'s imprisonment, but chiefly for the destruction of the people, and the Temple, maketh this lamentation, as Ps. 6:6.
- **d.** Jer. 45:4 Meaning, that God might destroy this people, because he had planted them.
- **e.** Jer. 45:5 Thinkest thou to have honor and credit? wherein he showeth his infirmity.
- **f.** Jer. 45:5 Read Jer. 21:9.

JER. 46

- **a.** Jer. 46:1 That is, nine nations, which are round about the land of Egypt.
- **b.** Jer. 46:2 Read 2 Kings 23:29 and 24:7; 2 Chron. 35:20.
- **c.** Jer. 46:3 He warneth the Egyptians to prepare themselves to war.
- **d.** Jer. 46:5 The Prophet had this vision of the Egyptians, which should be put to flight by the Babylonians at Carchemish.
- **e.** Jer. 46:6 The Babylonians shall discomfit them at the river Euphrates.
- **f.** Jer. 46:7 He derideth the boastings of the Egyptians, who thought by their riches and power to have overcome all the world, alluding to the river Nilus, which at certain times overfloweth the country of Egypt.
- **g.** Jer. 46:9 For these nations took part with the Egyptians.
- **h.** Jer. 46:10 He calleth the slaughter of God's enemies a sacrifice, because it is a thing that doth please him, Isa. 34:6.
- **i.** Jer. 46:10 That is, at Carchemish.
- **j.** Jer. 46:11 For at Gilead did grow most sovereign balm for wounds.
- **k.** Jer. 46:11 So called, because Egypt had not yet been overcome by the enemy.
- **l.** Jer. 46:11 He showeth that no salve or medicine can prevail whereas God giveth the wound.
- **m.** Jer. 46:16 As they that should repent that they helped the Egyptians.
- **n.** Jer. 46:17 He derideth them which shall impute their overthrow to lack of counsel and policy, or to fortune, and not observing of time: not considering that it is God's just judgment.
- **o.** Jer. 46:18 To wit, that the Egyptians shall be destroyed.
- **p.** Jer. 46:20 They have abundance of all things, and therefore are disobedient and proud.
- **q.** Jer. 46:21 As verse 9.
- **r.** Jer. 46:22 They shall be scarce able to speak for fear of the Chaldeans.
- **s.** Jer. 46:22 Meaning, Egypt.
- **t.** Jer. 46:23 That is, they shall slay the great and mighty men of power.
- **u.** Jer. 46:23 To wit, Nebuchadnezzar's army.
- **v.** Jer. 46:25 Some take the Hebrew word Amon for the King's name of No, that is, of Alexandria.
- **w.** Jer. 46:26 Meaning, that after the space of forty years Egypt should be restored, Isa. 19:23; Ezek. 29:13.
- **x.** Jer. 46:27 God comforteth all his that were in captivity, but specially the small Church of the Jews, whereof were Jer. and Baruch, which remained among the Egyptians: for the Lord never forsaketh his, Isa. 44:2; Jer. 30:10.
- **y.** Jer. 46:28 Read Jer. 10:14.

JER. 47

- **a.** Jer. 47:1 Which was also called Gaza, a city of the Philistines.
- **b.** Jer. 47:2 He meaneth the army of the Chaldeans, Isa. 8:7, 8.
- **c.** Jer. 47:3 The great fear shall take away their natural affection.
- **d.** Jer. 47:3 Their heart shall so fail them.
- **e.** Jer. 47:4 For the Caphtorims, which are also called Cappadocians, had destroyed in old time the Philistines, and dwelt in their land even to Gaza, Deut. 2:23.

Philistines, and to destroy Tyre, and Sidon, and all the rest that take their part: for the Lord will destroy the Philistines, the remnant of the isle of [e]Caphtor. **5** [f]Baldness is come upon Gaza: Ashkelon is cut up with the rest of their valleys. How long wilt [g]thou cut thyself? **6** O thou sword of the Lord, how long will it be or thou cease! turn again into thy scabbard, rest and be still. **7** How can it [h]cease, seeing the Lord hath given it a charge against Ashkelon, and against the sea bank? even there hath he appointed it.

48

The word of the Lord against the Moabites. 26 Because of their pride and cruelty.

1 Concerning Moab, thus saith the Lord of hosts, the God of Israel, Woe unto [a]Nebo: for it is wasted: Kirjathaim is confounded and taken: Misgab is confounded and afraid. **2** Moab shall boast no more of Heshbon: for they have devised evil against it. [b]Come, and let us destroy it, that it be no more a nation: also thou shalt be destroyed, [c]O Madmen, and the sword shall pursue thee. **3** A voice of crying shall be from Horonaim with desolation and great destruction. **4** Moab is destroyed: her little ones have caused their cry to be heard. **5** For at the going up of [d]Luhith, the mourner shall go up with weeping: for in the going down of Horonaim, the enemies have heard a cry of destruction. **6** Flee and save your lives, and be like unto the [e]heath in the wilderness. **7** For because thou hast trusted in thy [f]works and in thy treasures, thou shalt also be taken, and [g]Chemosh shall go forth into captivity with his Priests and his Princes together. **8** And the destroyer shall come upon all cities, and no city shall escape: the valley also shall perish and the plain shall be destroyed as the Lord hath spoken. **9** Give wings unto Moab, that it may flee and get away: for the cities thereof shall be desolate, without any to dwell therein. **10** [h]Cursed be he that doeth the work of the Lord [i]negligently, and cursed be he that keepeth back his sword from blood. **11** Moab hath been at rest from his youth, and he hath settled on his lees, and hath not been [j]poured from vessel to vessel, neither hath he gone into captivity: therefore his taste remained in him, and his scent is not changed. **12** Therefore behold, the days come, saith the Lord, that I will send unto him such as shall carry him away, and shall empty his vessels, and break their bottles. **13** And Moab shall be ashamed of Chemosh, as the house of Israel was ashamed of [k]Bethel their confidence. **14** How think you thus, We are mighty and strong men of war? **15** Moab is destroyed, and his cities [l]burnt up, and his chosen young men are gone down to slaughter, saith the King, whose name is, The Lord of hosts. **16** The destruction of Moab is ready to come, and his plague hasteth fast. **17** All ye that are about him, mourn for him, and all ye that know his name, say, [m]How is the strong staff broken, and the beautiful rod! **18** Thou daughter that dost inhabit Dibon, come down from thy glory, and sit in thirst: for the destroyer of Moab shall come upon thee, and he shall destroy thy strongholds. **19** Thou that dwellest in Aroer, stand by the way, and behold ask him that fleeth and that escapeth, and say, What is done? **20** [n]Moab is confounded: for it is destroyed, howl and cry, tell ye it in Arnon, that Moab is made waste, **21** And judgment is come upon the plain country, upon Holon and upon Jahzah, and upon Mephaath, **22** And upon Dibon, and upon Nebo, and upon the house of Diblathaim, **23** And upon Kirjathaim, and upon Beth Gamul, and upon Beth Meon, **24** And upon Kerioth, and upon Bozrah, and upon all the cities of the land of Moab far or near. **25** The [o]horn of Moab is cut off, and his arm is broken, saith the Lord. **26** Make ye him [p]drunken: for he magnified himself against the Lord: Moab shall [q]wallow in his vomit, and he also shall be in derision. **27** For didst not thou deride Israel, as though he had been found among thieves? for when thou speakest of him, thou art [r]moved. **28** O ye that dwell in Moab, leave the cities, and dwell in the rocks, and be like the dove that maketh her nest in the sides of the hole's mouth. **29** [1]We have heard the pride of Moab (he is exceeding proud) his stoutness, and his arrogancy, and his pride, and the haughtiness of his heart. **30** I know his wrath, saith the Lord, [s]but it shall not be so: and his dissimulations, for they do not right. **31** [t]Therefore will I howl for Moab, and I will cry out for all Moab: mine heart shall mourn for the men of Kir Heres. **32** O vine of Sibmah, I will weep for thee, as I wept for Jazer: thy plants are gone over the sea, they are come to the sea [u]of Jazer: the destroyer is fallen upon thy summer fruits, and upon thy vintage, **33** And joy, and gladness is taken from the plentiful field, and from the land of Moab: and I have caused wine to fail from the winepress: none shall tread with shouting: their shouting shall be no shouting. **34** From the cry of Heshbon unto Elealeh and unto Jahaz have they made their noise: from Zoar unto Horonaim, the [v]heifer of three years old shall go lowing: for the waters also of Nimrim shall be wasted. **35** Moreover, I will cause to cease in Moab, saith the Lord, him that offereth in the high places, and him that burneth incense to his gods. **36** Therefore mine heart shall sound for Moab like a [w]shawm, and mine heart shall sound like a shawm for the men of Kir Heres, because the riches that he hath gotten is perished. **37** [2]For every head shall be [x]bald, and every beard plucked: upon all the hands shall be cuttings, and upon the loins sackcloth. **38** And mourning shall be upon all the house tops of Moab, and in all the streets thereof: for I have broken Moab like a vessel wherein is no pleasure, saith the Lord. **39** They shall howl, saying, How is he destroyed? how hath Moab turned the back with shame? so shall Moab be a derision, and a fear to all them about him. **40** For thus saith the Lord, Behold, [y]he shall flee as an eagle, and shall spread his wings over Moab. **41** The cities are taken, and the strongholds are won, and the mighty men's hearts in Moab at that day shall be as the heart of a woman in travail. **42** And Moab shall be destroyed from being a people, because he hath set up himself against the Lord: **43** [z]Fear, and pit, and snare shall be upon thee, O inhabitant of Moab, saith the Lord. **44** He that escapeth from the fear, shall fall in the pit, and he that getteth up out of the pit, shall be taken in the snare: for I will bring upon it, even upon Moab the year of their visitation, saith the Lord. **45** They that fled, stood under the shadow [aa]of Heshbon, because of the force: for [ab]the fire came out of Heshbon, and a flame from Sihon, and devoured the corner of Moab, and the top of the seditious children. **46** Woe be unto thee, O Moab: the people of [ac]Chemosh perisheth: for thy sons are taken captives, and thy daughters led into captivity. **47** Yet will I bring again the captivity of Moab in the [ad]latter days, saith the Lord. Thus far of the judgment of Moab.

49

1 The word of the Lord against the Ammonites, 7 Edom, 23 Damascus, 28 Kedar, 34 and Elam.

1 Unto the children of [a]Ammon thus saith the Lord, Hath Israel no sons? or hath he none heir? Why then hath their king [b]possessed Gad? and his people dwelt in [c]his cities? **2** Therefore behold, the days come, saith the Lord, that I will cause a noise of war to be heard in [d]Rabbah of the Ammonites, and it shall be a desolate heap, and her daughters shall be burnt with fire: then shall Israel possess those that possessed him, saith the Lord. **3** Howl, O Heshbon, for Ai is wasted: cry ye daughters of Rabbah: gird you with sackcloth: mourn and run to and fro by the hedges: for their king shall go into captivity; and his Priests, and his Princes likewise. **4** Wherefore gloriest thou in the [e]valleys? thy valley floweth away, O rebellious daughter: she trusted in her treasures, saying, Who shall come unto me? **5** Behold, I will bring [f]a fear upon thee, saith the Lord God of hosts, of all those that be about thee, and ye shall be scattered every man [g]right forth, and none shall gather him that fleeth. **6** And [h]afterward I will bring again the captivity of the children of Ammon. **7** To Edom thus saith the Lord of hosts,

---

f. Jer. 47:5 They that pilled off their hair for sorrow and heaviness.
g. Jer. 47:5 As the heathen used in their mourning, which the Lord forbade his people to do, Deut. 14:1.
h. Jer. 47:7 Meaning, that it is not possible that the wicked should by any means escape or stay the Lord, when he will take vengeance.

JER. 48

a. Jer. 48:1 These were cities of the Moabites, which Nebuchadnezzar took before he went to fight against Necho king of Egypt.
b. Jer. 48:2 Thus shall the Babylonians encourage one another.
c. Jer. 48:2 Read Isa. 25:10.
d. Jer. 48:5 Horonaim and Luhith were two places whereby the Moabites should flee, Isa. 15:5.
e. Jer. 48:6 Hide yourselves in barren places, where the enemy will not pursue after you, Jer. 17:6.
f. Jer. 48:7 That is, the idols which are the works of thine hands. Some read, in thy possessions, for so the word may signify, as 1 Sam. 25:2.
g. Jer. 48:7 Both thy great idol and his maintainers shall be led away captives, so that they shall then know that it is in vain to look for help at idols, Isa. 15:2.
h. Jer. 48:10 He showeth that God would punish the Chaldeans, if they did not destroy the Egyptians, and that with a courage, and calleth this executing of his vengeance against his enemies, his work: though the Chaldeans sought another end, Isa. 10:11.
i. Jer. 48:10 Or, deceitfully.
j. Jer. 48:11 Hath not been removed as the Jews have, but have lived at ease, and as a wine that feedeth itself on his lees.
k. Jer. 48:13 As the calf of Bethel was not able to deliver the Israelites: no more shall Chemosh deliver the Moabites.
l. Jer. 48:15 Hebrew, gone up, or destroyed.
m. Jer. 48:17 How are they destroyed that put their trust in their strength and riches?
n. Jer. 48:20 Thus they that flee, shall answer.
o. Jer. 48:25 That is, his power and strength.
p. Jer. 48:26 He willed the Chaldeans to lay afflictions enough upon them, till they be like drunken men that fall down to their shame and are derided of all.
q. Jer. 48:26 Or, shall be full, or clap his hands.
r. Jer. 48:27 Thou rejoicest to hear of his misery.
s. Jer. 48:30 He shall not execute his malice against his neighbors.
t. Jer. 48:31 Read Isa. 16:7.
u. Jer. 48:32 Which city was in the utmost border of Moab: and hereby he signifieth that the whole land should be destroyed, and the people carried away.
v. Jer. 48:34 Read Isa. 15:5.
w. Jer. 48:36 Their custom was to play on flutes or instruments, heavy and grave tunes at burials and in the time of mourning, as Matt. 9:23.
x. Jer. 48:37 Or, shaven.
y. Jer. 48:40 That is, Nebuchadnezzar, as Jer. 49:22.
z. Jer. 48:43 He that escapeth one danger shall be taken of another, Isa. 24:17.
aa. Jer. 48:45 They fled thither, thinking to have succor of the Amorites.
ab. Jer. 48:45 The Amorites had destroyed the Moabites in times past, and now because of their power, the Moabites shall seek to them for help.
ac. Jer. 48:46 Which vaunted themselves of their idol, as though he could have defended them.
ad. Jer. 48:47 That is, they shall be restored by the Messiah.

JER. 48

1. Isa 16:6 **2.** Isa 15:2,3 / Ezek. 7:18

JER. 49

a. Jer. 49:1 They were separated from the Moabites by the river Arnon, and after that the ten tribes were carried away into captivity, they invaded the country of Gad.
b. Jer. 49:1 To wit, of the Ammonites.
c. Jer. 49:1 Meaning, of the Israelites.
d. Jer. 49:2 Which was one of the chief cities of the Ammonites, as were Heshbon and Ai: there was also a city called Heshbon among the Moabites.
e. Jer. 49:4 In thy plentiful country.
f. Jer. 49:5 Signifying, that power and riches cannot prevail, when as God will execute his judgments.
g. Jer. 49:5 That is, without looking back, and as everyone can find a way to escape.
h. Jer. 49:6 In the time of Christ, when the Gentiles shall be called.

Is wisdom no more in [i]Teman? is counsel perished from their children? is their wisdom vanished? 8 Flee, ye inhabitants of Dedan ([j]they are turned back, and have consulted to dwell) for I have brought the destruction of Esau upon him, and the time of his visitation. 9 If the [k]grape gatherers come to thee, would they not leave some grapes? if thieves come by night, they will destroy till they have enough. 10 For I have discovered Esau: I have uncovered his secrets, and he shall not be able to hide himself: his seed is wasted, and his brethren and his neighbors, and there shall be none to say, 11 Leave thy [l]fatherless children, and I will preserve them alive, and let thy widows trust in me. 12 For thus saith the Lord, [m]Behold, they whose judgment was not to drink of the cup, have assuredly drunken, and art thou he that shall escape free? thou shalt not go free, but thou shalt surely drink of it. 13 For I have sworn by myself, saith the Lord, that [n]Bozrah shall be waste, and for a reproach, and a desolation, and a curse, and all the cities thereof shall be perpetual desolations. 14 I have heard a rumor from the Lord, and an ambassador is sent unto the heathen, saying, Gather you together, and come against [o]her, and rise up to the battle. 15 For lo, I will make thee but small among the heathen, and despised among men. 16 Thy [p]fear, and the pride of thine heart hath deceived thee, thou that dwellest in the clefts of the rock, and keepest the height of the hill: though thou shouldest make thy nest as high as the eagle, I will bring thee down from thence, saith the Lord. 17 Also Edom shall be desolate: everyone that goeth by it, shall be astonished, and shall hiss at all the plagues thereof, 18 As in the overthrow of Sodom and of Gomorrah, and the places thereof near about, saith the Lord: no man shall dwell there, neither shall the sons of men remain in it. 19 Behold, [q]he shall come up like a lion from the swelling of Jordan unto the strong dwelling place: for I will make Israel to rest, even I will make [r]him to haste away from her, and who is a chosen man that I may appoint against her? for who is like me? and who will appoint me the time? and who is the [s]shepherd that will stand before me? 20 Therefore hear the counsel of the Lord that he hath devised against Edom, and his purpose that he hath conceived, against the inhabitants of Teman: surely the least [t]of the flock shall draw them out: surely [u]he shall make their habitations desolate with them. 21 The earth is moved at the noise of their fall: the cry of their voice is heard in the red sea. 22 Behold, he shall come up, and fly as the eagle, [v]and spread his wings over Bozrah, and at that day shall the heart of the strong men of Edom be as the heart of a woman in travail. 23 Unto [w]Damascus he saith, Hamath is confounded and Arpad, for they have heard evil tidings, and they are faint hearted as one on the fearful sea that can not rest: 24 Damascus is discouraged, and turneth herself to flight, [x]and fear hath seized her: anguish and sorrows have taken her as a woman in travail. 25 How is the glorious [y]city not reserved, the city of my joy? 26 Therefore her young men shall fall in her streets, and all her men of war shall be cut off in that day, saith the Lord of hosts. 27 And I will kindle a fire in the wall of Damascus, which shall consume the palaces of [z]Ben-Hadad. 28 Unto [aa]Kedar, and to the kingdoms of Hazor, which Nebuchadnezzar king of Babel shall smite, thus saith the Lord, Arise, and go up unto Kedar, and destroy the men of the East. 29 Their tents and their flocks shall they take away: yea, they shall take to themselves their [ab]curtains and all their vessels, and their camels, and they shall cry unto them, Fear is on every side. 30 Flee, get you far off ([ac]they have consulted to dwell) O ye inhabitants of Hazor, saith the Lord: for Nebuchadnezzar king of Babel hath taken counsel against you, and hath devised a purpose against you. 31 [ad]Arise, and get you up unto the wealthy nation that dwelleth without care, saith the Lord, which have neither gates nor bars, but dwell alone. 32 And their camels shall be a bootie, and the multitude of their cattle a spoil, and I will scatter them into all winds, and to the utmost corners, and I will bring their destruction from all the sides thereof, saith the Lord. 33 And Hazor shall be a dwelling for dragons, and desolation forever: there shall no man dwell there, nor the sons of men remain in it. 34 The words of the Lord that came to Jeremiah the Prophet, concerning [ae]Elam, in the beginning of the reign of Zedekiah king of Judah, saying, 35 Thus saith the Lord of hosts, Behold, I will break the [af]bow of Elam, even the chief of their strength. 36 And upon Elam I will bring the four winds from the four quarters of heaven, and will scatter them towards all these winds, and there shall be no nation, whither the fugitives of Elam shall not come. 37 For I will cause Elam to be afraid before their enemies, and before them that seek their lives, and will bring upon them a plague, even the indignation of my wrath, saith the Lord, and I will send the sword after them, till I have consumed them. 38 And I will set my [ag]throne in Elam, and I will destroy both the king and the princes from thence, saith the Lord: but [ah]in the latter days I will bring again the captivity of Elam, saith the Lord.

50

He prophesieth the destruction of Babylon, and the deliverance of Israel which was in captivity.

1 The word that the Lord spake concerning Babel, and concerning the land of the Chaldeans by the [a]ministry of Jeremiah the Prophet. 2 Declare among the nations, and publish it, and set up a standard, proclaim it and conceal it not: say, [b]Babel is taken, Bel is confounded, [c]Merodach is broken down: her idols are confounded, and their images are burst in pieces. 3 For out of the North [d]there cometh up a nation against her, which shall make her land waste, and none shall dwell therein: they shall flee, and depart, both man and beast. 4 In those days, and at that time, saith the Lord, the children of Israel shall [e]come, they, and the children of Judah together, going, and [f]weeping shall they go, and seek the Lord their God. 5 They shall ask the way to Zion, with their faces thitherward, saying, Come, and let us cleave to the Lord in a perpetual covenant that shall not be forgotten. 6 My people hath been as lost sheep: their [g]shepherds have caused them to go astray, and have turned them away to the mountains: they have gone from [h]mountain to hill, and forgotten their resting place. 7 All that found them have devoured them, and their enemies said, We offend not, because they have sinned against the Lord, [i]the habitation of justice, even the Lord the hope of their fathers. 8 [j]Flee from the midst of Babel, and depart out of the land of the Chaldeans, and be ye as the he goats [k]before the flock. 9 For lo, I will raise and cause to come up against Babel a multitude of mighty nations from the North country, and they shall set themselves in array against her, whereby she shall be taken: their arrows shall be as of a strong man, which is expert, for none shall return in vain. 10 And Chaldea shall be a spoil: all that spoil her, [l]shall be satisfied, saith the Lord. 11 Because you were glad and rejoiced in destroying mine heritage, and because ye are grown fat, as the calves in the grass, [m]and neighed like strong horses, 12 Therefore your mother shall be sore confounded, and she that bare you shall be ashamed, behold, the uttermost of the nations shall be a desert, a dry land, and a wilderness. 13 Because of the wrath of the Lord it shall not be inhabited, but shall be wholly desolate: everyone that goeth by Babel, shall be astonished, [n]and hiss at all her plagues. 14 [o]Put yourselves in array against Babel round about: all ye that bend the bow, shoot at her, spare no arrows: for she hath [p]sinned against the Lord. 15 Cry against her round about: she hath [q]given her hand: her foundations are fallen, and her walls are destroyed: for it is the vengeance of the Lord: take vengeance upon her: as she hath done, do unto her. 16 Destroy the [r]sower from Babel, and him that handleth the scythe in the time of harvest: because of the sword of the oppressor they shall turn everyone to his people, and they shall flee everyone to his own land. 17 Israel is like scattered sheep: the lions have dispersed them: first the king of [s]Assyria hath devoured him, and last

---

i. Jer. 49:7 Which was a city of Edom, called by the name of Teman Eliphaz' son, who came of Esau.
j. Jer. 49:8 The enemies that shall dissemble as though they fled away, shall turn back and invade your land, and possess it.
k. Jer. 49:9 Meaning, that God would utterly destroy them, and not spare one, though the grape gatherers leave some grapes, and thieves seek but till they have enough, Obad. 1:5.
l. Jer. 49:11 The destruction shall be so great, that there shall be none left to take care over the widows and the fatherless.
m. Jer. 49:12 I have not spared mine own people, and how should I pity thee?
n. Jer. 49:13 Which was a chief city of Edom.
o. Jer. 49:14 That is, Bozrah.
p. Jer. 49:16 Or, idol.
q. Jer. 49:19 To wit, Nebuchadnezzar after he hath overcome Judah, which is meant by the swelling of Jordan, shall come against mount Seir and Edom.
r. Jer. 49:19 That is, the Israelites, whom the Edomites kept as prisoners, to haste away from thence.
s. Jer. 49:19 The captain and governor of the army, meaning, Nebuchadnezzar.
t. Jer. 49:20 They shall not be able to resist his petty captains.
u. Jer. 49:20 To visit, the enemy.
v. Jer. 49:22 As Jer. 48:40, was said of Moab.
w. Jer. 49:23 Which was the chief city of Syria, whereby he meaneth the whole country.
x. Jer. 49:24 When she heard the sudden coming of the enemy.
y. Jer. 49:25 He speaketh this in the person of the king and of them of the country, who shall wonder to see Damascus the chief city destroyed.
z. Jer. 49:27 Who was king of Syria, 1 Kings 20:26, and had built these palaces, which were still called the palaces of Ben-Hadad.
aa. Jer. 49:28 Meaning, the Arabians, and their borderers.
ab. Jer. 49:29 Because they used to dwell in tents, he nameth the things that pertain thereunto.
ac. Jer. 49:30 The enemies will dwell in your places.
ad. Jer. 49:31 He showeth that they of Hazor will flee to the Arabians for succor, but that shall not avail them.
ae. Jer. 49:34 That is, Persia, so called of Elam the son of Shem.
af. Jer. 49:35 Because the Persians were good archers, he showeth that the thing wherein they put their trust, should not profit them.
ag. Jer. 49:38 I will place Nebuchadnezzar there, and in these prophecies Jer. speaketh of those countries, which should be subdued under the first of those four monarchies whereof Daniel maketh mention.
ah. Jer. 49:38 This may be referred to the Empire of Persians and Medes after the Chaldeans, or unto the time of Christ, as Jer. 48:47.

JER. 50

a. Jer. 50:1 Hebrew, hands.
b. Jer. 50:2 After that God had used the Babylonians' service to punish other nations, he showeth that their turn shall come to be punished.
c. Jer. 50:2 These were two of their chief idols.
d. Jer. 50:3 To wit, the Medes and the Persians.
e. Jer. 50:4 When Cyrus shall take Babel.
f. Jer. 50:4 Read Jer. 31:9.
g. Jer. 50:6 Their governors and ministers by their examples have provoked them to idolatry.
h. Jer. 50:6 They have committed idolatry in every place.
i. Jer. 50:7 For the Lord dwelt among them in his Temple, and would have maintained them by his justice against their enemies.
j. Jer. 50:8 When God shall deliver you by Cyrus.
k. Jer. 50:8 That is, most forward and without fear.
l. Jer. 50:10 Shall be made rich thereby.
m. Jer. 50:11 For joy of the victory, that ye had against my people.
n. Jer. 50:13 In sign of contempt and disdain.
o. Jer. 50:14 He speaketh to the enemies the Medes and Persians.
p. Jer. 50:14 Though the Lord called the Babylonians his servants, and their work his work in punishing his people, yet because they did it not to glorify God, but for their own malice, and to profit themselves, it is here called sin.
q. Jer. 50:15 Or, yielded, or made peace.
r. Jer. 50:16 Destroy her so that none be left to labor the ground, or to take the fruit thereof.
s. Jer. 50:17 Meaning, Tiglath-Pilesar, who carried away the ten tribes.
t. Jer. 50:17 He carried away the rest, to wit, Judah, and Benjamin.

this Nebuchadnezzar king of Babel hath broken his [t]bones. **18** Therefore thus saith the Lord of hosts the God of Israel, Behold, I will visit the king of Babel, and his land, as I have visited the King of Assyria. **19** And I will bring Israel again to his habitation: he shall feed on Carmel and Bashan, and his soul shall be satisfied upon the mount Ephraim and Gilead. **20** In those days, and at that time, saith the Lord, the iniquity of Israel shall be sought for, and there shall be none: and the sins of Judah, and they shall not be found: for I will be merciful unto them whom I reserve. **21** Go up against the land of the [u]rebels, even against it and against the inhabitants [1]of [v]Pekod: destroy, and lay it waste after them, saith the Lord, and do according to all that I have commanded thee. **22** A cry of battle is in the land, and of great destruction. **23** How is the [w]hammer of the whole world destroyed, and broken! how is Babel become desolate among the nations! **24** I have snared thee, and thou art taken, O Babel, and thou wast not aware: thou art found, and also caught, because thou hast striven against the Lord. **25** The Lord hath opened his treasure, and hath brought forth the weapons of his wrath: for this is the work of the Lord God of hosts in the land of the Chaldeans. **26** Come against her [x]from the utmost border: open her storehouses, tread on her as on sheaves, and destroy her utterly: let nothing of her be left. **27** Destroy all her [y]bullocks: let them go down to the slaughter. Woe unto them, for their day is come, and the time of their visitation. **28** The voice of them that [z]flee, and escape out of the land of Babel to declare in Zion, the vengeance of the Lord our God, and the vengeance of his Temple. **29** Call up the archers against Babel: all ye that bend the bow, besiege it round about: let none thereof escape: [2]recompense her according to her work, and according to all that she hath done, do unto her: for she hath been proud against the Lord, even against the holy One of Israel. **30** Therefore shall her young men fall in the streets, and all her men of war shall be destroyed in that day, saith the Lord. **31** Behold, I come unto thee, O proud man, saith the Lord God of hosts: for thy day is come, even the time that I will visit thee. **32** And the proud shall stumble and fall, and none shall raise him up: and I will kindle a fire in his cities, and it shall devour all round about him. **33** Thus saith the Lord of hosts, The children of Israel, and the children of Judah were oppressed together: and all that took them captives, held them, and would not let them go. **34** But their strong redeemer, whose Name is the Lord of hosts, he shall maintain their cause, that he may give rest to the land, [aa]and disquiet the inhabitants of Babel. **35** A sword is upon the Chaldeans, saith the Lord, and upon the inhabitants of Babel, and upon her princes, and upon her wise men. **36** A sword is upon the [ab]soothsayers, and they shall dote: a sword is upon her strong men, and they shall be afraid. **37** A sword is upon their horses, and upon their chariots, and upon all the multitude that are in the midst of her, and they shall be like women: a sword is upon her treasures, and they shall be spoiled. **38** A [ac]drought is upon her waters, and they shall be dried up: for it is the land of graven images, and they dote upon their idols. **39** Therefore the [ad]Ziims with the Iims shall dwell there, and [ae]the ostriches shall dwell therein: for it shall be no more inhabited, neither shall it be inhabited from generation unto generation. **40** As God destroyed [3]Sodom and Gomorrah with the places thereof near about, saith the Lord: so shall no man dwell there, neither shall the son of man remain therein. **41** Behold, a people shall come from the North, and a great nation, and many kings shall be raised up from [af]the coasts of the earth. **42** They shall hold the bow and the buckler: they are cruel and unmerciful: their voice shall roar like the sea, and they shall ride upon horses, and be put in array like men to the battle against thee, O daughter of Babel. **43** The king of Babel hath heard the report of them, and his hands [ag]waxed feeble: sorrow came upon him, even sorrow as of a woman in travail. **44** Behold, he [4]shall come up like a lion from the swelling of Jordan unto the strong habitation: for I will make Israel to rest, and I will make them to haste away from her: and who is a chosen man that I may appoint against her? for who is like me, and who will appoint me the time? and who is the [ah]shepherd that will stand before me? **45** Therefore hear the counsel of the Lord, that he hath devised against Babel, and his purpose that he hath conceived against the land of the Chaldeans: surely the least of the flock shall draw them out: surely he shall make their habitation desolate with them. **46** At the noise of the winning of Babel the earth is moved, and the cry is heard among the nations.

51

6 Why Babylon is destroyed. 41 The vain confidence of the Babylonians. 43 The vanity of idolaters. 59 Jeremiah giveth his book to Seraiah.

1 Thus saith the Lord, Behold, I will raise up against Babel, and against the inhabitants [a]that lift up their heart against me, a destroying [b]wind, **2** And will send unto Babel fanners that shall fan her, and shall empty her land, for in the day of trouble they shall be against her on every side. **3** Also to the bender that bendeth his bow, and to him that lifteth himself up in his brigandine, will I say, Spare not her young men, but destroy all her host. **4** Thus the slain shall fall in the land of the Chaldeans, and they that are thrust through in her streets. **5** For Israel hath been no [c]widow, nor Judah from his God, from the Lord of hosts, though their land was filled with sin against the holy one of Israel. **6** [d]Flee out of the midst of Babel, and deliver every man his soul: be not destroyed in her iniquity: for this is the time of the Lord's vengeance: he will render unto her a recompense. **7** Babel hath been as a golden cup in the [e]Lord's hand, that made all the earth drunken, the nations have drunken of her wine, therefore do the nations [f]rage. **8** [1]Babel is suddenly fallen, and destroyed: howl for her, bring balm for her sore, if she may be healed. **9** We would have cured Babel, but she could not be healed: forsake her, and let [g]us go everyone into his own country: for her judgment is come up into heaven, and is lifted up to the clouds. **10** The Lord hath brought forth our [h]righteousness: come and let us declare in Zion the work of the Lord our God. **11** Make bright the arrows: [i]gather the shields: the Lord hath raised up the spirit of the King of the Medes: for his purpose is against Babel to destroy it, because it is the [j]vengeance of the Lord, and the vengeance of his Temple. **12** Set up the standard upon the walls of Babel, make the watch strong: set up the watchmen: prepare the scouts: for the Lord hath both devised, and done that which he spake against the inhabitants of Babel. **13** O thou that dwellest upon many [k]waters, abundant in treasures, thine end is come, even the [l]end of thy covetousness. **14** The Lord of hosts hath sworn by [m,2]himself, saying, Surely I will fill thee with men, as with caterpillars, and they shall cry and shout against thee. **15** [3]He hath made the earth by his power, and established the world by his wisdom, and hath stretched out the heaven by his discretion. **16** He giveth by his voice the multitude of waters in the heaven, and he causeth the clouds to ascend from the ends of the earth, he turneth lightnings to rain, and bringeth forth the wind out of his treasures. **17** Every man is a beast by his own [n]knowledge: every founder is confounded by the graven image: for his melting is but falsehood, and there is no breath therein. **18** They are vanity, and the work of errors: in the time of their [o]visitation they shall perish. **19** The [p]portion of Jacob is not like them: for he is the maker of all things, and Israel is the rod of his inheritance: the Lord of hosts is his Name. **20** Thou art mine [q]hammer, and weapons of war: for with thee will I break the nations, and with thee will I destroy kingdoms, **21** And by thee will I break horse and horseman, and by thee will I break the chariot and him that rideth therein. **22** By thee also will I break man and woman, and by thee will I break old and young, and by thee will I break the young man and the maid. **23** I will also break by thee the shepherd and his flock, and by thee will I break the husbandman and his yoke of oxen, and by thee will I break the dukes and princes. **24** And I will render unto Babel, and to all the inhabitants of the Chaldeans all their evil, that they have done in Zion, even in your sight, saith the Lord. **25** Behold, I come unto thee, O destroying [r]mountain, saith the Lord, which destroyest all the earth: and I will stretch out mine hand upon thee, and roll thee down from the [s]rocks, and will make thee a burnt mountain. **26** They shall not take of thee a stone for a corner, nor a stone for foundations: but thou shalt be destroyed forever, saith the Lord. **27** Set up a standard in the land: blow the trumpets among the nations: prepare the nations against her: call up the kingdoms of [t]Ararat, Minni, and Ashkenaz against her, appoint the prince against her, cause horses to come up as the rough caterpillars. **28** Prepare against her the nations with the kings of the Medes, the dukes thereof, and the princes thereof, and all the land of his dominion. **29** And the land shall tremble and sorrow: for the device of the Lord shall be performed against Babel, to make the land of Babel waste without an inhabitant. **30** The strong men of Babel have ceased to fight: they have

---

u. Jer. 50:21 That is, Babylon: thus the Lord raised up Cyrus.
v. Jer. 50:21 Or, of them that should be visited.
w. Jer. 50:23 Nebuchadnezzar, who had smitten down all the princes and people of the world.
x. Jer. 50:26 Hebrew, from the end.
y. Jer. 50:27 Her princes and mighty men.
z. Jer. 50:28 Of the Jews which should be delivered by Cyrus.
aa. Jer. 50:34 He showeth that when God executeth his judgments against his enemies, that his Church shall then have rest.
ab. Jer. 50:36 Hebrew, liars.
ac. Jer. 50:38 For Cyrus did cut the river Euphrates, and divided the course thereof into many streams, so that it might be passed over as though there had been no water: which thing he did by the counsel of two of Belshazzar's captains, who conspired against their king, because he had gelded the one of them in despite, and slain the son of the other.
ad. Jer. 50:39 Read Isa. 13:21.
ae. Jer. 50:39 Hebrew, sons of the ostriches, or young.
af. Jer. 50:41 Meaning, that the Persians should gather their army of many nations.
ag. Jer. 50:43 Which is meant of Belshazzar, Dan. 5:6.
ah. Jer. 50:44 Read Jer. 49:19.

JER. 50
1. Ezek. 23:13
2. Rev. 18:6
3. Gen. 19:24 / Isa. 13:19
4. Jer. 49:19

JER. 51
a. Jer. 51:1 Or, of the land that riseth up.
b. Jer. 51:1 The Medes and Persians that shall destroy them as the wind doth the chaff.
c. Jer. 51:5 Though they were forsaken for a time, yet they were not utterly cast off as though their husbands were dead.
d. Jer. 51:6 He showeth that there remaineth nothing for them that abide in Babylon, but destruction, Jer. 17:6 and 48:6.
e. Jer. 51:7 By whom the Lord poured out the drink of his vengeance, to whom it pleased him.
f. Jer. 51:7 For the great afflictions that they have felt by the Babylonians.
g. Jer. 51:9 Thus the people of God exhort one another to go to Zion and praise God.
h. Jer. 51:10 In approving our cause and punishing our enemies.
i. Jer. 51:11 Or, fill, or multiply.
j. Jer. 51:11 For the wrong done to his people and to his Temple, Jer. 50:28.
k. Jer. 51:13 For the land of Chaldea was full of rivers, which ran into Euphrates.
l. Jer. 51:13 Or, measures.
m. Jer. 51:14 Hebrew, his soul.
n. Jer. 51:17 Read Jer. 10:14.
o. Jer. 51:18 When God shall execute his vengeance.
p. Jer. 51:19 That is, the true God of Israel is not like to these idols: for he can help when all things are desperate.
q. Jer. 51:20 He meaneth the Medes and Persians, as he did before call the Babylonians his hammer, Jer. 50:23.
r. Jer. 51:25 Not that Babylon stood on a mountain, but because it was strong and seemed invincible.
s. Jer. 51:25 From thy strongholds and fortresses.
t. Jer. 51:27 By these three nations he meaneth Armenia the higher, Armenia the lower, and Scythia: for Cyrus had gathered an army of divers nations.
u. Jer. 51:31 By turning the course of the river one side was made open and the reeds that did grow in the water were destroyed, which Cyrus did by the counsel of Gobria and Gabatha Belshazzar's captains.

remained in their holds: their strength hath failed, and they were like women: they have burnt her dwelling places, and her bars are broken. **31** A post shall run to meet the post, and a messenger to meet the messenger, to show the King of Babel, that his city is taken on a [u]side thereof, **32** And that the passages are stopped, and the reeds burnt with fire, and the men of war troubled. **33** For thus saith the Lord of hosts the God of Israel, The daughter of Babel is like a threshingfloor: the time of her threshing is come: yet a little while, and the time of her harvest [v]shall come. **34** Nebuchadnezzar the King of Babel hath [w]devoured me, and destroyed me: he hath made me an empty vessel: he swallowed me up like a dragon: and filled his belly with my delicates, and hath cast me out. **35** The spoil of me, and that which was left of me, is brought unto Babel, shall the inhabitant of Zion say: and my blood unto the inhabitants of Chaldea, shall Jerusalem say. **36** Therefore thus saith the Lord, Behold, I will maintain thy [x]cause, and take vengeance for thee, and I will dry up the sea, and dry up her springs. **37** And Babel shall be as heaps, a dwelling place for dragons, an astonishment, and an hissing, without an inhabitant. **38** They shall roar together like lions, and yell as the lion's whelps. **39** In their [y]heat I will make them feasts, and I will make them drunken that they may rejoice, and sleep a perpetual sleep, and not wake, saith the Lord. **40** I will bring them down like lambs to the slaughter, and like rams and goats. **41** How is [z]Sheshach taken! and how is the glory of the whole earth taken! how is Babel become an astonishment among the nations! **42** The [aa]sea is come up upon Babel: she is covered with the multitude of the waves thereof. **43** Her cities are desolate: the land is dry and a wilderness, a land wherein no man dwelleth, neither doth the son of man pass thereby. **44** I will also visit Bel in Babel, and I will bring out of his mouth, that which [ab]he hath swallowed up, and the nations shall run no more unto him, and the wall of Babel shall fall. **45** My people, go out of the midst of her, and deliver ye every man his soul from the fierce wrath of the Lord, **46** Lest your heart even faint, and ye fear the rumor that shall be heard in the land: the rumor shall come this year, and after that in the other [ac]year shall come a rumor, and cruelty in the land, and ruler against ruler. **47** Therefore behold, the days come, that I will visit the images of Babel, and the whole land shall be confounded, and all her slain shall fall in the midst of her. **48** Then the heaven and [ad]the earth, and all that is therein, shall rejoice for Babel: for the destroyers shall come unto her from the North, saith the Lord. **49** As Babel caused the [ae]slain of Israel to fall, so by Babel the slain of all the earth did fall. **50** Ye that [af]have escaped the sword, go away, stand not still: remember the Lord afar off, and let Jerusalem come into your mind. **51** We are [ag]confounded because we have heard reproach: shame hath covered our faces, for strangers are come into the Sanctuaries of the Lord's house. **52** Wherefore behold, the days come, saith the Lord, that I will visit her graven images, and through all her land the wounded shall groan. **53** Though Babel should mount up to [ah]heaven, and though she should defend her strength on high, yet from me shall her destroyers come, saith the Lord. **54** A sound of a cry cometh from Babel, and great destruction from the land of the Chaldeans, **55** Because the Lord hath laid Babel waste, and destroyed from her the great voice, and her waves shall roar like great waters, and a sound was made by their noise: **56** Because the destroyer is come upon her, even upon Babel, and her strong men are taken, their bows are broken: for the Lord God that recompenseth, shall surely recompense. **57** And I will [ai]make drunk her princes, and her wise men, her dukes, and her nobles, and her strong men: and they shall sleep a perpetual sleep, and not wake, saith the King, whose Name is the Lord of hosts. **58** Thus saith the Lord of hosts, The [aj]thick wall of Babel shall be broken, and her high gates shall be burnt with fire, and the people shall labor in vain, and the folk in the fire, for they shall be weary. **59** The word which Jeremiah the Prophet commanded Seraiah the son of Neriah, the son of Mahseiah, when he went with Zedekiah the king of Judah into Babel, in the [ak]fourth year of his reign, and this Seraiah was a peaceable Prince. **60** So Jeremiah wrote in a book all the evil that should come upon Babel, even all these things that are written against Babel. **61** And Jeremiah said to Seraiah, When thou comest unto Babel, and shalt see and shalt read all these words, **62** Then shalt thou say, O Lord, thou hast spoken against this place, to destroy it, that none should remain in it, neither man nor beast, but that it should be desolate forever. **63** And when thou hast made an end of reading this book, thou shalt bind a [al]stone to it, and cast it in the midst of Euphrates, **64** And shalt say, Thus shall Babel be drowned and shall not rise from the evil, that I will bring upon her: and they shall [am]be weary. Thus far are the words of Jeremiah.

52

4 Jerusalem is taken. 10 Zedekiah's sons are killed before his face, and his eyes put out. 13 The city is burned. 31 Jehoiachin is brought forth of prison, and fed like a king.

1 Zedekiah [1]was one and twenty years old when he began to reign, and he reigned eleven years in Jerusalem, and his mother's name was Hamutal, the daughter of Jeremiah of Libnah. **2** And he did evil in the eyes of the Lord, according to all that Jehoiakim had done. **3** [a]Doubtless because the wrath of the Lord was against Jerusalem and Judah, till he had cast them out from his presence, therefore Zedekiah rebelled against the king of Babel. **4** [2]But in the ninth year of his reign, in the tenth month the tenth day of the month came Nebuchadnezzar King of Babel, he and all his host against Jerusalem, and pitched against it, and built forts against it round about. **5** So the city was besieged unto the eleventh year of the king Zedekiah. **6** Now in the fourth month, the ninth day of the month, the famine was sore in the city, so that there was no more bread for the people of the land. **7** Then the city was broken up, and all the men of war fled, and went out of the city by night, by the [b]way of the gate between the two walls, which was by the King's garden: (now the Chaldeans were by the city round about) and they went by the way of the wilderness. **8** But the army of the Chaldeans pursued after the king, and took Zedekiah in the desert of Jericho, and all the host was scattered from him. **9** Then they took the King and carried him up unto the king of Babel to Riblah in the land of Hamath, [c]where he gave judgment upon him. **10** And the king of Babel slew the sons of Zedekiah before his eyes: he slew also all the princes of Judah in Riblah. **11** Then he put out the eyes of Zedekiah, and the king of Babel bound him in chains, and carried him to Babel, and put him in prison till the day of his death. **12** Now in the fifth month in the [d]tenth day of the month (which was the nineteenth year of the king Nebuchadnezzar King of Babel) came Nebuzaradan chief steward which [e]stood before the king of Babel in Jerusalem, **13** And burnt the House of the Lord, and the King's house, and all the houses of Jerusalem, and all the great houses burnt he with fire. **14** And all the army of the Chaldeans that were with the chief steward, brake down all the walls of Jerusalem round about. **15** Then Nebuzaradan the chief steward carried away captive certain of the poor of the people, and the residue of the people that remained in the city, and those that were fled, and fallen to the King of Babel, with the rest of the multitude. **16** But Nebuzaradan the chief steward left certain of the poor of the land, to dress the vines, and to till the land. **17** Also the [f]pillars of brass that were in the House of the Lord, and the bases, and the brazen Sea, that was in the House of the Lord, the Chaldeans brake, and carried all the brass of them to Babel. **18** The pots also and the [g]besoms, and the instruments of music, and the basins, and the incense dishes, and all the vessels of brass wherewith they ministered, took they away. **19** And the bowls, and the ashpans, and the basins, and the pots, and the candlesticks, and the incense dishes, and the cups, and all that was of gold, and that was of silver, took the chief steward away, **20** With the two pillars, one Sea, and twelve brazen bulls, that were under the bases, which King Solomon had made in the House of the Lord: the brass of all these vessels was without [h]weight. **21** And concerning the pillars, the height of one pillar was eighteen cubits, and a thread of twelve cubits did compass it, and the thickness thereof was four fingers: it was hollow. **22** And a chapiter of brass was upon it, and the height of one chapiter was five cubits with network, and pomegranates upon the chapiters round about, all of brass: the second pillar also, and the pomegranates were like

---

v. Jer. 51:33 When she shall be cut up and threshed.
w. Jer. 51:34 This is spoken in the person of the Jews bewailing their state and the cruelty of the Babylonians.
x. Jer. 51:36 Thus the Lord esteemed the injury done to his Church, as done to himself, because their cause is his.
y. Jer. 51:39 When they are inflamed with surfeiting and drinking, I will feast with them, alluding to Belshazzar's banquet, Dan. 5:2.
z. Jer. 51:41 Meaning, Babel, as Jer. 25:26.
aa. Jer. 51:42 The great army of the Medes and Persians.
ab. Jer. 51:44 That is, his gifts and presents which he had received as part of the spoil of other nations, and which the idolaters brought unto him from all countries.
ac. Jer. 51:46 Meaning, that Babylon should not be destroyed all at once, but little by little should be brought to nothing: for the first year came the tidings, the next year the siege, and in the third year it was taken: yet this is not that horrible destruction which the prophets threatened in many places: for that was after this when they rebelled and Darius overcame them by the policy of Zopyrus, and hanged three thousand gentlemen besides the common people.
ad. Jer. 51:48 All creatures in heaven and earth shall rejoice, and praise God for the destruction of Babylon the great enemy of his Church.
ae. Jer. 51:49 Babylon did not only destroy Israel, but many other nations.
af. Jer. 51:50 Ye that are now captives in Babylon.
ag. Jer. 51:51 He showeth how they should remember Jerusalem by lamenting the miserable affliction thereof.
ah. Jer. 51:53 For the walls were two hundred foot high.
ai. Jer. 51:57 I will so astonish them by afflictions that they shall not know which way to turn them.
aj. Jer. 51:58 The thickness of the wall was fifty foot thick.
ak. Jer. 51:59 This was not in the time of his captivity, but seven years before, when he went either to gratulate Nebuchadnezzar, or to entreat of some matters.
al. Jer. 51:63 St. John in his Revelation alludeth to this place, when he saith that the Angel took a millstone and cast it into the sea: signifying thereby the destruction of Babylon, Rev. 18:21.
am. Jer. 51:64 They shall not be able to resist, but shall labor in vain.

JER. 51
1. Isa. 21:9 / Rev. 14:8
2. Amos 6:8 / Jer. 10:12

JER. 52
a. Jer. 52:3 So the Lord punished sin by sin, and gave him up to his rebellious heart, till he had brought the enemy upon him to lead him away and his people.
b. Jer. 52:7 Read Jer. 39:4.
c. Jer. 52:9 Read 2 Kings 25:6; Jer. 39:5.
d. Jer. 52:12 In 2 Kings 25:8, it is called the seventh day, because the fire began then, and so continued to the tenth.
e. Jer. 52:12 That is, which was his servant, as 2 Kings 25:8.
f. Jer. 52:17 Of these pillars, read 1 Kings 7:15.
g. Jer. 52:18 Which were also made of brass, as 1 Kings 7:45.
h. Jer. 52:20 It was so much in quantity.
i. Jer. 52:23 But because of the roundness, no more could be seen but ninety and six.
j. Jer. 52:24 Which served in the high Priest's stead, if he had any necessary impediment.
k. Jer. 52:25 In 2 Kings 25:19, is read but of five: those were the most excellent, and the other two, which were not so noble, are not there mentioned with them.
l. Jer. 52:28 Which was the latter end of the seventh year of his reign, and the beginning of the eighth.
m. Jer. 52:29 In the latter end also of that year, and the beginning of the nineteenth.
n. Jer. 52:29 Hebrew, souls.

unto these. 23 And there were ninety and six pomegranates on a side: and all
the pomegranates upon the network were an [i]hundred round about. 24 And the
chief steward took Seraiah the chief Priest, and Zephaniah [j]the second Priest, and
the three keepers of the door. 25 He took also out of the city an Eunuch, which
had the oversight of the men of war, and [k]seven men that were in the King's presen-
ce, which were found in the city, and Sopher captain of the host, who mustered the
people of the land, and threescore men of the people of the land, that were found
in the midst of the city. 26 Nebuzaradan the chief steward took them, and brou-
ght them to the King of Babel to Riblah. 27 And the king of Babel smote them,
and slew them in Riblah, in the land of Hamath: thus Judah was carried away cap-
tive out of his own land. 28 This is the people, whom Nebuchadnezzar carried
away captive, in the [l]seventh year, even three thousand Jews, and three and twen-
ty. 29 In the [m]eighteenth year of Nebuchadnezzar, he carried away captive from
Jerusalem eight hundred thirty and two [n]persons. 30 In the three and twentieth
year of Nebuchadnezzar, Nebuzaradan the chief steward carried away captive of the
Jews seven hundred forty and five persons: all the persons were four thousand and
six hundred. 31 And in the seven and thirtieth year of the captivity of Jehoiachin
King of Judah, in the twelfth month, in the five and twentieth day of the month,
Evil-Merodach king of Babel, in the first year of his reign, [o]lifted up the head of
Jehoiachin king of Judah, and brought him out of prison, 32 And spake kindly
unto him, and set his throne above the throne of the Kings, that were with him in
Babel, 33 And changed his prison [p]garments, and he did continually eat bread
before him all the days of his life. 34 His portion was a [q]continual portion given
him of the king of Babel, every day a certain, all the days of his life until he died.

o. Jer. 52:31 That is, restored him to liberty and honor.
p. Jer. 52:33 And gave him princely apparel.
q. Jer. 52:34 That is he had allowance in the court, and thus at length he had rest and quietness because he obeyed Jer. the Prophet, whereas the others were cruelly ordered, that would not obey him.

JER. 52
1. 2 Kings 24:18 / 2 Chron. 39:11
2. 2 Kings 25:1 / Jer. 39:1

LAMENTATIONS

1 *The Prophet bewaileth the miserable estate of Jerusalem. 5 And showeth that they are plagued because of their sins. The first and second Chapter begin every verse according to the letters of the Hebrew Alphabet. The third hath three verses for every letter, and the fourth is as the first.*

1 How doth [a]the city remain solitary that was full of people? she is as a widow:
she that was great among the nations, [b]and princess among the provinces, is made
tributary. 2 She weepeth continually in the [c]night, and her tears run down by
her cheeks: among all her [d]lovers, she hath none to comfort her: all her friends have
dealt unfaithfully with her, and are her enemies. 3 Judah is carried away captive,
because [e]of affliction, and because of great servitude, she dwelleth among the hea-
then, and findeth no rest: all her persecutors took her in the straits. 4 The ways
of Zion lament, because no man cometh [f]to the solemn feasts, all her gates are deso-
late: her Priests sigh: her virgins are discomfited, and she is in [g]heaviness. 5 Her
adversaries [h]are the chief, and her enemies prosper: for the Lord hath afflicted her,
for the multitude of her transgressions, and her children are gone into captivity
before the enemy. 6 And from the daughter of Zion all her beauty is departed:
her princes are become [i]like harts that find no pasture, and they are gone without
strength before the pursuer. 7 Jerusalem remembered the days of her affliction,
and of her rebellion, and all her pleasant things that she had in times past, when
her people [j]fell into the hand of the enemy, and none did help her: the adversary
saw her, and did mock at her [k]Sabbaths. 8 Jerusalem hath grievously sinned,
therefore she is [l]in derision: all that honored her, despise her, because they have
seen her filthiness: yea, she sigheth, and turneth backward. 9 [m]Her filthiness
is in her skirts: she remembered not her last end, therefore she came down won-
derfully: she had no comforter: O Lord, behold mine affliction: for the enemy [n]is
proud. 10 The enemy hath stretched out his hand upon all her pleasant things:
for she hath seen the heathen enter into her Sanctuary, whom [o]thou didst com-
mand, that they should not enter into thy Church. 11 All her people sigh and
seek their bread: they have given their pleasant things for meat to refresh the soul:
see, O Lord, and consider: for I am become vile. 12 Have ye no regard, all ye
that pass by this way? behold and see, if there be any [p]sorrow like unto my sor-
row, which is done unto me wherewith the Lord hath afflicted me in the day of
his fierce wrath. 13 From above hath [q]he sent fire into my bones, which prevail
against them: he hath spread a net for my feet, and turned me back: he hath made
me desolate, and daily in heaviness. 14 The [r]yoke of my transgressions is bound
upon his hand: they are wrapped, and come up upon my neck: he hath made my
strength to fall: the Lord hath delivered me into their hands, neither am I able to
rise up. 15 The Lord hath trodden under foot all my valiant men in the midst
of me: he hath called an assembly against me to destroy my young men: the Lord
hath trodden [s]the winepress upon the virgin the daughter of Judah. 16 [1]For the-
se things I weep: mine eye, even mine eye casteth out water, because the comforter
that should refresh my soul, is far from me: my children are desolate, because the
enemy prevailed. 17 Zion stretcheth out her hands, and there is none to comfort
her: the Lord hath appointed the enemies of Jacob round about him: Jerusalem is
[t]as a menstruous woman in the midst of them. 18 The Lord is righteous: for I
have rebelled against his [u]commandment: hear, I pray you, all people, and behold
my sorrow: my virgins and my young men are gone into captivity. 19 I called for

LAM. 1
a. Lam. 1:1 The Prophet wondereth at the great judgment of God, seeing Jerusalem, which was so strong and so full of people, to be now destroyed and desolate.
b. Lam. 1:1 Which had chief rule over many provinces and countries.
c. Lam. 1:2 So that she taketh no rest.
d. Lam. 1:2 Meaning, the Egyptians and Assyrians, which promised help.
e. Lam. 1:3 For her cruelty toward the poor and oppression of servants, Jer. 34:11.
f. Lam. 1:4 As they used to come up with mirth and joy, Ps. 42:4.
g. Lam. 1:4 Hebrew, bitterness.
h. Lam. 1:5 That is, have rule over her, Deut. 28:41.
i. Lam. 1:6 As men pined away with sorrow and that have no courage.
j. Lam. 1:7 In her misery she considered the great benefits and commodities that she had lost.
k. Lam. 1:7 At her religion and serving of God, which was the greatest grief to the godly.
l. Lam. 1:8 Or, driven away.
m. Lam. 1:9 She is not ashamed of her sin, although it be manifest.
n. Lam. 1:9 Hebrew, hath magnified himself.
o. Lam. 1:10 God forbiddeth that the Ammonites and Moabites should enter into the Congregation of the Lord, and under them he comprehendeth all enemies, Deut. 23:3.
p. Lam. 1:12 Thus Jerusalem lamenteth moving others to pity her and to learn by her example.
q. Lam. 1:13 This declareth that we should acknowledge God to be the author of all our afflictions to the intent that we might seek unto him for remedy.
r. Lam. 1:14 Mine heavy sins are continually before his eyes, as he that tieth a thing to his hand for a remembrance.
s. Lam. 1:15 He hath trodden them underfoot as they tread grapes in the winepress.
t. Lam. 1:17 Which because of her pollution was separate from her husband, Lev. 15:19, and was abhorred for the time.
u. Lam. 1:18 Hebrew, mouth.
v. Lam. 1:19 That is, they died for hunger.
w. Lam. 1:22 Of desiring vengeance against the enemy, read Jer. 11:20 and 18:21.
x. Lam. 1:22 Or, gather them like grapes.

LAM. 1
1. Jer. 14:17 /Lam. 2:18

LAM. 2
a. Lam. 2:1 That is, brought her from prosperity to adversity.
b. Lam. 2:1 Hath given her a most sore fall.
c. Lam. 2:1 Alluding to the Temple, or to the Ark of the covenant, which was called the footstool of the Lord, because they should not set their minds so low, but lift up their hearts toward the heavens.
d. Lam. 2:3 Meaning, the glory and strength, as 1 Sam. 2:1.
e. Lam. 2:3 That is, his succor which he was wont to send us, when our enemies oppressed us.
f. Lam. 2:4 Showing that there is no remedy but destruction, where God is the enemy.
g. Lam. 2:7 As the people were accustomed to praise God to the solemn feasts with a loud voice, so now the enemies blaspheme him with shouting and cry.
h. Lam. 2:8 This is a figurative speech, as that was, when he said, the ways did lament, Lam. 1:4, meaning, that this sorrow was so great, that the insensible things had their part thereof.
i. Lam. 2:9 Or, find.
j. Lam. 2:11 Or, faint.
k. Lam. 2:12 Hebrew, wheat and wine.
l. Lam. 2:12 Hebrew, poured out the soul.
m. Lam. 2:13 Meaning, that her calamity was so evident, that it needed no witnesses.
n. Lam. 2:14 Because the false prophets called themselves Seers, as the others were called, therefore he showeth that they saw amiss, because they did not reprove the people's faults, but flattered them in their sins, which was the cause of their destruction.
o. Lam. 2:14 Or, burdens.
p. Lam. 2:20 Or, brought up in their own hands.
q. Lam. 2:22 Or, enemies, whom I feared.

my lovers, but they deceived me: my Priests and mine Elders perished in the city, while they [v]sought their meat to refresh their souls. **20** Behold, O Lord, how I am troubled: my bowels swell: mine heart is turned within me, for I am full of heaviness: the sword spoileth abroad, as death doeth at home. **21** They have heard that I mourn, but there is none to comfort me: all mine enemies have heard of my trouble, and are glad, that thou hast done it: thou wilt bring the day, that thou hast pronounced, and they shall be like unto me. **22** [w]Let all their wickedness come before thee: [x]do unto them, as thou hast done unto me, for all my transgressions: for my sighs are many, and mine heart is heavy.

2

Chapter 2

1 How hath the Lord [a]darkened the daughter of Zion in his wrath! and hath cast down from [b]heaven unto the earth the beauty of Israel, and remembered not his [c]footstool in the day of his wrath!

2 The Lord hath destroyed all the habitations of Jacob, and not spared: he hath thrown down in his wrath the strongholds of the daughter of Judah: he hath cast them down to the ground: he hath polluted the kingdom and the princes thereof. **3** He hath cut off in his fierce wrath all the [d]horn of Israel: he hath drawn back his [e]right hand from before the enemy, and there was kindled in Jacob like a flame of fire, which devoured round about. **4** He [f]hath bent his bow like an enemy: his right hand was stretched up as an adversary, and slew all that was pleasant to the eye in the Tabernacle of the daughter of Zion: he poured out his wrath like fire. **5** The Lord was as an enemy: he hath devoured Israel and consumed all his palaces: he hath destroyed his strongholds, and hath increased in the daughter of Judah lamentation and mourning. **6** For he hath destroyed his Tabernacle, as a garden he hath destroyed his Congregation: the Lord hath caused the feasts and Sabbaths to be forgotten in Zion, and hath despised in the indignation of his wrath, the King and the Priest. **7** The Lord hath forsaken his altar: he hath abhorred his Sanctuary: he hath given into the hand of the enemy the walls of her palaces: they have made a [g]noise in the House of the Lord, as in the day of solemnity. **8** The Lord hath determined to destroy the wall of the daughter of Zion: he stretched out a line: he hath not withdrawn his hand from destroying: therefore he made the rampart, [h]and the wall to lament: they were destroyed together. **9** Her gates are sunk to the ground: he hath destroyed and broken her bars: her King and her Princes are among the Gentiles: the Law is no more, neither can her Prophets [i]receive any vision from the Lord. **10** The Elders of the daughter of Zion sit upon the ground, and keep silence: they have cast up dust upon their heads: they have girded themselves with sackcloth: the virgins of Jerusalem hang down their heads to the ground. **11** Mine eyes do fail with tears: my bowels swell: my liver is poured upon the earth, for the destruction of the daughter of my people, because the children and sucklings [j]swoon in the streets of the city. **12** They have said to their mothers, Where is [k]bread and drink? when they swooned as the wounded in the streets of the city, and when they [l]gave up the ghost in their mother's bosom. **13** [m]What thing shall I take to witness for thee? What thing shall I compare to thee, O daughter Jerusalem? what shall I liken to thee, that I may comfort thee, O virgin daughter Zion? for thy breach is great like the sea: who can heal thee? **14** Thy Prophets have[n]looked out vain and foolish things for thee, and they have not discovered thine iniquity, to turn away thy captivity, but have looked out for thee false [o]prophecies, and causes of banishment. **15** All that pass by the way, clap their hands at thee: they hiss and wag their head upon the daughter Jerusalem, saying, Is this the city that men call, The perfection of beauty, and the joy of the whole earth? **16** All thine enemies have opened their mouth against thee: they hiss and gnash the teeth, saying, Let us devour it: certainly this is the day that we looked for: we have found and seen it. **17** [1]The Lord hath done that which he had purposed: he hath fulfilled his word that he had determined of old time: he hath thrown down, and not spared: he hath caused thine enemy to rejoice over thee, and set up the horn of thine adversaries. **18** Their heart [2]cried unto the Lord, O wall of the daughter Zion, let tears run down like a river, day and night: take thee no rest, neither let the apple of thine eye cease. **19** Arise, cry in the night: in the beginning of the watches, pour out thine heart like water before the face of the Lord: lift up thine hands toward him for the life of thy young children, that faint for hunger in the corners of all the streets. **20** Behold, O Lord, and consider to whom thou hast done thus: shall the women eat their fruit, and children of a [p]span long? shall the Priest and the Prophet be slain in the Sanctuary of the Lord? **21** The young and the old lie on the ground in the streets: my virgins and my young men are fallen by the sword: thou hast slain them in the day of thy wrath: thou hast killed, and not spared. **22** Thou hast called as in a solemn day my [q]terrors round about, so that in the day of the Lord's wrath none escaped nor remained: those that I have nourished and brought up, hath mine enemy consumed.

3

Chapter 3

1 I am the man that hath seen [a]affliction in the rod of his indignation.

2 He hath led me, and brought me into darkness, but not to light. **3** Surely he is turned against me: he turneth his hand against me all the day. **4** My flesh and my skin hath he caused to wax old, and he hath broken my bones. **5** He hath [b]built against me, and compassed me with gall and labor. **6** He hath set me in dark places, as they that be dead forever. **7** He hath hedged about me, that I cannot get out: he hath made my chains heavy. **8** Also when I cry and shout, he shutteth out my [c]prayer. **9** He hath [d]stopped up my ways with hewn stone, and turned away my paths. **10** [e]He was unto me as a bear lying in wait, and as a lion in secret places. **11** He hath stopped my ways, and pulled me in pieces: he hath made me desolate. **12** He hath bent his bow, and made me a mark for the arrow. **13** He caused [f]the arrows of his quiver to enter into my reins. **14** I was a derision to all my people, and their song all the day. **15** He hath filled me with bitterness, and made me drunken with [g]wormwood. **16** He hath also broken my teeth with stones, and hath covered me with ashes. **17** Thus my soul was far off from peace: I forgot prosperity, **18** And I said, My strength and my [h]hope is perished from the Lord, **19** Remembering mine affliction, and my mourning, the wormwood and the gall. **20** My soul hath them in remembrance, and is humbled [i]in me. **21** I consider this in mine heart: therefore have I hope. **22** It is the Lord's [j]mercies that we are not consumed, because his compassions fail not. **23** They are renewed [k]every morning: great is thy faithfulness. **24** The Lord is my [l]portion, saith my soul: therefore will I hope in him. **25** The Lord is good unto them that trust in him, and to the soul that seeketh him. **26** It is good both to trust, and to wait for the salvation of the Lord. **27** It is good for a man that he bear the yoke in his [m]youth. **28** He sitteth alone, [n]and keepeth silence, because he hath borne it upon him. **29** He putteth his [o]mouth in the dust, if there may be hope. **30** He giveth his cheek to him that smiteth him: he is filled full with reproaches. **31** For the Lord will not forsake forever. **32** But though he send affliction, yet will he have compassion according to the multitude of his mercies. **33** For he doth not [p]punish [q]willingly, nor afflict the children of men, **34** In stamping under his feet all the prisoners of the earth, **35** In overthrowing the right of a man before the face of the most High, **36** In subverting a man in his cause: the Lord [r]seeth it not. **37** Who is he then that saith, and it cometh to pass, and the Lord [s]commandeth it not? **38** Out of the mouth of the most High proceedeth not [t]evil and good? **39** Wherefore then is the living [u]man sorrowful? man suffereth for his sin. **40** Let us search and try our ways, and turn again to the Lord. **41** Let us lift up [v]our hearts with our hands unto God in the heavens. **42** We have sinned, and have rebelled, therefore thou hast not spared. **43** Thou hast covered us with wrath, and persecuted us: thou hast slain, and not spared. **44** Thou hast covered thyself with a cloud, that our prayer should not pass through. **45** Thou hast made us as the [1]offscouring and refuse in the midst of the people. **46** All our enemies have opened their mouth against us. **47** Fear, and a snare is come upon us with desolation and destruction. **48** Mine eye casteth out rivers of water, for the destruction of the daughter of my people. **49** Mine eye droppeth without stay, and ceaseth not, **50** Till the Lord look down, and behold from heaven. **51** Mine eye [w]breaketh mine heart because of all the daughters of my city. **52** Mine enemies chased me sore, like a bird, without cause. **53** They have shut up my life[x]in the dungeon, and cast a stone upon me. **54** Waters flowed over mine head, then thought I, I am destroyed. **55** I called upon thy Name, O Lord, out of the low dungeon. **56** Thou hast heard my voice: stop not thine ear from my sigh, and from my cry. **57** Thou drewest near in the day that I called upon thee: thou saidest, Fear not. **58** O Lord, thou hast maintained the cause of my [y]soul,

---

LAM. 2

1. Lev. 26:15,25 /Deut. 28:15,25

2. Jer. 14:17 / Lam. 1:16

LAM. 3

a. Lam. 3:1 The Prophet complaineth of the punishments and afflictions that he endured by the false prophets and hypocrites, when he declared the destruction of Jerusalem, as Jer. 20:1, 2.

b. Lam. 3:5 He speaketh this, as one that felt God's heavy judgment, which he greatly feared, and therefore setteth them out with this diversity of words.

c. Lam. 3:8 This is a great tentation to the godly when they see not the fruit of their prayers, and causeth them to think that they are not heard, which thing God useth to do, that they might pray more earnestly and the oftener.

d. Lam. 3:9 And keepeth me in hold as a prisoner.

e. Lam. 3:10 He hath no pity on me.

f. Lam. 3:13 Hebrew, sons.

g. Lam. 3:15 With great anguish and sorrow he hath made me to lose my sense.

h. Lam. 3:18 Thus with pain he was driven to and fro between hope and despair, as the godly ofttimes are, yet in the end the spirit getteth the victory.

i. Lam. 3:20 He showeth that God thus useth to exercise his, to the intent that hereby they may know themselves, and feel his mercies.

j. Lam. 3:22 Considering the wickedness of man, it is [a] marvel that any remaineth alive: but only that God for his own mercy's sake and for his promise, will ever have his Church to remain, though they be never so few in number, Isa. 1:9.

k. Lam. 3:23 We feel thy benefits daily.

l. Lam. 3:24 The godly put their whole confidence in God, and therefore look for none other inheritance, as Ps. 16:5.

m. Lam. 3:27 He showeth that we can never begin too timely to be exercised under the cross, that when the afflictions grow greater, our patience also by experience may be stronger.

n. Lam. 3:28 He murmureth not against God, but is patient.

o. Lam. 3:29 He humbleth himself as they that fall down with their face to the ground, and so with patience waiteth for succor.

p. Lam. 3:33 He taketh no pleasure in it, but doeth it of necessity for our amendment, when he suffereth the wicked to oppress the poor.

q. Lam. 3:33 Hebrew, with his heart.

r. Lam. 3:36 He doth not delight therein.

s. Lam. 3:37 He showeth that nothing is done without God's providence.

t. Lam. 3:38 That is, adversity and prosperity, Amos 3:6.

u. Lam. 3:39 When God afflicteth him.

v. Lam. 3:41 That is, both hearts and hands: for else to lift up the hands, is but hypocrisy.

w. Lam. 3:51 I am overcome with sore weeping for all my people.

x. Lam. 3:53 Read Jer. 37:16, how he was in the miry dungeon.

y. Lam. 3:58 Meaning, the cause wherefore his life was in danger.

and hast redeemed my life. **59** O Lord, thou hast seen my wrong, judge thou
my cause. **60** Thou hast seen all their vengeance, and all their devises against
me: **61** Thou hast heard their reproach, O Lord, and all their imaginations
against me. **62** The lips also of those that rose against me, and their whispering
against me continually. **63** Behold, their sitting down, and their rising up, how I
am their song. **64** [2]Give them a recompense, O Lord, according to the work of
their hands. **65** Give them [z]sorrow of heart even thy curse to them. **66** Perse-
cute with wrath and destroy them from under the heaven, O Lord.

4 *Chapter 4*

1 How is the [a]gold become so [b]dim? the most fine gold is changed,
and the stones of the Sanctuary are scattered in the corner of every street.
2 The noble [c]men of Zion comparable to fine gold, how are they esteemed as
earthen [d]pitchers, even the work of the hands of the potter! **3** Even the dragons
[e]draw out the breasts, and give suck to their young: but the daughter of my people
is become cruel like the [f]ostriches in the wilderness. **4** The tongue of the sucking
child cleaveth to the roof of his mouth for thirst: the young children ask bread, but
no man breaketh it unto them. **5** They that did feed delicately, perish in the stre-
ets: they that were brought up in scarlet, embrace the dung. **6** For the iniquity of
the daughter of my people is become greater than the sin of Sodom, that was [1]de-
stroyed as in a moment, and [g]none pitched camps against her. **7** Her [2]Nazirites
were purer than the snow, and whiter than the milk: they were more ruddy in body,
than the red precious stones: they were like polished sapphire. **8** Now their [h]visa-
ge is blacker than a coal: they cannot know them in the streets: their skin cleaveth
to their bones: it is withered like a stock. **9** They that be slain with the sword,
are better than they that are killed with hunger: for they fade away as they were
stricken through for the [i]fruits of the field. **10** The hands of the pitiful women
have sodden their own children, which were their meat in the destruction of the
daughter of my people. **11** The Lord hath accomplished his indignation: he hath
poured out his fierce wrath, he hath kindled a fire in Zion, which hath devoured
the foundations thereof. **12** The kings of the earth, and all the inhabitants of the
world would not have believed that the adversary and the enemy should have ente-
red into the gates of Jerusalem: **13** For the sins of her prophets, and the iniquities
of her priests, that have shed the blood of the just in the midst of [j]her. **14** They
have wandered as blind men[k]in the streets, and they were polluted with blood, so
that[l]they would not touch their garments. **15** But they cried unto them, Depart
ye polluted, depart, depart, touch not: therefore they fled away, and wandered:
they have said among the heathen, They shall no more dwell there. **16** The [m]an-
ger of the Lord hath scattered them, he will no more regard them: [n]they reverenced
not the face of the Priest, nor had compassion on the Elders. **17** While we waited
for our vain help, our eyes failed: for in our waiting we looked for [o]a nation that
could not save us. **18** They hunt our steps, that we cannot go in our streets: our
end is near, our days are fulfilled, for our end is come. **19** Our persecutors are
swifter than the eagles of the heaven: they pursued us upon the mountains, and
laid wait for us in the wilderness. **20** The [p]breath of our nostrils, the Anointed of
the Lord was taken in their nets, of whom we said, Under his shadow we shall be
preserved alive among the heathen. **21** Rejoice and be glad, [q]O daughter Edom:
that dwellest in the land of Uz, the cup also shall pass through unto thee: thou shalt
be drunken [r]and vomit. **22** Thy punishment is accomplished, O daughter Zion:
he [s]will no more carry thee away into captivity, but he will visit thine iniquity, O
daughter Edom, he will discover thy sins.

5 *The prayer of Jeremiah.*

1 Remember, O Lord, what is come upon us: [a]consider, and
behold our reproach. **2** Our inheritance is turned to the strangers, our houses
to the aliens. **3** We are fatherless, even without father, and our mothers are as
widows. **4** We have drunk our [b]water for money, and our wood is sold unto
us. **5** Our necks are under persecution: we are weary, and have no rest. **6** We
have given our [c]hands to the Egyptians, and to Assyria, to be satisfied with bre-
ad. **7** Our fathers have sinned, and are not, and we have borne [d]their ini-
quities. **8** Servants have ruled over us, none would deliver us out of their
hands. **9** We got our bread with the peril of our lives, because of the sword
[e]of the wilderness. **10** Our skin was black like as an oven because of the ter-
rible famine. **11** They defiled the women in Zion, and the maids in the cities
of Judah. **12** The princes are hanged up by [f]their hand: the faces of the Elders
were not had in honor. **13** They took the young men to grind, and the chil-
dren fell under [g]the wood. **14** The Elders have ceased from the [h]gate and the
young men from their songs. **15** The joy of our heart is gone, our dance is tur-
ned into mourning. **16** The crown of our head is fallen: woe now unto us, that
we have sinned. **17** Therefore our heart is heavy for these things, our [i]eyes are
dim, **18** Because of the mountain of Zion, which is desolate: the foxes run upon
it. **19** But thou, O Lord, remainest [j]forever: thy throne is from generation to
generation. **20** Wherefore dost thou forget us forever, and forsake us so long
time? **21** [k]Turn thou us unto thee, O Lord, and we shall be turned: renew our
days as of old. **22** But thou hast utterly rejected us: thou art exceedingly angry
against us.

---

z. Lam. 3:65 Or, an obstinate heart.

LAM. 3

1. 1 Cor. 4:13 **2.** Ps. 28:4

LAM. 4

a. Lam. 4:1 By the gold, he meaneth the princes, as by the stones he understandeth the Priests.
b. Lam. 4:1 Or, hid.
c. Lam. 4:2 Or, sons.
d. Lam. 4:2 Which are of small estimation, and have none honor.
e. Lam. 4:3 Though the dragons be cruel, yet they pity their young, and nourish them, which things Jerusalem doth not.
f. Lam. 4:3 The women forsake their children, as the ostrich doth her eggs, Job 39:17.
g. Lam. 4:6 Or, no strength was against her.
h. Lam. 4:8 They that were before most in God's favor, are now in greatest abomination unto him.
i. Lam. 4:9 For lack of food they pine away and consume.
j. Lam. 4:13 He meaneth that these things are come to pass therefore, contrary to all men's expectation.
k. Lam. 4:14 Some refer this to the blind men, which as they went, stumbled on the blood, whereof the city was full.
l. Lam. 4:14 Meaning, the heathen which came to destroy them, could not abide them.
m. Lam. 4:16 Or, face.
n. Lam. 4:16 That is, the enemies.
o. Lam. 4:17 He showeth two principal causes of their destruction: their cruelty and their vain confidence in man: for they trusted in the help of the Egyptians.
p. Lam. 4:20 Our king Josiah, in whom stood our hope of God's favor, and on whom depended our state and life, was slain, whom he calleth Anointed, because he was a figure of Christ.
q. Lam. 4:21 This is spoken by derision.
r. Lam. 4:21 Or, show thy nakedness.
s. Lam. 4:22 He comforteth the Church, by that after seventy years their sorrows shall have an end, whereas the wicked should be tormented forever.

LAM. 4

1. Gen. 19:25 **2.** Num. 6:2

LAM. 5

a. Lam. 5:1 This prayer as is thought, was made when some of the people were carried away captive, others, as the poorest remained, and some went into Egypt, and other places for succor: albeit it seemeth that the Prophet foreseeing their miseries to come, thus prayed.
b. Lam. 5:4 Meaning, their extreme servitude and bondage.
c. Lam. 5:6 We are joined in league and amity with them, or have submitted ourselves unto them.
d. Lam. 5:7 As our fathers have been punished for their sins: so we that are culpable of the same sins, are punished.
e. Lam. 5:9 Because of the enemy that came from the wilderness, and would not suffer us to go and seek our necessary food.
f. Lam. 5:12 That is, by the enemy's hand.
g. Lam. 5:13 Their slavery was so great, that they were not able to abide it.
h. Lam. 5:14 There were no more laws nor form of commonwealth.
i. Lam. 5:17 With weeping.
j. Lam. 5:19 And therefore thy covenant and mercies can never fail.
k. Lam. 5:21 Whereby is declared that it is not in man's power to turn to God, but is only his work to convert us, and thus God worketh in us before we can turn to him, Jer. 31:18.

EZEKIEL

1

1 The time wherein Ezekiel prophesied, in what place. 3 His kindred. 5 The vision of the four beasts. 26 The vision of the throne.

1 It came to pass in the [a]thirtieth year in the fourth month, and in the fifth day of the month (as I was among the captives by the river [b]Chebar) that the heavens were opened, and I saw visions of [c]GOD. **2** In the fifth day of the month (which was the fifth year of king Jehoiachin's captivity) **3** The word of the Lord came unto Ezekiel the Priest, the son of Buzi, in the land of the Chaldeans, by the river Chebar, where the [d]hand of the Lord was upon him. **4** And I looked, and behold, a [e]whirlwind came out of the North, a great cloud and a fire wrapped about it, and a brightness was about it, and in the midst thereof, to wit, in the midst of the fire came out as the likeness of [f]amber. **5** Also out of the midst thereof came the likeness of [g]four beasts, and this was their form: they had the appearance of a man, **6** And every one had four faces, and every one had four wings. **7** And their feet were straight feet, and the sole of their feet was like the soles of a calf's foot, and they sparkled like the appearance of bright brass. **8** And the hands of a man came out from under their wings in the four parts of them, and they four had their faces, and their wings. **9** They where [h]joined by their wings one to another, and when they went forth, they returned not, but every one went straight forward. **10** And the similitude of their faces was as [i]the face of a man: and they four had the face of a lion on the right side, and they four had the face of a bullock on the left side: they four also had the face of an Eagle. **11** Thus were their faces: but their wings were spread out above: two wings of every one were joined one to another, and two covered their bodies. **12** And every one went straight forward: they went whither their [j]spirit led them, and they returned not when they went forth. **13** The similitude also of the beasts, and their appearance was like burning coals of fire, and like the appearance of lamps: for the fire ran among the beasts, and the fire gave a glister, and out of the fire there went lightning. **14** And the beasts ran, and [k]returned like unto lightning. **15** Now as I beheld the beasts, behold, a wheel appeared upon the earth by the beasts, having four faces. **16** The fashion of the wheels and their work was like unto a [l]Chrysolite: and they four had one form, and their fashion and their work was as one wheel in another wheel. **17** When they went, they went upon their four sides, and they returned not when they went. **18** They had also [m]rings, and height, and were fearful to behold, and their rings were full of eyes, round about them four. **19** And when the beasts went, the wheels went with them: and when the beasts were lifted up from the earth, the wheels were lifted up. **20** Whither their spirit led them, they went, and thither did the spirit of the wheels lead them, and the wheels were lifted up besides them: for the spirit of the beasts was in the wheels. **21** When the beasts went, they went, and when they stood, they stood, and when they were lifted up from the earth, the wheels were lifted up besides them: for the spirit of the beasts was in the wheels. **22** And the similitude of the firmament upon the heads of the beasts was wonderful, like unto crystal spread over their heads above. **23** And under the firmament were their wings straight, the one toward the other: every one had two which covered them, and every one had two which covered their bodies. **24** And when they went forth, I heard the noise of their [n]wings, like the noise of great waters, and as the voice of the Almighty, even the voice of speech, as the noise of an host: even when they stood, they [o]let down their wings. **25** And there was a voice from the firmament that was over their heads, when they stood, and had let down their wings. **26** And above the firmament that was over their heads, was the fashion of a throne like unto a Sapphire stone, and upon the similitude of the throne was by appearance, as the similitude of a man above upon it. **27** And I saw as the appearance of amber, and as the similitude of fire [p]round about within it to look too, even from his loins upward: and to look too, even from his loins downward, I saw as a likeness of fire, and brightness round about it. **28** As the likeness of the bow, that is in the cloud in the day of rain, so was the appearance of the light round about. **29** This was the appearance of the similitude of the glory of the Lord: and when I saw it, I fell [q]upon my face, and I heard a voice of one that spake.

2

The Prophet is sent to call the people from their error.

1 And [a]he said unto me, [b]Son of man, stand up upon thy feet, and I will speak unto thee. **2** [c]And the Spirit entered into me, when he had spoken unto me, and set me upon my feet, so that I heard him that spake unto me. **3** And he said unto me, Son of Man, I send thee to the children of Israel, to a rebellious nation that hath rebelled against me: for they and their fathers have rebelled against me, even unto this very day. **4** For they are [d]impudent children, and stiff-hearted: I do send thee unto them, and thou shalt say unto them, Thus saith the Lord God. **5** But surely they will not hear, neither indeed will they cease: for they are a rebellious house: yet shall they know that [e]there hath been a Prophet among them. **6** And thou son of man, [f]fear them not, neither be afraid of their words, although rebels and thorns be with thee, and thou remainest with scorpions: fear not their words, nor be afraid at their looks, for they are a rebellious house. **7** Therefore thou shalt speak my words unto them: but surely they will not hear, neither will they indeed cease: for they are rebellious. **8** But thou son of man, hear what I say unto thee: be not thou rebellious, like this rebellious house: open thy mouth, and [g]eat that I give thee. **9** And when I looked up, behold, an hand was sent unto me, and lo, a roll of a book was therein. **10** And he spread it before me, and it was written within and without, and there was written therein, [h]Lamentations and mourning, and woe.

3

1 The Prophet being fed with the word of God and with the constant boldness of the spirit, is sent unto the people that were in captivity. 17 The office of true ministers.

1 Moreover he said unto me, Son of man, eat that thou findest: [a]eat this roll, and go, and speak unto the house of Israel. **2** So I opened my mouth, and he gave me this roll to eat. **3** And he said unto me, Son of man, cause thy belly to eat, and fill thy bowels with this roll that I give thee. Then did I eat, and it was in my mouth as sweet as honey. **4** And he said unto me, Son of man, go and enter into the house of Israel, and declare them my words. **5** For thou art not sent to a people of an [b]unknown tongue, or of an hard language, but to the house of Israel, **6** Not to many people of an unknown tongue, or of an hard language, whose words thou canst not understand: yet if I should send thee to them, they would obey thee. **7** But the house of Israel will not obey thee: for they will not obey me: yea, all the house of Israel are impudent and stiff-hearted. **8** Behold, I have made thy [c]face strong against their faces, and thy forehead hard against their foreheads. **9** I have made thy forehead as the adamant, and harder than the flint: fear them not therefore, neither be afraid at their looks: for they are a rebellious

---

EZEK. 1

- **a.** Ezek. 1:1 After that the book of the Law was found, which was the eighteenth year of the reign of Josiah, so that five and twenty years after this book was found, Jeconiah was led away captive with Ezek. and many of the people, who the first year after saw these visions.
- **b.** Ezek. 1:1 Which was a part of Euphrates so called.
- **c.** Ezek. 1:1 That is notable and excellent visions, so that it might be known, it was no natural dream, but came of God.
- **d.** Ezek. 1:3 That is, the spirit of prophecy, as Ezek. 3:22 and 37:1.
- **e.** Ezek. 1:4 By this diversity of words he signifieth the fearful judgment of God and the great afflictions that should come upon Jerusalem.
- **f.** Ezek. 1:4 Or, pale fellow.
- **g.** Ezek. 1:5 Which were the four Cherubims that represented the glory of God, as Ezek. 3:23.
- **h.** Ezek. 1:9 The wing of the one touched the wing of the other.
- **i.** Ezek. 1:10 Every Cherubim had four faces, the face of a man, and of a lion on the right side, and the face of a bullock and of an Eagle on the left side.
- **j.** Ezek. 1:12 Hebrew, whither their spirit or wings was to go.
- **k.** Ezek. 1:14 That is, when they had executed God's will: for afore they returned not till God had changed the state of things.
- **l.** Ezek. 1:16 The Hebrew word is tarshish meaning that the color was like the Cilician Sea, or a precious stone so called.
- **m.** Ezek. 1:18 Or, the trent.
- **n.** Ezek. 1:24 Which declared the swiftness and the fearfulness of God's judgments.
- **o.** Ezek. 1:24 Which signified that they had no power of themselves, but only waited to execute God's commandment.
- **p.** Ezek. 1:27 Whereby was signified a terrible judgment toward the earth.
- **q.** Ezek. 1:29 Considering the majesty of God, and the weakness of flesh.

EZEK. 2

- **a.** Ezek. 2:1 That is, the Lord.
- **b.** Ezek. 2:1 Meaning, man which is but earth and ashes, which was to humble him, and cause him to consider his own state, and God's grace.
- **c.** Ezek. 2:2 So that he could not abide God's presence, till God's Spirit did enter into him.
- **d.** Ezek. 2:4 Hebrew, hard of face.
- **e.** Ezek. 2:5 This declareth on the one part God's great affection toward his people, that notwithstanding their rebellion, yet he will send his Prophets among them, and admonisheth his ministers on the other part that they cease not to do their duty, though the people be never so obstinate: for the word of God shall be either to their salvation or greater condemnation.
- **f.** Ezek. 2:6 Read Jer. 1:17, he showeth that for none afflictions they should cease to do their duties.
- **g.** Ezek. 2:8 He doth not only exhort him to his duty, but also giveth him the means wherewith he may be able to execute it.
- **h.** Ezek. 2:10 He showeth what were the contents of this book: to wit, God's judgments against the wicked.

EZEK. 3

- **a.** Ezek. 3:1 Whereby is meant that none is meet to be God's messenger before he have received the word of God in his heart, as verse 10, and have a zeal thereunto, and delight therein, as Jer. 15:16; Rev. 10:10.
- **b.** Ezek. 3:5 Hebrew, deep lips.
- **c.** Ezek. 3:8 God promiseth his assistance to his ministers, and that he will give them boldness and constancy in their vocation, Isa. 50:7; Jer. 1:18; Mic. 3:8.

house. 10 He said moreover unto me, Son of man, [d]receive in thine heart all my words that I speak unto thee, and hear them with thine ears, 11 And go and enter to them that are led away captives unto the children of thy people, and speak unto them, and tell them, Thus saith the Lord God: but surely they will not hear, neither will they indeed cease. 12 Then the spirit took me up, and I heard behind me a noise of a great rushing, saying, [e]Blessed be the glory of the Lord out of his place. 13 I heard also the noise of the wings of the beasts, that touched one another, and the rattling of the wheels that were by them, even a noise of a great rushing. 14 So the spirit lifted me up, and took me away, and I [f]went in bitterness and indignation of my spirit, but the hand of the Lord was strong upon me. 15 Then I came to them that were led away captives to [g]Tel Abib, that dwelt by the river Chebar, and I sat where they sat, and remained there astonished among them [h]seven days. 16 And at the end of seven days, the word of the Lord came again unto me, saying, 17 Son of man, I have made thee a [i]watchman unto the house of Israel: therefore hear the word at my mouth, and give them warning from me 18 When I shall say unto the wicked, Thou shalt surely die, and thou givest not him warning, nor speakest to admonish the wicked of his wicked way, that he may live, the same wicked man shall die in his iniquity: but his blood will I require at thine hand. 19 Yet, if thou warn the wicked, and he turn not from his wickedness, nor from his wicked way, he shall die in his iniquity, but thou hast delivered thy soul. 20 Likewise if a [j]righteous man turn from his righteousness, and commit iniquity, I will lay a [k]stumbling block before him and he shall die, because thou hast not given him warning, he shall die in his sin, and his [l]righteous deeds, which he hath done, shall not be remembered: but his blood will I require at thine hand. 21 Nevertheless, if thou admonish that righteous man, that the righteous sin not, and that he doth not sin, he shall live because he is admonished: also thou hast delivered thy soul. 22 And the [m]hand of the Lord was there upon me, and he said unto me, Arise, and go into the [n]field, and I will there talk with thee. 23 So when I had risen up, and gone forth into the field, behold, the glory of the Lord stood there, as the [o]glory which I saw by the river Chebar, and I fell down upon my face. 24 Then the Spirit entered into me, which [p]set me up upon my feet, and spake unto me, and said to me, Come, and [q]shut thyself within thine house. 25 But thou, O son of man, behold, they shall put bands upon thee, and shall bind thee with them, and thou shalt not go out among them. 26 And I will make thy tongue [r]cleave to the roof of thy mouth, that thou shalt be dumb, and shalt not be to them as a man that rebuketh: for they are a rebellious house. 27 But when I shall have spoken unto thee, I will open thy mouth, and thou shalt say unto them, Thus saith the Lord God, He that heareth, let him hear, and he that leaveth off, [1]let him leave: for they are a rebellious house.

4

1 The besieging of the city of Jerusalem is signified. 9 The long continuance of the captivity of Israel. 16 An hunger is prophesied to come.

1 Thou also son of man, take thee a brick, and lay it before thee, and portray upon it the city, even Jerusalem, 2 And lay siege against it, and build a fort against it, and cast a mount against it, set the camp also against it, and lay engines of war against it round about. 3 Moreover, take an [a]iron pan, and set it for a wall of iron between thee and the city, and direct thy face toward it, and it shall be besieged, and thou shalt lay siege against it: this shall be a sign unto the house of Israel. 4 Sleep thou also upon thy left side, and lay the iniquity of the [b]house of Israel upon it: according to the number of the days, that thou shalt sleep upon it, thou shalt bear their iniquity. 5 For I have laid upon thee the years of their iniquity according to the number of the days, even three hundred and ninety days: so shalt thou bear the iniquity of the house of Israel. 6 And when thou hast accomplished them, sleep again upon thy [c]right side, and thou shalt bear the iniquity of the house of Judah forty days: I have appointed thee a day for a year, even a day for a year. 7 Therefore thou shalt direct thy face toward the siege of Jerusalem, and thine [d]arm shall be uncovered, and thou shalt prophesy against it. 8 And behold, I will lay [e]bands upon thee, and thou shalt not turn thee from one side to another, till thou hast ended the days of thy siege. 9 Thou shalt take also unto thee wheat, and barley, and beans, and lentils, and millet, [f]and fitches, and put them in one vessel, and make thee bread thereof according to the number of the days, that thou shalt sleep upon thy side: even [g]three hundred and ninety days shalt thou eat thereof. 10 And the meat, whereof thou shalt eat shall be by weight, even [h]twenty shekels a day: and from time to time shalt thou eat thereof. 11 Thou shalt drink also water by measure, even the sixth part of [i]an Hin: from time to time shalt thou drink. 12 And thou shalt eat it as barley cakes, and thou shalt bake it [j]in the dung that cometh out of man in their sight. 13 And the Lord said, So shall the children of Israel eat their defiled bread among the Gentiles, whither I will cast them. 14 Then said I, Ah, Lord God, behold, my soul hath not been polluted: for from my youth up, even unto this hour, I have not eaten of a thing dead or torn in pieces, neither came there any [k]unclean flesh in my mouth. 15 Then he said unto me, Lo, I have given thee bullocks [l]dung for man's dung, and thou shalt prepare thy bread therewith. 16 Moreover, he said unto me, Son of man, behold, I will break [m]the staff of bread in Jerusalem, and they shall eat bread by weight, and with care, and they shall drink water by measure, and with astonishment. 17 Because that bread and water shall fail, they shall be astonied one with another, and shall consume away for their iniquity.

5

The sign of the hairs, whereby is signified the destruction of the people.

1 And thou son of man, take thee a sharp knife, or take thee a barber's razor, and cause it [a]to pass upon thine head, and upon thy beard: then take thee balances to weigh, and divide the hair. 2 Thou shalt burn with fire the third part in the midst of the [b]city, when the days of the siege are fulfilled, and thou shalt take the other third part, and smite about it with a knife, and the last third part thou shalt scatter in the wind, and I will draw out a sword after them. 3 Thou shalt also take thereof a few in number, and bind them in thy [c]lap. 4 Then take of them again and cast them into the midst of the fire, and burn them in the fire: [d]for thereof shall a fire come forth into all the house of Israel. 5 Thus saith the Lord God, This is Jerusalem, I have set it in the midst of the nations and countries, that are round about her. 6 And she hath changed my [e]judgments into wickedness more than the nations, and my statutes more than the countries, that are round about her: for they have refused my judgments, and my statutes, and they have not walked in them. 7 Therefore thus saith the Lord God, Because your [f]multitude is greater than the nations that are round about you, and ye have not walked in my statutes, neither have ye kept my judgments: no, ye have not done according to the judgments of the nations, that are round about you. 8 Therefore thus saith the Lord God, Behold, I, even I come against thee, and will execute judgment in the midst of thee, even in the sight of the nations. 9 And I will do in thee that I never did before, neither will do anymore the like, because of all thine abominations. 10 For in the midst of thee, the fathers [1]shall eat their sons, and the sons shall eat their fathers, and I will execute judgment in thee, and the whole remnant of thee will I scatter into all the winds. 11 Wherefore as I live, saith the Lord God, Surely, because thou hast defiled my Sanctuary with all thy filthiness, and with all thine abominations, therefore will I also destroy thee, neither shall mine eye spare thee, neither will I have any pity. 12 The third part of thee shall die with the pestilence, and with famine shall they be consumed in the midst of thee: and another third part shall fall by the sword round about thee: and I will scatter the last third part into all winds, and I will draw out a sword after them. 13 Thus shall mine anger be accomplished, and I will cause my wrath to cease in them, and I will be [g]comforted: and they shall know, that I the Lord have

---

d. Ezek. 3:10 He showeth what is meant by the eating of the book, which is that the ministers of God may speak nothing as of themselves, but that only, which they have received of the Lord.
e. Ezek. 3:12 Whereby he signifieth, that God's glory should not be diminished, although he departed out of his Temple, for this declared that the city and Temple should be destroyed.
f. Ezek. 3:14 This showeth that there is ever an infirmity of the flesh which can never be ready to render full obedience to God, and also God's grace which ever assisteth his, and overcometh their rebellious affections.
g. Ezek. 3:15 Which was a place by Euphrates, where the Jews were prisoners.
h. Ezek. 3:15 Declaring hereby that God's ministers must with advisement and deliberation utter his judgments.
i. Ezek. 3:17 Of this read Ezek. 33:2.
j. Ezek. 3:20 If he that hath been instructed in the right way turn back.
k. Ezek. 3:20 I will give him up to a reprobate mind, Rom. 1:28.
l. Ezek. 3:20 Which seemed to have been done in faith, and were not.
m. Ezek. 3:22 That is, the Spirit of prophecy.
n. Ezek. 3:22 Or, valley.
o. Ezek. 3:23 Meaning, the vision of the Cherubims, and the wheels.
p. Ezek. 3:24 Read Ezek. 2:2.
q. Ezek. 3:24 Signifying, that not only he should not profit, but they should grievously trouble and afflict him.
r. Ezek. 3:26 Which declareth the terrible plague of the Lord, when God stoppeth the mouths of his ministers, and that all such are the rods of his vengeance that do it.

EZEK. 3

1. Rev. 22:11

EZEK. 4

a. Ezek. 4:3 Which signified the stubbornness and hardness of their heart.
b. Ezek. 4:4 Hereby he represented the idolatry and sin of the ten tribes (for Samaria was on his left hand from Babylon) and how they had remained therein three hundred and ninety years.
c. Ezek. 4:6 Which declared Judah, who had now from the time of Josiah slept in their sins forty years.
d. Ezek. 4:7 In token of a speedy vengeance.
e. Ezek. 4:8 The people should so straightly be besieged, that they should not be able, to turn them.
f. Ezek. 4:9 Meaning, that the famine should be so great, that they should be glad to eat whatsoever they could get.
g. Ezek. 4:9 Which were fourteen months that the city was besieged, and this was as many days as Israel sinned years.
h. Ezek. 4:10 Which make a pound.
i. Ezek. 4:11 Read Exod. 29:40.
j. Ezek. 4:12 Signifying hereby the great scarcity of fuel and matter to burn.
k. Ezek. 4:14 Much less such vile corruption.
l. Ezek. 4:15 To be as fire to bake thy bread with.
m. Ezek. 4:16 That is, the force and strength wherewith it should nourish, Isa. 3:1; Ezek. 5:17 and 14:13.

EZEK. 5

a. Ezek. 5:1 To shave thine head and thy beard.
b. Ezek. 5:2 To wit, of that city which he had portrayed upon the brick, Ezek. 4:1. By the fire and pestilence he meaneth the famine, wherewith one part perished during the siege of Nebuchadnezzar. By the sword, those that were slain whom Zedekiah fled, and those that were carried away captive. And by the scattering into the wind, those that fled into Egypt, and into other parts after the city was taken.
c. Ezek. 5:3 Meaning, that a very few should be left, which the Lord should preserve among all these storms, but not without troubles and trial.
d. Ezek. 5:4 Out of that fire which thou kindlest shall a fire come, which shall signify the destruction of Israel.
e. Ezek. 5:6 My word and law into idolatry and superstitions.
f. Ezek. 5:7 Because your idols are in greater number, and your superstitions more than among the professed idolaters, read Isa. 65:11, or he condemneth their ingratitude in respect of his benefits.
g. Ezek. 5:13 That is, I will not be pacified, till I be revenged, Isa. 1:24.

spoken it in my zeal, when I have accomplished my wrath in them. **14** Moreover, I will make thee waste, and abhorred among the nations that are round about thee, and in the sight of all that pass by. **15** So thou shalt be a reproach and shame, a chastisement and an astonishment unto the nations, that are round about thee, when I shall execute judgments in thee in anger and in wrath, and in sharp rebukes: I the Lord have spoken it. **16** When I shall send upon them the [h]evil [i]arrows of famine, which shall be for their destruction, and which I will send to destroy you: and I will increase the famine upon you, and will break your staff of bread. **17** [2]So I will send upon you famine, and evil beasts, and they shall spoil thee: and pestilence and blood shall pass through thee: and I will bring the sword upon thee: I the Lord have spoken it.

6

He showeth that Jerusalem shall be destroyed for their idolatry. 8 He prophesieth the repentance of the remnant of the people, and their deliverance.

1 Again the word of the Lord came unto me, saying, **2** Son of man, Set thy face towards the [1]mountains of Israel, and prophesy against them, **3** And say, Ye mountains of Israel, hear the word of the Lord God: thus saith the Lord God to the [a]mountains and to the hills, to the rivers and to the valleys, Behold, I, even I will bring a sword upon you, and I will destroy your high places: **4** And your altars shall be desolate, and your images of the [b]Sun shall be broken: and I will cast down your slain men before your idols. **5** And I will lay the dead carcasses of the children of Israel before their [c]idols, and I will [2]scatter your bones round about your altars. **6** In all your dwelling places the cities shall be desolate, and the high places shall be laid waste, so that your altars shall be made waste and desolate, and your idols shall be broken and cease, and your images of the Sun shall be cut in pieces, and your works shall be abolished. **7** And the slain shall fall in the midst of you, and ye shall know that I am the Lord. **8** Yet will I leave a remnant, [d]that you may have some that shall escape the sword among the nations, when you shall be scattered through the countries. **9** And they that escape of you, shall remember me among the nations, where they shall be in captivity, because I am grieved for their whorish hearts, which have departed from me, and for their eyes, which have gone a whoring after their idols, and they [e]shall be displeased in themselves for the evils which they have committed in all their abominations. **10** And they shall know that I am the Lord, and that I have not said in vain, that I would do this evil unto them. **11** Thus saith the Lord God, [f]Smite with thine hand, and stretch forth with thy foot, and say, Alas, for all the wicked abominations of the house of Israel: for they shall fall by the sword, by the famine, and by the pestilence. **12** He that is far off, shall die of the pestilence, and he that is near, shall fall by the sword, and he that remaineth and is besieged, shall die by the famine: thus will I accomplish my wrath upon them. **13** Then [g]ye shall know, that I am the Lord, when their slain men shall be among their idols round about their altars, upon every high hill in all the tops of the mountains, and under every green tree, and under every thick oak, which is the place where they did offer sweet savor to all their idols. **14** So will I [3]stretch mine hand upon them, and make the land waste and desolate [h]from the wilderness unto Diblath in all their habitations, and they shall know that I am the Lord.

7

The end of all the land of Israel shall suddenly come.

1 Moreover the word of the Lord came unto me, saying, **2** Also thou son of man, thus saith the Lord God, An end is come unto the land of Israel: the end is come upon the four corners of the land. **3** Now is the end come upon thee, and I will send my wrath upon thee, and will judge thee according to thy ways, and will lay upon thee all [a]thine abominations. **4** Neither shall mine eye spare thee, neither will I have pity: but I will lay thy ways upon thee: and thine abomination shall be in the midst of thee, and ye shall know that I am the Lord. **5** Thus saith the Lord God, [b]Behold, one evil, even one evil is come. **6** An end is come, the end is come, it [c]watched for thee: behold, it is come. **7** The [d]morning is come unto thee, that dwellest in the land: the time is come, the day of trouble is near, and not the [e]sounding again of the mountains. **8** Now I will shortly pour out my wrath upon thee, and fulfill mine anger upon thee: I will judge thee according to thy ways, and will lay upon thee all thine abominations. **9** Neither shall mine eye spare thee, neither will I have pity, but I will lay upon thee according to thy ways, and thine abominations shall be in the midst of thee, and ye shall know that I am the Lord that smiteth. **10** Behold, the day, behold, it is come: the morning is gone forth, the [f]rod flourisheth: [g]pride hath budded. **11** [h]Cruelty is risen up into a rod of wickedness: none of them shall remain, nor of their riches, nor of any of theirs, neither shall there be [i]lamentation for them. **12** The time is come, the day draweth near: let not the buyer [j]rejoice, nor let him that selleth [k]mourn: for the wrath is upon all the multitude thereof. **13** For he that selleth, shall not [l]return to that which is sold, although they were yet alive: for the [m]vision was unto all the multitude thereof, and they returned not, [n]neither doth any encourage himself in the punishment of his life. **14** [o]They have blown the trumpet, and prepared all, but none goeth to the battle: for my wrath is upon all the multitude thereof. **15** The sword is without, and the pestilence, and the famine within: he that is in the field, shall die with the sword, and he that is in the city, famine and pestilence shall devour him. **16** But they that flee away from them, shall escape, and shall be in the mountains, like the doves of the valleys: all they shall mourn, every one for his iniquity. **17** [1]All hands shall be weak, and all knees shall fall away as water. **18** [2]They shall also gird themselves with sackcloth, and fear shall cover them, and shame shall be upon all faces, and baldness upon their heads. **19** They shall cast their silver in the streets, and their gold shall be cast far off: their [3]silver and their gold cannot deliver them in the day of the wrath of the Lord: they shall not satisfy their souls, neither fill their bowels: for this ruin is for their iniquity. **20** He had also set the beauty of his [p]ornament in majesty: but they made images of their abominations, and of their idols therein: therefore have I set it far from them. **21** And I will give it into the hands of the [q]strangers to be spoiled, and to the wicked of the earth to be robbed, and they shall pollute it. **22** My face will I turn also from them, and they shall pollute my [r]secret place: for the destroyers shall enter into it, and defile it. **23** Make a [s]chain: for the land is full of the [t]judgment of blood, and the city is full of cruelty. **24** Wherefore I will bring the most wicked of the heathen, and they shall possess their houses: I will also make the pomp of the mighty to cease, and their [u]holy places shall be defiled. **25** When destruction cometh, they shall seek peace, and shall not have it. **26** Calamity shall come upon calamity, and rumor shall be upon rumor: then shall they seek a vision of the Prophet: but the Law shall perish from the Priest, and counsel from the Ancient. **27** The king shall mourn, and the prince shall be clothed with desolation, and the hands of the people in the land shall be troubled: I will do unto them according to their ways, and according to their judgments will I judge them, and they shall know that I am the Lord.

8

1 An appearance of the similitude of God. 3 Ezekiel is brought to Jerusalem in the spirit. 6 The Lord showeth the Prophet the idolatries of the house of Israel.

1 And in the [a]sixth year, in the [b]sixth month, and in the fifth day of the month, as I sat in mine house, and the Elders of Judah sat before me, the hand of the Lord God fell there upon me. **2** Then I beheld, and lo, there was a likeness, as the appearance of [c]fire, to look to, from his loins downward, and from his loins upward, as the appearance of brightness, and like unto amber. **3** And

---

h. Ezek. 5:16 Or, dangerous.
i. Ezek. 5:16 Which were the grasshoppers, mildew, and whatsoever were occasions of famine.

EZEK. 5
1. Lev. 26:29 /Deut. 28:53 / 2Kings 6:29 / Lam 4:10
2. Ezek. 14:13

EZEK. 6
a. Ezek. 6:3 He speaketh to all the places where the Israelites accustomed to commit their idolatries, threatening them destruction.
b. Ezek. 6:4 Read 2 Kings 23:11.
c. Ezek. 6:5 In contempt of their power and force, which shall neither be able to deliver you nor themselves.
d. Ezek. 6:8 He showeth that in all dangers God will preserve a few, which shall be as the seed of his Church and call upon his Name.
e. Ezek. 6:9 They shall be ashamed to see that their hope in idols was but vain, and so shall repent.
f. Ezek. 6:11 By these signs he would that the Prophet should signify the great destruction to come.
g. Ezek. 6:13 That is, all nations when you shall see my judgments.
h. Ezek. 6:14 Some read, more desolate than the wilderness of Diblath, which was in Syria, and bordered upon Israel, or from the wilderness, which was South unto Diblath, which was North: meaning, the whole country.

EZEK. 6
1. Ezek. 36:1
2. 2Kings 23:20
3. Ezek. 5:14

EZEK. 7
a. Ezek. 7:3 I will punish thee as thou hast deserved for thine idolatry.
b. Ezek. 7:5 Or, behold, evil cometh after evil.
c. Ezek. 7:6 He showeth that the judgments of God ever watch to destroy the sinners, which notwithstanding he delayeth till there be no more hope of repentance.
d. Ezek. 7:7 The beginning of his punishments is already come.
e. Ezek. 7:7 Which was a voice of joy and mirth.
f. Ezek. 7:10 The scourge is in a readiness.
g. Ezek. 7:10 That is, the proud tyrant Nebuchadnezzar, hath gathered his force and is ready.
h. Ezek. 7:11 This cruel enemy shall be a sharp scourge for their wickedness.
i. Ezek. 7:11 Their own affliction shall be so great, that they shall have no regard to lament for others.
j. Ezek. 7:12 For the present profit.
k. Ezek. 7:12 For he shall lose nothing.
l. Ezek. 7:13 In the year of the Jubilee, meaning that none should enjoy the privilege of the law, Lev. 25:13, for they should all be carried away captives.
m. Ezek. 7:13 This vision signified, that all should be carried away, and none should return for the Jubilee.
n. Ezek. 7:13 No man for all this endeavoreth himself, or taketh heart to repent for his evil life. Some read, for none shall be strengthened in his iniquity of his life: meaning, that they should gain nothing by flattering themselves in evil.
o. Ezek. 7:14 The Israelites made a brag, but their hearts failed them.
p. Ezek. 7:20 Meaning, the Sanctuary.
q. Ezek. 7:21 That is, of the Babylonians.
r. Ezek. 7:22 Which signifieth the most holy place, whereinto none might enter but the high Priest.
s. Ezek. 7:23 Signifying, that they should be bound and led away captives.
t. Ezek. 7:23 That is, of sins that deserve death.
u. Ezek. 7:24 Which was the Temple that was divided into three parts, Ps. 63:35.

EZEK. 7
1. Isa. 13:7 / Jer. 6:24
2. Is. 15:3 / Jer. 48:37
3. Prov. 11:4 / Zeph. 1:18 / Eccl. 5:8

EZEK. 8
a. Ezek. 8:1 Of the captivity of Jeconiah.
b. Ezek. 8:1 Which contained part of August, and part of September.
c. Ezek. 8:2 As Ezek. 1:27.

he stretched out the likeness of an hand, and took me by an hairy lock of mine
head, and the Spirit lifted me up between the earth and the heaven, and brought
me [d]by a Divine [e]vision to Jerusalem, into the entry of the inner [f]gate that lieth
toward the North, where remained the idol of [g]indignation, which provoked in-
dignation. **4** And behold, the glory of the God of Israel was there according to
the vision, that I saw [h]in the field. **5** Then said he unto me, Son of man, lift
up thine eyes now toward the North. So I lifted up mine eyes toward the Nor-
th, and behold, Northward, at the gate of the [i]altar, this idol of indignation was
in the entry. **6** He said furthermore unto me, Son of man, seest thou not what
they do? even the great abominations that the house of Israel commiteth here to
cause me to depart from [j]my Sanctuary? but yet turn thee and thou shalt see gre-
ater abominations. **7** And he caused me to enter at the gate of the court: and
when I looked, behold, an hole was in the wall. **8** Then said he unto me, Son
of man, dig now in the wall. And when I had dug in the wall, behold, there was a
door. **9** And he said unto me, Go in, and behold the wicked abominations that
they do here. **10** So I went in, and saw, and behold, there was every similitude
of creeping things, and [k]abominable beasts, and all the idols of the house of Israel
painted upon the wall round about. **11** And there stood before them seventy
[l]men of the Ancients of the house of Israel, and in the midst of them stood Jaaza-
niah, the son of Shaphan, with every man his censor in his hand, and the vapor
of the incense went up like [m]a cloud. **12** Then said he unto me, Son of man,
hast thou seen what the Ancients of the house of Israel [n]do in the dark, everyone
in the chamber of his imagery? for they say, The Lord seeth us not, the Lord hath
forsaken the earth. **13** Again he said also unto me, Turn thee again, and thou
shalt see greater abominations that they do. **14** And he caused me to enter into
the entry of the gate of the Lord's house, which was toward the North: and behold,
there sat women mourning for [o]Tammuz. **15** Then said he unto me, Hast thou
seen this, O son of man? Turn thee again, and thou shalt see greater abominations
than these. **16** And he caused me to enter into the inner court of the Lord's hou-
se, and behold, at the door of the Temple of the Lord, between the porch and the
altar were about five and twenty men with their backs toward the Temple of the
Lord, and their faces toward the East, and they worshipped the sun, toward the
East. **17** Then he said unto me, Hast thou seen this, O son of man? Is it a small
thing to the house of Judah to commit these abominations which they do here?
for they have filled the land with cruelty, and have returned to provoke me: and lo,
they have cast out [p]stink before their noses. **18** Therefore will I also execute my
wrath: mine eye shall not spare them, neither will I have pity, and [1]though they cry
in mine ears with a loud voice, yet will I not hear them.

9

1 The destruction of the city. 4 They that shall be saved, are marked. 8 A complaint of the Prophet for the destruction of the people.

1 He cried also with a loud voice in mine ears, saying, The visitations of [a]the
city draw near, and every man hath a weapon in his hand to destroy it. **2** And
behold, six [b]men came by the way of the high gate, which lieth toward the [c]North,
and every man a weapon in his hand to destroy it: and one man among them was
clothed with linen, with a writer's [d]inkhorn by his side, and they went in and stood
beside the brazen altar. **3** And the glory of the God of Israel was [e]gone up from
the Cherub, whereupon he was, and stood on the [f]door of the house, and he called
to the man clothed with linen, which had the writer's inkhorn by his side. **4** And
the Lord said unto him, Go through the midst of the city, even through the midst
of Jerusalem, and [g]set a mark upon the foreheads of them that [h]mourn, and cry
for all the abominations that be done in the midst thereof. **5** And to the other
he said, that I might hear, Go ye after him through the city, and smite: let your
eye spare none, neither have pity. **6** Destroy utterly the old, and the young, and
the maids, and the children, and the women, but touch no man, upon whom is
the [i]mark, and begin at my Sanctuary. Then they began at the [j]ancient men, whi-
ch were before the house. **7** And he said unto them, Defile the house, and fill
the courts with the slain, then go forth: and they went out and slew them in the
city. **8** Now when they had slain them, and I had escaped, I fell down upon my
face, and cried, saying, [k]Ah Lord God, wilt thou destroy all the residue of Israel,
in pouring out thy wrath upon Jerusalem? **9** Then said he unto me, The iniqui-
ty of the house of Israel, and Judah is exceeding great, so that the land is full of
[l]blood, and the city full of corrupt judgment: for they say, The Lord hath forsaken
the earth, and the Lord seeth us not. **10** As touching me also, mine eye shall
not spare them, neither will I have pity, but will recompense their ways upon their
heads. **11** And behold, the man clothed with linen which had the inkhorn by
his side, made report, and said, Lord, I have done as thou hast commanded me.

10

1 Of the man that took hot burning coals out of the middle of the wheels of the Cherubims. 8 A rehearsal of the vision of the wheels, of the beasts, and of the Cherubims.

1 And as I looked, behold in the [1]firmament that was above the head of the
[a]Cherubims there appeared upon them like unto the similitude of a throne, as it
were a sapphire stone. **2** And he spake unto the man clothed with linen, and
said, Go in between the wheels, even under the Cherub, and fill thine hands with
coals of fire from between the Cherubims, and scatter them over [b]the city. And he
went in my sight. **3** Now the Cherubims stood upon the right side of the house,
when the man went in, and the cloud filled the inner court. **4** Then the glory
of the Lord [c]went up from the Cherub, and stood over the door of the house, and
the house was filled with the cloud, and the court was filled with the brightness of
the Lord's glory. **5** And the [d]sound of the Cherubims' wings was heard into the
utter court, as the voice of the Almighty God, when he speaketh. **6** And when he
had commanded the man clothed with linen, saying, Take fire from between the
wheels, and from between the Cherubims, then he went in and stood beside the
wheel. **7** And one Cherub stretched forth his hand from between the Cherubims
unto the fire that was between the Cherubims, and took thereof, and put it into
the hands of him that was clothed with linen: who took it and went out. **8** And
there appeared in the Cherubims, the likeness of a man's hand under their win-
gs. **9** And when I looked up, behold, four wheels were beside the Cherubims,
one wheel by one Cherub, and another wheel by another Cherub, and the appea-
rance of the wheels was as the color of a [e]Chrysolite stone. **10** And their appea-
rance (for they were all four of one fashion) was as if one wheel had been in another
wheel. **11** When they went forth, they went upon their four sides, and they re-
turned not as they went: but to the place whither the first went, they went after it,
and they [f]turned not as they went. **12** And their whole body, and their [g]rings,
and their hands, and their wings, and the wheels were full of eyes round about,
even in the same four wheels. **13** And the Cherub cried to these wheels in mine
hearing, saying, O wheel. **14** And every beast had four faces: the first face was
the face of a Cherub, and the second face was the face of a man, and the third the
face of a lion, and the fourth the face of an Eagle. **15** And the Cherubims were
lifted up: [2]this is the beast that I saw at the river Chebar. **16** And when the Che-
rubims went, the wheels went by them: and when the Cherubims lifted up their
wings to mount up from the earth, the same wheels also turned not from beside
them. **17** When the Cherubims stood, they stood: and when they were lifted up,
they lifted themselves up also: for the [h]spirit of the beast was in them. **18** [i]Then
the glory of the Lord departed from above the door of the house, and stood upon
the Cherubims. **19** And the Cherubims lifted up their wings and mounted up
from the earth in my sight: when they went out, the wheels also were beside them:
and everyone stood at the entry of the gate of the Lord's House at the East side,
and the glory of the God of Israel was upon them on high. **20** [3]This is the [j]beast
that I saw under the God of Israel by the river Chebar, and I knew that they were
the Cherubims. **21** Every one had four faces, and every one four wings, and the
likeness of man's hands was under their wings. **22** And the likeness of their faces

---

d. Ezek. 8:3 Hebrew, in the visions of God.
e. Ezek. 8:3 Meaning, that he was thus carried in spirit, and not in body.
f. Ezek. 8:3 Which was the porch or the court where the people assembled.
g. Ezek. 8:3 So called, because it provoked God's indignation, which was the idol of Baal.
h. Ezek. 8:4 Read Ezek. 3:22.
i. Ezek. 8:5 That is, in the court where the people had made an altar to Baal.
j. Ezek. 8:6 For God will not be where idols are.
k. Ezek. 8:10 Which were forbidden in the Law, Lev. 11:4.
l. Ezek. 8:11 Thus they that should have kept all the rest in the fear, and true service of God, were the ringleaders of all abomination, and by their example pulled others from God.
m. Ezek. 8:11 It was in such abundance.
n. Ezek. 8:12 For besides their common idolatry they had particular service, which they had in secret chambers.
o. Ezek. 8:14 The Jews write, that this was a Prophet of the idols, who after his death was once a year mourned for in the night.
p. Ezek. 8:17 Declaring that the censings and service of the idolaters, are but infection and villainy before God.

EZEK. 8

1. Prov. 1:28 / Isa. 46:7 / Jer. 11:11 / Mic. 3:4

EZEK. 9

a. Ezek. 9:1 The time to take vengeance.
b. Ezek. 9:2 Which were Angels in the similitude of men.
c. Ezek. 9:2 Signifying, that the Babylonians should come from the North to destroy the city and the Temple.
d. Ezek. 9:2 To mark them that should be saved.
e. Ezek. 9:3 Which declared that he was not bound thereunto, neither would remain any longer, than there was hope that they would return from their wickedness and worship him aright.
f. Ezek. 9:3 Or, Threshold.
g. Ezek. 9:4 Or, mark with [x].
h. Ezek. 9:4 He showeth what is the manner of God's children, whom he marketh to salvation: to wit, to mourn and cry out against the wickedness, which they see committed against God's glory.
i. Ezek. 9:6 Thus in all his plagues the Lord preserveth his small number, which he marketh, as Exod. 12:12; Rev. 7:3, but the chief mark is the Spirit of adoption, wherewith the heart is sealed up to life everlasting.
j. Ezek. 9:6 Which were the chief occasion of all these evils, as Ezek. 8:11.
k. Ezek. 9:8 This declareth that the servants of God have a compassion, when they see his judgments executed.
l. Ezek. 9:9 That is, with all kinds of wickedness, read Isa. 1:15.

EZEK. 10

a. Ezek. 10:1 Which in Ezek. 1:5, he called the four beasts.
b. Ezek. 10:2 This signified, that the city should be burnt.
c. Ezek. 10:4 Meaning, that the glory of God should depart from the Temple.
d. Ezek. 10:5 Read Ezek. 1:24.
e. Ezek. 10:9 Read Ezek. 1:16.
f. Ezek. 10:11 Until they had executed God's judgments.
g. Ezek. 10:12 Or, trents.
h. Ezek. 10:17 There was one consent between the Cherubims and the wheels.
i. Ezek. 10:18 Read Ezek. 9:3.
j. Ezek. 10:20 That is, the whole body of the four beasts or Cherubims.

EZEK. 10

1. Ezek. 1:22
2. Ezek. 1:5
3. Ezek. 1:15

was the selfsame faces, which I saw by the river Chebar, and the appearance of the
Cherubims was the selfsame, and they went every one straight forward.

11

1 Who they were that seduced the people of Israel. 5 Against these he prophesieth, showing them how they shall be dispersed abroad. 19 The renewing of the heart cometh of God. 21 He threateneth them that lean unto their own counsels.

1 Moreover, the Spirit lifted me up, and brought me unto the East gate of
the Lord's house, which lieth Eastward, and behold, at the entry of the gate were
five and twenty men: among whom I saw Jaazaniah the son of Azzur, and Pe-
latiah the son of Benaiah, the princes of the people. **2** Then said he unto me,
Son of man, these are the men that imagine mischief, and devise wicked coun-
sel in this city. **3** For they say, [a]It is not near, let us build houses: this city is the
[b]caldron, and we be the flesh. **4** Therefore prophesy against them, son of man,
prophesy. **5** And the Spirit of the Lord fell upon me, and said unto me, Speak,
Thus saith the Lord, O ye house of Israel, this have ye said, and I know that which
riseth up of your minds. **6** Many have ye murdered in this city, and ye have filled
the streets thereof with the slain. **7** Therefore thus saith the Lord God, They that
ye have slain, and have laid in the midst of it, they are [c]the flesh, and this city is the
caldron, but I will bring you forth of the midst of it. **8** Ye have feared the sword,
and I will bring a sword upon you, saith the Lord God. **9** And I will bring you
out of the midst thereof, and deliver you into [d]the hands of strangers, and will exe-
cute judgments among you. **10** Ye shall fall by the sword, and I will judge you in
the border of [e]Israel, and ye shall know that I am the Lord. **11** This city shall not
be your caldron, neither shall ye be the flesh in the midst thereof, but I will judge
you in the border of Israel. **12** And ye shall know that I am the Lord: for ye have
not walked in my statutes, neither executed my judgments, but have done after the
manners of the heathen that are round about you. **13** And when I prophesied,
Pelatiah the son of [f]Benaiah died: then fell I down upon my face, and cried with a
loud voice, and said, Ah Lord God, wilt thou then utterly destroy all the remnant
of Israel? **14** Again the word of the Lord came unto me, saying, **15** Son of
man, thy [g]brethren, even thy brethren, the men of thy kindred, and all the house
of Israel, wholly are they unto whom the inhabitants of Jerusalem have said, De-
part ye far from the Lord: for the land is given us in possession. **16** Therefore say,
Thus saith the Lord God, Although I have cast them far off among the heathen,
and although I have scattered them among the countries, yet will I be to them
as a little [h]Sanctuary in the countries where they shall come. **17** Therefore say,
Thus saith the Lord God, I will gather you again from the people, and assemble
you out of the countries where ye have been scattered, and I will give you the land
of Israel. **18** And they shall come thither, and they shall take away all the idols
thereof, and all the abominations thereof from thence. **19** [1]And I will give them
one heart, and I will put a new spirit within their bowels: and I will take the [i]stony
heart out of their bodies, and will give them an heart of flesh, **20** That they
may walk in my statutes, and keep my judgments, and execute them: and they
shall be my people, and I will be their God. **21** But upon them, whose heart is
toward their idols, and whose affection goeth after their abominations, I will lay
their way upon their own heads saith the Lord God. **22** Then did the Cheru-
bims lift up their wings, and the wheels beside them, and the glory of the God of
Israel was upon them on high. **23** And the glory of the Lord went up from the
midst of the city, and stood upon the mountain which is toward the East side of
the city. **24** Afterward the Spirit took me up, and brought me in a vision by the
Spirit of God into Chaldea to them that were led away captives: so the vision that
I had seen, went up from me. **25** Then I declared unto them that were [j]led away
captives, all the things that the Lord had showed me.

12

1 The parable of the captivity. 18 Another parable whereby the distress of hunger and thirst is signified.

1 The word of the Lord also came unto me, saying, **2** Son of man, thou
dwellest in the midst of a rebellious house, which have eyes to see, and see [a]not:
they have ears to hear, and hear not: for they are a rebellious house. **3** Therefore
thou son of man, [b]prepare thy stuff to go into captivity, and go forth by day in their
sight: and thou shalt pass from thy place to another place in their sight, if it be pos-
sible that they may consider it: for they are a rebellious house. **4** Then shalt thou
bring forth thy stuff by day in their sight, as the stuff of him that goeth into cap-
tivity: and thou shalt go forth at even in their sight, as they that go forth into cap-
tivity. **5** Dig thou through the wall in their sight, and carry out thereby. **6** In
their sight shalt thou bear it upon thy shoulders and carry it forth in the dark:
thou shalt cover thy face that thou see not the earth: for I have set thee as a [c]sign
unto the house of Israel. **7** And as I was commanded, so I brought forth my stuff
by day, as the stuff of one that goeth into captivity: and by night I dug through
the wall with mine hand, and brought it forth in the dark, and I bore it upon my
shoulder in their sight. **8** And in the morning came the word of the Lord unto
me, saying, **9** Son of man, hath not the house of Israel, the rebellious house, said
unto thee, What [d]doest thou? **10** But say thou unto them, Thus saith the Lord
God, This [e]burden concerneth the chief in Jerusalem, and all the house of Israel
that are among them. **11** Say, I am your sign: like as I have done, so shall it be
done unto them: they shall go into bondage and captivity. **12** And the chiefest
that is among them, shall bear upon his shoulder in the dark, and shall go forth:
they shall dig through the wall, to carry out thereby: he shall cover his face, that he
see not the ground with his eyes. **13** My net also will I spread upon [f]him, and he
shall be taken in my net, and I will bring him to Babel to the land of the Chalde-
ans, yet shall he not see it, though he shall die there. **14** And I will scatter toward
every wind all that are about him to help him, and all his garrisons, and I will draw
out the sword after them. **15** And they shall know that I am the Lord, when I
shall scatter them among the nations, and disperse them in the countries. **16** But
I will leave a [g]little number of them from the sword, from the famine, and from the
pestilence, that they may declare all these abominations among the heathen, where
they come, and they shall know, that I am the Lord. **17** Moreover, the word of
the Lord came unto me, saying, **18** Son of man, eat thy bread with trembling,
and drink thy water with trouble, and with carefulness, **19** And say unto the
people of the land, Thus saith the Lord God of the inhabitants of Jerusalem, and
of the land of Israel, They shall eat their bread with carefulness, and drink their
water with desolation: for the land shall be desolate from her abundance, because
of the cruelty of them that dwell therein. **20** And the cities that are inhabited,
shall be left void, and the land shall be desolate, and ye shall know that I am the
Lord. **21** And the word of the Lord came unto me, saying, **22** Son of man,
what is that proverb that you have in the land of Israel, saying, The days [h]are pro-
longed, and all visions [i]fail? **23** Tell them therefore, Thus saith the Lord God, I
will make this proverb to cease, and they shall no more use it as a proverb in Israel:
but say unto them, The days are at hand, and the effect of every vision. **24** For
no vision shall be anymore in vain, neither shall there be any flattering divination
within the house of Israel. **25** For I am the Lord: I will speak, and that thing
that I shall speak, shall come to pass: it shall be no more prolonged: for in your
days, O rebellious house, will I say the thing, and will perform it, saith the Lord
God. **26** Again the word of the Lord came unto me, saying, **27** Son of man,
behold, they of the house of Israel say, The vision that he seeth, is for [j]many days
to come, and he prophesieth of the times that are far off. **28** Therefore say unto
them, Thus saith the Lord God, All my words shall no longer be delayed, but that
thing which I have spoken, shall be done, saith the Lord God.

13

2 The word of the Lord against false prophets, which teach the people the counsels of their own hearts.

1 And the word of the Lord came unto me, saying, **2** Son of man, prophesy
against the prophets of [1]Israel, that prophesy, and say thou unto them, that
prophesy out of their [a]own hearts, Hear the word of the Lord. **3** Thus saith
the Lord God, Woe unto the foolish Prophets that follow their own spirit, and
have seen nothing. **4** O Israel, thy Prophets are like the foxes [b]in the waste pla-
ces. **5** [c]Ye have not risen up in the gaps, neither made up the hedge for the house
of Israel, to stand in the battle in the day of the Lord. **6** They have seen vanity,

---

EZEK. 11

- **a.** Ezek. 11:3 Thus the wicked derided the Prophets, as though they preached but errors, and therefore gave themselves still to their pleasures.
- **b.** Ezek. 11:3 We shall not be pulled out of Jerusalem, till the hour of our death come, as the flesh is not taken out of the caldron till it be sod.
- **c.** Ezek. 11:7 Contrary to their vain confidence he showeth in what sense the city is the caldron: that is, because of the dead bodies that have been murdered therein, and so lie as flesh in the caldron.
- **d.** Ezek. 11:9 That is, of the Chaldeans.
- **e.** Ezek. 11:10 That is, in Riblah, read 2 Kings 25:6.
- **f.** Ezek. 11:13 It seemeth that this noble man died of some terrible death, and therefore the Prophet feared some strange judgment of God toward the rest of the people.
- **g.** Ezek. 11:15 They that remained still at Jerusalem thus reproached them that were gone into captivity, as though they were cast off and forsaken of God.
- **h.** Ezek. 11:16 They shall be yet a little Church: showing that the Lord will ever have some to call upon his Name, whom he will preserve and restore, though they be for a time afflicted.
- **i.** Ezek. 11:19 Meaning, the heart whereunto nothing can enter, and regenerate them anew, so that their heart may be soft, and ready to receive my graces.
- **j.** Ezek. 11:25 When Jeconiah was led away captive.

EZEK. 11

1. Jer. 32:39 /Ezek. 36:29

EZEK. 12

- **a.** Ezek. 12:2 That is, they receive not the fruit of that which they see and hear.
- **b.** Ezek. 12:3 Hebrew, make thee vessels to go into captivity.
- **c.** Ezek. 12:6 That as thou doest, so shall they do, and therefore in thee they shall see their own plague and punishment.
- **d.** Ezek. 12:9 Do not they deride thy doings?
- **e.** Ezek. 12:10 Or, prophecy.
- **f.** Ezek. 12:13 When the king shall think to escape by fleeing, I will take him in my net, as Ezek. 17:20 and 32:3.
- **g.** Ezek. 12:16 Which should bear his Name, and should be his Church, read Ezek. 11:16.
- **h.** Ezek. 12:22 Because they did not immediately see the prophecies accomplished, they contemned them as though they should never be fulfilled.
- **i.** Ezek. 12:22 Or, take none effect.
- **j.** Ezek. 12:27 That is, it shall not come to pass in our days, and therefore we care not for it: thus the wicked ever abuse God's patience and benignity.

EZEK. 13

- **a.** Ezek. 13:2 After their own fantasy, and not as having the revelation of the Lord, Jer. 23:16.
- **b.** Ezek. 13:4 Watching to destroy the vineyard.
- **c.** Ezek. 13:5 He speaketh to the governors, and true ministers that should have resisted them.
- **d.** Ezek. 13:7 Ye promised peace to this people, and now ye see their destruction, so that it is manifest, that ye are false prophets.

and lying divination, saying, The Lord saith it, and the Lord hath not sent them: and they have made others to hope that they would confirm the word of their prophecy. **7** Have ye not seen a vain vision? and have ye not spoken a lying divination? [d]ye say, The Lord saith it, albeit I have not spoken. **8** Therefore thus saith the Lord God, Because ye have spoken vanity and have seen lies, therefore behold, I am against you, saith the Lord God, **9** And mine hand shall be upon the Prophets that see vanity, and divine lies: they shall not be in the assembly of my people, neither shall they be written in the [e]writing of the house of Israel, neither shall they enter into the land of Israel: and ye shall know that I am the Lord God. **10** And therefore, because they have deceived my people, saying, [f]Peace, and there was no peace: and one built up a [g]wall, and behold, the others daubed it with untempered mortar, **11** Say unto them which daub it with untempered mortar, that it shall fall: for there shall come a great shower, and I will send hailstones, which shall cause it to fall, and a stormy wind shall break it. **12** Lo, when the wall is fallen, shall it not be said unto you, Where is the daubing wherewith ye have daubed it? **13** Therefore thus saith the Lord God, I will cause a stormy wind to break forth in my wrath, and a great shower shall be in mine anger, and hailstones in mine indignation to consume it. **14** So I will destroy the wall that ye have daubed with untempered mortar, and bring it down to the ground, so that the foundation thereof shall be discovered, and it shall fall, and ye shall be consumed in the midst thereof, and ye shall know, that I am the Lord. **15** Thus will I accomplish my wrath upon the wall, and upon them that have daubed it with [h]untempered mortar, and will say unto you, The wall is no more, neither the daubers thereof, **16** To wit, the Prophets of Israel, which prophesy upon Jerusalem, and see visions of peace for it, and there is no peace, saith the Lord God. **17** Likewise thou son of man, set thy face against the daughters of thy people, which prophesy out of their own heart: and prophesy thou against them, and say, **18** Thus saith the Lord God, Woe unto the women that sow [i]pillows under all armholes, and make veils upon the head of everyone that standeth up, to hunt souls: will ye hunt the souls of my people, and will ye give life to the souls that come unto you? **19** And will ye pollute me among my people for handfuls of [j]barley, and for pieces of bread to slay the souls of them that should not die, and [k]to give life to the souls that should not live, in lying to my people, that hear your lies? **20** Wherefore thus saith the Lord God, Behold, I will have to do with your pillows, wherewith ye hunt the [l]souls to make them to flee, and I will tear them from your arms, and will let the souls go, even the souls that ye hunt to make them to flee. **21** Your veils also will I tear, and deliver my people out of your hand, and they shall be no more in your hands to be hunted, and ye shall know that I am the Lord. **22** Because with your lies ye have made the heart of the [m]righteous sad, whom I have not made sad, and strengthened the hands of the wicked, that he should not return from his wicked way, by promising him life, **23** Therefore ye shall see no more vanity, nor divine divinations: for I will deliver my people out of your hand, and ye shall know that I am the Lord.

14

4 The Lord sendeth false Prophets for the ingratitude of the people. 22 He reserveth a small portion for his Church.

1 Then came certain of the Elders of Israel unto me, and [a]sat before me. **2** And the word of the Lord came unto me, saying, **3** Son of man, these men have set up their idols in their [b]heart, and put the stumbling block of their iniquity before their face: should I, being required, answer them? **4** Therefore speak unto them, and say unto them, Thus saith the Lord God, Every man of the house of Israel that setteth up his idols in his heart, and putteth the stumbling block of his iniquity before his face, and cometh to the [c]Prophet, I the Lord will answer him that cometh, according to the multitude [d]of his idols: **5** That [e]I may take the house of Israel in their own heart, because they are all departed from me through their idols. **6** Therefore say unto the house of Israel, Thus saith the Lord God, Return, and withdraw yourselves, and turn your faces from your idols, and turn your faces from all your abominations. **7** For everyone of the house of Israel, or of the stranger that sojourneth in Israel, which departeth from me, and setteth up his idols in his heart, and putteth the stumbling block of his iniquity before his face, and cometh to a Prophet, for to inquire of him for me, I the Lord will answer him [f]for myself, **8** And I will set my face against that man, and will make him an example and proverb, and I will cut him off from the midst of my people, and ye shall know that I am the Lord. **9** And if the Prophet be [g]deceived, when he hath spoken a thing, I the Lord have deceived that Prophet, and I will stretch out mine hand upon him, and will destroy him from the midst of my people of Israel. **10** And they shall bear their punishment: the punishment of the Prophet shall be even as the punishment of him that asketh, **11** That the house of [h]Israel may go no more astray from me, neither be polluted anymore with all their transgressions, but that they may be my people, and I may be their God, saith the Lord God. **12** The word of the Lord came again unto me, saying, **13** Son of man, when the land sinneth against me by committing a trespass, then will I stretch out mine hand upon it, [i]and will break the staff of the bread thereof, and will send famine upon it, and I will destroy man and beast forth of it. **14** Though these three men [j]Noah, Daniel, and Job were among them, they should deliver but their own souls by their [k]righteousness, saith the Lord God. **15** If I bring noisome beasts into the land and they spoil it, so that it be desolate, that no man may pass through, because of beasts, **16** Though these three men were in the midst thereof, As I live, saith the Lord God, they shall save neither sons nor daughters: they only shall be delivered, but the land shall be waste. **17** Or if I bring a sword upon this land, and say, Sword, go through the land, so that I destroy man and beast out of it, **18** Though these three men were in the midst thereof, As I live, saith the Lord God, they shall deliver neither sons nor daughters, but they only shall be delivered themselves. **19** Or if I send a pestilence into this land, and pour out my wrath upon it in blood, to destroy out of it man and beast, **20** And though Noah, Daniel and Job were in the midst of it, As I live, saith the Lord God, they shall deliver neither son nor daughter: they shall but deliver their own souls by their righteousness. **21** For thus saith the Lord God, How much more when I send my [1]four sore judgments upon Jerusalem, even the sword, and famine, and the noisome beast, and pestilence, to destroy man and beast out of it? **22** Yet behold, therein shall be left a [l]remnant of them that shall be carried away both sons and daughters: behold, they shall come forth unto you, and ye shall see their way, and their enterprises: and ye shall be comforted, concerning the evil that I have brought upon Jerusalem, even concerning all that I have brought upon it. **23** And they shall comfort you, when ye see their way and their enterprises: and ye shall know, that I have not done without cause all that I have done in it, saith the Lord God.

15

2 As the unprofitable wood of the vine tree is cast into the fire, so Jerusalem shall be burnt.

1 And the word of the Lord came unto me, saying, **2** Son of man, what cometh of the vine tree above all other trees? and of the vine branch, which is among the [a]trees of the forest? **3** Shall wood be taken thereof to do any work? or will men take a pin of it to hang any vessel thereon? **4** Behold, it is cast in the fire to be consumed: the fire consumeth both the ends of it, and the midst of it is burnt. Is it meet for any work? **5** Behold, when it was whole, it was meet for no work: how much less shall it be meet for any work, when the fire hath consumed it, and it is burnt? **6** Therefore thus saith the Lord God, as the vine tree, that is among the trees of the forest, which I have given to the fire to be consumed, so will I give the inhabitants of Jerusalem. **7** And I will set my face against them: they shall go out from one [b]fire, and another fire shall consume them: and ye shall know, that I am the Lord, when I set my face against them, **8** And when I make the land waste, because they have greatly offended, saith the Lord God.

---

e. Ezek. 13:9 That is, in the book of life, wherein the true Israelites are written.
f. Ezek. 13:10 Read Jer. 6:14.
g. Ezek. 13:10 Whereas the true Prophets prophesied the destruction of the city to bring the people to repentance, the false prophets spake the contrary, and flattered them in their vanities, so that what one false prophet said (which is here called the building of the wall) another false prophet would affirm, though he had neither occasion nor good ground to bear him.
h. Ezek. 13:15 Whereby is meant whatsoever man of himself setteth forth under the authority of God's word.
i. Ezek. 13:18 These superstitious women for lucre would prophesy and tell every man his fortune, giving them pillows to lean upon, and kerchiefs to cover their heads, to the intent they might the more allure them and bewitch them.
j. Ezek. 13:19 Will ye make my word to serve your bellies?
k. Ezek. 13:19 These sorcerers made the people believe that they could preserve life or destroy it, and that it should come to everyone according as they prophesied.
l. Ezek. 13:20 That is, to cause them to perish, and that they should depart from the body.
m. Ezek. 13:22 By threatening them that were godly, and upholding the wicked.

EZEK. 13

1. Ezek. 14:9

EZEK. 14

a. Ezek. 14:1 He showeth the hypocrisy of the idolaters, who will dissemble to hear the Prophets of God, though in their heart they follow nothing less than their admonitions, and also how by one means or other God doth discover them.
b. Ezek. 14:3 They are not only idolaters in heart, but also worship their filthy idols openly, which lead them in blindness, and cause them to stumble, and cast them out of God's favor, so that he will not hear them when they call unto him, read Jer. 10:15.
c. Ezek. 14:4 To inquire of things which the Lord hath appointed to come to pass.
d. Ezek. 14:4 As his abomination hath deserved: that is, he shall be led with lies according as he delighted therein, 2 Thess. 2:10.
e. Ezek. 14:5 That is, convince them by their own conscience.
f. Ezek. 14:7 Or, by myself.
g. Ezek. 14:9 The Prophet declareth that God for man's ingratitude raiseth up false prophets to seduce them that delight in lies rather than in the truth of God, and thus he punisheth sin by sin, 1 Kings 22:20, 22, and destroyeth as well those Prophets as that people.
h. Ezek. 14:11 Thus God's judgments against the wicked, are admonitions to the godly, to cleave unto the Lord, and not to defile themselves with like abominations.
i. Ezek. 14:13 Read Ezek. 4:16 and 5:17; Isa. 3:1.
j. Ezek. 14:14 Though Noah and Job were now alive, which in their time were most godly men (for at this time Daniel was in captivity with Ezek.) and so these three together should pray for this wicked people, yet would I not hear them, read Jer. 15:1.
k. Ezek. 14:14 Meaning, that a very few (which he calleth the remnant, verse 22) should escape these plagues, whom God hath sanctified and made righteous, so that this righteousness is a sign that they are the Church of God, whom he would preserve for his own sake.
l. Ezek. 14:22 Read Ezek. 5:3.

EZEK. 14

1. Ezek. 5:17

EZEK. 15

a. Ezek. 15:2 Which brings forth no fruit, no more than the other trees of the forest do: meaning that if Jerusalem, which bore the name of his Church, did not bring forth fruit it would be utterly destroyed.
b. Ezek. 15:7 Though they escape one danger, yet another will take them.

16

The Prophet declared the benefits of God toward Jerusalem. 15 Their unkindness. 46 He justifieth the wickedness of other people in comparison of the sins of Jerusalem. 49 The cause of the abominations, into which the Sodomites fell. 60 Mercy is promised to the repentant.

1 Again, the word of the Lord came unto me, saying, **2** Son of man, cause
Jerusalem to know her abominations, **3** And say, Thus saith the Lord God unto
Jerusalem, Thine habitation and thy kindred is of the land [a]of Canaan: thy father
was an Amorite, and thy mother an Hittite. **4** And in thy nativity when thou
wast [b]born, thy navel was not cut: thou wast not washed in water to soften thee:
thou wast not salted with salt, nor swaddled in clouts. **5** None eye pitied thee to
do any of these unto thee, for to have compassion upon thee, but thou wast cast
out in the open field to the contempt of thy person in the day that thou wast
born. **6** And when I passed by thee, I saw thee polluted in thine [c]own blood, and
I said unto thee, when thou wast in thy blood, Thou shalt live: even when thou
wast in thy blood, I said unto thee, Thou shalt live. **7** I have caused thee to mul-
tiply as the bud of the field, and thou hast increased and waxen great, and thou hast
gotten excellent ornaments: thy breasts are fashioned, thine hair is grown, whereas
thou wast naked and bare. **8** Now when I passed by thee, and looked upon thee,
behold, thy time was as the time of love, and I spread my skirts over thee, and co-
vered [d]thy filthiness: yea, I swear unto thee, and entered into a covenant with [e]thee,
saith the Lord God, and thou becamest mine. **9** Then washed I thee with [f]water:
yea, I washed away thy blood from thee, and I [g]anointed thee with oil. **10** I
clothed thee also with broidered work, and shod thee with badgers' skin, and I gir-
ded thee about with fine linen, and I covered thee with silk. **11** I decked thee
also with ornaments, and I put bracelets upon thine hands, and a chain on thy
neck. **12** And I put a frontlet upon thy face, and earrings in thine ears, and a
beautiful [h]crown upon thine head. **13** Thus wast thou decked with gold and sil-
ver, and thy raiment was of fine linen, and silk, and broidered work: thou didst eat
fine flour, and honey and oil, and thou wast very beautiful, and thou didst grow up
into a kingdom. **14** And thy name was spread among the heathen for thy beau-
ty: for it was perfect through my [i]beauty which I had set upon thee, saith the Lord
God. **15** Now thou didst [j]trust in thine own beauty, and playedst the harlot,
because of thy renown, and hast poured out [k]thy fornications on everyone that
passed by, thy desire was to him. **16** And thou didst take thy garments, and
deckedst thine high places with divers colors, [l]and playedst the harlot thereupon:
the like things shall not come, neither hath any done so. **17** Thou hast also taken
thy fair jewels made of my gold and of my silver, which I had given thee, and [m]ma-
dest to thyself images of men, and didst commit whoredom with them, **18** And
tookest thy broidered garments, and coveredst them: and thou hast set mine oil
and my perfume before them. **19** My meat also, which I gave thee, as fine flour,
oil and honey, wherewith I fed thee, thou hast even set it before them for a sweet
savor: thus it was, saith the Lord God. **20** Moreover thou hast taken thy sons and
thy daughters, whom thou hast borne unto me, and these hast thou sacrificed unto
them, to [n]be devoured: is this thy whoredom a small matter? **21** That thou hast
slain my children, and delivered them to cause them to pass through fire for
them? **22** And in all thine abominations and whoredoms thou hast not remem-
bered the days of thy youth, when thou wast naked and bare, and wast polluted in
thy blood. **23** And beside all thy wickedness (woe, woe unto thee, saith the Lord
God) **24** Thou hast also built unto thee an high place, and hast made thee an
high place in every street. **25** Thou hast built thine high place at every [o]corner of
the way, and hast made thy beauty to be abhorred: thou hast opened thy feet to
everyone that passed by, and multiplied thy whoredom. **26** Thou hast also com-
mitted fornication with the [p]Egyptians thy neighbors, which have great members,
and hast increased thy whoredom, to provoke me. **27** Behold, therefore I did
stretch out mine hand over thee, and will diminish thine ordinary, and deliver thee
unto the will of them that hate thee, even to the [q]daughters of the Philistines,
which are ashamed of thy wicked way. **28** Thou hast played the whore also with
the Assyrians, because thou wast insatiable: yea, thou hast played the harlot with
them, and yet couldest not be satisfied. **29** Thou hast moreover multiplied thy
fornication from the land of Canaan unto Chaldea, and yet thou wast not satisfied
herewith. **30** How weak is thine heart, saith the Lord God, seeing thou doest all
these things, even the work of a [r]presumptuous whorish woman? **31** In that
thou buildest thine high place in the corner of every way, and makest thine high
place in every street, and hast not been as an harlot [s]that despiseth a reward, **32** But
as a wife that playeth the harlot, and taketh others for her husband: **33** They give
gifts to all other whores, but thou givest gifts unto all thy lovers, and rewardest
them that they may come unto thee on every side for thy fornication. **34** And
the contrary is in thee from other women in thy fornications, neither the like for-
nication shall be after thee: for in that thou givest a reward and no reward is given
unto thee, therefore thou art contrary. **35** Wherefore, O harlot, hear the word of
the Lord. **36** Thus saith the Lord God, Because thy [t]shame was poured out, and
thy filthiness discovered through thy fornications with thy lovers, and with all the
idols of thine abominations, and by the blood of thy children, which thou didst
offer unto them, **37** Behold, therefore I will gather all [u]thy lovers, with whom
thou hast taken pleasure, and all them that thou hast loved, with all them that thou
hast hated: I will even gather them round about against thee, and will discover thy
filthiness unto them, that they may see all thy filthiness. **38** And I will judge thee
after the manner of them that are [v]harlots, and of them that shed blood, and I will
give thee the blood of wrath, and jealousy. **39** I will also give thee into their
hands, and they shall destroy thine high place, and shall break down thine high
places: they shall strip thee also out of thy clothes, and shall take thy fair jewels, and
leave thee naked and bare. **40** They shall also bring up a company against thee,
and they shall stone thee with stones, and thrust thee through with their
swords. **41** And they [l]shall burn up thine houses with fire, and execute judg-
ments upon thee in the sight of many women: and I will cause thee to cease from
playing the harlot, and thou shalt give no reward anymore. **42** So will I make my
wrath toward thee to rest, and my [w]jealousy shall depart from thee, and I will cease,
and be no more angry. **43** Because thou hast not remembered the days of thy
youth, but hast provoked me with all these things, behold, therefore I also have
[x]brought thy way upon thy head, saith the Lord God: yet hast not thou had consi-
deration of all thine abominations. **44** Behold, all that use proverbs, shall use
this proverb against thee, saying, As is the mother, [y]so is her daughter. **45** Thou
art thy mother's daughter, that hath cast off her husband and her children, and
thou art the sister of thy [z]sisters, which forsook their husbands and their children:
your mother is an Hittite, and your father an Amorite. **46** And thine elder sister
is Samaria, and her [aa]daughters, that dwell at thy left hand, and [ab]thy younger si-
ster, that dwelleth at thy right hand, is Sodom, and her daughters. **47** Yet hast
thou [ac]not walked after their ways, nor done after their abominations: but as it had
been a very little thing, thou wast corrupted more than they in all thy ways. **48** As
I live, saith the Lord God, Sodom thy sister hath not done, neither she nor her
daughters, as thou hast done and thy daughters. **49** Behold, this was the iniquity
of thy sister Sodom, [ad]pride, fullness of bread and abundance of idleness was in her,
and in her daughters: neither did she strengthen the hand of the poor and nee-
dy. **50** But they were haughty, and committed abomination before me: therefore
I took them away as pleased me. **51** Neither [ae]hath Samaria committed half of
thy sins, but thou hast exceeded them in thine abominations, and hast [af]justified
thy sisters in all thine abominations which thou hast done. **52** Therefore thou
which hast justified thy sisters, bear thine own shame for thy sins, that thou hast
committed more abominable than they which are more righteous than thou art: be
thou therefore confounded also, and bear thy shame, seeing that thou hast justified
thy sisters. **53** Therefore I will bring again [ag]their captivity, with the captivity of
Sodom, and her daughters, and with the captivity of Samaria, and her daughters:
even the captivity of thy captives in the midst of them, **54** That thou mayest bear

---

EZEK. 16

a. Ezek. 16:3 Thou boastest to be of the seed of Abraham, but thou art degenerate and followest the abominations of the wicked Canaanites, as children do the manners of their fathers, Isa. 1:4 and 57:3.
b. Ezek. 16:4 When I first brought thee out of Egypt, and planted thee in this land to be my Church.
c. Ezek. 16:6 Being thus in thy filthiness and forsaken of all men, I took thee and gave thee life: whereby is meant that before God wash his Church, and give life, there is nothing but filthiness and death.
d. Ezek. 16:8 These words, as blood, pollution, nakedness, and filthiness, are oftentimes repeated to beat down their pride, and to cause them to consider what they were before God received them to mercy, favored them and covered their shame.
e. Ezek. 16:8 That thou shouldest be a chaste wife unto me, and that I should maintain thee and endue thee with all graces.
f. Ezek. 16:9 I washed away thy sins.
g. Ezek. 16:9 I sanctified thee with mine holy Spirit.
h. Ezek. 16:12 Hereby he showeth how he saved his Church, enriched it, and gave it power and dominion to reign.
i. Ezek. 16:14 He declareth wherein the dignity of Jerusalem stood: to wit, in that that the Lord gave them of his beauty and excellency.
j. Ezek. 16:15 In abusing my gifts, and in putting thy confidence in thine own wisdom and dignity, which were the occasions of thine idolatry.
k. Ezek. 16:15 There was none idolatry so vile wherewith thou didst not pollute thyself.
l. Ezek. 16:16 This declareth how the idolaters put their chief delight in those things, which please the eyes and outward senses.
m. Ezek. 16:17 Thou hast converted my vessels and instruments, which I gave thee to serve me with, to the use of thine idols.
n. Ezek. 16:20 Meaning, by fire: read Lev. 18:21; 2 Kings 23:10.
o. Ezek. 16:25 Or, head.
p. Ezek. 16:26 He noteth the great impiety of this people, who first falling from God to seek help at strange nations, did also at length embrace their idolatry, thinking thereby to make their amity more strong.
q. Ezek. 16:27 Or, cities.
r. Ezek. 16:30 Or, that will bear rule.
s. Ezek. 16:31 Meaning, that some harlots contemn small rewards, but no lovers gave a reward to Israel, but they gave to all others: signifying that the idolaters bestow all their substance, which they receive of God for his glory, to serve their vile abominations.
t. Ezek. 16:36 Or, … parts.
u. Ezek. 16:37 Egyptians, Assyrians and Chaldeans, whom thou tookest to be thy lovers, shall come and destroy thee, Ezek. 23:9.
v. Ezek. 16:38 I will judge thee to death, as the adulterers and murderers.
w. Ezek. 16:42 I will utterly destroy thee, and so my jealousy shall cease.
x. Ezek. 16:43 I have punished thy faults, but thou wouldest not repent.
y. Ezek. 16:44 As were the Canaanites, and the Hittites and others your predecessors, so are you their successors.
z. Ezek. 16:45 That is, of Samaria and Sodom.
aa. Ezek. 16:46 That is, her cities.
ab. Ezek. 16:46 Hebrew, thy sister younger than thou.
ac. Ezek. 16:47 But done far worse.
ad. Ezek. 16:49 He allegeth these four vices, pride, excess, idleness and contempt of the poor, as four principal causes of such abomination, wherefore they were so horribly punished, Gen. 19:24.
ae. Ezek. 16:51 Which worshipped the calves in Bethel and Dan.
af. Ezek. 16:51 Thou art so wicked, that in respect of thee Sodom and Samaria were just.
ag. Ezek. 16:53 This he speaketh in comparison, seeing that he would restore Jerusalem when Sodom should be restored, that is, never: and this is meant of the greatest part of the Jews.
ah. Ezek. 16:54 In that thou hast showed thyself worse than they and yet thoughtest to escape punishment.

thine own shame, and mayest be confounded in all that thou hast done, in that thou hast [ah]comforted them. **55** And thy sister Sodom and her daughters shall return to their former state: Samaria also and her daughters shall return to their former state: [ai]when thou and thy daughters shall return to your former state. **56** For thy sister Sodom [aj]was not heard of [ak]by thy report in the day of thy pride, **57** Before thy wickedness was [al]discovered, as in that same time of the reproach of the daughters of Aram, and of all the daughters of the Philistines round about [am]her, which despise thee on all sides. **58** Thou hast borne therefore thy wickedness and thine abomination, saith the Lord. **59** For thus saith the Lord God, I might even deal with thee, as thou hast done: when thou didst despise the [an]oath, in breaking the covenant. **60** Nevertheless, I will [ao]remember my covenant made with thee in the days of thy youth, and I will confirm unto thee an everlasting Covenant. **61** Then thou shalt remember thy ways, and be ashamed, when thou shalt receive [ap]thy sisters, both thy elder and thy younger, and I will give them unto thee for daughters, but not [aq]by thy covenant. **62** And I will establish my covenant with thee, and thou shalt know that I am the Lord, **63** That thou mayest remember, and be [ar]ashamed, and never open thy mouth anymore: because of thy shame when I am pacified toward thee, for all that thou hast done, saith the Lord God.

17

The parable of the two Eagles.

1 And the word of the Lord came unto me, saying, **2** Son of man, put forth a parable and speak a proverb unto the house of Israel, **3** And say, Thus saith the Lord God, The great [a]eagle with great wings and long wings, and full of feathers, which had diverse colors, came unto Lebanon, and took the highest branch of the cedar, **4** And brake off the top of his twig, and carried it into the land of [b]merchants, and set it in a city of merchants. **5** He took also of the [c]seed of the land, and planted it in a fruitful ground: he placed it by great waters, and set it as a willow tree. **6** And it budded up, and was like [d]a spreading vine of [e]low stature, whose branches turned toward it, and the roots thereof were under it: so it became a vine, and it brought forth branches, and shot forth buds. **7** There was also [f]another great Eagle with great wings and many feathers, and behold, this vine did turn her roots toward it, and spread forth her branches toward it, that she might water it by the trenches of her plantation. **8** It was planted in a good soil by great [g]waters, that it should bring forth branches, and bear fruit, and be an excellent vine. **9** Say thou, Thus saith the Lord God, Shall it prosper? shall [h]he not pull up the roots thereof, and destroy the fruit thereof, and cause them to dry? all the leaves of her bud shall wither without great power, or many people, to pluck it up by the roots thereof. **10** Behold, it was planted: but shall it prosper? shall it not be dried up, and wither? [i]when the East wind shall touch it, it shall wither in the trenches, where it grew. **11** Moreover, the word of the Lord came unto me, saying, **12** Say now to this rebellious house, Know ye not what these things mean? tell them, behold, the king of Babel is come to Jerusalem, and hath taken [j]the king thereof and the princes thereof, and led them with him to Babel, **13** And hath taken one of the King's seed, and made a covenant with him, and hath taken [k]an oath of him: he hath also taken the princes of the land, **14** That the kingdom might be in subjection, and not lift itself up, but keep their covenant, and stand to it. **15** But he rebelled against him, and sent his ambassadors into Egypt, that they might give him horses, and much people: shall he prosper? shall he escape that doeth such things? or shall he break the covenant, and be delivered? **16** As I live, saith the Lord God, he shall die in the midst of Babel, in the place of the king that had made him king, whose oath he despised, and whose covenant made with him, he brake. **17** Neither shall Pharaoh with his mighty host, and great multitude of people, maintain him in the war, when they have cast up mounts, and built ramparts to destroy many persons. **18** For he hath despised the oath, and broken the covenant (yet lo, he had given [l]his hand) because he hath done all these things, he shall not escape. **19** Therefore, thus saith the Lord God, As I live, I will surely bring mine oath that he hath despised, and my covenant that he hath broken, upon his own head. **20** [1]And I will spread my net upon him, and he shall be taken in my net, and I will bring him to Babel, and will enter into judgment with him there for his trespass that he hath committed against me. **21** And all that flee from him with all his host, shall fall by the sword, and they that remain shall be scattered toward all the winds: and ye shall know that I the Lord have spoken it. **22** Thus saith the Lord God, I will also take off the top[m]of this high cedar, and will set it, and cut off the [n]top of the tender plant thereof, and I will plant it upon an high mountain and great. **23** Even in the high mountain of Israel will I plant it: and it shall bring forth boughs, and bear fruit, and be an excellent cedar, and under it shall remain all birds, and every [o]fowl shall dwell in the shadow of the branches thereof. **24** And all the [p]trees of the field shall know that I the Lord have brought down the high tree, and exalted the low tree: that I have dried up the green tree, and made the dry tree to flourish: I the Lord have spoken it, and have done it.

18

2 He showeth that every man shall bear his own sin. 21 To him that amendeth, salvation is promised. 24 Death is prophesied to the righteous, which turneth back from the right way.

1 The word of the Lord came unto me again, saying, **2** What mean ye that ye speak this proverb concerning the land of Israel, saying, [a]The fathers have eaten sour grapes, and the children's teeth are set on edge? **3** As I live, saith the Lord God, ye shall use this proverb no more in Israel. **4** Behold, all souls are mine, both the soul of the father, and also the soul of the son are mine: the soul that sinneth, it shall die. **5** But if a man be just, and do that which is lawful and right, **6** And hath not eaten [b]upon the mountains, neither hath lift up his eyes to the idols of the house of Israel, neither hath [1]defiled his neighbor's wife, neither hath [c]lain with a [2]menstruous woman, **7** Neither hath oppressed any, but hath restored the pledge to his debtor: he that hath spoiled none by violence, [3]but hath given his bread to the hungry, and hath covered the naked with a garment, **8** And hath not given forth upon [4]usury, neither hath taken any increase, but hath withdrawn his hand from iniquity, and hath executed true judgment between man and man, **9** And hath walked in my statutes, and hath kept my judgments to deal truly, he is just, he shall surely live, saith the Lord God. **10** If he beget a son, that is a [d]thief, or a shedder of blood, if he do anyone of these things, **11** Though he do not all these things, but either hath eaten upon the mountains, or defiled his neighbor's wife, **12** Or hath oppressed the poor and needy, or hath spoiled by violence, or hath not restored the pledge, or hath lifted up his eyes unto the idols, or hath committed abomination, **13** Or hath given forth upon usury, or hath taken increase, shall he live? he shall not live: seeing he hath done all these abominations, [e]he shall die the death, and his blood shall be upon him. **14** But if he beget a son, that seeth all his father's sins, which he hath done, and feareth, neither doeth such like, **15** That hath not eaten upon the mountains, neither hath lifted up his eyes to the idols of the house of Israel, nor hath defiled his neighbor's wife, **16** Neither hath oppressed any, nor hath withheld the pledge, neither hath spoiled by violence, but hath given his bread to the hungry, and hath covered the naked with a garment, **17** Neither hath withdrawn his hand from the afflicted, nor received usury nor increase, but hath executed my judgments, and hath walked in my statutes, he shall not die in the iniquity of his father, but he shall surely live. **18** His father, because he cruelly oppressed and spoiled his brother by violence, and hath not done good among his people, lo, even he dieth in his iniquity. **19** Yet say ye, Wherefore shall not the son bear the iniquity of the father? because the son hath

---

ai. Ezek. 16:55 Meaning, that it should never come to pass.
aj. Ezek. 16:56 Hebrew, was not a rumor in thy mouth.
ak. Ezek. 16:56 Thou wouldest not call her punishment to mind when thou wast aloft, to learn by her example to fear my judgments.
al. Ezek. 16:57 That is, till thou wast brought under by the Syrians and Philistines, 2 Chron. 28:19.
am. Ezek. 16:57 Which joined with the Syrians, or compassed about Jerusalem.
an. Ezek. 16:59 When thou brakest the covenant which was made between thee and me, as verse 8.
ao. Ezek. 16:60 That is, of mercy and love I will pity thee, and so stand to my covenant though thou hast deserved the contrary.
ap. Ezek. 16:61 Whereby he showeth that among the most wicked, he had ever some seed of his Church, which he would cause to fructify in due time: and here he declareth how he will call the Gentiles.
aq. Ezek. 16:61 But of my free mercy.
ar. Ezek. 16:63 This declareth what fruits God's mercies work in his, to wit, sorrow and repentance for their former life.

EZEK. 16

1. 2Kings 25:9

EZEK. 17

a. Ezek. 17:3 That is, Nebuchadnezzar, who hath great power, riches, and many countries under him, shall come to Jerusalem, and take away Jeconiah the King, as verse 12.
b. Ezek. 17:4 Meaning, to Babylon.
c. Ezek. 17:5 That is, Zedekiah, who was of the King's blood and was left at Jerusalem, and made King instead of Jeconiah, 2 Kings 24:17; Jer. 37:1.
d. Ezek. 17:6 This was Zedekiah's kingdom.
e. Ezek. 17:6 That is, might not have power to rebel against Babylon, as verse 14.
f. Ezek. 17:7 Meaning, the king of Egypt, of whom Zedekiah sought succor against Nebuchadnezzar.
g. Ezek. 17:8 They thought to be moistened by the waters of Nilus.
h. Ezek. 17:9 Shall not Nebuchadnezzar destroy it?
i. Ezek. 17:10 By this dry wind he meaneth the Babylonians.
j. Ezek. 17:12 That is, Jeconiah, 2 Kings 24:15.
k. Ezek. 17:13 For his subjection and obedience.
l. Ezek. 17:18 Because he took the Name of God in vain, and brake his oath which he had confirmed by giving his hand: therefore the Prophet declareth that God would not suffer such perjury and infidelity to escape punishment.
m. Ezek. 17:22 This promise is made to the Church which shall be as a small remnant, and as the top of a tree.
n. Ezek. 17:22 I will trim it, and dress it.
o. Ezek. 17:23 Both the Jews and Gentiles shall be gathered into it.
p. Ezek. 17:24 All the world shall know that I have plucked down the proud enemies, and set up my Church which was low and contemned.

EZEK. 17

1. Ezek. 12:13 / Ezek. 32:3

EZEK. 18

a. Ezek. 18:2 The people murmured at the chastisings of the Lord, and therefore used this proverb, meaning, that their fathers had sinned, and their children were punished for their transgressions, read Jer. 31:29.
b. Ezek. 18:6 If he hath not eaten of the flesh that hath been offered up to idols, to honor them thereby.
c. Ezek. 18:6 Hebrew, come near.
d. Ezek. 18:10 Or, a cruel man.
e. Ezek. 18:13 He showeth how the son is punished for his father's fault: that is, if he be wicked as his father was, and doth not repent, he shall be punished as his father was, or else not.
f. Ezek. 18:21 He joineth the observation of the commandments with repentance: for none can repent in deed, except he labor to keep the Law.
g. Ezek. 18:22 Or, not laid to his charge.
h. Ezek. 18:22 That is, in the fruits of his faith which declare that God doth accept him.
i. Ezek. 18:23 He speaketh this to commend God's mercy to poor sinners, who rather is ready to pardon than to punish, as his long suffering declareth, Ezek. 33:11. Albeit God in his

executed judgment and justice, and hath kept all my statutes, and done them, he shall surely live. **20** [5]The same soul that sinneth, shall die: the son shall not bear the iniquity of the father, neither shall the father bear the iniquity of the son, but the righteousness of the righteous shall be upon him, and the wickedness of the wicked shall be upon himself. **21** But if the wicked will return from all his sins that he hath committed, and keep all my [f]statutes, and do that which is lawful and right, he shall surely live, and shall not die. **22** All his transgressions that he hath committed, they shall not be [g]mentioned unto him, but in his [h]righteousness that he hath done, he shall live. **23** [i]Have I any desire that the wicked should die, saith the Lord God? [j]or shall he not live, if he return from his ways? **24** But if the righteous turn away from his righteousness, and commit iniquity, and do according to all the abominations that the wicked man doeth, shall he live? all his [k]righteousness that he hath done, shall not be mentioned: but in his transgression that he hath committed, and in his sin that he hath sinned, in them shall he die. **25** Yet ye say, The way of the Lord is not [l]equal: hear now, O house of Israel. Is not my way equal? or are not your ways unequal? **26** For when a righteous man turneth away from his righteousness, and commiteth iniquity, he shall even die for the same, he shall even die for his iniquity that he hath done. **27** Again, when the wicked turneth away from his wickedness that he hath committed, and doeth that which is lawful and right, he shall save his soul alive. **28** Because he considereth, and turneth away from all his transgressions that he hath committed, he shall surely live, and shall not die. **29** Yet saith the house of Israel, The way of the Lord is not equal. O house of Israel, are not my ways equal? or are not your ways unequal? **30** Therefore I will judge you, O house of Israel, everyone according to his ways, saith the Lord God: return therefore, and cause others to turn away from all your transgressions: so iniquity shall not be your destruction. **31** Cast away from you all your transgressions, whereby ye have transgressed and make [m]you a new heart and a new spirit: for why will ye die, O house of Israel? **32** For I desire not the death of him that dieth, saith the Lord God: cause therefore one another to return, and live ye.

19

1 The captivity of the kings of Judah signified by the lion's whelps and by the lion. 10 The prosperity of the city of Jerusalem that is past, and the misery thereof that is present.

1 Thou also take up a lamentation for the [a]princes of Israel, **2** And say, Wherefore lay thy [b]mother as a lioness among the lions? she nourished her young ones among the lion's whelps, **3** And she brought up one of her whelps, and it became a lion, and it learned to catch the prey, and it devoured men. **4** The [c]nations also heard of him, and he was taken in their nets, and they brought him in chains unto the land of Egypt. **5** Now when she saw that she had waited, and her hope was lost, she took another of her [d]whelps, and made him a lion. **6** Which went among the lions, and became a lion, and learned to catch the prey, and he devoured [e]men. **7** And he knew their widows, and he destroyed their cities, and the land was wasted, and all that was therein by the noise of his roaring. **8** Then the [f]nations set against him on every side of the countries, and laid their nets for him: so he was taken in their pit. **9** And they put him in prison and in chains, and brought him to the king of Babel, and they put him in holds, that his voice should no more be heard upon the mountains of Israel. **10** Thy [g]mother is like a vine in thy blood, planted by the waters: she brought forth fruit and branches by the abundant waters, **11** And she had strong rods for the scepters of them that bear rule, and her stature was exalted among the branches, and she appeared in her height with the multitude of her branches. **12** But she was plucked up in wrath: she was cast down to the ground, and the [h]East wind dried up her fruit: her branches were broken and withered: as for the rod of her strength, the fire consumed it. **13** And now she is planted in the wilderness in a dry and thirsty ground. **14** And fire is gone out [i]of a rod of her branches, which hath devoured her fruit, so that she hath no strong rod to be a scepter to rule: this is a lamentation, and shall be for a lamentation.

20

3 The Lord denieth that he will answer them when they pray, because of their wickedness. 33 He promiseth that his people shall return from captivity. 46 By the forest that should be burnt, is signified the burning of Jerusalem.

1 And in the [a]seventh year, in the fifth month, the tenth day of the month, came certain of the Elders of Israel to inquire of the Lord, and sat before me. **2** Then came the word of the Lord unto me, saying, **3** Son of man, speak unto the Elders of Israel, and say unto them, Thus saith the Lord God, Are ye come to inquire of me? as I live, saith the Lord God, when I am asked, I will not answer you. **4** Wilt thou judge them, son of man? wilt thou judge them? cause [b]them to understand the abominations of their fathers, **5** And say unto them, Thus saith the Lord God, In the day when I chose Israel, and [c]lifted up mine hand unto the seed of the house of Jacob, and made myself known unto them in the land of Egypt, when I lift up mine hand unto them, and said, I am the Lord your God, **6** In the day that I lifted up mine hand unto them, to bring them forth of the land of Egypt, into a land that I had provided for them, flowing with milk and honey, which is pleasant among all lands, **7** Then said I unto them, Let every man cast away the abominations of his eyes, [d]and defile not yourselves with the idols of Egypt: for I am the Lord your God. **8** But they rebelled against me, and would not hear me: for none cast away the abominations of [e]their eyes, neither did they forsake the idols of Egypt: then I thought to pour out mine indignation upon them, and to accomplish my wrath against them in the midst of the land of Egypt. **9** But I had respect to my [f]Name, that it should not be polluted before the heathen, among whom they were, and in whose sight I made myself known unto them in bringing them forth of the land of Egypt. **10** Now I carried them out of the land of Egypt, and brought them into the wilderness. **11** And I gave them my statutes, and declared my judgments unto them, [1]which if a man do, he shall live in them. **12** Moreover I gave them also my [2]Sabbaths to be a sign between me and them, that they might know that I am the Lord, that sanctify them. **13** But the house of Israel rebelled against me in the wilderness: they walked not in my statutes, and they cast away my judgments, which if a man do, he shall live in them, and my Sabbaths have they greatly polluted: then I thought to pour out mine indignation upon them [3]in the wilderness to consume them, **14** But I had respect to my name, that it should not be polluted before the [g]heathen in whose sight I brought them out. **15** Yet nevertheless, I lifted up mine hand unto them in the wilderness, that I would not bring them into the land, which I had given them, flowing with milk and honey, which was pleasant above all lands, **16** Because they cast away my judgments, and walked not in my statutes, but have polluted my [h]Sabbaths: for their heart went after their idols. **17** Nevertheless, mine eye spared them, that I would not destroy them, neither would I consume them in the wilderness. **18** But I said unto their children in the wilderness, Walk ye not in the ordinances of your [i]fathers, neither observe their manners, nor defile yourselves with their idols. **19** I am the Lord your God: walk in my statutes, and keep my judgments and do them, **20** And sanctify my Sabbaths, and they shall be a sign between me and you, that ye may know that I am the Lord your God. **21** Notwithstanding the children rebelled against me: they walked not in my statutes, nor kept my judgments to do them, which if a man do, he shall live in them, but they polluted my Sabbaths: then I thought to pour out mine indignation upon them, and to accomplish my wrath against them in the wilderness. **22** Nevertheless, I withdrew mine hand and had respect to my Name, that it should not be polluted before the heathen, in whose sight I brought them forth. **23** Yet I lifted up mine hand unto them in the wilderness, that I would scatter them among the heathen, and disperse them through the countries, **24** Because they had not executed my judgments, but had cast away my statutes, and had polluted my Sabbaths, and their eyes were after [j]their fathers'

---

eternal counsel appointed the death and damnation of the reprobate, yet the end of his counsel was not their death only, but chiefly his own glory. Also because he doth not approve sin, therefore it is here said that he would have them to turn away from it, that they might live.

j. Ezek. 18:23 Or, rather that he may return from his ways, and live.
k. Ezek. 18:24 That is, the false opinion that the hypocrites have of their righteousness.
l. Ezek. 18:25 In punishing the father with the children.
m. Ezek. 18:31 He showeth that man cannot forsake his wickedness, till his heart be changed, which is only the work of God.

EZEK. 18

1. Lev. 18:20
2. Lev. 20:18
3. Isa. 58:7 / Mat.. 25:35
4. Exod. 22:25 / Lev. 25:37 / Deut. 23:19 / Ps. 15:5
5. Deut. 24:16 / 2 Kings 4:6 / 2 Chron. 25:4

EZEK. 19

a. Ezek. 19:1 That is, Jehoahaz and Jehoiakim Josiah's sons, who for their pride and cruelty are compared unto lions.
b. Ezek. 19:2 To wit, Jehoahaz's mother, or Jerusalem.
c. Ezek. 19:4 By Pharaoh Necho king of Egypt, 2 Kings 23:33.
d. Ezek. 19:5 Which was Jehoiakim.
e. Ezek. 19:6 He slew of the prophets, and them that feared God, and ravished their wives.
f. Ezek. 19:8 Nebuchadnezzar with his great army which was gathered of divers nations.
g. Ezek. 19:10 He speaketh this in the reproach of this wicked king, in whose blood, that is, in the race of his predecessors, Jerusalem should have been blessed, according to God's promise, and flourished as a fruitful vine.
h. Ezek. 19:12 Meaning, that the Chaldeans should destroy them as the East wind doth the fruit of the vine.
i. Ezek. 19:14 Destruction is come by Zedekiah, who was the occasion of this rebellion.

EZEK. 20

a. Ezek. 20:1 Of the captivity of Jeconiah.
b. Ezek. 20:4 This declareth the great lenity and patience of God, which calleth sinners to repentance before he condemns them.
c. Ezek. 20:5 I sware that I would be their God, which manner of oath was observed from all antiquity, where they used to lift up their hands toward the heaven, acknowledging God to be the author of truth, and the defender thereof, and also the Judge of the heart, wishing that he should take vengeance, if they concealed anything which they knew to be truth.
d. Ezek. 20:7 God had forbidden them to make mention of the idols, Exod. 23:13; Ps. 16:4.
e. Ezek. 20:8 Which thing declareth the wickedness of man's heart, which judge God's service by their eyes and outward senses.
f. Ezek. 20:9 God had ever this respect to his glory, that he would not have his Name evil spoken of among the Gentiles for the punishment that his people deserved, in confidence whereof the godly ever prayed, as Exod. 32:12; Num. 14:13.
g. Ezek. 20:14 Who might thereby take an occasion to blaspheme my Name and to accuse me of lack of ability, or else that I had sought a means to destroy them more commodiously.
h. Ezek. 20:16 That is, my true religion, which I had commanded them, and gave themselves to serve me according to their own fantasies.
i. Ezek. 20:18 Whereby the holy Ghost confuteth them that say that they will follow the religion and example of their fathers, and not measure their doings by God's word whether they be approvable thereby or no.
j. Ezek. 20:24 Meaning, that they set their delight upon them.
k. Ezek. 20:25 Because they would not obey my laws, I gave them up to themselves, that they should obey their own fantasies, as verse 39; Rom. 1:21, 24.
l. Ezek. 20:26 I condemned those things, and counted them as abominable, which they thought had been excellent, and to

idols. 25 Wherefore I gave [k]them also statutes that were not good, and judgments, wherein they should not live. 26 And I polluted them in their own [l]gifts in that they caused to pass by the fire all that first openeth the womb, that I might destroy them, to the end that they might know that I am the Lord. 27 Therefore, son of man, speak unto the house of Israel and say unto them, Thus saith the Lord God, Yet in this your fathers have blasphemed me, though they had before grievously transgressed against me. 28 [m]For when I had brought them into the land, for the which I lifted up mine hand to give it to them, then they saw every high hill, and all the thick trees, and they offered there their sacrifices, and there they presented their offering of provocation: there also they made their sweet savor, and poured out there their drink offerings. 29 Then I said unto them, What is the high place whereunto ye go? And the name thereof was called [n]Bamah unto this day. 30 Wherefore, say unto the house of Israel, Thus saith the Lord God, Are ye not polluted [o]after the manner of your fathers? and commit ye not whoredom after their abominations? 31 For when you offer your gifts, and make your sons to pass through the fire, you pollute yourselves with all your idols unto this day: shall I answer you when I am asked, O house of Israel? As I live, saith the Lord God, [p]I will not answer you when I am asked. 32 Neither shall that be done that cometh into your mind: for ye say, we will be as the heathen, and as the families of the countries, and serve wood, and [q]stone. 33 As I live, saith the Lord God, I will surely rule you with a mighty hand, and with a stretched out arm, and in my wrath poured out, 34 And will bring you from the people, and will gather you out of the countries, wherein ye are scattered, with a mighty hand, and with a stretched out arm, and in my wrath poured out, 35 And I will bring you into the [r]wilderness of the people, and there will I plead with you face to face. 36 Like as I pleaded with your fathers in the wilderness of the land of Egypt, so will I plead with you, saith the Lord God. 37 And I will cause you to pass under the rod, and will bring you into the bond of the covenant. 38 And I will [s]choose out from among you the rebels, and them that transgress against me: I will bring them out of the land where they dwell, and they shall not enter into the land of Israel, and ye shall know that I am the Lord. 39 As for you, O house of Israel, thus saith the Lord God, [t]Go you, and serve everyone his idol, seeing that ye will not obey me, and pollute mine holy Name no more with your gifts, and with your idols. 40 For in mine holy mountain, even in the high mountain of Israel, saith the Lord God, there shall all the house of Israel, and all in the land serve me: there will I accept them, and there will I require your offerings, and the firstfruits of your oblations, with all your holy things. 41 I will accept your sweet savor, when I bring you from the people, and gather you out of the countries, wherein ye have been scattered, that I may be sanctified in you before the heathen. 42 And ye shall know that I am the Lord, when I shall bring you into the land of Israel, into the land for the which I lifted up mine hand to give it to your fathers. 43 And there shall ye remember your ways, and all your works, wherein ye have been defiled, and ye [u]shall judge yourselves worthy to be cut off, for all your evils, that ye have committed. 44 And ye shall know that I am the Lord, when I have respect unto you for my Name's sake, and not after your wicked ways, nor according to your corrupt works, O ye house of Israel, saith the Lord God. 45 Moreover, the word of the Lord came unto me, saying, 46 Son of man, Set thy face toward the way of Teman, and drop thy word toward [v]the South, and prophesy toward the forest of the field of the South, 47 And say to the forest of the South, Hear the word of the Lord: thus saith the Lord God, Behold, I will kindle a fire in thee, and it shall devour all the [w]green wood in thee, and all the dry wood: the continual flame shall not be quenched, and every face from the South to the North shall be burnt therein. 48 And all flesh shall see, that I the Lord have kindled it, and it shall not be quenched. Then said I, Ah Lord God, they say of me, Doth not he speak [x]parables?

21

3 He threateneth the sword and destruction to Jerusalem. 25 He showeth the fall of king Zedekiah. 29 He is commanded to prophesy the destruction of the children of Ammon. 30 The Lord threateneth to destroy Nebuchadnezzar.

1 The word of the Lord came to me again, saying,

2 Son of man, set thy face toward Jerusalem, [a]and drop thy word toward the holy places, and prophesy against the land of Israel, 3 And say to the land of Israel, Thus saith the Lord, Behold, I come against thee, and will draw my sword out of his sheath, and cut off from thee both the [b]righteous and the wicked. 4 Seeing then that I will cut off from thee both the righteous and wicked, therefore shall my sword go out of his sheath against all flesh from the South to the [c]North, 5 That all flesh may know that I the Lord have drawn my sword out of his sheath, and it shall not return anymore. 6 Mourn therefore thou son of man, as in the pain of thy [d]reins, and mourn bitterly before them. 7 And if they say unto thee, Wherefore mournest thou? Then answer, Because [e]of the bruit: for it cometh, and every heart shall melt, and all hands shall be weak, and all minds shall faint, and all knees shall fall away as water: behold, it cometh, and shall be done, saith the Lord God. 8 Again, the word of the Lord came unto me, saying, 9 Son of man, prophesy, and say, Thus saith the Lord God, say, A sword, a sword both sharp and furbished. 10 It is sharpened to make a sore slaughter, and it is furbished that it may [f]glitter: how shall we rejoice? for it contemneth the [g]rod of my son, as [h]all other trees. 11 And he hath given it to be furbished, that he may handle it: this sword is sharp, and is furbished that he may give it into the hand of the [i]slayer. 12 Cry and howl, son of man: for this shall come to my people, and it shall come unto all the princes of Israel: the terrors of the sword shall be upon my people, [j]smite therefore upon thy thigh. 13 For it is a trial, [k]and what shall this be, if the sword contemn even the rod? It shall be no more, saith the Lord God. 14 Thou therefore, son of man, prophesy and smite [l]hand to hand, and let the sword be doubled: let the sword that hath killed, return the third time: it is the sword of the great slaughter entering into their privy chambers. 15 I have brought the fear of the sword into all their gates to make their heart to faint, and to multiply their ruins. Ah, it is made bright, and it is dressed for the slaughter. 16 Get thee [m]alone: go to the right hand, or get thyself to the left hand, whithersoever thy face turneth. 17 I will also smite mine hands together, and will cause my wrath to cease. I the Lord have said it. 18 The word of the Lord came unto me again, saying, 19 Also thou son of man, appoint thee [n]two ways, that the sword of the King of Babel may come: both twain shall come out of one land, and choose a place, and choose it in the corner of the way of the city. 20 Appoint a way, that the sword may come to Rabbah of the Ammonites, and [o]to Judah in Jerusalem the strong city. 21 And the King of Babel stood at the [p]parting of the way, at the head of the two ways, consulting by divination, and made his arrows bright: he consulted with idols, and looked in [q]the liver. 22 At his right hand was the divination for Jerusalem to appoint captains to open their mouth in the slaughter, and to lift up their voice with shouting, to lay engines of war against the gates, to cast a mount, and to build a fortress. 23 And it shall be unto them [r]as a false divination in their sight for the oaths made unto them: [s]but he will call to remembrance their iniquity, to the intent they should be taken. 24 Therefore thus saith the Lord God, Because ye have made your iniquity to be remembered in discovering your rebellion, that in all your works your sins might appear: because, I say, that ye are come to remembrance, ye shall be taken with the hand. 25 And thou [t]Prince of Israel polluted, and wicked, whose day is come, when iniquity shall have an end, 26 Thus saith the Lord God, I will take away the [u]diadem, and take off the crown: this shall be no more the same: I will exalt the humble, and will abase him that is high. 27 I will overturn, overturn, overturn it, and it shall be no

---

have declared most zeal, Luke 16:15, for that which God required, as most excellent, that they gave to their idols.

m. Ezek. 20:28 Not only in the wilderness, when I brought them out of Egypt, but since I placed them in this land: which declareth how prompt man's heart is to idolatry, seeing that by no admonitions he can be drawn back.

n. Ezek. 20:29 Which signifieth an high place, declaring that they vaunted themselves of their idolatry, and were not ashamed thereof, though God had commanded them expressly that they should have no altar lifted upon high by stairs, Exod. 20:26.

o. Ezek. 20:30 Hebrew, in the way.

p. Ezek. 20:31 He showeth that the ingratitude of the people deserveth that God should cut them off, and that they should not have the comfort of his word.

q. Ezek. 20:32 He declareth that man of nature is wholly enemy unto God, and to his own salvation, and therefore God calleth him to the right way, partly by chastising, but chiefly by his mercy in forgiving his rebellion, and wickedness.

r. Ezek. 20:35 I will bring you among strange nations as into a wilderness, and there will visit you, and so call you to repentance, and then bring the godly home again, Isa. 65:9.

s. Ezek. 20:38 Signifying, that he will not burn the corn with the chaff, but choose out the wicked to punish them when he will spare his.

t. Ezek. 20:39 This is spoken to the hypocrites.

u. Ezek. 20:43 Your own consciences shall convict you after, that you have felt my mercies.

v. Ezek. 20:46 For Judah stood South from Babylon.

w. Ezek. 20:47 Both strong and weak in Jerusalem.

x. Ezek. 20:48 The people said that the Prophet spake darkly: therefore he desireth the Lord to give them a plain declaration thereof.

EZEK. 20

1. Lev. 18:5 / Rom. 10:5 / Gal. 3:12

2. Exod. 20:8 / Exod. 31:13 / Deut. 5:12

3. Num. 14:28,29 / Num. 26:65

EZEK. 21

a. Ezek. 21:2 Speak sensibly, that all may understand.

b. Ezek. 21:3 That is such which seem to have an outward show of righteousness, by observation of the ceremonies of the law.

c. Ezek. 21:4 Meaning, through all the land.

d. Ezek. 21:6 As though thou were in extreme anguish.

e. Ezek. 21:7 Because of the great noise of the army of the Chaldeans.

f. Ezek. 21:10 And so cause a fear.

g. Ezek. 21:10 Meaning, the scepter: showing that it will not spare the King, who should be as the son of God, and in his place.

h. Ezek. 21:10 That is, the rest of the people.

i. Ezek. 21:11 To wit, unto the army of the Chaldeans.

j. Ezek. 21:12 Read Jer. 31:19.

k. Ezek. 21:13 Ezek. moved with compassion, thus complaineth, fearing the destruction of the kingdom which God had confirmed to David and his posterity by promise, which promise God performed, although here it seemed to man's eye that it should utterly perish.

l. Ezek. 21:14 That is, encourage the sword.

m. Ezek. 21:16 Provide for thyself: for thou shalt see God's plague of all parts on this country.

n. Ezek. 21:19 This was spoken, because that when Nebuchadnezzar came against Judah, his purpose was also to go against the Ammonites: but doubting in the way, which enterprise to undertake first he consulted with his soothsayers, and so went against Judah.

o. Ezek. 21:20 That is, to the tribe of Judah that kept themselves in Jerusalem.

p. Ezek. 21:21 To know whether he should go against the Ammonites or them of Jerusalem.

q. Ezek. 21:21 He used conjuring and sorcery.

r. Ezek. 21:23 Because there was a league between the Jews, and the Babylonians, they of Jerusalem shall think nothing less than that this thing should come to pass.

s. Ezek. 21:23 That is, Nebuchadnezzar will remember the rebellion of Zedekiah, and so come upon them.

t. Ezek. 21:25 Meaning, Zedekiah, who practiced with the Egyptians to make himself high and able to resist the Babylonians.

u. Ezek. 21:26 Some refer this to the Priest's attire: for Jehozadak the Priest went into captivity with the king.

v. Ezek. 21:27 That is, unto the coming of Messiah: for though the Jews had some sign of government afterward under the Persians, Greeks and Romans, yet this restitution was not till

more until he [v]come, whose right it is, and I will give it him. **28** And thou, son of man, prophesy, and say, Thus saith the Lord God to the children of Ammon, and to their blasphemy: say thou, I say, The sword, the sword is drawn forth and furbished to the slaughter, to consume, because of the glittering, **29** While they see [w]vanity unto thee, and prophesied a lie unto thee to bring thee upon the necks of the wicked that are slain, whose day is come, when their iniquity shall have an end. **30** Shall I cause it to return into his sheath? I will judge thee in the place where thou wast created, even in the land of thine habitation. **31** And I will pour out mine indignation upon thee, and will blow against thee in the fire of my wrath, and deliver thee into the hand of beastly men, and skillful to destroy. **32** Thou shalt be in the fire to be devoured: thy blood shall be in the midst of the land, and thou shalt be no more remembered: for I the Lord have spoken it.

22

1 Jerusalem is reproved for cruelty. 25 Of the wicked doctrine of the false prophets and priests, and of their unsatiable covetousness. 26 The tyranny of rulers. 29 The wickedness of the people.

1 Moreover, the word of the Lord came unto me, saying, **2** Now thou son of man, wilt thou [a]judge, wilt thou judge this bloody city? wilt thou show her all her abominations? **3** Then say, Thus saith the Lord God, The city sheddeth blood in the midst of it, that her [b]time may come, and maketh idols against [c]herself, to pollute herself. **4** Thou hast offended in thy blood, that thou hast shed, and hast polluted thyself in thine idols, which thou hast made, and thou hast caused thy days to draw near, and art come unto thy term: therefore have I made thee a reproach to the heathen, and a mocking to all countries. **5** Those that be near, and those that be far from thee, shall mock thee, which art vile in [d]name and sore in affliction. **6** Behold, the princes of Israel everyone in thee was ready to his power, to shed blood. **7** In thee have they despised father and mother: in the midst of thee [e]have they oppressed the stranger: in thee have they vexed the fatherless and the widow. **8** Thou hast despised mine holy things, and hast polluted my Sabbaths. **9** In thee are men that carry tales to shed blood: in thee are they that eat upon the mountains: in the midst of thee they commit abomination. **10** [1]In thee have they discovered their fathers' shame: in thee have they vexed her that was polluted in her flowers. **11** And everyone [2]hath committed abomination with his neighbor's wife, and everyone hath wickedly defiled his daughter-in-law, and in thee hath every man forced his own sister, even his father's daughter. **12** In thee have they taken gifts to shed blood: thou hast taken usury and the increase, and thou hast defrauded thy neighbors by extortion, and hast forgotten me, saith the Lord God. **13** Behold, therefore I have [f]smitten mine hands upon thy covetousness, that thou hast used, and upon the blood, which hath been in the midst of thee. **14** Can thine heart endure, or can thine hands [g]be strong, in the days that I shall have to do with thee? I the Lord have spoken it, and will do it. **15** And I will scatter thee among the heathen, and disperse thee in the countries, and will cause thy [h]filthiness to cease from thee. **16** And thou shalt take thine [i]inheritance in thyself in the sight of the heathen, and thou shalt know that I am the Lord. **17** And the word of the Lord came unto me, saying, **18** Son of man, the house of Israel is unto me as [j]dross: all they are brass, and tin, and iron, and lead in the midst of the furnace: they are even the dross of silver. **19** Therefore thus saith the Lord God, Because ye are all as dross, behold, therefore I will gather you in the midst of Jerusalem. **20** As they gather silver and brass, and iron, and lead, and tin into the midst of the furnace, to blow the fire upon it to melt it, so will I gather you in mine anger and in my wrath, and will put you there [k]and melt you. **21** I will gather you, I say, and blow the fire of my wrath upon you, and you shall be melted in the midst thereof. **22** As silver is melted in the midst of the furnace, so shall ye be melted in the midst thereof, and ye shall know that I the Lord have poured out my wrath upon you. **23** And the word of the Lord came unto me, saying, **24** Son of man, say unto her, Thou art the land, that is unclean, [l]and not rained upon in the day of wrath. **25** There is a conspiracy [m]of her prophets in the midst thereof like a roaring lion, ravening the prey: they have devoured souls: they have taken the riches and precious things: they have made her many widows in the midst thereof. **26** Her Priests have broken my Law, and have defiled mine holy things: they have put no difference between the holy and profane, neither discerned between the unclean and the clean, and have hid their [n]eyes from my Sabbaths, and I am profaned among them. **27** Her princes in [3]the midst thereof are like wolves, ravening the prey to shed blood, and to destroy souls for their own covetous lucre. **28** And her [o]prophets have daubed them with untempered mortar, seeing vanities, and divining lies unto them, saying, Thus saith the Lord God, when the Lord had not spoken. **29** The people of the land have violently oppressed by spoiling and robbing, and have vexed the poor and the needy: yea, they have oppressed the stranger against right. **30** And I sought for a man among them, that should [p]make up the hedge, and stand in the gap before me for the land, that I should not destroy it, but I found none. **31** Therefore have I poured out mine indignation upon them, and consumed them with the fire of my wrath: their own ways have I rendered upon their heads, saith the Lord God.

23

Of the Idolatry of Samaria and Jerusalem, under the names of Oholah and Oholibah.

1 The word of the Lord came again unto me, saying, **2** Son of man, there were two women, the daughters of one [a]mother. **3** And they committed fornication in [b]Egypt, they committed fornication in their youth: there were their breasts pressed, and there they bruised the teats of their virginity. **4** And the names of [c]them were Oholah the elder, and Oholibah her sister: and they were mine, and they bare sons and daughters: thus were their names: Samaria is Oholah, and Jerusalem Oholibah. **5** And Oholah played the harlot [d]when [e]she was mine, and she was set on fire with her lovers, to wit, with the Assyrians her neighbors, **6** Which were clothed with blue silk, both captains and princes they were all pleasant young men, and horsemen riding upon horses. **7** Thus she committed her whoredom with them, even with all them that were the chosen men of Assyria, and with all on whom she doted, and defiled herself with all their idols. **8** Neither left she her fornications, learned of the Egyptians: for in her youth they [f]lay with her, and they bruised the breasts of her virginity, and poured their whoredom upon her. **9** Wherefore I delivered her into the hands of her lovers, even into the hands of the Assyrians, upon whom she doted. **10** These discovered her shame: they took away her sons and her daughters, and slew her with the sword, and she had an evil name among women: for [g]they had executed judgment upon her. **11** And when her sister Oholibah saw this, she marred herself with inordinate love more than she, and with her fornications more than her sister with her fornications. **12** She doted upon the Assyrians her neighbors, both captains and princes clothed with divers suits, horsemen riding upon horses: they were all pleasant young men. **13** Then I saw that she was defiled, and that they were both after one sort, **14** And that she increased her fornications: for when she saw men [h]painted upon the wall, the images of the Chaldeans painted with vermilion, **15** And girded with girdles upon their loins, and with dyed attire upon their heads (looking all like princes after the manner of the Babylonians in Chaldea, the land of their nativity) **16** As soon, I say, as she saw them, she doted upon them, and sent messengers unto them, into Chaldea. **17** Now when the Babylonians came to her into the bed of love, they defiled her with their fornication, and she was polluted with them, and her lust departed from them. **18** So she discovered her fornication, and disclosed her shame: then mine heart forsook her, like as mine heart had forsaken her sister. **19** Yet she increased her whoredom more, and called to remembrance the days of her youth wherein she had played the harlot in the land of Egypt. **20** For she doted upon their servants whose members are as the members of asses, and whose issue is like the issue of horses. **21** Thou calledst to remembrance the wickedness of thy youth, when thy teats were bruised by the Egyptians: therefore the paps of thy youth are thus. **22** Therefore, O Oholibah, thus saith the Lord God, Behold, I will raise up thy lovers against thee, from whom thine heart is departed, and I will bring them against thee on every

---

Christ's coming, and at length should be accomplished, as was promised, Gen. 49:10.

w. Ezek. 21:29 Though the Jews and Ammonites would not believe that thou, to wit, the sword, shouldest come upon them, and said, that the Prophets, which threatened, spake lies, yet thou shalt as surely come, as though thou werest already upon their necks.

EZEK. 22

a. Ezek. 22:2 Art thou ready to execute thy charge, which I commit unto thee against Jerusalem, that murdereth the Prophets and them that are godly?
b. Ezek. 22:3 That is, the time of her destruction.
c. Ezek. 22:3 To her own undoing.
d. Ezek. 22:5 Whose very name all men hate.
e. Ezek. 22:7 He meaneth hereby that there was no kind of wickedness which was not committed in Jerusalem, and therefore the plagues of God should speedily come upon her.
f. Ezek. 22:13 In token of my wrath and vengeance.
g. Ezek. 22:14 That is, able to defend thyself.
h. Ezek. 22:15 I will thus take away the occasion of thy wickedness.
i. Ezek. 22:16 Thou shalt be no more the inheritance of the Lord, but forsaken.
j. Ezek. 22:18 Which before was most precious.
k. Ezek. 22:20 Meaning, hereby that the godly should be tried, and the wicked destroyed.
l. Ezek. 22:24 Thou art like a barren land which the Lord plagueth with drought.
m. Ezek. 22:25 The false prophets have conspired together to make their doctrine more probable.
n. Ezek. 22:26 They have neglected my service.
o. Ezek. 22:28 They which should have reproved them, flattered them in their vices, and covered their doings with lies, Ezek. 13:10.
p. Ezek. 22:30 Which would show himself zealous in my cause by resisting vice, Isa. 59:16 and 63:5, and also pray unto me to withhold my plagues, Ps. 106:23.

EZEK. 22

1. Lev. 20:11,18
2. Jer. 5:8
3. Mic. 3:11 / Zeph. 3:3

EZEK. 23

a. Ezek. 23:2 Meaning, Israel and Judah, which came both out of one family.
b. Ezek. 23:3 They became idolaters after the manner of the Egyptians.
c. Ezek. 23:4 Oholah signifieth a mansion or dwelling in herself, meaning Samaria, which was the royal city of Israel and Oholibah signifieth my mansion in her, whereby is meant Jerusalem, where God's Temple was.
d. Ezek. 23:5 Hebrew, under me.
e. Ezek. 23:5 When the Israelites were named the people of God, they became idolaters, and forsook God, and put their trust in the Assyrians.
f. Ezek. 23:8 The holy Ghost useth these terms which seem strange to chaste ears, to cause this wicked vice of idolatry so to be abhorred, that … any should abide to hear the name thereof.
g. Ezek. 23:10 Meaning, the Assyrians.
h. Ezek. 23:14 This declareth that no words are able sufficiently to express the rage of idolaters, and therefore the holy Ghost here compareth them to those which in their raging love and filthy lusts dote upon the images and paintings of them after whom they lust.
i. Ezek. 23:23 These were the names of certain princes and captains under Nebuchadnezzar.
j. Ezek. 23:24 Hebrew, I will give judgment before them.
k. Ezek. 23:24 Or, laws.
l. Ezek. 23:25 They shall destroy thy princes and priests with the rest of thy people.

side, **23** To wit, the Babylonians, and all the Chaldeans, [i]Pekod, and Shoa, and Koa, and all the Assyrians with them: they were all pleasant young men, captains and princes: all they were valiant and renowned, riding upon horses. **24** Even these shall come against thee with chariots, wagons, and wheels, and with a multitude of people, which shall set against thee buckler and shield, and helmet round about, and [j]I will leave the punishment unto them, and they shall judge thee according to their [k]judgments. **25** And I will lay mine indignation upon thee, and they shall deal cruelly with thee: they shall cut off thy [l]nose and thine ears, and thy remnant shall fall by the sword: they shall carry away thy sons and thy daughters, and thy residue shall be devoured by the fire. **26** They shall also strip thee out of thy clothes, and take away thy fair jewels. **27** Thus will I make thy wickedness to cease from thee, and thy fornication out of the land of Egypt: so that thou shalt not lift up thine eyes unto them, nor remember Egypt anymore. **28** For thus saith the Lord God, Behold, I will deliver thee into the hand of them, whom thou hatest, even into the hands of them from whom thine heart is departed. **29** And they shall handle thee despitefully, and shall take away all thy [m]labor, and shall leave thee naked and bare, and the shame of thy fornications [n]shall be discovered, both thy wickedness, and thy whoredom. **30** I will do these things unto thee, because thou hast gone a whoring after the heathen, and because thou art polluted with their idols. **31** Thou hast walked in the way of thy sister: therefore will I give her [o]cup into thine hand. **32** Thus saith the Lord God, Thou shalt drink of thy sister's cup, deep and large: thou shalt be laughed to scorn and had in derision, because it containeth much. **33** Thou shalt be filled with [p]drunkenness and sorrow, even with the cup of destruction, and desolation, with the cup of thy sister Samaria. **34** Thou shalt even drink it, and wring it out to the dregs, and thou shalt break the shards thereof, and tear thine own breasts: for I have spoken it, saith the Lord God. **35** Therefore thus saith the Lord God, Because thou hast forgotten me, and cast me behind thy back, therefore thou shalt also bear thy wickedness and thy whoredom. **36** The Lord said moreover unto me, Son of man, wilt thou judge Oholah and Oholibah? and wilt thou declare to them their abominations? **37** For they have played the whores, and blood is in their hands, and with their idols have they committed adultery, and have also caused their sons, whom they bore unto me, to pass by the fire to be their [q]meat. **38** Moreover, thus have they done unto me: they have defiled my Sanctuary in the same day, and have profaned my Sabbaths. **39** For when they had slain their children to their idols, they came the same day into my Sanctuary to defile it: and lo, thus have they done in the midst of mine house. **40** And how much more is it that they sent for men to come from [r]far, unto whom a messenger was sent, and lo, they came? for whom thou didst wash thyself, and paintedst thine eyes, and deckedst thee with ornaments, **41** And satest [s]upon a costly bed, and a table prepared before it, whereupon thou hast set mine incense and mine oil. **42** And a voice of a multitude being at ease, was with her: and with the men to make the company great, were brought men of [t]Saba from the wilderness, which put bracelets upon their hands, and beautiful crowns upon their heads. **43** Then I said unto her that was old in adulteries, Now shall she and her fornications come to an end. **44** And they went in unto her as they go to a common harlot: so went they to Oholah and Oholibah the wicked women. **45** And the righteous men they shall judge them after the manner of [u]harlots, and after the manner of murderers: for they are harlots, and blood is in their hands. **46** Wherefore thus saith the Lord God, I will bring a multitude upon them, and will give them unto the tumult and to the spoil, **47** And the multitude shall stone them with stones, and cut them with their swords: they shall slay their sons, and their daughters, and burn up their houses with fire. **48** Thus will I cause wickedness to cease out of the land, that all [v]women may be taught not to do after your wickedness. **49** And they shall lay your wickedness upon you, and ye shall bear the sins of your idols, and ye shall know that I am the Lord God.

24

He showeth the destruction of Jerusalem by a parable of a seething pot. 16 The parable of Ezekiel's wife being dead.

1 Again in the [a]ninth year, in the tenth month, in the tenth day of the [b]month, came the word of the Lord unto me, saying, **2** Son of man, write thee the name of the day, even of this same day: for the King of Babel set himself against Jerusalem this same day. **3** Therefore speak a parable unto the rebellious house, and say unto them, Thus saith the Lord God, Prepare a [c]pot, prepare it, and also pour water into it. **4** Gather the [d]pieces thereof into it, even every good piece, as the thigh and the shoulder, and fill it with the chief bones. **5** Take one of the best sheep, and [e]burn also the [f]bones under it, and make it boil well, and seethe the bones of it therein, **6** Because the Lord God saith thus, Woe to the bloody city, even to the pot, [g]whose scum is therein, and whose scum is not gone out of it: bring it out [h]piece by piece: let no [i]lot fall upon it. **7** For her blood is in the midst of her: she set it upon an high [j]rock, and poured it not upon the ground to cover it with dust, **8** That it might cause wrath to arise, and take vengeance: even I have set her blood upon an high rock that it should not be covered. **9** Therefore thus saith the Lord God, [1]Woe to the bloody city, for I will make [k]the burning great. **10** Heap on much wood: [l]kindle the fire, consume the flesh, and cast in spice, and let the bones be burnt. **11** Then set it empty upon the coals thereof, that [m]the brass of it may be hot, and may burn, and that the filthiness of it may be molten in it, and that the scum of it may be consumed. **12** [n]She hath wearied herself with lies, and her great scum went not out of her: therefore her scum shall be consumed with fire. **13** Thou remainest in thy filthiness and wickedness: because I would [o]have purged thee, and thou wast not purged, thou shalt not be purged from thy filthiness, till I have caused my wrath to light upon thee. **14** I the Lord have spoken it: it shall come to pass, and I will do it: I will not go back, neither will I spare, neither will I repent: according to thy ways, and according to thy works shall [p]they judge thee, saith the Lord God. **15** Also the word of the Lord came unto me, saying, **16** Son of man, behold, I take away from thee the [q]pleasure of thine eyes with a plague: yet shalt thou neither mourn nor weep, neither shall thy tears run down. **17** Cease from sighing: make no mourning for the dead, and bind the tire of thine head upon thee, [r]and put on thy shoes upon thy feet, and cover not thy lips, and eat [s]not the bread of men. **18** So I spake unto the people in the morning, and at even my wife died: and I did in [t]the morning, as I was commanded. **19** And the people said unto me, Wilt thou not tell us what these things mean toward us that thou doest so? **20** Then I answered them, The word of the Lord came unto me, saying, **21** Speak unto the house of Israel, Thus saith the Lord God, behold, I will [u]pollute my Sanctuary, even the [v]pride of your power, the pleasure of your eyes, and your heart's desire, and your sons, and your daughters whom ye have left, shall fall by the sword. **22** And ye shall do as I have done: ye shall not cover your lips, neither shall ye eat the bread of men. **23** And your tire shall be upon your heads, and your shoes upon your feet: ye shall not mourn nor weep, but ye shall pine away for your iniquities, and mourn one toward another. **24** Thus Ezekiel is unto you a sign: according to all that he hath done, ye shall do: and when this cometh, ye shall know that I am the Lord God. **25** Also, thou son of man, shall it not be in the day when I take from them their power, the joy of their honor, the pleasure of their eyes, and the [w]desire of their heart, their sons and their daughters, **26** That he that escapeth in that day, shall come unto thee to tell thee that which he hath heard with his ears? **27** In that day shall thy mouth be opened to him which is escaped, and thou shalt speak, and be no more dumb, and thou shalt be a sign unto them, and they shall know that I am the Lord.

25

2 The word of the Lord against Ammon, which rejoiced at the fall of Jerusalem, 8 against Moab and Seir, Idumea and the Philistines.

1 The word of the Lord came again unto me, saying, **2** Son of man, set thy face against the Ammonites, and prophesy against them, **3** And say unto the Ammonites, Hear the word of the Lord God, Thus saith the Lord God, Because thou saidest, [a]Ha, ha, against my Sanctuary, when it was polluted, and against the land of Israel, when it was desolate, and against the house of Judah, when they went into captivity, **4** Behold, therefore I will deliver thee to the [b]men of the East

---

m. Ezek. 23:29 All thy treasures and riches which thou hast gotten by labor.
n. Ezek. 23:29 All the world shall see thy shameful forsaking of God to serve idols.
o. Ezek. 23:31 I will execute the same judgments and vengeance against thee, and that with greater severity.
p. Ezek. 23:33 Meaning, that its afflictions should be so great that they should cause them to lose their senses, and reason.
q. Ezek. 23:37 That is, to be sacrifices to their idols, read Ezek. 16:20.
r. Ezek. 23:40 They sent into other countries to have such as should teach the service of their idols.
s. Ezek. 23:41 He meaneth the altar that was prepared for the idols.
t. Ezek. 23:42 Which should teach the manner of worshipping their gods.
u. Ezek. 23:45 That is, worthy of death, read Ezek. 16:38.
v. Ezek. 23:48 Meaning, all other cities and countries.

EZEK. 24

a. Ezek. 24:1 Of Jeconiah's captivity, and of the reign of Zedekiah, 2 Kings 25:1.
b. Ezek. 24:1 Called Tebeth, which containeth part of December and part of January: in the which month and day Nebuchadnezzar besieged Jerusalem.
c. Ezek. 24:3 Whereby was meant Jerusalem.
d. Ezek. 24:4 That is the citizens, and the chief men thereof.
e. Ezek. 24:5 Or, heap.
f. Ezek. 24:5 Meaning, of the innocents, whom they had slain, who were the cause of the kindling of God's wrath against them.
g. Ezek. 24:6 Whose iniquities and wicked citizens there yet remain.
h. Ezek. 24:6 Signifying that they should not be destroyed all at once, but by little and little.
i. Ezek. 24:6 Spare none estate or condition.
j. Ezek. 24:7 The city showed her cruelty to all the world, and was not ashamed thereof, neither yet hid it.
k. Ezek. 24:9 Or, an heap of wood.
l. Ezek. 24:10 Meaning, that the city should be utterly destroyed, and that he would give the enemies an appetite thereunto.
m. Ezek. 24:11 Or, bottom.
n. Ezek. 24:12 The city hath flattered herself in vain.
o. Ezek. 24:13 I labored by sending my Prophets to call thee to repentance, but thou wouldest not.
p. Ezek. 24:14 That is, the Babylonians.
q. Ezek. 24:16 Meaning, his wife, in whom he delighted, as verse 18.
r. Ezek. 24:17 For in mourning they went bareheaded and barefooted, and also covered their lips.
s. Ezek. 24:17 That is, which the neighbors sent to them that mourned.
t. Ezek. 24:18 Meaning, the morning following.
u. Ezek. 24:21 By sending the Chaldeans to destroy it, as Ezek. 7:22.
v. Ezek. 24:21 Wherein you boast and delight.
w. Ezek. 24:25 Hebrew, lifting up of their souls.

EZEK. 24

1. Nah. 3:1 / Hab. 2:12

EZEK. 25

a. Ezek. 25:3 Because ye rejoiced when the enemy destroyed my city and Temple.
b. Ezek. 25:4 That is, to the Babylonians.

for a possession, and they shall set their [c]palaces in thee, and make their dwellings in thee: they shall eat thy fruit, and they shall drink thy milk: **5** And I will make [d]Rabbah a dwelling place for camels, and the Ammonites a sheepcote, and ye shall know that I am the Lord. **6** For thus saith the Lord God, Because thou hast clapped the hands, and stamped with the feet, and rejoiced in heart with all thy despite against the land of Israel, **7** Behold, therefore I will stretch out mine hand upon thee, and will deliver thee to be spoiled of the heathen, and I will root thee out from the people, and I will cause thee to be destroyed out of the countries, and I will destroy thee, and thou shalt know that I am the Lord. **8** Thus saith the Lord God, Because that Moab and Seir do say, Behold, the house of Judah is like unto all the heathen, **9** Therefore, behold, I will open the side of Moab, even of the cities [e]of his cities, I say, in his frontiers with the pleasant country, Beth Jeshimoth, Baal Meon, and Kirjathaim. **10** I will call the men of the East against the Ammonites, and will give them in possession, so that the Ammonites shall no more be remembered among the nations. **11** And I will execute judgments upon Moab, and they shall know that I am the Lord. **12** Thus saith the Lord God, because that Edom hath done evil by taking vengeance upon the house of Judah, and hath committed great offence, and revenged himself upon them, **13** Therefore thus saith the Lord God, I will also stretch out mine hand upon Edom, and destroy man and beast out of it, and I will make it desolate from Teman, and they of Dedan shall fall by the sword. **14** And I will execute my vengeance upon Edom by the hand of my people Israel, and they shall do in Edom according to mine anger, and according to mine indignation, and they shall know my vengeance, saith the Lord God. **15** Thus saith the Lord God, Because the Philistines have executed vengeance, and revenged themselves with a despiteful heart, to destroy it for the old hatred, **16** Therefore thus saith the Lord God, behold, I will stretch out mine hand upon the Philistines, and I will cut off the [f]Cherethims, and destroy the remnant of the seacoast. **17** And I will execute great vengeance upon them with rebukes of mine indignation, and they shall know that I am the Lord, when I shall lay my vengeance upon them.

26

1 He prophesieth that Tyre shall be overthrown, because it rejoiced at the destruction of Jerusalem. 15 The wondering and astonishment of the merchants for the destruction of Tyre.

1 And in the [a]eleventh year in the first day of the month, the word of the Lord came unto me, saying, **2** Son of man, because that Tyre hath said against Jerusalem, Aha, the [b]gate of the people is broken: it is turned unto me: for seeing she is desolate, I shall be [c]replenished, **3** Therefore thus saith the Lord God, Behold, I come against thee, O Tyre, and I will bring up many nations against thee, as the sea mounteth up with his waves. **4** And they shall destroy the walls of Tyre and break down her towers: I will also scrape her dust from her, and make her like the top of a rock. **5** Thou shalt be for the spreading of nets in the midst of the sea: for I have spoken it, saith the Lord God, and it shall be a spoil to the nations. **6** And her [d]daughters which are in the field, shall be slain by the sword, and they shall know that I am the Lord. **7** For thus saith the Lord God, Behold, I will bring upon Tyre Nebuchadnezzar king of Babel, a King of kings from the North, with horses and with chariots, and with horsemen, with a multitude and much people. **8** He shall slay with the sword thy daughters in the field, and he shall make a fort against thee, and cast a mount against thee, and lift up the buckler against thee. **9** He shall set engines of war before him against thy walls, and with his weapons break down thy towers. **10** The dust of his horses shall cover thee, for their multitude: thy walls shall shake at the noise of the horsemen, and of the wheels, and of the chariots, when he shall enter into thy gates as into the entry of a city that is broken down. **11** With the hooves of his horses shall he tread down all thy streets: he shall slay the people by the sword, and the [e]pillars of thy strength shall fall down to the ground. **12** And they shall rob thy riches, and spoil thy merchandise, and they shall break down thy walls, and destroy thy pleasant houses, and they shall cast thy stones and thy timber and thy dust into the midst of the water. **13** [1]Thus will I cause the sound of thy songs to cease, and the sound of thine harps shall be no more heard. **14** I will lay thee like the top of a rock: [f]thou shalt be for a spreading of nets: thou shalt be built no more: for I the Lord have spoken it, saith the Lord God. **15** Thus saith the Lord God to Tyre, Shall not the isles tremble at the sound of thy fall? and at the cry of the wounded, when they shall be slain and murdered in the midst of thee? **16** Then all the princes of the [g]sea shall come down from their thrones: they shall lay away their robes, and put off their broidered garments, and shall clothe themselves with astonishment: they shall sit upon the ground and be astonished at every moment, and be amazed at thee. **17** And they shall take up a lamentation for thee, and say to thee, How art thou destroyed, that wast inhabited [h]of the Sea men, the renowned city which was strong in the sea, both she and her inhabitants, which cause their fear to be on all that haunt therein! **18** Now shall the isles be astonished in the day of thy fall: yea, the isles that are in the sea, shall be troubled at thy departure. **19** For thus saith the Lord God, when I shall make thee a desolate city, like the cities that are not inhabited, and when I shall bring the deep upon thee, and great waters shall cover thee, **20** When I shall cast thee down with them that descend into the pit, with the people [i]of old time, and shall set thee in the low parts of the earth, like the old ruins, with them, I say, which go down to the pit, so that thou shalt not be inhabited, and I shall show my glory in the land of the [j]living. **21** I will [k]bring thee to nothing, and thou shalt be no more: though thou be sought for, yet shalt thou never be found again, saith the Lord God.

27

The Prophet bewaileth the desolation of Tyre, showing what were the riches, power and authority thereof in times past.

1 The word of the Lord came again unto me, saying, **2** Son of man, take up a lamentation for Tyre, **3** And say unto Tyre that is situated at the entry of the sea, which is the mart [a]of the people for many isles, Thus saith the Lord God, O Tyre, thou hast said, I am of perfect beauty. **4** Thy borders are in the [b]midst of the sea, and thy builders have made thee of perfect beauty. **5** They have made all thy ship boards of fir trees of [c]Senir: they have brought cedars from Lebanon, to make masts for thee. **6** Of the oaks of Bashan have they made thine ores: the company of the Assyrians have made thy banks of ivory, brought out of the isles of [d]Kittim. **7** Fine linen with broidered work, brought from Egypt, was spread over thee to be thy sail, blue silk and purple, brought from the isles of Elishah was thy covering. **8** The inhabitants of Sidon, and Arvad were thy mariners, O Tyre: thy wise men that were in thee, they were thy [e]pilots. **9** The ancients of Gebal, and the wise men thereof were in thee thy [f]caulkers, all the ships of the sea with their mariners were in thee to occupy thy merchandise. **10** They of Persia, and of Lud and of Put were in thine army: thy men of war they hanged the shield and helmet in thee: they set forth thy beauty. **11** The men of Arvad with thine army were upon thy walls round about, and the [g]Gammadims were in thy towers: they hanged their shields upon thy walls round about: they have made thy beauty perfect. **12** They of Tarshish were thy merchants for the multitude of all riches, for silver, iron, tin, and lead, which they brought to thy fairs. **13** They of [h]Javan, Tubal and Meshech were thy merchants, [i]concerning the lives of men, and they brought vessels of brass for thy merchandise. **14** They of the house of [j]Togarmah brought to thy fairs, horses and horsemen, and mules. **15** The men of Dedan were thy merchants: and the merchandise of many isles were in thine hands: they brought thee for a present, [k]horns, teeth, and peacocks. **16** They of Aram were thy merchants for the multitude of thy [l]wares: they occupied in thy fairs, with [m]emeralds, purple, and broidered work, and [n]fine linen, and coral, and pearl. **17** They of Judah and of the land of Israel were thy merchants: they brought for thy merchandise wheat of [o]Minnith, and Pannag, and honey, and oil, and [p]balm. **18** They of Damascus were thy merchants in the multitude of thy wares, for the multitude of all riches, as in the wine of Helbon and white wool. **19** They of Dan also and of Javan, going to and fro, occupied in thy fairs: iron work, cassia and calamus were among thy merchandise. **20** They of Dedan were thy merchants in precious clothes for the chariots. **21** They of Arabia, and all the princes of Kedar [q]occupied with thee, in lambs, and rams and goats: in these were thy merchants. **22** The merchants of Sheba, and Raamah were thy merchants: they occupied in thy fairs with the chief of all spices, and with all precious stones and

---

- **c.** Ezek. 25:4 They shall chase thee away, and take thy gorgeous houses to dwell in.
- **d.** Ezek. 25:5 Called also Philadelphin, which was the chief city of the Ammonites, and full of conduits, 2 Sam. 12:27.
- **e.** Ezek. 25:9 So that no power or strength should be able to resist the Babylonians.
- **f.** Ezek. 25:16 Which were certain garrisons of Philistines, whereby they ofttimes molested the Jews, of the Cherethims David also had a guard, 2 Sam. 8:18.

EZEK. 26

- **a.** Ezek. 26:1 Either of the captivity of Jeconiah, or of the reign of Zedekiah.
- **b.** Ezek. 26:2 That is, the famous city Jerusalem, whereunto all people resorted.
- **c.** Ezek. 26:2 My riches and fame shall increase: thus the wicked rejoice at their fall by whom they may have any profit or advantage.
- **d.** Ezek. 26:6 The towns that belonged unto her.
- **e.** Ezek. 26:11 For Tyre was much built by art and by labor of men was won out of the Sea. Some refer this unto the images of the noble men which they had erected up for their glory and renown.
- **f.** Ezek. 26:14 I will make thee so bare that thou shalt have nothing to cover thee.
- **g.** Ezek. 26:16 The governors and rulers of other countries that dwell by the sea: whereby he signifieth that her destruction should be so horrible, that all the world should hear thereof and be afraid.
- **h.** Ezek. 26:17 Meaning, merchants which by their traffic did enrich her wonderfully and increase her power.
- **i.** Ezek. 26:20 Which were dead long ago.
- **j.** Ezek. 26:20 Meaning, in Judea, when it shall be restored.
- **k.** Ezek. 26:21 Or, make thee a terror.

EZEK. 26

- **1.** Jer. 7:34

EZEK. 27

- **a.** Ezek. 27:3 Which servest all the world with thy merchandise.
- **b.** Ezek. 27:4 Hebrew, heart.
- **c.** Ezek. 27:5 This mountain was called Hermon, but the Amorites called it Senir, Deut. 3:9.
- **d.** Ezek. 27:6 Which is taken for Greece and Italy.
- **e.** Ezek. 27:8 Or, shipmasters.
- **f.** Ezek. 27:9 Meaning, that they built the walls of the city, which is here meant by the ship: and of these were the builders of Solomon's Temple, 1 Kings 5:18.
- **g.** Ezek. 27:11 That is, they of Cappadocia, or Pygmies and dwarfs, which were so called, because that out of the high towers they seemed little.
- **h.** Ezek. 27:13 Of Greece, Italy and Cappadocia.
- **i.** Ezek. 27:13 By selling slaves.
- **j.** Ezek. 27:14 Which are taken for a people of Asia minor.
- **k.** Ezek. 27:15 Meaning, Unicorn's horns, and Elephant's teeth.
- **l.** Ezek. 27:16 Or, works.
- **m.** Ezek. 27:16 Or, carbuncle.
- **n.** Ezek. 27:16 Or, silk.
- **o.** Ezek. 27:17 Where the best wheat grew.
- **p.** Ezek. 27:17 Or, turpentine, or, treacle.
- **q.** Ezek. 27:21 Or, were merchants whose merchandise passed through thine hands.

gold. **23** They of Haram and Canneh and Eden, the merchants of Sheba, Assyria and Chilmad were thy merchants. **24** These were thy merchants in all sorts of things, in raiment of blue silk, and of broidered work, and in coffers for the rich apparel, which were bound with cords: chains also were among thy merchandise. **25** The ships of Tarshish [r]were thy chief in thy merchandise, and thou wast replenished and made very glorious in the midst of the sea. **26** Thy [s]robbers have brought thee into great waters: the [t]East wind hath broken thee in the midst of the sea. **27** Thy riches and thy fairs, thy merchandise, thy mariners and pilots, thy caulkers, and the occupiers of thy merchandise, and all thy men of war that are in thee, and all thy multitude which is in the midst of thee, shall fall in the midst of the sea in the day of thy ruin. **28** The [u]suburbs shall shake at the sound of the cry of thy pilots. **29** And all that handle the oar, the mariners and all the pilots of the sea shall come down from their ships, and shall stand upon the land, **30** And shall cause their voice to be heard against thee, and shall cry bitterly, and shall cast dust upon their heads, and wallow themselves in the ashes. **31** They shall pluck off their hair for thee, and gird them with a sackcloth, and they shall weep for thee with sorrow of heart and bitter mourning. **32** And in their mourning, they shall take up a lamentation for thee, saying, What city is like Tyre so destroyed in the midst of the sea! **33** When thy wares went forth of the seas, thou filledst many people, and thou didst enrich the Kings of the earth with the multitude of thy riches and of thy merchandise. **34** When thou shalt be broken by the seas in the depths of the waters, thy merchandise and all thy multitude which was in the midst of thee, shall fall. **35** All the inhabitants of the isles shall be astonished at thee, and all their Kings shall be sore afraid and troubled in their countenance. **36** The merchants among the people shall hiss at thee: thou shalt be a terror, and never shalt be [v]anymore.

28

2 The word of God against the king of Tyre for his pride. 21 The word of the Lord against Sidon. 25 The Lord promises that he will gather together the children of Israel.

1 The word of the Lord came again unto me, saying, **2** Son of man, say unto the prince of Tyre, Thus saith the Lord God, because thine heart is exalted, and thou hast said, [a]I am a god, I sit in the seat of God in the midst of the sea, yet thou art but a man and not God, and [b]though thou didst think in thine heart, that thou wast equal with God, **3** Behold, thou art wiser than [c]Daniel: there is no secret that they can hide from thee. **4** With thy wisdom and thine understanding thou hast gotten thee riches, and hast gotten gold and silver into thy treasures. **5** By thy great wisdom and by thine occupying hast thou increased thy riches, and thine heart is lifted up because of thy riches. **6** Therefore thus saith the Lord God, Because thou didst think in thine heart, that thou wast equal with God, **7** Behold, therefore I will bring strangers upon thee, even the terrible nations: and they shall draw their swords against the beauty of thy wisdom, and they shall defile thy brightness. **8** They shall cast thee down to the pit, and thou shalt die the death of them, that are slain in the midst of the sea. **9** Wilt thou say then before him that slayeth thee, I am a god? but thou shalt be a man, and no god, in the hands of him that slayeth thee. **10** Thou shalt die the death of the [d]uncircumcised by the hands of strangers: for I have spoken it, saith the Lord God. **11** Moreover, the word of the Lord came unto me, saying, **12** Son of man, take up a lamentation upon the King of Tyre, and say unto him, Thus saith the Lord God, Thou sealest up the sum, and art full of [e]wisdom, and perfect in beauty. **13** Thou hast been in Eden the garden of God: every precious stone was in thy garment, the ruby, the topaz, and the [f]diamond, the chrysolite, the onyx, and the jasper, the sapphire, [g]emerald, and the carbuncle and gold: the workmanship of thy timbrels, and of thy pipes was prepared in thee in the day that thou wast created. **14** Thou art [h]the anointed Cherub, that covereth, and I have set thee [i]in honor: thou wast upon the holy mountain of God: thou hast walked in the midst of the [j]stones of fire. **15** Thou wast perfect in thy ways from the day that thou wast [k]created, till iniquity was found in thee. **16** By the multitude of thy merchandise, they have filled the midst of thee with cruelty, and thou hast sinned: therefore I will cast thee as profane out of the [l]mountain of God: and I will destroy thee, O covering Cherub, from the midst of the stones of fire. **17** Thine heart was lifted up because of thy beauty, and thou hast corrupted thy wisdom by reason of thy brightness: I will cast thee to the ground. I will lay thee before kings that they may behold thee. **18** Thou hast defiled thy [m]sanctification by the multitude of thine iniquities, and by the iniquity of thy merchandise: therefore will I bring forth a fire from the midst of thee, which shall devour thee: and I will bring thee to ashes upon the earth, in the sight of all them that behold thee. **19** All they that know thee among the people, shall be astonished at thee: thou shalt be [n]a terror, and never shalt thou be anymore. **20** Again the word of the Lord came unto me, saying, **21** Son of man, set thy face against Sidon, and prophesy against it, **22** And say, Thus saith the Lord God, Behold, I come against thee, O Sidon, and I will be [o]glorified in the midst of thee: and they shall know that I am the Lord, when I shall have executed judgments in her, and shall be sanctified in her. **23** For I will send into her pestilence, and blood into her streets, and the slain shall fall in the midst of her: [p]the enemy shall come against her with the sword on every side, and they shall know that I am the Lord. **24** And they shall be no more a pricking thorn unto the house of Israel, nor any grievous thorn of all that are round about them, and despised them, and they shall know that I am the Lord God. **25** Thus saith the Lord God, When I shall have gathered the house of Israel from the people where they are scattered, and shall be [q]sanctified in them in the sight of the heathen, then shall they dwell in the land, that I have given to my servant Jacob. **26** And they shall dwell safely therein, and shall build houses, and plant vineyards: yea, they shall dwell safely, when I have executed judgments upon all round about them that despise them, and they shall know that I am the Lord their God.

29

He prophesieth against Pharaoh and Egypt. 13 The Lord promiseth that he will restore Egypt after forty years. 18 Egypt is the reward of King Nebuchadnezzar for the labor which he took against Tyre.

1 In the [a]tenth year and in the tenth month, in the twelfth day of the month, the word of the Lord came unto me, saying, **2** Son of man, set thy face against Pharaoh the king of Egypt, and prophesy against him, and against all Egypt. **3** Speak, and say, Thus saith the Lord God, Behold, I come against thee, Pharaoh king of Egypt, the great [b]dragon, that lieth in the midst of his rivers, which hath said, The river is mine, and I have made it for myself. **4** But I will put [c]hooks in thy jaws, and I will cause the fish of thy rivers to stick unto thy scales, and I will draw thee out of the midst of thy rivers, and all the fish of thy rivers shall stick unto thy scales. **5** And I will leave thee in the wilderness, both thee and all the fish of thy rivers: thou shalt fall upon the open field: thou shalt not be brought together, nor gathered: for I have given thee for meat to the beasts of the field, and to the fowls of heaven. **6** And all the inhabitants of Egypt shall know that I am the Lord, because they have been a staff of [d]reed to the house of Israel. **7** When they took hold of thee with their hand, thou didst break and rent all their shoulder: and when they leaned upon thee, thou brakest and madest all their loins to [e]stand [f]upright. **8** Therefore thus saith the Lord God, Behold, I will bring a sword upon thee, and destroy man and beast out of thee. **9** And the land of Egypt shall be desolate, and waste, and they shall know that I am the Lord: because he hath said, [g]The river is mine, and I have made it, **10** Behold, therefore I come upon thee, and upon thy rivers, and I will make the land of Egypt utterly waste and desolate from the tower of Syene, even unto the borders of the [h]black Moors. **11** No foot of man shall pass by it, nor foot of beast shall pass by it, neither shall it be inhabited forty years. **12** And I will make the land of Egypt desolate in the midst of the countries that are desolate, and her cities shall be desolate among the cities that are desolate for forty years: and I will scatter the Egyptians among the nations, and will disperse them through the countries. **13** Yet thus saith the Lord God, [i]At the end of forty years will I gather the Egyptians from the people, where they were

---

r. Ezek. 27:25 Or, came in company toward thee.
s. Ezek. 27:26 Or, rowers.
t. Ezek. 27:26 That is, Nebuchadnezzar.
u. Ezek. 27:28 That is, the cities near about thee, as was Zidon, Arvad, and others.
v. Ezek. 27:36 Whereby is meant a long time: for it was prophesied to be destroyed but seventy years, Isa. 23:15.

EZEK. 28

a. Ezek. 28:2 I am safe that none can come to hurt me, as God is in the heaven.
b. Ezek. 28:2 Hebrew, though thou set thine heart as the heart of God.
c. Ezek. 28:3 Thus he speaketh by derision: for Daniel had declared notable signs of his wisdom in Babylon, when Ezek. wrote this.
d. Ezek. 28:10 Like the rest of the heathen and infidels, which are God's enemies.
e. Ezek. 28:12 He derideth the vain opinion and confidence that the Tyrians had in their riches, strength and pleasures.
f. Ezek. 28:13 Or, jasper.
g. Ezek. 28:13 Or, carbuncle.
h. Ezek. 28:14 He meaneth the royal state of Tyre, which for the excellency and glory thereof he compareth to the Cherubims which covered the Ark: and by this word anointed he signifieth the same.
i. Ezek. 28:14 I did thee this honor to make thee one of the builders of my Temple, which was when Hiram sent unto Solomon things necessary for the work.
j. Ezek. 28:14 To wit, among my people Israel, which shined as precious stones.
k. Ezek. 28:15 Which was when I first called thee to this dignity.
l. Ezek. 28:16 Thou shalt have no part among my people.
m. Ezek. 28:18 That is, the honor, whereunto I called them.
n. Ezek. 28:19 Or, brought to nothing.
o. Ezek. 28:22 By executing my judgments against thy wickedness.
p. Ezek. 28:23 That is, Nebuchadnezzar.
q. Ezek. 28:25 He showeth for what cause God will assemble his Church, and preserve it still, though he destroy his enemies: to wit, that they should praise him, and give thanks for his great mercies.

EZEK. 29

a. Ezek. 29:1 To wit, of the captivity of Jeconiah, or of the reign of Zedekiah. Of the order of these prophecies, and how the former sometimes standeth after the latter, read Jer. 27:1.
b. Ezek. 29:3 He compareth Pharaoh to a dragon which hideth himself in the river Nile, as Isa. 51:9.
c. Ezek. 29:4 I will send enemies against thee, which shall pluck thee, and thy people which trust in thee, out of thy sure places.
d. Ezek. 29:6 Read 2 Kings 18:21; Isa. 36:6.
e. Ezek. 29:7 Or, shake.
f. Ezek. 29:7 When they felt their hurt, they would stay no more upon thee, but stood upon their feet, and put their trust in others.
g. Ezek. 29:9 Thus God cannot suffer that man should arrogate anything to himself, or put his trust in anything save in him alone.
h. Ezek. 29:10 Hebrew, Cush, or Ethiopia.
i. Ezek. 29:14 Meaning, that they should not have full dominion, but be under the Persians, Greeks and Romans, and the cause is that the Israelites should no more put their trust in them, but learn to depend on God.
j. Ezek. 29:16 Lest I should by this means punish their sins.
k. Ezek. 29:17 Counting from the captivity of Jeconiah.
l. Ezek. 29:18 He took great pains at the siege of Tyre, and his army was sore handled.
m. Ezek. 29:18 Signifying that Nebuchadnezzar had more pains than profit, by the taking of Tyre.

scattered, **14** And I will bring again the captivity of Egypt, and will cause them to return into the land of Pathros, into the land of their habitation, and they shall be there a [l]small kingdom. **15** It shall be the smallest of the kingdoms, neither shall it exalt itself anymore above the nations: for I will diminish them, that they shall no more rule the nations. **16** And it shall be no more the confidence of the house of Israel, to bring their [j]iniquity to remembrance by looking after them, so shall they know that I am the Lord God. **17** In the [k]seven and twentieth year also in the first month, and in the first day of the month, came the word of the Lord unto me, saying, **18** Son of man, Nebuchadnezzar king of Babel caused his army to serve a great [l]service against Tyre: every head was made bald, and every shoulder was made bare: yet he had no wages, [m]nor his army for Tyre, for the service that he served against it. **19** Therefore thus saith the Lord God, Behold, I will give the land of Egypt unto Nebuchadnezzar the king of Babel, and he shall take her multitude, and spoil her spoil, and take her prey, and it shall be the wages for his army. **20** I have given him the land of Egypt for his labor, that he served [n]against it, because they wrought [o]for me, saith the Lord God. **21** In that day will I cause the horn of the house of Israel to grow, and I will give thee an open mouth in the midst of them, and they shall know that I am the Lord.

30

The destruction of Egypt and the cities thereof.

1 The word of the Lord came again unto me, saying,

2 Son of man, prophesy, and say, Thus saith the Lord God, Howl and cry, Woe be unto this day. **3** For the day is near, and the day of the Lord is at hand, a cloudy day, and it shall be the time of the heathen. **4** And the sword shall come upon Egypt, and fear shall be in Ethiopia, when the slain shall fall in Egypt, when they shall take away her multitude, and when her foundations shall be broken down. **5** [a]Ethiopia and Put, and Lud, and all the common people, and Chub, and the men of the land, that is in league, shall fall with them by the sword. **6** Thus saith the Lord, They also that maintain Egypt, shall fall, and the pride of her power shall come down: from the tower of [b]Syene shall they fall by the sword, saith the Lord God. **7** And they shall be desolate in the midst of the countries that are desolate, and her cities shall be in the midst of the cities that are wasted. **8** And they shall know that I am the Lord, when I have set a fire in Egypt, and when all her helpers shall be destroyed. **9** In that day shall there messengers go forth from me in ships, to make the careless Moors afraid, and fear shall come upon them, as in the day of Egypt: for lo, it cometh. **10** Thus saith the Lord God, I will also make the multitude of Egypt to cease by the hand of Nebuchadnezzar king of Babel. **11** For he and his people with him, even the terrible nations shall be brought to destroy the land: and they shall draw their swords against Egypt, and fill the land with the slain. **12** And I will make the rivers dry, and sell the land into the hands of the wicked, and I will make the land waste, and all that therein is by the hands of strangers: I the Lord have spoken it. **13** Thus saith the Lord God, I will also destroy the idols, and I will cause their idols to cease out of [c]Noph, and there shall be no more a prince of the land of Egypt, and I will send a fear in the land of Egypt. **14** And I will make Pathros desolate, and will set fire in [d]Zoan, and I will execute judgment in No. **15** And I will pour my wrath upon [e]Sin, which is the strength of Egypt: and I will destroy the multitude of [f]No. **16** And I will set fire in Egypt: Sin shall have great sorrow, and No shall be destroyed, and Noph shall have sorrows daily. **17** The young men of [g]Aven, and of [h]Pi Beseth shall fall by the sword: and these cities shall go into captivity. **18** At Tehaphnehes the day [i]shall restrain his light, when I shall break there the [j]bars of Egypt: and when the pomp of her power shall cease in her, the cloud shall cover her, and her daughters shall go into captivity. **19** Thus will I execute judgments in Egypt, and they shall know that I am the Lord. **20** And in the [k]eleventh year, in the first month, and in the seventh day of the month, the word of the Lord came unto me, saying, **21** Son of man, [l]I have broken the arm of Pharaoh king of Egypt: and lo, it shall not be bound up to be healed, neither shall they put a roll to bind it, and so make it strong to hold the sword. **22** Therefore thus saith the Lord God, Behold, I come against Pharaoh King of Egypt, and will break [m]his arm that was strong, but is broken, and I will cause the sword to fall out of his hand. **23** And I will scatter the Egyptians among the nations, and will disperse them through the countries. **24** And I will strengthen the arm of the king of Babel, and put my sword in his hand, but I will break Pharaoh's arms, and he shall cast out sighings, as the sighings of him that is wounded before him. **25** But I will strengthen the arms of the king of Babel, and the arms of Pharaoh shall fall down, and they shall know, that I am the Lord, [n]when I shall put my sword into the hand of the king of Babel, and he shall stretch it out upon the land of Egypt. **26** And I will scatter the Egyptians among the nations, and disperse them among the countries, and they shall know, that I am the Lord.

31

2 A comparison of the prosperity of Pharaoh with the prosperity of the Assyrians. 10 He prophesieth a like destruction to them both.

1 And in the [a]eleventh year, in the third month, and in the first day of the month the word of the Lord came unto me, saying, **2** Son of man, speak unto Pharaoh king of Egypt, and to his multitude, Whom art thou [b]like in thy greatness? **3** Behold, Assyria was like a cedar in Lebanon with fair branches, and with thick shadowing boughs, and shot up very high, and his top was among the thick boughs. **4** The waters nourished him, and the deep exalted him on high with her rivers running round about his plants, and sent out her [c]little rivers unto all the trees of the [d]field. **5** Therefore his height was exalted above all the trees of the field, and his boughs were multiplied, and his branches were long, because of the multitude of the waters, which the deep sent out. **6** All the fowls of the heavens made their nests in his boughs, and under his branches did all the beasts of the field bring forth their young, and under his shadow dwelt all mighty nations. **7** Thus was he fair in his greatness, and in the length of his branches: for his root was near great waters. **8** The cedars in the garden [e]of God could not hide him: no fir tree was like his branches: and the chestnut trees were not like his boughs: all the trees in the garden of God were not like unto him in his beauty. **9** I made him fair by the multitude of his branches: so that all the trees of Eden, that were in the garden of God, envied him. **10** Therefore thus saith the Lord God, Because [f]he is lifted up on high, and hath shot up his top among the thick boughs, and his heart is lifted up in his height, **11** I have therefore delivered him into the hands of the [g]mightiest among the heathen: he shall handle him, for I have cast him away for his wickedness. **12** And the strangers have destroyed him, even the terrible nations, and they have left him upon the mountains, and in all the valleys his branches are fallen, and his boughs are [h]broken by all the rivers of the land: and all the people of the earth are departed from his shadow, and have forsaken him. **13** Upon his ruin shall all the fowls of the heaven remain, and all the beasts of the field shall be upon his branches, **14** So that none of all the trees by the waters shall be exalted by their height, neither shall shoot up their top among the thick boughs, neither shall their leaves stand up in their height, which drink so much water: for they are all delivered unto death in the nether parts of the earth in the midst of the children of men among them that go down to the pit. **15** Thus saith the Lord God, In the day when he went down to hell, I caused them to mourn, and I [i]covered the deep for him, and I did restrain the floods thereof, and the great waters were stayed: I caused Lebanon to mourn for him, and all the trees of the field fainted. **16** I made the nations to shake at the sound of his fall, when I cast him down to hell, with them that descend into the pit, and all the excellent trees of Eden, and the best of Lebanon: even all that are nourished with waters, shall [j]be comforted in the nether parts of the earth. **17** They also went down to hell with him unto them that were slain with the sword, and his arm, and they that dwelt under his shadow in the midst of the heathen. **18** To whom [k]art thou thus like in glory and in greatness among the trees of Eden? yet thou shalt be cast down with the trees of Eden unto the nether parts of the earth: thou shalt sleep in the midst of the [l]uncircumcised, with them that be slain by the sword: this is Pharaoh and all his multitude, saith the Lord God.

32

2 The Prophet is commanded to bewail Pharaoh King of Egypt. 12 He prophesieth that destruction shall come unto Egypt through the King of Babylon.

1 And in the [a]twelfth year in the twelfth month, and in the first day of the month, the word of the Lord came unto me, saying, **2** Son of man, take up a lamentation for Pharaoh king of Egypt, and say unto him, Thou art like a [b]lion of

---

n. Ezek. 29:20 Or, in it.
o. Ezek. 29:20 Or, evil against me.

EZEK. 29
l. Jer. 46:26

EZEK. 30
a. Ezek. 30:5 By Put and Lud are meant Africa and Libya.
b. Ezek. 30:6 Which was a strong city of Egypt, Ezek. 29:10.
c. Ezek. 30:13 Or, Memphis, or Cairo.
d. Ezek. 30:14 Or, Tanis.
e. Ezek. 30:15 Or, Pelusium.
f. Ezek. 30:15 Or, Alexandria.
g. Ezek. 30:17 Or, Heliopolis.
h. Ezek. 30:17 Or, Pubastum.
i. Ezek. 30:18 Meaning, that there shall be great sorrow and affliction.
j. Ezek. 30:18 That is, the strength and force.
k. Ezek. 30:20 Of the captivity of Jeconiah, or of Zedekiah's reign.
l. Ezek. 30:21 For Nebuchadnezzar destroyed Pharaoh Necho at Carchemish, Jer. 46:26.
m. Ezek. 30:22 His force and power.
n. Ezek. 30:25 Whereby we see that tyrants have no power of themselves, neither can do anymore harm than God appointeth, and when he will they must cease.

EZEK. 31
a. Ezek. 31:1 Of Zedekiah's reign, or of Jeconiah's captivity.
b. Ezek. 31:2 Meaning, that he was not like in strength to the King of the Assyrians, whom the Babylonians overcame.
c. Ezek. 31:4 Many other nations were under their dominion.
d. Ezek. 31:4 Or, country.
e. Ezek. 31:8 Signifying, that there was no greater power in the world than his was.
f. Ezek. 31:10 Or, thou wast lifted up.
g. Ezek. 31:11 That is, of Nebuchadnezzar, who afterward was the monarch and only ruler of the world.
h. Ezek. 31:12 Hereby is signified the destruction of the power of the Assyrians by the Babylonians.
i. Ezek. 31:15 The deep waters that caused him to mount so high (meaning his great abundance and pomp) shall now lament as though they were covered with sackcloth.
j. Ezek. 31:16 To cause this destruction of the king of Assyria to seem more horrible, he setteth forth other kings and princes which are dead, as though they rejoiced at the fall of such a tyrant.
k. Ezek. 31:18 Meaning, that Pharaoh's power was nothing so great as his was.
l. Ezek. 31:18 Read Ezek. 28:10.

EZEK. 32
a. Ezek. 32:1 Which was the first year of the general captivity under Zedekiah.

the nations, and art as a [c]dragon in the sea: thou castedst out thy rivers [d]and troubledst the waters with thy feet, and stampedst in their rivers. **3** Thus saith the Lord God, [1]I will therefore spread my net over thee a great multitude of people, and they shall make thee come up into my net, **4** Then will I leave thee upon the land, and I will cast thee upon the open field, and I will cause all the fowls of the heaven to remain upon thee, and I will fill all the beasts of the field with thee. **5** And I will lay thy flesh upon the mountains, and fill the valleys [e]with thine height. **6** I will also water with thy blood the land wherein thou [f]swimmest, even to the mountains, and the rivers shall be full of thee. **7** And when I shall [g]put thee out, I will cover the heaven, and make the stars thereof dark: [2]I will cover the sun with a cloud, and the moon shall not give her light. **8** All the lights of heaven will I make dark for thee, and bring [h]darkness upon thy land, saith the Lord God. **9** I will also trouble the hearts of many people, when I shall bring thy destruction among the nations, and upon the countries which thou hast not known. **10** Yea, I will make many people amazed at thee, and their kings shall be astonished with fear for thee, when I shall make my sword to glitter against their faces, and they shall be afraid at every moment: every man for his own life in the day of thy fall. **11** For thus saith the Lord God, The sword of the king of Babel shall come upon thee. **12** By the swords of the mighty will I cause thy multitude to fall: they all shall be terrible nations, and they shall destroy the [i]pomp of Egypt, and all the multitude thereof shall be consumed. **13** I will destroy also all the beasts thereof from the great watersides, neither shall the foot of man trouble them anymore, nor the hooves of beasts trouble them. **14** Then will I make [j]their waters deep, and cause their rivers to run like oil, saith the Lord God. **15** When I shall make the land of Egypt desolate, and the country with all that is therein, shall be laid waste: when I shall smite all them which dwell therein, then shall they know that I am the Lord. **16** This is the mourning wherewith they shall lament her: the daughters of the nations shall lament her: they shall lament for Egypt, and for all her multitude, saith the Lord God. **17** In the twelfth year also in the fifteenth day of the month, came the word of the Lord unto me, saying, **18** Son of man, lament for the multitude of Egypt, and [k]cast them down, even them and the daughters of the mighty nations under the nether parts of the earth, with them that go down into the pit. **19** Whom dost thou pass [l]in beauty? go down and sleep with the uncircumcised. **20** They shall fall in the midst of them that are slain by the sword: [m]she is delivered to the sword: draw her down, and all her multitude. **21** The most mighty and strong shall speak to [n]him out of the midst of hell with them that help her: they are gone down, and sleep with the uncircumcised that be slain by the sword. **22** Assyria is there and all his company: their graves are about him: all they are slain and fallen by the sword. **23** Whose graves are made in the side of the pit, and his multitude are round about his grave: all they are slain and fallen by the sword, which caused fear to be in the land of the living. **24** There is [o]Elam and all his multitude round about his grave: all they are slain and fallen by the sword, which are gone down with the uncircumcised into the nether parts of the earth, which caused themselves to be feared in the land of the [p]living, yet have they borne their shame with them that are gone down to the pit. **25** They have made his bed in the midst of the slain with all his multitude: their graves are round about him: all these uncircumcised are slain by the sword: though they have caused their fear in the land of the living, yet have they borne their shame with them that go down to the pit: they are laid in the midst of them that be slain. **26** There is [q]Meshech, Tubal, and all their multitude: their graves are round about them: all these uncircumcised were slain by the sword, though they caused their fear to be in the land of the living. **27** And they shall not lie with the valiant [r]of the uncircumcised, that are fallen, which are gone down to the grave with their weapons of war, and have laid their swords under their heads, but their iniquity shall be upon their bones: because they were the fear of the mighty in the land of the living. **28** Yea, thou shalt be broken in the midst of the uncircumcised, and lie with them that are slain by the sword. **29** There is Edom, his kings, and all his princes, which with their strength are laid by them that were slain by the sword: they shall sleep with the uncircumcised, and with them that go down to the pit. **30** There be all the princes of the [s]North, with all the Sidonians, which are gone down with the slain, with their fear: they are ashamed of their strength, and the uncircumcised sleep with them that be slain by the sword, and bear their shame with them that go down to the pit. **31** Pharaoh shall see them, and he shall be [t]comforted over all his multitude: Pharaoh, and all his army shall be slain by the sword, saith the Lord God. **32** For I have caused my [u]fear to be in the land of the living: and he shall be laid in the midst of the uncircumcised with them, that are slain by the sword, even Pharaoh and all his multitude, saith the Lord God.

33

2 The office of the governors and ministers. 14 He strengtheneth them that despair, and boldeneth them with the promise of mercy. 30 The word of the Lord against the mockers of the Prophet.

1 Again, the word of the Lord came unto me, saying, **2** Son of man, speak to the children of thy people, and say unto them, When I bring the sword upon a land, if the people of the land take a man [a]from among them, and make him their [b]watchman, **3** If when he seeth the sword come upon the land, he blow the trumpet, and warn the people, **4** Then he that heareth the sound of the trumpet, and will not be warned, if the sword come, and take him away, his blood shall be upon his own head. **5** For he heard the sound of the trumpet, and would not be admonished: therefore his blood shall be upon him: but he that receiveth warning, shall save his life. **6** But if the watchman see the sword come, and blow not the trumpet, and the people be not warned: if the sword come, and take any person from among them, he is taken away for his [c]iniquity, but his blood will I require at the watchman's hand. **7** [1]So thou, O son of man, I have made thee a watchman unto the house of Israel: therefore thou shalt hear the word at my [d]mouth, and admonish them from me. **8** When I shall say unto the wicked, O wicked man, thou shalt die the death, if thou dost not speak and admonish the wicked of his way, that wicked man shall die for his iniquity, but his blood will I [e]require at thine hand. **9** Nevertheless, if thou warn the wicked of his way to turn from it, if he do not turn from his way, he shall die for his iniquity, but thou hast delivered thy soul. **10** Therefore, O thou son of man, speak unto the house of Israel, Thus ye speak and say, If our transgressions and our sins be upon us, and we are consumed because of them, [f]how should we then live? **11** Say unto them, As I live, saith the Lord God, [g]I desire not the death of the wicked, but that the wicked turn from his way and live: turn you, turn you from your evil ways, for why will ye die, O ye house of Israel? **12** Therefore thou son of man, say unto the children of thy people, The [h]righteousness of the righteous shall not deliver him in the day of his transgression, nor the wickedness of the wicked shall cause him to fall therein, in the day that he returneth from his wickedness, neither shall the righteous live for his righteousness in the day that he sinneth. **13** When I shall say unto the righteous, that he shall surely live, if he trust to his own righteousness, and commit iniquity, all his righteousness shall be no more remembered, but for his iniquity that he hath committed, he shall die for the same. **14** Again when I shall say unto the wicked, Thou shalt die the death, if he turn from his sin, and do that which is lawful and [i]right, **15** To wit, if the wicked restore the pledge, and give again that he had robbed, and walk in the statutes of life, without committing iniquity, he shall surely live, and not die. **16** None of his sins that he hath committed, shall be mentioned unto him: because he hath done that, which is lawful and right, he shall surely live. **17** Yet the children of thy people say, [2]The way of the Lord is not equal: but their own way is unequal. **18** When the righteous turneth from his righteousness, and committeth iniquity, he shall even die thereby. **19** But if the wicked return from his wickedness, and do that which is lawful and right, he shall live thereby. **20** Yet ye say, The way of the Lord is not equal, O ye house of Israel, I will judge you every one after his ways. **21** Also in the twelfth year of our [j]captivity, in the tenth month, and in the fifth day of the month, one that had escaped out of Jerusalem, came unto me, and said, The city is smitten. **22** Now the [k]hand of the Lord had been upon me in the evening afore he that had escaped, came, and had opened my mouth until he came to me in the morning: and when he had opened my [l]mouth, I was no more dumb. **23** Again the word of the Lord came unto me, and said, **24** Son of man, these that dwell in the desolate places of the land of Israel, talk and say, [m]Abraham was but one, and he possessed the land: but we are many, therefore the land shall be given us in possession. **25** Wherefore say unto

---

b. Ezek. 32:2 Thus the scriptures compare tyrants to cruel and huge beasts which devour all that be weaker than they, and such as they may overcome.
c. Ezek. 32:2 Or, whale.
d. Ezek. 32:2 Thou preparest great armies.
e. Ezek. 32:5 With heaps of the carcasses of thine army.
f. Ezek. 32:6 As Nile overfloweth Egypt, so will I make the blood of thine host to overflow it.
g. Ezek. 32:7 The word signifieth to be put out as a candle is put out.
h. Ezek. 32:8 By this manner of speech is meant the great sorrow that shall be for the slaughter of the king and his people.
i. Ezek. 32:12 This came to pass in less than four years after this prophecy.
j. Ezek. 32:14 To wit, of the Chaldeans thine enemies, which shall quietly enjoy all thy commodities.
k. Ezek. 32:18 That is, prophesy, that they shall be cast down: thus the Lord giveth his Prophets power both to plant and to destroy by his word, read Jer. 1:10.
l. Ezek. 32:19 Have not other kingdoms, more beautiful than thou, perished?
m. Ezek. 32:20 That is, Egypt.
n. Ezek. 32:21 To make the matter more sensible, he bringeth in Pharaoh whom the dead shall meet and marvel at him, read Isa. 14:9.
o. Ezek. 32:24 Meaning, the Persians.
p. Ezek. 32:24 Whom in his life all the world feared.
q. Ezek. 32:26 That is, the Cappadocians and Italians, or Spaniards, as Josephus writeth.
r. Ezek. 32:27 Which died not by cruel death, but by the course of nature, and are honorably buried with their coat armor, and signs of honor.
s. Ezek. 32:30 The Kings of Babylon.
t. Ezek. 32:31 As the wicked rejoice when they see others partakers of their miseries.
u. Ezek. 32:32 I will make the Egyptians afraid of me, as they caused others to fear them.

EZEK. 32

1. Ezek. 12:13 / Ezek. 17:20 **2.** Isa. 13:10 / Joel. 2:31 / Joel. 3:15 / Matt. 24:29

EZEK. 33

a. Ezek. 33:2 Or, of their coasts.
b. Ezek. 33:2 He showeth that the people ought to have continually governors and teachers which may have a care over them, and to warn them ever of the dangers which are at hand.
c. Ezek. 33:6 Signifying, that the wicked shall not escape punishment though the watchman be negligent: but if the watchman blow the trumpet, and then he will not obey, he shall deserve double punishment.
d. Ezek. 33:7 Which teacheth that he that receiveth not his charge at the Lord's mouth, is a spy, and not a true watchman.
e. Ezek. 33:8 The watchman must answer for the blood of all that perish through his negligence.
f. Ezek. 33:10 Thus the wicked when they hear God's judgments for their sins, despair of his mercies, and murmur.
g. Ezek. 33:11 Read Ezek. 18:23.
h. Ezek. 33:12 Read of this righteousness, Ezek. 18:21, 24.
i. Ezek. 33:14 Hereby he condemneth all them of hypocrisy, which pretend to forsake wickedness, and yet declare not themselves such by their fruits, that is, in obeying God's commandments, and by godly life.
j. Ezek. 33:21 When the Prophet was led away captive with Jeconiah.

them, Thus saith the Lord God, Ye eat with the [n]blood, and lifted up your eyes
toward your idols, and shed blood: should ye then possess the land? **26** Ye lean
upon your [o]swords, ye work abomination, and ye defile every one his neighbor's
wife: should ye then possess the land? **27** Say thus unto them, Thus saith the
Lord God, As I live, so surely they that are in the desolate places, shall fall by the
sword: and him that is in the open field, will I give unto the beasts to be devoured:
and they that be in the forts and in the caves, shall die of the pestilence. **28** For I
will lay the land desolate and waste, and the [3]pomp of her strength shall cease: and
the mountains of Israel shall be desolate, and none shall pass through. **29** Then
shall they know that I am the Lord, when I have laid the land desolate and waste,
because of all their abominations, that they have committed. **30** Also thou son
of man, the children of thy people that [p]talk of thee by the walls and in the doors
of houses, and speak one to another, everyone to his brother, saying, Come, I pray
you, and hear what is the word that cometh from the Lord. **31** For they come
unto thee, as the people useth to come: and my people sit before thee, and hear thy
words, but they will not do them: for with their mouths they make [q]jests, and their
heart goeth after their covetousness. **32** And lo, thou art unto them, as a [r]jesting
song of one that hath a pleasant voice, and can sing well: for they hear thy words,
but they do them not. **33** And when this cometh to pass (for lo, it will come)
then shall they know, that a Prophet hath been among them.

34

2 Against the shepherds that despised the flock of Christ, and seek their own reign. 7 The Lord saith that he will visit his dispersed flock, and gather them together. 23 He promiseth the true shepherd Christ, and with him peace.

1 And the word of the Lord came unto me, saying, **2** Son of man, prophesy
against the shepherds of Israel, prophesy and say unto them, Thus saith the Lord
God unto the shepherds, [1]Woe be unto the [a]shepherds of Israel, that feed themsel-
ves: should not the shepherds feed the flocks? **3** Ye eat the [b]fat, and ye clothe you
with the wool: ye kill them that are fed, but ye feed not the sheep. **4** The [c]weak
have ye not strengthened: the sick have ye not healed, neither have ye bound up
the broken, nor brought again that which was driven away, neither have ye sought
that which was lost, but with cruelty, and with rigor have ye ruled them. **5** And
they were scattered without a shepherd: and when they were dispersed, they were
[d]devoured of all the beasts of the field. **6** My sheep wandered through all the
mountains, and upon every high hill: yea, my flock was scattered through all the
earth, and none did seek or search after them. **7** Therefore ye shepherds, hear
the word of the Lord. **8** As I live, saith the Lord God, surely because my flock
was spoiled, and my sheep were devoured of all the beasts of the field, having no
shepherd, neither did my shepherds seek my sheep, but the shepherds fed them-
selves, and fed not my sheep, **9** Therefore, hear ye the word of the Lord, O ye
shepherds. **10** Thus saith the Lord God, Behold, I come against the shepherds,
and will require my sheep at their hands, and cause them to cease from feeding
the sheep: neither shall the shepherds feed themselves anymore: for I will deliver
thy sheep from [e]their mouths, and they shall no more devour them. **11** For thus
saith the Lord God, Behold, I will search my sheep, and seek them out. **12** As a
shepherd searcheth out his flock, when he hath been among his sheep that are scat-
tered, so will I seek out my sheep and will deliver them out of all places, where they
have been scattered in [f]the cloudy and dark day, **13** And I will bring them out
from the people, and gather them from the countries, and will bring them to their
own land, and feed them upon the mountains of Israel, by the rivers, and in all the
inhabited places of the country. **14** I will feed them in a good pasture, and upon
the high mountains of Israel shall their fold be: there shall they lie in a good fold,
and in fat pasture shall they feed upon the mountains of Israel. **15** I will feed
my sheep, and bring them to their rest, saith the Lord God. **16** I will seek that
which was lost, and bring again that which was driven away, and will bind up that
which was broken, and will strengthen the weak, but I will destroy the fat and the
[g]strong, and I will feed them with [h]judgment. **17** Also you my sheep, thus saith
the Lord God, Behold, I judge between sheep and sheep, between the rams and the
goats. **18** Seemeth it a small thing unto you to have eaten up the good [i]pasture,
but ye must tread down with your feet, the residue of your pasture? and to have
drunk of the deep waters, but ye must trouble the residue with your feet. **19** And
my sheep eat that which ye have trodden with your feet, and drink that which ye
have troubled with your feet. **20** Therefore thus saith the Lord God unto them,
Behold, I, even I will judge between the fat sheep and the lean sheep. **21** Becau-
se ye have thrust with side and with shoulder, and pushed all the weak with your
horns, till ye have scattered them abroad, **22** Therefore will I help my sheep, and
they shall no more be spoiled, and I will judge between sheep and sheep. **23** And
I will set up a shepherd over them, and he shall feed them, even my servant [j]David,
he shall feed them, and he shall be their shepherd. **24** And I the Lord will be
their God, and my servant David shall be the Prince among them, I the Lord have
spoken it. **25** And I will make with them a covenant of peace, and will cause the
evil beasts to cease out of the land, and they shall [k]dwell safely in the wilderness,
and sleep in the woods. **26** And I will set them, as a blessing, even round about
my mountains, and I will cause rain to come down in due season: and there shall
be rain of blessing. **27** And the [l]tree of the field shall yield her fruit, and the ear-
th shall give her fruit, and they shall be safe in their land, and shall know that I am
the Lord, when I have broken the cords of their yoke, and delivered them out of
the hands of those that served themselves of them. **28** And they shall no more be
spoiled of the heathen, neither shall the beasts of the land devour them, but they
shall dwell safely, and none shall make them afraid. **29** And I will raise up for
them a [m]plant of renown, and they shall be no more consumed with hunger in the
land, neither bear the reproach of the heathen anymore. **30** Thus shall they un-
derstand, that I the Lord their God am with them, and that they, even the house of
Israel are my people, saith the Lord God. **31** And ye my sheep, the sheep of my
pasture are men, and I am your God, saith the Lord God.

35

2 The destruction that shall come on mount Seir, because they troubled the people of Israel.

1 Moreover, the word of the Lord came unto me, saying, **2** Son of man, Set
thy face against mount [a]Seir, and prophesy against it, **3** And say unto it, Thus
saith the Lord God, Behold, O mount Seir, I come against thee, and I will stretch
out mine hand against thee, and I will make thee desolate and waste. **4** I will
lay thy cities waste, and thou shalt be desolate, and thou shalt know that I am the
Lord. **5** Because thou hast had a perpetual hatred, and hast put the children of
Israel to flight by the force of the sword in the time of their calamity, when their
[b]iniquity had an end, **6** Therefore as I live, saith the Lord God, I will prepare thee
unto blood, and blood shall pursue thee: except thou [c]hate blood, even blood shall
pursue thee. **7** Thus will I make mount Seir desolate and waste, and cut off from
it him that passeth out and him that returneth. **8** And I will fill his mountains
with his slain men: in thine hills, and in thy valleys, and in all thy rivers shall they
fall, that are slain with the sword. **9** I will make thee perpetual desolations, and
thy cities shall not [d]return, and ye shall know that I am the Lord. **10** Because
thou hast said, [e]These two nations and these two countries shall be mine, and we
will possess them (seeing the Lord was [f]there) **11** Therefore as I live, saith the
Lord God, I will even do according to thy [g]wrath, and according to thine indigna-
tion, which thou hast used in thine hatred against them: and I will make myself
known among [h]them, when I have judged thee. **12** And thou shalt know, that I
the Lord have heard all the blasphemies which thou hast spoken against the moun-
tains of Israel, saying, They lie waste, they are given us to be devoured. **13** Thus
with your mouths ye have boasted against me, and I have multiplied your words
against me: I have heard them. **14** Thus saith the Lord God, So shall all the
world rejoice, when I shall make thee desolate. **15** As thou didst rejoice at the
inheritance of the house of Israel, because it was desolate, so will I do unto thee:

---

k. Ezek. 33:22 I was endued with the Spirit of prophecy, Ezek. 8:1.
l. Ezek. 33:22 Whereby is signified that the ministers of God cannot speak till God give them courage, and open their mouths, Ezek. 24:27 and 29:21; Eph. 6:19.
m. Ezek. 33:24 Thus the wicked think themselves more worthy to enjoy God's promises than the Saints of God, to whom they were made: and would bind God to be subject to them, though they would not be bound to him.
n. Ezek. 33:25 Contrary to the Law, Lev. 17:14.
o. Ezek. 33:26 As they that are ready still to shed blood.
p. Ezek. 33:30 In derision.
q. Ezek. 33:31 This declareth that we ought to hear God's word with such zeal and affection, that we should in all points obey it, else we abuse the word to our own condemnation, and make of his ministers, as though they were jests to serve men's foolish fantasies.
r. Ezek. 33:32 Or, pleasant, and love song.

EZEK. 33
1. Ezek. 3:17
2. Ezek. 18:25
3. Ezek. 7:24 / Ezek. 24:21 / Ezek. 30:6,7

EZEK. 34
a. Ezek. 34:2 By the shepherds he meaneth the king, the Magistrates, Priests, and Prophets.
b. Ezek. 34:3 Ye seek to enrich yourselves by their commodities, and to spoil their riches and substance.
c. Ezek. 34:4 He describeth the office and duty of a good pastor, who ought to love and succor his flock, and not to be cruel toward them.
d. Ezek. 34:5 For lack of good government and doctrine they perished.
e. Ezek. 34:10 By destroying the covetous hirelings, and restoring true shepherds, whereof we have a sign so oft as God sendeth true preachers, who both by doctrine and life labor to feed his sheep in the pleasant pastures of his word.
f. Ezek. 34:12 In the day of their affliction and misery: and this promise is to comfort the Church in all dangers.
g. Ezek. 34:16 Meaning, such as lift up themselves above their brethren, and think they have no need to be governed by me.
h. Ezek. 34:16 That is, by putting difference between the good and the bad, and so give to either as they deserve.
i. Ezek. 34:18 By good pasture and deep waters is meant the pure word of God and the administration of justice, which they did not distribute to the poor till they had corrupted it.
j. Ezek. 34:23 Meaning Christ, of whom David was a figure, Jer. 30:9; Hos. 3:5.
k. Ezek. 34:25 This declareth that under Christ the flock should be truly delivered from sin, and hell, and so be safely preserved in the Church, where they should never perish.
l. Ezek. 34:27 The fruits of God's grace shall appear in great abundance in his Church.
m. Ezek. 34:29 That is, the rod that shall come out of the root of Jesse, Isa. 11:1.

EZEK. 34
1. Jer. 1:31

EZEK. 35
a. Ezek. 35:2 Where the Edomites dwelt.
b. Ezek. 35:5 When by their punishment I called them from their iniquity.
c. Ezek. 35:6 Except thou repent thy former cruelty.
d. Ezek. 35:9 To wit, to their former estate.
e. Ezek. 35:10 Meaning, Israel and Judah.
f. Ezek. 35:10 And so by fighting against God's people, they should go about to put him out of his own possession.
g. Ezek. 35:11 As thou hast done cruelly, so shalt thou be cruelly handled.
h. Ezek. 35:11 Showing that when God punisheth the enemies, the godly ought to consider that he hath a care over them, and so praise his Name: and also that the wicked rage as

thou shalt be desolate, O mount Seir, and all Idumea wholly, and they shall know that I am the Lord.

36

1 He promiseth to deliver Israel from the Gentiles. 22 The benefits done unto the Jews, are to be ascribed to the mercy of God, and not unto their deservings. 26 God reneweth our hearts that we may walk in his commandments.

1 Also thou son of man, prophesy unto the [1]mountains of Israel, and say, Ye mountains of Israel, hear the word of the Lord. **2** Thus saith the Lord God, Because the [a]enemy hath said against you, Aha, even the [b]high places of the world are ours in possession, **3** Therefore prophesy and say, Thus saith the Lord God, Because that they have made you desolate, and swallowed you up on every side that ye might be a possession unto the residue of the heathen, and ye are come unto the lips and [c]tongues of men, and unto the reproach of the people, **4** Therefore ye mountains of Israel, hear the word of the Lord God, Thus saith the Lord God to the mountains, and to the hills, to the rivers and to the valleys, and to the waste and desolate places, and to the cities that are forsaken, which are spoiled and had in derision of the residue of the heathen that are round about. **5** Therefore thus saith the Lord God, Surely in the fire of mine indignation have I spoken against the residue of the heathen, and against all Idumea, which have [d]taken my land for their possession, with the joy of all their heart, and with despiteful minds to cast it out for a prey. **6** Prophesy therefore upon the land of Israel, and say unto the mountains and to the hills, to the rivers, and to the valleys, Thus saith the Lord God, Behold, I have spoken in mine indignation and in my wrath, because ye have suffered the [e]shame of the heathen. **7** Therefore thus saith the Lord God, I have [f]lifted up mine hand, surely the heathen that are about you, shall bear their shame. **8** But you, O mountains of Israel, ye shall [g]shoot forth your branches, and bring forth your fruit to my people of Israel: for they are ready to come. **9** For behold, I come unto you, and I will turn unto you, and ye shall be tilled and sown. **10** And I will multiply the men upon you, even all the house of Israel wholly, and the cities shall be inhabited, and the desolate places shall be built. **11** And I will multiply upon you man and beast, and they shall increase, and bring fruit, and I will cause you to dwell after your old estate, and I will bestow benefits upon you more than [h]at the first, and ye shall know that I am the Lord. **12** Yea, I will cause men to walk upon [i]you, even my people Israel, and they shall possess [j]you, and ye shall be their inheritance, and ye shall no more henceforth deprive them of men. **13** Thus saith the Lord, Because they say unto you, Thou [k]land devourest up men, and hast been a waster of thy people, **14** Therefore thou shalt devour men no more, neither waste thy people henceforth, saith the Lord God, **15** Neither will I cause men to hear in thee the shame of the heathen anymore, neither shalt thou bear the reproach of the people anymore, neither shalt cause thy folk to fall anymore, saith the Lord God. **16** Moreover, the word of the Lord came unto me, saying, **17** Son of man, when the house of Israel dwelt in their own land, they defiled it by their own ways, and by their deeds: their way was before me as the filthiness of the menstruous. **18** Wherefore I poured my wrath upon them, for the blood that they had shed in the land, and for their idols, wherewith they had polluted it. **19** And I scattered them among the heathen, and they were dispersed through the countries: for according to their ways, and according to their deeds, I judged them. **20** [2]And when they entered unto the heathen, whither they went, they polluted mine holy Name, when they said of them, These are the people of the Lord, and are gone out of his land. **21** But I favored mine holy [l]Name, which the house of Israel had polluted among the heathen, whither they went. **22** Therefore say unto the house of Israel, Thus saith the Lord God, I do not this for your sakes, O house of Israel, but for mine [m]holy Name's sake, which ye polluted among the heathen, whither ye went. **23** And I will sanctify my great Name, which was polluted among the heathen, among whom you have polluted it, and the heathen shall know that I am the Lord, saith the Lord God, when I shall be sanctified in you before [n]their eyes. **24** For I will take you from among the heathen, and gather you out of all countries, and will bring you into your own land. **25** Then will I pour clean [o]water upon you, and ye shall be clean: yea, from all your filthiness, and from all your idols will I cleanse you. **26** [3]A new heart also will I give you, and a new spirit will I put within you, and I will take away the stony heart out of your body, and I will give you an heart of flesh. **27** And I will put my spirit within you, and cause you to walk in my statutes, and ye shall keep my judgments and do them. **28** And ye shall dwell in the land that I gave to your fathers, and ye shall be my people, and I will be your God. **29** I will also deliver you from all your filthiness, and I will call for [p]corn, and will increase it, and lay no famine upon you. **30** For I will multiply the fruit of the trees, and the increase of the field, that ye shall bear no more the reproach of famine among the heathen. **31** Then shall ye remember your own wicked ways, and your deeds that were not good, and shall judge yourselves worthy to have been [q]destroyed for your iniquities, and for your abominations. **32** Be it known unto you that I do not this for your sakes, saith the Lord God: therefore, O ye house of Israel, be ashamed and confounded for your own ways. **33** Thus saith the Lord God, What time as I shall have cleansed you from all your iniquities, I will cause you to dwell in the cities, and the desolate places shall be built. **34** And the desolate land shall be tilled, whereas it lay waste in the sight of all that passed by. **35** For they said, This waste land was like the garden of Eden, and these waste, and desolate, and ruinous cities were strong, and were inhabited. **36** Then the residue of the heathen, that are left round about you, shall [r]know that I the Lord build the ruinous places, and plant the desolate places: I the Lord have spoken it, and will do it. **37** Thus saith the Lord God, I will yet for this be sought of the house of Israel, to perform it unto them: I will increase them with men like a flock. **38** As the holy flock, as the flock of Jerusalem in their solemn feasts, so shall the desolate cities be filled with flocks of men, and they shall know that I am the Lord.

37

He prophesieth the bringing again of the people, being in captivity. 16 He showeth the union of the ten tribes with the two.

1 The hand of the Lord was upon me, and carried me out in the Spirit of the Lord, and set me down in the midst of the [a]field, which was full of [b]bones: **2** And he led me round about by them, and behold, they were very many in the open field, and lo, they were very dry. **3** And he said unto me, Son of man, can these bones live? And I answered, O Lord God, thou knowest. **4** Again he said unto me, Prophesy upon these bones, and say unto them, O ye dry bones, hear the word of the Lord. **5** Thus saith the Lord God unto these bones, Behold, I will cause breath to enter into you, and ye shall live. **6** And I will lay sinews upon you, and make flesh grow upon you, and cover you with skin, and put breath in you, that ye may live, and ye shall know that I am the Lord. **7** So I prophesied as I was commanded: and as I prophesied, there was a noise, and behold, there was a shaking, and the bones came together, bone to his bone. **8** And when I beheld, lo, the sinews, and the flesh grew upon them, and above the skin covered them, but there was no breath in them. **9** Then said he unto me, Prophesy unto the wind: prophesy, son of man, and say to the wind, Thus saith the Lord God, Come from the four [c]winds, O breath, and breathe upon these slain, that they may live. **10** So I prophesied as he had commanded me: and the breath came into them, and they lived, and stood up upon their feet, an exceeding great army. **11** Then he said unto me, Son of man, these bones are the whole house of Israel. Behold, they say, Our bones are dried, and our hope is gone, and we are clean cut off. **12** Therefore prophesy, and say unto them, Thus saith the Lord God, Behold, my people, I will open your graves, and cause you to come up out of your sepulchers, and bring you into the land of Israel, **13** And ye shall know that I am the Lord, [d]when I have opened your graves, O my people, and brought you up out of your sepulchers, **14** And shall put my Spirit in you, and ye shall live, and I shall place you in your own land: then ye shall know that I the Lord have spoken it, and performed it, saith the Lord. **15** The word of the Lord came again unto me, saying, **16** Moreover, thou son of man, take thee a piece of wood, and write upon it, Unto Judah, and to the children of Israel his companions: then take [e]another piece of wood, and write upon it, Unto Joseph the tree of Ephraim, and to all the house of Israel his companions, **17** And thou shalt join them one to another into one tree, and they shall be as one in thine hand. **18** And when the

---

though there were no God, till they feel his hand to their destruction.

EZEK. 36

a. Ezek. 36:2 That is, the Edomite.
b. Ezek. 36:2 That is, Jerusalem, which for God's promises was the chiefest of all the world.
c. Ezek. 36:3 Ye are made a matter of talk and derision to all the world.
d. Ezek. 36:5 They appointed with themselves to have it, and therefore came with Nebuchadnezzar against Jerusalem for this purpose.
e. Ezek. 36:6 Because you have been a laughingstock unto them.
f. Ezek. 36:7 By making a solemn oath, read Ezek. 20:5.
g. Ezek. 36:8 God declareth his mercies and goodness toward his Church, who still preserveth his, even when he destroyeth his enemies.
h. Ezek. 36:11 Which was accomplished under Christ, to whom all these temporal deliverances did direct them.
i. Ezek. 36:12 That is, upon the mountains of Jerusalem.
j. Ezek. 36:12 Or, thee.
k. Ezek. 36:13 This the enemies imputed as the reproach of the land, which God did for the sins of the people according to his just judgments.
l. Ezek. 36:21 And therefore would not suffer my Name to be had in contempt, as the heathen would have reproached me, if I had suffered my Church to perish.
m. Ezek. 36:22 This excludeth from man all dignity, and means to deserve anything by, seeing that God referreth the whole to himself, and that only for the glory of his holy Name.
n. Ezek. 36:23 Or, your.
o. Ezek. 36:25 That is, his spirit, whereby he reformeth the heart, and regenerateth his, Isa. 44:3.
p. Ezek. 36:29 Under the abundance of temporal benefits he concludeth the spiritual graces.
q. Ezek. 36:31 Ye shall come to true repentance, and think yourselves unworthy to be of the number of God's creatures, for your ingratitude against him.
r. Ezek. 36:36 He declareth that it ought not to be referred to the soil or plentifulness of the earth that any country is rich and abundant, but only to God's mercies, as his plagues and curses declare, when he maketh it barren.

EZEK. 36

1. Ezek. 6:2
2. Isa. 52:5 / Rom. 2:24
3. Jer. 32:39 / Ezek. 11:19

EZEK. 37

a. Ezek. 37:1 Or, valley.
b. Ezek. 37:1 He showeth by a great miracle that God hath power, and also will deliver his people from their captivity, inasmuch as he is able to give life to the dead bones, and bodies, and raise them up again.
c. Ezek. 37:9 Signifying, all parts whereas the Israelites were scattered: that is, the faithful shall be brought to the same unity of spirit and doctrine, wheresoever they are scattered through the world.
d. Ezek. 37:13 That is, when I have brought you out of those places, and towns where you are captives.
e. Ezek. 37:16 Which signifieth the joining together of the two houses, of Israel, and Judah.

children of thy people shall speak unto thee, saying, Wilt thou not show us what
thou meanest by these? **19** Thus shalt answer them, Thus saith the Lord God,
Behold, I will take the tree [f]of Joseph, which is in the hand of Ephraim, and the
tribes of Israel his fellows, and will put them with him even with the tree of Judah,
and make them one tree, and they shall be one in mine hand. **20** And the pie-
ces of wood whereon thou writest, shall be in thine hand, in their sight. **21** And
say unto them, Thus saith the Lord God, Behold, I will take the children of Israel
from among the heathen whither they be gone, and will gather them on every side,
and bring them into their own land. **22** And I will make them one people in the
land, upon the mountains of Israel, [1]and one king shall be king to them all: and
they shall be no more two peoples, neither be divided anymore henceforth into
two kingdoms. **23** Neither shall they be polluted anymore with their idols, nor
with their abominations, nor with any of their transgressions: but I will save them
out of all their dwelling places, wherein they have sinned, and will cleanse them: so
shall they be my people, and I will be their God. **24** And David my [2]servant shall
be king over them, and they shall all have one shepherd: they shall also walk in my
judgments, and observe my statutes, and do them. **25** And they shall dwell in
the [g]land, that I have given unto Jacob my servant, where your fathers have dwelt,
and they shall dwell therein, even they, and their sons, and their sons' sons forever,
and my servant David shall be their prince forever. **26** Moreover, I will make a
[3]covenant of peace with them: it shall be an everlasting covenant with them, and
I will place them, and multiply them, and will set my sanctuary among them fo-
revermore. **27** My tabernacle also shall be with them: yea, I will be their God,
and they shall be my people. **28** Thus the heathen shall know, that I the Lord do
sanctify Israel, when my Sanctuary shall be among them forevermore.

38

2 He prophesieth that Gog and Magog shall fight with great power against the people of God. 21 Their destruction.

1 And the word of the Lord came unto me, saying, **2** Son of men, set thy
face against [a]Gog, and against the land of Magog, the chief prince of Meshech and
Tubal, and prophesy against him, **3** And say, Thus saith the Lord God, Behold, I
come against thee, O Gog, the chief prince of Meshech and Tubal. **4** And I will
destroy thee, and put hooks in thy jaws, and I will bring thee forth and all thine
host, both horses and horsemen, all clothed with all sorts of armor, even a great
multitude with bucklers and shields, all [b]handling swords. **5** They of [c]Paras, of
Cush, and Put with them, even all they that bear shield and helmet. **6** [d]Gomer
and all his bands, and the house of Togarmah of the North quarters, and all his
bands, and much people with thee. **7** Prepare thyself, and make thee [e]ready,
both thou, and all thy multitude that are assembled unto thee, and be thou their
safeguard. **8** After many days thou shalt be visited: for in the latter years thou
shalt come into the land that hath been destroyed with the sword, and is gathered
out of many people upon the mountains of Israel, which have long lain waste: yet
[f]they have been brought out of the people, and they shall dwell all safe. **9** Thou
shalt ascend and come up like a tempest, and shalt be like a cloud to cover the
land, both thou, and all thy bands, and many people with thee. **10** Thus saith
the Lord God, Even at the same time shall many things come into thy mind, and
thou shalt think [g]evil thoughts. **11** And thou shalt say, I will go up to the land
that hath no walled towers: [h]I will go to them that are at rest and dwell in safety,
which dwell all without walls, and have neither bars nor gates, **12** Thinking to
spoil the prey, and to take a booty, to turn thine hand upon the desolate places that
are now inhabited, and upon the people that are gathered out of the nations whi-
ch have gotten cattle, and goods, and dwell in the midst of the land. **13** Sheba
and Dedan, and the merchants of Tarshish with all the lions thereof shall say unto
thee, [i]Art thou come to spoil the prey? hast thou gathered thy multitude to take a
booty? to carry away silver and gold, to take away cattle and goods, and to spoil a
great prey? **14** Therefore, son of man, prophesy, and say unto Gog, Thus saith
the Lord God, In that day, when my people of Israel [j]dwelleth safe shalt thou not
know it, **15** And come from thy place out of the North parts, thou and much
people with thee? all shall ride upon horses, even a great multitude and a mighty
army. **16** And thou shalt come up against my people of Israel, as a cloud to cover
the land, thou shalt be in the [k]latter days, and I will bring thee upon my land, that
the heathen may know me, when I [l]shall be sanctified in thee, O Gog, before their
eyes. **17** Thus saith the Lord God, Art not thou he, of whom I have spoken in
old time, [m]by the hand of my servants the Prophets of Israel which prophesied in
those days and years, that I would bring thee upon them? **18** At the same time
also when Gog shall come against the land of Israel, saith the Lord God, my wra-
th shall arise in mine anger. **19** For in mine indignation, and in the fire of my
wrath have I spoken it: surely at that time there shall be a great shaking in the land
of Israel, **20** So that the fishes of the Sea, and the fowls of the heaven, and the
beasts of the field, and all that move and creep upon the earth, and all the men that
are upon the earth, shall tremble at my presence, and the mountains shall be over-
thrown, and the [n]stairs shall fall, and every wall shall fall to the ground. **21** For
I will call for a sword against him [o]throughout all my mountains, saith the Lord
God: every man's sword shall be against his brother. **22** And I will plead against
him with pestilence, and with blood, and I will cause to rain upon him and upon
his bands, and upon the great people that are with him, a sore rain, and hailstones,
fire, and brimstone. **23** Thus will I be [1]magnified, and sanctified, and known in
the eyes of many nations, and they shall know, that I am the Lord.

39

1 He showeth the destruction of Gog, and Magog. 11 The graves of Gog and his host. 17 They shall be devoured of birds and beasts. 23 Wherefore the house of Israel is captive. 24 Their bringing again from captivity is promised.

1 Therefore thou son of man, prophesy against Gog, and say, Thus saith the
Lord God, Behold, I come against thee, O Gog, the chief prince of Meshech and
Tubal. **2** And I will destroy thee [a]and leave but the sixth part of thee, and will
cause thee to come up from the North parts, and will bring thee upon the moun-
tains of Israel: **3** And I will smite thy bow out of thy left hand, and I will cause
thine arrows to fall out of thy right hand. **4** Thou [b]shalt fall upon the mountains
of Israel, and all thy bands and the people, that is with thee: for I will give thee
unto the birds, and to every feathered fowl and beast of the field to be devou-
red. **5** Thou shalt fall upon the open field: for I have spoken it, saith the Lord
God. **6** And I will send a fire on Magog, and among them that dwell safely in the
[c]isles, and they shall know that I am the Lord. **7** So will I make mine holy Name
known in the midst of my people Israel, and I will not suffer them to pollute mine
holy Name anymore, and the heathen shall know that I am the Lord, the Holy one
of Israel. **8** Behold, [d]it is come, and it is done, saith the Lord God: and this is the
day whereof I have spoken. **9** And they that dwell in the cities of Israel shall [e]go
forth, and shall burn and set fire upon the weapons, and on the shields, and buck-
lers, upon the bows, and upon the arrows, and upon the staves in their hands, and
upon the spears, and they shall burn them with fire seven years. **10** So that they
shall bring no wood out of the field, neither cut down any out of the forests: for
they shall burn the weapons with fire, and they shall rob those that robbed them,
and spoil those that spoiled them, saith the Lord God. **11** And at the same time
will I give unto Gog [f]a place there for burial in Israel, even the valley, whereby men
go toward the East part of the sea: and it shall cause them that pass by, to stop their
[g]noses, and there shall they bury Gog with all his multitude: and they shall call it
the valley of [h]Hamon Gog. **12** [i]And seven months long shall the house of Israel
be burying of them, that they may cleanse the land. **13** Yea, all the people of the
land shall bury them, and they shall have a name, when I shall be glorified, saith
the Lord God. **14** And they shall choose out men to go continually through the
[j]land with them that travail, to bury those that remain upon the ground, to cle-
anse it: they shall search to the end of seven months. **15** And the travelers that
pass through the land, if any see a man's bone, then shall he set up a sign by it, till
the buriers have buried it in the valley of Hamon Gog. **16** And also the name

---

f. Ezek. 37:19 That is, the house of Israel.
g. Ezek. 37:25 Meaning, that the elect by Christ shall dwell in the heaven by Jerusalem, which is meant by the land of Canaan.

EZEK. 37
1. John 10:16
2. Isa. 40:11 / Jer. 23:5 / Ezek. 34:23 / Dan. 9:24
3. Ps. 109:4 / Ps. 116:2

EZEK. 38
a. Ezek. 38:2 Which was a people that came of Magog the son of Japheth, Gen. 10:2. Magog also here signifieth a certain country so that by these two countries which had the government of Greece and Italy, he meaneth the principal enemies of the Church, Rev. 20:8.
b. Ezek. 38:4 He showeth that the enemies should bend themselves against the Church, but it should be to their own destruction.
c. Ezek. 38:5 The Persians, Ethiopians and men of Africa.
d. Ezek. 38:6 Gomer was Japheth's son, and Togarmah the son of Gomer, and are thought to be they that inhabit Asia Minor.
e. Ezek. 38:7 Signifying, that all the people of the world should assemble themselves against the Church and Christ their head.
f. Ezek. 38:8 Or, it: meaning, the land of Israel.
g. Ezek. 38:10 That is, to molest and destroy the Church.
h. Ezek. 38:11 Meaning, Israel, which had now been destroyed, and was not yet built again: declaring hereby the simplicity of the godly, who seek not so much to fortify themselves by outward force, as to depend on the providence and goodness of God.
i. Ezek. 38:13 One enemy shall envy another because everyone shall think to have the spoil of the Church.
j. Ezek. 38:14 Shalt not thou spy thine occasions to come against my Church when they suspect nothing?
k. Ezek. 38:16 Meaning, in the last age, and from the coming of Christ unto the end of the world.
l. Ezek. 38:16 Signifying, that God will be sanctified by maintaining his Church, and destroying his enemies, as Ezek. 36:23 and 37:28.
m. Ezek. 38:17 Hereby he declareth that none affliction can come to the Church, whereof they have not been advertised aforetime, to teach them to endure all things with more patience, when they know that God hath so ordained.
n. Ezek. 38:20 All means whereby man should think to save himself, shall fail, the affliction in those days shall be so great, and the enemies' destruction shall be so terrible.
o. Ezek. 38:21 Against the people of Gog and Magog.

EZEK. 38
1. Ezek. 36:23 / Ezek. 37:28

EZEK. 39
a. Ezek. 39:2 Or, destroy thee with six plagues, as Ezek. 38:22.
b. Ezek. 39:4 Meaning, that by the virtue of God's word the enemy shall be destroyed wheresoever he assaileth his Church.
c. Ezek. 39:6 That is, among all nations where the enemies of my people dwell, seem they never so far separated.
d. Ezek. 39:8 That is, this plague is fully determined, in my counsel, and cannot be changed.
e. Ezek. 39:9 After this destruction the Church shall have great peace and tranquility, and burn all their weapons, because they shall no more fear the enemies, and this is chiefly meant of the accomplishment of Christ's kingdom when by their head Christ, all enemies shall be overcome.
f. Ezek. 39:11 Which declareth that the enemies shall have an horrible fall.
g. Ezek. 39:11 For the stink of the carcasses.
h. Ezek. 39:11 Or, the multitude of Gog.
i. Ezek. 39:12 Meaning, a long time.
j. Ezek. 39:14 Partly that the holy land should not be polluted, and partly for the compassion that the children of God have, even on their enemies.

of the city shall be [k]Hamonah: thus shall they cleanse the land. **17** And thou
son of man, thus saith the Lord God, Speak unto every feathered fowl, and to all
the beasts of the field, Assemble yourselves, and come: [l]gather yourselves on every
side to my sacrifice: for I do sacrifice a great sacrifice for you upon the mountains
of Israel, that ye may eat flesh, and drink blood. **18** Ye shall eat the flesh of the
valiant, and drink the blood of the princes of the earth, of the weathers, of the
lambs, and of the goats, and of bullocks, even of all fat beasts of Bashan. **19** And
ye shall eat fat till ye be full, and drink blood till ye be drunken of my sacrifice,
which I have sacrificed for you. **20** Thus you shall be filled at my table with
horses and chariots, with valiant men, and with all men of war, saith the Lord
God. **21** And I will set my glory among the heathen, and all the heathen shall
see my judgment, that I have executed, and mine hand, which I have laid upon
them. **22** So the house of Israel shall know, that I am the Lord their God from
that day and so forth. **23** And the heathen shall know that the house of Israel
went into captivity for [m]their iniquity, because they trespassed against me: therefo-
re hid I my face from them, and gave them into the hand of their enemies: so fell
they all by the sword. **24** According to their uncleanness, and according to their
transgressions have I done unto them, and hid my face from them. **25** There-
fore thus saith the Lord God, Now will I bring again the captivity of Jacob, and
have compassion upon the whole house of Israel, and will be jealous for mine holy
Name, **26** After that they have borne their shame, and all their transgression,
whereby they have transgressed against me, when they dwelt safely in their land,
and without fear of any. **27** When I have brought them again from the people,
and gathered them out of their enemies' lands, and am [1]sanctified in them in the
sight of many nations, **28** Then shall they know, that I am the Lord their God,
which caused them to be led into captivity among the heathen: but I have gathered
them unto their own land, and have left none of them anymore there, **29** Nei-
ther will I hide my face anymore from them: for I have poured out my Spirit upon
the house of Israel, saith the Lord God.

40

The restoring of the city and the Temple.

1 In the five and twentieth year of our being in captivity, in the
[a]beginning of the year, in the tenth day of the month, in the fourteenth year after
that the city was smitten, in the selfsame day, the hand of the Lord was upon me,
and brought me thither. **2** Into the land of Israel brought he me by [b]a divine vi-
sion, and set me upon a very high mountain, whereupon was as the building of a
city, toward the South. **3** And he brought me thither, and behold, there was a
[c]man, whose similitude was to look to, like brass, with a linen thread in his hand,
and a reed to measure with: and he stood at the gate. **4** And the man said unto
me, Son of man, behold with thine eyes, and hear with thine ears, and set thine
heart upon all that I shall show thee: for to the intent that they might be showed
thee, art thou brought hither: declare all that thou seest unto the house of Isra-
el. **5** And behold, I saw a wall on the outside of the house round about: and in
the man's hand was a reed to measure with, of six cubits long, by the cubit, and an
hand breadth: so he measured the breadth of the building with one reed, and the
height with one reed. **6** Then came he unto the gate which looketh toward the
East, and went up the stairs thereof, and measured the [d]post of the gate, which was
one reed broad, and [e]the other post of the gate, which was one reed broad. **7** And
every chamber was one reed long, and one reed broad, and between the chambers
were five cubits: and the post of the gate by the porch of the gate within was one
reed. **8** He measured also the porch of the gate within with one reed. **9** Then
measured he the porch of the gate of eight cubits and the [f]posts thereof, of two cu-
bits, and the porch of the gate was inward. **10** And the Chambers of the gate
Eastward, were three on this side, and three on that side: they three were of one
measure, and the posts had one measure on this side, and one on that side. **11** And
he measured the breadth of the entry of the gate ten cubits, and the height of the
gate thirteen cubits. **12** The space also before the chambers was one cubit on this
side and the space was one cubit on that side, and the chambers were six cubits on
this side, and six cubits on that side. **13** He measured then the gate from the roof
of a chamber to the top of the gate: the breadth was five and twenty cubits, door
against door. **14** He made also posts of threescore cubits, and the posts of the
court, and of the gate, had one measure round about. **15** And upon the forefront
of the entry of the gate unto the forefront of the porch of the gate within were fifty
cubits. **16** And there were narrow windows in the chambers, and in their posts
within the gate round about, and likewise to the arches: and the windows went
round about within: and upon the posts were palm trees. **17** Then brought he
me into the outward court, and lo, there were chambers, and a pavement made for
the court round about, and thirty chambers were upon the pavement. **18** And
the pavement was by the side of the gates over against the length of the gates, and
the pavement was beneath. **19** Then he measured the breadth from the forefront
of the lower gate without, unto the forefront of the court within, an hundred
cubits Eastward and Northward. **20** And the gate of the outward court, that lo-
oked toward the North, measured he after the length and breadth there-
of. **21** And the chambers thereof were three on this side, and three on that side,
and the posts thereof and the arches thereof were after the measure of the first gate:
the length thereof was fifty cubits, and the breadth five and twenty cubi-
ts. **22** And their windows, and their arches with their palm trees, were after the
measure of the gate that looketh toward the East, and the going up unto it had
seven steps, and the arches thereof were before them. **23** And the gate of the in-
ner court stood over against the gate toward the North, and toward the East, and
he measured from gate to gate an hundred cubits. **24** After that, he brought me
toward the South, and lo, there was a gate toward the South, and he measured the
posts thereof, and the arches thereof according to these measures. **25** And there
were windows in it, and in the arches thereof round about, like those windows: the
height was fifty cubits, and the breadth five and twenty cubits. **26** And there
were seven steps to go up to it, and the arches thereof were before them, and it had
palm trees, one on this side, and another on that side upon the post there-
of. **27** And there was a gate in the inner court toward the South, and he measu-
red from gate to gate toward the South an hundred cubits. **28** And he brought
me into the inner court by the South gate, and he measured the South gate, accor-
ding to these measures, **29** And the chambers thereof, and the posts thereof, and
the arches thereof according to these measures, and there were windows in it, and
in the arches thereof round about, it was fifty cubits long, and five and twenty cu-
bits broad. **30** And the arches round about were five and twenty cubits long, and
five cubits broad. **31** And the arches thereof were toward the utter Court, and
palm trees were upon the posts thereof, and the going up to it had eight
steps. **32** Again he brought me into the inner court toward the East, and he me-
asured the gate according to these measures. **33** And the chambers thereof, and
the posts thereof, and the arches thereof were according to these measures, and
there were windows therein, and in the arches thereof round about: it was fifty cu-
bits long, and five and twenty cubits broad. **34** And the arches thereof were
toward the utter court, and palm trees were upon the posts thereof, on this side and
on that side, and the going up to it had eight steps. **35** After he brought me to
the North gate, and measured it, according to these measures, **36** The chambers
thereof, the posts thereof, and the arches thereof, and there were windows therein
round about: the height was fifty cubits, and the breadth five and twenty cubi-
ts. **37** And the posts thereof were toward the utter court, and palm trees were
upon the posts thereof on this side, and on that side, and the going up to it had
eight steps. **38** And every chamber, and the entry thereof was under the posts of
the gates: there they washed the burnt offering. **39** And in the porch of the gate
stood two tables on this side, and two tables on that side, upon the which they slew
the burnt offering, and the sin offering, and the trespass offering. **40** And at the
side beyond the steps, at the entry of the North gate stood two tables, and on the
other side, which was at the porch of the gate were two tables. **41** Four tables
were on this side, and four tables on that side by the side of the gate even eight
tables whereupon they slew their sacrifice. **42** And the four tables were of hewn
stone for the burnt offering, of a cubit and an half long, and a cubit and an half
broad, and one cubit high: whereupon also they laid the instruments wherewith
they slew the burnt offering and the sacrifice. **43** And within were borders an
hand broad, fastened round about, and upon the tables lay the flesh of the offe-
ring. **44** And without the inner gate were the chambers of the singers in the in-
ner court, which was at the side of the North gate: and their prospect was toward
the South, and one was at the side of the East gate, having the prospect toward the
North. **45** And he said unto me, This chamber whose prospect is toward the
South is for the Priests, that have charge to keep the house. **46** And the chamber
whose prospect is toward the North, is for the Priests that have the charge to keep
the Altar: these are the sons of Zadok among the sons of Levi, which may come
near to the Lord to minister unto him. **47** So he measured the court an hundred
cubits long, and an hundred cubits broad, even four square: likewise the Altar that
was before the house. **48** And he brought me to the porch of the house, and me-
asured the posts of the porch, five cubits on this side, and five cubits on that side:
and the breadth of the gate was three cubits on this side, and three cubits on that
side. **49** The length of the porch was twenty cubits, and the breadth eleven cubi-
ts, and he brought me by the steps whereby they went up to it, and there were pil-
lars by the posts, one on this side and another on that side.

41

1 The disposition and order of the building of the Temple, and the other things thereunto belonging.

1 Afterward, he brought me to the Temple and measured the posts, six cu-
bits broad on the one side, and six cubits broad on the other side, which was the
breadth of the Tabernacle. **2** And the breadth of the entry was ten cubits, and
the sides of the entry were five cubits, on the one side, and five cubits on the other

k. Ezek. 39:16 Or, multitude.
l. Ezek. 39:17 Whereby he signifieth the horrible destruction that should come upon the enemies of his Church.
m. Ezek. 39:23 The heathen shall know that they overcame not my people by their strength, neither yet by the weakness of mine arm, but that this was for my people's sins.

EZEK. 39
1. Ezek. 36:23

EZEK. 40
a. Ezek. 40:1 The Jews counted the beginning of the year after two sorts: for their feasts, they began to count in March, and for their other affairs in September: so that this is to be understood of September.
b. Ezek. 40:2 Or, visions of God.
c. Ezek. 40:3 Which was an Angel in form of a man, that came to measure out this building.
d. Ezek. 40:6 Or, threshold.
e. Ezek. 40:6 Or, upper posts.
f. Ezek. 40:9 Or, pentises.

side, and he measured the length thereof forty cubits, and the breadth twenty cubits. **3** Then went he in, and measured the posts of the entry two cubits, and the entry six cubits, and the breadth of the entry seven cubits. **4** So he measured the length thereof twenty cubits, and the breadth twenty cubits before the Temple, and he said unto me, This is the most holy place. **5** After, he measured the wall of the house, six cubits, and the breadth of every chamber four cubits round about the house, on every side. **6** And the chambers were chamber upon chamber, three and thirty foot high, and they entered into the wall made for the chambers which was round about the house, that the posts might be fastened therein, and not be fastened in the wall of the house. **7** And it was large, and went round mounting upward to the chambers: for the stairs of the house was mounting upward, round about the house: therefore the house was larger upward: so they went up from the lowest chamber to the highest by the midst. **8** I saw also the house high round about: the foundations of the chambers were a full reed of six great cubits. **9** The thickness of the wall which was for the chamber without, was five cubits, and that which remained, was the place of the chambers that were within. **10** And between the chambers was the wideness of twenty cubits round about the House on every side. **11** And the doors of the chambers were toward the place that remained, one door toward the North, and another door toward the South, and the breadth of the place that remained, was five cubits round about. **12** Now the building that was before the separate place toward the West corner, was seventy cubits broad, and the wall of the building was five cubits thick round about, and the length ninety cubits. **13** So he measured the house an hundred cubits long, and the separate place and the building with the walls thereof were an hundred cubits long. **14** Also the breadth of the forefront of the house and of the separate place toward the East, was an hundred cubits. **15** And he measured the length of the building over against the separate place, which was behind it, and the chambers on the one side and on the other side an hundred cubits with the Temple within, and the arches of the court. **16** The posts and the narrow windows, and the chambers round about, on three sides over against the posts, ceiled with cedar wood round about, and from the ground up to the windows, and the windows were ceiled. **17** And from above the door unto the inner house and without, and by all the wall round about within and without it was ceiled according to the measure. **18** And it was made with Cherubims and palm trees, so that a palm tree was between a Cherub and a Cherub: and every Cherub had two faces. **19** So that the face of a man was toward the palm tree on the one side, and the face of a lion toward the palm tree on the other side: thus was it made through all the house round about. **20** From the ground unto above the door were Cherubims, and palm trees made as in the wall of the Temple. **21** The posts of the Temple were squared, and thus to look unto was the similitude and form of the Sanctuary. **22** The altar of wood was three cubits high, and the length thereof two cubits, and the corners thereof and the length thereof and the sides thereof were of wood. And he said unto me, This is the Table that shall be before the Lord. **23** And the Temple and the Sanctuary had two doors. **24** And the doors had two wickets, even two turning wickets, two wickets for one door, and two wickets for another door. **25** And upon the doors of the Temple there were made Cherubims and palm trees, like as was made upon the walls, and there were thick planks upon the forefront of the porch without. **26** And there were narrow windows and palm trees on the one side, and on the other side, by the sides of the porch, and upon the sides of the house, and thick planks.

42

Of the chambers of the Temple for the Priests, and the holy things.

1 Then brought he me into the utter court by the way toward the North, and he brought me into the chamber that was over against the separate place, and which was before the building toward the North. **2** Before the length of an hundred cubits, was the North door, and it was fifty cubits broad. **3** Over against the twenty cubits which were for the inner court, and over against the pavement, which was for the utter court, was chamber against chamber in three rows. **4** And before the chambers was a gallery of ten cubits wide, and within was a way of one cubit, and their doors toward the North. **5** Now the chambers above were narrower: for those chambers seemed to eat up these, to wit, the lower, and those that were in the midst of the building. **6** For they were in three rows, but had not pillars as the pillars of the court: therefore there was a difference from them beneath and from the middlemost, even from the ground. **7** And the wall that was without over against the chambers, toward the utter court on the forefront of the chambers, was fifty cubits long. **8** For the length of the chambers that were in the utter court, was fifty cubits: and lo, before the Temple were an hundred cubits. **9** And under these chambers was the entry, on the East side, as one goeth into them from the outward court. **10** The chambers were in the thickness of the wall of the court toward the East, over against the separate place, and over against the building. **11** And the way before them was after the manner of the chambers, which were toward the North, as long as they, and as broad as they: and all their entries were like, both according to their fashions, and according to their doors. **12** And according to the doors of the chambers, that were toward the South, was a door in the corner of the way, even the way directly before the wall toward the East, as one entereth. **13** Then said he unto me, The North chambers and the South chambers which are before the separate place, they be holy chambers wherein the Priests that approach unto the Lord, shall eat the most holy things: there shall they lay the most holy things, and the meat offering, and the sin offering, and the trespass offering: for the place is holy. **14** When the Priests enter therein, they shall not go out of the holy place into the utter court, but there they shall lay their garments wherein they minister: for they are holy, and shall put on other garments, and so shall approach to those things, which are for the people. **15** Now when he had made an end of measuring the inner house, he brought me forth toward the gate whose prospect is toward the East, and measured it round about. **16** He measured the East side with the measuring rod, five hundred reeds even with the measuring reed round about. **17** He measured also the North side, five hundred reeds, even with the measuring reed round about. **18** And he measured the South [a]side five hundred reeds with the measuring reed. **19** He turned about also to the West side, and measured five hundred reeds with the measuring reed. **20** He measured it by the four sides: it had a wall round about, five hundred reeds long, and five hundred broad to make a separation between the Sanctuary, and the profane place.

43

2 He seeth the glory of God going into the Temple, from whence it had before departed. 7 He mentioneth the idolatry of the children of Israel, for the which they were consumed and brought to naught. 9 He is commanded to call them again to repentance.

1 Afterward he brought me to the gate even the gate that turneth toward the East. **2** And behold, the glory of the God of Israel, came from out of the East, whose voice was like a noise of great waters, and the earth was made light with his glory. **3** And the vision which I saw was [1]like the vision, even as the vision that I saw [a]when I came to destroy the city: and the visions were like the vision that I saw by the river Chebar, and I fell upon my face. **4** And the [b]glory of the Lord came into the house by the way of the gate, whose prospect is toward the East. **5** So the Spirit took me up and brought me into the inner court, and behold, the glory of the Lord filled the house. **6** And I heard one speaking unto me out of the house: and there stood a man by me, **7** Which said unto me, Son of man this place is my throne, and the place of the soles of my feet, whereas I will dwell among the children of Israel forever, and the house of Israel shall no more [c]defile mine holy Name, neither they, nor their kings by their fornication, nor by the carcasses of [d]their kings in their high places. **8** Albeit they set their thresholds by my thresholds, and their posts by my posts (for there was but a wall between me and them) yet have they defiled mine holy Name with their abominations, that they have committed: wherefore I have consumed them in my wrath. **9** Now therefore let them put away their fornication, and the carcasses of their kings far from me, and I will dwell among them forever. **10** Thou son of man, show this House to the house of Israel, that they may be ashamed of their wickedness, and let them measure the pattern. **11** And if they be ashamed of all that they have done, show them the form of the house, and the pattern thereof, and the going out thereof, and the coming in thereof, and the whole fashion thereof, and all the ordinances thereof, and all the figures thereof, and all the laws thereof: and write it in their sight, that they may keep the whole fashion thereof, and all the ordinances thereof, and do them. **12** This is the [e]description of the house, It shall be upon the top of the mount: all the limits thereof round about shall be most holy. Behold, this is the description of the house. **13** And these are the measures of the Altar, after the cubits, the cubit is a cubit, and an hand breadth, even the bottom shall be a cubit, and the breadth a cubit, and the border thereof by the edge thereof round about shall be a span: and this shall be the height of the Altar. **14** And from the bottom which toucheth the ground to the lower piece shall be two cubits and the breadth one cubit, and from the little piece to the great piece shall be four cubits, and the breadth one cubit. **15** So the altar shall be four cubits, and from the altar upward shall be four horns. **16** And the altar shall be twelve cubits long and twelve broad, and foursquare in the four corners thereof. **17** And the frame shall be fourteen cubits long, and fourteen broad in the foursquare corners thereof, and the border about it shall be half a cubit, and the bottom thereof shall be a cubit about, and the steps thereof shall be turned toward the East. **18** And he said unto me, Son of man, thus saith the Lord God, These are the ordinances of the altar in the day when they shall make it to offer the burnt offering thereon, and to sprinkle blood thereon. **19** And thou shalt give to the Priests, and to the Levites that be of the seed of Zadok, which approach unto me, to minister unto me, saith the Lord God, a young bullock for a sin offering. **20** And thou shalt take of the blood thereof, and put it on the four horns of it, and on the four corners of the frame, and upon the border round about: thus shalt thou cleanse it, and reconcile

---

EZEK. 42

a. Ezek. 42:18 Or, wind.

EZEK. 43

a. Ezek. 43:3 When I prophesied the destruction of the city of the Chaldeans.

b. Ezek. 43:4 Which was departed afore, Ezek. 10:4 and 12:22.

c. Ezek. 43:7 By their idolatries.

d. Ezek. 43:7 He alludeth to Amnon and Manasseh, who were buried in their gardens near the Temple, and there had erected up monuments to their idols.

e. Ezek. 43:12 Hebrew, law.

f. Ezek. 43:26 Hebrew, fill his hand.

EZEK. 43

1. Ezek. 9:3

it. **21** Thou shalt take the bullock also of the sin offering, and burn it in the appointed place of the house without the Sanctuary. **22** But the second day thou shalt offer an he goat without blemish for a sin offering, and they shall cleanse the altar, as they did cleanse it with the bullock. **23** When thou hast made an end of cleansing it, thou shalt offer a young bullock without blemish, and a ram out of the flock without blemish. **24** And thou shalt offer them before the Lord, and the Priests shall cast salt upon them, and they shall offer them for a burnt offering unto the Lord. **25** Seven days shalt thou prepare every day an he goat for a sin offering: they shall also prepare a young bullock and a ram out of the flock without blemish. **26** Thus shall they seven days purify the altar, and cleanse it, and [f]consecrate it. **27** And when these days are expired upon the eighth day and so forth, the Priests shall make your burnt offerings upon the altar, and your peace offerings, and I will accept you, saith the Lord God.

44

He reproveth the people for their offense. 7 The uncircumcised in heart, and in the flesh. 9 Who are to be admitted to the service of the Temple, and who to be refused.

1 Then he brought me toward the gate of the outward Sanctuary, which turneth toward the East, and it was shut. **2** Then said the Lord unto me, This gate shall be [a]shut, and shall not be opened, and no man shall enter by it, because the Lord God of Israel hath entered by it, and it shall be shut. **3** It appertaineth to the Prince: the Prince himself shall sit in it to eat bread before the Lord: he shall enter by the way of the porch of that gate, and shall go out by the way of the same. **4** Then brought he me toward the North gate before the house: and when I looked, behold, the glory of the Lord, filled the house of the Lord, and I fell upon my face. **5** And the Lord said unto me, Son of man, [b]mark well and behold with thine eyes, and hear with thine ears, all that I say unto thee, concerning all the ordinances of the house of the Lord, and all the laws thereof, and mark well the entering in of the house with every going forth of the Sanctuary. **6** And thou shalt say to the rebellious, even to the house of Israel, Thus saith the Lord God, O house of Israel, ye have enough of all your abominations, **7** Seeing that ye have brought into my Sanctuary [c]strangers uncircumcised in heart, and uncircumcised in flesh, to be in my Sanctuary, to pollute mine house, when ye offer my bread, even fat, and blood: and they have broken my covenant, because of all your abominations. **8** For ye have not kept the [d]ordinances of mine holy things: but you yourselves have set others to take the charge of my Sanctuary. **9** Thus saith the Lord God, No stranger uncircumcised in heart, nor uncircumcised in flesh, shall enter into my Sanctuary, of any stranger that is among the children of Israel, **10** Neither yet the [e]Levites that are gone back from me, when Israel went astray, which went astray from me after their idols, but they shall bear their iniquity. **11** And they shall serve in my Sanctuary, and keep the gates of the House, and minister in the House: they shall slay the burnt offering and the sacrifice for the people: and they shall stand before them to serve them. **12** Because they served before their idols, and caused the house of Israel to fall into iniquity, therefore have I lifted up mine hand against them, saith the Lord God, and they shall bear their iniquity, **13** And they shall not come near unto me to do the office of the Priest unto me, neither shall they come near unto any of mine holy things in the most holy place, but they shall bear their shame, and their abominations, which they have committed. **14** And I will make them keepers of the watch of the House, for all the service thereof, and for all that shall be done therein. **15** But the Priests of the Levites, the sons of Zadok, that [f]kept the charge of my Sanctuary, when the children of Israel went astray from me, they shall come near to me to serve me, and they shall stand before me to offer me the fat and the blood, saith the Lord God. **16** They shall enter into my Sanctuary, and shall come near to my table, to serve me, and they shall keep my charge. **17** And when they shall enter in at the gates of the inner court, they shall be clothed with linen garments, and no wool shall come upon them while they serve in the gates of the inner court, and within. **18** They shall have linen bonnets upon their heads, and shall have linen breeches upon their loins: they shall not gird themselves in the sweating places. **19** But when they go forth into the utter court, even to the utter court to the people, they shall put off their garments, wherein they ministered, and lay them in the holy chambers, and they shall put on other garments: for they shall not sanctify the people with their garments. **20** They shall not also [g]shave their heads, nor suffer their locks to grow long, but round their heads. **21** [1]Neither shall any Priests drink wine when they enter into the inner court. **22** Neither shall they take for their [2]wives a widow, or her that is divorced: but they shall take maidens of the seed of the house of Israel, or a widow that hath been the widow of a Priest. **23** And they shall teach my people the difference between the holy and profane, and cause them to discern between the unclean and the clean. **24** And in controversy they shall stand to judge, and they shall judge it according to my judgments: and they shall keep my laws and my statutes in all mine assemblies, and they shall sanctify my Sabbaths. **25** [3]And they shall come at no dead person to defile themselves, except at their father or mother, or son or daughter, brother or sister, that hath had yet none husband: in these may they [h]be defiled. **26** And when he is cleansed, they shall reckon unto him seven days. **27** And when he goeth into the Sanctuary, unto the inner court, to minister in the Sanctuary, he shall offer his sin offering, saith the Lord God. **28** [4]And the Priesthood shall be their inheritance, yea, I am their inheritance: therefore shall ye give them no possession in Israel, for I am their possession. **29** They shall eat the meat offering, and the sin offering, and the trespass offering, and every dedicated thing in Israel shall be theirs. **30** [5]And all the first of all the firstborn, and every oblation, even all of every sort of your oblations shall be the Priest's. Ye shall also give unto the Priest the first of your dough, that he may cause the blessing to rest in thine house. **31** The Priests shall not eat of anything that is [6]dead, or torn, whether it be fowl or beast.

45

1 Out of the land of promise are there separate four portions, of which the first is given to the Priests and to the Temple, the second to the Levites, the third to the city, the fourth to the prince. 9 An exhortation unto the heads of Israel. 10 Of just weights and measures. 14 Of the firstfruits, etc.

1 Moreover, when ye shall divide the land for inheritance, ye shall offer an oblation unto the Lord an [a]holy portion of the land, five and twenty thousand reeds long, and ten thousand broad: this shall be holy in all the borders thereof round about. **2** Of this there shall be for the Sanctuary five hundred in length, with five hundred in breadth, all square round about, and fifty cubits round about for the suburbs thereof. **3** And of this measure shalt thou measure the length of five and twenty thousand, and the breadth of ten thousand: and in it shall be the Sanctuary, and the most holy place. **4** The holy portion of the land shall be the Priests, which minister in the Sanctuary, which came near to serve the Lord: and it shall be a place for their houses, and an holy place for the Sanctuary. **5** And in the five and twenty thousand of length, and the ten thousand of breadth shall the Levites that minister in the house, have their possession for twenty chambers. **6** Also ye shall appoint the possession of the city, five thousand broad, and five and twenty thousand long over against the oblation of the holy portion: it shall be for the whole house of Israel. **7** And a portion shall be for the prince on the one side, and on that side of the oblation of the holy portion, and of the possession of the city, even before the oblation of the holy portion, and before the possession of the city from the West corner Westward, and from the East corner Eastward, and the length shall be by one of the portions from the West border unto the East border. **8** In this land shall be his possession in Israel: and my princes shall no more oppress my people, and the rest of the land shall they give to the house of Israel, according to their tribes. **9** Thus saith the Lord God, Let it [b]suffice you, O princes of Israel: leave off cruelty and oppression, and execute judgment and justice: take away your exactions from my people, saith the Lord God. **10** Ye shall have just balances, and a true [c]Ephah, and a true Bath. **11** The Ephah and the Bath shall be equal: a Bath shall contain the tenth part of an Homer, and an Ephah the tenth part of an Homer: the equality thereof shall be after the Homer. **12** [1]And the shekel shall be twenty Gerahs, and twenty shekels, and [d]five and twenty shekels and fifteen shekels shall be your Mina. **13** This is the oblation that ye shall offer, the sixth part of an Ephah of an Homer of wheat, and ye shall give the sixth part of an Ephah of an Homer of Barley. **14** Concerning the ordinance of the oil, even of the Bath of oil, ye shall offer the tenth part of a Bath out of the Cor (ten Baths are an Homer: for ten Baths fill an Homer) **15** And one Lamb of two hundred sheep out of the fat pastures of Israel for a meat offering, and for a burnt offering and for peace offerings, to make reconciliation for them, saith the Lord God. **16** All the people of the land shall give this oblation for the prince in Israel. **17** And it shall be the prince's part to give burnt offerings, and meat offerings, and drink offerings in the solemn feasts and in the new moons, and in the Sabbaths, and in all the high feasts of the house of Israel: he shall prepare the sin offering, and the meat offering, and the burnt offering, and the peace offerings to make reconciliation for the house of Israel. **18** Thus saith the Lord God, In the first month, in the first day of the [e]month, thou shalt take a young bullock without blemish and cleanse the Sanctuary. **19** And the Priest shall take of the blood of the sin offering, and

---

EZEK. 44

- **a.** Ezek. 44:2 Meaning, from the common people, but not from the Priests, nor the Prince, read Ezek. 46:8,9.
- **b.** Ezek. 44:5 Hebrew, set thine hearts.
- **c.** Ezek. 44:7 For they had brought idolaters which were of other countries, to teach them their idolatry, Ezek. 23:40.
- **d.** Ezek. 44:8 Ye have not offered unto me according to my Law.
- **e.** Ezek. 44:10 The Levites which had committed idolatry, were put from their dignity and could not be received into the Priests' office, although they had been of the house of Aaron, but must serve in the inferior offices, as to watch and to keep the doors, read 2 Kings 23:9.
- **f.** Ezek. 44:15 Which observed the Law of God, and fell not to idolatry.
- **g.** Ezek. 44:20 As did the infidels and heathen.
- **h.** Ezek. 44:25 They may be at their burial, which was a defiling.

EZEK. 44

1. Lev. 10:9
2. Lev. 21:13,14
3. Lev. 21:1,2,11
4. Deut. 18:1 / Num. 18:20
5. Exod. 18:2 / Exod. 22:29 / Exod. 34:15 / Num. 3:13
6. Exod. 22:31 / Lev. 22:8

EZEK. 45

- **a.** Ezek. 45:1 Of all the land of Israel the Lord only requireth this portion for the Temple and for the Priests, for the city and for the Prince.
- **b.** Ezek. 45:9 The Prophet showeth that the heads must be first reformed afore any good order can be established among the people.
- **c.** Ezek. 45:10 Ephah and Bath were both of one quantity, save that Ephah contained in dry things that which Bath did in liquor, Lev. 5:11; 1 Kings 5:11.
- **d.** Ezek. 45:12 That is, three-score shekels make a weight called Mina, for he joineth these three parts to a Mina.
- **e.** Ezek. 45:18 Which was Nisan, containing part of March and part of April.
- **f.** Ezek. 45:19 Or, court.

put it upon the posts of the house, and upon the four [f]corners of the frame of the altar, and upon the posts of the gate of the inner court. **20** And so shalt thou do the seventh day of the month, for everyone that hath erred, and for him that is deceived: so shall you reconcile the house. **21** [2]In the first month in the fourteenth day of the month, ye shall have the Passover, a feast of seven days, and ye shall eat unleavened bread. **22** And upon that day, shall the prince prepare for himself and for all the people of the land, a bullock for a sin offering. **23** And in the seven days of the feast he shall make a burnt offering to the Lord, even of seven bullocks, and seven rams without blemish daily for seven days, and an he goat daily for a sin offering. **24** And he shall prepare a meat offering of an Ephah for a bullock, an Ephah for a ram, and an [g]Hin of oil for an Ephah. **25** In the seventh month, in the fifteenth day of the month, shall he do the like in the feast for seven days, according to the sin offering, according to the burnt offering, and according to the meat offering, and according to the oil.

46

1 The sacrifices of the Sabbath and of the new moon. 8 Through which doors they must go in, or come out of the Temple, etc.

1 Thus saith the Lord God, The gate of the inner court, that turneth toward the East, shall be shut the six working days: but on the Sabbath it shall be opened, and in the day of the new moon it shall be opened. **2** And the prince shall enter by the way of the porch of that gate without, and shall stand by the post of the gate, and the Priests shall make his burnt offering, and his peace offerings, and he shall worship at the threshold of the gate: after he shall go forth, but the gate shall not be shut till the evening. **3** Likewise the people of the land shall worship at the entry of this gate before the Lord on the Sabbaths, and in the new moons. **4** And the burnt offering that the prince shall offer unto the Lord on the Sabbath day, shall be six lambs without blemish, and a ram without blemish. **5** And the meat offering shall be an Ephah for a ram: and the meat offering for the lambs [a]a gift of his hand, and an Hin of oil to an Ephah. **6** And in the day of the new moon it shall be a young bullock without blemish, and six lambs and a ram: they shall be without blemish. **7** And he shall prepare a meat offering, even an Ephah for a bullock, and an Ephah for a ram, and for the lambs [b]according as his hand shall bring, and an Hin of oil to an Ephah. **8** And when the prince shall enter, he shall go in by the way of the porch of that gate, and he shall go forth by the way thereof. **9** But when the people of the land shall come before the Lord in the solemn feasts, he that entereth in by the way of the North gate to worship, shall go out by the way of the South gate: and he that entereth by the way of the South gate, shall go forth by the way of the North gate: he shall not return by the way of the gate whereby he came in, but they shall go forth over against it. **10** And the prince shall be in the midst of them: he shall go in when they go in, and when they go forth, they shall go forth together. **11** And in the feasts, and in the solemnities the meat offering shall be an Ephah to a bullock, and an Ephah to a ram, and to the lambs, the gift of his hand, and an Hin of oil to an Ephah. **12** Now when the prince shall make a free burnt offering, or peace offerings freely unto the Lord, one shall then open him the gate that turneth toward the East, and he shall make his burnt offering and his peace offerings, as he did on the Sabbath day: after he shall go forth, and when he is gone forth, one shall shut the gate. **13** Thou shalt daily make a burnt offering unto the Lord of a lamb of one year, without blemish: thou shalt do it every morning. **14** And thou shalt prepare a meat offering for it every morning, the sixth part of an Ephah, and the third part of an Hin of oil, to mingle with the fine flour: this meat offering shall be continually by a perpetual ordinance unto the Lord. **15** Thus shall they prepare the lamb, and the meat offering, and the oil every morning, for a continual burnt offering. **16** Thus saith the Lord God, If the prince give a gift of his inheritance unto any of his sons, it shall be his sons, and it shall be their possession by inheritance. **17** But if he give a gift of his inheritance to one of his servants, then it shall be his to the [c]year of liberty: after, it shall return to the Prince, but his inheritance shall remain to his sons for them. **18** Moreover the prince shall not [d]take of the people's inheritance, nor thrust them out of their possession: but he shall cause his sons to inherit of his own possession, that my people be not scattered every man from his possession. **19** After he brought me through the entry, which was at the side of the gate, into the holy chambers of the Priests, which stood toward the North: and behold, there was a place at the West side of them. **20** Then said he unto me, This is the place where the Priests shall seethe the trespass offering and the sin offering, where they shall bake the meat offering, that they should not bear them into the utter court, [e]to sanctify the people. **21** Then he brought me forth into the utter court, and caused me to go by the four corners of the court: and behold, in every corner of the court there was a court. **22** In the four corners of the court there were courts joined of forty cubits long, and thirty broad: these four corners were of one measure. **23** And there went a wall about them, even about those four, and kitchens were made under the walls round about. **24** Then said he unto me, This is the kitchen where the ministers of the house shall seethe the sacrifice of the people.

47

1 The vision of the waters that came out of the Temple. 13 The coasts of the land of promise, and the division thereof by tribes.

1 Afterward he brought me unto the door of the house: and behold, [a]waters issued out from under the threshold of the house Eastward: for the forefront of the house stood toward the East, and the waters ran down from under the right side of the house, at the South side of the altar. **2** Then brought he me out toward the North gate, and led me about by the way without unto the utter gate by the way that turneth Eastward: and behold, there came forth waters on the right side **3** And when the man that had the line in his hand, went forth Eastward, he measured a thousand cubits, and he brought me through the waters: the waters were to the ankles. **4** Again he measured a thousand and brought me through the waters: the waters were to the knees: again he measured a thousand, and brought me through: the waters were to the loins. **5** Afterward he measured a thousand, and it was a [b]river, that I could not pass over: for the waters were risen, and the waters did flow, as a river that could not be passed over. **6** And he said unto me, Son of man, hast thou seen this? Then he brought me, and caused me to return to the brink of the river: **7** Now when I turned, behold, at the brink of the river were very many [c]trees on the one side and on the other. **8** Then said he unto me, These waters issue out toward the East country, and run down into the plain, and shall go into one [d]sea: they shall run into another sea, and the waters shall be wholesome. **9** And everything that liveth, which moveth, wheresoever the rivers shall come, shall live, and there shall be a very great multitude of fish, because these waters shall come thither: [e]for they shall be wholesome, and everything shall live whither the river cometh. **10** And then the [f]fishers shall stand upon it, and from En Gedi even unto [g]En Eglaim, they shall spread out their nets: for their fish shall be according to their kinds, as the fish of [h]the main sea, exceeding many. **11** But [i]the miry places thereof, and the marshes thereof shall not be wholesome: they shall be made salt pits. **12** And by this river upon the brink thereof, on this side, and on that side shall grow all [j]fruitful trees, whose leaf shall not fade, neither shall the fruit thereof fail: it shall bring forth new fruit according to his months, because their waters run out of the Sanctuary: and the fruit thereof shall be meat, and the leaf thereof shall be for [k]medicine. **13** Thus saith the Lord God, This shall be the border, whereby ye shall inherit the land according to the twelve tribes [1]of Israel: Joseph shall have two portions. **14** And ye shall inherit it, one as well as another: [2]concerning the which I lifted up mine hand to give it unto your fathers, and this land shall fall unto you for inheritance. **15** And this shall be the border [l]of the land toward the North side, from the main sea toward Hethlon, as men go to Zedad: **16** Hamath, Berothah, Sibraim, which is between the border of Damascus, and the border of Hamath, and Hazar, Hatticon, which is by the coast of Hauran. **17** And the border from the sea shall be Hazar, Enan, and the border of Damascus, and the residue of the North Northward, and the border of Hamath: so shall be the North part. **18** But the East side shall ye measure from Hauran, and from Damascus, and from Gilead, and from the land of Israel by Jordan, and from the border unto the East sea: and so shall be the East part. **19** And the South side shall be toward Teman, from Tamar to the waters of [m]Meriboth in Kadesh, and the river to the main sea: so shall be the South part toward Teman. **20** The West part also shall be the great sea from the border, till a man come over against Hamath: this shall be the west part. **21** So shall ye divide this land unto you, according to the tribes of Israel. **22** And you shall divide it by lot for an inheritance unto you, and to the strangers that dwell among you, which shall beget children among you, and they shall be unto you, as born in the country among the children of Israel, [n]they shall part inheritance with you in the midst of the tribes of Israel. **23** And in what tribe the stranger dwelleth, there shall ye give him his inheritance, saith the Lord God.

---

g. Ezek. 45:24 Read Exod. 29:40.

EZEK. 45

1. Exod. 30:13 / Lev. 27:25 / Num. 3:47 **2.** Exod. 22 / Lev. 23:5

EZEK. 46

a. Ezek. 46:5 That is, as much as he will.
b. Ezek. 46:7 Meaning, as he shall think good.
c. Ezek. 46:17 Which was at the Jubilee, Lev. 25:9.
d. Ezek. 46:18 But be content with that portion that God hath assigned him, as Ezek. 45:8.
e. Ezek. 46:20 That the people should not have to do with those things which appertain to the Lord, and think it lawful for them to eat them.

EZEK. 47

a. Ezek. 47:1 Whereby are meant the spiritual graces that should be given to the Church under the kingdom of Christ.
b. Ezek. 47:5 Signifying that the graces of God should never decrease, but ever abound in his Church.
c. Ezek. 47:7 Meaning, the multitude of them that should be refreshed by the spiritual waters.
d. Ezek. 47:8 Showing that the abundance of these graces should be so great, that all the world should be full thereof, which is here meant by the Persian sea, or Genezareth, and the sea called Mediterranean, Zech. 14:8.
e. Ezek. 47:9 The waters which of nature are salt, and unwholesome shall be made sweet and comfortable.
f. Ezek. 47:10 Signifying, that when God bestoweth his mercies in such abundance, the ministers shall by their preaching win many.
g. Ezek. 47:10 Which were cities at the corners of the salt or dead sea.
h. Ezek. 47:10 They shall be here of all sorts, and in as great abundance as in the great Ocean where they are bred.
i. Ezek. 47:11 That is, the wicked and reprobate.
j. Ezek. 47:12 Or, tree for meat.
k. Ezek. 47:12 Or, for bruises and sores.
l. Ezek. 47:15 By the land of promise he signifieth the spiritual land whereof this was a figure.
m. Ezek. 47:19 Or, strife.
n. Ezek. 47:22 Meaning, that in this spiritual kingdom there should be no difference between Jew nor Gentile, but that all should be partakers of this inheritance in their head Christ.

EZEK. 47

1. Gen. 48:22 **2.** Gen. 12:7 / Gen. 13:15 / Gen 15:18 / Gen. 26:4 / Deut. 34:4

48

The lots of the tribes. 9 The parts of the possession of the Priests, of the Temple, of the Levites, of the city, and of the Prince are rehearsed.

1 Now these are the names of the [a]tribes. From the North side, to the coast toward Hethlon as one goeth to Hamath, Hazar, Enan, and the border of Damascus Northward the coast of Hamath, even from the East side to the West shall be a portion for Dan. **2** And by the border of Dan from the East side unto the West side, a portion for Asher. **3** And by the border of Asher from the East part even unto the West part, a portion for Naphtali. **4** And by the border of Naphtali from the East quarter unto the West side, a portion for Manasseh. **5** And by the border of Manasseh, from the East side unto the West side, a portion for Ephraim. **6** And by the border of Ephraim, from the East part even unto the West part, a portion for Reuben. **7** And by the border of Reuben, from the East quarter unto the West quarter, a portion for Judah. **8** And by the border of Judah from the East part unto the West part [b]shall be the offering which they shall offer of five and twenty thousand reeds broad, and of length as one of the other parts, from the East side unto the West side, and the Sanctuary shall be in the midst of it. **9** The oblation that ye shall offer unto the Lord, shall be of five and twenty thousand long, and of ten thousand the breadth. **10** And for them, even for the Priests shall be this holy oblation, toward the North five and twenty thousand long, and toward the West, ten thousand broad, and toward the East ten thousand broad, and toward the South five and twenty thousand long, and the Sanctuary of the Lord shall be in the midst thereof. **11** It shall be for the Priests that are sanctified of the sons of [1]Zadok, which have kept my charge, which went not astray, when the children of Israel went astray, as the Levites went astray. **12** Therefore this oblation of the land that is offered shall be theirs, as a thing most holy by the border of the Levites. **13** And over against the border of the Priests the Levites shall have five and twenty thousand long, and ten thousand broad: all the length shall be five and twenty thousand, and the breadth ten thousand. **14** And they shall not sell of it, neither change it, nor alienate the firstfruits of the land: for it is holy unto the Lord. **15** And the five thousand that are left in the breadth over against the five and twenty thousand, shall be a profane place for the city, for housing, and for suburbs, and the city shall be in the midst thereof. **16** And these shall be the measures thereof, the North part five hundred and four thousand, and the South part [c]five hundred and four thousand, and the East part five hundred and four thousand, and the West part five hundred and four thousand. **17** And the suburbs of the city shall be toward the North two hundred and fifty, and toward the South two hundred and fifty, and toward the East two hundred and fifty, and toward the West two hundred and fifty. **18** And the residue in length over against the oblation of the holy portion shall be ten thousand Eastward, and ten thousand Westward: and it shall be over against the oblation of the holy portion, and the increase thereof shall be for food unto them that serve in the city. **19** And they that serve in the city, shall be of all the tribes of Israel that shall serve therein. **20** All the oblation shall be five and twenty thousand with [d]five and twenty thousand: you shall offer this oblation foursquare for the Sanctuary, and for the possession of the city. **21** And the residue shall be for the prince on the one side and on the other of the oblation of the Sanctuary, and of the possession of the city, over against the five and twenty thousand of the oblation toward the East border, and Westward over against the five and twenty thousand toward the West border, over against shall be for the portion of the prince: this shall be the holy oblation, and the house of the Sanctuary shall be in the midst thereof. **22** Moreover, from the possession of the Levites, and from the possession of the city, that which is in the midst shall be the prince's: between the border [e]of Judah, and between the border of Benjamin shall be the Princes. **23** And the rest of the tribes shall be thus: from the East part unto the West part, Benjamin shall be a portion. **24** And by the border of Benjamin, from the East side unto the West side, Simeon a portion. **25** And by the border of Simeon from the East part unto the West part, Issachar a portion. **26** And by the border of Issachar, from the East side unto the West, Zebulun a portion. **27** And by the border of Zebulun, from the East part unto the West part, Gad a portion. **28** And by the border of Gad at the South side, toward [f]Temath, the border shall be even from [g]Tamar, unto the waters of Meribah in Kadesh, and to the [h]river, that runneth into the main sea. **29** This is the land, which ye shall distribute unto the tribes of Israel for inheritance, and these are their portions, saith the Lord God. **30** And these are the bounds of the city, on the North side five hundred, and four thousand measures. **31** And the gates of the city shall be after the names of the tribes of Israel, the gates Northward, one gate of Reuben, one gate of Judah, and one gate of Levi. **32** And at the East side five hundred and four thousand, and three gates, and one gate of Joseph, one gate of Benjamin, and one gate of Dan. **33** And at the South side, five hundred and four thousand measures, and three ports, one gate of Simeon, one gate of Issachar, and one gate of Zebulun. **34** At the West side, five hundred and four thousand, with their three gates, one gate of Gad, one gate of Asher, and one gate of Naphtali. **35** It was round about eighteen thousand measures, and the name of the city from that day shall be, [i]The Lord is there.

EZEK. 48

a. Ezek. 48:1 The tribes after that they entered into the land under Joshua, divided the land somewhat otherwise than is here set forth by this vision.
b. Ezek. 48:8 That is, the portion of the ground which they shall separate and appoint to the Lord, which shall be divided into three parts, for the Priests, for the Prince, and for the city.
c. Ezek. 48:16 Meaning, that it should be square.
d. Ezek. 48:20 Every way it shall be five and twenty thousand.
e. Ezek. 48:22 So that Judah was on the North side of the Prince's and Levites' portions, and Benjamin on the South side.
f. Ezek. 48:28 Which is here taken for Edom.
g. Ezek. 48:28 Which was Jericho the city of palm trees.
h. Ezek. 48:28 Meaning, Nile that runneth into the Sea, called Mediterranean.
i. Ezek. 48:35 Hebrew, Jehovah Shammah.

EZEK. 48

1. Ezek. 44:5

DANIEL

1 *1 The captivity of Jehoiakim king of Judah. 4 The king chooseth certain young men of the Jews to learn his law. 5 They have the king's ordinary appointed, 8 but they abstain from it.*

1 In the [a]third year of the reign of Jehoiakim king of Judah, came Nebuchadnezzar King of Babel unto Jerusalem and besieged it. **2** And the Lord gave Jehoiakim king of Judah into his hand with part of the vessels of the house of God, which he carried into the land of [b]Shinar, to the house of his god, and he brought the vessels into his god's treasury. **3** And the King spake unto [c]Ashpenaz the master of his [d]Eunuchs, that he should bring certain of the children of Israel, of the [e]King's seed, and of the princes: **4** Children in whom was no blemish, but well [f]favored, and instruct in all wisdom, and well seen in knowledge, and able to utter knowledge, and such as were able to stand in the king's palace, and whom they might [g]teach the learning, and the tongue of the Chaldeans. **5** And the king appointed them provision every day of a [h]portion of the king's meat, and of the wine, which he drank, so nourishing them [i]three years, that at the end thereof, they might stand [j]before the king. **6** Now among these were certain of the children of Judah, Daniel, Hananiah, Mishael and Azariah. **7** Unto whom the chief of the Eunuchs [k]gave other names: for he called Daniel, Belteshazzar, and Hananiah, Shadrach, and Mishael, Meshach, and Azariah, Abednego. **8** But Daniel had determined in his heart, that he would not [l]defile himself with the portion of the King's meat, nor with the wine which he drank: therefore he required the chief of the Eunuchs that he might not defile himself. **9** (Now God had brought Daniel into favor, and tender love with the chief of the Eunuchs.) **10** And the chief of the Eunuchs said unto Daniel, [m]I fear my lord the King, who hath appointed your meat and your drink: therefore if he see your faces worse liking than the other children which are of your sort, then shall you make me lose mine head unto the King. **11** Then said Daniel to Melzar, whom the chief of the Eunuchs had set over Daniel, Hananiah, Mishael, and Azariah, **12** Prove thy servants, I beseech thee, [n]ten days, and let them give us [o]pulse to eat, and water to drink. **13** Then let our countenances be looked upon before thee, and the countenances of the children that eat of the portion of the King's meat: and as thou seest, deal with thy servants. **14** So he consented to them in this matter, an proved them ten days. **15** And at the end of ten days, their [p]countenances appeared fairer, and in [q]better liking than all the children's, which did eat the portion of the King's meat. **16** Thus Melzar took away the portion of their meat, and the wine that they should drink, and gave them pulse. **17** As for these four children, God gave them knowledge, and understanding in all learning [r]and wisdom: also he gave Daniel understanding of all [s]visions and dreams. **18** Now when the time [t]was expired, that the King had appointed to bring them in, the chief of the Eunuchs brought them before Nebuchadnezzar. **19** And the King communed with them: and among them all was found none like Daniel, Hananiah, Mishael, and Azariah: therefore stood they before the king. **20** And in all matters of wisdom, and understanding that the King enquired of them, he found them ten times better than all the enchanters and astrologians that were in all his realm. **21** And Daniel was unto [u]the first year of king Cyrus.

2 *1 The dreams of Nebuchadnezzar. 13 The king commandeth all the wise men of Babylon to be slain, because they could not interpret his dream. 16 Daniel requireth time to solute the question. 24 Daniel is brought unto the king, and showeth him his dream, and the interpretation thereof. 44 Of the everlasting kingdom of Christ.*

1 And in the [a]second year of the reign of Nebuchadnezzar, Nebuchadnezzar dreamed [b]dreams wherewith his spirit was [c]troubled, and his [d]sleep was upon him. **2** Then the king commanded to call the enchanters, and the astrologians, and the sorcerers, and the [e]Chaldeans for to show the king his dreams: so they came and stood before the King. **3** And the king said unto them, I have dreamed a dream, and my spirit was troubled to know the dream. **4** Then spake the Chaldeans to the king in the [f]Aramite's language, O king, live forever: show thy servants thy dream, and we shall show the interpretation. **5** And the King answered and said to the Chaldeans, The thing is gone from me. If ye will not make me understand the dream with the interpretation thereof, ye [g]shall be drawn in pieces, and your houses shall be made a jakes. **6** But if ye declare the dream and the interpretation thereof, ye shall receive of me gifts and rewards, and great honor: therefore show me the dream and the interpretation of it. **7** They answered again, and said, Let the king show [h]his servants the dream, and we will declare the interpretation thereof. **8** Then the king answered, and said, I know certainly that ye [i]would gain the time, because ye see the thing is gone from me. **9** But if ye will not declare me the dream, there is but one judgment for you: for ye have prepared lying and corrupt words, to speak before me till the time be changed: therefore tell me the dream, that I may know, if ye can declare me the interpretation thereof. **10** Then the Chaldeans answered before the king, and said, There is no man upon earth that can declare the king's matter: yea, there is neither King nor Prince nor lord that asked such things at an enchanter, or astrologian, or Chaldean. **11** For it is a rare thing that the king requireth, and there is none other that can declare it before the king, except the gods whose dwelling is not with flesh. **12** For this cause the king was angry and in great fury, and commanded to destroy all the wise men of Babel. **13** And when sentence was given, the wise men were slain: and they [j]sought Daniel and his fellows to be put to death. **14** Then Daniel answered with

---

DAN. 1

a. Dan. 1:1 Read 2 Kings 24:1 and Jer. 25:1.
b. Dan. 1:2 Which was a plain by Babylon, where was the Temple of their great god, and is here taken for Babylon.
c. Dan. 1:3 Who was as master of the wards.
d. Dan. 1:3 He calleth them Eunuchs whom the King nourished and brought up to be rulers of other countries afterward.
e. Dan. 1:3 His purpose was to keep them as hostages, and that he might show himself victorious, and also by their good entreaty and learning of his religion, they might favor rather him than the Jews, and so to be able to serve him as governors in their land: moreover by this means the Jews might be better kept in subjection, fearing otherwise to procure hurt to these noble men.
f. Dan. 1:4 The King required three things, that they should be of noble birth, that they should be witty and learned, and that they should be of a strong and comely nature, that they might do him better service: this he did for his own commodity, therefore it is not to praise his liberality: yet in this he is worthy praise, that he esteemed learning, and knew that it was a necessary means to govern by.
g. Dan. 1:4 That they might forget their own religion, and country fashions to serve him the better to his purpose: yet it is not to be thought that Dan. did learn any knowledge that was not godly: in all points he refused the abuse of things and superstition, insomuch that he would not eat the meat which the King appointed him, but was content to learn the knowledge of natural things.
h. Dan. 1:5 That by their good entertainment they might learn to forget the mediocrity of their own people.
i. Dan. 1:5 To the intent that in this time they might both learn the manners of the Chaldeans, and also their tongue.
j. Dan. 1:5 As well to serve at the table, as in other offices.
k. Dan. 1:7 That they might altogether forget their religion: for the Jews gave their children names, which might ever put them in remembrance of some point of religion: therefore this was a great tentation and a sign of servitude, which they were not able to resist.
l. Dan. 1:8 Not that he thought any religion to be in the meat or drink, (for afterward he did eat) but because the king should not entice him by this sweet poison to forget his religion and accustomed sobriety, and that in his meat and drink he might daily remember of what people he was: and Dan. bringeth this in to show how God from the beginning assisted him with his Spirit, and at length called him to be a Prophet.
m. Dan. 1:10 He supposed they did this for their religion, which was contrary to the Babylonians, and therefore herein he representeth them, which are of no religion: for neither he would condemn theirs, nor maintain his own.
n. Dan. 1:12 Meaning, that within this space he might have the trial, and that no man should be able to discern it: and thus he spake, being moved by the Spirit of God.
o. Dan. 1:12 Not that it was a thing abominable to eat dainty meats, and to drink wine, as both before and after they did, but if they should have hereby been won to the King, and have refused their own religion, that meat and drink had been accursed.
p. Dan. 1:15 This bare feeding and that also of Moses, when he fled from the court of Egypt, declareth that we must live in such sobriety as God doth call us unto, seeing he will make it more profitable unto us than all dainties: for his blessing only sufficeth.
q. Dan. 1:15 Hebrew, fatter in flesh.
r. Dan. 1:17 Meaning, in the liberal sciences, and natural knowledge, and not in the magical arts which are forbidden, Deut. 18:11.
s. Dan. 1:17 So that he only was a Prophet and none of the others: for by dreams and visions God appeared to his Prophets, Num. 12:6
t. Dan. 1:18 Of the three years above mentioned, verse 5.
u. Dan. 1:21 That is, he was esteemed in Babylon as a Prophet so long as that commonwealth stood.

DAN. 2

a. Dan. 2:1 The father and the son were both called by this name, so that this is meant of the son, when he reigned alone: for he reigned also after a sort with his father.
b. Dan. 2:1 Not that he had many dreams, but because many matters were contained in this dream.
c. Dan. 2:1 Because it was so rare and strange a dream: that he had not had the like.
d. Dan. 2:1 He was so heavy with sleep, that he began to sleep again. Some read, and his sleep was broken from him.
e. Dan. 2:2 For all these Astrologers and sorcerers called themselves by this name of honor, as though all the wisdom and knowledge of the country depended upon them, and that all other countries were void of the same.
f. Dan. 2:4 That is, in the Syrian tongue which differed not much from the Chaldeans, save it seemed to be more eloquent, and therefore the learned used to speak it, as the Jewish writers do to this day.
g. Dan. 2:5 This is a just reward of their arrogance (which vaunted of themselves that they had the knowledge of all things) that they should be proved fools, and that to their perpetual shame and confusion.
h. Dan. 2:7 Herein appeared their ignorance, that notwithstanding their brags, yet were they not able to tell the dream, except he entered them into the matter, and therefore they would pretend knowledge where was but mere ignorance, and so as deluders of the people, they were worthy to die.
i. Dan. 2:8 Hebrew, redeem the time.
j. Dan. 2:13 Which declareth that God would not have his servant joined in the company of these sorcerers and Astrologers, whose arts were wicked, and therefore justly ought to die, though the king did it upon a rage and no zeal.
k. Dan. 2:14 Or, the captain of the guards.

counsel and wisdom to Arioch the king's [k]chief steward, which was gone forth to
put to death the wise men of Babel. **15** Yea, he answered and said unto Arioch
the king's captain, Why is the sentence so hasty from the king? Then Arioch decla-
red the thing to Daniel. **16** So Daniel went and desired the king that he would
give him leisure, and that he would show the king the interpretation there-
of. **17** Then Daniel went to his house, and showed the matter to Hananiah, Mi-
shael, and Azariah his companions, **18** That they should beseech the God of
heaven for grace in this secret, that Daniel and his fellows should not perish with
the rest of the wise men of Babel. **19** Then was the secret revealed unto Daniel
in a vision by night: therefore Daniel praised the God of heaven. **20** And Daniel
answered and said, [1]The Name of God be praised forever and ever: for wisdom and
strength are his. **21** And he changeth the times and seasons: he taketh away kin-
gs: he setteth up kings: he giveth wisdom unto the wise, and understanding to tho-
se that understand. **22** He discovereth the deep and secret things: he knoweth
what is in darkness, and the [l]light dwelleth with him. **23** I thank thee and praise
thee, O thou God of my [m]fathers, that thou hast given me wisdom and [n]strength,
and hast showed me now the thing that we desired of thee: for thou hast declared
unto us the king's matter. **24** Therefore Daniel went unto Arioch, whom the
King had ordained to destroy the wise men of Babel: he went and said thus unto
him, Destroy not [o]the wise men of Babel, but bring me before the king, and I will
declare unto the king the interpretation. **25** Then Arioch brought Daniel before
the king in all haste, and said thus unto him, I have found a man of the children of
Judah that were brought captives, that will declare unto the king the interpreta-
tion. **26** Then answered the king, and said unto Daniel, whose name was Belte-
shazzar, Art thou able to show me the dream which I have seen, and the interpre-
tation thereof? **27** Daniel answered in the presence of the king, and said, The
secret which the king hath demanded, can neither the wise, the astrologians, the
enchanters, nor the soothsayers declare unto the king. **28** But there is a God in
[p]heaven that revealeth secrets, and showeth the king Nebuchadnezzar what shall be
in the latter days. Thy dream, and the things which thou hast seen in thine head
upon thy bed, is this: **29** O king, when thou wast in thy bed, thoughts came into
thy mind, what should come to pass hereafter, and he that revealeth secrets, telleth
thee what shall come. **30** As [q]for me, this secret is not showed me for any wi-
sdom that I have more than any other living, but only to show the king the inter-
pretation, and that thou mightest know the thoughts of thine heart. **31** O king,
thou sawest, and behold, there was a great image: this great image whose glory was
so excellent, stood before thee, and the form therefore was terrible. **32** This ima-
ge's head was of fine [r]gold, his breast, and his arms of silver, his belly and his thighs
of brass, **33** His legs of iron, and his feet were part of iron, and part of
clay. **34** Thou beheldest it till a stone was cut without hands, which smote the
image upon his feet, that were of iron and clay, and brake them to pieces. **35** Then
was the iron, the clay, the brass, the silver and the gold broken all together, and
became like the chaff of the summer flowers, and the wind carried them away, that
no place was found for them: and the stone that smote the image, became a great
mountain, and filled the whole earth. **36** This is the dream, and we will declare
before the king the interpretation thereof. **37** O king, thou art a king of kings:
for the God of heaven hath given thee a kingdom, power, and strength, and
glory. **38** And in all places where the children of men dwell, the beasts of the
field, and the fowls of the heaven hath he given into thine hand, and hath made
thee ruler over them all: thou art [s]this head of gold. **39** And after thee shall rise
another kingdom, [t]inferior to thee, of silver, and another [u]third kingdom shall be
of brass, which shall bear rule over all the earth. **40** And the fourth kingdom
shall be strong as iron: for as iron breaketh in pieces, and subdueth all things, and
as iron bruiseth all these things, so shall it break in [v]pieces, and bruise all. **41** Whe-
reas thou sawest the feet and toes, part of potter's clay, and part of iron: the king-
dom shall be [w]divided, but there shall be in it of the strength of the iron, as thou
sawest the iron mixed with the clay, and earth. **42** And as the toes of the feet were
part of iron, and part of clay, so shall the kingdom be partly strong, and partly
broken. **43** And whereas thou sawest iron mixed with clay and earth, they shall
mingle themselves with [x]the seed of men: but they shall not join one with another,
as iron cannot be mixed with clay. **44** And in the days of these kings, shall the
God of heaven set up a kingdom, which [y]shall never be destroyed: and this king-
dom shall not be given to another people, but it shall break, and destroy all these
kingdoms, and it shall stand forever. **45** Whereas thou sawest, that the [z]stone
was cut of the mountain without hands, and that it brake in pieces the iron, the
brass, the clay, the silver, and the gold: so the great God hath showed the king, what
shall come to pass hereafter, and the dream is true, and the interpretation thereof
is sure. **46** Then the king Nebuchadnezzar fell upon his face, and [aa]bowed him-
self unto Daniel, and commanded that they should offer meat offerings, and sweet
odors unto him. **47** Also the King answered unto Daniel, and said, I know of a
truth that your [ab]God is a God of gods, and the Lord of kings, and the revealer of
secrets, seeing thou couldest open this secret. **48** So the king made Daniel a great
man, and gave him many and great [ac]gifts. He made him governor over the whole
province of Babel, and chief of the rulers, and above all the wise men of Ba-
bel. **49** Then Daniel [ad]made request to the King, and he set Shadrach, Meshach,
and Abednego over the charge of the province of Babel: but Daniel sat in the [ae]gate
of the king.

3

1 The king setteth up a golden image. 8 Certain are accused because they despised the king's commandment, and are put into a burning oven. 15 By belief in God they are delivered from the fire. 25 Nebuchadnezzar confesseth the power of God after the sight of the miracle.

1 Nebuchadnezzar the king made [a]an image of gold, whose height was thre-
escore cubits, and the breadth thereof six cubits: he set it up in the plain of Dura,
in the province of Babel. **2** Then Nebuchadnezzar the king sent forth to gather
together the nobles, the princes and the dukes, the judges, the receivers, the coun-
selors, the officers, and all the governors of the provinces, that they should come to
the [b]dedication of the image, which Nebuchadnezzar the [c]King had set up. **3** So
the nobles, princes, and dukes, the judges, the receivers, the counselors, the offi-
cers, and all the governors of the provinces were assembled unto the dedicating of
the image that Nebuchadnezzar the King had set up and they stood before the ima-
ge which Nebuchadnezzar had set up. **4** Then an herald cried aloud, Be it known
to you, O people, [d]nations, and languages, **5** That when ye hear the sound of the
cornet, trumpet, harp, sackbut, psaltery, dulcimer, and all instruments of music, ye
fall down, and worship the golden image, that Nebuchadnezzar the king hath set

---

l. Dan. 2:22 He showeth that man hath neither wisdom nor knowledge, but very dark blindness and ignorance of himself: for it cometh only of God, that man understandeth anything.
m. Dan. 2:23 To whom thou madest thy promise, and who lived in thy fear: whereby he excludeth all other gods.
n. Dan. 2:23 Meaning, power to interpret it.
o. Dan. 2:24 Whereby appeareth that many were slain, as verse 13, and the rest at Dan.'s offer were preserved on condition: not that Dan. favored their wicked profession, but that he had respect to equity, because the King proceeded according to his wicked affection, and not considering if their science were lawful or no.
p. Dan. 2:28 He affirmeth that man by reason and art is not able to attain to the cause of God's secrets, but the understanding only thereof must come of God: whereby he smiteth the king with a certain fear and reverence of God, that he might be the more apt to receive the high mysteries, that should be revealed.
q. Dan. 2:30 Because he had said that God only must reveal the signification of this dream, the King might have asked, why Dan. did enterprise to interpret it, and therefore he showeth that he was but God's minister and had no gifts, but such as God had given him to set forth his glory.
r. Dan. 2:32 By gold, silver, brass and iron, are meant the Chaldean, Persian, Macedonian and Roman kingdoms, which should successively rule all the world till Christ (which is here called the stone) come himself, and destroy the last: and this was to assure the Jews, that their affliction should not end with the empire of the Chaldeans, but that they should patiently abide the coming of Messiah, which should be at the end of this fourth monarchy.
s. Dan. 2:38 Dan. leaveth out the kingdom of the Assyrians, which was before the Babylonian, both because it was not a Monarchy and general empire, and also because he would declare the things that were to come, to the coming of Christ, for the comfort of the elect among these wonderful alterations, and he calleth the Babylonian kingdom the golden head, because in respect of the other three, it was the best, and yet it was of itself wicked and cruel.
t. Dan. 2:39 Meaning, the Persians which were not inferior in dignity, power, and riches, but were worse touching ambition, cruelty, and all kind of vice, showing that the world should grow worse and worse, till it was restored by Christ.
u. Dan. 2:39 That is, of the Macedonians shall be of brass, not alluding to the hardness thereof, but to the vileness in respect of silver.
v. Dan. 2:40 That is, the Roman empire shall subdue all these other aforenamed, which after Alexander were divided into the Macedonians, Grecians, Syrians and Egyptians.
w. Dan. 2:41 They shall have civil wars, and continual discords among themselves.
x. Dan. 2:43 They shall by marriages and affinities think to make themselves strong: yet shall they never be joined in hearts.
y. Dan. 2:44 His purpose is to show, that all the kingdoms of the world are transitory, and that the kingdom of Christ shall only remain forever.
z. Dan. 2:45 Meaning Christ, who was sent of God, and not set up by man, whose kingdom at the beginning should be small and without beauty to man's judgment, but should at length grow and fill the whole earth, which he calleth a great mountain, as verse 35. And this kingdom which is not only referred to the person of Christ, but also to the whole body of his Church, and to every member thereof, shall be eternal: for the Spirit that is in them is life eternal, Rom. 8:10.
aa. Dan. 2:46 Though this humbling of the king seemed to deserve commendation, yet because he joined God's honor with the Prophet's, it is to be reproved, and Dan. herein erred, if he suffered it: but it is credible that Dan. admonished him of his fault, and did not suffer it.
ab. Dan. 2:47 This confession was but a sudden motion, as it was also in Pharaoh, Exod. 9:28, but his heart was not touched, as appeared soon afterward.
ac. Dan. 2:48 Not that the Prophet was desirous of gifts or honor, but because by this means he might relieve his poor brethren, which were grievously oppressed in this their captivity, and also he received them, lest he should offend this cruel king, which willingly gave them.
ad. Dan. 2:49 He did not this for their private profit: but that the whole Church, which was then there in affliction, might have some release and ease by this benefit.
ae. Dan. 2:49 Meaning, that either he was a judge, or that he had the whole authority, so than none could be admitted to the king's presence, but by him.

DAN. 2
1. Ps. 113:2 / Ps. 115:18

DAN. 3
a. Dan. 3:1 Under pretence of religion, and holiness in making an image to his idol Bel, he sought his own ambition and vain glory: and this declareth that he was not toucheth with the true fear of God before but that he confessed him on a sudden motion as the wicked when they are overcome with the greatness of his works. The Greek interpreters write, that this was done eighteen years after the dream, and as may appear, the King feared lest the Jews by their religion, should have altered the state of his commonwealth, and therefore he meant to bring all to one kind of religion, and so rather sought his own quietness than God's glory.
b. Dan. 3:2 Showing that the idol is not known for an idol so long as he is with workmen: but when the ceremonies and customs are recited and used, and the consent of the people is there, then of a block they think they have made a god.
c. Dan. 3:2 This was sufficient with the wicked at all times to approve their religion, if the king's authority were alleged for the establishment thereof, not considering in the mean season what God's word did permit.
d. Dan. 3:4 These are the two dangerous weapons, wherewith Satan used to fight against the children of God, the consent of the multitude, and the cruelty of the punishment: for though some feared God, yet the multitude, which consented to the wickedness, astonied them: and here the King required,

up. **6** And whosoever falleth not down, and worshippeth, shall the same hour be cast into the midst of an hot fiery furnace. **7** Therefore as soon as all the people heard the sound of the cornet, trumpet, harp, sackbut, psaltery, and all instruments of music, all the people, nations, and languages fell down, and worshipped the golden image, that Nebuchadnezzar the king had set up. **8** By reason whereof at that same time came men of the Chaldeans, and grievously accused the Jews. **9** For they spake and said to the king Nebuchadnezzar, O King, live forever. **10** Thou, O King, hast made a decree, that every man that shall hear the sound of the cornet, trumpet, harp, sackbut, psaltery, and dulcimer, and all instruments of music, shall fall down, and worship the golden image. **11** And whosoever falleth not down, and worshippeth, that he should be cast into the midst of an hot fiery furnace. **12** There are certain Jews whom thou hast set over the charge of the province of Babel, [e]Shadrach, Meshach, and Abednego: these men, O King, have not regarded thy commandment, neither will they serve thy gods, nor worship the golden image that thou hast set up. **13** Then Nebuchadnezzar in his anger and wrath commanded that they should bring Shadrach, Meshach, and Abednego, so these men were brought before the king. **14** And Nebuchadnezzar spake, and said unto them, What disorder? will not you, Shadrach, Meshach, and Abednego, serve my god, nor worship the golden image that I have set up? **15** [f]Now therefore are ye ready when ye hear the sound of the cornet, trumpet, harp, sackbut, psaltery, and dulcimer, and all instruments of music, to fall down, and worship the image which I have made? for if ye worship it not, ye shall be cast immediately into the midst of an hot fiery furnace: for who is that God, that can deliver you out of mine hands? **16** Shadrach, Meshach, and Abednego answered and said to the King, O Nebuchadnezzar, we [g]are not careful to answer thee in this matter. **17** Behold, our God whom we serve, is [h]able to deliver us from the hot fiery furnace, and he will deliver us out of thine hand, O king. **18** But if not, be it known to thee, O king, that we will not serve thy gods, nor worship the golden image which thou hast set up. **19** Then was Nebuchadnezzar full of rage, and the form of his visage was changed against Shadrach, Meshach, and Abednego: therefore he charged and commanded that they should heat the furnace at once seven [i]times more than it was wont to be heated. **20** And he charged the most valiant men of war that were in his army, to bind Shadrach, Meshach, and Abednego, and to cast them into the hot fiery furnace. **21** So these men were bound in their coats, their hosen, and their cloaks, with their other garments, and cast into the midst of the hot fiery furnace. **22** Therefore, because the king's commandment was strait, that the furnace should be exceeding hot, the flame of the fire slew those men that brought forth Shadrach, Meshach and Abednego. **23** And these three men, Shadrach, Meshach and Abednego fell down bound into the midst of the hot fiery furnace. **24** Then Nebuchadnezzar the king was astonied, and rose up in haste, and spake, and said unto his counselors, Did not we cast three men bound into the midst of the fire? Who answered, and said unto him, It is true, O king. **25** And he answered, and said, Lo, I see four men loose, walking in the midst of the fire, and they have no hurt, and the form of the fourth is like the [j]son of God. **26** Then the King Nebuchadnezzar came near to the mouth of the hot fiery furnace, and spake and said, Shadrach, Meshach and Abednego, the servants of the high God, go forth and come hither: so Shadrach, Meshach and Abednego [k]came forth of the midst of the fire. **27** Then the nobles, princes, and dukes, and the king's counselors came together to see these men, because the fire had no power over their bodies: for not an hair of their head was burnt, neither were their coats changed, nor any smell of fire came upon them. **28** Wherefore Nebuchadnezzar spake and said, [l]Blessed be the God of Shadrach, Meshach and Abednego, who hath sent his Angel, and delivered his servants, that put their trust in him, and have changed the king's commandment, and yielded their bodies rather than they would serve or worship any god save their own God. **29** Therefore I make a decree that every people, nation, and language, which speak any [m]blasphemy against the God of Shadrach, Meshach, and Abednego, shall be drawn in pieces, and their houses shall be made a jakes, because there is no god that can deliver after this sort. **30** Then the King promoted Shadrach, Meshach and Abednego in the province of Babel. **31** Nebuchadnezzar king unto all people, nations and languages, that dwell in all the [n]world, Peace be multiplied unto you: **32** I thought it good to declare the signs and wonders, that the high God hath wrought toward me. **33** How great are his signs, and how mighty are his wonders! [o]his kingdom is an everlasting kingdom, and his dominion is from generation to generation.

4

2 Another dream of Nebuchadnezzar, which Daniel declareth. 29 The Prophet declareth how of a proud king, he should become as a beast. 31 After he confesseth the power of God, and is restored to his former dignity.

1 I Nebuchadnezzar being at [a]rest in mine house, and flourishing in my palace, **2** Saw a [b]dream, which made me afraid, and the thoughts upon my bed, and the visions of mine head troubled me. **3** Therefore made I a decree, that they should bring all the wise men of Babel before me, that they might declare unto me the interpretation of the dream. **4** So came the enchanters, the astrologians, the Chaldeans and the soothsayers, to whom I told the dream, but [c]they could not show me the interpretation thereof, **5** Till at the last Daniel came before me, (whose name was [d]Belteshazzar, according to the name of my god, which hath the spirit of the holy gods in him) and before him I told the dream, saying, **6** O Belteshazzar, [e]chief of the enchanters, because I know, that the spirit of the holy gods is in thee, and no secret troubleth thee, tell me the visions of my dream, that I have seen, and the interpretation thereof. **7** Thus were the visions of my head in my bed, and behold, I saw a [f]tree in the midst of the earth, and the height thereof was great: **8** A great tree and strong, and the height thereof reached unto heaven, and the sight thereof to the ends of all the earth. **9** The boughs thereof were fair and the fruit thereof much, and in it was meat for all: it made a shadow under it for the beasts of the field, and the fowls of the heaven dwelt in the boughs thereof, and all flesh fed of it. **10** I saw in the visions of mine head upon my bed, and behold, a [g]watchman and an holy one came down from heaven, **11** And cried aloud, and said thus, Hew down the tree, and break off his branches: shake off his leaves, and scatter his fruit, that the beasts may flee from under it, and the fowls from his branches. **12** Nevertheless, leave the stump of his roots in the earth, and with a band of iron and brass bind it among the grass of the field, and let it be wet with the dew of heaven, and let his portion be with the beasts among the grass of the field. **13** [h]Let his heart be changed from man's nature, and let a beast's heart be given unto him, and let seven times be passed over him. **14** [i]The sentence is according to the decree of the watchmen, and according to the word of the holy ones: the demand was answered, to the intent that living men may know, that the most High hath power over the kingdom of men, and giveth it to whomsoever he will, and appointeth over it the most abject among men. **15** This is the dream, that I King Nebuchadnezzar have seen: therefore thou, O Belteshazzar, declare the interpretation thereof: for all the wise men of my kingdom are not able to show me the interpretation: but thou art able, for the spirit of the holy gods is in thee. **16** Then Daniel (whose name was Belteshazzar) held his [j]peace by the space of one hour, and his thoughts troubled him, and the King spake and said, Belteshazzar, let neither the dream, nor the interpretation thereof trouble thee. Belteshazzar answered and said, My lord, the dream be to them that hate thee, and the interpretation thereof to thine enemies. **17** The tree that thou sawest, which was great and mighty, whose height reached unto the heaven, and the sight thereof through all the world, **18** Whose leaves were fair, and the fruit thereof much, and in it was meat for all, under the which the beasts of the field dwelt, and

---

not an inward consent, but an outward gesture, that the Jews might by little and little learn to forget their true religion.

e. Dan. 3:12 It seemeth that they named not Dan., because he was greatly in the king's favor, thinking if these three had been destroyed, they might have had better occasion to accuse Dan.: and this declareth that this policy of erecting this image was invented by the malicious flatterers which sought nothing but the destruction of the Jews, whom they accused of rebellion and ingratitude.

f. Dan. 3:15 Signifying that he would receive them to grace if they would now at the length obey his decree.

g. Dan. 3:16 For they should have done injury to God, if they should have doubted in this holy cause, and therefore they say, that they are resolved to die for God's cause.

h. Dan. 3:17 They ground on two points, first on the power and providence of God over them, and secondly on their cause, which was God's glory, and the testifying of his true religion with their blood, and so make open confession, that they will not so much as outwardly consent to idolatry.

i. Dan. 3:19 This declareth that the more that tyrants rage, and the more witty they show themselves inventing strange and cruel punishments, the more is God glorified by his servants to whom he giveth patience and constancy to abide the cruelty of their punishment: for either by delivereth them from death, or else for this life giveth them a better.

j. Dan. 3:25 For the Angels were called the sons of God, because of their excellency: therefore the king called this Angel whom God sent to comfort his in these great torments, the son of God.

k. Dan. 3:26 This commendeth their obedience unto God, that they would not for any fear depart out of this furnace, till the time appointed, as Noah remained in the ark, till the Lord called him forth.

l. Dan. 3:28 He was moved by the greatness of the miracle to praise God, but his heart was not touched. And here we see that miracles are not sufficient to convert men to God, but that doctrine most chiefly be adjoined, without the which there can be no faith.

m. Dan. 3:29 If this heathen king moved by God's Spirit would not see blasphemy unpunished, but made a law and set a punishment to such transgressors, much more ought all they that profess religion, take order that such impiety reign not, lest according as their knowledge and charge is greater, so they suffer double punishment.

n. Dan. 3:31 Meaning, so far as his dominion extended.

o. Dan. 3:33 Read Dan. 2:44.

DAN. 4

a. Dan. 4:1 There was no trouble that might cause me to dream, and therefore it came only of God.

b. Dan. 4:2 This was another dream besides that which he saw of the four Empires, for Dan. both declared what that dream was, and what it meant, and here he only expoundeth the dream.

c. Dan. 4:4 In that that he sent abroad to others, whose ignorance in times past he had experimented, and left Dan. which was ever ready at hand, it declareth the nature of the ungodly, which never seek to the servants of God, but for very necessity, and then they spare no flatterings.

d. Dan. 4:5 This no doubt was a great grief to Dan. not only to have his name changed, but to be called by the name of a vile idol, which thing Nebuchadnezzar did to make him forget the true religion of God.

e. Dan. 4:6 Which also was a great grief to the Prophet to be numbered among the sorcerers and men whose practices were wicked and contrary to God's word.

f. Dan. 4:7 By the tree is signified the dignity of a king whom God ordaineth to be a defense for all kind of men, and whose state is profitable for mankind.

g. Dan. 4:10 Meaning the Angel of God, which neither eateth nor sleepeth, but is ever ready to do God's will, and is not infected with man's corruption, but is ever holy: and in that that he commandeth to cut down this tree, he knew that it should not be cut down by man, but by God.

h. Dan. 4:13 Hereby he meaneth that Nebuchadnezzar should not only for a time lose his kingdom, but be like a beast.

i. Dan. 4:14 God hath decreed this judgment and the whole army of heaven have as it were subscribed unto it, like as also they desire the execution of his decree against all them that lift up themselves against God.

j. Dan. 4:16 He was troubled for the great judgment of God, which he saw ordained against the king, and so the Prophets used on the one part to denounce God's judgments for the zeal they bare to his glory, and on the other part to have compassion upon man, and also to consider that they should be

upon whose branches the fowls of the heaven did sit, **19** It is thou, O king, that art great and mighty: for thy greatness is grown, and reacheth unto heaven, and thy dominion to the ends of the earth. **20** Whereas the King saw a watchman, and an holy one that came down from heaven, and said, Hew down the tree, and destroy it, yet leave the stump of the roots thereof in the earth, and with a band of iron and brass bind it among the grass of the field, and let it be wet with the dew of heaven, and let his portion be with the beasts of the field, [k]till seven times pass over him. **21** This is the interpretation, O king, and it is the decree of the most High, which is come upon my lord the king, **22** That they shall drive thee from men, and thy dwelling shall be with the beasts of the field: they shall make thee to eat grass as the [l]oxen, and they shall wet thee with the dew of heaven: and seven times shall pass over thee, till thou know, that [m]the most High beareth rule over the kingdom of men, and giveth it to whomsoever he will. **23** Whereas they said, that one should leave the stump of the tree roots, thy kingdom shall remain unto thee: after that, thou shalt know, that the heavens have the rule. **24** Wherefore, O king, let my counsel be acceptable unto thee, and [n]break off thy sins by righteousness, and thine iniquities by mercy towards the poor: lo, let there be a [o]healing of thine error. **25** All these things shall come upon the king Nebuchadnezzar. **26** At the end of twelve [p]months, he walked in the royal palace of Babel. **27** And the king spake and said, Is not this great Babel that I have built for the house of the kingdom by the might of my power, and for the honor of my majesty? **28** While the word was in the king's mouth, a voice came down from heaven, saying, O king Nebuchadnezzar, to thee be it spoken, Thy kingdom is departed from thee, **29** And they shall drive thee from men, and thy dwelling shall be with the beasts of the field: they shall make thee to eat grass, as the oxen, and seven times shall pass over thee, until thou knowest, that the most High beareth rule over the kingdom of men, and giveth it unto whomsoever he will. **30** The very same hour was this thing fulfilled upon Nebuchadnezzar, and he was driven from men, and did eat grass as the oxen, and his body was wet with the dew of heaven, till his hairs were grown as eagles feathers, and his nails like birds claws. **31** And at the end of these [q]days, I Nebuchadnezzar lifted up mine eyes unto heaven, and mine understanding was restored unto me, and I gave thanks unto the most High, and I praised and honored him, that liveth forever, [l]whose power is an everlasting power, and his kingdom is from generation to generation. **32** And all the inhabitants of the earth are reputed as nothing: and according to his [r]will he worketh in the army of heaven, and in the inhabitants of the earth: and none can stay his hand, nor say unto him, What doest thou? **33** At the same time was mine understanding restored unto me, and I returned to the honor of my kingdom: my glory and my beauty was restored unto me, and my counselors and [s]my princes sought unto me, and I was established in my kingdom, and my glory was augmented toward me. **34** Now therefore I Nebuchadnezzar [t]praise, and extol and magnify the king of heaven, whose works are all truth, and his ways judgment: and those that walk in pride, he is able to abase.

5

5 Belshazzar king of Babylon seeth an handwriting on the wall. 8 The soothsayers called of the king, cannot expound the writing. 25 Daniel readeth it, and interpreteth it also. 30 The king is slain. 31 Darius enjoyeth the kingdom.

1 King [a]Belshazzar made a great feast to a thousand of his princes, and drank wine [b]before the thousand. **2** And Belshazzar [c]while he tasted the wine, commanded to bring him the golden and silver vessels, which his [d]father Nebuchadnezzar had brought from the Temple in Jerusalem, that the king and his princes, his wives, and his concubines might drink therein. **3** Then were brought the golden vessels, that were taken out of the Temple of the Lord's house at Jerusalem, and the king and his princes, his wives and his concubines drank in them. **4** They drank wine, and praised the [e]gods of gold, and of silver, of brass, of iron, of wood, and of stone. **5** At the same hour appeared fingers of a man's hand, which wrote over [f]against the candlestick upon the plaster of the wall of the king's palace, and the king saw the palm of the hand that wrote. **6** Then the king's countenance was changed, and his thoughts troubled him, so that the joints of his loins were loosed, and his [g]knees smote one against the other. **7** Wherefore the king cried loud, that they should bring [h]the astrologians, the Chaldeans and the soothsayers. And the king spake, and said to the wise men of Babel, Whosoever can read this writing, and declare me the interpretation thereof, shall be clothed with purple, and shall have a chain of gold about his neck, and shall be the third ruler in the kingdom. **8** Then came all the king's wise men, but they could neither read the writing, nor show the king the interpretation. **9** Then was king Belshazzar greatly troubled, and his countenance was changed in him, and his princes were astonied. **10** Now the [i]Queen by reason of the talk of the King and his princes, came into the banquet house, and the Queen spake, and said, O king, live forever: let not thy thoughts trouble thee, nor let thy countenance be changed. **11** There is a man in thy kingdom, in whom is the spirit of the holy gods, and in the days of thy father, light and understanding and wisdom like the wisdom of the gods, was found in him: whom the king Nebuchadnezzar thy father, the king, I say, thy father, made chief of the [j]enchanters, astrologians, Chaldeans, and soothsayers, **12** Because a more excellent spirit, and knowledge, and understanding (for he did expound dreams, and declare hard sentences, and dissolved doubts) were found in him, even in Daniel, whom the king named Belteshazzar: now let Daniel be called, and he will declare the interpretation. **13** Then was Daniel brought before the king, and the king spake and said unto Daniel, Art thou that Daniel, which art of the children of the captivity of Judah, whom my father the king brought out of Jewry? **14** Now I have heard of thee, that [k]the spirit of the holy gods is in thee, and that light and understanding, and excellent wisdom is found in thee. **15** Now therefore wise men and Astrologians have been brought before me, that they should read this writing, and show me the interpretation thereof: but they could not declare the interpretation of the thing. **16** Then heard I of thee, that thou couldest show interpretations, and dissolve doubts: now if thou canst read the writing, and show me the interpretation thereof, thou shalt be clothed with purple, and shall have a chain of gold about thy neck, and shalt be the third ruler in the kingdom. **17** Then Daniel answered, and said before the king, Keep thy rewards to thyself, and give thy gifts to another: yet I will read the writing unto the king, and show him the interpretation. **18** O king, hear thou, The most high God gave unto [l]Nebuchadnezzar thy father a kingdom, and majesty, and honor, and glory. **19** And for the majesty that he gave him, all people, nations, and languages trembled, and feared before him: he put to death whom he would: he smote whom he would: whom he would he set up, and whom he would he put down. **20** But when his heart was puffed up, and his mind hardened in pride, he was deposed from his kingly throne, and they took his honor from him. **21** And he was driven from the sons of men, and his heart was made like the beasts, and his dwelling was with the wild asses: they fed him with grass like oxen, and his body was wet with the dew of the heaven, till he knew that the most high God bare rule over the kingdom of men, and that he appointeth over it, whomsoever he pleaseth. **22** And thou his son, O Belshazzar, hast not humbled thine heart, though thou knewest all these things, **23** But hast lifted thyself up against the Lord of heaven, and they have brought the vessels of his House before thee, and thou and thy princes, thy wives and thy concubines have drunk wine in them, and thou hast praised the gods of silver and gold, of brass, iron, wood and stone, which neither see, neither hear, nor understand: and the God in whose hand thy breath is and all thy ways, him hast thou not glorified. **24** [m]Then was the palm of the hand sent from him, and hath written this writing. **25** And this is the writing that he hath written, [n]MENE, MENE, TEKEL UPHARSIN. **26** This

---

subject to God's judgments, if he did not regard them with pity.

k. Dan. 4:20 Whereby he meaneth a long space, as seven years. Some interpret seven months, and others seven weeks, but it seemeth he means of years.

l. Dan. 4:22 Not that his shape or form was changed into a beast, but that he was either stricken mad, and so avoided man's company, or was cast out for his tyranny, and so wandered among the beasts, and ate herbs and grass.

m. Dan. 4:22 Dan. showeth the cause why God thus punished him.

n. Dan. 4:24 Cease from provoking God to anger any longer by thy sins, that he may mitigate his punishment, if thou show by thine upright life that thou hast true faith and repentance.

o. Dan. 4:24 Suffer the errors of thy former life to be redressed.

p. Dan. 4:26 After that Dan. had declared this vision: and this his pride declareth that it is not in man to convert to God, except his Spirit move him: seeing that these terrible threatenings could not move him to repent.

q. Dan. 4:31 When the term of these seven years was accomplished.

r. Dan. 4:32 He confesseth God's will to be the rule of all justice, and a most perfect law, whereby he governeth both man and Angels and devils, so that none ought to murmur or ask a reason of his doings, but only to stand content therewith and give him the glory.

s. Dan. 4:33 By whom it seemeth that he had been put from his kingdom before.

t. Dan. 4:34 He doth not only praise God for his deliverance, but also confesseth his fault that God may only have the glory, and man the shame, and that he may be exalted and man cast down.

DAN. 5

1. Dan. 7:14 / Mic. 4:17 / Luke 1:33

DAN. 5

a. Dan. 5:1 Dan. reciteth this history of king Belshazzar, Evil-merodach's son, to show God's judgments against the wicked for the deliverance of his Church: and how the prophecy of Jeremiah was true, that they should be delivered after seventy years.

b. Dan. 5:1 The kings of the East parts then used to sit alone commonly, and disdained that any should sit in their company: and now to show his power, and how little he set by his enemy, which then besieged Babylon, he made a solemn banquet, and used excess in their company, which is meant here by drinking wine: thus the wicked are most dissolute and negligent, when their destruction is at hand.

c. Dan. 5:2 Or, overcome with wine.

d. Dan. 5:2 Meaning, his grandfather.

e. Dan. 5:4 In contempt of the true God, they praise their idols, not that they thought that the gold or silver were gods, but that there was a certain virtue and power in them to do them good, which is also the opinion of all idolaters.

f. Dan. 5:5 That it might the better be seen.

g. Dan. 5:6 So he that before contemned God, was moved by this sight to tremble for fear of God's judgments.

h. Dan. 5:7 Thus the wicked in their troubles seek many means, who draw them from God, because they seek not to him who is the only comfort in all afflictions.

i. Dan. 5:10 To wit, his grandmother Nebuchadnezzar's wife, which for her age was not before at the feast, but came thither when she heard of these strange news.

j. Dan. 5:11 Read Dan. 4:6, and this declareth that both this name was odious unto him, and also he did not use these vile practices, because he was not among them when all were called.

k. Dan. 5:14 For the idolaters thought that the Angels had power as God, and therefore had them in like estimation, as they had God, thinking that the spirit of prophecy and understanding came of them.

l. Dan. 5:18 Before he read the writing, he declareth to the king his great ingratitude toward God, who could not be moved to give him the glory, considering his wonderful work toward his grandfather, and so showeth that he doth not sin of ignorance but of malice.

m. Dan. 5:24 After that God had so long time deferred his anger, and patiently waited for thine amendment.

n. Dan. 5:25 This word is twice written for the certainty of the thing: showing that God had most surely counted: signifying also that God hath appointed a term for all kingdoms, and

is the interpretation of the thing, MENE, God hath numbered thy kingdom, and
hath finished it. **27** TEKEL, thou art weighed in the balance, and art found
[o]too light. **28** PERES, thy kingdom is divided and given to the Medes and Per-
sians. **29** Then at the commandment of Belshazzar they clothed Daniel with
purple, and put a chain of gold about his neck, and made a proclamation concer-
ning him that he should be the third ruler in the kingdom. **30** The same night
was Belshazzar the King of the Chaldeans slain. **31** And Darius [p]of the Medes
took the kingdom, being threescore and two years old.

6

1 Daniel is made ruler over the governors. 5 An act against Daniel. 16 He is put into a den of lions by the commandment of the king. 23 He is delivered by faith in God. 24 Daniel's accusers are put unto the lions. 25 Darius by a decree magnifieth the God of Daniel.

1 It pleased Darius to set over the kingdom [a]an hundred and twenty gover-
nors, which should be over the whole kingdom, **2** And over these three rulers,
(of whom Daniel was one) that the governors might give accompts unto them, and
the king [b]should have no damage. **3** Now this Daniel [c]was preferred above the
rulers, and governors, because the spirit was excellent in him, and the king thought
to set him over the whole realm. **4** Wherefore the rulers and governors [d]sought
an occasion against Daniel concerning the kingdom: but they could find none oc-
casion nor fault: for he was so faithful that there was no blame nor fault found in
him. **5** Then said these men, We shall not find an occasion against this Daniel,
except we find it against him concerning the Law of his God. **6** Therefore the
rulers and these governors went together to the king, and said thus unto him, King
Darius, live forever. **7** All the rulers of thy kingdom, the officers and governors,
the counselors and dukes have consulted together to make a decree for the king,
and to establish a statute, that whosoever shall ask a petition of any god or man for
thirty days save of thee, O king, he shall be cast into the den of lions. **8** Now, O
king, confirm the decree, and seal the writing, that it be not changed, according
to the law of the Medes and Persians, which altereth not. **9** Wherefore king Da-
rius [e]sealed the writing and the decree. **10** Now when Daniel understood that
he had sealed the writing, he went into his house, and his [f]window being open in
his chamber toward Jerusalem, he kneeled upon his knees three times a day, and
prayed and praised his God, as he did aforetime. **11** Then these men assembled,
and found Daniel praying, and making supplication unto his God. **12** So they
came and spake unto the king concerning the king's decree, Hast thou not sealed
the decree, that every man that shall make a request to any god or man within
thirty days, save to thee, O King, shall be cast into the den of lions? The King
answered, and said, The thing is true, according to the law of the Medes and Per-
sians, which altereth not. **13** Then answered they, and said unto the King, This
Daniel which is of the children of the captivity of Judah, regardeth not thee, O
king, nor the decree that thou hast sealed, but maketh his petition three times a
day. **14** When the King heard these words, he was sore displeased with himself,
and set his heart on Daniel, to deliver him: and he labored till the sun went down,
to deliver him. **15** Then these men assembled unto the king, and said unto the
King, Understand, O King, that the law of the Medes and Persians is, that no de-
cree nor statute which the king confirmeth, may be [g]altered. **16** Then the King
commanded, and they brought Daniel, and cast him into the den of lions: now the
king spake, and said unto Daniel, Thy God, whom thou always servest, even he
will deliver thee. **17** And a stone was brought, and laid upon the mouth of the
den, and the King sealed it with his own signet, and with the signet of his princes,
that the purpose might not be changed, concerning Daniel. **18** Then the king
went unto his palace, and remained fasting, neither were the instruments of music
brought before him, and his sleep went from him. **19** Then the king arose early
in the morning, and went in all haste unto the den of lions. **20** And when he
came to the den, he cried with a lamentable voice unto Daniel: and the king spake,
and said to Daniel, O Daniel the servant of the living God, is not thy God (whom
thou always servest) [h]able to deliver thee from the lions? **21** Then said Daniel
unto the King, O king, live forever. **22** My God hath sent his Angel and hath
shut the lion's mouths, and they have not hurt me: for [i]my justice was found out
before him: and unto thee, O king, I have done [j]no hurt. **23** Then was the King
exceeding glad for him, and commanded that they should take Daniel out of the
den: so Daniel was brought out of the den, and no manner of hurt was found upon
him, because he [k]believed in his God. **24** And by the commandment of the King
these men which had accused Daniel, were brought, and were [l]cast into the den
of lions, even they, their children, and their wives: and the lions had the mastery
of them, and brake all their bones a pieces, or ever they came at the ground of the
den. **25** Afterward King Darius wrote, Unto all people, nations and languages,
that dwell in all the world: Peace be multiplied unto you. **26** I make a decree,
that in all the dominion of my kingdom, men tremble and fear [m]before the God
of Daniel: for he is the [n]living God, and remaineth forever: and his kingdom shall
not perish, and his dominion shall be everlasting. **27** He rescueth and delivereth,
and he worketh signs and wonders in heaven and in earth: who hath delivered
Daniel from the power of the lions. **28** So this Daniel prospered in the reign of
Darius and in the reign of Cyrus of Persia.

7

3 A vision of four beasts is showed unto Daniel. 8 The ten horns of the fourth beast. 27 Of the everlasting kingdom of Christ.

1 In the first year of Belshazzar King of Babel, Daniel saw a dream, and the-
re were visions in his head, upon his bed: [a]then he wrote the dream, and declared
the sum of the matter. **2** Daniel spake and said, I saw in my vision by night,
and behold, the four winds of the heaven strove upon [b]the great sea: **3** And four
great beasts came up from the sea one divers from another. **4** The first was as a
[c]lion, and had eagle's wings: I beheld till the wings thereof were plucked off, and
it was lifted up from the earth, and set upon his feet as a man, and a man's heart
was given him. **5** And behold, another beast which was the second, was like a
[d]bear, and stood upon the [e]one side: and he had three ribs in his [f]mouth between
his teeth, [g]and they said thus unto him, Arise, and devour much flesh. **6** After
this, I beheld, and lo, there was another like a [h]leopard, which had upon his back
[i]four wings of a fowl: the beast had also four heads, and [j]dominion was given
him. **7** After this, I saw in the visions by night, and behold, the [k]fourth beast was
fearful and terrible and very strong. It had great [l]iron teeth: it devoured and brake
in pieces, and stamped [m]the residue under his feet: and it was unlike to the beasts
that were before it: for it had [n]ten horns. **8** As I considered the horns, behold,

---

that a miserable end shall come on all that raise themselves against him.

o. Dan. 5:27 Or, wanting.

p. Dan. 5:31 Cyrus his son-in-law gave him this title of honor, although Cyrus in effect had the dominion.

DAN. 6

a. Dan. 6:1 Read Esther 1:1.

b. Dan. 6:2 Or, not be troubled.

c. Dan. 6:3 This heathen king preferred Dan. a stranger to all his nobles and familiars, because the graces of God were more excellent in him than in others.

d. Dan. 6:4 Thus the wicked cannot abide the graces of God in others, but seek by all occasions to deface them, therefore against such assaults there is no better remedy than to walk upright in the fear of God, and to have a good conscience.

e. Dan. 6:9 Herein is condemned the wickedness of the king, who would be set up as a god, and passed not what wicked laws he approved for the maintenance of the same.

f. Dan. 6:10 Because he would not by his silence show that he consented to this wicked decree, he set open his windows toward Jerusalem, when he prayed: both to stir up himself with the remembrance of God's promises to his people, when they should pray toward that Temple, and also that others might see, that he would neither consent in heart nor deed for these few days to anything that was contrary to God's glory.

g. Dan. 6:15 Thus the wicked maintain evil laws by constancy and authority, which is ofttimes either lightness, or stubbornness, when as the innocents thereby perish, and therefore governors neither ought to fear, nor be ashamed to break such.

h. Dan. 6:20 This declareth that Darius was not touched with the true knowledge of God, because he doubted of his power.

i. Dan. 6:22 My just cause and uprightness in this thing wherein I was charged, is approved of God.

j. Dan. 6:22 For he did disobey the king's wicked commandment to obey God, and so did no injury to the king, who ought to command nothing whereby God should be dishonored.

k. Dan. 6:23 Because he committed himself wholly unto God whose cause he did defend, he was assured that nothing but good could come unto him: wherein we see the power of faith, as Heb. 11:33.

l. Dan. 6:24 This is a terrible example against all the wicked which do against their conscience make cruel laws to destroy the children of God, and also admonisheth Princes how to punish such when their wickedness is come to light: though not in every point, or with like circumstances, yet to execute true justice upon them.

m. Dan. 6:26 This proveth not that Darius did worship God aright, or else was converted: for then he would have destroyed all superstition and idolatry: and not only given God the chief place, but also have set him up, and caused him to be honored according to his word: but this was a certain confession of God's power, whereunto he was compelled by this wonderful miracle.

n. Dan. 6:26 Which hath not only life in himself, but is the only fountain of life, and quickeneth all things, so that without him there is no life.

DAN. 7

a. Dan. 7:1 Whereas the people of Israel looked for a continual quietness, after their seventy years, as Jeremiah had declared, he showeth that this rest shall not be a deliverance from all troubles, but a beginning, and therefore encourageth them to look for a continual affliction, till the Messiah be uttered and revealed, by whom they should have a spiritual deliverance, and all the promises be fulfilled: whereof they should have a certain token in the destruction of the Babylonian kingdom.

b. Dan. 7:2 Which signified that there should be horrible troubles and afflictions in the world in all corners of the world, and at sundry times.

c. Dan. 7:4 Meaning, the Assyrian and Chaldean empire, which was most strong and fierce in power, and most soon come to their authority, as though they had wings to fly: yet their wings were pulled by the Persians, and they went on their feet, and were made like other men, which is here meant by man's heart.

d. Dan. 7:5 Meaning, the Persians which were barbarous and cruel.

e. Dan. 7:5 They were small in the beginning and were shut up in the mountains and had no bruit.

f. Dan. 7:5 That is, destroyed many kingdoms, and was insatiable.

g. Dan. 7:5 To wit, the Angels by God's commandment, who by this means punished the ingratitude of the world.

h. Dan. 7:6 Meaning, Alexander the king of Macedonia.

i. Dan. 7:6 That is, his four chief captains, which had the empire among them after his death. Seleucus had Asia the great, Antigonus the less, Cassander and after him Antipater was king of Macedonia, and Ptolemy had Egypt.

j. Dan. 7:6 It was not of himself nor of his own power that he got all these countries: for his army contained but thirty thousand men, and he overcame in one battle Darius, which had ten hundred thousand, when he was so heavy with sleep, that his eyes were scarce open, as the stories report: therefore this power was given him of God.

k. Dan. 7:7 That is, the Roman Empire which was a monster, and could not be compared to any beasts, because the nature of none was able to express it.

l. Dan. 7:7 Signifying, the tyranny and greediness of the Romans.

m. Dan. 7:7 That which the Romans could not quietly enjoy in other countries, they would give it to other Kings and rulers, that at all times when they would, they might take it again: which liberality is here called the stamping of the rest under the feet.

n. Dan. 7:7 That is, sundry and divers provinces which were governed by the deputies and proconsuls, whereof everyone might be compared to a King.

o. Dan. 7:8 Which is meant of Julius Caesar, Augustus, Tiberius, Caligula, Claudius, and Nero, etc., who were as kings in effect, but because they could not rule, but by the consent of the Senate, their power is compared to a little horn. For there came up among them another little [o]horn, before whom there were [p]three of the first horns plucked away: and behold, in this horn were [q]eyes like the eyes of man, and a mouth speaking presumptuous things. **9** I beheld till the [r]thrones were set up, and the [s]Ancient of days did sit, whose garment was white as snow, and the hair of his head like the pure wool: his throne was like the fiery flame, and his wheels, as burning fire. **10** A fiery stream issued, and came forth from before him: thousand thousands ministered unto him, and ten thousand [t]thousands stood before him: the judgment was set, and the [u]books opened. **11** Then I beheld, [v]because of the voice of the presumptuous words which the horn spake: I beheld, even till the beast was slain, and his body destroyed, and given to the burning fire. **12** As [w]concerning the other beasts, they had taken away their dominion: yet their lives were prolonged for a certain time and season. **13** As I beheld in visions by night, behold, [x]one like the son of man came in the clouds of heaven, and [y]approached unto the Ancient of days, and they brought him before him. **14** And he gave him [z]dominion, and honor, and a kingdom, that all people, nations and languages should serve him: his dominion is an everlasting dominion, which shall never be taken away: and his dominion shall never be destroyed. **15** I Daniel was [aa]troubled in my spirit, in the midst of my body, and the visions of mine head made me afraid. **16** Therefore I came unto [ab]one of them that stood by, and asked him the truth of all this: so he told me, and showed me the interpretation of these things. **17** These great beasts which are four, are four kings, which shall arise out of the earth, **18** And they shall take the [ac]kingdom of the Saints of the [ad]most High, and shall possess the kingdom forever, even forever and ever. **19** After this, I would know the truth of the fourth beast, which was [ae]so unlike to all the others, very fearful, whose teeth were of iron, and his nails of brass: which devoured brake in pieces, and stamped the [af]residue under his feet. **20** Also to know of the ten horns that were in his head, and of the others which came up, before whom three fell, and of the horn that had eyes, and of the mouth that spake presumptuous things, whose [ag]look was more stout than his fellows. **21** I beheld, and the same [ah]horn made battle against the Saints, yea, and prevailed against them, **22** Until [ai]the Ancient of days came, and judgment was given to the Saints of the most High: and the time approached, that the Saints possessed the kingdom. **23** Then he said, The fourth beast shall be the fourth kingdom in the earth, which shall be unlike to all the kingdoms, and shall devour the whole earth, and shall tread it down and break it in pieces. **24** And the ten horns out of this kingdom are ten Kings that shall rise: and another shall rise after them, and he shall be unlike to the first, and he shall subdue [aj]three Kings, **25** And shall speak words against [ak]the most High, and shall consume the Saints of the most High, and think that he may [al]change times and laws, and they shall be given into his hand until a [am]time, and times, and the dividing of time. **26** But the [an]judgment shall sit, and they shall take away his dominion to consume and destroy it unto the end. **27** And the [ao]kingdom, and dominion, and the greatness of the kingdom under the whole heaven shall be given to the holy people of the most High, whose kingdom is an everlasting kingdom, and all [ap]powers shall serve and obey him. **28** Even this is the end of the matter, I Daniel had many [aq]cogitations which troubled me, and my countenance changed in me: but I kept the matter in mine heart.

8

A vision of a battle between a ram and a goat: 20 The understanding of the vision.

1 In the third year of the reign of king Belshazzar, a vision appeared unto me, even unto me Daniel, [a]after that which appeared unto me at the first. **2** And I saw in a vision, and when I saw it, I was in the palace of Shushan, which is in the province [b]of Elam, and in a vision me thought I was by the river of Ulai. **3** Then I looked up and saw, and behold, there stood before the river a [c]ram which had two horns, and these two horns were high: but one was [d]higher than another, and the highest came up last. **4** I saw the ram pushing against the West, and against the North, and against the South: so that no [e]beasts might stand before him, nor could deliver out of his hand, but he did what he listed, and became great. **5** And as I considered, behold, [f]a goat came from the West over the whole earth, and touched not the ground: and this goat had an [g]horn that appeared between his eyes. **6** And he came unto the ram that had the two horns, whom I had seen standing by the river, and ran unto him in his fierce rage. **7** And I saw him come unto the ram, and being moved against him, he [h]smote the ram, and brake his two horns: and there was no power in the ram to stand against him, but he cast him down to the ground, and stamped upon him, and there was none that could deliver the ram out of his power. **8** Therefore the goat waxed exceeding great, and when he was at the strongest, his great [i]horn was broken: and for it came up four that [j]appeared toward the four winds of the heaven. **9** And out of one of them came forth a [k]little horn, which waxed very great toward the [l]South, and toward the [m]East, and toward the [n]pleasant land. **10** Yea, it grew up unto the [o]host of heaven, and it cast down some of the host, and of the stars to the ground, and trode upon them, **11** And extolled himself against the [p]prince of the host, from whom the [q]daily sacrifice was taken away, and the place of his Sanctuary was cast down. **12** And [r]a time shall be given him over the daily

---

Muhammad came not of the Roman Empire, and the Pope hath no vocation of government: therefore this cannot be applied unto them, and also in this prophecy the Prophet's purpose is chiefly to comfort the Jews unto the revelation of Christ. Some take it for the whole body of Antichrist.

p. Dan. 7:8 Meaning, a certain portion of the ten horns: that is, a part from the whole estate was taken away. For Augustus took from the Senate the liberty of choosing the deputies to send into the provinces, and took the government of certain countries to himself.

q. Dan. 7:8 These Roman Emperors at the first used a certain humanity and gentleness, and were content that others, as the Consuls, and Senate, should bear the names of dignity, so that they might have the profit, and therefore in election and counsels would behave themselves according as did other Senators: yet against their enemies and those that would resist them, they were fierce and cruel, which is here meant by the proud mouth.

r. Dan. 7:9 Meaning, the places where God and his Angels should come to judge these Monarchies, which judgment should begin at the first coming of Christ.

s. Dan. 7:9 That is, God which was before all times, and is here described as man's nature is able to comprehend some portion of his glory.

t. Dan. 7:10 That is, an infinite number of Angels, which were ready to execute his commandment.

u. Dan. 7:10 This is meant of the first coming of Christ, when as the will of God was plainly revealed by his Gospel.

v. Dan. 7:11 Meaning, that he was astonied when he saw these Emperors in such dignity and pride, and so suddenly destroyed at the coming of Christ, when this fourth Monarchy was subject to men of other nations.

w. Dan. 7:12 As the three former Monarchies had an end at the time that God appointed, although they flourished for a time, so shall this fourth have, and they that patiently abide God's appointment, shall enjoy the promises.

x. Dan. 7:13 Which is meant of Christ, who had not yet taken upon him man's nature, neither was the son of David according to the flesh, as he was afterward: but appeared then in a figure, and that in the clouds: that is, being separate from the common sort of men by manifest signs of his divinity.

y. Dan. 7:13 To wit, when he ascend into the heavens, and his divine majesty appeared, and all power was given unto him, in respect of that that he was our Mediator.

z. Dan. 7:14 This is meant of the beginning of Christ's kingdom, when God the Father gave unto him all dominion, as to the Mediator, to the intent that he should govern here his Church in earth continually, till the time that he brought them to eternal life.

aa. Dan. 7:15 Through the strangeness of the vision.

ab. Dan. 7:16 Meaning, of the Angels, as verse 10.

ac. Dan. 7:18 Because Abraham was appointed heir of all the world, Rom. 4:13, and in him all the faithful, therefore the kingdom thereof is theirs by right, which these four beasts or tyrants should invade, and usurp until the world were restored by Christ: and this was to confirm them that were in troubles, that their afflictions should have an end at length.

ad. Dan. 7:18 That is, of the most high things, because God hath chosen them out of this world, that they should look up to the heavens, whereon all their hope dependeth.

ae. Dan. 7:19 For the other three Monarchies were governed by a King, and the Roman Empire by Consuls: the Romans changed their governors yearly, and the other Monarchies retained them for term of life: also the Romans were the strongest of all the others, and were never quiet among themselves.

af. Dan. 7:19 Read verse 7.

ag. Dan. 7:20 This is meant of the fourth beast, which was more terrible than the others.

ah. Dan. 7:21 Meaning the Roman Emperors, who were most cruel against the Church of God both of the Jews and of the Gentiles.

ai. Dan. 7:22 Till God showed his power in the person of Christ, and by the preaching of the Gospel gave unto his some rest, and so obtained a famous Name in the world, and were called the Church of God, or the kingdom of God.

aj. Dan. 7:24 Read the exposition hereof, verse 8.

ak. Dan. 7:25 That is, shall make wicked decrees and proclamations against God's word, and send throughout all their dominion, to destroy all that did profess it.

al. Dan. 7:25 These Emperors shall not consider that they have their power of God, but think it is in their own power to change God's laws and man's, and as it were the order of nature, as appeareth by Octavius, Tiberius, Caligula, Nero, Domitian, etc.

am. Dan. 7:25 God shall suffer them thus to rage against his Saints for a long time, which is meant by the time and times, but at length he will assuage these troubles, and shorten the time for his elect's sake, Matt. 24:22, which is here meant by the dividing of time.

an. Dan. 7:26 God by his power shall restore things that were out of order, and so destroy this little horn, that it shall never rise up again.

ao. Dan. 7:27 He showeth wherefore the beast should be destroyed, to wit, that his Church might have rest and quietness, which though they do not fully enjoy here, yet they have it in hope, and by the preaching of the Gospel enjoy the beginning thereof, which is meant by these words: Under the heaven: and therefore he here speaketh of the beginning of Christ's kingdom in this world, which kingdom the faithful have by the participation that they have with Christ their head.

ap. Dan. 7:27 That is, some of every sort that bear rule.

aq. Dan. 7:28 Though he had many motions in his heart which moved him to and fro to seek out this matter curiously, yet he was content with that which God revealed, and kept it in memory, and wrote it for the use of the Church.

DAN. 8

a. Dan. 8:1 After the general vision, he cometh to certain particular visions as touching the destruction of the Monarchy of the Persians, and Macedonians: for the ruin of the Babylonians was at hand, and also he had sufficiently spoken thereof.

b. Dan. 8:2 That is, of Persia.

c. Dan. 8:3 Which represented the kingdom of the Persians and Medes, which were joined together.

d. Dan. 8:3 Meaning, Cyrus, which after grew greater in power than Darius his uncle and father-in-law.

e. Dan. 8:4 That is, no kings or nations.

f. Dan. 8:5 Meaning, Alexander that came from Greece with great speed and expedition.

g. Dan. 8:5 Though he came in the name of all Greece, yet he bore the title and dignity of the general captain, so that the strength was attributed to him, which is meant by this horn.

h. Dan. 8:7 Alexander overcame Darius in two sundry battles, and so had the two kingdoms of the Medes and Persians.

i. Dan. 8:8 Alexander's great power was broken: for when he had overcome all the East, he thought to return toward Greece to subdue them that had rebelled, and so died by the way.

j. Dan. 8:8 That is, which were famous: for almost in the space of fifteen years there were fifteen divers successors before this monarchy was divided to these four, whereof Cassander had Macedonia, Seleucus Syria, Antigonus Asia the less, and Ptolemy Egypt.

k. Dan. 8:9 Which was Antiochus Epiphanes, who was of a servile and flattering nature, and also there were others between him and the kingdom, and therefore is here called the little horn, because neither princely conditions, nor any other thing was in him, why he should obtain this kingdom.

l. Dan. 8:9 That is, toward Egypt.

m. Dan. 8:9 Whereby he meaneth Ptolemeus.

n. Dan. 8:9 That is, Judea.

o. Dan. 8:10 Antiochus raged against the elect of God, and trode his precious stars under feet, which are so called, because they are separated from the world.

p. Dan. 8:11 That is, God, who governeth and maintaineth his Church.

q. Dan. 8:11 He labored to abolish all religion, and therefore cast God's service out of his Temple, which God had chosen as a little corner from all the rest of the world to have his Name there truly called upon.

r. Dan. 8:12 He showeth that their sins are the cause of these horrible afflictions: and yet comforteth them, in that he

sacrifice for the iniquity: and it shall [s]cast down the truth to the ground, and thus
shall it do, and prosper. **13** Then I heard one of the [t]Saints speaking, and one of
the Saints spake unto a certain one, saying, How long shall endure the vision of
the daily sacrifice, and the iniquity of the [u]desolation to tread both the Sanctuary
and the [v]army underfoot? **14** And [w]he answered me, Unto the [x]evening and
the morning, two thousand and three hundred: then shall the Sanctuary be clean-
sed. **15** Now when I Daniel had seen the vision, and sought for the meaning,
behold, there stood before me [y]like the similitude of a man. **16** And I heard a
man's voice between the banks of Ulai, which called, and said, Gabriel, [z]make this
man to understand the vision. **17** So he came where I stood: and when he came,
I was afraid, and fell upon my face: but he said unto me, Understand, O son of
man: for [aa]in the last time shall be the vision. **18** Now as he was speaking unto
me, I being asleep fell on my face to the ground: but he touched me, and set me up
in my place. **19** And he said, Behold, I will show thee what shall be in the last
[ab]wrath: for in the end of the time appointed it shall come. **20** The ram which
thou sawest having two horns, are the Kings of the Medes and Persians. **21** And
the goat is the King of Greece, and the great horn that is between his eyes, is the
first king. **22** And that that is broken, and four stood up for it, are four king-
doms, which shall stand up [ac]of that nation, but not [ad]in his strength. **23** And
in the end of their kingdom, when the rebellious shall be consumed, a King of
[ae]fierce countenance, and understanding dark sentences, shall stand up. **24** And
his power shall be mighty, but not [af]in his strength: and he shall destroy wonder-
fully, and shall prosper, and practice, and shall destroy the [ag]mighty, and the holy
people. **25** And through his [ah]policy also he shall cause craft to prosper in his
hand, and he shall extol himself in his heart, and by [ai]peace shall destroy many:
he shall also stand up against the [aj]prince of princes, but he shall be broken down
[ak]without hand. **26** And the vision of the [al]evening and the morning, which
is declared, is true: therefore seal thou up the vision, for it shall be after many
days. **27** And I Daniel was stricken and sick [am]certain days: but when I rose up, I
did the king's business, and I was astonished at the vision, but none understood it.

9

3 Daniel desireth to have that performed of God, which he had promised concerning the return of the people from their banishment in Babylon. 5 A true confession. 20 Daniel's prayer is heard. 21 Gabriel the Angel expoundeth unto him the vision of the seventy weeks. 24 The anointing of Christ. 25 The building again of Jerusalem. 26 The death of Christ.

1 In the first year of Darius the son of [a]Ahasuerus, of the seed of the Me-
des, which was made king over the [b]realm of the Chaldeans, **2** Even in the first
year of his reign, I Daniel understood by [c]books the number of the years, whe-
reof the Lord had spoken unto Jeremiah the Prophet, that he would accomplish
seventy years in the desolation of Jerusalem. **3** And I turned my face unto the
Lord God, and [d]sought by prayer and supplications with fasting and sackcloth and
ashes. **4** And I prayed unto the Lord my God, and made my confession, saying,
Oh Lord God which art [e]great and fearful, and keepest covenant and mercy toward
them which love [f]thee, and toward them that keep thy commandments, **5** We
have sinned and have committed iniquity, and have done wickedly, yea, we have re-
belled, and have departed from thy precepts, and from thy judgments. **6** For we
would not obey thy servants the Prophets, which spake in thy name to our kings,
to our princes, and to our fathers, and to all the people of the land. **7** O Lord, [g]ri-
ghteousness belongeth unto thee, and unto us [h]open shame, as appeareth this day
unto every man of Judah, and to the inhabitants of Jerusalem, yea, unto all Israel,
both near and far off, through all the country, whither thou hast driven them, be-
cause of their offences, that they have committed against thee. **8** O Lord, unto us
appertaineth open shame, to our [i]Kings, to our princes, and to our fathers, because
we have sinned against thee. **9** Yet compassion and forgiveness is in the Lord our
God, albeit we have rebelled against him. **10** For we have not obeyed the [j]voice
of the Lord our God, to walk in his laws, which he hath laid before us by the mini-
stry of his servants the Prophets. **11** Yea, all Israel have transgressed thy Law, and
are turned back, and have not heard thy voice: therefore the [k]curse is poured upon
us, and the oath that is written in the Law of Moses the servant of God, because
we have sinned against him. **12** And he hath confirmed his words, which he spa-
ke against us, and against our judges that [l]judged us, by bringing upon us a great
plague: for under the whole heaven hath not been the like, as hath been brought
upon Jerusalem. **13** All this plague is come upon us, as it is written in the Law of
Moses: yet made we not our prayer before the Lord our God, that we might turn
from our iniquities and understand thy truth. **14** Therefore hath the Lord [m]ma-
de ready the plague, and brought it upon us: for the Lord our God is righteous in
all his works which he doeth: for we would not hear his voice. **15** [l]And now, O
Lord our God, that hast brought thy people out of the land of Egypt with a mighty
hand, and hast gotten thee renown, as appeareth this day, we have sinned, we have
done wickedly. **16** O Lord, according to all thy [n]righteousness, I beseech thee,
let thine anger and thy wrath be turned away from thy city Jerusalem thine holy
Mountain: because of our sins, and for the iniquities of our fathers, Jerusalem and
thy people are a reproach to all that are about us. **17** Now therefore, O our God,
hear the prayer of thy servant, and his supplications, and cause thy face to [o]shine
upon thy Sanctuary, that lieth waste for the [p]Lord's sake. **18** O my God, incli-
ne thine ear and hear: open thine eyes, and behold our desolations, and the city
whereupon thy Name is called: for we do not present our supplications before thee
for our own [q]righteousness, but for thy great tender mercies. **19** O Lord hear,
O Lord forgive, O Lord [r]consider, and do it: defer not, for thine own sake, O my
God: for thy Name is called upon thy city, and thy people. **20** And while I was
speaking and praying, and confessing my sin, and the sin of my people Israel, and
did present my supplication before the Lord my God, for the holy Mountain of
my God, **21** Yea, while I was speaking in prayer, even the man [z]Gabriel, whom
I had seen before in the vision, came flying, and touched me about the time of the
evening oblation. **22** And he informed me, and talked with me, and said, O Da-
niel, I am now come forth to give thee knowledge and understanding. **23** At the
beginning of thy supplications the commandment came forth, and I am come to
show thee, for thou art greatly beloved: therefore understand the matter and con-
sider the vision. **24** Seventy [s]weeks are determined upon [t]thy people and upon
thine holy city, to finish the wickedness, and to seal up [u]the sins, and to reconcile
the iniquity, and to bring in everlasting righteousness, and to seal up the vision
and prophecy, and to anoint the most Holy. **25** Know therefore and understand
that from [v]the going forth of the commandment to bring again the people, and to
build Jerusalem, unto Messiah the Prince, shall be seven [w]weeks and [x]threescore
and two weeks, and the street shall be built again, and the wall even in a [y]troublous
time. **26** And after threescore and two [z]weeks, shall Messiah be slain, and shall

---

appointeth this tyrant a time, whom he would not suffer utterly to abolish his religion.

s. Dan. 8:12 This horn shall abolish for a time the true doctrine, and so corrupt God's service.

t. Dan. 8:13 Meaning, that he heard one of the Angels asking this question of Christ, whom he called a certain one, or a secret one, or a marvelous one.

u. Dan. 8:13 That is, the Jews' sins, which were cause of his destruction.

v. Dan. 8:13 That is, which suppresseth God's religion, and his people.

w. Dan. 8:14 Christ answered me for the comfort of the Church.

x. Dan. 8:14 That is, until so many natural days be past, which make 6 years, 3 months and an half: for so long under Antiochus was the Temple profaned.

y. Dan. 8:15 Which was Christ who in this manner declared himself to the old fathers, how he would be God manifest in flesh.

z. Dan. 8:16 This power to command the Angel, declared that he was God.

aa. Dan. 8:17 The effect of this vision shall not yet appear, but a long time after.

ab. Dan. 8:19 Meaning, that great rage which Antiochus should show against the Church.

ac. Dan. 8:22 That is, out of Greece.

ad. Dan. 8:22 They shall not have like power as had Alexander.

ae. Dan. 8:23 Noting that this Antiochus was impudent and cruel, and also crafty that he could not be deceived.

af. Dan. 8:24 That is, not like Alexander's strength.

ag. Dan. 8:24 Both the Gentiles that dwelt about him, and also the Jews.

ah. Dan. 8:25 Whatsoever he goeth about by his craft, he shall bring it to pass.

ai. Dan. 8:25 That is, under pretence of peace, or as it were in sport.

aj. Dan. 8:25 Meaning, against God.

ak. Dan. 8:25 For God would destroy him with a notable plague, and so comfort his Church.

al. Dan. 8:26 Read verse 14.

am. Dan. 8:27 For fear and astonishment.

DAN. 9

a. Dan. 9:1 Who was also called Astyages.

b. Dan. 9:1 For Cyrus led with ambition, went about wars in other countries, and therefore Darius had the title of the kingdom, though Cyrus was king in effect.

c. Dan. 9:2 For though he was an excellent Prophet, yet he daily increased in knowledge by reading of the Scriptures.

d. Dan. 9:3 He speaketh not of that ordinary prayer, which he used in his house thrice a day, but of a rare and vehement prayer, least their sins should cause God to delay the time of their deliverance prophesied by Jeremiah.

e. Dan. 9:4 That is, hast all power in thyself to execute thy terrible judgments against obstinate sinners, as thou art rich in mercy to comfort them which obey thy word and love thee.

f. Dan. 9:4 Hebrew, him.

g. Dan. 9:7 He showeth that whensoever God punisheth, he doeth it for just cause: and thus the godly never accuse him of rigor as the wicked do, but acknowledge that in themselves there is just cause why he should so entreat them.

h. Dan. 9:7 Hebrew, confusion of face.

i. Dan. 9:8 He doth not excuse the kings because of their authority, but prayeth chiefly for them as the chief occasions of these great plagues.

j. Dan. 9:10 He showeth that they rebel against God, which serve him not according to his commandment and word.

k. Dan. 9:11 As Deut. 27:15, or the curse confirmed by an oath.

l. Dan. 9:12 Or, governed us.

m. Dan. 9:14 Hebrew, watched upon the evil.

n. Dan. 9:16 That is, according to all thy merciful promises and the performance thereof.

o. Dan. 9:17 Show thyself favorable.

p. Dan. 9:17 That is, for thy Christ's sake in whom thou wilt accept all our prayers.

q. Dan. 9:18 Declaring, that the godly flee only unto God's mercies, and renounce their own works, when they seek for remission of their sins.

r. Dan. 9:19 Thus he could not content himself with any vehemence of words: for he was so led with a fervent zeal considering God's promise made to the city in respect of his Church, and for the advancement of God's glory.

s. Dan. 9:24 He alludeth to Jeremiah's prophecy: who prophesied that their captivity should be seventy years: but now God's mercy should sevenfold exceed his judgment, which should be four hundred and ninety years, even to the coming of Christ, and so then it should continue forever.

t. Dan. 9:24 Meaning, Dan.'s nation, over whom he was careful.

u. Dan. 9:24 To show mercy and to put sin out of remembrance.

v. Dan. 9:25 That is, from the time that Cyrus gave them leave to depart.

w. Dan. 9:25 These weeks make forty-nine years, whereof 46 are referred to the time of the building of the Temple, and three to the laying of the foundation.

x. Dan. 9:25 Counting from the sixth year of Darius, who gave the second commandment for the building of the Temple are 62 weeks, which make 434 years, which comprehend the time from the building of the Temple unto the baptism of Christ.

y. Dan. 9:25 Hebrew, in straits of time.

z. Dan. 9:26 In this least week of the seventy, shall Christ come and preach and suffer death.

aa. Dan. 9:26 He shall seem to have no beauty, nor to be of any estimation, as Isa. 53:2.

ab. Dan. 9:26 Meaning Titus, Vespasian's son, who should come and destroy both the Temple and the people without all hope of recovery.

ac. Dan. 9:27 By the preaching of the Gospel he confirmed his promise, first to the Jews, and after to the Gentiles.

[aa]have nothing, and the people of the [ab]prince that shall come, shall destroy the
city and the Sanctuary, and the end thereof shall be with a flood: and unto the end
of the battle it shall be destroyed by desolations. **27** And he [ac]shall confirm the
covenant with many for one week: and in the midst of the week he shall cause the
sacrifice and the oblation to [ad]cease, [ae]and for the overspreading of the abomina-
tions, he shall make it desolate, even until the consummation determined shall be
poured upon the desolate.

10

1 There appeareth unto Daniel a man clothed in linen, 11 which showeth him wherefore he is sent.

1 In the [a]third year of Cyrus King of Persia, a thing was revealed unto Daniel
(whose name was called Belteshazzar) and the word was true, but the time ap-
pointed was [b]long, and he understood the thing, and had understanding of the vi-
sion. **2** At the same time I Daniel was in heaviness for three weeks of days. **3** I
ate no pleasant bread, neither came flesh nor wine in my mouth, neither did I
anoint myself at all, till three weeks of days were fulfilled. **4** And in the four and
twentieth day of the [c]first month, as I [d]was by the side of that great river, even
Hiddekel, **5** And I lifted mine eyes, and looked, and behold, there was a man
[e]clothed in linen, whose loins were girded with fine gold of [1]Uphaz. **6** His body
also was like the Chrysolite, and his face (to look upon) like the lightning, and his
eyes as lamps of fire, and his arms and his feet were like in color to polished brass,
and the voice of his words was like the voice of a multitude. **7** And I Daniel alo-
ne saw the vision: for the men that were with me, saw not the vision: but a great
fear fell upon them, so that they fled away and hid themselves. **8** Therefore I was
left alone, and saw this great vision, and there remained no strength in me: for [f]my
strength was turned in me into corruption, and I retained no power. **9** Yet heard
I the voice of his words: and when I heard the voice of his words, I slept on my
face, and my face was toward the ground. **10** And behold, an [g]hand touched me,
which set me up upon my knees, and upon the palms of mine hands, **11** And
he said unto me, O Daniel, a man greatly beloved, understand the words that I
speak unto thee, and stand in thy place: for unto thee am I now sent. And when he
had said this word unto me, I stood trembling. **12** Then said he unto me, Fear
not, Daniel: for from the first day that thou didst set thine heart to understand,
and to humble thyself before thy God, thy words were heard, and I am come for
thy words. **13** But the [h]prince of the kingdom of Persia withstood me one and
twenty days: but lo, [i]Michael one of the chief princes, came to help me, and I re-
mained there by the Kings of Persia. **14** Now I am come to show thee what shall
come to thy people in the latter days: for yet the [j]vision is for many days. **15** And
when he spake these words unto me, I set my face toward the ground, and held
my tongue. **16** And behold, [k]one like the similitude of the sons of man touched
my lips: then I opened my mouth, and spake, and said unto him that stood be-
fore me, O my Lord, [l]by the vision my sorrows are returned upon me, and I have
retained no strength. **17** For how can the servant of this my Lord talk with my
Lord being such one? for as for me, straightway there remained no strength in me,
neither is there breath left in me. **18** Then there came again, and touched me,
one like the appearance of a man, and he strengthened me, **19** And said, O man,
greatly beloved, fear not: [m]peace be unto thee: be strong and of good courage. And
when he had spoken unto me, I [n]was strengthened, and said, Let my Lord speak:
for thou hast strengthened me. **20** Then said he, Knowest thou wherefore I am
come unto thee? but now will I return to fight with the Prince of Persia: and when I
am gone forth, lo, the [o]Prince of Greece shall come. **21** But I will show thee that
which is decreed in the Scripture of truth: [p]and there is none that holdeth with me
in these things, but Michael your prince.

11

A prophecy of the kingdoms, which should be enemies to the Church of God, as of Persia, 3 Of Greece, 5 of Egypt, 28 of Syria, 36 and of the Romans.

1 Also I, in the first year of Darius of the Medes, even I [a]stood to encourage
and to strengthen him. **2** And now will I show thee the truth. Behold, there shall
stand up yet [b]three kings in Persia, and the fourth shall be far richer than they all:
and by his strength, and by his riches he shall stir up [c]all against the realm of Gre-
ece. **3** But a [d]mighty King shall stand up, that shall rule with great dominion,
and do according to his pleasure. **4** And when he shall stand up, [e]his kingdom
shall be broken, [f]and shall be divided toward the [g]four winds of heaven: and not to
his [h]posterity, nor according to [i]his dominion, which he ruled: for his kingdom
shall be plucked up even to be for others besides [j]those. **5** And the [k]King of the
South shall be mighty, and one of [l]his princes, and shall prevail against him, and
bear rule: his dominion shall be a great dominion. **6** And in the end of years they
shall be joined together: for the King's [m]daughter of the South shall come to the
King of the North to make an agreement, but she shall not retain the power of the
[n]arm, neither shall [o]he continue, nor his [p]arm: but she shall be delivered to death,
and they that brought her, and he [q]that begat her, and he that comforted her, in
these times. **7** But out of the bud of her [r]roots shall one stand up in his stead,
[s]which shall come with an army, and shall enter into the fortress of the King of the
North, and do with them as he list, and shall prevail, **8** And shall also carry cap-
tives into Egypt their gods: with their molten images, and with their precious ves-
sels of silver and of gold, and he shall continue [t]more years than the king of the
North. **9** So the king of the South shall come into his kingdom, and shall return
into his own land. **10** Wherefore his [u]sons shall be stirred up, and shall assemble
a mighty great army: and one [v]shall come, and overflow, and pass through: then
shall he [w]return, and be stirred up at his fortress. **11** And the King of the South
shall be angry, and shall come forth, and fight with him, even with the king of the
North: for he shall set forth a great [x]multitude, and the multitude shall be given
into his hand. **12** Then the multitude shall be proud, and their heart shall be li-
fted up: for he shall cast down thousands: but he shall not still prevail, **13** For the
King of the North [y]shall return, and shall set forth a greater multitude than afore,

---

ad. Dan. 9:27 Christ accomplished this by his death and resurrection.

ae. Dan. 9:27 Meaning, that Jerusalem and the Sanctuary should be utterly destroyed for their rebellion against God, and their idolatry: or as some read, that the plague shall be so great, that they shall be all astonied at them.

DAN. 9

1. Exod. 14:28 **2.** Dan. 8:16

DAN. 10

a. Dan. 10:1 He noteth this third year, because at this time the building of the Temple began to be hindered by Cambyses Cyrus' son, when the father made war in Asia minor against the Scythians, which was a discouraging to the godly, and a great fear to Dan..

b. Dan. 10:1 Which is to declare that the godly should not hasten too much, but patiently to abide the issue of God's promise.

c. Dan. 10:4 Called Abib, which containeth part of March, and part of April.

d. Dan. 10:4 Being carried by the Spirit of prophecy to have the sight of this river Tigris.

e. Dan. 10:5 This was the Angel of God, which was sent to assure Dan. in this prophecy that followeth.

f. Dan. 10:8 The word also signifieth comeliness, or beauty, so that for fear he was like a dead man for deformity.

g. Dan. 10:10 Which declareth that when we are struck down with the majesty of God, we cannot rise, except he also lift us up with his hand, which is his power.

h. Dan. 10:13 Meaning, Cambyses who reigned in his father's absence, and did not only for this space hinder the building of the Temple, but would have further raged, if God had not sent me to resist him, and therefore have I stayed for the profit of the Church.

i. Dan. 10:13 Though God could by one Angel destroy all the world, yet to assure his children of his love, he sendeth forth double power, even Michael, that is, Christ Jesus the head of Angels.

j. Dan. 10:14 For though the Prophet Dan. should end and cease, yet his doctrine should continue till the coming of Christ, for the comfort of his Church.

k. Dan. 10:16 This was the same Angel that spake with him before in the similitude of a man.

l. Dan. 10:16 I was overcome with fear and sorrow, when I saw the vision.

m. Dan. 10:19 He declareth hereby that God would be merciful to the people of Israel.

n. Dan. 10:19 Which declareth that when God smiteth down his children, he doth not immediately lift them up at once (for now the Angel had touched him twice) but by little and little.

o. Dan. 10:20 Meaning, that he would not only himself bridle the rage of Cambyses, but also the other Kings of Persia by Alexander the King of Macedonia.

p. Dan. 10:21 For this Angel was appointed for the defense of the Church under Christ, who is the head thereof.

DAN. 10

1. Jer. 10:9

DAN. 11

a. Dan. 11:1 The Angel assureth Dan. that God hath given him power to perform these things, seeing he appointed him to assist Darius when he overcame the Chaldeans.

b. Dan. 11:2 Whereof Cambyses that now reigned, was the first, the second Smerdis, the third Darius the son of Hystaspis, and the fourth Xerxes, which all were enemies to the people of God, and stood against them.

c. Dan. 11:2 For he raised up all the East countries to fight against the Greeks, and albeit he had in his army nine hundred thousand men, yet in four battles he was discomfited and fled away with shame.

d. Dan. 11:3 That is, Alexander the great.

e. Dan. 11:4 For when his estate was most flourishing, he overcame himself with drink, and so fell into a disease: or as some write, was poisoned by Cassander.

f. Dan. 11:4 For his twelve chief Princes first divided his kingdom among themselves.

g. Dan. 11:4 After this his Monarchy was divided into four: for Seleucus had Syria, Antigonus Asia minor, Cassander the kingdom of Macedonia, and Ptolemy Egypt.

h. Dan. 11:4 Thus God revenged Alexander's ambition and cruelty in causing his posterity to be murdered, partly of the father's chief friends, and partly one of another.

i. Dan. 11:4 None of these four shall be able to be compared to the power of Alexander.

j. Dan. 11:4 That is, his posterity having no part thereof.

k. Dan. 11:5 To wit, Ptolemy king of Egypt.

l. Dan. 11:5 That is, Antiochus the son of Seleucus, and one of Alexander's princes shall be more mighty: for he should have both Asia and Syria.

m. Dan. 11:6 That is, Berenice the daughter of Ptolemy Philadelphus shall be given in marriage to Antiochus Theos, thinking by this affinity that Syria and Egypt should have a continual peace together.

n. Dan. 11:6 That force and strength shall not continue: for soon after Berenice and her young son after her husband's death, was slain of her stepson Seleucus Callinicus the son of Laodice, the lawful wife of Antiochus, but put away for this woman's sake.

o. Dan. 11:6 Neither Ptolemy nor Antiochus.

p. Dan. 11:6 Some read, seed, meaning, the child begotten of Berenice.

q. Dan. 11:6 Some read, she that begate her, and thereby understand her nurse, which brought her up: so that all they that were occasion of this marriage, were destroyed.

r. Dan. 11:7 Meaning, that Ptolemeus Euergetes after the death of his father Philadelphus should succeed in the kingdom being of the same stock that Berenice was.

s. Dan. 11:7 To revenge the sister's death against Antiochus Callinicus king of Syria.

t. Dan. 11:8 For this Ptolemy reigned six and forty years.

u. Dan. 11:10 Meaning, Seleucus and Antiochus the great, the sons of Callinicus, shall make war against Ptolemy Philopater the son of Philadelphus.

v. Dan. 11:10 For his elder brother Seleucus died, or was slain while the wars were preparing.

w. Dan. 11:10 That is, Philopater when he shall see Antiochus to take great dominions from him in Syria, and also ready to invade Egypt.

x. Dan. 11:11 For Antiochus had six thousand horsemen, and threescore thousand footmen.

y. Dan. 11:13 After the death of Ptolemy Philopater, who left Ptolemeus Epiphanes his heir.

and shall come forth (after certain years) with a mighty army, and great riches. **14** And at the same time there shall [z]many stand up against the king of the South: also the rebellious children of thy [aa]people shall exalt themselves to establish the vision, but they shall fall. **15** So the King of the North shall come, and cast up a mount, and take the strong city: and the arms of the South shall [ab]not resist, neither his chosen people, neither shall there be any strength to withstand. **16** But he that shall come, shall do unto him as he list, and none shall stand against him: and he shall stand in the [ac]pleasant land, which by his hand shall be consumed. **17** Again he shall [ad]set his face to enter with the power of his whole kingdom, and his confederates with him: thus shall he do, and he shall give him the [ae]daughter of women to destroy [af]her: but [ag]she shall not stand on his side, neither be for him. **18** After this shall he turn his face unto the [ah]isles, and shall take many, but a prince [ai]shall cause his shame to light upon him, besides that he shall cause his own shame to turn upon [aj]himself. **19** For he shall turn his face toward the forts of [ak]his own land: but he shall be overthrown and fall, and be no more [al]found. **20** [am]Then shall stand up in his place in the glory of the kingdom, one that shall raise taxes: but after few days he shall be destroyed, neither in [an]wrath, nor in battle. **21** And in his place shall stand up a [ao]vile person, to whom they shall not give the honor of the kingdom: but he shall come in peaceably and obtain the kingdom by flatteries. **22** And the [ap]arms shall be overthrown with a flood before him, and shall be broken: and also the prince of the [aq]covenant. **23** And after [ar]the league made with him, he shall work deceitfully: for he shall come up, and overcome with a [as]small people. **24** He shall enter into the quiet and plentiful province, and he shall do that which his fathers [at]have not done, nor his fathers' fathers: he shall divide among them the prey and the spoil, and the substance, yea, and he shall forecast his devices against the strongholds, even for a [au]time. **25** Also he shall stir up his power, and his courage against the King of the South with a great army, and the King of the South shall be stirred up to battle with a very great and mighty army: but he shall not [av]stand: for they shall forecast and practice against him. **26** Yea, they that feed of the portion of [aw]his meat, shall destroy him: and his army [ax]shall overflow: and many shall fall, and be slain. **27** And both these Kings' hearts shall be to do [ay]mischief, and they shall talk of deceit at one table: but it shall not avail: for [az]yet the end shall be at the time appointed. **28** Then shall he return into his land with great [ba]substance: for his heart shall be against the holy covenant: so shall he do and return to his own land. **29** At the time appointed he shall return, and come toward the South: but the last shall not be as the first. **30** For the ships [bb]of Chittim shall come against him: therefore he shall be sorry and return and fret against the holy covenant: so shall he do, he shall even return [bc]and have intelligence with them that forsake the holy covenant. **31** And arms [bd]shall stand on his part, and they shall pollute the Sanctuary [be]of strength, and shall take away the daily sacrifice, and they shall set up the abominable desolation. **32** And such as wickedly [bf]break the covenant, shall he cause to sin by flattery: but the people that do know their God, shall prevail and prosper. **33** And they that understand among the [bg]people, shall instruct many: [bh]yet they shall fall by sword, and by flame, by captivity and by spoil many days. **34** Now when they shall fall, they shall be holpen with a [bi]little help: but many shall cleave unto them [bj]feignedly. **35** And some of them [bk]of understanding shall fall to try them, and to purge, and to make them white, till the time be out: for there is a time appointed. **36** And the [bl]king shall do what him list: he shall exalt himself, and magnify himself against all, that is God, and shall speak marvelous things against the God of gods, and shall prosper, till the wrath [bm]be accomplished: for the determination is made. **37** Neither shall he regard the [bn]God of his fathers, nor the desires [bo]of women, nor care for any God: for he shall magnify himself above all. **38** But in his place shall he honor the [bp]god Mauzzim, and the god whom his fathers knew not, shall he honor with [bq]gold and with silver, and with precious stones, and pleasant things. **39** Thus shall he do in [br]the holds of Mauzzim with a strange god whom he shall acknowledge: he shall increase his glory, and shall cause them to rule over many, and shall divide the land for gain. **40** And at the end of time shall the king of the [bs]South push at him, and the king of the North shall come against him like a whirlwind with chariots, and with horsemen, and with many ships, and he shall enter into the countries, and shall overflow and pass through. **41** He shall enter also into the [bt]pleasant land, and many countries shall be overthrown: but these shall escape out of his hand, even Edom and Moab, and the chief of the children of Ammon. **42** He shall stretch forth his hands also upon the countries, and the land of Egypt shall not escape. **43** But he shall have power over the treasures of gold and of silver, and over all the precious things of Egypt, and of the Libyans, and of the black Mores where he shall pass. **44** But the tidings out of the East and the North shall [bu]trouble him: therefore he shall go forth [bv]with great wrath to destroy and root out many. **45** And he shall plant the tabernacles [bw]of his palace between the seas in the glorious and holy mountain, yet he shall come to his end, and none shall help him.

---

z. Dan. 11:14 For not only Antiochus came against him but also Philip King of Macedonia, and these two brought great power with them.

aa. Dan. 11:14 For under Onias which falsely alleged that place of Isa. 19:19, certain of the Jews retired with him into Egypt to fulfill this prophecy: also the Angel showeth that all these troubles which are in the Church, are by the providence and counsel of God.

ab. Dan. 11:15 The Egyptians were not able to resist Scopas Antiochus' captain.

ac. Dan. 11:16 He showeth that he shall not only afflict the Egyptians, but also the Jews, and shall enter into their country, whereof he admonisheth them before, that they may know that all these things came by God's providence.

ad. Dan. 11:17 This was the second battle that Antiochus fought against Ptolemy Epiphanes.

ae. Dan. 11:17 To wit, a beautiful woman which was Cleopatra Antiochus' daughter.

af. Dan. 11:17 For he regarded not the life of his daughter in respect of the kingdom of Egypt.

ag. Dan. 11:17 She shall not agree to his wicked counsel, but shall love her husband, as her duty requireth, and not seek his destruction.

ah. Dan. 11:18 That is, toward Asia, Greece, and those isles which are in the sea called Mediterranean: for the Jews called all countries isles which were divided from them by sea.

ai. Dan. 11:18 For whereas Antiochus was wont to contemn the Romans, and put their ambassadors to shame in all places, Atilius the Consul, or Lucius Scipio put him to flight, and caused his shame to turn on his own head.

aj. Dan. 11:18 By his wicked life, and obeying of foolish counsel.

ak. Dan. 11:19 For fear of the Romans he shall flee to his holds.

al. Dan. 11:19 For when as under the pretence of poverty he would have robbed the Temple of Jupiter Dodomeus, the countrymen slew him.

am. Dan. 11:20 That is, Seleucus shall succeed his father Antiochus.

an. Dan. 11:20 Not by foreign enemies, or battle, but by treason.

ao. Dan. 11:21 Which was Antiochus Epiphanes, who as is thought was the occasion of Seleucus his brother's death, and was of a vile, cruel and flattering nature, and defrauded his brother's son of the kingdom, and usurped the kingdom without the consent of the people.

ap. Dan. 11:22 He showeth that great foreign powers shall come to help the young son of Seleucus against his uncle Antiochus: and yet shall be overthrown.

aq. Dan. 11:22 Meaning, Ptolemais Philopater's son who was this child's cousin germane, and is here called the prince of the covenant, because he was the chief, and all others followed his conduct.

ar. Dan. 11:23 For after the battle Philometor and his uncle Antiochus made a league.

as. Dan. 11:23 For he came upon him at unawares, and when he suspected his uncle Antiochus nothing.

at. Dan. 11:24 Meaning, in Egypt.

au. Dan. 11:24 He will content himself with the small holds for a time, but ever labor by craft to attain to the chiefest.

av. Dan. 11:25 He shall be overcome with treason.

aw. Dan. 11:26 Signifying his princes and the chief about him.

ax. Dan. 11:26 Declaring that his soldiers shall brast out and venture their life to slay and to be slain for the safeguard of their prince.

ay. Dan. 11:27 The uncle and the nephew shall take truce, and banquet together, yet in their hearts they shall imagine mischief one against the other.

az. Dan. 11:27 Signifying, that it standeth not in the counsel of men to bring things to pass, but in the providence of God, who ruleth the Kings by a secret bridle, that they cannot do what they list themselves.

ba. Dan. 11:28 Which he shall take of the Jews in spoiling Jerusalem and the Temple, and this is told them before to move them to patience, knowing that all things are done by God's providence.

bb. Dan. 11:30 That is, the Roman power shall come against him: for P. Popilius the Ambassador appointed him to depart in the Romans' name, to which thing he obeyed, although with grief, and to revenge his rage he came against the people of God the second time.

bc. Dan. 11:30 With the Jews which shall forsake the covenant of the Lord: for first he was called against the Jews by Jason the high Priest, and this second time by Menelaus.

bd. Dan. 11:31 A great faction of the wicked Jews shall hold with Antiochus.

be. Dan. 11:31 So called because the power of God was nothing diminished, although this tyrant set up in the Temple the image of Jupiter Olympius, and so began to corrupt the pure service of God.

bf. Dan. 11:32 Meaning, such as bare the name of Jews, but indeed were nothing less, for they sold their souls, and betrayed their brethren for gain.

bg. Dan. 11:33 They that remain constant among the people shall teach others by their example, and edify many in the true religion.

bh. Dan. 11:33 Whereby he exhorteth the godly to constancy, although they should perish a thousand times, and though their miseries endure never so long.

bi. Dan. 11:34 As God will not leave his Church destitute, yet will he not deliver it all at once, but so help, as they may still seem to fight under the cross, as he did in the time of the Maccabees, whereof he here prophesieth.

bj. Dan. 11:34 That is, there shall be even of this small number many hypocrites.

bk. Dan. 11:35 To wit, of them that fear God and will lose their life for the defense of true religion. Signifying also that the Church must continually be tried and purged, and ought to look for one persecution after another: for God hath appointed the time: therefore we must obey.

bl. Dan. 11:36 Because the Angel's purpose is to show the whole course of the persecutions of the Jews unto the coming of Christ, he now speaketh of the Monarchy of the Romans which he noteth by the name of a King, who were without religion and condemned the true God.

bm. Dan. 11:36 So long the tyrants shall prevail as God hath appointed to punish his people: but he showeth that it is but for a time.

bn. Dan. 11:37 The Romans shall observe no certain form of religion as other nations, but shall change their gods at their pleasures, yea, contemn them and prefer themselves to their gods.

bo. Dan. 11:37 Signifying that they should be without all humanity: for the love of women is taken for singular or great love, as 2 Sam. 1:26.

bp. Dan. 11:38 That is, the god of power and riches: they shall esteem their own power above all their gods and worship it.

bq. Dan. 11:38 Under pretence of worshipping the gods, they shall enrich their city with the most precious jewels of all the world, because that hereby all men should have them in admiration for their power and riches.

br. Dan. 11:39 Although in their hearts they had no religion, yet they did acknowledge the gods, and worshipped them in their temples, lest they should have been despised as Atheists: but this was to increase their fame and riches: and when they got any country, they so made others the rulers thereof, that the profit ever came to the Romans.

bs. Dan. 11:40 That is, both the Egyptians and the Syrians shall at length fight against the Romans, but they shall be overcome.

bt. Dan. 11:41 The Angel forewarneth the Jews that when they should see the Romans invade them, and that the wicked should escape their hands, that then they should not think but that all this was done by God's providence, forasmuch as he warned them of it so long afore, and therefore he would still preserve them.

bu. Dan. 11:44 Hearing that Crassus was slain, and Antonius discomfited.

bv. Dan. 11:44 For Augustus overcame the Parthians, and recovered that which Antonius had lost.

bw. Dan. 11:45 The Romans after this reigned quietly throughout all countries, and from sea to sea, and in Judea: but at length for their cruelty God shall destroy them.

12

1 Of the deliverance of the Church by Christ.

1 And at that [a]time shall Michael stand up, the great prince, whi-
ch standeth for the children of thy people, and there shall be a time of trouble,
such as never was since there began to be a nation unto that same time: and at
that time thy people shall be delivered, everyone that shall be found written in
the book. 2 And many [b]of them that sleep in the dust of the earth, shall awake,
some to everlasting life, and some to shame and perpetual contempt. 3 And they
that be [c]wise, shall shine, as the brightness of the firmament: and they that [d]turn
many to righteousness, shall shine as the stars, forever and ever. 4 But thou, O
Daniel, [e]shut up the words, and seal the book [f]till the end of the time: many shall
run to and fro, and knowledge shall be increased. 5 Then I Daniel looked, and
behold, there stood other two, the one on this side of the brink of the [g]river, and
the other on that side of the brink of the river. 6 And one said unto the man
clothed in linen, which was upon the waters of the river, When shall be the end
of these wonders? 7 And I heard the man clothed in linen which was upon the
waters of the river, when he held up his [h]right hand, and his left hand unto hea-
ven, and sware by him that liveth forever, that it shall tarry for a [i]time two times
and an half: and when he shall have accomplished [j]to scatter the power of the holy
people, all these things shall be finished. 8 Then I heard it, but I understood it
not: then said I, O my Lord, what shall be the end of these things? 9 And he
said, Go thy way, Daniel: for the words are closed up, and sealed, till the end of
the time. 10 Many shall be purified, made white, and tried: but the wicked shall
do wickedly, and none of the wicked shall have understanding: but the wise shall
understand. 11 And from the time that the [k]daily sacrifice shall be taken away,
and the abominable desolation set up, there [l]shall be a thousand, two hundred and
ninety days. 12 Blessed is he that waiteth and cometh to the thousand, three
hundred and [m]five and thirty days. 13 But go [n]thou thy way till the end be: for
thou shalt rest and stand up in thy lot, at the end of the days.

DAN. 12

a. Dan. 12:1 The Angel here noteth two things: first that the Church shall be in great affliction and trouble at Christ's coming, and next that God will send his Angel to deliver it, whom here he calleth Michael, meaning Christ, which is published by the preaching of the Gospel.

b. Dan. 12:2 Meaning, all shall rise at the general resurrection, which thing he here nameth because the faithful should have ever respect to that: for in the earth there shall be no sure comfort.

c. Dan. 12:3 Who have kept the true fear of God and his religion.

d. Dan. 12:3 He chiefly meaneth the ministers of God's word, and next all the faithful which instruct the ignorant, and bring them to the true knowledge of God.

e. Dan. 12:4 Though the most part despise this prophecy, yet keep thou it sure and esteem it as a treasure.

f. Dan. 12:4 Till the time that God hath appointed for the full revelation of these things: and then many shall run to and fro to search the knowledge of these mysteries which things they obtain now by the light of the Gospel.

g. Dan. 12:5 Which was Tigris.

h. Dan. 12:7 Which was as were a double oath, and did the more confirm the thing.

i. Dan. 12:7 Meaning, a long time, a longer time, and at length a short time: signifying that their troubles should have an end.

j. Dan. 12:7 When the Church shall be scattered and diminished in such sort as it shall seem to have no power.

k. Dan. 12:11 From the time that Christ by his sacrifice shall take away the sacrifice and ceremonies of the Law.

l. Dan. 12:11 Signifying that the time shall be long of Christ's second coming, and yet the children of God ought not to be discouraged, though it be deferred.

m. Dan. 12:12 In this number he addeth a month and a half to the former number, signifying that it is not in man to appoint the time of Christ's coming, but that they are blessed that patiently abide his appearing.

n. Dan. 12:13 The Angel warneth the Prophet patiently to abide; till the time appointed come, signifying that he should depart this life, and rise again with the elect, when God had sufficiently humbled and purged his Church.

HOSEA

1

1 The time wherein Hosea prophesied. 2 The idolatry of the people. 10 The calling of the Gentiles. 11 Christ is the head of all people.

1 The word of the Lord that came unto Hosea the son of Beeri, in the days
[a]of Uzziah, Jotham, Ahaz, and Hezekiah, [b]kings of Judah, and in the days of Je-
roboam the son of Joash king of Israel. 2 At the beginning the Lord spake by
Hosea, and the Lord said unto Hosea, Go, take unto thee a wife [c]of fornications,
and children of fornications: for the land hath committed great whoredom, depar-
ting from the Lord. 3 So he went, and took [d]Gomer, the daughter of Diblaim,
which conceived and bare him a son. 4 And the Lord said unto him, Call his
name [e]Jezreel: for yet a little, and I will visit the blood of Jezreel upon the house of
[f]Jehu, and will cause to cease the kingdom of the house of Israel. 5 And at that
[g]day will I also break the bow of Israel in the valley of Jezreel. 6 She conceived
yet again, and bare a daughter, and God said unto him, Call her name [h]Lo-Ruha-
mah: for I will no more have pity upon the house of Israel: but I will utterly [i]take
them away. 7 Yet I will have mercy upon the house of Judah, and will [j]save them
by the Lord their God, and will not save them by bow, nor by sword, nor by batt-
le, by horses, nor by horsemen. 8 Now when she had weaned Lo-Ruhamah, she
conceived, and bare a son. 9 Then said God, Call his name [k]Lo-Ammi: for ye are
not my people: therefore will I not be yours. 10 Yet the number of the [l]children
of Israel shall be as the sand of the sea, which cannot be measured nor told: and in
the place where it was said unto them, Ye are not my people, it shall be said unto
them, Ye are the sons of the living God. 11 Then shall the children of Judah, and
the children of Israel be [m]gathered together, and appoint themselves one head, and
they shall come up out of the land: for great is the [n]day of Jezreel.

2

1 The people is called to repentance. 5 He showeth their idolatry and threateneth them except they repent.

1 Say unto your [a]brethren, Ammi, and to your sisters, Ruhamah, 2 Plead
with your [b]mother: plead with her: for she is not my wife, neither am I her hu-
sband: but let her take away her fornications out of her sight, and her adulteries
[c]from between her breasts. 3 Lest I strip her naked, and [d]set her as in the day that
she was [e]born, and make her as a wilderness, and leave her like a dry land, and slay
her for thirst. 4 And I will have no pity upon her children: for they be the [f]chil-
dren of fornication. 5 For their mother hath played the harlot: she that conceived
them, hath done shamefully: for she said, I will go after thy [g]lovers that give me my
bread and my water, my wool, and my flax, mine oil and my drink. 6 Therefore

---

HOSEA. 1

a. Hos. 1:1 Called also Azariah, who being a leper was disposed from his kingdom.

b. Hos. 1:1 So that it may be gathered by the reign of these four kings, that he preached above threescore years.

c. Hos. 1:2 That is, one that of long time hath accustomed to play the harlot: not that the Prophet did this thing in effect, but he saw this in a vision, or else was commanded by God to set forth under this parable or figure the idolatry of the Synagogue, and of the people her children.

d. Hos. 1:3 Gomer signifieth a consumption or corruption, and Diblaim clusters of figs, declaring that they were all corrupt like rotten figs.

e. Hos. 1:4 Meaning, that they should be no more called Israelites of the which name they boasted because Israel, did prevail with God: but that they were as bastard, and therefore should be called Jezreelites, that is scattered people, alluding to Jezreel, which was the chief city of the ten tribes under Ahab where Jehu shed so much blood, 2 Kings 10:8.

f. Hos. 1:4 I will be revenged upon Jehu for the blood that he shed in Jezreel: for albeit God stirred him up to execute his judgments, yet he did them for his own ambition, and not for the glory of God as the end declared: for he built up that idolatry which he had destroyed.

g. Hos. 1:5 When the measure of their iniquity is full, and I shall take vengeance and destroy all their policy and force.

h. Hos. 1:6 That is, not obtaining mercy: whereby he signifieth, that God's favor was departed from them.

i. Hos. 1:6 For the Israelites never returned after that they were taken captives by the Assyrians.

j. Hos. 1:7 For after their captivity he restored him miraculously by the means of Cyrus, Ezra 1:1.

k. Hos. 1:9 That is, not my people.

l. Hos. 1:10 Because they thought that God could not have been true in his promise except he had preserved them, he declareth though they were destroyed, yet the true Israelites, which are the sons of the promise, should be without number, which stand both of the Jews and the Gentiles, Rom. 9:26.

m. Hos. 1:11 To wit, after the captivity of Babylon when the Jews were restored, but chiefly this is referred to the time of Christ, who should be the head both of the Jews and Gentiles.

n. Hos. 1:11 The calamity and destruction of Israel shall be so great, that to restore them shall be as a miracle.

HOSEA. 2

a. Hos. 2:1 Seeing that I have promised you deliverance, it remaineth that you encourage one another to embrace the same, considering that ye are my people on whom I will have mercy.

b. Hos. 2:2 God showeth that the fault was not in him, but in their Synagogue, and their idolatries, that he forsook them, Isa. 50:1.

c. Hos. 2:2 Meaning, that their idolatry was so great, that they were not ashamed, but boasted of it, Ezek. 16:25.

d. Hos. 2:3 For though this people were as an harlot for their idolatries, yet he had left them with their apparel and dowry and certain signs of his favor, but if they continued still, he would utterly destroy them.

e. Hos. 2:3 When I brought her out of Egypt, Ezek. 16:4.

f. Hos. 2:4 That is, bastards and begotten in adultery.

g. Hos. 2:5 Meaning, the idol which they served, and by whom they thought they had wealth and abundance.

behold, I will stoop [h]thy way with thorns, and make an hedge, that she shall not find her paths. **7** Though she follow after her lovers, yet shall she not come at them: though she seek them, yet shall she not find them: then shall she say, [i]I will go and return to my first husband: for at that time was I better than now. **8** Now she did not know that I [j]gave her corn, and wine, and oil, and multiplied her silver and gold, which they bestowed upon Baal. **9** Therefore will I return, and take away [k]my corn in the time thereof, and my wine in the season thereof, and will recover my wool and my flax lent, to cover her shame. **10** And now will I discover her [l]lewdness in the sight of her lovers, and no man shall deliver her out of mine hand. **11** I will also cause all her mirth to cease, her feast days, her new moons, and her Sabbaths, and all her solemn feasts. **12** And I will destroy her vines and her fig trees, whereof she hath said, These are my rewards that my lovers have given me: and I will make them as a forest, and the wild beasts shall eat them. **13** And I will visit upon her the days of [m]Baal, wherein she burnt incense to them: and she decked herself with her [n]earrings and her jewels, and she followed her lovers, and forgot me, saith the Lord. **14** Therefore behold, I will [o]allure her, and bring her into the wilderness, and speak friendly unto her. **15** And I will give her her vineyards from thence, and the valley [p]of Achor for the door of hope, and she shall [q]sing there as in the days of her youth, and as in the day when she came up out of the land of Egypt. **16** And at that day, saith the Lord, thou shalt call me [r]Ishi, and shalt call me no more [s]Baali. **17** For I will take away the names of Baal out of her mouth, and they shall be no more remembered by their [t]names. **18** And in that day will I make a covenant for them with the [u]wild beasts, and with the fowls of the heaven, and with that that creepeth upon the earth: and I will break the bow, and the sword and the battle out of the earth: and will make them to sleep safely. **19** And I will marry thee unto me forever: yea, I will marry thee unto me in righteousness, and in judgment, and in mercy, and in compassion. **20** I will even marry thee unto me in [v]faithfulness, and thou shalt know the Lord. **21** And in that day I will hear, saith the Lord, I will even hear [w]the heavens, and they shall hear the earth, **22** And the earth shall hear the corn, and the wine, and the oil, and they shall hear Jezreel. **23** And I will sow her unto me in the earth, and I will have mercy upon her, that was not pitied, [1]and I will say to them which were not my people, Thou art my people. And they shall say, Thou art my God.

3

1 The Jews shall be cast off for their idolatry. 5 Afterward they shall return to the Lord.

1 Then said the Lord to me, [a]Go yet, and love a woman (beloved of her husband, and was an harlot) according to the love of the Lord toward the children of Israel: yet they looked to other gods, and [b]loved the wine bottles. **2** So [c]I bought her to me for fifteen pieces of silver, and for an homer of barley, and an half homer of barley. **3** And I said unto her, Thou shalt abide with [d]me many days: thou shalt not play the harlot, and thou shalt be to none other man, and I will be so unto thee. **4** For the children of Israel shall [e]remain many days without a king and without a [f]prince, and without an offering, and without an image, and without an Ephod, and without Teraphim. **5** Afterward shall the children of Israel convert and seek the Lord their God, and [g]David their king, and shall fear the Lord and his goodness in the latter days.

4

A complaint against the people and the priests of Israel.

1 Hear the word of the Lord, ye children of Israel: for the Lord [a]hath a controversy with the inhabitants of the land, because there is no truth, nor mercy, nor knowledge of God in the land. **2** By swearing, and lying, and killing, and stealing, and whoring, they break out, and [b]blood toucheth blood. **3** Therefore shall the land mourn, and everyone that dwelleth therein shall be cut off, with the beasts of the field, and with the fowls of the heaven, and also the fishes of the sea shall be taken away. **4** Yet [c]let none rebuke, nor reprove another: for thy people are as they that rebuke the Priest. **5** Therefore shalt thou fall in the [d]day, and the Prophet shall fall with thee in the night, and I will destroy thy [e]mother. **6** My people are destroyed for lack of knowledge: because [f]thou hast refused knowledge, I will also refuse thee that thou shalt be no Priest to me: and seeing [g]thou hast forgotten the Law of thy God, I will also forget thy children. **7** As they were [h]increased, so they sinned against me: therefore will I change their glory into shame. **8** [i]They eat up the sins of my people, and lift up their minds in their iniquity. **9** And there shall be like people like [j]priest: for I will visit their ways upon them, and reward them their deeds. **10** For they shall eat, and not have enough, they shall [k]commit adultery, and shall not increase, because they have left off to take heed to the Lord. **11** [l]Whoredom, and wine, and new wine take away their heart. **12** My [m]people ask counsel at their stocks, and their staff teacheth them: for the [n]spirit of fornications hath caused them to err, and they have gone a whoring from under their God. **13** They sacrifice upon the tops of the mountains, and burn incense upon the hills under the oaks, and the poplar tree, and the elm, because the shadow thereof is good: therefore your daughters shall be [o]harlots, and your spouses shall be whores. **14** I will not [p]visit your daughters when they are harlots: nor your spouses, when they are whores: for they themselves are separated with harlots, and sacrifice with whores: therefore the people that doth not understand, shall fall. **15** Though thou Israel, play the harlot, yet [q]let not Judah sin: come not ye unto [r]Gilgal, neither go ye up to [s]Beth Aven, nor swear, The Lord liveth. **16** For Israel is rebellious as an unruly heifer. Now the Lord will feed them as a [t]lamb in a large place. **17** Ephraim is joined to idols: let him alone. **18** Their drunkenness stinketh: they have committed whoredom: their rulers love to say with shame, [u]Bring ye. **19** The wind hath [v]bound them up in her wings, and they shall be ashamed of their sacrifices.

5

1 Against the Priests and rulers of Israel. 13 The help of man is in vain.

1 O ye Priests, hear this, and hearken ye, O house of Israel, and give ye ear, O house of the King: for judgment is toward you, because you have been a [a]snare on Mizpah, and a net spread upon Tabor. **2** Yet they were profound to decline to [b]slaughter, though I have been a [c]rebuker of them all. **3** I know [d]Ephraim, and Israel is not hid from me: for now, O Ephraim, thou art become an

---

h. Hos. 2:6 I will punish thee that then thou mayest try whether thine idols can help thee, and bring thee into such straightness that thou shalt have no lust to play the wanton.
i. Hos. 2:7 This he speaketh of the faithful, which are truly converted, and also showeth the use and profit of God's rods.
j. Hos. 2:8 This declareth that idolaters defraud God of his honor, when they attribute his benefits to their idols.
k. Hos. 2:9 Signifying, that God will take away his benefits when man by his ingratitude doth abuse them.
l. Hos. 2:10 That is, all her service, ceremonies and inventions whereby she worshipped her idols.
m. Hos. 2:13 I will punish her for her idolatry.
n. Hos. 2:13 By showing how harlots trim themselves to please others, he declareth how that superstitious idolaters set a great part of their religion, in decking themselves on their holy days.
o. Hos. 2:14 By my benefits in offering her grace and mercy, even in that place where she shall think herself destitute of all help and comfort.
p. Hos. 2:15 Which was a plentiful valley, and wherein they had great comfort when they came out of the wilderness, as Josh. 7:26, and is called the door of hope, because it was a departing from death and an entry into life.
q. Hos. 2:15 She shall then praise God as she did when she was delivered out of Egypt.
r. Hos. 2:16 That is, mine husband, knowing that I am joined to thee by an inviolable covenant.
s. Hos. 2:16 That is, my master: which name was applied to their idols.
t. Hos. 2:17 No idolatry shall once come into their mouth, but they shall serve me purely according to my word.
u. Hos. 2:18 Meaning, that he will so bless them that all creatures shall favor them.
v. Hos. 2:20 With a covenant that never shall be broken.
w. Hos. 2:21 Then shall the heaven desire rain for the earth which shall bring forth for the use of man.

HOSEA 2
1. Rom. 9:25 / 1 Pet. 2:10

HOSEA. 3
a. Hos. 3:1 Herein the Prophet representeth the person of God, which loved his Church before he called her, and did not withdraw the same when she gave herself to idols.
b. Hos. 3:1 That is, gave themselves wholly to pleasure, and could not take up, as they that are given to drunkenness.
c. Hos. 3:2 Yet I loved her and paid a small portion for her, lest she perceiving the greatness of my love, should have abused me, and not been under duty: for fifteen pieces of silver were but half the price of a slave, Exod. 21:32.
d. Hos. 3:3 I will try thee a long time as in thy widowhood whether thou wilt be mine or no.
e. Hos. 3:4 Meaning, not only all the time of their captivity, but also unto Christ.
f. Hos. 3:4 That is, they should neither have policy nor religion, and their idols also wherein they put their confidence, should be destroyed.
g. Hos. 3:5 This is meant of Christ's kingdom, which was promised unto David to be eternal, Ps. 72:17.

HOSEA. 4
a. Hos. 4:1 Because the people would not obey the admonitions of the Prophet, he citeth them before the judgment seat of God, against whom they chiefly offended, Isa. 7:13; Zech. 12:10; Mic. 6:1, 2.
b. Hos. 4:2 In every place appeareth a liberty to most heinous vices, so that one followeth in the neck of another.
c. Hos. 4:4 As though he would say that it were in vain to rebuke them: for no man can abide it: yea, they will speak against the prophets and priests whose office it is chiefly to rebuke them.
d. Hos. 4:5 Ye shall perish all together the one because he would not obey, and the other, because he would not admonish.
e. Hos. 4:5 That is, the Synagogue wherein thou boastest.
f. Hos. 4:6 That is, the Priests shall be cast off, because that for lack of knowledge, they are not able to execute their charge, and instruct others, Deut. 33:3; Mal. 2:7.
g. Hos. 4:6 Meaning, the whole body of the people, which were weary with hearing the word of God.
h. Hos. 4:7 The more I was beneficial unto them.
i. Hos. 4:8 To wit, the Priests seek to eat the people's offerings, and flatter them in their sins.
j. Hos. 4:9 Signifying, that as they have sinned together, so shall they be punished together.
k. Hos. 4:10 Showing that their wickedness shall be punished on all sorts: for though they think by the multitude of wives to have many children, yet they shall be deceived of their hope.
l. Hos. 4:11 In giving themselves to pleasures, they become like brute beasts.
m. Hos. 4:12 Thus he speaketh by derision in calling them his people, which now for their sins they were not: for they sought help of stocks and sticks.
n. Hos. 4:12 They are carried away with a rage.
o. Hos. 4:13 Because they take away God's honor, and give it to idols: therefore he will give them up to their lusts, that they shall dishonor their own bodies, Rom. 1:28.
p. Hos. 4:14 I will not correct your shame to bring you to amendment, but let you run headlong to your own damnation.
q. Hos. 4:15 God complaineth that Judah is infected, and willeth them to learn to return in time.
r. Hos. 4:15 For albeit the Lord had honored this place in time past by his presence, yet because it was abused by their idolatry, he would not that his people should resort thither.
s. Hos. 4:15 He calleth Bethel, that is, the house of God, Beth Aven, that is, the house of iniquity, because of their abominations set up there, signifying that no place is holy, where God is not purely worshipped.
t. Hos. 4:16 God will so disperse them, that they shall not remain in any certain place.
u. Hos. 4:18 They are so impudent in receiving bribes, that they will command men to bring them unto them.
v. Hos. 4:19 To carry them suddenly away.

HOSEA. 5
a. Hos. 5:1 The Priests and Princes caught the poor people in their snares, as the fowlers did the birds, in these two high mountains.

harlot, and Israel is defiled. **4** They will not give their minds to turn unto their God: for the spirit of fornication is in the midst of them, and they have not known the Lord. **5** And the [e]pride of Israel doth testify to his face: therefore shall Israel and Ephraim fall in their iniquity: Judah also shall fall with them. **6** They shall go with their sheep, and with their bullocks, to seek the Lord: but they shall not find him: for he hath withdrawn himself from them. **7** They have transgressed against the Lord: for they have begotten [f]strange children: now shall [g]a month devour them with their portions. **8** Blow ye the trumpet in Gibeah, and the shame in Ramah: cry out at Beth Aven, after thee, O [h]Benjamin. **9** Ephraim shall be desolate in the day of rebuke: among the tribes of Israel have I caused to [i]know the truth. **10** The princes of Judah were like them that [j]remove the bound: therefore will I pour out my wrath upon them like water. **11** Ephraim is oppressed and broken in judgment, because he willingly walked after the [k]commandment. **12** Therefore will I be unto Ephraim as a moth, and to the house of Judah as a rottenness. **13** When Ephraim saw his sickness, and Judah his wound, then went Ephraim unto [l]Assyria, and sent unto King [m]Jareb: yet could he not heal you, nor cure you of your wound. **14** For I will be unto Ephraim as a lion, and as a lion's whelp, to the house of Judah: I, even I will spoil and go away: I will take away, and none shall rescue it. **15** I will go, and return to my place, till they acknowledge their fault, and seek me: in their affliction, they will seek me diligently.

6

1 Affliction causeth a man to turn to God. 9 The wickedness of the Priests.

1 Come, and let [a]us return to the Lord: for he hath spoiled, and he will heal us: he hath wounded us, and he will bind us up. **2** After two days will [b]he revive us, and in the third day he will raise us up, and we shall live in his sight. **3** Then shall we have knowledge, and endeavor ourselves to know the Lord: his going forth is prepared as the morning, and he shall come unto us as the rain, and as the latter rain unto the earth. **4** O Ephraim, what shall I do unto thee? O Judah, how shall I entreat thee? for [c]your goodness is as a morning cloud, and as the morning dew it goeth away. **5** Therefore have I [d]cut down by the Prophets: I have slain them by the words of my mouth, and thy [e]judgments were as the light that goeth forth. **6** For I desired [f]mercy, and not sacrifice, and the knowledge of God more than burnt offerings. **7** But they [g]like men have transgressed the covenant: there have they trespassed against me. **8** [h]Gilead is a city of them that work iniquity, and is polluted with blood. **9** And as the thieves wait for a man, so the company of Priests murder in the way by consent: for they work mischief. **10** I have seen villainy in the house of Israel: there is the whoredom of Ephraim: Israel is defiled. **11** Yea, Judah hath set a [i]plant for thee, while I would return the captivity of my people.

7

1 Of the vices and wantonness of the people. 12 Of their punishment.

1 When I would have healed Israel, then the iniquity of Ephraim was discovered, and the wickedness of Samaria: for they have dealt falsely: and [a]the thief cometh in, and the robber spoileth without. **2** And they consider not in their hearts, that I remember all their wickedness: now their own inventions have beset them about: they are in my sight. **3** They make the [b]king glad with their wickedness, and the princes with their lies. **4** They are all adulterers, and as a very [c]oven heated by the baker, which ceaseth from raising up, and from kneading the dough until it be leavened. **5** This is the [d]day of our king: the princes have made him sick with flagons of wine: he stretcheth out his hand to scorners. **6** For they have made ready their heart like an oven while they lie in wait: their baker sleepeth all the night: in the morning it burneth as a flame of fire. **7** They are all hot as an oven, and have [e]devoured their judges: all their kings are fallen: there is none among them that calleth unto me. **8** Ephraim hath [f]mixed himself among the people. Ephraim is as a cake on the hearth not turned. **9** Strangers have devoured his strength, and he knoweth it not: yea, [g]gray hairs are here, and there upon him, yet he knoweth not. **10** And the pride of Israel testifieth to his face, and they do not return to the Lord their God, nor seek him for all this. **11** Ephraim also is like a dove deceived without [h]heart: they call to Egypt: they go to Assyria. **12** But when they shall go, I will spread my net upon them, and draw them down as the fowls of the heaven: I will chastise them as their [i]Congregation hath heard. **13** Woe unto them: for they have fled away from me: destruction shall be unto them, because they have transgressed against me: though I have [j]redeemed them, yet they have spoken lies against me. **14** And they have not cried unto me with their hearts, [k]when they howled upon their beds: [l]they assembled themselves for corn, and wine, and they rebel against me. **15** Though I have bound and strengthened their arm, yet do they imagine mischief against me. **16** They return, but not to the most high: they are like a deceitful bow: their princes shall fall by the sword, for the rage [m]of their tongues: this shall be their derision in the land of Egypt.

8

1 The destruction of Judah and Israel, because of their idolatry.

1 Set the trumpet to thy [a]mouth: he shall come as an eagle against the House of the Lord, because they have transgressed my covenant, and trespassed against my Law. **2** Israel shall [b]cry unto me, My God, we know thee. **3** Israel hath cast off the thing that is good: the enemy shall pursue him. **4** They have set up a [c]king, but not by me: they have made princes, and I knew it not: of their silver and their gold have they made them idols: therefore shall they be destroyed. **5** Thy calf, O Samaria, hath cast thee off: mine anger is kindled against them: how long will they be without [d]innocency! **6** [e]For it came even from Israel: the workman made it, therefore it is not God: but the calf of Samaria shall be broken in pieces. **7** For they have [f]sown the wind, and they shall reap the whirlwind: it hath no stalk: the bud shall bring forth no meal: if so be it brought forth, the strangers shall devour it. **8** Israel is devoured, now shall they be among the Gentiles as a vessel wherein is no pleasure. **9** For they are gone up to Assyria: they are as a [g]wild ass alone by himself: Ephraim hath hired lovers. **10** Yet though they have hired among the nations, now will I gather them and they shall sorrow a little for the [h]burden of the king and the princes. **11** Because Ephraim hath made many altars to sin, his altars shall be to sin. **12** I have written to them the great things of my Law: but they were counted as a [i]strange thing. **13** They sacrifice flesh for the sacrifices of mine offerings, and eat it: but the [j]Lord accepteth them not: now will he remember their iniquity, and visit their sins: they shall return to Egypt. **14** For Israel hath forgotten his maker, and buildeth Temples, and Judah hath increased strong cities: but I will send a fire upon his cities, and it shall devour the palaces thereof.

---

b. Hos. 5:2 Notwithstanding they seemed to be given altogether to holiness, and to sacrifices which here he calleth slaughter in contempt.
c. Hos. 5:2 Though I had admonished them continually by my Prophets.
d. Hos. 5:3 They boasted themselves not only to be Israelites, but also Ephraimites, because their king Jeroboam came of that tribe.
e. Hos. 5:5 Meaning, their contemning of all admonitions.
f. Hos. 5:7 That is, their children are degenerate, so that there is no hope in them.
g. Hos. 5:7 Their destruction is not far off.
h. Hos. 5:8 That is, all Israel comprehended under this part, signifying that the Lord's plagues should pursue them from place to place till they were destroyed.
i. Hos. 5:9 By the success they shall know that I have surely determined this.
j. Hos. 5:10 They have turned upside down all political order and all manner of religion.
k. Hos. 5:11 To wit, after king Jeroboam's commandment, and did not rather follow God.
l. Hos. 5:13 Instead of seeking for remedy at God's hand.
m. Hos. 5:13 Who was king of the Assyrians.

HOSEA. 6

a. Hos. 6:1 He showeth the people how they ought to turn to the Lord, that he might call back his plagues.
b. Hos. 6:2 Though he correct us from time to time, yet his help will not be far off, if we return to him.
c. Hos. 6:4 You seem to have a certain holiness and repentance, but it is upon the sudden, and as a morning cloud.
d. Hos. 6:5 I have still labored by my prophets, and as it were framed you to bring you to amendment, but all was in vain: for my word was not food to feed them, but a sword to slay them.
e. Hos. 6:5 My doctrine which I taught thee, was most evident.
f. Hos. 6:6 He showeth to what scope his doctrine tended, that they should join the obedience of God, and the love of their neighbor with outward sacrifices.
g. Hos. 6:7 That is, like light and weak persons.
h. Hos. 6:8 Which was the place where the Priests dwelt, and which should have been best instructed in my word.
i. Hos. 6:11 That is, doth imitate thine idolatry, and hath taken grafts of thy trees.

HOSEA. 7

a. Hos. 7:1 Meaning, that there was no one kind of vice among them, but that they were subject to all wickedness, both secret and open.
b. Hos. 7:3 They esteem their wicked king Jeroboam above God, and seek but how to flatter and please him.
c. Hos. 7:4 He compareth the rage of the people to a burning oven which the baker heateth, still till his dough be leavened and raised.
d. Hos. 7:5 They used all riot and excess in their feasts, and solemnities whereby their king was overcome with surfeit, and brought into diseases, and delighted in flatteries.
e. Hos. 7:7 By their occasion God hath deprived them of all good rulers.
f. Hos. 7:8 That is, he counterfeited the religion of the Gentiles, yet is but as a cake baked on the one side, and raw on the other, that is, neither thoroughly hot, nor thoroughly cold, but partly a Jew, and partly a Gentile.
g. Hos. 7:9 Which are a token of his manifold afflictions.
h. Hos. 7:11 That is, without all judgment, as they that cannot tell whether it is better to cleave only to God, or to seek the help of man.
i. Hos. 7:12 According to my curses made to the whole Congregation of Israel.
j. Hos. 7:13 That is, divers times redeemed them, and delivered them from death.
k. Hos. 7:14 When they were in affliction, and cried out for pain, they sought not unto me for help.
l. Hos. 7:14 They only seek their own commodity and wealth, and pass not for me their God.
m. Hos. 7:16 Because they boast of their own strength, and pass not what they speak against me and my servants, Ps. 73:9.

HOSEA. 8

a. Hos. 8:1 God encourageth the Prophet to signify the speedy coming of the enemy against Israel, which was once the people of God.
b. Hos. 8:2 They shall cry like hypocrites, but not from the heart, as their deeds declare.
c. Hos. 8:4 That is, Jeroboam by whom they sought their own liberty, and not to obey my will.
d. Hos. 8:5 That is, upright judgment and godly life.
e. Hos. 8:6 Meaning, the calf was invented by themselves, and of their fathers in the wilderness.
f. Hos. 8:7 Showing that their religion hath but a show, and in itself is but vanity.
g. Hos. 8:9 They never cease, but run to and fro to seek help.
h. Hos. 8:10 That is, for the king and the princes shall lay upon them: which means the Lord useth to bring them to repentance.
i. Hos. 8:12 Thus the idolaters count the word of God as strange in respect of their own inventions.
j. Hos. 8:13 Saying that they offer it to the Lord, but he accepteth no service, which he himself hath not appointed.

9

Of the hunger and captivity of Israel.

1 Rejoice not, O Israel for joy [a]as other people: for thou hast gone a whoring from thy God: thou hast loved [b]a reward upon every corn floor. **2** [c]The floor, and the winepress shall not feed them, and the new wine shall fail in her. **3** They will not dwell in the Lord's land, but Ephraim will return to Egypt, and they will eat unclean things in Assyria. **4** They shall not offer [d]wine to the Lord, neither shall their sacrifices be pleasant unto him: but they shall be unto them as the bread of mourners: all that eat thereof, shall be polluted: for their bread [e]for their souls shall not come into the house of the Lord. **5** What will ye do [f]then in the solemn day, and in the day of the feast of the Lord? **6** For lo, they are gone from [g]destruction: but Egypt shall gather them up, and Memphis shall bury them: the nettle shall possess the pleasant places of their silver, and the thorn shall be in their tabernacles. **7** The days of visitation are come: the days of recompense are come: Israel shall know it: [h]the Prophet is a fool: the spiritual man is mad, for the multitude of thine iniquity: therefore the hatred is great. **8** The watchman of Ephraim [i]should be with my God: but the Prophet is the snare of a fowler in all his ways, and hatred in the house of his God. **9** They [j]are deeply set: they are corrupt as in the days of Gibeah: therefore he will remember their iniquity, he will visit their sins. **10** I found Israel like [k]grapes in the wilderness: I saw your fathers as the first ripe in the fig tree at her first time: but they went to Baal Peor, and separated themselves unto that shame, and their abominations were according to [l]their lovers. **11** Ephraim their glory shall flee away like a bird: from the birth [m]and from the womb, and from the conception. **12** Though they bring up their children, yet I will deprive them from being men: yea, woe to them, when I depart from them. **13** Ephraim, as I saw, is as a tree [n]in Tyre planted in a cottage: but Ephraim shall bring forth his children to the murderer. **14** O Lord, give them: what wilt thou give them? give them a [o]barren womb and dry breasts. **15** All their wickedness is in [p]Gilgal: for there do I hate them: for the wickedness of their inventions, I will cast them out of mine House: I will love them no more: all their princes are rebels. **16** Ephraim is smitten, their root is dried up: they can bring no fruit: yea, though they bring forth, yet will I slay even the dearest of their body. **17** My God will cast them away, because they did not obey him: and they shall wander among the nations.

10

1 Against Israel and his idols. 14 His destruction for the same.

1 Israel is a [a]empty vine, yet hath it brought forth fruit unto itself, and according to the multitude of the fruit thereof he hath increased the altars: according to the [b]goodness of their land they have made fair images. **2** Their heart is [c]divided: now shall they be found faulty: he shall break down their altars; he shall destroy their images. **3** For now they shall say, We have no [d]King because we feared not the Lord: and what should a King do to us? **4** They have spoken words, swearing falsely in making [e]a covenant: thus [f]judgment groweth as wormwood in the furrows of the field. **5** The inhabitants of Samaria shall [g]fear because of the calf of Beth Aven: for the people thereof shall mourn over it, and the [h]Chemarims thereof, that rejoiced on it for the glory thereof, because it is departed from it. **6** It shall be also brought to Assyria, for a present unto king Jareb: Ephraim shall receive shame, and Israel shall be ashamed of his own counsel. **7** Of Samaria, the king thereof is destroyed, as the foam upon the water. **8** The high places also of [i]Aven shall be destroyed, even the sin of Israel: the thorn and the thistle shall grow upon their altars, and they shall say to the mountains, [l]Cover us, and to the hills, Fall upon us. **9** O Israel, thou hast [j]sinned from the days of Gibeah: there they [k]stood: the battle in Gibeah against the children of iniquity did not [l]touch them. **10** It is my desire [m]that I should chastise them, and the people shall be gathered against them, when they shall gather themselves in their two [n]furrows. **11** And Ephraim is as a heifer used to delight in [o]threshing: but I will pass by her [p]fair neck: I will make Ephraim to ride: Judah shall plow, and Jacob shall break his clods. **12** Sow to yourselves in righteousness: reap after the measure of mercy: [q]break up your fallow ground: for it is time to seek the Lord, till he come and rain righteousness upon you. **13** But you have plowed wickedness: ye have reaped iniquity: you have eaten the fruit of lies: because thou didst trust in thine own ways, and in the multitude of thy strong men, **14** Therefore shall a tumult arise among thy people, and all thy munitions shall be destroyed, as [r]Shalman destroyed Beth Arbel in the day of battle: the mother with the children was dashed in pieces. **15** So shall Bethel do unto you, because of your malicious wickedness: in a morning shall the king of Israel be destroyed.

11

1 The benefits of the Lord toward Israel. 5 Their ingratitude against him.

1 When Israel [a]was a child, then I loved him, and called my son out of Egypt. **2** They called them, but they [b]went thus from them: they sacrificed unto Baal, and burnt incense to images. **3** I led Ephraim also, as one should bear them in his arms: but they knew not that I healed them. **4** I led them with cords [c]of a man, even with bands of love, and I was to them, as he was taketh off the yoke from their jaws, and I laid the meat unto them. **5** He shall no more return into the land of Egypt: but Assyria shall be his [d]King, because they refused to convert. **6** And the sword shall fall on his cities, and shall consume his bars, and devour them, because of their own counsels. **7** And my people are bent to rebellion against me: though [e]they called them to the most high, yet none at all would exalt him. **8** [f]How shall I give thee up, Ephraim? how shall I deliver thee, Israel? how shall I make thee, as [g]Admah? how shall I set thee, as Zeboim? mine heart is turned within me: [h]my repentings are rouled together. **9** I will not execute the fierceness of my wrath: I will not return to destroy Ephraim: for I am God, and not man, the holy one in the midst of thee, and I will not [i]enter into the city. **10** They shall walk after the Lord: he shall roar like a lion: when he shall roar, then the children of the West shall fear. **11** [j]They shall fear as a sparrow out of Egypt, and as a dove out of the land of Assyria, and I will place them in their houses, saith the Lord. **12** Ephraim compasseth me about with lies, and the house of Israel with deceit: but Judah yet ruleth with [k]God, and is faithful with the Saints.

12

He admonisheth by Jacob's example to trust in God, and not in riches.

1 Ephraim is fed [a]with the wind, and followeth after the East wind: he increaseth daily lies and destruction, and they do make a covenant with Assyria, and [b]oil is carried into Egypt. **2** The Lord hath also a controversy with

---

HOSEA. 9

- **a.** Hos. 9:1 For though all other people should escape, yet thou shalt be punished.
- **b.** Hos. 9:1 Thou hast committed idolatry in hope of reward, and to have thy barns filled, Jer. 44:17, as an harlot that had rather live by playing the whore, than to be entertained of her own husband.
- **c.** Hos. 9:2 These outward things that thou seekest, shall be taken from thee.
- **d.** Hos. 9:4 All their doings both touching policy and religion, shall be rejected as things polluted.
- **e.** Hos. 9:4 The meat offering which they offered for themselves.
- **f.** Hos. 9:5 When the Lord shall take away all the occasions of serving him, which shall be the most grievous point of your captivity, when ye shall see yourselves cut off from God.
- **g.** Hos. 9:6 Though they think to escape by fleeing the destruction that is at hand, yet shall they be destroyed in the place whither they flee for succor.
- **h.** Hos. 9:7 Then they shall know that they were deluded by them, who challenged to themselves to be their prophets and spiritual men.
- **i.** Hos. 9:8 The Prophet's duty is to bring men to God, and not to be a snare to pull them from God.
- **j.** Hos. 9:9 This people is so rooted in their wickedness, that Gibeah which was like to Sodom, was never more corrupt, Judg. 19:22.
- **k.** Hos. 9:10 Meaning, that he so esteemed them and delighted in them.
- **l.** Hos. 9:10 They were as abominable unto me, as their lovers the idols.
- **m.** Hos. 9:11 Signifying, that God would destroy their children by these sundry means, and so consume them by little and little.
- **n.** Hos. 9:13 As they kept tender plants in their houses in Tyre to preserve them from the cold air of the sea, so was Ephraim at the first unto me, but now I will give him to the slaughter.
- **o.** Hos. 9:14 The Prophet seeing the great plagues of God toward Ephraim, prayeth to God to make them barren, rather than that this great slaughter should come upon their children.
- **p.** Hos. 9:15 The chief cause of their destruction is that they commit idolatry, and corrupt my Religion in Gilgal.

HOSEA. 10

- **a.** Hos. 10:1 Whereof though the grapes were gathered, yet ever as it gathered new strength, it increased new wickedness, so that the correction which should have brought them to obedience, did but utter their stubbornness.
- **b.** Hos. 10:1 As they were rich and had abundance.
- **c.** Hos. 10:2 To wit, from God.
- **d.** Hos. 10:3 The day shall come that God shall take away their king, and then they shall feel the fruit of their sins, and how they trusted in him in vain, 2 Kings 17:6, 7.
- **e.** Hos. 10:4 In promising to be faithful toward God.
- **f.** Hos. 10:4 Thus their integrity and fidelity, which they pretended, was nothing but bitterness and grief.
- **g.** Hos. 10:5 When the calf shall be carried away.
- **h.** Hos. 10:5 Chemarims were certain idolatrous priests, which did wear black apparel in their sacrifices, and cried with a loud voice: which superstition Elijah derided, 1 Kings 18:27, read 2 Kings 23:5.
- **i.** Hos. 10:8 This he speaketh in contempt of Bethel, read Hos. 4:15.
- **j.** Hos. 10:9 In those days wast thou as wicked as the Gibeonites, as God there partly declared: for thy zeal could not be good in executing God's judgments, seeing thine own deeds were as wicked as theirs.
- **k.** Hos. 10:9 To wit, to fight, or the Israelites remained in that stubbornness from that time.
- **l.** Hos. 10:9 The Israelites were not moved by their example to cease from their sins.
- **m.** Hos. 10:10 Because they are so desperate, I will delight to destroy them.
- **n.** Hos. 10:10 That is, when they have gathered all their strength together.
- **o.** Hos. 10:11 Wherein is pleasure, as in plowing is labor and pain.
- **p.** Hos. 10:11 I will lay my yoke upon her fat neck.
- **q.** Hos. 10:12 Read Jer. 4:4.
- **r.** Hos. 10:14 That is, Shalmaneser in the destruction of that city spared neither kind nor age.

HOSEA 10

- **1.** Isa. 2:19 / Luke 23:30 / Rev. 6:16; / Rev. 9:6

HOSEA. 11

- **a.** Hos. 11:1 While the Israelites were in Egypt, and did not provoke my wrath by their malice and ingratitude.
- **b.** Hos. 11:2 They rebelled and went a contrary way when the Prophets called them to repentance.
- **c.** Hos. 11:4 That is, friendly: and not as beasts or slaves.
- **d.** Hos. 11:5 Seeing they contemn all this kindness, they shall be led captive into Assyria.
- **e.** Hos. 11:7 To wit, the Prophets.
- **f.** Hos. 11:8 God considereth with himself, and that with a certain grief, how to punish them.
- **g.** Hos. 11:8 Which were two of the cities that were destroyed with Sodom, Deut. 29:23.
- **h.** Hos. 11:8 Meaning, that his love wherewith he first loved them, made him between doubt and assurance what to do: and herein appeareth his Fatherly affection: that his mercy toward his shall overcome his judgments, as he declareth in the next verse.
- **i.** Hos. 11:9 To consume thee, but will cause thee to yield, and so receive thee to mercy: and this is meant of the final number who shall walk after the Lord.
- **j.** Hos. 11:11 The Egyptians, and the Assyrians shall be afraid when the Lord maintaineth his people.
- **k.** Hos. 11:12 Governeth their state according to God's word, and doth not degenerate.

[c]Judah, and will visit Jacob, according to his ways: according to his works, will he recompense him. **3** He took his brother by the heel in the womb, and by his strength he had [d]power with God, **4** And had [e]power over the Angel, and prevailed: he wept and prayed unto him: [f]he found him in Bethel, and there he spake with us. **5** Yea, the Lord God of hosts, the Lord is himself his memorial. **6** Therefore turn thou to thy God: keep mercy and judgment, and hope still in thy God. **7** He is [g]Canaan: the balances of decree are in his hand: he loveth to oppress. **8** And Ephraim said, Notwithstanding I am rich, I have found me out riches in all my labors: they shall find none iniquity in me, [h]that were wickedness. **9** Though I am the Lord thy God, from the land of Egypt, yet will I make thee to dwell in the tabernacles, as in [i]the days of the solemn feast. **10** I have also spoken by the Prophets, and I have multiplied visions, and used similitudes by the ministry of the Prophets. **11** Is there [j]iniquity in Gilead? surely they are vanity: they sacrifice bullocks in Gilgal, and their altars are as heaps in the furrows of the field. **12** [k]And Jacob fled into the country of Aram, and Israel served for a wife, and for a wife he kept sheep, **13** And by a [l]Prophet the Lord brought Israel out of Egypt, and by a Prophet was he reserved. **14** But Ephraim provoked him with high places: therefore shall his blood be poured upon him, and his reproach shall his Lord reward him.

13

1 The abomination of Israel, 9 and cause of their destruction.

1 When Ephraim spake, there was [a]trembling: he [b]exalted himself in Israel, but he hath sinned in Baal, [c]and is dead. **2** And now they sin more and more, and have made them molten images of their silver, and idols according to their own understanding: they were all the work of the craftsmen: they say one to another while they sacrifice a [d]man, Let them kiss the calves. **3** Therefore they shall be as the morning cloud, and as the morning dew that passeth away, as the chaff that is driven with a whirlwind out of the floor, and as the smoke that goeth out of the chimney. **4** Yet I am the Lord thy God [e]from the land of Egypt, and thou shalt know no God but me: for there is no Savior beside me. **5** I did know thee in the wilderness, in the land of drought. **6** As in their pastures, so were they filled: they were filled, and their heart was exalted: therefore have they forgotten me. **7** And I will be unto them as a very lion, and as a leopard in the way of Assyria. **8** I will meet them, as a bear that is robbed of her whelps, and I will break the caul of their heart, and there will I devour them like a lion: the wild beasts shall tear them. **9** O Israel, one [f]hath destroyed thee, but in me is thine help. **10** [g]I am: where is thy king that should help thee in all thy cities? and thy judges, of whom thou saidest, Give me a king and princes? **11** I gave thee a king in mine anger, and I took him away in my wrath. **12** The iniquity of Ephraim is [h]bound up: his sin is hid. **13** The sorrows of a travailing woman shall come upon him: he is an unwise son, else would he not stand still at the time, even at the [i]breaking forth of the children.

14

I will redeem them from the power of the grave: I will deliver them from death: O [j]death, I will be thy death: O grave, I will be thy destruction: [k]repentance is hid from mine eyes.

15 Though he grew up among his brethren, an East wind shall come, even the wind of the Lord shall come up from the wilderness, and dry up his vein, and his fountain shall be dried up: he shall spoil the treasure of all pleasant vessels. **14 1** The destruction of Samaria. **2** He exhorteth Israel to turn to God, who requireth praise and thanks. **1** Samaria shall be desolate: for she hath rebelled against her God: they shall fall by the sword: their infants shall be dashed in pieces, and their women with child shall be ripped. **2** O Israel, [a]return unto the Lord thy God: for thou hast fallen by thine iniquity. **3** Take unto you words, and turn to the Lord, and say unto him, [b]Take away all iniquity, and receive us graciously: so will we render the calves of our [c]lips. **4** Assyria shall [d]not save us, neither will we ride upon horses, neither will we say anymore to the work of our hands, Ye are our gods: for in thee the fatherless findeth mercy. **5** [e]I will heal their rebellion: I will love them freely: for mine anger is turned away from him. **6** I will be as the dew unto Israel: he shall grow as the lily and fasten his roots, as the trees of Lebanon. **7** His branches shall spread, and his beauty shall be as the olive tree, and his smell as Lebanon. **8** They that dwell under his [f]shadow, shall return: they shall revive as the corn, and flourish as the vine: the scent thereof shall be as the wine of Lebanon. **9** Ephraim shall say, What have I to do anymore with idols? I [g]have heard him, and looked upon him: I am like a green fir tree: upon me is thy fruit found. **10** Who is [h]wise, and he shall understand these things? and prudent, and he shall know them? for the ways of the Lord are righteous and the just shall walk in them: but the wicked shall fall therein.

HOSEA. 12

a. Hos. 12:1 That is, flattereth himself with vain confidence.
b. Hos. 12:1 Meaning, presents to get friendship.
c. Hos. 12:2 Which in those points was like to Ephraim, but not in idolatries.
d. Hos. 12:3 Seeing that God did thus prefer Jacob their father, Judah's ingratitude was the more to be abhorred.
e. Hos. 12:4 Read Gen. 32:24-32.
f. Hos. 12:4 God found Jacob as he lay sleeping in Bethel, Gen. 28:12, and so spake with him there, that the fruit of that speech appertained to the whole body of the people, whereof we are.
g. Hos. 12:7 As for Ephraim he is more like the wicked Canaanites, than godly Abraham or Jacob.
h. Hos. 12:8 Thus the wicked measure God's favor by outward prosperity and like hypocrites cannot abide that any should reprove their doings.
i. Hos. 12:9 Seeing thou wilt not acknowledge my benefits, I will bring thee again to dwell in tents, as in the feast of the Tabernacles, which thou dost now contemn.
j. Hos. 12:11 The people thought that no man durst have spoken against Gilead, that holy place, and yet the Prophet saith, that all their religion was but vanity.
k. Hos. 12:12 If you boast of your riches and nobility, ye seem to reproach your father, who was a poor fugitive and servant.
l. Hos. 12:13 Meaning, Moses, whereby appeareth, that whatsoever they have, it cometh of God's free goodness.

HOSEA. 13

a. Hos. 13:1 He showeth the excellency and authority that this tribe had above all the rest.
b. Hos. 13:1 He made a king of his tribe.
c. Hos. 13:1 The Ephraimites are not far from destruction, and have lost their authority.
d. Hos. 13:2 The false prophets persuaded the idolaters to offer their children after the example of Abraham, and he showeth how they would exhort one another to the same, and to kiss and worship these calves which were their idols.
e. Hos. 13:4 He calleth them to repentance, and reproveth their ingratitude.
f. Hos. 13:9 Thy destruction is certain, and my benefits toward thee declare that it cometh not of me: therefore thine own malice, idolatry and vain confidence in men must needs be the cause thereof.
g. Hos. 13:10 I am all one, James 1:17.
h. Hos. 13:12 It is surely laid up to be punished, as Jer. 17:1.
i. Hos. 13:13 But would come out of the womb, that is out of this dangers wherein he is and not to tarry to be stifled.
j. Hos. 13:14 Meaning, that no power shall resist God when he will deliver his, but even in death will he give them life.
k. Hos. 13:14 Because they will not turn to me, I will change my purpose.

HOSEA. 14

a. Hos. 14:2 He exhorteth them to repentance to avoid all these plagues, willing them to declare by words their obedience and repentance.
b. Hos. 14:3 He showeth them how they ought to confess their sins.
c. Hos. 14:3 Declaring that this is the true sacrifice, that the faithful can offer, even thanks and praise, Heb. 13:15.
d. Hos. 14:4 We will leave off all vain confidence and pride.
e. Hos. 14:5 He declareth how ready God is to receive them that do repent.
f. Hos. 14:8 Whosoever join themselves to this people, shall be blessed.
g. Hos. 14:9 God showeth how prompt he is to hear his, when they repent, and to offer himself, as a protection and safeguard unto them, as a most sufficient fruit and profit.
h. Hos. 14:10 Signifying, that the true wisdom and knowledge consisteth in this even to rest upon God.

JOEL

1

1 A prophecy against the Jews. 2 He exhorteth the people to prayer and fasting for the misery that was at hand.

1 The word of the Lord that came to Joel the son of Pethuel. **2** Hear ye this,
O [a]Elders, and hearken ye all inhabitants of the land, whether [b]such a thing hath
been in your days, or yet in the days of your fathers. **3** Tell you your children
of it, and let your children show to their children, and their children, to another
generation. **4** That which is left of the palmerworm, hath the grasshopper eaten,
and the residue of the grasshopper hath the cankerworm eaten, and the residue of
the cankerworm hath the caterpillar eaten. **5** Awake ye [c]drunkards, and weep
and howl all ye drinkers of wine, because of the new wine, for it shall be pulled
from your mouth. **6** Yea, [d]a nation cometh upon my land, mighty and without
number, whose teeth are like the teeth of a lion, and he hath the jaws of a great
lion. **7** He maketh my vine waste, and pilleth off the bark of my fig tree: he ma-
keth it bare, and casteth it down: the branches thereof are made white. **8** Mourn
like a virgin girded with sackcloth, for the [e]husband of her youth. **9** The meat
offering and the drink offering is [f]cut off from the house of the Lord: the Priests
the Lord's ministers mourn. **10** The field is wasted: the land mourneth: for the
corn is destroyed: [g]the new wine is dried up, and the oil is decayed. **11** Be ye
ashamed, O husbandmen: howl, O ye vinedressers for the wheat and for the barley,
because the harvest of the field is perished. **12** The vine is dried up, and the fig
tree is decayed: the pomegranate tree and the palm tree, and the apple tree, even all
the trees of the field are withered: surely the joy is withered away from the sons of
men. **13** [h]Gird yourselves and lament ye Priests: howl ye ministers of the altar:
come, and lie all night in sackcloth, ye ministers of my God: for the meat offering,
and the drink offering is taken away from the house of your God. **14** Sanctify
you a fast: call a solemn assembly: gather the Elders, and all the inhabitants of the
land into the house of the Lord your God, and cry unto the Lord, **15** Alas: for
the day, for the [i]day of the Lord is at hand, and it cometh as a destruction from
the Almighty. **16** Is not the meat cut off before our eyes? and joy, and gladness
from the house of our God? **17** The seed is rotten under their clods: the garners
are destroyed: the barns are broken down, for the corn is withered. **18** How did
the beasts mourn! the herds of cattle pine away, because they have no pasture, and
the flocks of sheep are destroyed. **19** O Lord, to thee will I cry: for the fire hath
devoured the pastures of the wilderness, and the flame hath burnt up all the trees of
the field. **20** The beasts of the field cry also unto thee: for the river of waters are
dried up, and the [j]fire hath devoured the pastures of the wilderness.

2

He prophesieth of the coming and cruelty of their enemies. 13 An exhortation to move them to convert. 18 The love of God toward his people.

1 Blow [a]the trumpet in Zion, and shout in mine holy mountain, let all
the inhabitants of the land tremble: for the day of the Lord is come: for it is at
hand. **2** A [b]day of darkness, and of blackness, a day of clouds and obscurity, as
the morning spread upon the mountains, so is there a [c]great people, and a mighty:
there was none like it from the beginning, neither shall be anymore after it, unto
the years of many generations. **3** A fire devoureth before him, and behind him
a flame burneth up: the land is as the garden of [d]Eden before him, and behind
him a desolate wilderness, so that nothing shall escape him. **4** The beholding of
him is like the sight of horses, and like the horsemen, so shall they run. **5** Like
the noise of chariots in the tops of the mountains shall they leap, like the noise
of a flame of fire that devoureth the stubble, and as a mighty people prepared
to the battle. **6** Before his face shall the people tremble: all faces [e]shall gather
blackness. **7** They shall run like strong men, and go up to the wall like men of
war, and every man shall go forward in his ways, and they shall not stay in their
paths. **8** Neither shall one [f]thrust another, but everyone shall walk in his path:
and when they fall upon the sword, they shall not be wounded. **9** They shall run
to and fro in the city: they shall run upon the wall: they shall clime up upon the
houses, and enter in at the windows like the thief. **10** The earth shall tremble
before him, the heavens shall shake, the [g]sun and the moon shall be dark, and the
stars shall withdraw their shining. **11** And the Lord shall [h]utter his voice befo-
re his host: for his host is very great: for he is strong that doeth his word: [1]for the
day of the Lord is great and very terrible, and who can abide it? **12** Therefore
also now the Lord saith, Turn you unto me with all your heart, and with fasting,
and with weeping, and with mourning, **13** And [i]rent your heart, and not your
clothes: and turn unto the Lord your God, for he is gracious and merciful, slow to
anger, and of great kindness, and repenteth him of the evil. **14** Who knoweth,
if he will [j]return and repent and leave a blessing behind him, even a meat offering
and a drink offering unto the Lord your God? **15** Blow the trumpet in Zion,
sanctify a fast, call a solemn assembly. **16** Gather the people, sanctify the congre-
gation: gather the elders: assemble the [k]children, and those that suck the breasts:
let the bridegroom go forth of his chamber, and the bride out of her bride cham-
ber. **17** Let the Priests, the ministers of the Lord, weep between the porch and
the altar, and let them say, Spare thy people, O Lord, and give not thine heritage
into reproach, that the heathen should rule over them. [2]Wherefore should they say
among the people, Where is their God? **18** Then will the Lord be [l]jealous over
his land, and spare his people. **19** Yea, the Lord will answer and say unto his
people, Behold, I will send you corn and wine, and oil, and you shall be satisfied
therewith: and I will no more make you a reproach among the heathen. **20** But
I will remove far off from you the [m]Northern army, and I will drive him into a
land, barren and desolate with his face toward the [n]East sea, and his end to the ut-
most sea, and his stink shall come up, and his corruption shall ascend, because he
hath exalted himself to do this. **21** Fear not, O land, but be glad, and rejoice:
for the Lord will do great things. **22** Be not afraid, ye beasts of the field: for the
pastures of the wilderness are green for the tree beareth her fruit: the fig tree and
the vine do give their force. **23** Be glad then, ye children of Zion, and rejoice
in the Lord your God, for he hath given you the rain of [o]righteousness, [3]and he
will cause to come down for you the rain, even the first rain, and the latter rain in
the first month. **24** And the barns shall be full of wheat, and the presses shall
abound with wine and oil. **25** And I will render you the years that the grasshop-
per hath eaten, the cankerworm and the caterpillar and the palmerworm, my great
host which I sent among you. **26** So you shall eat and be satisfied and praise the
name of the Lord your God, that hath dealt marvelously with you: and my people
shall never be ashamed. **27** Ye shall also know that I am in the midst of Israel,
and that I am the Lord your God and none other, and my people shall never be
ashamed. **28** And afterward will I pour [p]out my Spirit upon all flesh: and your
sons and your daughters shall prophesy: your old men shall dream [q]dreams, and
your young men shall see visions. **29** And also upon the servants, and upon the
maids in those days will I pour my Spirit. **30** And I will show [r]wonders in the
heavens and in the earth: blood and fire, and pillars of smoke. **31** The [s]sun shall

---

JOEL. 1

a. Joel 1:2 Signifying the Princes, the Priests and the governors.
b. Joel 1:2 He calleth the Jews to the consideration of God's judgments, who had now plagued the fruits of the ground for the space of four years, which was for their sins, and to call them to repentance.
c. Joel 1:5 Meaning, that the occasion of their excess and drunkenness was taken away.
d. Joel 1:6 This was another plague wherewith God had punished them when he stirred up the Assyrians against them.
e. Joel 1:8 Mourn grievously, as a woman which hath lost her husband to whom she hath been married in her youth.
f. Joel 1:9 The tokens of God's wrath did appear in his Temple, insomuch as God's service was left off.
g. Joel 1:10 All comfort and substance for nourishment is taken away.
h. Joel 1:13 He showeth that the only means to avoid God's wrath, and to have all things restored, is unfeigned repentance.
i. Joel 1:15 We see by these great plagues that utter destruction is at hand.
j. Joel 1:20 That is, drought.

JOEL. 2

a. Joel 2:1 He showeth the great judgments of God, which are at hand, except they repent.
b. Joel 2:2 Of affliction and trouble.
c. Joel 2:2 Meaning, the Assyrians.
d. Joel 2:3 The enemy destroyed our plentiful country, wheresoever he cometh.
e. Joel 2:6 They shall be pale and black for fear, as Nah. 2:10.
f. Joel 2:8 For none shall be able to resist them.
g. Joel 2:10 Read Joel 2:31 and Isa. 13:10; Ezek. 32:7; Joel 3:15; Matt. 24:29.
h. Joel 2:11 The Lord shall stir up the Assyrians to execute his judgments.
i. Joel 2:13 Mortify your affections and serve God with pureness of heart, and not with ceremonies.
j. Joel 2:14 He speaketh this to stir up their slothfulness, and not that he doubted of God's mercies, if they did repent. How God repenteth, read Jer. 18:8.
k. Joel 2:16 That as all have sinned, so all may show forth signs of their repentance, that men seeing the children which are not free from God's wrath, might be the more lively touched with the consideration of their own sins.
l. Joel 2:18 If they repent he showeth that God will preserve and defend them with a most ardent affection.
m. Joel 2:20 That is, the Assyrians your enemies.
n. Joel 2:20 Called the salt sea, or Persian sea: meaning, that though his army were so great that it filled all from this sea to the sea called Mediterranean, yet he would scatter them.
o. Joel 2:23 That is, such as should come by just measure, and as was wont to be sent when God was reconciled with them.
p. Joel 2:28 That is, in greater abundance, and more generally than in times past: and this was fulfilled under Christ, when as God's graces, and his Spirit under the Gospel was abundantly given to the Church, Isa. 44:3; Acts 2:17; John 7:38, 39.
q. Joel 2:28 As they had visions and dreams in old time, so shall they now have clearer revelations.
r. Joel 2:30 He warneth the faithful what terrible things should come, to the intent that they should not look for continual quietness in this world, and yet in all these troubles he would preserve them.
s. Joel 2:31 The order of nature shall seem to be changed for the horrible afflictions that shall be in the world, Isa. 13:10; Ezek. 32:7; Joel 3:15; Matt. 24:29.

be turned into darkness, and the moon into blood, before the great and terrible day of the Lord come. **32** But whosoever shall call [t]on the Name of the Lord, shall be saved: for in mount Zion, and in Jerusalem shall be deliverance as the Lord hath said, and in the [u]remnant, whom the Lord shall call.

3

Of the judgment of God against the enemies of his people.

1 For behold, in [a]those days and in that time, when I shall bring again the captivity of Judah and Jerusalem, **2** I will also gather all nations, and will bring them down into the [b]valley of Jehoshaphat, and will plead with them there for my people, and for mine heritage Israel: whom they have scattered among the nations, and parted my land. **3** And they have cast lots for my people, and have given the child [c]for the harlot, and sold the girl for wine, that they might drink. **4** Yea, and [d]what have you to do with me, O Tyre and Sidon, and all the coasts of Philistia? will ye render me [e]a recompense? and if ye recompense me, swiftly and speedily will I render your recompense upon your head: **5** For ye have taken my silver and my gold, and have carried into your temples my goodly and pleasant things. **6** The children also of Judah and the children of Jerusalem have you sold unto the Grecians, that ye might send them far from their border. **7** Behold, I will raise them out of the place where ye have sold them, and will render your reward upon your own head. **8** And I will sell your sons and your daughters into the hand of the children of Judah, and they [f]shall send them to the Sabeans, to a people far off, for the Lord hath spoken it. **9** Publish this among the Gentiles: prepare war, wake up the mighty men: let all the men of war draw near and come up. **10** [g]Break your plowshares into swords, and your scythes into spears: let the weak say, I am strong. **11** Assemble yourselves, and come all ye heathen, and gather yourselves together round about: there shall the Lord cast down the mighty men. **12** Let the heathen be wakened, and come up to the valley of Jehoshaphat: for there will I sit to judge all the heathen round about. **13** Put in your [h]scythes, for the harvest is ripe, come, get you down, for the winepress is full: yea, the winepresses run over, for their wickedness is great. **14** O multitude, O multitude, come into the valley of threshing: for the day of the Lord is near in the valley of threshing. **15** The sun and moon shall be darkened, and the stars shall withdraw their light. **16** The Lord also shall roar out of Zion, and utter his voice from Jerusalem, and the heavens and the earth shall shake, but the Lord will be the [i]hope of his people, and the strength of the children of Israel. **17** So shall ye know that I am the Lord your God dwelling in Zion, mine holy Mountain: then shall Jerusalem be holy, and there shall no strangers go [j]through her anymore. **18** And in that day shall the mountains [k]drop down new wine, and the hills shall flow with milk, and all the rivers of Judah shall run with waters, and a fountain shall come forth of the House of the Lord, and shall water the valley of Shittim. **19** [l]Egypt shall be waste, and Edom shall be a desolate wilderness, for the injuries of the children of Judah, because they have shed innocent blood in their land. **20** But Judah shall dwell forever, and Jerusalem from generation to generation. **21** For I will [m]cleanse their blood, that I have not cleansed, and the Lord will dwell in Zion.

---

t. Joel 2:32 God's judgments are for the destruction of the infidels, and to move the godly to call upon the Name of God, who will give them salvation.
u. Joel 2:32 Meaning hereby the Gentiles, Rom. 10:13.

JOEL. 2
1. Jer. 30:7 / Amos 5:18 / Zeph. 1:!5
2. Ps. 79:10
3. Lev. 26:4 / Deut. 11:14

JOEL. 3
a. Joel 3:1 When I shall deliver my Church, which standeth of the Jews and of the Gentiles.
b. Joel 3:2 It appeareth that he alludeth to that great victory of Jehoshaphat, when as God without man's help destroyed the enemies, 2 Chron. 20:26, also he hath respect to this word Jehoshaphat which signifieth pleading or judgment, because God would judge the enemies of his Church, as he did there.
c. Joel 3:3 That which the enemy gat for the sale of my people, he bestowed upon harlots and drink.
d. Joel 3:4 He taketh the cause of his Church in hand against the enemy, as though the injury were done to himself.
e. Joel 3:4 Have I done you wrong, that ye will render me the like?
f. Joel 3:8 For afterward God sold them by Nebuchadnezzar and Alexander the great, for the love he bare to his people, and thereby they were comforted, as though the price had been theirs.
g. Joel 3:10 When I shall execute my judgments against mine enemies, I will cause everyone to be ready, and to prepare their weapons to destroy one another for my Church's sake.
h. Joel 3:13 Thus he shall encourage the enemies when their wickedness is full ripe, to destroy one another, which he calleth the valley of God's judgment.
i. Joel 3:16 God assureth his against all trouble, that when he destroyeth his enemies, his children shall be delivered.
j. Joel 3:17 The strangers shall no more destroy his Church: which if they do, it is the people, which by their sins make the breach for the enemy.
k. Joel 3:18 He promiseth to his Church abundance of graces, read Ezek. 47:1, which should water and comfort the most barren places, Amos 9:13.
l. Joel 3:19 The malicious enemies shall have no part of his graces.
m. Joel 3:21 He had suffered his Church hitherto to lie in their filthiness, but now he promiseth to cleanse them and to make them pure unto him.

AMOS

1

1 The time of the prophecy of Amos. 3 The word of the Lord against Damascus, 6 The Philistines, Tyre, Idumea, and Ammon.

1 The words of Amos, who was among the herdsmen at [a]Tekoa, which he saw upon Israel, in the days of Uzziah king of Judah, and in the days of [b]Jeroboam the son of Joash king of Israel, two years before the [c]earthquake. **2** And he said, The Lord shall roar from Zion, and utter his voice from Jerusalem, and the dwelling places of the shepherds shall perish, and the top [d]of Carmel shall wither. **3** Thus saith the Lord, For [e]three transgressions of Damascus, and for four, I will not turn to it, because they have [f]threshed Gilead with threshing instruments of iron. **4** Therefore will I send a fire into the house of Hazael, and it shall devour the [g]palaces of Ben-Hadad. **5** I will break also the bars of Damascus, and cut off the inhabitant of Bikeath-Aven: and him that holdeth the scepter out of Beth Eden, and the people of Aram shall go into captivity unto [h]Kir, saith the Lord. **6** Thus saith the Lord, For three transgressions of Gaza, and for four, I will not turn to it, because they [i]carried away prisoners the whole captivity to shut them up in Edom. **7** Therefore will I send a fire upon the walls of Gaza, and it shall devour the palaces thereof. **8** And I will cut off the inhabitant from Ashdod, and him that holdeth the scepter from Ashkelon, and turn mine hand to Ekron, and the remnant of the Philistines shall perish, saith the Lord God. **9** Thus saith the Lord, For three transgressions of Tyre, and for four, I will not turn to it, because they shut the whole captivity in Edom, and have not remembered the [j]brotherly covenant. **10** Therefore will I send a fire upon the walls of Tyre, and it shall devour the palaces thereof. **11** Thus saith the Lord, For three transgressions of Edom, and for four, I will not turn to it, because he did pursue his brother with the sword, and [k]did cast off all pity, and his anger spoiled him evermore, and his wrath watched him [l]always. **12** Therefore will I send a fire upon Teman, and it shall devour the places of Bozrah. **13** Thus saith the Lord, For three transgressions of the children of Ammon, and for four, I will not turn to it, because they [m]have ripped up the women with child of Gilead, that they might enlarge their border. **14** Therefore will I kindle a fire in the wall of Rabbah, and it shall devour the palaces thereof, with shouting in the day of battle, and with a tempest in the day of the whirlwind. **15** And their king shall go into captivity, he and his princes together, saith the Lord.

AMOS 1
a. Amos 1:1 Which was a town five miles from Jerusalem in Judea, but he prophesied in Israel.
b. Amos 1:1 In his days the kingdom of Israel did most flourish.
c. Amos 1:1 Which as Josephus writeth, was when Uzziah would have usurped the Priest's office, and therefore was smitten with the leprosy.
d. Amos 1:2 Whatsoever is fruitful and pleasant in Israel, shall shortly perish.
e. Amos 1:3 He showeth first that all the people round about should be destroyed for their manifold sins: which are meant by three and four, which make seven, because the Israelites should the more deeply consider God's judgments toward them.
f. Amos 1:3 If the Syrians shall not be spared for committing this cruelty against one city, it is not possible that Israel should escape punishment which hath committed so many and grievous sins against God and man.
g. Amos 1:4 The antiquity of their buildings shall not avoid my judgments, read Jer. 49:27.
h. Amos 1:5 Tiglath-Pileser led the Assyrians captive, and brought them to Cyrene, which he calleth here Kir.
i. Amos 1:6 They joined themselves with the Edomites their enemies, which carried them away captives.
j. Amos 1:9 For Esau (of whom came the Edomites) and Jacob were brethren, therefore they ought to have admonished them of their brotherly friendship, and not to have provoked them to hatred.
k. Amos 1:11 Hebrew, corrupt his compassions.
l. Amos 1:11 He was a continual enemy unto him.
m. Amos 1:13 He noteth the great cruelty of the Ammonites, that spared not the women, but most tyrannously tormented them, and yet the Ammonites came of Lot, who was of the household of Abraham.

2

Against Moab, Judah, and Israel.

1 Thus saith the Lord, For three transgressions of Moab, and for four, I will not turn to it, because it burnt the [a]bones of the king of Edom into lime. **2** Therefore will I send a fire upon Moab, and it shall devour the palaces of Kerioth, and Moab shall die with tumult, with shouting, and with the sound of a trumpet. **3** And I will cut off the judge out of the midst thereof, and will slay all the princes thereof with him, saith the Lord. **4** Thus saith the Lord, For three transgressions of Judah, and for four, [b]I will not turn to it, because they have cast away the Law of the Lord, and have not kept his commandments, and their lies caused them to err after the which their fathers have walked. **5** Therefore will I send a fire upon Judah, and it shall devour the palaces of Jerusalem. **6** Thus saith the Lord, For three transgressions of [c]Israel, and for four, I will not turn to it, because they sold the righteous for silver, and the poor for [d]shoes. **7** They gape over the head of the poor, in the [e]dust of the earth, and pervert the ways of the meek: and a man and his father will go in to a maid, to dishonor mine holy Name. **8** And they lie down upon clothes laid to pledge [f]by every altar: and they [g]drink the wine of the condemned in the house of their God. **9** Yet destroyed I the [h]Amorite before them, whose height was like the height of the cedars, and he was strong as the oaks: notwithstanding I destroyed his fruit from above, and his root from beneath. **10** Also I brought you up from the land of Egypt, and led you forty years through the wilderness, to possess the land of the Amorite. **11** And I raised up of your sons for Prophets, and of [i]your young men for Nazirites. Is it not even thus, O ye children of Israel, saith the Lord? **12** But ye gave the Nazirites wine to drink, and commanded the Prophets, saying, Prophesy not. **13** Behold, I am [j]pressed under you as a cart is pressed that is full of sheaves. **14** Therefore the flight shall perish from the [k]swift, and the strong shall not strengthen his force, neither shall the mighty save his life. **15** Nor he that handleth the bow shall stand, and he that is swift of foot, shall not escape, neither shall he that rideth the horse, save his life. **16** And he that is of a mighty courage among the strong men, shall flee away naked in that day, saith the Lord.

3

He reproveth the house of Israel of ingratitude. 11 For the which God will punish them.

1 Hear this word that the Lord pronounceth against you, O children of Israel, even against the whole family which I brought up from the land of Egypt, saying, **2** You [a]only have I known of all the families of the earth: therefore I will visit you for all your iniquities. **3** Can two walk together except they be [b]agreed? **4** Will a [c]lion roar in the forest, when he hath no prey? or will a lion's whelp cry out of his den, if he hath taken nothing? **5** [d]Can a bird fall in a snare upon the earth, where no fowler is? or will he take up the [e]snare from the earth, and have taken nothing at all? **6** Or [f]shall a trumpet be blown in the city, and the people be not afraid? or shall there [g]be evil in a city, and the Lord hath not done it? **7** Surely the Lord God will do nothing, but he [h]revealeth his secret unto his servants the Prophets. **8** The lion hath roared: who will not be afraid? the Lord God hath spoken, who can but [i]prophesy? **9** Proclaim in the palaces at [j]Ashdod, and in the palaces in the land of Egypt, and say, Assemble yourselves upon the mountains of Samaria: so behold the great tumults in the midst thereof, and the oppressed in the midst thereof. **10** For they know not to do right, saith the Lord: they store up violence, and robbery [k]in their palaces. **11** Therefore thus saith the Lord God, An adversary shall come even round about the country, and shall bring down thy strength from thee, and thy palaces shall be spoiled. **12** Thus saith the Lord, As the shepherd taketh [l]out of the mouth of the lion two legs, or a piece of an ear: so shall the children of Israel be taken out that dwell in Samaria in the corner of a bed: and in [m]Damascus, as in a couch. **13** Hear, and testify in the house of Jacob, saith the Lord God, the God of hosts. **14** Surely in the day that I shall visit the transgressions of Israel upon him, I will also visit the altars of Bethel, and the horns of the altar shall be broken off, and fall to the ground. **15** And I will smite the winter house with the summer house, and the houses of ivory shall perish, and the great houses shall be consumed, saith the Lord.

4

Against the governors of Samaria.

1 Hear this word, ye [a]kine of Bashan that are in the mountain of Samaria, which oppress the poor, and destroy the needy, and they say to their masters, [b]Bring, and let us drink. **2** The Lord God hath sworn by his holiness, that lo, the days shall come upon you, that he will take you away with [c]thorns, and your posterity with fish-hooks. **3** And ye shall go out at the breaches every cow forward: and ye shall cast yourselves out of the palace, saith the Lord. **4** Come to [d]Bethel, and transgress: to Gilgal, and multiply transgression, and bring your sacrifices in the morning, and your riches after three [e]years. **5** And offer a thanksgiving [f]of leaven, publish and proclaim the free offerings: for this [g]liketh you, O ye children of Israel, saith the Lord God. **6** And therefore have I given you [h]cleanness of teeth in all your cities, and scarceness of bread in all your places, yet have ye not returned unto me, saith the Lord. **7** And also I have withholden the rain from you, when there were yet three [i]months to the harvest, and I caused it to rain upon one city, and have not caused it to rain upon another city: one piece was rained upon, and the piece whereupon it rained not, withered. **8** So two or three cities wandered unto one city to drink water, but they were [j]not satisfied: yet have ye not returned unto me, saith the Lord. **9** I have smitten you with blasting and mildew: your great gardens and your vineyards, and your fig trees, and your olive trees did the palmerworm devour: yet have ye not returned unto me, saith the Lord. **10** Pestilence have I sent among you after the manner of [k]Egypt: your young men have I slain with the sword, and have taken away your horses: and I have made the stink of your tents to come up even into your nostrils, yet have ye not returned unto me, saith the Lord. **11** I have overthrown you, as God overthrew Sodom and Gomorrah: and ye were as a [l]firebrand plucked out of the burning, yet have ye not returned unto me, saith the Lord. **12** Therefore thus will I do unto thee, O Israel: and because I will do thus unto thee, prepare to [m]meet thy God, O Israel. **13** For lo, he that formeth the mountains, and createth the wind, and declareth unto man what is his thought: which maketh the morning darkness, and walketh upon the high places of the earth, the Lord God of hosts is his Name.

5

A lamentation for the captivity of Israel.

1 Hear ye this word, which I lift up upon you, even a lamentation of the house of Israel. **2** The [a]virgin Israel is fallen, and shall no more rise: she is left upon her land, and there is none to raise her up. **3** For thus saith the Lord God, The city which went out by a thousand, shall leave [b]an hundred: and that which went forth by an hundred, shall leave ten to the house of Israel. **4** For thus saith the Lord unto the house of Israel, Seek ye me, and ye shall live. **5** But seek not Bethel, nor enter into [c]Gilgal, and go not to Beersheba: for Gilgal shall go into captivity, and Bethel shall come to nought. **6** Seek the Lord, and ye shall live,

---

AMOS 2

a. Amos 2:1 For the Moabites were so cruel against the king of Edom, that they burnt his bones after that he was dead: which declared their barbarous rage, seeing they would revenge themselves of the dead.

b. Amos 2:4 Seeing the Gentiles that had not so far knowledge were thus punished, Judah which was so fully instructed of the Lord's will, might not think to escape.

c. Amos 2:6 If he spare not Judah unto whom his promises were made, much more he will not spare this degenerate kingdom.

d. Amos 2:6 They esteemed most vile bribes more than men's lives.

e. Amos 2:7 When they have spoiled him and thrown him unto the ground, they gape for his life.

f. Amos 2:8 Thinking by these ceremonies, that is, by sacrificing, and being near mine altar, they may excuse all their other wickedness.

g. Amos 2:8 They spoil others and offer thereof unto God, thinking that he will dispense with them, when he is made partaker of their iniquity.

h. Amos 2:9 The destruction of their enemies and his mercy toward them, should have caused their hearts to melt for love toward him.

i. Amos 2:11 Ye contemned my benefits, and abused my graces, and craftily went about to stop the mouths of my Prophets.

j. Amos 2:13 You have wearied me with your sins, Isa. 1:14.

k. Amos 2:14 None shall be delivered by any means.

AMOS 3

a. Amos 3:2 I have only chosen you to be mine among all other people, and yet you have forsaken me.

b. Amos 3:3 Hereby the Prophet signifieth that he speaketh not of himself, but as God guideth and moveth him, which is called the agreement between God and his Prophets.

c. Amos 3:4 Will God threaten by his Prophet, except there be some great occasion?

d. Amos 3:5 Can anything come without God's providence?

e. Amos 3:5 Shall his threatenings be in vain?

f. Amos 3:6 Shall the Prophets threaten God's judgments and the people not be afraid?

g. Amos 3:6 Doth any adversity come without God's appointment? Isa. 45:7.

h. Amos 3:7 God dealeth not with the Israelites, as he doeth with other people: for he ever warneth them before of his plagues by his Prophets.

i. Amos 3:8 Because the people ever murmured against the Prophets, he showeth that God's Spirit moved them so to speak as they did.

j. Amos 3:9 He calleth the strangers, as the Philistines and Egyptians, to be witness of God's judgments against the Israelites for their cruelty and oppression.

k. Amos 3:10 The fruit of their cruelty and theft appeareth by their great riches, which they have in their houses.

l. Amos 3:12 When the lion hath satiate his hunger, the shepherd findeth a leg or a rip of an ear, to show that the sheep have been worried.

m. Amos 3:12 Where they thought to have had a sure hold, and to have been in safety.

AMOS 4

a. Amos 4:1 Thus he calleth the princes and governors, which being overwhelmed with the great abundance of God's benefits, forgot God, and therefore he calleth them by the name of beasts and not of men.

b. Amos 4:1 They encourage such as have authority over the people to powle them, so that they may have profit by it.

c. Amos 4:2 He alludeth to fishers, which catch fish by hooks and thorns.

d. Amos 4:4 He speaketh this in contempt of them which resorted to those places, thinking that their great devotion and good intention had been sufficient to have bound God unto them.

e. Amos 4:4 Read Deut. 14:28.

f. Amos 4:5 As Lev. 7:13.

g. Amos 4:5 You only delight in these outward ceremonies and have none other respect.

h. Amos 4:6 That is, lack of bread and meat.

i. Amos 4:7 I stayed the rain till the fruits of the earth were destroyed with drought, and yet you would not consider it to return to me by repentance.

j. Amos 4:8 They could not find water enough where they had heard say it had rained.

k. Amos 4:10 As I plagued the Egyptians, Exod. 9:10.

l. Amos 4:11 You were almost all consumed, and a few of you wonderfully preserved, 2 Kings 14:26.

m. Amos 4:12 Turn to him by repentance.

AMOS 5

a. Amos 5:2 He so calleth them, because they so boasted of themselves or because they were given to wantonness and daintiness.

b. Amos 5:3 Meaning, that the tenth part should scarcely be saved.

c. Amos 5:5 In those places they worshipped new idols, which aforetime served for the true honor of God: therefore he saith that these shall not save them.

lest he break out like fire in the house of Joseph and devour it, and there be none to quench it in Bethel. **7** They turn [d]judgment to wormwood, and leave off righteousness in the earth. **8** He [e]maketh Pleiades, and Orion, and he turneth the shadow of death into the morning, and he maketh the day dark as night: he calleth the waters of the sea, and poureth them out upon the open earth: the Lord is his Name. **9** He strengtheneth the destroyer against the mighty, and the destroyer shall come against the fortress. **10** They have hated him [f]that rebuked in the gate: and they abhorred him that speaketh uprightly. **11** Forasmuch then as your treading is upon the poor, and [g]ye take from him burdens of wheat, ye have built houses of hewn stone, but ye shall not dwell in them: ye have planted pleasant vineyards, but ye shall not drink wine of them. **12** For I know your manifold transgressions, and your mighty sins: they afflict the just, they take rewards, and they oppress the poor in the gate. **13** Therefore [h]the prudent shall keep silence in that time, for it is an evil time. **14** Seek good and not evil, that ye may live: and the Lord God of hosts shall be with you, as you have spoken. **15** Hate the evil, and love the good, and establish judgment in the gate: it may be that the Lord God of hosts will be merciful unto the remnant of Joseph. **16** Therefore the Lord God of hosts, the Lord saith thus, Mourning shall be in all streets: and they shall say in all the high ways, Alas, alas: and they shall call the [i]husbandman to lamentation, and such as can mourn, to mourning. **17** And in all the vines shall be lamentation: for I will pass through thee, saith the Lord. **18** Woe unto you, that [j]desire the day of the Lord: what have you to do with it? the day of the Lord is darkness and not light, **19** As if a man did flee from a lion, and a bear met him: or went into the house, and leaned his hand on the wall, and a serpent bit him. **20** Shall not the day of the Lord be darkness, and not light, even darkness and no light in it? **21** I hate and abhor your feast days, and I will not smell in your solemn assemblies. **22** Though ye offer me burnt offerings and meat offerings, [k]I will not accept them: neither will I regard the peace offerings of your fat beasts. **23** Take thou away from me the multitude of thy songs (for I will not hear the melody of thy viols.) **24** And let judgment run down as [l]waters, and righteousness as a mighty river. **25** Have ye offered unto me sacrifices and offerings in the wilderness forty years, O house of Israel? **26** But you have born [m]Sikkuth your king, and Chiun your images, and the star of your gods which you made to yourselves. **27** Therefore will I cause you to go into captivity beyond Damascus, saith the Lord, whose Name is the God of hosts.

6

Against the princes of Israel living in pleasure.

1 Woe to [a]them that are at ease in Zion, and trust in the mountain of Samaria, [b]which were famous at the beginning of the nations: and the house of Israel came to them. **2** Go you unto Calneh, and see: and from thence go you to Hamath the great: then go down to Gath of the Philistines: be [c]they better than these kingdoms? or the border of their land greater than your border, **3** Ye that put far away the [d]evil day, and approach to the seat of iniquity? **4** They lie upon beds of ivory, and stretch themselves upon their beds, and eat the lambs of the flock, and the calves out of the stall. **5** They sing to the sound of the viol: they invent to themselves instruments of music like [e]David. **6** They drink wine in bowls, and anoint themselves with the chief ointments, but no man is [f]sorry for the affliction of Joseph. **7** Therefore now shall they go captive with the first that go captive, and [g]the sorrow of them that stretched themselves, is at hand. **8** [h]The Lord God hath sworn by himself, saith the Lord God of hosts, I abhor [i]the excellency of Jacob, and hate his palaces: therefore will I deliver up the city with all that is therein. **9** And if there remain ten men in one house, they shall die. **10** And his uncle [j]shall take him up and burn him, to carry out the bones out of the house, and shall say unto him, that is by the [k]sides of the house, Is there yet any with thee? And he shall say, None. Then shall he say, [l]Hold thy tongue: for we may not remember the Name of the Lord. **11** For behold, the Lord commandeth, and he will smite the great house with breaches, and the little house with clefts. **12** Shall horses [m]run upon the rock? or will one plow there with oxen? for ye have turned judgment into gall, and the fruit of righteousness into [n]wormwood. **13** Yet rejoice in a thing of nought: ye say, Have not we gotten us [o]horns by our own strength? **14** But behold, I will raise up against you a nation, O house of Israel, saith the Lord God of hosts: and they shall afflict you from the entering in of [p]Hamath unto the river of the wilderness.

7

God showeth certain visions, whereby he signifieth the destruction of the people of Israel. 10 The false accusation of Amaziah, 12 His crafty counsel.

1 Thus hath the Lord God showed unto me, and behold, he formed [a]grasshoppers in the beginning of the shooting up of the latter growth: and lo, it was in the latter growth [b]after the King's mowing. **2** And when they had made an end of eating the grass of the land, then I said, O Lord God, spare, I beseech thee: who shall raise up Jacob? for he is small. **3** So the Lord [c]repented for this. It shall not be, saith the Lord. **4** Thus also hath the Lord God showed unto me, and behold, the Lord God called to judgment by fire, [d]and it devoured the great deep, and did eat up a part. **5** Then said I, O Lord God, cease, I beseech thee: who shall raise up Jacob? for he is small. **6** So the Lord repented for this. This also shall not be, saith the Lord God. **7** Thus again he showed me, and behold, the Lord stood upon a wall made by line [e]with a line in his hand. **8** And the Lord said unto me, Amos, what seest thou? And I said, A line. Then said the Lord, Behold, I will set a line in the midst of my people Israel, and will pass by them no more. **9** And the high places of Isaac shall be desolate, and the temples of Israel shall be destroyed: and I will rise against the house of Jeroboam with the sword. **10** [f]Then Amaziah the Priest of Bethel sent to Jeroboam king of Israel, saying, Amos hath conspired against thee in the midst of the house of Israel: the land is not able to bear all his words. **11** For thus Amos saith, Jeroboam shall die by the sword, and Israel shall be led away captive out of their own land. **12** Also [g]Amaziah said unto Amos, O thou the Seer, go, flee thou away into the land of Judah, and there eat thy bread, and prophesy there. **13** But prophesy no more at Bethel: for it is the king's chapel, and it is the king's court. **14** Then answered Amos, and said to Amaziah, I was no [h]Prophet, neither was I a Prophet's son, but I was an herdsman, and a gatherer of wild figs. **15** And the Lord took me as I followed the flock, and the Lord said unto me, Go prophesy unto my people Israel. **16** Now therefore hear thou the word of the Lord. Thou sayest, Prophesy not against Israel, and speak nothing against the house of Isaac. **17** Therefore thus saith the Lord, [i]Thy wife shall be an harlot in the city, and thy sons and thy daughters shall fall by the sword, and thy land shall be divided by line: and thou shalt die in a polluted land, and Israel shall surely go into captivity forth of his land.

8

1 Against the rulers of Israel. 7 The Lord sweareth. 11 The famine of the word of God.

1 Thus hath the Lord God showed unto me, and behold, a basket of summer fruit. **2** And he said, Amos, what seest thou? And I said, A basket of [a]summer

---

d. Amos 5:7 Instead of judgment and equity they execute cruelty and oppression.
e. Amos 5:8 He describeth the power of God, Job 9:9.
f. Amos 5:10 They hate the Prophets, which reprove them in the open assemblies.
g. Amos 5:11 Ye take both his money and also his food, wherewith he should live.
h. Amos 5:13 God will so plague them that they shall not suffer the godly once to open their mouths to admonish them of their faults.
i. Amos 5:16 So that all degrees shall have matter of lamentation for the great plagues.
j. Amos 5:18 Thus he speaketh, because the wicked and hypocrites said they were content to abide God's judgments, whereas the godly tremble and fear, Jer. 30:7; Joel 2:2, 11; Zeph. 1:15.
k. Amos 5:22 Because ye have corrupted my true service, and remain obstinate in your vices, Isa. 1:11; Jer. 6:10.
l. Amos 5:24 Do your duty to God, and to your neighbor, and so ye shall feel his grace plentifully, if you show your abundant affections according to God's word.
m. Amos 5:26 That idol which you esteemed as your king, and carried about as you did Chiun, in which images you thought that there was a certain divinity.

AMOS 6

a. Amos 6:1 The Prophet threateneth the wealthy, which regarded not God's plagues nor menaces by his Prophets.
b. Amos 6:1 These two cities were famous by their first inhabitants the Canaanites: and seeing beforetime they did nothing avail them that were there born, why should you look that they should save you which were brought in to dwell in other men's possessions?
c. Amos 6:2 If God have destroyed these excellent cities in three divers kingdoms, as in Babylon, Syria, and of the Philistines, and hath brought their wide borders into a greater straightness than yours yet are, think you to be better, or to escape?
d. Amos 6:3 Ye that continue still in your wickedness, and think that God's plagues are not at hand, but give yourselves to all idleness, wantonness, and riot.
e. Amos 6:5 As he caused divers kinds of instruments to be made to serve God's glory, so these did contend to invent as many to serve their wanton affections and lusts.
f. Amos 6:6 They pitied not their brethren, whereof now many were slain and carried away captive.
g. Amos 6:7 Some read, the joy of them that stretch themselves, shall depart.
h. Amos 6:8 Read Jer. 51:14.
i. Amos 6:8 That is, the riches and pomp.
j. Amos 6:10 The destruction shall be so great, that none shall almost be left to bury the dead: and therefore they shall burn them at home, to carry out the burnt ashes with more ease.
k. Amos 6:10 That is, to some neighbor that dwelleth round about.
l. Amos 6:10 They shall be so astonished at this destruction, that they shall boast no more of the Name of God, and that they are his people: but they shall be dumb when they hear God's Name, and abhor it, as they that are desperate, or reprobate.
m. Amos 6:12 He compareth them to barren rocks, whereupon it is in vain to bestow labor: showing that God's benefits can have no place among them.
n. Amos 6:12 Read Amos 5:7.
o. Amos 6:13 That is, power and glory.
p. Amos 6:14 From one corner of the country to another.

AMOS 7

a. Amos 7:1 To devour the land: and he alludeth to the invading of the enemies.
b. Amos 7:1 After the public commandment for mowing was given: or as some read, when the king's sheep were shorn.
c. Amos 7:3 That is, stayed this plague at my prayer.
d. Amos 7:4 Meaning, that God's indignation was inflamed against the stubbornness of this people.
e. Amos 7:7 Signifying that this should be the last measuring of the people, and that he would defer his judgment no longer.
f. Amos 7:10 That is, when Amos had prophesied that the king should be destroyed: for the wicked Priest more for hatred he bare to the Prophet than for love toward the king, thought this accusation sufficient to condemn him, whereas none other could take place.
g. Amos 7:12 When this instrument of Satan was not able to compass his purpose by the king, he assayed by another practice, that was, to fear the Prophet, that he might depart, and not reprove their idolatry there openly, and so hinder his profit.
h. Amos 7:14 Thus he showeth by his extraordinary vocation, that God had given him a charge, which he must needs execute.
i. Amos 7:17 Thus God used to approve the authority of his Prophets, by his plagues and judgments against them which were malicious enemies, Jer. 28:12 and 29:21, 25, as this day he doeth against them that persecute the ministers of his Gospel.

AMOS 8

a. Amos 8:2 Which signified the ripeness of their sins, and the readiness of God's judgments.
b. Amos 8:3 There shall be none left to mourn for them.

fruit. Then said the Lord unto me, The end is come upon my people of Israel, I will pass by them no more. **3** And the songs of the Temple shall be howlings in that day, saith the Lord God: many dead bodies shall be in every place: they shall cast them forth with [b]silence. **4** Hear this, O ye that [c]swallow up the poor, that ye may make the needy of the land to fail, **5** Saying, When will the [d]new month be gone, that we may sell corn? and the Sabbath, that we may set forth wheat, and make [e]the Ephah small and the shekel great, and falsify the weights by deceit? **6** That we may buy the poor for silver, and the needy for shoes: yea, and sell the refuse of the wheat. **7** The Lord hath sworn by the excellency of Jacob, Surely, I will never forget any of their works. **8** Shall not the land tremble for this, and everyone mourn, that dwelleth therein? and it shall rise up wholly as a flood, and it shall be cast out, and [f]drowned as by the flood of Egypt. **9** And in that day, saith the Lord God, I will even cause the [g]Sun to go down at noon: I will darken the earth in the clear day. **10** And I will turn your feasts into mourning: and all your songs into lamentation: and I will bring sackcloth upon all loins, and baldness upon every head: and I will make it as the mourning of an only son, and the end thereof as a bitter day. **11** Behold, the days come, saith the Lord God, that I will send a famine in the Land, not a famine of bread, nor a thirst for water, but of hearing the word of the Lord. **12** And they shall wander from sea to sea, and from the North even unto the East shall they run to and fro to seek the [h]word of the Lord, and shall not find it. **13** In that day shall the fair virgins and the young men perish for thirst. **14** They that swear by the sin [i]of Samaria, and that say, Thy God, O Dan, liveth, and [j]the manner of Beersheba liveth, even they shall fall, and never rise up again.

9

Threatenings against the Temple, 2 And against Israel. 11 The restoring of the Church.

1 I saw the Lord standing upon the [a]Altar, and he said, Smite the lintel of the door, that the posts may shake: and cut them in pieces, even the [b]heads of them all, and I will slay the last of them with the sword: he that fleeth of them, shall not flee away: and he that escapeth of them, shall not be delivered. **2** Though they dig into the hell, thence shall mine hand take them: though they climb up to heaven, thence will I bring them down. **3** And though they hide themselves in the top of Carmel, I will search and take them out thence: and though they be hid from my sight in the bottom of the sea, thence will I command the [c]serpent, and he shall bite them. **4** And though they go into captivity before their enemies, thence will I command the sword, and it shall slay them: and I will set mine eyes upon them for evil, and not for good. **5** And the Lord God of hosts shall touch the land, and it shall melt away, and all that dwell therein shall mourn, and it shall rise up wholly like a flood, and shall be drowned as by the flood of Egypt. **6** He buildeth his [d]spheres in the heaven, and hath laid the foundation of his globe of elements in the earth: he calleth the waters of the sea, and poureth them out upon the open earth: the Lord is his Name. **7** Are ye not as the Ethiopians [e]unto me, O children of Israel, saith the Lord? have not I brought up Israel out of the land of Egypt? and the Philistines from [f]Caphtor, and Aram from Kir? **8** Behold, the eyes of the Lord God are upon the sinful kingdom, and I will destroy it clean out of the earth. Nevertheless I will not utterly [g]destroy the house of Jacob, saith the Lord. **9** For lo, I will command and I will sift the house of Israel among all nations, like as corn is sifted in a sieve: yet shall not the [h]least stone fall upon the earth. **10** But all the sinners of my people shall die by the sword, which say, The evil shall not come, nor hasten for us. **11** In that day will I raise up the [i]Tabernacle of David, that is fallen down, and close up the breaches thereof, and I will raise up his ruins, and I will build it, as in the days of old, **12** That they may possess the remnant of [j]Edom, and of all the heathen, because my Name is called upon them, saith the Lord, that doeth this. **13** Behold, the days come, saith the Lord, that the plowman shall [k]touch the mower, and the treader of grapes him that soweth seed: and the mountains shall [l]drop sweet wine, and all the hills shall melt. **14** [m]And I will bring again the captivity of my people of Israel: and they shall build the waste cities, and inhabit them, and they shall plant vineyards, and drink the wine thereof: they shall also make gardens, and eat the fruits of them. **15** And I will plant them upon their land, and they shall no more be pulled up again out of their land which I have given them, saith the Lord thy God.

---

c. Amos 8:4 By staying the sale of food, and necessary things which you have gotten into your own hands, and so cause the poor to spend quickly that little that they have, and at length for necessity to become your slaves.
d. Amos 8:5 When the dearth was once come they were so greedy of gain, that they thought the holy day to be an hindrance unto them.
e. Amos 8:5 That is, the measure small, and the price great.
f. Amos 8:8 That is, the inhabitants of the land shall be drowned, as Nile drowneth many when it overfloweth.
g. Amos 8:9 In the midst of their prosperity, I will send great affliction.
h. Amos 8:12 Whereby he showeth that they shall not only perish in body, but also in soul for lack of God's word, which is the food thereof.
i. Amos 8:14 For the idolaters did use to swear by their idols: which here he calleth their sin, as the Papists yet do by theirs.
j. Amos 8:14 That is, the common manner of worshipping, and the service or religion there used.

AMOS 9

a. Amos 9:1 Which was at Jerusalem: for he appeared not in the idolatrous places of Israel.
b. Amos 9:1 Both the chief of them and also the common people.
c. Amos 9:3 He showeth that God will declare himself enemy unto them in all places, and that his elements and all creatures shall be enemies to destroy them.
d. Amos 9:6 He declareth by the wonderful power of God, by the making of the heavens and the elements, that it is not possible for man to escape his judgments when he punisheth.
e. Amos 9:7 Am I more bound to you than to the Ethiopians, or black moors? yet have I bestowed upon you greater benefits.
f. Amos 9:7 Read Jer. 47:4.
g. Amos 9:8 Though he destroy the rebellious multitude, yet he will ever reserve the remnant his Church to call upon his Name.
h. Amos 9:9 Meaning, that none of his should perish in his wrath.
i. Amos 9:11 I will send the Messiah promised, and restore by him the spiritual Israel, Acts 15:16.
j. Amos 9:12 Meaning, that the very enemies as were the Edomites, and others should be joined with the Jews in one society, and body, whereof Christ should be the head.
k. Amos 9:13 Signifying, that there shall be great plenty of all things, so that when one kind of fruit is ripe, another should follow, and every one in course, Lev. 26:5.
l. Amos 9:13 Read Joel 3:18.
m. Amos 9:14 The accomplishment thereof is under Christ, when they are planted in this Church, out of the which they can never be pulled, after they are once grafted therein.

OBADIAH

1 *Obadiah*

1 The vision of Obadiah. Thus saith the Lord God against Edom,
[a]We have heard a rumor from the Lord, and an ambassador is sent among the
heathen: arise, and [b]let us rise up against her to battle. **2** Behold, I have made
thee small among the heathen: thou art utterly despised. **3** The [c]pride of thi-
ne heart hath deceived thee: thou that dwellest in the clefts of the rocks, who-
se habitation is high, that saith in his heart, Who shall bring me down to the
ground? **4** Though thou exalt thyself as the eagle, and make thy nest among the
stars, thence will I bring thee down, saith the Lord. **5** [d]Came thieves to thee or
robbers by night? how wast thou brought to silence? would they not have stolen
till they had enough? if the grape gatherers came to thee, would they not leave
some grapes? **6** How are the things of Esau sought up, and his treasures sear-
ched? **7** All the men of thy confederacy [e]have driven thee to the borders: the men
that were at peace with thee, have deceived thee, and prevailed against thee: they
that eat thy [f]bread, have laid a wound under thee: there is none understanding in
him. **8** Shall not I in that day, saith the Lord, even destroy the wise men out of
Edom, and understanding from the mount of Esau? **9** And thy strong men, O
Teman, shall be afraid, because everyone of the mount of Esau shall be cut off by
slaughter. **10** For thy cruelty against thy [g]brother Jacob, shame shall cover thee,
and thou shalt be cut off forever. **11** When thou stoodest [h]on the other side, in
the day that the strangers carried away his substance, and strangers entered into
his gates, and cast lots upon Jerusalem, even thou wast as one of them. **12** But
thou shouldest not have beholden the day of thy brother, in the day that he was
made [i]a stranger, neither shouldest thou have rejoiced over the children of Judah,
in the day of their destruction: thou shouldest not have spoken proudly in the day
of affliction. **13** Thou shouldest not have entered into the gate of my people in
the day of their destruction, neither shouldest thou have once looked on their af-
fliction in the day of their destruction, nor have laid hands on their substance in
the day of their destruction. **14** Neither shouldest thou have stood in the cros-
sways to cut off them, that should escape, neither shouldest thou have shut up
the remnant thereof in the day of affliction. **15** For the day [j]of the Lord is near,
upon all the heathen: as thou hast done, it shall be done to thee: thy reward shall
return upon thine head. **16** For as ye have [k]drunk upon mine holy Mountain,
so shall all the heathen drink continually: yea, they shall drink and swallow up,
and they shall be [l]as though they had not been. **17** But upon mount Zion shall
be deliverance, and it shall be holy, and the house of Jacob shall possess their pos-
sessions, **18** And the house of Jacob shall be [m]a fire, and the house of Joseph a
flame, and the house of Esau as stubble, and they shall kindle in them and devour
them: and there shall be no remnant of the house of Esau: for the Lord hath spoken
it. **19** And they shall possess the South side of the [n]mount of Esau, and the plain
of the Philistines: and they shall possess the fields of Ephraim, and the fields of Sa-
maria, and Benjamin shall have Gilead. **20** And the captivity of this host of the
children of Israel, which were among the [o]Canaanites, shall possess unto Zarepha-
th, and the captivity of Jerusalem, which is in Sepharad, shall possess the cities of
the South. **21** And they [p]that shall save, shall come up to mount Zion to judge
the mount of Esau, and the kingdom shall be the Lord's.

OBADIAH 1

a. Obadiah 1:1 God hath certainly revealed to his prophets, that he will raise up the heathen to destroy the Edomites, whereof the rumor is now published, Jer. 49:14.

b. Obadiah 1:1 Thus the heathen encourage themselves to rise against Edom.

c. Obadiah 1:3 Which despisest all others in respect of thyself, and yet art but an handful in comparison of others, and art shut up among the hills as separate from the rest of the world.

d. Obadiah 1:5 God will so destroy them that he will leave none, though thieves when they come, take but till they have enough, and they that gather grapes, ever leave some behind them, Jer. 49:9.

e. Obadiah 1:7 They in whom thou didst trust for to have help and friendship of them, shall be thine enemies and destroy thee.

f. Obadiah 1:7 That is, thy familiar friends and guests have by secret practices destroyed thee.

g. Obadiah 1:10 He showeth the cause why the Edomites were so sharply punished: to wit, because they were enemies to his Church, whom he now comforteth by punishing their enemies.

h. Obadiah 1:11 When Nebuchadnezzar came against Jerusalem, thou joinedest with him, and hadest part of the spoil, and so didst rejoice when my people, that is, thy brother were afflicted, whereas thou shouldest have pitied and helped thy brother.

i. Obadiah 1:12 When the Lord deprived them of their former dignity, and gave them to be carried into captivity.

j. Obadiah 1:15 When he will summon all the heathen, and send them to destroy thee.

k. Obadiah 1:16 That is, rejoiced and triumphed.

l. Obadiah 1:16 The Edomites shall be utterly destroyed, and yet in despite of all the enemies I will reserve my Church and restore it.

m. Obadiah 1:18 God attributeth this power, to consume his enemies, to his Church, which power is only proper to himself, as Isa. 10:17; Deut. 4:24; Heb. 12:29.

n. Obadiah 1:19 He describeth how the Church shall be enlarged and have great possessions: but this chiefly is accomplished under Christ, when as the faithful are made heirs and lords of all things by him which is their head.

o. Obadiah 1:20 By the Canaanites, the Jews mean the Dutchmen, and by Zarephath, France, and by Sepharad, Spain.

p. Obadiah 1:21 Meaning that God will raise up in his Church such as shall rule and govern for the defense of the same, and destruction of his enemies under Messiah, whom the Prophet calleth here, the Lord and head of this kingdom.

JONAH

1

3 Jonah fled when he was sent to preach. 4 A tempest ariseth, and he is cast into the sea for his disobedience.

1 The word of the Lord came [a]also unto Jonah the son of Amittai, saying, **2** Arise, and go to [b]Nineveh, that [c]great city, and cry against it: for their wickedness is come up before me. **3** But Jonah rose up to [d]flee into Tarshish, from the presence of the Lord, and went down to [e]Japho: and he found a ship going to Tarshish: so he paid the fare thereof, and went down into it, that he might go with them unto Tarshish, from the [f]presence of the Lord. **4** But the Lord sent out a great wind into the sea, and there was a mighty tempest in the sea, so that the ship was like to be broken. **5** Then the mariners were afraid, and cried every man unto his god, and cast the wares that were in the ship, into the sea, to lighten it of them: but Jonah was gone down [g]into the sides of the ship, and he lay down, and was fast asleep. **6** So the shipmaster came to him, and said unto him, What meanest thou, O sleeper? Arise, call upon thy [h]God, if so be that God will think upon us, that we perish not. **7** And they said everyone to his fellow, Come, and let us cast [i]lots, that we may know for whose cause this evil is upon us. So they cast lots, and the lot fell upon Jonah. **8** Then said they unto him, Tell us for whose cause this evil is upon us? What is thine occupation? and whence comest thou? which is thy country? and of what people art thou? **9** And he answered them, I am an Hebrew, and I fear the Lord God of heaven, which hath made the sea, and the dry land. **10** Then were the men exceedingly afraid, and said unto him, Why hast thou done this? (for the men knew that he fled from the presence of the Lord, because he had told them) **11** Then said they unto him, What shall we do unto thee, that the sea may be calm unto us? (for the sea wrought, and was troublous) **12** And he said unto them, Take me, and cast me into the sea: so shall the sea be calm unto you: for I know that for my sake this great tempest is upon you. **13** Nevertheless the men rowed to bring it to the land, but they could not: for the sea wrought, and was troublous against them. **14** Wherefore they cried unto the Lord, and said, [j]We beseech thee, O Lord, we beseech thee, let us not perish for this man's life, and lay not upon us innocent blood: for thou, O Lord, hast done as it pleased thee. **15** So they took up Jonah, and cast him into the sea, and the sea ceased from her raging. **16** Then the men [k]feared the Lord exceedingly, and offered a sacrifice unto the Lord, and made vows. **17** Now the Lord had prepared a great fish to swallow up Jonah: and Jonah was in the [l]belly of the fish three days and three nights.

2

1 Jonah is in the fish's belly. 2 His prayer. 10 He is delivered.

1 Then Jonah prayed unto the Lord his God [a]out of the fish's belly,

2 And said, I cried in mine affliction unto the Lord, and he heard me: out of the belly [b]of hell cried I, and thou heardest my voice. **3** For thou hadst cast me into the bottom in the midst of the sea, and the floods compassed me about: all thy surges, and all thy waves passed over me. **4** Then I said, I am [c]cast away out of thy sight: yet will I look again toward thine holy Temple. **5** The waters compassed me about unto the soul: the depth closed me round about, and the weeds were wrapped about mine head. **6** I went down to the bottom of the mountains: the earth with her bars was about me forever, yet hast thou brought up my [d]life from the pit, O Lord my God. **7** When my soul fainted within me, I remembered the Lord: and my prayer came unto thee into thine holy Temple. **8** They that wait upon lying [e]vanities, forsake their own [f]mercy. **9** But I will sacrifice unto thee with the voice of thanksgiving, and will pay that that I have vowed: salvation is of the Lord. **10** And the Lord spake unto the fish, and it cast out Jonah upon the dry land.

3

1 Jonah is sent again to Ninevah. 5 The repentance of the king of Ninevah.

1 And the word of the Lord came unto [a]Jonah the second time, saying, **2** Arise, go unto Nineveh that great city, and preach unto it the preaching which I bid thee. **3** So Jonah arose, and went to Nineveh according to the word of the Lord: now Nineveh was a [b]great and excellent city of three days journey. **4** And Jonah began to enter into the city a day's [c]journey, and he cried and said, Yet forty days, and Nineveh shall be overthrown. **5** So the people of Nineveh [d]believed God, and proclaimed a fast, and put on sackcloth, from the greatest of them, even to the least of them. **6** For word came unto the king of Nineveh, and he rose from his throne, and he laid his robe from him, and covered him with sackcloth, and sat in ashes. **7** And he proclaimed and said through Nineveh, (by the counsel of the king and his nobles) saying, Let neither man, nor [e]beast, bullock nor sheep taste anything, neither feed nor drink water. **8** But let man and beast put on sackcloth, and [f]cry mightily unto God: yea, let every man turn from his evil way, and from the wickedness that is in their hands. **9** [g]Who can tell if God will turn, and repent and turn away from his fierce wrath, that we perish not? **10** And God saw their [h]works that they turned from their evil ways: and [i]God repented of the evil that he had said that he would do unto them, and he did it not.

4

The great goodness of God toward his creatures.

1 Therefore it displeased [a]Jonah exceedingly, and he was angry. **2** And he prayed unto the Lord, and said, I pray thee, O Lord, was not this my saying, when I was yet in my country? therefore I prevented it to flee unto [b]Tarshish: for I knew, that thou art a gracious God, and merciful, slow to anger, and of great kindness, and repentest thee of the evil. **3** Therefore now, O Lord, take, I beseech thee, my life [c]from me: for it is better for me to die than to live. **4** Then said the Lord, Doest thou well to be [d]angry? **5** So Jonah went out of the city, and sat on the East side of the city, and there made him a booth, and sat under

---

JONAH 1

- **a.** Jonah 1:1 After that he had preached a long time in Israel: and so Ezekiel, after that for a time he had prophesied in Judah, he had visions in Babylon, Ezek. 1:1.
- **b.** Jonah 1:2 For seeing the great obstination of the Israelites, he sent his Prophet to the Gentiles, that they might provoke them to repentance, or at least make them inexcusable: for Nineveh was the chief city of the Assyrians.
- **c.** Jonah 1:2 For as authors write, it contained in circuit about eight and forty miles, and had a thousand and five hundred towers, and at this time there were an hundred and twenty thousand children therein, Jonah 4:11.
- **d.** Jonah 1:3 Whereby he declared his weakness, that would not promptly follow the Lord's calling, but gave place to his own reason, which persuaded him that he should nothing at all profit there, seeing he had done so small good among his own people, Jonah 4:2.
- **e.** Jonah 1:3 Which was the haven, and port to take shipping thither, called also Joppa.
- **f.** Jonah 1:3 From that vocation whereunto God had called him, and wherein he would have assisted him.
- **g.** Jonah 1:5 As one that would have cast off this care and solicitude by seeking rest and quietness.
- **h.** Jonah 1:6 As they had called on their idols, which declareth that idolaters have no stay nor certainty, but in their troubles seek they cannot tell to whom.
- **i.** Jonah 1:7 Which declareth that the matter was in great extremity and doubt, which thing was God's motion in them, for the trial of the cause: and this may not be done but in matters of great importance.
- **j.** Jonah 1:14 This declareth that the very wicked in their necessities flee unto God for succor and also that they are touched with a certain fear to shed man's blood, whereas they know no manifest sign of wickedness.
- **k.** Jonah 1:16 They were touched with a certain repentance of their life past, and began to worship the true God by whom they saw themselves so wonderfully delivered: but this was done for fear, and not of a pure heart and affection, neither according to God's word.
- **l.** Jonah 1:17 Thus the Lord would chastise his Prophet with a most terrible spectacle of death, and hereby also confirmed him of his favor and support in this his charge which was enjoined him.

JONAH 2

- **a.** Jonah 2:1 Being now swallowed up of death, and seeing no remedy to escape, his faith brast out unto the Lord, knowing that out of the very hell he was able to deliver him.
- **b.** Jonah 2:2 For he was now in the fish's belly as in a grave or place of darkness.
- **c.** Jonah 2:4 This declared what his prayer was, and how he labored between hope and despair, considering the neglect of his vocation, and God's judgments for the same: but yet in the end faith got the victory.
- **d.** Jonah 2:6 Thou hast delivered me from the belly of the fish and all these dangers, as it were raising me from death to life.
- **e.** Jonah 2:8 They that depend upon anything save on God alone.
- **f.** Jonah 2:8 They refuse their own felicity, and that goodness which they should else receive of God.

JONAH 3

- **a.** Jonah 3:1 This is a great declaration of God's mercy, that he receiveth him again, and sendeth him forth as his Prophet, which had before showed so great infirmity.
- **b.** Jonah 3:3 Read Jonah 1:2.
- **c.** Jonah 3:4 He went forward one day in the city, and preached, and so he continued till the city was converted.
- **d.** Jonah 3:5 For he declared that he was a Prophet sent to them from God to denounce his judgments against them.
- **e.** Jonah 3:7 Not that the dumb beasts had sinned or could repent, but that by their example man might be astonished, considering that for his sin the anger of God hanged over all creatures.
- **f.** Jonah 3:8 He willed that the men should earnestly call unto God for mercy.
- **g.** Jonah 3:9 For partly by the threatening of the Prophet, and partly by the motion of his own conscience, he doubted whether God would show them mercy.
- **h.** Jonah 3:10 That is, the fruits of their repentance, which did proceed of faith, which God had planted by the ministry of his Prophet.
- **i.** Jonah 3:10 Read Jer. 18:8.

JONAH 4

- **a.** Jonah 4:1 Because hereby he should be taken as a false prophet, and so the Name of God, which he preached, should be blasphemed.
- **b.** Jonah 4:2 Read Jonah 1:3.
- **c.** Jonah 4:3 Thus he prayed of grief fearing lest God's Name by this forgiveness might be blasphemed, as though he sent his Prophets forth to denounce his judgments in vain.
- **d.** Jonah 4:4 Wilt thou be judge when I do things for my glory, and when I do not?

it in the shadow [e]till he might see what should be done in the city. **6** And the Lord God prepared a [f]gourd, and made it to come up over Jonah, that it might be a shadow over his head, and deliver him from his grief. So Jonah was exceeding glad of the gourd. **7** But God prepared a worm when the morning rose the next day, and it smote the gourd, that it withered. **8** And when the sun did arise, God prepared also a fervent East wind: and the sun beat upon the head of Jonah, that he fainted and wished in his heart to die, and said, It is better for me to die than to live. **9** And God said unto Jonah, Doest thou well to be angry for the gourd? And he said, I do well to be [g]angry unto the death. **10** Then said the Lord, Thou hast had pity on the gourd for the which thou hast not labored, neither madest it grow, which came up in a night and perished in a night, **11** And should [h]not I spare Nineveh that great city, wherein are sixscore thousand persons, that [i]cannot discern between their right hand and their left hand, and also much cattle?

---

e. Jonah 4:5 For he doubted as yet whether God would show them mercy or not, and therefore after forty days he departed out of the city, looking what issue God would send.
f. Jonah 4:6 Which was a further means, to cover him from the heat of the sun, as he remained in his booth.
g. Jonah 4:9 This declareth the great inconveniences whereinto God's servants do fall when they give place to their own affections, and do not in all things willingly submit themselves to God.
h. Jonah 4:11 Thus God mercifully reproveth him which would pity himself, and this gourd, and yet would restrain God to show his compassion to so many thousand people.
i. Jonah 4:11 Meaning, that they were children and infants.

MICAH

1

1 The destruction of Judah and Jerusalem because of the idolatry.

1 The word of the Lord, that came unto Micah the [a]Moreshite in the days of Jotham, Ahaz, and Hezekiah kings of Judah, which he saw concerning Samaria, and Jerusalem. **2** Hear, [b]all ye people: hearken thou, O earth, and all that therein is, and let the Lord God be witness against you, even the Lord from his holy Temple. **3** For behold, the Lord cometh out of his place, and will come [c]down, and tread upon the high places of the earth. **4** And the mountains shall melt under him (so shall the valleys cleave) as wax before the fire, and as the waters that are poured downward. **5** For the wickedness of Jacob is all this, and for the sins of the house of Israel: what is the wickedness of Jacob? Is not [d]Samaria? and which are the high [e]places of Judah? Is not Jerusalem? **6** Therefore I will make Samaria as an heap of the field, and for the planting of a vineyard, and I will cause the stones thereof to tumble down into the valley, and I will discover the foundations thereof. **7** And all the graven images thereof shall be broken, and all the [f]gifts thereof shall be burnt with the fire, and all the idols thereof will I destroy: for she gathered it of the hire of an harlot, and they shall return [g]to the wages of an harlot. **8** Therefore I will mourn and howl: I will go without clothes, and naked: I will make lamentation like the dragons, and mourning as the ostriches. **9** For her plagues are grievous: for it is come into Judah: the enemy is come unto the gate of my people, unto Jerusalem. **10** Declare ye it not at [h]Gath, neither weep ye: for the house of [i]Aphrah roll thyself in the dust. **11** Thou that dwellest at [j]Shaphir, go together naked with shame: she that dwelleth at Zaanan, shall not come forth in the mourning of Beth Ezel: the enemy shall [k]receive of you for his standing. **12** For the inhabitant of Maroth waited for good, but evil came from the Lord unto the [l]gate of Jerusalem. **13** O thou inhabitant of Lachish, bind the chariot to the beasts [m]of price: she [n]is the beginning of the sin to the daughter of Zion: for the transgressions of Israel were found in thee. **14** Therefore shalt thou give presents to Moresheth [o]Gath: the houses of Achzib shall be as a lie to the kings of Israel. **15** Yet will I bring an [p]heir unto thee, O inhabitant of Mareshah, he shall come unto Adullam, [q]the glory of Israel. **16** Make thee bald: and shave thee for thy delicate children: enlarge thy baldness as the eagle, for they are gone into captivity from thee.

2

1 Threatenings against the wanton and dainty people. 6 They would teach the Prophets to preach.

1 Woe unto them that imagine iniquity, and work wickedness upon their beds: [a]when the morning is light they practice it, because their hand [b]hath power. **2** And they covet fields, and take them by violence, and houses, and take them away: so they oppress a man and his house, even man and his heritage. **3** Therefore thus saith the Lord, Behold, against this family have I devised a plague, whereout ye shall not pluck your necks, and ye shall not go so proudly, for this time is evil. **4** In that day shall they take up a parable against you, and lament with a doleful lamentation, and say, [c]We be utterly wasted: he hath changed the portion of my people: how hath he taken it away to restore it unto me? he hath divided our fields. **5** Therefore thou shalt have none that shall cast a cord by lot in [d]the congregation of the Lord. **6** [e]They that prophesy, Prophesy ye not. [f]They shall not prophesy to them, neither shall they take shame. **7** O thou that art named of the house of Jacob, is the Spirit of the Lord shortened? [g]are these his works? are not my works good unto him [h]that walketh uprightly? **8** But he that was [i]yesterday my people, is risen up on the other side, as against an enemy: they spoil the [j]beautiful garment from them that pass by peaceably, as though they returned from the war. **9** The women of my people have ye cast out from their pleasant houses, and from their children have ye taken away [k]my glory continually. **10** Arise and depart, for this is not your [l]rest: because it is polluted, it shall destroy you, even with a sore destruction. **11** If a man [m]walk in the spirit, and would lie falsely, saying, [n]I will prophesy unto thee of wine, and of strong drink, he shall even be the prophet of this people. **12** I will surely gather [o]thee wholly, O Jacob: I will surely gather the remnant of Israel: I will put them together as the sheep of Bozrah, even as the flock in the midst of their fold: the cities shall be full of brute of the men. **13** The [p]breaker up shall come up before them: they shall

---

MICAH 1

a. Micah 1:1 Born in Moresheth, a city of Judah.
b. Micah 1:2 Because of the malice and obstinacy of the people, whom he had so oft exhorted to repentance, he summoneth them to God's judgments, taking all creatures, and God himself to witness, that the preaching of his Prophets, which they have abused, shall be revenged.
c. Micah 1:3 Meaning hereby, that God will come to judgment against the strong cities and holds.
d. Micah 1:5 Samaria, which should have been an example to all Israel of true religion and justice, was the puddle, and stews of all idolatry and corruption, and boasted themselves of their father Jacob.
e. Micah 1:5 That is, the idolatry and infection.
f. Micah 1:7 Which they gathered by evil practices, and thought that their idols had enriched them therewith for their service unto them.
g. Micah 1:7 The gain that came by their idols shall be consumed as a thing of naught: for as the wages or riches of harlots are wickedly gotten, so are they vilely and speedily spent.
h. Micah 1:10 Lest the Philistines our enemies rejoice at our destruction.
i. Micah 1:10 Which was a city near to Jerusalem, Josh. 18:23, there called Ophrah, and signifieth dust: therefore he willeth them to mourn and roll themselves in the dust, for their dusty city.
j. Micah 1:11 These were cities whereby the enemy should pass as he came to Judah.
k. Micah 1:11 He shall not depart before he hath overcome you, and so you shall pay for his tarrying.
l. Micah 1:12 For Rabshakeh had shut up Jerusalem, that they could not send to succor them.
m. Micah 1:13 To flee away: for Sennacherib laid siege first to that city, and re-mained therein when he sent his captains and army against Jerusalem.
n. Micah 1:13 Thou first receivedst the idolatry of Jeroboam, and so didst infect Jerusalem.
o. Micah 1:14 Thou shalt bribe the Philistines thy neighbors, but they shall deceive thee, as well as they of Jerusalem.
p. Micah 1:15 He prophesieth against his own city: and because it signified an heritage, he saith that God would send an heir to possess it.
q. Micah 1:15 For so they thought themselves for the strength of their city.

MICAH 2

a. Micah 2:1 As soon as they rise, they execute their wicked devices of the night, and according to their power hurt others.
b. Micah 2:1 Hebrew, is in power.
c. Micah 2:4 Thus the Jews lament and say that there is no hope of restitution, seeing their possessions are divided among the enemies.
d. Micah 2:5 Ye shall have no more lands to divide as you had in times past, and as you used to measure them in the Jubilee.
e. Micah 2:6 Thus the people warn the prophets that they speak to them no more, for they cannot abide their threatenings.
f. Micah 2:6 God saith that they shall not prophesy, nor receive no more of their rebukes nor taunts.
g. Micah 2:7 Are these your works according to his Law?
h. Micah 2:7 Do not the godly find my words comfortable?
i. Micah 2:8 That is, aforetime.
j. Micah 2:8 The poor can have no commodity by them, but they spoil them, as though they were enemies.
k. Micah 2:9 That is, their substance and living, which is God's blessing, and as it were part of his glory.
l. Micah 2:10 Jerusalem shall not be your safeguard: but the cause of your destruction.
m. Micah 2:11 That is, show himself to be a Prophet.
n. Micah 2:11 He showeth what prophets they delight in, that is, in flatterers, which tell them pleasant tales, and speak of their commodities.
o. Micah 2:12 To destroy thee.
p. Micah 2:13 The enemy shall break their gates and walls, and lead them into Chaldea.

break out, and pass by the gate, and go out by it, and their king shall go before them, and the Lord shall be [q]upon their heads.

3

1 Against the tyranny of princes and false prophets.

1 And I said, Hear, I pray you, O heads of Jacob, and ye princes of the house of Israel: should not ye know [a]judgment? 2 But they hate the good, and love the evil: [b]they pluck off their skins from them, and their flesh from their bones. 3 And they eat also the flesh of my people, and flay off their skin from them, and they break their bones, and chop them in pieces, as for the pot, and as flesh within the caldron. 4 Then [c]shall they cry unto the Lord, but he will not hear them: he will even hide his face from them at that time, because they have done wickedly in their works. 5 Thus saith the Lord, Concerning the prophets that deceive my people, and [d]bite them with their teeth, and cry, peace, but if a man put not into their mouths, they prepare war against him. 6 Therefore [e]night shall be unto you for a vision, and darkness shall be unto you for a divination, and the Sun shall go down over the prophets, and the day shall be dark over them. 7 Then shall the Seers be ashamed, and the Soothsayers confounded: yea, they shall all cover [f]their lips, for they have none answer of God. 8 Yet notwithstanding I am full [g]of power by the Spirit of the Lord, and of judgment, and of strength to declare unto Jacob his transgression, and to Israel his sin. 9 Hear this, I pray you, ye heads of the house of Jacob, and princes of the house of Israel: they abhor judgment, and pervert all equity. 10 They build up Zion with [h]blood, and Jerusalem with iniquity, 11 The heads thereof judge for rewards, and the priests thereof teach for hire, and the prophets thereof prophesy for money: yet will they [i]lean upon the Lord and say, Is not the Lord among us? no evil can come upon us. 12 Therefore shall Zion for your sake be [j]plowed as a field, and Jerusalem shall be an heap, and the mountain of the house, as the high places of the forest.

4

1 Of the kingdom of Christ, and felicity of his Church.

1 But in the [a]last days it shall come to pass, that the mountain of the House of the Lord shall be prepared in the top of the mountains, and it shall be exalted above the [b]hills, and people shall flow unto it. 2 Yea, many nations shall come and say, Come, and let us go up to the Mountain of the Lord, and to the House of the God of Jacob, and he will [c]teach us his ways, and we will walk in his paths: for the Law shall go forth of Zion, and the word of the Lord from Jerusalem. 3 And he shall judge among many people, and [d]rebuke mighty nations afar off, and they shall break their swords into mattocks, and their spears into [e]scythes: nation shall not lift up a sword against nation, neither shall they [f]learn to fight anymore. 4 But they shall sit every man under his vine, and under his fig tree, and none shall make them afraid: for the mouth of the Lord of hosts hath spoken it. 5 For all people will walk [g]everyone in the name of his god, and we will walk in the Name of the Lord our God, forever and ever. 6 At the same day saith the Lord, will I gather her that halteth, and I will gather her that is cast out, and her that I have afflicted. 7 And I will make her that halteth, [h]a remnant, and her that was cast far off, a mighty nation, and the Lord shall reign over them in Mount Zion, from henceforth even forever. 8 And thou, O [i]tower of the flock, the stronghold of the daughter Zion, unto thee shall it come, even [j]the first dominion, and kingdom shall come to the daughter Jerusalem. 9 Now why dost thou cry out with lamentation? is [k]there no king in thee? is thy counselor perished? for sorrow hath taken thee, as a woman in travail. 10 Sorrow and mourn, O daughter Zion, like a woman in travail: for now shalt thou go forth of the city, and dwell in the field, and shalt go into Babel, but there shalt thou be delivered: there the Lord shall redeem thee from the hand of thine enemies. 11 Now also many nations are gathered against thee, saying, Zion shall be condemned, and our eye shall look upon Zion. 12 But they [l]know not the thoughts of the Lord: they understand not his counsel, for he shall gather them as the sheaves in the barn. 13 Arise and thresh, [m]O daughter Zion: for I will make thine horn iron, and I will make thine hooves brass, and thou shalt break in pieces many people: and I will consecrate their riches unto the Lord: and their substance unto the ruler of the whole world.

5

1 The destruction of Jerusalem. 2 The excellency of Bethlehem.

1 Now assemble thy garrisons, O daughter [a]of garrisons: he hath laid siege against us: they shall smite the judge of Israel with a rod upon the cheek. 2 And thou Bethlehem Ephrathah art [b]little to be among the thousands of Judah, yet out of thee shall he come forth unto me, that shall be the ruler in Israel: whose [c]goings forth have been from the beginning and from everlasting. 3 Therefore will he give them up, until the time that [d]she which shall bear, shall travail: then the remnant of their brethren shall return unto the children of Israel. 4 And he shall [e]stand, and feed in the strength of the Lord, and in the majesty of the Name of the Lord his God, and they shall dwell still: for now shall he be magnified unto the ends of the world. 5 And he [f]shall be our peace when Assyria shall come into our land: when he shall tread in our palaces, then shall we raise against him seven shepherds, and eight principal men. 6 And they shall destroy [g]Assyria with the sword, and the land of Nimrod with their swords: thus shall he [h]deliver us from Assyria, when he cometh into our land, and when he shall tread within our borders. 7 And the [i]remnant of Jacob shall be among many people, as a dew from the Lord, and as the showers upon the grass, that waiteth not for man, nor hopeth in the sons of Adam. 8 And the remnant of Jacob shall be among the Gentiles in the midst of many people, as the Lion among the beasts of the forest, and as the Lion whelp among the flocks of sheep, who when he goeth through, treadeth down and teareth in pieces, and none can deliver. 9 Thine hand shall be lifted up upon thine adversaries, and all thine enemies shall be cut off. 10 And it shall come to pass in that day, saith the Lord, that I will cut off thine [j]horses out of the midst of thee, and I will destroy thy chariots. 11 And I will cut off the cities of thy land, and overthrow all thy strongholds. 12 And I will cut off thine enchanters out of thine hand: and thou shalt have no more soothsayers. 13 Thine idols also will I cut off, and thine images out of the midst of thee: and thou shalt no more worship the work of thine hands. 14 And I will pluck up thy groves out of the midst of thee: so will I destroy thine enemies. 15 And I will execute a vengeance in my wrath and indignation upon the heathen, [k]which they have not heard.

---

q. Micah 2:13 To drive them forward, and to help their enemies.

MICAH 3

a. Micah 3:1 That thing which is just and lawful, both to govern my people aright, and also to discharge your own conscience.
b. Micah 3:2 The Prophet condemneth the wicked governors not only of covetousness, theft, and murder, but compareth them to wolves, lions, and most cruel beasts.
c. Micah 3:4 That is, when I shall visit their wickedness: for though I hear the godly before they cry, Isa. 65:24, yet I will not hear these though they cry, Isa. 1:15 and Ezek. 8:18; James 2:13; 1 Pet. 3:11, 12.
d. Micah 3:5 They devour all their substance, and then flatter them, promising that all shall go well, but if one restrain from their bellies, then they invent all ways to mischief.
e. Micah 3:6 As you have loved to walk in darkness, and to prophesy lies, so God shall reward you with gross blindness and ignorance, so that when all others shall see the bright beams of God's graces, ye shall as blind men grope as in the night.
f. Micah 3:7 When God shall discover them to the world, they shall be afraid to speak: for all shall know that they were but false prophets, and did belie the word of God.
g. Micah 3:8 The Prophet being assured of his vocation by the Spirit of God, setteth himself alone against all the wicked, showing how God both gave him gifts, ability and knowledge, to discern between good and evil, and also constancy to reprove the sins of the people, and not to flatter them.
h. Micah 3:10 They build them houses by bribery, which he calleth blood and iniquity.
i. Micah 3:11 They will say, that they are the people of God, and abuse his Name, as a pretence to cloak their hypocrisy.
j. Micah 3:12 Read Jer. 26:18.

MICAH 4

a. Micah 4:1 When Christ shall come, and the Temple shall be destroyed.
b. Micah 4:1 Read Isa. 2:2.
c. Micah 4:2 He showeth that there is no true Church, but where as the people are taught by God's pure word.
d. Micah 4:3 By his corrections and threatenings he will bring the people into subjection which are in the utmost corners of the world.
e. Micah 4:3 They shall abstain from all evil doing, and exercise themselves in godliness and in well doing to others.
f. Micah 4:3 Read Isa. 2:4
g. Micah 4:5 He showeth that the people of God ought to remain constant in their religion, albeit all the world should give themselves to their superstition and idolatry.
h. Micah 4:7 I will cause that Israel, which is now as one lame and halting, and so almost destroyed, shall live again, and grow into a great people.
i. Micah 4:8 Meaning, Jerusalem, where the Lord's flock was gathered.
j. Micah 4:8 The flourishing state of the kingdom, as it was under David and Solomon, which thing was accomplished to the Church by the coming of Christ.
k. Micah 4:9 In the mean season he showeth that they should endure great troubles and temptations when thy saw themselves neither to have king nor counsel.
l. Micah 4:12 He showeth that the faithful ought not to measure God's judgments by the brags and threatenings of the wicked, but thereby are admonished to lift up their hearts to God to call for deliverance.
m. Micah 4:13 God giveth his Church this victory, so oft as he overcometh their enemies: but the accomplishment thereof shall be at the last coming of Christ.

MICAH 5

a. Micah 5:1 He forewarneth them of the dangers that shall come before they enjoy these comforts, showing that forasmuch as Jerusalem was accustomed with her garrisons to trouble others, the Lord would now cause other garrisons to vex her, and that her rulers should be smitten on the face most contemptuously.
b. Micah 5:2 For so the Jews divided their country that for every thousand there was a chief captain: and because Bethlehem was not able to make a thousand, he calleth it little, but yet God will raise up his captain and governor therein: and thus it is not the least by reason of this benefit, as Matt. 2:6.
c. Micah 5:2 He showeth that the coming of Christ and all his ways were appointed of God from all eternity.
d. Micah 5:3 He compareth the Jews to women with child, who for a time should have great sorrows, but at length they should have a comfortable deliverance, John 16:21.
e. Micah 5:4 That is, Christ's kingdom shall be stable and everlasting, and his people as well the Gentiles as the Jews shall dwell in safety.
f. Micah 5:5 This Messiah shall be a sufficient safeguard for us, and though the enemy invade us for a time, yet shall God stir up many which shall be able to deliver us.
g. Micah 5:6 These whom God shall raise up for the deliverance of his Church, shall destroy all the enemies thereof, which are meant here by the Assyrians and Babylonians which were the chief at that time.
h. Micah 5:6 By these governors will God deliver us when the enemy cometh into our land.
i. Micah 5:7 This remnant or Church which God shall deliver shall only depend on God's power and defense, as doth the grass of the field, and not on the hope of man.
j. Micah 5:10 I will destroy all things wherein thou puttest thy confidence, as thy vain confidence and idolatry, and so will help thee.
k. Micah 5:15 It shall be so terrible that the like hath not been heard of.

6

An exhortation to the dumb creatures to hear the judgment against Israel being unkind. 6 What manner of sacrifices do please God.

1 Hearken ye now what the Lord saith, Arise thou, and contend before the [a]mountains, and let the hills hear thy voice. **2** Hear ye, O mountains, the Lord's quarrel, and ye mighty foundations of the earth: for the Lord hath a quarrel against his people, and he will plead with Israel. **3** O my people, what have I done unto thee? or wherein have I grieved thee? testify against me. **4** Surely I [b]brought thee up out of the land of Egypt, and redeemed thee out of the house of servants, and I have sent before thee, Moses, Aaron, and Miriam. **5** O my people, remember now what Balak king of Moab had devised, and what Balaam the son of Beor answered him, from [c]Shittim unto Gilgal, that ye may know the [d]righteousness of the Lord. **6** Wherewith [e]shall I come before the Lord, and bow myself before the high God? shall I come before him with burnt offerings, and with calves of a year old? **7** Will the Lord be pleased with thousands of rams, or with ten thousand rivers of oil? shall I give my [f]firstborn for my transgression, even the fruit of my body, for the sin of my soul? **8** He hath showed thee, O man, what is good, and what the Lord requireth of thee: [g]surely to do justly, and to love mercy, and to humble thyself, to walk with thy God. **9** The Lord's voice crieth unto the [h]city, and the man of wisdom shall see thy name: Hear the rod, and who hath appointed it. **10** Are yet the treasures of wickedness in the house of the wicked, and the scant measure, that is abominable? **11** Shall I justify the wicked balances, and the bag of deceitful weights? **12** For the rich men thereof [i]are full of cruelty, and the inhabitants thereof have spoken lies, and their tongue is deceitful in their mouth. **13** Therefore also will I make thee sick in smiting thee, and in making thee desolate, because of thy sins. **14** Thou shalt eat and not be satisfied, and [j]thy casting down shall be in the midst of thee, and thou [k]shalt take hold, but shalt not deliver, and that which thou deliverest, will I give up to the sword. **15** Thou shalt sow, but not reap: Thou shalt tread the olives, but thou shalt not anoint thee with oil, and make sweet wine, but shall not drink wine. **16** For the [l]statutes of Omri are kept, and all the manner of the house of Ahab, and ye walk in their counsels, that I should make thee waste, and the inhabitants thereof an hissing: therefore ye shall bear the reproach of my people.

7

1 A complaint for the small number of the righteous. 4 The wickedness of those times. 14 The prosperity of the Church.

1 Woe is me, for I am as the [a]Summer gatherings, and as the grapes of the vintage: there is no cluster to eat: my soul desired the first ripe fruits. **2** The good man is perished out of the earth, and there is none righteous among men: [b]they all lie in wait for blood: every man hunteth his brother with a net. **3** To make good for the evil of their hands, the prince asked, and the judge judgeth for a reward: therefore the [c]great man he speaketh out the corruption of his soul: so [d]they wrapped it up. **4** The best of them is as [e]a brier, and the most righteous of them is sharper than a thorn-hedge: the day of [f]thy watchmen and thy visitation cometh: then shall be their confusion. **5** Trust ye not in a friend, neither put ye confidence in a counselor: keep the doors of thy mouth from her that lieth in thy bosom. **6** For the son revileth the father: the daughter riseth up against her mother, the daughter-in-law against her mother-in-law, and a man's enemies are the men of his own house. **7** Therefore [g]I will look unto the Lord: I will wait for God my Savior: my God will hear me. **8** Rejoice not against me, [h]O mine enemy: though I fall, I shall arise, when I shall sit in darkness, the Lord shall be a light unto me. **9** I will bear the wrath of the Lord, because I have sinned against him, until he plead my cause, and execute judgment for me: then will he bring me forth to the light, and I shall see his righteousness. **10** Then she that is mine enemy, shall look upon it, and shame shall cover her, which said unto me, Where is the Lord thy God? Mine eyes shall behold her: now shall she be trodden down as the mire of the streets. **11** This is [i]the day, that thy walls shall be built: this day shall drive far away [j]the decree. **12** In this day also they shall come unto thee from [k]Assyria, and from the strong cities, and from the strongholds even unto the river, and from Sea to Sea, and from mountain to mountain. **13** Notwithstanding the land shall be desolate because of them that dwell therein, and for the fruits of [l]their inventions. **14** [m]Feed thy people with thy rod, the flock of thine heritage (which dwell solitary in the wood) as in the midst of Carmel: let them feed in Bashan and Gilead, as in old time. **15** [n]According to the days of thy coming out of the land of Egypt, will I show unto him marvelous things. **16** The nations shall see, and be confounded for all their power: they shall [o]lay their hand upon their mouth: [p]their ears shall be deaf. **17** They shall [q]lick the dust like a serpent: they shall move out of their holes like worms: they shall be afraid of the Lord our God, and shall fear because of thee. **18** Who is a God like unto thee, that taketh away iniquity, and [r]passeth by the transgression of the remnant of his heritage! He retaineth not his wrath forever, because mercy pleaseth him. **19** He will turn again, and have compassion upon us: he will subdue our iniquities, and cast all [s]their sins into the bottom of the sea. **20** Thou wilt perform thy [t]truth to Jacob, and mercy to Abraham, as thou hast sworn unto our fathers in old time.

MICAH 6

a. Micah 6:1 He took the high mountains and hard rocks to witness against the obstinacy of his people.
b. Micah 6:4 I have not hurt thee, but bestowed infinite benefits upon thee.
c. Micah 6:5 That is, remember my benefits from the beginning how I delivered you from Balaam's curse, and also spared you from Shittim, which was in the plain of Moab, till I brought you into the land promised.
d. Micah 6:5 That is, the truth of his promise and his manifold benefits toward you.
e. Micah 6:6 Thus the people by hypocrisy ask how to please God and are content to offer sacrifices, but will not change their lives.
f. Micah 6:7 There is nothing so dear to man, but the hypocrites will offer it unto God, if they think thereby to avoid his anger: but they will never be brought to mortify their own affections, and to give themselves willingly to serve God as he commandeth.
g. Micah 6:8 The Prophet in few words calleth them to the observation of the second Table, to know if they will obey God aright or no, saying that God hath prescribed them to do this.
h. Micah 6:9 Meaning, that when God speaketh to any city or nation, the godly will acknowledge his majesty and consider not the mortal man that bringeth the threatening, but God that sendeth it.
i. Micah 6:12 That is, of Jerusalem.
j. Micah 6:14 Thou shalt be consumed with inward grief and evils.
k. Micah 6:14 Meaning, that the city should go about to save her men, as they that lay hold on that which they would preserve.
l. Micah 6:16 You have received all the corruption and idolatry, wherewith the ten tribes were infected under Omri and Ahab his son: and to excuse your doings, you allege the King's authority by his statutes, and also wisdom and policy in so doing, but you shall not escape punishment: but as I have shown you great favor, and taken you for my people, so shall your plagues be accordingly, Luke 12:47.

MICAH 7

a. Micah 7:1 The Prophet taketh upon him the person of the earth, which complaineth that all her fruits are gone, so that none is left: that is, that there is no godly man remaining: for all are given to cruelty and deceit, so that none spareth his own brother.
b. Micah 7:2 He showeth that the prince, the judge, and the rich man are linked together all to do evil, and to cloak the doings one of another.
c. Micah 7:3 That is, the rich man that is able to give money, abstaineth from no wickedness nor injury.
d. Micah 7:3 These men agree among themselves and conspire with one consent to do evil.
e. Micah 7:4 They that are of most estimation and are counted most honest among them, are but thorns and briers to prick.
f. Micah 7:4 Meaning of the Prophets and governors.
g. Micah 7:7 The Prophet showeth that the only remedy for the godly in desperate evils, is to flee unto God for succor.
h. Micah 7:8 This is spoken in the person of the Church which calleth the malignant Church her enemy.
i. Micah 7:11 To wit, when God shall show himself a deliverer of his Church, and a destroyer of his enemies.
j. Micah 7:11 Meaning, the cruel empire of the Babylonians.
k. Micah 7:12 When the Church shall be restored, they that were enemies afore, shall come out of all the corners of the world unto her, so that neither holds, rivers, seas, nor mountains shall be able to let them.
l. Micah 7:13 Afore this grace appear, he showeth how grievously the hypocrites themselves shall be punished, seeing that the earth itself, which cannot sin shall be made waste because of their wickedness.
m. Micah 7:14 The Prophet prayeth to God to be merciful unto his Church, when they should be scattered abroad as in solitary places in Babylon, and to be beneficial unto them as in times past.
n. Micah 7:15 God promiseth to be favorable to his people, as he had been afore time.
o. Micah 7:16 They shall be as dumb men, and dare brag no more.
p. Micah 7:16 They shall be astonished and afraid to hear men speak, lest they should hear of their destruction.
q. Micah 7:17 They shall fall flat on the ground for fear.
r. Micah 7:18 As though he would not see it, but wink at it.
s. Micah 7:19 Meaning of his elect.
t. Micah 7:20 The Church is assured, that God will declare in effect the truth of his merciful promise, which he had made of old to Abraham, and to all that should apprehend the promise by faith.

NAHUM

1

Of the destruction of the Assyrians, and of the deliverance of Israel.

1 The [a]burden of Nineveh. [b]The book of the vision of Nahum the [c]Elkoshite. 2 God is [d]jealous, and the Lord revengeth: the Lord revengeth: even the Lord [e]of anger, the Lord will take vengeance on his adversaries, and he reserveth wrath for his enemies. 3 The [f]Lord is slow to anger, but he is great in power, and will not surely clear the wicked: the Lord hath his way in the whirlwind, and in the storm, and the clouds are the dust of his feet. 4 He rebuketh the sea, and drieth it, and he drieth up all the rivers: Bashan is wasted and Carmel, and the flower of Lebanon is wasted. 5 The mountains tremble for him, and the hills melt, and the earth is burnt at his sight, yea the world, and all that dwell therein. 6 [g]Who can stand before his wrath? or who can abide in the fierceness of his wrath? his wrath is poured out like fire, and the rocks are broken by him. 7 The Lord is good [h]and as a stronghold in the day of trouble, and he knoweth them that trust in him. 8 But passing over as with a flood, he will utterly destroy the [i]place thereof, and darkness shall pursue his enemies. 9 What do ye [j]imagine against the Lord? he will make an utter destruction: affliction shall not rise up the second time. 10 For he shall come as unto [k]thorns folden one in another, and as unto drunkards in their drunken-ness: they shall be devoured as stubble fully dried. 11 There [l]cometh one out of thee that imagineth evil against the Lord, even a wicked counselor. 12 Thus saith the Lord, Though they be [m]quiet, and also many, yet thus shall they be cut off when he shall pass by: though I have afflicted thee, I will afflict thee no more. 13 For now I will break his yoke from thee, and will burst thy bonds in sunder. 14 And the Lord hath given a commandment concerning thee that no more of thy name be [n]sown: out of the house of thy gods will I cut off the graven, and the molten image: I will make it thy grave for thee, for thou art vile. 15 [*l*]Behold upon the mountains the feet of him that declareth, and publisheth [o]peace: O Judah, keep thy solemn feasts, perform thy vows: for the wicked shall no more pass through thee: he is utterly cut off.

2

He describeth the victories of the Chaldeans against the Assyrians.

1 The [a]destroyer is come before thy face: keep the munition: look to the way: make thy loins strong: increase thy strength mightily. 2 For the Lord hath [b]turned away the glory of Jacob, as the glory of Israel: for the emptiers have emptied them out, and [c]marred their vine branches. 3 The shield of his mighty men is made red, [d]the valiant men are in scarlet: the chariots shall be as in the fire and flames in the day of his preparation, and [e]the fir trees shall tremble. 4 The chariots shall rage in the streets: they shall run to and fro in the highways: they shall seem like lamps: they shall shoot like the lightning. 5 [f]He shall remember his strong men: they shall stumble as they go: they shall make haste to the walls thereof, and the defense shall be prepared. 6 The gates of the rivers shall be opened, and the palace shall melt. 7 And Huzzab the Queen shall be led away captive, and her maids shall lead her as with the voice of doves, smiting upon their breasts. 8 But Nineveh is [g]of old like a pool of water: yet they shall flee away. Stand, stand, shall they cry: but none shall look back. 9 [h]Spoil ye the silver, spoil the gold: for there is none end of the store and glory of all the pleasant vessels. 10 [i]She is empty and void and waste, and the heart melteth, and the knees smite together, and sorrow is in all loins, and the faces [j]of them all gather blackness. 11 Where is the [k]dwelling of the lions, and the pasture of the lion's whelps? where the lion and the lioness waked, and the lion's whelp, and none made them afraid. 12 The lion did tear in pieces enough for his whelps, and worried for his lioness, and filled his holes with prey, and his dens with spoil. 13 Behold, I come unto thee saith the Lord of hosts, and I will burn her chariots in the [l]smoke, and the sword shall devour thy young lions, and I will cut off thy spoil from the earth, and the voice of thy [m]messengers shall no more be heard.

3

1 Of the fall of Ninevah. 8 No power can escape the hand of God.

1 O bloody city, it is all full of lies and robbery: [a]the prey departeth not. 2 The noise of a whip, [b]and the noise of the moving of the wheels, and the beating of the horses, and the leaping of the chariots. 3 The horseman lifteth up both the bright sword, and the glittering spear, and a multitude is slain, and the dead bodies are many: there is none end of their corpses: they stumble upon their corpses, 4 Because of the multitude of the fornications of the [c]harlot that is beautiful, and is a mistress of witchcraft, and selleth the people through her whoredom, and the nations through her witchcrafts. 5 Behold, I come upon thee, saith the Lord of hosts, and will discover thy skirts upon thy face, and will show the nations thy filthiness, and the kingdoms thy shame. 6 And I will cast filth upon thee, and make thee vile, and will set thee as a gazing stock. 7 And it shall come to pass, that all they that look upon thee, shall flee from thee, and say, Nineveh is destroyed, who will have pity upon her? where shall I seek comforters for thee? 8 Art thou better than [d]No, which was full of people? that lay in the rivers, and had the waters round about it? whose ditch was the sea, and her wall was from the sea? 9 Ethiopia and Egypt were her strength, and there was none end: Put and Lubim were [e]her helpers. 10 Yet was she carried away, and went into captivity: her young children also were dashed in pieces at the head of all the streets: and they cast lots for her noble men, and all her mighty men were bound in chains. 11 Also thou shalt be drunken: thou shalt hide thyself, and shalt seek help because of the enemy. 12 All thy strong cities shall be like fig trees with the first ripe figs: for if they be shaken, they fall into the mouth of the eater. 13 Behold, thy people within thee are women: the gates of thy land shall be opened unto thine enemies, and the fire shall devour thy bars. 14 Draw thee waters for the siege: fortify thy strongholds: go into the clay, and temper the mortar: make strong brick. 15 There shall the fire devour thee: the sword shall cut thee off: it shall eat thee up like the [f]locusts, though thou be multiplied like the

---

NAHUM 1

- **a.** Nahum 1:1 Read Isa. 13:1.
- **b.** Nahum 1:1 The vision or revelation, which God commanded Nahum to write concerning the Ninevites.
- **c.** Nahum 1:1 That is, born in a poor village in the tribe of Simeon.
- **d.** Nahum 1:2 Meaning, of his glory.
- **e.** Nahum 1:2 With his he is but angry for a time, but his anger never assuageth toward the reprobate, though for a time he defer it.
- **f.** Nahum 1:3 Thus the wicked would make God's mercy an occasion to sin, but the Prophet willeth them to consider his force and justice.
- **g.** Nahum 1:6 If all creatures be at God's commandment, and none is able to resist his wrath, shall man flatter himself, and think by any means to escape, when he provoketh his God to anger?
- **h.** Nahum 1:7 Lest the faithful should be discouraged by hearing the power of God, he showeth them that his mercy appertain unto them, and that he hath care over them.
- **i.** Nahum 1:8 Signifying, that God will suddenly destroy Nineveh, and the Assyrians, in such sort as they shall lie in perpetual darkness, and never recover their strength again.
- **j.** Nahum 1:9 He showeth that the enterprises of the Assyrians against Judah and the Church, were against God, and therefore he would so destroy them at once, that he should not need to return the second time.
- **k.** Nahum 1:10 Although the Assyrians think themselves like thorns that prick on all sides, yet the Lord will set fire on them, and as drunken men are not able to stand against any force, so they shall be nothing able to resist him.
- **l.** Nahum 1:11 Which may be understood either of Sennacherib, or of the whole body of the people of Nineveh.
- **m.** Nahum 1:12 Though they think themselves in most safety, and of greatest strength, yet when God shall pass by, he will destroy them: notwithstanding he comforteth his Church, and promiseth to make an end of punishing them by the Assyrians.
- **n.** Nahum 1:14 Meaning, Sennacherib, who should have no more children, but be slain in the house of his gods, 2 Kings 19:36, 37.
- **o.** Nahum 1:15 Which peace the Jews should enjoy by the death of Sennacherib.

NAHUM 1

- **l.** Rom. 10:15

NAHUM 2

- **a.** Nahum 2:1 That is, Nebuchadnezzar is in readiness to destroy the Assyrians: and the Prophet derideth the enterprises of the Assyrians which prepared to resist him.
- **b.** Nahum 2:2 Seeing God hath punished his own people Judah and Israel, he will now punish the enemies by whom he scourged them, read Isa. 10:12.
- **c.** Nahum 2:2 Signifying, that the Israelites were utterly destroyed.
- **d.** Nahum 2:3 Both to fear the enemy, and also that they themselves should not so soon espy blood one of another to discourage them.
- **e.** Nahum 2:3 Meaning, their spears should shake and crash together.
- **f.** Nahum 2:5 Then the Assyrians shall seek by all means to gather their power, but all things shall fail them.
- **g.** Nahum 2:8 The Assyrians will flatter themselves and say, that Nineveh is so ancient that it can never perish, and is as a fishpool, whose waters they that walk on the banks cannot touch, but they shall be scattered, and shall not look back though men would call them.
- **h.** Nahum 2:9 God commandeth the enemies to spoil Nineveh, and promiseth them infinite riches and treasures.
- **i.** Nahum 2:10 That is, Nineveh, and the men thereof shall be after this sort.
- **j.** Nahum 2:10 Read Joel 2:6.
- **k.** Nahum 2:11 Meaning, Nineveh, whose inhabitants were cruel like the Lions, and given to all oppression, and spared no violence or tyranny to provide for their wives and children.
- **l.** Nahum 2:13 That is, as soon as my wrath beginneth to kindle.
- **m.** Nahum 2:13 Signifying the heralds, which were accustomed to proclaim war. Some read, of thy gum teeth, wherewith Nineveh was wont to bruise the bones of the poor.

NAHUM 3

- **a.** Nahum 3:1 It never ceaseth to spoil and rob.
- **b.** Nahum 3:2 He showeth how the Chaldeans shall haste, and how courageous their horses shall be in beating the ground when they come against the Assyrians.
- **c.** Nahum 3:4 He compareth Nineveh to an harlot, which by her beauty and subtlety enticeth young men, and bringeth them to destruction.
- **d.** Nahum 3:8 Meaning, Alexandria, which was in league with so many nations, and yet was now destroyed.
- **e.** Nahum 3:9 Or, thine.
- **f.** Nahum 3:15 Signifying, that God's judgments should suddenly destroy the Assyrians, as these vermin are with rain or change of weather.

locusts, and multiplied like the grasshopper. **16** Thou hast multiplied thy merchants above the stars of heaven: the locust spoileth and flieth away. **17** Thy princes are as the grasshoppers, and thy captains as the great grasshoppers which remain in the hedges in the cold day: but when the sun ariseth, they flee away, and their place is not known where they are. **18** Thy [g]shepherds do sleep, O king of Assyria: thy strong men lie down: thy people is scattered upon the mountains, and no man gathereth them. **19** There is no healing of thy wound: thy plague is grievous: all that hear the brute of thee, shall clap the hands over thee: for upon [h]whom hath not thy malice passed continually?

g. Nahum 3:18 Thy princes and counselors.
h. Nahum 3:19 Meaning, that there was no people to whom the Assyrians had not done hurt.

HABAKKUK

1

1 A complaint against the wicked that persecute the just.

1 The burden, which Habakkuk the Prophet did see.

2 O Lord, how long shall I cry, and thou wilt not hear! even cry out unto thee [a]for violence, and thou wilt not help! **3** Why dost thou show me iniquity, and cause me to behold sorrow? for spoiling, and violence are before me: and there are that raise up strife and contention. **4** Therefore the Law is dissolved, and judgment doth never go forth: for the wicked doth [b]compass about the righteous: therefore [c]wrong judgment proceedeth. **5** Behold among the heathen, and regard, and wonder, and marvel: for I will work a work in your days: [d]ye will not believe it, though it be told you. **6** For lo, I raise up the Chaldeans, that bitter and furious nation, which shall go upon the breadth of the land to possess the dwelling places that are not theirs. **7** They are terrible and fearful: [e]their judgment, and their dignity shall proceed of themselves. **8** Their horses also are swifter than the leopards, and are more fierce than the wolves in the [1]evening: and their horsemen are many: and their horsemen shall come from far: they shall fly as the eagle hasting to meat. **9** They come all to spoil: for their faces shall be an [f]East wind, and they shall gather the captivity [g]as the sand. **10** And they shall mock the Kings, and the princes shall be a scorn unto them: they shall deride every stronghold: for they shall gather [h]dust, and take it. **11** Then shall they [i]take a courage, and transgress and do wickedly, imputing this their power unto their god. **12** Art not thou of old, O Lord my God, mine holy One? we shall not [j]die: O Lord, thou hast ordained them for judgment, and O God, thou hast established them for correction. **13** Thou art of pure eyes, and canst not see evil: thou canst not behold wickedness: wherefore dost thou look upon the transgressors, and holdest thy tongue, when the wicked devoureth the man, that is more righteous than he? **14** And makest men as the [k]fishes of the sea, and as the creeping things, that have no ruler over them? **15** They take up all with the angle: they catch it in their net, and gather it in their yarn, whereof they rejoice and are glad. **16** Therefore they sacrifice unto their [l]net, and burn incense unto their yarn, because by them their portion is fat, and their meat plenteous. **17** Shall they therefore stretch out their net, and not spare continually to slay [m]the nations?

2

1 A vision. 5 Against pride, covetousness, drunkenness, and idolatry.

1 I will stand upon my [a]watch, and set me upon the tower, and will look and see what he would say unto me, and what I shall answer to him that rebuketh me. **2** And the Lord answered me, and said, Write the vision, and make it plain upon tables, that he may run [b]that readeth it. **3** For the vision is yet for an appointed time, but at the [c]last it shall speak and not lie: though it tarry, wait: for it shall surely come, and shall not stay. **4** Behold, [d]he that lifteth up himself, his mind is not upright in him, but the just shall live by his faith, **5** Yea, indeed the proud man is as [e]he that transgresseth by wine: therefore shall he not endure, because he hath enlarged his desire as the hell, and is as death, and cannot be satisfied, but gathereth unto him all nations, and heapeth unto him all people. **6** Shall not all these take up a parable against him, and a taunting proverb against him, and say, Ho, he that increaseth that which is not his? [f]how long? and he that ladeth himself with thick clay? **7** Shall [g]they not rise up suddenly, that shall bite thee? and awake, that shall stir thee? and thou shalt be their prey? **8** Because thou hast spoiled many nations, all the remnant of the people shall spoil thee, because of men's blood, and for the wrong done in the land, in the city, and unto all that dwell therein. **9** Ho, he that coveteth an evil covetousness to his house, that he may set his nest on high, to escape from the power of evil. **10** Thou [h]hast consulted shame to thine own house, by destroying many people, and hast sinned against thine own soul. **11** For the [i]stone shall cry out of the wall, and the beam out of the timber shall answer it. **12** Woe unto him that buildeth a town with blood, and erecteth a city by iniquity. **13** Behold, is it not of the [j]Lord of hosts, that the people shall labor in the very fire? the people shall even weary themselves for very vanity. **14** For the earth shall [k]be filled with the knowledge of the glory of the Lord, as the waters cover the sea. **15** Woe unto him that giveth his neighbor [l]drink: thou joinest thine heat, and makest him drunken also, that thou mayest see their privities. **16** Thou art filled with shame [m]for glory: drink thou also, and be made naked: the cup of the Lord's right hand shall be turned unto thee, and shameful spewing shall be for thy glory. **17** For the [n]cruelty of Lebanon shall cover thee: so shall the spoil of the beasts, which made them afraid, because of men's blood, and for the wrong done in the land, in the city, and unto all that dwell therein. **18** What profiteth the [o]image? for the maker therefore hath made it an image, and a teacher of lies, though he that made it, trust therein, when he maketh dumb idols. **19** Woe unto him that saith to the wood, Awake, and to the dumb stone, Rise up, it shall teach thee: [p]behold, it is laid over with gold and silver, and

HABAKKUK 1

a. Hab. 1:2 The Prophet complaineth unto God, and bewaileth that among the Jews is left none equity and brotherly love: but instead hereof reigneth cruelty, theft, contention and strife.
b. Hab. 1:4 To suppress him, if any should show himself zealous of God's cause.
c. Hab. 1:4 Because the judges which should redress this excess, are as evil as the rest.
d. Hab. 1:5 As in times past you would not believe God's word, so shall ye not now believe the strange plagues which are at hand.
e. Hab. 1:7 They themselves shall be your judges in this cause, and none shall have authority over them to control them.
f. Hab. 1:9 For the Jews most feared this wind, because it destroyed their fruits.
g. Hab. 1:9 They shall be so many in number.
h. Hab. 1:10 They shall cast up mounts against it.
i. Hab. 1:11 The Prophet comforteth the faithful that God will also destroy the Babylonians, because they shall abuse this victory, and become proud and insolent, attributing the praise hereof to their idols.
j. Hab. 1:12 He assureth the godly of God's protection, showing that the enemy can do no more than God hath appointed, and also that their sins required such a sharp rod.
k. Hab. 1:14 So that the great devoureth the small, and the Chaldeans destroy all the world.
l. Hab. 1:16 Meaning, that the enemies flatter themselves, and glory in their own force, power and wit.
m. Hab. 1:17 Meaning, that they should not.

HABAKKUK 1

1. Zeph. 3:3

HABAKKUK 2

a. Hab. 2:1 I will renounce mine own judgment, and only depend on God to be instructed what I shall answer them that abuse my preaching, and to be armed against all temptations.
b. Hab. 2:2 Write it in great letters, that he that runneth may read it.
c. Hab. 2:3 Which contained the destruction of the enemy, and the comfort of the Church: which thing though God execute not according to man's hasty affections, yet the issue of both is certain at his time appointed.
d. Hab. 2:4 To trust in himself, or in any worldly thing, is never to be quiet: for the only rest is to stay upon God by faith, Rom. 1:17; Gal. 3:11; Heb. 10:38.
e. Hab. 2:5 He compareth the proud and covetous man to a drunkard that is without reason and sense, whom God will punish and make him a laughing stock to all the world: and this he speaketh for the comfort of the godly, and against the Chaldeans.
f. Hab. 2:6 Signifying, that all the world shall wish the destruction of tyrants, and that by their oppression and covetousness, they heap but upon themselves more heavy burdens: for the more they get, the more are they troubled.
g. Hab. 2:7 That is, the Medes and Persians, that should destroy the Babylonians?
h. Hab. 2:10 Signifying, that the covetous man is the ruin of his own house, when as he thinketh to enrich it by cruelty and oppression.
i. Hab. 2:11 The stones of the house shall cry, and say that they are built of blood, and the wood shall answer and say the same of itself.
j. Hab. 2:13 Meaning, that God will not defer his vengeance long, but will come and destroy all their labors, as though they were consumed with fire.
k. Hab. 2:14 In the destruction of the Babylonians his glory shall appear through all the world.
l. Hab. 2:15 He reproacheth thus the king of Babylon, who as he was drunken with covetousness and cruelty, so he provoked others to the same, and inflamed them by his rage, and so in the end brought them to shame.
m. Hab. 2:16 Whereas thou thoughtest to have glory of these thy doings, they shall turn to thy shame: for thou shalt drink of the same cup with others in thy turn.
n. Hab. 2:17 Because the Babylonians were cruel not only against other nations, but also against the people of God, which is meant by Lebanon and the beasts therein, he showeth that the like cruelty shall be executed against them.
o. Hab. 2:18 He showeth that the Babylonians' gods could nothing avail them, for they were but blocks or stones, read Jer. 10:8.
p. Hab. 2:19 If thou wilt consider what it is, and how that it hath neither breath nor life, but is a dead thing.

there is no breath in it. **20** But the Lord is in his holy Temple: let all the earth
keep silence before him.

3

2 A prayer for the faithful.

1 A prayer of Habakkuk the Prophet for the [a]ignorances.
2 [b]O Lord, I have heard thy voice, and was afraid: O Lord, revive thy [c]work in
the midst of the people, in the midst of the years make it known: in wrath remem-
ber mercy. **3** God cometh from [d]Teman, and the holy One from mount Paran,
Selah. His glory covereth the heavens, and the earth is full of his praise, **4** And
his brightness was as the light: [e]he had horns coming out of his hands, and the-
re was the hiding of his power. **5** Before him went the pestilence, and burning
coals went forth before his feet. **6** He stood and measured the earth: he beheld
and dissolved the nations, and the everlasting mountains were broken, and the an-
cient hills did bow: his [f]ways are everlasting. **7** [g]For his iniquity I saw the tents
of Cushan, and the curtains of the land of Midian did tremble. **8** Was the Lord
angry against the [h]rivers? or was thine anger against the floods? or was thy wrath
against the sea, that thou didst ride [i]upon thine horses? thy chariots brought sal-
vation. **9** Thy [j]bow was manifestly revealed, and the [k]oaths of the tribes were
a sure word, Selah, thou [l]didst cleave the earth with rivers. **10** The mountains
saw thee, and they trembled: the stream of the water [m]passed by: the deep made
a noise, and lifted up his hand on high. **11** The [n]sun and moon stood still in
their habitation: [o]at the light of thine arrows they went, and at the bright shining
of thy spears. **12** Thou trodest down the land in anger, and didst thresh the hea-
then in displeasure. **13** Thou wentest forth for the salvation of thy people, even
for salvation with thine [p]Anointed: thou hast wounded the head of the house of
the wicked, and discoveredst the foundations unto the [q]neck, Selah. **14** Thou
didst [r]strike through with his own staves the heads of his villages: they came out
as a whirlwind to scatter me: their rejoicing was as to devour the poor secret-
ly. **15** Thou didst walk in the sea with thine horses upon the heap of great wa-
ters. **16** When I [s]heard, my belly trembled: my lips shook at the voice: rottenness
entered into my bones, and I trembled in myself, that I might rest in [t]the day of
trouble: for when he cometh up [u]unto the people, he shall destroy them. **17** For
the fig tree shall not flourish, neither shall fruit be in the vines: the labor of the olive
shall fail, and the fields shall yield no meat: the sheep shall be cut off from the fold,
and there shall be no bullock in the stalls. **18** But I will rejoice in the Lord: I will
joy [v]in the God of my salvation. **19** The Lord God is my strength: he will make
my feet like hinds' feet, and he will make me to walk upon mine high places. [w]To
the chief singer on Neginoth.

HABAKKUK 3

- **a.** Hab. 3:1 The Prophet instructeth his people to pray unto God, not only for their great sins but also for such as they had committed of ignorance.
- **b.** Hab. 3:2 Thus the people were afraid when they heard God's threatenings, and prayed.
- **c.** Hab. 3:2 That is, the state of thy Church which is now ready to perish, before it come to half a perfect age, which should be under Christ.
- **d.** Hab. 3:3 Teman and Paran were near Sinai, where the Law was given: whereby is signified that his deliverance was as present now as it was then.
- **e.** Hab. 3:4 Whereby is meant a power that was joined with his brightness, which was hid to the rest of the world, but was revealed in mount Sinai to his people, Ps. 31:16.
- **f.** Hab. 3:6 Signifying, that God hath wonderful means, and ever had a marvelous power when he would deliver his Church.
- **g.** Hab. 3:7 The iniquity of the king of Syria in vexing thy people was made manifest by thy judgment, to the comfort of thy Church, Judg. 5:10, and also of the Midianites, which destroyed themselves, Judg. 7:22.
- **h.** Hab. 3:8 Meaning, that God was not angry with the waters, but that by this means he would destroy his enemies, and deliver his Church.
- **i.** Hab. 3:8 And so didst use all the elements as instruments for the destruction of thine enemies.
- **j.** Hab. 3:9 That is, thy power.
- **k.** Hab. 3:9 For he had not only made a covenant with Abraham, but renewed it with his posterity.
- **l.** Hab. 3:9 Read Num. 20:11.
- **m.** Hab. 3:10 He alludeth to the red sea and Jordan, which gave passage to God's people, and showed signs of their obedience as it were by the lifting up their hands.
- **n.** Hab. 3:11 As appeareth, Josh. 10:11.
- **o.** Hab. 3:11 According to thy commandment, the sun was directed by the weapons of thy people, that fought in thy cause, as though it durst not go forward.
- **p.** Hab. 3:13 Signifying, that there is no salvation, but by Christ.
- **q.** Hab. 3:13 From the top to the toe thou hast destroyed the enemies.
- **r.** Hab. 3:14 God destroyed his enemies both great and small with their own weapons, though they were never so fierce against his Church.
- **s.** Hab. 3:16 He returneth to that which he spake in the second verse, and showeth how he was afraid of God's judgments.
- **t.** Hab. 3:16 He showeth that the faithful can never have true rest, except they feel before the weight of God's judgments.
- **u.** Hab. 3:16 That is, the enemy, but the godly shall be quiet, knowing that all things shall turn to good unto them.
- **v.** Hab. 3:18 He declareth wherein standeth the comfort and joy of the faithful, though they see never so great afflictions prepared.
- **w.** Hab. 3:19 The chief singer upon the instruments of music, shall have occasion to praise God for this great deliverance of his Church.

ZEPHANIAH

1

4 Threatenings against Judah and Jerusalem, because of their idolatry.

1 The word of the Lord, which came unto Zephaniah the son of Cu-
shi, the son of Gedaliah, the son of Amariah, the son of Hezekiah, in the days of
[1]Josiah, the son of [2]Amon king of Judah. **2** I will surely destroy all things from
off the land, saith the Lord. **3** I will destroy man and beast: I will destroy the
[a]fowls of the heaven, and the fishes of the sea, and ruins shall be to the wicked,
and I will cut off man from off the land, saith the Lord. **4** I will also stretch out
mine hand upon Judah, and upon all the inhabitants of Jerusalem, and I will cut
off the remnant of Baal from this place, and the name of the [b]Chemarims with the
Priests, **5** And them that worship the host of heaven upon the housetops, and
them that worship and swear by the Lord, and swear by [c]Milcam. **6** And them
that are turned back from the Lord, and those that have not sought the Lord, nor
inquired for him. **7** Be still at the presence of the Lord God: for the day of the
Lord is at hand: for the Lord hath prepared a sacrifice, and hath sanctified his gue-
sts. **8** And it shall be in the day of the Lord's sacrifice, that I will visit the princes
and the king's children, and all such as are clothed with [d]strange apparel. **9** In
the same day also will I visit all those that [e]dance upon the threshold so proudly,
which fill their masters' houses by cruelty and deceit. **10** And in that day, saith
the Lord, there shall be a noise, and cry from the [f]fish gate, and an howling from
the second gate, and a great destruction from the hills. **11** Howl ye inhabitants
of [g]the low place: for the company of the merchants is destroyed: all they that bear
silver, are cut off. **12** And at that time will I search Jerusalem with [h]lights, and
visit the men that are frozen [i]in their dregs, and say in their hearts, The Lord will
neither do good nor do evil. **13** Therefore their goods shall be spoiled, and their
houses waste: [3]they shall also build houses, but not inhabit them, and they shall
plant vineyards, but not drink the wine thereof. **14** The great day of the Lord is
near: it is near, and hasteth greatly, even the voice of the day of the Lord: [j]the strong
man shall cry there bitterly. **15** [4]That day is a day of wrath, a day of trouble and
heaviness, a day of destruction and desolation, a day of obscurity and darkness,
a day of clouds and blackness, **16** A day of the trumpet and alarm against the
strong cities, and against the high towers. **17** And I will bring distress upon men,
that they shall walk like blind men, because they have sinned against the Lord, and
their blood shall be poured out as dust, and their flesh as the dung. **18** [5]Neither

---

ZEPHANIAH 1

- **a.** Zeph. 1:3 Not that God was angry with these dumb creatures, but because man was so wicked for whose cause they were created, God maketh them to take part of the punishments with him.
- **b.** Zeph. 1:4 Which were an order of superstitious priests appointed to minister in the service of Baal, and were as his peculiar chaplains, read 2 Kings 23:5; Hos. 10:5.
- **c.** Zeph. 1:5 He alludeth to their idol Molech which was forbidden, Lev. 20:2, yet they called him, their king, and made him as a god: therefore he here noteth them that will both say they worship God, and yet will swear by idols and serve them: which halting is here condemned, as Ezek. 20:39; 1 Kings 18:21; 2 Kings 17:33.
- **d.** Zeph. 1:8 Meaning, the courtiers, which did imitate the strange apparel of other nations to win their favor thereby, and to appear glorious in the eyes of all others, read Ezek. 23:14, 15.
- **e.** Zeph. 1:9 He meaneth the servants of the rulers which invade other men's houses, and rejoice and leap for joy, when they can get any prey to please their master withall.
- **f.** Zeph. 1:10 Signifying, that all the corners of the city of Jerusalem should be full of trouble.
- **g.** Zeph. 1:11 This is meant of the street of the merchants which was lower than the rest of the place about it.
- **h.** Zeph. 1:12 So that nothing shall escape me.
- **i.** Zeph. 1:12 By their prosperity they are hardened in their wickedness.
- **j.** Zeph. 1:14 They that trusted in their own strength and contemned the Prophets of God.

ZEPHANIAH 1

1. 2 Kings 22:1
2. 2 Kings 21:19
3. Deut. 28:30 / Amos 5:11
4. Jer. 30:7 / Joel 2:11 / Amos 5:18
5. Ezek. 7:19
6. Zeph. 3:1

their silver nor their gold shall be able to deliver them in the day of the Lord's wra-
th, but the [6]whole land shall be devoured by the fire of his jealousy: for he shall
make even a speedy riddance of all them that dwell in the land.

2

1 He moveth to return to God, 5 prophesying destruction against the Philistines, Moabites and others.

1 Gather [a]yourselves, even gather you, O nation not worthy to be lo-
ved, **2** Before the decree come forth, and ye be as chaff that passeth in a day,
and before the fierce wrath of the Lord come upon you, and before the day of the
Lord's anger come upon you. **3** Seek ye the Lord all the meek of the earth, whi-
ch [b]have wrought his judgment: seek righteousness, seek lowliness, if so be that ye
may be hid in the day of the Lord's wrath. **4** For [c]Gaza shall be forsaken, and
Ashkelon desolate: they shall drive out Ashdod at the noon day, and Ekron shall
be rooted up. **5** Woe unto the inhabitants of the sea [d]coast. the nation of the
Cherethims, the word of the Lord is against you: O Canaan, the land of the Phi-
listines, I will even destroy thee without an inhabitant. **6** And the sea coast shall
be dwellings and cottages for shepherds and sheepfolds. **7** And that coast shall be
for the [e]remnant of the house of Judah, to feed thereupon: in the houses of Ashke-
lon shall they judge toward night: for the Lord their God shall visit them, and
turn away their captivity. **8** I have heard the reproach of Moab, and the rebukes
of the children of Ammon, whereby they upbraided my people, and [f]magnified
themselves against their borders. **9** Therefore, as I live, saith the Lord of hosts,
the God of Israel, Surely Moab shall be as Sodom, and the children of Ammon as
Gomorrah, even the breeding of nettles, and salt pits, and a perpetual desolation,
the residue of my folk shall spoil them, and the remnant of my people shall pos-
sess them. **10** This shall they have for their pride, because they have reproached,
and magnified themselves against the Lord of host's people. **11** The Lord will be
terrible unto them: [g]for he will consume all the gods of the earth, and every man
shall worship him from his place, even all the isles of the heathen. **12** Ye Morians
also shall be slain by my sword with them. **13** And he will stretch out his hand
against the North, and destroy Assyria, and will make Nineveh desolate, and waste
like a wilderness. **14** And flocks shall lie in the midst of her, and all the beasts of
the nations, and the [h]pelican and the [i]owl shall abide in the upper posts of it: the
voice of birds shall sing in the windows, and desolations shall be upon the posts:
for the cedars are uncovered. **15** This is the [j]rejoicing city that dwelt careless, that
said in her heart, I am, and there is none besides me: how is she made waste, and
the lodging of the beasts! everyone that passeth by her shall hiss and wag his hand.

3

4 Against the governors of Jerusalem. 8 Of the calling of all the Gentiles. 13 A comfort to the residue of Israel.

1 Woe to her that is filthy and polluted, to the robbing [a]city. **2** She heard
not the voice: she received not correction: she trusted not in the Lord: she drew
not near to her God. **3** Her princes within her are as roaring [1]lions: her judges
are as [2]wolves in the evening, which [b]leave not the bones till the morrow. **4** Her
prophets are light, and wicked persons: her priests have polluted the Sanctuary:
they have wrested the Law. **5** The [c]just Lord is in the midst thereof: he will
do none iniquity: every morning doth he bring his judgment to light, he faileth
not: but the wicked will not learn to be ashamed. **6** I have [d]cut off the nations:
their towers are desolate: I have made their streets waste, that none shall pass by,
their cities are destroyed without man, and without inhabitant. **7** I said, surely
thou wilt fear me: thou wilt receive instruction: so their dwelling should not be
destroyed howsoever I visited them, but [e]they rose early, and corrupted all their
works. **8** Therefore [f]wait ye upon me, saith the Lord, until the day that I rise up
to the prey: for I am determined to gather the nations, and that I will assemble the
kingdoms to pour upon them mine indignation, even all my fierce wrath: for all
the earth shall be devoured with the fire of my jealousy. **9** Surely [g]then will I turn
to the people a pure language, that they may all call upon the name of the Lord to
serve him [h]with one consent. **10** From beyond the rivers of Ethiopia, the [i]dau-
ghter of my dispersed, praying unto me, shall bring me an offering. **11** In that
day shalt thou not be ashamed for [j]all thy works, wherein thou hast transgressed
against me: for then will I take away out of the midst of thee them that rejoice of
thy pride, and thou shalt no more be proud of mine holy mountain. **12** Then
will I leave in the midst of thee an humble and poor people: and they shall trust
in the Name of the Lord. **13** The remnant of Israel shall do none iniquity, nor
speak lies: neither shall a deceitful tongue be found in their mouth: for they shall
be fed and lie down, and none shall make them afraid. **14** Rejoice, O daughter
Zion: be ye joyful, O Israel: be glad and rejoice with all thine heart, O daughter
Jerusalem. **15** The Lord hath taken away thy [k]judgments: he hath cast out thine
[l]enemy: the king of Israel, even the Lord is in the midst of [m]thee: thou shalt see no
more evil. **16** In that day it shall be said to Jerusalem, Fear thou not, O Zion, let
not thine hands be faint. **17** The Lord thy God in the midst of thee is mighty:
he will save, he will rejoice over thee with joy: he will quiet himself in [n]his love: he
will rejoice over thee with joy. **18** After a certain time will I gather the afflicted
that were of thee, and them that bare the reproach for [o]it. **19** Behold, at that
time I will bruise all that afflict thee, and I will [p]save her that halteth, and gather
her that was cast out, and I will get them praise and fame in all the [q]lands of their
shame. **20** At that time will I bring you again, and then will I gather you: for I
will give you a name and a praise among all people of the earth, when I turn back
your captivity before your eyes, saith the Lord.

ZEPHANIAH 2

a. Zeph. 2:1 He exhorteth them to repentance, and willeth them to descend into themselves and gather themselves, lest they be scattered like chaff.
b. Zeph. 2:3 That is, which have lived uprightly and godly according as he prescribeth by his word.
c. Zeph. 2:4 He comforteth the faithful in that God would change his punishments from them unto the Philistines their enemies and other nations.
d. Zeph. 2:5 That is, Galilee: by these nations he meaneth the people that dwelt near to the Jews, and instead of friendship were their enemies: therefore he calleth them Canaanites whom the Lord appointed to be slain.
e. Zeph. 2:7 He showeth why God would destroy their enemies, because their country might be a resting place for his Church.
f. Zeph. 2:8 These nations presumed to take from the Jews that country which the Lord had given them.
g. Zeph. 2:11 When he shall deliver his people and destroy their enemies and Idols, his glory shall shine throughout all the world.
h. Zeph. 2:14 Read Isa. 34:11.
i. Zeph. 2:14 Or, hedgehog.
j. Zeph. 2:15 Meaning, Nineveh, which rejoicing so much of her strength and prosperity, should be thus made waste, and God's people delivered.

ZEPHANIAH 3

a. Zeph. 3:1 That is, Jerusalem.
b. Zeph. 3:3 They are so greedy that they eat up bones and all.
c. Zeph. 3:5 The wicked thus boasted that God was ever among them, but the Prophet answereth that that cannot excuse their wickedness: for God will not bear with their sins: yet that he did patiently abide and sent his Prophets continually to call them to repentance, but he profited nothing.
d. Zeph. 3:6 By the destruction of other nations he showeth that the Jews should have learned to fear God.
e. Zeph. 3:7 They were most earnest and ready to do wickedly.
f. Zeph. 3:8 Seeing ye will not repent, you shall look for my vengeance as well as other nations.
g. Zeph. 3:9 Lest any should think then that God's glory should have perished when Judah was destroyed, he showeth that he will publish his grace through all the world.
h. Zeph. 3:9 Hebrew, with one shoulder, as Hos. 6:9.
i. Zeph. 3:10 That is, the Jews shall come as well as the Gentiles: which is to be understood under the time of the Gospel.
j. Zeph. 3:11 For they shall have full remission of their sins, and the hypocrites which boasted of the Temple, which was also thy pride in times past, shall be taken from thee.
k. Zeph. 3:15 That is, the punishment for thy sin.
l. Zeph. 3:15 As the Assyrians, Chaldeans, Egyptians and other nations.
m. Zeph. 3:15 To defend thee as by thy sins thou hast put him away, and left thyself naked, as Exod. 32:25.
n. Zeph. 3:17 Signifying, that God delighteth to show his love and great affection toward his Church.
o. Zeph. 3:18 That is, them that were had in hatred and reviled for the Church, and because of their religion.
p. Zeph. 3:19 I will deliver the Church, which now is afflicted, as Mic. 4:6.
q. Zeph. 3:19 As among the Assyrians and Chaldeans which did mock them and put them to shame.

ZEPHANIAH 3

a. Ezek. 22:25,27 / Mic. 3:11
b. Hab. 1:8

HAGGAI

1

1 The time of the Prophecy of Haggai. 8 An exhortation to build the Temple again.

1 In the second year of king [a]Darius, in the sixth month, the first day of the month, came the word of the Lord (by the ministry of the Prophet Haggai) unto [b]Zerubbabel the son of Shealtiel, a prince of Judah, and to Jehoshua the son of Jehozadak the high Priest, saying, **2** Thus speaketh the Lord of hosts, saying, This people say, the time is not yet come, [c]that the Lord's house should be built. **3** Then came the word of the Lord by the ministry of the Prophet Haggai, saying, **4** Is it time for yourselves to dwell in your [d]ceiled houses, and this house lie waste? **5** Now therefore thus saith the Lord of hosts, Consider your own ways in your hearts. **6** [e]Ye have sown much, and bring in little: ye eat, but ye have not enough: ye drink, but ye are not filled: ye clothe you, but ye be not warm: and he that earneth wages, putteth the wages into a broken bag. **7** Thus saith the Lord of hosts, Consider your own ways in your hearts. **8** Go [f]up to the mountain, and bring wood, and build this House, and [g]I will be favorable in it, and I will [h]be glorified, saith the Lord. **9** Ye looked for much, and lo, it came to little: and when ye brought it home, I did blow [i]upon it. And why, saith the Lord of hosts? Because of mine House that is waste, and ye turn every man unto his own house. **10** Therefore the heaven over you stayed itself from dew, and the earth stayed her fruit. **11** And I called for a drought upon the land, and upon the mountains, and upon the corn, and upon the wine, and upon the oil, upon all that the ground bringeth forth: both upon men and upon cattle, and upon all the labor of the hands. **12** When Zerubbabel the son of Shealtiel, and Joshua the son of Jehozadak the high Priest, with all the remnant of the people, heard the [j]voice of the Lord their God, and the words of the Prophet Haggai (as the Lord their God had sent him) then the people did fear before the Lord. **13** Then spake Haggai the Lord's messenger in the Lord's message unto the people, saying, I am with you, saith the Lord. **14** And the Lord stirred up [k]the spirit of Zerubbabel the son of Shealtiel, a prince of Judah, and the spirit of Joshua the son of Jehozadak the high Priest, and the spirit of all the remnant of the people, and they came, and did the work in the House of the Lord of hosts their God.

2

He showeth that the glory of the second Temple shall exceed the first.

1 In the four and twentieth day of the sixth month, in the second year of king Darius, **2** In the seventh month, in the one and twentieth day of the month, came the word of the Lord by the ministry of the Prophet Haggai, saying, **3** Speak now to Zerubbabel the son of Shealtiel prince of Judah, and to Joshua the son of Jehozadak the high Priest, and to the residue of the people, saying, **4** Who is left among you that saw this [a]House in her first glory, and how do you see it now? is it not in your eyes, in comparison of it as nothing? **5** Yet now be of good courage, O Zerubbabel, saith the Lord, and be of good comfort, O Joshua, son of Jehozadak the high Priest: and be strong, all ye people of the land, saith the Lord, and [b]do it: for I am with you, saith the Lord of hosts. **6** According to the word that I covenanted with you, when ye came out of Egypt: so my Spirit shall remain among you, fear ye not. **7** For thus saith the Lord of hosts, [c]Yet a little while, and I will shake the heavens and the earth, and the sea, and the dry land: **8** And I will move all nations, and [d]the desire of all nations shall come, and I will fill this House with glory, saith the Lord of hosts. **9** The [e]silver is mine, and the gold is mine, saith the Lord of hosts. **10** The glory of this last House shall be greater than the first, saith the Lord of hosts: and in this place will I give [f]peace, saith the Lord of hosts. **11** In the four and twentieth day of the ninth month, in the second year of Darius, came the word of the Lord unto the Prophet Haggai, saying, **12** Thus saith the Lord of hosts, Ask now the Priests concerning the Law, and say, **13** If one bear [g]holy flesh in the skirt of his garment, and with his skirt do touch the bread or the pottage, or the wine, or oil, or any meat, shall it be holy? And the Priests answered and said, No. **14** Then said Haggai, If a polluted person touch any of these, shall it be unclean? And the Priests answered, and said, It shall be unclean. **15** Then answered Haggai, and said, So is this people, and so is this nation before me, saith the Lord: and so are all the works of their hands, and that which they offer here, is unclean. **16** And now, I pray you, consider in your minds: from this [h]day and afore, even afore a stone was laid upon a stone in the Temple of the Lord: **17** [i]Before these things were, when one came to an heap of twenty measures, there were but ten: when one came to the winepress, for to draw out fifty vessels out of the press, there were but twenty. **18** I smote you with blasting, and with mildew, and with hail, in all the labors of your hands: yet you turned not to me, saith the Lord. **19** Consider, I pray you, in your minds, from [j]this day, and afore, from the four and twentieth day of the ninth month, even from the day that the foundation of the Lord's Temple was laid: consider it in your minds. **20** Is the [k]seed yet in the barn? as yet the vine, and the fig tree, and the pomegranate, and the olive tree hath not brought forth: from this day will I bless you. **21** And again the word of the Lord came unto Haggai in the four and twentieth day of the month, saying, **22** Speak to Zerubbabel the prince of Judah, and say, I [l]will shake the heavens and the earth. **23** And I will overthrow the throne of kingdoms, and I will destroy the strength of the [m]kingdoms of the heathen, and I will overthrow the chariots, and those that ride in them, and the horse and the riders shall come down, every one by the sword of his brother. **24** In that day, saith the Lord of hosts, will I take thee, O Zerubbabel my servant, the son of Shealtiel, saith the Lord, and will make thee as a [n]signet: for I have chosen thee, saith the Lord of hosts.

HAGGAI 1

a. Haggai 1:1 Who was the son of Histaspis and the third king of the Persians, as some think.

b. Haggai 1:1 Because the building of the Temple began to cease, by reason that the people were discouraged by their enemies: and if these two notable men had need to be stirred up and admonished of their duties, what shall we think of other governors, whose doings are either against God, or very cold in his cause?

c. Haggai 1:2 Not that they condemned the building thereof, but they preferred policy and private profit to religion, being content with small beginnings.

d. Haggai 1:4 Showing that they sought not only their necessities, but their very pleasures before God's honor.

e. Haggai 1:6 Consider the plagues of God upon you for preferring your policies to his religion, and because ye seek not him first of all.

f. Haggai 1:8 Meaning, that they should leave off their own commodities, and go forward in the building of God's Temple, and in the setting forth of his religion.

g. Haggai 1:8 That is, I will hear your prayers according to my promise, 1 Kings 8:21, 29.

h. Haggai 1:8 That is, my glory shall be set forth by you.

i. Haggai 1:9 And so bring it to nothing.

j. Haggai 1:12 This declareth that God was the author of the doctrine, and that he was but the minister, as Exod. 14:31; Judg. 7:20; Acts 15:28.

k. Haggai 1:14 Which declareth that men are inept and dull to serve the Lord, neither can they obey his word or his messengers, before God reform their hearts, and give them new spirits, John 6:44.

HAGGAI 2

a. Haggai 2:4 For the people according as Isa. 30:19 and Ezek. 41:1, had prophesied, thought this Temple should have been more excellent than Solomon's Temple, which was destroyed by the Babylonians, but the Prophets meant the spiritual Temple, The Church of Christ.

b. Haggai 2:5 That is, go forward in building the Temple.

c. Haggai 2:7 He exhorteth them to patience though see not as yet this Temple so glorious as the Prophets had declared: for this should be accomplished in Christ, by whom all things should be renewed.

d. Haggai 2:8 Meaning, Christ whom all ought to look for and desire: or by desire he may signify all precious things, as riches, and such like.

e. Haggai 2:9 Therefore when his time cometh he can make all the treasures of the world to serve his purpose: but the glory of this second Temple doth not stand in material things, neither can be built.

f. Haggai 2:10 Meaning, all spiritual blessings and felicity purchased by Christ, Phil. 4:7.

g. Haggai 2:13 That is, the flesh of the sacrifices, whereby he signifieth that thing which of itself is good, cannot make another thing so: and therefore they ought not to justify themselves by their sacrifices and ceremonies: but contrary he that is unclean and not pure of heart, doth corrupt those things and make them detestable unto God, which else are good and godly.

h. Haggai 2:16 Consider how God did plague you with famine afore you began to build the Temple.

i. Haggai 2:17 That is, before the building was begun.

j. Haggai 2:19 From the time they began to build the Temple, he promiseth that God would bless them: and albeit as yet the fruit was not come forth, yet in the gathering they should have plenty.

k. Haggai 2:20 He exhorteth them to patience, and to abide till the harvest came, and then they should see God's blessings.

l. Haggai 2:22 I will make a change, and renew all things in Christ, of whom Zerubbabel here is a figure.

m. Haggai 2:23 Hereby he showeth that there shall be no let or hindrance, when God will make this wonderful restitution of his Church.

n. Haggai 2:24 Signifying that his dignity should be most excellent, which thing was accomplished in Christ.

ZECHARIAH

1

He exhorteth the people to return to the Lord, and to eschew the wickedness of their fathers. 16 He signifieth the restitution of Jerusalem and the Temple.

1 In the eighth month of the second year of [a]Darius, came the word of the Lord unto [b]Zechariah the son of Berechiah, the son of Iddo the Prophet, saying, **2** The Lord hath been [c]sore displeased with your fathers. **3** Therefore say thou unto them, Thus saith the Lord of hosts, [d]Turn ye unto me, saith the Lord of hosts, and I will turn unto you, saith the Lord of hosts. **4** Be ye not as your fathers, unto whom the former [1]Prophets have cried, saying, Thus saith the Lord of hosts, Turn you now from your evil ways, and from your wicked works: but they would not hear, nor hearken unto me, saith the Lord. **5** Your fathers, where [e]are they? and do the Prophets live forever? **6** But did not my words and my statutes, which I commanded by my servants the Prophets, take hold of [f]your fathers? and [g]they returned, and said, As the Lord of hosts hath determined to do unto us according to our own ways, and according to our works, so hath he dealt with us. **7** Upon the four and twentieth day of the eleventh month, which is the month [h]Shebat, in the second year of Darius, came the word of the Lord unto Zechariah the son of Berechiah, the son of Iddo the Prophet, saying, **8** I [i]saw by night, and behold [j]a man riding upon a red horse, and he stood among the myrtle trees that were in a bottom, and behind him were there [k]red horses speckled and white. **9** Then said I, O my Lord, what are these? And the Angel that talked with me, said unto me, I will show thee what these be. **10** And the man that stood among the myrtle trees, answered and said, These are they whom the Lord hath sent to go through the world. **11** And they answered the Angel of the Lord that stood among the myrtle trees, and said, We have gone through the world: and behold, all the world sitteth still and is at rest. **12** Then the [l]Angel of the Lord answered and said, O Lord of hosts, how long wilt thou be unmerciful to Jerusalem, and to the cities of Judah, with whom thou hast been displeased now these threescore and ten years? **13** And the Lord answered the Angel that talked with me, with good words and comfortable words. **14** So the Angel that communed with me, said unto me, Cry thou, and speak, thus saith the Lord of hosts, I am [m]jealous over Jerusalem and Zion with a great zeal, **15** And am greatly angry against the careless heathen: for I was angry but [n]a little, and they helped forward the affliction. **16** Therefore thus saith the Lord, I will return unto Jerusalem with tender mercy: mine house shall be built in it, saith the Lord of hosts, and a line [o]shall be stretched upon Jerusalem. **17** Cry yet, and speak, Thus saith the Lord of hosts, My cities shall yet [p]be broken with plenty: the Lord shall yet comfort Zion, and shall yet choose Jerusalem. **18** Then lifted I up mine eyes and saw, and behold, [q]four horns. **19** And I said unto the Angel that talked with me, What be these? And he answered me, These are the horns which have scattered Judah, Israel, and Jerusalem. **20** And the Lord showed me four [r]carpenters. **21** Then said I, What come these to do? And he answered, and said, These are the horns, which have scattered Judah, so that a man durst not lift up his head: but these are come to fray them, and to cast out the horns of the Gentiles, which lifted up their horn over the land of Judah to scatter it.

2

The restoring of Jerusalem and Judah.

1 I lifted up mine eyes again, and looked, and behold, a [a]man with a measuring line in his hand. **2** Then said I, Whither goest thou? And he said unto me, To measure Jerusalem, that I may see what is the breadth thereof, and what is the length thereof. **3** And behold, the Angel that talked with me, went forth, and another Angel went out to meet him, **4** And said unto him, Run, speak to this [b]young man, and say, [c]Jerusalem shall be inhabited without walls, for the multitude of men and cattle therein. **5** For I, saith the Lord, will be unto her a wall of [d]fire round about, and will [e]be the glory in the midst of her. **6** Ho, ho, come [f]forth, and flee from the land of the North, saith the Lord: for I have scattered you into the four [g]winds of the heaven, saith the Lord. **7** [h]Save thyself, O Zion, that dwellest with the daughter of Babel. **8** For thus saith the Lord of hosts, After this [i]glory hath he sent me unto the nations, which spoiled you: for he that toucheth you, toucheth the [j]apple of his eye. **9** For behold, I will lift up mine hand [k]upon them: and [l]they shall be a spoil to those that served them, and ye shall know that the Lord of hosts hath [m]sent me. **10** Rejoice and be glad, O daughter Zion: for lo, I come, and will dwell in the midst of thee, saith the Lord. **11** And many nations shall be joined to the Lord in that day, and shall be my people: and I will dwell in the midst of thee, and thou shalt know that the Lord of hosts hath sent me unto thee. **12** And the Lord shall inherit Judah his portion in the holy land, and shall choose Jerusalem again. **13** Let all flesh be still before the Lord: for he is raised up out of his holy place.

3

A prophecy of Christ and of his kingdom.

1 And he showed me Joshua the high Priest, [a]standing before the Angel of the Lord, and [b]Satan stood at his right hand to resist him. **2** And the [c]Lord said unto Satan, The Lord reprove thee, O Satan: even the Lord that hath chosen Jerusalem, reprove thee. Is not this a [d]brand taken out of the fire? **3** Now

---

ZECHARIA 1

- **a.** Zech. 1:1 Who was the son of Histaspis.
- **b.** Zech. 1:1 This was not that Zech., whereof is mentioned 2 Chron. 24:20, but had the same name, and is called the son of Berechiah, as he was, because he came of those progenitors, as of Joiada or Berechiah, and Iddo.
- **c.** Zech. 1:2 He speaketh this to fear them with God's judgments, that they should not provoke him as their fathers had done, whom he so grievously punished.
- **d.** Zech. 1:3 Let your fruits declare that you are God's people, and that he hath wrought in you by his Spirit, and mortified you: for else man hath no power to return to God, but God must convert him, as Jer. 31:18; Lam. 5:21; Isa. 21:8 and 31:6 and 45:21.
- **e.** Zech. 1:5 Though your fathers be dead, yet God's judgments in punishing them ought still to be before your eyes: and though the Prophets be dead, yet their doctrine remaineth forever, 2 Pet. 1:15.
- **f.** Zech. 1:6 Seeing ye saw the force of my doctrine in punishing your fathers, why do ye not fear the threatenings contained in the same, and declared by my Prophets?
- **g.** Zech. 1:6 As men astonished with my judgments, and not that they were touched with true repentance.
- **h.** Zech. 1:7 Which containeth part of January and part of February.
- **i.** Zech. 1:8 This vision signifieth the restoration of the Church: but as yet it should not appear to man's eyes, which is here meant by the night, by the bottom, and by the myrrh trees which are black, and give a dark shadow, yet he compareth God to a King, who hath his posts and messengers abroad by whom he still worketh his purpose and bringeth his matters to pass.
- **j.** Zech. 1:8 Who was the chief among the rest of the horsemen.
- **k.** Zech. 1:8 These signified the divers offices of God's Angels by whom God sometimes punisheth and sometimes comforteth and bringeth forth his works in divers sorts.
- **l.** Zech. 1:12 That is, Christ the mediator prayed for the salvation of his Church, which was now troubled, when all the countries about them were at rest.
- **m.** Zech. 1:14 Though for a time God defer his help and comfort from his Church, yet this declareth that he loveth them still most dearly, as a most merciful father his children, or an husband his wife, and when it is expedient for them, his help is ever ready.
- **n.** Zech. 1:15 In destroying the reprobate, I showed myself but a little angry toward my church, but the enemy would have destroyed them also, and considered not the end of my chastisements.
- **o.** Zech. 1:16 To measure out the buildings.
- **p.** Zech. 1:17 The abundance shall be so great, that the places of store shall not be able to contain these blessings that God will send, but shall even break for fullness.
- **q.** Zech. 1:18 Which signified all the enemies of the Church, East, West, North, South.
- **r.** Zech. 1:20 These Carpenters or Smiths are God's instruments, which with their mallets and hammers break these hard and strong horns which should overthrow the Church, and declare that none enemy's horn is so strong, but God hath an hammer to break it in pieces.

ZECHARIA 1

- **1.** Jer. 3:12 / Ezek. 18:30 / Hos. 14:2 / Joel. 2:12

ZECHARIA 2

- **a.** Zech. 2:1 This is the Angel who was Christ: for in respect of his office he is oftimes called an Angel, but in respect of his eternal essence, is God, and so called.
- **b.** Zech. 2:4 Meaning, himself Zech..
- **c.** Zech. 2:4 Signifying the spiritual Jerusalem and Church under Christ, which should be extended by the Gospel through all the world, and should need no material walls, nor trust in any worldly strength, but should be safely preserved and dwell in peace among all their enemies.
- **d.** Zech. 2:5 To defend my Church, to fear the enemies and to destroy them if they approach near.
- **e.** Zech. 2:5 In me they shall have their full felicity and glory.
- **f.** Zech. 2:6 He calleth to them, which partly for fear, and partly for their own case, remained still in captivity, and so preferred their own private commodities to the benefits of God promised in his Church.
- **g.** Zech. 2:6 As it was I that scattered you, so have I power to restore you.
- **h.** Zech. 2:7 By fleeing from Babylon, and coming to the Church.
- **i.** Zech. 2:8 Seeing that God had begun to show his grace among you by delivering you, he continueth the same still toward you, and therefore sendeth me his Angel and his Christ to defend you from your enemies, that they shall not hurt you, neither by the way nor at home.
- **j.** Zech. 2:8 Ye are so dear unto God, that he can no more suffer your enemies to hurt you, than a man can abide to be thrust in the eye, Ps. 17:8.
- **k.** Zech. 2:9 Upon the heathen your enemies.
- **l.** Zech. 2:9 They shall be your servants, as you have been theirs.
- **m.** Zech. 2:9 This must necessarily be understood of Christ, who being God equal with his Father, was sent as he was Mediator to dwell in his Church and to govern them.

ZECHARIA 3

- **a.** Zech. 3:1 He prayed to Christ the Mediator for the state of the Church.
- **b.** Zech. 3:1 Which declareth that the faithful have not only war with flesh and blood, but with Satan himself and spiritual wickedness, Eph. 6:12.
- **c.** Zech. 3:2 That is, Christ speaketh to God as the Mediator of his Church, that he would rebuke Satan: and here he showeth himself to be the continual preserver of his Church.
- **d.** Zech. 3:2 Meaning, that Joshua was wonderfully preserved in the captivity, and now Satan sought to afflict and trouble him when he was doing his office.

Joshua was clothed with [e]filthy garments, and stood before the Angel. **4** And he answered and spake unto those that stood before him, saying, Take away the [f]filthy garments from him. And unto him he said, Behold, I have [g]caused thine iniquity to depart from thee, and I will clothe thee with change of raiment. **5** And I said, Let them [h]set a fair diadem upon his head. So they set a fair diadem upon his head, and clothed him with garments, and the Angel of the Lord stood by. **6** And the Angel of the Lord testified unto Joshua, saying, **7** Thus saith the Lord of hosts, If thou wilt walk in my ways, and keep my watch, thou shalt also [i]judge mine house, and shalt also keep my [j]courts, and I will give thee place among [k]these that stand by. **8** Hear now, O Joshua the high Priest, thou and thy fellows that sit before thee: for they [l]are monstrous persons: but behold, I will bring forth the [m]Branch my servant. **9** For lo, the [n]stone that I have laid before Joshua: upon one stone shall be seven eyes: behold, I [o]will cut out the graving thereof, saith the Lord of hosts, and I will take [p]away the iniquity of this land in one day. **10** In that day, saith the Lord of hosts, shall ye call every man his neighbor under the [q]vine, and under the fig tree.

4

The vision of the golden candlestick, and the exposition thereof.

1 And the Angel that talked with me, came again and waked me, as a man that is raised out of his sleep, **2** And said unto me, What seest thou? And I said, I have looked, and behold, a [a]candlestick all of gold with a bowl upon the top of it, and his seven lamps therein, and seven [b]pipes to the lamps which were upon the top thereof, **3** And two olive trees over it, one upon the right side of the bowl, and the other upon the left side thereof. **4** So I answered and spake to the Angel that talked with me, saying, What are these my Lord? **5** Then the Angel that talked with me, answered and said unto me, Knowest thou not what these be? And I said, No, my Lord. **6** Then he answered and spake unto me, saying, This is the word of the Lord unto [c]Zerubbabel, saying, Neither by [d]an army nor strength, but by my Spirit, saith the Lord of hosts. **7** Who art thou, O [e]great mountain, before Zerubbabel? thou shall be a plain, and [f]he shall bring forth the headstone thereof, with shoutings, crying, Grace, grace unto it. **8** Moreover, the word of the Lord came unto me, saying, **9** The hands of Zerubbabel have laid the foundation of this house: his hands shall also finish it, and [g]thou shalt know that the Lord of hosts hath sent me unto you. **10** For who hath despised the day of the [h]small things? but they shall rejoice, and shall see the stone of [i]tin in the hand of Zerubbabel: [j]these seven are the eyes of the Lord, which go through the whole world. **11** Then answered I, and said unto him, What are these two olive trees upon the right and upon the left side thereof? **12** And I spake moreover, and said unto him, What be these two olive branches, which through the two golden pipes empty themselves into the gold? **13** And he answered me, and said, Knowest thou not what these be? And I said, No, my Lord. **14** Then said he, These are the two [k]olive branches, that stand with the ruler of the whole earth.

5

1 The vision of the flying book, signifying the curse of thieves, and such as abuse the Name of God. 6 By the vision of the measure is signified the bringing of Judah's afflictions into Babylon.

1 Then I turned me, and lifted up mine eyes and looked, and behold, a flying book. **2** And he said unto me, What seest thou? And I answered, I see a flying [a]book: the length thereof is twenty cubits, and the breadth thereof ten cubits. **3** Then said he unto me, This is the curse that goeth forth over the whole earth: for everyone that [b]stealeth, shall be cut off, as well on this [c]side, as on that: and everyone that [d]sweareth, shall be cut off, as well on this side, as on that. **4** I will bring it forth, saith the Lord of hosts, and it shall enter into the house of the thief, and into the house of him that falsely sweareth by my Name: and it shall remain in the midst of his house, and shall consume it, with the timber thereof, and stones thereof. **5** Then the Angel that talked with me, went forth, and said unto me, Lift up now thine eyes, and see what is this that goeth forth. **6** And I said, What is it? And he said, This is an [e]Ephah that goeth forth. He said moreover, This is the [f]sight of them through all the earth. **7** And behold, there was lifted up a [g]talent of lead: and this is a [h]woman that sitteth in the midst of the Ephah. **8** And he said, This is [i]wickedness, and he cast it into the midst of the Ephah, and he cast the weight of lead upon the mouth thereof. **9** Then I lifted mine eyes, and looked: and behold, there came out two [j]women, and the wind was in their wings (for they had wings like the wings of a stork) and they lifted up the Ephah between the earth and the heaven. **10** Then said I to the Angel that talked with me, Whither do these bear the Ephah? **11** And he said unto me, To build it an house in the land of Shinar, and it shall be [k]established and set there upon her own place.

6

By the four chariots he describeth the four Monarchies.

1 Again, I turned and lifted up mine eyes, and looked: and behold, there came four [a]chariots out from between [b]two mountains, and the mountains were mountains of brass. **2** In the first chariot were [c]red horses, and in the second chariot [d]black horses, **3** And in the third chariot [e]white horses, and in the fourth chariot, horses of [f]divers colors, and reddish. **4** Then I answered, and said unto the Angel that talked with me, What are these, my Lord? **5** And the Angel answered, and said unto me, These are the four [g]spirits of the heaven, which go forth from standing with the Lord of all the earth. **6** That with the black horse went forth into the land of the North, and the white went out after them, and they of divers colors went forth toward the [h]South country. **7** And the [i]reddish went out, and required to go, and pass through the world, and he said, Go, pass

---

e. Zech. 3:3 In respect of the glorious garments and precious stones that the Priests did wear before the captivity: and by this contemptible state the Prophet signifieth, that these small beginnings should be made excellent when Christ shall make the full restitution of his Church.

f. Zech. 3:4 See verse 3.

g. Zech. 3:4 He showeth of what apparel he speaketh, which is, when our filthy sins are taken away, and we are clad with God's mercies, which is meant of the spiritual restitution.

h. Zech. 3:5 The Prophet prayeth, that besides the raiment, the Priest might also have tyre for his head accordingly, that is, that the dignity of the Priesthood might be perfect: and this was fulfilled in Christ, who was both Priest and King: and here all such are condemned, that can content themselves with any mean reformation in religion, seeing the Prophet desireth the perfection, and obtaineth it.

i. Zech. 3:7 That is, have rule and government in my Church, as thy predecessors have had.

j. Zech. 3:7 Whereby he meaneth to have the whole charge and ministry of the Church.

k. Zech. 3:7 That is, the Angels, who represented the whole number of the faithful: signifying that all the godly should willingly receive him.

l. Zech. 3:8 Because they follow my word, they are contemned in the world, and esteemed as monsters, Isa. 8:18.

m. Zech. 3:8 That is, Christ, who did so humble himself, that not only he became the servant of God, but also the servant of men: and therefore in him they should have comfort, although in the world they were contemned, Isa. 11:1; Jer. 23:5 and 33:14, 15.

n. Zech. 3:9 He showeth that the ministers cannot build, before God lay the first stone, which is Christ, who is full of eyes, both because he giveth light unto all others, and that all ought to seek light at him, Zech. 4:10.

o. Zech. 3:9 That is, I will make perfect in all points, as a thing wrought by the hand of GOD.

p. Zech. 3:9 Though I have punished this land for a time, yet I will even now be pacified, and visit their sins no more.

q. Zech. 3:10 Ye shall then live in peace and quietness, that is, in the kingdom of Christ, Isa. 2:2; Mic. 4:4; Hag. 2:10.

ZECHARIA 4

a. Zech. 4:2 Which was ever in the midst of the Temple, signifying that the graces of God's spirit should shine there in most abundance, and in all perfection.

b. Zech. 4:2 Which conveyed the oil that dropped from the trees into the lamps, so that the light never failed: and this vision was to confirm the faithful that God had sufficient power in himself to continue his graces, and to bring his promise to pass though he had no help of man.

c. Zech. 4:6 Who was a figure of Christ and therefore this doctrine was directed to all the Church who are his body and members.

d. Zech. 4:6 He showeth that God's power only is sufficient to preserve his Church, though he use not man's help thereunto.

e. Zech. 4:7 He compareth the power of the adversaries to a great mountain, who thought the Jews nothing in respect of them, and would have hindered Zerubbabel, who represented Christ, whom the enemies daily labor to let in the building of his spiritual Temple, but all in vain.

f. Zech. 4:7 Though the enemies think to stay this building, yet Zerubbabel shall lay the highest stone thereof, and bring it to perfection, so that all the godly shall rejoice, and pray unto God that he would continue his grace and favor toward the Temple.

g. Zech. 4:9 Meaning, the Prophet, that I am Christ sent of my Father for the building and preservation of my spiritual Temple.

h. Zech. 4:10 Signifying, that all were discouraged at the small and poor beginnings of the Temple.

i. Zech. 4:10 Whereby he signifieth the plummet and line, that is, that Zerubbabel which represented Christ, should go forward with his building to the joy and comfort of the godly, though the world be against him, and though his for a while be discouraged, because they see not things pleasant to the eye.

j. Zech. 4:10 That is, God hath seven eyes: meaning, a continual providence, so that neither Satan nor any power in the world, can go about to bring anything to pass to hinder his work, Zech. 5:9.

k. Zech. 4:14 Which were ever green and full of oil, so that still they poured forth oil into the lamps: signifying, that God will continually maintain and preserve his Church, and endue it still with abundance and perfection of grace.

ZECHARIA 5

a. Zech. 5:2 Because the Jews had provoked God's plagues by contemning his word, and casting off all judgment and equity, he showeth that God's curses written in this book had justly light both on them and their fathers: but now if they would repent, God would send the same among the Chaldeans their former enemies.

b. Zech. 5:3 That is, useth any injury toward his neighbor.

c. Zech. 5:3 Meaning, wheresoever he be in the world.

d. Zech. 5:3 He that transgresseth the first table, and serveth not God aright but abuseth God's Name.

e. Zech. 5:6 Which was a measure in dry things, containing about ten pottels.

f. Zech. 5:6 That is, all the wickedness of the ungodly is in God's sight, which he keepeth in a measure, and can shut it or open it at his pleasure.

g. Zech. 5:7 To cover the measure.

h. Zech. 5:7 Which representeth iniquity, as in the next verse.

i. Zech. 5:8 Signifying, that Satan should not have such power against the Jews to tempt them, as he had in time past, but that God would shut up iniquity in a measure as in a prison.

j. Zech. 5:9 Which declared that God would execute his judgment by the means of the weak and infirm means.

k. Zech. 5:11 To remove the iniquity and affliction that came for the same from Judah, to place it forever in Babylon.

ZECHARIA 6

a. Zech. 6:1 By chariots here, as by horses afore, he meaneth the swift messengers of God to execute and declare his will.

b. Zech. 6:1 By the brazen mountains he meaneth the external counsel, and providence of God whereby he hath from before all eternity decreed what shall come to pass, and that which neither Satan nor all the world can alter.

c. Zech. 6:2 Which signified the great cruelty and persecution that the Church had endured under divers enemies.

d. Zech. 6:2 Signifying, that they had endured great afflictions under the Babylonians.

e. Zech. 6:3 These represented their state under the Persians, which restored them to liberty.

f. Zech. 6:3 Which signified, that God would sometimes give his Church rest, and pour his plagues upon their enemies, as he did in destroying Nineveh and Babylon, and others their enemies.

g. Zech. 6:5 Meaning, all the actions and motions of God's Spirit, which according to his unchangeable counsel he causeth to appear through all the world.

h. Zech. 6:6 That is, toward Egypt, and other countries there about.

i. Zech. 6:7 That is, they of divers colors, which ask [...], to signify that Satan hath no power to hurt or afflict, till God gives it him, Job 1:12.

through the world. So they went throughout the world. **8** Then cried he upon me, and spake unto me, saying, Behold, these that go toward the North country, have pacified my [j]spirit in the North country. **9** And the word of the Lord came unto me, saying, **10** Take of them of the captivity, even of Heldai, and of Tobijah, and Jedaiah, which are come from Babel, and come thou the same day, and go unto the house of [k]Josiah, the son of Zephaniah. **11** Take even silver, and gold, and make crowns, and set them upon the [l]head of Joshua, the son of Jehozadak the high Priest, **12** And speak unto him, saying, Thus speaketh the Lord of hosts, and saith, Behold, the man whose name is the [m]Branch, and he shall grow [n]up out of his place, and he shall [o]build the Temple of the Lord. **13** Even he shall build the Temple of the Lord, and he shall bear the [p]glory, and shall sit and rule upon his throne, and he shall be a Priest upon his throne, and the counsel of peace shall be between [q]them both. **14** And the crowns shall be to [r]Helem, and to Tobijah, and to Jedaiah, and to [s]Hen the son of Zephaniah, for a [t]memorial in the Temple of the Lord. **15** And they that are [u]far off, shall come and build in the Temple of the Lord, and ye shall know, that the Lord of hosts hath sent me unto you. And this shall come to pass, if ye will [v]obey the voice of the Lord your God.

7

5 The true fasting. 11 The rebellion of the people is the cause of their affliction.

1 And in the fourth year of King Darius, the word of the Lord came unto Zechariah in the fourth day of the ninth month, even in [a]Chislev, **2** For [b]they had sent unto the House of God Sharezer, and Regem-Melech and their men to pray before the Lord, **3** And to speak unto the Priests, which were in the House of the Lord of hosts, and to the Prophets, saying, Should I [c]weep in the fifth month, and [d]separate myself as I have done these so many [e]years? **4** Then came the word of the Lord of hosts unto me, saying, **5** Speak unto all the people of the land, and to the [f]Priests, and say, When ye fasted, and mourned in the fifth and seventh month, even the seventy years, did ye fast unto me? [g]do I approve it? **6** And when ye did eat, and when ye did drink, did ye not eat [h]for yourselves, and drink for yourselves? **7** Should ye not hear the words which the Lord [i]hath cried by the ministry of the former Prophets when Jerusalem was inhabited, and in prosperity, and the cities thereof round about her, when the South and the plain was inhabited? **8** And the word of the Lord came unto Zechariah, saying, **9** Thus speaketh the Lord of hosts, saying, [j]Execute true judgment, and show mercy and compassion, every man to his brother, **10** And oppress not the widow, nor the fatherless, the stranger nor the poor, and let none of you imagine evil against his brother in your heart. **11** But they refused to hearken, and [k]pulled away the shoulder, and stopped their ears, that they should not hear. **12** Yea, they made their hearts as an adamant stone, lest they should hear the Law and the words which the Lord of hosts sent in his [l]Spirit by the ministry of the former Prophets: therefore came a great wrath from the Lord of hosts. **13** Therefore it is come to pass, that as he cried, and they would not hear, so they cried, and I would not hear, saith the Lord of hosts. **14** But I scattered them among all the nations, whom they knew not: thus the land was desolate [m]after them, that no man passed through nor returned: for they laid the pleasant land [n]waste.

8

2 Of the return of the people unto Jerusalem, and of the mercy of God toward them. 16 Of good works. 20 The calling of the Gentiles.

1 Again the word of the Lord of hosts came to me, saying, **2** Thus saith the Lord of hosts, I was [a]jealous for Zion with great jealousy, and I was jealous for her with great wrath. **3** Thus saith the Lord, I will return unto Zion, and will dwell in the midst of Jerusalem: and Jerusalem shall be called a [b]city of truth, and the Mountain of the Lord of hosts, the holy Mountain. **4** Thus saith the Lord of hosts, There shall yet old [c]men and old women dwell in the streets of Jerusalem, and every man with his staff in his hand for very age. **5** And the streets of the city shall be full of boys and girls, playing in the streets thereof. **6** Thus saith the Lord of hosts, Though it be [d]impossible in the eyes of the remnant of this people in these days, should it therefore be impossible in my sight, saith the Lord of hosts? **7** Thus saith the Lord of hosts, Behold, I will deliver my people from the East country, and from the West country. **8** And I will bring them, and they shall [e]dwell in the midst of Jerusalem, and they shall be my people, and I will be their God in truth, and in righteousness. **9** Thus saith the Lord of hosts, Let your [f]hands be strong, ye that hear in these days these words by the mouth of the Prophets, which were in the day, that the foundation of the house of the Lord of hosts was laid, that the Temple might be built. **10** For before these days there was no hire for [g]man, nor any hire for beast, neither was there any peace to him that went out or came in because of the affliction: for I set all men, everyone against his neighbor. **11** But now, I will not entreat the residue of this people as aforetime, saith the Lord of hosts. **12** For the seed shall be prosperous: the vine shall give her fruit, and the ground shall give her increase, and the heavens shall give their dew: and I will cause the remnant of this people to possess all these things. **13** And it shall come to pass, that as ye were a curse among the heathen, O house of Judah, and house of Israel, so will I deliver you, and ye shall be a blessing: fear not, but let your hands be strong. **14** For thus saith the Lord of hosts, As I thought to punish [h]you, when your fathers provoked me unto wrath, saith the Lord of hosts, and repented not, **15** So again have I determined in these days [i]to do well unto Jerusalem, and to the house of Judah: fear ye not. **16** These are the things that ye shall do, Speak ye every man the truth unto his neighbor: execute judgment truly, and uprightly in your gates, **17** And let none of you imagine evil in your hearts against his neighbor, and love no false oath: for all these are the things that I hate, saith the Lord. **18** And the word of the Lord of hosts came unto me, saying, **19** Thus saith the Lord of hosts, The fast of the fourth month, and the fast of the fifth, and the fast of the seventh, and the fast of the [j]tenth, shall be to the house of Judah joy and gladness, and prosperous high feasts: therefore love the truth and peace. **20** Thus saith the Lord of hosts, That there shall yet come [k]people, and the inhabitants of great cities. **21** And they that dwell in one city, shall go to another, saying, [l]Up, let us go and pray before the Lord, and seek the Lord of hosts: I will go also. **22** Yea great people and mighty nations shall come to seek the Lord of hosts in Jerusalem, and to pray before the Lord. **23** Thus saith the Lord of hosts, In those days shall ten men take hold out of all languages of the nations, even take hold of the skirt of him that is a Jew, and say, We will go with you: for we have heard that God is with you.

---

j. Zech. 6:8 By punishing the Chaldeans mine anger ceased, and you were delivered.
k. Zech. 6:10 To receive of him and the other three, money to make the two crowns: which were men of great authority among the Jews, and doubted of the restitution of the kingdom, and of the Priesthood, and hurt others by their example.
l. Zech. 6:11 Because this could not be attributed to anyone according to the Law, therefore it followeth that Joshua must represent the Messiah, who was both Priest and king.
m. Zech. 6:12 Meaning, Christ, of whom Joshua was the figure: for in Greek they were both called Jesus.
n. Zech. 6:12 That is, of himself without the help of man.
o. Zech. 6:12 Which declareth, that none could build this Temple whereof Haggai speaketh, but only Christ: and therefore it was spiritual, and not material, Hag. 2:10.
p. Zech. 6:13 Whereof Joshua had but a shadow.
q. Zech. 6:13 The two offices of the kingdom, and Priesthood shall be so joined together, that they shall be no more dissevered.
r. Zech. 6:14 Who was also called Heldai.
s. Zech. 6:14 He was also called Joshiash.
t. Zech. 6:14 That they may acknowledge their infirmity, which looked that all things should have been restored incontinently: and of this their infidelity these two crowns shall remain as tokens, Acts 1:16.
u. Zech. 6:15 That is, the Gentiles by the preaching of the Gospel, shall help toward the building of the spiritual Temple.
v. Zech. 6:15 If ye will believe and remain in the obedience of faith.

ZECHARIA 7

a. Zech. 7:1 Which contained part of November and part of December.
b. Zech. 7:2 That is, the rest of the people that remained yet in Chaldea, sent to the Church at Jerusalem, for the resolution of these questions, because these feasts were consented upon by the agreement of the whole Church, the one in the month that the Temple was destroyed, and the other when Gedaliah was slain, Jer. 41:2.
c. Zech. 7:3 By weeping and mourning, appear what exercises they used in their fasting.
d. Zech. 7:3 That is, prepare myself with all devotion to his fast.
e. Zech. 7:3 Which was now since the time the Temple was destroyed.
f. Zech. 7:5 For there were both of the people, and of the Priests, which doubted as touching this controversy, besides them which as yet remained in Chaldea, and reason of it, as of one of the chief points of their religion.
g. Zech. 7:5 For they thought they had deserved toward God because of this fast, which they invented of themselves: and though fasting of itself be good, yet because they thought it a service toward God, and trusted therein, it is here reproved.
h. Zech. 7:6 Did ye not eat and drink for your own commodity and necessity, and so likewise ye did abstain according to your own fantasies, and not after the prescript of my Law.
i. Zech. 7:7 Hereby he condemneth their hypocrisy, which thought by their fasting to please God and by such things as they invented, and in the mean season would not serve him as he had commanded.
j. Zech. 7:9 He showeth that they did not fast with a sincere heart, but for hypocrisy, and that it was not done of a pure religion, because that they lacked these offices of charity, which should have declared that they were godly, Matt. 23:23.
k. Zech. 7:11 And would not carry the Lord's burden, which was sweet and easy, but would bear their own, which was heavy and grievous to the flesh, thinking to merit thereby: which similitude is taken of oxen, which shrink at the yoke, Neh. 9:29.
l. Zech. 7:12 Which declareth that they rebelled not only against the Prophets, but against the Spirit of God that spake in them.
m. Zech. 7:14 That is, after they were called captive.
n. Zech. 7:14 By their sins whereby they provoked God's anger.

ZECHARIA 8

a. Zech. 8:2 I loved my city with a singular love, so that I could not abide that any should do her any injury.
b. Zech. 8:3 Because she shall be faithful and loyal toward me her husband.
c. Zech. 8:4 Though their enemies did greatly molest and trouble them, yet God would come and dwell among them, and so preserve them so long as nature would suffer them to live, and increase their children in great abundance.
d. Zech. 8:6 He showeth wherein our faith standeth, that is, to believe that God can perform that which he hath promised, though it seem never so impossible to man, Gen. 18:14; Rom. 4:20.
e. Zech. 8:8 So that their return shall not be in vain: for God will accomplish his promise, and their prosperity shall be sure and stable.
f. Zech. 8:9 Let neither respect of your private commodities neither counsel of others, nor fear of enemies discourage you in the going forward with the building of the Temple, but be constant and obey the Prophets, which encourage you thereunto.
g. Zech. 8:10 For God cursed your work, so that neither man nor beast had profit of their labors.
h. Zech. 8:14 Read Ezek. 18:20.
i. Zech. 8:15 Which declareth that man cannot turn to God till he changes man's heart by his spirit, and so begin to do well, which is to pardon his sins and to give him his graces.
j. Zech. 8:19 Which fast was appointed when the city was besieged, and was the first fast of these four: and here the Prophet showeth, that if the Jews will repent, and turn wholly to God, they shall have no more occasion to fast, or to show signs of heaviness: for God will send them joy and gladness.
k. Zech. 8:20 He declareth the great zeal that God should give the Gentiles to come to his Church, and to join with the Jews in his true religion, which should be in the kingdom of Christ.

ZECHARIA 8

1. Isa. 2:2 / Mic. 4:1

9

The threatenings of the Gentiles. 9 The coming of Christ.

1 The burden of the word of the Lord in the land of [a]Hadrach: and Damascus shall be his [b]rest: when the [c]eyes of man, even of all the tribes of Israel shall be toward the Lord. **2** And Hamath also shall border [d]thereby: Tyre also and Sidon, though they be [e]very wise. **3** For Tyre did build herself a stronghold, and heaped up silver as the dust, and gold as the mire of the streets. **4** Behold, the Lord will spoil her, and he will smite her [f]power in the sea, and she shall be devoured with fire. **5** Ashkelon shall see it, and fear, and Gaza also shall be very sorrowful, and Ekron: for her countenance shall be ashamed, and the king shall perish from Gaza, and Ashkelon shall not be inhabited. **6** And the [g]stranger shall dwell in Ashdod, and I will cut off the pride of the Philistines. **7** And I will take away his blood out of his mouth, and his abominations from between his [h]teeth: but he that remaineth, even he shall be for our God, and he shall be as a prince in Judah, but [i]Ekron shall be as a Jebusite. **8** And I will camp about [j]mine House against the army, against him that passeth by, and against him that returneth, and no oppressor shall come upon them anymore: for now [k]have I seen with mine eyes. **9** Rejoice greatly, O daughter Zion: shout for joy, O daughter Jerusalem: behold, thy king cometh unto thee: [l]he is just, and saved himself, poor and riding upon an [m]ass, and upon a colt the foal of an ass. **10** And I will cut off the [n]chariots from Ephraim, and the horse from Jerusalem: the bow of the battle shall be broken, and he shall speak peace unto the heathen, and his dominion shall be from [o]sea unto sea, and from the [p]River to the end of the land. **11** [q]Thou also shall be saved through the blood of thy covenant. I have loosed thy [r]prisoners out of the pit wherein is no water. **12** Turn you to the [s]stronghold, ye [t]prisoners of hope: even today do I declare, that I will render the [u]double unto thee. **13** For Judah have I bent as a [v]bow for me: Ephraim's hand have I filled, and I have raised up thy sons, O Zion, against thy sons, O Greece, and have made thee as a giant's sword. **14** And the Lord shall be seen over them, and his arrow shall go forth as the lightning: and the Lord God shall blow the trumpet, and shall come forth with the whirlwinds of the South. **15** The Lord of hosts shall defend them, and they shall devour them, [w]and subdue them with sling stones, and they shall drink, and make a noise as through wine, and they shall be filled like bowls, and as the horns of the Altar. **16** And the Lord their God shall deliver them in that day as the flock of his people: for they shall be as the [x]stones of the crown lifted up upon his land. **17** For how great is his goodness! and how great is his beauty! corn shall make the young men cheerful, and new wine the maids.

10

1 The vanity of Idolatry. 3 The Lord promiseth to visit and comfort the house of Israel.

1 Ask you of the [a]Lord rain in the time of the latter rain: so shall the Lord make white clouds, and give you showers of rain, and to everyone grass in the field. **2** Surely the [b]idols have spoken vanity, and the soothsayers have seen a lie, and the dreamers have told a vain thing: they comfort in vain: therefore [c]they went away as sheep: they were troubled, because there was no shepherd. **3** My wrath was kindled against the shepherds, and I did visit the [d]goats: but the Lord of hosts will visit his flock the house of Judah, and will make them as [e]his beautiful horse in the battle. **4** Out [f]of him shall the corner come forth: out of him the nail, out of him ye bow of battle, and out of him every [g]appointer of tribute also. **5** And they shall be as the mighty men, which tread down their enemies in the mire of the streets in the battle, and they shall fight, because the Lord is with them, and the riders on horses shall be confounded. **6** And I will strengthen the house of Judah, and I will preserve the [h]house of Joseph, and I will bring them again, for I pity them: and they shall be as though I had not cast them off: for I am the Lord their God, and will hear them. **7** And they of Ephraim shall be as a giant: and their heart shall rejoice as through wine: yea, their children shall see it, and be glad: and their heart shall rejoice in the Lord. **8** I will [i]hiss for them: and gather them: for I have redeemed them: and they shall increase, as they have increased. **9** And I will [j]sow them among the people, and they shall remember me in far countries: and they shall live with their children and [k]turn again. **10** I will bring them again also out of the land of Egypt, and gather them out of Assyria: and I will bring them into the land of Gilead, and Lebanon, and place shall not be found for them. **11** And he [l]shall go into the sea with affliction, and shall smite the waves in the sea, and all the depths of the river shall dry up: and the pride of Assyria shall be cast down, and the scepter of Egypt shall depart away. **12** And I will strengthen them in the Lord, and they shall walk in his Name, saith the Lord.

11

The destruction of the Temple. 4 The care of the faithful is committed to Christ. 7 A grievous vision against Jerusalem and Judah.

1 Open thy doors, O [a]Lebanon, and the fire shall devour thy cedars. **2** Howl, [b]fir trees: for the cedar is fallen, because all the mighty are destroyed: howl ye, O oaks of Bashan, for the [c]defenced forest is cut down. **3** There is the voice of the howling of the shepherds: for their [d]glory is destroyed: the voice of the roaring of lion's whelps: for the pride of Jordan is destroyed. **4** Thus saith the Lord my God, Feed the sheep of the [e]slaughter. **5** They that possess them, slay them [f]and sin not: and they that sell them, say, [g]Blessed be the Lord: for I am rich, and their own shepherds spare them not. **6** Surely I will no more spare those that dwell in the land, saith the Lord: but lo, [h]I will deliver the men every one into his neighbor's hand, and into the hand of his [i]king: and they shall smite the land, and out of their hands I will not deliver them. **7** For I fed the sheep of slaughter, even the [j]poor of the flock, and I took unto me [k]two staves: the one I called Beauty, and the other I called Bands, and I fed the sheep. **8** [l]Three shepherds also I cut off in one month, and my soul loathed [m]them, and their soul abhorred me. **9** Then said I, I will not feed you: that that dieth, let it die: and that that perisheth, let it perish: and

---

ZECHARIA 9

a. Zech. 9:1 Whereby he meaneth Syria.

b. Zech. 9:1 God's anger shall abide upon their chief city, and not spare so much as that.

c. Zech. 9:1 When the Jews shall convert and repent, then God will destroy their enemies.

d. Zech. 9:2 That is, by Damascus: meaning, that Hamath or Antioch should be under the same rod and plague.

e. Zech. 9:2 He secretly showeth the cause of their destruction, because they deceived all others by their craft and subtlety, which they cloaked with this name of wisdom.

f. Zech. 9:4 Though they of Tyre think themselves invincible by reason of the sea that compass them round about, yet they shall not escape God's judgments.

g. Zech. 9:6 Meaning, that all should be destroyed, save a very few, that should remain as strangers.

h. Zech. 9:7 He promiseth to deliver the Jews when he shall take vengeance on their enemies for their cruelty and wrongs done to them.

i. Zech. 9:7 As the Jebusites had been destroyed, so should Ekron and all the Philistines.

j. Zech. 9:8 He showeth that God's power only shall be sufficient to defend his Church against all adversaries be they never so cruel, or assemble their power never so often.

k. Zech. 9:8 That is, God hath now seen the great injuries and afflictions wherewith they have been afflicted by their enemies.

l. Zech. 9:9 That is, he hath righteousness and salvation in himself for the use and commodity of his Church.

m. Zech. 9:9 Which declareth that they should not look for such a king as should be glorious in the eyes of man, but should be poor, and yet in himself have all power to deliver his: and this is meant of Christ, as Matt. 21:5.

n. Zech. 9:10 No power of man or creature shall be able to let this kingdom of Christ, and he shall peaceably govern them by his word.

o. Zech. 9:10 That is, from the red sea, to the sea, called Syriacum: and by these places which the Jews knew, he meant an infinite space and compass over the whole world.

p. Zech. 9:10 That is, from Euphrates.

q. Zech. 9:11 Meaning, Jerusalem, or the Church which is saved by the blood of Christ whereof the blood of the sacrifices was a figure, and is here called the covenant of the Church, because God made it with his Church: and left it with them for the love that he bare unto them.

r. Zech. 9:11 God showeth that he will deliver his Church out of all dangers, seem they never so great.

s. Zech. 9:12 That is, into the holy land where the city and the Temple are, where God will defend you.

t. Zech. 9:12 Meaning the faithful, which seemed to be in danger of their enemies on every side, and yet lived in hope that God would restore them to liberty.

u. Zech. 9:12 That is, double benefits and prosperity, in respect of that which your fathers enjoined from David's time to the captivity.

v. Zech. 9:13 I will make Judah and Ephraim, that is, my whole Church, victorious against all enemies, which he here meaneth by the Grecians.

w. Zech. 9:15 He promiseth that the Jews shall destroy their enemies, and have abundance and excess of all things, as there is abundance on the altar when the sacrifice is offered: Which things are not to move them to intemperancy, but to sobriety, and a thankful remembrance of God's great liberality.

x. Zech. 9:16 The faithful shall be preserved, and reverenced of all, that the very enemies shall be compelled to esteem them: for God's glory shall shine in them, as Josephus declareth of Alexander the great when he met Jadi the high Priest.

ZECHARIA 10

a. Zech. 10:1 The Prophet reproveth the Jews, because by their own infidelity they put back God's graces promised, and so famine came by God's just judgment: therefore to avoid this plague, he willeth them to turn to God, and to pray in faith to him, and so he will give them abundance.

b. Zech. 10:2 He calleth to remembrance God's punishments in times past, because they trusted not in him, but in their idols and sorcerers who ever deceived them.

c. Zech. 10:2 That is, the Jews went into captivity.

d. Zech. 10:3 Meaning, the cruel governors which did oppress the poor sheep, Ezek. 34:16, 17.

e. Zech. 10:3 He will be merciful to his Church and cherish them as a king or prince doth his best horse which shall be for his own use in war.

f. Zech. 10:4 Out of Judah shall the chief governor proceed, who shall be as a corner to uphold the building, and as a nail to fasten it together.

g. Zech. 10:4 Over their enemies.

h. Zech. 10:6 That is, the ten tribes, which should be gathered under Christ to the rest of the Church.

i. Zech. 10:8 Whereby he declareth the power of God, who needeth no great preparation when he will deliver his: for with a beck or hiss he can call them from all places suddenly.

j. Zech. 10:9 Though they shall yet be scattered and seem to be lost, yet it shall be profitable unto them: for there they shall come to the knowledge of my Name, which was accomplished under the Gospel, among whom it was first preached.

k. Zech. 10:9 Not that they should return into their country, but be gathered and joined in one faith by the doctrine of the Gospel.

l. Zech. 10:11 He alludeth to the deliverance of the people out of Egypt, whereas the Angel smote the floods and rivers.

ZECHARIA 11

a. Zech. 11:1 Because the Jews thought themselves so strong by reason of this mountain, that no enemy could come to hurt them, the Prophet showeth that when God sendeth the enemies, it shall show itself ready to receive them.

b. Zech. 11:2 Showing, that if the strong men were destroyed, the weaker were not able to resist.

c. Zech. 11:2 Seeing that Lebanon was destroyed, which was the strongest munition, the weaker places could not think to hold out.

d. Zech. 11:3 That is, the renown of Judah and Israel should perish.

e. Zech. 11:4 Which being now destinate to be slain, were delivered as out of the lion's mouth.

f. Zech. 11:5 Their governors destroy them without any remorse of conscience, or yet thinking that they do evil.

g. Zech. 11:5 He noteth the hypocrites, which ever have the Name of God in their mouths, though in their life and doings they deny God, attributing their gain to God's blessings, which cometh of the spoil of their brethren.

h. Zech. 11:6 I will cause one to destroy another.

i. Zech. 11:6 Their governors shall execute cruelty over them.

j. Zech. 11:7 That is, the small remnant, whom he thought worthy to show mercy unto.

k. Zech. 11:7 God showeth his great benefits toward his people to convince them of greater ingratitude, which would neither be ruled by his most beautiful order of government, neither continue in the bands of brotherly unity, and therefore he let the remnant eat, everyone the flesh of his neighbor. **10** And I took my staff, even Beauty, and brake it, that I might disannul my covenant, which I had made with all people. **11** And it was broken in that day: and so the [n]poor of the sheep that waited upon me, knew that it was the word of the Lord. **12** And I said unto them, If ye think it good, give me [o]my wages: and if no, leave off: so they weighed for my wages thirty pieces of silver. **13** And the Lord said unto me, Cast it unto the [p]potter: a goodly price, that I was valued at of them. And I took the thirty pieces of silver, and cast them to the potter in the house of the Lord. **14** Then brake I mine other staff: even the Bands, that I might dissolve the brotherhood between Judah and Israel. **15** And the Lord said unto me, Take to thee yet [q]the instruments of a foolish shepherd. **16** For lo, I will raise up a shepherd in the land, which shall not look for the thing that is lost, nor seek the tender lambs, nor heal that that is hurt, nor feed that that [r]standeth up, but he shall eat flesh of the fat, and tear their claws in pieces. **17** O idol shepherd that leaveth the flock: the sword shall be upon his [s]arm, and upon his right eye. His arm shall be clean dried up, and his right eye shall be utterly darkened.

12

Of the destruction and building again of Jerusalem.

1 The burden of the word of the Lord upon [a]Israel, saith the Lord, which spread the heavens, and laid the foundation of the earth, and formed the spirit of man within him. **2** Behold, I will make Jerusalem a [b]cup of poison unto all the people round about: and also with Judah will he be in the siege against Jerusalem. **3** And in that day will I make Jerusalem an heavy stone for all people: all that lift it up, shall be torn, though all the people of the earth be gathered together against it. **4** In that day, saith the Lord, I will smite every horse with astonishment, and his rider with madness, and I will open mine eyes upon the house of Judah, and will smite every horse of the people with blindness. **5** And the princes of Judah shall say in their hearts, The [c]inhabitants of Jerusalem shall be my strength in the Lord of hosts their God. **6** In that day will I make the princes of Judah like coals of fire among the wood, and like a firebrand in the sheaf, and they shall devour all the people round about on the right hand, and on the left: and Jerusalem shall be inhabited again in her own place, even in Jerusalem. **7** The Lord also shall preserve the [d]tents of Judah, as afore time: therefore the glory of the house of David shall not boast, nor the glory of the inhabitants of Jerusalem against Judah. **8** In that day shall the Lord defend the inhabitants of Jerusalem, and he that is feeble among them, in that day shall be as David: and the house of David shall be as God's house, and as the Angel of the Lord before them. **9** And in that day will I seek to destroy all the nations that come against Jerusalem. **10** And I will pour upon the house of David, and upon the inhabitants of Jerusalem, the Spirit of [e]grace and of compassion, and they shall look upon me, whom they have [f]pierced, and they shall lament for [g]him, as one mourneth for his only son, and be sorry for him as one is sorry for his firstborn. **11** In that day shall there be a great mourning in Jerusalem, as the [h]mourning of [i]Hadad Rimmon in the valley of Megiddo. **12** And the [j]land shall bewail every family [k]apart, the family of the [l]house of David apart, and their wives apart: the family of the house of Nathan apart, and their wives apart: **13** The family of the house of Levi apart, and their wives apart: the family of [m]Shemei apart, and their wives apart: **14** All the families that [n]remain, every family apart, and their wives apart.

13

1 Of the fountain of grace. 2 Of the clean riddance of idolatry. 3 The zeal of the godly against false prophets.

1 In that day there [a]shall be a fountain opened to the house of David, and to the inhabitants of Jerusalem, for sin and for uncleanness. **2** And in that day, saith the Lord of hosts, I will cut off the [b]names of the idols out of the land: and they shall no more be remembered: and I will cause the [c]prophets, and the unclean spirit to depart out of the land. **3** And when any shall yet [d]prophesy, his father and his mother that begat him, shall say unto him, Thou shalt not live: for thou speakest lies in the Name of the Lord: and his father and his mother that begat him, [e]shall thrust him through, when he prophesieth. **4** And in that day shall the prophets [f]be ashamed everyone of his vision, when he hath prophesied: neither shall they wear a rough garment to deceive. **5** But he shall say, I am no [g]Prophet: I am an husbandman: for man taught me to be an herdsman from my youth up. **6** And one shall say unto him, What are these [h]wounds in thine hands? Then he shall answer, Thus was I wounded in the house of my friends. **7** Arise, O sword, upon my [i]shepherd, and upon the man, that is my fellow, saith the Lord of hosts: smite the shepherd, and the sheep shall be scattered: and I will turn mine hand upon the little ones. **8** And in all the land, saith the Lord, [j]two parts therein shall be cut off, and die: but the third shall be left therein. **9** And I will bring that third part through the fire, and will fine them as the silver is fined, and will try them as gold is tried: they shall call on my Name, and I will hear them: I will say, It is my people, and they shall say, The Lord is my God.

14

8 Of the doctrine that shall proceed out of the Church, and of the restoration thereof.

1 Behold, the day of the Lord cometh, and thy spoil shall be [a]divided in the midst of thee. **2** For I will gather all nations against Jerusalem to battle, and the city shall be taken, and the houses spoiled, and the women defiled, and half of the city shall go into captivity, and the residue of the people shall not be cut off from the city. **3** Then the Lord shall go forth, and fight against those nations, as when he [b]fought in the day of battle. **4** And his feet shall stand in that day upon the [c]mount of olives, which is before Jerusalem on the Eastside, and the mount of olives shall cleave in the midst thereof: toward the East and toward the West there shall be a very great [d]valley, and half of the mountain shall remove toward the North, and half of the mountain toward the South. **5** And ye shall flee unto the [e]valley of the mountains: for the valley of the mountains shall reach unto Azal: yea, ye shall flee like as ye fled from the [f]earthquake, in the days of Uzziah king of Judah: and the Lord [g]my God shall come, and all the Saints with thee. **6** And in

---

breaketh both the one and the other. Some read, for Bands, Destroyers, but in verse 14 the first reading is confirmed.

l. Zech. 11:8 Whereby he showeth his care and diligence that he would suffer them to have no evil rulers, because they should consider his great love.

m. Zech. 11:8 Meaning, the people, because they would not acknowledge these great benefits of God.

n. Zech. 11:11 He showeth that the least part ever profit by God's judgments.

o. Zech. 11:12 Besides their ingratitude God accuseth them of malice and wickedness, which did not only forget his benefits, but esteemed them as things of naught.

p. Zech. 11:13 Showing that it was too little to pay his wages, which could scarce suffice to make a few tiles to cover the Temple.

q. Zech. 11:15 Signifying that they should have a certain kind of regiment and outward show of government: but in effect it should be nothing: for they should be wolves, and devouring beasts instead of shepherds.

r. Zech. 11:16 And is in health and sound.

s. Zech. 11:17 By the arms he signifieth strength, as he doth wisdom and judgments by the eye: that is, the plague of God shall take away both thy strength and judgment.

ZECHARIA 12

a. Zech. 12:1 That is, the ten tribes, which neglected God's benefit in delivering their brethren, and had rather remain in captivity, than to return home when God called them.

b. Zech. 12:2 Jerusalem shall be defended against all her enemies: so shall God defend all Judah also, and shall destroy the enemies.

c. Zech. 12:5 Every captain, that had many under him afore, shall now think that the small power of Jerusalem shall be sufficient to defend them against all enemies, because the Lord is among them.

d. Zech. 12:7 The people which are now as it were dispersed by the fields, and lie open to their enemies, shall be no less preserved by my power, than if they were under their kings (which is meant by the house of David) or in their defensed cities.

e. Zech. 12:10 They shall have the feeling of my grace by faith, and know that I have compassion on them.

f. Zech. 12:10 That is, whom they have continually vexed with their obstinacy, and grieved my Spirit, John 19:37, where it is referred to Christ's body, which here is referred to the Spirit of God.

g. Zech. 12:10 They shall turn to God by true repentance, whom before they had so grievously offended by their ingratitude.

h. Zech. 12:11 They shall lament and repent exceedingly for their offences against God.

i. Zech. 12:11 Which was the name of a town and place near to Megiddo where Josiah was slain, 2 Chron. 35:22.

j. Zech. 12:12 That is, in all places where the Jews shall remain.

k. Zech. 12:12 Signifying, that this mourning or repentance should not be a vain ceremony: but everyone touched with his own griefs, shall lament.

l. Zech. 12:12 Under these certain families he containeth all the tribes, and showeth that both the Kings and the Priests had by their sins pierced Christ.

m. Zech. 12:13 Called also Simeon.

n. Zech. 12:14 To wit, which were elected by grace, and preserved from the common destruction.

ZECHARIA 13

a. Zech. 13:1 He showeth what shall be the fruit of their repentance, to wit, remission of sins by the blood of Christ, which shall be a continual running fountain, and purge them from all uncleanness.

b. Zech. 13:2 He promiseth that God will also purge them from all superstition, and that their religion shall be pure.

c. Zech. 13:2 Meaning, the false prophets and teachers, who are the corrupters of all religion, whom the Prophet here calleth unclean spirits.

d. Zech. 13:3 That is, when they shall prophesy lies, and make God, who is the author of truth, a cloak thereunto.

e. Zech. 13:3 He showeth what zeal the godly shall have under the kingdom of Christ, Deut. 13:6, 9.

f. Zech. 13:4 God shall make them ashamed of their errors and lies, and bring them to repentance, and they shall no more wear Prophet's apparel to make their doctrine seem more holy.

g. Zech. 13:5 They shall confess their former ignorance, and be content to labor for their living.

h. Zech. 13:6 Hereby he showeth that though their parents and friends dealt more gently with them, and put them not to death, yet they would so punish their children, that became false prophets, that the marks and signs should remain forever.

i. Zech. 13:7 The Prophet warneth the Jews, that before this great comfort should come under Christ, there should be an horrible dissipation among the people: for their governors and pastors should be destroyed, and the people should be as scattered sheep: and the Evangelist applieth this to Christ, because he was the head of all Pastors, Matt. 26:31.

j. Zech. 13:8 The greatest part shall have no portion of these blessings, and yet they that shall enjoy them, shall be tried with great afflictions, so that it shall be known that only God's power and his mercies do preserve them.

ZECHARIAH 14

a. Zech. 14:1 He armeth the godly against the great tentations that should come, before they enjoyed this prosperous estate promised under Christ, that when these dangers should come, they might know that they were warned of them afore.

b. Zech. 14:3 As your fathers and you have had experience both at the red sea, and at all other times.

c. Zech. 14:4 By this manner of speech the Prophet showeth God's power and care over his Church, and how he will as it were by miracle save it.

d. Zech. 14:4 So that out of all the parts of the world, they shall see Jerusalem, which was before hid with this mountain: and this he meaneth of the spiritual Jerusalem the Church.

e. Zech. 14:5 He speaketh of the hypocrites, which could not abide God's presence, but should flee into all places, where they might hide them among the mountains.

f. Zech. 14:5 Read Amos 1:1.

g. Zech. 14:5 Because they did not credit the Prophet's words, he turneth to God and comforteth himself in that that he knew that these things should come, and saith, Thou, O God, with thine Angels wilt come to perform this great thing.

that day shall there be no clear light but dark. 7 And there shall be a day (it is known to the Lord) [h]neither day nor night, but about the evening time it shall be light. 8 And in that day shall there [i]waters of life go out from Jerusalem, half of them toward the East sea, and half of them toward the uttermost sea, and shall be, both in summer and winter. 9 And the Lord shall be King over all the earth: in that day shall there be one [j]Lord, and his Name shall be one. 10 All the land shall be turned [k]as a plain from Geba to Rimmon, toward the South of Jerusalem, and it shall be lifted up, and inhabited in her place: from Benjamin's gate unto the place of the first gate, unto the corner gate, and from the tower of Hananiel unto the king's winepresses. 11 And men shall dwell in it, and there shall be no more destruction, but Jerusalem shall be safely inhabited. 12 And this shall be the plague wherewith the Lord will smite all people, that have fought against Jerusalem: their flesh shall consume away, though they stand upon their feet, and their eyes shall consume in their holes, and their tongue shall consume in their mouth. 13 But in that day [l]a great tumult of the Lord shall be among them, and everyone shall take [m]the hand of his neighbor, and his hand shall rise up against the hand of his neighbor. 14 And Judah shall fight also against Jerusalem, and the arm of all the heathen shall be gathered round about, with [n]gold and silver, and great abundance of apparel. 15 Yet this shall be the plague of the horse, of the mule, of the camel and of the ass, and of all the beasts that be in these tents at this [o]plague. 16 But it shall come to pass that everyone that is left of all the nations, which came against Jerusalem, shall go up from year to year to worship the King the Lord of hosts, and to keep the feast of Tabernacles. 17 And who so will not come up of all the families of the earth unto Jerusalem to worship the King the Lord of hosts, even upon them shall come no rain. 18 And if the family of [p]Egypt go not up, and come not, it shall not rain upon them. This shall be the plague wherewith the Lord will smite all the heathen, that come not up to keep the feast of tabernacles. 19 This shall be the punishment of Egypt, and the punishment of all the nations that come not up to keep the feast of Tabernacles. 20 In that day shall there be written upon the [q]bridles of the horses, The holiness unto the Lord, and the [r]pots in the Lord's house shall be like the bowls before the altar. 21 Yea, every pot in Jerusalem and Judah shall be holy unto the Lord of hosts, [s]and all they that sacrifice, shall come and take of them, and seethe therein: and in that day there shall be no more the Canaanite in the house of the Lord of hosts.

h. Zech. 14:7 Signifying, that there should be great troubles in the Church, and that the time hereof is in the Lord's hands, yet at length (which is here meant by the evening) God would send comfort.
i. Zech. 14:8 That is, the spiritual graces of God, which should ever continue in most abundance.
j. Zech. 14:9 All idolatry and superstition shall be abolished, and there shall be one God, one faith, and one religion.
k. Zech. 14:10 This new Jerusalem shall be seen through all the world, and shall excel the first in excellency, wealth, and greatness.
l. Zech. 14:13 God will not only raise up war without, but sedition at home to try them.
m. Zech. 14:13 To hurt and oppress him.
n. Zech. 14:14 The enemies are rich, and therefore shall not come for a prey, but to destroy and shed blood.
o. Zech. 14:15 As the men should be destroyed, verse 12.
p. Zech. 14:18 By the Egyptians, which were greatest enemies to true religion, he meaneth all the gentiles.
q. Zech. 14:20 Signifying, that to what service they were put now (whether to labor, or to serve in war) they were now holy, because the Lord had sanctified them.
r. Zech. 14:20 As precious the one as the other, because they shall be sanctified.
s. Zech. 14:21 But all shall be pure and clean, and there shall neither be hypocrites, nor any that shall corrupt the true service of God.

MALACHI

1

A complaint against Israel, and chiefly the Priests.

1 The [a]burden of the word of the Lord to Israel by the ministry of Malachi. 2 I have loved you, saith the Lord: yet ye say, [b]Wherein hast thou loved us? Was not Esau Jacob's brother, saith the Lord? Yet I loved Jacob, 3 And I [c,d]hated Esau, and made his mountains waste, and his heritage a wilderness for dragons. 4 Though Edom say, We are impoverished, but we will return and build the desolate places: yet saith the Lord of hosts, They shall build, but I will destroy it, and they shall call them, The border of wickedness, and the people, with whom the Lord is angry forever. 5 And your eyes shall see it, and ye shall say, The Lord will be magnified upon the border of Israel. 6 A son honoreth his father, and a servant his master. If then I be a father, where is my honor? and if I be a master, where is my fear, saith the Lord of hosts unto you, [e]O Priests that despise my Name? and ye say, [f]Wherein have we despised thy Name? 7 Ye offer [g]unclean bread upon mine altar: and you say, Wherein have we polluted thee? in that ye say, The table of the Lord is not [h]to be regarded. 8 And if ye offer the blind for sacrifice, it is [i]not evil: and if ye offer the lame and sick, it is not evil: offer it now unto thy princes: will he be content with thee, or accept thy person, saith the Lord of hosts? 9 And now I pray you, [j]pray before God that he may have mercy upon us: this hath been by your means: will he regard [k]your persons, saith the Lord of hosts? 10 Who is there even among you [l]that would shut the doors, and kindle not fire on mine altar in vain? I have no pleasure in you, saith the Lord of hosts, neither will I accept an offering at your hand. 11 For from the rising of the sun unto the going down of the same, my Name is [m]great among the Gentiles, and in every place incense shall be offered unto my Name, and a pure offering: for my Name is great among the heathen, saith the Lord of hosts. 12 But ye have polluted it, in that ye say, [n]The table of the Lord is polluted, and the fruit thereof even his meat is not to be regarded. 13 Ye said also, Behold, it is a [o]weariness, and ye have snuffed at it, saith the Lord of hosts, and ye offered that which was torn, and the lame, and the sick: thus ye offered an offering: should I accept this of your hand, saith the Lord? 14 But cursed be the deceiver, which hath in his flock [p]a male, and voweth, and sacrificeth unto the Lord a corrupt thing: for I am a great king, saith the Lord of hosts, and my Name is terrible among the heathen.

2

1 Threatenings against the Priests, being seducers of the people.

1 And now, O ye [a]Priests, this commandment is for you. 2 If ye will not hear it, nor consider it in your heart, to give glory [b]unto my Name, saith the Lord of hosts, I will even send a curse upon you, and will curse your [c]blessings: yea, I have cursed them already, because ye do not consider it in your heart. 3 Behold, I will corrupt [d]your seed, and cast dung upon your faces, even the [e]dung of your solemn feasts, and you shall be like unto it. 4 And ye shall know,

MALACHI 1

a. Malachi 1:1 Read Isa. 13:1.
b. Malachi 1:2 Which declareth their great ingratitude that did not acknowledge this love, which was so evident, in that he chose Abraham from out of all the world, and next chose Jacob the younger brother of whom they came, and left Esau the elder.
c. Malachi 1:3 For beside here the signs of mine hatred appeared even when he was made servant unto his younger brother, being yet in his mother's belly, and also afterward in that he was put from his birthright, yet even now before your eyes the signs hereof are evident, in that that his country lieth waste and he shall never return to inhabit.
d. Malachi 1:3 Whereas ye my people, whom the enemy hated more than them, are by my grace and love toward you delivered, read Rom. 9:13.
e. Malachi 1:6 Besides the rest of the people he condemneth the Priests chiefly, because they should have reproved others for their hypocrisy, and obstinacy against God, and not have hardened them by their example to greater evils.
f. Malachi 1:6 He noteth their gross hypocrisy, which would not see their faults, but most impudently covered them, and so were blind guides.
g. Malachi 1:7 Ye receive all manner offerings for your own greediness, and do not examine whether they be according to my Law, or no.
h. Malachi 1:7 Not that they said thus, but by their doings they declared no less.
i. Malachi 1:8 You make it no fault: whereby he condemneth them, that think it sufficient to serve God partly as he hath commanded, and partly after man's fantasy: and so come not to the pureness of religion, which he requireth, and therefore in reproach he showeth them that a mortal man would not be content to be so served.
j. Malachi 1:9 He derideth the Priests who bare the people in hand that they prayed for them, and showeth that they were the occasion, that these evils came upon the people.
k. Malachi 1:9 Will God consider your office and state, seeing you are so covetous and wicked?
l. Malachi 1:10 Because the Levites who kept the doors did not try whether the sacrifices that came in, were according to the Law, God wisheth that they would rather shut the doors, than to receive such as were not perfect.
m. Malachi 1:11 God showeth that their ingratitude, and neglect of his true service shall be the cause of the calling of the Gentiles: and here the Prophet that was under the Law, framed his words to the capacity of the people, and by the altar and sacrifice he meaneth the spiritual service of God, which should be under the Gospel, when an end should be made to all these legal ceremonies by Christ's only sacrifice.
n. Malachi 1:12 Both the Priests and the people were infected with this error, that they passed not what was offered: for they thought that God was as well content with the lean, as with the fat: but in the mean season they showed not that obedience to God, which he required, and so committed both impiety, and also showed their contempt of God, and covetousness.
o. Malachi 1:13 The Priests and people were both weary with serving God, and passed not what manner of sacrifice and service they gave to God: for that which was least profitable, was thought good enough for the Lord.
p. Malachi 1:14 That is, hath ability to serve the Lord according to his word, and yet will serve him according to his covetous mind.

MALACHI 2

a. Malachi 2:1 He speaketh unto them chiefly, but under them he containeth the people also.
b. Malachi 2:2 To serve me according to my word.
c. Malachi 2:2 That is, the abundance of God's benefits.
d. Malachi 2:3 Your seed sown shall come to no profit.
e. Malachi 2:3 You boast of your holiness, sacrifices and feasts, but they shall turn to your shame and be as vile as dung.

that I have [f]sent this commandment unto you, that my covenant, which I made with Levi, might stand, saith the Lord of hosts. **5** My [g]covenant was with him of life and peace, and I [h]gave him fear, and he feared me, and was afraid before [i]my Name. **6** The Law of [j]truth was in his mouth, and there was no iniquity found in his lips: he walked with me in peace and equity, and did turn many away from iniquity. **7** For the Priest's [k]lips should preserve knowledge, and they should seek the Law at his mouth: for he is the [l]messenger of the Lord of hosts. **8** But ye are gone out of the way: ye have caused many to fall by the Law: ye have broken the covenant of Levi, saith the Lord of hosts. **9** Therefore have I also made you to be despised, and vile before all the people, because ye kept not my ways, but have been partial in the Law. **10** Have we not all one [m]father? hath not one God made us? why do we transgress everyone against his brother, and break the covenant of [n]our fathers? **11** Judah hath transgressed, and an abomination is committed in Israel and in Jerusalem: for Israel hath defiled the holiness of the Lord, which he loved, and hath married the [o]daughter of a strange god. **12** The Lord will cut off the man that doeth this: both the master and the servant out of the Tabernacle of Jacob, and him that [p]offereth an offering unto the Lord of hosts. **13** And this have ye done again, and [q]covered the altar of the Lord with tears, with weeping and with mourning: because the offering is no more regarded, neither received acceptably at your hands. **14** Yet ye say, [r]Wherein? Because the Lord hath been witness between thee and the wife of thy youth, against whom thou hast transgressed: yet is she thy [s]companion, and the wife of thy [t]covenant. **15** And did not [u]he make one? yet had he [v]abundance of spirit: and wherefore one? because he sought a godly [w]seed: therefore keep yourselves in your [x]spirit, and let none trespass against the wife of his youth. **16** If thou hatest her, [y]put her away, saith the Lord God of Israel, yet he covereth [z]the injury under his garment, saith the Lord of hosts: therefore keep yourselves in your spirit, and transgress not. **17** Ye have [aa]wearied the Lord with your words: yet ye say wherein have we wearied him? When ye say, Everyone that doeth [ab]evil, is good in the sight of the Lord, and he delighteth in them. Or where is the God of [ac]judgment?

3

1 Of the messenger of the Lord, John Baptist, and of Christ's office.

1 Behold, I will send my [a]messenger, and he shall prepare the way before me: and the [b]Lord whom ye seek, shall speedily come to his Temple: even the [c]messenger of the Covenant, whom ye desire: behold, he shall come, saith the Lord of hosts. **2** But who [d]may abide the day of his coming? and who shall endure, when he appeareth? for he is like a purging fire, and like fuller's soap. **3** And he shall sit down to try and fine the silver: he shall even fine the sons of [e]Levi and purify them as gold and silver, that they may bring offerings unto the Lord in righteousness. **4** Then shall the offerings of Judah and Jerusalem be acceptable unto the Lord, as in old time and in the years afore. **5** And I will come near to you to judgment, and I will be a swift witness against the soothsayers, and against the adulterers, and against false swearers, and against those that wrongfully keep back the hireling's wages, and vex the widow, and the fatherless, and oppress the stranger, and fear not me, saith the Lord of hosts. **6** For I am the Lord: I change not, and ye sons of Jacob [f]are not consumed. **7** From the days of your fathers, ye are gone away from mine ordinances, and have not kept them: [g]return unto me, and I will return unto you, saith the Lord of hosts: but ye said, Wherein shall we return? **8** Will a [h]man spoil his gods? yet have ye spoiled me: but ye say, Wherein have we spoiled thee? In [i]tithes and offerings. **9** Ye are cursed with a curse: for ye have spoiled me, even this whole nation. **10** Bring ye all the tithes into the storehouse, that there may be meat in my house, and prove me now herewith, saith the Lord of hosts, if I will not open the windows of heaven unto you, and pour you out a blessing [j]without measure. **11** And I will rebuke the [k]devourer for your sakes, and he shall not destroy the fruit of your ground, neither shall your vine be barren in the field, saith the Lord of hosts. **12** And all nations shall call you blessed: for ye shall be a pleasant land, saith the Lord of hosts. **13** Your words have been stout [l]against me, saith the Lord: yet ye say, What have we spoken against thee? **14** Ye have said, It is in vain to serve God: and what profit is it that we have kept his commandment, and that we walked humbly before the Lord of hosts? **15** Therefore we count the proud blessed: even they that work wickedness, are set up, and they that tempt God, yea, they are [m]delivered. **16** [n]Then spake they that feared the Lord, everyone to his neighbor, and the Lord hearkened and heard it, and a [o]book of remembrance was written before him for them that feared the Lord, and that thought upon his Name. **17** And they shall be to me, saith the Lord of hosts, in that day [p]that I shall do this, for a flock, and I will [q]spare them, as a man spareth his own son that serveth him. **18** Then shall you return, and discern between the righteous and wicked, between him that serveth God, and him that serveth him not.

4

The day of the Lord before the which Elijah should come.

1 For behold, the day cometh that shall [a]burn as an oven, and all the proud, yea, and all that do wickedly, shall be stubble, and the day that cometh, shall burn them up, saith the Lord of hosts, and shall leave them neither root nor branch. **2** But unto you that fear my name, shall the [b]sun of righteousness arise, and health shall be under his wings, and ye shall go [c]forth and grow up as fat calves. **3** And ye shall tread down the wicked: for they shall be dust under the soles of your feet in the day that I shall do this, saith the Lord of hosts. **4** [d]Remember the Law of Moses my servant, which I commanded unto him in Horeb for all Israel with the statutes and judgments. **5** Behold, I will send you [e]Elijah the Prophet before the coming of the great and [f]fearful day of the Lord. **6** And he shall [g]turn the heart of the fathers to the children, and the heart of the children to their fathers, lest I come and [h]smite the earth with cursing.

---

f. Malachi 2:4 The Priests objected against the Prophet that he could not reprove them, but he must speak against the Priesthood, and the office established of God by promise, but he showeth that the office is nothing slandered, when these villains and dung are called by their own names.
g. Malachi 2:5 He showeth what were the two conditions of the covenant made with the tribe of Levi on God's part, that he would give them long life and felicity, and on their part, that they should faithfully serve him according to his word.
h. Malachi 2:5 I prescribed Levi a certain Law to serve me.
i. Malachi 2:5 He served me and set forth my glory with all humilitude and submission.
j. Malachi 2:6 He showeth that the Priests ought to have knowledge to instruct others in the word of the Lord.
k. Malachi 2:7 He is as the treasure house of God's word, and ought to give to everyone according to their necessity, and not to reserve it for himself.
l. Malachi 2:7 Showing that whosoever doth not declare God's will, is not his messenger, and Priest.
m. Malachi 2:10 The Prophet accuseth the ingratitude of the Jews toward God and man: for seeing they were all born of one father Abraham, and God had elected them to be his holy people, they ought neither to offend God nor their brethren.
n. Malachi 2:10 Whereby they had bound themselves to God to be an holy people.
o. Malachi 2:11 They have joined themselves in marriage with them that are of another religion.
p. Malachi 2:12 That is, the Priest.
q. Malachi 2:13 Yet cause the people to lament, because that God doth not regard their sacrifices, so that they seem to sacrifice in vain.
r. Malachi 2:14 This is another fault, whereof he accuseth them, that is, that they broke the laws of marriage.
s. Malachi 2:14 As the one half of thyself.
t. Malachi 2:14 She that was joined to thee by a solemn covenant, and by the invocation of God's name.
u. Malachi 2:15 Did not God make man and woman as one flesh and not many?
v. Malachi 2:15 By his power and virtue he could have made many women for one man.
w. Malachi 2:15 Such as should be born in lawful and moderate marriage, wherein is no excess of lusts.
x. Malachi 2:15 Contain yourselves within your bounds, and be sober in mind, and bridle your affections.
y. Malachi 2:16 Not that he doth allow divorcement, but of two faults he showeth, which is the less.
z. Malachi 2:16 He thinketh it sufficient to keep his wife still, albeit he take others, and so as it were covereth his fault.
aa. Malachi 2:17 Ye murmur against God, because he heard not you as soon as ye called.
ab. Malachi 2:17 In thinking that God favored the wicked, and hath no respect to them that serve him.
ac. Malachi 2:17 Thus they blasphemed God in condemning his power and justice, because he judged not according to their fantasies.

MALACHI 3

a. Malachi 3:1 This is meant of John Baptist, as Christ expoundeth it, Luke 7:27.
b. Malachi 3:1 Meaning, Messiah, Ps. 40:1, 7; Dan. 9:17, 25.
c. Malachi 3:1 That is, Christ, by whom the covenant was made and ratified, who is called the Angel or messenger of the covenant, because he reconcileth us to his father and is Lord or king, because he hath the government of his Church.
d. Malachi 3:2 He showeth that the hypocrites which wish so much for the Lord's coming will not abide when he draweth near: for he will consume them, and purge his and make them clean.
e. Malachi 3:3 He beginneth at the Priests that they might be lights, and shine unto others.
f. Malachi 3:6 They murmured against God, because they saw not his help ever present to defend them: and therefore he accuseth them of ingratitude, and showeth that in that they are not daily consumed, it is a token, that he doth still defend them, and so his mercy toward them never changeth.
g. Malachi 3:7 Read Zech. 1:3.
h. Malachi 3:8 There are none of the heathen so barbarous, that will defraud their gods of their honor, or deal deceitfully with them.
i. Malachi 3:8 Whereby the service of God should have been maintained, and the Priests and the poor relieved.
j. Malachi 3:10 Not having respect how much ye need, but I will give you in all abundance: so that ye shall lack place to put my blessings in.
k. Malachi 3:11 Meaning, the caterpillar, and whatsoever destroyeth corn and fruits.
l. Malachi 3:13 The Prophet condemneth them of double blasphemy against God: first, in that they said that God had no respect to them that served him, and next, that the wicked were more in his favor than the godly.
m. Malachi 3:15 They are not only preferred to honor, but also delivered from dangers.
n. Malachi 3:16 After these admonitions of the Prophet, some were lively touched, and encouraged others to fear God.
o. Malachi 3:16 Both because the thing was strange that some turned to God in that great and universal corruption, and also that this might be an example of God's mercies to all penitent sinners.
p. Malachi 3:17 When I shall restore my Church according to my promise, they shall be as mine own proper goods.
q. Malachi 3:17 That is, forgive their sins, and govern them with my Spirit.

MALACHI 4

a. Malachi 4:1 He prophesieth of God's judgments against the wicked, who would not receive Christ, when as God should send him for the restoration of his Church.
b. Malachi 4:2 Meaning, Christ, who with his wings or beams of his grace should lighten and comfort his Church, Eph. 5:14, and he is called the sun of righteousness, because in himself he hath all perfection and also the justice of the Father dwelleth in him: whereby he regenerateth us unto righteousness, cleanseth us from the filth of this world, and reformeth us to the image of God.
c. Malachi 4:2 Ye shall be set at liberty, and increase in the joy of the Spirit, 2 Cor. 3:17.
d. Malachi 4:4 Because the time was come that the Jews should be destitute of Prophets until the time of Christ, because they should with more fervent minds desire his coming, the Prophet exhorteth them to exercise themselves diligently in studying the Law of Moses in the mean season, whereby they might continue in the true religion, and also be armed against all tentations.
e. Malachi 4:5 This Christ expoundeth of John Baptist, Matt. 11:13, 14, who both for his zeal, and restoring of religion, is aptly compared to Elijah.
f. Malachi 4:5 Which as it is true for the wicked, so doth it waken the godly, and call them to repentance.
g. Malachi 4:6 He showeth wherein John's office should stand: in the turning of men to God, and joining the father and children in one voice of faith: so that the father shall turn to the religion of his son which is converted to Christ, and the son shall embrace the faith of the true fathers, Abraham, Isaac, and Jacob.
h. Malachi 4:6 The second point of his office was to denounce God's judgments against them that would not receive Christ.

THE NEW TESTAMENT

THE HOLY GOSPEL OF JESUS CHRIST, ACCORDING TO

MATTHEW

1

1 That Jesus is that Messiah, the Savior promised to the Fathers. 18 The nativity of Christ.

1 The [a,b,1]book of the [c]generation of Jesus Christ the son of David, the [d]son
of Abraham. 2 [2]Abraham begat Isaac. [3]And Isaac begat Jacob. [4]And Jacob begat
Judah and his brethren. 3 [5]And Judah begat Perez, and Zerah of Tamar. And Pe-
rez begat Hezron. And Hezron begat Ram. 4 And Ram begat Amminadab. And
Amminadab begat Nahshon. And Nahshon begat Salmon. 5 And Salmon begat
[6]Boaz of Rahab. And Boaz begat Obed of Ruth. And Obed begat Jesse. 6 And
[7]Jesse begat David the King. And David the King begat Solomon of her that was
[8]the wife of Uriah. 7 And [9]Solomon begat Rehoboam. And Rehoboam begat
Abijah. And Abijah begat Asa. 8 And Asa begat Jehoshaphat. And Jehoshaphat
begat Joram. And Joram begat Uzziah. 9 And Uzziah begat Jotham. And Jotham
begat Ahaz. And Ahaz begat Hezekiah. 10 And [10]Hezekiah begat Manasseh.
And Manasseh begat Amon. And Amon begat Josiah. 11 And [11]Josiah begat
Jakim. And Jakim [e]begat Jeconiah and his brethren about the time they were car-
ried away to Babylon. 12 And after they were carried away into Babylon, [12]Je-
coniah begat Shealtiel. And [13]Shealtiel be-gat Zerubbabel. 13 And Zerubbabel
begat Abiud. And Abiud begat Eliakim. And Eliakim begat Azor. 14 And Azor
begat Zadok. And Zadok begat Achim. And Achim begat Eliud. 15 And Eliud
begat Eleazar. And Eleazar begat Matthan. And Matthan begat Jacob. 16 And
Jacob begat Joseph the husband of Mary, of whom was born Jesus, that is called
Christ. 17 So [f]all the generations from Abraham to David, are fourteen genera-
tions. And from David until they were carried away into Babylon, fourteen gene-
rations: and after they were carried away into Babylon until Christ, fourteen gene-
rations. 18 Now the birth of [g]Jesus Christ was thus, When as his mother Mary
was [14]betrothed to Joseph, before they came together, she was found with child of
the holy Ghost. 19 Then Joseph her husband being a just man, and not willing
to [15]make her a public example, was minded to put her away secretly. 20 But
while he thought these things, behold, the Angel of the Lord appeared unto him in
a dream, saying, Joseph, the son of David, fear not to [h]take Mary thy [i]wife: for that
which is [j]conceived in her, is of the holy Ghost. 21 And she shall bring [k]forth
a son, and thou shalt [16]call his name JESUS: for he shall [l,17]save his people from
their sins. 22 And all this was done that it might be fulfilled, which is spoken of
the Lord by the Prophet, saying, 23 [18]Behold, a [m]virgin shall be with child, and
shall bear a son, and they shall call his name Emmanuel, which is by interpretation,
God with us. 24 Then Joseph being raised from sleep, did as the Angel of the
Lord had enjoined him, and took his wife. 25 But he knew her not, [n]till she had
brought forth her first born son, and he called his name JESUS.

2

The wise men, who are the firstfruits of the Gentiles, worship Christ. 14 Joseph fled into Egypt with Jesus and his mother. 16 Herod slayeth the children.

1 When [a,1]Jesus then was born at Bethlehem in [b]Judea, in the days of Herod
the king, behold, there came [c]Wise men from the East to Jerusalem, 2 Saying,
Where is the King of the Jews that is born? for we have seen his star in the East, and
are come to worship him. 3 When king Herod heard this, he was [d]troubled, and
all Jerusalem with him. 4 And gathering together all the [e]chief Priests and [f]Scri-
bes of the people, he asked of them, where Christ should be born. 5 And they
said unto him, At Bethlehem in Judea: for so it is written by the Prophet, 6 [2]And
thou Bethlehem in the land of Judah, art not the [g]least among the Princes of Judah:
for out of thee shall come the governor that [h]shall feed my people Israel. 7 Then
Herod privily called the Wise men, and diligently inquired of them the time of
the star that appeared, 8 And sent them to Bethlehem, saying, Go, and search
diligently for the babe: and when ye have found him, bring me word again, that I
may come also, and worship him. 9 So when they had heard the king, they de-
parted: and lo, the star which they had seen in the East, went before them, till it
came and stood over the place where the babe was. 10 And when they saw the
star, they rejoiced with an exceeding great joy, 11 And went into the house, and
found the babe with Mary his mother, and [i]fell down, and worshipped him, and
opened their [j]treasures, and presented unto him gifts, even gold, and frankincense,
and myrrh. 12 And after they were [k]warned of God in a dream, that they should
not go again to Herod, they returned into their country another way. 13 [l]After
their departure, behold, the Angel of the Lord appeareth to Joseph in a dream,
saying, Arise, and take the babe and his mother, and flee into Egypt, and be there
till I bring thee word, for Herod will seek the babe to destroy him. 14 So he aro-
se and took the babe and his mother by night, and departed into Egypt. 15 And
was there unto the death of Herod, that it might be fulfilled, which is spoken of
the Lord by the [3]Prophet, saying, Out of Egypt have I called my son. 16 Then
Herod, seeing that he was mocked of the Wise men, was exceeding wroth, and sent
forth, and slew all the male children that were in Bethlehem, and in all the coasts
thereof from two years old and under, according to the time which he had dili-
gently searched out of the Wise men. 17 Then was that fulfilled which is spoken
[m]by the Prophet Jeremiah, saying, 18 [4]In Ramah was [n]a voice heard, mourning,
and weeping, and great howling: [o]Rachel weeping for her children, and would not
be comforted, because they were not. 19 [p]And when Herod was dead, behold,
an Angel of the Lord appeareth in a dream to Joseph in Egypt, 20 Saying, Ari-
se, and take the babe and his mother, and go into the land of Israel: for they are

---

MATT. 1

a. Matt. 1:1 Jesus Christ came of Abraham of the tribe of Judah, and of the stock of David as God promised.
b. Matt. 1:1 Rehearsal: As the Hebrews used to speak: as Gen. 5:1, The book of the generations.
c. Matt. 1:1 Of the ancestors of whom Christ came.
d. Matt. 1:1 Which Christ is also the son of Abraham.
e. Matt. 1:11 That is, the captivity fell in the days of Jakim and Jeconiah: for Jeconiah was born before their carrying away into captivity.
f. Matt. 1:17 All those which are reckoned up in this pedigree of David's stock, as they begat one another orderly in their degrees.
g. Matt. 1:18 Christ is the true Emmanuel, and therefore, Jesus (that is, Savior) is conceived in the Virgin by the holy Ghost, as it was foretold by the Prophets.
h. Matt. 1:20 Receive her at her parents' and kinsfolk's hands.
i. Matt. 1:20 Which was promised, and made sure to thee to be thy wife.
j. Matt. 1:20 Of the mother's substance by the holy Ghost.
k. Matt. 1:21 Christ is born of the same Virgin which never knew man: and is called Jesus of God himself, by the Angel.
l. Matt. 1:21 Deliver, and this showeth us the meaning of this name Jesus.
m. Matt. 1:23 There is in the Hebrew and Greek text, an article added, to point out the woman, and set her forth plainly: as you would say, that Virgin, or a certain virgin.
n. Matt. 1:25 This little word Till, in the Hebrew tongue, giveth us to understand also, that a thing shall not come to pass in time to come: as Michal had no children Till her death day, 2 Sam. 6:23. And in the last Chapter of this Evangelist: Behold, I am with you till the end of the world.

MATT. 1

1. Luke 3:23
2. Gen. 21:2
3. Gen. 25:14
4. Gen. 29:35
5. Gen. 38:27 / 1Chron. 2:5 / Ruth 4:18-19
6. Ruth 4:21
7. 1Sam. 16:1 / 1Sam. 17:12
8. 2Sam. 12:24
9. 1Kings 11:43 / 2Chron. 3:10-11
10. 2Kings 20:21 / 2Kings 28:11 / 1Chron. 3:13-15
11. 2Kings 23:34 / 2 Kings 24:1-6 / 2 Chron. 36:4-9
12. 1Chron. 3:16
13. 1Chron. 3:17 / Ezra 3:2 / Ezra 5:2
14. Luke 1:27
15. Deut. 14:1
16. Luke 1:31
17. Acts 4:12
18. Isa. 7:14

MATT. 2

a. Matt. 2:1 Christ a poor child, laid down in a crib, and nothing set by of his own people, receiveth notwithstanding a noble witness of his divinity from heaven, and of his kingly estate of strangers: which his own also unwittingly allow of, although they do not acknowledge him.
b. Matt. 2:1 For there was another in the tribe of Zebulun.
c. Matt. 2:1 Wise and learned men: It is a Persian word which they use in good part.
d. Matt. 2:3 Was much moved, for he was a stranger, and came to the kingdom by force: and the Jews were troubled: for wickedness is mad and raging.
e. Matt. 2:4 The chief priests, that is, such as were of Aaron's family, which were divided into four and twenty orders, 1 Chron. 14:5 and 2 Chron. 36:14.
f. Matt. 2:4 They that expound the Law to the people, for the Hebrews take this word of another, which signifieth as much as to expound and declare.
g. Matt. 2:6 Though thou be a small town, yet shalt thou be very famous and notable through the birth of the Messiah, who shall be born in thee.
h. Matt. 2:6 That shall rule and govern: for Kings are fitly called leaders and shepherds of the people.
i. Matt. 2:11 A kind of humble and lovely reverence.
j. Matt. 2:11 The rich and costly presents, which they brought him.
k. Matt. 2:12 God warned and told them of it, whereas they asked it not.
l. Matt. 2:13 Christ being yet scarce born, beginneth to be crucified for us, both in himself, and also in his members.
m. Matt. 2:17 For God speaketh by the mouth of the Prophets.
n. Matt. 2:18 A voice of lamenting, weeping, and howling.
o. Matt. 2:18 That is to say, All that compass about Bethlehem: for Rachel Jacob's wife, who died in childbirth, was buried in the way that leadeth to this town, which is also called Ephrathah, because of the fruitfulness of the soil, and plenty of corn.

dead which sought the babe's life. **21** Then he arose up, and took the babe and his mother, and came into the land of Israel. **22** But when he heard that Archelaus did reign in Judea instead of his father Herod, he was afraid to go thither: yet after he was warned of God in a dream, he turned aside into the parts of Galilee. **23** And went and dwelt in a city called Nazareth, that it might be fulfilled which was spoken by the Prophets, which was, That he should be called a Nazarite.

3

1 John preacheth. 4 His apparel and meat. 5 He baptizeth. 8 The fruits of repentance. 10 The axe at the root of the trees. 12 The fan and the chaff. 13 Christ is baptized.

1 And [1]in [a]those days, [b]John the Baptist came and preached in the [c]wilderness of Judea, **2** And said, [d]Repent: for the [e]kingdom of heaven is at hand. **3** For this is he of whom it is spoken by the Prophet Isaiah, saying, [2]The voice of him that crieth in the wilderness, Prepare ye the way of the Lord: [f]make his paths straight. **4** [3]And this John had his garment of camel's hair, and a girdle of a skin about his loins, his meat was also [g]locusts and wild honey. **5** [4]Then went out to him [h]Jerusalem and all Judea, and all the region round about Jordan, **6** And they were baptized of him in Jordan, [i]confessing their sins. **7** [j]Now when he saw many of the Pharisees, and of the Sadducees come to his baptism, he said unto them, [5]O generation of vipers, who hath forewarned you to flee from the anger to come? **8** [k]Bring forth therefore fruit worthy amendment of life, **9** [l]And [m]think not to say [n]with yourselves, [6]We have Abraham to our father: for I say unto you, that God is able even of these stones to raise up children unto Abraham. **10** And now also is the axe put to the root of the trees: [7]therefore every tree which bringeth not forth good fruit, is hewn down, and cast into the fire. **11** [o,8]Indeed I baptize you with water to [p]amendment of life, but he that cometh after me is mightier than I, whose shoes I am not worthy to bear, he will baptize you with the holy Ghost, and with fire. **12** [q]Which hath his fan in his hand, and will [r]make clean his floor, and gather his wheat into his garner, but will burn up the chaff with unquenchable fire. **13** [s,9]Then came Jesus from Galilee to Jordan unto John to be baptized of him. **14** But John earnestly put him back, saying, I have need to be baptized of thee, and comest thou to me? **15** Then Jesus answering, said to him, Let be now: for thus it becometh us to fulfill [t]all righteousness. So he suffered him. **16** And Jesus when he was baptized, came straight out of the water. And lo, the heavens were opened unto [u]him, and John saw the Spirit of God descending like a dove, and lighting upon him. **17** [v]And lo, a voice came from heaven, saying, [10]This is my beloved Son, in whom I am [w]well pleased.

4

1 Christ is tempted. 4 He vanquisheth the devil with Scripture. 11 The Angels minister unto him. 12 He preacheth repentance, and that himself is come. 18 The calling of Peter, Andrew. 21 James and John. 24 He preacheth the Gospel, and healeth the diseased.

1 Then [1]was [a]Jesus led aside of the Spirit into the wilderness, to be tempted of the devil. **2** And when he had fasted [b]forty days, and forty nights, he was afterward hungry. **3** Then came to him the tempter, and said, If thou be the Son of God, command that these stones be made bread. **4** But he answering, said, It is written, [2]Man shall not live by bread only, but by every word that proceedeth out of the mouth of God. **5** Then the devil took him up into the holy city, and set him on a [c]pinnacle of the Temple. **6** And said unto him, If thou be the Son of God, cast thyself down, for it is written, [3]that he will give his Angels charge over thee, and with their hands they shall lift thee up, lest at any time thou shouldest dash thy foot against a stone. **7** Jesus said unto him, It is written again, [4]Thou shalt not [d]tempt the Lord thy God. **8** Again the devil took him up into an exceeding high mountain, and showed him all the kingdoms of the world, and the glory of them, **9** And said to him, All these will I give thee, if thou wilt fall down, and worship me. **10** Then said Jesus unto him, Avoid Satan: for it is written, [5]Thou shalt worship the Lord thy God, and him only shalt thou serve. **11** [6]Then the devil left him: and behold, the Angels came, and ministered unto him. **12** [e,7]And when Jesus had heard that John was committed to prison, he returned into Galilee, **13** And leaving Nazareth, went and dwelt in [f]Capernaum, which is near the sea in the borders of Zebulun and Naphtali, **14** That it might be fulfilled which was spoken by Isaiah the Prophet, saying, **15** [8]The land of Zebulun, and the land of Naphtali by the way of the [g]sea, beyond Jordan, [h]Galilee of the Gentiles: **16** The people which sat in darkness, saw great light: and to them which sat in the region and shadow of death, light is risen up. **17** [9]From that time Jesus began to preach, and to say, Amend your lives: for the kingdom of heaven is at [i]hand. **18** [j]And Jesus walking by the sea of Galilee saw two brethren, Simon, which was called Peter, and Andrew his brother, casting a net into the sea (for they were fishers.) **19** [10]And he said unto them, Follow me, and I will make you fishers of men. **20** And they straightway leaving the nets, followed him. **21** And when he was gone forth from thence, he saw other two brethren, James the son of Zebedee, and John his brother in a ship with Zebedee their father, mending their nets, and he called them. **22** And they without tarrying, leaving the ship and their father, followed him. **23** So [k]Jesus went about all Galilee, teaching in [l]their [m]Synagogues, and preaching the Gospel of the [n]kingdom, and healing [o]every sickness, and every [p]disease among the people. **24** And his fame spread abroad through all Syria: and they brought unto him all sick people, that were taken with divers diseases, and [q]torments, and them that were possessed with devils, and those which were [r]lunatic, and those that had the [s]palsy: and he healed them. **25** And there followed him great multitudes out of Galilee, and Decapolis, and Jerusalem, and Judea, and from beyond Jordan.

5

1 Who are blessed. 13 The Apostles are the salt and light of the world. 14 The city set on an hill. 15 The candle. 16 Good works. 19 The fulfiling of Christ's commandments. 21 What killing is. 23 Reconciliation is set be-

---

p. Matt. 2:19 Christ is brought up in Nazareth, after the death of the tyrant by God's providence: that by the very name of the place, it might plainly appear to the world, that he is the Lord's true Nazarite.

MATT. 2

1. Luke 2:6
2. Mic. 5:2 / John 7:42
3. Hos. 11:1
4. Jer. 31:15

MATT. 3

a. Matt. 3:1 Not when Joseph went to dwell at Nazareth, but a great while after, about the space of 15 years: for in the 30 year of his age was Jesus baptized of John: therefore by those days is meant, at that time that Jesus remained as yet an inhabitant of the town of Nazareth.

b. Matt. 3:1 John, who through his singular holiness and rare austereness of life caused all men to cast their eyes upon him, prepareth the way for Christ following fast on his heels, as the Prophet Isaiah foretold, and delivereth the sum of the Gospel, which in short space after should be delivered more fully.

c. Matt. 3:1 In a hilly country, which was notwithstanding inhabited, for Zechariah dwelt there, Luke 1:40, and there was Joab's house, 1 Kings 2:34; and besides these, Joshua maketh mention of six towns that were in the wilderness, Josh. 15:62.

d. Matt. 3:2 The word in the Greek tongue signifieth a changing of our minds and heart from evil to better.

e. Matt. 3:2 The kingdom of Messiah, whose government shall be heavenly, and nothing but heavenly.

f. Matt. 3:3 Make him a plain and smooth way.

g. Matt. 3:4 Locusts were a kind of meat which certain of the East people use, which were therefore called devourers of Locusts.

h. Matt. 3:5 The people of Jerusalem.

i. Matt. 3:6 Acknowledging that they were saved only by free remission and forgiveness of their sins.

j. Matt. 3:7 There is nothing that stoppeth up the way of mercy and salvation against us so much as the opinion of our own righteousness doth.

k. Matt. 3:8 True repentance is an inward thing which hath its seat in the mind and heart.

l. Matt. 3:9 The faith of the fathers availeth their unbelieving children nothing at all: and yet for all that God playeth not the liar, nor dealeth unfaithfully in his league which he made with the holy fathers.

m. Matt. 3:9 Think not that you have any cause to be proud of Abraham.

n. Matt. 3:9 In your hearts.

o. Matt. 3:11 We may neither dwell upon the signs which God hath ordained as means to lead us unto our salvation, neither upon them: but we must climb up to the matter itself, that is to say, to Christ, who inwardly worketh that effectually, which is outwardly signified unto us.

p. Matt. 3:11 The outward sign putteth us in mind of this, that we must change our lives and become better, assuring us as by a seal, that we are engrafted into Christ; whereby our old man dieth and the new man riseth up, Rom. 6:4.

q. Matt. 3:12 The triumphs of the wicked shall end in everlasting torment.

r. Matt. 3:12 Will cleanse it thoroughly, and make a full riddance.

s. Matt. 3:13 Christ sanctified our baptism in himself.

t. Matt. 3:15 All such things as it hath appointed us to keep.

u. Matt. 3:16 To John.

v. Matt. 3:17 Christ's full consecration and authorizing to the office of mediatorship, is showed by the father's own voice, and a visible sign of the holy Ghost.

w. Matt. 3:17 The Greek word betokeneth a thing of great account, and such as highly pleaseth a man. So then the Father saith, that Christ only is the man whom when he beholdeth, look what opinion he had conceived of us, he layeth it clean aside.

MATT. 3

1. Mark 1:4 / Luke 3:3
2. Isa. 40:3 / Mark 1:3 / Luke 3:4 / John 1:23
3. Mark 1:6
4. Mark 1:5 / Luke 1:7
5. Matt. 12:34
6. John 8:39
7. Acts 13:26
8. Matt. 7:19
9. Mark 1:8 / Luke 5:16 / John 1:26 / Acts 1:5 / Acts 2:4 / Acts 8:17 / Acts 19:4-5
10. Mark 1:9 / Luke 3:21
11. Col. 1:13 / 2 Pet. 1:17

MATT. 4

a. Matt. 4:1 Christ was tempted all manner of ways and still overcometh, that we also through his virtue may overcome.

b. Matt. 4:2 Full forty days.

c. Matt. 4:5 The battlement wherewith the flat roof of the temple was compassed about, that no man might fall down: as was appointed by the Law, Deut. 22:8.

d. Matt. 4:7 Word for word, Thou shalt not go on still in tempting.

e. Matt. 4:12 When the Herald's mouth is stopped, the Lord revealeth himself, and bringeth full light into the darkness of this world, preaching free forgiveness of sins to them that repent.

f. Matt. 4:13 Which was a town a great deal more famous than Nazareth was.

g. Matt. 4:15 Of Tiberias, or because that country bended toward Tyre, which standeth upon the sea that cutteth the midst of the world.

h. Matt. 4:15 So called, because it bordered upon Tyre and Sidon, and because Solomon gave the king of Tyre twenty cities in that quarter, 1 Kings 9:11.

i. Matt. 4:17 Is come to you.

j. Matt. 4:18 Christ thinking by time, that he should at length depart from us, even at the beginning of his preaching getteth him disciples after an heavenly sort, men indeed poor, and utterly unlearned, and therefore such as might be least suspected witnesses of the truth of those things which they heard and saw.

k. Matt. 4:23 Christ assureth the hearts of the believers of his spiritual and saving virtue, by healing the diseases of the body.

l. Matt. 4:23 Their, that is, the Galileans'.

m. Matt. 4:23 Synagogues, the Jews' Churches.

n. Matt. 4:23 Of Messiah.

o. Matt. 4:23 Diseases of all kinds, but not every one: that is, as we say, some of every one.

p. Matt. 4:23 The word signifieth properly the weakness of the stomach: but here it is taken for those diseases which make men faint, and wear away, that have them.

q. Matt. 4:24 The word signifieth properly, the stone wherewith gold is tried: and by a borrowed kind of speech is applied to all kinds of examination by torture, when as by rough dealing and torments, we go about to draw out the truth of men, which otherwise they would not confess: and in this place it is taken for those diseases, which put sick men to great woe.

r. Matt. 4:24 Which at every full Moon, or other changes of the Moon, are shrewdly troubled and diseased.

*fore sacrifice. 27 Adultery. 29 The plucking out of the eye. 30 Cutting off of
the hand. 31 The bill of divorcement. 33 Not to swear. 44 To love our ene-
mies. 48 Perfectness.*

1 And when he saw the multitude, he went up into a mountain: and when
he was set, his disciples came to him. 2 [a]And he opened his mouth, and taught
them, saying, 3 [1]Blessed are the [b]poor in [c]spirit, for theirs is the kingdom of he-
aven. 4 [2]Blessed are they that mourn: for they shall be comforted. 5 [3]Blessed
are the meek: for they shall inherit the earth. 6 [4]Blessed are they which hunger
and thirst for righteousness: for they shall be filled. 7 Blessed are the merciful:
for they shall obtain mercy. 8 Blessed are the [d,5]pure in heart: for they shall
see God. 9 Blessed are the peacemakers: for they shall be called the children
of God. 10 Blessed are they [6]which suffer persecution for righteousness' sake;
for theirs is the kingdom of heaven. 11 [7]Blessed shall ye be when men revile
you, and persecute you, and say all manner of evil against you for my sake, fal-
sely. 12 Rejoice and be glad, for great is your reward in heaven: for so persecuted
they the Prophets which were before you. 13 [8]Ye [e]are the salt of the [f]earth: but
if the salt have lost his savor, wherewith shall it be [g]salted? It is thenceforth good
for nothing, but to be cast out, and to be trodden under foot of men. 14 Ye are
the [h]light of the world. A city that is set on an hill, cannot be hid. 15 [9]Neither
do men light a candle, and put it under a bushel, but on a candlestick, and it gi-
veth light unto all that are in the house. 16 [10]Let your light so shine before
men, that they may see your good works, and glorify your father which is in hea-
ven. 17 [i]Think not that I am come to destroy the Law, or the Prophets. I am not
come to destroy them, but to [j]fulfill them. 18 [11]For truly I say unto you, Till he-
aven and earth perish, one jot or one tittle of the Law shall not escape, till all things
be fulfilled. 19 [k,12]Whosoever therefore shall break one of these least command-
ments, and teach men so, he shall be called the [l]least in the kingdom of heaven: but
whosoever shall observe and teach them, the same shall be called great in the king-
dom of heaven. 20 For I say unto you, except your righteousness [13]exceed the ri-
ghteousness of the Scribes and Pharisees, ye shall not enter into the kingdom of he-
aven. 21 [m]Ye have heard that it was said unto them of the old time, [14]Thou shalt
not kill: for whosoever killeth shall be culpable of judgment. 22 But I say unto
you, whosoever is angry with his brother unadvisedly, shall be [n]culpable [o]of judg-
ment. And whosoever saith unto his brother, Raca, shall be worthy to be punished
by the [p]Council. And whosoever shall say, Fool, shall be worthy to be punished
with [q]hell [r]fire. 23 [s]If then thou bring thy gift to the [t]altar, and there remem-
berest that thy brother hath ought against thee, 24 Leave there thine offering
before the altar, and go thy way: first be reconciled to thy brother, and then come
and offer thy gift. 25 [u,15]Agree with thine adversary quickly, while thou art in
the way with him, lest thine adversary deliver thee to the Judge, and the Judge de-
liver thee to the sergeant, and thou be cast into prison. 26 Verily I say unto thee,
thou shalt not come out thence, till thou hast [v]paid the utmost farthing. 27 [w]Ye
have heard that it was said to them of old time, [16]Thou shalt not commit adul-
tery. 28 But I say unto you, that whosoever looketh on a woman to lust after
her, hath committed adultery with her already in his heart. 29 [17]Wherefore if
thy [x]right eye cause thee [y]to offend, pluck it out and cast it from thee: for better
it is for thee, that one of thy members perish, than that thy whole body should
be cast into hell. 30 Also if thy right hand make thee to offend, cut it off, and
cast it from thee: for better it is for thee, that one of thy members perish, than that
thy whole body should be cast into hell. 31 It hath been said also, [18]Whosoever
shall put away his wife, let him give her a bill of divorcement. 32 But I say unto
you, whosoever shall put away his wife (except it be for fornication) causeth her
to commit adultery: and whosoever shall marry her that is divorced, committeth
adultery. 33 [z]Again, ye have heard that it was said to them of old time, [19]Thou
shalt not forswear thyself, but shalt perform thine oaths to the Lord. 34 But I say
unto you, Swear not at all, neither by heaven, for it is the throne of God: 35 Nor
yet by the earth, for it is his footstool: neither by Jerusalem: for it is the city of the
great King. 36 Neither shalt thou swear by thine head, because thou canst not
make one hair white or black. 37 [20]But let your communication be [aa]Yea, yea:
Nay, nay. For whatsoever is more than these, cometh of [ab]evil. 38 [ac]Ye have he-
ard that it hath been said, An [21]eye for an eye, and a tooth for a tooth. 39 But I
say unto you, [22]Resist not evil: but whosoever shall smite thee on thy right cheek,
turn to him the other also. 40 And if any man will sue thee at the law, and take
away thy coat, let him have thy cloak also. 41 And whosoever will compel thee
to go a mile, go with him twain. 42 [23]Give to him that asketh, and from him
that would borrow of thee, turn not away. 43 Ye have heard that it hath been
said, [24]Thou shalt love thy neighbor, and hate thine enemy. 44 But I say unto
you, [25]Love your enemies: bless them that curse you: do good to them that hate
you, [26]and pray for them which hurt you, and persecute you, 45 [ad,27]That ye
may be the children of your father that is in heaven: for he maketh his sun to arise
on the evil and the good, and sendeth rain on the just and unjust. 46 For if ye
love them, which love you, what reward shall you have? Do not the Publicans even
the same? 47 And if ye be friendly to your brethren only, what singular thing do
ye? do not even the [ae]Publicans likewise? 48 Ye shall therefore be perfect, as your
Father which is in heaven, is perfect.

---

s. Matt. 4:24 Weak and feeble men, who have the parts of their body loosed, and so weakened, that they are neither able to gather them up together, nor put them out as they would.

MATT. 4

1. Mark 1:12 / Luke 4:1
2. Deut. 8:3
3. Ps. 91:11
4. Deut. 6:16
5. Deut. 16:13 / Deut. 10:20
6. Mark 1:13 / Luke 4:13
7. Mark 1:14 / Luke 4:14 / John 4:43
8. Isa. 9:1
9. Mark 1:15
10. Mark 1:16 / 1Cor. 1:27

MATT. 5

a. Matt. 5:2 Christ teacheth that the greatest joy and felicity is not in the commodities and pleasures of this life, but is laid up in heaven for them that willingly rest in the good will and pleasure of God, and endeavor to profit all men, although they be cruelly vexed, and troubled of the worldlings, because they will not fashion themselves to their manners.
b. Matt. 5:3 Under the name of poverty are all such miseries meant, as are joined with poverty.
c. Matt. 5:3 Whose minds and spirits are brought under, and tamed, and obey God.
d. Matt. 5:8 Fitly is this word Pure, joined with the heart, for as a bright and shining resemblance or image may be seen plainly in a clear and pure looking glass, even so doth the face (as it were) of the everlasting God, shine forth, and clear appears in a pure heart.
e. Matt. 5:13 The ministers of the word, especially (unless they will be the most caitiff of all) must needs lead others both by word and deed to this greatest joy and felicity.
f. Matt. 5:13 Your doctrine must be very sound and good, for if it be not so, it shall be naught set by, and cast away as a thing unsavory and vain.
g. Matt. 5:13 What shall you have to salt withal? And so are fools in the Latin tongue called saltless, as you would say, men that have no salt, or savor and taste in them.
h. Matt. 5:14 You shine and give light, by being made partakers of the true light.
i. Matt. 5:17 Christ came not to bring any new way of righteousness and salvation into the world, but to fulfill that in deed which was shadowed by the figures of the Law, by delivering men through grace from the curse of the Law: and moreover to teach the true use of obedience which the Law appointed, and to engrave in our hearts the force of obedience.
j. Matt. 5:17 That the prophecies may be accomplished.
k. Matt. 5:19 He beginneth with the true expounding of the Law, and setteth it against the old (but yet false) glosses of the Scribes: So far is he from abolishing the least commandment of his Father.
l. Matt. 5:19 He shall have no place in the Church.
m. Matt. 5:21 The true meaning of the first commandment.
n. Matt. 5:22 He speaketh of the judgment of God, and of the difference of sins, and therefore applieth his words to the form of civil judgments, which were then used.
o. Matt. 5:22 Of that judgment which was ruled by three men, who had the hearing and deciding of money matters, and such other small causes.
p. Matt. 5:22 By that judgment which stood of 23 Judges, who had the hearing and deciding of weighty affairs and matters of life and death: as the highest Judges of all, were to the number of 71, which had the hearing of most weighty affairs, as the matter of a whole tribe or of an high Priest, or of a false prophet.
q. Matt. 5:22 Whereas we read here, Hell, it is in the text itself, Gehenna, which is an Hebrew word made of two, and is as much to say, as the Valley of Hinnom, which otherwise the Hebrews called Tophet: it was a place where the Israelites were wont most cruelly to sacrifice their children to false gods, whereupon it was taken for a place appointed to torment the reprobates in Jer. 7:31.
r. Matt. 5:22 The Jews used four kinds of punishments, before their government was taken away by Herod, hanging, heading, stoning, and burning: this is it that Christ shot at, because burning was the greatest punishment, therefore in that he maketh mention of a judgment, a council, and a fire, he showeth that some sins are worse than other sins, but yet they are all such that we must give account for them, and will be punished for them.
s. Matt. 5:23 The covetous Pharisees taught that God was appeased by the sacrifices appointed in the Law, which they themselves devoured. But Christ on the contrary side denieth that God accepteth any man's offering, unless he maketh satisfaction to his brother whom he hath offended: and saith moreover, that these stubborn and stiffnecked despisers of their brethren, shall never escape the wrath and curse of God, before they have made full satisfaction to their brethren.
t. Matt. 5:23 He applieth all this speech to the state of his time, when as there was an altar standing in Jerusalem, and therefore they are very foolish, that gather hereupon, that we must build altars, and use sacrifices: but they are more fools, which draw that to purgatory, which is spoken of peacemaking and atonement one with another.
u. Matt. 5:25 Cut off all cause for enmity.
v. Matt. 5:26 Thou shalt be dealt withall to the utmost extremity.
w. Matt. 5:27 He is taken for an adulterer before God, whatsoever he be, that coveteth a woman: and therefore we must keep our eyes chaste, and all the members we have, yea, and we must eschew all occasions which might move us to evil, how dear soever it cost us.
x. Matt. 5:29 He nameth the right eye and the right hand, because the parts of the right side of our bodies are the chiefest, and the readiest to commit any wickedness.
y. Matt. 5:29 Word for word, do cause thee to offend: for sins are stumbling blocks as it were, that is to say, rocks which we are cast upon.
z. Matt. 5:33 The meaning of the third commandment against the froward opinion and judgment of the Scribes, which excused by oaths or indirect forms of swearing.
aa. Matt. 5:37 Whatsoever you vouch, vouch it barely, and whatsoever you deny, deny it barely without any more words.
ab. Matt. 5:37 From an evil conscience, or from the devil.
ac. Matt. 5:38 He showeth clean contrary to the doctrine of the Scribes, that the sum of the second table must be understood, that we may in no wise render evil for evil, but rather suffer double injury, and do well to them that are our deadly enemies.
ad. Matt. 5:45 A double reason: the one is taken of relatives, that children must be like their father: the other is taken of comparison, The children of God must be better, than the children of this world.
ae. Matt. 5:47 They that were the toll masters, and had the oversight of tributes and customs: a kind of men that the Jews hated to death, both because they served the Romans in these offices, (whose yokeful bondage they could hardly away withall) and also because these toll masters are for the most part given to covetousness.

MATT. 5

1. Luke 6:20
2. Isa. 61:2-3 / Luke 6:21
3. Ps. 37:11
4. Isa. 65:13
5. Ps. 24:4
6. 1Cor. 14:33 / 1Pet. 3:14
7. Acts 5:41 / 1Pet. 4:14
8. Mark 9:50 / Luke 14:34
9. Mark 4:21 / Luke 8:16 / Luke 11:33
10. 1Pet. 2:12
11. Luke 16:17
12. James 2:10
13. Luke 11:39
14. Exod. 20:13/ Deut. 5:17
15. Luke 12:58
16. Exod. 20:14 / Rom. 13:9
17. Matt. 18:8-9 / Mark 9:47
18. Matt 19:7 / Deut. 24:1 / Mark 10:4 / Luke 16:18 / 1Cor. 7:10
19. Exod. 20:7 / Lev. 19:12 / Deut. 5:11
20. James 5:12
21. Exod. 21:24 / Lev. 24:20 / Deut. 19:21
22. Luke 6:29 / Rom. 12:17 / 1Cor. 6:7
23. Deut. 15:8
24. Lev. 19:18
25. Luke 6:27
26. Luke 23:34 / Acts 7:60 / 1Cor. 4:13
27. Luke 6:35

6

1 Alms. 5 Prayer. 14 Forgiving our brother. 16 Fasting. 19 Our treasure. 20 We must succor the poor. 24 God and riches. 25 Careful seeking for meat and drink, and apparel, forbidden. 33 The kingdom of God and his righteousness.

1 Take heed that ye give not your [a]alms before men to be seen of them, or else ye shall have no [b]reward of your Father which is in heaven. **2** [1]Therefore when thou givest thine alms, thou shalt not make a trumpet to be blown before thee, as the [c]hypocrites do in the Synagogues and in the streets, to be praised of men. Verily I say unto you, they have their reward. **3** But when thou doest thine alms, let not thy left hand know what thy right hand doeth, **4** That thine alms may be in secret, and thy Father that seeth in secret, he will reward thee openly. **5** [d]And when thou prayest, be not as the hypocrites: for they love to stand and pray in the Synagogues, and in the corners of the streets, because they would be seen of men. Verily I say unto you, they have their reward. **6** But when thou prayest, enter into thy chamber: and when thou hast shut thy door, pray unto thy Father which is in secret, and thy Father which seeth in secret, shall reward thee openly. **7** Also when ye pray, use no [e]vain repetitions as the Heathen: for they think to be heard for their much babbling. **8** Be ye not like them therefore: for your Father knoweth whereof ye have need, before ye ask of him. **9** [f]After this manner therefore pray ye, [2]Our father which art in heaven, hallowed be thy name. **10** Thy kingdom come. Thy will be done even in earth as it is in heaven. **11** Give us this day our [g]daily bread. **12** And forgive us our debts, as we also forgive our debtors. **13** And lead us not into temptation, but deliver [3]us from [h]evil: for thine is the kingdom, and the power, and the glory for ever. Amen. **14** [i,4]For if ye do forgive men their trespasses, your heavenly Father will also forgive you. **15** But if ye do not forgive men their trespasses, no more will your father forgive you your trespasses. **16** [j]Moreover, when ye fast, look not sour as the hypocrites: for they [k]disfigure their faces, that they might seem unto men to fast. Verily I say unto you that they have their reward. **17** But when thou fastest, anoint thine head, and wash thy face, **18** That thou seem not unto men to fast, but unto thy Father which is in secret: and thy Father which seeth in secret, will reward thee openly. **19** [l]Lay not up treasures for yourselves upon the earth, where the moth and canker corrupt, and where thieves dig through and steal. **20** [5]But lay up treasures for yourselves in heaven, where neither the moth nor canker corrupteth, and where thieves neither dig through nor steal. **21** For where your treasure is, there will your heart be also. **22** [m,6]The light of the body is the eye: if then thine [n]eye be single, thy whole body shall be light. **23** But if thine eye be wicked, then all thy body shall be dark. Wherefore if the light that is in thee, be darkness, how great is that darkness? **24** [o,7]No man can serve [p]two masters: for either he shall hate the one, and love the other, or else he shall lean to the one, and despise the other. Ye cannot serve God and [q]riches. **25** [r,8]Therefore I say unto you, be not careful for your life, what ye shall eat, or what ye shall drink: nor yet for your body, what ye shall put on. Is not the life more worth than meat? and the body than raiment? **26** Behold the fowls of the [s]heaven: for they sow not, neither reap, nor carry into the barns, yet your heavenly Father feedeth them. Are ye not much better than they? **27** Which of you by [t]taking care is able to add one cubit unto his stature? **28** And why care ye for raiment? Learn how the Lilies of the field do grow: they [u]are not wearied, neither spin: **29** Yet I say unto you, that even Solomon in all his glory was not arrayed like one of these. **30** Wherefore if God so clothe the grass of the field which is today, and tomorrow is cast into the oven, shall he not do much more unto you, O ye of little faith? **31** Therefore take no thought, saying, What shall we eat? or what shall we drink? or wherewith shall we be clothed? **32** (For after all these things seek the Gentiles) for your heavenly Father knoweth that ye have need of all these things. **33** But seek ye first the kingdom of God, and his righteousness, and all these things shall be ministered unto you. **34** Care not then for the morrow, for the morrow shall care for itself: the day hath enough with his own grief.

7

1 We may not give judgment of our neighbors, 6 Nor cast that which is holy unto dogs. 13 The broad and strait way. 15 False prophets. 18 The tree and fruit. 24 The house built on a rock, 26 and on the sand.

1 Judge [a]not, that ye be not judged. **2** For with what [1]judgment ye judge, ye shall be judged, and with what measure ye mete, it shall be [2]measured unto you again. **3** And why seest thou the mote, that is in thy brother's eye, and perceivest not the beam that is in thine own eye? **4** [3]Or how sayest thou to thy brother, Suffer me to cast out the mote out of thine eye, and behold, a beam is in thine own eye? **5** Hypocrite, first cast out that beam out of thine own eye, and then shalt thou see clearly to cast out the mote out of thy brother's eye. **6** [b]Give ye not that which is holy to dogs, neither cast ye your [c]pearls before swine, lest they tread them under their feet, and turning again, all to rent you. **7** [d,4]Ask, and it shall be given you: seek, and ye shall find: knock, and it shall be opened unto you. **8** For whosoever asketh, receiveth: and he that seeketh, findeth: and to him that knocketh, it shall be opened. **9** For what man is there among you, which if his son ask him bread, would give him a stone? **10** Or if he ask fish, will he give him a serpent? **11** If ye then, which are evil, can give to your children good gifts, how much more shall your Father which is in heaven, give good things to them that ask him? **12** [e,5]Therefore whatsoever ye would that men should do to you: even so do ye to them: for this is the [f]Law and the Prophets. **13** [g,6]Enter in at the strait gate: for it is the wide gate, and broad way that leadeth to destruction: and many there be which go in thereat. **14** Because [h]the gate is strait, and the way narrow that leadeth unto life, and few there be that find it. **15** [i]Beware of false prophets, which come to you in sheep's clothing, but inwardly they are ravening wolves. **16** Ye shall know them by their fruits. [7]Do men gather grapes of thorns? or figs of thistles? **17** So every good tree bringeth forth good fruit, and a corrupt tree bringeth forth evil fruit. **18** A good tree cannot bring forth evil fruit, neither can a corrupt tree bring forth good fruit. **19** [8]Every tree that bringeth not forth good fruit, is hewn down, and cast into the fire. **20** Therefore by their fruits ye shall know them. **21** [j]Not everyone that saith unto me, Lord, Lord, shall enter into the kingdom of heaven, [9]but he that doeth my Father's will which is in heaven. **22** [10]Many will say to me in that day, Lord, Lord, have we not by thy [k]Name prophesied, and by thy name cast out devils? and by thy name done many [l]great works? **23** And then will I profess to them, [m,11]I never knew you, [12]depart from me [n]ye that work iniquity. **24** [o]Whosoever then heareth of me these words, [13]and doeth the same, I will liken him to a wise man, which hath builded his house on a rock: **25** And the rain fell, and the floods came, and the winds blew, and beat upon that house, and it fell not: for it was grounded on a rock, **26** But whosoever heareth these my words, and doeth them not, shall be likened unto a foolish man, which hath builded his house upon the sand: **27** And the rain fell, and the floods came, and the winds blew, and beat upon that house, and it fell, and the fall thereof was great. **28** [14]And it came to pass, when Jesus had ended these words,

---

MATT. 6

- **a.** Matt. 6:1 Ambition maketh alms vain.
- **b.** Matt. 6:1 This word, Reward, is always taken in the Scriptures for a free recompense, and therefore the schoolmen do fondly set it to be answerable to a deserving, which they call merit.
- **c.** Matt. 6:2 Counterfeits, for Hypocrites were players that played a part in a play.
- **d.** Matt. 6:5 He reprehendeth two foul faults in prayer, ambition, and vain babbling.
- **e.** Matt. 6:7 Long prayers are not condemned, but vain needless, and superstitious.
- **f.** Matt. 6:9 A true sum and form of all Christian prayers.
- **g.** Matt. 6:11 That, that is meet for our nature for our daily food, or such, as may suffice our nature and complexion.
- **h.** Matt. 6:13 From the Devil, or from all adversity.
- **i.** Matt. 6:14 They that forgive wrongs, to them sins are forgiven, but revenge is prepared for them that revenge.
- **j.** Matt. 6:16 Against such as hunt after a name of holiness, by fasting.
- **k.** Matt. 6:16 They suffer not their first hue to be seen, that is to say, they mar the natural color of their faces, that they may seem lean and palefaced.
- **l.** Matt. 6:19 Those men's labors are shown to be vain which pass not for the assured treasure of everlasting life, but spend their lives in scraping together frail and vain riches.
- **m.** Matt. 6:22 Men do maliciously and wickedly put out even the little light of nature that is in them.
- **n.** Matt. 6:22 The judgment of the mind: that as the body is with the eyes, so our whole life may be ruled with right reason, that is to say, with the Spirit of God wherewith we are lightened.
- **o.** Matt. 6:24 God will be worshipped of the whole man.
- **p.** Matt. 6:24 Which be at jar together, for if two agree, they are as one.
- **q.** Matt. 6:24 This word is a Syrian word, and signifieth all things that belong to money.
- **r.** Matt. 6:25 The froward carking carefulness for things of this life is corrected in the children of God by an earnest thinking upon the providence of God.
- **s.** Matt. 6:26 Of the air, or that live in the air: for in all tongues almost this word Heaven is taken for the air.
- **t.** Matt. 6:27 He speaketh of care which is joined with thought of mind, and hath for the most part difficult yoke with it.
- **u.** Matt. 6:28 By labor.

MATT. 6

1. Rom. 2:8
2. Luke 11:2
3. Matt. 13:19
4. Mark 11:25
5. Luke 12:33 / 1Tim 6:19
6. Luke 11:34
7. Luke 16:13
8. Luke 12:22 /Phil. 4:6 /1Tim. 6:8 / 1Pet. 5:7 / Ps. 55:23

MATT. 7

- **a.** Matt. 7:1 We ought to find fault one with another, but we must beware we do it not without cause, or to seem holier than they, or in hatred of them.
- **b.** Matt. 7:6 The stiffnecked and stubborn enemies of the Gospel are unworthy to have it preached unto them.
- **c.** Matt. 7:6 A pearl hath his name among the Grecians, for the orient brightness that is in it: and a pearl was in ancient time in great estimation among the Latins: for a pearl that Cleopatra had, was valued at two hundred and fifty thousand crowns, and the word is now borrowed from that, to signify the most precious heavenly doctrine.
- **d.** Matt. 7:7 Prayers are a sure refuge in all miseries.
- **e.** Matt. 7:12 A rehearsal of the meaning of the second table.
- **f.** Matt. 7:12 That is to say, the doctrine of the Law and Prophets.
- **g.** Matt. 7:13 Example of life must not be taken from a multitude.
- **h.** Matt. 7:14 The way is straight and narrow we must pass through this rough way, and suffer and endure, and be thronged, and to enter into life.
- **i.** Matt. 7:15 False teachers must be taken heed of, and they are known by false doctrine and evil living.
- **j.** Matt. 7:21 Even the best gifts that are, are nothing without godliness.
- **k.** Matt. 7:22 By Name here, is meant that mighty working power of God, which every man witnesseth that calleth upon him.
- **l.** Matt. 7:22 Properly powers: Now these excellent works wrought are called Powers, by occasion of these things which they bring to pass, for by them we understand, how mighty the power of God is.
- **m.** Matt. 7:23 This is not of ignorance, but because he will cast them away.
- **n.** Matt. 7:23 You that are given to all kind of wickedness, and seem to make an art of sin.
- **o.** Matt. 7:24 True godliness resteth only upon Christ, and therefore always remaineth invincible.

MATT. 7

1. Luke 6:37-38 / Rom. 2:1 / 1Cor. 4:3
2. Mark 4:24 /Luke 6:38
3. Luke 6:41
4. Matt. 21:22 /Mark 11:24 /Luke 11:9 / John 24:13 / John 16:23 / James 1:5
5. Luke 6:31 / Job 4:16
6. Luke 13:14
7. Luke 6:44
8. Matt. 3:10
9. Rom. 2:13
10. James 1:22
11. Luke 13:27
12. Ps. 6:8
13. Luke 6:47-48
14. Mark 4:22 /Luke 4:32

the people were astonished at his doctrine. **29** For he taught them as one having authority, and not as the Scribes.

8

1 The Leper cleansed. 5 The Centurion's faith. 11 The calling of the Gentiles, 12 and casting out of the Jews. 14 Peter's mother-in-law healed. 19 A Scribe desirous to follow Christ. 23 The tempest on the sea. 28 Two possessed with devils cured. 32 The devils go into swine.

1 Now when he was come down from the mountain, great multitudes followed him. **2** [a,1]And lo, there came a Leper and worshipped him, saying, Master, if thou wilt, thou canst make me clean. **3** And Jesus putting forth his hand, touched him, saying, I will, be thou clean: and immediately his leprosy was cleansed. **4** Then Jesus said unto him, See thou tell no man, but go, and show thyself unto the Priest, and offer the gift that [2]Moses commanded, for a witness to them. **5** [b,3]When Jesus was entered into Capernaum, there came unto him a Centurion, beseeching him, **6** And said, Master, my servant lieth sick at home of the palsy, and is grievously pained. **7** And Jesus said unto him, I will come and heal him. **8** But the Centurion answered, saying, Master, I am not worthy that thou shouldest come under my roof: but speak the word only, and my servant shall be healed. **9** For I am a man also under the authority of another, and have soldiers under me: and I say to one, Go, and he goeth: and to another, Come, and he cometh: and to my servant, Do this, and he doeth it. **10** When Jesus heard that, he marveled, and said to them that followed him, Verily, I say unto you, I have not found so great faith, even in Israel. **11** But I say unto you, that many shall come from the East and West, and shall [c]sit down with Abraham, and Isaac, and Jacob, in the kingdom of heaven. **12** And the children of the kingdom shall be cast out into [d]utter [4]darkness: there shall be weeping and gnashing of teeth. **13** Then Jesus said unto the Centurion, Go thy way, and as thou hast believed, so be it unto thee. And his servant was healed the same hour. **14** [e,5]And when Jesus came to Peter's house, he saw his wife's mother laid down, and sick of a fever. **15** And he touched her hand, and the fever left her: so she arose, and ministered unto them. **16** [6]When the Even was come, they brought unto him many that were possessed with devils: and he cast out the spirits with his word, and healed [f]all that were sick, **17** That it might be fulfilled, which was spoken by [7]Isaiah the Prophet, saying, He took our infirmities, and bare our sicknesses. **18** [8]And when Jesus saw great multitudes of people about him, he commanded them to go [g]over the water. **19** [h]Then came there a certain Scribe, and said unto him, Master, I will follow thee whithersoever thou goest. **20** But Jesus said unto him, The foxes have holes, and the birds of the heaven have [i]nests, but the Son of man hath not whereon to rest his head. **21** [j]And another of his disciples said unto him, Master, suffer me first to go, and bury my father. **22** But Jesus said unto him, Follow me, and let the dead bury the dead. **23** [k,9]And when he was entered into the ship, his disciples followed him. **24** And behold, there arose a great tempest in the sea, so that the ship was covered with waves: but he was asleep. **25** Then his disciples came, and awoke him, saying, Master, save us: we perish. **26** And he said unto them, Why are ye fearful, O ye of little faith? Then he arose, and rebuked the winds and the sea: and so there was a great calm. **27** And the men marveled, saying, What man is this, that both the winds and the sea obey him? **28** [l,10]And when he was come to the other side into the country of the Gergesenes, there met him two possessed with devils which came out of the graves very fierce, so that no man might go by that way. **29** And behold, they cried out, saying, Jesus the son of God, what have we to do with thee? Art thou come hither to torment us before the time? **30** Now there was [m]afar off from them, a great herd of swine feeding. **31** And the devils besought him, saying, If thou cast us out, suffer us to go into the herd of swine. **32** And he said unto them, Go. So they went out and departed into the herd of swine: and behold, the whole herd of swine ran headlong into the sea, and died in the water. **33** Then the herdmen fled: and when they were come into the city, they told all things, and what was become of them that were possessed with the devils, **34** And behold, all the city came out to meet Jesus: and when they saw him, they besought him to [n]depart out of their coasts.

9

1 One sick of the palsy, is healed. 5 Remission of sins. 9 Matthew called. 10 Sinners. 17 New wine. 18 The ruler's daughter raised. 20 A woman healed of a bloody issue. 28 Two blind men by faith receive sight. 32 A dumb man possessed is healed. 37 The harvest and workmen.

1 Then he [a]entered into a ship, and passed over, and came into his [b]own city. **2** And [1]lo, they brought to him a man sick of the palsy laid on a bed. And Jesus [c]seeing their faith, said to the sick of the palsy, Son be of good comfort: thy sins are forgiven thee. **3** And behold, certain of the Scribes said with themselves, This man [d]blasphemeth. **4** But when Jesus saw their thoughts, he said, Wherefore think ye evil things in your hearts? **5** For whether is it easier to say, Thy sins are forgiven thee, or to say, Arise, and walk? **6** And that ye may know that the Son of man hath authority in earth to forgive sins (then said he unto the sick of the palsy,) Arise, take up thy bed, and go to thine house. **7** And he arose, and departed to his own house. **8** So when the multitude saw it, they marveled, and glorified God, which had given such authority to men. **9** [e,2]And as Jesus passed forth from thence, he saw a man sitting at the [f]custom, named Matthew, and said to him, Follow me. And he arose, and followed him. **10** And it came to pass, as Jesus sat at meat in his house, behold, many Publicans and [g]sinners that came thither, sat down at the table with Jesus and his disciples. **11** And when the Pharisees saw that, they said to his disciples, Why eateth your Master with Publicans and sinners? **12** Now when Jesus heard it, he said unto them, The whole need not the Physician, but they that are sick. **13** But go ye and learn what this is, [3]I will have mercy, and not sacrifice: for I am not come to call the righteous, but the sinners to repentance. **14** [h,5]Then came the disciples of John to him, saying, Why do we and the Pharisees fast oft, and thy disciples fast not? **15** And Jesus said unto them, Can the [i]children of the marriage chamber mourn as long as the bridegroom is with them? But the days will come, when the bridegroom shall be taken from them, and then shall they fast. **16** Moreover, no man pieceth an old garment with a piece of [j]new cloth: for that that should fill it up, taketh away from the garment, and the breach is worse. **17** Neither do they put new wine into old vessels: for then the vessels would break, and the wine would be spilt, and the vessels would perish: but they put new wine into new vessels, and so are both preserved. **18** [k,6]While he thus spake unto them, behold, there came a certain ruler, and worshipped him, saying, My daughter is now deceased: but come and lay thine hand on her, and she shall live. **19** And Jesus arose and followed him with his disciples. **20** (And behold, a woman which was diseased with an issue of blood twelve years, came behind him, and touched the hem of his garment. **21** For she said in herself, If I may touch but his garment only, I shall be whole. **22** Then Jesus turned him about, and seeing her, did say, Daughter, be of good comfort: thy faith hath made thee whole. And the woman was made whole at that same moment.) **23** [l] Now when Jesus came into the ruler's house, and saw the [m]minstrels and the multitude making noise, **24** He said unto them, Get you hence: for the maid is not dead, but sleepeth. And they laughed him to scorn. **25** And when the multitude were put forth, he went in and took her by the hand, and the maid arose. **26** And this bruit went throughout all that land. **27** [n]And as Jesus departed thence, two blind men followed him, crying, and saying, O son of David, have mercy upon us. **28** And when he was come into the house, the blind came to him, and Jesus said unto them, Believe ye that I am able to do this? And they said unto him, Yea, Lord. **29** Then touched he their eyes, saying, According to your faith be it unto you. **30** And their eyes were opened, and Jesus gave them great charge, saying, See that no man know it. **31** But when they were departed, they spread abroad his fame throughout all that land. **32** [o,7]And as they went

---

MATT. 8

- **a.** Matt. 8:2 Christ in healing the leprous with the touching of his hand, showeth that he abhorreth no sinners that come unto him, be they never so unclean.
- **b.** Matt. 8:5 Christ by setting before them the example of the uncircumcised Centurion, and yet of an excellent faith, provoketh the Jews to emulation, and together forewarneth them of their casting off, and the calling of the Gentiles.
- **c.** Matt. 8:11 A Metaphor taken of banquets, for they that sit down together are fellows in the banquet.
- **d.** Matt. 8:12 Which are without the kingdom: For in the kingdom is light, and without the kingdom darkness.
- **e.** Matt. 8:14 Christ, in healing divers diseases, showeth that he was sent of his Father, that in him only we should seek remedy in all our miseries.
- **f.** Matt. 8:16 Of all sorts.
- **g.** Matt. 8:18 For Capernaum was situated upon the lake of Tiberias.
- **h.** Matt. 8:19 The true disciples of Christ must prepare themselves to all kind of miseries.
- **i.** Matt. 8:20 Word for word, shades made with boughs.
- **j.** Matt. 8:21 When God requireth our labor, we must leave off all our duty to men.
- **k.** Matt. 8:23 Although Christ seemeth oftentimes to neglect his, even in most extreme danger, yet in time convenient he assuageth all tempests, and bringeth them to the haven.
- **l.** Matt. 8:28 Christ came to deliver me from the miserable thraldom of Satan: but the world had rather lack Christ, than the vilest and least of their commodities.
- **m.** Matt. 8:30 Of an hill, as Mark and Luke witness: Now Gadara as Josephus recordeth, book 17 chapter 13, lived after the order of the Grecians, and therefore we may not marvel if there were swine there.
- **n.** Matt. 8:34 Where men live as swine, there doth not Christ tarry, but devils.

MATT. 8

- **1.** Mark 2:40 / Luke 5:12
- **2.** Lev. 14:3-4
- **3.** Luke 7:1
- **4.** Matt. 22:13
- **5.** Mark 1:29 / Luke 4:38
- **6.** Mark 1:32 / Luke 4:40
- **7.** Isa. 53:4/ 1Pet. 2:24
- **8.** Luke 9:57-58
- **9.** Mark 4:37 / Luke 8:23
- **10.** Mark 5:1-2 / Luke 26:27

MATT. 9

- **a.** Matt. 9:1 Sins are the causes of our afflictions, and Christ only forgiveth them if we believe.
- **b.** Matt. 9:1 Into Capernaum, for as Theophylact saith, Bethlehem brought him forth, Nazareth brought him up, and Capernaum was his dwelling place.
- **c.** Matt. 9:2 Knowing by a manifest sign.
- **d.** Matt. 9:3 To blaspheme, signifieth amongst the divines to speak wickedly: and amongst the more eloquent Grecians, to slander.
- **e.** Matt. 9:9 Christ calleth the humble sinners unto him, but he condemneth the proud hypocrites.
- **f.** Matt. 9:9 At the customer's table, where it was received.
- **g.** Matt. 9:10 The customers fellows which were placed by the Romans, after that Judea was brought into the form of a province, to gather the customs, and therefore of the rest of the Jews, they were called sinners, that is to say very vile men.
- **h.** Matt. 9:14 Against naughty emulation in matters indifferent.
- **i.** Matt. 9:15 An Hebrew kind of speech, for they that are admitted into a marriage chamber are as the nearest about the bridegroom.
- **j.** Matt. 9:16 Raw, which was never put to the fuller.
- **k.** Matt. 9:18 There is no evil so old and incurable, which Christ cannot heal by and by, if he be touched with true faith, but lightly as it were with the hand.
- **l.** Matt. 9:23 Even death itself giveth place to the power of Christ.
- **m.** Matt. 9:23 It appeareth that they used minstrels at their mournings.
- **n.** Matt. 9:27 By healing these two blind, Christ showeth that he is the light of the world.
- **o.** Matt. 9:32 An example of that power that Christ hath over the devil.

out, behold, they brought to him a dumb man possessed with a devil. **33** And
when the devil was cast out, the dumb spake: then the multitude marveled, saying,
The like was never seen in Israel. **34** But the Pharisees said, [8]He casteth out de-
vils, through the prince of devils. **35** And [9]Jesus went about all cities and towns,
teaching in their Synagogues, and preaching the Gospel of the kingdom, and hea-
ling every sickness and every disease among the people. **36** [p]But [10]when he saw
the multitude, he had compassion upon them, because they were dispersed, and
scattered abroad, as sheep having no shepherd. **37** Then said he to his disciples,
[11]Surely the harvest is great, but the laborers are few. **38** Wherefore pray the
Lord of the harvest, that he would [q]send forth laborers into his harvest.

10

1 The gift of healing given to the Apostles. 5 They are sent to preach the Gospel. 13 Peace. 14 Shaking off the dust. 18 Affliction. 22 Continuance unto the end. 23 Fleeing from persecution. 28 Fear. 29 Two sparrows. 30 Hairs of our head. 32 To acknowledge Christ. 34 Peace and the sword. 35 Variance. 37 Love of parents. 38 The cross. 39 To lose the life. 40 To receive a Preacher.

1 And [a,1]he called his twelve disciples unto him, and gave them power
against unclean spirits, to cast them out, and to heal every sickness, and every
disease. **2** Now the names of the twelve Apostles are these. The [b]first is Simon
called Peter, and Andrew his brother, James the son of Zebedee, and John his
brother, **3** Philip and Bartholomew: Thomas, and Matthew that Publican: James
the son of Alphaeus, and Lebbaeus whose surname was Thaddaeus: **4** Simon the
Canaanite, and Judas [c]Iscariot, who also betrayed him. **5** These twelve did Jesus
send forth, and commanded them, saying, Go not into the way of the Gentiles,
and into the cities of the Samaritans enter ye not: **6** But go rather [2]to the lost she-
ep of the house of Israel. **7** [d,3]And as ye go preach, saying, The kingdom of hea-
ven is at hand. **8** [e]Heal the sick: cleanse the lepers: raise up the dead: cast out the
devils. Freely ye have received, freely give. **9** [f,4]Possess [g]not gold, nor silver, nor
money in your girdles, **10** Nor a scrip for the journey, neither two coats, neither
shoes, nor a staff: [5]for the workman is worthy of his [h]meat. **11** [i]And into [6]what-
soever city or town ye shall come, inquire who is worthy in it, and there abide till
ye go thence. **12** And when ye come into an house, salute the same. **13** And if
the house be worthy, let your [j]peace come upon it: but if it be not worthy, let your
peace return to you. **14** [7]And whosoever shall not receive you, nor hear your
words, when ye depart out of that house, or that city, [8]shake off the dust of your
feet. **15** Truly I say unto you, it shall be easier for them of the land of Sodom and
Gomorrah in the day of judgment, than for that city. **16** [k,9]Behold, I send you as
[l]sheep in the midst of the wolves: be ye therefore wise as serpents, and [m]innocent
as doves. **17** But beware of [n]men, for they will deliver you up to the Councils,
and will scourge you in their Synagogues. **18** And ye shall be brought to the go-
vernors and kings for my sake, in witness to them, and to the Gentiles. **19** [10]But
when they deliver you up, take no thought how or what ye shall speak: for it shall
be given you in that hour, what ye shall say. **20** For it is not ye that speak, but the
spirit of your Father which speaketh in you. **21** And the [11]brother shall betray
the brother to death, and the father the son, and the children shall rise against their
parents, and shall cause them to die. **22** And ye shall be hated of all men for my
Name: [12]but he that endureth to the end, he shall be saved. **23** And when they
persecute you in this city, flee into another: for verily I say unto you, ye shall not
[o]go over all the cities of Israel, till the Son of man be come. **24** [13]The disciple is
not above his master, nor the servant above his Lord. **25** It is enough for the di-
sciple to be as his master is, and the servant as his Lord. [14]If they have called the ma-
ster of the house [p]Beelzebub, how much more them of his household? **26** [q]Fear
them not therefore: [15]for there is nothing covered, that shall not be disclosed, nor
hid, that shall not be known. **27** What I tell you in darkness, that speak ye in
light: and what ye hear in the ear, that preach ye on the [r]houses. **28** And [s]fear ye
not them which kill the body, but are not able to kill the soul: but rather fear him,
which is able to destroy both soul and body in hell. **29** Are not two sparrows
sold for a [t]farthing, and one of them shall not fall on the ground without your Fa-
ther? **30** [16]Yea, and all the hairs of your head are numbered. **31** Fear ye not
therefore, ye are of more value than many sparrows. **32** [u,17]Whosoever there-
fore shall confess me before men, him will I confess also before my Father which
is in heaven. **33** But whosoever shall deny me before men, him will I also deny
before my Father which is in heaven. **34** [v,18]Think not that I am come to send
peace into the earth, but the sword. **35** For I am come to set a man at variance
against his father, and the daughter against her mother, and the daughter-in-law
against her mother-in-law. **36** [19]And a man's enemies shall be they of his own
household. **37** [w,20]He that loveth father or mother more than me, is not wor-
thy of me. And he that loveth son, or daughter more than me, is not worthy of
me. **38** [21]And he that taketh not his cross, and followeth after me, is not wor-
thy of me. **39** [22]He that will find [x]his life, shall lose it: and he that loseth his
life for my sake, shall find it. **40** [y,23]He that receiveth you, receiveth me: and he
that receiveth me, receiveth him that sent me. **41** [z]He that receiveth a Prophet
in [aa]the name of a Prophet, shall receive a Prophet's reward: and he that receiveth
a righteous man, in the name of a righteous man, shall receive the reward of a ri-
ghteous man. **42** [24]And whosoever shall give unto one of these [ab]little ones to
drink a cup of cold water only, in the name of a disciple, verily I say unto you, he
shall not lose his reward.

11

2 John sendeth his disciples to Christ. 7 Christ's testimony of John. 13 The Law and the Prophets. 15 Christ and John. 21 Chorazin, Bethsaida. 25 The Gospel revealed to children. 28 They that are weary and laden.

1 And [a]it came to pass that when Jesus had made an end of [b]comman-
ding his twelve disciples, he departed thence to teach and to preach in [c]their ci-
ties. **2** [1]And when John heard in the prison the works of Christ, he sent two of
his disciples, and said unto him, **3** Art thou he that should come, or shall we
look for another? **4** And Jesus answering, said unto them, Go, and show John,
what things ye hear and see. **5** The blind receive sight, and the halt do walk: the
lepers are cleansed, and the deaf hear, the dead are raised up, [2]and the poor recei-
ve the Gospel. **6** And blessed is he that shall not be offended in me. **7** [d]And
as they departed, Jesus began to speak unto the multitude of John, What went ye
out into the wilderness to see? a reed shaken with the wind? **8** But what went ye
out to see? A man clothed in soft raiment? Behold they that wear soft clothing, are
in kings' houses. **9** But what went ye out to see? A Prophet? Yea, I say unto you,
and more than a Prophet. **10** For this is he of whom it is written, [3]Behold, I send
my messenger before thy face which shall prepare thy way before thee. **11** Ve-
rily I say unto you, Among them which are begotten of women, arose there not
a greater than John Baptist, notwithstanding, he that is the least in the [e]kingdom

---

p. Matt. 9:36 Although the ordinary pastors cease, yet Christ hath not cast off the care of his Church.

q. Matt. 9:38 Word for word, cast them out: for men are very slow in so holy a work.

MATT. 9

1. Mark 2:3 / Luke 5:18
2. Mark 2:14 /Luke 5:27
3. Hos. 6:6 / Matt. 12:7
4. 1Tim. 1:15
5. Mark 2:18 / Luke 5:33
6. Mark 5:22 / Luke 8:41
7. Luke 11:14
8. Matt. 12:24 /Mark 3:22 / Luke 11:15
9. Mark 6:34
10. Luke 10:2 / John 4:35-36

MATT. 10

a. Matt. 10:1 The Apostles are sent to preach the Gospel in Israel.

b. Matt. 10:2 Theophylact saith that Peter and Andrew are called the first, because they were first called.

c. Matt. 10:4 A man of Kerioth. Now Kerioth was in the tribe of Judah, Josh. 15:25.

d. Matt. 10:7 The sum of the Gospel: or preaching of the Apostles.

e. Matt. 10:8 Miracles are dependences of the word.

f. Matt. 10:9 The ministers of the word must cast away all cares that might hinder them the least wise that might be.

g. Matt. 10:9 For this journey, to wit, both that nothing might hinder them, and also that they might feel some taste of God's providence: for at their return back, the Lord asketh of them, whether they lacked anything by the way, Luke 22:35.

h. Matt. 10:10 God will provide you meat.

i. Matt. 10:11 Happy are they that receive the preaching of the Gospel: and unhappy are they, that refuse it.

j. Matt. 10:13 It is manner of speech taken from the Hebrews, whereby they meant all kind of happiness.

k. Matt. 10:16 Christ showeth how the ministers must behave themselves under the cross.

l. Matt. 10:16 You shall be in great dangers.

m. Matt. 10:16 You shall not so much as revenge an injury: and by the mixing of these beasts' natures together, he will not have our wisdom to be malicious, nor our simplicity mad, but a certain form of good nature as exquisitely framed of both of them, as may be.

n. Matt. 10:17 For in the cause of religion men are wolves one to another.

o. Matt. 10:23 Bring to an end, that is, you shall not have gone through all the cities of Israel, and preached in them.

p. Matt. 10:25 It was the idol of the Acronites, which we call the god of flies.

q. Matt. 10:26 Truth shall not always be hid.

r. Matt. 10:27 Openly, and in the highest places. For the tops of their houses were so made, that they might walk upon them, Acts 10:9.

s. Matt. 10:28 Though tyrants be never so raging and cruel, yet we may not fear them.

t. Matt. 10:29 The fourth part of an ounce.

u. Matt. 10:32 The necessity and reward of open confessing Christ.

v. Matt. 10:34 Civil dissentions follow the preaching of the Gospel.

w. Matt. 10:37 Nothing without exception is to be preferred before our duty to God.

x. Matt. 10:39 They are said to find their life, which deliver it out of danger: and this is spoken after the opinion of the people which think them clean lost that die, because they think not of the life to come.

y. Matt. 10:40 God is both author and revenger of his holy ministry.

z. Matt. 10:41 We shall lose nothing that we bestow upon Christ.

aa. Matt. 10:41 As a Prophet.

ab. Matt. 10:42 Which in the sight of the world are vile and abject.

MATT. 10

1. Mark 3:13-15 /Luke 9:1-2
2. Acts 13:46
3. Luke 10:9-11
4. Mark 6:8-9 /Luke 9:3 / Luke 22:35
5. 1Tim. 5:15
6. Luke 10:8
7. Mark 6:11 / Luke 9:5
8. Acts 13:51
9. Luke 10:3
10. Mark 13:11 /Luke 12:11
11. Luke 21:16
12. Mark 13:13
13. Luke 6:40 / John 13:16 / John 15:20
14. Matt. 12:24
15. Mark 4:22 / Luke 8:17 / Luke 12:1
16. 1Sam. 14:45 / 2Sam. 14:11 / Acts 27:34
17. Mark 8:38 / Luke 9:26 / Luke 12:8 / 2Tim. 2:12
18. Luke 12:51
19. Mic. 7:6
20. Luke 14:26
21. Matt. 16:24 / Mark 8:34 / Luke 9:25 / Luke 14:27
22. John 14:25
23. Luke 10:16 /John 13:20
24. Mark 9:41

MATT. 11

a. Matt. 11:1 Christ showeth by his works, that he is the promised Messiah.

b. Matt. 11:1 Of instructing them with precepts.

c. Matt. 11:1 The disciples' cities, that is to say, in Galilee, where many of them were born, Acts 2:7.

d. Matt. 11:7 What agreement, and what difference is betwixt the ministry of the Prophets, the preaching of John, and the full light of the Gospel, which Christ hath brought.

e. Matt. 11:11 In the new state of the Church where the true glory of God shineth: the persons are not compared together, but the kinds of doctrines, the preaching of John with the law and the Prophets, and again, the most clear preaching of the Gospel with John's.

of heaven, is greater than he. **12** And from [4]the time of John Baptist hitherto, the kingdom of God suffereth violence, and the violent take it by force. **13** For all the Prophets and the Law [f]prophesied unto John. **14** And if ye will receive it, this is [5]that Elijah, which was to come. **15** He that hath ears to hear let him hear. **16** [g,6]But whereunto shall I liken this generation? [h]It is like unto little children which sit in the markets, and call unto their fellows, **17** And say, We have piped unto you, and ye have not danced, we have mourned unto you, and ye have not lamented. **18** For John came neither eating nor drinking, and they say, He hath a devil. **19** The Son of men came eating and drinking, and they say, Behold a glutton and a drinker of wine, a friend unto Publicans and sinners: [i]but [j]wisdom is justified of her children. **20** [k,7]Then began he to upbraid the cities, wherein most of his great works were done, because they repented not. **21** Woe be to thee Chorazin: Woe be to thee Bethsaida: for if the great works which were done in you, had been done in Tyre and Sidon, they had repented long ago in sackcloth and ashes. **22** But I say to you, It shall be easier for Tyre and Sidon at the day of judgment, than for you. **23** And thou Capernaum, which art lifted up unto heaven, shalt be brought down to hell: for if the great works, which have been done in thee, had been done among them of Sodom, they had remained to this day. **24** But I say unto you, that it shall be easier for them of the land of Sodom in the day of judgment, than for thee. **25** [8]At that time Jesus answered and said, I give thee thanks, O Father, Lord of heaven and earth, because thou hast hid these things from the wise, and men of understanding, and hast [l]opened them unto babes. **26** It is [m]so, O Father, because thy [n]good pleasure was such. **27** [o,9]All things are given unto me of my Father: and [10]no man knoweth the Son, but the Father: neither knoweth any man the Father, but the Son, and he to whom the Son will reveal him. **28** Come unto me, all ye that are weary and laden, and I will ease you. **29** Take my yoke on you, and learn of me that I am meek and lowly in heart: and ye shall find [11]rest unto your souls. **30** [12]For my yoke is [p]easy, and my burden light.

12

1 The disciples pluck the ears of corn. 6 Mercy, sacrifice. 10 The withered hand is healed. 12 We must do good on the Sabbath. 22 The possessed is holpen. 25 A kingdom divided. 31 Sin, blasphemy. 33 The good or evil tree. 34 Vipers. 38 The Ninevites. 42 The Queen of Sheba. 48 The true mother and brethren of Christ.

1 At [a,1]that time Jesus went on a Sabbath day through the corn, and his disciples were an hungered, and began to pluck the ears of corn and to eat. **2** And when the Pharisees saw it, they said unto him, Behold, thy disciples do [2]that which is not lawful to do upon the Sabbath. **3** But he said unto them, [3]Have ye not read what David did when he was an hungered, and they that were with him? **4** How he went into the house of God, and did eat the [b]showbread, which was not lawful for him to eat, neither for them which were with him, but only for the [4]Priests? **5** Or have ye not read in the Law, how that on the Sabbath days the Priests in the Temple [c,5]break the Sabbath, and are blameless? **6** But I say unto you, that here is one greater than the Temple. **7** Wherefore if ye knew what this is, [6]I will have mercy and not sacrifice, ye would not have condemned the innocents. **8** For the son of man is Lord, even of the Sabbath. **9** [d,7]And he departed thence, and went into their Synagogue: **10** And behold, there was a man which had his hand dried up. And they asked him, saying, Is it lawful to heal upon a Sabbath day? that they might accuse him. **11** And he said unto them, What man shall there be among you, that hath a sheep, and if it fall on the Sabbath day into a pit, doth not take it and lift it out? **12** How much more then is a man better than a sheep? therefore, it is lawful to do well on a Sabbath day. **13** Then said he to the man, Stretch forth thine hand. And he stretched it forth, and it was made whole as the other. **14** [e]Then the Pharisees went out, and consulted against him, how they might destroy him. **15** But when Jesus knew it, he departed thence, and great multitudes followed him, and he healed them all, **16** And charged them in threatening wise, that they should not make him known, **17** That it might be fulfilled which was spoken by Isaiah the Prophet, saying, **18** [8]Behold my servant whom I have chosen, my beloved in whom my soul delighteth: I will put my Spirit on him, and he shall show [f]judgment to the Gentiles. **19** He shall not strive, nor cry, neither shall any man hear his voice in the streets. **20** A bruised reed shall he not break, and smoking flax shall he not quench, till he [g]bring forth judgment unto victory. **21** And in his Name shall the Gentiles trust. **22** [h,9]Then was brought to him one possessed with a devil, both blind and dumb, and he healed him, so that he which was blind and dumb, both spake and saw, **23** And all the people were amazed, and said, Is not this that son of David? **24** But when the Pharisees heard it, they said, [10]This man casteth the devils no otherwise out but through Beelzebub the prince of devils. **25** [i]But Jesus knew their thoughts, and said to them, Every kingdom divided against itself, is brought to naught, and every city or house divided against itself shall not stand. **26** So if Satan cast out Satan, he is divided against himself: how shall then his kingdom endure? **27** Also if I through Beelzebub cast out devils, by whom do your children cast them out? Therefore they shall be your judges. **28** But if I cast out devils by the Spirit of God, then is the kingdom of God come unto you. **29** Else how can a man enter into a strong man's house and spoil his goods, except he first bind the strong man, and then spoil his house? **30** He that is not with me, is against me: and he that gathereth not with me, scattereth. **31** [11]Wherefore I say unto you, Every sin and blasphemy shall be forgiven unto men: but the blasphemy against the holy Ghost shall not be forgiven unto men. **32** And whosoever shall speak a word against the son of man, it shall be forgiven him: [j]but whosoever shall speak against the holy Ghost, it shall not be forgiven him, neither in this world, nor in the world to come. **33** Either make the tree good, and his fruit good: or else make the tree evil, and his fruit evil: for the tree is known by the fruit. **34** [k]O generations of vipers, how can you speak good things, when ye are evil? For of the [12]abundance of the heart the mouth speaketh. **35** A good man out of the good treasure of his heart bringeth forth good things: and an evil man out of an evil treasure, bringeth forth evil things. **36** But I say unto you, that of every [l]idle word that men shall speak, they shall give account thereof at the day of judgment. **37** For by thy words thou shalt be justified, and by thy words thou shalt be condemned. **38** [m,13]Then answered certain of the Scribes and of the Pharisees, saying, Master, we would see a sign of thee. **39** But he answered and said to them, An evil and [n]adulterous generation seeketh a sign, but no sign shall be given unto it, save that sign of the Prophet Jonah. **40** [14]For as Jonah was three days and three nights in the whale's belly: so shall the son of man be three days and three nights in the heart of the earth. **41** [o]The men of Nineveh shall rise in judgment with this generation, and condemn it: for they [15]repented at the preaching of Jonah: and behold, a greater than Jonah is here. **42** [16]The Queen of the [p]South shall rise in judgment with this generation, and shall condemn it: for she came from the [q]utmost parts of the earth to hear the wisdom of Solomon: and behold, a greater than Solomon is here. **43** [17]Now when the unclean spirit is gone out of a man, he walketh throughout dry places, seeking rest, and findeth none. **44** Then he saith, I will return into mine house from whence I came: and when he is come, he findeth it empty, swept and garnished. **45** Then he goeth, and taketh unto him seven other spirits worse than himself, and they enter in, and dwell there: [18]and the end of that man is worse than the beginning. Even so shall it be with this wicked generation. **46** [r,19]While he yet spake to the multitude, behold, his mother, and his brethren stood without, desiring to speak with him. **47** Then one said unto him, Behold, thy mother and thy brethren stand without, desiring to speak with thee. **48** But he answered, and said to him that told him, Who is my mother, and who are my brethren? **49** [s]And he stretched forth his hand toward

---

f. Matt. 11:13 They prophesied of things to come, which are now present and clearly and plainly seen.
g. Matt. 11:16 There are none more stout and stubborn enemies of the Gospel, than they to whom it ought to be most acceptable.
h. Matt. 11:16 He blameth the frowardness of this age, by a proverb, in that they could be moved neither with rough, nor gentle dealing.
i. Matt. 11:19 That which the most part refuse, the elect and chosen embrace.
j. Matt. 11:19 Wise men do acknowledge the wisdom of the Gospel, when they receive it.
k. Matt. 11:20 The proud reject the Gospel offered unto them, to their great hurt and smart which turneth to the salvation of the simple.
l. Matt. 11:25 Through the ministry of Christ, who only showeth the truth of all things pertaining to God.
m. Matt. 11:26 This word showeth, that he contenteth himself in his father's counsel.
n. Matt. 11:26 God's will is the only rule of righteousness.
o. Matt. 11:27 There is no true knowledge of God, nor quietness of mind, but only in Christ alone.
p. Matt. 11:30 May easily be borne. For his commandments are not grievous, for all that is born of God overcometh the world, 1 John 5:4.

MATT. 11

1. Luke 7:18
2. Isa. 61:1 / Luke 4:18
3. Mal. 3:1 / Luke 7:28
4. Luke 16:16
5. Mal. 4:5
6. Luke 7:31
7. Luke 10:13
8. Luke 10:21
9. John 3:35
10. John 6:46
11. Jer. 6:16
12. 1 John 5:3

MATT. 12

a. Matt. 12:1 Of the true sanctifying of the Sabbath, and the abrogating of it.
b. Matt. 12:4 The Hebrews call it bread of faces, because it stood before the Lord all the weeks upon the golden table appointed to that service, Lev. 24:6.
c. Matt. 12:5 When the Priests do God's service upon the Sabbath day, yet they break not the Law: much less doth the Lord of the Sabbath break the Sabbath.
d. Matt. 12:9 The ceremonies of the Law are not against the love of our neighbor.
e. Matt. 12:14 How far and in what respect we may give place to the unbridled rage of the wicked.
f. Matt. 12:18 By judgment is meant a settled state because Christ was to publish true religion among the Gentiles, and to cast out superstition, which thing wheresoever it is done, the Lord is said to reign and judge there, that is to say, to govern and rule matters.
g. Matt. 12:20 He shall pronounce sentence and judgment, maugre the world and Satan, and show himself conqueror over all his enemies.
h. Matt. 12:22 A truth be it never so manifest, is subject to the slander of the wicked: yet notwithstanding it ought to be avouched stoutly.
i. Matt. 12:25 The kingdom of Christ and the kingdom of the devil cannot consist together.
j. Matt. 12:32 Of blasphemy against the holy Ghost.
k. Matt. 12:34 Hypocrites at the length betray themselves even by their own mouth.
l. Matt. 12:36 Vain and unprofitable trifles which the most part of men spend their lives in.
m. Matt. 12:38 Against froward desires of miracles.
n. Matt. 12:39 Bastard, which fell from Abraham's faith, or forsook the true worship of God.
o. Matt. 12:41 Christ teacheth by the sorrowful example of the Jews, that there are none more miserable than they which put out the light of the Gospel which was kindled in them.
p. Matt. 12:42 He meaneth the Queen of Sheba: whose country is South in respect of the land of Israel, 1 Kings 10.
q. Matt. 12:42 For Sheba is situated in the utmost coast of . . . Arabia at the mouth of the Arabian Sea.
r. Matt. 12:46 Christ teacheth by his own example, how that all things ought to be set apart in respect of God's glory.
s. Matt. 12:49 None are more near unto us, than they that are of the household of faith.

his disciples and said, Behold my mother, and my brethren. **50** For whosoever shall do my Father's will which is in heaven, the same is my brother and sister and mother.

13

1 The parable of the Sower. 11 and 34 Why Jesus spake in parables. 18 The exposition of the parable. 24 The parable of the tares. 31 Of the mustard seed. 33 Of the leaven. 44 Of the hidden treasure. 45 Of the pearl. 47 Of the draw net cast into the sea. 53 Christ is not received of his countrymen the Nazarites.

1 The [1]same day went Jesus out of the house, and sat by the sea side. **2** [a]And great multitudes resorted unto him, so that he went into a ship, and sat down: and the whole multitude stood on the shore. **3** Then he spake many things to them in parables, saying, Behold, a sower went forth to sow. **4** And as he sowed, some fell by the way side, and the fowls came and devoured them up. **5** And some fell upon stony ground, where they had not much earth, and anon they sprung up, because they had no depth of earth. **6** And when the sun was up, they were parched, and for lack of rooting withered away. **7** And some fell among thorns, and the thorns sprung up, and choked them. **8** And some again fell in good ground, and brought forth fruit, one corn an hundredfold, some sixtyfold, and another thirtyfold. **9** He that hath ears to hear, let him hear. **10** Then the disciples came, and said to him, Why speakest thou to them in parables? **11** [b]And he answered and said unto them, Because it is given unto you to know the secrets of the kingdom of heaven, but to them it is not given. **12** [2]For whosoever hath, to him shall be given, and he shall have abundance: but whosoever hath not, from him shall be taken away even that he hath. **13** Therefore speak I to them in parables, because they seeing, do not see: and hearing, they hear not, neither understand. **14** So in them is fulfilled the prophecy of Isaiah, which prophecy saith, [3]By hearing ye shall hear, and shall not understand, and seeing ye shall see, and shall not perceive. **15** For this people's heart is waxed fat, and their ears are dull of hearing, and with their eyes they have winked, lest they should see with their eyes, and hear with their ears, and should understand with their hearts, and should return, that I might heal them. **16** [c]But blessed are your eyes, for they see: and your ears, for they hear. **17** [4]For verily I say unto you, that many Prophets, and righteous men have desired to see those things which ye see, and have not seen them, and to hear those things which ye hear, and have not heard them. **18** [5]Hear ye therefore the parable of the Sower. **19** Whensoever any man heareth the word of that kingdom, and understandeth it not, that evil one cometh, and catcheth away that which was sown in his [d]heart: and this is he which hath received the seed by the way side. **20** And he that received seed in the stony ground, is he which heareth the word, and incontinently with joy receiveth it, **21** Yet hath he no root in himself, and endureth but a season: for as soon as tribulation or persecution cometh because of the word, by and by he is offended. **22** And he that received the seed among thorns, is he that heareth the word: but the care of this world, and the deceitfulness of riches choke the word, and he is made unfruitful. **23** But he that received the seed in the good ground, is he that heareth the word, and understandeth it, which also beareth fruit, and bringeth forth, some an hundredfold, some sixtyfold, and some thirtyfold. **24** [e]Another parable put he forth unto them, saying, The kingdom of heaven is like unto a man which sowed good seed in his field. **25** But while men slept, there came his enemy and sowed tares among the wheat, and went his way. **26** And when the blade was sprung up, and brought forth fruit, then appeared the tares also. **27** Then came the servants of the householder, and said unto him, Master, sowest thou not good seed in thy field? from whence then hath it tares? **28** And he said unto them, Some envious man hath done this. Then the servants said unto him, Wilt thou then that we go and gather them up? **29** But he said, Nay, lest while ye go about to gather the tares, ye pluck up also with them the wheat. **30** Let both grow together until the harvest, and in time of harvest I will say to the reapers, Gather ye first the tares, and bind them in sheaves to burn them: but gather the wheat into my barn. **31** [f,6]Another parable he put forth unto them, saying, The kingdom of heaven is like unto a grain of mustard seed, which a man taketh and soweth in his field: **32** Which indeed is the least of all seeds: but when it is grown, it is the greatest among herbs, and it is a tree, so that the birds of heaven come and build in the branches thereof. **33** [7]Another parable spake he to them, The kingdom of heaven is like unto leaven, which a woman taketh and hideth in three pecks of meal, till all be leavened. **34** [8]All these things spake Jesus unto the multitude in parables, and without parables spake he not unto them, **35** That it might be fulfilled, which was spoken by the Prophet, saying, [9]I will open my mouth in parables, and will utter the things which have been kept secret from the foundation of the world. **36** Then sent Jesus the multitude away, and went into the house. And his disciples came unto him, saying, Declare unto us the parable of the tares of that field. **37** [g]Then answered he, and said to them, He that soweth the good seed, is the son of man, **38** And the field is the world, and the good seed are the children of the kingdom, and the tares are the children of that wicked one. **39** And the enemy that soweth them, is the devil, [10]and the harvest is the end of the world, and the reapers be the Angels. **40** As then the tares are gathered and burned in the fire, so shall it be in the end of this world. **41** The Son of man shall send forth his Angels, and they shall gather out of his kingdom all things that offend, and them which do iniquity, **42** And shall cast them into a furnace of fire. There shall be wailing and gnashing of teeth. **43** [11]Then shall the just men shine as the sun in the kingdom of their father. He that hath ears to hear, let him hear. **44** [h]Again, the kingdom of heaven is like unto a treasure hid in the field, which when a man hath found, he hideth it, and for joy thereof departeth, and selleth all that he hath, and buyeth that field. **45** Again, the kingdom of heaven is like to a merchant man that seeketh good pearls, **46** Who having found a pearl of great price, went and sold all that he had and bought it. **47** [i]Again, the kingdom of heaven is like unto a draw net cast into the sea, that gathereth of all kinds of things. **48** Which, when it is full, men draw to land, and sit and gather the good into vessels, and cast the bad away. **49** So shall it be at the end of the world. The Angels shall go forth, and sever the bad from among the just, **50** And shall cast them into a furnace of fire: there shall be wailing and gnashing of teeth. **51** [j]Jesus said unto them, Understand ye all these things? They said unto him, Yea, Lord. **52** Then said he unto them, Therefore every Scribe which is taught unto the kingdom of heaven, is like unto an householder, which bringeth forth out of his treasure things both new and old. **53** And it came to pass, that when Jesus had ended these parables, he departed thence, **54** [k,12]And came into his own country, and taught them in their Synagogue, so that they were astonied, and said, Whence cometh this wisdom and great works unto this man? **55** Is not this the carpenter's son? Is not his mother called Mary, [13]and his brethren James and Joses, and Simon, and Judas? **56** And are not his sisters all with us? Whence then hath he all these things? **57** And they were offended with him. Then Jesus said to them, [14]A Prophet is not without honor, save in his own country, and in his own house. **58** And he did not many great works there, for their unbelief's sake.

14

1 Herod's judgment of Christ. 3 Wherefore John was bound, 10 and beheaded. 13 Jesus departeth. 18 Of the five loaves, etc. 23 Christ prayeth. 24 The Apostles tossed with the waves. 28 Faith. 30 Peter in jeopardy. 36 The hem of Christ's garment.

1 At [a,1]that time Herod the Tetrarch heard of the fame of Jesus, **2** And said unto his servants, This is that John Baptist, he is risen again from the dead,

---

MATT. 12

1. Mark 2:23 / Luke 6:1
2. Deut. 23:25
3. 1 Sam. 21:6
4. Exod. 29:33 / Lev. 8:31 / Lev. 24:9
5. Num. 28:9
6. Hos. 6:6-7 / Matt. 9:13
7. Mark 3:1 / Luke 6:6
8. Isa. 42:1
9. Luke 12:14
10. Matt. 9:34 / Mark 3:22 / Luke 11:15
11. Mark 3:28-29 / Luke 12:10 / 1 John 5:16
12. Luke 6:45
13. Matt. 16:1 / Luke 11:29 / 1 Cor. 1:22
14. Jonah 1:17
15. Jonah 3:5
16. 1 Kings 10:1 / 2 Chron. 9:1
17. Luke 11:24
18. Heb. 6:4-5 / Heb. 10:26 / 2 Pet. 2:20
19. Mark 3:31 / Luke 8:20

MATT. 13

a. Matt. 13:2 Christ showeth in putting forth this parable of the Sower, that the seed of life which is sown in the world, cometh not on so well in one as in another, and the reason is, for that men for the most part either do not receive it, or suffer it not to ripen.

b. Matt. 13:11 The gift of understanding and of faith is proper to the elect, and all the rest are blinded through the just judgment of God.

c. Matt. 13:16 The condition of the Church under and since Christ, is better than it was in the time of the Fathers under the Law.

d. Matt. 13:19 Though there be mention made of the heart yet this sowing is referred to hearing without understanding. For whether the seed be received in the heart or no, yet he that soweth, soweth to the heart.

e. Matt. 13:24 Christ showeth in another parable of the evil seed mixed with the good, that the Church shall never be free and quit from offences, both in doctrine and manners, until the day appointed for the restoring of all things to come, and therefore the faithful have to arm themselves with patience and constancy.

f. Matt. 13:31 God beginneth his kingdom with very small beginnings, to the end that by the growing on of it, beside the expectation and hope of all men, his mighty power and working may be the more set forth.

g. Matt. 13:37 He expoundeth the former parable of the good and evil seed.

h. Matt. 13:44 Few men understand how great the riches of the kingdom of heaven are, and no man can be partaker of them, but he that redeemeth them with the loss of all his goods.

i. Matt. 13:47 There are many in the Church, which notwithstanding are not of the Church, and therefore at length shall be cast out: but the full and perfect cleansing of them is deferred to the last day.

j. Matt. 13:51 They ought to be diligent, which have not only to be wise for themselves, but to dispense the wisdom of God to others.

k. Matt. 13:54 Men do not only sin of ignorance, but also wittingly and willfully lay stumbling blocks in their own ways, that when God calleth them, they may not obey, and so most plainly destroy and cast away themselves.

MATT. 13

1. Matthew 13:1 / Mark 4:1 / Luke 8:4-5
2. Matthew 13:12 / Matt. 25:19
3. Matthew 13:14 / Isa. 6:9 / Mark 4:12 / Luke 8:10 / John 12:40 / Acts 28:26 / Rom. 11:8
4. Matthew 13:17 / Luke 10:24
5. Matthew 13:18 / Mark 4:15 / Luke 8:11
6. Matthew 13:31 / Mark 4:30 / Luke 13:19
7. Matthew 13:33 / Luke 13:21
8. Matthew 13:34 / Mark 4:33-34
9. Matthew 13:35 / Ps. 78:2
10. Matthew 13:39 / Joel 3:13 / Rev. 14:15
11. Matthew 13:43 / Dan. 12:3
12. Matthew 13:54 / Mark 6:1 / Luke 4:6
13. Matthew 13:55 / John 6:42
14. Matthew 13:57 / Mark 6:4 / Luke 4:24 / John 4:44

MATT. 14

a. Matt. 14:1 Here is in John an example of an invincible courage, which all faithful Ministers of God's word ought to follow: in Herod, an example of tyrannous vanity, pride and cruelty, and to be short, of a courtly conscience, and of their insufferable slavery, which have once given themselves over to pleasures: in Herodias and her daughter, an example of whore-like wantonness, and womanlike cruelty.

b. Matt. 14:2 By works he meaneth that force and power, whereby works are wrought and not the works, as is seen oft before.

and therefore great [b]works are wrought by him. **3** [2]For Herod had taken John, and bound him, and put him in prison for Herodias' sake, his brother Philip's wife. **4** For John said unto him, It is not lawful for thee to have her. **5** And when he would have put him to death, he feared the multitude, because they counted him as a [4]Prophet. **6** But when Herod's birthday was kept, the daughter of Herodias danced before them, and pleased [c]Herod. **7** Wherefore he promised with an oath, that he would give her whatsoever she would ask. **8** And she being before instructed of her mother, said, Give me here John Baptist's head in a platter. **9** And the king was sorry: nevertheless, because of the oath, and them that sat with him at the table, he commanded it to be given her, **10** And sent, and beheaded John in the prison. **11** And his head was brought in a platter, and given to the maid, and she brought it unto her mother. **12** And his disciples came, and took up the body, and buried it, and went and told Jesus. **13** [5]And when Jesus heard it, he departed thence by ship into a desert place apart. And when the multitude had heard it, they followed him on foot out of the cities. **14** [d]And Jesus went forth and saw a great multitude, and was moved with compassion toward them, and he healed their sick. **15** And when even was come, [6]his disciples came to him, saying, This is a desert place, and the time is already past: let the multitude depart, that they may go into the towns, and buy them vittles. **16** But Jesus said to them, They have no need to go away: give ye them to eat. **17** Then said they unto him, We have here but five loaves, and two fishes. **18** And he said, Bring them hither to me. **19** And he commanded the multitude to sit down on the grass, and took the five loaves, and the two fishes, and looked up to heaven, and blessed, and brake, and gave the loaves to his disciples, and the disciples to the multitude. **20** And they did all eat, and were sufficed, and they took up of the fragments that remained, twelve baskets full. **21** And they that had eaten, were about five thousand men, beside women and little children. **22** And straightway Jesus compelled his disciples to enter into a ship, and to go over before him, while he sent the multitude away. **23** And as soon as he had sent the multitude away, he went up into a mountain alone to pray: and [7]when the evening was come, he was there alone. **24** [e]And the ship was now in the midst of the sea, and was tossed with waves: for it was a contrary wind. **25** And in the [f]fourth watch of the night, Jesus went unto them, walking on the sea. **26** And when his disciples saw him walking on the sea, they were troubled, saying, It is a [g]spirit, and cried out for fear. **27** But straightway Jesus spake unto them, saying, Be of good comfort, It is I: be not afraid. **28** [h]Then Peter answered him, and said, Master, if it be thou, bid me come unto thee on the water. **29** And he said, Come. And when Peter was come down out of the ship, he walked on the water to go to Jesus. **30** But when he saw a mighty wind, he was afraid: and as he began to sink, he cried, saying, Master, save me. **31** So immediately Jesus stretched forth his hand, and caught him, and said to him, O thou of little faith, wherefore didst thou doubt. **32** And as soon as they were come into the ship, the wind ceased. **33** Then they that were in the ship, came and worshipped him, saying, Of a truth thou art the Son of God. **34** [8]And when they were come over, they came into the land of [i]Gennesaret. **35** [j]And when the men of that place knew him, they sent out into all that country round about, and brought unto him all that were sick, **36** And besought him, that they might touch the hem of his garment only: and as many as touched it were made whole.

15

3 The commandments and traditions of men. 12 Offences. 13 The plant which is rooted up. 14 Blind leading the blind. 18 The heart. 22 The woman of Canaan. 26 The children's bread: whelps. 28 Faith. 32 4,000 men fed. 36 Thanksgiving.

1 Then [a]came to Jesus the Scribes and Pharisees, which were of Jerusalem, saying, **2** [1]Why do thy disciples transgress the tradition of the Elders? for they [b]wash not their hands when they eat bread. **3** [c]But he answered and said unto them, Why do ye also transgress the commandment of God by your tradition? **4** [2]For God hath commanded, saying, [d]Honor thy father and mother: [3]and he that curseth father or mother, let him die the death. **5** But ye say, [e]Whosoever shall say to father or mother, By the gift that is offered by me, thou mayest have profit, **6** Though he honor not his father, or his mother, shall be free: thus have ye made the commandment of God of no [f]authority by your tradition. **7** [g]O hypocrites, Isaiah prophesied well of you, saying, **8** [4]This people draweth near unto me with their mouth, and honoreth me with the lips, but their heart is far off from me. **9** But in vain they worship me, teaching for doctrines, men's precepts. **10** [h]Then he called the multitude unto him, and said to them, Hear and understand. **11** [5]That which goeth into the mouth, defileth not the man, but that which cometh out of the mouth that defileth the man. **12** Then came his disciples, and said unto him, Perceivest thou not, that the Pharisees are offended in hearing this saying? **13** But he answered and said, [6]Every plant which mine heavenly Father hath not planted, shall be rooted up. **14** Let them alone, they be the [7]blind leaders of the blind: and if the blind lead the blind, both shall fall into the ditch. **15** [8]Then answered Peter, and said to him, Declare unto us this parable. **16** Then said Jesus, Are ye yet without understanding? **17** Perceive ye not yet, that whatsoever entereth into the mouth, goeth into the belly, and is cast out into the draught? **18** But those things which proceed out of the mouth, come from the heart, and they defile the man. **19** For out of the heart [9]come evil thoughts, murders, adulteries, fornications, thefts, false testimonies, slanders. **20** These are the things which defile the man: but to eat with unwashed hands, defileth not the man. **21** [10]And Jesus went thence, and departed into the [i]coasts of Tyre and Sidon. **22** And behold, a woman a [j]Canaanite came out of the same coasts, and cried, saying unto him, Have mercy on me, O Lord, the son of David: my daughter is miserably vexed with a devil. **23** [k]But he answered her not a word. Then came to him his disciples, and besought him, saying, Send her away, for she crieth after us. **24** But he answered, and said, I am not sent, but unto the [11]lost sheep of the [l]house of Israel. **25** Yet she came, and worshipped him, saying, Lord help me. **26** And he answered, and said, It is not good to take the children's bread, and to cast it to whelps. **27** But she said, Truth, Lord: yet indeed the whelps eat of the crumbs, which fall from their master's table. **28** Then Jesus answered, and said unto her, O woman, great is thy faith: be it to thee, as thou desirest. And her daughter was made whole at that hour. **29** [m]So Jesus [12]went away from thence, and came near unto the sea of Galilee, and went up in a mountain and sat down there. **30** And great multitudes came unto him, [13]having with them, halt, blind, dumb, [n]maimed, and many others, and cast them down, at Jesus' feet, and he healed them. **31** Insomuch that the multitude wondered, to see the dumb speak, the maimed whole, the halt to go, and the blind to see: and they glorified the God of Israel. **32** [o,14]Then Jesus called his disciples unto him, and said, I have compassion on this multitude, because they have [p]continued with me already three days, and have nothing to eat: and I will not let them depart fasting, lest they faint in the way. **33** And his disciples said unto him, Whence should we get so much bread in the wilderness, as should suffice so great a multitude! **34** And Jesus said unto them, How many loaves have ye? And they said, Seven, and a few little fishes. **35** Then he commandeth the multitude [q]to sit down on the ground. **36** And took the seven loaves, and the fishes, and gave thanks, and brake them, and gave to his disciples, and the disciples to the multitude. **37** And they did all eat, and were sufficed, and they took up of the fragments

---

c. Matt. 14:6 There were three Herods: the first of them was Antipater's son, who is also called Ascalonius, in whose reign Christ was born, and he it was that caused the children to be slain. The second was called Antipas, Magnus his son, whose mother's name was Malthace or Martaca, and this was called Tetrarch, by reason of enlarging his dominion, when Archelaus was banished to Vienna in France. The third was Agrippa, Magnus his nephew by Aristobulus, and he it was that slew James.

d. Matt. 14:14 Christ refresheth a great multitude with five loaves and two little fishes, showing thereby, that they shall want nothing, which lay all things aside and seek the kingdom of heaven.

e. Matt. 14:24 We must sail even through mighty tempests, and Christ will never forsake us, so that we go whither he hath commanded us.

f. Matt. 14:25 By the fourth watch is meant the time near to day breaking: for in old time they divided the night into four watches, in which they scouted.

g. Matt. 14:26 A spirit, as it is here taken, is that which a man imagineth to himself vainly in his mind, persuading himself that he seeth something, and seeth nothing.

h. Matt. 14:28 By faith we tread under our feet even the tempests themselves, but yet by the virtue of Christ, which helpeth that virtue, which he of his mercy hath given.

i. Matt. 14:34 This Gennesaret was a lake nigh to Capernaum, which is also called the Sea of Galilee, and Tiberias, so that the country itself grew to be called by that name.

j. Matt. 14:35 In that that Christ healeth the sick, we are given to understand that we must seek remedy for spiritual diseases at his hands: and that we are bound not only to run ourselves, but also to bring others to him.

MATT. 14

1. Mark 6:14 / Luke 9:7
2. Mark 6:17 / Luke 3:19
3. Lev. 18:16 / Lev. 20:21
4. Matt. 21:26
5. Mark 6:32 / Luke 9:10
6. Mark 6:35 / Luke 9:12 / John 6:5
7. Mark 6:45-47 / John 6:16-18
8. Mark 6:54

MATT. 15

a. Matt. 15:1 None commonly are more bold contemners of God, than they whom God appointeth keepers of his law.

b. Matt. 15:2 Which they received of their ancestors from hand to hand, or their elders allowed, which were the governors of the Church.

c. Matt. 15:3 Their wicked boldness, in corrupting the commandments of God, and that upon the pretence of godliness, and usurping authority to make laws, is here reproved.

d. Matt. 15:4 By honor is meant all kinds of duties which children owe to their parents.

e. Matt. 15:5 The meaning is this: whatsoever I bestow upon the Temple, is to thy profit, for it is as good as if I gave it thee, for (as the Pharisees of our time say) it shall be meritorious for thee: for under this color of religion, they raked all to themselves, as though that he that had given anything to the Temple, had done the duty of a child.

f. Matt. 15:6 You made it of no power and authority as much as lay in you: for otherwise the commandments of God stand fast in the Church of God, in despite of the world and Satan.

g. Matt. 15:7 The same men are condemned for hypocrisy and superstition, because they made the kingdom of God to stand in outward things.

h. Matt. 15:10 Christ teacheth us that hypocrisy of false teachers which deceive our soul, is not to be borne withall, no not in indifferent matters, and there is no reason why their ordinary vocation should blind our eyes: otherwise we are like to perish with them.

i. Matt. 15:21 Coasts which were near to Tyre and Sidon, that is, in that quarter where Palestine bendeth toward Phoenicia, and the sea of Syria.

j. Matt. 15:22 Of the flock of the Canaanites, which dwelled in Phoenicia.

k. Matt. 15:23 In that that Christ doth sometimes as it were stop his ears against the prayers of his Saints, he doeth it for his glory and our profit.

l. Matt. 15:24 Of the people of Israel, which people was divided into tribes, but all those tribes came of one house.

m. Matt. 15:29 Christ ceaseth not to be beneficial even there where he is contemned, and in the midst of wolves he gathered together and fostereth his flock.

n. Matt. 15:30 Whose members were weakened with the palsy, or by nature, for afterward it is said, he healed them. Now Christ was wont to heal in this wise, that such members as were weak, he restored to health, and yet he could easily if he had would, have given them hands and feet and other members which wanted them.

o. Matt. 15:32 By doing again this miracle, Christ showeth that he will never be wanting to them that follow him, no not in the wilderness.

p. Matt. 15:32 Go not from my side.

q. Matt. 15:35 Word for word, to lie down backward, as rowers do when in rowing they draw their oars to them.

that remained, seven [r]baskets full. **38** And they that had eaten, were four thou-
sand men, beside women, and little children. **39** Then Jesus sent away the mul-
titude, and took ship, and came into the parts of Magdala.

16

1 The sign of Jonah. 6 The leaven of the Pharisees, 12 for their doctrine. 13 The people's opinion of Christ. 17 Faith cometh of God. 18 The rock. 19 The keys. 21 Christ foreshadoweth his death. 24 The forsaking of ourself, and the cross. 25 To lose the life.

1 Then [a,1]came the Pharisees and Sadducees, and did [b]tempt him, desi-
ring him to show them a sign from heaven. **2** But he answered, and said unto
them, When it is evening, ye say, Fair weather, for the sky is red. **3** [2]And in
the morning, ye say, Today shall be a tempest: for the sky is red and lowering. O
hypocrites, ye can discern the [c]face of the sky, and can ye not discern the signs of
the times? **4** [3]The wicked generation, and adulterous seeketh a sign, but there
shall no sign be given it, but [d]that sign of the Prophet [4]Jonah: so he left them,
and departed. **5** [e]And when his disciples were come to the other side, they had
[5]forgotten to take bread with them. **6** Then Jesus said unto them, Take heed
and beware of the leaven of the Pharisees and Sadducees. **7** And they reaso-
ned among themselves, saying, It is because we have brought no bread. **8** But
Jesus [f]knowing it, said unto them, O ye of little faith, why reason ye thus among
yourselves, because ye have brought no bread? **9** Do ye not yet perceive, nei-
ther remember the [g]five loaves, when there were [6]five thousand men, and how
many baskets took ye up? **10** Neither the seven loaves when there were [7]four
thousand men, and how many baskets took ye up? **11** Why [h]perceive ye not
that I [i]said not unto you concerning bread, that ye should beware of the leaven
of the Pharisees and Sadducees? **12** Then understood they that he had not said
that they should beware of the leaven of bread, but of the doctrine of the Phari-
sees, and Sadducees. **13** [j,8]Now when Jesus came into the coasts of [k]Caesarea
Philippi, he asked his disciples, saying, Whom do men say that I, the son of man,
am? **14** And they said, Some say, [l]John Baptist: and some, Elijah: and others, Je-
remiah, or one of the Prophets. **15** He said unto them, But whom say ye that I
am? **16** Then Simon Peter answered, and said, [9]Thou art that Christ, the son of
the living God. **17** [m]And Jesus answered, and said to him, Blessed art thou, Si-
mon, the son of Jonah: for [n]flesh and blood hath not revealed it unto thee, but my
Father which is in heaven. **18** [o]And I say also unto thee, that thou art [p,10]Peter,
and upon this rock I will build my Church: and the [q]gates of hell shall not overco-
me it. **19** [r]And I [11]will give unto thee the [s]keys of the Kingdom of heaven, and
whatsoever thou shalt [t]bind upon earth, shall be bound in heaven: and whatsoever
thou shalt loose on earth, shall be loosed in heaven. **20** [u]Then he charged his di-
sciples, that they should tell no man that he was Jesus that Christ. **21** [v]From that
time forth Jesus began to show unto his disciples, that he must go unto Jerusalem,
and suffer many things of the [w]Elders, and of the high Priests, and Scribes, and be
slain and be raised again the third day. **22** Then Peter [x]took him aside, and began
to rebuke him, saying, Master, pity thyself: this shall not be unto thee. **23** [y]Then
he turned back, and said unto Peter, Get thee behind me, [z]Satan: thou art an of-
fence unto me, because thou [aa]understandest not the things that are of God, but
the things that are of men. **24** [ab]Jesus then said to his disciples, [12]If any man will
follow me, let him forsake himself: and take up his cross, and follow me. **25** For
[13]whosoever will save his life, shall lose it: and whosoever shall lose his life for my
sake, shall [ac]find it. **26** [14]For what shall it profit a man though he should win the
whole world, if he lose his own soul? or what shall a man give for recompense of
his soul? **27** For the son of man shall come [ad]in the glory of his Father with his
Angels, and [15]then shall he give to every man according to his deeds. **28** [16]Verily
I say unto you, there be some of them that stand here, which shall not taste of de-
ath, till they have seen the Son of man come in his [ae]kingdom.

17

2 The transfiguration of Christ. 5 Christ ought to be heard. 12 Elijah. 13 John Baptist. 17 The unbelief of the Apostles. 20 The power of faith. 21 Prayer and fasting. 22 Christ foretelleth his passion. 24 He payeth tribute.

1 And [a,b,1]after six days, Jesus took Peter and James, and John his brother,
and brought them up into an high mountain apart, **2** And was [c]transfigured
before them: and his face did shine as the Sun, and his clothes were as white as
the light. **3** And behold, there appeared unto them Moses, and Elijah, talking
with him. **4** Then answered Peter, and said to Jesus, Master, it is good for us to
be here: if thou wilt, let us make here three tabernacles, one for thee, and one for
Moses, and one for Elijah. **5** While he yet spake, behold, a bright cloud sha-
dowed them: and behold, there came a voice out of the cloud, saying, [2]This is
[d]that my beloved Son, in whom I am well pleased: hear him. **6** And when the
disciples heard that, they [e]fell on their faces, and were sore afraid. **7** Then Jesus
came and touched them, and said, Arise, and be not afraid. **8** And when they
lifted up their eyes, they saw no man, save Jesus only. **9** And as they came down
from the mountain, Jesus charged them, saying, Show the [f]vision to no man, un-
til the Son of man rise again from the dead. **10** [3]And his disciples asked him,
saying, Why then say the Scribes that [4]Elijah must first come? **11** And Jesus
answered, and said unto them, Certainly Elijah must first come, and restore all
things. **12** But I say unto you, that Elijah is come already, and they knew him
not, but have done unto him whatsoever they would: likewise shall also the Son
of man suffer of them. **13** Then the disciples perceived that he spake unto them
of John Baptist. **14** [g,5]And when they were come to the multitude, there came

---

r. Matt. 15:37 A kind of vessel wrought with twigs.

MATT. 15

1. Mark 7:1
2. Exod. 20:12 / Deut. 5:16 / Eph. 6:2
3. Exod. 21:17 / Lev. 20:9 / Prov. 20:20
4. Isa. 29:13
5. Mark 7:18
6. John 15:2
7. Luke 6:39
8. Mark 7:10
9. Gen. 6:5 / Gen. 8:21 / Mark 7:21
10. Mark 7:24
11. Matt. 10:6
12. Mark 7:31
13. Isa. 35:5
14. Mark 8:1

MATT. 16

a. Matt. 16:1 The wicked which otherwise are at defiance one with another, agree well together against Christ, but do what they can, Christ beareth always the victory, and triumpheth over them.
b. Matt. 16:1 To try whether he could do that which they desired, but their purpose was naught, for they thought to find some thing in him by that means whereupon they might have just occasion to reprehend him: or else distrust and curiosity moved them so to do, for by such means also is God said to be tempted, that is to say, provoked to anger, as though men would strive with him.
c. Matt. 16:3 The outward show and countenance as it were of all things, is called in the Hebrews' tongue, a face.
d. Matt. 16:4 The article showeth the notableness of the deed.
e. Matt. 16:5 False teachers must be taken heed of.
f. Matt. 16:8 Not by others, but by virtue of his divinity.
g. Matt. 16:9 That five thousand men were filled with so many loaves?
h. Matt. 16:11 A demand or question joined with admiration.
i. Matt. 16:11 Said, for commanded.
j. Matt. 16:13 There are divers judgments and opinions of Christ, notwithstanding he is known of his alone.
k. Matt. 16:13 There were two Caesareas, the one called Stratonis upon the sea Mediterranean, which Herod built sumptuously in the honor of Octavius, Josephus, lib. 15. The other was Caesarea Philippi, which Herod the great the Tetrarch's son by Cleopatra built in the honor of Tiberius at the foot of Lebanon, Josephus, lib. 15.
l. Matt. 16:14 As Herod thought.
m. Matt. 16:17 Faith is of grace, not of nature.
n. Matt. 16:17 By this kind of speech is meant man's natural procreation upon the earth, the creature not being destroyed which was made, but deformed through sin: So then this is the meaning: this was not revealed to thee by any understanding of man, but God showed it thee from heaven.
o. Matt. 16:18 That is true faith, which confesseth Christ, the virtue whereof is invisible.
p. Matt. 16:18 Christ spoke in the Syrian tongue, and therefore used not this descanting betwixt Petros, which signifieth Peter, and Petra, which signifieth a rock, but in both places used this word Cephas: but his mind was that wrote in Greek, by the divers termination to make a difference between Peter, who is a piece of the building, and Christ the Petra, that is, the rock and foundation: or else he gave his name Peter, because of the confession of his faith, which is the Church's as well as his, as the old fathers witness: For so saith Theophylact, That confession which thou hast made, shall be the foundation of the believers.
q. Matt. 16:18 The enemies of the Church are compared to a strong kingdom, and therefore by Gates, are meant cities which are made strong with counsels and fortresses, and this is the meaning, whatsoever Satan can do by counsel or strength. So doth Paul, 2 Cor. 10:4, call them strongholds.
r. Matt. 16:19 The authority of the Church is from God.
s. Matt. 16:19 A metaphor taken of stewards which carry the keys: and here is set forth the power of the ministers of the word, as Isa. 22:22, and that power is common to all ministers, as Matt. 18:18, and therefore the ministers of the Gospel may rightly be called the key of the kingdom of heaven.
t. Matt. 16:19 They are bound whose sins are retained, heaven is shut against them, because they received not Christ by faith: on the other side, how happy are they, to whom heaven is open, which embrace Christ, and are delivered by him, and become fellow heirs with him.
u. Matt. 16:20 Men must first learn and then teach.
v. Matt. 16:21 The minds of men are in time to be prepared and made ready against the stumbling block of persecution.
w. Matt. 16:21 It was a name of dignity and not of age, and it is put for them, which were the Judges, which the Hebrews called Sanhedrin.
x. Matt. 16:22 Took him by the hand and led him aside, as they used to do, which meant to talk familiarly with one.
y. Matt. 16:23 Against a preposterous zeal.
z. Matt. 16:23 The Hebrews call him Satan, that is to say, an adversary, whom the Grecians call diabolos, that is to say, slanderer, or tempter: but it is spoken of them, that either of malice, as Judas, John 6:70, or of lightness and pride resist the will of God.
aa. Matt. 16:23 By this word we are taught that Peter sinned, through a false persuasion of himself.
ab. Matt. 16:24 No men provide worse for themselves, than they that love themselves more than God.
ac. Matt. 16:25 Shall gain himself: And this is his meaning, they that deny Christ to save themselves, do not only not gain that which they look for, but also lose the thing they would have kept, that is themselves, which loss is the greatest of all: but as for them that doubt not to die for Christ, it fareth far otherwise with them.
ad. Matt. 16:27 Like a King, as Matt. 6:29.
ae. Matt. 16:28 By his kingdom is understood the glory of his ascension, and what followeth thereof, Eph. 4:10, or the preaching of the Gospel, Mark 9:1.

MATT. 16

1. Matt. 12:38 / Mark 8:11
2. Luke 12:54
3. Matt. 12:39
4. Jonah 1:17
5. Mark 8:14 / Luke 2:1
6. Matt. 14:17 / John 6:9
7. Matt. 15:34
8. Mark 8:27 / Luke 9:18
9. Josh. 6:69
10. John 1:42
11. John 20:21
12. Matt. 10:38 / Mark 8:34 / Luke 9:23 / Luke 14:27
13. Matt. 10:39 / Mark 8:35 / Luke 9:24-26 / Luke 17:33
14. Job 12:25
15. Ps. 62:12 / Rom. 2:6
16. Mark 9:1 / Luke 9:27

MATT. 17

a. Matt. 17:1 Christ is in such sort humble in the Gospel, that in the mean season he is Lord both of heaven and earth.
b. Matt. 17:1 Luke reckoneth eight days, containing in that number the first and last, and Matt. speaketh but of them that were betwixt them.
c. Matt. 17:2 Changed into another hue.
d. Matt. 17:5 The article or the word, That, severeth Christ from other children. For he is God's natural Son, we by adoption, therefore he is called the first begotten among the brethren, because that although he be of right the only Son, yet is he chief among many in that he is the fountain and head of the adoption.
e. Matt. 17:6 Fell down flat on their faces and worshipped him, as Matt. 2:11.
f. Matt. 17:9 Which they saw: otherwise the word, used in this place is properly spoken of that which is seen in a dream.
g. Matt. 17:14 Men are unworthy of Christ his goodness, yet notwithstanding he regardeth them.
h. Matt. 17:14 As men that make supplications used to do.
i. Matt. 17:15 They that at certain times of the moon are troubled with the falling sickness, or any other kind of disease:

to him a certain man, and [h]fell down at his feet, **15** And said, Master, have pity on my son: for he is [i]lunatic, and is sore vexed: for oft times he falleth into the fire, and oft times into the water. **16** And I brought him to thy disciples, and they could not heal him. **17** Then Jesus answered, and said, O generation faithless, and crooked, how long now shall I be with you! how long now shall I suffer you! bring him hither to me. **18** And Jesus rebuked the devil, and he went out of him: and the child was healed at that hour. **19** [j]Then came the disciples to Jesus apart, and said, Why could not we cast him out? **20** And Jesus said unto them, Because of your unbelief: for [6]verily I say unto you, if ye have faith as much as is a grain of mustard seed, ye shall say unto this mountain, Remove hence to yonder place, and it shall remove: and nothing shall be impossible unto you. **21** [k]Howbeit this kind goeth not out, but by [l]prayer and fasting. **22** [m]And they [7]being in Galilee, Jesus said unto them, The Son of Man shall be delivered into the hands of men. **23** And they shall kill him, but the third day shall he rise again: and they were very sorry. **24** [n]And when they were come to Capernaum, they that received poll money, came to Peter, and said, Doth [o]not your Master [p]pay [q]poll money? **25** He said, Yes. And when he was come into the house, Jesus prevented him, saying, What thinkest thou, Simon? Of whom do the kings of the earth take tribute, or poll money? of their [r]children, or of strangers? **26** Peter said unto him, Of strangers. Then said Jesus unto him, Then are the children free. **27** Nevertheless, lest we should offend them: go to the sea, and cast in an angle, and take the first fish that cometh up, and when thou hast opened his mouth, thou shalt find a [s]piece of twenty pence: that take, and give it unto them for me and thee.

18

1 The greatest in the kingdom of God. 5 To receive a little child. 6 To give offence. 7 Offences. 9 The pulling out of the eye. 10 The Angels. 11 The lost sheep. 15 The telling of one his fault. 17 Excommunication. 21 We must always pardon the brother that repenteth. 23 The parable of the king that taketh an account of his servants.

1 The [1]same time the disciples came unto Jesus, saying, Who is the greatest in the kingdom of heaven? **2** [a]And Jesus called a [b]little child unto him, and set him in the midst of them, **3** And said, Verily I say unto you, except ye be [c,2]converted, and become as little children, ye shall not enter into the kingdom of heaven. **4** Whosoever therefore shall humble himself as this little child, the same is the greatest in the kingdom of heaven. **5** And whosoever shall receive one such little child in my Name, receiveth me. **6** [d,3]But whosoever shall offend one of these little ones which believe in me, it were better for him, that a millstone were hanged about his neck, and that he were drowned in the depth of the sea. **7** [e]Woe be unto the world because of offences, for it must needs be that [f]offences shall come, but woe be to that man by whom the offence cometh. **8** [4]Wherefore, if thy hand or thy foot cause thee to [g]offend, cut them off, and cast them from thee: it is better for thee to enter into life, halt, or maimed, than having two hands, or two feet, to be cast into everlasting fire. **9** And if thine eye cause thee to offend, pluck it out and cast it from thee: it is better for thee to enter into life with one eye, than having two eyes to be cast into hell fire. **10** [h]See that ye despise not one of these little ones: for I say unto you, that in heaven their [5]Angels always behold the face of my Father which is in heaven. **11** For [6]the Son of man is come to save that which was lost. **12** How think ye? [7]If a man have an hundred sheep, and one of them be gone astray, doth he not leave ninety and nine, and go into the mountains, and seek that which is gone astray? **13** And if so be that he find it, verily I say unto you, he rejoiceth more of that sheep, than of the ninety and nine which went not astray: **14** So is it not the will of your Father which is in heaven, that one of these little ones should perish. **15** [i,8]Moreover, if thy brother trespass against [j]thee, go and tell him his fault between thee and him alone: if he hear thee, thou hast won thy brother. **16** But if he hear thee not, take yet with thee one or two, that by the [k,9]mouth of two or three witnesses, every word may be [l]confirmed. **17** [m]And if he [n]refuse to hear them, tell it unto the [o]Church: and if he refuse to hear the Church also, let him be unto thee as an [p]heathen man, and a Publican. **18** Verily I say unto you, [10]Whatsoever ye bind on earth, shall be bound in heaven: and whatsoever ye loose on earth, shall be losed in heaven. **19** Again, verily I say unto you, that if two of you shall [q]agree in earth upon anything, whatsoever they shall desire, it shall be given them of my Father which is in heaven. **20** For where two or three are gathered together in my Name, there am I in the midst of them. **21** [r]Then came Peter to him, and said, Master, how oft shall my brother sin against me, and I shall forgive him? [12]unto seven times? **22** Jesus said unto him, I say not to thee, Unto seven times, but, Unto seventy times seven times. **23** Therefore is the kingdom of heaven likened unto a certain King, which would take an account of his servants. **24** And when he had begun to reckon, one was brought unto him, which ought him [s]ten thousand talents. **25** And because he had nothing to pay, his lord commanded him to be sold, and his wife, and his children, and all that he had, and the debt to be paid. **26** The servant therefore fell down, and [t]worshipped him, saying, Lord, [u]refrain thine anger toward me, and I will pay thee all. **27** Then that servant's lord had compassion, and loosed him, and forgave him the debt. **28** But when the servant was departed, he found one of his fellow servants which ought him an hundred pence, and he laid hands on him, and throttled him, saying, Pay me that thou owest. **29** Then his fellow servant fell down at his feet, and besought him, saying, Refrain thine anger toward me, and I will pay thee all. **30** Yet he would not, but went and cast him into prison, till he should pay the debt. **31** And when his other fellow servants saw what was done, they were very sorry, and came, and declared unto their lord all that was done. **32** Then his lord called him unto him, and said to him, O evil servant, I forgave thee all that debt, because thou prayedst me. **33** Oughtest not thou also to have had pity on thy fellow servant, even as I had pity on thee? **34** So his lord was wroth, and delivered him to the tormentors, till he should pay all that was due to him. **35** So likewise shall mine heavenly Father do unto you, except ye forgive from your hearts, each one to his brother their trespasses.

19

2 The sick are healed. 3 and 7 A bill of divorcement. 12 Eunuchs. 13 Children brought to Christ. 17 God only good. The commandments must be kept. 21 A perfect man. 23 A rich man. 26 Salvation cometh of God. 27 To leave all and follow Christ.

1 And [1]it came to pass, that when Jesus had finished these sayings, he [a]departed from Galilee, and came into the coasts of Judea beyond Jordan. **2** And great multitudes followed him, and he healed them there. **3** [b]Then came unto him the Pharisees tempting him, and saying to him, Is it lawful for a man to [c]put away

---

but in this place, we must so take it, that besides the natural disease, he had a devilish frenzy.

j. Matt. 17:19 Incredulity and distrust hinder and break the course of God's benefits.
k. Matt. 17:21 The remedy against distrust.
l. Matt. 17:21 To give us to understand the watchfulness and diligence of earnest prayer, which cannot be without sobriety.
m. Matt. 17:22 Our minds must be prepared more and more against the offence of the cross.
n. Matt. 17:24 In that that Christ doth willingly obey Caesar's edicts, he showeth that civil policy is not taken away by the Gospel.
o. Matt. 17:24 He denieth not, but he asketh.
p. Matt. 17:24 Ought he not to pay?
q. Matt. 17:24 They that were from twenty years of age to fifty, paid half a shekel of the Sanctuary, Exod. 30:13. This was an Attic didrachma which the Romans exacted, after they had subdued Judea.
r. Matt. 17:25 By children we must not understand subjects which pay tribute, but natural children.
s. Matt. 17:27 The word here used, is stater, which is in value 4 didrachmas; every drachma is about five pence.

MATT. 17

1. Mark 9:2 / Luke 9:28
2. Matt. 3:17 / 2 Pet. 1:17
3. Mark 9:11-12
4. Mal. 4:5 / Matt. 11:14
5. Mark 9:14 / Luke 9:38
6. Luke 17:6
7. Matt. 20:17 / Mark 9:3 / Luke 9:44 / Luke 7:24

MATT. 18

a. Matt. 18:2 Humbleness of mind is the right way to preeminence.
b. Matt. 18:2 A child in years.
c. Matt. 18:3 A kind of speech taken from the Hebrews, and it is as much as, repent.
d. Matt. 18:6 We ought to have great respect to our brethren be they never so base: and he that doeth otherwise, shall be sharply punished.
e. Matt. 18:7 A good man cannot but go through the midst of offences, yet he must cut off all occasion of offences.
f. Matt. 18:7 Lets and hindrances which stop the course of good works. The Greek word importeth thus much, things which we stumble at.
g. Matt. 18:8 See Matt. 5:29.
h. Matt. 18:10 The weaker that a man is, the greater care we ought to have of his salvation, as God teacheth us by his own example.
i. Matt. 18:15 We must labor for concord, not to revenge injuries.
j. Matt. 18:15 If his offence be such, that thou only knowest thy brother's offence.
k. Matt. 18:16 That is, by the word and witness the mouth is sometime taken for the word or speech, Num. 3:16, and also for a still witness, to wit, when the matter speaketh of itself, as in Matt. 21:16.
l. Matt. 18:16 Sure and certain.
m. Matt. 18:17 He that contemneth the judgment of the Church, contemneth God.
n. Matt. 18:17 Word for word, do not vouchsafe to hear, or make as though he did not hear.
o. Matt. 18:17 He speaketh not of any kind of policy, but of an Ecclesiastical assembly, for he speaketh afterward of the power of loosing and binding, which belonged to the Church, and he hath regard to the order used in those days, at what time the Elders had the judgment of Church matters in their hands, John 9:22 and 12:42 and 16:2, and used casting out of the Synagogue for a punishment, as we do now excommunication.
p. Matt. 18:17 Profane, and void of religion: such men, the Jews called Gentiles: whose company they shunned as they did the Publicans.
q. Matt. 18:19 This word is translated from the body to the mind, for it belongeth properly to song.
r. Matt. 18:21 They shall find God severe and not to be pleased, which do not forgive their brethren, although they have been diversly and grievously injured by them.
s. Matt. 18:24 Here is set down a very great sum of threescore hundred thousand crowns, and a small sum of ten crowns, that the difference may be the greater, for there is no proportion between them.
t. Matt. 18:26 This was a civil reverence which was very usual in the East.
u. Matt. 18:26 Yield not too much to thine anger against me: so is God called in the Scripture, slow to anger, that is to say, gentle and one that refraineth the storming of his mind, Ps. 86:5, patient and of great mercy.

MATT. 18

1. Mark 9:34 / Luke 9:46
2. Matt. 19:14 / 1 Cor. 14:20
3. Mark 9:42 / Luke 17:2
4. Matt. 5:29-30 / Mark 9:45
5. Ps. 34:8
6. Luke 19:10
7. Luke 15:4
8. Lev. 19:7 / Luke 17:3 / James 5:19
9. Deut. 19:15 / John 8:17 / 2 Cor. 13:1 / Heb. 10:28
10. 1 Cor. 5:4 / 2 Thess. 3:14
11. John 20:24
12. Luke 17:4

MATT. 19

a. Matt. 19:1 Passed over the water out of Galilee into the borders of Judea.
b. Matt. 19:3 The band of marriage ought not to be broken, unless it be for fornication.
c. Matt. 19:3 To send her a book of divorcement, see also Matt. 1:19.

his wife upon every occasion? **4** And he answered and said unto them, Have ye not read, [2]that he which made them at the beginning, made them male and female, **5** And said, [3]For this cause, shall a man leave father and mother, and [d]cleave unto his wife, and they which were [e]two, shall be one flesh? **6** Wherefore they are no more twain, but one flesh. Let not man therefore put asunder that, which God hath [f]coupled together. **7** [g]They said to him, Why did then [4]Moses command to give a bill of divorcement, and to put her away? **8** He said unto them, Moses, [h]because of the hardness of your heart, [i]suffered you to put away your wives: but from the beginning it was not so. **9** I say therefore unto you, [5]that whosoever shall put away his wife, except it be [j]for whoredom, and marry another, committeth adultery: and whosoever marrieth her which is divorced, doth commit adultery. **10** Then said his disciples to him, If the [k]matter be so between man and wife, it is not good to marry. **11** [l]But he said unto them, All men cannot [m]receive this thing, save they to whom it is given. **12** For there are some [n]eunuchs, which were so born of their mother's belly: and there be some eunuchs, which be gelded by men: and there be some eunuchs, which have [o]gelded themselves for the kingdom of heaven. He that is able to receive this, let him receive it. **13** [p,6]Then were brought unto him little children, that he should put his hands on them, and pray: and the disciples rebuked them. **14** But Jesus said, Suffer little children, and forbid them not to come to me: for of such is the kingdom of heaven. **15** And when he had put his hands on them, he departed thence. **16** [q,7]And behold, one came and said unto him, Good Master, what good thing shall I do, that I may have eternal life? **17** And he said unto him, Why called thou me good? there is none good but one, even God: but if thou wilt enter into life, keep the Commandments. **18** He said unto him, Which? And Jesus said, [8]These, Thou shalt not kill: Thou shalt not commit adultery: Thou shalt not steal: Thou shalt not bear false witness. **19** Honor thy father, and mother: and, Thou shalt love thy neighbor as thyself. **20** The young man said unto him, I have observed all these things from my youth. What lack I yet? **21** Jesus said unto him, If [r]thou wilt be perfect, go, sell that thou hast, and give it to the poor, and thou shalt have treasure in heaven, and come, and follow me. **22** And when the young man heard that saying, he went away sorrowful: for he had great possessions. **23** [s]Then Jesus said unto his disciples, Verily I say unto you, that a rich man shall hardly enter into the kingdom of heaven. **24** And again I say unto you, It is [t]easier for a [u]camel to go through the eye of a needle, than for a rich man to enter into the kingdom of God. **25** And when his disciples heard it, they were exceedingly amazed, saying, Who then can be saved? **26** And Jesus beheld them, and said unto them, With men this is impossible, but with God all things are possible. **27** [9]Then answered Peter, and said to him, Behold, we have forsaken all, and followed thee: what therefore shall we have? **28** [v]And Jesus said unto them, Verily I say to you, that when the Son of man shall sit in the throne of his Majesty, ye which followed me in the [w]regeneration, [10]shall sit also upon twelve thrones, and judge the twelve tribes of Israel. **29** And whosoever shall forsake houses, or brethren, or sisters, or father, or mother, or wife, or children, or lands, for my Name's sake, he shall receive an hundredfold more, and shall inherit everlasting life. **30** [x,11]But many that are first, shall be last, and the last shall be first.

20

1 Laborers hired into the vineyard. 15 The evil eye. 17 He foretelleth his passion. 20 Zebedee's sons. 22 The cup. 28 Christ is our minister. 30 Two blind men.

1 For the kingdom of heaven is like unto a certain [a]householder, which went out at the dawning of the day to hire laborers into his vineyard. **2** And he [b]agreed with the laborers for a penny a day, and sent them into his vineyard. **3** And he went out about the third hour, and saw others standing idle in the marketplace, **4** And said unto them, Go ye also into my vineyard, and whatsoever is right, I will give you: and they went their way. **5** Again he went out about the sixth and ninth hour, and did likewise. **6** And he went about the [c]eleventh hour, and found others standing idle, and said unto them, Why stand ye here all the day idle? **7** They said unto him, Because no man hath hired us. He said to them, Go ye also into my vineyard, and whatsoever is right, that shall ye receive. **8** And when even was come, the master of the vineyard said unto his steward, Call the laborers, and give them their hire, beginning at the last, till thou come to the first. **9** And they which were hired about the eleventh hour, came and received every man a penny. **10** Now when the first came, they supposed that they should receive more, but they likewise received every man a penny. **11** And when they had received it, they murmured against the master of the house, **12** Saying, These last have wrought but one hour, and thou hast made them equal unto us, which have borne the burden and heat of the day. **13** And he answered one of them, saying, Friend, I do thee no wrong: didst thou not agree with me for a penny? **14** Take that which is thine own, and go thy way: I will give unto this last, as much as to thee. **15** Is it not lawful for me to do as I will with mine own? Is thine eye [d]evil, because I am good? **16** [1]So the last shall be first, and the first last: for many are called, but few chosen. **17** [e,2]And Jesus went up to Jerusalem, and took the twelve disciples apart in the way, and said unto them, **18** [f]Behold, we go up to Jerusalem, and the Son of man shall be delivered unto the chief Priests, and unto the Scribes, and they shall condemn him to death, **19** [g]And [3]shall deliver him to the Gentiles, to mock, and to scourge, and to crucify him, but the third day he shall rise again. **20** [h,4]Then came to him the mother of Zebedee's children with her sons, worshipping him, and desiring a certain thing of him. **21** And he said unto her, What wouldest thou? She said to him, Grant that these my two sons may sit, the one at thy right hand, and the other at thy left hand in thy kingdom. **22** And Jesus answered, and said, Ye know not what ye ask. Are ye able to [i]drink of the cup that I shall drink of, and to be baptized with the [j]baptism that I shall be baptized with? they said to him, We are able. **23** And he said unto them, Ye shall drink indeed of my cup, and shall be baptized with the baptism, that I am baptized with, but to sit at my right hand, and at my left hand, is [k]not mine to give: but it shall be given to them for whom it is prepared of my Father. **24** [5]And when the other ten heard this, they disdained at the two brethren. **25** Therefore Jesus called them unto him, and said, Ye know that the lords of the Gentiles have [l]domination over them, and they that are great, exercise authority over them. **26** But it shall not be so among you: but whosoever will be great among you, let him be your servant. **27** And whosoever will be chief among you, let him be your servant. **28** [6]Even as the Son of man came not to be served, but to serve, and to give his life for the ransom of many. **29** [m,7]And as they departed from Jericho, a great multitude followed him. **30** And behold, two blind men, sitting

---

d. Matt. 19:5 The Greek word imported to be glued unto, whereby is signified that straight knot, which is between man and wife, as though they were glued together.

e. Matt. 19:5 They which were two, become as it were one: and this word flesh is by a figure taken for the whole man, or the body after the manner of the Hebrews.

f. Matt. 19:6 Hath made them yoke fellows, as the marriage itself is by a borrowed kind of speech called a yoke.

g. Matt. 19:7 Because political Laws are constrained to bear with some things, it followeth not by and by that God alloweth them.

h. Matt. 19:8 Being occasioned by reason of the hardness of your hearts.

i. Matt. 19:8 By a political law, not by the moral law: for this law is a perpetual law of God's justice, the other boweth and bendeth as the carpenter's Bevel.

j. Matt. 19:9 Therefore in these days the Laws that were made against adulterers were not regarded: for they should have needed no divorcement, if marriage had been cut asunder with punishment by death.

k. Matt. 19:10 If the matter stands so between man and wife, or in marriage.

l. Matt. 19:11 The gift of continency is peculiar, and therefore no man can set a Law to himself of perpetual continency.

m. Matt. 19:11 Receive and admit, as by translation we say, that a straight and narrow place is not able to receive many things.

n. Matt. 19:12 The word Eunuch is a general word, and hath divers kinds under it, as gelded men and barren men.

o. Matt. 19:12 Which abstain from marriage, and live continently through the gift of God.

p. Matt. 19:13 Infants and little children are contained in the free covenant of God.

q. Matt. 19:16 They neither know themselves nor the Law, that seek to be saved by the Law.

r. Matt. 19:21 The young man did not answer truly in saying that he had kept all the commandments: and therefore he layeth out an example of true charity before him, to show the disease that lay lurking in his mind.

s. Matt. 19:23 Rich men have need of a singular gift of God, to escape out of the snares of Satan.

t. Matt. 19:24 Word for word, it is of less labor.

u. Matt. 19:24 Theophylact noteth, that by this word is meant a cable rope, but Caninius allegeth out of the Talmuds that it is a proverb, and the word Camel, signifieth the beast itself.

v. Matt. 19:28 It is not lost, that is neglected for God's sake.

w. Matt. 19:28 The regeneration is taken for that day, wherein the elect shall begin to live a new life, that is to say, when they shall enjoy the heavenly inheritance, both in body and soul.

x. Matt. 19:30 To have begun well, and not to continue unto the end, doth not only not profit, but also hurteth very much.

MATT. 19

1. Mark 10:1
2. Gen. 1:27
3. Gen. 2:24 / 1 Cor. 6:16 / Eph. 5:31
4. Deut. 24:1
5. Matt. 5:32 / Mark 10:11 / Luke 16:18 / 1 Cor. 7:11
6. Mark 10:13 / Luke 18:15 / Matt. 18:2
7. Mark 10:27 / Luke 18:18
8. Exod. 20:13 / Deut. 5:16 / Rom. 13:9
9. Mark 10:28 / Luke 18:28
10. Luke 22:29
11. Matt. 26:16 / Mark 10:31 / Luke 13:30

MATT. 20

a. Matt. 20:1 God is bound to no man, and therefore he calleth whomsoever and whensoever he listeth. This only every man ought to take heed of, and hereupon bestow his whole endeavor, that he go forward and come to the mark without all stopping or staggering, and not curiously to examine other men's doings, or the judgments of God.

b. Matt. 20:2 Word for word, fell in time: it is a kind of speech taken from song.

c. Matt. 20:6 The last hour: for the day was twelve hours long, and the first hour began at the Sun rising.

d. Matt. 20:15 Naught, that is, to say, dost thou envy at my goodness towards them? for the Hebrews by an evil eye, meant envy, because such dispositions appear chiefly in the eyes, as above in Matt. 6:23. It is set to answer the word, single, and is taken there for corrupt: for whereas he said there before, verse 22, If thine eye be single, he addeth in verse 23, but if thine eye be wicked, or corrupt, the word being the same in that place, as it is here.

e. Matt. 20:17 Christ goeth to the cross necessarily, but yet willingly.

f. Matt. 20:18 They that least ought, are the greatest persecutors of Christ.

g. Matt. 20:19 The ignomy of the cross, is the sure way to the glory of everlasting life.

h. Matt. 20:20 The manner of the heavenly kingdom is quite contrary to the earthly kingdom.

i. Matt. 20:22 This is spoken by a figure, taking the cup, for that which is contained in the cup. And again the Hebrews understand by this word, Cup, sometime the manner of punishment which is rendered to sin, as Ps. 11:6, or the joy that is given to the faithful, as Ps. 23:5, and sometime a lot or condition, as Ps. 16:5.

j. Matt. 20:22 This is applied to afflictions, as David commonly useth.

k. Matt. 20:23 The almightiness of Christ his divinity is not shut out by this, but it showeth the debasing of himself by taking man's nature upon him.

l. Matt. 20:25 Somewhat sharply and roughly.

m. Matt. 20:29 Christ by healing these blind men with an only touch, showeth that he is the only light of the world.

n. Matt. 20:32 Himself, not by other men's means.

MATT. 20

1. Matt. 19:30 / Matt. 22:14 / Mark 10:31 / Luke 13:30
2. Mark 10:32 / Luke 18:31
3. John 18:32
4. Mark 10:35
5. Mark 10:41 / Luke 22:25
6. Phil. 2:7
7. Mark 10:46 / Luke 18:35

by the way side, when they heard that Jesus passed by, cried, saying, O Lord, the Son of David, have mercy on us. **31** And the multitude rebuked them, because they should hold their peace: but they cried the more, saying, O Lord, the Son of David, have mercy on us. **32** Then Jesus stood still, and [n]called them, and said, What will ye that I should do to you? **33** They said to him, Lord, that our eyes may be opened. **34** And Jesus moved with compassion, touched their eyes, and immediately their eyes received sight, and they followed him.

21

1 Christ rideth on an ass unto Jerusalem. 12 He casteth out the sellers. 13 The house of prayer. 19 The withered fig tree. 25 John's baptism. 28 Who do the will of God. 30 Publicans, Harlots. 33 God's vineyard. The Jews. 38 The son killed of the husbandmen. 42 The cornerstone.

1 And [a,1]when they drew near to Jerusalem, and were come to Bethphage, unto the mount of the Olives, then sent Jesus two disciples, **2** Saying to them, Go into the town that is over against you, and anon ye shall find an ass bound, and a colt with her: loose them, and bring them unto me. **3** And if any man say ought unto you, say ye, that the Lord hath need of them, and straightway [b]he will let them go. **4** All this was done that it might be fulfilled, which was spoken by the Prophet, saying, **5** [2]Tell ye the [c]daughter of Zion, Behold, thy King cometh unto thee, meek and sitting upon an ass, and a colt, the foal of an ass used to the yoke. **6** So the disciples went, and did as Jesus had commanded them, **7** And brought the ass and the colt, and put on them their [d]clothes, and set him [e]thereon. **8** And a great multitude spread their garments in the way: and others cut down branches from the trees, and strawed them in the way. **9** Moreover, the people that went before, and they also that followed, cried, saying, [f]Hosanna to the Son of David, [g]Blessed be he that cometh in the Name of the Lord, Hosanna thou which art in the highest heavens. **10** [3]And when he was come into Jerusalem, [h]all the city was moved, saying, Who is this? **11** And the people said, This is Jesus that Prophet of Nazareth in Galilee. **12** And Jesus went into the Temple of God, and cast out all them [4]that sold and bought in the Temple, and overthrew the tables of the moneychangers, and the seats of them that sold doves, **13** And said to them, It is written, [5]My house shall be called the house of prayer: but [6]ye have made it a den of thieves. **14** Then the blind, and the halt came to him, in the Temple, and he healed them. **15** [i]But when the chief Priests and Scribes saw the marvels that he did, and the children crying in the Temple, and saying, Hosanna to the Son of David, they disdained, **16** And said unto him, Hearest thou what these say? And Jesus said unto them, Yea: read ye never, [7]By the mouth of babes and sucklings thou hast [j]made perfect the praise? **17** [k]So he left them, and went out of the city unto Bethany, and lodged there. **18** [l]And [8]in the morning, as he returned into the city, he was hungry. **19** And seeing a fig tree in the way, he came to it, and found nothing thereon, but leaves only, and said to it, Never fruit grow on thee henceforward. And anon the fig tree withered. **20** And when his disciples saw it, they marveled, saying, How soon is the fig tree withered! **21** [m]And Jesus answered and said unto them, [9]Verily I say unto you, if ye have faith, and [n]doubt not, ye shall not only do that, which I have done to the fig tree, but also if ye say unto this mountain, Take thyself away, and cast thyself into the sea, it shall be done. **22** [10]And whatsoever ye shall ask in prayer, if ye believe, ye shall receive it. **23** [o,11]And when he was come into the Temple, the chief Priests, and the Elders of the people came unto him, as he was teaching, and said, By what [p]authority doest thou these things? and who gave thee this authority? **24** Then Jesus answered, and said unto them, I also will ask of you [q]a certain thing, which if ye tell me, I likewise will tell you by what authority I do these things. **25** The [r]baptism of John, whence was it? from [s]heaven, or of men? Then they [t]reasoned among themselves, saying, If we shall say, From heaven, he will say unto us, Why did ye not then believe him? **26** And if we say, Of men, we fear the multitude, [12]for all hold John as a Prophet. **27** Then they answered Jesus, and said, We can not tell. And he said unto them, Neither tell I you by what authority I do these things. **28** [u]But what think ye? A certain man had two sons, and came to the elder, and said, Son, go and work today in my vineyard. **29** But he answered, and said, I will not: yet afterward he repented himself, and went. **30** Then came he to the second, and said likewise. And he answered, and said, I will, Sir: yet he went not. **31** Whether of them twain did the will of the father? They said unto him, The first. Jesus said unto them, Verily I say unto you, that the Publicans and the harlots [v]go before you into the kingdom of God. **32** For John came unto you in the [w]way of righteousness, and ye believed him not: but the Publicans and the harlots believed him, and ye though ye saw it, were not moved with repentance afterward, that ye might believe him. **33** [x]Hear another parable, There was a certain householder, [13]which planted a vineyard, and hedged it round about, and made a winepress therein, and [y]built a tower, and let it out to husbandmen, and went into a strange country. **34** And when the time of the fruit drew near, he sent his servants to the husbandmen to receive the fruits thereof. **35** And the husbandmen took his servants and beat one, and killed another, and stoned another. **36** Again he sent other servants, more than the first: and they did the like unto them. **37** But last of all he sent unto them his own son, saying, They will reverence my son. **38** But when the husbandmen saw the son, they said among themselves, [14]This is the heir: come, let us kill him, and let us [z]take his inheritance. **39** So they took him, and cast him out of the vineyard, and slew him. **40** When therefore the Lord of the vineyard shall come, what will he do to those husbandmen? **41** They said unto him, He will [aa]cruelly destroy those wicked men, and will let out his vineyard unto other husbandmen, which shall deliver him the fruits in their seasons. **42** Jesus said unto them, Read ye never in the Scriptures, [15]The stone which the [ab]builders refused, the same is [ac]made the [ad]head of the corner? [ae]This was the Lord's doing, and it is marvelous in our eyes. **43** Therefore say I unto you, The kingdom of God shall be taken from you, and shall be given to a nation, which shall bring forth the [af]fruits thereof. **44** [16]And whosoever shall fall on this stone, he shall be broken: but on whomsoever it shall fall, it will [ag]dash him in pieces. **45** And when the chief Priests and Pharisees had heard his parables, they perceived that he spake of them. **46** [ah]And they seeking to lay hands on him, feared the people, because they took him as a Prophet.

22

2 The parable of the marriage. 9 The calling of the Gentiles. 11 The wedding garments, faith. 16 Of Caesar's tribute. 23 They question with Christ touching the resurrection. 32 God is of the living. 36 The greatest commandment. 37 To love God. 39 To love our neighbor. 42 Jesus reasoneth with the Pharisees touching the Messiah.

1 Then [a,1]Jesus answered, and spake unto them again in parables, saying, **2** The kingdom of heaven is like unto a certain king which married his son, **3** And sent forth his servants, to call them that were bidden to the wedding, but they would not come. **4** Again he sent forth other servants, saying,

---

MATT. 21

a. Matt. 21:1 Christ by his humility triumphing over the pride of this world, ascendeth to true glory by ignomy of the cross.
b. Matt. 21:3 He that shall say anything to you, shall let them go, to wit, the ass and the colt.
c. Matt. 21:5 The city of Zion. An Hebrew kind of speech, common in the lamentations of Jeremiah.
d. Matt. 21:7 Their uppermost garments.
e. Matt. 21:7 Upon their garments, not upon the ass and the colt.
f. Matt. 21:9 This was an ancient kind of crying which they used in the feast of Tabernacles, when they carried boughs according as God commanded, Lev. 23:40. And the word is corruptly made of two, for we should say, Hoshiangna, which is as much to say, as Save I pray thee.
g. Matt. 21:9 Well be it to him that cometh in the name of the Lord, that is to say, whom the Lord hath given us for our king.
h. Matt. 21:10 That is, all the men of Jerusalem were moved.
i. Matt. 21:15 Such as should be masters of godliness, are they that do most envy the glory of Christ: but in vain.
j. Matt. 21:16 Thou hast made most perfect. We read in David, Thou hast established or grounded, and if the matter be considered well, it is all one that the Evangelist saith, for that is stable and sure, which is most perfect.
k. Matt. 21:17 Christ doth so forsake the wicked, that yet he hath a consideration and regard of his Church.
l. Matt. 21:18 Hypocrites shall at length have their masks discovered, and their vizards plucked from their faces.
m. Matt. 21:21 How great the force of faith is.
n. Matt. 21:21 The Greek word signifieth a sticking or wavering of mind, so that we cannot tell which way to take.
o. Matt. 21:23 Against them which overstepping the doctrine, blind the calling and vocation to an ordinary succession going about by that false pretext, to stop Christ's mouth.
p. Matt. 21:23 Or, by what power.
q. Matt. 21:24 One word, that is to say, I will ask you in one word.
r. Matt. 21:25 John his preaching is called by a figure, Baptism, because he preached the baptism of repentance, etc., Mark 1:4; Acts 19:3.
s. Matt. 21:25 From God, and so it is plainly seen how these are set one against another.
t. Matt. 21:25 Beat their heads about it and mused, or laid their heads together.
u. Matt. 21:28 It is no new thing to see them to be the worst of all men, which ought to show the way of godliness to others.
v. Matt. 21:31 They make haste to the kingdom of God, and you slack so that at least wise you should have followed their example. Mark then that this word (go before) is improperly taken in this place, whereas no man followeth.
w. Matt. 21:32 Living uprightly, being of a good and honest conversation: For the Hebrews use this word, Way, for life and manners.
x. Matt. 21:33 Those men oftentimes are the cruelest enemies of the Church, to whose fidelity it is committed: But the vocation of God, is neither tied to time, place, nor person.
y. Matt. 21:33 Made the place strong: For a tower is the strongest place of a wall.
z. Matt. 21:38 Word for word, let us hold it fast.
aa. Matt. 21:41 A kind of proverb, showing what end the wicked are worthy of.
ab. Matt. 21:42 Master builders, which are chief builders of the house, that is, of the Church.
ac. Matt. 21:42 Began to be.
ad. Matt. 21:42 The chiefest stone in the corner is called the head of the corner, which beareth up the couplings or joints of the whole building.
ae. Matt. 21:42 That matter (in that the stone which was cast away, is made the head) is the Lord's doing, which we behold and greatly marvel at.
af. Matt. 21:43 They bring forth the fruits of the kingdom of God, which bring forth the fruits of the Spirit, and not of the flesh, Gal. 5.
ag. Matt. 21:44 As chaff used to be scattered with the wind, for he useth a word which signifieth properly, to separate the chaff from the corn with winnowing, to scatter it abroad.
ah. Matt. 21:46 The wicked can do nothing, but what God will.

MATT. 21

1. Mark 11:1 / Luke 19:29
2. Isa. 62:11 / Zech. 9:9 / John 12:15
3. Mark 11:11 / Luke 19:45 / John 2:13
4. Deut. 14:25
5. Isa. 56:6-7
6. Jer. 7:11 / Mark 11:17 / Luke 19:46
7. Ps. 8:2
8. Mark 21:12
9. Matt. 17:20
10. Matt. 7:7 / John 15:7 / 1 John 5:14
11. Mark 11:27-28 / Luke 20:1-2
12. Matt. 14:5 / Mark 6:20
13. Isa. 5:1 / Jer. 2:21 / Mark 12:1 / Luke 20:9
14. Matt. 26:3-4 / Matt. 27:1 / John 11:53
15. Ps. 118:22 / Acts 4:11 / Rom. 9:33
16. Isa. 8:14

MATT. 22

a. Matt. 22:1 Not all of the whole company of them that are called by the voice of the Gospel are the true Church before God: for the most part of them had rather follow the commodities of this life: and some do most cruelly persecute those that call them: but they are the true Church, which

Tell them which are bidden, Behold, I have prepared my dinner: mine oxen and my fatlings are [b]killed, and all things are ready: come unto the marriage. **5** But they made light of it, and went their ways, one to his farm, and another about his merchandise. **6** And the remnant took his servants, and entreated them sharply, and slew them. **7** [c]But when the king heard it, he was wroth, and sent forth his warriors, and destroyed those murderers, and burnt up their city. **8** Then said he to his servants, Truly the [d]wedding is prepared: but they which were bidden, were not worthy. **9** [e]Go ye therefore out into the highways, and as many as ye find, bid them to the marriage. **10** So those servants went out into the highways, and gathered together all that ever they found, both good and [f]bad: so the wedding was furnished with guests. **11** [g]Then the king came in, to see the guests, and saw there a man which had not on a wedding garment. **12** And he said unto him, Friend, how camest thou in hither, and hast not on a wedding garment? And he was [h]speechless. **13** Then said the king to the [i]servants, Bind him hand and foot: take him away, and cast him into utter darkness: [2]there shall be weeping and gnashing of teeth. **14** [3]For many are called, but few chosen. **15** [4]Then went the Pharisees and took counsel how they might [j]tangle him in talk. **16** And they sent unto him their disciples with the [k]Herodians, saying, Master, we know that thou art true, and teachest the way of God [l]truly, neither carest for any man: for thou considerest not the [m]person of men. **17** [n]Tell us therefore, how thinkest thou? Is it lawful to give [o]tribute unto Caesar, or not? **18** But Jesus perceived their wickedness, and said, Why tempt ye me, ye hypocrites? **19** Show me the tribute money. And they brought him a [p]penny. **20** And he said unto them, Whose is this image and superscription? **21** They said unto him, Caesar's. Then said he unto them, [5]Give therefore to Caesar, the things which are Caesar's, and give unto God, those things which are God's. **22** And when they heard it, they marveled, and left him, and went their way. **23** [q,6]The same day the Sadducees came to him, (which say that there is no resurrection) and asked him, **24** Saying, Master, [7]Moses said, If a man die, having no [r]children, his brother shall marry his wife by the right of alliance, and raise up seed unto his brother. **25** Now therefore were with us seven brethren, and the first married a wife, and deceased: and having no issue, left his wife unto his brother. **26** Likewise also the second, and the third, unto the seventh. **27** And last of all the woman died also. **28** Therefore in the resurrection, whose wife shall she be of the seven? for all had her. **29** Then Jesus answered, and said unto them, Ye are deceived, not knowing the Scriptures, nor the power of God. **30** For in the resurrection they neither marry wives, nor wives are bestowed in marriage, but are as the [s]Angels of God in heaven. **31** And concerning the resurrection of the dead, have ye not read what is spoken unto you of God, saying, **32** [8]I am the God of Abraham, and the God of Isaac, and the God of Jacob? God is not the God of the dead, but of the living. **33** And when the multitude heard it, they were astonied at his doctrine. **34** [t,9]But when the Pharisees had heard, that he had put the Sadducees to silence, they assembled together. **35** And [u]one of them, which was an expounder of the Law, asked him a question, tempting him, and saying, **36** Master, which is the great commandment in the Law? **37** Jesus said to him, [10]Thou shalt love the Lord thy God with all thine heart, with all thy [v]soul, and with all thy mind. **38** This is the first and the great commandment. **39** And the second is like unto this, [11]Thou shalt love thy [w]neighbor as thyself. **40** On these two commandments hangeth the whole Law and the Prophets. **41** [x,12]While the Pharisees were gathered together, Jesus asked them, **42** Saying, What think ye of Christ? [y]whose son is he? They said unto him, David's. **43** He said unto them, How then doth David in spirit, call him Lord, saying, **44** [13]The Lord said to my Lord, Sit at my right hand, till I make thine enemies thy footstool? **45** If then David call him Lord, how is he his son? **46** And none could answer him a word, neither durst any from that day forth ask him any more questions.

23

2 How the Scribes teaching the people the Law of Moses, behave themselves. 5 Their Phylacteries, and Fringes. 7 Greetings. 8 We are brethren. 9 The Father. 10 The servant. 13 To shut the kingdom of heaven. 14 To devour widow's houses. 15 A Proselyte. 16 To swear by the Temple. 23 To tithe the mint. 25 To cleanse the outside of the cup. 27 Painted sepulchers. 33 Serpents, vipers. 37 The Hen.

1 Then spake Jesus to the multitude, and to his disciples, **2** [a]Saying, The [1]Scribes and the Pharisees [b]sit in Moses' seat. **3** [c]All therefore whatsoever they bid you observe, that observe and do: but after their works do not: for they say, and do not. **4** [d,2]For they bind heavy burdens, and grievous to be borne, and lay them on men's shoulders, but they themselves will not move them with one of their fingers. **5** [e]All their works they do for to be seen of men: for they make their [f]phylacteries broad, and make long [g]the [3]fringes of their garments, **6** [4]And love the chief place at feasts, and to have the chief seats in the [h]assemblies, **7** And greetings in the markets, and to be called of men, Rabbi, [i]Rabbi. **8** [j,5]But be not ye [k]called, Rabbi: for [l]one is your doctor, to wit, Christ, and all ye are brethren. **9** And [6]call no man your [m]father upon the earth: for there is but one, your father which is in heaven. **10** Be not called [n]doctors: for one is your doctor, even Christ. **11** But he that is greatest among you, let him be your servant. **12** [7]For whosoever [o]will exalt himself, shall be brought low: and whosoever will humble himself, shall be exalted. **13** [p]Woe therefore be unto you, Scribes and Pharisees, [q]hypocrites, because ye shut up the kingdom of heaven before men: for ye yourselves go not in, neither suffer ye them that would [r]enter, to come in. **14** [s,8]Woe be unto you, Scribes and Pharisees, hypocrites: for ye devour widows' houses, even [t]under a color of long prayers: wherefore ye shall receive the greater damnation. **15** Woe be unto you, Scribes and Pharisees, hypocrites: for ye compass sea and [u]land to make one of your profession: and

---

obey when they are called, such as for the most part they are, whom the world despiseth.

b. Matt. 22:4 The word here used is commonly used in sacrifices, and is by translation used for other feasts also: for feasts and banquets were wont to be begun with sacrifices.

c. Matt. 22:7 A dreadful destruction of them that contemn Christ.

d. Matt. 22:8 The marriage feast.

e. Matt. 22:9 God doth first call us, when we think nothing of it.

f. Matt. 22:10 The general calling offereth the Gospel to all men: but their life is examined that enter in.

g. Matt. 22:11 In the small number which come at the calling, there are some castaways which do not confirm their faith with newness of life.

h. Matt. 22:12 Word for word, haltered, that is to say, he held his peace, as though he had had a bridle or an halter about his neck.

i. Matt. 22:13 To them that served the guests.

j. Matt. 22:15 Snare him in his words or talk. The Greek word is derived of snares which hunters lay.

k. Matt. 22:16 They which with Herod made a new religion patched together of the heathenish and the Jewish religion.

l. Matt. 22:16 Truly and sincerely.

m. Matt. 22:16 Thou art not moved with any appearance and outward show.

n. Matt. 22:17 The Christians must obey their Magistrates, although they be wicked and extortioners, but so far forth as the authority that God hath over us may remain safe unto him, and his honor be not diminished.

o. Matt. 22:17 The word that is used here, signifieth a valuing and rating of men's substance, according to the proportion whereof they paid tribute in those provinces which were subject to tribute, and it is here taken for the tribute itself.

p. Matt. 22:19 Before Matt. 17:24 there is mention made of a didrachma, and here, of a penny, whereas a didrachma is more by the seventh part than a penny: so that there seemeth to be a jar in these two places: but they may easily be recorded thus: The penny was paid to the Romans for tribute according to the proportion they were rated at, the drachma was paid of everyone to the Temple, which also the Romans took to themselves when they had subdued Judea.

q. Matt. 22:23 Christ voucheth the resurrection of the flesh against the Sadducees.

r. Matt. 22:24 Under which name are daughters also comprehended, but yet as touching the family and name of a man, because he that left daughters was in no better case, than if he had left no children at all, (for they were not reckoned in the family) by the name of children are Sons understood.

s. Matt. 22:30 He saith not that they shall be without bodies, for then they should not be men anymore, but they shall be as Angels, for they shall neither marry nor be married.

t. Matt. 22:34 The Gospel doth not abolish the precepts of the Law, but doth rather confirm them.

u. Matt. 22:35 A scribe, so saith Mark 12:28, now what a scribe is, see Matt. 2:4.

v. Matt. 22:37 The Hebrew text readeth, Deut. 6:5, with thine heart, soul, and strength: and in Mark 12:30 and Luke 10:27 we read with soul, heart, strength and thought.

w. Matt. 22:39 Another man.

x. Matt. 22:41 Christ proveth manifestly that he is David's son according to the flesh, but otherwise, David's Lord, and very God.

y. Matt. 22:42 Or, whose stock or family: for the Hebrews call a man's posterity, sons.

MATT. 22

1. Luke 14:16 / Rev. 19:9
2. Matt. 8:12 / Matt. 13:42 / Matt. 25:30
3. Matt. 20:16
4. Mark 12:13 / Luke 20:20
5. Mark 12:17 / Luke 20:25 / Rom. 13:7
6. Mark 12:18 / Luke 20:27 / Acts 23:8
7. Deut. 25:5
8. Exod. 3:6 / Mark 12:27
9. Mark 12:28
10. Deut. 6:5
11. Mark 12:31 / Rom. 13:9 / Gal. 5:14 / James 2:8
12. Mark 12:35 / Luke 10:41
13. Ps. 110:1

MATT. 23

a. Matt. 23:2 We ought to hear whatsoever any wicked teachers teach us purely out of the word of God, yet so that we eschew their evil manners.

b. Matt. 23:2 Because God appointed the order, therefore the Lord would have his word to be heard even from the mouth of hypocrites and hirelings.

c. Matt. 23:3 Provided always, that they deliver Moses his doctrine which they profess, which thing the Metaphor of the seat showeth, which they occupied as teachers of Moses his learning.

d. Matt. 23:4 Hypocrites for the most part are most severe exactors of those things which they themselves chiefly neglect.

e. Matt. 23:5 Hypocrites are ambitious.

f. Matt. 23:5 It was a thread, or ribbon of blue silk in the fringe of a corner, the beholding whereof made them to remember the laws and ordinances of God: and therefore was it called a Phylactery, as ye would say, a keeper, Num. 15:38; Deut. 6:8, which order the Jews afterward abused, as they do nowadays, which hang the St. John's Gospels about their necks: a thing condemned many years ago in the Council of Antioch.

g. Matt. 23:5 Word for word, Twisted tassels of thread which hung at the nethermost hems of their garments.

h. Matt. 23:6 When assemblies and Councils are gathered together.

i. Matt. 23:7 This word Rabbi, signifieth one that is above his fellows, and is as good as a number of them: and we may see by the repeating of it, how proud a rule it was. Now they were called Rabbi, which by the laying on of hands were uttered and declared to the world to be wise men.

j. Matt. 23:8 Modesty is a singular ornament of God's minsters.

k. Matt. 23:8 Seek not ambitiously after it: for our Lord doth not forbid us to give the Magistrate and our Masters the honor that is due to them, Augustine de sermone verbi Domine ex, Matt. 11.

l. Matt. 23:8 He seemeth to allude to a place of Isaiah, chapter 54:13, and Jer. 31:34.

m. Matt. 23:9 He shooteth at a fashion which the Jews used, for they called the Rabbis, our fathers.

n. Matt. 23:10 It seemeth that the Scribes did very greedily hunt after such titles, whom verse 16 he calleth blind guides.

o. Matt. 23:12 He seemeth to allude to the name of the Rabbis, for Rabbi signifieth one that is aloft.

p. Matt. 23:13 Hypocrites can abide none to be better than themselves.

q. Matt. 23:13 Christ when he reproveth any man sharply, uses this word, to give us to understand that there is nothing more detestable than hypocrisy and falsehood in religion.

r. Matt. 23:13 Which are even at the door.

s. Matt. 23:14 It is a common thing among hypocrites, to abuse the pretence of zeal to covetousness and extortion.

t. Matt. 23:14 Word for word, under a color of long praying. And this word, Even, noteth a double naughtiness in them: the one, that they devoured widows' goods: the other, that they did it under a color of godliness.

u. Matt. 23:15 The dry part: now that part of that earth is called dry, which the Lord hath given us to dwell upon.

v. Matt. 23:16 Is a debtor. Sins are called in the Syrian tongue, Debts, and it is certain that Christ spake in the Syrian tongue.

when he is made, ye make him twofold more the child of hell, than you yoursel-
ves. **16** Woe be unto you blind guides, which say, Whosoever sweareth by the
Temple, it is nothing: but whosoever sweareth by the gold of the Temple, he [v]of-
fendeth. **17** Ye fools and blind, Whether is greater, the gold, or the Temple that
[w]sanctifieth the gold? **18** And whosoever sweareth by the altar, it is nothing:
but whosoever sweareth by the offering that is upon it, offendeth. **19** Ye fools
and blind, whether is greater, the offering, or the altar which sanctifieth the of-
fering? **20** Whosoever therefore sweareth by the altar, sweareth by it, and by
all things thereon. **21** [9]And whosoever sweareth by the Temple, sweareth by it,
and by him that dwelleth therein. **22** [10]And he that sweareth by heaven, swe-
areth by the [x]throne of God, and by him that sitteth theron. **23** [y,11]Woe be to
you, Scribes and Pharisees, hypocrites: for ye tithe mint, and anise, and cummin,
and leave the weightier matters of the law, as judgment, and mercy and [z]fidelity.
These ought ye to have done, and not to have left the other. **24** Ye blind guides,
which strain out a gnat, and swallow a camel. **25** [aa]Woe be to you, [12]Scribes
and Pharisees, hypocrites: for ye make clean the utter side of the cup, and of the
platter: but within they are full of bribery and excess. **26** Thou blind Pharisee,
cleanse first the inside of the cup and platter, that the outside of them may be clean
also. **27** Woe be to you, Scribes and Pharisees, hypocrites: for ye are like unto
whited tombs, which appear beautiful outward, but are within full of dead men's
bones, and all filthiness. **28** So are ye also: for outward ye appear righteous unto
men, but within ye are full of hypocrisy and iniquity. **29** [ab,13]Woe be unto you,
Scribes and Pharisees, hypocrites: for ye build the tombs of the Prophets, and
garnish the sepulchers of the righteous, **30** And say, If we had been in the days
of our fathers, we would not have been partners with them in the blood of the
Prophets. **31** So then ye be witnesses unto yourselves, that ye are the children
of them that murdered the Prophets. **32** [ac]Fulfill ye also the measure of your fa-
thers. **33** O serpents, the generation of vipers, how should ye escape the damna-
tion of [ad]hell! **34** [ae]Wherefore behold, I send unto you Prophets, and wise men,
and Scribes, and of them ye shall kill and crucify: and of them shall ye scourge in
your Synagogues, and persecute from city to city, **35** [af]That upon you may come
all the righteous blood that was shed upon the earth, [14]from the blood of Abel
the righteous, unto the blood of Zechariah the son of [ag]Berechiah, [15]whom ye
slew between the Temple and the altar. **36** Verily I say unto you, all these things
shall come upon this generation. **37** [ah,16]Jerusalem, Jerusalem, which killest the
Prophets, and stonest them which are sent to thee, how often would I have [ai]gathe-
red thy children together, as the hen gathered her chickens under her wings, and ye
would not! **38** Behold, your habitation shall be left unto you desolate. **39** For
I say unto you, ye shall not see me henceforth till that ye say, Blessed is he that co-
meth in the Name of the Lord.

24

2 The destruction of the Temple. 4 The signs of Christ's coming. 12 Iniquity. 23 False Christs. 29 The signs of the end of the world. 31 The Angels. 32 The fig tree. 37 The days of Noah. 42 We must watch. 45 The servant.

1 And [1]Jesus went out, and departed from the Temple, and his disciples came
to him, to show him the building of the Temple. **2** [a]And Jesus said unto them,
See ye not all these things? Verily I say unto you, [2]there shall not be here left
a stone upon a stone, that shall not be cast down. **3** And as he sat upon the
mount of Olives, his disciples came unto him apart, saying, Tell us when these
things shall be, and what sign shall be of thy coming, and of the end of the wor-
ld. **4** [b]And Jesus answered, and said unto them, [3]Take heed that no man deceive
you. **5** For many shall come in my Name, saying, I am Christ, and shall deceive
many. **6** And ye shall hear of wars, and rumors of wars: see that ye be not [4]trou-
bled: for all these things must come to pass, but the [c]end is not yet. **7** For nation
shall rise against nation, and realm against realm, and there shall be famine, and
pestilence, and earthquakes in [d]divers places. **8** All these are but the beginning
of [e]sorrows. **9** [5]Then shall they deliver you up to be afflicted, and shall kill you,
and ye shall be hated of all nations for my Name's sake. **10** And then shall many
be offended, and shall betray one another, and shall hate one another. **11** And
many false prophets shall arise, and shall deceive many. **12** And because ini-
quity shall be increased, the love of many shall be cold. **13** [f,6]But he that en-
dureth to the end, he shall be saved. **14** And this [g]Gospel of the kingdom shall
be preached through the whole [h]world for a witness unto all nations, and then
shall the end come. **15** [i]When ye [7]therefore shall see the [j]abomination of de-
solation spoken of by [8]Daniel the Prophet, set in the holy place (let him that
readeth consider it.) **16** Then let them which be in Judea, flee into the moun-
tains. **17** Let him which is on the housetop, not come down to fetch anything
out of his house. **18** And he that is in the field, let not him return back to fetch
his [k]clothes. **19** And woe shall be to them that are with child, and to them that
give suck in those days. **20** But pray that your flight be not in the winter, nei-
ther on the [l,9]Sabbath day. **21** For then shall be great tribulation, such as was not
from the beginning of the world to this time, nor shall be. **22** And except [m]those
days should be shortened, there should no [n]flesh be saved: but for the elect's sake
those days shall be shortened. **23** [10]Then if any man shall say unto you, Lo, here
is Christ, or there, believe it not. **24** For there shall arise false Christs, and false
prophets, and [o]shall show great signs and wonders, so that if it were possible, they
should deceive the very elect. **25** Behold, I have told you before. **26** Where-
fore if they shall say unto you, Behold, he is in the desert, go not forth: Behold,
he is in the secret places, believe it not. **27** For as the lightning cometh out of
the East, and is seen into the West, so shall also the coming of the Son of man
be. **28** [p,11]For wheresoever a dead [q]carcass is, thither will the Eagles be gathered
together. **29** [r,12]And immediately after the tribulations of those days shall the
sun be darkened, and the moon shall not give her light, and the stars shall fall from
heaven, and the powers of heaven shall be shaken. **30** And then shall appear the
[s]sign of the Son of man in heaven: and then shall all the [t]kindreds of the earth
[u]mourn, [13]and they shall see the Son of man [v]come in the clouds of heaven with
power and great glory. **31** [14]And he shall send his Angels with a great sound of a
trumpet, and they shall gather together his elect, from the [w]four winds, and from
the one end of the heavens unto the other. **32** [x]Now learn the parable of the fig
tree: when her bough is yet [y]tender, and it putteth forth leaves, ye know that sum-
mer is near. **33** So likewise ye, when ye see all these things, know that the king-
dom of God is near, even at the doors. **34** Verily I say unto you, this [z]generation
shall not pass, till all these things be done. **35** [aa,15]Heaven and earth shall pass
away: but my words shall not pass away. **36** [ab]But of that day and hour knoweth

---

w. Matt. 23:17 Causeth the gold to be counted holy, which is dedicated to an holy use.
x. Matt. 23:22 If heaven be God's throne, then he is no doubt above all this world.
y. Matt. 23:23 Hypocrites are careful in trifles, and neglect the greatest things of purpose.
z. Matt. 23:23 Faithfulness in keeping of promises.
aa. Matt. 23:25 Hypocrites are too much careful of outward things, and the inward they utterly contemn.
ab. Matt. 23:29 Hypocrites when they go most about to cover their wickedness, then do they by the just judgment of God, shame themselves.
ac. Matt. 23:32 A proverb used of the Jews, which hath this meaning, Go ye on also and follow your ancestors, that at length your wickedness may come to the full.
ad. Matt. 23:33 See also Matt. 5:22.
ae. Matt. 23:34 Hypocrites be cruel.
af. Matt. 23:35 The end of them which persecute the Gospel, under the pretence of zeal.
ag. Matt. 23:35 Of Joiada, who was also called Berechiah, that is, blessed of the Lord.
ah. Matt. 23:37 Where the mercy of God was greatest, there was greatest wickedness and rebellion, and at length the most sharp judgments of God.
ai. Matt. 23:37 He speaketh of the outward ministry, and as he was promised for the saving of this people, so was he also careful for it, even from the time that the promise was made to Abraham.

MATT. 23

1. Neh. 8:4
2. Luke 11:46 / Acts 15:10
3. Num. 15:38 / Deut. 12:12 / Mark 12:38
4. Luke 11:43 / Luke 20:46
5. James 3:1
6. Mal. 1:6
7. Luke 14:11 / Luke 18:14
8. Mark 12:40 / Luke 20:47
9. 1 Kings 8:13 / 2 Chron. 6:2
10. Matt. 5:34
11. Luke 11:42
12. Luke 12:39
13. Matt.5:22
14. Gen. 4:8
15. 2 Chron. 24:21
16. Luke 13:34

MATT. 24

a. Matt. 24:2 The destruction of the city, and especially of the Temple is foretold.
b. Matt. 24:4 The Church shall have a continual conflict with infinite miseries and offences, and that more is, with false prophets, until the day of victory and triumph cometh.
c. Matt. 24:6 That is, when those things are fulfilled, yet the end shall not come.
d. Matt. 24:7 Everywhere.
e. Matt. 24:8 Word for word, of great torments, like unto women in travail.
f. Matt. 24:13 The Gospel shall be spread abroad, rage the devil never so much: and they which do constantly believe, shall be saved.
g. Matt. 24:14 Joyful tidings of the kingdom of heaven.
h. Matt. 24:14 Through all that part that is dwelt in.
i. Matt. 24:15 The Kingdom of Christ shall not be abolished when the city of Jerusalem is utterly destroyed, but shall be stretched out even to the end of the world.
j. Matt. 24:15 The abomination of desolation, that is to say, which all men detest and cannot abide, by reason of the foul and shameful filthiness of it: and he speaketh of the idols that were set up in the Temple, or as others think, he meant the morning of the doctrine in the Church.
k. Matt. 24:18 This betokeneth the great fear that shall be.
l. Matt. 24:20 It was not lawful to take a journey on the Sabbath day; Josephus, book 13.
m. Matt. 24:22 Those things which befell the people of the Jews, in the 34 years, when as the whole land was wasted, and at length the city of Jerusalem taken, and both it and their Temple destroyed, are mixed with those which shall come to pass before the last coming of our Lord.
n. Matt. 24:22 The whole nation should utterly be destroyed: and this word Flesh is by a figure taken for man, as the Hebrews used to speak.
o. Matt. 24:24 Shall openly lay forth great signs for men to behold.
p. Matt. 24:28 The only remedy against the furious rage of the world, is to be gathered and joined to Christ.
q. Matt. 24:28 Christ, who will come with speed and his presence will be with a majesty to whom all shall flock even as Eagles.
r. Matt. 24:29 Everlasting damnation shall be the end of the security of the wicked, and everlasting bliss, of the miseries of the godly.
s. Matt. 24:30 The exceeding glory and majesty, which shall bear witness, that Christ the Lord of heaven and earth draweth near to judge the world.
t. Matt. 24:30 All nations: and he alludeth to the dispersion which we read of, Gen. 10 and 11, or to the dividing of the people of Israel.
u. Matt. 24:30 They shall be in such sorrow, that they shall strike themselves: and it is transferred to the mourning.
v. Matt. 24:30 Sitting upon the clouds, as he was taken up into heaven.
w. Matt. 24:31 From the four quarters of the world.
x. Matt. 24:32 If God hath prescribed a certain order to nature, much more hath he done so to his eternal judgments, but the wicked understand it not, or rather make a mock at it: but the godly do mark it, and wait for it.
y. Matt. 24:32 When his tenderness showeth that the sap which is the life of the tree, is come from the root into the bark.
z. Matt. 24:34 This age: this word generation or Age, being used for the men of this age.
aa. Matt. 24:35 The Lord doth now begin the judgment, which he will make an end of in the latter day.
ab. Matt. 24:36 It is sufficient for us to know that God hath appointed a latter day for the restoring of all things, but when it shall be, it is hidden from us all, for our profit, that we may be so much the more watchful, that we be not taken as they were in old time in the flood.

no man, no not the Angels of heaven, but my father only. **37** But as the days of Noah were, so likewise shall the coming of the Son of man be. **38** [16]For as in the days before the flood, they did [ac]eat and drink, marry, and give in marriage, unto the day that Noah entered into the Ark, **39** And knew nothing, till the flood came, and took them all away, so shall also the coming of the Son of man be. **40** [ad,17]Then two shall be in the fields, the one shall be received, and the other shall be refused. **41** [ae]Two women shall be grinding at the mill: the one shall be received, and the other shall be refused. **42** [af,18]Watch therefore: for ye know not what hour your master will come. **43** [19]Of this be sure, that if the good man of the house knew at what watch the thief would come, he would surely watch, and not suffer his house to be dug through. **44** Therefore be ye also ready: for in the hour that ye think not, will the Son of man come. **45** [20]Who then is a faithful servant and wise, whom his master hath made ruler over his household, to give them meat in season? **46** Blessed is that servant, whom his master when he cometh, shall find so doing. **47** Verily I say unto you, he shall make him ruler over all his goods. **48** But if that evil servant shall say in his heart, My master doth defer his coming, **49** And begin to smite his fellows, and to eat, and to drink with the drunken, **50** That servant's master will come in a day, when he looketh not for him, and in an hour that he is not aware of, **51** And will [ag]cut him off, and give him his portion with hypocrites: [21]there shall be weeping and gnashing of teeth.

25

1 The virgins looking for the Bridegroom. 13 We must watch. 14 The talents delivered unto the servants. 24 The evil servants. 30 After what sort the last judgment shall be. 41 The cursed.

1 Then [a]the kingdom of heaven shall be likened unto ten virgins, which took their lamps, and [b]went forth to meet the bridegroom. **2** And five of them were wise, and five foolish. **3** The foolish took their lamps, but took no oil with them. **4** But the wise took oil in their vessels with their lamps. **5** Now while the bridegroom tarried long, all [c]slumbered and slept. **6** And at midnight there was a cry made, Behold, the bridegroom cometh: go out to meet him. **7** Then all those virgins arose and trimmed their lamps. **8** And the foolish said to the wise, Give us of your oil, for our lamps are out. **9** But the wise answered, saying, Not so, lest there will not be enough for us and you: but go ye rather to them that sell, and buy for yourselves. **10** And while they went to buy, the bridegroom came: and they that were ready, went in with him to the wedding, and the gate was shut. **11** Afterwards came also the other virgins, saying, Lord, Lord, open to us. **12** But he answered, and said, Verily I say unto you, I know you not. **13** [1]Watch therefore: for ye know neither the day, nor the hour, when the son of man will come. **14** [d,2]For the kingdom of heaven is as a man that going into a strange country, called his servants, and delivered to them his goods. **15** And unto one he gave five talents, and to another two, and to another one, to every man after his own [e]ability, and straightway went from home. **16** Then he that had received the five talents, went and occupied with them, and gained other five talents. **17** Likewise also he that received two, he also gained other two. **18** But he that received that one, went and dug it in the earth, and hid his master's money. **19** But after a long season, the master of those servants came, and reckoned with them. **20** Then came he that had received five talents, and brought other five talents, saying, Master, thou deliveredst unto me five talents: behold, I have gained with them other five talents. **21** Then his master said unto him, It is well done good servant and faithful, Thou hast been faithful in little, I will make thee ruler over much: [f]enter into thy master's joy. **22** Also he that had received two talents, came, and said, Master, thou deliveredst unto me two talents: behold, I have gained two other talents more. **23** His master said unto him, It is well done good servant, and faithful, Thou hast been faithful in little, I will make thee ruler over much: enter into thy master's joy. **24** Then he that had received the one talent, came, and said, Master, I knew that thou wast an hard man, which reapest where thou sowedst not, and gatherest where thou strawedst not: **25** I was therefore afraid, and went, and hid thy talent in the earth: behold, thou hast thine own. **26** And his master answered, and said unto him, Thou evil servant, and slothful, thou knewest that I reap where I sowed not, and gather where I strawed not. **27** Thou oughtest therefore to have put my money to the [g]exchangers, and then at my coming should I have received mine own with vantage. **28** Take therefore the talent from him, and give it unto him which hath ten talents. **29** [3]For unto every man that hath, it shall be given, and he shall have abundance, and from him that hath not, even that he hath shall be taken away. **30** Cast therefore that unprofitable servant into utter [4]darkness: there shall be weeping and gnashing of teeth. **31** [h]And when the Son of man cometh in his glory and all the holy Angels with him, then shall he sit upon the throne of his glory, **32** And before him shall be gathered all nations, and he shall separate them one from another as a shepherd separateth the sheep from the goats. **33** And he shall set the sheep on his right hand, and the goats on the left. **34** Then shall the king say to them on his right hand, Come ye [i]blessed of my father: take the inheritance of the kingdom prepared for you from the foundation of the world. **35** [5]For I was an hungered, and ye gave me meat: I thirsted, and ye gave me drink: I was a stranger, and ye took me in unto you. **36** I was naked, and ye clothed me: I was [6]sick, and ye visited me: I was in prison, and ye came unto me. **37** Then shall the righteous answer him, saying, Lord, when saw we thee an hungered, and fed thee? or athirst, and gave thee drink? **38** And when saw we thee a stranger, and took thee in unto us? or naked, and clothed thee? **39** Or when saw we thee sick, or in prison, and came unto thee? **40** And the king shall answer, and say unto them, Verily I say unto you, inasmuch as ye have done it unto one of the least of these my brethren, ye have done it to me. **41** Then shall he say to them on the left hand, [7]Depart from me ye cursed, into everlasting fire, which is prepared for the devil and his angels. **42** For I was an hungered, and ye gave me no meat: I thirsted, and ye gave me no drink: **43** I was a stranger, and ye took me not in unto you: I was naked, and ye clothed me not: sick, and in prison, and ye visited me not. **44** Then shall they also answer him, saying, Lord, when saw we thee an hungered, or athirst, or a stranger, or naked, or sick, or in prison, and did not minister unto thee? **45** Then shall he answer them, and say, Verily I say unto you, inasmuch as ye did it not to one of the least of these, ye did it not to me. **46** [8]And these shall go into everlasting pain, and the righteous into life eternal.

26

3 The consultation of the Priests against Christ. 6 His feet are anointed. 15 Judas selleth him. 26 The institution of the supper, 34 and 36 Peter's denial: Christ is heavy. 47 He is betrayed with a kiss. 57 He is led to Caiaphas. 64 He confesseth himself to be Christ. 67 They spit at him.

1 And [a,1]it came to pass, when Jesus had finished all these sayings, he said unto his disciples, **2** [b]Ye know that after two days is the Passover, and the Son of man shall be delivered to be crucified. **3** [2]Then assembled together the chief Priests, and the Scribes, and the Elders of the people into the hall of the high Priest called Caiaphas: **4** And consulted together that they might take Jesus by subtilty, and kill him. **5** But they said, Not on the [c]feast day, lest any uproar be among the people. **6** [d,3]And when Jesus was in Bethany, in the house of Simon the

---

ac. Matt. 24:38 The word which the Evangelist useth, expresseth the matter more fully than ours doth: for it is a word which is proper to brute beasts: and his meaning is, that in those days men shall be given to their bellies like unto brute beasts: for otherwise it is no fault to eat and drink.

ad. Matt. 24:40 Against them that persuade themselves that God will be merciful to all men, and do by that means give over themselves to sin, that they may in the meanwhile live in pleasure void of all care.

ae. Matt. 24:41 The Greek women and the Barbarians did grind and bake. (Plutarch, book Problem)

af. Matt. 24:42 An example of the horrible carelessness of men in those things whereof they ought to be most careful.

ag. Matt. 24:51 To wit, from the rest, or will cut him into two parts, which was a most cruel kind of punishment, wherewith as Justin Martyr witnesseth, Isaiah the Prophet was executed by the Jews: the like kind of punishment we read of, 1 Sam. 15:33 and Dan. 3:29.

MATT. 24

1. Mark 13:1 / Luke 21:5-6
2. Luke 19:44
3. Eph. 5:6 / Col. 2:18
4. Eph. 5:6 / Col. 2:18
5. Matt. 10:17 / Luke 21:12 / John 15:20 / John 16:2
6. 1 Thess. 3:13 / 2 Tim. 2:5
7. Mark 13:14 / Luke 21:20
8. Dan. 9:27
9. Acts 1:12
10. Mark 13:21 / Luke 17:23
11. Luke 17:37
12. Mark 13:14 / Luke 21:25 / Isa. 13:10 / Ezek. 32:7 / Joel 2:31 / Joel 3:15
13. Rev. 1:7 / Dan. 7:13
14. 1 Cor. 15:52 / 1 Thess. 4:16
15. Mark 13:31
16. Luke 17:26 / Gen. 7:1 / 1 Pet. 3:20
17. Luke 17:36
18. Mark 13:35
19. Luke 12:39 / 1 Thess. 5:2 / Rev. 16:15
20. Luke 12:42
21. Matt. 13:42 / Matt. 25:30

MATT. 25

a. Matt. 25:1 We must desire strength at God's hand, which may serve us as a torch while we walk through this darkness, to bring us to our desired end: otherwise if we become slothful and negligent as weary of our pains and travail, we shall be shut out of the doors.

b. Matt. 25:1 The pomp of bridals was wont for the most part to be kept in the night seasons, and that by damsels.

c. Matt. 25:5 Their eyes being heavy with sleep.

d. Matt. 25:14 Christ witnesseth that there shall be a long time between his departure to his father, and his coming again to us, but yet notwithstanding that, he will at that day take an account not only of the rebellious and obstinate, how they have bestowed that which they received of him, but also of his household servants, which have not through slothfulness employed those gifts which he bestowed upon them.

e. Matt. 25:15 According to the wisdom and skill in dealing, which was given them.

f. Matt. 25:21 Come, and receive the fruit of goodness, now the Lord's joy is doubled, John 15:11, that my joy may remain in you, and your joy be fulfilled.

g. Matt. 25:27 Table mates which have their shop bulks or tables set abroad, where they let out money to usury.

h. Matt. 25:31 A lively setting forth of the everlasting judgment which is to come.

i. Matt. 25:34 Blessed and happy, upon whom my Father hath most abundantly bestowed his benefits.

MATT. 25

1. Matt. 24:42 / Mark 13:35
2. Luke 19:12-13
3. Matt. 13:12 / Mark 4:25 / Luke 8:18 / Luke 19:26
4. Matt. 8:12 / Matt. 22:13
5. Isa. 58:7 / Ezek. 18:7
6. Eccl. 7:35
7. Ps. 6:8 / Matt. 7:13 / Luke 13:27
8. Dan. 12:2 / John 5:29
9.

MATT. 26

a. Matt. 26:1 Christ witnesseth by his voluntarily going to death, that he will make full satisfaction for the sin of Adam, by his obedience.

b. Matt. 26:2 God himself and not men, appointed the time that Christ should be crucified in.

c. Matt. 26:5 By the word Feast, is meant the whole feast of unleavened bread: the first and eighth day whereof were so holy, that they might do no manner of work therein, though the whole company of the Sanhedrin determined otherwise: And yet it came to pass through God's providence, that Christ suffered at that time, to the end that all the people of Israel might be witnesses of his everlasting sacrifice.

d. Matt. 26:6 By this sudden work of a sinful woman, Christ giveth the guests to understand of his death and burial which was nigh: the favor whereof shall bring life to all sinners which flee unto him. But Judas taketh an occasion hereby to accomplish his wicked purpose and counsel.

e. Matt. 26:7 For these things were done before Christ came to Jerusalem: and yet some think that the Evangelists recite two histories.

leper, 7 [e]There came unto him a woman, which had a [f]box of very costly ointment, and poured it on his head, as he sat at the table. 8 And when his [g]disciples saw it, they had indignation, saying, What needed this [h]waste? 9 For this ointment might have been sold for much, and been given to the poor. 10 [i]And Jesus knowing it, said unto them, Why trouble ye the woman? for she hath wrought a good work upon me. 11 [j,4]For ye have the poor always with you, but me shall ye not have always. 12 For [k]in that she poured this ointment on my body, she did it to bury me. 13 Verily I say unto you, wheresoever this Gospel shall be preached throughout all the world, there shall also this that she hath done, be spoken of for a memorial of her. 14 [5]Then one of the twelve, called Judas Iscariot, went unto the chief Priests, 15 And said, What will ye give me, and I will deliver him unto you, and they appointed unto him thirty pieces of silver. 16 And from that time, he sought opportunity to betray him. 17 [l,6]Now [m]on the first day of the feast of unleavened bread, the disciples came to Jesus, saying unto him, Where wilt thou that we prepare for thee to eat the Passover? 18 And he said, Go ye into the city to such a man, and say to him, The master saith, My time is at hand: I will keep the Passover at thine house with my disciples. 19 And the disciples did as Jesus had given them charge, and made ready the Passover. 20 [7]So when the even was come, he [n]sat down with the twelve. 21 And as they did eat, he said, [8]Verily, I say unto you, that one of you shall betray me. 22 And they were exceeding sorrowful, and began every one of them to say unto him, Is it I, Master? 23 And he answered and said, [9]He that [o]dippeth his hand with me in the dish, he shall betray me. 24 Surely the Son of man goeth his way, as it is written of him: but woe be to that man, by whom the Son of man is betrayed: it had been good for that man, if he had never been born. 25 Then Judas [p]which betrayed him, answered, and said, Is it I, master? He said unto him, Thou hast said it. 26 [q,10]And as they did eat, Jesus took the bread, and when he had [r]blessed, he brake it, and gave it to the disciples, and said, Take, eat: [s]this is my body. 27 Also he took the cup, and when he had given thanks, he gave it them, saying, Drink ye [t]all of it. 28 [u]For this is my blood of the [v]new Testament that is shed for many, for the remission of sins. 29 I say unto you that I will not drink henceforth of this fruit of the vine until that day, when I shall drink it new with you in my Father's kingdom. 30 And when they had sung [w]a Psalm, they went out into the mount of Olives. 31 [x,11]Then said Jesus unto them, All ye shall be offended by me this night: for it is written, I [12]will smite the shepherd, and the sheep of the flock shall be scattered. 32 But [13]after I am risen again, I will go before you into Galilee. 33 But Peter answered, and said unto him, Though that all men should be offended by thee, yet will I never be offended. 34 [14]Jesus said unto him, Verily I say unto thee, that this night, before the cock crow, thou shalt deny me thrice. 35 Peter said unto him, Though I should die with thee, I will in no case deny thee. Likewise also said all the disciples. 36 [y,15]Then went Jesus with them into a place which is called Gethsemane, and said unto his disciples, Sit ye here, while I go, and pray yonder. 37 And he took unto him Peter, and the two sons of Zebedee, and began to wax sorrowful, and [z]grievously troubled. 38 [aa]Then said Jesus unto them, My soul is very heavy, even unto the death: tarry ye here, and watch with me. 39 So he went a little further, and fell on his face, and prayed, saying, O my Father, if it be possible, [ab]let this [ac]cup pass from me: nevertheless, not as I will, but as thou wilt. 40 [ad]After, he came unto the disciples, and found them asleep, and said to Peter, What? could ye not watch with me one hour? 41 Watch, and pray, that ye enter not into temptation: the spirit indeed is ready, but the flesh is weak. 42 Again he went away the second time, and prayed, saying, O my Father, if this cup cannot pass away from me, but that I must drink it, thy will be done. 43 And he came and found them asleep again, for their eyes were heavy. 44 So he left them, and went away again, and prayed the third time, saying the same words. 45 Then came he to his disciples, and said unto them, Sleep henceforth, and take your rest: behold, the hour is at hand, and the Son of man is given into the hands of sinners. 46 [ae]Rise, let us go: behold, he is at hand that betrayeth me. 47 [16]And while he yet spake, lo, Judas one of the twelve came, and with him a great multitude with swords and staves, [af]from the high Priests and Elders of the people. 48 Now he that betrayed him, had given them a token, saying, Whomsoever I shall kiss, that is he, lay hold on him. 49 And forthwith he came to Jesus, and said, God save thee, Master, and kissed him. 50 [ag]Then Jesus said unto him, [ah]Friend, wherefore art thou come? Then came they, and laid hands on Jesus, and took him. 51 And behold, one of them which were with Jesus, stretched out his hand, and drew his sword, and struck a servant of the high Priest, and smote off his ear. 52 [ai]Then said Jesus unto him, Put up thy sword into his place: [17]for all that [aj]take the sword, shall perish with the sword. 53 [ak]Either thinkest thou, that I cannot now pray to my Father, and he will give me more than twelve legions of Angels? 54 [al]How then should the [18]Scriptures be fulfilled, which say, that it must be so? 55 The same hour said Jesus to the multitude, Ye be come out as it were against a thief, with swords and staves to take me: I sat daily teaching in the Temple among you, and ye took me not. 56 But all this was done, that the Scriptures of the Prophets might be fulfilled. [19]Then all the disciples forsook him, and fled. 57 [am,20]And they took Jesus, and led him to [an]Caiaphas the high Priest, where the Scribes and the Elders were assembled. 58 And Peter followed him afar off unto the high Priest's [ao]hall, and went in and sat with the servants to see the end. 59 Now [21]the chief Priests and the Elders, and all the whole Council sought false witness against Jesus, to put him to death. 60 But they found none, and though many false witnesses came, yet found they none: but at the last came two false witnesses, 61 And said, This man said, [22]I can destroy the Temple of God, and build it in three days. 62 Then the chief Priest arose, and said to him, Answerest thou nothing? [ap]What is the matter that these men witness against thee? 63 But Jesus held his peace. Then the chief Priest answered, and said to him, I charge thee swear unto us by the living God, to tell us, If thou be that Christ the son of God, or no. 64 [23]Jesus said to him, Thou hast said it: nevertheless I say unto you, [aq]Hereafter shall ye see the Son of man, sitting [ar]at the right hand of

---

f. Matt. 26:7 These boxes were of alabaster, which in old time men made hollow to put in ointments: for some write, that alabaster keepeth ointment without corruption, Pliny, book 13, chapter 1.

g. Matt. 26:8 This is a figure called Synecdoche: for it is said but of Judas that he was moved thereat, John 12:4.

h. Matt. 26:8 Unprofitable spending.

i. Matt. 26:10 We ought not rashly to condemn that which is not orderly done.

j. Matt. 26:11 Christ, who was once anointed in his own person, must always be anointed in the poor.

k. Matt. 26:12 In that she poured this ointment upon my body, she did it to bury me.

l. Matt. 26:17 Christ verily purposing to bring us into our country out of hand, and so to abrogate the figure of the Law, fulfilleth the Law, neglecting the contrary tradition and custom of the Jews, and there withall showeth that all things shall so come to pass by the ministry of men, that the secret counsel of God shall govern them.

m. Matt. 26:17 This was the fourteenth day of the first month: and the first day of unleavened bread should have been the fifteenth, but because this day's evening (which after the manner of the Romans was referred to the day before) did belong by the Jews' manner to the day following, therefore it is called the first day of unleavened bread.

n. Matt. 26:20 Because the Law appointed them to be shod, and have their staffs in their hands, as though they were in haste, thereby it is to be gathered that they sat not down when they did eat the Passover, but stood, for otherwise when they went to meat, they put off their shoes: therefore he speaketh here in this place, not of the Passover, but of the Supper, which was celebrated after that the Passover was solemnly done.

o. Matt. 26:23 That is to say, whom I vouchsafed to come to my table, alluding to the place, Ps. 41:9, which is not so to be understood, as though at the selfsame instant that the Lord spake these words, Judas had his hand in the dish (for that had been an undoubted token) but it is meant of his tabling and eating with them.

p. Matt. 26:25 Whose head was about nothing then but to betray him.

q. Matt. 26:26 Christ minding forthwith to fulfill the promises of the old covenant, instituteth a new covenant with new figures.

r. Matt. 26:26 Mark saith, Had given thanks: and therefore blessing is not a consecrating, with a conjuring kind of murmuring and force of words: and yet the bread and the wine are changed, not in nature, but in quality, for they become undoubted tokens of the body and blood of Christ, not of their own nature or force of words, but by Christ his institution, which must be recited and laid forth, that faith may find what to lay hold on, both in the word and in the elements.

s. Matt. 26:26 This is a figurative speech, which is called Metonymy: that is to say, the putting of one name for another—so calling the bread his body, which is the sign and sacrament of his body: and yet notwithstanding, it is so a figurative and changed kind of speech, that the faithful do receive Christ indeed with all his gifts (though by a spiritual means) and become one with him.

t. Matt. 26:27 Therefore they which took away the cup from the people, did against Christ his institution.

u. Matt. 26:28 To wit, this cup or wine, is my blood Sacramentally, as Luke 22:20.

v. Matt. 26:28 Or covenant, that is to say, whereby the new league and covenant is made, for in making of leagues, they used pouring of wine, and shedding of blood.

w. Matt. 26:30 When they had made an end of their solemn singing, which some think was six Psalms, beginning at Ps. 112 to 117.

x. Matt. 26:31 Christ being more careful of his disciples, than of himself, forewarneth them of their flight, and putteth them in better comfort.

y. Matt. 26:36 Christ having regard to the weakness of his disciples, leaving all the rest in safety, taketh with him but three to be witnesses of his anguish, and goeth of purpose into the place appointed to betray him in.

z. Matt. 26:37 The word which he useth, signifieth great sorrow, and marvelous and deadly grief: which thing, as it betokeneth the truth of man's nature, which shunneth death as a thing that entered in against nature, so it showeth that though Christ were void of sin, yet he sustained this horrible punishment, because he felt the wrath of God kindled against us for sins, which he revenged and punished in his person.

aa. Matt. 26:38 Christ a true man, going about to suffer the punishment which was due unto us, for forsaking of God is forsaken of his own: he hath a terrible conflict with the horror and fear of the curse of God: out of which he escaping as a conqueror, causeth us not to be afraid anymore of death.

ab. Matt. 26:39 Let it pass me, and not touch me.

ac. Matt. 26:39 That is, which is at hand, and is offered and prepared for me: a kind of speech which the Hebrews use, for the wrath of God, and the punishment he sendeth. See also Matt. 20:22.

ad. Matt. 26:40 An example of the carelessness of man.

ae. Matt. 26:46 Christ offereth himself willingly to be taken, that in so obeying willingly, he might make satisfaction for the willful fall of man.

af. Matt. 26:47 Sent from the high Priests.

ag. Matt. 26:50 Christ is taken that we might be delivered.

ah. Matt. 26:50 Christ reprehendeth Judas tauntingly, and rebuketh him sharply, for he knew well enough for what cause he came.

ai. Matt. 26:52 Our vocation must be the rule of our zeal.

aj. Matt. 26:52 They take the sword to whom the Lord hath not given it, that is to say, they which use the sword, and are not called to it.

ak. Matt. 26:53 Christ was taken, because he was willing to be taken.

al. Matt. 26:54 By this questioning he answereth a sly objection, for they might have asked him why he did not in this his great extremity of danger, call to his Father for aid: but to this he answereth by a question.

am. Matt. 26:57 Christ being innocent is condemned of the high Priest for that wickedness whereof we are guilty.

an. Matt. 26:57 From Annas to Caiaphas, before whom the multitude was assembled, John 18:13.

ao. Matt. 26:58 The word here used, signifieth properly an open large room before an house, as we see in Kings' palaces and noble men's houses: we call it a court, for it is open to the air, and by a figure Synecdoche is taken for the house itself.

ap. Matt. 26:62 How cometh it to pass that these men witness against thee?

aq. Matt. 26:64 This word distinguisheth his first coming from the latter.

ar. Matt. 26:64 Sitting with God in like and equal honor at the right hand of his power, that is, in greatest power: for the right hand signifieth among the Hebrews, that that is mighty and of great power.

as. Matt. 26:64 Clouds of heaven, see also Matt. 24:30.

the power of God, and come in the [as]clouds of the heaven. **65** Then the high
Priest [at]rent his clothes, saying, He hath blasphemed, what have we any more need
of witnesses: behold, now ye have heard his blasphemy. **66** What think ye? They
answered, and said, He is guilty of death. **67** [24]Then spat they in his face, and
buffeted him, and others smote him with rods, **68** Saying, Prophesy to us, O
Christ, Who is he that smote thee? **69** [au,25]Peter [av]sat without in the hall, and a
maid came to him, saying, Thou also wast with Jesus of Galilee: **70** But he de-
nied before them all, saying, I wot not what thou sayest. **71** And when he went
out into the porch, another maid saw him, and said unto them that were there,
This man was also with Jesus of Nazareth. **72** And again he denied with an oath,
saying, I know not the man. **73** So after a while, came unto him they that stood
by, and said unto Peter, Surely thou art also one of them: for even thy speech
bewrayeth thee. **74** Then began he to [aw]curse himself, and to swear, saying, I
know not the man. And immediately the cock crew. **75** Then Peter remembered
the words of Jesus, which had said unto him, Before the cock crow thou shalt deny
me thrice. So he went out, and wept bitterly.

27

2 He is delivered bound to Pilate. 5 Judas hangeth himself. 19 Pilate's wife. 20 Barabbas is asked. 24 Pilate washeth his hands. 29 Christ is crowned with thorns. 34 He is crucified. 40 Reviled. 50 He giveth up the Ghost. 57 He is buried. 62 The soldiers watch him.

1 When the [1]morning was come, all the chief Priests, and the Elders of the pe-
ople took counsel against Jesus, to put him to death. **2** And led him away bound,
and delivered him unto Pontius Pilate the governor. **3** [a]Then when Judas whi-
ch betrayed him, saw that he was condemned, he repented himself, and brought
again the thirty pieces of silver to the chief Priests, and Elders, **4** Saying, I have
sinned, betraying the innocent blood. But they said, What is that to us? see thou to
it. **5** And when he had cast down the silver pieces in the Temple, he [b]departed,
and went, [2]and hanged himself. **6** And the chief Priests took the silver pieces,
and said, It is not lawful for us to put them into the [c]treasure, because it is the price
[d]of blood. **7** And they took counsel, and bought with them a potter's field, for
the burial of [e]strangers. **8** Wherefore that field is called, [3]The field of blood, until
this day. **9** (Then was fulfilled that which was spoken by [f]Jeremiah the Prophet,
saying, [g,4]And they took thirty silver pieces, the price of him that was valued,
whom they of the children of Israel valued. **10** And they gave them for the pot-
ter's field, as the Lord appointed me.) **11** [h,5]And Jesus stood before the governor,
and the governor asked him, saying, Art thou that King of the Jews? Jesus said unto
him, Thou sayest it. **12** And when he was accused of the chief Priests, and El-
ders, he answered nothing. **13** Then said Pilate unto him, Hearest thou not how
many things they lay against thee? **14** But he answered him not to one word,
insomuch that the governor marveled greatly. **15** [i]Now at the feast the governor
was wont to deliver unto the people a prisoner whom they would. **16** And they
had then a notable prisoner called Barabbas. **17** When they were then gathered
together, Pilate said unto them, Whether will ye that I let loose unto you Barabbas,
or Jesus which is called Christ? **18** (For he knew well, that for envy they had deli-
vered him. **19** Also when he was set down upon the judgment seat, his wife sent
to him, saying, Have thou nothing to do with that just man: for I have suffered
many things this day in a dream by reason of him.) **20** [6]But the chief Priests and
the elders had persuaded the people that they should ask Barabbas, and should
destroy Jesus. **21** Then the governor answered, and said unto them, Whether of
the twain will ye that I let loose unto you? And they said, Barabbas. **22** Pilate
said unto them, What shall I do then with Jesus, which is called Christ? They all
said to him, Let him be crucified. **23** Then said the governor, But what evil hath
he done? Then they cried the more, saying, Let him be crucified. **24** [j]When Pi-
late saw that he availed nothing, but that more tumult was made, he took water
and [k]washed his hands before the multitude, saying, I am innocent of the [l]blood
of this just man: look you to it. **25** Then answered all the people, and said, [m]His
blood be on us, and on our children. **26** Thus let he Barabbas loose unto them,
and scourged Jesus, and delivered him to be crucified. **27** [7]Then the soldiers of
the governor took Jesus into the common hall, and gathered about him the whole
band, **28** [n]And they stripped him, and [o]put about him a [p]scarlet robe, **29** And
platted a crown of thorns, and put it upon his head, and a reed in his right hand,
and bowed their knees before him, and mocked him, saying, God save thee, King
of the Jews, **30** And spitted upon him, and took a reed, and smote him on the
head. **31** Thus when they had mocked him, they took the robe from him, and
put his own raiment on him, and let him away to crucify him. **32** [8]And as they
came out, they found a man of Cyrene, named Simon: him they [q]compelled to
bear his cross. **33** [r,9]And when they came unto the place called Golgotha (that is
to say, the place of dead men's skulls) **34** [s]They gave him vinegar to drink, min-
gled with gall: and when he had tasted thereof, he would not drink. **35** [t]And
when they had crucified him, they parted his garments, and did cast lots, that it
might be fulfilled, which was spoken by the Prophet, [10]They divided my garments
among them, and upon my vesture did cast lots. **36** And they sat and watched
him there. **37** [u]They set up also over his head his cause written, THIS IS JESUS
THE KING OF THE JEWS. **38** [v]And there were two thieves crucified with
him, one on the right hand, and another on the left. **39** [w]And they that passed
by, reviled him, wagging their heads, **40** And saying, [11]Thou that destroyest the
Temple, and buildest it in three days, save thyself: if thou be the Son of God, come
down from the cross. **41** Likewise also the high Priests mocking him, with the
Scribes, and Elders, and Pharisees, said, **42** He saved others, but he cannot save
himself: if he be the king of Israel, let him now come down from the cross, and
we will believe in him. **43** [12]He trusted in God, let him deliver him now, if he
will have him: for he said, I am the Son of God. **44** The self same thing also the
[x]thieves which were crucified with him, cast in his teeth. **45** [y]Now from the sixth
hour was there darkness over all the land, unto the ninth hour. **46** And about the
ninth hour Jesus cried with loud voice, saying, [13]Eli, Eli, lama sabachthani? that is,
My God, my God, why hast thou [z]forsaken me? **47** And some of them that sto-
od there, when they heard it, said, This man calleth [aa]Elijah. **48** And straightway
one of them ran, and took [14]a sponge and filled it with vinegar, and put it on a
reed, and gave him to drink. **49** Others said, Let be: let us see if Elijah will come
and save him. **50** [ab]Then Jesus cried again with a loud voice, and yielded up the
ghost. **51** [ac]And behold, [15]the [ad]veil of the Temple was rent in twain, from the
top to the bottom, and the earth did quake, and the stones were cloven. **52** And
the [ae]graves did open themselves, and many bodies of the Saints, which slept, aro-
se, **53** And came out of the graves after his resurrection, and went into the holy

---

at. Matt. 26:65 This was an usual matter among the Jews: for so were they bound to do, when they heard any Israelite to blaspheme God, and it was a tradition of their Talmud in the book of the Magistrates, in the title, of the four kinds of death.

au. Matt. 26:69 Peter by the wonderful providence of God appointed to be a witness of all these things, is prepared to the example of singular constancy, by the experience of his own incredulity.

av. Matt. 26:69 That is, without the place where the Bishop sat, but not without the house, for afterward he went from thence into the porch.

aw. Matt. 26:74 He swore and cursed himself.

MATT. 26

1. Mark 14:1 / Luke 22:1
2. John 11:47
3. Mark 14:3 / John 11:2
4. Deut. 15:11
5. Mark 14:10
6. Mark 14:12 / Luke 22:7
7. Luke 22:14
8. Mark 14:18 / John 13:21
9. Ps. 41:9
10. 1 Cor. 11:24
11. Mark 14:27 / John 16:32 / John 18:8
12. Zech. 13:7
13. Mark 14:28 / Mark 16:7
14. John 13:38 / Mark 14:30
15. Luke 22:39
16. Mark 14:43 / Luke 22:47 / John 18:3
17. Gen. 9:6 / Rev. 13:10
18. Isa. 35:10
19. Matt. 26:31
20. Mark 14:53 / Luke 22:54 / John 18:14
21. Mark 14:55
22. John 2:19
23. Matt. 16:27 / Rom. 14:20 / 2 Thess. 4:14
24. Isa. 30:6
25. Mark 14:66 / Luke 22:55 / John 18:29

MATT. 27

a. Matt. 27:3 An example of the horrible judgment of God, as well against them which sell Christ, as against them which buy Christ.

b. Matt. 27:5 Out of men's sights.

c. Matt. 27:6 The treasury of the Temple.

d. Matt. 27:6 Of life and death.

e. Matt. 27:7 Strangers and guests, whom the Jews could not abide to be joined unto, no not after they were dead.

f. Matt. 27:9 Seeing this prophecy is read in Zech. 11:12, it cannot be denied, but Jeremiah's name crept into the text, either through the Printer's fault, or some other's ignorance: it may be also that it came out of the margin, by reason of the abbreviation of the letters, the one being iou, and the other zou, which are not much unlike: but in the Syrian text the Prophet's name is not set down at all.

g. Matt. 27:9 The Evangelist doth not follow the Prophet's words, but his meaning, which he showeth to be fulfilled.

h. Matt. 27:11 Christ holdeth his peace when he is accused, that we may not be accused: acknowledging our guiltiness, and therewithall his own innocence.

i. Matt. 27:15 Christ is first quitted of the same Judge, before he be condemned, that we might see how the just died for the unjust.

j. Matt. 27:24 Christ being quit by the testimony of the Judge himself, is notwithstanding condemned by the same to quit us before God.

k. Matt. 27:24 It was a manner in old time, when any man was murdered, and in other slaughters, to wash their hands in water, to declare themselves guiltless.

l. Matt. 27:24 Of the murder; an Hebrew kind of speech.

m. Matt. 27:25 If there be any offence committed in slaying him, let us and our posterity smart for it.

n. Matt. 27:28 Christ suffereth that reproach which was due to our sins; notwithstanding in the meantime by the secret providence of God, he is entitled King by them which did him that reproach.

o. Matt. 27:28 They cast a cloak about him, and wrapped it about him, for it lacked sleeves.

p. Matt. 27:28 John and Mark make mention of a purple robe, which is also a very pleasant red. But these profane and malapert saucy soldiers clad Jesus in this array, to mock him withall, who was indeed a true King.

q. Matt. 27:32 They compelled Simon to bear his burdensome cross, whereby it appeareth that Jesus was so sore handled before, that he fainted by the way, and was not able to bear his cross throughout: for John writeth that he did bear the cross, to wit, at the beginning.

r. Matt. 27:33 He is led out of the city, that we may be brought into the heavenly kingdom.

s. Matt. 27:34 Christ found no comfort anywhere, that in him we might be filled with all comfort.

t. Matt. 27:35 He is made a curse, that in him we may be blessed: he is spoiled of his garments, that we might be enriched by his nakedness.

u. Matt. 27:37 He is pronounced the true Messiah, even of them of whom he is rejected.

v. Matt. 27:38 Christ began then to judge the world, when after his judgment he hung betwixt two thieves.

w. Matt. 27:39 To make full satisfaction for us, Christ suffereth and overcometh, not only the torments of the body, but also the most horrible torments of the mind.

x. Matt. 27:44 This is spoken by the figure Synecdoche, for there was but one of them that did revile him.

y. Matt. 27:45 Heaven itself is darkened for very horror, and Jesus crieth out from the depth of hell, and in the meanwhile he is mocked.

z. Matt. 27:46 To wit, in this misery: and this crying out is proper to his humanity, which notwithstanding was void of sin, but yet felt the wrath of God which is due to our sins.

aa. Matt. 27:47 They allude to Elijah's name, not for want of understanding the tongue, but of a profane impudence and sauciness, and he repeated these words, to the end that this better harping upon the name might be understood.

ab. Matt. 27:50 Christ after he had overcome other enemies, at length provoked and setteth upon death itself.

ac. Matt. 27:51 Christ, when he is dead, showeth himself to be God almighty, even his enemies confessing the same.

ad. Matt. 27:51 Which divided the holiest of all.

ae. Matt. 27:52 That is to say, the stones clave asunder, and the graves did open themselves, to show by this token, that death was overcome: and the resurrection of the dead followed

city, and appeared unto many. **54** When the Centurion, and they that were with him, watching Jesus, saw the earth quake, and the things that were done, they feared greatly, saying, Truly this was the Son of God. **55** And many women were there, beholding him afar off, which had followed Jesus from Galilee, ministering unto him. **56** Among whom was Mary Magdalene, and Mary the mother of James, and Joses, and the mother of Zebedee's sons. **57** [af,16]And when the even was come, there came a rich man of Arimathea, named Joseph, who had also himself been Jesus' disciple. **58** He went to Pilate, and asked the body of Jesus. Then Pilate commanded the body to be delivered. **59** So Joseph took the body, and wrapped it in a clean linen cloth, **60** And put it in his new tomb, which he had hewn out in a rock, and rolled a great stone to the door of the sepulcher, and departed. **61** And there was Mary Magdalene, and the other Mary, sitting over against the sepulcher. **62** [ag]Now the next day that followed the Preparation of the Sabbath, the high Priests and Pharisees assembled to Pilate, **63** And said, Sir, we remember that that deceiver said, while he was yet alive, Within three days I will rise. **64** Command therefore, that the sepulcher be made sure until the third day, lest his Disciples come by night, and steal him away, and say unto the people, He is risen from the dead: so shall the last error be worse than the first. **65** Then Pilate said unto them, Ye have a [ah]watch: go, and make it sure, as ye know. **66** And they went, and made the sepulcher sure, with the watch, and sealed the stone.

28

1 The women go to the sepulcher. 2 The Angel. 9 The women see Christ. 18 He sendeth his Apostles to preach.

1 Now [1]in [a]the [b]end of the Sabbath, when the first day of the week [c]began to dawn, Mary Magdalene, and the other Mary, came to see the sepulcher. **2** And behold, there was a great earthquake: for the Angel of the Lord descended from heaven, and came and rolled back the stone from the door, and sat upon it. **3** And his [d]countenance was like lightning, and his raiment white as snow. **4** And for fear of him, the keepers were astonied, and became as dead men. **5** But the Angel answered, and said to the women, Fear [e]ye not: for I know that ye seek Jesus which was crucified: **6** He is not here, for he is risen, as he said: come, see the place where the Lord was laid, **7** And go quickly, and tell his disciples that he is risen from the dead: and behold, he goeth before you into Galilee: there ye shall see him: lo, I have told you. **8** So they departed quickly from the sepulcher, with fear and great joy, and did run to bring his disciples word. **9** [f]And as they went to tell his disciples, behold, Jesus also met them, saying, God save you. And they came, and took him by the feet, and worshipped him. **10** Then said Jesus unto them, Be not afraid. Go, and tell my brethren, that they go into Galilee, and there shall they see me. **11** [g]Now when they were gone, behold, some of the watch came into the city, and showed unto the high Priests all the things that were done. **12** And they gathered them together with the Elders, and took counsel, and gave large money unto the soldiers, **13** Saying, Say, His disciples came by night, and stole him away while we slept. **14** And if this matter [h]come before the governor to be heard, we will persuade him, and so use the matter that you shall not need to care, **15** So they took the money, and did as they were taught: and this saying is noised among the Jews unto this day. **16** [i]Then the eleven disciples went into Galilee, into a mountain, where Jesus had appointed them. **17** And when they saw him, they worshipped him: but some doubted. **18** And Jesus came, and spake unto them, saying, [2]All power is given unto me, in heaven, and in earth. **19** [j,3]Go therefore, and teach all nations, baptizing them [k]in the Name of the Father, and the Son, and the holy Ghost, **20** Teaching them to observe all things, whatsoever I have commanded you: and lo, [4]I am with you [l]alway, until the end of the world, Amen.

---

the resurrection of Christ, as appeareth by the next verse following.

af. Matt. 27:57 Christ is buried, not privately or by stealth, but by the governor's consent by a famous man, in a place not far distant, in a new sepulcher, so that it cannot be doubted of his death.

ag. Matt. 27:62 The keeping of the sepulcher is committed to Christ's own murderers, that there might be no doubt of his resurrection.

ah. Matt. 27:65 The soldiers of the garrison, which were appointed to keep the Temple.

MATT. 27

1. Mark 15:1 / Luke 22:66 / John 18:28
2. Acts 1:18
3. Acts 1:19
4. Zech. 11:12
5. Mark 15:2 / Luke 23:3 / John 18:33
6. Mark 15:11 / Luke 23:18 / John 18:40 / Acts 3:14
7. Mark 15:26 / John 19:2
8. Mark 15:21 / Luke 23:26
9. Mark 15:22 / John 19:17
10. Ps. 22:18 / Mark 15:24
11. John 2:19
12. Ps. 22:8
13. Ps. 22:1
14. Ps. 69:21
15. 2 Chron. 3:14
16. Mark 15:42 / Luke 13:50 / John 19:38

MATT. 28

a. Matt. 28:1 Christ having put death to flight in the sepulcher, riseth by his own power, as straightway the Angel witnesseth.

b. Matt. 28:1 At the going out of the Sabbath, that is, about daybreak after the Roman's count, which reckon the natural day, from the sun rising to the next sun rising: and not as the Hebrews, which count from evening to evening.

c. Matt. 28:1 When the morning after the first day after the Sabbath began to dawn: and that first day is the same, which we now call Sunday or the Lord's day.

d. Matt. 28:3 The beams of his eyes, and by the figure Synecdoche, for the countenance.

e. Matt. 28:5 The word (Ye) is spoken with force to confirm the women, now that the soldiers were afraid.

f. Matt. 28:9 Christ appeareth himself after his resurrection, and sending the women to his disciples, showeth that he hath not forgotten them.

g. Matt. 28:11 The more the sun shineth, the more are the wicked blinded.

h. Matt. 28:14 For it was to be feared, that it would be brought to the governor's ears.

i. Matt. 28:16 Christ appeareth also to his Disciples, whom he maketh Apostles.

j. Matt. 28:19 The sum of the Apostleship is, the publishing of the doctrine received of Christ throughout all the world, and the ministering of the Sacraments: the efficacy of which things hangeth not of the ministers, but of the Lord.

k. Matt. 28:19 Calling upon the name of the Father, the Son, and the holy Ghost.

l. Matt. 28:20 Forever: and this place is meant of the manner of the presence of his spirit, by means whereof he maketh us partakers both of himself and of all his benefits, but is absent from us in body.

MATT. 28

1. Mark 16:5 / John 20:11
2. Heb. 1:2 / Matt. 11:27 / John 17:2
3. Mark 16:15
4. John 14:16

THE HOLY GOSPEL OF JESUS CHRIST, ACCORDING TO MARK

1

4 John baptizeth. 6 His apparel and meat. 9 Jesus is baptized. 12 He is tempted. 14 He preacheth the Gospel, 21 and 29 he teacheth in the Synagogues. 23 He healeth one that had a devil. 29 Peter's mother-in-law. 32 Many diseased persons. 40 The leper.

1 The beginning of the Gospel of Jesus Christ, the Son of God: 2 [a]As it is
written in the [b]Prophets, [1]Behold, [c]I send my messenger [d]before thy face, which
shall prepare thy way before thee. 3 [2]The voice of him that crieth in the wilder-
ness, is, Prepare the way of the Lord: make his paths straight. 4 [e,3]John did bap-
tize in the wilderness, and preach the [f]baptism of amendment of life, for remission
of sins. 5 And all the country of Judea, and they of Jerusalem went out unto him,
and were all baptized of him in the river Jordan, confessing their sins. 6 [4]Now
John was clothed with camel's hair, and with a girdle of a skin about his loins: and
he did eat [5]locusts and wild honey, 7 [g,6]And preached, saying, A stronger than I
cometh after me, whose shoe's latchet I am not worthy to [h]stoop down, and unlo-
ose. 8 Truth it is, I have [i]baptized you with water: but he will baptize you with
the holy Ghost. 9 [j,7]And it came to pass in those days, that Jesus came from Na-
zareth, a city of Galilee, and was baptized of John in Jordan. 10 [k]And as soon as
[l]he was come out of the water, John saw the heavens cloven in twain, and the holy
Ghost descending upon him like a dove. 11 Then there was a voice from hea-
ven, saying, Thou art my beloved Son, in whom I am [m]well pleased. 12 [n,8]And
immediately the Spirit [o]driveth him into the wilderness. 13 And he was the-
re in the wilderness forty days, and was tempted of Satan: he was also with the
wild beasts, and the Angels ministered unto him. 14 [p,9]Now after that John
was committed to prison, Jesus came into Galilee, preaching the Gospel of the
kingdom of God, 15 And saying, The time is fulfilled, and the kingdom of God
is at hand: repent and believe the Gospel. 16 [q,10]And as he walked by the sea
of Galilee, he saw Simon and Andrew his brother, casting a net into the sea (for
they were fishers.) 17 Then Jesus said unto them, Follow me, and I will make
you to be fishers of men. 18 And straightway they forsook their nets, and fol-
lowed him. 19 [r]And when he had gone a little further thence, he saw James
the son of Zebedee, and John his brother, as they were in the ship, mending their
nets. 20 And anon he called them: and they left their father Zebedee in the ship
with his hired servants, and went their way after him. 21 So [11]they entered into
[s]Capernaum: and straightway on the Sabbath day he entered into the Synagogue,
and taught. 22 And they were astonied at his doctrine, [12]for he taught them as
one that had authority, and not as the Scribes. 23 [t]And there was in their Syna-
gogue a man [u]in whom was an unclean spirit, and he cried out, 24 Saying, Ah,
what have we to do with thee, O [v]Jesus of Nazareth? Art thou come to destroy us?
I know thee what thou art, even thou [w]holy one of God. 25 And Jesus rebuked
him, saying, Hold thy peace, and come out of him. 26 And the unclean spirit
[x]tare him, and cried with a loud voice, and came out of him. 27 And they were
all amazed, so that they demanded [y]one of another, saying, What thing is this?
what new doctrine is this? for he [z]commandeth even the foul spirits with authority,
and they obey him. 28 And immediately his fame spread abroad throughout all
the region [aa]bordering on Galilee. 29 [ab,13]And as soon as they were come out
of the Synagogue, they entered into the house of Simon and Andrew, with James
and John. 30 And Simon's wife's mother lay sick of a fever, and anon they told
him of her. 31 And he came and took her by the hand, and lifted her up, and
the fever forsook her by and by, and she ministered unto them. 32 And when
even was come, at what time the Sun setteth, they brought to him all that were
diseased, and them that were possessed with devils. 33 And the whole city was
gathered together at the door. 34 And he healed many that were sick of divers
diseases: and he cast out many devils, and [ac]suffered not the devils to say that
they knew him. 35 And in the morning very early before day, Jesus arose and
went out into a solitary place, and there prayed. 36 And Simon, and they that
were with him, followed carefully after him. 37 And when they had found him,
they said unto him, All men seek for thee. 38 Then he said unto them, Let us
go into the [ad]next towns, that I may preach there also: for I came out for that
purpose. 39 And he preached in their Synagogues, throughout all Galilee, and
cast the devils out. 40 [ae,14]And there came a leper to him, beseeching him, and
kneeled down unto him, and said to him, If thou wilt, thou canst make me cle-
an. 41 And Jesus had compassion, and put forth his hand, and touched him, and
said to him, I will: be thou clean. 42 And as soon as he had spoken, immediately
the leprosy departed from him, and he was made clean. 43 And after he had gi-
ven him a straight commandment, he sent him away forthwith, 44 [af]And said
unto him, See thou say nothing to any man, but get thee hence, and show thyself
to the [ag,15]Priest, and offer for thy cleansing those things which Moses comman-
ded, for a testimonial unto them. 45 But when he was departed, [16]he began to
tell many things, and to publish the matter: so that Jesus could no more openly
enter into the city, but was without in desert places: and they came to him from
every quarter.

2

3 and 4 One sick of the palsy, having his sins forgiven him, is healed. 14 Matthew is called. 19 Fastings and afflictions are foretold. 23 The Disciples pluck the ears of corn. 26 The showbread.

1 After [a,1]a few days, he entered into Capernaum again, and it was noised that
he was in the [b]house. 2 And anon many gathered together, insomuch, that the
[c]places about the door could not receive any more: and he preached the word unto
them. 3 And there came unto him, that brought one sick of the palsy, borne of
four men. 4 And because they could not come near unto him for the multitude,

---

MARK. 1

a. Mark 1:2 John goeth before Christ, as it was forespoken by the Prophets.
b. Mark 1:2 This is the figure Metonymy, whereby is meant the books of the Prophets, Malachi and Isaiah.
c. Mark 1:2 The Prophet useth the present tense, when he speaketh of a thing to come, being as a sure of it, as if he saw it.
d. Mark 1:2 A metaphor taken from the usage of kings, which used to have ushers go before them.
e. Mark 1:4 The sum of John's doctrine, or rather Christ's, is remission of sins and amendment of life.
f. Mark 1:4 The Jews used many kinds of washings: but here is spoken of a peculiar kind of washing, which hath all the parts of true baptism, amendment of life, and forgiveness of sins.
g. Mark 1:7 John and all ministers cast their eyes upon Christ the Lord.
h. Mark 1:7 The Evangelist his meaning was to express the condition of the basest servant.
i. Mark 1:8 He showeth that all the force of baptism proceedeth from Christ, who baptizeth within.
j. Mark 1:9 Christ doth consecrate our baptism in himself.
k. Mark 1:10 The vocation of Christ from heaven, as head of the Church.
l. Mark 1:10 John that went down into the water with Christ.
m. Mark 1:11 See also Matt. 3:17.
n. Mark 1:12 Christ being tempted overcometh.
o. Mark 1:12 Here is no violent and forcible driving out meant: but the divine power claddeth Christ (who had lived until this time as a private man) with a new person, and prepareth him to the combat that was at hand, and to his ministry.
p. Mark 1:14 After that John is taken, Christ showeth himself fully.
q. Mark 1:16 The calling of Simon and Andrew.
r. Mark 1:19 The calling of James and John.
s. Mark 1:21 From the city Nazareth.
t. Mark 1:23 He preacheth that doctrine, by which alone Satan is driven out of the world, which also he confirmeth by a miracle.
u. Mark 1:23 Word for word, a man in an unclean spirit, that is to say, possessed with an evil spirit.
v. Mark 1:24 He was born in Bethlehem, but through the error of the people, he was called a Nazarene, because he was brought up in Nazareth.
w. Mark 1:24 He alludeth to that name that was written in the golden plate which the high Priest wore, Exod. 28:36.
x. Mark 1:26 See also Mark 9:20.
y. Mark 1:27 As men amazed.
z. Mark 1:27 By his own authority, or as a Lord.
aa. Mark 1:28 Not only into Galilee, but also into the countries bordering upon it.
ab. Mark 1:29 By healing of divers diseases, he showeth that he hath brought true life into the world.
ac. Mark 1:34 For it belongeth not to the devils to preach the Gospel, Acts 16:18.
ad. Mark 1:38 Villages which were as cities.
ae. Mark 1:40 By healing the leprous, he showeth that he came for this cause, to wipe out the sins of the world with his touching.
af. Mark 1:44 He witnesseth that he was not moved with ambition, but with the only desire of his Father's glory, and love toward poor sinners.
ag. Mark 1:44 All the posterity of Aaron might judge of a leper.

MARK. 1

1. Mal. 3:1
2. Isa. 40:3 / Luke 3:4 / John 1:15
3. Matt. 3:1
4. Matt. 3:4
5. Lev. 11:22
6. Matt. 3:11 / Luke 3:16 / John 1:26 / Acts 1:5 / Acts 2:4 / Acts 2:11 / Acts 2:16 / Acts 19:4
7. Matt. 3:13 / Luke 3:21 / John 1:33
8. Matt. 4:1 / Luke 4:1 / Heb. 2:18
9. Matt. 4:12 / Luke 4:14 / John 4:13
10. Matt. 4:18 / Luke 5:2
11. Matt. 4:13 / Luke 4:32
12. Matt. 7:28 / Luke 4:32
13. Matt. 8:14 / Luke 4:38
14. Matt. 8:2 / Luke 5:12
15. Lev. 14:4
16. Luke 5:15

MARK. 2

a. Mark 2:1 Christ showeth by healing this man, which was sick of the palsy, that men recover in him through faith only, all their strength which they have lost.
b. Mark 2:1 In the house where he used to remain, for he chose Capernaum to dwell in, and left Nazareth.
c. Mark 2:2 Neither the house nor the entry was able to hold them.
d. Mark 2:4 They brake up the upper part of the house, which was plain, and let down the man that was sick of the palsy, into the lower part where Christ preached, for they could not otherwise come into his sight.

they uncovered the roof of the house where he was: and when they had broken it
open, they [d]let down the [e]bed, wherein the sick of the palsy lay. **5** Now when
Jesus saw their faith, he said to the sick of the palsy, Son, thy sins are forgiven
thee. **6** And there were certain of the Scribes sitting there, and [f]reasoning in their
hearts, **7** Why doth this man speak such blasphemies? [2]who can forgive sins, but
God only? **8** And immediately, when Jesus perceived in his spirit, that thus they
reasoned with themselves, he said unto them, Why reason ye these things in your
hearts? **9** Whether is it easier to say to the sick of the palsy, Thy sins are forgiven
thee? or to say, Arise, take up thy bed, and walk? **10** But that ye may know, that
the Son of man hath authority in earth to forgive sins, he said unto the sick of the
palsy, **11** I say unto thee, Arise, and take up thy bed, and get thee hence into thi-
ne own house. **12** And by and by he arose, and took up his bed, and went forth
before them all, insomuch that they were all [g]amazed, and glorified God, saying,
We never saw such a thing. **13** [h]Then he went forth again toward the sea, and all
the people resorted unto him, and he taught them. **14** [3]And as Jesus passed by,
he saw [i]Levi the son of Alphaeus sit at the receipt of custom, and said unto him,
Follow me. And he arose and followed him. **15** And it came to pass, as Jesus sat
at table in his house, many Publicans and sinners sat at table also with Jesus, and
his disciples: for there were many that followed him. **16** And when the Scribes
and Pharisees saw him eat with the Publicans and sinners, they said unto his disci-
ples, How is it, that he eateth and drinketh with Publicans and sinners? **17** Now
when Jesus heard it, he said unto them, The whole have no need of the Physi-
cian, but the sick. [4]I came not to call the righteous, but the sinners to repentan-
ce. **18** [j,5]And the disciples of John, and the Pharisees did fast, and came and said
unto him, Why do the disciples of John, and of the Pharisees fast, and thy disciples
fast not? **19** And Jesus said unto them, Can the children of the marriage cham-
ber fast, while the bridegroom is with them? as long as they have the bridegroom
with them, they cannot fast. **20** But the days will come, when the bridegroom
shall be taken from them, and then shall they fast in those days. **21** Also no man
soweth a piece of new cloth in an old garment: for else the new piece that filled it
up, taketh away somewhat from the old, and the breach is worse. **22** Likewise,
no man putteth new wine into old vessels: for else the new wine breaketh the ves-
sels, and the wine runneth out, and the vessels are lost; but new wine must be put
into new vessels. **23** [k,6]And it came to pass as he went through the corn on the
[l]Sabbath day, that his disciples, as they went on their way, began to pluck the ears
of corn. **24** And the Pharisees said unto him, Behold, why do they on the Sab-
bath day, that which is not lawful? **25** And he said to them, Have ye never read
what [7]David did when he had need, and was an hungered, both he, and they that
were with him? **26** How he went into the house of God, in the days of [m]Abiathar
the high [8]Priest, and did eat the Showbread, which were not lawful to eat, but for
the Priests, and gave also to them which were with him? **27** And he said to them,
The Sabbath was made for man, and not man for the Sabbath. **28** Wherefore the
Son of man is Lord, even of the [n]Sabbath.

3

1 The withered hand is healed. 6 The Pharisees consult with the Herodians. 10 Many are healed by touching Christ. 11 At his sight the devils fall down before him. 14 The twelve Apostles. 24 The kingdom divided against itself. 29 Blasphemy against the holy Ghost. 33 Christ's parents.

1 And [a,1]he entered again into the Synagogue, and there was a man which had
a [b]withered hand. **2** And they watched him, whether he would heal him on the
Sabbath day, that they might accuse him. **3** Then he said unto the man which
had the withered hand, Arise: stand forth in the midst. **4** And he said to them, Is
it lawful to do a good deed on the Sabbath day, or to do evil? to save the [c]life, or to
kill? but they held their peace. **5** Then he looked round about on them [d]angrily,
mourning also for the [e]hardness of their hearts, and said to the man, Stretch for-
th thine hand. And he stretched it out: and his hand was restored, as whole as the
other. **6** [f]And the Pharisees departed, and straightway gathered a council with
the [g]Herodians against him, that they might destroy him. **7** But Jesus avoided
with his disciples to the sea: and a great multitude followed him from Galilee, and
from Judea, **8** And from Jerusalem, and from Idumea, and [h]beyond Jordan: and
they that dwelled about Tyre and Sidon, when they had heard what great things he
did, came unto him in great number. **9** And he commanded his disciples, that a
little ship should [i]wait for him, because of the multitude, lest they should throng
him. **10** For he had healed many, insomuch that they pressed upon him to touch
him, as many as had [j]plagues. **11** And when the [k]unclean spirits saw him, they
fell down before him, and cried, saying, Thou art the Son of God. **12** And he
sharply rebuked them, to the end they should not utter him. **13** [2]Then he went
up into a mountain, and called unto him whom he would, and they came unto
him. **14** [l]And he [m]appointed twelve, that they should be with him, and that he
might send them to preach. **15** And that they might have power to heal sicknes-
ses, and to cast out devils: **16** And the first was Simon, and he named Simon, Pe-
ter, **17** Then James the son of Zebedee, and John James' brother (and surnamed
them Boanerges, which is, The sons of thunder.) **18** And Andrew, and Philip,
and Bartholomew, and Matthew, and Thomas, and James the son of Alphaeus, and
[n]Thaddaeus, and Simon the Canaanite, **19** And Judas Iscariot, who also betrayed
him, and they came [o]home. **20** And the multitude assembled again, so that they
could not so much as eat bread. **21** [p]And when his [q]kinsfolks heard of it, they
went out to lay hold on him: for they said that he was beside himself. **22** [3]And
the Scribes which came down from Jerusalem, said, He hath Beelzebub, and throu-
gh the prince of the devils he casteth out devils. **23** But he called them unto
him, and said unto them in parables, How can Satan drive out Satan? **24** For
if a kingdom be divided against itself, that kingdom cannot stand. **25** Or if
a house be divided against itself, that house cannot continue. **26** So if [r]Satan
make insurrection against himself, and be divided, he cannot endure, but is at an
end. **27** No man can enter into a strong man's house, and take away his goods,
except he first bind that strong man, and then spoil his house. **28** [s,4]Verily I say
unto you, all sins shall be forgiven unto the children of men, and blasphemies,
wherewith they blaspheme: **29** But he that blasphemeth against the holy Ghost,
shall never have forgiveness, but is culpable of eternal damnation. **30** [t]Because
they said, He had an unclean spirit. **31** [5]Then came his [u]brethren and mother
and stood without, and sent unto him, and called him. **32** And the people sat
about him, and they said unto him, Behold, thy mother, and thy brethren seek
for thee without. **33** But he answered them, saying, Who is my mother and my
brethren? **34** [v]And he looked round about on them, which sat in compass about
him, and said, Behold my mother and my brethren. **35** For whosoever doeth the
will of God, he is my brother, my sister, and my mother.

4

4 The parable of the sower. 14 And the meaning thereof. 18 Thorns. 21 The candle. 26 Of him that sowed, and then slept. 31 The grain of mustard seed. 38 Christ sleepeth in the ship.

1 And [1]he began again to teach by the [a]seaside, and there gathered unto him
a great multitude, so that he entered into a ship, and sat [b]in the sea, and all the

---

e. Mark 2:4 The word signifieth the worst kind of bed, whereupon men used to lay down themselves at noontide, and such other times, to refresh themselves: we call it a couch.
f. Mark 2:6 In their minds disputing upon that matter, on both sides.
g. Mark 2:12 Word for word, past themselves, or out of their wits.
h. Mark 2:13 The Gospel offendeth the proud, and saveth the humble.
i. Mark 2:14 Matthew's other name.
j. Mark 2:18 The superstitious and hypocrites do rashly put the sum of godliness in things indifferent, and are here for three causes reprehended. First, for that not considering what every man's strength is able to bear, they rashly make all manner of laws concerning such things, without all discretion.
k. Mark 2:23 Secondarily, for that they make no difference between the laws which God made concerning the same things, and laws that are made of things which are utterly unlawful.
l. Mark 2:23 Word for word, on the Sabbaths, that is, on the holy days.
m. Mark 2:26 In 1 Sam. 21:1 he is called Ahimelech and his son Abiathar, but by conference of other places, it is plain, that both of them had two names. See also 1 Chron. 24:6; 2 Sam. 8:17; 2 Sam. 15:29; 1 Kings 2:26; 2 Kings 25:18.
n. Mark 2:28 Hath the Sabbath day in his power, and may rule as him listeth.

MARK. 2

1. Matt. 9:1 / Luke 5:28
2. John 14:4 / Isa. 43:25
3. Matt. 9:9 / Luke 5:27
4. 1 Tim. 1:13
5. Matt. 9:14 / Luke 5:33
6. Matt. 12:1 / Luke 6:1
7. 1 Sam. 21:6
8. Exod. 29:53 / Lev. 3:31 / Lev. 24:9

MARK. 3

a. Mark 3:1 Thirdly, for that they preferred the ceremonial Law (which was but an appendant to the moral Law) before the moral Law: whereas contrariwise, they should have learned out of this, the true use of the ceremonial Law.
b. Mark 3:1 That is, unprofitable and dead.
c. Mark 3:4 A figurative speech, by the figure Synecdoche. For this kind of saying, To save the life, is as much, as to save the man.
d. Mark 3:5 Men, when they have wrong done unto them, are angry, but not without vice, but Christ is angry without vice, neither is he sorry so much for the injury that is done to his own person, as for their wickedness: and therefore he had pity upon them, and for that cause is he said to have mourned.
e. Mark 3:5 As though their heart had been so closed up, and grown together, that wholesome doctrine could prevail no more with them.
f. Mark 3:6 The more the truth is kept under, the more it cometh out.
g. Mark 3:6 See also Matt. 22:16.
h. Mark 3:8 Which Josephus calleth stony or rocky.
i. Mark 3:9 Should always be ready for him.
j. Mark 3:10 Diseases wherewith God scourgeth men as it were with whips.
k. Mark 3:11 In them whom they had entered into: or by the figure called Metonymy, for them which were vexed with unclean spirits.
l. Mark 3:14 The twelve Apostles are set apart to be trained up to the office of the Apostleship.
m. Mark 3:14 Chose and appointed out twelve to be familiar and conversant with him.
n. Mark 3:18 Whom Luke also calleth Judas: and for difference's sake, the other Judas is called Iscariot.
o. Mark 3:19 The disciples whom Christ had taken to be of his train and to live with him, come home to his house, to be with him always after.
p. Mark 3:21 None are worse enemies of the Gospel, than they that least ought.
q. Mark 3:21 Word for word, they that were of him, that is, his kinfolks: for they that were mad, were brought to their kinsmen.
r. Mark 3:26 Satan's imps or . . . .
s. Mark 3:28 They only are without hope of salvation, which do maliciously oppugn Christ, whom they know.
t. Mark 3:30 These are the words of the Evangelist.
u. Mark 3:31 Under this name Brother, the Hebrews understand all that are of the same stock and kindred.
v. Mark 3:34 The spiritual kindred is far otherwise to be accounted of, than the carnal or fleshly.

MARK. 3

1. Matt. 12:9 / Luke 6:6
2. Mark 6:7 / Matt. 10:1 / Luke 9:1
3. Matt. 9:34 / Matt. 12:24 / Luke 11:15
4. Matt. 18:31 / Luke 12:10 / John 5:16
5. Matt. 12:46 / Luke 8:19

MARK. 4

a. Mark 4:1 Seaside of Tiberias.
b. Mark 4:1 In a ship which was launched into the sea.

people was by the seaside on the land. **2** And he taught them many things in pa-
rables, and said unto them in his doctrine, **3** [c]Hearken: Behold, there went out
a sower to sow. **4** And it came to pass as he sowed, that some fell by the wayside,
and the fowls of the heaven came, and devoured it up. **5** And some fell on stony
ground, where it had not much earth, and by and by sprang up, because it had not
depth of earth. **6** But as soon as the Sun was up, it was burnt up, and because
it had not root, it withered away. **7** And some fell among the thorns, and the
thorns grew up, and choked it, so that it gave no fruit. **8** Some again fell in good
ground, and did yield fruit that sprung up, and grew, and it brought forth, some
thirtyfold, some sixtyfold, and some an hundredfold. **9** Then he said unto them,
He that hath ears, to hear, let him hear. **10** And when he was [d]alone, they that
were [e]about him with the twelve, asked him of the parable. **11** And he said unto
them, To you it is given to know the mystery of the kingdom of God: but unto
them that are [f]without, all things be done in parables, **12** [2]That they seeing, may
see, and not discern: and they hearing, may hear, and not understand, lest at any
time they should turn, and their sins should be forgiven them. **13** Again he said
unto them, Perceive ye not this parable? how then should ye understand all other
parables? **14** The sower soweth the word. **15** And these are they that receive
the seed by the wayside, in whom the word is sown: but when they have heard it,
Satan cometh immediately, and taketh away the word that was sown in their he-
arts. **16** And likewise they that receive the seed in stony ground, are they, which
when they have heard the word, straightway receive it with gladness. **17** Yet have
they no root in themselves, and endure but a time: for when trouble and persecu-
tion ariseth for the word, immediately they be offended. **18** Also they that recei-
ve the seed among the thorns, are such as hear the word: **19** But the cares [g]of this
world, and the [3]deceitfulness of riches, and the lusts of other things enter in, and
choke the word, and it is unfruitful. **20** But they that have received seed in good
ground, are they that hear the word, and receive it, and bring forth fruit: one corn
thirty, another sixty, and some an hundred. **21** [h]Also he said unto them, [4]Co-
meth the candle in, to be put under a bushel, or under the bed, and not to be put
in a candlestick? **22** [5]For there is nothing hid, that shall not be opened, neither is
there a secret, but that it shall come to light. **23** If any man have ears to hear, let
him hear. **24** [i]And he said unto them, Take heed what ye hear. [6]With what me-
asure you mete, it shall be measured unto you: and unto you that hear, shall more
be given. **25** [7]For unto him that hath, shall it be given, and from him that hath
not, shall be taken away even that he hath. **26** [j]Also he said, So is the kingdom
of God, as if a man should cast seed in the ground. **27** And [k]should sleep, and
rise up night and day, and the seed should spring and grow up, he [l]not knowing
how. **28** For the earth bringeth forth fruit [m]of itself, first the blade, then the ears,
after that full corn in the ears. **29** And as soon as the fruit showeth itself, anon he
putteth in the sickle, because the harvest is come. **30** [n,8]He said moreover, Whe-
reunto shall we liken the kingdom of God? or with what comparison shall we com-
pare it? **31** It is like a grain of mustard seed, which when it is sown in the earth,
is the least of all seeds that be in the earth: **32** But after that it is sown, it groweth
up, and is greatest of all herbs, and beareth great branches, so that the fowls of the
heaven may build under the shadow of it. **33** And [9]with many such parables he
preached the word unto them, [o]as they were able to hear it. **34** And without pa-
rables spake he nothing unto them: but he [p]expounded all things to his disciples
apart. **35** [10]Now the same day when even was come, he said unto them, Let us
pass over unto the other side. **36** And they left the multitude, and took him as
he was in the ship, and there was also with him other little ships. **37** [q]And there
arose a great storm of wind, and the waves dashed into the ship, so that it was now
full. **38** And he was in the stern asleep on a pillow: and they awoke him, and said
to him, Master, carest thou not that we perish? **39** And he arose up, and rebuked
the wind, and said unto the sea, Peace, and be still. So the wind ceased, and it was
a great calm. **40** Then he said unto them, [r]Why are ye so fearful? how is it that
ye have no faith? **41** And they feared exceedingly, and said one to another, Who
is this, that both the wind and sea obey him?

5

2 One possessed is healed. 7 The devil acknowledgeth Christ. 9 A Legion of devils. 13 entered into swine. 22 Jairus's daughter. 25 A woman is healed of a bloody issue. 26 Physicians. 34 Faith. 39 Sleep.

1 And [a,1]they came over to the other side of the sea into the country of the
[b]Gadarenes. **2** And when he was come out of the ship, there met him inconti-
nently out of the graves, a man [c]which had an unclean spirit: **3** Who had his abi-
ding among the graves, and no man could bind him, no not with chains: **4** Be-
cause that when he was often bound with fetters and chains, he plucked the chains
asunder, and brake the fetters in pieces, neither could any man tame him. **5** And
always both night and day he cried in the mountains, and in the graves, and struck
himself with stones. **6** And when he saw Jesus afar off, he ran, and worshipped
him, **7** And cried with a loud voice, and said, What have I to do with thee, Jesus
the Son of the most High God? I [d]will that thou swear to me by God, that thou
torment me not. **8** (For he said unto him, Come out of the man, thou uncle-
an spirit.) **9** And he asked him, What is thy name? and he answered, saying,
My name is Legion: for we are many. **10** And he [e]prayed him instantly, that he
would not send them away out of the country. **11** Now there was there in the
[f]mountains a great heard of swine, feeding. **12** And all the devils besought him,
saying, Send us into the swine, that we may enter into them. **13** And inconti-
nently Jesus gave them leave. Then the unclean spirits went out and entered into
the swine, and the herd ran headlong from the high bank into the [g]sea, (and there
were about two thousand swine) and they were choked up in the sea. **14** And the
swineherds fled, and told it in the city, and in the country, and they came out to
see what it was that was done. **15** And they came to Jesus, and saw him that had
been possessed with the devil, and had the legion, sit both clothed, and in his right
mind: and they were afraid. **16** And they that saw it, told them, what was done
to him that was possessed with the devil, and concerning the swine. **17** Then
they began to pray him, that he would depart from their coasts. **18** And when he
was come into the ship, he that had been possessed with the devil, prayed him that
he might be with him. **19** Howbeit, Jesus would not suffer him, but said unto
him, Go thy way home to thy friends, and show them what great things the Lord
hath done unto thee, and how he hath had compassion on thee. **20** So he de-
parted, and began to publish in Decapolis, what great things Jesus had done unto
him: and all men did marvel. **21** And when Jesus was come over again by ship
unto the other side, a great multitude gathered together to him, and he was near
unto the sea. **22** [2]And [h]behold, there came one of the rulers of the Synagogue,
whose name was Jairus: and when he saw him, he fell down at his feet, **23** And
besought him instantly, saying, My little daughter lieth at point of death: I pray
thee that thou wouldest come and lay thine hands on her, that she may be healed,
and live. **24** Then he went with him, and a great multitude followed him and
thronged him. **25** ([i]And there was a certain woman, which was diseased with
an issue of blood twelve years, **26** And had suffered many things of many phy-
sicians, and had spent all that she had, and it availed her nothing, but she became
much worse. **27** When she had heard of Jesus, she came in the press behind, and
touched his garment. **28** For she said, if I may but touch his clothes, I shall be
whole. **29** And straightway the course of her blood was dried up, and she felt in
her body, that she was healed of that plague. **30** And immediately when Jesus
did know in himself the virtue that went out of him, he turned him round about
in the press, and said, Who hath touched my clothes? **31** And his disciples said
unto him, Thou seest the multitude throng thee, and sayest thou, Who did touch
me? **32** And he looked round about, to see her that had done that. **33** And
the woman feared and trembled: for she knew what was done in her, and she came
and fell down before him, and told him the whole truth. **34** And he said to her,
Daughter, thy faith hath made thee whole: go in peace, and be whole of thy pla-
gue.) **35** While he yet spake, there came from the same ruler of the Synagogue's
house certain which said, Thy daughter is dead: why diseasest thou the master any
further? **36** [j]As soon as Jesus heard that word spoken, he said unto the ruler of

---

c. Mark 4:3 The selfsame doctrine of the Gospel is sown everywhere, but it hath not like success indeed through the fault of man, but yet by the just judgment of God.
d. Mark 4:10 Word for word, solitary.
e. Mark 4:10 They that followed him at the heels.
f. Mark 4:11 That is to say, to strangers, and such as are none of ours.
g. Mark 4:19 Which pertain to this life.
h. Mark 4:21 Although the light of the Gospel be rejected of the world, yet it ought to be lighted, if it were for no other cause than this, that the wickedness of the world might be made manifest.
i. Mark 4:24 The more liberally that we communicate such gifts as God hath given us with our brethren, the more bountiful will God be toward us.
j. Mark 4:26 The Lord soweth and reapeth after a manner unknown to men.
k. Mark 4:27 That is, when he hath done sowing, should pass the time both day and night, nothing doubting, but that the seed would spring which groweth both day and night.
l. Mark 4:27 It is the part of the ministers, to labor the ground with all diligence, and commend the success to God: for that mighty working whereby the seed cometh to blade and ear, is secret and only known by the fruit.
m. Mark 4:28 By a certain power which moveth itself.
n. Mark 4:30 God far otherwise than men use, beginneth with the least, and endeth with the greatest.
o. Mark 4:33 According to the capacity of the hearers.
p. Mark 4:34 Word for word, Loosed, as you would say, read them the hard riddles.
q. Mark 4:37 They that sail with Christ, although he seems to sleep never so soundly when they are in danger, yet they are preserved of him in time convenient, being awakened.
r. Mark 4:40 How cometh it to pass that you have no faith?

MARK. 4

1. Matt. 13:1 / Luke 8:4
2. Isa. 6:9 / Matt. 13:14 / Luke 8:10 / John 12:40 / Acts 28:26 / Rom. 11:8
3. 1 Tim. 6:17
4. Mark 5:15 / Luke 8:16 / Luke 11:33
5. Matt. 10:26 / Luke 8:17 / Luke 12:2
6. Matt. 7:2 / Luke 6:38
7. Matt. 13:12 / Matt. 25:29 / Luke 8:18 / Luke 19:26
8. Matt. 13:31 / Luke 13:19
9. Matt. 8 / Matt. 13:34
10. Matt. 8:23 / Luke 8:22

MARK. 5

a. Mark 5:1 Many have the virtue of Christ in admiration, and yet they will not redeem it with the loss of the least thing they have.
b. Mark 5:1 See also Matt. 8:30.
c. Mark 5:2 Word for word, in an unclean spirit: now they are said to be in the spirit, because the spirit holdeth them fast locked up, and as it were bound.
d. Mark 5:7 That is, assure me by an oath, that thou will not vex me.
e. Mark 5:10 That devil that played the messenger for his fellows.
f. Mark 5:11 This whole country is for the greater part of it very hilly, for the mountains of Galeed run through it.
g. Mark 5:13 Strabo in the sixteenth book saith that in Gadaris there is a standing pool of very naughty water, which if beasts taste of, they shed their hair, nails, or hooves and horns.
h. Mark 5:22 The whole company assembled not disorderly, but in every Synagogue there were certain men which governed the people.
i. Mark 5:25 Jesus being touched with true faith although it be but weak, doth heal us by his virtue.
j. Mark 5:36 Fathers apprehend by faith the promises of life even for their children.

the Synagogue, Be not afraid: only believe. **37** And he suffered no man to follow
him save Peter and James, and John the brother of James. **38** So he came unto
the house of the ruler of the Synagogue, and saw the tumult, and them that wept
and wailed greatly. **39** And he went in, and said unto them, Why make ye this
trouble, and weep? the child is not dead, but sleepeth. **40** [k]And they laughed
him to scorn: but he put them all out, and took the father, and the mother of the
child, and them [l]that were with him, and entered in where the child lay, **41** And
took the child by the hand, and said unto her, Talitha cumi, which is by interpre-
tation, Maiden, I say unto thee, arise. **42** And straightway the maiden arose,
and walked: for she was of the age of twelve years, and they were astonied out of
measure. **43** And he charged them straitly that no man should know of it, and
commanded to give her meat.

6

3 Christ preaching in his country, his own condemn him. 6 The unbelief of the Nazarites. 7 The Apostles are sent. 13 They cast out devils: they anoint the sick with oil. 14 Herod's opinion of Christ. 18 The cause of John's imprisonment. 22 Dancing. 27 John beheaded, 29 buried. 30 The Apostles return from preaching. 34 Christ teacheth in the desert. 37 He feedeth the people with five loaves. 48 The Apostles are troubled on the sea. 56 The sick that touch Christ's garment, are healed.

1 And [a,1]he departed thence, and came into his own country, and his disci-
ples followed him. **2** And when the Sabbath was come, he began to teach in the
Synagogue, and many that heard him, were astonied, and said, From whence hath
this man these things? and what wisdom is this that is given unto him, that even
such [b]great works are done by his hands? **3** Is not this that carpenter Mary's son,
the brother of James and Joses, and of Judas and Simon? and are not his [c]sisters
here with us? And they were offended in him. **4** And Jesus said unto them, A
[2]Prophet is not without [d]honor, but in his own country, and among his own kin-
dred, and in his own house. **5** And he [e]could there do no great works, save that
he laid his hands upon a few sick folk, and healed them. **6** And he marveled at
their unbelief, [3]and went about by the towns on every side, teaching. **7** [f,4]And he
called unto him the twelve, and began to send them forth two and two, and gave
them power over unclean spirits, **8** [g]And commanded them that they should
take nothing for their journey, save a staff only: neither scrip, neither bread, neither
money in their girdles: **9** But that they should be shod with [h,5]sandals, and that
they should not put on [i]two coats, **10** And he said unto them, Wheresoever ye
shall enter into an house, [j]there abide till ye depart thence. **11** [k,6]And whosoever
shall not receive you, nor hear you, when ye depart thence, [7]shake off the dust that
is under your feet, for a witness unto them. Verily I say unto you, It shall be easier
for Sodom, or Gomorrah at the day of Judgment, than for that city. **12** And they
went out, and preached, that men should amend their lives. **13** And they cast
out many devils: and they [l,8]anointed many that were sick, with oil, and healed
them. **14** [m,9]Then King Herod heard of him (for his Name was made manifest)
and said, John Baptist is risen again from the dead, and therefore great [n]works are
wrought by him. **15** Others said, It is Elijah, and some said, It is a Prophet, or as
one of [o]those Prophets. **16** [10]So when Herod heard it, he said, It is John whom
[p]I beheaded: he is risen from the dead. **17** For Herod himself had sent forth,
and had taken John, and bound him in prison for Herodias' sake, which was his
brother Philip's wife, because he had married her. **18** For John said unto Herod,
[11]It is not lawful for thee to have thy brother's wife. **19** Therefore Herodias [q]laid
wait against him: and would have killed him, but she could not: **20** For Herod
feared John, knowing that he was a just man, and an holy, and reverenced him,
and when he heard him, he did many things, and heard him [r]gladly. **21** But the
time being convenient, when Herod on his birthday made a banquet to his prin-
ces and captains, and chief estates of Galilee: **22** And the daughter [s]of the same
Herodias came in, and danced, and pleased Herod, and them that sat at table to-
gether, the King said unto the maid, Ask of me what thou wilt, and I will give it
thee. **23** And he swore unto her, Whatsoever thou shalt ask of me, I will give it
thee, even unto the half of my kingdom. **24** [12]So [t]she went forth, and said to
her mother, What shall I ask? And she said, John Baptist's head. **25** Then she
came in straightway with haste unto the King, and asked, saying, I would that
thou shouldest give me even now in a charger the head of John Baptist. **26** Then
the King was very sorry: yet for his oath's sake, and for their sakes which sat at
table with him, he would not refuse her. **27** And immediately the King sent the
[u]hangman, and gave charge that his head should be brought in. So he went and
beheaded him in the prison, **28** And brought his head in a charger, and gave
it to the maid, and the maid gave it to her mother. **29** And when his disciples
heard it, they came and took up his body, and put it in a tomb. **30** [13]And the
Apostles gathered themselves together to Jesus, and told him all things, both what
they had done, and what they had taught. **31** [v]And he said unto them, Come ye
apart into the wilderness, and rest a while: for there were many comers and goers,
that they had not leisure to eat. **32** [14]So they went by ship out of the way into a
desert place. **33** But the people saw them when they departed, and many knew
him, and ran afoot thither out of all cities, and came thither before them, and as-
sembled unto him. **34** [15]Then Jesus went out, and saw a great multitude, and
had compassion on them, because they were like sheep which had no shepherd:
[16]and he began to teach them many things. **35** [17]And when the day was now far
spent, his disciples came unto him, saying, This is a desert place, and now the day
is far passed. **36** Let them depart, that they may go into the country and towns
about, and buy them bread: for they have nothing to eat. **37** But he answered,
and said unto them, Give ye them to eat. And they said unto him, [w]Shall we go,
and buy [x]two hundred pennies worth of bread, and give them to eat? **38** [18]Then
he said unto them, How many loaves have ye? go and look. And when they knew
it, they said, Five, and two fishes. **39** So he commanded them to make them all
sit down by [y]companies upon the green grass. **40** Then they sat down by [z]rows,
by hundreds, and by fifties. **41** And he took the five loaves, and the two fishes,
and looked up to heaven, and gave thanks, and broke the loaves, and gave them
to his disciples to set before them, and the two fishes he divided among them
all. **42** So they did all eat, and were satisfied. **43** And they took up twelve
baskets full of the fragments, and of the fishes. **44** And they that had eaten, were
about five thousand men. **45** [aa]And straightway he caused his disciples to go
into the ship, and to go before unto the other side unto Bethsaida, while he sent
away the people. **46** Then as soon as he had sent [ab]them away, he departed into
a mountain to pray. **47** [19]And when even was come, the ship was in the midst
of the sea, and he alone on the land. **48** And he saw them troubled in rowing,
(for the wind was contrary unto them) and about the fourth watch of the night, he
came unto them, walking upon the sea, and would have passed by them. **49** And
when they saw him walking upon the sea, they supposed it had been a spirit, and
cried out. **50** For they all saw him, and were sore afraid: but anon he talked with
them, and said unto them, Be ye of good comfort: it is I, be not afraid. **51** Then
he went up unto them into the ship, and the wind ceased, and they were [ac]much
more amazed in themselves, and marveled. **52** For they had not [ad]considered the
matter of the loaves, because their hearts were hardened. **53** [20]And they came
over, and went into the land of Gennesaret, and arrived. **54** [ae]So when they were
come out of the ship, straightway they knew him, **55** And ran about throughout
all that region round about, and began to carry hither and thither in couches all
that were sick, where they heard that he was. **56** And whithersoever he entered

---

k. Mark 5:40 Such as mock and scorn Christ, are unworthy to be witnesses of his goodness.
l. Mark 5:40 The three disciples.

MARK. 5

1. Matt. 8:28 / Luke 8:16 **2.** Matt. 9:15 / Luke 8:41

MARK. 6

a. Mark 6:1 The faithless world doth no whit at all diminish the virtue of Christ, but wittingly and willingly depriveth itself of the efficacy of it, being offered unto them.
b. Mark 6:2 The word signifieth powers, or virtues, whereby are meant those wonderful works that Christ did, which showed and set forth the virtue and power of his Godhead to all the world, Matt. 7:22.
c. Mark 6:3 After the manner of the Hebrews, who by brethren and sisters, understand all their kinfolks.
d. Mark 6:4 Not only that hath that honor which of right is due to him taken from him, but also evil spoken of and misreported.
e. Mark 6:5 That is, he would not: for we must needs have faith, if we will receive the works of God.
f. Mark 6:7 The disciples are prepared to that general Apostleship, by a peculiar sending forth.
g. Mark 6:8 Faithful Pastors ought not to have their minds set, no not on things that are necessary for this life, if they may be an hindrance unto them, be it never so little.
h. Mark 6:9 The word signifieth properly women's shoes.
i. Mark 6:9 That is, they should take no change of garments with them, that they might be lighter for this journey, and make more speed.
j. Mark 6:10 That is, change not your inns in this short journey.
k. Mark 6:11 The Lord is a most severe revenger of his servants.
l. Mark 6:13 That oil was a token and a sign of this marvelous virtue: and seeing that the gift of healing is ceased a good while since, the ceremony which is yet retained of some is to no purpose.
m. Mark 6:14 The Gospel confirmeth the godly, and vexeth the wicked.
n. Mark 6:14 This word signifieth Powers, whereby is meant the power of working miracles.
o. Mark 6:15 Of the old Prophets.
p. Mark 6:16 Commanded to be beheaded.
q. Mark 6:19 Sought all means to do him hurt.
r. Mark 6:20 The tyrant was very well content to hear sentence pronounced against him, but the seed fell upon stony places.
s. Mark 6:22 Which the same Herodias had not by Herod Antipas, but by Philip, and Josephus calleth her Salome.
t. Mark 6:24 For women used not to sit at table with men.
u. Mark 6:27 The word signifieth one that beareth a dart, and the king's guard was so called, because they did bear darts.
v. Mark 6:31 Such as follow Christ shall want nothing, no not in the wilderness, but shall have abundance. And how wicked a thing is it, not to look for this transitory life at his hand-s,who giveth everylasting life?
w. Mark 6:37 This declareth that there is an horrible disorder among the people, where the true preaching of God's word wanteth.
x. Mark 6:37 Which is about five pounds sterling.
y. Mark 6:39 Word for word, by banquets, after the manner of the Hebrews, who have no distributives, as Mark 6:7. Now he calleth the rows of the sitters, banquets.
z. Mark 6:40 The word signifieth the beds in a garden, and it is word for word, by beds and beds, meaning thereby that they sat down in rows one by another, as beds in a garden.
aa. Mark 6:45 The faithful servants of God after their little labor, are subject to great tempest, which Christ doth so moderate being present in power, although absent in body, that he bringeth them to an happy haven, at such time and by such means, as they looked not for: A lively image of the Church tossed to and fro in this world.
ab. Mark 6:46 His disciples.
ac. Mark 6:51 They were so far from leaving to be amazed, when they knew that it was no spirit, that they were much more astonished than ever they were before, when they saw the wind and the seas obey his commandment.
ad. Mark 6:52 Either they perceived not, or had not well considered that miracle of the five loaves, insomuch that that virtue of Christ was no less strange to them, than if they had not been present at that miracle which was done but a little before.
ae. Mark 6:54 Christ being rejected in his own country, and arriving upon a sudden amongst them of whom he was not looked for, is received to their profit.

into towns, or cities, or villages, they laid their sick in the streets, and prayed him that they might touch at the least the edge of his garment. And as many as touched [af]him, were made whole.

7

2 The Apostles are found fault with, for eating with unwashed hands. 4 The Pharisees' traditions about washings, Hypocrites. 8 Men's traditions more set by than God's. 10 Parents must be honored. 15 The things that do indeed defile a man. 25 The woman of Canaan. 32 The deaf dumb man is healed.

1 Then [a,1]gathered unto him the Pharisees, and certain of the Scribes which came from Jerusalem. **2** And when they saw some of his disciples [b]eat meat with [c]common hands, (that is to say, unwashen) they complained. **3** (For the Pharisees, and all the Jews, except they wash their hands oft, eat not, [d]holding the traditions of the Elders. **4** And when they come from the [e]market, except they wash, they eat not: and many other things there be, which they have taken upon them to observe, as the washing of cups, and [f]pots, and of brazen vessels, and of beds.) **5** Then asked him the Pharisees and Scribes, Why [g]walk not thy disciples according to the tradition of the Elders, but eat meat with unwashen hands? **6** [h]Then he answered and said unto them, Surely [2]Isaiah hath prophesied well of you, hypocrites, as it is written, This people honoreth me with lips, but their heart is far away from me. **7** [i]But they worship me in vain, teaching for doctrines the commandments of men. **8** [j]For ye lay the Commandments of God apart, and observe the tradition of men, as the washing of pots and of cups, and many other such like things ye do. **9** [k]And he said unto them, Well ye reject the commandment of God, that ye may observe your own tradition. **10** For Moses said, [3]Honor thy father and thy mother: and [4]Whosoever shall speak evil of father or mother, let him [l]die the death. **11** But ye say, If a man say to father or mother, Corban, that is, By the gift that is offered by me, thou mayest have profit, he shall be free. **12** So ye suffer him no more to do anything for his father, or his mother. **13** Making the word of God of none authority, by your tradition which ye have ordained: and ye do many such like things. **14** [5]Then he calleth the whole multitude unto him, and said unto them, Hearken you all unto me, and understand. **15** There is nothing without a man, that can defile him, when it entereth into him: but the things which proceed out of him, are they which defile the man. **16** If any have ears to hear, let him hear. **17** And when he came into an house, away from the people, his disciples asked him concerning the parable. **18** And he said unto them, What? are ye without understanding also? Do ye not know that whatsoever thing from without entereth into a man, cannot defile him, **19** Because it entered not into his heart, but into the belly, and goeth out into the draught which is the [m]purging of all meats? **20** Then he said, That which cometh out of man, that defileth man. **21** [6]For from within, even out of the heart of men, proceed evil thoughts, adulteries, fornications, murders, **22** Thefts, [n]covetousness, wickedness, deceit, uncleanness, a [o]wicked eye, backbiting, pride, foolishness. **23** All these evil things come from within, and defile a man. **24** [p,7]And from thence he rose, and went into the [q]borders of Tyre and Sidon, and entered into an house, and would that no man should have known: but he could not be hid. **25** For a certain woman, whose little daughter had an unclean spirit, heard of him, and came, and fell at his feet, **26** (And the woman was a [r]Greek, a [s]Syro-Phoenician by nation) and she besought him that he would cast out the devil out of her daughter. **27** But Jesus said unto her, Let the children first be fed: for it is not good to take the children's bread, and to cast it unto [t]whelps. **28** Then she answered, and said unto him, [u]Truth, Lord: yet indeed the whelps eat under the table of the children's crumbs. **29** Then he said unto her, For this saying go thy way: the devil is gone out of thy daughter. **30** And when she was come home to her house, she found the devil departed, and her daughter lying on the bed. **31** [v]And he departed again from the coasts of Tyre and Sidon, and came unto the sea of Galilee, through the midst of the coasts of [w]Decapolis. **32** And they brought unto him one that was deaf and stammered in his speech, and prayed him to put his hand upon him. **33** Then he took him aside from the multitude, and put his fingers in his ears, and did spit, and touched his tongue. **34** And looking up to heaven, he sighed, and said unto him, Ephphatha, that is, Be opened. **35** And straightway his ears were opened, and the string of his tongue was loosed, and he spake plain. **36** And he commanded them that they should tell no man: but how much soever he forbade them, the more a great deal they published it, **37** And were beyond measure astonied, saying, He hath done all things well: [8]He maketh both the deaf to hear, and the dumb to speak.

8

1 The miracle of the seven loaves. 11 The Jews seek signs. 15 To beware of the leaven of the Pharisees. 22 A blind man healed. 27 The people's sundry opinions of Christ. 29 The Apostles acknowledge Christ. 31 He foretelleth his death. 33 Peter, Satan. 35 To save and lose the life. 38 To be ashamed of Christ.

1 In [1]those days, when there was a very great multitude, and had nothing to eat, Jesus called his disciples to him, and said unto them, **2** I have compassion on the multitude, because they have now continued with me three days, and have nothing to eat. **3** And if I send them away fasting to their own houses, they would [a]faint by the way: for some of them came from far. **4** Then his disciples answered him, Whence can a man satisfy these with bread here in the wilderness? **5** And he asked them, How many loaves have ye? And they said, Seven. **6** Then he commanded the multitude to sit down on the ground: and he took the seven loaves, and gave thanks, brake them, and gave to his disciples to set before them, and they did set them before the people. **7** They had also a few small fishes: and when he had given thanks, he commanded them also to be set before them, **8** So they did eat, and were sufficed, and they took up of the broken meat that was left, seven baskets full. **9** (And they that had eaten, were about four thousand) so he sent them away. **10** [2]And anon he entered into a ship with his disciples, and came into the parts of Dalmanutha. **11** [b,3]And the Pharisees [c]came forth, and began to dispute with him, seeking of him a sign from heaven, and tempting him. **12** Then he [d]sighed deeply in his spirit, and said, Why doth this generation seek a sign? Verily I say unto you, [e]a sign shall not be given unto this generation. **13** So he left them, and went into the ship again, and departed to the other side. **14** [4]And they had forgotten to take bread, neither had they in the ship with them, but one loaf. **15** [f]And he charged them, saying, Take heed, and beware of the leaven of the Pharisees, and of the leaven of Herod. **16** [g]And they reasoned among themselves, saying, It is, because we have no bread. **17** And when Jesus knew it, he said unto them, Why reason you thus, because ye have no bread? perceive ye not yet, neither understand? have ye your hearts yet hardened? **18** Have ye eyes, and see not? and have ye ears, and hear not? and do ye not remember? **19** [5]When I brake the five loaves among five thousand, how many baskets full of broken meat took ye up? They said unto him, Twelve. **20** And when I brake seven among four thousand, how many baskets full of the leavings of broken meat took ye up? And they said, Seven. **21** Then he said unto them,

---

af. Mark 6:56 Or, the hem of the garment.

MARK. 6

1. Matt. 13:54 / Luke 4:16
2. Matt. 13:57 / Luke 4:24 / John 4:44
3. Matt. 4:23 / Luke 13:22
4. Mark 3:14 / Matt. 10:1 / Luke 9:1
5. Acts 12:3
6. Matt. 10:14 / Luke 9:5
7. Acts 13:51 / Acts 18:6
8. James 5:14
9. Matt. 14:1 / Luke 9:7
10. Luke 3:19

MARK. 7

a. Mark 7:1 None do more resist the wisdom of God, than they that should be wisest, and that upon a zeal of their own traditions: for men do not please themselves more in anything than in superstition, that is to say, in a worship of God fondly devised of themselves.
b. Mark 7:2 Word for word, eat bread: a kind of speech which the Hebrews use, taking bread for all kinds of food.
c. Mark 7:2 For the Pharisees would not eat their meat with unwashed hands, because they thought that their hands were defiled with common handling of things, Matt. 15:11, 12.
d. Mark 7:3 Observing diligently.
e. Mark 7:4 That is to say, from civil affairs and worldly, they go not to meat, unless they wash themselves first.
f. Mark 7:4 By these words are understood all kinds of vessels, which are appointed for our daily use.
g. Mark 7:5 Why live they not? a kind of speech taken from the Hebrews: for amongst them, the way is taken for trade of life.
h. Mark 7:6 Hypocrisy is always joined with superstition.
i. Mark 7:7 The more earnest the superstitious are, the more they are mad, in promising themselves God's favor by their deserts.
j. Mark 7:8 The devices of superstitious men do not only not fulfill the Law of God (as they blasphemously persuade themselves) but also do utterly take it away.
k. Mark 7:9 True Religion, which is clean contrary to superstition, consisteth in spiritual worship: and all enemies of true Religion, although they seem to have taken deep root, shall be plucked up.
l. Mark 7:10 Without hope of pardon, he shall be put to death.
m. Mark 7:19 For that that goeth into the draught, purgeth all meats.
n. Mark 7:22 All kind of craftiness whereby men profit themselves by other men's losses.
o. Mark 7:22 Cankered malice.
p. Mark 7:24 That which the proud do reject when it is offered unto them, that same do the modest and humble sinners as it were violently wring out.
q. Mark 7:24 Into the uttermost coasts of Palestine, which were next to Tyre and Sidon.
r. Mark 7:26 By profession, profane.
s. Mark 7:26 Neighbor or near to Damascus.
t. Mark 7:27 He useth this word Whelps rather than the word Dogs, that he may seem to speak more contumaciously.
u. Mark 7:28 As if she said, it is as thou sayest Lord, for it is enough for the whelps, if they can but gather up the crumbs that are under the table: therefore I crave the crumbs, and not the children's bread.
v. Mark 7:31 As the Father created us to this life in the beginning in his only Son, so doth he also in him alone renew us unto everlasting life.
w. Mark 7:31 It was a little country, and so called of ten cities, which the four governments do run between and compass, Pliny, book 3, chap. 8.

MARK. 7

1. Matt. 15:2
2. Isa. 29:14
3. Exod. 10:12 / Deut. 5:26 / Eph. 6:2
4. Exod. 11:17 / Lev. 20:9 / Prov. 20:20
5. Matt. 15:10
6. Gen. 6:5 / Gen. 8:21
7. Matt. 15:21
8. Gen. 1:31

MARK. 8

a. Mark 8:3 Word for word, they will fall in sunder, or be dissolved, for when men fall in a swound, their sinews fall one from another.
b. Mark 8:11 The stubborn enemies of the doctrine of the Gospel, giving no credit to the miracles already done require new: but Christ being angry with them, doth utterly forsake them.
c. Mark 8:11 A common kind of speech, which the Hebrews use, whereby is meant that the Pharisees went from their houses of purpose, to encounter with him.
d. Mark 8:12 These sighs came even from the heart root, for the Lord was very much moved with these men's so great infidelity.
e. Mark 8:12 Word for word, If a sign be given: It is a cut kind of speech very common among the Hebrews: wherein some such words as these must be understood. Let me be taken for a liar, or some such like. And when they speak out the whole, they say, The Lord do thus and thus by me.
f. Mark 8:15 We must especially take heed of them which corrupt the word of God, what degree soever they be of, either in the Church, or in civil policy.
g. Mark 8:16 They that have their minds fixed on earthly things, are utterly blind in heavenly things, although they be never so plainly set forth unto them.
h. Mark 8:21 How cometh it to pass, that you understand not these things which are so plain and evident?
i. Mark 8:22 A true image of our regeneration, which Christ separating us from the world, worketh and accomplisheth by little and little in us.

[h]How is it that ye understand not? **22** [i]And he came to Bethsaida, and they
brought a blind man unto him, and desired him to touch him. **23** Then he took
the blind by the hand, and led him out of the town, and spat in his eyes, and put
his hands upon him, and asked him, if he saw ought. **24** And he looked up, and
said, I [j]see men: for I see them walking like trees. **25** After that, he put his hands
again upon his eyes, and made him [k]look again. And he was restored to his sight,
and saw every man afar off clearly. **26** [l]And he sent him home to his house,
saying, Neither go into the town, nor tell it to any in the town. **27** [m,6]And Jesus
went out, and his disciples into the towns of Caesarea Philippi. And by the way
he asked his disciples, saying unto them, Whom do men say that I am? **28** And
they answered, Some say, John Baptist: and some, Elijah: and some, one of the
Prophets. **29** And he said unto them, But whom say ye that I am? Then Peter
answered, and said unto him, Thou art that Christ. **30** [n]And he sharply charged
them, that concerning him they should tell no man. **31** [o]Then he began to teach
them that the son of man must suffer many things, and should be reproved of the
Elders, and of the high Priests, and of the Scribes, and be slain, and within three
days rise again. **32** [p]And he spake that thing boldly. Then Peter took him aside,
and began to rebuke him. **33** Then he turned back and looked on his disciples,
and rebuked Peter, saying, Get thee behind me, Satan: for thou [q]understandest not
the things that are of God, but the things that are of men. **34** [r]And he called the
people unto him with his disciples, and said unto them, [7]Whosoever will follow
me, let him forsake himself, and take up his cross, and follow me. **35** For whoso-
ever will [8]save his life, shall lose it: but whosoever shall lose his life for my sake and
the Gospel's, he shall save it. **36** [s]For what shall it profit a man, though he should
win the whole world, if he lose his soul? **37** Or what exchange shall a man give
for his soul? **38** [9]For whosoever shall be ashamed of me, and of my words among
this adulterous and sinful generation, of him shall the Son of man be ashamed also,
when he cometh in the glory of his Father with the holy Angels.

9

2 Christ's transfiguration. 7 Christ must be heard. 11 Of Elias and John Baptist. 14 The possessed healed. 23 Faith can do all things. 31 Christ foretelleth his death. 33 Who is greatest among the Apostles. 36 Christ taketh a child in his arms. 42 To offend. 50 Salt. Peace.

1 And [1]he said unto them, Verily I say unto you, that there be some of them
that stand here, which shall not taste of death till they have seen the [a]kingdom
of God come with power. **2** [b,2]And six days after, Jesus taketh unto him Pe-
ter, and James, and John, and carrieth them up into an high mountain out of
the way alone, and his shape was changed before them. **3** And his raiment did
[c]shine, and was very white as snow, so white as no fuller can make upon the ear-
th. **4** And there appeared unto them Elijah with Moses, and they were talking
with Jesus. **5** Then Peter answered, and said to Jesus, Master, it is good for us to
be here: let us make also three tabernacles, one for thee, and one for Moses, and
one for Elijah. **6** Yet he knew not what he said: for they were [d]afraid. **7** And
there was a cloud that shadowed them, and a voice came out of the cloud, saying,
[3]This is my beloved Son: hear him. **8** And suddenly they looked round about,
and saw no more any man save Jesus only with them. **9** [e,4]And as they came
down from the mountain, he charged them, that they should tell no man what
they had seen, save when the Son of man were risen from the dead again. **10** So
they [f]kept that matter to themselves, and [g]demanded one of another, what the ri-
sing from the dead again should mean. **11** [h]Also they asked him, saying, Why
say the Scribes, that [5]Elijah must first come? **12** And he answered, and said unto
them, Elijah verily shall first come, and restore all things: and [6]as it is written of
the Son of man, he must suffer many things, and be set at nought. **13** But I
say unto you, that Elijah is come, (and they have done unto him whatsoever they
would) as it is written of him. **14** [i,7]And when he came to his disciples, he saw a
great multitude about them, and the Scribes disputing with them. **15** And strai-
ghtway all the people, when they beheld him, were amazed, and ran to him, and
saluted him. **16** Then he asked the Scribes, What dispute you among yoursel-
ves? **17** And one of the company answered, and said, Master, I have brought my
son unto thee, which hath a dumb spirit: **18** And wheresoever he taketh him, he
[j]teareth him, and he foameth, and gnasheth his teeth, and pineth away: and I spa-
ke to thy disciples, that they should cast him out, and they could not. **19** Then
he answered him, and said, O faithless generation, how long now shall I be with
you! how long now shall I suffer you! Bring him unto me. **20** So they brought
him unto him: and as soon as the spirit [k]saw him, he tare him, and he fell down
on the ground wallowing and foaming. **21** Then he asked his father, How long
time is it since he hath been thus? And he said, Of a child. **22** And oft times he
casteth him into the fire, and into the water to destroy him: but if thou canst do
anything, help us, and have compassion upon us. **23** And Jesus said unto him,
If thou canst believe it, [l]all things are possible to him that believeth. **24** And
straightway the father of the child crying with tears, said, Lord, I believe: help
my unbelief. **25** When Jesus saw that the people came running together, he re-
buked the unclean spirit, saying unto him, Thou dumb and deaf spirit, I charge
thee come out of him, and enter no more into him. **26** [m]Then the spirit cried,
and rent him sore, and came out, and he was as one dead, insomuch that many
said, He is dead. **27** But Jesus took his hand, and lifted him up, and he aro-
se. **28** [n]And when he was come into the house, his disciples asked him secretly,
Why could not we cast him out? **29** And he said unto them, This kind can by no
other means come forth, but by prayer and fasting. **30** [8]And they departed then-
ce, and [o]went together through Galilee, and he would not that any should have
known it. **31** [p]For he taught his disciples, and said unto them, The Son of man
shall be delivered into the hands of men, and they shall kill him, but after that he is
killed, he shall rise again the third day. **32** But they understood not that saying,
and were afraid to ask him. **33** [q,9]After, he came to Capernaum: and when he
was in the [r]house, he asked them, What was it that ye disputed among you by the
way? **34** And they held their peace: for by the way they reasoned among them-
selves, who should be the chiefest. **35** And he sat down and called the twelve,
and said to them, If any man desire to be first, the same shall be last of all, and
servant unto all. **36** And he took a little child, and set him in the midst of them,
and took him in his arms, and said unto them, **37** Whosoever shall receive one
of such little children in my Name, receiveth me: and whosoever receiveth me, re-
ceiveth not [s]me, but him that sent me. **38** [t,10]Then John answered him, saying,
Master, we saw one casting out devils by thy Name, which followeth not us, and
we forbade him, because he followeth us not. **39** [11]But Jesus said, Forbid him
not: for there is no man that can do a miracle by my Name, that can lightly speak
evil of me. **40** For whosoever is not against us, is on our part. **41** [12]And who-
soever shall give you a cup of water to drink for my Name's sake, because ye belong
to Christ, verily I say unto you, he shall not lose his reward. **42** [u,13]And whoso-
ever shall offend one of these little ones, that believe in me, it were better for him
rather, that a millstone were hanged about his neck, and that he were cast into the
sea. **43** [14]Wherefore if thine hand cause thee to offend, cut it off: it is better for
thee to enter into life, maimed, than having two hands, to go into hell, into the
fire that never shall be quenched, **44** [15]Where their [v]worm dieth not, and the
fire never goeth out. **45** Likewise, if thy foot cause thee to offend, cut it off: it is
better for thee to go halt into life, than having two feet, to be cast into hell, into
the fire that never shall be quenched, **46** Where their worm dieth not, and the
fire never goeth out. **47** And if thine eye cause thee to offend, pluck it out: it is

---

j. Mark 8:24 He perceived some moving of men, when he could not discern their bodies.

k. Mark 8:25 He commanded him again, to try indeed, whether he could see well or no.

l. Mark 8:26 Christ will not have his miracles to be separated from his doctrine.

m. Mark 8:27 Many praise Christ, which yet notwithstanding spoil him of his praise.

n. Mark 8:30 Christ hath appointed his times to the preaching of the Gospel: and therefore here defers it to a more commodious time, lest sudden haste should rather hinder than further the mystery of his coming.

o. Mark 8:31 Christ suffered all that he suffered for us, not unwillingly neither unawares, but foreknowing it, and willingly.

p. Mark 8:32 None are more mad than they that are wise beside the word of God.

q. Mark 8:33 This is not godly, but worldly wisdom.

r. Mark 8:34 The disciples of Christ must bear stoutly what burden soever the Lord layeth upon them, and subdue the affections of the flesh.

s. Mark 8:36 They are the most foolish of all men which purchase the enjoying of this life with the loss of everlasting bliss.

MARK. 8

1. Matt. 15:32
2. Matt. 15:39
3. Matt. 16:1
4. Matt. 16:5
5. John 6:11
6. Matt. 16:13 / Luke 9:18
7. Matt. 10:38 / Matt. 28:24 / Luke 9:23 / Luke 14:27
8. Matt. 10:39 / Matt. 16:25 / Luke 9:24 / Luke 17:33
9. Matt. 10:33 / Luke 8:26 / Luke 12:9

MARK. 9

a. Mark 9:1 When he shall begin his kingdom through the preaching of the Gospel: that is to say, after the resurrection.

b. Mark 9:2 The heavenly glory of Christ, which should within a short space be abased upon the cross, is avouched by visible signs, by the presence and talk of Elijah and Moses, and by the voice of the Father himself, before three of his disciples, which are witnesses against whom lieth no exception.

c. Mark 9:3 Did sparkle as it were.

d. Mark 9:6 They were beside themselves for fear.

e. Mark 9:9 The Lord hath appointed his time for the publishing of the Gospel.

f. Mark 9:10 Even very hardly as it were.

g. Mark 9:10 They questioned not together touching the general resurrection which shall be in the latter day, but they understood not what he meant by that which he spake of his own peculiar resurrection.

h. Mark 9:11 The foolish opinion of the Rabbis is here repelled touching Elijah's coming, which was that either Elijah should rise again from the dead, or that his soul should enter into some other body.

i. Mark 9:14 Christ showeth by a miracle even to the unworthy, that he is come to bridle the rage of Satan.

j. Mark 9:18 Vexed him inwardly, as the colic useth to do.

k. Mark 9:20 So soon as Jesus had looked upon the boy that was brought unto him, the devil began to rage after his manner.

l. Mark 9:23 There is nothing but Christ can and will do it, for them that believe in him.

m. Mark 9:26 The nearer that the virtue of Christ is, the more outrageously doth Satan rage.

n. Mark 9:28 We have need of faith, and therefore of prayer and fasting, to cast Satan out of his old possession.

o. Mark 9:30 He and his disciples together.

p. Mark 9:31 Christ forewarneth us with great diligence, to the end we should not be oppressed with sudden calamities, but the slothfulness of man is wonderful.

q. Mark 9:33 Only humility doth exalt.

r. Mark 9:33 Where he was wont to make his abode.

s. Mark 9:37 He doth not only receive me, but also him that sent me.

t. Mark 9:38 God who is the author of an ordinary vocation, worketh also extraordinarily so oft as it pleaseth him. But an extraordinary vocation is tried by the doctrine and the effects.

u. Mark 9:42 God is so severe a revenger of offenses, that it is better to suffer any loss, than to be an occasion of offense unto any.

v. Mark 9:44 Their worm which shall be cast into that flame.

better for thee to go into the kingdom of God with one eye, than having two eyes,
to be cast into hell fire, **48** Where their worm dieth not, and the fire never goeth
out. **49** [w]For every man shall be [x]salted with fire: and [16]every sacrifice shall be
salted with salt. **50** [17]Salt is good: but if the salt be unsavory, wherewith shall it
be seasoned? have salt in yourselves, and have peace one with another.

10

9 The wife, only for fornication, is to be put away. 13 Little children are brought to Christ. 17 A rich man asketh Jesus, how he may possess eternal life. 28 The Apostles forsook all things for Christ's sake. 33 Christ foreshoweth his death. 35 Zebedee's sons' request. 46 Blind Bartimaeus healed.

1 And [1]he [a]arose from thence, and went into the coasts of Judea by the far side
of Jordan, and the people resorted unto him again, and as he was wont, he taught
them again. **2** Then the Pharisees came and asked him, if it were lawful for a
man to put away his wife, and tempted him. **3** And he answered, and said unto
them, What did [2]Moses command you? **4** And they said, Moses suffered to wri-
te a bill of divorcement, and to put her away. **5** [b]Then Jesus answered, and said
unto them, For the hardness of your heart he wrote this [c]precept unto you. **6** But
at the beginning of the creation [3]God made them male and female: **7** [4]For this
cause shall man leave his father and mother, and cleave unto his wife. **8** And they
twain shall be one flesh: so that they are no more twain, but one flesh. **9** [5]The-
refore, what God hath coupled together, let not man separate. **10** And in the
house his disciples asked him again of that matter. **11** And he said unto them,
[6]whosoever shall put away his wife and marry another, commiteth adultery [d]a-
gainst her. **12** And if a woman put away her husband, and be married to another,
she commiteth adultery. **13** [e,7]Then they brought little children to him, that he
should touch them, and his disciples rebuked those that brought them. **14** But
when Jesus saw it, he was displeased, and said to them, Suffer the little children to
come unto me, and forbid them not: for of such is the kingdom of God. **15** Ve-
rily I say unto you, Whosoever shall not receive the kingdom of God [f]as a little
child, he shall not enter therein. **16** And he took them up in his arms, and put
his hands upon them, and blessed them. **17** [g]And when he was gone out on the
way, there came one [8]running, and kneeled to him, and asked him, Good Master,
what shall I do, that I may possess eternal life? **18** Jesus said to him, Why callest
thou me good? there is none good but one, even God. **19** Thou knowest the
commandments, [9]Thou shalt not commit adultery. Thou shalt not kill. Thou shalt
not steal. Thou shalt not bear false witness. Thou shalt [h]hurt no man. Honor thy
father and mother. **20** Then he answered, and said to him, Master, all these thin-
gs have I observed from my youth. **21** And Jesus looked upon him, and loved
him, and said unto him, One thing is lacking unto thee. Go and sell all that thou
hast, and give to the poor, and thou shalt have treasure in heaven, and come, follow
me, and take up the cross. **22** But he was sad at that saying, and went away sor-
rowful: for he had great possessions. **23** And Jesus looked round about, and said
unto his disciples, How hardly do they that have riches, enter into the kingdom
of God! **24** And his disciples were afraid at his words. But Jesus answered again,
and said unto them, Children, how hard is it for them that trust in riches, to enter
into the kingdom of God! **25** It is easier for a camel to go through the eye of a
needle, than for a rich man to enter into the kingdom of God. **26** And they were
much more astonied, saying with themselves, Who then can be saved? **27** But
Jesus looked upon them, and said, With men it is impossible, but not with God:
for with God all things are possible. **28** [i,10]Then Peter began to say unto him,
Lo, we have forsaken all, and have followed thee. **29** Jesus answered, and said,
Verily I say unto you, there is no man that hath forsaken house, or brethren, or
sisters, or father, or mother, or wife, or children, or lands for my sake and the Go-
spels, **30** But he shall receive an [j]hundredfold, now at this present, houses, and
brethren, and sisters, and mothers, and children, and lands [k]with persecutions, and
in the world to come, eternal life. **31** [11]But many that are first, shall be last, and
the last, first. **32** [l,12]And they were in the way going up to Jerusalem, and Jesus
went before them, and they were troubled, and as they followed, they were afraid,
and Jesus took the twelve again, and began to tell them what things should come
unto him, **33** Saying, Behold, we go up to Jerusalem, and the Son of man shall
be delivered unto the high Priests, and to the Scribes, and they shall condemn him
to death, and shall deliver him to the Gentiles. **34** And they shall mock him,
and scourge him, and spit upon him, and kill him: but the third day he shall rise
again. **35** [m,13]Then James and John the sons of Zebedee came unto him, saying,
Master, [n]we would that thou shouldest do for us that we desire. **36** And he said
unto them, What would ye I should do for you? **37** And they said to him, Grant
unto us, that we may sit, one at thy right hand, and the other at thy left hand in
thy glory. **38** But Jesus said unto them, Ye know not what ye ask. Can ye drink
of the cup that I shall drink of, and be baptized with the baptism that I shall be
baptized with? **39** And they said unto him, We can. But Jesus said unto them, Ye
shall drink indeed of the cup that I shall drink of, and be baptized with the baptism
wherewith I shall be baptized: **40** But to sit at my right hand and at my left, is
not mine to give, but it shall be given to them for whom it is prepared. **41** And
when the ten heard that, they began to disdain at James and John. **42** [o]But
Jesus called them unto him, and said to them, [14]Ye know that [p]they which are
princes among the Gentiles, have domination over them, and they that be great
among them, exercise authority over them. **43** But it shall not be so among you:
but whosoever will be great among you, shall be your servant. **44** And who-
soever will be chief of you, shall be the servant of all. **45** For even the Son of
man came not to be served, but to serve, and to give his life for the ransom of
many. **46** [q,15]Then they came to Jericho: and as he went out of Jericho with his
disciples, and a great multitude, Bartimaeus the son of Timaeus, a blind man, sat
by the wayside, begging. **47** And when he heard that it was Jesus of Nazareth,
he began to cry, and to say, Jesus the Son of David, have mercy on me. **48** And
many rebuked him, because he should hold his peace: but he cried much more,
O Son of David, have mercy on me. **49** Then Jesus stood still, and commanded
him to be called: and they called the blind, saying unto him, Be of good comfort:
arise, he calleth thee. **50** So he threw away his cloak, and rose, and came to Je-
sus. **51** And Jesus answered, and said unto him, What wilt thou that I do unto
thee? And the blind said unto him, Lord, that I may receive sight. **52** Then Jesus
said unto him, Go thy way: thy faith hath saved thee. And by and by he received
his sight, and followed Jesus in the way.

11

1 Christ entereth into Jerusalem riding on an ass. 13 The fruitless fig tree is cursed. 15 Sellers and buyers are cast out of the Temple. 23 The force of faith. 24 Faith in prayer. 25 The brother's offenses must be pardoned. 27 The Priests ask by what authority he wrought those things that he did. 30 Whence John's baptism was.

1 And [a,1]when they came near to Jerusalem, to Bethphage and Bethany unto
the mount of Olives, he sent forth two of his disciples, **2** And said unto them,
Go your ways into that town that is over against you, and as soon as ye shall en-
ter into it, ye shall find a colt tied, whereon never man sat: loose him, and bring
him. **3** And if any man say unto you, Why do ye this? Say that the Lord hath
need of him, and straightway he will send him hither. **4** And they went their
way, and found a colt, tied by the door without, in a place where two ways met,
and they loosed him. **5** Then certain of them, that stood there, said unto them,
What do ye loosing the colt? **6** And they said unto them, as Jesus had com-
manded them: So they let them go. **7** [2]And they brought the colt to Jesus, and
cast their garments on him, and he sat upon him. **8** And many spread their
garments in the way: others cut down branches off the trees, and strawed them
in the way. **9** And they that went before, and they that followed, cried, saying,
Hosanna: [b]blessed be he that cometh in the Name of the Lord. **10** [c]Blessed be

---

w. Mark 9:49 We must be seasoned and powdered by God, both that we may be acceptable sacrifices unto him: and also that we being knit together, may season one another.

x. Mark 9:49 That is, shall be consecrated to God, being seasoned with the incorruptible word.

MARK. 9

1. Matt. 6:28 / Luke 9:27
2. Matt. 17:1 / Luke 9:28
3. Matt. 3:17 / Matt. 27:5 / Mark 1:11
4. Matt. 17:9
5. Mal. 4:5
6. Isa. 13:4
7. Matt. 17:14 / Luke 9:38
8. Matt. 17:21 / Luke 9:22
9. Matt. 18:1 / Luke 9:46
10. Luke 9:49
11. 1 Cor. 12:3
12. Matt. 10:42
13. Matt. 18:5 / Luke 17:1
14. Matt. 5:29 / Matt. 18:8
15. Isa. 66:24
16. Lev. 2:13
17. Matt. 5:13 / Luke 14:34

MARK. 10

a. Mark 10:1 That is to say, departed and went from thence: for in the Hebrew tongue, sitting and dwelling are all one, and so are rising and going forth.

b. Mark 10:5 God did never allow those divorces, which the Law did tolerate.

c. Mark 10:5 See also Matt. 19. For Moses gave them no commandment to put away their wives, but rather made a good provision for the wives against the stubborn hardness of their husbands.

d. Mark 10:11 Whom he putteth away, for he is an adulterer by keeping company with another.

e. Mark 10:13 God of his goodness comprehendeth in the covenant not only the fathers, but the children also: and therefore he blesseth them.

f. Mark 10:15 We must in malice become children, if we will enter into the kingdom of heaven.

g. Mark 10:17 Two things are chiefly to be eschewed of them which earnestly seek eternal life: that is to say, an opinion of their merits or deservings, which is not only understood, but condemned by the due consideration of the Law: and the love of riches, which turneth aside many, from that race wherein they ran with a good courage.

h. Mark 10:19 Neither by force nor deceit, nor any other means whatsoever.

i. Mark 10:28 To neglect all things in comparison of Christ, is a sure way unto eternal life, so that we fall not away by the way.

j. Mark 10:30 An hundredfold as much, if we look to the true use and commodities of this life, so that we measure them after the will of God, and not after the wealth itself, and our greedy desire.

k. Mark 10:30 Even in the midst of persecutions.

l. Mark 10:32 The disciples are again prepared to patience, not to be overcome by the foretelling unto them of his death, which was at hand, and therewithall of life which should most certainly follow.

m. Mark 10:35 We must first strive, before we triumph.

n. Mark 10:35 We pray thee.

o. Mark 10:42 The Magistrates according to God's appointment, rule over their subjects: but the Pastors are not called to rule, but to serve, according to the example of the Son of God himself, who went before them, for so much as he also was a Minister of his Father's will.

p. Mark 10:42 They to whom it is decreed and appointed.

q. Mark 10:46 Christ only, being called upon by faith, healeth our blindness.

MARK. 10

1. Matt. 19:2
2. Deut. 24:1
3. Gen. 2:27 / Matt. 9:4
4. Gen. 2:24 / 1 Cor. 6:16 / Eph. 5:3
5. 1 Cor. 7:10
6. Matt. 5:30 / Matt. 19:9 / Luke 16:18
7. Matt. 19:13 / Luke 13:15
8. Matt. 19:16 / Luke 18:18
9. Exod. 20:13
10. Matt. 19:27 / Luke 18:28
11. Matt. 19:30 / Luke 13:30
12. Matt. 20:17 / Luke 18:31
13. Matt. 20:20
14. Luke 22:25
15. Matt. 20:29 / Luke 18:35

MARK. 11

a. Mark 11:1 A lively image of the spiritual kingdom of Christ on earth.

b. Mark 11:9 Well be it to him that cometh to us from God, or that is sent of God.

the kingdom that cometh in the Name of the Lord of our father David: Hosanna, O thou which art in the highest heavens. **11** [3]So Jesus entered into Jerusalem, and into the Temple: and when he had looked about on all things, and now it was evening, he went forth unto Bethany with the twelve. **12** [4]And on the morrow when they were come out from Bethany, he was hungry. **13** [d]And seeing a fig tree afar off, that had leaves, he went to see if he might find anything thereon: but when he came unto it, he found nothing but leaves: for the time of figs was not yet. **14** Then Jesus answered, and said to it, Never man eat fruit of thee hereafter while the world standeth: and his disciples heard it. **15** [e]And they came to Jerusalem, and Jesus went into the Temple, and began to cast out them that sold and bought in the Temple, and overthrew the tables of the moneychangers, and the seats of them that sold doves. **16** Neither would he suffer that any man should carry a [f]vessel through the Temple. **17** And he taught, saying unto them, Is it not written, [5]Mine house shall be [g]called the house of prayer unto all nations? [6]but you have made it a den of thieves. **18** And the Scribes and high Priests heard it, and sought how to destroy him: for they feared him, because the whole multitude was astonied at his doctrine. **19** But when even was come, Jesus went out of the city. **20** [h,7]And in the morning as they journeyed together, they saw the fig tree dried up from the roots. **21** Then Peter remembered, and said unto him, Master, behold, the fig tree which thou cursedst, is withered. **22** And Jesus answered, and said unto them, Have [i]the faith of God. **23** For verily I say unto you, that whosoever shall say unto this mountain, Be thou taken away, and cast into the sea, and shall not waver in his heart, but shall believe that those things which he saith, shall come to pass, whatsoever he saith, shall be done to him. **24** [8]Therefore I say unto you, Whatsoever ye desire when ye pray, believe that [j]ye shall have it, and it shall be done unto you. **25** [9]But when [k]ye shall stand, and pray, forgive, if ye have anything against any man, that your Father also which is in heaven, may forgive you your trespasses. **26** For if you will not forgive, your Father which is in heaven, will not pardon you your trespasses. **27** [l,10]Then they came again to Jerusalem: and as he walked in the Temple, there came to him the high Priests, and the Scribes, and the Elders, **28** And said unto him, By what authority doest thou these things? and who gave thee this authority, that thou shouldest do these things? **29** Then Jesus answered, and said unto them, I will also ask you a certain thing, and answer ye me, and I will tell you by what authority I do these things. **30** The baptism of John, was it from heaven, or of men? answer me. **31** And they thought with themselves, saying, If we shall say, From heaven, he will say, Why then did ye not believe him? **32** [m]But if we say, Of men, we fear the people: for all men counted John that he was a Prophet indeed. **33** Then they answered, and said unto Jesus, We cannot tell. And Jesus answered, and said unto them, Neither will I tell you by what authority I do these things.

12

Of the vineyard. 10 Christ the stone refused of the Jews. 12 Of tribute to be given to Caesar. 18 The Sadducees denying the resurrection. 28 The first commandment. 31 To love God and the neighbor is better than sacrifices. 36 Christ David's son. 38 To beware of the Scribes and Pharisees. 42 The poor widow.

1 And [a]he began to speak unto them in [b]parables, [1]A certain man planted a vineyard, and compassed it with an hedge, and dug a pit for the winepress, and built a tower in it, and let it out to husbandmen, and went into a strange country. **2** [c]And at the time, he sent to the husbandmen a servant, that he might receive of the husbandmen of the fruit of the vineyard. **3** But they took him, and beat him, and sent him away empty. **4** And again he sent unto them another servant, and at him they cast stones, and brake his head, and sent him away shamefully handled. **5** And again he sent another, and him they slew, and many others, beating some, and killing some. **6** Yet had he one son, his dear beloved: him also he sent the last unto them, saying, They will reverence my son. **7** But the husbandmen said among themselves, This is the heir: come, let us kill him, and the inheritance shall be ours. **8** So they took him, and killed him, and cast him out of the vineyard. **9** What shall then the Lord of the vineyard do? He will come and destroy these husbandmen, and give the vineyard to others. **10** Have ye not read so much as this Scripture, [2]The stone which the builders did refuse, is made the head of the corner. **11** This was done of the Lord, and it is marvelous in our eyes. **12** Then they [d]went about to take him, but they feared the people: for they perceived that he spake that parable against them: therefore they left him, and went their way. **13** [e,3]And they sent unto him certain of the Pharisees, and of the Herodians, that they might take him in his talk. **14** And when they came, they said unto him, Master, we know that thou art true, and carest for no man: for thou [f]considerest not the person of men, but teachest the [g]way of God truly, Is it lawful to give tribute to Caesar, or not? **15** Should we give it, or should we not give it? but he knew their hypocrisy, and said unto them, Why tempt ye me? Bring me a penny, that I may see it. **16** So they brought it, and he said unto them, Whose is this image and superscription? and they said unto him, Caesar's. **17** Then Jesus answered, and said unto them, [4]Give to Caesar the things that are Caesar's, and to God, those that are God's: and they marveled at him. **18** [h,5]Then came the Sadducees unto him, (which say, there is no resurrection) and they asked him, saying, **19** Master, [6]Moses wrote unto us, If any man's brother die, and leave his wife, and leave no children, that his brother should take his wife, and raise up seed unto his brother. **20** There were seven brethren, and the first took a wife, and when he died, left no issue. **21** Then the second took her, and he died, neither did he yet leave issue, and the third likewise: **22** So these seven had her, and left no issue: last of all the wife died also. **23** In the resurrection then, when they shall rise again, whose wife shall she be of them? for seven had her to wife. **24** Then Jesus answered, and said unto them, Are ye not therefore deceived, because ye know not the Scriptures, neither the power of God? **25** For when they shall rise again from the dead, neither men marry, nor wives are married, but are as the Angels which are in heaven. **26** And as touching the dead, that they shall rise again, have ye not read in the book of Moses how in the bush God spake unto him, saying, I [7]am the God of Abraham, and the God of Isaac, and the God of Jacob? **27** God is not the God of the dead, but the God of the living. Ye are therefore greatly deceived. **28** [i,8]Then came one of the Scribes that had heard them disputing together, and perceiving that he had answered them well, he asked him, Which is the first commandment of all? **29** Jesus answered him, The first of all the commandments is, [9]Hear, Israel, The Lord our God is the only Lord. **30** Thou shalt therefore love the Lord thy God with all thine heart, and with all thy soul, and with all thy mind, and with all thy strength: this is the first commandment. **31** And the second is like, that is, [10]Thou shalt love thy neighbor as thyself. There is none other commandment greater than these. **32** Then that Scribe said unto him, Well, Master, thou hast said the truth, that there is one God, and that there is none but he, **33** And to love him with all the heart, and with all the understanding, and with all the soul, and with all the strength, and to love his neighbor as himself, is more than all whole burnt offerings and sacrifices. **34** Then when Jesus saw that he answered discreetly, he said unto him, Thou art not far from the kingdom of God. And no man after that durst ask him any question. **35** [j,11]And Jesus answered and said teaching in the Temple, How say the Scribes that Christ is the son of David? **36** For David himself said by [k]the holy Ghost, [12]The Lord said to my Lord, Sit at my right hand, till I make thine enemies thy footstool. **37** Then David himself calleth him Lord: by what means is he then his son? and much people heard him gladly. **38** [l,13]Moreover he said unto them in [m]his doctrine, Beware of the Scribes which love to go in [n]long robes, and love salutations in the markets, **39** And the chief seats in the Synagogues, and the first rooms at feasts, **40** Which [14]devour widows' houses, even under a color of long prayers. These shall receive the greater damnation. **41** [o,15]And as Jesus sat over against the treasury, he beheld how the people [p]cast money into the

---

c. Mark 11:10 Happy and prosperous.
d. Mark 11:13 An example of that vengeance which hangeth over the heads of hypocrites.
e. Mark 11:15 Christ showeth indeed, that he is the true King and high Priest, and therefore the revenger of the divine service of the Temple.
f. Mark 11:16 That is, any profane instrument, of which those fellows had a number, that made the court of the Temple a marketplace.
g. Mark 11:17 Shall openly be so accounted and taken.
h. Mark 11:20 The force of faith is exceeding great, and charity is ever joined with it.
i. Mark 11:22 The faith of God is that assured faith and trust which we have in him.
j. Mark 11:24 Word for word, that you receive it speaking in the time that now is, to show the certainty of the thing and the performance indeed.
k. Mark 11:25 When you shall appear before the altar.
l. Mark 11:27 The Gospel hath been assaulted long time since, under the pretense of an ordinary successsion.
m. Mark 11:32 A reward of an evil conscience to be afraid of those, of whom they should and might have been feared.

MARK. 11

1. Matt. 21:1 / Luke 18:29
2. John 12:24
3. Matt. 21:10 / Luke 19:45
4. Matt. 21:19
5. Isa. 56:7
6. Jer. 7:13
7. Matt. 21:19
8. Matt. 7:7 / Luke 11:9
9. Matt. 6:14
10. Matt. 21:23 / Luke 20:1

MARK. 12

a. Mark 12:1 The calling of God is not tied either to place, person, or time, without exception.
b. Mark 12:1 This word Parable, which the Evangelists use, doth not only signify a comparing of things together, but also dark speeches and allegories.
c. Mark 12:2 When the fruits of the ground used to be gathered.
d. Mark 12:12 They were greedy and very desirous.
e. Mark 12:13 The Gospel joineth the authority of the Magistrate with the service of God.
f. Mark 12:14 Thou dost not so judge by outward appearance, that the truth is thereby darkened any whit at all.
g. Mark 12:14 The way whereby we come to God.
h. Mark 12:18 The resurrection of the body is avouched against the foolish ignorance and malice of the Sadducees.
i. Mark 12:28 Sacrifices and outward worship, never pleased God, unless such necessary duties as we owe to God and our neighbors went afore.
j. Mark 12:35 Christ proveth his Godhead even out of David himself, of whom he came according to the flesh.
k. Mark 12:36 Word for word, in the holy Ghost, and there is a great force in this kind of speech, whereby is meant that it was not so much David, as the holy Ghost that spake, who did in a manner possess David.
l. Mark 12:38 The manners of ministers are not rashly to be followed as an example.
m. Mark 12:38 While he taught them.
n. Mark 12:38 The word is a stole, which is a kind of woman's garment, long even down to the heels, and is taken generally, for any garment made for comeliness, but in this place it seemeth to signify that fringed garment mentioned in Deut. 22:11.
o. Mark 12:41 The doing of our duties, which God alloweth, is not esteemed according to the outward value, but to the inward affects of the heart.
p. Mark 12:41 Money of any kind of metal, as the Romans used, who in the beginning did stamp or coin brass, and after used it for current money.

MARK. 12

1. Isa. 5:1 / Jer. 2:2 / Matt. 21:33 / Luke 20:9
2. Ps. 118:22 / Isa. 28:16 / Matt. 21:42 / Acts 4:11 / Rom. 9:33 / 1 Pet. 2:8
3. Matt. 22:15 / Luke 20:20
4. Rom. 13:7
5. Matt. 22:23 / Luke 20:27
6. Deut. 25:5 / Matt. 22:24
7. Exod. 3:6 / Matt. 22:32
8. Matt. 22:35
9. Deut. 6:4
10. Lev. 19:18 / Matt. 22:39 / Rom. 13:9 / Gal. 5:14 / James 2:8
11. Matt. 22:41 / Luke 20:41
12. Ps. 110:1
13. Mark 23:6 / Luke 11:43 / Luke 20:43
14. Matt. 23:14 / Luke 20:47
15. Luke 21:1

treasury, and many rich men cast in much. **42** And there came a certain poor widow, and she threw in two mites, which make a quadrin. **43** Then he called unto him his disciples, and said unto them, Verily I say unto you, that this poor widow hath cast more in, than all they which have cast into the treasury. **44** For they all did cast in of their superfluity: but she of her poverty did cast in all that she had, even all her living.

13

Of the destruction of Jerusalem. 9 Persecutions for the Gospel. 10 The Gospel must be preached to all nations. 26 Of Christ's coming to judgment. 33 We must watch and pray.

1 [1]And [a]as he went out of the Temple, one of his disciples said unto him, Master, see what manner stones, and what manner buildings are here. **2** [2]Then Jesus answered and said unto him, Seest thou these great buildings? there shall not be left one stone upon a stone, that shall not be thrown down. **3** And as he sat on the mount of Olives, over against the Temple, Peter, and James, and John, and Andrew asked him secretly, **4** Tell us, when shall these things be? and what shall be the sign when all these things shall be fulfilled? **5** And Jesus answered them, and began to say, [3]Take heed lest any man deceive you. **6** For many shall come in my Name, saying, I am Christ, and shall deceive many. **7** Furthermore when ye shall hear of wars, and rumors of wars, be ye not troubled, for such things must needs be: but the end shall not be yet. **8** For nation shall rise against nation, and kingdom against kingdom, and there shall be earthquakes in divers quarters, and there shall be famine and troubles: these are the beginnings of sorrows. **9** But take ye heed to yourselves: for they shall deliver you up to the Councils, and to the Synagogues: ye shall be beaten, and brought before rulers and kings for my sake, for a [b]testimonial unto them. **10** And the Gospel must first be published among all nations. **11** [4]But when they lead you, and deliver you up, [c]be not careful before hand, [d]neither study what ye shall say: but what is given you at the same time, that speak: for it is not you that speak, but the holy Ghost. **12** Yea, and the brother shall deliver the brother to death, and the father the son, and the children shall rise against their parents, and shall cause them to die. **13** And ye shall be hated of all men [e]for my Name's sake: but whosoever shall endure unto the end, he shall be saved. **14** [5]Moreover, when ye shall see the abomination of desolation (spoken of by [6]Daniel the Prophet) [f]set where it ought not, (let him that readeth, consider it) then let them that be in Judea, flee into the mountains. **15** And let him that is upon the house, not come down into the house, neither enter therein, to fetch anything out of his house. **16** And let him that is in the field, not turn back again to take his garment. **17** Then woe shall be to them that are with child, and to them that give suck in those days. **18** Pray therefore that your flight be not in the winter. **19** For [g]those days shall be such tribulation, as was not from the beginning of the creation which God created unto this time, neither shall be. **20** And except that the Lord had shortened those days, no flesh should be saved: but for the elect's sake, which he hath chosen, he hath shortened those days. **21** Then [7]if any man say to you, Lo, here is Christ, or lo, he is there, believe it not. **22** For false Christs shall rise, and false prophets, and shall show signs and wonders, to deceive if it were possible the very elect. **23** But take ye heed: behold, I have showed you all things before. **24** Moreover in those days, after that tribulation, [8]the sun shall wax dark, and the moon shall not give her light, **25** And the stars of heaven shall fall: and the powers which are in heaven, shall shake. **26** And then shall they see the Son of man, coming in the clouds, with great power and glory. **27** [9]And he shall then send his Angels, and shall gather together his elect from the four winds, and from the utmost part of the earth to the utmost part of heaven. **28** Now learn a parable of the fig tree. When her bough is yet tender, and it bringeth forth leaves, ye know that summer is near. **29** So in like manner, when ye see these things come to pass, know that the kingdom of God is near, even at the doors. **30** Verily I say unto you, that this generation shall not pass, till all these things be done. **31** Heaven and earth shall pass away, but my words shall not pass away. **32** [h]But of that day and hour knoweth no man, no, not the Angels which are in heaven, neither the Son himself, but the Father. **33** [10]Take heed: watch, and pray: for ye know not when the time is. **34** For the Son of man is as a man going into a strange country, and leaveth his house, and giveth authority to his servants, and to every man his work, and commandeth the porter to watch. **35** Watch ye therefore, (for ye know not when the master of the house will come, at even, or at midnight, at the cock crowing, or in the dawning,) **36** Lest if he come suddenly, he should find you sleeping. **37** And those things that I say unto you, I say unto all men, Watch.

14

1 The Priests' conspiracy against Christ. 3 The woman pouring oil on Christ's head. 12 The preparing of the Passover. 22 The institution of the Supper. 41 Christ delivered into the hands of men. 43 Judas betrayeth him with a kiss. 53 Christ is before Caiaphas. 66 Peter's denial.

1 And [a,1]two days after followed the feast of the Passover, and of unleavened bread: and the high Priests, and Scribes sought how they might take him by craft, and put him to death. **2** But they said, Not in the feast day, lest there be any tumult among the people. **3** [2]And when he was in Bethany in the house of Simon the leper, as he sat at table, there came a woman having a box of ointment of Spikenard, very costly, and she brake the box, and poured it on his head. **4** [b]Therefore some disdained among themselves, and said, To what end is this waste of ointment? **5** For it might have been sold for more than [c]three hundred pence, and been given unto the poor, and they murmured against her. **6** But Jesus said, Let her alone: Why trouble ye her? she hath wrought a good work on me. **7** [d]For ye have the poor with you always, and when ye will ye may do them good, but me ye shall not have always. **8** [e]She hath done that she could: she came aforehand to anoint my body to the burying. **9** Verily I say unto you, wheresoever this Gospel shall be preached throughout the whole world, this also that she hath done, shall be spoken of in remembrance of her. **10** [f,3]Then Judas Iscariot, one of the twelve, went away unto the high Priests, to betray him unto them. **11** And when they heard it, they were glad, and promised that they would give him money: therefore he sought how he might conveniently betray him. **12** [g,4]Now the first day of unleavened bread, [h]when [i]they sacrificed the [j]Passover, his disciples said unto him, Where wilt thou that we go and prepare, that thou mayest eat the Passover? **13** Then he sent forth two of his disciples, and said unto them, Go ye into the city, and there shall a man meet you bearing a pitcher of water: follow him. **14** And whithersoever he goeth in, say ye to the good man of the house, The master saith, Where is the lodging where I shall eat the Passover with my disciples? **15** And he will show you an [k]upper chamber which is large, trimmed and prepared: there make it ready for us. **16** So his disciples went forth, and came to the city, and found as he had said unto them, and made ready the Passover. **17** And at even he came with the twelve. **18** [l,5]And as they sat at table and did eat, Jesus said, Verily I say unto you, that one of you shall betray me, which eateth with me. **19** Then they began to be sorrowful and to say to him one by one, Is it I? And another, Is it I? **20** And he answered and said unto them, It is one of the twelve that [m]dippeth with me in the platter. **21** Truly the Son of man goeth his way, as it is written of him: [6]but woe be to that man, by whom the Son of man is betrayed: it had been good for that man, if he had never been born. **22** [7]And as they did eat, Jesus took the bread, and when he had given thanks, he brake it and gave it to them, and said, Take, eat, this is my body. **23** Also he took the cup, and when he had given thanks, gave it to them: and they all drank of it. **24** And he said unto them, This is my blood of that new Testament which is shed for many. **25** Verily I say unto you, I will drink no more of the fruit of the vine until that day, that I drink it new in the kingdom of God. **26** And when they had sung a Psalm, they went out to the mount of Olives. **27** [n,8]Then Jesus said unto them, All ye shall be offended by me this night: for it is written, [9]I will smite the shepherd, and the sheep shall be scattered. **28** But after that I am risen,

---

MARK. 13

- **a.** Mark 13:1 The destruction of the Temple, city, and whole nation is aforetold, and the troubles of the Church, but yet there are annexed many comforts, and last of all, the end of the world is described.
- **b.** Mark 13:9 The hearing of you preaching shall be a most evident witness against them, so that they shall not be able to pretend ignorance.
- **c.** Mark 13:11 We are not forbidden to think beforehand, but pensive carefulness whereby men discourage themselves, which proceedeth from distrust, and want of confidence and sure hope of God's assistance: that carefulness we are willed to beware of, see also Matt. 6:27.
- **d.** Mark 13:11 By any kind of artificial and cunning kind of tale what to speak.
- **e.** Mark 13:13 For me.
- **f.** Mark 13:14 When the heathen and profane people shall not only enter into the Temple, and defile both it and the city, but also clean destroy it.
- **g.** Mark 13:19 This is a kind of speech which the Hebrews use, and it hath a great force in it, for it giveth us to understand that in all that time one misery shall so follow upon another, as if the time itself were very misery itself: So the Prophet Amos, 5:20 saith, that the day of the Lord shall be darkness.
- **h.** Mark 13:32 The latter day is not curiouly to be searched for which the Father alone knoweth: but let us rather take heed, that it come not upon us unaware.

MARK. 13

1. Matt.24:1 / Luke 21:5
2. Luke 19:43
3. Eph. 5:6 / 2 Thess. 2:3
4. Matt. 10:19 / Luke 12:11 / Luke 21:14
5. Matt. 24:15 / Luke 21:20
6. Dan. 9:27
7. Matt. 24:23 / Luke 17:23 / Luke 21:8
8. Isa. 13:10 / Ezek. 52:7 / Joel 2:10 / Joel 3:15
9. Matt. 24:31
10. Matt. 24:23

MARK. 14

- **a.** Mark 14:1 By the will of God, against the counsel of men, it came to pass that Christ should be put to death upon the solemn day of the Passover, that in all respects the truth might agree to the figure.
- **b.** Mark 14:4 Rash judgments are frustrated before God.
- **c.** Mark 14:5 Which is about six pounds English.
- **d.** Mark 14:7 Christ suffered himself to be anointed once or twice for certain considerations: but his will is to be daily anointed in the poor.
- **e.** Mark 14:8 This woman by the secret instinct of the Spirit, anointing Christ, setteth before men's eyes, his death and burial which were at hand.
- **f.** Mark 14:10 Covetousness cloaked with a zeal of charity, is an occasion to betray and crucify Christ.
- **g.** Mark 14:12 Christ being made subject to the Law for us, doth celebrate the Passover according to the Law: and therewithall by a miracle showeth that notwithstanding he in the flesh shall straightway suffer, yet that he is God.
- **h.** Mark 14:12 That is, upon which day, and at the evening of the same day, which was the beginning of the fifteenth, see also Matt. 26:17.
- **i.** Mark 14:12 They used to sacrifice.
- **j.** Mark 14:12 This is spoken thus, by the figure Metonymy, which is usual in sacraments, and by the Passover is meant the Paschal lamb.
- **k.** Mark 14:15 The Greek word signifieth that part of the house that is highest from the ground, to what use soever it be put, but because they used to sup in that part of the house, they called it a supping chamber.
- **l.** Mark 14:18 The figure of the law, which is by and by to be fulfilled, is abrogated: and in place thereof are put figures of the new covenant answerable unto them, which shall continue to the world's end.
- **m.** Mark 14:20 That useth to eat meat with me.
- **n.** Mark 14:27 Christ foretelleth how he shall be forsaken of his, but yet that he will never forsake them.

I will go into [10]Galilee before you. **29** [o]And Peter said unto him, Although all
men should be offended at thee, yet would not I. **30** Then Jesus said unto him,
Verily I say unto thee, this day, even in this night before the cock crow twice, thou
shalt deny me thrice. **31** But he said [p]more earnestly, If I should die with thee, I
will not deny thee: likewise also said they all. **32** [q,11]After, they came into a place
named Gethsemane: then he said to his disciples, Sit ye here, till I have
prayed. **33** And he took with him Peter, and James, and John, and he began to
be troubled, and in great heaviness, **34** And said unto them, My soul is very he-
avy, even unto the death: tarry here, and watch. **35** So he went forward a little,
and fell down on the ground, and prayed, that if it were possible, that hour might
pass from him, **36** And he said, [r]Abba, Father, all things are possible unto thee:
take away this cup from me: nevertheless not that I will, but that thou wilt, be
done. **37** [s]Then he came, and found them sleeping, and said to Peter, Simon,
sleepest thou? couldest not thou watch one hour? **38** Watch ye, and pray, that ye
enter not into temptation: the spirit indeed is ready, but the flesh is weak. **39** And
again he went away, and prayed, and spake the same words. **40** And he returned,
and found them asleep again: for their eyes were heavy: neither knew they what
they should answer him. **41** And he came the third time, and said unto them,
Sleep henceforth, and take your rest: it is enough: the hour is come: behold, the
Son of man is delivered into the hands of sinners. **42** Rise up: let us go: lo, he
that betrayeth me, is at hand. **43** [t,12]And immediately while he yet spake, came
Judas that was one of the twelve, and with him a great multitude with swords and
staves from the high Priests, and Scribes, and Elders. **44** And he that betrayed
him, had given them a token, saying, Whomsoever I shall kiss, he it is: take him
and lead him away [u]safely. **45** And as soon as he was come, he went straightway
to him, and said, Hail Master, and kissed him. **46** Then they laid their hands on
him, and took him. **47** And [v]one of them that stood by, drew out a sword, and
smote a servant of the high Priest, and cut off his ear. **48** And Jesus answered,
and said to them, Ye be come out as against a thief, with swords and with staves, to
take me. **49** I was daily with you, teaching in the Temple, and ye took me not:
but this is done that the Scriptures should be fulfilled. **50** Then they [w]all forsook
him, and fled. **51** [x]And there followed him a certain young man, clothed in [y]li-
nen upon his bare body, and the young men caught him. **52** But he left his linen
cloth, and fled from them naked. **53** [13]So they led Jesus away to the high Priest,
and to him came [z]together all the high Priests, and the Elders, and the Scri-
bes. **54** And Peter followed him afar off, even into the hall of the high Priest, and
sat with the servants, and warmed himself at the fire. **55** [aa]And the [14]high Prie-
sts, and all the Council sought for witness against Jesus, to put him to death, but
found none. **56** For many bare false witness against him, but their witness agreed
not together. **57** Then there arose certain, and bare false witness against him,
saying, **58** We heard him say, [15]I will destroy this Temple made with hands, and
within three days I will build another, made without hands. **59** But their witness
yet agreed not together. **60** Then the high Priest stood up amongst them, and
asked Jesus, saying, Answerest thou nothing? what is the matter that these bear wi-
tness against thee? **61** But he held his peace, and answered nothing. Again the
high Priest asked him, and said unto him, Art thou that Christ the son of the [ab]
Blessed? **62** And Jesus said, I am he, [16]and ye shall see the Son of man sit at the
right hand of the power of God, and come in the clouds of heaven. **63** Then the
high Priest rent his clothes, and said, What have we anymore need of witnes-
ses? **64** Ye have heard the blasphemy: what think ye? And they all condemned
him to be worthy of death. **65** [ac]And some began to spit at him, and to cover his
face, and to beat him with fists, and to say unto him, Prophesy. And the sergeants
smote him with their rods. **66** [ad,17]And as Peter was beneath in the hall, there
came one of the maids of the high Priest. **67** And when she saw Peter warming
himself, she looked on him, and said, Thou wast also with Jesus of Naza-
reth. **68** But he denied it, saying, I know him not, neither wot I what thou
sayest. Then he went out into the porch, and the cock crew. **69** [18]Then [ae]a maid
saw him again, and began to say to them that stood by, This is one of them. **70** But
he denied it again: and anon after, they that stood by, said again to Peter, Surely
thou art one of them: for thou art of Galilee, and thy speech is like. **71** And he
began to curse, and swear, saying, I know not this man of whom ye spe-
ak. **72** [19]Then the second time the cock crew, and Peter remembered the word
that Jesus had said unto him, Before the cock crow twice, thou shalt deny me thri-
ce, and weighing that with himself, he wept.

15

1 Of the things Christ suffered under Pilate. 11 Barabbas is preferred before Christ. 15 Pilate delivereth Christ to be crucified. 17 He is crowned with thorns. 19 They spit on him, and mock him. 21 Simon of Cyrene carrieth Christ's cross. 27 Christ is crucified between two thieves. 26 He is railed at. 37 He giveth up the ghost. 43 Joseph burieth him.

1 And [a,1]anon in the dawning, the high Priests held a Council with the El-
ders, and the Scribes, and the whole Council, and bound Jesus, and led him away,
and [b]delivered him to Pilate. **2** Then Pilate asked him, Art thou the King of the
Jews? And he answered, and said unto him, Thou sayest it. **3** And the high Priests
accused him of many things. **4** [2]Wherefore Pilate asked him again, saying, An-
swered thou nothing? behold how many things they witness against thee. **5** But
Jesus answered no more at all, so that Pilate marveled. **6** Now at the feast, Pi-
late [c]did deliver a prisoner unto them, whomsoever they would desire. **7** Then
there was one named Barabbas, which was bound with his fellows, that had made
insurrection, who in the insurrection had committed murder. **8** And the peo-
ple cried aloud, and began to desire that he would do as he had ever done unto
them. **9** Then Pilate answered them, and said, Will ye that I let loose unto you
the King of the Jews? **10** For he knew that the high Priests had delivered him
of envy. **11** But the high Priests had moved the people to desire that he would
rather deliver Barabbas unto them. **12** And Pilate answered, and said again
unto them, What will ye then that I do with him, whom ye call the King of
the Jews? **13** And they cried again, Crucify him. **14** Then Pilate said unto
them, But what evil hath he done? And they cried the more fervently, Crucify
him. **15** So Pilate willing to content the people, loosed them Barabbas, and deli-
vered Jesus, when he had scourged him, that he might be crucified. **16** Then the
soldiers led him away into the hall, which is the common hall, and called together
the whole band, **17** [d]And clad him with purple, and platted a crown of thorns,
and put it about his head, **18** And began to salute him, saying, Hail, King of
the Jews. **19** And they smote him on the head with a reed, and spat upon him,
and bowed the knees, and did him reverence. **20** And when they had mocked
him, they took the purple off him, and put his own clothes on him, and led him
out to crucify him. **21** [3]And they [e]compelled one that passed by, called Simon
of Cyrene (which came out of the country, and was father of Alexander and Rufus)
to bear his cross. **22** [f,4]And they brought him to a place named Golgotha, whi-
ch is by interpretation, the place of dead mens' skulls. **23** And they gave him to
drink wine mingled with myrrh: but he received it not. **24** [g,5]And when they

---

o. Mark 14:29 Here is set forth in an excellent person, a most sorrowful example of man's rashness and weakness.
p. Mark 14:31 That doubling of words, setteth out more plainly Peter's vehement affirmation.
q. Mark 14:32 Christ suffering for us in that flesh which he took upon him for our sakes, the most horrible terrors of the curse of God, receiveth the cup at his Father's hands, which he being just, doth straightway drink of for the unjust.
r. Mark 14:36 This doubling of the word was used in those days, when their languages were so mixed together: for this word, Abba, is a Syrian word.
s. Mark 14:37 An horrible example of the sluggishness of men, even in the disciples whom Christ had chosen.
t. Mark 14:43 As men did willingly spoil God their Creator of his praise in forsaking and betraying him: so Christ willingly going about to make satisfaction for this ruin, is forsaken for his own, and betrayed by one of his familiars as a thief, that the punishment might be agreeable to the sin, and we who are very traitors, forsakers, and sacrilegers might be delivered out of the devil's snare.
u. Mark 14:44 So diligently, that he escape not out of your hands.
v. Mark 14:47 That is, Peter.
w. Mark 14:50 All his disciples.
x. Mark 14:51 Under pretence of godliness, all things are lawful to such as do violence against Christ.
y. Mark 14:51 Which he cast about him, when he hearing that stir in the night suddenly ran forth: whereby we may understand with how great licentiousness these villains violently set upon him.
z. Mark 14:53 The highest council was assembled, because Christ was accused as a blasphemer and a false prophet: for as for the other crime of treason, it was forged against him by the Priests, to enforce Pilate by that means to condemn him.
aa. Mark 14:55 Christ, who was so innocent that he could not be oppressed, no not by false witnesses, is at the length, for confessing God to be his father, condemned of impiety before the high Priest: that we, who denied God and were indeed wicked, might be quit before God.
ab. Mark 14:61 Of God, who is most worthy of all praise?
ac. Mark 14:65 Christ suffering all kinds of reproach for our sakes, getteth everlasting glory to them that believe in him.
ad. Mark 14:66 An heavy example of the frailness of man, together with a most comfortable example of the mercy of God, who giveth the spirit of repentance and faith to his elect.
ae. Mark 14:69 If we compare the Evangelists diligently together, we shall perceive that Peter was known of many through the maiden's report: yea, and in Luke, when the second denial is spoken of, there is a manservant mentioned, and not a maid.

MARK. 14
1. Matt. 26:2 / Luke 22:1
2. Matt. 26:6 / John 12:2
3. Matt. 26:14 / Luke 22:4
4. Matt. 26:17 / Luke 2:28
5. Ps. 41:20 / Matt. 26:20-23 / Luke 22:14 / John 13:18-21
6. Acts 1:16
7. Matt. 26:26 / 1 Cor. 11:24
8. John 16:32
9. Zech. 13:7
10. Mark 16:7
11. Matt. 26:36 / Luke 22:39
12. Matt. 26:47 / Luke 22:47 / John 18:3
13. Matt. 26:57 / Luke 32:54 / John 18:24
14. Matt. 26:59
15. John 9:19
16. Matt. 24:39
17. Matt. 26:69 / Luke 22:55 / John 18:25
18. Matt. 26:71 / Luke 22:58
19. Matt. 26:75 / John 13:38

MARK. 15
a. Mark 15:1 Christ being bound before the judgment seat of an earthly judge, in open assembly is condemned as guilty unto the death of the cross, not for his own sins, (as appeareth by the judge's own words) but for all ours, that we most guilty creatures being delivered from the guiltiness of our sins, might be quitted before the judgment seat of God, even in the open assembly of the Angels.
b. Mark 15:1 It was not lawful for them to put any man to death, for all causes of life and death were taken away from them, first by Herod the great, and afterward by the Romans, about forty years before the destruction of the Temple, and therefore they deliver Jesus to Pilate.
c. Mark 15:6 Used Pilate to deliver.
d. Mark 15:17 Christ going about to take away the sins of men, who went about to usurp the throne of God himself, is condemned as one that hunted after the kingdom, and mocked with a false show of a kingdom, that we on the other side, who shall indeed be eternal kings, might receive the crown of glory at God's own hand.
e. Mark 15:21 The rage of the wicked hath no measure, but in the mean season, even the weakness of Christ, being in pain under the heavy burden of the cross, doth manifestly show that a lamb is led to be sacrificed.
f. Mark 15:22 Christ is led out of the walls of the earthly Jerusalem, into a foul place of dead men's carcasses, as a man most unclean, not touching himself, but touching our sins, which were laid upon him, to the end that we being made clean by his blood, might be brought into the heavenly Sanctuary.
g. Mark 15:24 Christ hangeth naked upon the cross, and as the most wickedest caitiff that ever was, most vilely reproved: that we being clothed with his righteousness, and blessed with his curses, and sanctified by his only oblation, may be taken up into heaven.

had crucified him, they parted his garments, casting lots for them, what every man should have. **25** And it was the third hour when they crucified him. **26** And the title of his cause was written above, THAT KING OF THE JEWS. **27** They crucified also with him two thieves, the one on the right hand, and the other on his left. **28** Thus the Scripture was fulfilled, which saith, [6]And he was counted among the wicked. **29** And they that went by, railed on him, wagging their heads, and saying, [7]Hey, thou that destroyest the Temple, and buildest it in three days, **30** Save thyself, and come down from the cross. **31** Likewise also even the high Priests mocking, said among themselves with the Scribes, He saved other men, himself he cannot save. **32** Let Christ the king of Israel now come down from the cross, that we may see, and believe. They also that were crucified with him, reviled him. **33** Now when the sixth hour was come, [h]darkness arose over [i]all the land until the ninth hour. **34** And at the [j]ninth hour Jesus cried with a loud voice, saying, Eloi, [8]Eloi, lama-sabachthani? which is by interpretation, My God, my God, why hast thou forsaken me? **35** And some of them that stood by, when they heard it, said, Behold, he calleth Elijah. **36** And one ran, and filled a [9]sponge full of vinegar, and put it on a reed, and gave him to drink, saying, Let him alone: let us see if Elijah will come, and take him down. **37** And Jesus cried with a loud voice, and gave up the ghost. **38** And the veil of the Temple was rent in twain, from the top to the bottom. **39** Now when the Centurion, which stood over against him, saw that he thus crying gave up the ghost, he said, Truly this man was the Son of God. **40** [k]There were also women which beheld afar off, among whom was Mary Magdalene, and Mary the mother of James the less, and of Joses, and Salome, **41** Which also when he was in Galilee, [10]followed him, and ministered unto him, and many other women which came up with him unto Jerusalem. **42** [11]And now when the night was come (because it was the day of the preparation that is before the Sabbath) **43** [12]Joseph of Arimathea, an [l]honorable counselor, which also looked for the kingdom of God, came, and went in [m]boldly unto Pilate, and asked the body of Jesus. **44** And Pilate marveled, if he were already dead, and called unto him the Centurion, and asked of him whether he had been any while dead. **45** And when he knew the truth of the Centurion, he gave the body to Joseph: **46** Who bought a linen cloth, and took him down, and wrapped him in the linen cloth, and laid him in a tomb that was hewn out of a rock, and rolled a stone unto the door of the sepulcher: **47** And Mary Magdalene, and Mary Joses' mother, beheld where he should be laid.

16

1 Of Christ's resurrection. 9 He appeareth to Mary Magdalene and others. 15 He sendeth his Apostles to preach. 19 His ascension.

1 And [1]when the Sabbath day was past, Mary Magdalene, and Mary the mother of James and Salome, bought sweet ointments, that they might come and anoint him. **2** Therefore early in the morning, the first day of the week, they came unto the sepulcher, when the Sun was now risen. **3** And they said one to another, Who shall roll us away the stone from the door of the sepulcher? **4** And when they [a]looked, they saw that the stone was rolled away (for it was a very great one) **5** [2]So they went into the [b]sepulcher, and saw a young man sitting at the right side, clothed in a long white robe: and they were sore troubled. **6** But he said unto them, Be not so troubled: ye seek Jesus of Nazareth, which hath been crucified: he is risen, he is not here: behold the place where they put him. **7** But go your way, and tell his disciples, and Peter, that he will go before you into Galilee: there shall ye see him, [3]as he said unto you. **8** And they went out quickly, and fled from the sepulcher: for they trembled, and were amazed: neither said they anything to any man: for they were afraid. **9** [c]And when Jesus was risen again, early the first day of the week, he appeared first to Mary Magdalene, [4]out of whom he had cast seven devils: **10** And she went and told them that had been with him, which mourned and wept. **11** And when they heard that he was alive, and had appeared to her, they believed it not. **12** [d,5]After that, he appeared unto two of them in another form, as they walked and went into the country. **13** And they went and told it to the remnant, neither believed they them. **14** [e,6]Finally, he appeared unto the eleven as they sat together, and reproached them for their unbelief and hardness of heart, because they believed not them which had seen him, being risen up again. **15** [f]And he said unto them, [7]Go ye into all the world, and preach the Gospel to [g]every creature. **16** He that shall believe and be baptized, shall be saved: [8]but he that will not believe, shall be damned. **17** And these tokens shall follow them that believe, [9]In my Name they shall cast out devils, and [10]shall speak with [h]new tongues, **18** [11]And shall take away serpents, and if they shall drink any deadly thing, it shall not hurt them: [12]they shall lay their hands on the sick, and they shall recover. **19** [i,13]So after the Lord had spoken unto them, he was received into heaven, and sat at the right hand of God. **20** And they went forth, and preached everywhere. And the [14]Lord wrought with them, and confirmed [j]the word with signs that followed. Amen.

---

h. Mark 15:33 How angry God was against our sin, which he punished in our surety, his son, it appeareth by this horrible darkness.

i. Mark 15:33 By this word, land, he meaneth Palestine: so that the strangeness of the wonder, is so much the more set forth in that, that at the feast of the Passover, and in the full moon, when the Sun shined over all the rest of the world and at midday that corner of the world, wherein so wicked an act was committed, was overcovered with most gross darkness.

j. Mark 15:34 Christ striving mightily with Satan, with sin, and with death, all three armed with the horrible curse of God, grievously tormented in body hanging upon the cross, and in soul plunged in the depth of hell, yet he riddeth himself, crying with a mighty voice: and notwithstanding the wound which he received of death in that that he died, yet by smiting both things above and things beneath, by renting of the veil of the Temple, and by the testimony wrung out of them which murdered him, he showeth evidently unto the rest of his enemies which are as yet obstinate, and mock at him, that he shall be known out of hand to be conqueror and Lord of all.

k. Mark 15:40 Christ to the great shame of men which forsook the Lord, chose women for his witnesses, which beheld all this whole action.

l. Mark 15:43 A man of great authority, of the counsel of the Sanhedrin, or else taken into counsel by Pilate.

m. Mark 15:43 If we consider what danger Joseph cast himself into, we shall perceive how bold he was.

MARK. 15

1. Matt. 27:1 / Luke 22:66 / John 18:19
2. Matt. 27:12 / Luke 23:3 / John 18:35
3. Matt. 27:32 / Luke 23:26
4. Matt. 27:33 / Luke 23:33 / John 19:17
5. Luke 23:34
6. Isa. 53:12
7. John 2:19
8. Ps. 22:1 / Matt. 27:46
9. Ps. 69:22
10. Luke 8:2
11. Matt. 27:57
12. Luke 23:50 / John 19:38

MARK. 16

a. Mark 16:4 When they cast their eyes toward the sepulchre.

b. Mark 16:5 Into the cave out where the sepulchre was cut out.

c. Mark 16:9 Christ himself appeareth to Mary Magdalene to upbraid the disciples' incredulity.

d. Mark 16:12 Christ appeareth to two other disciples, and at length to the eleven.

e. Mark 16:14 The Evangelist considered not the order of the time, but the course of his history, which he divided into three parts: The first showeth how he appeared to the women, the second, to his Disciples, the third, to his Apostles, and therefore he saith, Finally.

f. Mark 16:15 The Apostles are appointed, and their office is limited unto them, which is to preach that which they heard of him, and to minister the Sacraments, which Christ hath instituted, having besides power to do miracles.

g. Mark 16:15 Not to the Jews only, nor in Judea only, but to all men, and everywhere: and so must all the Apostles do.

h. Mark 16:17 Strange tongues, such as they knew not before.

i. Mark 16:19 Christ having accomplished his office on earth, ascendeth into heaven, from whence (the doctrine of his Apostles being confirmed with signs) he will govern his Church, unto the world's end.

j. Mark 16:20 To wit, the doctrine: therefore doctrine must go before, and signs must follow after.

MARK. 16

1. Luke 24:1 / John 20:1
2. Matt. 18:1 / John 20:12
3. Mark 11:28 / Matt. 16:32
4. John 20:16 / Luke 8:2
5. Luke 24:13
6. Luke 24:36 / John 20:19
7. Matt. 28:19
8. John 12:45
9. Acts 16:18
10. Acts 2:4 / Acts 10:46
11. Acts 28:5
12. Acts 28:8
13. Luke 24:51
14. Heb. 2:4

THE HOLY GOSPEL OF JESUS CHRIST, ACCORDING TO

LUKE

1 *Luke: Preface 5 Zacharias and Elizabeth. 15 What an one John should be. 20 Zacharias stricken dumb, for his incredulity. 26 The Angel saluteth Mary, and foretelleth Christ's nativity. 39 Mary visited Elizabeth. 46 Mary's song. 68 The song of Zacharias, showing that the promised Christ is come. 76 The office of John.*

1 Forasmuch as [a]many have [b]taken in hand to set forth the story of those things, whereof we are fully persuaded, **2** [c]As they have delivered them unto us, which from the beginning saw them themselves, and were ministers of the word, **3** It seemed good also to me ([d]most noble Theophilus) as soon as I had searched out perfectly all things [e]from the beginning, to write unto thee thereof from point to point, **4** That thou mightest [f]acknowledge the certainty of those things whereof thou hast been instructed. **5** In [g]the [h]time of [i]Herod King of Judea, there was a certain Priest named Zacharias, of the [j,1]course of Abijah: and his wife was of the daughters of Aaron, and her name was Elizabeth. **6** Both were [k]just before God, and [l]walked in all the [m]commandments and ordinances of the Lord, [n]without reproof. **7** And they had no child, because that Elizabeth was barren: and both were well stricken in age. **8** And it came to pass, as he executed the Priest's office before God, as his course came in order, **9** [2]According to the custom of the Priest's office, his lot was to burn incense, when he went into the [o]Temple of the Lord. **10** And the whole multitude of the people were without in prayer, [3]while the incense was burning. **11** Then appeared unto him an Angel of the Lord, standing at the right side of the Altar of incense. **12** And when Zacharias saw him, he was troubled, and fear fell upon him. **13** But the Angel said unto him, Fear not, Zacharias: for thy prayer is heard, and thy wife Elizabeth shall bear thee a son, and thou shalt call his name John. **14** And thou shalt have joy and gladness, and many shall rejoice at his birth. **15** For he shall be great in the [p]sight of the Lord, and shall neither drink wine, nor [q]strong drink: and he shall be filled with the holy Ghost, even from his mother's womb. **16** [4]And many of the children of Israel shall he [r]turn to their Lord God. **17** [5]For he shall go [s]before him [t]in the spirit and power of Elijah, to turn the [u]hearts of the fathers to the children, and the disobedient to the [v]wisdom of the just men, to make ready a people prepared for the Lord. **18** Then Zacharias said unto the Angel, Whereby shall I know this? for I am an old man, and my wife is of a great age. **19** And the Angel answered, and said unto him, I am Gabriel [w]that stand in the presence of God, and am sent to speak unto thee, and to show thee these good tidings. **20** And behold, thou shalt be dumb, and not be able to speak, until the day that these things be done, because thou believest not my words, which shall be fulfilled in their season. **21** Now the people waited for Zacharias, and marveled that he tarried so long in the Temple. **22** And when he came out, he could not speak unto them: then they perceived that he had seen a vision in the Temple: for he made signs unto them, and remained dumb. **23** And it came to pass, when the days of his office were fulfilled, that he departed to his own house. **24** And after those days, his wife Elizabeth conceived, and hid herself five months, saying, **25** Thus hath the Lord dealt with me, in the days wherein he looked on me, to take from me my rebuke among men. **26** [x]And in the sixth month, the Angel Gabriel was sent from God unto a city of Galilee, named Nazareth, **27** [6]To a virgin affianced to a man whose name was Joseph, of the [y]house of David, and the virgin's name was Mary. **28** And the Angel went in unto her, and said, Hail thou that art [z]freely beloved: the Lord is with thee: [aa]blessed art thou among women. **29** And when she saw him, she was [ab]troubled at his saying, and thought what manner of salutation that should be. **30** Then the Angel said unto her, Fear not, Mary: for thou hast [ac]found favor with God. **31** [7]For lo thou shalt conceive in thy womb, and bear a son, [8]and shalt call his Name Jesus. **32** He shall be great, and shall be [ad]called the Son of the most High, and the Lord God shall give unto him the throne of his father David. **33** [9]And he shall reign over the house of Jacob forever, and of his kingdom shall be none end. **34** Then said Mary unto the Angel, [ae]How shall this be, seeing [af]I know not man? **35** And the Angel answered, and said unto her, The holy Ghost [ag]shall come upon thee, and the power of the most High shall overshadow thee: therefore also that [ah]Holy thing which shall be born of thee, shall be [ai]called the Son of God. **36** And behold, thy [aj]cousin, Elizabeth, she hath also conceived a son in her old age: and this is her [ak]sixth month, which was called barren. **37** For with God shall nothing be impossible. **38** Then Mary said, Behold the servant of the Lord: be it unto me according to thy word. So the Angel departed from her. **39** [al]And Mary arose in those days, and went into the [am]hill country with haste to a [an]city of Judah, **40** And entered into the house of Zacharias, and saluted Elizabeth. **41** And it came to pass, as Elizabeth heard the salutation of Mary, the babe [ao]sprang in her belly, and Elizabeth was filled with the holy Ghost. **42** And she cried with a loud voice, and said, Blessed art thou among women, because [ap]the fruit of thy womb is blessed. **43** And whence

LUKE 1

a. Luke 1:1 Luke commendeth the witnesses that saw this history.

b. Luke 1:1 Many took it in hand, but did not perform: Luke wrote his Gospel before Matthew and Mark.

c. Luke 1:2 Luke was not an eyewitness, and therefore it was not he to whom the Lord appeared when Cleopas saw him: and he was taught not only by Paul, but by others of the Apostles also.

d. Luke 1:3 It is most mighty, and therefore Theophilus was a very honorable man, and in place of great dignity.

e. Luke 1:3 Luke began his Gospel a great deal farther off, than the others did.

f. Luke 1:4 Have fuller knowledge of those things, which before thou knewest but meanly.

g. Luke 1:5 John who was another Elijah, and appointed to be herald of Christ, coming of the stock of Aaron, and of two famous and blameless parents, hath showed in his conception, which was against the course of nature, a double miracle, to the end that men should be more readily stirred up to the hearing of his preaching, according to the forewarning of the Prophets.

h. Luke 1:5 Word for word, in the days: so speak the Hebrews, giving us to understand, how short and frail a thing the power of princes is.

i. Luke 1:5 Herod the great.

j. Luke 1:5 For the posterity of Aaron was divided into courses.

k. Luke 1:6 The true mark of righteousness is, to be liked and allowed of in the judgment of God.

l. Luke 1:6 Lived, so speak the Hebrews, for our life is as a way, wherein we must walk, until we come to the mark.

m. Luke 1:6 In all the moral and ceremonial law.

n. Luke 1:6 Whom no man could justly reprove: now so it is, that the fruits of justification are set forth here, and not the cause, which is faith only, and nothing else.

o. Luke 1:9 The Temple was one, and the Court another, for Zacharias went out of the Court or outward room, where all the people were, and therefore are said to be without, into the temple.

p. Luke 1:15 So speak the Hebrews when it signified a rare kind of excellency: so is it said of Nimrod, Gen. 10:9. He was a valiant hunter before God.

q. Luke 1:15 Any drink that may make drunken.

r. Luke 1:16 Shall be a means to bring many to repentance, and turn themselves to the Lord from whom they fell.

s. Luke 1:17 As they used to go before kings, and when you see them, you know the king is not far off.

t. Luke 1:17 This is spoken by the figure Metonymy, taking the spirit, for the gift of the spirit, as you would say, the cause, for that that cometh of the cause.

u. Luke 1:17 By this figure Synecdoche, he showeth that he shall take away all kinds of enmities, which used to breed great troubles and turmoils amongst men.

v. Luke 1:17 Wisdom and goodness are two of the chiefest causes which make men to reverence and honor their fathers.

w. Luke 1:19 That appears, for so the Hebrews use this word (to stand) meaning that they are ready to do his commandment.

x. Luke 1:26 The Angel serving the Lord which should be born, is sent to the virgin Mary, in whom the Son of the most high promised to David, is conceived by the virtue of the holy Ghost.

y. Luke 1:27 As much is to be said of Mary, otherwise Christ had not been of the stock, not the son of David.

z. Luke 1:28 It might be rendered word for word, full of favor and grace, and he showeth straight after, laying out plainly unto us, what that favor is, in that he saith, the Lord is with thee.

aa. Luke 1:28 Of God.

ab. Luke 1:29 Moved at the strangeness of the matter.

ac. Luke 1:30 So speak the Hebrews, saying, that men have found favor, which are in favor.

ad. Luke 1:32 He shall be declared so to be, for he was the Son of God from everlasting, but was made manifest in the flesh in his time.

ae. Luke 1:34 The greatness of the matter causeth the Virgin to ask this question, not that she distrusteth any whit at all, for she asketh only of the manner of the conceiving, so that it is plain she believed all the rest.

af. Luke 1:34 So speak the Hebrews, signifying by this modest kind of speech the company of man and wife together, and this is the meaning of it: how shall this be, forseeing, I shall be Christ his mother, I am very sure. I shall not know any man: for the godly virgin had learned by the Prophets, that the Messiah should be born of a Virgin.

ag. Luke 1:35 That is, the holy Ghost shall cause thee to conceive by his mighty power.

ah. Luke 1:35 That pure thing and void of all spot of uncleanness: for he that was to take away sin, must needs be void of sin.

ai. Luke 1:35 Declared and showed to the world, to be the Son of God.

aj. Luke 1:36 Though Elizabeth were of the tribe of Levi, yet she might be Mary's cousin: for whereas it was forbidden by the Law, for maidens to be married to men of other tribes, this could not let, but that the Levites might take them wives out of any tribe: for the Levites had no portion allotted them, when the land was divided among the people.

ak. Luke 1:36 This is now the sixth month from the time when she conceived.

al. Luke 1:39 Elizabeth being great with child with John, and Mary with Christ, by the inspiration of the holy Ghost, do rejoice each for other.

am. Luke 1:39 Which is on the South side of Jerusalem.

an. Luke 1:39 That is to say, Hebron: which was in times past called Kirjath Arba, which was one of the towns, that was given to the Levites, in the tribe of Judah, and is said to be in the mountains of Judah, Josh. 14:15 and 21:11.

ao. Luke 1:41 This was no ordinary nor usual kind of moving.

ap. Luke 1:42 Christ is blessed in respect of his humanity.

cometh this to me, that the mother of my Lord should come to me? 44 For lo,
as soon as the voice of thy salutation sounded in mine ears, the babe sprang in my
belly for joy. 45 And blessed is she that believed: for those things shall be perfor-
med, which were told her from the Lord. 46 [aq]Then Mary said, My soul magni-
fieth the Lord, 47 And my spirit rejoiceth in God my Savior. 48 For he hath
[ar]looked on the [as]poor degree of his servant: for behold, from henceforth shall all
ages call me blessed, 49 Because he that is mighty hath done for me great things,
and holy is his Name. 50 And his mercy is from generation to generation on
them [at]that fear him. 51 [10]He that showed strength with his [au]arm: [11]he hath
[av]scattered the proud in the [aw]imagination of their hearts. 52 [12]He hath [ax]put
down the mighty from their seats, and exalted them of [ay]low degree. 53 [13]He
hath filled the [az]hungry with good things, and sent away the rich emp-
ty. 54 [ba,14]He hath upholden Israel his servant to be mindful of his mer-
cy, 55 ([15]As he hath [bb]spoken to our fathers, to wit, to Abraham and his seed)
forever. 56 And Mary abode with her about three months: after, she returned to
her own house. 57 [bc]Now Elizabeth's time was fulfilled, that she should be deli-
vered, and she brought forth a son. 58 And her neighbors and cousins heard tell
how the Lord had showed his great mercy upon her, and they [16]rejoiced with
her. 59 And it was so that on the eighth day they came to circumcise the babe,
and called him Zacharias, after the name of his father. 60 But his mother answe-
red, and said, Not so, but he shall be called John. 61 And they said unto her,
There is none of thy kindred that is named with this name. 62 Then they made
signs to his father, how he would have him called. 63 So he asked for writing
tablets, and wrote, saying, His name is John, and they marveled all. 64 And his
mouth was opened immediately, and his tongue, [bd]and he spake and praised
God. 65 Then fear came on all them that dwelt near unto them, and all [be]these
words were noised abroad throughout all the hill country of Judea. 66 And all
they that heard them, [bf]laid them up in their hearts, saying, What manner child
shall this be! and the [bg]hand of the Lord was with him. 67 [bh]Then his father Za-
charias was filled with the holy Ghost, and prophesied, saying, 68 Blessed be the
Lord God of Israel, because he hath [bi]visited [17]and [bj]redeemed his peo-
ple, 69 [18]And hath raised up the [bk]horn of salvation unto us, in the house of his
servant David, 70 [19]As he spake by the mouth of his holy Prophets, which were
since the world began, saying, 71 That he would send us deliverance from our
enemies, and from the hands of all that hate us, 72 That he might show mercy
towards our fathers: and [bl]remember his holy covenant, 73 [20]And the oath, whi-
ch he sware to our father Abraham. 74 Which was, that he would grant unto us,
that we being delivered out of the hands of our enemies, should serve him without
fear, 75 All the days of our life, in [21]holiness and righteousness [bm]before
him. 76 And thou, [bn]babe, shalt be called the Prophet of the most High: for
thou shalt go before the face of the Lord to prepare his ways, 77 And to [bo]give
knowledge of salvation unto his people, by the [bp]remission of their sins, 78 Throu-
gh the tender mercy of our God, whereby [22]the [bq]dayspring from on high hath
visited us, 79 To give light to them that sit in darkness, and in the shadow of
death, and to guide our feet into the way of [br]peace. 80 And the child grew, and
waxed strong in spirit, and was in the wilderness, till the day came that he should
show himself unto Israel.

2

Augustus Caesar taxeth all the world. 7 Christ is born. 13 The Angels' Song. 21 Christ is circumcised. 22 Mary purified. 28 Simeon taketh Christ in his arms. 29 His Song. 36 Anna the Prophetess. 40 The child Christ. 46 Jesus disputeth with the doctors.

1 And [a]it came to pass in those days, that there came a decree from Augustus
Caesar, that all the [b]world should be [c]taxed. 2 (This first taxing was made when
Quirinius was governor of Syria.) 3 Therefore went all to be taxed, every man
to his own city. 4 And Joseph also went up from Galilee out of a city called Na-
zareth, into Judea, unto the [d]city of [1]David, which is called Bethlehem (because
he was of the house and lineage of David,) 5 To be taxed with Mary that was
given him to wife, which was with child. 6 And so it was, that while they were
there, the days were accomplished that she should be delivered. 7 And she brou-
ght forth her first begotten son, and wrapped him in swaddling clothes, and laid
him in a cratch, because there was no room for them in the inn. 8 [e]And there
were in the same country shepherds, [f]abiding in the field, and keeping watch by
night over their flock. 9 And lo, the Angel of the Lord [g]came upon them, and
the glory of the Lord shone about them, and they were sore afraid. 10 Then
the Angel said unto them, Be not afraid: for behold, I bring you glad tidings of
great joy, that shall be to all the people, 11 That is, that unto you is born this
day in the city of David, a Savior, which is Christ the Lord. 12 And this shall
be a sign to you, Ye shall find the babe swaddled, and laid in a cratch. 13 And
straightway there was with the Angel [h]a multitude of heavenly soldiers, praising
God, and saying, 14 Glory be to God in the high heavens, and peace in ear-
th, and toward men [i]good will. 15 And it came to pass when the Angels were
gone away from them into heaven, that the shepherds said one to another, Let us
go then unto Bethlehem, and see this thing that is come to pass, which the Lord
hath showed unto us. 16 So they came with haste, and found both Mary and
Joseph and the babe laid in the cratch. 17 And when they had seen it, they pu-
blished abroad the thing that was told them of that child. 18 And all that heard
it, wondered at the things which were told them of the shepherds. 19 But Mary
kept all those sayings, and pondered them in her heart. 20 And the shepherds
returned glorifying and praising God, for all that they had heard and seen, as it
was spoken unto them. 21 [j,2]And when the eight days were accomplished, that
they should circumcise the child, his name was then called [3]Jesus, which was na-
med of the Angel, before he was conceived in the womb. 22 [k,4]And when the
days of [l]her purification, after the Law of Moses, were accomplished, they brought
him to Jerusalem, to present him to the Lord, 23 (As it is written in the Law of
the Lord, [5]Every man child that first openeth the womb, shall be called holy to the
Lord,) 24 And to give an oblation, [6]as it is commanded in the Law of the Lord,
a pair of turtledoves, or two young pigeons. 25 [m]And behold, there was a man
in Jerusalem, whose name was Simeon: this man was just, and feared God, and
waited for the consolation of Israel, and the [n]holy Ghost was upon him. 26 And
it was declared to him from God by the holy Ghost, that he should not see death,
before he had seen that Anointed of the Lord. 27 And he came by the motion
of the spirit into the Temple, and when the [o]parents brought in the babe Jesus, to
do for him after the custom of the Law. 28 Then he took him in his arms, and
praised God, and said, 29 Lord, now [p]lettest thou thy servant depart in peace,

---

aq. Luke 1:46 Christ the redeemer of the afflicted, and revenger of the proud, of long time promised to the fathers, is now at length exhibited indeed.
ar. Luke 1:48 Hath freely and graciously loved.
as. Luke 1:48 Word for word, My baseness, that is, my base estate: so that the Virgin vaunteth not her deserts, but the grace of God.
at. Luke 1:50 To them that live godly and religiously, so speak the Hebrews.
au. Luke 1:51 That is, an heaping up of words more than needed, which the Hebrews use very much, and the arm is taken for strength.
av. Luke 1:51 Even as the wind doth the chaff.
aw. Luke 1:51 He hath scattered them, and the imagination of their hearts; or by and through the imagination of their own hearts: so that their wicked counsel turned to their own destruction.
ax. Luke 1:52 The mighty and rich men.
ay. Luke 1:52 Such as none account is made of, and are vile in men's eyes, which are indeed the poor in spirit, that is, such as challenge nothing to themselves in the sight of God.
az. Luke 1:53 Them that are brought to extreme poverty.
ba. Luke 1:54 He hath holpen up Israel with his arm, being clean cast down.
bb. Luke 1:55 Promised.
bc. Luke 1:57 John's nativity is set out with new miracles.
bd. Luke 1:64 was restored to its former state, is read in some copies.
be. Luke 1:65 All this that was said and done.
bf. Luke 1:66 Thought upon them diligently and earnestly, and as it were, printed them in their hearts.
bg. Luke 1:66 That is, the present favor of God, and a singular kind of virtue appeared in him.
bh. Luke 1:67 John scarce born, by the authority of the holy Ghost, is appointed to his office.
bi. Luke 1:68 That he hath showed himself mindful of his people, insomuch that he came down from heaven himself, to visit us in person, and to redeem us.
bj. Luke 1:68 Hath paid the ransom, that is to say, the price of our redemption.
bk. Luke 1:69 This word Horn in the Hebrew tongue signifieth might, and it is a Metaphor, taken from beasts, that fight with their horns: and by raising up the might of Israel, is meant, that the kingdom of Israel was defended, and the enemies thereof laid on the ground, even then when the strength of Israel seemed to be utterly decayed.
bl. Luke 1:72 Declared indeed that he was mindful.
bm. Luke 1:75 To God's good liking.
bn. Luke 1:76 Though thou be at this present never so little.
bo. Luke 1:77 Open the way.
bp. Luke 1:77 Forgiveness of sins, is the means whereby God saveth us, Rom. 4:7.
bq. Luke 1:78 Or bud, or branch; he alludeth unto the places in Jer. 23:5; Zech. 3:8 and 6:12, and he is called a bud from on high, that is, sent from God unto us, and not as other buds which bud out of the earth.
br. Luke 1:79 Into the way which leadeth us to true happiness.

LUKE 1

1. 1 Chron. 24:1
2. Exod. 30:7
3. Lev. 16:17
4. Mal. 4:5
5. Matt. 11:14
6. Matt. 1:18
7. Isa. 7:14
8. Luke 2:21 / Matt. 1:21
9. Dan. 7:14, 27 / Mic. 4:7
10. Isa. 51:9 / Ps. 33:10
11. Isa. 29:15
12. 1 Sam. 2:6
13. Ps. 24:10
14. Isa. 30:18 / Isa. 41:8 / Isa. 54:5 / Jer. 31:5-20
15. Gen. 17:19 / Gen. 22:17 / Ps. 132:12
16. Luke 1:14
17. Luke 2:30 / Matt. 1:21
18. Ps. 131:18
19. Jer. 23:6 / Jer. 30:10
20. Gen. 22:16 / Jer. 31:33 / Heb. 9:13-17
21. 1 Pet. 1:15
22. Zech. 3:8 / Zech. 6:12 / Mal. 4:2

LUKE 2

a. Luke 2:1 Christ the son of God, taking upon him the form of a servant, and making himself of no reputation, is poorly born in a stable: and by the means of Augustus the mightiest prince in the world (thinking nothing less) hath his cradle prepared in Bethlehem, as the Prophets forewarned.
b. Luke 2:1 So far as the Empire of the Romans did stretch.
c. Luke 2:1 That is, the inhabitants of every city should have their names taken, and their goods rated at a certain value, that the Emperor might understand, how rich every country, city, family, and house was.
d. Luke 2:4 Which David was born, and brought up in.
e. Luke 2:8 The Angels themselves declare to poor shepherds (nothing regarding the pride of the mighty) the Godhead and office of the child lying in the crib.
f. Luke 2:8 Lodging without doors, and open in the air.
g. Luke 2:9 Came suddenly upon them, when they thought of no such matter.
h. Luke 2:13 Whole armies of Angels, which compass the Majesty of God round about, as it were soldiers.
i. Luke 2:14 God's ready, good, infinite, and gracious favor toward men.
j. Luke 2:21 Christ the head of the Church, made subject to the Law, to deliver us from the curse of the Law, (as the Name of Jesus doth well declare) being circumcised, doth ratify and seal in his own flesh, the circumcision of the fathers.
k. Luke 2:22 Christ, upon whom all our sins were laid, being offered to God, according to the Law, doth purify both Mary and us all in himself.
l. Luke 2:22 This is meant, for the fulfilling of the Law: for otherwise the virgin was not defiled, nor unclean, by the birth of this child.
m. Luke 2:25 Simeon doth openly in the Temple foretell the deaf, of the coming of Messiah, of the casting out of the greatest part of Israel, and of the calling of the Gentiles.
n. Luke 2:25 He was endued with the gifts of the holy Ghost, and this is spoken by the figure Metonymy.
o. Luke 2:27 Joseph and Mary: and so he speaketh, as it was commonly taken.
p. Luke 2:29 Lettest me depart out of this life, to be joined to my fathers.
q. Luke 2:29 As thou promised me.

according to thy [q]word, **30** For [r]mine eyes have seen thy [s]salvation, **31** Which thou hast prepared [t]before the face of all people, **32** A light to be revealed to the Gentiles, and the glory of thy people Israel. **33** And Joseph and his mother marveled at those things, which were spoken touching him. **34** And Simeon blessed them, and said unto Mary his mother, Behold, this child is [u]appointed for the [v,7]fall and rising again of many in Israel, and for a [w]sign which shall be spoken against, **35** (Yea and a sword shall [x]pierce through thy soul) that the thoughts of many hearts may be opened. **36** [y]And there was a Prophetess, one Anna the daughter of Phanuel, of the tribe of Asher, which was of a great age, after she had lived with an husband seven years from her virginity: **37** And she was widow about fourscore, and four years, and went not out of the Temple, but served God with fastings and prayers night and day. **38** She then coming at the same instant upon them, confessed likewise the Lord, and spake of him to all that looked for redemption in Jerusalem. **39** And when they had performed all things, according to the Law of the Lord, they returned into Galilee to their own city Nazareth. **40** And the child grew, and waxed strong in Spirit, [z]and was filled with wisdom, and the grace of God was with him. **41** [aa]Now his parents went to Jerusalem, every year, [8]at the feast of the Passover. **42** And when he was twelve years old, and they were come up to Jerusalem, after the custom of the feast, **43** And had finished the days thereof, as they returned, the child Jesus remained in Jerusalem, and Joseph knew not, nor his mother, **44** But they supposing that he had been in the company, went a day's journey, and sought him among their kinsfolk, and acquaintances. **45** And when they found him not, they turned back to Jerusalem, and sought him. **46** And it came to pass three days after, that they found him in the Temple, sitting in the midst of the doctors, both hearing them, and asking them questions: **47** And all that heard him, were astonied at his understanding and answers. **48** [ab]So when they saw him, they were amazed, and his mother said unto him, Son, why hast thou thus dealt with us? behold, thy father and I have sought thee with very heavy hearts. **49** Then said he unto them, How is it that ye sought me? knew ye not that I must go about my Father's business? **50** But they understood not the word that he spake to them. **51** [ac]Then he went down with them, and came to Nazareth, and was subject to them: and his mother kept all these sayings in her heart. **52** And Jesus increased in wisdom, and stature, and in favor with God and men.

3

3 John exhorteth to repentance. 15 His testimony of Christ. 20 Herod putteth him in prison. 21 Christ is baptized. 23 His pedigree.

1 Now [a]in the fifteenth year of the reign of Tiberius Caesar, Pontius Pilate being governor of Judea, and Herod being Tetrarch of Galilee, and his brother Philip Tetrarch of Iturea, and of the country of Trachonitis, and Lysanias the Tetrarch of Abilene, **2** ([1]When [b]Annas and Caiaphas were the high Priests) the word of God came unto John, the son of Zacharias in the wilderness. **3** [2]And he came into all the coasts about Jordan, preaching the baptism of repentance for the remission of sins, **4** As it is written in the book of the sayings of Isaiah the Prophet, which saith, [3]The voice of him that crieth in the wilderness is, Prepare ye the way of the Lord: make his paths straight. **5** Every valley shall be filled, and every mountain and hill shall be brought low, and crooked things shall be made straight, and the rough ways shall be made smooth. **6** And all flesh shall see the salvation of God. **7** Then said he to the people that were come out to be baptized of him, [4]O generations of vipers, who hath forewarned you to flee from the wrath to come? **8** Bring forth therefore fruits worthy amendment of life, and begin not to say with yourselves, We have Abraham to our Father: for I say unto you, that God is able of these stones to raise up children unto Abraham. **9** Now also is the axe laid unto the root of the trees: therefore every tree which bringeth not forth good fruit, shall be hewn down, and cast into the fire. **10** Then the people asked him, saying, What shall we do then? **11** And he answered, and said unto them, [5]He that hath two coats, let him part with him that hath none: and he that hath meat, let him do likewise. **12** Then came there Publicans also to be baptized, and said unto him, Master, what shall we do? **13** And he said unto them, Require no more than that which is [c]appointed unto you. **14** The soldiers likewise demanded of him, saying, And what shall we do? And he said unto them, Do violence to no man, neither accuse any falsely, and be content with your [d]wages. **15** [e]As the people waited, and all men mused in their hearts of John, if he were not that Christ. **16** John answered, and said to them all, [6]Indeed I baptize you with water, but one stronger than I, cometh, whose shoe's latchet I am not worthy to unloose: he will baptize you with the holy Ghost, and with fire. **17** [f]Whose fan is in his hand, and he will make clean his floor, and will gather the wheat into his garner, but the chaff will he burn up with fire that never shall be quenched. **18** Thus then exhorting with many other things, he preached unto the people. **19** [g,7]But when Herod the Tetrarch was rebuked of him, for Herodias his brother Philip's wife, and for all the evils which Herod had done, **20** He added yet this above all, that he shut up John in prison. **21** [h,8]Now it came to pass, as all the people were baptized, and that Jesus was baptized and did pray, that the heaven was opened: **22** And the holy Ghost came down in a bodily shape like a dove upon him, and there was a voice from heaven, saying, Thou art my beloved Son: in thee I am well pleased. **23** [i]And Jesus himself began to be about thirty years of age, being as men supposed the son of Joseph, which was the son of Heli, **24** The son of Matthat, the son of Levi, the son of Melchi, the son of Janna, the son of Joseph, **25** The son of Mattathiah, the son of Amos, the son of Nahum, the son of Esli, the son of Naggai, **26** The son of Maath, the son of Mattathiah, the son of Semei, the son of Joseph, the son of Judah, **27** The son of Joannas, the son of Rhesa, the son of Zerubbabel, the son of Shealtiel, the son of Neri, **28** The son of Melchi, the son of Addi, the son of Cosam, the son of Elmodam, the son of Er, **29** The son of Jose, the son of Eliezer, the son of Jorim, the son of Matthat, the son of Levi, **30** The son of Simeon, the son of Judah, the son of Joseph, the son of Jonan, the son of Eliakim, **31** The son of Melea, the son of Menan, the son of Mattathah, the son of Nathan, the son of David, **32** The son of Jesse, the son of Obed, the son of Boaz, the son of Salmon, the son of Nahshon, **33** The son of Amminadab, the son of Ram, the son of Hezron, the son of Perez, the son of Judah, **34** The son of Jacob, the son of Isaac, the son of Abraham, the son of Terah, the son of Nahor, **35** The son of Serug, the son of Reu, the son of Peleg, the son of Eber, the son of Shelah, **36** The son of Cainan, the son of Arphaxad, the son of Shem, the son of Noah, the son of Lamech, **37** The son of Methuselah, the son of Enoch, the son of Jared, the son of Mahalalel, the son of Cainan, **38** The son of Enosh, the son of Seth, the son of Adam, the son of God.

4

1 Of Christ's temptation, and fasting. 16 He teacheth in Nazareth to the great admiration of all. 24 A Prophet that teacheth in his own country is condemned. 33 One possessed of the devil is cured. 38 Peter's mother-in-law is healed, 40 and divers sick persons are restored to health. 41 The devils acknowledge Christ.

1 And [a]Jesus full of the holy Ghost returned from Jordan, and was led by that Spirit into the wilderness, **2** [1]And was there forty days tempted of the devil, and in those days he did eat nothing, but when they were ended, he afterward was hungry. **3** [b]Then the devil said unto him, If thou be the son of God, command this stone, that it be made bread. **4** But Jesus answered him, saying, It is written, [2]That man shall not live by bread only, but by every word of God. **5** Then the devil took him up into an high mountain, and showed him all the kingdoms of the world, in the twinkling of an eye. **6** And the devil said unto him, All this [c]power will I give thee, and the glory of those kingdoms: for that is [d]delivered to

---

r. Luke 2:30 That is, for I have seen with my very eyes: for he saw before in mind, as it is said of Abraham, He saw my day, and rejoiced.
s. Luke 2:30 That, wherein thy salvation is contained.
t. Luke 2:31 As a sign set up in an high place, for all men to look upon.
u. Luke 2:34 Is appointed and set of God for a mark.
v. Luke 2:34 Fall of the reprobate, which perish through their own default: and for the rising of the elect, unto whom God shall give faith to believe.
w. Luke 2:34 That is, a mark, which all men shall strive earnestly to hit.
x. Luke 2:35 Shall wound and grieve most sharply.
y. Luke 2:36 Another witness besides Simeon, against whom no exception may be brought, inviting all men to the receiving of the Messiah.
z. Luke 2:40 As Christ grew up in age, so the virtue of his Godhead showed itself more and more.
aa. Luke 2:41 The Scribes and Pharisees are stirred up to hear the wisdom of Christ in his time, by an extraordinary deed.
ab. Luke 2:48 All duties which we owe to men as they were not to be neglected, so are they according to our vocation, not to be preferred before the glory of God.
ac. Luke 2:51 Christ very man is made like unto us in all things, except sin.

LUKE 2

1. John 7:42
2. Gen. 17:12 / Lev. 12:3 / John 7:22
3. Luke 1:31 / Matt. 1:22
4. Lev. 12:6
5. Exod. 13:2 / Num. 8:16
6. Lev. 12:6
7. Isa. 8:14 / Rom. 9:32 / 1 Pet. 2:8
8. Deut. 16:1

LUKE 3

a. Luke 3:1 John cometh at the time foretold of the Prophets, and layeth the foundation of the Gospel which is exhibited unto us, setting forth the true observing of the Law, and free mercy in Christ, which cometh after him, using also baptism the effectual sign both of regeneration and also of forgiveness of sins.
b. Luke 3:2 Josephus calleth him Ananus.
c. Luke 3:13 Require no more than that sum that is appointed for the tribute money.
d. Luke 3:14 Which was paid them partly in money, and partly in victual.
e. Luke 3:15 If we would rightly, and fruitfully receive the sacraments, we must neither rest in the signs, neither in him that ministereth the signs, but lift up our eyes to Christ, who is the author of the sacraments, and the giver of that which is represented by the sacraments.
f. Luke 3:17 The Gospel is the fan of the world.
g. Luke 3:19 John's preaching is confirmed with his death.
h. Luke 3:21 Our baptism is sanctified in the head of the Church, and Christ also is pronounced, by the voice of the Father, to be our everlasting King, Priest, and Prophet.
i. Luke 3:23 The stock of Christ, according to the flesh, is brought by order even to Adam, and so to God, that it might appear, that he only it was, whom God promised to Abraham and David, and appointed from everlasting to his Church, which is gathered together of all sorts of men.

LUKE 3

1. Acts 4:6
2. Matt. 3:2 / Mark 1:4
3. Isa. 40:3 / John 1:25
4. Matt. 3:7
5. James 2:15 / 1 John 3:17
6. Matt. 3:11 / Mark 1:3 / John 1:26 / Acts 1:5 / Acts 8:4 / Acts 11:16 / Acts 19:4
7. Matt. 14:3 / Mark 6:17
8. Matt. 3:13 / Mark 1:9 / John 1:32

LUKE 4

a. Luke 4:1 Christ being carried away (as it were out of the world, into the desert) after the fast of forty days, and the overcoming of Satan thrice, coming as it were suddenly from heaven, beginneth his office.
b. Luke 4:3 Christ being stirred up of Satan, first to distrust in God, secondly to the desire of riches and honor, and lastly to a vain confidence of himself, overcometh him thrice by the word of God.
c. Luke 4:6 By this word power, are the kingdoms themselves meant, which have the power: and so it is spoken by the figure Metonymy.

me: and to whomsoever I will, I give it. **7** If thou therefore wilt worship me, they
shall be all [e]thine. **8** But Jesus answered him, and said, Hence from me, Satan:
for it is written, [3]Thou shalt worship the Lord thy God, and him alone thou shalt
serve. **9** Then he brought him to Jerusalem, and set him on a pinnacle of the
Temple, and said unto him, If thou be the Son of God, cast thyself down from
hence, **10** For it is written, [4]That he will give his Angels charge over thee to keep
thee: **11** And with their hands they shall lift thee up, lest at anytime thou shoul-
dest dash thy foot against a stone. **12** And Jesus answered, and said unto him,
It is said, [5]Thou shalt not tempt the Lord thy God. **13** And when the devil had
ended all the temptation, he departed from him for a little season. **14** And Je-
sus returned by the power of the spirit into Galilee: and there went a fame of him
throughout all the region round about: **15** For he taught in their Synagogues,
and was honored of all men. **16** [f,6]And he came to Nazareth where he had been
brought up, and (as his custom was) went into the Synagogue on the Sabbath day,
and stood up to read. **17** And there was delivered unto him the book of the
Prophet Isaiah: and when he had [g]opened the book, he found the place, where it
was written, **18** [7]The Spirit of the Lord is upon me, because he hath anointed
me, that I should preach the Gospel to the poor: he hath sent me, that I should heal
the brokenhearted, that I should preach deliverance to the captives, and recovering
of sight to the blind, that I should set at liberty them that are bruised: **19** And
that I should preach the acceptable year of the Lord. **20** And he closed the book,
and gave it again to the minister, and sat down: and the eyes of all that were in the
Synagogue were fastened on him. **21** Then he began to say unto them, This day
is the Scripture fulfilled in your ears. **22** [h]And all [i]bare him witness, and [j]won-
dered at the [k]gracious words, which proceeded out of his mouth, and said, Is not
this Joseph's son? **23** Then he said unto them, Ye will surely say unto me this
Proverb, Physician, heal thyself: whatsoever we have heard done in Capernaum,
do it here likewise in thine own country. **24** And he said, Verily I say unto you,
[8]No Prophet is accepted in his own country. **25** But I tell you of a truth, many
widows were in Israel in the days of [9]Elijah, when heaven was shut three years
and six months, when great famine was throughout all the [l]land: **26** But unto
none of them was Elijah sent, save into Zarephath, a city of Sidon, unto a certain
widow. **27** Also many lepers were in Israel, in the time of [10]Elisha the Prophet:
yet none of them was made clean, saving Naaman the Syrian. **28** [m]Then all that
were in the Synagogue, when they heard it, were filled with wrath, **29** And rose
up, and thrust him out of the city, and led him unto the edge of the hill, where-
on their city was built, to cast him down headlong. **30** But he passed through
the midst of them, and went his way, **31** [11]And came down into Capernaum a
city of Galilee, and there taught them on the Sabbath days. **32** [12]And they were
astonied at his doctrine: for his word was with authority. **33** [13]And in the Sy-
nagogue there was a man which had a spirit of an unclean devil, which cried with
a loud voice, **34** [n]Saying, Oh, what have we to do with thee, thou Jesus of Na-
zareth? art thou come to destroy us? I know who thou art, even the Holy one of
God. **35** And Jesus rebuked him, saying, Hold thy peace, and come out of him.
Then the devil throwing him in the midst of them, came out of him, and hurt him
nothing at all. **36** So fear came on them all, and they spake among themselves,
saying, What thing is this: for with authority and power he commandeth the foul
spirits, and they come out? **37** And the fame of him spread abroad throughout
all the places of the country round about. **38** [o,14]And he rose up, and came out
of the Synagogue, and entered into Simon's house. And Simon's wife's mother was
taken with a great fever, and they required him for her. **39** Then he stood over
her, and rebuked the fever, and it left her, and immediately she arose, and ministe-
red unto them. **40** Now at the Sun setting, all they that had sick folks of divers
diseases, brought them unto him, and he laid his hands on everyone of them, and
healed them. **41** [p,15]And devils also came out of many, crying, and saying, Thou
art that Christ that Son of God: but he rebuked them, and suffered them not to
say that they knew him to be that Christ. **42** [q]And when it was day, he departed,
and went forth into a desert place, and the people sought him, and came to him,
and kept him that he should not depart from them. **43** But he said unto them,
Surely I must also preach the kingdom of God to other cities: for therefore am I
sent. **44** And he preached in the Synagogues of Galilee.

5

1 Christ teacheth out of the ship. 6 Of the draught of fish. 12 The Leper. 16 Christ prayeth in the desert. 18 One sick of the palsy. 27 Levi the Publican. 34 The fastings and afflictions of the Apostles after Christ's ascension. 36,37,38 Fainthearted and weak disciples are likened to old bottles and worn garments.

1 Then [a,1]it came to pass, as the people [b]pressed upon him to hear the word
of God, that he stood by the lake of Gennesaret, **2** And saw two ships stand by
the lakeside, but the fishermen were gone out of them, and were washing their
nets. **3** And he entered into one of the ships, which was Simon's, and required
him that he would thrust off a little from the land: and he sat down, and taught the
people out of the ship. **4** Now when he had left speaking, he said unto Simon,
Launch out into the deep, and let down your nets to make a draught. **5** Then
Simon answered, and said unto him, [c]Master, we have travailed sore all night,
and have taken nothing: nevertheless at thy word I will let down the net. **6** And
when they had so done, they enclosed a great multitude of fishes, so that their net
brake. **7** And they beckoned to their partners, which were in the other ship,
that they should come and help them, who came then, and filled both the ships,
that they did sink. **8** Now when Simon Peter saw it, he fell down at Jesus knees,
saying, Lord, go from me: for I am a sinful man. **9** For he was utterly astonied,
and all that were with him, for the draught of fishes which they took. **10** And
so was also James and John the sons of Zebedee, which were companions with
Simon. Then Jesus said unto Simon, Fear not: from henceforth thou shalt catch
men. **11** And when they had brought the ships to land, they forsook all, and fol-
lowed him. **12** [d,2]Now it came to pass, as he was in a certain city, behold, there
was a man full of leprosy, and when he saw Jesus, he fell on his face, and besought
him, saying, Lord, if thou wilt, thou canst make me clean. **13** So he stretched
forth his hand, and touched him, saying, I will, be thou clean. And immediately
the leprosy departed from him. **14** And he commanded him that he should tell
it no man: but Go, saith he, and show thyself to the Priest, and offer for thy cle-
ansing, as [3]Moses hath commanded, for a witness unto them. **15** [e]But so much
more went there a fame abroad of him, and great multitudes came together to hear,
and to be healed of him of their infirmities. **16** But he kept himself apart in the
wilderness, and prayed. **17** [f]And it came to pass, on a certain day, as he was te-
aching, that the Pharisees and doctors of the Law sat by, which were come out of
every town of Galilee, and Judea, and Jerusalem, and the power of the Lord [g]was
in him, to heal them. **18** [4]Then behold, men brought a man lying in a bed, whi-
ch was taken with a palsy, and they sought means to bring him in, and to lay him
before him. **19** And when they could not find by what way they might bring
him in, because of the press, they went up on the house, and let him down throu-
gh the tiling, bed and all, in the midst before Jesus. **20** And when he saw their
faith, he said unto him, Man, thy sins are forgiven thee. **21** Then the Scribes and
the Pharisees began to reason, saying, Who is this that speaketh blasphemies? Who
can forgive sins, but God only? **22** But when Jesus perceived their reasoning he
answered, and said unto them, What reason ye in your hearts? **23** Whether is
easier to say, Thy sins are forgiven thee, or to say, Rise and walk? **24** But that ye
may know that the Son of man hath authority to forgive sins in earth, (he said unto
the sick of the palsy) I say to thee, Arise: take up thy bed, and go into thine hou-
se. **25** And immediately he rose up before them, and took up his bed whereon he
lay, and departed to his own house, praising God. **26** And they were all amazed,
and praised God, and were filled with fear, saying, Doubtless we have seen stran-
ge things today. **27** [h,5]And after that, he went forth and saw a Publican named

---

d. Luke 4:6 That is surely so, for he is prince of the world yet not absolutely, and is the sovereign over it, but by sufferance, and way of entreaty, and therefore he saith not true, that he can give it to whom he will.

e. Luke 4:7 Out of an high place, which had a goodly champion country underneath it, he showed him the situation of all countries.

f. Luke 4:16 Who Christ is, and wherefore he came, he showeth out of the prophet Isaiah.

g. Luke 4:17 Their books in those days were rolled up as scrolls upon a ruler: and so Christ unrolled, or unfolded it, which is here called opened.

h. Luke 4:22 Familiarity causeth Christ to be contemned, and therefore he oftentimes goeth to strangers.

i. Luke 4:22 Approved those things, which he spake, with common consent and voice: for the word, witness, signifieth in this place, and many others to allow and approve a thing with open confession.

j. Luke 4:22 Not only the doctors, but also the common people were present at this conference of the Scriptures: and besides that their mother tongue was used, for else how could the people have wondered? Paul appointed the same order in the Church at Corinth, 1 Cor. 14.

k. Luke 4:22 Words full of the mighty power of God, which appeared in all his doings as well, and allured men marvelously unto him, Ps. 45:2, grace is poured into thy lips.

l. Luke 4:25 Land of Israel, see Mark 15:38.

m. Luke 4:28 The more sharply the world is rebuked, the more it rageth openly: but the life of the godly is not simply subject to the pleasure of the wicked.

n. Luke 4:34 Christ astonisheth not only men, be they never so blockish, but even the demons also, whether they will or no.

o. Luke 4:38 In that, that Christ healeth the diseases of the body with his word only, he proveth that he is God Almighty, sent for man's salvation.

p. Luke 4:41 Satan, who is a continual enemy to the truth, ought not to be heard, no not then, when he speaketh the truth.

q. Luke 4:42 No color of zeal ought to hinder us in the race of our vocation.

LUKE 4

1. Matt. 4:1 / Mark 1:12
2. Deut. 8:3 / Matt. 4:4
3. Deut. 6:13 / Deut. 10:20
4. Ps. 91:12
5. Deut. 6:16
6. Matt. 13:54 / Mark 6:1 / John 4:43
7. Isa. 61:1
8. John 4:44
9. 1 Kings 17:9 / James 5:17
10. 2 Kings 5:14
11. Matt. 4:13 / Mark 1:21
12. Matt. 7:29 / Mark 1:22
13. Mark 1:23
14. Matt. 8:14 / Mark 1:30
15. Mark 1:35

LUKE 5

a. Luke 5:1 Christ advertiseth the four disciples, which he had taken unto him, of the office of the Apostleship, which should hereafter be committed unto them.

b. Luke 5:1 Did as it were lie upon him, so desirous they were to see him, and hear him, and therefore he taught them out of a ship.

c. Luke 5:5 The word signifieth him that hath rule over anything.

d. Luke 5:12 Christ by healing the leper with his only touch, and sending him to the Priest, witnesseth that it is he, through whom and by whom, apprehended by faith, all we which are unclean, according to the Law, by the witness of God himself, are pronounced to be pure and clean.

e. Luke 5:15 Christ had rather be famous by his doctrine, than by miracles, and therefore he departeth from them that seek him, as a physician of the body, and not as the author of salvation.

f. Luke 5:17 Christ in healing him that was sick of the palsy, showeth the cause of all diseases, and the remedy.

g. Luke 5:17 The mighty power of Christ's Godhead, showed itself in him, at that time.

h. Luke 5:27 The Church is a company of sinners through the grace of Christ repentant, which banquet with him, to the great offence of the proud and envious worldlings.

i. Luke 5:33 It is the point of hypocrites and ignorant men to put an holiness in fasting, and in things indifferent.

j. Luke 5:34 Laws generally made without any consideration of circumstances, for fasting and other things of like sort, are not only tyrannous, but very hurtful in the Church.

Levi, sitting at the receipt of custom, and said unto him, Follow me. **28** And he left all, rose up, and followed him. **29** Then Levi made him a great feast in his own house, where there was a great company of Publicans, and of others that sat at table with them. **30** But they that were Scribes and Pharisees among them, murmured against his disciples, saying, Why eat ye and drink ye with Publicans and sinners? **31** Then Jesus answered, and said unto them, They that are whole, need not the Physician, but they that are sick. **32** [6]I came not to call the righteous, but sinners to repentance. **33** [i,7,8]Then they said unto him, Why do the disciples of John fast often, and pray, and the disciples of the Pharisees also, but thine eat and drink? **34** [j]And he said unto them, Can ye make the children of the wedding chamber to fast, as long as the bridegroom is with them? **35** But the days will come, even when the bridegroom shall be taken away from them: then shall they fast in those days. **36** Again he spake also unto them a parable, No man putteth a piece of a new garment into an old vesture: for then the new renteth it, and the piece taken out of the new, agreeth not with the old. **37** Also no man poureth new wine into old vessels: for then the new wine will break the vessels, and it will run out, and the vessels will perish: **38** But new wine must be poured into new vessels: so both are preserved. **39** Also no man that drinketh old wine, straightway desireth new: for he saith, The old is more profitable.

6

1 The disciples pull the ears of corn on the Sabbath. 6 Of him that had a withered hand. 13 The election of the Apostles. 20 The blessings and curses. 27 We must love our enemies. 46 With what fruit the word of God is to be heard.

1 And [a,1]it came to pass on a second solemn Sabbath, that he went through the corn fields, and his disciples [b]plucked the ears of corn, and did eat, and rubbed them in their hands. **2** And certain of the Pharisees said unto them, Why do ye that which is not lawful to do on the Sabbath days? **3** Then Jesus answered them, and said, [2]Have ye not read this, that David did when he himself was an hungered, and they which were with him, **4** How he went into the house of God, and took, and ate the showbread, and gave also to them which were with him, which was not lawful to eat, but for the [3]Priests only? **5** And he said unto them, The Son of man is Lord also of the Sabbath day. **6** [c,4]It came to pass also on another Sabbath, that he entered into the Synagogue, and taught, and there was a man, whose right hand was dried up. **7** And the Scribes and Pharisees watched him, whether he would heal on the Sabbath day, that they might find an accusation against him. **8** But he knew their thoughts, and said to the man which had the withered hand, Arise, and stand up in the midst. And he arose, and stood up. **9** Then said Jesus unto them, I will ask you a question, Whether is it lawful on the Sabbath days to do good, or to do evil? to save life, or to [d]destroy? **10** And he beheld them all in compass, and said unto the man, Stretch forth thine hand. And he did so, and his hand was restored again, as whole as the other. **11** Then they were filled full of madness, and communed one with another, what they might do to Jesus. **12** And it came to pass in those days, that he went into a mountain to pray, and [e]spent the night in prayer to God. **13** And when it was day, [5]he called his disciples, and of them he chose twelve which also he called Apostles: **14** (Simon whom he named also Peter, and Andrew his brother, James and John, Philip and Bartholomew, **15** Matthew and Thomas: James the son of Alphaeus, and Simon called Zealous, **16** Judas James' brother, and Judas Iscariot, which also was the traitor.) **17** Then he came down with them, and stood in a plain place with the company of his disciples, and a great multitude of people out of all Judea, and Jerusalem, and from the [f]sea coast of Tyre and Sidon, which came to hear him, and to be healed of their diseases: **18** And they that were vexed with foul spirits, and they were healed. **19** And the whole multitude sought to touch him: for there went virtue out of him, and healed them all: **20** [g,6]And he lifted up his eyes upon his disciples, and said, Blessed be ye poor: for yours is the kingdom of God. **21** [7]Blessed are ye that hunger now: for ye shall be satisfied: [8]blessed are ye that weep now: for ye shall laugh. **22** [9]Blessed are ye when men hate you, and when [h]they separate you, and revile you, and put out your name as evil, for the Son of man's sake. **23** Rejoice ye in that day, and [i]be glad: for behold, your reward is great in heaven: for after this manner their fathers did to the Prophets: **24** [10]But woe be to you that are rich: for ye have [j]received your consolation. **25** [11]Woe be to you that are full: for ye shall hunger. Woe be to you that now laugh: for ye shall wail and weep. **26** Woe be to you when all men speak well of you: for so did their fathers to the false prophets. **27** [k,12]But I say unto you which hear, Love your enemies: do well to them which hate you. **28** Bless them that curse you, and pray for them which hurt you. **29** [13]And unto him that smiteth thee on the one cheek, offer also the other, [14]and him that taketh away thy cloak, forbid not to take thy coat also. **30** Give to every man that asketh of thee: and of him that taketh away the things that be thine, ask them not again. **31** [15]And as ye would that men should do to you, so do ye to them likewise. **32** [16]For if ye love them which love you, [l]what thank shall ye have? for even the sinners love those that love them. **33** And if ye do good for them which do good for you, what thank shall ye have? for even the sinners do the same. **34** [17]And if ye lend to them of whom ye hope to receive, what thank shall ye have? for even the sinners lend to sinners, to receive the like. **35** Wherefore love ye your enemies, and do good, and lend, [m]looking for nothing again, and your reward shall be great, and ye shall be the children of [18]the most High: for he is kind unto the unkind, and to the evil. **36** Be ye therefore merciful, as your Father also is merciful. **37** [n,19]Judge not, and ye shall not be judged: condemn not, and ye shall not be condemned: [o]forgive, and ye shall be forgiven. **38** Give, and it shall be given unto you: [20]a good measure, [p]pressed down, shaken together and running over shall men give into your bosom: for with what measure ye mete, with the same shall men mete to you again. **39** [q]And he spake a parable unto them, [21]Can the blind lead the blind? shall they not both fall into the ditch? **40** [22]The disciple is not above the master: but whosoever will be a perfect disciple, shall be as his master. **41** [r,23]And why seest thou a mote in thy brother's eye, and considerest not the beam that is in thine own eye? **42** Either how canst thou say to thy brother, Brother, let me pull out the mote that is in thine eye, when thou seest not the beam that is in thine own eye? Hypocrite, cast out the beam out of thine own eye first, and then shalt thou see perfectly to pull out the mote that is in thy brother's eye. **43** [s,24]For it is not a good tree that bringeth forth evil fruit: neither an evil tree, that bringeth forth good fruit. **44** [25]For every tree is known by his own fruit: [26]for neither of thorns gather men figs, nor of bushes gather they grapes. **45** A good man out of the good treasure of his heart bringeth forth good; and an evil man out of the evil treasure of his heart bringeth forth evil: for of the abundance of the heart his mouth speaketh. **46** [27]But why call ye me Lord, Lord, and do not the things that I speak? **47** [t]Whosoever cometh to me, and heareth my words, and doeth the same, I will show you to whom he is like: **48** He is like a man which built an house, and dug deep, and laid the foundation on a rock: and when the waters arose, the flood beat upon that house, and could not shake it: for it was grounded upon a rock. **49** But he that heareth and doeth not, is like a man that built an house upon the earth without foundation, against which the flood did beat, and it fell by and by: and the fall of that house was great.

LUKE 5

1. Matt. 4:18 / Mark 1:16
2. Matt. 8:2 / Mark 1:40
3. Lev. 14:4
4. Matt. 9:2 / Mark 2:3
5. Matt. 9:9 / Mark 2:14
6. 1 Tim. 1:15
7. Matt. 9:14
8. Mark 2:18

LUKE 6

a. Luke 6:1 Christ showeth against the superstitious, who stick in every trifle, that the Law of the very Sabbath, was not given to be kept without exception: much less that the salvation of man should consist in the outward keeping of it.
b. Luke 6:1 Epiphanius noteth well in his treatise, where he confuteth Ebion, that the time, when the disciples plucked the ears of the corn, was in the feast of unleavened bread: Now, whereas in these feasts which were kept many days together, as the feast of Tabernacles, and the Passover, their first day and their last were of like solemnity, Lev. 23. Luke fitly calleth the last day the second Sabbath, though Theophylact understandeth it of any other of them, that followed the first.
c. Luke 6:6 Charity is the rule of all ceremonies.
d. Luke 6:9 Whoso helpeth not his neighbor when he can, he killeth him.
e. Luke 6:12 In that, that Christ useth earnest and long prayer, in choosing twelve of his own company, to the office of the Apostleship, he showeth how religiously we ought to behave ourselves in the choice of Ecclesiastical persons.
f. Luke 6:17 From all the seacoast, which is called Syro-Phoenecia.
g. Luke 6:20 Christ teacheth against all Philosophers, and especially the Epicureans, that the chiefest felicity of man is laid up in no place here on earth, but in heaven: and that persecution for righteousness' sake, is the right way unto it.
h. Luke 6:22 Cast you out of their Synagogues, as John expoundeth it, John 16:2, which is the sharpest punishment the Church hath, if so be the Elders judge rightfully, and by the word of God.
i. Luke 6:23 Leaps (as cattle do, which are provender pricked) for exceeding joy.
j. Luke 6:24 That is, you reap now of your riches, all the commodities and blessings you are ever likely to have, and therefore, you have not to look for any other reward, Matt. 6:2.
k. Luke 6:27 Christian charity, which differeth much from the worldly, doth not only not revenge injuries, but comprehended even our most grievous enemies, and that for our Father's sake, which is in heaven: so far is it, from seeking its own profit in doing well.
l. Luke 6:32 What is there in this your work, that is to be accounted of? for if you look to have commodity by loving, seek those commodities, which are commodities indeed: love your enemies, and so you shall show to the world that you look for those commodities, which come from God.
m. Luke 6:35 When you will lend, do it only to benefit and pleasure withall, and not for hope, to receive the principal again.
n. Luke 6:37 Brotherly reprehension must not proceed of curiosity, nor churlishness, nor malice, but they must be just, moderate, and loving.
o. Luke 6:37 He speaketh not here of civil judgments, and therefore by the word, forgive, is meant that good nature, which the Christians use in suffering and pardoning wrongs.
p. Luke 6:38 These are borrowed kinds of speeches taken from them which use to measure dry things, as corn and such like, who use a frank kind of dealing therein, and thrust it down and shake it together, and press it and heap it.
q. Luke 6:39 Unskillful reprehenders hurt both themselves and others: for such as the master is, such is the scholar.
r. Luke 6:41 Hypocrites, which are very severe reprehenders of others, are very quick of sight to spy other men's faults, but very blind to see their own.
s. Luke 6:43 He is a good man, not that is skillful to reprehend others, but he that proveth his uprightness in word and deed.
t. Luke 6:47 Affliction doth at the length discern true godliness from false and feigned.

LUKE 6

1. Matt. 12:1 / Mark 2:23
2. 1 Sam. 21:6
3. Exod. 29:39 / Lev. 8:31 / Lev. 24:9
4. Matt. 12:19 / Mark 3:1
5. Luke 9:1 / Matt. 10:1 / Mark 13:3 / Mark 6:7
6. Matt. 5:3
7. Isa. 65:13
8. Isa. 61:3
9. Matt. 5:11
10. Amos 6:1
11. Isa. 65:13
12. Matt. 5:44
13. Matt. 5:39
14. 1 Cor. 6:7
15. Matt. 7:12
16. Matt. 5:46
17. Matt. 5:42 / Deut. 15:8
18. Matt. 5:45
19. Matt. 7:1
20. Matt. 7:2 / Mark 4:24
21. Matt. 15:14
22. Matt. 10:24 / John 13:16 / John 15:20
23. Matt. 7:3
24. Matt. 7:17
25. Matt. 12:33
26. Matt. 7:16
27. Matt. 7:21 / Rom. 2:13 / James 2:21

7

1 Of the Centurion's servant. 9 The Centurion's faith. 11 The widow's son raised from death at Nain. 19 John sendeth his disciples to Christ. 33 His peculiar kind of living. 37 The sinful woman washeth Jesus' feet.

1 When [a,1]he had ended all his sayings in the audience of the people, he entered into Capernaum. **2** And a certain Centurion's servant was sick and ready to die, which was dear unto him. **3** And when he heard of Jesus, he sent unto him the Elders of the Jews, beseeching him that he would come, and heal his servant. **4** So they came to Jesus, and besought him instantly, saying that he was worthy that he should do this for him: **5** For he loveth, said they, our nation, and he hath built us a Synagogue. **6** Then Jesus went with them: but when he was now not far from the house, the Centurion sent friends to him, saying unto him, Lord, trouble not thyself: for I am not worthy that thou shouldest enter under my roof: **7** Wherefore I thought not myself worthy to come unto thee: but say the word, and my servant shall be whole: **8** For I likewise am a man set under authority, and have under me soldiers, and I say unto one, Go, and he goeth: and to another, Come, and he cometh: and to my servant, Do this, and he doeth it. **9** When Jesus heard these things, he marveled at him, and turned him, and said to the people that followed him, I say unto you, I have not found so great faith, no not in Israel. **10** And when they that were sent, turned back to the house, they found the servant that was sick, whole. **11** [b]And it came to pass the day after, that he went into a city called [c]Nain, and many of his disciples went with him, and a great multitude. **12** Now when he came near to the gate of the city, behold, there was a dead man carried out, who was the only begotten son of his mother, which was a widow, and much people of the city was with her. **13** And when the Lord saw her, he had compassion on her, and said unto her, Weep not. **14** And he went and touched the coffin (and they that bare him, stood still) and he said, Young man, I say unto thee, Arise. **15** And he that was dead, sat up, and began to speak, and he delivered him to his mother. **16** Then there came a fear on them all, and they glorified God, saying, A great Prophet is risen among us, and God hath visited his people. **17** And this rumor of him went forth throughout all Judea, and throughout all the region round about. **18** [d]And the disciples of John showed him of all these things. **19** So John called unto him two certain men of his disciples, and sent them to Jesus, saying, Art thou he that should come, or shall we wait for another? **20** And when the men were come unto him, they said, John Baptist hath sent us unto thee, saying, Art thou he that should come, or shall we wait for another? **21** And [e]at that time, he cured many of their sicknesses, and plagues, and of evil spirits, and unto many blind men he gave sight freely. **22** And Jesus answered, and said unto them, Go your ways and show John, what things ye have seen and heard, that the blind see, the halt go, the lepers are cleansed, the deaf hear, the dead are raised, and the poor receive the Gospel. **23** And blessed is he, that shall not be offended in me. **24** [f]And when the messengers of John were departed, he began to speak unto the people of John, What went ye out into the wilderness to see? A reed shaken with the wind? **25** But what went ye out to see? A man clothed in soft raiment? behold, they which are gorgeously appareled, and live delicately, are in Kings' courts. **26** But what went ye forth to see? A Prophet? yea, I say to you, and greater than a Prophet. **27** This is he of whom it is written, [2]Behold, I send my messenger before thy face, which shall prepare thy way before thee. **28** For I say unto you, there is no greater Prophet than John, among them that are begotten of women: nevertheless, he that is the least in the kingdom of God, is greater than he. **29** Then all the people that heard, and the Publicans [g]justified God, being baptized with the baptism of John. **30** But the Pharisees and the expounders of the Law despised the counsel of God [h]against themselves, and were not baptized of him. **31** [i,3]And the Lord said, Whereunto shall I liken the men of this generation? and what thing are they like unto? **32** They are like unto little children sitting in the marketplace, and crying one to another, and saying, We have piped unto you, and ye have not danced: we have mourned to you, and ye have not wept. **33** For John Baptist came neither eating bread, nor drinking wine: and ye say, He hath the devil. **34** The Son of man is come, and eateth, and drinketh: and ye say, Behold, a man which is a glutton, and a drinker of wine, a friend of Publicans and sinners: **35** But wisdom is justified of all her children. **36** [j]And one of the Pharisees desired him that he would eat with him: and he went into the Pharisee's house, and sat down at table. **37** And behold, a woman in the city, which was a sinner, when she knew that Jesus sat at table in the Pharisee's house, she brought a box of ointment. **38** [4]And she stood at his feet behind him weeping, and began to wash his feet with tears, and did wipe them with the hairs of her head, and kissed his feet, and anointed them with the ointment. **39** [k]Now when the Pharisee which bade him, saw it, he spake within himself, saying, If this man were a Prophet, he would surely have known who, and what manner of woman this is which toucheth him: [l]for she is a sinner. **40** [m]And Jesus answered, and said unto him, Simon, I have somewhat to say unto thee. And he said, Master, say on. **41** There was a certain lender which had two debtors: the one ought five hundred pence, and the other fifty: **42** When they had nothing to pay, he forgave them both: Which of them therefore, tell me, will love him most? **43** Simon answered, and said, I suppose that he to whom he forgave most. And he said unto him, Thou hast truly judged. **44** Then he turned to the woman, and said unto Simon, Seest thou this woman? I entered into thine house, and thou gavest me no water to my feet: but she hath washed my feet with tears, and wiped them with the hairs of her head. **45** Thou gavest me no kiss: but she, since the time I came in, hath not ceased to kiss my feet. **46** Mine head with oil thou didst not anoint: but she hath anointed my feet with ointment. **47** Wherefore I say unto thee, many sins are forgiven her: [n]for she loved much. To whom a little is forgiven, he doth love a little. **48** And he said unto her, Thy sins are forgiven thee. **49** And they that sat at table with him, began to say within themselves, Who is this that even forgiveth sins? **50** And he said to the woman, Thy faith hath saved thee: [o]go in peace.

8

1 Women that minister unto Christ of their substance. 4 The parable of the sower. 16 The candle. 19 Christ's mother and brethren. 22 He rebuked the winds. 26 Of Legion. 37 The Gadarenes reject Christ. 41 Jairus's daughter healed. 43 The woman delivered from the issue of blood. 52 Weeping for the dead.

1 And it came to pass afterward, that he himself went through every city and town, preaching and publishing the kingdom of God, and the twelve were with him, **2** And certain women, which were healed of evil spirits, and infirmities, as [1]Mary which was called Magdalene, out of whom went seven devils, **3** And Joanna the wife of Chuza Herod's steward, and Susanna, and many others which ministered unto him of their substance. **4** [a,2]Now when much people were gathered together, and were come unto him out of all cities, he spake by a parable. **5** A sower went out to sow his seed, and as he sowed, some fell by the wayside, and it was trodden under feet, and the fowls of heaven devoured it up. **6** And some fell on the stones, and when it was sprung up, it withered away, because it lacked moistness. **7** And some fell among thorns, and the thorns sprang up with it, and choked it. **8** And some fell on good ground, and sprang up, and bare fruit, an hundredfold. And as he said these things, he cried, He that hath ears to hear, let him hear. **9** Then his disciples asked him, demanding what parable that was. **10** And he said, Unto you it is given to know the [b]secrets of the kingdom of God, but to others in parables, that when [3]they see, they should not see, and when they hear, they should not understand. **11** [4]The parable is this, The seed is the word of God. **12** And they that are beside the way, are they that hear: afterward cometh the devil, and taketh away the word out of their hearts, lest they should believe, and be saved. **13** But they that are on the stones, are they which when they have heard, receive the word with joy: but they have no roots: which for a while believe, but in the time of temptation go away. **14** And that which fell among thorns, are they which have heard, and after [c]their departure are choked with cares and with riches, and voluptuous living, and [d]bring forth no fruit. **15** But that which fell in good ground, are they which with an [e]honest and good heart hear the word, [f]and keep it, and bring forth fruit with patience. **16** [g,5]No man when he hath lighted a candle, covereth it under a vessel, neither putteth it under the bed,

---

LUKE 7

- **a.** Luke 7:1 Christ admonisheth the Jews, by setting before them the example of the Centurion, that for their obstinacy and rebellion, he will go to the Gentiles.
- **b.** Luke 7:11 Christ avoucheth openly his power over death.
- **c.** Luke 7:11 Nain is the name of a town in Galilee, which was situated on the other side of Kishon, which falleth into the sea of Galilee.
- **d.** Luke 7:18 John sendeth from the prison his unbelieving disciples, to Christ himself, to be confirmed.
- **e.** Luke 7:21 When John's disciples came to Christ.
- **f.** Luke 7:24 That which the Prophets showed long before, John showeth at hand: and Christ himself doth present it daily unto us, in the Gospel, but for the most part in vain, for that many seek nothing else, but foolish toys and vain glory.
- **g.** Luke 7:29 Said that he was just, good, faithful, and merciful.
- **h.** Luke 7:30 To their own hurt.
- **i.** Luke 7:31 What way soever God followeth in offering us the Gospel, the most part of men procure offences unto themselves: yet notwithstanding some Church is gathered together.
- **j.** Luke 7:36 Proud men deprive themselves of the benefits of the presence of Christ, even then when he is at home with them in their houses; which the humble and base do enjoy.
- **k.** Luke 7:39 Rashness is the fellow of pride.
- **l.** Luke 7:39 The Pharisee respecteth the Law, which holdeth them defiled, that touch the defiled.
- **m.** Luke 7:40 To love Christ, is a sure and perpetual witness of remission of sins.
- **n.** Luke 7:47 That is, saith Theophylact, she hath showeth her faith abundantly: and Basil in his sermon of Baptism saith, He that oweth much, hath much forgiven him, that he may love much more: And therefore Christ's saying is so plain by the similitude , that it is a wonder to see the enemies of the truth draw and rack this place so soundly to establish their meritorious works: for the greater sum a man hath forgiven him, the more he loveth him that hath been so gracious to him: And this woman showeth by duties of love, how great the benefit was she had received: and therefore the charity that is here spoken of, is not to be taken for the cause, but as a sign: for Christ saith not as the Pharisees did, that she was a sinner, but beareth her witness that the sins of her life past are forgiven her.
- **o.** Luke 7:50 He confirmeth the benefit which he had bestowed with a blessing.

LUKE 7

1. Matt. 8:5
2. Matt. 3:1
3. Matt. 11:16
4. Mark 15:42 / John 20:11

LUKE 8

- **a.** Luke 8:4 The selfsame Gospel is sown everywhere, but not with like fruit, and that through the only fault of men themselves.
- **b.** Luke 8:10 Those things are called secret, which may not be uttered: for the word used here, is as much as we say in our tongue, to hold a man's peace.
- **c.** Luke 8:14 That is, so soon as they have heard the word, they go about their business.
- **d.** Luke 8:14 They bring not forth perfect and full fruit to the ripening: or, they begin, but they bring not to an end.
- **e.** Luke 8:15 Which seeketh not only to seem such a one, but is so indeed: so that this word, Honest, respecteth the outward life, and the word, good, is referred to the good gifts of the mind.
- **f.** Luke 8:15 With much ado: for the devil and the flesh fight against the spirit of God, which is a new guest.
- **g.** Luke 8:16 That that every man hath received in private, he ought to bestow to the use and profit of all men.

but setteth it on a candlestick, that they that enter in, may see the light. **17** [6]For nothing is secret, that shall not be evident: neither anything hid, that shall not be known, and come to light. **18** [h]Take [i]heed therefore how ye hear: for [7]whosoever hath, to him shall be given: and whosoever hath not, from him shall be taken even that [j]which it seemeth that he hath. **19** [k,8]Then came to him his mother and his brethren, and could not come near to him for the press. **20** And it was told him by certain which said, Thy mother and thy brethren stand without, and would see thee. **21** But he answered, and said unto them, My mother and my brethren are these which hear the word of God, and do it. **22** [l,9]And it came to pass on a certain day, that he went into a ship with his disciples, and he said unto them, Let us go over unto the other side of the lake. And they launched forth. **23** And as they sailed, he fell [m]asleep, and there came down a storm of wind on the lake, and [n]they were filled with water, and were in jeopardy. **24** Then they went to him, and awoke him, saying, Master, Master, we perish. And he arose, and rebuked the wind, and the waves of water: and they ceased, and it was calm. **25** Then he said unto them, Where is your faith? and they feared, and wondered among themselves, saying, Who is this that commandeth both the winds and water, and they obey him! **26** [10]So they sailed unto the region of the Gadarenes, which is over against Galilee. **27** [o]And as he went out to land, there met him a certain man out of the city, which had devils long time, and he wore no garment, neither abode in house, but in the graves. **28** And when he saw Jesus, he cried out, and fell down before him, and with a loud voice said, What have I to do with thee, Jesus the son of God the most High? I beseech thee torment me not. **29** For he commanded the foul spirit to come out of the man: (for oft times he had caught him: therefore he was bound with chains, and kept in fetters: but he brake the bands, [p]and was carried of the devil into wildernesses.) **30** Then Jesus asked him, saying, What is thy name? and he said, Legion, because many devils were entered into him. **31** And they besought him, that he would not command them to go out into the deep. **32** And there was thereby an herd of many swine feeding on an hill: and the devils besought him, that he would suffer them to enter into them. So he suffered them. **33** Then went the devils out of the man, and entered into the swine: and the herd was carried with violence from a steep down place into the lake, and was choked. **34** When the herdsmen saw what was done, they fled: and when they were departed, they told it in the city and in the country. **35** Then they came out to see what was done, and came to Jesus, and found the man, out of whom the devils were departed, sitting at the feet of Jesus, clothed, and in his right mind: and they were afraid. **36** They also which saw it, told them by what means he that was possessed with the devil, was healed. **37** Then the whole multitude of the country about the Gadarenes, besought him that he would depart from them: for they were taken with a great fear: and he went into the ship, and returned. **38** Then the man, out of whom the devils were departed, besought him that he might be with him: but Jesus sent him away, saying, **39** Return into thine own house, and show what great things God hath done to thee. So he went his way, and preached [q]throughout all the city, what great things Jesus had done unto him. **40** And it came to pass, when Jesus was come again, that the people [r]received him: for they all waited for him. **41** [s,11]And behold, there came a man named Jairus, and he was the ruler of the Synagogue, who fell down at Jesus' feet, and besought him that he would come into his house. **42** For he had but a daughter only, about twelve years of age, and she lay a dying (and as he went, the people thronged him. **43** And a woman having an issue of blood, twelve years long, which had spent all her [t]substance upon physicians, and could not be healed of any: **44** When she came behind him, she touched the hem of his garment, and immediately her issue of blood stanched. **45** Then Jesus said, Who is it that hath touched me? When every man denied, Peter said and they that were with him, Master, the multitude thrust thee, and tread on thee, and sayest thou, Who hath touched me? **46** And Jesus said, Someone hath touched me: for I perceive that virtue is gone out of me. **47** When the woman saw that she was not hid, she came trembling, and fell down before him, and told him before all the people: for what cause she had touched him, and how she was healed immediately. **48** And he said unto her, Daughter, be of good comfort: thy faith hath saved thee: go in peace.) **49** While he yet spake, there came one from the ruler of the Synagogue's house, which said to him, Thy daughter is dead: disease not the Master. **50** When Jesus heard it, he answered him, saying, Fear not: believe only, and she shall be saved. **51** And when he went into the house, he suffered no man to go in with him, save Peter, and James, and John, and the father and mother of the maid. **52** And all wept, and [u]sorrowed for her: but he said, Weep not: for she is not dead, but sleepeth. **53** And they laughed him to scorn, knowing that she was dead. **54** So he thrust them all out, and took her by the hand, and cried, saying, Maid, arise. **55** And her spirit came again, and she [v]rose straightway: and he commanded to give her meat. **56** Then her parents were astonied: but he commanded them that they should tell no man what was done.

9

1 The Apostles are sent to preach. 7 and 19 The common people's opinion of Christ. 12 Of the five loaves and two fishes. 20 The Apostle's confession. 24 To lose the life. 35 We must hear Christ. 39 The possessed of a spirit. 46 Strife among the Apostles for the Primacy. 49 One casting out devils in Christ's Name. 52 The Samaritans will not receive Christ. 55 Revenge forbidden. 57, 59, 61 Of three that would follow Christ, but on divers conditions.

1 Then [a,1]called he his twelve disciples together, and gave them power and authority over all devils, and to heal diseases. **2** [2]And he sent them forth to preach the kingdom of God, and to cure the sick. **3** And he said to them, [3]Take nothing to your journey, neither staves, nor scrip, neither bread, nor silver, neither have two coats apiece. **4** And whatsoever house ye enter into, there [b]abide, and thence depart. **5** And how many soever will not receive you, when ye go out of that city, [4]shake off the very dust from your feet for a testimony against them. **6** And they went out, and went through every town preaching the Gospel, and healing everywhere. **7** [c,5]Now Herod the Tetrarch heard of all that was done by him: and he [d]doubted, because that it was said of some, that John was risen again from the dead: **8** And of some, that Elijah had appeared: and of some, that one of the old Prophets was risen again. **9** Then Herod said, John have I beheaded: who then is this of whom I hear such things? and he desired to see him. **10** [e,6]And when the Apostles returned, they told him what great things they had done. [7]Then he took them to him, and went aside into a [f]solitary place, near to the city called Bethsaida. **11** But when the people knew it, they followed him: and he received them, and spake unto them of the kingdom of God, and healed them that had need to be healed. **12** [8]And when the day began to wear away, the twelve came, and said unto him, Send the people away, that they may go into the towns and villages round about, and lodge, and get meat: for we are here in a desert place. **13** But he said unto them, Give ye them to eat. And they said, We have no more but five loaves and two fishes, [g]except we should go and buy meat for all this people. **14** For they were about five thousand men. Then he said to his disciples, Cause them to sit down by fifties in a company. **15** And they did so, and caused all to sit down. **16** Then he took the five loaves, and the two fishes, and looked up to heaven, and [h]blessed them, and brake, and gave to the disciples, to set before the people. **17** So they did all eat, and were satisfied: and there was taken up of that remained to them, twelve baskets full of broken meat. **18** [i,9]And it came to pass, as he was [j]alone praying, his disciples were with

---

h. Luke 8:18 Heavenly gifts are lost with niggardliness, and increase with liberality.
i. Luke 8:18 That is, with what minds you come to hear the word, and how you behave yourselves when you have heard it.
j. Luke 8:18 Either to himself, or to others, or to both: for there are none so proud, as these fellows, if it were possible to see that, that they cloke: neither are there that deceive the simple more than they do.
k. Luke 8:19 There is no knot of flesh and blood, among men so nigh and strait, as the band which is between Christ, and them who embrace him with a true faith.
l. Luke 8:22 It is expedient for us sometimes to come into extreme danger, as though Christ passed not for us, that we may have a better trial, both of his power, and also of our weakness.
m. Luke 8:23 Jesus fell on sleep: and it appeareth, that he was very fast on sleep, because they called twice before he awoke.
n. Luke 8:23 Not the disciples, but the ship.
o. Luke 8:27 Christ showeth, by casting out a Legion of devils by his word only, that his heavenly virtue was appointed to deliver men from the slavery of the devil: but foolish men will not for the most part redeem this so excellent grace freely offered unto them, with the least loss of their pelting pelf.
p. Luke 8:29 By force and violence, as a horse when he is spurred.
q. Luke 8:39 To wit, the city of the Gadarenes: and though Mark says that he preached it in Decapolis, they differ not, for Pliny recordeth, lib. 5, chap. 18, that Gadara is a town of Decapolis, so that Decapolis was partly on this side Jordan, and partly on the other side.
r. Luke 8:40 The multitude was glad he was come again, and rejoiced greatly.
s. Luke 8:41 Christ showeth by a double miracle, that he is Lord both of life and death.
t. Luke 8:43 All that she had to live upon.
u. Luke 8:52 The word signifieth to beat and strike, and is transferred to the mournings and lamentations, that are at burials, at which times men use such kind of behavior.
v. Luke 8:55 The corpse was laid out, and the wench received life, and rose out of the bed, that all the world might see, she was not only restored to life, but also void of all sickness.

LUKE 8

1. Mark 16:9
2. Matt. 13:3 / Mark 4:1
3. Isa. 6:9 / Matt. 13:14 / Mark 4:12 / John 12:40 / Acts 28:26 / Rom. 11:8
4. Matt. 13:8 / Mark 4:15
5. Luke 12:33 / Matt. 5:15 / Mark 4:21
6. Matt. 10:26 / Mark 4:22 / Luke 12:2
7. Matt. 13:12 / Matt. 25:29 / Mark 4:25 / Luke 19:26
8. Matt. 12:46 / Mark 3:32
9. Matt. 8:23 / Mark 4:36
10. Matt. 8:28 / Mark 5:1
11. Matt. 9:18 / Mark 5:22

LUKE 9

a. Luke 9:1 The twelve Apostles are sent forth at the only commandment of Christ, and furnished with the power of the holy Ghost: both that none of the Israelites might pretend ignorance, and also that they might be better prepared to their general ambassy.
b. Luke 9:4 When you depart out of any city, depart from thence where you first took up your lodging: so that in few words, the Lord forbiddeth them to change their lodgings: for this publishing of the Gospel, was as it were a thorough passage, that none of Judea might pretend ignorance, as though he had not heard that Christ was come.
c. Luke 9:7 So soon as the world heareth tidings of the Gospel, it is divided into divers opinions, and the tyrants especially are afraid.
d. Luke 9:7 He stuck as it were fast in the mire.
e. Luke 9:10 They shall lack nothing that follow Christ, no not in the wilderness.
f. Luke 9:10 The word signifieth a desert: note this was not in the town Bethsaida, but part of the fields belonging to the town.
g. Luke 9:13 This is unperfectly spoken, and therefore we must understand something, as this, we cannot give them to eat, unless we go and buy, etc.
h. Luke 9:16 He gave God thanks for these loaves and fishes, and withall prayed him to feed this so great a multitude with so small a quantity, and to be short, that this whole banquet might be to the glory of God.
i. Luke 9:18 Although the world be tossed up and down, betwixt divers errors, yet we ought not to contemn the truth, but be so much the more desirous to know it, and be more constant to confess it.
j. Luke 9:18 Alone from the people.

him: and he asked them, saying, Whom say the people that I am? **19** They an-
swered, and said, John Baptist: and others say, Elijah: and some say, that one of
the old Prophets is risen again. **20** And he said unto them, But whom say ye
that I am? Peter answered, and said: That Christ of God. **21** And he warned and
commanded them, that they should tell that to no man, **22** [k]Saying, [10]The Son
of man must suffer many things, and be reproved of the Elders, and of the high
Priests and Scribes, and be slain, and the third day rise again. **23** [11]And he said
to them all, If any man will come after me, let him deny himself, and take up his
cross [l]daily, and follow me. **24** [12]For whosoever will save his life, shall lose it: and
whosoever shall lose his life for my sake, the same shall save it. **25** [13]For what
advantageth it a man, if he win the whole world, and destroy himself, or lose him-
self? **26** [14]For whosoever shall be ashamed of me, and of my words, of him shall
the Son of man be ashamed, when he shall come in his glory, and in the glory of
the Father, and of the holy Angels. **27** [15]And I tell you of a surety, there be some
standing here, which shall not taste of death, till they have seen the kingdom of
God. **28** [m,16]And it came to pass about an eight days after those words, that he
took Peter and John, and James, and went up into a mountain to pray. **29** And
as he prayed, the fashion of his countenance was changed, and his garment was
white and glistered. **30** And behold, two men talked with him, which were Mo-
ses and Elijah: **31** Which appeared in glory, and told of his [n]departing, which
he should accomplish at Jerusalem. **32** But Peter and they that were with him,
were heavy with sleep, and when they awoke, they saw his glory, and the two men
standing with him. **33** And it came to pass, as they departed from him, Peter
said unto Jesus, Master, it is good for us to be here: let us therefore make three ta-
bernacles, one for thee, and one for Moses, and one for Elijah, and wist not what
he said. **34** While he thus spake, there came a cloud and overshadowed them,
and they feared when they were entering into the cloud. **35** [17]And there came
a voice out of the cloud, saying, This is that my beloved Son, hear him. **36** And
when the voice was past, Jesus was found alone: and they kept it close, and told no
man in [o]those days any of those things which they had seen. **37** [p]And it came
to pass on the next day, as they came down from the mountain, much people met
him. **38** [18]And behold, a man of the company cried out, saying, Master, I bese-
ech thee, behold my son: for he is all that I have. **39** And lo, a spirit taketh him,
and suddenly he crieth, and he teareth him, that he foameth, and hardly departeth
from him, when he hath [q]bruised him. **40** Now I have besought thy disciples
to cast him out, but they could not. **41** Then Jesus answered and said, O gene-
ration faithless, and crooked, how long now shall I be with you, and suffer you?
bring thy son hither. **42** And while he was yet coming, the devil rent him, and
tore him: and Jesus rebuked the unclean spirit, and healed the child, and delivered
him to his father. **43** [r]And they were all amazed at the mighty power of God:
and while they all wondered at all things which Jesus did, he said unto his disci-
ples, **44** [s]Mark these words diligently: [19]for it shall come to pass, that the son
of man shall be delivered into the hands of men. **45** But they understood not
that word: for it was hid from them, so that they could not perceive it: and they
feared to ask him of that word. **46** [t,20]Then there arose a disputation among
them, which of them should be the greatest. **47** When Jesus saw the thoughts of
their hearts, he took a little child, and set him by him, **48** And said unto them,
Whosoever receiveth this little child in my Name, receiveth me: and whosoever
shall receive me, receiveth him that sent me: for he that is least among you all, he
shall be great. **49** [u,21]And John answered and said, Master, we saw one casting
out devils in thy Name, and we forbad him, because he followeth thee not with
us. **50** Then Jesus said unto him, Forbid ye him not: for he that is not against
us, is with us. **51** [v]And it came to pass, when the days were accomplished, that
he should be received up, he [w]settled himself fully to go to Jerusalem, **52** And
sent messengers before him: and they went and entered into a town of the Sa-
maritans, to prepare him lodging. **53** But they would not receive him, because
his behavior was as though he would go to Jerusalem. **54** [x]And when his disci-
ples, James and John saw it, they said, Lord, wilt thou that we command, that
fire come down from heaven, and consume them, even as [22]Elijah did? **55** But
Jesus turned about, and rebuked them, and said, Ye know not of what [y]spirit ye
are. **56** For the Son of man is not come to destroy men's lives, but to save them.
Then they went to another town. **57** [z]And it came to pass that as they went in
the way, [23]a certain man said unto him, I will follow thee, Lord, whithersoever
thou goest. **58** And Jesus said unto him, The foxes have holes, and the birds of
the heaven nests, but the Son of man hath not whereon to lay his head. **59** [aa]
But he said unto another, Follow me. And the same said, Lord, suffer me first to
go and bury my father. **60** And Jesus said unto him, Let the dead bury [ab]their
dead: but go thou, and preach the kingdom of God. **61** [ac]Then another said, I
will follow thee, Lord: but let me first go bid them farewell, which are at mine hou-
se. **62** And Jesus said unto him, No man that putteth his hand to the plough,
and looketh back, is apt to the kingdom of God.

10

1 The seventy disciples. 10 The unthankful cities charged with impiety. 17 The disciples returning home, are warned to be humble. 29, 30 Who is our neighbor. 38 Of Martha and her sister Mary.

1 After [a,1]these things, the Lord appointed other seventy also, and sent them,
two and two before him into every city and place, whither he himself should
come. **2** And he said unto them, [2]The harvest is great, but the laborers are few:
pray therefore the Lord of the harvest to send forth laborers into his harvest. **3** [b,3]
Go your ways: behold, I send you forth as lambs among wolves. **4** Bear no bag,
neither scrip, nor shoes, and [4]salute [c]no man by the way. **5** [5]And into whatso-
ever house ye enter, first say, Peace be to this house. **6** And if [d]the son of peace
be there, your peace shall rest upon him, if not, it shall turn to you again. **7** And
in that house [e]tarry still, eating and drinking such things as by them shall be set
before you: [6]for the laborer is worthy of his wages. Go not from house to hou-
se. **8** [7]But into whatsoever city ye shall enter, if they receive you, [f]eat such thin-
gs as are set before you, **9** And heal the sick that are there, and say unto them,
The kingdom of God is come near unto you. **10** [g]But into whatsoever city ye
shall enter, if they will not receive you, go your ways out into the streets of the
same, and say, **11** Even the very [8]dust, which cleaveth on us of your city, we
wipe off against you: notwithstanding know this, that the kingdom of God was
come near unto you. **12** For I say to you, that it shall be easier in that day for
them of Sodom, than for that city. **13** [9]Woe be to thee, Chorazin: woe be to
thee, Bethsaida: for if the miracles had been done in Tyre and Sidon, which have
been done in you, they had a great while agone repented, sitting in sackcloth and
ashes. **14** Therefore it shall be easier for Tyre, and Sidon, at the judgment, than
for you. **15** And thou, Capernaum, which art exalted to heaven, shalt be thrust
down to hell. **16** [10]He that heareth you, heareth me: and he that despiseth you,
despiseth me: and he that despiseth me, despiseth him that sent me. **17** [h]And
the seventy turned again with joy, saying, Lord, even the devils are subdued to
us [i]through thy Name. **18** And he said unto them, I saw Satan, like lightning,

---

k. Luke 9:22 Christ himself attained to the heavenly glory by the cross and invincible patience.
l. Luke 9:23 Even as one day followeth another, so doth one cross follow another, and the cross is by the figure Metonymy, taken for the miseries of this life: for to be hanged, was the sorest and cruelest punishment that was amongst the Jews.
m. Luke 9:28 Lest the disciples of Christ should be offended at the debasing himself in his flesh, he teacheth them that it is voluntary, showing therewithall for a space the brightness of his glory.
n. Luke 9:31 What death he should die in Jerusalem.
o. Luke 9:36 Until Christ was risen again from the dead.
p. Luke 9:37 Christ is offended with nothing so much as with incredulity, although he bears with it for a time.
q. Luke 9:39 As it fareth in the falling sickness.
r. Luke 9:43 We have no cause to promise ourselves rest and quietness in this world, seeing that they themselves which seemed to fawn upon Christ, do shortly after crucify him.
s. Luke 9:44 Give diligent ear unto them, and when you have once heard them, see that you keep them.
t. Luke 9:46 The end of ambition is ignomy; but the end of modest obedience is glory.
u. Luke 9:49 Extraordinary things are neither rashly to be allowed, nor condemned.
v. Luke 9:51 Christ goeth willingly to death.
w. Luke 9:51 Word for word: he hardened his face, that is, he resolved with himself to die, and therefore ventured upon his journey, and cast away all fear of death, and went on.
x. Luke 9:54 We must take heed of the immoderateness of zeal, and fond imitation, even in good causes, that whatsoever we do, we do it to God's glory, and the profit of our neighbor.
y. Luke 9:55 So speak the Hebrews, that is, you know not what will, mind, and counsel you are of: so the gifts of God are called the spirit, because they are given of God's Spirit, and so are they, that are contrary to them, which proceed of the wicked spirit, as the spirit of covetousness, of pride, and madness.
z. Luke 9:57 Such as follow Christ, must prepare themselves, to suffer all discommodities.
aa. Luke 9:59 The calling of God ought to be preferred, without all controversy before all duties that we owe to men.
ab. Luke 9:60 Who notwithstanding that they live in this frail life of man, yet are strangers from the true life, which is everlasting and heavenly.
ac. Luke 9:61 Such as follow Christ, must at once renounce all worldly cares.

LUKE 9

1. Matt. 10:1 / Mark 3:13 / Mark 6:7
2. Matt. 10:7
3. Matt. 10:9 / Mark 6:8
4. Luke 10:11 / Matt. 10:14 / Mark 6:11 / Acts 13:51
5. Matt. 14:1 / Mark 6:14
6. Mark 6:30
7. Matt. 14:13 / Mark 6:32
8. Matt. 14:15 / Mark 6:35 / John 6:5
9. Matt. 16:13 / Mark 8:27
10. Matt. 17:22 / Mark 8:31
11. Luke 14:27 / Matt. 10:38 / Matt. 16:24 / Mark 8:34
12. Luke 17:33 / Matt. 16:39 / Matt. 16:25 / John 12:25
13. Matt. 16:26 / Mark 8:36
14. Luke 12:9 / Matt. 10:33 / Mark 8:38 / 2 Tim. 2:12
15. Matt. 16:28 / Mark 9:1
16. Matt. 17:2 / Mark 9:2
17. 2 Pet. 1:17
18. Matt. 17:14 / Mark 9:17
19. Matt. 17:22 / Mark 9:31
20. Matt. 18:1 / Mark 9:35
21. Mark 9:38
22. 2 Kings 1:10 / 2 Kings 12:13
23. Matt. 8:19

LUKE 10

a. Luke 10:1 The seventy are sent as the second forewarners, of the coming of Christ.
b. Luke 10:3 The faithful ministers of the word are in this world as lambs among wolves: but if they be diligent to do their duty, he that sent them will also preserve them.
c. Luke 10:4 This is spoken after the manner of a figure, which men use, when they put down more in words, than is meant: usually among the Hebrews, when they command a thing to be done speedily without delay, as 2 Kings 4:29: for otherwise courteous and gentle salutations, are points of Christian duty: as for the calling it was but for a season.
d. Luke 10:6 So speak the Hebrews: that is, he that favoreth the doctrine of peace and embraceth it.
e. Luke 10:7 Take up your lodging in that house, which ye first enter into, that is, be not careful for commodious lodging, as men do which purpose to stay long in a place: for here is not instituted that solemn preaching of the Gospel, which was used afterward ,when the Churches were settled: but these are sent abroad to all the coasts of Judea, to give them to understand, that the last Jubilee is at hand.
f. Luke 10:8 Content yourselves with that meat that is set before you.
g. Luke 10:10 God is a most severe revenger of the ministry of his Gospel.
h. Luke 10:17 Neither the gift of miracles, neither what else soever excellent gift, but only our election giveth us occasion of true joy: and the only publishing of the Gospel is the destruction of Satan.
i. Luke 10:17 For Christ's disciples used no absolute authority, but wrought such miracles as they did, by calling upon Christ's Name.
j. Luke 10:18 Paul placeth the devil and his angels, in the air, Eph. 6:12, and he is said to be cast down from thence by force when his power is abolished by the voice of the Gospel.
k. Luke 10:19 Shall do you wrong.

[j]fall down from heaven. **19** Behold, I give unto you power to tread on Serpen-
ts, and Scorpions, and over all the power of the enemy, and nothing shall [k]hurt
you. **20** Nevertheless, in this rejoice not, that the spirits are subdued unto you:
but rather rejoice, because your names are written in heaven. **21** [l]That same hour
rejoiced Jesus in the spirit, and said, I confess unto thee, Father, Lord of heaven
and earth, that thou hast hid these things from the [m]wise and understanding, and
hast revealed them to babes: even so, Father, because it so pleased thee. [n] **22** [o]All
things are given me of my Father: and no man knoweth who the son is, but the
Father: neither who the Father is, save the Son, and he to whom the Son will re-
veal him. **23** [p]And he turned to his disciples, and said secretly, [11]Blessed are
the eyes, which see that ye see. **24** For I tell you that many Prophets and Kin-
gs have desired to see those things, which ye see, and have not seen them: and to
hear those things which ye hear, and have not heard them. **25** [q,12]Then behold,
[r]a certain Lawyer stood up, and tempted him, saying, Master, what shall I do to
inherit eternal life? **26** And he said unto him, What is written in the Law? how
readest thou? **27** And he answered and said, [13]Thou shalt love thy Lord God
with all thine heart, and with all thy soul, and with all thy strength, and with all
thy thought, [14]and thy neighbor as thyself. **28** Then he said unto him, Thou hast
answered right: this do, and thou shalt live. **29** [s]But he willing to [t]justify himself,
said unto Jesus, Who is then my neighbor? **30** And Jesus answered, and said, A
certain man went down from Jerusalem to Jericho, and fell among thieves, and
they robbed him of his raiment, and wounded him, and departed, leaving him half
dead. **31** Now so it fell out, that there came down a certain Priest that same way,
and when he saw him, he passed by on the other side. **32** And likewise also a Le-
vite, when he was come near to the place, went and looked on him, and passed by
on the other side. **33** Then a certain Samaritan, as he journeyed, came near unto
him, and when he saw him, he had compassion on him, **34** And went to him,
and bound up his wounds and poured in oil and wine, and put him on his own
beast, and brought him to an Inn, and made provision for him. **35** And on the
morrow when he departed, he took out two pence, and gave them to the host, and
said unto him, Take care of him, and whatsoever thou spendest more, when I come
again, I will recompense thee. **36** Which now of these three, thinkest thou, was
neighbor unto him that fell among the thieves? **37** And he said, He that showed
mercy on him. Then said Jesus unto him, Go, and do thou likewise. **38** [u]Now it
came to pass, as they went, that he entered into a certain town, and a certain wo-
man named Martha, received him into her house. **39** And she had a sister cal-
led Mary, which also sat at Jesus' feet, and heard his preaching. **40** But Martha
was cumbered about much serving, and came to him, and said, Master, dost thou
not care that my sister hath left me to serve alone? bid her therefore, that she help
me. **41** And Jesus answered, and said unto her, Martha, Martha, thou carest, and
art troubled about many things: **42** But one thing is needful, Mary hath chosen
the good part, which shall not be taken away from her.

11

1 He teacheth his Apostles to pray. 14 The dumb devil driven out. 27 A woman of the company lifted up her voice. 29 The Jews require signs. 37 He being feasted of the Pharisee, reproveth the outward show of holiness.

1 And so it was, that as he was praying in a certain place, when he ceased,
one of his disciples said unto him, Lord, teach us to pray, as John also taught his
disciples. **2** [1]And he said unto them, When ye pray, say, [a]Our Father which art
in heaven, hallowed be thy Name. Thy kingdom come: Let thy will be done, even
in earth, as it is in heaven: **3** Our daily bread give us [b]for the day: **4** And for-
give us our sins: for even we forgive every man that is indebted to us: And lead us
not into temptation: but deliver us from evil. **5** [c]Moreover he said unto them,
Which of you shall have a friend, and shall go to him at midnight, and say unto
him, Friend, lend me three loaves? **6** For a friend of mine is come out of the way
to me, and I have nothing to set before him: **7** And he within should answer,
and say, Trouble me not: the door is now shut, and my children are with me in
bed: I cannot rise and give them to thee. **8** I say unto you, Though he would
not arise and give him, because he is his friend, yet doubtless because of his [d]im-
portunity, he would rise and give him as many as he needed. **9** [2]And I say unto
you, Ask, and it shall be given you: seek, and ye shall find: knock, and it shall be
opened unto you. **10** [3]For everyone that asketh, receiveth: and he that seeketh,
findeth: and to him that knocketh, it shall be opened. **11** [4]If a son shall ask
bread of any of you that is a father, will he give him a stone? or if he ask a fish,
will he for a fish give him a serpent? **12** Or if he ask an egg, will he give him a
scorpion? **13** If ye then which are evil, can give good gifts unto your children,
how much more shall your heavenly Father give the holy Ghost to them that desi-
re him? **14** [5]Then he cast out a devil which was dumb: and when the devil was
gone out, the dumb spake, and the people wondered. **15** [e]But some of them
said, [6]He casteth out devils through Beelzebub the chief of the devils. **16** And
others tempted him, seeking of him a sign from heaven. **17** [f]But he knew their
thoughts, and said unto them, [7]Every kingdom divided against itself, shall be de-
solate, and an house divided against an house, falleth. **18** So if Satan also be di-
vided against himself, how shall his kingdom stand, because ye say that I cast out
devils [g]through Beelzebub? **19** If I through Beelzebub cast out devils, by whom
do your children cast them out? Therefore shall they be your judges. **20** But if I
by the [h]finger of God cast out devils, doubtless the kingdom of God is come unto
you. **21** When a strong man armed keepeth his [i]palace, the things that he pos-
sesseth, are in peace. **22** But when a stronger than he cometh upon him, and
overcometh him: he taketh from him all his armor wherein he trusted, and divi-
deth his spoils. **23** [j]He that is not with me, is against me: and he that gathereth
not with me, scattereth. **24** [k,8]When the unclean spirit is gone out of a man, he
walketh through dry places, seeking rest: and when he findeth none, he saith, I will
return unto mine house whence I came out. **25** And when he cometh, he fin-
deth it swept and garnished. **26** Then goeth he, and taketh to him seven other
spirits worse than himself: and they enter in, and dwell there: [9]so the last state of
that man is worse than the first. **27** [l]And it came to pass as he said these things,
a certain woman of the company lifted up her voice, and said unto him, Blessed is
the womb that bare thee, and the paps which thou hast sucked. **28** But he said,
Yea, rather blessed are they that hear the word of God, and keep it. **29** [m,10]And
when the people were gathered thick together, he began to say, This is a wicked
generation: they seek a sign, and there shall no sign be given them, but the sign
of Jonah the Prophet. **30** For as Jonah was a sign to the Ninevites: so shall also
the son of man be to this generation. **31** [12]The Queen of the South shall rise in
judgment, with the men of this generation, and shall condemn them: for she came
from the utmost parts of the earth to hear the wisdom of Solomon, and behold,
a greater than Solomon is here. **32** The men of Nineveh shall rise in judgment
with this generation, and shall condemn it: for they [13]repented at the preaching of
Jonah: and behold, a greater than Jonah is here. **33** [n,14]No man when he hath
lighted a candle, putteth it in a privy place, neither under a bushel: but on a cand-
lestick, that they which come in, may see the light. **34** [15]The light of the body is
the eye: therefore when thine eye is single, then is thy whole body light: but if thine
eye be evil, then thy body is dark. **35** Take heed therefore, that the light which
is in thee, be not darkness. **36** If therefore thy whole body shall be light, having
no part dark, then shall all be light, even as when a candle doth light thee with the
brightness. **37** [o]And as he spake, a certain Pharisee besought him to dine with
him: and he went in, and sat down at the table. **38** And when the Pharisee saw it,
he marveled that he had not first washed before dinner. **39** [16]And the Lord said
to him, Indeed ye Pharisees make clean the outside of the cup, and of the platter:
but the inward part is full of ravening and wickedness. **40** Ye fools, did not he
that made that which is without, make that which is within also? **41** Therefore,
give alms [p]of those things which you have, and behold, all things shall be clean
unto you. **42** [q]But woe be to you, Pharisees: for ye [r]tithe the mint and the rue,

---

l. Luke 10:21 The Church is contemptible, if we behold the outward face of it, but the wisdom of God is not so marvelous, in any thing, as in it.
m. Luke 10:21 Of this world.
n. Luke 10:21 Then he turned to his disciples, and said, Is read in some copies.
o. Luke 10:22 Whosoever seeketh the Father without the Son, wandereth out of the way.
p. Luke 10:23 The difference of the old Testament and the new consisteth in the measure of revelation.
q. Luke 10:25 Faith doth not take away, but establisheth the doctrine of the Law.
r. Luke 10:25 One of them that professed himself to be learned in the rites and laws of Moses.
s. Luke 10:29 All they are comprehended in the name of our neighbor, by the Law, whomsoever we may help.
t. Luke 10:29 That is, to vouch his righteousness, or show, that he was just, that is, void of all faults: and James 5:1 useth the word of justification in this sense.
u. Luke 10:38 Christ careth not to be entertained delicately, but to be heard diligently, that is it which he especially requireth.

LUKE 10
1. Matt. 10:1
2. Matt. 9:37
3. Matt. 10:16
4. 2 Kings 4:29
5. Matt. 10:12 / Mark 6:10
6. Deut. 24:14 / Matt. 10:10 / 1 Tim. 5:18
7. Matt. 10:11
8. Luke 9:5 / Acts 33:51 / Acts 18:6
9. Matt. 11:21
10. Matt. 10:40 / John 13:20
11. Matt. 13:16
12. Matt. 22:35 / Mark 12:28
13. Deut. 6:5
14. Lev. 19:18

LUKE 11
a. Luke 11:2 A form of true prayer.
b. Luke 11:3 That is, as much as is needful for us this day, whereby we are not debarred to have an honest care for the maintenance of our lives; but that carping care, which killeth a number of men, is cut off and restrained.
c. Luke 11:5 We must pray with faith.
d. Luke 11:8 Word for word, impudency: but that impudency which is spoken of here, is not to be found fault withall, but is very commendable before God, for he liketh well of such importunity.
e. Luke 11:15 An example of horrible blindness, and such as cannot be healed, when as upon an evil conscience, and pretended malice, the power of God is blasphemed.
f. Luke 11:17 The true way to know the true Christ, from the false, is this, that the true Christ hath no accord or agreement with Satan: And it remaineth that after we know him, we acknowledge him.
g. Luke 11:18 By the name and power of Beelzebub.
h. Luke 11:20 That is, by the power of God: so it is said, Exod. 8:19.
i. Luke 11:21 The word signifieth properly an open and void room before an house, and so by translation is taken for noblemen's houses.
j. Luke 11:23 Against indifferent men, and such as love to have a mean, which seek means to reconcile Christ and Satan together.
k. Luke 11:24 He that doth not continue, is in worse case, than he that never began.
l. Luke 11:27 Christ seeketh not praise in himself, but in our salvation.
m. Luke 11:29 They that are fond desireres of miracles, instead of miracles shall receive punishment.
n. Luke 11:33 Our minds are therefore lightened with the knowledge of God, that we should give light unto others, and therefore our chiefest labor ought to be to pray for that light.
o. Luke 11:37 The service of God consisteth not in outward cleanliness, and devised rites or ceremonies, but in the spiritual righteousness of the heart, and charity.
p. Luke 11:41 That is, according to your abilities as who would say, instead of your extortions, which hindered you, that you could not eat cleanly, use charity, and accordingly as your ability shall serve you, be good to the poor, and so shall that, that is within the platter, be sanctified though the platter be unwashed.
q. Luke 11:42 It is the propense of hypocrites, to stand stoutly for little trifles, and let pass greater matters.

and [s]all manner herbs, and pass over [t]judgment and the love of God: these ought
ye to have done, and not to have left the other undone. 43 [u,17]Woe be to you,
Pharisees: for ye love the uppermost seats in the Synagogues, and greetings in the
markets. 44 [v]Woe be to you, Scribes and Pharisees hypocrites: [18]for ye are as gra-
ves which appear not, and the men that walk over them, perceive not. 45 [w]Then
answered one of the Lawyers, and said unto him, Master, thus saying thou put-
test us to rebuke also. 46 And he said, Woe be to you also, ye Lawyers: [19]for
ye lade men with burdens grievous to be borne, and ye yourselves touch not the
burdens with one of your fingers. 47 [x]Woe be to you: [20]for ye build the sepul-
chers of the Prophets, and your fathers killed them. 48 Truly [y]ye bear witness,
and allow the deeds of your fathers: for they killed them, and ye build their se-
pulchers. 49 Therefore said the wisdom of God, I will send them Prophets and
Apostles, and of them they shall slay, and [z]persecute away, 50 That the blood of
all the Prophets, [aa]shed from the foundation of the world, may be required of this
generation, 51 From the blood of [21]Abel unto the blood of [22]Zechariah, which
was slain between the altar and the Temple: verily I say unto you, it shall be requi-
red of this generation. 52 [ab]Woe be to you, Lawyers: for ye have [ac]taken away
the key of knowledge: ye entered not in yourselves, and them that came in, ye for-
bade. 53 [ad]And as he said these things unto them, the Scribes and Pharisees be-
gan to urge him sore, and to [ae]provoke him to speak of many things, 54 Laying
wait for him, and seeking to catch something of his mouth, whereby they might
accuse him.

12

1 The leaven of the Pharisee. 5 Who is to be feared. 8 To confess Christ. 16 The parable of the rich man whose land was very fertile. 21 Not to care for earthly things. 31 But to seek the kindom of God. 39 The thief in the night. 51 Debate for the Gospel's sake.

1 In [a,1]the meantime, there gathered together [b]an innumerable multitu-
de of people, so that they trod one another: and he began to say unto his disci-
ples first, Take heed to yourselves of the leaven of the Pharisees, which is hypo-
crisy. 2 [2]For there is nothing covered, that shall not be revealed: neither hid,
that shall not be known. 3 Wherefore whatsoever ye have spoken in darkness,
it shall be heard in the light: and that which ye have spoken in the ear, in secret
places, shall be preached on the houses. 4 [c,3]And I say unto you, my friends,
be not afraid of them that kill the body, and after that are not able to do anymo-
re. 5 But I will [d]forewarn you, whom ye shall fear: fear him which after he hath
killed, hath power to cast into hell: yea, I say unto you, him fear. 6 Are not five
sparrows bought for two farthings, and yet not one of them is forgotten before
God? 7 [4]Yea, and all the hairs of your head are numbered: fear not therefore:
ye are more of value than many sparrows. 8 [e,5]Also I say unto you, Whosoever
shall confess me before men, him shall the Son of man confess also before the An-
gels of God. 9 But he that shall deny me before men, shall be denied before the
Angels of God. 10 [6]And whosoever shall speak a word against the Son of man,
it shall be forgiven him: but unto him that shall blaspheme the holy Ghost, it shall
not be forgiven. 11 [f,7]And when they shall bring you unto the Synagogues, and
unto the rulers and Princes, take no thought how, or what thing ye shall answer,
or what ye shall speak. 12 For the holy Ghost shall teach you in the same hour,
what ye ought to say. 13 [g]And one of the company said unto him, Master, bid
my brother divide the inheritance with me. 14 And he said unto him, Man, who
made me a judge, or a divider over you? 15 Wherefore he said unto them, Take
heed, and beware of [h]covetousness: for though a man have abundance, yet his [i]life
standeth not in his riches. 16 [j]And he put forth a parable unto them, saying, The
[k]ground of a certain rich man brought forth fruits plenteously. 17 Therefore he
[l]thought with himself, saying, What shall I do, because I have no room where I
may lay up my fruits? 18 And he said, This will I do, I will pull down my barns,
and build greater, and therein will I gather all my fruits, and my goods. 19 And
I will say to my soul, Soul, thou hast much goods laid up for many years, live at
ease, eat, drink, and [m]take thy pastime. 20 But God said unto him, O fool, this
night will they fetch away thy soul from thee: then whose shall those things be
which thou hast provided? 21 So is he that gathereth riches [n]to himself, and is
not rich in God. 22 [o]And he spake unto his disciples, Therefore I say unto you,
[8]Take no thought for your life, what ye shall eat: neither for your body, what ye
shall put on. 23 The life is more than meat: and the body more than the rai-
ment. 24 Consider the ravens: for they neither sow nor reap: which neither have
storehouse nor barn, and yet God feedeth them: how much more are ye better
than fowls? 25 And which of you with taking thought, can add to his stature one
cubit? 26 If ye then be not able to do the least thing, why take ye thought for
the remnant? 27 Consider the lilies how they grow: they labor not, neither spin
they: yet I say unto you, that Solomon himself in all his royalty was not clothed
like one of these. 28 If then God so clothe the grass which is today in the field,
and tomorrow is cast into the oven, how much more will he clothe you, O ye of
little faith? 29 Therefore ask not what ye shall eat, or what ye shall drink, neither
[p]hang you in suspense. 30 For all such things the people of the world seek for:
and your Father knoweth that ye have need of these things. 31 [q]But rather seek
ye after the kingdom of God, and all these things shall be cast upon you. 32 [r]Fe-
ar not, little flock: for it is your Father's pleasure to give you the kingdom. 33 [s,-
9]Sell that ye have, and give [t]alms: make you bags which wax not old: a treasure that
can never fail in heaven, where no thief cometh neither moth corrupteth. 34 For
where your treasure is, there will your hearts be also. 35 [u,10]Let your loins be
girded about, and your lights burning, 36 And ye yourselves like unto men that
wait for their master, when he will return from the wedding, that when he cometh
and knocketh, they may open unto him immediately. 37 Blessed are those ser-
vants, whom the Lord when he cometh shall find waking: verily I say unto you, he
will gird himself about, and make them to sit down at table, and will come forth,
and serve them. 38 And if he come in the second watch, or come in the third

---

r. Luke 11:42 You decide by God's Law that the tenth part is due to be paid.
s. Luke 11:42 Of all kind of herbs some, as Augustine expoundeth it in his Enchiridion to Laurence, chap. 99, where he showeth in like sort how that place of Paul, 1 Tim. 2:4, God will have all men to be saved, is to be expoundeth after the same manner.
t. Luke 11:42 That is to say, that that is right and reason to do: for this word, Judgment, containeth the commandments of the second table, and the other words, The love of God, contain the first.
u. Luke 11:43 Hypocrisy and ambition are commonly joined together.
v. Luke 11:44 Hypocrites deceive men with an outward show.
w. Luke 11:45 Hypocrites are very severe against other men, but think all things lawful to themselves.
x. Luke 11:47 Hypocrites honor those saints when they are dead, whom they most cruelly persecute, when they were alive.
y. Luke 11:48 When you persecute God's servants, like mad men, even as your fathers did, though you color it with a pretence of godliness, yet notwithstanding, in that you beautify the sepulchers of the Prophets, what do you else, but glory in your fathers' cruelty, and set up monuments (as it were) in glory and triumph of it?
z. Luke 11:49 They shall so vex them and trouble them, that at length they shall banish them.
aa. Luke 11:50 That you may be called to an account for it, yea, and be punished, for the shedding of that blood of the Prophet.
ab. Luke 11:52 They have of long time chiefly hindered the people, from entering into the knowledge of God, which ought to be the doorkeepers of the Church.
ac. Luke 11:52 You have hidden and taken away, so that it cannot be found anywhere.
ad. Luke 11:53 The more the world is reprehended, the worse it is, and yet must we not betray the truth.
ae. Luke 11:53 They proposed many questions to him, to draw something out of his mouth, which they might traitorously carp at.

LUKE 11

1. Matt. 6:9
2. Matt. 7:7 / Matt. 21:22 / Mark 11:24 / John 14:13 / John 16:23 / James 1:5
3. Matt. 7:8
4. Matt. 7:9
5. Matt. 9:32 / Matt. 12:22
6. Matt. 9:34 / Matt. 12:24 / Mark 3:22
7. Matt. 12:25 / Mark 3:24
8. Matt. 12:43
9. Heb. 6:4 / 2 Pet. 2:20
10. Matt. 12:38-39
11. Jonah 1:12
12. 1 Kings 10:1 / 2 Chron. 9:1
13. Jonah 3:5
14. Luke 8:16 / Matt. 5:15 / Mark 4:21
15. Matt. 6:22
16. Matt. 23:25
17. Luke 20:26 / Matt. 23:6 / Mark 12:38-39
18. Matt. 23:27
19. Matt. 23:4 / Acts 15:10
20. Matt. 23:29
21. Gen. 4:8
22. 2 Chron. 24:21

LUKE 12

a. Luke 12:1 The faithful teachers of God's word, which are appointed by him for his people, must both take good heed of them, which corrupt the purity of doctrine with goodly glosses, and also take pains through the help of Christ, to set forth sincere doctrine, openly and without fear.
b. Luke 12:1 Word for word, ten thousands of people, a certain number for an uncertain.
c. Luke 12:4 Although hypocrites have princes to execute their cruelty, yet there is no cause why we could be afraid of them, the least iota that may be, seeing they can do nothing, but what pleaseth God, and God wills not anything that may be against the salvation of his elect.
d. Luke 12:5 He warneth them of dangers that presently hang over their heads, for those that come upon the sudden, do make the greater wound.
e. Luke 12:8 Great is the reward of a constant confession: and horrible is the punishment of the denying of Christ, yea impossible to be called back again shall the punishment be, if upon set purpose, both with mouth and heart we blaspheme a known truth.
f. Luke 12:11 It is a great and hard conflict to confess the truth, yet he that can do all things, and is almighty, will not be wanting to the weakest which strive and contend in his appointed time.
g. Luke 12:13 Christ would not for three causes be a judge to divide an inheritance. First, for that he would not foster up and cherish the fleshly opinion that the Jews had of Messiah: Secondly for that he would distinguish the civil governance, from the Ecclesiastical: Thirdly, to teach us to beware of them which abuse the show of the gospel, and also the name of ministers, to their own private commodities.
h. Luke 12:15 By covetousness is meant, that greedy desire to get, commonly with other men's hurt.
i. Luke 12:15 God is the author and preserver of man's life; goods are not.
j. Luke 12:16 There are none more mad, than rich men which hang upon their riches.
k. Luke 12:16 Or rather country, for here is set forth a man that possesseth not a piece of ground only, but an whole country, as they do, which join house to house, and field to field, Isa. 5:8.
l. Luke 12:17 Made his reckoning within himself, which is the property of covetous churls that spend their life in those trifles.
m. Luke 12:19 Be merry and make good cheer.
n. Luke 12:21 Caring for no man but for himself, and minding to trust in himself.
o. Luke 12:22 An earnest thinking upon the providence of God, is a present remedy against the most foolish and pining carefulness of men for this life.
p. Luke 12:29 A Metaphor taken of things that hang in the air, for they that are careful for this worldly life, and hang upon the arm of man, have always wavering and doubtful minds, swaying sometimes this way, and sometimes that way.
q. Luke 12:31 They shall lack nothing, which are careful for the kingdom of heaven.
r. Luke 12:32 It is a foolish thing not to look for small things, at his hands, which giveth us freely the greatest things.
s. Luke 12:33 A godly bountifulness is a ready way to get true riches.
t. Luke 12:33 This is the figure Metonymy, for by this word, Alms, is meant that compassion and friendliness of an heart that tendereth the misery and poor estate of man, and showeth forth itself by some gift, and hath the name given it in the Greek tongue, of mercy and compassion: and therefore he is said to give alms, who parteth with some thing to another, and giveth to the poor, showing thereby, that he pitieth their poor estate.
u. Luke 12:35 The life of the faithful servants of God, in this world is a certain watchful peregrination, having the light of the word going before it.

watch, and shall find them so, blessed are those servants. **39** [11]Now understand
this, that if the good man of the house had known at what hour the thief would
have come, he would have watched, and would not have suffered his house to be
dug through. **40** [v]Be ye also prepared therefore: for the Son of man will come at
an hour when ye think not. **41** Then Peter said unto him, Master, tellest thou
this parable unto us, or even to all? **42** And the Lord said, Who is a faithful
steward and wise, whom the master shall make ruler over his household, to give
them their [w]portion of meat in season? **43** Blessed is that servant, whom his ma-
ster when he cometh, shall find so doing. **44** Of a truth, I say unto you, that he
will make him ruler over all that he hath. **45** But if that servant say in his heart,
My master doth defer his coming, and shall begin to smite the servants, and mai-
dens, and to eat and drink, and to be drunken, **46** The master of that servant
will come in a day when he thinketh not, and at an hour when he is not aware
of, and will cut him off, and give him his portion with the unbelievers. **47** And
that servant that knew his master's will, and prepared not himself, neither did ac-
cording to his will, shall be beaten with many stripes. **48** But he that knew it
not, and yet did commit things worthy of stripes, shall be beaten with few stri-
pes: for unto whomsoever much is given, of him shall be much required, and to
whom men much commit, [x]the more of him will they ask. **49** [y]I am come to
put fire on the earth, and what is my desire, if it be already kindled? **50** Notwi-
thstanding I must be baptized with a baptism, and how am I grieved till it be en-
ded? **51** [12]Think ye that I am come to give peace on earth? I tell you, nay, but
rather debate. **52** For from henceforth there shall be five in one house divided,
three against two, and two against three. **53** The father shall be divided against
the son, and the son against the father: the mother against the daughter, and the
daughter against the mother: the mother-in-law against her daughter-in-law, and
the daughter-in-law against her mother-in-law. **54** [z,13]Then said he to the peo-
ple, When ye see a cloud [aa]rise out of the West, straightway ye say, A shower co-
meth: and so it is. **55** And when ye see the South wind blow, ye say, that it will
be hot: and it cometh to pass. **56** Hypocrites, ye can discern the face of the earth,
and of the sky: but why discern ye not this time? **57** [ab]Yea, and why judge ye not
of yourselves what is right? **58** [14]While thou goest with thine adversary to the
ruler, as thou art in the way, give diligence in the way, that thou mayest be delivered
from him, lest he draw thee to the judge, and the judge deliver thee to the [ac]jailer,
and the jailer cast thee into prison. **59** I tell thee, thou shalt not depart thence,
till thou hast paid the utmost mite.

13

Of the Galileans, 4 and those that were slain under Siloam. 6 The fig tree that bare no fruit. 11 The woman vexed with the spirit of infirmity, that is, with a disease brought on her by Satan, is healed. 19 The parable of the grain of mustard seed. 21 Of leaven. 23 How few shall be saved. 31 Herod that Fox.

1 There [a]were certain men present at the same season, that showed him of the
Galileans, whose blood [b]Pilate had mingled with their sacrifices. **2** And Jesus an-
swered, and said unto them, Suppose ye, that these Galileans were greater sinners
than all the other Galileans, because they have suffered such things? **3** I tell you,
nay: but except ye amend your lives, ye shall all likewise perish. **4** Or think you
that those eighteen, upon whom the tower in [c]Siloam fell, and slew them, were sin-
ners above all men that dwell in Jerusalem? **5** I tell you, nay: but except ye amend
your lives, ye shall all likewise perish. **6** [d]He spake also this parable, A certain
man had a fig tree, planted in his vineyard: and he came and sought fruit thereon,
and found none. **7** Then said he to the dresser of his vineyard, Behold, this three
years have I come and sought fruit of this fig tree, and find none: cut it down: why
keepeth it also the ground [e]barren? **8** And he answered, and said unto him, Lord,
let it alone this year also, till I dig round about it, and dung it. **9** And if it bear
fruit, well: if not, then after thou shalt cut it down. **10** [f]And he taught in one of
the Synagogues on the Sabbath day. **11** And behold, there was a woman which
had a [g]spirit of infirmity eighteen years, and was bowed together, and could not
lift up herself in any wise. **12** When Jesus saw her, he called her to him, and said
to her, Woman, thou art [h]loosed from thy disease. **13** And he laid his hands on
her, and immediately she was made straight again, and glorified God. **14** [i]And
the [j]ruler of the Synagogue answered with indignation, because that Jesus healed
on the Sabbath day, and said unto the people, There are six days in which men
ought to work: in them therefore come and be healed, and not on the Sabbath
day. **15** Then answered him the Lord, and said, Hypocrite, doth not each one
of you on the Sabbath day loose his ox or his ass from the stall, and lead him away
to the water? **16** And ought not this daughter of Abraham, whom Satan had
bound, lo, eighteen years, be loosed from this bond on the Sabbath day? **17** And
when he said these things, all his adversaries were ashamed: but all the people rejoi-
ced at all the excellent things that were done by him. **18** [1]Then said he, What
is the kingdom of God like? or whereto shall I compare it? **19** [k]It is like a grain
of mustard seed, which a man took and sowed in his garden, and it grew, and
waxed a great tree, and the fowls of the heaven made nests in the branches there-
of. **20** [2]And again he said, Whereunto shall I liken the kingdom of God? **21** It
is like leaven, which a woman took, and hid in three pecks of flour, till all was
leavened. **22** [l,3]And he went through all cities and towns, teaching, and jour-
neying towards Jerusalem. **23** Then said one unto him, Lord, are there few that
shall be saved? And he said unto them, **24** [4]Strive to enter in at the strait gate:
for many, I say unto you, will seek to enter in, and shall not be able. **25** When
the good man of the house is risen up, and hath shut to the door, and ye began to
stand without, and to knock at the door, saying, Lord, Lord, open to us, and he
shall answer and say unto you, I know you not whence ye are, **26** [m]Then shall
ye begin to say, We have eaten and drunk in thy presence, and thou hast taught in
our streets. **27** [5]But he shall say, I tell you, I know you not whence ye are: depart
from me, all ye workers of iniquity. **28** [n]There shall be weeping and gnashing of
teeth, when ye shall see Abraham, and Isaac, and Jacob, and all the Prophets in the
kingdom of God, and yourselves thrust out at doors. **29** Then shall come many
from the [o]East, and from the West, and from the North, and from the South, and
shall sit at Table in the kingdom of God. **30** [6]And behold, there are last, whi-
ch shall be first, and there are first, which shall be last. **31** [p]The same day there
came certain Pharisees, and said unto him, Depart, and go hence: for Herod will
kill thee. **32** Then said he unto them, Go ye and tell that [q]fox, Behold, I cast
out devils, and will heal still [r]today, and tomorrow, and the third day I shall be
[s]perfected. **33** [t]Nevertheless I must walk today, and tomorrow, and the day fol-
lowing: for it cannot be that a Prophet should perish out of Jerusalem. **34** [7]O
Jerusalem, Jerusalem, which killest the Prophets, and stonest them that are sent to
thee, how often would I have gathered thy children together, as the hen gathered
her [u]brood under her wings, and ye would not. **35** Behold, your house is left
unto you desolate: and verily I tell you, ye shall not see me until the time come that
ye shall say, Blessed is he that cometh in the name of the Lord.

---

v. Luke 12:40 None have more need to watch, than they that have some degree of honor in the household of God.
w. Luke 12:42 That is, every month such measure of corn as was appointed them.
x. Luke 12:48 More than of him to whom so much was not given.
y. Luke 12:49 The Gospel is the only cause of peace between the goodly, and so is it the occasion of great trouble among the wicked.
z. Luke 12:54 Men which are very quick of sight in earthly things, are blind in those things which pertain to the heavenly life, and that through their own malice.
aa. Luke 12:54 Which appeareth, and gathereth itself together in that part of the air.
ab. Luke 12:57 Men that are blinded with the love of themselves, and therefore are detestable and stubborn, shall bear the reward of their folly.
ac. Luke 12:58 To him that had to demand and gather the amerciaments which they were condemned unto that had wrongfully troubled men: moreover, the magistrate's officers make them which are condemned, pay that, that they owe, yea, and oftentimes if they be obstinate, they do not only take the cost and charge of them, but also imprison them.

LUKE 12

1. Matt. 16:5 / Mark 8:14
2. Matt. 10:26 / Mark 4:22
3. Matt. 20:28
4. 1 Sam. 14:45 / Acts 27:34
5. Luke 9:26 / Matt. 10:32 / Mark 8:38 / 2 Tim. 1:12
6. Matt. 17:31 / Mark 3:28 / 1 John 5:15
7. Matt. 10:19 / Mark 13:11
8. Matt. 6:25 / 1 Pet. 5:7 / Ps. 55:22
9. Matt. 6:20
10. 1 Pet. 1:13
11. Matt. 24:43 / Rev. 26:15 / Rev. 3:3
12. Matt. 10:34
13. Matt. 16:2
14. Matt. 15:25

LUKE 13

a. Luke 13:1 We must not rejoice at the just punishment of others, but rather be instructed thereby to repentance.
b. Luke 13:1 Pontius Pilate was governor of Judea, almost ten years, and about the fourth year of his government, which might be about the fifteenth year of Tiberius' reign, Christ finished the work of our redemption by his death.
c. Luke 13:4 To wit, in the place, or river: for Siloam was a small river, from whence the conduits of the city came, whereof John 9:7 and Isa. 8:6, and therefore it was a tower or castle, built upon the conduit side, which fell down suddenly, and killed some.
d. Luke 13:6 Great and longsuffering is the patience of God, but yet so that at length he executed judgment.
e. Luke 13:7 Maketh the ground barren in that part, which otherwise were good for vines.
f. Luke 13:10 Christ came to deliver us from the bands of Satan.
g. Luke 13:11 Troubled with a disease which Satan brought.
h. Luke 13:12 For Satan had the woman bound, as if she had been in chains, insomuch that for eighteen years space she could not hold up her head.
i. Luke 13:14 A lively image of hypocrisy, and reward thereof.
j. Luke 13:14 One of the rulers of the Synagogue, for it appeareth by Mark 5:22 and Acts 13:15 that there were many rulers of the Synagogue.
k. Luke 13:19 God beginneth his kingdom with small beginnings, that the unlooked for proceeding of it may better set forth his power.
l. Luke 13:22 Against them which had rather err with many, than go right with a few, and by that means through their own slowness, are shut out of the kingdom of God.
m. Luke 13:26 He is in vain in the Church, which is not of the Church, which thing the cleanness of life showeth.
n. Luke 13:28 The casting off of the Jews, and the calling of the Gentiles is foretold.
o. Luke 13:29 From all the quarters of the world, and these are four of the chiefest.
p. Luke 13:31 We must go forward in the case of our calling, through the midst of terrors, whether they be true or fained.
q. Luke 13:32 That deceitful and treacherous man.
r. Luke 13:32 That is, a small time, and Theophylact saith, it is a proverb: or else, by Today, we may understand the time that now is, and by Tomorrow, the time to come, meaning thereby all the time of his ministry and office.
s. Luke 13:32 To wit, when the sacrifice for sin is ended.
t. Luke 13:33 There are nowhere more cruel enemies of the godly, than they which are within the Sanctuary and Church itself: but God seeth it, and will in his time have an account of it.
u. Luke 13:34 Word for word, the nest: now the brood of chickens is the nest.

LUKE 13

1. Matt. 13:31 / Mark 4:31
2. Matt. 13:33
3. Matt. 9:35 / Mark 6:6
4. Matt. 7:13
5. Mark 7:23 / Mark 25:41 / Ps. 6:8
6. Matt. 19:30 / Matt. 20:16 / Mark 10:31
7. Matt. 23:37

14

The dropsy healed on the Sabbath. 8 The chief place: at banquets. 12 The poor must be called to our feasts. 16 Of those that were bid to the great supper. 23 Some compelled to come in. 28 One about to build a tower.

1 And [a]it came to pass that when he was entered into the house of [b]one of
the chief Pharisees on the Sabbath day, to eat bread, they watched him. **2** And
behold, there was a certain man before him, which had the dropsy. **3** Then Jesus
answering, spake unto the Lawyers and Pharisees, saying, Is it lawful to heal on the
Sabbath day? **4** And they held their peace. Then he took him, and healed him,
and let him go, **5** And answered them, saying, Which of you shall have an ass,
or an ox fallen into a pit, and will not straightway pull him out on the Sabbath
day? **6** And they could not answer him again to those things. **7** [c]He spake also
a parable to the guests, when he marked how they chose out the chief rooms, and
said unto them, **8** When thou shalt be bidden of any man to a wedding, set not
thyself down in the chiefest place, lest a more honorable man than thou be bidden
of him, **9** And he that bade both him and thee, come, and say to thee, Give this
man room, and thou then begin with shame to take the lowest room. **10** [1]But
when thou art bidden, go and sit down in the lowest room, that when he that bade
thee, cometh, he may say unto thee, Friend, sit up higher: then shalt thou have
worship in the presence of them that sit at table with thee. **11** [2]For whosoever
exalteth himself, shall be brought low, and he that humbleth himself, shall be exal-
ted. **12** [d]Then said he also to him that had bidden him, [3]When thou makest a
dinner or a supper, call not thy friends, nor thy brethren, neither thy kinsmen,
nor the rich neighbors, lest they also bid thee again, and a recompense be made
thee. **13** But when thou makest a feast, call the poor, the maimed, the lame and
the blind, **14** And thou shalt be blessed, because they cannot recompense thee:
for thou shalt be recompensed at the resurrection of the just. **15** Now when one
of them that sat at table heard these things, he said unto him, Blessed is he that
eateth bread in the kingdom of God. **16** Then said he to him, [4]A certain man
made a great supper, and bade many, **17** And sent his servant at supper time to
say to them that were bidden, Come: for all things are now ready. **18** [e]But they
all with [f]one mind began to make excuse: The first said unto him, I have bought a
farm, and I must needs go out and see it: I pray thee have me excused. **19** And
another said, I have bought five yoke of oxen, and I go to prove them: I pray thee
have me excused. **20** And another said, I have married a wife, and therefore I
cannot come. **21** So that servant returned, and showed his master these things.
Then was the good man of the house angry, and said to his servant, Go out quickly
into the [g]streets and lanes of the city, and bring in hither the poor, and the maimed,
and the halt, and the blind. **22** And the servant said, Lord, it is done as thou hast
commanded, and yet there is room. **23** Then the master said to the servant, Go
out into the highways, and hedges, and compel them to come in, that mine house
may be filled. **24** For I say unto you, that none of those men which were bidden,
shall taste of my supper. **25** [h]Now there went great multitudes with him, and he
turned and said unto them, **26** [5]If any man come to me, and [i]hate not his father,
and mother, and wife, and children, and brethren, and sisters: yea, and his own
life also, he cannot be my disciple. **27** [j,6]And whosoever beareth not his cross,
and cometh after me, cannot be my disciple. **28** For which of you minding to
build a tower, [k]sitting not down before, and counteth the cost, whether he have
sufficient to perform it, **29** Lest that after he hath laid the foundation, and is not
able to perform it, all that behold it, begin to mock him, **30** Saying, This man
began to build, and was not able to make an end. **31** Or what King going to
make war against another King, sitteth not down first, and taketh counsel, whether
he be able with ten thousand, to meet him that cometh against him with twenty
thousand? **32** Or else while he is yet a great way off, he sendeth an ambassage,
and desireth peace. **33** So likewise, whosoever he be of you, that forsaketh not all
that he hath, he cannot be my disciple. **34** [l,7]Salt is good: but if salt have lost his
savor, wherewith shall it be salted? **35** It is neither meet for the land, nor yet for
the dunghill, but men cast it out. He that hath ears to hear, let him hear.

15

The parable of the lost sheep. 8 Of the groat, 12 And of the prodigal son.

1 Then [a]resorted unto [b]him [c]all the Publicans and sinners, to hear him. **2** The-
refore the Pharisees and Scribes murmured, saying, He receiveth sinners, and ea-
teth with them. **3** Then spake he this parable to them, saying, **4** [1]What man
of you having an hundred sheep, if he lose one of them, doth not leave ninety and
nine in the wilderness, and go after that which is lost, until he find it? **5** And
when he hath found it, he layeth it on his shoulders with joy. **6** And when he
cometh home, he calleth together his friends and neighbors, saying unto them,
Rejoice with me: for I have found my sheep which was lost. **7** I say unto you,
that likewise joy shall be in heaven for one sinner that converteth, more than for
ninety and nine just men, which need none amendment of life. **8** Either what
woman having ten groats, if she lose one groat, doth not light a candle, and sweep
the house, and seek diligently till she find it? **9** And when she hath found it, she
calleth her friends, and neighbors, saying, Rejoice with me: for I have found the
groat which I had lost. **10** Likewise I say unto you, there is joy in the presence
of the Angels of God, for one sinner that converteth. **11** [d]He said moreover, A
certain man had two sons, **12** And the younger of them said to his father, Father,
give me the portion of the goods that falleth to me. So he divided unto them his
substance. **13** So not many days after, when the younger son had gathered all
together, he took his journey into a far country, and there he wasted his goods with
riotous living. **14** Now when he had spent all, there arose a great dearth throu-
ghout that land, and he began to be in necessity. **15** Then he went and clave to
a citizen of that country, and he sent him to his farm, to feed swine. **16** And he
would fain have filled his belly with the husks that the swine ate: but no man gave
them him. **17** [e]Then he came to himself, and said, How many hired servants
at my father's have bread enough, and I die for hunger? **18** I will rise and go
to my father, and say unto him, Father, I have sinned against [f]heaven, and before
thee, **19** And am no more worthy to be called thy son: make me as one of thine
hired servants. **20** So he arose and came to his father, and when he was yet a great
way off, his father saw him, and had compassion, and ran and fell on his neck, and
kissed him. **21** [g]And the son said unto him, Father, I have sinned against heaven,
and before thee, and am no more worthy to be called thy son. **22** Then the father
said to his servants, Bring forth the best robe, and put it on him, and put a ring on
his hand, and shoes on his feet, **23** And bring the fat calf, and kill him, and let
us eat, and be merry: **24** For this my son was dead, and is alive again: and he was
lost, but he is found. And they began to be merry. **25** [h]Now the elder brother
was in the field, and when he came and drew near to the house, he heard melody,
and dancing, **26** And called one of his servants, and asked what those things me-
ant. **27** And he said unto him, Thy brother is come, and thy father hath killed
the fat calf, because he hath received him safe and sound. **28** Then he was angry,
and would not go in: therefore came his father out, and entreated him. **29** But
he answered, and said to his father, Lo, these many years have I done thee service,
neither brake I at anytime thy commandment, and yet thou never gavest me a kid
that I might make merry with my friends. **30** But when this thy son was come,
which hath devoured thy goods with harlots, thou hast for his sake killed the fat
calf. **31** And he said unto him, Son thou art ever with me, and all that I have, is
thine. It was meet that we should make merry, and be glad: for this thy brother was
dead, and is alive again: and he was lost, but he is found.

LUKE 14

- **a.** Luke 14:1 The Law of the very Sabbath ought not to hinder the offices of charity.
- **b.** Luke 14:1 Either one of the Elders, whom they called the Sanhedrin, or one of the chiefs of the Synagogue, John 7:48, for this word Pharisee was the name of a sect, though it appears by the whole history that the Pharisees were in great credit.
- **c.** Luke 14:7 The reward of pride is ignomy and the reward of true modesty is glory.
- **d.** Luke 14:12 Against them which lavish out their goods either ambitiously, or for hope of recompence, whereas Christian charity respecteth only the glory of God, and the profit of our neighbor.
- **e.** Luke 14:18 The most part even of them to whom God hath revealed himself are so mad, that such helps as they have received of God, they willingly turn into lets and hindrances.
- **f.** Luke 14:18 As of set purpose, and a thing agreed upon before, for though they allege several causes, yet all of them agree in this, that they have their excuses, that they may not come to supper.
- **g.** Luke 14:21 Wide and broad quarters.
- **h.** Luke 14:25 Even those affections, which are of themselves worthy of praise and commendation, must be ruled and ordered, that godliness may have the upper hand and preeminence.
- **i.** Luke 14:26 If the matter stands between God and him, as Theophylact saith: and therefore these words are not spoken simply, but by comparison.
- **j.** Luke 14:27 The true followers of Christ must at once build and fight, and therefore be ready and prepared to suffer all kinds of miseries.
- **k.** Luke 14:28 At home, and casteth all his costs before he begin the work.
- **l.** Luke 14:34 The disciples of Christ must be wise, both for themselves and for others: otherwise they become the most foolish of all.

LUKE 14

1. Prov. 25:7
2. Luke 28:14 / Matt. 23:12
3. Prov. 3:27 / Job 4:7
4. Matt. 22:8 / Rev. 19:9
5. Matt. 10:47
6. Luke 9:23 / Matt. 16:24 / Mark 8:34
7. Matt. 5:13 / Mark 9:50

LUKE 15

- **a.** Luke 15:1 Or, draw near.
- **b.** Luke 15:1 We must not despair of them, which have gone out of the way, but according to the example of Christ, we must take great pains about them.
- **c.** Luke 15:1 Some Publicans and sinners came to Christ from all quarters.
- **d.** Luke 15:11 Men by their voluntary falling from God, having spoiled themselves of the benefits which they received of him, cast themselves headlong into infinite calamities: but God of his singular goodness, offering himself freely to them, whom he called to repentance, through the greatness of their misery wherewith they were tamed, doth not only gently receive them, but also enricheth them with far greater gifts, and blesseth them with the chiefest bliss.
- **e.** Luke 15:17 The beginning of repentance is the acknowledging of the mercy of God, which stirreth us to hope well.
- **f.** Luke 15:18 Against God, because he is said to dwell in heaven.
- **g.** Luke 15:21 In true repentance there is a feeling of our sins, joined with sorrow and shame, from whence springeth a confession, after which followeth forgiveness.
- **h.** Luke 15:25 Such as truly fear God, desire to have all men to be their fellows.

LUKE 15

1. Matt. 18:12

16

1 The parable of the steward accused to his master. 13 To serve two masters. 16 The law and the Prophets. 19 Of Dives and Lazarus.

1 And he said also unto his disciples, [a]There was a certain rich man, which had a steward, and he was accused unto him, that he wasted his goods. **2** And he called him, and said unto him, How is it that I hear this of thee? Give an account of thy stewardship: for thou mayest be no longer steward. **3** Then the steward said within himself, What shall I do? for my master taketh away from me the stewardship. I cannot dig, and to beg I am ashamed. **4** I know what I will do, that when I am put out of the stewardship, they may receive me into their houses. **5** Then called he unto him everyone of his master's debtors, and said unto the first, How much owest thou unto my master? **6** And he said, An hundred measures of oil. And he said to him, Take thy writing, and sit down quickly, and write fifty. **7** Then said he to another, How much owest thou? And he said, An hundred measures of wheat. Then he said to him, Take thy writing and write fourscore. **8** And the Lord commended [b]the unjust steward, because he had done wisely. Wherefore the [c]children of this world are in their generation wiser than the children of light. **9** And I say unto you, Make you friends with the riches [d]of iniquity, that when ye shall want, they may receive you into everlasting [e]habitations. **10** [f]He that is faithful in the least, he is also faithful in much: and he that is unjust in the least, is unjust also in much. **11** If then ye have not been faithful in the wicked riches, who will trust you in the [g]true treasure? **12** And if ye have not been faithful in [h]another man's goods, who shall give you that which is yours? **13** [i,1]No servant can serve two masters: for either he shall hate the one, and love the other: or else he shall lean to the one, and despise the other. Ye cannot serve God and riches. **14** All these things heard the Pharisees also which were covetous, and they scoffed at him. **15** [j]Then he said unto them, Ye are they, which justify yourselves before men: but God knoweth your hearts: for that which is highly esteemed among men, is abomination in the sight of God. **16** [k,2]The Law and the Prophets endured until John: and since that time the kingdom of God is preached, and every man presseth into it. **17** [3]Now it is more easy that heaven and earth should pass away, than that one tittle of the Law should fall. **18** [4]Whosoever putteth away his wife, and marrieth another, commiteth adultery: and whosoever marrieth her [l]that is put away from her husband, commiteth adultery. **19** [m]There was a certain rich man, which was clothed in [n]purple and fine linen, and fared well and delicately every day. **20** Also there was a certain beggar named Lazarus, which was laid at his gate full of sores, **21** And desired to be refreshed with the crumbs that fell from the rich man's table: yea, and the dogs came and licked his sores. **22** And it was so that the beggar died, and was carried by the Angels into Abraham's bosom. The rich man also died, and was buried. **23** And being in hell in torments, [o]he lifted up his eyes, and saw Abraham afar off, and Lazarus in his bosom. **24** Then he cried, and said, Father Abraham, have mercy on me, and send Lazarus that he may dip the tip of his finger in water, and cool my tongue: for I am tormented in this flame. **25** But Abraham said, Son, remember that thou in thy lifetime receivedst thy pleasures, and likewise Lazarus pains: now therefore is he comforted, and thou art tormented. **26** Besides all this, between you and us there is a great gulf set, so that they which would go from hence to you, cannot: neither can they come from thence to us. **27** [p]Then he said, I pray thee therefore father, that thou wouldest send him to my father's house, **28** (For I have five brethren) that he may testify unto them, lest they also come into this place of torment. **29** Abraham said unto him, They have Moses and the Prophets: let them hear them. **30** And he said, Nay, father Abraham: but if one came unto them from the dead, they will amend their lives. **31** Then he said unto him, If they hear not Moses and the Prophets, neither will they be persuaded, though one rise from the dead again.

17

1 Offenses. 3 We must forgive him that trespasseth against us. 10 We are unprofitable servants. 11 Of the ten lepers. 20 Of the coming of the kingdom of heaven. 33 False Christs. 36 After what manner Christ's coming shall be.

1 Then said he to his disciples, [a,1]It cannot be avoided, but that offences will come, but woe be to him by whom they come. **2** It is better for him that a great millstone were hanged about his neck, and that he were cast into the sea, then that he should offend one of these little ones. **3** [b]Take heed to yourselves: if thy brother trespass against thee, rebuke him: and if he repent, forgive him. **4** [2]And though he sin against thee seven times in a day, and seven times in a day turn again to thee, saying, it repenteth me, thou shalt forgive him. **5** [c]And the Apostles said unto the Lord, Increase our faith. **6** And the Lord said, [3]If ye had faith, as much as is [d]a grain of mustard seed, and should say unto this mulberry tree, Pluck thyself up by the roots, and plant thyself in the sea, it should even obey you. **7** [e]Who is it also of you, that having a servant plowing or feeding cattle, would say unto him by and by, when he were come from the field, Go, and sit down at table, **8** And would not rather say to him, Dress wherewith I may sup, and gird thyself, and serve me, till I have eaten and drunken, and afterward eat thou, and drink thou? **9** Doth he thank that servant, because he did that which was commanded unto him? I trow not. **10** [f]So likewise ye, when ye have done all those things, which are commanded you, say, We are unprofitable servants: we have done that which was our duty to do. **11** [g]And so it was when he went to Jerusalem, that he passed through the midst of Samaria, and Galilee. **12** And as he entered into a certain town, there met him ten men that were lepers, which stood afar off. **13** And they lifted up their voices and said, Jesus, Master, have mercy on us. **14** And when he saw them, he said unto them, [4]Go, show yourselves unto the Priests. And it came to pass, that as they went, they were cleansed. **15** Then one of them, when he saw that he was healed, turned back, and with a loud voice praised God, **16** And fell down on his face at his feet, and gave him thanks: and he was a Samaritan. **17** And Jesus answered, and said, Are there not ten cleansed? but where are the nine? **18** There is none found that returned to give God praise, save this stranger. **19** And he said unto him, Arise, go thy way, thy faith hath saved thee. **20** [h]And when he was demanded of the Pharisees, when the kingdom of God should come, he answered them, and said, The kingdom of God cometh not with [i]observation. **21** Neither shall men say, Lo here, or lo there: for behold, the kingdom of God is [j]within you. **22** [k]And he said unto the disciples, the days will come, when ye shall desire to see [l]one of the days of the Son of man, and ye shall not see it. **23** [m,5]Then they shall say to you, Behold here, or behold there: but go not thither, neither follow them. **24** For as the lightning that lighteneth out of the one part under heaven, shineth unto the other part under heaven, so shall the Son of man be in his day. **25** But first must he suffer many things and be reproved of this generation. **26** [n,6]And as it was in the days of Noah, so shall

---

LUKE 16

a. Luke 16:1 Seeing that men oftentimes purchase friendship to themselves, by other men's costs, it is a shame for us, if with a free and liberal bestowing of the goods which the Lord hath given us to that purpose, we do not please him, nor procure the good will of our neighbors, seeing that by this only means, riches, which are oftentimes occasions of sin, are turned to another end and purpose.

b. Luke 16:8 This parable doth not approve the steward's naughty dealing, for it was every theft: but parables are set forth, to show a thing covertly, and as it were under a figure to represent the truth, though it agree not thoroughly with the matter itself: so that Christ meaneth by this parable to teach us, that worldly men are more heady in the affairs of this world, than the children of God are careful for everlasting life.

c. Luke 16:8 Men that are given to this present life, contrary to whom the children of light are set: St. Paul calls those spiritual, and the other carnal.

d. Luke 16:9 This is not spoken of goods that are evil gotten, for God will have our bountifulness to the poor, proceed and come from a good fountain: but he calleth those riches of iniquity, which men use naughtily.

e. Luke 16:9 To wit, the poor Christians: for they are the inheritors of these Tabernacles, Theophylact.

f. Luke 16:10 We ought to take heed that for abusing our earthly function and duty, we be not deprived of heavenly gifts: for how can they use spiritual gifts aright, who abuse worldly things?

g. Luke 16:11 That is, heavenly and true riches: which are contrary to worldly and flitting substance.

h. Luke 16:12 In worldly goods, which are called other men's, because they are committed to our credit.

i. Luke 16:13 No man can love God and riches together.

j. Luke 16:15 Our sins are not hidden to God, although they be hidden to men, yea although they be hidden to them whose sins they are.

k. Luke 16:16 The Pharisees despised the excellency of the new Covenant, in respect of the old, being ignorant of the perfect righteousness of the Law, and how false expounders they were of the Law, Christ declareth by the seventh Commandment.

l. Luke 16:18 They that gather by this place, that a man cannot be married again after that he hath put away his wife for adultery, while she liveth, reason fondly: for Christ speaketh of those divorces which the Jews used, of which sort we cannot take the divorcement for adultery, for adulterers were put to death by the law.

m. Luke 16:19 The end of the poverty and misery of the godly, shall be everlasting joy: as the end of riotousness and cruel pride of the rich shall be everlasting misery, without all hope of mercy.

n. Luke 16:19 Very gorgeously and sumptuously, for purple garments were costly, and this fine linen which was a kind of linen that came out of Achaia, was as dear as gold.

o. Luke 16:23 Heavenly and spiritual things are expressed, and set forth under colors and resemblances fit for our senses.

p. Luke 16:27 Seeing that we have a most sure rule to live by, laid forth unto us in the word of God, rashly and vainly do men seek for other revelation.

LUKE 16

1. Matt. 6:24
2. Matt. 11:1
3. Matt. 5:18
4. Matt. 5:32 / Matt. 19:9 / 1 Cor. 7:11

LUKE 17

a. Luke 17:1 The Church is of necessity subject to offences, but the Lord will not suffer them unpunished, if any of the least be offended.

b. Luke 17:3 Our reprehensions must be just, and proceed of love and charity.

c. Luke 17:5 God will never be utterly lacking to the Godly (although he be not so perfectly with them, as they would) even in those difficulties, which cannot be overcome by man's reason.

d. Luke 17:6 If you had no more faith, but the quantity of the grain of mustard seed.

e. Luke 17:7 Seeing that God may challenge unto himself of right, both us and all that is ours, he can be debtor unto us for nothing, although we labor manfully even unto death.

f. Luke 17:10 The most perfect keeping of the Law, which we can perform, deserves no reward.

g. Luke 17:11 Christ doeth well even unto such, as will be unthankful, but the benefits of God profit them only to salvation, which are thankful.

h. Luke 17:20 The kingdom of God is not marked of many, although it be most present before their eyes: because they fondly persuade themselves, that it is joined with outward pomp.

i. Luke 17:20 With any outward pomp and show of majesty, to be known by: for there were otherwise many plain and evident tokens, whereby men might have understood, that Christ was the Messiah, whose kingdom was so long looked for: but he speaketh in this place of those signs which the Pharisees dreamed of, which looked for an earthly kingdom of Messiah.

j. Luke 17:21 You look about for Messiah as though he were absent, but he is amongst you in the midst of you.

k. Luke 17:22 We oftentimes neglect those things when they be present, which we afterward desire when they are gone, but in vain.

l. Luke 17:22 The time will come that you shall seek for the Son of man, with great sorrow of heart, and shall not find him.

m. Luke 17:23 Christ forewarneth us that false Christs shall come, and that his glory shall suddenly be spread far and wide through the world, after that the ignomy of the cross is put out and extinguished.

n. Luke 17:26 The world shall be taken unawares with the sudden judgment of God: and therefore the faithful ought to watch continually.

it be in the days of the Son of man. **27** They ate, they drank, they married wi-
ves, and gave in marriage unto the day that Noah went into the Ark: and the flood
came, and destroyed them all. **28** [7]Likewise also as it was in the days of Lot: They
ate, they drank, they bought, they sold, they planted, they built. **29** But in the
day that Lot went out of Sodom, it rained fire and brimstone from heaven, and
destroyed them all. **30** After these examples shall it be in the day when the son of
man revealed. **31** [o]At that day he that is upon the house, and his stuff in the hou-
se, let him not come down to take it out: and he that is in the field likewise, let him
not turn back to that he left behind. **32** [8]Remember Lot's wife. **33** [9]Whosoe-
ver will seek to save his soul, shall loose it: and whosoever shall loose it, shall [p]get it
life. **34** [10]I tell you, in that night there shall be two in one bed: the one shall be
received, and the other shall be left. **35** Two women shall be grinding together,
the one shall be taken, and the other shall be left. **36** Two shall be in the field:
one shall be received, and another shall be left. **37** [q]And they answered, and said
to him, Where, Lord? And he said unto them, [11]Wheresoever the body is, thither
shall also the eagles be gathered together.

18

2 The parable of the unrighteous Judge and the widow. 10 Of the Pharisee and the Publican. 15 Children are of the kingdom of heaven. 22 To sell all and give to the poor. 28 The Apostles forsake all. 31 Christ foretelleth his death. 35 The blind man receiveth sight.

1 And [a]he spake also a parable unto them, to this end, that they [1]ought always
to pray, and not to [b]wax faint, **2** [c]Saying, there was a judge in a certain city, whi-
ch feared not God, neither reverenced man. **3** And there was a widow in that
city, which came unto him, saying, Do me justice against mine adversary. **4** And
he would not of a long time: but afterward he said with himself, Though I fear not
God, nor reverence man, **5** Yet because this widow troubleth me, I will do her
right, lest at the last she come and [d]make me weary. **6** And the Lord said, Hear
what the unrighteous judge saith. **7** Now shall not God avenge his elect, which
cry day and night unto him, yea, though [e]he suffer long for them? **8** I tell you
he will avenge them quickly: but when the Son of man cometh, shall he find faith
on the earth? **9** [f]He spake also this parable unto certain which trusted in them-
selves that they were just, and despised others. **10** Two men went up into the
Temple to pray: the one a Pharisee, and the other a Publican. **11** [g]The Pharisee
stood and prayed thus with himself, O God, I thank thee that I am not as other
men, extortioners, unjust, adulterers, or even as this Publican. **12** I fast twice
in the week: I give tithe of all that ever I possess. **13** But the Publican standing
[h]afar off, would not lift up so much as his eyes to heaven, but smote his breast,
saying, O God, be merciful to me a sinner. **14** I tell you, this man departed to
his house, justified rather than the other: [2]for every man that exalteth himself shall
be brought low, and he that humbleth himself shall be exalted. **15** [i,3]They brou-
ght unto him also babes that he should touch them. [j]And when his disciples saw
it, they rebuked them. **16** [k]But Jesus [l]called them unto him, and said, Suffer
the babes to come unto me, and forbid them not: for of such is the kingdom of
God. **17** [m]Verily I say unto you, whosoever receiveth not the kingdom of God
as a babe, he shall not enter therein. **18** [4]Then a certain ruler asked him, saying,
Good Master, what ought I do, to inherit eternal life? **19** And Jesus said unto
him, Why callest thou me good? none is good, save one, even God. **20** Thou
knowest the commandments, [5]Thou shalt not commit adultery: Thou shalt not
kill: Thou shalt not steal: Thou shalt not bear false witness: Honor thy father and
thy mother. **21** [n]And he said, All these have I kept from my youth. **22** Now
when Jesus heard that, he said unto him, yet lackest thou one thing, Sell all that
ever thou hast, and distribute unto the poor, and thou shalt have treasure in he-
aven, and come follow me. **23** But when he heard those things, he was very
heavy: for he was marvelous rich. **24** [o]And when Jesus saw him very sorrowful,
he said, With what difficulty shall they that have riches, enter into the kingdom
of God! **25** Surely it is easier for a camel to go through a needle's eye, than for
a rich man to enter into the kingdom of God. **26** Then said they that heard it,
And who then shall be saved? **27** And he said, The things which are impossible
with men, are possible with God. **28** [6]Then Peter said, Lo, we have left all, and
have followed thee. **29** [p]And he said unto them, Verily I say unto you, there is
no man that hath left house, or parents, or brethren, or wife, or children for the
kingdom of God's sake, **30** Which shall not receive much more in this world,
and in the world to come life everlasting. **31** [q,7]Then Jesus took unto him the
twelve, and said unto them, Behold, we go up to Jerusalem, and all things shall be
fulfilled to the Son of man, that are written by the Prophets. **32** For he shall be
delivered unto the Gentiles, and shall be mocked, and shall be spiteful entreated,
and shall be spitted on. **33** And when they have scourged him, they will put
him to death: but the third day he shall rise again. **34** But they understood [r]no-
ne of these things, and this saying was hid from them, neither perceived they the
things, which were spoken. **35** [s,8]And it came to pass, that as he was come near
unto Jericho, a certain blind man sat by the wayside, begging. **36** And when he
heard the people pass by, he asked what it meant. **37** And they said unto him,
that Jesus of Nazareth passed by. **38** Then he cried, saying, Jesus the Son of Da-
vid, have mercy on me. **39** [t]And they which went before, rebuked him that he
should hold his peace, but he cried much more, O Son of David have mercy on
me. **40** And Jesus stood still, and commanded him to be brought unto him.
And when he was come near, he asked him, **41** Saying, What wilt thou that I
do unto thee? And he said, Lord, that I may receive my sight. **42** And Jesus said
unto him, Receive thy sight: thy faith hath saved thee. **43** Then immediately he
received his sight, and followed him, praising God: and all the people, when they
saw this, gave praise to God.

19

2 Zacchaeus the Publican. 13 Ten pieces of money delivered to servants to occupy withall. 19 Jesus entereth into Jerusalem. 41 He foretelleth the destruction of the ciy with tears. 45 He casteth the sellers out of the Temple.

1 Now [a]when Jesus entered and passed through Jericho, **2** Behold, there
was a man named Zacchaeus, which was the [b]chief receiver of the tribute, and he
was rich. **3** And he sought to see Jesus, who he should be, and could not for the
press, because he was of a low stature. **4** Wherefore he ran before, and climbed
up into a wild fig tree, that he might see him: for he should come that way. **5** And
when Jesus came to the place, he looked up, and saw him, and said unto him, Zac-
chaeus, come down at once: for today I must abide at thine house. **6** Then he
came down hastily, and received him joyfully. **7** [c]And when all they saw it, they
murmured, saying, that he was gone in to lodge with a sinful man. **8** [d]And Zac-
chaeus stood forth, and said unto the Lord, Behold, Lord, the half of my goods I
give to the poor: and if I have taken from any man by [e]forged cavillation, I resto-
re him fourfold. **9** Then Jesus said to him, This day is salvation come unto this
house, forasmuch as he is also become the [f]son of Abraham. **10** [1]For the son
of man is come to seek, and to save that which was lost. **11** [g]And while they

---

o. Luke 17:31 We must take good heed, that neither distrust, nor the enticements of this world, nor any respect of friendship hinder us the least that may be.
p. Luke 17:33 That is, shall save it, so Matthew expoundeth it: for the life that is here spoken of, is everlasting salvation.
q. Luke 17:37 The only way to continue is to cleave to Christ.

LUKE 17
1. Matt. 18:7 / Mark 9:42
2. Matt. 18:28
3. Matt. 17:20
4. Lev. 14:2
5. Matt. 24:23 / Mark 13:21
6. Gen. 7:5 / Matt. 24:38 / 1 Pet. 3:20
7. Gen. 19:24
8. Gen. 19:26
9. Luke 9:24 / Matt. 10:39 / Mark 8:35 / John 12:25
10. Matt. 24:41
11. Matt. 24:28

LUKE 18
a. Luke 18:1 God will have us to continue in prayer, not to weary us, but to exercise us, therefore we must so strive with impatience, that long delay cause us not to break off the course of our prayers.
b. Luke 18:1 Yield to afflictions, and adversities, as they do which are out of heart.
c. Luke 18:2 He doth not compare things that are equal together, but the less with the greater: If a man get his right at a most unrighteous judge's hands, much more shall the prayers of the godly prevail before God.
d. Luke 18:5 Word for word, beat me down with her blows, and it is a metaphor taken of wrestlers, who beat their adversaries with their fists or clubs: so do they that are importunate beat the judge's ears with their crying out, even as it were with blows.
e. Luke 18:7 Though he seems slow in revenging the injury done to his.
f. Luke 18:9 Two things especially make our prayers void and of none effect: confidence of our own righteousness, and the contempt of others: and an humble heart is contrary to both these.
g. Luke 18:11 Although we confess that whatsoever we have, we have it of God, yet are we despised of God, as proud and arrogant, if we put never so little trust in our own works before God.
h. Luke 18:13 Far from the Pharisee in a lower place.
i. Luke 18:15 The children were tender and young, in that they were brought, which appeareth more evidently in that, that they were infants, which is to be marked against them that are enemies to the baptizing of children.
j. Luke 18:15 To judge or think of Christ after the reason of our flesh, is the cause of infinite corruptions.
k. Luke 18:16 The children also of the faithful are comprehended in the free covenant of God.
l. Luke 18:16 Them that carried the children, whom the disciples drove away.
m. Luke 18:17 Childlike innocence is an ornament of Christians.
n. Luke 18:21 The enticement of riches carrieth away many from the right way.
o. Luke 18:24 To be both rich and godly, is a singular gift of God.
p. Luke 18:29 They become the richest of all, which refuse not to be poor for Christ's sake.
q. Luke 18:31 As sure and certain as persecution is, so sure is the glory which remaineth for the conquerors.
r. Luke 18:34 Hereby we see how ignorant the disciples were.
s. Luke 18:35 Christ showeth by a visible miracle, that he is the light of the world.
t. Luke 18:39 The more stops and lets that Satan layeth in our way, even by them which profess Christ's Name, so much the more ought we to go forward.

LUKE 18
1. Rom. 12:12 / 1 Thess. 5:17
2. Luke 14:11 / Matt. 23:12
3. Matt. 19:13 / Mark 10:13
4. Matt. 19:16 / Mark 10:17
5. Exod. 20:30
6. Matt. 19:27 / Mark 10:28
7. Matt. 20:17 / Mark 10:32
8. Matt. 20:29 / Mark 10:46

LUKE 19
a. Luke 19:1 Christ preventeth them with his grace especially which seemed to be furthest from it.
b. Luke 19:2 The overseer and head of the Publicans which were there together: for the Publicans were divided into companies: as we may gather by many places of Cicero his orations.
c. Luke 19:7 The world forsaketh the grace of God, and yet is unwilling that it should be bestowed upon others.
d. Luke 19:8 The example of true repentance, is known by the effect.
e. Luke 19:8 By falsely accusing any man: and this agreeth most fitly to the master of the customer's person: for commonly they have this trade among them when they rob and spoil the commonweal, they have nothing in their mouths, but the profit of the commonweal, and under that color they play the thieves, insomuch that if men reprove and go about to redress their robbery, and spoiling, they cry out, the commonwealth is hindered.
f. Luke 19:9 Beloved of God, one that walketh in the steps of Abraham's faith: and we gather that salvation came to that house, because they received the blessing as Abraham had, for all of the household were circumcised.
g. Luke 19:11 We must patiently wait for the judgment of God, which shall be revealed in his time.
h. Luke 19:13 There are three sorts of men in the Church: the one sort fall from Christ whom they see not; the other, which according to their vocation, bestow the gifts which they have

heard these things, he continued and spake a parable, because he was near to Jerusalem, and because also they thought that the kingdom of God should shortly appear. **12** He said therefore, [2]A certain noble man went into a far country, to receive for himself a kingdom, and so to come again. **13** [h]And he called his ten servants, and delivered them ten pieces of money, and said unto them, Occupy till I come. **14** Now his citizens hated him, and sent an ambassage after him, saying, We will not have this man to reign over us. **15** And it came to pass, when he was come again, and had received his kingdom, that he commanded the servants to be called to him, to whom he gave his money, that he might know what every man had gained. **16** Then came the first, saying, Lord, [i]thy piece hath increased ten pieces. **17** And he said unto him, Well, good servant: because thou hast been faithful in a very little thing, take thou authority over ten cities. **18** And the second came, saying, Lord, thy piece hath increased five pieces. **19** And to the same he said, Be thou also ruler over five cities. **20** [j]So the other came, and said, Lord, behold thy piece, which I have laid up in a napkin: **21** For I feared thee, because thou art a straight man: thou takest up that thou laidst not down, and reapest that thou didst not sow. **22** Then he said unto him, Of thine own mouth will I judge thee, O evil servant. Thou knewest that I am a straight man, taking up that I laid not down, and reaping that I did not sow. **23** Wherefore then gavest not thou my money into the [k]bank, that at my coming I might have required it with vantage? **24** And he said to them that stood by, Take from him that piece, and give it him that hath ten pieces. **25** (And they said unto him, Lord, he hath ten pieces.) **26** [3]For I say unto you, that unto all them that have, it shall be given: and from him that hath not, even that he hath, shall be taken from him. **27** Moreover, those mine enemies, which would not that I should reign over them, bring hither, and slay them before me. **28** And when he had thus spoken, [l]he went forth before, ascending up to Jerusalem. **29** [m,4]And it came to pass, when he was come near to Bethphage, and Bethany, besides the mount which is called the mount of Olives, he sent two of his disciples, **30** Saying, Go ye to the town which is before you, wherein as soon as ye are come, ye shall find a colt tied, whereon never man sat: loose him, and bring him hither. **31** And if any ask you, why ye loose him, thus shall ye say unto him, Because the Lord hath need of him. **32** So they that were sent, went their way, and found it as he had said unto them. **33** And as they were loosing the colt, the owners thereof said unto them, Why loose ye the colt? **34** And they said, The Lord hath need of him. **35** [5]So they brought him to Jesus, and they cast their garments on the colt, and set Jesus thereon. **36** And as he went, they spread their clothes in the way. **37** And when he was now come near to the going down of the mount of Olives, the whole multitude of the disciples began to rejoice, and to praise God with a loud voice, for all the great works that they had seen, **38** Saying, Blessed be the King that cometh in the Name of the Lord: peace in heaven, and glory in the highest places. **39** [n]Then some of the Pharisees of the company said unto him, Master, rebuke thy disciples. **40** But he answered, and said unto them, I tell you, that if these should hold their peace, the stones would cry. **41** [o,6]And when he was come near, he beheld the City, and wept for it, **42** [p]Saying, [q]O if thou hadst even known [r]at the least in this [s]thy day those things, which belong unto thy [t]peace! but now are they hid from thine eyes. **43** For the days shall come upon thee, that thine enemies shall cast a trench about thee, and compass thee round, and keep thee in on every side, **44** And shall make thee even with the ground, and thy children which are in thee, and they shall not leave in thee a stone upon a stone, because thou knewest not [u]that season of thy visitation. **45** [v,7]He went also into the Temple, and began to cast out them that sold therein, and them that bought, **46** Saying unto them, It is written, [8]Mine house is the house of prayer, [9]but ye have made it a den of thieves. **47** And he taught daily in the Temple. And the high Priests and the Scribes, and the chief of the people sought to destroy him. **48** But they could not find what they might do to him: for all the people hanged upon him when they heard him.

20

4 From whence John's Baptism was. 9 The wickedness of the Priests is noted by the parable of the vineyard and the husbandmen. 21 To give tribute to Caesar. 27 He convinceth the Sadducees denying the resurrection. 41 How Christ is the son of David.

1 And [a,1]it came to pass, that on one of those days, as he taught the people in the Temple, and preached the Gospel, the high Priests and the Scribes came upon him, with the Elders, **2** And spake unto him, saying, Tell us by what authority thou doest these things, or who is he that hath given thee this authority? **3** And he answered, and said unto them, I also will ask you one thing: tell me therefore: **4** The baptism of John, was it from heaven, or of men? **5** And they reasoned within themselves, saying, If we shall say, From heaven, he will say, Why then believed ye him not? **6** But if we shall say, Of men, all the people will stone us: for they be persuaded that John was a Prophet. **7** Therefore they answered, that they could not tell whence it was. **8** Then Jesus said unto them, Neither tell I you, by what authority I do these things. **9** [b,2]Then began he to speak to the people this parable, A certain man planted a vineyard, and let it forth to husbandmen: and went into a strange country, for a great time. **10** And at the time convenient he sent a servant to the husbandmen, that they should give him of the fruit of the vineyard: but the husbandmen did beat him, and sent him away empty. **11** Again he sent yet another servant: and they did beat him, and foul entreated him, and sent him away empty. **12** Moreover he sent the third, and him they wounded, and cast out. **13** Then said the Lord of the vineyard, What shall I do? I will send my beloved son: it may be that they will do reverence when they see him. **14** But when the husbandmen saw him, they reasoned with themselves, saying, This is the heir: come, let us kill him, that the inheritance may be ours. **15** So they cast him out of the vineyard, and killed him. What shall the Lord of the vineyard therefore do unto them? **16** He will come and destroy these husbandmen, and will give out his vineyard to others. But when they heard it, they said, God forbid. **17** And he beheld them, and said, What meaneth this then that is written, [3]The stone that the builders refused, that is made the head of the corner? **18** Whosoever shall fall upon that stone, shall be broken: and on whomsoever it shall fall, it will grind him to powder. **19** Then the high Priests, and the Scribes the same hour went about to lay hands on him (but they feared the people) for they perceived that he had spoken this parable against them. **20** [c,4]And they [d]watched him, and sent forth [e]spies, which should feign themselves just men [f]to take him in his talk, and to deliver him unto the power and [g]authority of the governor. **21** And they asked him, saying, Master, we know that thou sayest, and teachest right, neither dost thou accept [h]any man's person, but teachest the way of God truly. **22** Is it lawful for us to give Caesar tribute or no? **23** But he perceived their [i]craftiness, and said unto them, Why tempt ye me? **24** Show me a penny. Whose image and superscription hath it? They answered, and said, Caesars. **25** Then he said unto them, [5]Give then unto Caesar the things which are Caesar's, and to God those which are God's. **26** And they could not reprove his saying before the people: but they marveled at his answer, and held their peace. **27** [j,6]Then came to him certain of the Sadducees (which deny that there is any resurrection) and they asked him, **28** Saying, Master, [7]Moses wrote unto us, If any man's brother die having a wife, and he die without children, that his brother should take his wife, and raise up seed unto his brother. **29** Now there were seven brethren, and the first took a wife, and he died without children. **30** And the second took the wife, and he died childless. **31** Then the third took her: and so likewise the seven died, and left no children. **32** And last of all, the woman died also. **33** Therefore at the resurrection, whose wife of them shall she be? for seven had her to wife. **34** Then Jesus answered, and said unto them, The [k]children of this world marry wives, and are married. **35** But they which shall be counted worthy to enjoy that world, and the resurrection from the dead, neither marry wives, neither are married. **36** For they can die no more, forasmuch as they are equal unto the Angels,

---

received of God, to his glory with great pains and diligence: the third live idly, and do no good. As for the first, the Lord when he cometh will justly punish them in his time: the other he will bless, according to the pains which they have taken: and as for the slothful and idle persons, he will punish them as the first.

i. Luke 19:16 This was a piece of money, which the Grecians used, and was in value about an hundred pence, which is about ten crowns.

j. Luke 19:20 Against them which spend their life idly in deliberating, and otherwise, in contemplation.

k. Luke 19:23 To the bankers and changers.

l. Luke 19:28 The disciples staggered and stayed at the matter, but Christ goeth on boldly though death were before his eyes.

m. Luke 19:29 Christ showeth in his own person, that his kingdom is not of this world.

n. Luke 19:39 When they linger which ought to be the chiefest preachers and setters forth of the kingdom of God, he will raise up others extraordinarily, in despite of them.

o. Luke 19:41 Christ is not simply delighted with the destruction, no not of the wicked.

p. Luke 19:42 Christ breaketh off his speech, which showeth partly how he was moved with compassion for the destruction of the city, that was like to ensue: and partly to upbraid them for their treachery and stubbornness against him, such as hath not lightly been heard of.

q. Luke 19:42 At least wise thou, O Jerusalem, to whom this message was properly sent.

r. Luke 19:42 If after the slaying of so many Prophets, and so oft refusing me the Lord of the Prophets, now especially in this my last coming to thee, thou hadst had any regard to thyself.

s. Luke 19:42 The fit and commodious time is called the day of this city.

t. Luke 19:42 That is, those things wherein thy happiness standeth.

u. Luke 19:44 That is, this very instant wherein God visited thee.

v. Luke 19:45 Christ showeth after his entry into Jerusalem by a visible sign, that it is his office enjoined him of his Father to purge the Temple.

LUKE 19

1. Matt. 18:11
2. Matt. 25:14
3. Luke 8:18 / Matt. 13:12 / Matt. 25:29 / Mark 4:25
4. Matt. 21:1 / Mark 11:1
5. Matt. 21:7 / John 12:14
6. Luke 21:6 / Matt. 24:1 / Mark 13:1
7. Matt. 21:13
8. Mark 11:17
9. Isa. 56:7 / Jer. 7:11

LUKE 20

a. Luke 20:1 The Pharisees being overcome with the truth of Christ's doctrine, move a question about his outward calling, and are overcome by the witness of their own conscience.

b. Luke 20:9 It is no new thing to have them the chiefest enemies of Christ and his servants, which are conversant in the very Sanctuary of God's holy place: but at length they shall not escape unpunished.

c. Luke 20:20 The last refuge that false prophets have to destroy the true Prophets, is to lay sedition, and treason to their charge.

d. Luke 20:20 A fit time to take him in.

e. Luke 20:20 Whom they had deceitfully hired.

f. Luke 20:20 That they might take some hold in his talk and thereby forge some false accusation against him.

g. Luke 20:20 To put him to death.

h. Luke 20:21 Thou are not moved by favor of any: and by person he meaneth outward circumstances, which if a man have respect unto, he will not judge alike of them that are indeed alike.

i. Luke 20:23 Craftiness is a certain diligence and witness to do evil, gotten by much use and great practice in matters.

j. Luke 20:27 The resurrection of the flesh is avouched against the Sadducees.

k. Luke 20:34 They are called here in this place, the children of this world, which live in this world: and not they, that wholly

and are the sons of God, since they are the [l]children of the resurrection. **37** And
that the dead shall rise again, even [8]Moses showed it besides the bush, when he
said, The Lord is the God of Abraham, and the God of Isaac, and the God of Ja-
cob. **38** For he is not the God of the dead, but of them which live: for all [m]live
unto him. **39** Then certain of the Scribes answered, and said, Master, thou hast
well said. **40** And after that, durst they not ask him anything at all. **41** [n,9]Then
said he unto them, How say they that Christ is David's son? **42** And David him-
self saith in the book of the Psalms, [10]The Lord said unto my Lord, Sit at my right
hand, **43** Till I shall make thine enemies thy footstool. **44** Seeing David called
him Lord, how is he then his son? **45** Then in the audience of all the people he
said unto his disciples, **46** [o,11]Beware of the Scribes, which willingly go in long
robes, and love salutations in the markets, and the highest seats in the assemblies,
and the chief rooms at feasts: **47** Which devour widow's [p]houses, and in show
make long prayers: These shall receive greater damnation.

21

1 The widow's liberality above her riches. 5 Of the time of the destruction of the Temple, 19 and Jerusalem. 25 The signs going before the last judgment.

1 And [a,1]as he beheld, he saw the rich men which cast their gifts into the
treasury.
2 And he saw also a certain poor widow which cast in thither two mi-
tes: **3** And he said, Of a truth I say unto you, that this poor widow hath cast in
more than they all. **4** For they all have of their superfluity cast into the offerings
of God: but she of her penury hath cast in all the living that she had. **5** [b,2]Now
as some spake of the Temple, how it was garnished with goodly stones, and with
[c]consecrated things, he said, **6** Are these the things that ye look upon? the days
will come wherein a stone shall not be left upon a stone, that shall not be thrown
down. **7** Then they asked him, saying, Master, but when shall these things be?
and what sign shall there be when these things shall come to pass? **8** [3]And he
said, Take heed, that ye be not deceived: for many will come [d]in my Name, saying,
I am Christ, and the time draweth near: follow ye not them therefore. **9** [e]And
when ye hear of wars and seditions, be not afraid: for these things must first come,
but the end followeth not by and by. **10** Then said he unto them, Nation shall
rise against nation, and kingdom against kingdom, **11** [4]And great earthquakes
shall be in divers places, and hunger, and pestilence, and fearful things, and gre-
at signs shall there be from heaven. **12** But before all these, they shall lay their
hands on you, and persecute you, delivering you up to the assemblies, and into
prisons, and bring you before Kings and rulers for my Name's sake. **13** And this
shall turn to you, for a [f]testimonial. **14** [5]Lay it up therefore in your hearts, that
ye cast not beforehand what ye shall answer. **15** For I will give you a mouth,
and wisdom where against all your adversaries shall not be able to speak nor re-
sist. **16** Yea, ye shall be betrayed also of your parents and of your brethren, and
kinsmen, and friends, and some of you shall they put to death. **17** And ye shall
be hated of all men for my Name's sake. **18** [6]Yet there shall not one hair of your
heads perish. **19** By your patience [g]possess your souls. **20** [h,7]And when ye see
Jerusalem besieged with soldiers, then understand that the desolation thereof is
near. **21** Then let them which are in Judea, flee to the mountains: and let them
which are in the midst thereof, depart out: and let not them that are in the coun-
try, enter therein: **22** For these be the days of vengeance, to fulfill all things that
are written. **23** But woe be to them that be with child, and to them that give
suck in those days: for there shall be great distress in this land, and [i]wrath over this
people, **24** And they shall fall on the [j]edge of the sword, and shall be led captive
into all nations, and Jerusalem shall be trodden under foot of the Gentiles, until
the time of the Gentiles be fulfilled. **25** [k,8]Then there shall be signs in the sun,
and in the moon, and in the stars, and upon the earth trouble among the nations,
with perplexity: the sea and the waters shall roar. **26** [l]And men's hearts shall fail
them for fear and for looking after those things which shall come on the world:
for the powers of heaven shall be shaken. **27** And then shall they see the Son of
man come in a cloud, with power and great glory. **28** And when these things
begin to come to pass, then look up, and lift up your heads: [9]for your redemption
draweth near. **29** [m]And he spake to them a parable, Behold, the fig tree, and all
trees, **30** When they now shoot forth, ye seeing them, know of your own selves,
that summer is then near. **31** So likewise ye, when ye see these things come to
pass, know ye that the kingdom of God is near. **32** Verily I say unto you, This
age shall not pass, till all these things be done: **33** Heaven and earth shall pass
away, but my words shall not pass away. **34** [10]Take heed to yourselves, lest at any
time your hearts be oppressed with surfeiting and drunkenness, and cares of this
life, and lest that day come on you at unawares, **35** For as a snare shall it come
[n]on all them that dwell on the face of the whole earth. **36** Watch therefore, and
pray continually, that ye may be counted worthy to escape all these things that
shall come to pass, and that ye may [o]stand before the son of man. **37** Now in
the daytime he taught in the Temple, and at night he went out, and abode in the
mount, that is called the mount of Olives. **38** And all the people came in the
morning to him, to hear him in the Temple.

22

3 Judas selleth Christ. 7 The Apostles prepare the Passover. 24 They strive who shall be chiefest. 31 Satan desireth them. 35 Christ showeth that they wanted nothing. 42 He prayeth in the mount. 44 He sweateth blood. 50 Malchus's ear cut off and healed. 57, 58, 60 Peter denieth Christ thrice. 63 Christ is mocked and strooken. 69 He confesseth himself to be the Son of God.

1 Now [1]the [a]feast of unleavened bread drew near, which is called the Passo-
ver. **2** And the high Priests and Scribes sought how they might kill him: for they
feared the people. **3** [b,2]Then entered Satan into Judas, who was called Iscariot,
and was of the number of the twelve. **4** And he went his way, and communed
with the high Priests and [c]captains, how he might betray him to them. **5** So
they were glad, and agreed to give him money. **6** And he consented, and sought
opportunity to betray him unto them, when the people were [d]away. **7** [e,3]Then
came the day of unleavened bread, when the Passover [f]must be sacrificed. **8** And
he sent Peter and John, saying, Go and prepare us the [g]Passover that we may eat
it. **9** And they said to him, Where wilt thou, that we prepare it? **10** Then he said
unto them, Behold, when ye be entered into the city, there shall a man meet you,
bearing a pitcher of water: follow him into the house that he entereth in, **11** And
say unto the good man of the house, The Master saith unto thee, Where is the lo-
dging where I shall eat my Passover with my disciples? **12** Then he shall show
you a great high chamber trimmed: there make it ready. **13** So they went, and
found as he had said unto them, and made ready the Passover. **14** [h,4]And when
the [i]hour was come, he sat down, and the twelve Apostles with him. **15** Then
he said unto them, I have earnestly desired to eat this Passover with you, before I
[j]suffer. **16** For I say unto you, Henceforth I will not eat of it anymore, until it be

---

are given to the world, as before Luke 16:8, which are contrary to the children of light.

l. Luke 20:36 That is, men partakers of the resurrection, for as we say truly, that they shall live indeed, which shall enjoy everlasting bliss, so do they rise indeed, which rise to life, though if this word resurrection, be taken generally, it belongeth also to the wicked which shall rise to condemnation, which is not properly life, but death.

m. Luke 20:38 That is, before him: a notable saying, the godly do not die, though they die here on earth.

n. Luke 20:41 Christ is so the son of David according to the flesh, that he is also his Lord (because he is the everlasting son of God) according to the spirit.

o. Luke 20:46 We must avoid the example of the ambitious and covetous pastors.

p. Luke 20:47 This is spoken by the figure Metonymy, houses, for the goods and substance.

LUKE 20

1. Matt. 21:25 / Mark 11:27
2. Matt. 21:33 / Mark 12:1 / Isa. 5:1 / Jer. 2:21
3. Ps. 118:22 / Isa. 28:16 / Acts 4:11 / Rom. 9:33 / 1 Pet. 2:8
4. Matt. 22:16 / Matt. 12:13
5. Rom. 13:7
6. Matt. 22:23 / Mark 12:18
7. Deut. 25:5
8. Exod. 3:6
9. Matt. 22:44 / Mark 12:35
10. Ps. 110:1
11. Luke 11:43 / Matt. 23:6 / Mark 12:38

LUKE 21

a. Luke 21:1 The poor may exceed in bounty and liberality even the richest, according to God's judgment.

b. Luke 21:5 The destruction of the Temple is foretold, that that true spiritual building may be built up, whose head builders must and ought to be circumspect.

c. Luke 21:5 There were things that were hanged upon walls and pillars.

d. Luke 21:8 Using my Name.

e. Luke 21:9 The true Temple of God is built up even in the midst of incredible tumults, and most sharp miseries, through invincible patience, so that the end thereof cannot be but most happy.

f. Luke 21:13 This shall be the end of your troubles and afflictions, they shall be witnesses both before God and man, as well of the treacherous and cruel dealing of your enemies, as also of your constancy: A noble saying, that the afflictions of the godly and holy men pertains to the witness of the truth.

g. Luke 21:19 Though you are compassed about on all sides with many miseries, yet notwithstanding be valiant and courageous, and bear out these things manfully.

h. Luke 21:20 The final destruction of the whole city is foretold.

i. Luke 21:23 By wrath, those things are meant, which God sendeth when he is displeased.

j. Luke 21:24 Word for word, mouth, for the Hebrews call the edge of a sword the mouth, because the edge biteth.

k. Luke 21:25 When the times are expired, appointed for the salvation of the Gentiles and punishment of the Jews: And so he passeth from the destruction of Jerusalem, to the history of the latter judgment.

l. Luke 21:26 After divers tempests, the Lord will at the length plainly appear to deliver his Church.

m. Luke 21:29 We must be sober and watchful both day and night for the Lord's coming, that we be not taken at unawares.

n. Luke 21:35 On all men wheresoever they be.

o. Luke 21:36 You may so appear that you will abide the countenance and sentence of the Judge without fear.

LUKE 21

1. Mark 12:42
2. Luke 19:43 / Matt. 24:1 / Mark 13:1
3. Eph. 5:6 / 2 Thess. 2:3
4. Matt. 24:7 / Mark 13:18
5. Luke 12:12 / Matt. 10:19 / Mark 13:11
6. Matt. 10:30
7. Dan. 9:27 / Matt. 14:15 / Mark 13:14
8. Isa. 13:10 / Ezek. 31:7 / Matt. 24:29 / Mark 13:14
9. Rom. 8:27
10. Rom. 13:13

LUKE 22

a. Luke 22:1 Christ is taken upon the day of the Passover, rather by the providence of his Father, than by the will of men.

b. Luke 22:3 God by his wonderful providence, causeth him to be the minister of our salvation, who was the author of our destruction.

c. Luke 22:4 They that had the charge of keeping the Temple, which were none of the Priests and Bishops, as appeareth by verse 52 of this Chapter.

d. Luke 22:6 Without tumult, unwitting to the people which used to follow him: and therefore indeed they watched their time, when they knew he was alone in the garden.

e. Luke 22:7 Christ teacheth his disciples by a manifest miracle, that although he be going to be crucified, yet nothing is hid from him: and therefore that he goeth willingly to death.

f. Luke 22:7 By the order appointed by the Law.

g. Luke 22:8 The lamb which was the figure of the Passover: And this is spoken by the figure metonymy, which is very usual in the matter of the Sacraments.

h. Luke 22:14 Christ having ended the Passover according to the order of the Law, forewarneth them that this shall be his last banquet with them, after the manner and necessity of this life.

i. Luke 22:14 The evening and twilight, at what time this supper was to be kept.

j. Luke 22:15 I am put to death.

fulfilleth in the kingdom of God. **17** And he took the cup, and gave thanks, and
said, Take this, and divide it among you: **18** For I say unto you, I will not drink
of the fruit of the vine, until the kingdom of God be come. **19** [k,5]And he took
bread, and when he had given thanks, he brake it, and gave to them, saying, This is
my body, which is given for you: do this in the remembrance of me. **20** Likewi-
se also after supper he took the cup, saying, This [l]cup is [m]that new Testament in
my blood, which is shed for you. **21** [n,6]Yet behold, the [o]hand of him that be-
trayeth me, is with me at the table. **22** [p]And truly the Son of man goeth as it
is appointed: but woe be to that man by whom he is betrayed. **23** Then they
began to inquire among themselves which of them it should be, that should do
that. **24** [q,7]And there arose also a strife among them, which of them should seem
to be the greatest. **25** But he said unto them, The kings of the Gentiles reign over
them, and they that bear rule over them, are called [r]bountiful. **26** But ye shall
not be so: but let the greatest among you be as the least: and the chiefest as he that
serveth. **27** For who is greater, he that sitteth at table, or he that serveth? is not
he that sitteth at table? And I am among you as he that serveth. **28** [s]And ye are
they which have continued with me in my tentations. **29** Therefore I appoint
unto you a kingdom, as my Father hath appointed unto me, **30** [8]That ye may
eat, and drink at my table, in my kingdom, and sit on seats, and judge the twelve
tribes of Israel. **31** [t]And the Lord said, Simon, Simon, behold, [9]Satan hath desi-
red you, [u]to winnow you as wheat. **32** [v]But I have prayed for thee, that thy faith
fail not: therefore when thou art converted, strengthen thy brethren. **33** [w,10]And
he said unto him: Lord, I am ready to go with thee into prison, and to dea-
th. **34** But he said, I tell thee, Peter, the cock shall not crow this day, before thou
hast thrice denied that thou knewest me. **35** And he said unto them, [11]When
I sent you without bag, and scrip, and shoes, lacked ye anything? And they said,
Nothing. **36** [x]Then he said to them, But now he that hath a bag, let him take
it, and likewise a scrip: and he that hath none, let him sell his coat, and buy a
sword. **37** For I say unto you, That yet the same which is written, must be per-
formed in me, [12]Even with the wicked was he numbered: for doubtless those thin-
gs which are written of me, have an end. **38** And they said, Lord, behold, here
are two swords. And he said unto them, It is enough. **39** [13]And he came out,
and went (as he was wont) to the mount of Olives: and his disciples also followed
him. **40** [y,14]And when he came to the place, he said to them, Pray, lest ye en-
ter into tentation. **41** [z]And he was drawn aside from them about a stone's cast,
and kneeled down, and prayed, **42** Saying, Father, If thou wilt, take away this
cup from me: nevertheless, not my will, but thine be done. **43** And there appe-
ared an Angel unto him from heaven, comforting him. **44** But being in an [aa]a-
gony, he prayed more earnestly: and his sweat was like [ab]drops of blood, trickling
down to the ground. **45** [ac]And he rose up from prayer, and came to his disciples,
and found them sleeping for heaviness. **46** And he said unto them, Why sleep
ye? rise and pray, lest ye enter into tentation. **47** [ad,15]And while he yet spake,
behold, a company, and he that was called Judas one of the twelve, went before
them, and came near unto Jesus to kiss him. **48** And Jesus said unto him, Judas,
betrayest thou the Son of man with a kiss? **49** [ae]Now when they which were
about him, saw what would follow, they said unto him, Lord, shall we smite with
the sword? **50** And one of them smote a servant of the high Priest, and struck
off his right ear. **51** Then Jesus answered, and said, Suffer them thus far: and he
touched his ear, and healed him. **52** [af]Then Jesus said unto the high Priests, and
captains of the Temple, and the Elders which were come to him, Be ye come out as
unto a thief with swords and staves? **53** When I was daily with you in the Tem-
ple, ye stretched not forth the hands against me: but this is your very hour, and the
[ag]power of darkness. **54** [16]Then took they him, and led him, and brought him to
the high Priest's house. [ah]And Peter followed afar off. **55** [17]And when they had
kindled a fire in the midst of the hall, and were set down together, Peter also sat
down among them. **56** And a certain maid beheld him as he sat by the fire, and
having well looked on him, said, This man was also with him. **57** But he denied
him, saying, Woman, I know him not. **58** And after a little while, another man
saw him, and said, Thou art also of them. But Peter said, Man, I am not. **59** And
about the space of an hour after, a certain other affirmed, saying. Verily, even this
man was with him: for he is also a Galilean. **60** And Peter said, Man, I know not
what thou sayest. And immediately while he yet spake, the cock crew. **61** Then
the Lord turned back, and looked upon Peter: and Peter remembered the word
of the Lord, how he had said unto him, [18]Before the cock crow, thou shalt deny
me thrice. **62** And Peter went out, and wept bitterly. **63** [ai,19]And the men
that held Jesus, mocked him, and struck him. **64** And when they had blindfol-
ded him, they smote him on the face, and asked him, saying, Prophesy who it is
that smote thee. **65** And many other things blasphemously spake they against
him. **66** [aj,20]And as soon as it was day, the Elders of the people, and the high
Priests and the Scribes came together, and led him into their Council, **67** Saying,
Art thou that Christ? tell us. And he said unto them, If I tell you, ye will not believe
it. **68** And if also I ask you, you will not answer me, nor let me go. **69** Here-
after shall the Son of man sit at the right hand of the power of God. **70** Then
said they all, Art thou then the Son of God? And he said to them, Ye say, that I
am. **71** Then said they, What need we any further witness? for we ourselves have
heard it of his own mouth.

23

1 He is accuseth before Pilate. 7 He is sent to Herod. 11 He is mocked. 24 Pilate yieldeth him up to the Jews' request. 27 The women bewail him. 33 He is crucified. 39 One of the thieves revileth him. 43 The other is saved by faith. 45 He dieth. 53 He is buried.

1 Then [a]the whole multitude of them arose, and led him unto Pilate. **2** And
they began to accuse him, saying, We have found this man [b]perverting the nation,
[1]and forbidding to pay tribute to Caesar, saying, That he is Christ a King. **3** [2]And
Pilate asked him, saying, Art thou the King of the Jews? And he answered him, and
said, Thou sayest it. **4** Then said Pilate to the high Priests, and to the people, I
find no fault in this man. **5** But they were the more fierce, saying, He moveth
the people, teaching throughout all Judea, beginning at Galilee, even to this pla-
ce. **6** [c]Now when Pilate heard of Galilee, he asked whether the man were a Ga-
lilean. **7** And when he knew that he was of [d]Herod's jurisdiction, he sent him
to Herod, which was also at Jerusalem in those days. **8** And when Herod saw
Jesus, he was exceedingly glad: for he was desirous to see him of a long season,
because he had heard many things of him, and trusteth to have seen some sign
done by him. **9** Then questioned he with him of many things: but he answered
him nothing. **10** The high Priests also and Scribes stood forth and accused him

---

k. Luke 22:19 Christ establisheth his new Covenant, and his communicating with us with new signs.

l. Luke 22:20 Here is a double Metonymy: for first the vessel is taken for that which is contained in the vessel, as the cup, for the wine which is within the cup. Then the wine is called the Covenant or Testament, whereas indeed it is but the sign of the Testament, or rather of the blood of Christ, whereby the Testament was made: neither is it a vain sign, though it be not all one with the thing that it representeth.

m. Luke 22:20 This word, that, showeth the excellency of the Testament, and answereth to the place of Jeremiah, Chapter 31:31, where the new Testament is promised.

n. Luke 22:21 Christ showeth again that he goeth to death willingly, although he be not ignorant of Judas's treason.

o. Luke 22:21 That is, his practice , so use the Hebrews to speak, 2 Kings 14:19.Is not the hand of Joab in this matter?

p. Luke 22:22 Although the decree of God's providence comes necessarily to pass, yet it excuseth not the fault of the instruments.

q. Luke 22:24 The Pastors are not called to rule, but to serve.

r. Luke 22:25 Have great titles, for so it was the custom to honor Princes with some great titles.

s. Luke 22:28 Such as are partakers of the afflictions of Christ, shall also be partakers of his kingdom.

t. Luke 22:31 We must always think upon the wait that Satan layeth for us.

u. Luke 22:31 To toss you and scatter you, and also to cast you out.

v. Luke 22:32 It is through the prayers of Christ, that the elect do never utterly fall away from the faith: and that for this cause, that they should stir up one another.

w. Luke 22:33 Christ showeth that faith differeth much from a vain security, in setting before us the grievous example of Peter.

x. Luke 22:36 All this talk is by way of an allegory, as if he said, O my friends and fellow soldiers, you have lived hitherto as it were in peace: but now there is a most sharp battle at hand to be fought, and therefore you must lay all other things aside, and think upon furnishing yourselves in armor. And what this armor is, he showeth by his own example, when he prayed afterward in the garden, and reproved Peter for striking with the sword.

y. Luke 22:40 Christ hath made death acceptable unto us, by overcoming in our name, all the horrors of death, which had joined with them the curse of God.

z. Luke 22:41 Prayers are a sure succor against the most perilous assaults of our enemies.

aa. Luke 22:44 This agony showeth that Christ strove much, and was in great distress: for Christ strove not only with the fears of death, as other men used to do, for so many martyrs might seem more constant than Christ, but with the fearful judgment of his angry Father, which is the fearfullest thing in the world: and the matter was, for that he took the burden of all our sins upon himself.

ab. Luke 22:44 These do not only show that Christ was true man, but other things also which the goodly have to consider of, wherein redemption of all mankind is contained in the son of God his debasing himself to the state of a servant: such things as no man can sufficiently declare.

ac. Luke 22:45 Men are utterly sluggish, even in their greatest dangers until Christ stir them up.

ad. Luke 22:47 Christ is willingly betrayed and taken, that by his obedience he might deliver us which were guilty for the betraying of God's glory.

ae. Luke 22:49 That zeal which carrieth us out of the bounds of our vocation, pleaseth not Christ.

af. Luke 22:52 Even the very fear of them which took Christ, proveth partly their evil conscience, and partly also that all these things were done by God's providence.

ag. Luke 22:53 The power that was given to darkness, to oppress the light for a season.

ah. Luke 22:54 We have to behold in Peter an example both of the fragility of man's nature, and of the singular goodness of God toward his elect.

ai. Luke 22:63 Christ bare the shame that was due to our sins.

aj. Luke 22:66 Christ is wrongfully condemned of blasphemy before the high Priest's judgment seat, that we might be quit before God from the blasphemy which we deserved.

LUKE 22

1. Matt. 26:1-5 / Mark 14:10
2. Matt. 26:14 / Mark 14:10
3. Matt. 26:17 / Mark 14:13
4. Matt. 26:10 / Mark 14:17
5. Matt. 26:16 / Mark 14:22 / 1 Cor. 11:24
6. Matt. 26:21 / Mark 14:18 / Ps. 41:9
7. Matt. 20:25 / Mark 10:42
8. Matt. 19:28
9. 1 Pet. 5:8
10. Matt. 26:34 / Mark 14:39 / John 13:38
11. Matt. 10:9
12. Isa. 63:12
13. Matt. 26:36 / Mark 14:32 / John 18:1
14. Matt. 26:14 / Mark 14:38
15. Matt. 26:47 / Mark 14:43 / John 18:3
16. Matt. 26:58
17. Matt. 26:38,59 / Mark 14:66 / John 18:25
18. Matt. 26:34 / John 13:38
19. Matt. 26:67 / Mark 14:65
20. Matt. 27:1 / Mark 15:1 / John 18:28

LUKE 23

a. Luke 23:1 Christ, who is now ready to suffer for the sedition, which we raised in this world, is first of all pronounced guiltless, that it might appear that he suffered not for his own sins (which were none) but for ours.

b. Luke 23:2 Corrupting the people, and leading them into errors.

c. Luke 23:6 Christ is a laughingstock to princes, but to their great smart.

d. Luke 23:7 This was Herod Antipas the Tetrarch, in the time of whose governance, which was almost the space of 22 years, John the Baptist preached and was put to death, and Jesus Christ also died and rose again, and the Apostles began to preach, and divers things were done at Jerusalem almost seven years after Christ's death. This Herod was sent into banishment to Lyons, about the second year of Gaius Caesar.

vehemently. **11** And Herod with his [e]men of war, despised him, and mocked
him, and arrayed him in white, and sent him again to Pilate. **12** [f]And the same
day Pilate and Herod were made friends together: for before they were enemies
one to another. **13** [g]Then Pilate called together the high Priests, and the [h]rulers,
and the people, **14** [3]And said unto them, Ye have brought this man unto me, as
one that perverted the people: and behold, I have examined him before you, and
have found no fault in this man, of those things whereof ye accuse him: **15** No,
nor yet Herod: for I sent you to him: and lo, nothing worthy of death is done of
him. **16** [i]I will therefore chastise him, and let him loose. **17** (For of necessity
he must have let one loose unto them at the feast.) **18** Then all the multitude cri-
ed at once, saying, Away with him, and deliver unto us Barabbas: **19** Which for
a certain insurrection made in the city, and murder, was cast in prison. **20** Then
Pilate spake again to them, willing to let Jesus loose. **21** But they cried, saying,
Crucify, crucify him. **22** [j]And he said unto them the third time, But what evil
hath he done? I find no cause of death in him: I will therefore chastise him, and let
him loose. **23** But they were instant with loud voices, and required that he mi-
ght be crucified: and the voices of them and of the high Priests prevailed. **24** So
Pilate gave sentence, that it should be as they required. **25** And he let loose unto
them him that for insurrection and murder was cast into prison, whom they de-
sired, and delivered Jesus to do with him what they would. **26** [k,4]And as they
led him away, they caught one Simon of Cyrene, coming out of the field, and
on him they laid the cross, to bear it after Jesus. **27** [l]And there followed him a
great multitude of people, and of women, which women bewailed and lamented
him. **28** But Jesus turned back unto them, and said, Daughters of Jerusalem,
weep not for me, but weep for yourselves, and for your children. **29** For behold,
the days will come, when men shall say, Blessed are the barren, and the wombs
that never bare, and the paps which never gave suck. **30** Then shall they begin to
say to the mountains, [5]Fall on us: and to the hills, Cover us. **31** [6]For if they do
these things to a [m]green tree, what shall be done to the dry? **32** [7]And there were
two others, which were evildoers, led with him to be slain. **33** [n]And when they
were come to the place, which is called Calvary, there they crucified him, and the
evildoers: one at the right hand, and the other at the left. **34** [o]Then said Jesus,
Father, forgive them: for they know not what they do. And they parted his raiment,
and cast lots. **35** And the people stood, and beheld: and the rulers mocked him
with them, saying, He saved others: let him save himself, if he be that Christ the
[p]Chosen of God. **36** The soldiers also mocked him, and came and offered him
vinegar, **37** And said, If thou be the King of the Jews, save thyself. **38** [q]And
a superscription was also written over him, in Greek letters, and in Latin, and in
Hebrew, THIS IS THAT KING OF THE JEWS. **39** [r]And [s]one of the evildoers,
which were hanged, railed on him, saying, If thou be that Christ, save thyself and
us. **40** But the other answered, and rebuked him, saying, Fearest thou not God,
seeing thou art in the same condemnation? **41** We are indeed righteously here:
for we receive things worthy of that we have done: but this man hath done nothing
[t]amiss. **42** And he said unto Jesus, Lord, remember me, when thou comest into
thy kingdom. **43** Then Jesus said unto him, Verily I say unto thee, today shalt
thou be with me in [u]Paradise. **44** [v]And it was about the sixth hour: and there
was a darkness over all the land, until the ninth hour. **45** [w]And the Sun was dar-
kened, and the veil of the Temple rent through the midst. **46** And Jesus cried
with a loud voice, and said, [8]Father, into thine hands I commend my spirit. And
when he thus had said, he gave up the ghost. **47** [x]Now when the Centurion saw
what was done, he glorified God, saying, Of a surety this man was just. **48** And
all the people that came together to that sight, beholding the things which were
done: smote their breasts, and returned. **49** [y]And all his acquaintances stood
afar off, and the women that followed him from Galilee, beholding these thin-
gs. **50** [z,9]And behold, there was a man named Joseph, which was a counselor, a
good man and a just. **51** He did not consent to the counsel and deed of them,
which was of Arimathea, a city of the Jews: who also himself waited for the king-
dom of God. **52** He went unto Pilate, and asked the body of Jesus, **53** And
took it down, and wrapped it in a linen cloth, and laid it in a tomb hewn out
of a rock, wherein was never man yet laid. **54** And that day was the prepara-
tion, and the Sabbath [aa]drew on. **55** [ab]And the women also that followed after,
which came with him from Galilee, beheld the sepulcher, and how his body was
laid. **56** And they returned and prepared odors, and ointments, and resteth the
Sabbath day according to the commandment.

24

The women come to the sepulchre. 9 They report that which they heard of the Angels, unto the Apostles. 13 Christ doth accompany two going to Emmaus. 27 He expoundeth the Scriptures unto them. 39 He offereth himself to his Apostles to be handled. 49 He promiseth the holy Ghost. 51 He is carried up into heaven.

1 Now the [a,1]first day of the week [b]early in the morning, they came unto the
sepulcher, and brought the odors which they had prepared, and certain women
with them. **2** And they found the stone rolled away from the sepulcher, **3** And
went in, but found not the body of the Lord Jesus. **4** And it came to pass, that
as they were amazed thereat, behold, two men suddenly stood by them in shining
vestures. **5** And as they were afraid, and bowed down their faces to the earth,
they said to them, Why seek ye him that liveth, among the dead? **6** He is not
here, but is risen: remember [2]how he spake unto you, when he was yet in Gali-
lee, **7** Saying, that the Son of man must be delivered into the hands of sinful
men, and be crucified, and the third day rise again. **8** And they remembered his
words, **9** [c]And returned from the sepulcher, and told all these things unto the
eleven, and to all the remnant. **10** Now it was Mary Magdalene, and Joanna,
and Mary the mother of James, and other women with them which told these
things unto the Apostles. **11** But their words seemed unto them as a feigned
thing, neither believed they them. **12** [d,3]Then arose Peter and ran unto the se-
pulcher, and [e]looked in and saw the linen clothes laid by themselves, and departed
wondering in himself at that which was come to pass. **13** [f,4]And behold two of
them went that same day to a town which was from Jerusalem about threescore
furlongs, called Emmaus. **14** And they talked together of all these things that
were done. **15** And it came to pass, as they communed together, and reasoned,
that Jesus himself drew near, and went with them. **16** [g]But their eyes were hol-
den, that they could not know him. **17** And he said unto them, What man-
ner of communications are these that ye have one to another as ye walk and are
sad? **18** And [h]the one (named Cleopas) answered and said unto him, Art thou
only a stranger in Jerusalem, and hast not known the things which are come to
pass therein in these days? **19** And he said unto them, What things? And they
said unto him, Of Jesus of Nazareth, which was a Prophet, mighty indeed and in
word before God, and all people, **20** [i]And how the high Priests, and our rulers
delivered him to be condemned to death, and have crucified him. **21** But we
trusted that it had been he that should have delivered Israel, and as touching all
these things, today is the third day, that they were done. **22** Yea, and certain wo-
men among us made us astonied, which came early unto the sepulcher. **23** And
when they found not his body, they came, saying, that they had also seen a vision
of Angels, which said, that he was alive. **24** Therefore certain of them which
were with us, went to the sepulcher, and found it even so as the women had said,

---

e. Luke 23:11 Accompanied with his nobles and soldiers which followed him from Galilee.

f. Luke 23:12 The hatred of godliness joineth the wicked together.

g. Luke 23:13 Christ is quit the second time, even of him of whom he is condemned, that it might appear, how he being just, redeemed us which were unjust.

h. Luke 23:13 Those whom the Jews called the Sanhedrin.

i. Luke 23:16 The wisdom of the flesh, of two evils chooseth the less, but God curseth such counsels.

j. Luke 23:22 Christ is quit the third time, before he was condemned once, that it might appear, how that our sins were condemned in him.

k. Luke 23:26 An example of the outrageousness and disorder of the soldiers.

l. Luke 23:27 The triumph of the wicked hath a most horrible end.

m. Luke 23:31 As if he said, If they do thus to me that am fruitful, and always flourishing, and who lives forever by reason of my Godhead, what will they do to you, that are unfruitful and void of all lively righteousness?

n. Luke 23:33 Christ became accursed for us upon the Cross, suffering the punishment which they deserved that would be God's.

o. Luke 23:34 Christ in praying for his enemies, showeth that he is both the sacrifice and the Priest.

p. Luke 23:35 Whom God loveth more than all others.

q. Luke 23:38 Pilate at unawares is made a preacher of the kingdom of Christ.

r. Luke 23:39 Therefore either we must take that spoken by Synecdoche which Matthew saith, or that both of them mocked Christ. But one of them at length overcome with the great patience of God, brake forth into that confession worthy all memory.

s. Luke 23:39 Christ, in the midst of the humbling of himself upon the cross, showeth indeed that he hath both power of life to save the believers, and of death to revenge the rebellious.

t. Luke 23:41 More than he ought.

u. Luke 23:43 God made the visible paradise to the East part of the world: but that which we behold with the eyes of our mind is the place of everlasting joy and salvation through the goodness and mercy of God, a most pleasant rest of the souls of the godly, and most quiet and joyful dwelling.

v. Luke 23:44 Christ being even at the point of death, showeth himself to be God almighty, even to the blind.

w. Luke 23:45 Christ entereth stoutly into the very darkness of death, for to overcome death even within his most secret places.

x. Luke 23:47 Christ causeth his very enemies to give honorable witness on his side, so oft as it pleaseth him.

y. Luke 23:49 Christ gathereth together, and defendeth his little flock in the midst of the tormentors.

z. Luke 23:50 Christ through his famous burial confirmeth the truth both of his death, and resurrection, by the plain and evident witness of Pilate.

aa. Luke 23:54 Word for word, dawning, as now beginning, for the light of the former day drew toward the going down, and that was the day of preparation for the feast which was to be kept the day following.

ab. Luke 23:55 Christ, being set upon by the devil and all his instruments, and being even, in death's mouth, setteth weak women in his foreward, minding straightways to triumph over those terrible enemies without any great endeavor.

LUKE 24

a. Luke 24:1 Poor silly women, even beside their expectation are chosen to be the first witnesses of the resurrection, that there might be no suspicion either of deceit or violence.

b. Luke 24:1 Very early as Mark saith: or as John saith, while it was yet dark, that is, when it was yet scarce the dawning of the day.

c. Luke 24:9 The cowardly and dastardly minds of the disciples is upbraided by the stout courage of women, (so wrought by God's great mercy) to show that the kingdom of God consisteth in an extraordinary power.

d. Luke 24:12 Christ useth the incredulity of his disciples, to the fuller setting forth of the truth of his resurrection, lest they should seem to have believed that too lightly, which they preached afterward to all the world.

e. Luke 24:12 As it were holding down his head, and bowing his neck, looked diligently in.

f. Luke 24:13 The resurrection is proved by two other witnesses, which saw it, and that it was no forged thing framed of purpose in their own brains, all the circumstances do declare.

g. Luke 24:16 Were held back and stayed, God so appointing it, no doubt: and therefore his body was not invisible, but their eyes were dimmed.

h. Luke 24:18 Some of the old fathers think that the other disciple was this our Evangelist, but Epiphanius writing against the Saturnilians, saith it was Nathanael, but all these are uncertainties.

i. Luke 24:20 It appeareth by the converting of the forewarnings of the Prophets, that all those things are true and certain, which the Evangelists have put down in writing of Christ.

but him they saw not. **25** Then he said unto them, O fools and slow of heart to
believe all that the Prophets have spoken! **26** Ought not Christ to have suffered
these things, and to enter into his glory? **27** And he began at Moses, and at all
the Prophets, and interpreted unto them in all the Scriptures the things which were
written of him. **28** And they drew near unto the town, which they went to, but
he made as though he would have gone further. **29** But they constrained him,
saying, Abide with us, for it is towards night, and the day is far spent. So he went
in to tarry with them. **30** And it came to pass, as he sat at table with them, he
took the bread, and blessed, and brake it, and gave it to them. **31** Then their eyes
were opened, and they knew him: and he was [j]no more seen of them. **32** And
they said between themselves, Did not our hearts burn within us, while he talked
with us by the way, and when he opened to us the Scriptures? **33** And they rose
up the same hour, and returned to Jerusalem, and found the eleven gathered to-
gether, and them that were with them, **34** Which said, The Lord is risen inde-
ed, and hath appeared to Simon. **35** Then they told what things were done in
the way, and how he was known of them in [k]breaking of bread. **36** [l,5]And as
they spake these things, Jesus himself stood in the midst of them, and said unto
them, Peace be to you. **37** But they were abashed and afraid, supposing that
they had seen a spirit. **38** Then he said unto them, Why are ye troubled? and
wherefore do [m]doubts arise in your hearts? **39** Behold mine hands and my feet:
for it is I myself: handle me, and see: for a spirit hath not flesh and bones, as ye
see me have. **40** And when he had thus spoken, he showed them his hands and
feet. **41** And while they yet believed not for joy, and wondered, he said unto
them, Have ye here any meat? **42** And they gave him a piece of a broiled fish,
and of an honeycomb, **43** And he took it, and did eat before them. **44** [n]And
he said unto them, These are the words, which I spake unto you while I was yet
with you, that all must be fulfilled which are written of me in the Law of Moses,
and in the Prophets, and in the Psalms. **45** Then opened he their understanding,
that they might understand the Scriptures, **46** And said unto them, Thus is it
written, and thus it behooved Christ to suffer, and to rise again from the dead the
third day, **47** And that repentance, and remission of sins should be preached in
his Name among all nations, [o]beginning at Jerusalem. **48** Now ye are witnes-
ses of these things. **49** And behold, I do send the [6]promise of my Father upon
you: but tarry ye in the city of Jerusalem, [p]until ye be endued with power from
on high. **50** [q]Afterward he lead them out into Bethany, and lifted up his hands,
and blessed them. **51** And it came to pass, that as he blessed them, [7]he departed
from them, and was carried up into heaven. **52** And they worshipped him, and
returned to Jerusalem with great joy, **53** And were continually in the Temple,
praising, and lauding God. Amen.

---

j. Luke 24:31 Suddenly taken away, and therefore we may not imagine that he was there in such a body as could not be seen, but believe indeed that he changed his place.
k. Luke 24:35 When he brake bread, which that people used, and as the Jews use yet at this day at the beginning of their meals, and say a prayer.
l. Luke 24:36 The Lord himself showeth by certain and necessary signs, that he was risen again, and that in the same body which he took upon him.
m. Luke 24:38 Divers and doubtful thoughts which fall oft into men's heads, when any strange thing falleth out, whereof there is no great likelihood.
n. Luke 24:44 The preaching of the Gospel, which was promised to the Prophets and performed in his time, is committed unto the Apostles: the sum whereof, is repentance and remission of sins.
o. Luke 24:47 The Apostles who are the preachers of the Gospel beginning at Jerusalem.
p. Luke 24:49 Until the holy Ghost comes down from heaven upon you.
q. Luke 24:50 Christ ascendeth into heaven, and departing bodily from his disciples, filleth their hearts with the holy Ghost.

LUKE 24
1. Mark 16:1 / John 20:1
2. Luke 9:22 / Matt. 17:23 / Mark 9:31
3. John 20:6
4. Mark 16:12
5. Mark 16:14 / John 20:19
6. John 15:26 / Acts 1:4
7. Mark 16:19 / Acts 1:9

THE HOLY GOSPEL OF JESUS CHRIST, ACCORDING TO JOHN

1

That Word begotten of God before all worlds, 2 and which was ever with the Father, 14 is made man. 6, 7 For what end John was sent from God. 15 His preaching of Christ's office. 19, 20 The record that he bare given out unto the Priests. 40 The calling of Andrew, 42 of Peter, 43 Philip, 45 and Nathanael.

1 In [a]the [b]beginning [c]was [d]that Word, and that Word was [e]with God, and
that [f]Word was God. **2** This same was in the beginning with God. **3** [g,1]All
[h]things were made by it, and [i]without it [j]was made nothing that was made. **4** [k]In
it [l]was life, and that life was [m]the light of men. **5** [n]And that light shineth in the
wilderness, and the darkness [o]comprehendeth it not. **6** [p,2]There was a man sent
from God, whose name was John. **7** This same came for a witness, to bear wit-
ness of that light, that all men [q]through him might believe. **8** He was not [r]that
light, but was sent to bear witness of that light. **9** [s]This was [t]that true light, which
lighteth every man that cometh into the world. **10** [u]He was in the world, and
the world was [3]made by him: and the world knew him not. **11** He came [v]unto
his own, and his own received him not. **12** [w]But as many as received him, to
them he gave [x]prerogative to be the sons of God, even to them that believe in his
Name, **13** Which are born not of blood, nor of the [y]will of the flesh, nor of the
will of man, but of God. **14** [z,4]And that Word was made [aa]flesh, and [ab]dwelt

---

JOHN. 1
a. John 1:1 The Son of God is of one, and the selfsame eternity or everlastingness, and of one and the selfsame essence or nature, with the Father.
b. John 1:1 From his beginning, as the Evangelist saith, 1 John 1:1, as though he said, that the world began not then to have his being, when God began to make all that was made: for the word was even then when all things that were made, began to be made, and therefore he was before the beginning of all things.
c. John 1:1 Had his being.
d. John 1:1 This word, That, pointeth out unto us a peculiar and choice thing above all other, and putteth a difference between this Word, which is the Son of God, and the Laws of God, which otherwise also are called the word of God.
e. John 1:1 This word (With) putteth out the distinction of persons to us.
f. John 1:1 This word (Word) is the first in order in the sentence, and is that which the learned call (Subjectum:) and this word (God) is the latter in order, and the same which the learned call (Predicatum.)
g. John 1:3 The son of God declareth that same his everlasting Godhead, both by the creating of all things, and also by the preserving of them, and especially by the excellent gifts of reason and understanding, wherewith he that beautified man above all other creatures.
h. John 1:3 Paul expoundeth this place, Col. 1:15 and 16.
i. John 1:3 That is, as the Father did work, so did the Son work with him: for he was fellow worker with him.
j. John 1:3 Of all those things which were made, nothing was made without him.
k. John 1:4 That is, by him: and it is spoken after the manner of the Hebrews, meaning thereby that by his force and working power all life cometh to the world.
l. John 1:4 To wit, even then, when all things are made by him, for else he would have said, Life is in him, and not life was.
m. John 1:4 That force of reason and understanding, which is kindled in our minds to acknowledge him, the author of so great a benefit.
n. John 1:5 The light of men is turned into darkness, but yet so that there is clearness enough to make them without excuse.
o. John 1:5 They could not perceive nor reach unto it, to receive any light of it, no, they did not so much as acknowledge him.
p. John 1:6 There is another more full manifestation of the Son of God, to the consideration whereof men are in good time stirred up, even by John's voice, who is as it were the herald of Christ.
q. John 1:7 Through John.
r. John 1:8 That light which we spake of, to wit, Christ, who only can lighten our darkness.
s. John 1:9 When as the Son of God saw, that man did not acknowledge him by his works, although they were endued with understanding (which he had given to them all) he exhibited himself unto his people to be seen of them with their corporal eyes: yet neither so did they acknowledge him, nor receive him.
t. John 1:9 Who only and properly deserveth to be called the light, for he shineth of himself and borroweth light of none.
u. John 1:10 That person of the Word, was made manifest even at that time when the world was made.
v. John 1:11 The Word showed himself again, when he came in the flesh.
w. John 1:12 The Son being shut out of the most of his people, and acknowledged but of a few, doth regenerate them by his own virtue and power, and receiveth them into that honor which is common to all the children of God, that is to be the sons of God.
x. John 1:12 He vouchsafed to give them this prerogative to take them to be his children.
y. John 1:13 Of that gross and corrupt nature of man, which is throughout the Scriptures set as enemy to the Spirit.
z. John 1:14 That Son, who is God from everlasting, took upon him man's nature, that one and the selfsame might be both God and man, which manifestly appeared to many witnesses, that saw him amongst whom he was conversant, and unto whom by sure and undoubted arguments he showed both his natures.
aa. John 1:14 That is, man: so that the part is taken for the whole, by the figure Synecdoche: for he took upon him all our whole nature, that is to say, a true body, and a true soul.

among us, (and we [5]saw the [ac]glory thereof, [ad]as the glory of the only begotten Son
of the Father) [ae]full of grace and truth. **15** [af]John bare witness of him, and cried,
saying, This was he of whom I said, He that cometh [ag]after me, was [ah]before me:
for he was better than I. **16** [ai,6]And of his fullness have all we received, and [aj]gra-
ce for grace. **17** For the Law was given by Moses, but grace and truth came by
Jesus Christ. **18** [ak,7]No man hath seen God at any time: that only begotten Son,
which is in the [al]bosom of the Father, he hath [am]declared him. **19** [an]Then this
is the record of John, when the Jews sent Priests and Levites from Jerusalem to ask
him, Who art thou? **20** And he [ao]confessed and [ap]denied not, and said plainly,
I am not that Christ. **21** And they asked him, What then? Art thou Elijah? And
he said, [aq]I [8]am not. Art thou [ar]that Prophet? And he answered, No. **22** Then
said they unto him, Who art thou, that we may give an answer to them that sent
us? What sayest thou of thyself? **23** He said, [9]I am the voice of him that crieth
in the wilderness, Make straight the way of the Lord, as said the Prophet Isa-
iah. **24** [as]Now they which were sent, were of the Pharisees. **25** And they asked
him, and said unto him, [at]Why baptizest thou then, if thou be not that Christ,
neither Elijah, nor that Prophet? **26** John answered them, saying, I baptize with
water: but there is one [au]among you, whom ye know not. **27** [10]He it is that co-
meth after me, which was before me, whose shoe latchet I am not worthy to unlo-
ose. **28** These things were done in Bethabara beyond Jordan, where John did
baptize. **29** [av]The next day John seeth Jesus coming unto him, and saith, Behold
[aw]that Lamb of God, which [ax]taketh away the [ay]sin of the world. **30** This is he
of whom I said, After me cometh a man, which was before me: for he was better
than I. **31** And [az]I knew him not: but because he should be declared to Israel,
therefore am I come, baptizing with water. **32** [ba]So John bare record, saying,
I beheld, [11]that Spirit come down from heaven, like a dove, and it abode upon
him, **33** And I knew him not: but he that sent me to baptize with water, he
said unto me, Upon whom thou shalt see that Spirit come down, and tarry still
on him, that is he which baptizeth with the holy Ghost. **34** And I saw, and bare
record that this is [bb]that Son of God. **35** [bc]The next day, John stood again, and
two of his disciples. **36** [bd]And he beheld Jesus walking by, and said, Behold
that Lamb of God. **37** [be]And the two disciples heard him speak, and followed
Jesus. **38** Then Jesus turned about, and saw them follow, and said unto them,
What seek ye? And they said unto him, Rabbi, (which is to say by interpretation,
Master) [bf]where dwellest thou? **39** He said unto them, Come, and see. They
came and saw where he dwelt, and abode with him that day: for it was about the
[bg]tenth hour. **40** Andrew, Simon Peter's brother, was one of the two which had
heard it of John, and that followed him. **41** The same found his brother Simon
first, and said unto him, We have found that Messiah which is by interpretation,
that [bh]Christ. **42** And he brought him to Jesus. And Jesus beheld him, and said,
Thou art Simon the son of Jonah: thou shalt be called Cephas, which is by inter-
pretation a stone. **43** The day following, Jesus would go into Galilee, and found
Philip, and said unto him, Follow me. **44** Now Philip was of Bethsaida, the
city of Andrew and Peter. **45** [bi]Philip found Nathanael, and said unto him, We
have found him of whom [12]Moses did write in the Law, and the [13]Prophets, Jesus
that Son of Joseph, that was of Nazareth. **46** [bj]Then Nathanael said unto him,
Can there any good thing come out of Nazareth? Philip said to him, Come, and
see. **47** [bk]Jesus saw Nathanael coming to him, and said of him, Behold indeed an
Israelite, in whom is no guile. **48** [bl]Nathanael said unto him, Whence knewest
thou me? Jesus answered, and said unto him, Before that Philip called thee, when
thou wast under the fig tree, I saw thee. **49** Nathanael answered, and said unto
him, Rabbi, thou art that Son of God: thou art that King of Israel. **50** Jesus an-
swered, and said unto him, Because I said unto thee, I saw thee under the fig tree,
believest thou? thou shalt see greater things than these. **51** And he said unto
him, Verily, verily, I say unto you, Hereafter shall ye see heaven open, and the An-
gels of God [bm,14]ascending, and descending upon that Son of man.

2

1 Christ turneth water into Wine, 11 which was the beginning of his miracles. 12 He goeth down to Capernaum: 13 from thence he goeth up to Jerusalem, 15 and casteth the merchandise out of the Temple. 19 He foretelleth that the Temple, that is, his body shall be destroyed of the Jews. 23 Many believe in him, seeing the miracles which he did.

1 And [a]the [b]third day, was there a marriage in Cana a town of Galilee, and
the mother of Jesus was there. **2** And Jesus was called also, and his disciples unto
the marriage. **3** [c]Now when the wine failed, the mother of Jesus said unto him,
They have no wine. **4** Jesus said unto her, Woman, what have I to do with thee?
mine [d]hour is not yet come. **5** His mother said unto the servants, Whatsoever
he saith unto you, do it. **6** And there were set there, six [e]waterpots of stone, after
the manner of the purifying of the Jews, containing two or three [f]firkins apie-
ce. **7** And Jesus said unto them, Fill the waterpots with water. Then they filled
them up to the brim. **8** Then he said unto them, Draw out now, and bear unto
the governor of the feast. So they bare it. **9** Now when the governor of the feast
had tasted the water that was made wine, (for he knew not whence it was, but the
servants, which drew the water, knew) the governor of the feast called the bridegro-
om, **10** And said unto him, All men at the beginning set forth good wine, and

---

ab. John 1:14 For a season, and when that was ended, he went up into heaven: for the word which he useth, is taken from tents: and yet notwithstanding, his absence from us in body is not such, but that he is always present with us, though not in flesh, yet by the virtue of his Spirit.

ac. John 1:14 The glory which he speaketh of here, is that manifestation of Christ's majesty, which was as it were laid open before our eyes when the Son of God appeared in flesh.

ad. John 1:14 This word (as) doth not in this place betoken a likeness, but the truth of the matter, for his meaning is this, that we saw such a glory, as beseemed and was meet for the true and only begotten Son of God, who is Lord and King over all the world.

ae. John 1:14 He was not only a partaker of grace and truth, but was full of the very substance of grace and truth.

af. John 1:15 John is a faithful witness of the excellency of Christ.

ag. John 1:15 That is, He before whom I am sent to prepare him the way: so that these words are referred to the time of his calling, and not of his age, for John was six months older than he.

ah. John 1:15 This sentence hath in it a turning of the reason as we call it, as who would say, a setting of that first which should be last, and that last which should be first: for in plain speech this it is: He that cometh after me, is better than I am, for he was before me. The like kind of turning the reason we find in Luke 7:47: many sins are forgiven her, because she loved much, which is thus much to say, she loved much, because many sins are forgiven her.

ai. John 1:16 Christ is the most plentiful fountain of all goodness, but then he poured out his gifts most bountifully, when as he exhibited and showed himself to the world.

aj. John 1:16 That is grace upon grace, as a man would say graces heaped one upon another.

ak. John 1:18 That true knowledge of God proceedeth only from Jesus Christ.

al. John 1:18 Who is nearest to his Father, not only in respect of his love towards him, but by the bond of nature, and for that union or oneness that is between them, whereby the Father and the Son are one.

am. John 1:18 Revealed him, and showed him unto us, whereas before he was hid under the shadows of the Law, so that the quickness of the sight of our minds was not able to perceive him: for whosoever seeth him, seeth the Father also.

an. John 1:19 John is neither the Messiah, nor like to any of the other Prophets, but is the herald of Christ, who is now present.

ao. John 1:20 He did acknowledge him, and spake of him plainly and openly.

ap. John 1:20 This repeating of the one and the selfsame thing, though in divers words, is used much of the Hebrews, and it hath great force: for they used to speak one thing twice, to set it out more certainly and plainly.

aq. John 1:21 The Jews thought that Elijah should come again before the days of Messiah, and they took the ground of that their opinion out of Mal. 4:5, which place is to be understood of John, Matt. 11:14. And yet John denieth that he is Elijah, answering them indeed according as they meant.

ar. John 1:21 They inquire of some great Prophet, and not of Christ, for John denied before, that he is Christ, for they thought that some great Prophet should be sent like unto Moses, wresting to that purpose that place of Deut. 18:15, which is to be understood of all the company of the Prophets and ministers, which have been and shall be to the end, and especially of Christ, who is the head of all Prophets.

as. John 1:24 Christ is the author of baptism, and not John: and therefore the force thereof consisteth not in John, who is the minister, but wholly in Christ the Lord.

at. John 1:25 Hereby we may prove that the Jews knew there should be some change in religion under Messiah.

au. John 1:26 Whom all the world seeth not, and is even amongst you.

av. John 1:29 The body and truth of all the sacrifices of the Law, to make satisfaction for the sin of the world, is in Christ.

aw. John 1:29 This word (That) which is added, hath great force in it, not only to set forth the worthiness of Christ, and so to separate him from the Lamb which was a figure of him, and from all other sacrifices of the Law, but also to bring into our mind the Prophecies of Isaiah and others.

ax. John 1:29 This word of the present time signifieth a continual act, for the Lamb hath this virtue proper unto him, and forever, to take away the sins of the world.

ay. John 1:29 That is, that root of sins, to wit, our corruption, and so consequently, the fruits of sin, which are commonly called in the plural number sins.

az. John 1:31 I never knew him by face before.

ba. John 1:32 Christ is proved to be the Son of God, by the coming down of the holy Ghost, by the Father's voice, and by John's testimony.

bb. John 1:34 This word (That) pointeth out unto us some excellent thing, and maketh a difference between Christ and others, whom Moses and the Prophets commonly call the sons of God, or the sons of the most high.

bc. John 1:35 John gathered disciples, not to himself, but to Christ.

bd. John 1:36 Christ is set before us to follow not as a vain shadow, but as our Mediator.

be. John 1:37 In this first gathering of the disciples we have shown unto us, that the beginning of salvation is from God, who calleth us unto his Son by the ministry of his servants: whom (so preventing us) we must also hear, and follow him home, that being instructed by him, we may also instruct others.

bf. John 1:38 Where is thy lodging?

bg. John 1:39 The night grew on.

bh. John 1:41 That is, anointed, and King after the manner of the Jewish people.

bi. John 1:45 The good endeavors even of the unlearned, God doth so allow, that he maketh them masters to the learned.

bj. John 1:46 We must especially take heed of false presumptions, which shut up against us the entrance to Christ.

bk. John 1:47 Simple uprightness discerneth the true Israelites from the false.

bl. John 1:48 The end of miracles is to set before us Christ the Almighty, and also the only author of our salvation, that we may apprehend him by faith.

bm. John 1:51 By these words the power of God is signified which should appear in his ministry by the angels serving him as the head of the Church.

JOHN. 1

1. Col. 1:16
2. Matt. 3:1 / Mark 1:4 / Luke 3:2
3. Heb. 11:3
4. Matt. 1:16
5. Matt. 17:2 / 2 Pet. 1:17
6. Col. 1:19 / Col. 2:9
7. 1 Tim. 6:16 / 1 John 4:12
8. Acts 13:25
9. Isa. 40:3 / Matt. 3:3 / Luke 3:4
10. Matt. 3:11 / Mark 1:7 / Luke 3:16 / Acts 1:5 / Acts 11:16 / Acts 19:4
11. Matt. 3:16 / Mark 1:10 / Luke 3:22
12. Gen. 49:10 / Deut. 18:18
13. Isa. 4:2 / Isa. 40:10 / Isa. 45:8 / Jer. 25:5 / Jer. 33:14 / Ezek. 24:43 / Ezek. 37:24 / Dan. 9:24
14. Gen. 28:12

JOHN. 2

a. John 2:1 Christ declaring openly in an assembly by a notable miracle, that he hath power over the nature of things, to feed man's body, leadeth the minds of all men, to his spiritual and saving virtue and power.

b. John 2:1 After the talk which he had with Nathanael, or after that he departured from John, or after that he came into Galilee.

c. John 2:3 Christ is careful enough of our salvation, and therefore hath no need of others to put him in mind of it.

d. John 2:4 Mine appointed time.

e. John 2:6 These were vessels appointed for water, wherein they washed themselves.

f. John 2:6 Every firkin contained an hundred pounds, at twelve ounces the pound: Whereby we gather that Christ helped them with a thousand and eight hundred pounds of wine.

when men have [g]well drunk, then that which is worse: but thou hast kept back the good wine until now. **11** This beginning of miracles did Jesus in Cana a town of Galilee, and showed forth his glory: and his disciples believed on him. **12** After that, he went down into Capernaum, he and his mother, and his [h]brethren, and his disciples: but they continued not many days there. **13** [i]For the Jews' Passover was at hand. Therefore Jesus went up to Jerusalem. **14** [j]And he found in the Temple those that sold oxen, and sheep, and doves, and changers of money sitting there. **15** Then he made a scourge of small cords and drove them all out of the Temple with the sheep and oxen, and poured out the changers' money, and overthrew their tables, **16** And said unto them that sold doves, Take these things hence: make not my father's house, an house of merchandise. **17** And his disciples remembered, that it was written, [1]The [k]zeal of thine house hath eaten me up. **18** [l]Then answered the Jews, and said unto him, What [m]sign showest thou unto us, that thou doest these things? **19** Jesus answered, and said unto them, [2]Destroy this Temple, and in three days I will raise it up again. **20** Then said the Jews, Forty and six years was this Temple a building, and wilt thou rear it up in three days? **21** But he spake of the [n]temple of his body. **22** As soon therefore as he was risen from the dead, his disciples remembered that he thus said unto them: and they believed the Scriptures, and the word which Jesus had said. **23** Now when he was at Jerusalem at the Passover in the feast, many believed in his Name, when they saw his miracles which he did. **24** [o]But Jesus did not commit himself unto them, because he knew them all. **25** [p]And had no need that any should testify of man, for he knew what was in man.

3

1 Christ teacheth Nicodemus the very principles of Christian regeneration. 14 The serpent in the wilderness. 23 John baptizeth, 27 and teacheth his, that he is not Christ.

1 There [a]was now a man of the Pharisees, named Nicodemus, a [b]ruler of the Jews. **2** This man came to Jesus by night, and said unto him, Rabbi, we know that thou art a [c]teacher come from God, for no man could do these miracles that thou doest, [d]except God were with him. **3** [e]Jesus answered and said unto him, Verily verily I say unto thee, Except a man be born again, he cannot [f]see the [g]kingdom of God. **4** Nicodemus said unto him, How [h]can a man be born which is old? can he enter into his mother's womb again, and be born? **5** Jesus answered, Verily, verily I say unto thee, except that a man be born of water and of the Spirit, he cannot enter into the kingdom of God. **6** That which is born of the flesh, is [i]flesh: and that that is born of the Spirit, is spirit. **7** Marvel not that I said to thee, Ye must be born again. **8** The wind bloweth where it [j]listeth, and thou hearest the sound thereof, but canst not tell whence it cometh, and whither it goeth: so is every man that is born of the Spirit. **9** [k]Nicodemus answered, and said unto him, How can these things be? **10** Jesus answered, and said unto him, Art thou a teacher of Israel, and knowest not these things? **11** Verily, verily I say unto thee, We speak that we know, and testify that we have seen: but ye receive not our [l]witness. **12** If when I tell you earthly things, ye believe not, how should ye believe, If I shall tell you of heavenly things? **13** For no [m]man [n]ascendeth up to heaven, but he that had descended from heaven, [o]that Son of man which [p]is in heaven. **14** [1]And as Moses lifted up the serpent in the wilderness, so must that Son of man be lifted up, **15** That whosoever believeth in him, should not perish, but have eternal life. **16** [q,2]For God so loveth the world, that he hath given his only begotten Son, that whosoever believeth [r]in him, should not perish, but have everlasting life. **17** [s,3]For God sent not his Son into the world, that he should [t]condemn the world, but that the [u]world through him might be saved. **18** He that believeth in him, is not condemned: but he that believeth not, is condemned already, because he hath not believed in the Name of that only begotten Son of God. **19** [v,4]And this is the [w]condemnation, that that light came into the world, and men loved darkness rather than that light, because their deeds were evil. **20** For every man that evil doeth, hateth the light, neither cometh to light, lest his deeds should be reproved. **21** But he that [x]doeth truth, cometh to the light, that his deeds might be made manifest, that they are wrought [y]according to God. **22** After these things came Jesus, and his disciples into the land of Judea, and there tarried with them, and [5]baptized. **23** And John also baptized in Aenon besides Salim, because there was much water there: and they came and were baptized. **24** For John was not yet cast into prison. **25** [z]Then there arose a question between John's disciples and the Jews, about purifying. **26** And they came unto John, and said unto him, Rabbi, he that was with thee beyond Jordan, to whom [6]thou barest witness, behold, he baptizeth, and all men come to him. **27** John answered, and said, A man [aa]can receive nothing, except it be given him from heaven. **28** Ye yourselves are my witnesses, that [7]I said, I am not that Christ, but that I am sent before him. **29** He that hath the bride, is the bridegroom: but the friend of the bridegroom which standeth and heareth him, rejoiceth greatly, because of the bridegroom's voice. This my joy therefore is fulfilled. **30** He must increase, but I must decrease. **31** He that is come from on high, is above all: he that is of the earth, is of the [ab]earth, and [ac]speaketh of the earth: he that is come from heaven, is above all. **32** And what he hath [ad]seen and heard, that he testifieth: but [ae]no man receiveth his testimony. **33** He that hath receiveth his testimony, hath sealed that [8]God is true. **34** For he whom God hath sent, speaketh the words of God: for God giveth him not the Spirit by measure. **35** The Father loveth the Son, and hath [af,9]given all things into his hand. **36** [10]He that believeth in the Son, hath everlasting life, and he that obeyeth not the Son, shall not [ag]see life, but the wrath of God abideth on him.

---

g. John 2:10 Word for word, are drunken. Now this speech, to be drunken, is not always taken in evil part in the Hebrew tongue, but signifieth sometime such store, and plentiful use of wine, as doth not pass measure, as Gen. 43:34.
h. John 2:12 That is, his cousins.
i. John 2:13 Christ being made subject to the Law for us, satisfieth the Law of the Passover.
j. John 2:14 Christ being ordained to purge the Church, doth with great zeal begin his office both of Priest and Prophet.
k. John 2:17 Zeal in this place is taken for a wrathful indignation and displeasure of the mind, conceived of some naughty and evil dealing towards them whom we love well.
l. John 2:18 Against them which so bind God to an ordinary calling which they themselves most shamefully abuse, that they will not admit an extraordinary, which God confirmeth from heaven, (and they although in vain would have it extinguished) unless it be sealed with outward and bodily miracles.
m. John 2:18 With what miracle dost thou confirm it, that we may see that heavenly power and virtue, which giveth thee authority to speak and do thus?
n. John 2:21 That is, of his body.
o. John 2:24 It is not good crediting them, which stand only upon miracles.
p. John 2:25 Christ is the searcher of hearts, and therefore true God.

JOHN. 2
1. Ps. 69:9
2. Matt. 26:61 / Matt. 27:40 / Mark 14:58 / Mark 15:29

JOHN. 3
a. John 3:1 There are none sometimes more unlearned, than the learned: but as well the learned as the unlearned must desire wisdom of Christ only.
b. John 3:1 A man of great estimation, and a ruler amongst the Jews.
c. John 3:2 We know that thou art sent from God to teach us.
d. John 3:2 But he in whom some part of the excellency of God appeareth. And if Nicodemus had known Christ aright, he would not only have said that God was with him, but in him: as Paul doth, 2 Cor. 1:19.
e. John 3:3 The beginning of Christianity consisteth in this, that we know ourselves not only to be corrupt in part, but to be wholly dead in sin: so that our nature hath need to be created anew, as touching the qualities thereof: which can be done by no other virtue, but by the divine and heavenly, whereby we were first created.
f. John 3:3 That is, go in, or enter, as he expounded himself afterward, verse 5.
g. John 3:3 The Church: for Christ showeth in this place, how we come to be citizens, and to have ought to do in the city of God.
h. John 3:4 How can I that am old, be born again? for he answereth, as if Christ's words belonged to none but to him.
i. John 3:6 That is, fleshly, to wit, wholly unclean and under the wrath of God: and therefore this word (Flesh) signifieth the corrupt nature of man: contrary to which is the Spirit, that is, the man ingrafted into Christ through the grace of the holy Ghost, whose nature is everlasting and immortal, though the strife of the flesh remaineth.
j. John 3:8 With free and wandering blasts, as it listeth.
k. John 3:9 The secret mystery of our regeneration which cannot be comprehended by man's capacity, is perceived by faith, and that in Christ only, because that he is both God on earth, and man in heaven, that is to say, in such sort man, that he is God also, and therefore almighty: and in such sort God, that he is man also, and therefore his power is manifest unto us.
l. John 3:11 You handle doubtful things, and such as you have no certain author for, and yet men believe you: but I teach those things that are of a truth and well known, and you believe me not.
m. John 3:13 Only Christ can teach us heavenly things for no man ascendeth, etc.
n. John 3:13 That is, hath any spiritual light and understanding, or ever had, but only that Son of God, which came down to us.
o. John 3:13 Whereas he is said to have come down from heaven, that must be understood of his Godhead, and of the manner of his conception: for Christ's birth upon the earth was heavenly, and not earthly, for he was conceived by the holy Ghost.
p. John 3:13 That which is proper to the divinity of Christ, is here spoken of whole Christ, to give us to understand that he is but one person, wherein two natures are united, and this kind of speech men call, the communicating of proprieties.
q. John 3:16 Nothing else but the free love of the Father, is the beginning of our salvation, and Christ is he in whom our righteousness and salvation is resident: and faith is the instrument or mean whereby we apprehend it, and life everlasting is that which is set before us to apprehend.
r. John 3:16 It is not all one to believe in a thing, and to believe of a thing, for we may not believe (in anything) save only in God, but we may believe (of anything) whatsoever, this saith Nazianzene in his oration of the Spirit.
s. John 3:17 Not Christ, but the despising of Christ doth condemn.
t. John 3:17 That is, to be the cause of the condemning of the world, for indeed sins are the cause of death, but Christ shall judge the quick and the dead.
u. John 3:17 Not only the people of the Jews, but whosoever shall believe in him.
v. John 3:19 Only wickedness is the cause, why men refuse the light that is offered them.
w. John 3:19 That is, the cause of condemnation, which sticketh fast in men, unless through God's great benefit they be delivered from it.
x. John 3:21 That is, he that leadeth an honest life, and void of all craft and deceit.
y. John 3:21 That is, with God, God as it were going before.
z. John 3:25 Satan inflameth the disciples of John with a fond emulation of their master, to hinder the course of the Gospel: but John being mindful of his office, doth not only break off their endeavors, but also taketh occasion thereby to give testimony of Christ, how that in him only the Father hath set forth life everlasting.
aa. John 3:27 What mean you to go about to better my state? this is every man's lot and portion that they cannot better themselves one iota.
ab. John 3:31 Is nothing else but man, a piece of work and of the slime of the earth.
ac. John 3:31 Savoreth of nothing but corruption, ignorance, dullness, etc.
ad. John 3:32 What he knoweth fully and perfectly.
ae. John 3:32 That is, very few.
af. John 3:35 Committed them to his power and will.
ag. John 3:36 Shall not enjoy.

JOHN. 3
1. Num. 31:9 / John 12:32
2. 1 John 4:9
3. John 1:39 / John 12:47
4. John 1:9
5. John 4:1
6. John 1:34
7. John 1:20
8. Rom. 3:4
9. Matt. 11:27
10. 1 John 5:10

4

6 Jesus being weary, asketh drink of the woman of Samaria. 21 He teacheth the true worship. 26 He confesseth that he is the Messiah, 32 His meat. 39 The Samaritans believe in him. 46 He healeth the Ruler's son.

1 Now [a]when the Lord knew, how the Pharisees had heard, that Jesus made [1]and baptized more disciples than John, **2** (Though Jesus himself baptized not: but his disciples.) **3** He left Judea, and departed again into Galilee. **4** And he must needs go through Samaria. **5** [b]Then came he to a city of Samaria called Sychar, near unto the possession that [2]Jacob gave to his son Joseph. **6** And there was Jacob's Well. Jesus then wearied in the journey, sat [c]thus on the Well: it was about the [d]sixth hour. **7** There came a woman of Samaria to draw water. Jesus said unto her, Give me drink. **8** For his disciples were gone away into the city, to buy meat. **9** Then said the woman of Samaria unto him, How is it, that thou being a Jew, askest drink of me, which am a woman of Samaria? For the Jews [e]meddle not with the Samaritans. **10** Jesus answered and said unto her, If thou knewest [f]that gift of God, and who it is that saith to thee, Give me drink, thou wouldest have asked of him, and he would have given thee [g]water of life. **11** The woman said unto him, Sir, thou hast nothing to draw with, and the Well is deep: from whence then hast thou that water of life? **12** Art thou greater than our father Jacob, which gave us the Well, and he himself drank thereof, and his sons, and his cattle. **13** Jesus answered, and said unto her, Whosoever drinketh of this water, shall thirst again: **14** But whosoever drinketh of the water that I shall give him, shall never be more athirst: but the water that I shall give him, shall be in him a well of water, springing up into everlasting life. **15** The woman said unto him, Sir, give me of that water, that I may not thirst, neither come hither to draw. **16** Jesus said unto her, Go, call thine husband, and come hither. **17** The woman answered, and said, I have no husband. Jesus said unto her, thou hast well said, I have no husband. **18** For thou hast had five husbands, and he whom thou now hast, is not thine husband: that saidest thou truly. **19** The woman said unto him, Sir, I see that thou art a Prophet. **20** [h]Our fathers worshipped in this [i]mountain, and ye say, that in [3]Jerusalem is the place where men ought to worship. **21** Jesus said unto her, Woman, believe me, the hour cometh, when ye shall neither in this mountain, nor at Jerusalem worship the Father. **22** Ye worship that which ye [4]know not: we worship that which we know: for salvation is of the Jews. **23** But the hour cometh, and now is, when the true worshippers shall worship the Father in [j]Spirit and Truth: for the Father requireth even such to worship him. **24** [5]God is a [k]Spirit, and they that worship him, must worship him in Spirit and Truth. **25** The woman said unto him, I know well that Messiah shall come, which is called Christ: when he is come, he will tell us all things. **26** Jesus said unto her, I am he, that speak unto thee. **27** And upon that, came his disciples, and marveled that he talked with a woman: yet no man said unto him, What askest thou? or why talkest thou with her. **28** The woman then left her waterpot, and went her way into the city, and said to the men, **29** Come, see a man which hath told me all things that ever I did: is not he that Christ? **30** Then they went out of the city, and came unto him. **31** In the meanwhile, the disciples prayed him, saying, Master, eat. **32** [l]But he said unto them, I have meat to eat, that ye know not of. **33** Then said the disciples between themselves, Hath any man brought him meat? **34** Jesus said unto them, My meat is that I may do the will of him that sent me, and finish his work. **35** [m]Say not ye, There are yet four months, and then cometh harvest? Behold, I say unto you, Lift up your eyes, and look on the regions: [6]for they are white already unto harvest. **36** [n]And he that reapeth, receiveth reward, and gathered fruit unto life eternal, that both he that soweth, and he that reapeth might rejoice together. **37** For herein is the [o]saying true, that one soweth and another reapeth. **38** I sent you to reap that, whereon ye bestowed no labor: other men labored, and ye are entered into their labors. **39** [p]Now many of the Samaritans of that city believed in him, for the saying of the woman which testified, He hath told me all things that ever I did. **40** Then when the Samaritans were come unto him, they besought him, that he would tarry with them: and he abode there two days. **41** And many more believed because of his own word. **42** And they said unto the woman, Now we believe, not because of thy saying: for we have heard him ourselves, and know that this is indeed that Christ the Savior of the world. **43** [q]So two days after he departed thence, and went into [r]Galilee. **44** For Jesus himself had [7]testified, that a Prophet hath none honor in his own country. **45** Then when he was come into Galilee, the Galileans received him, which had seen all the things that he did at Jerusalem at the feast: for they went also to the feast. **46** [s]And Jesus came again into [8]Cana a town of Galilee, where he had made of water wine. And there was a certain [t]ruler, whose son was sick at Capernaum. **47** When he heard that Jesus was come out of Judea into Galilee, he went unto him, and besought him that he would go down, and heal his son: for he was even ready to die. **48** Then said Jesus unto him, Except ye see signs and wonders, ye will not believe. **49** The ruler said unto him, Sir, go down before my son dies. **50** Jesus said unto him, Go thy way, thy son liveth: and the man believed the word that Jesus had spoken unto him, and went his way. **51** And as he was now going down, his servants met him, saying, Thy son liveth. **52** Then inquired he of them the hour when he began to amend. And they said unto him, Yesterday the seventh hour the fever left him. **53** Then the father knew that it was the same hour in the which Jesus had said unto him, Thy son liveth. And he believed, and all his household. **54** This second miracle did Jesus again, after he was come out of Judea into Galilee.

5

2 One lying at the pool, 5 is healed of Christ on the Sabbath. 10 The Jews that rashly find fault with that his deed, 17 he convinceth with the authority of his Father, 19, 20 He proveth his divine power by many reasons, 45 and with Moses' testimony.

1 After [1]that, there was a feast of the Jews, and Jesus went to Jerusalem. **2** [a]And there is at Jerusalem by the place of the sheep, a [b]pool called in Hebrew [c]Bethesda, having five porches: **3** In the which lay a great multitude of sick folk, of blind, halt, and withered, waiting for the moving of the water. **4** For an Angel went down at a certain season into the pool, and troubled the water: whosoever then first, after the stirring of the water, stepped in, was made whole of whatsoever disease he had. **5** And a certain man was there, which had been diseased eight and thirty years. **6** When Jesus saw him lie, and knew that he now long time had been diseased, he said unto him, Wilt thou be made whole? **7** The sick man answered him, Sir, I have no man, when the water is troubled, to put me into the pool: but while I am coming, another steppeth down before me. **8** Jesus said unto him, Rise: take up thy bed, and walk. **9** And immediately the man was made whole, and took up his bed, and walked: and the same day was the Sabbath. **10** [d]The Jews therefore said to him that was made whole, It is the Sabbath day: [2]it is not lawful for thee to carry thy bed. **11** He answered them, He that made me whole he said unto me, Take up thy bed, and walk. **12** Then asked they him, What man is that which said unto thee, Take up thy bed, and walk? **13** And he that was healed, knew not who it was: for Jesus had conveyed himself away from the multitude that was in that place. **14** And after that, Jesus found him in the Temple, and said unto him, Behold, thou art made whole: sin no more, lest a worse thing come unto thee. **15** The man departed, and told the Jews that it was Jesus that had made him whole. **16** And therefore the Jews did persecute Jesus, and sought to slay him, because he had done these things on the

---

JOHN. 4

- **a.** John 4:1 This measure is to be kept in doing of our duty, that neither by fear we be terrified from going forward, neither by rashness procure or pluck dangers upon our heads.
- **b.** John 4:5 Christ leaving the proud Pharisees, communicateth the treasures of everlasting life with a poor sinful woman, and stranger, refelling the gross errors of the Samaritans, and defending the true service of God, which was delivered to the Jews, but yet so, that he calleth both of them back to himself as one whom only all the fathers, and also all the ceremonies of the Law did regard, and had a respect unto.
- **c.** John 4:6 Even as he was weary, or because he was weary.
- **d.** John 4:6 It was almost noon.
- **e.** John 4:9 There is no familiarity nor friendship, between the Jews and the Samaritans.
- **f.** John 4:10 By this word (That) we are given to understand, that Christ speaketh of some excellent gift, that is to say, even of himself, whom his Father offered to this woman.
- **g.** John 4:10 This everlasting water, that is to say, the exceeding love of God, is called living, or of life, to make a difference between it, and the water that should be drawn out of a well: and these metaphors are very much used of the Jews, Jer. 2:13; Joel 3:18; Zech. 13:11.
- **h.** John 4:20 All the religion of superstitious people, standeth for the most part, upon two pillars, but very weak, that is to say upon the examples of the fathers perverted, and a foolish opinion of outward things: against which errors we have to set the word and nature of God.
- **i.** John 4:20 The name of this mountain is Gerizim, whereupon Sanabaletta the Cushite built a Temple by Alexander of Macedonia's leave, after the victory of Issica, and made there Manasses his son-in-law high priest, Josephus, book 11.
- **j.** John 4:23 This word (Spirit) is to be taken here, as it is set against that commandment, which is called carnal, Heb. 7:16, as the commandment is considered in itself: and so he speaketh of (Truth) not as we set it against a lie, but as we take it in respect of the outward ceremonies of the Law: which did only shadow that which Christ performed indeed.
- **k.** John 4:24 By the word (Spirit) he meaneth the nature of the Godhead, and not the third person in the Trinity.
- **l.** John 4:32 We may have care of our bodies, but yet so, that we prefer willingly and freely the occasion which is offered us to enlarge the kingdom of God, before all necessities of this life whatsoever.
- **m.** John 4:35 When the spiritual corn is ripe, we must not linger: for so the children of this world would condemn us.
- **n.** John 4:36 The doctrine of the Prophets was as it were a sowing time: and the doctrine of the Gospel, as the harvest, and there is an excellent agreement between them both, and the ministers of them both.
- **o.** John 4:37 That proverb.
- **p.** John 4:39 The Samaritans do most joyfully embrace that which the Jews most stubbornly rejected.
- **q.** John 4:43 The despisers of Christ deprive themselves of his benefit: yet Christ prepareth a place for himself.
- **r.** John 4:43 Into the towns and villages of Galilee: for he would not make abode in his country of Nazareth, because they despised him, and where (as the other Evangelists write) the efficacy of his benefits was hindered through their marvelous stiffneckedness.
- **s.** John 4:46 Although Christ be absent in body, yet he worketh mightily in the believers by his word.
- **t.** John 4:46 Some of Herod's courtiers, for though Herod was not a king, but a Tetrarch, yet the lofty name only except, he was a king, or at least the people called him a king.

JOHN. 4

1. John 3:22
2. Gen. 33:19 / Gen. 48:22 / John 24:32
3. Deut. 12:6
4. 2 Kings 17:29
5. 2 Cor. 3:27
6. Matt. 9:37 / Luke 10:2
7. Matt. 13:57 / Mark 6:4 / Luke 4:24
8. John 2:1, 12

JOHN. 5

- **a.** John 5:2 There is no disease so old, which Christ cannot heal.
- **b.** John 5:2 Whereof cattle drank, and used to be plunged in; whereof there could not be but great store at Jerusalem.
- **c.** John 5:2 That is to say, the house of pouring out, because great store of water was poured out into that place.
- **d.** John 5:10 True religion is no more cruelly assaulted by any means, than by the pretence of religion itself.
- **e.** John 5:17 The work of God was never the breach of the Sabbath: but the works of Christ are the works of the Father, both because they are one God, and also because the Father doth not work but in the Son.
- **f.** John 5:18 That is, his only and no man's else, which they gather by that, that he saith, (And I work) applying this word (work) to himself, which is proper to God, and therefore maketh himself equal to God.
- **g.** John 5:19 Not only without his Father's authority, but also without his mighty working and power.

Sabbath day. **17** [e]But Jesus answered them, My father worketh hitherto, and I
work. **18** [3]Therefore the Jews sought the more to kill him: not only because he
had broken the Sabbath: but said also that God was [f]his Father, and made himself
equal with God. **19** Then answered Jesus, and said unto them, Verily, verily I
say unto you, The Son can do nothing [g]of himself, save that he [h]seeth the Father
do: for whatsoever things he doeth, the same things doeth the Son [i]in like man-
ner. **20** For the Father loveth the Son, and showeth him all things, whatsoever
he himself doeth, and he will show him greater works than these, that ye should
marvel. **21** [j]For likewise as the Father raiseth up the dead, and quickeneth them,
so the Son quickeneth whom he will. **22** For the Father [k]judgeth [l]no man, but
hath committed all judgment unto the Son, **23** Because that all men should
honor the Son, as they honor the Father: he that honoreth not the Son, the same
honoreth not the Father which hath sent him. **24** [m]Verily, verily I say unto you,
he that heareth my word, and believeth him that sent me, hath everlasting life, and
shall not come into condemnation, but hath passed from death to life. **25** [n]Ve-
rily, verily I say unto you, the hour shall come, and now is, when the dead shall
hear the voice of the Son of God: and they that hear it shall live. **26** For as the
Father hath life in himself, so likewise hath he given to the Son to have life in him-
self. **27** And hath given him [o]power also to execute judgment, in that he is the
[p]Son of man. **28** [q]Marvel not at this: for the hour shall come, in the which all
that are in the graves, shall hear his voice. **29** [r]And they shall come [s]forth, [4]that
have done good, unto the [t]resurrection of life: but they that have done evil, unto
the resurrection of condemnation. **30** [u]I can [v]do nothing of mine own self: [w]as
I hear, I judge: and my judgment is just, because I seek not mine own will, but the
will of the Father who hath sent me. **31** If I [5]should bear witness of myself, my
witness were not [x]true. **32** [6]There is another that beareth witness of me, and I
know that the witness, which he beareth of me, is true. **33** [y,7]Ye sent unto John,
and he bore witness unto the truth. **34** But I receive not the record of man: ne-
vertheless these things I say, that ye might be saved. **35** He was a burning and
a shining candle: and ye would for [z]a season have rejoiced in his light. **36** But I
have greater witness than the witness of John: for the works which the Father hath
given me to finish, the same works that I do, bear witness of me, that the Father
sent me. **37** And the [8]Father himself, which hath sent me, beareth witness of me.
Ye have not heard his voice at any time, [9]neither have ye seen his shape. **38** And
his word have you not abiding in you: for whom he hath sent, him ye believed
not. **39** [10]Search the Scriptures: for in them ye think to have eternal life, and
they are they which testify of me. **40** But ye will not come to me, that ye might
have life. **41** I receive not the praise of men. **42** But I know you, that ye have
not the [aa]love of God in you. **43** I am come in my Father's Name, and ye receive
me not: if another shall come in his own name, him will ye receive. **44** How can
ye believe, which receive honor one of another, and seek not the [11]honor that co-
meth of God alone? **45** [ab]Do not think that I will accuse you to my Father: there
is one that accuseth you, even Moses, in whom ye trust. **46** For had ye believed
Moses, ye would have believed me: for he [12]wrote of me. **47** But if ye believe not
his writings, how shall ye believe my words.

6

5 Five thousand are fed with five loaves and two fishes. 15 Christ goeth apart from the people. 17 As his disciples were rowing, 19 he cometh to them walking on the water. 26 He reasoneth of the true 27 and everlasting, 35 bread of life. 42, 52 The Jews murmur, 60 and many of the disciples, 66 depart from him. 69 The Apostles confess him to be the Son of God.

1 After these things, Jesus went his way [a]over the sea of Galilee, which is
Tiberias. **2** And a great multitude followed him, because they saw his mi-
racles, which he did on them that were diseased. **3** Then Jesus went up into
a mountain, and there he sat with his disciples. **4** Now the Passover a [1]feast
of the Jews was near. **5** [b,2]Then Jesus lift up his eyes, and seeing that a gre-
at multitude came unto him, he said unto Philip, Whence shall we buy bread,
that these might eat? **6** (And this he said to prove him: for he himself knew
what he would do.) **7** Philip answered him, Two hundred pennyworth of bre-
ad is not sufficient for them, that everyone of them may take a little. **8** Then
said unto him one of his disciples, Andrew, Simon Peter's brother, **9** There is
a little boy here, which hath five barley loaves, and two fishes: but what are they
among so many? **10** And Jesus said, Make the people sit down. (Now there was
much grass in that place.) Then the men sat down, in number about five thou-
sand. **11** And Jesus took the bread, and gave thanks, and gave to the disciples,
and the disciples to them that were set down: and likewise of the fishes as much
as they would. **12** And when they were satisfied, he said unto his disciples, Ga-
ther up the broken meat which remaineth, that nothing be lost. **13** Then they
gathered it together, and filled twelve baskets with the broken meat of the five
barley loaves, which remained unto them that had eaten. **14** Then the men,
when they had seen the miracle that Jesus did, said, This is of a truth that Prophet
that should come into the world. **15** [c]When Jesus therefore perceived that they
would come, and take him to make him a king, he departed again into a mountain
himself alone. **16** [d]When even was now come, his disciples went down unto the
sea, **17** [3]And entered into a ship, and went over the sea, [e]towards Capernaum:
and now it was dark, and Jesus was not come to them. **18** And the Sea arose with
a great wind that blew. **19** And when they had rowed about five and twenty, or
thirty furlongs, they saw Jesus walking on the sea, and drawing near unto the ship:
so they were afraid. **20** But he said unto them, It is I: be not afraid. **21** Then
[f]willingly they received him into the ship, and the ship was by and by at the land,
whither they went. **22** The day following, the people which stood on the other
side of the sea, saw that there was none other ship there, save that one, where into
his disciples were entered, and that Jesus went not with his disciples in the ship, but
that his disciples were gone alone, **23** And that there came other ships from Ti-
berias near unto the place where they ate the bread, after the Lord had given than-
ks. **24** Now when the people saw that Jesus was not there, neither his disciples,
they also took shipping, and came to Capernaum, seeking for Jesus. **25** And
when they had found him on the other side of the sea, they said unto him, Rab-
bi, when camest thou hither? **26** [g]Jesus answered them, and said, Verily, verily
I say unto you, Ye seek me not, because ye saw the miracles, but because ye ate of
the loaves, and were filled. **27** [h]Labor not for the meat which perisheth, but for
the meat that endureth unto everlasting life, which the Son of man shall give unto
you: for him hath [4]God the Father [i]sealed. **28** Then said they unto him, What
shall we do, that we might work the [j]works of God? **29** [k]Jesus answered, and
said unto them, [l,5]This is the work of God, that ye believe in him, whom he hath
sent. **30** [m]They said therefore unto him, What sign showest thou then, that we
may see it, and believe thee? what dost thou work? **31** Our fathers did eat Manna
in the desert, as it is [6]written, He gave them bread from heaven to eat. **32** [n]Then

---

h. John 5:19 This must be understood of Christ's person, which consisteth of two natures, and not simply of his Godhead: so then he saith that his Father moveth and governeth him in all things, but yet notwithstanding, when he saith he worketh with his Father, he voucheth his Godhead.

i. John 5:19 In like sort, jointly and together. Not for that the Father doeth some things, and then the son worketh after him, and doeth the like, but because the might and power of the Father and the Son do work equally and jointly together.

j. John 5:21 The Father maketh no man partaker of everlasting life, but in Christ, in whom only also he is truly worshipped.

k. John 5:22 This word (judgeth) is taken by the figure Synecdoche, for all government.

l. John 5:22 These words are not so to be taken, as though they simply denied that God governeth the world, but as the Jews imagined it, which separate the Father from the Son, whereas indeed, the Father doth not govern the world but only in the person of his Son, being made manifest in the flesh: so saith he afterward, verse 30, that he came not to do his own will: that his doctrine is not his own, John 7:16, that the blind man and his parents sinned not, etc., John 9:3.

m. John 5:24 The Father is not worshipped but by his Son's word apprehended by faith, which is the only way that leadeth to eternal life.

n. John 5:25 We are all dead in sin and cannot be quickened by any other means, than by the word of Christ apprehended by faith.

o. John 5:27 That is, high and sovereign power to rule and govern all things, insomuch that he hath power of life and death.

p. John 5:27 That is, he shall not only judge the world as he is God, but also as he is man, he received this of his Father to be judge of the world.

q. John 5:28 All shall appear before the judgment seat of Christ at length to be judged.

r. John 5:29 Faith and infidelity shall be judged by their fruits.

s. John 5:29 Of their graves.

t. John 5:29 To that resurrection which had life everlasting following it: against which is set the resurrection of condemnation: that is, which condemnation followeth.

u. John 5:30 The father is the author and approver of all things which Christ doeth.

v. John 5:30 See verse 22.

w. John 5:30 As my father directeth me, who dwelleth in me.

x. John 5:31 Faithful, that is, worthy to be credited, see John 8:14.

y. John 5:33 Christ is declared to be the only Savior by John's voice, and infinite miracles, and by the testimonies of all the Prophets. But the world notwithstanding being addicted to false prophets, and desirous to seem religious, seeth none of all these things.

z. John 5:35 A little while.

aa. John 5:42 Love toward God.

ab. John 5:45 This denial doth not put away that which is here said, but correcteth it, as if Christ said, the Jews shall have no sorer an accuser than Moses.

JOHN. 5

1. Lev. 23:3 / Deut. 16:1
2. Jer. 17:22
3. John 7:19
4. Matt. 25:41
5. John 8:14
6. Matt. 3:17
7. John 1:27
8. Matt. 3:15 / Matt. 17:5
9. Deut. 4:12
10. Acts 17:11
11. John 12:43
12. Gen. 3:15 / Gen. 22:18 / Gen 49:10 / Deut. 18:15

JOHN. 6

a. John 6:1 Not that he cut over the lake of Tiberias, but by reason of the large creeks, his sailing made his journey the shorter: therefore he is said to have gone over the sea, when as he passed over from one side of the creek to the other.

b. John 6:5 They that follow Christ do sometimes hunger, but they are never destitute of help.

c. John 6:15 Christ is not only not delighted, but also greatly offended with a preposterous worship.

d. John 6:16 The godly are often in peril and danger, but Christ cometh to them in time, even in the midst of the tempests, and bringeth them to the heaven.

e. John 6:17 In Mark 6:45 they are willed to go before to Bethsaida, for Bethsaida was in the way to Capernaum.

f. John 6:21 They were afraid at the first, but when they knew his voice, they became new men, and took him willingly into the ship, whom they had shunned and fled from before.

g. John 6:26 They that seek the kingdom of heaven lack nothing: notwithstanding the Gospel is not the food of the belly, but of the mind.

h. John 6:27 Bestow your labor and pain.

i. John 6:27 That is, whom God the Father hath distinguished from all other men by planting his own virtue in him, as though he had sealed him with his seal, that he might be a lively pattern and representer of him: and that more is, installed him to this office, to reconcile us men to God, and bring us to everlasting life, which is only proper to Christ.

j. John 6:28 Which please God: for they think that everlasting life hangeth upon the condition of fulfilling the Law: therefore Christ calleth them back to faith.

k. John 6:29 Men torment themselves in vain, when they go about to please God without faith.

l. John 6:29 That is, this is the work that God requireth, that you believe in me, and therefore he calleth them back to faith.

m. John 6:30 The spiritual virtue of Christ is contemned of them which are desirous of earthly miracles.

n. John 6:32 Christ, who is the true and only author and giver of eternal life, was signified unto the fathers, in Manna.

Jesus said unto them, Verily, verily I say unto you, Moses gave you not [o]that bread
from heaven, but my Father giveth you that true bread from heaven. **33** For the
bread of God is he which cometh down from heaven, and giveth life unto the wor-
ld. **34** Then they said unto him, Lord, evermore give us this bread. **35** And
Jesus said unto them, I am that bread [p]of life: he that cometh to me, shall not hun-
ger, and he that believeth in me, shall never thirst. **36** But I said unto you, that ye
also have seen me, and believe not. **37** [q]All that the Father giveth me, shall come
to me: and him that cometh to me, I cast not away. **38** For I came down from
heaven, not to do mine [r]own will, but his will which hath sent me. **39** And this
is the Father's will which hath sent me, that of all which he hath given me, I should
lose nothing, but should raise it up again at the last day. **40** And this is the will
of him that sent me, that every man which [s]seeth the Son, and believeth in him,
should have everlasting life: and I will raise him up at the last day. **41** [t]The Jews
then murmured at him because he said, I am that bread, which is come down from
heaven. **42** And they said, [7]Is not this Jesus that son of Joseph, whose father and
mother we know? how then saith he, I came down from heaven? **43** Jesus then
answered, and said unto them, Murmur not among yourselves. **44** No man can
come to me, except the Father, which hath sent me, draw him: and I will raise him
up at the last day. **45** It is written in the [u,8]Prophets, And they shall be all [v]taught
of God. Every man therefore that hath heard, and hath learned of the Father, co-
meth unto me: **46** [9]Not that any man hath seen the Father, [w]save he which is of
God, he hath seen the Father. **47** Verily, verily I say unto you, he that believeth
in me, hath everlasting life. **48** [x]I am that bread of life. **49** [10]Your fathers did
eat Manna in the wilderness, and are dead. **50** [y]This is that bread, which cometh
down from heaven, that he which eateth of it, should not die. **51** [z]I am that [aa]li-
ving bread, which came down from heaven: if any man [ab]eat of this bread, he shall
live forever: and the bread that I will give is my flesh, which I will give for the life
of the world. **52** [ac]Then the Jews strove among themselves, saying, How can this
man give us his flesh to eat? **53** Then Jesus said unto them, Verily, verily I say
unto you, Except ye eat the flesh of the Son of man, and drink his blood, ye have
[ad]no life in you. **54** Whosoever [11]eateth my flesh, and drinketh my blood, hath
eternal life, and I will raise him up at the last day. **55** For my flesh is meat indeed,
and my blood is drink indeed. **56** He that eateth my flesh, and drinketh my blo-
od, dwelleth in me, and I in him. **57** As [ae]that living Father hath sent me, so live
I by the [af]Father, and he that eateth me, even he shall live by me. **58** This is that
bread which came down from heaven: not as your fathers have eaten Manna, and
are dead. He that eateth of this bread, shall live forever. **59** These things spake he
in the Synagogue, as he taught in Capernaum. **60** [ag]Many therefore of his disci-
ples (when they heard this) said, This is an hard saying: who can hear it? **61** But
Jesus knowing in himself, that his disciples murmured at this, said unto them,
Doth this offend you? **62** What then if ye should see that Son of man ascend up
[12]where he was before? **63** [ah]It is the [ai]spirit that quickeneth: the flesh profiteth
nothing: the words that I speak unto you, are spirit and life. **64** But there are
some of you that believe not: for Jesus knew from the beginning, which they were
that believed not, and who should betray him. **65** And he said, Therefore said I
unto you, that no man can come unto me, except it be given unto him of my Fa-
ther. **66** [aj]From that time, many of his disciples went back, and walked no more
with him. **67** Then said Jesus to the twelve, Will ye also go away? **68** Then
Simon Peter answered him, Master, to whom shall we go? thou hast the words of
eternal life: **69** And we believe and know that thou art that Christ that Son of
the living God. **70** [ak]Jesus answered them, Have not I [13]chosen you twelve, and
one of you is a devil? **71** Now he spake it of Judas Iscariot the son of Simon: for
he it was that should betray him, though he was one of the twelve.

7

2 Christ, after his cousins were gone up to the feast of Tabernacles, 10 goeth thither privily. 12 The people's sundry opinions of him. 14 He teacheth in the Temple. 32 The Priests command to take him. 41 Strife among the multitude about him, 47 and between the Pharisees and the officers that were sent to take him, 50 and Nicodemus.

1 After these things, Jesus walked in Galilee, and would not walk in Judea:
for the Jews sought to kill him. **2** Now the Jews' [a,1]feast of the Tabernacles was
at hand. **3** [b]His brethren therefore said unto him, Depart hence, and go into Ju-
dea, that thy disciples may see thy works that thou doest. **4** For there is no man
that doeth anything secretly, and he himself seeketh to be famous. If thou doest
these things, show thyself to the world. **5** For as yet his [c]brethren believed not
in him. **6** [d]Then Jesus said unto them, My time is not yet come: but your time
is always ready. **7** The world cannot hate you: but me it hateth, because I testify
of it, that the works thereof are evil. **8** Go ye up unto this feast: I will not go up
yet unto this feast: [2]for my time is not yet fulfilled. **9** These things he said unto
them, and abode still in Galilee. **10** [e]But as soon as his brethren were gone up,
then went he also up unto the feast, not openly, but as it were privily. **11** Then
the Jews sought him at the feast, and said, Where is he? **12** And much murmu-
ring was there of him among the people. Some said, He is a good man: others said,
Nay: but he deceiveth the people. **13** Howbeit no man spake [f]openly of him for
fear of the Jews. **14** [g]Now when [h]half the feast was done, Jesus went up into the
Temple, and taught. **15** And the Jews marveled, saying, How knoweth this man
the Scriptures, seeing that he never learned! **16** [i]Jesus answered them, and said,
[j]My doctrine is not mine, but his that sent me. **17** If any man will do his will,
he shall know of the doctrine, whether it be of God, or whether I speak of my-
self. **18** [k]He that speaketh of himself, seeketh his own glory: but he that seeketh
his glory that sent him, the same is true, and no unrighteousness is in him. **19** [l,3]
Did not Moses give you a Law, and yet none of you keepeth the Law? [4]Why go
ye about to kill me? **20** The people answered, and said, Thou hast a devil: who
goeth about to kill thee? **21** [m]Jesus answered, and said unto them, I have done
one work, and ye all marvel. **22** [5]Moses therefore gave unto you circumcision,

---

o. John 6:32 He denieth that Manna was that true heavenly bread, and saith that he himself is that true bread, because he feedeth unto the true and everlasting life. And as for that, that Paul 1 Cor. 10 calleth Manna spiritual food, it maketh nothing against this place, for he joineth the thing signified with the sign: but in this whole disputation, Christ dealeth with the Jews after their own opinion and conceit of the matter, and they had no further consideration of the Manna, but in that it fed the belly.

p. John 6:35 Which have life, and give life.

q. John 6:37 The gift of faith proceedeth from the free election of the Father in Christ, after which followeth necessarily everlasting life: Therefore faith in Christ Jesus is a sure witness of our election, and therefore of our glorification, which is to come.

r. John 6:38 See John 5:22.

s. John 6:40 Seeing and believing are joined together: for there is another kind of seeing, which is general, which the devils have, for they see: but here he speaketh of that kind of seeing, which is proper to the elect.

t. John 6:41 Flesh cannot perceive spiritual things, and therefore the beginning of our salvation cometh from God, who changeth our nature, so that we being inspired of him, may abide to be instructed and saved by Christ.

u. John 6:45 In the book of the Prophets, for the old Testament was divided by them into three several parts, into the Law the Prophets, and the Holy writ.

v. John 6:45 To wit, they shall be children of the Church, for so the Prophet Isaiah expoundeth it, Isa. 54:13, that is to say, ordained to life, Acts 13:48, and therefore the knowledge of the heavenly truth, is the gift and work of God, and standeth not in any power of man.

w. John 6:46 If the son only hath seen the Father, then it is he only that can teach and instruct us truly.

x. John 6:48 The true use of Sacraments, is to ascend from them to the thing itself, that is to Christ: and by the partaking of whom only, we get everlasting life.

y. John 6:50 He pointed out himself when he spake these words.

z. John 6:51 Christ being sent from the Father, is the selfsame unto us for the getting and keeping of everlasting life, that bread and flesh, yea meat and drink are to the use of this transitory life.

aa. John 6:51 Which giveth life to the world.

ab. John 6:51 That is to say, whosoever is partaker of Christ indeed, who is our food.

ac. John 6:52 Flesh cannot put a difference between fleshly eating which is done by the help of the teeth, and spiritual eating which consisteth in faith, and therefore is condemneth that which it understandeth not: yet notwithstanding the truth must be preached and taught.

ad. John 6:53 If Christ be present, life is present, but when Christ is absent, then is death present.

ae. John 6:57 In that that Christ is man, he receiveth that power which quickeneth and giveth life to them that are his, of his Father: and he addeth this word (That) to make a difference between him and all other fathers.

af. John 6:57 Christ his meaning is, that though he be man, yet his flesh can give life, not of the own nature, but because that flesh of his liveth by the Father, that is to say, death suck and draw out of the Father, that power which it hath to give life.

ag. John 6:60 The reason of man cannot comprehend the uniting of Christ and his members: therefore let it worship and reverence that which is better than itself.

ah. John 6:63 The flesh of Christ doth therefore quicken us, because that he that is man, is God: which mystery is only comprehended by faith, which is the gift of God, properly only to the elect.

ai. John 6:63 Spirit, that is, that power which floweth from the Godhead, causeth the flesh of Christ, which otherwise were nothing but flesh, but to live in itself, and to give life to us.

aj. John 6:66 Such is the malice of men, that they take occasion of their own destruction, even of the very doctrine of salvation (unless it be a few, which believe through the singular gift of God.)

ak. John 6:70 The number of the professors, of Christ is very small, and among them also there be some hypocrites, and worse than all others.

JOHN. 6

1. Lev. 23:7 / Deut. 16:2
2. Matt. 14:16 / Mark 6:37 / Luke 9:13
3. Matt. 14:25 / Mark 6:47
4. John 1:32 / Mark 3:17 / Mark 7:3 / John 17:3
5. 1 John 3:23
6. Exod. 16:14 / Num. 11:7 / Ps. 78:25
7. Matt. 13:55
8. Isa. 54:13 / Jer. 31:13
9. Matt. 11:17
10. Exod. 16:15
11. 1 Cor. 11:27
12. John 3:13
13. Matt. 26:16

JOHN. 7

a. John 7:2 This feast was so called, because of the booths and tents which they pight of divers kinds of boughs, and sat under them seven days together; all which time the feast lasted.

b. John 7:3 The grace of God cometh not by inheritance, but it is a gift that cometh other ways, whereby it cometh to pass, that oftentimes the children of God suffer more affliction by their own kinsfolk than by strangers.

c. John 7:5 His kinsfolk: for so use the Hebrews to speak.

d. John 7:6 We must not follow the foolish desires of our friends.

e. John 7:10 An example of horrible confusion in the very bosom of the Church. The Pastors oppress the people with terrors and fear: the people seek Christ, when he appeareth not: when he offereth himself, they neglect him. Some also that know him condemn him rashly: a very few think well of him, and that in secret.

f. John 7:13 Or, boldly and freely: for the chief of the Jews sought nothing so much, as to bury his fame and name.

g. John 7:14 Christ striveth with goodness against the wickedness of the world: in the mean season the most part of men take occasion of offense even by that fame, whereby they ought to have been stirred up to embrace Christ.

h. John 7:14 About the fourth day of the feast.

i. John 7:16 Therefore are there few to whom the Gospel favoreth well, because the study of godliness is very rare.

j. John 7:16 See John 5:22, and he speaketh this after the opinion of the Jews, as if he said, My doctrine is not mine, that is, it is not his whom you take to be a man as others are, and therefore set light by him, but it is his that sent me.

k. John 7:18 The true doctrine of salvation differeth from the false in this, that the same setteth forth the glory of God, and this by puffing up of men darkeneth the glory of God.

l. John 7:19 None do more confidently boast themselves to be the defenders of the Law of God, than they that do most impudently break it.

m. John 7:21 The Sabbath day (which is here set before us for a rule of all ceremonies) was not appointed to hinder but to further and practice God's works: amongst which the love of our neighbor is the chiefest.

n. John 7:23 That is to say, if the law of circumcision which Moses gave, be of so great accompt amongst you, that you doubt not to circumcise upon the Sabbath, do you rightly reprove me for healing a man thoroughly?

(not because it is of Moses, but of the [6]fathers) and ye on the Sabbath day circumcise a man. **23** If a man on the Sabbath receive circumcision, that the [n]Law of Moses should not be broken, be ye angry with me, because I have made a man every whit whole on the Sabbath day? **24** [o,7]Judge not [p]according to the appearance, but judge righteous judgment. **25** [q]Then said some of them of Jerusalem, Is not this he whom they go about to kill? **26** And behold, he speaketh openly, and they say nothing to him: do the rulers know indeed that this is indeed that Christ? **27** [r]Howbeit we know this man whence he is: but when that Christ cometh, no man shall know whence he is. **28** [s]Then cried Jesus in the Temple as he taught, saying, Ye both know me, and know whence I am: yet am I not come of myself, but he that sent me, is true, whom ye know not. **29** But I know him: for I am of him, and he hath sent me. **30** [t]Then they sought to take him, but no man laid hands on him, because his hour was not yet come. **31** Now many of the people believed on him, and said, When that Christ cometh, will he do more miracles than this man hath done? **32** [u]The Pharisees heard that the people murmured these things of him, and the Pharisees, and high Priests sent officers to take him. **33** Then said Jesus unto them, Yet am I a little while with you, and then go I unto him that sent me. **34** [8]Ye shall seek me, and shall not find me, and where I am, can ye not come. **35** Then said the Jews among themselves, Whither will he go, that we shall not find him? Will he go unto them that are [v]dispersed among the Greeks, and teach the Greeks? **36** What saying is this that he said, Ye shall seek me, and shall not find me? and where I am, can ye not come? **37** [w]Now in the [x]last and [9]great day of the feast, Jesus stood and cried, saying, If any man thirst, let him come unto me, and drink. **38** He that believeth in me, [10]as saith the [y]Scripture, out of his belly shall flow rivers of water of life. **39** ([11]This spake he of the Spirit, which they that believed in him, should receive: for the [z]holy Ghost was not yet given, because that Jesus was not yet [aa]glorified.) **40** [ab]So many of the people, when they heard this saying, said, [12]Of a truth this is that Prophet: **41** Others said, This is that Christ: and some said, But shall that Christ come out of Galilee? **42** [13]Saith not the Scripture that that Christ shall come of the seed of David, and out of the town of Bethlehem, where David was? **43** So was there dissension among the people for him. **44** And some of them would have taken him, but no man laid hands on him. **45** [ac]Then came the officers to the high Priests and Pharisees, and they said unto them, Why have ye not brought him? **46** The officers answered, Never man spake like this man. **47** Then answered them the Pharisees, Are ye also deceived? **48** [ad]Doth any of the rulers, or of the Pharisees believe in him? **49** But this people, which know not the Law, are cursed, **50** Nicodemus said unto them, ([14]he that came to Jesus by night, and was one of them.) **51** Doth our Law judge a man before it hear him, [15]and know [ae]what he hath done? **52** They answered, and said unto him, Art thou also of Galilee? Search and look: for out of Galilee ariseth no Prophet. **53** [af]And every man went unto his own house.

8

3 The woman taken in adultery, 11 hath her sins forgiven her. 12 Christ the light of the world. 19 The Pharisees ask where his Father is. 39 The sons of Abraham. 42 The sons of God, 44 The devil the father of lying. 56 Abraham saw Christ's day.

1 And Jesus went unto the mount of Olives,

2 And early in the morning came again into the Temple, and all the people came unto him, and he sat down and taught them. **3** [a]Then the Scribes and the Pharisees brought unto him a woman taken in adultery, and set her in the midst, **4** And said unto him, Master, we found this woman committing adultery even in the very act. **5** [1]Now Moses in our Law commanded, that such should be stoned: what sayest thou therefore? **6** And this they said to tempt him, that they might have, whereof to accuse him. But Jesus stooped down, and with his finger wrote on the ground, **7** [b]And while they continued asking him, he lifted himself up, and said unto them, [2]Let him that is among you without sin, cast the first stone at her. **8** And again he stooped down, and wrote on the ground. **9** And when they heard it, being accused by their own conscience, they went out, one by one, beginning at the eldest even to the last: so Jesus was left alone, and the woman standing in the midst. **10** [c]When Jesus had lifted up himself again, and saw no man, but the woman, he said unto her, Woman, where are those thine accusers? hath no man condemned thee? **11** She said, No man, Lord. And Jesus said, Neither do I condemn thee: go and sin no more. **12** [d]Then spake Jesus again unto them, saying, I [3]am that light of the world: he that followeth me, shall not walk in darkness, but shall have that light of life. **13** [e]The Pharisees therefore said unto him, [f]Thou bearest record of thyself: thy record is not true. **14** [4]Jesus answered, and said unto them, [g]Though I bear record of myself, yet my record is true: for I know whence I come, and whither I go: but ye cannot tell whence I came, and whither I go. **15** Ye judge after the flesh: I [h]judge no man. **16** And if I also judge, my judgment is true, for I am not alone, but I, and the Father, that sent me. **17** And it is also written in your Law, [5]that the testimony of two men is true. **18** [i]I am one that bear witness of myself, and the Father that sent me beareth witness of me. **19** [j]Then said they unto him, Where is that Father of thine? Jesus answered, Ye neither know me, nor the Father of mine. If ye had known me, ye should have known that Father of mine also. **20** These words spake Jesus in the [k]treasury, as he taught in the Temple, and no man laid hands on him: [l]for his hour was not yet come. **21** [m]Then said Jesus again unto them, I go my way, and ye shall seek me, and shall die in your sins, Whither I go, can ye not come. **22** Then said the Jews, Will he kill himself, because he saith, Whither I go, can ye not come? **23** And he said unto them, Ye are from beneath, I am from above: ye are of this world, I am not of this world. **24** I said therefore unto you, That ye shall die in your sins: for except ye believe, that I am he, ye shall die in your sins. **25** [n]Then said they unto him, Who art thou? And Jesus said unto them, Even [o]the same thing that I said unto you from the beginning. **26** [p]I have many things to say, and to judge of you: but he that sent me, is true, and the things that I have heard of him, those speak I to the world. **27** [q]They understood not that he spake to them of the Father. **28** Then said Jesus unto them, When ye have lifted up the Son of man, then shall ye know that I am he, and that I do nothing of myself, but as my Father hath taught me, so I spake these things. **29** For he that sent me, is with me: the Father hath not left me alone, because I do always those things that please him. **30** As he spake these things, many believed in him. **31** [r]Then said Jesus to the Jews which believed in him, If ye continue in my word, ye are verily my disciples, **32** And shall know the truth, and the truth

---

o. John 7:24 We must judge according to the truth of things, lest the persons of men do turn us and carry us away.
p. John 7:24 By the show that I make: for I seem to be but an abject and rascal of Galilee, and a carpenter's son, whom no man maketh account of: but mark the matter itself well, and judge the tree by the fruit.
q. John 7:25 Many do marvel that the endeavors of the enemies of God have no success: yet in the mean season they do not acknowledge the virtue and power of God.
r. John 7:27 Men are very wise to procure stops and stays to themselves.
s. John 7:28 The truth of Christ doth not hang upon the judgment of man.
t. John 7:30 The wicked cannot do what they list, but what God hath appointed.
u. John 7:32 As the kingdom of God increaseth, so increaseth the rage of his enemies, till at length they in vain seek for those blessings absent, which they despised when they were present.
v. John 7:35 Word for word, (to the dispersion of the Gentiles or Greeks) and under the name of the Greeks he understandeth the Jews which were dispersed amongst the Gentiles.
w. John 7:37 There are two principles of our salvation: the one is to be thoroughly touched with a true feeling of our extreme poverty: the other to seek in Christ only (whom we catch hold on by faith) the abundance of all good things.
x. John 7:37 The last day of the feast of Tabernacles, that as, the eighth day, was as high a day, as the first.
y. John 7:38 This is not read word for word in any place, but it seemeth to be taken out of many places where mention is made of the gifts of the holy Ghost, as Joel 2; Isa. 44, but especially in Isa. 55.
z. John 7:39 What is meant by the holy Ghost, he expressed a little before, speaking of the Spirit which they that believed in him should receive. So that by the name of holy Ghost, are meant the virtues and mighty workings of the holy Ghost.
aa. John 7:39 That is, those things were not yet seen and perceived, which were to show and set forth the glory of the only begotten.
ab. John 7:40 There is contention even in the Church itself about the chief point of religion: neither hath Christ any more cruel enemies than those that occupy the seat of truth: yet can they not do what they would.
ac. John 7:45 God from heaven scorneth such as are his son's enemies.
ad. John 7:48 False Pastors are so fond and foolish that they esteem the Church of God according to the multitude and outward show.
ae. John 7:51 What he hath committed, who is accused.
af. John 7:53 There is no counsel against the Lord.

JOHN. 7

1.	Lev. 13:34	**9.**	Lev. 23:5
2.	John 8:20	**10.**	Deut. 18:15
3.	Exod. 24:3	**11.**	Joel 2:28 / Acts 2:17
4.	John 5:12	**12.**	Deut. 18:15
5.	Lev. 12:3	**13.**	Mic. 5:2 / Matt. 2:5
6.	Gen. 17:10	**14.**	John 3:2
7.	Deut. 1:16	**15.**	Deut. 17:8 / Deut. 19:15
8.	John 13:33		

JOHN. 8

a. John 8:3 While the wicked go about to make a snare for good men, they make a snare for themselves.
b. John 8:7 Against hypocrites which are very severe judges against other men, and flatter themselves in their own sins.
c. John 8:10 Christ would not take upon him the civil Magistrates office: he contented himself to bring sinners to faith and repentance.
d. John 8:12 The world which is blind in itself cannot come to have ray light but in Christ only.
e. John 8:13 Christ is without all exception the best witness of the truth, for he was sent by his Father for that purpose, and was by him approved to the world by infinite miracles.
f. John 8:13 Thou bearest witness of thyself which thing by all men's opinion, is naught: and for a man to commend himself is very discommendable.
g. John 8:14 That which he denied afore, John 5:31, must be taken by a manner of granting, for in that place he framed himself somewhat to the humor of his hearers, which acknowledged nothing in Christ but his humanity, and therefore he was content they should set light by his own witness, unless it were otherwise confirmed. But in this place he standeth for the maintenance of his Godhead, and praiseth his Father, who is his witness, and agreeth with him.
h. John 8:15 I do now only teach you, I condemn no man: but yet if I list to do it, I might lawfully do it, for I am not alone, but my Father is with me.
i. John 8:18 The Godhead is plainly distinguished from the manhood, else there were not two witnesses: for the party accused is not taken for a witness.
j. John 8:19 No man can know God, but in Christ only.
k. John 8:20 This was some place appointed for the gathering of the offerings.
l. John 8:20 We live and die at the pleasure of God and not of men: Therefore this one thing remaineth that we go forward constantly in our vocation.
m. John 8:21 Because that men do naturally abhor heavenly things, no man can be a fit disciple of Christ, unless the Spirit of God frame him: in the mean season notwithstanding, the world must of necessity perish, because it refuseth the life that is offered unto it.
n. John 8:25 He shall at length know who Christ is, which will diligently hear, what he saith.
o. John 8:25 That is, I am Christ, and the savior, for so I told you from the beginning that I was.
p. John 8:26 God is the revenger of Christ's doctrine despised.
q. John 8:27 Even the contempt of Christ maketh for his glory: which thing his enemies shall feel at length to their great smart.
r. John 8:31 The true disciples of Christ continue in his doctrine, that profiting more and more in the knowledge of the truth, they may be delivered from the most grievous burden of sin, into the true liberty of righteousness and life.

shall [s]make you free. **33** [t]They answered him, We be [u]Abraham's seed, and were
never bond to any man: why sayest thou then, Ye shall be made free? **34** Jesus
answered them, Verily, verily I say unto you, that whosoever committeth sin, is the
[6]servant of sin. **35** And the servant abideth not in the house forever: but the Son
abideth forever. **36** If that Son therefore shall make you free, ye shall be free in-
deed. **37** [v]I know that ye are Abraham's seed, but ye seek to kill me, because my
word hath no place in you. **38** I speak that which I have seen with my Father:
and ye do that which ye have seen with your Father. **39** They answered, and
said unto him, Abraham is our father. Jesus said unto them, If ye were Abraham's
children, ye would do the works of Abraham. **40** But now ye go about to kill
me, a man that have told you the truth, which I have heard of God: this did not
Abraham. **41** Ye do the works of your father. Then said they to him, We are
not born of fornication: we have one Father, which is God. **42** Therefore Jesus
said unto them, If God were your Father, then would ye love me: for I proceeded
forth, and came from God, neither came I of myself, but he sent me. **43** Why
do ye not understand my [w]talk? because ye cannot hear my word. **44** [7]Ye are
of your father the devil, and the lusts of your father ye will do: he hath been a
murderer from the [x]beginning, and [y]abode not in the [z]truth, because there is no
truth in him. When he speaketh a lie, then speaketh he of his [aa]own: for he is a
liar, and the [ab]father thereof. **45** And because I tell you the truth, ye believe me
not. **46** [ac]Which of you can rebuke me of sin? and if I say the truth, why do ye
not believe me? **47** [8]He that is of God heareth God's words: ye therefore hear
them not, because ye are not of God. **48** [ad]Then answered the Jews, and said
unto him, Say we not well that thou art a Samaritan, and hast a devil? **49** Je-
sus answered, I have not a devil, but I honor my Father, and ye have dishonored
me. **50** And I seek not mine own praise: but there is one that [ae]seeketh it, and
judgeth. **51** [af]Verily, verily I say unto you, If a man keep my word, he shall never
[ag]see death. **52** [ah]Then said the Jews to him, Now know we that thou hast a de-
vil. Abraham is dead, and the Prophets: and thou sayest, If a man keep my word, he
shall never taste of death. **53** Art thou greater than our father Abraham, which is
dead? and the Prophets are dead: whom makest thou thyself? **54** [ai]Jesus answe-
red, If I honor myself, mine honor is [aj]nothing worth: it is my Father that honoreth
me, whom ye say, that he is your God. **55** [ak]Yet ye have not known him: but I
know him, and if I should say I know him not, I should be a liar like unto you: but
I know him, and keep his word. **56** [al]Your father Abraham [am]rejoiced to see my
[an]day, and he [ao]saw it, and was glad. **57** Then said the Jews unto him, Thou art
not yet fifty years old, and hast thou seen Abraham? **58** Jesus said unto them,
Verily, verily I say unto you, before Abraham was, I [ap]am. **59** [aq]Then took they
up stones to cast at him, but Jesus hid himself, and went out of the Temple: And
he passed through the midst of them, and so went his way.

9

1 Christ giveth sight on the Sabbath day, to him that was born blind. 13 Whom, after he had long reasoned against the Pharisees, 22, 35 and was cast out of the Synagogue, 36 Christ endueth with the knowledge of the everlasting light.

1 And [a]as Jesus passed by, he saw a man which was blind from his birth.
2 And his disciples asked him, saying, Master, who did sin, this man, or his
parents, that he was born blind? **3** Jesus answered, [b]Neither hath this man sin-
ned, nor his parents, but that the works of God should be showed on him. **4** [c]I
must work the works of him that sent me, while it is [d]day: the night cometh when
no man can work. **5** As long as I am in the world, [1]I am the light of the wor-
ld. **6** [e]As soon as he had thus spoken, he spat on the ground, and made clay of
the spittle, and anointed the eyes of the blind with the clay, **7** And said unto
him, Go wash in the pool of Siloam (which is by interpretation, Sent.) He went
his way therefore and washed, and came again seeing. **8** [f]Now the neighbors
and they that had seen him before, when he was blind, said, Is not this he that
sat and begged? **9** Some said, This is he: and others said, He is like him: but he
himself said, I am he. **10** Therefore they said unto him, How were thine eyes
[g]opened? **11** He answered, and said, The man that is called Jesus, made clay,
and anointed mine eyes, and said unto me, Go to the pool of Siloam and wash.
So I went and washed, and received sight. **12** Then they said unto him, Whe-
re is he? He said, I cannot tell. **13** They brought to the Pharisees him that was
once blind. **14** And it was the Sabbath day, when Jesus made the clay, and ope-
ned his eyes. **15** Then again the Pharisees also asked him, how he had received
sight. And he said unto them, He laid clay upon mine eyes, and I washed, and do
see. **16** [h]Then said some of the Pharisees, This man is not of God, because he
keepeth not the Sabbath day. Others said, How can a man that is a sinner, do such
miracles? and there was a dissension among them. **17** Then spake they unto the
blind again, What sayest thou of him, because he hath opened thine eyes? And he
said, He is a Prophet. **18** Then the Jews did not believe him (that he had been
blind, and received his sight) until they had called the parents of him that had
received sight. **19** And they asked them, saying, Is this your son, whom ye say
was born blind? How doth he now see then? **20** His parents answered them,
and said, We know that this is our son, and that he was born blind: **21** But
by what means he now seeth, we know not: or who hath opened his eyes, can
we not tell: he is old enough: ask him: he shall answer for himself. **22** These
words spake his parents, because they feared the Jews: for the Jews had ordained
already, that if any man did confess that he was Christ, he should be excommu-
nicated out of the Synagogue. **23** Therefore said his parents, He is old enough:
ask him. **24** Then again called they the man that had been blind, and said unto
him, [i]Give glory unto God: we know that this man is a [j]sinner. **25** Then he an-
swered, and said, Whether he be a sinner or no, I cannot tell: one thing I know,
that I was blind, and now I see. **26** Then said they to him again, What did he to
thee? how opened he thine eyes? **27** He answered them, I have told you already,
and ye have not heard it: wherefore would ye hear it again? will ye also be his di-
sciples? **28** [k]Then reviled they him, and said, Be thou his disciple: we be Moses'
disciples. **29** We know that God spake with Moses: but this man we know not
from whence he is. **30** The man answered, and said unto them, Doubtless, this
is a marvelous thing, that ye know not whence he is, and yet he hath opened mine
eyes. **31** Now we know that God heareth not sinners: but if any man be a wor-
shipper of God, and doeth his will, him heareth he. **32** Since the world began,
was it not heard, that any man opened the eyes of one that was born blind. **33** If
this man were not of God, he could have done nothing. **34** They answered, and
said unto him, [l]Thou art altogether born in sins, and dost thou teach us? so they

---

s. John 8:32 From the slavery of sin.
t. John 8:33 Some of the multitude, not they that believed: for this is not the speech of men that consent unto him but of men that are against him.
u. John 8:33 Born and begotten of Abraham.
v. John 8:37 Our wicked manners declare, that we are plainly born of a devilish nature, But we are changed, and made of the household of God, according to the covenant which he made with Abraham by Christ only, apprehended and laid hold on by faith: which faith is known by a godly and honest life.
w. John 8:43 Or, language: as though he said, you do no more understand what I say, than if I spake in a strange and unknown language to you.
x. John 8:44 From the beginning of the world: for as soon as man was made, the devil cast him headlong into death.
y. John 8:44 That is, continued not constantly, or remained not.
z. John 8:44 That is, in faithfulness, and uprightness, that is, kept not his creation.
aa. John 8:44 Even of his own head, and of his own brain or disposition.
ab. John 8:44 The author thereof.
ac. John 8:46 Christ did thoroughly execute the office, that his Father enjoined him.
ad. John 8:48 The enemies of Christ make their bravery for a while, but the Father will appear at his time to revenge the reproach that is done unto him in the person of his son.
ae. John 8:50 That is, that will revenge both your despising of me, and of him.
af. John 8:51 The only doctrine of the Gospel apprehended by faith, is a sure remedy against death.
ag. John 8:51 That is, he shall not feel it: for even in the midst of death, the faithful see life.
ah. John 8:52 Against them which abuse the glory of the Saints, to darken Christ's glory.
ai. John 8:54 There is nothing farther off from all ambition than Christ, but his Father hath set him above all things.
aj. John 8:54 This is spoken by manner of a grant: as if he had said, Be it so, let this report which I give of myself, be of no force: yet there is another that glorifieth me, that is, that honoreth my Name.
ak. John 8:55 There is no right knowledge of God, without Christ, neither any right knowledge of Christ without his word.
al. John 8:56 The virtue of Christ showed itself through all former ages in the Fathers, for they saw in the promises, that he should come, and did very joyfully lay hold on him with a lively faith.
am. John 8:56 Was very desirous.
an. John 8:56 A day is a space that a man liveth in, or doeth any notable act, or suffereth any great thing.
ao. John 8:56 With the eyes of faith, Heb. 11:13.
ap. John 8:58 Christ as he was God, was before Abraham: and he was the Lamb slain from the beginning of the world.
aq. John 8:59 Zeal without knowledge, breaketh out at length into a most open madness: and yet the wicked cannot do what they list.

JOHN. 8

1. Lev. 20:10
2. Deut. 17:7
3. John 1:5 / John 9:5
4. John 5:31
5. Deut. 17:6 / Deut. 19:15 / Matt. 18:16 / 2 Cor. 13:1 / Heb. 10:28
6. Rom. 6:20 / 2 Pet. 2:19
7. 1 John 3:8
8. John 4:6

JOHN. 9

a. John 9:1 Sin is the beginning even of all bodily diseases, and yet doth it not follow, that God always respecteth their sins, whom he most sharply punisheth.
b. John 9:3 Christ reasoneth here, as his disciples thought, which presuppose that there come no diseases but for sins only: whereupon he answereth that there was another cause of this man's blindness, and that was, that God's his work might be seen.
c. John 9:4 The works of Christ are as it were a light, which lighten the darkness of the world.
d. John 9:4 By (day) is meant the light, that is, the lightsome, doctrine of the heavenly truth: and by (night) is meant the darkness which cometh by the obscurity of the same doctrine.
e. John 9:6 Christ healing the man born blind, by taking the sign of clay, and afterward the sign of the fountain of Siloam (which signifieth Sent) showeth that as he at the beginning made man, so doth he again restore both his body and soul: and yet so, that he himself cometh first of his own accord to heal us.
f. John 9:8 A true image of all men, who as they are of nature blind, do neither themselves receive the light that is offered unto them, nor suffer it in others, and yet make a great ado amongst themselves.
g. John 9:10 This is an Hebrew kind of speech, for they call a man's eyes shut, when they cannot receive any light: And therefore they are said to have their eyes opened, which of blind men are made to see.
h. John 9:16 Religion is not assaulted by any means more than by pretence of Religion: but the more it is pressed down, the more it riseth up.
i. John 9:24 A solemn order, whereby men were constrained in old time to acknowledge their fault before God, as if they should say, Consider thou art before God, who knoweth the whole matter, and therefore see thou reverence his majesty, and do him this honor, rather to confess the whole matter openly, than to lie before him, Josh. 7:19; 1 Sam. 6:5.
j. John 9:24 He is called a sinner in the Hebrew tongue, which is a wicked man, and maketh as it were an art of sins.
k. John 9:28 Proud wickedness must needs at length break forth, which in vain lieth hid under a zeal of godliness.
l. John 9:34 Thou art naught even from the cradle, and as we use to say, there is nothing in thee but sin.

cast him out. **35** [m]Jesus heard that they had cast him out: and when he had
found him, he said unto him, Dost thou believe in the Son of God? **36** He an-
swered, and said, Who is he, Lord, that I might believe in him? **37** And Jesus said
unto him, Both thou hast seen him, and he it is that talketh with thee. **38** Then
he said, Lord, I believe, and worshipped him. **39** [n]And Jesus said, I am come
unto [o]judgment into this world, that they [p]which see not, might see: and that they
[2]which see, might be made blind. **40** And some of the Pharisees which were with
him, heard these things, and said unto him, Are we blind also? **41** Jesus said unto
them, If ye were blind, ye should not have sin: but now ye say, We see: therefore
your sin remaineth.

10

1 Christ proveth that the Pharisees are the evil shepherds, 8 and by many reasons, that himself 11, 14 is the good shepherd: 19 And thereof dissension ariseth. 31 They take up stones, 39 and go about to take him, but he escapeth.

1 Verily, [a]verily I say unto you, He that entereth not in by the door into the
sheepfold, but climbeth up another way, he is a thief and a robber. **2** But he that
goeth in by the door, is the shepherd of the sheep. **3** To him the [b]porter openeth,
and the sheep hear his voice, and he calleth his own sheep by name, and leadeth
them out. **4** And when he hath sent forth his own sheep, he goeth before them,
and the sheep follow him: for they know his voice. **5** And they will not follow a
stranger, but they flee from him: for they know not the voice of strangers. **6** This
[c]parable spake Jesus unto them: but they understood not what things they were
which he spake unto them. **7** Then said Jesus unto them again, Verily, verily I
say unto you, I am that door of the sheep. **8** [d]All that [e]ever came before me, are
thieves and robbers: but the sheep did not hear them. **9** [f]I am that door: by me
if any man enter in, he shall be saved, and shall [g]go in, and go out, and find pa-
sture. **10** The thief cometh not, but for to steal, and to kill, and to destroy: I am
come that they might have life, and have it in abundance. **11** [1]I am that good
shepherd: that good shepherd giveth his life for his sheep. **12** But an hireling,
and he which is not the shepherd, neither the sheep are his own, seeth the wolf co-
ming, and he leaveth the sheep, and fleeth, and the wolf catcheth them, and scatte-
reth the sheep. **13** So the hireling fleeth, because he is an hireling, and careth not
for the sheep. **14** I am that good shepherd, and know mine, and am known of
mine. **15** As the Father [h]knoweth me, so know I the Father: and I lay down my
life for my sheep. **16** [i]Other sheep I have also, which are not of this fold: them
also must I bring, and they shall hear my voice: and [2]there shall be [j]one sheepfold,
and one shepherd. **17** [k]Therefore doth my Father love me, because [l,3]I lay down
my life, that I might take it again. **18** No man taketh it from me, but I lay it
down of myself: I have power to lay it down, and have power to take it again: this
[4]commandment have I received of my Father. **19** [m]Then there was a dissension
again among the Jews for these sayings. **20** And many of them said, He hath a
devil, and is mad: why hear ye him? **21** Others said, These are not the words of
him that hath a devil: can the devil open the eyes of the blind? **22** And it was at
Jerusalem the feast of the [n]Dedication, and it was winter. **23** [o]And Jesus walked
in the Temple, in Solomon's porch. **24** Then came the Jews round about him,
and said unto him, How long dost thou make us to doubt? If thou be that Christ,
tell us plainly. **25** [p]Jesus answered them, I told you, and ye believe not: the works
that I do in my Father's Name, they bear witness of me. **26** [q]But ye believe not:
[r]for ye are not of my sheep, as I said unto you. **27** My sheep hear my voice, and I
know them, and they follow me, **28** And I give unto them eternal life, and they
shall never perish, neither shall any pluck them out of mine hand. **29** My Father
which gave them me, is greater than all, and none is able to take them out of my
Father's hand. **30** I and my Father are one. **31** [s,5]Then the Jews again took up
stones, to stone him. **32** Jesus answered them, Many good works have I showed
you from my [t]Father: for which of these works do ye stone me? **33** The Jews an-
swered him, saying, For the good work we stone thee not, but for blasphemy, and
that thou being a man, makest thyself God. **34** Jesus answered them, Is it not
written in your Law, [6]I said, Ye are gods? **35** If he called them gods, unto whom
the word of God was given, and the Scripture cannot be [u]broken, **36** Say ye of
him, whom the Father hath sanctified, and sent into the world, Thou blasphemest,
because I said, I am the Son of God? **37** If I do not the works of my Father, belie-
ve me not. **38** But if I do, then though ye believe not me, yet believe the works,
that ye may know and believe, that the Father is in me, and I in him. **39** [v]A-
gain they went about to take him: but he escaped out of their hands, **40** And
went again beyond Jordan, into the place where John first baptized, and there abo-
de. **41** And many resorted unto him, and said, John did no miracle: but all thin-
gs that John spake of this man, were true. **42** And many believed in him there.

11

1 Christ, to show that he is, 25 the life and the resurrection, 14 cometh to Lazarus being dead, 17, 34 and buried, 43 and raiseth him up. 47 As the Priests were consulting together, 49 Caiaphas 50 prophecieth that one must die for the people. 56, 57 They command to seek Christ out, and to take him.

1 And [a]a certain man was sick, named Lazarus of Bethany, the [b]town of
Mary, and her sister Martha. **2** (And it was that [1]Mary which anointed the
Lord with ointment, and wiped his feet with her hair, whose brother Lazarus was
sick.) **3** Therefore his sisters sent unto him, saying, Lord, behold, he whom thou
lovest, is sick. **4** When Jesus heard it, he said, This sickness is not unto [c]death,
but for the glory of God, that the Son of God might be glorified thereby. **5** Now
Jesus loved Martha and her sister, and Lazarus. **6** [d]And after he had heard that
he was sick, yet abode he two days still in the same place where he was. **7** Then
after that, said he to his disciples, Let us go into Judea again. **8** [e]The disciples said
unto him, Master, the Jews lately sought to [2]stone thee, and dost thou go thither
again? **9** Jesus answered, Are there not [f]twelve hours in the day? If a man walk in
the day, he stumbleth not, because he seeth the light of this world. **10** But if a
man walk in the night, he stumbleth, because there is no light in him. **11** The-
se things spake he, and after, he said unto them, Our friend Lazarus [g]sleepeth:
but I go to wake him up. **12** Then said his disciples, Lord, if he sleep, he shall
be safe. **13** Howbeit, Jesus spake of his death: but they thought that he had
spoken of the natural sleep. **14** Then said Jesus unto them plainly, Lazarus is
dead. **15** And I am glad for your sakes, that I was not there, that ye may believe:

---

m. John 9:35 Most happy is their state, which are cast furthest out of the Church of the wicked (which proudly boast themselves of the name of the Church) that Christ may come never to them.
n. John 9:39 Christ doth lighten all them by the preaching of the Gospel, which acknowledge their own darkness, but such as seem to themselves to see clearly enough, those he altogether blindeth: of which sort are they oftentimes, which have the highest place in the Church.
o. John 9:39 With great power and authority, to do what is righteous and just: as if he said, These men take upon them to govern the people of God after their own lusts, as though they saw all things, and no man but they: but I will rule far otherwise than these men do: for whom they account for blind men, them I will lighten, and such as take themselves to be wisest, them will I drown in most gross darkness of ignorance.
p. John 9:39 In these words (of seeing and not seeing) there is a secret taunting and check to the Pharisees: for they thought all men blind but themselves.

JOHN. 9

1. John 1:9 / John 8:12 / John 12:35
2. John 3:17 / John 12:47

JOHN. 10

a. John 10:1 Seeing that by Christ only we have access to the Father, there are neither other true shepherds, than those which come to Christ themselves, and bring others thither also, neither is any to be thought the true sheepfold, but that which is gathered to Christ.
b. John 10:3 In those days they used to have a servant always sitting at the door, and therefore he speaketh after the manner of those days.
c. John 10:6 This word (parable) which the Evangelist useth here, signifieth a dark kind of speech, when words are taken from their natural meaning, to signify another thing to us.
d. John 10:8 It maketh no matter, how many, neither how old the false teachers there have been.
e. John 10:8 These large terms must be applied to the matter he speaketh of. And therefore when he calleth himself the door, he calleth all them thieves and robbers which take upon them this name of Door, which none of the Prophets can, for they showed the sheep, that Christ was the door.
f. John 10:9 Only Christ is the true Pastor, and that only is the true Church, which acknowledgeth him to be properly their only Pastor: To him are opposite thieves which feed not the sheep, but kill them: and hirelings also, which forsake the flock in time of danger, because they feed it only for their own profit and gains.
g. John 10:9 That is, shall live safely: so use the Jews to speak, as Deut. 26:6, and yet there is a peculiar alluding to the shepherd's office.
h. John 10:15 Loveth me, alloweth me.
i. John 10:16 The calling of the Gentiles.
j. John 10:16 The certain mark of the Catholic Church throughout all the world, which hath one head, that is Christ, the only keeper and only shepherd of it.
k. John 10:17 Christ is by the decree of the Father, the only true shepherd of the true Church, for he willingly gave his life for his sheep, and by his own power rose again to life.
l. John 10:17 He speaketh in the time that now is because Christ's whole life was as it were a perpetual death.
m. John 10:19 The Gospel discovereth hypocrisy, and therefore the world must needs rage when it cometh forth.
n. John 10:22 The feast of the Dedication was instituted by Judas Maccabeus and his brethren, after the restoring of God's true religion, by the casting out of Antiochus his garrison, 1 Macc. 4:59.
o. John 10:23 The unbelievers and proud men accuse the Gospel of darkness, which darkness indeed is within themselves.
p. John 10:25 The doctrine of the Gospel is proved from heaven by two witnesses: both by the purity of the doctrine, and by miracles.
q. John 10:26 It is no marvel that there do but a few believe, seeing that all men are by nature untamed beasts: yet notwithstanding God hath his, which he turneth into sheep, and commiteth them unto his Son, and preserveth them against the cruelty of all wild beasts.
r. John 10:26 He giveth a reason why they believed not, to wit, because they are none of his sheep.
s. John 10:31 Christ proveth his dignity by divine works.
t. John 10:32 Through my Father's authority and power.
u. John 10:35 Void and of none effect.
v. John 10:39 Christ fleeth danger, not of mistrust, nor for fear of death, nor that he would be idle, but to gather a Church in another place.

JOHN. 10

1. Isa. 40:11 / Ezek. 34:23
2. Ezek. 37:22
3. Isa. 53:7
4. Acts 2:24
5. John 8:59
6. Ps. 82:6

JOHN. 11

a. John 11:1 Christ in restoring the stinking carcass of his friend to life, showeth an example both of his mighty power, and also of his singular good will toward men: which is also an image of the resurrection to come.
b. John 11:1 Where his sisters dwelt.
c. John 11:4 That is to say, sent for the purpose to kill him.
d. John 11:6 In that, that God seemeth sometimes to linger in helping of us, he doeth it both for his glory, and for our salvation, as the falling out of the matter in the end, plainly proveth.
e. John 11:8 This only is the sure and right way to life, to follow God boldly without fear, who calleth us and shineth before us in the darkness of this world.
f. John 11:9 All things are fitly wrought and brought to pass in their season.
g. John 11:11 The Jews used a milder kind of speech, and called death a sleep, whereupon in other languages the place of burial where the dead are laid, waiting for the resurrection, is called a sleeping place.

but let us go unto him. **16** Then said Thomas (which is called Didymus) unto
his fellow disciples, Let us also go, that we may die with him. **17** Then came Je-
sus, and found that he had lain in the grave four days already. **18** (Now Bethany
was near unto Jerusalem, about fifteen furlongs off.) **19** [h]And many of the Jews
were come to Martha and Mary to comfort them for their brother. **20** Then
Martha, when she heard that Jesus was coming, went to meet him: but Mary sat
still in the house. **21** Then said Martha unto Jesus, Lord, if thou hadst been here,
my brother had not been dead. **22** But now I know also, that whatsoever thou
askest of God, God will give it thee. **23** Jesus said unto her, Thy brother shall [i]ri-
se again. **24** Martha said unto him, I know that he shall rise again [3]in the resur-
rection at the last day. **25** Jesus said unto her, I am the resurrection and the life:
[4]he that believeth in me, though he were dead yet shall he live. **26** And whosoever
liveth, and believeth in me, shall never die: Believest thou this? **27** She said unto
him, Yea, Lord, I believe that thou art that Christ that Son of God, which should
come into the world. **28** And when she had so said, she went her way, and called
Mary her sister secretly, saying, The Master is come, and calleth for thee. **29** And
when she heard it, she arose quickly, and came unto him. **30** For Jesus was not
yet come into the town, but was in the place where Martha met him. **31** The
Jews then which were with her in the house, and comforted her, when they saw
Mary, that she rose up hastily, and went out, followed her, saying, She goeth unto
the grave, to weep there. **32** Then when Mary was come where Jesus was, and
saw him, she fell down at his feet, saying unto him, Lord, if thou hadst been here,
my brother had not been dead. **33** [j]When Jesus therefore saw her weep, and the
Jews also weep which came with her, he [k]groaned in the spirit, and was troubled
in himself, **34** And said, Where have ye laid him? They said unto him, Lord,
come and see. **35** And Jesus wept. **36** Then said the Jews, behold, how he
loved him. **37** And some of them said, [5]Could not he which opened the eyes
of the blind, have made also, that this man should not have died? **38** Jesus the-
refore again groaned in himself, and came to the grave. And it was a cave, and a
stone was laid upon it. **39** Jesus said, Take ye away the stone. Martha the sister of
him that was dead, said unto him, Lord, he stinketh already for he hath been dead
four days. **40** Jesus said unto her, Said I not unto thee, that if thou didst believe,
thou shouldest see the glory of God? **41** Then they took away the stone from
the place where the dead was laid. And Jesus lifted up his eyes, and said, Father, I
thank thee, because thou hast heard me. **42** I know that thou hearest me always,
but because of the people that stand by, I said it, that they may believe, that thou
hast sent me. **43** As he had spoken these things, he cried with a loud voice, La-
zarus, come forth. **44** Then he that was dead, came forth, bound hand and foot
with bands, and his face was bound with a napkin. Jesus said unto them, Loose
him, and let him go. **45** Then many of the Jews, which came to Mary, and had
seen the things, which Jesus did, believed in him. **46** [l]But some of them went
their way to the Pharisees, and told them what things Jesus had done. **47** Then
gathered the high Priests, and the Pharisees a [m]council, and said, What shall we
do? For this man doeth many miracles. **48** If we let him thus alone, all men will
believe in him, and the Romans will come and [n]take away both our place, and the
nation. **49** [o]Then one of them named Caiaphas, which was the high Priest that
same year, said unto them, Ye perceive nothing at all, **50** [6]Nor yet do you consi-
der that it is expedient for us, that one man die for the people, and that the whole
nation perish not. **51** [p]This spake he not of himself: but being high Priest that
same year, he prophesied that Jesus should die for that nation: **52** And not for
that nation only, but that he should gather together in one the children of God,
which [q]were scattered. **53** Then from that day forth they consulted together, to
put him to death. **54** [r]Jesus therefore walked no more openly among the Jews,
but went thence unto a country near to the wilderness, into a city called Ephraim,
and there continued with his disciples. **55** And the Jews' Passover was at hand,
and many went out of the country up to Jerusalem before the Passover, to purify
themselves. **56** Then sought they for Jesus, and spake among themselves, as they
stood in the Temple, What think ye, that he cometh not to the feast? **57** Now
both the high Priests and the Pharisees had given a commandment, that if any man
knew where he were, he should show it, that they might take him.

12

2 As Christ is at supper with Lazarus, 3 Mary anointeth his feet. 5 Judas findeth fault with her. 7 Christ defendeth her. 10 The Priests would put Lazarus to death. 12 As Christ cometh to Jerusalem. 18 The people meet him. 22 The Greeks desire to see him. 42 The chief rulers that believe in him, but for fear do not confess him, 44 he exhorteth to faith.

1 Then [1]Jesus, six days before the Passover, came to Bethany, where Lazarus
was, who died, whom he had raised from the dead. **2** There they made him
a supper, and Martha served: but Lazarus was one of them that sat at the table
with him. **3** Then took Mary a pound of ointment of Spikenard very costly, and
anointed Jesus' feet, and wiped his feet with her hair, and the house was filled with
the savor of the ointment. **4** Then said one of his disciples, even Judas Iscariot,
Simon's son, which should betray him: **5** [a]Why was not this ointment sold for
three hundred pence, and given to the poor? **6** Now he said thus, not that he
cared for the poor, but because he was a thief, and [2]had the bag, and bore that whi-
ch was given. **7** [b]Then said Jesus, Let her alone: against the day of my burying
she kept it. **8** For the poor always ye have with you, but me ye shall not have
always. **9** [c]Then much people of the Jews knew that he was there: and they came,
not for Jesus' sake only, but that they might see Lazarus also, whom he had raised
from the dead. **10** The high Priests therefore consulted, that they might put La-
zarus to death also, **11** because that for his sake many of the Jews went away, and
believed in Jesus. **12** [3]On the morrow a great multitude that were come to the
feast, when they heard that Jesus should come to Jerusalem, **13** Took branches of
palm trees, and went forth to meet him, and cried, Hosanna, Blessed is the King of
Israel that cometh in the Name of the Lord. **14** And Jesus found a young ass, and
sat thereon, as it is written, **15** [4]Fear not, daughter of Zion: behold, thy King
cometh sitting on an ass's colt. **16** But his disciples understood not these things
at the first: but when Jesus was glorified, then remembered they, that these things
were written of him, and that they had done these things unto him. **17** The peo-
ple therefore that was with him, bare witness that he called Lazarus out of the grave
and raised him from the dead. **18** Therefore met him the people also, because
they heard that he had done this miracle. **19** [d]And the Pharisees said among
themselves, Perceive ye how ye prevail nothing? Behold, the world goeth after
him. **20** Now there were certain Greeks among them that [e]came up to wor-
ship at the feast. **21** And they came to Philip, which was of Bethsaida in Galilee,
and desired him, saying, Sir, we would see that Jesus. **22** Philip came and told
Andrew: and again Andrew and Philip told Jesus. **23** And Jesus answered them,
saying, The hour is come, that the Son of man must be glorified. **24** [f]Verily, verily
I say unto you, Except the wheat corn fall into the ground and [g]die, it abideth alo-
ne: but if it die, it bringeth forth much fruit. **25** [5]He that loveth his life, shall lose
it, and he that hateth his life in this world, shall keep it unto life eternal. **26** [6]If
any man serve me, let him follow me: for where I am, there shall my servant be:
and if any man serve me, him will my father honor. **27** [h]Now is my soul trou-
bled: and what shall I say? Father, save me from this [i]hour: but therefore came I
unto this hour. **28** Father, [j]glorify thy Name. Then came there a voice from he-
aven, saying, I have both glorified it, and will glorify it again. **29** Then said the
people that stood by, and heard, that it was a thunder: others said, An Angel spake
to him. **30** [k]Jesus answered, and said, This voice came not because of me, but for
your sakes. **31** Now is the judgment of this world: now shall the prince of this

---

h. John 11:19 God who is the maker of nature, doth not condemn natural affections, but showeth that they ought to be examined by the rule of faith.
i. John 11:23 That is, shall recover life again.
j. John 11:33 Christ took upon him together with our flesh all affections of man (sin only excepted) and amongst them especially mercy and compassion.
k. John 11:33 These are tokens that he was greatly moved, but yet they were without sin: and these affections are proper to man's nature.
l. John 11:46 The last point of hard and iron-like stubbornness is this, to proclaim open war against God, and yet ceaseth not to make a presence both of godliness and of the profit of the commonwealth.
m. John 11:47 The Jews called the council Sanhedrin: and the word that John useth is Synedri.
n. John 11:48 That is, take away from us by force: for at that time, though the high Priest's authority was greatly lessened and decayed, yet there was some kind of government left among the Jews.
o. John 11:49 The raging and mad company of the false Church, persuade themselves that they cannot be in safety, unless he is taken away, who only upholdeth the Church: And so likewise judgeth the wisdom of the flesh in worldly affairs, which is governed by the spirit of giddiness or madness.
p. John 11:51 Christ doth sometimes so turn the tongues, even of the wicked, that in cursing, they bless.
q. John 11:52 For they were not gathered together in one country, as the Jews were, but to be gathered from all quarters, from the East to the West.
r. John 11:54 We may give place to the rage of the wicked, when it is expedient so to do, but yet in such sort, that we swerve not from God's vocation.

JOHN. 11
1. John 12:3 / Matt. 26:7
2. John 7:30 / John 8:59 / John 10:33
3. John 5:29 / Luke 14:14
4. John 6:35
5. John 9:6
6. John 18:14

JOHN. 12
a. John 12:5 An horrible example in Judas of a mind blinded with covetousness, and yet pretending godliness.
b. John 12:7 This Extraordinary anointing, which was for a sign, is so allowed of God, that he witnesseth how he will not be worshipped with outward pomp, or costly service, but with alms.
c. John 12:9 When the light of the Gospel showeth itself, some are found to be curious, and others (which left ought) to be open enemies: others in a rage honor him, whom they will straightway fall from: and very few do so reverently receive him as they ought: Notwithstanding Christ beginneth his spiritual kingdom in the midst of his enemies.
d. John 12:19 Even they which go about to oppress Christ, are made instruments of his glory.
e. John 12:20 After the solemn custom: the Greeks were first so called by the name of the country of Greece, where they dwelt: but afterward, all that were not of the Jew's religion, but worshipped false gods, and were also called Heathens, were called by this name.
f. John 12:24 The death of Christ is as it were a sowing, which seemeth to be a dying to the corn, but indeed is the cause of a far greater harvest: and such as is the condition of the head, so shall it be of the members.
g. John 12:24 A wheat corn dieth when it is changed by virtue of the ground, and becometh a root of a fruitful blade.
h. John 12:27 Whilst Christ went about to suffer all the punishment which is due to our sins, and whilst his divinity did not yet show his might and power so far as this satisfaction might thoroughly wrought, now when he is stricken with the great fear of the curse of God, he crieth out and prayeth , and desireth to be released: yet notwithstanding he preferreth the will and glory of his Father before all things, whose obedience the Father alloweth even from heaven.
i. John 12:27 To wit, of death that is now at hand.
j. John 12:28 So then the Father's glory is Christ's glory.
k. John 12:30 Christ foretelleth to the deaf, the manner of his death, the overcoming of the devil and the world, and in conclusion his triumph.

world be cast out. 32 [7]And I, if I were [l]lift up from the earth, will draw [m]all men
unto me. 33 Now this said he, signifying what death he should die. 34 The
people answered him, We have heard out of the [8]Law, that that Christ bideth fo-
rever: and how sayest thou, that that Son of man must be lift up? Who is that Son
of man? 35 [n]Then Jesus said unto them, Yet a little while is [9]the light with you:
walk while ye have that light, lest the darkness come upon you: for he that walketh
in the dark, knoweth not whither he goeth. 36 While ye have that light, believe
in that light, that ye may be the [o]children of the light. These things spake Jesus, and
departed, and hid himself from them. 37 [p]And though he had done so many
miracles before them, yet believed they not on him, 38 That the saying of Isaiah
the Prophet might be fulfilled, that he said, [10]Lord, who believed our report? and
to whom is the [q]arm of the Lord revealed? 39 Therefore could they not believe,
because that Isaiah saith again, 40 [11]He hath blinded their eyes, and hardened
their heart, that they should not see with their eyes, nor understand with their he-
art, and should be converted, and I should heal them. 41 These things said Isaiah
when he saw his glory, and spake of him. 42 [r]Nevertheless, even among the chief
rulers, many believed in him: but because of the Pharisees they did not confess
him, lest they should be cast out of the Synagogue. 43 [12]For they loved the prai-
se of men, more than the praise of God. 44 [s]And Jesus cried, and said, He that
believeth in me, believeth [t]not in me, but in him that sent me. 45 And he that
seeth me, seeth him that sent me. 46 I [13]am come a light into the world, that
whosoever believeth in me, should not abide in darkness. 47 [14]And if any man
hear my words, and believe not, I judge him not: for I came not to judge the world,
but to save the world. 48 He that refuseth me, and receiveth not my words, hath
one that judgeth him: [15]the word that I have spoken, it shall judge him in the last
day. 49 For I have not spoken of myself: but the father which sent me, he gave
me a commandment what I should say, and what I should speak. 50 And I know
that his commandment is life everlasting: the things therefore that I speak, I speak
them so as the Father said unto me.

13

4 Christ rising from supper, 14 to command humility to his Apostles, washeth their feet. 21 He noteth the traitor Judas, 26 with an evident token. 34 He commendeth charity. 37, 38 He foretelleth Peter of his denial.

1 Now [a,1]before the feast of the Passover, when Jesus knew that his hour was
come, that he should depart out of this world unto the Father, forasmuch as he
loved his [b]own which were in the world, unto the end he loved them. 2 And
when supper was done (and that the devil had now put in the heart of Judas Isca-
riot, Simon's son, to betray him.) 3 Jesus knowing that the Father had given
all things into his [c]hands, and that he was come forth from God, and went to
God, 4 He [d]riseth from Supper, and layeth aside his upper garments, and took
a towel, and girded himself. 5 After that, he poured water into a basin, and be-
gan to wash the disciples' feet, and to wipe them with the towel, wherewith he
was girded. 6 Then came he to Simon Peter, who said to him, Lord, dost thou
wash my feet? 7 Jesus answered and said unto him, What I do, thou knowest
not now: but thou shalt know it hereafter. 8 Peter said unto him, Thou shalt
never wash my feet. Jesus answered him, If I wash thee not, thou shalt have [e]no
part with me. 9 Simon Peter said unto him, Lord, not my feet only, but also the
hands and the head. 10 Jesus said to him, He that is washed, needeth not, save
to wash his feet, but is clean every whit: and ye are [2]clean, but not all. 11 For he
knew who should betray him: therefore said he, Ye are not all clean. 12 So after
he had washed their feet, and had taken his garments, and was set down again, he
said unto them, Know ye what I have done to you? 13 Ye call me Master, and
Lord, and ye say well: for so am I. 14 If I then your Lord, and Master, have
washed your feet, ye also ought to wash one another's feet. 15 For I have given
you an example, that ye should do, even as I have done to you. 16 Verily, verily
I say unto you, [3]The servant is not greater than his master, neither the [f]ambassa-
dor greater than he that sent him. 17 If ye know these things, blessed are ye if
ye do them. 18 [g]I speak not of you all: I know whom I have chosen: but it is
that the Scripture might be fulfilled, [4]He that eateth bread with me, hath lift up
his heel against me. 19 From henceforth tell I you before it come, that when it is
come to pass, ye might believe that I am he. 20 [5]Verily, verily I say unto you, If
I send any, he that receiveth him, receiveth me, and he that receiveth me, receiveth
him that sent me. 21 When Jesus had said these things, he was troubled in the
Spirit, and [h]testified, and said, Verily, verily I say unto you, that one of you shall
betray me. 22 [6]Then the disciples looked one on another, doubting of whom he
spake. 23 Now there was one of his disciples, which [i]leaned on Jesus' bosom,
whom Jesus loved. 24 To him beckoned therefore Simon Peter, that he should
ask who it was of whom he spake. 25 He then as he leaned on Jesus' breast, said
unto him, Lord, who is it? 26 Jesus answered, He it is, to whom I shall give a
sop, when I have dipped it: and he wet a sop, and gave it to Judas Iscariot, Simon's
son. 27 And after the sop, Satan entered into him. Then said Jesus unto him,
That thou doest, do quickly. 28 But none of them that were at table, knew, for
what cause he spake it unto him. 29 For some of them thought because Judas
had the bag, that Jesus had said unto him, Buy those things that we have need of
against the feast: or that he should give something to the poor. 30 As soon then
as he had received the sop, he went immediately out, and it was night. 31 [j]When
he was gone out, Jesus said, [k]Now is the son of man glorified, and God is glorified
in him. 32 If God be glorified in him, God shall also glorify him in himself, and
shall straightway glorify him. 33 [l]Little children, yet a little while am I with you:
ye shall seek me, but as I said unto the [7]Jews, Whither I go, can ye not come: also
to you say I now. 34 [8]A new commandment give I unto you, that ye love one
another: as I have loved you, that ye also love one another. 35 By this shall all
men know, that ye are my disciples, if ye have love one to another. 36 [m]Simon
Peter said unto him, Lord, whither goest thou? Jesus answered him, Whither I go,
thou canst not follow me now: but thou shalt follow me afterward. 37 Peter said
unto him, Lord, why can I not follow thee now? [9]I will lay down my life for thy
sake. 38 Jesus answered him, Wilt thou lay down thy life for my sake? Verily,
verily I say unto thee, The cock shall not crow, till thou have denied me thrice.

14

He comforteth his disciples, 2, 7 declaring his divinity and the fruit of his death, 16 promising the comforter, 17 even the holy Spirit, 26 whose office he setteth out. 27 He promiseth his peace.

1 Let [a]not your heart be troubled: ye believe in God, believe also in me. 2 In
my Father's house are many dwelling places: if it were not so, [b]I would have told
you: I go to [c]prepare a place for you. 3 [d]And if I go to prepare a place for you,
I will [e]come again, and receive you unto myself, that where I am, there may ye

---

l. John 12:32 Christ used a word, which hath a double meaning: for it signifieth either to lift up, or to rid out of the way, for his meaning was to put them in mind of his death, but the Jews seem to take it another way.

m. John 12:32 Chrysostom and Theophylact refer this word, All, to all nations: that is, not to the Jews only.

n. John 12:35 Unmeasurable is the mercy of God, but an horrible judgment followed, if it be contemned.

o. John 12:36 That is, partakers of light.

p. John 12:37 Faith is not of nature, but of grace.

q. John 12:38 The arm of the Lord, is the Gospel, which is the power of God to salvation to all that believe: And therefore the arm of the Lord is not revealed to them, whose hearts the Lord hath not opened.

r. John 12:42 Such as believe, are not only few in number, if they be compared with the unbelievers, but also the most of those few (yea and that especially the chiefest) do fear men more than God.

s. John 12:44 The sum of the Gospel, and therefore of salvation, which Christ witnessed in the midst of Jerusalem, by his crying out, is this: to rest upon Christ through faith, as the only Savior appointed and given us of the Father.

t. John 12:44 This word Not, doth not take any whit of this from Christ which is here spoken of, but is in way of correction rather, as if he said, He that believeth in me, doth not so much believe in me, as in him that sent me. So is it in Mark 9:37.

JOHN. 12

1. Matt. 26:17 / Mark 14:3
2. John 13:29
3. Matt. 21:8 / Mark 11:8 / Luke 19:35
4. Ezek. 9:9
5. Matt. 10:39 / Matt. 16:25 / Mark 8:35 / Luke 9:24 / Luke 17:33
6. John 17:34
7. John 3:14
8. Ps. 89:36 / Ps. 110:4 / Ps. 117:2 / Isa. 40:8 / Ezek. 37:25
9. John 1:9
10. Isa. 53:1 / Rom. 10:16
11. Isa. 6:9 / Matt. 13:14 / Mark 4:12 / Luke 8:10 / Acts 28:26 / Rom. 11:8
12. John 5:44
13. John 3:19 / John 9:39
14. John 3:17
15. Mark 16:16

JOHN. 13

a. John 13:1 Christ no less certain of the victory, than of the combat which was at hand, using the sign of washing the feet, doth partly thereby give an example of singular modesty, and his great love toward his Apostles in this notable act, being like very shortly to depart from them: and partly witnesseth unto them, that it is he only which washeth away the filth of his people, and that by little and little, in their time and season.

b. John 13:1 Them of his household, that is, his Saints.

c. John 13:3 Into his power.

d. John 13:4 In that he is said to rise, it argueth that there was a space between the ceremonies of the Passover, and this washing of feet, at what time it seemeth that the Supper was instituted.

e. John 13:8 Unless thou suffer me to wash thee, thou shalt have no part in the kingdom of heaven.

f. John 13:16 The word signifieth an Apostle which is anyone that is sent from another.

g. John 13:18 The betraying of Christ was not casual, or a thing that happened by chance, but the Father so ordained the cause of our salvation, to reconcile us unto himself in his Son, and the Son did willingly and voluntarily obey the Father.

h. John 13:21 He affirmed it openly, and sealed it.

i. John 13:23 John's leaning was such, that sitting down in his bed, his head was toward Jesus' head: so that it was an easy matter for him to touch Jesus' bosom: for it is certain that in old time men used not to sit at the table, but to lie down: on the one side.

j. John 13:31 We have to consider the glorifying of Christ in his ignominy.

k. John 13:31 This verse and the next following, are a most plain and evident testimony of the divinity of Christ.

l. John 13:33 The eternal glory shall flow by little and little from the head into the members. But in the meantime, we must take good heed that we pass over the race of this life in brotherly love.

m. John 13:36 An heavy example of rash trust and confidence.

JOHN. 13

1. Matt. 26:2 / Mark 14:1 / Luke 12:1
2. John 15:3
3. John 15:20 / Matt. 10:24 / Luke 6:40
4. Ps. 41:9
5. Matt. 10:40 / Luke 10:16
6. Matt. 26:21 / Mark 14:18 / Luke 22:21
7. John 7:34
8. Lev. 19:18 / Matt. 22:39 / John 15:12 / 1 John 4:21
9. Matt. 26:33 / Mark 14:29 / Luke 22:33

JOHN. 14

a. John 14:1 He believeth in God that believeth in Christ, and there is no other way to confirm our minds in greatest distresses.

b. John 14:2 That is, if it were not so as I tell you, to wit, unless there were place enough not only for me, but for you also in my father's house, I would not thus deceive you with a vain hope, but I would have told you so plainly.

c. John 14:2 All the speech is by way of an allegory, whereby the Lord comforteth his own, declaring unto them his departure into heaven, which is, not to reign there alone, but to go before, and prepare a place for them.

d. John 14:3 Christ went not away from us: to the end to forsake us, but rather that he might at length take us up with him into heaven.

e. John 14:3 These words are to be referred to the whole Church, and therefore the Angels said to the disciples when they were astonished, What stand you gazing up into heaven? This Jesus shall so come as you saw him go up, Acts 1:11, and in

be also. 4 [f]And whither I go, ye know, and the way ye know. 5 Thomas said
unto him, Lord, we know not whither thou goest: how can we then know the
way? 6 Jesus said unto him, I am [g]that Way, and that Truth, and that Life. No
man cometh unto the Father, but by me. 7 [h]If ye had known me, ye should
have known my Father also: and from henceforth ye know him, and have seen
him. 8 Philip said unto him, Lord, show us thy Father, and it sufficeth us. 9 Je-
sus said unto him, I have been so long time with you, and hast thou not known
me, Philip? he that hath seen me, hath seen my Father: how then sayest thou, Show
us thy Father? 10 [i]Believest thou not, that I am in the Father, and the Father is
in me? The words that I speak unto you, I speak not of myself: but the Father that
dwelleth in me, he doeth the works. 11 Believe me, that I am in the Father,
and the Father is in me: at the least, believe me for the very works' sake. 12 [j]Ve-
rily, verily I say unto you, he that believeth in me, the works that I do, he shall
do also, and [k]greater than these shall he do: for I go unto my Father. 13 [1]And
whatsoever ye ask in my Name, that will I do, that the Father may be glorified
in the Son. 14 If ye shall ask anything in my Name, I will do it. 15 [l]If ye
love me, keep my commandments. 16 And I will pray the Father, and he shall
give you another Comforter, that he may abide with you forever, 17 Even the
[m]Spirit of truth, whom the [n]world cannot receive, because it seeth him not, nei-
ther knoweth him: but ye know him: for he dwelleth with you, and shall be in
you. 18 I will not leave you fatherless: but I will come to you. 19 Yet a little
while, and the world shall see me no more, but ye shall see me: because I live, ye
shall live also. 20 At that day shall ye know that I am [o]in my Father, and you in
me, and I in you. 21 He that hath my commandments, and keepeth them: is he
that loveth me: and he that loveth me, shall be loved of my Father: and I will love
him, and will [p]show mine own self to him. 22 [q]Judas said unto him, (not Isca-
riot) Lord, what is the cause that thou wilt show thyself unto us, and not unto the
world? 23 Jesus answered, and said unto him, If any man love me, he will keep
my word, and my Father will love him, and we will come unto him, and will dwell
with him. 24 He that loveth me not, keepeth not my words, and the word whi-
ch ye hear, is not mine, but the Father's which sent me. 25 [r]These things have I
spoken unto you, being present with you. 26 [2]But the Comforter, which is the
holy Ghost, whom the Father will send in my Name, he shall teach you all things,
and bring all things to your remembrance, which I have told you. 27 [s]Peace I
leave with you: my peace I give unto you: not as the world giveth, give I unto you.
Let not your heart be troubled, nor fear. 28 [t]Ye have heard how I said unto you,
I go away, and will come unto you. If ye loved me, ye would verily rejoice, because
I said, I go unto the Father: for the Father [u]is greater than I. 29 And now have
I spoken unto you, before it come, that when it is come to pass, ye might belie-
ve. 30 [v]Hereafter will I not speak many things unto you: for the prince of this
world cometh, and hath [w]nought in me, 31 But it is that the world may know
that I love my Father: and as the Father hath commanded me, so I do. Arise, let
us go hence.

15

1 By the parable of the vine, 2 and the branches, 5, 6 he declareth how the disciples may bear fruit. 12, 17 He commendeth mutual love. 18 He exhorteth them to bear afflictions patiently, 20 by his own example.

1 I [a]am that true vine, and my Father is that husbandman. 2 [1]Every bran-
ch that beareth not fruit in me, he taketh away: and everyone that beareth fruit,
he purgeth it, that it may bring forth more fruit. 3 [2]Now are ye clean through
the word, which I have spoken unto you. 4 Abide in me, and I in you: as the
branch cannot bear fruit of itself, except it abide in the vine, no more can ye,
except ye abide in me. 5 I am that vine: ye are the branches: he that abideth in
me, and I in him, the same bringeth forth much fruit: for without me can ye do
nothing. 6 [3]If a man abide not in me, he is cast forth as a branch, and withe-
reth: and men gather them, and cast them into the fire, and they burn. 7 [b,4]If ye
abide in me, and my words abide in you, ask what ye will, and it shall be done to
you. 8 [c]Herein is my Father glorified, that ye bear much fruit, and be made my
disciples. 9 [d]As the father hath loved me, so have I loved you: [e]continue in that
my love. 10 If ye shall keep my commandments, ye shall abide in my love, as I
have kept my Father's commandments, and abide in his love. 11 These things
have I spoken unto you, that my joy might remain in you, and that your joy mi-
ght be full. 12 [5]This is my commandment, that ye love one another, as I have
loved you. 13 Greater love than this hath no man, when any man bestoweth
his life for his friends. 14 Ye are my friends, if ye do whatsoever I command
you. 15 [f]Henceforth call I you not servants: for the servant knoweth not what
his master doeth: but I have called you friends: for all things that I have heard of
my Father, have I made known to you. 16 [g]Ye [h]have not chosen me, but I have
chosen you, and ordained you, [6]that ye go and bring forth fruits, and that your
fruit remain, that whatsoever ye shall ask of the Father in my Name, he may give
it you. 17 These things command I you, that ye love one another. 18 [i]If the
world hate you, ye know that it hated me before you. 19 If ye were of the wor-
ld, the world would love his own: but because ye are not of the world, but I have
chosen you out of the world, therefore the world hateth you. 20 Remember the
word that I said unto you, [7]The servant is not greater than his master. [8]If they have
persecuted me, they will persecute you also: if they have kept my word, they will
also keep yours. 21 [j]But [9]all these things will they do unto you for my Name's
sake, because they have not known him that sent me. 22 [k]If I had not come and
spoken unto them, they should not have had sin: but now have they no cloak for
their sin. 23 He that hateth me, hateth my Father also. 24 If I had not done
works among them which none other man did, they had not had sin: but now have
they both seen, and have hated both me, and my Father. 25 But it is that the
word might be fulfilled, that is written in their [l]Law, [10]They hated me without a
cause. 26 [m]But when that Comforter shall come, [11]whom I will send unto you
from the Father, even the Spirit of truth, which proceedeth of the Father, he shall
testify of me. 27 And ye shall witness also, because ye have been with me from
the beginning.

---

all places of the Scripture, the full comfort of the Church is referred to that day when God shall be all in all, and is therefore called the day of redemption.

f. John 14:4 Christ only is the way to true and everlasting life, for he it is in whom the Father hath revealed himself.

g. John 14:6 This saying showeth unto us both the nature, the will and office of Christ.

h. John 14:7 It is plain by this place, that to know God, and to see God, is all one: Now whereas he said before, that no man saw God at any time, that it is to be understood thus, without Christ: or were it not through Christ, no man could ever see, nor saw God at any time: for as Chrysostom saith, the Son is a very short and easy setting forth of the father's nature unto us.

i. John 14:10 The majesty of God showeth itself most evidently, both in Christ's doctrine and deeds.

j. John 14:12 The approving of the virtue of Christ is not included within his own person, but it is spread through the body of his whole Church.

k. John 14:12 That is, not I only do them, but I can also give other men power to do greater.

l. John 14:15 He loveth Christ aright, which obeyeth his commandments: and because the same is accompanied with an infinite sort of miseries, although he be absent in body, yet doth he comfort his with the present virtue of the holy Ghost, whom the world despiseth, because it knoweth him not.

m. John 14:17 The holy Ghost is called the Spirit of truth ,of the effect which he worketh, because he inspireth the truth into us, whereas otherwise he hath truth in himself.

n. John 14:17 Worldly men.

o. John 14:20 The Son is in the Father after such sort, that he is of one selfsame substance with the Father, but he is in his disciples in a certain respect as an aider and helper of them.

p. John 14:21 I will show myself to him, and be known of him, as if he saw me with his eyes: but this showing of himself is not bodily, but spiritually, yet so plain as none can be more.

q. John 14:22 We must not ask why the Gospel is revealed to some rather than to others, but we must rather take heed, that we embrace Christ who is offered unto us, and that we truly love him, that is to say, that we give ourselves wholly to his obedience.

r. John 14:25 It is the office of the holy Ghost to imprint in the midst of the elect in their times and seasons, that which Christ once spake.

s. John 14:27 All true felicity cometh to us by Christ alone.

t. John 14:28 So far is it, that we should be sorry for the departing of Christ, from us according to the flesh, that we should rather rejoice for it, seeing that all the blessing of the members dependeth upon the glorifying of the head.

u. John 14:28 This is spoken in that, that he is Mediator, for so the Father is greater than he, inasmuch as the person to whom request is made, is greater than he that maketh the request.

v. John 14:30 Christ goeth to death not unwillingly, but willingly, not as yielding to the devil, but obeying his Father's decree.

w. John 14:30 As who would say, Satan will by and by set upon me with all the might he can, but he hath no power over me, neither shall he find any such thing in me as he thinketh he shall.

JOHN. 14

1. John 16:23 / Matt. 7:7 / Mark 11:24 / James 1:5
2. John 15:26

JOHN. 15

a. John 15:1 We are of nature dry and fit for nothing but the fire: Therefore that we may live and be fruitful, we must first be grafted into Christ, as it were into a vine by the Father's hand: and then be daily shred with a continual meditation of the word and the cross; otherwise it shall not avail any man at all to have been grafted, unless he cleave fast unto the vine, and so draw juice out of it.

b. John 15:7 He abideth in Christ, which resteth in his doctrine, and therefore bringeth forth good fruit: And the Father will deny such an one nothing.

c. John 15:8 As who would say, Herein shall my Father be glorified, and herein also shall you be my disciples, if you bring forth much fruit.

d. John 15:9 The love of the Father towards the Son, and of the Son towards us, and ours towards God and our neighbor, are joined together with an inseparable knot: and there is nothing more sweet and pleasant than it is. Now this love showeth itself by its effects: a most perfect example whereof, Christ himself exhibited unto us.

e. John 15:9 That is, in that love, wherewith I love you: which love is on both parts.

f. John 15:15 The doctrine of the Gospel (as it is uttered by Christ's own mouth) is a most perfect and absolute declaration of the counsel of God, which pertaineth to our salvation, and is committed unto the Apostles.

g. John 15:16 Christ is the author and preserver of the ministry of the Gospel, even to the world's end, but the ministers have above all things need of prayer and brotherly love.

h. John 15:16 This place teacheth us plainly, that our salvation cometh from the only favor and gracious goodness of the everlasting God towards us, and of nothing that we do or can deserve.

i. John 15:18 It ought not only not to fear, but rather confirm the faithful ministers of Christ, when they shall be hated of the world as their Master was.

j. John 15:21 The hatred that the world beareth against Christ, proceedeth of the blockishness of the mind, which notwithstanding is voluntary blind, so that the world can pretend no excuse to cover their fault.

k. John 15:22 As who would say, If I had not come, these men would not have stuck to have said still before God's judgment seat, that they are religious, and void of sin: but seeing I came to them, and they clean refuse me, they can have no cloak for their wickedness.

l. John 15:25 Sometime by this word, Law, are meant the five books of Moses, but in this place, the whole Scripture: for the place alleged is in the Psalms.

m. John 15:26 Against the rage of the wicked, we shall stand surely by the inward testimony of the holy Ghost: But the holy Ghost speaketh no otherwise, than he spake by the mouth of the Apostles.

JOHN. 15

1. Matt. 15:13
2. John 13:10
3. Col. 2:23
4. 1 John 3:22
5. John 13:34 / 1 Thess. 4:9 / 1 John 3:11 / 1 John 4:21
6. Matt. 28:19
7. John 13:16 / Matt. 10:24
8. Matt. 24:9
9. John 16:4
10. Ps. 35:19
11. John 14:26 / Luke 24:49

16

1 He foretelleth the disciples of persecution. 7 He promiseth the Comforter, and declareth his office. 21 He compareth the affliction of his, to a woman that travaileth with child.

1 These [a]things have I said unto you, that ye should not be offended. **2** They shall excommunicate you: yea the time shall come, that whosoever killeth you, will think that he doeth God service. **3** And these things will they do unto you, because they have not known the Father, nor me. **4** [1]But these things have I told you, that when the hour shall come, ye might remember, that I told you them. And these things said I not unto you from the beginning, because I was with you. **5** But now I go my way to him that sent me, and none of you asketh me, Whither goest thou? **6** But because I have said these things unto you, your hearts are full of sorrow. **7** [b]Yet I tell you the truth, It is expedient for you that I go away: for if I go not away, that Comforter will not come unto you: but if I depart, I will send him unto you, **8** [c]And when he is come, he will [d]reprove the [e]world of sin, and of righteousness, and of judgment. **9** Of sin, because they believed not in me: **10** Of [f]righteousness, because I go to my Father, and ye shall see me no more. **11** Of [g]judgment, [h]because the prince of this world is judged. **12** [i]I have yet many things to say unto you, but ye cannot bear them now. **13** Howbeit, when he is come which is the spirit of truth, he will lead you into all truth: for he shall not speak of himself, but whatsoever he shall hear, shall he speak, and he will show you the things to come. **14** [j]He shall glorify me: for he shall receive of mine, and shall show it unto you. **15** All things that the Father hath, are mine: therefore said I, that he shall take of mine, and show it unto you. **16** [k]A [l]little while, and ye shall not see me: and again a little while, and ye shall see me: [m]for I go to the Father. **17** Then said some of his disciples among themselves, What is this that he saith unto us, A little while, and ye shall not see me, and again a little while, and ye shall see me, and, For I go to the Father. **18** They said therefore, What is this that he saith, A little while? we know not what he saith. **19** Now Jesus knew that they would ask him, and said unto them, Do ye inquire among yourselves, of that I said, A little while, and ye shall not see me: and again, a little while, and ye shall see me? **20** Verily, verily I say unto you, that ye shall weep and lament, and the world shall rejoice, and ye shall sorrow, but your sorrow shall be turned to joy. **21** A woman when she travaileth hath sorrow because her hour is come: but as soon as she is delivered of the child, she remembereth no more the anguish, for joy that a man is born into the world. **22** And ye now therefore are in sorrow: but I will see you again, and your hearts shall rejoice, and your joy shall no man take from you. **23** And in that day shall ye ask me nothing. [2]Verily, verily I say unto you, whatsoever ye shall ask the Father in my Name, he will give it you. **24** Hitherto have ye asked nothing in my Name: ask, and ye shall receive, that your joy may be full. **25** [n]These things have I spoken unto you in parables: but the time will come, when I shall no more speak to you in parables: but I shall show you plainly of the Father. **26** [o]At that day shall ye ask in my Name, and I say not unto you, that I will pray unto the Father for you: **27** For the Father himself loveth you, because ye have loved me, [3]and have believed that I came out from God. **28** I am come out from the Father, and came into the world: again I leave the world, and go to the Father. **29** [p]His disciples said unto him, Lo, now speakest thou plainly, and thou speakest no parable. **30** Now know we that thou knowest all things, and needest not that any man should ask thee. By this we believe, that thou art come out from God. **31** Jesus answered them, Do you believe now? **32** [q,4]Behold, the hour cometh, and is already come, that ye shall be scattered every man into his own, and shall leave me alone: But I am not alone: for the Father is with me. **33** [r]These things have I spoken unto you, that [s]in me ye might have peace: in the world ye shall have affliction, but be of good comfort: I have overcome the world.

17

1 Christ prayeth that his glory together with his Father's may be made manifest. 9 He Prayeth for his Apostles, 20 and for all believers.

1 These [a]things spake Jesus, and lift up his eyes to heaven, and said, [b]Father, that hour is come: glorify thy Son, that thy Son also may glorify thee, **2** [1]As thou hast given him power over [c]all flesh, that he should give eternal life to all them that thou hast given him. **3** And this is life eternal, that they know thee to be the [d]only very God, and whom thou hast sent, Jesus Christ. **4** I have glorified thee on the earth: I have finished the work which thou gavest me to do. **5** And now glorify me, thou Father, with thine own self, with the glory which I had with thee before the world was. **6** [e]I have declared thy Name unto the men which thou gavest me out of the world: [f]thine they were, and thou [g]gavest them me, and they have kept thy word. **7** [2]Now they know that all things whatsoever thou hast given me, are of thee. **8** For I have given unto them the words which thou gavest me, and they have received them, and have known surely that I came out from thee, and have believed that thou hast sent me. **9** I pray for them: I pray not for the world, but for them which thou hast given me: for they are thine. **10** And all mine are thine, and thine are mine, and I am glorified in them. **11** And now am I no more in the world, but these are in the world, and I come to thee. Holy Father, keep them in thy Name, even them whom thou hast given me, that they may be [h]one as we are. **12** While I was with them in the world, I kept them in thy Name: those that thou gavest me, have I kept, and none of them is lost, but the child of perdition, that the [3]Scripture might be fulfilled. **13** And now come I to thee, and these things speak I in the world, that they might have my joy fulfilled in themselves. **14** I have given them thy word, and the world hath hated them, because they are not of the world, as I am not of the world. **15** [i]I pray not that thou shouldest take them out of the world, but that thou keep them from evil. **16** They are not of the world, as I am not of the world. **17** [j]Sanctify them with thy truth: thy word is truth. **18** [k]As thou didst send me into the world, so have I sent them into the world. **19** And for their sakes sanctify I myself, that they also may be sanctified through the [l]truth. **20** [m]I pray not for these alone, but for them also which shall believe in me, through their word, **21** That they all

---

JOHN. 16

a. John 16:1 The ministers of the Gospel must look for all manner of reproaches, not only of them which are open enemies, but even of them also which seem to be of the same household, and the very pillars of the Church.
b. John 16:7 The absence of Christ, according to the flesh, is profitable to the Church, that we may wholly depend upon his spiritual power.
c. John 16:8 The Spirit of God worketh so mightily by the preaching of the word, that he constraineth the world, will it, nill it, to confess its own unrighteousness, and Christ's righteousness and almightiness.
d. John 16:8 He will so reprove the world, that the worldlings shall be able to present no excuse.
e. John 16:8 He respecteth the time that followed his ascension, when as all gainsayers were manifestly reproved through the pouring out of the holy Ghost upon the Church: So that the very enemies of Christ were reproved of sin, in that they were constrained to confess that they were deceived, in that they believed not, and therefore they said to Peter, Acts 2, Men and brethren, what shall we do?
f. John 16:10 Of Christ himself: For when the world shall see, that I have poured out the holy Ghost, they shall be constrained to confess that I was just, and was not condemned of my Father, when I went out of this world.
g. John 16:11 Of that authority and power, which I have both in heaven and earth.
h. John 16:11 That is, because they shall then understand and know indeed, that I have overcome the devil, and do govern the world, when all men shall see, that they set themselves against you in vain, for I will arm you with that heavenly power, whereby you may destroy every high thing which is lifted up against the knowledge of God, 2 Cor. 10:12.
i. John 16:12 The doctrine of the Apostles proceeded from the holy Ghost, and is most perfect.
j. John 16:14 The holy Ghost bringeth no new doctrine, but teacheth that which was uttered by Christ's own mouth, and imprinteth it in our minds.
k. John 16:16 The grace of the holy Ghost is a most lively glass, wherein Christ is truly beholden with the most sharpsighted eyes of faith, and not with the bleared eyes of the flesh: whereby we feel a continual joy even in the midst of sorrows.
l. John 16:16 When a little time is once past.
m. John 16:16 For I pass to eternal glory, so that I shall be much more present with you, than I was before: for then you shall feel indeed what I am, and what I am able to do.
n. John 16:25 The holy Ghost which was poured upon the Apostles after the Ascension of Christ, instructed both them in all chiefest mysteries and secrets of our salvation, and also by them the Church, and will also instruct it to the end of the world.
o. John 16:26 The sum of the worship of God, is the invocation of the Father in the Name of the Son the Mediator, who is already heard for us, for whom he hath abased himself, and is now also glorified.
p. John 16:29 Faith and foolish security differ very much.
q. John 16:32 Neither the wickedness of the world, neither the weakness of his own can diminish anything of the virtue of Christ.
r. John 16:33 The surety and stay of the Church dependeth only upon the victory of Christ.
s. John 16:33 That in me you might be thoroughly quieted. For by (peace) is meant in this place, that quiet state of mind, which is clean contrary to disquietness and heaviness.

JOHN. 16

1. John 15:21
2. John 14:13 / Matt. 7:7 / Matt. 21:22 / Mark 12:24 / Luke 11:9 / James 1:5
3. John 17:8
4. Matt. 26:31 / Mark 14:27

JOHN. 17

a. John 17:1 Jesus Christ the everlasting high Priest being ready straightway to offer up himself, doth by solemn prayers consecrate himself to God the Father as a sacrifice: and us together with himself. Therefore this prayer was from the beginning, is, and shall be to the end of the world, the foundation and ground of the Church of God.
b. John 17:1 He first declareth, that as he came into the world to the end that the Father might show in him, being apprehended by faith, his glory in saving his elect, so he applied himself to that only: and therefore desireth of the Father, that he would bless the work which he hath finished.
c. John 17:2 Over all men.
d. John 17:3 He calleth the Father the only very God, to set him against all false gods, and not to shut out himself and the holy Ghost, For straightway he joineth the knowledge of the Father and the knowledge of himself together, and according to his accustomed manner, setteth forth the whole Godhead in the person of the father: So is the Father alone said to be King, immortal, wise, and dwelling in the light which no man can attain unto, invisible, Rom. 16:17; 1 Tim. 1:17.
e. John 17:6 First of all he prayeth for those his disciples, by whom he would have the rest to be gathered together, commendeth them unto the Father, (having once rejected the whole company of the reprobate) because he received them of him into his custody, and for that they embracing his doctrine, shall have so many and so mighty enemies, that there is no way for them to be in safety, but by his help only.
f. John 17:6 He showeth hereby that everlasting election and choice, which was hidden in the good will and pleasure of God, which is the groundwork of our salvation.
g. John 17:6 He showeth how the everlasting and hidden purpose of God is declared in Christ, by whom we are justified and sanctified, if we lay hold of him by faith, that at length we may come to the glory of the election.
h. John 17:11 He prayeth that his people may peaceably agree and be joined together in one, that as the Godhead is one, so they may be of one mind and one consent together.
i. John 17:15 He showeth what manner of deliverance he meaneth: not that they should be in no danger, but that they being preserved from all, might prove by experience that the doctrine of salvation is true, which they received at his mouth to deliver to others.
j. John 17:17 That is, make them holy: and that is said to be holy, which is dedicated and made proper to God only.
k. John 17:18 He addeth moreover, that the Apostles have a vocation common with him, and therefore that they must be holden up by the selfsame virtue to give up themselves wholly to God, whereby he being first, did consecrate himself to the Father.
l. John 17:19 The true and substantial sanctification of Christ, is set against the outward purifyings.
m. John 17:20 Secondarily he offereth to God the Father, all his, that is, how many soever shall believe in him by the doctrine of the Apostles: that as he cleaveth unto the Father receiving from him all fullness, so they being joined with him, may

may be one, as thou, O Father, art in me, and I in thee: even that they may be also
one in us, that the world may believe that thou hast sent me. 22 And the glory
that thou gavest me, I have given them, that they may be one, as we are one, 23 I
in them, and thou in me, that they may be made perfect in one, and that the
world may know that thou hast sent me, and hast loved them as thou hast loved
me. 24 [4]Father, I will that they which thou hast given me, be with me even whe-
re I am, that they may behold that my glory, which thou hast given me: for thou
lovedst me before the foundation of the world. 25 O righteous Father, the world
also hath not known thee, but I have known thee, and these have known, that thou
hast sent me. 26 [n]And I have declared unto them thy Name, and will declare
it, that the love wherewith thou hast loved me, may be in them, and I in them.

18

By Christ's power, whom Judas betrayeth, 6 the soldiers are cast down to the ground. 13 Christ is led to Annas, and from him to Caiaphas. 22, 23 His answer to the officer that smote him with a rod. 28 Being delivered to Pilate, 36 he declareth his kingdom.

1 When [a]Jesus had spoken these things, he went forth with his disciples over
the brook [1]Kidron, where was a garden, into the which he entered, and his disci-
ples. 2 And Judas which betrayed him knew also the place: for Jesus ofttimes
resorted thither with his disciples. 3 [b,2]Judas then, after he had received a band
of men and officers of the high Priests, and of the Pharisees, came thither with lan-
terns and torches, and weapons. 4 [c]Then Jesus, knowing all things that should
come unto him, went forth and said unto them, Whom seek ye? 5 They answe-
red him, Jesus of Nazareth. Jesus said unto them, I am he. Now Judas also which
betrayed him, stood with them. 6 As soon then as he had said unto them, I am
he, they went away backwards, and fell to the ground. 7 Then he asked them
again, Whom seek ye? And they said, Jesus of Nazareth. 8 [d]Jesus answered, I
said unto you, that I am he: therefore if ye seek me, let these go their way. 9 This
was that the word might be fulfilled which he spake, [3]Of them which thou gavest
me, have I lost none. 10 [e]Then Simon Peter having a sword, drew it, and smo-
te the high Priest's servant, and cut off his right ear. Now the servants name was
Malchus. 11 Then said Jesus unto Peter, Put up thy sword into the sheath: shall
I not drink of the cup which my Father hath given me? 12 Then the band and
the captain, and the officers of the Jews took Jesus, and bound him. 13 [f]And led
him away to [4]Annas first (for he was father-in-law to Caiaphas, which was the high
Priest that same year.) 14 [5]And Caiaphas was he, that gave counsel to the Jews,
that it was expedient that one man should die for the people. 15 [g,6]Now Simon
Peter followed Jesus, and another disciple, and that disciple was known of the high
Priest: therefore he went in with Jesus into the hall of the high Priest. 16 But Pe-
ter stood at the door without. Then went out the other disciple which was known
unto the high Priest, and spake to her that kept the door, and brought in Pe-
ter. 17 Then said the maid that kept the door, unto Peter, Art not thou also one
of this man's disciples? He said, I am not. 18 And the servants and officers stood
there, which had made a fire of coals: for it was cold, and they warmed themselves.
And Peter also stood among them, and warmed himself. 19 ([h]The high Priest
then asked Jesus of his disciples, and of his doctrine, 20 Jesus answered him,
I spake openly to the world: I ever taught in the Synagogue and in the Temple,
whither the Jews resort continually, and in secret have I said nothing. 21 Why
askest thou me? ask them which heard me what I said unto them: behold, they
know what I said. 22 When he had spoken these things, one of the officers
which stood by, smote Jesus with his rod, saying, Answerest thou the high Priest
so? 23 Jesus answered him, If I have evil spoken, bear witness of the evil: but if
I have well spoken, why smitest thou me? 24 [7]Now Annas had sent him bound
unto Caiaphas the high Priest.) 25 [i,8]And Simon Peter stood and warmed him-
self, and they said unto him, Art not thou also of his disciples? He denied it, and
said, I am not. 26 One of the servants of the high Priest, his cousin whose ear
Peter smote off, said, Did not I see thee in the garden with him? 27 Peter then
denied again, and immediately the cock crew. 28 [j,9]Then led they Jesus from
[k]Caiaphas into the common hall. Now it was morning, and they themselves went
not into the common hall, lest they should be [10]defiled, but that they might eat
the Passover. 29 Pilate then went out unto them, and said, What accusation
bring ye against this man? 30 They answered, and said unto him, If he were
not an evil doer, we would not have delivered him unto thee. 31 Then said Pi-
late unto them, Take ye him, and judge him after your own Law. Then the Jews
said unto him, [l]It is not lawful for us to put any man to death. 32 It was that
the word of Jesus [11]might be fulfilled which he spake, [m]signifying what death he
should die. 33 [12]So Pilate entered into the common hall again, and called Je-
sus, and said unto him, Art thou the king of the Jews? 34 Jesus answered him,
Sayest thou that of thyself, or did others tell it thee of me? 35 Pilate answered,
Am I a Jew? Thine own nation, and the high Priest have delivered thee unto me.
What hast thou done? 36 [n]Jesus answered, My kingdom is not of this world: if
my kingdom were of this world, my servants would surely fight, that I should not
be delivered to the Jews: but now is my kingdom not from hence. 37 Pilate then
said unto him, Art thou a King then? Jesus answered, Thou sayest that I am a King:
for this cause am I born, and for this cause came I into the world, that I should bear
witness unto the truth: everyone that is of the truth, heareth my voice. 38 [o]Pilate
said unto him, [p]What is truth? And when he had said that, he went out again unto
the Jews, and said unto them, I find in him no cause at all. 39 [13]But you have a
custom that I should deliver you one loose at the Passover: will ye then that I loose
unto you the King of the Jews? 40 [14]Then [q]cried they all again, saying, Not him,
but Barabbas: now this Barabbas was a murderer.

19

Pilate, when Christ was scourged, 2 and crowned with thorns, 4 was desirous to let him loose: 8 but being overcome with the outrage of the Jews, 16 he delivereth him to be crucified. 26 Jesus committeth his mother to the disciple. 30 Having tasted vinegar, he dieth: 34 and being dead, his side is pierced with a spear. 40 He is buried.

1 Then [1]Pilate took Jesus and [a]scourged him. 2 And the soldiers plat-
ted a crown of thorns, and put it on his head, and they put on him a purple
garment, 3 And said, Hail King of the Jews. And they smote him with their
rods. 4 [b]Then Pilate went forth again, and said unto them, Behold, I bring him
forth to you, that ye may know, that I find no fault in him at all. 5 Then came
Jesus forth wearing a crown of thorns, and a purple garment. And Pilate said unto
them, Behold the man. 6 Then when the high Priests and officers saw him, they
cried, saying, [c]Crucify, crucify him. Pilate said unto them, Take ye him, and cruci-
fy him: for I find no fault in him. 7 The Jews answered him, We have a law, and
by our law he ought to die, because he made himself the Son of God. 8 [d]When
Pilate then heard that word, he was the more afraid, 9 And went again into the
common hall, and said unto Jesus, Whence art thou? But Jesus gave him none
answer. 10 Then said Pilate unto him, Speakest thou not unto me? Knowest
thou not that I have power to crucify thee, and have power to loose thee? 11 Je-
sus answered, Thou couldest have no power at all against me, except it were gi-
ven thee from above: therefore he that delivered me unto thee, hath the greater
sin. 12 From thenceforth Pilate sought to loose him, but the Jews cried, saying,
If thou deliver him, thou art not Caesar's friend: for whosoever maketh himself a
King, speaketh against Caesar. 13 [e]When Pilate heard this word, he brought

---

receive life from him, and at length being together beloved in him, may also with him enjoy everlasting glory.

n. John 17:26 He communicateth with his by little and little, the knowledge of the Father, which is most full in Christ the Mediator, that they may in him be beloved of the Father, with the selfsame love wherewith he loveth the Son.

JOHN. 17

1. Matt. 28:18
2. John 16:27
3. Ps. 109:7
4. John 12:26

JOHN. 18

a. John 18:1 Christ goeth of his own accord into a garden, which his betrayer knew, to be taken: that by his obedience he might take away the sin that entered into the world by one man's rebellion, and that in a garden.

b. John 18:3 Christ, who was innocent, was taken as a wicked person, that we which are wicked might be let go as innocent.

c. John 18:4 Christ's person (but not his virtue) was bound of the adversaries, when and how he would.

d. John 18:8 Christ doth not neglect the office of a good pastor, no not in his greatest danger.

e. John 18:10 We ought to contain the zeal we bear to God, within the bounds of our vocation.

f. John 18:13 Christ is brought before an earthly high Priest to be condemned for our blasphemies, that we might be acquitted of the everlasting high Priest himself.

g. John 18:15 A lively example of the fragility of man even in the best, when they be once left to themselves.

h. John 18:19 Christ defendeth his cause but slenderly, not that he would withdraw himself from death, but to show that he was condemned as an innocent.

i. John 18:25 After that men have once fallen, they cannot only not lift themselves by their own strength, but also they fall more and more into worse, until they be raised up again, by a new virtue of God.

j. John 18:28 The Son of God is brought before the judgment seat of an earthly and profane man, in whom there is found much less wickedness, than in the princes of the people of God: A lively image of the wrath of God against sin, and therewithal of his great mercy, and least of all, of his most severe judgment against the stubborn contemners of his grace when it is offered unto them.

k. John 18:28 From Caiaphas's house.

l. John 18:31 For judgments of life and death were taken from them forty years before the destruction of the temple.

m. John 18:32 For Christ had foretold that he should be crucified.

n. John 18:36 Christ avoucheth his spiritual kingdom, but rejecteth a worldly.

o. John 18:38 It was requisite that Christ should be pronounced innocent, but notwithstanding (in that that he took upon him our person) was to be condemned as a most wicked man.

p. John 18:38 He speaketh this disdainfully and scoffingly, and not by way of asking a question.

q. John 18:40 Word for word, made a great and foul voice.

JOHN. 18

1. Matt. 26:36 / Mark 14:32 / Luke 22:39
2. Matt. 26:47 / Mark 14:43 / Luke 22:47
3. John 17:12
4. Luke 3:2
5. John 11:50
6. Matt. 26:58 / Mark 14:54 / Luke 22:54
7. Matt. 26:57 / Luke 21:54
8. Matt. 16:69 / Mark 14:59 / Luke 22:55
9. Matt. 27:2 / Mark 15:1 / Luke 23:1
10. Acts 10:28 / Acts 11:3
11. Matt. 20:19
12. Matt. 27:11 / Mark 15:2 / Luke 23:3
13. Matt. 27:15 / Mark 15:6 / Luke 23:17
14. Acts 3:14

JOHN. 19

a. John 19:1 The wisdom of the flesh, chooseth of two evils the least, but God curseth that same wisdom.

b. John 19:4 Christ is again acquitted by the same mouth wherewith he is afterward condemned.

c. John 19:6 They will have him crucified, whom by an old custom of theirs, they should have stoned and hanged up as convict of blasphemy: but they desire to have him crucified after the manner of the Romans.

d. John 19:8 Pilate's conscience fighteth for Christ, but straightway it yieldeth, because it is not upholden with the singular virtue of God.

e. John 19:13 Pilate condemneth himself first, with the same mouth wherewith he afterward condemneth Christ.

f. John 19:13 Gabbatha signifieth an high place, as judgment seats are.

g. John 19:16 Christ fasteneth Satan, sin and death to the cross.

Jesus forth, and sat down in the judgment seat in a place called the pavement, and in Hebrew, [f]Gabbatha. **14** And it was the Preparation of the Passover, and about the sixth hour: and he said unto the Jews, Behold your King. **15** But they cried, Away with him, away with him, crucify him. Pilate said unto them, Shall I crucify your King? The high Priests answered, We have no King but Caesar. **16** [g]Then delivered he him unto them, to be crucified. [2]And they took Jesus, and led him away. **17** And he bare his own cross, and came into a place named of dead men's skulls, which is called in Hebrew, Golgotha: **18** Where they crucified him, and two other with him, on either side one, and Jesus in the midst. **19** [h]And Pilate wrote also a title, and put it on the cross, and it was written, JESUS OF NAZARETH THE KING OF THE JEWS. **20** This title then read many of the Jews: for the place where Jesus was crucified, was near to the city: and it was written in Hebrew, Greek, and Latin. **21** Then said the high Priests of the Jews to Pilate, Write not, The King of the Jews, but that he said, I am the King of the Jews. **22** Pilate answered, What I have written, I have written. **23** [i]Then the [3]soldiers, when they had crucified Jesus, took his garments (and made four parts, to every soldier a part) and his coat: and the coat was without seam woven from the top throughout. **24** Therefore they said one to another, Let us not divide it, but cast lots for it, whose it shall be. This was that the Scripture might be fulfilled, which saith, [4]They parted my garments among them, and on my coat did cast lots. So the soldiers did these things indeed. **25** [j]Then stood by the cross of Jesus his mother, and his mother's sister, Mary the wife of Clopas, and Mary Magdalene. **26** And when Jesus saw his mother, and the disciple standing by, whom he loved, he said unto his mother, Woman, behold thy son. **27** Then said he to the disciple, Behold thy mother: and from that hour, the disciple took her home unto him. **28** [k]After, when Jesus knew that all things were performed, that the [5]Scripture might be fulfilled, he said, I thirst. **29** And there was set a [l]vessel full of vinegar: and they filled a sponge with vinegar: and put it about an Hyssop stalk, and put it to his mouth. **30** Now when Jesus had received of the vinegar, he said, It is finished, and bowed his head, and gave up the ghost. **31** [m]The Jews then (because it was the Preparation, that the bodies should not remain upon the cross on the Sabbath day: for that Sabbath was an high day) besought Pilate that their legs might be broken, and that they might be taken down. **32** Then came the soldiers and brake the legs of the first, and of the other, which was crucified with Jesus. **33** But when they came to Jesus, and saw that he was dead already, they brake not his legs. **34** [n]But one of the soldiers with a spear [o]pierced his side, and forthwith came there out blood and water. **35** And he that saw it, bare record, and his record is true: and he knoweth that he saith true, that ye might believe it. **36** For these things were done, that the Scripture should be fulfilled, [6]Not a bone of him shall be broken. **37** And again another Scripture saith, [7]They shall see him whom they have thrust through. **38** [p,8]And after these things, Joseph of Arimathea (who was a disciple of Jesus, but secretly for fear of the Jews) besought Pilate that he might take down the body of Jesus. And Pilate gave him license. He came then and took Jesus' body. **39** And there came [9]also Nicodemus (which first came to Jesus by night) and brought of myrrh and aloes mingled together about an hundred pounds. **40** Then took they the body of Jesus, and wrapped it in linen clothes with the odors, as the manner of the Jews is to bury. **41** And in that place where Jesus was crucified, was a garden, and in the garden a new sepulcher, wherein was [q]never man yet laid. **42** There then laid they Jesus, because of the Jews' Preparation day, for the sepulcher was near.

20

1 Mary bringeth word that Christ is risen: 3 Peter and John 4 run to see it. 15 Jesus appeareth to Mary, 19 and to the disciples that were together in the house, 25 Thomas, before faithless, 29 now believeth.

1 Now [a,1]the first day of the week came Mary Magdalene, early when it was yet dark, unto the sepulcher, and saw the stone taken away from the tomb. **2** Then she ran, and came to Simon Peter, and to the other disciple, whom Jesus loved, and said unto them, They have taken away the Lord out of the sepulcher, and we know not where they have laid him. **3** Peter therefore went forth, and the other disciple, and they came unto the sepulcher. **4** So they ran both together, but the other disciple did outrun Peter, and came first to the sepulcher. **5** And he stooped down, and saw the linen clothes lying: yet went he not in. **6** Then came Simon Peter following him, and went into the sepulcher, and saw the linen clothes lie, **7** And the kerchief that was upon his head, not lying with the linen clothes, but wrapped together in a place by itself. **8** Then went in also the other disciple, which came first to the sepulcher, and he saw it, and believed. **9** For as yet they knew not the Scripture, That he must rise again from the dead. **10** And the disciples went away again unto their own home. **11** [2]But Mary stood [b]without at the sepulcher weeping: and as she wept, she bowed herself into the sepulcher, **12** [c]And saw two Angels in [d]white, sitting, the one at the head, and the other at the feet, where the body of Jesus had lain. **13** And they said unto her, Woman, why weepest thou? She said unto them, They have taken away [e]my Lord, and I know not where they have laid him. **14** [f]When she had thus said, she turned herself back, and saw Jesus standing, and knew not that it was Jesus. **15** Jesus saith unto her, Woman, why weepest thou? whom seekest thou? She supposing that he had been the gardener, said unto him, Sir, if thou hast borne him hence, tell me where thou hast laid him, and I will take him away. **16** Jesus saith unto her, Mary. She turned herself, and said unto him, Rabboni, which is to say, Master. **17** [g]Jesus saith unto her, Touch me not: for I am not yet ascended to my Father: but go to my [h]brethren, and say unto them, I ascend unto [i]my Father, and to your Father, and to my God, and your God. **18** Mary Magdalene came and told the disciples that she had seen the Lord, and that he had spoken these things unto her. **19** [j,3]The same day then at night, which was the first day of the week, and when the [k]doors were shut where the disciples were assembled for fear of the Jews, came Jesus and stood in the midst, and said to them, Peace be unto you. **20** And when he had so said, he showed unto them his hands, and his side. Then were the disciples glad when they had seen the Lord. **21** [4]Then said Jesus to them again, Peace be unto you: as my Father sent me, so send I you. **22** And when he had said that, he breathed on them, and said unto them, Receive the holy Ghost. **23** [l]Whosoever's sins ye remit, they are remitted unto them: and whosoever's sins ye retain, they are retained. **24** [m]But Thomas one of the twelve, called Didymus, was not with them when Jesus came. **25** The other disciples therefore said unto him, We have seen the Lord: but he said unto them, Except I see in his hands the print of the nails, and put my finger into the print of the nails, and put mine hand into his side, I will not believe it. **26** And eight days after, again his disciples were within, and Thomas with them. Then came Jesus, when the doors were shut, and stood in the midst, and said, Peace be unto you. **27** After said he to Thomas, Put thy finger here, and see mine hands, and put forth thine hand, and put it into my side, and be not faithless, but faithful. **28** Then Thomas answered, and said unto him, Thou art my Lord, and my God. **29** [n]Jesus said unto him, Thomas, because thou hast seen me, thou believest: blessed are they that have not seen, and have believed. **30** [o,5]And many other signs also did Jesus in the presence of his disciples, which are not written in this book. **31** But these things are

---

h. John 19:19 Christ sitting upon the throne of the cross, is openly written everlasting king of all people, with his own hand, whose mouth condemned him for usurping a kingdom.

i. John 19:23 Christ signifieth by the division of his garments amongst the bloody butchers (his coat except, that hath no seam) that it shall come to pass, that he will shortly divide his benefits, and enrich his very enemies throughout the world: but so notwithstanding that the treasure of his Church shall remain whole.

j. John 19:25 Christ is a perfect example of all righteousness, not only in the keeping of the first, but also of the second table.

k. John 19:28 Christ, when he hath taken the vinegar, yieldeth up the Ghost, drinking up indeed that most bitter and sharp cup of his Father's wrath in our name.

l. John 19:29 Galatinus witnesseth out of the book called Sanhedrin, that the Jews were wont to give them that were executed, vinegar mixed with frankincense to drink, to make their brains somewhat troubled: so charitably the Jews provided for the poor men's consciences which were executed.

m. John 19:31 The body of Christ which was dead for a season (because it so pleased him) is wounded, but the least bone of it is not broken: and such is the state of his mystical body.

n. John 19:34 Christ being dead upon the cross, witnesseth by a double sign, that he only is the true satisfaction, and the true washing for the believers.

o. John 19:34 This wound was a most manifest witness of the death of Christ: for the water that issued out by this wound, gave us plainly to understand, that the weapon pierced the very skin that compasseth the heart, which is the vessel that containeth that water, and that being once wounded, that creature which is so pierced and stricken, cannot choose but die.

p. John 19:38 Christ is openly buried, and in a famous place, Pilate writing and suffering it, and that by men which did favor Christ, in such wise, that yet before that day, they never openly followed him: so that by his burial, no man can justly doubt either of his death, or resurrection.

q. John 19:41 That no man might cavil at his resurrection, as though some other that had been buried there, had risen, Theophylact.

JOHN. 19

1. Matt. 27:27 / Mark 15:16
2. Matt. 27:31 / Mark 15:25 / Luke 23:26
3. Matt. 27:35 / Mark 15:24
4. Ps. 22:18
5. Ps. 69:22
6. Exod. 12:46 / Num. 9:12
7. Zech. 12:10
8. Matt. 27:57 / Mark 15:42 / Luke 23:50
9. John 3:2

JOHN. 20

a. John 20:1 Mary Magdalene, Peter and John are the first witnesses of the resurrection: and such as cannot justly be suspected, for that they themselves could scarcely be persuaded of it, so far is it off, that they should invent it of set purpose.

b. John 20:11 That is, without the cave, which the sepulchre was cut out of.

c. John 20:12 Two Angels are made witnesses of the Lord's resurrection.

d. John 20:12 In white clothing.

e. John 20:13 Many speak as the common people use to speak: for they speak of a dead carcass, as they do of a whole man.

f. John 20:14 Jesus witnesseth by his presence, that he is truly risen.

g. John 20:17 Christ which is risen, is not to be sought in this world according to the flesh, but in heaven by faith, whither he is gone before us.

h. John 20:17 By his brethren he meaneth his disciples: for in the next verse following, it is said, that Mary told his disciples.

i. John 20:17 He calleth God his Father because he is his Father naturally in the Godhead, and he saith your Father, because he is our Father by grace, through the adoption of the sons of God: that is, by taking us of his free grace to be his sons, Epiphanius.

j. John 20:19 Christ in that that he presented himself before his disciples suddenly through his divine power, when the gates were shut, doth fully assure them both of his resurrection, and also of their Apostleship, inspiring them with the holy Ghost, who is the director of the ministry of the Gospel.

k. John 20:19 Either the doors opened to him of their own accord, or the very walls themselves were a passage for him.

l. John 20:23 The publishing of the forgiveness of sins by faith in Christ, and the setting forth and denouncing the wrath of God in retaining the sins of the unbelievers, is the sum of the preaching of the Gospel.

m. John 20:24 Christ draweth out of the unbelief of Thomas, a certain and sure testimony of his resurrection.

n. John 20:29 True faith dependeth upon the mouth of God, and not upon fleshly eyes.

o. John 20:30 To believe in Christ, the Son of God, and our only Savior, is the end of the doctrine of the Gospel, and especially of the history of the resurrection.

written that ye might believe, that Jesus is that Christ that Son of God, and that in
believing ye might have life through his Name.

21

1 Jesus appeareth to his disciples as they were fishing, 6, 7 whom they know by a miraculous draught of fishes. 15 He committeth the charge of the sheep to Peter, 18 and foretelleth him of the manner of his death.

1 After these things, [a]Jesus showed himself again to his disciples at the sea of
Tiberias: and thus showed he himself: **2** There were together Simon Peter, and
Thomas, which is called Didymus, and Nathanael of Cana in Galilee, and the sons
of Zebedee, and two others of his disciples. **3** Simon Peter said unto them, I go
a fishing. They said unto him, We also will go with thee. They went their way and
entered into a ship straightway, and that night caught they nothing. **4** But when
the morning was now come, Jesus stood on the shore: nevertheless the disciples
knew not that it was Jesus. **5** Jesus then said unto them, Sirs, have ye any meat?
They answered him, No. **6** Then he said unto them, Cast out the net on the ri-
ght side of the ship, and ye shall find. So they cast out, and they were not able at all
to draw it, for the multitude of fishes. **7** Therefore said the disciple whom Jesus
loved, unto Peter, It is the Lord. When Simon Peter heard that it was the Lord, he
girded his [b]coat to him (for he was naked) and cast himself into the sea. **8** But
the other disciples came by ship, (for they were not far from land, but about two
hundred cubits) and they drew the net with fishes. **9** As soon then as they were
come to land, they saw hot coals, and fish laid thereon, and bread. **10** Jesus said
unto them, Bring of the fishes, which ye have now caught. **11** Simon Peter step-
ped forth and drew the net to land full of great fishes, an hundred, fifty and three:
and albeit there were so many, yet was not the net broken. **12** Jesus said unto
them, Come, and dine. And none of the disciples durst ask him, Who art thou?
seeing they knew that he was the Lord. **13** Jesus then came and took bread and
gave them, and fish likewise. **14** This is now the third time that Jesus showed
himself to his disciples, after that he was risen again from the dead. **15** [c]So
when they had dined, Jesus said to Simon Peter, Simon the son of Jonah, lovest
thou me more than these? He said unto him, Yea, Lord, thou knowest that I love
thee. He said unto him, Feed my lambs. **16** He said to him again the second
time, Simon the son of Jonah, lovest thou me? He said unto him, Yea, Lord, thou
knowest that I love thee. He said unto him, Feed my sheep. **17** He said unto him
[d]the third time, Simon the son of Jonah, lovest thou me? Peter was sorry becau-
se he said to him the third time, Lovest thou me? and said unto him, Lord, thou
knowest all things: thou knowest that I love thee. Jesus said unto him, Feed my
sheep. **18** [e]Verily, verily I say unto thee, When thou wast young, thou [f]girdedst
thyself, and walkedst whither thou wouldest: but when thou shalt be old, thou
shalt stretch forth thine hands, and another shall [g]gird thee, and lead thee without
thou wouldest [h]not. **19** And this spake he signifying by what [i]death he should
glorify God. And when he had said this, he said to him, Follow me. **20** [j]Then
Peter turned about, and saw the disciple whom JESUS loved, following, which had
also [1]leaned on his breast at supper, and had said, Lord, which is he that betrayeth
thee? **21** When Peter therefore saw him, he said to Jesus, Lord, what shall this
man do? **22** Jesus said unto him, If I will that he tarry till I come, what is it to
thee? follow thou me. **23** Then went this word abroad among the brethren, that
this disciple should not die. Yet Jesus said not to him, He shall not die: but if I
will that he tarry till I come, what is it to thee? **24** [k]This is that disciple, which
testifieth of these things, and wrote these things, and we know that his testimony
is true. **25** [2]Now there are also many other things which Jesus did, the which if
they should be written every one, I suppose the world could not contain the books
that should be written, Amen.

JOHN. 20

1. Mark 16:1 / Luke 24:1
2. Matt. 28:1 / Mark 16:5
3. Mark 16:14 / Luke 24:36 / 1 Cor. 15:5
4. Matt. 28:18
5. John 21:25

JOHN. 21

a. John 21:1 In that, that Christ here is not only present, but also eateth with his disciples, he giveth a most full assurance of his resurrection.

b. John 21:7 It was a linen garment, which could not let his swimming.

c. John 21:15 Peter by his triple confession is restored into his former degree from whence he fell by his triple denial: and therewithal is advertised, that he is indeed a pastor, which showeth his love to Christ in feeding his sheep.

d. John 21:17 It was meet that he that had denied him thrice, should confess him thrice, that Peter might neither doubt of the forgiveness of his so grievous a sin, nor of his restoring to the office of the Apostleship.

e. John 21:18 The violent death of Peter is foretold.

f. John 21:18 They that took far journeys, especially in the East country, and in those places where the people used long garments, had need to be girded and trussed up.

g. John 21:18 He meant that kind of girding which is used toward captives, when they are bound fast with cords and chains, as who would say, Now thou girdest thyself as thou thinkest best, to go whither thou listest, but the time will be, when thou shall not gird thee with a girdle, but another shall bind thee with chains, and carry thee whither thou wouldest not.

h. John 21:18 Not that Peter suffered ought for the truth of God against his will: for we read that he came with joy and gladness when he returned from the Council where he was whipped: but because this will cometh not from the flesh, but from the gift of the Spirit which is given us from above, therefore he showeth there should be a certain striving and conflict or repugnancy, which also is in us, in all our sufferances as touching the flesh.

i. John 21:19 That is, that Peter should die by a violent death.

j. John 21:20 We must take heed, that while we cast our eyes upon others, we neglect not that which is enjoined us.

k. John 21:24 The history of Christ is true and warily written: not for the curiosity of men, but for the salvation of the godly.

JOHN. 21

1. John 13:23
2. John 20:30

THE

ACTS

OF THE HOLY APOSTLES, WRITTEN BY LUKE THE EVANGELIST

1

1 Luke tieth this history to his Gospel. 9 Christ being taken into heaven. 10 The Apostles, 11 being warned by the Angels, 12 to return, 14 and give themselves to prayer. 15 By Peter's motion, 18 into Judas the traitor's place. 26 Matthias is chosen.

1 I have made the [a]former treatise, O Theophilus, of all that Jesus began to [b]do and teach, **2** Until the day that he was taken up, after that he through the holy Ghost, had given commandments unto the Apostles, whom he had chosen: **3** [c]To whom also he presented himself alive after that he had suffered, by many [d]infallible tokens, being seen of them by the space of forty days, and speaking of those things which appertained to the kingdom of God. **4** [1]And when he had [e]gathered them together, he commanded them that they should not depart from Jerusalem, but to wait for the promise of the Father, [2]which said he, ye have heard of me. **5** [3]For John indeed baptized with water, but ye shall be baptized [f]with the holy Ghost within these few days. **6** [g]When they therefore were come together they asked of him, saying, Lord, wilt thou at this time [h]restore the kingdom to Israel? **7** And he said unto them, It is not for you to know the times, or the [i]seasons, which the Father hath put in his own power. **8** [4]But ye shall receive power of the holy Ghost, when he shall come on you: and ye shall be witnesses unto me both in Jerusalem and in all Judea, and in Samaria, and unto the uttermost part of the earth. **9** [j,5]And when he had spoken these things, while they beheld, he was taken up: for a cloud took him up out of their sight. **10** And while they looked steadfastly toward heaven, as he went, behold, two men stood by them in white apparel. **11** Which also said, Ye men of Galilee, why stand ye gazing into heaven? This Jesus which is taken up [k]from you into heaven, shall so come, as ye have seen him go into heaven. **12** Then returned they unto Jerusalem from the mount that is called the mount of Olives, which is near to Jerusalem, being from it a Sabbath [l]day's journey. **13** [m]And when they were [n]come in, they went up into an upper chamber, where abode both Peter and James, and John, and Andrew, Philip, and Thomas, Bartholomew, and Matthew, James the son of Alphaeus, and Simon Zealot, and Judas James's brother. **14** These all [o]continued with [p]one accord in [q]prayer and supplication with the [r]women, and Mary the mother of Jesus, and with his [s]brethren. **15** [t]And in those days Peter stood up in the midst of the disciples, and said (now the number of [u]names that were in one place were about an hundred and twenty.) **16** [v]Ye men and brethren, this scripture must needs have been fulfilled, Which the [6]holy Ghost by the mouth of David spake before of Judas, which [7]was guide to them that took Jesus. **17** For he was numbered with us, and had obtained fellowship in this ministration. **18** He therefore hath [w]purchased a field with the reward of iniquity: and when he had [x]thrown down himself headlong, he brast asunder in the midst, and all his bowels gushed out. **19** And it is known unto all the inhabitants of Jerusalem, insomuch, that that field is called in their own language, Akel Dama, that is, The field of blood. **20** For it is written in the book of Psalms, [9]Let his habitation be void, and let no man dwell therein: [10]also, Let another take his [y]charge. **21** [z]Wherefore of these men which have companied with us, all the time that the Lord Jesus was [aa]conversant among us, **22** Beginning from the baptism of John unto the day that he was taken up [ab]from us, must one of them be made a witness with us of his resurrection. **23** [ac]And they [ad]presented two, Joseph called Barsabas, whose surname was Justus, and Matthias. **24** And they prayed, saying, Thou Lord, which knowest the hearts of all men, show whether of these two thou hast chosen, **25** That he may take the [ae]room of this ministration and Apostleship, from which Judas hath [af]gone astray, to go to his own place. **26** Then they gave forth their lots: and the lot fell on Matthias, and he was by a common consent counted with the eleven Apostles.

2

1 The Apostles 4 filled with the holy Ghost 8 speak with divers tongues: 12 They are thought to be drunk, 15 but Peter disproveth that. 34 He teacheth that Christ is the Messiah: 37 And seeing the hearers astonied, 38 he exhorteth them to repentance.

1 And [a]when the day of Pentecost was [b]come, they were [c]all with one accord in one place. **2** And suddenly there came a sound from heaven, as of a rushing and mighty wind, and it filled all the house where they sat. **3** And there appeared unto them cloven tongues, like fire, and it sat upon each of them. **4** And they

---

ACTS 1

- **a.** Acts 1:1 A passing over from the history of the Gospel, that is, from the history of the sayings and doings of Christ, unto the acts of the Apostles.
- **b.** Acts 1:1 The acts of Jesus are the miracles and doings which showed his Godhead, and his most perfect holiness and example of his doctrine.
- **c.** Acts 1:3 Christ did not straightway ascend into heaven after his resurrection: because he would thoroughly prove his resurrection: and with his presence confirm his Apostles in the doctrine, which they had heard.
- **d.** Acts 1:3 He calleth those infallible tokens, which are otherwise termed necessary: now in that Christ spake, and walked, and ate, and was felt of many, these are sure signs and tokens that he truly rose again.
- **e.** Acts 1:4 They were dispersed here and there, but he gathereth them together that they might altogether be witnesses of his resurrection.
- **f.** Acts 1:5 Either of the Father, or of me: so that either the Father or Christ is set here against John, as the holy Ghost is against the water, as things answerable the one to the other.
- **g.** Acts 1:6 We must fight before we triumph: and we ought not curiously to search after those things, which God hath not revealed.
- **h.** Acts 1:6 To the old and ancient state.
- **i.** Acts 1:7 That is, the fit occasions that serve to doing of matters which the Lord hath appointed to bring things to pass in.
- **j.** Acts 1:9 After that Christ had promised the full virtue of the holy Ghost, wherewith he would govern his Church, although he should be absent in body, he took up his body from us into heavenly tabernacles, there to continue until the latter day of judgment, as the Angels witness.
- **k.** Acts 1:11 That is, out of your sight.
- **l.** Acts 1:12 About two miles.
- **m.** Acts 1:13 Ecclesiastical assemblies to hear the word, and to make common prayer, were first instituted and kept in private houses by the Apostles.
- **n.** Acts 1:13 They went into the house, which the Church hath chosen at that time to be a receipt for the whole assembly.
- **o.** Acts 1:14 The Greek word signified an invincible constancy, and steadiness.
- **p.** Acts 1:14 It is to good purpose, that this concord is mentioned: for those prayers are most acceptable to God which are made with agreeing minds and wills.
- **q.** Acts 1:14 The disciples prayed for the sending of the holy Ghost, and also to be delivered from present dangers wherewith they were beset.
- **r.** Acts 1:14 For it was behoovable to have the wives confirmed, who were afterward to be partakers of the dangers with their husbands.
- **s.** Acts 1:14 With his kinfolks.
- **t.** Acts 1:15 Peter is made the mouth and interpreter of the whole company of the Apostles, either by secret revelation of the holy Ghost, or by express judgment of the Congregation.
- **u.** Acts 1:15 Because men are commonly billed and enrolled by their names.
- **v.** Acts 1:16 Peter preventeth the offense that might be taken of the falling away of Judas the betrayer, showing that all things which came unto him, were foretold by God.
- **w.** Acts 1:18 Luke considered not Judas's purpose, but that that followed of it, and so we used to say, that a man hath procured himself harm, not that his will and purpose was so, but in respect of that which followed.
- **x.** Acts 1:18 The Greek words signify thus much, that Judas fell down flat and was rent in sunder in the middle, with a marvelous huge noise.
- **y.** Acts 1:20 His office and ministry David wrote these words against Doeg the King's herdsman: And these words, Shepherd, Sheep, and Flock, are put over to the Church office and ministry, so that the Church and the offices thereof are called by these names.
- **z.** Acts 1:21 The Apostles deliberate upon nothing, but first they consult and take advisement by God's word: and again they do nothing that concerneth and is behoovable for the whole body of the Congregation, without making the Congregation privy unto it.
- **aa.** Acts 1:21 Word for word, went in and out, which kind of speech betokeneth as much in the Hebrew tongue, as the exercising of a public and painful office, when they speak of such as are in any public office, Deut. 31:2; 1 Chron. 27:1.
- **ab.** Acts 1:22 From our company.
- **ac.** Acts 1:23 Apostles must be chosen immediately from God, and therefore after prayers, Matthias is chosen by lot, which is as it were GOD'S own voice.
- **ad.** Acts 1:23 Openly, and by the voices of all the whole company.
- **ae.** Acts 1:25 That he may be fellow and partaker of this ministry.
- **af.** Acts 1:25 Departed from, or fallen from: And it is a Metaphor taken from the way: For callings are signified by the name of ways, with the Hebrews.

ACTS 1

1. Luke 24:49
2. John 14:25
3. Matt. 3:11; Mark 1:8; Luke 3:16; Acts 2:2; Acts 11:16; Acts 19:4
4. Acts 2:2
5. Luke 24:51
6. Ps. 41:9
7. John 13:27
8. Matt. 27:5
9. Ps. 69:26
10. Ps. 109:7

ACTS 2

- **a.** Acts 2:1 The Apostles being gathered together on a most solemn feast day in one place, that it might evidently appear to all the world, that they had all one office, one Spirit, one faith, are by a double sign from heaven authorized, and anointed with all the most excellent gifts of the holy Ghost and especially with an extraordinary and necessary gift of tongues.
- **b.** Acts 2:1 Word for word, was fulfilled: that is, was begun, as Luke 2:21. For the Hebrews say that a day, or a year is fulfilled or ended, when the former days or years are ended, and the other begun, Jer. 25:12. And it shall come to pass, that when seventy years are fulfilled, I will visit, etc. For the Lord did not

were all filled with the holy Ghost, and began to speak with [d]other tongues, as the
[e]Spirit gave them utterance. 5 And there were dwelling at Jerusalem Jews, men
that feared God, of every nation under heaven. 6 Now when this was noised, the
multitude came together and were astonied, because that every man heard them
speak his own language. 7 And they wondered all, and marveled, saying among
themselves, Behold, are not all these which speak, of Galilee? 8 [f]How then hear
we every man our own language, wherein we were born? 9 Parthians, and Medes,
and Elamites, and the inhabitants of Mesopotamia, and of Judea, and of Cappado-
cia, of Pontus, and Asia, 10 And of Phrygia, and Pamphylia, of Egypt, and of the
parts of Libya, which is beside Cyrene, and strangers of Rome, and [g]Jews, and Pro-
selytes, 11 Cretes, and Arabians: we heard them speak in our own tongues the
wonderful works of God. 12 [h]They were all then amazed, and doubted, saying
one to another, What may this be? 13 And others [i]mocked, and said, They are
full of new wine. 14 But Peter standing with the eleven, [j]lifted up his voice, and
said unto them, Ye men of Judea, and ye all that inhabit Jerusalem, be this known
unto you, and hearken unto my words. 15 For these are not drunken, as ye sup-
pose, since it is but the [k]third hour of the day. 16 But this is that, which was
spoken by the [l]Prophet [1]Joel, 17 [m]And it shall be in the last days, saith God,
I will pour out of my Spirit upon [n]all [o]flesh, and your sons, and your daughters
shall prophesy, and your young men shall see visions, and your old men shall dre-
am dreams. 18 And on my servants, and on mine handmaids I will pour out of
my Spirit in those days, and they shall prophesy. 19 And I will show wonders in
heaven above, and tokens in the earth beneath, blood, and fire, and the vapors of
smoke. 20 The Sun shall be turned into darkness, and the moon into blood, be-
fore that great and notable day of the Lord come. 21 [p]And it shall be, that who-
soever shall [q]call on the Name of the Lord, shall be saved. 22 [r]Ye men of Israel,
hear these words, JESUS of Nazareth, a man [s]approved of God among you with
great works, and wonders, and signs, which God did by him in the midst of you,
as ye yourselves also know: 23 Him, I say, being delivered by the determinate
counsel, and [t]foreknowledge of God, after you had taken, with wicked [u]hands you
have crucified and [v]slain. 24 [w]Whom God hath raised up, and loosed the [x]sor-
rows of death, because it was impossible that he should be holden of it. 25 For
David saith concerning him, [2]I beheld the Lord always before me: for he is at my
right hand, that I should not be shaken. 26 Therefore did mine heart rejoice,
and my tongue was glad, and moreover also my flesh shall rest in hope, 27 Be-
cause thou wilt not [y]leave my soul in grave, neither wilt suffer thine Holy one to
see corruption. 28 Thou hast [z]showed me the ways of life, and shalt make me
full of joy with thy countenance. 29 Men and brethren, I may boldly speak unto
you of the Patriarch David, [3]that he is both dead and buried, and his sepulcher
remaineth with us unto this day. 30 Therefore, seeing he was a Prophet, and
knew that God had [aa,4]sworn with an oath to him, that of the fruit of his loins he
would raise up Christ concerning the flesh, to set him upon his throne. 31 He
knowing this before, spake of the resurrection of Christ, that [5]his soul should not
be left in grave, neither his flesh should see corruption. 32 [ab]This Jesus hath
God raised up, whereof we all are witnesses. 33 Since then that he by the [ac]ri-
ght hand of God hath been exalted, and hath received of his Father the promise
of the holy Ghost, he hath shed forth this which ye now see and hear. 34 For
David is not ascended into heaven, but he saith, [6]The Lord said to my Lord, Sit
at my right hand, 35 Until I make thine enemies thy footstool. 36 Therefo-
re, let all the house of Israel know for a surety, that God hath [ad]made him both
Lord, and Christ, this Jesus, I say, whom ye have crucified. 37 Now when they
heard it, they were pricked in their hearts, and said unto Peter and the other Apo-
stles, Men and brethren, what shall we do? 38 [ae]Then Peter said unto them,
Amend your lives, and be baptized every one of you in the Name of Jesus Christ
for the remission of sins: and ye shall receive the gift of the holy Ghost. 39 For
the [af]promise is made unto you, and to your children, and to all that are afar off,
even as many as the Lord our God shall call. 40 [ag]And with many other words
he besought and exhorted them, saying, Save yourselves from this froward genera-
tion. 41 [ah]Then they that gladly received his word, were baptized, and the same
day there were added to the Church about three thousand souls. 42 [ai]And they
continued in the Apostles' doctrine, and [aj]fellowship, and [ak]breaking of bread, and
prayers. 43 [al]And fear came upon every soul: and many wonders and signs were
done by the Apostles. 44 [am]And all that believed, were in one place, and had
all things common. 45 And they sold their possessions, and goods, and parted
them to all men, as everyone had need. 46 [an]And they continued daily with one
accord in the Temple, and breaking bread at home, did eat their meat together with
gladness and singleness of heart, 47 Praising God, and had favor with all the pe-
ople: and the Lord added to the Church from day to day, such as should be saved.

3

1 Peter goeth into the Temple with John, 2 healeth the cripple. 9 To the people gathered together to see the miracle, 12 he expoundeth the mystery of our salvation through Christ, 14 accusing their ingratitude, 19 and requiring the repentance.

1 Now [a]Peter and John went up together into the Temple, at the ninth hour
of prayer. 2 And a certain man which was a cripple from his mother's womb
was carried, whom they laid daily at the gate of the Temple called Beautiful, to
ask alms of them that entered into the Temple, 3 Who seeing Peter and John,
that they would enter into the Temple, desiring to receive an alms. 4 And Pe-
ter earnestly beholding him with John, said, Look on us. 5 And he [b]gave heed
unto them, trusting to receive some thing of them. 6 Then said Peter, Silver and
gold have I none, but such as I have, that give I thee: In the Name of Jesus Christ
of Nazareth, rise up and walk. 7 And he took him by the right hand, and lifted
him up, and immediately his feet and ankle bones received strength. 8 And he
leaped up, stood, and walked, and entered with them into the temple, walking
and leaping, and praising God. 9 And all the people saw him walk, and praising

---

bring home his people after the seventieth year was ended, but in the seventieth year. Now the day of Pentecost was the fiftieth day after the feast of the Passover.

c. Acts 2:1 The twelve Apostles, which were to be the Patriarchs as it were of the Church.

d. Acts 2:4 He calleth them other tongues, which were not the same which the Apostles used commonly, and Mark calleth them new tongues.

e. Acts 2:4 Hereby were understood that the Apostles used not now one tongue, and then another by haphazard and at all adventure, or as fantastical men used to do, but with good consideration of their hearers: and to be short, that they spake nothing but as the holy Ghost governed their tongues.

f. Acts 2:8 Not that they spake with one voice, and many languages were heard, but that the Apostles spake with strange tongues: for else the miracle had rather been in the hearers, whereas now it is in the speakers, Nazianzen in his oration of Whitsunday.

g. Acts 2:10 By Jews, he meaneth them that were both Jews by birth, and Jews by profession of religion though they were born in other places: and they were Proselytes, which were Gentiles born and embraced the Jews' religion.

h. Acts 2:12 God's word pierceth some so, that it driveth them to seek out the truth, and it doth so choke others, that it forceth them to be witnesses of their own impudency.

i. Acts 2:13 The word which he useth here, signifieth such a kind of mocking which is reproachful and contumelious: And by this reproachful mocking we see, that there is no miracle so great and excellent, which the wickedness of man dareth not speak evil of.

j. Acts 2:14 Peter's boldness is to be marked, wherein the grace of the holy Ghost is to be seen, even straight after the beginning.

k. Acts 2:15 After the sun rising, which may be about seven or eight of the clock with us.

l. Acts 2:16 There is nothing that can dissolve questions and doubts, but testimonies taken out of the Prophets: for men's reasons may be overturned, but God's voice cannot be overturned.

m. Acts 2:17 Peter setting the truth of God against the false accusations of men, showeth in himself and in his fellows, that that is fulfilled which Joel spake concerning the full giving of the holy Ghost in the latter days: which grace also is offered to the whole Church, to their certain and undoubted destruction, which do contemn it.

n. Acts 2:17 All without exception, both upon the Jews and Gentiles.

o. Acts 2:17 That is, men.

p. Acts 2:21 The chiefest use of all the gifts of the holy Ghost, is to bring men to salvation by faith.

q. Acts 2:21 This word, Call on, signifieth in holy Scriptures, an earnest praying and craving for help at God's hand.

r. Acts 2:22 Christ being innocent, was by God's providence crucified of wicked men.

s. Acts 2:22 Who is by those works which God wrought by him, so manifestly approved and allowed of, that no man can gainsay him.

t. Acts 2:23 God's everlasting knowledge going before, which can neither be separated from his determinate counsel, as the Epicureans say, neither yet be the cause of evil: for God in his everlasting and unchangeable counsel, appointed the wicked act of Judas to an excellent end: and God doeth that well which the instruments do ill.

u. Acts 2:23 God's counsel doth not excuse the Jews, whose hands were wicked.

v. Acts 2:23 The fault is said to be theirs, by whose counsel and egging forward it is done.

w. Acts 2:24 Christ (as David foretold) did not only rise again, but also was in the grave void of all corruption.

x. Acts 2:24 The dead that was full of sorrow both of body and mind: therefore when death appeared conqueror and victor over those sorrows, Christ is rightly said to have overcome those sorrows of death, when as being dead, he overcame death, to live forever with his Father.

y. Acts 2:27 Thou wilt not suffer me to remain in grave.

z. Acts 2:28 Thou hast opened me the way to the true life.

aa. Acts 2:30 Had sworn solemnly.

ab. Acts 2:32 Peter witnesseth that Jesus Christ is the appointed everlasting King, which he proveth manifestly by the gifts of the holy Ghost,and the testimony of David.

ac. Acts 2:33 Might and power of God.

ad. Acts 2:36 Christ is said to be made, because he was advanced to that dignity: and therefore it is not spoken of his nature, but of his state and dignity.

ae. Acts 2:38 Repentance and remission of sins in Christ, are two principles of the Gospel, and therefore of our salvation: and they are obtained by the promises apprehended by faith, and are ratified in us by Baptism, wherewith is joined the virtue of the holy Ghost.

af. Acts 2:39 The word that is used here, giveth us to understand that it was a free gift.

ag. Acts 2:40 He is truly joined to the Church which separateth himself from the wicked.

ah. Acts 2:41 A notable example of the virtue of the holy Ghost: but such as are of age, are not baptized before they make confession of their faith.

ai. Acts 2:42 The marks of the true Church of the doctrine of the Apostles, the duties of charity, the pure and simple administration of the Sacraments, and true invocation used of all the faithful.

aj. Acts 2:42 Communicating of goods, and all other duties of charity, as is showed afterward.

ak. Acts 2:42 The Jews used thin loaves, and therefore they did rather brake them than cut them: So by breaking of bread, they understood that living together and the banquets which they used to keep. And when they kept their love feasts, they used to celebrate the Lord's Supper, which even in these days began to be corrupted, and Paul amendeth it, 1 Cor. 11.

al. Acts 2:43 So oft as the Lord thinketh it expedient, he bridleth the rage of strangers that the Church may be planted, and have some refreshing.

am. Acts 2:44 Charity maketh all things common concerning the use, according as necessity requireth.

an. Acts 2:46 The faithful came together at the beginning with great fruit, not only to the hearing of the word, but also to meat.

ACTS 2

1. Joel 2:28; Isa. 24:3
2. Ps. 16:9
3. 1 Kings 2:10; Acts 13:36
4. Ps. 132:11
5. Ps. 16:10; Acts 13:35
6. Ps. 110:1

ACTS 3

a. Acts 3:1 Christ in healing a man that was born lame, and well known to all men, both in place and time very famous, by the hands of his Apostles, doth partly confirm them which believed, and partly also calleth others to believe.

b. Acts 3:5 Both with heart and eyes.

God. **10** And they knew him, that it was he which sat for the alms at the Beautiful gate of the Temple: and they were amazed, and sore astonied at that which was come unto him. **11** And as the cripple which was healed, [c]held Peter and John, all the people ran amazed unto them in the porch which is called Solomon's. **12** [d]So when Peter saw it, he answered unto the people, Ye men of Israel, why marvel ye at this? or why look ye so steadfastly on us, as though by our own power or godliness, we had made this man go? **13** The God of Abraham, and Isaac, and Jacob, the [1]God of our fathers hath glorified his Son Jesus, whom ye betrayed, and denied in the presence of Pilate, when he had judged him to be delivered. **14** But ye denied the Holy one and the just, and desired a murderer to be given you, **15** And killed the Lord [e]of life, whom God hath raised from the dead, whereof we are witnesses. **16** And his Name hath made this man sound, whom ye see and know, through faith in his Name: [f]and the faith which is by him, hath given to him this perfect health of his whole body in the presence of you all. **17** [g]And now brethren, I know that through ignorance ye did it, as did also your governors. **18** But those things, which God before had showed [h]by the mouth of all his Prophets, that Christ should suffer, he hath thus fulfilled. **19** Amend your lives therefore, and turn, that your sins may be put away, when the time of refreshing shall come from the presence of the Lord. **20** And he shall send Jesus Christ, which before was preached unto you. **21** [i]Whom the heaven must contain until the time that all things be restored, which God had spoken by the mouth of all his holy Prophets since the world began. **22** [2]For Moses said unto the Fathers, The Lord your God shall raise up unto you [j]a Prophet, even of your brethren, like unto me: ye shall hear him in all things whatsoever he shall say unto you. **23** For it shall be that every person which shall not hear that Prophet, shall be destroyed out of the people. **24** Also all the Prophets [k]from Samuel, and thenceforth as many as have spoken, have likewise foretold of these days. **25** [l]Ye are the [m]children of the Prophets, and of the covenant, which God hath made unto our fathers, saying to Abraham, [3]Even in thy seed shall all the kindreds of the earth be blessed. **26** First unto you hath God [n]raised up his Son Jesus, and him he hath sent to bless you, in turning everyone of you from your iniquities.

4

1 Peter and John, 3 are taken and brought before the council, 7 and 19 They speak boldly in Christ's cause. 24 The disciples pray unto God. 32 Many sell their possessions. 36 Of whom Barnabas is one.

1 And [a]as they spake unto the people, the Priests and the [b]Captain of the Temple, and the Sadducees came upon them. **2** Taking it grievously that they taught the people, and preached in Jesus' Name the resurrection from the dead. **3** And they laid hands on them, and put them in hold, until the next day, for it was now eventide. **4** Howbeit many of them which heard the word, believed, and the [c]number of the men was about five thousand. **5** And it came to pass on the morrow, that their [d]rulers, and Elders, and Scribes, were gathered together at Jerusalem, **6** And Annas the chief Priest, and Caiaphas, and John, and Alexander, and as many as were of the [e]kindred of the high Priest. **7** [f]And when they had set them before them, they asked, By what power, or in what [g]Name have ye done this? **8** Then Peter full of the holy Ghost, said unto them, Ye rulers of the people, and Elders of Israel, **9** [h]For as much as we this day are examined, of the good deed done to the impotent man, to wit, by what means he is made whole, **10** [i]Be it known unto you all, and to all the people of Israel, that by the Name of Jesus Christ of Nazareth, whom ye have crucified, whom God raised again from the dead, even by him doth this man stand here before you, whole. **11** [1]This is the stone cast aside of you builders, which is become the head of the corner. **12** Neither is there salvation in any other: for among men there is [j]given none other [k]Name [l]under heaven, whereby we must be saved. **13** [m]Now when they saw the boldness of Peter and John, and understood that they were unlearned men and without [n]knowledge, they marveled, and knew them, that they had been with Jesus: **14** And beholding also the man which was healed standing with them, they had nothing to say against it. **15** Then they commanded them to go aside out of the Council, and [o]conferred among themselves, **16** [p]Saying, What shall we do to these men? for surely a manifest sign is done by them, and it is openly known to all them that dwell in Jerusalem: and we cannot deny it. **17** But that it be noised no farther among the people, let us threaten and charge them, that they speak henceforth to no man in this Name. **18** So they called them, and commanded them, that in no wise they should speak or teach in the Name of Jesus. **19** [q]But Peter and John answered unto them, and said, Whether it be right in the sight of God, to obey you rather than God, judge ye. **20** For we cannot but speak the things which we have seen and heard. **21** [r]So they threatened them, and let them go, and found nothing how to punish them, because of the people: for all men praised God for that which was done. **22** For the man was above forty years old, on whom this miracle of healing was showed. **23** [s]Then as soon as they were let go, they came to their fellows, and showed all that the high Priests and Elders had said unto them. **24** [t]And when they heard it, they lifted up their voices to God with one accord, and said, O Lord, thou art the God which had made the heaven, and the earth, the sea, and all things that are in them. **25** [2]Which by the mouth of thy servant David hast said, Why did the Gentiles rage, and the people imagine vain things? **26** The kings of the earth assembled, and the rulers came together against the Lord, and against his Christ. **27** For doubtless, against thine holy Son Jesus, whom thou hadst anointed, both Herod and Pontius Pilate, with the Gentiles and the [u]people of Israel gathered themselves together. **28** To [v]do whatsoever [w]thine hand, and thy counsel had determined before to be done. **29** And now, O Lord, behold their threatenings, and grant unto thy servants with all boldness to speak thy word, **30** So that thou stretch forth thine hand that healing, and signs, and wonders may be done by the Name of thine holy Son Jesus. **31** [x]And when as they had prayed, the place was shaken where they were assembled together, and they were all filled with the holy Ghost, and they spake the word of God boldly. **32** [y]And the multitude of them that believed, were of [z]one heart, and of one soul: neither any of them said, that anything of that which he possessed, was his own, but they had all things [3]common. **33** And with great power gave the Apostles witness of the resurrection of the Lord Jesus: and great grace was upon them all. **34** [aa]Neither was there any among them, that lacked: for as many as were possessors of lands or houses, sold them, and brought the price of the things

---

c. Acts 3:11 Either because he loved them, who had healed him: or because he feared that if he once let them go out of his sight, he should be lame again.
d. Acts 3:12 Miracles are appointed to convince the unbelievers, and therefore they do wickedly abuse them, who standeth amazed either at the miracles themselves, or at the instruments and means which it pleaseth God to use, take an occasion to establish idolatry and superstition by that, which God hath provided for the knowledge of his true worship, that is, Christianity.
e. Acts 3:15 Who hath life in himself, and giveth life to others.
f. Acts 3:16 Because he believed on him being raised from the dead, whose Name he heard of by us.
g. Acts 3:17 It is best of all to receive Christ so soon as he is offered unto us: but such as have neglected so great a benefit through man's weakness, have yet repentance for a means. As for the ignominy of the cross, we have to set against that, the decree and purpose of God, foretold by the Prophets, of Christ, how that first of all he should be crucified here upon earth, and then he should appear from heaven the judge and restorer of all things, that all believers might be saved, and all unbelievers utterly perish.
h. Acts 3:18 Though there were many Prophets, yet he speaketh but of one mouth, to show unto us the consent and agreement of the Prophets.
i. Acts 3:21 Or, be taken up into heaven.
j. Acts 3:22 This promise was of an excellent and singular Prophet.
k. Acts 3:24 At what time the kingdom of Israel was established.
l. Acts 3:25 The Jews that believe are the first begotten in the kingdom of God.
m. Acts 3:25 For whom the Prophets were specially appointed.
n. Acts 3:26 Given to the world, or raised from the dead, and advanced to his kingdom.

ACTS 3

1. Acts 5:30
2. Deut. 18:15; Acts 7:37
3. Gen. 12:3; Gal. 3:8

ACTS 4

a. Acts 4:1 None are commonly more diligent or bolder enemies of the Church, than such as profess themselves to be head builders: but the more they rage, the more constantly the faithful servants of God do continue.
b. Acts 4:1 The Jews had certain garrisons for the guard and safety of the Temple and holy things, Matt. 26:65. These garrisons had a Captain, such as Eleazarus Ananias, the high Priest's son was, in the time of the war that was in Judea, being a very impudent and proud young man, Josephus, lib. 2, of the taking of Judea.
c. Acts 4:4 While they thought to diminish the number, they increased them.
d. Acts 4:5 These were they that made the Sanhedrin, which were all of the tribe of Judah, until Herod used that cruelty against David's stock.
e. Acts 4:6 Of whom the high Priests were wont to be chosen and made, the execution of the yearly office being now changed them.
f. Acts 4:7 Against such as brag of a succession of persons, without a succession of doctrine, and by that means beat down the true ministers of the word, so far forth as they are able.
g. Acts 4:7 By what authority.
h. Acts 4:9 Wolves which succeed true pastors plead their own cause, and not God's neither the Churches'.
i. Acts 4:10 He is indeed a true Shepherd, that teacheth his sheep to hang upon Christ only, as upon one that is not dead, but hath conquered death, and hath all rule in his own hand.
j. Acts 4:12 Of God.
k. Acts 4:12 There is no other man, or no other power and authority whatsoever: which kind of speech being usual among the Jews, rose upon this, that when we are in danger, we call upon them at whose hands we look for help.
l. Acts 4:12 Anywhere: and this setteth forth unto us the largeness of Christ's kingdom.
m. Acts 4:13 The good liberty and boldness of the servants of God doeth yet thus much good that such as lay hid under a vizard of zeal, do at length bewray themselves to be indeed wicked men.
n. Acts 4:13 The word used here, is Idiot, which being spoken in comparison had to a Magistrate, betokeneth a private man, but when we speak of sciences and studies, it signifieth one that is unlearned: and in accompt of honor and estimation it importeth one of base degree, and no estimation.
o. Acts 4:15 Laid their heads together.
p. Acts 4:16 He that flattereth himself in ignorance, cometh at length to do open wickedness, and that against his own conscience.
q. Acts 4:19 We must so obey men to whom we are subject, that especially and before all things we obey God.
r. Acts 4:21 So far off are the wicked from doing what they list, that contrariwise God useth even that to the setting forth of his glory, which he giveth them leave to do.
s. Acts 4:23 The Apostles communicate their troubles with the Congregation.
t. Acts 4:24 We ought neither to be afraid of the threatenings of our enemies, neither yet foolishly condemn their rage and madness against us: but we have to set against their force and malice, an earnest thinking upon the power and good will of God (both which we do manifestly behold in Christ) and so flee to the aid and succor of our Father.
u. Acts 4:27 Although the people of Israel was but one people, yet the plural number is here used, not so much for the twelve tribes, every one of which made a people, as for the great multitude of them, as though many nations had assembled themselves together, as Judg. 5:14.
v. Acts 4:28 The wicked execute God's counsel, though they think nothing of it, but they are not therefore without fault.
w. Acts 4:28 Thou hadst determined of thine absolute authority and power.
x. Acts 4:31 God witnesseth to his Church by a visible sign, that it is he that will establish it by shaking the powers both of heaven and earth.
y. Acts 4:32 An example of the true Church, wherein there is consent as well in doctrine as in charity one towards another: And the Pastors deliver true doctrine both sincerely, and constantly.
z. Acts 4:32 They agreed both in counsel, will, and purposes.

that were sold, 35 And laid it down at the Apostles' feet, and it was distributed
unto every man, according as he had need. 36 Also Joses which was called of the
Apostles, Barnabas (that is by interpretation, the son of consolation) being a Levite,
and of the country of Cyprus, 37 Where as he had land, sold it, and brought the
money, and laid it down at the Apostles' feet.

5

1 Ananias for his deceit in keeping back part of price, 5 falleth down dead, 10 and likewise Sapphira his wife. 12 Through divers the Apostles' miracles, 14 the faith is increased. 18 The Apostles that were imprisoned, 19 are delivered by an Angel, 26 and being before the Synod of the Priests, 36 through Gamaliel's counsel they are kept alive, 40 and beaten: 41 They glorify God.

1 But [a]a certain man named Ananias, with Sapphira his wife, sold a posses-
sion, 2 And [b]kept away part of the price, his wife also being of counsel, and
brought a certain part, and laid it down at the Apostles' feet. 3 Then said Peter,
Ananias, why hath Satan [c]filled thine heart, that thou shouldest [d]lie unto the holy
Ghost, and keep away part of the price of this possession? 4 While it remained,
appertained it not unto thee? and after it was sold, was it not in thine own power?
how is it that thou hast [e]conceived this thing in thine heart? thou hast not lied
unto men, but unto God. 5 Now when Ananias heard these words, he fell down,
and gave up the ghost. Then great fear came on all them that heard these thin-
gs. 6 And the young men rose up, and took him up, and carried him out, and bu-
ried him. 7 And it came to pass about the space of three hours after, that his wife
came in, ignorant of that which was done. 8 And Peter said unto her, Tell me,
sold ye the land for so much? And she said, Yea, for so much. 9 Then Peter said
unto her, Why have ye agreed together, to [f]tempt the Spirit of the Lord? behold,
the feet of them which have buried thine husband, are at the [g]door, and shall carry
thee out. 10 Then she fell down straightway at his feet, and yielded up the ghost:
and the young men came in, and found her dead, and carried her out, and buried
her by her husband. 11 [h]And great fear came on all the Church, and on as many
as heard these things. 12 Thus by the hands of the Apostles were many signs and
wonders showed among the people (and they were all with one accord in Solomon's
porch. 13 And of the other durst no man join himself to them: nevertheless the
people [i]magnified them. 14 Also the number of them that believed in the Lord,
both of men and women, grew more and more) 15 Insomuch that they brought
the sick into the streets, and laid them on beds and couches, that at the leastway the
shadow of Peter, when he came by, might shadow some of them. 16 There came
also a multitude out of the cities round about unto Jerusalem, bringing sick folks,
and them which were vexed with unclean spirits, who were all healed. 17 [j]Then
the chief Priest rose up, and all they that were with him (which was the [k]sect of the
Sadducees) and were full of indignation, 18 And laid hands on the Apostles, and
put them in the common prison. 19 [l]But the Angel of the Lord by night ope-
ned the prison doors, and brought them forth, and said, 20 [m]Go your way, and
stand in the Temple, and speak to the people, all the [n]words of this life. 21 [o]So
when they heard it, they entered into the Temple early in the morning, and taught.
And the chief Priest came, and they that were with him, and called the Council
together, and all the Elders of the children of Israel, and sent to the prison, to cau-
se them to be brought. 22 But when the officers came, and found them not in
the prison, they returned and told it, 23 Saying, Certainly we found the prison
shut as sure as was possible, and the keepers standing without, before the doors:
but when we had opened, we found no man within. 24 Then when the chief
Priest and the captain of the Temple, and the high Priests heard these things, they
doubted of them, whereunto this would grow. 25 [p]Then came one and showed
them, saying, Behold, the men that ye put in prison, are standing in the Temple,
and teach the people. 26 [q]Then went the captain with the officers, and brought
them without violence (for they feared the people, lest they should have been sto-
ned.) 27 And when they had brought them, they set them before the Council,
and the chief Priest asked them, 28 [r]Saying, Did we not straightly command
you, that ye should not teach in this name? and behold, ye have filled Jerusalem
with your doctrine, and ye would [s]bring this man's blood upon us. 29 [t]Then
Peter and the Apostles answered, and said, We ought rather to obey God than
men. 30 [u]The [1]God of our fathers hath raised up Jesus whom ye slew, and han-
ged on a tree. 31 Him hath God lifted up with his right hand, to be a Prince and
a Savior, to give repentance to Israel, and forgiveness of sins. 32 [v]And we are his
witnesses concerning these things which we say: yea, and the holy Ghost, whom
God hath given to them that obey him. 33 Now when they heard it, they [w]brast
for anger, and consulted to slay them. 34 [x]Then stood there up in the Council
a certain Pharisee named Gamaliel, a doctor of the Law, honored of all the peo-
ple, and commanded to put the Apostles forth a little space, 35 And said unto
them, Men of Israel, take heed to yourselves, what ye intend to do touching these
men. 36 [y]For before these times, rose up Theudas [z]boasting himself, to whom
resorted a number of men, about a four hundred, who was slain: and they all whi-
ch obeyed him were scattered, and brought to naught. 37 After this man, arose
up Judas of Galilee, in the days of the tribute, and drew away much people after
him: he also perished, and all that obeyed him, were scattered abroad. 38 And
now I say unto you, [aa]Refrain yourselves from these men, and let them alone: for
if this counsel, or this work be of [ab]men, it will come to naught: 39 But if it be
of God, ye cannot destroy it, lest ye be found even fighters against God. 40 And
to him they agreed, and called the Apostles: and when they had beaten them,
they commanded that they should not speak in the Name of Jesus, and let them
go. 41 [ac]So they departed from the Council, rejoicing, that they were counted
worthy to suffer rebuke for his Name. 42 And daily in the [ad]Temple, and from
house to house they ceased not to teach, and preach Jesus Christ.

6

1 The Apostles, 3 appoint the office of Deaconship, 5 to seven chosen men: 8 Of whom Stephen, full of faith, is one: 12 He is taken, 13 and accused as a transgressor of Moses' Law.

1 And [a]in those days, as the number of the disciples grew, there arose a mur-
muring of the [b]Grecians towards the Hebrews, because their widows were ne-
glected in the [c]daily ministering. 2 [d]Then the twelve called the multitude of
the disciples together, and said, It is not [e]meet that we should leave the word of
God to serve the [f]tables. 3 [g]Wherefore brethren, look you out among you seven
men of honest report, and full of the holy Ghost, and of wisdom, which we may
appoint to this business. 4 And we will give ourselves continually to prayer, and
to the ministration of the word. 5 And the saying pleased the whole multitude:
and they chose Stephen a man full of faith and of the holy Ghost, and [1]Philip, and
Prochorus, and Nicanor, and Timon, and Parmenas, and Nicolas a Proselyte of

---

aa. Acts 4:34 True charity helpeth the necessity of the poor with its own loss: but so, that all things be done well and orderly.

ACTS 4

1. Ps. 118:12; Isa. 28:16; Matt. 21:42; Mark 12:10; Luke 21:17; Rom. 9:33; 1 Pet. 2:7
2. Ps. 2:1
3. Acts 2:44

ACTS 5

a. Acts 5:1 Luke showeth by contrary examples, how great a sin hypocrisy is, especially in them which under a false pretence and cloak of zeal would seem to shine and be chief in the Church.
b. Acts 5:2 Craftily took away.
c. Acts 5:3 Fully possessed.
d. Acts 5:3 For when they had appointed that farm or possession for the Church, they stuck not at it to keep away a part of the price, as though they had had to do with men, and not with God, and therefore he saith afterward that they tempted God.
e. Acts 5:4 Hereby is declared an advised and purposed deceit, and the fault of the man in admitting the devil's suggestions.
f. Acts 5:9 Look how oft men do things with an evil conscience; so oft they pronounce sentence against themselves, and as much as in them lieth, provoke God to anger, as of set purpose, minding to try whether he be just and almighty or no.
g. Acts 5:9 Are at hand.
h. Acts 5:11 The Lord by his marvelous virtue bridleth some, that they may not hurt the Church: other some he awe and fear: and other some he allureth unto him.
i. Acts 5:13 Highly praised them.
j. Acts 5:17 The more that the Church increaseth, the more increaseth the rage of Satan, and therefore they proceed from threatenings, to prisoning.
k. Acts 5:17 The word which is used here, is Heresy, which signifieth a choice, and so is taken for a right form of learning, or faction, or study and course of life, which the Latins call a sect: at the first this word was indifferently used, but at length, it came to be taken only in evil part, whereupon came the name of Heretic, which is taken for one that goeth astray from sound and wholesome doctrine after such sort, that he setteth light by the judgment of God and his Church, and continueth in his opinion, and breaketh the peace of the Church.
l. Acts 5:19 Angels are made servants of the servants of God.
m. Acts 5:20 God doth therefore deliver his, that they may more stoutly provoke his enemies.
n. Acts 5:20 Words, whereby the way unto life is showed.
o. Acts 5:21 God mocketh his enemies' attempts from above.
p. Acts 5:25 The more openly that Christ's virtue showeth itself, the more increaseth the madness of his enemies which conspire against him.
q. Acts 5:26 Tyrants which fear not God, are constrained to fear his servants.
r. Acts 5:28 It is the property of tyrants to set out their own commandments as right and reason, be they never so wicked.
s. Acts 5:28 Make us guilty of murdering, that man whom yet they will not vouchsafe to name.
t. Acts 5:29 We ought to obey no man, but so far forth as obeying him, we may obey God.
u. Acts 5:30 Christ is appointed and indeed declareth Prince and preserver of his Church in despite of his enemies.
v. Acts 5:32 It is not sufficient for us that there is a right end, but we must also according to our vocation go on forward till we come unto it.
w. Acts 5:33 This reckoneth that they were in a most vehement rage, and marvelously disquieted in mind, for it is a borrowed kind of speech taken from them which are harrishly cut in sunder with a saw.
x. Acts 5:34 Christ findeth defenders of his cause even in the very routs of his enemies, so oft as he thinketh it needful.
y. Acts 5:36 In matters of religion we must take good heed that we attempt nothing under a color of zeal, beside our vocation.
z. Acts 5:36 To be of some fame.
aa. Acts 5:38 He dissuadeth his fellows from murdering the Apostles, neither doth he think it good to refer the matter to the Roman Magistrate, for the Jews could abide nothing worse, than to have the tyranny of the Romans confirmed.
ab. Acts 5:38 If it be counterfeit and devised.
ac. Acts 5:41 The Apostles, accustomed to suffer and bear words, are at length inured to bear stripes, yet so, that by that means they become stronger.
ad. Acts 5:42 Both publicly and privately.

ACTS 5

1. Acts 3:13

ACTS 6

a. Acts 6:1 When Satan has assailed the Church without, and that to small purpose and in vain, he assaileth it within, with civil dissension and strife betwixt themselves: but the Apostles take occasion thereby to set order in the Church.
b. Acts 6:1 Of their parts which of Grecians became religious Jews.
c. Acts 6:1 In the bestowing of alms according to their necessity.
d. Acts 6:2 The office of preaching the word and dispensing the goods of the Church, are different one from another, and not rashly to be joined together, as the Apostles do here institute: And the Apostles do not choose so much as the Deacons without the consent of the Church.
e. Acts 6:2 It is such a matter, as we may in no wise accept of it.
f. Acts 6:2 Banquets though by the name of tables, other offices are also meant, which are annexed to it, such as pertain to the care of the poor.
g. Acts 6:3 In choosing of Deacons (and much more of Ministers) there must be examination both of their learning and manners of life.

Antioch, 6 [h]Which they set before the Apostles: and they prayed, and [i]laid their
hands on them. 7 [j]And the word of God increased, and the number of the disci-
ples was multiplied in Jerusalem greatly, and a great company of the Priests were
obedient to the [k]faith. 8 [l]Now Stephen full of faith and [m]power, did great won-
ders and miracles among the people. 9 [n]Then there arose certain of the [o]Synago-
gue, which are called Libertines, and Cyrenians, and of Alexandria, and of them of
Cilicia, and of Asia, and disputed with Stephen. 10 [p]But they were not able to
resist the wisdom, and the Spirit by the which he spake. 11 Then they suborned
men, which said, We have heard him speak blasphemous words against Moses,
and God. 12 [q]Thus they moved the people and the Elders, and the Scribes: and
running upon him, caught him, and brought him to the Council, 13 [r]And set
forth false witnesses, which said, This man ceaseth not to speak blasphemous words
against this holy place, and the Law. 14 For we have heard him say, that this
Jesus of Nazareth shall destroy this place, and shall change the ordinances which
Moses gave us. 15 And as all that sat in the Council looked steadfastly on him,
they [s]saw his face as it had been the face of an Angel.

7

1 Stephen pleading his cause, showeth that God chose the Fathers, 20 before Moses was born, 42 and before the Temple was built: 44 And that all outward ceremonies were ordained according to the heavenly Pattern. 54 The Jews gnashing their teeth, 59 stone him.

1 Then [a]said the chief Priest, Are these things so? 2 [b]And he said, Ye men,
brethren, and Fathers, hearken, [1]That God of [c]glory appeared unto our father
Abraham, while he was in [d]Mesopotamia, before he dwelt in Haran, 3 And said
unto him, Come out of thy country, and from thy kindred, and come into the land
which I shall show thee. 4 Then came he out of the land of the Chaldeans, and
dwelt in Haran. And after that his father was dead, God brought him from thence
into this land, wherein ye now dwell, 5 And he gave him none inheritance in it,
[e]no not the breadth of a foot: yet he [f]promised that he would give it to him for a
possession, and to his [2]seed after him, when as yet he had no child. 6 But God
spake thus, that his seed should be a sojourner in a strange land: and that they
should keep it in bondage, and entreat it evil [g]four hundred years. 7 But the na-
tion to whom they shall be in bondage, will I judge, saith God: and after that, they
shall come forth and serve me in this place. 8 [3]He gave him also the covenant of
circumcision: and to Abraham begat [4]Isaac, and circumcised him the eighth day:
and Isaac begat [5]Jacob, and Jacob the twelve [6]Patriarchs. 9 [h]And the Patriarchs
moved with envy, sold [7]Joseph into Egypt: but God was [i]with him, 10 And de-
livered him out of all his afflictions, and [8]gave him [j]favor and wisdom in the sight
of Pharaoh king of Egypt, who made him governor over Egypt, and over his who-
le house. 11 Then came there a famine over all the land of Egypt and Canaan,
and great affliction, that our fathers found no sustenance. 12 But when [9]Jacob
heard that there was corn in Egypt, he sent our fathers first: 13 [10]And at the
second time Joseph was known of his brethren, and Joseph's kindred was made
known unto Pharaoh. 14 Then sent Joseph and caused his father to be brou-
ght, and all his kindred, even threescore and fifteen souls. 15 So [11]Jacob went
down into Egypt, and he [12]died, and our fathers, 16 And were [k]removed into
Shechem, and were put in the sepulcher, that Abraham had bought [13]for money
of the sons of Hamor, son of Shechem. 17 But when the time of the promise
drew near, which God had sworn to Abraham, the people [14]grew and multiplied in
Egypt, 18 Till another King arose, which knew not Joseph. 19 The same [l]de-
alt subtly with our kindred, and evil entreated our fathers, and made them to cast
out their young children, that they should not remain alive. 20 [15]The same time
was Moses born and was [m]acceptable unto God: which was nourished up in his
father's house three months. 21 And when he was cast out, Pharaoh's daughter
took him up, and nourished him for her own son. 22 And Moses was learned in
all the wisdom of the Egyptians, and was mighty in words and in deeds. 23 Now
when he was full forty years old, it came into his heart to visit his brethren, the
children of Israel. 24 [16]And when he saw one of them suffer wrong, he defended
him, and avenged his quarrel that had the harm done to him, and smote the Egyp-
tian. 25 For he supposed his brethren would have understood, that God by his
hand should give them deliverance: but they understood it not. 26 [17]And the
next day, he showed himself unto them as they strove, and would have set them at
one again, saying, Sirs, ye are brethren: why do ye wrong one to another? 27 But
he that did his neighbor wrong, thrust him away, saying, Who made thee a prince,
and a judge over us? 28 Wilt thou kill me, as thou didst the Egyptian yester-
day? 29 Then fled Moses at that saying, and was a stranger in the land of Midian,
where he begat two sons. 30 And when forty years were expired, there appea-
red to him in the [18]wilderness of mount Sinai, an [n]Angel of the Lord in a flame
of fire, in a bush. 31 And when Moses saw it, he wondered at the sight: and as
he drew near to consider it, the voice of the Lord came unto him, saying, 32 I
am the God of thy fathers, the God of Abraham, and the God of Isaac, and the
God of Jacob. Then Moses trembled, and durst not behold it. 33 Then the Lord
said to him, Put off thy shoes from thy feet: for the place where thou standest, is
holy ground. 34 I have seen, I have seen the affliction of my people, which is in
Egypt, and I have heard their groaning, and am come down to deliver them: and
now come, and I will send thee into Egypt. 35 This Moses whom they forsook,
saying, Who made thee a prince and a judge? the same God sent for a prince, and
a deliverer by the [o]hand of the Angel which appeared to him in the bush. 36 He
[19]brought them out, doing wonders, and miracles in the land of Egypt, and in the
Red Sea, and in the wilderness [20]forty years. 37 [p]This is that Moses, which said
unto the children of Israel, [21]A Prophet shall the Lord your God raise up unto you,
even of your brethren, like unto me: him shall ye hear. 38 [22]This is he that was in
the Congregation, in the wilderness with the Angel, which spake to him in mount
Sinai, and with our fathers, who received the lively oracles to give unto us. 39 To
whom our fathers would not obey, but refused, and in their hearts turned back
again into Egypt, 40 Saying unto Aaron, [23]Make us gods that may go before
us: for we know not what is become of this Moses that brought us out of the land
of Egypt. 41 And they made a [q]calf in those days, and offered sacrifice unto the
idol, and rejoiced in the works of their own hands. 42 Then God turned him-
self away, and [r]gave them up to serve the [s]host of heaven, as it is written in the
book of the Prophets, [24]O house of Israel, have ye offered to me slain beasts and
sacrifices by the space of forty years in the wilderness? 43 And ye [t]took up the
Tabernacle of Moloch, and the star of your god Remphan, figures, which ye made
to worship them: therefore I will carry you away beyond Babylon. 44 [u]Our fa-
thers had the Tabernacle of [v]witness in the wilderness, as he had appointed, spe-
aking unto [25]Moses, that he should make it according to the fashion that he had
seen. 45 [26]Which tabernacle also our fathers [w]received, and brought in with Je-
sus into the [x]possession of the Gentiles, which God drove out [y]before our fathers,
unto the days of David: 46 [27]Who found favor before God, and desired that he

---

h. Acts 6:6 The ancient Church did with laying on of hands, as it were consecrate to the Lord, such as were lawfully elected.
i. Acts 6:6 This ceremony of laying on of hands came from the Jews, who used this order both in public affairs, and offering of sacrifices, and also in private prayers and blessings, as appeareth Gen. 28, and the Church observed this ceremony, 1 Tim. 5:22; Acts 8:17, but here is no mention made either of cream, or shaving, or raising, or crossing, etc.
j. Acts 6:7 An happy end of temptation.
k. Acts 6:7 This is the figure Metonymy, meaning by faith, the doctrine of the Gospel which engendereth faith.
l. Acts 6:8 God exerciseth his Church first with evil words and slanders, then with imprisonments, afterward with scourgings, and by these means prepareth it in such sort, that at length he causeth it to encounter with Satan and the world, even to bloodshed and death, and that with good success.
m. Acts 6:8 Excellent and singular gifts.
n. Acts 6:9 Schools and Universities were of old time addicted to false pastors, and were the instruments of Satan to blow abroad and defend false doctrines.
o. Acts 6:9 Of the company and College as it were.
p. Acts 6:10 False teachers, because they will not be overcome, flee from disputations to manifest and open slandering and false accusations.
q. Acts 6:12 The first bloody persecution of the Church of Christ began and sprang from a Council of Priests by the suggestion of the University doctors.
r. Acts 6:13 An example of cavillers or false accusers, which gather false conclusions of things that are well uttered and spoken.
s. Acts 6:15 Hereby it appeareth that Stephen had an excellent and goodly countenance, having a quiet and settled mind, a good conscience, and sure persuasion that his cause was just: for seeing he was to speak before the people, God beautified his countenance, to the end that with the very beholding of him, the Jews' minds might be pierced and amazed.

ACTS 6

1. Acts 21:8

ACTS 7

a. Acts 7:1 Stephen is admitted to plead his cause, but to this end and purpose, that under a cloak, and color of Law, he might be condemned.
b. Acts 7:2 Stephen witnesseth unto the Jews, that he acknowledgeth the true fathers, and the only true God: and showeth moreover, that they are more ancient than the Temple, with all that service appointed by the Law, and therefore they ought to lay another foundation of true religion, that is to say, the free covenant that God made with the fathers.
c. Acts 7:2 That mighty God full of glory and majesty.
d. Acts 7:2 When he saith afterward, verse 4, that Abraham came out of Chaldea, it is evident that Mesopotamia contained Chaldea which was near unto it, and bordering upon it, and so writeth Plinius, book 6, chap. 27.
e. Acts 7:5 Not so much ground as to set his foot upon.
f. Acts 7:5 The promise of the possession was certain and belonged to Abraham, though his posterity enjoyed it a great while after his death: and this is the figure Synecdoche.
g. Acts 7:6 There are reckoned four hundred years, from the beginning of Abraham's progeny, which was at the birth of Isaac: and four hundred and thirty years which are spoken of by Paul, Gal. 3:17, from the time that Abraham and his father departed together out of Ur of the Chaldeans.
h. Acts 7:9 Stephen reckoneth up diligently the horrible mischiefs of some of the Fathers, to teach the Jews that they ought not rashly to rest in the authority or examples of the Fathers.
i. Acts 7:9 By this kind of speech, is meant the peculiar favor that God showeth men: for he seemeth to be away from them, whom he helpeth not, and on the other side, he is with them whom he delivereth out of whatsoever great troubles.
j. Acts 7:10 Gave him favor in Pharaoh's sight for his wisdom.
k. Acts 7:16 The Patriarchs the sons of Jacob, though there be mention made of no more than Joseph, Josh. 24:32.
l. Acts 7:19 He devised a subtle invention against our stock, in that he commanded all the males to be cast out.
m. Acts 7:20 That child was born through God's merciful goodness and favor, to be of a goodly and fair countenance.
n. Acts 7:30 Now he calleth the Son of God an Angel, for he is the Angel of great counsel, and therefore, straightway after he showeth him, saying to Moses, I am that God of thy Fathers, etc.
o. Acts 7:35 By the power.
p. Acts 7:37 He acknowledgeth Moses for the lawgiver, but so that he proveth by his own witness, that the Law had respect to a more perfect thing, that is to say, to the prophetic office which tended to Christ, the head of all Prophets.
q. Acts 7:41 This was the superstition of the Egyptians' idolatry: for they worshipped Apis a strange and marvelous calf, and made goodly images of Kine, Herodias, lib. 2.
r. Acts 7:42 Being destitute and void of his Spirit, he gave them up to Satan, and wicked lusts to worship stars.
s. Acts 7:42 By the host of heaven, here he meaneth not the Angels, but the moon and sun and other stars.
t. Acts 7:43 You took it upon your shoulders and carried it.
u. Acts 7:44 Moses indeed erected a Tabernacle, but that was to call them back to that form which he had seen in the mountain.
v. Acts 7:44 That is, of the covenant.
w. Acts 7:45 Delivered from hand to hand.

might find a tabernacle for the God of Jacob. **47** [z,28]But Solomon built him an
house. **48** Howbeit the most High [29]dwelleth not in temples made with hands,
as saith the Prophet, **49** [30]Heaven is my throne, and earth is my footstool: what
house will ye build for me, saith the Lord? or what place is it that I should rest
in? **50** Hath not mine hand made all these things? **51** [aa,31]Ye stiff-necked and
of [ab]uncircumcised hearts and ears, ye have always resisted the holy Ghost: as your
fathers did, so do you. **52** Which of the Prophets have not your fathers persecu-
ted? and they have slain them, which showed before of the coming of that Just, of
whom ye are now the betrayers and murderers, **53** [32]Which have received the
law by the [ac]ordinance of Angels, and have not kept it. **54** [ad]But when they he-
ard these things, their hearts brast for anger, and they gnashed at him with their
teeth. **55** [ae]But he being full of the holy Ghost, looked steadfastly into heaven,
and saw the glory of God, and Jesus [af]standing at the right hand of God, **56** And
said, Behold, I see the heavens open, and the Son of man standing at the right
hand of God. **57** [ag]Then they gave a shout with a loud voice, and stopped their
ears, and [ah]ran upon him violently all at once, **58** And cast him out of the city,
and stoned him: and the [ai]witnesses laid down their clothes at a young man's feet,
named Saul. **59** And they stoned Stephen, who called on God, and said, Lord
Jesus receive my spirit. **60** [aj]And he kneeled down, and cried with a loud voice,
Lord, [ak]lay not this sin to their charge. And when he had thus spoken, he [al]slept.

8

2 The godly make lamentation for Stephen. 3 Saul maketh havoc of the Church. 5 Philip preacheth Christ at Samaria. 9 Simon Magus, 13 his covetousness reproved. 26 Philip 27 cometh to the Ethiopian Eunuch, 38 and baptizeth him.

1 And [a]Saul consented to his death. And at that time, there was a great perse-
cution against the Church which was at Jerusalem, and they were all scattered abro-
ad throughout the regions of Judea and of Samaria, except the Apostles. **2** [b]Then
certain men fearing God, [c]carried Stephen among them, to be buried, and made
great lamentation for him. **3** [d]But Saul made havoc of the Church, and entered
into every house, and drew out both men and women, and put them into pri-
son. **4** Therefore they that were scattered abroad, went to and fro preaching the
word. **5** [e]Then came Philip into the city of Samaria, and preached Christ unto
them. **6** And the people gave heed unto those things which Philip spake, with
one accord, hearing and seeing the miracles which he did. **7** For unclean spiri-
ts crying with a loud voice, came out of many that were possessed of them: and
many taken with palsies, and that halted, were healed. **8** And there was great joy
in that city. **9** [f]And there was before in the city, a certain man called Simon, whi-
ch used [g]witchcraft, and [h]bewitched the people of Samaria, saying that he himself
was some great man, **10** To whom they gave heed from the least to the grea-
test, saying, This man is that great power of God. **11** And they gave heed unto
him, because that of long time he had bewitched them with sorceries. **12** But
as soon as they believed Philip, which preached the things that concerned the
kingdom of God, and the Name of Jesus Christ, they were baptized both men
and women. **13** [i]Then Simon himself believed also, and was baptized, and
continued with Philip, and wondered, when he saw the signs and great miracles
which were done. **14** [j]Now when the Apostles, which were at Jerusalem, heard
say, that Samaria had received the word of God, they sent unto them Peter and
John. **15** Which when they were come down, prayed for them, that they might
receive the [k]holy Ghost. **16** (For as yet he was fallen down on none of them,
but they were baptized only in the Name of the Lord Jesus.) **17** Then laid they
their hands on them, and they received the holy Ghost. **18** [l]And when Simon
saw that through laying on of the Apostles' hands the holy Ghost was given, he
offered them money, **19** Saying, Give me also this power, that on whomsoever
I lay the hands, he may receive the holy Ghost. **20** [m]Then said Peter unto him,
Thy money perish with thee, because thou thinkest that the gift of God may be
obtained with money. **21** Thou hast neither part nor fellowship in this [n]business:
for thine heart is not [o]right in the sight of God. **22** [p]Repent therefore of this thy
wickedness, and pray God, that if it be possible, the thought of thine heart may
be forgiven thee. **23** For I see that thou art in the [q]gall of bitterness, and in the
[r]bond of iniquity. **24** Then answered Simon, and said, Pray ye to the Lord for
me, that none of these things which ye have spoken, come upon me. **25** So they,
when they had testified and preached the word of the Lord, returned to Jerusalem,
and preached the Gospel in many towns of the Samaritans. **26** [s]Then the Angel
of the Lord spake unto Philip, saying, Arise, and go toward the South unto the way
that goeth down from Jerusalem unto Gaza, which is waste. **27** And he arose
and went on: and behold, a certain Eunuch of Ethiopia, Candace the Queen of
the Ethiopians' [t]chief Governor, who had the rule of all her treasure, and came to
Jerusalem to worship. **28** And as he returned sitting in his chariot, he read Isa-
iah the Prophet. **29** Then the Spirit said unto Philip, Go near and join thyself to
yonder chariot. **30** And Philip ran thither, and heard him read the Prophet Isa-
iah, and said, But understandest thou what thou readest? **31** And he said, How
can I, except I had [u]a guide? And he desired Philip, that he would come up and sit
with him. **32** [v]Now the place of the Scripture which he read, was this, [I]He was
lead as a sheep to the slaughter: and like a lamb dumb before his shearer, so opened
he not his mouth. **33** In his [w]humility his judgment hath been exalted: but who
shall declare his [x]generation? for his life is taken from the earth. **34** Then the Eu-
nuch answered Philip, and said, I pray thee, of whom speaketh the Prophet this?
of himself, or of some other man? **35** Then Philip opened his mouth, and began
at the same Scripture, and preached unto him Jesus. **36** And as they went on
their way, they came unto a certain water, and the Eunuch said, See, here is water:
what doth let me to be baptized? **37** [y]And Philip said unto him, If thou believest
with all thine heart, thou mayest. Then he answered, and said, [z]I believe that that
Jesus Christ is that Son of God. **38** Then he commanded the chariot to stand
still: and they went down both into the water, both Philip and the Eunuch, and he

---

x. Acts 7:45 By the figure Metonymy, for the countries which the Gentiles possessed.

y. Acts 7:45 God drove them out, that they should yield up the possession of those countries to our fathers, when they entered into the land.

z. Acts 7:47 Solomon built a Temple, according to God's commandment, but not with any such condition, that the Majesty of God should be enclosed therein.

aa. Acts 7:51 Stephen moved with the zeal of God, at length judgeth his own judges.

ab. Acts 7:51 They are of uncircumcised hearts, which lie drowned still in the sins of nature, and stick fast in them: for otherwise all the Jews were circumcised as touching the flesh, and therefore there were two kinds of circumcision, Rom. 2:28.

ac. Acts 7:53 By the ministry of Angels.

ad. Acts 7:54 The more Satan is pressed, the more he brasteth out into an open rage.

ae. Acts 7:55 The nearer that the Martyrs approach to death, the nearer they beholding Christ, do rise up even into heaven.

af. Acts 7:55 Ready to confirm him in the confession of the truth, and to receive him to him.

ag. Acts 7:57 The zeal of hypocrites and superstitious people, breaketh out at length into most open madness.

ah. Acts 7:57 This was done in a rage and fury: for at that time the Jews could put no man to death by law, as they confess before Pilate, saying that it was not lawful for them to put any man to death, and therefore it is reported by Josephus, lib. 20, that Ananus a Sadducee slew James the brother of the Lord, and for so doing, was accused before Albinus the President of the country.

ai. Acts 7:58 It was appointed by the Law, that the witnesses should cast the first stones, Deut. 17:7.

aj. Acts 7:60 Faith and charity never forsake the true servants of God, even to the last breath.

ak. Acts 7:60 The word which he useth here noteth out such a kind of imputing or laying to one's charge, as remaineth firm, and steady forever, never to be remitted.

al. Acts 7:60 See 1 Thess. 4:13.

ACTS 7

1. Gen. 12:4
2. Gen. 15:13
3. Gen. 17:9
4. Gen. 21:3
5. Gen. 25:14
6. Gen. 29:33; Gen. 30:5; Gen. 35:23
7. Gen. 37:18
8. Gen. 41:37
9. Gen. 42:1
10. Gen. 45:4
11. Gen. 46:5
12. Gen. 49:33
13. Gen. 23:16
14. Exod. 1:7
15. Exod. 2:2
16. Exod. 2:11
17. Exod. 2:13
18. Exod. 3:2
19. Exod. 7–10; 13–14
20. Exod. 16:1–3
21. Deut. 18:15; Acts 3:22
22. Exod. 19:2
23. Exod. 32:1
24. Amos 5:25
25. Exod. 25:40; Heb. 8:5
26. Josh. 3:14
27. 2 Sam. 7:2; Ps. 132:5
28. 1 Chron. 17:12; 1 Kings 6:1
29. Acts 17:24
30. Isa. 66:1
31. Jer. 9:26; Ezek. 44:9
32. Exod. 19:16; Gal. 3:19

ACTS 8

a. Acts 8:1 Christ useth the rage of his enemies to the spreading forth and enlarging of his kingdom.

b. Acts 8:2 The godly mourn for Stephen after his death, and bury him, showing therein an example of singular faith and charity: but no man prayeth to him.

c. Acts 8:2 Amongst all the duties of charity which the godly use, there is no mention made of shrining up of relics.

d. Acts 8:3 The dispersion or scattering abroad of the faithful, is the joining together of Churches.

e. Acts 8:5 Philip, who was before a Deacon in Jerusalem, is made of God extraordinarily an Evangelist.

f. Acts 8:9 Christ overcometh Satan so oft as he listeth, and carrieth him about as it were in a triumph in the sight of them, whom he deceived and bewitched.

g. Acts 8:9 The word which is used in this place was at the first taken in good part, and is borrowed out of the Persians' language, who call their wise men by that name, but afterward it was taken in evil part.

h. Acts 8:9 He had so allured the Samaritans with his witchcrafts, that as blind and mad harebrains they were wholly addicted to him.

i. Acts 8:13 The wicked and the very reprobate are constrained oftentimes to taste of the good gift of God, but they cast it up again forthwith.

j. Acts 8:14 Peter not chief, but as an ambassador sent from the whole company of the Apostles, and John his companion according to the authority which was committed unto them, confirm and build up the Churches of Samaria, whose foundation had been laid afore by Philip.

k. Acts 8:15 Those excellent gifts, which are necessary, especially for them that were to be appointed rulers and governors of the Church.

l. Acts 8:18 Ambition and covetousness do at length pluck the hypocrites out of their dens.

m. Acts 8:20 They are the successors of Simon Magus, and not of Simon Peter, which either buy or sell holy things.

n. Acts 8:21 In this doctrine which I preach.

o. Acts 8:21 Is not upright in deed, and without dissembling.

p. Acts 8:22 We must hope well even of the vilest sinners, so long and so far forth as we may.

q. Acts 8:23 He calleth the inward malice of the heart, and that venomous and devilish wickedness wherewith this Magician was wholly replenished, the gall of bitterness: and he is said to be in the gall as though he were wholly overwhelmed with gall, and buried in it.

r. Acts 8:23 Entangled in the bonds of iniquity.

s. Acts 8:26 Christ who calleth freely whom he listeth, doth now use Philip who thought on no such matter, to instruct and baptize the Eunuch at unawares, and by this means extendeth the limits of his kingdom even into Ethiopia.

t. Acts 8:27 A man of great wealth and authority with Candaces: Now this word Candaces is a common name to all the Queens of Ethiopia.

u. Acts 8:31 To show me the way how to understand it.

v. Acts 8:32 Those things which seem most to come by chance or fortune (as men term it) are governed by the secret providence of God.

w. Acts 8:33 The Hebrew text readeth it thus, Out of a narrow strait, and out of judgment was he taken: whereby the narrow strait, he meaneth the grave and the very bands of death, and by judgment, the punishment which was laid upon him, and the miserable state which Christ took upon him for our sakes, in bearing his Father's wrath.

x. Acts 8:33 How long his age shall last: for Christ having once risen from the dead, dieth no more, Rom. 6:9.

y. Acts 8:37 Profession of faith is requisite in baptizing of them which are of years, and therefore it is evident that we are not then first ingrafted into Christ, when we are baptized, but being already ingrafted are then confirmed.

z. Acts 8:37 The sum of the confession which is necessary for baptism.

baptized him. **39** And as soon as they were come up out of the water, the Spirit
of the Lord caught away Philip, that the Eunuch saw him no more: so he went on
his way rejoicing. **40** But Philip was found at Azotus, and he walked to and fro
preaching in all the cities, till he came to Caesarea.

9

*2 Saul going towards Damascus, 4 is stricken down to the ground of the
Lord: 10 Ananias is sent 18 to baptize him. 23 The laying away of the
Jews, 25 he escapeth, being let down through the wall. 33 Peter cureth Aeneas of
the palsy, 36 and by him Tabitha being dead, 40 is restored to life.*

1 And [a,1]Saul yet [b]breathing out threatenings and slaughter against the di-
sciples of the Lord, went unto the high Priest, **2** And desired of him letters to
Damascus to the Synagogues, that if he found any that were of that [c]way, (either
men or women) he might bring them bound unto Jerusalem. **3** Now as he jour-
neyed, it came to pass that as he was come near to Damascus, [2]suddenly there shi-
ned round about him a light from heaven. **4** And he fell to the earth, and heard
a voice saying to him, Saul, Saul, why persecutest thou me? **5** And he said, Who
art thou, Lord? And the Lord said, I am Jesus whom thou persecutest: it is [d]hard
for thee to kick against pricks. **6** He then both trembling and astonied, said,
Lord, what wilt thou that I do? And the Lord said unto him, Arise, and go into
the city, and it shall be told thee what thou shalt do. **7** The men also which jour-
neyed with him, [e]stood amazed, hearing his [f]voice, but seeing no man. **8** And
Saul arose from the ground, and opened his eyes, but saw no man. Then led they
him by the hand, and brought him into Damascus, **9** Where he was three days
without sight, and neither ate nor drank. **10** And there was a certain disciple at
Damascus named Ananias, and to him said the Lord in a vision, Ananias. And he
said, Behold, I am here Lord. **11** Then the Lord said unto him, Arise, and go
into the street which is called Straight, and seek in the house of Judas after one
called Saul of [g]Tarsus: for behold, he prayeth. **12** (And he saw in a vision a man
named Ananias coming in to him, and putting his hands on him, that he might
receive his sight.) **13** Then Ananias answered, Lord, I have heard by many of this
man, how much evil he hath done to thy saints at Jerusalem. **14** Moreover here
he hath authority of the high Priests, to bind all that call on thy Name. **15** Then
the Lord said unto him, Go thy way: for he is a [h]chosen vessel unto me, to bear
my Name before the Gentiles, and Kings, and the children of Israel. **16** For I
will [i]show him, how many things he must suffer for my Name's sake. **17** Then
Ananias went his way, and entered into [j]that house, and put his hands on him, and
saith, Brother Saul, the Lord hath sent me (even Jesus that appeared unto thee in
the way as thou camest) that thou mightest receive thy sight, and be filled with the
holy Ghost. **18** And immediately there fell from his eyes as it had been scales,
and suddenly he received sight, and arose, and was baptized, **19** And received
meat, and was strengthened. So was Saul certain days with the disciples which were
at Damascus. **20** [k]And straightway he preached Christ in the Synagogues, that
he was that Son of God. **21** So that all that heard him were amazed, and said,
Is not this he, that made havoc of them which called on this Name in Jerusalem,
and came hither for that intent, that he should bring them bound unto the high
Priests? **22** [l]But Saul increased the more in strength, and confounded the Jews
which dwelt at Damascus, [m]confirming that this was that Christ. **23** [n]And after
that many days were fulfilled, the Jews took counsel to kill him, **24** But their
laying await was known of Saul: now they [3]watched the gates day and night, that
they might kill him. **25** [o]Then the disciples took him by night, and put him
through the wall, and let him down by a rope in a basket. **26** [p]And when Saul
was come to Jerusalem, he assayed to join himself with the disciples: but they were
all afraid of him, and believed not that he was a disciple. **27** But Barnabas took
him, and brought him to the Apostles, and declared to them, how he had seen the
Lord in the way, and that he had spoken unto him, and how he had spoken bol-
dly at Damascus in the Name of Jesus. **28** [q]And he was conversant [r]with them
at Jerusalem, **29** And spake boldly in the Name of the Lord Jesus, and spake
and disputed against the [s]Grecians: but they went about to slay him. **30** [t]But
when the brethren knew it, they brought him to Caesarea, and sent him forth to
Tarsus. **31** [u]Then had the Churches rest through all Judea, and Galilee, and Sa-
maria, and were [v]edified, and walked in the fear of the Lord, and were multiplied
by the comfort of the holy Ghost. **32** [w]And it came to pass, as Peter walked
throughout all quarters, he came also to the saints which dwelt at Lydda. **33** And
there he found a certain man named Aeneas, which had kept his couch eight ye-
ars, and was sick of the palsy. **34** Then said Peter unto him, Aeneas, Jesus Christ
maketh thee whole: arise and truss thy couch together. And he arose immedia-
tely. **35** And all that dwelt at [x]Lydda and Sharon, saw him, and turned to the
Lord. **36** [y]There was also at Joppa a certain woman, a disciple named Tabitha
(which by interpretation is called Dorcas) she was full of good works and alms
which she did. **37** And it came to pass in those days, that she was sick and died:
and when they had washed her, they laid her in an upper chamber. **38** Now fo-
rasmuch as Lydda was near to Joppa, and the disciples had heard that Peter was
there, they sent unto him two men, desiring that he would not delay to come unto
them. **39** Then Peter arose and came with them: and when he was come, they
brought him into the upper chamber, where all the widows stood by him weeping,
and showing the coats and garments, which Dorcas made, while she was with
them. **40** But Peter put them all forth, and kneeled down, and prayed, and tur-
ned him to the body, and said, Tabitha, arise. And she opened her eyes, and when
she saw Peter, sat up. **41** Then he gave her the hand and lifted her up, and called
the Saints and widows, and restored her alive. **42** And it was known throughout
all Joppa, and many believed in the Lord. **43** And it came to pass, that he tarried
many days in Joppa with one Simon a Tanner.

10

*1 Cornelius 4 at the Angel's commandment, 5 sendeth for Peter. 11
Who also by a vision, 15, 20 is taught not to despise the Gentiles. 34
He preacheth the Gospel to Cornelius and his household. 45 Who having received
the holy Ghost, 47 are baptized.*

1 Furthermore [a]there was a certain man in Caesarea called Cornelius, a cap-
tain of the band called the Italian band, **2** A [b]devout man, and one that feared
God with [c]all his household, which gave much alms to the people, and prayed God
continually. **3** He saw in a vision evidently (about the ninth hour of the day) an
Angel of God coming in to him, and saying unto him, Cornelius. **4** But when he
looked on him, he was afraid, and said, [d]What is it, Lord? and he said unto him,
Thy prayers and thine alms are [e]come up into [f]remembrance before God. **5** Now
therefore send men to Joppa, and call for Simon, whose surname is Peter. **6** He
lodgeth with one Simon a Tanner, whose house is by the sea side: he shall tell thee
what thou oughtest to do. **7** And when the Angel which spake unto Cornelius,
was departed, he called two of his servants, and a soldier that feared God, one of
them that waited on him, **8** And told them all things, and sent them to Jop-
pa. **9** On the morrow as they went on their journey, and drew near unto the city,
Peter went up upon the house to pray, about the sixth hour. **10** Then waxed he
an hungered, and would have eaten: but while they made something ready, he fell
into a [g]trance. **11** And he saw heaven opened, and a certain vessel come down
unto him, as it had been a great sheet, knit at the [h]four corners, and was let down

---

ACTS 8

1. Isa. 53:7

ACTS 9

- **a.** Acts 9:1 Saul (who is also Paul) persecuting Christ most cruelly, who did as it were flee before him, falleth into his hands, and is overcome: and with a singular example of the goodness of God, instead of punishment which he justly deserved for his cruelty, is not only received to favor, but is also even by the mouth of God appointed an Apostle, and is confirmed by the ministry and witness of Ananias.
- **b.** Acts 9:1 This is a token that Saul's stomach boiled and cast out great threatenings to murder the disciples.
- **c.** Acts 9:2 Any trade of life which a man taketh himself unto, the Jews call a way.
- **d.** Acts 9:5 This is a proverb which is spoken of them that through their own stubbornness hurt themselves.
- **e.** Acts 9:7 Stood still and could not go one step forward, but abode amazed as if they had been very stones.
- **f.** Acts 9:7 They heard Paul's voice: for afterwards it is said in flattering, that they heard not his voice that speak: as beneath, Acts 22:9. But others go about to set these places at one which seem to be at ajar, after this sort, to wit, that they heard a sound of a voice, but no perfect voice.
- **g.** Acts 9:11 Tarsus was a city of Cilicia near unto Anchiala, which two cities Sardanapalus is said to have built in one day.
- **h.** Acts 9:15 To bear my name in.
- **i.** Acts 9:16 I will show him plainly.
- **j.** Acts 9:17 Into Judas's house.
- **k.** Acts 9:20 Paul beginneth straightways to execute the office which was enjoined him, never consulting with flesh and blood.
- **l.** Acts 9:22 Paul striveth not with his own authority alone, but with the testimonies of the Prophets.
- **m.** Acts 9:22 By conferring places of the Scripture together, as cunning craftsman do, when they make up anything, they use to gather all parts together, to make them agree fitly one with another.
- **n.** Acts 9:23 Paul, who was before a persecutor, hath now persecution laid before himself, but yet afar off.
- **o.** Acts 9:25 We are not forbidden to avoid and eschew the dangers and conspiracies that the enemies of God lay for us, so that we swerve not from our vocation.
- **p.** Acts 9:26 In ancient times no man was rashly or lightly received into the number of and amongst the sheep of Christ, much less to be a pastor.
- **q.** Acts 9:28 The constant servants of God must look for danger after danger: yet God watcheth for them.
- **r.** Acts 9:28 With Peter and James, for he saith that he saw none of the Apostles but them, Gal. 1:18-19.
- **s.** Acts 9:29 See Acts 6:1.
- **t.** Acts 9:30 The ministers of the word may change their place, by the advice and counsel of the congregation and Church.
- **u.** Acts 9:31 The end of persecution is the building of the Church, so that we will patiently wait for the Lord.
- **v.** Acts 9:31 This is a borrowed kind of speech, which signifieth establishment and increase.
- **w.** Acts 9:32 Peter's Apostleship is confirmed by healing of the man that was sick of the palsy.
- **x.** Acts 9:35 Lydda was a city of Palestine, and Sharon a Champion country and a place of good pasturage between Caesarea of Palestine and the mountain Tabor, and the lake of Gennesaret, which extendeth itself in great length beyond Joppa.
- **y.** Acts 9:36 Peter declareth evidently by raising up a dead body through the Name of Christ, that he preacheth the glad tidings of life.

ACTS 9

1. Rom. 9:3; Gal. 1:13
2. Acts 22:6; 1 Cor. 15:8
3. 2 Cor. 11:31

ACTS 10

- **a.** Acts 10:1 Peter consecrateth the firstfruits of the Gentiles to God by the means of two miracles.
- **b.** Acts 10:2 So that he worshipped one God, and was no idolater, and neither could be void of faith in Christ, because he was a devout man but as yet he knew not that he was come.
- **c.** Acts 10:2 This is a great commendation to this man, that he labored to have all his household and familiar friends and acquaintances to be religious and godly.
- **d.** Acts 10:4 What wilt thou with me, Lord? for he settleth himself to hear.
- **e.** Acts 10:4 This is a borrowed kind of speech, which the Hebrews use very much, taken from sacrifices, and applied to prayers: for it is said of whole burnt sacrifices, that the smoke and savor of them goeth up into God's nostrils: so do our prayers as a sweet-smelling sacrifice which the Lord taketh great pleasure in.
- **f.** Acts 10:4 That is, insomuch that they will not suffer God as it were, to forget thee: for so doth the Scripture use oftentimes to prattle with us as nurses do with little children, when they frame their tongues to speak.

to the earth. 12 Wherein were [i]all manner of [j]four footed beasts of the earth,
and wild beasts and [k]creeping things, and fowls of the heaven. 13 And there
came a voice to him, Arise, Peter: kill, and eat. 14 [l]But Peter said, Not so, Lord:
for I have never eaten anything that is polluted, or unclean. 15 And the voice
spake unto him again the second time, The things that God hath purified, [m]pol-
lute thou not. 16 This was so done thrice: and the vessel was drawn up again
into heaven. 17 Now while Peter doubted in himself what this vision which he
had seen, meant, behold, the men which were sent from Cornelius, had inquired
for Simon's house, and stood at the gate, 18 And called, and asked, whether Si-
mon, which was surnamed Peter, were lodged there. 19 And while Peter thought
on the vision, the Spirit said unto him, Behold, three men seek thee. 20 Arise
therefore, and get thee down, and go with them, and doubt nothing: For I have
sent them. 21 Then Peter went down to the men, which were sent unto him
from Cornelius, and said, Behold, I am he whom ye seek: what is the cause whe-
refore ye are come? 22 And they said, Cornelius the captain, a just man, and
one that feareth God, and of good report among all the nation of the Jews, was
warned from heaven by an holy Angel to send for thee into his house, and to
hear thy words. 23 Then called he them in, and lodged them: and the next
day, Peter went forth with them, and certain brethren from Joppa accompanied
him. 24 And the day after, they entered into Caesarea. Now Cornelius waited
for them, and had called together his kinsmen, and special friends. 25 [n]And it
came to pass as Peter came in, that Cornelius met him, and fell down at his feet,
and worshipped him. 26 But Peter took him up, saying, Stand up: for even I
myself am a man. 27 And as he talked with him, he came in, and found many
that were come together. 28 And he said unto them, Ye know that it is an un-
lawful thing for a man that is a Jew, to company, or come unto one of another
nation: but God hath showed me, that I should not call any man polluted, or un-
clean. 29 Therefore came I unto you without saying nay, when I was sent for.
I ask therefore, for what intent have ye sent for me? 30 Then Cornelius said,
Four days ago, about [o]this hour, I fasted, and at the ninth hour I prayed in mine
house, and behold, a man stood before me in bright clothing, 31 [p]And said,
Cornelius, thy prayer is heard, and thine alms are had in remembrance in the si-
ght of God. 32 [q]Send therefore to Joppa, and call for Simon, whose surname is
Peter (he is lodged in the house of Simon a Tanner by the Seaside) who when he
cometh, shall speak unto thee. 33 Then sent I for thee immediately, and thou
hast well done to come. Now therefore are we all here present before God to hear
all things that are commanded thee of God. 34 [r]Then Peter opened his mouth,
and said, Of a truth I perceive, that [s,1]God is no respecter of persons. 35 But
in every nation he that [t]feareth him, and worketh righteousness, is accepted with
him. 36 Ye [u]know the word which God hath sent to the children of Israel, pre-
aching peace by Jesus Christ, which is Lord of all: 37 [v]Even the word which
came through all Judea, [2]beginning in Galilee, after the Baptism which John pre-
ached: 38 To wit, how God [w]anointed Jesus of Nazareth with the holy Ghost,
and with power: who went about doing good, and healing all that were oppressed
of the devil: for God was with him. 39 And we are witnesses of all things which
he did both in the land of the Jews, and in Jerusalem, whom they slew, hanging
him on a tree. 40 Him God raised up the third day, and caused that he was
showed openly: 41 Not to all the people, but unto the witnesses [x]chosen befo-
re of God, even to us which did eat and drink with him, after he arose from the
dead. 42 And he commanded us to preach unto the people, and to testify, that it
is he that is ordained of God a judge of quick and dead. 43 To him also give all
the [3]Prophets witness, that through his Name all that believe in him, shall receive
remission of sins. 44 [y]While Peter yet spake these words, the holy Ghost fell on
all them which heard the word. 45 So they of the circumcision, which believed,
were astonied, as many as came with Peter, because that on the Gentiles also was
poured out the gift of the holy Ghost. 46 For they heard them speak with ton-
gues, and magnify God. Then answered Peter, 47 [z]Can any man forbid water,
that these should not be baptized, which have received the holy Ghost, as well as
we? 48 So he commanded them to be baptized in the Name of the Lord. Then
prayed they him to tarry certain days.

11

2 Peter being accused for going to the Gentiles, 5 defendeth himself. 22 Barnabas is sent to Antioch, 26 where the disciples are called Christians: 28 and there Agabas foretelleth a famine to come.

1 Now [a]the Apostles and the brethren that were in Judea, heard, that the
Gentiles had also received the word of God. 2 And when Peter was come up
to Jerusalem, they of the circumcision contended against him, 3 Saying, Thou
wentest into men uncircumcised, and hast eaten with them. 4 Then Peter began,
and expounded the thing in order to them, saying, 5 I was in the city of Jop-
pa, praying, and in a trance I saw this vision, A certain vessel coming down as it
had been a great sheet, let down from heaven by the four corners, and it came to
me, 6 Toward the which when I had fastened mine eyes, I considered, and saw
four footed beasts of the earth, and wild beasts, and creeping things, and fowls
of the heaven. 7 Also I heard a voice, saying unto me, Arise, Peter: slay and
eat. 8 And I said, God forbid, Lord: for nothing polluted or unclean hath at
anytime entered into my mouth. 9 But the voice answered me the second time
from heaven, The things that God hath purified, pollute thou not. 10 And this
was done three times, and all were taken up again into heaven. 11 Then behold,
immediately there were three men already come unto the house where I was, sent
from Caesarea unto me. 12 And the Spirit said unto me, that I should go with
them, without doubting: moreover these six brethren came with me, and we en-
tered into the man's house. 13 And he showed us, how he had seen an Angel in
his house, which stood and said to him, Send men to Joppa, and call for Simon,
whose surname is Peter. 14 He shall speak words unto thee, whereby both thou
and all thine house shall be saved. 15 And as I began to speak, the holy Ghost
fell on them, [1]even as upon us at the beginning. 16 Then I remembered the
word of the Lord, how he said, [2]John baptized with water, but ye shall be baptized
with the holy Ghost. 17 For as much then as God gave them a like gift, as he
did unto us, when we believed in the Lord Jesus Christ, who was I, that I could
let God? 18 [b]When they heard these things, they held their peace, and glori-
fied God, saying, Then hath God also to the Gentiles granted repentance unto
life. 19 [c]And they which were [3]scattered abroad because of the affliction that
arose about Stephen, went throughout till they came unto Phonicia and Cyprus,
and [d]Antioch, preaching the word to no man, but unto the Jews only. 20 [e]Now
some of them were men of Cyprus and of Cyrene, which when they were come
into Antioch, spake unto the Grecians, and preached the Lord Jesus. 21 And
the hand of the Lord was with them, so that a great number believed and tur-
ned unto the Lord. 22 [f]Then tidings of those things came unto the ears of the
Church, which was in Jerusalem, and they sent forth Barnabas, that he should
go unto Antioch. 23 Who when he was come and had seen the grace of God,
was glad, and exhorted all, that with purpose of heart they would continue in
the Lord. 24 For he was a good man, and full of the holy Ghost, and faith and
much people joined themselves unto the Lord. 25 [g]Then departed Barnabas to
Tarsus to seek Paul: 26 And when he had found him, he brought him unto
Antioch: and it came to pass that a whole year they were conversant with the
Church, and taught much people, insomuch that the disciples were first called
Christians in Antioch. 27 [h]In those days also came Prophets from Jerusalem

---

g. Acts 10:10 For though Peter stand not amazed as one that is tongue tied, but talketh with God, and is instructed in his mysteries, yet his mind was far otherwise than it was wont to be, but shortly returned to the old bent.
h. Acts 10:11 So that it seemed to be a foursquare sheet.
i. Acts 10:12 Here is this word (All) which is general, plainly put for an indefinite and uncertain, that is to say, for some of all sorts, not for all of every sort.
j. Acts 10:12 That is, such as were meet for men's use.
k. Acts 10:12 What is meant by the creeping things, see Lev. 11.
l. Acts 10:14 Peter profiteth daily in the knowledge of the benefit of Christ, yea, after that he had received the holy Ghost.
m. Acts 10:15 Do not thou hold them as unprofitable.
n. Acts 10:25 Religious adoration or worship agreeth only to God: but civil worship is given to the Ministers of the word, although not without danger.
o. Acts 10:30 He meaneth not the selfsame hour, but the like, that is, about nine of the clock the other day, as it was then nine when he spake to Peter.
p. Acts 10:31 Cornelius's faith showeth forth itself by prayer and charity.
q. Acts 10:32 As faith cometh by hearing, so is it nourished and groweth up by the same.
r. Acts 10:34 Distinction of nations is taken away by the coming of Christ: And it is evidently seen by faith and righteousness, who is agreeable to him, or whom he accepteth.
s. Acts 10:34 That God judgeth not after the outward appearance.
t. Acts 10:35 By the fear of God, the Hebrews understand the whole service of God: whereby we perceive that Cornelius was not void of faith, no more than they were which lived before Christ's time: and therefore they deal foolishly, which build preparative works and free will upon this place.
u. Acts 10:36 God gave the Israelites to understand, that whosoever liveth godly, is acceptable to God, of what nation soever he be, for he preached peace to men through Jesus Christ, who is Lord not of one nation only, that is, of the Jews, but of all.
v. Acts 10:37 The sum of the Gospel (which shall be made manifest at the latter day when Christ himself shall sit as judge both of the quick and the dead) is this, that Christ promised to the Fathers, and exhibited in his time with the mighty power of God, (which was by all means showed) and at length crucified to reconcile us to God, did rise again the third day, that whosoever believeth in him should be saved through the remission of sins.
w. Acts 10:38 This style is taken from an old custom of the Jews, who used to anoint their Kings and Priests, whereupon it grew, to call them anointed, upon whom God bestowed gifts and virtues.
x. Acts 10:41 This choosing of the Apostles is properly given to God: for though God be president in the lawful election of ministers, yet there is in this place a secret opposition and setting of God's choosing, and men voice the one against the other, for the Apostles are immediately appointed of God, and the Church Ministers by means.
y. Acts 10:44 The Spirit of God sealeth that in the heart of the hearers, which the minister of the word speaketh by the commandment of God, as it appeareth by the effects.
z. Acts 10:47 Baptism doth not sanctify or make them holy which receive it, but sealeth up and confirmeth their sanctification.

ACTS 10

1. Deut. 10:17; 2 Chron. 19:7; Job 34:19; Rom. 2:11; Gal. 2:6; Eph. 6:9; Col. 3:25; 1 Pet. 1:17
2. Luke 4:14
3. Jer. 31:34; Mic. 7:18; Acts 15:9

ACTS 11

a. Acts 11:1 Peter being without cause reprehended of the unskillful and ignorant, doth not object that he ought not to be judged of any, but openly giveth an account of his doing.
b. Acts 11:18 Such as ask a question of the truth which they know not, ought to be quietly heard, and must also quietly yield to the declaration thereof.
c. Acts 11:19 The scattering abroad of the Church of Jerusalem is the cause of the gathering together of many other Churches.
d. Acts 11:19 He speaketh of Antioch which was in Syria and bordered upon Cilicia.
e. Acts 11:20 The Church of Antioch, the new Jerusalem of the Gentiles was extraordinarily called.
f. Acts 11:22 The Apostles do not rashly condemn an extraordinary vocation, but yet they judge it by the effects.
g. Acts 11:25 There was no contention amongst the Apostles either of usurping, or of holding places and degrees.
h. Acts 11:27 God doth so wrap up his Church with the wicked, in his scourges and plagues which he sendeth upon the earth, that notwithstanding he provideth for it conveniently.

unto Antioch. 28 And there stood up one of them named Agabus, and signified
by the Spirit, that there should be great famine throughout all the world, which
also came to pass under Claudius Caesar. 29 [i]Then the disciples every man ac-
cording to his ability, purposed to send [j]succor unto the brethren which dwelt in
Judea. 30 Which thing they also did, and sent it to the Elders by the hand of
Barnabas and Saul.

12

*Herod killeth James with the sword, 4 And imprisoneth Peter, 8
whom the Angel delivereth. 20 Herod being offended with them of
Tyrus, 21 is pacified: 22 And taking the honor due to God, to himself, 23 he is
eaten with worms, and so dieth.*

1 Now [a]about that time, [b]Herod the king stretched forth his hand to vex
certain of the Church, 2 And he [c]killed James the brother of John with the
sword. 3 [d]And when he saw that it pleased the Jews, he proceeded further,
to take Peter also (then were the days of unleavened bread.) 4 [e]And when he
had caught him, he put him in prison, and delivered him to four quaternions of
soldiers to be kept, intending after the Passover to bring him forth to the peo-
ple. 5 [f]So Peter was kept in prison, but earnest prayer was made of the Church
unto God for him. 6 And when Herod would have brought him out unto the
people, the same night slept Peter between two soldiers, bound with two chains,
and the keepers before the door, kept the prison. 7 [1]And behold the Angel of the
Lord came upon them, and a light shined in the [g]house, and he smote Peter on
the side, and raised him up, saying, Arise quickly. And his chains fell off from his
hands. 8 And the Angel said unto him, Gird thyself, and bind on thy sandals.
And so he did. Then he said unto him, Cast thy garment about thee, and follow
me. 9 So Peter came out and followed him, and knew not that it was true, which
was done by the Angel, but thought he had seen a vision. 10 Now when they
were past the first and the second watch, they came unto the iron gate that leadeth
unto the city, which opened to them by its own accord, and they went out, and
passed through one street, and by and by the Angel departed from him. 11 And
when Peter was come to himself, he said, Now I know for a truth, that the Lord
hath sent his Angel, and hath delivered me out of the hand of Herod, and from all
the waiting for of the people of the Jews. 12 [h]And as he considered the thing, he
came to the house of Mary, the mother of John, whose surname was Mark, where
many were gathered together, and prayed. 13 [i]And when Peter knocked at the
entry door, a maid [j]came forth to hearken, named Rhoda, 14 But when she
knew Peter's voice, she opened not the entry door for gladness, but ran in, and told
how Peter stood before the entry. 15 But they said unto her, Thou art mad. Yet
she affirmed it constantly, that it was so. Then said they, It is his Angel. 16 But
Peter continued knocking, and when they had opened it, and saw him, they were
astonied. 17 [k]And he beckoned unto them with the hand, to hold their peace,
and told them how the Lord had brought him out of the prison. And he said,
Go show these things unto James and to the brethren: and he departed and went
into another place. 18 [l]Now as soon as it was day, there was no small trouble
among the soldiers, what was become of Peter. 19 And when Herod had sou-
ght for him, and found him not, he examined the keepers, and commanded them
to be led to be punished. And he went down from Judea to Caesarea, and the-
re abode. 20 [m]Then Herod was angry with them of Tyre and Sidon, but they
came all with one accord unto him, and persuaded Blastus the King's Chamber-
lain, and they desired peace, because their country was nourished by the King's
land. 21 And upon a day appointed, Herod arrayed himself in royal apparel, and
sat on the judgment seat, and made an oration unto them. 22 [n]And the people
gave a shout, saying, The voice of God, and not of man. 23 [o]But immediately
the Angel of the Lord smote him, because he [p]gave not glory unto God, so that he
was eaten of worms, and gave up the ghost. 24 [q]And the [r]word of God grew, and
multiplied. 25 So Barnabas and Saul returned from Jerusalem, when they had
fulfilled their office, and took with them John, whose surname was Mark.

13

*2 The holy Ghost commandeth that Paul and Barnabas be separated unto
him. 6 At Paphos, 8 Elymas the sorcerer 11 is stricken blind: 14
From whence being come to Antioch, 17 They preach the Gospel, 45 the Jews
vehemently withstanding them.*

1 There [a]were also in the Church that was at Antioch, certain Prophets and
teachers, as Barnabas, and Simeon called Niger, and Lucius of Cyrene, and Ma-
naen (which had been brought up with [b]Herod the Tetrarch) and Saul. 2 Now
as they [c]ministered to the Lord, and fasted, the holy Ghost said, Separate me Bar-
nabas and Saul, for the work whereunto I have [d]called them. 3 [e]Then fasted
they and prayed, and laid their hands on them, and let them go. 4 [f]And they
after they were sent forth of the holy Ghost, came down unto [g]Seleucia, and from
thence they sailed to Cyprus. 5 And when they were at Salamis, they preached
the word of God in the Synagogues of the Jews: and they had also John to their
minister. 6 So when they had gone throughout the isle unto Paphos, they found
a certain sorcerer, a false prophet, being a Jew, named Bar-Jesus, 7 Which was
with the Deputy Sergius Paulus, a prudent man. He called unto him Barnabas and
Saul, and desired to hear the word of God. 8 [h]But Elymas the sorcerer, (for so
is his name by interpretation) withstood them, and sought to turn away the De-
puty from the faith. 9 Then Saul (which also is called Paul) being full of the holy
Ghost, set his eyes on him, 10 [i]And said, O full of all subtlety and all [j]mischief,
the child of the devil, and enemy of all righteousness, wilt thou not cease to pervert
the straight ways of the Lord? 11 Now therefore behold, the [k]hand of the Lord
is upon thee, and thou shalt be blind, and not see the sun for a season. And imme-
diately there fell on him a mist and a darkness, and he went about, seeking some to
lead him by the hand. 12 Then the Deputy when he saw what was done, belie-
ved, and was astonied at the doctrine of the Lord. 13 [l]Now when Paul and they
that were with him were departed by ship from Paphos, they came to Perga a city of
Pamphylia: then John departed from them, and returned to Jerusalem. 14 But
when they departed from Perga, they came to Antioch a city of [m]Pisidia, and went
into the Synagogue on the Sabbath day, and sat down. 15 [n]And after the lectu-
re of the Law and Prophets, the rulers of the Synagogue sent unto them, saying,
Ye men and brethren, if ye [o]have any word of exhortation for the people, say
on. 16 [p]Then Paul stood up and beckoned with the hand, and said, Men of Isra-
el, and ye that fear God, hearken. 17 The God of this people of Israel chose our
fathers, and [q]exalted the people when they dwelt in the land of [1]Egypt, and with
an [r,2]high arm brought them out thereof. 18 And about the time [3]of forty years,
suffered he their manners in the wilderness. 19 And he destroyed seven nations
in the land of Canaan, and [4]divided their land to them by lot. 20 Then afterward

---

- **i.** Acts 11:29 All Congregations or Churches make one body.
- **j.** Acts 11:29 That is, that thereof the Deacons might succor the poor: for it behooved to have all these things done orderly, and decently, and therefore it is said, that they sent these things to the Elders, that is, to the governors of the Church.

ACTS 11

1. Acts 2:4
2. Acts 1:5; Acts 19:4; Matt. 3:11; Mark 1:8; Luke 3:16; John 1:26
3. Acts 8:1

ACTS 12

- **a.** Acts 12:1 God giveth his Church a truce, but for a little time.
- **b.** Acts 12:1 This name Herod was common to all them that came of the stock of Herod Ascalonites, whose surname was Magnus: but he that is spoken of here, was nephew to Herod the great son to Aristobulus, and father to that Agrippa who is spoken of afterward.
- **c.** Acts 12:2 Violently, his cause being not once heard.
- **d.** Acts 12:3 It is an old fashion of tyrants to procure the favor of the wicked, with the blood of the godly.
- **e.** Acts 12:4 The tyrants and wicked make a gallows for themselves, even then when they do most according to their own will and fantasy.
- **f.** Acts 12:5 The prayers of the godly overturn the counsel of tyrants, obtain Angels of God, break the prison, unloose chains, put Satan to flight and preserve the Church.
- **g.** Acts 12:7 In the prison.
- **h.** Acts 12:12 Holy meeting in the night as well of men as women (when they cannot be suffered in the day time) are allowable by the example of the Apostles.
- **i.** Acts 12:13 We obtain more of God, than we dare well hope for.
- **j.** Acts 12:13 Out of the place where they were assembled, but not out of the house.
- **k.** Acts 12:17 We may sometimes give place to the rage of the wicked, but yet so that our diligence which ought to be used in God's business, be not a whit slackened.
- **l.** Acts 12:18 Evil counsel falleth out in the end to the hurt of the devisers of it.
- **m.** Acts 12:20 A miserable and shameful example of the end of the enemies of the Church.
- **n.** Acts 12:22 The flattery of the people, maketh fools fain.
- **o.** Acts 12:23 God resisteth the proud.
- **p.** Acts 12:23 Josephus recordeth, that this king did not repress those flatterers' tongues, and therefore at his death he complained and cried out of their vanity.
- **q.** Acts 12:24 Tyrants build up the Church by plucking it down.
- **r.** Acts 12:24 They that heard the word of God.

ACTS 12

1. Acts 5:19

ACTS 13

- **a.** Acts 13:1 Paul with Barnabas is again the second time appointed Apostle of the Gentiles, not of man, neither by man, but by an extraordinary commandment of the holy Ghost.
- **b.** Acts 13:1 The same was Antipas, which put John Baptist to death.
- **c.** Acts 13:2 While they were busy doing their office, that is, as Chrysostom expoundeth it, while they were preaching.
- **d.** Acts 13:2 The Lord is said to call (whereof this word (calling) cometh, which is usual in the Church) when he causeth that to be, which was not, whether you refer it to the matter itself or to any quality or thing about the matter: and it groweth of this, because when things begin to be, then they have some name: as God's mighty power is also declared thereby, who spake the word, and things were made.
- **e.** Acts 13:3 Fast, and solemn prayers were used before the laying on of hands.
- **f.** Acts 13:4 Paul and his companions do at the first bring Cyprus to the subjection and obedience of Christ.
- **g.** Acts 13:4 Seleucia was a city of Cilicia, so called of Seleucus one of Alexander's successors.
- **h.** Acts 13:8 The devil maketh the conquest of Christ more glorious, in that that he setteth himself against him.
- **i.** Acts 13:10 The sorcerer which was stricken of Paul with a corporal punishment (although extraordinarily) showeth an example to lawful magistrates, how they ought to punish them which wickedly and obstinately hinder the course of the Gospel.
- **j.** Acts 13:10 He noteth out such a fault, as whoso hath it, runneth headlong and with great desire to all kinds of wickedness with the least motion in the world.
- **k.** Acts 13:11 His power which he showeth in striking and beating down his enemies.
- **l.** Acts 13:13 An example in one and the selfsame company both of singular constancy, and also of great weakness.
- **m.** Acts 13:14 This putteth a difference betwixt it, and Antioch which was in Syria.
- **n.** Acts 13:15 In the Synagogue of the Jews (according to the pattern whereof Christian Congregations were instituted) first the Scriptures were read, then such as were learned were licensed by the rulers of the Synagogue to speak and expound.
- **o.** Acts 13:15 Word for word, If there be any word in you: and this is a kind of speech taken from the Hebrews, whereby is meant, that the gifts of God's grace are in us, as it were in treasure houses, and that they are not ours, but God's: In like sort saith David, Thou hast put a new song in my mouth, Ps. 40:1.
- **p.** Acts 13:16 God bestowed many peculiar benefits upon his chosen Israel, but this especially, that he promised them the everlasting redeemer.
- **q.** Acts 13:17 Advanced and brought to honor.
- **r.** Acts 13:17 Openly and with much force, breaking in pieces the enemies of his people.

he gave unto them [5]Judges about [s]four hundred and fifty years, unto the time of
Samuel the Prophet. **21** So after that, they desired a [6]King, and God gave unto
them [7]Saul, the son of Cis, a man of the tribe of Benjamin, by the space of [t]forty
years. **22** And after he had taken him away, he raised up [8]David to be their King,
of whom he witnessed, saying, I have found David the son of Jesse, a man after
mine own heart, which will do all things that I will. **23** [u]Of this man's seed hath
God [9]according to his promise raised up to Israel, the Savior Jesus: **24** When
[10]John had first preached [v]before his coming the baptism of repentance to all the
people of Israel. **25** And when John had fulfilled his course, he said, [11]Whom ye
think that I am, I am not he: but behold, there cometh one after me, whose shoe
of his feet I am not worthy to loose. **26** [w]Ye men and brethren, children of the
generation of Abraham, and whosoever among you feareth God, to you is the word
of this salvation sent. **27** [x]For the inhabitants of Jerusalem, and their rulers, be-
cause they knew him not, nor yet the words of the Prophets, which are read every
Sabbath day, they have fulfilled them in condemning him. **28** And though they
found no cause of death in him, [12]yet desired they Pilate to kill him. **29** And
when they had fulfilled all things that were written of him, they took him down
from the tree, and put him in a sepulcher. **30** [y]But God [13]raised him up from
the dead. **31** And he was seen many days of them, which came up with him
from Galilee to Jerusalem, which are his witnesses unto the people. **32** And we
declare unto you, that touching the promise made unto the fathers, **33** God hath
fulfilled it unto us their children, in that he [z]raised up Jesus, [aa]even as it is written
in the second Psalm, [14]Thou art my Son: this day have I begotten thee. **34** Now
as concerning that he raised him up from the dead, no more to return to corrup-
tion, he hath said thus, [15]I will give you the holy things of David, [ab]which are
faithful. **35** [ac]Wherefore he saith also in another place, [16]Thou wilt not suffer
thine holy one to see corruption. **36** Howbeit, David after he had served his
time by the counsel of God, he [17]slept, and was laid with his fathers, and saw
corruption. **37** But he whom God raised up, saw no corruption. **38** [ad]Be it
known unto you therefore, men and brethren, that through this man is preached
unto you the forgiveness of sins. **39** And from [ae]all things, from which ye could
not be justified by the Law of Moses, by him everyone that believeth, is justi-
fied. **40** [af]Beware therefore lest that come upon you, which is spoken of in the
Prophets, **41** [18]Behold, ye despisers, and wonder, and vanish away: for I work
a work in your days, a work which ye shall not believe, if a man would declare
it you. **42** [ag]And when they were come out of the Synagogue of the Jews, the
Gentiles besought, that they would preach these words to them the next Sabbath
day. **43** Now when the congregation was dissolved, many of the Jews and [ah]Pro-
selytes that feared God, followed Paul and Barnabas, which spake unto them, and
exhorted them to continue in the grace of God. **44** And the next Sabbath day
came almost the whole city together, to hear the word of God. **45** [ai]But when
the Jews saw the people, they were full of envy, and spake against those things,
which were spoken of Paul, contrarying them, and railing on them. **46** [aj]Then
Paul and Barnabas spake boldly, and said, It was necessary that the word of God
should first have been spoken unto you: but seeing ye put it from you, and [ak]jud-
ge yourselves unworthy of everlasting life, lo, we turn to the Gentiles. **47** For so
hath the Lord commanded us, saying, [19]I have made thee a light of the Gentiles,
that thou shouldest be the salvation unto the end of the world. **48** And when the
Gentiles heard it, they were glad, and glorified the word of the Lord: and as many
as were [al]ordained unto eternal life, believed. **49** Thus the word of the Lord was
published throughout the whole country. **50** [am]But the Jews stirred certain [an]de-
vout and honorable women, and the chief men of the city, and raised persecution
against Paul and Barnabas, and expelled them out of their coasts. **51** [ao]But they
[20]shook off the dust of their feet against them, and came unto Iconium. **52** And
the disciples were filled with joy, and with the holy Ghost.

14

1 Paul and Barnabas 5 are persecuted at Iconium: 6 At Lystra Paul 10 healeth a cripple: 13 They are about to do sacrifice unto them, 18 but they forbid it. 19 Paul by the persuasion of certain Jews, is stoned: 23 From thence passing through divers Churches, 26 they return to Antioch.

1 And [a]it came to pass in [b]Iconium, that they went both together into the
Synagogue of the Jews, and so spake, that a great multitude both of the Jews and
of the Grecians believed. **2** And the [c]unbelieving Jews stirred up, and corrupted
the minds of the Gentiles against the brethren. **3** [d]So therefore they abode there
a long time, and spake boldly in the Lord, which gave testimony unto the word
of his grace, and caused signs and wonders to be done by their hands. **4** But the
multitude of the city was divided: and some were with the Jews, and some with
the Apostles. **5** And when there was an assault made both of the Gentiles, and of
the Jews with their rulers, to do them violence, and to stone them, **6** They were
ware of it, and [e]fled unto Lystra, and Derbe, cities of Lycaonia, and unto the region
round about, **7** And there preached the Gospel. **8** [f]Now there sat a certain man
at Lystra, impotent in his feet, which was a cripple from his mother's womb, who
had never walked. **9** He heard Paul speak: who beholding him and perceiving
that he had faith to be healed, **10** Said with a loud voice, Stand upright on thy
feet. And he leaped up, and walked. **11** Then when the people saw what Paul had
done, they lifted up their voices, saying in the speech of Lycaonia, Gods are come
down to us in the likeness of men. **12** And they called Barnabas, Jupiter: and
Paul Mercurius, because he was the chief speaker. **13** Then Jupiter's Priest, which
was before their city, brought bulls with garlands unto the [g]gates, and would have
sacrificed with the people. **14** But when the Apostles, Barnabas and Paul heard
it, they rent their clothes, and ran in among the people, crying, **15** [h]And saying,
O men, why do ye these things? We are even men subject to the [i]like passions
that ye be, and preach unto you, that ye should turn from these [j]vain things unto
the living God, [1]which made heaven and earth, and the sea, and all things that in
them are: **16** [k]Who in times past [l,2]suffered all the Gentiles to walk in their own
ways. **17** Nevertheless, he left not himself without witness, in that he did good
and gave us rain from heaven, and fruitful seasons, filling our hearts with food,
and gladness. **18** And speaking these things, scarce appeased they the multitude,
that they had not sacrificed unto them. **19** [m]Then there came certain Jews from
Antioch and Iconium, which when they had persuaded the people, [3]stoned Paul,
and drew him out of the city, supposing he had been dead. **20** Howbeit, as the

---

s. Acts 13:20 There were from the birth of Isaac unto the destruction of the Canaanites under the governance of Joshua four hundred and seven and forty years, and therefore he addeth in this place, this word, About, for there want three years, but the Apostle useth the whole greater number.

t. Acts 13:21 In this space of forty years must the time of Samuel be reckoned with the days of Saul: for the kingdom did as it were swallow up his government.

u. Acts 13:23 He proveth by the witness of John, that Jesus is that Savior which should come of David.

v. Acts 13:24 John as an Herald, did not show Christ's coming afar off as the other Prophets did, but hard at hand, and entered on his journey.

w. Acts 13:26 Christ was promised and sent properly to the Jews.

x. Acts 13:27 All things came to pass to Christ, which the Prophets foretold of Messiah: so that hereby also it appeareth that he is the true and only Savior: and yet notwithstanding they are not to be excused which did not only not receive him, but also persecute him most cruelly although he was innocent.

y. Acts 13:30 We must set the glory of the resurrection against the shame of the cross, and grave. And the resurrection is proved as well by witnesses which saw it, as by the testimonies of the Prophets.

z. Acts 13:33 For then he appeared plainly and manifestly as that only Son of God, when as he left off his weakness, and came out of the grave, having conquered death.

aa. Acts 13:33 If Christ had tarried in death, he had not been the true Son of God, neither had the covenant, which was made with David, been sure.

ab. Acts 13:34 The Greeks call those holy things, which the Hebrews call gracious bounties: and they are called David's bounties in the passive signification, because God bestowed them upon David: Moreover, they are termed faithful, after the manner of speech which the Hebrews use, who terms those things faithful, which are steady and sure such as never alter nor change.

ac. Acts 13:35 The Lord was so in grave, that he felt no corruption.

ad. Acts 13:38 Christ was sent to give them free remission of sins, which were condemned by the Law.

ae. Acts 13:39 Whereas the ceremonies of the Law could not absolve you from your sins, this man doth absolve you, if you lay hold on him by faith.

af. Acts 13:40 The benefits of God turn to the utter undoing of them that contemn them.

ag. Acts 13:42 The Gentiles go before the Jews into the kingdom of heaven.

ah. Acts 13:43 Which had forsaken their heathenish religion, and embraced the religion set forth by Moses.

ai. Acts 13:45 The favor of one selfsame Gospel is unto the reprobate and unbelievers, death, and to the elect and such as believe, life.

aj. Acts 13:46 The Gospel is published to the Gentiles by the express commandment of God.

ak. Acts 13:46 By this your doing you do as it were, pronounce sentence against yourselves, and judge yourselves.

al. Acts 13:48 Therefore either all were not appointed to everlasting life, or else all should have believed: but because that is not so, it followeth, that some certain were ordained, and therefore God did not only foreknow, but also foreordain, that neither faith nor the effects of faith should be the cause of his ordaining or appointment, but his ordaining the cause of faith.

am. Acts 13:50 Such is the craft and subtlety of the enemies of the Gospel, that they abuse the simplicity of some which are not altogether evil men, to execute their cruelty.

an. Acts 13:50 Such as embraced Moses' Law.

ao. Acts 13:51 The wickedness of the world cannot let God to gather his Church together, and to foster and cherish it, when it is gathered together.

ACTS 13

1. Exod. 1:9
2. Exod. 13:14
3. Exod. 16:1
4. Josh. 14:1
5. Judg. 3:9
6. 1 Sam. 8:5
7. 1 Sam. 9:15; 1 Sam. 10:1
8. 1 Sam. 16:13
9. Ps. 89:21; Isa. 11:1
10. Mal. 3:1; Matt. 3:2; Mark 1:2; Luke 3:2
11. Matt. 3:11; Mark 1:7; John 1:20
12. Matt. 27:22; Mark 15:13; Luke 23:20; John 19:6
13. Matt. 28:2; Mark 16:6; Luke 24:6; John 20:19
14. Ps. 2:7; Heb. 1:5; Heb. 5:5
15. Isa. 55:3
16. Ps. 16:11; Acts 2:31
17. 1 Kings 2:10; Acts 2:29
18. Hab. 1:5
19. Isa. 49:6
20. Matt. 20:14; Mark 6:11; Luke 9:5; Acts 18:6

ACTS 14

a. Acts 14:1 We ought to be no less constant in preaching of the Gospel, than the perverseness of the wicked is obstinate in persecuting of it.

b. Acts 14:1 Iconium was a city of Lycaonia.

c. Acts 14:2 Which obeyed not the doctrine.

d. Acts 14:3 We ought not to leave our places and give place to threatenings, neither to open rage, but when there is no other remedy, and that not for our own quietness' sake, but that the Gospel of Christ may be spread further abroad.

e. Acts 14:6 It is lawful sometimes to flee dangers, in time convenient.

f. Acts 14:8 It is an old subtlety of the devil, either to cause the faithful servants of God to be banished at once, or to be worshipped for idols: and that chiefly taking occasion by miracles wrought by them.

g. Acts 14:13 Of the house where Paul and Barnabas were.

h. Acts 14:15 That is also called idolatry, which giveth to creatures, be they never so holy and excellent, that which is proper to the only one God, that is invocation or calling upon.

i. Acts 14:15 Men, as ye are, and partakers of the selfsame nature of man as you.

j. Acts 14:15 He calleth idols vain things, after the manner of the Hebrews.

k. Acts 14:16 Custom, be it never so old, doth not excuse the idolaters.

l. Acts 14:16 Suffered them to live as they listed, prescribing and appointing them no kind of religion.

m. Acts 14:19 The devil when he is brought to the last cast, at length rageth openly, but in vain, even then when he seemeth to have the upper hand.

disciples stood round about him, he arose up, and came into the city, and the next day he departed with Barnabas to Derbe. **21** [n]And after they had preached the glad tidings of the Gospel to that city, and had taught many, they returned to Lystra, and to Iconium, and to Antioch. **22** [o]Confirming the disciples hearts, and exhorting them to continue in the faith, affirming that we must through many afflictions enter into the kingdom of God. **23** [p]And when they had ordained them Elders by election in every Church, and prayed, and fasted, they commended them to the Lord in whom they believed. **24** [q]Thus they went throughout Pisidia, and came to Pamphylia. **25** And when they had preached the word in Perga, they came down to [r]Attalia, **26** And thence sailed to [s]Antioch, [4]from whence they had been commended unto the grace of God, to the work, which they had fulfilled. **27** And when they were come and had gathered the Church together, they rehearsed all the things that God had done by them, and how he had opened the door of faith unto the Gentiles. **28** So there they abode a long time with the disciples.

15

1 Certain go about to bring in circumcision at Antioch: 6 About which matter the Apostles consult: 19 and what must be done 23 they declare by letters. 36 Paul and Barnabas 39 are at great variance.

1 Then [a]came down [b]certain from Judea, and taught the brethren, saying, Except ye be circumcised after the manner of Moses, ye cannot be saved. **2** [c]And when there was great dissension, and disputation by Paul and Barnabas against them, they ordained that Paul and Barnabas, and certain others of them, should go up to Jerusalem unto the Apostles and Elders about this question. **3** Thus [d]being brought forth by the Church, they passed through Phoenicia and Samaria, declaring the conversion of the Gentiles, and they brought great joy unto all the brethren. **4** And when they were come to Jerusalem, they were received of the Church, and of the Apostles and Elders, and they declared what things God had done by them. **5** But said they, certain of the sect of the Pharisees, which did believe, rose up, saying that it was needful to circumcise them, and to command them to keep the Law of Moses. **6** [e]Then the Apostles and Elders came together to look to this matter. **7** And when there had been great disputation, Peter rose up, and said unto them, [f,1]Ye men and brethren, ye know that a [g]good while ago, among us God chose out me, that the Gentiles by my mouth should hear the word of the Gospel, and believe. **8** And God which knoweth the hearts, bare them witness, in giving unto them the holy Ghost even as he did unto us. **9** And he put no [h]difference between us and them, after that [i,2]by faith he had purified their hearts. **10** [j]Now therefore, why [k]tempt ye God, to [3]lay a yoke on the disciples' necks, which neither our fathers, nor we were able to bear? **11** But we believe, through the grace of the Lord Jesus Christ to be saved, even as they do. **12** [l]Then all the multitude kept silence, and heard Barnabas and Paul, which told what signs and wonders God had done among the Gentiles by them. **13** And when they held their peace, [m]James answered, saying, Men and brethren, hearken unto me. **14** [n]Simeon hath declared, how God first did visit the Gentiles, to take of them a people unto his Name. **15** And to this agree the words of the Prophets, as it is written, **16** [4]After this I will return, and will build again the Tabernacle of David, which is fallen down, and the ruins thereof will I build again, and I will set it up. **17** That the residue of men might seek after the Lord, and all the Gentiles upon whom my Name is called, saith the Lord which doeth all these things. **18** From the beginning of the world, God [o]knoweth all his works. **19** [p]Wherefore my sentence is, that we trouble not them of the Gentiles that are turned to God, **20** But that we send unto them, that they abstain themselves from [q]filthiness of idols, and fornication, and that is strangled, and from blood. **21** For Moses of old time hath in every city them that preach him, seeing he is read in the Synagogues every Sabbath day. **22** [r]Then it seemed good to the Apostles and Elders with the whole Church to send chosen men of their own company to Antioch with Paul and Barnabas: to wit, Judas whose surname was Barsabas, and Silas, which were chief men among the brethren, **23** And wrote letters by them after this manner, THE APOSTLES, and the Elders, and the brethren, Unto the brethren which are of the Gentiles in Antioch, and in Syria, and in Cilicia, send greeting. **24** [s]Forasmuch as we have heard, that certain which [t]went out from us, have troubled you with words, and [u]cumbered your minds, saying, Ye must be circumcised and keep the Law: to whom we gave no such commandment, **25** It seemed therefore good to us, when we were come together with one accord, to send chosen men unto you, with our beloved Barnabas and Paul. **26** Men that have [v]given up their lives for the Name of our Lord Jesus Christ. **27** We have therefore sent Judas and Silas, which shall also tell you the same things by mouth. **28** [w]For it seemed good to the [x]holy Ghost, and [y]to us, to lay no more burden upon you, than these [z]necessary things. **29** [aa]That is, that ye abstain from things offered to idols, and blood, and that that is strangled, and from fornication: from which if ye keep yourselves, ye shall do well. Fare ye well. **30** [ab]Now when they were departed, they came to Antioch, and after that they had assembled the multitude, they delivered the Epistle, **31** And when they had read it, they rejoiced for the consolation. **32** And Judas and Silas being Prophets, exhorted the brethren with many words, and strengthened them. **33** And after they had tarried there a space, they were let go in [ac]peace of the brethren unto the Apostles. **34** Notwithstanding Silas thought good to abide there still. **35** Paul also and Barnabas continued in Antioch, teaching and preaching with many others the word of the Lord. **36** [ad]But after certain days, Paul said unto Barnabas, Let us return and visit our brethren in every city, where we have preached the word of the Lord, and see how they do. **37** [ae]And Barnabas counseled to take with them John, called Mark. **38** But Paul thought it not meet to take him unto their company, which departed from them from Pamphylia, and went not with them to the work. **39** [af]Then were they so [ag]stirred, that they departed asunder one from the other, so that Barnabas took Mark, and sailed unto Cyprus. **40** And Paul chose Silas and departed, being commended of the brethren unto the grace of God. **41** And he went through Syria and Cilicia, establishing the Churches.

---

n. Acts 14:21 We must go forward in our vocation through a thousand deaths.
o. Acts 14:22 It is the office of the ministers, not only to teach, but also to confirm them that are taught, and prepare them to the cross.
p. Acts 14:23 The Apostles committed the Churches which they had planted, to proper and peculiar Pastors, which they made not rashly, but with prayers and fastings going before: neither did they thrust them upon Churches through bribery or lordly superiority, but chose and placed them by the voice of the congregation.
q. Acts 14:24 Paul and Barnabas having made an end of their peregrination, and being returned to Antioch, do render an account to the Congregation or Church.
r. Acts 14:25 Attalia was a sea city of Pamphylia, near to Lycia.
s. Acts 14:26 Antioch of Syria.

ACTS 14

1. Gen. 1:1; Ps. 146:5; Rev. 14:7
2. Ps. 81:13; Rom. 1:24
3. 2 Cor. 11:25
4. Acts 13:3

ACTS 15

a. Acts 15:1 The Church is at length troubled with dissension within itself, and the trouble riseth of the proud and stubborn wits of certain evil men: The first strife was concerning the office of Christ, whether we be saved by his only righteousness apprehended by faith, or we have need also to observe the Law.
b. Acts 15:1 Epiphanius is of opinion that this was Cerinthus.
c. Acts 15:2 Meetings of Congregations were instituted to suppress heresies, whereunto certain were sent by common consent in the name of all.
d. Acts 15:3 Courteously and lovingly brought on their way by the Church, that is, by certain appointed by the Church.
e. Acts 15:6 The matter is first handled, both parts being heard in the assembly of the Apostles and ancients, and after is communicated with the people.
f. Acts 15:7 God himself in calling of the Gentiles which are uncircumcised, did teach that our salvation doth consist in faith without the worship appointed by the Law.
g. Acts 15:7 Word for word, of old time, that is, even from the first time that we were commanded to preach the Gospel, and straightways after that the holy Ghost came down upon us.
h. Acts 15:9 He put no difference between us and them, as touching the benefit of his free favor.
i. Acts 15:9 Christ pronounceth them Blessed, which are pure of heart: and here we are plainly taught that men are made such by faith.
j. Acts 15:10 Peter passing from the Ceremonies to the Law itself in general, showeth that none could be saved, if salvation were to be sought for by the Law, and not by grace only in Jesus Christ; because that no man could ever fulfil the Law, neither Patriarch, nor Apostle.
k. Acts 15:10 Why tempt ye God, as though he could not save by faith?
l. Acts 15:12 A true pattern of a lawful Council, where God's truth only reigneth.
m. Acts 15:13 The son of Alphaeus, who is called the Lord's brother.
n. Acts 15:14 James confirmeth the calling of the Gentiles, out of the word of God, therein agreeing to Peter.
o. Acts 15:18 And therefore nothing cometh to pass by fortune, but by God's appointment.
p. Acts 15:19 In matters indifferent we may so far bear with the weakness of our brethren, as they may have time to be instructed.
q. Acts 15:20 From sacrifices or from feasts which were kept in idols' Temples.
r. Acts 15:22 In a lawful Synod, neither they which are appointed and chosen Judges, appoint and determine anything tyrannously or upon a lordliness, neither doth the common multitude set themselves tumultuously against them, which sit as Judges by the word of God: as the like order also is held in publishing and ratifying those things which have been so determined and agreed upon.
s. Acts 15:24 The Council of Jerusalem concludeth, that they trouble men's consciences, which teach us to seek salvation in any other means than in Christ only, apprehended by faith, from whence soever they come, and whomsoever they pretend to be author of their vocation.
t. Acts 15:24 From our congregation.
u. Acts 15:24 A borrowed kind of speech taken of them which pull down that that was built up: and it is a very usual metaphor in the Scriptures: to say the Church is built, for, the Church is planted and stablished.
v. Acts 15:26 Have greatly hazarded their lives.
w. Acts 15:28 That is, a lawful Council, which the holy Ghost ruleth.
x. Acts 15:28 First they made mention of the holy Ghost, that it may not seem to be any man's work.
y. Acts 15:28 Not that men have any authority of themselves, but to show the faithfulness that they used in their ministry and labor.
z. Acts 15:28 This was no precise necessity, but in respect of the state of that time, that the Gentiles and the Jews might more peaceably live together with less occasion of quarrel.
aa. Acts 15:29 Charity is required even in things indifferent.
ab. Acts 15:30 It is requisite for all people to know certainly what to hold in matters of faith and religion, and not that the Church by ignorance and knowing nothing, should depend upon the pleasure of a few.
ac. Acts 15:33 This is an Hebrew kind of speech, which is as much to say, as the brethren wished them all prosperous success, and the Church dismissed them with good leave.
ad. Acts 15:36 Congregations or Churches do easily degenerate, unless they be diligently seen unto, and therefore went these Apostles to oversee such as they had planted, and for this cause also Synods were instituted and appointed.
ae. Acts 15:37 A lamentable example of discord between excellent men and very great friends, yet not for profane or their private affairs, neither yet for doctrine.
af. Acts 15:39 God useth the faults of his servants to the profit and building of his Church, yet we have to take heed, even in the best matters that we pass not measure in our heat.
ag. Acts 15:39 They were in great heat: but herein we have to consider the force of God's counsel: for by this means it came to pass, that the doctrine of the Gospel was exercised in many places.

ACTS 15

1. Acts 10:20; Acts 11:13
2. Acts 10:43; 1 Cor. 1:2
3. Matt. 23:4
4. Amos 9:11

16

1 Paul having circumcised Timothy, 12 being at Philippi, 14 instructed Lydia in the faith. 16 The spirit of divination, 18 is by him cast out: 20 and for that cause 22 they are whipped, 24 and imprisoned. 26 Through an earthquake, 27 the prison doors are opened. 31, 32 The Gaoler receiveth the faith.

1 Then [a]came he to Derbe and to Lystra: and behold, a certain disciple was
there, named [1]Timothy, a woman's son, which was a [b]Jewess and believed, but his
father was a Grecian, 2 Of whom the brethren which were at Lystra and Ico-
nium, [c]reported well. 3 [d]Therefore Paul would that he should go forth with him,
and took and circumcised him, because of the Jews, which were in those quarters:
for they knew all that his father was a Grecian. 4 [e]And as they went through the
cities, they delivered them [f]the decrees to keep, ordained of the Apostles and Elders
which were at Jerusalem. 5 And so were the Churches established in the faith,
and increased in number daily. 6 [g]Now when they had gone throughout Phry-
gia, and the region of Galatia, they were [h]forbidden of the holy Ghost, to preach
the word in Asia. 7 Then came they to Mysia, and sought to go into Bithynia:
but the Spirit suffered them not. 8 Therefore they passed through Mysia, and
came down to Troas, 9 [i]Where a vision appeared to Paul in the night. There sto-
od a man of Macedonia, and prayed him, saying, Come into Macedonia, and help
us. 10 [j]And after he had seen the vision, immediately we prepared to go into
Macedonia, being assured that the Lord had called us to preach the Gospel unto
them. 11 Then went we forth from Troas, and with a straight course came to Sa-
mothrace, and the next day to Neapolis. 12 And from thence to Philippi, which
is the chief city in the parts of Macedonia, and whose inhabitants came from Rome
to dwell there: and we were in that city abiding certain days. 13 [k]And on the Sab-
bath day we went out of the city, besides a river, where they were wont to [l]pray: and
we sat down, and spake unto the women, which were come together. 14 [m]And
a certain woman named Lydia, a seller of purple, of the city of the Thyatirians,
which worshipped God, heard us: whose heart the Lord opened, that she atten-
ded unto the things, which Paul spake. 15 [n]And when she was baptized, and
her household, she besought us, saying, If ye have judged me to be faithful to the
Lord, come into mine house, and abide there: and she constrained us. 16 [o]And
it came to pass that as we went to prayer, a certain maid having a spirit [p]of divi-
nation, met us, which gat her masters much vantage with divining. 17 She fol-
lowed Paul and us, and cried, saying, These men are the servants of the most high
God, which show unto you the way of salvation. 18 And this did she [q]many
days: but Paul being grieved, turned about, and said to the spirit, I command
thee in the Name of Jesus Christ, that thou come out of her. And he came out
the same hour. 19 [r]Now when her masters saw that the hope of their gain was
gone, they caught Paul and Silas, and drew them into the marketplace unto the
Magistrates. 20 [s]And brought them to the governors, saying, These men which
are Jews trouble our city, 21 [t]And preach ordinances, which are not lawful for us
to receive, neither to observe, seeing we are Romans. 22 [u]The people also rose
up together against them, and the governors rent their clothes, and commanded
them to be beaten with rods. 23 And when they had beaten them sore, they cast
them into prison, commanding the Gaoler to keep them surely, 24 Who having
received such commandment, cast them into the inner prison, and made their feet
[v]fast in the stocks. 25 [w]Now at midnight Paul and Silas prayed, and sung Psal-
ms unto God: and the prisoners heard them. 26 And suddenly there was a great
earthquake, so that the foundation of the prison was shaken: and by and by all the
doors opened, and every man's bands were loosed. 27 [x]Then the keeper of the
prison waked out of his sleep, and when he saw the prison doors open, he drew
out his sword and would have killed himself, supposing the prisoners had been
fled. 28 [y]But Paul cried with a loud voice, saying, Do thyself no harm: for we all
are here. 29 Then he called for a light, and leaped in, and came trembling, and
fell down before Paul and Silas. 30 And brought them out, and said, Sirs, what
must I do to be saved? 31 And they said, Believe in the Lord Jesus Christ, and
thou shalt be saved, and thine household. 32 And they preached unto him the
word of the Lord, and to all that were in the house. 33 [z]Afterward he took them
the same hour of the night, and washed their stripes, and was baptized with all that
belonged unto him straightway. 34 And when he had brought them into his
house, he set meat before them, and rejoiced that he with all his household belie-
ved in God. 35 [aa]And when it was day, the governors sent the sergeants, saying,
Let those men go. 36 Then the keeper of the prison told these words unto Paul,
saying, The governors have sent to loose you: now therefore get you hence, and go
in peace. 37 [ab]Then said Paul unto them, After that they have beaten us openly
uncondemned, which are Romans, they have cast us into prison, and now would
they put us out privily? nay verily: but let them come and bring us out. 38 [ac]And
the sergeants told these words unto the governors, who feared when they heard that
they were Romans. 39 Then came they and prayed them, and brought them out,
and desired them to depart out of the city. 40 [ad]And they went out of the prison,
and entered into the house of Lydia: and when they had seen the brethren, they
comforted them, and departed.

17

1 Paul at Thessalonica 3 preaching Christ, 6, 7 is entertained of Jason: 10 He is sent to Berea: 15 from thence coming to Athens, 19 in Mars' street 23 he preacheth the living God to them unknown, 34 and so many are converted unto Christ.

1 Now [a]as they passed through Amphipolis, and Apollonia, they came to
Thessalonica, where was a Synagogue of the Jews. 2 And Paul, as his manner
was, went in unto them, and three Sabbath days disputed with them by the Scrip-
tures, 3 [b]Opening, and alleging that Christ must have suffered, and risen again
from the dead, and this is Jesus Christ, whom said he, I preach to you. 4 And
some of them believed, and joined in company with Paul and Silas: also of
the Grecians that feared God a great multitude, and of the chief women not a
few. 5 [c]But the Jews which believed not, moved with envy, took unto them cer-
tain [d]vagabonds and wicked fellows, and when they had assembled the multitude,
they made a tumult in the city, and made assault against the house of Jason, and
sought to bring them out to the people. 6 But when they found them not, they
drew Jason and certain brethren unto the heads of the city, crying, These are they
which have subverted the state of the [e]world, and here they are, 7 Whom Jason
hath received, and these all do against the decrees of Caesar, saying, that there is
another King one Jesus. 8 Then they troubled the people, and the heads of the
city, when they heard these things. 9 Notwithstanding when they had received
sufficient [f]assurance of Jason and of the others, they let them go. 10 [g]And the
brethren immediately sent away Paul and Silas by night unto Berea, which when
they were come thither, entered into the Synagogue of the Jews. 11 [h]These were
also more [i]noble men than they which were at Thessalonica, which received the
word with all readiness, and searched the Scriptures daily, whether those things
were so. 12 Therefore many of them believed, and of honest women, which

---

ACTS 16

- **a.** Acts 16:1 Paul himself doth not receive Timothy into the ministry without sufficient testimony, and allowance of the brethren.
- **b.** Acts 16:1 Paul in his latter Epistle to Timothy, commendeth the godliness of Timothy's mother and grandmother.
- **c.** Acts 16:2 Both for his godliness and honesty.
- **d.** Acts 16:3 Timothy is circumcised, not simply for any necessity, but in respect of the time only to win the Jews.
- **e.** Acts 16:4 Charity is to be observed in things indifferent so that regard be had both of the weak, and the quietness of the Church.
- **f.** Acts 16:4 These decrees which he spake of in the former chapter.
- **g.** Acts 16:6 God appointeth certain and determinate times to open and set forth his truth, that both the election and the calling may proceed of grace.
- **h.** Acts 16:6 He showeth not why they were forbidden, but only that they were forbidden, teaching us to obey and not to inquire.
- **i.** Acts 16:9 They are the ministers of the Gospel, by whom he helpeth such as were like to perish.
- **j.** Acts 16:10 The Saints did not easily believe every vision.
- **k.** Acts 16:13 God beginneth his kingdom in Macedonia by the conversion of a woman, and so showeth that there is no exception of persons in the Gospel.
- **l.** Acts 16:13 Where they were wont to assemble themselves.
- **m.** Acts 16:14 The Lord only openeth the heart to hear the word which is preached.
- **n.** Acts 16:15 An example of a godly housewife.
- **o.** Acts 16:16 Satan transformeth himself into an Angel of light, and coveteth to enter by undermining, but Paul openly letteth him, and casteth him out.
- **p.** Acts 16:16 This is a proper note of Apollo, which was wont to give answers to them that asked him.
- **q.** Acts 16:18 Paul made no haste to this miracle, for he did all things as he was led by the Spirit.
- **r.** Acts 16:19 Covetousness of lucre and gain is an occasion of persecuting the truth. In the mean season, God sparing Timothy, calleth Paul and Silas as the stronger, to battle.
- **s.** Acts 16:20 Covetousness pretendeth a desire of common peace and godliness.
- **t.** Acts 16:21 It is an argument of the devil, to urge the authority of ancestors without any distinction.
- **u.** Acts 16:22 An Example of evil Magistrates to obey the fury and rage of the people.
- **v.** Acts 16:24 Because he would be more sure of them, he set them fast in the stocks.
- **w.** Acts 16:25 The prayers of the godly do shake both heaven and earth.
- **x.** Acts 16:27 The merciful Lord, so oft as he listeth, draweth men to life, even through the midst of death, and whereas justly they deserved great punishment, he showeth them great mercy.
- **y.** Acts 16:28 In means which are especially extraordinary, we ought not to move our foot forward, unless that God goes before us.
- **z.** Acts 16:33 God with one selfsame hand woundeth and healeth, when it pleaseth him.
- **aa.** Acts 16:35 Shame and confusion is in process of time, the reward of wicked and unjust Magistrates.
- **ab.** Acts 16:37 We must not render injury for injury, and yet notwithstanding it is lawful for us to use such helps as God giveth us, to bridle the outrageousness of the wicked, that they hurt not others in like sort.
- **ac.** Acts 16:38 The wicked are not moved with the fear of God, but with the fear of men: and by that means also God provideth for his, when it is needful.
- **ad.** Acts 16:40 We may eschew dangers, so that we never neglect our duty.

ACTS 16

- **1.** Rom. 16:21; Phil. 2:19; 1 Thess. 3:2

ACTS 17

- **a.** Acts 17:1 The casting out of Silas and Paul, was the saving of many others.
- **b.** Acts 17:3 Christ is therefore the Mediator, because he was crucified and rose again: much less is he to be rejected, because the cross is ignominious.
- **c.** Acts 17:5 Although the zeal of the unfaithful seems never so goodly, yet at length it is found to have neither truth nor equity: But yet the wicked cannot do what they list, for even among themselves God stirreth up some, whose help he useth to the deliverance of his.
- **d.** Acts 17:5 Certain companions which do nothing but walk the streets, wicked men, to be hired for every man's money, to do any mischief, such as we commonly call the rascals and very sinks and dunghill knaves of all towns and cities.
- **e.** Acts 17:6 Into what country and place soever they come, they cause sedition and tumult.
- **f.** Acts 17:9 When Jason had put them in good assurance that they should appear.
- **g.** Acts 17:10 That is indeed the wisdom of the Spirit, which always setteth the glory of God before itself as a mark whereunto it directeth itself, and never swerveth from it.

were Grecians, and men not a few. **13** [j]But when the Jews of Thessalonica knew,
that the word of God was also preached of Paul at Berea, they came thither also,
and moved the people. **14** [k]But by and by the brethren sent away Paul to go as
it were to the sea: but Silas and Timothy abode there still. **15** [l]And they that did
conduct Paul, [m]brought him unto Athens: and when they had received a com-
mandment unto Silas and Timothy that they should come to him at once, they
departed. **16** [n]Now while Paul waited for them at Athens, his spirit was [o]stirred
in him, when he saw the city subject to [p]idolatry. **17** Therefore he disputeth
in the Synagogue with the Jews, and with them that were religious, and in the
market daily with [q]whomsoever he met. **18** [r]Then certain Philosophers of the
Epicureans, and of the Stoics, disputed with him, and some said, What will this
[s]babbler say? Others said, He seemeth to be a setter forth of strange gods (becau-
se he preached unto them Jesus, and the resurrection.) **19** And they took him,
and brought him into [t]Mars' street, saying, May we not know, what this new
doctrine, whereof thou speakest, is? **20** For thou bringest certain strange things
unto our ears: we would know therefore what these things mean. **21** [u]For all the
Athenians and strangers which dwelt there, gave themselves to nothing else, but
either to tell, or to hear some news. **22** [v]Then Paul stood in the midst of Mars'
street, and said, Ye men of Athens, I perceive that in all things ye are too [w]supersti-
tious. **23** For as I passed by, and beheld your [x]devotions, I found an altar whe-
rein was written, UNTO THE [y]UNKNOWN GOD. Whom ye then ignorantly
worship, him show I unto you. **24** [z]God that made the world, and all things that
are therein, seeing that he is Lord of heaven and earth, [1]dwelleth not in temples
made with hands. **25** [2]Neither is worshipped with men's hands, as though he
needed anything, seeing he giveth to all life and breath and all things, **26** [aa]And
hath made of [ab]one blood all mankind, to dwell on all the face of the earth, and
hath assigned the seasons which were ordained before, and the bounds of their
habitation, **27** That they should seek the Lord, if so be they might have [ac]gro-
ped after him, and found him, though doubtless he be not far from every one of
us. **28** For in him we live, and move, and have our being, as also certain of your
own Poets have said: For we are also his generation. **29** [3]Forasmuch then, as we
are the generation of God, we ought not to think that the Godhead is like unto
gold, or silver, or stone [ad]graven by art and the invention of man. **30** [ae]And
the time of this ignorance God regarded not: but now he admonisheth all men
everywhere to repent. **31** Because he hath appointed a day in the which he will
judge the world in righteousness, by that man whom he hath appointed, where-
of he hath given an [af]assurance to all men, in that he hath raised him from the
dead. **32** [ag]Now when they had heard of the resurrection from the dead, some
mocked, and others said, We will hear thee again of this thing. **33** And so Paul
departed from among them. **34** Howbeit certain men clave unto Paul, and belie-
ved: among whom was also Dionysius Areopagite, and a woman named Damaris,
and others with them.

18

As Paul at Corinth 6 taught the Gentiles, 9 the Lord comforteth him. 12 He is accused before Gallio, 16 but in vain: 18 From thence he saileth to Syria, 19 and so to Ephesus. 23 At Galatia and Phrygia he strengtheneth the disciples. 24 Apollos being more perfectly instructed by Aquila, 28 preacheth Christ with great efficacy.

1 After [a]these things, Paul departed from Athens, and came to Corin-
th, **2** And found a certain Jew named [1]Aquila, born in Pontus, lately come from
Italy, and his wife Priscilla (because that [b]Claudius had commanded all Jews to de-
part from Rome) and he came unto them. **3** And because he was of the same craft,
he abode with them and wrought (for their craft was to make tents.) **4** [c]And he
disputed in the Synagogue every Sabbath day, and [d]exhorted the Jews, and the Gre-
cians. **5** Now when Silas and Timothy were come from Macedonia, Paul, [e]forced
in spirit, testified to the Jews that Jesus was the Christ. **6** [f]And when they resisted
and blasphemed, he [2]shook his raiment, and said unto them, Your [g]blood be upon
your own head: I am clean: from henceforth will I go unto the Gentiles. **7** So he
departed thence, and entered into a certain man's house, named Justus, a worship-
per of God, whose house joined hard to the Synagogue. **8** And [3]Crispus the chief
ruler of the Synagogue, believed in the Lord with all his household: and many of
the Corinthians hearing it, believed and were baptized. **9** [h]Then said the Lord to
Paul in the night by a vision, Fear not, but speak, and hold not thy peace. **10** For
I am with thee, and no man shall lay hands on thee to hurt thee: for I have much
people in this city. **11** So he [i]continued there a year and six months, and taught
the word of God among them. **12** [j]Now when Gallio was deputy of [k]Achaia,
the Jews arose with one accord against Paul, and brought him to the judgment
seat, **13** Saying, This fellow persuadeth men to worship God otherwise than the
Law appointeth. **14** And as Paul was about to open his mouth, Gallio said unto
the Jews, If it were a matter of wrong, or an evil deed, O ye Jews, I would according
to [l]reason maintain you. **15** But if it be a question of [m]words and [n]names, and of
your Law, look ye to it yourselves: for I will be no judge of those things. **16** And
he drove them from the judgment seat. **17** Then took all the Grecians Sosthenes
the chief ruler of the Synagogue, and beat him before the judgment seat: but Gallio
cared nothing for those things. **18** [o]But when Paul had tarried there yet a good
while, he took leave of the brethren, and sailed into Syria, (and with him Priscil-
la and Aquila) after that [p]he had shorn his head in [q]Cenchrea: for he had made a
[4]vow. **19** Then he came to Ephesus, and left them there: but he entered into the
Synagogue and disputed with the Jews. **20** [r]Who desired him to tarry a longer
time with them: but he would not consent, **21** But bade them farewell, saying, I
must needs keep this feast that cometh, in Jerusalem: but I will return again unto
you, [s,5]if God will. So he sailed from Ephesus. **22** And when he came down to
Caesarea, he went up to Jerusalem: and when he had saluted the Church, he went
down unto Antioch. **23** Now when he had tarried there a while, he departed,
and went through the country of Galatia and Phrygia by order, strengthening all

---

h. Acts 17:11 The Lord setteth out in one moment, and in one people, divers examples of his unsearchable wisdom, to cause them to fear him.
i. Acts 17:11 He compareth the Jews, with the Jews.
j. Acts 17:13 Satan hath his, who are zealous for him, and that even such, as least of all ought.
k. Acts 17:14 There is neither counsel, nor fury, nor madness, against the Lord.
l. Acts 17:15 The sheep of Christ do also watch for their pastor's health and safety, but yet in the Lord.
m. Acts 17:15 It is not for nought that the Jews of Berea were so commended, for they brought Paul safe from Macedonia to Athens, and there is in distance betwixt those two, all Thessalia, and Boeotia, and Attica.
n. Acts 17:16 In comparing the wisdom of God with man's wisdom, men scoff and mock at that which they understand not: And God useth the curiosity of fools to gather together his elect.
o. Acts 17:16 He could not forbear.
p. Acts 17:16 Slavishly given to Idolatry: Pausanias writeth that there were more Idols in Athens, than in all Greece, yea they had altars dedicated to Shame, and Fame, and Lust, whom they made goddesses.
q. Acts 17:17 Whomsoever Paul met with, that would suffer him to talk with him, he reasoned with him, so thoroughly did he burn with the zeal of God's glory.
r. Acts 17:18 Two sects especially of the Philosophers do set themselves against Christ: the Epicureans, which make a mock and scoff at all religions, and the Stoics, which determine upon matters of religion according to their own brains.
s. Acts 17:18 Word for word, seed gatherer: a borrowed kind of speech taken of birds which spoil corn, and is applied to them which without all art bluster out such knowledge as they have gotten by hearing this man and that man.
t. Acts 17:19 This was a place called as you would say, Mars hill, where the judges sat which were called Areopagus, upon weighty affairs, which in old time arraigned Socrates, and afterward condemned him of impiety.
u. Acts 17:21 The wisdom of man is vanity.
v. Acts 17:22 The idolaters themselves minister most strong and forcible arguments against their own superstition.
w. Acts 17:22 To stand in too peevish and servile a fear of your gods.
x. Acts 17:23 Whatsoever men worship for religion's sake, that we call devotion.
y. Acts 17:23 Pausanias in his Atticis, maketh mention of the altar which the Athenians had dedicated to unknown gods: and Laertius in his Epimenides maketh mention of an altar that had no name entitled.
z. Acts 17:24 It is a most foolish and vain thing to compare the Creator with the creature, to limit him within a place, which can be comprehended in no place, and to think to allure him with gifts, of whom all men have received all things whatsoever they have: And these are the fountains of all idolatry.
aa. Acts 17:26 God is wonderful in all his works, but especially in the work of man: not that we should stand amazed at his works, but that we should lift up our eyes to the workman.
ab. Acts 17:26 Of one stock and one beginning.
ac. Acts 17:27 For as blind men we could not seek out God, but only by groping wise, before the true light came and lightened the world.
ad. Acts 17:29 Which stuff, as gold, silver, stones, are customably graven as a man's wit can devise, for men will not worship that gross stuff as it is, unless by some art it have gotten some shape upon it.
ae. Acts 17:30 The oldness of the error doth not excuse them that err, but it commendeth and setteth forth the patience of God: who notwithstanding will be a just judge to such as contemn him.
af. Acts 17:31 By declaring Christ to be the judge of the world through the resurrection from the dead.
ag. Acts 17:32 Men, to show forth their vanity, are diversely affected and moved with one selfsame Gospel, which notwithstanding ceaseth not to be effectual in the elect.

ACTS 17

1. Acts 7:48
2. Ps. 50:8
3. Isa. 40:19

ACTS 18

a. Acts 18:1 The true ministers are so far from seeking their own profit, that they do willingly depart from their right, rather than the course of the Gospel should be hindered in the least wise that might be.
b. Acts 18:2 Suetonius recordeth that Rome banished the Jews, because they were always at disquiet, and that by Christ's means.
c. Acts 18:4 The truth ought always to be freely uttered, yet notwithstanding the doctrine may be so moderated, as occasion of the profit that the people take thereby, shall require.
d. Acts 18:4 Exhorted so that he persuaded, and so the word signifieth.
e. Acts 18:5 Was very much grieved in mind: whereby is signified the great earnestness of his mind, which was greatly moved: for Paul was so zealous, that he clean forgot himself, and with a wonderful courage gave himself to preach Christ.
f. Acts 18:6 Although we have assayed all means possible, and yet in vain, we must not leave off from our work, but forsake the rebellious, and go to them that be more obedient.
g. Acts 18:6 This is a kind of speech taken from the Hebrews, whereby he meaneth, that the Jews are cause of their own destruction: and as for him, that he is without fault in forsaking them and going to other nations.
h. Acts 18:9 God doth avouch and maintain the constancy of his servants.
i. Acts 18:11 Word for word, sat, whereupon they in former time, took the name of their Bishop's seat: but Paul sat, that is, continued teaching the word of God: and this kind of seat belongeth nothing to them which never saw their seats with a mind to teach in them.
j. Acts 18:12 The wicked are never weary of evil doing, but the Lord mocketh their endeavors marvelously.
k. Acts 18:12 That is, of Greece, yet the Romans did not call him Deputy of Greece, but of Achaia, because the Romans brought the Greeks into subjection by the Achaians, which in those days were Princes of Greece, as Pausanias recordeth.
l. Acts 18:14 As much as in right I could.
m. Acts 18:15 As if a man have not spoken well, as the case of your religion standeth.
n. Acts 18:15 For this profane man thinketh that the controversy of religion, is but a brawl about words, and for no matter of substance.
o. Acts 18:18 Paul is made all to all, to win all to Christ.
p. Acts 18:18 That is, Paul.
q. Acts 18:18 Cenchrea was an haven of the Corinthians.
r. Acts 18:20 The Apostles were carried about not by the will of man, but by the leading of the holy Ghost.
s. Acts 18:21 So we should promise nothing without this clause, for we know not what the day following will bring forth.

the disciples. **24** [t]And a certain Jew named [6]Apollos, born at Alexandria, came to
Ephesus, an eloquent man, and [u]mighty in the Scriptures. **25** The same was in-
structed in the way of the Lord, and he spake fervently in the Spirit, and taught di-
ligently the things of the Lord, and knew but the baptism of John only. **26** And
he began to speak boldly in the Synagogue. Whom when [7]Aquila and Priscilla
had heard, they took him unto them, and expounded unto him the [v]way of God
more perfectly. **27** And when he was minded to go into Achaia, the brethren
exhorting him, wrote to the disciples to receive him: and after he was come thither,
he helped them much which had believed through [w]grace. **28** For mightily he
confuted publicly the Jews, with great vehemency, showing by the Scriptures, that
Jesus was that Christ.

19

*Certain disciples at Ephesus, 3 having only received John's baptism, 2
and know not the visible gifts of the holy Ghost, wherewith God had be-
autified his Son's kingdom, 5 are baptized in the Name of Jesus. 13 The Jewish
exorcists 16 are beaten of the devil. 19 Conjuring books are burnt. 24 Demetri-
us 29 raiseth sedition against Paul.*

1 And [a]it came to pass, while Apollos was at Corinth, that Paul when he
passed through the upper coasts, came to Ephesus, and found certain disci-
ples, **2** And said unto them, Have ye received the [b]holy Ghost since ye believed?
And they said unto him, We have not so much as heard whether there be an holy
Ghost. **3** [c]And he said unto them, Unto [d]what were ye then baptized? And they
said, Unto [e]John's baptism. **4** Then said Paul, [1]John verily baptized with the
baptism of repentance, saying unto the people, that they should believe in him,
which should come after him, that is, in Christ Jesus. **5** And when they heard it,
they were baptized in the Name of the Lord Jesus. **6** So Paul laid his hands upon
them, and the holy Ghost came on them, and they spake the tongues, and prophe-
sied. **7** And all the men were about twelve. **8** Moreover he went into the Sy-
nagogue, and spake boldly for the space of three months, disputing and exhorting
to the things that appertain to the kingdom of God. **9** [f]But when certain were
hardened, and disobeyed, speaking evil of the [g]way of God before the multitude,
he departed from them, and separated the disciples, and disputed daily in the
school of one [h]Tyrannus. **10** And this was done by the space of two years, so
that all they which dwelt in Asia, heard the word of the Lord Jesus, both Jews and
Grecians. **11** And God wrought no small miracles by the hands of Paul, **12** So
that from his body were brought unto the sick, kerchiefs, or handkerchiefs, and
the diseases departed from them, and the evil spirits went out of them. **13** [i]Then
certain of the vagabond Jews, [j]exorcists took in hand to name over them which
had evil spirits, the name of the Lord Jesus, saying, We adjure you by Jesus, whom
Paul preacheth. **14** (And there were certain sons of Sceva a Jew, the Priest, about
seven which did this.) **15** And the evil spirit answered, and said, Jesus I acknow-
ledge, and Paul I know: but who are ye? **16** And the man in whom the evil spirit
was, ran on them, and overcame them, and [k]prevailed against them, so that they
fled out of that house, naked and wounded. **17** And this was known to all the
Jews and Grecians also which dwelt at Ephesus, and fear came on them all, and the
Name of the Lord Jesus was magnified, **18** [l]And many that believed, came and
[m]confessed, and showed their works. **19** Many also of them which used curious
arts, brought their books, and burned them before all men: and they counted the
price of them, and found it [n]fifty thousand pieces of silver. **20** So the word of
God grew mightily, and prevailed. **21** [o]Now when these things were accompli-
shed, Paul purposed by the [p]Spirit to pass through Macedonia and Achaia, and to
go to Jerusalem, saying, After I have been there, I must also see Rome. **22** So
sent he into Macedonia two of them that ministered unto him, Timothy, and
Erastus, but he remained in Asia for a season. **23** [q]And the same time there
arose no small trouble about that way. **24** For a certain man named Demetrius
a silversmith, which made silver [r]temples of Diana, brought great gains unto the
craftsmen, **25** Whom he called together, with the workmen of like things, and
said, Sirs, ye know that by this craft we have our goods: **26** Moreover ye see and
hear, that not alone at Ephesus, but almost throughout all Asia this Paul hath per-
suaded, and turned away much people, saying, That they be not Gods which are
made with hands. **27** So that not only this thing is dangerous unto us, that this
our [s]portion shall be reproved, but also that the temple of the great goddess Diana
should be nothing esteemed, and that it would come to pass that her magnificence,
which all Asia and the world worshippeth, should be destroyed. **28** Now when
they heard it, they were full of wrath, and cried out, saying, Great is Diana of the
Ephesians. **29** And the whole city was full of confusion, and they rushed into
the common place with one assent, and caught [2]Gaius, and [3]Aristarchus, men of
Macedonia, and Paul's companions of his journey. **30** And when Paul would
have entered in unto the people, the disciples suffered him not. **31** [t]Certain also
of the chief of Asia, which were his friends, sent unto him, desiring him that he
would not present himself in the Common place. **32** Some therefore cried one
thing, and some another: for the assembly was out of order, and the more part
knew not wherefore they were come together. **33** And some of the company
drew forth Alexander, the Jews thrusting him forwards. Alexander then becko-
ned with the hand, and would have excused the matter to the people. **34** [u]But
when they knew that he was a Jew, there arose a shout almost for the space of two
hours, of all men, crying, Great is Diana of the Ephesians. **35** [v]Then the town
clerk when he had stayed the people, said, Ye men of Ephesus, what man is it that
knoweth not how that the city of the Ephesians is a worshipper of the great god-
dess Diana, and of the image, which [w]came down from Jupiter? **36** Seeing then
that no man can speak against these things, ye ought to be appeased, and to do
nothing rashly. **37** For ye have brought hither these men, which have neither
committed sacrilege, neither do blaspheme your goddess. **38** Wherefore, if De-
metrius and the craftsmen which are with him, have a [x]matter against any man,
the [y]law is open, and there are [z]Deputies: let them accuse one another. **39** But if
ye inquire anything concerning other matters, it may be determined in a [aa]lawful
assembly. **40** For we are even in jeopardy to be accused of this day's sedition,
forasmuch as there is no cause, whereby we may give a reason of this concourse of
people. **41** And when he had thus spoken, he let the assembly depart.

20

*1 Paul appointed to go to Macedonia: 7 In Troas preaching until mid-
night, 9 Eutychus fell down dead out of a window, 10 he raised him
to life: 15 At Miletus, 17 Having called the Elders of Ephesus together, 23 he
declareth what things shall come upon himself, 28 and others.*

1 Now [a]after the tumult was appeased, Paul called the disciples unto him,
and embraced them, and departed to go into Macedonia. **2** And when he had
gone through those parts, and had exhorted them with [b]many words, he came into
Greece. **3** [c]And having tarried there three months, because the Jews laid wait for
him, as he was about to sail into Syria, he purposed to return through Macedo-
nia. **4** And there accompanied him into Asia, Sopater of Berea, and of them of
Thessalonica, Aristarchus, and Secundus, and Gaius of Derbe, and Timothy, and
of them of Asia, Tychicus, and Trophimus. **5** These went before, and tarried us at

---

t. Acts 18:24 Apollos, a godly and learned man, refuseth not to profit in the school of a base and abject handicraftsman, and also of a woman: and so becometh an excellent minister of the Church.

u. Acts 18:24 Very well instructed in the knowledge of the Scriptures.

v. Acts 18:26 The way that leadeth to God.

w. Acts 18:27 Through God's gracious favor, or by those excellent gifts which God hath bestowed upon him.

ACTS 18

1. Rom. 16:3
2. Acts 13:51; Matt. 10:14
3. 1 Cor. 1:14
4. Num. 16:18; Acts 21:24
5. 1 Cor. 4:19; James 4:15
6. 1 Cor. 1:12
7. Rom. 16:3

ACTS 19

a. Acts 19:1 Paul being nothing offended at the rudeness of the Ephesians, planted a Church among them.

b. Acts 19:2 Those excellent gifts of the holy Ghost, which were in those days in the Church.

c. Acts 19:3 John did only begin to instruct the disciples whom Christ should make perfect.

d. Acts 19:3 In what doctrine then are you taught and instructed?

e. Acts 19:3 To be baptized into John's baptism, is to profess the doctrine which John preached and sealed with his baptism.

f. Acts 19:9 For a man to separate himself and others from infidels which are utterly desperate, it is not to divide the Church, but rather to unite it and make it one.

g. Acts 19:9 By this word Way, the Hebrews understand any kind of life, and here it is taken for Christianity.

h. Acts 19:9 This was a man's proper name.

i. Acts 19:13 Satan is constrained to give witness against himself.

j. Acts 19:13 So were they called which cast out devils by conjuring them in the Name of God: and in the beginning of the Church, they which had the gift of working miracles, and laid their hands on them that were possessed with devils, were also so called.

k. Acts 19:16 He prevailed against them, though they strove never so much.

l. Acts 19:18 Conjuring and sorcery is condemned by open testimony, and by the authority of the Apostle.

m. Acts 19:18 Confessed their errors, and detested them openly, being terrified with the fear of the judgment of God: and what is this to ear shrift?

n. Acts 19:19 They that make the least value of it, reckon it to be about eight hundred pounds English.

o. Acts 19:21 Paul is never weary.

p. Acts 19:21 By the motion of God's Spirit: therefore we may not say that Paul ran hand over head to death, but as the Spirit of God led him.

q. Acts 19:23 Gain cloaked with a show of religion is the very cause wherefore idolatry is stoutly and stubbornly defended.

r. Acts 19:24 These were certain counterfeit temples with Diana's picture in them which they bought that worshipped her.

s. Acts 19:27 As if he said, If Paul go on thus as he hath begun to confute the opinion which men have of Diana's image, all this our gain will come to nought.

t. Acts 19:31 There ought to be in all Christians and especially in the Ministers, an invincible constancy, which may not by any storms or assaults be overcome, which notwithstanding must suffer itself modestly to be governed by wisdom.

u. Acts 19:34 Instead of reason, the idolaters are sufficiently contented with their own madness and outcries, and those are the greatest defenses that they have.

v. Acts 19:35 An example of a political man who redeemeth peace and quietness with lies, which Paul would never have done.

w. Acts 19:35 The Ephesians believed superstitiously, that the image of Diana came down from heaven to them.

x. Acts 19:38 Have ought to accuse any man of.

y. Acts 19:38 For there are certain days appointed for civil causes and matters of judgment, and the Deputies sit.

z. Acts 19:38 By the Deputies are meant also the Deputies' Substitutes, that is, such as did sit for them.

aa. Acts 19:39 He speaketh of a lawful assembly, not only to except against the disordered hurly-burly of the people, but also against all meeting and coming together which was not by order: for there were certain days appointed to call the people together in.

ACTS 19

1. Acts 1:5; Acts 2:2; Acts 11:16; Matt. 3:11; Mark 1:8; Luke 3:16; John 1:26
2. Rom. 16:23; 1 Cor. 1:14
3. Col. 4:10

ACTS 20

a. Acts 20:1 Paul departed from Ephesus by the consent of the Church, not to be idle or at rest, but to take pains in another place.

b. Acts 20:2 For after so great trouble there was need of a long exhortation.

c. Acts 20:3 A froward zeal is the guider and instructor to murders: and we are not debarred by the wisdom of God to prevent the endeavors of wicked men.

Troas. 6 And we sailed forth from Philippi, after the days of unleavened bread,
and came unto them to Troas in five days, where we abode seven days. 7 [d]And
the [e]first day of the week, the disciples being come together to break bread, Paul
preached unto them, ready to depart on the morrow, and continued the preaching
unto midnight. 8 [f]And there were many lights in an upper chamber, where they
were gathered together. 9 And there sat in a window a certain young man, na-
med Eutychus, fallen into a dead sleep: and as Paul was long preaching, he over-
come with sleep, fell down from the third loft, and was taken up dead. 10 But
Paul went down, and laid himself upon him, and embraced him, saying, Trouble
not yourselves: for his life is in him. 11 Then when Paul was come up again,
and had broken bread, and eaten, having spoken a long while till the dawning of
the day, he so departed. 12 And they brought the boy alive, and they were not a
little comforted. 13 Then we went before to ship, and sailed unto the city Assos,
that we might receive Paul there: for so had he appointed, and would himself go
afoot. 14 Now when he was come unto us to Assos, and we had received him,
we came to Mitylene. 15 And we sailed thence, and came the next day over
against Chios, and the next day we arrived at Samos, and tarried at Trogyllium:
the next day we came to Miletus. 16 [g]For Paul had determined to sail by Ephe-
sus, because he would not spend the time in Asia: for he hasted to be, if he could
possible, at Jerusalem, at the day of Pentecost. 17 Wherefore from [h]Miletus,
he sent to Ephesus, and called the Elders of the Church. 18 [i]Who when they
were come to him, he said unto them, Ye know from the first day that I came into
Asia, after what manner I have been with you at all seasons, 19 Serving the Lord
with all modesty, and with many tears, and temptations, which came unto me by
the layings await of the Jews, 20 And how I kept [j]back nothing that was pro-
fitable, but have showed you, and taught you openly and throughout every hou-
se. 21 Witnessing both to the Jews, and to the Grecians the repentance toward
God, and faith toward our Lord Jesus Christ. 22 [k]And now behold, I go [l]bound
in the Spirit unto Jerusalem, and know not what things shall come unto me the-
re, 23 Save that the holy Ghost witnesseth in every city, saying, that bonds and
afflictions abide me. 24 But I pass not at all, neither is my life dear unto myself,
so that I may fulfill my course with joy, and the ministration which I have recei-
ved of the Lord Jesus, to testify the Gospel of the grace of God. 25 And now
behold, I know that henceforth ye all, through whom I have gone preaching the
kingdom of God, shall see my face no more. 26 Wherefore I take you to record
this day, that I am [m]pure from the blood of all men. 27 [n]For I have kept nothing
back, but have showed you all the counsel of God. 28 Take heed therefore unto
yourselves, and to all the flock, whereof the holy Ghost hath made you Overseers
to [o]feed the Church of God which [p]he hath purchased with [q]that his own blo-
od. 29 [r]For I know this, that after my departing shall grievous wolves enter in
among you, not sparing the flock. 30 Moreover of your own selves shall men
arise speaking perverse things, to [s]draw disciples after them. 31 Therefore wa-
tch, and remember, that by the space of three years I ceased not to warn everyone,
both night and day with tears. 32 [t]And now brethren, I commend you to God,
and to the word of his grace, which is able to build further, and to give you an
[u]inheritance, among all them, which are sanctified. 33 [v]I have coveted no man's
silver, nor gold, nor apparel. 34 Yea, ye know, that these hands have ministered
unto my [1]necessities, and to them that were with me. 35 I have showed you all
things, how that so laboring, ye ought to [w]support the weak, and to remember the
words of the Lord Jesus, how that he said, It is a blessed thing to give, rather than
to receive. 36 And when he had thus spoken, he kneeled down, and prayed with
them all. 37 [x]Then they wept all abundantly, and fell on Paul's neck, and kissed
him, 38 Being chiefly sorry for the words which he spake, That they should see
his face no more. And they accompanied him unto the ship.

21

1 Paul goeth toward Jerusalem: 8 at Caesarea he talketh with Philip the Evangelist: 10 Agabus foretelleth him of his bonds. 17 After he came to Jerusalem, 26 and into the Temple, 27 The Jews laid hands on him: 32 Lysias the captain taketh him from them.

1 And [a]as we launched forth, and were departed from them, we came with
a straight course unto Cos, and the day following unto the Rhodes, and from
thence unto Patara. 2 And we found a ship that went over unto Phoenicia, and
went aboard, and set forth. 3 And when we had discovered Cyprus, we left it
on the left hand, and sailed toward Syria, and arrived at Tyre: for there the ship
unladed the burden. 4 And when we had found disciples, we tarried there seven
days. And they told Paul through the [b]Spirit, that he should not go up to Jerusa-
lem. 5 But when the days were ended, we departed and went our way, and they
all accompanied us with their wives and children, even out of the city: and we kne-
eled down on the shore, prayed. 6 Then when we had embraced one another, we
took ship, and they returned home. 7 And when we had ended the course from
Tyre, we arrived at Ptolemais, and saluted the brethren, and abode with them one
day. 8 And the next day, Paul and we that were with him, departed, and came
unto Caesarea: and we entered into the house of [1]Philip the Evangelist, which was
one of the [c]seven Deacons, and abode with him. 9 Now he had four daughters,
virgins, which did [d]prophesy. 10 And as we tarried there many days, there came
a certain Prophet from Judea, named Agabus. 11 And when he was come unto
us, he took Paul's girdle, and bound his own hands and feet, and said, Thus saith
the holy Ghost, So shall the Jews at Jerusalem bind the man that owneth this girdle,
and shall deliver him into the hands of the Gentiles. 12 And when we had heard
these things, both we and others of the same place besought him that he would not
go up to Jerusalem. 13 Then Paul answered, and said, What do ye weeping and
breaking mine heart? For I am ready not to be bound only, but also to die at Jerusa-
lem for the Name of the Lord Jesus. 14 [e]So when he would not be persuaded, we
ceased, saying, The will of the Lord be done. 15 And after those days we trussed
up our fardels, and went up to Jerusalem. 16 There went with us also certain of
the disciples of Caesarea, and brought with them one Mnason of Cyprus, an old
disciple, with whom we should lodge. 17 And when we were come to Jerusalem,
the brethren received us gladly. 18 And the next day Paul went in with us unto
James: and all the Elders were there assembled. 19 [f]And when he had embraced
them, he told by order all things, that God had wrought among the Gentiles by his
ministration. 20 [g]So when they heard it, they glorified God, and said unto him,
Thou seest, brother, how many thousand Jews there are which believe, and they
are all zealous of the Law: 21 Now they are informed of thee, that thou teachest
all the Jews, which are among the Gentiles, to forsake Moses, and sayest that they
ought not to circumcise their sons, neither to live after the customs. 22 What
is then to be done? the multitude must needs come together: for they shall hear
that thou art come. 23 Do therefore this that we say to thee. We have four men,
which have made a vow, 24 Them take, and [h]purify thyself with them, and [i]con-
tribute with them, that they may [2]shave their heads: and all shall know, that those
things, whereof they have been informed concerning thee, are nothing, but that
thou thyself also walkest and keepest the Law. 25 For as touching the Gentiles,
which believe, we have written, and determined that they observe no such thing,
but that they keep themselves from things offered to idols, and from blood, and

---

d. Acts 20:7 Assemblies in the nighttime cannot be justly condemned, neither ought, when the cause is good.
e. Acts 20:7 Word for word, the first day of the Sabbath, that is upon the Lord's day: so that by this place, and by 1 Cor. 16:2, it is not amiss gathered, that in those days the Christians were wont to assemble themselves solemnly together upon that day.
f. Acts 20:8 The devil minding to trouble the Church with a great offense, giveth Paul a singular occasion to confirm the Gospel.
g. Acts 20:16 Paul an earnest and diligent follower of Christ, making haste to his bonds without any ceasing or stopping in his race, doth first of all as it were make his testament, wherein he giveth an account of his former life, defendeth the doctrine which he taught, and exhorteth the Pastors of the Church to persevere and go forward with continuance in their office.
h. Acts 20:17 According as the situation of these places is set forth, that distance between Ephesus and Miletus was about 400 furlongs, which maketh almost fifty Dutch miles.
i. Acts 20:18 A lively image of a true pastor.
j. Acts 20:20 I refrained not to speak, neither dissembled in any respect whatsoever, either for fear or lucre's sake.
k. Acts 20:22 He testifieth that he goeth to his bonds by the commandment of God.
l. Acts 20:22 He calleth that motion of the holy Ghost, which forced him to take his journey to Jerusalem, the bond of the Sprit, whom he followed with all his heart.
m. Acts 20:26 If you do perish, yet there shall be no fault in me, see Acts 18:6.
n. Acts 20:27 The doctrine of the Apostles is most perfect and absolute.
o. Acts 20:28 To keep it, to feed it, and govern it.
p. Acts 20:28 A notable sentence for Christ's Godhead: which showeth plainly in his person, how that by reason of the joining together of the two natures in his own person, that which is proper to one is spoken of the other being taken in the derivative, and not in the primitive: which in old time the godly fathers termed a communicating or fellowship of proprieties, that is to say, a making common of that to two, which belongeth but to one.
q. Acts 20:28 This word, That showeth the excellency of this blood.
r. Acts 20:29 A prophecy of pastors that should straightway degenerate into wolves against such as boast and brag only of a succession of persons.
s. Acts 20:30 This is a great misery, to want the presence of such a shepherd, but greater to have wolves enter in.
t. Acts 20:32 The power of God, and his free promises revealed in his word, are the props and upholders of the ministry of the Gospel.
u. Acts 20:32 As children, and therefore of free love and good will.
v. Acts 20:33 Pastors must before all things beware of covetousness.
w. Acts 20:35 As it were by reaching out the hand to them, which otherwise are about to slip and fall away, and so to stay them.
x. Acts 20:37 The Gospel doth not take away natural affections, but ruleth and bridleth them in good order.

ACTS 20

1. 1 Cor. 4:12; 1 Thess. 2:9; 2 Thess. 3:8

ACTS 21

a. Acts 21:1 Not only men simply, but even our friends, and such as are endued with the Spirit of God, do sometimes go about to hinder the course of our vocation: but it is our part to go forward without all stopping or staggering, after that we are sure of our calling from God.
b. Acts 21:4 They foretold through the Spirit what danger hanged over Paul's head, and this they did as Prophets: but of a fleshly affection they frayed him from going to Jerusalem.
c. Acts 21:8 He speaketh of the seven Deacons which he mentioned before, Acts 6.
d. Acts 21:9 They had a peculiar gift of foretelling things to come.
e. Acts 21:14 The will of God bridleth all affections in them which earnestly seek the glory of God.
f. Acts 21:19 God is to be praised, who is the Author of all good sayings and deeds.
g. Acts 21:20 In things indifferent (of which sort were not the traditions of the Pharisees, but the ceremonies of the Law, until such time as Christian liberty was more fully revealed to the Jews) charity willeth us to conform or apply ourselves willingly so far as we may, to our brethren which do not stubbornly, and maliciously, resist the truth, but are not thoroughly instructed especially if the question be of a whole multitude.
h. Acts 21:24 That is, consecrate thyself: for he speaketh not here of the unclean, but of such as were subject to the vow of the Nazarites.
i. Acts 21:24 That it may be known, that thou wast not only present at the vow, but also a chief man in it: and therefore it is said afterwards, that Paul declared the days of purification: for although the charges for the Nazarites' offerings were

from that that is strangled, and from fornication. **26** Then Paul took the men, and the next day was purified with them, and entered into the Temple, [j]declaring the accomplishment of the days of the purification, until that an offering should be offered for everyone of them. **27** [k]And when the seven days were almost ended, the Jews which were of Asia (when they saw him in the Temple) moved all the people, and laid hands on him, **28** Crying, Men of Israel, help: this is the man that teachest all men everywhere against the people, and the Law, and this place: moreover, he hath brought Grecians into the Temple, and hath polluted this holy place. **29** For they had seen before Trophimus an Ephesian with him in the city, whom they supposed that Paul had brought into the Temple. **30** Then all the city was moved, and the people ran together: and they took Paul, and drew him out of the Temple, and forthwith the doors were shut. **31** [l]But as they went about to kill him, tidings came unto the chief captain of the band, that all Jerusalem was on an uproar. **32** Who immediately took soldiers and Centurions, and ran down unto them: and when they saw the chief captain and the soldiers, they left beating of Paul. **33** Then the chief Captain came near and took him, and commanded him to be bound with two chains, and demanded who he was, and what he had done. **34** And one cried this, another that, among the people. So when he could not know the certainty for the tumult, he commanded him to be led into the castle. **35** And when he came unto the grieces, it was so that he was borne of the soldiers, for the violence of the people. **36** For the multitude of the people followed after, crying, Away with him. **37** And as Paul should have been led into the castle, he said unto the chief captain, May I speak unto thee? Who said, Canst thou speak Greek? **38** Art not thou the [m]Egyptian who before these days raised a sedition, and led out into the wilderness four thousand men that were murderers? **39** Then Paul said, Doubtless, I am a man which am a Jew, and citizen of Tarsus, a famous city of Cilicia, and I beseech thee, suffer me to speak unto the people. **40** And when he had given him license, Paul stood on the grieces, and beckoned with the hand unto the people, and when there was made great silence, he spake unto them in the Hebrew tongue, saying,

22

1 Paul yieldeth a reason of his faith, 22 and the Jews heard him awhile: 23 But so soon as they cried out, 24 He is commanded to be scourged and examined, 27 and so declareth that he is citizen of Rome.

1 Ye men, brethren and fathers, hear my defense now towards you. **2** (And when they heard that he spake in the Hebrew tongue to them, they kept the more silence, and he said,) **3** [a]I am verily a man, which am a Jew, born in Tarsus in Cilicia, but brought up in this city at the [b]feet of Gamaliel, and instructed according to the perfect manner of the Law of the fathers, and was zealous toward God, as ye all are this day. **4** And I persecuted this way unto the death, binding and delivering into prison both men and women. **5** As also the chief Priest doth bear me witness, and all the company of the Elders: of whom also I received letters unto the brethren, and went to Damascus to bring them which were there, bound unto Jerusalem, that they might be punished. **6** And so it was, as I journeyed, and was come near unto Damascus about noon, that suddenly there shone from heaven a great light round about me. **7** So I fell unto the earth, and heard a voice, saying unto me, Saul, Saul, why persecutest thou me? **8** Then I answered, Who art thou, Lord? And he said to me, I am Jesus of Nazareth, whom thou persecutest. **9** Moreover they that were with me, saw indeed a light and were afraid: but they heard not the voice of him that spake unto me. **10** Then I said, What shall I do, Lord? And the Lord said unto me, Arise, and go into Damascus: and there it shall be told thee of all things, which are appointed for thee to do. **11** So when I could not see for the glory of that light, I was led by the hand of them that were with me, and came into Damascus. **12** And one Ananias a godly man, as pertaining to the Law, having good report of all the Jews which dwelt there, **13** Came unto me, and stood, and said unto me, Brother Saul, receive thy sight: and that same hour I looked upon him. **14** And he said, The God of our fathers hath appointed thee, that thou shouldest know his will, and shouldest see that Just one, and shouldest hear the voice of his mouth. **15** For thou shalt be his witness unto all men, of the things which thou hast seen and heard. **16** Now therefore why tarriest thou? Arise, and be baptized, and wash away thy sins, in calling on the Name of the Lord. **17** And it came to pass, that when I was come again to Jerusalem, and prayed in the Temple, I was in a trance, **18** And saw him, saying unto me, Make haste, and get thee quickly out of Jerusalem: for they will not receive thy witness concerning me. **19** Then I said, Lord, they know that I prisoned, and beat in every Synagogue them that believed in thee. **20** And when the blood of thy martyr Stephen was shed, I also stood by, and consented unto his death, and kept the clothes of them that [c]slew him. **21** Then he said unto me, Depart: for I will send thee far hence unto the Gentiles. **22** [d]And they heard him unto this word, but then they lifted up their voices, and said, Away with such a fellow from the earth: for it is not meet that he should live. **23** And as they [e]cried and cast off their clothes, and threw dust into the air, **24** [f]The chief captain commanded him to be led into the castle, and bade that he should be scourged, and examined, that he might know wherefore they cried so on him. **25** [g]And as they bound him with thongs, Paul said unto the Centurion that stood by, Is it lawful for you to scourge one that is a Roman, and not condemned? **26** Now when the Centurion heard it, he went, and told the chief captain, saying, Take heed what thou doest: for this man is a Roman. **27** Then the chief captain came, and said to him, Tell me, art thou a Roman? And he said, Yea. **28** And the chief captain answered, With a great sum obtained I this freedom. Then Paul said, But I was so born. **29** Then straightway they departed from him, which should have examined him: and the chief captain also was afraid, after he knew that he was a [h]Roman, and that he had bound him. **30** On the next day, because he would have known the certainty wherefore he was accused of the Jews, he loosed him from his bonds, and commanded the high Priests and all their Council to come together: and he brought Paul, and set him before them.

23

1 As Paul pleadeth his cause, 2 Ananias commandeth them to smite him. 7 Dissension among his accusers. 11 God encourageth him. 14 The Jews laying wait for Paul, 17 is declared unto the chief captain. 24 He sendeth him to Felix the Governor.

1 And [a]Paul beheld earnestly the Council, and said, Men and brethren, I have in all good conscience served God until this day. **2** [b]Then the high Priest Ananias commanded them that stood by, to smite him on the mouth. **3** [c]Then said Paul to him, God [d]will smite thee, thou [e]whited wall: for thou sittest to judge me according to the Law, and [f]transgressing the Law, commandest thou me to be smitten? **4** And they that stood by, said, Revilest thou God's high Priest? **5** [g]Then said Paul, I knew not brethren, that he was the high Priest: for it is written, [1]Thou shalt not speak evil of the ruler of thy people. **6** [h]But when Paul perceived that the one part were of the Sadducees, and the other of the Pharisees, he cried in the Council, Men and brethren, [2]I am a Pharisee, the son of a Pharisee: I am accused of the hope and resurrection of the dead. **7** [i]And when he had said this, there was a dissension between the Pharisees and the Sadducees, so that the multitude was divided. **8** [j,3]For the Sadducees say that there is no resurrection, neither [k]Angel, nor spirit: but the Pharisees confess both. **9** [l]Then there was a great cry: and the [m]Scribes of the Pharisees' part rose up, and strove, saying, We find none evil in this man: but if a spirit or an Angel hath spoken to him, let us not fight against God. **10** [n]And when there was a great dissension, the chief captain, fearing lest Paul should have been pulled in pieces of them, commanded the soldiers to go down, and take him from among them, and to bring him into the castle. **11** Now the night following, the Lord stood by him, and said, Be of good courage, Paul, for as thou hast testified of me in Jerusalem, so must thou bear witness also at Rome. **12** [o]And when the day was come, certain of the Jews made an assembly, and bound themselves [p]with a curse, saying, that they would neither

---

appointed, yet they might add somewhat unto them, Num. 6:21.

j. Acts 21:26 The Priests were to be advertised of the accomplishment of the days of the purification, because there were sacrifices to be offered the same day that their vow was ended.

k. Acts 21:27 A preposterous zeal is the cause of great confusion, and great mischiefs.

l. Acts 21:31 God findeth some even amongst the wicked and profane themselves, to hinder the endeavors of the rest.

m. Acts 21:38 Touching this Egyptian which assembled thirty thousand men, read Josephus, book 2, chap. 12.

ACTS 21

1. Acts 6:5 **2.** Acts 18:18; Num. 6:18

ACTS 22

a. Acts 22:3 Paul making a short declaration of his former life, proveth both his vocation and doctrine to be of God.

b. Acts 22:3 That is, his daily hearer: the reason of this speech is this: for that they which teach, sit commonly in the higher place speaking to their scholars which sit upon forms beneath: and therefore he saith, at the feet of Gamaliel.

c. Acts 22:20 This is properly spoken: for Stephen was murdered of a sort of cutthroats, not by order of justice, but by open force: for at that time the Jews could not put any man to death by Law.

d. Acts 22:22 Stout and stubborn pride will neither itself embrace the truth, neither suffer others to receive it.

e. Acts 22:23 The description of a seditious hurly-burly, and of an harebrained and mad multitude.

f. Acts 22:24 The wisdom of the flesh doth not consider what is just, but what is profitable, and therewithall measure the profit, according as it appeareth presently.

g. Acts 22:25 There is no cause why we may not use those lawful means which God giveth us, to repel, or put away an injury.

h. Acts 22:29 Not by Nation, but by the law of his city.

ACTS 23

a. Acts 23:1 Paul against the false accusations of his enemies, setteth a good conscience, for proof whereof, he repeateth the whole course of his life.

b. Acts 23:2 Hypocrites are constrained at length to betray themselves by their intemperance.

c. Acts 23:3 It is lawful for us to complain of injuries, and to summon the wicked to the judgment seat of God, so that we do it without hatred, and with a quiet and peaceable mind.

d. Acts 23:3 It appeareth plainly by the Greek plural, that Paul did not curse the high Priest, but only pronounce the punishment of God against him.

e. Acts 23:3 This is a vehement and sharp speech, but yet not reproachful: For the godly may speak roundly, and yet be void of the bitter affection of a sharp and angry mind.

f. Acts 23:3 For the Law commandeth the judge to hear the person that is accused patiently, and to pronounce the sentence advisedly.

g. Acts 23:5 We must willingly and from the heart give honor to Magistrates, although they be tyrants.

h. Acts 23:6 We may lawfully sometimes set the wicked together by the ears, that they may leave off to assault us, so that it be with no hindrance of the truth.

i. Acts 23:7 The concord of the wicked is weak although they conspire together to oppress the truth.

j. Acts 23:8 It is an old heresy of the Sadducees, to deny the substance of Angels and souls, and therewithall the resurrection of the dead.

k. Acts 23:8 Natures that want bodies.

l. Acts 23:9 The Lord when it pleaseth him, findeth defenders of his cause, even amongst his enemies.

m. Acts 23:9 The Scribes' office was a public office, and the name of the Pharisees was the name of a sect.

n. Acts 23:10 God will not forsake his to the end.

eat nor drink till they had killed Paul. **13** And they were more than forty, which had made this conspiracy. **14** And they came to the chief Priests and Elders, and said, We have bound ourselves with a solemn curse, that we will eat nothing, until we have slain Paul. **15** Now therefore, [q]ye and the Council, signify to the chief captain, that he bring him forth unto you tomorrow, as though you would know something more perfectly of him, and we, or ever he come near will be ready to kill him. **16** But when Paul's sister's son heard of their laying await, he went, and entered into the castle, and told Paul. **17** [r]And Paul called one of the Centurions unto him, and said, Take this young man hence unto the chief captain: for he hath a certain thing to show him. **18** So he took him, and brought him to the chief captain, and said, Paul the prisoner called me unto him, and prayed me to bring this young man unto thee, which hath something to say unto thee. **19** Then the chief captain took him by the hand, and went apart with him alone, and asked him, What hast thou to show me? **20** And he said, The Jews have conspired to desire thee, that thou wouldest bring forth Paul tomorrow into the Council, as though they would inquire somewhat of him more perfectly: **21** But let them not persuade thee: for there lie in wait for him of them, more than forty men, which have bound themselves with a curse, that they will neither eat nor drink, till they have killed him: and now are they ready, and wait for thy promise. **22** [s]The chief captain then let the young man depart, after he had charged him to utter it to no man, that he had [t]showed him these things. **23** And he called unto him two certain Centurions, saying, Make ready two hundred soldiers, that they may go to Caesarea, and horsemen threescore and ten, and two hundred with darts, at the third hour of the night: **24** And let them make ready an horse, that Paul being set on, may be brought safe unto Felix the governor. **25** And he wrote an Epistle in this manner: **26** [u]Claudius Lysias unto the most noble governor Felix sendeth greeting. **27** As this man was taken of the Jews, and should have been killed of them, I came upon them with a garrison, and rescued him, perceiving that he was a Roman. **28** And when I would have known the cause wherefore they accused him, I brought him forth into their Council. **29** There I perceived that he was accused of questions of their Law, but had no crime worthy of death, or of bonds. **30** And when it was showed me, how that the Jews laid wait for the man, I sent him straightway to thee, and commanded his accusers to speak before thee the things that they had against him. Farewell. **31** Then the soldiers as it was commanded them, took Paul, and brought him by night to Antipatris, **32** And the next day, they left the horsemen to go with him, and returned into the Castle. **33** Now when they came to Caesarea, they delivered the Epistle to the governor, and presented Paul also unto him. **34** So when the Governor had read it, he asked of what province he was: and when he understood that he was of Cilicia, **35** I will hear thee, said he, when thine accusers also are come, and commanded him to be kept in Herod's judgment hall.

24

2 Tertullus accuseth Paul: 10 He answereth for himself: 21 He preacheth Christ to the governor and his wife. 26 Felix hopeth, but in vain, to receive a bribe, 27 who going from his office, leaveth Paul in prison.

1 Now [a]after five days, Ananias the high Priest came down with the Elders, and with Tertullus a certain orator, which appeared before the governor against Paul. **2** And when he was called forth, Tertullus began to accuse him, saying, Seeing that we have obtained great quietness [b]through thee, and that many [c]worthy things are done unto this nation through thy providence, **3** We acknowledge it wholly, and in all places, most noble Felix, with all thanks. **4** But that I be not tedious unto thee, I pray thee, that thou wouldest hear us of thy courtesy a few words. **5** Certainly we have found this man a [d]pestilent fellow, and a mover of sedition among all the Jews throughout the world, and a [e]chief maintainer of the sect of the [f]Nazarenes: **6** And hath gone about to pollute the Temple: therefore we took him, and would have judged him according to our Law: **7** But the chief captain Lysias came upon us, and with great violence took him out of our hands, **8** Commanding his accusers to come to thee: of whom thou mayest (if thou wilt inquire) know all these things whereof we accuse him. **9** And the Jews likewise [g]affirmed, saying that it was so. **10** [h]Then Paul, after that the governor had beckoned unto him that he should speak, answered, I do the more gladly answer for myself, forasmuch as I know that [i]thou hast been oft many years a judge unto this nation, **11** Seeing that thou mayest know, that there are but twelve days since I came up to worship in Jerusalem. **12** And they neither found me in the Temple, disputing with any man, neither making uproar among the people, neither in the Synagogues, nor in the city. **13** Neither can they [j]prove the things, whereof they now accuse me. **14** [k]But this I confess unto thee, that after the way (which they call [l]heresy) so worship I the God of my fathers, believing all things which are written in the Law and the Prophets, **15** And have hope towards God, that the resurrection of the dead, which they themselves look for also, shall be both of just and unjust. **16** And herein I endeavor myself to have always a clear conscience toward God and toward men. **17** [m]Now after many years, I came and brought alms to my nation and offerings, **18** At [n]what time, certain Jews of [o]Asia found me purified in the Temple, neither with multitude, nor with tumult. **19** Who ought to have been present before thee, and accuse me, if they had ought against me. **20** Or let these themselves say, if they have found any unjust thing in me, while I stood in the [p]Council, **21** Except it be for this one voice, that I cried standing among them, Of the resurrection of the dead am I accused of you this day. **22** [q]Now when Felix heard these things, he deferred them, and said, When I shall more [r]perfectly know the things which concern this way, by the coming of Lysias the chief Captain, I will decide your matter. **23** [s]Then he commanded a Centurion to keep Paul, and that he should have ease, and that he should forbid none of his acquaintance to minister unto him, or to come unto him. **24** And after certain days, came Felix with his wife [t]Drusilla, which was a Jewess, and he called forth Paul, and heard him of the faith in Christ. **25** And as he disputed of righteousness and temperance, and of the judgment to come, Felix trembled, and answered, Go thy way for this time, and when I have convenient time, I will call for thee. **26** He hoped also that money should have been given him of Paul, that he might loose him: wherefore he sent for him the oftener, and communed with him. **27** [u]When two years were expired, Porcius Festus came into Felix's room, and Felix willing to [v]get favor of the Jews, left Paul bound.

25

1 Festus succeeding Felix, 6 commandeth Paul to be brought forth. 11 Paul appealeth unto Caesar. 14 Festus openeth Paul's matter to king Agrippa, 23 and bringeth him before him, 27 that he may understand his cause.

1 When [a]Festus was then come into the province, after three days he went up from Caesarea unto Jerusalem. **2** Then the high Priest, and the chief of the Jews appeared before him against Paul: and they besought him, **3** And desired favor against him, that he would send for him to Jerusalem: and they laid wait to kill him by the way. **4** But Festus answered, that Paul should be kept at Caesarea, and that he himself would shortly depart thither. **5** Let them therefore, said he, which among you are able, come down with us: and if there be any wickedness in the man, let them accuse him. **6** [b]Now when he had tarried among them no more than ten days, he went down to Caesarea, and the next day sat in the judgment seat, and commanded Paul to be brought. **7** And when he was come, the Jews which were come from Jerusalem, stood about him and laid many and grievous

---

o. Acts 23:12 Such as are carried away with a foolish zeal, think that they may lie and murder, and do whatsoever mischief they list.
p. Acts 23:12 They cursing and banning themselves, promised.
q. Acts 23:15 Ye and the Senate requiring the same to be done, lest that the Tribune should think that it was demanded of him at some private man's suit.
r. Acts 23:17 The wisdom of the Spirit must be joined with simplicity.
s. Acts 23:22 There is no counsel against the Lord and his servants.
t. Acts 23:22 Greek, that thou hast showed these things to me.
u. Acts 23:26 Lysias is suddenly made by the Lord Paul's patron.

ACTS 23

1. Exod. 22:27
2. Acts 14:22; Phil. 3:5
3. Matt. 22:23

ACTS 24

a. Acts 24:1 Hypocrites, when they cannot do what they would do by force and deceit, at length they go about to compass it by a show of Law.
b. Acts 24:2 Felix ruled that province with great cruelty and covetousness, and yet Josephus recordeth that he did many worthy things, as that he took Eleazar the captain of certain cutthroats, and put that deceiving wretch the Egyptian to flight, which caused great troubles in Judea.
c. Acts 24:2 He useth a word which the Stoics defined to be a perfect duty and behavior.
d. Acts 24:5 Word for word, a plague.
e. Acts 24:5 As you would say, a ringleader, or ensign bearer.
f. Acts 24:5 So they called the Christians scoffingly of the town's name where they thought that Christ was born, whereupon it came that Julian the Apostate called him Galilean.
g. Acts 24:9 Confirmed Tertullus's saying.
h. Acts 24:10 Tertullus by the devil's rhetoric beginneth with flattery, maketh an end with lies: but Paul using heavenly eloquence, and but a simple beginning casteth off from himself the crime of sedition, wherewith he was burdened, with a simple denial.
i. Acts 24:10 Paul pleaded his cause two years before Felix departed out of the province, Acts 27, but he had governed Trachonite, and Batanea, and Galavnite, before that Claudius made him governor of Judea: Josephus in the History of the Jewish War, lib. 2, chap. 11.
j. Acts 24:13 They cannot lay forth before thee and prove by good reasons.
k. Acts 24:14 Paul goeth in the cause of Religion from a state conjectural to a state of quality not only not denying that objected against him, but also proving it to be true, to be heavenly and from God, and to be the oldest of all religions.
l. Acts 24:14 Here this word, Heresy, or sect, is taken in good part.
m. Acts 24:17 Paul in conclusion telleth the thing which was done, truly, which Tertullus had before divers ways corrupted.
n. Acts 24:18 And while I was busy about those things.
o. Acts 24:18 Hereby it appeareth that these of Asia were Saul's enemies, and those that stirred up the people against him.
p. Acts 24:20 Whither the Tribune brought me.
q. Acts 24:22 The Judge suspendeth his sentence, because the matter is doubtful.
r. Acts 24:22 Felix could not judge whether he had done wickedly in the matters of his religion or no, until he had better understanding of that way which Paul professed: and as for other matters touching the sedition, he thinketh good to defer it till he hears Lysias, and therefore he gave Paul somewhat more liberty.
s. Acts 24:23 God is a most faithful keeper of his servants, and the force of the truth is wonderful, even amongst men which are otherwise profane.
t. Acts 24:24 This Drusilla was Agrippa's sister, of whom Luke speaketh afterward, a very harlot and licentious woman, and being the wife of Azizus king of the Emesens, who was circumcised, departed from him, and went to Felix, the brother of one Pallas, who was sometime Nero's bondman.
u. Acts 24:27 In a naughty mind that is guilty to itself, although, sometimes there be some show of equity, yet by and by, it will be extinguished: but in the mean season we have need to patience, and that continual.
v. Acts 24:27 For whereas he had behaved himself very wickedly in the province, had it not been for favor of his brother Pallas, he should have died for it: so that we may gather hereby why he would have pleasured the Jews.

ACTS 25

a. Acts 25:1 Satan's Ministers are subtle and diligent in seeking all occasions: but God who watcheth for his, hindereth all their counsels easily.
b. Acts 25:6 We may repel an injury justly, but not with injury.

complaints against Paul, whereof [c]they could make no plain proof, **8** Forasmuch
as he answered, that he had neither offended anything against the law of the Jews,
neither against the temple, nor against Caesar. **9** [d]Yet Festus willing to get favor
of the Jews, answered Paul and said, Wilt thou go up to Jerusalem, and there be
judged of these things before me? **10** Then said Paul, I stand at Caesar's judg-
ment seat, where I ought to be judged: to the Jews I have done no wrong, as thou
very well knowest. **11** For if I have done wrong, or committed anything worthy
of death, I refuse not to die: but if there be none of these things, whereof they ac-
cuse me, no man, to pleasure them, can deliver me to them: I appeal unto Cae-
sar. **12** Then when Festus had spoken with the Council, he answered, Hast thou
appealed unto Caesar? unto Caesar shalt thou go. **13** [e]And after certain days,
King [f]Agrippa and Bernice came down to Caesarea to salute Festus. **14** And
when they had remained there many days, Festus declared Paul's cause unto the
king, saying, There is a certain man left in prison by Felix, **15** Of whom when
I came to Jerusalem, the high Priests and Elders of the Jews informed me, and de-
sired to have judgment against him. **16** To whom I answered, that it is not the
manner of the Romans for favor to [g]deliver any man to the death, before that he
which is accused, have the accusers before him, and have place to defend himself,
concerning the crime. **17** Therefore when they were come hither, without de-
lay the day following I sat on the judgment seat, and commanded the man to be
brought forth. **18** Against whom when the accusers stood up, they brought no
crime of such things as I supposed: **19** [h]But had certain questions against him
of their own [i]superstitions, and of one Jesus which was dead, whom Paul affirmed
to be alive. **20** And because I doubted of such manner of question, I asked him
whether he would go to Jerusalem, and there be judged of these things. **21** But
because he appealed to be reserved to the examination of Augustus, I comman-
ded him to be kept, till I might send him to Caesar. **22** [j]Then Agrippa said
unto Festus, I would also hear the man myself. Tomorrow, said he, thou shalt hear
him. **23** And on the morrow when Agrippa was come, and Bernice with great
[k]pomp, and were entered into the Common hall with the chief captains and chief
men of the city, at Festus's commandment Paul was brought forth. **24** And Fe-
stus said, King Agrippa, and all men which are present with us, ye see this man,
about whom all the multitude of the Jews have called upon me, both at Jerusa-
lem, and here, crying, that he ought not to live any longer. **25** Yet have I found
nothing worthy of death, that he hath committed: nevertheless, seeing that he hath
appealed to Augustus, I have determined to send him. **26** Of whom I have no
certain thing to write unto my [l]lord: wherefore I have brought him forth unto you,
and especially unto thee, King Agrippa, that after examination had, I might have
somewhat to write. **27** For me thinketh it unreasonable to send a prisoner, and
not to show the causes which are laid against him.

26

2 Paul in the presence of Agrippa, 4 declareth his life from his childhood, 16 and his calling, 21 with such efficacy of words 28 that almost he persuaded him to Christianity. 30 But he and his company depart doing nothing in Paul's matter.

1 Then Agrippa said unto Paul, Thou art permitted to speak for thyself. So
Paul stretched forth the hand, and answered for himself. **2** [a]I think myself happy,
King Agrippa, because I shall answer this day before thee of all the things whereof
I am accused of the Jews: **3** Chiefly, because thou hast knowledge of all customs,
and questions which are among the Jews: wherefore I beseech thee to hear me pa-
tiently. **4** [b]As touching my life from my childhood, and what it was from the
beginning among mine own nation at Jerusalem, know all the Jews, **5** Which
[c]knew me heretofore, even from my [d]Elders (if they would testify) that after the
[e]most straight sect of our religion, I lived a Pharisee. **6** [f]And now I stand and
am accused for the hope of the promise made of God unto our fathers. **7** Whe-
reunto our twelve tribes instantly serving God day and night, hope to come: for
the which hope's sake, O King Agrippa, I am accused of the Jews. **8** [g]Why
should it be thought a thing incredible unto you, that God should raise again the
dead? **9** I also verily thought in myself, that I ought to do many contrary things
against the Name of Jesus of Nazareth. **10** [1]Which thing I also did in Jerusalem:
for many of the Saints I shut up in prison, having received authority of the High
Priests, and when they were put to death, I gave my [h]sentence. **11** And I puni-
shed them throughout all the Synagogues, and [i]compelled them to blaspheme and
being more mad against them, I persecuted them, even unto strange cities. **12** At
which time, even as I went to [2]Damascus with authority, and commission from the
high Priests, **13** At midday, O king, I saw in the way a light from heaven pas-
sing the brightness of the sun, shine round about me, and them which went with
me. **14** So when we were all fallen to the earth, I heard a voice speaking unto
me, and saying in the Hebrew tongue, Saul, Saul, why persecutest thou me? It is
hard for thee to kick against pricks. **15** Then I said, Who art thou, Lord? And
he said, I am Jesus whom thou persecutest. **16** But rise and stand up on thy feet:
for I have appeared unto thee for this purpose to appoint thee a minister and a wit-
ness, both of the things which thou hast seen, and of the things in the which I will
appear unto thee, **17** Delivering thee from this people, and from the Gentiles,
unto whom now I send thee, **18** [j]To open their eyes, that they may turn from
darkness to light, and from the power of Satan unto God, that they may receive
forgiveness of sins, and inheritance among them, which are sanctified by faith in
me. **19** [k]Wherefore, King Agrippa, I was not disobedient unto the heavenly vi-
sion, **20** [3]But showed first unto them of Damascus, and at Jerusalem, and throu-
ghout all the coasts of Judea, and then to the Gentiles, that they should repent and
turn to God, and do works worthy amendment of life. **21** For this cause the
Jews caught me in the [4]Temple, and went about to kill me. **22** [l]Nevertheless, I
obtained help of God, and continue unto this day, witnessing both to [m]small and
to great, saying none other things, than those which the Prophets and Moses did
say should come, **23** To wit, that Christ should [n]suffer, and that he should be the
[o]first that should rise from the dead, and should show [p]light unto this people, and
to the Gentiles. **24** [q]And as he thus answered for himself, Festus said with a loud
voice, Paul, thou art beside thyself, much learning doth make thee mad. **25** But
he said, I am not mad, O noble Festus, but I speak the words of truth, and sober-
ness. **26** For the king knoweth of these things, before whom also I speak boldly:
for I am persuaded that none of these things are hidden from him: for this thing
was not done in a [r]corner. **27** [s]O King Agrippa, believest thou the Prophets? I
know that thou believest. **28** Then Agrippa said unto Paul, Almost thou per-
suadest me to become a Christian. **29** Then Paul said, [t]I would to God that not
only thou, but also all that hear me today, were both almost, and altogether such as
I am, except these bonds. **30** [u]And when he had thus spoken, the king rose up,
and the governor, and Bernice, and they that sat with them. **31** And when they
were gone apart, they talked between themselves, saying, This man doeth nothing
worthy of death, nor of bonds. **32** Then said Agrippa unto Festus, This man mi-
ght have been loosed, if he had not appealed unto Caesar.

27

1 Paul 7, 9 foretelleth the peril of the voyage, 11 but he is not believed. 14 They are tossed to and fro with the tempest, 22, 41 and suffer shipwreck: 34 Yet all safe and sound 44 escape to land.

1 Now [a]when it was concluded, that we should sail into Italy, they delivered
both Paul, and certain other prisoners unto a Centurion, named Julius, of the
band of Augustus. **2** And [1]we entered into a ship of Adramyttium, purposing
to sail by the coasts of Asia, and launched forth, and had Aristarchus of Macedo-
nia, a Thessalonian, with us. **3** And the next day we arrived at Sidon: and Julius
courteously entreated Paul, and gave him liberty to go unto his friends, that they
might refresh him. **4** And from thence we launched, and sailed hard by Cyprus,
because the winds were contrary. **5** Then sailed we over the sea by Cilicia, and

---

c. Acts 25:7 They could not prove them certainly and with undoubted reasons.
d. Acts 25:9 God doth not only turn away the counsel of the wicked, but also turneth it upon their own heads.
e. Acts 25:13 Festus thinking no such thing, even before kings, bringing to light the wickedness of the Jews, and Paul's innocence, doth marvelously confirm the Church of God.
f. Acts 25:13 This Agrippa was Agrippa's son, whose death Luke spake of before, and Bernice was his sister.
g. Acts 25:16 The Romans used not to deliver any man to be punished before, etc.
h. Acts 25:19 The profane and wicked take an occasion to condemn the true doctrine by reason of private controversies and contentions of men betwixt themselves: but the truth nevertheless abideth in the mean season safe and sure.
i. Acts 25:19 This profane man calleth the Jews' religion, superstition, and that before king Agrippa, but no marvel: for the rulers of provinces by reason of the majesty of the empire of Rome, used to prefer themselves before kings.
j. Acts 25:22 That is fulfilled in Paul, which the Lord before had told to Ananias of him, Acts 9:15.
k. Acts 25:23 Gorgeously like a Prince.
l. Acts 25:26 To Augustus. Good Princes refused this name at the first, to wit, to be called Lords, but afterwards they admitted it, as we read of Traianus.

ACTS 26

a. Acts 26:2 To have a skillful judge, is a great and singular gift of God.
b. Acts 26:4 Paul divideth the history of his life into two times: for the first [he] calleth his adversaries witnesses: for the latter, the fathers and prophets.
c. Acts 26:5 What I was, and where, and how I lived.
d. Acts 26:5 That my parents were Pharisees.
e. Acts 26:5 The sect of the Pharisees was the most exquisite amongst all the sects of the Jews, for it was better than all the rest.
f. Acts 26:6 There are three chief and principal witnesses of true doctrine, God, the true Fathers, and the consent of the Church.
g. Acts 26:8 He proveth the resurrection of the dead, first by the power of God, then by the resurrection of Christ: whereof he is a sufficient witness.
h. Acts 26:10 I consented to, and allowed of their doing: for he was not a judge.
i. Acts 26:11 By extreme punishment.
j. Acts 26:18 The end of the Gospel is to save them which are brought to the knowledge of Christ, and are justified and sanctified in him being laid hold on by faith.
k. Acts 26:19 Paul allegeth God to be author of the office of his Apostleship, and his grace as a witness.
l. Acts 26:22 Christ is the end of the Law and the Prophets.
m. Acts 26:22 To everyone.
n. Acts 26:23 That Christ should not be such a king as the Jews dreamed of, but one appointed to bear our miseries, and the punishment of our sins.
o. Acts 26:23 The first of them which are raised from the dead.
p. Acts 26:23 Life, yea, and that a most blessed life which shall be endless: and this is set against darkness, which almost in all tongues signifieth sometimes death, and sometimes misery and calamity.
q. Acts 26:24 The wisdom of God is madness to fools, yet notwithstanding we must boldly avouch the truth.
r. Acts 26:26 Secretly, and privately.
s. Acts 26:27 Paul as it were forgetting himself that he stood a prisoner to defend his cause, he forgetteth not the office of his Apostleship.
t. Acts 26:29 I would to God that not only almost, but thoroughly and altogether both thou and all that hear me this day, might be made as I am, my bonds only except.
u. Acts 26:30 Paul is solemnly quit, and yet not dismissed.

ACTS 26

1. Acts 8:3
2. Acts 9:2
3. Acts 9:22, 26; Acts 13:4
4. Acts 21:30

ACTS 27

a. Acts 27:1 Paul with many other prisoners, and through the midst of many deaths, is brought to Rome, but yet by God's

Pamphilia, and came to Myra, a city in Lycia. **6** And there the Centurion found a ship of Alexandria, sailing into Italy, and put us therein. **7** And when we had sailed slowly many days, and scarce were come against Cnidus, because the wind suffered us not, we sailed hard by Candia, near to [b]Salmone, **8** And with much ado sailed beyond it, and came unto a certain place called the Fair Havens, near unto the which was the city Lasea. **9** [c]So when much time was spent, and sailing was now jeopardous, because also the [d]Fast was now passed, Paul exhorted them, **10** And said unto them, Sirs, I see that this voyage will be with hurt, and much damage, not of the lading and ship only, but also of our lives. **11** [e]Nevertheless the Centurion believed rather the governor and the master of the ship, than those things which were spoken of Paul. **12** And because the haven was not commodious to winter in, many took counsel to depart thence, if by any means they might attain to Phoenix, there to winter, which is an haven of Crete, and lieth toward the Southwest and by West, and Northwest and by West. **13** And when the Southern wind blew softly, they supposing to attain their purpose, loosed nearer, and sailed by Crete. **14** But anon after, there arose by [f]it a stormy wind called [g]Euroclydon. **15** And when the ship was caught, and could not resist the wind, we let her go, and were carried away. **16** And we ran under a little Isle named Clauda, and had much ado to get the boat. **17** Which they took up and used all help, undergirding the ship, fearing lest they should have fallen into Syrtis, and they strake sail, and so were carried. **18** [h]The next day when we were tossed with an exceeding tempest, they lightened the ship. **19** And the third day we cast out with our own hands the tackling of the ship. **20** And when neither sun nor stars in many days appeared, and no small tempest lay upon us, all hope that we should be saved, was then taken away. **21** [i]But after long abstinence, Paul stood forth in the midst of them, and said, Sirs, ye should have hearkened to me, and not have loosed from Candia: so should ye have gained this hurt and loss. **22** But now I exhort you to be of good courage: for there shall be no loss of any man's life among you, save of the ship only. **23** For there stood by me this night the Angel of God, whose I am, and whom I serve. **24** Saying, Fear not, Paul: for thou must be brought before Caesar: and lo, God hath given unto thee freely, all that sail with thee. **25** [j]Wherefore, Sirs, be of good courage: for I believe God, that it shall be so as it hath been told me. **26** Howbeit, we must be cast into a certain Island. **27** [k]And when the fourteenth night was come, as we were carried to and fro in the [l]Adriatic sea about midnight, the shipmen deemed that some country [m]approached unto them. **28** And sounded, and found it twenty fathoms: and when they had gone a little further, they sounded again, and found fifteen fathoms. **29** Then fearing lest they should have fallen into some rough places, they cast four anchors out of the stern, and wished that the day were come. **30** [n]Now as the mariners were about to flee out of the ship, and had let down the boat into the sea under a color as though they would have cast anchors out of the foreship. **31** [o]Paul said unto the Centurion and the soldiers, Except these abide in the ship, ye cannot be safe. **32** Then the soldiers cut off the ropes of the boat, and let it fall away. **33** [p]And when it began to be day, Paul exhorted them all to take meat, saying, This is the fourteenth day that ye have tarried, and continued fasting, receiving nothing: **34** Wherefore I exhort you to take meat: for this is for your safeguard: for there shall not an [q]hair fall from the head of any of you. **35** And when he had thus spoken, he took bread, and gave thanks to God in presence of them all, and brake it, and began to eat. **36** Then were they all of good courage, and they also took meat. **37** Now we were in the ship in all two hundred threescore and sixteen souls. **38** And when they had eaten enough, they lightened the ship, and cast out the wheat into the sea. **39** [r]And when it was day, they knew not the country, but they spied a certain [s]creek with a bank, into the which they were minded (if it were possible) to thrust in the ship. **40** So when they had taken up the anchors, they committed the ship unto the sea, and loosed the rudder bonds, and hoisted up the main sail to the wind, and drew to the shore. **41** And when they fell into a place, where [t]two seas met, they thrust in the ship: and the forepart stuck fast, and could not be moved, but the hinder part was broken with the violence of the waves. **42** [u]Then the soldiers' counsel was to kill the prisoners, lest any of them, when he had swam out, should flee away. **43** [v]But the Centurion willing to save Paul, stayed them from this counsel, and commanded that they that could swim, should cast themselves first into the sea, and go out to land: **44** [w]And the others, some on boards, and some on certain pieces of the ship: and so it came to pass, that they came all safe to land.

28

2 The Barbarians' courtesy towards Paul and his company. 3 A viper on Paul's hand: 6 He shaketh it off without harm: 8 Publius 9 and others are by him healed. 11 They depart from Malta, 16 and come to Rome. 17 Paul openeth to the Jews, 20 the cause of his coming: 22 He preacheth Jesus 30 two years.

1 And when they were come safe, then they knew that the Isle was called [a]Malta. **2** And the Barbarians showed us no little kindness, for they kindled a fire, and received us everyone, because of the present shower, and because of the cold. **3** [b]And when Paul had gathered a number of sticks, and laid them on the fire, there came a viper out of the heat, and leaped on his hand. **4** [c]Now when the Barbarians saw the worm hang on his hand, they said among themselves, This man surely is a murderer, whom, though he hath escaped the sea, yet [d]Vengeance hath not suffered to live. **5** But he shook off the worm into the fire, and felt no harm. **6** Howbeit they waited when he should have [e]swollen, or fallen down dead suddenly: [f]but after they had looked a great while, and saw no inconvenience come to him, they changed their minds, and said, That he was a God. **7** [g]In the same quarters, the chief man of the Isle (whose name was Publius) had possessions: the same received us, and lodged us three days courteously. **8** And so it was, that the father of Publius lay sick of the fever, and of a bloody flix: to whom Paul entered in, and when he prayed, he laid his hands on him, and healed him. **9** [h]When this then was done, others also in the Isle, which had diseases, came to him, and were healed, **10** [i]Which also did us great honor: and when we departed, they laded us with things necessary. **11** [j]Now after three months we departed in a ship of Alexandria, which had wintered in the Isle, whose [k]badge was Castor and Pollux. **12** And when we arrived at Syracuse, we tarried there three days. **13** And from thence we set a compass, and came to Rhegium: and after one day, the South wind blew, and we came the second day to Puteoli: **14** [l]Where we found brethren, and were desired to tarry with them seven days, and so we went toward Rome. **15** [m]And from thence when the brethren heard of us, they came to meet us at the [n]Market of Appius, and at the three taverns, whom when Paul saw, he thanked God, and waxed bold. **16** So when we came to Rome, the Centurion delivered the prisoners to the general Captain: but Paul was suffered to dwell by [o]himself with a soldier that kept him. **17** [p]And the third day after, Paul calleth the chief of the Jews together, and when they were come, he said unto them, Men and brethren, though I have committed nothing against the people, or Laws of the fathers, yet was I delivered prisoner from Jerusalem into the hands of the Romans. **18** Who when they had examined me, would have let me go, because there was no cause of death in me. **19** [q]But when the Jews spake contrary, I was constrained to appeal unto Caesar, not because I had ought to accuse my nation of. **20** For this cause therefore have I called for you to see you, and to speak with

---

own hand as it were, and set forth and commended unto the world with many singular testimonies.

b. Acts 27:7 Which was an high hill of Candia.

c. Acts 27:9 God's providence taketh not away the causes which God useth as means, but rather ordereth and disposeth their right use even then when he openeth an extraordinary issue.

d. Acts 27:9 This is meant of the Jews' fast, which they keep in the feast of expiation, as we read Lev. 23:27, which fell in the seventh month which we call October, and is not good for navigation, or sailing.

e. Acts 27:11 Men cast themselves willingly into an infinite sort of dangers, when they choose to follow their own wisdom, rather than God speaking by the mouth of his servants.

f. Acts 27:14 By Candia, from whose shore our ship was driven by that means.

g. Acts 27:14 Northeast wind.

h. Acts 27:18 The end proveth that none provide worse for themselves, than they which commit themselves to be governed only by their own wisdom.

i. Acts 27:21 God spareth the wicked for a time, for his elect and chosen's sake.

j. Acts 27:25 The promise is made effectual through faith.

k. Acts 27:27 We attain and come to the promised and sure salvation through the midst of tempests and death itself.

l. Acts 27:27 For Ptolemy writeth, that the Adriatic Sea beateth upon the East shore of Cilicia.

m. Acts 27:27 That they drew near to some country.

n. Acts 27:30 There is none so foul an act, whereupon distrust and an evil conscience do not enforce men.

o. Acts 27:31 Although the performing of God's promises doth not simply depend upon second causes, yet they make themselves unworthy of God's bountifulness, which do not embrace those means which God offereth them, either upon rashness or distrust.

p. Acts 27:33 When the world trembleth, the faithful alone be not only quiet, but confirm others by their example.

q. Acts 27:34 This is a proverb which the Hebrews use, whereby is meant, that they shall be safe, and not one of them perish.

r. Acts 27:39 Then are tempests most of all to be feared and looked for, when the port or haven is nearest.

s. Acts 27:39 A creek is a sea within land, as the Adriatic Sea, and the Persian Sea.

t. Acts 27:41 So is Isthmus called, because the sea toucheth it on both sides.

u. Acts 27:42 There is nowhere more unfaithfulness and unthankfulness than in unbelievers.

v. Acts 27:43 God findeth even amongst his enemies them whose help he useth to preserve his.

w. Acts 27:44 The goodness of God overcometh man's malice.

ACTS 27

1. 2 Cor. 11:15

ACTS 28

a. Acts 28:1 That is it which at this day we call Malta.

b. Acts 28:3 The godly are sure to have danger upon danger, but they have always a glorious issue.

c. Acts 28:4 Although adversity be the punishment of sin, yet seeing that God in punishing of men doth not always respect sin, they judge rashly, which either do not wait for the end, or do judge and esteem of men according to prosperity or adversity.

d. Acts 28:4 Right and reason.

e. Acts 28:6 The Greek word signifieth, to be inflamed, or to swell: moreover Dioscorides in book 6, chap. 38, witnesseth, that the biting of a viper causeth a swelling of the body, and so saith Nicander, in his remedies against poisons.

f. Acts 28:6 There is nothing more unconstant, every way, than they which are ignorant of true religion.

g. Acts 28:7 It never yet repented any man, that received the servant of God, were he never so miserable and poor.

h. Acts 28:9 Although Paul were a captive, yet the virtue of God was not captive.

i. Acts 28:10 God doeth well to strangers for his children's sake.

j. Acts 28:11 Idols do not defile the Saints, which do in no wise consent unto them.

k. Acts 28:11 So they used to deck the forepart of their ships, whereupon the ships were called by such names.

l. Acts 28:14 God boweth and bendeth the hearts even of profane men, as it pleaseth him to favor his.

m. Acts 28:15 God never suffereth his to be afflicted above their strength.

n. Acts 28:15 Appius way, was a pavement made by Appius the blind with the help of his soldiers, long and broad, and running out toward the sea, and there were three taverns in it.

o. Acts 28:16 Not in a common prison, but in a house which he hired for himself.

p. Acts 28:17 Paul in every place remembereth himself to be an Apostle.

you: for that hope of Israel's sake, I am bound with this chain. 21 Then they said
unto him, We neither received letters out of Judea concerning thee, neither came
any of the brethren that showed or spake any evil of thee. 22 But we will hear
of thee what thou thinkest: for as concerning this sect, we know that everywhere
it is spoken against. 23 [r]And when they had appointed him a day, there came
many unto him into his lodging, to whom he expounded, [s]testifying the kingdom
of God, and persuading them those things that concern Jesus, both out of the Law
of Moses, and out of the Prophets, from morning to night. 24 [t]And some were
persuaded with the things which were spoken, and some believed not. 25 The-
refore when they agreed not among themselves, they departed, after that Paul
had spoken one word, to wit, Well spake the holy Ghost by Isaiah the Prophet
unto our fathers, 26 [u]Saying, [1]Go unto this people, and say, By hearing ye shall
hear, and shall not understand, and seeing ye shall see, and not perceive. 27 For
the heart of this people is waxed fat, and their ears are dull of hearing, and with
their eyes have they [v]winked, lest they should see with their eyes, and hear with
their ears, and understand with their hearts, and should return that I might heal
them. 28 [w]Be it known therefore unto you, that this salvation of God is sent to
the Gentiles, and they shall hear it. 29 [x]And when he had said these things, the
Jews departed, and had great reasoning among themselves. 30 [y]And Paul remai-
ned two years full in an house hired for himself, and received all that came in unto
him, 31 Preaching the kingdom of God, and teaching those things which con-
cern the Lord Jesus Christ, with all boldness of speech, without let.

---

q. Acts 28:19 We may use the means which God giveth us, but so that we seek the glory of God, and not ourselves.
r. Acts 28:23 The law and the Gospel agree well together.
s. Acts 28:23 By good reasons, and proved that the kingdom of God foretold them by the Prophets, was come.
t. Acts 28:24 The Gospel is a savor of life to them that believe, and a savor of death to them that be disobedient.
u. Acts 28:26 The unbelievers do willingly resist the truth, and yet not by chance.
v. Acts 28:27 They made as though they saw not that which they saw against their wills: yea they did see, but they would not see.
w. Acts 28:28 The unbelief of the reprobate and castaways cannot cause the truth of God to be of none effect.
x. Acts 28:29 Not the Gospel, but the contempt of the Gospel is the cause of strife and debate.
y. Acts 28:30 The word of God cannot be bound.

ACTS 28
1. Isa. 6:9; Matt. 13:14; Mark 14:12; Luke 8:10; John 12:40; Rom. 11:8

THE EPISTLE OF THE APOSTLE PAUL TO THE ROMANS

1

1 He first showeth on what authority his Apostleship standeth. 15 Then he commendeth the Gospel, 16 by which God setteth out his power to those that are saved, 17 by faith, 21 but were guilty of wicked unthankfulness to God: 26 For which his wrath was worthily powered on them, 29 so that they ran headlong to all kinds of sin.

1 PAUL [a]a [b,c]servant of JESUS Christ called to be an [d]Apostle, [1,e]put apart
to preach the Gospel of God, 2 (Which he had promised afore by his Prophets
in the holy Scriptures) 3 [f]Concerning his [g]Son Jesus Christ our Lord (which was
[h]made of the seed of David [i]according to the flesh, 4 And [j]declared [k]mightily to
be the Son of God, touching the Spirit of sanctification by the resurrection from
the dead) 5 [l]By whom we have received [m]grace and Apostleship (that [n]obedience
might be given unto the faith) for his name [o]among all the Gentiles, 6 Among
whom ye be also the [p]called of Jesus Christ: 7 To all you that be at Rome beloved
of God, called to be Saints: [q]Grace be with you, and peace from God our Father,
and from the Lord Jesus Christ. 8 [r]First I thank my God through Jesus Christ
for you all, because your faith is [s]published throughout the [t]whole world. 9 For
God is my witness (whom I serve in my [u]spirit in the [v]Gospel of his Son) that wi-
thout ceasing I make mention of you. 10 Always in my prayers, beseeching that
by some means, one time or other I might have a prosperous journey by the will
of God, to come unto you. 11 For I long to see you, that I might bestow among
you some spiritual gift, that you might be strengthened: 12 That is, that [w]I mi-
ght be comforted together with you, through our mutual faith, both yours and
mine. 13 Now my brethren, I would that ye should not be ignorant, how that I
have oftentimes purposed to come unto you (but have been let hitherto) that I mi-
ght have some fruit also among you, as I have among the other Gentiles. 14 I am
debtor both to the Grecians, and to the Barbarians, both to the wise men and to
the unwise. 15 Therefore, as much as in me is, I am ready to preach the Gospel
to you also that are at [x]Rome. 16 For I am not ashamed of the Gospel of Christ:
[y]for it is the [z]power of God unto salvation to everyone that believeth, to the Jew
first, and also to the [aa]Grecian. 17 [ab]For by it the righteousness of God is reve-
aled from [ac]faith to faith: [ad]as it is written, [2]The just shall live by faith. 18 [ae]For
the wrath of God is revealed from heaven against [af]all ungodliness, and unrighteou-
sness of men, which withhold the [ag]truth in unrighteousness. 19 [ah]Forasmuch

---

ROM. 1
a. Rom. 1:1 The first part of the Epistle containing a most profitable preface unto verse 16.
b. Rom. 1:1 He moving the Rom. to give diligent ear unto him in that he showeth that he cometh not in his own name, but as God's messenger unto the Gentiles, entreateth with them of the weightiest matter, that is promised long since by God, by many fit witnesses, and now at length performed indeed.
c. Rom. 1:1 A Minister, for this word servant, is not taken in this place, as set against this word, Freeman, but declareth his ministry and office.
d. Rom. 1:1 Whereas he said before in a general term, that he was a minister, now he cometh to a more special name, and saith that he is an Apostle, and that he took not upon him this office of his own lead, but being called of God, and therefore in this his writing to the Romans, doeth nothing but his duty.
e. Rom. 1:1 Appointed of God to preach the Gospel.
f. Rom. 1:3 By declaring the sum of the doctrine of the Gospel, he stirreth up the Rom. to good consideration of the matter whereof he entreateth: So then he showeth that Christ (who is the very substance and sum of the Gospel) is the only son of God the Father, who as touching his humanity, is made of the seed of David, but touching his divine and spiritual nature, whereby he sanctified himself, is begotten of the Father from everlasting, as by his mighty resurrection manifestly appeareth.
g. Rom. 1:3 This is a plain testimony of the person of Christ, that he is but one, and of his two natures, and their properties.
h. Rom. 1:3 Which took flesh of the virgin, David's daughter.
i. Rom. 1:3 As he is man: for this word Flesh, by the figure Synecdoche, is taken for man.
j. Rom. 1:4 Showed and made manifest.
k. Rom. 1:4 The divine and mighty power is set against the weakness of the flesh, for that overcame death.
l. Rom. 1:5 Of whom.
m. Rom. 1:5 This marvelous liberal and gracious gift, which is given me, the least of all the Saints, to preach, etc., Eph. 3:8.
n. Rom. 1:5 That men through faith might obey God.
o. Rom. 1:5 For his Name's sake.
p. Rom. 1:6 Which through God's goodness, are Christ's.
q. Rom. 1:7 God's free good will: by peace, the Hebrews mean a prosperous success in all things.
r. Rom. 1:8 He procureth their favorable patience, in that he reckoneth up their true commendation, and his true Apostolic good will toward them, confirmed by taking God himself to witness.
s. Rom. 1:8 Because your faith is such, that it is commended in all Churches.
t. Rom. 1:8 In all Churches.
u. Rom. 1:9 Very willingly and with all my heart.
v. Rom. 1:9 In preaching his Son.
w. Rom. 1:12 Though Paul were never so excellent, yet by teaching the Church, he might be instructed by it.
x. Rom. 1:15 He meaneth all them that dwelt in Rome, though some of them were not Romans, see the end of the epistle.
y. Rom. 1:16 The second part of the Epistle unto the beginning of Chap. 9. Now the whole end and purpose of the disputation is this: that is to say: to show that there is but one way to attain unto salvation (which is set forth unto us of God in the Gospel, without any difference of nations) and that is Jesus Christ apprehended by faith.
z. Rom. 1:16 God's mighty and effectual instrument to save men by.
aa. Rom. 1:16 When this word Grecian, is set against this word Jew, then doth it signify a Gentile.
ab. Rom. 1:17 The confirmation of the former proposition: we are taught in the Gospel that we are justified before God by faith which increaseth daily: and therefore also saved.
ac. Rom. 1:17 From faith which increaseth daily.
ad. Rom. 1:17 The proof as well of the first as the second proposition, out of Habakkuk, who attributeth and giveth unto faith both justice and life before God.
ae. Rom. 1:18 Another confirmation of that principal question: All men being considered in themselves or without Christ, are guilty both of [ungodliness], and also unrighteousness, and therefore are subject to condemnation: Therefore must they needs seek righteousness in some other.
af. Rom. 1:18 Against all kinds of ungodliness.
ag. Rom. 1:18 By truth, Paul meaneth all the light that is left in man since his fall, not as though they being led thereby were able to come into favor with God, but that their own reason might condemn them of wickedness both against God and man.

as that, which may be known of God, is manifest in [ai]them, for God hath showed it unto them. **20** For the invisible things of him, that is, his eternal power and Godhead, are seen by the creation of the world, being [aj]considered in his works, to the intent that they should be without excuse: **21** Because that when they knew God, they [ak]glorified him not as God, neither were thankful, but became [al]vain in their thoughts, and their foolish heart was full of darkness. **22** When they [am]professed themselves to be wise, they became fools. **23** For they turned the glory of the [an]incorruptible God to the similitude of the image of a corruptible man, and of birds, and four footed beasts, and of creeping things. **24** [ao]Wherefore [ap]also God [aq]gave them up to their hearts lusts, unto uncleanness, to defile their own bodies between themselves: **25** Which turned the truth of God unto a lie, and worshipped and served the creature, forsaking the Creator which is blessed forever, Amen. **26** For this cause God gave them up to vile affections: for even their women did change the natural use into that which is against nature. **27** And likewise also the men left the natural use of the woman, and burned in their lust one toward another, and man with man wrought filthiness, and received in themselves such [ar]recompense of their error, as was meet. **28** [as]For as they regarded not to acknowledge God, even so God delivered them up unto a [at]reprobate mind, to do those things which are not convenient, **29** Being full of all unrighteousness, fornication, wickedness, covetousness, maliciousness, full of envy, of murder, of debate, of deceit, taking all things in the evil part, whisperers, **30** Backbiters, haters of God, doers of wrong, proud, boasters, inventors of evil things, disobedient to parents, without understanding, [au]covenant breakers, without natural affection, such as can never be appeased, merciless. **31** Which men, though they knew the [av]Law of God, how that they which commit such things are worthy of death, yet not only do the same, but also [aw]favor them that do them.

2

1 He bringeth all before the judgment seat of God. 12 The excuse the Gentiles might pretend, 14 of ignorance, he taketh quite away. 17 He urgeth the Jews with the written Law, 23 in which they boasted. 27 And so maketh both Jew and Gentile alike.

1 Therefore [a]thou art inexcusable, O man, whosoever thou art that condemnest: for in that thou condemnest another, thou condemnest thyself: for thou that condemnest, doest the same things. **2** But we [b]know that the judgment of God is according to [c]truth, against them which commit such things. **3** And thinkest thou this, O thou man, that condemnest them which do such things, and doest the same, that thou shalt escape the judgment of God? **4** [d]Or despisest thou the riches of his bountifulness, and patience, and long sufferance, not knowing that the bountifulness of God leadeth thee to repentance? **5** But thou, after thine hardness, and heart that cannot repent, [1,e]heapest up as a treasure unto thyself wrath against the day of wrath, and of the declaration of the just judgment of God, **6** [2,f]Who will reward every man according to his works: **7** That is, to them which through patience in well doing, seek [g]glory, and honor, and immortality, everlasting life: **8** But unto them that are contentious, and disobey the [h]truth, and obey unrighteousness, shall be [i]indignation and wrath. **9** Tribulation and anguish shall be upon the soul of every man that doeth evil: of the Jew first, and also of the Grecian. **10** But to every man that doeth good, shall be glory, and honor, and peace: to the Jew first, and also to the Grecian. **11** For there is [j]no respect of persons with God. **12** [k]For as many as have sinned without the Law, shall perish also without the Law: and as many as have sinned in the Law, shall be judged by the Law, **13** [l](For the hearers of the Law are not righteous before God: but the doers of the Law shall be [m]justified. **14** [n]For when the Gentiles which have [o]not the Law, do by [p]nature the things contained in the Law, they having not the Law, are a Law unto themselves, **15** Which show the effect of the Law [q]written in their hearts, their conscience also bearing witness and their thoughts accusing one another, or excusing.) **16** [r]At the day when God shall judge the secrets of men by Jesus Christ, according to [s]my Gospel. **17** [t]Behold, thou art called a Jew, and restest in the Law, and gloriest in God, **18** And knowest his will, and [u,v]triest the things that dissent from it, in that thou art instructed by the Law: **19** And persuadest thyself that thou art a guide of the blind, a light of them which are in darkness, **20** An instructor of them which lack discretion, a teacher of the unlearned, which hast the [w]form of knowledge, and of the truth in the [x]law. **21** Thou therefore, which teachest another, teachest thou not thyself? thou that preachest, A man should not steal, dost thou steal? **22** Thou that sayest, A man should not commit adultery, dost thou commit adultery? thou that abhorrest idols, committest thou sacrilege? **23** Thou that gloriest in the Law, through breaking the Law, dishonorest thou God? **24** For the Name of God is blasphemed among the Gentiles through you, [3]as it is written. **25** [y]For circumcision verily is profitable, if thou do the Law: but if thou be a transgressor of the Law, thy circumcision is made uncircumcision. **26** Therefore [z]if the uncircumcision keep the ordinances of the Law, shall not his [aa]uncircumcision be counted for circumcision? **27** And shall not [ab]uncircumcision which is by nature (if it keep the Law) condemn thee which by the [ac]letter and circumcision art a transgressor of the Law? **28** For he is not a Jew, which is one [ad]outward: neither is that circumcision, which is outward in the flesh: **29** But he is a Jew which is one within, and the circumcision is of the heart, in the [ae]spirit, not in the letter, whose praise is not of men, but of God.

---

ah. Rom. 1:19 Their ungodliness he proveth hereby, that although all men have a most clear and evident glass wherein to behold the everlasting and almighty nature of God, even in his creatures, yet have they fallen away from those principles to most foolish and sound devices of their own brains, in consituting and appointing the service of God.
ai. Rom. 1:19 In their hearts.
aj. Rom. 1:20 Thou seest not God, and yet thou acknowledgest him as God by his works, Cicero.
ak. Rom. 1:21 They did not honor him with that honor, and service, which was meet for his everlasting power and Godhead.
al. Rom. 1:21 As if he said, became so mad of themselves.
am. Rom. 1:22 Or thought themselves.
an. Rom. 1:23 For the true God they took another.
ao. Rom. 1:24 The unrighteousness of men he setteth forth first, in this, that even against nature following their lusts, they defiled themselves one with another, by the just judgment of God.
ap. Rom. 1:24 The contempt of religion, is the fountain of all mischief.
aq. Rom. 1:24 As a just judge.
ar. Rom. 1:27 A meet reward for their deserts.
as. Rom. 1:28 He proveth the unrighteousness of man by a large rehearsal of many kinds of wickedness, from which (if not from all, yet at the least from many of them) no man is altogether free.
at. Rom. 1:28 Into a mad and froward mind, whereby it cometh to pass, that the conscience being once put out, and having almost no more remorse of sin, men run headlong into all kinds of mischief.
au. Rom. 1:30 Unmindful of their covenants and bargains.
av. Rom. 1:31 By the Law of God he meaneth that which the Philosophers called the Law of nature, and the Lawyers themselves termed the Law of nations.
aw. Rom. 1:31 Are fellows and partakers with them in their wickedness, and besides that, commend them which do amiss.

ROM. 1
1. Acts 13:1
2. Hab. 2:4

ROM. 2
a. Rom. 2:1 He convinceth them which would seem to be exempt out of the number of other men, because they reprehend other men's faults, and saith that they are least of all to be excused, for if they were well and narrowly searched (as God surely doth) they themselves would be found guilty in those things which they reprehend, and punish in others: so that in condemning others they pronounce sentence against themselves.
b. Rom. 2:2 Paul allegeth no places of Scripture, for he reasoneth generally against all men: but he bringeth such reasons as every man is persuaded of in his mind, so that the devil himself is not able to pluck them clean out.
c. Rom. 2:2 Considering and judging things aright, and not by any outward show.
d. Rom. 2:4 A vehement and grievous crying out against them that please themselves, because they see more than others do, and yet are no whit better than others are.
e. Rom. 2:5 Whilst thou givest thyself to pleasures, thinking to increase thy goods, thou shalt find God's wrath.
f. Rom. 2:6 The ground of the former disputation, That both the Jews and Gentiles have together need of righteousness.
g. Rom. 2:7 Glory which followeth good works, which he layeth not out before us, as though there were any that could attain to salvation by his own strength, but, by laying this condition of salvation before us, which no man can perform, to bring men to Christ, who alone justified the believers, as he himself concludeth, Rom. 2:21-22, following.
h. Rom. 2:8 By truth, he meaneth that knowledge which we have of nature.
i. Rom. 2:8 God's indignation against sinners, which shall quickly be kindled.
j. Rom. 2:11 God doth not measure men either by their blood, or by their country, either to receive them, or to cast them away.
k. Rom. 2:12 He applieth that general accusation of mankind particularly both to the Gentiles, and to the Jews.
l. Rom. 2:13 He preventeth an objection which might be made by the Jews, whom the Law doth not excuse, but condemns, because that not the hearing of the Law, but the keeping of the Law doth justify.
m. Rom. 2:13 Shall be pronounced just before God's judgment seat: which is true indeed, if any such could be found that had fulfilled the law: but seeing Abraham was not justified by the Law, but by faith, it followeth that no man can be justified by works.
n. Rom. 2:14 He preventeth an objection which might be made by the Gentiles, who although they have not the Law of Moses, yet they have no reason whereby they may excuse their wickedness in that they have somewhat written in their hearts instead of a Law, as men that forbid, and punish some things as wicked, and command and commend other some as good.
o. Rom. 2:14 Not simply, but in comparison of the Jews.
p. Rom. 2:14 Command honest things, and forbid dishonest.
q. Rom. 2:15 This knowledge is a natural knowledge.
r. Rom. 2:16 God deferreth many judgments, which notwithstanding he will execute at their convenient time by Jesus Christ, with a most straight examination, not only of words and deeds, but of thoughts also, be they never so hidden or secret.
s. Rom. 2:16 As this my doctrine witnesseth, which I am appointed to preach.
t. Rom. 2:17 He proveth by the testimony of David, and the other Prophets, that God bestowed greatest benefits upon the Jews, in giving them also the Law, but that they are the most unthankful and unkindest of all men.
u. Rom. 2:18 Canst try and discern what things swerve from God's will.
v. Rom. 2:18 Or allowest the things that are excellent.
w. Rom. 2:20 The way to teach and frame others in the knowledge of the truth.
x. Rom. 2:20 As though he said, that the Jews under a color of an outward serving of God, challenged all to themselves, when as indeed, they did nothing less than observe the Law.
y. Rom. 2:25 He precisely preventeth their objection, which set an holiness in circumcision, and the outward observation of the Law: So that he showeth that the outward circumcision, if it be separated from the inward, doth not only not justify, but also condemns them that are indeed circumcised, of whom requireth that, which is signifieth, that is to say, cleanness of the heart and the whole life, according to the commandment of the Law, so that if there be a man uncircumcised according to the flesh, who is circumcised in heart, he is far better and more to be more accounted of, than any Jew that is circumcised according to the flesh only.
z. Rom. 2:26 This is the figure Metonymy, for, if the uncircumcised.
aa. Rom. 2:26 The state and condition of the uncircumcised.
ab. Rom. 2:27 He which is uncircumcised by nature and blood.
ac. Rom. 2:27 Paul useth oftentimes to set the letter against the Spirit: but in this place, the circumcision which is according to the letter, is the cutting off of the foreskin, but the circumcision of the Spirit, is the circumcision of the heart, that is to say, the spiritual end of the ceremony, is true holiness and righteousness whereby the people of God is known from profane and heathenish men.
ad. Rom. 2:28 By the outward ceremony only.
ae. Rom. 2:29 Whose force is inward, and in the heart.

ROM. 2
1. James 5:3
2. Ps. 62:12 / Matt. 16:27 / Rev. 22:12
3. Isa. 52:5 / Ezek. 36:20

3 *1 He giveth the Jews some 2 preferment, for the covenant's sake, 4 but yet such, as wholly dependeth on God's mercy. 9 That both Jews and Gentiles are sinners, 11 he proveth by Scriptures: 19 and showing the use of the Law, 28 he concludeth that we are justified by faith.*

1 What [a]is then the preferment of the Jew? or what is the profit of circumcision? **2** Much every manner of way: for [b]chiefly, because unto them were of credit committed the [c]oracles of God. **3** For what, though some did not [d]believe? shall their unbelief make the [e]faith of God without effect? **4** God forbid: yea, let God be true, and every man a liar, as it is written, That thou mightest be [f]justified in thy words, and overcome, [g]when thou art judged. **5** [h]Now if our [i]unrighteousness commend the righteousness of God, what shall we say? is God unrighteous which punisheth? (I speak as [j]a man.) **6** God forbid: (else how shall God judge the world?) **7** [k]For if the [l]verity of God hath more abounded through my lie unto his glory, why am I yet condemned as a sinner? **8** And (as we are blamed, and as some affirm, that we say) why do we not evil, that good may come thereof? whose damnation is just. **9** [m]What then? are we more excellent? No, in no wise: for we have already proved, that all, both Jews and Gentiles are [n]under sin, **10** As it is written, [1]There is none righteous no not one. **11** There is none that understandeth: there is none that seeketh God. **12** They have all gone out of the way: they have been made altogether unprofitable: there is none that doeth good, no not one. **13** [2]Their throat is an open sepulcher: they have used their tongues to deceit: [3]the poison of asps is under their lips. **14** [4]Whose mouth is full of cursing and bitterness. **15** [5]Their feet are swift to shed blood. **16** Destruction and calamity are in their ways: **17** And the [o]way of peace they have not known. **18** [6]The fear of God is not before their eyes. **19** [p]Now we know that whatsoever the [q]law saith, it saith it to them which are under the law, that [r]every mouth may be stopped, and all the world be [s]subject to the judgment of God. **20** Therefore by the [t]works of the Law shall no [u]flesh be [v]justified in his [w]sight: for by the Law cometh the knowledge of sin. **21** [x]But now is the righteousness of God made manifest without the Law, having witness of the Law, and of the Prophets, **22** [y]To wit, the righteousness of God by the faith of [z]Jesus Christ, unto all, and upon all that believe. **23** For there is no difference: for all have sinned, and are deprived of the [aa]glory of God, **24** [ab]And are justified [ac]freely by his grace, through the redemption that is in Christ Jesus, **25** [ad]Whom God hath set forth to be a reconciliation through faith in his [ae]blood to declare his righteousness, by the forgiveness of the sins that [af]are passed, **26** Through the [ag]patience of God, to show at [ah]this time his righteousness, that he might be [ai]just, and a [aj]justifier of him which is of the [ak]faith of Jesus. **27** [al]Where is then the rejoicing? It is excluded. By what [am]Law? of works? Nay: but by the Law of faith. **28** Therefore we conclude, that a man is justified by faith, without the works of the Law. **29** [an]God, is he the God of the [ao]Jews only, and not of the Gentiles also? Yes, even of the Gentiles also. **30** For it is one God, who shall justify [ap]circumcision of faith, and uncircumcision through faith. **31** [aq]Do we then make the Law of [ar]none effect through faith? God forbid: yea, we [as]establish the Law.

4 *1 He proveth that which he said before of faith, by the example of Abraham, 3, 6 and the testimony of the Scripture: and ten times in the Chapter he beateth upon this word, Imputation.*

1 What [a]shall we say then, that Abraham our father hath found concerning the [b]flesh? **2** [c]For if Abraham were justified by works, he hath wherein to rejoice, but not with God. **3** [d]For what saith the Scripture? Abraham believed God, and it was counted to him for righteousness. **4** [e]Now to him that [f]worketh, the wages is not [g]counted by favor, but by debt: **5** But to him that worketh not, but believeth in him that [h]justifieth the ungodly, his faith is counted for righteousness. **6** [i]Even as David declareth the blessedness of the man, unto whom God imputeth righteousness without works, saying, **7** Blessed are they whose iniquities are forgiven, and whose sins are covered. **8** Blessed is the man to whom the Lord imputeth not sin. **9** [j]Came this [k]blessedness then upon the circumcision only, or upon the uncircumcision also? For we say, that faith was imputed unto Abraham for righteousness. **10** [l]How was it then imputed? when he was circumcised, or uncircumcised? not when he was circumcised, but when he was uncircumcised. **11** [m]After, he received the [n]sign of circumcision, as the [o]seal of the

---

ROM. 3

a. Rom. 3:1 The first meeting with, or preventing an objection of the Jews: what then, have the Jews no more preferment than the Gentiles? yes, that have they, saith the Apostle, on God's behalf: for he committed the tables of the covenant to them, so that the unbelief of a few, cannot cause the whole nation without exception to be cast away of God, who is true, and who also useth their unworthiness to commend and set forth his goodness.
b. Rom. 3:2 The Jews' state and condition was chiefest.
c. Rom. 3:2 Words.
d. Rom. 3:3 Break the covenant.
e. Rom. 3:3 The faith that God gave.
f. Rom. 3:4 That thy justice might be plainly seen.
g. Rom. 3:4 Forasmuch as thou showest forth an evident token of thy righteousness, constancy and faith, by preserving him who had broken his covenant.
h. Rom. 3:5 Another prevention, issuing out of the former answer: that the justice of God is in such sort commended and set forth by our unrighteousness, that therefore God forgetteth not that he is the judge of the world, and therefore a most severe revenger of unrighteousness.
i. Rom. 3:5 Treachery, and all the fruits thereof.
j. Rom. 3:5 Therefore I speak not these words in mine own person, as though I thought so, but this is the talk of man's wisdom, which is not subject to the will of God.
k. Rom. 3:7 A third objection which addeth somewhat to the former, If sins do turn to the glory of God, they are not only not to be punished, but we ought rather to give ourselves to them: which blasphemy Paul contending himself to curse and detest, pronounceth just punishment against such blasphemers.
l. Rom. 3:7 The truth and constancy.
m. Rom. 3:9 Another answer to the first objection: that the Jews, if they be considered in themselves, are no better than other men are: as it has been long since pronounced by the mouth of the Prophets.
n. Rom. 3:9 Are guilty of sin.
o. Rom. 3:17 An innocent and peaceable life.
p. Rom. 3:19 He proveth that this grievous accusation which is uttered by David and Isaiah, doth properly concern the Jews.
q. Rom. 3:19 The law of Moses.
r. Rom. 3:19 A conclusion of all the former disputation, from verse 8 of the first Chapter. Therefore saith the Apostle, No man can hope to be justified by any Law, whether it be that general Law, or the particular Law of Moses, and therefore to be saved: seeing it appeareth (as we have already proved) by comparing the Law and man's life together, that all men are sinners, and therefore worthy of condemnation in the sight of God.
s. Rom. 3:19 Be found guilty before God.
t. Rom. 3:20 By that that the Law can by us be performed.
u. Rom. 3:20 Flesh is here taken for man, as in many other places, and furthermore hath here a greater force: for it is put to show the contrariety betwixt God and man: as if you would say, Man who is nothing else but a piece of flesh defiled with sin, and God who is most pure and most perfect in himself.
v. Rom. 3:20 Absolved before the judgment seat of God.
w. Rom. 3:20 A secret setting of the righteousness which is before men, be they never so just, against the justice which can stand before God: now there is no righteousness can stand before God, but the righteousness of Christ only.
x. Rom. 3:21 Therefore saith the Apostle, Lest that men should perish, God doth now exhibit that, which he promised of old, that is to say, a way whereby we may be justified and saved before him without the Law.
y. Rom. 3:22 The matter, as it were of this righteousness, is Christ Jesus apprehended by faith, and for this end offered to all people, as without him all people are shut out from the kingdom of God.
z. Rom. 3:22 Which we give to Jesus Christ, or which resteth upon him.
aa. Rom. 3:23 By the Glory of God, is meant that mark which we all shoot at, that is, everlasting life, which standeth in that we are made partakers of the glory of God.
ab. Rom. 3:24 Therefore this righteousness touching us, is altogether freely given, for it standeth upon those things which we have not done ourselves, but such as Christ hath suffered for our sakes, to deliver us from sin.
ac. Rom. 3:24 Of his free gift, and mere liberality.
ad. Rom. 3:25 God then is the author of that free justification, because it pleaseth him: and Christ is he, which suffered punishment for our sins, and in whom we have remission of them: and the means whereby we apprehend Christ, is faith. To be short, the end is the setting forth of the goodness of God, that by this means it may appear, that he is merciful indeed, and constant in his promises, as he that freely, and of mere grace justifieth the believers.
ae. Rom. 3:25 This name of Blood, calleth us back to the figure of the old sacrifices, the truth and substance of which sacrifices is in Christ.
af. Rom. 3:25 Of those sins which we committed when we were his enemies.
ag. Rom. 3:26 Through his patience, and suffering nature.
ah. Rom. 3:26 To wit, when Paul wrote this.
ai. Rom. 3:26 That he might be found exceeding true and faithful.
aj. Rom. 3:26 Making him just, and without blame by imputing Christ's righteousness unto him.
ak. Rom. 3:26 Of the number of them which by faith lay hold upon Christ: contrary to whom, are they which look to be saved by circumcision, that is, by the Law.
al. Rom. 3:27 An argument to prove this conclusion, that we are justified by faith without works, taken from the end of Justification. The end of Justification is the glory of God alone: therefore we are justified by faith without works: for if we were justified either by our own works only, or partly by faith, and partly by works, the glory of this justification should not be wholly given to God.
am. Rom. 3:27 By what doctrine? now the doctrine of works hath [this] condition joined with it, If thou doest: and the doctrine of faith hath this condition, If thou believest.
an. Rom. 3:29 Another argument of an absurdity: if justification depended upon the Law of Moses, then should God be a Savior to the Jews only. Again: if he should save the Jews after one sort, and the Gentiles after another, he should not be one and like himself. Therefore he will justify both of them after one selfsame manner, that is to say, by faith. Moreover, this argument must be joined to that which followeth next, that this conclusion may be firm and evident.
ao. Rom. 3:29 God is said to be their God, after the manner of the Scripture, whom he loveth and tendereth.
ap. Rom. 3:30 The circumcised.
aq. Rom. 3:31 The taking away of an objection: yet it is not the Law taken away therefore, but is rather established, as it shall be declared in [its] proper place.
ar. Rom. 3:31 Vain, void, to no purpose, and of no force.
as. Rom. 3:31 We make it effectual and strong.

ROM. 3

1. Ps. 14:1-3 / Ps. 53:1-3
2. Ps. 5:10
3. Ps. 140:3
4. Ps. 10:7
5. Isa. 59:7
6. Ps. 36:1

ROM. 4

a. Rom. 4:1 A new argument of great weight, taken from the example of Abraham the father of all believers: And this is the proposition: if Abraham be considered in himself by his works, he hath deserved nothing wherein to rejoice with God.
b. Rom. 4:1 By works, as appeareth in the next verse.
c. Rom. 4:2 A preventing of an objection: Abraham may well rejoice and extol himself amongst men, but not with God.
d. Rom. 4:3 A confirmation of the proposition: Abraham was justified by imputation of faith, therefore freely without any respect of his works.
e. Rom. 4:4 The first proof of the confirmation, taken of contraries: to him that deserveth anything by his labor, the wages is not counted by favor, but by debt: but to him that hath done nothing, but believeth in him which promiseth freely, faith is imputed.
f. Rom. 4:4 To him that hath deserved anything by his work.
g. Rom. 4:4 Is not reckoned nor given him.
h. Rom. 4:5 That maketh him which is wicked in himself, just in Christ.
i. Rom. 4:6 Another proof of the same confirmation: David putteth blessedness in free pardon of sins, therefore justification also.
j. Rom. 4:9 A new proposition: that this manner of justification belongeth both to uncircumcised, and also to the circumcised, as is declared in the person of Abraham.
k. Rom. 4:9 This saying of David, wherein he pronounceth them blessed.
l. Rom. 4:10 He proveth that it belongeth to the uncircumcised (for there was no doubt of the circumcised) in this sort: Abraham was justified in uncircumcision, therefore this justification belongeth also to the uncircumcised. Nay, it does not appertain to the circumcised in respect of the circumcision, much less are the uncircumcised shut out for their uncircumcision.
m. Rom. 4:11 A preventing of an objection: why then was Abraham circumcised, if he were already justified? That the gift of righteousness (saith he) might be confirmed in him.
n. Rom. 4:11 Circumcision, which is a sign: as we say, the Sacrament of Baptism, for Baptism which is a Sacrament.

righteousness of the faith which he had, when he was uncircumcised, [p]that he should be the father of all them that believe, not being circumcised, that righteousness might be imputed to them also. **12** [q]And the father of circumcision, not unto them only which are of the circumcision, but unto them also that walk in the steps of the faith of our father Abraham which he had when he was uncircumcised. **13** [r]For the promise that he should be the [s]heir of the world, was not given to Abraham, or to his seed, through the [t]Law, but through the righteousness of faith. **14** [u]For if they which are of the [v]Law, be heirs, faith is made void, and the promise is made of none effect. **15** [w]For the Law causeth wrath: for where no Law is, there is no transgression. **16** [x]Therefore it is by faith, that it might come by grace, and the promise might be sure to all the [y]seed, [z]not to that only which is of the Law: but also to that which is of the faith of Abraham who is the father of us all, **17** (As it is written, I have made thee a [aa]father of many nations) even before [ab]God whom he believed, who [ac]quickeneth the dead, and [ad]calleth those things which be not, as though they were. **18** [ae]Which Abraham above hope, believed under hope, that he should be the father of many nations: according to that which was spoken to him, So shall thy seed be. **19** And he [af]not weak in the faith, considered not his own body, which was now [ag]dead, being almost an hundred years old, neither the deadness of Sarah's womb. **20** Neither did he doubt of the promise of God through unbelief, but was strengthened in the faith, and gave [ah]glory to God, **21** Being [ai]fully assured that he which had promised, was also able to do it. **22** And therefore it was imputed to him for righteousness. **23** [aj]Now is it not written for him only, that it was imputed to him for righteousness, **24** But also for us, to whom it shall be imputed for righteousness, which believe in him that raised up Jesus our Lord from the dead, **25** Who was delivered to death for our [ak]sins, and is risen again for our justification.

5

1 He amplifieth 2 Christ's righteousness, which is laid hold on by faith, 5 who was given for the weak, 8 and sinful. 14 He compareth Christ with Adam. 17 Death with Life, 20 and the Law with Grace.

1 Then being [a]justified by faith, we have peace toward God through our Lord Jesus Christ. **2** [1,b]By whom also through faith we have [c]had this access into this grace [d]wherein we [e]stand, [f]and [g]rejoice under the hope of the glory of God. **3** [h]Neither that only, but also we [2]rejoice in tribulations, [i]knowing that tribulation bringeth forth patience. **4** And patience experience, and experience hope. **5** [j]And hope maketh not ashamed, because the [k]love of God is shed abroad in our hearts by the holy Ghost, which is given unto us. **6** [l]For Christ, when we were yet of no strength, at his [m]time died for the [3]ungodly. **7** [n]Doubtless one will scarce die [o]for a righteous man: but yet for a good man it may be that one dare die. **8** But God [p]setteth out his love towards us, seeing that while we were yet [q]sinners, Christ died for us. **9** Much more then, being now justified by his blood, we shall be saved from [r]wrath through him. **10** For if when we were enemies, we were reconciled to God by the death of his Son, much more being reconciled, we shall be saved by his life, **11** [s]And not only so, but we also rejoice in God through our Lord Jesus Christ, by whom we have now received the atonement. **12** [t]Wherefore, as by [u]one man [v]sin entered into the world, and death by sin, and so death went over all men: [w]in whom all men have sinned. **13** [x]For unto the [y]time of the Law was sin in the world, but sin is not [z]imputed, while there is no law. **14** [aa]But death reigned from Adam to Moses, even over [ab]them also that sinned not after the like [ac]manner of the transgression of Adam, [ad]which was the figure of him that was to come. **15** [ae]But yet the gift is not so as is the offense: for if through the offense of [af]that one, many be dead, much more the grace of God, and the gift by grace, which is by one man Jesus Christ, hath abounded unto many. **16** [ag]Neither is the gift so, as that which entered in by one that sinned: for the fault came of one offense unto condemnation: but the gift is of many offenses to [ah]justification. **17** [ai]For if by the offense of one, death reigned through one, much more shall they which receive that abundance of grace, and of that gift of that righteousness, [aj]reign in life through one, that is, Jesus Christ. **18** [ak]Likewise then, as by the offense of one, the fault came on all men to condemnation, so by the justifying of one, the benefit abounded toward all men to the [al]justification of

---

o. Rom. 4:11 Circumcision was called before a sign, in respect of the outward ceremony: now Paul showeth the force and substance of that sign, that is, to what end it is used, to wit, not only to signify, but also to seal up the righteousness of faith, whereby we come to possess Christ himself: for the holy Ghost worketh that inwardly indeed, which the Sacraments being joined with the word, do represent.

p. Rom. 4:11 An applying of the example of Abraham to the uncircumcised believers, whose father also he maketh Abraham.

q. Rom. 4:12 An applying of the same example, to the circumcised believers, whose father Abraham is, but yet by faith.

r. Rom. 4:13 A reason why the seed of Abraham is to be esteemed by faith, because that Abraham himself through faith was made partaker of that promise, whereby he was made the father of all nations.

s. Rom. 4:13 That all the nations of the world should be his children: or by the world may be understood the land of Canaan.

t. Rom. 4:13 For works that he had done, or upon this condition that he should fulfill the Law.

u. Rom. 4:14 A double confirmation of that reason: the one is, that the promise cannot be apprehended by the Law, and therefore it should be frustrated: the other, that the condition of faith should be joined in vain to that promise which should be apprehended by works.

v. Rom. 4:14 If they be heirs which have fulfilled the Law.

w. Rom. 4:15 A reason of the first confirmation, why the promise cannot be apprehended by the Law: because that the Law doth not reconcile God and us, but rather denounceth his anger against us, forsomuch as no man can observe it.

x. Rom. 4:16 The conclusion of this argument. The salvation and justification of all the posterity of Abraham (that is, of the Church which is gathered together of all people) proceedeth of faith, which layeth hold on the promise made unto Abraham, and which promise Abraham himself first of all laid hold on.

y. Rom. 4:16 To all the believers.

z. Rom. 4:16 That is to say, not only of them which believe and are also circumcised according to the Law, but of them also which without circumcision, and in respect of faith only, are counted amongst the children of Abraham.

aa. Rom. 4:17 This fatherhood is spiritual, depending only upon the virtue of God, who made the promise.

ab. Rom. 4:17 Before God, that is, by a spiritual kindred, which had place before God, and maketh us acceptable to God.

ac. Rom. 4:17 Who restored to life.

ad. Rom. 4:17 With whom these things are already, which as yet are not in deed, as he that can with a word make what he will of nothing.

ae. Rom. 4:18 A description of true faith, wholly resting in the power of God, and his good will, set forth in the example of Abraham.

af. Rom. 4:19 Very strong and constant.

ag. Rom. 4:19 Void of strength, and unmeet to get children.

ah. Rom. 4:20 Acknowledged and praised God, as most gracious and true.

ai. Rom. 4:21 A description of true faith.

aj. Rom. 4:23 The rule of justification is always one, both in Abraham and in all the faithful: that is to say, faith in God, who after that there was made a full satisfaction for our sins in Christ our mediator, raised him from the dead, that we also being justified, might be saved in him.

ak. Rom. 4:25 To pay the ransom for our sins.

ROM. 5

a. Rom. 5:1 Another argument taken of the effects: we are justified with that, which truly appeaseth our conscience before God but faith in Christ doth appease our conscience, and not the Law, as it was before said, therefore by faith we are justified, and not by the Law.

b. Rom. 5:2 Whereas quietness of conscience is attributed to faith, it is to be referred to Christ, who is the giver of faith itself, and in whom faith itself is effectual.

c. Rom. 5:2 We must here know, that we have yet still this same effect of faith.

d. Rom. 5:2 By which grace, that is, by which gracious love and good will, or that state whereunto we are graciously taken.

e. Rom. 5:2 We stand steadfast.

f. Rom. 5:2 A preventing of an objection against them which beholding the daily miseries and calamities of the Church, think that the Christians dream, when they brag of their felicity: to whom the Apostle answereth, that their felicity is laid up under hope of another place: which hope is so certain and sure, that they do not less rejoice for that happiness, than if they did presently enjoy it.

g. Rom. 5:2 Our minds are not only quiet and settled, but also we are marvelously glad and conceive great joy for that heavenly inheritance which waiteth for us.

h. Rom. 5:3 Tribulation itself giveth us divers and sundry ways occasion to rejoice, much less doth it make us miserable.

i. Rom. 5:3 Afflictions accustom us to patience, and patience assureth us of the goodness of God, and this experience confirmeth, and fostereth our hope, which never deceiveth us.

j. Rom. 5:5 The ground of hope is an assured testimony of the conscience, by the gift of the holy Ghost, that we are beloved of God, and this is nothing else but that which we call faith: whereof it followeth, that through faith our consciences are quieted.

k. Rom. 5:5 Wherewith he loveth us.

l. Rom. 5:6 A sure comfort in adversity, that our peace and quietness of conscience be not troubled: for he that so loved them that were of no strength, and while they were yet sinners, that he died for them, how can he neglect them being now sanctified and living in him?

m. Rom. 5:6 In time fit and convenient, which the father hath appointed.

n. Rom. 5:7 An amplifying of the love of God towards us, so that we cannot doubt of it, which delivereth Christ to death for the unjust, and for them of whom he could receive no commodity, and (that more is) for his very enemies. How can it be then that Christ being now alive, should not save them from destruction, whom by his death he justifieth and reconcileth?

o. Rom. 5:7 In the stead of some just man.

p. Rom. 5:8 He setteth out his love unto us, that in the midst of our afflictions we may know assuredly, he will be present with us.

q. Rom. 5:8 While sin reigned in us.

r. Rom. 5:9 From affliction and destruction.

s. Rom. 5:11 He now passeth over to the other part of justification, which consisteth in the free imputation of the obedience of Christ: so that to the remission of sins there is added moreover and besides, the gift of Christ's righteousness imputed or put upon us by faith, which swalloweth up that unrighteousness which flowed from Adam into us, and all the fruits thereof: so that in Christ we do not only cease to be unjust, but we begin also to be just.

t. Rom. 5:12 From Adam, in whom all have sinned, both guiltiness and death (which is the punishment of the guiltiness) came upon all.

u. Rom. 5:12 By Adam, who is compared with Christ, like to him in this, that both of them make those who are theirs, partakers of that they have into: but they are unlike in this, that Adam deriveth sin into them that are his, even of nature, and that to death: but Christ maketh them that are his, partakers of his righteousness by grace, and that unto life.

v. Rom. 5:12 By sin is meant that disease which is ours by inheritance, and men commonly call it original sin: for so he useth to call that sin in the singular number, whereas, if he speaks of the fruits of it, he useth the plural number, calling them sins.

w. Rom. 5:12 That is, in Adam.

x. Rom. 5:13 That this is so, that both guiltiness and death began not after the giving and transgressing of Moses' Law, it appeareth manifestly by that, that men died before that Law was given: for in that they died, sin, which is the cause of death, was then: and in such sort, that it was also imputeth: whereupon it followeth that there was then some Law, the breach whereof was the cause of death.

y. Rom. 5:13 Even from Adam to Moses.

z. Rom. 5:13 Where there is no Law made, no man is punished as faulty and guilty.

aa. Rom. 5:14 But that this Law was not that universal Law, and that death did not proceed from any actual sin of everyone particularly, it appeareth hereby, that the very infants which neither could ever know nor transgress that natural Law, are notwithstanding dead as well as Adam.

ab. Rom. 5:14 Our infants.

ac. Rom. 5:14 Not after that sort as they sin that are of more years, following their lusts: but yet the whole posterity was corrupt in Adam, when as he wittingly and willingly sinned.

ad. Rom. 5:14 Now the first Adam answereth the latter, who is Christ, as it is afterward declared.

ae. Rom. 5:15 Adam and Christ are compared together in this respect, that both of them do give and yield to theirs, that which is their own: but herein first they differ, that Adam by nature hath spread his fault to the destruction of many, but Christ's obedience hath by grace overflowed many.

af. Rom. 5:15 That is, Adam.

ag. Rom. 5:16 Another inequality consisteth in this, that by Adam's one offense men are made guilty, but the righteousness of Christ imputed unto us freely, doth not only absolve us from that one fault, but from all others.

ah. Rom. 5:16 To the sentence of absolution, whereby we are quit, and pronounced righteous.

ai. Rom. 5:17 The third difference is, that the righteousness of Christ being imputed unto us by grace, is of greater power to bring life, than the offense of Adam is to addict his posterity to death.

aj. Rom. 5:17 Be partakers of true and everlasting life.

ak. Rom. 5:18 Therefore to be short, as by one man's offense, the guiltiness came on all men, to make them subject to death: so on the contrary side, the righteousness of Christ, which

life. **19** [am]For as by one man's [an]disobedience [ao]many were made sinners, so by
that obedience of that one, shall many also be made righteous. **20** [ap]Moreover,
the Law [aq]entered thereupon, that the offense should abound: nevertheless, where
sin abounded, there grace [ar]abounded much more: **21** That as sin had reigned
unto death, so might grace also reign by righteousness unto eternal life through
Jesus Christ our Lord.

6

1 He cometh to sanctification, without which, that no man putteth on Christ's righteousness, he proveth 4 by an argument taken of Baptism, 12 and thereupon exhorteth to holiness of life, 16 briefly making mention of the Law transgressed.

1 What [a]shall we say then? Shall we continue still in [b]sin, that grace may
abound? God forbid. **2** [c]How shall we, that are [d]dead to sin, live yet the-
rein? **3** [e]Know ye not, that [1]all we which have been baptized into [f]Jesus Christ,
have been baptized into his death? **4** [2]We are buried then with him by baptism
into his death, that like as Christ was raised up from the dead [g]to the glory of the
Father, so [h]we also should [3]walk in newness of life. **5** [4,i]For if we be planted
with him to the [j]similitude of his death, even so shall we [k]be to the similitude
of his resurrection, **6** Knowing this, that our [l]old man is crucified with [m]him,
that the body of [n]sin might be destroyed, that henceforth we should not [o]ser-
ve sin, **7** [p]For he that is dead, is freed from sin. **8** Wherefore, if we be dead
with Christ, we believe that we shall live also with him, **9** Knowing that Christ
being raised from the dead, dieth no more: death hath no more dominion over
him. **10** For in that he died, he died [q]once to sin: but in that he liveth, he liveth
to [r]God. **11** Likewise think ye also, that ye are dead to sin, but are alive to God
in Jesus Christ our Lord. **12** [s]Let not sin [t]reign therefore in your mortal body,
that ye should obey it in the lusts thereof: **13** Neither [u]give ye your [v]members,
as [w]weapons of unrighteousness unto sin: but give yourselves unto God, as they
that are alive from the dead, and give your members as weapons of righteousness
unto God. **14** [x]For sin shall not have dominion over you: for ye are not under
the Law, but under grace. **15** [y]What then? shall we sin, because we are not under
the Law, but under grace? God forbid. **16** [5]Know ye not, that to whomsoever ye
give yourselves as servants to obey, his servants ye are to whom ye obey, whether it
be of sin unto death, or of obedience unto righteousness? **17** [z]But God be than-
ked, that ye have been the servants of sin, but ye have obeyed from the heart unto
the [aa]form of the doctrine, whereunto ye were delivered. **18** Being then made
free from sin, ye are made the servants of righteousness. **19** I speak after the
manner of man, because of the infirmity of your flesh: for as ye have given your
members servants to uncleanness and to iniquity, to commit iniquity, so now give
your members servants unto righteousness in holiness. **20** For when ye were the
servants of sin, ye were [ab]freed from righteousness. **21** [ac]What fruit had ye then
in those things, whereof ye are now ashamed? For the [ad]end of those things is dea-
th. **22** But now being freed from sin, and made servants unto God, ye have your
fruit in holiness, and the end, everlasting life. **23** [ae]For the wages of sin is death:
but the gift of God is eternal life, through Jesus Christ our Lord.

7

1 He declareth what it is, to be no more under the Law, 2 by an example taken of the Law of marriage, 7, 12 And lest the Law should seem faulty, 14 he proveth, that our sin is the cause, 2, 5 that the same is an occasion of death, 17 which was given us unto life. 21 He setteth out the battle between the flesh and the spirit.

1 Know [a]ye not, brethren, (for I speak to them that know the Law) that the
Law hath dominion over a man as long as he liveth? **2** [1]For the woman which is
in subjection to a man, is bound by the Law to the man, while he liveth: but if the
man be dead, she is delivered from the Law of the man. **3** So then, if while the
man liveth, she taketh another man, she shall be [b]called an [2]adulteress: but if the
man be dead, she is free from the Law, so that she is not an adulteress, though she
take another man. **4** [c]So ye, my brethren, are dead also to the Law by the [d]body
of Christ, that ye should be unto another, even unto him that is raised up from the
dead, that we should bring forth [e]fruit unto [f]God. **5** [g]For when we [h]were in the
flesh, the [i]affections of sins, which were by the [j]law, had [k]force in our members, to
bring forth fruit unto death, **6** But now we are delivered from the Law, he [l]being
dead [m]in whom we were [n]holden, that we should serve in [o]newness of Spirit, and
not in the oldness of the [p]letter. **7** [q]What shall we say then? Is the Law sin? God

---

by God's mercy is imputed to all believers, justifieth them, that they may become partakers of everlasting life.

al. Rom. 5:18 Not only because our sins are forgiven us, but also because the righteousness of Christ is imputed unto us.

am. Rom. 5:19 The ground of this whole comparison is this, that these two men are set as two stocks or roots, so that out of the one, sin by nature, out of the other, righteousness by grace doth spring forth upon others.

an. Rom. 5:19 So then, sin entered not into us only by following the steps of our forefather, but we take corruption of him by inheritance.

ao. Rom. 5:19 This word, Many, is set against this word, A few.

ap. Rom. 5:20 A preventing of an objection: why then did the Law of Moses enter thereupon? that men might be so much the more guilty, and the benefit of God in Christ Jesus be so much the more glorious.

aq. Rom. 5:20 Beside that disease which all men were infected withall by being defiled with one man's sin, the Law entered.

ar. Rom. 5:20 Grace was poured so plentifully from heaven, that it did not only countervail sin, but above measure passed it.

ROM. 5

1. Eph. 2:18
2. James 1:2
3. Heb. 9:15 / 1 Pet. 3:18

ROM. 6

a. Rom. 6:1 He passeth now to another benefit of Christ, which is called sanctification or regeneration.

b. Rom. 6:1 In that corruption: for though the guiltiness of sin be not imputed to us, yet the corruption remaineth still in us: the which Sanctification that followeth Justification killeth by little and little.

c. Rom. 6:2 The benefits of Justification and Sanctification, are always joined together inseparably, and both of them proceed from Christ, by the grace of God: Now sanctification is the abolishing of sin, that is, of our natural corruption, into whose place succeedeth the cleanness and pureness of nature reformed.

d. Rom. 6:2 They are said of Paul to be dead to sin, which are in such sort made partakers of the virtue of Christ, that that natural corruption is dead in them, that is, the force of it is put out, and it bringeth not forth his bitter fruits: and on the other side, they are said to live to sin, which are in the flesh, that is, whom the spirit of God hath not delivered from the slavery of the corruption of nature.

e. Rom. 6:3 There are three parts of this Sanctification, to wit, the dead of the old man or sin, his burial, and the resurrection of the new man, descending into us from the virtue of the death, burial, and resurrection of Christ, of which benefit our baptism is the sign and pledge.

f. Rom. 6:3 To the end that growing up in one with him, we should receive his strength to quench sin in us, and to make us new men.

g. Rom. 6:4 That Christ himself being discharged of his infirmity and weakness, might live in glory with God forever.

h. Rom. 6:4 And we which are his members rise for this end, that being made partakers of the selfsame virtue, we should begin to lead a new life, as though we were already in heaven.

i. Rom. 6:5 The death of sin and the life of righteousness, or our ingrafting into Christ, and growing up into one with him, cannot be separated by any means, neither in death nor life, whereby it followeth, that no man is sanctified, which lived still to sin, and therefore is no man made partaker of Christ by faith, which repenteth not, and turneth not from his wickedness: for as he said before, the Law is not subverted, but established by faith.

j. Rom. 6:5 Insomuch as by the means of the strength which cometh from him to us, we so die to sin as he is dead.

k. Rom. 6:5 For we become every day more perfect than others: for we shall never be perfectly sanctified, as long as we live here.

l. Rom. 6:6 All our whole nature, as we are conceived and born into this world with sin, which is called old, partly by comparing that old Adam with Christ, and partly also in respect of the deformation of our corrupt nature, which we change with a new.

m. Rom. 6:6 Our corrupt nature is attributed to Christ, not in deed, but by imputation.

n. Rom. 6:6 That naughtiness which sticketh fast in us.

o. Rom. 6:6 The end of sanctification which we shoot at, and shall at length come to, to wit when God shall be all in all.

p. Rom. 6:7 He proveth it by the effects of death, using a comparison of Christ the head with his members.

q. Rom. 6:10 Once for all.

r. Rom. 6:10 With God.

s. Rom. 6:12 An exhortation to contend and strive with corruption and all the effects thereof.

t. Rom. 6:12 By reigning, Saint Paul meaneth that chiefest and high rule, which no man striveth against, and if any do, yet it is in vain.

u. Rom. 6:13 To sin, as to a Lord or tyrant.

v. Rom. 6:13 Your mind and all the powers of it.

w. Rom. 6:13 As instruments to commit wickedness withall.

x. Rom. 6:14 He granteth that sin is not yet so dead in us that it is utterly extinct: but he promised victory to them that contend manfully, because we have the grace of God given us which worketh so, that the Law is not now in us the power and instrument of sin.

y. Rom. 6:15 To be under the law and under sin, signify all one, in respect of them which are not sanctified, as on the contrary side, to be under grace and righteousness, agree to them that are regenerate. Now these are contraries, so that one cannot agree with the other: Therefore let righteousness expel sin.

z. Rom. 6:17 By nature we are slaves to sin, and free from righteousness, but by the grace of God we are made servants to righteousness, and therefore free from sin.

aa. Rom. 6:17 This kind of speech hath a force in it: for he meaneth thereby that the doctrine of the Gospel is like a certain mold which we are cast into to be framed and fashioned like unto it.

ab. Rom. 6:20 Righteousness had no rule over you.

ac. Rom. 6:21 An exhortation to the study of righteousness and hatred of sin, the contrary ends of both, being set down before us.

ad. Rom. 6:21 The reward or payment.

ae. Rom. 6:23 Death is the punishment due to sin, but we are sanctified freely, unto life everlasting.

ROM. 6

1. Gal. 3:27
2. Col. 2:12
3. Eph. 4:23 / Col. 3:3 / Heb. 12:1 / 1 Pet. 2:1
4. 1 Cor. 6:14 / 2 Tim. 2:11
5. John 1:34 / 2 Pet. 2:19

ROM. 7

a. Rom. 7:1 By propounding the similitude of a marriage, he compareth the state of man both before and after regeneration together. The law of matrimony, saith he, is this, that so long as the husband liveth, the marriage abideth in force, but if he be dead, the woman may marry again.

b. Rom. 7:3 That is, she shall be an adulteress, by the consent and judgment of all men.

c. Rom. 7:4 An application of the similitude thus. So, saith he, doth it fare with us: for now we are joined to the spirit as it were to the second husband, by whom we must bring forth new children: we are dead in respect of the first husband, but in respect of the latter we are as it were raised from the dead.

d. Rom. 7:4 That is, in the body of Christ, to give us to understand how straight and near that fellowship is betwixt Christ and his members.

e. Rom. 7:4 He calleth the children, which the wife hath by her husband, fruit.

f. Rom. 7:4 Which are acceptable to God.

g. Rom. 7:5 A declaration of the former saying: for the concupiscences (saith he) which the law stirred up in us, were in us as it were an husband, of whom we brought forth very deadly and cursed children. But now since that husband is dead, and so consequently being delivered from the force of that killing law, we have passed into the governance of the spirit, so that we bring forth now, not those rotten and dead, but lively children.

h. Rom. 7:5 When we were in the state of the first marriage, which he calleth in the next verse following the oldness of the letter.

i. Rom. 7:5 The motions that egged us to sin, which show their force even in our minds.

j. Rom. 7:5 He saith not, of the law, but by the law, because they spring of sin which dwelleth within us, and take occasion to work thus in us, by reason of the restraint that the law maketh, not that the fault is in the law, but in ourselves.

k. Rom. 7:5 Wrought their strength.

l. Rom. 7:6 As if he said, The bond which bound us, is dead, and vanished away, insomuch, that sin which held us, hath not now wherewith to hold us.

m. Rom. 7:6 For this husband is within us.

n. Rom. 7:6 Satan is an unjust possessor, for he brought us in bondage of sin and himself deceitfully: and yet notwithstanding so long as we are sinners, we sin willingly.

forbid. Nay, I knew not sin, but by the Law: for I had not known [r]lust, except the Law had said, [3]Thou shalt not lust. **8** But sin took an occasion by the commandment, and wrought in me all manner of concupiscence: for without the Law sin is [s]dead. **9** [t]For I once was alive, without the [u]law: but when the commandment [v]came, sin revived, **10** But I [w]died: and the same commandment which was ordained unto life, was found to be unto me unto death. **11** For sin took occasion by the commandment, and deceived me, and thereby slew me. **12** [x]Wherefore the Law is [4]holy, and that [y]commandment is holy, and just, and good. **13** [z]Was that then which is good, [aa]made death unto me? God forbid: but sin, that it might [ab]appear sin, wrought death in me by that which is good, that sin might be [ac]out of measure sinful by the commandment. **14** [ad]For we know that the Law is spiritual, but I am carnal, sold under sin. **15** [ae]For I [af]allow not that which I do: for what I [ag]would, that do I not: but what I hate, that do I. **16** If I do then that which I would not, I consent to the Law, that it is good. **17** Now then, it is no more I, that do it, but [ah]sin that dwelleth in me. **18** [ai]For I know, that in me, that is, in my flesh, dwelleth no good thing: for to will is present with me: but I find [aj]no means to perform that which is good, **19** For I do not the good thing, which I would, but the evil, which I would not, that do I. **20** Now if I do that I would not, it is no more I that do it, but the sin that dwelleth in me. **21** [ak]I find then that when I would do good, I am thus yoked, that evil is present with me. **22** For I delight in the Law of God, concerning the [al]inner man. **23** But I see another Law in my members, rebelling against the law of my [am]mind, and leading me captive unto the law of sin, which is in my members. **24** [an]O [ao]wretched man that I am, who shall deliver me from the body of this death! **25** I [ap]thank God through Jesus Christ our Lord. Then I [aq]myself in my mind serve the Law of God, but in my flesh the law of sin.

8

1 He concludeth that there is no condemnation to them, who are grafted in Christ through his Spirit, 3 howsoever they be as yet burdened with sins: 9 For they live through that Spirit, 14 Whose testimony, 15 driveth away all fear, 28 and relieveth our present miseries.

1 Now [a]then there is no condemnation to them that are in Christ Jesus, which [b]walk not after the [c]flesh, but after the Spirit. **2** [d]For the [e]Law of the Spirit of [f]life which is in [g]Christ Jesus, hath [h]freed me from the Law of sin and of death. **3** [i]For (that that was [j]impossible to the Law, inasmuch as it was weak, because of the [k]flesh) God sending his own Son, in the similitude of [l]sinful flesh, and for [m]sin, [n]condemned sin in the flesh, **4** That that [o]righteousness of the Law might be fulfilled [p]in us, which walk not after the flesh, but after the Spirit. **5** [q]For they that are after the [r]flesh, savor the things of the flesh: but they that are after the Spirit, the things of the Spirit. **6** [s]For the wisdom of the flesh is death: but the wisdom of the Spirit is life and peace, **7** [t]Because the wisdom of the flesh is enmity against God: [u]for it is not subject to the Law of God, neither indeed can be. **8** [v]So then they that are in the flesh, cannot please God. **9** [w]Now ye are not in the flesh, but

---

o. Rom. 7:6 As becometh them, which after the death of their old husband are joined to the spirit: as whom the spirit of God hath made new men.

p. Rom. 7:6 By the letter he meaneth the law, in respect of that old condition: for before that our will be framed by the holy Ghost, the law speaketh but to deaf men, and therefore it is dumb and dead to us, as touching the fulfilling of it.

q. Rom. 7:7 An objection: what then? are the law and sin all one, and do they agree together? nay, saith he: Sin is reproved and condemned by the law. But because sin cannot abide to be reproved, and was not in a manner felt until it was provoked and stirred up by the law, it taketh occasion thereby to be more outrageous, and yet by no fault of the law.

r. Rom. 7:7 By the word, Lust, in this place he meaneth not evil lusts themselves, but the fountain from whence they spring: for the very heathen philosophers themselves condemned wicked lusts, though somewhat darkly, but as for the fountain of them, they could not so much as suspect it, and yet it is the very seat of the natural and unclean spot and filth.

s. Rom. 7:8 Though sin be in us, yet it is not known for sin, neither doth it so rage, as it rageth after that the law is known.

t. Rom. 7:9 He setteth himself before us for an example, in whom all men may behold, first what they are of nature before they earnestly think upon the law of God: to wit, blockish, and ready to sin and wickedness, without all true sense and feeling of sin, then what manner of persons they become, when their conscience is reproved by the testimony of the law, to wit, stubborn, and more inflamed with the desire of sin, than ever they were before.

u. Rom. 7:9 When I knew not the law, then me thought I lived in deed: for my conscience never troubled me, because it knew not my disease.

v. Rom. 7:9 When I began to understand the commandment.

w. Rom. 7:10 In sin, or by sin.

x. Rom. 7:12 The conclusion: That the law of itself is holy, but all the fault is in us which abuse the law.

y. Rom. 7:12 Touching not coveting.

z. Rom. 7:13 The proposition: That the Law is not the cause of death, but our corrupt nature, being therewith not only discovered, but also stirred up, and took occasion thereby to rebel, as which, the more that things are forbidden it, the more it desireth them, and from hence cometh guiltiness, and occasion of death.

aa. Rom. 7:13 Beareth it the blame of my death?

ab. Rom. 7:13 That sin might show itself to be sin, and bewray itself to be that, which is in deed.

ac. Rom. 7:13 As evil as it could, showing all the venom it could.

ad. Rom. 7:14 The cause of this matter, is this: Because that the Law requireth a heavenly pureness, but men, such as they be born, are bondslaves of corruption, which they willingly serve.

ae. Rom. 7:15 He setteth himself, being regenerate, before us, for an example, in whom may easily appear the strife of the Spirit and the flesh, and therefore of the Law of God, and our wickedness. For since that the Law in a man not regenerate bringeth forth death only, therefore in him it may easily be accused: but seeing that in a man which is regenerate, it bringeth forth good fruit, it doth better appear that evil actions proceed not from the Law, but from sin, that is, from our corrupt nature: And therefore the Apostle teacheth also, what the true use of the Law is, in reproving sin in the regenerate, unto the end of the chapter, as a little before (to wit, from the seventh verse unto this fifteenth) he declared the use of it in them which are not regenerate.

af. Rom. 7:15 The deeds of my life, saith he, answer not, nay they are contrary to my will: Therefore by the consent of my will with the Law, and repugnancy with the deeds of my life, it appeareth evidently, that the Law and a right ruled do persuade one thing, but corruption which hath her seat also in the regenerate, another thing.

ag. Rom. 7:15 It is to be noted, that one selfsame man is said to will and not to will, in divers respects: to wit, he is said to will, in that, that he is regenerate by grace: and not to will, in that, that he is not regenerate, or in that, that he is such an one as he was born. But because the part which is regenerate, at length becometh conqueror, therefore Paul sustaining the part of the regenerate, speaketh in such sort as if the corruption which sinneth willingly, were something without a man: although afterward he granteth that this evil is in his flesh, or in his members.

ah. Rom. 7:17 That natural corruption, which cleaveth fast even to them that are regenerate, and not clean conquered.

ai. Rom. 7:18 This vice, or sin, or law of sin, doth wholly possess those men which are not regenerate, and hindereth them or holdeth them back that are regenerate.

aj. Rom. 7:18 This doth indeed agree to that man, whom the grace of God hath made a new man: for where the Spirit is not, how can there be any strife there.

ak. Rom. 7:21 The conclusion: As the Law of God exhorteth to goodness, so doth the Law of sin (that is, the corruption wherein we are born) force us to wickedness: but the Spirit, that is, our mind, in that that it is regenerate, consenteth with the Law of God: but the flesh, that is, the whole natural man, is bondslave to the Law of sin. Therefore to be short, wickedness and death are not of the Law, but of sin, which reigneth in them that are not regenerate: for they neither will, nor do good, but will, and do evil: But in them that are regenerate, it striveth against the Spirit or law of the mind, so that they cannot either live so well as they would, or be so void of sin as they would.

al. Rom. 7:22 The inner man, and the new man are all one, and are answerable and set as contrary to the old man: neither doth this word, Inner man, signify man's mind and reason, and the old man, the powers that are under them, as the Philosophers imagine, but by the outward man is meant whatsoever is either without or within a man, from top to toe, so long as that man is not born anew by the grace of God.

am. Rom. 7:23 The law of the mind in this place, is not to be understood of the mind as it is naturally, and as our mind is from our birth, but of the mind which is renewed by the Spirit of God.

an. Rom. 7:24 It is a miserable thing to be yet in part subject to sin, which of its own nature maketh us guilty of death: but we must cry to the Lord, who will by death itself at length make us conquerors as we are already conquerors in Christ.

ao. Rom. 7:24 Wearied with miserable and continual conflict.

ap. Rom. 7:25 He recovereth himself, and showeth us that he resteth only in Christ.

aq. Rom. 7:25 This is the true perfection of them that are born anew, to confess that they are imperfect.

ROM. 7

1. 1 Cor. 7:32
2. Matt. 5:32
3. Exod. 20:17 / Deut. 5:21
4. 1 Tim. 1:8

ROM. 8

a. Rom. 8:1 A conclusion of all the former disputation from Rom 1:16 even to this place: Seeing that we being justified by faith in Christ, do obtain remission of sins and imputation of righteousness, and are also sanctified, it followeth hereof, that they that are grafted into Christ by faith, are out of all fear of condemnation.

b. Rom. 8:1 The fruits of the Spirit, or effects of sanctification, which is begun in us, do not ingraft us into Christ, but do declare that we are grafted into him.

c. Rom. 8:1 Follow not the flesh for their guide: for he is not said to live after the flesh, that hath the holy Ghost for his guide, though sometimes he step away.

d. Rom. 8:2 A preventing of an objection: seeing that the virtue of the spirit which is in us, is so weak, how may we gather thereby, that there is no condemnation to them that have that virtue? because saith he, that virtue of the quickening spirit which is so weak in us, is most perfect and most mighty in Christ, and being imputed unto us which believe, causeth us to be so accounted of, as though there were no relics of corruption, and death in us. Therefore hitherto Paul disputed of remission of sins, and imputation of fulfilling the Law, and also of sanctification which is begun in us: but now he speaketh of the perfect imputation of Christ's manhood, which part was necessarily required to the full appeasing of our consciences: for our sins are defaced by the blood of Christ, and the guiltiness of our corruption is covered with the imputation of Christ's obedience: and the corruption itself (which the Apostle calleth sinful sin) is healed in us by little and little, by the gift of sanctification, but yet it lacketh besides that another remedy, to wit, the perfect sanctification of Christ's own flesh, which also is to us imputed.

e. Rom. 8:2 The power and authority of the spirit, against which is set the tyranny of sin.

f. Rom. 8:2 Which mortifieth the old man, and quickeneth the new man.

g. Rom. 8:2 To wit, absolutely and perfectly.

h. Rom. 8:2 For Christ's sanctification being imputed unto us, perfecteth our sanctification which is begun in us.

i. Rom. 8:3 He useth no argument here, but expoundeth the mystery of sanctification, which is imputed unto us: for because, that the virtue of the law was not such (and that by reason of the corruption of our nature) that it could make man pure and perfect: and for that it rather kindled the disease of sin, than did put it out and extinguish it, therefore God clothed his Son with flesh like unto our sinful flesh, wherein he utterly abolished our corruption, that being accounted thoroughly pure and without fault in him apprehended and laid hold on by faith, we might be found to have fully that singular perfection which the Law requireth, and therefore that there might be no condemnation in us.

j. Rom. 8:3 Which is not proper to the Law, but cometh by our fault.

k. Rom. 8:3 In man not born anew, whose disease the law could not heal it.

l. Rom. 8:3 Of man's nature which was corrupt through sin, until he sanctified it.

m. Rom. 8:3 To abolish sin in our flesh.

n. Rom. 8:3 Showed that sin hath no right in us.

o. Rom. 8:4 The very substance of the law of God might be fulfilled, or that same which the law requireth, that we may be found just before God: for if with our justification there be joined that sanctification which is imputed to us, we are just, according to the perfect form which the Lord requireth.

p. Rom. 8:4 He returneth to that which he said, that the sanctification which is begun in us, is a sure testimony of our ingrafting into Christ, which is a most plentiful fruit of a godly and honest life.

q. Rom. 8:5 A reason why to walk after the flesh, agreeth not to them which are grafted in Christ, but to walk after the spirit agreeth and is meet for them: because, saith he, that they which are after the flesh, savor the things of the flesh, but they that are after the spirit, the things of the spirit.

r. Rom. 8:5 They that live as the flesh leadeth them.

s. Rom. 8:6 He proveth the consequent: because that whatsoever the flesh savoreth, that engendereth death: and whatsoever the spirit savoreth, that tendeth to joy and life everlasting.

t. Rom. 8:7 A reason and proof, why the wisdom of the flesh is death: because, saith he, it is the enemy of God.

u. Rom. 8:7 A reason why the wisdom of the flesh is enemy to God: because it neither will neither can be subject to him. And by flesh he meaneth a man not regenerate.

v. Rom. 8:8 The conclusion: therefore they that walk after the flesh, cannot please God: whereby it followeth, that they are not ingrafted into Christ.

w. Rom. 8:9 He cometh to the others, to wit, to them which walk after the spirit, of whom we have to understand contrary

in the Spirit, because the spirit of God dwelleth in you: but if any man hath not
the Spirit of Christ, the same is not his. 10 [x]And if Christ be in you, the [y]body
is dead, because of sin: but the Spirit is life for righteousness sake. 11 [z]But if the
Spirit of him that raised up Jesus from the dead, dwell in you, he that raised up
Christ from the dead, shall also quicken your mortal bodies, by his Spirit that [aa]
dwelleth in you. 12 [ab]Therefore brethren, we are debtors not to the flesh, to live
after the flesh: 13 [ac]For if ye live after the flesh, ye shall die: but if ye mortify the
deeds of the body by the Spirit, ye shall live. 14 [ad]For as many as are led by the
Spirit of God, they are the sons of God. 15 [ae]For ye have not received the [af]Spirit
of bondage, to [ag]fear again: but ye have received the Spirit of [ah]adoption, whereby
we cry, Abba, Father. 16 The same Spirit beareth witness with our spirit, that we
are the children of God. 17 [ai]If we be children, we are also [aj]heirs, even the heirs
of God, and heirs annexed with Christ: [ak]if so be that we suffer with him, that we
may also be glorified with him. 18 [al]For I [am]count that the afflictions of this pre-
sent time are not worthy of the glory, which shall be showed unto us. 19 [an]For
the fervent desire of the [ao]creature waiteth when the sons of God shall be revea-
led, 20 Because the creature is subject to [ap]vanity, not of its [aq]own will, but by
reason [ar]of him, which hath subdued it under [as]hope, 21 Because the creature
also shall be delivered from the [at]bondage of corruption into the glorious liberty of
the sons of God. 22 For we know that every creature groaneth with us also, and
[au]travaileth in pain together unto this present. 23 [av]And not only the creature,
but we also which have the firstfruits of the Spirit, even we do sigh in [aw]ourselves,
waiting for the adoption, even [ax,1]the redemption of our body. 24 [ay]For we are
saved by hope: but [az]hope that is seen, is not hope: for how can a man hope for that
which he seeth? 25 But if we hope for that we see not, we do with patience abide
for it. 26 [ba]Likewise the Spirit also [bb]helpeth our infirmities: for we know not
what to pray as we ought: but the Spirit itself maketh [bc]request for us with sighs,
which cannot be expressed. 27 But he that searcheth the hearts, knoweth what
is the [bd]meaning of the Spirit: for he maketh request for the Saints, [be]according to
the will of God. 28 [bf]Also we know that [bg]all things work together for the best
unto them that love God, even to them that are called of his [bh]purpose. 29 For
those which he knew before, he also predestinated to be made like to the image
of his Son, that he might be the firstborn among many brethren. 30 Moreover,
whom he [bi]predestinated, them also he called, and whom he called, them also he
justified, and whom he justified, them he also glorified. 31 [bj]What shall we then
say to these things? If God be on our side, who can be against us? 32 Who spa-
red not his own Son, but gave him for us all to death, how shall he not with him
[bk]give us all things also? 33 [bl]Who shall lay anything to the charge of God's
chosen? it is [bm]God that justifieth. 34 Who shall condemn? it is Christ which is
dead: yea, or rather, which is risen again, who is also at the right hand of God, and
maketh request also for us. 35 Who shall separate us from the love of [bn]Christ?
shall tribulation or anguish, or persecution, or famine, or nakedness, or peril, or
sword? 36 As it is written, [2]For thy sake are we killed all day long: we are coun-
ted as sheep for the slaughter: 37 [bo]Nevertheless, in all these things we are more
than conquerors through him that loved us. 38 For I am persuaded that neither
death, nor life, nor Angels, nor principalities, nor powers, nor things present, nor
things to come, 39 Nor height, nor depth, nor any other creature, shall be able
to separate us from the love of God, which is in Christ Jesus our Lord.

9

1 He answereth an objection, that might be brought on the Jews' behalf, 7 and telleth of two sorts of Abraham's children, 15 and that God worketh all things in this matter according to his will, 20 even as the potter doth. 24, 30 He proveth as well the calling of the Gentiles, 31 as also the rejecting of the Jews, 25, 27 by the testimony of the Prophets.

1 I say [a]the truth in Christ, I lie not, my conscience bearing me witness in
the holy Ghost, 2 That I have great heaviness, and continual sorrow in mine he-
art. 3 For I would wish myself to be [b]separate from Christ, for my brethren that
are my kinsmen according to the [c]flesh, 4 Which are the Israelites, to whom per-
taineth the adoption, and the [d]glory, and the [1,e]Covenants, and the giving of the
[f]Law, and the [g]service of God, and the [h]promises. 5 Of whom are the fathers,
and of whom concerning the flesh, Christ came, who is [i]God over all, blessed fore-
ver, Amen. 6 [2,j]Notwithstanding it cannot be that the word of God should take
none effect: for all they are not [k]Israel, which are of Israel: 7 Neither are they

---

things to the former: and first of all he defineth what it is to be in the spirit, or to be sanctified: to wit, to have the spirit of God dwelling in us; then he declareth, that sanctification is so joined and knit to our grafting in Christ, that it can by no means be separated.

x. Rom. 8:10 He confirmeth the faithful against the relics of flesh and sin, granting that they are yet (as appeareth by the corruption which is in them) touching one of their parts (which he calleth the body, that is to say, a lump) which is not yet purged from the earthly filthiness in death: but therewithall willing them to doubt nothing of the happy success of their combat, because that even the little spark of the Spirit, (that is, of the grace of regeneration) which appeareth to be in them by the fruits of righteousness, is the seed of life.

y. Rom. 8:10 The flesh, or all that which as yet sticketh fast in the clefts of sin, and death.

z. Rom. 8:11 A confirmation of the former sentence. You have the selfsame Spirit, which Christ hath: Therefore at length it shall die the same in you, that it did in Christ, to wit, when all infirmities being utterly laid aside, and death overcome, it shall clothe you with heavenly glory.

aa. Rom. 8:11 By the virtue and power of it, which showed the same might first in our head, and daily worketh in his members.

ab. Rom. 8:12 An exhortation to oppress the flesh daily more and more by the virtue of the Spirit of regeneration, because (saith he) you are debtors unto God, forsomuch as you have received so many benefits of him.

ac. Rom. 8:13 Another reason of the profit that ensueth: for such as strive and fight valiantly, shall have everlasting life.

ad. Rom. 8:14 A confirmation of this reason: they be the children of God, which are governed by his Spirit, therefore shall they have life everlasting.

ae. Rom. 8:15 He declareth and expoundeth by the way, in these two verses, by what right this name, to be called the children of God, is given to the believers: because saith he, they have received the grace of the Gospel, wherein God showeth himself, not (as before in the publishing of the Law) terrible and fearful, but a most benign and loving father in Christ, so that with great boldness we call him Father, that holy Ghost sealing this adoption in our hearts by faith.

af. Rom. 8:15 By the Spirit is meant the holy Ghost, whom we are said to receive, when he worketh in our minds.

ag. Rom. 8:15 Which fear is stirred up in our minds, by the preaching of the Law.

ah. Rom. 8:15 Which sealeth our adoption in our minds, and therefore openeth our mouths.

ai. Rom. 8:17 A proof of the consequent of the confirmation: because that he which is the Son of God, doth enjoy God with Christ.

aj. Rom. 8:17 Partakers of our father's goods, and that freely, because we are children by adoption.

ak. Rom. 8:17 Now Paul teacheth by what way the sons of God do come to that felicity, to wit, by the cross, as Christ himself did: and therewithall openeth unto them fountains of comfort: as first, that we have Christ a companion and fellow of our afflictions: secondly, that we shall be also his followers in that everlasting glory.

al. Rom. 8:18 Thirdly that this glory which we look for, doth a thousand parts surmount the misery of our afflictions.

am. Rom. 8:18 All being well considered, I gather.

an. Rom. 8:19 Fourthly, he plainly teacheth us that we shall certainly be renewed from that confusion and horrible deformation of the whole world, which cannot be continual, as it was not at the beginning: But as it had a beginning by the sin of man, for whom it was made by the ordinance of God, so shall it at length be restored with the elect.

ao. Rom. 8:19 All this world.

ap. Rom. 8:20 Is subject to a vanishing and flitting state.

aq. Rom. 8:20 Not by their natural inclination.

ar. Rom. 8:20 That they should obey the Creator's commandment, whom it pleased to show by their fickle estate, how greatly he was displeased with man.

as. Rom. 8:20 God would not make the world subject to everlasting curse, for the sin of man, but gave it hope that it should be restored.

at. Rom. 8:21 From the corruption which they are now subject to, they shall be delivered and changed into that blessed state of incorruption, which shall be revealed when the sons of God shall be advanced to glory.

au. Rom. 8:22 By this word is meant, not only exceeding sorrow, but also the fruit that followeth of it.

av. Rom. 8:23 Fifthly, if the rest of the world looks for a restoring, groaning as it were for it, and that not in vain, let it not grieve us also to sigh, yea, let us be more certainly persuaded of our redemption to come, forasmuch as we have the firstfruits of the Spirit.

aw. Rom. 8:23 Even from the bottom of our hearts.

ax. Rom. 8:23 That last restoring, which shall be the accomplishment of our adoption.

ay. Rom. 8:24 Sixthly, hope is necessarily joined with faith: seeing then that we believe those things, which we are not yet in possession of, and hope respected not the thing that is present, we must therefore hope and patiently wait for that which we believe shall come to pass.

az. Rom. 8:24 This is spoken by the figure Metonymy: Hope, for that which is hoped for.

ba. Rom. 8:26 Seventhly, There is no cause why we should faint under the burden of afflictions, seeing that prayers minister unto us a most sure help, which cannot be frustrated, seeing they proceed from the spirit of God which dwelleth in us.

bb. Rom. 8:26 Beareth our burden, as it were that we faint not under it.

bc. Rom. 8:26 Provoketh us to prayers, and telleth us as it were within, what we shall say, and how we shall groan.

bd. Rom. 8:27 What sobs and sighs proceed from the instinct of his Spirit.

be. Rom. 8:27 Because he teacheth the godly to pray according to God's will.

bf. Rom. 8:28 Eighthly, we are not afflicted, either by chance or to our harm, but by God's providence for our great profit, who as he chose us from the beginning, so hath he predestined us to be made like to the image of his Son: and therefore will bring us in his time, being called and justified, to glory, by the cross.

bg. Rom. 8:28 Not only afflictions, but whatsoever else.

bh. Rom. 8:28 He calleth that, Purpose, which God hath from everlasting appointed with himself according to his good will and pleasure.

bi. Rom. 8:30 He useth the time past, for the time present, as the Hebrews use, who sometimes set down the thing that is to come, by the time that is past, to signify the certainty of it: and he hath also regard to God's continual working.

bj. Rom. 8:31 Ninethly, we have no cause to fear that the Lord will not give us whatsoever is profitable for us, seeing that he hath not spared his own Son to save us.

bk. Rom. 8:32 Give us freely.

bl. Rom. 8:33 A most glorious and comfortable conclusion of the whole second part of this Epistle, that is, of the treatise of justification. There are no accusers that we have need to be afraid of before God, seeing that God himself absolveth us as just: and therefore much less need we to fear damnation, seeing that we rest upon the death and resurrection, the almighty power and defense of Jesus Christ. Therefore what can there be so weighty in this life, or of so great force and power, that might seize us, as though we might fall from the love of God, wherewith he loveth us in Christ: Surely nothing. Seeing that it is in itself most constant and sure, and also in us being confirmed by steadfast faith.

bm. Rom. 8:33 Who pronounceth us not only guiltless, but also perfectly just in his Son.

bn. Rom. 8:35 Wherewith Christ loveth us.

bo. Rom. 8:37 We are not only not overcome with so great and many miseries and calamities, but also more than conquerors in all of them.

ROM. 8

1. Luke 21:28 **2.** Ps. 44:22

ROM. 9

a. Rom. 9:1 The third part of this Epistle, even to the twelfth Chapter, wherein Paul ascendeth to the higher causes of faith: and first of all because he purposed to speak much of the casting off of the Jews, he useth an insinuation, declaring by a double or triple oath, and by witnessing of his great desire towards their salvation, his singular love towards them, and therewithall granting unto them all their prerogatives.

b. Rom. 9:3 The Apostle loved his brethren so entirely, that if it have been possible he would have been ready to have redeemed the casting away of the Israelites, with the loss of his own soul forever: for this word separate, betokeneth as much in this place.

c. Rom. 9:3 Being brethren by flesh, as of one nation and country.

d. Rom. 9:4 The ark of the covenant, which was a token of God's presence.

e. Rom. 9:4 The tables of the covenant: and this is spoken by the figure Metonymy.

f. Rom. 9:4 Of the judicial Law.

g. Rom. 9:4 The ceremonial Law.

h. Rom. 9:4 Which were made to Abraham and to his posterity.

i. Rom. 9:5 A most manifest testimony of the Godhead and divinity of Christ.

all children, because they are the seed of Abraham: [3,l]but, In [m]Isaac shall thy seed be called: **8** [n]That is, they which are the children of the [o]flesh, are not the children of God: but the [4]children of the [p]promise, are counted for the seed. **9** [q]For this is a word of promise, [5]In this same time will I come, and Sarah shall have a son. **10** [r]Neither he only felt this, but also [6]Rebecca, when she had conceived by one, even by our father Isaac. **11** For ere the children were born, and when they had neither done good nor evil (that the [s]purpose of God might [t]remain according to election, not by works, but by him that calleth.) **12** [u]It was said unto her, [7]The Elder shall serve the younger. **13** As it is written, [8]I have loved Jacob, and have hated Esau. **14** [v]What shall we say then? Is there [w]unrighteousness with God? God forbid. **15** [x]For he saith to Moses, [9]I will [y]have mercy on him, to whom I will show mercy: and will have [z]compassion on him, on who I will have compassion. **16** [aa]So then it is not in him that [ab]willeth, nor in him that runneth, but in God that showeth mercy. **17** [ac]For the [ad]Scripture saith unto Pharaoh, [10]For this same purpose have [ae]I stirred thee up, that I might [af]show my power in thee, and that my Name might be declared throughout all the earth. **18** [ag]Therefore he hath mercy on whom he [ah]will, and whom he will he hardeneth. **19** [ai]Thou wilt say then unto me, Why doth he yet complain? for who hath resisted his will? **20** [aj]But, O man, who art thou which pleadest against God? [ak]shall the [11]thing [al]formed say to him that formed it, Why hast thou made me thus? **21** [12,am]Hath not the potter power of the clay to make of the same lump one [an]vessel to [ao]honor, and another unto [ap]dishonor? **22** [aq]What and if God would, to show his wrath, and to make his power known, suffer with long patience the [ar]vessels of wrath, prepared to [as]destruction? **23** And that he might declare the [at]riches of his glory upon the vessels of mercy, which he hath prepared unto glory? **24** [au]Even us whom he hath called, not of the [av]Jews only, but also of the Gentiles. **25** [aw]As he saith also in Hosea, [13]I will call them, My people, which were not my people: and her, Beloved, which was not beloved. **26** And it shall be in the place where it was said unto them, [14]Ye are not my people, that there they shall be called, The children of the living God. **27** [ax]Also Isaiah crieth concerning Israel, [15]Though the number of the children of Israel were as the sand of the sea, yet shall but a remnant be saved. **28** For he will make his account, and gather it into a [ay]short sum with righteousness: for the Lord will make a short count in the earth. **29** [16]And as Isaiah said before, Except the Lord of [az]hosts had left us a [ba]seed, we had been made as Sodom, and had been like to Gomorrah. **30** [bb]What shall we say then? That the Gentiles which followed [bc]not

---

j. Rom. 9:6 He entereth into the handling of predestination by a kind of preventing an objection: How may it be, that Israel is cast off, but that therewithall we must also make the covenant which God made with Abraham and his seed, frustrate and void? He answereth therefore, that God's word is true, although that Israel be cast off: for the election of the people of Israel is so general and common, that notwithstanding the same, God chooseth by his secret counsel, such as it pleaseth him. So then this is the proposition and state of this Treatise: The grace of salvation is offered generally in such sort, that notwithstanding it, the efficacy thereof pertaineth only to the elect.

k. Rom. 9:6 Israel in the first place, is taken for Jacob: and in the second, for the Israelites.

l. Rom. 9:7 The first proof is taken from the example of Abraham's own house, wherein Isaac only was counted the son, and that by God's ordinance: although that Ishmael also was born of Abraham, and circumcised before Isaac.

m. Rom. 9:7 Isaac shall be thy true and natural son, and therefore heir of thy blessing.

n. Rom. 9:8 A general application of the former proof or example.

o. Rom. 9:8 Which are born of Abraham by the course of nature.

p. Rom. 9:8 Which are born by virtue of the promise.

q. Rom. 9:9 A reason of that application: Because that Isaac was born by the virtue of the promise, and therefore he was not chosen, nay he was not at all, but by the free will of God: whereby it followeth that the promise is the fountain of predestination, and not the flesh from which promise the particular election proceedeth: that is, that the elect be born elect: and not that they be first born and then afterward elected, in respect of God who doth predestinate.

r. Rom. 9:10 Another forcible proof, taken from the example of Esau and Jacob, which were both born of the same Isaac, which was the son of promise, of one mother, and at one birth, and not at divers as Ishmael and Isaac were: and yet notwithstanding, Esau being cast off, only Jacob was chosen: and that before their birth, that neither any goodness of Jacob's might be thought to be the cause of his election, neither any wickedness of Esau, of his casting away.

s. Rom. 9:11 God's decree, which proceedeth of his mere good will, whereby it pleased him to choose one, and refuse the other.

t. Rom. 9:11 Paul saith not, might be made, but being made, might remain. Therefore they are deceived which make foreseen faith the cause of election, and foreknown infidelity, the cause of reprobation.

u. Rom. 9:12 He proveth the casting away of Esau by that, that he was made servant to his brother: and proveth the choosing of Jacob by that that he was made Lord of his brother, although his brother were the first begotten. And lest that any man might take this saying of God, and refer it to external things, the Apostle showeth out of Malachi, who is a good interpreter of Moses, that the servitude of Esau was joined with the hatred of God, and the Lordship of Jacob with the love of God.

v. Rom. 9:14 The first objection: If God doth love or hate upon no consideration of worthiness or unworthiness, then [is] he unjust, because he may love them which are unworthy, and hate them that are worthy. The Apostle detesteth this blasphemy, and afterward answereth it severally, point by point.

w. Rom. 9:14 Man's will knoweth no other causes of love or hatred, but those that are in the persons, and thereupon this objection riseth.

x. Rom. 9:15 He answereth first touching them which are chosen to salvation in choosing of whom, he denieth that God may seem unjust, although he choose and predestinate to salvation, them that are not yet born, without any respect of worthiness: because he bringeth not the chosen to the appointed end, but by the means of his mercy, which is a cause next under predestination. Now mercy presupposeth misery, and again misery presupposeth sin or voluntary corruption of mankind, and corruption presupposeth a pure and perfect creation. Moreover mercy is showed by her degrees: to wit, by calling, by faith, by justification and sanctification, so that at length we come to glorification, as the Apostle will show afterward. Now all these things, orderly following the purpose of God, do clearly prove that he can by no means seem unjust in loving and saving his.

y. Rom. 9:15 I will be merciful and favorable to whom I list to be favorable.

z. Rom. 9:15 I will have compassion on whomsoever I list to have compassion.

aa. Rom. 9:16 The conclusion of the answer: Therefore God is not unjust in choosing and saving of his free goodness, such as it pleaseth him: as he also answered Moses, when he prayed for all the people.

ab. Rom. 9:16 By will, he meaneth the thought and endeavor of heart, and by running, good works: to neither of which he giveth the praise, but only to the mercy of God.

ac. Rom. 9:17 Now he answereth concerning the reprobate or them whom God hateth being not yet born, and hath appointed to destruction, without any respect of unworthiness. And first of all he proveth this to be true, by alleging the testimony of God himself touching Pharaoh, whom he stirred up to this purpose, that he might be glorified in his hardening and just punishing.

ad. Rom. 9:17 God so speaketh unto Pharaoh in the Scripture, or, the Scripture bringeth in God, so speaking to Pharaoh, Exodus 9:16.

ae. Rom. 9:17 Brought thee into this world.

af. Rom. 9:17 Secondly, he bringeth the end of God's counsel, to show that there is no unrighteousness in him. Now this chiefest end, is not properly and simply the destruction of the wicked, but God's glory which appeareth in their rightful punishment.

ag. Rom. 9:18 A conclusion of the full answer to the first objection: therefore seeing that God doth not save them whom he freely chose according to his good will and pleasure, but by justifying and sanctifying them by his grace, his counsel in saving them cannot seem unjust. And again, there is not injustice in the everlasting counsel of God touching the destruction of them whom he listeth to destroy, for that he hardeneth before he destroyeth: Therefore the third answer for the maintenance of God's justice is the everlasting counsel of reprobation, consisteth in this word Hardening: which notwithstanding he concealed in the former verse, because the History of Pharaoh was well known. But the force of the word is great: for Hardening, which is set against Mercy, presupposeth the same things that mercy did, to wit, a voluntary corruption, wherein the reprobate are hardened: and again corruption presupposeth a perfect state of creation. Moreover, this hardening also is voluntary, for God so hardeneth being offended with corruption, that he useth their own will whom he hardeneth, to the executing of that judgment. Then follow the fruits of Hardening, to wit, unbelief and sin, which are the true and proper causes of the condemnation of the reprobate. Why doth he then appoint to destruction? because he will: why doth he harden? because they are corrupt: why doth he condemn? because they are sinners. Where is then unrighteousness? Nay, if he should destroy all after this same sort, to whom should he do injury?

ah. Rom. 9:18 Whom it pleased him to appoint, to show his favor upon.

ai. Rom. 9:19 Another objection but only for the reprobate, rising upon the former answer. If God do appoint to everlasting destruction, such as he listeth, and if that cannot be hindered notwithstanded that he hath once decreed, how doth he justly condemn them, which perish by his will?

aj. Rom. 9:20 The Apostle doth not answer that it is not God's will, or that God doth not either reject or elect according to his pleasure, which thing the wicked call blasphemy, but he rather granteth, his adversary both the antecedents, to wit, that it is God's will, and that it must of necessity so fall out, yet he denieth that God is therefore to be thought an unjust revenger of the wicked: for seeing it appeareth by manifest proof that this is the will of God and his doing, what impudency is it for man, which is but dust and ashes to dispute with God, and as it were to call him into judgment? Now if any man say that the doubt is not so dissolved and answered, I answer, that there is no surer demonstration in any matter, because it is grounded upon this principle, That the will of God is the rule of righteousness.

ak. Rom. 9:20 An amplification of the former answer, taken from a comparison, whereby also it appeareth that God's determined counsel is set of Paul the highest of all causes, so that it dependeth not upon any respect of second causes, but doth rather frame and direct them.

al. Rom. 9:20 This similitude agreeth very fitly in the first creation of mankind.

am. Rom. 9:21 Alluding to the creation of Adam, he compareth mankind not yet made (but in the Creator's mind) to a lump of clay: whereof afterward God made and doth daily make, according as he purposed from everlasting both such as should be elect, and such as should be reprobate, as also this word, making, declareth.

an. Rom. 9:21 Whereas in the objection propounded, mention was only made of vessels to dishonor: yet he speaketh of the other also in this answer, for that he proveth the Creator to be just in either of them, as the rule of contraries doth require.

ao. Rom. 9:21 To honest uses.

ap. Rom. 9:21 Seeing then, that in the name of dishonor, the ignomy of everlasting death is signified, they speak with Paul, which say, that some are made of God to most just destruction: and they [that] are offended with this kind of speech bewray their own folly.

aq. Rom. 9:22 The second answer is this, that God, moreover and besides that he doth justly decree whatsoever he doth decree, useth that moderation in executing of his decrees, as declareth his singular lenity even in the reprobate in that, that he suffereth them a long time, and permitteth them to enjoy many and singular benefits, until at length he justly condemns them: and that to good end and purpose, to wit, to show himself to be an enemy and revenger of wickedness, that it may appear what power he is of by these severe judgments, and finally by comparison of contraries to set forth indeed, how great his mercy is towards the elect.

ar. Rom. 9:22 By vessels, the Hebrews understand all kinds of instruments.

as. Rom. 9:22 Therefore again, we may say with Paul that some men are made of God the Creator to destruction.

at. Rom. 9:23 The unmeasurable and marvelous greatness.

au. Rom. 9:24 Having established the doctrine of the eternal predestination of God on both parts: that is, as well of the reprobate, as of the elect, he cometh now to show the use of it, teaching us that we ought not to seek the testimony of it in the secret counsel of God, but by the vocation which is made manifest and set forth in the Church, propounding unto us the example of the Jews and Gentiles, that the doctrine may be better perceived.

av. Rom. 9:24 He saith not that all and every one of the Jews are called, but some of the Jews, and some of the Gentiles.

aw. Rom. 9:25 Our vocation or calling is free and of grace, even as our predestination is: and therefore there is no cause why either our own unworthiness, or the unworthiness of our ancestors should cause us to think that we are not the elect and chosen of God, if we be called of him, and so embrace through faith the salvation that is offered us.

ax. Rom. 9:27 Contrariwise, Neither any outward general calling, neither any worthiness of our ancestors is a sufficient witness of election, unless by faith and belief we answer God's calling: which thing came to pass in the Jews, as the Lord had forewarned.

ay. Rom. 9:28 God purposeth to bring the unkind and unthankful people to an extreme fewness.

az. Rom. 9:29 Armies, by which word the chiefest power that is, is given to God.

ba. Rom. 9:29 Even a very few.

bb. Rom. 9:30 The declaration and manifestation of our election, is our calling apprehended by faith, as it came to pass in the Gentiles.

bc. Rom. 9:30 So then, the Gentiles had no works to prepare and procure God's mercy beforehand: and as for that, that the Gentiles attained to that which they sought not for, the mercy of God is to be thanked for it: and in that the Jews attained not that which they sought after, they can thank none for it but themselves, because they sought it not aright.

righteousness, have attained unto righteousness, even the righteousness which is of
faith. **31** [bd]But Israel which followed the Law of righteousness, could not attain
unto the Law of righteousness. **32** Wherefore? Because they sought it not by fai-
th, but as it were by the [be]works of the Law: for they have stumbled at the stum-
bling stone, **33** As it is written, [17]Behold, I lay in Zion a stumbling stone, and a
rock to make men fall: and everyone that believeth in him, shall not be ashamed.

10

1 He handleth the effects of election, 3 that some refuse, and some embrace. 4 Christ, who is the end of the Law. 15 He showeth that Moses foretold the calling of the Gentiles, 20 and Isaiah the hardening of the Jews.

1 Brethren, [a]mine hearts desire and prayer to God for Israel is, that they mi-
ght be saved. **2** For I bear them record that they have the zeal of God, but not
according to knowledge. **3** [b]For they, [c]being ignorant of the righteousness of
God, and going about to [d]establish their own righteousness, have not submitted
themselves to the righteousness of God. **4** [1,e]For Christ is the [f]end of the Law for
righteousness unto [g]everyone that believeth. **5** [h]For Moses thus describeth the
righteousness which is of the Law, [2]That the man which doeth these things, shall
live thereby. **6** But the righteousness which is of faith, speaketh on this wise,
[3,i]Say not in thine heart, Who shall ascend into heaven? (that is to bring Christ
from above.) **7** Or, Who shall descend into the deep? (that is to bring Christ
again from the dead.) **8** [j]But what saith it? [4]The [k]word is near thee, even in thy
mouth, and in thine heart. This is the word of faith which we preach. **9** [l]For if
thou shalt [m]confess with thy mouth the Lord Jesus, and shalt believe in thine he-
art, that [n]God raised him up from the dead, thou shalt be saved: **10** For with
the heart man [o]believeth unto righteousness, and with the mouth man confesseth
to salvation. **11** [p]For the Scripture saith, [5]Whosoever [q]believeth in him, shall
not be ashamed. **12** For there is no difference between the Jew and the Grecian:
for he that is Lord over all, is rich unto all that call on him. **13** [6,r]For whosoever
shall call upon the Name of the Lord, shall be saved. **14** But how shall they call
on him, in whom they have not believed? [s]and how shall they believe in him, of
whom they have not heard? and how shall they hear without a preacher? **15** And
how shall they preach, except they be sent? as it is written, [7]How beautiful are the
feet of them which bring glad tidings of peace, and bring glad tidings of good
things! **16** [t]But they have not [u]all obeyed the Gospel: for Isaiah saith, [8]Lord,
who hath believed our report? **17** [v]Then faith is by hearing, and hearing by
the [w]word of God. **18** [x]But I demand, Have they not heard? [9]No doubt their
sound went out through all the earth, and their words into the ends of the wor-
ld. **19** [y]But I demand, Did not Israel know God? First Moses saith, [10]I will pro-
voke you to envy by a [z]nation that is not my nation, and by a foolish nation I will
anger you. **20** [11]And Isaiah is [aa]bold, and saith, I was found of them that sought
me not, and have been made manifest to them that asked not after me. **21** And
unto Israel he saith, All the day long have I stretched forth mine hand unto a diso-
bedient, and gainsaying people.

11

1 Lest the casting off of the Jews should be limited according to the outward appearance, 4 he showeth that Elijah was in times past decieved: 16 and that, seeing they have an holy root, 23 many of them likewise shall be holy. 18, 24 He exhorteth the Gentiles to be humble, 33 and crieth out, that God's judgments are unsearchable.

1 I Demand then, [a]Hath God cast away his people? God forbid: for [b]I also
am an Israelite, of the seed of Abraham, of the tribe of Benjamin. **2** [c]God hath
not cast away his people which he [d]knew before. [e]Know ye not what the Scriptu-
re saith of Elijah, how he communeth with God against Israel, saying, **3** [1]Lord,
they have killed thy Prophets, and dug down thine Altars: and I am left alone,
and they seek my life? **4** But what saith the answer of God to him? [2]I have
[f]reserved unto myself seven thousand men, which have not bowed the knee to
[g]Baal. **5** Even so then, at this present time is there a remnant according to the
[h]election of grace. **6** [i]And if it be of grace, it is [j]no more of works: or else were
grace no more grace: but if it be of works, it is no more grace: or else were work
no more work. **7** What then? Israel hath not obtained that he sought: but the
election hath obtained it, and the rest have been [k]hardened, **8** [l]According as it
is written, [3]God hath given them the spirit of [m]slumber: eyes that they [n]should

---

bd. Rom. 9:31 The pride of men is the cause that they condemn vocation, so that the cause of their damnation need not to be sought for any other where but in themselves.

be. Rom. 9:32 Seeking to come by righteousness, they followed the Law of righteousness.

ROM. 19

1. Rom. 2:17 / Eph. 2:12
2. Rom. 2:28
3. Gen. 21:12 / Heb. 11:18
4. Gal. 4:28
5. Gen. 18:10
6. Gen. 25:21
7. Gen. 25:23
8. Mal. 1:2
9. Exod. 33:19
10. Exod. 9:16
11. Isa. 45:9
12. Jer. 18:6
13. Hos. 2:23 / 1 Pet. 2:10
14. Hos. 1:10
15. Isa. 20:21
16. Isa. 1:9
17. Ps. 118:22 / Isa. 8:14 / Isa. 28:16 / 1 Pet. 2:6

ROM. 10

a. Rom. 10:1 Purposing to set forth in the Jews an example of marvelous obstinacy, he useth an insinuation.

b. Rom. 10:3 The first entrance into the vocation unto salvation, is to renounce our own righteousness: the next is, to embrace that righteousness by faith, which God freely offereth us the Gospel.

c. Rom. 10:3 The ignorance of the Law which we ought to know, excuseth none before God, especially it excuseth not them that are of his household.

d. Rom. 10:3 Ignorance hath always pride joined with it.

e. Rom. 10:4 The proof: The Law itself hath respect unto Christ, that such as believe in him should be saved. Therefore the calling to salvation by the works of the law is vain and foolish, but Christ is offered for salvation to every believer.

f. Rom. 10:4 The end of the Law is to justify them that keep the Law: but seeing we do not observe the Law through the fault of our flesh, we attain not unto this end: but Christ salveth this disease, for he fulfilled the Law for us.

g. Rom. 10:4 Not only to the Jews, but also to the Gentiles.

h. Rom. 10:5 That the Law regardeth and tendeth to Christ, that is a manifest proof, for that is propoundeth such a condition, as can be and is fulfilled of none but Christ only: which being imputed unto us by faith, our conscience is quieted, so that now no man can ask, Who can ascend up into heaven, or bring us from hell, seeing the Gospel teacheth that both of these is done by Christ, and that for their sakes, which with true faith embrace him which calleth them.

i. Rom. 10:6 Think not with thyself, as men that are staggering use to do.

j. Rom. 10:8 Vocation cometh by the word preached.

k. Rom. 10:8 By the word, Moses understood the Law which the Lord published with his own voice: and Paul applied it to the preaching of the Gospel which was the perfection of the Law.

l. Rom. 10:9 That is indeed true faith which is settled not only in the head, but also in the heart of man, whereof also we give testimony, by our outward life, and which tendeth to Christ as to our alone and only Savior, even as he setteth forth himself in his word.

m. Rom. 10:9 If thou profess plainly, sincerely, and openly, that thou takest Jesus only to be thy Lord and Savior.

n. Rom. 10:9 The Father, who is said to have raised the Son from the dead: and this is not spoken to shut out the divinity of the Son, but to set forth the Father's counsel touching our redemption in the resurrection of the Son.

o. Rom. 10:10 Faith is said to justify, and furthermore seeing the confession of the mouth is an effect of faith, and confession is the way to come to salvation, it followeth that faith is also said to save.

p. Rom. 10:11 Now he proveth the other part which he propounded afore in the fourth verse, to wit, that Christ calleth whomsoever he listeth without any difference, and this he confirmeth by a double testimony.

q. Rom. 10:11 To believe in God is to yield and consent to God's promise of our salvation by Christ, and that not only in general, but when we know that the promises pertain to us whereupon riseth a sure trust.

r. Rom. 10:13 True calling upon the Name of God is the testimony of true faith, and true faith of true vocation or calling, and true calling, of true election.

s. Rom. 10:14 That is, true faith which seeketh God in his word, and that preached according as God hath appointed in the Church.

t. Rom. 10:16 Wheresover faith is, there is also the word, but not contrariwise, wheresoever the word is, there is faith also: for many refuse and reject the word.

u. Rom. 10:16 He speaketh this because of the Jews.

v. Rom. 10:17 A conclusion of the former gradation: we must ascend from faith, to our vocation, as by our vocation we came to the testimony of our election.

w. Rom. 10:17 By God's Commandment.

x. Rom. 10:18 An objection: If calling be a testimony of election, were not the Jews called? why should I not … that, saith the Apostle, seeing that there is no nation which hath not been called? much less can I say, that the Jews were not called.

y. Rom. 10:19 The defender and maintainer of the Jews' cause goeth on still to ask, whether the Jews also knew not God which called them. Isaiah (saith the Apostle) denieth it: and witnesseth that the Gospel was translated from them to the Gentiles, because the Jews neglected it. And therewithall the Apostle teacheth, that that outward and universal calling, which is set forth by the creation of the world, sufficeth not to the knowledge of God: yea, and that the particular also which is by the word of God, is of itself of small or no efficacy, unless it be apprehended or laid hold on by faith, by the gift of God: otherwise by unbelief it is made unprofitable, and that by the only fault of man, who can pretend no ignorance.

z. Rom. 10:19 He calleth all profane people, a nation that is no nation, that they are not said to live but to die, which are appointed for everlasting condemnation.

aa. Rom. 10:20 Speaketh without fear.

ROM. 10

1. Gal. 3:24
2. Lev. 18:5 / Ezek. 20:11 / Gal. 3:12
3. Deut. 30:12
4. Deut. 30:14
5. Isa. 28:16
6. Joel 2:32
7. Isa. 52:7 / Nah. 1:15
8. Isa. 53:1 / John 12:38
9. Ps. 19:3
10. Deut. 32:21
11. Isa. 65:1

ROM. 11

a. Rom. 11:1 Now the Apostle showeth how this doctrine is to be applied to others, abiding still in his propounded cause. Therefore he teacheth us that all the Jews in particular are not cast away, and therefore we ought not to pronounce rashly of private persons, whether they be of the number of the elect or not.

b. Rom. 11:1 The first proof, I am a Jew, and yet elected, therefore we may and ought fully to resolve upon our election, as hath been before said: but of another man's we cannot be so certainly resolved, and yet ours may cause us to hope well of others.

c. Rom. 11:2 The second proof: Because that God is faithful in his league or Covenant, although men be unfaithful: So then seeing that God hath said, that he will be the God of his unto a thousand generations, we must take heed, that we think not that the whole race and offspring is cast off, by reason of the unbelief of a few, but rather, that we hope well of every member of the Church, because of God's league and Covenant.

d. Rom. 11:2 Which he loved and chose from everlasting.

e. Rom. 11:2 The third proof, taken from the answer that was made to Elijah: even then also, when there appeared openly to the face of the world no elect, yet God knew his elect and chosen, and of them also good store and number. Whereupon this also is concluded, that we ought not rashly to pronounce of any man as of a reprobate, seeing that the Church is oftentimes brought to that state, that even the most watchful and sharp-sighted pastors think it to be clean extinct and put out.

f. Rom. 11:4 He speaketh of remnants and reserved people which were chosen from everlasting, and not of remnants that should be chosen afterward: for they are not chosen, because they were not idolaters, but therefore they were not idolaters, because they were chosen and elect.

g. Rom. 11:4 Baal signifieth as much as Master or patron, or one in whose power another is, which name the idolaters at this day give their idols, naming them patrons, and patronesses or Ladies.

h. Rom. 11:5 The election of grace, is not whereby men chose grace, but whereby God chose us of his grace and goodness.

i. Rom. 11:6 Although that all be not elect and chosen, yet let them that are elected, remember that they are freely chosen, and let them that stubbornly refuse the grace and free mercy of God, impute it unto themselves.

j. Rom. 11:6 This saying beateth down flat to the ground all the doctrine of all kinds and manner of works, whereby our justifiers of themselves do teach, that works are either wholly or partly the cause of our justification.

k. Rom. 11:7 See Mark 3:5.

l. Rom. 11:8 And yet this hardness of heart cometh not but by God's just decree and judgment, and yet without fault, whom as he so punisheth the unthankful by taking from them all sense and perseverance and by doubling their darkness, that the benefits of God which are offered unto them, do redound to their just destruction.

m. Rom. 11:8 A very dead sleep which taketh away all sense.

n. Rom. 11:8 That is, eyes unjust to see.

not see, and ears that they should not hear unto this day. 9 And David saith,
[4,o]Let their table be made a snare, and a net, and a stumbling block, even for a
recompense unto them. 10 Let their eyes be darkened that they see not, and
bow down their back always. 11 [p]I demand then, Have they stumbled, that they
should fall? God forbid: but through their fall, salvation cometh unto the Gentiles,
to provoke them to follow them. 12 Wherefore if the fall of them be the [q]riches
of the world, and the diminishing of them the riches of the Gentiles, how much
more shall their [r]abundance be? 13 [s]For in that I speak to you Gentiles, inasmu-
ch as I am the Apostle of the Gentiles, I [t]magnify mine office, 14 To try if by any
means I might provoke them of my flesh to follow them, and might save some of
them. 15 For if the casting away of them be the reconciling of the world, what
shall the receiving be, [u]but life from the dead? 16 [v]For if the [w]firstfruits be holy,
so is the whole lump: and if the [x]root be holy, so are the branches. 17 [5,y]And
though some of the branches be broken off, and thou being a wild Olive tree,
wast grafted in [z]for them, and made [aa]partaker of the root and fatness of the Olive
tree: 18 [ab]Boast not thyself against the branches: and if thou boast thyself, thou
bearest not the root, but the root thee. 19 Thou wilt say then, The branches are
broken off, that I might be grafted in. 20 Well: through unbelief they are broken
off, and thou standest by faith: be not high-minded, but [ac]fear. 21 For if God
spared not the [ad]natural branches, take heed, lest he also spare not thee. 22 [ae-]
Behold therefore the [af]bountifulness, and severity of God: toward them which have
fallen, severity: but toward thee, bountifulness, if thou continue in his [ag]bountiful-
ness: or else thou shalt also be cut off. 23 [ah]And they also, if they abide not still
in unbelief, shall be grafted in: for God is able to graft them in again. 24 For if
thou wast cut out of the Olive tree, which was wild by [ai]nature, and was grafted
contrary to nature in a [aj]right Olive tree, how much more shall they that are by
nature, be grafted in their own Olive tree? 25 [ak]For I would not, brethren, that
ye should be ignorant of this secret (lest ye should be arrogant in [al]yourselves) that
partly obstinacy is come to Israel, until the fullness of the Gentiles be [am]come
in. 26 And so all Israel shall be saved, as it is written, [6]The deliverer shall come
out of Zion, and shall turn away the ungodliness from Jacob. 27 And this is my
covenant to them, [7]When I shall take away their sins. 28 [an]As concerning the
[ao]Gospel, they are enemies for your sakes: but as touching the [ap]election, they are
beloved for the fathers' sakes. 29 [aq]For the gifts and calling of God are without
repentance. 30 [ar]For even as ye in times past have not believed God, yet have
now obtained mercy through their unbelief: 31 Even so now have they not be-
lieved by the mercy showed unto you, that they also may obtain mercy. 32 For
God hath shut up [as]all in unbelief, that he might have mercy on all. 33 [at]O the
deepness of the riches, both of the wisdom, and knowledge of God! how unsear-
chable are his [au]judgments, and his [av]ways past finding out! 34 [8,aw]For who hath
known the mind of the Lord? or who was his counselor? 35 Or who hath given
unto him [ax]first, and he shall be recompensed? 36 For of him, and through him,
and for [ay]him are all things: to him be glory forever. Amen.

12

1 He exhorteth 2 to that worship which is acceptable to God, 9 to love unfained, 14, 20 even towards our enemies.

1 I Beseech [a]you therefore brethren, [b]by the mercies of God, that ye [c]give up
your [d]bodies a [e]living sacrifice, holy, acceptable unto God, which is your [f]reaso-
nable serving of God. 2 [g]And fashion not yourselves like unto this world, but be
ye changed by the renewing of your [h]mind, that ye may [i]prove what that good,
and acceptable and perfect will of God is. 3 [i]For I [j]say through the grace that is
given unto me, to everyone that is among you, that no man [k]presume to under-
stand above that which is meet to understand, but that he understand according

---

o. Rom. 11:9 As unhappy birds are enticed to death by that which is their sustenance, so did that only thing turn to the Jews' destruction, out of which they sought life, to wit, the Law of God, for the preposterous zeal whereof they refused the Gospel.

p. Rom. 11:11 God appointed this casting out of the Jews, that it might be an occasion to call the Gentiles: and again might turn this calling of the Gentiles, to be an occasion to restore the Jews, to wit, that they being inflamed and provoked by emulation of the Gentiles, might themselves at length embrace the Gospel. And hereby we may learn, that the severity of God serveth as well for the setting forth of his glory as his mercy doth, and also that God prepares himself a way to mercy, by his severity, so that we ought not rashly to despair of any man, nor proudly triumph over other men, but rather provoke them to an holy emulation, that God may be glorified in them also.

q. Rom. 11:12 By riches he meaneth the knowledge of the Gospel to everlasting life: and by the world, all nations dispersed throughout the whole world.

r. Rom. 11:12 Of the Jews, when the whole nation without exception shall come to Christ.

s. Rom. 11:13 He witnesseth by his own example, that he goeth before all others in this behalf.

t. Rom. 11:13 I make noble and famous.

u. Rom. 11:15 It shall come to pass that when the Jews come to the Gospel, the world shall as it were come quicken again, and rise up from death to life.

v. Rom. 11:16 The nation of the Jews being considered in their stock and root, that is, in Abraham, is holy, although that many of the branches be cut off. Therefore in judging of our brethren, we must not stick in their unworthiness, to think that they are at once all cast off, but we ought to consider the root of the Covenant, and rather go back to their ancestors which were faithful, that we may know that the blessing of the Covenant resteth in some of their posterity, as we also find proof hereof in ourselves.

w. Rom. 11:16 He alludeth to the firstfruits of the loaves by the offering whereof all the whole crop of corn was sanctified, and they might vie the rest of the year following with good conscience.

x. Rom. 11:16 Abraham.

y. Rom. 11:17 There is no cause why the Gentiles which have obtained mercy, should triumph over the Jews which condemn the grace of God, seeing they are grafted into the Jews' ancestors. But let them rather take heed that that also be not found in them which is worthily condemned in the Jews. And hereof also this general doctrine may be gathered and taken, that we ought to be studious of God's glory, even in respect of our neighbors: so far ought we to be from bragging and glorying, for that, that we are preferred before others by a singular grace.

z. Rom. 11:17 In place of those boughs which are broken off.

aa. Rom. 11:17 It is against the common course of husbandry, that the barren juice of the imp is changed with the juice of the good tree.

ab. Rom. 11:18 We may rejoice in the Lord, but so that we despise not the Jews, whom we ought rather to provoke to that good striving with us.

ac. Rom. 11:20 See that thou stand in awe of God modestly and carefully.

ad. Rom. 11:21 He calleth them natural, not because they had any holiness of nature, but because they were born of them, whom the Lord set apart for himself from, other nations, by his league and covenant which he freely made with them.

ae. Rom. 11:22 Seeing the matter itself declareth that election cometh not by inheritance (although the fault be in men, and not in God, why the blessing of God is not perpetual) we must take good heed, that that be not found in ourselves, which we think blameworthy in others, for the election is sure, but they that are truly elect and ingrafted, are not proud in themselves with contempt of others, but with due reverence to God, and love towards their neighbor, run to the mark which is set before them.

af. Rom. 11:22 The tender and loving heart.

ag. Rom. 11:22 In that state which God's bountifulness hath advanced thee unto: and we must mark here, that he speaketh not of the election of every private man, which remaineth steadfast forever, but of the election of the whole nation.

ah. Rom. 11:23 Many are now for a season cut off, that is, are without the root, which in their time shall be grafted in: and again there are a great sort, which after a sort, and touching the outward show, seem to be ingrafted, which notwithstanding through their own fault afterward are cut off and clean cast away: which thing is especially to be considered in nations and peoples, as in the Gentiles and Jews.

ai. Rom. 11:24 Understand nature, not as it was first made, but as it was corrupted in Adam, and so derived from him to his posterity.

aj. Rom. 11:24 Into the people of the Jews which God had sanctified of his mere grace: and he speaketh of the whole nation, not of every one part.

ak. Rom. 11:25 The blindness of the Jews is neither so universal that the Lord hath no elect in that nation, neither shall it be continual: for there shall be a time wherein they also (as the Prophets have forewarned) shall effectually embrace that which they do now so stubbornly for the most part reject and refuse.

al. Rom. 11:25 That ye be not proud within yourselves.

am. Rom. 11:25 Into the Church.

an. Rom. 11:28 Again, that he may join the Jews and Gentiles together as it were in one body, and especially may teach what duty the Gentiles owe to the Jews, he beateth this into their heads, that the nation of the Jews is not utterly cast off without hope of recovery.

ao. Rom. 11:28 Forasmuch as they received it not.

ap. Rom. 11:28 In that, that God respecteth not what they deserve, but what he promised to Abraham.

aq. Rom. 11:29 The reason or proof: because the covenant made with that nation of life everlasting, cannot be frustrate and vain.

ar. Rom. 11:30 Another reason, because that although that they which are hardened, are worthily punished, yet hath not this stubbornness of the Jews so come to pass properly for an hatred to that nation, but that an entry might as it were be opened to bring in the Gentiles, and afterward the Jews being inflamed with emulation of this mercy which is showed to the Gentiles, might themselves also be partakers of the same benefit, and so it might appear that both Jews and Gentiles are saved, only by the free mercy and grace of God, which could not have been so manifest, if at the beginning, God had brought all together into the Church, or if he had saved the nation of the Jews without this interruption.

as. Rom. 11:32 Both Jews and Gentiles.

at. Rom. 11:33 The Apostle crieth not as astonished with this wonderful wisdom of God, which he teacheth us, ought to be religiously reverenced, and not curiously and profanely to be searched beyond the compass of that that God hath revealed unto us.

au. Rom. 11:33 The course that he holdeth in governing all things both generally and particularly.

av. Rom. 11:33 The order of his counsels and doings.

aw. Rom. 11:34 He bridleth three manner of ways, the wicked boldness of man: First, because that God is above all, most wise, and therefore it is very absurd, and plainly godless to measure him by our folly. Moreover, because he is debtor to no man, and therefore no man can complain of injury done unto him. Thirdly, because all things are made for his glory, and therefore we must refer all things to his glory, much less may we contend and debate the matter with him.

ax. Rom. 11:35 This saying overthroweth the doctrine of foreseen works and merits.

ay. Rom. 11:36 To wit, for God, to whose glory all things are referred, not only things that were made, but especially his new works which he worketh in his elect.

ROM. 11

1. 1 Kings 19:10
2. 1 Kings 19:18
3. Isa. 6:9 / Isa. 29:10 / Matt. 13:14 / John 12:40 / Acts 28:26
4. Ps. 69:23
5. Jer. 11:6
6. Isa. 59:20
7. Isa. 27:9
8. Job 41:2 / Isa. 40:13 / 1 Cor. 2:16

ROM. 12

a. Rom. 12:1 The fourth part of this Epistle, which after the finishing of the chief points of Christian doctrine, consisteth in declaring of precepts of Christian life. And first of all he giveth general precepts and grounds: the chiefest whereof is this that every man consecrate himself wholly to the spiritual service of God, and do as it were sacrifice himself, trusting to the grace of God.

b. Rom. 12:1 By this preface he showeth that God's glory is the utmost end of all our doings.

c. Rom. 12:1 In times past the sacrifices were presented before the altar, but now the altar is everywhere.

d. Rom. 12:1 Yourselves: in times past, other bodies than our own, now our own must be offered.

e. Rom. 12:1 In times past, dead sacrifices were offered, but now we must offer such as have the spirit of life in them.

f. Rom. 12:1 Spiritual.

g. Rom. 12:2 The second precept is this, That we take not other men's opinions or manners for a rule of life, but that we wholly renouncing this world, set before us as our mark, the will of God, as it is manifested and opened unto us in his word.

h. Rom. 12:2 Why then there is no place left for reason, which the heathen Philosophers place as a Queen in a Castle, nor for man's free will, which the Popish Schoolmen dream on, if the mind must be renewed. See Eph. 1:18 and 2:5 and 4:17 and Col. 1:21.

i. Rom. 12:3 Thirdly he admonisheth us very earnestly, that every man keep himself within the bounds of his vocation, and that every man be wise according to the measure of grace that God hath given him.

j. Rom. 12:3 I charge.

k. Rom. 12:3 That he please not himself too much, as they do, which persuade themselves they know more than indeed they do.

to [l]sobriety, as God hath dealt to every man the [2]measure of [m]faith. 4 [n]For as we have many members in one body, and all members have not one office, 5 So we being many, are one body in Christ, and every one, one anothers members. 6 [3,o]Seeing then that we have gifts that are divers, according to the grace that is given unto us, whether we have prophecy, let us prophesy according to the [p]portion of faith. 7 Or an office, let us wait on the office: or he that [q]teacheth, on teaching: 8 Or he that [r]exhorteth, on exhortation: he that [s]distributeth, let him do it [4]with simplicity: he that [t]ruleth, with diligence: he that [u]showeth mercy, with cheerfulness. 9 [v]Let love be without dissimulation. [5]Abhor that which is evil, and cleave unto that which is good. 10 [6]Be affectioned to love one another with brotherly love. In giving honor, go one before another. 11 Not slothful to do service, fervent in spirit [w]serving the Lord, 12 [x]Rejoicing in hope, patient in tribulation, [7]continuing in prayer. 13 [8,y]Distributing unto the [z]necessities of the Saints: [9]giving yourselves to hospitality. 14 [10]Bless them which persecute you: bless, I say, and curse not. 15 Rejoice with them that rejoice, and weep with them that weep. 16 Be like affectioned one towards another: [11]be not high-minded: but make yourselves equal to them of the [aa]lower sort: be not [ab]wise in yourselves. 17 [12]Recompense to no man evil for evil: procure things honest in the sight of all men. 18 [13]If it be possible, as much as in you is, have peace with all men. 19 Dearly beloved, [14]avenge not yourselves, but give place unto wrath: for it is written, [15]Vengeance is mine: I will repay, saith the Lord. 20 [16]Therefore if thine enemy hunger, feed him: if he thirst, give him drink: for in so doing thou shalt heap [ac]coals of fire on his head. 21 Be not overcome of evil, but overcome evil with goodness.

13

1 He willeth that we submit ourselves to Magistrates: 8 To love our neighbor: 13 To love uprightly, 14 and to put on Christ.

1 Let [1,a]every [b]soul be subject unto the higher [c]powers: [d]for there is no power but of God: and the powers that be, are [e]ordained of God. 2 Whosoever therefore resisteth the power, resisteth the ordinance of God: and they that resist, shall receive to themselves condemnation. 3 [f]For Magistrates are not to be feared for good works, but for evil. [g]Wilt thou then be without fear of the power? do well: so shalt thou have praise of the same. 4 For he is the minister of God for thy wealth: [h]but if thou do evil, fear: for he beareth not the sword for nought: for he is the minister of God to [i]take vengeance on him that doeth evil. 5 [j]Wherefore ye must be subject, not because of wrath only, but [k]also for conscience sake. 6 [l]For, for this cause ye pay also tribute: for they are God's ministers, applying themselves for the same thing. 7 [2]Give to all men therefore their duty: tribute, to whom ye owe tribute: custom, to whom custom: fear, to whom [m]fear: honor, to whom ye owe [n]honor. 8 [o]Owe nothing to any man, but to love one another: [p]for he that loveth another, hath fulfilled the [q]Law. 9 For this, [3]Thou shalt not commit adultery, Thou shalt not kill, Thou shalt not steal, Thou shalt not bear false witness, Thou shalt not covet: and if there be any other commandment, it is [r]briefly comprehended in this saying, even in this, [4]Thou shalt love thy neighbor as thyself. 10 Love doeth not evil to his neighbor: therefore is love the [5]fulfilling of the Law. 11 [s]And that, considering the season, that it is now time that we should arise from sleep: for now is our salvation nearer, than when we believed it. 12 The night is past, and the day is [t]at hand, let us therefore cast away the works [u]of darkness, and let us put on the armor of light, 13 So that we walk honestly, as in the day: not in [6]gluttony, and drunkenness, neither in chambering and wantonness, nor in strife and envying. 14 [7]But [v]put ye on the Lord JESUS CHRIST, and take no thought for the flesh, to fulfill the lust of it.

14

1 He willeth that we so deal with the weak in faith, 2, 5 that through our fault they be not offended. 10 And on the other side he commandeth them not rashly to judge of the stronger: 19 That within the bounds of edification 20 and charity. 22 Christian liberty may conflict.

1 Him [a]that is weak in the faith, [b]receive unto you, but not for [c]controversies of disputations. 2 [d]One [e]believeth that he may eat of all things: and another, which is weak, eateth herbs. 3 [f]Let not him that eateth, despise him that eateth

---

l. Rom. 12:3 We will be sober if we take not that upon us, which we have not, and if we brag not of that we have.
m. Rom. 12:3 By faith he meaneth the knowledge of God in Christ, and the gifts which the holy Ghost poureth upon the faithful.
n. Rom. 12:4 There is a double reason of the precept going afore: the one is because God hath not committed everything to be done of every man: and therefore, he doeth backwardly, and not only unprofitably, but also to the great disprofit of others, wearieth himself and others, which passeth the bounds of his vocation: the other is, for that this diversity and inequality of vocations and gifts, redoundeth to our commodity seeing that the same is therefore instituted and appointed, that we should be bound one to another. Whereupon it followeth that no man ought to be grieved thereat, seeing that the use of every private gift is common.
o. Rom. 12:6 That which he spake before in general, he applieth particularly to the holy functions, wherein men offend with greater danger. And he divideth them into two sorts, to wit, into Prophets, and Deacons, and again he divideth the Prophets into doctors, and Pastors. And of Deacons he maketh three sorts: to wit, the one to be such as (as it were) treasurers of the Church coffers, whom he calleth properly Deacons: the other to be the governors of discipline, who are called Seniors or Elders: the third to be such as properly served in the help of the poor, of which sort the company of widows were.
p. Rom. 12:6 That every man observe the measure of that which is revealed unto him.
q. Rom. 12:7 Whose office only is to expound the Scriptures.
r. Rom. 12:8 Who in other places is called the Pastor.
s. Rom. 12:8 To wit, the alms, that he distribute them faithfully, and without respect of person.
t. Rom. 12:8 The Elders of the Church.
u. Rom. 12:8 They that are busied about tending on the poor, must do it with cheerfulness, lest they add sorrow to sorrow.
v. Rom. 12:9 Now he cometh to the duties of the second Table, which he deriveth from charity, which is as it were the fountain of them all. And he defineth Christian charity by sincerity, hatred of evil, earnest study of good things, good affection to help our neighbor, and whose final end is, the glory of God.
w. Rom. 12:11 This piece is well put in, for it maketh difference between Christian duties, and Philosophical duties.
x. Rom. 12:12 He reckoneth up divers other virtues together with their effects, to wit, hope, patience in tribulation, equanimity, continuance in prayer, liberality towards the saints, hospitality, moderation of mind, even in helping our enemies, a selfsame feeling with others as well in adversity as prosperity, modesty, endeavor to maintain honest concord so nigh as we may with all men, which cannot be extinguished by any man's injuries.
y. Rom. 12:13 A true rule of charity, when we are no less touched with other men's wants, than with our own, and having that feeling, help them as much as we can.
z. Rom. 12:13 Not upon pleasure, and needless duties, but upon necessary uses.
aa. Rom. 12:16 There is nothing that doth so much break concord as ambition, when as every man loatheth a base estate, and seeketh ambitiously to be aloft.
ab. Rom. 12:16 Be not puffed up, with opinion of your own wisdom.
ac. Rom. 12:20 After this sort doth Solomon point out the wrath of God which hangeth over a man.

ROM. 12
1. Eph. 5:17 / 1 Thess. 4:3
2. 1 Cor. 12:11 / Eph. 4:7
3. 1 Pet. 4:10
4. Matt. 6:2 / 2 Cor. 9:7
5. Amos 5:15
6. Eph. 4:2 / 1 Pet. 2:17
7. 1 Pet. 5:8
8. Luke 18:1 / 1 Cor. 16:1
9. Heb. 13:2 / 1 Pet. 4:13
10. Matt. 5:44
11. Prov. 3:7 / Isa. 5:21
12. Prov. 20:22 / Matt. 5:39 / 2 Cor. 8:11 / 1 Pet. 3:9
13. Heb. 12:14
14. Eccl. 2:18 / Matt. 5:39
15. Deut. 32:35 / Heb. 10:30
16. Prov. 24:22

ROM. 13
a. Rom. 13:1 Now he showeth severally, what subjects owe to their Magistrates, to wit, obedience: From which he showeth that no man is free: and in such sort that it is not only due to the highest Magistrate himself, but also even to the basest, which hath any office under him.
b. Rom. 13:1 Yea, though an Apostle, though an Evangelist, though a Prophet: Chrysostom. Therefore the tyranny of the Pope over all kingdoms must down to the ground.
c. Rom. 13:1 A reason taken of the nature of the thing itself: For to what purpose are they placed in higher degree, but that the inferior should be subject unto them?
d. Rom. 13:1 Another argument of great force: Because God is author of this order: so that such as are rebels ought to know, that they make war with God himself: wherefore they cannot but purchase to themselves great misery and calamity.
e. Rom. 13:1 Be distributed: for some are greater, some smaller.
f. Rom. 13:3 The third argument taken from the end wherefore they were made, which is most profitable: for that God by this means preserveth the good and bridleth the wicked: by which words the Magistrates themselves are put in mind of that duty which they owe to their subjects.
g. Rom. 13:3 An excellent way to bear this yoke, not only without grief, but also with great profit.
h. Rom. 13:4 God hath armed the Magistrate even with a revenging sword.
i. Rom. 13:4 By whom God revengeth the wicked.
j. Rom. 13:5 The conclusion: We must obey the magistrate, not only for fear of punishment, but much more because that (although the Magistrate have no power over the conscience of man, yet seeing he is God's minister) he cannot be resisteth by any good conscience.
k. Rom. 13:5 So far as lawfully we may: for if unlawful things be commanded us, we must answer as Peter teacheth us, It is better to obey God than men.
l. Rom. 13:6 He reckoneth up the chiefest things wherein consisteth the obedience of subjects.
m. Rom. 13:7 Obedience, and that from the heart.
n. Rom. 13:7 Reverence, (which as reason is) we must give to the Magistrate.
o. Rom. 13:8 He showeth how very few judgments need to be executed, to wit, if we so order our life, as no man may justly require anything of us, besides that only that we owe one to another, by the perpetual law of charity.
p. Rom. 13:8 He commendeth charity, as an abridgement of the whole Law.
q. Rom. 13:8 He hath not only done one commandment, but performed generally that which the Law commandeth.
r. Rom. 13:9 For the whole Law commandeth nothing else, but that we love God and our neighbor. But seeing Paul speaketh here of the duties we owe one to another, we must restrain this word, Law to the second Table.
s. Rom. 13:11 An application taken of the circumstance of the time: which also itself putteth us in mind of our duty, seeing that this remaineth after that the darkness of ignorance and wicked affections by the knowledge of God's truth be driven out of us, that we order our life according to that certain and sure rule of all righteousness and honesty, being fully grounded upon the virtue of the Spirit of Christ.
t. Rom. 13:12 In other places we are said to be in the light, but yet so, that it appeareth not as yet what we are, for as yet we see but as it were in the twilight.
u. Rom. 13:12 That kind of life, which they lead, that flee the light.
v. Rom. 13:14 To put on Christ, is to possess Christ, to have him in us, and us in him.

ROM. 13
1. Titus 3:1 / 1 Pet. 2:13
2. Matt. 22:11
3. Exod. 20:14 / Deut. 5:18
4. Lev. 19:11 / Matt. 21:39 / Mark 12:31 / Gal. 5:14 / James 1:8
5. 1 Tim. 1:1
6. Luke 21:34
7. Gal. 5:16 / 1 Pet. 2:11

ROM. 14
a. Rom. 14:1 Now he showeth how we ought to behave ourselves toward our brethren in matters and things indifferent, offending in the use of them, not of malices or damnable superstition, but for lack of knowledge of the benefit of Christ. And thus he teacheth that they are to be instructed gently and patiently, and so that we apply ourselves to their ignorance in such matters according to the rule of charity.
b. Rom. 14:1 Do not for a matter or thing that is indifferent, and such as you may do or not do, shun his company, but take him to you.
c. Rom. 14:1 To make him by your doubtful and uncertain disputations go away more in doubt than he came, or start back with a troubled conscience.
d. Rom. 14:2 He propoundeth for an example, the difference of meats, which some thought was necessarily to be observed as a thing prescribed by the Law (not knowing that it was taken away) whereas on the contrary side, such as had profited in the knowledge of the Gospel, knew well that this schoolmastership of the Law was abolished.
e. Rom. 14:2 Knows by faith.
f. Rom. 14:3 In such a matter, saith the Apostle, Let neither them which know their liberty, proudly despise their weaker brother, neither let the unlearned crabbedly or frowardly condemn that, that they understand not.
g. Rom. 14:3 The first reason: Because that seeing both he that eateth and he that eateth not, is notwithstanding the member of Christ, neither he which eateth not, can justly

not: and let not him which eateth not, condemn him that eateth: for [g]God hath
received him. **4** [1,h]Who art thou that condemnest another man's servant? he
standeth or falleth to his own master: yea, he shall be established: for God is able
to make him stand. **5** [i]This man esteemeth one day above another day, and
another man counteth every day alike: [j]let [k]every man be fully persuaded in his
mind. **6** [l]He that [m]observeth the day, observeth it to the Lord: and he that ob-
serveth not the day, observeth it not to the [n]Lord. He that [o]eateth, eateth to the
Lord: [p]for he giveth God thanks: and he that eateth [q]not, eateth not to the Lord,
and giveth God thanks. **7** [r]For none of us liveth to [s]himself, neither doth any
die to himself. **8** For whether we live, we live unto the Lord: or whether we die,
we die unto the Lord: whether we live therefore, or die, we are the Lords. **9** For
Christ therefore died and rose again, and revived, that he might be Lord both of
the dead and the quick. **10** [t]But why dost thou condemn thy brother? or why
dost thou despise thy brother? [2]for we shall all appear before the judgment seat of
Christ. **11** For it is written, [u]I [3]live, saith the Lord, and every knee shall bow to
me, and all tongues shall [v]confess unto God. **12** So then everyone of us shall
give accounts of himself to God. **13** [w]Let us not therefore judge one another
anymore: but use your judgment rather in [x]this that no man put an occasion to
fall, or a stumbling block before his brother. **14** [y]I know, and am persuaded
through the [z]Lord Jesus, that there is nothing unclean of [aa]itself: but unto him that
judgeth anything to be unclean, to him it is unclean. **15** But if thy brother be
grieved for the meat, now walkest thou not charitably: [4,ab]destroy not him with
thy meat, for whom [ac]Christ died. **16** [ad]Cause not your commodity to be evil
spoken of. **17** [ae]For the kingdom of God, is not meat nor drink, but righteou-
sness, and peace, and joy in the holy Ghost. **18** For whosoever in [af]these thin-
gs serveth Christ, is acceptable unto God, and is approved of men. **19** [ag]Let
us then follow those things which concern peace, and wherewith one may edify
another. **20** Destroy not the work of God for meat's sake: [5]all things indeed are
pure: but it is evil for the man which eateth with offense. **21** [6]It is good neither
to eat flesh, nor to drink wine, nor anything whereby thy brother stumbleth, or
is offended, or made weak. **22** [ah]Hast thou [ai]faith? have it with thyself befo-
re God: blessed is he that condemneth not himself in that thing which he [aj]al-
loweth. **23** For he that [ak]doubteth, is condemned if he eat, because he eateth not
of faith: and whatsoever is not of faith, is sin.

15

1 The stronger must employ their strength to strengthen the weak. 5 By Christ's example, 7 who received 8 not only the Jews, 10 but also the Gentiles. 15 The cause why he wrote this Epistle.

1 We [a]which are strong, ought to bear the infirmities of the weak, and not
to [b]please ourselves. **2** Therefore let every man please his neighbor in that that
is [c]good to edification. **3** [d]For Christ also would not please himself, but as it is
written, [1]The rebukes of them which rebuke thee, fell on me. **4** [e]For whatso-
ever things are written [f]aforetime, are written for our learning, that we through
patience, and comfort of the [g]Scriptures might have hope. **5** [h]Now the God of
patience and consolation give you that ye be [2]like-minded one towards another,
according to Christ Jesus, **6** That ye with one mind, and with one mouth may
praise God, even the Father of our Lord Jesus Christ. **7** Wherefore receive ye
one another, as Christ also [i]received us to the glory of God. **8** [j]Now I say, that
Jesus Christ was a minister of the [k]circumcision, for the [l]truth of God, to confirm
the promises made unto the fathers. **9** [m]And let the Gentiles praise God, for his
mercy, as it is written, [3]For this cause I will [n]confess thee among the Gentiles, and
sing unto thy Name. **10** And again he saith, [4]Rejoice, ye Gentiles with his peo-
ple. **11** And again, [5]Praise the Lord, all ye Gentiles, and laud ye him all people
together. **12** And again Isaiah saith, [6]There shall be a root of Jesse, and he that
shall rise to reign over the Gentiles, in him shall the Gentiles trust. **13** [o]Now the
God of [p]hope fill you with [q]all joy, and peace in believing, that ye may abound in
hope, through the power of the holy Ghost. **14** [r]And I myself also am persuaded

---

be condemned, neither he which eateth be justly condemned: Now the first proposition is declared in the sixth verse following.

h. Rom. 14:4 Another reason which hangeth upon the former: why the ruder and more unlearned ought not to be contemned of the more skillful, as men without hope of salvation: Because, saith the Apostle, he that is ignorant today, may be endued tomorrow with further knowledge, so that he also may stand sure: Therefore it belongeth to God, and not unto man, to pronounce the sentence of condemnation.

i. Rom. 14:5 Another example of the difference of days according to the law.

j. Rom. 14:5 He setteth against this contempt, and hasty or rash judgments, a continual desire to profit, that the strong may be certainly persuaded of their liberty, of what manner and sort it is, and how they ought to use it: and again the weak may daily profit, lest either they abuse the gift of God, or these please themselves in their infirmity.

k. Rom. 14:5 That he may say in his conscience, that he knoweth and is persuaded by Jesus Christ, that nothing is unclean of itself, and this persuasion must be grounded upon the word of God.

l. Rom. 14:6 A reason taken from the nature of indifferent things, which a man may with good conscience do and omit: for seeing that the difference of days and meats was appointed by God, how could they, which as yet understood not the abrogating of the Law, and yet otherwise acknowledged Christ as their Savior, with good conscience neglect that which they knew was commanded of God? And on the contrary side, they that knew the benefit of Christ in this behalf, did with good conscience neither observe days nor meats. Therefore saith the Apostle, verse 10, Let not the strong condemn the weak for these things, seeing that the weak brethren are brethren notwithstanding. Now if any man would draw this doctrine to these our times and ages, let them know that the Apostle speaketh of such things indifferent, as they which thought them not to be indifferent, had a ground in the Law, and were deceived by simple ignorance: and not of malice (for to such the Apostles yielded not, no not for a moment) nor superstition, but of a religious fear of God.

m. Rom. 14:6 Observeth precisely.

n. Rom. 14:6 God shall judge whether he do well or no: And therefore you should rather strive about this, how every one of you will be allowed of God, than to think upon other men's doings.

o. Rom. 14:6 He that maketh no difference of meats.

p. Rom. 14:6 So the Apostle showeth that he speaketh of the faithful, both strong and weak. But what if we have to do with infidels? Then must we here take heed of two things, as also is declared in the Epistle to the Corinthians. The one is, that we count not their superstitions among things indifferent, as they did which sat down to meat in Idols' Temples: the other is, that then also when the matter is indifferent (as to buy a thing offered to idols, in the butcher's shambles, and to eat it at home in a private banquet) we wound not the conscience of our weak brother.

q. Rom. 14:6 He that toucheth not meats which he taketh to be unclean by the Law.

r. Rom. 14:7 We must not stick, saith he, in the meat itself, but in the use of the meat, so that he is justly to be reprehended that liveth so, that he casteth not his eyes upon God. For both our life and our death is dedicated to him, and for this cause Christ hath properly died, and not simply, that we might eat this meat or that.

s. Rom. 14:7 Hath respect to himself only, which the Hebrews utter after this sort, Doeth well to his own soul.

t. Rom. 14:10 The conclusion: we must leave to God his right: and therefore in matters, which according as the conscience if affected, are either good or evil, the strong must not despise their weak brethren, much less condemn them. But this consequent cannot be taken of equal force in the contrary, to wit, that the weak should not judge the strong, because the weak do not know, that they which do not observe a day, and eat, observe it not to the Lord, and eat to the Lord, as the strong men know, that the weak which observe a day and eat not, observe the day to the Lord, and eat not to the Lord.

u. Rom. 14:11 This is a form of an oath, proper to God only, for he and none but he liveth, and hath his being of himself.

v. Rom. 14:11 Shall acknowledge me from God.

w. Rom. 14:13 After that he hath concluded what is not to be done, he showeth what is to be done: to wit, we must take heed that we do not utterly cast down with abusing our liberty, our brother who is not yet strong.

x. Rom. 14:13 He rebuketh by this way, these malicious judgers of others, which occupy their heads about nothing, but to find fault with their brethren's life, whereas they should rather bestow their wits upon this, that they do not with their disdainfulness either cast their brethren clean down, or give them some offense.

y. Rom. 14:14 The preventing of an objection: It is true that the schoolmastership of the Law is taken away by the benefit of Christ, to such as know it, but yet notwithstanding we have to consider in the use of this liberty what is expedient, that we may have regard of our weak brother, seeing that our liberty is not lost thereby.

z. Rom. 14:14 By the Spirit of the Lord Jesus, or by the Lord Jesus, who I am sure brake down the wall at his coming.

aa. Rom. 14:14 By nature.

ab. Rom. 14:15 It is the part of a cruel mind to make more account of meat, than of our brother's salvation. Which thing they do, that presume to eat with offense of any brother, and so give him occasion to go back from the Gospel.

ac. Rom. 14:15 Another argument: We must follow Christ's example: who was so far from destroying the weak with meat, that he gave his life for them.

ad. Rom. 14:16 Another argument: for that by this means the liberty of the Gospel is evil spoken of, as though it openeth the way to attempt any thing whatsoever, and boldeneth us to all things.

ae. Rom. 14:17 A general reason, and the ground of all the other arguments: The kingdom of heaven consisteth not in these outward things, but in the study of righteousness, and peace, and comfort of the holy Ghost.

af. Rom. 14:18 He that liveth peaceably, and doeth righteously, through the holy Ghost.

ag. Rom. 14:19 A general conclusion: The use of this liberty, yea and our whole life, ought to be referred to the edifying of one another, insomuch that we esteem that thing unlawful by reason of the offense of our brother, which is of itself pure and lawful.

ah. Rom. 14:22 He giveth a double warning in these matters, one, which pertaineth to the strong, that he which hath obtained a sure knowledge of this liberty, keep that treasure to the end he may use it wisely and profitably as hath been said: the other which respecteth the weak, that they do nothing rashly by other men's example with a wavering conscience, for that cannot be done without sin, whereof we are not persuaded by the word of God, that he liketh, and approveth it.

ai. Rom. 14:22 He showed before verse 14 what he meaneth by faith, to wit, for a man to be certain and out of doubt in matters and things indifferent.

aj. Rom. 14:22 Embraceth.

ak. Rom. 14:23 Reasoneth with himself.

ROM. 14

1. James 4:12
2. 2 Cor. 1:10
3. Isa. 45:23 / Phil. 2:10
4. 1 Cor. 8:11
5. Titus 1:15
6. 2 Cor. 8:13

ROM. 15

a. Rom. 15:1 Now the Apostle reasoneth generally of tolerating or bearing with the weak by all means, so far forth as may be for their profit.

b. Rom. 15:1 And despise others.

c. Rom. 15:2 For his profit and edification.

d. Rom. 15:3 A confirmation taken of the example of Christ, who suffered all things to bring not only the weak, but also his most cruel enemies, overcoming them with patience, to his Father.

e. Rom. 15:4 The preventing of an objection: Such things as are cited out of the examples of the ancients, are propounded unto us to this end and purpose, that according to the example of our Fathers, we should in patience and hope bear one with another.

f. Rom. 15:4 By Moses and the Prophets.

g. Rom. 15:4 The Scriptures are said to teach and comfort, because God useth them to teach and comfort his people withall.

h. Rom. 15:5 We must take an example of patience, of God that both the weak and the strong serving God with a mutual consent, may bring one another to God, as Christ also received us unto himself, although we were never so unworthy.

i. Rom. 15:7 He did not disdain us, but received us of his own accord, to make us partakers of God's glory.

j. Rom. 15:8 An applying of the example of Christ to the Jews, whom he vouchsafed this honor for the promises which he made unto their fathers, although they were never so unworthy, that he executed the office of a minister amongst them with marvelous patience. Therefore much less ought the Gentiles despise them for certain faults, whom the Son of God so much esteemed.

k. Rom. 15:8 Of the circumcised Jews, for as long as he lived, he never went out of their quarters.

l. Rom. 15:8 That God might be seen to be true.

m. Rom. 15:9 An applying of the same to the Gentiles, whom also the Lord of his incomprehensible goodness had regard of, so that they are not to be condemned of the Jews as strangers.

n. Rom. 15:9 I will openly profess, and set forth thy Name.

o. Rom. 15:13 He sealeth up as it were all the former treatise with prayers, wishing all that to be given them of the Lord, that he had commanded them.

p. Rom. 15:13 In whom we hope.

q. Rom. 15:13 Abundantly and plentifully.

r. Rom. 15:14 The conclusion of the Epistle, wherein he first excuseth himself, that he hath written somewhat at large unto them, rather to warn them, than to teach them, and that of

of you, my brethren, that [s]ye also are full of goodness, and filled with all knowledge, and are able to admonish one another. **15** Nevertheless, brethren, I have somewhat boldly after a sort written unto you, as one that putteth you in remembrance, through the grace that is given me of God, **16** That I should be the minister of Jesus Christ toward the Gentiles, ministering the Gospel of God, that the [t]offering up of the Gentiles might be acceptable, being sanctified by the holy Ghost. **17** [u]I have therefore whereof I may rejoice in Christ Jesus in those things which pertain to God. **18** For I dare not speak of anything, which [v]Christ hath not wrought by me, to make the Gentiles obedient in word and deed, **19** With the [w]power of signs and wonders, by the power of the spirit of God: so that from Jerusalem, and round about unto Illyricum, I have caused to abound the Gospel of Christ. **20** Yea, so I enforced myself to preach the Gospel, not where Christ was named, lest I should have built on another man's foundation. **21** But as it is written, [7]To whom he was not spoken of, they shall see him, and they that heard not, shall understand him. **22** [8,x]Therefore also I have been oft let to come unto you: **23** But now seeing I have no more place in these quarters, and also have [9]been desirous many years agone to come unto you, **24** When I shall take my journey into Spain, I will come to you: for I trust to see you in my journey, and to be brought on my way thitherward by you, after that I have been somewhat filled with your company. **25** But now go I to Jerusalem, to [y]minister unto the Saints. **26** For it hath pleased them of Macedonia and Achaia, to make a certain distribution unto the poor Saints which are at Jerusalem. **27** [z]For it hath pleased them, and their debtors are they: [10]for if the Gentiles be made partakers of their spiritual things, their duty is also to [aa]minister unto them in carnal things. **28** When I have therefore performed this, and have [ab]sealed them this [ac]fruit, I will pass by you into Spain. **29** [ad]And I know when I come, that I shall come to you with abundance of the blessing of the Gospel of Christ. **30** Also brethren, I beseech you for our Lord Jesus Christ's sake, and for the [ae]love of the spirit, that ye would strive with me by prayers to God for me, **31** That I may be delivered from them which are disobedient in Judea, and that my service which I have to do at Jerusalem, may be accepted of the Saints, **32** That I may come unto you with joy by the will of God, and may with you be refreshed. **33** Thus the God of peace be with you all. Amen.

16

1 He commendeth Phoebe. 3 He sendeth greeting to many. 17 And warneth to beware of them which are the causes of division.

1 I [a]Commend unto you Phoebe our sister, which is a servant of the Church of Cenchrea: **2** That ye receive her in the [b]Lord, as it becometh Saints, and that ye assist her in whatsoever business she needeth of your aid: for she hath given hospitality unto many, and to me also. **3** Greet [1]Priscilla, and Aquila, my fellow helpers in Christ Jesus. **4** (Which have for my life laid down their own neck. Unto whom not I only give thanks, but also all the Churches of the Gentiles.) **5** Likewise greet the [c]Church that is in their house. Salute my beloved Epaenetus, which is the [d]firstfruits of Achaia in Christ. **6** Greet Mary which bestowed much labor on us. **7** Salute Andronicus and Junia my cousins and fellow prisoners, which are notable among the Apostles, and were in [e]Christ before me. **8** Greet Amplias my beloved in the Lord. **9** Salute Urbanus our fellow helper in Christ, and Stachys my beloved. **10** Salute Apelles approved in Christ. Salute them which are of Aristobulus' friends. **11** Salute Herodion my kinsman. Greet them which are of the friends of Narcissus which are in the Lord. **12** Salute Tryphena and Tryphosa, which women labor in the Lord. Salute the beloved Persis, which woman hath labored much in the Lord. **13** Salute Rufus chosen in the Lord, and his mother and mine. **14** Greet Asyncritus, Phlegon, Hermas, Patrobas, Mercurius, and the brethren which are with them. **15** Salute Philologus and Julia, Nereus, and his sister, and Olympas and all the Saints which are with them. **16** Salute one another with an [2]holy [f]kiss. The Churches of Christ salute you. **17** [g]Now I beseech you brethren, [h]mark them diligently which cause division and offenses, contrary to the doctrine which ye have learned, and [3]avoid them. **18** For they that are such, serve not the Lord Jesus Christ but their own bellies, and with [i]fair speech and flattering deceive the hearts of the simple. **19** [j]For your obedience is come abroad among all: I am glad therefore of you: but yet I would have you [k]wise unto that which is good, and [l]simple concerning evil. **20** [m]The God of peace shall tread Satan under your feet shortly. The grace of our Lord Jesus Christ be with you. **21** [4,n]Timothy my helper, and Lucius and Jason, and Sosipater my kinsmen, salute you. **22** I Tertius, which [o]wrote out this Epistle, salute you in the Lord. **23** Gaius mine host, and of the whole Church saluteth you. Erastus the steward of the city saluteth you, and Quartus a brother. **24** [p]The grace of our Lord Jesus Christ be with you all, Amen. **25** [5,q]To him now that is of power to establish you according to my Gospel, and preaching of Jesus Christ, [6]by the revelation of the [r]mystery, which was kept secret since the world began: **26** (But now is opened, and [s]published among all nations by the Scriptures of the Prophets, at the commandment of the everlasting God for the obedience of faith.) **27** To God, I say, only wise, be praise through Jesus Christ for ever. Amen. Written to the Romans from Corinth, and sent by Phoebe, servant of the Church which is at Cenchrea.

---

necessity, by reason of his vocation, which bindeth him peculiarly to the Gentiles.

s. Rom. 15:14 Of your own accord, and of yourselves.
t. Rom. 15:16 By the offering up of the Gentiles, he meaneth the Gentiles themselves, whom he offered to God as a sacrifice.
u. Rom. 15:17 He commendeth his Apostleship highly by the effects, but yet so that moreover and besides that he speaketh all things truly, he giveth all the glory to God as the only author: and doth not properly respect himself, but this rather: that men might less doubt of the truth of the doctrine which he propoundeth unto them.
v. Rom. 15:18 Christ was so with me in all things, and by all means, that if I would never so fain, yet I cannot say, what he hath done by me to bring the Gentiles to obey the Gospel.
w. Rom. 15:19 In the first place this word, Power, signifieth the force, and working of the wonders in piercing men's minds: and in the latter, it signifieth God's mighty power which was the worker of those wonders.
x. Rom. 15:22 He writeth at large to the Romans, and that familiarly, his singular good will towards them, and the state of his affairs, but so, that he swerveth not an iota from the end of Apostolical doctrine: for he declareth nothing but that which appertaineth to his office, and is godly: and commending by a little digression as it were, the liberality of the Churches of Macedonia, he provoketh them modestly to follow their godly deed.
y. Rom. 15:25 Doing, his duty for the Saints, to carry them that money which was gathered for their use.
z. Rom. 15:27 Alms are voluntary, but yet such as we owe by the law of charity.
aa. Rom. 15:27 To serve the turns.
ab. Rom. 15:28 Performed it faithfully, and sealed it as it were with my ring.
ac. Rom. 15:28 This money which was gathered for the use of the poor: which alms is very fitly called fruit.
ad. Rom. 15:29 He promiseth them through the blessing of God, not to come empty unto them: and requiring of them the duty of prayers, he showeth what thing we ought chiefly to rest upon in all difficulties and adversities.
ae. Rom. 15:30 For that mutual communion, wherewith the holy Ghost hath tied our hearts and minds together.

ROM. 15

1. Ps. 69:10
2. 1 Cor. 1:10
3. Ps. 18:50
4. Deut. 32:43
5. Ps. 117:1
6. Isa. 11:10
7. Isa. 52:15
8. Rom. 1:11
9. 1 Thess. 2:17
10. 1 Cor. 6:21

ROM. 16

a. Rom. 16:1 Having made an end of the whole disputation, he cometh now to familiar commendations and salutations, and that to good consideration and purpose, to wit, that the Rom. might know, who are most to be honored and made account of amongst them, and also whom they ought to set before them to follow: and therefore he attributeth unto every of them peculiar and singular testimonies.
b. Rom. 16:2 For Christ's sake, which is proper to the Christians, for the heathen Philosophers have resemblances of the same virtues.
c. Rom. 16:5 The company of the faithful, for in so great a city as that was, there were divers companies.
d. Rom. 16:5 For he was the first of Achaia that believed in Christ: and this kind of speech is an allusion to the ceremonies of the Law.
e. Rom. 16:7 Ingrafted by faith.
f. Rom. 16:16 He calleth that an holy kiss, which proceedeth from an heart that is full of that holy love: now this is to be referred to the manner used in those days.
g. Rom. 16:17 As by namely describing them, which were worthy of commendation, he sufficiently declared when they ought to hear and follow, so doth he now point out unto them whom they ought to take heed of, yet he nameth them not, for that it was not needful.
h. Rom. 16:17 Warily and diligently, as though you should scout out for your enemies in a watch tower.
i. Rom. 16:18 The word which he useth, signifieth a promising which performeth nothing, and if thou hearest any such, thou mayest assure thyself that he that promiseth thee is more careful of thy matters, than of his own.
j. Rom. 16:19 Simplicity must be joined with wisdom.
k. Rom. 16:19 Furnished with the knowledge of the truth, and wisdom, that you may embrace good things, and eschew evil, beware of the deceits and snares of false prophets, and resist them openly: and this place doth plainly destroy the Papists' faith of credit, whereas they maintain it to be sufficient for one man to believe as another man believeth, without further knowledge, or examination what the matter is, or what ground it hath: using these daily speeches, We believe as our fathers believed, and we believe as the Church believeth.
l. Rom. 16:19 As men that know no way to deceive, much less to deceive in deed.
m. Rom. 16:20 We must fight, with a certain hope of victory.
n. Rom. 16:21 He annexeth salutations, partly to renew mutual friendship, and partly to the end that this Epistle might be of some weight with the Romans, having the confirmation of so many that subscribed unto it.
o. Rom. 16:22 Wrote it as Paul uttered it.
p. Rom. 16:24 Now taking his leave of them this third time, he wisheth that unto them, whereupon dependeth all the force of the former doctrine.
q. Rom. 16:25 He setteth forth the power and wisdom of God with great thanksgiving, which especially appears in the Gospel, and maketh mention also of the calling of the Gentiles to confirm the Rom. in the hope of this salvation.
r. Rom. 16:25 That secret and hidden thing, that is to say, the calling of the Gentiles.
s. Rom. 16:26 Offered and exhibited to all nations to be known.

ROM. 16

1. Acts 18:3
2. 1 Cor. 16:20 / 2 Cor. 13:2 / 1 Pet. 5:14
3. 2 John 10
4. Acts 16:1 / Phil. 2:29
5. Eph. 3:20
6. Eph. 3:9 / Col. 2:26 2 Tim. 1:10 / Titus 1:2

THE FIRST EPISTLE OF APOSTLE PAUL TO THE CORINTHIANS

1 *After the salutation, 10 which in effect is an exhortation. 12 He reprehendeth the Corinthians' sects and divisions, 17 and calleth them from pride to humility: 20 For overthrowing all worldly wisdom. 23, 25 he advanceth only the preaching of the cross.*

1 Paul [a]called to be an [b]Apostle of Jesus Christ, through the will of God, and our brother [c]Sosthenes, **2** [d]Unto the Church of God, which is at Corinth, to them that are [1,e]sanctified in [f]Christ Jesus, [2]Saints by [g]calling, [3]with all that [h]call on the Name of our Lord Jesus Christ in every place, both their Lord, and ours: **3** [i]Grace be with you, and peace from God our Father, and from the Lord Jesus Christ. **4** [j]I thank my God always on your behalf for the grace of God, which is given you in Jesus Christ. **5** That in all things ye are made rich in him [k]in [l]all kind of speech, and in all knowledge: **6** [m]As the testimony of Jesus Christ hath been [n]confirmed in you: **7** So that ye are not destitute of any gift: [4,o]waiting for the [p]appearing of our Lord Jesus Christ. **8** [5,q]Who shall also confirm you unto the end, that ye may be [r]blameless in the day of our Lord Jesus Christ. **9** [6]God is [s]faithful, by whom ye are called unto the fellowship of his son Jesus Christ our Lord. **10** [t]Now I beseech you, brethren, by the Name of our Lord Jesus Christ, that [u]ye all speak one thing, and that there be no dissensions among you: but be ye [v]knit together in one mind, and in one judgment. **11** [w]For it hath been declared unto me, my brethren, of you by them that are of the house of Chloe, that there are contentions among you. **12** Now [x]this I say, that every one of you saith, I am Paul's, and I am [7]Apollos's, and I am Cephas's and I am Christ's. **13** [y]Is Christ divided? was [z]Paul crucified for you? either were ye [aa]baptized into the name of Paul? **14** [ab]I thank God, that I baptized none of you, but [8]Crispus, and Gaius, **15** Lest any should say, that I had baptized into mine own name. **16** I baptized also the household of Stephanas: furthermore know I not, whether I baptized any other. **17** [ac]For CHRIST sent me not to baptize, but to preach the Gospel, [ad]not with [9,ae]wisdom of words, lest the [af]cross of Christ should be made of none effect. **18** For that [ag]preaching of the cross is to them that perish, foolishness: but unto us, which are saved, it is the [10,ah]power of God. **19** [ai]For it is written, [11]I will destroy the wisdom of the wise, and will cast away the understanding of the prudent. **20** Where is the wise? where is the [aj]Scribe? where is the [ak]disputer of this world? hath not God made the wisdom of

1 CORINTHIANS 1

a. 1 Cor. 1:1 The inscription of the Epistle, wherein he chiefly goeth about to procure the good will of the Corinthians towards him, yet notwithstanding so, that always he letteth them to wit, that he is the servant of God, and not of men.

b. 1 Cor. 1:1 If he be an Apostle, then he must be heard, although he sometimes reprehend them sharply, seeing he hath not his own cause in hand, but is a messenger that bringeth the commandments of Christ.

c. 1 Cor. 1:1 He joineth Sosthenes with himself, that this doctrine might be confirmed by two witnesses.

d. 1 Cor. 1:2 It is a Church of God, although it hath great faults in it, so that it obey them which admonish it.

e. 1 Cor. 1:2 A true definition of the Catholic Church, which is one.

f. 1 Cor. 1:2 The father sanctifieth us, that is to say, separateth us from the wicked, in giving us to his Son, that he may be in us, and we in him.

g. 1 Cor. 1:2 Whom God of his gracious goodness and mere love hath separated for himself: or whom God hath called to holiness: the first of these two expositions showeth from whence our sanctification cometh, and the second showeth to what end it tendeth.

h. 1 Cor. 1:2 He is said properly to call on God, who crieth unto the Lord when he is in danger, and craveth help at his hands: and by the figure Synecdoche it is taken for all the service of God: and therefore to call upon Christ's Name, is to acknowledge and take him for very God.

i. 1 Cor. 1:3 The foundation and the life of the Church, is Christ Jesus given of the Father.

j. 1 Cor. 1:4 Going about to condemn many vices, he beginneth with a true commendation of their virtues, lest he might seem after to descend to chiding being moved with malice or envy: yet so, that he referreth all to God as the author of them, and that in Christ. That the Corinthians might be more ashamed to profane and abuse the holy gifts of God.

k. 1 Cor. 1:5 He toucheth that by name, which they most abused.

l. 1 Cor. 1:5 Seeing that while we live here, we know but in part and prophesy in part, this word All must be refrained to the present state of the faithful: and by speech he meaneth not a vain kind of babbling, but the gift of holy eloquence, which the Corinthians abused.

m. 1 Cor. 1:6 He showeth that the true use of these gifts consisteth herein that the mighty power of Christ might thereby be set forth in them, that hereafter it might evidently appear how wickedly they abused them to glory and ambition.

n. 1 Cor. 1:6 By those excellent gifts of the holy Ghost.

o. 1 Cor. 1:7 He saith by the way, that there is no cause why they should please themselves so much in those gifts which they had received, seeing that those were nothing in comparison of them which are to be looked for.

p. 1 Cor. 1:7 He speaketh of the last coming of Christ.

q. 1 Cor. 1:8 He testifieth that he hopeth well of them hereafter, that they may more patiently abide his reprehension afterward. And yet together therewithall showeth, that as well the beginning as the accomplishing of our salvation is only the work of God.

r. 1 Cor. 1:8 He calleth them blameless, not whom man never found fault with, but with whom no man can justly find fault, that is to say, them which are in Christ Jesus, in whom there is no condemnation. See Luke 1:6.

s. 1 Cor. 1:9 True and constant, who doth not only call us, but giveth us the gift of perseverance also.

t. 1 Cor. 1:10 Having made an end of the preface, he cometh to the matter itself, beginning with the most grave obtestation, as though they should hear Christ himself speaking and not Paul.

u. 1 Cor. 1:10 The first part of this Epistle, wherein his purpose is to call back the Corinthians to brotherly concord, and to take away all occasion of discord. So then this first part concerneth the taking away of schisms. Now a schism is when men which otherwise agree and consent together in doctrine, do yet separate themselves one from another.

v. 1 Cor. 1:10 Knit together, as a body that consisteth of all his parts fitly knit together.

w. 1 Cor. 1:11 He beginneth his reprehension and chiding by taking away of an objection: for that be understood by good witnesses, that there were many factions among them. And therewithall he openeth the cause of dissensions, because that some did hang on one doctor, some on another, and some were so addicted to themselves, that they neglected all doctors and teachers, calling themselves the disciples of Christ only, shutting forth their teachers.

x. 1 Cor. 1:12 The matter I would say to you, is this.

y. 1 Cor. 1:13 The first reason why schisms ought to be eschewed: because Christ formeth by that means, to be divided and torn in pieces, who cannot be the head of two divers and disagreeing bodies, being himself one.

z. 1 Cor. 1:13 Another reason: Because they cannot without great injury to God so hang of men as of Christ: which thing no doubt they do, which allow whatsoever some man speaketh, even for his person's sake: as these men allowed one selfsame Gospel being uttered of one man, and did loathe it being uttered of another man. So that these factions were called by the names of their teachers. Now Paul setteth down his own name not only to grieve no man, but also to showeth it he pleadeth not his own cause.

aa. 1 Cor. 1:13 The third reason taken of the form and end of Baptism, wherein we make a promise to Christ, calling on also the Name of the Father and the holy Ghost. Therefore although a man does not fall from the doctrine of Christ, yet if he hang upon some certain teachers, and despise others, he forsaketh Christ: for if he hold Christ his only master, he would hear him, teaching by whomsoever.

ab. 1 Cor. 1:14 He protesteth that he speaketh so much the more boldly of these things, because that through God's providence he is void of all suspicion of challenging disciples unto himself, and taking them from others. Whereby we may understand that not the scholars only, but the teachers also are here reprehended, which gathered themselves flocks apart.

ac. 1 Cor. 1:17 The taking away of an objection: that he gave not himself to baptize many amongst them: not for the contempt of Baptism, but because he was chiefly occupied in delivering the doctrine, and committed them that received his doctrine to others to be baptized, whereof he had store. And so he declared sufficiently how far he was from all ambition: whereas on the other side they whom he reprehendeth, as though they gathered disciples unto themselves and not to Christ, bragged most ambitiously of numbers, which they had baptized.

ad. 1 Cor. 1:17 Now he turneth himself to the doctors themselves, which pleased themselves in brave and ambitious eloquence, to the end that they might draw more disciples after them. He confesseth plainly that he was unlike unto them, opposing gravely as it became an Apostle, his example against their perverse judgments: So that this is another place of this Epistle, touching the observing of a godly simplicity, both in words and sentences in teaching of the Gospel.

ae. 1 Cor. 1:17 With eloquence: which Paul casteth off from him not only, as not necessary, but also as flat contrary to the office of his Apostleship: and yet had Paul his kind of eloquence, but it was heavenly, not of man, and void of painted words.

af. 1 Cor. 1:17 The reason why he used not the pomp of words and painted speech: because it was God's will to bring the world to his obedience by that way, whereby the most idots amongst men might understand, that this work was done of God himself without the art of man. Therefore as salvation is set forth unto us in the Gospel by the cross of Christ, then which nothing is more contemptible, and more far from life, so God would have the manner of the preaching of the cross most different from those means, with which men do use to draw and entice others, either to hear or believe: therefore it pleased him by a certain kind of most wise folly, to triumph over the most foolish wisdom of the world, as he had said before by Isaiah: that he would. And hereby this we may gather, that both those doctors which were puffed up with ambitious eloquence, and also their hearers strayed far away from the end and mark of their vocation.

ag. 1 Cor. 1:18 The preaching of Christ crucified, or the kinds of speech which we use.

ah. 1 Cor. 1:18 It is that wherein he declareth his marvelous power in saving his elect, which would not so evidently appear, if it hanged upon any help of man: for so man might attribute that to himself, which is proper only to the cross of Christ.

ai. 1 Cor. 1:19 The Apostle proveth that this ought not only not to seem strange, seeing that it was foretold so long before, but declareth further, that God is wont to punish the pride of the world in such sort, which so pleaseth itself in its own wisdom: and therefore that that is vain, yea a thing of nothing, and such as God rejecteth as unprofitable, which they so carefully labored for, and made so great account of.

aj. 1 Cor. 1:20 Where art thou, O thou learned fellow, and thou that spendeth thy days in turning thy books?

ak. 1 Cor. 1:20 Thou that spendeth all thy time in seeking out the secret things of this world, and in expounding all hard questions: and thus triumpheth he against all the men of this world, for there was not one of them that could so much as dream upon this secret and hidden mystery.

this world foolishness? 21 [al]For seeing the [am]world by wisdom knew not God in the [an]wisdom of GOD, [ao]it pleased God by the [ap]foolishness of preaching to save them that believe: 22 [12,aq]Seeing also that the Jews require a sign, and the Grecians seek after wisdom. 23 But we preach Christ crucified: unto the Jews, even a stumbling block, and unto the Grecians, foolishness: 24 But unto them which are called, both of the Jews and Grecians, we preach Christ, the power of God, and the wisdom of God. 25 For the foolishness of God is wiser than men, and the weakness of God is stronger than men. 26 [ar]For brethren, you see your [as]calling, how that not many wise men [at]after the flesh, not many mighty, not many noble are called. 27 But God hath chosen the foolish things of the world to confound the wise, and God hath chosen the weak things of the world, to confound the mighty things, 28 And vile things of the world, and things which are despised, hath God chosen, and things which [au]are not, to bring to [av]nought things that are. 29 That no [aw]flesh should rejoice in his presence. 30 But ye are [ax]of him in Christ Jesus, [ay]who of God is made unto us wisdom and righteousness, and sanctification, and redemption. 31 That, according as it is written, [13,az]He that rejoiceth, let him rejoice in the Lord.

2

1 He setteth down a platform of his preaching, 4 which was base in respect of man's wisdom, 7, 13 but noble in respect of the spiritual power and efficacy. 14 And so concludeth that flesh and blood cannot rightly judge thereof.

1 And [a]I, brethren, when I came to you, came not with [1]excellency of words, or of wisdom, showing unto you the [b]testimony of God. 2 For I [c]esteemed not to know any thing among you, save Jesus Christ, and him crucified. 3 [2]And I was among you in [d]weakness, and in fear, and in much trembling. 4 Neither stood my word, and my preaching in the [3]enticing speech of man's wisdom, [e]but in plain [f]evidence of the Spirit and of power. 5 [g]That your faith should not be in the wisdom of men, but in the power of God. 6 [h]And we speak wisdom among them that are [i]perfect: not the wisdom of this world, neither of the [j]princes of this world, which come to nought. 7 [k]But we speak the wisdom of God in a [l]mystery, even the hid wisdom, [m]which God had determined before the world, unto our glory. 8 [n]Which none of the princes of this world hath known: for had they known it, they would not have crucified the [o]Lord of glory. 9 [p]But as it is written, [4]The things which eye hath not seen, neither ear hath heard, neither came into [q]man's heart, are, which God hath prepared for them that love him. 10 [r]But God hath revealed them unto us by his Spirit: for the spirit [s]searcheth all things, yea, the deep things of God. 11 [t]For what man knoweth the things of a man, save the [u]spirit of a man, which is in him? even so the things of God knoweth no man, but the Spirit of God. 12 Now we have receiveth not the [v]spirit of the world, but the Spirit, which is of God, [w]that we might [x]know the things that are given to us of God. 13 [y]Which things also we speak, not in the [5]words which man's wisdom teacheth, but which the holy Ghost teacheth, [z]comparing spiritual things with spiritual things. 14 [aa]But the [ab]natural man perceiveth not the things of the Spirit of God: for they are foolishness unto him, neither can he know them, because they are [ac]spiritually discerned. 15 [ad]But he that is spiritual, [ae]discerneth all things: yet [af]he himself is judged of [ag]no man. 16 [6,ah]For who hath known the mind of the Lord, that he might [ai]instruct him? But we have the [aj]mind of Christ.

---

al. 1 Cor. 1:21 He showeth that the pride of men was worthily punished of GOD, because they would not behold God, as meet was they should; in the most clear glass of the wisdom of the world, which is the workmanship of the world.

am. 1 Cor. 1:21 By the world he meaneth all men which are not born anew, but remain as they were, when they were first born.

an. 1 Cor. 1:21 In the workmanship of this world, which hath the marvelous wisdom of God engraved in it, so that every man may behold it.

ao. 1 Cor. 1:21 The goodness of God is wonderful, for while he goeth about to punish the pride of the world, he is very provident and careful, for the salvation of it, and teacheth men to become fools, that they may be wise to God.

ap. 1 Cor. 1:21 So calleth the preaching of the Gospel as the enemies supposed it: but in the mean season he taunteth them very sharply, who had rather charge God with folly, than acknowledge their own and crave pardon for it.

aq. 1 Cor. 1:22 A declaration of that which he said that the preaching of the Gospel, is foolish. It is foolish, saith he, to them whom God had not endued with new light, that is to say, to all men, being considered in themselves: for the Jews require miracles, and the Greeks arguments, which they may comprehend by their wit and wisdom: and therefore they do not only not believe the Gospel, but also they mock at it. Notwithstanding in this foolish preaching, there is the great virtue and wisdom of God, but such as those only which are called, do perceive. God showing most plainly, that even then when mad men think him most foolish, he is far wiser than they are: and that he surmounteth all their might and power, when he useth most vile and abject things, as it hath appeared in the fruit of the preaching of the Gospel.

ar. 1 Cor. 1:26 A confirmation taken of those things which came to pass at Corinth, where the Church especially consisted of the basest and common people, insomuch that the philosophers of Greece were driven to shame, when they saw that they could do nothing with their wisdom and eloquence, in comparison of the Apostles, whom notwithstanding they called idiots and unlearned. And herewithall doth he beat down their pride, for God did not prefer them before those noble and wise men because they should be proud, but that they might be constrained even whether they would or not, to rejoice in the Lord, by whose mercy, although they were, the most abject of all, they had obtained in Christ, both this wisdom, and all things necessary to salvation.

as. 1 Cor. 1:26 What way the Lord hath taken in calling you.

at. 1 Cor. 1:26 After that kind of wisdom which men make account of, as though there were none else: who because they are carnal, know not spiritual wisdom.

au. 1 Cor. 1:28 Which in man's judgment are almost nothing.

av. 1 Cor. 1:28 To show that they are vain and unprofitable, and nothing worth, see Rom. 3:31.

aw. 1 Cor. 1:29 Flesh is oft as we see, taken for the whole man: and he ruleth this word flesh, very fitly, to set the weak and miserable condition of man with the majesty of God, one against the other.

ax. 1 Cor. 1:30 Whom he cast down before, now he lifteth up, yea, higher then all men: yet so, that he showeth them all their worthiness is without themselves, that is, standeth in Christ, and that of God.

ay. 1 Cor. 1:30 He teacheth that especially and above all things, the Gospel ought not to be contemned, seeing it containeth the chiefst things that are to be desired, to wit, true wisdom, the true way to obtain righteousness, the true way to live honestly and godly, the true deliverance from all miseries and calamities.

az. 1 Cor. 1:31 Let him yield all to God and give him thanks: and so by this place is man's free will beaten down, which the Papist so dream of.

1 CORINTHIANS 1

1. Acts 15:9 / 1 Thess. 4:7
2. Rom. 1:7 / Eph. 1:1 / Col. 1:22 / 1 Tim. 1:9 / Titus 2:3
3. 2 Tim. 1:21
4. Titus 2:11 / Phil. 3:20
5. 1 Thess. 3:13 / 1 Thess. 5:23
6. 1 Thess. 5:24
7. Acts 18:24
8. Acts 18:8
9. 1 Cor. 2:13 / 2 Pet. 1:16
10. Rom. 1:16
11. Isa. 29:14
12. Matt. 12:38
13. Jer. 9:24 / 2 Cor. 10:17

1 CORINTHIANS 2

a. 1 Cor. 2:1 He returneth to 1 Cor. 1:17, that is to say, to his own example: confessing that he used not amongst them either excellency of words, or enticing speech of man's wisdom, but with great simplicity of speech, both knew and preached Jesus Christ crucified, humble and abject, as touching the flesh.

b. 1 Cor. 2:1 The Gospel.

c. 1 Cor. 2:2 I purposed not to profess any other knowledge, but the knowledge of Christ and him crucified.

d. 1 Cor. 2:3 He setteth weakness, against excellency of words, and therefore joineth with it fear and trembling, which are the companions of true modesty, not such fear and trembling as terrify the conscience, but such as are contrary to vanity and pride.

e. 1 Cor. 2:4 He turneth that now to the commendation of his ministry, which he had granted to his adversaries: for his virtue and power which they knew well enough, was so much the more excellent, because it had no worldly help joined with it.

f. 1 Cor. 2:4 By plain evidence he meaneth such a proof, as is made by certain and necessary reasons.

g. 1 Cor. 2:5 And he telleth the Corinthians, that he did it for their great profit, because they might thereby know manifestly, that the Gospel was from heaven. Therefore he privately rebuketh them, because that in seeking vain ostentation, they willingly deprived themselves of the greatest help of their faith.

h. 1 Cor. 2:6 Another argument taken of the nature of the thing, that is, of the Gospel, which is true wisdom, but known to them only which are desirous of perfection: and is unsavory to them which otherwise excel in the world, but yet vainly and frailly.

i. 1 Cor. 2:6 Those are called perfect here, not which had gotten perfection already, but such as tend to it, as Phil. 3:15, so that perfect, is set against weak.

j. 1 Cor. 2:6 They that are wiser, richer, or mightier than other men are.

k. 1 Cor. 2:7 He showeth the cause why this wisdom cannot be perceived of those excellent worldly writes: to wit, because indeed it is so deep that they cannot attain unto it.

l. 1 Cor. 2:7 Which men could not so much as dream of.

m. 1 Cor. 2:7 He taketh away an objection: if it be so hard, when and how is it known? God, saith he, determined with himself from the beginning, that which his purpose was to bring forth at this time out of his secrets for the salvation of men.

n. 1 Cor. 2:8 He taketh away another objection: why then, how cometh it to pass, that this wisdom was so rejected of men of highest authority, that they crucified Christ himself? Paul answereth: because they knew not Christ such as he was.

o. 1 Cor. 2:8 That mighty God, full of true majesty and glory: Now this place hath in it a most evident proof of the divinity of Christ, and of his joining of the two natures in one, which hath this in it, that that which is proper to the manhood alone, is vouched of the Godhead joined with the manhood: which kind of speech is called of the old fathers, a making common of things belonging to someone, with other to whom they do not belong.

p. 1 Cor. 2:9 Another objection: But how could it be that those witty men could not perceive this wisdom? Paul answereth: Because we preach those things which pass all man's understanding.

q. 1 Cor. 2:9 Man cannot so much as think of them, much less conceive them with his senses.

r. 1 Cor. 2:10 A question: if it surmount the capacity of men, how can it be understood of any man, or how can you declare and preach it? by a peculiar lightening by God's Spirit, wherewith whosoever is inspired, he can enter even to the very secrets of God.

s. 1 Cor. 2:10 There is nothing so secret and hidden in God, but the Spirit of God peereth into it.

t. 1 Cor. 2:11 He setteth that forth by a similitude, which he spake of the inspiration of the Spirit. As the force of man's wit searcheth out things pertaining to man, so doth our mind by that power of the holy Ghost, understand heavenly things.

u. 1 Cor. 2:11 The mind of man, which is endued with ableness to understand and judge.

v. 1 Cor. 2:12 The Spirit which we have received, doth not teach us things of this world, but lifteth us up to God, and this place teacheth us against the Papists, what faith is, from whence it cometh, and what force it is of.

w. 1 Cor. 2:12 That which he spake generally, he restraineth now to those things which God hath opened unto us of our salvation in Christ: lest that any man should separate the Spirit from the preaching of the word and Christ: or should think that those fantastical men are governed by the Spirit of God, which wandering besides the word, thrust upon us their vain imaginations for the secrets of God.

x. 1 Cor. 2:12 This word know is taken here in his proper sense, for true knowledge, which the Spirit of God worketh in us.

y. 1 Cor. 2:13 Now he returneth to his purpose, and concludeth the argument which he began verse 6, and it is thus: the words must be applied to the matter, and the matter must be set forth with words which are meet and convenient for it: now this wisdom is spiritual and not of man, and therefore it must be delivered by a spiritual kind of teaching, and not by enticing words of man's eloquence, that the simple, and yet wonderful majesty of the holy Ghost may therein appear.

z. 1 Cor. 2:13 Applying the words unto the matter, to wit, that as we teach spiritual things, so must our kind of teaching be spiritual.

aa. 1 Cor. 2:14 Again he preventeth an offence or stumbling block: how cometh it to pass that so few allow these things? This is not to be marveled at, sayeth the Apostle, seeing that men in their natural powers as they termed them are not endued with that faculty, whereby spiritual things are discerned which faculty cometh another way and therefore they accompt spiritual wisdom as folly: and it is as if he should say, It is no marvel that blind men cannot judge of colors, seeing that they lack the light of their eyes, and therefore light is to them as darkness.

ab. 1 Cor. 2:14 The man that hath no further light of understanding than that which he brought with him, even from his mother's womb, as Jude defineth it, Jude 19.

ac. 1 Cor. 2:14 By the virtue of the holy Ghost.

ad. 1 Cor. 2:15 He amplifieth the matter by contraries.

ae. 1 Cor. 2:15 Understandeth and discerneth.

3

1 He yieldeth a reason why he preached small matters unto them: 4 He showeth how they ought to esteem of Ministers: 6 The minister's office. 10 A true form of edifying. 16 He warneth the Corinthians, that they be not drawn away to profane things, 18 through the proud wisdom of the flesh.

1 And [a]I could not speak unto you, brethren, as unto spiritual men, but as
unto [b]carnal, even as unto babes in Christ. 2 I gave you milk to drink, and not
[c]meat: for ye were not yet [d]able to bear it, neither yet now are ye able. 3 For ye
are yet carnal: for whereas there is among you envying, and strife, and divisions, are
ye not carnal, and walk as [e]men? 4 For when one saith, I am Paul's, and another,
I am Apollos's, are ye not carnal? 5 [f]Who is Paul then? and who is Apollos, but
the ministers by whom ye believed, and as the Lord gave to every man? 6 [g]I
have planted, Apollos watered, but God gave the increase. 7 So then, neither is
he that planteth anything, neither he that watereth, but God that giveth the in-
crease. 8 And he that planteth, and he that watereth, are one, [1]and every man
shall receive his wages, according to his labor. 9 For we together are God's [h]la-
borers: ye are God's husbandry, and God's building. 10 According to the grace
of God given to me, as a skillful master builder, I have laid the foundation, and
another buildeth thereon: [i]but let every man take heed how he buildeth upon
it. 11 [j]For other foundation can no man lay, than that which is laid, which is
Jesus Christ. 12 [k]And if any man build on this foundation, gold, silver, precious
stones, timber, hay, or stubble, 13 [l]Every man's work shall be made manifest: for
the day shall declare it, because it shall be revealed by the fire: and the fire shall
try every man's work of what sort it is. 14 If any man's work, that he hath built
upon, abide, he shall receive wages. 15 If any man's work burn, he shall lose,
but [m]he shall be saved himself: nevertheless yet as it were by the fire. 16 [2,n]K-
now ye not that ye are the Temple of God, and that the Spirit of God dwelleth
in you? 17 If any man [o]destroy the Temple of God, him shall God destroy: for
the Temple of God is holy, which ye are. 18 [p]Let no man deceive himself: If
any man among you seem to be wise in this world, let him be a fool, that he may
be wise. 19 For the wisdom of this world is foolishness with God: for it is writ-
ten, [3]He [q]catcheth the wise in their own craftiness. 20 [4]And again, The Lord
knoweth that the thoughts of the wise be vain. 21 [r]Therefore let no man [s]rejoice
in men: for all things are [t]yours. 22 Whether it be Paul, or Apollos, or Cephas,
or the [u]world, or life, or death, whether they be things present, or things to come,
even all are yours, 23 And ye Christ's, and Christ God's.

4

1 Bringing in the definition of a true Apostle, 7 he showeth that humility ought rather to be an honor than a shame unto him. 9 He bringeth in proof, whereby it may evidently appear, 10 that he neither had care of glory, 11 nor of his belly. 17 He commendeth Timothy.

1 Let [a]a [b]man so think of us, as of the ministers of Christ, and disposers of
the secrets of God: 2 [c]And as for the rest, it is required of the disposers, that
every man be found faithful. 3 [d]As touching me, I pass very little to be judged
of you, [e]or of man's [f]judgment: no, [g]I judge not mine own self. 4 For I know

---

af. 1 Cor. 2:15 The wisdom of the flesh, saith Paul, determined nothing certainly, no not in its own affairs, much less can it discern strange, that is, spiritual things. But the Spirit of God, wherewith spiritual men are endued, can be deceived by no means, and therefore be reproved of no man.

ag. 1 Cor. 2:15 Of no man: for when the Prophets are judged of the Prophets, it is the Spirit that judges, and not the man.

ah. 1 Cor. 2:16 A reason of the former saying: for he is called spiritual, which hath learned that by the virtue of the Spirit, which Christ hath taught us. Now if that which we have learned of that Master, could be reproved of any man, he must needs be wiser than God: whereupon it followeth, that they are not only foolish, but also wicked, which think that they can devise something that is either more perfect, or that they can teach the wisdom of God a better way than they knew or taught, which undoubtedly, were endued with God's Spirit.

ai. 1 Cor. 2:16 Lay his head to his, and teach him what he should do.

aj. 1 Cor. 2:16 We are endued with the Spirit of Christ, who openeth unto us those secrets, which by all other means are unsearchable, and also all truth whatsoever.

1 CORINTHIANS 2

1.	1 Cor. 1:17	**4.**	Isa. 64:4
2.	Acts 18:1	**5.**	1 Cor. 1:17 / 2 Pet. 1:16
3.	1 Cor. 1:17 / 2 Pet. 1:16	**6.**	Isa. 40:13 / Rom. 11:34

1 CORINTHIANS 3

a. 1 Cor. 3:1 Having declared the worthiness of heavenly wisdom, and of the Gospel, and having generally condemned the blindness of man's mind, now at length he applieth it particularly to the Corinthians, calling them carnal, that is, such in whom as yet the flesh prevaileth against the spirit. And he bringeth a double testimony of it: first, for that he had proved them to be such, insomuch that he dealt with them no otherwise than with ignorant men, and such as are almost babes in the doctrine of godliness; and secondly, because they showed indeed by these dissensions, which sprang up by reason of the ignorance of the virtue of the Spirit, and heavenly wisdom, that they had profited very little or nothing.

b. 1 Cor. 3:1 He calleth them carnal, which are as yet ignorant, and therefore to express it the better, he termeth them babes.

c. 1 Cor. 3:2 Substantial meat, or strong meat.

d. 1 Cor. 3:2 To be fed by me with substantial meat: therefore as the Corinthians grew up in age, so the Apostle nourished them by teaching first with milk, then with strong meat, which difference was only but in the manner of teaching.

e. 1 Cor. 3:3 By the square and compass of man's wit and judgment.

f. 1 Cor. 3:5 After that he hath sufficiently reprehended ambitious teachers, and their foolish esteemers, now he showeth how the true ministers are to be esteemed, that we attribute not unto them, more or less than we ought to do. Therefore he teacheth us, that they are they by whom we are brought to faith and salvation, but yet as the ministers of God, and such as do nothing of themselves, but God so working by them as it pleaseth him to furnish them with his gifts. Therefore we have not to mark or consider what minister it is that speaketh, but what is spoken: and we must depend only upon him which speaketh by his servants.

g. 1 Cor. 3:6 He beautifieth the former sentence, with two similitudes: first comparing the company of the faithful, to a field which God maketh fruitful, when it is sowed and watered through the labor of his servants: next, by comparing it to a house, which indeed the Lord buildeth, but by the hands of his workmen, some of whom, he useth in laying the foundation, others in building of it up. Now, both these similitudes tend to this purpose, to show that all things are wholly accomplished by God's only authority and might, so that we must only have an eye to him. Moreover, although that God useth some in the better part of the work, we must not therefore contemn others, in respect of them, and much less may we divide, or set them apart, as these factious men did seeing that all of them labor in God's business, and in such sort, that they serve to finish one selfsame work, although by a divers manner of working, insomuch that they need one another's help.

h. 1 Cor. 3:9 Serving under him: Now they which serve under another, do nothing by their own strength, but as it is given them by grace, which grace maketh them fit to that service. See 1 Cor. 15:10; 2 Cor. 3:6, and all the increase that cometh by their labor, doth so proceed from God, that no part of the praise of it may be given to the under servant.

i. 1 Cor. 3:10 Now he speaketh to the teachers themselves, who succeeded him in the Church of Corinth, and in their person, to all that were after or shall be Pastors of Congregations, seeing that they succeed into the labor of the Apostles, which were planters and chief builders. Therefore he warneth them first, that they persuade not themselves that they may build after their own fantasy, that is, that they may propound and set forth anything in the Church, either in matter, or in kind of teaching, different from the Apostles which were the chief builders.

j. 1 Cor. 3:11 Moreover, he showeth what this foundation is, to wit, Christ Jesus, from which they may not turn away one iota in the building up of this building.

k. 1 Cor. 3:12 Thirdly, he showeth that they must take heed that the upper part of the building be answerable to the foundation, that is, that admonitions, exhortations, and whatsoever pertaineth to the edifying of the flock, be answerable to the doctrine of Christ, as well in matter as in form: which doctrine is compared to gold, silver, and precious stones: of which matter, Isaiah also and John in the Revelation build the heavenly city. And to these are opposite, wood, hay, stubble, that is to say, curious and vain questions or decrees: and besides to be short, all that kind of teaching which serveth to ostentation. For false doctrines, whereof he speaketh not here, are not said properly to be built upon this foundation, unless peradventure in show only.

l. 1 Cor. 3:13 He testifieth, as indeed the truth is, that all are not good builders, no not some of them which stand upon this one and only foundation: but howsoever this work of evil builders, saith he, stand for a season, yet shall it not always deceive, because that the light of the truth appearing at length, as day shall dissolve this darkness, and show what it is. And as that stuff is tried by the fire, whether it be good or not, so will God in his time by the touch of his Spirit and word, try all buildings, and so shall it come to pass, that such as be found pure and sound, shall still continue so, to the praise of the workman; but they that are otherwise, shall be consumed, and vanish away, and so shall the workman be frustrated of the hope of his labor, which pleased himself in a thing of nought.

m. 1 Cor. 3:15 He taketh not away hope of salvation from the unskillful and foolish builders, which hold fast the foundation, of which sort were those Rhetoricians rather than pastors of Corinth: but he addeth an exception, that they must notwithstanding suffer this trial of their work, and also abide the loss of their vain labors.

n. 1 Cor. 3:16 Continuing still in the metaphor of a building, he teacheth us that this ambition is not only vain, but also sacrilegious: For he saith that the Church is as it were the Temple of God, which God hath as it were consecrated unto himself by his Spirit. Then turning himself to these ambitious men: he showeth that they profane the Temple of God, because those vain arts wherein they please themselves so much, are as he teacheth, so many pollutions of the holy doctrine of God, and the purity of the Church. Which wickedness shall not be suffered unpunished.

o. 1 Cor. 3:17 Defileth it, and maketh it unclean, being holy: and surely they do defile it, by Paul's judgment, which by fleshly eloquence defile the purity of the Gospel.

p. 1 Cor. 3:18 He concludeth by the contrary, that they profess pure wisdom in the Church of God, which refuse and cast away all those vanities of men, and if they be mocked of the world, it is sufficient for them that they be wise according to the wisdom of God, and as he will have them to be wise.

q. 1 Cor. 3:19 Be they never so crafty, yet the Lord will take them when he shall discover their treachery.

r. 1 Cor. 3:21 He returneth to the proposition of verse 2, first warning the hearers, that henceforward they esteem not as lords, those whom God hath appointed to be ministers, and not lords of their salvation, which thing they do, that depend upon men, and not upon God, that speaketh by them.

s. 1 Cor. 3:21 Please himself.

t. 1 Cor. 3:21 Helps, appointeth for your benefit.

u. 1 Cor. 3:22 He passeth from the persons to the things themselves, that his argument may be more forcible, yea, he ascendeth from Christ to the Father, to show us that we rest ourselves no not in Christ himself, in that that he is man, but because he carrieth us up even to the Father, as Christ witnesseth of himself everywhere, that he was sent of his Father, that by this band we may be all knit with God himself.

1 CORINTHIANS 3

1.	Ps. 62:12 / Gal. 6:5	**3.**	Job 5:13
2.	1 Cor. 6:19 / 2 Cor. 6:16	**4.**	Ps. 44:11

1 CORINTHIANS 4

a. 1 Cor. 4:1 He concludeth the duty of the hearers towards their ministers: that they esteem them not as lords: and yet notwithstanding, that they give ear unto them, as to them that are sent from Christ, sent I say to this end and purpose, that they may receive as it were at their hands, the treasure of salvation which is drawn out of the secrets of God.

b. 1 Cor. 4:1 Every man.

c. 1 Cor. 4:2 Last of all, he warneth the ministers that they also behave themselves not as lords, but as faithful servants, because they must render an account of their stewardship unto God.

d. 1 Cor. 4:3 Because in reprehending others, he set himself for an example, he useth a preoccupation or preventing of an objection, and using the gratuity of an Apostle, he showeth that he careth not for the contrary judgments that they have of him, in that they esteemed him as a vile person, because he did not set forth himself as they did. And he bringeth good reasons why he was nothing moved with the judgments which they had of him.

e. 1 Cor. 4:3 First, because that that which men judge in these cases of their own brains, is no more to be accounted of, than when the unlearned do judge of wisdom.

f. 1 Cor. 4:3 Word for word, Day, after the manner of speech of the Cilicians.

g. 1 Cor. 4:3 Secondly, saith he, how can you judge how much or how little I am to be accounted of, seeing that I myself which know myself better than you do, and which dare profess that I have walked in my vocation with a good conscience, dare not yet notwithstanding challenge anything to myself? for I know that I am not unblameable, all this notwithstanding: much less therefore should I please myself as you do.

nothing by myself, yet am I not thereby justified: but he that judgeth me, is the [h]Lord. **5** [i]Therefore [1]judge nothing before the time, until the Lord come, who will lighten things that are hid in darkness, and make the counsels of the hearts manifest: and then shall every man have [j]praise of God. **6** [k]Now these things, brethren, I have figuratively applied unto mine own self and Apollos, for your sakes, that ye might learn [l]by us, that no man presume above that which is written, that one swell not against another for any man's cause. **7** [m]For who separateth thee? and what hast thou, that thou hast not received? if thou hast received it, why rejoicest thou, as though [n]thou hadst not received it? **8** [o]Now ye are full: now ye are made rich: ye reign as kings without us, and would to God ye did reign, that we also might reign with you. **9** For I think that God hath set forth us the last Apostles, as men appointed to death, for we are made a [p]gassing stock unto the world, and to the Angels, and to men. **10** We are fools for Christ's sake, and ye are wise in Christ: we are weak, and ye are strong: ye are honorable, and we are despised. **11** Unto this hour we both hunger, and thirst, and are naked, and are buffeted, and have no certain dwelling place, **12** [2]And labor, working with our own hands: we are reviled, and yet we bless: we are persecuted, and suffer it. **13** [3]We are evil spoken of, and we pray: we are made as the [q]filth of the world, the offscouring of all things, unto this time. **14** [r]I write not these things to shame you, but as my beloved children I admonish you. **15** For though ye have ten thousand instructors in Christ, yet have ye not many fathers: for in Christ Jesus I have begotten you through the Gospel. **16** Wherefore, I pray you, be followers of me. **17** For this cause have I sent unto you Timothy, which is my beloved son, and faithful in the Lord, which shall put you in remembrance of my [s]ways in Christ as I teach everywhere in every Church. **18** [t]Some are puffed up as though I would not come unto you. **19** But I will come to you shortly, [4]if the Lord will, and I will know, not the [u]words of them which are puffed up, but the power. **20** For the kingdom of God is not in word, but in power. **21** [v]What will ye? shall I come unto you with a rod, or in love, and in the [w]spirit of meekness?

5

1 That they have winked at him who committed incest with his mother-in-law, 2, 6 he showeth should cause them rather to be ashamed, than to rejoice: 10 Such kind of wickedness is to be punished with excommunication, 12 lest others be infected with it.

1 It [a]is heard certainly that there is fornication among you: and such fornication as is not once named among the Gentiles, that one should have his father's wife. **2** [b]And ye are puffed up, and have not rather sorrowed, that he which hath done this deed, might be put from among you. **3** [c]For I verily as absent in body, but present in [d]spirit, have determined already as though I were present, that he that hath thus done this thing, **4** When ye are gathered together, and my spirit, in the [e]Name of our Lord Jesus Christ, that such one, I say, [f]by the power of our Lord Jesus Christ, **5** [g]Be [h]delivered unto Satan, for the [i]destruction of the flesh, that the spirit may be saved in the day of the Lord Jesus. **6** [j]Your rejoicing [k]is not good: know ye not that a little leaven leaveneth the whole lump? **7** [l]Purge out therefore the old leaven, that ye may be a new [m]lump, as ye are unleavened: for Christ our [n]Passover is sacrificed for us. **8** Therefore let us keep the [o]feast, not with old leaven, neither in the leaven of maliciousness and wickedness: but with the unleavened bread of sincerity and truth. **9** [p]I wrote unto you in an Epistle, that ye should not company together with fornicators, **10** And not [q]altogether with the fornicators of this world, or with the covetous, or with extortioners, or with idolaters: for then ye must go out of the world. **11** But now I have written unto you, that ye company not together: if any that is called a brother, be a fornicator, or covetous, or an idolater, or a railer, or a drunkard, or an extortioner, with such one eat not. **12** [r]For what have I to do to judge them also which are without? do ye not judge them that are within? **13** But God judgeth them that are without. Put away therefore from among yourselves that wicked man.

6

1 He inveigheth against their contention in law matters, 6 wherewith they vexed one another under judges that were infidels, to the reproach of the Gospel, 9 and then sharply threateneth fornicators.

1 Dare [a,b]any of you, having business against another, be judged [c]under the unjust, [d]and not under the Saints? **2** [e]Do ye not know that the Saints shall judge the world? If the world then shall be judged by you, are ye unworthy to judge the smallest matters? **3** Know ye not that we shall judge the Angels? how much more things that pertain to this life? **4** [f]If then ye have [g]judgments of things pertaining to this life, set them up which are [h]least esteemed in the Church. **5** [i]I speak it to your shame. Is it so that there is not a wise man among you? no, not one, that can

---

h. 1 Cor. 4:4 I permit myself to the Lord's judgment.
i. 1 Cor. 4:5 A third reason proceeding of a conclusion as it were, out of the former reasons. It is God's office, to esteem every man according to his value, because he knoweth the secrets of the heart, which men for the most part are ignorant of. Therefore this judgment pertaineth not to you.
j. 1 Cor. 4:5 One could not be praised above the rest, but the other should be blamed: and he mentioneth praise rather than dispraise, for that the beginning of this sore was this, that they gave more to some men than meet was.
k. 1 Cor. 4:6 Having rejected their judgment, he setteth forth himself again as a singular example of modesty, as one which concealing in this Epistle those factious teacher's names, doubted not to put down his own name and Apollos' in their place, and took upon him, as it were, their shame: so far was he from preferring himself to any.
l. 1 Cor. 4:6 By our example, which chose rather to take other men's faults upon us, than to carpe any by name.
m. 1 Cor. 4:7 He showeth a good means to bridle pride: first, if thou consider how rightly thou exemptest thyself out of the number of others, seeing thou art a man thyself: again, if thou consider that although thou have something more than other men have, yet thou hast it not but by God's bountifulness. And what wise man is he that will brag of another's goodness, and that against God?
n. 1 Cor. 4:7 There is nothing then in us of nature, that is worthy of commendation: but all that we have, we have it of grace, which the Pelagians and half Pelagians will not confess.
o. 1 Cor. 4:8 He descendeth to a most grave mock, to cause these ambitious men to blush even against their wills.
p. 1 Cor. 4:9 He that will take a right view how like Paul and the Pope are, who lyingly boasteth that he is his successor, let him compare the delicates of the Popish court with Saint Paul's state, as we see it here.
q. 1 Cor. 4:13 Such as by sweeping is gathered together.
r. 1 Cor. 4:14 Moderating the sharpness of his mock, he putteth them in mind to remember of whom they were begotten in Christ, and that they should not doubt to follow him for an example, although he seem vile according to the outward show, in respect of others, yet mighty by the efficacy of God's Spirit, as they had trial thereof in themselves.
s. 1 Cor. 4:17 What way and rule I follow everywhere in teaching the Churches.
t. 1 Cor. 4:18 Last of all he descendeth also to Apostolic threatenings, but yet chiding them as a father, lest by their disorder he be constrained to come to punish some among them.
u. 1 Cor. 4:19 By words, he meaneth their painted and colored kind of eloquence, against which he setteth the virtue of the Spirit.
v. 1 Cor. 4:21 A passing over to another part of this Epistle, wherein he reprehended more sharply a very heinous offence, showing the use of ecclesiastical correction.
w. 1 Cor. 4:21 Meekly affected towards you.

1 CORINTHIANS 4

1. Matt. 7:1
2. Acts 20:34 / 1 Thess. 2:9 / 2 Thess. 3:8
3. Matt. 5:44 / Luke 23:34 / Acts 7:60
4. Acts 19:21 / James 4:15

1 CORINTHIANS 5

a. 1 Cor. 5:1 They are greatly to be reprehended which by suffering of wickedness, set forth the Church of God to be mocked and scorned as the infidels.
b. 1 Cor. 5:2 There are none more proud, than they that least know themselves.
c. 1 Cor. 5:3 Excommunication ought not to be committed to one man's power, but must be done by the authority of the whole Congregation, after that the matter is diligently examined.
d. 1 Cor. 5:3 In mind, thought, and will.
e. 1 Cor. 5:4 Calling upon Christ his Name.
f. 1 Cor. 5:4 There is no doubt but that judgment is ratified in heaven, wherein Christ himself sitteth as Judge.
g. 1 Cor. 5:5 The excommunicate is delivered to the power of Satan, in that, that he is cast out of the house of God.
h. 1 Cor. 5:5 What it is to be delivered to Satan, the Lord himself declareth when he saith, Let him be unto thee as an Heathen and Publican, Matt 18:17, that is to say, to be disfranchised, and put out of the right and liberty of the city of Christ, which is the Church, without which Satan is lord and master.
i. 1 Cor. 5:5 The end of excommunication is not to cast away the excommunicate, that he should utterly perish, but that he may be saved, to wit, that by this means his flesh may be tamed, that he may learn to live to the Spirit.
j. 1 Cor. 5:6 Another end of excommunication is, that others be not infected, and therefore it must of necessity be retained in the Church, that the one be not infected by the other.
k. 1 Cor. 5:6 Is naught, and not grounded upon good reason, as though you were excellent, and yet there is such wickedness found amongst you.
l. 1 Cor. 5:7 By alluding to the ceremony of the Passover, he exhorteth them to cast out that unclean person from amongst them. In times past, saith he, it was not lawful for them which did celebrate the Passover, to eat leavened bread: insomuch that he was holden as unclean and unworthy to eat the Passover, whosoever had but tasted of leaven. Now our whole life must be as it were the feast of unleavened bread, wherein all they that are partakers of that immaculate Lamb which is slain, must cast out both of themselves, and also out of their houses and Congregations all impurity.
m. 1 Cor. 5:7 By lump he meaneth the whole body of the Church, every member whereof must be unleavened bread, that is, be renewed in spirit, by plucking away the old corruption.
n. 1 Cor. 5:7 The Lamb of our Passover.
o. 1 Cor. 5:8 Let us lead our whole life, as it were a continual feast, honestly and uprightly.
p. 1 Cor. 5:9 Now he speaketh more generally; and that which he spake before of the incestuous person, he showeth that it pertaineth to others, which are known to be wicked, and such as through their naughty life are a slander to the Church, which ought also by lawful order be cast out of the community of the Church. And making mention of eating meat, either he meaneth those feasts of love whereat the Supper of the Lord was received, or else their common usage and manner of life which is rightly to be taken, lest any man should think that either matrimony were broken by excommunication, or such duties hindered and cut off thereby, as we owe one to another: children to their parents, subjects to their rulers, servants to their masters, and neighbor to neighbor, to win one another to God.
q. 1 Cor. 5:10 If you should utterly abstain from such men's company, you should go out of the world: therefore I speak of them which are in the very bosom of the Church, which must be called home by discipline, and not of them which are without, with whom we must labor by all means possible, to bring them to Christ.
r. 1 Cor. 5:12 Such as are false brethren, ought to be cast out of the Congregation: as for them which are without, they must be left to the judgment of God.

1 CORINTHIANS 6

a. 1 Cor. 6:1 The third question is of civil judgments: Whether it be lawful for one faithful to draw another faithful before the judgment seat of an infidel? He answereth that it is not lawful, for offense sake, for it is not evil of itself.
b. 1 Cor. 6:1 As if he said, Are ye become so impudent, that you are not ashamed to make the Gospel a laughingstock to profane men?
c. 1 Cor. 6:1 Before the unjust.
d. 1 Cor. 6:1 He addeth that he doth not forbid that one neighbor may go to law with another, if need so require, but yet under holy judges.
e. 1 Cor. 6:2 He gathereth by a comparison that the faithful cannot seek to infidels to be judged, without great injury done to the Saints, seeing that God himself will make the Saints judges of the world, and of the devils, with his Son Christ: much more ought they to judge these light and small causes: which may be by equity, and good conscience, determineth.
f. 1 Cor. 6:4 The conclusion, wherein he prescribeth a remedy for this mischief: to wit, if they end their private affairs betwixt themselves by chosen arbiters out of the Church: for which matter and purpose, the least of you, saith he, is sufficient. Therefore he condemneth not judgment seats, but showeth what is expedient for the circumstance of the time, and that without any diminishing of the right of the magistrate: for he speaketh not of judgments which are practiced between the faithful and the infidels, neither of public judgments, but of controversies which may be ended by private arbiters.
g. 1 Cor. 6:4 Courts and places of judgments.
h. 1 Cor. 6:4 Even the most abject among you.

judge between his brethren? **6** But a brother goeth to law with a brother, and that under the infidels. **7** [j]Now therefore there is altogether [k]infirmity in you, that ye go to law one with another: [1,l]why rather suffer ye not wrong? why rather sustain ye not harm? **8** [2]Nay, ye yourselves do wrong, and do harm, and that to your brethren. **9** Know ye not that the unrighteous shall not inherit the kingdom of God? [m]Be not deceived: neither fornicators, nor idolaters, nor adulterers, nor wantons, nor buggerers, **10** Nor thieves, nor covetous, nor drunkards, nor railers, nor extortioners shall inherit the kingdom of God. **11** And such were [3]some of you: but ye are washed, but ye are sanctified, but ye are justified, in the [n]Name of the Lord Jesus, and by the Spirit of our God. **12** [4,o,p]All things are lawful unto me, but all things are not profitable. I may do all things, but I will not be brought under the [q]power of any thing. **13** [r]Meats are ordained for the belly, and the belly for the meats: but God shall destroy both it, and them. Now the body is not for fornication, but for the Lord, and the Lord for the body. **14** And God hath also raised up the Lord, and [5]shall raise us up by his power. **15** [s]Know ye not, that your bodies are the members of Christ? shall I then take the members of Christ, and make them the members of an harlot? God forbid. **16** [t]Do ye not know, that he which coupleth himself with an harlot, is one body? [6]for [u]two, saith he, shall be one flesh. **17** But he that is joined unto the Lord, is one spirit. **18** [v]Flee fornication: every sin that a man doeth, is without the body: but he that commiteth fornication, sinneth against his own body. **19** [w]Know ye not, that [7]your body is the temple of the holy Ghost, which is in you, whom ye have of God? and [x]ye are not your own. **20** [8]For ye are bought for a price: therefore glorify God in your body, and in your spirit: for they are God's.

7

Entreating here of marriage, 4 which is a remedy against fornication, 10 and may not be broken, 18, 20 he willeth every man to live contented with his lot. 25 He showeth what the end of virginity should be, 35 and who ought to marry.

1 Now [a]concerning the things [b]whereof ye wrote unto me, It were [c]good for a man not to touch a woman. **2** Nevertheless, to avoid fornication, let every man have his wife, and let every woman have her own husband. **3** [1,d]Let the husband give unto the wife [e]due benevolence, and likewise also the wife unto the husband. **4** [f]The wife hath not the power of her own body, but the husband: and likewise also the husband hath not the power of his own body, but the wife. **5** Defraud not one another, [g]except it be with consent for a time, that ye may [h]give yourselves to fasting and prayer, and again come together, that Satan tempt you not for your incontinency. **6** [i]But I speak this by permission, not by commandment. **7** For I [j]would that all men were even as I myself am: but every man hath his proper gift of God, one after this manner, and another after that. **8** [k]Therefore I say unto the [l]unmarried, and unto the widows, It is good for them if they abide even as I do. **9** But if they cannot abstain, let them marry: for it is better to marry than to [m]burn. **10** [2,n]And unto the married I command, not I, but the Lord, Let not the wife depart from her husband. **11** But and if she depart, let her remain unmarried, or be reconciled unto her husband, and let not the husband put away his wife. **12** [o]But to the remnant I speak, and not the Lord, If any brother have a wife that believeth not, if she be content to dwell with him, let him not forsake her. **13** And the woman which hath an husband that believeth not, if he be content to dwell with her, let her not forsake him. **14** [p]For the unbelieving husband is [q]sanctified to the [r]wife, and the unbelieving wife is sanctified to the [s]husband, else were your children unclean: but now are they [t]holy. **15** [u]But if the unbelieving depart, let him depart: a brother or a sister is not in subjection in [v]such things: [w]but God hath called us in peace. **16** For what knowest thou, O wife, whether thou shalt save thine husband?

---

i. 1 Cor. 6:5 He applieth the general proposition to a particular, always calling them back to this, to take away from them that false opinion of their own excellency, from whence all these mischiefs sprang.

j. 1 Cor. 6:7 Now he goeth further also, and although by granting them private arbiters out of the Congregation of the faithful, he doth not simply condemn, but rather establish private judgments, so that they be exercised without offense, yet he showeth that if they were such as they ought to be, and as it were to be wished, they should not need to use that remedy neither.

k. 1 Cor. 6:7 A weakness of mind which is said to be in them that suffer themselves to be overcome of their lusts, and it is a fault that squareth greatly from temperance and moderation, so that he nippeth them which could not put up an injury done unto them.

l. 1 Cor. 6:7 This pertaineth chiefly to the other part of the reprehension, to wit, that they went to law even under infidels, whereas they should rather have suffered any loss, than to have given that offense. But yet this is generally true, that we ought rather depart from our right, than try the uttermost of the Law hastily, and upon an affection to revenge an injury. But the Corinthians cared for neither, and therefore he saith that they must repent, unless they will be shut out of the inheritance of God.

m. 1 Cor. 6:9 Now he prepareth himself to pass over to the fourth treatise of this Epistle, which concerneth matters indifferent: debating this matter first, how men may well use women or not: which question hath three branches, fornication, matrimony, and a single life. As for fornication, he utterly condemneth it. And marriage he commandeth to some, as a good and necessary remedy for them, to others he leaveth it free: And others some he dissuadeth from it, not as unlawful, but as discommodious, and that not without exception. As for singleness of life under which also I comprehend virginity he enjoineth it to no man: yet he persuadeth men unto it, but not for itself, but for another respect, neither all men nor without exception. And being about to speak against fornication, he beginneth with a general reprehension of those vices, wherewith that rich and riotous city most abounded: warning and teaching them earnestly, that repentance is unseparably joined with forgiveness of sins, and sanctification with justification.

n. 1 Cor. 6:11 In Jesus.

o. 1 Cor. 6:12 Secondly, he showeth that the Corinthians do simply offend in matters indifferent. First, because they abused them: next, because they used indifferent things, without any discretion, seeing the use of them ought to be brought to the rule of charity: and that he doth not use them aright, which immoderately abuseth them, and so becometh a slave unto them.

p. 1 Cor. 6:12 Whatever: but this general word must be restrained to things that are indifferent.

q. 1 Cor. 6:12 He is in subjection to things that are indifferent, whatsoever he be that thinketh he may not be without them, which is a flattering kind of slavery under a color of liberty, which sealeth upon such men.

r. 1 Cor. 6:13 Secondarily, because they counted many things for indifferent which were of themselves unlawful, as fornication, which they numbered amongst mere natural and lawful desires, as well as meat and drink: Therefore the Apostle showeth, that they are utterly unlike: for meats, saith he, were made for the necessary use of man's life, which is not perpetual. For both meats, and all this manner of nourishing are quickly abolished. But we must not so think of the uncleanness of fornication, for which the body is not made, but on the contrary side is ordained to pureness, as appeareth by this, that is consecrated to Christ, even as Christ also is given us of his Father, to quicken our bodies with that virtue wherewith he also rose again.

s. 1 Cor. 6:15 A declaration of the former argument by contraries, and the applying of it.

t. 1 Cor. 6:16 A proof of the same argument: a harlot and Christ are clean contrary, so are the flesh and the Spirit: therefore he that is one with an harlot which is done by carnal copulation of their bodies cannot be one with Christ, which unity is pure and spiritual.

u. 1 Cor. 6:16 Moses doth not speak these words of fornication, but of marriage: but seeing that fornication is the corrupting of marriage, and both of them is a carnal and fleshly copulation, we cannot say that the Apostle abuseth his testimony. Again, Moses hath not this word Two but it is very well expresseth both here and in Matt. 29:5, because he speaketh only but of man and wife: whereupon the opinion of them that vouch it to be lawful to have many wives, is beaten down: for he that companieth with many, is sundered as it were into many parts.

v. 1 Cor. 6:18 Another argument why fornication is to be eschewed, because it defileth the body with a peculiar kind of filthiness.

w. 1 Cor. 6:19 The third argument: Because a fornicator is sacrilegious, for that our bodies are consecrate to God.

x. 1 Cor. 6:19 The fourth argument: Because we are not our own men, to give ourselves to any other, much less to Satan and the flesh, seeing that God himself hath bought us, and that with a great price, to the end that both in body and soul, we should serve to his glory.

1 CORINTHIANS 6

1. Matt. 5:39 / Luke 6:29 / Rom. 12:19
2. 1 Thess. 4:6
3. Titus 3:3
4. 1 Cor. 10:23
5. Rom. 6:5
6. Gen. 2:24 / Matt. 19:5 / Mark 10:8 / Eph. 5:31
7. 1 Cor. 3:17 / 2 Cor. 6:16
8. 1 Cor. 7:13 / 1 Pet. 1:18

1 CORINTHIANS 7

a. 1 Cor. 7:1 He teacheth concerning marriage, that although a single life hath his commodities, which he will declare afterwards, yet that marriage is necessary for the avoiding of fornication: but so that neither one man may have many wives, or any wife many husbands.

b. 1 Cor. 7:1 Touching those matters whereof you wrote unto me.

c. 1 Cor. 7:1 Commodious, and as we say expedient. For marriage bringeth many griefs with it, and that by reason of the corruption of our first estate.

d. 1 Cor. 7:3 Secondly, he showeth that the parties married, must with singular affection entirely love one the other.

e. 1 Cor. 7:3 This word due containeth all kind of benevolence, though he speak more of one sort than of the other, in that that followeth.

f. 1 Cor. 7:4 Thirdly, he warneth them that they are each in other's power, as touching the body, so that they may not defraud one another.

g. 1 Cor. 7:5 He addeth an exception: unless the one abstain from the other by mutual consent, that they may the better give themselves to prayer, wherein notwithstanding, he warneth them to consider what is expedient, lest by this long breaking off as it were from marriage, they bestirred up to incontinency.

h. 1 Cor. 7:5 Do nothing else.

i. 1 Cor. 7:6 Fifthly, he teacheth that marriage is not simply necessary for all men, but for them which have not the gift of continency, and this gift is by a peculiar grace of God.

j. 1 Cor. 7:7 I wish.

k. 1 Cor. 7:8 Sixthly, he giveth the selfsame admonition touching the second marriage, to wit, that a single life is to be allowed, but for such as have the gift of continency: otherwise they ought to marry again, that their conscience may be at peace.

l. 1 Cor. 7:8 This whole place is flat against them which condemn second marriages.

m. 1 Cor. 7:9 So to burn with lust, that either the will yieldeth to the temptation, or else we cannot call upon God with a quiet conscience.

n. 1 Cor. 7:10 Seventhly, he forbiddeth contentions and the publishing of divorces for he speaketh not here of the fault of whoredom, which was then death even by the law of the Romans also whereby he affirmeth that the hand of marriage is not dissolved, and that from Christ's mouth.

o. 1 Cor. 7:12 Eighthly, he affirmeth that those marriages which are already contracted between a faithful and an unfaithful or infidel, are firm, so that the faithful may not forsake the unfaithful.

p. 1 Cor. 7:14 He answereth an objection: But the faithful is defiled by the society of the unfaithful. The Apostle denieth that, and proveth that the faithful man with good conscience may use the vessel of his unfaithful wife, by this that their children which are born of them, are accounted holy that is, contained within the promise for it is said to all the faithful, I will be thy God, and the God of thy seed.

q. 1 Cor. 7:14 The godliness of the wife is of more force, to cause their coupling together to be accounted holy, than the infidelity of the husband is, to profane the marriage.

r. 1 Cor. 7:14 The infidel is not sanctified or made holy in his own person, but in respect of his wife, he is sanctified to her.

s. 1 Cor. 7:14 To the faithful husband.

t. 1 Cor. 7:14 This place destroyeth the opinion of them that would not have children to be baptized, and their opinion also, that make baptism the very cause of salvation. For the children of the faithful are holy, by virtue of the covenant, even before Baptism, and baptism is added as the seal of that holiness.

u. 1 Cor. 7:15 He answereth to a question: what if the unfaithful forsake the faithful? then is the faithful free, saith he, because he is forsaken of the unfaithful.

v. 1 Cor. 7:15 When any such thing falleth out.

w. 1 Cor. 7:15 Lest any man upon pretence of this liberty should give occasion to the unfaithful to depart, he giveth to understand, that marriage contracted with an infidel, ought peaceably to be kept, that if it be possible the infidel may be won to the faith.

Or what knowest thou, O man, whether thou shalt save thy wife? **17** [x]But as God hath distributeth to every man, as the Lord [y]hath called every one, so let him walk: and so ordain I in all Churches. **18** [z]Is any man called being circumcised? let him not [aa]gather his uncircumcision: is any called uncircumcised? let him not be circumcised. **19** Circumcision is nothing, and uncircumcision is nothing, but the keeping of the commandments of God. **20** [3]Let every man abide in the same vocation wherein he was called. **21** Art thou called being a servant? [ab]care not for it: but if yet thou mayest be free, use it rather. **22** For he that is called in the [ac]Lord, being a servant, is the Lord's freeman: likewise also he that is called being free, is Christ's servant. **23** [4,ad]Ye are bought with a price: be not the servants of men. **24** [ae]Brethren, let every man, wherein he was called, therein abide with [af]God. **25** [ag]Now concerning virgins, I have no commandment of the Lord: but I give mine [ah]advise, as [ai]one that hath obtained mercy of the Lord to be faithful. **26** I suppose then [aj]this to be good for the [ak]present necessity: I mean that it is good for a man so to be. **27** Art thou bound unto a wife? seek not to be loosed: art thou loosed from a wife? seek not a wife. **28** But if thou takest a wife, thou sinnest not: and if a virgin marry, she sinneth not: nevertheless, such shall have trouble in the [al]flesh: but I [am]spare you. **29** And this I say, brethren, because the time is [an]short, hereafter that both they which have wives, be as though they had none: **30** And they that [ao]weep, as though they wept not: and they that rejoice, as though they rejoiced not: and they that buy, as though they possessed not: **31** And they that use this [ap]world, as though they used it not: for the [aq]fashion of this world goeth away. **32** And I would have you without care. The unmarried careth for things of the Lord, how he may please the Lord. **33** But he that is married, [ar]careth for the things of the world, how he may please his wife. **34** There is difference also between a virgin and a wife: the unmarried woman careth for the things of the Lord, that she may be holy, both in body and in [as]spirit: but she that is married, careth for the things of the world, how she may please her husband. **35** And this I speak for your own [at]commodity, not to tangle you in a snare, but that ye follow that which is honest, and that ye may cleave fast unto the Lord without separation. **36** [au]But if any man think that it is uncomely for his virgin, if she pass the flower of her age, and need so require, let him do what he will, he [av]sinneth not: let them be married. **37** Nevertheless, he that standeth firm in his [aw]heart, that he hath no [ax]need, but hath power over his own will, and hath so decreed in his heart, that he will keep his virgin, he doeth well. **38** So then he that giveth her to marriage, doeth well, but he that giveth her not to marriage, doeth [ay]better. **39** [az]The wife is bound by the [ba]law, as long as her husband [5]liveth: but if her husband be dead, she is at liberty to marry with whom she will, only in the [bb]Lord. **40** But she is more blessed, if she so abide in my judgment: [6]and I think that I have also the Spirit of God.

8

1 From this place unto the end of the tenth Chapter, he willeth them not to be at the Gentiles' profane banquets. 13 He restraineth the abuse of Christian liberty, 11 and showeth that knowledge must be tempered with charity.

1 And as [a]touching things sacrificed unto idols, we know that we [b]all have knowledge: knowledge [c]puffeth up, but love [d]edifieth. **2** Now, if any man think that he knoweth anything, he knoweth nothing, yet as he ought to know. **3** But if any man love God, the same is known of him. **4** [e]Concerning therefore the eating of things sacrificed unto [f]idols, we know that an idol is [g]nothing in the world, and that there is none other God but one. **5** For though there be that are called gods, whether in heaven, or in earth as there be many gods, and many lords. **6** Yet unto us there is but one God, which is that Father, [h]of whom are all things, and we [i]in him, and [1,j]one Lord Jesus Christ, [k]by whom are all things, and we by him. **7** [l]But every man hath not that knowledge: for [m]many having [n]conscience of the idol, until this hour, eat as a thing sacrificed unto the idol, and so their conscience being weak, is defiled. **8** [o]But meat maketh us not acceptable to God, for neither if we eat, have we the more: neither if we eat not, have we the

---

x. 1 Cor. 7:17 Taking occasion by that which he said of the bondage and liberty of matrimony, he digresseth to a general doctrine concerning the outward state and condition of man's life, as Circumcision and uncircumcision, servitude and liberty: warning every man generally to live with a contented mind in the Lord, what state or condition forever he be in, because that those outward things, as to be circumcised or uncircumcised, to be bond or free, are not of the substance as they term it of the kingdom of heaven.

y. 1 Cor. 7:17 Hath bound him to a certain kind of life.

z. 1 Cor. 7:18 Notwithstanding he giveth us to understand, that in these examples all are not like sort: because that circumcision is not simply of itself to be desired, but such as are bound may desire to be free. Therefore herein only they are equal, that the kingdom of God consisteth not in them, and therefore these are no hindrance to obey God.

aa. 1 Cor. 7:18 He is said to gather his uncircumcision, who by the help of a Chirurgeon recovereth an upper skin: which is done by the drawing the skin with an instrument, to make it to cover the nut. Celsus in book 7, chapter 25.

ab. 1 Cor. 7:21 As though this calling were too unworthy a calling for Christ.

ac. 1 Cor. 7:22 He that is in state of a servant, and is called to be a Christian.

ad. 1 Cor. 7:23 He showeth the reason of the unlikeness, because that he that desireth to be circumcised, maketh himself subject to man's tradition, and not to God. And this may be much more understood of superstitions, which some do foolishly accompt for things indifferent.

ae. 1 Cor. 7:24 A repetition of the general doctrine.

af. 1 Cor. 7:24 So purely and from the heart, that your doings may be approved before God.

ag. 1 Cor. 7:25 He enjoineth virginity to no man, yet he persuadeth and praiseth it for another respect, to wit, both for the necessity of the present time, because the faithful could scarce abide in any place, and use the commodities of this present life, and therefore such as were not troubled with families, might be the readier: and also for the cares of this life, which marriage draweth with it necessity, so that they cannot but have their minds distracteth: and this hath place in women especially.

ah. 1 Cor. 7:25 The circumstances considered, this I counsel you.

ai. 1 Cor. 7:25 It is I that speak this which I am minded to speak: and the truth is, I am a man, but yet worthy credit, for I have obtained of the Lord to be such an one.

aj. 1 Cor. 7:26 To remain a virgin.

ak. 1 Cor. 7:26 For the necessity which the Saints are daily subject unto, who are continually tossed up and down, so that their estate may seem most unfit for marriage, were it not that the weakness of the flesh enforced them to it.

al. 1 Cor. 7:28 By the flesh he understandeth what things forever belong to this present life, for marriage bringeth with it many discommodities: so that he bendeth more to a sole life, not because it is a service more agreeable to God than marriage is, but for those discommodities, which if it were possible he would wish all men to be void of, that they might give themselves to God only.

am. 1 Cor. 7:28 I would your weakness were provided for.

an. 1 Cor. 7:29 For we are now in the latter end of the world.

ao. 1 Cor. 7:30 By weeping, the Hebrews understand all adversity, and be joy, all prosperity.

ap. 1 Cor. 7:31 Those things which God giveth us here.

aq. 1 Cor. 7:31 The guise, the shape, and fashion: whereby he showeth us, that there is nothing in this world that continueth.

ar. 1 Cor. 7:33 They that are married, have their wits drawn hither and thither, and therefore if any man have the gift of continency, it is more commodious for him to live alone: but they that are married may care for the things of the Lord also, Clement, Strom. 3.

as. 1 Cor. 7:34 Mind.

at. 1 Cor. 7:35 He meaneth that he will enforce no man either to marry or not to marry, but to show them barely what kind of life is most commodious.

au. 1 Cor. 7:36 Now he turneth himself to the Parents, in whose power and authority their children are, warning them that according to the former doctrine they consider what is meet and convenient for their children, that they neither deprive them of the necessary remedy against incontinency, nor constrain them to marriage, whereas neither their will doth lead them, nor any necessity urgeth them. And again he praiseth virginity, but of itself, and not in all.

av. 1 Cor. 7:36 He doeth well: for so he expoundeth it verse 38.

aw. 1 Cor. 7:37 Resolved with himself.

ax. 1 Cor. 7:37 That the weakness of his daughter enforceth him not, or any other matter, that that he may safely keep her a virgin still.

ay. 1 Cor. 7:38 Provideth more commodiously for his children, and that not simply, but by reason of such conditions as are before mentioned.

az. 1 Cor. 7:39 That which he spake of a widower, he speaketh now of a widow, to wit, that she may marry again, so that she do it in the fear of God: and yet he dissembleth not, but saith, that if she remain still a widow, she shall be void of many cares.

ba. 1 Cor. 7:39 By the law of marriage.

bb. 1 Cor. 7:39 Religiously, and in the fear of God.

1 CORINTHIANS 7

1. 1 Pet. 3:7
2. Matt. 5:32 / Matt. 19:9 / Mark 10:11-12 / Luke 16:18
3. 1 Tim. 6:1
4. 1 Cor. 6:20 / 1 Pet. 18:19
5. Rom. 7:1
6. 1 Thess. 4:8

1 CORINTHIANS 8

a. 1 Cor. 8:1 He entereth to entreat of another kind of things indifferent, to wit, of things offered to idols, or the use or flesh so offered and sacrificed. And first of all he removeth all those things which the Corinthians pretended in using things offered to idols without any respect. First of all they affirmed that this difference of meats was for unskillful men, but as for them, they knew well enough the benefit of Christ, which causeth all these things to be clean to them that are clean. Be it so saith Paul: be it that we are all sufficiently instructed in the knowledge of Christ. I say notwithstanding that we must not simply rest in this knowledge. The reason is that unless our knowledge be tempered with charity, it doth not only not avail, but also doeth much hurt, because it is the mystery of pride: nay, it doth not so much as discern the name of godly knowledge, if it be separate from the love of God and therefore from the love of our neighbor.

b. 1 Cor. 8:1 This general word is to be abridged as appeareth verse 7, for there is a kind of taunt in it, as we may perceive by the next verse.

c. 1 Cor. 8:1 Ministereth occasion of vanity and pride, because it is void of charity.

d. 1 Cor. 8:1 Instructed our neighbor.

e. 1 Cor. 8:4 The application of that answer to things offered to idols: I grant, saith he that an idol is indeed a vain imagination, and that there is but one God and Lord, herefore that meat cannot be made holy or profane by the idol: but it followeth not therefore that a man may without respect use those meats as any other.

f. 1 Cor. 8:4 This word idol in this place is taken for an image which is made to present some godhead, that worship might be given unto it: whereupon came the word idolatry that is to say, Image service.

g. 1 Cor. 8:4 It is a vain dream.

h. 1 Cor. 8:6 When the Father is distinguished from the Son, He is named the beginning of all things.

i. 1 Cor. 8:6 We have our being in him.

j. 1 Cor. 8:6 But as the Father is called Lord, so is the Son, God therefore this word One doth not respect the persons, but the natures.

k. 1 Cor. 8:6 This word By doth not signify the instrumental cause, but the efficient: For the Father and the Son work together, which is not so to be taken, that we make two causes, seeing they have both but one nature though they be distinct persons.

l. 1 Cor. 8:7 The reason why that followeth not, is this: because there are many men which do not know that which you know. Now the judgments of outward things depend not only upon your conscience, but upon the conscience of them that behold you, and therefore your actions must be applied not only to your knowledge, but also to the ignorance of your brethren.

m. 1 Cor. 8:7 An applying of the reason, There are many which cannot eat of things offered to idols, but with a wavering conscience, because they think them to be unclean: therefore if by thy example they enterprise to do that which inwardly they thinketh displeaseth God, their conscience is defiled with this eating, and thou hast been the occasion of this mischief.

n. 1 Cor. 8:7 By conscience of the idol, he meaneth the secret judgment that they had within themselves,whereby they thought all things unclean, that were offered to idols, and therefore they could not use them with good conscience. For this force hath conscience, that if it be good, it maketh things indifferent good, and if it be evil, it maketh them evil.

o. 1 Cor. 8:8 A preventing of an objection: Why then, shall we therefore be deprived of our liberty? Nay saith the Apostle, you shall lose no part of Christianity although you abstain for your brethren's sake, as also if you receive the meat, it maketh you no whit the more holy, for our commendation before God consisteth not in meats: but to use our liberty with offense of our brethren, is an abuse of liberty, the true use whereof is clean contrary, to wit, so to use it, as in using of it we have consideration of our weak brethren.

p. 1 Cor. 8:10 Another plainer explication of the same reason, propounding the example of the sitting down at the table in the idol's temple, which thing the Corinthians did evil accompt of among things indifferent, because it is simply less. **9** But take heed lest by any means this power of yours be an occasion of falling, to them that are weak. **10** [p]For if any man see thee which hast knowledge, sit at table in the idols' temple, shall not the conscience of him which is weak, be boldened, to eat those things which are sacrificed to idols? **11** [q]And through thy knowledge shall the [2]weak brother perish, for whom Christ died. **12** [r]Now when ye sin so against the brethren, and wound their weak conscience, ye sin against Christ. **13** [3,s]Wherefore if meat offend my brother, I will eat no flesh while the world standeth, that I may not offend my brother.

9

1 He declareth, that from the liberty which the Lord gave him, 15 he willingly abstained, 18, 22 lest in things indifferent he should offend any. 24 He showeth that our life is like unto a race.

1 Am [a]I not an Apostle? am I not free? [b]have I not seen Jesus Christ our Lord? are ye not my work [c]in the Lord? **2** If I be not an Apostle unto others, yet doubtless I am unto you: for ye are the [d]seal of mine Apostleship in the Lord. **3** [e]My defense to him that [f]examine me, is this, **4** [g]Have we not power to [h]eat and to drink? **5** Or have we not power to lead about a wife being a [i]sister, as well as the rest of the Apostles, and as the brethren of the Lord, and Cephas? **6** Or I only and Barnabas, have not we power [j]not to work? **7** [k]Who [l]goeth a warfare any time at his own cost? who planteth a vineyard, and eateth not of the fruit thereof? or who feedeth a flock, and eateth not of the milk of the flock? **8** [m]Say I these things [n]according to man? saith not the Law the same also? **9** For it is written in the Law of Moses, [1]Thou shalt not muzzle the mouth of the ox that treadeth out the corn: doth God take care for [o]oxen? **10** Either saith he it not altogether for our sakes? For our sakes no doubt it is written, that he which eareth, should ear in hope, and that he that thresheth in hope, should be partaker of his hope. **11** [2,p]If we have sown unto you spiritual things, is it a great thing if we reap your carnal things? **12** [q]If others with you be partakers of this [r]power, are not we rather? nevertheless, we have not used this power: but suffer all things, that we should not hinder the Gospel of Christ. **13** [s]Do ye not know, that they which minister about the [3]holy things, eat of the [t]things of the Temple? and they which wait at the altar, are [u]partakers with the altar? **14** So also hath the Lord ordained, that they which preach the Gospel, should live [v]of the Gospel. **15** But I have used none of these things: [w]neither wrote I these things, that it should be so done unto me: for it were better for me to die, than that any man should make my rejoicing vain. **16** For though I preach the Gospel, I have nothing to rejoice of: for necessity is laid upon me, and woe is unto me, if I preach not the Gospel. **17** For if I do it willingly, I have a reward, but if I do it against my will, notwithstanding the dispensation is committed unto me. **18** What is my reward then? verily that when I preach the Gospel, I make the Gospel of Christ [x]free, that I abuse not mine authority in the Gospel. **19** For though I be free from all men, yet have I made myself servant unto all men, that I may win the more. **20** [4]And unto the Jews, I become as a Jew, that I may win the Jews: to them that are under the [y]Law, as though I were under the Law, that I may win them that are under the Law: **21** To them that are without Law, as though I were without Law, when I am not without Law as pertaining to God, but am in the Law through Christ that I may win them that are without Law: **22** To the weak I become as weak, that I may win the weak: I am made all things to [z]all men, that I might by all means save some. **23** And this I do for the Gospel's sake, that I might be partaker thereof with [aa]you. **24** [ab]Know ye not, that they which run in a race, run all, yet one receiveth the prize? so run that ye may obtain. **25** And every man that proveth masteries, [ac]abstaineth from all things: and they do it to obtain a corruptible crown: but we for an incorruptible. **26** I therefore so run, not as uncertainly: so fight I, not as one that beateth the air. **27** But I beat down my [ad]body, and bring it into subjection, lest by any means after that I have preached to others, I myself should be [ae]reproved.

10

1 If God spared not the Jews, neither will he spare those who are of like condition, 3, 4 touching the outward signs of his grace. 14 That it is absurd, that such should be partakers of the table of the devils, who are partakers of the Lord's Supper. 24 To have consideration of our neighbor in things indifferent.

1 Moreover, [a]brethren, I would not that ye should be ignorant, that all our [b]fathers were under [1]that cloud, and all passed through that [2]sea, **2** [c]And were all

---

forbidden for the circumstance of the place, although offense do cease, as it shall be declared in his place.

q. 1 Cor. 8:11 An amplification of the argument taken both of comparison and contraries: Thou wretched man, saith he, pleasing thyself with thy knowledge which indeed is none for if thou haddest true knowledge, thou wouldest not sit down to meat in idol's temple wilt thou destroy thy brother, hardening his weak conscience by this example to do evil, for whose salvation Christ himself has died?

r. 1 Cor. 8:12 Another amplification: Such offending of our weak brethren redoundeth unto Christ, and therefore let not these men think that they have to do only with their brethren.

s. 1 Cor. 8:13 The conclusion, which Paul conceiveth in his own person, that he might not seem to exact that of others, which he will not be first subject unto himself. I had rather saith he abstain forever from all kind of flesh, than give occasion of sin to any of my brethren, much less would I refuse in any certain place or time for my brother's sake not to eat flesh offered to idols.

1 CORINTHIANS 8

1. John 13:13 / 1 Cor. 12:3 **3.** Rom. 14:21
2. Rom. 14:15

1 CORINTHIANS 9

a. 1 Cor. 9:1 Before he proceedeth any further in his proposed manner of things offered to idols he would show the cause of all this mischief, and also take it away: to wit, that the Corinthians thought themselves not bound to depart from an iota of their liberty for any man's pleasure. Therefore he propoundeth himself for an example and that in a matter almost necessary. And yet he speaketh generally of both, but first of his own person. If saith he you allege for yourselves that you are free, and therefore will use your liberty, am I not also free, seeing I am an Apostle?

b. 1 Cor. 9:1 He proveth his Apostleship by the effects, in that that he was appointed of Christ himself, and the authority of his function was sufficiently confirmed to him amongst them by their conversion. And all these things he setteth before their eyes, to make them ashamed for that they would not in the least wise that might be, debase themselves, for the weak's sake, whereas the Apostle himself did all that he could to win them to God when they were utterly reprobate and without God.

c. 1 Cor. 9:1 By the Lord.

d. 1 Cor. 9:2 As a seal whereby it appeareth sufficiently that God is the author of my Apostleship.

e. 1 Cor. 9:3 He addeth this by the way, as if he would say, So far it is off, that you may doubt of my Apostleship, that I use it to refute them which call it into controversy, by opposing those things which the Lord hath done by me amongst you.

f. 1 Cor. 9:3 Which like Judges examine me and my doings.

g. 1 Cor. 9:4 Now touching the matter itself, he saith, Seeing that I am free, and truly an Apostle, why may not I I say not, eat of all things offered to idols but be maintained by my labors, yea and keep my wife also, as the residue of the apostles lawfully do, as by name, John and James, the Lord's cousins, and Peter himself?

h. 1 Cor. 9:4 Upon the expense of the Church?

i. 1 Cor. 9:5 One that is a Christian and a true believer?

j. 1 Cor. 9:6 Not to live by the work of our hands?

k. 1 Cor. 9:7 That he may not seem to burden the Apostles, he showeth that it is just that they do, by an argument of comparison, seeing that soldiers live by their wages, and husbandmen by the fruits of their labors, and shepherds by that that cometh of their flocks.

l. 1 Cor. 9:7 Useth to go a warfare?

m. 1 Cor. 9:8 Secondly he bringeth forth the authority of God's institution by an argument of comparison.

n. 1 Cor. 9:8 Have I no better ground than the common custom of men?

o. 1 Cor. 9:9 Was it God's proper drift to provide for oxen, when he made this Law? for otherwise there is not the smallest thing in the world, but God hath a care of it.

p. 1 Cor. 9:11 An assumption of the arguments with an amplification, for neither in so doing do we require a reward meet for our deserts.

q. 1 Cor. 9:12 Another argument of great force: others are nourished amongst you, therefore it was lawful for me, yea rather for me than any other: and yet I refused it, and had rather still suffer any discommodity, than the Gospel of Christ should be hindered.

r. 1 Cor. 9:12 The word signifieth a right and interest, whereby he giveth us to understand that the ministers of the word must of right and duty be found of the Church.

s. 1 Cor. 9:13 Last of all he bringeth forth the express Law concerning the nourishing of the Levites, which privilege notwithstanding he will not use.

t. 1 Cor. 9:13 This is spoken by the figure Metonymy, for, of those things that are offered in the temple.

u. 1 Cor. 9:13 Are partakers with the altar in dividing the sacrifice.

v. 1 Cor. 9:14 Because they preach the Gospel. It followed by this place, that Paul gat no living, neither would have any other man get, by any commodity of masses, or any other such superstitious trumperies.

w. 1 Cor. 9:15 He taketh away occasion of suspicion by the way, that it might not be thought that he wrote this as though he challenged his wages that was not paid him. Nay saith him, I had rather die, than not continue in this purpose to preach the Gospel freely. For I am bound to preach the Gospel, seeing that the Lord hath enjoined me this office: but unless I do it willingly and for the love of God, nothing is to be allowed that I do. If I had rather that the Gospel should be evil spoken of, than that I should not require my wages, then would it appear that I took these pains not so much for the Gospel's sake, as for my gains and advantages. But I say, this were not to use, but abuse my right and liberty. Therefore not only in this thing, but also in all others as much as I could I am made all things to all men, that I might win them to Christ, and might together with them be won to Christ.

x. 1 Cor. 9:18 By taking nothing of them to whom I preach it.

y. 1 Cor. 9:20 The word Law in this place, must be restrained to the ceremonial Law.

z. 1 Cor. 9:22 In matters that are indifferent, which may be done or not done with a good conscience: as if he said, I changed myself into all fashions, that by all means, I might save some.

aa. 1 Cor. 9:23 That both I and they to whom I preach the Gospel, may receive fruit by the Gospel.

ab. 1 Cor. 9:24 He bringeth in another cause of this mischief, to wit, that they were given to gluttony, for there were solemn banquets of sacrifices, and the riot of the Priests was always too much celebrated and kept. Therefore it was hard for them which were accustomed to righteousness, especially when they pretended the liberty of the Gospel, to be restrained from these banquets: but contrarywise, the Apostle calleth them by a pleasant similitude, and also by his own example, to sobriety and mortification of the flesh, showing that they cannot be fit to run or wrestle as then the games of Isthmians were which pamper up their bodies, and therefore affirming that they can have no reward, unless they take another course and trade of life.

ac. 1 Cor. 9:25 Useth a most exquisite diet.

ad. 1 Cor. 9:27 The old man which striveth against the spirit.

ae. 1 Cor. 9:27 This word Reproved is not set as contrary to the word Elect but as contrary to the word Approved when we see one by experience not to be such an one as he ought to be.

1 CORINTHIANS 9

1. Deut. 25:4 / 1 Tim. 5:18 **3.** Deut. 18:1
2. Rom. 15:27 **4.** Acts 16:3 / Gal. 2:3

1 CORINTHIANS 10

a. 1 Cor. 10:1 He setteth out that which he said, laying before them an example of the horrible judgment of God against them which had in effect the selfsame pledges, of the same adoption and salvation that we have: and yet notwithstanding when they gave themselves to idols' feasts, perished in the wilderness, being horribly and manifoldly punished. Now, moreover and besides that these things are fitly spoken against them which frequented idols' feasts, the same also seems to be alleged to this end and purpose, because many men are thus minded, that those things are not of such great weight, that God will be angry with them if they use them, so that they frequent Christian assemblies and be baptized, and receive the Communion, and confess Christ.

b. 1 Cor. 10:1 Paul speaketh thus in respect of the covenant, and not in respect of the persons, saving in general.

c. 1 Cor. 10:2 In effect the Sacrament of the old fathers were all one with ours, for they respected Christ only who offered himself unto them in divers shadows.

[d]baptized unto [e]Moses, in that cloud, and in that sea, **3** [3]And did all eat the [f]sa-
me spiritual [g]meat, **4** [4]And did all drink the same spiritual drink for they drank
of the spiritual Rock that [h]followed them: and the Rock was [i]Christ. **5** But
with many of them God was not pleased: for they were [5]overthrown in the wil-
derness. **6** [j]Now these things are our [k]examples, to the intent that we should
not lust after evil things [6]as they also lusted. **7** Neither be ye idolaters as were
some of them, as it is written, [7]The people sat down to eat and drink, and rose
up to play. **8** Neither let us commit fornication, as some of them committed
fornication, and fell in one [8]day three and twenty thousand. **9** Neither let us
tempt [l]Christ, as some of them also tempted him, and [9]were destroyed of ser-
pents. **10** Neither murmur ye, as some of them [10]also murmured, and were
destroyed of the destroyer. **11** Now all these things came unto them for exam-
ples, and were written to admonish us, upon whom the [m]ends of the world are
come. **12** [n]Wherefore, let him that thinketh he standeth, take heed lest he
fall. **13** There hath no temptation taken you, but such as appertaineth to [o]man:
and God is faithful, which will not suffer you to be tempted above that you be
able, but will even [p]give the issue with the temptation, that ye may be able to bear
it. **14** Wherefore my beloved, flee from idolatry. **15** [q]I speak as unto them
which have understanding: judge ye what I say. **16** The cup of [r]blessing which
we bless, is it not the [s]communion of the blood of Christ? The bread which we
break, is it not the communion of the body of Christ? **17** For we that are many,
are one bread and one body, because we all are partakers of one bread. **18** Behold
Israel, which is after the [t]flesh: are not they which eat of the sacrifices [u]partakers
of the Altar? **19** What say I then? that the idol is anything? or that that which
is sacrificed to idols, is anything? **20** Nay, but that the things which the Gen-
tiles sacrifice, they sacrifice to devils, and not unto God: and I would not that ye
should have [v]fellowship with the devils. **21** Ye cannot drink the cup of the Lord,
and the [w]cup of the devils. Ye cannot be partakers of the Lord's table, and of the
table of the devils. **22** Do we provoke the Lord to anger? are we stronger than
he? **23** [11,x,y]All things are lawful for me, but all things are not expedient: all
things are lawful for me, but all things edify not. **24** Let no man seek his own,
but every man another's wealth. **25** [z]Whatsoever is sold in the [aa]shambles, eat
ye, and ask no question for conscience sake. **26** [12]For the earth is the Lord's, and
[ab]all that therein is. **27** If any of them which believe not, call you to a feast, and
if ye will go, whatsoever is set before you, eat, asking no question for conscience
sake. **28** But if any man say unto you, This is sacrificed unto idols, eat it not,
because of him that showed it, and for the conscience for the earth is the Lord's,
and all that therein is. **29** And the conscience, I say, not thine, but of that other:
[ac]for why should my liberty be condemned of another man's conscience? **30** For
if I through God's [ad]benefit be partaker, why am I evil spoken of, for that where-
fore I give thanks? **31** [13,ae]Whether therefore ye eat, or drink, or whatsoever ye
do, do all to the glory of God. **32** Give none offence, neither to the Jews, nor to
the Grecians, nor to the Church of God: **33** Even as I please all men in all thin-
gs, not seeking mine own profit, but the profit of many, that they might be saved.

11

1 He blameth the Corinthians for that in their holy assemblies, 4 men do pray having their heads covered, 6 and women bareheaded: and because their meetings tended to evil, 21 who mingled profane banquets with the holy Supper of the Lord, 23 which he required to be celebrated according to Christ's institution.

1 Be [1]ye followers of me, even as I am of Christ: **2** [a]Now brethren, I com-
mend you, that ye remember all my things, and keep the ordinances, as I de-
livered them to you. **3** [b]But I will that ye know, that Christ is the [2]head of
every man: and the man is the woman's head: and God is [c]Christ's head. **4** [d]E-
very [e]man praying or prophesying having anything on his head, dishonoreth his
head. **5** [f]But every woman that prayeth or prophesieth bareheaded, dishonoreth
her head: [g]for it is even one very thing, as though she were shaven. **6** Therefore if
the woman be not covered, let her also be shorn: and if it be shame for a woman to
be shorn or shaven, let her be covered. **7** [h]For a man ought not to cover his head:
forasmuch as he is the [3]image and glory of God: but the woman is the glory of the
man. **8** [i]For the man is not of the woman, but the woman of the man. **9** [4,j]For
the man was not created for the woman's sake: but the woman for the man's
sake. **10** [k]Therefore ought the woman to have [l]power on her head, because of

---

d. 1 Cor. 10:2 All of them were baptized with the outward sign, but not in deed, wherewith God cannot be charged, but they themselves.

e. 1 Cor. 10:2 Moses being their guide.

f. 1 Cor. 10:3 The same that we do.

g. 1 Cor. 10:3 Manna, which was a spiritual meat to the believers, which in faith lay hold upon Christ who is the true meat.

h. 1 Cor. 10:4 Of the river and running Rock, which followed the people.

i. 1 Cor. 10:4 Did sacramentally signify Christ, so that together with the sign, there was the thing signified, and the truth itself: for God doth not offer a bare sign, but the thing signifieth by the sign, together with it which is to be received with faith.

j. 1 Cor. 10:6 An amplifying of the example against them which are carried away with their lusts beyond the bounds which God has measured out. For this is the beginning of all evil, as of idolatry which hath gluttony a companion unto it fornication, rebelling against Christ, murmuring, and such like, which God punished most sharply in that old people, to the end that we which succeed them, and have a more full declaration of the will of God, might by that means take better heed.

k. 1 Cor. 10:6 Some read figures: which signified our sacraments: for circumcision was to the Jews a seal of righteousness, and to us a lively pattern of Baptism, and so in the other Sacraments.

l. 1 Cor. 10:9 To tempt Christ, is to provoke him to a combat as it were which those men do, who abuse the knowledge that he hath given them, and make it to serve for a cloak for their lusts and wickedness.

m. 1 Cor. 10:11 This our age is called the end, for it is the shutting up of all ages.

n. 1 Cor. 10:12 In conclusion, he descendeth to the Corinthians themselves, warning them that they please not themselves, but rather that they prevent the subtleties of Satan. Yet he useth an insinuation, and comforteth them, that he may not seem to make them altogether like to those wicked idolaters and contemners of Christ, which perished in the wilderness.

o. 1 Cor. 10:13 Which cometh of weakness.

p. 1 Cor. 10:13 He that would have you tempted for your profit's sake, will give you an issue to escape out of the temptation.

q. 1 Cor. 10:15 Now returning to those idols' feasts, that he may not seem to dally at all, first he promiseth that he will use no other reasons than such as they knew very well themselves. And he useth an induction borrowed of the agreement that is the things themselves. The holy banquets of the Christians are pledges, first of all of the community that they have with Christ, and next, one with another. The Israelites also do ratify in the sacrifices, their mutual conjunction in one selfsame religion: therefore so do the idolaters also join themselves with their idols or devils rather for idols are nothing in those solemn banquets, whereupon it followeth, that that table is a table of devils, and therefore you must eschew it: for you cannot be partakers of the Lord and of idols together, much less may such banquets be accounted for things indifferent. Will ye then strive with God? and if you do, think you that you shall get the upper hand?

r. 1 Cor. 10:16 Of thanksgiving: whereupon, that holy banquet was called Eucharist, that is, a thanksgiving.

s. 1 Cor. 10:16 A most effectual pledge and note of our knitting together with Christ, and ingrafting to him.

t. 1 Cor. 10:18 That is, as yet observe their ceremonies.

u. 1 Cor. 10:18 Are consenting and guilty, both of that worship and sacrifice.

v. 1 Cor. 10:20 Have anything to do with the devils, or enter into that society which is begun on the devil's name.

w. 1 Cor. 10:21 The heathen and profane people were wont to shut up and make an end of their feasts which they kept to the honor of their gods, in offering meat offerings and drink offerings to them, with banquets and feastings.

x. 1 Cor. 10:23 Coming to another kind of things offered to idols, he repeateth that general rule, that in the use of things indifferent we ought to have consideration not of ourselves only, but of our neighbors, and therefore these are many things which of themselves are lawful, which may be evil done of us, because of offense to our neighbor.

y. 1 Cor. 10:23 See 1 Cor. 6:13.

z. 1 Cor. 10:25 An applying of the rule to the present matter: Whatsoever is sold in the shambles, you may indifferently buy it as it were at the Lord's hand, and eat it either at home with the faithful, or being called home to the unfaithful, to wit, in a private banquet: but yet with this exception, unless any man is present which is weak, whose conscience may be offended, by setting meats offered to idols before them: for then you ought to have consideration of their weakness.

aa. 1 Cor. 10:25 The flesh that was sacrificed, was used to be sold in the shambles, and the price returned to the priests.

ab. 1 Cor. 10:26 All those things whereof it is full.

ac. 1 Cor. 10:29 A reason: for we must take heed that our liberty be not evil spoken of, and that the benefit of God which we ought to use with thanksgiving be not changed into impiety, and that through our fault, if we choose rather to offend the conscience of the weak, than to yield a little of our liberty in a matter of no importance, and so give occasion to the weak to judge in such sort of us, and of Christian liberty. And the Apostle taketh these things upon his own person, that the Corinthians may have so much the less occasion to oppose anything against him.

ad. 1 Cor. 10:30 If I may through God's benefits eat this meat, or that meat, why should I through my fault, cause that benefit of God to turn to my blame?

ae. 1 Cor. 10:31 The conclusion: We must order our lives in such sort, that we seek not ourselves, but God's glory, and so the salvation of as many as we may, wherein the Apostle flicketh not to propound himself to the Corinthians even his own flock as an example, but so that he calleth them back to Christ, unto whom he himself hath regard.

1 CORINTHIANS 10

1. Exod. 13:21 / Num. 9:19
2. Exod. 14:22
3. Exod. 16:15
4. Exod. 17:6 / Num. 20:19 / Num. 21:16
5. Num. 26:65
6. Num. 11:4 / Num. 26:64 / Ps. 106:14
7. Exod. 32:6
8. Num. 25:9
9. Num. 21:6 / Ps. 106:14
10. Num. 14:37 / Judg. 3:24
11. 1 Cor. 6:12
12. Ps. 24:1
13. Col. 3:17

1 CORINTHIANS 11

a. 1 Cor. 11:2 The fifth treatise of this epistle concerning the right ordering of public assemblies, containing three points, to wit, of the comely apparel of men and women, of the order of the Lord's supper, and of the right use of spiritual gifts. But going about to reprehend certain things, he beginneth notwithstanding with a general praise of them, calling those particular laws of comeliness and honesty, which belong to the ecclesiastical policy, traditions: which afterward they called Canons.

b. 1 Cor. 11:3 He setteth down God, in Christ our mediator, for the end and mark not only of doctrine, but also of ecclesiastical comeliness. Then applying it to the question proposed, touching the comely apparel both of men and women in public assemblies, he declareth that the woman is one degree beneath the man by the ordinance of God, and that the man is so subject to Christ, that the glory of God ought to appear in him for the preeminence of the sex.

c. 1 Cor. 11:3 In that, that Christ is our mediator.

d. 1 Cor. 11:4 Hereof he gathereth that if men do either pray or preach in public assemblies having their heads covered which was then a sign of subjection they did as it were spoil themselves of their dignity, against God's ordinance.

e. 1 Cor. 11:4 It appeareth that this was a political law serving only for the circumstances of the time that Paul lived in, by this reason, because in these our days for a man to speak bareheaded in an assembly, is a sign of subjection.

f. 1 Cor. 11:5 And in like sort he concludeth, that women which show themselves in public and ecclesiastical assemblies without the sign and token of their subjection, that is to say, uncovered, shame themselves.

g. 1 Cor. 11:5 The first argument taken from the common sense of man, forsomuch as nature teacheth women, that it is dishonest for them to come abroad bareheaded, seeing that she hath given them thick and long hair, which they do so diligently trim and deck, that they can in no wise abide to have it shaven.

h. 1 Cor. 11:7 The taking away of an objection: Have not men also hair given to them? I grant, saith the Apostle, but there is another matter in it: For man was made to this end and purpose, that the glory of God should appear in his rule and authority: but the woman was made, that by profession of her obedience, she might more honor her husband.

i. 1 Cor. 11:8 He proveth the inequality of the woman, by that, that the man is the matter whereof woman was first made.

j. 1 Cor. 11:9 Secondly, by that, that the woman was made for man, and not the man for the woman's sake.

k. 1 Cor. 11:10 The conclusion: Women must be covered, to show by this external sign their subjection.

l. 1 Cor. 11:10 A covering which is a token of subjection.

the [m]Angels. **11** [n]Nevertheless, neither is the man without the woman, neither
the woman without the man [o]in the Lord. **12** For as the woman is of the man,
so is the man also by the woman: but all things are of God. **13** [p]Judge in your-
selves, Is it comely that a woman pray unto God uncovered? **14** Doth not nature
itself teach you, that if a man have long hair, it is a shame unto him? **15** But if a
woman have long hair, it is a praise unto her: for her hair is given her for a [q]cove-
ring. **16** [r]But if any man list to be contentious, we have no such custom, neither
the Churches of God. **17** [s]Now in this that I declare, I praise you not, that ye
come together, not with profit, but with hurt. **18** [t]For first of all, when ye come
together in the Church, I hear that there are dissensions among you: and I believe
it to be true in some part. **19** [u]For there must be heresies even among you, that
they which are [v]approved among you, might be known. **20** When ye come to-
gether therefore into one place, this is [w]not to eat the Lord's Supper. **21** For every
man when they should eat, taketh his own supper [x]afore, and one is hungry, and
another is drunken. **22** [y]Have ye not houses to eat and to drink in? despise ye the
Church of God, and shame them that have not? what shall I say to you? shall I prai-
se you in this? I praise you not. **23** [z]For I have received of the Lord that which I
also have delivered unto you, to wit, That the Lord Jesus in the night when he was
betrayed, took bread. **24** [5]And when he had given thanks, he brake it, and said,
Take, eat: this is my body, which is [aa]broken for you: this do ye in remembrance
of me. **25** After the same manner also he took the cup, when he had supped,
saying, This cup is the New Testament in my blood: this do as oft as ye drink it,
in remembrance of me. **26** For as often as ye shall eat this bread, and drink this
cup, ye show the Lord's death till he come. **27** [ab]Wherefore, whosoever shall eat
this bread, and drink the cup of the Lord [ac]unworthily, shall be guilty of the body
and blood of the Lord. **28** [6,ad]Let [ae]every man therefore examine himself, and
so let them eat of this bread, and drink of this cup. **29** For he that eateth and
drinketh unworthily, eateth and drinketh his own damnation, because he [af]discer-
neth not the Lord's body. **30** [ag]For this cause many are weak, and sick among
you, and many sleep. **31** For if we would [ah]judge ourselves, we should not be
judged. **32** But when we are judged, we are chastened of the Lord, because we
should not be condemned with the world. **33** [ai]Wherefore, my brethren, when
ye come together to eat, tarry one for another. **34** [aj]And if any man be hungry,
let him eat at home, that ye come not together unto condemnation. [ak]Other things
will I set in order when I come.

12

1 To draw away the Corinthians from contention and pride, he showeth that spiritual gifts are therefore diversely bestowed, 7 that the same being jointly to each other employed, 12 we may grow up together into one body of Christ in such equal proportion and measure, 20 as the members of man's body do.

1 Now [a]concerning spiritual gifts, brethren, I would not have you [b]igno-
rant. **2** [c]Ye know that ye were [d]Gentiles, and were carried away unto the dumb
idols, as ye were led. **3** [e]Wherefore I declare unto you, that no man [1]speaking
by the spirit of God, calleth Jesus [2,f]execrable: also no man can say that Jesus is the
Lord, but by the holy Ghost. **4** [g]Now there are diversities of gifts, but the [h]same
Spirit. **5** And there are diversities of administrations, but the same Lord. **6** And
there are diversities of [i]operations, but God is the same which worketh all in
all. **7** But the manifestation of the Spirit is [j]given to every man, to [k]profit wi-
thal. **8** [l]For to one is given by the Spirit the word of [m]wisdom: and to another
the word of knowledge, by the same Spirit: **9** And to another is given faith by
the same Spirit: and to another the gifts of healing, by the same Spirit: **10** And to
another the [n]operations of great works: and to another, [o]prophecy: and to another,
the [p]discerning of spirits: and to another, diversities of tongues: and to another,
the interpretation of tongues. **11** [3]And all these things worketh one and the sel-
fsame Spirit, distributing to every man severally [q]as he will. **12** [r]For as the body
is one, and hath many members, and all the members of the body, which is one,
though they be many, yet are but one body: [s]even so is [t]Christ. **13** For by one
Spirit are we all baptized into [u]one body, whether we be Jews, or Grecians, whether
we be bond, or free, and have been all made to [v]drink into one Spirit. **14** [w]For

---

m. 1 Cor. 11:10 What this meaneth, I do not yet understand.

n. 1 Cor. 11:11 A digression which the Apostle useth, lest that which he spake of the superior tie of men, and the lower degrees of women in consideration of the policy of the Church, should be so taken as though there were no measure of this inequality. Therefore he teacheth that men have in such sort the preeminence, that God made them not alone, but women also: and woman was so made of man, that men also are born by the means of women, and this ought to put them in mind to observe the degree of every sex, in such sort that mutual conjunction may be cherished.

o. 1 Cor. 11:11 By the Lord.

p. 1 Cor. 11:13 He urgeth the argument taken from the common sense of nature.

q. 1 Cor. 11:15 To be a covering for her, and such a covering as should procure another.

r. 1 Cor. 11:16 Against such as are stubbornly contentious we have to oppose this, that the Churches of God are not contentious.

s. 1 Cor. 11:17 He passeth now to the next treatise concerning the right administration of the Lord's Supper. And the Apostle useth this sharper preface that the Corinthians might understand, that whereas they observed generally the Apostle's commandments, yet they foully neglected them in a matter of greatest importance.

t. 1 Cor. 11:18 To celebrate the Lord's Supper aright, it is required that there be not only consent of doctrine, but also of affections, that it be not profaned.

u. 1 Cor. 11:19 Although that schisms and heresies proceed from the devil, are evil, and yet they come not by chance, nor without cause, and they turn to the profit of the elect.

v. 1 Cor. 11:19 Whom experience hath taught to be of sound Religion and godliness.

w. 1 Cor. 11:20 This is an usual kind of speech, whereby the Apostle denieth that flatly, which many did not well.

x. 1 Cor. 11:21 Eateth his meat and tarrieth not till other come.

y. 1 Cor. 11:22 The Apostle thinketh it good to take away the love feasts, for their abuse, although they had been a long time, and with commendation used in Churches, and were appointed and instituted by the Apostles.

z. 1 Cor. 11:23 We must take a true form of keeping the Lord's Supper, out of the institution of it, the parts whereof are these, touching the Pastors, to show forth the Lord's death, by preaching his word: to bless the bread and the wine by calling upon the name of God, and together with prayers to declare the institution thereof, and finally to deliver the bread broken to be eaten, and the cup received to be drunk with thanksgiving. And touching the flock, that every man examine himself, that is to say, to prove both his knowledge, and also faith and repentance: to show forth the Lord's death, that is, in true faith to yield unto his word and institution: and last of all, to take the bread at the Minister's hand, and to eat it and to drink the wine, and give God thanks: This was Paul's and the Apostles' manner of ministering.

aa. 1 Cor. 11:24 This word Broken noteth out unto us Christ his manner of death, for although his legs were not broken, as the thieves legs were, yet was his body very sore tormented, and torn, and bruised.

ab. 1 Cor. 11:27 Whoever contemn the holy Sacrament: that is, use them not aright, are guilty not of the bread and wine, but of the thing itself, that is of Christ, and shall be grievously punished for it.

ac. 1 Cor. 11:27 Otherwise then meet is such mysteries should be handled.

ad. 1 Cor. 11:28 The examination of a man's self, is of necessity required in the Supper and therefore they ought not to be admitted unto it, which cannot examine themselves: as children, furious and mad men, also such as either have no knowledge of Christ, or not sufficient, although they profess Christian Religion: and others such like.

ae. 1 Cor. 11:28 This place beateth down the faith of credit, or unwrapped faith, which the Papists maintain.

af. 1 Cor. 11:29 He is said to discern the Lord's body, that hath consideration of the worthiness of it, and therefore cometh to eat of this meat with great reverence.

ag. 1 Cor. 11:30 The profaning of the body and blood of the Lord in his mysteries is sharply punished of him, and therefore such a mischief ought diligently to be prevented by judging and correcting of a man's self.

ah. 1 Cor. 11:31 Try and examine ourselves, by faith and repentance, separating yourselves from the wicked.

ai. 1 Cor. 11:33 The Supper of the Lord is a common action of the whole Church, and therefore there is no place, for private suppers.

aj. 1 Cor. 11:34 The Supper of the Lord was instituted not to feed the belly but to feed the soul with the communion of Christ, and therefore it ought to be separate from common banquets.

ak. 1 Cor. 11:34 Such things as pertain to order, as place, time, form of prayers, and other such like, the Apostle took order for in Congregations according to the consideration of times, places and persons.

1 CORINTHIANS 11

1. 2 Thess. 3:9
2. Eph. 5:23
3. Gen. 1:26 / Gen. 5:1 / Gen. 9:6 / Col. 3:10
4. Gen. 2:22
5. Matt. 25:26 / Mark 14:21 / Luke 22:19
6. 1 Cor. 13:5

1 CORINTHIANS 12

a. 1 Cor. 12:1 Now he entereth into the third part of this treatise, touching the right use of spiritual gifts, wherein he giveth the Corinthians plainly to understand that they abused them: for they that excelled, bragged ambitiously of them, and so robbed God of the praise of his gifts: and having no consideration of their brethren abused to a vain ostentation, and so robbed the Church of the use of those gifts. On the other side, the inferior sort envied the better, and went about to make a departure, so that all that body was as it were scattered and rent in pieces. So then he going about to remedy these abuses, willeth them first to consider diligently, that they have not these gifts of themselves, but from the free grace and liberality of God, to whose glory they ought to bestow them all.

b. 1 Cor. 12:1 Ignorant to what purpose those gifts are given you.

c. 1 Cor. 12:2 He proveth the same by comparing their former state with that wherein they were at this time endued with those excellent gifts.

d. 1 Cor. 12:2 As touching God's service and the Covenant, mere strangers.

e. 1 Cor. 12:3 The conclusion: Know you therefore, that you cannot so much as move your lips to honor Christ withall, but by the grace of the holy Ghost.

f. 1 Cor. 12:3 Doth curse him, only any means whatsoever diminish his glory.

g. 1 Cor. 12:4 In the second place, he layeth another foundation, to wit, that these gifts are divers, as the functions also are divers, and their offices divers, but that one selfsame Spirit Lord and God is the giver of all these gifts, and that to one end, to wit, for the profit of all.

h. 1 Cor. 12:4 The Spirit is plainly distinguished from the gifts.

i. 1 Cor. 12:6 So Paul endeth that inward force which cometh from the holy Ghost, and maketh men fit to wonderful things.

j. 1 Cor. 12:7 The holy Ghost openeth and showeth himself freely in giving of these gifts.

k. 1 Cor. 12:7 To the use and benefit of the Church.

l. 1 Cor. 12:8 He declareth this manifold diversity, and reckoneth up the chiefest gifts, beating that into their heads, which he said before, to wit, that all these things proceeded from one selfsame Spirit.

m. 1 Cor. 12:8 Wisdom is a most excellent gift, very requisite, not only for them which teach, but also for them that exhort and comfort, which thing is proper to the Pastor's office, as the word of knowledge agreeth to the Doctors.

n. 1 Cor. 12:10 By operation he meaneth those great workings of God's mighty power, which pass and excel amongst his miracles, as the delivery of his people Israel by the hand of Moses: that which he did by Elijah against the Priests of Baal, in sending down fire from heaven to consume his sacrifice: and that which he did by Peter in the matter of Ananias and Sapphira.

o. 1 Cor. 12:10 Foretelling of things to come.

p. 1 Cor. 12:10 Whereby false prophets are known from true, wherein Peter passed Philip in discovering Simon Magus, Acts 8:20.

q. 1 Cor. 12:11 He addeth moreover something else, to wit, that although these gifts are unequal, yet they are most wisely divided, because the will of the Spirit of God is the rule of this distribution.

r. 1 Cor. 12:12 He setteth forth his former saying by a similitude taken from the body: This saith he, is manifestly seen in the body, whose members are divers, but yet so knit together, that they make but one body.

s. 1 Cor. 12:12 The applying of the similitude. So must we also think, saith he, of the mystical body of Christ: for all we that believe, whether we be Jews or Gentiles, are by one selfsame Baptism joined together with our head, that by that means, there may be framed one body compact of many members: and we have drunk one selfsame spirit, that is to say, a spiritual feeling, perseverance and motion common to us all, out of one cup.

t. 1 Cor. 12:12 Christ joined together with his Church.

u. 1 Cor. 12:13 To become one body with Christ.

v. 1 Cor. 12:13 By one quickening drink of the Lord's blood, we are made partakers of his only Spirit.

w. 1 Cor. 12:14 He amplifieth that which followed of the similitudes, as if he should say, The unity of the body is not

the body also is not one member, but many. **15** [x]If the foot would say, Because
I am not the hand, I am not of the body, is it therefore not of the body? **16** And
if the ear would say, Because I am not the eye, I am not of the body, is it therefore
not of the body? **17** [y]If the whole body were an eye, where were the hearing? If
the whole were hearing, where were the smelling? **18** But now hath God dispo-
sed the members every one of them in the body at his own pleasure. **19** For if
they were all one member, where were the body? **20** But now are there many
members, yet but one body. **21** [z]And the eye cannot say unto the hand, I have
no need of thee: nor the head again to the feet, I have no need of you. **22** Yea,
much rather those members of the body, which seem to be [aa]more feeble, are ne-
cessary. **23** And upon those members of the body, which we think most unho-
nest, put we more [ab]honesty on: and our uncomely parts have more comeliness
on. **24** For our comely parts need it not: but God hath tempered the body to-
gether: and hath given the more honor to that part which lacked, **25** Lest there
should be any division in the body: but that the members should have the same
[ac]care one for another. **26** [ad]Therefore if one member suffer, all suffer with it: if
one member be had in honor, all the members rejoice with it. **27** Now ye are
the body of Christ, and members for your [ae]part. **28** [4]And God hath ordained
some in the Church: as first Apostles, secondly Prophets, thirdly teachers, then
them that do miracles: after that, the gifts of healing, [af]helpers, [ag]governors, diver-
sity of tongues. **29** Are all Apostles? are all Prophets? are all teachers? **30** Are
all doers of miracles? have all the gifts of healing? do all speak with tongues? do
all interpret? **31** [ah]But desire you the best gifts, and I will yet show you a more
excellent way.

13

1 He showeth that there are gifts so excellent, which in God's sight are not corrupt, if Charity be away: 4 and therefore he digresseth unto the commendation of it.

1 Though [a]I speak with the tongues of men and [b]Angels, and have not love,
I am as sounding brass, or a [c]tinkling cymbal. **2** And though I had the gift of
prophecy, and knew all secrets and all knowledge, yea, if I had all [d]faith, so that
I could remove [1]mountains, and had not love, I were nothing. **3** And though I
feed the poor with all my goods, and though I give my body, that I be burned, and
have not love, it profiteth me nothing. **4** [e]Love [f]suffereth long: it is bountiful:
love envieth not: love doth not boast itself: it is not puffed up: **5** It doth [g]no un-
comely thing: it seeketh not her own thing: it is not provoked to anger: it thinketh
no evil: **6** It rejoiceth not in iniquity, but [h]rejoiceth in the truth: **7** It suffereth
all things: it believeth all things: it hopeth all things: it endureth all things. **8** [i]Lo-
ve doth never fall away, though that prophesyings be abolished, or the tongues
cease, or [j]knowledge vanish away. **9** [k]For we know in [l]part, and we prophesy
in part. **10** But when that which is perfect, is come, then that which is in part
shall be abolished. **11** [m]When I was a child, I spake as a child: I understood as
a child, I thought as a child: but when I became a man, I put away childish thin-
gs. **12** [n]For [o]now we see through a glass darkly: but then shall we see face to
face. Now I know in part: but then shall I know even as I am known. **13** [p]And
now abideth faith, hope and love, even these three: but the chiefest of these is love.

14

1 He commendeth the gifts of prophecying: 7 and by a similitude taken of musical instruments, 12 he teacheth the true use of interpreting the Scriptures: 17 he taketh away the abuse: 34 And forbiddeth women to speak in the Congregation.

1 Follow [a]after love, and covet spiritual gifts, and rather that ye may
[b]prophesy. **2** [c]For he that speaketh a strange [d]tongue, speaketh not unto men,
but unto God: for no man heareth him: howbeit in the [e]spirit he speaketh se-
cret things. **3** But he that prophesieth, speaketh unto men to [f]edifying, and to

---

only not left by this diversity of members, but also it could not be a body, if it did not consist of many, and those were divers members.

x. 1 Cor. 12:15 Now he buildeth his doctrine upon the foundations which he had laid: and first of all he continueth in his purposed similitude, and afterward he goeth to the matter barely and simply. And first of all he speaketh unto them which would have separated themselves from those whom they envied, because they had not such excellent gifts as they: now this is, saith he, as if the foot should say it were not of the body, because it is not the hand: or the ear, because it is not the eye. Therefore all parts ought rather to defend the unity of the body, being coupled together to serve one the other.

y. 1 Cor. 12:17 Again, speaking to them, he showeth them that if that should come to pass which they desire, to wit, that all should be equal one to another, there would follow a destruction of the whole body, yea, and of themselves: for it could not be a body, unless it were made of many members knit together, and divers one from another. And that no man might find fault with this division as unequal, he addeth that God himself hath coupled all these together. Therefore all must remain coupled together, that the body may remain in safety.

z. 1 Cor. 12:21 Now on the other side, he speaketh unto them which were endued with more excellent gifts, willing them not to despise the inferiors as unprofitable, and as though they served to no use: for God, saith he, hath in such sort tempered this inequality, that the more excellent and beautiful members can in no wise lack the more abject and such as we are ashamed of, and that they should have more care to see unto them, and to cover them: that by this means the necessity which is on both parts, might keep the whole body in peace and concord: that although if each part be considered apart, they are of divers degrees and conditions, yet because they are joined together, they have a community both in commodities and discommodities.

aa. 1 Cor. 12:22 Of the smallest and vilest offices, and therefore finally accounted of, of the rest.

ab. 1 Cor. 12:23 We more carefully cover them.

ac. 1 Cor. 12:25 Should bestow their operations and offices to the profit and preservation of the whole body.

ad. 1 Cor. 12:26 Now he applieth the same doctrine to the Corinthians without any allegory, warning them that seeing there are divers functions and divers gifts, it is their duty, not to offend one against another, either by envy or ambition, but rather that they being joined together in love and charity one with another, every one of them bestow to the profit of all, that which he hath received, according as his ministry doth require.

ae. 1 Cor. 12:27 For all churches wheresoever they are dispersed through the whole world, are divers members of one body.

af. 1 Cor. 12:28 The offices of Deacons.

ag. 1 Cor. 12:28 He setteth forth the order of Elders, which were the maintainers of the Church's discipline.

ah. 1 Cor. 12:31 He teacheth them that are ambitious and envious, a certain holy ambition and envy, to wit, if they give themselves to the best gifts, and such as are most profitable to the Church, and so if they contend to excel one another in love, which surpasseth all other gifts.

1 CORINTHIANS 12

1. Mark 9:31
2. John 13:15 / 1 Cor. 8:6 / Phil. 2:11
3. Rom. 12:3 / Eph. 4:7
4. Eph. 4:11

1 CORINTHIANS 13

a. 1 Cor. 13:1 He reasoneth first of Charity, the excellency whereof he first showeth by this, that without it, all other gifts are as nothing before God which thing he proveth partly by an induction, and partly also by an argument taken of the end, wherefor those gifts are given. For to what purpose are those gifts, but to God's glory, and the profit of the Church, as is before proved? so that those gifts, without Charity, have no right use.

b. 1 Cor. 13:1 A very earnest kind of amplifying a matter, as if he said, If there were any tongues of Angels, and I had them, and did not use them to the benefit of my neighbor, it were nothing else but a vain and prattling type of babbling.

c. 1 Cor. 13:1 That giveth a rude and no certain sound.

d. 1 Cor. 13:2 By faith, he meaneth the gift of doing miracles, and not that faith which justified, which cannot be void of Charity as the other may.

e. 1 Cor. 13:4 He describeth the force and nature of charity, partly by a comparison of contraries, and partly by the effects of itself: whereby the Corinthians may understand, both how profitable it is in the Church, and how necessary and also how far they are from it: and therefore how vainly and without cause they are proud.

f. 1 Cor. 13:4 Word for word deferreth wrath.

g. 1 Cor. 13:5 It is not contumelious.

h. 1 Cor. 13:6 Rejoice that righteousness in the righteous. For the Hebrews mean by truth, righteousness.

i. 1 Cor. 13:8 Again he commendeth the excellency of charity, in that that it shall never be abolished in the Saints, whereas the other gifts which are necessary for the building up of the Church, so long as we live here, shall have no place in the world to come.

j. 1 Cor. 13:8 The way to get knowledge by prophesying.

k. 1 Cor. 13:9 The reason: Because we are now in the state, that we have need to learn daily, and therefore we have need of those helps, to wit, of the gift of tongues, and knowledge, and also of those that teach them. But to what purpose serve they then, when we have obtained and gotten the full knowledge of God, which serve now but for them which are imperfect, and go by degrees to perfection?

l. 1 Cor. 13:9 We learn imperfectly.

m. 1 Cor. 13:11 He setteth forth that that he said, by an excellent similitude, comparing this life to our infancy or childhood, wherein we stagger and stammer rather than speak, and think and understand but childish things, and therefore have need of such things as may form and frame our tongue and mind: But when we become men, to what purpose should we desire that stammering, those childish toys, and such like things, whereby our childhood is framed by little and little?

n. 1 Cor. 13:12 The applying of the similitude of our childhood to this present life, wherein we darkly behold heavenly things, according to the small measure of light which is given us, through the understanding of tongues, and hearing the teachers and ministers of the Church: of our man's age and strength, to that heavenly and eternal life, wherein when we behold God himself present, and are lightened with his full and perfect light, to what purpose should we desire the voice of man, and those worldly things which are most imperfect? But yet then, shall all the Saints be knit both with God, and between themselves with most fervent love, and therefore charity shall not be abolished, but perfected, although it shall not be showeth forth and entertained by such manner of duties as peculiarly and only belong to the infirmity of this life.

o. 1 Cor. 13:12 All this must be understood by comparison.

p. 1 Cor. 13:13 The conclusion: As if the Apostle should say, Such therefore shall be our condition then: but now we have three things, and they remain sure if we be Christ's as without which true religion cannot consist, to wit, faith, hope, and charity. And among these, charity is the chiefest, because it ceaseth not in the life to come as the rest do, but is perfected and accomplished. For seeing that faith and hope tend to things which are promised, and are to come, when we have presently gotten them, to what purpose should we have faith and hope? but yet there at length shall we truly and perfectly love both God, and one another.

1 CORINTHIANS 13

1. Matt. 17:20

1 CORINTHIANS 14

a. 1 Cor. 14:1 He inferreth now that, that he spake before: Therefore seeing charity is the chiefest of all, before all things set it before you as chief and principal: and so esteem those things as most excellent: which profit the greater part of men: as prophecy that is to say, the gifts of teaching and applying the doctrine, which was contemned in respect of other gifts, although it be chiefest and most necessary for the Church and not those which for a show seem to be marvelous as the gifts of tongues, when a man was suddenly endued with the knowledge of many tongues, which made men greatly amazed, and yet of itself was not greatly to any use, unless there were an interpreter.

b. 1 Cor. 14:1 What prophecy is, he showeth in the third verse.

c. 1 Cor. 14:2 He reprehendeth their perverse judgment touching the gift of tongues. For why was it given? to wit, to the intent that the mysteries of God might be the better known to a greater sort. Thereby it is evident that Prophecy, whereunto the gift of tongues ought to serve, is better than this: and therefore the Corinthians did judge amiss, in that they made more account of the gift of tongues, than of prophesying: because forsooth the gift of tongues was a thing more to be bragged of. And hereupon followed another abuse of the gift of tongues, in that the Corinthians used tongues in the Congregation, without an interpreter. Which thing although it might be done to some profit of him, that spake them, yet he corrupted the right use of that gift, because there came thereby no profit to the hearers: and common assemblies were instituted and appointed not for any private man's commodity, but for the profit of the whole company.

d. 1 Cor. 14:2 A strange language, which no man can understand without an interpreter.

e. 1 Cor. 14:2 By that inspiration which he has received of the Spirit, which notwithstanding he abuseth, when he speaketh mysteries which none of the company can understand.

f. 1 Cor. 14:3 Which may further men in the study of godliness.

exhortation, and to comfort. **4** He that speaketh strange language, edifieth himself: but he that prophesieth, edifieth the [g]Church. **5** I would that ye all spake strange languages, but rather that ye prophesied: for greater is he that prophesieth, than he that speaketh diverse tongues, except he expound it, that the Church may receive edification. **6** And now, brethren, if I come unto you speaking diverse tongues, what shall I profit you, except I speak to you, either by revelation, or by knowledge, or by prophesying, or by doctrine? **7** [h]Moreover things without life which give a sound, whether it be a pipe or an harp, except they make a distinction in the sounds, how shall it be known what is piped or harped? **8** And also if the trumpet give an uncertain sound, who shall prepare himself to battle? **9** So likewise you, by the tongue, except ye utter words that have [i]signification, how shall it be understood what is spoken? for ye shall speak in the air. **10** [j]There are so many kinds of voices as it cometh to pass in the world, and none of them is dumb. **11** Except I know then the power of the voice, I shall be unto him that speaketh a Barbarian, and he that [k]speaketh, shall be a Barbarian unto me. **12** [l]Even so, forasmuch as ye covet spiritual gifts, seek that ye may excel unto the edifying of the Church. **13** Wherefore, let him that speaketh a strange tongue, [m]pray that he may interpret. **14** [n]For [o]if I pray in a strange tongue, my [p]spirit prayeth: but mine understanding is [q]without fruit. **15** What is it then? I will pray with the spirit, but I will pray with the [r]understanding also: I will sing with the spirit: but I will sing with the understanding also. **16** [s]Else, when thou blessest with the [t]spirit, how shall he that [u]occupieth the room of the unlearned, say [v]Amen, at thy giving of thanks, seeing he knowest not what thou sayest? **17** For thou verily givest thanks well, but the other is not edified. **18** [w]I thank my God, I speak languages more than ye all. **19** Yet had I rather in the Church to speak [x]five words with mine understanding, that I might also instruct others, than ten thousand words in a strange tongue. **20** [y]Brethren, be not [1]children in understanding, but as concerning maliciousness be children, but in understanding be of a ripe age. **21** In the [z]Law it is written, [2]By men of other tongues, and by other languages will I speak unto this people: yet so shall they not hear me, saith the Lord. **22** [aa]Wherefore strange tongues are for a sign, not to them that believe, but to them that believe not: but prophesying serveth not for them that believe not, but for them which believe. **23** [ab]If therefore, when the whole Church is come together in one, and all speak strange tongues, there come in they that are [ac]unlearned, or they which believe not, will they not say, that ye are out of your wits? **24** But if all prophesy, and there come in one that believeth not, or one unlearned, he is rebuked of all men, and is judged of all, **25** And so are the secrets of his heart made manifest, and so he will fall down on his face and worship God, and say plainly that God is in you indeed. **26** [ad]What is to be done then, brethren? when ye come together, according as every one of you hath a Psalm, or hath doctrine, or hath a tongue, or hath revelation, or hath interpretation, let all things be done unto edifying. **27** [ae]If any man speak a strange tongue, let it be by two, or at the most, by three, and that by course, and let one interpret. **28** But if there be no interpreter, let him keep silence in the Church, which speaketh languages, and let him speak to himself, and to God. **29** [af]Let the Prophets speak, two or three, and let the others judge. **30** And if anything be revealed to another that sitteth by, let the first hold his peace. **31** For ye may all prophesy one by one, that all may learn, and all may have comfort. **32** And the [ag]spirits of the Prophets are subject to the Prophets. **33** For God is not the author of confusion, but of peace, as we see in all the Churches of the Saints. **34** [3,ah]Let your women keep silence in the Churches: for it is not permitted unto them to speak: but they ought to be subject, as also [4]the Law saith. **35** And if they will learn anything, let them ask their husbands at home: for it is a shame for women to speak in the Church. **36** [ai]Came the word of God out from you? either came it unto you only? **37** If any man think himself to be a Prophet, or [aj]spiritual, let him acknowledge, that the things that I write unto you, are the commandments of the Lord. **38** [ak]And if any man be ignorant, let him be ignorant. **39** [al]Wherefore, brethren, covet to prophesy, and forbid not to speak languages. **40** Let all things be done honestly, and by order.

15

1 The Gospel that Paul preached. 3 The death and resurrection of Christ. 8 Paul saw Christ. 9 He had persecuted that Church, whereof afterward he was made a minister. 12 Christ first rose again, and we all shall rise by him. 26 The last enemy, death. 29 To be baptized for dead. 32 At Ephesus Paul fought with beasts. 35 How the dead are raised. 45 The first Adam. The last Adam, 47 The first and second man. 51 We shall all be changed, we shall not all sleep. 55 Death's sting. 57 Victory. 58 Constancy and steadfastness.

1 Moreover [1,a]brethren, I declare unto you the Gospel which I preached unto you, which ye have also received, and wherein ye [b]continue, **2** And whereby ye are saved, if ye keep in memory, after what manner I preached it unto you, [c]except ye have believed in vain. **3** For first of all, I delivered unto you that which I received, how that Christ died for our sins, according to the [2]Scriptures, **4** And that he was buried, and that he arose the third day, according to the [3]Scriptures, **5** [4]And that he was seen of Cephas, then of the [d]twelve. **6** After that, he was seen of more than five hundred brethren at [e]once: whereof many remain unto this present, and some also are asleep. **7** After that, he was seen of James: then of all the Apostles. **8** [5,f]And last of all he was seen also of me, as of one born out of due time. **9** [6]For I am the least of the Apostles, which am not meet to be called an Apostle, because I persecuted the Church of God. **10** [7]But by the grace of God I am that I am: and his grace which is in me, was not in vain: but I labored more abundantly than they all: yet not I, but the grace of God which is with me. **11** Wherefore, whether it were I, or they, so we preach, and so have ye believed. **12** [g]Now if it be preached, that Christ is risen from the dead, how

---

g. 1 Cor. 14:4 The company.
h. 1 Cor. 14:7 He setteth forth that which he said, by a similitude, which he borroweth and taketh from instruments of music, which although they speak not perfectly, yet they are distinguished by their sounds, that they may be the better used.
i. 1 Cor. 14:9 That do fitly utter the matter itself.
j. 1 Cor. 14:10 He proveth that interpretation is necessarily to be joined with the gift of tongues, by the manifold variety of languages, insomuch that if one speak to another without an interpreter, it is as if he spake not.
k. 1 Cor. 14:11 As the Papists in all their sermons and they that ambitiously pour out some Hebrew or Greek words in the Pulpit before the unlearned people, thereby to get them a name of vain learning.
l. 1 Cor. 14:12 The conclusion: if they will excel in those spiritual gifts, as it is meet, they must seek the profit of the Church, and therefore they must not use gift of tongues, unless there is an interpreter to expound the strange and unknown tongue, whether it be himself that speaketh, or another interpreter.
m. 1 Cor. 14:13 Pray for the gift of interpretation.
n. 1 Cor. 14:14 A reason: Because it is not sufficient for us to speak so in the Congregation, that we ourselves do worship God in spirit, that is, according to the gift that we have received, but we must also be understood of the company, lest that be unprofitable to others which we have spoken.
o. 1 Cor. 14:14 If I pray, when the church is assembled together, in a strange tongue.
p. 1 Cor. 14:14 The gift and inspiration which the spirit giveth me, doeth his part, but only to myself.
q. 1 Cor. 14:14 No fruit cometh to the Church by my prayers.
r. 1 Cor. 14:15 So that I may be understood of others, and may instruct others.
s. 1 Cor. 14:16 Another reason: Seeing that the whole Congregation must agree to him that speaketh, and also witness this agreement, how shall they give their assent or agreement which know not what is spoken?
t. 1 Cor. 14:16 Only without all consideration of the hearers.
u. 1 Cor. 14:16 He that sitteth as a private man.
v. 1 Cor. 14:16 So then one uttered the prayers, and all the company answered, Amen.
w. 1 Cor. 14:18 He propoundeth himself for an example, both that they may be ashamed of their foolish ambition, and also that he may eschew all suspicion of envy.
x. 1 Cor. 14:19 A very few words.
y. 1 Cor. 14:20 Now he reproveth them freely for their childish folly, which see not how this gift of tongues which was given to the profit of the Church, is turned by their ambition into an instrument of cursing, seeing that this same also is contained amongst the punishments wherewith God punished the stubbornness of his people, that he dispersed them amongst strangers whose language they understood not.
z. 1 Cor. 14:21 By the Law he understandeth all the whole Scripture.
aa. 1 Cor. 14:22 The conclusion: Therefore the gift of tongues serveth to punish the unfaithful and unbelievers, unless it be referred to prophecy that is to say, to the interpretation of Scripture and that that which is spoken, be by the means understood of the hearers.
ab. 1 Cor. 14:23 Another argument: The gift of tongues without prophecy is not only unprofitable to the faithful: but also doth very much hurt as well to them as to the unfaithful which should be won in the public assemblies. For by this means it cometh to pass, that the faithful seem to others to be mad, much less can the unfaithful be instructed thereby.
ac. 1 Cor. 14:23 See Acts 4:13.
ad. 1 Cor. 14:26 The conclusion: The edifying of the Congregation is a rule and square of the right use of all spiritual gifts.
ae. 1 Cor. 14:27 The manner how to use the gift of tongues. It may be lawful for one or two, or at the most three, to use the gift of tongues, one after another in an assembly, so that there be some to expound the same: but if there are none to expound, let him that hath that gift, speak to himself alone.
af. 1 Cor. 14:29 The manner of prophesying: Let two or three propound, and let the other judge of that that is propounded, whether it be agreeable to the word of God or no: If in this examination the Lord give any man nought to speak, let them give him leave to speak. Let every man be admitted to prophesy, severally and in his order, so far forth as it is required for the edifying of the Church. Let them be content to be subject to each other's judgment.
ag. 1 Cor. 14:32 The doctrine which the Prophets bring which are inspired with God's Spirit.
ah. 1 Cor. 14:34 Women are commanded to be silent in public assemblies, and they are commanded to ask of their husbands at home.
ai. 1 Cor. 14:36 A general conclusion of the treatise of the right use of spiritual gifts in assemblies: with a sharp reprehension, lest the Corinthians might alone seem to themselves to be wise.
aj. 1 Cor. 14:37 Skillful in knowing and judging spiritual things.
ak. 1 Cor. 14:38 The Church ought not to care for such as be stubbornly ignorant, and will not abide to be taught, but to go forward notwithstanding in those things which are right.
al. 1 Cor. 14:39 Prophecy ought simply to be retained and kept in Congregations, the gift of tongues is not to be forbidden, but all things must be done orderly.

1 CORINTHIANS 14

1. Matt. 28:3
2. Isa. 28:11
3. 1 Tim. 2:12
4. Gen. 3:16

1 CORINTHIANS 15

a. 1 Cor. 15:1 The sixth treatise of this Epistle, concerning the resurrection: and he useth a transition, or passing over from one matter to another, showing first that he bringeth no new thing, to the end that the Corinthians might understand that they had begun to swerve from the right course: and next that he goeth not about to entreat of a trifling matter, but of another chief point of the Gospel, which if it be taken away, their faith must needs come to nought. And so at the length he beginneth this treatise at Christ's resurrection, which is the ground and foundation of ours, and confirmeth it first by the testimony of the Scriptures, and by the witness of the Apostles, and of more than five hundred brethren, and last of all his own.
b. 1 Cor. 15:1 In the profession whereof you continue yet.
c. 1 Cor. 15:2 Which is very absurd, and cannot be, but that they believe, must reap the fruit of faith.
d. 1 Cor. 15:5 Of those twelve picked and chosen Apostles, which were commonly called twelve, though Judas was put out of the number.
e. 1 Cor. 15:6 Not fewer all times, but together and at one instant.
f. 1 Cor. 15:8 He maintaineth by the way, the authority of his Apostleship, which was requisite to be in good credit among the Corinthians, that this Epistle might be of force and weight amongst them. In the mean season he compareth himself to such sort after a certain divine art with certain others, that he maketh himself inferior to them all.
g. 1 Cor. 15:12 The first argument to prove that there is a resurrection from the dead: Christ is risen again, therefore the dead shall rise again.

say some among you, that there is no resurrection of the dead? **13** [h]For if the-
re be no resurrection of the dead, then is Christ not risen: **14** [i]And if Christ be
not risen, then is our preaching vain, and your faith is also vain. **15** And we are
found also false witnesses of God: for we have testified of God, that he hath raised
up Christ: whom he hath not raised up, if so be the dead be not raised. **16** [j]For
if the dead be not raised, then is Christ not raised. **17** And if Christ be not rai-
sed, your faith is vain: [k]ye are [l]yet in your sins. **18** [m]And so they which are asle-
ep in Christ, are perished. **19** [n]If in this life only we have hope in Christ, we
are of all men the most miserable. **20** [o]But now is Christ risen from the dead,
[p]and was made the [8,q]firstfruits of them that slept. **21** [r]For since by man came
death, by man came also the resurrection of the dead. **22** For as in Adam all
die, even so in Christ shall all be [s]made alive. **23** [t]But every man in his [9]own
order: the firstfruits is Christ, afterward, they that are of Christ, at his coming
shall rise again. **24** [u]Then shall be the [v]end, when he hath delivered up the kin-
gdom to God, even the Father, when he hath put down [w]all rule, and all authority
and power. **25** For he must reign [10]till he hath put all his enemies [x]under his
feet. **26** The [y]last enemy that shall be destroyed, is death. **27** [11]For he hath
put down all things under his feet. And when he saith that all things are subdued
to him, it is manifest that he is excepted, which did put down all things under
him. **28** And when all things shall be subdued unto him, [z]then shall the Son
also himself be subject unto him, that did subdue all things under him, that [aa]God
may be all in all. **29** [ab]Else what shall they do which are baptized [ac]for dead? if
the dead rise not at all, why are they then baptized for dead? **30** [ad]Why are we
also in jeopardy every hour? **31** By your [ae]rejoicing which I have in Christ Jesus
our Lord, I die daily. **32** [af]If I have fought with beasts at Ephesus [ag]after the
manner of men, what advantageth it me, if the dead be not raised up? [12,ah]let us
[ai]eat and drink: for tomorrow we shall die. **33** [aj]Be not deceived: evil speakings
corrupt good manners. **34** Awake to live righteously, and sin not: for some have
not the knowledge of God, I speak this to your shame. **35** [ak]But some man will
say, How are the dead raised up? and with what body come they forth? **36** [al]O
fool, that which thou sowest, is not quickened, except it die. **37** And that which
thou sowest, thou sowest not that body that shall be, but bare corn as it falleth,
of wheat, or of some other. **38** [am]But God giveth it a body at his pleasure, even
to every seed his own body. **39** All flesh is not the same flesh, but there is one
flesh of men, and another flesh of beasts, and another of fishes, and another of
birds: **40** There are also heavenly bodies, and earthly bodies: but the glory of
the heavenly is one, and the glory of the earthly is another. **41** There is another
glory of the sun, and another glory of the moon, and another glory of the stars: for
one star differeth from another star in glory. **42** [an]So also is the resurrection of
the dead. The body is [ao]sown in corruption, and is raised in incorruption. **43** It
is sown in [ap]dishonor, and is raised in glory: it is sown in weakness, and is raised
in [aq]power. **44** [ar]It is sown a natural body, and is raised a spiritual body: there
is a natural body, and there is a spiritual body. **45** [as]As it is also written, The
[at]first man [13]Adam was made a living soul: and the last Adam was made a [au]-
quickening spirit. **46** [av]Howbeit that was not first which is spiritual: but that
which is natural, and afterward that which is spiritual. **47** The first man is of
the earth, [aw]earthly: the second man is the Lord from [ax]heaven. **48** [ay]As is the
earthly, such are they that are earthly: and as is the heavenly, such are they also

---

h. 1 Cor. 15:13 The second by an absurdity, If there is no resurrection of the dead, then is not Christ risen again.

i. 1 Cor. 15:14 The proof of that absurdity by other absurdities: If Christ be not risen again, the preaching of the Gospel is in vain, and the credit that you gave unto it is vain, and we are liars.

j. 1 Cor. 15:16 He repeateth the same argument taken of an absurdity, purposing to show how faith is in vain if the resurrection of Christ be taken away.

k. 1 Cor. 15:17 First, seeing death is the punishment of sin, in vain should we believe that our sins were forgiven us, if they remain: but they do remain, if Christ rose not from death.

l. 1 Cor. 15:17 They are yet in their sins, which are not sanctified, nor have obtained remission of their sins.

m. 1 Cor. 15:18 Secondly, unless that this be certain that Christ rose again, all they which died in Christ, are perished. So then what profit cometh of faith?

n. 1 Cor. 15:19 The third argument, which is also taken from an absurdity: for unless there be another life, wherein such as trust and believe in Christ shall be blessed, they were the most miserable of all creatures, because in this life they are the most miserable.

o. 1 Cor. 15:20 A conclusion of the former argument: Therefore Christ is risen again.

p. 1 Cor. 15:20 He putteth the last conclusion for the first proposition of the argument that followeth. Christ is risen again, Therefore shall we the faithful for of them he speaketh rise again: Then followeth the first reason of this consequent: for Christ is set forth unto us, to be considered of, not as a private man apart and by himself, but as the firstfruits: And he taketh that which was known, to all men, to wit, that the whole heap is sanctified in the firstfruits.

q. 1 Cor. 15:20 He alludeth to the firstfruits of corn, the offering whereof sanctified the rest of the fruits.

r. 1 Cor. 15:21 Another confirmation of the same consequent: for Christ is to be considered as opposite to Adam, that as from one man Adam, sin came over all, so from one man Christ, life cometh unto all: that is to say, that all the faithful, as they die, because by nature they were born of Adam, so because in Christ they are made the children of God by grace, they are quickened and restored to life by him.

s. 1 Cor. 15:22 Shall rise by the virtue of Christ.

t. 1 Cor. 15:23 He doeth two things together: for he showeth that the resurrection is in such sort common to Christ with all his members, that notwithstanding he far passeth them, both in time for he was the first that rose again from the dead and also in honor, because that from him and in him is all our life and glory. Then by this occasion he passeth in the next argument.

u. 1 Cor. 15:24 The fourth argument, wherewith also he confirmeth the others, hath a most sure ground, to wit, because that God must reign. And this is the manner of his reign, that the Father will be showed to be King in his Son who was made man, to whom all things are made subject the promiser only except to the end that the Father may afterward triumph in his Son the conqueror. And he maketh two parts of this reign and dominion of the Son, wherein the Father's glory consisteth: to wit, the overcoming of his enemies whereof some must be deprived of all power, as Satan and all the wicked, be they never so proud and mighty, and others must be utterly abolished as death and a plain and full delivery of the godly from all enemies, that by this means God may fully set forth the body of the Church, cleaving fast to their head Christ, his kingdom and glory as a king in his subjects. Moreover he putteth the first degree of this kingdom in the resurrection of the Son, who is the head: and the perfection, in the full conjunction of the members with the head, which shall be in the latter day. Now all these tend to this purpose, to show that unless the dead do rise again, neither the Father can be King above all, neither Christ be Lord of all: for neither should the power of Satan and death be overcome, nor the glory of God be full in his Son, nor his Son in his members.

v. 1 Cor. 15:24 The shutting up and finishing of all things.

w. 1 Cor. 15:24 All his enemies which shall be spoiled of all the power they have.

x. 1 Cor. 15:25 Christ is considered here, as he appeared in the form of a servant, in which respect he ruleth the Church as head, and that because this power was given him of his Father.

y. 1 Cor. 15:26 The shutting up of the argument, which is taken from the whole to the part: for if all his enemies shall be put under his feet, then must it needs be that death also shall be subdued under him.

z. 1 Cor. 15:28 Not because the Son was not subject to his Father before, but because his body, that is to say, the Church which is here in distress, and not yet wholly partaker of his glory, is not yet fully perfect, and also because the bodies of the saints which be in the graves shall not be glorified until the resurrection: but Christ as he is God, hath us subject to him as his Father hath, but as he is Priest, he is subject to his father together with us. Augustine, book 1, chap. 8, of the Trinity.

aa. 1 Cor. 15:28 By this high kind of speech, is set forth an incomprehensible glory which floweth from God, and shall fill all of us, as we are joined together with our head, but yet so, that our head shall always reserve his preeminence.

ab. 1 Cor. 15:29 The fifth argument taken of the end of Baptism, to wit, because that they which are baptized, are baptized for dead, that is to say, that they may have a remedy against death because that Baptism is a token of regeneration.

ac. 1 Cor. 15:29 They that are baptized, to this end and purpose, that death may be put out in them, or to rise again from the dead, whereof baptism is a seal.

ad. 1 Cor. 15:30 The sixth argument: Unless there be a resurrection of the dead, why should the Apostles so daily cast themselves into danger of so many deaths?

ae. 1 Cor. 15:31 As though he said, I die daily, as all the miseries I suffer can well witness, which I may truly boast of, that I have suffered amongst you.

af. 1 Cor. 15:32 The taking away of an objection: but thou Paul, didst ambitiously, as commonly men are wont to do, when thou didst fight with beasts at Ephesus: That is very like, saith Paul, for what could that advantage me, were it not for the glory of eternal life which I hope for?

ag. 1 Cor. 15:32 Not upon any godly motion, nor casting mine eyes upon God, but carried away with vain glory, or a certain headiness.

ah. 1 Cor. 15:32 The seventh argument which dependeth upon the last: if there be no resurrection of the dead, why do we give ourselves to anything else, save to eating and drinking?

ai. 1 Cor. 15:32 These are speeches that Epicureans use.

aj. 1 Cor. 15:33 The conclusion with a sharp exhortation, that they take heed of the naughty company of certain: from whence he showeth that this mischief sprang: warning them to be wise with sobriety unto righteousness.

ak. 1 Cor. 15:35 Now that he hath proved the resurrection, he discovereth their doltishness, in that they scoffingly demanded, how it could be that the dead should rise again, and if they did rise again, they asked mockingly, what manner of bodies they should have. Therefore he sendeth these fellows which seemed to themselves to be marvelous wise and witty, to be instructed of poor rude husbandmen.

al. 1 Cor. 15:36 Thou mightest have learned either of these, saith Paul, by daily experience: for seeds are sown, and rot, and yet notwithstanding so far it is off, that they perish, that contrarywise they grow up far more beautiful: and whereas they are sown naked and dry, they spring up green from death by the virtue of God: and doth it seem incredible to thee that our bodies should rise from corruption, and that endued with a far more excellent quality?

am. 1 Cor. 15:38 We see a diversity both in one and the selfsame thing which hath now one form and then another, and yet keepeth its own kind, as it is evident in a grain which is sown bare, but springeth up far after another sort: and also in divers kinds of one selfsame sort, as amongst beasts: and also among things of divers sorts, as the heavenly bodies and the earthly bodies: which also differ very much one from another. Therefore there is no cause why we should reject either the resurrection of the bodies, or changing of them into a better state, as a thing impossible, or strange.

an. 1 Cor. 15:42 He maketh three manner of qualities of the bodies being raised: Incorruption, to wit, because they shall be sound, and altogether of a nature that cannot be corrupt: Glory, because they shall be adorned with beauty and honor: Power, because they shall continue everlasting without meat, drink, and all other helps, without which this frail life cannot keep itself from corruption.

ao. 1 Cor. 15:42 Is buried, and man is hid as seed in the ground.

ap. 1 Cor. 15:43 Void of honor, void of glory, and beauty.

aq. 1 Cor. 15:43 Freed from the former weakness, whereas it is subject to such alteration and change, that it cannot maintain itself without meat and drink, and such otherlike helps.

ar. 1 Cor. 15:44 He showeth perfectly in one word, this change of the quality of the body by the resurrection, when he saith, that of a natural body, it shall become a spiritual body, which two qualities being clean different, the one from the other, he straightway expoundeth and setteth forth diligently.

as. 1 Cor. 15:45 That is called a natural body, which is quickened and maintained by a living soul only, such as Adam was, of whom all we are born naturally: and that is said to be a spiritual, which together with the soul is quickened with a far more excellent virtue: to wit, with the Spirit of God, which descendeth from Christ the second Adam unto us.

at. 1 Cor. 15:45 Adam is called the first man, because he is the root as it were from which we spring: and Christ is the latter man: because he is the beginning of all them that are spiritual, and in him we are all comprehended.

au. 1 Cor. 15:45 Christ is called a Spirit, by reason of that most excellent nature, that is to say, God who dwelleth in him bodily, as Adam is called a living soul, by reason of the soul which is the best part in him.

av. 1 Cor. 15:46 Secondly he willeth the order of this double state or quality to be observed, that the natural was first, Adam being created of the clay of the earth: and the spiritual followed and came upon it, to wit, when the Lord being sent from heaven, endued our flesh which was prepared and made fit for him, with the fulness of the Godhead.

aw. 1 Cor. 15:47 Wallowing in dirt, and wholly given to an earthly nature.

ax. 1 Cor. 15:47 The Lord is said to come down from heaven by that kind of speech, whereby that which is proper to one is touched of another.

ay. 1 Cor. 15:48 He applieth both the earthly naturalness of Adam if I may so say to our bodies, so long as they are naturally conversant on earth, to wit, in this life, and in the grave: and also the spirituality of Christ to the same our

that are heavenly. **49** And as we have born the [az]image of the earthly, so shall
we bear the image of the heavenly. **50** [ba]This say I, brethren, that [bb]flesh and
blood cannot inherit the kingdom of God, neither doth corruption inherit incor-
ruption. **51** [bc]Behold, I show you a [bd]secret thing, We shall not all sleep, but
we shall all be changed, **52** In [be]a moment, in the twinkling of an eye at the last
[14]trumpet: for the trumpet shall blow, and the dead shall be raised up incorrupti-
ble, and we shall be changed. **53** For this corruptible must put on incorruption:
and this mortal must put on immortality. **54** So when this corruptible hath put
on incorruption, and this mortal hath put on immortality, then shall be brought to
pass the saying, that is written, [15]Death is swallowed up into victory. **55** O death
where is thy sting? O grave where is thy victory? **56** The sting of death is sin: and
the strength of sin is the Law. **57** [16]But thanks be unto God, which hath given
us victory through our Lord Jesus Christ. **58** [bf]Therefore my beloved brethren,
be ye steadfast, unmovable, abundant always in the work of the Lord, forasmuch
as ye know that your labor is not in vain in the [bg]Lord.

16

1 He exhorteth them to help the poor brethren of Jerusalem: 10 Then he commendeth Timothy, 13 and so with a friendly exhortation, 19 and commendations, endeth the Epistle.

1 Concerning [a]the gathering for the Saints, as I have ordained in the Chur-
ches of Galatia, so do ye also. **2** Every [b]first day of the week, let every one of you
put aside by himself, and lay up as God hath [c]prospered him, that then there be no
gatherings when I come. **3** And when I am come, whomsoever ye shall allow by
[d]letters, them will I send to bring your liberality unto Jerusalem. **4** [e]And if it be
meet that I go also, they shall go with me. **5** Now I will come unto you, after I
have gone through Macedonia for I will pass through Macedonia. **6** And it may
be that I will abide, yea, or winter with you, that ye may bring me on my way, whi-
thersoever I go. **7** For I will not see you now in my passage, but I trust to abide
a while with you, if the Lord permit. **8** And I will tarry at Ephesus until Pente-
cost. **9** For a great door and [f]effectual is opened unto me, and there are many
adversaries. **10** Now if Timothy come, see that he be [g]without fear with you: for
he worketh the work of the Lord, even as I do. **11** Let no man therefore despise
him: but convey him forth [h]in peace, that he may come unto me: for I looked for
him with the brethren. **12** As touching our brother Apollos, I greatly desired
him to come unto you with the brethren: but his mind was not at all to come at
this time: howbeit he will come when he shall have convenient time. **13** Watch
ye: stand fast in the faith: quit you like men, and be strong. **14** Let all your things
be done in love. **15** Now brethren, I beseech you ye know the house of [i]Stepha-
nas, that it is the firstfruits of Achaia, and that they have [j]given themselves to mini-
ster unto the Saints. **16** That ye be [k]obedient even unto such, and to all that help
with us and labor. **17** I am glad of the coming of Stephanas, and Fortunatus, and
Achaicus: for they have supplied the want of you. **18** For they have comforted
my [l]spirit and yours: [m]acknowledge therefore such men. **19** The Churches of
Asia salute you: Aquila and Priscilla with the Church that is in their house, salu-
te you greatly in the Lord. **20** All the brethren greet you. Greet ye one another
with an [1]holy kiss. **21** The salutation of me Paul with mine own hand. **22** If
any man love not the Lord Jesus Christ, let him be had in execration [n]maran-a-
tha. **23** The grace of our Lord Jesus Christ be with you. **24** My love be with
you all in Christ Jesus, Amen. The first Epistle to the Corinthians, written from
Philippi, and sent by Stephanas, and Fortunatus, and Achaicus, and Timothy.

---

bodies, after that they are risen again: and he saith, that that goeth before and this shall follow.

az. 1 Cor. 15:49 Not a vain and false image, but such an one as had the truth with it indeed.

ba. 1 Cor. 15:50 The conclusion: We cannot be partakers of the glory of God, unless we put off all that gross and filthy nature of our bodies subject to corruption, that the same body may be adorned with incorruptible glory.

bb. 1 Cor. 15:50 Flesh and blood are taken here for a living body, which cannot attain to incorruption, unless it put off corruption.

bc. 1 Cor. 15:51 He goeth further, declaring that it shall come to pass that they which shall be found alive in the latterday, shall not descend into that corruption of the grave, but shall be renewed with a sudden change, which change is very requisite: and that the certain enjoying of the benefit and victory of Christ, is deferred unto that latter time.

bd. 1 Cor. 15:51 A thing that hath been hid, and never known hitherto, and therefore worthy that you give good care unto it.

be. 1 Cor. 15:52 He showeth us that the time shall be very short.

bf. 1 Cor. 15:58 An exhortation taken from the profit that ensueth, that seeing they understand that the glory of the other life is laid up for faithful workmen, they continue and stand fast in the truth of the doctrine of the resurrection of the dead.

bg. 1 Cor. 15:58 Through the Lord's help and goodness working in us.

1 CORINTHIANS 15

1. Gal. 1:11
2. Isa. 53:5 / 1 Pet. 2:24
3. Jonah 2:1
4. John 20:19
5. Acts 9:5
6. Eph. 3:8
7. Eph. 3:7
8. Col. 1:18 / Rev. 1:5
9. 1 Thess. 4:13
10. Ps. 110:1 / Acts 2:34 / Heb. 1:13 / Heb. 10:13
11. Ps. 8:6 / Heb. 2:8
12. Isa. 22:13
13. Gen. 2:7
14. Matt. 24:31 / 1 Thess. 4:16
15. Hos. 13:14 / Heb. 2:4
16. 1 John 5:5

1 CORINTHIANS 16

a. 1 Cor. 16:1 Collections in old time were made by the Apostles appointment the first day of the week, on which day the manner was then to assemble themselves.

b. 1 Cor. 16:2 Which in times past was called Sunday, but now is called the Lord's day.

c. 1 Cor. 16:2 That every man bestow, according to the ability that God hath blessed him with.

d. 1 Cor. 16:3 Which you shall give them to carry.

e. 1 Cor. 16:4 The residue of the Epistle is spent in writing of familiar matters, yet so that all things be referred to his purposed mark, that is to say, to the glory of God, and the edifying of the Corinthians.

f. 1 Cor. 16:9 Very fit and convenient to do great things by.

g. 1 Cor. 16:10 Without any just occasion of fear.

h. 1 Cor. 16:11 Safe and sound, and that with all kinds of courtesy.

i. 1 Cor. 16:15 Stephanas is the name of a man and not of a woman.

j. 1 Cor. 16:15 Given themselves wholly to the ministry.

k. 1 Cor. 16:16 That you honor and reverence them, be obedient to them and be content to be ruled by them, as meet as you should, seeing they have bestowed themselves, and their goods to help you withall.

l. 1 Cor. 16:18 Mine heart.

m. 1 Cor. 16:18 Take them for such men as they are indeed.

n. 1 Cor. 16:22 By these words, are betokened the secret kind of curse and excommunication that was amongst the Jews: and the words are as much as to say, as our Lord cometh: So that his meaning may be this, Let him be accursed even to the coming of the Lord, that is to say, to his death's day, even for ever.

1 CORINTHIANS 16

a. 1 Cor. 16:20 : Rom. 16:16; 1 Cor. 3:2; 1 Pet. 3:14

THE SECOND EPISTLE OF APOSTLE PAUL TO THE

CORINTHIANS

1

1 He beginneth with the praise of afflictions, 8 declaring what he hath sufferred in Asia, 10 and how happily God assisted him. 17 He saith it was not upon any lightness, that he came not, according to his promise.

1 PAUL [a]an Apostle of JESUS Christ, by the will of God, and our brother Timothy, to the Church of God, which is at Corinth, with all the Saints, which are in all Achaia: **2** Grace be with you, and peace from God, our Father, and from the Lord Jesus Christ. **3** [1,b,c]Blessed be God, even the Father of our Lord Jesus Christ, the Father of [d]mercies, and the God of all comfort, **4** Which comforteth us in all our tribulation, [e]that we may be able to comfort them which are in any affliction by the comfort wherewith we ourselves are comforted of God. **5** For as the [f]sufferings of Christ abound in us, so our consolation aboundeth through Christ. **6** [g]And whether we be afflicted, it is for your consolation and salvation, which is [h]wrought in the enduring of the same sufferings, which we also suffer: or whether we be comforted, it is for your consolation and salvation. **7** And our hope is steadfast concerning you, in as much as we know, that as ye are partakers of the sufferings, so shall ye be also of the consolation. **8** [i]For brethren, we would not have you ignorant of our affliction, which came unto us in Asia, how we were pressed out of measure passing strength, so that we altogether [j]doubted even of life. **9** Yea, we received the sentence of death in [k]ourselves, because we should not rest in ourselves, but in God, which raised the dead. **10** Who delivered us from so [l]great a death, and doth deliver us: in whom we trust, that yet hereafter he will deliver us. **11** [2,m]So that ye labor together in prayer for us, [n]that for the gift bestowed upon us for many, thanks may be given by many persons for us. **12** [o]For our rejoicing is this, the testimony of our conscience, that in simplicity and godly [p]pureness, and not in fleshly wisdom, but by the [q]grace of God we have had our conversation in the world, and most of all to youwards. **13** For we write [r]none other things unto you, than that ye read or else that ye acknowledge, and I trust ye shall acknowledge unto the [s]end. **14** Even as ye have acknowledged us partly, that we are your [t]rejoicing, even as ye are ours, in the [u]day of our Lord Jesus. **15** And in this confidence was I minded first to come unto you, that ye might have had a [v]double grace, **16** And to pass by you into Macedonia, and to come again out of Macedonia, unto you, and to be led forth toward Judea of you. **17** [w]When I therefore was thus minded, did I use lightness? or mind I those things which I mind, according to the [x]flesh, that with me should be, [y]Yea, yea, and Nay, nay? **18** [z]Yea, God is [aa]faithful, that our word toward you, was not Yea, and Nay? **19** [ab]For the Son of God Jesus Christ, who was preached among you by us, that is, by me, and Silvanus, and Timothy, [ac]was not Yea, and Nay: but in [ad]him it was Yea. **20** [ae]For all the promises of God in him are Yea, and are in [af]him Amen, unto the glory of God through [ag]us. **21** [ah]And it is God which established us with you in Christ, and hath anointed us. **22** Who hath also sealed us, and hath given the [ai]earnest of the Spirit in our hearts. **23** [aj]Now, I call God for a record unto my [ak]soul, that to spare you, I came not as yet unto Corinth. **24** [al]Not that we have dominion over your faith, but we are helpers of your [am]joy: for by faith ye stand.

2

1 He excuseth his not coming unto them, 2 and privily reprehendeth them: 4 He showeth that such is his affection towards them, 5 that he never rejoiceth but when they are merry. 6 Perceiving the adulterer whom he commanded to be delivered up to Satan to repent, he requesteth that they forgive him. 13 He mentioneth his going into Macedonia.

1 But I determined thus in myself, that I would not come again to you in [a]heaviness. **2** For if I make you sorry, who is he then that should make me glad, but the same which is made sorry by me? **3** And I wrote this same thing unto you, lest when I came, I should take heaviness of them of whom I ought to rejoice: this [b]confidence have I in you all, that my joy is the joy of you all. **4** For in great affliction, and anguish of heart I wrote unto you with many tears: not that ye

---

2 CORINTHIANS 1

- **a.** 2 Cor. 1:1 See the declaration of such salutations in the former Epistles.
- **b.** 2 Cor. 1:3 He beginneth after his manner with thanksgiving, which notwithstanding otherwise than he was wont he applieth to himself: beginning his Epistle with the setting forth of the dignity of his Apostleship, constrained as it should seem by their importunity, which took an occasion to despise him by reason of his miseries. But he answereth that he is not so afflicted, but that his comforts do exceed his afflictions, showing the ground of them, even the mercy of God the Father in Jesus Christ.
- **c.** 2 Cor. 1:3 To him be praise and glory given.
- **d.** 2 Cor. 1:3 Most merciful.
- **e.** 2 Cor. 1:4 The Lord doth comfort us to this end and purpose, that we may so much the more surely comfort others.
- **f.** 2 Cor. 1:5 The miseries which we suffer for Christ, or which Christ suffereth in us.
- **g.** 2 Cor. 1:6 He denieth that either his afflictions wherewith he was often afflicted, or the consolations which he received of God, may justly be despised, seeing that the Cor. both might and ought to take great occasion to be confirmed by either of them.
- **h.** 2 Cor. 1:6 Although salvation be given us freely, yet because there is a way appointed us wherewith we must come to it, which is the race of an innocent and upright life, which we must run, therefore we are said to work our salvation, Phil. 2:12. And because it is God only that of his free good will worketh all things in us, therefore is he said to work the salvation in us by those selfsame things by which we must pass to everlasting life, after that we have once overcome all encumbrances.
- **i.** 2 Cor. 1:8 He witnesseth that he is not only not ashamed of his afflictions, but that he desireth also to have all men know the greatness of them, and also his delivery from them, although it be not yet perfect.
- **j.** 2 Cor. 1:8 I know not at all what to do, neither did I see by man's help which way to save my life.
- **k.** 2 Cor. 1:9 I was resolved within myself to die.
- **l.** 2 Cor. 1:10 From these great dangers.
- **m.** 2 Cor. 1:11 That he may not seem to boast himself, he attributeth all to God, and therewith also confesseth that he attributeth much to the prayers of the faithful.
- **n.** 2 Cor. 1:11 The end of the afflictions of the Saints, is the glory of God, and therefore they ought to be precious unto us.
- **o.** 2 Cor. 1:12 Secondly he putteth away another slander, to wit, that he was a light man, and such a one as was not lightly to be credited, seeing that he promised to come unto them, and came not. And first he speaks of the simplicity of his mind, and sincerity, which they know both by his voice when he was present, and they ought to acknowledge it also in his letters, being absent: and moreover he protesteth that he will never be otherwise.
- **p.** 2 Cor. 1:12 With clearness, and holy and true plainness of mind, as God himself can witness.
- **q.** 2 Cor. 1:12 Trusting to that very wisdom, which God of his free goodness hath given me from heaven.
- **r.** 2 Cor. 1:13 He saith he writeth barely and simply: for he that writeth in colored sort, is rightly said to write otherwise than we read: and this he saith the Cor. shall know and like of very well.
- **s.** 2 Cor. 1:13 Perfectly.
- **t.** 2 Cor. 1:14 Paul's rejoicing in the Lord was, that he had won the Cor.: and they themselves rejoiced that such an Apostle was their instructor, and taught them so purely and sincerely.
- **u.** 2 Cor. 1:14 When he shall sit as judge.
- **v.** 2 Cor. 1:15 Another benefit.
- **w.** 2 Cor. 1:17 He putteth away their slander and false report by denying it, and first of all in that divers went about to persuade the Cor., that in the preaching of the Gospel, Paul agreed not to himself: for this was the matter and the case.
- **x.** 2 Cor. 1:17 As men do, which will rashly promise anything, and change their purpose at every turning of an hand.
- **y.** 2 Cor. 1:17 That I should say and unsay a thing?
- **z.** 2 Cor. 1:18 He calleth God to witness, and for judge of his constancy in preaching and teaching one selfsame Gospel.
- **aa.** 2 Cor. 1:18 True, and of whose faithfulness it were horrible wickedness to doubt.
- **ab.** 2 Cor. 1:19 He joineth also with himself, his fellows as witnesses, with whom he fully consented in teaching one selfsame thing, to wit, one selfsame Christ.
- **ac.** 2 Cor. 1:19 Was not divers and wavering.
- **ad.** 2 Cor. 1:19 That is in God.
- **ae.** 2 Cor. 1:20 Last of all he declareth the sum of his doctrine, to wit, that all the promises of salvation are sure and ratified in Christ.
- **af.** 2 Cor. 1:20 Christ is set also forth to exhibit and fulfill them all most assuredly, and without all doubt.
- **ag.** 2 Cor. 1:20 Through our ministry.
- **ah.** 2 Cor. 1:21 He attributeth the praise of this constancy, only to the grace of God, through the holy Ghost, and therewithall concludeth that they cannot doubt of his faith, and his fellows, without doing injury to the Spirit of God, seeing that they themselves do know all this to be true.
- **ai.** 2 Cor. 1:22 An earnest, is, whatsoever is given to confirm a promise.
- **aj.** 2 Cor. 1:23 Now coming to the matter, he sweareth, that he did not only, not lightly alter his purpose of coming to them, but rather that he came not unto them for this cause, that he might not be constrained to deal more sharply, with them being present, than he would.
- **ak.** 2 Cor. 1:23 Against myself and to the danger of mine own life.
- **al.** 2 Cor. 1:24 He removeth all suspicion of arrogance, declaring that he speaketh not as a Lord unto them, but as a servant, appointed of God to comfort them.
- **am.** 2 Cor. 1:24 He setteth the joy and peace of conscience, which God is author of, against tyrannous fear, and therewithall showeth the end of the Gospel.

2 CORINTHIANS 1

- **1.** Eph. 1:3 / 1 Pet. 1:3
- **2.** Rom. 15:30

2 CORINTHIANS 2

- **a.** 2 Cor. 2:1 Causing grief amongst you, which he should have done if he had come to them before they had repented them.
- **b.** 2 Cor. 2:3 For I trusted that you would take that out of the way forewith, which you knew I was discontented with, considering how you are persuaded that my joy is your joy.
- **c.** 2 Cor. 2:5 He passeth to another part of this Epistle: which notwithstanding is put amongst the first, whereunto he returneth afterward, and he handleth the releasing and unloosing of the incestuous person, because he seemed to have given sufficient testimony of his repentance: showing the true use of excommunication, to wit, that it proceed not of

should be made sorry, but that ye might perceive the love which I have, specially unto you. **5** [c]And if any hath caused sorrow, the same hath not made [d]me sorry, but [e]partly lest I should more [f]charge him you all. **6** It is sufficient unto the same man, that he was rebuked of many. **7** So that now contrariwise ye ought rather to [g]forgive him, and comfort him, lest the same should be swallowed up with overmuch heaviness. **8** Wherefore, I pray you, that you would [h]confirm your love towards him. **9** For this cause also did I write: that I might know the proof of you, whether ye would be obedient in all things. **10** To whom ye forgive anything, I forgive also: for verily if I forgave anything, to whom I forgave it, for your sakes forgave I it in the [i]sight of Christ, **11** Lest Satan should circumvent us: for we are not ignorant of his [j]enterprises. **12** [k]Furthermore, when I came to Troas to preach Christ's Gospel, and a door was opened unto me of the Lord, **13** I had no rest in my spirit, because I found not Titus my brother, but took my leave of them, and went away into Macedonia. **14** Now thanks be unto God, which always maketh us to triumph in Christ, and maketh manifest the [l]savor of his knowledge by us in every place. **15** [m]For we are unto God the sweet savor of Christ, in them that are saved, and in them which perish. **16** To the one we are the savor of death, unto death, and to the other the savor of life, unto life: [n]and who is sufficient for these things? **17** [1]For we are not as many, which make [o]merchandise of the word of God: but as of sincerity, but as of God in the sight of God speak we in Christ.

3

1 He desireth no other commendation, 3 than their continuing in the faith. 6 He is a minister not of the letter, but of the Spirit. 8 He showeth the difference of the Law, and the Gospel, 13 that the brightness of the Law doth rather dim the sight than lighten it: 18 But the Gospel doth make manifest God's countenance unto us.

1 Do we begin to praise ourselves again? or need we as some others, Epistles of recommendation unto you, or letters of recommendation from you? **2** Ye are our epistle, written in our hearts, which is understood and read of all men, **3** In that ye are [a]manifest, to be the Epistle of Christ, [b]ministered by us, and written, not with ink, but with the Spirit of the [c]living God, [d]not in tables of stone, but in fleshly tables of the heart. **4** And such [e]trust have we through Christ to God: **5** Not that we are sufficient of ourselves, to think anything, as of ourselves: but our [f]sufficiency is of God, **6** [g]Who also hath made us able ministers of the New Testament, not of the [h]letter, but of the Spirit: for the letter killeth, but the Spirit giveth life. **7** If then the ministration of death written with letters [i]and engraven in stones, was [j]glorious, so that the children of Israel could not behold the face of Moses, for the glory of his countenance which glory is gone away. **8** How shall not the [k]ministration of the Spirit be more glorious? **9** For if the ministry of condemnation was glorious, much more doth the ministration of [l]righteousness exceed in glory. **10** For even that which was glorified, was not glorified in this point, that is, as touching the exceeding glory. **11** For if that they should be [m]abolished, was glorious, much more shall that which remaineth be glorious. **12** [n]Seeing then that we have such trust, we use great boldness of speech. **13** [1,o]And we are not as Moses, which put a veil upon his face, that the children of Israel should not look unto the [p]end of that which should be abolished. **14** Therefore their minds are hardened: for until this day remaineth the same covering untaken away in the reading of the old Testament, which veil in Christ is put away. **15** But even unto this day, when Moses is read, the veil is laid over their hearts. **16** Nevertheless when their heart shall be turned to the Lord, the veil shall be taken away. **17** Now the [q]Lord is the [2]Spirit, and where the Spirit of the Lord is, there is liberty. **18** [r]But we all behold as in a mirror the glory of the Lord with open face, and are changed into the same image, from glory to glory, as by the Spirit of the Lord.

4

1 He showeth that he hath so labored in preaching the Gospel, 4 That such are even blinded of Satan, who do not perceive the brightness thereof, 7 that the same is carried in earthen vessels, 10 who are subject to many miseries: 16 and therefore he exhorteth them by his own example to be courageous, 17 and condemn this present life.

1 Therefore, [a]seeing that we have this ministry, as we have received mercy, we [b]faint not: **2** But have cast from us the [c]cloaks of shame, and walk not in craftiness, neither handle we the word of God [d]deceitfully: but in declaration of the truth we approve ourselves to every man's conscience in the sight of God. **3** [e]If the Gospel be then hid, it is hid to them that are lost. **4** In whom the god of this world hath blinded the minds, that is, of the infidels, that the [f]light of the glorious Gospel of Christ, which is the [g]image of God, should not shine unto them. **5** [h]For we preach not ourselves, but Christ Jesus the Lord, and ourselves your servants for [i]Jesus' sake. **6** For God [1,j]that commanded the light to shine out of darkness, is he which hath shined in our hearts, to give the [k]light of the knowledge of the glory of God in the face of Jesus Christ. **7** [l]But we have this

---

hatred, but of love, and so ends lest if we keep no measure, we serve Satan the devil.

d. 2 Cor. 2:5 As if he said, All that sorrow is so clean wiped away, as though he had never felt it.

e. 2 Cor. 2:5 As for me saith Paul I have no more to do with him.

f. 2 Cor. 2:5 Lest I should overcharge him, who is burdened enough of himself, which I would be glad were taken from him.

g. 2 Cor. 2:7 That whereas before you punished him sharply, you would now forgive him.

h. 2 Cor. 2:8 That at my entreaty, you would declare by the consent of the whole Church, that you take him again for a brother.

i. 2 Cor. 2:10 Truly and from the heart.

j. 2 Cor. 2:11 Of his mischievous counsel and devilish will.

k. 2 Cor. 2:12 He returneth to the confirmation of his Apostleship, and bringeth forth the testimonies, both of his labor, and also of God's blessing.

l. 2 Cor. 2:14 He alludeth to the anointing of the Priests, and the incense of the sacrifices.

m. 2 Cor. 2:15 He denieth that ought should be taken away from the dignity of his Apostleship, because they saw evidently that it was not received with like success in every place, nay rather very many rejected and detested him, seeing that he preacheth Christ, not only as a Savior of them that believe, but also as a Judge of them that condemn him.

n. 2 Cor. 2:16 Again, he putteth away all suspicion of arrogance, attributing all things that he did, to the virtue of God, whom he serveth sincerely, and without all dishonest affection: whereof he maketh them witnesses even to verse 6 of the next chapter.

o. 2 Cor. 2:17 We do not handle it craftily and covetously, or less sincerely than we ought: and he useth a metaphor which is taken from hucksters, which used to play the false harlots with whatsoever cometh into their hands.

2 CORINTHIANS 2

1. 2 Cor. 4:2

2 CORINTHIANS 3

a. 2 Cor. 3:3 The Apostle frameth his speech wisely, that by little and little he may come from the commendation of the person, to the matter itself.

b. 2 Cor. 3:3 Which I took pains to write as it were.

c. 2 Cor. 3:3 By the way he setteth the virtue of God, against the ink wherewith Epistles are commonly written, to show that it was wrought by God.

d. 2 Cor. 3:3 He alludeth by the way, to the comparison of the outward ministry of the Priesthood of Levi, with the ministry of the Gospel, and the Apostolic ministry, which he handleth afterward more fully.

e. 2 Cor. 3:4 This boldness we show, and thus gloriously may we boast of the worthiness and fruit of our ministry.

f. 2 Cor. 3:5 In that we are fit and meet to make other men partakers of so great a grace.

g. 2 Cor. 3:6 He amplifieth his ministry and his fellows: that is to say, the ministry of the Gospel, comparing it with the ministry of the Law, which he considereth in the person of Moses, by whom the Law was given: against whom he setteth Christ the author of the Gospel. Now this comparison is taken from the very substance of the ministry. The Law is as it were a writing of itself dead, and without efficacy: but the Gospel, or new covenant, is as it were the very virtue of God itself, in renewing, justifying, and saving men. The Law propoundeth death, accusing all men of unrighteousness: The Gospel offereth and giveth righteousness and life. The governance of the Law served for a time to the promise: The Gospel remaineth to the end of the world. Therefore what is the glory of that in comparison of the majesty of this?

h. 2 Cor. 3:6 Not of the Law, but of the Gospel.

i. 2 Cor. 3:7 Imprinted and engraven: so that by this place we may plainly perceive, that the Apostle speaketh not of the ceremonies of the Law, but even of the ten commandments.

j. 2 Cor. 3:7 This word Glory, betokeneth a brightness, and a majesty, which was bodily in Moses, but spiritually in Christ.

k. 2 Cor. 3:8 Whereby God offereth, yea and giveth the Spirit, not as a dead thing, but a quickening Spirit, working life.

l. 2 Cor. 3:9 To wit, of Christ, which being imputed to us as our own, we are not only not condemned, but also we are crowned as righteous.

m. 2 Cor. 3:11 The Law, yea, and the ten commandments themselves, together with Moses, is abolished, if we consider the ministry of Moses apart by itself.

n. 2 Cor. 3:12 He showeth wherein standeth this glory of the preaching of the Gospel, to wit, in that that it setteth forth plainly and evidently, that which the Law showeth darkly, for it sent them that heard it to be healed of Christ, which was to come, after it had wounded them.

o. 2 Cor. 3:13 He expoundeth by the way the allegory of Moses' covering, which was a token of the darkness and weakness that is in men, which were rather dulled by the bright shining of the Law, then lightened, which covering was taken away by the coming of Christ, who lighteneth the hearts, and turneth them to the Lord, that we may be brought from the slavery of this blindness, and set in the liberty of the light, by the virtue of Christ's Spirit.

p. 2 Cor. 3:13 Into the very bottom of Moses' ministry.

q. 2 Cor. 3:17 Christ is that spirit which taketh away that covering, by working in our hearts, whereunto also the Law itself called us, though in vain, because it speaketh to dead men, until the spirit quickeneth us.

r. 2 Cor. 3:18 Going forwards in the allegory of the covering, he compareth the Gospel to a glass, which although it be most bright and sparkling, yet doth it not only not dazzle their eyes, which look in it, as the law doth, but also transformeth them with its beams, so that they also be partakers of the glory and shining of it, to lighten others: as Christ said unto his, You are the light of the world, whereas he himself was the only light. We are also commanded in another place, to shine as candles before the world, because we are partakers of God's Spirit. But Paul speaketh here properly, of the ministers of the Gospel, as it appeareth both by that that goeth before, and that that cometh after, and that, setting them his own example and his fellows.

2 CORINTHIANS 3

1. Exod. 34:34 **2.** Job 4:14

2 CORINTHIANS 4

a. 2 Cor. 4:1 Now he plainly witnesseth that both he and his fellows through the mercy of God do their vocation and duty uprightly and sincerely, neglecting all dangers.

b. 2 Cor. 4:1 Though we are broken in pieces with miseries and calamities, yet we yield not.

c. 2 Cor. 4:2 Subtlety, and all kinds of deceit, which men hunt after, as it were dens and lurking holes, to cover their shameless dealings withall.

d. 2 Cor. 4:2 This is it that in the former Chapter he called, making merchandise of the word of God.

e. 2 Cor. 4:3 An objection: Many hear the Gospel, and yet are no more lightened thereby than by the preaching of the Law. He answereth, The fault is in the men themselves, whose eyes Satan plucketh out, who ruleth in this world. And yet notwithstanding doth he and his fellows set forth the most clear light of the Gospel to be seen and beholden, seeing that Christ whom only they preach, is he in whom only God will be known, and as it were seen.

f. 2 Cor. 4:4 The light of plain and lightsome preaching, which telleth forth the glory of Christ.

g. 2 Cor. 4:4 In whom the Father setteth forth himself to be seen and beholden.

h. 2 Cor. 4:5 He removeth according to his accustomed manner, all suspicion of ambition: avouching that he teacheth faithfully, but as a servant, and witnessing that all this light which he and his fellows give to others, proceedeth from the Lord.

i. 2 Cor. 4:5 To preach this selfsame Jesus to you.

j. 2 Cor. 4:6 Which made only with his word.

k. 2 Cor. 4:6 That being lightened of God, we should in like sort give that light to others.

l. 2 Cor. 4:7 He taketh away a stumbling block, by which was darkened, amongst some, the bright shining of the ministry of the Gospel, to wit, because the Apostles were the most

treasure in earthen vessels, [m]that the excellency of that power might be of God, and not of us. **8** We are afflicted on every side, yet are we not in distress: we are in doubt, but yet we despair not. **9** We are persecuted, but not forsaken: cast down, but we perish not. **10** [n]Everywhere we bear about in our body the [o]dying of the Lord Jesus, that the life of Jesus might also be made manifest in our bodies. **11** For we which [p]live, are always delivered unto death for Jesus' sake, that the life also of Jesus might be made manifest in our [q]mortal flesh. **12** [r]So then death worketh in us, and life in you. **13** [s]And because we have the same [t]spirit of faith, according as it is written, [2]I believed, and therefore have I spoken, we also believe, and therefore speak, **14** Knowing that he which hath raised up the Lord Jesus, shall raise us up also by Jesus, and shall set us with you. **15** [u]For all things are for your sakes, [v]that that most plenteous grace by the thanksgiving of many, may redound to the praise of God. **16** Therefore we faint not, [w]but though our outward man perish, yet the inward man is [x]renewed daily. **17** For our [y]light affliction which is but for a moment, causeth unto us a far most excellent and an eternal weight of [z]glory: **18** While we look not on the things which are seen, but on the things which are not seen for the things which are seen, are temporal: but the things which are not seen, are eternal.

5

1 He continueth in the same argument, 5 touching the certain hope of salvation 7 through faith, 12 not to praise himself, 14 seeing he hath God and his Church before his eyes, 17 and esteemeth nothing, but newness of life in Christ.

1 For [a]we know that if our earthly house of this tabernacle be destroyed, we have a building given of God, that is, an house not made with hands, but eternal in the heavens. **2** For therefore we sigh, desiring to be [b]clothed with our house, which is from [c]heaven. **3** [d]Because that if we be clothed, we shall not be found [1]naked. **4** For indeed we that are in this tabernacle, sigh and are burdened because we would not be unclothed, but would be clothed upon, that mortality might be swallowed up of life. **5** And he that hath [e]created us for this thing, is God, who also hath given unto us the earnest of the Spirit. **6** [f]Therefore we are always [g]bold, though we know that while we are at home in the body, we are absent from the Lord. **7** For we walk by [h]faith, and not by sight. **8** Nevertheless, we are [i]bold, and love rather to remove out of the body, and to dwell with the Lord. **9** Wherefore also we [j]covet, that both dwelling at home, and removing from home, we may be acceptable to him. **10** [2,k]For we must all [l]appear before the judgment seat of Christ, that every man may receive the things which are done in his body, according to that he hath done, whether it be good or evil. **11** [m]Knowing therefore that [n]terror of the Lord, we persuade men, and we are made manifest unto God, and I trust also that we are made manifest in your consciences. **12** [o]For we praise not ourselves again unto you, but give you an occasion to rejoice of us that ye may have to answer against them, which rejoice in the [p]face, and not in the heart. **13** [q]For whether we be out of our wit, we are it to God: or whether we be in our right mind, we are it unto you. **14** [r]For that love of Christ [s]constraineth us, **15** Because we thus judge, that if [t]one be dead for all, then were all dead, and he died for all, that they which live, should not henceforth [u]live unto themselves, but unto him which died for them, and rose again. **16** [v]Wherefore, henceforth know we no man after the flesh, [w]yea though we had known Christ after the flesh, yet not henceforth know we him no more. **17** [x]Therefore if any man be in Christ, let him be a [y]new creature. [3]Old things are passed away: behold, all things are become new. **18** [z]And all things are of God, which hath reconciled us unto himself by Jesus Christ, and hath given unto us the ministry of reconciliation. **19** For God was in Christ, and reconciled the world to himself, not imputing their sins unto them, and hath [aa]committed to us the word of reconciliation. **20** Now then are we ambassadors for Christ: as though God did beseech you through us, we pray you in Christ's stead, that ye be reconciled to God. **21** For he hath made him to be [ab]sin for us, which [ac]knew no sin, that we should be made the [ad]righteousness of God in him.

---

miserable of all men, Paul answereth that he and his fellows are as it were earthen vessels, but yet there is in them a most precious treasure.

m. 2 Cor. 4:7 He bringeth marvelous reasons, why the Lord doth so afflict his chiefest servants, to the end saith he that all men may perceive that they stand not by any man's virtue, but by the singular virtue of God, in that they die a thousand times, but never perish.

n. 2 Cor. 4:10 An amplification of the former sentence, wherein he compareth his afflictions to a daily death, and the virtue of the Spirit of God in Christ, to life, which oppresseth that death.

o. 2 Cor. 4:10 So Paul calleth that miserable estate and condition, that the faithful, but especially the minsters, are in.

p. 2 Cor. 4:11 Which live, that life, to wit, by the Spirit of Christ, amongst so many and so great miseries.

q. 2 Cor. 4:11 Subject to that miserable condition.

r. 2 Cor. 4:12 A very cunning conclusion: as if he would say, Therefore to be short, we die, that you may live by our death, for that they ventured into all those dangers for the building of the Church's sake, and they ceased not to confirm all the faithful with the examples of their patience.

s. 2 Cor. 4:13 He declareth the former sentence, showing that he and his fellows die in a sort to purchase life to others, but yet notwithstanding they are partakers of the same life with them: because they themselves do first believe that, which they propound to others to believe, to wit, that they also shall be saved together with them in Christ.

t. 2 Cor. 4:13 The same faith by the inspiration of the same Spirit.

u. 2 Cor. 4:15 He showeth how this constancy is preserved in them, to wit, because they respect God's glory, and the salvation of the Churches committed unto them.

v. 2 Cor. 4:15 When it shall please God to deliver me, and restore me to you, that exceeding benefit which shall be poured upon me, shall in like sort redound to the glory of God, by the thanksgiving of many.

w. 2 Cor. 4:16 He addeth as it were a triumphant song, how that he is outwardly afflicted, but inwardly he profiteth daily: and passeth not at all for all the miseries that may be sustained in this life, in comparison of that most constant and eternal glory.

x. 2 Cor. 4:16 Gathereth new strength, that the outward man be not overcome with the miseries which come freshly one upon the neck of another, being maintained and upholden with the strength of the inward man.

y. 2 Cor. 4:17 Afflictions are not called light, as though they were light of themselves, but because they pass away quickly, when as indeed our whole life is of no long continuance.

z. 2 Cor. 4:17 Which remaineth forever firm and stable, and can never be shaken.

2 CORINTHIANS 4

1. Gen. 1:3 **2.** Ps. 116:10

2 CORINTHIANS 5

a. 2 Cor. 5:1 Taking occasion by the former comparison, he compareth this miserable body, as it is in this life, to a frail and brickle tabernacle, against which he setteth the heavenly Tabernacle, so terming that sure and everlasting condition of this same body glorified in heaven, insomuch, saith he, that we are not only not addicted to this tabernacle, but also do with sobs and sighs desire rather that tabernacle. And so this place also concerning the glory to come, is put within the treatise of the dignity of the ministry, as the other was, whereof we spake in the beginning of the second Chapter.

b. 2 Cor. 5:2 He calleth the glory of immortality, which we shall be as it were clothed with, a garment.

c. 2 Cor. 5:2 Heavenly, not that the substance of it is heavenly, but for the glory of it.

d. 2 Cor. 5:3 An exposition of the former saying: We do not without cause, desire to be clad with the heavenly house, that is, with that everlasting and immortal glory, as with a garment: for when we depart hence, we shall not remain naked, having once cast off the covering of this body, but we shall take our bodies again, which shall put on as it were another garment besides: and therefore we sigh not for the weariness of this life, but for the desire of a better life. Neither is this desire in vain, for we are made to that life, the pledge whereof we have, even the Spirit of adoption.

e. 2 Cor. 5:5 He meaneth that first creation, to give us to understand, that our bodies were made to this end, that they should be clothed with heavenly immortality.

f. 2 Cor. 5:6 He inferreth upon that sentence which went next before, thus, Therefore, seeing that we know by the Spirit, that we are strangers so long as we are here, we patiently suffer this tarriance for we are now so with God, that we behold him but by faith, and are therefore now absent from him but so that we aspire and have a longing always to him: therefore also we behave ourselves so, that we may be acceptable to him, both while we live here, and when we go from hence to him.

g. 2 Cor. 5:6 He calleth them bold which are always resolved with a quiet and settled mind to suffer what dangers soever, nothing doubting, but their end shall be happy.

h. 2 Cor. 5:7 Faith of those things which we hope for, and not having God presently in our view.

i. 2 Cor. 5:8 And yet we are in such sort bold and do so pass on our pilgrimage with a valiant and quiet mind, that yet notwithstanding, we had rather depart hence to the Lord.

j. 2 Cor. 5:9 And seeing it is so, we strive to live so, that both in this our pilgrimage here we may please him, and that at length we may be received home to him.

k. 2 Cor. 5:10 That no man might think it to pertain to all, which he spoke of that heavenly glory, he addeth, that every one shall first render an account of his pilgrimage, after that he is departed from hence.

l. 2 Cor. 5:10 We must all appear personally, and inquiry shall be made of us, that all may see, how we have lived.

m. 2 Cor. 5:11 Now he passeth over, and taking occasion of the former sentence, returneth to 4:16, confirming his own sincerity and his fellows'.

n. 2 Cor. 5:11 That terrible judgment.

o. 2 Cor. 5:12 He removeth all suspicion of pride, by a new reason, because it is behoovable, not for his part, but for theirs, that his Apostleship be counted sincere against the vain ostentation of a few others.

p. 2 Cor. 5:12 In outward disguising, and that colored show of man's wisdom and eloquence, and not in true godliness, which is sealed in the heart.

q. 2 Cor. 5:13 The meaning is: Even when I am mad as some men think of me while I seem as a fool to boast myself, I do it for your profit, no less than when I preach the Gospel simply unto you.

r. 2 Cor. 5:14 He goeth forward in putting away all suspicion of desire of estimation and boasting: for the love of Christ, saith he, compelleth us hereunto, that seeing he died for us all, which were dead when as we lived to ourselves that is, while we were yet given to these earthly affections we in like sort should consecrate our whole life which we have received of him, to him to wit being endued with the holy Ghost to this end and purpose, that we should meditate upon nothing but that which is heavenly.

s. 2 Cor. 5:14 Possesseth us wholly.

t. 2 Cor. 5:15 He speaketh here of sanctification, whereby it cometh to pass that Christ liveth in us.

u. 2 Cor. 5:15 See Romans, chapters 6 and 7.

v. 2 Cor. 5:16 He showeth what it is, not to live to ourselves, but to Christ, to wit, to know no man according to the flesh, that is to say, to be so conversant amongst men, as not to care for those worldly and carnal things, as they do which respect a man's stock, his country, form, glory, riches, and such like, wherein men commonly dote, and weary themselves.

w. 2 Cor. 5:16 An amplification: This is, saith he, so true, that we do not now think carnally of Christ himself, who hath now left the world, and therefore must be considered of us spiritually.

x. 2 Cor. 5:17 An exhortation for every man which is renewed with the spirit of Christ, to meditate heavenly things, and not earthly.

y. 2 Cor. 5:17 As a thing made anew of God, for though a man be not newly created when God giveth him the spirit of regeneration, but only his qualities are changed, yet notwithstanding it pleased the holy Ghost to speak so, to teach us, that we must attribute all things to the glory of God: not that we are as stocks or blocks: but because God creates in us, both the will to will well, and the power to do well.

z. 2 Cor. 5:18 He commendeth the excellency of the ministry of the Gospel, both by the authority of God himself, who is the author of that ministry, and also by the excellency of the doctrine of it: for it announceth atonement with God, by free forgiveness of our sins, and justification offered unto us in Christ, and that so lovingly and liberally, that God himself doth after a sort pray men by the mouth of his ministers, to have consideration of themselves, and not to despise so great a benefit. And when he so saith, he plainly reprehendeth them which falsely challenged to themselves the name of pastors.

aa. 2 Cor. 5:19 Used our labor and travail.

ab. 2 Cor. 5:21 A sinner, not in himself, but by imputation of the guilt of all our sins to him.

ac. 2 Cor. 5:21 Who was clean void of sin.

ad. 2 Cor. 5:21 Righteous before God, and that with righteousness which is not essential to us, but being essential in Christ, God imputeth it to us through faith.

2 CORINTHIANS 5

1. Rev. 16:15 **3.** Isa. 43:19 / Rev. 21:5
2. Rom. 14:10

6

1 He exhorteth them to lead their lives as it becometh Christians, 5 neither to be dismayed in tribulations, 9 nor puffed up with glory: 14 to avoid all uncleanness, 16 considering that they are the temples of the living God.

1 So [a]we therefore as workers together beseech you, that ye receive not the grace of God in vain. **2** [b]For he saith, [1]I have heard thee in a time [c]accepted, and in the day of salvation have I succored thee: behold now the accepted time, behold now the day of salvation. **3** [d]We give no occasion of offence in anything, that our ministry should not be reprehended. **4** But in all things we [e]approve ourselves as [2]the ministers of God, [f]in much patience, in afflictions, in necessities, in distresses. **5** In stripes, in prisons, in [g]tumults, in labors, **6** [h]By watchings, by fastings, by purity, by knowledge, by long suffering, by kindness, by the holy Ghost, by love unfeigned, **7** By the [i]word of truth, by the [j]power of God, by the [k]armor of righteousness on the right hand, and on the left, **8** By honor, and dishonor, by evil report, and good report, as deceivers, and yet true: **9** As unknown, and yet known: as dying, and behold, we live, as chastened, and yet not killed: **10** As sorrowing, and yet always rejoicing: as poor, and yet making many rich: as having nothing, and yet possessing all things. **11** [l]O Corinthians, our mouth is [m]open unto you, our heart is made large. **12** Ye are not [n]kept strait in us, but ye are kept strait in your own [o]bowels. **13** Now for the same recompense, I speak as to my children, Be you also enlarged. **14** [p]Be not unequally yoked with the infidels: for what fellowship hath righteousness with unrighteousness? and what communion hath light with darkness? **15** And what concord hath Christ with Belial? or what [q]part hath the believer with the infidel? **16** And what agreement hath the Temple of God with idols? [3]for ye are the Temple of the [r]living God: as God hath said, [4]I will [s]dwell among them, and walk there: and I will be their God, and they shall be my people. **17** [5]Wherefore come out from among them, and separate yourselves, saith the Lord, and touch none unclean thing, and I will receive you. **18** [6]And I will be a Father unto you, and ye shall be my sons and daughters, saith the Lord Almighty.

7

1 Lest by overmuch urging them he should dismay their tender minds, 2 he proveth that all that he said, 4 proceeded of the great good will he bare unto them: 8 and therefore they should not be offended, that he made them sorry, 10 and brought them to repentance not to be repented of.

1 Seeing then we have these promises, dearly beloved, let us cleanse ourselves from all filthiness of the [a]flesh and spirit, and finish our sanctification in the fear of God. **2** [b,c]Receive us: we have done wrong to no man: we have corrupted no man: we have defrauded no man. **3** I speak it not to your [d]condemnation: for I have said before, that ye are in our hearts, to die and live together. **4** I use great boldness of speech toward you: I rejoice greatly in you: I am filled with comfort, and am exceeding joyous in all our tribulation. **5** For when we were come into Macedonia, our flesh had no rest, but we were troubled on every side, fightings without, and terrors within. **6** But God, that comforteth the [e]abject, comforted us at the [f]coming of Titus: **7** And not by his coming only, but also by the consolation wherewith he was comforted of you, when he told us your great desire, your mourning, your fervent mind to me-ward, so that I rejoiced much more. **8** [g]For though I made you sorry with a letter, I repent not, though I did repent: for I perceive that the same Epistle made you sorry, though it were but for a season. **9** I now rejoice, not that ye were sorry, but that ye sorrowed to [h]repentance: for ye sorrowed godly, so that in nothing ye were hurt by us. **10** For [i]godly sorrow causeth repentance unto salvation, not to be repented of: but the worldly sorrow causeth death. **11** For behold, this thing that ye have been godly sorry, what great care hath it wrought in you: yea, what clearing of yourselves: yea, what indignation: yea, what fear: yea, how great desire: yea, what a zeal: yea, what revenge: in all things ye have showed yourselves, that ye are pure in this matter. **12** Wherefore, though I wrote unto you, I did not it for his cause that had done the wrong, neither for his cause that had the injury, but that our care toward you in the [j]sight of God might appear unto you. **13** Therefore we were comforted, because ye were comforted: but rather we rejoiced much more for the joy of Titus, because his spirit was refreshed by you all. **14** For if that I have boasted anything to him of you, I have not been ashamed: but as I have spoken unto you all things in truth, even so our boasting unto Titus was true. **15** And his inward affection is more abundant toward you, when he remembereth the obedience of you all, and how with fear and trembling ye received him. **16** I rejoice therefore that I may put my confidence in you in all things.

8

1 He exhorteth them by the example of the Macedonians, 9 and also even of Christ himself, 14 to be liberal towards the saints: 16 for which purpose, he showeth that Titus, 18 and another brother came unto them.

1 We [a]do you also to wit, brethren, of the [b]grace of God bestowed upon the Churches of Macedonia. **2** Because in [c]great trial of affliction their joy abounded, and their most extreme poverty abounded unto their rich liberality. **3** For to their power I bear record yea, and beyond their power they were [d]willing. **4** And prayed us with great instance that we would receive the [e]grace, and fellowship of the ministering which is toward the Saints. **5** [f]And this they did, not as we looked for: but gave their own selves, first to the Lord, and after unto us by the will of God, **6** That we should exhort Titus, that as he had begun, so he would also accomplish the same grace among you also. **7** Therefore, as ye abound in everything, in faith and word, and knowledge, and in all diligence, and in your love towards us, even so see that ye abound in this grace also. **8** [g]This say I not by commandment, but because of the [h]diligence of others: therefore prove I the [i]naturalness of your love. **9** [j]For ye know the grace of our Lord Jesus Christ, that he being rich, for your sakes became poor, that ye through his poverty might be

---

2 CORINTHIANS 6

- **a.** 2 Cor. 6:1 Men do not only need the ministry of the Gospel, before they have received grace, that they may be partakers of it, but also after they have received grace, that they may continue in it.
- **b.** 2 Cor. 6:2 In that that grace is offered, it is of the grace of God, who hath appointed times and seasons to all things, that we may take occasion when it is offered.
- **c.** 2 Cor. 6:2 Which I of my free mercy and love towards you, . . . appointed, at which time God poured out that his marvelous love upon us.
- **d.** 2 Cor. 6:3 He showeth the Cor. a pattern of a true minister, in his own example, and Timothy and Silvanus, to the end, that as he purposed from the beginning he might procure authority to himself and his like.
- **e.** 2 Cor. 6:4 Declare and show indeed.
- **f.** 2 Cor. 6:4 He first of all reckoneth up those things which are neither always in the ministers, nor without exception, unless it be according to the affection of the mind, patience only except, which also is one of the virtues which ought to be always in a good minister.
- **g.** 2 Cor. 6:5 In tossing to and fro, finding no place of rest and quietness.
- **h.** 2 Cor. 6:6 Secondly, he reckoneth up such virtues as are necessary, and ought always to be in them, and whereby as by good armor, all lets and hindrances may be overcome.
- **i.** 2 Cor. 6:7 Preaching of the Gospel.
- **j.** 2 Cor. 6:7 Power to work miracles, and to bring under the wicked.
- **k.** 2 Cor. 6:7 Uprightness.
- **l.** 2 Cor. 6:11 Going about to rebuke them, he saith first, that he dealeth with them sincerely and with an open and plain heart, and therewithall complaineth that they do not the like in loving again their Father.
- **m.** 2 Cor. 6:11 The opening of the mouth and heart, betokeneth a most earnest affection in him that speaketh, as it fareth commonly with them that are in some great joy.
- **n.** 2 Cor. 6:12 You are in mine heart, as in an house, and that no narrow or strait house, for I have opened my whole heart to you, but you are inwardly straitlaced to me-ward.
- **o.** 2 Cor. 6:12 After the manner of the Hebrews, he calleth those tender affections which rest in the heart, bowels.
- **p.** 2 Cor. 6:14 Now he rebuked them boldly, for that they became fellows with infidels in outward idolatry, as though it were a thing indifferent. And this is the fourth part of this Epistle, the conclusion whereof is, that such as the Lord has vouchsafed the name of his children, must keep themselves pure, not only in mind, but also in body, that they may wholly be holy unto the Lord.
- **q.** 2 Cor. 6:15 What can there be between them?
- **r.** 2 Cor. 6:16 He setteth the living God against idols.
- **s.** 2 Cor. 6:16 God dwelleth with us, because Christ is become God with us.

2 CORINTHIANS 6

1.	Isa. 49:8	**4.**	Lev. 26:11
2.	1 Cor. 4:1	**5.**	Isa. 52:11
3.	1 Cor. 3:16 / 1 Cor. 6:19	**6.**	Jer. 31:1

2 CORINTHIANS 7

- **a.** 2 Cor. 7:1 Both of body and soul, that by this means the sanctification may be perfect, consisting in both the parts thereof.
- **b.** 2 Cor. 7:2 He returneth again from that admonition to his own person, opposing the testimonies both of his faithfulness and also of his continual good will towards them.
- **c.** 2 Cor. 7:2 Let me have some place amongst you, that I may teach you.
- **d.** 2 Cor. 7:3 To condemn you of unkindness or treachery.
- **e.** 2 Cor. 7:6 Whose hearts are cast down, and are very far spent.
- **f.** 2 Cor. 7:6 With those things which Titus told me of you at his coming, to wit, how fruitfully you read over my letters, moreover and besides that, I am exceedingly refreshed with his presence.
- **g.** 2 Cor. 7:8 An objection: But thou hast handled us roughly. The Apostle answereth that he used not this toughness without grief. And he addeth moreover, that he is also glad now that he drove them to that sorrow, although it was against his will, since it was so profitable unto them: for there is a sorrow not only praiseworthy, but also necessary, to wit, whereby repentance groweth by certain degrees, for the which repentance he praiseth them highly. And this is the fifth part of this Epistle.
- **h.** 2 Cor. 7:9 Insomuch that that sorrow did you much good toward the amending of your lewdness and sins.
- **i.** 2 Cor. 7:10 Godly sorrow is when we are not terrified with the fear of punishment, but because we feel we have offended God our most merciful Father: contrary to this, there is another sorrow, that only feareth punishment, or when a man is vexed for the loss of some worldly goods: the fruit of the first, repentance, and the fruit of the second, is desperation, unless the Lord helps speedily.
- **j.** 2 Cor. 7:12 It was not colored nor counterfeit, but such as I dare stand to before God.

2 CORINTHIANS 8

- **a.** 2 Cor. 8:1 The sixth part of this epistle containing divers exhortations to stir up the Cor. to liberality, wherewith the poverty of the Church of Jerusalem might be holpen in time convenient. And first of all he setteth out before them the example of the Churches of Macedonia, which otherwise were brought by great misery to extreme poverty, to the end that they should follow them.
- **b.** 2 Cor. 8:1 The benefit that God bestowed upon the Churches.
- **c.** 2 Cor. 8:2 For those manifold afflictions wherewith the Lord tried them, did not only not quail their joyful readiness, but also made it much more excellent, and famous.
- **d.** 2 Cor. 8:3 Of their own accord they were liberal.
- **e.** 2 Cor. 8:4 He calleth that, Grace, that other men would have called a burden. And this verse is to be expounded by the sixth verse.
- **f.** 2 Cor. 8:5 He amplifieth the forwardness of the Macedonians, in this, that they also desired Paul to stir up the Cor. to accomplish the giving of alms, by sending again of Titus unto them.
- **g.** 2 Cor. 8:8 Thirdly he warneth them that they deceive not their expectation which they have conceived of them.
- **h.** 2 Cor. 8:8 At the request of the Macedonians.
- **i.** 2 Cor. 8:8 Then appeareth the naturalness of our love, when as in deed and that frankly and freely we help our brethren, even for Christ's sake.
- **j.** 2 Cor. 8:9 The fourth argument taken from the example of Christ.

made rich. 10 [k]And I show my mind herein: for this is expedient for you, which
have begun not to do only, but also to [l]will, a year ago. 11 Now therefore per-
form to do it also, that as there was a readiness to will, even so ye may perform it
of that which ye have. 12 [m]For if there be first a willing mind, it is accepted ac-
cording to that a man hath, and not according to that he hath not. 13 [n]Neither
is it that other men should be eased and you grieved: But upon [o]like condition,
at this time your abundance supplieth their lack: 14 That also their abundan-
ce may be for your lack, that there may be equality. 15 As it is written, [1]He
that gathered much, had nothing over, and he that gathered little, had not the
less. 16 [p]And thanks be unto God, which had put in the heart of Titus the same
care for you. 17 Because he accepted the exhortation, yea, he was so careful that
of his own accord he went unto you. 18 And we have sent also with him the
brother, whose praise is [q]in the Gospel throughout all the Churches. 19 And not
so only, but is also chosen of the Churches to be a fellow in our journey, concerning
this [r]grace that is ministered by us unto the glory of the same Lord, and declaration
of your prompt mind. 20 Avoiding this, that no man should blame us in this [s]a-
bundance that is ministered by us, 21 [2]Providing for honest things, not only be-
fore the Lord, but also before men. 22 And we have sent with them our brother,
whom we have ofttimes proved to be diligent in many things, but now much more
diligent, for the great confidence, which I have in you. 23 Whether any do in-
quire of Titus, he is my fellow and helper to you-ward: or of our [t]brethren, they
are messengers of the Churches, and the [u]glory of Christ. 24 Wherefore show
toward them, and before the [v]Churches the proof of your love, and of the rejoicing
that we have of you.

9

1 Why, albeit he think well of their ready wills, 3 yet earnestly exhorteth them, 4 he yieldeth a reason: 6 He compareth alms to seed sowing, 10 which God doth repay with great gain.

1 For [a]as touching the ministering to the Saints, it is superfluous for me to
write unto you. 2 For I know your readiness of mind, whereof I boast myself of
you unto them of Macedonia, and say, that Achaia was prepared a year ago, and
your zeal hath provoked many. 3 Now have I sent the brethren, lest our rejoicing
over you should be in vain in this behalf, that ye as I have said be ready. 4 Lest
if they of Macedonia come with me, and find you unprepared, we that we may
not say, you should be ashamed in this my [b]constant boasting. 5 Wherefore, I
thought it necessary to exhort the brethren to come before unto you, and to finish
your benevolence appointed afore, that it might be ready, and come as of benevo-
lence, and not as of [c]niggardliness. 6 [d]This yet remember, that he which soweth
sparingly, shall reap also sparingly, and he that soweth liberally, shall reap also li-
berally. 7 As every man [e]wisheth in his heart, so let him give, not [1,f]grudgingly,
or of [g]necessity: for God loveth a cheerful giver. 8 And God is able to make all
[h]grace to abound toward you, that ye always having all sufficiency in all things,
may abound in [i]every good work, 9 [2]As it is written, He hath sparsed abroad
and hath given to the poor: his benevolence remaineth for [j]ever. 10 Also he
that findeth seed to the sower, will minister likewise bread for food, and multiply
your seed, and increase the [k]fruits of your benevolence. 11 That on all parts ye
may be made rich unto all liberality, which causeth through us thanksgiving unto
God. 12 [l]For the ministration of this service not only supplieth the necessities of
the Saints, but also abundantly causeth many to give thanks to God, 13 Which
by the [m]experiment of this ministration praise God for your [n]voluntary submis-
sion to the Gospel of Christ, and for your liberal distribution to them, and to all
men. 14 And in their prayer for you, to long after you greatly, for the abundant
grace of God in you. 15 [o]Thanks therefore be unto God for his unspeakable gift.

10

2 He showeth with what confidence, 4 with what weapons, 6 and with what revenge he is armed against the cavillations of the wicked, 7 and that, when he is present, his deeds have no less power, 11 than his words have force when he is absent.

1 Now [a]I Paul myself beseech you by the meekness, and [b]gentleness of Christ,
which when I am present among you am base, but am bold toward you being ab-
sent: 2 And this I require you, that I need not to be bold when I am present, with
that same confidence, wherewith I think to be bold against some, which esteem us
as though we walked [c]according to the flesh. 3 [d]Nevertheless, though we walk in
the flesh, yet we do not war after the flesh. 4 For the weapons of our warfare are
not [e]carnal, but mighty through [f]God, to cast down holds. 5 Casting down the
imaginations, and every high thing that is exalted against the knowledge of God,
[g]and bringing into captivity every thought to the obedience of Christ, 6 And
having ready the vengeance against all disobedience, when your obedience is ful-
filled. 7 [h]Look ye on things after the [i]appearance? If any man trust in himself
that he is Christ's, let him consider this again of [j]himself, that as he is Christ's, even
so are we Christ's. 8 For though I should boast somewhat more of our autho-
rity, which the Lord hath given us for edification, and not for your destruction, I
should have no shame. 9 This I say, that I may not seem as it were to fear you
with letters. 10 For the letters, saith [k]he, are sore and strong, but his bodily
presence is weak, and his speech is of no value. 11 Let such one think this, that
such as we are in word by letters, when we are absent, such will we be also in deed,
when we are present. 12 [l]For we [m]dare not make ourselves of the number, or to
compare ourselves to them, which praise themselves: but they understand not that
they measure themselves with [n]themselves, and [o]compare themselves with them-
selves. 13 But we will not rejoice of things, which are not within our [p]measure,

---

k. 2 Cor. 8:10 He taketh good heed that he seem not to wrest it out of them by constraint, for unless it be voluntary, God doth not accept it.

l. 2 Cor. 8:10 Not only to do, but also to do willingly: for he noteth out a ready willingness without any enforcement by any other men; much less came it of ambition and vainglory.

m. 2 Cor. 8:12 Against such as use to excuse themselves, because they are not rich, as though it were only proper to rich men to help the poor.

n. 2 Cor. 8:13 Christian liberality is mutual, that proportion may be ob-served.

o. 2 Cor. 8:13 That like as now in your abundance you help others, which are poor, with some part of your goods, so should others in like sort bestow some of theirs upon you.

p. 2 Cor. 8:16 He commendeth Titus and his two companions for many causes, both that their credit might not be suspected, as though he had sent them slyly to spoil the Churches, and also that they might be so much the readier to contribute.

q. 2 Cor. 8:18 In the preaching of the Gospel.

r. 2 Cor. 8:19 These alms which are bestowed for the relief of the Church of Jerusalem.

s. 2 Cor. 8:20 In this plentiful liberality of the Churches, which is committed to our trust.

t. 2 Cor. 8:23 Titus's two companions.

u. 2 Cor. 8:23 By whom the glory of Christ is set forth.

v. 2 Cor. 8:24 All Churches shall be witnesses of this your godly dealing, in whose presence you are, for so much as you see the messengers whom they have chosen by all their consents, and sent them unto you.

2 CORINTHIANS 8

1. Exod. 16:18 **2.** Rom. 12:17

2 CORINTHIANS 9

a. 2 Cor. 9:1 He wisely meeteth with the suspicion which the Cor. might conceive, as though the Apostle in urging them so carefully, should doubt of their good will. Therefore he witnesseth that he doeth it not to teach them that they ought to help the Saints, seeing that he had become surety for them to the Macedonians, but only to stir them up which were running of themselves to the end that all things might both be in a better readiness, and also be more plentiful.

b. 2 Cor. 9:4 The word which he useth, signifieth such a stayedness and settledness of mind, as cannot be moved with any terror or fear.

c. 2 Cor. 9:5 As from covetous men.

d. 2 Cor. 9:6 Alms must be given neither niggardly, nor with a loathful mind, or hardly: But as frank and free alms is compared to a sowing which hath a most plentiful harvest of most abundant blessing following it.

e. 2 Cor. 9:7 Determineth and appointeth freely with himself.

f. 2 Cor. 9:7 With a sparing and niggardly heart.

g. 2 Cor. 9:7 Against his will, as loath to be evil reported of.

h. 2 Cor. 9:8 All God's bountiful liberality.

i. 2 Cor. 9:8 To help others by all means possible, in doing them good in their necessities.

j. 2 Cor. 9:9 Is everlasting: Now David speaketh of a man that feareth God, and loveth his neighbor, who shall never want saith he to give to others.

k. 2 Cor. 9:10 There is none so good an inheritance to the godly, as bountifulness is.

l. 2 Cor. 9:12 Another excellent and double fruit of liberality towards the Saints, is this: that it giveth occasion to praise God, and that our faith is also thereby made manifest.

m. 2 Cor. 9:13 By this proof of your liberality in this helping and succoring of them.

n. 2 Cor. 9:13 In showing with one consent, that you acknowledge that only Gospel which you have willingly submitted yourselves unto, declaring thereby, that you agree with the Church of Jerusalem.

o. 2 Cor. 9:15 Lest by his great commendation and praise, the Cor. should be puffed up, he shutteth up this exhortation, with this exclamation.

2 CORINTHIANS 9

1. Rom. 12:8 **2.** Ps. 112:9

2 CORINTHIANS 10

a. 2 Cor. 10:1 He returneth to the defense of his Apostleship, but so that he useth this authority therein: for he warneth them earnestly and gravely, using also terrible threatenings to show themselves such as are apt to be instructed. And he refelleth certain proud men which made no better accompt of him, than of a bragging Thraso, in that he used to be sharp against them when he was absent, because they saw no great majesty in him after the manner of men, and besides, had proved his lenity, notwithstanding that in his absence, he had written to them sharply. Therefore first of all he professeth that he was gentle and moderate, but after the example of Christ: but if they continue, still to despise his gentleness, he protesteth unto them that he will show indeed how far they are deceived, which make that accompt of the office of an Apostle, that they do of worldly offices, that is, according to the outward appearance.

b. 2 Cor. 10:1 That nature which is inclined to mercy, rather than to rigor of justice.

c. 2 Cor. 10:2 As though I had no other aid and help than that which outwardly I seem to have: and therefore Paul setteth his flesh, that is, his weak condition and state, against his spiritual and Apostolic dignity.

d. 2 Cor. 10:3 Secondly he witnesseth, that although he be like unto other men, yet he cometh furnished with that strength, which no holds of man can match, whether they resist by craft and deceit, or by force and might, because he warrioreth with divine weapons.

e. 2 Cor. 10:4 Are not such as men get them authority withall one of another, and do great acts.

f. 2 Cor. 10:4 Stand upon that infinite power of God.

g. 2 Cor. 10:5 An amplification of this spiritual virtue, which in such sort conquereth the enemies be they never so crafty and mighty, that it bringeth some of them by repentance unto Christ, and justly revengeth others, that are stubbornly obstinate, separating them from the others which suffer themselves to be ruled.

h. 2 Cor. 10:7 He beateth into their heads that same matter, with great weight of words and sentences.

i. 2 Cor. 10:7 Do ye judge of things according to the outward show.

j. 2 Cor. 10:7 Not being told of it by me.

k. 2 Cor. 10:10 He noteth out someone that was the seeds man of this speech.

l. 2 Cor. 10:12 Being constrained to refel the foolish brags of certain ambitious men, he witnesseth, that they are able to bring nothing, but that they falsely persuade themselves of themselves: and as for himself, although he brags of excellent things, yet he will not pass the bounds which God hath measured him out, according whereunto he came even unto them in preaching the Gospel of Christ, and trusteth that he shall go further, when they have so profited that he shall not need to tarry any longer amongst them to instruct them. And hereunto is added an amplification, in that he never succeeded other men in their labors.

m. 2 Cor. 10:12 This is spoken after a taunting sort.

n. 2 Cor. 10:12 Upon a vain persuasion that they have of themselves, they take upon them they care not what.

o. 2 Cor. 10:12 They condemn all others, and measure all their doings only by themselves.

p. 2 Cor. 10:13 Of those things which God hath not measured to me.

[1]but according to the measure of the line, whereof God hath distributed unto us
a measure to attain even unto you. **14** For we stretch not ourselves beyond our
measure, as though we had not attained unto you: for even to you also have we
come in preaching the Gospel of Christ. **15** Not boasting of things which are
[q]without our measure: that is, of other men's labors: and we hope, when your faith
shall increase, to be magnified by you according to your line abundantly, **16** And
to preach the Gospel in those regions which are beyond you: not to rejoice in [r]a-
nother man's line: that is, in the things that are prepared already. **17** [2,s]But let
him that rejoiceth, rejoice in the Lord. **18** For he that praiseth himself, is not
allowed, but he whom the Lord praiseth.

11

2 He testifieth that for the great loves sake he beareth to the Corinthians, he is compelled 5 to utter his own praises: 9 and that he bestowed his labor on them without any reward, 13 that the false apostles should not surpass him in anything, 22 whom he far excelled in those things which are praiseworthy indeed.

1 Would [a]to God, ye could suffer a little my foolishness, and indeed, ye suf-
fer me. **2** For I am jealous over you, with [b]godly jealousy: for I have prepared
you for one husband, to [c]present you as a pure virgin to Christ: **3** But I fear
lest as the [1]serpent beguiled Eve through his subtlety, so your minds should be
[d]corrupt from the simplicity that is in [e]Christ: **4** [f]For if he that cometh, prea-
cheth [g]another Jesus whom we have not preached: or if ye receive another spirit
whom ye have not received: either another Gospel which ye have not received, ye
might well have suffered him. **5** Verily I suppose that I was not inferior to the
very chief Apostles. **6** [h]And though I be [i]rude in speaking, yet I am not so in
knowledge, but among you we have been made manifest to the uttermost, in all
things. **7** [j]Have I committed an offence, because I abased myself, that ye might
be exalted, and because I preached to you the Gospel of God freely? **8** I robbed
other Churches, and took wages of them to do you service. **9** And when I was
present with you, and had need, [2]I was not slothful to the hindrance of any man:
for that which was lacking unto me, the brethren which came from Macedonia,
supplied, and in all things I kept, [k]and will keep myself, that I should not be grie-
vous unto you. **10** The [l]truth of Christ is in me, that this rejoicing shall not be
[m]shut up against me in the regions of Achaia. **11** Wherefore? because I love you
not? God knoweth. **12** But what I do, that will I do, that I may cut away occa-
sion from them which desire occasion, that they might be found like unto us in
that wherein they [n]rejoice. **13** [o]For such false apostles are deceitful workers, and
transform themselves into the Apostles of Christ. **14** And no marvel: for Satan
himself is transformed into an Angel of [p]light. **15** Therefore it is no great thing,
though his ministers transform themselves, as though they were the ministers of
righteousness, whose end shall be according to their works. **16** [q]I say again, Let
no man think that I am foolish, or else take me even as a fool, that I also may boast
myself a little. **17** That I speak, I speak it not after the Lord: but as it were fooli-
shly, in this my great boasting. **18** Seeing that many rejoice after the flesh, I will
rejoice also. **19** For ye suffer fools gladly, because that ye are wise. **20** [r]For ye
suffer, even if a man bring you into bondage, if a man devour you, if a man take
your goods, if a man exalt himself, if a man smite you on the face. **21** I speak as
concerning the [s]reproach: as though that we had been [t]weak: but wherein any man
is bold I speak foolishly I am bold also. **22** They are Hebrews, [3]so am I: they are
Israelites, so am I: they are the seed of Abraham, so am I. **23** They are the mi-
nisters of Christ I speak as a fool I am [u]more: in labors more abundant: in stripes
above measure: in prison more plenteously: in [v]death oft. **24** Of the Jews [w]five
times received I forty stripes save one. **25** I was [x]thrice [4]beaten with rods: I was
[5]once stoned: I suffered thrice [6]shipwreck: night and day have I been in the deep
sea. **26** In journeying I was often, in perils of waters, in perils of robbers, in pe-
rils of mine own nation, in perils among the Gentiles, in perils in the city, in perils
in wilderness, in perils in the sea, in perils among false brethren, **27** In weari-
ness and [y]painfulness, in watching often, in hunger and thirst, in fastings often, in
cold and in nakedness. **28** [z]Beside the things which are outward, I am cumbered
daily, and have the care of all the Churches. **29** Who is weak, and I am not weak?
Who is offended, and I burn not? **30** [aa]If I must needs rejoice, I will rejoice of
mine infirmities. **31** The God, even the Father of our Lord Jesus Christ, which
is blessed for evermore, knoweth that I lie not. **32** In [7]Damascus the governor of
the people under King Aretas, laid watch in the city of the Damascenes, and would
have caught me. **33** But at a window was I let down in a basket through the wall,
and escaped his hands.

12

1 He doth even unwillingly make rehearsal, 3 of the heavenly visions, 4 that were revealed unto him, 6 for which though he might indeed glory, yet he will not, 10 being privy of his own infirmities: 11 but they drive him to this kind of folly, 20 in that they give ear to certain vainglorious persons, who draw them from Christ.

1 It [a]is not expedient for me no doubt to rejoice: for I will come to visions
and revelations of the Lord. **2** I know a man [b]in Christ above fourteen years ago,
whether he were in the body, I cannot tell, or out of the body, I cannot tell: God
knoweth which was taken up into the [c]third heaven. **3** And I know such a man
whether in the body, or out of the body, I cannot tell: God knoweth. **4** How
that he was taken up into [d]Paradise, and heard words which [e]cannot be spoken,
which are not [f]possible for man to utter. **5** [g]Of such a man will I rejoice: of

---

q. 2 Cor. 10:15 As though God had divided the whole world among the Apostles, to be husbanded.

r. 2 Cor. 10:16 In countries which other men have prepared and husbanded with the preaching of the Gospel.

s. 2 Cor. 10:17 He somewhat mitigateth that which he spake of himself and therewith also prepareth the Cor. to hear other things, witnessing that he seeketh nothing else but to approve himself to God, whose glory he only seeketh.

2 CORINTHIANS 10

1. Eph. 4:7
2. Jer. 9:24 / 1 Cor. 1:31

2 CORINTHIANS 11

a. 2 Cor. 11:1 He granteth that after a sort he playeth the fool in this vaunting of things, but he addeth that he doeth it against his will, for their profit because he seeth them deceived by certain vain and crafty men, through the craft and subtlety of Satan.

b. 2 Cor. 11:2 He speaketh as a woer, but yet as one that seeketh them not for himself, but for God.

c. 2 Cor. 11:2 To marry you together.

d. 2 Cor. 11:3 This place is to be marked against them which loathe that plain and pure simplicity of the Scriptures, in comparison of the colors and paintings of man's eloquence.

e. 2 Cor. 11:3 Which is meet for them that are in Christ.

f. 2 Cor. 11:4 He showeth that they deceive themselves, if they look to receive of any other man, either a more excellent Gospel, or more excellent gifts of the holy Ghost.

g. 2 Cor. 11:4 A more perfect doctrine of Jesus Christ.

h. 2 Cor. 11:6 He refuteth the slanders of those Thrasoes. I grant, saith he, that I am not so eloquent an Orator, but yet they cannot take away the knowledge of the Gospel from me, whereof you have had good proof, and that every manner of way.

i. 2 Cor. 11:6 Paul lacked not the kind of eloquence which is meet for a man, and fit for the Gospel, but he willingly wanted that painted kind of speech, which too many nowadays hunt after and follow.

j. 2 Cor. 11:7 Another slander, to wit, that he was a rascal, and lived by the labor of his own hands. But herein, saith the Apostle, what can you lay against me, but that I was content to take any pains for your sakes, and when I lacked, to travail for my living with mine own hands in part, and partly also when poverty constrained me, I chose rather otherwise to seek my sustenance, than to be any burden to you, although I preached the Gospel unto you?

k. 2 Cor. 11:9 An amplification: so far is he from being ashamed of this act, that he hath also resolved with himself to do no otherwise hereafter amongst them, to the intent that it may always be truly said, that he taught in Achaia for nothing: not that he disdaineth the Cor., but that these Thrasoes may never find the occasion which they have already sought for, and he in the mean season may set something before them to follow, that at length they may truly say, that they are like to Paul.

l. 2 Cor. 11:10 This is a form of an oath, as if he said, let me not be thought to have any truth in me.

m. 2 Cor. 11:10 Shall be always open to me.

n. 2 Cor. 11:12 Paul's adversaries sought all occasions they could, to be equal to him. And therefore seeing they had rather eat up the Cor., than preach to them for nothing, they sought another occasion, to wit, to make Paul to take something: which thing if he had done, then hoped they by that means to be equal to him: for they made such a show of zeal and knowledge, and set it forth with such a glossing kind of eloquence, that some of them even despised Paul: but he showeth that all this is nothing but colors and painting.

o. 2 Cor. 11:13 Now at length he pointeth out these fellows in their colors, forewarning that it will come to pass, that they will at length betray themselves, what countenance soever they make of zeal that they have to God's glory.

p. 2 Cor. 11:14 By light is meant the heavenly glory, whereof the Angels are partakers.

q. 2 Cor. 11:16 He goeth forward boldly, and using a vehement Irony of kind of taunting, desireth the Cor. to pardon him, if for a time he contend as a fool before them being wise, with those jolly fellows touching those eternal things, to wit, touching his stock, his ancestors and valiant acts.

r. 2 Cor. 11:20 Before he cometh to the matter, he toucheth the Cor., who persuading themselves to very wise men, did not mark in the mean season that those false apostles abused their simplicity for advantage.

s. 2 Cor. 11:21 As if he said, in respect of that reproach which they do unto you I speak it which surely is as evil as if they did beat you.

t. 2 Cor. 11:21 Paul is called weak, in that he seemeth to the Cor. a vile and abject man, a beggarly artificer, a most wretched and miserable idiot, whereas notwithstanding therein God's mighty power was made manifest.

u. 2 Cor. 11:23 Paul being honorable indeed, defendeth his ministry openly, not for his own sake, but because he saw his doctrine come into hazard.

v. 2 Cor. 11:23 In danger of present death.

w. 2 Cor. 11:24 He alludeth to that that is written, Deut. 25:3, and moreover this place showeth us, that Paul suffered many things which Luke passed over.

x. 2 Cor. 11:25 Of the Roman Magistrates.

y. 2 Cor. 11:27 Painfulness is a troublesome sickness, as when a man who is weary and would rest, he is constrained to fall to new labor.

z. 2 Cor. 11:28 He addeth this in conclusion further, that the Cor. might be ashamed to despise him, upon whose care almost all Churches depended, as it was plainly seen by experience.

aa. 2 Cor. 11:30 He turneth that against the adversaries, which they objected against him: as if he should say, They allege my calamities, to take away my authority from me: but if I would boast myself, I would take no better argument: and God himself is my witness that I devise and forge nothing.

2 CORINTHIANS 11

1. Gen. 3:4
2. 2 Cor. 12:13
3. Phil. 3:5
4. Acts 16:23
5. Acts 14:19
6. Acts 27:14
7. Acts 9:24

2 CORINTHIANS 12

a. 2 Cor. 12:1 He goeth forward in his purpose, and because those bragging mates boasted of revelations, he reckoneth up those things which lift him up above the common capacity of men: but he useth a preface, and excuseth himself advisedly.

b. 2 Cor. 12:2 I speak this in Christ, that is, be it spoken without vainglory, for I seek nothing but Christ Jesus only.

c. 2 Cor. 12:2 Into the highest heaven: for we need not to dispute subtly upon the word Third but yet this place is to be marked against them which make heaven to be everywhere.

d. 2 Cor. 12:4 So the Grecians name that which we call a park, that is to say, a place where trees are planted, and wild beasts kept, by which name they that translated the old Testament out of the Hebrew into Greek, called the garden Eden, whereunto Adam was put straight after his creation, as a most delicate and pleasant place. And hereunto grew it, that that blessed seat of the glory of God is called by that name.

e. 2 Cor. 12:4 Which no man is able to utter.

f. 2 Cor. 12:4 Which the Saints themselves are not by any means able to express, because it is God himself. Thus doth Clement Alexandria expound this place, Strom. 5.

g. 2 Cor. 12:5 To remove all suspicion of ambition he witnesseth that he braggeth not of those things as his own, but as

myself will I not rejoice, except it be of mine infirmities. 6 For though I would rejoice, I should not be a fool, for I will say the truth: but I refrain, lest any man should think of me above that he seeth in me, or that he heareth of me. 7 [h]And lest I should be exalted out of measure through the abundance of revelations, there was given unto me a [i]prick in the flesh, the messenger of [j]Satan to buffet me, because I should not be exalted out of measure. 8 For this thing I besought the Lord [k]thrice, that it might depart from me. 9 And he said unto me, My grace is sufficient for thee: for my power is made perfect through weakness. [l]Very gladly therefore will I rejoice rather in mine infirmities, that the power of Christ may [m]dwell in me. 10 Therefore I take [n]pleasure in infirmities, in reproaches, in necessities, in persecutions, in anguish for Christ's sake: for when I am weak, then am I strong. 11 I was a fool to boast myself: ye have compelled me: [o]for I ought to have been commended of you: for in nothing was I inferior unto the very chief Apostles, though I be nothing. 12 The [p]signs of an Apostle were wrought among you with all patience, with signs, and wonders and great works. 13 For what is it, wherein ye were inferiors unto other Churches, [1]except that I have not been [q]slothful to your hindrance? forgive me this wrong. 14 Behold, the third time I am ready to come unto you, and yet will I not be slothful to your hindrance: for I seek not yours, but you: for the children ought not to lay up for the fathers, but the fathers for the children. 15 And I will most gladly bestow, and will be bestowed for your souls: though the more I love you, the less I am loved. 16 [r]But be it that I charged you not: yet for as much as I was crafty, I took you with guile. 17 Did I pill you by any of them whom I sent unto you? 18 I have desired Titus, and with him I have sent a brother: did Titus pill you of any things? walked we not in the selfsame spirit? walked we not in the same steps? 19 [s]Again, think ye that we excuse ourselves unto you? we speak before God in [t]Christ. But we do all things, dearly beloved, for your edifying. 20 [u]For I fear lest when I come, I shall not find you such as I would: and that I shall be found unto you such as ye would not: and lest there be strife, envying, wrath, contentions, backbitings, whisperings, swellings, and discord. 21 I fear lest when I come again, my God abase me among you, and I shall bewail many of them which have sinned already, and have not repented of the uncleanness, and fornication, and wantonness which they have committed.

13

1 Coming the third time, 2 he denounceth the sharper vengeance toward them, 4 who have a perfect trial of the power of Christ in his Apostleship: 7 At length he prayeth for their repentance, 11 And wisheth them prosperity.

1 Lo this is the third time that I come unto you. [1]In the mouth of two or three witnesses shall every word stand. 2 I told you before, and tell you before: as though I had been present the second time, so write I now being absent to them, which heretofore have sinned, and to all others, that if I come again, I will not spare, 3 [a]Seeing that ye seek experience of Christ, that speaketh in me, which toward you is not weak, but is [b]mighty in you. 4 For though he was crucified concerning [c]his infirmity, yet liveth he through the power of God. And we no doubt are weak in him, but we shall live with him, through the power of God toward you. 5 [2,d]Prove yourselves whether ye are in the faith: examine yourselves: know ye not your own selves, how that Jesus Christ is in you, except ye be reprobates? 6 [e]But I trust that ye shall know that we are not reprobates. 7 Now I pray unto God that ye do none evil, not that we should seem approved, but that ye should do that which is honest: though we be as [f]reprobates. 8 For we cannot do anything against the truth, but for the truth. 9 For we are glad when we are weak, and that ye are strong: this also we wish for, even your [g]perfection. 10 Therefore write I these things being absent, lest when I am present, I should use sharpness, according to the power which the Lord hath given me, to edification, and not to destruction. 11 [h]Finally brethren, fare ye well: be perfect: be of good comfort: be of one mind: live in peace, and the God of love and peace shall be with you. 12 [i]Greet one another with an [3]holy kiss. All the Saints salute you. 13 The grace of our Lord Jesus Christ, and the love of God, and the communion of the holy Ghost be with you all, Amen. The second Epistle to the Corinthians, written from Philippi, a city in Macedonia, and sent by Titus and Lucas.

---

out of himself, and yet notwithstanding faineth nothing, lest by this occasion other men should attribute more unto him than indeed he is: and therefore he had rather glory in his miseries.

h. 2 Cor. 12:7 An excellent doctrine: why God will have even his best servants to be vexed of Satan and by all kinds of temptations, to wit, lest they should be too much puffed up, and also that they may be made perfect by that continual exercise.

i. 2 Cor. 12:7 He meaneth concupiscence, that sticketh fast in us, as it were a prick, insomuch that it constrained Paul himself being regenerate, to cry out, I do not that good that I would, etc. And he calleth it a prick, by a borrowed kind of speech taken from thorns, or stumps, which are very dangerous and hurtful for the feet, if a man walks through woods that are cut down.

j. 2 Cor. 12:7 Which setteth those lusts on fire.

k. 2 Cor. 12:8 Oft.

l. 2 Cor. 12:9 He concludeth, that he will only see his miseries against the vain brags of the false apostles, and therewith also excuseth himself, for that by their importunity, he was constrained to speak so much of these things as he did: to wit, because that if his Apostleship were subverted his doctrine must needs fall.

m. 2 Cor. 12:9 That I might feel the virtue of Christ more and more: For the weaker that our tabernacles are, the more doth Christ's virtue appear in them.

n. 2 Cor. 12:10 I do not only take them patiently and with a good heart, but also I take great pleasure in them.

o. 2 Cor. 12:11 Again he maketh the Cor. witnesses of those things whereby God had sealed his Apostleship amongst them, and again he desireth by certain arguments, how far he is from all covetousness, and also how he is affectioned towards them.

p. 2 Cor. 12:12 The arguments whereby it may well appear, that I am indeed an Apostle of Jesus Christ.

q. 2 Cor. 12:13 I was not slothful in getting my living with mine own hands, that I might not be burdensome to you.

r. 2 Cor. 12:16 He putteth away another most grievous slander, to wit, that he did subtly and by others, make his gain and profit of them.

s. 2 Cor. 12:19 He concludeth, that he writeth not these things unto them, as though he needed to defend himself, for he is guilty of nothing: but because it is behoovable for them to doubt nothing of his fidelity who instructed them.

t. 2 Cor. 12:19 As it becometh him to speak truly and sincerely, that professeth himself to be in Christ, that is to say, to be a Christian.

u. 2 Cor. 12:20 Having confirmed his authority unto them, he rebuketh them sharply, and threateneth them also like an Apostle, showing that he will not spare them hereafter, unless they repent, seeing that this is the third time that he hath warned them.

2 CORINTHIANS 12

1. 2 Cor. 11:9

2 CORINTHIANS 13

a. 2 Cor. 13:3 A most sharp reprehension, for that, while they despise the Apostle's admonitions, they tempt Christ's own patience: and also while they condemn him as wretched and miserable, they lay nothing herein against him, which is not common to him with Christ.

b. 2 Cor. 13:3 And will be most mighty to be revenged of you, when need shall be.

c. 2 Cor. 13:4 As touching that base form of a servant which he took upon him when he abased himself.

d. 2 Cor. 13:5 He confirmeth that which he spake of the virtue of God appearing in his ministry, and he gathereth by the mutual relation between the people's faith and the minister's preaching, that they must either reverence his Apostleship, upon whose doctrine their faith is grounded, or they must condemn themselves of infidelity, and must confess themselves not to be of Christ's body.

e. 2 Cor. 13:6 He mitigateth that sharpness, trusting that they will show themselves towards their faithful Apostle, apt and willingly to be taught: adding this moreover, that he passeth not for his own fame and estimation, so that he may serve to their salvation, which is the only mark that he shooteth at.

f. 2 Cor. 13:7 In men's judgment.

g. 2 Cor. 13:9 That all things may be in good order amongst you, and the members of the Church restored into their place, which have been shaken and out of place.

h. 2 Cor. 13:11 A brief exhortation, but yet such an one as comprehendeth all the parts of a Christian man's life.

i. 2 Cor. 13:12 He saluteth them familiarly, and in conclusion wisheth well unto them.

2 CORINTHIANS 13

1. Deut. 19:17 / Matt. 18:16 / John 8:17 / Heb. 10:28

2. 1 Cor. 11:28

3. 1 Cor. 16:20

THE EPISTLE OF THE APOSTLE PAUL TO THE

GALATIANS

1

1 Straight after the salutation, 6 He reprehendeth the Galatians for revolting, 9 from his Gospel, 15 which he received from God, 17 before he had communicated with any of the Apostles.

1 Paul [a]an Apostle not [b]of men, neither by [c]man, [1]but by [d]Jesus Christ, and God the Father which hath raised him from the dead. **2** And all the brethren which are with me unto the Churches of Galatia: **3** Grace be with you, and peace from God the Father, and from our Lord Jesus Christ, **4** [e]Which gave himself for our sins, that he might deliver us [2]from this present evil [f]world according to the will of God even our Father, **5** To whom be glory forever and ever, Amen. **6** [g]I marvel that ye are so soon [h]removed away unto another Gospel, from him that had called you in the grace of Christ, **7** [i]Which is not another Gospel, save that there be some which trouble you, and intend to [j]pervert the Gospel of Christ. **8** But though that we, or an Angel from heaven preach unto you otherwise than that which we have preached unto you, let him be [k]accursed. **9** As we said before, so say I now again, If any man preach unto you otherwise than that ye have received, let him be accursed. **10** [l]For now preach I [m]man's doctrine, or God's? or go I about to please men? for if I should yet please men, I were not the servant of Christ. **11** [3,n]Now I certify you, brethren, that the Gospel which was preached of me, was not after man. **12** For neither received I it of man, neither was I taught it, but by the [o]revelation of Jesus Christ. **13** [p]For ye have heard of my conversation in time past, in the Jewish religion, how that [4]I persecuted the Church of God extremely, and wasted it, **14** And profited in the Jewish religion above many of my companions of mine own nation, and was much more zealous of the [q]traditions of my fathers. **15** But when it pleased God which had [r]separated me from my mother's womb, and called me by his grace. **16** To reveal his Son [s]in me, that I should preach him [5]among the Gentiles immediately, [t]I communicated not with [u]flesh and blood: **17** Neither came I again to Jerusalem to them which were Apostles before me, but I went into Arabia, and turned again unto Damascus. **18** Then after three years I came again to Jerusalem, to visit Peter, and abode with him fifteen days. **19** And none other of the Apostles saw I, save James the Lord's brother. **20** Now the things which I write unto you, behold, I witness [v]before God, that I lie not. **21** After that, I went into the coasts of Syria and Cilicia: for I was unknown by face unto the Churches of Judea which were in Christ. **22** But they had heard only some say, He which persecuted us in time past, now preacheth the [w]faith which before he destroyed. **23** And they glorified God for me.

2

1 That the Apostles did nothing disagree from his Gospel, 3 he declareth by the example of Titus being uncircumcised, 11 and also by his . . . the same against Peter's dissimulation. 17 And so he passeth to the handling of our free justification by Christ, etc.

1 Then [a]fourteen years after, I went up again to Jerusalem with Barnabas, and took with me Titus also. **2** And I went up by revelation, and declared unto them that Gospel which I preach among the Gentiles, but particularly to them that were the chief, lest by any means I should run, or had run [b]in vain: **3** But neither yet Titus which was with me, though he were a Grecian, was compelled to be circumcised, **4** To wit, for the [c]false brethren which were craftily sent in, and crept in privily to spy out our liberty which we have in Christ Jesus, that they might bring us into bondage. **5** To whom we gave not place by [d]subjection for an hour, that the [e]truth of the Gospel might continue with [f]you. **6** But by them which seemed to be great, I was not taught whatsoever they were in time passed, I am nothing the better: [1]God accepteth no man's person for they that are the chief, did add nothing to me above that I had. **7** But contrariwise, when they saw that the Gospel over the [g]uncircumcision was committed unto me, as the Gospel over the circumcision

---

GALATIANS 1

- **a.** Gal. 1:1 A salutation comprehending in few words, the sum of the Apostle's doctrine, and also besides straightway from the beginning, showing the gravity meet for the authority of an Apostle, which he had to maintain against the false apostles.
- **b.** Gal. 1:1 He showeth who is the author of the minister generally: for herein the whole ministry agreeth, that whether they be Apostles, or Shepherds, or Doctors, they are appointed of God.
- **c.** Gal. 1:1 He toucheth the instrumental cause: for this is a peculiar prerogative to the Apostles, to be called immediately from Christ.
- **d.** Gal. 1:1 Christ no doubt is man, but he is God also, and head of the Church, and in this respect to be exempted out of the number of men.
- **e.** Gal. 1:4 The sum of the true Gospel is this, that Christ by his only offering, saveth us being chosen out from the world, by the free decree of God the Father.
- **f.** Gal. 1:4 Out of that most corrupt state which is without Christ.
- **g.** Gal. 1:6 The first part of the Epistle wherein he witnesseth that he is an Apostle, nothing inferior to those chief disciples of Christ, and wholly agreeing with them, whose names the false apostles did abuse. And he beginneth with chiding, reproving them of lightness for that they have ear so easily unto them which perverted them and drew them away to a new Gospel.
- **h.** Gal. 1:6 He useth the passive voice, to cast the fault upon the false apostles, and he useth the time that now is, to give them to understand, that it was not already done, but in doing.
- **i.** Gal. 1:7 He warneth them in time to remember that there are not many Gospels, and therefore whatsoever these false apostles pretend which had the Law, Moses and the Fathers in their mouths, yet they are in deed so many corruptions of the true Gospel, insomuch that he himself, yea, and the very Angels themselves, and therefore much more these false apostles ought to be holden accursed, if they go about to change the least iota that may be in the Gospel, that he delivered to them before.
- **j.** Gal. 1:7 For there is nothing more contrary to faith or free justification, than justification by the Law, or by our deserving.
- **k.** Gal. 1:8 See Rom. 9:3.
- **l.** Gal. 1:10 A confirmation taken both from the nature of the doctrine itself, and also from that manner which he useth in teaching: for neither saith he, did I teach those things which pleased men as these men do which put part of salvation in external things, and works of the Law, neither went I about to procure any man's favor. And therefore the matter itself showeth that that doctrine which I delivered unto you, is heavenly.
- **m.** Gal. 1:10 He toucheth the false apostles who had nothing but men in their mouths, and he, though he would derogate nothing from the Apostles, preacheth God and not men.
- **n.** Gal. 1:11 A second argument to prove that this doctrine is heavenly, because he had it from heaven, from Jesus Christ himself, without any man's help, wherein he excelleth them whom Christ taught here on earth after the manner of men.
- **o.** Gal. 1:12 This place is to be understood of an extraordinary revelation, for otherwise the Son alone revealed his Gospel by his Spirit, although by the ministry of men, which Paul shutteth out here.
- **p.** Gal. 1:13 He proveth that he was extraordinarily taught of Christ himself, by the history of his former life, which the Gal. themselves know well enough: for saith he, it is well known in what school I was brought up, even from a child, to wit, amongst the deadly enemies of the Gospel. And no man may cavil and say that I was a scholar of the Pharisees in name only and not in deed, no man is ignorant, how that I excelled in Pharisaism, and was suddenly made of a Pharisee, an Apostle of the Gentiles, so that I had no space to be instructed of men.
- **q.** Gal. 1:14 He calleth them the traditions of his Fathers, because he was not only a Pharisee himself, but also had a Pharisee to his father.
- **r.** Gal. 1:15 He speaketh of God's everlasting predestination, whereby he appointed him to be an Apostle, whereof he maketh three degrees, the everlasting counsel of God, his appointing from his mother's womb, and his calling: here is no mention at all, we see, of works foreseen.
- **s.** Gal. 1:16 To me, and this is a kind of speech which the Hebrews use, whereby this is given us to understand, that this gift cometh from God.
- **t.** Gal. 1:16 Because it might be objected, that indeed he was called of Christ in the way, but afterwards was instructed of the Apostles and others, whose names as I said before the false apostles abused to destroy his Apostleship, as though he delivered another Gospel than the true Apostles did, and as though he were not of their number, which are to be credited without exception: therefore Paul answereth, that he began straightway after his calling to preach the Gospel at Damascus and in Arabia, and was not from that time in Jerusalem but only fifteen days, where he saw only Peter and James, and afterwards, he began to teach in Syria and Cilicia, with the consent and approbation of the Churches of the Jews, which knew him only by name, so far off was it, that he was there instructed of men.
- **u.** Gal. 1:16 With any man in the world.
- **v.** Gal. 1:20 This is a kind of an oath.
- **w.** Gal. 1:22 The doctrine of faith.

GALATIANS 1

1. Titus 1:3
2. Luke 1:74
3. 1 Cor. 15:1
4. Acts 9:8
5. Eph. 3:8

GALATIANS 2

- **a.** Gal. 2:1 Now he showeth how he agreeth with the Apostles with whom he granteth that he conferred touching his Gospel which he taught among the Gentiles, fourteen years after his conversion, and they allowed it in such sort, that they constrained not his fellow Titus to be circumcised, although some tormented themselves therein, which traitorously laid wait against him, but in vain: neither did they add the least iota that might be to the doctrine which he had preached, but contrariwise they gave to him and Barnabas the right hands of fellowship and acknowledged them as Apostles appointed of the Lord to the Gentiles.
- **b.** Gal. 2:2 Unfruitfully, for as touching his doctrine, Paul doubted not of it, but because there were certain reports cast abroad of him, that he was of another opinion than the rest of the Apostles were, which thing might have hindered the course of the Gospel, therefore he labored to remedy this sore.
- **c.** Gal. 2:4 Which by deceit, and counterfeit holiness crept in amongst the faithful.
- **d.** Gal. 2:5 By submitting ourselves to them, and betraying our own liberty.
- **e.** Gal. 2:5 The true and sincere doctrine of the Gospel, which remained safe from being corrupt with any of these men's false doctrines.
- **f.** Gal. 2:5 Under the Gal.' name, he understandeth all nations.
- **g.** Gal. 2:7 Among the Gentiles, as Peter had to preach it among the Jews.

was unto Peter: **8** For he that was mighty by Peter in the Apostleship over the circumcision, was also mighty by me toward the Gentiles. **9** And when James, and Cephas, and John, knew of the grace that was given unto me, which are [h]counted to be pillars, they gave to me and to Barnabas the right [i]hands of fellowship, that we should preach unto the Gentiles, and they unto the circumcision, **10** Warning only that we should remember the poor: which thing also I was diligent to do. **11** And when Peter was come to Antioch, I withstood him to his [j]face: for he was to be condemned. **12** [k]For before that certain came from James, he ate with the Gentiles: but when they were come, he withdrew and separated himself, fearing them which were of the circumcision. **13** And the other Jews played the hypocrites likewise with him, insomuch that Barnabas was [l]led away with them by that their hypocrisy. **14** But when I saw, that they went not the [m]right way to the [n]truth of the Gospel, I said unto Peter before all men, If thou being a Jew, livest as the Gentiles, and not like the Jews, why [o]constrainest thou the Gentiles to do like the Jews? **15** [p]We which are Jews [q]by nature, and not [r]sinners of the Gentiles, **16** Know that a man is not justified by the works of the Law, but by the faith [s]of Jesus Christ, even we, I say, have believed in Jesus Christ, that we might be justified by the faith of Christ, and not by the works of the Law, because that by the works of the Law, [t]no flesh shall be justified. **17** [2,u]If then while [v]we seek to be made righteous by Christ, we ourselves are found sinners, is Christ therefore the minister of sin? God forbid. **18** For if I build again the things that I have destroyed, I make myself a trespasser. **19** For I through the Law am dead to the [w]Law, that I might live unto God. **20** I am crucified with Christ, but I live, yet not [x]I anymore, but Christ liveth in me: and in that I now live in the [y]flesh, I live by the faith in the Son of God, who hath loved me, and given himself for me. **21** [z]I do not abrogate the grace of God: for if righteousness be by the Law, then Christ died without a [aa]cause.

3

1 He rebuketh them, for suffering themselves to be drawn from the grace of free justification in Christ, most lively set out unto them. 6 He bringeth in Abraham's example, 10 declaring the effects, 21 and causes of the giving of the Law.

1 [a]O foolish Galatians, who hath bewitched you, that ye should not obey the truth, to whom Jesus Christ before was described in your [b]sight, and among you crucified? **2** This only would I learn of you, Received ye the [c]Spirit by the works of the Law, or by the hearing of [d]faith preached? **3** [e]Are ye so foolish, that after ye have begun in the Spirit, ye would now be made perfect by the [f]flesh? **4** [g]Have ye suffered so many things in vain? if so be it be even in vain. **5** [h]He therefore that ministereth to you the Spirit, and worketh miracles among you, doeth he it through the works of the Law, or by the hearing of faith preached? **6** [i]Yea rather as [j]Abraham believed God, and it was [1]imputed to him for righteousness. **7** [k]Know ye therefore, that they which are of faith, the same are the children of Abraham. **8** [l]For the Scripture foreseeing, that God would justify the Gentiles through faith, preached before the Gospel unto Abraham, saying, [2,m]In thee shall all the Gentiles be [n]blessed. **9** [o]So then they which be of faith, are blessed with [p]faithful Abraham. **10** [q]For as many as are of the works of the Law, are under the curse: [r]For it is written, [3]Cursed is every man that continueth not in all things, which are written in the book of the Law, to do them. **11** [s]And that no man is justified by the Law in the sight of God, it is evident: [4]for the just shall live by faith. **12** [t]And the Law is not of faith: but [5]the man that shall do those things, shall live in them. **13** [u]Christ hath redeemed us from the curse of the Law, made a curse for us, [v]for it is written, [6,w]Cursed is everyone that hangeth on tree. **14** [x]That the blessing of Abraham might come on the Gentiles through Christ Jesus, that we might receive the promise of the Spirit through faith. **15** [y]Brethren, I speak as [z]men do: [7]though it be but a man's covenant, when it is [aa]confirmed, yet no man

---

h. Gal. 2:9 Whom alone and only, these men count for pillars of the Church, and whose name they abuse to deceive you.
i. Gal. 2:9 They gave us their hand in token that we agreed wholly in the doctrine of the Gospel.
j. Gal. 2:11 Before all men.
k. Gal. 2:12 Another most vehement proof of his Apostleship, and also of that doctrine, which he had delivered concerning free justification by faith only because that for this thing only he reprehended Peter at Antioch, who offended herein, in that for a few Jews' sakes which came from Jerusalem he played the Jew, and offended the Gentiles which had believed.
l. Gal. 2:13 By example rather than by judgment.
m. Gal. 2:14 Word for word, with a right foot which he setteth against halting and dissembling which is backward.
n. Gal. 2:14 He calleth the truth of the Gospel both the doctrine itself, and also the use of doctrine, which we call the practice.
o. Gal. 2:14 He saith they were constrained, which played the Jews by Peter's example.
p. Gal. 2:15 The second part of this Epistle, the state whereof is this: we are justified by faith in Christ Jesus without the works of the Law: which thing he propoundeth in such sort, that first of all he meeteth with an objection, for I also saith he am a Jew, that no man may say against me, that I am an enemy to the Law and afterward, he confirmeth it by the express witness of David.
q. Gal. 2:15 Although we be Jews, yet we preach justification by faith because we know undoubtedly, that no man can be justified by the Law.
r. Gal. 2:15 So the Jews called the Gentiles, because they were strangers from God's covenant.
s. Gal. 2:16 In Jesus Christ.
t. Gal. 2:16 No man, and in this word flesh there is a great vehemence, whereby is meant that the nature of man is utterly corrupt.
u. Gal. 2:17 Before he goeth any further, he meeteth with their objection, which abhorred this doctrine of free justification by faith, because say they, men are by this means withdrawn from the study of good works. And in this sort is the objection, If sinners should be justified through Christ by faith without the Law Christ should approve sinners, and should as it were exhort them thereunto by his ministry. Paul answereth that this consequence is false, because that Christ destroyeth sin in the believers: For so saith he do men flee unto Christ, through the terror and fear of the Law that being quit from the curse of the Law and justified, they may be saved by him, that together therewithall, he beginneth in them by little and little, that strength and power of his which destroyeth sin: to the end that this old man being abolished by the virtue of Christ crucified, Christ may live in them, and they may consecrate themselves to God. Therefore if any man give himself to sin after he hath received the Gospel, let him not accuse Christ nor the Gospel, but himself, for that he destroyeth the work of God in himself.
v. Gal. 2:17 He goeth from justification to sanctification, which is another benefit we receive by Christ, if we lay hold on him by faith.
w. Gal. 2:19 The Law that terrifieth the conscience, bringeth us to Christ, and he only causeth us to die to the Law indeed, because that by making us righteous, he taketh away from us the terror of conscience, and by sanctifying us, causeth through the mortifying of lust in us, that it cannot take such occasion to sin by the restraint which the Law maketh, as it did before, Rom. 7:10-11.
x. Gal. 2:20 The same that I was before.
y. Gal. 2:20 In this mortal body.
z. Gal. 2:21 The second argument taken of an absurdity: If men may be justified by the Law, then was it not necessary for Christ to die.
aa. Gal. 2:21 For there was no cause why he should do so.

GALATIANS 2

1. Deut. 10:17 / 2 Chron. 19:7 / Job 34:19 / Acts 10:34 / Rom. 2:11 / Eph. 6:9 / Col. 3:25 / 1 Pet. 1:17
2. Rom. 3:19

GALATIANS 3

a. Gal. 3:1 The third reason or argument taken of those gifts of the holy Ghost, wherewith they were endued from heaven after they had heard and believed the Gospel by Paul's ministry: which seeing they were so evident to all men's eyes, that they were as it were lively images, wherein they might behold the truth of the doctrine of the Gospel, no less than if they had beheld with their eyes Christ himself crucified, in whose only death they ought to have their trust, he marvelleth how it could be that they could be so bewitched by the false apostles.
b. Gal. 3:1 Christ was laid before you, so notably and so plainly, that you had his lively image as it were represented before your eyes, as if he had been crucified before you.
c. Gal. 3:2 Those spiritual graces and gifts, which were a seal as it were to the Gal., that the Gospel which was preached to them was true.
d. Gal. 3:2 Of the doctrine of faith.
e. Gal. 3:3 The fourth argument mixed with the former and it is double, If the Law is to be joined with faith, this were not to go forward, but backward, seeing that those spiritual gifts which were bestowed upon you, are more excellent than any that could proceed from yourselves. And moreover, it should follow, that the Law is better than Christ, because it should perfect and bring to end that which Christ began only.
f. Gal. 3:3 By the flesh he meaneth the ceremonies of the Law, against which he setteth the Spirit, that is, the spiritual working of the Gospel.
g. Gal. 3:4 An exhortation by manner of upbraiding, that they do not in vain suffer so many conflicts.
h. Gal. 3:5 He repeateth the third argument which was taken of the effects, because he had interlaced certain other arguments by the way.
i. Gal. 3:6 The first argument which is of great force, and hath three grounds, The first, That Abraham was justified by faith, to wit, by free imputation of righteousness according to the promise apprehended by faith, as Moses doth most plainly witness.
j. Gal. 3:6 See Rom. 4.
k. Gal. 3:7 The second, that the sons of Abraham must be esteemed and accounted of by faith.
l. Gal. 3:8 The third, that all people that believe, are without exception, comprehended in the promise of the blessing.
m. Gal. 3:8 A proof of the first and second grounds, out of the words of Moses.
n. Gal. 3:8 Blessing in this place, signifieth the free promise by faith.
o. Gal. 3:9 The conclusion of the fifth argument: Therefore as Abraham is blessed by faith, so are all his children that is to say, all the Gentiles that believe blessed, that is to say, freely justified.
p. Gal. 3:9 With faithful Abraham, and not by faithful Abraham, to give us to understand that the blessing cometh not from Abraham, but from him, by whom Abraham and all his posterity is blessed.
q. Gal. 3:10 The sixth argument, the conclusion whereof is also in the former verse taken of contraries, thus, They are accursed which are of the works of the Law, that is to say, which value their righteousness by the performance of the Law. Therefore they are blessed which are of faith, that is, they which have righteousness by faith.
r. Gal. 3:10 A proof of the former sentence or proposition: and the proposition of this argument is this: Cursed is he that fulfilleth not the whole Law.
s. Gal. 3:11 The second proposition with the conclusion: But no man fulfilleth the Law. Therefore no man is justified by the Law, or else, which seek righteousness by the works of the Law. And there is annexed also this manner of proof of the second proposition, to wit, Righteousness and life are attributed to faith, Therefore no man fulfilleth the Law.
t. Gal. 3:12 Here is a reason shown of the former consequence: Because the law promiseth life to all that keep it, and therefore if it be kept, it justifieth and giveth life. But the Scripture attributing righteousness and life to faith, taketh it from the Law, seeing that faith justifieth by imputation, and the Law by the performing of the work.
u. Gal. 3:13 A preventing of an objection: How then can they be blessed, whom the Law pronounceth to be accursed? Because Christ sustained the curse which the Law laid upon us, that we might be quit from it.
v. Gal. 3:13 A proof of the answer by the testimony of Moses.
w. Gal. 3:13 Christ was accursed for us, because he bare the curse that was due to us, to make us partakers of his righteousness.
x. Gal. 3:14 A conclusion of all that was said before in the handling of the fifth and sixth reasons, to wit, that both the Gentiles are made partakers of the free blessing of Abraham in Christ, and also that the Jews themselves, of whose number the Apostle counteth himself to be, cannot obtain that promised grace of the Gospel, which he calleth the Spirit, but only by faith. And the Apostle doth severally apply the conclusion, both to the one and the other, preparing himself a way, to the next argument, whereby he declareth, that the one only seed of Abraham, which is made of all peoples can no otherwise be joined and grow up together, but by faith in Christ.
y. Gal. 3:15 He putteth forth two general rules before the next argument, which is the seventh in order: That one is, that it is not lawful to break covenants and contracts which are justly made and according to Law amongst men, neither may anything be added unto them: The other is, that God did so make a covenant with Abraham, that he would gather together his children which consist both of Jews and Gentiles into one body as appeareth by that which hath been said before. For he did not say, that he would be the God of Abraham and of his seeds, which things notwithstanding should have been said, if he had many and divers seeds, as the Gentiles apart and the Jews apart, but that he would be the God of Abraham, and of his seed, as of one.

doth abrogate it, or addeth anything thereto, **16** Now to Abraham and his seed
were the promises made. He saith not, and to the seeds, as speaking of many: but,
And to thy seed, as of one, [ab]which is [ac]Christ. **17** [ad]And this I say, that the co-
venant that was confirmed afore of God [ae]in respect of Christ, the [af]Law which was
four hundred and thirty years after, cannot disannul, that it should make the pro-
mise of none effect. **18** [ag]For if the [ah]inheritance be of the Law, it is no more by
the promise, but God gave it freely unto Abraham by promise. **19** [ai]Wherefore
then serveth the Law? It was added because of the [aj]transgressions, [ak]till the seed
came, unto the which the promise was made: [al]and it was [am]ordained by [an]Angels
in the hand of a Mediator. **20** Now a Mediator is not a Mediator of one: [ao]but
God is one. **21** [ap]Is the Law then against the promises of God? God forbid: For
if there had been a Law given which could have given life, surely righteousness
should have been by the Law. **22** But the [aq]Scripture hath [8]concluded [ar]all under
sin, that the [as]promise by the faith of Jesus Christ should be given to them that be-
lieve. **23** [at]But before faith came, we were kept under the Law, as under a garri-
son, and shut up unto [au]that faith, which should afterward be revealed. **24** Whe-
refore the Law was our schoolmaster to bring us to Christ, that we might be made
righteous by faith. **25** But after that faith is come, we are no longer under a scho-
olmaster. **26** [av]For ye are all the sons of God by faith, in Christ Jesus. **27** [aw]For
all ye that are [ax]baptized into Christ, have [ay]put on Christ. **28** There is neither
Jew nor Grecian: there is neither bond nor free: there is neither male nor female:
for ye are all [az]one in Christ Jesus. **29** And if ye be Christ's, then are ye Abraham's
seed, and heirs by promise.

4

1 Being delivered from the bondage of the Law, 4 by Christ's coming, who is the end thereof, 9 it is very absurd to slide back to beggarly ceremonies: 13 He calleth them again therefore to the purity of the doctrine of the Gospel, 21 confirming his discourse with a fine allegory.

1 Then [a]I say, that the heir as long as he is a child, differeth nothing from a
servant, though he be Lord of all, **2** But is under tutors and governors, [b]until
the time appointed of the Father. **3** Even so we, when we were children, were
in bondage under the [c]rudiments of the world. **4** [d]But when the [e]fullness of
time was come, God sent forth his Son made of a [f]woman, and made under the
Law, **5** That he might redeem them which were under the Law, that we [1]might
receive the [g]adoption of the sons. **6** [h]And because ye are sons, God hath [i]sent
forth the [j]Spirit of his Son into your hearts, which crieth, Abba, Father. **7** Whe-
refore, thou art no more a [k]servant, but a son: now if thou be a son, thou art also
the [l]heir of God through Christ. **8** [m]But even then, when ye knew not God,
ye did service unto them, which by nature are not gods: **9** But now seeing ye
know God, yea, rather are known of God, how turn ye again unto impotent and
[n]beggarly rudiments, whereunto as from the beginning ye will be in bondage [o]a-
gain? **10** Ye observe days, and months, and times, and years. **11** I am in fear of
you, lest I have bestowed on you labor in vain. **12** [p]Be ye as I for I am even as you
brethren, I beseech you: ye have not hurt me at all. **13** And ye know, how throu-
gh [q]infirmity of the flesh, I preached the Gospel unto you at the first. **14** And
the [r]trial of me which was in my flesh, ye despised not, neither abhorred: but ye
received me as an Angel of God, yea, as [s]Christ Jesus. **15** [t]What was then your

---

z. Gal. 3:15 I will use an example which is common among you, that you may be ashamed you give not so much to God's covenants, as you do to man's.

aa. Gal. 3:15 Authentical, as we call it.

ab. Gal. 3:16 He putteth forth the sum of the seventh argument, to wit, that both the Jews and the Gentiles grow together into one body of the seed of Abraham, in Christ only, so that all are one in Christ, as it is afterward declared, verse 21.

ac. Gal. 3:16 Paul speaketh not of Christ's person, but of two peoples, which grew together in one, in Christ.

ad. Gal. 3:17 The eighth argument taken of comparison, thus: If a man's covenant being authentical be firm and strong, much more God's covenant. Therefore the Law was not given to abrogate the promise made to Abraham, which had respect to Christ, that is to say, the end whereof did hang of Christ.

ae. Gal. 3:17 Which tendeth to Christ.

af. Gal. 3:17 An enlarging of that argument, thus: Moreover and besides that the promise is of itself firm and strong, it was also confirmed with the prescription of long time, to wit, of 430 years, so that it could in no wise be broken.

ag. Gal. 3:18 An objection: We grant that the promise was not abrogated by the covenant of the Law, and therefore we join the Law with the promise. Nay, saith the Apostle, these two cannot stand together, to wit, that the inheritance should both be given by the Law and also by promise, for the promise is free: whereby it followeth, that the Law was not given to justify, for by that means the promise should be broken.

ah. Gal. 3:18 By this word inheritance is meant the right of the seed, which is, that God should be our God, that is to say, that by virtue of the covenant that was made with faithful Abraham, we that be faithful, might by that means be blessed of God as well as he.

ai. Gal. 3:19 An objection which riseth of the former answer: If the inheritance be not by the Law at the least in part then why was the Law given, after that the promise was made? Therefore saith the Apostle, to reprove men of sin, and so teach them to look unto Christ, in whom at length that promise of saving all people together should be fulfilled, and not that the Law was given to justify men.

aj. Gal. 3:19 That men might understand, by discovering of their sins, by the only grace of God, which he revealed to Abraham, and that in Christ.

ak. Gal. 3:19 Until the partition wall was broken down, and that full seed sprang up, framed of two peoples, both of Jews and Gentiles: for by this word Seed, we may not understand, Christ alone by himself, but coupled and joined together with his body.

al. Gal. 3:19 A confirmation of the former answer taken from the manner and form of giving the Law: for it was given by Angels, striking a great terror into all, and by Moses a Mediator coming between. Now they that are one, need no Mediator, but they that are twain at the least, and that are at variance one with another. Therefore the Law itself and the Mediator, were witnesses of the wrath of God, and not that God would by this means reconcile men to himself, and abolish the promise, or add the Law unto the promise.

am. Gal. 3:19 Commanded and given, or proclaimed.

an. Gal. 3:19 By the service and ministry.

ao. Gal. 3:20 A taking away of an objection, lest any man might say, that sometimes by consent of the parties which have made a covenant, something is added to the covenant, or the former covenants are broken. This, saith the Apostle, cometh to pass in God, who is always one, and the selfsame, and like himself.

ap. Gal. 3:21 The conclusion uttered by a manner of asking a question, and it is the same that was uttered before, verse 17, but proceeding of another rule: so that the argument is new, and is this: God is always like unto himself: Therefore the Law was not given to abolish the promises. But it should abolish them if it gave life, for by that means it should justify, and therefore it should abolish that justification which was promised to Abraham and to his seed by faith. Nay it was rather given to bring to light the guiltiness of all men, to the end that all believers fleeing to Christ promised, might be freely justified in him.

aq. Gal. 3:22 By this word, Scripture, he meaneth the Law.

ar. Gal. 3:22 All men, and whatsoever cometh from man.

as. Gal. 3:22 In every one of these words, there lieth an argument against the merits of works, for all these words, promise, faith, Christ, might be given, to believers, are against merits, and not one of them can stand with deserving works.

at. Gal. 3:23 Now there followeth another handling of the second part of this Epistle: the state whereof is this: Although the Law that is, the whole government of God's house according to the Law does not justify, is it therefore to be abolished, seeing that Abraham himself was circumcised, and his posterity held still the use of Moses' Law? Paul affirmeth that it ought to be abolished, because it was instituted for that end and purpose, that is should be as it were a schoolmaster and keeper to the people of God, until the promise appeared in deed, that is to say, Christ, and the Gospel manifestly published with great efficacy of the Spirit.

au. Gal. 3:23 The cause why we were kept under the Law, is set down here.

av. Gal. 3:26 Because age changeth not the condition of servants, he addeth that we are free by condition, and therefore, seeing we are out of our childhood, we have no more need of a keeper and Schoolmaster.

aw. Gal. 3:27 Using a general particle, lest the Jews at the least should not think themselves bound with the band of the Law, he pronounceth that Baptism is common to all believers, because it is a pledge of our delivery in Christ, as well to the Jews as to the Grecians, that by this means all may be truly one in Christ, that is to say, that promised seed to Abraham and inheritors of everlasting life.

ax. Gal. 3:27 He setteth Baptism secretly against circumcision, which the false apostles so much bragged of.

ay. Gal. 3:27 The Church must put on Christ, as it were a garment, and be covered with him, that it may be thoroughly holy, and without blame.

az. Gal. 3:28 You are all as one: and so in this great knot and conjunction signified.

GALATIANS 3

1. Gen. 15:6 / Rom. 4:3 / James 2:23
2. Gen. 12:3 / Acts 3:25
3. Deut. 27:26
4. Hab. 2:4 / Rom. 1:17 / Heb. 10:10
5. Lev. 18:5
6. Lev. 21:13
7. Heb. 9:17
8. Rom. 3:9

GALATIANS 4

a. Gal. 4:1 He declareth that by another double similitude, which he said before concerning the keeper and schoolmaster. For he saith, that the Law, that is, the whole government of God's house according to the Law was as it were a tutor or overseer appointed for a time, until such time as that protection and overseeing which was but for a time, being ended, we should at length come to be at our own liberty, and should live as children, and not as servants. Moreover, he showeth by the way, that that governance of the Law, was as it were an ABC, and as certain principles in comparison of the doctrine of the Gospel.

b. Gal. 4:2 This is added, because he that is always under a tutor or governor, may hardly be counted a freeman.

c. Gal. 4:3 The Law is called rudiments, because that by the Law God instructed his Church as it were by rudiments, and afterward poured out his holy Spirit most plentifully in the time of the Gospel.

d. Gal. 4:4 He uttereth and declareth many things at once, to wit, that this tutorship was ended at his time, that curious men may leave to ask, why that schoolmastership lasted so long. And moreover, that we are not sons by nature, but by adoption, and that in that Son of God, who therefore took upon him our flesh, that we might be made his brethren.

e. Gal. 4:4 The time is said to be full, when all parts of it are past and ended, and therefore Christ could not have come either sooner or later.

f. Gal. 4:4 He calleth Mary a woman, in respect of the sex, and not as the word is used in a contrary sense to a virgin still.

g. Gal. 4:5 The adoption of the sons of God, is from everlasting, but is revealed and showed in the time appointed for it.

h. Gal. 4:6 He showeth that we are in such sort free and set at liberty, that in the mean season we must be governed by the Spirit of Christ, which reigning in our hearts, may teach us the true service of the Father. But this is not to serve, but rather to enjoy true liberality, as it cometh sons and heirs.

i. Gal. 4:6 By that that followeth he gathereth that that went before: for if we have his spirit, we are his sons, and if we are his sons, then are we free.

j. Gal. 4:6 The holy Ghost, who is both of the Father and of the Son: but there is a peculiar reason why he is called the Spirit of the Son, to wit, because the holy Ghost sealeth up our adoption in Christ, and maketh us a full assurance of it.

k. Gal. 4:7 The word, servant, is not taken here for one that liveth in sin, which is proper to the infidels, but for one that is yet under the ceremonies of the Law, which is proper to the Jews.

l. Gal. 4:7 Partaker of this blessing.

m. Gal. 4:8 He applieth the former doctrine to the Gal., with a peculiar reprehension: for in comparison of them, the Jews might have pretended some excuse as men that were born and brought up in that service of the Law. But seeing the Gal. were taken and called out of idolatry to Christian liberty: what pretence might they have to go back to those impotent and beggarly rudiments?

n. Gal. 4:9 They are called impotent and beggarly ceremonies, being considered apart by themselves without Christ: and again, for that by that means they gave good testimony that they were beggars in Christ, when as notwithstanding, for men, to fall back from Christ to ceremonies, is nothing else, but to cast away riches, and to follow beggarly.

o. Gal. 4:9 By going backward.

p. Gal. 4:12 He mitigateth and qualifieth those things wherein he might have seemed to have spoken somewhat sharply, very artificially and divinely, declaring his good will towards them in such sort, that the Gal. could not but either be utterly desperate when they read these things, or acknowledge their own lightness with tears, and desire pardon.

q. Gal. 4:13 Many afflictions.

r. Gal. 4:14 Those daily troubles wherewith the Lord tried me amongst you.

s. Gal. 4:14 For my ministry's sake.

t. Gal. 4:15 What a talk was there abroad in the world amongst men, how happy you were?

felicity? for I bear you record, that if it had been possible, ye would have plucked out your own eyes, and have given them unto me. **16** Am I therefore become your enemy, because I tell you the truth? **17** They are jealous over you [u]amiss: yea, they would exclude you, [v]that ye should altogether love them. **18** But it is a good thing to love [w]earnestly always in a good thing, and not only when I am present with you, **19** My little children, of whom I travail in birth again, until Christ be formed in you. **20** And I would I were with you now, that I might [x]change my voice: for I am in doubt of you. **21** [y]Tell me, ye that [z]will be under the Law, do ye not hear the Law? **22** For it is written, that Abraham had two sons, [2]one by a servant, and [3]one by a free woman. **23** But he which was of the servant, was born after the [aa]flesh: and he which was of the free woman, was born by [ab]promise. **24** By the which things another thing is meant: for [ac]these mothers are the [ad]two Testaments, the one which is Hagar of mount [ae]Sinai, which gendereth unto bondage. **25** For Hagar or Sinai is a mountain in Arabia, and it [af]answered to Jerusalem which now is and [ag]she is in bondage with her children. **26** But Jerusalem, which is [ah]above, is free: which is the mother of us all. **27** [ai]For it is written, [4]Rejoice thou barren that bearest no children: break forth, and cry, thou that travailest not: for the [aj]desolate hath many more children, than she which hath an husband. **28** [5]Therefore, brethren, we are after the [ak]manner of Isaac, children of the [al]promise. **29** But as then he that was born after the [am]flesh, persecuted him that was born after the [an]Spirit, even so it is now. **30** But what saith the Scripture? [6]Put out the servant and her son: for the son of the servant shall not be heir with the son of the free woman. **31** [ao]Then brethren, we are not children of the servant, but of the free woman.

5

1 Having declared that we came of the free woman, he showeth the price of that freedom, 13 and how we should use the same, 16 that we may obey the Spirit, 19 and resist the flesh.

1 Stand fast therefore in the liberty wherewith Christ hath made us free, and be not entangled again with the yoke of bondage. **2** [1,a]Behold, I Paul say unto you, that if ye be [b]circumcised, Christ shall profit you nothing. **3** For I testify again to every man, which is circumcised, that he is bound to keep the whole Law. **4** Ye are [2,c]abolished from Christ: whosoever are [d]justified by the Law, ye are fallen from grace. **5** [e]For we through the [f]Spirit wait for the hope of righteousness through faith. **6** [g]For in Jesus Christ neither circumcision availeth anything, neither [h]uncircumcision, [i]but [j]faith which worketh by love. **7** [k]Ye did run well: who did let you, that ye did not obey the truth? **8** [l]It is not the persuasion of [m]him that calleth you. **9** [3,n]A little leaven doth leaven the whole lump. **10** [o]I have trust in you through the Lord, that ye will be none otherwise minded: but he that troubleth you, shall bear his condemnation, whosoever he be. **11** [p]And brethren, if I yet preach circumcision, why do I yet suffer persecution? Then is the slander of the cross abolished. **12** [q]Would to God they were even cut off which do [r]disquiet you. **13** For brethren, ye have been called unto liberty: [s]only use not your liberty as an occasion unto the flesh, but by love serve one another. **14** [t]For [u]all the Law is fulfilled in one word, which is this, [4]Thou shalt love thy neighbor as thyself. **15** [v]If ye bite and devour one another, take heed lest ye be consumed one of another. **16** [w]Then I say, [5]Walk in the Spirit, and ye shall not fulfill the lusts of the flesh. **17** For the [x]flesh lusteth against the Spirit, and the Spirit against the flesh: and these are contrary one to another, so that ye cannot do the same things that ye would. **18** And if ye be led by the Spirit, ye are not under the Law. **19** [y]Moreover the works of the flesh are manifest, which are adultery, fornication, uncleanness, wantonness, **20** Idolatry, witchcraft, hatred, debate, emulations, wrath, contentions, seditions, heresies, **21** Envy, murders, drunkenness, gluttony, and such like, whereof I tell you before, as I also have told you before, that they which do such things, shall not inherit the kingdom of God. **22** But the [z]fruit of the Spirit is love, joy, peace, longsuffering, gentleness, goodness, faith, **23** Meekness, temperancy: [aa]against such there is no law. **24** For they that are Christ's, have crucified the flesh with the affections and the lusts. **25** If we [ab]live in the Spirit, let us also walk in the Spirit. **26** [ac]Let us not be desirous of vainglory, provoking one another, envying one another.

---

u. Gal. 4:17 For they are jealous over you for their own commodity.
v. Gal. 4:17 That they may convey all your love from me to themselves.
w. Gal. 4:18 He setteth his own true and good love, which he earnestly bent towards them, against the naughty vicious love of the false apostles.
x. Gal. 4:20 Use other words among you.
y. Gal. 4:21 Because the false apostles always urged this, that unless the Gentiles were circumcised, Christ could profit them nothing at all, and this dissension of them which believed of the circumcision against them which believed of the uncircumcision, was full of offense: the Apostle, after divers arguments whereby he hath refuted their error, bringeth forth an allegory, wherein he saith the holy Ghost did shadow not unto us, all these mysteries: to wit, that it should come to pass, that two sorts of sons should have Abraham a father common to them both, but not with like success: for as Abraham begat Ishmael, by the common course of nature, of Hagar his bondmaid and a stranger, and begat Isaac of Sarah a free woman by the virtue of the promise and by grace only, and the first was not only not heir, but also persecuted the heir: So there are two covenants, and as it were two sons born to Abraham of those two covenants, as it were of two mothers. The one was made in Sinai, without the land of promise according to which covenant Abraham's children according to the flesh were begotten: to wit, the Jews which seek righteousness by that covenant, that is, by the Law: but they are not heirs, nay they shall at length be cast out of the house, as they that persecute the true heirs. The other was made in that high Jerusalem or in Zion to wit, by the sacrifice of Christ which begetteth children of promise, to wit, believers by the virtue of the holy Ghost which children as Abraham do rest themselves in the free promise, and they only by the right of children shall be partakers of the father's inheritance, and those servants shall be shut out.
z. Gal. 4:21 That desire so greatly.
aa. Gal. 4:23 As all men are, and by the common course of nature.
ab. Gal. 4:23 By virtue of the promise, which Abraham laid hold on for himself and his true seed, for otherwise Abraham and Sarah were past begetting and bearing children.
ac. Gal. 4:24 These do represent and shadow forth.
ad. Gal. 4:24 They are called two covenants, one of the old Testament, and another of the New: which were not two indeed, but in respect of the times, and the diversity of the government.
ae. Gal. 4:24 He maketh mention of Sinai, because that covenant was made in that mountain, of which mountain Hagar was a shadow.
af. Gal. 4:25 Look how the case standeth betwixt Hagar and her children, even so standeth it between Jerusalem and hers.
ag. Gal. 4:25 That is, Sinai.
ah. Gal. 4:26 Which is excellent, and of great account.
ai. Gal. 4:27 He showeth that in this allegory, he hath followed the steps of Isaiah, who foretold that the Church should be made and consist of the children of barren Sarah, that is to say, of them which only spiritually should be made Abraham's children by faith, rather than of fruitful Hagar, even then foreshowing the casting off of the Jews, and calling of the Gentiles.
aj. Gal. 4:27 She that is destroyed and wasted.
ak. Gal. 4:28 After the manner of Isaac who is the first begotten of the heavenly Jerusalem, as Israel is of the slavish Synagogue.
al. Gal. 4:28 That seed, unto which the promise belongeth.
am. Gal. 4:29 By the common course of nature.
an. Gal. 4:29 By the virtue of God's promise and after a spiritual manner.
ao. Gal. 4:31 The conclusion of the former allegory, that we by no means procure and call back again the slavery of the Law, seeing that the children of the bondmaid shall not be heirs.

GALATIANS 4

1. Rom. 8:15
2. Gen. 16:15
3. Gen. 21:1
4. Isa. 54:1
5. Rom. 8:9
6. Gen. 21:10

GALATIANS 5

a. Gal. 5:2 Another obtestation wherein he plainly witnesseth that justification of works, and justification of faith cannot stand together, because no man can be justified by the Law, but he that doth fully and perfectly fulfill it. And he taketh the example of circumcision, because it was the ground of all the service of the Law, and was chiefly urged of the false Apostles.
b. Gal. 5:2 Circumcision is in other places called the seal of righteousness, but here we must have consideration of the circumstance of the Baptism come in place of circumcision. And moreover Paul reasoneth according to the opinion that his enemies had of it, which made circumcision a piece of their salvation.
c. Gal. 5:4 That is, as he himself expoundeth it afterwards, ye are fallen from grace.
d. Gal. 5:4 That is, seek to be justified by the Law, for in deed no man is justified by the Law.
e. Gal. 5:5 He privily compareth the new people with the old: for it is certain that they also did ground all their hope of justification and life in faith and not in circumcision, but so, that their faith was wrapped in the external and ceremonial worship: but our faith is bare and content with spiritual worship.
f. Gal. 5:5 Through the Spirit, which engendereth faith.
g. Gal. 5:6 He addeth a reason for that now circumcision is abolished, seeing that Christ is exhibited unto us with full plenty of spiritual circumcision.
h. Gal. 5:6 He maketh mention also of uncircumcision, lest the Gentiles should please themselves in it, as the Jews do in circumcision.
i. Gal. 5:6 The taking away of an objection: If all that worship of the Law be taken away, wherein then shall we exercise ourselves? In charity, saith Paul: for faith, whereof we speak, cannot be idle, nay it bringeth forth daily fruits of charity.
j. Gal. 5:6 So is true faith distinguished from counterfeit faith: for charity is not joined to faith as a fellow cause, to help forward our justification with faith.
k. Gal. 5:7 Again he chideth the Gal., but with an admiration, and therewithall a praise of their former race, to the end that he may make them more ashamed.
l. Gal. 5:8 He playeth the part of an Apostle with them, and useth his authority, denying that that doctrine can come from God which is contrary to his.
m. Gal. 5:8 Of God.
n. Gal. 5:9 He addeth this, that he may not seem to contend upon a trifle, warning them diligently by a similitude which he borroweth of leaven, as Christ himself also did not to suffer the purity of the Apostolical doctrine, to be infected with the least corruption that may be.
o. Gal. 5:10 He mitigateth the former reprehension, casting the fault upon the false Apostles, against whom he denounceth the horrible judgment of God.
p. Gal. 5:11 He willeth them to consider how that he seeketh not his own profit in this matter, seeing that he could eschew the hatred of men, if he would join Judaism with Christianity.
q. Gal. 5:12 An example of a true Pastor inflamed with the zeal of God's glory and love of his flock.
r. Gal. 5:12 For they that preach the Law, cause men's consciences always to tremble.
s. Gal. 5:13 The third part of this Epistle, showing that the right use of Christian liberty consisteth in this, that being delivered from the slavery of sin and the flesh, and being obedient to the Spirit, we should serve unto one another's salvation through love.
t. Gal. 5:14 He propoundeth the love of our neighbor, as a mark whereunto all Christians ought to refer all their actions, and thereunto he citeth the testimony of the Law.
u. Gal. 5:14 This particle All must be restrained to the second table.
v. Gal. 5:15 An exhortation to the duties of charity, by the profit that ensueth thereof, because that no men provide worse for themselves, than they that hate one another.
w. Gal. 5:16 He acknowledgeth the great weakness of the godly, for that they are but in part regenerate: but he willeth them to remember that they are endued with the Spirit of God, which hath delivered them from the slavery of sin, and so of the Law so far forth as it is the virtue of sin, that they should not give themselves to lusts.
x. Gal. 5:17 For the flesh dwelleth even in the regenerate man, but the Spirit reigneth although not without great strife, as is largely set forth, Rom. 7.
y. Gal. 5:19 He setteth out that particularly, which he spake generally, reckoning up some chief effects of the flesh, and opposing them to the fruits of the Spirit, that no man may pretend ignorance.
z. Gal. 5:22 Therefore, they are not the fruits of free will, but so far forth as our will is made free by grace.
aa. Gal. 5:23 Lest that any man should object, that Paul played the Sophister, as one who urging the Spirit, urgeth nothing but that which the Law commandeth, he showeth that he requireth not that liberal and outward obedience, but spiritual, which proceedeth not from the Law, but from the Spirit of Christ, which doth beget us again, and must and ought to be the ruler and guider of life.

6

1 Now he entreateth particularly of charity toward such as offend, 6 toward the Minsters of the word, 10 and those that are of the household of faith: 12 Not like unto such who have a counterfeit zeal of the Law, 13 glorying in the mangling of the flesh, 14 and not in the cross of Christ.

1 Brethren, [a]If a man be [b]suddenly taken in any offense, ye which are [c]spiri-
tual, [d]restore such one with the [e]spirit of meekness, [f]considering thyself, lest thou
also be tempted. **2** [g]Bear ye one another's burden, and so fulfill the [h]Law of
Christ. **3** For if any man seem to himself, that he is somewhat, when he is nothing,
he deceiveth himself in his imagination. **4** But let every man prove his own work:
and then shall he have rejoicing in himself only and not in another. **5** [1,i]For every
man shall bear his own burden. **6** [j]Let him that is taught in the word, make him
that hath taught him, partaker of [k]all his [2]goods. **7** [l]Be not deceived: God is
not mocked: for whatsoever a man soweth, that shall he also reap. **8** For he that
soweth to his [m]flesh, shall of the flesh reap corruption: but he that soweth to the
spirit, shall of the spirit reap life everlasting. **9** [3,n]Let us not therefore be weary of
well doing: for in due season we shall reap, if we faint not. **10** [o]While we have
therefore time, let us do good unto all men, but especially unto them, which are
of the household of faith. **11** [p]Ye see how large a letter I have written unto you
with mine own hand. **12** As many as desire to make a [q]fair show in the [r]flesh,
they constrain you to be circumcised, only because they would not suffer persecu-
tion for the [s]cross of Christ. **13** For they themselves which are circumcised keep
not the Law, but desire to have you circumcised, that they might rejoice in [t]your
flesh. **14** [u]But God forbid that I should [v]rejoice, but in the cross of our Lord Je-
sus Christ, whereby the world is crucified unto me, and I unto the world. **15** For
in Christ Jesus neither circumcision availeth anything, nor uncircumcision, but a
new creature. **16** And as many as walk according to this rule, peace shall be upon
them, and mercy, and upon the [w]Israel of God. **17** [x]From henceforth let no man
put me to business: for I bear, in my body the [y]marks of the [z]Lord Jesus. **18** [aa]-
Brethren, the grace of our Lord Jesus Christ be with your [ab]spirit, Amen. Unto
the Galatians written from Rome.

---

ab. Gal. 5:25 If we be indeed endued with the quickening Spirit, which causeth us to die to sin, and live to God, let us show it in our deeds, that is, by holiness of life.

ac. Gal. 5:26 He addeth peculiar exhortations according as he knew the Gal. subject to divers vices: and first of all he warneth them to take heed of ambition, which vice hath two fellows, backbiting and envy, out of which two it cannot be but many contentions must needs arise.

GALATIANS 5

1. Acts 15:1
2. 1 Cor. 1:17
3. 1 Cor. 5:6
4. Lev. 19:18 / Matt. 22:39 / Mark 12:31 / Rom. 13:9 / James 2:8
5. Rom. 13:14 / 1 Pet. 2:11

GALATIANS 6

a. Gal. 6:1 He condemneth importunate rigor, because that brotherly reprehensions ought to be moderated and tempered by the spirit of meekness.

b. Gal. 6:1 Through the malice of the flesh and the devil.

c. Gal. 6:1 Which are upholden by the virtue of God's Spirit.

d. Gal. 6:1 Labor to fill up that that is wanting in him.

e. Gal. 6:1 This is a kind of speech which the Hebrews use, giving to understand thereby, that all good gifts come from God.

f. Gal. 6:1 He toucheth the fore: for they commonly are most severe judges, which forget their own infirmities.

g. Gal. 6:2 He showeth that this is the end of reprehensions, to raise up our brother which is fallen, and not proudly to oppress him. Therefore everyone must seek to have commendation of his own life by approving of himself, and not by reprehending others.

h. Gal. 6:2 Christ, in plain and flat words, calleth the commandment of charity, his commandment.

i. Gal. 6:5 A reason wherefore men ought to have the greatest eye upon themselves, because that every man shall be judged before God according to his own life, and not by comparing himself with other men.

j. Gal. 6:6 It is meet that masters should be sound by their scholars, so far forth as they are able.

k. Gal. 6:6 Of whatsoever he hath, according to his ability.

l. Gal. 6:7 He commendeth liberality towards the poor, and first of all chideth them which were not ashamed to pretend this and that, and all because they would not help their neighbors, as though they could deceive God: and afterward compareth alms to a spiritual sowing, which shall have a most plentiful harvest, so that it shall be very profitable: and compareth covetous niggardliness to a carnal sowing, whereof nothing can be gathered but such things as fade away, and perish by and by.

m. Gal. 6:8 To the commodities of this present life.

n. Gal. 6:9 Against such as are liberal at the beginning, but continue not, because the harvest seemeth to be deferred very long, as though the seed time and the harvest were at one instant.

o. Gal. 6:10 They that are of the household of faith, that is, such as are joined with us in the profession of one selfsame religion, ought to be preferred before all others, yet so notwithstanding that our liberality extends to all.

p. Gal. 6:11 The fourth and last part of the Epistle, wherein he returneth to his principal end and purpose: to wit, that the Gal. should not suffer themselves to be led out of the way by the false apostles: and he pointeth out those false apostles in their colors, reproving them of ambition, as men that do not that which they do, for any affection and zeal they have to the Law, but only for this purpose, that they may purchase themselves favor amongst their own sort, by the circumcision of the Gal..

q. Gal. 6:12 He setteth a far show against the truth.

r. Gal. 6:12 In keeping of ceremonies.

s. Gal. 6:12 For the preaching of him that was crucified.

t. Gal. 6:13 That they have entangled you in Judaism, and yet he harpeth on the form of circumcision.

u. Gal. 6:14 He sticketh not to compare himself with them, showing that on the contrary part he rejoiceth in those afflictions which he suffereth for Christ's sake, and as he is despised of the world, so doth he in like sort esteem the world as naught: which is the true circumcision of a true Israelite.

v. Gal. 6:14 When Paul useth this word in good sense of part, it signifieth to rest a man's self wholly in a thing, and to content himself therewith.

w. Gal. 6:16 Upon the true Israel, whose praise is of God and not of men, Rom. 2:19.

x. Gal. 6:17 Continuing still in the same metaphor, he opposeth his miseries and the marks of those stripes which he bare for Christ's sake, against the scar of the outward circumcision, as a true mark of his Apostleship.

y. Gal. 6:17 Marks which are burnt into a man's flesh, as they used in old times, to mark their servants that had run away from them.

z. Gal. 6:17 For it importeth much, whose marks we bear: for the cause maketh the Martyr, and not the punishment.

aa. Gal. 6:18 Taking his farewell of them, he wisheth them grace, and the Spirit against the deceits of the false apostles, who labored to beat those outward things into their brains.

ab. Gal. 6:18 With your minds and hearts.

GALATIANS 6

1. 1 Cor. 3:18
2. 1 Cor. 9:7
3. 2 Thess. 3:13

THE EPISTLE OF THE APOSTLE PAUL TO THE

EPHESIANS

1

1 After the salutation, 4 he entreateth of the free election of God, 5 and adoption. 7, 13 from whence man's salvation floweth, as from the true and natural fountain: and because so high a mystery cannot be understood, 16 he prayeth that the full, 20 knowledge of Christ, may by God be reavealed unto the Ephesians.

1 Paul [a]an Apostle of Jesus Christ by the will of God, to the [1]Saints, which
are at Ephesus, and to the [b]faithful in Christ Jesus: **2** Grace be with you, and
peace from God our Father, and from the Lord Jesus Christ. **3** [2,c]Blessed be
God, [d]and the Father of our Lord Jesus Christ, [e]which hath blessed us, with [f]all
spiritual blessing in [g]heavenly things in [h]Christ, **4** [i]As he hath chosen us in [j]him,
before the foundation of the world, [k]that we [l]should [m]be holy, and without bla-
me [n]before him in love: **5** [o]Who hath predestinated us, to be adopted through
Jesus Christ [p]in himself, according to the good pleasure of his will. **6** [q]To the
[r]praise of the glory of his grace, [s]wherewith he hath made us freely accepted in his
beloved. **7** [t]By whom we have redemption through his blood, even the forgive-
ness of sins, according to his rich grace: **8** [u,v]Whereby he hath been abundant
toward us in [w]all wisdom and understanding, **9** And hath opened unto us the
[x]mystery of his will [y]according to his good pleasure, which he hath purposed in
him, **10** [z]That in the dispensation of the fullness of the times, he might [aa]ga-
ther together in one all things, both which are in heaven, and which are in earth,
even in Christ: **11** [ab]In whom also we are chosen when we were predestinated
according to the purpose of him, which worketh [ac]all things after the counsel of
his own will, **12** That we, which [ad]first trusted in Christ, should be unto the
praise of his glory: **13** [ae]In whom also ye have trusted, after that ye heard the
[af]word of truth, even the Gospel of your salvation, wherein also after that ye belie-
ved, ye were [ag]sealed with the holy [ah]Spirit of promise, **14** Which is the earnest
of our inheritance, for the [ai]redemption of that liberty purchased unto the praise
of his glory. **15** [aj]Therefore also after that I heard of the faith, which ye have in
the Lord Jesus, and love toward all the Saints, **16** I cease not to give thanks for
you, making mention of you in my prayers, **17** [ak]That the God of our Lord Jesus
Christ, that Father of [al]glory, might give unto you the Spirit of wisdom, and reve-
lation through the [am]knowledge of him, **18** That the eyes of your understanding
may be lightened, that ye may know what the [an]hope is of his calling, and what
the riches of his glorious inheritance is in the Saints, **19** [ao]And what is the excee-
ding greatness of his power toward us, which believe, [3]according to the working of
his mighty power, **20** [ap]Which he wrought in Christ, when he raised him from
the dead, and set him at his [aq]right hand in the heavenly places, **21** Far above
all principality, and power, and might, and domination, and every [ar]Name, that is
named, not in this world only, but also in that that is to come, **22** [as]And hath
made all things subject under his feet, and hath given him over all things to be the
[at]head to the Church, **23** Which is his body, even the [au]fullness of him that fil-
leth all in all things.

EPHESIANS 1

a. Eph. 1:1 The inscription and salutation, whereof we have spoken in the former Epistles.

b. Eph. 1:1 This is the definition of the Saints, showing what they are.

c. Eph. 1:3 The first part of the Epistle, wherein he handleth all the parts of our salvation, propounding the example of the Ephesians, and using divers exhortations, and beginning after his manner with thanksgiving.

d. Eph. 1:3 The efficient cause of our salvation is God, not considered confusedly and generally, but as the father of our Lord Jesus Christ.

e. Eph. 1:3 The next final cause, and in respect of us, is our salvation, all things being bestowed upon us which are necessary to our salvation, which kind of blessings is heavenly and proper to the elect.

f. Eph. 1:3 With all kind of gracious and bountiful goodness which is heavenly indeed, and from God only.

g. Eph. 1:3 Which God our Father gave us from his high throne from above: or because the Saints have those gifts bestowed on them, which belong properly to the citizens of heaven.

h. Eph. 1:3 The matter of our salvation is Christ, in whom only we are endued with spiritual blessing and unto salvation.

i. Eph. 1:4 He declareth the efficient cause, or by what means God the Father saveth us in his Son: Because saith he, he chose us from everlasting in his Son.

j. Eph. 1:4 To be adopted in him.

k. Eph. 1:4 He expoundeth the next final cause, which he maketh double, to wit, sanctification and justification, whereof he will speak hereafter. And hereby also two things are to be noted, to wit, that holiness of life cannot be separated from the grace of election: and again what pureness forever is in us, is the gift of God, who hath freely of his mercy chosen us.

l. Eph. 1:4 Then God did not choose us, because we were, or otherwise should have been holy, but to the end we should be holy.

m. Eph. 1:4 Being clothed with Christ's righteousness.

n. Eph. 1:4 Truly and sincerely.

o. Eph. 1:5 Another plainer exposition of the efficient cause, and also of eternal election, whereby God is saith to have chosen us in Christ, to wit, because it pleased him to appoint us out when we were not yet born, whom he would make to be his children by Jesus Christ: so that there is no reason here of our election to be sought, but in the free mercy of God, neither is faith which God foresaw, the cause of predestination, but the effect.

p. Eph. 1:5 God respecteth nothing, either that present is, or that is to come, but himself only.

q. Eph. 1:6 The uttermost and chiefest final cause is the glory of God the Father, who saveth us freely in his Son.

r. Eph. 1:6 That as his bountiful goodness deserveth all praise, so also it should be set forth and published.

s. Eph. 1:6 Another final cause more near, is our justification, while that he freely accounteth us for just in his Son.

t. Eph. 1:7 An expounding of the material cause, how we are made acceptable to God in Christ, for it is he only, whose sacrifice by the mercy of God is imputed unto us, for the forgiveness of sin.

u. Eph. 1:8 Now he cometh at length to the formal cause, that is to say, to vocation or preaching of the Gospel, whereby God executeth that eternal counsel of our free reconciliation and salvation in Christ. And putting in place of the Gospel all wisdom and understanding, he showeth how excellent it is.

v. Eph. 1:8 By which gracious goodness and bountifulness.

w. Eph. 1:8 In perfect and sound wisdom.

x. Eph. 1:9 For unless the Lord had opened unto us that mystery, we could never have so much as dreamed of it ourselves.

y. Eph. 1:9 Not only the election, but also the vocation proceedeth of meer grace.

z. Eph. 1:10 The Father exhibiteth and gave Christ, who is the head of all the elect unto the world, at that time which was convenient, according as he most wisely disposed all times from everlasting. And Christ is he in whom all the elect from the beginning of the world, otherwise wandering and separated from God are gathered together: of which some were then in heaven when he came into the earth, to wit, such as by faith in him to come, were gathered together and others being found upon the earth, were gathered together of him, and the rest are daily gathered together.

aa. Eph. 1:10 The faithful are said to be gathered together in Christ, because they are joined together with him through faith, and become as it were one man.

ab. Eph. 1:11 He applieth severally the benefit of vocation to the believing Jews, going back to the very fountain, that even they also may not attribute their salvation neither to themselves, nor to their stock, nor to any other thing, but to the only grace and mercy of God, both because they were called, and also because they were first called.

ac. Eph. 1:11 All things are attributed to the grace of God without exception, and yet for all that, we are not stocks, for he giveth us grace both to will and to be able to do those things that are good, Phil. 2:13.

ad. Eph. 1:12 He speaketh of the Jews.

ae. Eph. 1:13 Now he maketh the Eph. or rather all the Gentiles equal to the Jews, because that notwithstanding they came last, yet being called by the same Gospel, they embraced it by faith, and were sealed up with the same spirit, which is the pledge of election, until the inheritance itself be seen, that in them also the glory of God might shine forth, and be manifested.

af. Eph. 1:13 That word which is truth indeed, because it cometh from God.

ag. Eph. 1:13 This is a borrowed kind of speech taken of a seal, which being put to anything, maketh a difference between those things that are authentical, and others that are not.

ah. Eph. 1:13 With that Spirit, which bringeth not the Law, but the promise of free adoption.

ai. Eph. 1:14 Full and perfect.

aj. Eph. 1:15 He returneth to the former gratulation, concluding two things together of those things that went before: the first is, that all good things come to us from God the Father in Christ, and by Christ, that for them he may be praised of us. The second is that all those things which he bringeth to two heads, to wit, faith and charity are increased in us by certain degrees, so that we must desire increase of his grace from whom we have the beginning, and of whom we hope for the end.

ak. Eph. 1:17 The causes of faith are God the Father lightening our minds with his holy spirit, that we may embrace Christ opened unto us in the Gospel, to the obtaining of everlasting life, and the setting forth of God's glory.

al. Eph. 1:17 Full of majesty.

am. Eph. 1:17 For it is not enough for us to have known God once, but we must know him every day more and more.

an. Eph. 1:18 What blessings they are which he calleth you to hope for whom he calleth to Christ.

ao. Eph. 1:19 The excellency of faith is declared by the effects, because the mighty power of God is set forth and shown therein.

ap. Eph. 1:20 The Apostle willeth us to behold in our most glorious Christ with the eye of faith, that most excellent power and glory of God, whereof all the faithful are partakers, although it be as yet very dark in us, by reason of the ignominy of the cross and the weakness of the flesh.

aq. Eph. 1:20 To be set on God's right hand, is to be partaker of the sovereignty which he hath over all creatures.

ar. Eph. 1:21 Everything whatsoever it be, or above all things be they of never such power or excellency.

as. Eph. 1:22 That we should not think that that excellent glory of Christ is a thing wherewith we have nought to do, he witnesseth, that he was appointed of God the Father the head of all the Church, and therefore the body must be joined to his head, which otherwise should be a maimed thing without the members: which notwithstanding is not of necessity seeing that the Church is rather quickeneth and sustained by the only virtue of Christ, so far off is it, that he needeth the fullness thereof but of the infinite goodwill and pleasure of God, who vouchsafeth to join us to his Son.

at. Eph. 1:22 Insomuch that there is nothing but is subject to him.

au. Eph. 1:23 For the love of Christ is so great toward the Church, that though he do fully satisfy all with all things, yet he esteemeth himself but a maimed and unperfect head, unless he have the Church joined to him as his body.

2

1 The better to set out the grace of Christ, he useth a comparison, calling them to mind, 5 that they were altogether castaways and aliants, 8 that they are saved by grace, 13 and brought near, 16 by reconciliation through Christ, 17 published by the Gospel.

1 And [1,a]you hath he quickened, that were [b]dead in [c]trespasses and sins, **2** [d]Wherein, in times past ye walked, [e]according to the course of this world, and [f]after the prince that ruleth in the air, even the spirit, that now [g]worketh in the [h]children of disobedience, **3** [i]Among whom we also had our conversation in time past in the lusts of our [j]flesh, in fulfilling the will of the flesh, and of the mind, and [k]were by nature the [l]children of wrath, as well as [m]others. **4** [n]But God which is rich in mercy, through his great love wherewith he loved us, **5** Even when we were dead by sins, hath quickened us together in Christ, by whose grace ye are saved, **6** And hath raised us up [o]together, and made us sit together in the heavenly places in Christ Jesus, **7** That he might show in the ages to come the exceeding riches of his grace through his kindness toward us in Christ Jesus. **8** For by [p]grace are ye saved through faith, and that not of yourselves: it is the gift of God, **9** [q]Not of works, lest any man should boast himself. **10** For we are [r]his workmanship created in Christ Jesus unto good works, which God hath ordained, that we should walk in them. **11** [s]Wherefore remember that ye being in time past Gentiles in the flesh, and [t]called uncircumcision of them, which are [u]called circumcision in the flesh, made with hands, **12** That ye were, I say, at that time [v]without Christ, and were [w]aliens from the commonwealth of Israel, and were [2]strangers from the covenants of promise, and had no hope, and were without God in the world. **13** [x]But now in Christ Jesus, ye which once were far off, are made near by the blood of Christ. **14** [y]For he is our peace, which hath made of both one, and hath broken the stop of the partition wall, **15** [3]In abrogating through his flesh the hatred, that is, the Law of commandments which standeth in ordinances, for to make of twain one new man in himself, so making peace, **16** And that he might reconcile both unto God in [z]one body by his cross, and [aa]slay hatred thereby, **17** [ab]And came, and preached peace to you which were afar off, and to them that were near. **18** For [ac]through him we both have an entrance unto the Father by one Spirit. **19** [ad]Now therefore ye are no more strangers and foreigners: but citizens with the Saints, and of the household of God. **20** [ae]And are built upon the foundation of the Apostles and Prophets, Jesus Christ himself being the [af]chief cornerstone, **21** In whom all the building [ag]coupled together, groweth unto an holy Temple in the Lord. **22** In whom ye also are built together to be the habitation of God by the Spirit.

3

1 He declareth that therefore he suffered many things of the Jews, 3 because he preached the mystery touching the salvation of the Gentiles, 8 at God's commandment. 13 After he desired the Ephesians not to faint for his afflictions. 14 And for this cause he prayeth unto God, 18 that they may understand the great love of Christ.

1 For [a]this cause, I Paul am the [b]prisoner of Jesus Christ for you Gentiles. **2** If ye have heard of the dispensation of the grace of God, which is given me to youward, **3** That is, that God by revelation hath showed this mystery unto me as I wrote above in few words, **4** Whereby when ye read, ye may know mine understanding in the mystery of Christ **5** Which in [c]other ages was not opened unto the sons of men, as it is now revealed unto his holy Apostles and Prophets by the Spirit, **6** That the Gentiles should be inheritors also, and of the same body, and partakers of his promise in Christ by the Gospel, **7** Whereof I am made a minister by the gift of the grace of God given unto me through the effectual working of his power. **8** Even unto me the least of all Saints is this grace given, that I should preach among the Gentiles, the unsearchable riches of Christ, **9** And to make clear unto all men what the fellowship of the mystery is, which from the beginning of the world hath been hid in God, who hath created all things by Jesus Christ, **10** [d]To the intent, that now unto principalities and powers in heavenly places, might be known by the Church the [e]manifold wisdom of God, **11** According to the [f]eternal purpose, which he wrought in Christ Jesus our Lord: **12** By whom we have boldness and entrance with confidence, by faith in him. **13** Wherefore I desire that ye faint not at my tribulations for your sakes, which is your glory. **14** [g]For this cause I bow my knees unto the Father of our Lord Jesus Christ, **15** Of whom is named the whole [h]family in heaven and in earth **16** That he might grant you according to the [i]riches of his glory, that ye may be strengthened by his Spirit in the [j]inner man, **17** That Christ may dwell in your hearts by faith: **18** That ye, being rooted and grounded in [k]love, may be able to comprehend with all Saints, [l]what is the breadth, and length, and depth, and height: **19** And to know the [m]love of Christ, which [n]passeth knowledge,

---

EPHESIANS 1

1. 1 Cor. 1:2
2. 1 Cor. 1:3 / 1 Pet. 1:3
3. Eph. 3:7 / Col. 2:12

EPHESIANS 2

a. Eph. 2:1 He declareth again the greatness of God's good will, by comparing that miserable state wherein we are born, with that dignity whereunto we are advanced by God the Father in Christ. So he describeth that condition in such sort, that he saith, that touching spiritual motions we are not only born half dead, but wholly and altogether dead.

b. Eph. 2:1 See Rom. 6:2. So then he calleth them dead, which are not regenerate: for as the immortality of them which are damned, is no life, so this knitting together of body and soul is properly no life, but death in them which are not ruled by the Spirit of God.

c. Eph. 2:1 He showeth the cause of death, to wit, sins.

d. Eph. 2:2 He proveth by the effects that all were spiritually dead.

e. Eph. 2:2 He proveth this evil to be universal, insomuch as all are slaves of Satan.

f. Eph. 2:2 At the pleasure of the prince.

g. Eph. 2:2 Men are therefore slaves to Satan, because they are willingly rebellious against God.

h. Eph. 2:2 They are called the children of disobedience, which are given to disobedience.

i. Eph. 2:3 After that he hath severally condemned the Gentiles, he confesseth that the Jews, amongst whom he numbereth himself, are not a whit better.

j. Eph. 2:3 By the name of flesh in the first place, he meaneth the whole man, which he divideth into two parts: into the flesh, which is the part that the Philosophers term without reason, and into the thought, which they call reasonable: so that he leaveth nothing in man half dead, but concludeth that the whole man is of nature the son of wrath.

k. Eph. 2:3 The conclusion: All men are born subject to the wrath and curse of God.

l. Eph. 2:3 Men are said to be children of wrath passively, that is to say, guilty of everlasting death by the judgment of God, who is angry with them.

m. Eph. 2:3 Profane people which knew not God.

n. Eph. 2:4 Now hereof followeth another member of the comparison, declaring our excellency, to wit, that by the virtue of Christ we are delivered from that death, and made partakers of eternal life, to the end that at length we may reign with him. And by divers and sundry means he beateth this into their heads, that the efficient cause of this benefit is the free mercy of God: and Christ himself is the material cause: and faith is the instrument which also is the free gift of God: and the end is God's glory.

o. Eph. 2:6 To wit, as he addeth afterward in Christ, for as yet this is not fulfilled in us, but only in our head, by whose spirit we have begun to die to sin, and live to God, until that work be fully brought to an end: but yet the hope is certain, for we are as sure of that we look for: as we are of that we have received already.

p. Eph. 2:8 So then, Grace, that is to say, the gift of God, and faith, do stand one with another, to which two these are contrary, To be saved by ourselves, or by our works. Therefore what mean they which would join together things of so contrary nature?

q. Eph. 2:9 He taketh away expressly and namely from our works the praise of justification, seeing that the good works themselves are the effects of grace in us.

r. Eph. 2:10 He speaketh here of grace, and not of nature: therefore be the works never so good, look what they are, they are it of grace.

s. Eph. 2:11 Applying the former doctrine to the Gentiles, he showeth that they were not only as the Jews, by nature, but also after an especial sort, strangers and without God: and therefore they ought so much the rather remember that same so great a benefit of God.

t. Eph. 2:11 You were called no otherwise than Gentiles, that all the world might witness of your uncleanness.

u. Eph. 2:11 Of the Jews which were known from you by the mark of circumcision, the mark of the covenant.

v. Eph. 2:12 He beginneth first with Christ, who was the end of all the promises.

w. Eph. 2:12 You had no right or title, to the common wealth of Israel.

x. Eph. 2:13 Christ is the only bond of the Jews and Gentiles, whereby they be reconciled to God.

y. Eph. 2:14 As by the ceremonies and worship appointed by the Law, the Jews were divided from the Gentiles, so now Christ, having broken down the partition wall, joineth them both together, both in himself, and betwixt themselves, and to God. Whereby it followeth, that whosoever established the ceremonies of the Law, maketh the grace of Christ void and of none effect.

z. Eph. 2:16 He alludeth to the sacrifices of the Law, which represented that true and only sacrifice.

aa. Eph. 2:16 For he destroyed death by death, and fastened it as it were to the cross.

ab. Eph. 2:17 The preaching of the Gospel is an effectual instrument of this grace, common as well to the Jews as to the Gentiles.

ac. Eph. 2:18 Christ is the gate as it were, by whom we come to the Father, and the holy Ghost is as it were our lodes man who leadeth us.

ad. Eph. 2:19 The conclusion: The Gentiles are taken into the fellowship of salvation. And he describeth the excellency of the Church, calling it the city and house of God.

ae. Eph. 2:20 The Lord committed the doctrine of salvation, first to the Prophets, and then to the Apostles, the end whereof and matter as it were and substance, is Christ. Therefore that is indeed the true and Catholic Church, which is builded upon Christ by the Prophets and Apostles, as a spiritual temple consecrated to God.

af. Eph. 2:20 That is, the head of the building, for the foundations are as it were the heads of the buildings.

ag. Eph. 2:21 So that God is the workman not only of the foundation, but also of the whole building.

EPHESIANS 2

1. Col. 2:13
2. Rom. 9:4
3. Col. 2:14

EPHESIANS 3

a. Eph. 3:1 He maintaineth his Apostleship against the offense of the cross, whereon also he taketh an argument to confirm himself, affirming that he was not only appointed an Apostle by the mercy of God, but was also particularly appointed to the Gentiles, to call them on every side to salvation: because God had so determined it from the beginning, although he deferred a great while the manifestation of that his counsel.

b. Eph. 3:1 These words, The prisoner of Jesus Christ, are taken passively, that is to say I Paul am cast into prison for maintaining the glory of Christ.

c. Eph. 3:5 He meaneth not that none knew the calling of the Gentiles before, but because very few knew of it, and they that did know it, as the Prophets, had it revealed unto them very darkly, and under figures.

d. Eph. 3:10 The unlooked for calling of the Gentiles, was as it were a glass to the heavenly Angels, wherin they might behold the marvellous wisdom of God.

e. Eph. 3:10 God never had but one way only, to save men by: but it had divers fashions and forms.

f. Eph. 3:11 Which was before all beginnings.

g. Eph. 3:14 He teacheth by his own example, that the efficacy of the doctrine dependeth upon the grace of God, and therefore we ought to join prayers with the preaching and hearing of the word: which are needful not only to them which are younglings in religion, but even to the oldest also, that they growing up more and more by faith in Christ, being confirmed with all spiritual gifts, may be grounded and rooted in the knowledge of that immeasurable love, wherewith God the Father hath loved us in Christ, seeing that the whole family, whereof part is already received into heaven, and part is yet here on earth, dependeth upon that adoption of the heavenly Father, in his only Son.

h. Eph. 3:15 All that whole people which hath but one household Father, and that is the Church which is adopted in Christ.

i. Eph. 3:16 According to the greatness of his mercy.

j. Eph. 3:16 See Rom. 7:22.

k. Eph. 3:18 Wherewith God loveth us, which is the root of our election.

l. Eph. 3:18 How perfect that work of Christ is in every part.

m. Eph. 3:19 Which God hath showeth us in Christ.

that ye may be filled with all [o]fullness of God. **20** [p]Unto him therefore that is
able to do exceeding abundantly above all that we ask or think, according to the
power that worketh in us, **21** Be praise in the Church by Christ Jesus, throu-
ghout all generations forever, Amen.

4

These three last Chapters contain precepts of manners. 1 He exhorteth them to mutual love. 7 Sundry gifts are therefore bestowed of God, 16 that the Church may be built up. 18 He calleth them from the vanity of infidels, 25 from lying, 29 and from filthy talk.

1 I therefore, [a]being prisoner in the Lord, pray you that ye walk worthy of
the [b]vocation whereunto ye are called, **2** [c]With all humbleness of mind, and
meekness, with [d]long suffering, supporting one another through love, **3** [e]En-
deavoring to keep the unity of the Spirit in the bond of peace. **4** [f]There is one
body, and one Spirit, even as ye are called in one hope of your vocation. **5** The-
re is one Lord, one Faith, one Baptism. **6** One God and Father of all, which is
[g]above all, and [h]through all, and [i]in you all. **7** [j]But unto every one of us is gi-
ven grace according to the measure of the [k]gift of Christ. **8** Wherefore he sai-
th, When he ascended upon high, he led [l]captivity captive, and gave gifts unto
men. **9** Now, in that he ascended, what is it but that he had also descended first
into the [m]lowest parts of the earth? **10** He that descended, is even the same that
ascended, far above all heavens, that he might [n]fill [o]all things. **11** [p]He therefore
gave some to be [q]Apostles, and some [r]Prophets, and some [s]Evangelists, and some
[t]Pastors, and Teachers, **12** [u]For the repairing of the Saints, for the work of the
ministry, and for the edification of the [v]body of Christ, **13** [w]Till we all meet
together in the [x]unity of faith and that acknowledging of the Son of God unto a
perfect man, and unto the measure of the [y]age the fullness of Christ, **14** [z]That
we henceforth be no more children, [aa]wavering and carried about with every wind
of doctrine, by the [ab]deceit of men, and with craftiness, whereby they lay in [ac]wait
to deceive. **15** [ad]But let us follow the truth in love, and in all things, grow up
into him, which is the head, that is, Christ. **16** By whom all the body being
coupled and knit together by every joint, for the furniture thereof according to the
[ae]effectual power, which is in the measure of every part receiveth [af]increase of the
body, unto the edifying of itself in [ag]love. **17** [ah]This I say therefore and testify in
the Lord, that ye henceforth walk not as [1]other Gentiles walk, in [ai]vanity of their
mind. **18** Having their understanding darkened, and being strangers from the
[aj]life of God through the ignorance that is in them, because of the hardness of their
heart: **19** Which being [ak]past feeling, have given themselves unto wantonness,
to work all uncleanness, even with [al]greediness. **20** [am]But ye have not so lear-
ned Christ, **21** If so be ye have heard him, and have been taught by him, [an]as
the truth is in Jesus, **22** [2]That is, that ye cast off, concerning the conversation in
time past, [ao]that old man, which is corrupt through the deceivable lusts, **23** And
be renewed in the [ap]spirit of your mind, **24** And put on the new man, which
[aq]after God is created unto [ar]righteousness, and [as]true holiness. **25** [at]Wherefore
cast off lying, and speak every man truth unto his neighbor: for we are members
one of another. **26** [au]Be [av]angry, but sin not: let not the sun go down [aw]upon
your wrath, **27** Neither give place to the devil. **28** [ax]Let him that stole, steal
no more: but let him rather labor, and work with his hands the thing which is [ay]
good, that he may have to give unto him that needeth. **29** [az]Let no [ba]corrupt
communication proceed out of your mouths: but that which is good to the use of
edifying, that it may minister [bb]grace unto the hearers. **30** [bc]And grieve not the
holy Spirit of God, by whom ye are sealed unto the day of redemption. **31** Let all
bitterness, and anger, and wrath, crying, and evil speaking be put away from you,
with all maliciousness. **32** Be ye courteous one to another, and tender hearted,
freely forgiving one another, [bd]even as God for Christ's sake, freely forgave you.

- **n.** Eph. 3:19 Which passeth all the capacity of man's wit, to comprehend it fully in his mind: for otherwise who so hath the Spirit of God, perceiveth so much according to the measure that God hath given him as is sufficient to salvation.
- **o.** Eph. 3:19 So that we have abundantly in us, whatsoever things are required to make us perfect with God.
- **p.** Eph. 3:20 He breaketh forth into a thanksgiving, whereby the Eph. also may be confirmed to hope for anything of God.

EPHESIANS 4

- **a.** Eph. 4:1 Another part of the Epistle containing precepts of Christian life, the sum whereof is this, that every man behave himself as it is meet for so excellent grace of God.
- **b.** Eph. 4:1 By this is meant the general calling of the faithful, which is this, to be holy, as our God is holy.
- **c.** Eph. 4:2 Secondly, he commendeth meekness of the mind, which is shown forth by bearing one with another.
- **d.** Eph. 4:2 See Matt. 18:25.
- **e.** Eph. 4:3 Thirdly, he requireth perfect agreement, but yet such as is knit with the band of the holy Ghost.
- **f.** Eph. 4:4 An argument of great weight, for an earnest entertaining of brotherly love and charity one with another, because we are made one body as it were of one God, and Father, by one Spirit, worshipping one Lord with one faith, and consecrated to him with one Baptism, and hope for one selfsame glory, whereunto we are called. Therefore whosoever breaketh charity, breaketh all these things asunder.
- **g.** Eph. 4:6 Who only hath the chief authority over the Church.
- **h.** Eph. 4:6 Who only poureth forth his providence, through all the members of the Church.
- **i.** Eph. 4:6 Who only is joined together with us in Christ.
- **j.** Eph. 4:7 He teacheth us, that we indeed are all one body, and that all good gifts proceed from Christ only, who reigneth in heaven having mightily conquered all his enemies from whence he heapeth all gifts upon his Church: but yet notwithstanding these gifts are diversely and sundry ways divided according to his will and pleasure, and therefore every man ought to be content with that measure that God hath given him, and to bestow it to the common profit of the whole body.
- **k.** Eph. 4:7 Which Christ hath given.
- **l.** Eph. 4:8 A multitude of captives.
- **m.** Eph. 4:9 Down to the earth, which is the lowest part of the world.
- **n.** Eph. 4:10 Fill with his gifts.
- **o.** Eph. 4:10 The Church.
- **p.** Eph. 4:11 First of all he reckoneth up the Ecclesiastical functions, which are partly extraordinary and for a season, as Apostles, Prophets, Evangelists, and partly ordinary and perpetual, as Pastors and Doctors.
- **q.** Eph. 4:11 The Apostles were those twelve, unto whom Paul was afterward added, whose office was to plant Churches throughout all the world.
- **r.** Eph. 4:11 The Prophet's office was one of the chiefest, which were men of marvellous wisdom, and some of them could foretell things to come.
- **s.** Eph. 4:11 These the Apostles used as fellows in the execution of their office, being not able to answer all places themselves.
- **t.** Eph. 4:11 Pastors are they which govern the Church, and Teachers are they which govern the Schools.
- **u.** Eph. 4:12 He showeth the end of Ecclesiastical functions, to wit, that by the ministry of men all the Saints may so grow up together, that they may make one mystical body of Christ.
- **v.** Eph. 4:12 The Church.
- **w.** Eph. 4:13 The use of this ministry is perpetual so long as we are in this world, that is, until that time that having put off the flesh, and thoroughly and perfectly agreeing betwixt ourselves, we shall be joined with Christ our head. Which thing is done by that knowledge of the Son of God increasing in us, and he himself by little and little growing up in us until we come to be a perfect man, which shall be in the world to come, when God shall be all in all.
- **x.** Eph. 4:13 In that most near conjunction which is knit and fastened together by faith.
- **y.** Eph. 4:13 Christ is said to grow up to full age, not in himself, but in us.
- **z.** Eph. 4:14 Betwixt our childhood that is to say, a very weak state, while as we do yet altogether waiver and our perfect age, which we shall have at length in another world, there is a mean, to wit, our youth, and steady going forward to perfection.
- **aa.** Eph. 4:14 He compareth them which rest not themselves upon the word of God, to little boats which are tossed hither and thither with the doctrines of men, as it were with contrary winds, and therewithall forewarneth them that it cometh to pass not only by the lightness of man's brain, but also by the craftiness of certain, which make as it were an art of it.
- **ab.** Eph. 4:14 With those uncertain chances which toss men to and fro.
- **ac.** Eph. 4:14 By the deceit of those men which are very well practised in deceiving of others.
- **ad.** Eph. 4:15 By earnest affection of the truth and love, we grow up into Christ: for he being effectual by the ministry of his word, which as the vital spirit doth so quicken the whole body, that it nourisheth all the limbs thereof according to the measure and proportion of each one quickeneth and cherisheth his Church, which consisteth of divers functions, as of divers members, and preserveth the proportion of every one. And thereof it followeth that neither this body can live without Christ, neither can any man grow up spiritually, which separateth himself from the other members.
- **ae.** Eph. 4:16 Of Christ, who in manner of the soul, quickeneth all the members.
- **af.** Eph. 4:16 Such increase as is meet the body should have.
- **ag.** Eph. 4:16 Charity is the knitting of the limbs together.
- **ah.** Eph. 4:17 He descendeth to the fruits of Christian doctrine, and reasoneth first upon the principles of manners and actions, setting down a most grave comparison between the children of God, and them which are not regenerate. For in these men, all the powers of the mind are corrupted and their mind is given to vanity, and their senses are darkened with most gross mistiness, and their affections are so accustomed by little and little to wickedness, that at length they run headlong into all uncleanness, being utterly destitute of all judgment.
- **ai.** Eph. 4:17 If the noblest parts of the soul be corrupt, what is man but corruption only?
- **aj.** Eph. 4:18 Whereby God liveth in them.
- **ak.** Eph. 4:19 Void of all judgment.
- **al.** Eph. 4:19 They strove to pass one another as though there had been some gain to be gotten by it.
- **am.** Eph. 4:20 Here followeth the contrary part touching men which are regenerate by the true and lively knowledge of Christ, which have other principles of their doings far different, to wit, holy and honest desires, and a mind clean changed by the virtue of the holy Ghost, from whence proceed also like effects, as a just and holy life indeed.
- **an.** Eph. 4:21 As they have learned which acknowledge Christ indeed, and in good earnest.
- **ao.** Eph. 4:22 Yourselves.
- **ap.** Eph. 4:23 Where there ought to have been the greatest force of reason, there is the greatest corruption of all which wasteth all things.
- **aq.** Eph. 4:24 After the image of God.
- **ar.** Eph. 4:24 The effect and end of the new creation.
- **as.** Eph. 4:24 Not fained nor counterfeit.
- **at.** Eph. 4:25 He commendeth severally certain peculiar Christian virtues, and first of all he requireth truth that is to say, sincere manners condemning all deceit and dissembling, because we are born one for another.
- **au.** Eph. 4:26 He teacheth us to bridle our anger in such sort, that although it be not, yet that it break not out, and that it be straightway quenched before we sleep, lest Satan taking occasion to give us evil counsel through the wicked counselor, destroy us.
- **av.** Eph. 4:26 If it so fall out, that you be angry, yet sin not: that is, bridle your anger, and do not wickedly put that in execution, which you have wickedly conceived.
- **aw.** Eph. 4:26 Let not the night come upon you in your anger, that is, make atonement quickly for all matters.
- **ax.** Eph. 4:28 He descendeth from the heart to the hands condemning theft: and because that men which give themselves to this wickedness use to pretend poverty, he showeth that labor is a good remedy against poverty, which God blesseth in such sort that they which labor have always some overplus to help others so far is it from this, that they are constrained to steal other men's goods.
- **ay.** Eph. 4:28 By laboring in things that are holy, and profitable to his neighbor.
- **az.** Eph. 4:29 He bridleth the tongue also, teaching us so to temper our talk, that our hearer's mind be not only not destroyed, but also instructed.
- **ba.** Eph. 4:29 Word for word, rotten.
- **bb.** Eph. 4:29 By grace he meaneth that, whereby men may profit to the going on forward godliness and love.
- **bc.** Eph. 4:30 A general precept against all excess of affections which dwell in the part of the mind, which they call, Angry, and he setteth against them the contrary means. And useth a most vehement preface, how we ought to take heed that we grieve not the holy Spirit of God through our immoderateness and intemperance, who dwelleth in us to this end, to moderate all our affections.
- **bd.** Eph. 4:32 An argument taken from the example of Christ, most grave and vehement, both for pardoning of those injuries which have been done unto us by our greatest enemies, and much more for having consideration of the miserable, and using moderation and gentle behavior towards all men.

EPHESIANS 4

1. Rom. 1:21
2. Col. 3:8

5

3 Lest, in those vices which he reprehended, they should set light by his admonitions, 5 he terrifieth them by denouncing severe judgment, 8 and stirreth them forward: 15 Then he defendeth from general lessons of manners, 22 to the particular duties of wives, 25 and husbands.

1 Be ye therefore followers of God, as dear children, **2** [1]And walk in love, even as Christ hath loved us, and hath given himself for us, to be an offering and a sacrifice of a sweet smelling savor to God. **3** [2,a]But fornication, and all uncleanness, or covetousness, let it not be once named among you, as it becometh Saints, **4** Neither filthiness, neither foolish talking, neither [b]jesting, which are things not comely, but rather giving of thanks. **5** [c]For this ye know, that no whoremonger, neither unclean person, nor covetous person, which is an [d]idolater, hath any inheritance in the kingdom of Christ, and of God. **6** [3]Let no man deceive you with vain words: for, for such things cometh the wrath of God upon the children of disobedience. **7** [e]Be not therefore companions with them. **8** For ye were once darkness, but are now [f]light in the Lord: walk as children of light. **9** For the fruit of the [g]Spirit is in all goodness, and righteousness, and truth. **10** Approving that which is pleasing to the Lord. **11** And have no fellowship with the unfruitful works of darkness, but even [h]reprove them rather. **12** For it is shame even to speak of the things which are done of them in secret. **13** But all things when they are reproved of the light, are manifest: for it is light that maketh all things manifest. **14** Wherefore [i]he saith, Awake thou that sleepest, and stand up from the [j]dead, and Christ shall give thee light. **15** [k]Take heed therefore that ye walk circumspectly, not as fools, but as [4]wise, **16** [l]Redeeming the season: for the [m]days are evil. **17** [5]Wherefore, be ye not unwise, but understand what the will of the Lord is. **18** [n]And be not drunk with wine, wherein is [o]excess: but be fulfilled with the Spirit, **19** Speaking unto yourselves in Psalms, and hymns, and spiritual songs, singing and making melody to the Lord in your [p]hearts, **20** Giving thanks always for all things unto God even the Father, in the Name of our Lord Jesus Christ, **21** [q]Submitting yourselves one to another in the fear of God. **22** [6,r]Wives, submit yourselves unto your husbands, [s]as unto the Lord. **23** [7,t]For the husband is the wife's head, even as Christ is the head of the Church, [u]and the same is the Savior of his body. **24** [v]Therefore as the Church is in subjection to Christ, even so let the wives be to their husbands in everything. **25** [8,w]Husbands, love your wives, even as Christ loved the Church, and gave himself for it, **26** [x]That he might [y]sanctify it, and cleanse it by the washing of water through the [z]word, **27** That he might make it unto himself a glorious Church, [aa]not having spot or wrinkle, or any such thing: but that it should be holy and without blame. **28** [ab]So ought men to love their wives, as their own bodies: he that loveth his wife, loveth himself. **29** For no man ever yet hated his [ac]own flesh, but nourished and cherisheth it, even as the Lord doth the Church. **30** For we are members of his body, [ad]of his flesh, and of his bones. **31** [9]For this cause shall a man leave father and mother, and shall [ae]cleave to his wife, and they twain shall be one flesh. **32** [af]This is a great secret, but I speak concerning Christ, and concerning the Church. **33** [ag]Therefore everyone of you, do ye so: let everyone love his wife, even as himself, and let the wife see that she fear her husband.

6

1 He showeth the duties of children, 5 servants, 9 and masters: 10 Then he speaketh of the fierce battle that the faithful have, 12 and what weapons we must use in the same: 21 In the end he commendeth Tychicus.

1 Children, [1,a]obey your parents [b]in the [c]Lord: [d]for this is right. **2** [2,e]Honor thy father and mother [f]which is the first commandment with [g]promise **3** That it may be well with thee, and that thou mayest live long on earth. **4** [h]And ye, fathers, provoke not your children to wrath: but bring them up in instruction and [i]information of the Lord. **5** [3,j]Servants, be obedient unto them that are your masters, [k]according to the flesh, with [l]fear and trembling in singleness of your hearts, as unto Christ, **6** Not with service to the eye, as men pleasers, but as the servants of Christ, [m]doing the will of God from the heart. **7** With good will, serving the [n]Lord, and not men. **8** [o]And know ye that whatsoever good thing any man doeth, that same shall he receive of the Lord, whether he be bond or free, **9** [p]And ye masters, do the same things unto them, putting away threatening: and know that even your master also is in heaven, neither is there [4,q]respect of person with him. **10** [r]Finally, my brethren, be strong in the Lord, and in the power of his might. **11** Put on the whole armor of God, that ye may be able to

---

EPHESIANS 5

- **a.** Eph. 5:3 Now he cometh to another kind of affections, which is in that part of the mind, which men call covetous or desirous: and he reprehended fornication, covetousness, and jesting, very sharply.
- **b.** Eph. 5:4 Jests which men cast one at another: that no lightness be seen, nor evil example given, nor any offense moved by evil words or backbiting.
- **c.** Eph. 5:5 Because these sins are such that the most part of men count them not for sins, he awaketh the godly, to the end they should so much the more take heed to themselves from them, as most hurtful plagues.
- **d.** Eph. 5:5 A bondslave to idolatry, for the covetous man thinketh that his life standeth in his goods.
- **e.** Eph. 5:7 Because we are not so ready to anything as to follow evil examples, therefore the Apostle warneth the godly to remember always that the others are but as it were darkness, and that they themselves are as it were light. And therefore the others commit all villany as men are wont in the dark but they ought not only not to follow their examples, but also as the property of the light is reprove their darkness, and to walk so having Christ that true light going before them as it becometh wise men.
- **f.** Eph. 5:8 The faithful are called light, both because they have the true light in them which lighteneth them, and also because they give light to others, insomuch, that their honest conversation reproveth the life of wicked men.
- **g.** Eph. 5:9 By whose force we are made light in the Lord.
- **h.** Eph. 5:11 Make them open to all the world, by your good life.
- **i.** Eph. 5:14 The Scripture, or God in the Scripture.
- **j.** Eph. 5:14 He speaketh of the death of sin.
- **k.** Eph. 5:15 The worse and more corrupt that the manners of this world are, the more watchful ought we to be against all occasions, and respect nothing but the will of God.
- **l.** Eph. 5:16 This is a metaphor taken from the merchants: who prefer the least profit that may be, before all their pleasures.
- **m.** Eph. 5:16 The times are troublesome and sharp.
- **n.** Eph. 5:18 He setteth the sober and holy assemblies of the faithful, against the dissolute bankers of the unfaithful, in which the praises of the only Lord must ring, be it in prosperity or adversity.
- **o.** Eph. 5:18 All kind of riot, joined with all manner of filthiness and shamefulness.
- **p.** Eph. 5:19 With an earnest affection of the heart, and not with the tongue only.
- **q.** Eph. 5:21 A short repetition of the end whereunto all things ought to be referred, to serve one another for God's sake.
- **r.** Eph. 5:22 Now he descendeth to a family, dividing orderly all the parts of a family. And he saith that the duty of wives consisteth herein, to be obedient to their husbands.
- **s.** Eph. 5:22 The first argument, for they cannot be disobedient to their husbands, but they must resist God also, who is the author of this subjection.
- **t.** Eph. 5:23 A declaration of the former saying: Because God hath made the man head of the woman in matrimony, as Christ is the head of the Church.
- **u.** Eph. 5:23 Another argument: Because the good estate of the wife dependeth of the man, so that this submission is not only just, but also very profitable: as also the salvation of the Church is of Christ, although far otherwise.
- **v.** Eph. 5:24 The conclusion of the wives' duty towards their husbands.
- **w.** Eph. 5:25 The husbands' duty towards their wives, is to love them as themselves, of which love, the love of Christ toward his Church is a lively pattern.
- **x.** Eph. 5:26 Because many men pretend the infirmities of their wives to excuse their own hardness and cruelty, the Apostle willeth us to mark what manner of Church Christ gat, when he joined it to himself, and how he doth not only not loathe all her filth and uncleanness, but ceaseth not to wipe the same away with his cleanness, until he have wholly purged it.
- **y.** Eph. 5:26 Make it holy.
- **z.** Eph. 5:26 Through the promise of free justification and sanctification in Christ, received by faith.
- **aa.** Eph. 5:27 The Church, as it is considered in itself, shall not be without wrinkle, before it come to the mark it shooteth at: for while it is in this life, it runneth in a race: but if it be considered in Christ, it is clean and without wrinkle.
- **ab.** Eph. 5:28 Another argument: Every man loveth himself, even of nature: therefore he striveth against nature that loveth not his wife: he proveth the consequent, first by the mystical knitting of Christ and the Church together, and then by the ordinance of God, who saith, that man and wife are as one, that is, not to be divided.
- **ac.** Eph. 5:29 His own body.
- **ad.** Eph. 5:30 He alludeth to the making of the woman, which signifieth our coupling together with Christ, which is wrought by faith, but is sealed by the Sacrament of the Supper.
- **ae.** Eph. 5:31 See Matt. 19:5
- **af.** Eph. 5:32 That no man might dream of natural conjunction or knitting of Christ and his Church together such as the husbands and the wives is he showeth that it is secret, to wit, spiritual and such as far differeth from the common capacity of man: as which consisteth by the virtue of the Spirit, and not of the flesh by faith, and by no natural band.
- **ag.** Eph. 5:33 The conclusion both of the husband's duty toward his wife, and of the wife's toward her husband.

EPHESIANS 5

- **a.** Eph. 5:2 : John 13:14; John 15:12
- **2.** Eph. 4:29 / Col. 3:5 / 1 Thess. 2:17
- **3.** Matt. 24:4 / Mark 13:5 / Luke 21:8 / 2 Thess. 2:3
- **4.** Col. 4:5
- **5.** Rom. 12:2 / 1 Thess. 4:3
- **6.** Col. 3:18 / Titus 2:5 / 1 Pet. 3:1
- **7.** 1 Cor. 11:3
- **8.** Col. 3:19
- **9.** Gen. 2:14 / Matt. 19:5 / Mark 10:7 / 1 Cor. 6:16

EPHESIANS 6

- **a.** Eph. 6:1 He cometh to another part of a family, and showeth that the duty of the children toward their parents, consisteth in obedience unto them.
- **b.** Eph. 6:1 The first argument: because God hath so appointed: whereupon it followeth also, that children are so far forth bound to obey their parents, as they may not swerve from the true worship of God.
- **c.** Eph. 6:1 For the Lord is author of all fatherhood, and therefore we must yield such obedience as he will have us.
- **d.** Eph. 6:1 The second argument: because this obedience is most just.
- **e.** Eph. 6:2 A proof of the first argument.
- **f.** Eph. 6:2 The third argument, taken of the profit that ensueth thereby: because the Lord vouchsafed this commandment amongst the rest, of a special blessing.
- **g.** Eph. 6:2 With a special promise: for otherwise the second commandment hath a promise of mercy to a thousand generations, but that promise is general.
- **h.** Eph. 6:4 It is the duty of fathers to use their fatherly authority moderately, and to God's glory.
- **i.** Eph. 6:4 Such information and precepts, as being taken out of God's book are holy and acceptable to him.
- **j.** Eph. 6:5 Now he ascendeth to the third part of a family, to wit, to the duty both of the masters and of the servants. And he showeth that the duty of servants consisteth in a hearty love and reverence to their master.
- **k.** Eph. 6:5 He mitigateth the sharpness of service, in that they are spiritually free, notwithstanding the same, and yet that spiritual freedom taketh not away corporal service, insomuch that they cannot be Christ's, unless they serve their masters willingly and faithfully, so far forth as they may with safe conscience.
- **l.** Eph. 6:5 With careful reverence: for slavish fear is not allowable, much less in Christian servants.
- **m.** Eph. 6:6 To cut off occasion of all pretences, he teacheth us that it is God's will that some are either born or made servants, and therefore they must respect God's will, although their service be never so hard.
- **n.** Eph. 6:7 Being moved with a reverence so Godward, as though ye served God himself.
- **o.** Eph. 6:8 Although they serve unkind and cruel masters, yet the obedience of servants is no less acceptable to God, than the obedience of them that are free.
- **p.** Eph. 6:9 It is the duty of masters to use the authority that they have over their servants modestly, and holily, seeing that they in another respect have a common master, which is in heaven, who will judge both the bond and the free.
- **q.** Eph. 6:9 Either of freedom or bondage.
- **r.** Eph. 6:10 He concludeth the other part of this Epistle with a grave exhortation, that all be ready, and fight constantly, trusting to spiritual weapons, until their enemies be clean put to flight. And first of all, he warneth us to take the armor of God, whereby only our enemy may be dispatched.
- **s.** Eph. 6:12 Secondly he declareth that our chiefest and mightiest enemies are invisible, that we may not think that our chiefest conflict is with men.

stand against the assaults of the devil. **12** [s]For we wrestle not against flesh and [t]blood, but against [5,u]principalities, against powers, and against the worldly governors, the princes of the darkness of this world, against spiritual wickedness, which are in the high places. **13** [v]For this cause take unto you the whole armor of God, that ye may be able to resist in the [w]evil day, and having finished all things, stand fast. **14** Stand therefore, and your loins girded about with verity, and having on the breastplate of righteousness, **15** And your feet shod with the [x]preparation of the Gospel of peace. **16** Above all, take the shield of Faith, wherewith ye may quench all the fiery darts of the wicked, **17** And take the helmet of Salvation, and the sword of the Spirit, which is the word of God. **18** And pray always with all manner prayer and supplication in the [y]spirit: and watch thereunto with all perseverance and supplication for all Saints, **19** And for me, that utterance may be given unto me, that I may open my mouth boldly to publish the secret of the Gospel, **20** Whereof I am the ambassador in bonds, that therein I may speak boldly, as I ought to speak. **21** [z]But that ye may also know mine affairs, and what I do, Tychicus my dear brother and faithful minister in the Lord, shall show you of all things. **22** Whom I have sent unto you for the same purpose, that ye might know mine affairs, and that he might comfort your hearts. **23** Peace be with the brethren, and love with faith from God the Father, and from the Lord Jesus Christ. **24** Grace be with all them which love our Lord Jesus Christ, to their [aa]immortality, Amen. Written from Rome unto the Ephesians, and sent by Tychicus.

---

t. Eph. 6:12 Against men, which are of a frail and brittle nature, against which are set spiritual subtleties, more mighty than the other by a thousand parts.

u. Eph. 6:12 He giveth these names to the evil angels, reason of the effects which they work: not that they are able to do the same of themselves, but because God giveth them the bridle.

v. Eph. 6:13 He showeth that these enemies are put to flight with the only armor of God, to wit, with uprightness of conscience, a godly and holy life, knowledge of the Gospel, faith, and to be short, with the word of God, and using daily earnest prayer for the health of the Church, and especially, for the constance of the true, godly, and valiant ministers of the word.

w. Eph. 6:13 See Eph. 5:16.

x. Eph. 6:15 That the preparation of the Gospel may be as it were shoes to you: and it is very fitly called the Gospel of peace, for that, seeing we have to go to God through most dangerous ranks of enemies, this may encourage us to go on manfully, in that we know by the doctrine of the Gospel, that we take our journey to God, who is at peace with us.

y. Eph. 6:18 That holy prayers may proceed from the holy Spirit.

z. Eph. 6:21 A familiar and very amiable declaration of his state, together with a solemn prayer, wherewith Paul is wont to end his Epistles.

aa. Eph. 6:24 To life everlasting.

EPHESIANS 6

1. Col. 3:20

2. Exod. 20:12 / Deut. 5:16 / Matt. 15:4 / Mark 7:10

3. Col. 3:22 / Titus 2:9 / 1 Pet. 2:18

4. Deut. 10:17 / 2 Chron. 16:7 / Job 34:19 / Acts 10:34 / Rom. 2:11 / Gal. 2:6 / Col. 3:25 / 1 Pet. 1:17

5. Eph. 2:2

THE EPISTLE OF THE APOSTLE PAUL TO THE PHILIPPIANS

---

1 *3 Having testified his godly and tender affection towards the Philippians, 12 he entreateth of himself and his bands: 22 And pricketh them forward by his own example, 27 and exhorteth them to unity, 28 and patience.*

1 Paul [a]and Timothy the servants of JESUS CHRIST, to all the Saints in Christ Jesus, which are at Philippi, with the [b]Bishops, and Deacons: **2** Grace be with you, and peace from God our Father, and from the Lord Jesus Christ: **3** I thank my God, having you in perfect memory, **4** Always in all my prayers for all you, praying with gladness **5** Because of the [c]fellowship which ye have in the Gospel, from the [d]first day unto now. **6** And I am persuaded of this same thing, that he that hath begun this good work in you, will perform it until the [e]day of Jesus Christ, **7** As it becometh me so to judge of you all, because I have you in remembrance, that both in my [f]bands, and in my defense, and confirmation of the Gospel you all were partakers of my [g]grace. **8** [h]For God is my record, how I long after you all from the very heart root in Jesus Christ. **9** [i]And this I pray that your love may abound yet more and more in knowledge, and in all judgment, **10** That ye may allow those things which are best, that ye may be pure, and without offense, until the day of Christ, **11** Filled with the [j]fruits of righteousness, which are by Jesus Christ unto the glory and praise of God. **12** [k]I would ye understood, brethren, that the things which have come unto me, are turned rather to the furthering of the Gospel, **13** So that my bands [l]in Christ are famous throughout all the [m]judgment hall, and in all other places. **14** Insomuch that many of the brethren in the Lord are boldened through my bands, and dare more frankly speak the [n]Word. **15** Some preach Christ even through envy and strife, and some also of good will. **16** The one part preacheth Christ of contention, and not [o]purely, supposing to add more affliction to my bands. **17** But the others of love, knowing that I am set for the defense of the Gospel. **18** [p]What then: yet Christ is preached all manner ways, whether it be under a [q]pretence, or sincerely: and I therein joy: yea, and will joy. **19** For I know that this shall turn to my salvation through your prayer, and by the help of the Spirit of Jesus Christ, **20** [r]As I fervently look for, and hope, that in nothing I shall be ashamed, but that with all confidence, as always, so now Christ shall be magnified in my body, whether it be by life or by death. **21** For Christ is to me both in life and in death advantage. **22** [s]And whether to live in the [t]flesh were profitable for me, and what to choose I know not. **23** For I am distressed between both, desiring to be loosed and to be with Christ, which is best of all. **24** Nevertheless, to abide in the flesh, is more needful for you. **25** And this am I sure of, that I shall abide, and with you all continue, for your furtherance and joy of your faith, **26** That ye may more abundantly rejoice in JESUS CHRIST for me, by my coming to you again. **27** [u]Only let your conversation be as it becometh the Gospel of Christ,

---

PHILIPPIANS 1

a. Phil. 1:1 The mark whereat he shooteth in this Epistle, is to confirm the Phil. by all means possible, not only not to faint, but also to go forward. And first of all, he commendeth their former doings, to exhort them to go forward: which thing he sayeth, he hopeth fully they will do, and that by the testimony of their lively charity, but in the mean season he referreth all things to the grace of God.

b. Phil. 1:1 By the Bishops are meant both the Pastors, which have the dispensation of the word and the Elders, that govern: and by Deacons are meant those that were stewards of the treasury of the Church and had to look unto the poor.

c. Phil. 1:5 Because that you also are made partakers of the Gospel.

d. Phil. 1:5 Ever since I knew you.

e. Phil. 1:6 The Spirit of God will not forsake you unto the very latter end, until your mortal bodies shall appear before the judgment of Christ, to be glorified.

f. Phil. 1:7 A true proof of a true knitting together with Christ.

g. Phil. 1:7 He calleth his bands, grace, as though he had received some singular benefit.

h. Phil. 1:8 He declareth his good will towards them, therewithall showing by what means chiefly they may be confirmed, to wit, by continual prayer.

i. Phil. 1:9 He showeth what thing we ought chiefly desire, to wit, first of all, that we may increase in the true knowledge of God so that we may be able to discern things that differ one from another and also in charity, that even to the end we may give ourselves to good works indeed, to the glory of God by Jesus Christ.

j. Phil. 1:11 If righteousness be the tree, and good works the fruits, then must the papists needs be deceived, when they say that works are the cause of righteousness.

k. Phil. 1:12 He preventeth the offense that might come by his persecution, whereby divers took occasion to disgrace his Apostleship. To whom he answereth, that God hath blesseth his imprisonment in such wise, that he is by that means become more famous, and the dignity of the Gospel by this occasion is greatly enlarged, although not with like affection in all men, yet indeed.

l. Phil. 1:13 For Christ's sake.

m. Phil. 1:13 In the Emperor's court.

n. Phil. 1:14 The Gospel is called the Word, to set forth the excellence of it.

o. Phil. 1:16 Not with a pure mind: for otherwise their doctrine was pure.

p. Phil. 1:18 He showeth by setting forth his own example, that the end of our affliction is true joy: and that through the virtue of the Spirit of Christ, which he giveth to them that ask it.

q. Phil. 1:18 Under a goodly color and show: for they made Christ a cloak for their ambition and envy.

r. Phil. 1:20 We must continue even to the end, with great confidence, having nothing before our eyes but Christ's glory only, whether we live or die.

s. Phil. 1:22 An example of a true shepherd, who maketh more acount how he may profit his sheep, than he doth of any commodity of his own whatsoever.

t. Phil. 1:22 To live in this mortal body.

u. Phil. 1:27 Having set down those things before, in manner of a Preface, he descendeth now to exhortations, warning them first of all, to consent both in doctrine and mind, and afterward, that being thus knit together with those common bands, they continue through the strength of faith to bear all adversity in such sort, that they admit nothing unworthy the profession of the Gospel.

that whether I come and see you, or else be absent, I may hear of your matters, that ye [v]continue in one spirit, and in one mind, fighting together through the faith of the Gospel. **28** [w]And in nothing fear your adversaries, which is to them a token of perdition, and to you of salvation, and that of God. **29** [x]For unto you it is given for Christ, that not only ye should believe in him, but also suffer for his sake, **30** [y]Having the same fight, which ye saw in me, and now hear to be in me.

2

1 He exhorteth them above all things, 3 to humility, 6 and that by the example of Christ. 19 He promiseth to send Timothy shortly unto them, 26 and excuseth the long tarrying of Epaphroditus.

1 [a]If there be therefore any consolation in [b]Christ, if any comfort of love, if any fellowship of the Spirit, if any [c]compassion and mercy, **2** Fulfill my joy, that ye be like minded, having the [d]same love, being of one accord, and of one judgment, **3** That nothing be done through contention or vainglory, but that in meekness of mind every man esteem others better than himself. **4** Look not every man on his own things, but every man also on the things of other men. **5** [e]Let the same mind be in you that was even in Christ Jesus, **6** Who being in the [f]form of God, [g]thought it no robbery to be [h]equal with God: **7** But he made himself of [i]no reputation, and took on him the [j]form of a servant, and was made like unto men, and was found in shape as a man. **8** He humbled himself, and became obedient unto the death, even the death of the cross. **9** [k]Wherefore God hath also highly exalted him, and given him a [l]name above every name. **10** That at the Name of Jesus should [m]every knee bow, both of things in heaven, and things in earth, and things under the earth. **11** And that [n]every tongue should confess that Jesus Christ is the Lord, unto the glory of God the Father. **12** [o]Wherefore my beloved, as ye have always obeyed me, not as in my presence only, but now much more in mine absence, so [p]make an end of your own salvation with fear and trembling. **13** [q]For it is God which worketh in you both [r]the will and the deed, even of his good pleasure. **14** [s]Do all things without [1]murmuring and reasonings, **15** [t]That ye may be blameless, and pure, and the sons of God without rebuke in the midst of a naughty and crooked nation, among whom ye shine as [2]lights in the world, **16** Holding forth the [u]word of life, [v]that I may rejoice in the day of Christ, that I have not run in vain, neither have labored in vain. **17** Yea, and though I be offered up upon the [w]sacrifice, and service of your faith, I am glad, and rejoice with you all. **18** For the same cause also be ye glad, and rejoice with me. **19** [x]And I trust in the Lord Jesus, to send [3]Timothy shortly unto you, that I also may be of [y]good comfort, when I know your state. **20** For I have no man like-minded, who will faithfully care for your matters. **21** [4]For [z]all seek their own, and not that which is Jesus Christ's. **22** But ye know the proof of him, that as a son with the father, he hath served with me in the Gospel. **23** Him therefore I hope to send as soon as I know how it will go with me, **24** And I trust in the Lord, that I also myself shall come shortly. **25** But I supposed it necessary to send my brother Epaphroditus unto you my companion in labor, and fellow soldier, even your messenger, and he that ministered unto me such things as I wanted. **26** For he longed after all you, and was full of heaviness, because ye had heard that he had been sick. **27** And no doubt he was sick, very near unto death: but God had mercy on him, and not on him only, but on me also, lest I should have sorrow upon sorrow. **28** I sent him therefore the more diligently, that when ye should see him again, ye might rejoice, and I might be the less sorrowful. **29** Receive him therefore in the Lord with all gladness, and make much of such: **30** Because that for the [aa]work of Christ he was near unto death, and regarded not his life, to fulfill that service which was lacking on your part toward me.

3

2 He refuteth the vain boastings of the false apostles, 7 and setteth Christ against them. 10 He setteth out the force and nature of faith, 15 that laying all things aside, they may be partakers of the Cross of Christ, 18 the enemies whereof, he noteth out.

1 Moreover, [a]my brethren, rejoice in the Lord. [b]It grieveth me not to write the [c]same things to you, and for you it is a sure thing. **2** Beware of dogs: beware of evil workers: beware of the [d]concision. **3** [e]For we are the circumcision, which worship God in the spirit, and rejoice in Christ Jesus, and have no confidence [f]in the flesh: **4** [g]Though I might also have confidence in the flesh. If any other man thinketh that he hath whereof he might trust in the flesh, much more I, **5** Circumcised the eighth day, of the kindred of Israel, of the tribe of Benjamin, [1]an Hebrew of the Hebrews, [2]by the Law a Pharisee. **6** Concerning zeal, I persecuted the Church: touching the righteousness which is in the Law, I was unrebukeable. **7** But the things that were [h]vantage unto me, the same I counted loss for Christ's sake. **8** Yea, doubtless I think [i]all things but loss for the excellent knowledge sake of Christ Jesus my Lord, for whom I have counted all things loss, and do judge them to be dung, that I might [j]win Christ, **9** And might be found in [k]him, that is, [l]not having mine own righteousness, which is of the Law, but that which is through the faith of Christ, even the righteousness which is of God through faith, **10** [m]That I may [n]know him, and the virtue of his resurrection, and the [o]fellowship of his afflictions, and be made conformable unto his death, **11** If by any means I might attain unto the [p]resurrection of the dead: **12** Not as though I had already attained to it, either were already perfect:

- **v.** Phil. 1:27 The word signifieth, to stand fast, and it is proper to wrestlers, that stand fast, and shrink not a foot.
- **w.** Phil. 1:28 We ought not to be discouraged, but rather encouraged by the persecutions which the enemies of the Gospel imagine and practice against us: seeing that they are certain witnesses from God himself, both of our salvation, and of the destruction of the wicked.
- **x.** Phil. 1:29 He proveth that his saying, that persecution is a token of our salvation, because it is a gift of God to suffer for Christ, which gift he bestoweth upon his own, as he doth the gift of faith.
- **y.** Phil. 1:30 Now he showeth for what purpose he made mention of his afflictions.

PHILIPPIANS 2

- **a.** Phil. 2:1 A most earnest request to remove all those things, whereby that great and special consent and agreement is commonly broken, to wit, contention and pride, whereby it cometh to pass, that they separate themselves one from another.
- **b.** Phil. 2:1 Any Christian comfort.
- **c.** Phil. 2:1 If any feeling of inward love.
- **d.** Phil. 2:2 Like love.
- **e.** Phil. 2:5 He setteth before them a most perfect example of all modesty and sweet conversation, Christ Jesus, whom we ought to follow with all our might: who abased himself so far for our sakes, although he be above all, that he took upon him the form of a servant, to wit, our flesh willingly, subject to all infirmities, even to the death of the cross.
- **f.** Phil. 2:6 Such as God himself is, and therefore God, for there is none in all parts like to God, but God himself.
- **g.** Phil. 2:6 Christ, that glorious and everlasting God, knew that he might rightfully and lawfully not appear in the base flesh of man, but remain with majesty meet for God: yet he chose rather to debase himself.
- **h.** Phil. 2:6 If the Son be equal to the Father, then is there of necessity an equality, which Arrius, that Heretic, denieth: and if the Son be compared with the Father, then is there a distinction of persons, which Sabellius, that heretic, denieth.
- **i.** Phil. 2:7 He brought himself from all things, as it were to nothing.
- **j.** Phil. 2:7 By taking our manhood upon him.
- **k.** Phil. 2:9 He showeth the most glorious event of Christ's submission, to teach us, that modesty is the true way to true praise and glory.
- **l.** Phil. 2:9 Dignity and renown, and the matter with it.
- **m.** Phil. 2:10 All creatures shall at length be subject to Christ.
- **n.** Phil. 2:11 Every nation.
- **o.** Phil. 2:12 The conclusion: We must go on to salvation with humility and submission, by the way of our vocation.
- **p.** Phil. 2:12 He is said to make an end of his salvation, which runneth in the race of righteousness.
- **q.** Phil. 2:13 A most sure and grounded argument against pride, for that we have nothing in us praiseworthy but it cometh of the free gift of God, and is without us, for we have no ability or power, so much as to will well much less to do well but only of the free mercy of God.
- **r.** Phil. 2:13 Why then, we are not stocks, but yet we do not will well of nature, but only because God hath made of our naughty will a good will.
- **s.** Phil. 2:14 He describeth modesty by the contrary effects of pride, teaching us, that it is far both from all malicious, and close or inward hatred and also from open contentions and brawlings.
- **t.** Phil. 2:15 To be short, he requireth a life without fault, and pure, that being lightened with the word of God, they may shine in the darkness of this world.
- **u.** Phil. 2:16 The Gospel is called the word of life, because of the effects which it worketh.
- **v.** Phil. 2:16 Again he pricketh them forward, setting before them his true Apostolic care that he had of them, comforting them moreover, to the end they should not be sorry for the greatness of his afflictions, no not although he should die to make perfect their oblation with his blood, as it were with a drink offering.
- **w.** Phil. 2:17 As if he said, I brought you Phil. to Christ, my desire is that you present yourselves a lively sacrifice to him, and then shall it not grieve me to be offered up as a drink offering, to accomplish this your spiritual offering.
- **x.** Phil. 2:19 Moreover he confirmeth their minds both by sending back Epaphroditus unto them, whose fidelity towards them, and great pains in helping him, he commendeth: and also promising to send Timothy shortly unto them, by whose presence they shall receive great commodity, and hoping also to come himself shortly unto them, if God wills.
- **y.** Phil. 2:19 May be confirmed in my joy of mind.
- **z.** Phil. 2:21 The most part.
- **aa.** Phil. 2:30 He calleth it here the work of Christ, to visit Christ, being poor and in bands in the person of Paul.

PHILIPPIANS 2

1. 1 Pet. 4:9
2. Matt. 5:14
3. Acts 16:1
4. 1 Cor. 10:24

PHILIPPIANS 3

- **a.** Phil. 3:1 A conclusion of those things which have been before said, to wit, that they go forward cheerfully in the Lord.
- **b.** Phil. 3:1 A preface to the next admonition that followeth, to take good heed and beware of false apostles, which join Circumcision with Christ, that is to say, justification by works, with free justification by faith and beat into men's heads the ceremonies which are abolished: for true exercises of godliness and charity. And he calleth them dogs as profane barkers, and evil workmen, because they neglected true works and did not teach the true use of them. To be short, he calleth them Concision, because in urging Circumcision, they cut off themselves and others from the Church.
- **c.** Phil. 3:1 Which you have oftentimes heard of me.
- **d.** Phil. 3:2 He alludeth to Circumcision, of the name whereof while they boasted, they cut asunder the Church.
- **e.** Phil. 3:3 He showeth that we ought to use true circumcision, to wit, the circumcision of the heart, that cutting off all wicked affections by the virtue of Christ, we may serve God in purity of life.
- **f.** Phil. 3:3 In outward things, which pertain nothing to the soul.
- **g.** Phil. 3:4 He doubteth not to prefer himself even according to the flesh, before those perverse hote urgers of the Law, that all men may know that he doth with good judgment of mind, lightly esteem all those outward things: forsomuch as he lacketh nothing which hath Christ, nay, the confidence of our works cannot stand with the free justification in Christ by faith.
- **h.** Phil. 3:7 Which is accounted for vantage.
- **i.** Phil. 3:8 He shutteth out all works, as well those that go before, as those that come after faith.
- **j.** Phil. 3:8 That in their place I might get Christ, and of a poor man become rich: so far off am I from losing anything.
- **k.** Phil. 3:9 In Christ: for they that are found without Christ, are subject to condemnation.
- **l.** Phil. 3:9 That is, to be in Christ, to be found not in a man's own righteousness, but clothed with the righteousness of Christ imputed to him.
- **m.** Phil. 3:10 This is the end of righteousness by faith touching us, that by the virtue of his resurrection we may scape from death.
- **n.** Phil. 3:10 That I may feel him indeed, and have a trial of him.
- **o.** Phil. 3:10 The way to that eternal salvation is to follow Christ's steps, by afflictions and persecutions, until we come to Christ himself, who is our mark whereat we shoot, and receive that reward whereunto God calleth us in him. And the Apostle setteth these true exercises of godliness

but I follow, if that I may comprehend that for whose sake also I am [q]comprehen-
ded of Christ Jesus. **13** Brethren, I count not myself, that I have attained to it,
but one thing I do: I forget that which is behind, and endeavor myself unto that
which is before, **14** And follow hard toward the mark, for the prize of the high
calling of God in Christ Jesus. **15** [r]Let us therefore as many as be [s]perfect, be
thus minded: and if ye be otherwise minded, God shall reveal even the same unto
you. **16** Nevertheless, in that whereunto we are come, let us proceed by one
rule, that we may mind one thing. **17** Brethren, be followers of me, and look
on them, which walk so, as ye have us for an example. **18** [3,t] For many walk,
of whom I have told you often, and now tell you weeping, that they are the ene-
mies of the cross of Christ: **19** Whose [u]end is damnation, whose God is their
belly, and whose [v]glory is to their shame, which mind earthly things. **20** [w]But
our conversation is in heaven, from whence also we look for the [4]Savior, even the
Lord Jesus Christ, **21** Who shall change our vile body, that it may be fashioned
like unto his glorious body, according to the working, whereby he is able even to
subdue all things unto himself.

4

1 From particular exhortations, 4 he cometh to general. 10 He saith that he took such joy in their readiness to liberality, 12 that he will patiently bear the want.

1 Therefore, [a]my brethren, beloved and longed for, my joy and my [b]crown, so
continue in the [c]Lord, ye beloved. **2** [d]I pray Euodia, and beseech Syntyche, that
they be of one accord in the Lord. **3** Yea, and I beseech thee, faithful yokefellow,
help those women, which labored with me in the Gospel, with Clement also, and
with other my fellow laborers, whose names are in the [1,e]book of life. **4** [f]Rejoi-
ce in the [g]Lord always, again I say, rejoice. **5** [h]Let your [i]patient mind be known
unto all men. [j]The Lord is at hand. **6** [k]Be nothing careful, but in all things
let your requests be showed unto God in prayer and supplication with [l]giving of
thanks. **7** And the [m]peace of God which passeth all understanding, shall pre-
serve your [n]hearts and minds in Christ Jesus. **8** [o]Furthermore, brethren, what-
soever things are true, whatsoever things [p]are honest, whatsoever things are just,
whatsoever things are pure, whatsoever things are worthy love, whatsoever things
are of good report, if there be any virtue, or if there be any praise, think on the-
se things. **9** Which ye have both learned and received, and heard, and seen in
me: those things do, and the God of peace shall be with you. **10** [q]Now I rejoi-
ce also in the Lord greatly, that now at the last your care for me springeth afresh,
wherein notwithstanding ye were careful, but ye lacked opportunity. **11** I speak
not because of [r]want: for I have learned in whatsoever state I am, therewith to be
content. **12** And I can be [s]abased, and I can abound: everywhere in all things
I am [t]instructed, both to be full, and to be hungry, and to abound, and to have
want. **13** I am able to do all things through the help of Christ, which stren-
gtheneth me. **14** Notwithstanding ye have well done, that ye did communicate
to mine affliction. **15** [u]And ye Philippians know also that in the [v]beginning of
the Gospel, when I departed from Macedonia, no Church communicated with
me, concerning the matter of giving and receiving, but ye only. **16** For even
when I was in Thessalonica, ye sent once, and afterward again for my necessi-
ty. **17** [w]Not that I desire a gift: but I desire the fruit which may further your
reckoning. **18** Now I have received all, and have plenty: I was even filled, after
that I had received of Epaphroditus that which came from you, an [x]odor that
smelleth sweet, a sacrifice acceptable and pleasant to God. **19** And my God shall
fulfill all your necessities through his riches with glory in Jesus Christ. **20** Unto
God even our Father be praise for evermore, Amen. **21** Salute all the Saints in
Christ Jesus. The brethren, which are with me, greet you. **22** All the Saints salute
you, and most of all they which are of [y]Caesar's household. **23** The grace of our
Lord Jesus Christ be with you all, Amen. Written to the Philippians from Rome,
and sent by Epaphroditus.

---

against those vain ceremonies of the Law, wherein the false apostles put the sum of godliness.

p. Phil. 3:11 To life everlasting, which followeth the resurrection of the Saints.

q. Phil. 3:12 For we run not, but so far forth, as we are laid hold on of Christ, that is, as God giveth us strength, and showeth us the way.

r. Phil. 3:15 The conclusion of this exhortation standing upon three members: The one is, that such as have profited in the truth of this doctrine, should continue in it. The second is, that if there be any which are yet ignorant and understand not these things, and doubt of the abolishing of the Law, they should cause no trouble, and should be gently born withall, until they also be instructed of the Lord. The third is, that they esteem the false apostles by their fruits: wherein he doubteth not to set forth himself for an example.

s. Phil. 3:15 He said before that he was not perfect. So that in this place he calleth them perfect, which have somewhat profited in the knowledge of Christ and the Gospel, whom he setteth against the rude and ignorant, as he expoundeth himself in the next verse following.

t. Phil. 3:18 He painteth out the false apostles in their colors, not upon malice or ambition, but with sorrow and tears, to wit, because that being enemies of the Gospel for that is joined with affliction they regard nothing else, but the commodities of this life: that is to say, that flowing in peace, and quietness, and all worldly pleasures, they may live in great estimation amongst men, whose miserable end he forewarned them of.

u. Phil. 3:19 Reward.

v. Phil. 3:19 Which they hunt after at men's hands.

w. Phil. 3:20 He setteth against these fellows, true pastors which neglect earthly things, and aspire to heaven only, where they know, that even in their bodies they shall be clothed with that eternal glory, by the virtue of God.

PHILIPPIANS 3

1. 2 Cor. 11:22 **2.** Acts 23:6 **3.** Rom. 16:17 **4.** 1 Cor. 1:7 / Titus 2:13

PHILIPPIANS 4

a. Phil. 4:1 A rehearsal of the conclusion: That they manfully continue, until they have gotten the victory, trusting to the Lord's strength.

b. Phil. 4:1 My honor.

c. Phil. 4:1 In that concord, whereof the Lord is the band.

d. Phil. 4:2 He also calleth on some by name, partly, because they needed private exhortation, and partly also to stir up others, to be more prompt and ready.

e. Phil. 4:3 God is said after the manner of men, to have a book, wherein the names of his elect are written, to whom he will give everlasting life. Ezekiel calleth it the writing of the house of Israel, and the secret of the Lord, Ezek. 13:9.

f. Phil. 4:4 He addeth particular exhortations: and the first is, that the joy of the Phil. be not hindered by any afflictions that the wicked imagine and work against them.

g. Phil. 4:4 So is the joy of the world distinguisheth from our joy.

h. Phil. 4:5 The second is not taking all things in good part, they behave themselves moderately with all men.

i. Phil. 4:5 Your quiet and settled mind.

j. Phil. 4:5 The taking away of an objection: We must not be disquieted through impatience, seeing that God is at hand to give us remedy in time against all our miseries.

k. Phil. 4:6 The third is, that we be not too careful for anything, but with sure confidence give God thanks, and crave of him whatsoever we have need of, that with a quiet conscience we may wholly and with all our hearts submit ourselves to him.

l. Phil. 4:6 So David began very oft with tears, but ended with thanksgiving.

m. Phil. 4:7 That great quietness of mind, which God only giveth in Christ.

n. Phil. 4:7 He divideth the mind into the heart, that is, into that part which is the seat of the will and affections, and into the higher part, whereby we understand and reason of matters.

o. Phil. 4:8 A general conclusion, that as they have been taught both in word and example, so they frame their lives to the rule of all holiness and righteousness.

p. Phil. 4:8 Whatsoever things are such as do beautify and set you out with a holy gravity.

q. Phil. 4:10 He witnesseth that their liberality was acceptable to him, wherewith they did help him in his extreme poverty: but yet so moderating his words, that he might declare himself void of all suspicion of dishonesty, and that he hath a mind contented both with prosperity and adversity, and to be short, that he reposeth himself in the only will of God.

r. Phil. 4:11 As though I passed for my want.

s. Phil. 4:12 He useth a general word, and yet he speaketh but of one kind of cross, which is poverty, for commonly poverty bringeth all kinds of discommodity with it.

t. Phil. 4:12 This is a metaphor taken from holy things or sacrifices, for our life is like a sacrifice.

u. Phil. 4:15 He witnesseth that he remembereth also their former benefits, and again putteth away sinistrous suspicion of immoderate desire, in that that he received nought of any else.

v. Phil. 4:15 At that beginning when I preached the Gospel amongst you.

w. Phil. 4:17 He witnesseth again, that he alloweth well of their benefit not so much for his own sake as for theirs, because they gave it not so much to him, as they offered it to God as a sacrifice, whereof the Lord himself will not be forgetful.

x. Phil. 4:18 He alludeth to the sweet smelling savors that were offered in the old Law.

y. Phil. 4:22 Such as belong to the Emperor Nero.

PHILIPPIANS 4

1. Rev. 3:5 / Rev. 10:8 / Rev. 21:27

THE EPISTLE OF THE APOSTLE PAUL TO THE COLOSSIANS

1

1 After the salutation, 4 he praiseth them the more, to make them attentive unto him. 7 He reporteth the testimony of the doctrine which they heard of Epaphras. 13 He magnifieth God's grace towards them, 20 and showeth that all the parts of our salvation consist in Christ alone.

1 Paul an Apostle of Jesus Christ, by the [a]will of God, and Timothy our brother, **2** To them which are at [b]Colosse, Saints and faithful brethren in Christ: Grace be with you, and peace from God our Father, and from the Lord Jesus Christ. **3** [c]We give thanks to God even the [d]Father of our Lord Jesus Christ, always praying for you: **4** Since we heard of your faith in Christ Jesus, and of your love toward all Saints. **5** For the [e]hope's sake, which is laid up for you in heaven, whereof ye have heard before by the word of truth, which is the Gospel, **6** Which is come unto you, even as it is unto all the world, and is fruitful as it is also among you from the day that ye heard and truly knew the grace of God, **7** As ye also learned of Epaphras our dear fellow servant, which is for you a faithful minister of Christ: **8** [f]Who hath also declared unto us your love in the [g]Spirit. **9** For this cause we also, since the day we heard of it, cease not to pray for you, and to desire that ye might be fulfilled with knowledge of [h]his will in all wisdom, and spiritual understanding. **10** That ye might walk worthy of the Lord, and please him in all things, being fruitful in all good works, and increasing in the knowledge of God, **11** [i]Strengthened with all might through his glorious power, unto all patience, and longsuffering with [j]joyfulness, **12** [k]Giving thanks unto the [l]Father, which hath made us meet to be partakers of the inheritance of the Saints in [m]light, **13** Who hath delivered us from the power of darkness, and hath translated us into the kingdom [1]of his dear Son, **14** [n]In whom we have redemption through his blood, that is, the forgiveness of sins. **15** [o]Who is the [2]image of the invisible God, [p]the first begotten of every creature. **16** [3]For by him were all things created which are in heaven, and which are in earth, things visible and invisible: whether they be [q]Thrones, or Dominions, or Principalities, or Powers, all things were created by him, and for him. **17** And he is before all things, and in him all things consist. **18** [r]And he is the head of the body of the Church: he is the beginning, [4]and the [s]first begotten of the dead, that in all things he might have the preeminence. **19** [5]For it pleased the Father, that in him should [t]all fullness dwell. **20** [u]And through peace made by that blood of that his cross, to reconcile to himself through him, through him, I say, [v]all things, both which are in earth, and which are in heaven. **21** [w]And you which were in times past strangers and enemies, because your minds were set in evil works, hath [x]he now also reconciled, **22** In that body of his [y]flesh through death, to make you holy and unblameable, and without fault in his sight. **23** [z]If ye continue, grounded and established in the faith, and be not moved away from the hope of the Gospel, whereof ye have heard, and which hath been preached to [aa]every creature, which is under heaven, [ab]whereof I Paul am a minister. **24** Now rejoice I in my sufferings [ac]for you, and fulfill the [ad]rest of the afflictions of Christ in my flesh, for his body's sake, which is the Church, **25** [ae]Whereof I am a minister, according to the dispensation of God, which is given me unto youward, to fulfill the word of God, **26** [6]Which is the mystery hid since the world began, and from all ages, but now is made manifest to his [af]Saints, **27** To whom God [ag]would make known what is the riches of his glorious mystery among the Gentiles, which riches is Christ in you, the hope of glory, **28** [ah]Whom we preach, admonishing every man, and teaching every man in [ai]all wisdom, that we may present every man perfect in Christ Jesus. **29** Whereunto I also labor and strive, according to his working which worketh in me mightily.

2

4 He condemneth, as vain, whatsoever is without Christ, 11 entreating specially of circumcision, 16 of abstinence from meats, 18 and of worshipping of Angels. 20 That we are delivered from the traditions of the Law through Christ.

1 For I [a]would ye knew what great fighting I have for your sakes, and for them of Laodicea, and for as many as have not seen my [b]person in the flesh. **2** [c]That

---

COLOSSIANS 1

a. Col. 1:1 By the free bountifulness of God.
b. Col. 1:2 Colosse is situated in Phrygia, not far from Hierapolis and Laodicea, on that side that they bend toward Lycia and Pamphylia.
c. Col. 1:3 He commendeth the doctrine that was delivered them by Epaphras, and their readiness in receiving it.
d. Col. 1:3 We cannot otherwise consider of God to our salvation, but as he is Christ's Father, in whom we are adopted.
e. Col. 1:5 For the glory that is hoped for.
f. Col. 1:8 He declareth his good will towards them, telling them that they must not still remain at one stay but go on further both in the knowledge of the Gospel, and also in the true use of it.
g. Col. 1:8 Your spiritual love, or your love which cometh from the Spirit.
h. Col. 1:9 God's will.
i. Col. 1:11 The gift of continuance is not of us, but it proceedeth from the virtue of God, which he doth freely give us.
j. Col. 1:11 It must not be unwilling, and as it were drawn out of us by force, but proceed from a merry and joyful mind.
k. Col. 1:12 Having ended the preface, he goeth to the matter itself, that is to say, to an excellent description although it be but short of whole Christianity, which is fitly divided into three treatises: for first of all he expoundeth the true doctrine, according to the order of the causes, beginning from this verse to the 24. And from thence he beginneth to apply the same to the Col. with divers exhortations to verse 6 of the second Chapter. And last of all in the third place even to the third Chapter, he refuteth the corruption of true doctrine.
l. Col. 1:12 The efficient cause of our salvation is the only mercy of God the Father, who maketh us meet to be partakers of eternal life, delivering us from the darkness wherein we were born, and bringing us to the light of the knowledge of the glory of his Son.
m. Col. 1:12 In that glorious and heavenly kingdom.
n. Col. 1:14 The matter itself of our salvation, is Christ the Son of God, who hath obtained remission of sins for us by the offering up of himself.
o. Col. 1:15 A lively description of the person of Christ, whereby we understand that in him only, God showeth himself to be seen: who was begotten of the Father before anything was made, that is, from everlasting, by whom also all things that are made, were made without any exception, by whom also they do consist, and whose glory they serve.
p. Col. 1:15 Begotten before anything was made: and therefore the everlasting Son of the everlasting Father.
q. Col. 1:16 He setteth forth the Angels with glorious names, that by the comparison of most excellent spirits we may understand how far passing the excellence of Christ, in whom only we have to content ourselves, and let go all Angels.
r. Col. 1:18 Having gloriously declared the excellent dignity of the person of Christ, he describeth his office and function, to wit, that he is that same to the Church, that the head is to the body, that is to say, the prince and governor of it, and the very beginning of true life, as who rising first from death, he is the Author of eternal life, so that he is above all, in whom only there is most plentiful abundance of all good things, which is poured out upon the Church.
s. Col. 1:18 Who so rose again that he shall die no more, and who raiseth others from death to life by his power.
t. Col. 1:19 Most plentiful abundance of all things pertaining to God.
u. Col. 1:20 Now he teacheth how Christ executed that office which his Father joined him, to wit, by suffering the death of the cross which was joined with the curse of God according to his decree, that by this sacrifice he might reconcile his Father all men as well them which believed in him to come, and were already under this hope gathered into heaven, as them which should upon the earth believe in him afterwards. And thus is justification described of the Apostle, which is one and the chiefest part of the benefit of Christ.
v. Col. 1:20 The whole Church.
w. Col. 1:21 Sanctification is another work of God in us by Christ, in that that he restored us which hated God extremely, and were wholly and willingly given to sin to his gracious favor, in such sort, that he therewithall purifieth us with his holy Spirit, and consecrateth us to righteousness.
x. Col. 1:21 The Son.
y. Col. 1:22 In that fleshly body, to give us to understand that his body was not a fantastical body, but a true body.
z. Col. 1:23 This second treatise of this part of the Epistle, wherein he exhorteth the Col. not to suffer themselves by any means to be moved from this doctrine, showing and declaring that there is nowhere any other true Gospel.
aa. Col. 1:23 To all men: whereby we learn that the Gospel was not shut up within the corners of Judea alone.
ab. Col. 1:23 He purchased authority to this doctrine by his Apostleship, and taketh a most sure proof thereof, of his afflictions which he suffereth for Christ's Name to instruct the Churches with these examples of patience.
ac. Col. 1:24 For your profit and commodity.
ad. Col. 1:24 The afflictions of the Church are said to be Christ's afflictions, by reason of that fellowship and knitting together, that the body and the head have the one with the other, not that there is any more need to have the Church redeemed, but that Christ showeth his power in the daily weakness of his, and that for the comfort of the whole body.
ae. Col. 1:25 He bringeth another proof of his Apostleship, to wit, that God is the author of it, by whom also he was appointed peculiarly Apostle of the Gentiles, to the end that by this means, that same might be fulfilled by him, which the Prophets foretold of the calling of the Gentiles.
af. Col. 1:26 Whom he chose to sanctify unto himself in Christ: moreover he sayeth that the mystery of our redemption was hidden since the world began, except it were revealed unto a few, who also were taught it extraordinarily.
ag. Col. 1:27 This Paul bridleth the curiosity of men.
ah. Col. 1:28 He protesteth that he doth faithfully execute his Apostleship in every place, bringing men unto Christ only, through the Lord's plentiful blessings of his labors.
ai. Col. 1:28 Perfect and sound wisdom, which is perfect in itself, and shall in the end make them perfect that follow it.

COLOSSIANS 1

1. Matt. 3:17 / Matt. 17:5 / 2 Pet. 1:17
2. Heb. 1:3
3. John 1:3
4. Rev. 1:5 / 1 Cor. 15:20
5. John 1:14 / Col. 2:9
6. Rom. 16:25 / Eph. 3:9 / 2 Tim. 1:10 / Titus 1:2 / 1 Pet. 1:20

COLOSSIANS 2

a. Col. 2:1 The taking away of an objection, in that that he visited not the Colossians, nor the Laodiceans, he did it not of any negligence but is so much the more careful for them.
b. Col. 2:1 Me present in body.

[d]their hearts might be comforted, and they knit together in love, and in all ri-
ches of the [e]full assurance of understanding, to know the mystery of God, even
the Father, and of Christ: 3 In whom are hid all the treasures of [f]wisdom and
knowledge. 4 [g]And this I say, lest any man should beguile you with [h]enticing
words: 5 [1]For though I be absent in the flesh, yet am I with you in the spirit,
rejoicing and beholding your [i]order, and your [j]steadfast faith in Christ. 6 As ye
have therefore [k]received Christ Jesus the Lord, so walk in him. 7 Rooted and
built in him, and established in the faith, as ye have been taught, abounding the-
rein with thanksgiving: 8 [l]Beware lest there be any man that [m]spoil you throu-
gh philosophy, and vain deceit, [n]through the traditions of men, [o]according to the
[p]rudiments of the world, [q]and not after Christ. 9 [r]For [s]in him [t]dwelleth [u]all
the fullness of the Godhead [v]bodily. 10 And ye are complete in him, which is
the head of all principality and power. 11 [w]In whom also ye are circumcised
with [2]circumcision made without hands, by putting off the [x]sinful body of the fle-
sh, through the circumcision of Christ, 12 [y]In that ye are [3,z]buried with [aa]him
through baptism, [ab]in whom ye are also raised up together through the faith of
the operation of [ac]God, which raised him from the dead. 13 [4,ad]And you which
were dead in sins, [ae]and in the uncircumcision of your flesh, hath he quickened
together with him, forgiving you all your trespasses, 14 [af]And putting out the
[5,ag]handwriting of ordinances that was against us, which was contrary to us, he
even took it out of the way, and fastened it upon the cross, 15 And hath spoiled
the [ah]Principalities, and Powers, and hath [ai]made a show of them openly, and hath
triumphed over them in the [aj]same cross. 16 [ak]Let no man therefore condemn
you in meat and drink, or in respect of an holy day, or of the new moon, or of the
Sabbath days, 17 Which are but a shadow of things to come: but the [al]body is
in Christ. 18 [am]Let no man at his pleasure bear rule over you by [an]humbleness
of mind, and worshipping of Angels, [ao]advancing himself in those things whi-
ch he never saw, [ap,aq]rashly puffed up with his fleshly mind, 19 [ar]And holdeth
not the [as]head, whereof all the body furnished and knit together by joints and
bands, increaseth with the increasing of [at]God. 20 [au]Wherefore if ye be dead
with Christ from the ordinances of the world, why, [av]as though ye lived in the
world, are ye burdened with traditions? 21 [aw]As, Touch not, Taste not, Handle
not. 22 [ax]Which all perish with the using, [ay]and are after the commandments
and doctrines of men. 23 [az]Which things have indeed a show of [ba]wisdom, in
[bb]voluntary religion and humbleness of mind, and in [bc]not sparing the body, whi-
ch are things of no value, since they pertain to the [bd]filling of the flesh.

3

1 Against earthly exercises, which the false apostles urged, 2 he setteth heavenly: 5 and beginneth with the mortifying of the flesh, 8 whence he draweth particular exhortations, 18 and particular duties which depend on each man's calling.

1 If [a]ye then [b]be [c]risen with Christ, [d]seek those things which are above, where
Christ sitteth at the right hand of God. 2 Set your affections on things which
are above, and not on things which are on the [e]earth. 3 [f]For ye are dead, [g]and
your life is hid with Christ in God. 4 When Christ which is our life, shall appear,

---

c. Col. 2:2 He concludeth shortly the sum of the former doctrine, to wit, that the whole sum of true wisdom and most secret knowledge of God, consisteth in Christ only, and that this is the use of it touching men, that they being knit together in love, rest themselves happily in the knowledge of so great a goodness, until they come fully to enjoy it.

d. Col. 2:2 Whom he never saw.

e. Col. 2:2 Of that understanding, which bringeth forth certain and undoubted persuasion in our minds.

f. Col. 2:3 There is no true wisdom without Christ.

g. Col. 2:4 A passing over to the treatise following against the corruptions of Christianity.

h. Col. 2:4 With a framed kind of talk made to persuade.

i. Col. 2:5 The manner of your Ecclesiastical discipline.

j. Col. 2:5 Doctrine.

k. Col. 2:6 So then Christ hangeth not upon men's traditions.

l. Col. 2:8 He bringeth all corruptions to three kinds: The first is that, which resteth of vain and curious speculations, and yet beareth a show of a certain subtle wisdom.

m. Col. 2:8 This is a word of war, and it is as much as to drive or carry away a spoil or booty.

n. Col. 2:8 The second which is manifestly superstitious and vain, and standeth only upon custom and fained inspirations.

o. Col. 2:8 The third kind was of them which joined the rudiments of the world, that is to say, the ceremonies of the Law with the Gospel.

p. Col. 2:8 Principles and rulers, wherewith God ruled his Church, as it were under a schoolmaster.

q. Col. 2:8 A general confutation of all corruptions is this, that that must needs be a false religion, which addeth anything to Christ.

r. Col. 2:9 A reason: Because only Christ God and man, is most perfect, and passeth far above all things, so that whosoever hath him, may require nothing more.

s. Col. 2:9 By these words, is showed a distinction of the natures.

t. Col. 2:9 This word Dwelleth noteth out unto us the joining together of those natures, so that of God and Man, is one Christ.

u. Col. 2:9 These words set down most perfect Godhead to be in Christ.

v. Col. 2:9 The knitting together of God and man, is substantial and essential.

w. Col. 2:11 Now he dealeth perfecty against the third kind, that is to say, against them which urged the Jewish religion: and first of all, he denieth that we have need of the Circumcision of the flesh, seeing that without it we are circumcised within, by the virtue of Christ.

x. Col. 2:11 These many words are used to show what the old man is, whom Paul in other places calleth the body of sin.

y. Col. 2:12 The taking away of an objection: we need not so much as the eternal sign which our fathers had, seeing that our baptism is a most effectual pledge and witness, of that inward restoring and renewing.

z. Col. 2:12 See Rom. 6:4.

aa. Col. 2:12 So then all the force of the matter cometh not from the very deed done, that is to say, it is not the dipping of us into the water by a Minister that maketh us to be buried with Christ, as the Papists say, that even for the very act's sake, we become verily Christians, but it cometh from the virtue of Christ, for the Apostle addeth the resurrection of Christ and faith.

ab. Col. 2:12 One end of Baptism is the death and burial of the old man, and that by the mighty power of God only, whose virtue we lay hold on by faith, in the death and resurrection of Christ.

ac. Col. 2:12 Through faith which cometh from God.

ad. Col. 2:13 Another end of Baptism is, that we which were dead in sin, might obtain free remission of sins and eternal life through faith in Christ who died for us.

ae. Col. 2:13 A new argument which lieth in these few words, and it is thus: Uncircumcision was no hindrance to you, why you being justified in Christ should not obtain life therefore you need not circumcision to the argument of salvation.

af. Col. 2:14 He speaketh now more generally against the whole service of the Law, and showeth by two reasons that it is abolished: First, to what purpose should he that hath obtained remission of all his sins in Christ require those helps of the Law? Secondly, because that if a man do rightly consider those rites, he shall find that they were so many testimonies of our guiltiness, whereby we manifestly witnessed as it were by our own handwriting that we deserved damnation. Therefore did Christ put out that handwriting by his coming and fastening it to the cross, triumphed over all our enemies, were they never so mighty. Therefore to what end and purpose should we now use those ceremonies, as though we were still guilty of sin, and subject to the tyranny of our enemies?

ag. Col. 2:14 Abolishing the rites and ceremonies.

ah. Col. 2:15 Satan and his angels.

ai. Col. 2:15 As a conqueror made by a show of those captives, and put them to shame.

aj. Col. 2:15 The cross was as a chariot of triumph. No conqueror could have triumphed so gloriously in his chariot, as Christ did upon the cross.

ak. Col. 2:16 The conclusion: wherein also he nameth certain kinds, as the difference of days and meats, and proveth by a new argument that we are not bond unto them: to wit, because those things were shadows of Christ to come but we possess him now exhibited unto us.

al. Col. 2:17 The body as a thing of substance and pith, he setteth against shadows.

am. Col. 2:18 He disputeth against the first kind of corruptions, and setteth down the worshipping of Angels for an example: which kind of false religion he confuteth, first this way: because that they which being in such a worship, attribute that unto themselves which is proper only to God, to wit, authority to bind men's consciences with religion, although they seem to bring in these things by humbleness of mind.

an. Col. 2:18 By a foolish humbleness of mind: for otherwise humbleness is a virtue. For these Angel worshippers blamed such of pride, as would go straight to God, and use no other under means besides Christ.

ao. Col. 2:18 Secondly, because they rashly thrust upon them for oracles, those things which they neither saw nor heard, but devised of themselves.

ap. Col. 2:18 Thirdly, because these things have no other ground, whereupon they are built, but only the opinion of men, which please themselves without all measure in their own duties.

aq. Col. 2:18 Without reason.

ar. Col. 2:19 The fourth argument, which is of great weight, because they spoil Christ of his dignity, who only is sufficient both to nourish, and also to increase his whole body.

as. Col. 2:19 Christ.

at. Col. 2:19 With the increasing which cometh from God.

au. Col. 2:20 Now last of all he fighteth against the second kind of corruptions, that is to say, against mere superstitions, invented of men, which partly deceive the simplicity of some with their craftiness, and partly with very foolish superstitions, and to be laughed at: as when godliness, remission of sins, or any such like virtue is put in some certain kind of meat and such like things, which the inventors of such rites themselves understand not, because indeed it is not. And he useth an argument taken of comparison. If by the death of Christ who establisheth a new covenant with his blood, you be delivered from those external rites wherewith it pleased the Lord to prepare the world, as it were by certain rudiments to that full knowledge of true religion, why would ye be burdened with traditions, I wrote not what, as though ye were citizens of this world, that is to say, as though ye depended upon this life, and earthly things? Now this is the cause why before verse 8 he followed another order than he doth in the confutation: because he showeth thereby what degrees false religions came into the world, to wit, beginning first by curious speculations of the wise after which in process of time succeeded gross superstition, against which mischiefs the Lord set at length that service of the Law, which some abused in like sort: but in the confutation he began with the abolishing of the Law service, that he might show by comparison, that those false services ought much more to be taken away.

av. Col. 2:20 As though your felicity stood in these earthly things, and the kingdom of God were not rather spiritual.

aw. Col. 2:21 An imitation in the person of these superstitious men, rightly expressing their nature and use of speech.

ax. Col. 2:22 Another argument: The spiritual and inward kingdom of God cannot consist in these outward things, and such as perish with the using.

ay. Col. 2:22 The third argument: Because God is not the author of these traditions, and therefore they do not bind the conscience.

az. Col. 2:23 The taking away of an objection. These things have a goodly show, because men by this means, seem to worship God with a good mind and humble themselves, and neglect the body, which the most part of men curiously pamper up and cherish: but yet notwithstanding the things themselves are of no value, for so much as they pertain not to things that are spiritual and everlasting, but to the nourishment of the flesh.

ba. Col. 2:23 Which seem indeed to be some exquisite thing, and so wise devices as though they came from heaven.

bb. Col. 2:23 Hence sprang the works of supererogation, as the Papists term them, that is to say, needless works, as though men performed more than is commanded them, which was the beginning and the very ground whereon Monks' merits were brought in.

bc. Col. 2:23 A lively description of Monkery.

bd. Col. 2:23 Seeing they stand in meat and drink, wherein the kingdom of God doth not stand.

COLOSSIANS 2

1. 1 Cor. 5:3
2. Rom. 2:29
3. Rom. 6:4 / Eph. 1:19
4. Eph. 2:1
5. Eph. 2:15

COLOSSIANS 3

a. Col. 3:1 Another part of this Epistle, wherein he taketh occasion by the reason of those vain exercises, to show the duty of a Christian life: which is an ordinary thing with him after he hath once set down the doctrine itself.

b. Col. 3:1 Our renewing or new birth, which is wrought in us by being partakers of the resurrection of Christ, is the fountain of all holiness, out of which sundry arms or rivers do afterwards flow.

c. Col. 3:1 For if we be partakers of Christ, we are carried as it were into another life, where we shall need neither meat nor drink, for we shall be like unto the Angels.

d. Col. 3:1 The end and mark which all the duties of Christian life shoot at, is to enter into the kingdom of heaven, and to give ourselves to those things which lead us thither, that is to true godliness, and not to those outward and corporal things.

e. Col. 3:2 So he calleth that show of religion, which he spake of in the former Chapter.

then shall ye also appear with him in glory. **5** [1,h] Mortify therefore your [i]members which are on the earth, fornication, uncleanness, the inordinate affection, evil concupiscence, and covetousness which is idolatry. **6** For the which things' sake the wrath of God [j]cometh on the children of disobedience. **7** Wherein ye also walked once, when ye lived in them. **8** But now put ye away even all these things, wrath, anger, maliciousness, cursed speaking, filthy speaking, out of your mouth. **9** Lie not one to another: [k]seeing that ye have put off the old man with his works, **10** And have put on the new, [l]which is renewed in [m]knowledge after the image of him that created him, **11** [n]Where is neither Grecian nor Jew, circumcision nor uncircumcision, Barbarian, Scythian, bond, free: But Christ is all, and in all things. **12** Now therefore as the elect of God, holy and beloved, [o]put on the [p]bowels of mercies, kindness, humbleness of mind, meekness, longsuffering: **13** Forbearing one another, and forgiving one another, if any man have a quarrel to another: even as Christ forgave, even so do ye. **14** And above all these things put on love, which is the [q]bond of perfectness. **15** And let the peace of God [r]rule in your hearts, to the which ye are called in [s]one body, and be ye thankful: **16** Let the word of Christ dwell in you plenteously in all wisdom, teaching and admonishing your own selves, in [t]Psalms, and hymns, and spiritual songs, singing with a grace in your hearts to the Lord, **17** [2]And whatsoever ye shall do, in word or deed, do all in the [u]Name of the Lord Jesus, giving thanks to God even the Father by him. **18** [3,v]Wives, submit yourselves unto your husbands, as it is [w]comely in the Lord. **19** [4,x]Husbands, love your wives, and be not bitter unto them. **20** [5,y]Children, obey your parents in [z]all things: for that is well pleasing unto the Lord. **21** [aa]Fathers, provoke not your children to anger, lest they be discouraged. **22** [6,ab] Servants, be obedient unto them that are your masters according to the flesh, in all things, not with eye service as men pleasers, but in singleness of heart, fearing God. **23** And whatsoever ye do, do it heartily, as to the Lord, and not to men, **24** Knowing that of the Lord ye shall receive the [ac]reward of the inheritance: for ye serve the Lord Christ. **25** [ad]But he that doeth wrong, shall receive for the wrong that he hath done: and there is no respect of persons.

4

2 He returneth to general exhortations, 3 touching prayer and gracious speech, 7and so endeth with greetings and commendations.

1 Ye masters, do unto your servants, that which is just and equal, knowing that ye also have a master in heaven. **2** [1,a,b]Continue in prayer, and watch in the same with thanksgiving, **3** [2,c]Praying also for us, that God may open unto us the [d]door of utterance, to speak the mystery of Christ: wherefore I am also in bonds, **4** That I may utter it, as it becometh me to speak. **5** [3,e]Walk [f]wisely toward them that are without, and redeem the [g]season. **6** [h]Let your speech be [i]gracious always, and powdered with [j]salt, that ye may know how to answer every man. **7** Tychicus our beloved brother and faithful minister, and fellow servant in the Lord, shall declare unto you my whole state: **8** Whom I have sent unto you for the same purpose that he might know your state, and might comfort your hearts, **9** With Onesimus a faithful and a beloved brother, who is one of you. They shall show you of all things here. **10** Aristarchus my prison fellow saluteth you, and Marcus, Barnabas's cousin touching whom ye received commandments: If he come unto you, receive him. **11** And Jesus which is called Justus, which are of the circumcision. These [k]only are my work-fellows unto the [l]kingdom of God, which have been unto my consolation. **12** Epaphras the servant of Christ, which is one of you, saluteth you, and always striveth for you in prayers, that ye may stand perfect, and full in all the will of God. **13** For I bear him record, that he hath a great zeal for you, and for them of Laodicea, and them of Hierapolis, **14** [4]Luke the beloved physician greeteth you, and Demas. **15** Salute the brethren which are of Laodicea, and Nymphas, and the Church which is in his house. **16** And when this Epistle is read of you, cause that it be read in the Church of the Laodiceans also, and that ye likewise read the Epistle written from Laodicea, **17** And say to Archippus, Take heed to the ministry, that thou hast received in the Lord, that thou fulfill it. **18** The salutation by the hand of me Paul. Remember my bands. Grace be with you, Amen. Written from Rome to the Colossians, and sent by Tychicus, and Onesimus.

---

f. Col. 3:3 A reason taken of the efficient causes and others: you are dead as touching the flesh, that is, touching the old nature which seeketh after all transitory things, and on the other side, you have begun to live according to the Spirit, therefore give yourselves to spiritual and heavenly, and not to carnal and earthly things.

g. Col. 3:3 The taking away of an objection: while we are yet in this world, we are subject to many miseries of this life, so that the life that is in us, is as it were hidden: yet notwithstanding we have the beginnings of life and glory, the accomplishment whereof which lieth now in Christ's and in God's hand, shall be assuredly and manifestly performed in that glorious coming of the Lord.

h. Col. 3:5 Let not your dead nature be any more effectual in you, but let your living nature be effectual. Now the force of nature is known by the motions. Therefore let the affections of the flesh die in you, and let the contrary motions which are spiritual, live. And he reckoneth up a great long scroll of vices, and their contrary virtues.

i. Col. 3:5 The motions and lusts that are in us, are in this place very properly called members, because that the reason and will of man corrupted, doth use them as the body doth his members.

j. Col. 3:6 Useth to come.

k. Col. 3:9 A definition of our new birth taken of the parts thereof, which are the putting off of the old man, that is to say, of the wickedness which is in us by nature, and the restoring, and repairing of the new man, that is to say, of pureness which is given us by grace: but both of them are but begun in us in this present life, and by certain degrees finished: the one dying in us by little and little, and the other coming to the perfection of another life, by little and little.

l. Col. 3:10 Newness of life consisteth in knowledge, which transformeth man to the image of God his maker, that is to say, to the sincerity and pureness of the whole soul.

m. Col. 3:10 He speaketh of an effectual knowledge.

n. Col. 3:11 He telleth them again, that the Gospel doth not respect those external things, but true justification and sanctification in Christ only, which have many fruits, as he reckoneth them up here: But commendeth two things especially, to wit, godly concord, and continual study of God's word.

o. Col. 3:12 So put on, that you never put off.

p. Col. 3:12 Those most tender affections of exceeding compassion.

q. Col. 3:14 Which bindeth and knitteth together all the duties that pass from man to man.

r. Col. 3:15 Rule and govern all things.

s. Col. 3:15 You are joined together into one body through God's goodness, that you might help one another as fellow members.

t. Col. 3:16 By Psalms he meaneth all godly songs, which were written upon divers occasions, and by hymns, all such as contain the praise of God, and by spiritual songs, other more peculiar and artificious songs which were also in praise of God, but they were made fuller of music.

u. Col. 3:17 Call upon the name of Christ, when you do it, or, do it to Christ's praise and glory.

v. Col. 3:18 He goeth from precepts which concern the whole civil life of man, to precepts pertaining to every man's family, and requireth of wives, subjection in the Lord.

w. Col. 3:18 For those wives do not well, that do not set God in Christ before them in their love, but this Philosophy knoweth not.

x. Col. 3:19 He requireth of husbands, that they love their wives, and use them gently.

y. Col. 3:20 He requireth of children, that according to God's Commandment they be obedient to their parents.

z. Col. 3:20 In the Lord, and so is it expounded, Eph. 5:19.

aa. Col. 3:21 Of parents, that they be gentle towards their children.

ab. Col. 3:22 Of servants that fearing God himself to whom their obedience is acceptable, they reverently, faithfully, and from the heart, obey their masters.

ac. Col. 3:24 For that that you shall have duly obeyed your masters, the time shall come, that you shall be made sons of servants, and then shall you know this of a surety, which shall be when you are made partakers of the heavenly inheritance.

ad. Col. 3:25 He requireth of masters that being mindful how that they themselves also shall render an account before that heavenly Lord and Master, which will revenge wrongful doings without any respect of masters or servants, they show themselves just and upright with equity, unto their servants.

COLOSSIANS 3

1. Eph. 5:3
2. 1 Cor. 10:31
3. Eph. 5:22
4. 1 Pet. 3:1
5. Eph. 6:1
6. Eph. 6:5 / Titus 2:9 / 1 Pet. 2:8

COLOSSIANS 4

a. Col. 4:2 He addeth certain general exhortations and at length endeth his Epistle with divers familiar and godly salutations.

b. Col. 4:2 Prayers must be continual and earnest.

c. Col. 4:3 Such as minister the word, must especially be commended to the prayers of the Church.

d. Col. 4:3 An open and free mouth to preach the Gospel.

e. Col. 4:5 In all parts of our life, we ought to have good consideration even of them which are without the Church.

f. Col. 4:5 Advisedly and circumspectly.

g. Col. 4:5 Seek occasion to win them, although you lose of your own by it.

h. Col. 4:6 Our speech and talk must be applied to the profit of the hearers.

i. Col. 4:6 Framed to the profit of your neighbor.

j. Col. 4:6 Against this is set filthy communication, as Eph. 4:29.

k. Col. 4:11 Why then, Peter was not at that time at Rome.

l. Col. 4:11 In the Gospel.

COLOSSIANS 4

1. Luke 18:1 / 1 Thess. 5:17
2. Eph. 6:18 / 2 Thess. 3:1
3. Eph. 5:15
4. 2 Tim. 4:11

THE FIRST EPISTLE OF THE APOSTLE PAUL TO THE
THESSALONIANS

1 *1 He therefore beginneth with thanksgiving, 4 to put them in mind that whatsoever was praiseworthy in them, it came of God's goodness: 7 and that they are ensamples unto others.*

1 Paul, and Silvanus, and Timothy, unto the Church of the Thessalonians, which is in God the Father, and in the Lord Jesus Christ: Grace be with you, and peace from God our Father, and from the Lord Jesus Christ. **2** [a]We give God thanks always for you all, making mention of you in our prayers. **3** [b]Without ceasing, remembering your effectual faith, and diligent love, and the patience of your hope in our Lord Jesus Christ, in the sight of God, even our Father, **4** Knowing, beloved brethren, that ye are [c]elect of God. **5** [d]For our Gospel was not unto you in word only, but also in power, and in the holy Ghost, and in [e]much assurance, as ye know after what manner we were among you for your sakes. **6** [f]And ye became followers of us, and of the Lord, and received the word in much affliction, with [g]joy of the holy Ghost, **7** So that ye were as ensamples to all that believe in Macedonia and in Achaia. **8** For from you sounded out the word of the Lord, not in Macedonia and in Achaia only: but your faith also which is toward God, spread abroad in all quarters, that we need not to speak anything. **9** For [h]they themselves show of us what manner of entering in we had unto you, [i]and how ye turned to God from idols, to serve the living and true God. **10** And to look for his son from heaven, whom he raised from the dead, even Jesus which delivereth us from [j]that wrath to come.

2 *1 He declareth how faithfully he preacheth the Gospel unto them, 5 seeking neither gain, 6 nor praise of men: 10 and he proveth the same by their own testimony: 14 that they did courageously bear persecution of their countrymen: 17 that he desireth very much to see them.*

1 For [a]ye yourselves know, brethren, that our entrance in unto you was not in vain, **2** [b]But even after that we had suffered before, and were shamefully entreated at [1]Philippi, as ye know we were bold in [c]our God, to speak unto you the Gospel of God, with much striving. **3** [d]For our exhortation was not by deceit, nor [e]by uncleanness, nor by guile. **4** [f]But as we were [g]allowed of God, that the Gospel should be committed unto us, so we speak, not as they that please men, but God, which [h]approveth our hearts: **5** Neither yet did we ever use flattering words, as ye know, nor colored covetousness, God is record. **6** [i]Neither sought we praise of men, neither of you, nor of others, when we might have been [j]chargeable, as the Apostles of Christ. **7** But we were [k]gentle among you, even as a nurse cherisheth her children. **8** [l]Thus being affectioned toward you, our good will was to have dealt unto you, not the Gospel of God only, but also our own souls, because ye were dear unto us. **9** [m]For ye remember, brethren, [2]our labor and travail: for we labored day and night, because we would not be chargeable unto any of you, and preached unto you the Gospel of God. **10** [n]Ye are witnesses, and God also, how holily, and justly, and unblameably we behaved ourselves among you that believe. **11** [o]As ye know how that we exhorted you, and comforted, and besought every one of you, as a father his children. **12** [p]That ye [3]would walk worthy of God, who hath called you unto his kingdom and glory. **13** [q]For this cause also thank we God without ceasing, that when ye received the word of God, which ye heard of us, ye received it not as the word of men, but as it is indeed the word of God, which also worketh in you that believe. **14** [r]For brethren, ye are become followers of the Churches of God, which in Judea are in [s]Christ Jesus, because ye have also suffered the same things of your own [t]country men, even as they have of the Jews, **15** [u]Who both killed the Lord Jesus and their own Prophets, and have persecuted us away, [v]and God they please not, and are contrary to [w]all men, **16** And forbid us to preach unto the Gentiles, that they might be saved, to [x]fulfill their sins always: for the [y]wrath of God is come on them to the utmost. **17** [z]Forasmuch, brethren, as we [aa]were kept from you for a season, concerning sight, but not in the heart, we enforced the more to see your face with great desire. **18** Therefore we would have come unto you I Paul, at least once or twice but Satan hindered us. **19** For what is our hope or joy, or crown of rejoicing? are not even you it in the presence of our Lord Jesus Christ at his coming? **20** Yea, ye are our glory and joy.

3 *1 To show his affection towards them, he sendeth Timothy unto them: 6 He is so moved by the report of their prosperous state, 9 that he cannot give sufficient thanks, 11 and therefore he breaketh out into prayer.*

---

1 THESSALONIANS 1

a. 1 Thess. 1:2 An example of a right Christian rejoicing: whereby also we learn, that such as have great gifts in them are in two sorts bridled, to wit, if they consider that they have received all from God, and that continuance must be desired at his hands, whereunto also the whole Epistle exhorteth the Thessalonians.
b. 1 Thess. 1:3 He commendeth them for three special gifts, effectual faith, continual love, and patient hope: to the end they might be ashamed being endued with such excellent gifts, not to continue in God's election.
c. 1 Thess. 1:4 Word for word, that your election is of God.
d. 1 Thess. 1:5 Another reason why they ought in no wise start back but continue to the end, because they cannot doubt of his doctrine which hath been so many ways confirmed unto them, even from heaven as they themselves did well know.
e. 1 Thess. 1:5 Paul showeth by two things, that there followed very great fruits of his preaching, to wit, by these gifts of the holy Ghost, and that certain assurance which was thoroughly settled in their minds, as appeared by their willing bearing of the cross.
f. 1 Thess. 1:6 Another reason: Because even to that day, they embraced the Gospel with great cheerfulness, insomuch that they were an example to all their neighbors: so that it should be more shame for them to faint in the mid-race.
g. 1 Thess. 1:6 With joy which cometh from the holy Ghost.
h. 1 Thess. 1:9 All the believers.
i. 1 Thess. 1:9 It is no true conversion to forsake idols, unless a man therewithall worship the true and living God in Christ the only redeemer.
j. 1 Thess. 1:10 This word That is not put here without cause: and by wrath is meant that revenge and punishment, wherewith the Lord will judge the world at length in his terrible wrath.

1 THESSALONIANS 2

a. 1 Thess. 2:1 That which he touched before shortly concerning his Apostleship, he handleth now more at large, and to that end and purpose which we spake of.
b. 1 Thess. 2:2 The virtues of a true Pastor are freely, and without fear to preach the Gospel, even in the midst of dangers.
c. 1 Thess. 2:2 Through God his gracious help.
d. 1 Thess. 2:3 To teach pure doctrine faithfully and with a pure heart.
e. 1 Thess. 2:3 By any wicked and naughty kind of dealing.
f. 1 Thess. 2:4 To approve his conscience to God, being free from all flattery and covetousness.
g. 1 Thess. 2:4 Seeing there is this difference between the judgments of God and the judgments of men, that when men choose, they respect the qualities of those things which stand before them, but God findeth the reason of his counsel only in himself, it followeth, that seeing we are not able to think a good thought, that whomsoever he first chooseth to those holy callings, he maketh them able, and doth not find them able. And therefore in that we are allowed of God, it hangeth upon his mercy.
h. 1 Thess. 2:4 Which liketh and alloweth them.
i. 1 Thess. 2:6 To submit himself even to the basest, to win them, and to eschew all pride.
j. 1 Thess. 2:6 When I might lawfully have lived upon the expenses of the Church.
k. 1 Thess. 2:7 We were not rough, but easy, and gentle, as a nurse that is neither ambitious nor covetous, but taketh all pains as patiently, as if she were a mother.
l. 1 Thess. 2:8 To have the flock that is committed unto him in more estimation than his own life.
m. 1 Thess. 2:9 To depart with his own rights rather than to be chargeable to his sheep.
n. 1 Thess. 2:10 To excel others in example of godly life.
o. 1 Thess. 2:11 To exhort and comfort with a fatherly mind and affection.
p. 1 Thess. 2:12 To exhort all men diligently and earnestly to lead a godly life.
q. 1 Thess. 2:13 Having approved his ministry, he commendeth again to that end and purpose that I spake of the cheerfulness of the Thessalonians, which was answerable to his diligence in preaching, and their manly patience.
r. 1 Thess. 2:14 He confirmeth them in their afflictions which they suffered of their own people, because they were afflicted of their own countrymen: which came as well saith he to the Churches of the Jews, as to them: and therefore they ought to take it in good part.
s. 1 Thess. 2:14 Which Christ hath gathered together.
t. 1 Thess. 2:14 Even of them which are of the same country, and the same town that you are of.
u. 1 Thess. 2:15 He preventeth an offense which might be taken, for that the Jews especially above all others persecuted the Gospel. That is no new thing, sayeth he, seeing they slew Christ himself and his Prophets, and have banished me also.
v. 1 Thess. 2:15 He foretelleth the utter destruction of the Jews, lest any man should be moved by their rebellion.
w. 1 Thess. 2:15 For the Jews would neither enter into the kingdom of God themselves, nor suffer others to enter in.
x. 1 Thess. 2:16 Until the wickedness of theirs which they have by inheritance as it were of their fathers, be grown so great that the measure of their iniquity being filled, God may come forth to wrath.
y. 1 Thess. 2:16 The judgments of God being angry, which indeed appeared shortly after in the destruction of the city of Jerusalem, whither many resorted even out of divers provinces, when it was besieged.
z. 1 Thess. 2:17 He meeteth with an objection, why he came not to them straightway being in so great misery, I desired oftentimes saith he and it lay not in me, but Satan hindered my endeavors, and therefore I sent Timothy my faithful companion unto you, because you are most dear to me.
aa. 1 Thess. 2:17 Were kept asunder from you, and as it were orphans.

1 THESSALONIANS 2

1. Acts 16:12
2. Acts 20:34 / 1 Cor. 4:12 / 2 Thess. 3:8
3. Eph. 4:1 / Phil. 1:27 / Col. 1:10

1 Wherefore since we could no longer forbear, we thought it good to remain at Athens alone, 2 [1]And have sent Timothy our brother and minister of God, and our labor fellow in the Gospel of Christ, to establish you, and to comfort you touching your faith, 3 That no man should be moved with these afflictions: [a]for ye yourselves know, that we are appointed thereunto. 4 For verily when we were with you, we told you before that we should suffer tribulations, even as it came to pass, and ye know it. 5 Even for this cause, when I could no longer forbear, I sent him that I might know of your faith, lest the tempter had tempted you in any sort, and that our labor had been in vain. 6 [b]But now lately when Timothy came from you unto us, and brought us good tidings of your faith and love, and that ye have good remembrance of us always, desiring to see us, as we also do you, 7 Therefore brethren, we had consolation in you, in all our affliction and necessity through your faith. 8 For now are we [c]alive, if ye stand fast in the Lord. 9 For what thanks can we recompense to God again for you, for all the joy wherewith we rejoice for your sakes before our God, 10 Night and day, [2]praying exceedingly, that we might see your face, and might [d]accomplish that which is lacking in your faith? 11 Now God himself, even our Father, and our Lord Jesus Christ, guide our journey unto you. 12 [e]And the Lord increase you, and make you abound in love one toward another, and toward all men, even as we do toward you: 13 [3]To make your hearts stable and unblameable in holiness before God even our Father, at the coming of our Lord Jesus Christ with all his Saints.

4

1 He exhorteth them 3 to holiness, 9 and brotherly love. 13 He forbiddeth them to sorrow after to manner of infidels. 15 He setteth out the history of our resurrection.

1 And [a]furthermore we beseech you, brethren, and exhort you in the Lord Jesus, that ye [b]increase more and more, as ye have received of us, how ye ought to walk, and to please God. 2 For ye know what commandments we gave you by the Lord Jesus. 3 [1,c]For this is the will of God even your [d]sanctification, and that ye should abstain from fornication, 4 [e]That everyone of you should know, how to possess his vessel in holiness and honor, 5 [f]And not in the lust of concupiscence, even as the Gentiles which know not God: 6 [2,g]That no man oppress or defraud his brother in any matter: for the Lord is avenger of all such things, as we also have told you beforetime, and testified. 7 [3]For God hath not called us unto uncleanness, but unto holiness. 8 He therefore that [h]despiseth these things, despiseth not man, but God who hath even given you his holy Spirit. 9 [i]But as touching brotherly love, ye need not that I write unto you: [4]for ye are taught of God to love one another. 10 Yea, and that thing verily ye do unto all the brethren, which are throughout all Macedonia: but we beseech you brethren, that ye increase more and more, 11 [j]And that ye study to be quiet, and to meddle with your own business, [k]and to work with your own hands, as we commanded you. 12 That ye may behave yourselves honestly toward them that are without, and that nothing be lacking unto you. 13 [l]I would not brethren, have you ignorant [m]concerning them [n]which are asleep, that ye sorrow not even as others which have no hope. 14 [o]For if we believe that Jesus is dead, and is risen, even so them which sleep in [p]Jesus, will God [q]bring with him. 15 [r]For this say we unto you by the [s]word of the Lord, that [t]we which live, and are remaining in the coming of the Lord, shall not prevent them which sleep. 16 For the Lord himself shall descend from heaven with a [u]shout, and with the voice of the Archangel, and [5]with the trumpet of God: and the dead in Christ shall rise first: 17 Then shall we which live and remain, be [v]caught up with them also in the clouds, to meet the Lord in the air: and so shall we ever be with the Lord. 18 Wherefore, comfort yourselves one another with these words.

5

1 Condemning the curious searching for the seasons of Christ's coming, 6 he warneth them to be ready daily to receive him: 11 And so giveth them sundry good lessons.

1 But [a]of the times and [b]seasons, brethren, ye have no need that I write unto you. 2 For ye yourselves know perfectly, that the day of the Lord shall come, even as a thief in the night. 3 For when they shall say, Peace and safety, then shall come upon them sudden destruction, as the travail upon a woman with child, and they shall not escape. 4 [c]But ye, brethren, are not in darkness, that that day shall come on you, as it were a thief. 5 Ye are all the children of light, and the children of the day: we are not of the night, neither of darkness. 6 Therefore let us not sleep as do others, but let us watch and be sober. 7 For they that sleep, sleep in the night, and they that be drunken, are drunken in the night. 8 [d]But let us which are of the day, be sober, [1]putting on the breastplate of faith and love, and the hope of salvation for an helmet. 9 [e]For God hath not appointed us unto wrath, but to obtain salvation by the means of our Lord Jesus Christ. 10 [f]Which died for us, that whether we wake or sleep, we should live together with him. 11 [g]Wherefore exhort one another, and edify one another, even as ye do. 12 [h]Now we beseech you brethren, that ye [i]acknowledge them which labor among you, and are over you in the [j]Lord, and admonish you. 13 That ye have them in singular love for [k]their work's sake. [l]Be at peace among yourselves. 14 [m]We desire you, brethren, admonish them that are [n]out of order: comfort the feebleminded: bear with the weak: be patient toward all men. 15 [2,o]See that none recompense evil for evil unto any man: but ever follow that which is good, both toward yourselves, and toward all men. 16 [p]Rejoice

---

1 THESSALONIANS 3

- **a.** 1 Thess. 3:3 The will of God, who calleth his on this condition, to bring them to glory by affliction is a most sure remedy against all affliction.
- **b.** 1 Thess. 3:6 Because they have hitherto gone so well forward, he exhorteth them again to make an end of the rest of the journey, seeing that therein also they shall do him their Apostle a great pleasure.
- **c.** 1 Thess. 3:8 For now you cannot otherwise think me safe and in good case, unless you go forward in religion and faith.
- **d.** 1 Thess. 3:10 Paul was constrained through the importunate dealing of the enemies to leave the building which he had scarce begun: And for that cause he had left Silas and Timothy in Macedonia, and when Timothy came to Athens to him, he sent him back again straightway. So that he desireth to see the Thessalonians, that he may thereby thoroughly accomplish their faith and religion, that was as yet imperfect.
- **e.** 1 Thess. 3:12 Another part of the Epistle, wherein he speaketh of the duties of a Christian life. And he showeth that the perfection of a Christian life consisteth in two things, to wit, in charity toward all men, and inward purity of the heart, the accomplishment whereof notwithstanding is deferred to the next coming of Christ, who will then perfect his work by the same grace, wherewith he began it in us.

1 THESSALONIANS 3

- **1.** Acts 16:1
- **2.** Rom. 1:10 / Rom. 15:23
- **3.** 1 Thess. 5:23 / 1 Cor. 1:8

1 THESSALONIANS 4

- **a.** 1 Thess. 4:1 Divers exhortations, the ground whereof is this, to be mindful of those things, which they have heard of the Apostle.
- **b.** 1 Thess. 4:1 That ye labor to excel more and more, and daily pass yourselves.
- **c.** 1 Thess. 4:3 This is the sum of those things, which he delivered them, to dedicate themselves wholly to God. And he condemneth plainly all filthiness through lust, because it is altogether contrary to the will of God.
- **d.** 1 Thess. 4:3 See John 19:17.
- **e.** 1 Thess. 4:4 Another reason, because it defileth the body.
- **f.** 1 Thess. 4:5 The third, because the Saints are discerned from them which know not God, by honesty and purity.
- **g.** 1 Thess. 4:6 Secondly, he reprehendeth all violent oppression and immoderate desire, and showeth most severely as the Prophet of God, that God will revenge such wickedness.
- **h.** 1 Thess. 4:8 These commandments which I gave you.
- **i.** 1 Thess. 4:9 Thirdly, he requireth a ready mind to all manner of lovingkindness, and exhorteth them to profit more and more in that virtue.
- **j.** 1 Thess. 4:11 He condemneth unquiet brains, and such as are curious in matters which appertain not unto them.
- **k.** 1 Thess. 4:11 He rebuketh idleness and slothfulness, which vices whosoever are given unto, fall into other wickedness, to the great offense of the Church.
- **l.** 1 Thess. 4:13 The third part of the Epistle, which is interlaced among the former exhortations which he returneth unto afterward wherein he speaketh of mourning for the dead, and the manner of the resurrection, and of the latter day.
- **m.** 1 Thess. 4:13 We must take heed that we do not immoderately bewail the dead, that is, as they used to do which think that they are utterly perished.
- **n.** 1 Thess. 4:13 A confirmation: for death is but a sleep of the body for he speaketh of the faithful until the Lord cometh.
- **o.** 1 Thess. 4:14 A reason of the confirmation, for seeing that the head is risen, the members also shall rise, and that by the virtue of God.
- **p.** 1 Thess. 4:14 They die in Christ, which continue in faith, whereby they are grafted into Christ, even to the last gasp.
- **q.** 1 Thess. 4:14 Will call their bodies out of their graves, and join their souls to them again.
- **r.** 1 Thess. 4:15 The manner of the resurrection shall be thus: The bodies of the dead shall be as it were raised out of sleep, at the sound of the trumpet of God, Christ himself shall descend from heaven. The Saints for he speaketh properly of them which shall then be found alive together with the dead which shall rise, shall be taken up into the clouds to meet the Lord, and shall be in perpetual glory with him.
- **s.** 1 Thess. 4:15 In the Name of the Lord, as though he himself speaks unto you.
- **t.** 1 Thess. 4:15 He speaketh of these things, as though he should be one of them whom the Lord shall find alive at his coming, because that time is uncertain, and therefore every one of us ought to be in such a readiness, as if the Lord were coming at every moment.
- **u.** 1 Thess. 4:16 The word which the Apostle useth here, signifieth properly that encouragement which mariners use one to another, when they altogether with one shout put forth their oars and row together.
- **v.** 1 Thess. 4:17 Suddenly and in the twinkling of an eye.

1 THESSALONIANS 4

- **1.** Rom. 12:2 / Eph. 5:17
- **2.** 1 Cor. 6:8
- **3.** 1 Cor. 1:2
- **4.** John 13:43 / John 15:11 / 1 John 2:8 / 1 John 4:22
- **5.** 1 Cor. 15:52

1 THESSALONIANS 5

- **a.** 1 Thess. 5:1 The day that God hath appointed for his judgment, we know not. But this is sure that it shall come upon men when they look for nothing less.
- **b.** 1 Thess. 5:1 See Acts 1:7.
- **c.** 1 Thess. 5:4 Returning to exhortations he warneth us which are lightened with the knowledge of God, that it is our duty not to live securely in deliciousness, lest we be suddenly taken in a dead sleep in pleasures, but contrarywise to have an eye to the Lord, and not suffer ourselves to be oppressed with the cares of this world, for that is meet for the darkness of the night, and this for the light.
- **d.** 1 Thess. 5:8 We must fight with faith and hope, much less ought we lie carelessly snorting.
- **e.** 1 Thess. 5:9 He pricketh us forward by seeing most certain hope of victory before us.
- **f.** 1 Thess. 5:10 The death of Christ is a pledge of our victory, for therefore he died, that we might be partakers of his life or virtue, yea even while we live here.
- **g.** 1 Thess. 5:11 We must not only watch ourselves, but we are also bound to stir up and to confirm one another.
- **h.** 1 Thess. 5:12 We must have great consideration of them which are appointed to the ministry of the word, and government of the Church by God, and do their duty.
- **i.** 1 Thess. 5:12 That you acknowledge and take them for such as they are, that is to say, men worthy to be greatly accounted of among you.
- **j.** 1 Thess. 5:12 In those things which pertain to God's service: so is the Ecclesiastical function distinguished from civil authority, and true shepherds from wolves.
- **k.** 1 Thess. 5:13 So then, where this cause ceaseth, there must the honor cease.
- **l.** 1 Thess. 5:13 This maintenance of mutual concord, is especially to be looked unto.
- **m.** 1 Thess. 5:14 We must have consideration of every man, and as the disease is, so must the remedy be used.
- **n.** 1 Thess. 5:14 That keep not their rank or standing.
- **o.** 1 Thess. 5:15 Charity ought not to be overcome with any injuries.
- **p.** 1 Thess. 5:16 A quiet and appeased mind, is nourisheth with continual prayers, respecting the will of God.

evermore. 17 [3]Pray continually. 18 In all things, give thanks, for this is the
[q]will of God in Christ Jesus toward you. 19 [r]Quench not the Spirit. 20 De-
spise not [s]prophesying. 21 Try all things, and keep that which is good. 22 [t]Ab-
stain from all [u]appearance of evil. 23 Now the very God of peace [v]sanctify you
throughout: and I pray God that your whole spirit and soul and body, may be kept
blameless unto the coming of our Lord Jesus Christ. 24 [4,w,x]Faithful is he which
calleth you, which will also [y]do it. 25 [z]Brethren, pray for us. 26 Greet all the
brethren with an holy kiss. 27 I charge you in the Lord, that this Epistle be read
unto all the brethren the Saints. 28 The grace of our Lord Jesus Christ be with
you, Amen. The first Epistle unto the Thessalonians written from Athens.

q. 1 Thess. 5:18 An acceptable thing to God and such as he liketh well of.

r. 1 Thess. 5:19 The sparks of the Spirit of God that are kindled in us, are nourished by daily hearing the word of God: but true doctrine must be diligently distinguished from false.

s. 1 Thess. 5:20 The expounding of the word of God.

t. 1 Thess. 5:22 A general conclusion, that we waiting for the coming of Christ, do give ourselves to pureness both in mind, will, and body, through the grace and strength of the Spirit of God.

u. 1 Thess. 5:22 Whatsoever hath but the very show of evil, abstain from it.

v. 1 Thess. 5:23 Separate you from the world, and make you holy to himself through his spirit, in Christ in whom only you shall attain unto that true peace.

w. 1 Thess. 5:24 The good will and power of God is a sure confirmation against all difficulties, whereof we have a sure witness in our vocation.

x. 1 Thess. 5:24 Always one and ever like himself, who performeth in deed whatsoever he promiseth: and an effectual calling is nothing else but a right declaring and true setting forth of God's will: and therefore the salvation of the elect is safe and sure.

y. 1 Thess. 5:24 Who will also make you perfect.

z. 1 Thess. 5:25 The last part of the Epistle, wherein with most weighty charge, he commendeth both himself and this Epistle unto them.

1 THESSALONIANS 5

1. Isa. 59:17 / Eph. 6:17
2. Prov. 17:13 / Prov. 20:22 / Matt. 5:39 / Rom. 12:17 / 1 Pet. 3:9
3. Luke 18:1
4. 1 Cor. 1:9

THE SECOND EPISTLE OF THE APOSTLE PAUL TO THE

THESSALONIANS

1

3 He commendeth the increase of faith and charity, 4 and the patience of the Thessalonians: 6 And describing God's vengeance against such as oppress the godly, 10 he teacheth the godly to wait for the last judgment.

1 Paul and Silvanus, and Timothy, unto the Church of the Thessalonians, whi-
ch is in God our Father, and in the Lord Jesus Christ: 2 Grace be with you, and
peace from God our Father, and from the Lord Jesus Christ. 3 [1,a]We ought to
thank God always for you, brethren, as it is meet, because that your faith [b]groweth
exceedingly, and the love of every one of you toward another, aboundeth, 4 So
that we ourselves rejoice of you in the Churches of God, because of your patience
and faith in all your persecutions and tribulations that ye suffer. 5 [2,c]Which is
a manifest token of the righteous judgment of God, that ye may be counted wor-
thy of the kingdom of God, for the which ye also suffer. 6 [d]For it is a righteous
thing with God, to recompense tribulation to them that trouble you, 7 And to
you which are troubled, rest [e]with us, [3,f]when the Lord Jesus shall show himself
from heaven with his mighty Angels, 8 In flaming fire, rendering vengeance unto
them, [g]that do not know God, and which obey not unto the Gospel of our Lord
Jesus Christ, 9 Which shall be punished with everlasting perdition from the pre-
sence of the Lord, and from the glory of his power, 10 When he shall come to be
glorified in his Saints, and to be made marvelous in all them that believe [h]because
our testimony toward you was believed in that day. 11 [i]Wherefore, we also pray
always for you, that our God may make you worthy of [j]this calling, and fulfill [k]all
the good pleasure of his goodness, and the [l]work of faith with power. 12 That
the Name of our Lord Jesus Christ may be glorified in you, and ye in him, accor-
ding to the grace of our God, and of the Lord Jesus Christ.

2

2 He showeth that the day of the Lord shall not come, till there be a departure from the faith, 3 and that Antichrist be revealed, 8 whose destruction he setteth out, 15 and thereupon exhorteth to constancy.

1 Now [a]we beseech you, brethren, by the coming of our Lord Jesus Christ,
and by our [b]assembling unto him, 2 [c]That ye be not suddenly moved from your
mind, nor troubled neither by [d]spirit, nor by [e]word, nor by [f]letter, as it were from
us, as though the day of Christ were at hand. 3 Let no man deceive you by
any means: [g]for that day shall not come, except there come a departing first, and
that [h]that man of sin be disclosed, even the son of perdition. 4 Which is an
adversary, and [i]exalteth himself against all that is called God, or that is worship-
ped: [j]so that he doth sit as God in the Temple of God, showing himself that he
is God. 5 [k]Remember ye not, that when I was yet with you, I told you these
things? 6 And now ye know [l]what withholdeth, that he might be revealed in

2 THESSALONIANS 1

a. 2 Thess. 1:3 The first part of the Epistle, wherein he rejoiceth that through the grace of God, they have manfully sustained all the assaults of their enemies, wherein he confirmeth them moreover showing with what gifts they must chiefly fight, to wit, with faith and charity, which must daily increase.

b. 2 Thess. 1:3 That whereas it grew us before, it doth also receive some increase every day more and more.

c. 2 Thess. 1:5 He openeth the fountain of all true comfort, to wit, that in afflictions, which we suffer of the wicked for righteousness sake, we may behold as it were in a glass the testimony of that judgment to come, and the end therefore most acceptable to us, and most sharp to his enemies.

d. 2 Thess. 1:6 A proof: God is just, therefore he will worthily punish the unjust, and will do away the miseries of his people.

e. 2 Thess. 1:7 He confirmeth them also by the way, by this means, that the condition both of this present state and the state to come, is common to him with them.

f. 2 Thess. 1:7 A most glorious description of the second coming of Christ, to be set against all the miseries of the godly, and the triumphs of the wicked.

g. 2 Thess. 1:8 There is no knowledge of God unto salvation, without the Gospel of Christ.

h. 2 Thess. 1:10 The children of God shall be counted by the faith which they have in the Gospel, which is preached unto them by the Apostles.

i. 2 Thess. 1:11 Seeing that we have the mark set before us, it remaineth that we go unto it. And we go to it, by certain degrees of causes: first by the free love and good pleasure of God, by virtue whereof all other inferior causes work: from thence proceedeth the free calling to Christ, and from calling, faith, whereupon followeth both the glorifying of Christ in us, and us in Christ.

j. 2 Thess. 1:11 By calling he meaneth not the very act of calling, but that selfsame thing whereunto we are called, which is the glory of that heavenly kingdom.

k. 2 Thess. 1:11 Which he determined long since, only upon his gracious and merciful goodness toward you.

l. 2 Thess. 1:11 So then, faith is an excellent work of God in us: and we see here plainly that the Apostle leaveth nothing to free will, to make it checkmate with God's working therein, as the Papists dream.

2 THESSALONIANS 1

1. 1 Thess. 1:2
2. Jude 6
3. 1 Thess. 4:16

2 THESSALONIANS 2

a. 2 Thess. 2:1 The second part of the Epistle, containing an excellent prophecy of the state of the Church, which shall be from the Apostles' times unto the latter day of judgment.

b. 2 Thess. 2:1 If we think earnestly upon that immeasurable glory, which we shall be partakers of with Christ, it will be an excellent remedy for us against wavering, and impatience, so that neither the glistering of the world shall allure us, nor the dreadful sight of the cross dismay us.

c. 2 Thess. 2:2 We must take heed of false prophets, especially in this matter, which go about to deceive, and that for the most part, after three sorts: for either they brag of fained prophetical revelations, or they bring conjectures and reasons of their own, or use counterfeit writings.

d. 2 Thess. 2:2 By dreams and fables, which men pretend to be spiritual revelations.

e. 2 Thess. 2:2 Either by word of mouth, or by books written.

f. 2 Thess. 2:2 Either by forged letters, or falsely glossed upon.

g. 2 Thess. 2:3 The Apostle foretelleth that before the coming of the Lord, there shall be a throne set up clean contrary to Christ's glory, wherein that wicked man shall sit, and transfer all things that appertain to God, to himself, and many shall fall away from God to him.

h. 2 Thess. 2:3 By speaking of one, he pointed out the body of the tyrannous and persecuting Church.

i. 2 Thess. 2:4 All men know who he is that saith he can shut up heaven and open it at his pleasure, and took upon him to be Lord and master above all Kings and Princes, before whom Kings and Princes fall down and worship, honoring that Antichrist as a god.

j. 2 Thess. 2:4 He foretelleth that Antichrist, that is, whosoever he be that shall occupy that seat that falleth away from God shall not reign without the Church, but in the very bosom of the Church.

k. 2 Thess. 2:5 This prophecy was continually declared to the Ancient Church, but it was neglected of them that followed.

l. 2 Thess. 2:6 What hindereth and stayeth.

his time. 7 [m]For the mystery of iniquity doth already work: [n]only he which
now [o]withholdeth, shall let till he be taken out of the way. 8 [p]And then shall
[q]that wicked man be revealed, [1]whom the Lord shall [r]consume with the [s]Spirit
of his mouth, and shall abolish with the brightness of his coming, 9 [t]Even him
whose coming is by the effectual working of Satan, with all power, and signs, and
[u]lying wonders, 10 And in all deceivableness of unrighteousness, among them
that perish, because they received not the love of the truth, that they might be sa-
ved. 11 And therefore God shall send them [v]strong delusion, that they should
believe lies, 12 That all they might be damned which believed not the truth, but
[w]had pleasure in unrighteousness. 13 [x]But we ought to give thanks always to
God for you, brethren beloved of the Lord, because that God hath from the begin-
ning chosen you to salvation, through [y]sanctification of the Spirit, and the [z]faith of
truth, 14 Whereunto he called you by our [aa]Gospel, to obtain the glory of our
Lord Jesus Christ. 15 [ab]Therefore, brethren, stand fast and keep the instructions,
which ye have been taught, either by word, or by our Epistle. 16 Now the same
Jesus Christ our Lord, and our God, even the Father, which hath loved us, and
hath given us everlasting consolation and good hope through grace, 17 Comfort
your hearts, and stablish you in every word and good work.

3

1 He desireth them to further the preaching of the Gospel with their prayers, 6 and to withdraw themselves from those, who through idleness, 11 and curiosity pervert good order: 14 Whom he excludeth from the company of the faithful.

1 Furthermore, [a]brethren, [1]pray for us, that the word of the Lord may have
free passage and be glorified, even as it is with you. 2 And that we may be deli-
vered from [b]unreasonable and evil men: [c]for all men have not faith. 3 But the
Lord is faithful, which will stablish you, and keep you from [d]evil. 4 [e]And we are
persuaded of you through the Lord, that ye both do, and will do the things whi-
ch we warn you of. 5 [f]And the Lord guide your hearts to the love of God, and
the waiting for of Christ. 6 [g]We warn you, brethren, in the Name of our Lord
Jesus Christ, that ye withdraw yourselves from every brother that walked inordi-
nately, and not after the instruction, which he received of us. 7 [h]For ye yoursel-
ves know, [2]how ye ought to follow us: [3]for we behaved not ourselves inordinately
among you, 8 Neither took we bread of any man for nought: but we wrought
with labor and travail night and day, because we would not be chargeable to any
of you. 9 Not because we have not authority, but that we might make ourselves
an ensample unto you to follow us. 10 For even when we were with you, this we
warned you of, that if there were any, which would not work, that he should not
[i]eat. 11 For we hear, that there are some which walk among [j]you inordinately,
and work not at all, [k]but are busybodies. 12 [l]Therefore them that are such, we
warn and exhort by our Lord Jesus Christ, that they work with quietness, and eat
their own bread. 13 [m]And ye, brethren, be not weary in well doing. 14 [n]If
any man obey not this our saying in this letter, note him, and have no [o]company
with him, [p]that he may be ashamed. 15 [q]Yet count him not as an enemy, but
admonish him as a brother. 16 [r]Now the Lord himself of peace give you peace
always by all means. The Lord be with you all. 17 [s]The salutation of me Paul,
with mine own hand, which is the token in every Epistle: so I write, 18 The
grace of our Lord Jesus Christ be with you all, Amen. The second Epistle to the
Thessalonians, written from Athens.

---

m. 2 Thess. 2:7 Even in the Apostles' time the first foundations of the Apostolical seat were laid, but yet so, that they deceived men.
n. 2 Thess. 2:7 He foretelleth that when the empire of Rome is taken away, the seat that falleth away from God shall succeed and shall hold his place, as the old writers, Tertullian, Chrysostomes and Jerome do expound it.
o. 2 Thess. 2:7 He which is now in authority and ruleth all, to wit, the Roman Empire.
p. 2 Thess. 2:8 That wickedness shall at length be detected by the word of the Lord, and utterly be abolished by Christ's coming.
q. 2 Thess. 2:8 Word for word, that lawless fellow: that is to say, he that shall tread God's law clean underfoot.
r. 2 Thess. 2:8 Bring to nought.
s. 2 Thess. 2:8 With his word: for the true Ministers of the word are as a mouth, whereby the Lord breatheth out that mighty and everlasting word, which shall break his enemies in sunder, as it were an iron rod.
t. 2 Thess. 2:9 He foretelleth that Satan will bestow all his might and power, and use all false miracles that he can to establish that seat, and that with great success, because the wickedness of the world doeth so deserve it: yet so, that only the unfaithful shall perish through his deceit.
u. 2 Thess. 2:9 Which are partly false, and partly wrought to establish a falsehood.
v. 2 Thess. 2:11 A most mighty working to deceive them.
w. 2 Thess. 2:12 They liked lies so well, that they had pleasure in them which is the greatest madness that may be.
x. 2 Thess. 2:13 The elect shall stand steadfast and safe from all these mischiefs. Now election is known by these testimonies: Faith is gathered by sanctification: faith, by that that we accord unto the truth: truth by calling through the preaching of the Gospel: from whence we come at length to a certain hope of glorification.
y. 2 Thess. 2:13 To sanctify you.
z. 2 Thess. 2:13 Faith which layeth hold not upon lies, but upon the truth of God, which is the Gospel.
aa. 2 Thess. 2:14 By our preaching.
ab. 2 Thess. 2:15 The conclusion remaineth then, that we continue in the doctrine which was delivered unto us by the mouth and writings of the Apostles, through the free good will of God, which comforteth us with an invincible hope, and also in all godliness our whole life long.

2 THESSALONIANS 2

1. Isa. 11:4

2 THESSALONIANS 3

a. 2 Thess. 3:1 He addeth now consequently according to his manner, divers admonitions: The first of them is, that they make prayers for the increase and free passage of the Gospel, and for the safety of the faithful ministers of the same.
b. 2 Thess. 3:2 Which have no care of their duty.
c. 2 Thess. 3:2 It is no marvel that the Gospel is hated of so many, seeing that faith is a rare gift of God. Notwithstanding, the Church shall never be destroyed by the multitude of the wicked, because it is grounded and stayed upon the faithful promise of God.
d. 2 Thess. 3:3 From Satan's snares, or from evil.
e. 2 Thess. 3:4 The second admonition is, that they follow always the doctrine of the Apostles as a rule for their life.
f. 2 Thess. 3:5 Thirdly, he diligently and earnestly admonisheth them of two things which are given us by the only grace of God, to wit, of charity, and a watchful mind to the coming of Christ.
g. 2 Thess. 3:6 Fourthly, he saith, that idle and lazy persons ought not to be relieved of the Church, nay, that they are not to be suffered.
h. 2 Thess. 3:7 Lest he might seem to deal harshly with them, he setteth forth himself as an example, who besides his travail in preaching labored with his hands, which he saith he was not simply bound to do.
i. 2 Thess. 3:10 What shall we do then with those idle bellied Monks, and sacrificing Priests? A Monk saith Socrates, book 8, of his Tripartite history which worketh not with hands, is like a thief.
j. 2 Thess. 3:11 How great a fault idleness is, he declareth by that that God created no man in vain or to no purpose, neither is there any unto whom he hath not allotted as it were a certain standing and room. Whereupon it followeth, that the order which God hath appointed, is troubled by the idle, yea, broken, which is great sin and wickedness.
k. 2 Thess. 3:11 He reprehendeth a vice which is joined with the former, whereupon follow an infinite sort of mischiefs: to wit, that there are none more busy in other men's matters than they which neglect their own.
l. 2 Thess. 3:12 The Lord commandeth, and the Apostles pray in the name of Christ, first that no men be idle, and next, that every man do quietly and carefully see to do his duty in that office and calling wherein the Lord hath placed him.
m. 2 Thess. 3:13 We must take heed that some men's unworthiness cause us not to be slacker in well doing.
n. 2 Thess. 3:14 Excommunication is a punishment for the obstinate.
o. 2 Thess. 3:14 We must have no familiarity nor fellowship with the excommunicate.
p. 2 Thess. 3:14 The end of the excommunication is not the destruction, but the salvation of the sinner, that at least through shame he may be driven in repentance.
q. 2 Thess. 3:15 We must so eschew familiarity with the excommunicate, that we diligently seek all occasions and means that may be to bring them again into the right way.
r. 2 Thess. 3:16 Prayers are the seals of all exhortations.
s. 2 Thess. 3:17 The Apostle subscribeth his letters with his own hand, that false letters might not be brought and put in place of true.

2 THESSALONIANS 3

1. Eph. 6:19 / Col. 4:3
2. 1 Cor. 11:1
3. 1 Thess. 4:11

THE FIRST EPISTLE OF THE APOSTLE PAUL TO THE

TIMOTHY

1

Setting forth a perfect pattern of a true Pastor, whose office especially consisteth in teaching, 4 he warneth him that vain questions set apart, he teach those things, 5 which further charity and faith: 12 and that his authority be not condemned, 14 he showeth what an one he is made through the grace of God.

1 Paul [a]an Apostle of Jesus Christ, by the [b]commandment of God our Sa-
vior, and of our Lord Jesus Christ our hope, **2** Unto Timothy my natural son
in the faith: Grace, [c]mercy, and peace from God our Father, and from Christ Je-
sus our Lord. **3** [d]As I besought thee to abide still in Ephesus, when I departed
into Macedonia, so do, that thou mayest warn some, that they teach none other
doctrine, **4** [e]Neither that they give heed to fables and [f]genealogies which are en-
dless, which breed questions rather than godly edifying which is by faith. **5** [1,g]
For the end of the [h]commandment is [i]love out of a pure heart, and of a good con-
science, and of faith unfeigned. **6** [j]From the which things some have erred, and
have turned unto vain jangling. **7** [k]They would be doctors of the Law, and yet
understand not what they speak, neither whereof they affirm. **8** [l]And we know,
that the Law is good, if a man use it lawfully. **9** [m]Knowing this, that the Law
is not given unto a [n]righteous man, but unto the lawless and disobedient, to the
ungodly, and to [o]sinners, to the unholy, and to the profane, to murderers of fa-
thers and mothers, to manslayers, **10** To whoremongers, to buggerers, to men-
stealers, to liars, to the perjured, and if there be any other thing that is contrary
to wholesome doctrine, **11** [p]Which is according to the glorious Gospel of the
blessed God, [q]which is committed unto me. **12** [r]Therefore I thank him which
hath made me [s]strong, that is, Christ Jesus our Lord: for he counted me faithful,
and put me in his service: **13** When before I was a [t]blasphemer, and a persecu-
tor, and an oppressor: but I was received to mercy: for I did it ignorantly through
unbelief. **14** But the grace of our Lord was exceeding abundant [u]with faith and
love, which is in Christ Jesus. **15** [v]This is a [w]true saying, and by all means wor-
thy to be received, that [2]Christ Jesus came into the world to save sinners, of whom
I am chief. **16** Notwithstanding for this cause was I received to mercy, that Jesus
Christ should first show on me all long suffering unto the ensample of them, whi-
ch shall in time to come believe in him unto eternal life. **17** [x]Now unto the king
everlasting, immortal, invisible, unto God [y]only wise, be honor, and glory, for ever,
and ever, Amen. **18** [z]This commandment commit I unto thee, son Timothy,
according to the prophecies, which went before upon thee, that thou [aa]by them
shouldest fight a good fight, **19** Having [ab]faith and a good conscience, [ac]whi-
ch some have put away, and as concerning faith, have made shipwreck. **20** Of
whom is Hymenaeus, and Alexander, [3,ad]whom I have [ae]delivered unto Satan, that
they might [af]learn not to blaspheme.

2

He exhorteth them to make public prayers for all men, 4, 5 and that for two causes, 8 and therefore he willeth all men in all places to pray, 9 and declareth in what apparel, 11 and with what modesty, women ought to behave themselves in holy assemblies.

1 I [a]Exhort therefore, that first of all supplications, prayers, intercessions,
and giving of thanks be made for all men, **2** For Kings, and for all that are
in authority, [b]that we may lead a quiet and a peaceable life, in all godliness,
and [c]honesty. **3** For this is good and acceptable in the sight of God our Sa-
vior. **4** [d]Who will that all men shall be saved, and come unto the acknowled-
ging of the truth. **5** [e]For there is one God, and one Mediator between God and
man, which is the [f]man Christ Jesus, **6** Who gave himself a ransom for all men,
[g]to be that testimony in due time, **7** [i]Whereunto I am ordained a preacher and
an Apostle I speak the truth in Christ, and lie not even a teacher of the Gentiles

---

1 TIMOTHY 1

- **a.** 1 Tim. 1:1 First of all, he avoucheth his own free vocation, and also Timothy's, that the one might be confirmed by the other: and therewithal he declareth the sum of the Apostolical doctrine, to wit, the mercy of God in Christ Jesus apprehended by faith, the end whereof is yet hoped for.
- **b.** 1 Tim. 1:1 Or, ordinance.
- **c.** 1 Tim. 1:2 There is as much difference betwixt mercy and grace, as is betwixt the effect, and the cause: For grace is that free good will of God, whereby he chose us in Christ, and mercy is that free justification which followeth it.
- **d.** 1 Tim. 1:3 This whole Epistle consisteth in admonitions, wherein all the duties of a faithful Pastor are lively set out. And the first admonition is this, that no innovation be made either in the Apostle's doctrine itself, or in the manner of teaching it.
- **e.** 1 Tim. 1:4 The doctrine is corrupted not only by false opinions, but also by vain and curious speculations: the declaration and utterance whereof can nothing help our faith.
- **f.** 1 Tim. 1:4 He noteth out one kind of vain question.
- **g.** 1 Tim. 1:5 The second admonition is, that the right use and practice of the doctrine must be joined with the doctrine. And that consisteth in pure charity, and a good conscience, and true faith.
- **h.** 1 Tim. 1:5 Of the Law.
- **i.** 1 Tim. 1:5 There is neither love without a good conscience, nor a good conscience without faith, nor faith without the word of God.
- **j.** 1 Tim. 1:6 That which he spake before generally of vain and curious controversies, he applieth to them, which pretending a zeal of the Law, dwelled upon outward things, and never made an end of babbling of foolish trifles.
- **k.** 1 Tim. 1:7 There are none more unlearned, and more impudent in usurping the name of holiness, than foolish sophistical babblers.
- **l.** 1 Tim. 1:8 The taking away of an objection. He condemneth not the Law, but requireth the right use and practice of it.
- **m.** 1 Tim. 1:9 He indeed escapeth the curse of the Law, and therefore doth not abhor it, who fleeing and eschewing those things which the Law condemneth, giveth himself with all his heart to observe it: and not he that maketh a vain babbling of outward and curious matters.
- **n.** 1 Tim. 1:9 And such a one is he, whom the Lord hath endued with true doctrine, and with the holy Ghost.
- **o.** 1 Tim. 1:9 To such as make an art as it were of sinning.
- **p.** 1 Tim. 1:11 He setteth against fond and vain babbling, not only the Law, but the Gospel also, which condemneth not, but greatly commendeth the wholesome doctrine contained in the commandments of God, and therefore he calleth it a glorious Gospel, and the Gospel of the blessed God, the virtue whereof these babblers knew not.
- **q.** 1 Tim. 1:11 A reason why neither any other Gospel is to be taught than he hath taught in the Church, neither after any other sort, because there is no other Gospel besides that which God committed to him.
- **r.** 1 Tim. 1:12 He maintaineth of necessity his Apostleship against some that did carp at his former life, debasing himself, even to hell, to advance Christ's only mercy, wherewith he abolished all those his former doings.
- **s.** 1 Tim. 1:12 Which gave me strength, not only when I had no will to do well, but also when I was wholly given to evil.
- **t.** 1 Tim. 1:13 These are the preparative works which Paul braggeth of.
- **u.** 1 Tim. 1:14 He proveth this change by the effects, for that, that he that was a profane man, is become a believer: and he that did most outrageously persecute Christ, burneth now in love towards him.
- **v.** 1 Tim. 1:15 He turneth the reproach of the adversaries upon their own head, showing that this singular example of the goodness of God, redoundeth to the commodity of the whole Church.
- **w.** 1 Tim. 1:15 Worthy to be believed.
- **x.** 1 Tim. 1:17 He breaketh out into an exclamation, even for very zeal of mind, for that he cannot satisfy himself in amplifying the grace of God.
- **y.** 1 Tim. 1:17 See John 17:3.
- **z.** 1 Tim. 1:18 The conclusion of both the former fatherly admonitions, to wit, that Timothy striving manfully against all lets, being called to the ministry according to many prophecies which went before of him, should both maintain the doctrine which he had received, and keep also a good conscience.
- **aa.** 1 Tim. 1:18 By the help of them.
- **ab.** 1 Tim. 1:19 Wholesome and sound doctrine.
- **ac.** 1 Tim. 1:19 Whosoever keep not a good conscience, do lose also by little and little the gift of understanding: which he proveth by two most lamentable examples.
- **ad.** 1 Tim. 1:20 Such as fall from God, and his religion, are not to be suffered in the Church, but rather ought to be excommunicated.
- **ae.** 1 Tim. 1:20 Cast out of the Church, and so delivered them to Satan.
- **af.** 1 Tim. 1:20 That by their smart they might learn what it is to blaspheme.

1 TIMOTHY 1

1. Rom. 13:10
2. Matt. 4:13 / Mark 2:17
3. 1 Cor. 5:5

1 TIMOTHY 2

- **a.** 1 Tim. 2:1 Having dispatched those things which pertain to doctrine, he speaketh now in the second place of the other part of the ministry of the word, to wit, of public prayers. And first of all declaring this question, for whom we ought to pray: he teacheth that we must pray for all men, and especially for all manner of magistrates, which thing was at that time somewhat doubted of, seeing that kings, yea and the most part of magistrates were at that time enemies of the Church.
- **b.** 1 Tim. 2:2 An argument taken of the end: to wit, because that magistrates are appointed to this end, that men might peaceably and quietly live in all godliness and honesty, and therefore must we commend them especially to God, that they may faithfully execute so necessary an office.
- **c.** 1 Tim. 2:2 This word containeth all kind of duty, which is to be used amongst men in all their affairs.
- **d.** 1 Tim. 2:4 Another argument, why Churches or Congregations ought to pray for all men, without any difference of nation, kind, age, or order: to wit, because the Lord by calling of all sorts, yea, sometimes those that are greatest enemies to the Gospel, will have his Church gathered together after this sort, and therefore prayers to be made for all.
- **e.** 1 Tim. 2:5 God would not else be manifested to be the only God of all men, unless he would show his goodness in saving of all sorts of men: neither should Christ be seen to be the only mediator between God and all sorts of men, by having taken upon him that nature of man which is common to all men, unless he had satisfied for all sorts of men, and made intercession for all.
- **f.** 1 Tim. 2:5 Christ Jesus which was made man.
- **g.** 1 Tim. 2:6 A confirmation, because that even to the Gentiles in the secret of salvation now opened and made manifest the Apostle himself being appointed properly to this office, which he doth faithfully and sincerely execute.
- **h.** 1 Tim. 2:7 Faithfully and sincerely: and by faith he meaneth wholesome and sound doctrine, and by truth, an upright and sincere handling of it.
- **i.** 1 Tim. 2:8 He hath spoken of the persons for whom we must pray: and now he teacheth that the difference of

in [h]faith and verity. **8** [i]I will therefore that the men pray, everywhere [j]lifting up
pure hands without [k]wrath, or [l]doubting. **9** [2,m]Likewise also the women, that
they array themselves in comely apparel, with shamefastness and modesty, not with
braided hair, or gold, or pearls, or costly apparel, **10** But as becometh women
that profess the fear of God with good works. **11** Let the woman learn in silence
with all subjection. **12** [3]I permit not a woman to teach, [n]neither to usurp au-
thority over the man, but to be in silence. **13** [o]For [4]Adam was first formed, then
Eve. **14** [5,p]And Adam was not [q]deceived, but the woman was deceived, and was
in the transgression. **15** [r]Notwithstanding, through bearing of children she shall
be saved, if they continue in faith, and love, and holiness with modesty.

3

2 He setteth out Bishops, 8 and Christian deacons with their wives, 12 children and family, 15 he calleth the Church the house of God.

1 This [a]is a true saying, [b]If any man [c]desire the office of a Bishop, he desi-
reth a worthy work. **2** [1]A Bishop therefore must be unreproveable, the husband
of one [d]wife, watching, temperate, modest, harborous, apt to teach, **3** Not [e]gi-
ven to wine, no striker, not given to filthy lucre, but gentle, no fighter, not cove-
tous. **4** One that can rule his own house honestly, having children under obe-
dience with all honesty. **5** For if any cannot rule his own house, how shall he care
for the Church of God? **6** He may not be a young scholar, lest he being puffed
up fall into the [f]condemnation of the devil. **7** He must also be well reported of,
even of them which are without, lest he fall into rebuke, and the snare of the de-
vil. **8** [g]Likewise must [h]Deacons be grave, not double tongued, not given unto
much wine, neither to filthy lucre, **9** [2]Having the [i]mystery of the faith in pure
conscience. **10** And let them first be proved, then let them minister, if they be
found blameless. **11** [j]Likewise their wives must be honest, not evil speakers, but
sober, and faithful in all things. **12** [k]Let the Deacons be the husbands of one
wife, and such as can rule their children well, and their own households. **13** For
they that have ministered well, get themselves a good [l]decree, and [m]great liberty in
the faith, which is in Christ Jesus. **14** [n]These things write I unto thee, trusting to
come very shortly unto thee. **15** But if I tarry long, that thou mayest yet know,
how thou oughtest to behave thyself in the [o]house of God, which is the Church of
the living God, the [p]pillar and ground of truth. **16** [q]And without controversy,
great is the mystery of godliness, which is, God is manifested in the flesh, [r]justified
in the Spirit, seen of Angels, preached unto the Gentiles, believed on in the world,
and received up in glory.

4

1 He condemneth as well false doctrine, 3 of marriage and the choice of meats, 7 as also profane fables: 8 and commendeth the godly exercise, 13 and the daily reading of the Scriptures.

1 Now [a]the Spirit speaketh evidently, that in the latter times some shall de-
part from the [b]faith, and shall give heed unto spirits of error, and doctrines of de-
vils, **2** [c]Which speak lies through [d]hypocrisy, and have their [e]consciences burned
with an hot iron, **3** [f]Forbidding to marry, and commanding to abstain from
meats [g]which God hath created [h]to be received [i]with giving thanks of them which
believe and know the truth. **4** [j]For every creature of God is good, and nothing
ought to be refused, if it be received with thanksgiving. **5** [k]For it is [l]sanctified by
the [m]word of God, and prayer. **6** [n]If thou put the brethren in remembrance of
these things, thou shalt be a good minister of Jesus Christ, which hast been nou-
rished up in the words of faith, and of good doctrine which thou hast continually
[o]followed. **7** [p]But cast away profane, and old wives' fables, [q]and exercise thyself
unto [r]godliness. **8** [s]For bodily exercise profiteth little: but godliness is profitable
unto all things, which hath the promise of the life present, and of that that is to
come. **9** [t]This is a true saying, and by all means worthy to be received. **10** For
therefore we labor and are rebuked, because we trust in the living God, which
is the Savior of all men, specially of those that believe. **11** These things warn

---

places is taken away: for in times past, one only nation, and in one certain place, came together to public service: but now Churches or Congregations are gathered together everywhere orderly and decently and men come together to serve God publicly with common prayer, neither must we strive for the nation or for the purification of the body, or for the place, but for the mind, to have it clean from all offense, and full of sure trust and confidence.

j. 1 Tim. 2:8 He putteth the sign for the thing itself, the lifting up of hands, for the calling upon God.

k. 1 Tim. 2:8 Without these griefs and offenses of the mind, which hinder us from calling upon God with a good conscience.

l. 1 Tim. 2:8 Doubting which is against faith, James 1:6.

m. 1 Tim. 2:9 Thirdly he appointeth women to learn in the public assemblies with silence and modesty, being comely appareled without any riot or excess in their apparel.

n. 1 Tim. 2:12 The first argument, why it is not lawful for women to teach in the Congregation, because by this means they should be placed above men, for they should be their masters: which is against God's ordinance.

o. 1 Tim. 2:13 He proveth this ordinance of God, whereby the woman is subject to man, first by that, that God made the woman after man, for man's sake.

p. 1 Tim. 2:14 Then because that after sin God enjoined the woman this punishment, for that the man was deceived by her.

q. 1 Tim. 2:14 Adam was deceived, but through his wife's means, and therefore she is worthily for this cause subject to her husband, and ought to be.

r. 1 Tim. 2:15 He addeth a comfort by the way, that their subjection hindereth not but that women may be saved as well as men, if they behave themselves in those burdens of marriage holily and modestly, with faith and charity.

1 TIMOTHY 2

1. 2 Tim. 1:11
2. 1 Pet. 3:3
3. 1 Cor. 14:34
4. Gen. 1:27 / Gen. 27:21
5. Gen. 3:6

1 TIMOTHY 3

a. 1 Tim. 3:1 Having dispatched the treatise, as well of doctrine and of the manner of handling of it, as also of public prayer, he now in the third place cometh to the persons themselves, speaking first of Pastors and afterward of Deacons, and he useth a preface, that the Church may know that these be certain and sure rulers.

b. 1 Tim. 3:1 A Bishopric or the ministry of the word is not an idle dignity, but a work and that an excellent work: and therefore a Bishop must be furnished with many virtues both at home and abroad. Wherefore it be requisite before he be chosen, to examine well his learning, his gifts, and ableness, and his life.

c. 1 Tim. 3:1 He speaketh not here of ambitious seeking, than the which there cannot be a worse fault in the Church, but general of the mind, and disposition of man, framed and disposed to help and edify the Church of God, when and wheresoever it shall please the Lord.

d. 1 Tim. 3:2 Therefore he that shutteth out married men from the office of Bishops, only because they are married, is Antichrist.

e. 1 Tim. 3:3 A common tippler, and one that will sit by it.

f. 1 Tim. 3:6 Lest by reason that he is advanced to that degree, he take occasion to be proud, which will undo him, and so he fall into the same condemnation that the devil himself is fallen into.

g. 1 Tim. 3:8 Likewise the Deacons must first be proved that there may be a good trial of their honesty, truth, sobriety, mind, void of covetousness, that they are well instructed in the doctrine of faith, and to be short, of their good conscience and integrity.

h. 1 Tim. 3:8 These are they that had to see to the poor.

i. 1 Tim. 3:9 The doctrine of the Gospel, which is a mystery indeed: for flesh and blood do not reveal it.

j. 1 Tim. 3:11 Regard must be had also to the Pastors' and Deacons' wives.

k. 1 Tim. 3:12 They that have more wives than one at one time, must neither be called to be ministers, nor to be Deacons.

l. 1 Tim. 3:13 Honor and estimation.

m. 1 Tim. 3:13 Bold and assured confidence without fear.

n. 1 Tim. 3:14 Paul purposing to add many peculiar things pertaining to the daily office of a Pastor, speaketh first a word or two concerning his coming to Timothy, that he would be so much the more careful, lest at his coming he might be reproved of negligence.

o. 1 Tim. 3:15 The Pastor hath always to think, how that he is occupied in the house of the living God, wherein the treasure of the truth is kept.

p. 1 Tim. 3:15 To wit, in respect of men: for the Church resteth upon that cornerstone, Christ, and is the preserver of the truth, but not the mother.

q. 1 Tim. 3:16 There is nothing more excellent than this truth, whereof the Church is the keeper and preserver here amongst men, the ministry of the word being appointed to that end and purpose: for it teacheth us the greatest matters that may be thought of, to wit, that God is become visible in the person of Christ by taking our nature upon him, whose Majesty notwithstanding in so great weakness was manifested many ways, insomuch that the sight of it pierced the very Angels: and to conclude, he being preached unto the Gentiles was received of them, and is now placed above in glory unspeakable.

r. 1 Tim. 3:16 The power of the Godhead showeth itself so marvelously in that weak flesh of Christ, that though he were a weak man, yet all the world knoweth he was, and is God.

1 TIMOTHY 3

1. Titus 2:6
2. 1 Tim. 1:19

1 TIMOTHY 4

a. 1 Tim. 4:1 He setteth against that true doctrine, false opinions, which he foretelleth that certain which shall fall away from God and his religion, shall bring in by the suggestion of Satan, and so that a great number shall give ear to them.

b. 1 Tim. 4:1 From the true doctrine of God.

c. 1 Tim. 4:2 Although heretics counterfeit holiness never so much, yet they have no conscience.

d. 1 Tim. 4:2 For they will as it were practice the art of disguised persons and players, that we may not think they will lie lurking in some one corner, or keep any resemblance of shamefastness.

e. 1 Tim. 4:2 Whose conscience waxed so hard, that there grew an hard fleshiness over it, and so became to have a canker on it, and now at length required of very necessity to be burned with an hot iron.

f. 1 Tim. 4:3 He setteth down two kinds of this false doctrine, to wit, the Law of sole life, and difference of meats.

g. 1 Tim. 4:3 He proveth that he justly called such doctrines devilish, first, because the teachers of them make laws of things which are not their own: for have they created the meats?

h. 1 Tim. 4:3 Secondly, because they overthrow with their decrees, the end wherefore they were created of God, to wit, that we should use them.

i. 1 Tim. 4:3 Thirdly, for that by this means they rob God of his glory, who will be honored in the use of them. And herewithal the Apostle declareth that we must use the liberality of God soberly, and with a good conscience.

j. 1 Tim. 4:4 He setteth an Apostolical rule, for taking away the difference of meats, against that false doctrine.

k. 1 Tim. 4:5 He useth God's benefits rightly, which acknowledge the giver of them by his word, and calleth upon him.

l. 1 Tim. 4:5 It is so made pure and holy in respect of us, so that we may use it with a good conscience, as received at the Lord's hand.

m. 1 Tim. 4:5 We confess and acknowledge that God is the maker and giver of those creatures which we use. Secondly, that we are of the number of those, who through Christ's benefit have recovered that right over all creatures, which Adam lost by his fall. Thirdly, by our prayers we crave of the Lord, that we may use those meats with a good conscience, which we receive at his hands. Fourthly, we make an end of our eating and drinking, with thanksgiving and prayer: and so are our meats sanctified to us.

n. 1 Tim. 4:6 The conclusion with an exhortation to Timothy, to propound these things diligently to the Churches, which he had sucked of the Apostle, even in a manner from the teat.

o. 1 Tim. 4:6 Never departing from the side of it.

p. 1 Tim. 4:7 He setteth again true doctrine not only against that false and apostatical doctrine, but also against all vain and curious subtleties.

q. 1 Tim. 4:7 It is not only requisite that the minister of the word be sound in doctrine, but also that his life be godly and religious.

r. 1 Tim. 4:7 In the true serving of God.

s. 1 Tim. 4:8 Godliness consisteth in spiritual exercise, and not in outward austereness of life, which though it be something to be accounteth of, if it be rightly used, yet is it in no wise comparable with godliness: For it profiteth not of itself, but through the benefit of another, but this hath the promise both of the life present, and of that that is to come.

t. 1 Tim. 4:9 He goeth a little from his matter, and showeth that they which give themselves to godliness, although they are afflicted and reproached, are notwithstanding not to be counted miserable as other men are, because they are not afflicted for that cause that other men are, and the end of them both is far different one from the other. For how can God forsake his, which is bountiful even towards his enemies? And he willeth that this doctrine be well beaten into their heads.

and teach. **12** [u]Let no man despise thy youth, but be unto them that believe, an ensample, in word, in conversation, in love, in spirit, in faith and in pureness. **13** [v]Till I come, give attendance to reading, to exhortation, and to doctrine. **14** Despise not the gift that is in thee, which was given thee by prophecy with the laying on of the hands of the company of the Eldership. **15** These things exercise, and give thyself unto them, that it may be seen how thou profitest among all men. **16** Take heed unto thyself, and unto learning: continue therein: for in doing this thou shalt both [w]save thyself, and them that hear thee.

5

1 Having set down a manner how to rebuke all degrees. 5 He entreateth of widows, who then were chosen for the service of the Church: 17 Then he cometh to Elders, 23 and speaketh somewhat touching the health of the body.

1 Rebuke [a]not an elder, but exhort him as a father, and the younger men as brethren, **2** The elder women as mothers, the younger as sisters, with all pureness. **3** [b,c]Honor widows, which are widows indeed. **4** [d]But if any widow have children or nephews let them learn first to show godliness [e]toward their own house, and [f]to recompense their kindred: [g]for that is an honest thing, and acceptable before God. **5** [h]And she that is a widow indeed and left alone, trusteth in God, and continueth in supplications and prayers night and day. **6** [i]But she that liveth in pleasure, is dead, while she liveth. **7** These things therefore warn them of, that they may be blameless. **8** If there be any that provideth not for his own, and namely for them of his household, he denieth the faith, and is worse than an infidel. **9** [j]Let not a widow be taken into the number under threescore years old, that hath been the wife of [k]one husband. **10** And well reported of for good works: if she have nourished her children, if she have lodged the strangers, if she have [l]washed the Saints' feet, if she have ministered unto them which were in adversity, if she were continually given unto every good work. **11** [m]But [n]refuse the younger widows: for when they have begun to wax wanton against Christ, they will marry. **12** Having damnation, because they have broken the first faith. **13** [o]And likewise also being idle they learn to go about from house to house: yea they are not only idle, but also prattlers and busybodies, speaking things which are not comely. **14** [p]I will therefore that the younger women marry, and bear children, and govern the house, and give none occasion to the adversary to speak evil. **15** For certain are already turned back after Satan. **16** [q]If any faithful man or faithful woman have widows, let them minister unto them, and let not the Church be charged, that there may be sufficient for them that are widows indeed. **17** [r]The Elders that rule well, let them be had in [s]double honor, [t]specially they which labor in the word and doctrine. **18** For the Scripture saith, [1]Thou shalt not muzzle the mouth of the ox that treadeth out the corn: and, [2]The laborer is worthy of his wages. **19** [u]Against an Elder receive none accusation, but under two or three witnesses. **20** [v]Them that sin, rebuke openly, that the rest also may fear. **21** [3,w]I charge thee before God and the Lord Jesus Christ, and the elect Angels, that thou observe these things, without preferring one to another, and do nothing partially. **22** [x]Lay hands [y]suddenly on no man, neither be partaker of other men's sins; keep thyself pure. **23** [z]Drink no longer water, but use a little wine for thy stomach's sake, and thine often infirmities. **24** [aa]Some men's sins are open before hand, and go before unto judgment: but some men's follow after. **25** [ab]Likewise also the good works are manifest before hand, and they that are otherwise, cannot be hid.

6

1 He showeth the duty of servants: 10 and what a mischievous evil coveteousness is: 13 and having spoken somewhat of rich men, he once again forbiddeth Timothy, 20 to cumber himself with vain babblings.

1 Let [a]as many servants as are under the yoke, count their masters worthy of all honor, [b]that the Name of God, and his doctrine be not evil spoken of. **2** [c]And they which have believing masters, let them not despise them, because they are brethren, but rather do service, because they are faithful, and beloved, and [d]partakers of the benefit. [e]These things teach and exhort. **3** [f]If any man teach otherwise, and consenteth not to the wholesome words of our Lord Jesus Christ, and to the doctrine which is according to godliness, **4** He is puffed up and knoweth nothing, but doteth about questions and [g]strive of words, whereof cometh envy, strife, railings, evil surmisings, **5** Froward [h]disputations of men of corrupt minds and destitute of the truth, which think that gain is godliness: from such separate thyself. **6** [i]But godliness is great gain, if a man be content with that he hath. **7** [j]For we brought nothing into the world, and it is certain, that we can carry nothing out. **8** Therefore when we have food and raiment, let us therewith be content. **9** [k]For they that will be rich, fall into tentation and snares, and into many foolish and noisome lusts, which drown men in perdition

---

u. 1 Tim. 4:12 Now he returneth to that exhortation, showing which are the virtues of a Pastor, whereby he may come to be reverenced, although he be but young, to wit, such speech and life as are witnesses of charity, zeal, faith, and purity, but here is no mention made of the crosier staff, ring, cloak, and such other foolish and childish toys.

v. 1 Tim. 4:13 The private exercise of Pastors, is continual reading of the Scriptures, whence out they may draw matter of wholesome doctrine and exhortation, both to themselves and to others.

w. 1 Tim. 4:16 Faith is by hearing, and hearing by preaching: and therefore the ministers of the word are so said to save themselves and others, for that in them the Lord hath put the word of reconciliation.

1 TIMOTHY 5

a. 1 Tim. 5:1 Of keeping measure in private reprehensions according to the degrees of ages and kinds.

b. 1 Tim. 5:3 The Apostle giveth these rules touching the care of widows.

c. 1 Tim. 5:3 Have care of those widows which have need of help.

d. 1 Tim. 5:4 Widows' children and nephews must take care for their parents, according to their ability.

e. 1 Tim. 5:4 The first reason, because that, that which they bestow upon theirs, they bestow it upon themselves.

f. 1 Tim. 5:4 Another, because nature itself teacheth us to recompense our parents.

g. 1 Tim. 5:4 The third: because this dutifulness pleaseth God.

h. 1 Tim. 5:5 The second rule: Let the church have care of such as are widows indeed, that is to say, such as are poor and destitute of help of their own friends, and live godly and religiously.

i. 1 Tim. 5:6 The third rule: Let widows that live in pleasure, and neglect the care of their own family, be holden and accompted as fallers away from God and his religion, and worse than very infidels.

j. 1 Tim. 5:9 The fourth rule: Let none under threescore years old, be taken into the number of widows, to serve the Congregations or Churches, and such as are free from all reproach of unchastity, and are well reported of for their diligence, charity, and integrity.

k. 1 Tim. 5:9 That hath had no more husbands, but one at one time.

l. 1 Tim. 5:10 This is spoken in respect of the manner of those countries.

m. 1 Tim. 5:11 The first reason why younger widows are not to be admitted to this ministry, to wit, because for the lightness of their age, they will at length shake off the burden that Christ hath laid upon them, and think rather upon marrying again: and so will forsake the ministry whereunto they had bound themselves.

n. 1 Tim. 5:11 Take them not into the college of widows.

o. 1 Tim. 5:13 Another reason: because they are for the most part prattlers and busybodies, and gadders up and down, neglecting their charge and duty.

p. 1 Tim. 5:14 The fifth rule: Let younger widows marry and govern their houses godly.

q. 1 Tim. 5:16 The sixth rule: Let the faithful help their widows at their own charges as much as they can, and let not the Congregation be burdened with these expenses.

r. 1 Tim. 5:17 Now he giveth rules, and showeth how he ought to behave himself with the Elders, that is to say, with the Pastors and such as have the governance in the discipline of the Church, which is president of their company. The first rule: Let the Church or Congregation see unto this especially, as God himself hath commanded, that the Elders that do their duty well, be honestly maintained.

s. 1 Tim. 5:17 We must be more careful for them, than for the rest.

t. 1 Tim. 5:17 There were two kinds of Elders, the one attended upon the government only, and looked to the manners of the Congregation; the other did beside that, attend upon preaching and prayers, to and for the Congregation.

u. 1 Tim. 5:19 The second rule: Let no accusation be admitted against an Elder, but under two or three witnesses.

v. 1 Tim. 5:20 The third rule: Let the Elders so convicted be rebuked openly, that they may be an example to others.

w. 1 Tim. 5:21 The fourth rule: Let sincerity be used without any prejudice or respect of persons in Ecclesiastical proceedings, especially against the Elders because God himself is there present, and the Lord Jesus Christ with a multitude of Angels.

x. 1 Tim. 5:22 The fifth rule: Let the minister lay hands suddenly on no man. Let him not be faulty herein either by favoring any man's folly, or perverse affection: If ought be done otherwise than well of his fellows, let him keep his conscience pure.

y. 1 Tim. 5:22 As much as in thee lieth do not rashly admit any whatsoever, to any Ecclesiastical function.

z. 1 Tim. 5:23 The sixth rule: Let the Elders have indifferent consideration of their health, in the manner of their diet.

aa. 1 Tim. 5:24 Because hypocrites sometimes creep into the ministry although there be never so great diligence used, the Apostle willeth the Pastors not to be troubled therefore, or slack any whit of their diligence in trying and examining, because the Lord hath appointed a time to discover the faults of such men, and it is our parts to take heed that we offend not therein.

ab. 1 Tim. 5:25 Another comfort belonging to them, which sometimes are slandered and misreported of.

1 TIMOTHY 5

1. Deut. 25:4 / 1 Cor. 9:9
2. Matt. 10:10 / Luke 10:7
3. 1 Tim. 6:13

1 TIMOTHY 6

a. 1 Tim. 6:1 He addeth also rules for the servants' duty towards their masters: whereupon no doubt there were many questions then moved by them which took occasion by the Gospel to trouble the common state. And this is the first rule: Let servants that are come to the faith, and have infidels to their masters, serve them notwithstanding with great fidelity.

b. 1 Tim. 6:1 The reason: lest God should seem by the Doctrine of the Gospel to stir up men to rebellion and all wickedness.

c. 1 Tim. 6:2 The second rule: Let not servants that are come to the faith, and have also masters of the same profession and religion, abuse the name of brotherhood, but let them so much the rather obey them.

d. 1 Tim. 6:2 Let this be sufficient, that as touching those things which pertain to everlasting life, they are partakers of the same good will and love of God, as their masters themselves are.

e. 1 Tim. 6:2 A general conclusion, that these things ought not only to be simply taught, but must with exhortations be diligently beaten into their heads.

f. 1 Tim. 6:3 He condemneth severely, and excommunicateth or casteth out of the Church as proud men, such as content not themselves with Christ's doctrine, that is to say, the doctrine of godliness but weary both themselves and others in vain questions, for all other things are vain because they content not themselves in Christ's doctrine: and as lying deceivers, because they savor or sound of nothing but vanity: as mad men, because they trouble themselves so much in matters of nothing: as mischievous plagues, for that they cause great contentions, and corrupt men's minds and judgment: to be short, as profane and wicked, because they abuse the precious name of godliness and religion to filthy lucre.

g. 1 Tim. 6:4 Striving about words, and not about matter: and by words he meaneth all those things which have no pith in them, and whereby we can reap no profit.

h. 1 Tim. 6:5 Such as we see in those shameless schools of Popery, which are nothing else but vain babbling and prating.

i. 1 Tim. 6:6 He turneth away fitly the name of gain and lucre, confessing that godliness is great gain, but far after another sort, to wit, because it bringeth true sufficience.

j. 1 Tim. 6:7 He mocketh their folly, which do so greedily gape after frail things, that they can in no wise be satisfied, and yet notwithstanding they cannot enjoy that excess.

k. 1 Tim. 6:9 He frayeth Timothy from covetousness after another sort, to wit, because it draweth with it an infinite sort of lusts, and those very hurtful, wherewith covetous men do torment themselves so far forth, that in the end they cast away from them their faith and salvation.

and destruction. **10** For the desire of money is the root of all evil, which while some lusted after they erred from the faith, and [l]pierced themselves through with many sorrows. **11** [m]But thou, O [n]man of God, flee these things, and follow after righteousness, godliness, faith, love, patience, and meekness. **12** Fight the good fight of faith: lay hold of eternal life, whereunto thou art also called, and hast professed a good profession before many witnesses. **13** [1,o]I charge thee in the sight of God, who quickeneth all things, and before Jesus Christ, which under Pontius Pilate [2]witnessed a good confession. **14** That thou keep this commandment without spot, and unrebukeable, until the appearing of our Lord Jesus Christ, **15** Which in due time he shall show, that is [3,p] blessed and Prince only, the King of kings and Lord of lords. **16** Who only hath immortality, and dwelleth in the light that none can attain unto, [4]whom never man saw, neither can see, unto whom be honor and power everlasting, Amen. **17** [q]Charge them that are rich in [r]this world, that they be not high minded, and that they [5]trust not in uncertain riches, but in the [s]living God, which giveth us abundantly all things to enjoy. **18** That they do good, and be rich in good works, and be ready to distribute, and communicate, **19** [6,t]Laying up in store for themselves a good foundation against the time to come, that they may obtain eternal life. **20** [u]O Timothy, keep that which is committed unto thee, and avoid profane and vain babblings, and oppositions of science falsely so called, **21** Which while some [v]profess, they have erred concerning the faith. Grace be with thee, Amen. The first Epistle to Timothy, written from Laodicea, which is the chiefest city of Phrygia Pacatiana.

l. 1 Tim. 6:10 Sorrow and grief do as it were pierce through the mind of man, and are the harvest and true fruits of covetousness.
m. 1 Tim. 6:11 A peculiar exhortation to divers virtues, wherewith it behooveth the Pastors especially to be furnished.
n. 1 Tim. 6:11 Whom the Spirit of God ruleth.
o. 1 Tim. 6:13 A most earnest request and charge, to observe and keep all the premises faithfully, with our eyes set upon the coming of Jesus Christ, whose glory we have to set against the vain glistering of this world, and his power, against all the terrors of the wicked.
p. 1 Tim. 6:15 He heapeth many words together, to one purpose: whereby he voucheth the power of God, which if we stick fast unto, we shall not be moved out of our standings.
q. 1 Tim. 6:17 He addeth for an overplus as it were a sharp admonition to the rich, that they chiefly take heed of two mischiefs, to wit, of pride, and deceitful hope, against which he setteth three excellent virtues, hope in the living God, liberality towards their neighbor, and gentle conditions.
r. 1 Tim. 6:17 In things pertaining to this life, with whom those men are compared which are rich in good works.
s. 1 Tim. 6:17 Who only is, and that everlasting: for he setteth the frail nature of riches against God.
t. 1 Tim. 6:19 The praise of liberality by the effects thereof: because it is a sure testimony of the Spirit of God which dwelleth in us, and therefore of the salvation that shall be given us.
u. 1 Tim. 6:20 He rehearseth the chiefest of all the former exhortations, which ought to be deeply imprinted in the minds of all ministers of the word, to wit, that they eschew all vain babblings of sophistry and continue in the simplicity of sincere doctrine.
v. 1 Tim. 6:21 Not only in word, but also in countenance and gesture: to be short, while their behavior was such that even when they held their peace, they would make men believe their heads were occupied about nothing but high and weighty matters, even then they erred concerning the faith.

1 TIMOTHY 6
1. 1 Tim. 5:21
2. Matt. 27:11 / John 18:37
3. 2 Thess. 1:11 / Rev. 17:14 / Rev. 19:10
4. John 1:18
5. Mark 4:19 / Luke 12:15
6. Matt. 6:2

THE SECOND EPISTLE OF THE APOSTLE PAUL TO THE TIMOTHY

1

3 He commendeth Timothy's faith, 6 and exhorteth him to go on faithfully in the charge committed unto him: 8 and that neither for his bonds, 15 nor the revolting of others, he faint. 11 He triumpheth of his Apostleship. 14 He willeth him to have care of the thing committed unto him, 16 and praiseth Onesiphorus.

1 Paul an Apostle of Jesus Christ by the will of God, [a]according to the promise of life which is in Christ Jesus, **2** To Timothy my beloved son: Grace, mercy and peace from God the Father, and from Jesus Christ our Lord. **3** [b]I thank God, [1]whom I serve from mine [c]elders with pure conscience, that without ceasing I have remembrance of thee in my prayers night and day. **4** Desiring to see thee, mindful of thy tears, that I may be filled with joy: **5** When I call to remembrance the unfeigned faith that is in thee, which dwelt first in thy grandmother Lois, and in thy mother Eunice, and am assured that it dwelleth in thee also. **6** [d]Wherefore, I put thee in remembrance that thou [e]stir up the gift of God which is in thee, by the putting on of mine hands. **7** For God hath not given to us the Spirit of [f]fear, but of power, and of love, and of a sound mind. **8** [g]Be not therefore ashamed of the testimony of our Lord, neither of me [h]his prisoner: but be partaker of the afflictions of the [i]Gospel according to the [j]power of God, **9** [k]Who hath saved us, and called us with an [2]holy calling, not according to our [3]works, but according to his own purpose and grace, which was [l]given to us through Christ Jesus [m]before the [4]world was, **10** But is now made manifest by that appearing of our Savior Jesus Christ, who hath abolished death, and hath brought life and immortality unto [n]light through the Gospel. **11** [5,o]Whereunto I am appointed a preacher, and Apostle, and a teacher of the Gentiles. **12** [p]For the which cause I also suffer these things, [q]but I am not ashamed: for I know whom I have believed, and I am persuaded that he is able to keep that which I have committed to him against that day. **13** [r]Keep the true pattern of the wholesome words, which thou hast heard of me in faith and love which is in Christ Jesus. **14** [s]That worthy thing, which was committed to thee, keep [t]through the holy Ghost, which dwelleth in us. **15** [u]This thou knowest, that all they which are in Asia, be turned from me: of which sort are Phygellus and Hermogenes. **16** The Lord give mercy unto

2 TIMOTHY 1
a. 2 Tim. 1:1 Sent of God to preach that life which he promised in Christ Jesus.
b. 2 Tim. 1:3 The chiefest mark that he shooteth at in this Epistle, is to confirm Timothy to continue constantly and manfully even to the end, setting first before him the great good will he beareth him, and then reckoning up the excellent gifts which God would as it were have to be by inheritance in Timothy, and his ancestors, which might so much the more make him bound to God.
c. 2 Tim. 1:3 From Abraham, Isaac and Jacob: for he speaketh not of Pharisaism, but of Christianism.
d. 2 Tim. 1:6 He warneth us to set the invincible power of the Spirit, which God hath given us, against those storms which may and do come upon us.
e. 2 Tim. 1:6 The gift of God is as it were a certain lively flame kindled in our hearts, which the flesh and the devil go about to put out: and therefore we on the contrary side must labor as much as we can to foster and keep it burning.
f. 2 Tim. 1:7 To pierce us through, and terrify us, as men whom the Lord will destroy.
g. 2 Tim. 1:8 He proveth that the ignominy or shame of the cross is not only not to be ashamed of, but also that it is glorious and most honorable: first, because the Gospel wherefore the godly are afflicted, is the testimony of Christ: and secondly, because at length the great virtue and power of God appeareth in them.
h. 2 Tim. 1:8 For his sake.
i. 2 Tim. 1:8 The Gospel after a sort is said to be afflicted in them that preach it.
j. 2 Tim. 1:8 Through the power of God.
k. 2 Tim. 1:9 He showeth with how great benefits God hath bound us to maintain boldly and constantly his glory which is joined with our salvation, and reckoneth up the causes of our salvation, to wit, that free and eternal purpose of God to save us in Christ which was to come, whereby it should come to pass, that we should at length be freely called of God by the preaching of the Gospel, to Christ the destroyer of death and author of immortality.
l. 2 Tim. 1:9 He sayeth that that grace was given us from everlasting, unto which we were predestinate from everlasting. So that the doctrine of foreseen faith and foreseen works, is clean contrary to the doctrine which preached and teacheth the grace of God.
m. 2 Tim. 1:9 Before that course of years, which hath run on ever since the beginning of the world.
n. 2 Tim. 1:10 Hath caused life and immortality to appear.
o. 2 Tim. 1:11 That is, the Gospel which the Apostle preached.
p. 2 Tim. 1:12 He confirmeth his Apostleship by a strange argument, to wit, because the world could not abide it, and therefore it persecuted him that preached it.
q. 2 Tim. 1:12 By setting his own example before us, he showeth us how it may be, that we shall not be ashamed of the cross of Christ, to wit, if we be sure that God both can and will keep the salvation which he hath as it were laid up in store by himself for us against that day.
r. 2 Tim. 1:13 He showeth wherein he ought to be most constant, to wit, both in the doctrine itself, the abridgment whereof is faith and charity, and next in the manner of teaching it, a lively pattern and shape whereof Timothy knew in the Apostle.
s. 2 Tim. 1:14 An amplification, taken of the dignity of so great a benefit committed of the ministers.
t. 2 Tim. 1:14 The taking away of an objection. It is a hard thing to do it, but the Spirit of God is mighty, who hath inwardly endued us with his virtue.
u. 2 Tim. 1:15 He preventeth an offense which arose by the means of certain that fell from God and the religion, and uttereth also their names, that they might be known of all men. But he setteth against them the singular faith of one man, that one only good example might counterpoise and weigh down all evil examples.

the house of Onesiphorus: for he oft refreshed me, and was not ashamed of my chain, **17** But when he was at Rome, he sought me out very diligently, and found me. **18** The Lord grant unto him, that he may find mercy with the Lord at that day, and in how many things he hath ministered unto me at Ephesus, thou knowest very well.

2

2 The better to set out perseverance in the Christian warfare, 3 he taketh similitudes, 4 from soldiers, 6 and from husbandmen. 10 He showeth that his bonds are for the profit of the Saints: 15 Then he warneth Timothy to divide the word of truth aright, 17 to beware of the examples of the wicked, 22 and to do all things modestly.

1 Thou [a]therefore, my son, be strong in the grace that is in Christ Jesus. **2** And what things thou hast heard of me, by [b]many witnesses, the same deliver to faithful men, which shall be able to teach others also. **3** [c]Thou therefore suffer affliction as a good soldier of Jesus Christ. **4** No man that warreth, entangleth himself with the affairs of [d]this life, because he would please him that hath chosen him to be a soldier. **5** [e]And if any man also strive for a mastery, he is not crowned, except he strive as he ought to do. **6** [f]The husbandman must labor before he receive the fruits. **7** [g]Consider what I say: and the Lord give thee understanding in all things. **8** [h]Remember that Jesus Christ, made of the seed of David, was raised again from the dead according to my Gospel, **9** [i]Wherein I suffer trouble as an evil doer, even unto bonds: but the word of God is not bound. **10** Therefore I suffer all things for the elect's sake, that they might also obtain the salvation which is in Christ Jesus, with eternal glory. **11** [j]It is a true saying, For if we be [1,k]dead together with him: we also shall live together with him. **12** If we suffer, we shall also reign together with him: [2]if we deny him, he also will deny us. **13** If [3]we believe not, yet abideth he faithful: he cannot deny himself. **14** Of these things put them in remembrance, and [l]protest before the Lord, that they strive not about words, which is to no profit, but to the perverting of the hearers. **15** [m]Study to show thyself approved unto God a workman that needeth not to be ashamed, dividing the word of truth [n]aright. **16** [o]Stay profane, and vain babblings: [p]for they shall increase unto more ungodliness. **17** And their word shall fret as a canker: of which sort is Hymenaeus and Philetus. **18** Which as concerning the truth have erred from the mark, saying that the resurrection is past already, and do destroy the faith of certain. **19** [q]But the foundation of God remaineth sure, and hath this seal, The Lord knoweth who are his: and, Let everyone that [r]calleth on the Name of Christ, depart from iniquity. **20** [s]Notwithstanding in a great house are not only vessels of gold and of silver, but also of wood and of earth, [4]and some for honor, and some unto dishonor. **21** If any man therefore [t]purge himself from these, he shall be a vessel unto honor, sanctified, and meet for the Lord, and prepared unto every good work. **22** [u]Flee also the lusts of youth, and follow after righteousness, faith, love, and [v]peace, with them that [5]call on the Lord with pure heart, **23** [6]And put away foolish and unlearned questions, knowing that they engender strife. **24** But the servant of the Lord must not strive, but must be gentle toward all men, apt to teach, [w]suffering the evil, **25** Instructing them with meekness that are [x]contrary minded, proving if God at any time will give them repentance, that they may acknowledge the truth, **26** And come to amendment out of that snare of the devil, of whom they are taken prisoners, to do his will.

3

1 He foretelleth the dangerous times that are to ensue: 9 but with the certain hope of victory, 10 he encourageth him to the combat, 14 setting out especially the trial of sound doctrine.

1 This [a]know also, that in the [1]last days shall come perilous times. **2** For men shall be lovers of their own selves, covetous, boasters, proud, cursed speakers, disobedient to parents, unthankful, [b]unholy, **3** Without natural affection, truce breakers, false accusers, intemperate, fierce, no lovers at all of them which are good, **4** Traitors, heady, high-minded, lovers of pleasures more than lovers of God, **5** Having a show of godliness, but have denied the power thereof: [c]turn away therefore from such. **6** For of this sort are they which creep into houses, and lead captive simple women laden with sins, and led with divers lusts, **7** Which women are ever learning, and are never able to come to the acknowledging of the truth. **8** [2]And as Jannes and Jambres withstood Moses, so do these also resist the truth, men of corrupt minds, reprobate concerning the faith. **9** [d]But they shall prevail no longer: for their madness shall be evident unto all men, as theirs also was. **10** [e]But thou hast [f]fully known my doctrine, manner of living, purpose, faith, longsuffering, love, patience, **11** Persecutions, and afflictions which came unto me at [g]Antioch, at Iconium, and at Lystra, which persecutions I suffered: but from them all the Lord delivered me. **12** Yea, and all that will live godly in Christ Jesus, shall suffer persecution. **13** But the evil men and deceivers shall wax [h]worse and worse, deceiving, and being deceived. **14** But continue thou in the things which thou hast learned, and which are committed unto thee, knowing of whom thou hast learned them: **15** And that thou hast known the holy Scriptures of a child, which are able to make thee wise unto salvation, through the faith which is in Christ Jesus. **16** [3,i]For the whole Scripture is given by inspiration of God, and is profitable to teach, to convince, to correct, and to instruct in righteousness, **17** That the [j]man of God may be absolute, being made perfect unto all good works.

---

2 TIMOTHY 1

1. Acts 22:3
2. 1 Cor. 1:2
3. Titus 3:5
4. Rom. 16:25 / Eph. 1:4 / Col. 1:26 / Titus 1:2
5. 1 Tim. 2:7

2 TIMOTHY 2

a. 2 Tim. 2:1 The conclusion of the former exhortation, which hath also added unto it a declaration how that they do not keep that worthy thing that is committed unto them which keep it to themselves, but they rather which do most freely communicate it with others, to the end that many may be partakers of it, without any man's loss or hindrance.

b. 2 Tim. 2:2 When many were by, which can bear witness of these things.

c. 2 Tim. 2:3 Another admonition: That the ministry of the word is a spiritual warfare, which no man can so travail in, that he may please his captain, unless he forgo and part with all hindrances which might draw him away from it.

d. 2 Tim. 2:4 With affairs of household, or other things that belong to other ordinary businesses.

e. 2 Tim. 2:5 The third admonition: The ministry is like to a game or justing, wherein men strive for the victory, and no man is crowned unless he strive according to the laws which are prescribed, be they never so hard and painful.

f. 2 Tim. 2:6 Another similitude tending to the same end: no man may look for the harvest, unless he first take pains to plow and sow his ground.

g. 2 Tim. 2:7 All these things cannot be understood, and much less practiced, unless we ask of God and he gives us understanding.

h. 2 Tim. 2:8 He confirmeth plainly two principles of our faith, which are always assaulted of heretics, the one whereof to wit, that Christ is the true Messiah made man of the seed of David is the ground of our salvation: and the other is the highest part of it, to wit, that he is risen again from the dead.

i. 2 Tim. 2:9 The taking away of an objection: Truth it is, that he is kept in prison, as an evildoer, yet there is no cause, why therefore some should go about to derogate credit from his Gospel, seeing that notwithstanding God did bless his ministry, nay rather, that example of this his captivity and patience did sundry ways confirm the Church in the hope of a better life.

j. 2 Tim. 2:11 The fourth admonition: we ought not to contend upon words and questions, which are not only unprofitable, but also for the most part hurtful: but rather upon this, how we may frame ourselves to all manner of patience, and to die also with Christ that is to say, for Christ's Name because that is the plain way to the most glorious life: as contrariwise the falling away of men can diminish no part of the truth of God, although by such means, they procure most certain destruction to themselves.

k. 2 Tim. 2:11 If we be afflicted with Christ, and for Christ's sake.

l. 2 Tim. 2:14 Call God to witness, or as a Judge: as Moses, Joshua, Samuel, and Paul himself did, Acts 20.

m. 2 Tim. 2:15 The fifth admonition: A minister must not be an idle disputer, but a faithful steward in dividing aright the word of truth, insomuch that he must stop the mouths of other vain babblers.

n. 2 Tim. 2:15 By adding nothing to it, neither overslipping anything, neither mangling it, nor renting it in sunder, nor wresting of it: but marking diligently what his hearers are able to hear, and what is fit to edifying.

o. 2 Tim. 2:16 Mark and watch, and see they creep not on further.

p. 2 Tim. 2:16 He discovereth the subtlety of Satan, who beginning with these principles draweth us by little and little to ungodliness through the means of that wicked and profane babbling, still creeping on: which he proveth by the horrible example of them that taught that, the resurrection was already past.

q. 2 Tim. 2:19 A digression: wherein he salveth that offense that rose by their falling away: showing first, that the elect are out of all danger of any such falling away: secondly, that they are known to God and not to us: and therefore it is no marvel if we count hypocrites oftentimes for true brethren: but we must take heed that we be not like them, but rather that we be indeed, such as we are said to be.

r. 2 Tim. 2:19 That serveth and worshippeth him, and is as it were named of him, a faithful man or Christian.

s. 2 Tim. 2:20 The taking away of an objection: it is no dishonor to the good man of the house, that he hath not in a great house all vessels of one sort and for one service, but we must look to this, that we be found vessels prepared to honor.

t. 2 Tim. 2:21 By these words is meant the execution of the matter, and not the cause: for in that we purge ourselves, it is not to be attribueth to any free will that is in us, but to God, who freely and wholly worketh in us a good and an effectual will.

u. 2 Tim. 2:22 Returning to the matter from whence he digressed, verse 16, he warneth him to exercise himself in weighty matters, and such as pertain to godliness.

v. 2 Tim. 2:22 The sixth admonition: We must above all things eschew all bitterness of mind both in teaching all men, and also in calling them back which have gone out of the way.

w. 2 Tim. 2:24 To win them through our patient bearing with them, but not to please them or excuse them in their wickedness.

x. 2 Tim. 2:25 He meaneth such as do not yet see the truth.

2 TIMOTHY 2

1. Rom. 6:5
2. Matt. 10:33 / Mark 8:38
3. Rom. 3:3 / Rom. 9:6
4. Rom. 9:21
5. 1 Cor. 1:2
6. 1 Tim. 1:4 / 1 Tim. 4:7 / Titus 3:9

2 TIMOTHY 3

a. 2 Tim. 3:1 The seventh admonition: we may not hope for any Church in this world without corruption: but there shall be rather great abundance of most wicked men, even in the very bosom of the Church, which notwithstanding shall make a show and countenance of great holiness and charity.

b. 2 Tim. 3:2 Which make no account, either of right or honesty.

c. 2 Tim. 3:5 We must not dally with such men as resist the truth not of simple ignorance, but of a perverse mind, which thing appeareth by their fruits which he painteth out here lively but we must rather turn away from them.

d. 2 Tim. 3:9 He addeth a comfort: The Lord will at length pluck off all their vizards.

e. 2 Tim. 3:10 That we be not deceived by such hypocrites, we must set before us the virtues of the holy servants of God, and we must not be afraid of persecution, which they suffered willingly, and which always followeth true godliness. But we must especially hold fast the doctrine of the Apostles, the sum whereof is this, that we are saved through faith in Christ Jesus.

f. 2 Tim. 3:10 Thou knowest thoroughly, not only what I taught and did, but also how I was minded and disposed.

g. 2 Tim. 3:11 Which is in Pisidia.

h. 2 Tim. 3:13 Their wickedness shall daily increase.

i. 2 Tim. 3:16 The eighth admonition, which is most precious: A Pastor must be wise by the word of God only: wherein we have perfectly delivered unto us, whatsoever pertaineth either to discern, know and establish true opinions, and to confute false, and furthermore, to correct evil manners, and to frame good.

j. 2 Tim. 3:17 The Prophets and expounders of God's will, are properly and peculiarly called, Men of God.

4

1 He chargeth him to preach the Gospel with all diligence, 3 in that so
miserable a time: 6 that his death is hard at hand, 8 yet so, that as a
conqueror he maketh haste to a glorious triumph. 10 He showeth the cause why he
sendeth for Timothy, 11 even by reason of his present state.

1 I [a]Charge thee therefore before God, and before the Lord Jesus Christ, which
shall judge the quick and dead at that his appearing, and in his kingdom, **2** Prea-
ch the word: be instant, in season, and out of season: improve, rebuke, exhort with
all longsuffering and doctrine. **3** [b]For the time will come when they will not suf-
fer wholesome doctrine: but having their ears itching, shall after their own lusts get
them an heap of teachers, **4** And shall turn their ears from the truth, and shall be
given unto [c]fables. **5** [d]But watch thou in all things: suffer adversity: do the work
of an Evangelist: [e]cause thy ministry to be thoroughly liked of. **6** [f]For I am now
ready to be [g]offered, and the time of my departing is at hand. **7** I have fought a
good fight, and have finished my course: I have kept the faith. **8** For henceforth
is laid up for me the crown of righteousness, which the Lord the righteous Jud-
ge shall give me at that day: and not to me only, but unto all them also that love
that his appearing. **9** [h]Make speed to come unto me at once: **10** For Demas
hath forsaken me, and hath [i]embraced this present world, and is departed unto
Thessalonica. Crescens is gone to Galatia, Titus unto Dalmatia. **11** [1]Only Luke
is with me. Take Mark and bring him with thee: for he is profitable unto me to
minister. **12** And Tychicus have I sent to Ephesus. **13** The cloak that I left at
Troas with Carpus, when thou comest, bring with thee, and the books, but special-
ly the parchments. **14** Alexander the coppersmith hath done me much evil: the
Lord reward him according to his works. **15** Of whom be thou ware also: for he
withstood our preaching sore. **16** At my first answering no man assisted me, but
all forsook me: I pray God, that it may not be laid to their charge. **17** Notwi-
thstanding the Lord assisted me, and strengthened me, that by me the preaching
might be fully believed, and that all the Gentiles should hear: and I was delivered
out of the mouth of the [j]lion. **18** And the Lord will deliver me from every [k]evil
work, and will preserve me unto his [l]heavenly kingdom: to whom be praise for ever
and ever, Amen. **19** Salute Prisca and Aquila, and the [2]household of Onesipho-
rus. **20** Erastus abode at Corinth: Trophimus I left at Miletus sick. **21** Make
speed to come before winter. Eubulus greeteth thee, and Pudens, and Linus, and
Claudia, and all the brethren. **22** The Lord Jesus Christ be with thy Spirit. Grace
be with you, Amen. The second Epistle written from Rome unto Timothy, the
first Bishop elected of the Church of Ephesus, when Paul was presented the second
time before the Emperor Nero.

---

2 TIMOTHY 3

1. 1 Tim. 4:1 / 2 Pet. 3:3 / Jude 18
2. Exod. 7:11
3. 2 Pet. 1:20

2 TIMOTHY 4

a. 2 Tim. 4:1 The principal and chief of all admonitions, being therefore proposed with a most earnest charge, is this: That the word of God be propounded with a certain holy importunity, as necessity requireth: but so, that a good and true ground of the doctrine be laid, and the vehemency be tempered with all holy meekness.
b. 2 Tim. 4:3 Faithful Pastors in times past took all occasions they could, because men were very prompt and ready to return to their fables.
c. 2 Tim. 4:4 To false and unprofitable doctrines, which the world is now so bewitched withal, that it had rather the open light of the truth were utterly put out, when it would come out of darkness.
d. 2 Tim. 4:5 The wickedness and falling away of the world, ought to cause faithful ministers to be so much the more careful.
e. 2 Tim. 4:5 Prove and show by good and substantial proof, that thou art the true minister of God.
f. 2 Tim. 4:6 He foretelleth his death to be at hand, and setteth before them an excellent example, both of invincible constancy and sure hope.
g. 2 Tim. 4:6 To be offered for a drink offering: and he alludeth to the pouring out of blood or wine which was used in sacrifices.
h. 2 Tim. 4:9 The last part of the Epistle, setting forth grievous complaints against certain, and examples of singular godliness in every place, and of a mind never wearied.
i. 2 Tim. 4:10 Contented himself with this world.
j. 2 Tim. 4:17 Of Nero.
k. 2 Tim. 4:18 Preserve me pure from committing anything unworthy my Apostleship.
l. 2 Tim. 4:18 To make me partaker of his kingdom.

2 TIMOTHY 4

1. Col. 4:10,14
2. 2 Tim. 1:16

THE EPISTLE OF PAUL TO

TITUS

1

6 He showeth what kind of men ought to be chosen Ministers: 10 how vain babblers' mouths should be stopped: 12 and through this occasion he toucheth the nature of the Cretans, 14 and the Jews, who put boldness in outward things.

1 Paul [a]a [b]servant of God, and an Apostle of Jesus Christ, according to the
faith of God's [c]elect, [d]and the acknowledging of the truth, which is according
unto godliness. 2 Unto the [e]hope of eternal life, which God that cannot lie,
hath [f]promised before the [1,g]world began: 3 [h]But hath made his word manifest
in due time through the preaching, which is [2]committed unto me according to
the commandment of God our [i]Savior: 4 [j]To Titus my natural son according
to the common faith, [k]Grace, mercy, and peace from God the Father, and from
the Lord Jesus Christ our Savior. 5 [l]For this cause left I thee in Crete, that thou
shouldest continue to redress the things that remain, and shouldest ordain Elders
in every city as I ap-pointed thee. 6 [3]If any be unreproveable, the husband of one
wife, having faithful children, which are not slandered of riot, neither are [m]disobe-
dient. 7 [n]For a Bishop must be unreproveable, as God's [o]steward, not [p]froward,
not angry, not given to wine, no striker, not given to filthy lucre, 8 But harbe-
rous, one that loveth goodness, [q]wise, righteous, holy, temperate, 9 [r]Holding fast
that faithful word according to doctrine, [s]that he also may be able to exhort with
wholesome doctrine, and convince them that say against it. 10 [t]For there are
many disobedient and vain talkers and deceivers of minds, chiefly they of the [u]Cir-
cumcision, 11 Whose mouths must be stopped, which subvert whole houses,
teaching things which they ought not, for filthy lucre's sake. 12 [v]One of them-
selves, even one of their own Prophets said, The Cretans are always liars, evil beasts,
slow bellies. 13 This witness is true: wherefore convince them [w]sharply, that they
may be sound in the faith. 14 And not taking heed to [4]Jewish fables and com-
mandments of men, that turn away from the truth. 15 [x]Unto the pure [5]are all
things pure, but unto them that are defiled, and unbelieving, is nothing pure, but
even their [y]minds and consciences are defiled. 16 They profess that they know
God, but by works they deny him, and are abominable and disobedient, and unto
every good work reprobate.

2

2 He setteth out the duties of sundry persons and states, 6 and willeth him to instruct the Church in manners. 11 He draweth an argument from the end of our redemption, 12 which is, that we live godly and uprightly.

1 But [a]speak thou the things which become wholesome doctrine, 2 [b]That
the elder men be watchful, grave, temperate, sound in the faith, in love, and in pa-
tience: 3 The elder women likewise, that they be in such behavior as becometh
holiness, not false accusers, not subject to much wine, but teachers of honest thin-
gs. 4 That they may instruct the young women to be sober minded, that they
love their husbands, that they love their children, 5 That they be temperate,
chaste, [c]keeping at home, good and [1]subject unto their husbands, that the word
of God be not evil spoken of. 6 Exhort young men likewise, that they be sober
minded. 7 [d]In all things show thyself an example of good works with uncorrupt
doctrine, with [e]gravity, integrity, 8 And with the wholesome word, which can-
not be condemned, that he which withstandeth, may be ashamed, having nothing
concerning you to speak evil of. 9 [2,f]Let servants be subject to their masters, and
please them in all [g]things, not answering again, 10 Neither pickers, but that they
show all good faithfulness, that they may adorn the doctrine of God our Savior in
all things. 11 [3,h]For that grace of God, that bringeth salvation unto all men, hath
appeared, 12 And teacheth us, that we should deny ungodliness and [i]worldly lu-
sts, and that we should live soberly and righteously, and godly in this present wor-
ld, 13 [j]Looking for that blessed hope, and appearing of that glory of that mighty
God, and of our Savior Jesus Christ. 14 Who gave himself for us, that he might
redeem us from all iniquity, and purge us to be a [k]peculiar people unto himself,
zealous of good works. 15 These things speak, and exhort, and convince with all
[l]authority. See that no man despise thee.

3

1 He willeth that all generally be put in mind to reverence such as be in authority: 3 That they remember their former life, and attribute all justification unto grace. 9 And if any brabbler withstand these things, 10 he willeth that he be rejected.

1 Put [a]them in remembrance that they [1]be subject to the principalities and
powers, and that they be obedient, and ready to every good work. 2 That they
speak evil of no man, that they be no fighters, but soft, showing all meekness unto
all men. 3 [2,b] For we ourselves also were in times past unwise, disobedient, decei-
ved, serving the lusts and divers pleasures, living in maliciousness and envy, hate-
ful, and hating one another. 4 But when that bountifulness and that love of God
our Savior toward man appeared, 5 [3]Not by the works of [c]righteousness, which
we had done, but according to his mercy he saved us, by the washing of the new

---

TITUS 1

- **a.** Titus 1:1 He voucheth his Apostleship, not for Titus, but for the Cretans' sake both by the testimony of his outward calling, and by his consent wherein he agreeth with all the elect from the beginning of the world.
- **b.** Titus 1:1 Minister, as Christ himself, in that that he was a minister and head of the Prophets, is called a servant, Isa. 43:10.
- **c.** Titus 1:1 Of those whom God hath chosen.
- **d.** Titus 1:1 The faith wherein all the elect consent, is the true and sincere knowledge of God, tending to this end, that worshipping God aright that they at length obtain life everlasting according to the promise of God, who is true, which promise was exhibited to Christ in due time according to his eternal purpose.
- **e.** Titus 1:2 Hope is the end of faith.
- **f.** Titus 1:2 Freely, and of his mere liberality.
- **g.** Titus 1:2 See 2 Tim. 1:9.
- **h.** Titus 1:3 This truth is no other where to be sought, but in the preaching of the Apostle.
- **i.** Titus 1:3 This word Savior doth not only signify a preserver of life, but also a giver of life.
- **j.** Titus 1:4 The Apostle moveth the Cretans to hear Titus, by setting forth his consent and agreement with him in the faith, and therewithal showeth by what special note we may distinguish true ministers from false.
- **k.** Titus 1:4 There is but one way of salvation, common both to the Pastor and the flock.
- **l.** Titus 1:5 The first admonition, to ordain Elders in every city.
- **m.** Titus 1:6 This word is proper to horses and oxen, which will not abide the yoke.
- **n.** Titus 1:7 The second admonition, what faults pastors whom he comprehended afore under the word Elders ought to be void of, and what virtues they ought to have.
- **o.** Titus 1:7 Whom the Lord hath appointed steward of his gifts.
- **p.** Titus 1:7 Not hard conditioned, and evil to please.
- **q.** Titus 1:8 Circumspect, of a sound judgment, and of a singular example of moderation.
- **r.** Titus 1:9 The third admonition: The Pastor must hold fast that doctrine, which the Apostles delivered, and pertaineth to salvation, leaving all curious and vain matters.
- **s.** Titus 1:9 The fourth admonition: To apply the knowledge of true doctrine unto use, which consisteth in two things, to wit, in governing them which show themselves apt to learn, and confuting the obstinate.
- **t.** Titus 1:10 An applying of the general proposition to a particular: The Cretans above all others need sharp reprehensions: both because their minds are naturally given to lies and slothfulness, and also because of certain covetous Jews, which under a color of godliness joined partly certain vain traditions, and partly old ceremonies with the Gospel.
- **u.** Titus 1:10 Of the Jews, or rather of those Jews, which went about to join Christ and the Law together.
- **v.** Titus 1:12 Epimenides, who was counted a Prophet amongst them. Look upon Laertius and Cicero in his first book of Divination.
- **w.** Titus 1:13 Roughly and plainly, and go not about the bush with them.
- **x.** Titus 1:15 He showeth in few words, that purity consisteth not in any external worship, and that that is according to the old Law, as in difference of meats, and washing, and other such things which are abolished but in the mind and conscience: and whosoever teach otherwise, know not what is true religion indeed, and also are nothing less than that they would seem to be.
- **y.** Titus 1:15 If our minds and conscience be unclean, what cleanness is there in us before regeneration?

TITUS 1

1. Rom. 16:25 / Eph. 3:9 / Col. 1:26 / 2 Tim. 1:9 / 1 Pet. 1:20
2. Gal. 1:1
3. 1 Tim. 3:2
4. 1 Tim. 1:4
5. Rom. 14:20

TITUS 2

- **a.** Titus 2:1 The fifth admonition: The doctrine must not only be generally pure, but also be applied to all ages and orders of men, according to the diversity of circumstances.
- **b.** Titus 2:2 What are the chiefest virtues for old and young, both men and women: and how they ought to be stirred up unto them continually.
- **c.** Titus 2:5 No gadders up and down.
- **d.** Titus 2:7 The sixth admonition: That both the Pastor's life and doctrine must be sound.
- **e.** Titus 2:7 Not such a gravity as may drive men from coming to the minister, but such as may cause them to come in most reverent and honest sort.
- **f.** Titus 2:9 The seventh admonition, of servants' duty toward their masters.
- **g.** Titus 2:9 Which may be done without offense to God.
- **h.** Titus 2:11 The eighth admonition belonging to all the godly, that seeing God calleth all men to the Gospel, and Christ hath so justified us, that he hath also sanctified us, we must all of us give ourselves to true godliness and righteousness, setting before us a sure hope of that immeasurable glory: which thing must in such sort be beaten into their heads, that the gainsayers also must be reproved, by the authority of the mighty God.
- **i.** Titus 2:12 Lusts of the flesh, which belong to the present state of this life and world.
- **j.** Titus 2:13 Christ is here most plainly called that mighty God, and his appearance and coming is called by the figure Metonymy, our hope.
- **k.** Titus 2:14 As it were a thing peculiarly laid up for himself.
- **l.** Titus 2:15 With all authority possible.

TITUS 2

1. Eph. 5:23
2. Eph. 6:5 / Col. 3:22 / 1 Pet. 2:18
3. 1 Cor. 1:2 / Col. 1:22

birth, and the renewing of the [d]holy Ghost, **6** Which he shed on us abundantly,
through Jesus Christ our Savior, **7** That we, being justified by his grace, should
be made heirs according to the hope of eternal life. **8** [e]This is a true saying, and
these things I will thou shouldest affirm, that they which have believed God, mi-
ght be careful to show forth [f]good works. These things are good and profitable
unto men. **9** [4]But stay foolish questions, and genealogies, and contentions, and
brawlings about the Law: for they are unprofitable and vain. **10** [g]Reject him that
is an heretic, after once or twice admonition, **11** Knowing that he that is such,
is perverted, and sinneth, being damned of his own self. **12** [h]When I shall send
Artemas unto thee, or Tychicus, be diligent to come to me unto Nicopolis: for I
have determined there to winter. **13** Bring Zenas the expounder of the Law,
and Apollos on their journey diligently, that they lack nothing. **14** And let ours
also learn to show forth good works for necessary uses, that they be not unfrui-
tful. **15** All that are with me, salute thee. Greet them that love us in the faith.
Grace be with you all. Amen. To Titus, elect the first Bishop of the Church of
the Cretans, written from Nicopolis in Macedonia.

TITUS 3

- **a.** Titus 3:1 He declareth particularly and severally, that which he said before generally, noting out certain chief and principal duties, which men owe to men, and especially subjects to their magistrates.
- **b.** Titus 3:3 He confirmeth again the former exhortation, by propounding the free benefit of our regeneration, the pledge whereof is our Baptism.
- **c.** Titus 3:5 Word for word, of works which are done in righteousness: and this place doth fully refute the doctrine of merits.
- **d.** Titus 3:5 Which the virtue of the holy Ghost worketh.
- **e.** Titus 3:8 Again with great earnestness he beateth into our heads, how that we ought to give ourselves, to true godliness, and eschew all vain questions, which serve to nothing but to move strife and debate.
- **f.** Titus 3:8 Give themselves earnestly unto good works.
- **g.** Titus 3:10 The ministers of the word must at once cast off heretics, that is, such as stubbornly and seditiously disquiet the Church, and will give no ear to Ecclesiastical admonitions.
- **h.** Titus 3:12 Least of all, he writeth a word or two of private matters and commendeth certain men.

TITUS 3

1. Rom. 15:1 / 1 Pet. 2:13
2. 1 Cor. 6:11
3. 2 Tim. 1:9
4. 1 Tim. 1:4 / 1 Tim. 4:7 / 2 Tim. 2:23

THE EPISTLE OF PAUL TO PHILEMON

1 *Paul handling a base and small matter, yet according to his manner mounteth aloft unto God. 8 Sending again to Philemon his vagabond and thievish servant, he entreateth pardon for him, and very gravely preacheth of Christian equity.*

1 Paul a prisoner of Jesus Christ, and our brother Timothy, unto Philemon
our dear friend, and fellow helper, **2** And to our dear sister Apphia, and to Ar-
chippus our fellow soldier, and to the Church that is in thine house: **3** Grace be
with you, and peace from God our Father, and from the Lord Jesus Christ. **4** I
[1]give thanks to my God, making mention always of thee in my prayers, **5** When
I hear of thy love and faith, which thou hast toward the Lord Jesus, and toward all
Saints. **6** That the [a]fellowship of thy faith may be made effectual, and that what-
soever good thing is in you through Christ Jesus, may be [b]known. **7** For we have
great joy and consolation in thy love, because by thee, brother, the Saints [c]bowels
are comforted. **8** Wherefore, though I be very bold in Christ to command thee
that which is convenient, **9** [d]Yet for love's sake I rather beseech thee, though I
be as I am, even Paul aged, and even now a prisoner for Jesus Christ. **10** I bese-
ech thee for my son [2]Onesimus, whom I have begotten in my bonds, **11** Whi-
ch in times past was to thee unprofitable, but now profitable both to thee and to
me. **12** Whom I have sent again: thou therefore receive him, that is mine own
[e]bowels, **13** Whom I would have received with me, that in thy stead he might
have ministered unto me in the bonds of the Gospel. **14** But without thy mind
would I do nothing, that thy benefit should not be as it were of [f]necessity, but wil-
lingly. **15** It may be that he therefore [g]departed for [h]a season, that thou shoul-
dest receive him forever, **16** Not now as a servant, but above a servant, even as
a brother beloved, specially to me: how much more then unto thee, both in the
[i]flesh and in the Lord? **17** If therefore thou count our things common, receive
him as myself. **18** If he hath hurt thee, or oweth thee ought, that put on my
accounts. **19** I Paul have written this with mine own hand: I will recompense
it, albeit I do not say to thee, that thou owest moreover unto me even thine own
self. **20** [j]Yea, brother, let me obtain this pleasure of thee in the Lord: comfort my
bowels in the Lord. **21** Trusting in thine obedience, I wrote unto thee knowing
that thou wilt do even more than I say, **22** Moreover also prepare me lodging:
for I trust through your prayers I shall be freely given unto you. **23** There salute
thee Epaphras my fellow prisoner in Christ Jesus, **24** Mark, Aristarchus, Demas
and Luke, my fellow helpers. **25** The grace of our Lord Jesus Christ be with your
spirit, Amen. Written from Rome to Philemon, and sent by Onesimus a servant.

PHILEMON 1

- **a.** Philemon 1:6 By fellowship of faith, he meaneth those duties of charity which are bestowed upon the Saints, and flow forth of an effectual faith.
- **b.** Philemon 1:6 That by this means all men may perceive how rich you are in Christ, to wit, in faith, charity, and all bountifulness.
- **c.** Philemon 1:7 Because thou didst so dutifully and cheerfully refresh the Saints, that they conceived inwardly a marvelous joy: for by this word Bowels is meant not only the inward feeling of wants and miseries that men have one of another's state, but also that joy and comfort which entereth into the very bowels, as though the heart were refreshed and comforted.
- **d.** Philemon 1:9 An example of a Christian exercise and commendation for another man.
- **e.** Philemon 1:12 As mine own son, and as if I had begotten him of mine own body.
- **f.** Philemon 1:14 That thou mightest not seem to have lent me thy servant upon constraint, but willingly.
- **g.** Philemon 1:15 Thus he assuageth the harder kind of speech, which is to say, he ran away.
- **h.** Philemon 1:15 For a little time.
- **i.** Philemon 1:16 Because he is thy servant, as other servants are, and because he is the Lord's servant, so that thou must needs love him both for the Lord's sake, and for thine own sake.
- **j.** Philemon 1:20 Good brother let me obtain this benefit at thine hand.

PHILEMON 1

1. 1 Thess. 1:2 / 2 Thess. 1:3
2. Col. 4:9

THE EPISTLE TO THE
HEBREWS

The drift and end of this Epistle, is to show that Jesus Christ the Son of God both God and man, is that true eternal and only Prophet, King, and high Priest, that was shadowed by the figures of the old Law, and is now indeed exhibited: of whom the whole Church ought to be taught, governed and sanctified.

1

2 To show that the doctrine which Christ brought, is most excellent, in that it is the knitting up of all prophecies, 4 he advanceth him above the Angels: 10 And proveth by divers testimonies of the Scripture, that he far passeth all others.

1 At [a]sundry times and in divers manners God spake in the old time to
our fathers by the Prophets: in these [b]last days he hath spoken unto us by his
[c]Son, **2** [d]Whom he hath made [e]heir of all things, by whom also he made the
[f]worlds, **3** [1]Who being the [g]brightness of the glory, and the engraved form of his
[h]person, and [i]bearing up all things by his mighty word: [j]hath by himself purged our
sins: and [k]sitteth at the right hand of the Majesty in the highest places, **4** [l]And
is made so much more excellent than the Angels, inasmuch as he hath obtained
a more excellent [m]Name than they. **5** [n]For unto which of the Angels said he at
any time, [2]Thou art my Son, [o]this day begat I thee? and again, I [3]will be his Father,
and he shall be my Son: **6** And [p]again, when he bringeth in his first begotten
Son into the world, he saith, [4]And let all the Angels of God worship him. **7** And
of the Angels he saith, [5]He maketh the spirits his [q]messengers, and his ministers a
flame [r]of fire. **8** But unto the Son he saith, [6]O God, thy [s]throne is forever [t]and
ever: the scepter of thy kingdom is a [u]scepter of righteousness. **9** Thou hast loved
righteousness and [v]hated iniquity. Wherefore God, even thy God, hath [w]anoin-
ted thee with the oil of gladness, above thy [x]fellows. **10** And, [7]Thou, Lord, in
the beginning hast [y]established the earth, and the heavens are the works of thine
hands. **11** They shall perish, but thou dost remain, and they all shall wax old as
doth a garment, **12** And as a vesture shalt thou fold them up, and they shall be
changed: but thou art the same, and thy years shall not fail. **13** Unto which also
of the Angels said he at any time, [8]Sit at my right hand, till I make thine enemies
thy footstool? **14** Are they not all [z]ministering spirits, sent forth to minister, for
their sakes which shall be heirs of salvation?

2

1 Thereof he inferreth, that good heed must be given to Christ's doctrine: 9 And he setteth him out unto us even as our brother in our flesh, that we may with a good will yield up ourselves wholly unto him.

1 Wherefore [a]we ought diligently to give heed to the things which [b]we have
heard, lest at any time we [c]run out. **2** For if the [d]word spoken by Angels was
steadfast, and every transgression, and disobedience received a just recompense
of reward, **3** How shall we escape if we neglect so great salvation, [e]which at
the first began to be preached by the Lord, and afterward was confirmed unto
us by [f]them that heard him. **4** [1]God bearing witness thereto, both with [g]signs
and wonders, and with divers miracles, and gifts of the holy Ghost, according to
his own will? **5** [h]For he hath not put in subjection unto the Angels the [i]world
to come, whereof we speak. **6** [j]But [2]one in a certain place witnessed, saying,
[k]What is man, that thou shouldest be mindful of him? or the [l]son of man, that
thou wouldest consider him? **7** Thou [m]madest him a little inferior to the Angels:
thou crownedst him with [n]glory and honor, and hast set him above the works of
thine hands. **8** [3]Thou hast put all things in subjection under his feet. And in that
he hath put all things in subjection under him, he left nothing that should not be
subject unto him. [o]But we yet see not all things subdued unto him, **9** [p]But we
[q]see Jesus crowned with glory and honor, [4]which was made little [r]inferior to the
Angels, [s]through the [t]suffering of death, that by God's grace he might [u]taste dea-
th for [v]all men. **10** [w]For it became [x]him, for whom are all these things, and by

---

HEBREWS 1

a. Hebrews 1:1 The first part of the general proposition of this Epistle: the Son of God is indeed that Prophet or teacher, which hath actually now performed that that God after a sort and in shadows signified by his Prophets, and hath fully opened his Father's will to the world.

b. Hebrews 1:1 So that the former declaration made by the Prophets was not full, and nothing must be added to this latter.

c. Hebrews 1:1 Which one Son is God and man.

d. Hebrews 1:2 The second part of the same proposition: The same Son is appointed by the Father to be our King and Lord, by whom also he made all things, and in whom only he setteth forth his glory, yea and himself also to be beholden of us, who beareth up and sustaineth all things by his will and pleasure.

e. Hebrews 1:2 Possessor and equal compartner of all things with the Father.

f. Hebrews 1:2 That is, whatsoever hath been at any time, is, or shall be.

g. Hebrews 1:3 He in whom that glory and Majesty of the Father shineth, who is otherwise infinite, and cannot be beholden.

h. Hebrews 1:3 His father's person.

i. Hebrews 1:3 Sustaineth, defendeth and cherisheth.

j. Hebrews 1:3 The third part of the same proposition. The same Son executed the office of the high Priest in offering up himself, and is our only and most mighty Mediator in heaven.

k. Hebrews 1:3 This showeth that the savor of that his sacrifice is not only most acceptable to the Father, but also is everlasting, and furthermore how far this high Priest passeth all the other high Priests.

l. Hebrews 1:4 Before he cometh to declare the office of Christ, he setteth forth the excellency of his person, and first of all he showeth him so to be man, that therewithal he is God also.

m. Hebrews 1:4 Dignity and honor.

n. Hebrews 1:5 He proveth and confirmeth the dignity of Christ manifested in the flesh by these six evident testimonies, whereby it appeareth that he far passeth all Angels, insomuch that he is called both Son, and God, in verses 5, 6, 7, 10, 13.

o. Hebrews 1:5 The Father begat the Son from everlasting, but that everlasting generation was made manifest and represented to the world in his time, and therefore he addeth this word Today.

p. Hebrews 1:6 The Lord was not content to have spoken it once, but repeateth it in another place.

q. Hebrews 1:7 Cherub, Ps 18:11.

r. Hebrews 1:7 Seraph, Isa. 6:2.

s. Hebrews 1:8 The throne is proper to the Prince, and not to the servant.

t. Hebrews 1:8 For everlasting, for this doubling of the word increaseth the signification of it beyond all measure.

u. Hebrews 1:8 The government of thy kingdom is righteous.

v. Hebrews 1:9 This kind of rehearsing in which the Jews use contraries, hath great force in it.

w. Hebrews 1:9 In that, that the word became flesh, by pouring the holy Ghost upon him without measure.

x. Hebrews 1:9 For he is the head and we are his members.

y. Hebrews 1:10 Madest the earth firm and sure.

z. Hebrews 1:14 By that name by which we commonly call Princes' messengers, he here calleth the spirits.

HEBREWS 1

1. Col. 1:15
2. Ps. 2:7 / Heb. 5:5
3. 2 Sam. 7:14
4. Ps. 97:7
5. Ps. 104:4
6. Ps. 55:7
7. Ps. 102:25
8. Ps. 110:1 / 1 Cor. 15:25 / Heb. 10:12,13

HEBREWS 2

a. Hebrews 2:1 Now as it were pausing with himself and showing to what end and purpose all these things were spoken, to wit, to understand by the excellency of Christ above all creatures, that his doctrine, majesty and Priesthood is most perfect, he useth an exhortation taken from a comparison.

b. Hebrews 2:1 He maketh himself an hearer.

c. Hebrews 2:1 They are said to let the word run out, which hold it not fast when they have heard it.

d. Hebrews 2:2 The Law which appointed punishment for the offenders: and which Paul saith was given by Angels, Gal. 3:19, and Stephen, Acts 7:53.

e. Hebrews 2:3 If the breach and trangression of the word spoken by Angels was not suffered unpunished, much less shall it be lawful for us to neglect the Gospel which the Lord of Angels preached, and was confirmed by the voice of the Apostles, and with so many signs and wonders from heaven, and especially with so great and mighty working of the holy Ghost.

f. Hebrews 2:3 By the Apostles.

g. Hebrews 2:4 This is the true end of miracles. Now they are called signs, because they appear one thing, and represent another: and they are called wonders, because they represent some strange and unaccustomed things and virtues, because they give us a glimpse of God's mighty power.

h. Hebrews 2:5 If it were an heinous matter to contemn the Angels which are but servants, much more heinous is it to contemn that most mighty King of the restored world.

i. Hebrews 2:5 The world to come, whereof Christ is Father, Isa. 9:6, or the Church, which as a new world, was to be gathered together by the Gospel.

j. Hebrews 2:6 He showeth that the use of this kingly dignity consisteth herein, that men might not only in Christ recover that dignity which they have lost, but also might be through him advanced above all things, which dignity of men David describeth most excellently.

k. Hebrews 2:6 What is there in man that thou shouldest have so great regard of him, and do him that honor?

l. Hebrews 2:6 He calleth all the citizens of that heavenly kingdom as they are considered in themselves, before that God giveth them the liberty, of that city in Christ, Man, and Son of man.

m. Hebrews 2:7 This is the first honor of the citizens of the world to come, that they are next to the Angels.

n. Hebrews 2:7 For they shall be in very great honor, when they shall be partakers of the kingdom. And he speaketh of the thing that shall be, as though it were already, because it is so certain.

o. Hebrews 2:8 An objection: But where is this so great rule and dominion?

p. Hebrews 2:9 The answer: this is already fulfilled in Jesus Christ our head, who was for a time for our sakes inferior to the Angels, being made man: but now is advanced into most high glory.

q. Hebrews 2:9 By his virtue and power which appeareth manifestly in the Church.

r. Hebrews 2:9 Who abased himself for a season, and took upon him the position of a servant.

s. Hebrews 2:9 He showeth the cause of this subjection, to wit, to taste of death for our sakes, that so doing the part of a redeemer, he might not only be our Prophet and King, but also our high Priest.

t. Hebrews 2:9 That he might die.

u. Hebrews 2:9 Feel death.

v. Hebrews 2:9 Herein consisteth the force of the argument: for we could not at length be glorified with him, unless he was abased for us even all the faithful. And by this occasion the Apostle cometh to the other part of the declaration of Christ's person, wherein he proveth him to be in such sort God, and he is also man.

w. Hebrews 2:10 He proveth moreover by other arguments, why it behooveth the Son of God who is true God as he proveth a little before to become man notwithstanding, subject to all miseries, sin only except.

whom are all these things, [y]seeing that he brought many children unto glory, [z]that he should consecrate the [aa]Prince of their salvation through afflictions. **11** [ab]For he that [ac]sanctifieth, and they which are sanctified, are all of [ad]one: wherefore he is not ashamed to call them brethren, **12** [ae]Saying, [5]I will declare thy Name unto my brethren: in the midst of the Church will I sing praises to thee. **13** [af]And again, [6]I will put my [ag]trust in him. And again, [7,ah]Behold, here am I, and the children which God hath given me. **14** Forasmuch then as the children are [ai]partakers of flesh and blood, he also himself likewise took part with them, that he might destroy [8]through death, him that had the [aj]power of death, that is, the [ak]devil, **15** And that he might deliver all them, which for fear of [al]death were all their lifetime subject to bondage. **16** [am]For he in no sort took on him the [an]Angels' nature, but he took on him the [ao]seed of Abraham. **17** [ap]Wherefore in [aq]all things it behooved him to be made like unto his brethren, that he might be [ar]merciful, and a [as]faithful high Priest in things concerning God, that he might make reconciliation for the sins of the people. **18** For in that he suffered, and was [at]tempted, he is able to succor them that are tempted.

3

1 Now he showeth how far inferior Moses is to Christ, 5, 6 even so much as the servant to the Master: and so he bringeth in certain exhortations and threatenings taken out of David, 8 against such as either stubbornly resist, 12 or else are very slow to obey.

1 Therefore, [a]holy brethren, partakers of the heavenly vocation, consider the [b]Apostle and high Priest of our [c]profession Christ Jesus: **2** [d]Who was faithful to him that hath [e]appointed him, [f]even as [1]Moses was in all his house. **3** [g]For this man is counted worthy of more glory than Moses, inasmuch as he which hath builded the house, hath more honor than the house. **4** For every house is builded of some man, and he that hath built all things, is God. **5** [h]Now Moses verily was faithful in all his house, as a servant, for a witness of the things which should be spoken after. **6** But Christ is as the Son, over his own house, [i]whose [j]house we are, if we hold fast that [k]confidence and that rejoicing of that hope unto the end. **7** Wherefore, as the holy Ghost saith, [2]Today if ye [l]shall hear his voice, **8** Harden not your hearts, as in the [m]provocation, according to the day of the temptation in the wilderness, **9** Where your fathers tempted me, proved me, and saw my works forty years long. **10** Wherefore I was grieved with that generation, and said, They [n]err ever in their heart, neither have they known my ways. **11** Therefore I swear in my wrath, If they shall enter into my rest. **12** [o]Take heed brethren, lest at any time there be in any of you an evil heart, and unfaithful, to depart away from the living God. **13** But exhort one another daily, [p]while it is called today, lest any of you be hardened through the deceitfulness of sin. **14** [q]For we are made partakers of Christ, if we keep sure unto the end that [r]beginning, wherewith we are upholden, **15** [s]So long as it is said, Today if ye hear his voice, harden not your hearts, as in the provocation. **16** For some when they heard, provoked him to anger: howbeit, not all that came out of Egypt by Moses. **17** But with whom was he displeased forty years? Was he not displeased with them that sinned, [3]whose carcasses fell in the wilderness? **18** And to whom swear he that they should not enter into his rest, but unto them that obeyed not? **19** So we see that they could not enter in, because of unbelief.

4

1 He joineth exhortation with threatening, lest they, even as their fathers were be deprived of the rest offered unto them, 11 but that they endeavor to enter into it. 14 And so he beginneth to entreat of Christ's Priesthood.

1 Let us fear therefore, lest at any time by forsaking the promise of entering into his rest, any of you should seem to be deprived. **2** [a]For unto us was the Gospel preached as also unto them: but the word that they heard, profited not them, because it was not [b]mixed with faith in those that heard it. **3** [c]For we which have believed, do enter into rest, as he said to the other, [1]As I have sworn in my wrath, If they shall enter into my rest: although the works were finished from the foundation of the world. **4** For he spake in a certain place of the seventh day on

---

x. Hebrews 2:10 God.

y. Hebrews 2:10 First of all, because the Father, to whose glory all these things are to be referred, purposed to bring many sons unto glory. And how could he have men for his sons, unless his only begotten Son had become brother to men?

z. Hebrews 2:10 Secondly, The Father determined to bring those sons to glory, to wit, out of that ignominy wherein they lay before. Therefore the Son should not have been seen plainly to be made man, unless he had been made like unto other men, that he might come to glory in the selfsame way, by which he should bring others: yea rather, it became him which was Prince of the salvation of others, to be consecrated above others, through those afflictions, Prophet, King, and Priest, which are the parts of that principality for the salvation of others.

aa. Hebrews 2:10 The Chieftain, who as he is chiefest in dignity, so is he the first begotten from among the dead, amongst many brethren.

ab. Hebrews 2:11 The ground of both the former arguments: for neither should we be sons through him, neither could he be consecrated through afflictions, unless he hath been made man like unto us. But because this Sonhood dependeth not upon nature only, for no man is accompted the son of God, unless that besides that he is a son of a man, he be also Christ's brother, which is by sanctification, that is, by becoming one with Christ, who sanctifieth us through faith therefore the Apostle maketh mention of the sanctifier, to wit, of Christ, and of them that are sanctified, to wit, of all the faithful, whom therefore Christ vouchsafeth to call brethren.

ac. Hebrews 2:11 He useth the time that now is, to show us that we are yet still going on, and increasing in this sanctification, and by sanctification he meaneth our separation from the rest of the world, our cleansing from sin, and our dedication wholly unto God, all which Christ alone worketh in us.

ad. Hebrews 2:11 One, of one selfsame nature of man.

ae. Hebrews 2:12 That which he taught before of the incarnation of the sanctifier, he applieth to the prophetical office.

af. Hebrews 2:13 He applieth the same to the kingly power of Christ in delivering his from the power of the devil and death.

ag. Hebrews 2:13 I will commit myself to him, and to his defense.

ah. Hebrews 2:13 This Isaiah speaketh of himself and his disciples, but betokening thereby all ministers, as also his disciples signify the whole Church. And therefore seeing Christ is the head of the Prophets and ministers, these words are more rightly verified of him, than of Isaiah.

ai. Hebrews 2:14 Are made of flesh and blood which is a frail and brittle nature.

aj. Hebrews 2:14 The devil is said to have the power of death, because he is the author of sin: and from sin cometh death, and for this cause he eggeth us daily to sin.

ak. Hebrews 2:14 He speaketh of one as of the Prince, joining to him secretly all his angels.

al. Hebrews 2:15 By death thou must understand here that death which is joined with the wrath of God, as it must needs be, if it be without Christ, then there can be nothing devised more miserable.

am. Hebrews 2:16 He expoundeth those words of flesh and blood, showing that Christ is true man, and not by turning his divine nature, but by taking on man's nature. And he nameth Abraham, respecting the promises made to Abraham in this behalf.

an. Hebrews 2:16 The nature of Angels.

ao. Hebrews 2:16 The very nature of man.

ap. Hebrews 2:17 He applieth the same to the Priesthood, for which he should not have benefit, unless he had become man, and that like unto us in all things, sin only except.

aq. Hebrews 2:17 Not only as touching nature, but qualities also.

ar. Hebrews 2:17 That he might be truly touched with the feeling of our miseries.

as. Hebrews 2:17 Doing his office sincerely.

at. Hebrews 2:18 Was tried and egged to wickedness by the devil.

HEBREWS 2

1. Mark 16:20
2. Ps. 8:6
3. 1 Cor. 15:27
4. Phil. 2:8
5. Ps. 22:25
6. Ps. 18:2
7. Isa. 1:18
8. Hos. 13:14 / 1 Cor. 15:55

HEBREWS 3

a. Hebrews 3:1 Having laid the foundation, that is to say, declared and proved both the natures of one selfsame Christ, he giveth him three offices, to wit, the office of a Prophet, king, and Priest: and as touching the office of teaching and governing, compareth them with Moses and Joshua, unto verse 14 of the next Chapter, and with Aaron touching the Priesthood. And he propoundeth that which he purposeth to speak of, with a most grave exhortation, that all our faith may tend to Christ, as to the only everlasting teacher, governor, and high Priest.

b. Hebrews 3:1 The Ambassador or messenger, as Rom. 1:5, he is called the minister of circumcision.

c. Hebrews 3:1 Of the doctrine of the Gospel which we profess.

d. Hebrews 3:2 He confirmeth this exhortation with two reasons, first of all because Christ Jesus was appointed such an one of God: secondly, because he thoroughly executed the offices that his Father enjoined him.

e. Hebrews 3:2 Apostle and high Priest.

f. Hebrews 3:2 Now he cometh to the comparison with Moses, and he maketh them like one to the other in this, that they were both appointed rulers over God's house, and executed faithfully their office: but by and by after he showeth that there is great unlikeness in that similitude.

g. Hebrews 3:3 The first comparison: The builder of the house is better than the house itself, therefore is Christ better than Moses. The reason of the consequent is this: because the builder of this house is God, which cannot be attributed to Moses: and therefore Moses was not properly the builder, but a part of the house: but Christ as Lord and God, made all this house.

h. Hebrews 3:5 Another comparison: Moses was a faithful servant in this house, that is, in the Church, seeing the Lord that was to come, but Christ ruleth and governeth his house as Lord.

i. Hebrews 3:6 He applieth the former doctrine to this end, exhorting all men by the words of David to hear the Son himself speak, and to give full credit to his words, seeing that otherwise they cannot enter into that eternal rest.

j. Hebrews 3:6 To wit, Christ's.

k. Hebrews 3:6 He calleth that excellent effect of faith whereby we cry, Abba, that is, Father confidence, and to confidence he joineth hope.

l. Hebrews 3:7 So that God was to speak once again after Moses.

m. Hebrews 3:8 In the day that they vexed the Lord, or strove with him.

n. Hebrews 3:10 They are brutish and mad.

o. Hebrews 3:12 Now weighing the words of David, he showeth first by this word, Today that we must not neglect the occasion while we have it: for that word is not to be restrained to David's time, but it comprehendeth all the time wherein God calleth us.

p. Hebrews 3:13 While today lasteth, that is to say, so long as the Gospel is offered to us.

q. Hebrews 3:14 Now he considereth these words, If you hear his voice, etc., showing that they are spoken and meant of the hearing of faith, against which he setteth hardening through unbelief.

r. Hebrews 3:14 That beginning of trust and confidence: and after the manner of the Hebrews, he calleth that beginning, which is chiefest.

s. Hebrews 3:15 So long as this voice soundeth out.

HEBREWS 3

1. Num. 12:7
2. Ps. 95:8 / Heb. 4:7
3. Num. 14:37

HEBREWS 4

a. Hebrews 4:2 By these words, His voice, he showeth that David meant the preaching of Christ, who was then also preached, for Moses and the Prophets respected none other.

b. Hebrews 4:2 He compareth the preaching of the Gospel to drink, which being drunk, that is to say, heard, profiteth nothing, unless it be tempered with faith.

c. Hebrews 4:3 Lest any man should object, that those words were meant of the Land of Canaan, and of Moses' doctrine, and therefore cannot well be drawn to Christ, and to eternal life, the Apostle showeth that there are two manner of rests spoken of in the Scriptures: the one, of the seventh day, wherein God is said to have rested from all his works: the other is said to be that same, whereinto Joshua led the people: but this rest is not the last rest whereto we are called and that he proveth by two reasons. For seeing that David so long time after, speaking to the people which were then placed in the land of Canaan, useth these words, Today, and threateneth them still that they shall not enter into the rest of God, which refuseth then the voice of God that sounded in their ears, we must needs say that he meant another time than the time of Moses, and another rest than the rest of the land of Canaan: And that is, that everlasting rest, wherein we begin to live to God, after that the race of this life ceaseth: as God resteth the seventh day from those his works, that is to say, from making the world. Moreover, the Apostle therewithal signifieth that the way to this rest,

this wise, [2]And God did rest the seventh day from all his works. **5** And in this place again, If they shall enter into my rest. **6** Seeing therefore it remaineth that some must enter thereinto, and they to whom it was first preached, entered not therein for unbelief's sake: **7** Again he appointed in David a certain day, by To-day, after so long a time, saying, as it is said, [3]This day, if ye hear his voice, harden not your hearts. **8** For if [d]Jesus had given them rest, then would he not after this have spoken of another day. **9** There remaineth therefore a rest to the people of God. **10** [e]For he that is entered into his rest, hath also ceased from his own works, as God did from his. **11** [f]Let us study therefore to enter into that rest, lest [g]any man fall after the same example of disobedience. **12** [h]For the [i]word of God is [j]lively, and mighty in operation, and sharper than any two edged sword, and entereth through, even unto the dividing asunder of the [k]soul and the [l]spirit, and of the joints, and the marrow, and is a discerner of the thoughts, and the intents of the heart. **13** Neither is there any creature, which is not manifest in [m]his sight: but all things are naked and open unto his eyes, with whom we have to do. **14** [n]Seeing then that we have a great high Priest, which is entered into heaven, even Jesus the Son of God, let us [o]hold fast our profession. **15** [p]For we have not an high Priest, which cannot be touched with the feeling of our infirmities, but was in all things tempted in like sort, yet without sin. **16** Let us therefore go boldly unto the throne of grace, that we may receive mercy, and find grace to help in time of need.

5

1 First he showeth the duty of the high Priest: 5 Secondly, that Christ is appointed of God to be our high Priest, 7 and that he hath fulfilled all things belonging thereunto.

1 For [a]every high Priest is taken from among men, and is ordained for men, in things pertaining to God, [b]that he may offer both [c]gifts and [d]sacrifices for sins. **2** Which is [e]able sufficiently to have compassion [f]on them that are ignorant, and that are out of the way, because that he also is [g]compassed with infirmity, **3** And for the same sake he is bound to offer for sins, as well for his own part, as for the peoples. **4** [1,h]And no man taketh this honor unto himself, but he that is called of God, as was Aaron. **5** So likewise Christ took not to himself this honor to be made the high Priest, but he that said unto him, [2]Thou art my son, this day begat I thee, gave it him. **6** As he also in another place speaketh, [3]Thou art a Priest forever, after the [i]order of Melchizedek, **7** [j]Who in the [k]days of his flesh did offer up prayers and supplications, with strong crying and tears unto him, that was able to [l]save him from death, and was also heard in that which he feared. **8** And though he were the Son, yet [m]learned he obedience, by the things which he suffered. **9** [n]And being [o]consecrated, was made the author of eternal salvation unto all them that obey him: **10** And is called of God an high Priest after the order of Melchizedek. **11** [p]Of whom we have many things to say, which are hard to be uttered, because ye are dull of hearing. **12** [q]For when as concerning the time ye ought to be teachers, yet have ye need again that we teach you what are the first principles of the word of God: and are become such as have need of milk, and not of strong meat. **13** For everyone that useth milk, is inexpert in the [r]word of righteousness: for he is a babe. **14** But strong meat belongeth to them that are of age, which through long custom have their [s]wits exercised, to discern both good and evil.

6

1 He briefly toucheth the childish slothfulness of the Hebrews, 4 and terrifieth them with severe threatenings: 7 He stirreth them up to endeavor in time to go forward: 9 He hopeth well of them: 13 He allegeth Abraham's example: 17 and compareth faith that taketh hold on the word, 19 unto an anchor.

1 Therefore, leaving the doctrine of the [a]beginning of Christ, let us be led forward unto perfection, [b]not laying again the foundation of repentance from dead works, and of faith toward God, **2** Of the doctrine of baptisms, and laying on of hands, and of the resurrection from the dead, and of eternal judgment. **3** And this will we do if God permit. **4** [1,c] For it is [d]impossible that they which were once lightened, and have [e]tasted of the heavenly gift, and were made partakers of the holy Ghost, **5** And have tasted of the good word of God, and of the powers of the world to come, **6** If they fall away, should be renewed again by repentance: seeing they [f]crucify again to themselves the Son of God, and make a mock of him. **7** [g]For the earth which drinketh in the rain that cometh oft upon it, and bringeth forth herbs meet for them by whom it is dressed, receiveth blessing of God. **8** But that which beareth thorns and briars, is reproved, and is near unto cursing, whose end is to be burned. **9** [h]But beloved, we have persuaded ourselves better things of you, and such as accompany salvation, though we thus speak. **10** [i]For God is not unrighteous, that he should forget your work, and labor of love, which ye showed toward his Name, in that ye have ministered unto the Saints, and yet minister. **11** And we desire that every one of you show the same diligence, to the full assurance of hope unto the end, **12** [j]That ye be not slothful, but followers of them, which through faith and patience, inherit the promises. **13** [k]For when God made the promise to Abraham, because he had no greater to swear by, he swore by himself, **14** Saying, [2]Surely I will [l]abundantly bless thee, and multiply thee marvelously. **15** And so after that he had tarried patiently, he enjoyed the promise. **16** For men verily swear by him that is greater

---

which Moses and the land of Canaan and all that order of the Law did shadow, is opened in the Gospel only.

d. Hebrews 4:8 He speaketh of Joshua the son of Nun: and as the land of Canaan was a figure of our true rest, so was Joshua a figure of Christ.

e. Hebrews 4:10 As God rested the seventh day, so must we rest from our works, that is, from such as proceed from our corrupt nature.

f. Hebrews 4:11 He returneth to an exhortation.

g. Hebrews 4:11 Lest any man become a like example of infidelity.

h. Hebrews 4:12 An amplification taken from the nature of the word of God, the power whereof is such, that it entereth even to the deepest and most inward and secret parts of the heart, wounding them deadly that are stubborn, and plainly quickening the believers.

i. Hebrews 4:12 The doctrine of God which is preached both in the Law and in the Gospel.

j. Hebrews 4:12 He calleth the word of God lively by reason of the effects it worketh in them, to whom it is preached.

k. Hebrews 4:12 He calleth that the soul, which hath the affections resident in it.

l. Hebrews 4:12 By the spirit he meaneth that nobelest part which is called the mind.

m. Hebrews 4:13 In God's sight.

n. Hebrews 4:14 Now he entereth into the comparison of Christ's Priesthood with Aaron's, and declareth even in the very beginning the marvelous excellency of this Priesthood, calling him the Son of God and placing him in the seat of God in heaven, plainly and evidently setting him against Aaron's Priests, and the transitory tabernacle: which comparisons he setteth forth afterward more at large.

o. Hebrews 4:14 And let it not go out of your hands.

p. Hebrews 4:15 Lest he might seem by this great glory of our high Priest, to stay and stop us from going unto him, he addeth straightways after, that he is notwithstanding our brother indeed, as he proved it also before and that he accounteth all our miseries, as his own, to call us boldly to him.

HEBREWS 4

1. Ps. 95:11

2. Gen. 2:2 / Deut. 5:14

3. Heb. 3:7

HEBREWS 5

a. Hebrews 5:1 The first part of the first comparison of Christ's high Priesthood, with Aaron's: Other high Priests are taken from among men, and are called after the order of men.

b. Hebrews 5:1 The first part of the second comparison, Others as weak: are made high Priests, to the end that feeling the same infirmity in themselves which is in all the rest of the people, they should in their own and the people's name offer gifts and sacrifices, which are witnesses of common faith, and repentance.

c. Hebrews 5:1 Offering of things without life.

d. Hebrews 5:1 Beasts which were killed, but especially in the sacrifices for sins and offenses.

e. Hebrews 5:2 Fit and meet.

f. Hebrews 5:2 On them that are sinful: for in the Hebrew tongue, under ignorance and error is every sin meant, even that sin that is voluntary.

g. Hebrews 5:2 For that he himself beareth about with him a nature subject to the same discommodities and vices.

h. Hebrews 5:4 The third comparison which is whole: The others are called of God, and so was Christ, but in another order than Aaron: for Christ is called the Son, begotten of God, and a Priest forever after the order of Melchizedek.

i. Hebrews 5:6 After the likeness or manner as it is afterward declared, Heb. 7:15.

j. Hebrews 5:7 The other part of the second comparison: Christ being exceedingly afflicted and exceedingly merciful, asked not for his sins, for he had none, but for his fear, and obtained his request, and offered himself for all his.

k. Hebrews 5:7 While he lived here with us in our weak and frail nature.

l. Hebrews 5:7 To deliver him from death.

m. Hebrews 5:8 He learned indeed what it is to have a Father, whom a man must obey.

n. Hebrews 5:9 The other part of the first comparison: Christ was consecrate of God the Father as the author of our salvation, and an high Priest forever, and therefore he is so a man that notwithstanding he is far above all men.

o. Hebrews 5:9 See Heb. 2:10.

p. Hebrews 5:11 A digression, until he comes to the beginning of the seventh chapter: wherein he partly holdeth the Hebrews in the diligent consideration of those things which he hath said, and partly prepareth them to the understanding of those things whereof he will speak.

q. Hebrews 5:12 An example of an Apostolic chiding.

r. Hebrews 5:13 In the word that teacheth righteousness.

s. Hebrews 5:14 All their power whereby they understand and judge.

HEBREWS 5

1. 1 Chron. 13:10 / 1 Chron. 23:13

2. Ps. 2:7 / Heb. 1:5

3. Ps. 110:4 / Heb. 7:17

HEBREWS 6

a. Hebrews 6:1 The first principles of Christian religion, which we call the Catechism.

b. Hebrews 6:1 Certain principles of a Catechism, which comprehend the sum of the doctrine of the Gospel, were given in few words and briefly to the rude and ignorant, to wit, the profession of repentance and faith in God: the articles of which doctrine, were demanded of them which were not as yet received members of the Church, at the days appointed for Baptism: and of the children of the faithful which were baptized in their infancy: when hands were laid upon them. And of those articles, two are by name recited: the resurrection of the flesh, and the eternal judgment.

c. Hebrews 6:4 He addeth a vehemency to his exhortation, and a most sharp threatening of the certain destruction that shall come to them which fall from God and his religion.

d. Hebrews 6:4 He speaketh of a general backsliding, and such as do altogether fall away from the faith, and not of sins which are committed through the frailty of man against the first and the second table.

e. Hebrews 6:4 We must mark the force of this word, for it is one thing to believe as Lydia did, whose heart God opened, Acts 16:13, and another thing to have some taste.

f. Hebrews 6:6 As men that hate Christ, and as though they crucified him again make him a mocking stock to all the world, and that to their own destruction, as Julian the Apostate or backslider did.

g. Hebrews 6:7 He setteth forth the former threatening with a similitude.

h. Hebrews 6:9 He mitigateth and assuageth all that sharpness, hoping better of them to whom he writeth.

i. Hebrews 6:10 He praiseth them for their charity, thereby encouraging them to go forward, and to hold out to the end.

j. Hebrews 6:12 He showeth what virtues chiefly they have need of to go forward constantly, and also to profit: to wit, of charity, and patience: and lest any man should object and say, that these things are impossible to be done, he willeth them to set before themselves the examples of their ancestors, and to follow them.

k. Hebrews 6:13 Another prick to prick them forward: Because the hope of the inheritance is certain, if we continue to the end, for God hath not only promised it, but also promised it with an oath.

l. Hebrews 6:14 I will heap up benefits most plentifully upon thee.

m. Hebrews 6:17 More than was needful, were it not for the wickedness of men which believe not God, no though he swear.

than themselves, and an oath for confirmation is among them an end of all strife. 17 So God, willing more [m]abundantly to show unto the heirs of promise the stableness of his counsel, bound himself by an oath, 18 That by two immutable things, wherein it is impossible that God should lie, we might have strong consolation, which have our refuge to lay hold upon that hope that is set before us, 19 [n]Which hope we have, as an anchor of the soul, but sure and steadfast, and it entereth into that which is within the veil. 20 [o]Whither the forerunner is for us entered in, even Jesus that is made an high Priest forever after the order of Melchizedek.

7

1 He hath hitherto stirred them up, to mark diligently what things are to be considered in Melchizedek, 15 wherein he is like unto Christ. 20 Wherefore the Law should give place to the Gospel.

1 For this [a]Melchizedek [1]was King of Salem, the Priest of the most high God, who met Abraham, as he returned from the slaughter of the Kings, and [b]blessed him: 2 To whom also Abraham gave the tithe of all things: who first is by interpretation King of righteousness: after that, he is also King of Salem, that is, King of peace, 3 [c]Without father, without mother, without kindred, and hath neither beginning of his days, neither end of life: but is likened unto the Son of God, and continueth a Priest forever. 4 [d]Now consider how great this man was, unto whom even the Patriarch Abraham gave the tithe of the spoils. 5 For verily they which are the children of Levi, which receive the office of the Priesthood, have a [2]commandment to take, according to the Law, tithes of the people that is, of their brethren though they [e]came out of the loins of Abraham. 6 But he whose kindred is not counted among them, received tithes of Abraham, and blessed him that had the promises. 7 And [f]without all contradiction the less is blessed of the greater. 8 And here men that die, receive tithes: but there he receiveth them, of whom it is witnessed, that he liveth. 9 [g]And to say as the thing is, Levi also which receiveth tithes, payeth tithes in Abraham. 10 For he was yet in the loins of his father Abraham, when Melchizedek met him. 11 [h]If therefore [i]perfection had been by the Priesthood of the Levites for under it the Law was established to the people what needed it furthermore, that another Priest should rise after the order of Melchizedek, and not to be called after the order of Aaron? 12 [j]For if the Priesthood be changed, then of necessity must there be a change of the [k]Law. 13 For he of whom these things are spoken, pertaineth unto another tribe, whereof no man [l]served at the altar. 14 For it is evident, that our Lord sprung out of Judah, concerning the which tribe Moses spake nothing, touching the Priesthood. 15 [m]And it is yet a more evident thing, because that after the similitude of Melchizedek, there is risen up another Priest, 16 [n]Which is not made Priest after the [o]Law of the carnal commandment, but after the power of the endless life. 17 For he testifieth thus, [3]Thou art a Priest forever, after the order of Melchizedek. 18 [p]For the [q]commandment that went afore, is disannulled, because of the weakness thereof, and unprofitableness. 19 For the Law made nothing perfect, but the bringing in of a better hope made perfect, whereby we draw near unto God. 20 [r]And forasmuch as it is not without an oath for these are made Priests without an oath: 21 But this is made with an oath by him that said unto him, [4]The Lord hath sworn, and will not repent, Thou art a Priest forever, after the order of Melchizedek. 22 By so much is Jesus made a surety of a better Testament. 23 [s]And among them many were made Priests, because they were not suffered to endure, by the reason of death. 24 But this man, because he endureth ever, hath a Priesthood, which [t]cannot pass from one to another. 25 Wherefore, he is [u]able also perfectly to save them that come unto God by him, seeing he ever liveth, to make intercession for them. 26 [v]For such an high Priest it became us to have, which is holy, harmless, undefiled, separate from sinners, and made higher than the heavens: 27 Which needeth not daily as those high Priests to offer up sacrifice, [5]first for his own sins, and then for the peoples: [w]for [x]that did he [y]once, when he offered up himself. 28 For the Law maketh men high Priests, which have infirmity: but the [z]word of the oath [aa]that [ab]was since the Law, maketh the Son, who is consecrated for evermore.

8

1 To prove more certainly that the ceremonies of the Law are abrogated, 5 he showeth that they were appointed to serve the heavenly pattern. 8 He bringeth in the place of Jeremiah, 13 to prove the amendment of the old covenant.

1 Now [a]of the things which we have spoken, this is the sum, that we have such an high Priest, that sitteth at the right hand of the throne of the Majesty in heavens, 2 [b]And is a minister of the [c]Sanctuary, [d]and of that [e]true Tabernacle which the Lord pitched, and not man. 3 [f]For every high Priest is ordained to offer both gifts and sacrifices: wherefore it was of necessity, that this man should have somewhat also to offer. 4 [g]For he were not a Priest, if he were on the earth, seeing there are Priests that according to the Law offer gifts, 5 Who serve unto the

---

n. Hebrews 6:19 He likeneth hope to an anchor: because that even as an anchor being cast into the bottom of the sea, stayeth the whole ship, so doth hope also enter even into the very secret places of heaven. And he maketh mention of the Sanctuary, alluding to the old tabernacle, and by this means returneth to the comparisons of the Priesthood of Christ with the Levitical.

o. Hebrews 6:20 He repeateth David's words, wherein all those comparisons whereof he hath before made mention, are signified, as he declareth in all the next chapter.

HEBREWS 6

1. Heb. 10:26 / Matt. 12:45 / 2 Pet. 1:10 **2.** Gen. 12:2 / Gen. 17:1 / Gen. 22:17

HEBREWS 7

a. Hebrews 7:1 Declaring those words, According to the order of Melchizedek, whereupon that comparison standeth of the Priesthood of Christ with the Levitical: first Melchizedek himself is considered as the figure of Christ, and these are the hands of that comparison, Melchizedek was a King and a Priest: and such an one indeed is Christ alone. He was a King of peace and righteousness: such an one indeed is Christ alone.

b. Hebrews 7:1 With a solemn and Priestly blessing.

c. Hebrews 7:3 Another figure: Melchizedek set before us to be considered as one without beginning and without ending, for neither his father, nor his mother, nor his ancestors, nor his death are written of: and such an one indeed is the Son of God, to wit, an everlasting Priest: as he is God, without mother wonderfully begotten: as he is man, without father wonderfully conceived.

d. Hebrews 7:4 Another figure: Melchizedek in consideration of his Priesthood was above Abraham, for he took tenths of him, and blessed him as a Priest: Such an one indeed is Christ, upon whom dependeth even Abraham's sanctification, and all the believers, and whom all men ought to worship and reverence as the author of all.

e. Hebrews 7:5 Were begotten by Abraham.

f. Hebrews 7:7 He speaketh of the public blessing which the Priests used.

g. Hebrews 7:9 A double amplification: The first, that Melchizedek took the tenths, as one immortal to wit, in respect, that he is the figure of Christ, for his death is in no place made mention of, and David setteth him forth as an everlasting Priest but the Levitical Priests, as mortal men, for they succeed one another: the second, that Levi himself was tithed in Abraham by Melchizedek. Therefore the Priesthood of Melchizedek that is, Christ's who is pronounced to be an everlasting Priest according to his order is more excellent than the Levitical.

h. Hebrews 7:11 The third treatise of this Epistle, wherein after he hath proved Christ to be a King, a Prophet, and a Priest, he now handleth distinctly the condition and excellency of all these offices, showing that all these were but shadows in all other, but in Christ they are true and perfect. And he beginneth with the Priesthood, wherewith also the former treatise ended, that by this means all the parts and members of this disputation, may better hang together. And first of all he proveth that the Levitical Priesthood was imperfect because another Priest is promised a long time after according to another order, that is to say, of another manner of rule and fashion.

i. Hebrews 7:11 If the priesthood of Levi could have made any man perfect.

j. Hebrews 7:12 He showeth how that by the institution of the new Priesthood, not only the imperfection of the Priesthood of Levi was declared, but also that it was changed for this: for these two cannot stand together, because that first appointment of the tribe of Levi, did shut forth the tribe of Judah, and made it also inferior to Levi: and this latter doth place the Priesthood in the tribe of Judah.

k. Hebrews 7:12 Of the institution of Aaron.

l. Hebrews 7:13 Had anything to do about the altar.

m. Hebrews 7:15 Lest any man might object, that the Priesthood indeed was translated from Levi to Judah, but yet notwithstanding the same remaineth still, he both weigheth and expoundeth these words of David, forever, according to the order of Melchizedek, whereby also a divers institution of priesthood is well perceived.

n. Hebrews 7:16 He proveth the diversity and excellency of the institution of Melchizedek's Priesthood, by this, that the priesthood of the Law did stand upon an outward and bodily anointing: but the sacrifice of Melchizedek is set out to be everlasting and more spiritual.

o. Hebrews 7:16 Not after the ordination, which commandeth frail and transitory things, as was done in Aaron's consecration, and all that whole Priesthood.

p. Hebrews 7:18 Again, that no man might object that the last Priesthood was added to make a perfect one, by the coupling of them both together, he proveth that the first was abrogated by the latter as unprofitable, and that by the nature of them both. For how could those corporal and transitory things sanctify us, either of themselves, or being joined with another?

q. Hebrews 7:18 The ceremonial law.

r. Hebrews 7:20 Another argument whereby he proveth that the Priesthood of Christ is better than the Priesthood of Levi, because his was established with an oath, but theirs was not so.

s. Hebrews 7:23 Another argument tending to the same purpose. The Levitical Priests as mortal men could not be everlasting, but Christ as he is everlasting, so hath he also an everlasting Priesthood making most effectual intercession for them which by him come unto God.

t. Hebrews 7:24 Which cannot pass away.

u. Hebrews 7:25 He is fit and meet.

v. Hebrews 7:26 Another argument: There are required in an high Priest innocency, and perfect pureness, which may separate him from sinners, for whom he offereth. But the Levitical high Priests shall not be found to be such, for they offer first for their own sins: But Christ only is such a one; and therefore the true and only high Priest.

w. Hebrews 7:27 Another argument which notwithstanding he handleth afterward: The Levitical Priests offered sacrifice after sacrifice, first for themselves, and then for the people. But Christ offered not for himself, but for others, not sacrifices, but himself, not oftentimes, but once. And this ought not to seem strange; saith he, forsomuch as they are weak, but this man is consecrated an everlasting Priest, and that by an oath.

x. Hebrews 7:27 That sacrifice which he offered.

y. Hebrews 7:27 It was so done, that it needeth not be repeated or offered again anymore.

z. Hebrews 7:28 The commandment of God which was bound with an oath.

aa. Hebrews 7:28 Another argument taken of the time: former things are taken away by the latter.

ab. Hebrews 7:28 Exhibited.

HEBREWS 7

1. Gen. 14:18 **2.** Num. 18:21 **3.** Ps. 110:4 / Heb. 5:6 **4.** Ps. 110:4 **5.** Lev. 16:11

HEBREWS 8

a. Hebrews 8:1 He briefly repeateth that, whereunto all these things are to be referred, to wit, we have a far other high Priest than those Levitical high Priests are, even such an one as sitteth at the right hand of the most high God in heaven.

b. Hebrews 8:2 They of Levi were high Priests in an earthly sanctuary, but Christ is in the heavenly.

c. Hebrews 8:2 Of heaven.

d. Hebrews 8:2 They of Levi exercised their Priesthood in a frail tabernacle, but Christ beareth about with him a far other tabernacle, to wit, his body which God himself made to be everlasting, as it shall afterward be declared, Heb. 9:11.

e. Hebrews 8:2 Of his body.

f. Hebrews 8:3 He bringeth a reason why it must needs be that Christ should have a body which he calleth a tabernacle which the Lord pight and not man to wit, that he might have what to offer: for otherwise he could not be an high Priest. And the selfsame body is both the tabernacle and the sacrifice.

g. Hebrews 8:4 He giveth a reason why he said that our high Priest is in the heavenly sanctuary and not in the earthly: because, saith he, if he were now on the earth, he could not minister in the earthly sanctuary, seeing there are yet

pattern and shadow of heavenly things, as Moses was warned by God when he was
about to finish the Tabernacle. [1]See, said he, that thou make all things according
to the pattern, showed to thee in the mount. **6** [h]But now our high Priest hath
obtained a more excellent office, inasmuch as he is the Mediator of a better Testa-
ment, which is established upon better promises. **7** [i]For if that first Testament
had been unblameable, no place should have been sought for the second. **8** For
in rebuking them he saith, [2]Behold, the days will come, saith the Lord, when I
shall make with the [j]house of Israel, and with the house of Judah a new Testa-
ment: **9** Not like the Testament that I made with their fathers, in the day that I
took them by the hand, to lead them out of the land of Egypt: for they continued
not in my Testament, and I regarded them not, saith the Lord. **10** For this is
the Testament that I will make with the house of Israel, After those days, saith the
Lord, I will put my Laws in their mind, and in their heart I will write them, and I
will be their God, and they shall be my people. **11** And they shall not teach every
man his neighbor, and every man his brother, saying, Know the Lord: for all shall
know me, from the least of them to the greatest of them. **12** For I will be merci-
ful to their unrighteousness, and I will remember their sins and their iniquities no
more. **13** [k]In that he saith a new Testament, he hath abrogated the old: now that
which is disannulled and waxed old, is ready to vanish away.

9

2 Comparing the form of the Tabernacle, 10 and the ceremonies of the Law, 11 unto the truth set out in Christ, 15 he concludeth that now there is no more need of another Priest, 24 because Christ himself had fulfilled these duties under the new covenant.

1 Then [a]the first Testament had also ordinances of religion, and a [b]worl-
dly Sanctuary, **2** For the first Tabernacle was made, wherein was the candlesti-
ck, and the table, and the showbread, which Tabernacle is called the Holy pla-
ces. **3** And after the [c]second veil was the Tabernacle, which is called the [d]Holiest
of all, **4** Which had the golden censer, and the Ark of the Testament overlaid
round about with gold, wherein the golden pot, which had Manna, was, and [1]Aa-
ron's rod that had budded, and the [2]tables of the Testament. **5** [3]And over the Ark
were the glorious Cherubims, shadowing the [e]mercy seat: of which things we will
not now speak particularly. **6** [f]Now when these things were thus ordained, the
Priest went always into the first Tabernacle, and accomplished the service. **7** But
into the second went the [4]high Priest alone, once every year, not without blood
which he offered for himself, and for the [g]ignorances of the people. **8** [h]Whereby
the holy Ghost this signified, that the way into the Holiest of all was not yet ope-
ned, while as yet the first tabernacle was standing, **9** [i]Which was a figure [j]for
that present time, wherein were offered gifts and sacrifices that could not make
holy, concerning the conscience, him that did the service, **10** [k]Which only sto-
od in meats and drinks, and divers washings, and carnal rites, [l]which were enjoi-
ned, until the time of reformation. **11** [m]But Christ being come an high Priest
of good things to come, [n]by a [o]greater and a more perfect Tabernacle, not made
with hands, that is, not of this building, **12** [p]Neither by the blood of [q]goats and
calves: but by his own blood entered he in once unto the holy place, and obtai-
ned eternal redemption for us. **13** [5,r]For if the blood of bulls and of goats, and
the ashes of an heifer, sprinkling them that are unclean, sanctifieth as touching
the [s]purifying of the flesh, **14** How much more shall the [6]blood of Christ whi-
ch through the eternal Spirit offered himself without fault to God, [7]purge your
conscience from [t]dead works, to serve the living God? **15** [u]And for this cause
is he the Mediator of the new Testament, that through [8]death which was for the
redemption of the transgressions that were in the former Testament, they which
were called, might receive the promise of eternal inheritance. **16** [v]For where a
Testament is, there must be the death of him that made the Testament. **17** [9]For
the Testament is confirmed when men are dead: for it is yet of no force as long as
he that made it, is alive. **18** [w]Wherefore, neither was the first ordained without
blood. **19** For when Moses had spoken every precept to the people, [x]according
to the Law, he took the blood of calves and of goats, with water and purple wool
and hyssop, and [y]sprinkled both the book, and all the people, **20** [10]Saying, This
is the blood of the Testament, which God hath appointed unto you. **21** More-
over, he sprinkled likewise the Tabernacle with blood also, and all the ministering
vessels, **22** And almost all things are by the Law purged with blood, and without
shedding of blood is no remission. **23** It was then necessary, that the [z]similitudes
of heavenly things should be purified with such things: but the heavenly things
themselves are purified with better sacrifices than are these. **24** [aa]For Christ is
not entered into the holy places that are made with hands, which are similitudes
of the true Sanctuary: but is entered into very heaven, to appear now in the sight
of God for us, **25** [ab]Not that he should offer himself often, as the high Priest
entered into the Holy place every year with others' blood, **26** [ac]For then must

---

Levitical Priests, which are appointed for him, that is to say, to be patterns of that perfect example. And to what purpose should the patterns serve when the true and original example is present.

h. Hebrews 8:6 He entereth into the comparison of the old and transitory Testament or covenant being but for a time, whereof the Levitical Priests were mediators with the new the everlasting Mediator whereof is Christ, to show that this is not only better than that in all respects, but also that that was abrogated by this.

i. Hebrews 8:7 He proveth by the testimony of Jeremiah, that there is a second Testament or covenant, and therefore that the first was not perfect.

j. Hebrews 8:8 He calleth it an house, as it were one family of the whole kingdom: for whereas the kingdom of David was divided into two factions, the Prophet giveth us to understand that through the new Testament they shall be joined together again in one.

k. Hebrews 8:13 The conclusion: Therefore by the latter and the new, the first and old is taken away, for it could not be called new if it differed not from the old. And again that same is at length taken away: which is subject to corruption, and therefore imperfect.

HEBREWS 8

1. Exod. 15:40 / Acts 7:44 **2.** Jer. 31:31-34 / Rom. 11:17 / Heb. 10:16

HEBREWS 9

a. Hebrews 9:1 A division of the first Tabernacle which he calleth worldly, that is to say, transitory and earthly into two parts, to wit, into the holy places and the Holiest of all.

b. Hebrews 9:1 An earthy and a flitting.

c. Hebrews 9:3 He calleth it the second veil, not because there were two veils, but because it was behind the Sanctuary or the first Tabernacle.

d. Hebrews 9:3 The holiest Sanctuary.

e. Hebrews 9:5 The Hebrews call the cover of the Ark of the covenant, the mercy seat, whom both the Greeks and we follow.

f. Hebrews 9:6 Now he cometh to the sacrifices which he divideth into those daily sacrifices, and that yearly and solemn sacrifice, with the which the high Priest only, but once every year entering into the Holiest of all with blood, offered for himself and the people.

g. Hebrews 9:7 For the sins. See Heb. 5:2.

h. Hebrews 9:8 Of that yearly rite and ceremony he gathereth that the way was not by such sacrifices opened into heaven, which was shadowed by the Holiest of all. For why did the high Priest alone enter in thither, shutting out all other, and that to offer sacrifices there both for himself and for others, and after did shut the Holiest of all again?

i. Hebrews 9:9 An objection: If the way were not opened into heaven by those sacrifices that is to say, If the worshippers were not purged by them why then were those ceremonies used? to wit, that men might be called back to that spiritual example, that is to say, to Christ, who should correct all those things at his coming.

j. Hebrews 9:9 For that time that that figure had to last.

k. Hebrews 9:10 Another reason why they could not make clean the conscience of the worshipper, to wit, because they were outward and carnal or corporal things.

l. Hebrews 9:10 For they were as you would say a burden, from which Christ delivered us.

m. Hebrews 9:11 Now he entereth into the declaration of the figures, and first of all comparing the Levitical high Priest with Christ, that is to say, the figure with the thing itself he attributeth to Christ the administration of good things to come, that is, everlasting, which those carnal things had respect unto.

n. Hebrews 9:11 Another comparison of the first corruptible Tabernacle with the latter that is to say, with the human nature of Christ which is the true incorruptible Temple of God, whereinto which the Son of GOD entered, as the Levitical high Priests into the other which was frail and transitory.

o. Hebrews 9:11 By a more excellent and better.

p. Hebrews 9:12 Another comparison of the blood of sacrifices with Christ. The Levitical high Priests entering by their holy places into the Sanctuary, offered corruptible blood for one year only: but Christ entering into that holy body of his, entered by it into heaven itself, offering his own most pure blood for an everlasting redemption: For one selfsame Christ answereth both to the high Priest, and the Tabernacle, and the sacrifices, and offering themselves, as the truth to the figures, so that Christ is both the high Priest, and Tabernacle, and Sacrifice, yea, all these both truly, and forever.

q. Hebrews 9:12 For in this yearly sacrifice of reconciliation, there were two kinds of sacrifices, the one a goat, the other a heifer, or calf.

r. Hebrews 9:13 If the outward sprinkling of blood and ashes of beasts, was a true and effectual sign of purifying and cleansing, how much more shall the thing itself and the truth being present, which in times past was shadowed by those external Sacraments, that is to say, his blood which is in such sort man's blood, that is also the blood of the Son of God, and therefore hath an everlasting virtue of purifying and cleansing, does it?

s. Hebrews 9:13 He considereth the signs apart, being separate from the thing itself.

t. Hebrews 9:14 From sins which proceed from death, and bring forth nothing but death.

u. Hebrews 9:15 The conclusion of the former argument: therefore seeing the blood of beasts did not purge sins, the new Testament which was before time promised, whereunto those outward things had respect, is now indeed established, by the virtue whereof all transgressions might be taken away, and heaven indeed opened unto us: whereof it followeth that Christ shed his blood also for the Fathers: For he was shadowed by those old ceremonies, otherwise, unless they had served to represent him, they had been nothing at all profitable. Therefore this Testament is called the latter, not concerning the virtue of it, that is to say, remission of sins but in respect of that time, wherein the thing itself was finished, that is to say, wherein Christ was indeed exhibited to the world, and fulfilled all things which were necessary to our salvation.

v. Hebrews 9:16 A reason why the Testament must be established by the death of the Mediator, because this Testament hath the condition of a Testament or gift, which is made effectual by death, and therefore that it might be effectual, it must needs be that he that made the Testament, should die.

w. Hebrews 9:18 There must be a proportion between those things which purify, and those which are purified: Under the Law all those figures were earthly, the Tabernacle, the book, the vessels, the sacrifices, although they were the figures of heavenly things. Therefore it was requisite that all those should be purified with some matter and ceremony of the same nature, to wit, with the blood of beasts, with water, wool, hyssop. But under Christ all things are heavenly, an heavenly tabernacle, an heavenly sacrifice, an heavenly people, an heavenly doctrine, and heaven itself is set open before us for an eternal habitation. Therefore all these things are sanctified in like sort, to wit, with the everlasting offering of the quickening blood of Christ.

x. Hebrews 9:19 As the Lord had commanded.

y. Hebrews 9:19 He useth to sprinkle.

z. Hebrews 9:23 The similitudes of heavenly things were earthly, and therefore they were to be set forth with earthly things, as with the blood of beasts, and wool, and hyssop. But under Christ all things are heavenly, and therefore they could not but be sanctified with the offering of his lively blood.

aa. Hebrews 9:24 Another double comparison: the Levitical high Priest entered into the Sanctuary, which was made indeed by the commandment of God, but yet with men's hands, that it might be a pattern of another more excellent, to wit, of the heavenly place. But Christ entered even into heaven itself. Again, he appeared before the Ark, but Christ before God the Father himself.

ab. Hebrews 9:25 Another double comparison: the Levitical high Priest offered other blood, but Christ offered his own: he every year once iterated his offering: Christ offering himself but once, abolished sin altogether, both of the former ages and of the ages to come.

ac. Hebrews 9:26 An argument to prove that Christ's offering ought not to be repeated: Seeing that sins were to be purged from the beginning of the world, and it is proved that sins cannot be purged, but by the only blood of Christ: he must needs have died oftentimes since the beginning of the world. But a man can die but once: therefore Christ's oblation which was once done in the latter days, neither could nor can be repeated. Seeing then it is so, surely the virtue of it

he have often suffered since the foundation of the world but now in the [ad]end of the world hath he been made manifest, once to put away [ae]sin by the sacrifice of himself. **27** And as it is appointed unto men that they shall [af]once die, and after that cometh the judgment: **28** So [11]Christ was once offered to take away the sins of [ag]many, [ah]and unto them that look for him, shall he appear the second time without sin unto salvation.

10

1 He proveth that the sacrifices of the Law were imperfect, 2 because they were yearly renewed. 5 But that the sacrifice of Christ is one, and perpetual, 6 he proveth by David's testimony: 19 Then he addeth an exhortation, 29 and severely threateneth them that reject the grace of Christ. 36 In the end he praiseth patience, 38 that cometh of faith.

1 For [a]the law having the shadow of good things to [b]come, and not the very image of the things, can never with those sacrifices, which they offer year by year continually, sanctify the comers thereunto. **2** For would they not then have ceased to have been offered, because that the offerers once purged, should have had no more conscience of sins? **3** But in those sacrifices there is a remembrance again of sins every year. **4** For it is impossible that the blood of bulls and goats should take away sins. **5** [c]Wherefore when he [d]cometh into the world, he saith, [1]Sacrifice and offering thou wouldest not: but a [e]body hast thou ordained me. **6** In burnt offerings, and sin offerings thou hast had no pleasure. **7** Then I said, Lo, I come in the beginning of the book it is written of me that I should do thy will, O God. **8** Above, when he said, Sacrifice and offering, and burnt offerings, and sin offerings, thou wouldest not have, neither hadst pleasure therein which are offered by the Law. **9** Then said he, Lo, I come to do thy will, O God, he taketh away the [f]first, that he may stablish the second. **10** By the which will we are sanctified, even by the offering of the body of Jesus Christ once made. **11** [g]And every Priest [h]standeth daily ministering, and ofttimes offereth one manner of offering, which can never take away sins: **12** But this man after he had offered one sacrifice for sins, [2]sitteth forever at the right hand of God, **13** [i]And from henceforth tarrieth, [3]till his enemies be made his footstool. **14** For with one offering hath he consecrated forever them that are sanctified. **15** [j]For the holy Ghost also beareth us record: for after that he had said before, **16** [4]This is the Testament that I will make unto them after those days, saith the Lord, I will put my Laws in their heart, and in their minds I will write them. **17** And their sins and iniquities will I remember [k]no more. **18** Now where remission of these things is, there is no more offering for [l]sin. **19** [m]Seeing therefore, brethren, that by the blood of Jesus we may be bold to enter into the Holy place, **20** By the new and living way, which he hath prepared for us, through the veil, that is, his [n]flesh: **21** And seeing we have an high Priest, which is over the house of God, **22** [o]Let us draw near with a [p]true heart in assurance of faith, our [q]hearts being pure from an evil conscience, **23** And washed in our bodies with [r]pure water, let us keep the profession of our hope, without wavering, for he is faithful that promised. **24** And let us consider one another, to provoke unto love, and to good works, **25** Not forsaking the fellowship that we have among ourselves, as the manner of some is: but let us exhort one another, [s]and that so much the more, because ye see that the day draweth near. **26** [5]For if we sin [t]willingly after that we have received and acknowledged that truth, there remaineth no more sacrifice for sins, **27** But a fearful looking for of judgment, and violent fire, which shall devour the [u]adversaries. **28** [v]He that despiseth Moses' Law, dieth without mercy [6]under two, or three witnesses: **29** Of how much sorer punishment suppose ye shall he be worthy, which treadeth under foot the Son of God, and counteth the blood of the Testament as an unholy thing, wherewith he was sanctified, and doeth despite the Spirit of grace? **30** [w]For we know him that hath said, [7]Vengeance belongeth unto me: I will recompense, saith the Lord. And again, The Lord shall [x]judge his people. **31** It is a fearful thing to fall into the hands of the living God. **32** [y]Now call to remembrance the days that are passed, in the which, after ye had received light ye endured a great fight in afflictions, **33** Partly while ye were made a [z]gazing stock both by reproaches and afflictions, and partly while ye became [aa]companions of them which were so tossed to and fro. **34** For both ye sorrowed with me for my bonds, and suffered with joy the spoiling of your goods, knowing in yourselves how that ye have in heaven a better, and an enduring [ab]substance. **35** Cast not away therefore your confidence which hath great recompense of reward. **36** For ye have need of patience, that after ye have done the will of God, ye might receive the promise. **37** For yet a very [ac]little while, and he that shall come, will come, and will not tarry. **38** [8,ad]Now the just shall live by faith: but if any withdraw himself, my soul shall have no pleasure in him. **39** But we are not they which withdraw ourselves unto perdition, but follow faith unto the conservation of the soul.

---

extendeth both to sins that were before, and to sins that are after his coming.

ad. Hebrews 9:26 In the latter days.

ae. Hebrews 9:26 That whole root of sin.

af. Hebrews 9:27 He speaketh of the natural state and condition of man: For as for Lazarus and certain others that died twice, that was no usual thing but extraordinary, and for them that shall be changed, their changing is a kind of death, 1 Cor. 15:51.

ag. Hebrews 9:28 Thus the general promise is restrained to the elect only: and we have to seek the testimony of our election: not in the secret counsel of God, but in the effects that our faith worketh, and so we must climb up from the lowest step to the highest, there to find such comfort as is most certain, and shall never be moved.

ah. Hebrews 9:28 Shortly by the way he setteth out Christ as Judge, partly to terrify them, which do not rest themselves in the only oblation of Christ once made, and partly to keep the faithful in their duty, that they will go not back.

HEBREWS 9

1. Num. 7:10
2. 1 Kings 8:9 / 2 Chron. 5:10
3. Exod. 21:22
4. Exod. 30:10 / Lev. 16:2
5. Lev. 16:14 / Num. 19:4
6. 1 Pet. 1:19 / 1 John 1:7 / Rev. 1:5
7. Luke 1:74
8. Rom. 5:6 / 1 Pet. 3:18
9. Gal. 3:15
10. Exod. 24:8
11. Rom. 5:8 / 1 Pet. 3:18

HEBREWS 10

a. Hebrews 10:1 He preventeth a privy objection. Why then were those sacrifices offered? The Apostle answereth first touching that yearly sacrifice which was the solemnest of all, wherein saith he there was made every year a remembrance again of all former sins. Therefore that sacrifice had no power to sanctify: for to what purpose should those sins which are purged be repeated again, and wherefore should new sins come to be repeated every year, if those sacrifices did abolish sin?

b. Hebrews 10:1 Of things which are everlasting, which were promised to the Fathers, and exhibited in Christ.

c. Hebrews 10:5 A conclusion following of those things that went before, and comprehending also the other sacrifices. Seeing that the sacrifices of the Law could not do it, therefore Christ speaking of himself as of our high Priest manifested in the flesh, witnesseseth evidently that God resteth not in the sacrifices, but in the obedience of his Son our high Priest, in which obedience he offered up himself once to his Father for us.

d. Hebrews 10:5 The Son of God is said to come into the world, when he was made man.

e. Hebrews 10:5 It is word for word in the Hebrew text, Thou hast pierced mine ears through, that is, thou hast made me obedient, and willing to hear.

f. Hebrews 10:9 That is the sacrifices, to establish the second, that is, the will of God.

g. Hebrews 10:11 A conclusion, with the other part of the comparison. The Levitical high Priest repeateth the same sacrifices daily in his sanctuary: whereupon which it followeth that neither those sacrifices, neither those offerings, neither those high Priests could take away sins. But Christ, having offered one sacrifice once for the sins of all men, and having sanctified his own forever, sitteth at the right hand of the Father, having all power in his hands.

h. Hebrews 10:11 At the altar.

i. Hebrews 10:13 He preventeth a privy objection, to wit, that yet notwithstanding we are subject to sin and death, whereunto the Apostle answereth, that the full efficacy of Christ's virtue hath not yet showed itself, but shall at length appear when he will at once put to flight all his enemies, with whom as yet we strive.

j. Hebrews 10:15 Although there do yet remain in us relics of sin, yet the work of our sanctification which is to be perfected, hangeth upon the selfsame sacrifice which never shall be repeated: and that the Apostle proveth by alledging again the testimonies of Jeremiah, thus, Sin is taken away by the new Testament, seeing the Lord saith that it shall come to pass, that according to the form of it, he will no more remember our sins: Therefore we need now no purging sacrifice to take away that which is already taken away, but we must rather take pains, that we may now through faith be partakers of that sacrifice.

k. Hebrews 10:17 Why then, where is the fire of Purgatory, and that Popish distinction of the fault and the punishment?

l. Hebrews 10:18 He said well, for sin: for there remaineth another offering, to wit, of thanksgiving.

m. Hebrews 10:19 The sum of the former treatise: We are not shut out now of the holy place, as the Fathers were, but we have an entrance into the true holy place that is, into heaven seeing that we are purged with the blood not of beasts, but of Jesus. Neither as in times past, doth the high Priest shut us out by setting the veil against us, but through the veil, which is his flesh, he hath brought us into heaven itself, being present with us, so that we have now truly an high Priest, which is over the house of God.

n. Hebrews 10:20 So Christ's flesh showeth us the Godhead as it were under a veil, for otherwise we were not able to abide the brightness of it.

o. Hebrews 10:22 A most grave exhortation, wherein which he showeth how that sacrifice of Christ may be applied to us: to wit, by faith, which also he describeth, by the consequence, to wit, by sanctification of the Spirit, which causeth us surely to hope in God, and to procure by all means possible one another's salvation, through the love that is in us one toward another.

p. Hebrews 10:22 With no double and counterfeit heart, but with such an heart as is truly and indeed given to God.

q. Hebrews 10:22 This is it which the Lord saith, Be ye holy, for I am holy.

r. Hebrews 10:23 With the grace of the holy Ghost.

s. Hebrews 10:25 Having mentioned the last coming of Christ, he stirreth up the godly to the meditation of an holy life, and cites the faithless fallers from God, to the fearful judgment seat of the judge, because they wickedly rejected him in whom only salvation consisteth.

t. Hebrews 10:26 Without any cause or occasion, or show of occasion.

u. Hebrews 10:27 For it is another matter to sin through the frailty of man's nature, and another thing to proclaim war as it were to God as to an enemy.

v. Hebrews 10:28 If the breach of the Law of Moses was punished by death, how much more worthy death is it to fall away from Christ?

w. Hebrews 10:30 The reason of all these things is, because God is a revenger of such as despise him: otherwise he should not rightly govern his Church. Now there is nothing more horrible then the wrath of the living God.

x. Hebrews 10:30 Rule or govern.

y. Hebrews 10:32 As he terrified the fallers away from God so doth he now comfort them that are constant and stand strongly setting before them the success of their former fights, so stirring them up to a sure hope of a full and ready victory.

z. Hebrews 10:33 You were brought forth to be ashamed.

aa. Hebrews 10:33 In taking their miseries, to be your miseries.

ab. Hebrews 10:34 Goods and riches.

ac. Hebrews 10:37 He will come within this very little while.

ad. Hebrews 10:38 He commendeth the excellency of a sure faith by the effect, because it is the only way to life, which sentence he setteth forth and amplifieth by setting the contrary against it.

HEBREWS 10

1. Ps. 40:7
2. Heb. 1:13 / Ps. 110:1 / 1 Cor. 15:25
3. Heb. 1:13
4. Jer. 31:33 / Rom. 11:27 / Heb. 8:8
5. Heb. 6:4
6. Deut. 19:15 / Matt. 18:16 / John 8:17 / 2 Cor. 13:1
7. Deut. 32:35 / Rom. 12:19
8. Hab. 2:4 / Rom. 1:17 / Gal. 3:11

11

1 He declareth in the whole Chapter, that the Fathers, which from the beginning of the world were approved of God, attained salvation no other way than by faith, that the Jews may know that by the same only, they are knit unto the Fathers in an holy union.

1 Now [a]faith is the grounds of things which are hoped for, and the evidence of things which are not seen. 2 [b]For by it our [c]elders were well reported of. 3 [1,d]Through faith we understand that the world was ordained by the word of God, so that the things which we [e]see, are not made of things which did appear. 4 [f]By faith Abel [2]offered unto God a greater sacrifice than Cain, by [3]the which he obtained witness that he was righteous, God testifying of his gifts: by the which faith also he being dead, yet speaketh. 5 [g]By faith was [4]Enoch translated, that he should not [h]see death: neither was he found: for God had translated him: for before he was translated, he was reported of, that he had pleased God. 6 But without faith it is impossible to please him: for he that cometh to God, must believe that God is, and that he is a [i]rewarder of them that seek him. 7 [j]By faith [5]Noah being warned of God of the things which were as yet not seen, moved with reverence, prepared the Ark to the saving of his household, through the which Ark he condemned the world, and was made heir of the righteousness, which is by faith. 8 [k]By faith [6]Abraham, when he was called, obeyed God, to go out into a place, which he should afterward receive for inheritance, and he went out, not knowing whither he went. 9 By faith he abode in the land of promise, as in a strange country, as one that dwelt in tents with Isaac and Jacob heirs with him of the same promise. 10 For he looked for a city having a [l]foundation, whose builder and maker is God. 11 Through faith [7]Sarah also received strength to conceive seed, and was delivered of a child when she was past age, because she judged him faithful which had promised. 12 And therefore sprang thereof one, even of one which was [m]dead, so many as the stars of the sky in multitude, and as the sand of the sea shore which is innumerable. 13 All these died in [n]faith, and received not the [o]promises, but saw them afar off, and believed them, and [p]received them thankfully, and confessed that they were strangers and pilgrims on the earth. 14 For they that say such things, declare plainly, that they seek a country. 15 And if they had been mindful of that country, from whence they came out, they had leisure to have returned. 16 But now they desire a better, that is an heavenly: wherefore God is not ashamed of them to be called their God: for he hath prepared for them a city. 17 By faith [8]Abraham offered up Isaac, when he was [q]tried, and he that had received the [r]promises, offered his only begotten son. 18 To whom it was said, [9]In Isaac shall thy seed be called. 19 For he considered that God was able to raise him up even from the dead: from [s]whence he received him also after [t]a sort. 20 [u]By faith [10]Isaac blessed Jacob and Esau, concerning things to come. 21 [v]By faith [11]Jacob when he was a dying, blessed both the sons of Joseph, and [12]leaning on the end of his staff, worshipped God. 22 [w]By faith [13]Joseph when he died, made mention of the departing of the children of Israel, and gave commandment of his bones. 23 [14,x] By faith Moses when he was born, was hid three months of his parents, because they saw he was a proper child, neither [y]feared they the king's [15]commandment. 24 By faith [16]Moses when he was come to age, refused to be called the son of Pharaoh's daughter, 25 And chose rather to suffer adversity with the people of God, than to enjoy the [z]pleasures of sin for a season, 26 Esteeming the rebuke of Christ greater riches, than the treasures of Egypt: for he had respect unto the recompense of the reward. 27 By faith he forsook Egypt, and feared not the fierceness of the king: for he endured, as he that saw him which is invisible. 28 Through faith he ordained the [17]Passover and the effusion of blood, lest he that destroyed the first born, should touch them. 29 [aa]By faith they [18]passed through the red sea as by dry land, which when the Egyptians had assayed to do, they were swallowed up. 30 [ab]By faith the [19]walls of Jericho fell down after they were compassed about seven days. 31 [ac]By faith the [ad]harlot [20]Rahab perished not with them which obeyed not, when [21]she had received the spies [ae]peaceably. 32 [af]And what shall I more say? for the time would be too short for me to tell of [22]Gideon, of [23]Barak, and of [24]Samson, and of [25]Jephthah, also of David, and Samuel, and of the Prophets: 33 Which through faith subdued kingdoms, wrought righteousness, obtained the [ag]promises, stopped the mouths of lions, 34 Quenched the violence of fire, escaped the edge of the sword, of weak were made strong, waxed valiant in battle, turned to flight the armies of the aliens. 35 The [ah]women received their dead raised to life: others also were [ai]racked, and would not be delivered, that they might receive a better resurrection. 36 And others have been tried by mockings and scourgings, yea, moreover by bonds, and imprisonment. 37 They were stoned, they were hewn asunder, they were tempted, they were slain with the sword, they wandered up and down in [aj]sheep's skins, and in goats' skins, being destitute, afflicted, and tormented: 38 Whom the world was not worthy of: they wandered in wildernesses and mountains, and dens, and caves of the earth. 39 [ak]And these all through faith obtained good report, and received [al]not the promise, 40 God providing a better thing for us, that they [am]without us should not be made perfect.

12

1 He doth not only by the examples of the Fathers before recited, exhort them to patience and constancy, 3 but also by the example of Christ. 11 That the chastenings of God cannot be rightly judged by the outward sense of our flesh.

1 Wherefore, [1,a]let us also, seeing that we are compassed with so great a cloud of witnesses, cast away everything that presseth down, and the sin that [b]hangeth so fast on: let us run with patience the race that is set before us, 2 [c,d]Looking unto Jesus the author and finisher of our faith, who for the [e]joy that was set before him, endured the cross, and despised the shame, and is set at the right hand of the throne of God. 3 [f]Consider therefore him that endureth such speaking against of sinners, lest ye should be wearied and faint in your minds. 4 [g]Ye have not yet resisted unto blood, striving against sin. 5 [h]And ye have forgotten the consolation, which speaketh unto you as unto children, [2]My son, despise not the chastening of the Lord, neither faint when thou art rebuked of him. 6 For whom the Lord loveth, he chasteneth: and he scourgeth every son that he receiveth. 7 If ye endure chastening, God offered himself unto you as unto sons: for what son is it whom the father chasteneth not? 8 If therefore ye be without correction, whereof all are partakers, then are ye bastards, and not sons. 9 [i]Moreover we

---

HEBREWS 11

a. Hebrews 11:1 An excellent description of faith by the effects, because it representeth things which are but yet in hope, and setteth as it were before our eyes things that are invisible.
b. Hebrews 11:2 He showeth that the Fathers ought to be accounted of, by this virtue.
c. Hebrews 11:2 That is, those Fathers of whom we came: and whose authority and example ought to move us very much.
d. Hebrews 11:3 He showeth the propriety of faith, by setting unto us most piked examples of such as from the beginning of the world excelled in the Church.
e. Hebrews 11:3 So that the world which we see, was not made of any matter that appeared or was before, but of nothing.
f. Hebrews 11:4 Abel.
g. Hebrews 11:5 Enoch.
h. Hebrews 11:5 That he should not die.
i. Hebrews 11:6 This reward is not referred to our merits, but to the free promise, as Paul teacheth in Abraham the father of all the faithful, Rom. 4:4.
j. Hebrews 11:7 Noah.
k. Hebrews 11:8 Abraham and Sarah.
l. Hebrews 11:10 This foundation is set against their tabernacle.
m. Hebrews 11:12 As unlikely to bear children, as if she had been stark dead.
n. Hebrews 11:13 In faith, which they had while they lived, and followed them even to their grave.
o. Hebrews 11:13 This is the figure Metonymy, for the things promised.
p. Hebrews 11:13 For the Patriarchs were wont when they received the promises, to profess their religion, by building of altars, and calling on the name of the Lord.
q. Hebrews 11:17 Tried of the Lord.
r. Hebrews 11:17 Although the promises of life were made in that only begotten Son Isaac, yet he appointed him to die, and so against hope he believed in hope.
s. Hebrews 11:19 From which death.
t. Hebrews 11:19 For there was not the true and very death of Isaac, but as it were the death, by means whereof he seemed also as it were to have risen again.
u. Hebrews 11:20 Isaac.
v. Hebrews 11:21 Jacob.
w. Hebrews 11:22 Joseph.
x. Hebrews 11:23 Moses.
y. Hebrews 11:23 They were not afraid to bring him up.
z. Hebrews 11:25 Such pleasures as he could not enjoy, but he must needs provoke God's wrath against him.
aa. Hebrews 11:29 The red sea.
ab. Hebrews 11:30 Jericho.
ac. Hebrews 11:31 Rahab.
ad. Hebrews 11:31 A notable example of God's goodness.
ae. Hebrews 11:31 Courteously and friendly, so that she did not only not hurt them, but also kept them safe.
af. Hebrews 11:32 Gideon, Barak and other Judges and Prophets.
ag. Hebrews 11:33 The fruit of the promises.
ah. Hebrews 11:35 He seemeth to mean the story of that woman of Zarephath, whose son Elijah raised again from death, and the Shunammite, whose son Elisha restored to his mother.
ai. Hebrews 11:35 He meaneth that persecution which Antiochus wrought.
aj. Hebrews 11:37 In vile and rough clothing, so were the saints brought to extreme poverty, and constrained to live like beasts in wildernesses.
ak. Hebrews 11:39 An amplification taken of the circumstance of the time: their faith is so much the more to be marveled at, by how much the promises of things to come were more dark, yet at length were indeed exhibited to us, so that their faith and ours is as one, as is also their consecration and ours.
al. Hebrews 11:39 But saw Christ afar off.
am. Hebrews 11:40 For their salvation did hang upon Christ, who was exhibited in our days.

HEBREWS 11

1. Gen. 1:1 / John 1:10
2. Gen. 4:4
3. Matt. 23:35
4. Gen. 5:25
5. Gen. 6:13
6. Gen. 12:4
7. Gen. 17:19 / Gen. 21:2
8. Gen. 22:10
9. Gen. 21:12 / Rom. 9:7
10. Gen. 27:28,39
11. Gen. 48:15
12. Gen. 47:31
13. Gen. 50:25
14. Exod. 2:2 / Acts 7:22
15. Exod. 1:16
16. Exod. 2:11
17. Exod. 12:27
18. Exod. 14:21
19. Josh. 6:20
20. Josh. 6:23
21. Josh. 2:1
22. Judg. 6:11
23. Judg. 4:6
24. Judg. 13:24
25. Judg. 11:1 / Judg. 12:7

HEBREWS 12

a. Hebrews 12:1 An applying of the former examples, whereby we ought to be stirred up to run the whole race, casting away all stops and impediments.
b. Hebrews 12:1 For sin besiegeth us on all sides, so that we cannot escape out.
c. Hebrews 12:2 He setteth before us, as the mark of this race, Jesus himself our captain, who willingly overcame all the roughness of the same way.
d. Hebrews 12:2 As it were upon the mark of our faith.
e. Hebrews 12:2 Whereas he had all kind of blessedness in his hand and power, yet suffered willingly the ignominy of the cross.
f. Hebrews 12:3 An amplification taken of the circumstance of the person, and the things themselves, which he compareth betwixt themselves: for how great is Jesus in comparison of us, and how far more grievous things did he suffer than we?
g. Hebrews 12:4 He taketh an argument of the profit which cometh to us by God's chastisements, unless we be in fault. First of all because sin, or that rebellious wickedness of our flesh, is by this means turned.
h. Hebrews 12:5 Secondly, because they are testimony of his fatherly good will toward us, insomuch that they show themselves to be bastards, which cannot abide to be chastened of God.
i. Hebrews 12:9 Thirdly, if all men yield this right to fathers, to whom next after God we owe this life, that they may rightfully correct their children, shall we not be much more

have had the fathers of our bodies which corrected us, and we gave them reveren-
ce: should we not much rather be in subjection unto the father of spirits, that we
might live? **10** [j]For they verily for a few days chastened us after their own ple-
asure, but he chastened us for our profit, that we might be partakers of his holi-
ness. **11** Now no chastising for the present seemeth to be joyous, but grievous:
but afterward, it bringeth the quiet fruit of righteousness, unto them which are
thereby exercised. **12** [k]Wherefore lift up your hands which [l]hang down, and
your weak knees, **13** And make [m]straight steps unto your feet, lest that whi-
ch is halting, be turned out of the way, but let it rather be healed. **14** [3,n]Fol-
low peace with all men, and holiness, without the which no man shall see the
Lord. **15** [o]Take heed, that no man fall away from the grace of God: let no [p]root
of bitterness spring up and trouble you, lest thereby many be defiled. **16** [q]Let
there be no fornicator, or profane person as [4]Esau, which for one portion of meat
sold his birthright. **17** [5]For ye know how that afterward also when he would
have inherited the blessing, he was rejected: for he found no [r]place to repentan-
ce, though he sought that blessing with tears. **18** [s]For ye are not come unto the
[6]mount that might be [t]touched, nor unto burning fire, nor to blackness and dar-
kness, and tempest, **19** Neither unto the sound of a trumpet, and the voice of
words, which they that heard it, excused themselves, [7]that the word should not be
spoken to them any more. **20** For they were not able to abide that which was
commanded, [8]yea, though a beast touch the mountain, it shall be stoned, or thrust
through with a dart: **21** And so terrible was the [u]sight which appeared, that Mo-
ses said, I fear and quake. **22** But ye are come unto the mount Sion, and to the
city of the living God, the celestial Jerusalem, and to the company of innumerable
Angels. **23** And to the assembly and congregation of the first born, which are
written in heaven, and to God the judge of all, and to the spirits of just and [v]per-
fect men, **24** And to Jesus the Mediator of the new Testament, and to the blood
of sprinkling that speaketh better things than that of Abel. **25** [w]See that ye de-
spise not him that speaketh: for if they escaped not which refused him, that spake
on earth: much more shall we not escape, if we turn away from him that speaketh
from heaven. **26** [x]Whose voice then shook the earth, and now hath declared,
saying, [9]Yet [y]once more will I shake, not the earth only, but also heaven. **27** And
this word, Yet once more, signifieth the removing of those things which are shaken,
as of things which are made with hands, that the things which are not shaken, may
remain. **28** [z]Wherefore seeing we receive a kingdom, which cannot be shaken,
let us have grace whereby we may so serve God, that we may please him with [aa]re-
verence and [ab]fear. **29** For [10]even our God is a consuming fire.

13

1 He giveth good lessons not only for manners, 7 but also for doctrine.

1 Let [1,a]brotherly love continue. **2** [2]Be not forgetful to enter-
tain strangers: for thereby some have [3]received Angels into their houses unawa-
res. **3** Remember them that are in bonds, as though ye were bound with them:
and them that are in affliction, as [b]if ye were also afflicted in the body. **4** [c]Mar-
riage is honorable among all, and the bed undefiled: but whoremongers and adul-
terers God will judge. **5** [d]Let your conversation be without covetousness, and
be content with those things that ye have, for [e]he hath said, **6** [4]I will not fail
thee, neither forsake thee: **7** So that we may boldly say, [5]The Lord is mine hel-
per, neither will I fear what [f]man can do unto me. **8** [g]Remember them which
have the oversight of you, which have declared unto you the word of God: who-
se faith follow, considering what hath been the end of their conversation. [h]Jesus
Christ yesterday, and today, the same also is forever. **9** Be not carried about with
divers and strange doctrines: [i]for it is a good thing that the heart be stablished
with grace, and not with [j]meats, which have not profited them that have been
[k]occupied therein. **10** [l]We have an [m]altar, whereof they have no authority to eat,
which [n]serve in the Tabernacle. **11** [6]For the bodies of those beasts whose blo-
od is brought into the holy place by the high Priest for sin, are burnt without the
camp. **12** Therefore even Jesus, that he might sanctify the people with his own
blood, suffered without the gate. **13** [o]Let us go forth to him therefore out of the
camp, bearing his reproach. **14** [7]For here have we no continuing city: but we
seek one to come. **15** [p]Let us therefore by him offer the sacrifice of praise always
to God, that is, the [8]fruit of the lips, which confess his Name. **16** To do good,
and to distribute forget not: for with such sacrifices God is pleased. **17** [q]Obey
them that have the oversight of you, and submit yourselves: for they watch for your
souls, as they that must give accounts, that they may do it with joy, and not with
grief: for that is unprofitable for you. **18** [r]Pray for us, for we are assured that we
have a good conscience in all things, desiring to live honestly. **19** And I desire
you somewhat the more earnestly, that ye so do, that I may be restored to you
more quickly. **20** The God of peace that brought again from the dead our Lord
Jesus, the great shepherd of the sheep, through the blood of the everlasting Cove-
nant, **21** Make you [s]perfect in all good works, to do his will, [t]working in you
that which is pleasant in his sight through Jesus Christ, to whom be praise forever
and ever, Amen. **22** I beseech you also, brethren, suffer the words of exhortation:
for I have written unto you in few words. **23** Know that our brother Timothy is
delivered, with whom if he come shortly I will see you. **24** Salute all them that
have the oversight of you, and all the Saints. They of Italy salute you. **25** Grace
be with you all, Amen. Written to the Hebrews from Italy, and sent by Timothy.

---

subject to that our Father, who is the Author of the spiritual and everlasting life?

j. Hebrews 12:10 An amplification of the same argument: Those fathers have corrected us after their fancy, for some frail and transitory profit: but God chasteneth and instructeth us for our singular profit, to make us partakers of his holiness: which thing although these our senses do not presently perceive, yet the end of the matter proveth it.

k. Hebrews 12:12 The conclusion, we must go forward courageously and keep always a right course, and as far forth as we may without any staggering or stumbling.

l. Hebrews 12:12 The description of a man that is out of heart and clean discouraged.

m. Hebrews 12:13 Keep a right course, and so, that you show example of good life for others to follow.

n. Hebrews 12:14 We must live in peace, and holiness with all men.

o. Hebrews 12:15 We must study to edify one another, both in doctrine and example of life.

p. Hebrews 12:15 That no heresy, or backsliding be an offense.

q. Hebrews 12:16 We must eschew fornication, and a profane mind, that is, such a mind, as giveth not to God his due honor, which wickedness how severely God will at length punish, the horrible example of Esau teacheth us.

r. Hebrews 12:17 There was no place left for his repentance: and it appeareth by the effects, what his repentance was, for when he was gone out of his father's sight, he threatened his brother to kill him.

s. Hebrews 12:18 Now he applieth the same exhortation, to the Prophetical and kingly office of Christ compared with Moses, after this sort, If the majesty of the Law was so great, how great think you that the glory of Christ and the Gospel is? And this comparison he declareth also particularly.

t. Hebrews 12:18 Which might be touched with hands, which was of a gross and earthly matter.

u. Hebrews 12:21 The shape and form which he saw, which was no counterfeit and forged shape, but a true one.

v. Hebrews 12:23 So he calleth them that are taken up into heaven, although one part of them sleep in the earth.

w. Hebrews 12:25 The applying of the former comparison, If it were not lawful to contemn his word which spake on the earth, how much less his voice which is from heaven?

x. Hebrews 12:26 He compareth the steadfast majesty of the Gospel, wherewith the whole world was shaken, and even the very frame of heaven was as it were astonished, with the small and vanishing sound of the governance by the Law.

y. Hebrews 12:26 It appeareth evidently in this that the Prophet speaketh of the calling of the Gentiles, that these words must be referred to the kingdom of Christ.

z. Hebrews 12:28 A general exhortation to live reverently and religiously under the most happy subjection of so mighty a king, who as he blesseth his most mightily, so doth he most severely revenge the rebellious. And this is the sum of a Christian life, respecting the first table.

aa. Hebrews 12:28 By reverence is meant that honest shamefastness which keepeth them in their duties.

ab. Hebrews 12:28 Religious and godly fear.

HEBREWS 12

1. Rom. 6:4 / Col. 3:8 / Eph. 4:24 / 1 Pet. 2:1
2. Prov. 3:11
3. Rom. 12:18
4. Gen. 25:33
5. Gen. 27:38
6. Exod. 19:16
7. Exod. 20:19
8. Exod. 19:12
9. Hag. 2:7
10. Deut. 4:24

HEBREWS 13

a. Hebrews 13:1 He cometh to the second table, the sum whereof is charity, especially toward strangers and such as are afflicted.

b. Hebrews 13:3 Be so much touched, as if their misery were yours.

c. Hebrews 13:4 He commendeth chaste matrimony in all sorts of men, and threateneth utter destruction from God, against whoremongers and adulterers.

d. Hebrews 13:5 Covetousness is condemned, against which is set a contented mind with that which the Lord hath given.

e. Hebrews 13:5 Even the Lord himself.

f. Hebrews 13:7 He setteth man against God.

g. Hebrews 13:8 We have to set before us the examples of valiant Captains, whom we ought diligently to follow.

h. Hebrews 13:8 He repeateth the sum of the doctrine, to wit, the only ground of all precepts of manners, and that is this: That we ought to quiet and content ourselves in Christ only: for there was yet never any man saved without the knowledge of him, neither is at this day saved, neither shall be saved hereafter.

i. Hebrews 13:9 He toucheth them which mixed an external worship, and especially the difference of meats, with the Gospel, which doctrine he plainly condemneth as clean repugnant to the benefit of Christ.

j. Hebrews 13:9 By this one kind which concerneth the difference of clean and unclean meats, we have to understand all the ceremonial worship.

k. Hebrews 13:9 Which observed the difference of them superstitiously.

l. Hebrews 13:10 He refuteth their error by an apt and fit comparison. They which in times past served the Tabernacle, did not eat of the sacrifices whose blood was brought for sin into the holy place by the high Priest. Moreover these sacrifices did represent Christ our offering. Therefore they cannot be partakers of him which serve the Tabernacle, that is, such as stand in the service of the Law: but let not us be ashamed to follow him out of Jerusalem, from whence he was cast out and suffered: for in this also Christ, who is the truth, answereth that figure, in that he suffered without the gate.

m. Hebrews 13:10 By the Altar, he meaneth the offering.

n. Hebrews 13:10 Whereof they cannot be partakers which stubbornly retain the rites of the Law.

o. Hebrews 13:13 He goeth on further in this comparison, and showeth that this also signified unto us, that the godly followers of Christ must as it were go out of the world, bearing his cross.

p. Hebrews 13:15 Now that those corporal sacrifices are taken away, he teacheth us that the true sacrifices of confession remain, which consist partly in giving of thanks, and partly in liberality, with which sacrifices indeed God is now delighted.

q. Hebrews 13:17 We must obey the warnings and admonitions of our Ministers and Elders, which watch for the salvation of the souls which are committed unto them.

r. Hebrews 13:18 The last part of this Epistle, wherein he commendeth his ministry to the Hebrews, and wisheth them continuance and increase of graces from the Lord: and excuseth himself in that he hath used but few words to comfort them, having spent the Epistle in disputing: and saluteth certain brethren familiarly and friendly.

s. Hebrews 13:21 Make you fit or meet.

t. Hebrews 13:21 Hence cometh that saying of the Fathers, that God crowneth his works in us.

HEBREWS 13

1. Rom. 12:10
2. 1 Pet. 4:9
3. Gen. 18:3 / Gen. 19:3
4. Josh. 1:5
5. Ps. 118:6
6. Lev. 4:11 / Lev. 6:30 / Lev. 16:17
7. Mic. 2:10
8. Hos. 14:3

THE [a]GENERAL EPISTLE OF

JAMES

1

4 He entreateth of patience, 6 of faith, 10 and of lowliness of mind in rich men. 13 That tentations come not of God for our evil, 17 because he is the author of all goodness. 21 In what manner the word of life must be received.

1 James a servant of God, and of the Lord Jesus Christ, to the twelve Tribes,
which are [b]scattered abroad, salutation. 2 [c]My brethren, [d]count it exceeding joy,
[e]when ye fall into divers tentations, 3 [1,f]Knowing that the [g]trying of your faith
bringeth forth patience, 4 [h]And let patience have her perfect work, that ye may
be perfect and entire, lacking nothing. 5 [i]If any of you lack [j]wisdom, let him ask
of God, which giveth to all men liberally, and reproacheth no man, and it shall be
given him. 6 [2]But let him ask in faith, and [k]waver not: [l]for he that wavereth, is
like a wave of the sea, tossed of the wind, and carried away. 7 Neither let that
man think that he shall receive anything of the Lord. 8 A double minded man
is unstable in [m]all his ways. 9 [n]Let the brother of [o]low degree rejoice in that he
is exalted: 10 [p]Again, he that is [q]rich, in that he is made low: [r]for as the flower
of the grass, shall he [3]vanish away. 11 For as when the sun riseth with heat, then
the grass withereth, and his flower falleth away, and the goodly shape of it peri-
sheth: even so shall the rich man wither away in all his [s]ways. 12 [t,4]Blessed is
the man, that endureth [u]tentation: for when he is tried, he shall receive the crown
of life, which the Lord hath promised to them that love him. 13 [v]Let no man
say when he is [w]tempted, I am tempted of God: [x]for God cannot be tempted with
evil, neither tempteth he any man. 14 But every man is tempted, when he is
drawn away by his own concupiscence, and is enticed. 15 Then when lust hath
conceived, it bringeth forth [y]sin, and sin when it is finished, bringeth forth dea-
th. 16 [z]Err not my dear brethren. 17 Every good giving and every perfect gift
is from above, and cometh down from the [aa]Father of lights, with whom is no va-
riableness, neither [ab]shadow of turning. 18 [ac]Of his own [ad]will begat he us with
the word of truth, that we should be as the [ae]firstfruits of his creatures. 19 Whe-
refore my dear brethren, let every man be swift to hear, slow to speak, and slow
to wrath. 20 For the wrath of man doth not accomplish the [af]righteousness of
God. 21 Wherefore lay apart all filthiness, and superfluity of maliciousness, and
receive with [ag]meekness the word that is grafted in you, which is able to save your
souls. 22 [5,ah]And be ye doers of the word, and not hearers only, [ai]deceiving
your own selves. 23 [aj]For if any hear the word, and do it not, he is like unto a
man, that beholdeth his [ak]natural face in a glass. 24 For when he hath conside-
red himself, he goeth his way, and forgetteth immediately what manner of one he
was. 25 But who so looketh in the perfect law of liberty, and continueth therein,
he not being a forgetful hearer, but a doer of the work, shall be blessed in his [al]de-
ed. 26 [am]If any man among you seem religious, and refraineth not his tongue,
but deceiveth his [an]own heart, this man's religion is vain. 27 [ao]Pure religion and
undefiled before God, even the Father, is this, to [ap]visit the fatherless, and widows
in their adversity, and to keep himself unspotted of the world.

2

1 He sayeth, that to have respect of persons is not agreeable to Christ's faith, 14 which to profess in words is not enough, unless 15 we show it also in deeds of mercy and charity, 21 after the example of Abraham.

1 My [a]brethren, have not the faith of our [b]glorious Lord Jesus Christ [1]in re-
spect of persons. 2 For if there come into your company a man with a gold ring,
and in goodly apparel, and there come in also a poor man in vile raiment, 3 And
ye have a respect to him that weareth the gay clothing; and say unto him, Sit thou
here in a [c]goodly place, and say unto the poor, Stand thou there, or sit here un-
der my footstool, 4 Are ye not partial in [d]your selves, and are become Judges
of evil thoughts? 5 [e]Hearken my beloved brethren, hath not God chosen the

---

JAMES 1

- **a.** TITLE - That is, written to no one man, city or country, but to all the Jews generally, being now dispersed.
- **b.** James 1:1 To all the believing Jews, of what Tribe soever they be, and are dispersed through the whole world.
- **c.** James 1:2 The first place or part touching comfort in afflictions, wherein we ought not be cast down and be fainthearted, but rather rejoice and be glad.
- **d.** James 1:2 Seeing their condition was miserable in that scattering abroad, he doth well to begin as he doth.
- **e.** James 1:2 The first argument, because our faith is tried through afflictions: which ought to be most pure, for so it is behoovable for us.
- **f.** James 1:3 The second, Because patience, far passing and most excellent virtue, is by this means engendered in us.
- **g.** James 1:3 That wherewith your faith is tried, to wit, those manifold temptations.
- **h.** James 1:4 The third argument propounded in manner of an exhortation, that true and continual patience may be discerned from fained and for a time. The cross is as it were the instrument wherewith God doth polish and refine us. Therefore the work and effect of afflictions, is the perfecting of us in Christ.
- **i.** James 1:5 An answer to a privy objection: It is easily said, but it is not so easily done. He answereth that we need in this case a far other manner of wisdom, than the wisdom of man, to judge those things best for us, which are most contrary to the flesh: but yet we shall easily obtain this gift of wisdom, if we ask it rightly, that is, with a sure confidence of God, who is most bountiful and liberal.
- **j.** James 1:5 By wisdom he meaneth the knowledge of that doctrine whereof mention was made before, to wit, wherefore we are afflicted of God, and what fruit we have to reap of affliction.
- **k.** James 1:6 Why then what need other Mediator?
- **l.** James 1:6 A digression or going aside from his matter, against prayers which are conceived with a doubting mind, whereas we have a certain promise of God, and this is that second part of the Epistle.
- **m.** James 1:8 In all his thoughts and his deeds.
- **n.** James 1:9 He returneth to his purpose, repeating the proposition, which is, that we must rejoice in the cross, for it doth not press us down, but exalt us.
- **o.** James 1:9 Who is afflicted with poverty, or contempt, or with any kind of calamity.
- **p.** James 1:10 Before he concludeth, he giveth a doctrine contrary to the former: to wit, how we ought to use prosperity, which is plenty of all things: to wit, so that no man therefore please himself, but be so much the more void of pride.
- **q.** James 1:10 Who hath all things at his will.
- **r.** James 1:10 An argument taken of the very nature of the things themselves, for that they are most vain and uncertain.
- **s.** James 1:11 Whatsoever he either purposeth in his mind, or doeth.
- **t.** James 1:12 The conclusion: Therefore we must patiently bear the cross: and he addeth a fourth argument, which comprehendeth the sum of all the former, to wit, because we come by this way to the crown of life, but yet of grace according to the promise.
- **u.** James 1:12 Affliction whereby the Lord trieth him.
- **v.** James 1:13 The third part of this Epistle, wherein he descendeth from outward tentations, that is, from afflictions, whereby God trieth us, to inward, that is, to those lusts whereby we are stirred up to do evil. The sum is this: Every man is the author of these temptations to himself, and not God: for we bear about in our bosoms that wicked corruption, which taketh occasions by what means soever, to stir up evil motions in us, whence out at length proceed wicked doing, and in conclusion followeth death the just reward of them.
- **w.** James 1:13 When he is provoked to do evil.
- **x.** James 1:13 Here is a reason showed, why God cannot be the author of evil doing in us, because he desireth not evil.
- **y.** James 1:15 By sin is meant in this place actual sin.
- **z.** James 1:16 Another reason taken of contraries: God is the author of all goodness, and so, that he is always like himself; how then can he be thought to be author of evil?
- **aa.** James 1:17 From him who is the fountain and author of all goodness.
- **ab.** James 1:17 He goeth on in the metaphor: for the sun by his manifold and sundry kinds of turning, maketh hours, days, months, years, light and darkness.
- **ac.** James 1:18 The fourth part concerning the excellency and fruit of the word of God. The sum is this: we must hear the word of God most carefully and diligently, seeing it is the seed, wherewith God of his free favor and love hath begotten us unto himself, picking us out of the number of his creatures. And the Apostle condemneth two faults, which do greatly trouble us in this matter, to wit, for that we so please ourselves, that we had rather speak ourselves than hear God speaking: yea, we snuff and are angry when we are reprehended: against which faults, he setteth a peaceable and quiet mind, and such an one as is desirous of purity.
- **ad.** James 1:18 This is it which Paul calleth gracious favor, and good will, which is the fountain of our salvation.
- **ae.** James 1:18 As it were an holy kind of offering, taken out of the residue of man.
- **af.** James 1:20 That which God appointeth.
- **ag.** James 1:21 By meekness, he meaneth modesty, and whatsoever is contrary to an haughty and proud stomach.
- **ah.** James 1:22 Another admonition. Therefore is God's word heard, that we may frame our lives according to the prescript thereof.
- **ai.** James 1:22 He addeth reasons, and those most weighty: first, because they that do otherwise, do very much hurt themselves.
- **aj.** James 1:23 Secondly, because they lose the chiefest use of God's word, which correct not by it the faults that they know.
- **ak.** James 1:23 He alludeth to that natural spot, to which is contrary that purity whereunto we are born again, the lively image whereof we behold in the Law.
- **al.** James 1:25 Behaving himself so: for works do show faith.
- **am.** James 1:26 The third admonition: The word of God prescribeth a rule not only to do well, but also to speak well.
- **an.** James 1:26 The fountain of all brabbling, and cursed speaking, and sauciness, is this, that men know not themselves.
- **ao.** James 1:27 The fourth: the true service of God standeth in charity toward our neighbors especially such as need others' help, as the fatherless and widows, and purity of life.
- **ap.** James 1:27 To have a care of them, and to help them as much as we can.

JAMES 1

1. Rom. 5:3
2. Matt. 7:7 / Mark 11:24 / Luke 11:9 / John 14:13 / John 16:23
3. Isa. 40:6 / 1 Pet. 2:24
4. Job 5:17
5. Matt. 7:21 / Rom. 2:13

JAMES 2

- **a.** James 2:1 The fifth: Charity which proceedeth from a true faith, cannot stand with the accepting of persons: which he proveth plainly by setting forth their example, who with the reproach or disdain of the poor, honor the rich.
- **b.** James 2:1 For if we knew what Christ's glory is, and esteemed it as we ought to do, there would not be such respect of persons as there is.
- **c.** James 2:3 In a worshipful and honorable place.
- **d.** James 2:4 Have ye not which you ought not to do by this means with yourselves judged one man to be preferred before another?
- **e.** James 2:5 He showeth that they are perverse and naughty Judges, which prefer the rich before the poor, by that that God on the contrary side preferreth the poor, whom he hath enriched with true riches, before the rich.
- **f.** James 2:5 The needy and wretched, and if we measure it after the opinion of the world the veriest abjects of all men.
- **g.** James 2:6 Secondly, he proveth them to be mad men: for that the rich men are rather to be holden execrable and cursed, considering that they persecute the Church, and blaspheme Christ: for he speaketh of wicked and profane

[f]poor of this world, that they should be rich in faith, and heirs of the kingdom
which he promised to them that love him? **6** But ye have despised the poor.
[g]Do not the rich oppress you by tyranny, and do they not draw you before the
judgment seats? **7** Do not they blaspheme the worthy Name after which ye be
[h]named? **8** [i]But if ye fulfill the [j]royal Law according to the Scripture, which
saith, Thou shalt love thy neighbor as thyself, ye do well. **9** But if ye regard the
persons, ye commit sin, and are rebuked of the Law, as transgressors. **10** [k]For
whosoever shall keep the whole Law, and yet faileth in one point, he is guilty
of [l]all. **11** [m]For he that said, Thou shalt not commit adultery, said also, Thou
shalt not kill. Now though thou doest none adultery, yet if thou killest, thou art
a transgressor of the Law. **12** [n]So speak ye, and so do, as they that shall be jud-
geth by the Law of liberty. **13** For there shall be condemnation merciless to him
that showeth not [o]mercy, and mercy rejoiceth against condemnation. **14** [p]What
availeth it my brethren, though a man saith, he hath faith, when he hath no works?
can that faith save him? **15** [q]For if a brother or a sister be naked and destitute of
daily food, **16** And one of you say unto them, Depart in peace: warm yoursel-
ves, and fill your bellies, notwithstanding ye give them not those things, which are
needful to the body, what helpeth it? **17** Even so the faith, if it have no works,
is dead in itself. **18** But [r]some man might say, Thou hast the faith, and I have
works: show me thy faith out of thy works, and I will show thee my faith by my
works. **19** [s]Thou believest that there is one God: thou doest well: the devils also
believe it, and tremble. **20** [t]But wilt thou understand, O thou vain man, that the
faith which is without works, is dead? **21** Was not Abraham our father [u]justified
through works, [2]when he offered Isaac his son upon the altar? **22** Seest thou not
that the faith [v]wrought with his works? and through the works was the faith made
[w]perfect. **23** And the Scripture was [x]fulfilled which saith, [3]Abraham believed
God, and it was imputed unto him for righteousness: and he was called the friend
of God. **24** [y]Ye see then how that of works a man is [z]justified, and not of [aa]fai-
th only. **25** [ab]Likewise also was not [4]Rahab the harlot justified through works,
when she had received the messengers, and sent them out another way? **26** [ac]For
as the body without the spirit is dead, even so the faith without works is dead.

3

2 To show that a Christian man must govern his tongue with the bridle of faith and charity, 6 he declareth the commodities and mischiefs that ensue thereof: 15 and how much man's wisdom 17 differeth from heavenly.

1 My [a]brethren, be not many masters, [b]knowing that we [c]shall receive the
greater condemnation. **2** For in many things we [d]sin all. [e]If any man sin not
in word, he is a perfect man, and able to bridle all the body. **3** [f]Behold, we put
bits into the horses' mouths, that they should obey us, and we turn about all their
body. **4** Behold also the ships, which though they be so great, and are driven of
fierce winds, yet are they turned about with a very small rudder, whithersoever the
governor listeth. **5** Even so the tongue is a little member, and boasteth of great
things: [g]behold, how great a thing a little fire kindleth. **6** And the tongue is fire,
yea, a [h]world of wickedness: so is the tongue set among our members, that it defi-
leth the whole body, and [i]setteth on fire the course of nature, and it is set on fire of
hell. **7** For the whole nature of beasts, and of birds, and of creeping things, and
things of the sea is tamed, and hath been tamed of the nature of man. **8** But the
tongue can no man tame. It is an unruly evil, full of deadly poison. **9** [j]Therewith
bless we God even the Father, and therewith curse we men, which are made after
the [k]similitude of God. **10** [l]Out of one mouth proceedeth blessing and cursing:
my brethren, these things ought not so to be. **11** Doth a fountain send forth
at one place sweet water and bitter? **12** Can the fig tree, my brethren, bring
forth olives, either a vine figs? so can no fountain make both salt water and swe-
et. **13** [m]Who is a wise man and endued with knowledge among you? let him
show by good conversation his works in meekness of wisdom. **14** But if ye have
bitter envying and strife in your hearts, rejoice not, neither be liars against the
truth. **15** This wisdom descendeth not from above, but is earthly, sensual, and
devilish. **16** For where envying and strife is, there is sedition, and all manner of
evil works. **17** But the wisdom that is from above, is first pure, then peaceable,
gentle, easy to be entreated, full of [n]mercy and good fruits, without judging, and
without hypocrisy. **18** [o]And the fruit of righteousness is sown in peace, of them
that make peace.

4

1 He reckoneth up the mischiefs that proceed of the works of the flesh. 7 He exhorteth to humility, 8 and to purge the heart 3 from pride, 10 backbiting, 14 and the forgetfulness of our own infirmity.

1 From [a]whence are wars and contentions among you? are they not hence,
even of your pleasures, that fight in your members? **2** Ye lust, and have not:
ye envy, and desire immoderately, and cannot obtain: ye fight, and war, and get
nothing, [b]because ye ask not. **3** Ye ask, and receive not, because ye ask amiss,
that ye might lay the same on your pleasures. **4** [c]Ye adulterers and adulteresses,

---

rich men, such as the most part of them have been always, against whom he setteth the poor and abject.

h. James 2:7 Word for word, which is called upon of you.

i. James 2:8 The conclusion: Charity which God prescribeth cannot agree with the accepting of persons, seeing that we must walk in the King's highway.

j. James 2:8 The Law is said to be royal and like the King's highway, for that it is plain and without turnings, and that the Law calleth everyone our neighbor, without respect, whom we may help by any kind of duty.

k. James 2:10 A new argument to prove the same conclusion: They do not love their neighbors, which neglect some, and ambitiously honor others: for he doth not obey God, which cutteth off from the commandments of God that that is not so commodious for him, nay he is rather guilty generally for the breach of the whole Law, although he observe the residue.

l. James 2:10 Not that all sins are equal, but because he that breaketh one tittle of the Law, offendeth the majesty of the Lawgiver.

m. James 2:11 A proof: because the Lawmaker is always one and the selfsame, and the body of the Law cannot be divided.

n. James 2:12 The conclusion of the whole treatise: we are upon this condition delivered from the curse of the Law by the mercy of God, that in like sort we should maintain and cherish charity and goodwill one towards another, and whoso doth not so, shall not taste of the grace of God.

o. James 2:13 He that is hard and currish against his neighbor, or else helpeth him not, he shall find God an hard and rough Judge to himselfward.

p. James 2:14 The fifth place which hangeth very well with the former treatise, touching a true and lively faith. And the proposition of this place is this: faith which bringeth not forth works, is not that faith whereby we are justified, but an image of faith: or else this, they are not justified by faith, which show not the effects of faith.

q. James 2:15 The first reason taken of a similitude: If a man say to one that is hungry, Fill thy belly, and yet giveth him nothing, this shall not be true charity: so if a man say he believeth, and bringeth forth no works of his faith, this shall not be a true faith, but a certain dead thing set out with the name of faith, whereof no man hath to brag, unless he will openly incur reprehension, seeing that the cause is understood by the effects.

r. James 2:18 Nay, thus may every man beat down the pride.

s. James 2:19 Another reason taken of an absurdity: If such a faith were the true faith whereby we are justified, the devils should be justified: for they have that, but yet notwithstanding they tremble, and are not justified therefore, neither is that faith a true faith.

t. James 2:20 The third reason from the example of Abraham, who no doubt had a true faith: but he in offering his son, showed himself to have that faith which was not void of works, and therefore he received a true testimony when it was said, that faith was imputed to him for righteousness.

u. James 2:21 Was he not by his works known and found to be justified? for he speaketh not here of the causes of justification, but by what effects we may know that a man is justified.

v. James 2:22 Was effectual and fruitful with good works.

w. James 2:22 That the faith was declared to be a true faith, and that by works.

x. James 2:23 Then was the Scripture fulfilled, when it appeared plainly, how truly it was written of Abraham.

y. James 2:24 The conclusion: he is only justified that hath that faith which hath works following it.

z. James 2:24 Is proved to be just.

aa. James 2:24 Of that dead and fruitless faith which you boast of.

ab. James 2:25 A fourth reason taken from a like example of Rahab the harlot, who also proved by her works that she was justified by a true faith.

ac. James 2:26 The conclusion repeated again: faith which bringeth not forth fruits and works, is not faith, but a dead carcass.

JAMES 2

1. Lev. 9:15 / Deut. 1:17 / Deut. 16:29 / Prov. 24:23

2. Gen. 22:10

3. Gen. 15:6 / Rom. 4:3 / Gal. 3:6

4. Josh. 2:1

JAMES 3

a. James 3:1 The sixth part or place: Let no man usurp as most men ambitiously do authority to judge and censure others righteously.

b. James 3:1 A reason: Because they provoke God's severity against themselves, which do so curiously and rigorously condemn others, being themselves guilty and faulty.

c. James 3:1 Unless we surcease from this masterlike and proud finding fault with others.

d. James 3:2 Or, stumble.

e. James 3:2 The seventh place, touching the bridling of the tongue, joined with the former, so that it is manifest that there is no man which may not justly be found fault withal, seeing it is a rare virtue to bridle the tongue.

f. James 3:3 He showeth by two similitudes the one taken from the bridles of horses, the other from the rudders of ships, how great matters may be brought to pass by the good moderation of the tongue.

g. James 3:5 On the contrary part he showeth how great discommodities arise by the intemperance of the tongue, throughout the whole world, to the end that men may so much the more diligently give themselves to moderate it.

h. James 3:6 An heap of all mischiefs.

i. James 3:6 It is able to set the whole world on fire.

j. James 3:9 Amongst other faults of the tongue, the Apostle chiefly reproveth backbiting and speaking evil of our neighbors, even in them especially which otherwise will seem godly and religious.

k. James 3:9 He denieth by two reasons, that God can be praised by that man, that useth cursed speaking, or to backbite: first because man is the image of God, which whosoever reverenceth not doth not honor God himself.

l. James 3:10 Secondly, because the order of nature which God hath set in things, will not suffer things that are so contrary the one to the other, to stand the one with the other.

m. James 3:13 The eighth part which hangeth with the former, touching meekness of mind, against which he setteth envy and a contentious mind. And in the beginning he stoppeth the mouth of the chief fountain of all these mischiefs, to wit, a false persuasion of wisdom, whereas notwithstanding there is no true wisdom, but that is heavenly, and frameth our minds to all kinds of true moderation and simplicity.

n. James 3:17 He setteth mercy against the fierce and cruel nature of man, and showeth that heavenly wisdom bringeth forth good fruits, for he that is heavenly wise, referreth all things to God's glory, and the profit of his neighbor.

o. James 3:18 Because the world persuadeth itself that they are miserable which live peaceably and simply, on the contrary side the Apostle pronounceth that they shall at the length reap the harvest of peaceable righteousness.

JAMES 4

a. James 4:1 He goeth on forward in the same argument, condemning certain other causes of wars and contentions, to wit, unbridled pleasures and immoderate lusts, by their effects, for so much as the Lord doth worthily make them void, so that they bring nothing else to them in whom they are but incurable torments.

b. James 4:2 He reprehendeth them by name, which are not ashamed to go about to make God the minister and helper of their lusts and pleasures, in asking things which either are of themselves unlawful, or being lawful, ask them to wicked purposes and uses.

c. James 4:4 Another reason why such unbridled lusts and pleasures are utterly to be condemned, to wit, because that he that giveth himself to the world, divorceth himself from God, and breaketh the band of that holy and spiritual marriage.

know ye not that the amity of the world is the enmity of God? Whosoever there-
fore will be a friend of the world, maketh himself the enemy of God. 5 [d]Do ye
think that the Scripture saith in vain, The spirit that dwelleth in us, lusteth after
envy? 6 But the Scripture offereth more grace, and therefore saith, [1]God resisteth
the proud, and giveth grace to the humble. 7 [2,e]Submit yourselves to God: resist
the devil, and he will flee from you. 8 Draw near to God, and he will draw near
to you. Cleanse your hands, ye sinners, and purge your hearts, ye double min-
ded. 9 [f]Suffer afflictions, and sorrow ye, and weep: let your laughter be turned
into mourning, and your joy into [g]heaviness. 10 [3]Cast down yourselves before
the Lord, and he will lift you up. 11 [h]Speak not evil one of another, brethren.
He that speaketh evil of his brother, or he that condemneth his brother, speaketh
evil of the Law, and condemneth the Law: and if thou condemnest the Law, thou
art not an observer of the Law, but a judge. 12 There is one Lawgiver, which is
able to save, and to destroy, [4]Who art thou that judgest another man? 13 [i]Go to
now, ye that say, Today or tomorrow we will go into such a city, and continue there
a year, and buy and sell, and get gain, 14 And yet ye cannot tell what shall be
tomorrow. For what is your life? It is even a vapor that appeareth for a little time,
and afterward vanisheth away. 15 For that ye ought to say, [5]If the Lord will, and
if we live, we will do this or that. 16 But now ye rejoice in your boastings: all
such rejoicing is evil. 17 [j]Therefore to him that knoweth how to do well, and
doeth it not, to him it is sin.

5

1 He threateneth the rich with God's severe judgment, for their pride, 7 that the poor hearing the miserable end of the rich, 8 may patiently bear afflictions, 11 as Job did, 14 even in their distresses.

1 Go [a]to now, ye rich men: weep, and howl for your miseries that shall
come upon you. 2 Your riches are corrupt, and your garments are moth ea-
ten. 3 Your gold and silver is cankered, and the rust of them shall be a witness
against you, and shall eat your flesh, as it were fire. Ye have heaped up treasure for
the last days. 4 Behold, the hire of the laborers, which have reaped your fields
which is of you kept back by fraud crieth, and the cries of them which have rea-
ped, are entered into the [b]ears of the Lord of hosts. 5 Ye have lived in pleasure on
the earth, and in wantonness. Ye have [c]nourished your hearts, as in a [d]day of slau-
ghter. 6 Ye have condemned, and have killed the just, and he hath not resisted
you. 7 [e]Be patient therefore, brethren, unto the coming of the Lord. [f]Behold,
the husbandman waiteth for the precious fruit of the earth, and hath long patience
for it, until he receive the former, and the latter rain. 8 Be ye also patient there-
fore, and settle your hearts: for the coming of the Lord draweth near. 9 [g,h]Gru-
dge not one against another, brethren, lest ye be condemned: [i]behold, the judge
standeth before the door. 10 [j]Take, my brethren, the Prophets for an example
of suffering adversity, and of long patience, which have spoken in the name of the
Lord. 11 Behold, we count them blessed which endure. Ye have heard of the
patience of Job, and have known what [k]end the Lord made. For the Lord is very
pitiful and merciful. 12 [l]But before all things, my brethren, [1]swear not, neither
by heaven, nor by earth, nor by any other oath: but let [m]your yea, be yea, and your
nay, nay, lest ye fall into condemnation. 13 [n]Is any among you afflicted? Let him
pray. Is any merry? Let him sing. 14 [o]Is any sick among you? Let him call for
the Elders of the Church, and let them pray for him, and anoint him with [2,p]oil
in the [q]Name of the Lord. 15 And the prayer of faith shall save the sick, and
the Lord shall raise him up: and if he have committed [r]sins, they shall be forgiven
him. 16 [s]Acknowledge your faults one to another, and pray one for another,
that ye may be healed: [t]for the prayer of a righteous man availeth much, if it be
fervent. 17 [3]Elijah was a man subject to like passions as we are, and he prayed
earnestly that it might not rain, and it rained not on the earth for three years and
six months. 18 And he prayed again: and the heaven gave rain, and the earth
brought forth her fruit. 19 [u]Brethren, [4]If any of you hath erred from the truth,
and some man hath [v]converted him, 20 Let him know that he which hath con-
verted the sinner from going astray out of his way, shall save a soul from death, and
shall hide a multitude of sins.

---

d.

e. James 4:5 The taking away of an objection: Indeed our minds run headlong into these vices, but we ought so much the more diligently take heed of them: which care and study shall not be in vain, seeing that God resists the stubborn, and giveth that grace to the modest and humble that surmounteth all those vices.

f. James 4:7 The conclusion: We must set the contrary virtues against those vices, and therefore whereas we obeyed the suggestions of the devil, we must submit our minds to God, and resist the devil, with a certain and assured hope of victory: To be short, we must employ ourselves to come near unto God by purity and sincerity of life.

g. James 4:9 He goeth on in the same comparison of contraries, and setteth against those profane joys with an earnest sorrow of mind, and against pride and arrogance, holy modesty.

h. James 4:9 By this word the Greeks meant an heaviness joined with shamefastness, which is to be seen in a cast down countenance, and settled as it were upon the ground.

i. James 4:11 He reprehended most sharply another double mischief of pride: the one is in that the proud and arrogant will have other men to live according to their will and pleasure and therefore they do most arrogantly condemn whatsoever pleaseth them not: which thing cannot be done without great injury to our only Lawmaker, for by this means his Laws are found fault withal, as not circumspectly enough written, and men challenge that unto themselves which properly belongeth to God alone, in that they lay a Law upon men's consciences.

j. James 4:13 The other fault is this: that men do so confidently determine upon these and those matters and businesses, as though that every moment of their life did not depend of God.

k. James 4:17 The conclusion of all the former treatise: The knowledge of the will of God doth not only nothing at all profit, unless the life be answerable unto it, but also maketh the sins far more grievous.

JAMES 4

1. Prov. 3:34 / 1 Pet. 5:5
2. Eph. 4:27
3. 1 Pet. 5:6
4. Rom. 14:4
5. 1 Cor. 4:19

JAMES 5

a. James 5:1 He denounceth utter destruction to the wicked and profane rich men, and such as are drowned in their riotousness, mocking at their foolish confidence when as there is nothing indeed more vain than such things.

b. James 5:4 The Lord who is more mighty than ye are, hath heard them.

c. James 5:5 Ye have pampered up yourselves.

d. James 5:5 The Hebrews call a day that is appointed to solemn banqueting, a day of slaughter or feasting.

e. James 5:7 He applieth that to the poor, which he spake against the rich, warning them to wait for the Lord's coming patiently, who will revenge the injuries which the rich men do them.

f. James 5:7 The taking away of an objection: Although his coming serve to linger, yet at the least we must follow the husbandmen, who do patiently wait for the times that are proper for the fruits of the earth. And again, God will not defer the least iota of the time that he hath appointed.

g. James 5:9 He commendeth Christian patience, so that whereas others through impatience use to accuse one another, the faithful on the contrary side complain not, although they receive injury.

h. James 5:9 By grudging, he meaneth a certain inward complaining which betokeneth impatience.

i. James 5:9 The conclusion: The Lord is at the door, who will defend his own, and revenge his enemies, and therefore we need not to trouble ourselves.

j. James 5:10 Because most men are wont to object, that it is good to repel injuries by what means soever, he setteth against that, the examples of the Fathers, whose patience had a most happy end, because God as a most bountiful Father, never forsaketh his.

k. James 5:11 What end the Lord gave.

l. James 5:12 Because even the best men sometimes through impatience break out into oaths sometimes lesser, sometimes greater, the Apostle warneth us to detest such wickedness, and to accustom our tongues to simple and true talk.

m. James 5:12 That that you have to say or affirm, speak or affirm it simply, and without an oath: and that that you will deny, deny it simply and flatly.

n. James 5:13 He showeth the best remedy against all afflictions, to wit, prayers which have their place both in sorrow and joy.

o. James 5:14 He showeth peculiarly, to what physicians especially we must go, when we are diseased, to wit, to the prayers of the Elders, which then also could cure the body, for so much as the gift of healing was then in force and take away the chiefest cause of sickness and diseases, by obtaining for the sick through their prayers and exhortations, remission of sins.

p. James 5:14 This was a sign of the gift of healing: and now seeing we have the gift no more, the sign is no longer necessary.

q. James 5:14 By calling on the Name of the Lord.

r. James 5:15 He hath reason in making mention of sins, for diseases are for the most part sent because of sins.

s. James 5:16 Because God pardoneth their sins which confess and acknowledge them, and not theirs which justify themselves, therefore the Apostle addeth, that we ought freely to confer one with another touching those inward diseases, that we may help one another with our prayers.

t. James 5:16 He commendeth prayers by the effects that come of them, that all men may understand that there is nothing more effectual than they are, so that they proceed from a pure mind.

u. James 5:19 The taking away of an objection: All reprehensions are not condemned, seeing that on the contrary part there is nothing more acceptable to God, than to call into the way a brother that was wandering out of the way.

v. James 5:19 Hath called him back from his way.

JAMES 5

1. Matt. 5:34
2. Mark 6:13
3. 1 Kings 17:1 / 1 Kings 18:45 / Luke 4:25
4. Matt. 8:15

THE FIRST EPISTLE GENERAL OF

PETER

1

1 He extolleth God's mercy showed in Christ, which we lay hold on by faith, and possess through hope: 10 whereof the Prophets foretold. 13 He exhorteth 15 to renounce the world, 23 and their former life, and so wholly yield themselves to God.

1 PETER an Apostle of JESUS CHRIST, to the strangers that dwell here
and there throughout Pontus, Galatia, Cappadocia, Asia and Bithynia, 2 [a]Elect
according to the [b]foreknowledge of God the Father unto [c]sanctification of the
Spirit, through obedience and sprinkling of the blood of Jesus Christ: Grace and
peace be multiplied unto you. 3 Blessed be God, even the Father of our Lord
Jesus Christ, which according to his abundant mercy hath begotten us again unto
a [d]lively hope by the resurrection of Jesus Christ from the dead, 4 To an inhe-
ritance immortal and undefiled, and that withereth not, reserved in heaven for
us, 5 [e]Which are kept by the power of God through faith unto salvation, which
is prepared to be showed in the [f]last time. 6 Wherein ye rejoice, though now for
a season if need require ye are in heaviness, through manifold tentations, 7 That
the trial of your faith, being much more precious than gold that perisheth thou-
gh it be tried with fire might be found unto your praise, and honor and glory at
the [g]appearing of Jesus Christ: 8 Whom ye have not seen, and yet love him, in
whom now, though ye see him not, yet do you believe, and rejoice with joy un-
speakable and glorious, 9 Receiving the [h]end of your faith, even the salvation of
your souls. 10 [i]Of the which salvation the Prophets have inquired and searched,
which prophesied of the grace that should come unto you, 11 Searching when
or what time the Spirit which testified before of Christ which was in them, should
declare the sufferings that should come unto Christ, and the glory that should fol-
low. 12 Unto whom it was revealed, that not unto themselves, but unto us they
should minister the things, which are showed unto you by them which have pre-
ached unto you the Gospel by the holy Ghost [j]sent down from heaven, the which
things the Angels desire to behold. 13 [k]Wherefore [l]gird up the loins of your
mind: be sober, [m]and trust [n]perfectly on that grace [o]that is brought unto you, [p]in
the revelation of Jesus Christ, 14 [q]As obedient children, not fashioned yoursel-
ves unto the former lusts of your ignorance: 15 But as he which hath called you,
is holy, so be ye holy in [1]all manner of conversation, 16 [r]Because it is written,
[2]Be ye holy, for I am holy. 17 [s]And if ye [t]call him Father, which without [3]respect
of person judgeth according to every man's work, pass the time of your dwelling
here in fear. 18 [u]Knowing that ye were not redeemed with corruptible things,
as silver and gold, from your vain conversation, received by the traditions of the
fathers, 19 [4]But with the precious blood of Christ, as of a Lamb undefiled, and
without spot. 20 [v]Which was [5]ordained before the [w]foundation of the world,
but was declared in the last times for your sakes, 21 Which by his means do be-
lieve in God that raised him from the dead, and gave him glory, that your faith
and hope might be in God. 22 [x]Having purified your souls in obeying the truth
through the Spirit, to [6]love brotherly without feigning, love one another with a
pure heart fervently: 23 Being born anew, not of mortal seed, but of immortal,
by the word of God, who liveth and endureth forever. 24 [y]For all [7,z]flesh is as
grass, and all the glory of man is as the flower of grass. The grass withereth, and the
flower falleth away. 25 [aa]But the word of the Lord endureth forever: and this is
the word which is preached among you.

2

He exhorteth the newborn in faith, to lead their lives answerable to the same: 6 and lest their faith should stagger, he bringeth in that which was foretold touching Christ. 11 Then he willeth them to be obedient to Magistrates, 21 and that they patiently bear adversity after Christ's example.

1 Wherefore, [1,a]laying aside all maliciousness, and all guile, and dissimula-
tion, and envy, and all evil speaking, 2 [b]As [c]newborn babes desire that sincere

---

1 PETER 1

- **a.** 1 Peter 1:2 Peter purposing to speak of the duties of a Christian life, reasoneth first of the principles and beginning of all Christian actions, rising far higher than nature, and carrying us also far above the same. For he showeth that we which are otherwise of nature sinners, were through the free mercy of God the Father first chosen from everlasting: then according to that everlasting decree were by a certain second creation made his sons in Christ his only begotten, by whose Spirit we are inwardly changed, and by whose blood we also are reconciled, to the end, that as Christ himself rose again from the dead, we also might be received into that same heavenly and everlasting glory.
- **b.** 1 Peter 1:2 Or according to the purpose of God, who never altereth nor changeth the same.
- **c.** 1 Peter 1:2 That being set apart from the rest of the wicked world, through the working of the holy Ghost, they should be consecrate to God, Eph. 1:5.
- **d.** 1 Peter 1:3 Everlasting hope.
- **e.** 1 Peter 1:5 Now he showeth by what way we come unto that glory, to wit, through all kinds of afflictions, wherein notwithstanding faith maketh us so secure, that we are not only not overcome with sorrow, but also through the beholding of God himself who otherwise is invisible with the eyes of faith are unspeakably joyful: because all such things, as they are but for a time, so are they not applied unto us to destroy us, but as it were by fire to purge us, and to make us perfect, that at the length we may obtain salvation.
- **f.** 1 Peter 1:5 This is that time which Daniel calleth the time of the end, when as that great restoring of all things shall be, which all creatures look for. Rom. 8:19.
- **g.** 1 Peter 1:7 He speaketh of the second coming of Christ.
- **h.** 1 Peter 1:9 Or, reward.
- **i.** 1 Peter 1:10 He putteth a difference between true faith, that is to say, that faith which only hath an eye to the doctrine of the Prophets and Apostles, and false faith: Afterward he maketh two degrees of one and the selfsame faith, according to the manner of the divers revelations, when as indeed it is but one only faith: Thirdly, he saith, that the preaching of the Apostles is the fulfilling of the preaching of the Prophets, although the latter end of it be as yet looked for of the very Angels.
- **j.** 1 Peter 1:12 He alludeth to the prophecy of Joel, which was exhibited upon the day of Pentecost, in the Apostles, as it were in the firstfruits of the holy Ghost, which this same our Peter declareth, Acts 2:6.
- **k.** 1 Peter 1:13 He goeth from faith to hope, which is indeed a companion that cannot be sundered from faith: and he useth an argument taken of comparison: We ought not to be wearied in looking for so excellent a thing, which the very Angels wait for with great desire.
- **l.** 1 Peter 1:13 This is a borrowed speech, taken of a common usage amongst them: for by reason that they wore long garments, they could not travel unless they girded up themselves: and hence it is that Christ said, Let your loins be girded up.
- **m.** 1 Peter 1:13 He setteth forth very briefly, what manner of hope ours ought to be, to wit, continual, until we enjoy the thing we hope for: then, what we have to hope for, to wit, grace that is, free salvation revealed to us in the Gospel, and not that, that men do rashly and fondly promise to themselves.
- **n.** 1 Peter 1:13 Soundly and sincerely.
- **o.** 1 Peter 1:13 An argument to stir up our minds, seeing that God doth not wait till we seek him, but causeth so great a benefit to be brought even unto us.
- **p.** 1 Peter 1:13 He setteth out the end of faith, lest any man should promise himself, either sooner or later that full salvation, to wit, the later coming of Christ: and therewithal warneth us, not to measure the dignity of the Gospel according to the present state, seeing that that which we are now, is not yet revealed.
- **q.** 1 Peter 1:14 He passeth from faith and hope, to the fruits of them both, which are understood in the name of obedience: And it consisteth in two things, in renouncing our lusts, and living godly: which lusts have their beginning of that blindness wherein all men are born: but holiness proceedeth from the grace and favor of GOD, which adopteth us, and therefore regenerateth us, that the father and the children may be of one disposition.
- **r.** 1 Peter 1:16 He showeth that sanctification doth necessarily follow adoption.
- **s.** 1 Peter 1:17 As before he distinguished true faith and hope from false, so doth he now obedience, setting the quick and sharp sight of God, against an outward mask, and earnest reverence against vain severity.
- **t.** 1 Peter 1:17 If you will be called the sons of that Father.
- **u.** 1 Peter 1:18 An exhortation, wherein he setteth forth the excellency and greatness of the benefit of God the Father, in sanctifying us by the death of his own Son. And he partly setteth the purifyings of the Law against the thing itself, that is, against the blood of Christ, and partly also men's traditions which he condemneth as utterly vain and superstitious, be they never so old and ancient.
- **v.** 1 Peter 1:20 The taking away of an objection: what was done to the world before that Christ was sent into the world? was there no holiness before, and was there no Church? The Apostle answereth, that Christ was ordained and appointed to redeem and deliver mankind, before that mankind was: much less was there any Church without him before his coming into the flesh: yet we are happiest above the rest, to whom Christ was exhibited indeed, in this that he having suffered and overcome death for us, doth now most effectually work in us by the virtue of his Spirit, to create in us faith, hope, and charity.
- **w.** 1 Peter 1:20 From everlasting.
- **x.** 1 Peter 1:22 He commendeth the practice of obedience, that is, charity: earnestly beating into their heads again, that he speaketh not of any common charity, and such as proceedeth from that our corrupt nature, but of that whose beginning is the Spirit of God, which purifieth our souls through the word laid hold on by faith, and engendereth also in us a spiritually and everlasting life, as God is most pure and truly living.
- **y.** 1 Peter 1:24 A reason why we have need of this heavenly generation, to wit, because that men, be their glory never so great, are of nature void of all true and sound goodness.
- **z.** 1 Peter 1:24 The word flesh showeth the weakness of our nature, which is chiefly to be considered in the flesh itself.
- **aa.** 1 Peter 1:25 Again, lest any man should seek that spiritual force and virtue in fained imaginations, the Apostle calleth us back to the word of God: teaching us furthermore, that there is no other word of the Lord to be looked for, than this which is preached, in which only we must trust.

1 PETER 1

1. Luke 1:75
2. Lev. 11:44 / Lev. 19:2 / Lev. 20:7
3. Deut. 10:17 / Rom. 2:11 / Gal. 2:6
4. 1 Cor. 6:20 / 1 Cor. 7:13 / Heb. 9:14 / 1 John 1:7 / Rev. 1:5
5. Rom. 16:25 / Eph. 3:9 / Col. 1:26 / 2 Tim. 1:10 / Titus 1:2
6. 1 Pet. 2:17 / Rom. 2:10 / Eph. 4:2
7. Isa. 40:6 / James 1:10

1 PETER 2

- **a.** 1 Peter 2:1 Having laid for the foundation the Spirit of God effectually working by the word, and having built thereupon three virtues which are the grounds of all Christian actions, to wit, faith, hope, and charity: now he proceedeth to a general exhortation, the first member whereof is, that we flee all show, both of secret and also open malice.
- **b.** 1 Peter 2:2 The second is, that being newly begotten and born of the new seed of the incorrupt word drawing and sucking greedily the same word as milk, we should more and more as it were grow up in that spiritual life. And he calleth it, Sincere, not only because it is a most pure thing, but also that we should take heed of them which corrupt it.

milk of the word, that ye may grow thereby, **3** [d]Because ye [e]have tasted that the Lord is bountiful. **4** [f]To whom coming as unto a living stone, disallowed of men, but chosen of God and precious, **5** Ye also as lively stones, be made a spiritual house, [g]an holy [2]Priesthood to offer up spiritual sacrifices acceptable to God by Jesus Christ. **6** [h]Wherefore also it is contained in the Scripture, [3]Behold, I put in Zion a chief cornerstone, elect and precious, and he that believeth therein, shall not be ashamed. **7** [i]Unto you therefore which believe, it is precious: but unto them which be disobedient, the [4]stone which the builders disallowed, the same is made the head of the corner, **8** And a [5]stone to stumble at, and a rock of offence, even to them which stumble at the word, being disobedient, unto the which thing they were even ordained. **9** [j]But ye are a chosen generation, a royal [6]Priesthood, an holy nation, a people set at liberty, that ye should show forth the virtues of him that hath called you out of darkness into his marvelous light, **10** [7]Which in time past were not a people, yet are now the people of God: which in time past were not under mercy, but now have obtained mercy. **11** [k]Dearly beloved, [l]I beseech you, as strangers and pilgrims, [8,m]abstain from fleshly lusts [n]which fight against the soul, **12** [9,o] And have your conversation honest among the Gentiles, that they which speak evil of you as of evil doers, [p]may by your good [10]works which they shall see, glorify God in the day of [q]visitation. **13** [11,r] Therefore submit yourselves unto [s]all manner ordinance of man [t]for the Lord's sake, [u]whether it be unto the King, as unto the superior, **14** Or unto governors, as unto them that are sent of him, [v]for the punishment of evil doers, and for the praise of them that do well. **15** [w]For so is the will of God, that by well doing ye may put to silence the ignorance of the foolish men. **16** As free, and not as having the liberty for a cloak of maliciousness, but as the servants of God. **17** [x,y]Honor all men: [12]love [z]brotherly fellowship: fear God: honor the King. **18** [13,aa]Servants, be subject to your masters with all fear, not only to the good and courteous, but also to the froward. **19** [14,ab]For this is thankworthy, if a man for [ac]conscience toward God endure grief, suffering wrongly. **20** For what praise is it, if when ye be buffeted for your faults, ye take it patiently? but and if when ye do well, ye suffer wrong and take it patiently, this is acceptable to God. **21** [ad]For hereunto ye are called: for Christ also suffered for you, leaving you an [ae]example that ye should follow his steps, **22** [15]Who did no sin, neither was there guile found in his mouth. **23** Who when he was reviled, reviled not again: when he suffered, he threatened not, but [af]committed it to him [ag]that judgeth righteously. **24** [16,ah]Who his own self bare our sins in his body on the tree, that we being dead to sin, should live in righteousness: by whose stripes ye were healed. **25** For ye were as sheep going astray: but are now returned unto the Shepherd and Bishop of your souls.

3

1 That Christian women should not contemn their husbands, though they be infidels. 6 He bringeth in examples of godly Women. 8 General exhortations, 14 patiently to bear persecutions, 15 and boldly to yield a reason of their faith. 18 Christ's example.

1 Likewise [1,a]let the wives be subject to their husbands, [b]that even they which obey not the word, may without the word be won by the conversation of the wives. **2** While they behold your pure conversation which is with fear: **3** [2,c]Whose appareling let it not be that outward, with braided hair, and gold put about, or in putting on of apparel: **4** But let it be the [d]hidden man of the heart, which consisteth in the incorruption of a meek and quiet spirit, which is [e]before God a thing much set by. **5** [f]For even after this manner in time past did the holy women, which trusted in God, tire themselves, and were subject to their husbands. **6** As Sarah obeyed Abraham, and [3]called him Sir: whose daughters ye are, while ye do well, [g]not being afraid of any terror. **7** [4,h]Likewise ye husbands, [i]dwell with them as men of [j]knowledge, [k]giving [l]honor unto the woman, as unto the weaker [m]vessel,

---

c. 1 Peter 2:2 As becometh new men.

d. 1 Peter 2:3 He commendeth that spiritual nourishment for the sweetness and profit of it.

e. 1 Peter 2:3 Or, do taste.

f. 1 Peter 2:4 He goeth on forward in the same exhortation, and useth another kind of borrowed speech, alluding to the Temple. Therefore he saith, that the company of the faithful is as it were a certain holy and spiritual building, built of lively stones, the foundation whereof is Christ, as a lively stone sustaining all that are joined unto him with his living virtue, and knitting them together with himself, although this so great a treasure be neglected of men.

g. 1 Peter 2:5 Going forward in the same similitude, he compareth us now to Priests placed to this end in that spiritual temple, that we should serve him with spiritual worship, that is, with holiness and righteousness: but as the temple, so is the Priesthood built upon Christ, in whom only all our spiritual offerings are accepted.

h. 1 Peter 2:6 He proveth it by the testimony of the Prophet Isaiah.

i. 1 Peter 2:7 By setting the most blessed condition of the believers, and the most miserable of the rebellious one against another, he pricketh forward the believers, and triumpheth over the others: and also preventeth an offense which ariseth hereof, that none do more resist this doctrine of the Gospel, than they which are chiefest amongst the people of God, as were at that time that Peter wrote these things, the Priests and Elders, and Scribes. Therefore he answereth first of all that there is no cause why any man should be astonished at this their stubbornness, as though it were a strange matter, seeing that we have been forewarned so long before, that it should so come to pass: and moreover, that it pleased God to create and make certain to this selfsame purpose, that the Son of God might be glorified in their just condemnation. Thirdly, for that the glory of Christ is hereby set forth greatly, whereas notwithstanding Christ remaineth the sure head of his Church, and they that stumble at him, cast down and overthrow themselves, and not Christ. Fourthly, although they be created to this end and purpose, yet their fall and decay is not to be attributeth to God, but to their own obstinate stubbornness which cometh between God's decree, and the execution thereof or their condemnation, and is the true and proper cause of their destruction.

j. 1 Peter 2:9 The contrary member, to wit, he describeth the singular excellency of the elect: and also lest any man should doubt whether he be chosen or not, the Apostle calleth us back to the effectual calling, that is, to the voice of the Gospel sounding both in our ears and minds by the outward preaching and Sacraments, whereby we may certainly understand that everlasting decree of our salvation, which otherwise is most secret and hidden and that through the only mercy of God, who freely chooseth and calleth us. Therefore this only remaineth, sayeth he, that by all means possible we set forth so great goodness of the most mighty God.

k. 1 Peter 2:11 He returneth to that general exhortation.

l. 1 Peter 2:11 A reason why we ought to live holily, to wit, because we are citizens of heaven, and therefore we ought to live according to the Laws not of this world, which is most corrupt, but of the heavenly city, although we be strangers in the world.

m. 1 Peter 2:11 Another argument: The children of God live not according to the flesh, that is, according to that corrupt nature, but according to the spirit. Therefore fleshly motions ought not to bear rule in us.

n. 1 Peter 2:11 The third argument: for although those lusts flatter us, yet they cease not to fight against our salvation.

o. 1 Peter 2:12 The fourth argument, taken of the profit of so doing: for by this means also we provide for our good name and estimation, whilest we compel them at length to change their minds, which speak evil of us.

p. 1 Peter 2:12 The fifth argument, which also is of great force: Because the glory of God is greatly set forth by that means, whilst by example of our honest life, even the most profane men are brought unto God, and submit themselves unto him.

q. 1 Peter 2:12 When God shall also have mercy on them.

r. 1 Peter 2:13 That which he spoke generally, he now expoundeth by parts, describing severally every man's duty. And first of all he speaketh of obedience which is due both to the Laws, and also to the Magistrates both higher and lower.

s. 1 Peter 2:13 By ordinance, is meant the framing and ordering of civil government: which he calleth ordinance of man, not because man invented it, but because it is proper to men.

t. 1 Peter 2:13 The first argument: because the Lord is the author and revenger of this policy of men, that is, which is set amongst men: and therefore the true servants of the Lord must above all others be diligent observers of this order.

u. 1 Peter 2:13 He preventeth a cavil which is made by some, that say they will obey Kings and the higher magistrates, and yet contemn their ministers: as though their ministers were not armed with their authority which sent them.

v. 1 Peter 2:14 The second argument taken of the end of this order, which is not only most profitable, but also very necessary: seeing that by this means virtue is rewarded, and vice punished: wherein the quietness and happiness of this life consisteth.

w. 1 Peter 2:15 He declareth the first argument more amply, showing that Christian liberty doth amongst all things least, or not at all consist herein, to wit, to cast off the bridle of Laws, as at that time some altogether unskillful in the kingdom of God reported but rather in this, that living holily according to the will of God, we should make manifest to all men, that the Gospel is not a cloak for sin and wickedness, seeing we are in such sort free, that yet we are still the servants of God, and not of sin.

x. 1 Peter 2:17 He divideth the civil life of man, by occasion of those things of which he spake into two general parts: to wit, into those duties which private men owe to private men, and especially the faithful to the faithful, and into that subjection whereby inferiors are bound to their superiors: but so, that Kings be not made equal to God, seeing that fear is due to God, and honor to Kings.

y. 1 Peter 2:17 Be charitable and dutiful towards all men.

z. 1 Peter 2:17 The assembly and fellowship of the brethren, as Zech. 11:14.

aa. 1 Peter 2:18 He goeth to the duty of servants towards their masters, which he describeth with these bounds, that servants submit themselves willingly and not by constraint, not only to the good and courteous, but also to the froward and sharp masters.

ab. 1 Peter 2:19 The taking away of an objection: Indeed the condition of servants is hard, especially if they have froward masters: but this their subjection shall be so much the more acceptable to God, if his will prevails more with servants, than the masters' injuries.

ac. 1 Peter 2:19 Because he maketh a conscience of it to offered God, by whose good will and appointment, he knoweth this burden is laid upon him.

ad. 1 Peter 2:21 He mitigateth the grievousness of servitude, while he showeth plainly that Christ died also for servants, that they should bear so much the more patiently this inequality betwixt men which are of one selfsame nature, moreover setting before them Christ that Lord of Lords for an ensample, he signifieth that they cannot but seem too delicate, which show themselves more grieved in bearing of injuries, than Christ himself who was most just, and most sharply of all afflicted, and yet was most patient.

ae. 1 Peter 2:21 A borrowed kind of speech taken of painters and schoolmasters.

af. 1 Peter 2:23 He showeth them a remedy against injuries, to wit, that they commend their cause to God, by the ensample of Christ.

ag. 1 Peter 2:23 He seemeth now to turn his speech to masters, which have also themselves a master and judge in heaven: who will justly revenge the injuries that are done to servants without any respect of persons.

ah. 1 Peter 2:24 He calleth the servants back from the consideration of the injuries which they are constrained to bear, to think upon the greatness, and the end of the benefit received of Christ.

1 PETER 2

1. Rom. 6:4 / Eph. 4:23 / Col. 3:8 / Heb. 12:1
2. Rev. 1:6
3. Isa. 28:16 / Rom. 9:33
4. Ps. 118:21 / Matt. 21:41 / Acts 4:11
5. Isa. 8:14 / Rom. 9:33
6. Exod. 19:6
7. Hos. 2:23 / Rom. 9:25
8. Rom. 13:14 / Gal. 5:16
9. 1 Pet. 3:16
10. Matt. 5:16
11. Rom. 13:1
12. 1 Pet. 1:12 / Rom. 12:10
13. Eph. 5:6 / Col. 3:22
14. 2 Cor. 7:10
15. Isa. 53:9 / 1 John 3:5
16. Isa. 53:5 / Matt. 8:17

1 PETER 3

a. 1 Peter 3:1 In the third place he setteth forth the wives' duty to their husbands, commanding them to be obedient.

b. 1 Peter 3:1 He speaketh namely of them which had husbands that were not Christians, which ought so much the more be subject to their husbands, that by their honest and chaste conversation they may give them to the Lord.

c. 1 Peter 3:3 He condemneth the riot and excess of women and setteth forth their true appareling such as is precious before God: to wit, the inward and incorruptible which consisteth in a meek and quiet spirit.

d. 1 Peter 3:4 Who hath his seat fastened in the heart: so that the hid man is set against the outward decking of the body.

e. 1 Peter 3:4 Precious indeed, and so taken of God.

f. 1 Peter 3:5 An argument taken of the example of women, and especially of Sarah who was the mother of all believers.

g. 1 Peter 3:6 Because women are of nature fearful, he giveth them to understand, that he requireth of them that subjection, which is not wrung out of them either by force or fear.

[n]even as they which are heirs together of the [o]grace of life, [p]that your prayers be not interrupted. **8** [q]Finally, be ye all of one mind: one suffer with another: love as brethren: be pitiful, be courteous. **9** [5,r]Not rendering evil for evil, neither rebuke for rebuke: but contrariwise bless, [s]knowing that ye are thereunto called, that ye should be heirs of blessing. **10** [6,t]For if any man long after life, and to [u]see good days, let him refrain his tongue from evil, and his lips that they speak no guile. **11** [7]Let him eschew evil and do good: let him seek peace and follow after it. **12** For the eyes of the Lord are over the righteous, and his ears are open unto their prayers: and the [v]face of the Lord is against them that do evil. **13** [w]And who is it that will harm you, if ye follow that which is good? **14** [8]Notwithstanding blessed are ye, if ye suffer for righteousness' sake. [x]Yea, [9]fear not their [y]fear, neither be troubled. **15** But [z]sanctify the Lord God in your hearts, [aa]and be ready always to give an answer to every man that asketh you a reason of the hope that is in you, with meekness and reverence. **16** Having a good conscience, that when they speak evil of you as of evil doers, they may be ashamed which slander your good conversation in Christ. **17** [ab]For it is better if the will of God be so that ye suffer for well doing, than for evil doing. **18** [10,ac]For Christ also hath once suffered for sins, [ad]the just for the unjust, [ae]that he might bring us to God, [af]and was put to death concerning the [ag]flesh, but was quickened by the spirit. **19** [ah]By [ai]the which he also went, and preached unto the [aj]spirits that are in prison. **20** Which were in time passed disobedient, when [ak]once the long suffering of God abode in the days of [11]Noah, while the Ark was preparing, wherein few, that is, eight [al]souls were saved in the water. **21** [am]Whereof the baptism that now is, answering that figure, which is not a putting away of the filth of the flesh, but a confident demanding with a good conscience maketh to [an]God saveth us also [ao]by the resurrection of Jesus Christ. **22** Which is at the right hand of God, gone into heaven, to whom the Angels, and Powers, and might are subject.

4

1 He bringeth in Christ's example, and applieth it, 6 to the mortifying of the flesh, especially commending Charity: 12 And so entreateth of patience. 19 That it is necessary that correction begin at the Church.

1 Forasmuch [a]then as Christ hath suffered for us in the flesh, arm yourselves likewise with the same mind, which is, that he which hath suffered in the flesh, hath ceased from sin, **2** That he hence forward should live as much time as [b]remaineth in the flesh not after the lusts of men, but after the will of God. **3** [1,c]For it is sufficient for us that we have spent the time past of the life, after the lust [d]of the Gentiles walking in wantonness, lusts, drunkenness, in gluttony, drinkings, and in abominable idolatries. **4** [e]Wherein it seemeth to them [f]strange, that ye run not with them unto the same excess of riot: therefore speak they evil of you. **5** Which shall give account to him, that is ready to judge quick and dead. **6** [g]For unto this purpose was the Gospel preached also unto the dead, that they might be condemned according to men in the flesh, but might live according to God in the spirit. **7** [h]Now the end of all things is at hand. Be ye therefore sober, and watching in prayer. **8** [i]But above all things have fervent love among you: [2]for love shall cover the multitude of sins. **9** [j]Be ye [3]harberous one to another, without grudging. **10** [k,4]Let every man as he hath received the gift, minister the same one to another, [l]as good disposers of the manifold grace of God. **11** [m]If any man speak,

---

h. 1 Peter 3:7 He teacheth husbands also their duties, to wit, that the more understanding and wisdom they have, the more wisely and circumspectly they behave themselves.

i. 1 Peter 3:7 Do all the duties of wedlock.

j. 1 Peter 3:7 The more wisdom the husband hath, the more circumspectly he must behave himself in bearing those commodities, which through the woman's weakness ofttimes cause trouble both to the husband and the wife.

k. 1 Peter 3:7 The second argument, because the wife notwithstanding that she is weaker by nature than the man, is an excellent instrument of the man made to far most excellent uses: whereupon it followeth that she is not therefore to be neglected because she is weak, but on the contrary part she ought to be so much the more cared for.

l. 1 Peter 3:7 Having an honest care of her.

m. 1 Peter 3:7 The woman is called a vessel after the manner of the Hebrews, because the husband useth her as his fellow and helper to live faithfully before God.

n. 1 Peter 3:7 The third argument: for that they are equal in that which is the chiefest (that is to say, in the benefit of eternal life) which otherwise are unequal as touching the governance and conversation at home, and therefore they are not to be despised although they be weak.

o. 1 Peter 3:7 Of that gracious and free benefit whereby we have everlasting life given us.

p. 1 Peter 3:7 The fourth argument: All brawlings and chidings must be eschewed, because they hinder prayers and the whole service of God whereunto both the husband and wife are equally called.

q. 1 Peter 3:8 He returneth to common exhortations and commendeth concord and whatsoever things pertain to the maintenance of peace and mutual love.

r. 1 Peter 3:9 We must not only not recompense injury for injury, but we must also recompense them with benefits.

s. 1 Peter 3:9 An argument taken of comparison: Seeing that we ourselves are called of God whom we offend so often, to so great a benefit (so far is he from revenging the injuries which we do unto him) shall we rather make ourselves unworthy of so great bountifulness, than forgive one another's faults? And from this verse to the end of the chapter, there is a digression or going from the matter he is in hand with, to exhort us valiantly to bear afflictions.

t. 1 Peter 3:10 A secret objection: But this our patience shall be nothing else but a fleshing and hardening of the wicked in their wickedness, to make them to set upon us more boldly, and to destroy us. (Nay saith the Apostle by the words of David) to live without doing hurt, and to follow after peace when it fleeth away, is the way to the happy and quiet peace. And if so be any man be afflicted for doing justly, the Lord maketh all things, and will in his time deliver the godly, which cry unto him, and will destroy the wicked.

u. 1 Peter 3:10 Lead a blessed and happy life.

v. 1 Peter 3:12 This word (Face) after the manner of the Hebrews, is taken for (anger.)

w. 1 Peter 3:13 The second argument: when the wicked are provoked, they are more wayward: therefore they must rather be overcome with good turns: And if they cannot be gotten by that means also, yet notwithstanding we shall be blessed, if we suffer for righteousness' sake.

x. 1 Peter 3:14 A most certain counsel in afflictions, be they never so terrible, to be of a constant mind, and to stand fast. But how shall we attain unto it? If we sanctify God in our minds and hearts, that is to say, if we rest upon him, as one that is Almighty, that loveth mankind, that is good and true indeed.

y. 1 Peter 3:14 Be not dismayed as they are.

z. 1 Peter 3:15 Give him all praise and glory, and hang only on him.

aa. 1 Peter 3:15 He will have us when we are afflicted for righteousness' sake, to be careful not for redeeming of our life, either with denying, or renouncing the truth, or with like violence, or any such means: but rather to give an account of our faith boldly, and yet with a meek spirit, and full to godly reverence, that the enemies may not have anything justly to object, but may rather be ashamed of themselves.

ab. 1 Peter 3:17 A reason which standeth upon two general rules of Christianity, which notwithstanding all men allow not of. The one is, if we must needs suffer afflictions, it is better to suffer wrongfully than rightfully: the other is this, because we are so afflicted, not by hap, but by the will of our God.

ac. 1 Peter 3:18 A proof of either of the rules, by the example of Christ himself our chief pattern who was afflicted, not for his own sins (which were none) but for ours, and that according to his Father's decree.

ad. 1 Peter 3:18 An argument taken of comparison: Christ the just suffered for us that are unjust, and shall it grieve us who are unjust to suffer for the just's cause?

ae. 1 Peter 3:18 Another argument being partly taken of things coupled together, to wit, because Christ bringeth us to his Father that same way that he went himself, and partly from the cause efficient: to wit, because Christ is not only set before us for an example to follow, but also he holdeth us up by his virtue in all the difficulties of this life, until he bring us to his Father.

af. 1 Peter 3:18 Another argument taken of the happy end of these afflictions, wherein also Christ goeth before us both in example and virtues, as one who suffered most grievous torments even unto death, although but in one part only of him, to wit, in the flesh or man's nature, but yet became conqueror by virtue of his divinity.

ag. 1 Peter 3:18 As touching his manhood, for his body was dead, and his soul felt the sorrows of death.

ah. 1 Peter 3:19 A secret objection: Christ indeed might do this, but what is that to us? yet (saith the Apostle) for Christ hath showed forth this virtue in all ages both to the preservation of the godly, were they never so few and miserable, and to revenge the rebellion of his enemies, as it appeareth by the history of the flood: for Christ is he which in those days (when God through his patience appointed a time of repentance to the world) was present not in corporal presence, but by his divine virtue, preaching repentance even by the mouth of Noah himself who then prepared the Ark, to those disobedient spirits which are now in prison waiting for the full recompence of their rebellion, and saved those few (that is, eight only persons) in the water.

ai. 1 Peter 3:19 By the virtue of which Spirit, that is to say of the divinity: therefore this word, Spirit, cannot in this place be taken for the soul, unless we say, that Christ was raised up again, and quickened by the virute of his soul.

aj. 1 Peter 3:19 He calleth them Spirits, in respect of his time, not in respect of the time that they were in the flesh.

ak. 1 Peter 3:20 This word (once) showeth that there was a furthermost day appointed, and if that were once past, there should be no more.

al. 1 Peter 3:20 Men.

am. 1 Peter 3:21 A proportional applying of the former example to the times which followed the coming of Christ: for that preservation of Noah in the waters was a figure of our Baptism, not as though that material water of Baptism saveth us, as those waters which bare up the Ark saved Noah, but because Christ with his inward virtue, which the outward Baptism shadoweth, preserveth us being washed, so that we may call upon God with a good conscience.

an. 1 Peter 3:21 The conscience being sanctified may freely call upon God.

ao. 1 Peter 3:21 That selfsame virtue, whereby Christ rose again, and now being carried into heaven, hath received all power, doth at this day defend and preserve us.

1 PETER 3

1.	Col. 3:18 / Eph. 5:22	**6.**	Ps. 34:13
2.	Tim. 2:9	**7.**	Isa. 1:16
3.	Gen. 18:12	**8.**	Matt. 5:10
4.	1 Cor. 7:3	**9.**	Isa. 8:12,13
5.	Prov. 17:13 / Prov. 20:21 / Matt. 5:39 / Rom. 12:17 / 1 Thess. 5:15	**10.**	Rom. 5:6 / Heb. 9:15
		11.	Gen. 6:14 / Matt. 24:33 / Luke 17:26

1 PETER 4

a. 1 Peter 4:1 Having ended his digression and sliding from his matter, now he returneth to the exhortation which he brake off, taking occasion by that which he said touching the death, and resurrection of Christ, so defining our sanctification, that to be sanctified, is all one as to suffer in the flesh, that is to say: to leave off from our wickedness and viciousness: and to rise again to God, that is to say, to be renewed, by the virtue of the holy Ghost, that we may lead the rest of our life which remaineth, after the will of God.

b. 1 Peter 4:2 So much of this present life as remaineth yet to be passed over.

c. 1 Peter 4:3 By putting us in mind of the dishonesty of our former life led in the filth of sin, he calleth us to earnest repentance.

d. 1 Peter 4:3 Wickedly and licentiously after the manner of the Gentiles.

e. 1 Peter 4:4 That we be not moved with the enemies' perverse and slanderous judgments of us, we have to set against them that last judgment of God which remaineth for them, for none, whether they be then found living, or were dead before, shall escape it.

f. 1 Peter 4:4 They think it a new and strange matter.

g. 1 Peter 4:6 A digression because he made mention of the last general judgement. And he preventeth an objection, that seeing Christ came very lately, they may seem to be excusable which died before. But this the Apostle denieth, for saith he this selfsame Gospel was preached unto them also: for he speaketh unto the Jews and that to the same end that I now preach it unto you, to wit, that the flesh being abolished and put away that is to say, that wicked and naughty corruption which reigneth in men they should suffer themselves to be governed by the virtue of the Spirit of God.

h. 1 Peter 4:7 He returneth to his purpose, using an argument taken from the circumstance of the time, because the last end is at hand, and therefore we must so much the more diligently watch and pray with true sobriety of mind.

i. 1 Peter 4:8 He commendeth charity of one toward another, because it doth as it were bury a multitude of sins, and therefore preserveth and maintaineth peace and concord: for they that love one another, do easily forgive one another their offense.

j. 1 Peter 4:9 Of all the duties of charity, he commendeth one, namely, which was at that time most necessary, to wit, hospitality, which he will have to be voluntary and most courteous and bountiful.

k. 1 Peter 4:10 He showeth the use of charity, to wit, that every man bestow that gift which he hath received to the profit of his neighbor.

l. 1 Peter 4:10 A reason, because that what gift soever we have we have received it of God upon this condition, to be his disposers and stewards.

let him speak as the words of God. If any man minister, let him do it as of the abi-
lity which God ministereth, that God in all things may be glorified through Jesus
Christ, to whom is praise and dominion forever, and ever, Amen. **12** [n]Dearly
beloved, think it not [o]strange [p]concerning the fiery trial, which is among you to
prove you as though some strange thing were come unto you. **13** [q]But rejoi-
ce, inasmuch as ye are partakers of Christ's sufferings, that when his glory shall
appear, ye may be glad and rejoice. **14** [5,r]If ye be railed upon for the Name of
Christ, blessed are ye: for the [s]spirit of glory and of God resteth upon you: which
on their part is evil spoken of, but on your part is glorified. **15** [t]But let none of
you suffer as a murderer, or as a thief, or an evil doer, or as a busybody in other
men's matters. **16** But if any man suffer as a Christian, let him not be ashamed:
but let him glorify God in this behalf. **17** [u]For the time is come that judgment
must begin at the house of God. [v]If it first begin at us, what shall the end be of
them which obey not the Gospel of God? **18** [6]And if the righteous scarcely be
saved, where shall the ungodly and the sinner appear? **19** [w]Wherefore let them
that suffer according to the will of God, commit their souls to him in well doing,
as unto a faithful Creator.

5

1 He warneth the Elders not to usurp authority over the Church, 5 willing the younger sort to be willing to be taught, and to be modest, 8 to be sober and watchful to resist the cruel adversary.

1 The [a]Elders which are among you, [b]I beseech which am also an Elder, and
a witness of the sufferings of Christ, and also a partaker of the glory that shall be
revealed, **2** [c,d]Feed the [e]flock of God, [f]which dependeth upon you, [g]caring for it
not by constraint, but willingly: not for filthy lucre, but of a ready mind: **3** Not
as though ye were Lords over God's [h]heritage, but that ye may be examples to
the flock. **4** [i]And when that chief Shepherd shall appear, ye shall receive an in-
corruptible crown of glory. **5** [j]Likewise ye younger submit yourselves unto the
Elders, and submit yourselves every man, one to another: [1]deck yourselves inwar-
dly in lowliness of mind: [k]for [2]God resisteth the proud, and giveth grace to the
humble. **6** Humble [3]yourselves therefore [l]under the mighty hand of God, that
he may exalt you in due time. **7** [4]Cast all your care on him: for he careth for
you. **8** [m]Be sober, and watch: for [5]your adversary the devil as a roaring lion
walketh about, seeking whom he may devour: **9** Whom resist steadfast in the
faith, [n]knowing that the same afflictions are accomplished in your [o]brethren which
are in the world. **10** [p]And the God of all grace, which hath called us unto his
eternal glory by Christ Jesus, after that ye have suffered a little, make you perfect,
confirm, strengthen, and establish you. **11** To him be glory and dominion fore-
ver and ever, Amen. **12** [q]By Silvanus a faithful brother unto you, as I suppose,
have I written briefly, exhorting and testifying how that this is the true grace of
God, wherein ye stand. **13** [r]The Church that is at [s]Babylon elected together with
you, saluteth you, and Mark my son. **14** Greet ye one another with the [6] kiss of
love. Peace be with you all which are in Christ Jesus, Amen.

---

m. 1 Peter 4:11 He reckoneth up two kinds of these gifts as chief, to wit, the office of teaching in the Church, and the other Ecclesiastical functions, wherein two things specially are to be observed, to wit, that the pure word of God be taught, and whatsoever is done, be referred to the glory of God the Father, in Christ, as to the proper mark.

n. 1 Peter 4:12 Because the cross is joined with the sincere profession of Religion, the Apostle fitly repeateth that which he touched before, warning us not to be troubled at persecutions and afflictions, as a new and strange thing.

o. 1 Peter 4:12 As though some new thing had befallen you, which you never thought of before.

p. 1 Peter 4:12 The first reason: Because the Lord meaneth not to consume us with this fire as it were but to purge us of our dross, and make us perfect.

q. 1 Peter 4:13 Another reason: Because the afflictions of the godly and the wicked differ very much, and chiefly in three points. First, because the godly communicate with Christ in their afflictions, and therefore shall in their time be partakers also of his glory.

r. 1 Peter 4:14 Secondly, because that although the infidels think far otherwise, who in afflicting the godly, blaspheme God, yet the godly in that they are so railed upon, are honored of God with the true spiritual glory, and their adoption sealed in them by the Spirit of God.

s. 1 Peter 4:14 By Spirit he meaneth the gifts of the Spirit.

t. 1 Peter 4:15 The third difference: for the godly are not afflicted for their evil doings, but for righteousness' sake as Christians: whereby it cometh to pass that the cross, seeing it is a testimony unto them of faith and righteousness, ministereth unto them not an occasion of sorrow, but of unspeakable joy: now the Apostle propoundeth the third difference under the form of an exhortation.

u. 1 Peter 4:17 The third reason because the Lord of all the world being especially careful for them of his household, doth therefore chastise them first of all, yet so that he kepeth a measure in his greatest severity: And as he hath always used to do heretofore, so doth he now specially when as he exhibited himself in person to his Church.

v. 1 Peter 4:17 Lest the godly should be offended and stumble at that vain shadow of felicity of the wicked, as though God were not the governor of the world, for that the wicked are in good case, and the godly in evil, the Apostle teacheth by an argument of a comparison of them together, that God who spareth not his own, but nurtureth them under the cross, will at length in his time handle the rebellious and wicked far otherwise, whom he hath appointed to utter destruction.

w. 1 Peter 4:19 The conclusion: Seeing the godly are not afflicted by chance, but by the will of God, they ought not to despair, but go forward, notwithstanding in the way of holiness and well doing, commending themselves to God their faithful Creator, that is to say, their Father.

1 PETER 4

1.	Eph. 4:22	**4.**	Rom. 12:6 / Phil 2:14
2.	Prov. 10:12	**5.**	Matt. 10
3.	Rom. 12:13 / Heb. 13:2	**6.**	Prov. 2:31

1 PETER 5

a. 1 Peter 5:1 He describeth peculiarly the office of the Elders, that is to say, of them that have the care of the Church.

b. 1 Peter 5:1 He useth a preface touching the circumstance of his own person: to wit, that he as their companion, communeth with them not of matters which he knoweth not, but wherein he is as well experienced as any, and propoundeth unto them no other condition but that which he himself hath sustained before them, and doth still take the same pains, and also hath one selfsame hope together with them.

c. 1 Peter 5:2 The first rule: He that is a shepherd, let him feed the flock.

d. 1 Peter 5:2 He saith not, Offer for the quick and dead, and sing patched shreds in a strange tongue, but Feed.

e. 1 Peter 5:2 The second: Let the shepherd consider, that the flock is not his, but God's.

f. 1 Peter 5:2 The third: Let not the shepherds invade other men's flocks, but let them feed that which God hath committed unto them.

g. 1 Peter 5:2 Let the shepherds govern the Church with the word and example of godly and unblamable life, not by constraint but willingly, not for filthy lucre, but of a ready mind, not as Lords over God's portion and heritage, but as his ministers.

h. 1 Peter 5:3 Which is the Christian people.

i. 1 Peter 5:4 That the shepherds' minds be not overcome either with the wickedness of men, or their cruelty, he warneth them to cast their eyes continually upon that chief Shepherd, and the crown which is laid up for them in heaven.

j. 1 Peter 5:5 He commendeth many peculiar Christian virtues, and especially modesty: which admonition all of us stand in need of, but especially the younger sort, by reason of the outwardness and pride of that age.

k. 1 Peter 5:5 Because pride seemeth to many, to be the way unto the glory of this life, the Apostle witnesseth on the contrary side, that ignominy and shame is the reward of pride, and glory the reward of modesty.

l. 1 Peter 5:6 Because those proud and lofty spirits threaten the modest and humble, the Apostle warneth us to set the power of God against the vanity of proud men, and to hang wholly upon his providence.

m. 1 Peter 5:8 The cruelty of Satan, who seeketh by all means to devour us, is overcome by watchfulness and faith.

n. 1 Peter 5:9 The persecutions which Satan stirreth up are neither new nor proper to any one man, but from old and ancient time common to the whole Church, and therefore we must suffer that patiently wherein we have such and so many fellows of our conflicts and combats.

o. 1 Peter 5:9 Amongst your brethren which are dispersed throughout the world.

p. 1 Peter 5:10 He sealeth up as it were with a seal the former exhortation with a solemn prayer, again willing them to ask increase of strength at his hands of whom they had the beginning, and hope to have the accomplishment, to wit, of God the Father in Jesus Christ in whom we are sure of the glory of eternal life.

q. 1 Peter 5:12 Continuance and perseverance in the doctrine of the Apostles, is the only ground and foundation of Christian strength: Now the sum of the Apostles' doctrine, is salvation freely given of God.

r. 1 Peter 5:13 Familiar salutations.

s. 1 Peter 5:13 In that famous city of Assyria, where Peter the Apostle of the circumcision then was.

1 PETER 5

1.	Rom. 12:10	**5.**	Luke 22:31
2.	James 4:6	**6.**	Rom. 16:16 / 1 Cor. 16:20 / 2 Cor. 13:11
3.	James 4:10		
4.	Ps. 55:23 / Matt. 6:25 / Luke 12:22		

THE SECOND EPISTLE GENERAL OF

PETER

1

3 Having spoken of the bountifulness of God, 5 and of the virtues of faith. 6 He exhorteth them to holiness of life. 12 And that his counsel may be the more effectual. 14 He showeth that his death is at hand, 16 and that himself did see the power of Christ, which he opened unto them.

1 Simon [a]Peter a servant and an Apostle of Jesus Christ, to you which have
obtained like precious faith with us by the [b]righteousness of our God and Savior
Jesus Christ. 2 Grace and peace be multiplied to you, [c]through the acknowle-
dging of God, and of Jesus Christ our Lord, 3 [d]According as his [e]divine power
hath given unto us all things that pertain unto [f]life and godliness, through the
[g]acknowledging of him that hath called us unto glory and virtue. 4 [h]Whereby
most great and precious promises are given unto us, that by them ye should be par-
takers of the [i]divine nature, in that ye flee the corruption, which is in the [j]world
through [k]lust. 5 [l]Therefore give even all diligence thereunto: [m]join moreover vir-
tue with your faith: and with virtue, knowledge: 6 [n]And with knowledge, tem-
perance: and with temperance, patience: and with patience, godliness: 7 And
with godliness, brotherly kindness: and with brotherly kindness, love. 8 [o]For if
these things be among you, and abound, they will make you that ye neither shall
be idle, nor unfruitful in the acknowledging of our Lord Jesus Christ: 9 For he
that hath not these things, is blind, and [p]cannot see far off, and hath forgotten that
he was purged from his old sins. 10 [q]Wherefore, brethren, give rather diligen-
ce to make your calling and election sure: for if ye do these things, ye shall never
fall. 11 For by this means an entering shall be ministered unto you abundantly
into the everlasting kingdom of our Lord and Savior Jesus Christ. 12 [r]Where-
fore, I will not be negligent to put you always in remembrance of these things,
though that ye have knowledge, and be established in the present truth. 13 For
I think it meet as long as I am in this [s]tabernacle, to stir you up by putting you in
remembrance, 14 Seeing I know that the time is at hand that I must lay down
this my tabernacle, even as our Lord Jesus Christ hath [1]showed me. 15 [2]I will
endeavor therefore always, that ye also may be able to have remembrance of these
things after my departing. 16 [3,t]For we followed not deceivable fables, when we
opened unto you the power, and coming of our Lord Jesus Christ, but with our
eyes we saw his majesty: 17 For he received of God the Father honor and glory,
when there came such a voice to him from that excellent Glory, [4]This is my belo-
ved Son, in whom I am well pleased. 18 And this voice we heard when it came
from heaven being with him in the holy mount. 19 [u]We have also a most sure
word of the Prophets, [v]to the which ye do well that ye take heed, as unto a light
that shineth in a dark place, until the [w]day dawns, and the [x]day star arise in your
hearts. 20 [5,y]So that ye first know this, that no prophecy of the [z]Scripture is of
any [aa]private interpretation: 21 For the prophecy came not in old time by the
will of man: but [ab]holy men of God spake as they were [ac]moved by the holy Ghost.

2

1 He foretelleth them of false teachers, 13 whose wicked sleights and destruction he declareth. 12 He compareth them to bruit beasts, 17 and to wells without water, 20 because they seek to withdraw men from God to their old filthiness.

1 But [a]there were false prophets also among the [b]people, even as there shall
be false teachers among you: which privily shall bring in damnable heresies, even
denying the Lord that hath bought them, and bring upon themselves swift dam-
nation. 2 [c]And many shall follow their destructions, by whom the way of truth
shall be evil spoken of. 3 [d]And through covetousness shall they with feigned
words make [e]merchandise of you, [f]whose condemnation long since resteth not,
and their destruction slumbereth not. 4 For if God spared not the [1]Angels that
had sinned, but cast them down into [g]hell, and delivered them into [h]chains of
darkness, to be kept unto damnation: 5 Neither hath spared the [i]old world, but
saved [2]Noah the eighth person a [j]preacher of righteousness, and brought in the
Flood upon the world of the ungodly, 6 And [3]turned the cities of Sodom and
Gomorrah into ashes, condemned them and overthrew them, and made them an
ensample unto them that after should live ungodly, 7 And delivered just Lot
vexed with the uncleanly conversation of the wicked: 8 For he being righteous,
and dwelling among them, in [k]seeing and hearing, [l]vexed his righteous soul from

---

2 PETER 1

a. 2 Peter 1:1 A salutation wherein he giveth them to understand that he dealeth with them as Christ's ambassador, and otherwise agreeth with them in one selfsame faith which is grounded upon the righteousness of Jesus Christ our God and Savior.
b. 2 Peter 1:1 In that God standing to his promises, showed himself faithful, and therefore just unto us.
c. 2 Peter 1:2 Faith is the acknowledging of God and Christ, from whence all our blessedness issueth and showed.
d. 2 Peter 1:3 Christ setteth forth himself to us plainly in the Gospel, and that by his only power, and giveth us all things which are requisite both to eternal life, wherein he hath appointed to glorify us, and also to godliness, in that he doth furnish us with true virtue.
e. 2 Peter 1:3 He speaketh of Christ, whom he maketh God, and the only Savior.
f. 2 Peter 1:3 Unto salvation.
g. 2 Peter 1:3 This is the sum of true Religion, to be led by Christ to the Father, as it were by the hand.
h. 2 Peter 1:4 An explication of the former sentence, declaring the causes of so great benefits, to wit, God and his free promise, from whence all these benefits proceed, I say, these most excellent benefits, whereby we are delivered from the corruption of the world, that is, from the wicked lusts which we carry about us and are made, after a sort, like unto God himself.
i. 2 Peter 1:4 By the divine nature, he meaneth not the substance of the Godhead, but the partaking of these qualities whereby the image of God is restored in us.
j. 2 Peter 1:4 In men.
k. 2 Peter 1:4 For lust is the fear of corruption, and hath his fear even in our very bowels and inmost parts.
l. 2 Peter 1:5 Having laid the foundation that is, having declared the causes of our salvation and especially of our sanctification now he beginneth to exhort us to give our minds wholly to the true use of this grace. And he beginneth with faith without which nothing can please God, and he warneth us to have it full fraught with virtue that is to say with good and godly manners, being joined with the knowledge of God's will, without which there is neither faith neither any true virtue.
m. 2 Peter 1:5 Supply also, and support or aid.
n. 2 Peter 1:6 He reckoneth up certain and other principal virtues, whereof some pertain to the first Table of the Law, others to the last.
o. 2 Peter 1:8 As those fruits do spring from the true knowledge of Christ, so in like sort the knowledge itself is fostered, and groweth by bringing forth such fruits, insomuch that he that is unfruitful did either never know the true light, or hath forgotten the gift of sanctification which he hath received.
p. 2 Peter 1:9 He that hath not an effectual knowledge of God in him, is blind as touching the kingdom of God, for he cannot see things that are afar off, that is to say, heavenly things.
q. 2 Peter 1:10 The conclusion: Therefore seeing our calling and election is approved by those fruits, and is confirmed in us, and moreover seeing this is the only way to the everlasting kingdom of Christ, it remaineth that we cast our minds wholly that way.
r. 2 Peter 1:12 An amplifying of the conclusion joined with a modest excuse, wherein he declareth his love towards them, and foretelleth them of his death, which is at hand.
s. 2 Peter 1:13 In this body.
t. 2 Peter 1:16 Another amplification taken both of the great certainty and also excellency of this doctrine, as whereof our Lord Jesus Christ the Son of God is author, whose glory the Apostle himself both saw and heard.
u. 2 Peter 1:19 The truth of the Gospel is hereby also manifest, in that it agreeth wholly with the foretellings of the Prophets.
v. 2 Peter 1:19 The doctrine of the Apostles doth not shut out the doctrine of the Prophets, for they confirm each other by each other's testimonies, but the Prophets were as candles which gave light unto the blind, until the brightness of the Gospel began to shine.
w. 2 Peter 1:19 A more full and open knowledge than was under the shadows of the Law.
x. 2 Peter 1:19 That clearer doctrine of the Gospel.
y. 2 Peter 1:20 The Prophets are to be read, but so that we ask of God the gift of interpretation: for he that is the author of the writings of the Prophets, is also the interpreter of them.
z. 2 Peter 1:20 He joineth the Scripture and prophecy together to distinguish true prophecies from false.
aa. 2 Peter 1:20 For all interpretation cometh from God.
ab. 2 Peter 1:21 The godly interpreters and messengers.
ac. 2 Peter 1:21 Inspired of God: and these their motions were in very good order, and not such as were the motions of the profane soothsayers, and foretellers of things to come.

2 PETER 1

1. John 21:18
2. 1 Cor. 1:17
3. 1 Cor. 2:1
4. Matt. 17:5
5. 2 Tim. 3:16

2 PETER 2

a. 2 Peter 2:1 As in times past there were two kinds of Prophets, the one true, the other false, so Peter fortelleth them that there shall be some true and some false teachers in the Church, insomuch that Christ himself shall be denied by some, who notwithstanding shall call him redeemer.
b. 2 Peter 2:1 Under the Law, while the state and policy of the Jews was yet standing.
c. 2 Peter 2:2 There shall not only be heresies, but also many followers of them.
d. 2 Peter 2:3 Covetousness for the most part is a companion of heresy, and maketh merchandise even of souls.
e. 2 Peter 2:3 They will abuse you, and sell you as they sell cattle in a Fair.
f. 2 Peter 2:3 A comfort for the godly: God who cast the Angels that fell away from him headlong into the darkness of hell, at length to be judged, and who destroyed the old world with the flood, and preserved Noah the eight person, and who burned Sodom, and saved Lot, will deliver his elect from these errors, and will utterly destroy those unrighteous.
g. 2 Peter 2:4 So the Greeks called the deep dungeon under the earth, which should be appointed to torment the souls of the wicked in.
h. 2 Peter 2:4 Bound them with darkness as it were with chains: and by darkness, he meaneth that most miserable state of life, that is full of horror.
i. 2 Peter 2:5 Which was before the Flood: not that God made a new world, but because the world seemed new.
j. 2 Peter 2:5 For he ceased not for the space of an hundred and twenty years to warn the wicked both by word and deed, what wrath of God hanged over their heads.
k. 2 Peter 2:8 Which way soever he looked and turned his ears.
l. 2 Peter 2:8 He had a troubled soul, and being vehemently grieved, lived a painful life.

day to day with their unlawful deeds. 9 The Lord [m]knoweth to deliver the godly out of tentation, and to reserve the unjust unto the day of judgment under punishment: 10 [n]And chiefly them that walk after the flesh, in the lust of uncleanness, and despise government, which are bold, and stand in their own conceit, and fear not to speak evil of them that are in [o]dignity. 11 Whereas the Angels which are greater both in power and might, give not railing judgment against them before the Lord. 12 [p]But these as natural brute beasts, led with sensuality and [q]made to be taken, and destroyed, speak evil of those things which they know not, and shall perish through their own [r]corruption. 13 And shall receive the wages of unrighteousness, as they which count it pleasure daily to live deliciously. [s]Spots they are and blots, delighting themselves in their deceivings, [t]in feasting with you. 14 [u]Having eyes full of adultery, and that cannot cease to sin, beguiling unstable souls, they have hearts exercised with covetousness, they are the children of curse: 15 Which forsaking the right way, have gone astray following the way of [4]Balaam, the son of Beor, which loved the wages of unrighteousness. 16 But he was rebuked for his iniquity: for the dumb beast speaking with man's voice forbade the foolishness of the Prophet. 17 [5,v]These are [w]wells without water, and clouds carried about with a tempest, to whom the [x]black darkness is reserved forever. 18 For in speaking [y]swelling words of vanity, they [z]beguile with wantonness through the lusts of the flesh them that were [aa]clean escaped from them which are wrapped in error, 19 Promising unto them liberty, and are themselves the [6]servants of corruption: for of whomsoever a man is overcome, even unto the same is he in bondage. 20 [7,ab] For if they, after they have escaped from the filthiness of the world, through the acknowledging of the Lord, and of the Savior Jesus Christ, are yet tangled again therein, and overcome, the latter end is worse with them than the beginning. 21 For it had been better for them not to have acknowledged the way of righteousness, than after they have acknowledged it, to turn from the holy commandment given unto them. 22 But it is come unto them according to the true proverb, [8]The dog is returned to his own vomit: and the sow that was washed, to the wallowing in the mire.

3

1 He showeth that he writeth the same things again. 2 Because they must often be stirred up, 3 because dangers hang over their heads through certain mockers. 8 Therefore he warneth the godly that they do not after the judgment of the flesh, 12 appoint the day of the Lord, 14 but that they think it always at hand, 15 in which doctrine he showeth that Paul agreeth with him.

1 This [a]second Epistle I now write unto you, beloved, wherewith I stir up, and warn your pure minds, 2 To call to remembrance the words, which were told before of the holy Prophets, and also the commandment of us the Apostles of the Lord and Savior. 3 [1,b]This first understand, that there shall come in the last days, [c]mockers, which will walk after their lusts, 4 [d]And say, Where is the promise of his coming? for since the Fathers died, all things continue alike from the beginning of the creation. 5 [e]For this they willingly know not, that the heavens were of old, and the [f]earth that was of the water, and by the water, by the word of God. 6 [g]Wherefore the world that then was, perished, overflowed with the [h]water. 7 [i]But the heavens and earth, which are now, are kept by the same word in store, and reserved unto fire against the day of condemnation, and of the destruction of ungodly men. 8 [j]Dearly beloved, be not ignorant of this one thing, that one day is with the Lord, [2]as a thousand years, and a thousand years as one day. 9 [k]The Lord of that promise is not slack as some men count slackness [l]but is patient toward us, and [3]would have no man to perish, but would all men to come to repentance. 10 [m]But the day [4]of the Lord will come as a thief in the night, in the which the heavens shall pass away with a [n]noise, and the elements shall melt with heat, and the earth with the works that are therein shall be burnt up. 11 [o]Seeing therefore that all these things must be dissolved, what manner persons ought ye to be in holy conversation and godliness, 12 Looking for, and [p]hasting unto the coming of that day of God, by the which the heavens being on fire, shall be dissolved, and the elements shall melt with heat? 13 But we look for [5]new heavens, and a new earth, according to his promise, [q]wherein dwelleth righteousness. 14 Wherefore, beloved, seeing that ye look for such things, be diligent that ye may be found of him in [r]peace, without spot and blameless. 15 [6]And suppose that the long suffering of our Lord is salvation, [s]even as our beloved brother Paul according to the wisdom given unto him wrote to you. 16 As one that in all his Epistles speaketh of these things: [t]among the [u]which, some things are hard to be understood, which they that are unlearned and unstable, wrest, as they do also other Scriptures unto their own destruction. 17 Ye therefore beloved, seeing ye know these things before, beware, lest ye be also plucked away with the error of the wicked, and fall from your own steadfastness. 18 But grow in grace, and in the knowledge of our Lord and Savior Jesus Christ: to him be glory both now and for evermore. Amen.

---

m. 2 Peter 2:9 Hath been long practiced in saving and delivering the righteous.

n. 2 Peter 2:10 He goeth to another sort of corrupt men, which notwithstanding are within the bosom of the Church, which are wickedly given, and do seditiously speak evil of the authority of Magistrates, which the Angels themselves that minister before God, do not dispraise A true and lively description of the Romish Clergy as they call it.

o. 2 Peter 2:10 Princes and great men, be they never so high in authority.

p. 2 Peter 2:12 A lively painting out of the same persons, wherein they are compared to beasts, which are made to snare themselves to destruction, while they give themselves to fill their bellies: For there is no greater ignorance than is in these men, although they most impudently find fault with those things which they know not: and it shall come to pass that they shall destroy themselves as beasts, with those pleasures wherewith they are delighted, and dishonor and defile the company of the godly.

q. 2 Peter 2:12 Made to this end, to be a prey to others: so do these men willingly cast themselves into Satan's snares.

r. 2 Peter 2:12 Their own wicked manners shall bring them to destruction.

s. 2 Peter 2:13 Or, little rocks.

t. 2 Peter 2:13 When as by being amongst the Christians in the holy banquets which the Church keepeth, they would seem by that means to be true members of the Church, yet they are indeed but blots on the Church.

u. 2 Peter 2:14 He condemneth those men, as showing even in their behavior and countenance an inmeasurable lust, as making merchandise of the souls of light persons, as men exercised in all the crafts of covetousness, to be short, as men that sell themselves for money to curse the Sons of God after Balaam's example, whom the dumb beast reproved.

v. 2 Peter 2:17 Another note whereby they may be well known what manner of men they are, because they have inwardly nothing but either utterly vain or very hurtful, although they make a show of some great goodness: but they shall not escape unpunished for it, because under pretence of false liberty, they draw men into most miserable slavery of sin.

w. 2 Peter 2:17 Which boast of knowledge, and have nothing in them.

x. 2 Peter 2:17 Most gross darkness.

y. 2 Peter 2:18 They deceive men with vain and swelling words.

z. 2 Peter 2:18 They take them as fishes are taken with the hook.

aa. 2 Peter 2:18 Unfeignedly and indeed clean departed from Idolatry.

ab. 2 Peter 2:20 It were better never to have known the way of righteousness, than to turn back from it to the old filthiness: and men that do so are compared to dogs and swine.

2 PETER 2

1. Job 4:18 / Jude 6
2. Gen. 7:1
3. Gen. 19:13,14
4. Num. 22:23
5. Jude 12
6. John 8:34 / Rom. 6:20
7. Matt. 12:45 / Heb. 6:4
8. Prov. 16:11

2 PETER 3

a. 2 Peter 3:1 The remedy against those wicked enemies both of true doctrine and holiness, is to be sought for by the continual meditation of the writings of the Prophets and Apostles.

b. 2 Peter 3:3 He voucheth the second coming of Christ against the Epicureans by name.

c. 2 Peter 3:3 Monstrous men, who will seem wise by their contempt of God, and wicked boldness.

d. 2 Peter 3:4 The reason which these mockers pretend because the course of nature is all one as it was from the beginning: therefore the world is from everlasting, and shall be forever.

e. 2 Peter 3:5 He setteth against them the creation of heaven and earth by the word of God, which these men are willingly ignorant of.

f. 2 Peter 3:5 Which appeared when the waters were gathered together into one place.

g. 2 Peter 3:6 Secondly, he setteth against them the universal flood which was the destruction, as it were of the whole world.

h. 2 Peter 3:6 For the waters returning into their former place this world, that is to say, this beauty of the earth which we see, and all living creatures which live upon the earth perished.

i. 2 Peter 3:7 Thirdly, he pronounceth that it shall not be harder for God to burn heaven and earth with fire in that day which is appointed for the destruction of the wicked, which thing he will also do than it was for him in times past to make them with his only word and afterward to overwhelm them with water.

j. 2 Peter 3:8 The taking away of an objection: in that he seemeth to defer this judgment a long season, in respect of us it is true, but not before God with whom there is no time either long or short.

k. 2 Peter 3:9 The Lord will surely come, because he hath promised: and that neither sooner nor later than he hath promised.

l. 2 Peter 3:9 A reason why the latter day cometh not out of hand, because God doth patiently wait till the elect are brought to repentance, that none of them may perish.

m. 2 Peter 3:10 A very short description of the least distinction of the world, but in such sort as nothing could be spoken more gravely.

n. 2 Peter 3:10 With the violence as it were of a hissing storm.

o. 2 Peter 3:11 An exhortation to purity of life, setting before us that horrible judgment of God both to bridle our wantonness, and also to comfort us, so that we be found watching and ready to meet him at his coming.

p. 2 Peter 3:12 He requireth patience of us, yet such patience as is not slothful.

q. 2 Peter 3:13 In which heavens.

r. 2 Peter 3:14 That you may try to your profit, how gentle and peaceable he is.

s. 2 Peter 3:15 Paul's Epistles are allowed by the express testimony of Peter.

t. 2 Peter 3:16 There be certain of these things obscure and dark, whereof the unlearned take occasion to overthrow some men that stand not fast, wrestling the testimonies of the Scripture to their own destruction. But this is the remedy against such deceit, to labor that we may daily more and more grow up and increase in the knowledge of Christ.

u. 2 Peter 3:16 That is to say, among the which things: for he disputeth not here whether Paul's Epistles be plain or dark, but saith, that amongst those things which Paul hath written of his Epistles, and Peter himself in these two of his own, there are some things which cannot be easily understood, and therefore are of some drawn to their own destruction: and this he saith to make us more attentive and diligent, and not remove us from the reading of holy things, for to what end should they have written vain speculations?

2 PETER 3

1. 1 Tim. 4:1 / 1 Tim. 3:1 / Jude 18
2. Ps. 90:4
3. Ezek. 8:32 / Ezek. 33:11 / 1 Tim. 2:4
4. Matt. 24:44 / 1 Thess. 5:2 / Rev. 3:3 / Rev. 16:15
5. Isa. 65:17 / Isa. 66:22 / Rev. 21:1
6. Rom. 2:4

THE FIRST EPISTLE GENERAL OF

JOHN

1

1 He testifieth that he bringeth the eternal word, wherein is life, 5 and light. 9 God will be merciful unto the faithful, if groaning under the burden of their sins, they learn to flee unto his mercy.

1 That [a]which was from the beginning, which we have [b]heard, which we have seen with these our eyes, which we have looked upon, and these hands of ours have handled of that [c]word of life, 2 For that life was made manifest, and we have seen it, and bear witness, and [d]show unto you that eternal life, which was with the Father, and was made manifest unto us. 3 That I say, which we have seen and heard declare we unto you, [e]that ye may also have fellowship with us, and that our fellowship also may be with the Father and with his Son Jesus Christ. 4 And these things write I unto you, that your joy may be full. 5 [f]This then is the message, which we have heard of him, and declare unto you, that God [1]is light, and in him is no darkness. 6 If we say that we have fellowship with him, and walk in darkness, we lie, and do not truly. 7 But if we walk in the [g]light as he is in the light, we have fellowship one with another, [h]and the [2]blood of Jesus Christ his Son cleanseth us from all sin. 8 [3,i] If we say that we have no sin, we [j]deceive ourselves, and [k]truth is not in us. 9 [l]If we acknowledge our sins, he is [m]faithful and just, to [n]forgive us our sins, and to cleanse us from all unrighteousness. 10 [o]If we say, we have not sinned, we make him [p]a liar, and his [q]word is not in us.

2

1 He declareth that Christ is our mediator and advocate, 3 and showeth that the knowledge of God consisteth in holiness of life, 12 which appertaineth to all sorts, 14 that depend on Christ alone: 15 Then having exhorteth them to contemn the world, 18 he giveth warning that Antichrists be avoided, 24 and that the known truth be stood unto.

1 My [a]little children, these things write I unto you, that ye sin not: and if any man sin, we have an [b]Advocate with the Father, Jesus Christ, the Just. 2 And he is the [c]reconciliation for our sins: and not for ours only, but also for the sins of the [d]whole world. 3 [e]And hereby we are sure that we [f]know him, [g]if we keep his commandments. 4 [h]He that saith, I know him, and keepeth not his commandments, is a liar, and the truth is not in him. 5 [i]But he that keepeth his word, in him is the [j]love of God perfect indeed: hereby we know that we are in [k]him. 6 [l]He that saith he remaineth in him, ought even so to walk as he hath walked. 7 [m]Brethren, I write no new commandment unto you, but an old commandment, which ye have had from the beginning: this old commandment is that word, which ye have heard from the beginning. 8 [n]Again, a new commandment I write unto you, that [o]which is true in him: and also in you: for the darkness is past, and that true light now shineth. 9 [p]He that saith that he is in that light, and hateth his brother, is in darkness, until this time. 10 [1]He that loveth his brother, abideth in that light, and there is no occasion of evil in him. 11 But he that hateth his brother, is in darkness, and walketh in darkness, and knoweth not whither he goeth, because that darkness hath blinded his eyes. 12 [q]Little children, [r]I write unto you, because your sins are forgiven you for his [s]Name's sake. 13 [t]I write unto you, fathers, because ye have known him that is from the beginning. [u]I write unto you, young men, because ye have overcome that wicked one. [v]I write unto you, little children, because ye have known the Father. 14 [w]I have written unto you fathers, because ye have known him that is from the beginning. I have written unto you, young men, because ye are strong, and the word of God abideth in you, and ye have overcome that wicked one. 15 [x]Love not this [y]world, neither the things that are in this world. If any man love this world, the [z]love of the Father is not in him. 16 For all that is in this world, as the lust of the flesh, the lust of

---

1 JOHN 1

a. 1 John 1:1 He beginneth with the description of the person of Christ, whom he maketh one and not two: and him both God from everlasting for he was with the Father from the beginning, and is that eternal life and also made true man, whom John himself and his companions, both heard and beheld, and handled.

b. 1 John 1:1 I heard him speak, I saw him myself with mine eyes, I handled with mine hands him that is very God, being made very man, and not I alone, but others also that were with me.

c. 1 John 1:1 That same everlasting word, by whom all things are made, and in whom only there is life.

d. 1 John 1:2 Being sent by him: and that doctrine is rightly said to be showed, for no man could so much as have thought of it, if it had not been thus showed.

e. 1 John 1:3 The use of this doctrine is this, that all of us being coupled and joined together with Christ by faith, might become the Sons of God, in which thing only consisteth all happiness.

f. 1 John 1:5 Now he entereth into a question, whereby we may understand that we are joined together with Christ, to wit, if we be governed with his light, which is perceived by the ordering of our life. And thus he reasoneth, God is in himself most pure light, therefore he agreeth with them, which are lightsome, but with them which are of the darksome he hath no fellowship.

g. 1 John 1:7 God is said to be light of his own nature, and to be in light, that is to say, in that everlasting infinite blessedness: and we are said to walk in light, in that the beams of that light do shine unto us in the world.

h. 1 John 1:7 A digression or going from the matter he is in with, to the remission of sins: for this our sanctification which walk in the light, is a testimony of our joining and knitting together, with Christ: but because this our light is very dark, we must needs obtain another benefit in Christ, to wit, that our sins may be forgiven us being sprinkled with his blood: and this in conclusion is the prop and stay of our salvation.

i. 1 John 1:8 There is none but needeth this benefit, because there is none that is not a sinner.

j. 1 John 1:8 This place doth fully refute that perfectness, and works of supererogation which the Papists dream of.

k. 1 John 1:8 So then John speaketh not thus for modesty's sake, as some say, but because it is so indeed.

l. 1 John 1:9 Therefore the beginning of salvation is to acknowledge our wickedness, and to require pardon from him who freely forgiveth all sins, because he hath promised so to do, and he is faithful and just.

m. 1 John 1:9 So then our salvation hangeth upon the free promise of God, who because he is faithful and just, will perform that which he hath promised.

n. 1 John 1:9 Where are then our merits? for this is our true felicity.

o. 1 John 1:10 A rehearsal of the former sentence: wherein he condemned all of sin without exception, insomuch that if any man persuade himself otherwise, he doth as much as in him lieth, make the word of God himself vain and to no purpose, yea he maketh God a liar, for to what end either in times past needed sacrifices or now Christ and the Gospel, if we be not sinners?

p. 1 John 1:10 They do not only deceive themselves, but also are blasphemous against God.

q. 1 John 1:10 His doctrine shall have no place in us, that is, in our hearts.

1 JOHN 1

1. John 8:12

2. Heb. 9:28 / 1 Pet. 1:19 / Rev. 1:5

3. 1 Kings 8:46 / 2 Chron. 6:36 / Prov. 20:9

1 JOHN 2

a. 1 John 2:1 It followeth not hereof that we must give our wicked nature the bridle, or sin so much the more freely, because our sins are cleansed away by the blood of Christ but we must rather so much more diligently resist sin. And yet we must not despair because of our weakness, for we have an Advocate and a purger, Christ Jesus the just, and therefore acceptable unto his father.

b. 1 John 2:1 In that he nameth Christ he shutteth forth all other.

c. 1 John 2:2 Reconciliation and intercession go together, to give us to understand that he is both advocate and high Priest.

d. 1 John 2:2 For men of all sorts, of all ages and all places, so that this benefit belongeth not to the Jews only, of whom he speaketh, as appeareth 1 John 2:7, but also to other nations.

e. 1 John 2:3 He returneth to the testimony of our conjunction with God, to wit, to sanctification, declaring what it is to walk in the light, to wit, to keep God's commandments whereby it followeth that holiness doth not consist in those things which men have devised, neither in a vain profession of the Gospel.

f. 1 John 2:3 This must be understood of such a knowledge, as hath faith with it, and not of a common knowledge.

g. 1 John 2:3 For the tree is known by the fruit.

h. 1 John 2:4 Holiness, that is, a life ordered according to the prescript of God's commandments how weak soever they be, is of necessity joined with faith, that is, with the true knowledge of the Father in the Son.

i. 1 John 2:5 He that keepeth God's commandments loveth God indeed. He that loveth God, is in God, or is joined together with God. Therefore he that keepeth his commandments, is in him.

j. 1 John 2:5 Wherewith we love God.

k. 1 John 2:5 He meaneth our conjunction with Christ.

l. 1 John 2:6 He that is one with Christ must needs live his life, that is, must walk in his steps.

m. 1 John 2:7 The Apostle going about to expound the commandment of charity one toward another, telleth first, that when he urgeth holiness bringeth no new trade of life as they use to do which devise traditions, one after another but putteth them in mind of the same Law which God gave in the beginning, to wit, by Moses, at that time that God began to give Laws to his people.

n. 1 John 2:8 He addeth that the doctrine indeed is old, but it is now after a sort new both in respect of Christ, and also of us: in whom he through the Gospel, engraveth his Law effectually, not in tables of stone, but in our minds.

o. 1 John 2:8 Which thing to wit, that the doctrine is new of which I write unto you is true in him and in you.

p. 1 John 2:9 Now he cometh to the second Table, that is, to charity one towards another, and denieth that that man hath true light in him, or is indeed regenerate and the son of God, which hateth his brother: and such an one wandereth miserably in darkness, brag he of never so great knowledge of God, for that wittingly and willingly he casteth himself headlong into hell.

q. 1 John 2:12 He returneth again from sanctification to remission of sins, because that free reconciliation in Christ is the ground of our salvation, whereupon afterwards sanctification must be built as upon a foundation.

r. 1 John 2:12 Therefore I write unto you, because you are of their number whom God hath reconciled to himself.

s. 1 John 2:12 For his own sake: And in that he nameth Christ, he shutteth out all others, whether they be in heaven or earth.

t. 1 John 2:13 He showeth that this doctrine agreeth to all ages, and first of all speaking to old men, he showeth that Christ and his doctrine are passing ancient, and therefore they be delighted with old things, nothing ought to be more acceptable unto them.

u. 1 John 2:13 He advertiseth young men, if they be desirous to show their strength that they have a most glorious combat set here before them, to wit, Satan the worst enemies, who must be overcome: willing them to be as sure of the victory as if they had already gotten it.

v. 1 John 2:13 Finally, he showeth to children, that true Father, from whom they have to look for all good things, is set forth unto them in the Gospel.

w. 1 John 2:14 He addeth afterward in like order, as many exhortations, as if he should say, Remember your fathers: as I wrote even now, that the everlasting Son of God is revealed to us. Remember ye young men, that that strength whereby I said that you put Satan to flight, is given you by the word of God, which dwelleth in you.

the eyes, and the pride of life is not of the Father, but is of this world. 17 [aa]And this world passeth away, and the lust thereof: but he that fulfilleth the will of God, abideth ever. 18 [ab,ac]Little children, [ad]it is the last time, [ae]and as ye have heard that Antichrist shall come, even now there are many Antichrists: whereby we know that it is the last time. 19 [af]They went out from us, but they were not of us: for if they had been of us, [ag]they should have continued with us. [ah]But this cometh to pass, that it might appear, that they are not all of us. 20 [ai]But ye have an [aj]ointment from that [ak]Holy one, and know all things. 21 [al]I have not written unto you, because ye know not the truth: but because ye know it, and that no lie is of the truth. 22 [am]Who is a liar, but he that denieth that Jesus is [an]that Christ? the same is that Antichrist that denieth the Father and the Son. 23 [ao]Whosoever denieth the Son, the same hath not the Father. 24 [ap]Let therefore abide in you that same which ye have heard from the beginning. If that which ye have heard from the beginning, shall remain in you, ye shall also continue in the Son, and in the Father. 25 And this is the promise that he hath promised us, even that eternal life. 26 [aq]These things have I written unto you, concerning them that deceive you. 27 But that [ar]anointing which ye received of him, dwelleth in you: and ye [as]need not that any man teach you: but as the same [at]anointing teacheth you of all things, and it is true and is not lying, and as it taught you, ye shall abide in him. 28 [au]And now, little children, abide in him, that when he shall appear, we may be bold, and not be ashamed before him, at his coming. 29 [av]If ye know that he is righteous, know ye that he which doeth righteously, is born of him.

3

1 Setting down the inestimable glory of this that we are God's sons, 7 he showeth that newness of life must be testifieth by good works, whereof charity is a manifest token. 19 Of faith, 22 and praying unto God.

1 Behold, [a,b]what love the Father hath given to us, that we should be [c]called the sons of God: [d]For this cause this world knoweth you not, because it knoweth not him. 2 [e]Dearly beloved, now are we the sons of God, but yet it is not made manifest what we shall be: and we know that when he shall be made manifest: we shall be [f]like him: for we shall see him [g]as he is. 3 [h]And every man that hath this hope in him purgeth himself, even [i]as he is pure. 4 [j]Whosoever [k]commiteth sin, transgresseth also the Law: for [l]sin is the transgression of the Law. 5 [m]And ye know that he was made manifest, that he might [1]take away our sins, and in him is no sin. 6 Whosoever abideth in him, sinneth not: whosoever [n]sinneth, hath not seen him, neither hath known him. 7 [o]Little children, let no man deceive you, he that doeth righteousness, is righteous, as he is righteous. 8 [p]He that [2]commiteth sin, is of the [q]devil: for the devil [r]sinneth from the [s]beginning: for this purpose was made manifest that Son of God, that he might loose the works of the devil. 9 Whosoever is born of God sinneth not: for his [t]seed remaineth in him, neither can he sin, because he is born of God. 10 [u]In this are the children of God known, and the children of the devil: whosoever doeth not righteousness, is not of God, [v]neither he that loveth not his brother. 11 [w]For this is the message that ye heard from the beginning, that [3]we should love one another, 12 [x]Not as [4,y]Cain which was of that wicked one, and slew his brother: [z]and wherefore slew he him? because his own works were evil, and his brother's good. 13 Marvel not my brethren, though this world hate you. 14 [aa]We know that we are [ab]translated from death unto life, because we love the brethren: [5]he that loveth not his brother, abideth in death. 15 [ac]Whosoever hateth his brother, is a manslayer: and ye know that no manslayer hath eternal life abiding in him. 16 [6,ad]Hereby have we perceived love, that he laid down his life for us: therefore we ought also to lay down our lives for the brethren. 17 [7,ae]And whosoever hath this [af]world's good, and seeth his brother have need, and [ag]shutteth up his compassion from

---

x. 1 John 2:15 The world which is full of wicked desires, lusts or pleasures, and pride, is utterly hated of our heavenly Father. Therefore the Father and the world cannot be loved together: and this admonition is very necessary for green and flourishing youth.

y. 1 John 2:15 He speaketh of the world, as it agreeth not with the will of God, for otherwise God is said to love the world with an infinite love, John 3:16, that is to say, those whom he chose out of the world.

z. 1 John 2:15 Wherewith the Father is loved.

aa. 1 John 2:17 He showeth how much better it is to obey the Father's will, than the lusts of the world, by both their natures and unlike event.

ab. 1 John 2:18 Now he turneth himself to little children, which notwithstanding are well instructed in the sum of religion, and willeth them by divers reasons to shake off slothfulness, which is too too familiar with that age.

ac. 1 John 2:18 He useth this word little not because he speaketh to children, but to allure them the more by using such sweet words.

ad. 1 John 2:18 First, because the last time is at hand, so that the matter suffereth no delay.

ae. 1 John 2:18 Secondly because Antichrists, that is, such as fall from God, are already come, even as they heard that they should come. And it was very requisite to warn that unheedy and wariless age of that danger.

af. 1 John 2:19 A digression against certain offenses and stumbling blocks, whereat that rude age especially might stumble and be shaken. Therefore that they should not be terrified with the soul falling back of certain, first he maketh plain unto them, that although such as fall from God and his religion, had place in the Church, yet they were never of the Church, because the Church is the company of the elect which cannot perish, and therefore cannot fall from Christ.

ag. 1 John 2:19 So then the elect can never fall from grace.

ah. 1 John 2:19 Secondly, he showeth that these things fall out to the profit of the Church, that hypocrites may be plainly known.

ai. 1 John 2:20 Thirdly, he comforteth them to make them stand fast, insomuch as they are anointed by the holy Ghost with the true knowledge of salvation.

aj. 1 John 2:20 The grace of the holy Ghost, and this is a borrowed kind of speech taken from the anointings used in the Law.

ak. 1 John 2:20 From Christ who is peculiarly called holy.

al. 1 John 2:21 The taking away of an objection. He wrote not these things as to men which are ignorant of religion, but rather as to them which do well know the truth, yet so far forth that they are able to discern truth from falsehood.

am. 1 John 2:22 He showeth now plainly the false doctrine of the Antichrists, to wit, that either they fight against the person of Christ, or his office or both together, and at once. And they that do so do in vain boast and brag of God, for that in denying the Son the Father also is denied.

an. 1 John 2:22 Is the true Messiah.

ao. 1 John 2:23 They then are deceived themselves, and also do deceive others, which say that the Turks and other infidels worship the same God that we do.

ap. 1 John 2:24 The whole preaching of the Prophets and Apostles is contrary to that doctrine: Therefore it is utterly to be cast away and this wholly to be holden and kept, which leadeth us to seek eternal life in the free promise, that is to say, in Christ alone, who is given to us of the Father.

aq. 1 John 2:26 The same Spirit which endueth the elect with the knowledge of the truth, and sanctifieth them, giveth them therewithal the gift of perseverance, to continue to the end.

ar. 1 John 2:27 The Spirit which you have received of Christ, and which hath led you into all truth.

as. 1 John 2:27 You are not ignorant of these things, and therefore I teach them not as things that were never heard of, but call them to your remembrance as things which you do know.

at. 1 John 2:27 He commendeth both the doctrine which they had embraced, and also highly praiseth their faith and the diligence of such as taught them, yet so, that he taketh nothing from the honor due to the holy Ghost.

au. 1 John 2:28 The conclusion both of the whole exhortation, and also of the former treatise.

av. 1 John 2:29 A passing over to the treatise following, which tendeth to the same purpose, but yet is more ample, and handleth the same matter after another order: for before he taught us to go up from the effects to the cause, and in this that followeth, he goeth down from the causes to the effects. And this is the sum of the argument: God is the fountain of all righteousness: and therefore they that give themselves to righteousness, are known to be born of him, because they resemble God the Father.

1 JOHN 2

1. 1 John 3:14

1 JOHN 3

a. 1 John 3:1 He beginneth to declare this agreement between the Father and the Son at the highest cause, to wit, at that free love of God towards us, wherewith he so loveth us, that he also adopteth us to be his children.

b. 1 John 3:1 What a gift of how great love.

c. 1 John 3:1 That we should be the sons of God, and so that all the world may perceive we are so.

d. 1 John 3:1 Before he declareth this adoption, he saith two things: the one, that this so great a dignity is not to be esteemed, according to the judgment of the flesh, because it is unknown to the world, for the world knoweth not God the Father himself.

e. 1 John 3:2 The other: This dignity is not fully made manifest to ourselves, much less to strangers, but we are sure of the accomplishment of it, insomuch that we shall be like to the Son of God himself, and shall enjoy his sight indeed, such as he is now: but yet notwithstanding this is deferred until his next coming.

f. 1 John 3:2 Like, but not equal.

g. 1 John 3:2 For now we see as in a glass, 1 Cor. 13:12.

h. 1 John 3:3 Now he describeth this adoption, the glory whereof as yet consisteth in hope by the effect, to wit, because that whosoever is made the Son of God, endeavoreth to resemble the Father in purity.

i. 1 John 3:3 This word signifieth a likeness, but not in equality.

j. 1 John 3:4 The rule of this purity can from no whence else be taken but from the Law of God, the transgression whereof is that which is called sin.

k. 1 John 3:4 Giveth not himself to pureness.

l. 1 John 3:4 A short definition of sin.

m. 1 John 3:5 An argument taken from the material cause of our salvation: Christ in himself is most pure, and he came to take away our sins, by sanctifying us with the holy Ghost. Therefore, whosoever is truly partaker of Christ doth not give himself to sin: and so contrariwise he that giveth himself to sin knoweth not Christ.

n. 1 John 3:6 He is said to sin, that giveth not himself to pureness, and in him sin reigneth, but sin is said to dwell in the faithful, and not to reign in them.

o. 1 John 3:7 Another argument of things coupled together: He that liveth justly, is just, and resembleth Christ that is just, and by that is known to be the son of God.

p. 1 John 3:8 An argument taken of contraries: the devil is the author of sin, and therefore he is of the devil, or is ruled by the inspiration of the devil that serve sin: and if he be the devil's son, then is he not God's son: for the devil and God are so contrary the one to the other, that even the Son of God was sent to destroy the works of the devil. Therefore on the contrary side, whosoever resists sin, is the Son of God, being born again of his spirit as of new seed, insomuch that of necessity he is now delivered from the slavery of sin.

q. 1 John 3:8 Resembleth the devil, as the child doth the father, and is governed by his spirit.

r. 1 John 3:8 He saith not sinned, but sinneth, for he did nothing else but sin.

s. 1 John 3:8 From the very beginning of the world.

t. 1 John 3:9 The holy Ghost is so called of the effect he worketh, because by his virtue and mighty working, as it were by seed, we are made new men.

u. 1 John 3:10 The conclusion, by a wicked life they are known which are governed by the spirit of the Devil, and by a pure life, which are God's children.

v. 1 John 3:10 He beginneth to commend charity towards the brethren, as another mark of the Sons of God.

w. 1 John 3:11 The first reason, taken of the authority of God, which giveth the commandment.

x. 1 John 3:12 An amplification, taken of the contrary example of Cain, which slew his brother.

y. 1 John 3:12 He bringeth forth a very fit and very old example, wherein we may behold both the nature of the sons of God, and of the sons of the devil, and what state and condition remaineth for us in this world: and what shall be the end of both at length.

z. 1 John 3:12 A short digression: Let us not marvel that we are hated by the world for doing our duty, for such was the condition of Abel who was a just person: and who would not rather be like him than Cain?

aa. 1 John 3:14 The second reason: Because charity is a testimony that we are translated from death to life: and therefore hatred towards the brethren is a testimony of death, and whosoever nourished it, doth as it were foster death in his bosom.

ab. 1 John 3:14 Love is a token that we are translated from death to life, for as such as by the effects the cause is known.

ac. 1 John 3:15 A confirmation: Whosoever is a murderer, is in eternal death, who so hateth his brother, is a murderer, therefore he is in death. And thereupon followeth the contrary. He that loveth his brother, hath passed to life, for indeed we are born dead.

ad. 1 John 3:16 Now he showeth how far Christian charity extendeth, even so far, that according to the example of Christ, every man forget himself, to provide for and help his brethren.

ae. 1 John 3:17 He reasoneth by comparison: For if we are bound even to give our life for our neighbors, how much more are we bound to help our brothers' necessity with our goods and substance?

af. 1 John 3:17 Wherewith this life is sustained.

ag. 1 John 3:17 Openeth not his heart to him, nor helpeth him willingly and cheerfully.

him, how dwelleth the love of God in him? **18** [ah]My little children, let us not love in word, neither in tongue only, but in deed and in truth. **19** [ai]For thereby we know that we are of the truth, [aj]and shall before him assure our hearts. **20** For [ak]if our hearts condemn us, God is greater than our heart, and knoweth all things. **21** [al]Beloved, if our heart condemn us not, then have we boldness toward God. **22** [8,am]And whatsoever we ask, we receive of him, because we keep his commandments, and do those things which are pleasing in his sight. **23** [9]This is then his commandment, that we believe in the Name of his Son Jesus Christ, and love one another, as he gave commandment. **24** [10]For he that keepeth his commandments, dwelleth in him, and he in him: and hereby we know that he abideth in us, even by that [an]Spirit which he hath given us.

4

1 Having spoken somewhat touching the trying of spirits: 4 For some speak after the world, 5 and some after God. 7 He returneth to charity, 11, 19 and by the example of God he exhorteth to brotherly love.

1 Dearly [a]beloved, believe not every [b]spirit, but try the spirits whether they are of God: for many false Prophets are gone out into the world. **2** [c]Hereby shall ye know the Spirit of God, [d]Every spirit which confesseth that [e]Jesus Christ is come in the [f]flesh is of God. **3** And every spirit that confesseth not that Jesus Christ is come in the flesh, is not of God: but this is the spirit of Antichrist, of whom ye have heard, how that he should come, and now already he is in this world. **4** [g]Little children, ye are of God, and have overcome them: for greater is he that is in you, than he that is in this world. **5** [h]They are of this world, therefore spake they of this world, and this world heareth them. **6** [i]We are of God, [1]he that knoweth God, heareth us: he that is not of God heareth us not. Hereby know we the [j]Spirit of truth, and the spirit of error. **7** [k]Beloved, let us love one another: [l]for love cometh of God, and everyone that loveth is born of God, and knoweth God. **8** He that loveth not, knoweth not God, [m]for God is [n]love. **9** [2]Herein was that love of God made manifest amongst us, because God sent that his only begotten Son into this world, that we might live through him. **10** Herein is that love, not that we loved God, but that he loved us, and sent his Son to be a reconciliation for our sins. **11** [o]Beloved, if God so loved us, we ought also to love one another. **12** [3,p]No man hath seen God at any time. If we love one another, God dwelleth in us, and his love is [q]perfect in us. **13** Hereby know we, that we dwell in him, and he in us: because he hath given us of his Spirit. **14** [r]And we have seen, and do testify, that the Father sent the Son to be the Savior of the world. **15** Whosoever [s]confesseth that Jesus is the Son of God, in him dwelleth God, and he in God. **16** And we have known, and believed the love that God hath in us, [t]God is love, and he that dwelleth in love, dwelleth in God, and God in him. **17** [u]Herein is that love perfect in us, that we should have boldness in the day of judgment: for [v]as he is, even so are we in this world. **18** There is no [w]fear in love, but perfect love casteth out fear: for fear hath painfulness: and he that feareth, is not perfect in love. **19** [x]We love him, because he loved us first. **20** [y]If any man say, I love God, and hate his brother, he is a liar: [z]for how can he that loveth not his brother whom he hath seen, love God whom he hath not seen? **21** [4,aa]And this commandment have we of him, that he that loveth God, should love his brother also.

5

1 He showeth that brotherly love and faith are things inseparable: 10 And that there is no faith towards God, but by believing in Christ: 14 Hence proceedeth calling upon God with assurance: 16 and also that our prayers be available for our brethren.

1 Whosoever [a]believeth that Jesus is that [b]Christ, is born of God: and everyone that loveth him, which begat, loveth [c]him also which is begotten of him. **2** [d]In this we know that we love the children of God, when we love God, and keep his [e]commandments. **3** [f]For this is the love of God, that we keep his commandments: [g]and his [1]commandments are not [h]burdenous. **4** [i]For all that is born of God, overcometh this world: [j]and this is that victory that [k]hath overcome this

---

ah. 1 John 3:18 Christian charity standeth not in words, but in deed, and proceedeth from a sincere affection.

ai. 1 John 3:19 He commendeth charity by a triple effect: for first of all, by it we know that we are indeed the sons of God, as he showeth before.

aj. 1 John 3:19 Therefore it cometh that we have a quiet conscience, as on the contrary side he that thinketh that he hath God for a judge, because he is guilty to himself, either he is never or else very rare quiet: for God hath a far quicker sight than we, and judgeth more severely.

ak. 1 John 3:20 If an evil conscience convinceth us, much more ought the judgments of God contemn us, who knoweth our hearts better than we ourselves do.

al. 1 John 3:21 A third effect also riseth out of the former, that in these miseries we are sure to be heard, because we are the sons of God, as we understand by the grace of sanctification which is proper to the elect.

am. 1 John 3:22 The conclusion: That faith in Christ, and love one towards another, are things joined together, and therefore the outward testimonies of sanctification must and do answer that inward testimony of the Spirit given unto us.

an. 1 John 3:24 He meaneth the Spirit of sanctification whereby we are born anew, and live unto God.

1 JOHN 3

1. Isa. 53:6,9 / 2 Pet. 2:22,24
2. John 8:44
3. John 13:34 / John 15:12
4. Gen. 4:8
5. 1 John 2:10 / Lev. 9:17
6. John 15:13 / Eph. 5:2
7. Luke 3:11
8. Matt. 21:22 / John 15:7 / John 16:25 / 1 John 5:14
9. John 6:23 / John 17:3
10. John 13:34 / John 15:10

1 JOHN 4

a. 1 John 4:1 Taking occasion by the name of the Spirit, lest love and charity should be separated from the worship of God, which chiefly dependeth of his true knowledge, he returneth to that which he spake in the second Chapter touching the taking heed of Antichrists. And he will have us here to take heed of two things, the one is, that seeing there be many false prophets, we do not lightly give credit to every man: the other is, that because many men teach false things, we should not therefore believe any. We must then observe a mean, that we may be able to discern the Spirit of God, which are altogether to be followed from impure spirits which are to be eschewed.

b. 1 John 4:1 This is spoken by the figure Metonymy, and it is as if he had said, Believe not everyone that saith that he hath a gift of the holy Ghost to do the office of a Prophet.

c. 1 John 4:2 He giveth a certain and perpetual rule to know the doctrine of Antichrist by, to wit, if either the divine or human nature of Christ, or the true uniting of them together be denied: or if the least jot that may be, be derogate from his office who is our only King, Prophet, and everlasting high Priest.

d. 1 John 4:2 He speaketh simply of the doctrine, and not of the person.

e. 1 John 4:2 The true Messiah.

f. 1 John 4:2 Is true man.

g. 1 John 4:4 He comforteth the elect with a most sure hope of victory: but yet so, that he teacheth them that they fight not with their own virtue, but with the virtue and power of God.

h. 1 John 4:5 He bringeth a reason: why the world receiveth these teachers more willingly than the true: to wit, because they breathe out nothing but that which is worldly: which is another note also to know the doctrine of Antichrist by.

i. 1 John 4:6 He testifieth unto them that his doctrine and the doctrine of his fellows, is the assured word of God, which of necessity we have boldly to set against all the mouths of the whole world, and thereby discern the truth from falsehood.

j. 1 John 4:6 True Prophets against whom are set false Prophets, that is, such as err themselves, and lead others into error.

k. 1 John 4:7 He returneth to the commending of brotherly love and charity.

l. 1 John 4:7 The first reason: Because it is a very divine thing: and therefore very meet for the sons of God: so that whosoever is void of it, cannot be said to know God aright.

m. 1 John 4:8 A confirmation: For it is the nature of God to love men, whereof we have a most manifest proof above all others: in that that of his only free and infinite goodwill towards us his enemies, he delivered unto death not a common man, but his own Son, yea, his only begotten Son, to the end that we being reconciled through his blood, might be made partakers of his everlasting glory.

n. 1 John 4:8 In that he called God, Love he saith more than if he had said that he loveth us infinitely.

o. 1 John 4:11 Another reason by comparison: if God so loved us, shall not we his children love one another.

p. 1 John 4:12 A third reason: Because God is invisible, therefore by this effect of his Spirit, to wit, by charity, he is understood, yea, and to be not out of us, but joined with us, and in us, in whom he is so effectually working.

q. 1 John 4:12 Is surely in us, in deed and in truth.

r. 1 John 4:14 He underlayeth this charity with another foundation, to wit, faith in Jesus, which joineth us indeed with him, even as charity witnesseth that we are joined with him. Furthermore he testifieth of Christ, as who had seen him with his eyes.

s. 1 John 4:15 With such a confession as cometh from true faith and is accompanied with love, so that there be an agreement of all things.

t. 1 John 4:16 A fourth reason: God is the fountain and wellspring of charity, yea, charity itself: therefore whosoever abideth in it, hath God with him.

u. 1 John 4:17 Again as a little before he commendeth love, for that seeing that by our agreement with God in this thing, we have a certain testimony of our adoption, it cometh thereby to pass, that without fear we look for that latter day of judgment, so that trembling and that torment of conscience is cast out by this love.

v. 1 John 4:17 This signifieth all likeness, not equality.

w. 1 John 4:18 If we understand by love, that we are in God, and God in us, that we are sons, and that we know God, and that everlasting life is in us: he concludeth aright that we may well gather peace and quietness thereby.

x. 1 John 4:19 Lest any man should think that that peace of conscience proceedeth from our love as from the cause, he goeth back to the fountain, to wit, to the free love, wherewith God loveth us although we deserved and do deserve his wrath. And hereof springeth another double charity, which both are tokens and witnesses of that first, to wit, that, wherewith we love God who loved us first, and then for his sake our neighbors also.

y. 1 John 4:20 As he showed that the love of our neighbor cannot be separate from the love wherewith God loveth us, because this last engendereth the other: so he denieth that the other kind of love wherewith we love God, can be separate from the love of our neighbor: whereof it followeth, that they lie impudently which say they worship God, and yet regard not their neighbor.

z. 1 John 4:20 The first reason taken of comparison, why we cannot hate our neighbor and love God, to wit, because that he that cannot love his brother, whom he seeth, how can he love God whom he seeth not?

aa. 1 John 4:21 A second reason, why God cannot be hated and our neighbor loved, because the selfsame Lawmaker commanded both to love him and our neighbor.

1 JOHN 4

1. John 8:47
2. John 3:16
3. John 1:18 / 1 Tim. 6:16
4. John 13:34 / John 15:12

1 JOHN 5

a. 1 John 5:1 He goeth on forward in the same argument, showing how both those loves come into us from the love wherewith God loveth us, to wit, by Jesus our Mediator laid hold on by faith, in whom we are made the children of God, and do love the Father of whom we are so begotten and also our brethren which are begotten with us.

b. 1 John 5:1 Is the true Messiah.

c. 1 John 5:1 By one he meaneth all the faithful.

d. 1 John 5:2 The love of our neighbor doth so hang upon the love wherewith we love God, that this last must needs go before the first, whereof it followeth, that that is not to be called love when men agree together to do evil, neither that, when as in loving our neighbors, we respect not God's commandments.

e. 1 John 5:2 There is no love where there is no true doctrine.

f. 1 John 5:3 The reason: for to love God is to keep his commandments, which being so, and seeing that both the loves are commanded of one and the selfsame lawmaker as he taught before it followeth also that we do not love our neighbor, when we break God's commandments.

g. 1 John 5:3 Because experience teacheth us that there is no ability in our flesh, neither yet will to perform God's commandments, therefore lest the Apostle should seem, by so often putting them in mind of the keeping of the commandments of God, to require things that are impossible, he pronounceth that the commandments of God are not in such sort grievous or burdensome, that we can be oppressed with the burden of them.

h. 1 John 5:3 To them that are regenerate, that is to say, born anew, which are led by the Spirit of God, and are through grace delivered from the curse of the Law.

i. 1 John 5:4 A reason: Because by regeneration we have gotten strength to overcome the world, that is to say, whatsoever striveth against the commandments of God.

j. 1 John 5:4 He declareth what that strength is, to wit, Faith.

k. 1 John 5:4 He useth the time that is past to give us to understanding, that although we be in the battle, yet

world even our [l]faith. 5 [2,m]Who is it that overcometh this world, but he which
believeth that Jesus is that Son of God? 6 [n]This is that Jesus Christ that came by
water and blood: [o]not by water only, but by water and blood: and it is that [p]Spirit
that beareth witness: for that Spirit is truth. 7 For there are three, which bear
record in heaven, the Father, the [q]Word, and the holy Ghost: and these three are
[r]one. 8 And there are three, which bear record in the earth, the Spirit, and the
Water and the Blood: and these three agree in one. 9 [s]If we receive the witness of
men, the witness of God is greater: for [t]this is the witness of God, which he testified
of his Son. 10 [3,u]He that believeth in that Son of God, hath the witness in him-
self: he that believeth not God, hath made him a liar, because he believed not the
record, that God witnessed of that his Son. 11 [v]And this is that record, to wit,
that God hath given unto us eternal life, and this life is in that his Son. 12 He
that hath that Son, hath that life: and he that hath not that Son of God, hath not
that life. 13 [w]These things have I written unto you, that believe in the name of
that Son of God, that ye may know that ye have eternal life, and that ye may belie-
ve in the Name of that Son of God. 14 [x]And this is that assurance that we have
in him, [4]that if we ask anything according to his will, he heareth us. 15 And if
we know that he heareth us, whatsoever we ask, we know that we have the peti-
tions, that we have desired of him. 16 [y]If any man see his brother sin a sin that is
not unto death, let him [z]ask, and he shall give him life for them that sin not unto
death. [5]There is a sin unto death, I say not that thou shouldest pray for it. 17 [aa]
All unrighteousness is sin, but there is a sin not unto death. 18 [ab]We know that
whosoever is born of God, sinneth not: but he that is begotten of God keepeth
himself, and that wicked one toucheth him not. 19 [ac]We know that we are of
God, and this whole world lieth in wickedness. 20 But we know that that Son of
God is [6]come, and hath given us a mind to know him, which is true, and we are in
him that is true, that is, in that his Son Jesus Christ, the same is that very [ad]God,
and that eternal life. 21 [ae]Little children, keep yourselves from idols, Amen.

---

undoubtedly we shall be conquerors, and are most certain of the victory.

l. 1 John 5:4 Which is the instrumental cause, and as a mean and hand whereby we lay hold on him who indeed doth perform this, that is, hath and doth overcome the world, Even Christ Jesus.

m. 1 John 5:5 Moreover he declareth two things, the one what true faith is, to wit, that which resteth upon Jesus Christ the Son of God alone: whereupon followeth the other, to wit, that this strength is not proper to faith, but by faith as an instrument is drawn from Jesus Christ the Son of God.

n. 1 John 5:6 He proveth the excellency of Christ, in whom only all things are given us by six witnesses, three heavenly, and three earthly, which wholly and fully agree together. The heavenly witnesses are: the Father who sent the Son, the word itself which became flesh, and the holy Ghost. The earthly witnesses are, water, that is, our sanctification blood, that is, our justification the Spirit, that is, acknowledge of God the Father in Christ by faith through the testimony of the holy Ghost.

o. 1 John 5:6 He warneth us not to separate water from blood, that is, sanctification from justification, or righteousness begun, from righteousness imputed for we stand not upon sanctification but so far forth as it is a witness of Christ's righteousness imputed unto us: and although this imputation of Christ's righteousness be never separated from sanctification, yet it is only the matter of our salvation.

p. 1 John 5:6 Our spirit, which is the third witness, testifies that the holy Ghost is truth; that is to say, that that is true which he telleth us, to wit, that we are the sons of God.

q. 1 John 5:7 See John 8:13, 14.

r. 1 John 5:7 Agree in one.

s. 1 John 5:9 He showeth by an Argument of comparison, of what great weight the heavenly testimony is, that the Father hath given of the Son, unto whom agreeth both the Son himself and the holy Ghost.

t. 1 John 5:9 I conclude this aright: for that testimony which I said is given in heaven, cometh from God, who so setteth forth his Son.

u. 1 John 5:10 He proveth the sureness of the earthly witnesses by every man's conscience, having that testimony in itself, which conscience he saith cannot be deceived, because it consenteth the heavenly testimony, which the Father giveth of the Son: For otherwise the Father must needs be a liar, if the conscience, which accordeth and assenteth to the Father should lie.

v. 1 John 5:11 Now at length he showeth what this testimony is, that is confirmed with so many witnesses: to wit, that life or everlasting felicity, is the mere, and only gift of God, which is in the Son, and proceedeth from him unto us, which by faith are joined with him, so that without him life is nowhere to be found.

w. 1 John 5:13 The conclusion of the Epistle wherein he showeth first of all, that even they which already believe, do stand in deed of this doctrine, to the end that they may grow more and more in faith, that is to say, to the end that they may be daily more and more certified of their salvation in Christ through faith.

x. 1 John 5:14 Because we do not yet in effect obtain that which we hope for, the Apostle joineth invocation or prayer with faith, which he will have to proceed from faith, and moreover to be conceived in such sort, that nothing be asked but that which is agreeable to the will of God: and such prayers cannot be vain.

y. 1 John 5:16 We have to make prayers not only for ourselves, but also for our brethren which do sin, that their sins be not unto them, to death: and yet he excepteth that sin, which is never forgiven, or the sin against the holy Ghost, that is to say, an universal and willful falling away from the known truth of the Gospel.

z. 1 John 5:16 This is as much as if he said, Let him desire the Lord to forgive him, and he will forgive him being so desired.

aa. 1 John 5:17 The taking away of an objection: Indeed all iniquity is comprehended under the name of sin, but yet we must not despair therefore, because every sin is not deadly, and without hope of remedy.

ab. 1 John 5:18 A reason why not all, nay rather why no sin is mortal to some: to wit, because they be born of God, that is to say, made the sons of God in Christ, and being endued with his Spirit, they do not serve sin, neither are deadly wounded of Satan.

ac. 1 John 5:19 Every man must particularly apply to himself the general promises, that we may certainly persuade ourselves, that whereas all the world is by nature lost, we are freely made the sons of God, by the sending of Jesus Christ his Son unto us, of whom we are lightened with the knowledge of the true God, and everlasting life.

ad. 1 John 5:20 The divinity of Christ is most plainly proved by this place.

ae. 1 John 5:21 He expresseth a plain precept of taking heed of idols: which he setteth against the only true God, that with this seal as it were he might seal up all the former doctrine.

1 JOHN 5

1. Matt. 11:30
2. 1 Cor.15:57
3. John 3:16
4. 1 John 3:22
5. Matt. 12:31 / Mark 3:29
6. Luke 24:45

THE SECOND EPISTLE OF

JOHN

1 *This Epistle is written to a woman of great renown, 4 who brought up her children in the fear of God: 6 he exhorteth her to continue in Christian charity, 7 that she accompany not with Antichrists, 10 but avoid them.*

1 The Elder to the [a]elect [b]Lady, and her children, [c]whom I love in the truth:
and not I only, but also all that have known the truth, **2** For the truth's sake whi-
ch dwelleth in us, and shall be with us forever: **3** Grace be with you, mercy and
peace from God the Father, and from the Lord Jesus Christ the Son of the Father,
with [d]truth and love. **4** [e]I rejoiced greatly, that I found of thy children walking in
[f]truth, as we have received a commandment of the Father. **5** And now beseech I
thee, Lady, not as writing a new commandment unto thee, but the same which we
had from the beginning that we [1]love one another. **6** And this is that love that we
should walk after his commandments. This commandment is, that as ye have heard
from the beginning, ye should walk in it. **7** [g]For many deceivers are entered into
this world, which confess not that Jesus Christ is come in the flesh. He that is such
one, is a deceiver and an Antichrist. **8** [h,i]Look to yourselves, that we lose not the
things, which we have done, but that we may receive a full reward. **9** Whosoever
transgresseth, and abideth not in the doctrine of Christ, hath not God. He that
continueth in the doctrine of Christ, he hath both the Father and the Son. **10** [j]If
there come any unto you, and bring not this doctrine, [2]receive him not to house,
neither bid him Godspeed. **11** For he that biddeth him Godspeed, is partaker of
his evil deeds. Although I had many things to write unto you, yet would I not write
with paper and ink: but I trust to come unto you, and speak mouth to mouth, that
our joy may be full. **12** The sons of thine elect sister greet thee, Amen.

---

2 JOHN 1

a. 2 John 1:1 This is no proper name, but to be taken as the word soundeth, that is to say to the worthy and noble Lady.
b. 2 John 1:1 Excellent and honorable Dame.
c. 2 John 1:1 The bond of Christian conjunction or linking together, is the true and constant profession of the truth.
d. 2 John 1:3 With true knowledge, which hath always love joined with it, and following it.
e. 2 John 1:4 This true profession consisteth both in love one toward another which the Lord hath commanded, and also especially in wholesome and sound doctrine, which also is delivered unto us: for the commandment of God is a sound and sure foundation both of the rule of manners and of doctrine, and these cannot be separated the one from the other.
f. 2 John 1:4 According as the truth directeth them.
g. 2 John 1:7 Antichrists fighting against the person and office of Christ, were already crept into the Church in the time of the Apostles.
h. 2 John 1:8 He that maketh shipwreck of doctrine, loseth all.
i. 2 John 1:8 Beware and take good heed.
j. 2 John 1:10 We ought to have nothing to do with them that defend perverse doctrine.

2 JOHN 1

1. John 15:12
2. Rom. 16:17

THE THIRD EPISTLE OF

JOHN

1 *He commendeth Gaius for hospitality, 9 and reprehendeth Diotrephes for vainglory: 10 he exhorteth Gaius to continue in well doing: 12 and in the end commendeth Demetrius.*

1 The [a]Elder unto the beloved Gaius whom I love in the truth. **2** Beloved, I
wish chiefly that thou prosperedst and faredst well as thy soul prospereth. **3** For
I rejoiceth greatly when the brethren came and testified of the truth that is in thee,
how thou walkest in the truth. **4** I have no greater joy than [b]these, that is, to hear
that my sons walk in verity. **5** Beloved, thou doest [c]faithfully, whatsoever thou
doest to the brethren, and to strangers, **6** Which bore witness of thy love before
the Churches, Whom if thou [d]bringest on their journey as it seemeth according to
God, thou shalt do well, **7** Because that for his Name's sake they went forth, and
took nothing of the Gentiles. **8** We therefore ought to receive such, that we mi-
ght be [e]helpers to the truth. **9** [f]I wrote unto the Church, but Diotrephes which
loveth to have the preeminence among them, receiveth us not. **10** Wherefore if I
come, I will call to your remembrance his deeds which he doeth, prattling against
us with malicious words, and not therewith content, neither he himself receiveth
the brethren, but forbideth them that would, and thrusteth them out of the Chur-
ch. **11** Beloved, follow not that which is evil, but that which is good: he that
doeth well is of God: but he that doeth evil, hath not [g]seen God. **12** Demetrius
hath good report of all men, and of the truth itself: yea, and we ourselves bear re-
cord, and ye know that our record is true. **13** I have many things to write: but I
will not with ink and pen write unto thee: **14** For I trust I shall shortly see thee,
and we shall speak mouth to mouth. Peace be with thee. The friends salute thee.
Greet thy friends by name.

---

3 JOHN 1

a. 3 John 1:1 An example of a Christian gratulation.
b. 3 John 1:4 Than these joys.
c. 3 John 1:5 As becometh a believer and a Christian.
d. 3 John 1:6 He commendeth to Gaius either those selfsame men whom he had entertained before, returning now again to him about the affairs of the Church, or else some other which had like business.
e. 3 John 1:8 That we ourselves may help somewhat to the preaching of the truth.
f. 3 John 1:9 Ambition and covetousness, two pestilent plagues especially in them which have any Ecclesiastical function are condemned in Diotrephes' person.
g. 3 John 1:11 Hath not known God.

THE GENERAL EPISTLE OF

JUDE

1 *3 He warneth the godly to take heed of such men, 4 that make the grace*
of God a cloak for their wantonness: 5 and that they shall not escape un-
punished, for the contempt of that grace, 6, 7 he proveth by three examples: 14
and allegeth the prophecy of Enoch: 20 Finally he showeth the godly a means to
overthrow all the snares of those deceivers.

1 Jude a servant of Jesus Christ, and [a]brother of James, to them which are
called and sanctified [b]of God the Father, and [c]reserved to Jesus Christ: **2** Mercy
unto you, and peace and love be multiplied. **3** [d]Beloved, when I gave all dili-
gence to write unto you of the [e]common salvation, it was needful for me to write
unto you, to exhort you, that ye should earnestly [f]contend for the maintenance of
the faith, which was [g]once given unto the Saints. **4** [h]For there are certain men
crept in, which were before of old ordained to this condemnation: [i]ungodly men
they are, which turn the grace of our God into wantonness, and [1]deny God the
only Lord, and our Lord Jesus Christ. **5** [j]I will therefore put you in remembran-
ce, forasmuch as ye once knew this, how that the Lord, after that he had delivered
the people out of Egypt, [2]destroyed them afterward which believed not. **6** [k]The
[3]Angels also which kept not their first estate, but left their own habitation, he
hath reserved in everlasting chains under darkness unto the judgment of the great
day. **7** As [4]Sodom and Gomorrah, and the cities about them, which in like man-
ner as they did, [l]committed fornication, and followed [m]strange flesh, are set forth
for an example, and suffer the vengeance of eternal fire. **8** Likewise notwith-
standing these [n]sleepers also defile the flesh, [o]and despise [p]government, and speak
evil of them that are in authority. **9** [q]Yet Michael the Archangel, when he strove
against the devil, and disputed about the body of Moses, durst not blame him with
cursed speaking, but said, The Lord rebuke thee. **10** [r]But these speak evil of tho-
se things, which they know not: and whatsoever things they know naturally as bea-
sts, which are without reason, in those things they corrupt themselves. **11** [s]Woe
be unto them: for they have followed the way [5]of Cain, and are cast away by the
deceit [6]of Balaam's wages, and perish in the gainsaying [7]of Korah. **12** [t]These are
rocks in your [u]feasts of charity, when they feast with you, without [v]all fear, fee-
ding themselves: [8]clouds they are without water, carried about of winds, corrupt
trees and without fruit, twice dead, and plucked up by the roots. **13** They are
the raging waves of the sea, foaming out their own shames: they are wandering
stars, to whom is reserved the [w]blackness of darkness forever. **14** And Enoch
also the seventh from Adam, prophesied of such, saying, [9]Behold, the Lord [x]co-
meth with thousands of his Saints, **15** To give judgment against all men, and
to rebuke all the ungodly among them of all their wicked deeds, which they have
ungodly committed, and of all their cruel speakings, which wicked sinners have
spoken against him. **16** These are murmurers, complainers, walking after their
own lusts: [10]whose mouths speak proud things, having men's persons in admira-
tion, because of advantage. **17** [y]But, ye beloved, remember the words which
were spoken before of the Apostles of our Lord Jesus Christ: **18** How that they
told you that there should be mockers [11]in the last time, which should walk after
their own ungodly lusts. **19** [z]These are they that separate themselves from others,
natural, having not the Spirit. **20** But, ye beloved, edify yourselves in your most
holy faith, praying in the holy Ghost. **21** And keep yourselves in the love of
God, looking for the mercy of our Lord Jesus Christ, unto eternal life. **22** [aa]And
have compassion of some, in putting difference: **23** And others save with [ab]fear,
pulling them out of the fire, and hate even that [ac]garment which is spotted by the
flesh. **24** [ad]Now unto him that is able to keep you that ye fall not, and to pre-
sent you faultless before the presence of his glory with joy, **25** That is, to God
only wise, our Savior be glory, and majesty, and dominion, and power, both now
and forever, Amen.

JUDE 1

- **a.** Jude 1:1 This is put to make a difference between him and Judas Iscariot.
- **b.** Jude 1:1 By God the Father.
- **c.** Jude 1:1 Set apart by the everlasting counsel of God, to be delivered to Christ to be kept.
- **d.** Jude 1:3 The end and mark whereat he shooteth in this Epistle is that he confirmeth the godly against certain wicked men, both in wholesome doctrine and good manners.
- **e.** Jude 1:3 Of those things that pertain to the salvation of all of us.
- **f.** Jude 1:3 That ye should defend the faith by all the might you can, both by true doctrine and good example of life.
- **g.** Jude 1:3 Which was once so given, that it may never be changed.
- **h.** Jude 1:4 It is by God's providence and not by chance, that many wicked men creep into the Church.
- **i.** Jude 1:4 He condemneth this first in them, that they take a pretense or occasion to wax wanton, by the grace of God: which cannot be, but the chief empire of Christ must be abrogated, in that such men give up themselves to Satan: as at this time the sect of the Anabaptists doth, which they call Libertines.
- **j.** Jude 1:5 He setteth forth the horrible punishment of them which have abuseth the grace of God to follow their own lusts.
- **k.** Jude 1:6 The fall of the Angels was most sincerely punished, how much more then will the Lord punish wicked and faithless men?
- **l.** Jude 1:7 Following the steps of Sodom and Gomorrah.
- **m.** Jude 1:7 Thus he covertly setteth forth their horrible and monstrous lusts.
- **n.** Jude 1:8 Which are so blockish and void of reason as if all their senses and wits were in a most dead sleep.
- **o.** Jude 1:8 Another most pernicious doctrine of theirs, in that they take away the authority of Magistrates, and speak evil of them, as at this day the Anabaptists do.
- **p.** Jude 1:8 It is a greater matter to despise government, than the governors, that is to say, the matter itself, than the persons.
- **q.** Jude 1:9 An argument of comparison, Michael one of the chiefest Angels, was content to deliver Satan, although as most cursed enemy, to the judgment of God to be punished: and these perverse men are not ashamed to speak evil of the powers which are ordained of God.
- **r.** Jude 1:10 The conclusion.These men are in a double fault, to wit, both for their rash folly in condemning some, and for their impudent and shameless contempt of that knowledge, which when they had gotten, yet notwithstanding they lived as brute beasts, serving their bellies.
- **s.** Jude 1:11 He foretelleth their destruction, because they resemble or show forth Cain's shameless malice, Balaam's filthy covetousness, and to be short, Korah's seditious and ambitious head.
- **t.** Jude 1:12 He rebuketh most sharply with many other notes and marks, both their dishonesty or filthiness, and their sauciness, but especially their vain bravery of words, and most vain pride, joining herewithal a most grave and heavy threatening out of a most ancient prophecy of Enoch touching the judgment to come.
- **u.** Jude 1:12 The feasts of charity were certain banquets, which the brethren that were members of the Church kept altogether, as Tertullian setteth them forth in his Apology, Chap. 3:9.
- **v.** Jude 1:12 Impudently, without all reverence either to God or man.
- **w.** Jude 1:13 Most gross darkness.
- **x.** Jude 1:14 The present time for the time to come.
- **y.** Jude 1:17 The rising up of such monsters was spoken of before, that we should not be troubled at the newness of the matter.
- **z.** Jude 1:19 It is the property of Antichrists to separate themselves from the godly, because they are not governed by the Spirit of God: and contrariwise it is the property of Christians to edify one another through godly prayers both in faith and also in love until the mercy of Christ appears to their full salvation.
- **aa.** Jude 1:22 Among them which wander and go astray, the godly have to use this choice, that they handle some of them gently, and that others some being even in the very flame, they endeavor to save with severe and sharp instruction of the present danger: yet so, that they do in such sort abhor the wicked and dishonest, that they eschew even the least contagion that may be.
- **ab.** Jude 1:23 By fearing them, and holding them back with godly severity.
- **ac.** Jude 1:23 An amplification taken from the forbidden things of the Law which did defile.
- **ad.** Jude 1:24 He commendeth them to the grace of God, declaring sufficiently that it is God only that can give us that constancy which he requireth of us.

JUDE 1

1. 2 Pet. 2:1
2. Num. 14:37
3. 2 Pet. 2:4
4. Gen. 19:24
5. Gen. 4:8
6. Num. 22:21 / 2 Pet. 2:15
7. Num. 16:1
8. 2 Pet. 2:17
9. Rev. 1:7
10. Ps. 17:10
11. 1 Tim. 4:1 / 2 Tim. 3:1 / 2 Pet. 3:3

THE
REVELATION
OF SAINT JOHN THE APOSTLE

1 *2 He declareth what kind of doctrine is here handled, 8 even his that is the beginning and ending. 12 Then the mystery of the seven Candlesticks and stars, 20 is expounded.*

1 The [a,b]Revelation of [c]Jesus Christ, which God gave unto him, to show unto
his servants things which must shortly be done: which he sent, and showed by
his Angel unto his servant John, **2** Who bare record of the word of God, and
of the testimony of Jesus Christ, and of all things that he saw. **3** Blessed is he
that readeth, and they that hear the words of this prophecy, and keep those things
which are written therein: for the time is at hand. **4** [d]John to the seven Chur-
ches which are in Asia, Grace be with you, and peace [e]from him, [f]Which [1]is, and
Which was, and Which is to come, and from [g]the [h]seven Spirits which are before
his Throne, **5** And from Jesus Christ [i]which is that [2]faithful witness, and [3]that
first begotten of the dead, and that Prince of the Kings of the earth, unto him that
loved us, and washed us from our sins in his [4]blood, **6** And made us [5]Kings and
Priests unto God even his Father, to him, I say, be glory, and dominion for ever-
more, Amen. **7** Behold, he cometh with [6]clouds, and every [j]eye shall see him:
yea, even they which pierced him through: and all kindreds of the earth shall wail
before him, Even so, Amen. **8** [k]I [7]am [l]Alpha and Omega, the beginning and the
ending, saith the Lord, Which is, and Which was, and Which is to come, even
the Almighty. **9** [m]I John even your brother and companion in tribulation, and
in the kingdom and patience of Jesus Christ, was in the [n]Isle called Patmos, for
the word of God, and for the witnessing of Jesus Christ. **10** And I was ravished
in [o]spirit on the [p]Lord's day, and heard behind me a great voice, as it had been of
a trumpet, **11** Saying, I am Alpha and Omega, that first and that last: and that
which thou seest write in a book, and send it unto the seven Churches which are in
Asia, unto Ephesus, and unto Smyrna, and unto Pergamos, and unto Thyatira, and
unto Sardis, and unto Philadelphia, and unto Laodicea. **12** [q]Then I turned back
to [r]see the voice that spake with me: [s]and when I was turned, I saw seven golden
candlesticks, **13** And in the midst of the seven candlesticks, one like unto the son
of man, clothed with a garment down to the feet, and girded about the paps with
a golden girdle. **14** His head and hairs were white as white wool, and as snow,
and his eyes were as a flame of fire, **15** And his feet like unto fine brass burning
as in a furnace: and his voice as the sound of many waters. **16** And he had in his
right hand seven stars: and out of his mouth went a sharp two edged sword, and
his face shone as the sun shineth in his strength. **17** [t]And when I saw him, I fell
at his feet as dead: [u]then he laid his right hand upon me, saying unto me, Fear not:
[v]I am that [8]first and that last, **18** And am alive, but I was dead: and behold, I am
alive for evermore, Amen: and I have the keys of hell and of death. **19** [w]Write
these things which thou hast seen, and the things which are, and the things which
shall come hereafter. **20** [x]The mystery of the seven stars which thou sawest in
my right hand, and the seven golden candlesticks, is this, The seven stars are the
[y]Angels of the seven Churches: and the seven candlesticks which thou sawest, are
the seven Churches.

REVELATION 1

a. Revelation 1:1 This Chapter hath two principal parts, the title or inscription, which standeth instead of an exordium: and a narration going before the whole prophecy of this book: The inscription is double, general and particular. The general containeth the kind of prophecy, the author, and, matter, instruments, and manner of communicating the same, in the first verse: the most religious faithfulness of the Apostle as public witness, verse 2. And the use of communicating the same taken from the promise of God, and from the circumstance of the time, the third verse.

b. Revelation 1:1 An opening of a secret and hid thing.

c. Revelation 1:1 Which the Son opened to us out of his Father's bosom by Angels.

d. Revelation 1:4 This is the particular or singular inscription wherein salutation is written unto certain Churches by name, which represent the Church Catholic: and the certainty and the truth of the same is declared, from the Author thereof, unto the eighth verse.

e. Revelation 1:4 That is, from God the Father, eternal, immortal, immutable: whose unchangeableness S. John declareth by a form of speech which is undeclined. For there is no incongruity in this place, where, of necessity the words must be attempted unto the mysteries, not the mysteries corrupted or impaired by the word.

f. Revelation 1:4 By these three times, Is, Was and shall be, is signified this word Jehovah, which is the proper name of God.

g. Revelation 1:4 That is, from the holy Ghost which proceedeth from the Father and the Son. This Spirit is one in person according to his subsistence: but in communication of his virtue, and in demonstration of his divine works in those seven Churches, doth so perfectly manifest himself, as if there were many Spirits, every one perfectly working in his own Church, wherefore after Rev. 5:6, they are called the seven horns and seven eyes of the Lamb, as much to say, as his most absolute power and wisdom: and Rev. 3:1. Christ is said to have there seven Spirits of God, and Rev. 4:5, it is said, that seven lamps do burn before his throne, which also are those seven Spirits of God. That this place ought to be so understood, it is thus proved. For first grace and peace is asked by prayer of this Spirit, which is a divine work, and an action incommunicable, in respect of the most high Deity. Secondly, he is placed between the Father and the Son, as set in the same degree of dignity and operation with them. Besides he is before the throne as of the same substance with the Father and the Son: as the seven eyes and seven horns of the Lamb. Moreover, these spirits are never said to adore God, as all other things are. Finally, that is the power whereby the Lamb opened the book, and loosed the seven seals thereof when none could be found amongst all creatures by whom the book might be opened, Rev. 5. Of these things long ago, Master John Luide of Oxford wrote learnedly unto me. Now the holy Ghost is set in order of words before Christ, because there was in that which followeth, a long process of speech to be used concerning Christ.

h. Revelation 1:4 These are the seven spirits, which are, afterward, Rev. 5:6, called the horns and eyes of the Lamb, and are now made as a guard waiting upon God.

i. Revelation 1:5 A most ample and grave commendation of Christ, first from his offices the Priesthood and kingdoms, secondly from his benefits, as his love toward us, and washing us with his blood, in this verse, and communication of his kingdom and Priesthood with us: thirdly from his eternal glory and power, which always is to be celebrated of us, verse 6. Finally from the accomplishment of all things once to be effected by him, at his second coming, what time he shall openly destroy the wicked, and comfort the godly in the truth, verse 7.

j. Revelation 1:7 All men.

k. Revelation 1:8 A confirmation of the salutation aforegoing, taken from the words of God himself: in which he avoucheth his operation in every single creature, the immutable eternity that is in himself, and his omnipotence in all things: and concludeth in the unity of his own essence, that Trinity of persons, which was before spoken of.

l. Revelation 1:8 I am he before whom there is nothing, yea, by whom everything that is made, was made and shall remain though all they should perish.

m. Revelation 1:9 The narration opening the way to the declaring of the authority and calling of Saint John the Evangelist in this singular Revelation, and to procure faith, and credit unto this prophecy. This is the second part of this Chapter consisting of a proposition and an exposition. The proposition showeth, first who was called unto this Revelation, in what place, and how occupied, verse 9. Then at what time and by what means, namely, by the spirit and the word, and that on the Lord's day, which day ever since the resurrection of Christ, was consecrated for Christians unto the religion of the Sabbath: that is to say, to be a day of rest, verse 10. Thirdly, who is the author that calleth him, and what is the sum of his calling.

n. Revelation 1:9 Patmos is one of the isles of Sporas whither John was banished as some write.

o. Revelation 1:10 This is that holy ravishment expressed, wherewith the prophets were ravished, and being as it were carried out of the world were conversant with God, and so Ezekiel saith often that he was carried from place to place of the Lord's Spirit and that the Spirit of the Lord fell upon him.

p. Revelation 1:10 He calleth it the Lord's day, which Paul calleth the first day of the week, 1 Cor. 16:2.

q. Revelation 1:12 The exposition, declaring the third and last point of the proposition (for the other points are evident of themselves) wherein is spoken first of the author of his calling unto verse 17. Secondly of the calling itself unto the end of the Chap. And first of all the occasion is noted in this verse, in that S. John turned himself towards the vision: after is set down the description of the author in the verses following, Rev. 1:13–16.

r. Revelation 1:12 To see him whose voice I had heard.

s. Revelation 1:12 The description of the Author, which is Christ: by the candlesticks that standeth about him, that is the Churches that stand before him, and depend upon his direction, in this verse: by his properties, that he is one furnished with wisdom and dexterity to the achieving of great things, verse 13, and ancient gravity and most excellent sight of the eye, verse 14, with strength invincible and with a mighty word, verse 15. By his operations, that he ruleth the ministry of his servants in the Church, giveth the effect thereunto by the sword of his word, and enlightening all things with his countenance, doth most mightily provide for everyone by his divine providence, verse 16.

t. Revelation 1:17 A religious fear that goeth before the calling of the Saints, and their full confirmation to take upon them the vocation of God.

u. Revelation 1:17 A divine confirmation is this calling partly by sign and partly by word of power.

v. Revelation 1:17 A most elegant description of this calling contained in three things, which are necessary unto a just vocation: first the authority of him that calleth, for that he is the beginning and end of all things, in this verse, for that he is eternal and omnipotent, verse 18. Secondly, the sum of this prophetical calling, and revelation, verse 19. Lastly a declaration of those persons unto whom this prophecy is by the commandment of God directed in the description thereof, verse 20.

w. Revelation 1:19 The sum of this prophecy, that the Apostle must write whatsoever he should see, adding nothing, nor taking away anything, as verse 2. Hereof there are two parts: one is a narration of those things which are, that is, which then were at that time contained in the second and third Chapters, the other part is of those things which were to come, contained in the rest of this book.

x. Revelation 1:20 That is, the things which [were] mystical, signified by the particulars of the vision beforegoing.

y. Revelation 1:20 By the Angels he meaneth the Ministers of the Church.

REVELATION 1

1. Exod. 3:14
2. Ps. 89:38
3. 1 Cor. 15:21 / Col. 1:18
4. Heb. 9:14 / 1 Pet. 1:29 / 1 John 1:9
5. 1 Pet. 2:5
6. Isa. 3:14 / Matt. 24:30 / Jude 14
7. Rev. 21:6 / Rev. 22:13
8. Isa. 41:4

2

1 John is commanded to write those things which the Lord knew necessary to the Churches of Ephesus. 8 Of the Smyrnians, 12 of Pergamos, 18 and of Thyatira, as that they keep those things which they received of the Apostles.

1 [a]Unto the Angel of the Church of Ephesus write, [b]These things saith he that
holdeth the seven stars in his right hand, and walketh in the midst of the seven
golden candlesticks. **2** [c]I know thy works, and thy labor, and thy patience, and
how thou canst not bear with them which are evil, and hast examined them which
say they are Apostles, and are not, and hast found them liars. **3** And thou wast
burdened, and hast patience, and for my Name's sake hast labored, and hast not
fainted. **4** Nevertheless, I have somewhat [d]against thee, because thou hast left thy
first love. **5** Remember therefore from whence thou art fallen, and repent and do
the first works: or else I will come against thee shortly, and will remove thy candle-
stick out of his place, except thou amend. **6** But this thou hast that thou hatest
the works of the Nicolaitans, which I also hate. **7** [e]Let him that hath an ear hear
what the Spirit saith unto the Churches: To him that overcometh, will I give to eat
of the tree of life which is in [f]the midst of the [g]Paradise of God. **8** [h]And unto
the Angel of the Church of the [i]Smyrnians write, These things saith he that is first
and last, which was dead and is alive. **9** [j]I know thy works and tribulation, and
poverty but thou art rich and I know the blasphemy of them, which say they are
Jews, and are not, but are the Synagogue of Satan. **10** Fear none of those things,
which thou shalt suffer: behold, it shall come to pass, that the devil shall cast some
of you into prison, that ye may be tried, and ye shall have [k]tribulation ten days: be
thou faithful unto the death, and I will give thee the crown of life. **11** [l]Let him
that hath an ear hear what the Spirit saith unto the Churches. He that overcometh
shall not be hurt [m]of the second death. **12** [n]And to the Angel of the Church,
which is at [o]Pergamos write, Thus saith he which hath that sharp sword with two
edges. **13** [p]I know thy works, and where thou dwellest, even where Satan's thro-
ne is, and thou keepest my Name, and hast not denied my faith, even in [q]those
days when Antipas my faithful martyr was slain among you, where Satan dwel-
leth. **14** But I have a few things against thee, because thou hast there them that
maintain the doctrine of [1]Balaam, which taught Balak to put a stumbling block be-
fore the children of Israel, that they should [r]eat of things sacrificed unto idols, and
commit fornication. **15** Even so hast thou them that maintain the doctrine of
the [s]Nicolaitans, which thing I hate. **16** Repent thyself, or else I will come unto
thee shortly, and will fight against them with the sword of my mouth. **17** [t]Let
him that hath an ear, hear what the spirit saith unto the Churches. To him that
overcometh, will I give to eat [u]of the [v]Manna that is hid, and will give him a
[w,x]white stone, and in the stone a new [y]name written, which no man knoweth,
saving he that receiveth it. **18** And unto [z]the Angel of the Church which is at
Thyatira write, These things saith the Son of God, which hath his eyes like unto a
flame of fire, and his feet like fine brass. **19** I know [aa]thy works and thy love, and
[ab]service and faith, and thy patience, and thy works, and that they are more at the
last, than at the first. **20** Notwithstanding, I have a few things against thee, that
thou sufferest the woman Jezebel which calleth herself a prophetess, to teach and to
deceive my servants, to make them commit [ac]fornication and to eat meat sacrificed
unto idols. **21** And I gave her space to repent of her fornication, and she repen-
ted not. **22** Behold, I will cast her into a bed, and them that commit fornication
with her, into great affliction, except they repent them of their works. **23** And
I will kill her children with death, and all the Churches shall know that I am he
which [2]search the reins and hearts: and I will give unto every one of you according
unto your works. **24** And unto you I say, the rest of them of Thyatira, As many
as have not this learning, neither have known the [ad]deepness of Satan as they spe-
ak I will [ae]put upon you none other burden, **25** But that which ye have already,
hold fast till I come. **26** [af]For he that overcometh and keepeth my words unto
the end, to him will I give [ag]power over nations. **27** [3]And he shall rule them with
a rod of iron: and as the vessels of a potter, shall they be broken: **28** Even as I re-
ceived of my Father, so will I give him [ah]the morning Star. **29** Let him that hath
an ear, hear what the Spirit saith to the Churches.

3

1 The first Epistle sent to the Pastors of the Church of Sardis, 7 of Philadelphia, 14 And of the Laodiceans, 16 that they be not lukewarm, 20 but endeavor to further God's glory.

1 [a]And write unto the Angel of the Church which is at [b]Sardis, These thin-
gs saith he that hath the seven Spirits of God, and the seven stars, [c]I know thy
works: for thou hast a [d]name that thou livest, but thou art dead. **2** Be awake,
and strengthen the things which remain, that are [e]ready to die: for I have not
found thy work perfect before God. **3** Remember therefore, how thou hast re-
ceived and heard, and hold fast and repent. [1]If therefore thou wilt not watch,
I will come on thee as a thief, and thou shalt not know what hour I will come
upon thee. **4** Notwithstanding thou hast a few names yet in Sardis, [f]which have

---

REVELATION 2

- **a.** Revelation 2:1 The former part of this book is comprised in a narration of those things which then were as S. John taught us, Rev. 1:19, it belongeth wholly to instruction and in these next two Chapters, containeth seven places according to the number and condition of those Churches which were named before, Rev. 1:11, figured verse 12, distributed most aptly into their Pastors and flocks, verse 20, which verse of that Chap. is as it were a passage unto the first part. Every one of the seven places hath three principal members, an Exordium taken from the person of the Author: a Proposition, in which is praise and commendation of that which is good, reprehension of that which is evil: an instruction containing either an exhortation alone, or withal a dissuasion opposite unto it, and a conclusion stirring unto attention by divine promises. And this first place is unto the Pastors of the Church of Ephesus.
- **b.** Revelation 2:1 The exordium wherein are contained the special praises of Christ Jesus the Author of this prophecy, out of verses 16 and 13 of the first Chapter.
- **c.** Revelation 2:2 The proposition, first condemning the Pastor of this Church, verses 2, 3, then reproving him, verse 4, after informing him and withal threatening that he will translate the Church to another place, verse 5. This commutation or threat Christ mitigateth by a kind of correction, calling to mind the particular virtue and piety of the Church, which God never leaveth without recompense, verse 6. Concerning the Nicolaitans see after upon verse 11.
- **d.** Revelation 2:4 To deal with thee for.
- **e.** Revelation 2:7 The conclusion, containing a commandment of attention and a promise of everlasting life, shadowed out in a figure of which, Gen. 2:9.
- **f.** Revelation 2:7 That is, in Paradise after the manner of the Hebrew phrase.
- **g.** Revelation 2:7 Thus Christ speaketh as the Mediator.
- **h.** Revelation 2:8 The second place is unto the Pastors of the Church of the Smyrnians. The exordium is taken out of verses 17 and 18 of the first Chap.
- **i.** Revelation 2:8 Smyrna was one of the cities of Ionia in Asia.
- **j.** Revelation 2:9 The proposition of praise is in this verse and of exhortation joined with promise, is in the next verse.
- **k.** Revelation 2:10 That is, of ten years. For so commonly both in this book and in Daniel, years are signified by the name of days: that God thereby might declare, that the space of time is appointed by him, and the same very short. Now because Saint John wrote this book in the end of Domitian the Emperor his reign, as Justin and Ireneus do witness, it is altogether necessary that this should be referred unto that persecution which was done by the authority of the Emperor Trajan: who began to make havoc of the Christian Church in the tenth year of his reign, as the Historiographers do write: and his bloody persecution continued until Adrian the Emperor had succeeded in his place: the space of which time is precisely ten years, which are here mentioned.
- **l.** Revelation 2:11 The conclusions as verse 7.
- **m.** Revelation 2:11 See Rev. 20:6.
- **n.** Revelation 2:12 The third place is unto the Pastors of Pergamos. The Exordium is taken out of verse 16 of the first Chapter.
- **o.** Revelation 2:12 Pergamos was the name of a famous city in old time in Asia, where the Kings of the Attalians were always resident.
- **p.** Revelation 2:13 The proposition of praise is in this verse, of reprehension in the two following, and of exhortation joined with a conditional threat, verse 16. Now this Antipas was the Angel or minister of the Church of Pergamos, as Aretas writeth.
- **q.** Revelation 2:13 The faith of them of Pergamos is so much the more highly commended because they remained constant even in the very heat of persecution.
- **r.** Revelation 2:14 That which is here spoken of things offered to idols, is meant of the same kind which Paul speaketh of, 1 Cor. 10:13.
- **s.** Revelation 2:15 Which follow the footsteps of Balaam, and such as are abandoned unto all filthiness, as he showed in the verse foregoing, and is here signified by a note of similitude. And thus also must the next verse be understood. For this matter especially Ireneus must be consulted withal.
- **t.** Revelation 2:17 The conclusion, standing of exhortation as before, and of promise.
- **u.** Revelation 2:17 He alludeth to that sermon which we read of John 6, and to the place we find, Ps. 105:40.
- **v.** Revelation 2:17 Aretas writeth, that such a stone was wont to be given to wrestlers at games, or else that such stones did in old times witness the quitting of a man.
- **w.** Revelation 2:17 The bread of life, invisible, spiritual, and heavenly, which is kept secretly with God, from before all eternity.
- **x.** Revelation 2:17 Which is a sign and witness of forgiveness and remission of sins, of righteousness and true holiness, and of purity uncorrupted, after that the old man is killed.
- **y.** Revelation 2:17 A sign and testimony of newness of life in righteousness and true holiness, by putting on the new man, whom none doth inwardly know, save the spirit of man which is in himself, the praise whereof is not of man, but of God, Rom. 2:28.
- **z.** Revelation 2:18 The fourth place is unto the Pastors of Thyatira. The exordium is taken out of verses 14 and 15 of the first Chapter.
- **aa.** Revelation 2:19 The proposition of praise is in this verse: of reprehension, for they tolerated with them, the doctrine of ungodliness and unrighteousness, is verse 20, the authors whereof though they were called back of God, yet repented not verse 21, whereunto is added a most heavy threatening, verses 22 and 23, of a conditional promise, and of exhortation to hold fast the truth, is in the two verses following.
- **ab.** Revelation 2:19 So he calleth those offices of charity which are done to the saints.
- **ac.** Revelation 2:20 By Fornication, is often in the Scripture idolatry meant.
- **ad.** Revelation 2:24 He pointeth out the bragging of certain men, which boasted of their deep, that is, plentiful and common knowledge, which notwithstanding is devilish.
- **ae.** Revelation 2:24 I will speak no worse thing against you, being content to have showed you what I require to be in you.
- **af.** Revelation 2:26 The conclusion, wherein Christ assureth unto his servants the communion of his Kingdom and glory, in this verse and the next following, and commandeth an holy attention in the last verse.
- **ag.** Revelation 2:26 That is, I will make him a King by communion with me, and my fellow heir, as it is promised, Matt. 19:28 and 25:34; Rom. 8:17 and 1 Cor. 6:3; Eph. 2:6 and 1 Tim. 2:12.
- **ah.** Revelation 2:28 The brightness of greatest glory and honor nearest approaching unto the light of Christ, who is the Son of righteousness, and our head, Matt. 4.

REVELATION 2

1. Num. 24:14 / Num. 25:1
2. 1 Sam. 16:7 / Ps. 7:10 / Jer. 11:20 / Jer. 17:10
3. Ps. 2:9

REVELATION 3

- **a.** Revelation 3:1 The fifth place is unto the Pastors of Sardis. The exordium is taken out of verses 4 and 16 of the first Chap.
- **b.** Revelation 3:1 Sardis is the name of a most flourishing and famous City, where the Kings of Lydia kept their courts.
- **c.** Revelation 3:1 The proposition of reproof is in this verse: of exhortation joined with a threatening in the two verses that follow, and of qualification by way of correction unto the comfort of the good which yet remained there, verse 4.
- **d.** Revelation 3:1 Thou art said to live, but art dead indeed.
- **e.** Revelation 3:2 Other things, whose state is such, that they are now going, and unless they be confirmed, will perish forthwith.
- **f.** Revelation 3:4 That is, who have with all religion guarded themselves from sin and moral contagion, even from the very show of evil, as S. Jude exhorteth, verse 23.
- **g.** Revelation 3:4 Pure from all spot and shining with glory. So it is to be understood always hereafter as in the next verse.
- **h.** Revelation 3:4 They are meet and fit, to wit, because they are justified in Christ, as they have truly showed it: for he is righteous that worketh righteousness: but so, as the tree bringeth forth fruit. See Rom. 8:18.

not defiled their garments: and they shall walk with me in [g]white: for they are [h]worthy. 5 He [i]that overcometh, shall be clothed in white array, and I will not put out his Name out of the [2]book of life, but I will confess his name before my Father, and before his Angels. 6 Let him that hath an ear, hear what the Spirit saith unto the Churches. 7 [j]And write unto the Angel of the Church which is of Philadelphia, These things saith he that is Holy, and True, which hath the [k]key of David, which openeth and no man shutteth, and shutteth and no man openeth. 8 [l]I know thy works: behold I have set before thee an open door, and no man can shut it: for thou hast a little strength and hast kept my word, and hast not denied my Name. 9 Behold, I will make them [m]of the Synagogue of Satan, which call themselves Jews, and are not, but do lie: behold, I say, I will make them that they shall come [n]and worship before thy feet, and shall know that I have loved thee. 10 Because thou hast [o]kept the word of my patience, therefore I will deliver thee from the hour of tentation, which will come upon all the world, to try them that dwell upon the earth. 11 Behold, I come shortly: hold that which thou hast, that no man take thy crown. 12 [p]Him that overcometh, will I make a pillar in the Temple of my God, and he shall go no more out: [q]and I will write upon him the Name of my God, and the name of the city of my God, which is the new Jerusalem, which cometh down out of heaven from my God, and I will write upon him my new Name. 13 Let him that hath an ear, hear what the Spirit saith unto the Churches. 14 [r]And unto the Angel of the Church of the Laodiceans write, These things saith [s]Amen, the faithful and true witness, that [t]beginning of the creatures of God. 15 [u]I know thy works, that thou art neither cold nor hot: I would thou werest cold or hot. 16 Therefore because thou art lukewarm, and neither cold nor hot, it will come to pass, that I shall spew thee out of my mouth. 17 For thou sayest, I am rich, and increased with goods, and have need of nothing, and knowest not how thou art wretched and miserable, [v]and poor, and blind, and naked. 18 I counsel thee to buy of me gold tried by the fire, that thou mayest be made rich: and white raiment, that thou mayest be clothed, and that thy filthy nakedness do not appear: and anoint thine eyes with eye salve, that thou mayest see. 19 As many as I love, [3]I rebuke and chasten: be [w]zealous therefore and amend. 20 Behold, I stand at the door, and knock, [x]If any man hear my voice, and open the door, I will come in unto him, and will sup with him, and he with me. 21 [y]To him that overcometh, will I grant to sit with me in my throne, even as I overcame, and sit with my Father in his throne. 22 Let him that hath an ear, hear what the Spirit saith unto the Churches.

4

1 Another vision containing the glory of God's Majesty: 3 which is magnified of the four beasts, 10 and the four and twenty Elders.

1 After [a]this I looked, and behold, a door was open in heaven, and the first voice which I heard, was as it were of a trumpet talking with me, saying, Come up hither, and I will show thee things which must be done hereafter. 2 And [b]immediately I was ravished [c]in the spirit, [d]and behold, a throne was set in heaven, and one sat upon the throne. 3 [e]And he that sat, was to look upon, like unto a Jasper stone, and a sardine, and there was a rainbow round about the throne, in sight like to an emerald. 4 [f]And round about the throne were four and twenty seats, and upon the seats I saw four and twenty Elders sitting, clothed in white raiment, and had on their heads crowns of gold. 5 [g]And out of the throne proceeded lightnings, and thunderings and voices, and there were seven lamps of fire burning before the throne, which are the seven spirits of God. 6 [h]And before the throne there was a Sea of glass like unto crystal: and in the midst of the throne, and round about the throne were four beasts, full of eyes before and behind. 7 And the first beast was like a lion, and the second beast like a calf, and the third beast had a face as a man, and the fourth beast was like a flying Eagle. 8 And the [i]four beasts had each one of them six wings about him, and they were full of eyes within, and they ceased not [j]day nor night, saying, Holy, holy, holy, Lord God Almighty, Which was, and which is, and which is to come. 9 And when those beasts [k]gave glory, and honor, and thanks to him that sat on the throne, which liveth forever and ever, 10 [l]The four and twenty Elders fell down before him that sat on the throne, and worshipped him that liveth for evermore, and cast their crowns before the throne, saying, 11 [m]Thou art [1]worthy, O Lord, [n]to receive glory, and honor, and power: for thou hast created all things, and for thy will's sake they are, and have been created.

5

1 The book sealed with seven seals, 3 which none could open. 6 That Lamb of God, 9 is thought worthy to open, 12 even by the consent of all the company of heaven.

1 [a]And I saw in the [b]right hand of him that sat upon the throne, [c]a book written within, and on the backside sealed with seven seals. 2 And I saw a strong Angel which preached with a loud voice, Who is worthy to open the book, and to loose the seals thereof? 3 [d]And no man in heaven nor in earth, neither under the

---

i. Revelation 3:5 The conclusion standing upon a promise and a commandment as before.

j. Revelation 3:7 The sixth place is unto the Pastors of Philadelphia. The exordium is taken out of verse 18 of the first chapter.

k. Revelation 3:7 All power of rule in commanding and forbidding, delivering and punishing. And the house of David is the Church, and the continual promise of David's Kingdom belongeth to Christ.

l. Revelation 3:8 The proposition of praise is in this verse, of promises, to bring home again them that wander, verse 9, and to preserve the godly, verse 10, and of exhortation, verse 11.

m. Revelation 3:9 I will bring them to that case.

n. Revelation 3:9 That is, fall down and worship either thee civilly, or Christ religiously at thy feet (and thus I had rather take it) whether here in the Church (which seemeth more proper to the argument of this place) or there in the world to come. For Christ verily shall fulfill his word.

o. Revelation 3:10 Because thou hast been patient and constant, as I would my servants should be.

p. Revelation 3:12 The conclusion, which containeth a promise and a commandment.

q. Revelation 3:12 That is, the new man shall be turned after his Father, Mother, and head Christ.

r. Revelation 3:14 The seventh place is unto the pastors of the Church of Laodicea. The exordium is taken out of verse 15 of the first chapter.

s. Revelation 3:14 Amen soundeth as much in the Hebrew tongue, as Truly, or Truth itself.

t. Revelation 3:14 Of whom all things that are made, have their beginning.

u. Revelation 3:15 The proposition of reproof is in this verse, whereunto is adjoined a threatening, verse 16, with a confirmation declaring the same, verse 17, and of exhortation unto faith and repentance, verses 18, 19, whereunto is added a conditional promise, verse 20.

v. Revelation 3:17 The spiritual misery of men is metaphorically expressed in three points: unto which are matched as correspondent those remedies which are offered, verse 18.

w. Revelation 3:19 Zeal is set against them which are neither hot nor cold.

x. Revelation 3:20 This must be taken after the manner of an allegory, as John 14:23.

y. Revelation 3:21 The conclusion, consisting of a promise, as Rev. 2:26, and of an exhortation. Hitherto hath been the first part of the book of the Apocalypse.

REVELATION 3

1. Rev. 16:15 / 1 Thess. 5:2 / 2 Pet. 3:10
2. Rev. 20:12 / Rev. 21:27 / Phil. 5:3
3. Prov. 3:12 / Heb. 22:5

REVELATION 4

a. Revelation 4:1 Hereafter followeth the second part of this book, altogether prophetical, foretelling those things which were to come, as was said before, Rev. 1:19. This is divided into two histories: one common unto the whole world, unto Chapter 9: and another singular of the Church of God, thence unto chapter 22. And these histories are said to be described in several books, Rev. 5:1 and 10:2. Now this verse is as it were a passage from the former part unto this second: where it is said, that the heaven was opened, that is, that heavenly things were unlocked, and that a voice as of a trumpet sounded in heaven to stir up the Apostle, and call him to the understanding of things to come. The first history hath two parts: one the causes of things done, and of this whole Revelation, in that and the next chapter. Another of the acts done, in the next 4 chapters. The principal causes according to the distinction of persons in the vanity of divine essence, and according to the economy or dispensation thereof, are two. One the beginning, which none can approach unto, that is, God the Father, of whom is spoken in this chapter. The other, the Son, who is the mean cause, easy to be approached unto us, in respect that he is God and man in one person: of whom, Rev. 5.

b. Revelation 4:2 The manner of revelation, as before, 1:10.

c. Revelation 4:2 See Rev. 1:12.

d. Revelation 4:2 A description of God the Father, and of his glory in the heavens, framed unto the manner of men, by his office, nature, company, attending, effect, instruments and events that follow afterwards. In this verse, he is presented in office a judge, as Abraham said, Gen. 18, which is declared by his throne, as an ensign of judgment, and his sitting thereupon.

e. Revelation 4:3 By his nature, in that he is the Father, most glorious in his own person, and with his glory overshining all other things.

f. Revelation 4:4 By the company attending about him in that, as that most high Judge, he is accompanied with the most honorable attendance of Prophets and Apostles, both of the old and new Church, whom Christ hath made to be Priests and Kings, Rev. 1:6 and 5:10.

g. Revelation 4:5 By effects, in that most mightily he speaketh all things by his voice and word, as Ps. 29:3, and with the light of his spirit and providence peruseth and passes through all.

h. Revelation 4:6 By instruments used, in that he both hath a most ready treasury, and as it were a workhouse excellently furnished with all things, unto the executing of his will, which things flow from his commandment, as is repeated, Rev.15:2. And hath also the Angels most ready administers of his counsels and pleasure unto all parts of the world, continually watching (in this verse) working by reason otherwise than the instruments, without life last mentioned, courageous as lions, mighty as bulls, wise as men, swift as eagles, verse 7, most apt unto all purposes, as furnished with wings on every part, most piercing of sight, and finally pure and perfect Spirits, always in continual motion, verse 8.

i. Revelation 4:8 Every beast had six wings.

j. Revelation 4:8 By events, in that for all the causes before mentioned God is glorified both of Angels, as holy, Judge, omnipotent, eternal and immutable, verse 8, and also after their example he is glorified of holy men (verse 9) in sign and in speech, verses 10, 11.

k. Revelation 4:9 God is said to have glory, honor, kingdom, and such like given unto him, when we godly and reverently set forth that which is properly and only his.

l. Revelation 4:10 Three signs of divine honor given unto God, prostration or falling down, adoration and casting their crowns before God, in which the godly, though made kings by Christ, do willingly empty themselves of all glory, moved with a religious respect for the majesty of God.

m. Revelation 4:11 The sum of their speech: that all glory must be given unto God: the reason, because he is the eternal beginning of all things, from whose only will they have their being and are governed: and finally in all respects are that which they are.

n. Revelation 4:11 That is, that thou shouldest challenge the same to thyself alone. But as for us, we are unworthy, that even by thy goodness we should be made partakers of this glory. And hitherto hath been handled the principal cause unapproachable, which is God.

REVELATION 4

1. Rev. 5:12

REVELATION 5

a. Revelation 5:1 A passing unto the second principal cause, which is the Son of God, God and man, the mediator of all, as the eternal word of God the Father manifested in the flesh. This chapter hath two parts: one that prepareth the way unto the Revelation, by rehearsal of the occasions that did occur in the first four verses. Another, the history of the Revelation of Christ, thence unto the end of the chapter.

b. Revelation 5:1 That is, in the very right hand of God.

c. Revelation 5:1 Here are showed the occasions for which this principal cause, and this Revelation was also necessary: the same are three, the first a present vision of the book of the counsels of God, concerning the government of this whole world, which book is said to be laid up with the Father as it were in his hand: but shut and unknown unto all creatures, in this verse. The second is a religious desire of the Angels of God to understand the mysteries of this book, verse 2, whereof see 1 Pet. 1:12. The third is a lamentation of Saint John and all the godly, moved by the same desire, verse 4, when they saw that it was a thing impossible for any creature to effect: which is declared in the third verse.

earth, was able to open the book, neither to look thereon. **4** Then I wept much,
because no man was found worthy to open, and to read the book, neither to look
thereon. **5** [e]And one of the Elders said unto me, Weep not: behold, that [1,f]Lion
which is of the tribe of Judah, that root of David, hath obtained to open the book,
and to loose the seven seals thereof. **6** Then I beheld, and lo, [g]in the midst of
the throne, and of the four beasts, and in the midst of the Elders stood a Lamb, as
though he had been killed, which had seven horns, and seven eyes, which are the
seven spirits of God, sent into all the world. **7** [h]And he came, and took the book
out of the right hand of him that sat upon the throne. **8** [i]And when he hath
taken the book, the four beasts, and the four and twenty Elders fell down before
the Lamb, having every one [j]harps and golden vials full of odors, which are the
[k]prayers of the Saints, **9** And they sung a [l]new [m]song, saying, [n]Thou art worthy
to take the book, and to open the seals thereof, because thou wast killed, and hast
redeemed us to God by thy blood out of every kindred, and tongue, and people,
and nation. **10** And hast made us unto our God [2]Kings, and Priests, and we
shall reign on the earth. **11** [o]Then I beheld, and I heard the voice of many An-
gels round about the throne, and about the beasts and the Elders, [p]and there were
[3,q]ten thousand times ten thousand, and thousand thousands, **12** Saying with a
loud voice, Worthy is the Lamb that was killed, to [r]receive power, and riches, and
wisdom, and strength, and honor, and glory, and praise. **13** [s]And all the creatu-
res which are in heaven, and on the earth, and under the earth, and in the sea, and
all that are in them, heard I saying, Praise, and honor, and glory, and power be unto
him, that sitteth upon the throne, and unto the Lamb for evermore. **14** [t]And the
four beasts said, Amen, and the four and twenty Elders fell down and worshipped
him that liveth for evermore.

6

1 The Lamb openeth the first seal of the book. 3 The second, 5 the third, 7 the fourth, 9 the fifth, 12 and the sixth, and then arise murders, famine, pestilence, outcries of Saints, earthquakes, and divers strange sights in heaven.

1 [a]After I beheld when the Lamb had opened one of the seals, and I heard one
of the four beasts say, as it were the noise of thunder, Come and see. **2** Therefore
[b]I beheld, and lo, there was a white horse, and he that sat on him, had a bow, and
a crown was given unto him, and he went forth conquering that he might overco-
me. **3** And [c]when he had opened the second seal, I heard the second beast say,
Come and see. **4** And there went out another horse, that was red, and power was
given to him that sat thereon to take peace from the earth, and that they should kill
one another, and there was given unto him a great sword. **5** [d]And when he had
opened the third seal, I heard the third beast say, Come and see. Then I beheld, and
lo, a black horse, and he that sat on him, had balances in his hand. **6** And I heard
a voice in the midst of the four beasts say, A [e]measure of wheat for a penny, and
three measures of barley for a penny, [f]and oil, and wine hurt thou not. **7** [g]And
when he had opened the fourth seal, I heard the voice of the fourth beast say,
Come and see. **8** And I looked, and behold, a pale horse, and his name that sat
on him was Death, and Hell followed after him, and power was given unto them
over the fourth part of the earth, to kill with sword, and with hunger, and with
death, and with beasts of the earth. **9** [h]And when he had opened the fifth seal,
I saw under the altar the souls of them that were killed for the word of God, and
for the testimony which they maintained. **10** And they cried with a loud voice,
saying, How long, Lord, which art holy and true! dost not thou judge and aven-
ge our blood on them, that dwell on the earth? **11** And long [i]white robes were
given unto every one, and it was said unto them, that they should rest for a little
season until their fellow servants, and their brethren that should be killed even as
they were, were [j]fulfilled. **12** [k]And I beheld when he had opened the sixth seal,
and lo, there was a great earthquake, and the Sun was as black as [l]sackcloth of hair,
and the Moon was like blood. **13** And the stars of heaven fell unto the earth,
as a fig-tree casteth her green figs, when it is shaken of a mighty wind. **14** And
heaven departed away, as a scroll, when it is rolled, and every mountain and isle
were moved out of their places. **15** [m]And the kings of the earth, and the great
men, and the rich men, and the chief captains, and the mighty men, and every
bondman, and every free man, hid themselves in dens, and among the rocks of

---

d. Revelation 5:3 Thus neither of them that are in heaven, nor of them which are in the earth, etc. And this I like better. Now this enumeration of parts is sufficient to the denying of the whole. For of the creatures one sort is in heaven above the earth: another in the earth: and another under the earth in the sea, as is after declared, verse 13.

e. Revelation 5:5 The second part of this chapter, in which is set down the Revelation of the Son, as before was said. This part containeth first an history of the manner how God prepared S. John to understand this Revelation in this verse. Secondly, the Revelation of the Son himself unto verse 7. Thirdly, the accidents of this Revelation, in the rest of the chapter. The manner now, is here described in two sorts, one from without him, by speech in this verse. Another within, by opening the eyes of S. John (which before were held) that he might see, in the verse following.

f. Revelation 5:5 That is, the most mighty and most approved Prince: according to the use of the Hebrew speech.

g. Revelation 5:6 The sum of this Revelation: Christ the mediator taketh and openeth the book, verses 6, 7. Therefore in his Revelation is described the person of Christ, in this verse. His fact, in the next verse. The person is thus described, Christ, the mediator between God, Angels and men, as the eternal word of God, and our redeemer: as the Lamb of God, standing as slain, and making intercession for us by the virtue and merit of his everlasting sacrifice, is armed with the Spirit of God, in his own person, that is, with the power and wisdom of God essentially unto the government of this whole world.

h. Revelation 5:7 The fact of Christ the Mediator, that he cometh unto the throne of the Father, of which Rev. 4, and taketh the book out of his hand to open it. For that he opened it, it is first expressed, Rev. 6:1, etc.

i. Revelation 5:8 Now follow in the end the accidents of the Revelation last spoken of that all the holy Angels, and men did sing unto him: both the chief, verses 9, 10, and common order of Angels, verses 11, 12, and of all things created, verse 13, the princes of both sorts agreeing thereunto, verse 14.

j. Revelation 5:8 The symbols or signs of praise, sweet in savor, and acceptable unto God. See Rev. 8:3.

k. Revelation 5:8 See Rev. 9:3.

l. Revelation 5:9 No common song.

m. Revelation 5:9 That is composed according to the present matter: the Lamb having received the book, as it were with his feet, and opened it with his horns, as is said in the Canticles.

n. Revelation 5:9 The song of the Nobles or Princes standing by the throne, consisting of a publication of the praise of Christ, and a confirmation of the same from his benefits, both which we have received of himself (as are the suffering of his death, our redemption upon the cross by his blood in this verse: and our communion with him in Kingdom and Priesthood, which long ago he hath granted unto us with himself) and which we hereafter hope to obtain, as our kingdom to come in Christ, in the verse following.

o. Revelation 5:11 The consent of the common order of Angels, answering in melody unto their Princes that stood by the throne.

p. Revelation 5:11 A number finite, but almost infinite for one infinite indeed, as Dan. 7:10.

q. Revelation 5:11 By this is meant a great number.

r. Revelation 5:12 To have all praise given to him, as to the mightiest and wisest, etc.

s. Revelation 5:13 The consent of all the common multitude of the creatures.

t. Revelation 5:14 A confirmation of the praise beforegoing, from the contestation of the Nobles, expressed in word and signs, as once or twice before this.

REVELATION 5

1. Gen. 49:6
2. Rev. 1:6 / 1 Pet. 2:9
3. Dan. 7:10

REVELATION 6

a. Revelation 6:1 This is the second part of this first history (which I said was common and of the whole world) of the works of God in the government of all things. Of this part there are generally 3 members, the foresignifying, the caution, and the execution of all the evils which God poureth out upon this world, which hath most hardly deserved of him. The foresignifying is set down in this chapter, the caution for preserving the Church, is in the next chapter, and the execution is described, Rev. 8:9. In every part of the foresignifying, there are three branches: the several and express calling of S. John, to prepare himself to take knowledge of the things that were to be showed unto him in the opening of the seals: the sign and the word expounding the sign: And albeit the express calling of S. John, be used only in four of the signs, yet the same is also to be understood in the rest that follow. The author of the foresignifying is the Lamb, as that word of the Father made the Mediator, opening the seals of the book. The instruments are the Angels in most of the visions, who expound the sign and words thereof. Now this first verse containeth an express calling of S. John to mark the opinion of the first seal.

b. Revelation 6:2 The first sign joined with declaration, is that God for the sins, and horrible rebellion of the world, will invade the same: and first of all as afar off, with his darts of pestilence most suddenly, mightily, and gloriously, bear down the same as judge, and triumph over it as conqueror.

c. Revelation 6:3 The second sign joined with words of declaration (after the express calling of S. John as before) is that God being provoked unto wrath by the obstinacy and hardheartedness of the world not repenting for the former plague, as setting upon the same hand, will kindle the fire of debate amongst men, and will destroy the inhabitants of this world, one by the sword of another.

d. Revelation 6:5 The third sign with declaration, is that God will destroy the world with famine, withdrawing all provision: which is by the figure Synecdoche comprehended in wheat, barley, wine and oil.

e. Revelation 6:6 Hereby is signified what great scarcity of corn there was, for the word here used is a kind of measure of dry things, which is in quantity but the eighth part of a bushel, which was an ordinary portion to be given servants for their stint of meat for one day.

f. Revelation 6:6 I had rather distinguish and read the words thus, and the wine and the oil thou shalt not deal unjustly. In this sense likewise the wine and the oil shall be sold a very little for a penny. Thou shalt not deal unjustly, namely, when thou shalt measure out a very little for a great price: so is the place evident: otherwise that is most true, which the wise man saith, that whoso withholdeth the corn shall be cursed of the people, Prov. 11:26.

g. Revelation 6:7 The fourth sign joined with words of declaration, is, that God will addict the fourth part of the world indifferently, unto death and hell, or the grave by all those means at once, by which before severally and in order he had recalled their minds unto amendment. Unto these are also added the wild and cruel beasts of the earth, out of Lev. 26:22. Thus doth God according to his wisdom dispense the treasures of his power, justly towards all, mercifully towards the good, and with patience or longsufferance towards his enemies.

h. Revelation 6:9 The fifth sign is that the holy martyrs which are under the altar, whereby they are sanctified, that is, received into the trust and tuition of Christ (into whose hands they are committed) shall cry out for the justice of God, in an holy zeal to advance his kingdom and not of any private perturbation of the mind, in this and the next verse, and that God will, in deed, sign and word comfort them, verse 11.

i. Revelation 6:11 As before 3:4.

j. Revelation 6:11 Until their number be fulfilled.

k. Revelation 6:12 The sixth sign, the narration whereof hath two parts, the sign, and the event. The sign is, that the earth, heaven, and the things that are in them for the horror of the sins of the world upon those most heavy foretellings of God, and complaints of the Saints shall be shaken most vehemently, trembling in horrible manner, and losing their light in this verse: falling from on high, verse 13, withdrawing themselves and flying away for the greatness of the trouble, verse 14. So boldly do all creatures depend upon the will of God, and content themselves in his glory.

l. Revelation 6:12 So they called in old time those woven works that were of hair.

m. Revelation 6:15 The event of the sign aforegoing: that there is no man that shall not be astonished at that general commotion, fly away for fear and hide himself in this verse, and wish unto himself most bitter death for exceeding horror of the wrath of God, and of the Lamb, at which before he was astonished. Now this perplexity is not of the godly, but of the wicked, whose portion is in this life, as the Psalmist speaketh, Ps. 17:14. Not that sorrow which is according unto God, which worketh repentance unto salvation, whereof a man shall never repent him, but that worldly sorrow that bringeth death, 2 Cor. 7:9, as their wishings do declare: for this history is of the whole world, severed from the history of the Church, as I have showed before, Rev. 4:1.

n. Revelation 6:16 These are words of such as despair of their escape: of which despair there are two arguments, the presence of God and the Lamb provoked to wrath against the world in this verse, and the conscience of their own weakness, whereby men feel that they are no way able to stand in the day of the wrath of God, verse 17, as it is said, Isa. 14:27.

the mountains, 16 And said to the mountains and rocks, [n,1]Fall on us, and hide us from the presence of him that sitteth on the throne, and from the wrath of the Lamb. 17 For the great day of his wrath is come, and who can stand?

7

1 The Angels coming to hurt the earth, 3 are stayed until the elect of the Lord, 5 of all tribes were sealed. 13 Such as suffered persecution for Christ's sake, 16 have great felicity, 17 and joy.

1 And [a]after that, I saw four Angels stand on the [b]four corners of the earth, holding the four winds of the earth, that the winds should not blow on the earth, neither on the sea, [c]neither on any tree. 2 [d]And I saw [e]another Angel come up from the East, which had the seal of the living God, and he cried with a loud voice to the four Angels to whom power was given to hurt the earth, and the sea, saying, 3 Hurt ye not the earth, neither the sea, neither the trees, till we have sealed the servants of our God in their foreheads. 4 And I heard the number of them, which were sealed, and there were sealed [f]an hundred and four and forty thousand of all the tribes of the children of Israel. 5 Out of the tribe of Judah were sealed twelve thousand. Of the tribe of Reuben were sealed twelve thousand. Of the tribe of Gad were sealed twelve thousand. 6 Of the tribe of Asher were sealed twelve thousand. Of the tribe of Naphtali were sealed twelve thousand. Of the tribe of Manasseh were sealed twelve thousand. 7 Of the tribe of Simeon were sealed twelve thousand. [g]Of the tribe of [h]Levi were sealed twelve thousand. Of the tribe of Issachar were sealed twelve thousand. Of the tribe of Zebulun were sealed twelve thousand. 8 Of the tribe of [i]Joseph were sealed twelve thousand. Of the tribe of Benjamin were sealed twelve thousand. 9 After these things I beheld, and lo, a great multitude, [j]which no man could number, of all nations and kindreds, and people, and tongues [k]stood before the throne, and before the Lamb, clothed with long white robes, and palms in their hands. 10 [l]And they cried with a loud voice, saying, Salvation cometh of our God, that sitteth upon the throne, and of the Lamb. 11 And all the Angels stood round about the throne, and about the Elders, and the four beasts, and they fell before the throne on their faces, and worshipped God, 12 Saying, Amen, Praise and glory, and wisdom, and thanks, and honor, and power, and might, be unto our God for evermore, Amen. 13 [m]And one of the Elders spake, saying unto me, What are these which are arrayed in long white robes? and whence came they? 14 And I said unto him, Lord, thou knowest. And he said unto me, [n]These are they which came out of great tribulation, and have washed their long robes, and have made their long robes white in the blood of the Lamb. 15 Therefore are they in the presence of the throne of God, and serve him [o]day and night in his Temple, and he that sitteth on the throne will dwell [p]among them. 16 [1]They shall hunger no more, neither thirst anymore, neither shall the sun light on them, neither any heat. 17 For the Lamb, which is in the midst of the throne, shall govern them, and shall lead them unto the lively fountains of waters, and [2]God shall wipe away all tears from their eyes.

8

1 After the opening of the seventh seal, 3 the Saints' prayers are offered up with odors. 6 The seven Angels come forth with trumpets. 7 The four first blow, and fire falleth on the earth, 8 the sea is turned into blood, 10, 11 the waters wax bitter. 12 and the stars are darkened.

1 [a]And when he had opened the seventh seal, there was silence in heaven about half an hour. 2 [b]And I saw the seven Angels, which [c]stood before God, and to them were given seven trumpets. 3 [d]Then another Angel came and stood before the Altar, having a golden censer, and much odors was given unto him, that he should offer with the prayers of all Saints upon the golden Altar, which is before the throne. 4 And the smoke of the odors with the prayers of the Saints, [e]went up before God, out of the Angel's hand. 5 And the Angel took the censer, and filled it with fire of the Altar, and cast it into the earth, and there were voices, and thunderings, and lightnings, and earthquake. 6 [f]Then the seven Angels, which had the seven trumpets, prepared themselves to blow the trumpets. 7 [g]So the first Angel blew the trumpet, and there was hail and fire mingled with blood, and they were cast into the earth, and the third part of trees was burnt, and all green grass was burnt. 8 [h]And the second Angel blew the trumpet, and as it were a great mountain, burning with fire, was cast into the sea, and the third part of the sea became blood. 9 And the third part of the creatures, which were in the sea, and had life, died, and the third part of ships were destroyed. 10 [i]Then the third Angel blew the trumpet, and there fell a great star from heaven, burning like

---

REVELATION 6

1. Isa. 2:19 / Hos. 10:8 / Luke 23:30

REVELATION 7

a. Revelation 7:1 The second member of this part, is a preventing of danger as we distinguished the same before, Chap. 6:1, that is of the caution whereby God took care before hand and provided for his that after the example of the Israelites of old, Exod. 8:13, the faithful might be exempted from the plagues of this wicked world. This whole place is a certain interlocution and bringing in for this whole chapter by occasion of the prediction and argument of the sixth seal. For first that evil is prevented in the elect unto verse 9. Then thanks are given by the elect for that cause, verses 10, 11, 12. Lastly, the accomplishment of the thing is set forth unto the end of the chapter. The first verse is a transition speaking of the Angels which keep these inferior parts from all evil, until God do command. For (as it is excellently figured by Ezek. 11:12) their faces and their wings are reached upwards, continually waiting upon and beholding the countenance of God for their direction: and every [one] of them goeth into that part that is right before his face, whithesoever the Spirit shall go, they go, they step not out of the way, that is, they depart not so much as a foot breadth from the path commanded them of God.

b. Revelation 7:1 On the four quarters or coasts of the earth.

c. Revelation 7:1 That is, neither into the air, into which the tops of trees are advanced.

d. Revelation 7:2 Now God provideth against the danger of his elect by commandment, verses 2 and 3, and by sign or figure, both for those of the nation of the Jews, thence unto verse 8, and also of the Gentiles, verse 9.

e. Revelation 7:2 Not only another, or differing in number from the common Angels of God, but also in essence, office, and operation excelling all Angels: that is, Christ Jesus the eternal Angel or word of God, and mediator of the covenant. So hereafter Rev. 8:3 and 10:1, 5.

f. Revelation 7:4 That is, of the Jews a number certain in itself before God, and such as may be numbered of us: for which cause also the same is here set down as certain. But of the elect which are of the Gentiles, the number indeed is in itself certain with God, but of us not possibly to be numbered, as God, Gen. 15:5, and often elsewhere, and Isaiah figured most excellently, Isa. 49 and 60. This therefore is spoken with respect, when a certain number is put for one uncertain. Confer this with verse 6.

g. Revelation 7:7 Here the tribe of Levi is reckoned up in common with the rest, because all the Israelites were equally made Priests with them in Christ by his Priesthood, Rev. 1:6, and 5:10, and Rom. 12:1, and 1 Pet. 2:9. The name of Dan is not mentioned because the Danites long before forsaking the worship of God, were fallen away from the fellowship of God's people unto the part of the Gentiles, which evil many ages before Jacob foresaw, Gen. 49:18, for which cause also there is no mention made of this tribe in the first book of the Chronicles.

h. Revelation 7:7 He skipped Dan, and reckoneth Levi.

i. Revelation 7:8 Of Ephraim, who was Joseph's other son, and had the birthright given him, whereof he is called Joseph.

j. Revelation 7:9 See before upon verse 4.

k. Revelation 7:9 As Priests, Kings and glorious conquerors by martyrdom: which things are noted by their proper signs in this verse.

l. Revelation 7:10 The praise of God celebrated first by the holy men, in this verse, then by the heavenly Angels in the two verses following.

m. Revelation 7:13 A passage over unto the expounding of the vision, of which the Angel inquireth of S. John to stir him up withal, in this verse and John in the form of speech, both acknowledgeth his own ignorance, attributing knowledge unto the Angel, and also in most modest manner requesteth the expounding of the vision.

n. Revelation 7:14 The exposition of the vision, wherein the Angel telleth first the acts of the Saints, that is, their sufferings and work of faith in Christ Jesus, in this verse. Secondly their glory, both present, which consisteth in two things, that they minister unto God, and that God protecteth them, verse 15, and to come, in their perfect deliverance from all annoyances, verse 16, and in participation of all good things which even the memory of former evils shall never be able to diminish, verse 17. The cause efficient, and which containeth all these things is only one, the Lamb of God, the Lord, the Mediator, and the Savior Christ Jesus.

o. Revelation 7:15 He alludeth to the Levites, which served day and night, for else there is no night in heaven.

p. Revelation 7:15 Or, upon them, whereby is meant God's defense and protection, as it were towards them, who are as safe, as men in the Lord's tent.

REVELATION 7

1. Isa. 49:10
2. Isa. 25:8 / Rev. 11:4

REVELATION 8

a. Revelation 8:1 He returneth to the history of the seals of the book, which the Lamb openeth. The seventh seal is the next foresignification, and a precise commandment of the execution of the most heavy judgments of God upon this wicked world: which foresignification being understood by the seal, all things in heaven are silent, and in horror through admiration until commandment of execution be severally given of God unto the ministers of his wrath. So he passeth unto the third member of which I spake before in Rev. 6:1, which is of the execution of those evils wherewith God most justly determined to afflict the world.

b. Revelation 8:2 Now followeth the third branch of the common history, as even now I said: which is the execution of the judgments of God upon the world. This is first generally prepared unto verse 6, then by several parts expoundeth according to the order of those that administered the same unto the end of the Chap. following. Unto the preparation of this execution are declared these things: first, who were the administers and instruments thereof in this verse. Secondly, what is the work both of the Prince of Angels giving order for this execution, thence unto verse 5, and of his administers in verse 6. The administers of the execution are said to be seven Angels: their instruments, trumpets, whereby they should as it were sound the alarm at the commandment of God. They are propounded seven in number, because it pleased God not at once to pour out his wrath upon the rebellious world, but at divers times, and by piecemeal, and in slow order, and as with an unwilling mind to exercise his judgments upon his creatures, so long called upon both by word and signs if happily they had learned to repent.

c. Revelation 8:2 Which appear before him as his ministers.

d. Revelation 8:3 This is the great Emperor, the Lord Jesus Christ our King and Savior: who both maketh intercession to God the Father for the Saints, filling the heavenly Sanctuary with most sweet odor, and offering up their prayers, as the Calves and burnt sacrifices of their lips, in this verse: in such sort as every one of them (so powerful is that sweet savor of Christ, and the efficacy of his sacrifice) are held in reconcilement with God and themselves made most acceptable unto him, verse 4. And then also out of his treasury, and from the same sanctuary poureth forth upon the world the fire of his wrath, adding also divine tokens thereto: and by that means (as of old the Heralds of Rome were wont to do) he proclaimeth war against the rebellious world.

e. Revelation 8:4 Our prayers are nothing worth, unless that true and sweet savor of that only oblation be especially and before all things with them, that is to say, unless we being first of all justified through faith in his Son, be acceptable unto him.

f. Revelation 8:6 This is the work of the administers. The Angels the administers of Christ, only by sounding trumpet and voice (for they are only as Heralds) do effectual call forth the instruments of the wrath of God, through his power. Hitherto have been things general. Now followeth the narration of things particular, which the Angels fix in number wrought in their order set out in verse 19 of the next chap., and is concluded with the declaration of the event which followed upon these things done in the world, and in chapters 10 and 11.

g. Revelation 8:7 The first execution at the sound of the first Angel upon the earth, that is, the inhabitants of the earth (by Metonymy) and upon all the fruits thereof: as the comparing of this verse with the second member of verse 9 doth not obscurely declare.

h. Revelation 8:8 The second execution, upon the sea in this verse and all things that are there in the next verse.

i. Revelation 8:10 The third execution upon the floods and fountains, that is, upon all fresh waters, in this verse: the effect whereof is, that many are destroyed with the bitterness of waters, in the verse following.

j. Revelation 8:11 This is spoken by Metaphor of the name of a most bitter herb, and commonly known, unless perhaps a man following those that note the derivation of words had rather expound it adjectively, for that which by reason or bitterness cannot be drunk, or which maketh the liquor

a torch, and it fell into the third part of the rivers, and into the fountains of waters. **11** And the name of the star is called [j]wormwood: therefore the third part of the waters became wormwood, and many men died of the waters, because they were made bitter. **12** [k]And the fourth Angel blew the trumpet, and the third part of the sun was smitten, and the third part of the moon, and the third part of the stars, so that the third part of them was darkened: and the day was smitten, that the third part of it could not shine, and likewise the night. **13** [l]And I beheld, and heard one Angel flying through the midst of heaven, saying with a loud voice, Woe, woe, woe to the inhabitants of the earth, because of the sounds to come of the trumpet of the three Angels, which were yet to blow the trumpets.

9

1 The fifth Angel bloweth his trumpet, 3 and spoiling locusts come out. 13 The sixth Angel bloweth, 16 and bringeth forth horsemen, 20 to destroy mankind.

1 And the [a]fifth Angel blew the trumpet, and I saw a [b]star fall from heaven unto the earth, [c]and to him was given the key of the [d]bottomless pit. **2** [e]And he opened the bottomless pit, and there arose the smoke of the pit, the smoke of a great furnace, and the sun, and the air were darkened by the smoke of the pit. **3** [f]And there came out of the smoke Locusts upon the earth, and unto them was given power, as the scorpions of the earth have power. **4** [g]And it was commanded them that they should not hurt the grass of the earth, neither any green thing, neither any tree: but only those men which have not the seal of God in their foreheads. **5** And to them was commanded that they should not kill them, but that they should be vexed five months, and that their pain should be as the pain that cometh of a scorpion, when he hath stung a man. **6** [l]Therefore in those days shall men seek death, and shall not find it, and shall desire to die, and death shall flee from them. **7** [h]And the form of the locusts was like unto horses prepared unto the battle, and on their heads were as it were crowns, like unto gold, and their faces were like the faces of men. **8** And they had hair as the hair of women, and their teeth were as the teeth of lions. **9** And they had habergeons, like unto habergeons of iron, and the sound of their wings was like the sound of chariots when many horses run unto battle. **10** And they had tails like unto scorpions, and there were stings in their tails, and their power was to hurt men five months. **11** [i]And they have a king over them, which is the Angel of the bottomless pit, whose name in Hebrew is Abaddon, and in Greek he is named Apollyon, that is, destroying. **12** [j]One woe is past, and behold, yet two woes come after this. **13** [k]Then the sixth Angel blew the trumpet, [l]and I heard a voice from the [m]four horns of the golden altar, which is before God, **14** Saying to the sixth Angel, which had the trumpet, [n]Loose the four Angels, which are bound in the great river Euphrates. **15** [o]And the four Angels were loosed, which were prepared at an hour, at a day, at a month, and at a year to slay the third part of men. **16** And the number of horsemen of war were twenty thousand times ten thousand: for I heard the number of them. **17** And thus I saw the horses in a vision, and them that sat on them, having fiery habergeons, and of hyacinth, and of brimstone, and the heads of the horses were as the heads of lions, and out of their mouths went forth fire, and smoke, and brimstone. **18** Of these three was the third part of men killed, that is, of the fire, and of the smoke, and of the brimstone, which came out of their mouths. **19** For their power is in their mouths, and in their tails: [p]for their tails were like unto serpents, and had heads wherewith they hurt. **20** [q]And the

---

into which is poured more bitter than that any man can drink the same.

k. Revelation 8:12 The fourth execution upon these lightsome bodies of heaven, which minister unto this inferior world.

l. Revelation 8:13 A lamentable prediction or foretelling of those parts of the divine execution which are yet behind: which also is a passage unto the argument of the next Chapter. Of all these things in a manner Christ himself expressly foretold in Luke 12:24, and they are common plagues generally denounced, without particular note of time.

REVELATION 9

a. Revelation 9:1 The first execution upon the wicked men inhabiting the earth (as a little before the Angel said) wrought by the infernal powers, is declared in this place unto the eleventh verse. And after the sixth execution thence unto the nineteenth verse. And lastly is showed the common event that followed the former execution in the world, in the two last verses.

b. Revelation 9:1 That is, that the Angel of God glittering with glory, as a star fell down from heaven. Whether thou take him for Christ, who hath the keys of hell himself, and by Princely authority, Rev. 1:18, or whether for some inferior Angel, who hath the same key permitted unto him, and occupieth it ministerially, or by office of his ministry, here, and Rev. 21, so the word falling, is taken, Gen. 14:10, and 24:64, and Heb. 6:6.

c. Revelation 9:1 The key was given to his star. For those powers of wickedness are thrust down into hell, and bound with chains of darkness: and are there kept unto damnation, unless God for a time do let them loose, 2 Pet. 2:4; Jude 1:6, and of this book, Rev. 20:20, the history of which chapter hath agreement of time with this present chapter.

d. Revelation 9:1 By the bottomless pit, he meaneth the deepest darkness of hell.

e. Revelation 9:2 Unto this is added, the smoke of the hellish and infernal spirits, all dark, and darkening all things in heaven and in earth. The spiritual darknesses are the causes of all disorder and confusion. For the devil at a time certain (whereof the fifth verse) sent these darknesses into his kingdom, that he might at once and with one impression overthrow all things, and pervert if it were possible the elect themselves. By this darkness all spiritual light, both active as of the Sun, and passive, as of the air which is lightened by the Sun, is taken away: and this is that which goeth before the spirits: it followeth of the spirits themselves.

f. Revelation 9:3 A description of the malignant spirits invading the world, taken from their nature, power, form and order. From their nature, for that they are like unto certain locusts, in quickenness, subtlety, hurtfulness, number, and such like in this verse. From their power, for that they are as the scorpions of the earth, of a secret force to do hurt. For our battle is not here with flesh and blood, but with powers, etc., Eph. 6:12. This place of the power of the Devils generally noted in this verse, is particularly declared afterwards in the three next verses.

g. Revelation 9:4 Here that power of the devils is particularly described according to their actions and effects of the same. Their actions are said to be bounded by the counsel of God: both because they hurt not all men, but only the reprobate (for the godly and elect, in whom there is any part of a better life, God guardeth by his decree) whom Christ shall not have sealed, in this verse: and also because they neither had all power not at all times, no not over those that are their own, but limited in manner and time, by the prescript of God, verse 5. So their power to afflict the godly, is none, and for the wicked is limited in act and in effect by the will of God: for the manner was prescribed unto them that they should not slay, but torment the wretched world. The time is for five months or for an hundred and fifty days, that is, for so many years in which the devils have indeed mightily perverted all things in the world: and yet without that public and unpunished license of killing, which afterward they usurped when the sixth Angel had blown his trumpet, as shall be said upon verse 13. Now this space is to be accounted from the end of that thousand years mentioned, Rev. 20:3, and that is from the Popedom of that Gregory the seventh, a most monstrous Necromancer, who before was called Hildebrandus Senensis: for this man being made altogether of impiety and wickedness, as a slave of the devil, whom he served, was the most wicked firebrand of the world: he excommunicated the Emperor Henry the fourth: went about by all manner of treachery to set up and put down empires and kingdoms as liked himself: and doubted not to set Rodolph the Swedon over the Empire instead of Henry before named, sending unto him a Crown with this verse annexed unto it: Petra dedit Petro, Petrus diadema Rodolpho: that is, The Rock to Peter gave the crown, and Peter Rodolph doth renown. Finally, he so finely bestirred himself in his affairs, as he miserably set all Christendom on fire, and conveyed over unto his successors the burning brand of the same: who enraged with like ambition, never ceased to nourish that flame, and to enkindle it more and more: whereby Cities, Commonwealths, and whole kingdoms set together by the ears amongst themselves by most expert cut-throats, came to ruin, whiles they miserably wounded one another. This term of an hundred and fifty years, taketh end in the time of Gregory the ninth, or Hugolinus Anagniensis (as he was before called) who caused to be compiled by one Raimond his chaplain and confessor, the body of Decretals, and by sufferance of the Kings and Princes to be published in the Christian world, and established for a law. For by this sleight at length the Popes arrogated unto themselves license to kill whom they would, whiles others were unawares: and without fear established a butchery out of many of the wicked Canons of the Decretals, which the trumpet of the fifth Angel had expressly forbidden, and had hindered until this time. The effects of the bloody actions are declared upon the sixth verse: that the miserable world languishing in so great calamities, should willingly run together unto death, and prefer the same before life, by reason of the grievousness of the miseries that oppressed them.

h. Revelation 9:7 The form of these hellish spirits and administers, is shadowed out by signs and visible figures in this sort: that they are very expert and swift: that wheresoever they are in the world, the kingdom of theirs: that they manage all their affairs with cunning and skill, in this verse, that making show of mildness and tender affection to draw on men withal, they most impudently rage in all mischief: that they are most mighty to do hurt, Verse 8, that they are freed from being hurt of any man, as armed with the color of religion, and sacred authority of privilege, that they fill all things with horror, Verse 9, that they are fraudulent: that they are venomous and extremely noisome, though their power be limited, Verse 10. All which things are properly in the infernal powers, and communicated by them unto their ministers and vassals.

i. Revelation 9:11 The order of the powers of maliciousness: that they are subject to one infernal King, whom thou mayest call in English, The Destroyer: who driveth the whole world both Jews and Gentiles into the destruction that belongeth unto himself. And I cannot tell whether this name belongeth unto the Etymological interpretation of Hildebrand, by a figure often used in the holy Scripture: which albeit it may otherwise be turned of the Germans (as the sense of compound words is commonly ambiguous) yet in very deed it signifieth as much as if thou shouldest call him the firebrand, that is, he that setteth on fire those that be faithful unto him.

j. Revelation 9:12 A passage unto the next point, and the history of the time following.

k. Revelation 9:13 The sixth execution done upon the world by the tyrannical powers thereof working in the four parts of the earth, that is in most cruel manner executing their tyrannous dominion through the whole world, and killing the miserable people without punishment, which before was not lawful for them to do in that sort, as I showed upon the fourth verse. This narration has two parts: a commandment from God, in verse 14, and execution of the commandment, in the verse following.

l. Revelation 9:13 The commandment given by Christ himself, who is governor over all.

m. Revelation 9:13 He alludeth to the altar of incense, which stood in the Court which the Priests were in, over against the Ark of the Covenant, having a veil betwixt them.

n. Revelation 9:14 As if he should have said, These hitherto have been so bound by the power of God, that they could not freely run upon all men as themselves lusted, but were stayed and restrained at that great flood of Euphrates, that is, in their spiritual Babylon (for this is a Paraphrase of the spiritual Babylon by the limits of the spiritual Babylon long since overthrown) that they might not commit those horrible slaughters which they long breathed after. Now go to: let loose those four Angels, that is, administers of the wrath of God, in that number that is convenient to the slaughtering of the four quarters of the world: stir them up and give them the bridle, that rushing of that Babylon of theirs, which is the seat of the wicked ones, they may fly upon all the world, therein to rage, and most licentiously to exercise their tyranny, as God hath ordained. This was done when Gregory the ninth by public authority established for law his own Decretals, by which he might freely lay trains for the life of simple men. For who is it that seeth not that the laws Decretal most of them are as snares to catch souls withal? Since that time (O good God!) how great slaughters have there been? how great massacres? All histories are full of them: and this our age aboundeth with most horrible and monstrous examples of the same.

o. Revelation 9:15 The execution of the commandment is in two points: one, that those butchers are let loose, that out of their tower of the spiritual Babylon they might with fury run abroad through all the world, as well the thief of that crew which are most prompt unto all assays, in this verse: as their multitudes, both most copious, of which a number certain is named for a number infinite, Verse 16, and in themselves by all means fully furnished to hide and to hurt, Verse 17, as being armed with fire, smoke and brimstone, as appeareth in the color of their armor, which dazzleth the eyes of all men: and have the strength of Lions to hurt withal, from which (as out of their mouth) the fiery, smoky, and stinking darts of the Pope are shot out, Verse 18. The other point is, that these butchers have effected the commandment of God by fraud and violence, in the two verses following.

p. Revelation 9:19 That is, they [are] harmful every way: on what part soever thou put thine hand unto them or they touch thee, they do hurt. So the former are called Scorpions, Verse 3.

q. Revelation 9:20 Now remaineth the event (as I said upon the first verse) which followed of so many and so grievous

remnant of the men which were not killed by these plagues, repented not of the
works of their hands that they should not worship devils, and [2]idols of gold, and of
silver, and of brass, and of stone, and of wood, which neither can see, neither hear,
nor go. **21** Also they repented not of their murder, and of their sorcery, neither
of their fornication, nor of their theft.

10

Another Angel appeareth with a cloud, 2 holding a book open, 3 and crieth out. 8 A voice from heaven commandeth John to take the book. 10 He eateth it.

1 And [a]I saw [b]another mighty Angel come down from heaven, clothed with
a cloud, and the rainbow upon his head, and his face was as the sun, and his feet
as pillars of fire. **2** And he had in his hand a [c]little book open, and he put his
right foot upon the sea, and his left on the earth, **3** And cried with a loud voice,
as when a lion roareth: and when he had cried, seven thunders uttered their voi-
ces. **4** [d]And when the seven thunders had uttered their voices, I was about to
write: but I heard a voice from heaven, saying unto me, [e]Seal up those things whi-
ch the seven thunders have spoken, and write them not. **5** And the Angel which
I saw stand upon the sea, and upon the earth, [f]lift up his hand to heaven, **6** And
sware by him that liveth for evermore, which created heaven, and the things that
therein are, and the earth, and the things that therein are, and the sea, and the thin-
gs that therein are, [g]that [h]time should be no more. **7** But in the days of the [i]voice
of the seventh Angel, when he shall begin to blow the trumpet, even the mystery
of God shall be finished, as he hath declared to his servants the Prophets. **8** [j]And
the voice which I heard from heaven, spake unto me again, and said, Go, and take
the little book which is open in the hand of the Angel, which standeth upon the
sea, and upon the earth. **9** So I went unto the Angel, and said to him, Give me
the little book. And he said unto me, Take it, and eat it up, and it shall make thy
belly bitter, but it shall be in thy mouth as sweet as honey. **10** Then I took the
little book out of the Angel's hand, and ate it up, and it was in my mouth as swe-
et as honey: but when I had eaten it, my belly was bitter. **11** [k]And he said unto
me, Thou must prophesy again among the people and nations, and tongues, and
to many Kings.

11

1 The temple is commanded to be measured. 3 The Lord stirred up two witnesses, 7 whom the beast murdereth, 9 and no man burieth them. 11 God raiseth them to life, 12 and calleth them up to heaven, 13 the wicked are terrified, 15 by the trumpet of the seventh Angel the resurrection, 18 and judgment is described.

1 [a]Then was given me a reed like unto a rod, and the Angel stood by, saying,
Rise and [b]mete the Temple of God, and the Altar, and them that worship the-
rein. **2** [c]But the [d]Court which is without the Temple [e]cast out, and mete it
not: for it is given unto the [f]Gentiles, and the holy city shall they tread under
foot, [g]two and forty Months. **3** But [h]I will give power unto my two witnesses
and they shall [i]prophesy a thousand two hundred and threescore days, clothed in

---

judgments in the most wicked world: namely an impenitent affirmation of the ungodly in their impiety and unrighteousness, though they feel themselves most vehemently pressed with the hand of God: for their obstinate ungodliness is showed in this verse: and their unrighteousness in the verse following. Hitherto hath been the general history of things to be done universal in the whole world: which because it doth not so much belong to the Church of Christ, is therefore not so expressly distinguished by certainty of time and other circumstances, but is woven, as they say with a slight hand. Also there is none other cause why the history of the seventh Angel is passed over in this place, than for that the same more properly appertaineth unto the history of the Church. But this is more diligently set out according to the time thereof, Rev. 11 and 16, as shall appear upon those places.

REVELATION 9

1. Rev. 6:16 / Isa. 2:19 / Hos. 10:8
2. Ps. 115:4 / Ps. 135:25

REVELATION 10

a. Revelation 10:1 Now Saint John passeth unto the other Prophetical history, which is of the Church of God, as I showed that this book should be distinguished, Rev. 4:1. This story reacheth hence unto the two and twentieth Chapter. And this whole Chapter is but a transition from the common history of the world unto that which is particular of the Church. There are in this transition or passage, two preparatives as it were, unto this Church story comprised in this whole Chapter. One is the authority of Christ revealing his mysteries, and calling his servants unto the seventh verse. The other is Saint John's calling, proper unto this place, and prepared from before unto the end of this chapter. Authority is given unto this Revelation by these things: First, by the appearing from heaven in this habit and countenance, strong, ready, glorious, surveying all things by his providence and governing them by his omnipotence, the first verse. Secondly, that he brought not by chance, but out of a book, this open Revelation, set forth unto the eye, to signify the same unto the sea, and land, as the Lord over all, the second Verse. Thirdly, that he offered the same not whispering or muttering in a corner (as false prophets do) but crying out with a loud voice unto them which sleep, and with a lionish and terrible noise roused the secure: the very thunders themselves giving testimony thereunto, the third Verse. Lastly, for that he confirmed all by an oath, Verses 5, 6, 7.

b. Revelation 10:1 Christ Jesus, see the seventh Chapter and the second verse.

c. Revelation 10:2 Namely, a special book of the affairs of God's Church. For the book that containeth things belonging [unto] the whole world, is said to be kept with the Creator, the fifth Chapter and the first verse, but the book of the Church, with the Redeemer: and out of this book is taken the rest of the history of this Apocalypse.

d. Revelation 10:4 A godly care is laudable, but must be joined with knowledge. Therefore nothing is to be taken in hand, but by calling: which must be expected and waiting for of the godly.

e. Revelation 10:4 Keep them close.

f. Revelation 10:5 This was a gesture used of one that sweareth, which men do nowadays use.

g. Revelation 10:6 Neither time itself, nor the things that are in time: but that the world to come is at hand which is altogether of eternity and beyond all times.

h. Revelation 10:6 There shall never be anymore time.

i. Revelation 10:7 Whereof Rev. 11:15 and 16:17.

j. Revelation 10:8 The other part of this Chapter, concerning the particular calling of Saint John to the receiving of the prophecy following which is enjoined him, first by sign in three verses, then in plain words in the last verse. Unto the setting forth of the sign belong these things: That Saint John is taught from heaven to demand the book of the Prophecy in this verse: for these motions and desires God doth inspire: that demanding the book, he is charged to take it in a figurative manner, the use whereof also is expounded, the ninth verse, (as in the second Chapter of Ezekiel and the ninth verse) whence this similitude is borrowed: lastly, for that Saint John at the commandment of Christ took the book, and found by experience that the same as proceeding from Christ was most sweet, but in that it foretelleth the afflictions of the Church it was most bitter unto his spirit.

k. Revelation 10:11 A simple and plain declaration of the sign before going, witnessing the divine calling of S. John, and laying upon him the necessity thereof.

REVELATION 11

a. Revelation 11:1 The authority of the intended revelation being declared, together with the necessity of that calling, which was particularly imposed upon Saint John: hereafter followeth the history of the estate of Christ's Church both conflicting or warfaring, and overcoming in Christ. For both the true Church of Christ is said to fight against that which is falsely so called over the which Antichrist ruleth. Christ Jesus overthrowing Antichrist by the spirit of his mouth: and Christ is said to overcome most gloriously until he shall slay the Antichrist by the appearance of his coming, as the Apostle excellently teacheth, 2 Thess. 2:8. So this history hath two parts. One of the state of the Church conflicting with temptations, until Chapter 16. The other of the state of the same Church obtaining victory, thence unto Chapter 20. The first part hath two members most conveniently distributed into their times, whereof the first containeth an history of the Christian Church for 1260 years, what time the Gospel of Christ was as it were taken up from amongst men into heaven: the second containeth an history of the same Church unto the victory perfected. And these two members are briefly, though distinctly propounded in this Chapter, but are both of them more at large discussed after in due order. For we understand the state of the Church conflicting out of Chapters 12 and 13 and of the same growing out of afflictions out of Chapters 14, 15 and 16. Neither did Saint John at unawares join together the history of these two times in this Chapter, because here is spoken of prophecy, which all confess to be one just and innumerable in the Church, and which Christ commanded to be continual. The history of the former time reacheth unto verse 14: the latter is set down in the rest of this Chapter. In the former are showed these things: the calling of the servants of God in 4 verses: the conflicts which the faithful must undergo in their calling, for Christ and his Church, thence unto verse 10, and their resurrection and receiving up into heaven unto verse 14. In the calling of the servants of God are mentioned two things: the begetting and setting of the Church in two verses, and the education thereof in two verses. The begetting of the Church is here commended unto S. John by sign and by speech: the sign is a measuring rod, and the speech a commandment to measure the Temple of God, that is, to reduce the same unto a new form: because the Gentiles are already entered into the Temple of Jerusalem, and shall shortly defile and overthrow the same utterly.

b. Revelation 11:1 Either that of Jerusalem which was a figure of the Church of Christ, or that heavenly Example, whereof verse 19, but the first liketh me better and the things following do agree thereunto. The sense therefore is, Thou seest all things in God's house almost from the passion of Christ to be disordered: and that not only the city of Jerusalem but also the court of the Temple is trampled underfoot by the nations, and by profane men whether Jews or strangers: and that only the Temple, that is, the body of the Temple, with the Altar, and a small company of good men which truly worship God, do now remain, whom God doth sanctify and confirm by his presence. Measure therefore this, even this true Church, or rather the true type of the true Church, omitting the rest and so describe all things from me that the true Church of Christ may be as it were a very little center, and the Church of Antichrist as the circle of the center, every way in length and breadth compassing about the same, that by way of prophecy thou mayest so declare openly, that the state of the Temple of God and the faithful which worship him, that is, of the Church, is much more straight than the Church of Antichrist.

c. Revelation 11:2 As if he should say, it belongeth nothing unto them to judge those which are without, 1 Cor. 5:12, which be innumerable: look unto those of the household only, or unto the house of the living God.

d. Revelation 11:2 He speaketh of the outward court, which was called the peoples court, because all men might come into that.

e. Revelation 11:2 That is counted to be cast out, which in measuring is refused as profane.

f. Revelation 11:2 To profane persons wicked and unbelievers, adversaries unto the Church.

g. Revelation 11:2 Or a thousand and two hundred and threescore days as is said in the next verse: that is a thousand two hundred and threescore years, a day for a year as often in Ezekiel and Daniel, which thing I noted before, 2:10. The beginning of these thousand two hundred and threescore years, we account from the passion of Christ, whereby (the partition wall being broken down) we were made of two one, Eph. 2:14. I say one flock under one Shepherd, John 10:16 and the end of these years precisely falleth into the Popedom of Boniface the eighth who a little before the end of the year of Christ a thousand two hundred ninety four, entered the Popedom of Rome, in the feast of S. Lucie (as Bergomensis saith) having put in prison his predecessor Coelestinus, whom by fraud, under color of oracle, he deceived: for which cause, that well said of him, Intravit ut vulpes, regnavit ut leo, mortuus est ut canis. That is, he entered like a fox, reigned like a lion, and died like a dog. For if from a thousand two hundred ninety four years thou shalt take the age of Christ which he lived on the earth, thou shalt find there remaineth 1260 years, which are mentioned in this place and many others.

h. Revelation 11:3 I had rather translate it illud than illam, the Temple than the city: for God saith, I will give that Temple, and commit it unto my two witnesses, that is unto the Ministers of the word, who are few indeed, weak and contemptible: but yet two, that is, of such a number as one of them may help another, and one confirm the testimony of another unto all men, that from the mouth of two or three witnesses every word may be made good amongst men, 2 Cor. 13:1.

i. Revelation 11:3 They shall exercise their office enjoined by me by the space of those thousand two hundred and sixty years, in the midst of afflictions though never so lamentable which is figuratively showed by the mourning garment.

sackcloth. **4** These [j]are two olive trees, and two candlesticks, standing before the
God of the earth. **5** [k]And if any man will hurt them, fire proceedeth out of their
mouths and devoureth their enemies: for if any man would hurt them, thus must
he be killed. **6** These have power to shut heaven, that it rain not in the days of
their prophesying, and have power over waters to turn them into blood, and to
smite the earth with all manner plagues, as often as they will. **7** [l]And when they
have [m]finished their testimony, [n]the beast that cometh out of the bottomless pit,
shall make war against them, and shall [o]overcome them, and kill them, **8** And
their corpses shall lie in the [p]streets of the great city, which [q]spiritually is called So-
dom and Egypt, [r]where our Lord also was crucified. **9** And they of the people
and kindreds, and tongues, and Gentiles, shall see their corpses [s]three days and an
half, and shall not suffer their carcasses to be put in graves. **10** And they that
dwell upon the earth, [t]shall rejoice over them and be glad, and shall send gifts one
to another, for these two Prophets [u]vexed them that dwelt on the earth. **11** [v]But
after [w]three days and an half, [x]the spirit of life coming from God, shall enter into
them, and they [y]shall stand up upon their feet: and great fear shall come upon
them which saw them. **12** And they shall hear a great voice from heaven, saying
unto them, [z]Come up hither: And they shall ascend up to heaven in a cloud, [aa]
and their enemies shall see them. **13** [ab]And the same hour shall there be a great
earthquake, and the tenth part of the city shall fall, and in the earthquake shall be
slain in number seven thousand: and the remnant were sore feared, [ac]and [ad]ga-
ve glory to God of heaven. **14** [ae]The second woe is past, and behold, the third
woe will come anon. **15** [af]And the seventh Angel blew the trumpet, and there
were great voices in heaven, saying, [ag]The kingdoms of the world are our Lord's,
and his Christ's, and he shall reign for evermore. **16** [ah]Then the four and twen-
ty Elders, which sat before God on their seats, fell upon their faces and worship-
ped God. **17** Saying, We give thee thanks, Lord God Almighty, Which art, and
which wast, and which art to come: for thou hast received thy great might, and
hast obtained thy kingdom. **18** [ai]And the Gentiles were angry, and thy wrath is
come, and the time of the dead, that they should be judged, and that thou shoul-
dest give reward unto thy servants the Prophets, and to thy Saints, and to them that
fear thy Name, to small and great, and shouldest destroy them, which destroy the
earth. **19** Then the Temple of God was [aj]opened in heaven, and there was seen
in the Temple the Ark of his covenant: and there were lightnings, and voices, and
thunderings, and earthquake, and much hail.

12

1 A woman 2 appeareth travailing with child, 4 whose child the dragon would devour, 7 but Michael overcometh him 9 and casteth him out, 13 and the more he is cast down and vanquished, the more fiercely he exercised his subtleties.

1 And [a]there appeared a great wonder in heaven: [b]A woman clothed with
the Sun, and the Moon was under her feet, and upon her head a crown of twelve
Stars. **2** And [c]she was with child, and cried travailing in birth, and was pained

---

j. Revelation 11:4 That is, the ordinary and perpetual instruments of spiritual grace, peace and light in my Church, which God by his only power preserved in this Temple. See Zech. 4:3.

k. Revelation 11:5 The power and efficacy of the holy ministry, and which is truly Evangelical, is declared both in earth and in heaven, protecting the administers thereof, and destroying the enemies in this verse, virtue indeed divine most mightily showing itself forth in heaven, earth and the sea, verse 6, as it described, 2 Cor. 10:4, according to the promise of Christ, Mark 16:17. And this is the second place (as I said before) of the combats which the servants of God must needs undergo in the executing of their calling, and of the things that follow the same combats. In the combats or conflicts are these things: to overcome, in these two verses: to be overcome and killed, verse 7. After the slaughter follow these things, that the carcasses of the godly are laid abroad, verse 8 being unburied, are made a matter of scorn together of cursing and bitter execrations, verse 9, and that therefore gratulations are publicly and privately made, verse 10.

l. Revelation 11:7 That is, when they have spent those thousand two hundred and sixty years, mentioned verses 2 and 3, in publishing their testimony according to their office.

m. Revelation 11:7 When they have done their message.

n. Revelation 11:7 Of which after Rev. 13. That beast is the Roman Empire, made long ago of civil, Ecclesiastical: the chief head whereof was then Boniface the eighth, as I said before: who lifted up himself in so great arrogancy (saith the author of Falsciculus temporum) that he called himself Lord of the whole world, as well in temporal causes as in spiritual: There is an extant of that matter, written by the same Boniface most arrogantly, shall I say, or most wickedly, ca. unam sanctam, extra de majoritate & obedientia, and in the sixth of the Decretals (which is from the same author) many things are found of the same argument.

o. Revelation 11:7 He shall persecute most cruelly the holy men, and put them to death, and shall wound and pierce through with cursings both their names and writings. And that this was done to very many godly men by Boniface and others, the histories do declare, especially since the time that the odious and condemned name amongst the multitude first of the brethren Waldenses or Lugdunenses, then also of the Fratricels, was pretended, that good men might with more approbation be massacred.

p. Revelation 11:8 - That is, openly at Rome: where at that time was a most great concourse of people, the year of Jubilee being then first ordained by Boniface unto the same end, in the year of Christ a thousand three hundred, example whereof is read, Rev. 1. Extra, de penitentys & remissionibus. So by one act he committed double injury against Christ, both abolishing his truth by the restoring of the type of the Jubilee, and triumphing over his members by most wicked superstitions. O religious heart! Now that we should understand the things of Rome, Saint John himself is the author, both after in the seventeenth Chapter almost throughout, and also in the circumscription now next following, when he saith, it is that great City (as Rev. 17; 18 he calleth it) and is spiritually termed Sodom and Egypt: that spiritually (for that must here again be repeated from before) Christ was there crucified. For the two first appellations signify spiritual wickednesses: the latter signifieth the show and pretence of good, that is, of Christian and sound religion. Sodom signifieth most licentious impiety and injustice: Egypt most cruel persecution of the people of God: and Jerusalem signifieth the most confident glorying of that city, as it were in true religion, being yet full of falsehood and ungodliness. Now who is ignorant that these things do rather, and more agree unto Rome than unto any other city? The commendations of the City of Rome for many years past are publicly notorious, which are not for me to gather. This only I will say that he long since did very well see what Rome is, who taking his leave thereof, used these verses: ***Roma vale, vidi, Satis est vidisse: revertar, Quumleno, meretrix, scurra, cinadus ero. Now farewell Rome, I have thee seen: It was enough to see: I will return when as I mean, bawd, harlot knave to be.***

q. Revelation 11:8 After a most secret kind of meaning and understanding.

r. Revelation 11:8 Namely in his members, as also he said unto Saul, Acts 9:5.

s. Revelation 11:9 That is, for three years and a half for so many years Boniface lived after his Jubilee as Bergomensis witnesseth.

t. Revelation 11:10 So much the more shall they by this occasion exercise the jollity of their Jubilee.

u. Revelation 11:10 The gospel of Christ, in the affliction of the world, and the ministry thereof, the savor of death unto death to those that perish, 2 Cor. 2:16.

v. Revelation 11:11 The third place as noted I before, is of the rising again of the Prophets from the dead, and their carrying up into heaven. For their resurrection is showed in this verse: their calling and lifting up into heaven, in the verse following.

w. Revelation 11:11 That is, what time God shall destroy that wicked Boniface.

x. Revelation 11:11 That is, the Prophets of God shall in a sort rise again, not the same in person (as they say) but in spirit, that is in the power and efficacy of their ministry, which S. John expressed before verses 5 and 6. And so the prophecy that is spoken of Elijah, is interpreted by the Angel to be understood of John the Baptist, Luke 1:17. For the same Boniface himself, who sought to kill and destroy them, was by the fire of God's mouth (which the holy ministry showeth and exhibiteth) devoured and died miserably in prison, by the endeavor of Satra Columensis, and Nogaretus a french knight, whom Philip the fair King of France sent into Italy but with a small power.

y. Revelation 11:11 That is, the most grievous heat of afflictions and persecution shall stay for a while, for the great amaze that shall arise upon that sudden and unlooked for judgment of God.

z. Revelation 11:12 They were called by God into heaven and taken out of this malignant world, into the heavenly Church, which also lieth hidden here in the earth, to exercise their calling secretly: as of whom this wretched world was unworthy, Heb. 11:38. For the Church of the wicked is by comparison called the earth or the world: and the Church of the godly heaven. So in ancient time amongst the godly Israelites: so amongst the Jews in the days of Manasseh and other Kings, when the earth refused the heirs of heaven, we read that they lay hidden as heaven in the earth.

aa. Revelation 11:12 Yet could they not hinder the secret ones of the Lord (as the Psalmist called them, Ps 83:4) but they that went on forward in his work.

ab. Revelation 11:13 Bergomensis saith, in the year of our Lord 1301, this year a blazing star foretelling great calamity to come, appeared in heaven, in which year upon the feast of S. Andrew, so great an earthquake arose, as never before: which also continuing, by times, for many days, overthrew many stately houses. This saith he of the year next following the Jubilee: which S. John so many ages before, expressed word for word.

ac. Revelation 11:13 They were indeed broken with present astonishment of mind, but did not earnestly repent as they ought to have done.

ad. Revelation 11:13 Glorified God by confessing his name.

ae. Revelation 11:14 He passeth unto the second history: which is the second part of this Chapter. S. John calleth these the second and third woes, having respect unto Rev. 9:12.

af. Revelation 11:15 Of whose sounding the trumpet Christ expressly foretold, Rev. 10:7, and this is the second part of this Chapter, containing a general history of the Christian Church, from the time of Boniface 8 unto the consummation of the victory declared by voice from heaven. In this history there are three branches: a preparation by the sound of the Angels trumpet: a narration by the voice of heavenly Angels and Elders: and a confirmation by sign.

ag. Revelation 11:15 The narration hath two parts: an acclamation of the heavenly creatures, in this verse, and both an adoration by all the Elders, verse 16, and also a most ample thanksgiving, verses 17, 18. The sense of the acclamation is, Now the Lord is entered on his kingdom, and hath restored his Church, in which most mightily recovered from the profanation of the Gentiles, he may glorify himself. Namely, that which the Lord ordained when first he ordained his Church, that the faith of the Saints doth now behold as accomplished.

ah. Revelation 11:16 As before, 7:11. This giving of thanks is altogether of the same content with the words going before.

ai. Revelation 11:18 A speech of the Hebrew language, as much to say, as Gentiles being angry thine inflamed wrath came upon them and showed itself from heaven, occasioned by their anger and fury.

aj. Revelation 11:19 This is the confirmation of the next prophecy before going by signs exhibited in heaven, and that of two sorts, whereof some are visible, as the passing away of the heaven, the opening of the Temple, the Ark of the covenant appearing in the Temple, and testifying the glorious presence of God, and the lightning: others apprehended by ear and such dull senses which bear witness in heaven and in earth to the truth of the judgments of God.

REVELATION 12

a. Revelation 12:1 Hitherto hath been the general prophecy comprehended in 2 parts, as I showed upon Rev. 11. Now shall be declared the first part of this prophecy, in this and the next chapter and the latter part in chapters 14, 15 and 16. Unto the first part, which is of the conflicting or militant Church belong 2 things. The beginning and the progress of the same in conflicts and Christian combats. Of which two, the beginning or upspring of the Church is described in this Chap. and the progress thereof in the Chap. following. The beginning of the Christian Church, we define to be from the first moment of her the conception of Christ, until the time wherein this Church was as it were weaned and taken away from the breast or milk of her Mother: which is the time when the Church of the Jews with their city and Temple was overthrown by the judgment of God. So we have in this chapter the story of 60 years and upwards. The parts of this chapter are three. The first is, the history of the conception and bearing in womb, in 4 verses. The second, an history of the birth from verse 5 unto verse 12. The third is, of the woman that had brought forth,unto the end of the chapter. And these several parts have every one their conflicts. Therefore in that first part are two things contained, one, the conception and bearing in womb in two verses: and another of the lying in wait of the Dragon against that should be brought forth, in the next 2 verses. In the first point are these things, the description of the mother, verse 1, and the dolors of childbirth, verse 2, all showed unto John from heaven.

b. Revelation 12:1 A type of the true and holy Church, which then was in the nation of the Jews. This Church (as is the state of the holy Church Catholic) did in itself shine about with glory given of God, trod under feet mutability and changeableness, and possessed the kingdom of heaven as the heir thereof.

c. Revelation 12:2 For this is that barren woman that brought not forth, of which Isa. 45:1, and Gal. 4:27, she cried out for good cause, and was tormented at that time, when in the judgment of all she seemed near unto death, and in

ready to be delivered. **3** And there appeared another wonder in heaven: [d]for
behold, a great red dragon having [e]seven heads, and ten [f]horns, and seven crowns
upon his heads: **4** [g]And his tail drew the third part of the stars of heaven, and
cast them to the earth. And the dragon [h]stood before the woman, which was ready
to be delivered, [i]to devour her child, when she had brought it forth. **5** [j]So she
brought forth a man [k]child, which should rule all nations with a rod of iron: and
that her child was taken up unto God and to his throne. **6** [l]And the woman fled
into the wilderness, where she hath a place prepared of God, that [m]they should
feed her there a thousand, two hundred and threescore days. **7** And there was a
battle in heaven, [n]Michael and his Angels, fought against the dragon, and the dra-
gon fought and his angels. **8** [o]But they prevailed not, neither was their [p]place
found anymore in heaven. **9** And the great dragon that old serpent, called the
devil and Satan, was cast out, which deceiveth all the world: he was even cast into
the earth, and his angels were cast out with him. **10** Then I heard a loud voice
in heaven, saying, [q]Now is salvation, and strength, and the kingdom of our God,
and the power of his Christ: for the accuser of our brethren is cast down, which
accused them before our God day and night. **11** But they overcame him by that
blood of that Lamb, and by that word of their testimony, and they [r]loved not their
lives unto the death. **12** Therefore rejoice, ye heavens, and ye that dwell in them.
Woe to the inhabitants of the earth, and of the sea: for the devil is come down unto
you, which hath great wrath, knowing that he hath but a short time. **13** And
when [s]the dragon saw that he was cast unto the earth, he persecuted the woman
which had brought forth the man child. **14** [t]But to the woman were given two
wings of a great Eagle, that she might fly into the wilderness, into her [u]place whe-
re she is nourished for a [v]time, and times, and half a time, from the presence of
the serpent. **15** [w]And the serpent cast out of his mouth water after the woman,
like a flood, that he might cause her to be carried away of the flood, **16** [x]But
the earth helped the woman, and the earth opened her mouth, and swallowed
up the flood, which the dragon had cast out of his mouth. **17** [y]Then the dra-
gon was wroth with the woman, and went and made war with the remnant of her
seed, which keep the commandments of God, and have the testimony of Jesus
Christ. **18** [z]And I stood on the sea sand.

13

1 The beast with many heads is described 12 which draweth the most part of the world to idolatry. 13 The other beast rising out of the earth, 15 giveth power unto him.

1 And I [a]saw a beast rise [b]out of the sea, having seven heads, and [c]ten horns,
and upon his horns were ten crowns, and [d]upon his head [e]the name of bla-
sphemy. **2** And the beast which I saw was [f]like a leopard, and his feet like a bear,

---

means ready to give up the ghost by reason of her weakness and poverty.

d. Revelation 12:3 That is the devil or Satan (as is declared verse 9,) mighty, angry, and full of wrath.

e. Revelation 12:3 Thereby to withstand those seven Churches spoken of, that is the Catholic Church, and that with kingly furniture and tyrannical magnificence: signified by the crowns set upon his heads, and if the same without controversy belonged unto him by proper right: as also he boasted unto Christ, Matt. 4:9. See after, upon Rev. 13:1.

f. Revelation 12:3 More than are the horns of the Lamb, or than the Churches are: so well furnished doth the tyrant brag himself to be, unto all manner of mischief.

g. Revelation 12:4 After the description of Satan followeth this action, that is, his battle offered unto the Church partly to that which is visible wherein the wheat is mingled with the chaff, and the good fish with that which is evil: a good part thereof, though in appearance it shined as the Stars shine in heaven, he is said to thrust down out of heaven and to pervert: for if it were possible he would pervert even the elect, Matt. 24:24, and partly to the elect members of the holy Catholic Church in the second part of this verse. Many therefore of the members of this visible Church (saith S. John) he overthrew and triumphed upon them.

h. Revelation 12:4 He withstood that elect Church of the Jews which was now ready to bring forth the Christian Church, and watched for that she should bring forth. For the whole Church, and whole body is compared unto a woman: and a part of the Church unto that which is brought forth as we have noted at large upon, Cant. 7:6.

i. Revelation 12:4 Christ mystical (as they call him) that is the whole Church, consisting of the person of Christ as the head, and of the body united thereunto by the Spirit, so is the name of Christ taken, 1 Cor. 12:12.

j. Revelation 12:5 The second history of the Church delivered of child: in which first the consideration of the child born, and of the Mother is described in 2 verses: secondly the battle of the Dragon against the young child, and the victory obtained against him 3 verses following: last of all is sung a song of victory, unto verse 12. Now S. John in consideration of the child born, noteth two things: for he describeth him, and his station or place in this verse.

k. Revelation 12:5 That is, Christ the head of the Church (the beginning, root and foundation whereof is the same Christ) endowed with kingly power, and taken up into heaven out of the jaws of Satan (who as a serpent did bite him upon the cross) that sitting upon the celestial throne he might reign over all.

l. Revelation 12:6 The Church of Christ which was of the Jews, after his assumption into heaven, hid itself in the world as in a wilderness, trusting in the only defense of God, as witnesseth S. Luke in the Acts of the Apostles.

m. Revelation 12:6 Namely the Apostles, and servants of God ordained to feed with the word of life, the Church collected both of the Jews and Gentiles, unless that any man will take the word alerent impersonally after the use of the Hebrews instead, of aleretur, but I like the first better. For he hath respect unto those two Prophets, of whom Rev. 11:3, as for the meaning of the 1260 days, look the same place.

n. Revelation 12:7 Christ is the Prince of Angels, and head of the Church, who beareth that iron rod, the fifth verse. See the notes upon Daniel, Dan. 12:1. In this verse a description of the battle and of the victory in the two verses following. The Psalmist had respect unto this battle, Ps. 68:9, and Paul, Eph. 4:1 and Col. 2:15.

o. Revelation 12:8 The description of the victory, by denying of the thing in this verse, and by affirming the contrary in the next verse. As that Satan gained nothing in heaven but was by the power of God thrown down into the world, whereof he is the prince, Christ himself and his elected members standing still by the throne of God.

p. Revelation 12:8 They were cast out, so that they were never seen anymore in heaven.

q. Revelation 12:10 The song of victory or triumph containing first, a proposition of the glory of God and of Christ showed in that victory: secondly, it containeth a reason of the same proposition taken from the effects, as that the enemy is overcome in battle in this verse, and that the godly are made conquerors (and more than conquerors, Rom. 8:37) verse 11. Thirdly, a conclusion wherein is an exhortation unto the Angels, and the Saints, and unto the world, a prophecy of great misery, and of destruction procured by the devil against mankind, lest himself should shortly be miserable alone, verse 12.

r. Revelation 12:11 He is said in the Hebrew tongue, to love his life that esteemeth nothing more precious than his life: and on the other side, he is said not to love his life, who doubteth not to hazard it, wheresoever need requireth.

s. Revelation 12:13 The third part: an history of the woman delivered, consisting of two members, the second battle of Satan against the Christian Church of the Jewish nation, in four verses: and the battle intended against the seed thereof, that is against the Church of the Gentiles, which is called holy, by reason of the Gospel of Christ in the two last verses.

t. Revelation 12:14 That is, being strengthened with divine power: and taught by oracle, she fled swiftly from the assault of the devil, and from the common destruction of Jerusalem, and went into a solitary City beyond Jordan called Pella, as Eusebius telleth in the first Chapter of the third book of his Ecclesiastical history, which place God had commanded her by Revelation.

u. Revelation 12:14 Into that place where God had appointed her.

v. Revelation 12:14 That is, for three years and a half: so the same speech is taken, Dan. 7:15. This space of time is reckoned in manner from that last and most grievous rebellion of the Jews, unto the destruction of the city and Temple, for their destrution or falling away, began in the twelfth year of Nero, before the beginning whereof, many foresigns and predictions were showed from heaven, as Josephus writeth, lib. 7, chap. 12, and Hegesippus, lib. 5, chap. 44, amongst which this is very memorable, that in the feast of Pentecost, not only a great sound and noise was heard in the Temple, but also a great voice was heard of many out of the Sanctuary which cried out to all, Let us depart hence. Now three years and a half after this defection was begun of the Jews, and those wonders happened, the City was taken by force, the Temple overthrown, and the place forsaken of God: and this compass of time Saint John noted in this place.

w. Revelation 12:15 That is, he inflamed the Romans and the nations, that they persecuting the Jewish people with cruel arms might by the same occasion invade the Church of Christ, now departed from Jerusalem and out of Judea. For it is an usual thing in Scripture that the raging tumults of the nations, should be compared unto waters.

x. Revelation 12:16 That is, there was offered in their place other Jews, unto the Romans and nations raging against that people: and it came to pass thereby that the Church of God was saved whole from that violence, that most raging flood of persecution which the Dragon vomited out being altogether spent in the destruction of those other Jews.

y. Revelation 12:17 Being set on fire by this means, he began to be more mad, and because he perceived that his purpose against the Christian Church of the Jewish remnant was come to nought, he resolved to fall upon her seed, that is, the Church gathered also by God of the Gentiles, and the holy members of the same. And this is that other branch, as I said upon verse 13, in which the purpose of Satan is showed, verse 17, and his attempt, verse 18.

z. Revelation 12:18 That is, a most mighty tempest, that he rushed upon the whole world (whose prince he is) to raise the floods and provoke the nations, that they might with their furious bellows toss up and down, drive here and there, and finally destroy the Church of Christ with the holy members of the same. But the providence of God resisted his attempt, that he might favor the Church of the Gentiles, yet tender and as it were green. The rest of the story of the Dragon is excellently prosecuted by the Apostle S. John hereafter in the twentieth chapter. For here the Dragon endeavoring to do mischief, was by God cast into prison.

REVELATION 13

a. Revelation 13:1 The Apostle having declared the springing up of the Christian Church and the state of the Church from which ours taketh her beginning, doth now pass unto the story of the progress thereof, as I showed in the entrance of the former Chapter. And this history of the progress of the Church, and the battles thereof, is set down in this Chapter, but distinctly in two parts, one is of the civil Roman Empire, unto the tenth verse. Another of the body Ecclesiastical or prophetical, thence unto the end of the chapter. In the former part are showed these things: First the state of that Empire, in four verses: then the acts thereof in three verses: after the effect, which is exceeding great glory, verse 8. And last of all is commended the use: and the instruction of the godly against the evils that shall come from the same, verses 9, 10. The history of the state containeth a most ample description of the beast, first entire, verses 1, 2, and then restored after hurt, verses 3, 4.

b. Revelation 13:1 On the sand whereof stood the devil practicing new tempests against the Church, in the verse next beforegoing: what time the Empire of Rome was endangered by domestical dissensions, and was mightily tossed, having ever and anon new heads, and new Emperors. See in the seventeenth chapter and the eighth verse.

c. Revelation 13:1 Having the same instruments of power, providence, and most expert government which the Dragon is said to have had in Rev. 12:3.

d. Revelation 13:1 We read in chapter 12 and third verse, that the Dragon had seven crowns set upon seven heads: because the thief announceth himself to be proper Lord and Prince of the world: but this beast is said to have ten crowns set upon several, not heads, but horns: because the beast is beholden for all unto the Dragon, verse 2, and doth not otherwise reign them by law of subjection given by him, namely that he employ his horns against the Church of God. The speech is taken from the ancient custom and form of dealing in such case: by which they that were absolute kings did wear the diadem upon their heads: but their vassals and such as reigned by grace from them, wore the same upon their hoods: for so they might commodiously lay down their diadems when they came into the presence of their Sovereigns: as also their Elders are said, when they adored God which sat upon the throne, to have cast down their crowns before him, chap. 4, verse 10.

e. Revelation 13:1 - Contrary to that which God of old commanded should be written in the head piece of the high Priest, that is, Sanctitas Jehova, Holiness unto the Lord. The name of blasphemy imposed by the Dragon, is (as I think) that which S. Paul saith in chapter 2 of his 2 Epistle to the Thessalonians, verse 4. He sitteth as God, and boasteth himself to be God. For this name of blasphemy both the Roman Emperors did then challenge unto themselves, as Suetonius and Dion do report of Caligula and Domitian: and after them the Popes of Rome did with full mouth profess the same of themselves, when they challenged unto themselves sovereignty in holy things: of which kind of sayings the sixth book of the Decretals, the Clementines, and the Extravagants, are very full. For these men were not content with that which Anglicus wrote in his Poetria (the beginning whereof is, Papa stupor mundi. The Pope is the wonder of the world. Nec Deus es, nec homo, sed neuter es inter utrunque. Thou art not God, nay art thou man, but neuter mixed of both: as the gloss witnesseth upon the sixth book: but they were bold to take unto themselves the very name of God, and to accept it given of other: according as almost an hundred and twenty years since, there was made for Sixtus the fourth, when he should first enter into Rome

and his mouth as the mouth of a Lion: [g]and the dragon gave him his power and
his throne, and great authority. 3 [h]And I saw one of his heads as it were woun-
ded to death, but his deadly wound was healed, and all the world wondered and
followed the beast. 4 And they worshipped the dragon which gave power unto
the beast, and they worshipped the beast, saying, Who is like unto the beast! who
is able to war with him! 5 [i]And there was given unto him a mouth, that spake
great things and blasphemies, and power was given unto him, [j]to do two and for-
ty months. 6 And he opened his mouth unto blasphemy against God, to bla-
spheme his Name, [k]and his tabernacle, [l]and them that dwell in heaven. 7 And
it was given unto him to make war with the Saints, and to overcome them, and
power was given him over every kindred, and tongue, and nation. 8 Therefore
all that dwell upon the earth, shall worship him, [m]whose names are not written
in the book of life of that Lamb, which was slain from the beginning of the wor-
ld. 9 [n]If any man have an ear let him hear. 10 If any lead into captivity, he shall
go into captivity: [l]if any kill with a sword, he must be killed by a sword: here is
the patience and the faith of the Saints. 11 [o]And I beheld, another beast coming
out of the earth, [p]which had two horns like the Lamb, but he spake like the dra-
gon. 12 [q]And he did all that the first beast could do before him, and he caused
the earth and them which dwell therein, [r]to worship the first beast whose deadly
wound was healed. 13 [s]And he did great wonders, so that he made fire to come
down from heaven on the earth, in the sight of men. 14 And deceived them that
dwell on the earth by the signs which were permitted to him to do in the sight of
the beast, saying to them that dwell on the earth, that they should make the [t]ima-
ge of the [u]beast, which had the wound of a sword, and did live. 15 [v]And it was
permitted to him to give a [w]spirit unto the image of the beast, so that the image of
the beast should speak, and should cause that as many as would not worship the
image of the beast should be killed. 16 [x]And he made all, both small and great,
rich and poor, free and bond, to receive [y]a [z]mark in their right hand or in their fo-
reheads. 17 And that no man might [aa]buy or sell, save he that had the [ab]mark or
the name of the beast or the number of his name. 18 [ac]Here is wisdom. Let him
that hath wit, count the number of the beast: for it is the [ad]number of a man, and
his number is six hundred threescore and six.

---

in his dignity Papal, a Pageant of triumph, and cunningly fixed upon the gate of the city he should enter at, having written upon it this blasphemous verse: ***Oraclo vocis mundi moderaris habenas, Et merito in terris crederis esse deus. By oracle of thine own voice the world thou governest all, And worthily a God on earth, men think, and do thee call.*** These and six hundred the like who can impute unto that modesty whereby good men of old would have themselves called the servants of the servants of God, verily either this is a name of blasphemy, or there is none at all.

f. Revelation 13:2 Swift as the Leopard, easily clasping all things, as the bear doth with his foot, and tearing and devouring all things with the mouth as doth the Lion.

g. Revelation 13:2 That is, he lent the same unto the beast to use, when he perceived that himself could not escape, but must needs be taken by the hand of the Angel, and cast into the bottomless pit, Rev. 20, yet did not he abandon the same utterly from himself, but that he might use it as long as he could.

h. Revelation 13:3 This is the other place that pertaineth to the description of the beast of Rome: that besides that natural dignity and amplitude of the Roman Empire, which was shadowed in the two former verses, there was added this also as miraculous, that one head was wounded as it were unto death, and was healed again, as from heaven, in the sight of all men. This head was Nero the Emperor, in whom the race of the Caesars fell from imperial dignity, and the government of the Commonweal was translated unto others: in whose hands the Empire was so cured and recovered unto health, as he seemed unto all so much the more deeply rooted and grounded fast, than ever before. And hence followed those effects, which are next spoken of: First an admiration of certain power, as it were sacred and divine sustaining the Empire and governing it: Secondly the obedience and submission of the whole earth in this verse: Thirdly, the adoration of the Dragon, and most wicked worshipping of Devils, confirmed by the Roman Emperors: Lastly, the adoration of the beast himself, who grew into so great estimation, as that both the name and worship of a God was given unto him, the fourth verse. Now there were two causes which brought in the minds of men this religion: the show of excellency, which bringeth with it reverence: and the show of power invincible, which bringeth fear. Who is like (say they) unto the beast? Who shall be able to fight with him?

i. Revelation 13:5 The second member containing an history of the acts of the beast, as I said verse 1. The history of them is concluded in two points, the beginning and the manner of them. The beginning is the gift of the Dragon, who put and inspired into the beast both his impiety against God and his eminity and injustice against all men, especially against the godly and those that were of the household of faith, the fifth verse. The manner of the acts or actions done, is of two sorts both impious in mind, and blasphemous in speech against God, his Church and the godly, verse six, and also most cruel and injurious in deeds, even such as were done of most raging enemies and of most insolent and proud conquerors, the seventh verse.

j. Revelation 13:5 Namely his actions and manner of dealing. As concerning those two and forty months, I have spoken of them before in the twelfth Chapter and second verse.

k. Revelation 13:6 That is, the holy Church, the true house of the living God.

l. Revelation 13:6 That is, the godly in several who hid themselves from his cruelty. For this bloody beast surcharged those holy souls most falsely with innumerable accusations for the Name of Christ, as we read in Justin Martyr, Tertullian, Arnobius, Minutius, Eusebius, Augustine, and others: which example the latter times followed most diligently in destroying the flock of Christ and we in our own memory have found by experience to our incredible grief. Concerning heaven, see the eleventh Chapter and twelfth verse.

m. Revelation 13:8 That is, such as are not from everlasting elect in Christ Jesus. For this is that Lamb slain, of which the fifth Chapter, verse six. These words I do with Aretas distinguish in this manner: Whose names are not written even from the laying of the foundation of the world, in the book of life, of the Lamb slain. And this distinction is confirmed by a like place hereafter, Rev. 17:8.

n. Revelation 13:9 The conclusion of this speech of the first beast, consisting of two parts, An exhortation to attentive audience in this verse: and a foretelling, which partly containeth threatenings against the wicked, and partly comforts for those which in patience and faith shalt wait for that glorious coming of our Lord and Savior Christ, the tenth verse.

o. Revelation 13:11 The second member of the vision, concerning the ecclesiastical dominion, which in Rome succeeded that which was politic, and is in the power of the corporation of false Prophets, and of the forgers of false doctrine. Wherefore the same body or corporation is called of S. John by the name of false prophet, Rev. 6:13, 19 and 20. The form of this beast is first described in this verse, then his acts, in the verses following, and the whole speech is concluded in the last verse. This beast is by his breed a Son of the earth (as they say) obscurely born, and by little and little creeping up out of his abject estate.

p. Revelation 13:11 That is, in show he resembled the Lamb (for what is more mild or more humble than to be the servant of the servants of God) but in deed he played the part of the Dragon, and of the Wolf, Matt. 7:15. For even Satan changeth himself into an Angel of light, 2 Cor. 11:14, and what should his honest disciples and servants do?

q. Revelation 13:12 The history of the acts of this beast containeth in sum three things, hypocrisy, the witness of miracles and tyranny: of which the first is noted in this verse, the second in the 3 verses following: the third in the sixteenth and seventeenth verses. His hypocrisy is most full of leasing, whereby he abuseth both the former beast and the whole world: in that albeit he hath by his cunning, as it were by lime made of the former beast a most miserable … or anatomy, usurped all his authority unto himself and most impudently exerciseth the same in the sight and view of him: yet he carrieth himself so, as if he honored him with most high honor, and did in very truth cause him to be honored of all men.

r. Revelation 13:12 - For unto this beast of Rome, which of civil Empire is made an Ecclesiastical hierarchy, are given divine honors, and divine authority so far as he is believed to be above the Scriptures, which the gloss upon the Decretals declareth by this devilish verse, ***Articulos solvit, synodumque facit generalem, That is, He changeth the Articles of faith, and giveth authority to general Counsels.*** Which is spoken of the Papal power. So the beast is by birth, foundation, feat, and finally substance, one: only the Pope hath altered the form and manner thereof being himself the head both of that tyrannical Empire, and also of the false Prophets, for the Empire hath he taken unto himself, and thereunto hath added this cunning device. Now these words, whose deadly wound was cured are put here for distinction sake, as also sometimes afterwards: that even at that time the godly readers of this prophecy might by this sign be brought to see the things as present: as if it were said, that they might adore this very Empire that now is, whose head we have seen in our own memory to have been cut off, and to be cured again.

s. Revelation 13:13 The second point of the things done by the beast, is the credit of great wonders or miracles, appertaining to the strength of this impiety: of which signs some were given from above, as it is said, that fire was sent down from heaven by false sorcery, in this verse. Others were showed here below in the sight of the beast to establish idolatry, and deceive souls, which part S. John setteth forth beginning (as they say) at that which is last, in this manner: First the effect is declared in these words, He deceiveth the inhabitants of the earth, Secondly the common manner of working in two sorts, one of miracles. For the signs that were given him to do in the presence of the beasts: the other of the words added to the signs, and teaching the idolatry confirmed by those signs, Saying unto the inhabitants of the earth, that they should make an image unto the beasts which, etc. Thirdly, a special manner is declared: That is given unto him to put life into the image of the beast: and that such a kind of quickening, that the same both speaketh by answer unto those that ask counsel of it, and also pronounceth death against all those that do not obey nor worship it: all which things oftentimes by false miracles through the procurement and inspiration of the Devil, have been effected and wrought in images. The histories of the Papists are full of examples of such miracles, the most of them feigned, many also done by the devil in images: as of old in the serpent, Gen. 3:1. By which examples is confirmed, not the authority of the beast, but the truth of God, and of these prophecies.

t. Revelation 13:14 That is, images by enallage or change of the number: for the worship of them ever since the second Council of Nice, hath been ordained in the Church by public credit, and authority contrary unto the Law of God.

u. Revelation 13:14 In the Greek the word is in the Dative case, as much to say, as unto the worship, honor and obeying of the beast: for by this maintenance of images this Pseudoprophetical beast doth mightily profit the beast of Rome, of whom long ago he received them. Wherefore the same is hereafter very fitly called the image of the beast, for that images have their beginning from the beast, and have their form or manner from the will of the beast, and have their end and use fixed in the profit and commodity of the beast.

v. Revelation 13:15 And of this miracle of the images of the beast (that is, which the beast hath ordained to establish idolatry) which miraculously speak and give judgment, or rather marvelously, by the fraud of the false prophets, the Papists books are full fraughted.

w. Revelation 13:15 To give life as Jannes and Jambres imitated the wonders that Moses wrought.

x. Revelation 13:16 The third place, is a most wicked and most insolent tyrrany as was said before, usurped over the persons of men in this verse: and over their goods and actions, in the next verse. For he is said, both to bring upon all persons a tyrannous servitude, that as bondslaves they might serve the beast: and also to exercise over all their goods and actions, a peddler-like abuse of indulgences and dispensations (as they term them) amongst their friends, and against others to use most violent interdictions, and to shoot out cursings, even in natural and civil, private and public contracts, wherein all good faith ought to have place.

y. Revelation 13:16 That is, their Chrism, by which in the Sacrament (as they call it) of Confirmation, they make servile unto themselves, the persons and doings of men, signing them in their forehead and hands: and as for the sign left by Christ (of which Rev. 7:3) and the holy Sacrament of Baptism they make as void. For whom Christ hath joined unto himself by Baptism, this beast maketh challenge unto them by her greasy Chrism, which he doubteth not to prefer over Baptism, both in authority and efficacy.

z. Revelation 13:16 The mark of the name of the beast.

aa. Revelation 13:17 That is, have any traffic or intercourse with men, but they only those which have this anointing and consecration of Clearkely tonsure, as they call it. Read Gratian de Consecratione, distinct. s. c. omnes, cap. Spiritus, etc. of these matters.

ab. Revelation 13:17 Here the false Prophets do require three things, which are set down in the order of their greatness, a character, a name and the number of the name. The meaning is, that man that hath not first their anointing and clerical tonsure or shaving: secondly holy orders, by reserving whereof is communicated the same of the beast: or finally hath not attained that high degree of Pontifical knowledge, and of the Law (as they call it) Canonical, and hath not as it were made up in account and cast the number of the mysteries thereof: for in these things consisteth the number of that name of the beast. And this is excellently set forth in the next verse.

ac. Revelation 13:18 That is in this number of the beast consisteth that Popish wisdom, which unto them seemeth the greatest of all others. In these words S. John expoundeth that saying which went before of the number of the beast, what it hath above his mark or acconisance and his name. These things, saith S. John, the mark and the name of the beast, do easily happen unto any man: but to have the number of the beast, is wisdom: that is, only the wise and such as have understanding, can come by that number for they must be most illuminated doctors that attain thereunto, as the words following do declare.

ad. Revelation 13:18 How great and of what denomination this number of the beast is, by which the beast accounted his wisdom, S. John declareth in these words. Dost thou

14 *1 The Lamb standeth on mount Zion: 4 with his chaste worshippers. 6 One Angel preacheth the Gospel. 8 Another foretelleth the fall of Babylon: 9 the third warneth that the beast be avoided. 13 A voice from heaven pronounceth them happy who die in the Lord. 16 The Lord's sickle thrust into the harvest, 18 and into the vintage.*

1 Then I looked, and lo, a Lamb [a]stood on mount Zion, and with him an
[b]hundred forty and four thousand, having his Father's [c]Name written in their fo-
reheads. **2** And I heard a voice from heaven as the sound of many waters, and as
the sound of a great thunder: and I heard the voice of harpers, harping with their
harps. **3** And they sung as it were a new song before the throne, and before the
four beasts, and the Elders: and no man could learn that song, but the hundred,
forty and four thousand, which were bought from the earth. **4** These are they
which are not defiled with women: for they are virgins: these follow the Lamb whi-
thersoever he goeth: these are bought from men, being the firstfruits unto God,
and unto the Lamb. **5** And in their mouths was found no guile: for they are wi-
thout spot before the throne of God. **6** [d]Then I saw [e]another Angel fly in the
midst of heaven, having an everlasting Gospel to preach unto them that dwell on
the earth, and to every nation and kindred, and tongue, and people, **7** [f,1]Saying
with a loud voice, Fear God, and give glory to him: for the hour of his judgment
is come: and worship him that made [2]heaven and earth, and the sea and the foun-
tains of waters. **8** And there followed another Angel, saying, [3]Babylon that gre-
at city is fallen, it is fallen: for she made all nations to drink of the wine of the
[g]wrath of her fornication. **9** And the third Angel followed them, saying with a
loud voice, [h]If any man worship the beast and his image, and receive his mark in
his forehead, or on his hand, **10** The same shall drink of the wine of the wrath
of God, yea, of the pure wine, which is poured into the cup of his wrath, and he
shall be tormented in fire and brimstone before the holy Angels, and before the
Lamb. **11** And the smoke of their torment shall ascend evermore: and they shall
have no rest day nor night, which worship the beast and his name. **12** [i]Here is
the patience of Saints: here are they that keep the commandments of God, and the
faith of Jesus. **13** Then I heard a voice from heaven, saying unto me, Write, The
dead which die [j]in the Lord, are fully blessed. Even so saith the Spirit: for they rest
from their labors, and their [k]works follow them. **14** [l]And I looked, and behold,
[m]a white cloud, and upon the cloud one sitting like unto the Son of man, [n]having
on his head a golden crown, and in his hand a [o]sharp sickle. **15** [p]And another
Angel came out of the Temple, crying with a loud voice to him that sat on the
cloud, [4]Thrust in thy sickle and reap, for the time is come to reap: for the [5]harvest
of the earth is ripe. **16** And he that sat on the cloud, thrust in his sickle on the
earth, and the earth was reaped. **17** [q]Then another Angel came out of the Tem-
ple, which is in heaven, having also a sharp sickle. **18** And another Angel came
out from the altar, which had power over fire, and cried with a loud cry to him that
had the sharp sickle, and said, Thrust in thy sharp sickle, and gather the clusters of
the vineyard of the earth: for her grapes are ripe. **19** And the Angel thrust in his
sharp sickle on the earth, and cut down the vines of the vineyard of the earth, and
cast them into that great winepress of the wrath of God. **20** And the winepress
was trodden without the city, [r]and blood came out of the winepress, unto the horse
bridles, by the space of a thousand and six hundred furlongs.

---

demand how great it is? it is so great, that it occupieth the whole man: he is always learning, and never cometh to the knowledge thereof: he must be a man indeed that doth attain unto it. Askest thou of what denomination it is? verily it standeth of six throughout and perfectly ariseth of all the parts thereof in their several denominations (as they term them) it standeth of six by units, tens, hundreds, etc. so as there is no one part in the learning and order Pontifical, which is not either referred unto the head, and as it were the top thereof, or contained in the same: so fitly do all things in this hierarchy agree one with another, and with their head. Therefore that cruel beast Boniface the eighth doth commend by the number of six those Decretals which he perfected, in the proem of the sixth book. Which book (saith he) being to be added unto five other books of the same volume of Decretals, we thought good to name Sextum the sixth: that the same volume by addition thereof containing a senary, or the number of six books (which is a number perfect) may yield a perfect form of managing all things, and perfect discipline of behavior. Here therefore is the number of the beast, who poureth from himself all his parts and bringeth them all back again unto himself by his discipline in most wise and cunning manner. If any man desire more of this, let him read the gloss upon that place. I am not ignorant that other interpretations are brought upon this place: but I thought it my duty, with the good favor of all and without the offense of any, to propound mine opinion in this point. And for this cause especially, for that it seemed unto me neither profitable, nor like to be true, that the number of the beast, or of the name of the beast should be taken as the common sort of interpreters do take it. For this number of the beast teacheth, giveth out, imprinteth, as a public mark of such as be his, and esteemeth that mark above all others as the mark of those whom he loveth best. Now those other expositions seem rather to be far removed from this property and condition of that number: whether you respect the name Latinus or Titan, or another. For these the beast doth not teach, nor give forth nor imprint, but most diligently forbiddeth to be taught, and audaciously denieth: he approveth not these, but reproveth them: and hateth them that think so of this number, with an hatred, greater than that of Vatinius.

REVELATION 13

1. Gen. 9:6 / Matt. 26:52

REVELATION 14

a. Revelation 14:1 The history of the Church of Christ being finished for more than a thousand and three hundred years, at which time Boniface the eighth lived as before hath been said, there remaineth the rest of the history of the conflicting or militant Church, from thence unto the time of the last victory in three chapters. For first of all, as the foundation of the whole history, is described the standing of the lamb with his army and retinue in five verses, after his worthy acts which he hath done, and yet doth in most mighty manner, whilst he overthroweth Antichrist with the spirit of his mouth, in the rest of this chapter, and in the two following. Unto the description of the Lamb, are propounded three things: his situation, place and attendance: for the rest are expounded in the former visions, especially upon the fifth chapter.

b. Revelation 14:1 As ready girt to do his office (as Acts 6:56) in the midst of the Church which aforetime mount Zion did prefigure.

c. Revelation 14:1 As before 7:2. This retinue of the Lamb is described first by divine mark (as before 7:2) in this verse. Then by divine occupation, in that all and every one in his retinue most vehemently and sweetly (verse 2) do glorify the Lamb with a special song before God and his elect Angels: which song flesh and blood cannot hear, nor understand, verse 3. Lastly by their deeds done before, and their sanctification in that they were virgins, pure from spiritual and bodily fornication that is, from impiety and unrighteousness, that they followed the Lamb as a guide unto all godness, and cleaved unto him that they are holy unto him as of grace redeemed by him: that in truth and in simplicity of Christ, they have exercised all these things, sanctimony of life, the direction of the Lamb, a thankful remembrance of the redemption by him: finally (to conclude in a word) that they are blameless before the Lord, verses 4, 5.

d. Revelation 14:6 The other part (as I said in the first verse) is of the acts of the Lamb, the manner whereof is delivered in two sorts, of his speech, and of his facts. His speeches are set forth unto verse 13 of this chapter, and his facts unto chapter 16. In the speech of the Lamb, which is the word of the Gospel, are taught in this place, these things: The service of the godly consisting inwardly of reverence towards God, and outwardly of the glorifying of him: the visible sign of which is adoration, verse 7. The overthrowing of wicked Babylon, verse 8, and the fall of every one of the ungodly which worship the beast, verses 9, 10, 11. Finally, the state of the holy servants of God both present, verse 11, and to come, most blessed, according to the promise of God, verse 15.

e. Revelation 14:6 This Angel is a type or figure of the good and faithful servants of God, whom God especially from that time of Boniface the eighth, hath raised up to the publishing of the Gospel of Christ, both by preaching and by writing. So God first, near unto the time of the same Boniface, used Peter Cassiodorus an Italian: after, Arnold de villa nova, a Frenchman, then Occam, Dante, Petrarch, after that Johannes de rupe casa, a Franciscan: after again, John Wycliff an Englishman, and so continually one or another unto the restoring of the truth and enlarging of his Church.

f. Revelation 14:7 That is, Babylon is destroyed by the sentence and judgment of God: the execution whereof S. John described, chap. 18. And this voice of the ministers of Christ hath continued since the time that Babylon (which is Rome) hath by deliberate counsel and manifest malice oppugned the light of the Gospel offered from God.

g. Revelation 14:8 Of her fornication, whereby God was provoked to wrath.

h. Revelation 14:9 That is, shall not worship God alone, but shall transfer his divine honor unto this beast, whether he doeth it with his heart or counterfeiting in show. For he (saith Christ) that denieth me before men, him will I deny before my Father, and his Angels, Matt. 10:32. And this is that voice of the holy ministry; which at this time is very much used of the holy and faithful servants of God. For having now sufficiently found out the public obstinacy of Babylon they labor not any longer to thunder out as against the same but to save some particular members by terror (as S. Jude speaketh) and to pluck them out of the public flame, or else by a vehement commiseration of their state to lead them away, they set before them eternal death, into which they rush unawares, unless in good time they return unto God, but the godly which are of their own flock, they exhort unto patience, obedience, and faith in the Lord Jesus, and charge them to give light by their good example, of good life unto others.

i. Revelation 14:12 The patience, sanctification and justification by faith: the consequence whereof are rest, felicity, and glory eternal, in the heavenly fellowship of God and his Angels.

j. Revelation 14:13 That is for the Lord.

k. Revelation 14:13 By works, is meant the reward which followeth good works.

l. Revelation 14:14 The second part of this Chapter, as I said, verse 1. Of the acts and doings of Christ in overthrowing of Antichrist and his Church by the Spirit of his divine mouth: seeing that having been called back by word both publicly and privately unto his duty, and admonished of his most certain ruin: he yet ceaseth not to maintain and protect his own adherents, that they may do him service: and to afflict the godly with most barbarous persecutions. Of those things which Christ doeth, there are two kinds: one common or general in the rest of this chapter, another particular against that savage and rebellious beast and his worshippers in chapters 15 and 16. That common kind, is the calamity of wars spread abroad through the whole earth, and filling all things with blood, and that without respect of any person. This is figured or shadowed out in two types, of the harvest and vintage. Since the time that the light of the Gospel began to shine out, and since prophecy or preaching by the grace of God was raised up again, how horrible wars have been kindled in the world? how much human flesh hath been thrown to the earth by this divine reaping? how much blood (alas for woe) hath overflown for these hundred years almost? all history do cry out, and this our age (if ever before) is now in horror, by reason of the rage of the sickle which Antichrist calleth for. In this place is the first type, that is of the harvest.

m. Revelation 14:14 Declaring his fierceness by his color, like unto that which is in the white or milk circle of heaven.

n. Revelation 14:14 As one that shall reign from God, and occupy place of Christ in this miserable execution.

o. Revelation 14:14 That is, a most fit and commodious instrument of Execution, destroyed all by hewing and thrusting through, for who may stand against God?

p. Revelation 14:15 Christ giveth a commandment in this verse. And the Angel executeth in the next verse.

q. Revelation 14:17 The other type (as I said, verse14) is the vintage: the manner whereof is one with that which went before, if thou except this, that the grape gathering is more exact in seeking out everything, than is the harvest labor. This is therefore a more grievous judgment, both because it succeedeth the other, and because it is understood to be executed with great diligence.

r. Revelation 14:20 That is, it overflowed very deep, and very far and wide: the speech is by hyperbole or excessive, to signify the greatness of the slaughter. And these be those pleasant fruits forsooth, of the contempt of Christ, and desiring of Antichrist rather than him, which the miserable, mad, and blind world doth at this time reap.

REVELATION 14

1. Ps. 14:5,6
2. Acts 14:15
3. Isa. 21:9 / Jer. 51:8 / Rev. 18:2
4. Joel 3:13
5. Matt. 13:39

15

1 The seven Angels having the seven last plagues. 3 They that conquered the beast praise God. 6 To the seven Angels, 7 seven vials full of God's wrath are delivered.

1 And [a]I saw another sign in heaven, great and marvelous, seven [b]Angels ha-
ving the seven last plagues: for by them is fulfilled the wrath of God. 2 [c]And I
saw [d]as it were a glassy sea, mingled with fire, and [e]them that had gotten victory
of the beast, and of his image, and of his mark, and of the number of his name,
[f]stand at the glassy sea, having the harps of God, 3 And they sung [g]the song of
Moses the [h]servant of God, and the song of the Lamb, saying, [i]Great and mar-
velous are thy works, Lord God Almighty: just and true are thy [1,j]ways, King of
Saints. 4 [2]Who shall not fear thee, O Lord, and glorify thy name! for thou only
art holy, and all nations shall come and worship before thee: for thy judgments are
made manifest. 5 [k]And after that, I looked, and behold, the Temple of the taber-
nacle of Testimony was open in heaven. 6 And the seven Angels came out of the
Temple, which had the [l]seven plagues, clothed in [m]pure and bright linen, and ha-
ving their breasts [n]girded with golden girdles. 7 And therefore [o]four beasts gave
unto the seven Angels seven golden vials full of the wrath of God which lived for
evermore. 8 And the temple was full of the smoke of the glory of God and of his
power, and [p]no man was able to enter into the Temple, till the seven plagues of the
seven Angels were fulfilled.

16

2 And 17 the Angels pour out the seven vials of God's wrath given unto them, and so divers plagues arise in the world, 18 to terrify the wicked, 19 and the inhabitants of the great city.

1 And [a]I heard a great voice out of the Temple, saying to the seven Angels,
Go your ways, and poured out the seven vials of the wrath of God upon the
earth. 2 [b]And the first went and poured out his vial upon the earth: and the-
re fell a noisome and a grievous sore upon the men which had the [c]mark of the
beast, and upon them which worshipped his image. 3 [d]And the second Angel
poured out his vial upon the sea, and it [e]became as the blood of a dead man: and
every living thing died in the sea. 4 [f]And the third Angel poured out his vial
upon the rivers and fountains of waters, and they became blood. 5 And I heard
the Angel of the waters say, Lord, thou art just, which art, and which wast: and
Holy, because thou hast judged these things. 6 For they shed the blood of the
Saints, and Prophets, and therefore hast thou given them blood to drink: for they
are worthy. 7 [g]And I heard another out of the Sanctuary say, Even so, Lord God
almighty, true and righteous are thy judgments. 8 [h]And the fourth Angel pou-
red out his vial on the sun, and it was given to him to torment men with heat of
fire, 9 And men boiled in great heat, and blasphemed the Name of God, which
hath power over these plagues, and they repented not to give him glory. 10 [i]And
the fifth Angel poured out his vial upon the throne of the beast, and the kingdom
waxed dark, and they gnawed their tongues for sorrow. 11 And blasphemed the
God of heaven for their pains, and for their sores, and repented not of their wor-
ks. 12 [j]And the sixth Angel poured out his vial upon the great river [k]Euphrates,
and the [l]water thereof dried up, [m]that the way of the Kings of the East should be
prepared. 13 And I saw [n]three unclean spirits [o]like frogs come out of the mouth
of that [p]dragon, and out of the mouth of that [q]beast, and out of the mouth of
that [r]false prophet. 14 For they are the spirits of devils, working miracles, to go
unto the kings of the earth, and of the whole world, to gather them to the batt-
le of that great day of God Almighty. 15 [s,1]Behold I come as a thief. Blessed is
he that watcheth, and keepeth his garments, lest he walk naked, and men see his
filthiness. 16 [t]And they gathered them together into a place called in Hebrew,
[u]Armageddon. 17 [v]And the seventh Angel poured out his vial into the [w]air: and
there came a loud voice out of the Temple of heaven from [x]the throne, saying, [y]It

---

REVELATION 15

- **a.** Revelation 15:1 This is that other place of the acts of Christ, as I noted before, 14:14. Now therefore is showed a singular work of the judgment of God belonging to the overthrow of Antichrist and his forces of which divine work the preparation is described in this Chapter and the execution in the next. The preparation is first set down generally and in type in this verse: and is after particularly set forth in the rest of the Chapter.
- **b.** Revelation 15:1 Of which Rev. 8:9, in pouring forth in the plagues of the world: for even these plagues do for the most part agree with those.
- **c.** Revelation 15:2 There are two parts of the narration: one the confession of the Saints glorifying God, when they saw that preparation of the judgments of God, unto verse 4: another the vocation, instruction, and confirmation of those instruments which God hath ordained for the execution of his judgments, in 4 other verses.
- **d.** Revelation 15:2 This part of the vision alludeth unto the sea or large vessel of brass in which the Priests washed themselves in the entrance of the Temple: for in the entrance of the heavenly Temple (as it is called, verse 5) is said to have been a sea of glass, most lightsome and clear, unto the commodity of choice mixed with fire, that is, as containing the treasury of the judgments of God, which he bringeth forth and dispenseth according to his own pleasure: for out of the former, the Priests were cleansed of old and out of this the ungodly are destroyed now, Rev. 4:6.
- **e.** Revelation 15:2 That is, the Godly martyrs of Christ, who shall not give place even in miracles unto that beast: of these, see before, Rev. 13:17 and 14:9, 10.
- **f.** Revelation 15:2 Glorified God, from the particular observation of the weapons and instruments of God's wrath, floating in the sea of glass.
- **g.** Revelation 15:3 That song of triumph which is Exod. 15:2.
- **h.** Revelation 15:3 So is Moses called for honor's sake, as it is set forth, Deut. 34:10.
- **i.** Revelation 15:3 This song hath two parts, one a confession, but particular in this verse, and general, in the beginning of the next verse: another, a narration of causes belonging to the confession, whereof one kind is eternal in itself, and most present unto the godly in that God is both holy, and alone God, another kind is future and to come, in that the elect taken out of the Gentiles (that is, out of the wicked ones and unbelieving: as Rev. 11:2) were to be brought unto the same state of happiness by the magnificence of the judgment of God, in the next verse.
- **j.** Revelation 15:3 Thy doings.
- **k.** Revelation 15:5 The second part of the narration (as was [noted,] verse 2) wherein first the authority of the whole argument and matter thereof is figured by a forerunning type of a temple opened in heaven, as Rev. 11:19, namely that all those things are divine and of God, that proceed from thence, in this verse. Secondly, the administers or executors, come forth out of the Temple, verse 6. Thirdly, they are furnished with instruments of the judgments of God, and weapons fit for the manner of the same judgments, verse 7. Finally they are confirmed by testimony of the visible glory of God, in the last verse. A like testimony whereunto was exhibited of old in the Law, Exod. 40:34.
- **l.** Revelation 15:6 That is, commandments to inflict those seven plagues. Here is the figure called Metonymy.
- **m.** Revelation 15:6 Which was in old time a sign of the kingly or princely dignity.
- **n.** Revelation 15:6 That is, girding was a sign of diligence, and the girdle of gold was a sign of sincerity and trustiness in taking in charge the commandments of God.
- **o.** Revelation 15:7 Of these before, Rev. 4:7.
- **p.** Revelation 15:8 None of those seven Angels might resume, till he had performed fully the charge committed unto him according to the decree of God.

REVELATION 15

1. Ps. 145:17 **2.** Jer. 10:7

REVELATION 16

- **a.** Revelation 16:1 In the former Chapter was set down the preparation unto the work of God: here is delivered the execution thereof. And in this discourse of the execution, is a general commandment, in this verse, then a particular recital in order of the execution done by every of the seven Angels, in the rest of the chapter. This special execution against Antichrist and his crew, doth in manner agree unto that which was generally done upon the whole world, Rev. 8 and 9, and belongeth (if my conjecture fail me not) unto the same time. Yet herein they do differ one from another, that this was particularly effected upon the Princes and ringleaders of the wickedness of the world, the other generally against the whole world being wicked. And therefore these judgments are figured more grievous than those.
- **b.** Revelation 16:2 The history of the first Angel, whose plague upon the earth, is described almost in the same words with that sixth plague of the Egyptians, Exod. 9:9. But it doth signify a spiritual ulcer, and that torture or butchery of conscience seared with an hot iron, which accuseth the ungodly within and both by truth of the word (the light whereof God hath now so long showed forth) and by bitterness stirreth up and forceth out the sword of God's wrath.
- **c.** Revelation 16:2 See Rev. 13:16
- **d.** Revelation 16:3 The history of the second Angel who troubleth and molesteth the seas, that he may stir up the conscience of men sleeping in their wickedness. See Rev. 8:8.
- **e.** Revelation 16:3 It was turned into rotten and filthy blood, such as is in dead bodies.
- **f.** Revelation 16:4 The history of the third Angel striking the rivers, in this verse who proclaiming the justice of God, commendeth the same by a most grave comparison of the sins of men with the punishment of God: which is common to this place and that which went before. Wherefore also this praising is attributed to the Angel of the waters, a name common to the second and third Angels according as both of them are said to be sent against the waters, albeit, the one of the sea the other of the rivers, in two verses.
- **g.** Revelation 16:7 A confirmation of the praise before going, out of the sanctuary of God, whether immediately by Christ, or by some of his Angels, for Christ also is called another Angel, Rev. 3:8; 7:2; 12:1.
- **h.** Revelation 16:8 The history of the fourth Angel, who throweth the plague upon the heaven and upon the Sun, of which Luke 21:26 the effects whereof are noted two. The one peculiar, that it shall scorch men with heat, in this verse. The other proceeding accidentally from the former, that their fury shall so much the more be enraged against God in the next verse, when yet (O wonderful mercy and patience of God) all other creatures are first stricken often and grievously by the hand of God before mankind by whom he is provoked: as the things beforegoing [do] declare.
- **i.** Revelation 16:10 The story of the first Angel, who striketh the kingdom of the beast with two plagues abroad with darkness, within which biles and dolors most grievous, throughout his whole kingdom, that thereby he might wound the conscience of the wicked, and punish that most perverse obstinacy of the idolaters, whereof arose perturbation, and thence a furious indignation and desperate madness, raging against God and hurtful unto itself.
- **j.** Revelation 16:12 The story of the sixth Angel, divided into his act, and the event thereof. The act is, that the Angel did cast out of his mouth the plague of a most glowing heat, wherewith even the greatest floods, and which most were wont to swell and overflow (as Euphrates) were dried up by the counsel of God in this verse. The event is, that the mere madness wherewith the wicked are enraged, that they may scorn the judgments of God, and abuse them furiously to serve their own turn, and to the executing of their own wicked outrage.
- **k.** Revelation 16:12 The bound of the spiritual Babylon, and to the fortresses of the same, Rev. 9:14.
- **l.** Revelation 16:12 So the Church of the ungodly, and kingdom of the beast is said to be left naked, all the defenses whereof, in which they put their trust being taken away from it.
- **m.** Revelation 16:12 That is, that even they which dwell further off, may with more commodity make haste unto that sacrifice which the Lord hath appointed.
- **n.** Revelation 16:13 That is, every of them bent their whole force, and conspired that by wonders, word and work, they might bring into the same destruction all Kings, Princes and Potentates of the world, cursedly bewitched of them by their spirits, and teachers of the vanity and impurity of the beast that committed fornication with the kings of the earth. And this is a right description of our times.
- **o.** Revelation 16:13 Croaking with all importunity, and continually day and night provoking and calling forth to arms, as the trumpets, and furies of wars: as is declared in the next verse.
- **p.** Revelation 16:13 That is, the devil, as Rev. 11:3
- **q.** Revelation 16:13 Whereof Rev. 13:1.
- **r.** Revelation 16:13 That is, of that other beast, of which Rev. 13:11, for so he is called also Rev. 19:20 and 20:10.
- **s.** Revelation 16:15 A parenthesis for admonition in which God warneth his holy servants who rest in the expectation of Christ, always to address their minds unto his coming, and to look unto themselves, that they be not shamefully made naked and circumvented of these unclean spirits, and so they be miserable unprepared at the coming of their Lord.
- **t.** Revelation 16:16 Namely the Angel, who holily according to the commandment of God was to do sacrifice: notwithstanding that those impure spirits do the same wickedly as servants not unto God, but unto that beast that hath seven heads.
- **u.** Revelation 16:16 That is, (to say nothing of other expositions) the mountain itself, or mountain places of Megiddo. Now it is certain by the holy Scripture, that Megiddo is a city and territory in the tribe of Manasseh, bordering upon Issachar and Asher, and was made famous by that lamentable overthrow of king Josiah, whereof 2 Kings 23:30; 2 Chron. 37:22; Zech. 12:11. In this mountain country God

is done. **18** [z]And there were voices, and thunderings, and lightnings, and there
was a great earthquake, such as was not since men were upon the earth, even so mi-
ghty an earthquake. **19** [aa]And the great city was divided into three parts: and the
cities of the nations [ab]fell: and that great [ac]Babylon came in remembrance before
God, [2]to give unto her the cup of the wine of the fierceness of his wrath. **20** And
every isle fled away, and the mountains [ad]were not [ae]found. **21** [af]And there fell
a great hail, like [ag]talents out of heaven upon the men, and men blasphemed God,
because of the plague of the hail: for the plague thereof was exceeding great.

17

1 That great whore is described, 2 with whom the Kings of the earth committed fornication. 6 She is drunken with the blood of Saints. 7 The mystery of the woman, and the beast that carried her, expounded. 11 Their destruction. 14 The Lamb's victory.

1 Then [a]there came one of the seven Angels, which had the seven vials, and
talked with me, saying unto me, Come: I will show [b]thee the [c]damnation of the
great whore that sitteth upon many waters, **2** With whom have committed for-
nication the kings of the earth, and the inhabitants of the earth are drunken with
the wine of her fornication. **3** [d]So he carried me away into the wilderness in the
Spirit, and I saw a woman sit upon a [e]scarlet colored beast, full of names of bla-
sphemy, which had seven heads, and ten horns. **4** And [f]the woman was arrayed
[g]in purple and scarlet, and gilded with gold, and precious stones, and pearls, [h]and
had a cup of gold in her hand full of abomination, and filthiness of her fornica-
tion. **5** [i]And in her forehead was a name written, A mystery, [j]that great Babylon
that mother of whoredoms, and abominations of the earth. **6** [k]And I saw the
woman drunken with the blood of Saints, and with the blood of the Martyrs of JE-
SUS: and when I saw her, [l]I wondered with great marvel. **7** [m]Then the Angel said
unto me, Wherefore marvelest thou? I will show thee the mystery of that woman,
and of that beast that beareth her, which hath seven heads and ten horns. **8** [n]The
beast that thou hast seen, [o]was and is not, and [p]shall ascend out of the bottomless
pit, and shall go into perdition, and they that dwell on the earth, shall wonder
whose names are not written in the book of life from the foundation of the world
[q]when they behold the beast that was, and is not, and yet is. **9** [r]Here is the mind
that hath wisdom, The [s]seven heads [t]are seven mountains, whereon the woman sit-
teth: [u]they are also seven Kings. **10** [v]Five are fallen, [w]and one is, [x]and another is
not yet come: and when he cometh, he must continue a short space. **11** [y]And the

---

saith by figure and type, that the kings of the peoples which serve the beast shall meet together: because the Gentiles did always cast that lamentable overthrow in the teeth of the Church of the Jews unto their great reproach: and therefore were persuaded that that place should be most fortunate unto them (as they speak) and unfortunate unto the godly: but God here pronounceth, that that reproach of the Church, and confidence of the ungodly shall by himself be taken away, in the selfsame places where the nations persuaded themselves, they should mightily exult and triumph against God and his Church.

v. Revelation 16:17 The story of the seventh Angel unto the end of the chapter, in which first is showed by figure and speech, the argument of this plague, in this verse: and then is declared the execution thereof in the verses following.

w. Revelation 16:17 From whence he might move the heaven above and the earth beneath.

x. Revelation 16:17 That is, from him that sitteth on the throne, by the figure called Metonymy.

y. Revelation 16:17 That is, Babylon is undone, as is showed verse 16 and in the Chapters following. For the first onset (as I might say) of this denunciation, is described in this Chapter: and the last containing a perfect victory is described in those that follow.

z. Revelation 16:18 Now is declared the execution (as is said in verse 27) and the things that shall last come to pass in heaven and in earth, before the overthrow of the beast of Babylon: both generally, verse 18, and particularly in the cursed city, and such as have any familiarity therewith, in the 3 last verses.

aa. Revelation 16:19 That seat or standing place of Antichrist.

ab. Revelation 16:19 Of all such as cleave unto Antichrist, and fight against Christ.

ac. Revelation 16:19 That harlot, of whom in the Chapter next following. Now this phrase to come into remembrance is after the common use of the Hebrew speech, but borrowed from men, attributed unto God.

ad. Revelation 16:20 That is, were seen no more, or were no more extant. A borrowed Hebraism.

ae. Revelation 16:20 Appeared not, which the Hebrews utter after this sort, were not, Gen. 5:24.

af. Revelation 16:21 The manner of the particular execution, most evidently testifying the wrath of God by the original and greatness thereof: the event whereof is the same with that which is, Rev. 9:12, and that which hath been mentioned in this Chapter, from the execution of the fourth Angel hitherto, that is to say, an incorrigible pertinency of the world in their rebellion, and an heart that cannot repent, verses 9 and 11.

ag. Revelation 16:21 As it were about the weight of a talent was threescore pound, that is, six hundred groats, whereby is signified a marvelous and strange kind of weight.

REVELATION 16

1. Matt. 24:43 / Mark 14:16 / Mark 15:13 / Luke 12:39 **2.** Jer. 25:15

REVELATION 17

a. Revelation 17:1 The state of the Church militant being declared, now followeth the state of the Church overcoming and getting victory, as I showed before in the beginning of chapter 10. The state is set forth in 4 chapters. As in the place beforegoing I noted, that in that history the order of time was not always exactly observed, so the same is to be understood in this history, that it is distinguished according to the persons of which it treateth, and that in the several stories of the persons is severely observed in the time thereof. For first is delivered the story of Babylon destroyed, in this and the next chap. (for this Babylon out of all doubt shall perish before the 2 beasts and the Dragon). Secondly is delivered the destruction of both the two beasts, chap. 19. And lastly of the Dragon, chap. 20, in the story of the spiritual Babylon are distinctly set forth the state thereof in this chap. and the overthrow done from God, chap. 18. In this verse and that which followeth is a transition or passage unto the first argument, consisting of a particular calling of the Prophet (as often heretofore) and a general proposition.

b. Revelation 17:1 That is, the damnable harlot, by a figure of speech called hypallage. For S. John as yet had not seen her. Although another interpretation may be borne, yet I like this better.

c. Revelation 17:1 The sentence that is pronounced against this harlot.

d. Revelation 17:3 Henceforth is propounded the type of Babylon, and the state thereof in 4 verses. After a declaration of the type, in the rest of this chap., in the type are described two things, the beast (of whom chap. 13), in verse 3, and the woman that sitteth upon the beast, verses 4, 5, 6. The beast in process of time hath gotten somewhat more than was expressed in the former vision. First in that it is not read before that he was appareled in scarlet, a robe imperial and of triumph. Secondly, in that this is full of names of blasphemy: the other carried the name of blasphemy only in his head. So God did teach that this beast is much increased in impiety and injustice and doth in this last age, triumph in both these more insolently and proudly than ever before.

e. Revelation 17:3 A scarlet color, that is, with a red and purple garment: and surely it was not without cause that the Romish clergy were so much delighted with this color.

f. Revelation 17:4 That harlot, the spiritual Babylon, which is Rome. She is described by her attire, profession and deeds.

g. Revelation 17:4 In attire most glorious, triumphant, most rich, and most gorgeous.

h. Revelation 17:4 In profession, the nourisher of all, in this verse, and teaching her mysteries unto all, verse 5, setting forth all things most magnificently: but indeed most pernicious besotting miserable men with her cup, and bringing upon them a deadly giddiness.

i. Revelation 17:5 Deceiving with the title of religion, and public inscription of mystery: which the beast in times past did not bear.

j. Revelation 17:5 An exposition: in which S. John declareth what manner of woman this is.

k. Revelation 17:6 In manner of deeds: She is red with blood, and sheddeth it most licentiously, and therefore is colored with the blood of the Saints, as on the contrary part. Christ is set forth imbrued with the blood of his enemies; Isa. 3:1.

l. Revelation 17:6 A passage unto the second part of this chapter, by occasion given of S. John, as the words of the Angel do show, in the next verse.

m. Revelation 17:7 The second part or place, as I said, verse 1. The narration of the vision, promised in this verse, and delivered in the verse following. Now there is delivered first a narration of the beast and his story, unto verse 14. After, of the harlot, unto the end of the chap.

n. Revelation 17:8 The story of the beast hath a triple description of him. The first is a distinction of this beast from all that ever hath been at any time: which distinction is contained in this verse: The second is a delineation or painting out of the beast by things present, by which he might even at that time be known of the godly, and this delineation is according to his heads, verses 2, 10, 11. The third is an historical foretelling of things to come, and to be done by him: and these are ascribed unto his horns, verses 12, 13, 14. This beast is that Empire of Rome, of which I spake, chap. 13:11, according to the mutations and changes whereof which then had already happened, the holy Ghost hath distinguished and set out the same. The Apostle distinguisheth this beast from all others in these words. The beast which thou sawest, was and is not. For so I expound the words of the Apostle for evidence's sake as I will further declare in the notes following.

o. Revelation 17:8 The meaning is, that beast which thou sawest before (Rev. 13:1) and which yet thou hast now seen, was, (I say was) even from Julius Caesar in respect of beginning, rising up, station, glory, dominion, manner and stock, from the house of Julius: and yet is not now the same, if thou look unto the house and stock for the dominion of this family was translated unto another, after the death of Nero from the other unto a third, from a third unto a fourth, and so forth was varied and altered by innumerable changes. Finally, the Empire is one, as it were one beast: but exceedingly varied by kindreds, families, and persons. It was therefore (saith S. John) in the kindred or house of Julius: and now it is not in that kindred, but translated unto another.

p. Revelation 17:8 As if he should say, Also the same that is, shall shortly not be: but shall ascend out of the depth, or out of the sea (as was said, Rev. 13:1) that is, shall be a new stock from amongst the nations without difference, and shall in the same state go unto destruction or ruin, and perish: and so shall successively new Princes or Emperors come and go, arise and fall, the body of the beast remaining still, but tossed with so many and often alterations, as no man can but marvel that this beast was able to stand and hold out, in so many mutations. Verily no Empire that ever was tossed with so many changes, and as it were with so many tempests of the sea, ever continued so long.

q. Revelation 17:8 That is as many as have not learned the providence of God, according to the faith of the Saints, shall marvel at these grievous and often changes when they shall consider, the selfsame beast, which is the Roman Empire, to have been, not to be, and to be and still molested with perpetual mutation, and yet in the same to stand and continue. This in mine opinion is the most simple exposition of this place, and confirmed by the event of the things themselves. Although by the last change also, by which the Empire, that before was civil became Ecclesiastical, is not obscurely signified by these words: of which two, the first exercised cruelty upon the bodies of the saints: the other also upon their souls: the first by human order and policy, the other under the color of the law of God, and of Religion, raged and imbrued itself with the blood of the godly.

r. Revelation 17:9 An exhortation preparing unto audience, by the same argument, with that of Christ: He that hath ears to hear, let him hear. Wherefore, for mine own part, I had rather read in this place, Let there be here a mind, etc. So the Angel passeth fully unto the second place of this description.

s. Revelation 17:9 Very children know what that seven hilled city is, which is so much spoken of, and whereof Virgil thus reporteth, And compasseth seven towers in one wall: that city it is, which when John wrote these things had rule over the kings of the earth: It was and is not, and yet it remaineth this day, but it is declining to destruction.

t. Revelation 17:9 This is the painting out of the beast by things present (as I said before) whereby S. John endeavored to describe the same, that he might both be known of the godly in that age, and be further observed and marked of posterity afterwards. This delineation hath one type, that is, his heads, but a double description or application of the type: one permanent from the nature of itself, the other changeable, by the working of men. The description permanent, is by the seven hills, in this verse, the other that fleeteth, is from the seven kings, verses 10, 11. And here it is worthy to be observed, that one type hath sometimes two or more applications, as seemeth good unto the holy Ghost to express either one thing by divers types, or divers things by one type. So I noted before, of the seven spirits, Rev. 1:4. Now this woman that sitteth upon seven hills, is the city of Rome, called in times past of the Greeks, … i. of seven tops or crests, and of Varro, septiceps, i. of her seven heads (as here) of seven heads, and of others, septicollis, i. standing upon seven hills.

u. Revelation 17:9 The beginning of these Kings or Emperors is almost the same with the beginning of the Church of Christ, which I showed before, Rev. 11:1. Namely from the year 35, after the passion of Christ, what time the Temple and Church of the Jews was overthrown. In which year it came to pass by the providence of God that that saying The beast was and is not, was fulfilled before that the destruction of the Jews immediately following came to pass. That was the year from the building of the city of Rome, 109, from which year S. John both numbered the Emperors which hitherto hath been, when he wrote these things, and foretelleth two others next to come: and that with this

beast that was, and is not, is even [z]the eighth, and is [aa]one of the seven, and [ab]all
go into destruction. **12** [ac]And the ten horns which thou sawest, are [ad]ten kings,
which yet have not received a kingdom, but shall receive power, as Kings [ae]at one
hour with the beast. **13** [af]These have one mind, and shall give their power and
authority unto the beast. **14** These shall fight with the [ag]Lamb, and the Lamb
shall overcome them: [1]for he is Lord of Lords, and King of Kings: and they that
are on his side, called, and chosen, and faithful. **15** [ah]And he said unto me, The
waters which thou sawest, where the whore sitteth, [ai]are people, and multitudes,
and nations, and tongues. **16** And the ten [aj]horns which thou sawest upon the
beast, are they that shall hate the whore, and shall make her desolate, and naked,
and shall eat her flesh, and burn her with fire. **17** [ak]For God hath put in their
hearts to fulfill his will, and to do with one consent for to give their kingdom unto
the beast, until the words of God be fulfilled. **18** And that woman which thou
sawest, is that [al]great city which reigned over the kings of the earth.

18

2 The horrible destruction of Babylon set out. 11, 16, 18 The merchants of the earth, who were enriched with the pomp and luxuriousness of it, weep and wail: 20 but all the elect rejoice for that just vengeance of God.

1 [a]And after these things, I saw another [b]Angel come down from heaven, ha-
ving great power, so that the earth was lightened with his glory, **2** And he cried
out mightily with a loud voice, [c]saying, [1]It is fallen, it is fallen, Babylon that great
city, and is become the habitation of devils, and the hold of all foul spirits, and a
cage of every unclean and hateful bird. **3** For all nations have drunken of the
wine of the wrath of her fornication, and the kings of the earth have committed
fornication with her, and the merchants of the earth are waxed rich of the abun-
dance of her pleasures. **4** [d]And I heard another voice from heaven say, [e]Go out
of her, my people, that ye be not [f]partakers of her sins, and that ye receive not of
her plagues: **5** For her sins are [g]come up into heaven, and God hath remembered
her iniquities. **6** [h]Reward her, even as she hath rewarded you, and give her dou-
ble according to her works: and in the cup that she hath filled to you, fill her the
double. **7** Inasmuch as she glorified herself, and lived in pleasure, so much give
ye to her torment and sorrow: for she saith [i]in her heart, I sit being a queen, and
am [j]no widow, and shall [k]see no mourning. **8** Therefore shall her plagues come
at [l]one day, death, and sorrow, and famine, and she shall be burnt with fire: for
that God which condemneth her, is a strong Lord, **9** And the [m]kings of the earth
shall bewail her, and lament for her, which have committed fornication, and lived
in pleasure with her, when they shall see that smoke of that her burning, **10** And
shall stand afar off for fear of her torment, saying, Alas, alas, that great city Babylon,
that mighty city: for in one hour is thy judgment come. **11** [n]And the merchants
of the earth shall weep and wail over her: for no man buyeth their ware anymo-
re. **12** The ware of gold, and silver, and of precious stone, and of pearls, and of
fine linen, and of purple, and of silk, and of scarlet, and of all manner of Thynewo-
od, and of all vessels of ivory, and of all vessels of most precious wood, and of brass,
and of iron, and of marble, **13** And of cinnamon, and odors, and ointments, and
frankincense, and wine, and oil, and fine flour, and wheat, and beasts, and sheep,
and horses, and chariots, and servants, and souls of men. **14** [o]And the [p]apples
that thy soul lusted after, are departed from thee, and all things which were fat and
excellent, are departed from thee, and thou shalt find them no more. **15** The
merchants of these things which were waxed rich, shall stand afar off from her, for
fear of her torment, weeping and wailing. **16** And saying, Alas, alas, that great
city, that was clothed in fine linen and purple, and scarlet, and gilded with gold,
and precious stones, and pearls. **17** [q]For in one hour so great riches are come to
desolation. And every shipmaster, and all the people that occupy ships and ship-
men, and whosoever traffic on the sea, shall stand afar off. **18** And cry, when
they see that smoke of that her burning, saying, What city was like unto this great

---

purpose, that when this particular prediction of foretelling of things to come, should take effect the truth of all other predictions in the Church might be the more confirmed. Which sign God of old mentioned this in the Law, Deut. 18, and Jeremiah confirmeth, Jer. 28:8.

v. Revelation 17:10 Whose names are these: the first, Servius Sulpicius Galba, who was the seventh Emperor of the people of Rome, the second Marcus Salvius Otho, the third Aulus Vitellius, the fourth, Titus Flavius Vespasianus, the fifth, Titus Vespasianus his son of his own name.

w. Revelation 17:10 Flavius Domitian son of the first Vespasian. For in the latter end of his days S. John wrote these things, as witnesseth Irenaus, Lib. 5 adversus hareses.

x. Revelation 17:10 Nerua. The Empire being now translated from the family of Flavius. This man reigned only one year, four months, and nine days, as the history writers do tell.

y. Revelation 17:11 This is spoken by the figure synecdoche, as much to say as that head of the beast which was and is not, because it is cut off, and Nerua in so short time extinguished. How many heads there were, so many beasts there seemed to be in one. See the like speech in Rev. 13.3

z. Revelation 17:11 Nerua Traianus, who himself in divers respects is called here the seventh and the eighth.

aa. Revelation 17:11 Though in number and order of succession he be the eighth, yet he is reckoned together with one of these heads, because Nerua and he were one head. For this man obtained authority together with Nerua, and was Consul with him, when Nerua left his life.

ab. Revelation 17:11 Namely, to molest with persecutions the Churches of Christ, as the histories do accord, and I have briefly noted, Rev. 2:10.

ac. Revelation 17:12 The third place of this description as I said, verse 18, is a prophetical prediction of things to come which the beast should do, as in the words following S. John doth not obscurely signify, saying, which have not yet received the kingdom, etc. For there is an Antithesis or opposition between these kings, and those that went before. And first the persons are described, in this verse, then their deeds in the two verses following.

ad. Revelation 17:12 That is, arising with their kingdoms out of the Roman beast: at such time as that political Empire began by the craft of the Popes greatly to fall.

ae. Revelation 17:12 Namely, with the second beast whom we called before a false prophet, which beast, ascending out of the earth got unto himself all the authority and power of the first beast, and exerciseth the same before his face, as was said, Rev. 14:11, 12. For when the political Empire of the West began to bow downwards, there both arose those ten kings, and the second beast took the opportunity offered to usurp unto himself all the power of the former beast. These kings long ago, many have numbered and described to be ten and a great part of the events plainly testifieth the same in this our age.

af. Revelation 17:13 That is, by consent and agreement, that they may conspire with the beast, and depend upon his beck. Their story is divided into three parts, counsels, acts, and events. The counselors some of them consist in communicating of judgments and affections: and some in communicating of power, which they are said to have given unto this beast in this verse.

ag. Revelation 17:14 With Christ and his Church, as the reason following doth declare, and here are mentioned the facts and the events which followed for Christ's sake, and for the grace of God the Father towards those that are called, elected, and are his faithful ones in Christ.

ah. Revelation 17:15 This is the other member of the narration as I said verse 7, belonging unto the harlot, showed in the vision, verse 3. In this history of the harlot, these 3 things are distinctly propounded, what is her magnificence in this verse, what is her fall, and by whom it shall happen unto her, in the two verses following: and lastly, who that harlot is, in the last verse. This place which by order of nature should have been the first, is therefore made the last, because it was more fit to be joined with the next Chap.

ai. Revelation 17:15 That is, as unconstant and variable as the waters. Upon this foundation sitteth this harlot as Queen, a vain person upon that which is vain.

aj. Revelation 17:16 The ten Kings as verse 12. The accomplishment of this fact and event, is daily increased in this our age by the singular providence and most mighty government of God. Wherefore the facts are propounded in this verse, and the cause of them in the verses following.

ak. Revelation 17:17 A reason rendered from the chief efficient cause, which is the providence of God, by which alone S. John by inversion of order affirmeth to have come to pass, both that the Kings should execute upon the harlot, that which pleased God, and which he declared in the verse next beforegoing: and also that by one consent and counsel, they should give their kingdom unto the beast, etc., verses 13, 14. For as these being blinded have before depended upon the beck of the beast that lifteth up the harlot, so it is said that afterward it shall come to pass, that they shall turn back, and shall fall away from her when their hearts shall be turned into better state by the grace and mercy of God.

al. Revelation 17:18 That is, Rome that great City, or only City (as Justinian calleth it) the King and head whereof was then the Emperor, but now the Pope, since that the condition of the beast was changed.

REVELATION 17

1. Rev. 19:16 / 1 Tim. 6:15

REVELATION 18

a. Revelation 18:1 The second place (as I said before, 17:1) of the history of Babylon, is of the woeful fall and ruin of that whore of Babylon. This historical prediction concerning her, is threefold. The first a plain and simple foretelling of her ruin in three verses, the second a figurative prediction by the circumstances, thence, unto verse 20. The third, a confirmation of the same by sign or wonder, unto the end of the Chapter.

b. Revelation 18:1 Either Christ the eternal word of God the Father (as often elsewhere) or a created Angel, and one deputed unto this service: but thoroughly furnished with greatness of power, and with light of glory, as the ensign of power.

c. Revelation 18:2 The prediction or foretelling of her ruin, containing both the fall of Babylon, in this verse, and the cause thereof uttered by way of allegory concerning her spiritual and carnal wickedness, that is, her most great impiety and injustice, in the next verse: her fall is first simply declared of the Angel: and then the greatness thereof is showed here by the events, when he saith it shall be the seat and habitation of devils, of wild beasts and of cursed souls, as of old, Isa. 13:21, and often elsewhere.

d. Revelation 18:4 The second prediction, which is of the circumstances of the ruin of Babylon: of these there are two kinds: one going before it: as that beforehand the godly are delivered unto the ninth verse: the other following upon her ruin, namely the lamentation of the wicked and rejoicing of the godly, unto the twentieth verse.

e. Revelation 18:4 Two circumstances going before the ruin, are commanded in this place: one is, that the godly depart out of Babylon: as I mentioned, chapter 12, to have been done in time past, before the destruction of Jerusalem: this charge is given here, and in the next verse. The other is, that every one of them occupy themselves in their own place, in executing the judgment of God, as it was commanded the Levites of old, Exod. 32:27, and that they sanctify their hands unto the Lord, verses 6, 7, 8.

f. Revelation 18:4 Of his commandment there are two causes to avoid the contagion of sin, and to shun the participation of those punishments that belong thereunto.

g. Revelation 18:5 He useth a word which signifieth the following of sins one after another, and rising one another in such sort, that they grew at length to such an heap that they came up even to heaven.

h. Revelation 18:6 The provocation of the godly, and the commandment of executing the judgments of God, stand upon three causes which are here expressed: the unjust wickedness of the whore of Babylon, in this verse her cursed pride opposing itself against God, which is the fountain of all evil actions, verse 7, and her most just damnation by the sentence of God, verse 8.

i. Revelation 18:7 With herself.

j. Revelation 18:7 I am full of people and mighty.

k. Revelation 18:7 I shall taste of none.

l. Revelation 18:8 Shortly and at one instant.

m. Revelation 18:9 The circumstances following the fall of Babylon, or the consequences thereof (as I distinguished them, verse 4) are two. Namely the lamentation of the wicked unto verse 19: and the rejoicing of the godly, verse 20. This most sorrowful lamentation, according to the person of them that lament, hath three members, the first whereof is the mourning of the kings and mighty men of the earth, in two verses. The second is the lamentation of the merchants that traffic by land thence unto verse 16. The third is the wailing of those that merchandise by sea, verses 16, 17, 18. In every [one] of these the cause and manner of their mourning is described in order, according to the condition of those [that] mourn, with observation of that which best agreeth unto them.

n. Revelation 18:11 The lamentation of those that trade by land, as I distinguished immediately before.

o. Revelation 18:14 An apostrophe, or turning of the speech by imitation, used for more vehemence, as if those merchants, after the manner of mourners should in passionate speech speak unto Babylon, though now utterly fallen and overthrown. So Isa. 12:9, and in many other places.

p. Revelation 18:14 By this is meant that season which is next before the fall of the leaf, at what season fruits ripen, and the word signifieth such fruits as are longed for.

q. Revelation 18:17 The manner of mourning used by them that trade by sea.

r. Revelation 18:20 The other consequent unto the other ruin of Babylon, is the exultation or rejoicing of the godly in heaven and in earth, as was noted, verse 9.

city? **19** And they shall cast dust on their heads, and cry, weeping, and wailing, and say, Alas, alas that great city, wherein were made rich all that had ships on the sea by her coastlines: for in one hour she is made desolate. **20** [r]O heaven, rejoice of her, and ye holy Apostles and Prophets: for God hath punished her, to be revenged on her for your sakes. **21** [s]Then a mighty Angel took up a stone, like a great millstone, [2]and cast it into the sea, saying, With such violence shall that great city Babylon be cast and shall be found no more. **22** [t]And the voice of harpers, and musicians and of pipers, and trumpeters shall be heard no more in thee, and no craftsman, of whosoever craft he be, shall be found anymore in thee: and the sound of a millstone shall be heard no more in thee. **23** And the light of a candle shall shine no more in thee: and the voice of the bridegroom and of the bride shall be heard no more in thee: for thy merchants were the great men of the earth: and with thine enchantment were deceived all nations. **24** And in her was found the [u]blood of the Prophets [v]and of the Saints, and of all that were slain upon the earth.

19

1 The heavenly company praise God for avenging the blood of his servants on the whore. 9 They are written blessed, that are called to the Lamb's supper. 10 The Angel will not be worshipped. 11 That mighty King of Kings appeareth from heaven. 19 The battle, 20 wherein the beast is taken, and cast into the burning lake.

1 And [a]after these things I heard a great voice of a great multitude in heaven, saying, [b,c]Hallelujah, salvation, and glory, and honor, and power be to the Lord our God. **2** For true and righteous are his judgments: for he hath condemned the great whore which did corrupt the earth with her fornication, and hath avenged the blood of his servants shed by her hand. **3** And again they said, [d]Hallelujah: and that her smoke rose up for evermore. **4** And the four and twenty Elders, and the four beasts fell down, and worshipped God that sat on the throne, saying, Amen, Hallelujah. **5** [e]Then a voice came out of the [f]throne, saying, Praise our God, all ye his servants, and ye that fear him, both small and great. **6** And I heard [g]like a voice of a great multitude, and as the voice of many waters, and as the voice of strong thunderings, saying, Hallelujah: for the Lord that God that Almighty one hath reigned. **7** Let us be glad and rejoice, and give glory to him: for the marriage of the Lamb is come, and his wife hath made [h]herself ready. **8** And to her was granted, that she should be arrayed with [i]pure fine linen and shining, for the fine [j]linen is the [k]righteousness of Saints. **9** [l]Then he said unto me, Write, [1]Blessed are they which are called unto the Lamb's supper. And he said unto me, These words of God are true. **10** [m]And I fell before his feet, [2]to worship him, but he said unto me, See thou do it not: I am thy fellow servant, and one of thy brethren, which have the [n]testimony of Jesus, Worship God: for the testimony of [o]Jesus is the Spirit of prophecy. **11** [p]And I saw [q]heaven open, and behold a white horse, and he that sat upon him was called faithful and true, and he judgeth and fighteth righteously. **12** And his eyes were as a flame of fire, and on his head were many crowns: and he had a name written, that no man knew but himself. **13** And he was clothed with a garment dipped in blood, and his name is called, THE WORD OF GOD. **14** [r]And the hosts which were in heaven, followed him upon white horses, clothed with fine linen white and pure. **15** [s]And out of his mouth went out a sharp sword, that with it he should smite the heathen: for he shall [3]rule them with a rod of iron, for he it is that treadeth the winepress of the fierceness and wrath of Almighty God. **16** [t]And he hath upon his garment, and upon his thigh, a name written, [4]THE KING OF KINGS AND LORD OF LORDS. **17** [u]And I saw an Angel stand in the [v]sun who cried with a loud voice, saying, to all the fowls that did fly by [w]the midst of heaven, come, and gather yourselves together unto the supper of the great God, **18** That ye may eat the flesh of kings, and the flesh of high captains, and the flesh of mighty men, and the flesh of horses, and of them that sit on them, and the flesh of all freemen, and bondmen, and of small and great. **19** [x]And I saw the beast, and the kings of the earth, and their hosts gathered together to make battle against him that sat on the horse, and against his army. **20** But the beast [y]was taken, and with him [z]that false Prophet that wrought miracles before him, whereby he deceived them that received the beast's mark, and them that worshipped his image. These both were alive cast into a lake of fire burning with brimstone. **21** And the remnant were slain with the sword of him that sitteth upon the horse, which cometh out of his mouth, and all the fowls were filled full with their flesh.

20

1 The Angel 2 bindeth Satan for a thousand years. 8 Being loosed, he stirreth up Gog and Magog, that is, privy and open enemies against the Saints, 11 but the vengeance of the Lord cutting off their insolency. 12 The books are opened, by which the dead are judged.

1 And [a]I saw an Angel come down from heaven, having the key [b]of the bottomless pit, and a great chain in his hand. **2** And he took the dragon that old serpent, which is the devil and Satan, and he bound him [c]a thousand years: **3** And cast him into the bottomless pit, and he shut him up, and sealed the door upon

---

s. Revelation 18:21 The third prediction, as I said verse 1, standing of a sign, and the interpretation thereof: the interpretation thereof is in 2 sorts, first by a simple propounding of the thing itself, in this verse, and then by declaration of the events in the verses following.

t. Revelation 18:22 The events are two, the one of them opposite unto the other for amplification sake. There shall be, saith he, in Babylon no mirth nor joy at all, in this and the next verse, but all heavy and lamentable things from the bloody slaughters of the righteous and the vengeance of God coming upon it for the same.

u. Revelation 18:24 That is shed by bloody massacres, and calling for vengeance.

v. Revelation 18:24 That is, proved and found out, as if God had appointed a just inquiry, concerning the impiety, unnaturalness and injustice of those men.

REVELATION 18

1. Rev. 14:8 / Isa. 21:9 / Jer. 51:8 **2.** Jer. 51:63

REVELATION 19

a. Revelation 19:1 This chapter hath in sum two parts, one transitory or of passage unto the things that follow unto verse 10, another historical of the victory of Christ gotten against both the beasts unto the end of the chapter, which I said was the second history of this argument, Rev. 17:1. The transition hath two places, one of praising God for the overthrow done unto Babylon in 4 verses, and another likewise of praise, and Prophetical, for the coming of Christ unto his kingdom, and his most royal marriage with his Church, thence unto the tenth verse. The former praise has three branches, distinguished after the ancient manner of those that sing: … , that is, an invitation or provokement in 2 verses, … , a response or answer in the third verse, and … , a close or joining together in harmony: all which I thought good of purpose to distinguish in this place, lest any man should with Porphyrius, or other like dogs, object to Saint John of the heavenly Church, a childish and idle repetition of speech.

b. Revelation 19:1 Praise the Lord.

c. Revelation 19:1 The proposition of praise with exhortation in this verse, and the cause thereof, in the next verse.

d. Revelation 19:3 The song of the Antiphony or response, containing an amplification of the praise of God, from the perpetual and most certain testimony of his divine judgment as was done at Sodom and Gomorrah, Gen. 19.

e. Revelation 19:5 The second place of praise as I said verse 1, which first is commanded from God in this verse: and then is in most ample manner pronounced of the creatures, both because they see that kingdom of Christ to come, which most they desire, verse 6, also because they see that the Church is called forth to be brought home: into the house of her husband by holy marriage unto the fellowship of his kingdom, verses 7, 8. Wherefore S. John is commanded to write in a book the Epiphonema , or acclamation joined with a divine testimony, verse 9.

f. Revelation 19:5 Out of the temple from God, as Rev. 11:19.

g. Revelation 19:6 Without the Temple in heaven.

h. Revelation 19:7 Namely unto that holy marriage both herself in person in this verse and also furnished of her spouse with marriage gifts princely and divine is adorned and prepared in the next verse.

i. Revelation 19:8 As an ensign of Kingly and priestly dignity: which dignity Christ bestoweth upon us, Rev. 1:6.

j. Revelation 19:8 This is a gift given by the husband for marriage sake and a most choice ornament, which Christ bestoweth upon us, as upon his spouse.

k. Revelation 19:8 Good works which are lively testimonies of faith.

l. Revelation 19:9 Namely the Angel, as appeareth by the next verse.

m. Revelation 19:10 The particular history of this verse is brought in by occasion, and as it were besides the purpose, that Saint John might make a public example of his own infirmity, and of the modest sanctimony of the Angel, who hath renounced for himself the divine honors, and recalled all the servants of God, unto the worship of him alone: as also Rev. 22:8.

n. Revelation 19:10 Which are commanded to bear witness of Jesus.

o. Revelation 19:10 For Jesus is the mark that all the prophecies shoot at.

p. Revelation 19:11 The second place of this Chapter (as I said verse 1) is of the victory gotten by Christ against both the beasts: in which first Christ is described as one ready to fight, unto verse 16, then is showed the battle to be begun, thence unto verse 18: lastly is set forth the victory unto the end of the Chapter. In this place do shine most excellent properties of Christ as our heavenly Judge and revenger, according to his person, company, effects, and names.

q. Revelation 19:11 Properties belonging to his person, that he is heavenly, judge, faithful, true, just, in this verse, searching out all things ruling over all, to be searched out of none, verse 12, the trumpet, and the very essential word of God, verse 13.

r. Revelation 19:14 The company or retinue of Christ, holy, innumerable, heavenly, judicial, royal and pure.

s. Revelation 19:15 The effects of Christ prepared unto battle, that with his mouth he striketh the Gentiles, ruleth and destroyeth.

t. Revelation 19:16 The name agreeing unto Christ according to the former properties, expressed after the manner of the Hebrews.

u. Revelation 19:17 The second member as I said, verse 11. A reproachful calling forth of his enemies unto battle: in which not themselves (for why should they be called forth of the king of the world, or provoked being his subjects? for that is not comely) but in their hearing, the birds of the air are called to eat their carcasses.

v. Revelation 19:17 That is, openly, and in sight of all, as Num. 25:4 and 2 Sam. 12:11.

w. Revelation 19:17 That is, through this inferior heaven, and which is nearer unto us: a Hebrew phrase.

x. Revelation 19:19 The third member (as was said, verse 11) of the victory obtained by Christ. Unto this apppertaineth two things: his bucking with the beast and his forces in this verse: and the event most magnificent, described after the manner of men, in the verses following. All these things are plain.

y. Revelation 19:20 Namely, that beast with seven heads, of which before, Rev. 13:1 and 17:3.

z. Revelation 19:20 That is, that beast with two heads, of which Rev. 13:11. See also Rev. 16:14.

REVELATION 19

1. Matt. 22:2 **2.** Rev. 22:8 **3.** Ps. 2:9 **4.** Rev. 17:14 / 1 Tim. 6:15

REVELATION 20

a. Revelation 20:1 Now followeth the third place of the prophetical history, which is of the victory whereby Christ overcame the dragon, as I note, Rev. 7:1. This place must necessarily be joined with the end of chapter 12 and be applied unto the just understanding thereof. This chapter hath two parts, one of the dragon overcome, unto verse 10, the other of the resurrection and last judgment unto the end of the chapter. The history of the dragon is double: First of the first victory after which he was bound by Christ unto verse 6. The second is of the last victory, whereby he has thrown down into everlasting punishment, thence unto verse 10. This first history happened in the first time of the Christian Church, when the dragon thrown down from heaven by Christ, went about to molest the new birth of the Church in the earth, Rev. 12:17, 18. For which cause I gave warning, that this story of the Dragon must be annexed unto that place.

b. Revelation 20:1 That is of hell, whither God threw down the Angels which had sinned, and bound them in chains of darkness to be kept unto damnation, 2 Pet. 2:4; Jude 6.

c. Revelation 20:2 The first whereof (continuing this history with the end of chapter 12) is the 36 year from the passion of Christ, when the Church of the Jews being overthrown,

him, that he should deceive the people [d]no more till the thousand years were fulfilled: for after that he must be loosed for [e]a little season. **4** [f]And I saw [g,h]seats: and they sat upon them, and judgment was given unto them, and I saw the souls of them that were [i]beheaded for the witness of Jesus, and for the word of God, and which [j]did not worship the beast, neither his image, neither had taken his mark upon their foreheads or on their hands: and they lived, and reigned with Christ a thousand years. **5** [k]But the rest of the dead men [l]shall not live again, until the thousand years be finished: this is the first resurrection. **6** Blessed and holy is he, that hath part in the first resurrection: for on such the [m]second death hath no power: but they shall be the Priests of God and of Christ, [n]and shall reign with him a thousand years. **7** [o]And when the [p]thousand years are expired, Satan shall be loosed out of his prison, **8** [q]And shall go out to deceive the people, which are in the four quarters of the earth: even [1]Gog and Magog, to gather them together to battle, whose number is as the sand of the Sea. **9** And they went up into the [r]plain of the earth, and they compassed the tents of the Saints about, and the beloved city: but [s]fire came down from God out of heaven, and devoured them. **10** [t]And the devil that deceived them, was cast into a lake of fire and brimstone, where that beast and that false prophet are, and shall be tormented even day and night for evermore. **11** [u]And I saw a great [v]white throne, and one that sat on it, [w]from whose face fled away both the earth and heaven, and their place was no more found. **12** And I saw the dead, both great and small stand before [x]God: and the [y]books were opened, and [2]another book was opened, which is the book [z]of life, and the dead were judged of those things, which were written in the books, according to their works. **13** [aa]And the sea gave up her dead, which were in her, and death and hell delivered up the dead, which were in them: and they were judged every man according to their works. **14** [ab]And death, and hell were cast into the lake of fire: this is the second death. **15** And whosoever was not found written in the book of life, was cast into the lake of fire.

21

2 He describeth new Jerusalem descending from heaven, 6 The bride the Lamb's wife, 12 and the glorious building of the city, 19 garnished with precious stones, 22 whose Temple the Lamb is.

1 And [a]I saw [1]a new heaven, and a new earth: for the [2]first heaven, and the first earth were passed away, and there was no more sea. **2** [b]And I John saw the holy city new Jerusalem come down from God out of heaven, prepared as a bride trimmed for her husband. **3** [c]And I heard a great voice out of heaven, saying, Behold, the Tabernacle of God is with men, and he will dwell with them: and they shall be his people, and God himself shall be their God with them. **4** [3]And God shall wipe away all tears from their eyes, and there shall be no more death, neither sorrow, neither crying, neither shall there be anymore pain: for the first things are passed. **5** [d]And he that sat upon the throne, said, [4]Behold, I make all things new, and he said unto me, Write: for these things are faithful and true. **6** And he said unto me, [5,e]It is done, I am Alpha and Omega, the beginning and the end: I will give to him that is athirst, of the well of the water of life freely. **7** He that overcometh, shall inherit all things, and I will be his God, and he shall be my Son. **8** But the fearful and unbelieving, and the abominable and murderers, and whoremongers, and sorcerers, and idolaters, and all liars shall have their [f]part in the lake which burneth with fire and brimstone, which is the second death. **9** [g]And there came unto me one of the seven Angels, which had the seven vials full of the seven last plagues, and talked with me, saying, Come: I will show thee the bride the Lamb's wife. **10** And he carried me away in the spirit to a great and [h]an high mountain, and he showed me [i]that great city, that holy Jerusalem, descending out of heaven from God, **11** Having the glory of God, and her shining was like unto a stone most precious, as a jasper stone clear as crystal, **12** [j]And had a great wall and high, and had [k]twelve gates, and at the gates [l]twelve Angels, and the names written which are the twelve tribes of the children of Israel. **13** On the East part there were three gates, and on the North side three gates, on the South side three gates, and on the West side three gates. **14** And the wall of the city had [m]twelve foundations, and in them the names of the Lamb's twelve Apostles. **15** [n]And he that walked with me, had a golden reed, to measure the city withal, and the gates thereof, and the wall thereof. **16** [o]And the city lay [p]foursquare, and the length is as large as the breadth of it, and he measured the city with the reed, twelve thousand furlongs: and the length, and the breadth, and the height of it are equal. **17** And he measured the wall thereof an hundred forty and four cubits, by the measure of man, that is, of the [q]Angel. **18** [r]And the building of the wall of it

---

Satan assayed to invade the Christian Church gathered of the Gentiles, and to destroy part of her seed, Rev. 12:17. The thousandth year falleth precisely upon the times of that wicked Hildebrand, who was called Gregory the seventh a most damnable Necromancer and sorcerer, whom Satan used as an instrument when he was loosed out of bonds, thenceforth to annoy the Saints of God with most cruel persecutions, and the whole world with dissentions, and most bloody wars: as Benno the Cardinal reporteth at large. This is the first victory gotten over the dragon in the earth.

d. Revelation 20:3 Namely, with that public and violent deceit which he attempted before, Chapter 12, and which after a thousand years (alack for woe) he most mightily procured in the Christian world.

e. Revelation 20:3 Which being once expired, the second battle and victory shall be, of which verses 7, 8.

f. Revelation 20:4 A description of the common state of the Church of Christ in earth in that space of a thousand years, for which the devil was in bonds: in which first the authority, life, and common honor of the godly, is declared, verse 4. Secondly, newness of life is preached unto others by the Gospel, after that space, verse 5. Finally, he concludeth with promises, verse 6.

g. Revelation 20:4 For judgment was committed to them, as to members joined to the head, not [that] Christ's office was given over [to] them.

h. Revelation 20:4 This was a type of the authority of the good and faithful servants of God in the Church, taken from the manner of men.

i. Revelation 20:4 Of the Martyrs, which suffered in those first times.

j. Revelation 20:4 Of the Martyrs which suffered after that both the beasts were now risen up, Chapter 13, for these three things are expounded.

k. Revelation 20:5 Whoever shall lie dead in sin, and not know the truth of God.

l. Revelation 20:5 They shall not be renewed with that newness of the life by the enlightening of the Gospel of the glory of Christ. For this is the first resurrection, by which the souls of the godly do rise from their death. In the second resurrection their bodies shall rise again.

m. Revelation 20:6 That whereby both body and soul, that is, the whole man is addicted and delivered unto eternal death. So Rev. 2:11.

n. Revelation 20:6 A return unto the intended history, by resuming the words which are in the end of the fourth verse.

o. Revelation 20:7 The second history, of the latter victory of Christ, as was said verse 1. In which are summarily described the work, overthrow and eternal punishment of Satan.

p. Revelation 20:7 Of which I spake, verse 2. Then therefore shall be given unto him liberty to rage against the Church, and to molest the Saints for the sins of men: unto whom the faithful shall have associated themselves more than was meet, tasting with them of their impurity of doctrine and life.

q. Revelation 20:8 The work or act of Satan (which is the first member as I distinguished in the verse beforegoing) to deceive the whole world, even unto the uttermost nations thereof: to arm them against the people of God, in this verse, and to besiege and oppress the Church, with his whole strength, in the verse following.

r. Revelation 20:9 As if he said insomuch that the whole face of the earth, how great soever it is was filled.

s. Revelation 20:9 The wrath of God, consuming the adversaries, and overthrowing all their enterprises, Heb. 10:27. And this is the second member mentioned, verse 7, the overthrow of Satan.

t. Revelation 20:10 The third member, eternal destruction against those that are overcome: as I noted in the same place.

u. Revelation 20:11 The second part of this Chapter, in which is described the judge, in this verse, and the last judgment in the verse following.

v. Revelation 20:11 That is, a tribunal seat most Princelike and glorious: for so doth the Greek word also signify.

w. Revelation 20:11 That is, Christ, before whom when he cometh unto judgment, heaven and earth shall perish for the greatness of his majesty, 2 Pet. 3:7, 10, etc.

x. Revelation 20:12 That is, Christ the judge, 2 Cor. 5:10.

y. Revelation 20:12 As it were, our books of reckoning or accompts: that is, the testimony of our conscience, and of our works, which by no means can be avoided. This is spoken after the manner of men.

z. Revelation 20:12 The book of the eternal decree of God, in which God the Father hath elected in Christ according to the good pleasure of his will, those that shall be heirs of life. This also is spoken according to the manner of men.

aa. Revelation 20:13 This is a prevention or an answer to an objection: for happily some man will say, but they are dead, whom the sea, death and the grave hath consumed, how shall they appear before the judge? S. John answereth by resurrection from death, whereunto all things (however repugnant) shall minister and serve at the commandment of God, as Dan. 12.

ab. Revelation 20:14 The last enemy which is death shall be abolished by Christ (that he may no more make any attempt against us), 1 Cor. 15:16, and death shall feed upon the reprobate in hell for evermore, according to the righteous judgment of God, in the next verse.

REVELATION 20

1. Ezek. 39:2
2. Rev. 3:5 / Rev. 21:27 / Phil. 4:3

REVELATION 21

a. Revelation 21:1 Now followeth the second part of the history prophetical (as I said, Rev. 1 and 11:1) of the future estate of the Church in heaven after the last judgment, unto the fifth verse of the next chapter, in this are two things briefly declareth. The station, seat, or place thereof, verse 1. Then her state and condition in the verses following. Before the state of the Church described, is set down the state of the whole world, that there shall be a new heaven, and a new earth, as Isa. 65:17 and 66:12 and 2 Pet. 3:13, and this is the seat or place of the Church, in which righteousness shall dwell.

b. Revelation 21:2 The state of this glorious Church is first described generally, unto verse 8 and then specially and by parts, in the verses following. The general description consisteth in a vision showed afar off, verse 2, and in speech spoken from heaven. In the general these things are common that the Church is holy, new, the workmanship of God, heavenly, most glorious, the spouse of Christ, and partaker of this glory in this verse.

c. Revelation 21:3 The Church is described by the speech first of an Angel, in two verses, then of God himself in 4 verses. The Angel's speech describeth the glory of the Church by the most familiar cohabitation of God therewith, by communication of all manner [of] good things according to the covenant, in this verse: and by removing or putting far away of all evil things in the verse following.

d. Revelation 21:5 In the speech of God himself describing the Church, is first a certain exordium, or entrance, verse 5. Then followeth a magnificent description of the Church, by the present and future good things of the same in 3 verses following. In the exordium God challengeth to himself the restoring of all the creatures of which verse 1 and witnesseth the calling of S. John unto the writing of these things, in this verse.

e. Revelation 21:6 The description of the Church is of three sorts, by the abolishing of old things: by the being of present things in God, that is of things eternal and by the communication of all good things with the godly, verse 6. If so be they shall strive manfully, verse 7. But the reprobate are excluded from thence, verse 8.

f. Revelation 21:8 Their lot, and inheritance as it were.

g. Revelation 21:9 A transition unto the particular describing of the heavenly Church by the express calling of Saint John in this verse, and his rapting up by the Spirit, in confirmation of the truth of God in the verse following.

h. Revelation 21:10 He meaneth the place and stately seat of the Church, shadowed out in a mountain.

i. Revelation 21:10 A type of that Church which is one, ample, or Catholic, holy celestial, built of God, in this verse: and glorious in the verse following. This type propounded generally, is after particularly declared, verse 12, etc.

j. Revelation 21:12 A particular description (as I noted, verse 2) of the celestial Church. First, by the essential parts of the same, under the similitude of a city to verse 12. Secondly, from foreign accidents, unto the end of the chapter. Thirdly, by the effects, in the beginning of the next chapter, the essential parts are noted the matter and the form in the whole work: of these the superficies and foundation of the wall are entire parts (as they use to be called) which parts are first described in figure, unto verse 14 and afterward more exactly.

k. Revelation 21:12 According to the number of the tribes, of which chap. 7. For here the outward part is attributed unto the old Testament, and the foundation of the new Testament.

was of jasper: and the city was pure gold, like unto clear glass. **19** And the foundations of the wall of the city were garnished with all manner of precious stones: the first foundation was jasper: the second of Sapphire: the third of a Chalcedony: the fourth of an Emerald: **20** The fifth of a Sardonyx: the sixth of a Sardius: the seventh of a Chrysolite: the eight of a Beryl: the ninth of a Topaz: the tenth of a Chrysoprase: the eleventh of a Jacinth: the twelfth an Amethyst. **21** And the twelve gates were twelve pearls, and every gate is of one pearl, and the [s]street of the city is pure gold, as shining glass. **22** And I saw no Temple therein: for the Lord God Almighty and the Lamb are the Temple of it. **23** [6,t]And their city hath no need of the Sun, neither of the Moon to shine in it: for the glory of God did light it: and the Lamb is the light of it. **24** [7]And the people which are saved, shall walk in the light of it: and the kings of the earth shall bring their glory and honor unto it. **25** [8]And the gates of it shall not be shut by day: for there shall be no night there. **26** And the glory and honor of the Gentiles shall be brought unto it. **27** And there shall enter into it none unclean thing, neither whatsoever worketh abomination or lies: but they which are written in the Lamb's [9]book of life.

22

1 The river of water of life is showed, 2 and the tree of life: 6, 7 Then followeth the conclusion of this prophecy, 8 where John declareth, that the things herein contained are most true. 13 And now the third time repeateth these words, All things come from him, who is the beginning and the end.

1 And [a]he showed me a pure river of water of life, clear as crystal, proceeding out of the throne of God, and of the Lamb. **2** In the midst of the street of it, and of either side of the river was the tree of life, which bare twelve manner of fruits, and gave fruit every month: and the leaves of the tree served to heal the nations with. **3** And there shall be no more curse, but the throne of God and of the Lamb shall be in it, and his servants shall serve him. **4** And they shall see his face, and his Name shall be in their foreheads. **5** [1]And there shall be no night there, and they need no candle, neither light of the Sun: for the Lord God giveth them light, and they shall reign for evermore. **6** [b]And he said unto me, These words are faithful and true: and the Lord God of the holy Prophets sent his Angel to show unto his servants the things which must shortly be fulfilled. **7** Behold, I come shortly. Blessed is he that keepeth the words of the prophecy of this book. **8** And I am John, which saw and heard these things: and when I had heard and seen, [2]I fell down to worship before the feet of the Angel which showed me these things. **9** But he said unto me, See thou do it not: for I am thy fellow servant, and of thy brethren the Prophets, and of them which keep the words of this book: worship God. **10** [c]And he said unto me, [d]Seal not the words of the prophecy of this book: for the time is at hand. **11** [e]He that is unjust, let him be unjust still: and he which is filthy, let him be filthy still: and he that is righteous, let him be righteous still: and he that is holy, let him be holy still. **12** [f]And behold, I come shortly, and my reward is with me, [3]to give to every man according as his work shall be. **13** I am [4]Alpha and Omega, the beginning and the end, the first and the last. **14** Blessed are they, that do his Commandments, [g]that their right may be in the tree of Life, and may enter in through the gates into the City. **15** For without shall be dogs and enchanters, and whoremongers, and murderers, and idolaters, and whosoever loveth or maketh lies. **16** [h]I Jesus have sent mine Angel, to testify unto you these things in the Churches: I am the root and the generation of David, and the bright morning star. **17** And the Spirit and the bride say, Come. And let him that heareth say, Come: and let him that is athirst, come: and [5]let whosoever will, take of the water of life freely. **18** [i]For I protest unto every man that heareth the words of the prophecy of this book, If any man shall add unto these things, God shall add unto him the plagues that are written in this book. **19** And if any man shall diminish of the words of the book of this prophecy, God shall take away his part out of the book of life, and out of the holy City, and from those things which are written in this book. **20** [j]He which testifieth these things, saith, Surely I come quickly, Amen. Even so, come Lord Jesus. **21** [k]The grace of our Lord Jesus Christ be with you all, AMEN. THE END

---

l. Revelation 21:12 He meaneth the Prophets, who are the messengers of God, and watchmen of the Church.

m. Revelation 21:14 That is, foundation stones, according to the number of the gates, as is showed verse 19.

n. Revelation 21:15 A transition unto a more exquisite description of the parts of the Church, by finding out the measure of the same by the Angel that measured them.

o. Revelation 21:16 The measure and form most equal, in 2 verses.

p. Revelation 21:16 A foursquared figure hath equal sides, and outright corners, and therefore the Greeks call by this name those things that are steady, and of continuance and perfect.

q. Revelation 21:17 He addeth this, because the Angel had the shape of a man.

r. Revelation 21:18 The matter most precious and glittering which the presence of God maketh most glorious.

s. Revelation 21:21 By street, he meaneth the broadest place of the city.

t. Revelation 21:23 The second form of particular description (as I said, verse 12) from foreign and outward accidents: which are these, Light from God himself, in this verse, glory from men, verse 24, perfect security from all harm, verse 25. Finally such truth and incorruption of glory (verse 26) as can bear and abide with it, nothing that is inglorious, the last verse.

REVELATION 21

1. Isa. 65:17 / Isa. 66:22
2. 2 Pet. 3:13
3. Rev. 7:17 / Isa. 15:8
4. Isa. 43:19 / 2 Cor. 5:17
5. Rev. 1:8 / Rev. 22:13
6. Isa. 10:19
7. Isa. 60:3
8. Isa. 60:11
9. Rev. 2:3 / Rev. 20:12 / Phil. 4:3

REVELATION 22

a. Revelation 22:1 Here is absolved and finished the description of the celestial Church (as I showed before, Rev. 21:12) by the effects in 5 verses, and then this book is concluded in the rest of the chapter. The effects proceeding from God, who dwelleth in the Church are these: the everlasting grace of God in this verse, the eternal living of the godly, as Rev. 2:7, the eternal fruits which the godly bring forth unto God, themselves and others, verse 2, freedom and immunity from all evil, God himself taking pleasure in his servants and they likewise in their God, verse 3. The beholding and sight of God, and sealing of the faithful from all eternity, verse 4, the light of God, and an everlasting kingdom and glory, verse 5.

b. Revelation 22:6 The whole book is concluded and made up by a confirmation, and a salutation. The confirmation hath three places: The words of the Angel unto verse 15, the words of Christ: verses 16, 17, and the obtestation made by S. John from divine authority, thence unto verse 20. By speech of the Angel this prophecy is confirmed unto verse 8 and then he speaketh of the use of this book in the verses following. The prophecy is first confirmed by the Angel from the nature thereof, that it is faithful and true. Secondly from the nature of the efficient cause, both principal which is God, and instrumental, which is the Angel in this verse. Thirdly from the promises of God concerning his coming to effect all these things, and concerning our salvation, verse 7. Fourthly, from the testification of S. John himself, verse 8. The rest of the speech of the angel tending to the same and S. John interrupted or brake off by his unadvised act of worshipping him, in the same verse which the Angel forbidding, teacheth him that adoration must be given not to him, but only to God, as for himself, that he is of such nature and office, as he may not be adored: which thing also was in like manner done, Rev. 16:10.

c. Revelation 22:10 The Angel returneth unto his former speech: in which he teacheth the use of this book, both towards ourselves, in this and the next verse and in respect of God for declaration of his truth, thence unto verse 15.

d. Revelation 22:10 That is, propound this prophecy openly unto all, and conceal no part of it. The contrary whereunto is commanded, Isa. 8:6 and Dan. 8:26.

e. Revelation 22:11 An objection prevented. But there will be some that will abuse this occasion unto evil, and will wrest this Scripture unto their own destruction, as Peter saith. What then saith the Angel, the mysteries of God must not therefore be concealed, which it hath pleased him to communicate unto us. Let them be hurtful unto others, let such be more and more vile in themselves, whom this Scripture doth not please: yet others shall be further conformed thereby unto righteousness and true holiness. The care and reformation of these may not be neglected, because of the voluntary and malicious offense of others.

f. Revelation 22:12 The second place belonging unto the use of this book, as I said, verse 10. Also (saith God by the Angel) though there should be no use of this book unto men: yet it shall be of this use unto me, that it is a witness of my truth unto my glory, who will come shortly to give and execute just judgment, in this verse: who have taught that all these things have their being in me, in verse 13, and have denounced blessedness unto my servants in the Church, verse 14, and reprobation unto the ungodly, verse 15.

g. Revelation 22:14 The blessedness of the godly set down by their title and interest thereunto: and their fruit in the same.

h. Revelation 22:16 The second place of confirmation, as I said, is the speech of Christ, ratifying the vocation of S. John, and the authority of his calling and testimony, both from the condition of his own person being God and man, in whom all the promises of God are Yea and Amen, 2 Cor. 1:20: and also from the testification of other persons, by the acclamation of the holy Ghost, who here is as it were an honorable assistant of the marriage of the Church as the spouse: and of every of the godly as members: and finally from the thing present, that of their own knowledge and accord they are called forth unto the participation of the good things of God, verse 17.

i. Revelation 22:18 The obtestation of Saint John (which is the third place of the confirmation, as was noted, verse 6) joined with a curse of execration, to preserve the truth of this book entire and uncorrupted, in two verses.

j. Revelation 22:20 A divine confirmation or sealing of the obtestation: first from Christ avouching the same, and denouncing his coming against all those that shall put their sacrilegious hands hereunto: then from Saint John himself, who by a most holy prayer calleth Christ to take vengeance of them.

k. Revelation 22:21 The salutation Apostolical, which is the other place of the conclusion, as I said, verse 6, and is the end of almost every Epistle: which we wish unto the Church, and to all the holy and elect members thereof in Christ Jesus our Lord, until his coming to judgment, Come Lord Jesus, and do it. Amen, again, Amen.

REVELATION 22

1. Isa. 60:19
2. Rev. 19:10
3. Rom. 2:6
4. Rev. 1:8 / Rev. 21:6 / Isa. 41:44 / Isa. 34:6
5. Isa. 55:1

THE

APOCRYPHA BIBLE

APOCRYPHA BOOK OF
TOBIT

The Book of Tobit

1 _**1** The book of the words of Tobit, son of Tobiel, the son of Ananiel, the son of Aduel, the son of Gabael, of the seed of Asael, of the tribe of Nephthali; **2**. Who in the time of Enemessar king of the Assyrians was led captive out of Thisbe, which is at the right hand of that city, which is called properly Nephthali in Galilee above Aser. **3**.I Tobit have walked all the days of my life in the ways of truth and justice, and I did many almsdeeds to my brethren, and my nation, who came with me to Nineve, into the land of the Assyrians. **4**.And when I was in mine own country, in the land of Israel being but young, all the tribe of Nephthali my father fell from the house of Jerusalem, which was chosen out of all the tribes of Israel, that all the tribes should sacrifice there, where the temple of the habitation of the most High was consecrated and built for all ages. **5**.Now all the tribes which together revolted, and the house of my father Nephthali, sacrificed unto the heifer Baal. **6**.But I alone went often to Jerusalem at the feasts, as it was ordained unto all the people of Israel by an everlasting decree, having the firstfruits and tenths of increase, with that which was first shorn; and them gave I at the altar to the priests the children of Aaron. **7**.The first tenth part of all increase I gave to the sons of Aaron, who ministered at Jerusalem: another tenth part I sold away, and went, and spent it every year at Jerusalem: **8**.And the third I gave unto them to whom it was meet, as Debora my father's mother had commanded me, because I was left an orphan by my father. **9**. Furthermore, when I was come to the age of a man, I married Anna of mine own kindred, and of her I begat Tobias. **10**. And when we were carried away captives to Nineve, all my brethren and those that were of my kindred did eat of the bread of the Gentiles. **11**. But I kept myself from eating; **12**. Because I remembered God with all my heart. **13**. And the most High gave me grace and favour before Enemessar, so that I was his purveyor. **14**. And I went into Media, and left in trust with Gabael, the brother of Gabrias, at Rages a city of Media ten talents of silver. **15**. Now when Enemessar was dead, Sennacherib his son reigned in his stead; whose estate was troubled, that I could not go into Media. **16**. And in the time of Enemessar I gave many alms to my brethren, and gave my bread to the hungry, **17**. And my clothes to the naked: and if I saw any of my nation dead, or cast about the walls of Nineve, I buried him. **18**. And if the king Sennacherib had slain any, when he was come, and fled from Judea, I buried them privily; for in his wrath he killed many; but the bodies were not found, when they were sought for of the king. **19**. And when one of the Ninevites went and complained of me to the king, that I buried them, and hid myself; understanding that I was sought for to be put to death, I withdrew myself for fear. **20**. Then all my goods were forcibly taken away, neither was there any thing left me, beside my wife Anna and my son Tobias. **21**. And there passed not five and fifty days, before two of his sons killed him, and they fled into the mountains of Ararath; and Sarchedonus his son reigned in his stead; who appointed over his father's accounts, and over all his affairs, Achiacharus my brother Anael's son. **22**. And Achiacharus intreating for me, I returned to Nineve. Now Achiacharus was cupbearer, and keeper of the signet, and steward, and overseer of the accounts: and Sarchedonus appointed him next unto him: and he was my brother's son.

2 _**1** Now when I was come home again, and my wife Anna was restored unto me, with my son Tobias, in the feast of Pentecost, which is the holy feast of the seven weeks, there was a good dinner prepared me, in the which I sat down to eat. **2**.And when I saw abundance of meat, I said to my son, Go and bring what poor man soever thou shalt find out of our brethren, who is mindful of the Lord; and, lo, I tarry for thee. **3**.But he came again, and said, Father, one of our nation is strangled, and is cast out in the marketplace. **4**.Then before I had tasted of any meat, I started up, and took him up into a room until the going down of the sun. **5**.Then I returned, and washed myself, and ate my meat in heaviness, **6**.Remembering that prophecy of Amos, as he said, Your feasts shall be turned into mourning, and all your mirth into lamentation. **7**.Therefore I wept: and after the going down of the sun I went and made a grave, and buried him. **8**.But my neighbours mocked me, and said, This man is not yet afraid to be put to death for this matter: who fled away; and yet, lo, he burieth the dead again. **9**. The same night also I returned from the burial, and slept by the wall of my courtyard, being polluted and my face was uncovered: **10**. And I knew not that there were sparrows in the wall, and mine eyes being open, the sparrows muted warm dung into mine eyes, and a whiteness came in mine eyes: and I went to the physicians, but they helped me not: moreover Achiacharus did nourish me, until I went into Elymais. **11**. And my wife Anna did take women's works to do. **12**. And when she had sent them home to the owners, they paid her wages, and gave her also besides a kid. **13**. And when it was in my house, and began to cry, I said unto her, From whence is this kid? is it not stolen? render it to the owners; for it is not lawful to eat any thing that is stolen. **14**. But she replied upon me, It was given for a gift more than the wages. Howbeit I did not believe her, but bade her render it to the owners: and I was abashed at her. But she replied upon me, Where are thine alms and thy righteous deeds? behold, thou and all thy works are known.

3 _**1** Then I being grieved did weep, and in my sorrow prayed, saying, **2**.O Lord, thou art just, and all thy works and all thy ways are mercy and truth, and thou judgest truly and justly for ever. **3**.Remember me, and look on me, punish me not for my sins and ignorances, and the sins of mg fathers, who have sinned before thee: **4**.For they obeyed not thy commandments: wherefore thou hast delivered us for a spoil, and unto captivity, and unto death, and for a proverb of reproach to all the nations among whom we are dispersed. **5**.And now thy judgments are many and true: deal with me according to my sins and my fathers': because we have not kept thy commandments, neither have walked in truth before thee. **6**.Now therefore deal with me as seemeth best unto thee, and command my spirit to be taken from me, that I may be dissolved, and become earth: for it is profitable for me to die rather than to live, because I have heard false reproaches, and have much sorrow: command therefore that I may now be delivered out of this distress, and go into the everlasting place: turn not thy face away from me. **7**.It came to pass the same day, that in Ecbatane a city of Media Sara the daughter of Raguel was also reproached by her father's maids; **8**.Because that she had been married to seven husbands, whom Asmodeus the evil spirit had killed, before they had lain with her. Dost thou not know, said they, that thou hast strangled thine husbands? thou hast had already seven husbands, neither wast thou named after any of them. **9**. Wherefore dost thou beat us for them? if they be dead, go thy ways after them, let us never see of thee either son or daughter. **10**. Whe she heard these things, she was very sorrowful, so that she thought to have strangled herself; and she said, I am the only daughter of my father, and if I do this, it shall be a reproach unto him, and I shall bring his old age with sorrow unto the grave. **11**. Then she prayed toward the window, and said, Blessed art thou, O Lord my God, and thine holy and glorious name is blessed and honourable for ever: let all thy works praise thee for ever. **12**. And now, O Lord, I set I mine eyes and my face toward thee, **13**. And say, Take me out of the earth, that I may hear no more the reproach. **14**. Thou knowest, Lord, that I am pure from all sin with man, **15**. And that I never polluted my name, nor the name of my father, in the land of my captivity: I am the only daughter of my father, neither hath he any child to be his heir, neither any near kinsman, nor any son of his alive, to whom I may keep myself for a wife: my seven husbands are already dead; and why should I live? but if it please not thee that I should die, command some regard to be had of me, and pity taken of me, that I hear no more reproach. **16**. So the prayers of them both were heard before the majesty of the great God. **17**. And Raphael was sent to heal them both, that is, to scale away the whiteness of Tobit's eyes, and to give Sara the daughter of Raguel for a wife to Tobias the son of Tobit; and to bind Asmodeus the evil spirit; because she belonged to Tobias by right of inheritance. The selfsame time came Tobit home, and entered into his house, and Sara the daughter of Raguel came down from her upper chamber.

4 _**1** In that day Tobit remembered the money which he had committed to Gabael in Rages of Media, **2**.And said with himself, I have wished for death; wherefore do I not call for my son Tobias that I may signify to him of the money before I die? **3**.And when he had called him, he said, My son, when I am dead, bury me; and despise not thy mother, but honour her all the days of thy life, and do that which shall please her, and grieve her not. **4**.Remember, my son, that she saw many dangers for thee, when thou wast in her womb: and when she is dead, bury her by me in one grave. **5**.My son, be mindful of the Lord our God all thy days, and let not thy will be set to sin, or to transgress his commandments: do uprightly all thy life long, and follow not the ways of unrighteousness. **6**.For if thou deal truly, thy doings shall prosperously succeed to thee, and to all them that live justly. **7**.Give alms of thy substance; and when thou givest alms, let not thine eye be envious, neither turn thy face from any poor, and the face of God shall not be turned away from thee. **8**.If thou hast abundance give alms accordingly: if thou have but a little, be not afraid to give according to that little: **9**. For thou layest up a good treasure for thyself against the day of necessity. **10**. Because that alms do deliver from death, and suffereth not to come into darkness. **11**. For alms is a good gift unto all that give it in the sight of the most High. **12**. Beware of all whoredom, my son, and chiefly take a wife of the seed of thy fathers, and take not a strange woman to wife, which is not of thy father's tribe: for we are the children of the prophets, Noe, Abraham, Isaac, and Jacob: remember, my son, that our fathers from the beginning, even that they all married wives of their own kindred, and were blessed in their children, and their seed shall inherit the land. **13**. Now therefore, my son, love thy brethren, and despise not in thy heart thy brethren, the sons and daughters of thy people, in not taking a wife of them: for in pride is destruction and much trouble, and in lewdness is decay and great want: for lewdness is the mother of famine. **14**. Let not the wages of any man, which hath wrought for thee, tarry with thee, but give him it out of hand: for if thou serve God, he will also repay thee: be circumspect my son, in all things thou doest, and be wise in all thy conversation. **15**. Do that to no man which thou hatest: drink not wine to make thee drunken: neither let drunkenness go with thee in thy journey. **16**. Give of thy bread to the hungry, and of thy garments to them that are naked; and according to thine abundance give alms: and let not thine eye be envious, when thou givest alms. **17**. Pour out thy bread on the burial of the just, but give nothing to the wicked. **18**. Ask counsel of all that are wise, and despise not any counsel that is profitable. **19**. Bless the Lord thy God alway, and desire of him that thy ways may be directed, and that all thy paths and counsels may prosper: for every nation hath not counsel; but the Lord himself giveth all good things, and he humbleth whom he will, as he will; now therefore, my son, remember my commandments, neither let them be put out of thy mind. **20**. And now I signify this to they that I committed ten talents to Gabael the son of Gabrias at Rages in Media. **21**. And fear not, my son, that we are made poor: for thou hast much wealth, if thou fear God, and depart from all sin, and do that which is pleasing in his sight.

5 _1 Tobias then answered and said, Father, I will do all things which thou hast commanded me: **2**.But how can I receive the money, seeing I know him not? **3**.Then he gave him the handwriting, and said unto him, Seek thee a man which may go with thee, whiles I yet live, and I will give him wages: and go and receive the money. **4**.Therefore when he went to seek a man, he found Raphael that was an angel. **5**.But he knew not; and he said unto him, Canst thou go with me to Rages? and knowest thou those places well? **6**.To whom the angel said, I will go with thee, and I know the way well: for I have lodged with our brother Gabael. **7**.Then Tobias said unto him, Tarry for me, till I tell my father. **8**.Then he said unto him, Go and tarry not. So he went in and said to his father, Behold, I have found one which will go with me. Then he said, Call him unto me, that I may know of what tribe he is, and whether he be a trusty man to go with thee. **9**. So he called him, and he came in, and they saluted one another. **10**. Then Tobit said unto him, Brother, shew me of what tribe and family thou art. **11**. To whom he said, Dost thou seek for a tribe or family, or an hired man to go with thy son? Then Tobit said unto him, I would know, brother, thy kindred and name. **12**. Then he said, I am Azarias, the son of Ananias the great, and of thy brethren. **13**. Then Tobit said, Thou art welcome, brother; be not now angry with me, because I have enquired to know thy tribe and thy family; for thou art my brother, of an honest and good stock: for I know Ananias and Jonathas, sons of that great Samaias, as we went together to Jerusalem to worship, and offered the firstborn, and the tenths of the fruits; and they were not seduced with the error of our brethren: my brother, thou art of a good stock. **14**. But tell me, what wages shall I give thee? wilt thou a drachm a day, and things necessary, as to mine own son? **15**. Yea, moreover, if ye return safe, I will add something to thy wages. **16**. So they were well pleased. Then said he to Tobias, Prepare thyself for the journey, and God send you a good journey. And when his son had prepared all things far the journey, his father said, Go thou with this man, and God, which dwelleth in heaven, prosper your journey, and the angel of God keep you company. So they went forth both, and the young man's dog with them. **17**. But Anna his mother wept, and said to Tobit, Why hast thou sent away our son? is he not the staff of our hand, in going in and out before us? **18**. Be not greedy to add money to money: but let it be as refuse in respect of our child. **19**. For that which the Lord hath given us to live with doth suffice us. **20**. Then said Tobit to her, Take no care, my sister; he shall return in safety, and thine eyes shall see him. **21**. For the good angel will keep him company, and his journey shall be prosperous, and he shall return safe. **22**. Then she made an end of weeping.

6 _1 And as they went on their journey, they came in the evening to the river Tigris, and they lodged there.

2.And when the young man went down to wash himself, a fish leaped out of the river, and would have devoured him. **3**.Then the angel said unto him, Take the fish. And the young man laid hold of the fish, and drew it to land. **4**.To whom the angel said, Open the fish, and take the heart and the liver and the gall, and put them up safely. **5**.So the young man did as the angel commanded him; and when they had roasted the fish, they did eat it: then they both went on their way, till they drew near to Ecbatane. **6**.Then the young man said to the angel, Brother Azarias, to what use is the heart and the liver and the gal of the fish? **7**.And he said unto him, Touching the heart and the liver, if a devil or an evil spirit trouble any, we must make a smoke thereof before the man or the woman, and the party shall be no more vexed. **8**.As for the gall, it is good to anoint a man that hath whiteness in his eyes, and he shall be healed. **9**. And when they were come near to Rages, **10**. The angel said to the young man, Brother, to day we shall lodge with Raguel, who is thy cousin; he also hath one only daughter, named Sara; I will speak for her, that she may be given thee for a wife. **11**. For to thee doth the right of her appertain, seeing thou only art of her kindred. **12**. And the maid is fair and wise: now therefore hear me, and I will speak to her father; and when we return from Rages we will celebrate the marriage: for I know that Raguel cannot marry her to another according to the law of Moses, but he shall be guilty of death, because the right of inheritance doth rather appertain to thee than to any other. **13**. Then the young man answered the angel, I have heard, brother Azarias that this maid hath been given to seven men, who all died in the marriage chamber. **14**. And now I am the only son of my father, and I am afraid, lest if I go in unto her, I die, as the other before: for a wicked spirit loveth her, which hurteth no body, but those which come unto her; wherefore I also fear lest I die, and bring my father's and my mother's life because of me to the grave with sorrow: for they have no other son to bury them. **15**. Then the angel said unto him, Dost thou not remember the precepts which thy father gave thee, that thou shouldest marry a wife of thine own kindred? wherefore hear me, O my brother; for she shall be given thee to wife; and make thou no reckoning of the evil spirit; for this same night shall she be given thee in marriage. **16**. And when thou shalt come into the marriage chamber, thou shalt take the ashes of perfume, and shalt lay upon them some of the heart and liver of the fish, and shalt make a smoke with it: **17**. And the devil shall smell it, and flee away, and never come again any more: but when thou shalt come to her, rise up both of you, and pray to God which is merciful, who will have pity on you, and save you: fear not, for she is appointed unto thee from the beginning; and thou shalt preserve her, and she shall go with thee. Moreover I suppose that she shall bear thee children. Now when Tobias had heard these things, he loved her, and his heart was effectually joined to her.

7 _1 And when they were come to Ecbatane, they cameto the house of Raguel, and Sara met them: and after they had saluted one another, she brought them into the house. **2**.Then said Raguel to Edna his wife, How like is this young man to Tobit my cousin! **3**.And Raguel asked them, From whence are ye, brethren? To whom they said, We are of the sons of Nephthalim, which are captives in Nineve. **4**.Then he said to them, Do ye know Tobit our kinsman? And they said, We know him. Then said he, Is he in good health? **5**.And they said, He is both alive, and in good health: and Tobias said, He is my father. **6**.Then Raguel leaped up, and kissed him, and wept, **7**.And blessed him, and said unto him, Thou art the son of an honest and good man. But when he had heard that Tobit was blind, he was sorrowful, and wept. **8**.And likewise Edna his wife and Sara his daughter wept. Moreover they entertained them cheerfully; and after that they had killed a ram of the flock, they set store of meat on the table. Then said Tobias to Raphael, Brother Azarias, speak of those things of which thou didst talk in the way, and let this business be dispatched. **9**. So he communicated the matter with Raguel: and Raguel said to Tobias, Eat and drink, and make merry: **10**. For it is meet that thou shouldest marry my daughter: nevertheless I will declare unto thee the truth. **11**. I have given my daughter in marriage te seven men, who died that night they came in unto her: nevertheless for the present be merry. But Tobias said, I will eat nothing here, till we agree and swear one to another. **12**. Raguel said, Then take her from henceforth according to the manner, for thou art her cousin, and she is thine, and the merciful God give you good success in all things. **13**. Then he called his daughter Sara, and she came to her father, and he took her by the hand, and gave her to be wife to Tobias, saying, Behold, take her after the law of Moses, and lead her away to thy father. And he blessed them; **14**. And called Edna his wife, and took paper, and did write an instrument of covenants, and sealed it. **15**. Then they began to eat. **16**. After Raguel called his wife Edna, and said unto her, Sister, prepare another chamber, and bring her in thither. **17**. Which when she had done as he had bidden her, she brought her thither: and she wept, and she received the tears of her daughter, and said unto her, **18**. Be of good comfort, my daughter; the Lord of heaven and earth give thee joy for this thy sorrow: be of good comfort, my daughter.

8 _1 And when they had supped, they brought Tobias in unto her. **2**.And as he went, he remembered the words of Raphael, and took the ashes of the perfumes, and put the heart and the liver of the fish thereupon, and made a smoke therewith. **3**.The which smell when the evil spirit had smelled, he fled into the utmost parts of Egypt, and the angel bound him. **4**.And after that they were both shut in together, Tobias rose out of the bed, and said, Sister, arise, and let us pray that God would have pity on us. **5**.Then began Tobias to say, Blessed art thou, O God of our fathers, and blessed is thy holy and glorious name for ever; let the heavens bless thee, and all thy creatures. **6**.Thou madest Adam, and gavest him Eve his wife for an helper and stay: of them came mankind: thou hast said, It is not good that man should be alone; let us make unto him an aid like unto himself. **7**.And now, O Lord, I take not this my sister for lush but uprightly: therefore mercifully ordain that we may become aged together. **8**.And she said with him, Amen. **9**. So they slept both that night. And Raguel arose, and went and made a grave, **10**. Saying, I fear lest he also be dead. **11**. But when Raguel was come into his house, **12**. He said unto his wife Edna. Send one of the maids, and let her see whether he be alive: if he be not, that we may bury him, and no man know it. **13**. So the maid opened the door, and went in, and found them both asleep, **14**. And came forth, and told them that he was alive. **15**. Then Raguel praised God, and said, O God, thou art worthy to be praised with all pure and holy praise; therefore let thy saints praise thee with all thy creatures; and let all thine angels and thine elect praise thee for ever. **16**. Thou art to be praised, for thou hast made me joyful; and that is not come to me which I suspected; but thou hast dealt with us according to thy great mercy. **17**. Thou art to be praised because thou hast had mercy of two that were the only begotten children of their fathers: grant them mercy, O Lord, and finish their life in health with joy and mercy. **18**. Then Raguel bade his servants to fill the grave. **19**. And he kept the wedding feast fourteen days. **20**. For before the days of the marriage were finished, Raguel had said unto him by an oath, that he should not depart till the fourteen days of the marriage were expired; **21**. And then he should take the half of his goods, and go in safety to his father; and should have the rest when I and my wife be dead.

9

_**1** Then Tobias called Raphael, and said unto him, **2**.Brother Azarias, take with thee a servant, and two camels, and go to Rages of Media to Gabael, and bring me the money, and bring him to the wedding. **3**.For Raguel hath sworn that I shall not depart. **4**.But my father counteth the days; and if I tarry long, he will be very sorry. **5**.So Raphael went out, and lodged with Gabael, and gave him the handwriting: who brought forth bags which were sealed up, and gave them to him. **6**.And early in the morning they went forth both together, and came to the wedding: and Tobias blessed his wife.

10

_**1** Now Tobit his father counted every day: and when the days of the journey were expired, and they came not, **2**.Then Tobit said, Are they detained? or is Gabael dead, and there is no man to give him the money? **3**.Therefore he was very sorry. **4**.Then his wife said unto him, My son is dead, seeing he stayeth long; and she began to wail him, and said, **5**.Now I care for nothing, my son, since I have let thee go, the light of mine eyes. **6**.To whom Tobit said, Hold thy peace, take no care, for he is safe. **7**.But she said, Hold thy peace, and deceive me not; my son is dead. And she went out every day into the way which they went, and did eat no meat on the daytime, and ceased not whole nights to bewail her son Tobias, until the fourteen days of the wedding were expired, which Raguel had sworn that he should spend there. Then Tobias said to Raguel, Let me go, for my father and my mother look no more to see me. **8**.But his father in law said unto him, Tarry with me, and I will send to thy father, and they shall declare unto him how things go with thee. **9**. But Tobias said, No; but let me go to my father. **10**. Then Raguel arose, and gave him Sara his wife, and half his goods, servants, and cattle, and money: **11**. And he blessed them, and sent them away, saying, The God of heaven give you a prosperous journey, my children. **12**. And he said to his daughter, Honour thy father and thy mother in law, which are now thy parents, that I may hear good report of thee. And he kissed her. Edna also said to Tobias, The Lord of heaven restore thee, my dear brother, and grant that I may see thy children of my daughter Sara before I die, that I may rejoice before the Lord: behold, I commit my daughter unto thee of special trust; where are do not entreat her evil.

11

_**1** After these things Tobias went his way, praising God that he had given him a prosperous journey, and blessed Raguel and Edna his wife, and went on his way till they drew near unto Nineve. **2**.Then Raphael said to Tobias, Thou knowest, brother, how thou didst leave thy father: **3**.Let us haste before thy wife, and prepare the house. **4**.And take in thine hand the gall of the fish. So they went their way, and the dog went after them. **5**.Now Anna sat looking about toward the way for her son. **6**.And when she espied him coming, she said to his father, Behold, thy son cometh, and the man that went with him. **7**.Then said Raphael, I know, Tobias, that thy father will open his eyes. **8**.Therefore anoint thou his eyes with the gall, and being pricked therewith, he shall rub, and the whiteness shall fall away, and he shall see thee. **9**. Then Anna ran forth, and fell upon the neck of her son, and said unto him, Seeing I have seen thee, my son, from henceforth I am content to die. And they wept both. **10**. Tobit also went forth toward the door, and stumbled: but his son ran unto him, **11**. And took hold of his father: and he strake of the gall on his fathers' eyes, saying, Be of good hope, my father. **12**. And when his eyes began to smart, he rubbed them; **13**. And the whiteness pilled away from the corners of his eyes: and when he saw his son, he fell upon his neck. **14**. And he wept, and said, Blessed art thou, O God, and blessed is thy name for ever; and blessed are all thine holy angels: **15**. For thou hast scourged, and hast taken pity on me: for, behold, I see my son Tobias. And his son went in rejoicing, and told his father the great things that had happened to him in Media. **16**. Then Tobit went out to meet his daughter in law at the gate of Nineve, rejoicing and praising God: and they which saw him go marvelled, because he had received his sight. **17**. But Tobias gave thanks before them, because God had mercy on him. And when he came near to Sara his daughter in law, he blessed her, saying, Thou art welcome, daughter: God be blessed, which hath brought thee unto us, and blessed be thy father and thy mother. And there was joy among all his brethren which were at Nineve. **18**. And Achiacharus, and Nasbas his brother's son, came: **19**. And Tobias' wedding was kept seven days with great joy.

12

_**1** Then Tobit called his son Tobias, and said untohim, My son, see that the man have his wages, which went with thee, and thou must give him more. **2**.And Tobias said unto him, O father, it is no harm to me to give him half of those things which I have brought: **3**.For he hath brought me again to thee in safety, and made whole my wife, and brought me the money, and likewise healed thee. **4**.Then the old man said, It is due unto him. **5**.So he called the angel, and he said unto him, Take half of all that ye have brought and go away in safety. **6**.Then he took them both apart, and said unto them, Bless God, praise him, and magnify him, and praise him for the things which he hath done unto you in the sight of all that live. It is good to praise God, and exalt his name, and honourably to shew forth the works of God; therefore be not slack to praise him. **7**.It is good to keep close the secret of a king, but it is honourable to reveal the works of God. Do that which is good, and no evil shall touch you. **8**.Prayer is good with fasting and alms and righteousness. A little with righteousness is better than much with unrighteousness. It is better to give alms than to lay up gold: **9**. For alms doth deliver from death, and shall purge away all sin. Those that exercise alms and righteousness shall be filled with life: **10**. But they that sin are enemies to their own life. **11**. Surely I will keep close nothing from you. For I said, It was good to keep close the secret of a king, but that it was honourable to reveal the works of God. **12**. Now therefore, when thou didst pray, and Sara thy daughter in law, I did bring the remembrance of your prayers before the Holy One: and when thou didst bury the dead, I was with thee likewise. **13**. And when thou didst not delay to rise up, and leave thy dinner, to go and cover the dead, thy good deed was not hid from me: but I was with thee. **14**. And now God hath sent me to heal thee and Sara thy daughter in law. **15**. I am Raphael, one of the seven holy angels, which present the prayers of the saints, and which go in and out before the glory of the Holy One. **16**. Then they were both troubled, and fell upon their faces: for they feared. **17**. But he said unto them, Fear not, for it shall go well with you; praise God therefore. **18**. For not of any favour of mine, but by the will of our God I came; wherefore praise him for ever. **19**. All these days I did appear unto you; but I did neither eat nor drink, but ye did see a vision. **20**. Now therefore give God thanks: for I go up to him that sent me; but write all things which are done in a book. **21**. And when they arose, they saw him no more. **22**. Then they confessed the great and wonderful works of God, and how the angel of the Lord had appeared unto them.

13

_**1** Then Tobit wrote a prayer of rejoicing, and said, Blessed be God that liveth for ever, and blessed be his kingdom. **2**.For he doth scourge, and hath mercy: he leadeth down to hell, and bringeth up again: neither is there any that can avoid his hand. **3**.Confess him before the Gentiles, ye children of Israel: for he hath scattered us among them. **4**.There declare his greatness, and extol him before all the living: for he is our Lord, and he is the God our Father for ever. **5**.And he will scourge us for our iniquities, and will have mercy again, and will gather us out of all nations, among whom he hath scattered us. **6**. If ye turn to him with your whole heart, and with your whole mind, and deal uprightly before him, then will he turn unto you, and will not hide his face from you. Therefore see what he will do with you, and confess him with your whole mouth, and praise the Lord of might, and extol the everlasting King. In the land of my captivity do I praise him, and declare his might and majesty to a sinful nation. O ye sinners, turn and do justice before him: who can tell if he will accept you, and have mercy on you? **7**.I will extol my God, and my soul shall praise the King of heaven, and shall rejoice in his greatness. **8**.Let all men speak, and let all praise him for his righteousness. **9**. O Jerusalem, the holy city, he will scourge thee for thy children's works, and will have mercy again on the sons of the righteous. **10**. Give praise to the Lord, for he is good: and praise the everlasting King, that his tabernacle may be builded in thee again with joy, and let him make joyful there in thee those that are captives, and love in thee for ever those that are miserable. **11**. Many nations shall come from far to the name of the Lord God with gifts in their hands, even gifts to the King of heaven; all generations shall praise thee with great joy. **12**. Cursed are all they which hate thee, and blessed shall all be which love thee for ever. **13**. Rejoice and be glad for the children of the just: for they shall be gathered together, and shall bless the Lord of the just. **14**. O blessed are they which love thee, for they shall rejoice in thy peace: blessed are they which have been sorrowful for all thy scourges; for they shall rejoice for thee, when they have seen all thy glory, and shall be glad for ever. **15**. Let my soul bless God the great King. **16**. For Jerusalem shall be built up with sapphires and emeralds, and precious stone: thy walls and towers and battlements with pure gold. **17**. And the streets of Jerusalem shall be paved with beryl and carbuncle and stones of Ophir. **18**. And all her streets shall say, Alleluia; and they shall praise him, saying, Blessed be God, which hath extolled it for ever.

14 _1 So Tobit made an end of praising God. 2.And he was eight
and fifty years old when he lost his sight, which was restored to him
after eight years: and he gave alms, and he increased in the fear of the Lord God,
and praised him. 3.And when he was very aged he called his son, and the sons
of his son, and said to him, My son, take thy children; for, behold, I am aged, and
am ready to depart out of this life. 4.Go into Media my son, for I surely believe
those things which Jonas the prophet spake of Nineve, that it shall be overthrown;
and that for a time peace shall rather be in Media; and that our brethren shall lie
scattered in the earth from that good land: and Jerusalem shall be desolate, and
the house of God in it shall be burned, and shall be desolate for a time; 5.And
that again God will have mercy on them, and bring them again into the land,
where they shall build a temple, but not like to the first, until the time of that
age be fulfilled; and afterward they shall return from all places of their captivity,
and build up Jerusalem gloriously, and the house of God shall be built in it for
ever with a glorious building, as the prophets have spoken thereof. 6.And all
nations shall turn, and fear the Lord God truly, and shall bury their idols. 7.So
shall all nations praise the Lord, and his people shall confess God, and the Lord
shall exalt his people; and all those which love the Lord God in truth and justice
shall rejoice, shewing mercy to our brethren. 8.And now, my son, depart out of
Nineve, because that those things which the prophet Jonas spake shall surely come
to pass. 9. But keep thou the law and the commandments, and shew thyself
merciful and just, that it may go well with thee. 10. And bury me decently,
and thy mother with me; but tarry no longer at Nineve. Remember, my son, how
Aman handled Achiacharus that brought him up, how out of light he brought
him into darkness, and how he rewarded him again: yet Achiacharus was saved,
but the other had his reward: for he went down into darkness. Manasses gave
alms, and escaped the snares of death which they had set for him: but Aman fell
into the snare, and perished. 11. Wherefore now, my son, consider what alms
doeth, and how righteousness doth deliver. When he had said these things, he
gave up the ghost in the bed, being an hundred and eight and fifty years old; and
he buried him honourably. 12. And when Anna his mother was dead, he buried
her with his father. But Tobias departed with his wife and children to Ecbatane to
Raguel his father in law, 13. Where he became old with honour, and he buried
his father and mother in law honourably, and he inherited their substance, and
his father Tobit's. 14. And he died at Ecbatane in Media, being an hundred and
seven and twenty years old. 15. But before he died he heard of the destruction
of Nineve, which was taken by Nabuchodonosor and Assuerus: and before his
death he rejoiced over Nineve.

APOCRYPHA BOOK OF JUDITH

The Book of Judith

1 _1 In the twelfth year of the reign of Nabuchodonosor, who reigned in
Nineve, the great city; in the days of Arphaxad, which reigned over the
Medes in Ecbatane, 2 And built in Ecbatane walls round about of stones hewn
three cubits broad and six cubits long, and made the height of the wall seventy
cubits, and the breadth thereof fifty cubits: 3 And set the towers thereof upon
the gates of it an hundred cubits high, and the breadth thereof in the founda-
tion threescore cubits: 4 And he made the gates thereof, even gates that were
raised to the height of seventy cubits, and the breadth of them was forty cubits,
for the going forth of his mighty armies, and for the setting in array of his fo-
otmen: 5 Even in those days king Nabuchodonosor made war with king Ar-
phaxad in the great plain, which is the plain in the borders of Ragau. 6 And
there came unto him all they that dwelt in the hill country, and all that dwelt
by Euphrates, and Tigris and Hydaspes, and the plain of Arioch the king of the
Elymeans, and very many nations of the sons of Chelod, assembled themselves
to the battle. 7 Then Nabuchodonosor king of the Assyrians sent unto all that
dwelt in Persia, and to all that dwelt westward, and to those that dwelt in Cilicia,
and Damascus, and Libanus, and Antilibanus, and to all that dwelt upon the sea
coast, 8 And to those among the nations that were of Carmel, and Galaad, and
the higher Galilee, and the great plain of Esdrelom, 9 And to all that were in
Samaria and the cities thereof, and beyond Jordan unto Jerusalem, and Betane,
and Chelus, and Kades, and the river of Egypt, and Taphnes, and Ramesse, and
all the land of Gesem, 10 Until ye come beyond Tanis and Memphis, and to all
the inhabitants of Egypt, until ye come to the borders of Ethiopia. 11 But all
the inhabitants of the land made light of the commandment of Nabuchodonosor
king of the Assyrians, neither went they with him to the battle; for they were not
afraid of him: yea, he was before them as one man, and they sent away his ambas-
sadors from them without effect, and with disgrace. 12 Therefore Nabuchodo-
nosor was very angry with all this country, and sware by his throne and kingdom,
that he would surely be avenged upon all those coasts of Cilicia, and Damascus,
and Syria, and that he would slay with the sword all the inhabitants of the land
of Moab, and the children of Ammon, and all Judea, and all that were in Egypt,
till ye come to the borders of the two seas. 13 Then he marched in battle array
with his power against king Arphaxad in the seventeenth year, and he prevailed in
his battle: for he overthrew all the power of Arphaxad, and all his horsemen, and
all his chariots, 14 And became lord of his cities, and came unto Ecbatane, and
took the towers, and spoiled the streets thereof, and turned the beauty thereof into
shame. 15 He took also Arphaxad in the mountains of Ragau, and smote him
through with his darts, and destroyed him utterly that day. 16 So he returned
afterward to Nineve, both he and all his company of sundry nations being a very
great multitude of men of war, and there he took his ease, and banqueted, both
he and his army, an hundred and twenty days.

2 _1 And in the eighteenth year, the two and twentieth day of the first
month, there was talk in the house of Nabuchodonosor king of the As-
syrians that he should, as he said, avenge himself on all the earth. 2 So he
called unto him all his officers, and all his nobles, and communicated with them
his secret counsel, and concluded the afflicting of the whole earth out of his own
mouth. 3 Then they decreed to destroy all flesh, that did not obey the com-
mandment of his mouth. 4 And when he had ended his counsel, Nabuchodo-
nosor king of the Assyrians called Holofernes the chief captain of his army, which
was next unto him, and said unto him. 5 Thus saith the great king, the lord of
the whole earth, Behold, thou shalt go forth from my presence, and take with
thee men that trust in their own strength, of footmen an hundred and twenty
thousand; and the number of horses with their riders twelve thousand. 6 And
thou shalt go against all the west country, because they disobeyed my command-
ment. 7 And thou shalt declare unto that they prepare for me earth and water:
for I will go forth in my wrath against them and will cover the whole face of the
earth with the feet of mine army, and I will give them for a spoil unto them: 8 So
that their slain shall fill their valleys and brooks and the river shall be filled with
their dead, till it overflow: 9 And I will lead them captives to the utmost parts
of all the earth. 10 Thou therefore shalt go forth. and take beforehand for me
all their coasts: and if they will yield themselves unto thee, thou shalt reserve them
for me till the day of their punishment. 11 But concerning them that rebel, let
not thine eye spare them; but put them to the slaughter, and spoil them whereso-
ever thou goest. 12 For as I live, and by the power of my kingdom, whatsoever
I have spoken, that will I do by mine hand. 13 And take thou heed that thou
transgress none of the commandments of thy lord, but accomplish them fully, as
I have commanded thee, and defer not to do them. 14 Then Holofernes went
forth from the presence of his lord, and called ail the governors and captains, and
the officers of the army of Assur; 15 And he mustered the chosen men for the
battle, as his lord had commanded him, unto an hundred and twenty thousand,
and twelve thousand archers on horseback; 16 And he ranged them, as a great
army is ordered for the war. 17 And he took camels and asses for their car-
riages, a very great number; and sheep and oxen and goats without number for
their provision: 18 And plenty of victual for every man of the army, and very
much gold and silver out of the king's house. 19 Then he went forth and all
his power to go before king Nabuchodonosor in the voyage, and to cover all the
face of the earth westward with their chariots, and horsemen, and their chosen
footmen. 20 A great number also sundry countries came with them like locusts,
and like the sand of the earth: for the multitude was without number. 21 And
they went forth of Nineve three days' journey toward the plain of Bectileth,
and pitched from Bectileth near the mountain which is at the left hand of the
upper Cilicia. 22 Then he took all his army, his footmen, and horsemen and
chariots, and went from thence into the hill country; 23 And destroyed Phud
and Lud, and spoiled all the children of Rasses, and the children of Israel, which
were toward the wilderness at the south of the land of the Chellians. 24 Then he
went over Euphrates, and went through Mesopotamia, and destroyed all the high
cities that were upon the river Arbonai, till ye come to the sea. 25 And he took
the borders of Cilicia, and killed all that resisted him, and came to the borders of

Japheth, which were toward the south, over against Arabia. **26** He compassed also all the children of Madian, and burned up their tabernacles, and spoiled their sheepcotes. **27** Then he went down into the plain of Damascus in the time of wheat harvest, and burnt up all their fields, and destroyed their flocks and herds, also he spoiled their cities, and utterly wasted their countries, and smote all their young men with the edge of the sword. **28** Therefore the fear and dread of him fell upon all the inhabitants of the sea coasts, which were in Sidon and Tyrus, and them that dwelt in Sur and Ocina, and all that dwelt in Jemnaan; and they that dwelt in Azotus and Ascalon feared him greatly.

3 _**1** So they sent ambassadors unto him to treat of peace, saying, **2** Behold, we the servants of Nabuchodonosor the great king lie before thee; use us as shall be good in thy sight. **3** Behold, our houses, and all our places, and all our fields of wheat, and flocks, and herds, and all the lodges of our tents lie before thy face; use them as it pleaseth thee. **4** Behold, even our cities and the inhabitants thereof are thy servants; come and deal with them as seemeth good unto thee. **5** So the men came to Holofernes, and declared unto him after this manner. **6** Then came he down toward the sea coast, both he and his army, and set garrisons in the high cities, and took out of them chosen men for aid. **7** So they and all the country round about received them with garlands, with dances, and with timbrels. **8** Yet he did cast down their frontiers, and cut down their groves: for he had decreed to destroy all the gods of the land, that all nations should worship Nabuchodonosor only, and that all tongues and tribes should call upon him as god. **9** Also he came over against Esdraelon near unto Judea, over against the great strait of Judea. **10** And he pitched between Geba and Scythopolis, and there he tarried a whole month, that he might gather together all the carriages of his army.

4 _**1** Now the children of Israel, that dwelt in Judea, heard all that Holofernes the chief captain of Nabuchodonosor king of the Assyrians had done to the nations, and after what manner he had spoiled all their temples, and brought them to nought. **2** Therefore they were exceedingly afraid of him, and were troubled for Jerusalem, and for the temple of the Lord their God: **3** For they were newly returned from the captivity, and all the people of Judea were lately gathered together: and the vessels, and the altar, and the house, were sanctified after the profanation. **4** Therefore they sent into all the coasts of Samaria, and the villages and to Bethoron, and Belmen, and Jericho, and to Choba, and Esora, and to the valley of Salem: **5** And possessed themselves beforehand of all the tops of the high mountains, and fortified the villages that were in them, and laid up victuals for the provision of war: for their fields were of late reaped. **6** Also Joacim the high priest, which was in those days in Jerusalem, wrote to them that dwelt in Bethulia, and Betomestham, which is over against Esdraelon toward the open country, near to Dothaim, **7** Charging them to keep the passages of the hill country: for by them there was an entrance into Judea, and it was easy to stop them that would come up, because the passage was straight, for two men at the most. **8** And the children of Israel did as Joacim the high priest had commanded them, with the ancients of all the people of Israel, which dwelt at Jerusalem. **9** Then every man of Israel cried to God with great fervency, and with great vehemency did they humble their souls: **10** Both they, and their wives and their children, and their cattle, and every stranger and hireling, and their servants bought with money, put sackcloth upon their loins. **11** Thus every man and women, and the little children, and the inhabitants of Jerusalem, fell before the temple, and cast ashes upon their heads, and spread out their sackcloth before the face of the Lord: also they put sackcloth about the altar, **12** And cried to the God of Israel all with one consent earnestly, that he would not give their children for a prey, and their wives for a spoil, and the cities of their inheritance to destruction, and the sanctuary to profanation and reproach, and for the nations to rejoice at. **13** So God heard their prayers, and looked upon their afflictions: for the people fasted many days in all Judea and Jerusalem before the sanctuary of the Lord Almighty. **14** And Joacim the high priest, and all the priests that stood before the Lord, and they which ministered unto the Lord, had their loins girt with sackcloth, and offered the daily burnt offerings, with the vows and free gifts of the people, **15** And had ashes on their mitres, and cried unto the Lord with all their power, that he would look upon all the house of Israel graciously.

5 _**1** Then was it declared to Holofernes, the chief captain of the army of Assur, that the children of Israel had prepared for war, and had shut up the passages of the hill country, and had fortified all the tops of the high hills and had laid impediments in the champaign countries: **2** Wherewith he was very angry, and called all the princes of Moab, and the captains of Ammon, and all the governors of the sea coast, **3** And he said unto them, Tell me now, ye sons of Chanaan, who this people is, that dwelleth in the hill country, and what are the cities that they inhabit, and what is the multitude of their army, and wherein is their power and strength, and what king is set over them, or captain of their army; **4** And why have they determined not to come and meet me, more than all the inhabitants of the west. **5** Then said Achior, the captain of all the sons of Ammon, Let my lord now hear a word from the mouth of thy servant, and I will declare unto thee the truth concerning this people, which dwelleth near thee, and inhabiteth the hill countries: and there shall no lie come out of the mouth of thy servant. **6** This people are descended of the Chaldeans: **7** And they sojourned heretofore in Mesopotamia, because they would not follow the gods of their fathers, which were in the land of Chaldea. **8** For they left the way of their ancestors, and worshipped the God of heaven, the God whom they knew: so they cast them out from the face of their gods, and they fled into Mesopotamia, and sojourned there many days. **9** Then their God commanded them to depart from the place where they sojourned, and to go into the land of Chanaan: where they dwelt, and were increased with gold and silver, and with very much cattle. **10** But when a famine covered all the land of Chanaan, they went down into Egypt, and sojourned there, while they were nourished, and became there a great multitude, so that one could not number their nation. **11** Therefore the king of Egypt rose up against them, and dealt subtilly with them, and brought them low with labouring in brick, and made them slaves. **12** Then they cried unto their God, and he smote all the land of Egypt with incurable plagues: so the Egyptians cast them out of their sight. **13** And God dried the Red sea before them, **14** And brought them to mount Sina, and Cades- Barne, and cast forth all that dwelt in the wilderness. **15** So they dwelt in the land of the Amorites, and they destroyed by their strength all them of Esebon, and passing over Jordan they possessed all the hill country. **16** And they cast forth before them the Chanaanite, the Pherezite, the Jebusite, and the Sychemite, and all the Gergesites, and they dwelt in that country many days. **17** And whilst they sinned not before their God, they prospered, because the God that hateth iniquity was with them. **18** But when they departed from the way which he appointed them, they were destroyed in many battles very sore, and were led captives into a land that was not their's, and the temple of their God was cast to the ground, and their cities were taken by the enemies. **19** But now are they returned to their God, and are come up from the places where they were scattered, and have possessed Jerusalem, where their sanctuary is, and are seated in the hill country; for it was desolate. **20** Now therefore, my lord and governor, if there be any error against this people, and they sin against their God, let us consider that this shall be their ruin, and let us go up, and we shall overcome them. **21** But if there be no iniquity in their nation, let my lord now pass by, lest their Lord defend them, and their God be for them, and we become a reproach before all the world. **22** And when Achior had finished these sayings, all the people standing round about the tent murmured, and the chief men of Holofernes, and all that dwelt by the sea side, and in Moab, spake that he should kill him. **23** For, say they, we will not be afraid of the face of the children of Israel: for, lo, it is a people that have no strength nor power for a strong battle **24** Now therefore, lord Holofernes, we will go up, and they shall be a prey to be devoured of all thine army.

6 _**1** And when the tumult of men that were about the council was ceased, Holofernes the chief captain of the army of Assur said unto Achior and all the Moabites before all the company of other nations, **2** And who art thou, Achior, and the hirelings of Ephraim, that thou hast prophesied against us as to day, and hast said, that we should not make war with the people of Israel, because their God will defend them? and who is God but Nabuchodonosor? **3** He will send his power, and will destroy them from the face of the earth, and their God shall not deliver them: but we his servants will destroy them as one man; for they are not able to sustain the power of our horses. **4** For with them we will tread them under foot, and their mountains shall be drunken with their blood, and their fields shall be filled with their dead bodies, and their footsteps shall not be able to stand before us, for they shall utterly perish, saith king Nabuchodonosor, lord of all the earth: for he said, None of my words shall be in vain. **5** And thou, Achior, an hireling of Ammon, which hast spoken these words in the day of thine iniquity, shalt see my face no more from this day, until I take vengeance of this nation that came out of Egypt. **6** And then shall the sword of mine army, and the multitude of them that serve me, pass through thy sides, and thou shalt fall among their slain, when I return. **7** Now therefore my servants shall bring thee back into the hill country, and shall set thee in one of the cities of the passages: **8** And thou shalt not perish, till thou be destroyed with them. **9** And if thou persuade thyself in thy mind that they shall be taken, let not thy countenance fall: I have spoken it, and none of my words shall be in vain. **10** Then Holofernes commanded his servants, that waited in his tent, to take Achior, and bring him to Bethulia, and deliver him into the hands of the children of Israel. **11** So his servants took him, and brought him out of the camp into the plain, and they went from the midst of the plain into the hill country, and came unto the fountains that were under Bethulia. **12** And when the men of the city saw them, they took up their weapons, and went out of the city to the top of the hill: and every man that used a sling kept them from coming up by casting of stones against them. **13** Nevertheless having gotten privily under the hill, they bound Achior, and cast him down, and left him at the foot of the hill, and returned to their lord. **14** But the Israelites descended from their city, and came unto him, and loosed him, and brought him to Bethulia, and presented him to the governors of the city: **15** Which were in those days Ozias the son of Micha, of the tribe of Simeon, and Chabris the son of Gothoniel, and Charmis the son of Melchiel. **16** And they called together all the ancients of the city, and all their youth ran together, and their women, to the assembly, and they set Achior in the midst of all their people. Then Ozias asked him of that which was done. **17** And he answered and declared unto them the words of the council of Holofernes, and all the words that he had spoken in the midst of the princes of Assur, and whatsoever Holofernes had spoken proudly against the house of Israel. **18** Then the people fell down and worshipped God, and cried unto God. saying, **19** O Lord God of heaven, behold their pride, and pity the low estate of our nation, and look upon the face of those that are sanctified unto thee this day. **20** Then they comforted Achior, and praised him greatly. **21** And Ozias took him out of the assembly unto his house, and made a feast to the elders; and they called on the God of Israel all that night for help.

7 _**1** The next day Holofernes commanded all his army, and all his people which were come to take his part, that they should remove their camp against Bethulia, to take aforehand the ascents of the hill country, and to make war against the children of Israel. **2** Then their strong men removed their camps in that day, and the army of the men of war was an hundred and seventy thousand footmen, and twelve thousand horsemen, beside the baggage, and other men that were afoot among them, a very great multitude. **3** And they camped in the valley near unto Bethulia, by the fountain, and they spread themselves in breadth over Dothaim even to Belmaim, and in length from Bethulia unto Cynamon, which is over against Esdraelon. **4** Now the children of Israel, when they saw the multitude of them, were greatly troubled, and said every one to his neighbour, Now will these men lick up the face of the earth; for neither the high mountains, nor the valleys, nor the hills, are able to bear their weight. **5** Then every man took up his weapons of war, and when they had kindled fires upon their towers, they remained and watched all that night. **6** But in the second day Holofernes brought forth all his horsemen in the sight of the children of Israel which were in Bethulia, **7** And viewed the passages up to the city, and came to the fountains of their waters, and took them, and set garrisons of men of war over them, and he himself removed toward his people. **8** Then came unto him all the chief of the children of Esau, and all the governors of the people of Moab, and the captains of the sea coast, and said, **9** Let our lord now hear a word, that there be not an overthrow in thine army. **10** For this people of the children of Israel do not trust in their spears, but in the height of the mountains wherein they dwell, because it is not easy to come up to the tops of their mountains. **11** Now therefore, my lord, fight not against them in battle array, and there shall not so much as one man of thy people perish. **12** Remain in thy camp, and keep all the men of thine army, and let thy servants get into their hands the fountain of water, which issueth forth of the foot of the mountain: **13** For all the inhabitants of Bethulia have their water thence; so shall thirst kill them, and they shall give up their city, and we and our people shall go up to the tops of the mountains that are near, and will camp upon them, to watch that none go out of the city. **14** So they and their wives and their children shall be consumed with fire, and before the sword come against them, they shall be overthrown in the streets where they dwell. **15** Thus shalt thou render them an evil reward; because they rebelled, and met not thy person peaceably. **16** And these words pleased Holofernes and all his servants, and he appointed to do as they had spoken. **17** So the camp of the children of Ammon departed, and with them five thousand of the Assyrians, and they pitched in the valley, and took the waters, and the fountains of the waters of the children of Israel. **18** Then the children of Esau went up with the children of Ammon, and camped in the hill country over against Dothaim: and they sent some of them toward the south, and toward the east over against Ekrebel, which is near unto Chusi, that is upon the brook Mochmur; and the rest of the army of the Assyrians camped in the plain, and covered the face of the whole land; and their tents and carriages were pitched to a very great multitude. **19** Then the children of Israel cried unto the Lord their God, because their heart failed, for all their enemies had compassed them round about, and there was no way to escape out from among them. **20** Thus all the company of Assur remained about them, both their footmen, chariots, and horsemen, four and thirty days, so that all their vessels of water failed all the inhibitants of Bethulia. **21** And the cisterns were emptied, and they had not water to drink their fill for one day; for they gave them drink by measure. **22** Therefore their young children were out of heart, and their women and young men fainted for thirst, and fell down in the streets of the city, and by the passages of the gates, and there was no longer any strength in them. **23** Then all the people assembled to Ozias, and to the chief of the city, both young men, and women, and children, and cried with a loud voice, and said before all the elders, **24** God be judge between us and you: for ye have done us great injury, in that ye have not required peace of the children of Assur. **25** For now we have no helper: but God hath sold us into their hands, that we should be thrown down before them with thirst and great destruction. **26** Now therefore call them unto you, and deliver the whole city for a spoil to the people of Holofernes, and to all his army. **27** For it is better for us to be made a spoil unto them, than to die for thirst: for we will be his servants, that our souls may live, and not see the death of our infants before our eyes, nor our wives nor our children to die. **28** We take to witness against you the heaven and the earth, and our God and Lord of our fathers, which punisheth us according to our sins and the sins of our fathers, that he do not according as we have said this day. **29** Then there was great weeping with one consent in the midst of the assembly; and they cried unto the Lord God with a loud voice. **30** Then said Ozias to them, Brethren, be of good courage, let us yet endure five days, in the which space the Lord our God may turn his mercy toward us; for he will not forsake us utterly. **31** And if these days pass, and there come no help unto us, I will do according to your word. **32** And he dispersed the people, every one to their own charge; and they went unto the walls and towers of their city, and sent the women and children into their houses: and they were very low brought in the city.

8 _**1** Now at that time Judith heard thereof, which wasthe daughter of Merari, the son of Ox, the son of Joseph, the son of Ozel, the son of Elcia, the son of Ananias, the son of Gedeon, the son of Raphaim, the son of Acitho, the son of Eliu, the son of Eliab, the son of Nathanael, the son of Samael, the son of Salasadal, the son of Israel. **2** And Manasses was her husband, of her tribe and kindred, who died in the barley harvest. **3** For as he stood overseeing them that bound sheaves in the field, the heat came upon his head, and he fell on his bed, and died in the city of Bethulia: and they buried him with his fathers in the field between Dothaim and Balamo. **4** So Judith was a widow in her house three years and four months. **5** And she made her a tent upon the top of her house, and put on sackcloth upon her loins and ware her widow's apparel. **6** And she fasted all the days of her widowhood, save the eves of the sabbaths, and the sabbaths, and the eves of the new moons, and the new moons and the feasts and solemn days of the house of Israel. **7** She was also of a goodly countenance, and very beautiful to behold: and her husband Manasses had left her gold, and silver, and menservants and maidservants, and cattle, and lands; and she remained upon them. **8** And there was none that gave her an ill word; ar she feared God greatly. **9** Now when she heard the evil words of the people against the governor, that they fainted for lack of water; for Judith had heard all the words that Ozias had spoken unto them, and that he had sworn to deliver the city unto the Assyrians after five days; **10** Then she sent her waitingwoman, that had the government of all things that she had, to call Ozias and Chabris and Charmis, the ancients of the city. **11** And they came unto her, and she said unto them, Hear me now, O ye governors of the inhabitants of Bethulia: for your words that ye have spoken before the people this day are not right, touching this oath which ye made and pronounced between God and you, and have promised to deliver the city to our enemies, unless within these days the Lord turn to help you. **12** And now who are ye that have tempted God this day, and stand instead of God among the children of men? **13** And now try the Lord Almighty, but ye shall never know any thing. **14** For ye cannot find the depth of the heart of man, neither can ye perceive the things that he thinketh: then how can ye search out God, that hath made all these things, and know his mind, or comprehend his purpose? Nay, my brethren, provoke not the Lord our God to anger. **15** For if he will not help us within these five days, he hath power to defend us when he will, even every day, or to destroy us before our enemies. **16** Do not bind the counsels of the Lord our God: for God is not as man, that he may be threatened; neither is he as the son of man, that he should be wavering. **17** Therefore let us wait for salvation of him, and call upon him to help us, and he will hear our voice, if it please him. **18** For there arose none in our age, neither is there any now in these days neither tribe, nor family, nor people, nor city among us, which worship gods made with hands, as hath been aforetime. **19** For the which cause our fathers were given to the sword, and for a spoil, and had a great fall before our enemies. **20** But we know none other god, therefore we trust that he will not dispise us, nor any of our nation. **21** For if we be taken so, all Judea shall lie waste, and our sanctuary shall be spoiled; and he will require the profanation thereof at our mouth. **22** And the slaughter of our brethren, and the captivity of the country, and the desolation of our inheritance, will he turn upon our heads among the Gentiles, wheresoever we shall be in bondage; and we shall be an offence and a reproach to all them that possess us. **23** For our servitude shall not be directed to favour: but the Lord our God shall turn it to dishonour. **24** Now therefore, O brethren, let us shew an example to our brethren, because their hearts depend upon us, and the sanctuary, and the house, and the altar, rest upon us. **25** Moreover let us give thanks to the Lord our God, which trieth us, even as he did our fathers. **26** Remember what things he did to Abraham, and how he tried Isaac, and what happened to Jacob in Mesopotamia of Syria, when he kept the sheep of Laban his mother's brother. **27** For he hath not tried us in the fire, as he did them, for the examination of their hearts, neither hath he taken vengeance on us: but the Lord doth scourge them that come near unto him, to admonish them. **28** Then said Ozias to her, All that thou hast spoken hast thou spoken with a good heart, and there is none that may gainsay thy words. **29** For this is not the first day wherein thy wisdom is manifested; but from the beginning of thy days all the people have known thy understanding, because the disposition of thine heart is good. **30** But the people were very thirsty, and compelled us to do unto them as we have spoken, and to bring an oath upon ourselves, which we will not break. **31** Therefore now pray thou for us, because thou art a godly woman, and the Lord will send us rain to fill our cisterns, and we shall faint no more. **32** Then said Judith unto them, Hear me, and I will do a thing, which shall go throughout all generations to the children of our nation. **33** Ye shall stand this night in the gate, and I will go forth with my waitingwoman: and within the days that ye have promised to deliver the city to our enemies the Lord will visit Israel by mine hand. **34** But enquire not ye of mine act: for I will not declare it unto you, till the things be finished that I do. **35** Then said Ozias and the princes unto her, Go in peace, and the Lord God be before thee, to take vengeance on our enemies. **36** So they returned from the tent, and went to their wards.

9

_1 Judith fell upon her face, and put ashes upon her head, and uncovered
the sackcloth wherewith she wasclothed; and about the time that the
incense of that evening was offered in Jerusalem in the house of the Lord Judith
cried with a loud voice, and said, **2** O Lord God of my father Simeon, to
whom thou gavest a sword to take vengeance of the strangers, who loosened the
girdle of a maid to defile her, and discovered the thigh to her shame, and polluted
her virginity to her reproach; for thou saidst, It shall not be so; and yet they did
so: **3** Wherefore thou gavest their rulers to be slain, so that they dyed their bed
in blood, being deceived, and smotest the servants with their lords, and the lords
upon their thrones; **4** And hast given their wives for a prey, and their daughters
to be captives, and all their spoils to be divided among thy dear children; which
were moved with thy zeal, and abhorred the pollution of their blood, and called
upon thee for aid: O God, O my God, hear me also a widow. **5** For thou hast
wrought not only those things, but also the things which fell out before, and
which ensued after; thou hast thought upon the things which are now, and which
are to come. **6** Yea, what things thou didst determine were ready at hand, and
said, Lo, we are here: for all thy ways are prepared, and thy judgments are in thy
foreknowledge. **7** For, behold, the Assyrians are multiplied in their power; they
are exalted with horse and man; they glory in the strength of their footmen; they
trust in shield, and spear, and bow, and sling; and know not that thou art the Lord
that breakest the battles: the Lord is thy name. **8** Throw down their strength
in thy power, and bring down their force in thy wrath: for they have purposed to
defile thy sanctuary, and to pollute the tabernacle where thy glorious name resteth
and to cast down with sword the horn of thy altar. **9** Behold their pride, and
send thy wrath upon their heads: give into mine hand, which am a widow, the
power that I have conceived. **10** Smite by the deceit of my lips the servant with
the prince, and the prince with the servant: break down their stateliness by the
hand of a woman. **11** For thy power standeth not in multitude nor thy might
in strong men: for thou art a God of the afflicted, an helper of the oppressed,
an upholder of the weak, a protector of the forlorn, a saviour of them that are
without hope. **12** I pray thee, I pray thee, O God of my father, and God of the
inheritance of Israel, Lord of the heavens and earth, Creator of the waters, king
of every creature, hear thou my prayer: **13** And make my speech and deceit to
be their wound and stripe, who have purposed cruel things against thy covenant,
and thy hallowed house, and against the top of Sion, and against the house of the
possession of thy children. **14** And make every nation and tribe to acknowledge
that thou art the God of all power and might, and that there is none other that
protecteth the people of Israel but thou.

10

_1 Now after that she had ceased to cry unto the God of Israel, and
bad made an end of all these words. **2** She rose where she had fallen
down, and called her maid, and went down into the house in the which she abode
in the sabbath days, and in her feast days, **3** And pulled off the sackcloth which
she had on, and put off the garments of her widowhood, and washed her body
all over with water, and anointed herself with precious ointment, and braided the
hair of her head, and put on a tire upon it, and put on her garments of gladness,
wherewith she was clad during the life of Manasses her husband. **4** And she
took sandals upon her feet, and put about her her bracelets, and her chains, and
her rings, and her earrings, and all her ornaments, and decked herself bravely,
to allure the eyes of all men that should see her. **5** Then she gave her maid a
bottle of wine, and a cruse of oil, and filled a bag with parched corn, and lumps
of figs, and with fine bread; so she folded all these things together, and laid them
upon her. **6** Thus they went forth to the gate of the city of Bethulia, and found
standing there Ozias and the ancients of the city, Chabris and Charmis. **7** And
when they saw her, that her countenance was altered, and her apparel was chan-
ged, they wondered at her beauty very greatly, and said unto her. **8** The God,
the God of our fathers give thee favour, and accomplish thine enterprizes to the
glory of the children of Israel, and to the exaltation of Jerusalem. Then they wor-
shipped God. **9** And she said unto them, Command the gates of the city to
be opened unto me, that I may go forth to accomplish the things whereof ye
have spoken with me. So they commanded the young men to open unto her,
as she had spoken. **10** And when they had done so, Judith went out, she, and
her maid with her; and the men of the city looked after her, until she was gone
down the mountain, and till she had passed the valley, and could see her no
more. **11** Thus they went straight forth in the valley: and the first watch of
the Assyrians met her, **12** And took her, and asked her, Of what people art
thou? and whence comest thou? and whither goest thou? And she said, I am a
woman of the Hebrews, and am fled from them: for they shall be given you to be
consumed: **13** And I am coming before Holofernes the chief captain of your
army, to declare words of truth; and I will shew him a way, whereby he shall go,
and win all the hill country, without losing the body or life of any one of his
men. **14** Now when the men heard her words, and beheld her countenance,
they wondered greatly at her beauty, and said unto her, **15** Thou hast saved thy
life, in that thou hast hasted to come down to the presence of our lord: now there-
fore come to his tent, and some of us shall conduct thee, until they have delivered
thee to his hands. **16** And when thou standest before him, be not afraid in
thine heart, but shew unto him according to thy word; and he will entreat thee
well. **17** Then they chose out of them an hundred men to accompany her and
her maid; and they brought her to the tent of Holofernes. **18** Then was there a
concourse throughout all the camp: for her coming was noised among the tents,
and they came about her, as she stood without the tent of Holofernes, till they
told him of her. **19** And they wondered at her beauty, and admired the children
of Israel because of her, and every one said to his neighbour, Who would despise
this people, that have among them such women? surely it is not good that one
man of them be left who being let go might deceive the whole earth. **20** And
they that lay near Holofernes went out, and all his servants and they brought her
into the tent. **21** Now Holofernes rested upon his bed under a canopy, which
was woven with purple, and gold, and emeralds, and precious stones. **22** So
they shewed him of her; and he came out before his tent with silver lamps going
before him. **23** And when Judith was come before him and his servants they all
marvelled at the beauty of her countenance; and she fell down upon her face, and
did reverence unto him: and his servants took her up.

11

_1 Then said Holofernes unto her, Woman, be of good comfort,
fear not in thine heart: for I never hurt any that was willing to serve
Nabuchodonosor, the king of all the earth. **2** Now therefore, if thy people that
dwelleth in the mountains had not set light by me, I would not have lifted up
my spear against them: but they have done these things to themselves. **3** But
now tell me wherefore thou art fled from them, and art come unto us: for thou
art come for safeguard; be of good comfort, thou shalt live this night, and here-
after: **4** For none shall hurt thee, but entreat thee well, as they do the servants
of king Nabuchodonosor my lord. **5** Then Judith said unto him, Receive the
words of thy servant, and suffer thine handmaid to speak in thy presence, and I
will declare no lie to my lord this night. **6** And if thou wilt follow the words
of thine handmaid, God will bring the thing perfectly to pass by thee; and my
lord shall not fail of his purposes. **7** As Nabuchodonosor king of all the earth
liveth, and as his power liveth, who hath sent thee for the upholding of every
living thing: for not only men shall serve him by thee, but also the beasts of the
field, and the cattle, and the fowls of the air, shall live by thy power under Na-
buchodonosor and all his house. **8** For we have heard of thy wisdom and thy
policies, and it is reported in all the earth, that thou only art excellent in all the
kingdom, and mighty in knowledge, and wonderful in feats of war. **9** Now as
concerning the matter, which Achior did speak in thy council, we have heard his
words; for the men of Bethulia saved him, and he declared unto them all that he
had spoken unto thee. **10** Therefore, O lord and governor, respect not his word;
but lay it up in thine heart, for it is true: for our nation shall not be punished, nei-
ther can sword prevail against them, except they sin against their God. **11** And
now, that my lord be not defeated and frustrate of his purpose, even death is
now fallen upon them, and their sin hath overtaken them, wherewith they will
provoke their God to anger whensoever they shall do that which is not fit to be
done: **12** For their victuals fail them, and all their water is scant, and they have
determined to lay hands upon their cattle, and purposed to consume all those
things, that God hath forbidden them to eat by his laws: **13** And are resolved to
spend the firstfruits of the the tenths of wine and oil, which they had sanctified,
and reserved for the priests that serve in Jerusalem before the face of our God; the
which things it is not lawful for any of the people so much as to touch with their
hands. **14** For they have sent some to Jerusalem, because they also that dwell
there have done the like, to bring them a licence from the senate. **15** Now when
they shall bring them word, they will forthwith do it, and they shall be given to
thee to be destroyed the same day. **16** Wherefore I thine handmaid, knowing all
this, am fled from their presence; and God hath sent me to work things with thee,
whereat all the earth shall be astonished, and whosoever shall hear it. **17** For thy
servant is religious, and serveth the God of heaven day and night: now therefore,
my lord, I will remain with thee, and thy servant will go out by night into the val-
ley, and I will pray unto God, and he will tell me when they have committed their
sins: **18** And I will come and shew it unto thee: then thou shalt go forth with
all thine army, and there shall be none of them that shall resist thee. **19** And I
will lead thee through the midst of Judea, until thou come before Jerusalem; and
I will set thy throne in the midst thereof; and thou shalt drive them as sheep that
have no shepherd, and a dog shall not so much as open his mouth at thee: for
these things were told me according to my foreknowledge, and they were declared
unto me, and I am sent to tell thee. **20** Then her words pleased Holofernes and
all his servants; and they marvelled at her wisdom, and said, **21** There is not
such a woman from one end of the earth to the other, both for beauty of face,
and wisdom of words. **22** Likewise Holofernes said unto her. God hath done
well to send thee before the people, that strength might be in our hands and de-
struction upon them that lightly regard my lord. **23** And now thou art both
beautiful in thy countenance, and witty in thy words: surely if thou do as thou
hast spoken thy God shall be my God, and thou shalt dwell in the house of king
Nabuchodonosor, and shalt be renowned through the whole earth.

12

_1 Then he commanded to bring her in where hisplate was set; and
bade that they should prepare for her of his own meats, and that she
should drink of his own wine. **2** And Judith said, I will not eat thereof, lest
there be an offence: but provision shall be made for me of the things that I have
brought. **3** Then Holofernes said unto her, If thy provision should fail, how
should we give thee the like? for there be none with us of thy nation. **4** Then
said Judith unto him As thy soul liveth, my lord, thine handmaid shall not spend
those things that I have, before the Lord work by mine hand the things that he

hath determined. **5** Then the servants of Holofernes brought her into the tent, and she slept till midnight, and she arose when it was toward the morning watch, **6** And sent to Holofernes, saying, Let my lord now command that thine handmaid may go forth unto prayer. **7** Then Holofernes commanded his guard that they should not stay her: thus she abode in the camp three days, and went out in the night into the valley of Bethulia, and washed herself in a fountain of water by the camp. **8** And when she came out, she besought the Lord God of Israel to direct her way to the raising up of the children of her people. **9** So she came in clean, and remained in the tent, until she did eat her meat at evening. **10** And in the fourth day Holofernes made a feast to his own servants only, and called none of the officers to the banquet. **11** Then said he to Bagoas the eunuch, who had charge over all that he had, Go now, and persuade this Hebrew woman which is with thee, that she come unto us, and eat and drink with us. **12** For, lo, it will be a shame for our person, if we shall let such a woman go, not having had her company; for if we draw her not unto us, she will laugh us to scorn. **13** Then went Bagoas from the presence of Holofernes, and came to her, and he said, Let not this fair damsel fear to come to my lord, and to be honoured in his presence, and drink wine, and be merry with us and be made this day as one of the daughters of the Assyrians, which serve in the house of Nabuchodonosor. **14** Then said Judith unto him, Who am I now, that I should gainsay my lord? surely whatsoever pleaseth him I will do speedily, and it shall be my joy unto the day of my death. **15** So she arose, and decked herself with her apparel and all her woman's attire, and her maid went and laid soft skins on the ground for her over against Holofernes, which she had received of Bagoas far her daily use, that she might sit and eat upon them. **16** Now when Judith came in and sat down, Holofernes his heart was ravished with her, and his mind was moved, and he desired greatly her company; for he waited a time to deceive her, from the day that he had seen her. **17** Then said Holofernes unto her, Drink now, and be merry with us. **18** So Judith said, I will drink now, my lord, because my life is magnified in me this day more than all the days since I was born. **19** Then she took and ate and drank before him what her maid had prepared. **20** And Holofernes took great delight in her, and drank more wine than he had drunk at any time in one day since he was born.

13

_**1** Now when the evening was come, his servants made haste to depart, and Bagoas shut his tent without, and dismissed the waiters from the presence of his lord; and they went to their beds: for they were all weary, because the feast had been long. **2** And Judith was left along in the tent, and Holofernes lying along upon his bed: for he was filled with wine. **3** Now Judith had commanded her maid to stand without her bedchamber, and to wait for her. coming forth, as she did daily: for she said she would go forth to her prayers, and she spake to Bagoas according to the same purpose. **4** So all went forth and none was left in the bedchamber, neither little nor great. Then Judith, standing by his bed, said in her heart, O Lord God of all power, look at this present upon the works of mine hands for the exaltation of Jerusalem. **5** For now is the time to help thine inheritance, and to execute thine enterprizes to the destruction of the enemies which are risen against us. **6** Then she came to the pillar of the bed, which was at Holofernes' head, and took down his fauchion from thence, **7** And approached to his bed, and took hold of the hair of his head, and said, Strengthen me, O Lord God of Israel, this day. **8** And she smote twice upon his neck with all her might, and she took away his head from him. **9** And tumbled his body down from the bed, and pulled down the canopy from the pillars; and anon after she went forth, and gave Holofernes his head to her maid; **10** And she put it in her bag of meat: so they twain went together according to their custom unto prayer: and when they passed the camp, they compassed the valley, and went up the mountain of Bethulia, and came to the gates thereof. **11** Then said Judith afar off, to the watchmen at the gate, Open, open now the gate: God, even our God, is with us, to shew his power yet in Jerusalem, and his forces against the enemy, as he hath even done this day. **12** Now when the men of her city heard her voice, they made haste to go down to the gate of their city, and they called the elders of the city. **13** And then they ran all together, both small and great, for it was strange unto them that she was come: so they opened the gate, and received them, and made a fire for a light, and stood round about them. **14** Then she said to them with a loud voice, Praise, praise God, praise God, I say, for he hath not taken away his mercy from the house of Israel, but hath destroyed our enemies by mine hands this night. **15** So she took the head out of the bag, and shewed it, and said unto them, behold the head of Holofernes, the chief captain of the army of Assur, and behold the canopy, wherein he did lie in his drunkenness; and the Lord hath smitten him by the hand of a woman. **16** As the Lord liveth, who hath kept me in my way that I went, my countenance hath deceived him to his destruction, and yet hath he not committed sin with me, to defile and shame me. **17** Then all the people were wonderfully astonished, and bowed themselves and worshipped God, and said with one accord, Blessed be thou, O our God, which hast this day brought to nought the enemies of thy people. **18** Then said Ozias unto her, O daughter, blessed art thou of the most high God above all the women upon the earth; and blessed be the Lord God, which hath created the heavens and the earth, which hath directed thee to the cutting off of the head of the chief of our enemies. **19** For this thy confidence shall not depart from the heart of men, which remember the power of God for ever. **20** And God turn these things to thee for a perpetual praise, to visit thee in good things because thou hast not spared thy life for the affliction of our nation, but hast revenged our ruin, walking a straight way before our God. And all the people said; So be it, so be it.

14

_**1** Then said Judith unto them, Hear me now, my brethren, and take this head, and hang it upon the highest place of your walls. **2** And so soon as the morning shall appear, and the sun shall come forth upon the earth, take ye every one his weapons, and go forth every valiant man out of the city, and set ye a captain over them, as though ye would go down into the field toward the watch of the Assyrians; but go not down. **3** Then they shall take their armour, and shall go into their camp, and raise up the captains of the army of Assur, and shall run to the tent of Holofernes, but shall not find him: then fear shall fall upon them, and they shall flee before your face. **4** So ye, and all that inhabit the coast of Israel, shall pursue them, and overthrow them as they go. **5** But before ye do these things, call me Achior the Ammonite, that he may see and know him that despised the house of Israel, and that sent him to us as it were to his death. **6** Then they called Achior out of the house of Ozias; and when he was come, and saw the head of Holofernes in a man's hand in the assembly of the people, he fell down on his face, and his spirit failed. **7** But when they had recovered him, he fell at Judith's feet, and reverenced her, and said, Blessed art thou in all the tabernacles of Juda, and in all nations, which hearing thy name shall be astonished. **8** Now therefore tell me all the things that thou hast done in these days. Then Judith declared unto him in the midst of the people all that she had done, from the day that she went forth until that hour she spake unto them. **9** And when she had left off speaking, the people shouted with a loud voice, and made a joyful noise in their city. **10** And when Achior had seen all that the God of Israel had done, he believed in God greatly, and circumcised the flesh of his foreskin, and was joined unto the house of Israel unto this day. **11** And as soon as the morning arose, they hanged the head of Holofernes upon the wall, and every man took his weapons, and they went forth by bands unto the straits of the mountain. **12** But when the Assyrians saw them, they sent to their leaders, which came to their captains and tribunes, and to every one of their rulers. **13** So they came to Holofernes' tent, and said to him that had the charge of all his things, Waken now our lord: for the slaves have been bold to come down against us to battle, that they may be utterly destroyed. **14** Then went in Bagoas, and knocked at the door of the tent; for he thought that he had slept with Judith. **15** But because none answered, he opened it, and went into the bedchamber, and found him cast upon the floor dead, and his head was taken from him. **16** Therefore he cried with a loud voice, with weeping, and sighing, and a mighty cry, and rent his garments. **17** After he went into the tent where Judith lodged: and when he found her not, he leaped out to the people, and cried, **18** These slaves have dealt treacherously; one woman of the Hebrews hath brought shame upon the house of king Nabuchodonosor: for, behold, Holofernes lieth upon the ground without a head. **19** When the captains of the Assyrians' army heard these words, they rent their coats and their minds were wonderfully troubled, and there was a cry and a very great noise throughout the camp.

15

_**1** And when they that were in the tents heard, they were astonished at the thing that was done. **2** And fear and trembling fell upon them, so that there was no man that durst abide in the sight of his neighbour, but rushing out all together, they fled into every way of the plain, and of the hill country. **3** They also that had camped in the mountains round about Bethulia fled away. Then the children of Israel, every one that was a warrior among them, rushed out upon them. **4** Then sent Ozias to Betomasthem, and to Bebai, and Chobai, and Cola and to all the coasts of Israel, such as should tell the things that were done, and that all should rush forth upon their enemies to destroy them. **5** Now when the children of Israel heard it, they all fell upon them with one consent, and slew them unto Chobai: likewise also they that came from Jerusalem, and from all the hill country, (for men had told them what things were done in the camp of their enemies) and they that were in Galaad, and in Galilee, chased them with a great slaughter, until they were past Damascus and the borders thereof. **6** And the residue that dwelt at Bethulia, fell upon the camp of Assur, and spoiled them, and were greatly enriched. **7** And the children of Israel that returned from the slaughter had that which remained; and the villages and the cities, that were in the mountains and in the plain, gat many spoils: for the multitude was very great. **8** Then Joacim the high priest, and the ancients of the children of Israel that dwelt in Jerusalem, came to behold the good things that God had shewed to Israel, and to see Judith, and to salute her. **9** And when they came unto her, they blessed her with one accord, and said unto her, Thou art the exaltation of Jerusalem, thou art the great glory of Israel, thou art the great rejoicing of our nation: **10** Thou hast done all these things by thine hand: thou hast done much good to Israel, and God is pleased therewith: blessed be thou of the Almighty Lord for evermore. And all the people said, So be it. **11** And the people spoiled the camp the space of thirty days: and they gave unto Judith Holofernes his tent, and all his plate, and beds, and vessels, and all his stuff: and she took it and laid it on her mule; and made ready her carts, and laid them thereon. **12** Then all the women of Israel ran together to see her, and blessed her, and made a dance among them for her: and she took branches in her hand, and gave also to the women that were with her. **13** And they put a garland of olive upon her and her maid that was with her, and she went before all the people in the

dance, leading all the women: and all the men of Israel followed in their armour
with garlands, and with songs in their mouths.

16 _1 Then Judith began to sing this thanksgiving in all Israel, and all
the people sang after her this song of praise. **2** And Judith said,
Begin unto my God with timbrels, sing unto my Lord with cymbals: tune unto
him a new psalm: exalt him, and call upon his name. **3** For God breaketh the
battles: for among the camps in the midst of the people he hath delivered me out
of the hands of them that persecuted me. **4** Assur came out of the mountains
from the north, he came with ten thousands of his army, the multitude whereof
stopped the torrents, and their horsemen have covered the hills. **5** He bragged
that he would burn up my borders, and kill my young men with the sword, and
dash the sucking children against the ground, and make mine infants as a prey,
and my virgins as a spoil. **6** But the Almighty Lord hath disappointed them by
the hand of a woman. **7** For the mighty one did not fall by the young men,
neither did the sons of the Titans smite him, nor high giants set upon him: but
Judith the daughter of Merari weakened him with the beauty of her countenan-
ce. **8** For she put off the garment of her widowhood for the exaltation of those
that were oppressed in Israel, and anointed her face with ointment, and bound her
hair in a tire, and took a linen garment to deceive him. **9** Her sandals ravished
his eyes, her beauty took his mind prisoner, and the fauchion passed through his
neck. **10** The Persians quaked at her boldness, and the Medes were daunted at
her hardiness. **11** Then my afflicted shouted for joy, and my weak ones cried
aloud; but they were astonished: these lifted up their voices, but they were over-
thrown. **12** The sons of the damsels have pierced them through, and wounded
them as fugatives' children: they perished by the battle of the Lord. **13** I will
sing unto the Lord a new song: O Lord, thou art great and glorious, wonderful in
strength, and invincible. **14** Let all creatures serve thee: for thou spakest, and
they were made, thou didst send forth thy spirit, and it created them, and there is
none that can resist thy voice. **15** For the mountains shall be moved from their
foundations with the waters, the rocks shall melt as wax at thy presence: yet thou
art merciful to them that fear thee. **16** For all sacrifice is too little for a sweet
savour unto thee, and all the fat is not sufficient for thy burnt offering: but he that
feareth the Lord is great at all times. **17** Woe to the nations that rise up against
my kindred! the Lord Almighty will take vengeance of them in the day of judg-
ment, in putting fire and worms in their flesh; and they shall feel them, and weep
for ever. **18** Now as soon as they entered into Jerusalem, they worshipped the
Lord; and as soon as the people were purified, they offered their burnt offerings,
and their free offerings, and their gifts. **19** Judith also dedicated all the stuff of
Holofernes, which the people had given her, and gave the canopy, which she had
taken out of his bedchamber, for a gift unto the Lord. **20** So the people conti-
nued feasting in Jerusalem before the sanctuary for the space of three months and
Judith remained with them. **21** After this time every one returned to his own
inheritance, and Judith went to Bethulia, and remained in her own possession,
and was in her time honourable in all the country. **22** And many desired her,
but none knew her all the days of her life, after that Manasses her husband was
dead, and was gathered to his people. **23** But she increased more and more in
honour, and waxed old in her husband's house, being an hundred and five years
old, and made her maid free; so she died in Bethulia: and they buried her in the
cave of her husband Manasses. **24** And the house of Israel lamented her seven
days: and before she died, she did distribute her goods to all them that were ne-
arest of kindred to Manasses her husband, and to them that were the nearest of
her kindred. **25** And there was none that made the children of Israel any more
afraid in the days of Judith, nor a long time after her death.

APOCRYPHA BOOK OF ESTHER

The Book of Esther

1 _1 Now it came to pass in the days of Ahasuerus, (this [is] Ahasuerus
which reigned, from India even unto Ethiopia, [over] an hundred and
seven and twenty provinces:) **2** [That] in those days, when the king Ahasuerus
sat on the throne of his kingdom, which [was] in Shushan the palace, **3** In the
third year of his reign, he made a feast unto all his princes and his servants; the
power of Persia and Media, the nobles and princes of the provinces, [being] before
him: **4** When he shewed the riches of his glorious kingdom and the honour of
his excellent majesty many days, [even] an hundred and fourscore days. **5** And
when these days were expired, the king made a feast unto all the people that
were present in Shushan the palace, both unto great and small, seven days, in
the court of the garden of the king's palace; **6** [Where were] white, green, and
blue, [hangings,] fastened with cords of fine linen and purple to silver rings and
pillars of marble: the beds [were of] gold and silver, upon a pavement of red, and
blue, and white, and black, marble. **7** And they gave [them] drink in vessels of
gold, (the vessels being diverse one from another,) and royal wine in abundance,
according to the state of the king. **8** And the drinking [was] according to the
law; none did compel: for so the king had appointed to all the officers of his
house, that they should do according to every man's pleasure. **9** Also Vashti
the queen made a feast for the women [in] the royal house which [belonged]
to king Ahasuerus. **10** On the seventh day, when the heart of the king was
merry with wine, he commanded Mehuman, Biztha, Harbona, Bigtha, and Aba-
gtha, Zethar, and Carcas, the seven chamberlains that served in the presence of
Ahasuerus the king, **11** To bring Vashti the queen before the king with the
crown royal, to shew the people and the princes her beauty: for she [was] fair to
look on. **12** But the queen Vashti refused to come at the king's commandment
by [his] chamberlains: therefore was the king very wroth, and his anger burned
in him. **13** Then the king said to the wise men, which knew the times, (for
so [was] the king's manner toward all that knew law and judgment: **14** And
the next unto him [was] Carshena, Shethar, Admatha, Tarshish, Meres, Marsena,
[and] Memucan, the seven princes of Persia and Media, which saw the king's face,
[and] which sat the first in the kingdom;) **15** What shall we do unto the queen
Vashti according to law, because she hath not performed the commandment of
the king Ahasuerus by the chamberlains? **16** And Memucan answered before
the king and the princes, Vashti the queen hath not done wrong to the king only,
but also to all the princes, and to all the people that [are] in all the provinces of
the king Ahasuerus. **17** For [this] deed of the queen shall come abroad unto
all women, so that they shall despise their husbands in their eyes, when it shall
be reported, The king Ahasuerus commanded Vashti the queen to be brought in
before him, but she came not. **18** [Likewise] shall the ladies of Persia and Media
say this day unto all the king's princes, which have heard of the deed of the queen.
Thus [shall there arise] too much contempt and wrath. **19** If it please the king,
let there go a royal commandment from him, and let it be written among the laws
of the Persians and the Medes, that it be not altered, That Vashti come no more
before king Ahasuerus; and let the king give her royal estate unto another that is
better than she. **20** And when the king's decree which he shall make shall be pu-
blished throughout all his empire, (for it is great,) all the wives shall give to their
husbands honour, both to great and small. **21** And the saying pleased the king
and the princes; and the king did according to the word of Memucan: **22** For
he sent letters into all the king's provinces, into every province according to the
writing thereof, and to every people after their language, that every man should
bear rule in his own house, and that [it] should be published according to the
language of every people.

2 _1 After these things, when the wrath of king Ahasuerus was appeased,
he remembered Vashti, and what she had done, and what was decreed
against her. **2** Then said the king's servants that ministered unto him, Let there
be fair young virgins sought for the king: **3** And let the king appoint officers in
all the provinces of his kingdom, that they may gather together all the fair young
virgins unto Shushan the palace, to the house of the women unto the custody
of Hege the king's chamberlain, keeper of the women; and let their things for
purification be given [them:] **4** And let the maiden which pleaseth the king be
queen instead of Vashti. And the thing pleased the king; and he did so. **5** [Now]
in Shushan the palace there was a certain Jew, whose name [was] Mordecai, the
son of Jair, the son of Shimei, the son of Kish, a Benjamite; **6** Who had been
carried away from Jerusalem with the captivity which had been carried away with
Jeconiah king of Judah, whom Nebuchadnezzar the king of Babylon had carried
away. **7** And he brought up Hadassah, that [is,] Esther, his uncle's daughter:
for she had neither father nor mother, and the maid [was] fair and beautiful;
whom Mordecai, when her father and mother were dead, took for his own dau-
ghter. **8** So it came to pass, when the king's commandment and his decree was
heard, and when many maidens were gathered together unto Shushan the palace,
to the custody of Hegai, that Esther was brought also unto the king's house, to
the custody of Hegai, keeper of the women. **9** And the maiden pleased him,
and she obtained kindness of him; and he speedily gave her her things for puri-

fication, with such things as belonged to her, and seven maidens, [which were] meet to be given her, out of the king's house: and he preferred her and her maids unto the best [place] of the house of the women. **10** Esther had not shewed her people nor her kindred: for Mordecai had charged her that she should not shew [it.] **11** And Mordecai walked every day before the court of the women's house, to know how Esther did, and what should become of her. **12** Now when every maid's turn was come to go in to king Ahasuerus, after that she had been twelve months, according to the manner of the women, (for so were the days of their purifications accomplished, [to wit,] six months with oil of myrrh, and six months with sweet odours, and with [other] things for the purifying of the women;) **13** Then thus came [every] maiden unto the king; whatsoever she desired was given her to go with her out of the house of the women unto the king's house. **14** In the evening she went, and on the morrow she returned into the second house of the women, to the custody of Shaashgaz, the king's chamberlain, which kept the concubines: she came in unto the king no more, except the king delighted in her, and that she were called by name. **15** Now when the turn of Esther, the daughter of Abihail the uncle of Mordecai, who had taken her for his daughter, was come to go in unto the king, she required nothing but what Hegai the king's chamberlain, the keeper of the women, appointed. And Esther obtained favour in the sight of all them that looked upon her. **16** So Esther was taken unto king Ahasuerus into his house royal in the tenth month, which [is] the month Tebeth, in the seventh year of his reign. **17** And the king loved Esther above all the women, and she obtained grace and favour in his sight more than all the virgins; so that he set the royal crown upon her head, and made her queen instead of Vashti. **18** Then the king made a great feast unto all his princes and his servants, [even] Esther's feast; and he made a release to the provinces, and gave gifts, according to the state of the king. **19** And when the virgins were gathered together the second time, then Mordecai sat in the king's gate. **20** Esther had not [yet] shewed her kindred nor her people; as Mordecai had charged her: for Esther did the commandment of Mordecai, like as when she was brought up with him. **21** In those days, while Mordecai sat in the king's gate, two of the king's chamberlains, Bigthan and Teresh, of those which kept the door, were wroth, and sought to lay hand on the king Ahasuerus. **22** And the thing was known to Mordecai, who told it unto Esther the queen; and Esther certified the king [thereof] in Mordecai's name. **23** And when inquisition was made of the matter, it was found out; therefore they were both hanged on a tree: and it was written in the book of the chronicles before the king.

3

_**1** After these things did king Ahasuerus promote Haman the son of Hammedatha the Agagite, and advanced him, and set his seat above all the princes that [were] with him. **2** And all the king's servants, that [were] in the king's gate, bowed, and reverenced Haman: for the king had so commanded concerning him. But Mordecai bowed not, nor did [him] reverence. **3** Then the king's servants, which [were] in the king's gate, said unto Mordecai, Why transgressest thou the king's commandment? **4** Now it came to pass, when they spake daily unto him, and he hearkened not unto them, that they told Haman, to see whether Mordecai's matters would stand: for he had told them that he [was] a Jew. **5** And when Haman saw that Mordecai bowed not, nor did him reverence, then was Haman full of wrath. **6** And he thought scorn to lay hands on Mordecai alone; for they had shewed him the people of Mordecai: wherefore Haman sought to destroy all the Jews that [were] throughout the whole kingdom of Ahasuerus, [even] the people of Mordecai. **7** In the first month, that [is,] the month Nisan, in the twelfth year of king Ahasuerus, they cast Pur, that [is,] the lot, before Haman from day to day, and from month to month, [to] the twelfth [month,] that [is,] the month Adar. **8** And Haman said unto king Ahasuerus, There is a certain people scattered abroad and dispersed among the people in all the provinces of thy kingdom; and their laws [are] diverse from all people; neither keep they the king's laws: therefore it [is] not for the king's profit to suffer them. **9** If it please the king, let it be written that they may be destroyed: and I will pay ten thousand talents of silver to the hands of those that have the charge of the business, to bring [it] into the king's treasuries. **10** And the king took his ring from his hand, and gave it unto Haman the son of Hammedatha the Agagite, the Jews' enemy. **11** And the king said unto Haman, The silver [is] given to thee, the people also, to do with them as it seemeth good to thee. **12** Then were the king's scribes called on the thirteenth day of the first month, and there was written according to all that Haman had commanded unto the king's lieutenants, and to the governors that [were] over every province, and to the rulers of every people of every province according to the writing thereof, and [to] every people after their language; in the name of king Ahasuerus was it written, and sealed with the king's ring. **13** And the letters were sent by posts into all the king's provinces, to destroy, to kill, and to cause to perish, all Jews, both young and old, little children and women, in one day, [even] upon the thirteenth [day] of the twelfth month, which [is] the month Adar, and [to take] the spoil of them for a prey. **14** The copy of the writing for a commandment to be given in every province was published unto all people, that they should be ready against that day. **15** The posts went out, being hastened by the king's commandment, and the decree was given in Shushan the palace. And the king and Haman sat down to drink; but the city Shushan was perplexed.

4

_**1** When Mordecai perceived all that was done, Mordecai rent his clothes, and put on sackcloth with ashes, and went out into the midst of the city, and cried with a loud and a bitter cry; **2** And came even before the king's gate: for none [might] enter into the king's gate clothed with sackcloth. **3** And in every province, whithersoever the king's commandment and his decree came, [there was] great mourning among the Jews, and fasting, and weeping, and wailing; and many lay in sackcloth and ashes. **4** So Esther's maids and her chamberlains came and told [it] her. Then was the queen exceedingly grieved; and she sent raiment to clothe Mordecai, and to take away his sackcloth from him: but he received [it] not. **5** Then called Esther for Hatach, [one] of the king's chamberlains, whom he had appointed to attend upon her, and gave him a commandment to Mordecai, to know what it [was,] and why it [was.] **6** So Hatach went forth to Mordecai unto the street of the city, which [was] before the king's gate. **7** And Mordecai told him of all that had happened unto him, and of the sum of the money that Haman had promised to pay to the king's treasuries for the Jews, to destroy them. **8** Also he gave him the copy of the writing of the decree that was given at Shushan to destroy them, to shew [it] unto Esther, and to declare [it] unto her, and to charge her that she should go in unto the king, to make supplication unto him, and to make request before him for her people. **9** And Hatach came and told Esther the words of Mordecai. **10** Again Esther spake unto Hatach, and gave him commandment unto Mordecai; **11** All the king's servants, and the people of the king's provinces, do know, that whosoever, whether man or woman, shall come unto the king into the inner court, who is not called, [there is] one law of his to put [him] to death, except such to whom the king shall hold out the golden sceptre, that he may live: but I have not been called to come in unto the king these thirty days. **12** And they told to Mordecai Esther's words. **13** Then Mordecai commanded to answer Esther, Think not with thyself that thou shalt escape in the king's house, more than all the Jews. **14** For if thou altogether holdest thy peace at this time, [then] shall there enlargement and deliverance arise to the Jews from another place; but thou and thy father's house shall be destroyed: and who knoweth whether thou art come to the kingdom for [such] a time as this? **15** Then Esther bade [them] return Mordecai [this answer,] **16** Go, gather together all the Jews that are present in Shushan, and fast ye for me, and neither eat nor drink three days, night or day: I also and my maidens will fast likewise; and so will I go in unto the king, which [is] not according to the law: and if I perish, I perish. **17** So Mordecai went his way, and did according to all that Esther had commanded him.

5

_**1** Now it came to pass on the third day, that Esther put on [her] royal [apparel,] and stood in the inner court of the king's house, over against the king's house: and the king sat upon his royal throne in the royal house, over against the gate of the house. **2** And it was so, when the king saw Esther the queen standing in the court, [that] she obtained favour in his sight: and the king held out to Esther the golden sceptre that [was] in his hand. So Esther drew near, and touched the top of the sceptre. **3** Then said the king unto her, What wilt thou, queen Esther? and what [is] thy request? it shall be even given thee to the half of the kingdom. **4** And Esther answered, If [it seem] good unto the king, let the king and Haman come this day unto the banquet that I have prepared for him. **5** Then the king said, Cause Haman to make haste, that he may do as Esther hath said. So the king and Haman came to the banquet that Esther had prepared. **6** And the king said unto Esther at the banquet of wine, What [is] thy petition? and it shall be granted thee: and what [is] thy request? even to the half of the kingdom it shall be performed. **7** Then answered Esther, and said, My petition and my request [is;] **8** If I have found favour in the sight of the king, and if it please the king to grant my petition, and to perform my request, let the king and Haman come to the banquet that I shall prepare for them, and I will do to morrow as the king hath said. **9** Then went Haman forth that day joyful and with a glad heart: but when Haman saw Mordecai in the king's gate, that he stood not up, nor moved for him, he was full of indignation against Mordecai. **10** Nevertheless Haman refrained himself: and when he came home, he sent and called for his friends, and Zeresh his wife. **11** And Haman told them of the glory of his riches, and the multitude of his children, and all [the things] wherein the king had promoted him, and how he had advanced him above the princes and servants of the king. **12** Haman said moreover, Yea, Esther the queen did let no man come in with the king unto the banquet that she had prepared but myself; and to morrow am I invited unto her also with the king. **13** Yet all this availeth me nothing, so long as I see Mordecai the Jew sitting at the king's gate. **14** Then said Zeresh his wife and all his friends unto him, Let a gallows be made of fifty cubits high, and to morrow speak thou unto the king that Mordecai may be hanged thereon: then go thou in merrily with the king unto the banquet. And the thing pleased Haman; and he caused the gallows to be made.

6

_**1** On that night could not the king sleep, and he commanded to bring the book of records of the chronicles; and they were read before the king. **2** And it was found written, that Mordecai had told of Bigthana and Teresh, two of the king's chamberlains, the keepers of the door, who sought to lay hand on the king Ahasuerus. **3** And the king said, What honour and dignity hath been done to Mordecai for this? Then said the king's servants that ministered unto him, There is nothing done for him. **4** And the king said, Who [is] in the court? Now Haman was come into the outward court of the king's house, to speak unto the king to hang Mordecai on the gallows that he had prepared for him. **5** And the king's servants said unto him, Behold, Haman standeth in the court. And the king said, Let him come in. **6** So Haman came in. And the king said unto him, What shall be done unto the man whom the king delighteth to honour? Now Haman thought in his heart, To whom would the king delight to do honour more than to myself? **7** And Haman answered the king, For the man whom the king delighteth to honour, **8** Let the royal apparel be brought which the king [useth] to wear, and the horse that the king rideth upon, and the crown royal which is set upon his head: **9** And let this apparel and horse be delivered to the hand of one of the king's most noble princes, that they may array the man [withal] whom the king delighteth to honour, and bring him on horseback through the street of the city, and proclaim before him, Thus shall it be done to the man whom the king delighteth to honour. **10** Then the king said to Haman, Make haste, [and] take the apparel and the horse, as thou hast said, and do even so to Mordecai the Jew, that sitteth at the king's gate: let nothing fail of all that thou hast spoken. **11** Then took Haman the apparel and the horse, and arrayed Mordecai, and brought him on horseback through the street of the city, and proclaimed before him, Thus shall it be done unto the man whom the king delighteth to honour. **12** And Mordecai came again to the king's gate. But Haman hasted to his house mourning, and having his head covered. **13** And Haman told Zeresh his wife and all his friends every [thing] that had befallen him. Then said his wise men and Zeresh his wife unto him, If Mordecai [be] of the seed of the Jews, before whom thou hast begun to fall, thou shalt not prevail against him, but shalt surely fall before him. **14** And while they [were] yet talking with him, came the king's chamberlains, and hasted to bring Haman unto the banquet that Esther had prepared.

7 _**1** So the king and Haman came to banquet with Esther the queen. **2** And the king said again unto Esther on the second day at the banquet of wine, What [is] thy petition, queen Esther? and it shall be granted thee: and what [is] thy request? and it shall be performed, [even] to the half of the kingdom. **3** Then Esther the queen answered and said, If I have found favour in thy sight, O king, and if it please the king, let my life be given me at my petition, and my people at my request: **4** For we are sold, I and my people, to be destroyed, to be slain, and to perish. But if we had been sold for bondmen and bondwomen, I had held my tongue, although the enemy could not countervail the king's damage. **5** Then the king Ahasuerus answered and said unto Esther the queen, Who is he, and where is he, that durst presume in his heart to do so? **6** And Esther said, The adversary and enemy [is] this wicked Haman. Then Haman was afraid before the king and the queen. **7** And the king arising from the banquet of wine in his wrath [went] into the palace garden: and Haman stood up to make request for his life to Esther the queen; for he saw that there was evil determined against him by the king. **8** Then the king returned out of the palace garden into the place of the banquet of wine; and Haman was fallen upon the bed whereon Esther [was.] Then said the king, Will he force the queen also before me in the house? As the word went out of the king's mouth, they covered Haman's face. **9** And Harbonah, one of the chamberlains, said before the king, Behold also, the gallows fifty cubits high,which Haman had made for Mordecai, who had spoken good for the king, standeth in the house of Haman. Then the king said, Hang him thereon. **10** So they hanged Haman on the gallows that he had prepared for Mordecai. Then was the king's wrath pacified.

8 _**1** On that day did the king Ahasuerus give the house of Haman the Jews' enemy unto Esther the queen. And Mordecai came before the king; for Esther had told what he [was] unto her. **2** And the king took off his ring, which he had taken from Haman, and gave it unto Mordecai. And Esther set Mordecai over the house of Haman. **3** And Esther spake yet again before the king, and fell down at his feet, and besought him with tears to put away the mischief of Haman the Agagite, and his device that he had devised against the Jews. **4** Then the king held out the golden sceptre toward Esther. So Esther arose, and stood before the king, **5** And said, If it please the king, and if I have found favour in his sight, and the thing [seem] right before the king, and I [be] pleasing in his eyes, let it be written to reverse the letters devised by Haman the son of Hammedatha the Agagite, which he wrote to destroy the Jews which [are] in all the king's provinces: **6** For how can I endure to see the evil that shall come unto my people? or how can I endure to see the destruction of my kindred? **7** Then the king Ahasuerus said unto Esther the queen and to Mordecai the Jew, Behold, I have given Esther the house of Haman, and him they have hanged upon the gallows, because he laid his hand upon the Jews. **8** Write ye also for the Jews, as it liketh you, in the king's name, and seal [it] with the king's ring: for the writing which is written in the king's name, and sealed with the king's ring, may no man reverse. **9** Then were the king's scribes called at that time in the third month, that [is,] the month Sivan, on the three and twentieth [day] thereof; and it was written according to all that Mordecai commanded unto the Jews, and to the lieutenants, and the deputies and rulers of the provinces which [are] from India unto Ethiopia, an hundred twenty and seven provinces, unto every province according to the writing thereof, and unto every people after their language, and to the Jews according to their writing, and according to their language. **10** And he wrote in the king Ahasuerus' name, and sealed it with the king's ring, and sent letters by posts on horseback, [and] riders on mules, camels, [and] young dromedaries: **11** Wherein the king granted the Jews which [were] in every city to gather themselves together, and to stand for their life, to destroy, to slay, and to cause to perish, all the power of the people and province that would assault them, [both] little ones and women, and [to take] the spoil of them for a prey, **12** Upon one day in all the provinces of king Ahasuerus, [namely,] upon the thirteenth [day] of the twelfth month, which [is] the month Adar. **13** The copy of the writing for a commandment to be given in every province [was] published unto all people, and that the Jews should be ready against that day to avenge themselves on their enemies. **14** [So] the posts that rode upon mules [and] camels went out, being hastened and pressed on by the king's commandment. And the decree was given at Shushan the palace. **15** And Mordecai went out from the presence of the king in royal apparel of blue and white, and with a great crown of gold, and with a garment of fine linen and purple: and the city of Shushan rejoiced and was glad. **16** The Jews had light, and gladness, and joy, and honour. **17** And in every province, and in every city, whithersoever the king's commandment and his decree came, the Jews had joy and gladness, a feast and a good day. And many of the people of the land became Jews; for the fear of the Jews fell upon them.

9 _**1** Now in the twelfth month, that [is,] the month Adar, on the thirteenth day of the same, when the king's commandment and his decree drew near to be put in execution, in the day that the enemies of the Jews hoped to have power over them, (though it was turned to the contrary, that the Jews had rule over them that hated them;) **2** The Jews gathered themselves together in their cities throughout all the provinces of the king Ahasuerus, to lay hand on such as sought their hurt: and no man could withstand them; for the fear of them fell upon all people. **3** And all the rulers of the provinces, and the lieutenants, and the deputies, and officers of the king, helped the Jews; because the fear of Mordecai fell upon them. **4** For Mordecai [was] great in the king's house, and his fame went out throughout all the provinces: for this man Mordecai waxed greater and greater. **5** Thus the Jews smote all their enemies with the stroke of the sword, and slaughter, and destruction, and did what they would unto those that hated them. **6** And in Shushan the palace the Jews slew and destroyed five hundred men. **7** And Parshandatha, and Dalphon, and Aspatha, **8** And Poratha, and Adalia, and Aridatha, **9** And Parmashta, and Arisai, and Aridai, and Vajezatha, **10** The ten sons of Haman the son of Hammedatha, the enemy of the Jews, slew they; but on the spoil laid they not their hand. **11** On that day the number of those that were slain in Shushan the palace was brought before the king. **12** And the king said unto Esther the queen, The Jews have slain and destroyed five hundred men in Shushan the palace, and the ten sons of Haman; what have they done in the rest of the king's provinces? now what [is] thy petition? and it shall be granted thee: or what [is] thy request further? and it shall be done. **13** Then said Esther, If it please the king, let it be granted to the Jews which [are] in Shushan to do to morrow also according unto this day's decree, and let Haman's ten sons be hanged upon the gallows. **14** And the king commanded it so to be done: and the decree was given at Shushan; and they hanged Haman's ten sons. **15** For the Jews that [were] in Shushan gathered themselves together on the fourteenth day also of the month Adar, and slew three hundred men at Shushan; but on the prey they laid not their hand. **16** But the other Jews that [were] in the king's provinces gathered themselves together, and stood for their lives, and had rest from their enemies, and slew of their foes seventy and five thousand, but they laid not their hands on the prey, **17** On the thirteenth day of the month Adar; and on the fourteenth day of the same rested they, and made it a day of feasting and gladness. **18** But the Jews that [were] at Shushan assembled together on the thirteenth [day] thereof; and on the fourteenth thereof; and on the fifteenth [day] of the same they rested, and made it a day of feasting and gladness. **19** Therefore the Jews of the villages, that dwelt in the unwalled towns, made the fourteenth day of the month Adar [a day of] gladness and feasting, and a good day, and of sending portions one to another. **20** And Mordecai wrote these things, and sent letters unto all the Jews that [were] in all the provinces of the king Ahasuerus, [both] nigh and far, **21** To stablish [this] among them, that they should keep the fourteenth day of the month Adar, and the fifteenth day of the same, yearly, **22** As the days wherein the Jews rested from their enemies, and the month which was turned unto them from sorrow to joy, and from mourning into a good day: that they should make them days of feasting and joy, and of sending portions one to another, and gifts to the poor. **23** And the Jews undertook to do as they had begun, and as Mordecai had written unto them; **24** Because Haman the son of Hammedatha, the Agagite, the enemy of all the Jews, had devised against the Jews to destroy them, and had cast Pur, that [is,] the lot, to consume them, and to destroy them; **25** But when [Esther] came before the king, he commanded by letters that his wicked device, which he devised against the Jews, should return upon his own head, and that he and his sons should be hanged on the gallows. **26** Wherefore they called these days Purim after the name of Pur. Therefore for all the words of this letter, and [of that] which they had seen concerning this matter, and which had come unto them, **27** The Jews ordained, and took upon them, and upon their seed, and upon all such as joined themselves unto them, so as it should not fail, that they would keep these two days according to their writing, and according to their [appointed] time every year; **28** And [that] these days [should be] remembered and kept throughout every generation, every family, every province, and every city; and [that] these days of Purim should not fail from among the Jews, nor the memorial of them perish from their seed. **29** Then Esther the queen, the daughter of Abihail, and Mordecai the Jew, wrote with all authority, to confirm this second letter of Purim. **30** And he sent the letters unto all the Jews, to the hundred twenty and seven provinces of the kingdom of Ahasuerus, [with] words of peace and truth, **31** To confirm these days of Purim in their times [appointed,] according as Mordecai the Jew and Esther the queen had enjoined them, and as they had decreed for themselves and for their seed, the matters of the fastings and their cry. **32** And the decree of Esther confirmed these matters of Purim; and it was written in the book.

10 _**1** And the king Ahasuerus laid a tribute upon the land, and [upon] the isles of the sea. **2** And all the acts of his power and of his might, and the declaration of the greatness of Mordecai, whereunto the king advanced him, [are] they not written in the book of the chronicles of the kings of Media and Persia? **3** For Mordecai the Jew [was] next unto king Ahasuerus, and great among the Jews, and accepted of the multitude of his brethren, seeking the wealth of his people, and speaking peace to all his seed.

APOCRYPHA BOOK OF WISDOM

The Book of Wisdomor... The Wisdom of Solomon

1 _**1** Love righteousness, ye that be judges of the earth: think of the Lord with a good (heart,) and in simplicity of heart seek him. **2** For he will be found of them that tempt him not; and sheweth himself unto such as do not distrust him. **3** For froward thoughts separate from God: and his power, when it is tried, reproveth the unwise. **4** For into a malicious soul wisdom shall not enter; nor dwell in the body that is subject unto sin. **5** For the holy spirit of discipline will flee deceit, and remove from thoughts that are without understanding, and will not abide when unrighteousness cometh in. **6** For wisdom is a loving spirit; and will not acquit a blasphemer of his words: for God is witness of his reins, and a true beholder of his heart, and a hearer of his tongue. **7** For the Spirit of the Lord filleth the world: and that which containeth all things hath knowledge of the voice. **8** Therefore he that speaketh unrighteous things cannot be hid: neither shall vengeance, when it punisheth, pass by him. **9** For inquisition shall be made into the counsels of the ungodly: and the sound of his words shall come unto the Lord for the manifestation of his wicked deeds. **10** For the ear of jealousy heareth all things: and the noise of murmurings is not hid. **11** Therefore beware of murmuring, which is unprofitable; and refrain your tongue from backbiting: for there is no word so secret, that shall go for nought: and the mouth that belieth slayeth the soul. **12** Seek not death in the error of your life: and pull not upon yourselves destruction with the works of your hands. **13** For God made not death: neither hath he pleasure in the destruction of the living. **14** For he created all things, that they might have their being: and the generations of the world were healthful; and there is no poison of destruction in them, nor the kingdom of death upon the earth: **15** (For righteousness is immortal:) **16** But ungodly men with their works and words called it to them: for when they thought to have it their friend, they consumed to nought, and made a covenant with it, because they are worthy to take part with it.

2 _**1** For the ungodly said, reasoning with themselves, but not aright, Our life is short and tedious, and in the death of a man there is no remedy: neither was there any man known to have returned from the grave. **2** For we are born at all adventure: and we shall be hereafter as though we had never been: for the breath in our nostrils is as smoke, and a little spark in the moving of our heart: **3** Which being extinguished, our body shall be turned into ashes, and our spirit shall vanish as the soft air, **4** And our name shall be forgotten in time, and no man shall have our works in remembrance, and our life shall pass away as the trace of a cloud, and shall be dispersed as a mist, that is driven away with the beams of the sun, and overcome with the heat thereof. **5** For our time is a very shadow that passeth away; and after our end there is no returning: for it is fast sealed, so that no man cometh again. **6** Come on therefore, let us enjoy the good things that are present: and let us speedily use the creatures like as in youth. **7** Let us fill ourselves with costly wine and ointments: and let no flower of the spring pass by us: **8** Let us crown ourselves with rosebuds, before they be withered: **9** Let none of us go without his part of our voluptuousness: let us leave tokens of our joyfulness in every place: for this is our portion, and our lot is this. **10** Let us oppress the poor righteous man, let us not spare the widow, nor reverence the ancient gray hairs of the aged. **11** Let our strength be the law of justice: for that which is feeble is found to be nothing worth. **12** Therefore let us lie in wait for the righteous; because he is not for our turn, and he is clean contrary to our doings: he upbraideth us with our offending the law, and objecteth to our infamy the transgressings of our education. **13** He professeth to have the knowledge of God: and he calleth himself the child of the Lord. **14** He was made to reprove our thoughts. **15** He is grievous unto us even to behold: for his life is not like other men's, his ways are of another fashion. **16** We are esteemed of him as counterfeits: he abstaineth from our ways as from filthiness: he pronounceth the end of the just to be blessed, and maketh his boast that God is his father. **17** Let us see if his words be true: and let us prove what shall happen in the end of him. **18** For if the just man be the son of God, he will help him, and deliver him from the hand of his enemies. **19** Let us examine him with despitefulness and torture, that we may know his meekness, and prove his patience. **20** Let us condemn him with a shameful death: for by his own saying he shall be respected. **21** Such things they did imagine, and were deceived: for their own wickedness hath blinded them. **22** As for the mysteries of God, they kn ew them not: neither hoped they for the wages of righteousness, nor discerned a reward for blameless souls. **23** For God created man to be immortal, and made him to be an image of his own eternity. **24** Nevertheless through envy of the devil came death into the world: and they that do hold of his side do find it.

3 _**1** But the souls of the righteous are in the hand of God, and there shall no torment touch them. **2** In the sight of the unwise they seemed to die: and their departure is taken for misery, **3** And their going from us to be utter destruction: but they are in peace. **4** For though they be punished in the sight of men, yet is their hope full of immortality. **5** And having been a little chastised, they shall be greatly rewarded: for God proved them, and found them worthy for himself. **6** As gold in the furnace hath he tried them, and received them as a burnt offering. **7** And in the time of their visitation they shall shine, and run to and fro like sparks among the stubble. **8** They shall judge the nations, and have dominion over the people, and their Lord shall reign for ever. **9** They that put their trust in him shall understand the truth: and such as be faithful in love shall abide with him: for grace and mercy is to his saints, and he hath care for his elect. **10** But the ungodly shall be punished according to their own imaginations, which have neglected the righteous, and forsaken the Lord. **11** For whoso despiseth wisdom and nurture, he is miserable, and their hope is vain, their labours unfruitful, and their works unprofitable: **12** Their wives are foolish, and their children wicked: **13** Their offspring is cursed. Wherefore blessed is the barren that is undefiled, which hath not known the sinful bed: she shall have fruit in the visitation of souls. **14** And blessed is the eunuch, which with his hands hath wrought no iniquity, nor imagined wicked things against God: for unto him shall be given the special gift of faith, and an inheritance in the temple of the Lord more acceptable to his mind. **15** For glorious is the fruit of good labours: and the root of wisdom shall never fall away. **16** As for the children of adulterers, they shall not come to their perfection, and the seed of an unrighteous bed shall be rooted out. **17** For though they live long, yet shall they be nothing regarded: and their last age shall be without honour. **18** Or, if they die quickly, they have no hope, neither comfort in the day of trial. **19** For horrible is the end of the unrighteous generation.

4 _**1** Better it is to have no children, and to have virtue: for the memorial thereof is immortal: because it is known with God, and with men. **2** When it is present, men take example at it; and when it is gone, they desire it: it weareth a crown, and triumpheth for ever, having gotten the victory, striving for undefiled rewards. **3** But the multiplying brood of the ungodly shall not thrive, nor take deep rooting from bastard slips, nor lay any fast founda-

tion. **4** For though they flourish in branches for a time; yet standing not last,
they shall be shaken with the wind, and through the force of winds they shall be
rooted out. **5** The imperfect branches shall be broken off, their fruit unprofi-
table, not ripe to eat, yea, meet for nothing. **6** For children begotten of unlawful
beds are witnesses of wickedness against their parents in their trial. **7** But thou-
gh the righteous be prevented with death, yet shall he be in rest. **8** For honou-
rable age is not that which standeth in length of time, nor that is measured by
number of years. **9** But wisdom is the gray hair unto men, and an unspotted life
is old age. **10** He pleased God, and was beloved of him: so that living among
sinners he was translated. **11** Yea speedily was he taken away, lest that wicke-
dness should alter his understanding, or deceit beguile his soul. **12** For the
bewitching of naughtiness doth obscure things that are honest; and the wandering
of concupiscence doth undermine the simple mind. **13** He, being made perfect
in a short time, fulfilled a long time: **14** For his soul pleased the Lord: therefore
hasted he to take him away from among the wicked. **15** This the people saw,
and understood it not, neither laid they up this in their minds, That his grace and
mercy is with his saints, and that he hath respect unto his chosen. **16** Thus the
righteous that is dead shall condemn the ungodly which are living; and youth that
is soon perfected the many years and old age of the unrighteous. **17** For they
shall see the end of the wise, and shall not understand what God in his counsel
hath decreed of him, and to what end the Lord hath set him in safety. **18** They
shall see him, and despise him; but God shall laugh them to scorn: and they shall
hereafter be a vile carcase, and a reproach among the dead for evermore. **19** For
he shall rend them, and cast them down headlong, that they shall be speechless;
and he shall shake them from the foundation; and they shall be utterly laid waste,
and be in sorrow; and their memorial shall perish. **20** And when they cast up
the accounts of their sins, they shall come with fear: and their own iniquities shall
convince them to their face.

5

_**1** Then shall the righteous man stand in great boldness before the face of
such as have afflicted him, and made no account of his labours. **2** When
they see it, they shall be troubled with terrible fear, and shall be amazed at the
strangeness of his salvation, so far beyond all that they looked for. **3** And they
repenting and groaning for anguish of spirit shall say within themselves, This was
he, whom we had sometimes in derision, and a proverb of reproach: **4** We fools
accounted his life madness, and his end to be without honour: **5** How is he
numbered among the children of God, and his lot is among the saints! **6** There-
fore have we erred from the way of truth, and the light of righteousness hath not
shined unto us, and the sun of righteousness rose not upon us. **7** We wearied
ourselves in the way of wickedness and destruction: yea, we have gone through
deserts, where there lay no way: but as for the way of the Lord, we have not known
it. **8** What hath pride profited us? or what good hath riches with our vaunting
brought us? **9** All those things are passed away like a shadow, and as a post that
hasted by; **10** And as a ship that passeth over the waves of the water, which
when it is gone by, the trace thereof cannot be found, neither the pathway of the
keel in the waves; **11** Or as when a bird hath flown through the air, there is no
token of her way to be found, but the light air being beaten with the stroke of her
wings and parted with the violent noise and motion of them, is passed through,
and therein afterwards no sign where she went is to be found; **12** Or like as
when an arrow is shot at a mark, it parteth the air, which immediately cometh
together again, so that a man cannot know where it went through: **13** Even so
we in like manner, as soon as we were born, began to draw to our end, and had
no sign of virtue to shew; but were consumed in our own wickedness. **14** For
the hope of the Godly is like dust that is blown away with the wind; like a thin
froth that is driven away with the storm; like as the smoke which is dispersed here
and there with a tempest, and passeth away as the remembrance of a guest that
tarrieth but a day. **15** But the righteous live for evermore; their reward also is
with the Lord, and the care of them is with the most High. **16** Therefore shall
they receive a glorious kingdom, and a beautiful crown from the Lord's hand:
for with his right hand shall he cover them, and with his arm shall he protect
them. **17** He shall take to him his jealousy for complete armour, and make the
creature his weapon for the revenge of his enemies. **18** He shall put on righte-
ousness as a breastplate, and true judgment instead of an helmet. **19** He shall
take holiness for an invincible shield. **20** His severe wrath shall he sharpen for a
sword, and the world shall fight with him against the unwise. **21** Then shall the
right aiming thunderbolts go abroad; and from the clouds, as from a well drawn
bow, shall they fly to the mark. **22** And hailstones full of wrath shall be cast as
out of a stone bow, and the water of the sea shall rage against them, and the floods
shall cruelly drown them. **23** Yea, a mighty wind shall stand up against them,
and like a storm shall blow them away: thus iniquity shall lay waste the whole
earth, and ill dealing shall overthrow the thrones of the mighty.

6

_**1** Hear therefore, O ye kings, and understand; learn, ye that be jud-
ges of the ends of the earth. **2** Give ear, ye that rule the people, and
glory in the multitude of nations. **3** For power is given you of the Lord, and
sovereignty from the Highest, who shall try your works, and search out your
counsels. **4** Because, being ministers of his kingdom, ye have not judged aright,
nor kept the law, nor walked after the counsel of God; **5** Horribly and speedily
shall he come upon you: for a sharp judgment shall be to them that be in high
places. **6** For mercy will soon pardon the meanest: but mighty men shall be
mightily tormented. **7** For he which is Lord over all shall fear no man's person,
neither shall he stand in awe of any man's greatness: for he hath made the small
and great, and careth for all alike. **8** But a sore trial shall come upon the mi-
ghty. **9** Unto you therefore, O kings, do I speak, that ye may learn wisdom, and
not fall away. **10** For they that keep holiness holily shall be judged holy: and
they that have learned such things shall find what to answer. **11** Wherefore set
your affection upon my words; desire them, and ye shall be instructed. **12** Wi-
sdom is glorious, and never fadeth away: yea, she is easily seen of them that love
her, and found of such as seek her. **13** She preventeth them that desire her, in
making herself first known unto them. **14** Whoso seeketh her early shall have
no great travail: for he shall find her sitting at his doors. **15** To think therefo-
re upon her is perfection of wisdom: and whoso watcheth for her shall quickly
be without care. **16** For she goeth about seeking such as are worthy of her,
sheweth herself favourably unto them in the ways, and meeteth them in every
thought. **17** For the very true beginning of her is the desire of discipline; and
the care of discipline is love; **18** And love is the keeping of her laws; and the
giving heed unto her laws is the assurance of incorruption; **19** And incorrup-
tion maketh us near unto God: **20** Therefore the desire of wisdom bringeth to
a kingdom. **21** If your delight be then in thrones and sceptres, O ye kings of
the people, honour wisdom, that ye may reign for evermore. **22** As for wisdom,
what she is, and how she came up, I will tell you, and will not hide mysteries
from you: but will seek her out from the beginning of her nativity, and bring
the knowledge of her into light, and will not pass over the truth. **23** Neither
will I go with consuming envy; for such a man shall have no fellowship with wi-
sdom. **24** But the multitude of the wise is the welfare of the world: and a wise
king is the upholding of the people. **25** Receive therefore instruction through
my words, and it shall do you good.

7

_**1** I myself also am a mortal man, like to all, and the offspring of him that
was first made of the earth, **2** And in my mother's womb was fashioned
to be flesh in the time of ten months, being compacted in blood, of the seed of
man, and the pleasure that came with sleep. **3** And when I was born, I drew in
the common air, and fell upon the earth, which is of like nature, and the first voice
which I uttered was crying, as all others do. **4** I was nursed in swaddling clothes,
and that with cares. **5** For there is no king that had any other beginning of bir-
th. **6** For all men have one entrance into life, and the like going out. **7** Whe-
refore I prayed, and understanding was given me: I called upon God, and the
spirit of wisdom came to me. **8** I preferred her before sceptres and thrones, and
esteemed riches nothing in comparison of her. **9** Neither compared I unto her
any precious stone, because all gold in respect of her is as a little sand, and silver
shall be counted as clay before her. **10** I loved her above health and beauty, and
chose to have her instead of light: for the light that cometh from her never goeth
out. **11** All good things together came to me with her, and innumerable riches
in her hands. **12** And I rejoiced in them all, because wisdom goeth before them:
and I knew not that she was the mother of them. **13** I learned diligently, and
do communicate her liberally: I do not hide her riches. **14** For she is a treasure
unto men that never faileth: which they that use become the friends of God,
being commended for the gifts that come from learning. **15** God hath granted
me to speak as I would, and to conceive as is meet for the things that are given
me: because it is he that leadeth unto wisdom, and directeth the wise. **16** For
in his hand are both we and our words; all wisdom also, and knowledge of wor-
kmanship. **17** For he hath given me certain knowledge of the things that are,
namely, to know how the world was made, and the operation of the elemen-
ts: **18** The beginning, ending, and midst of the times: the alterations of the
turning of the sun, and the change of seasons: **19** The circuits of years, and
the positions of stars: **20** The natures of living creatures, and the furies of wild
beasts: the violence of winds, and the reasonings of men: the diversities of plants
and the virtues of roots: **21** And all such things as are either secret or manifest,
them I know. **22** For wisdom, which is the worker of all things, taught me:
for in her is an understanding spirit holy, one only, manifold, subtil, lively, clear,
undefiled, plain, not subject to hurt, loving the thing that is good quick, which
cannot be letted, ready to do good, **23** Kind to man, steadfast, sure, free from
care, having all power, overseeing all things, and going through all understanding,
pure, and most subtil, spirits. **24** For wisdom is more moving than any motion:
she passeth and goeth through all things by reason of her pureness. **25** For she
is the breath of the power of God, and a pure influence flowing from the glory
of the Almighty: therefore can no defiled thing fall into her. **26** For she is the
brightness of the everlasting light, the unspotted mirror of the power of God,
and the image of his goodness. **27** And being but one, she can do all things: and
remaining in herself, she maketh all things new: and in all ages entering into holy
souls, she maketh them friends of God, and prophets. **28** For God loveth none
but him that dwelleth with wisdom. **29** For she is more beautiful than the sun,
and above all the order of stars: being compared with the light, she is found before
it. **30** For after this cometh night: but vice shall not prevail against wisdom.

8

_**1** Wisdom reacheth from one end to another mightily: and sweetly doth
she order all things. **2** I loved her, and sought her out from my youth,
I desired to make her my spouse, and I was a lover of her beauty. **3** In that she

is conversant with God, she magnifieth her nobility: yea, the Lord of all things himself loved her. 4 For she is privy to the mysteries of the knowledge of God, and a lover of his works. 5 If riches be a possession to be desired in this life; what is richer than wisdom, that worketh all things? 6 And if prudence work; who of all that are is a more cunning workman than she? 7 And if a man love righteousness her labours are virtues: for she teacheth temperance and prudence, justice and fortitude: which are such things, as en can have nothing more profitable in their life. 8 If a man desire much experience, she knoweth things of old, and conjectureth aright what is to come: she knoweth the subtilties of speeches, and can expound dark sentences: she foreseeth signs and wonders, and the events of seasons and times. 9 Therefore I purposed to take her to me to live with me, knowing that she would be a counsellor of good things, and a comfort in cares and grief. 10 For her sake I shall have estimation among the multitude, and honour with the elders, though I be young. 11 I shall be found of a quick conceit in judgment, and shall be admired in the sight of great men. 12 When I hold my tongue, they shall bide my leisure, and when I speak, they shall give good ear unto me: if I talk much, they shall lay their hands upon their mouth. 13 Moreover by the means of her I shall obtain immortality, and leave behind me an everlasting memorial to them that come after me. 14 I shall set the people in order, and the nations shall be subject unto me. 15 Horrible tyrants shall be afraid, when they do but hear of me; I shall be found good among the multitude, and valiant in war. 16 After I am come into mine house, I will repose myself with her: for her conversation hath no bitterness; and to live with her hath no sorrow, but mirth and joy. 17 Now when I considered these things in myself, and pondered them in my heart, how that to be allied unto wisdom is immortality; 18 And great pleasure it is to have her friendship; and in the works of her hands are infinite riches; and in the exercise of conference with her, prudence; and in talking with her, a good report; I went about seeking how to take her to me. 19 For I was a witty child, and had a good spirit. 20 Yea rather, being good, I came into a body undefiled. 21 Nevertheless, when I perceived that I could not otherwise obtain her, except God gave her me; and that was a point of wisdom also to know whose gift she was; I prayed unto the Lord, and besought him, and with my whole heart I said,

9

_1 O God of my fathers, and Lord of mercy, who hast made all things with thy word, 2 And ordained man through thy wisdom, that he should have dominion over the creatures which thou hast made, 3 And order the world according to equity and righteousness, and execute judgment with an upright heart: 4 Give me wisdom, that sitteth by thy throne; and reject me not from among thy children: 5 For I thy servant and son of thine handmaid am a feeble person, and of a short time, and too young for the understanding of judgment and laws. 6 For though a man be never so perfect among the children of men, yet if thy wisdom be not with him, he shall be nothing regarded. 7 Thou hast chosen me to be a king of thy people, and a judge of thy sons and daughters: 8 Thou hast commanded me to build a temple upon thy holy mount, and an altar in the city wherein thou dwellest, a resemblance of the holy tabernacle, which thou hast prepared from the beginning. 9 And wisdom was with thee: which knoweth thy works, and was present when thou madest the world, and knew what was acceptable in thy sight, and right in thy commandments. 10 O send her out of thy holy heavens, and from the throne of thy glory, that being present she may labour with me, that I may know what is pleasing unto thee. 11 For she knoweth and understandeth all things, and she shall lead me soberly in my doings, and preserve me in her power. 12 So shall my works be acceptable, and then shall I judge thy people righteously, and be worthy to sit in my father's seat. 13 For what man is he that can know the counsel of God? or who can think what the will of the Lord is? 14 For the thoughts of mortal men are miserable, and our devices are but uncertain. 15 For the corruptible body presseth down the soul, and the earthy tabernacle weigheth down the mind that museth upon many things. 16 And hardly do we guess aright at things that are upon earth, and with labour do we find the things that are before us: but the things that are in heaven who hath searched out? 17 And thy counsel who hath known, except thou give wisdom, and send thy Holy Spirit from above? 18 For so the ways of them which lived on the earth were reformed, and men were taught the things that are pleasing unto thee, and were saved through wisdom.

10

_1 She preserved the first formed father of the world, that was created alone, and brought him out of his fall, 2 And gave him power to rule all things. 3 But when the unrighteous went away from her in his anger, he perished also in the fury wherewith he murdered his brother. 4 For whose cause the earth being drowned with the flood, wisdom again preserved it, and directed the course of the righteous in a piece of wood of small value. 5 Moreover, the nations in their wicked conspiracy being confounded, she found out the righteous, and preserved him blameless unto God, and kept him strong against his tender compassion toward his son. 6 When the ungodly perished, she delivered the righteous man, who fled from the fire which fell down upon the five cities. 7 Of whose wickedness even to this day the waste land that smoketh is a testimony, and plants bearing fruit that never come to ripeness: and a standing pillar of salt is a monument of an unbelieving soul. 8 For regarding not wisdom, they gat not only this hurt, that they knew not the things which were good; but also left behind them to the world a memorial of their foolishness: so that in the things wherein they offended they could not so much as be hid. 9 Rut wisdom delivered from pain those that attended upon her. 10 When the righteous fled from his brother's wrath she guided him in right paths, shewed him the kingdom of God, and gave him knowledge of holy things, made him rich in his travels, and multiplied the fruit of his labours. 11 In the covetousness of such as oppressed him she stood by him, and made him rich. 12 She defended him from his enemies, and kept him safe from those that lay in wait, and in a sore conflict she gave him the victory; that he might know that goodness is stronger than all. 13 When the righteous was sold, she forsook him not, but delivered him from sin: she went down with him into the pit, 14 And left him not in bonds, till she brought him the sceptre of the kingdom, and power against those that oppressed him: as for them that had accused him, she shewed them to be liars, and gave him perpetual glory. 15 She delivered the righteous people and blameless seed from the nation that oppressed them. 16 She entered into the soul of the servant of the Lord, and withstood dreadful kings in wonders and signs; 17 Rendered to the righteous a reward of their labours, guided them in a marvellous way, and was unto them for a cover by day, and a light of stars in the night season; 18 Brought them through the Red sea, and led them through much water: 19 But she drowned their enemies, and cast them up out of the bottom of the deep. 20 Therefore the righteous spoiled the ungodly, and praised thy holy name, O Lord, and magnified with one accord thine hand, that fought for them. 21 For wisdom opened the mouth of the dumb, and made the tongues of them that cannot speak eloquent.

11

1 She prospered their works in the hand of the holy prophet. 2 They went through the wilderness that was not inhabited, and pitched tents in places where there lay no way. 3 They stood against their enemies, and were avenged of their adversaries. 4 When they were thirsty, they called upon thee, and water was given them out of the flinty rock, and their thirst was quenched out of the hard stone. 5 For by what things their enemies were punished, by the same they in their need were benefited. 6 For instead of of a perpetual running river troubled with foul blood, 7 For a manifest reproof of that commandment, whereby the infants were slain, thou gavest unto them abundance of water by a means which they hoped not for: 8 Declaring by that thirst then how thou hadst punished their adversaries. 9 For when they were tried albeit but in mercy chastised, they knew how the ungodly were judged in wrath and tormented, thirsting in another manner than the just. 10 For these thou didst admonish and try, as a father: but the other, as a severe king, thou didst condemn and punish. 11 Whether they were absent or present, they were vexed alike. 12 For a double grief came upon them, and a groaning for the remembrance of things past. 13 For when they heard by their own punishments the other to be benefited, they had some feeling of the Lord. 14 For whom they respected with scorn, when he was long before thrown out at the casting forth of the infants, him in the end, when they saw what came to pass, they admired. 15 But for the foolish devices of their wickedness, wherewith being deceived they worshipped serpents void of reason, and vile beasts, thou didst send a multitude of unreasonable beasts upon them for vengeance; 16 That they might know, that wherewithal a man sinneth, by the same also shall he be punished. 17 For thy Almighty hand, that made the world of matter without form, wanted not means to send among them a multitude of bears or fierce lions, 18 Or unknown wild beasts, full of rage, newly created, breathing out either a fiery vapour, or filthy scents of scattered smoke, or shooting horrible sparkles out of their eyes: 19 Whereof not only the harm might dispatch them at once, but also the terrible sight utterly destroy them. 20 Yea, and without these might they have fallen down with one blast, being persecuted of vengeance, and scattered abroad through the breath of thy power: but thou hast ordered all things in measure and number and weight. 21 For thou canst shew thy great strength at all times when thou wilt; and who may withstand the power of thine arm? 22 For the whole world before thee is as a little grain of the balance, yea, as a drop of the morning dew that falleth down upon the earth. 23 But thou hast mercy upon all; for thou canst do all things, and winkest at the sins of men, because they should amend. 24 For thou lovest all the things that are, and abhorrest nothing which thou hast made: for never wouldest thou have made any thing, if thou hadst hated it. 25 And how could any thing have endured, if it had not been thy will? or been preserved, if not called by thee? 26 But thou sparest all: for they are thine, O Lord, thou lover of souls.

12

_1 For thine incorruptible Spirit is in all things. 2 Therefore chastenest thou them by little and little that offend, and warnest them by putting them in remembrance wherein they have offended, that leaving their wickedness they may believe on thee, O Lord. 3 For it was thy will to destroy by the hands of our fathers both those old inhabitants of thy holy land, 4 Whom thou hatedst for doing most odious works of witchcrafts, and wicked sacrifices; 5 And also those merciless murderers of children, and devourers of man's flesh, and the feasts of blood, 6 With their priests out of the midst of their idolatrous crew, and the parents, that killed with their own hands souls destitute of help: 7 That the land, which thou esteemedst above all other, might receive a worthy colony of God's children. 8 Nevertheless even those thou sparedst as men, and didst send wasps, forerunners of thine host, to destroy them by little and little. **9** Not that thou wast unable to bring the ungodly under the hand of the righteous in battle, or to destroy them at once with cruel beasts, or with one rough word: **10** But executing thy judgments upon them by little and little, thou gavest them place of repentance, not being ignorant that they were a naughty generation, and that their malice was bred in them, and that their cogitation would never be changed. **11** For it was a cursed seed from the beginning; neither didst thou for fear of any man give them pardon for those things wherein they sinned. **12** For who shall say, What hast thou done? or who shall withstand thy judgment? or who shall accuse thee for the nations that perish, whom thou made? or who shall come to stand against thee, to be revenged for the unrighteous men? **13** For neither is there any God but thou that careth for all, to whom thou mightest shew that thy judgment is not unright. **14** Neither shall king or tyrant be able to set his face against thee for any whom thou hast punished. **15** Forsomuch then as thou art righteous thyself, thou orderest all things righteously: thinking it not agreeable with thy power to condemn him that hath not deserved to be punished. **16** For thy power is the beginning of righteousness, and because thou art the Lord of all, it maketh thee to be gracious unto all. **17** For when men will not believe that thou art of a full power, thou shewest thy strength, and among them that know it thou makest their boldness manifest. **18** But thou, mastering thy power, judgest with equity, and orderest us with great favour: for thou mayest use power when thou wilt. **19** But by such works hast thou taught thy people that the just man should be merciful, and hast made thy children to be of a good hope that thou givest repentance for sins. **20** For if thou didst punish the enemies of thy children, and the condemned to death, with such deliberation, giving them time and place, whereby they might be delivered from their malice: **21** With how great circumspection didst thou judge thine own sons, unto whose fathers thou hast sworn, and made covenants of good promises? **22** Therefore, whereas thou dost chasten us, thou scourgest our enemies a thousand times more, to the intent that, when we judge, we should carefully think of thy goodness, and when we ourselves are judged, we should look for mercy. **23** Wherefore, whereas men have lived dissolutely and unrighteously, thou hast tormented them with their own abominations. **24** For they went astray very far in the ways of error, and held them for gods, which even among the beasts of their enemies were despised, being deceived, as children of no understanding. **25** Therefore unto them, as to children without the use of reason, thou didst send a judgment to mock them. **26** But they that would not be reformed by that correction, wherein he dallied with them, shall feel a judgment worthy of God. **27** For, look, for what things they grudged, when they were punished, that is, for them whom they thought to be gods; [now] being punished in them, when they saw it, they acknowledged him to be the true God, whom before they denied to know: and therefore came extreme damnation upon them.

13 _1 Surely vain are all men by nature, who are ignorant of God, and could not out of the good things that are seen know him that is: neither by considering the works did they acknowledge the workmaster; **2** But deemed either fire, or wind, or the swift air, or the circle of the stars, or the violent water, or the lights of heaven, to be the gods which govern the world. **3** With whose beauty if they being delighted took them to be gods; let them know how much better the Lord of them is: for the first author of beauty hath created them. **4** But if they were astonished at their power and virtue, let them understand by them, how much mightier he is that made them. **5** For by the greatness and beauty of the creatures proportionably the maker of them is seen. **6** But yet for this they are the less to be blamed: for they peradventure err, seeking God, and desirous to find him. **7** For being conversant in his works they search him diligently, and believe their sight: because the things are beautiful that are seen. **8** Howbeit neither are they to be pardoned. **9** For if they were able to know so much, that they could aim at the world; how did they not sooner find out the Lord thereof? **10** But miserable are they, and in dead things is their hope, who call them gods, which are the works of men's hands, gold and silver, to shew art in, and resemblances of beasts, or a stone good for nothing, the work of an ancient hand. **11** Now a carpenter that felleth timber, after he hath sawn down a tree meet for the purpose, and taken off all the bark skilfully round about, and hath wrought it handsomely, and made a vessel thereof fit for the service of man's life; **12** And after spending the refuse of his work to dress his meat, hath filled himself; **13** And taking the very refuse among those which served to no use, being a crooked piece of wood, and full of knots, hath carved it diligently, when he had nothing else to do, and formed it by the skill of his understanding, and fashioned it to the image of a man; **14** Or made it like some vile beast, laying it over with vermilion, and with paint colouring it red, and covering every spot therein; **15** And when he had made a convenient room for it, set it in a wall, and made it fast with iron: **16** For he provided for it that it might not fall, knowing that it was unable to help itself; for it is an image, and hath need of help: **17** Then maketh he prayer for his goods, for his wife and children, and is not ashamed to speak to that which hath no life. **18** For health he calleth upon that which is weak: for life prayeth to that which is dead; for aid humbly beseecheth that which hath least means to help: and for a good journey he asketh of that which cannot set a foot forward: **19** And for gaining and getting, and for good success of his hands, asketh ability to do of him, that is most unable to do any thing.

14 _1 Again, one preparing himself to sail, and about to pass through the raging waves, calleth upon a piece of wood more rotten than the vessel that carrieth him. **2** For verily desire of gain devised that, and the workman built it by his skill. **3** But thy providence, O Father, governeth it: for thou hast made a way in the sea, and a safe path in the waves; **4** Shewing that thou canst save from all danger: yea, though a man went to sea without art. **5** Nevertheless thou wouldest not that the works of thy wisdom should be idle, and therefore do men commit their lives to a small piece of wood, and passing the rough sea in a weak vessel are saved. **6** For in the old time also, when the proud giants perished, the hope of the world governed by thy hand escaped in a weak vessel, and left to all ages a seed of generation. **7** For blessed is the wood whereby righteousness cometh. **8** But that which is made with hands is cursed, as well it, as he that made it: he, because he made it; and it, because, being corruptible, it was called god. **9** For the ungodly and his ungodliness are both alike hateful unto God. **10** For that which is made shall be punished together with him that made it. **11** Therefore even upon the idols of the Gentiles shall there be a visitation: because in the creature of God they are become an abomination, and stumblingblocks to the souls of men, and a snare to the feet of the unwise. **12** For the devising of idols was the beginning of spiritual fornication, and the invention of them the corruption of life. **13** For neither were they from the beginning, neither shall they be for ever. **14** For by the vain glory of men they entered into the world, and therefore shall they come shortly to an end. **15** For a father afflicted with untimely mourning, when he hath made an image of his child soon taken away, now honoured him as a god, which was then a dead man, and delivered to those that were under him ceremonies and sacrifices. **16** Thus in process of time an ungodly custom grown strong was kept as a law, and graven images were worshipped by the commandments of kings. **17** Whom men could not honour in presence, because they dwelt far off, they took the counterfeit of his visage from far, and made an express image of a king whom they honoured, to the end that by this their forwardness they might flatter him that was absent, as if he were present. **18** Also the singular diligence of the artificer did help to set forward the ignorant to more superstition. **19** For he, peradventure willing to please one in authority, forced all his skill to make the resemblance of the best fashion. **20** And so the multitude, allured by the grace of the work, took him now for a god, which a little before was but honoured. **21** And this was an occasion to deceive the world: for men, serving either calamity or tyranny, did ascribe unto stones and stocks the incommunicable name. **22** Moreover this was not enough for them, that they erred in the knowledge of God; but whereas they lived in the great war of ignorance, those so great plagues called they peace. **23** For whilst they slew their children in sacrifices, or used secret ceremonies, or made revellings of strange rites; **24** They kept neither lives nor marriages any longer undefiled: but either one slew another traiterously, or grieved him by adultery. **25** So that there reigned in all men without exception blood, manslaughter, theft, and dissimulation, corruption, unfaithfulness, tumults, perjury, **26** Disquieting of good men, forgetfulness of good turns, defiling of souls, changing of kind, disorder in marriages, adultery, and shameless uncleanness. **27** For the worshipping of idols not to be named is the beginning, the cause, and the end, of all evil. **28** For either they are mad when they be merry, or prophesy lies, or live unjustly, or else lightly forswear themselves. **29** For insomuch as their trust is in idols, which have no life; though they swear falsely, yet they look not to be hurt. **30** Howbeit for both causes shall they be justly punished: both because they thought not well of God, giving heed unto idols, and also unjustly swore in deceit, despising holiness. **31** For it is not the power of them by whom they swear: but it is the just vengeance of sinners, that punisheth always the offence of the ungodly.

15 _1 But thou, O God, art gracious and true, longsuffering, and in mercy ordering all things, **2** For if we sin, we are thine, knowing thy power: but we will not sin, knowing that we are counted thine. **3** For to know thee is perfect righteousness: yea, to know thy power is the root of immortality. **4** For neither did the mischievous invention of men deceive us, nor an image spotted with divers colours, the painter's fruitless labour; **5** The sight whereof enticeth fools to lust after it, and so they desire the form of a dead image, that hath no breath. **6** Both they that make them, they that desire them, and they that worship them, are lovers of evil things, and are worthy to have such things to trust upon. **7** For the potter, tempering soft earth, fashioneth every vessel with much labour for our service: yea, of the same clay he maketh both the vessels that serve for clean uses, and likewise also all such as serve to the contrary: but what is the use of either sort, the potter himself is the judge. **8** And employing his labours lewdly, he maketh a vain god of the same clay, even he which a little before was made of earth himself, and within a little while after returneth to the same, out when his life which was lent him shall be demanded. **9** Notwithstanding his care is, not that he shall have much labour, nor that his life is short: but striveth to excel goldsmiths and silversmiths, and endeavoureth to do like the workers in brass, and counteth it his glory to make counterfeit things. **10** His heart is ashes, his hope is more vile than earth, and his life of less value than clay: **11** Forasmuch as he knew not his Maker, and him that inspired into him an active soul, and breathed in a living spirit. **12** But they counted our life a pastime, and our time here a market for gain: for, say they, we must be getting every way, though it be by evil means. **13** For this man, that of earthly matter

maketh brittle vessels and graven images, knoweth himself to offend above all
others. **14** And all the enemies of thy people, that hold them in subjection,
are most foolish, and are more miserable than very babes. **15** For they counted
all the idols of the heathen to be gods: which neither have the use of eyes to
see, nor noses to draw breath, nor ears to hear, nor fingers of hands to handle;
and as for their feet, they are slow to go. **16** For man made them, and he that
borrowed his own spirit fashioned them: but no man can make a god like unto
himself. **17** For being mortal, he worketh a dead thing with wicked hands: for
he himself is better than the things which he worshippeth: whereas he lived once,
but they never. **18** Yea, they worshipped those beasts also that are most hateful:
for being compared together, some are worse than others. **19** Neither are they
beautiful, so much as to be desired in respect of beasts: but they went without the
praise of God and his blessing.

16

_**1** Therefore by the like were they punished worthily, and by the mul-
titude of beasts tormented. **2** Instead of which punishment, dealing
graciously with thine own people, thou preparedst for them meat of a strange
taste, even quails to stir up their appetite: **3** To the end that they, desiring food,
might for the ugly sight of the beasts sent among them lothe even that, which
they must needs desire; but these, suffering penury for a short space, might be
made partakers of a strange taste. **4** For it was requisite, that upon them exer-
cising tyranny should come penury, which they could not avoid: but to these it
should only be shewed how their enemies were tormented. **5** For when the
horrible fierceness of beasts came upon these, and they perished with the stings of
crooked serpents, thy wrath endured not for ever: **6** But they were troubled for
a small season, that they might be admonished, having a sign of salvation, to put
them in remembrance of the commandment of thy law. **7** For he that turned
himself toward it was not saved by the thing that he saw, but by thee, that art the
Saviour of all. **8** And in this thou madest thine enemies confess, that it is thou
who deliverest from all evil: **9** For them the bitings of grasshoppers and flies
killed, neither was there found any remedy for their life: for they were worthy to
be punished by such. **10** But thy sons not the very teeth of venomous dragons
overcame: for thy mercy was ever by them, and healed them. **11** For they were
pricked, that they should remember thy words; and were quickly saved, that not
falling into deep forgetfulness, they might be continually mindful of thy good-
ness. **12** For it was neither herb, nor mollifying plaister, that restored them to
health: but thy word, O Lord, which healeth all things. **13** For thou hast power
of life and death: thou leadest to the gates of hell, and bringest up again. **14** A
man indeed killeth through his malice: and the spirit, when it is gone forth, re-
turneth not; neither the soul received up cometh again. **15** But it is not possi-
ble to escape thine hand. **16** For the ungodly, that denied to know thee, were
scourged by the strength of thine arm: with strange rains, hails, and showers, were
they persecuted, that they could not avoid, and through fire were they consu-
med. **17** For, which is most to be wondered at, the fire had more force in the
water, that quencheth all things: for the world fighteth for the righteous. **18** For
sometime the flame was mitigated, that it might not burn up the beasts that were
sent against the ungodly; but themselves might see and perceive that they were
persecuted with the judgment of God. **19** And at another time it burneth even
in the midst of water above the power of fire, that it might destroy the fruits of
an unjust land. **20** Instead whereof thou feddest thine own people with angels'
food, and didst send them from heaven bread prepared without their labour, able
to content every man's delight, and agreeing to every taste. **21** For thy suste-
nance declared thy sweetness unto thy children, and serving to the appetite of
the eater, tempered itself to every man's liking. **22** But snow and ice endured
the fire, and melted not, that they might know that fire burning in the hail, and
sparkling in the rain, did destroy the fruits of the enemies. **23** But this again did
even forget his own strength, that the righteous might be nourished. **24** For the
creature that serveth thee, who art the Maker increaseth his strength against the
unrighteous for their punishment, and abateth his strength for the benefit of such
as put their trust in thee. **25** Therefore even then was it altered into all fashions,
and was obedient to thy grace, that nourisheth all things, according to the desire
of them that had need: **26** That thy children, O Lord, whom thou lovest, might
know, that it is not the growing of fruits that nourisheth man: but that it is thy
word, which preserveth them that put their trust in thee. **27** For that which
was not destroyed of the fire, being warmed with a little sunbeam, soon melted
away: **28** That it might be known, that we must prevent the sun to give thee
thanks, and at the dayspring pray unto thee. **29** For the hope of the unthankful
shall melt away as the winter's hoar frost, and shall run away as unprofitable water.

17

_**1** For great are thy judgments, and cannot be expressed: therefore
unnurtured souls have erred. **2** For when unrighteous men thought
to oppress the holy nation; they being shut up in their houses, the prisoners of
darkness, and fettered with the bonds of a long night, lay [there] exiled from the
eternal providence. **3** For while they supposed to lie hid in their secret sins, they
were scattered under a dark veil of forgetfulness, being horribly astonished, and
troubled with [strange] apparitions. **4** For neither might the corner that held
them keep them from fear: but noises [as of waters] falling down sounded about
them, and sad visions appeared unto them with heavy countenances. **5** No
power of the fire might give them light: neither could the bright flames of the stars
endure to lighten that horrible night. **6** Only there appeared unto them a fire
kindled of itself, very dreadful: for being much terrified, they thought the things
which they saw to be worse than the sight they saw not. **7** As for the illusions
of art magick, they were put down, and their vaunting in wisdom was reproved
with disgrace. **8** For they, that promised to drive away terrors and troubles from
a sick soul, were sick themselves of fear, worthy to be laughed at. **9** For though
no terrible thing did fear them; yet being scared with beasts that passed by, and
hissing of serpents, **10** They died for fear, denying that they saw the air, whi-
ch could of no side be avoided. **11** For wickedness, condemned by her own
witness, is very timorous, and being pressed with conscience, always forecasteth
grievous things. **12** For fear is nothing else but a betraying of the succours whi-
ch reason offereth. **13** And the expectation from within, being less, counteth
the ignorance more than the cause which bringeth the torment. **14** But they
sleeping the same sleep that night, which was indeed intolerable, and which came
upon them out of the bottoms of inevitable hell, **15** Were partly vexed with
monstrous apparitions, and partly fainted, their heart failing them: for a sudden
fear, and not looked for, came upon them. **16** So then whosoever there fell
down was straitly kept, shut up in a prison without iron bars, **17** For whether
he were husbandman, or shepherd, or a labourer in the field, he was overtaken,
and endured that necessity, which could not be avoided: for they were all bound
with one chain of darkness. **18** Whether it were a whistling wind, or a melo-
dious noise of birds among the spreading branches, or a pleasing fall of water
running violently, **19** Or a terrible sound of stones cast down, or a running
that could not be seen of skipping beasts, or a roaring voice of most savage wild
beasts, or a rebounding echo from the hollow mountains; these things made them
to swoon for fear. **20** For the whole world shined with clear light, and none
were hindered in their labour: **21** Over them only was spread an heavy night,
an image of that darkness which should afterward receive them: but yet were they
unto themselves more grievous than the darkness.

18

_**1** Nevertheless thy saints had a very great light, whose voice they hea-
ring, and not seeing their shape, because they also had not suffered the
same things, they counted them happy. **2** But for that they did not hurt them
now, of whom they had been wronged before, they thanked them, and besought
them pardon for that they had been enemies. **3** Instead whereof thou gavest
them a burning pillar of fire, both to be a guide of the unknown journey, and an
harmless sun to entertain them honourably. **4** For they were worthy to be depri-
ved of light and imprisoned in darkness, who had kept thy sons shut up, by whom
the uncorrupt light of the law was to be given unto the world. **5** And when they
had determined to slay the babes of the saints, one child being cast forth, and
saved, to reprove them, thou tookest away the multitude of their children, and
destroyedst them altogether in a mighty water. **6** Of that night were our fathers
certified afore, that assuredly knowing unto what oaths they had given credence,
they might afterwards be of good cheer. **7** So of thy people was accepted both
the salvation of the righteous, and destruction of the enemies. **8** For wherewith
thou didst punish our adversaries, by the same thou didst glorify us, whom thou
hadst called. **9** For the righteous children of good men did sacrifice secretly, and
with one consent made a holy law, that the saints should be like partakers of the
same good and evil, the fathers now singing out the songs of praise. **10** But on
the other side there sounded an ill according cry of the enemies, and a lamentable
noise was carried abroad for children that were bewailed. **11** The master and the
servant were punished after one manner; and like as the king, so suffered the com-
mon person. **12** So they all together had innumerable dead with one kind of de-
ath; neither were the living sufficient to bury them: for in one moment the noblest
offspring of them was destroyed. **13** For whereas they would not believe any
thing by reason of the enchantments; upon the destruction of the firstborn, they
acknowledged this people to be the sons of God. **14** For while all things were
in quiet silence, and that night was in the midst of her swift course, **15** Thine
Almighty word leaped down from heaven out of thy royal throne, as a fierce man
of war into the midst of a land of destruction, **16** And brought thine unfeigned
commandment as a sharp sword, and standing up filled all things with death; and
it touched the heaven, but it stood upon the earth. **17** Then suddenly visions
of horrible dreams troubled them sore, and terrors came upon them unlooked
for. **18** And one thrown here, and another there, half dead, shewed the cause
of his death. **19** For the dreams that troubled them did foreshew this, lest they
should perish, and not know why they were afflicted. **20** Yea, the tasting of
death touched the righteous also, and there was a destruction of the multitude
in the wilderness: but the wrath endured not long. **21** For then the blameless
man made haste, and stood forth to defend them; and bringing the shield of his
proper ministry, even prayer, and the propitiation of incense, set himself against
the wrath, and so brought the calamity to an end, declaring that he was thy ser-
vant. **22** So he overcame the destroyer, not with strength of body, nor force of
arms, but with a word subdued him that punished, alleging the oaths and cove-
nants made with the fathers. **23** For when the dead were now fallen down by
heaps one upon another, standing between, he stayed the wrath, and parted the
way to the living. **24** For in the long garment was the whole world, and in the
four rows of the stones was the glory of the fathers graven, and thy Majesty upon
the daidem of his head. **25** Unto these the destroyer gave place, and was afraid
of them: for it was enough that they only tasted of the wrath.

19 1 As for the ungodly, wrath came upon them without mercy unto the end: for he knew before what they would do; **2** How that having given them leave to depart, and sent them hastily away, they would repent and pursue them. **3** For whilst they were yet mourning and making lamentation at the graves of the dead, they added another foolish device, and pursued them as fugitives, whom they had intreated to be gone. **4** For the destiny, whereof they were worthy, drew them unto this end, and made them forget the things that had already happened, that they might fulfil the punishment which was wanting to their torments: **5** And that thy people might pass a wonderful way: but they might find a strange death. **6** For the whole creature in his proper kind was fashioned again anew, serving the peculiar commandments that were given unto them, that thy children might be kept without hurt: **7** As namely, a cloud shadowing the camp; and where water stood before, dry land appeared; and out of the Red sea a way without impediment; and out of the violent stream a green field: **8** Wherethrough all the people went that were defended with thy hand, seeing thy marvellous strange wonders. **9** For they went at large like horses, and leaped like lambs, praising thee, O Lord, who hadst delivered them. **10** For they were yet mindful of the things that were done while they sojourned in the strange land, how the ground brought forth flies instead of cattle, and how the river cast up a multitude of frogs instead of fishes. **11** But afterwards they saw a new generation of fowls, when, being led with their appetite, they asked delicate meats. **12** For quails came up unto them from the sea for their contentment. **13** And punishments came upon the sinners not without former signs by the force of thunders: for they suffered justly according to their own wickedness, insomuch as they used a more hard and hateful behaviour toward strangers. **14** For the Sodomites did not receive those, whom they knew not when they came: but these brought friends into bondage, that had well deserved of them. **15** And not only so, but peradventure some respect shall be had of those, because they used strangers not friendly: **16** But these very grievously afflicted them, whom they had received with feastings, and were already made partakers of the same laws with them. **17** Therefore even with blindness were these stricken, as those were at the doors of the righteous man: when, being compassed about with horrible great darkness, every one sought the passage of his own doors. **18** For the elements were changed in themselves by a kind of harmony, like as in a psaltery notes change the name of the tune, and yet are always sounds; which may well be perceived by the sight of the things that have been done. **19** For earthly things were turned into watery, and the things, that before swam in the water, now went upon the ground. **20** The fire had power in the water, forgetting his own virtue: and the water forgat his own quenching nature. **21** On the other side, the flames wasted not the flesh of the corruptible living things, though they walked therein; neither melted they the icy kind of heavenly meat that was of nature apt to melt. **22** For in all things, O Lord, thou didst magnify thy people, and glorify them, neither didst thou lightly regard them: but didst assist them in every time and place.

APOCRYPHA BOOK OF SIRACH

The Wisdom of Jesus the Son of Sirach, or Ecclesiasticus

A Prologue made by an uncertain Author

This Jesus was the son of Sirach, and grandchild to Jesus of the same name with him: this man therefore lived in the latter times, after the people had been led away captive, and called home a again, and almost after all the prophets. Now his grandfather Jesus, as he himself witnesseth, was a man of great diligence and wisdom among the Hebrews, who did not only gather the grave and short sentences of wise men, that had been before him, but himself also uttered some of his own, full of much understanding and wisdom. When as therefore the first Jesus died, leaving this book almost perfected, Sirach his son receiving it after him left it to his own son Jesus, who, having gotten it into his hands, compiled it all orderly into one volume, and called it

Wisdom, intituling it both by his own name, his father's name, and his grandfather's; alluring the hearer by the very name of Wisdom to have a greater love to the study of this book. It containeth therefore wise sayings, dark sentences, and parables, and certain particular ancient godly stories of men that pleased God; also his prayer and song; moreover, what benefits God had vouchsafed his people, and what plagues he had heaped upon their enemies. This Jesus did imitate Solomon, and was no less famous for wisdom and learning, both being indeed a man of great learning, and so reputed also.

The Prologue of the Wisdom of Jesus the Son of Sirach. Whereas many and great things have been delivered unto us by the law and the prophets, and by others that have followed their steps, for the which things Israel ought to be commended for learning and wisdom; and whereof not only the readers must needs become skilful themselves, but also they that desire to learn be able to profit them which are without, both by speaking and writing: my grandfather

Jesus, when he had much given himself to the reading of the law, and the prophets, and other books of our fathers, and had gotten therein good judgment, was drawn on also himself to write something pertaining to learning and wisdom; to the intent that those which are desirous to learn, and are addicted to these things, might profit much more in living according to the law. Wherefore let me intreat you to read it with favour and attention, and to pardon us, wherein we may seem to come short of some words, which we have laboured to interpret. For the same things uttered in Hebrew, and translated into another tongue, have not the same force in them: and not only these things, but the law itself, and the prophets, and the rest of the books, have no small difference, when they are spoken in their own language. For in the eight and thirtieth year coming into Egypt, when Euergetes was king, and continuing there some time, I found a book of no small learning: therefore I thought it most necessary for me to bestow some diligence and travail to interpret it; using great watchfulness and skill in that space to bring the book to an end, and set it forth for them also, which in a strange country are willing to learn, being prepared before in manners to live after the law.

1 1 All wisdom cometh from the Lord, and is with him for ever. **2** Who can number the sand of the sea, and the drops of rain, and the days of eternity? **3** Who can find out the height of heaven, and the breadth of the earth, and the deep, and wisdom? **4** Wisdom hath been created before all things, and the understanding of prudence from everlasting. **5** The word of God most high is the fountain of wisdom; and her ways are everlasting commandments. **6** To whom hath the root of wisdom been revealed? or who hath known her wise counsels? **7** [Unto whom hath the knowledge of wisdom been made manifest? and who hath understood her great experience?] **8** There is one wise and greatly to be feared, the Lord sitting upon his throne. **9** He created her, and saw her, and numbered her, and poured her out upon all his works. **10** She is with all flesh according to his gift, and he hath given her to them that love him. **11** The fear of the Lord is honour, and glory, and gladness, and a crown of rejoicing. **12** The fear of the Lord maketh a merry heart, and giveth joy, and gladness, and a long life. **13** Whoso feareth the Lord, it shall go well with him at the last, and he shall find favour in the day of his death. **14** To fear the Lord is the beginning of wisdom: and it was created with the faithful in the womb. **15** She hath built an everlasting foundation with men, and she shall continue with their seed. **16** To fear the Lord is fulness of wisdom, and filleth men with her fruits. **17** She filleth all their house with things desirable, and the garners with her increase. **18** The fear of the Lord is a crown of wisdom, making peace and perfect health to flourish; both which are the gifts of God: and it enlargeth their rejoicing that love him. **19** Wisdom raineth down skill and knowledge of understanding standing, and exalteth them to honour that hold her fast. **20** The root of wisdom is to fear the Lord, and the branches thereof are long life. **21** The fear of the Lord driveth away sins: and where it is present, it turneth away wrath. **22** A furious man cannot be justified; for the sway of his fury shall be his destruction. **23** A patient man will tear for a time, and afterward joy shall spring up unto him. **24** He will hide his words for a time, and the lips of many shall declare his wisdom. **25** The parables of knowledge are in the treasures of wisdom: but godliness is an abomination to a sinner. **26** If thou desire wisdom, keep the commandments, and the Lord shall give her unto thee. **27** For the fear of the Lord is wisdom and instruction: and faith and meekness are his delight. **28** Distrust not the fear of the Lord when thou art poor: and come not unto him with a double heart. **29** Be not an hypocrite in the sight of men, and take good heed what thou speakest. **30** Exalt not thyself, lest thou fall, and bring dishonour upon thy soul, and so God discover thy secrets, and cast thee down in the midst of the congregation, because thou camest not in truth to the fear of the Lord, but thy heart is full of deceit.

2

1 My son, if thou come to serve the Lord, prepare thy soul for tempta-
tion. 2 Set thy heart aright, and constantly endure, and make not haste
in time of trouble. 3 Cleave unto him, and depart not away, that thou mayest
be increased at thy last end. 4 Whatsoever is brought upon thee take cheerfully,
and be patient when thou art changed to a low estate. 5 For gold is tried in the
fire, and acceptable men in the furnace of adversity. 6 Believe in him, and he
will help thee; order thy way aright, and trust in him. 7 Ye that fear the Lord,
wait for his mercy; and go not aside, lest ye fall. 8 Ye that fear the Lord, believe
him; and your reward shall not fail. 9 Ye that fear the Lord, hope for good,
and for everlasting joy and mercy. 10 Look at the generations of old, and see;
did ever any trust in the Lord, and was confounded? or did any abide in his fear,
and was forsaken? or whom did he ever despise, that called upon him? 11 For
the Lord is full of compassion and mercy, longsuffering, and very pitiful, and
forgiveth sins, and saveth in time of affliction. 12 Woe be to fearful hearts,
and faint hands, and the sinner that goeth two ways! 13 Woe unto him that is
fainthearted! for he believeth not; therefore shall he not be defended. 14 Woe
unto you that have lost patience! and what will ye do when the Lord shall visit
you? 15 They that fear the Lord will not disobey his Word; and they that love
him will keep his ways. 16 They that fear the Lord will seek that which is well,
pleasing unto him; and they that love him shall be filled with the law. 17 They
that fear the Lord will prepare their hearts, and humble their souls in his si-
ght, 18 Saying, We will fall into the hands of the Lord, and not into the hands
of men: for as his majesty is, so is his mercy.

3

1 Hear me your father, O children, and do thereafter, that ye may be
safe. 2 For the Lord hath given the father honour over the children, and
hath confirmed the authority of the mother over the sons. 3 Whoso honoureth
his father maketh an atonement for his sins: 4 And he that honoureth his mother
is as one that layeth up treasure. 5 Whoso honoureth his father shall have joy of
his own children; and when he maketh his prayer, he shall be heard. 6 He that
honoureth his father shall have a long life; and he that is obedient unto the Lord
shall be a comfort to his mother. 7 He that feareth the Lord will honour his fa-
ther, and will do service unto his parents, as to his masters. 8 Honour thy father
and mother both in word and deed, that a blessing may come upon thee from
them. 9 For the blessing of the father establisheth the houses of children; but
the curse of the mother rooteth out foundations. 10 Glory not in the dishonour
of thy father; for thy father's dishonour is no glory unto thee. 11 For the glory
of a man is from the honour of his father; and a mother in dishonour is a reproach
to the children. 12 My son, help thy father in his age, and grieve him not as
long as he liveth. 13 And if his understanding fail, have patience with him; and
despise him not when thou art in thy full strength. 14 For the relieving of thy
father shall not be forgotten: and instead of sins it shall be added to build thee
up. 15 In the day of thine affliction it shall be remembered; thy sins also shall
melt away, as the ice in the fair warm weather. 16 He that forsaketh his father
is as a blasphemer; and he that angereth his mother is cursed: of God. 17 My
son, go on with thy business in meekness; so shalt thou be beloved of him that is
approved. 18 The greater thou art, the more humble thyself, and thou shalt find
favour before the Lord. 19 Many are in high place, and of renown: but myste-
ries are revealed unto the meek. 20 For the power of the Lord is great, and he is
honoured of the lowly. 21 Seek not out things that are too hard for thee, neither
search the things that are above thy strength. 22 But what is commanded thee,
think thereupon with reverence, for it is not needful for thee to see with thine
eyes the things that are in secret. 23 Be not curious in unnecessary matters:
for more things are shewed unto thee than men understand. 24 For many are
deceived by their own vain opinion; and an evil suspicion hath overthrown their
judgment. 25 Without eyes thou shalt want light: profess not the knowledge
therefore that thou hast not. 26 A stubborn heart shall fare evil at the last; and
he that loveth danger shall perish therein. 27 An obstinate heart shall be laden
with sorrows; and the wicked man shall heap sin upon sin. 28 In the punish-
ment of the proud there is no remedy; for the plant of wickedness hath taken root
in him. 29 The heart of the prudent will understand a parable; and an attentive
ear is the desire of a wise man. 30 Water will quench a flaming fire; and alms
maketh an atonement for sins. 31 And he that requiteth good turns is mindful
of that which may come hereafter; and when he falleth, he shall find a stay.

4

1 My son, defraud not the poor of his living, and make not the needy eyes
to wait long. 2 Make not an hungry soul sorrowful; neither provoke a
man in his distress. 3 Add not more trouble to an heart that is vexed; and defer
not to give to him that is in need. 4 Reject not the supplication of the afflicted;
neither turn away thy face from a poor man. 5 Turn not away thine eye from
the needy, and give him none occasion to curse thee: 6 For if he curse thee in
the bitterness of his soul, his prayer shall be heard of him that made him. 7 Get
thyself the love of the congregation, and bow thy head to a great man. 8 Let
it not grieve thee to bow down thine ear to the poor, and give him a friendly
answer with meekness. 9 Deliver him that suffereth wrong from the hand of
the oppressor; and be not fainthearted when thou sittest in judgment. 10 Be
as a father unto the fatherless, and instead of an husband unto their mother: so
shalt thou be as the son of the most High, and he shall love thee more than thy
mother doth. 11 Wisdom exalteth her children, and layeth hold of them that
seek her. 12 He that loveth her loveth life; and they that seek to her early shall
be filled with joy. 13 He that holdeth her fast shall inherit glory; and whereso-
ever she entereth, the Lord will bless. 14 They that serve her shall minister to
the Holy One: and them that love her the Lord doth love. 15 Whoso giveth
ear unto her shall judge the nations: and he that attendeth unto her shall dwell
securely. 16 If a man commit himself unto her, he shall inherit her; and his
generation shall hold her in possession. 17 For at the first she will walk with
him by crooked ways, and bring fear and dread upon him, and torment him with
her discipline, until she may trust his soul, and try him by her laws. 18 Then
will she return the straight way unto him, and comfort him, and shew him her
secrets. 19 But if he go wrong, she will forsake him, and give him over to his
own ruin. 20 Observe the opportunity, and beware of evil; and be not ashamed
when it concerneth thy soul. 21 For there is a shame that bringeth sin; and
there is a shame which is glory and grace. 22 Accept no person against thy
soul, and let not the reverence of any man cause thee to fall. 23 And refrain
not to speak, when there is occasion to do good, and hide not thy wisdom in her
beauty. 24 For by speech wisdom shall be known: and learning by the word
of the tongue. 25 In no wise speak against the truth; but be abashed of the
error of thine ignorance. 26 Be not ashamed to confess thy sins; and force not
the course of the river. 27 Make not thyself an underling to a foolish man;
neither accept the person of the mighty. 28 Strive for the truth unto death,
and the Lord shall fight for thee. 29 Be not hasty in thy tongue, and in thy
deeds slack and remiss. 30 Be not as a lion in thy house, nor frantick among
thy servants. 31 Let not thine hand be stretched out to receive, and shut when
thou shouldest repay.

5

1 Set thy heart upon thy goods; and say not, I have enough for my
life. 2 Follow not thine own mind and thy strength, to walk in the
ways of thy heart: 3 And say not, Who shall controul me for my works? for
the Lord will surely revenge thy pride. 4 Say not, I have sinned, and what
harm hath happened unto me? for the Lord is longsuffering, he will in no wise
let thee go. 5 Concerning propitiation, be not without fear to add sin unto
sin: 6 And say not His mercy is great; he will be pacified for the multitude of
my sins: for mercy and wrath come from him, and his indignation resteth upon
sinners. 7 Make no tarrying to turn to the Lord, and put not off from day to
day: for suddenly shall the wrath of the Lord come forth, and in thy security thou
shalt be destroyed, and perish in the day of vengeance. 8 Set not thine heart
upon goods unjustly gotten, for they shall not profit thee in the day of calami-
ty. 9 Winnow not with every wind, and go not into every way: for so doth the
sinner that hath a double tongue. 10 Be stedfast in thy understanding; and let
thy word be the same. 11 Be swift to hear; and let thy life be sincere; and with
patience give answer. 12 If thou hast understanding, answer thy neighbour; if
not, lay thy hand upon thy mouth. 13 Honour and shame is in talk: and the
tongue of man is his fall. 14 Be not called a whisperer, and lie not in wait with
thy tongue: for a foul shame is upon the thief, and an evil condemnation upon
the double tongue. 15 Be not ignorant of any thing in a great matter or a small.

6

1 Instead of a friend become not an enemy; for [thereby] thou shalt inherit
an ill name, shame, and reproach: even so shall a sinner that hath a double
tongue. 2 Extol not thyself in the counsel of thine own heart; that thy soul be
not torn in pieces as a bull [straying alone.] 3 Thou shalt eat up thy leaves, and
lose thy fruit, and leave thyself as a dry tree. 4 A wicked soul shall destroy him
that hath it, and shall make him to be laughed to scorn of his enemies. 5 Swe-
et language will multiply friends: and a fairspeaking tongue will increase kind
greetings. 6 Be in peace with many: nevertheless have but one counsellor of a
thousand. 7 If thou wouldest get a friend, prove him first and be not hasty to
credit him. 8 For some man is a friend for his own occasion, and will not abide
in the day of thy trouble. 9 And there is a friend, who being turned to enmity,
and strife will discover thy reproach. 10 Again, some friend is a companion
at the table, and will not continue in the day of thy affliction. 11 But in thy
prosperity he will be as thyself, and will be bold over thy servants. 12 If thou be
brought low, he will be against thee, and will hide himself from thy face. 13 Se-
parate thyself from thine enemies, and take heed of thy friends. 14 A faithfull
friend is a strong defence: and he that hath found such an one hath found a
treasure. 15 Nothing doth countervail a faithful friend, and his excellency is in-
valuable. 16 A faithful friend is the medicine of life; and they that fear the Lord
shall find him. 17 Whoso feareth the Lord shall direct his friendship aright: for
as he is, so shall his neighbour be also. 18 My son, gather instruction from thy
youth up: so shalt thou find wisdom till thine old age. 19 Come unto her as
one that ploweth and soweth, and wait for her good fruits: for thou shalt not toil
much in labouring about her, but thou shalt eat of her fruits right soon. 20 She
is very unpleasant to the unlearned: he that is without understanding will not
remain with her. 21 She will lie upon him as a mighty stone of trial; and he
will cast her from him ere it be long. 22 For wisdom is according to her name,
and she is not manifest unto many. 23 Give ear, my son, receive my advice, and
refuse not my counsel, 24 And put thy feet into her fetters, and thy neck into
her chain. 25 Bow down thy shoulder, and bear her, and be not grieved with
her bonds. 26 Come unto her with thy whole heart, and keep her ways with
all thy power. 27 Search, and seek, and she shall be made known unto thee:

and when thou hast got hold of her, let her not go. **28** For at the last thou shalt
find her rest, and that shall be turned to thy joy. **29** Then shall her fetters be a
strong defence for thee, and her chains a robe of glory. **30** For there is a golden
ornament upon her, and her bands are purple lace. **31** Thou shalt put her on
as a robe of honour, and shalt put her about thee as a crown of joy. **32** My son,
if thou wilt, thou shalt be taught: and if thou wilt apply thy mind, thou shalt be
prudent. **33** If thou love to hear, thou shalt receive understanding: and if thou
bow thine ear, thou shalt be wise, **34** Stand in the multitude of the elders; and
cleave unto him that is wise. **35** Be willing to hear every godly discourse; and
let not the parables of understanding escape thee. **36** And if thou seest a man
of understanding, get thee betimes unto him, and let thy foot wear the steps of
his door. **37** Let thy mind be upon the ordinances of the Lord and meditate
continually in his commandments: he shall establish thine heart, and give thee
wisdom at thine owns desire.

7

1 Do no evil, so shall no harm come unto thee. **2** Depart from the
unjust, and iniquity shall turn away from thee. **3** My son, sow not
upon the furrows of unrighteousness, and thou shalt not reap them seven-
fold. **4** Seek not of the Lord preeminence, neither of the king the seat of ho-
nour. **5** justify not thyself before the Lord; and boast not of thy wisdom before
the king. **6** Seek not to be judge, being not able to take away iniquity; lest at
any time thou fear the person of the mighty, an stumblingblock in the way of thy
uprightness. **7** Offend not against the multitude of a city, and then thou shalt
not cast thyself down among the people. **8** Bind not one sin upon another;
for in one thou shalt not be unpunished. **9** Say not, God will look upon the
multitude of my oblations, and when I offer to the most high God, he will accept
it. **10** Be not fainthearted when thou makest thy prayer, and neglect not to
give alms. **11** Laugh no man to scorn in the bitterness of his soul: for there
is one which humbleth and exalteth. **12** Devise not a lie against thy brother;
neither do the like to thy friend. **13** Use not to make any manner of lie: for
the custom thereof is not good. **14** Use not many words in a multitude of
elders, and make not much babbling when thou prayest. **15** Hate not laborious
work, neither husbandry, which the most High hath ordained. **16** Number not
thyself among the multitude of sinners, but remember that wrath will not tarry
long. **17** Humble thyself greatly: for the vengeance of the ungodly is fire and
worms. **18** Change not a friend for any good by no means; neither a faithful
brother for the gold of Ophir. **19** Forego not a wise and good woman: for her
grace is above gold. **20** Whereas thy servant worketh truly, entreat him not evil.
nor the hireling that bestoweth himself wholly for thee. **21** Let thy soul love
a good servant, and defraud him not of liberty. **22** Hast thou cattle? have an
eye to them: and if they be for thy profit, keep them with thee. **23** Hast thou
children? instruct them, and bow down their neck from their youth. **24** Hast
thou daughters? have a care of their body, and shew not thyself cheerful toward
them. **25** Marry thy daughter, and so shalt thou have performed a weighty mat-
ter: but give her to a man of understanding. **26** Hast thou a wife after thy mind?
forsake her not: but give not thyself over to a light woman. **27** Honour thy
father with thy whole heart, and forget not the sorrows of thy mother. **28** Re-
member that thou wast begotten of them; and how canst thou recompense them
the things that they have done for thee? **29** Fear the Lord with all thy soul,
and reverence his priests. **30** Love him that made thee with all thy strength,
and forsake not his ministers. **31** Fear the Lord, and honor the priest; and give
him his portion, as it is commanded thee; the firstfruits, and the trespass offering,
and the gift of the shoulders, and the sacrifice of sanctification, and the firstfruits
of the holy things. **32** And stretch thine hand unto the poor, that thy blessing
may be perfected. **33** A gift hath grace in the sight of every man living; and for
the dead detain it not. **34** Fail not to be with them that weep, and mourn with
them that mourn. **35** Be not slow to visit the sick: for that shall make thee to
be beloved. **36** Whatsoever thou takest in hand, remember the end, and thou
shalt never do amiss.

8

1 Strive not with a mighty man' lest thou fall into his hands. **2** Be not
at variance with a rich man, lest he overweigh thee: for gold hath de-
stroyed many, and perverted the hearts of kings. **3** Strive not with a man that
is full of tongue, and heap not wood upon his fire. **4** Jest not with a rude man,
lest thy ancestors be disgraced. **5** Reproach not a man that turneth from sin,
but remember that we are all worthy of punishment. **6** Dishonour not a man
in his old age: for even some of us wax old. **7** Rejoice not over thy greatest
enemy being dead, but remember that we die all. **8** Despise not the discourse
of the wise, but acquaint thyself with their proverbs: for of them thou shalt learn
instruction, and how to serve great men with ease. **9** Miss not the discourse
of the elders: for they also learned of their fathers, and of them thou shalt learn
understanding, and to give answer as need requireth. **10** Kindle not the coals of
a sinner, lest thou be burnt with the flame of his fire. **11** Rise not up [in anger]
at the presence of an injurious person, lest he lie in wait to entrap thee in thy
words **12** Lend not unto him that is mightier than thyself; for if thou lendest
him, count it but lost. **13** Be not surety above thy power: for if thou be surety,
take care to pay it. **14** Go not to law with a judge; for they will judge for him
according to his honour. **15** Travel not by the way with a bold fellow, lest he be-
come grievous unto thee: for he will do according to his own will, and thou shalt
perish with him through his folly. **16** Strive not with an angry man, and go not
with him into a solitary place: for blood is as nothing in his sight, and where there
is no help, he will overthrow thee. **17** Consult not with a fool; for he cannot
keep counsel. **18** Do no secret thing before a stranger; for thou knowest not
what he will bring forth. **19** Open not thine heart to every man, lest he requite
thee with a shrewd turn.

9

1 Be not jealous over the wife of thy bosom, and teach her not an evil
lesson against thyself. **2** Give not thy soul unto a woman to set her
foot upon thy substance. **3** Meet not with an harlot, lest thou fall into her
snares. **4** Use not much the company of a woman that is a singer, lest thou
be taken with her attempts. **5** Gaze not on a maid, that thou fall not by those
things that are precious in her. **6** Give not thy soul unto harlots, that thou lose
not thine inheritance. **7** Look not round about thee in the streets of the city,
neither wander thou in the solitary place thereof. **8** Turn away thine eye from
a beautiful woman, and look not upon another's beauty; for many have been
deceived by the beauty of a woman; for herewith love is kindled as a fire. **9** Sit
not at all with another man's wife, nor sit down with her in thine arms, and
spend not thy money with her at the wine; lest thine heart incline unto her, and
so through thy desire thou fall into destruction. **10** Forsake not an old friend;
for the new is not comparable to him: a new friend is as new wine; when it is
old, thou shalt drink it with pleasure. **11** Envy not the glory of a sinner: for
thou knowest not what shall be his end. **12** Delight not in the thing that the
ungodly have pleasure in; but remember they shall not go unpunished unto their
grave. **13** Keep thee far from the man that hath power to kill; so shalt thou not
doubt the fear of death: and if thou come unto him, make no fault, lest he take
away thy life presently: remember that thou goest in the midst of snares, and that
thou walkest upon the battlements of the city. **14** As near as thou canst, guess
at thy neighbour, and consult with the wise. **15** Let thy talk be with the wise,
and all thy communication in the law of the most High. **16** And let just men
eat and drink with thee; and let thy glorying be in the fear of the Lord. **17** For
the hand of the artificer the work shall be commended: and the wise ruler of the
people for his speech. **18** A man of an ill tongue is dangerous in his city; and he
that is rash in his talk shall be hated.

10

1 A wise judge will instruct his people; and the government of a pru-
dent man is well ordered. **2** As the judge of the people is himself,
so are his officers; and what manner of man the ruler of the city is, such are all
they that dwell therein. **3** An unwise king destroyeth his people; but through
the prudence of them which are in authority the city shall be inhabited. **4** The
power of the earth is in the hand of the Lord, and in due time he will set over it
one that is profitable. **5** In the hand of God is the prosperity of man: and upon
the person of the scribe shall he lay his honour. **6** Bear not hatred to thy nei-
ghbour for every wrong; and do nothing at all by injurious practices. **7** Pride is
hateful before God and man: and by both doth one commit iniquity. **8** Because
of unrighteous dealings, injuries, and riches got by deceit, the kingdom is transla-
ted from one people to another. **9** Why is earth and ashes proud? There is not a
more wicked thing than a covetous man: for such an one setteth his own soul to
sale; because while he liveth he casteth away his bowels. **10** The physician cut-
teth off a long disease; and he that is to day a king to morrow shall die. **11** For
when a man is dead, he shall inherit creeping things, beasts, and worms. **12** The
beginning of pride is when one departeth from God, and his heart is turned away
from his Maker. **13** For pride is the beginning of sin, and he that hath it shall
pour out abomination: and therefore the Lord brought upon them strange cala-
mities, and overthrew them utterly. **14** The Lord hath cast down the thrones of
proud princes, and set up the meek in their stead. **15** The Lord hath plucked
up the roots of the proud nations, and planted the lowly in their place. **16** The
Lord overthrew countries of the heathen, and destroyed them to the foundations
of the earth. **17** He took some of them away, and destroyed them, and hath
made their memorial to cease from the earth. **18** Pride was not made for men,
nor furious anger for them that are born of a woman. **19** They that fear the
Lord are a sure seed, and they that love him an honourable plant: they that regard
not the law are a dishonourable seed; they that transgress the commandments are
a deceivable seed. **20** Among brethren he that is chief is honorable; so are they
that fear the Lord in his eyes. **21** The fear of the Lord goeth before the obtai-
ning of authority: but roughness and pride is the losing thereof. **22** Whether he
be rich, noble, or poor, their glory is the fear of the Lord. **23** It is not meet to
despise the poor man that hath understanding; neither is it convenient to magnify
a sinful man. **24** Great men, and judges, and potentates, shall be honoured;
yet is there none of them greater than he that feareth the Lord. **25** Unto the
servant that is wise shall they that are free do service: and he that hath knowledge
will not grudge when he is reformed. **26** Be not overwise in doing thy business;
and boast not thyself in the time of thy distress. **27** Better is he that laboureth,
and aboundeth in all things, than he that boasteth himself, and wanteth bre-
ad. **28** My son, glorify thy soul in meekness, and give it honour according to
the dignity thereof. **29** Who will justify him that sinneth against his own soul?
and who will honour him that dishonoureth his own life? **30** The poor man is
honoured for his skill, and the rich man is honoured for his riches. **31** He that

is honoured in poverty, how much more in riches? and he that is dishonourable in riches, how much more in poverty?

11 1 Wisdom lifteth up the head of him that is of low degree, and maketh him to sit among great men. 2 Commend not a man for his beauty; neither abhor a man for his outward appearance. 3 The bee is little among such as fly; but her fruit is the chief of sweet things. 4 Boast not of thy clothing and raiment, and exalt not thyself in the day of honour: for the works of the Lord are wonderful, and his works among men are hidden. 5 Many kings have sat down upon the ground; and one that was never thought of hath worn the crown. 6 Many mighty men have been greatly disgraced; and the honourable delivered into other men's hands. 7 Blame not before thou hast examined the truth: understand first, and then rebuke. 8 Answer not before thou hast heard the cause: neither interrupt men in the midst of their talk. 9 Strive not in a matter that concerneth thee not; and sit not in judgment with sinners. 10 My son, meddle not with many matters: for if thou meddle much, thou shalt not be innocent; and if thou follow after, thou shalt not obtain, neither shalt thou escape by fleeing. 11 There is one that laboureth, and taketh pains, and maketh haste, and is so much the more behind. 12 Again, there is another that is slow, and hath need of help, wanting ability, and full of poverty; yet the eye of the Lord looked upon him for good, and set him up from his low estate, 13 And lifted up his head from misery; so that many that saw from him is peace over all the 14 Prosperity and adversity, life and death, poverty and riches, come of the Lord. 15 Wisdom, knowledge, and understanding of the law, are of the Lord: love, and the way of good works, are from him. 16 Error and darkness had their beginning together with sinners: and evil shall wax old with them that glory therein. 17 The gift of the Lord remaineth with the ungodly, and his favour bringeth prosperity for ever. 18 There is that waxeth rich by his wariness and pinching, and this his the portion of his reward: 19 Whereas he saith, I have found rest, and now will eat continually of my goods; and yet he knoweth not what time shall come upon him, and that he must leave those things to others, and die. 20 Be stedfast in thy covenant, and be conversant therein, and wax old in thy work. 21 Marvel not at the works of sinners; but trust in the Lord, and abide in thy labour: for it is an easy thing in the sight of the Lord on the sudden to make a poor man rich. 22 The blessing of the Lord is in the reward of the godly, and suddenly he maketh his blessing flourish. 23 Say not, What profit is there of my service? and what good things shall I have hereafter? 24 Again, say not, I have enough, and possess many things, and what evil shall I have hereafter? 25 In the day of prosperity there is a forgetfulness of affliction: and in the day of affliction there is no more remembrance of prosperity. 26 For it is an easy thing unto the Lord in the day of death to reward a man according to his ways. 27 The affliction of an hour maketh a man forget pleasure: and in his end his deeds shall be discovered. 28 Judge none blessed before his death: for a man shall be known in his children. 29 Bring not every man into thine house: for the deceitful man hath many trains. 30 Like as a partridge taken [and kept] in a cage, so is the heart of the proud; and like as a spy, watcheth he for thy fall: 31 For he lieth in wait, and turneth good into evil, and in things worthy praise will lay blame upon thee. 32 Of a spark of fire a heap of coals is kindled: and a sinful man layeth wait for blood. 33 Take heed of a mischievous man, for he worketh wickedness; lest he bring upon thee a perpetual blot. 34 Receive a stranger into thine house, and he will disturb thee, and turn thee out of thine own.

12 1 When thou wilt do good know to whom thou doest it; so shalt thou be thanked for thy benefits. 2 Do good to the godly man, and thou shalt find a recompence; and if not from him, yet from the most High. 3 There can no good come to him that is always occupied in evil, nor to him that giveth no alms. 4 Give to the godly man, and help not a sinner. 5 Do well unto him that is lowly, but give not to the ungodly: hold back thy bread, and give it not unto him, lest he overmaster thee thereby: for [else] thou shalt receive twice as much evil for all the good thou shalt have done unto him. 6 For the most High hateth sinners, and will repay vengeance unto the ungodly, and keepeth them against the mighty day of their punishment. 7 Give unto the good, and help not the sinner. 8 A friend cannot be known in prosperity: and an enemy cannot be hidden in adversity. 9 In the prosperity of a man enemies will be grieved: but in his adversity even a friend will depart. 10 Never trust thine enemy: for like as iron rusteth, so is his wickedness. 11 Though he humble himself, and go crouching, yet take good heed and beware of him, and thou shalt be unto him as if thou hadst wiped a lookingglass, and thou shalt know that his rust hath not been altogether wiped away. 12 Set him not by thee, lest, when he hath overthrown thee, he stand up in thy place; neither let him sit at thy right hand, lest he seek to take thy seat, and thou at the last remember my words, and be pricked therewith. 13 Who will pity a charmer that is bitten with a serpent, or any such as come nigh wild beasts? 14 So one that goeth to a sinner, and is defiled with him in his sins, who will pity? 15 For a while he will abide with thee, but if thou begin to fall, he will not tarry. 16 An enemy speaketh sweetly with his lips, but in his heart he imagineth how to throw thee into a pit: he will weep with his eyes, but if he find opportunity, he will not be satisfied with blood. 17 If adversity come upon thee, thou shalt find him there first; and though he pretend to help thee, yet shall he undermine thee. 18 He will shake his head, and clap his hands, and whisper much, and change his countenance.

13 1 He that toucheth pitch shall be defiled therewith; and he that hath fellowship with a proud man shall be like unto him. 2 Burden not thyself above thy power while thou livest; and have no fellowship with one that is mightier and richer than thyself: for how agree the kettle and the earthen pot together? for if the one be smitten against the other, it shall be broken. 3 The rich man hath done wrong, and yet he threateneth withal: the poor is wronged, and he must intreat also. 4 If thou be for his profit, he will use thee: but if thou have nothing, he will forsake thee. 5 If thou have any thing, he will live with thee: yea, he will make thee bare, and will not be sorry for it. 6 If he have need of thee, he will deceive thee, and smile upon thee, and put thee in hope; he will speak thee fair, and say, What wantest thou? 7 And he will shame thee by his meats, until he have drawn thee dry twice or thrice, and at the last he will laugh thee to scorn afterward, when he seeth thee, he will forsake thee, and shake his head at thee. 8 Beware that thou be not deceived and brought down in thy jollity. 9 If thou be invited of a mighty man, withdraw thyself, and so much the more will he invite thee. 10 Press thou not upon him, lest thou be put back; stand not far off, lest thou be forgotten. 11 Affect not to be made equal unto him in talk, and believe not his many words: for with much communication will he tempt thee, and smiling upon thee will get out thy secrets: 12 But cruelly he will lay up thy words, and will not spare to do thee hurt, and to put thee in prison. 13 Observe, and take good heed, for thou walkest in peril of thy overthrowing: when thou hearest these things, awake in thy sleep. 14 Love the Lord all thy life, and call upon him for thy salvation. 15 Every beast loveth his like, and every man loveth his neighbor. 16 All flesh consorteth according to kind, and a man will cleave to his like. 17 What fellowship hath the wolf with the lamb? so the sinner with the godly. 18 What agreement is there between the hyena and a dog? and what peace between the rich and the poor? 19 As the wild ass is the lion's prey in the wilderness: so the rich eat up the poor. 20 As the proud hate humility: so doth the rich abhor the poor. 21 A rich man beginning to fall is held up of his friends: but a poor man being down is thrust away by his friends. 22 When a rich man is fallen, he hath many helpers: he speaketh things not to be spoken, and yet men justify him: the poor man slipped, and yet they rebuked him too; he spake wisely, and could have no place. 23 When a rich man speaketh, every man holdeth his tongue, and, look, what he saith, they extol it to the clouds: but if the poor man speak, they say, What fellow is this? and if he stumble, they will help to overthrow him. 24 Riches are good unto him that hath no sin, and poverty is evil in the mouth of the ungodly. 25 The heart of a man changeth his countenance, whether it be for good or evil: and a merry heart maketh a cheerful countenance. 26 A cheerful countenance is a token of a heart that is in prosperity; and the finding out of parables is a wearisome labour of the mind.

14 1 Blessed is the man that hath not slipped with his mouth, and is not pricked with the multitude of sins. 2 Blessed is he whose conscience hath not condemned him, and who is not fallen from his hope in the Lord. 3 Riches are not comely for a niggard: and what should an envious man do with money? 4 He that gathereth by defrauding his own soul gathereth for others, that shall spend his goods riotously. 5 He that is evil to himself, to whom will he be good? he shall not take pleasure in his goods. 6 There is none worse than he that envieth himself; and this is a recompence of his wickedness. 7 And if he doeth good, he doeth it unwillingly; and at the last he will declare his wickedness. 8 The envious man hath a wicked eye; he turneth away his face, and despiseth men. 9 A covetous man's eye is not satisfied with his portion; and the iniquity of the wicked drieth up his soul. 10 A wicked eye envieth [his] bread, and he is a niggard at his table. 11 My son, according to thy ability do good to thyself, and give the Lord his due offering. 12 Remember that death will not be long in coming, and that the covenant of the grave is not shewed unto thee. 13 Do good unto thy friend before thou die, and according to thy ability stretch out thy hand and give to him. 14 Defraud not thyself of the good day, and let not the part of a good desire overpass thee. 15 Shalt thou not leave thy travails unto another? and thy labours to be divided by lot? 16 Give, and take, and sanctify thy soul; for there is no seeking of dainties in the grave. 17 All flesh waxeth old as a garment: for the covenant from the beginning is, Thou shalt die the death. 18 As of the green leaves on a thick tree, some fall, and some grow; so is the generation of flesh and blood, one cometh to an end, and another is born. 19 Every work rotteth and consumeth away, and the worker thereof shall go withal. 20 Blessed is the man that doth meditate good things in wisdom, and that reasoneth of holy things by his understanding. ing. 21 He that considereth her ways in his heart shall also have understanding in her secrets. 22 Go after her as one that traceth, and lie in wait in her ways. 23 He that prieth in at her windows shall also hearken at her doors. 24 He that doth lodge near her house shall also fasten a pin in her walls. 25 He shall pitch his tent nigh unto her, and shall lodge in a lodging where good things are. 26 He shall set his children under her shelter, and shall lodge under her branches. 27 By her he shall be covered from heat, and in her glory shall he dwell.

15 1 He that feareth the Lord will do good, and he that hath the know-
ledge of the law shall obtain her. 2 And as a mother shall she meet
him, and receive him as a wife married of a virgin. 3 With the bread of under-
standing shall she feed him, and give him the water of wisdom to drink. 4 He
shall be stayed upon her, and shall not be moved; and shall rely upon her, and
shall not be confounded. 5 She shall exalt him above his neighbours, and in the
midst of the congregation shall she open his mouth. 6 He shall find joy and a
crown of gladness, and she shall cause him to inherit an everlasting name. 7 But
foolish men shall not attain unto her, and sinners shall not see her. 8 For she is
far from pride, and men that are liars cannot remember her. 9 Praise is not se-
emly in the mouth of a sinner, for it was not sent him of the Lord. 10 For praise
shall be uttered in wisdom, and the Lord will prosper it. 11 Say not thou, It is
through the Lord that I fell away: for thou oughtest not to do the things that he
hateth. 12 Say not thou, He hath caused me to err: for he hath no need of the
sinful man. 13 The Lord hateth all abomination; and they that fear God love
it not. 14 He himself made man from the beginning, and left him in the hand
of his counsel; 15 If thou wilt, to keep the commandments, and to perform
acceptable faithfulness. 16 He hath set fire and water before thee: stretch forth
thy hand unto whether thou wilt. 17 Before man is life and death; and whether
him liketh shall be given him. 18 For the wisdom of the Lord is great, and he is
mighty in power, and beholdeth all things: 19 And his eyes are upon them that
fear him, and he knoweth every work of man. 20 He hath commanded no man
to do wickedly, neither hath he given any man licence to sin.

16 1 Desire not a multitude of unprofitable children, neither delight in
ungodly sons. 2 Though they multiply, rejoice not in them, except
the fear of the Lord be with them. 3 Trust not thou in their life, neither respect
their multitude: for one that is just is better than a thousand; and better it is to
die without children, than to have them that are ungodly. 4 For by one that
hath understanding shall the city be replenished: but the kindred of the wicked
shall speedily become desolate. 5 Many such things have I seen with mine eyes,
and mine ear hath heard greater things than these. 6 In the congregation of
the ungodly shall a fire be kindled; and in a rebellious nation wrath is set on
fire. 7 He was not pacified toward the old giants, who fell away in the strength
of their foolishness. 8 Neither spared he the place where Lot sojourned, but
abhorred them for their pride. 9 He pitied not the people of perdition, who
were taken away in their sins: 10 Nor the six hundred thousand footmen, who
were gathered together in the hardness of their hearts. 11 And if there be one
stiffnecked among the people, it is marvel if he escape unpunished: for mercy and
wrath are with him; he is mighty to forgive, and to pour out displeasure. 12 As
his mercy is great, so is his correction also: he judgeth a man according to his
works 13 The sinner shall not escape with his spoils: and the patience of the
godly shall not be frustrate. 14 Make way for every work of mercy: for every
man shall find according to his works. 15 The Lord hardened Pharaoh, that
he should not know him, that his powerful works might be known to the wor-
ld. 16 His mercy is manifest to every creature; and he hath separated his light
from the darkness with an adamant. 17 Say not thou, I will hide myself from
the Lord: shall any remember me from above? I shall not be remembered among
so many people: for what is my soul among such an infinite number of creatu-
res? 18 Behold, the heaven, and the heaven of heavens, the deep, and the earth,
and all that therein is, shall be moved when he shall visit. 19 The mountains
also and foundations of the earth be shaken with trembling, when the Lord lo-
oketh upon them. 20 No heart can think upon these things worthily: and who
is able to conceive his ways? 21 It is a tempest which no man can see: for the
most part of his works are hid. 22 Who can declare the works of his justice? or
who can endure them? for his covenant is afar off, and the trial of all things is in
the end. 23 He that wanteth understanding will think upon vain things: and
a foolish man erring imagineth follies. 24 by son, hearken unto me, and learn
knowledge, and mark my words with thy heart. 25 I will shew forth doctrine in
weight, and declare his knowledge exactly. 26 The works of the Lord are done
in judgment from the beginning: and from the time he made them he disposed
the parts thereof. 27 He garnished his works for ever, and in his hand are the
chief of them unto all generations: they neither labour, nor are weary, nor cease
from their works. 28 None of them hindereth another, and they shall never
disobey his word. 29 After this the Lord looked upon the earth, and filled it
with his blessings. 30 With all manner of living things hath he covered the face
thereof; and they shall return into it again.

17 1 The Lord created man of the earth, and turned him into it
again. 2 He gave them few days, and a short time, and power also
over the things therein. 3 He endued them with strength by themselves, and
made them according to his image, 4 And put the fear of man upon all flesh,
and gave him dominion over beasts and fowls. 5 They received the use of the five
operations of the Lord, and in the sixth place he imparted them understanding,
and in the seventh speech, an interpreter of the cogitations thereof. 6 Counsel,
and a tongue, and eyes, ears, and a heart, gave he them to understand. 7 Withal
he filled them with the knowledge of understanding, and shewed them good and
evil. 8 He set his eye upon their hearts, that he might shew them the greatness
of his works. 9 He gave them to glory in his marvellous acts for ever, that they
might declare his works with understanding. 10 And the elect shall praise his
holy name. 11 Beside this he gave them knowledge, and the law of life for an
heritage. 12 He made an everlasting covenant with them, and shewed them his
judgments. 13 Their eyes saw the majesty of his glory, and their ears heard his
glorious voice. 14 And he said unto them, Beware of all unrighteousness; and
he gave every man commandment concerning his neighbour. 15 Their ways
are ever before him, and shall not be hid from his eyes. 16 Every man from
his youth is given to evil; neither could they make to themselves fleshy hearts
for stony. 17 For in the division of the nations of the whole earth he set a
ruler over every people; but Israel is the Lord's portion: 18 Whom, being his
firstborn, he nourisheth with discipline, and giving him the light of his love doth
not forsake him. 19 Therefore all their works are as the sun before him, and
his eyes are continually upon their ways. 20 None of their unrighteous deeds
are hid from him, but all their sins are before the Lord 21 But the Lord being
gracious and knowing his workmanship, neither left nor forsook them, but spa-
red them. 22 The alms of a man is as a signet with him, and he will keep the
good deeds of man as the apple of the eye, and give repentance to his sons and
daughters. 23 Afterwards he will rise up and reward them, and render their
recompence upon their heads. 24 But unto them that repent, he granted them
return, and comforted those that failed in patience. 25 Return unto the Lord,
and forsake thy sins, make thy prayer before his face, and offend less. 26 Turn
again to the most High, and turn away from iniquity: for he will lead thee out
of darkness into the light of health, and hate thou abomination vehement-
ly. 27 Who shall praise the most High in the grave, instead of them which live
and give thanks? 28 Thanksgiving perisheth from the dead, as from one that
is not: the living and sound in heart shall praise the Lord. 29 How great is the
lovingkindness of the Lord our God, and his compassion unto such as turn unto
him in holiness! 30 For all things cannot be in men, because the son of man is
not immortal. 31 What is brighter than the sun? yet the light thereof faileth;
and flesh and blood will imagine evil. 32 He vieweth the power of the height of
heaven; and all men are but earth and ashes.

18 1 He that liveth for ever Hath created all things in general. 2 The
Lord only is righteous, and there is none other but he, 3 Who go-
verneth the world with the palm of his hand, and all things obey his will: for he
is the King of all, by his power dividing holy things among them from profa-
ne. 4 To whom hath he given power to declare his works? and who shall find
out his noble acts? 5 Who shall number the strength of his majesty? and who
shall also tell out his mercies? 6 As for the wondrous works of the Lord, there
may nothing be taken from them, neither may any thing be put unto them,
neither can the ground of them be found out. 7 When a man hath done, then
he beginneth; and when he leaveth off, then he shall be doubtful. 8 What is
man, and whereto serveth he? what is his good, and what is his evil? 9 The
number of a man's days at the most are an hundred years. 10 As a drop of
water unto the sea, and a gravelstone in comparison of the sand; so are a thou-
sand years to the days of eternity. 11 Therefore is God patient with them, and
poureth forth his mercy upon them. 12 He saw and perceived their end to be
evil; therefore he multiplied his compassion. 13 The mercy of man is toward
his neighbour; but the mercy of the Lord is upon all flesh: he reproveth, and
nurtureth, and teacheth and bringeth again, as a shepherd his flock. 14 He
hath mercy on them that receive discipline, and that diligently seek after his ju-
dgments. 15 My son, blemish not thy good deeds, neither use uncomfortable
words when thou givest any thing. 16 Shall not the dew asswage the heat? so
is a word better than a gift. 17 Lo, is not a word better than a gift? but both
are with a gracious man. 18 A fool will upbraid churlishly, and a gift of the
envious consumeth the eyes. 19 Learn before thou speak, and use physick or
ever thou be sick. 20 Before judgment examine thyself, and in the day of vi-
sitation thou shalt find mercy. 21 Humble thyself before thou be sick, and in
the time of sins shew repentance. 22 Let nothing hinder thee to pay thy vow
in due time, and defer not until death to be justified. 23 Before thou prayest,
prepare thyself; and be not as one that tempteth the Lord. 24 Think upon
the wrath that shall be at the end, and the time of vengeance, when he shall
turn away his face. 25 When thou hast enough, remember the time of hunger:
and when thou art rich, think upon poverty and need. 26 From the morning
until the evening the time is changed, and all things are soon done before the
Lord. 27 A wise man will fear in every thing, and in the day of sinning he will
beware of offence: but a fool will not observe time. 28 Every man of understan-
ding knoweth wisdom, and will give praise unto him that found her. 29 They
that were of understanding in sayings became also wise themselves, and poured
forth exquisite parables. 30 Go not after thy lusts, but refrain thyself from thine
appetites. 31 If thou givest thy soul the desires that please her, she will make
thee a laughingstock to thine enemies that malign thee. 32 Take not pleasure
in much good cheer, neither be tied to the expence thereof. 33 Be not made a
beggar by banqueting upon borrowing, when thou hast nothing in thy purse: for
thou shalt lie in wait for thine own life, and be talked on.

19 1 A labouring man that A is given to drunkenness shall not be rich: and
he that contemneth small things shall fall by little and little. 2 Wine
and women will make men of understanding to fall away: and he that cleaveth

to harlots will become impudent. **3** Moths and worms shall have him to heri-
tage, and a bold man shall be taken away. **4** He that is hasty to give credit is
lightminded; and he that sinneth shall offend against his own soul. **5** Whoso
taketh pleasure in wickedness shall be condemned: but he that resisteth pleasures
crowneth his life. **6** He that can rule his tongue shall live without strife; and
he that hateth babbling shall have less evil. **7** Rehearse not unto another that
which is told unto thee, and thou shalt fare never the worse. **8** Whether it be
to friend or foe, talk not of other men's lives; and if thou canst without offence,
reveal them not. **9** For he heard and observed thee, and when time cometh he
will hate thee. **10** If thou hast heard a word, let it die with thee; and be bold, it
will not burst thee. **11** A fool travaileth with a word, as a woman in labour of a
child. **12** As an arrow that sticketh in a man's thigh, so is a word within a fool's
belly. **13** Admonish a friend, it may be he hath not done it: and if he have done
it, that he do it no more. **14** Admonish thy friend, it may be he hath not said
it: and if he have, that he speak it not again. **15** Admonish a friend: for many
times it is a slander, and believe not every tale. **16** There is one that slippeth in
his speech, but not from his heart; and who is he that hath not offended with his
tongue? **17** Admonish thy neighbour before thou threaten him; and not being
angry, give place to the law of the most High. **18** The fear of the Lord is the first
step to be accepted [of him,] and wisdom obtaineth his love. **19** The knowle-
dge of the commandments of the Lord is the doctrine of life: and they that do
things that please him shall receive the fruit of the tree of immortality. **20** The
fear of the Lord is all wisdom; and in all wisdom is the performance of the law,
and the knowledge of his omnipotency. **21** If a servant say to his master, I will
not do as it pleaseth thee; though afterward he do it, he angereth him that nou-
risheth him. **22** The knowledge of wickedness is not wisdom, neither at any
time the counsel of sinners prudence. **23** There is a wickedness, and the same
an abomination; and there is a fool wanting in wisdom. **24** He that hath small
understanding, and feareth God, is better than one that hath much wisdom, and
transgresseth the law of the most High. **25** There is an exquisite subtilty, and
the same is unjust; and there is one that turneth aside to make judgment appear;
and there is a wise man that justifieth in judgment. **26** There is a wicked man
that hangeth down his head sadly; but inwardly he is full of deceit, **27** Casting
down his countenance, and making as if he heard not: where he is not known, he
will do thee a mischief before thou be aware. **28** And if for want of power he be
hindered from sinning, yet when he findeth opportunity he will do evil. **29** A
man may be known by his look, and one that hath understanding by his counte-
nance, when thou meetest him. **30** A man's attire, and excessive laughter, and
gait, shew what he is.

20

1 There is a reproof that is not comely: again, some man holdeth
his tongue, and he is wise. **2** It is much better to reprove, than
to be angry secretly: and he that confesseth his fault shall be preserved from
hurt. **3** How good is it, when thou art reproved, to shew repentance! for so shalt
thou escape wilful sin. **4** As is the lust of an eunuch to deflower a virgin; so is he
that executeth judgment with violence. **5** There is one that keepeth silence, and
is found wise: and another by much babbling becometh hateful. **6** Some man
holdeth his tongue, because he hath not to answer: and some keepeth silence,
knowing his time. **7** A wise man will hold his tongue till he see opportunity: but
a babbler and a fool will regard no time. **8** He that useth many words shall be
abhorred; and he that taketh to himself authority therein shall be hated. **9** The-
re is a sinner that hath good success in evil things; and there is a gain that turneth
to loss. **10** There is a gift that shall not profit thee; and there is a gift whose
recompence is double. **11** There is an abasement because of glory; and there
is that lifteth up his head from a low estate. **12** There is that buyeth much for
a little, and repayeth it sevenfold. **13** A wise man by his words maketh him
beloved: but the graces of fools shall be poured out. **14** The gift of a fool shall
do thee no good when thou hast it; neither yet of the envious for his necessity: for
he looketh to receive many things for one. **15** He giveth little, and upbraideth
much; he openeth his mouth like a crier; to day he lendeth, and to morrow will
he ask it again: such an one is to be hated of God and man. **16** The fool saith, I
have no friends, I have no thank for all my good deeds, and they that eat my bread
speak evil of me. **17** How oft, and of how many shall he be laughed to scorn!
for he knoweth not aright what it is to have; and it is all one unto him as if he had
it not. **18** To slip upon a pavement is better than to slip with the tongue: so the
fall of the wicked shall come speedily. **19** An unseasonable tale will always be in
the mouth of the unwise. **20** A wise sentence shall be rejected when it cometh
out of a fool's mouth; for he will not speak it in due season. **21** There is that
is hindered from sinning through want: and when he taketh rest, he shall not be
troubled. **22** There is that destroyeth his own soul through bashfulness, and
by accepting of persons overthroweth himself. **23** There is that for bashfulness
promiseth to his friend, and maketh him his enemy for nothing. **24** A lie is a
foul blot in a man, yet it is continually in the mouth of the untaught. **25** A thief
is better than a man that is accustomed to lie: but they both shall have destruction
to heritage. **26** The disposition of a liar is dishonourable, and his shame is ever
with him. **27** A wise man shall promote himself to honour with his words:
and he that hath understanding will please great men. **28** He that tilleth his
land shall increase his heap: and he that pleaseth great men shall get pardon for
iniquity. **29** Presents and gifts blind the eyes of the wise, and stop up his mouth
that he cannot reprove. **30** Wisdom that is hid, and treasure that is hoarded up,
what profit is in them both? **31** Better is he that hideth his folly than a man that
hideth his wisdom. **32** Necessary patience in seeking ing the Lord is better than
he that leadeth his life without a guide.

21

1 My son, hast thou sinned? do so no more, but ask pardon for thy
former sins. **2** Flee from sin as from the face of a serpent: for if thou
comest too near it, it will bite thee: the teeth thereof are as the teeth of a lion,
slaying the souls of men. **3** All iniquity is as a two edged sword, the wounds
whereof cannot be healed. **4** To terrify and do wrong will waste riches: thus
the house of proud men shall be made desolate. **5** A prayer out of a poor man's
mouth reacheth to the ears of God, and his judgment cometh speedily. **6** He
that hateth to be reproved is in the way of sinners: but he that feareth the Lord
will repent from his heart. **7** An eloquent man is known far and near; but a man
of understanding knoweth when he slippeth. **8** He that buildeth his house with
other men's money is like one that gathereth himself stones for the tomb of his
burial. **9** The congregation of the wicked is like tow wrapped together: and the
end of them is a flame of fire to destroy them. **10** The way of sinners is made
plain with stones, but at the end thereof is the pit of hell. **11** He that keepeth
the law of the Lord getteth the understanding thereof: and the perfection of the
fear of the Lord is wisdom. **12** He that is not wise will not be taught: but there
is a wisdom which multiplieth bitterness. **13** The knowledge of a wise man shall
abound like a flood: and his counsel is like a pure fountain of life. **14** The inner
parts of a fool are like a broken vessel, and he will hold no knowledge as long as he
liveth. **15** If a skilful man hear a wise word, he will commend it, and add unto
it: but as soon as one of no understanding heareth it, it displeaseth him, and he
casteth it behind his back. **16** The talking of a fool is like a burden in the way:
but grace shall be found in the lips of the wise. **17** They enquire at the mouth
of the wise man in the congregation, and they shall ponder his words in their
heart. **18** As is a house that is destroyed, so is wisdom to a fool: and the know-
ledge of the unwise is as talk without sense. **19** Doctrine unto fools is as fetters
on the feet, and like manacles on the right hand. **20** A fool lifteth up his voice
with laughter; but a wise man doth scarce smile a little. **21** Learning is unto a
wise man as an ornament of gold, and like a bracelet upon his right arm. **22** A
foolish man's foot is soon in his [neighbour's] house: but a man of experience is
ashamed of him. **23** A fool will peep in at the door into the house: but he that
is well nurtured will stand without. **24** It is the rudeness of a man to hearken
at the door: but a wise man will be grieved with the disgrace. **25** The lips of
talkers will be telling such things as pertain not unto them: but the words of such
as have understanding are weighed in the balance. **26** The heart of fools is in
their mouth: but the mouth of the wise is in their heart. **27** When the ungodly
curseth Satan, he curseth his own soul. **28** A whisperer defileth his own soul,
and is hated wheresoever he dwelleth.

22

1 A slothful man is compared to a filthy stone, and every one will hiss
him out to his disgrace. **2** A slothful man is compared to the filth
of a dunghill: every man that takes it up will shake his hand. **3** An evilnurtured
man is the dishonour of his father that begat him: and a [foolish] daughter is born
to his loss. **4** A wise daughter shall bring an inheritance to her husband: but she
that liveth dishonestly is her father's heaviness. **5** She that is bold dishonoureth
both her father and her husband, but they both shall despise her. **6** A tale out of
season [is as] musick in mourning: but stripes and correction of wisdom are never
out of time. **7** Whoso teacheth a fool is as one that glueth a potsherd together,
and as he that waketh one from a sound sleep. **8** He that telleth a tale to a fool
speaketh to one in a slumber: when he hath told his tale, he will say, What is the
matter? **9** If children live honestly, and have wherewithal, they shall cover the
baseness of their parents. **10** But children, being haughty, through disdain and
want of nurture do stain the nobility of their kindred. **11** Weep for the dead,
for he hath lost the light: and weep for the fool, for he wanteth understanding:
make little weeping for the dead, for he is at rest: but the life of the fool is worse
than death. **12** Seven days do men mourn for him that is dead; but for a fool
and an ungodly man all the days of his life. **13** Talk not much with a fool, and
go not to him that hath no understanding: beware of him, lest thou have trouble,
and thou shalt never be defiled with his fooleries: depart from him, and thou
shalt find rest, and never be disquieted with madness. **14** What is heavier than
lead? and what is the name thereof, but a fool? **15** Sand, and salt, and a mass
of iron, is easier to bear, than a man without understanding. **16** As timber girt
and bound together in a building cannot be loosed with shaking: so the heart that
is stablished by advised counsel shall fear at no time. **17** A heart settled upon a
thought of understanding is as a fair plaistering on the wall of a gallery. **18** Pales
set on an high place will never stand against the wind: so a fearful heart in the
imagination of a fool cannot stand against any fear. **19** He that pricketh the eye
will make tears to fall: and he that pricketh the heart maketh it to shew her know-
ledge. **20** Whoso casteth a stone at the birds frayeth them away: and he that up-
braideth his friend breaketh friendship. **21** Though thou drewest a sword at thy
friend, yet despair not: for there may be a returning [to favour.] **22** If thou hast
opened thy mouth against thy friend, fear not; for there may be a reconciliation:
except for upbraiding, or pride, or disclosing of secrets, or a treacherous wound:
for for these things every friend will depart. **23** Be faithful to thy neighbour in
his poverty, that thou mayest rejoice in his prosperity: abide stedfast unto him in

the time of his trouble, that thou mayest be heir with him in his heritage: for a mean estate is not always to be contemned: nor the rich that is foolish to be had in admiration. **24** As the vapour and smoke of a furnace goeth before the fire; so reviling before blood. **25** I will not be ashamed to defend a friend; neither will I hide myself from him. **26** And if any evil happen unto me by him, every one that heareth it will beware of him. **27** Who shall set a watch before my mouth, and a seal of wisdom upon my lips, that I fall not suddenly by them, and that my tongue destroy me not?

23

1 O Lord, Father and Governor of all my whole life, leave me not to their counsels, and let me not fall by them. **2** Who will set scourges over my thoughts, and the discipline of wisdom over mine heart? that they spare me not for mine ignorances, and it pass not by my sins: **3** Lest mine ignorances increase, and my sins abound to my destruction, and I fall before mine adversaries, and mine enemy rejoice over me, whose hope is far from thy mercy. **4** O Lord, Father and God of my life, give me not a proud look, but turn away from thy servants always a haughty mind. **5** Turn away from me vain hopes and concupiscence, and thou shalt hold him up that is desirous always to serve thee. **6** Let not the greediness of the belly nor lust of the flesh take hold of me; and give not over me thy servant into an impudent mind. **7** Hear, O ye children, the discipline of the mouth: he that keepeth it shall never be taken in his lips. **8** The sinner shall be left in his foolishness: both the evil speaker and the proud shall fall thereby. **9** Accustom not thy mouth to swearing; neither use thyself to the naming of the Holy One. **10** For as a servant that is continually beaten shall not be without a blue mark: so he that sweareth and nameth God continually shall not be faultless. **11** A man that useth much swearing shall be filled with iniquity, and the plague shall never depart from his house: if he shall offend, his sin shall be upon him: and if he acknowledge not his sin, he maketh a double offence: and if he swear in vain, he shall not be innocent, but his house shall be full of calamities. **12** There is a word that is clothed about with death: God grant that it be not found in the heritage of Jacob; for all such things shall be far from the godly, and they shall not wallow in their sins. **13** Use not thy mouth to intemperate swearing, for therein is the word of sin. **14** Remember thy father and thy mother, when thou sittest among great men. Be not forgetful before them, and so thou by thy custom become a fool, and wish that thou hadst not been born, and curse they day of thy nativity. **15** The man that is accustomed to opprobrious words will never be reformed all the days of his life. **16** Two sorts of men multiply sin, and the third will bring wrath: a hot mind is as a burning fire, it will never be quenched till it be consumed: a fornicator in the body of his flesh will never cease till he hath kindled a fire. **17** All bread is sweet to a whoremonger, he will not leave off till he die. **18** A man that breaketh wedlock, saying thus in his heart, Who seeth me? I am compassed about with darkness, the walls cover me, and no body seeth me; what need I to fear? the most High will not remember my sins: **19** Such a man only feareth the eyes of men, and knoweth not that the eyes of the Lord are ten thousand times brighter than the sun, beholding all the ways of men, and considering the most secret parts. **20** He knew all things ere ever they were created; so also after they were perfected he looked upon them all. **21** This man shall be punished in the streets of the city, and where he suspecteth not he shall be taken. **22** Thus shall it go also with the wife that leaveth her husband, and bringeth in an heir by another. **23** For first, she hath disobeyed the law of the most High; and secondly, she hath trespassed against her own husband; and thirdly, she hath played the whore in adultery, and brought children by another man. **24** She shall be brought out into the congregation, and inquisition shall be made of her children. **25** Her children shall not take root, and her branches shall bring forth no fruit. **26** She shall leave her memory to be cursed, and her reproach shall not be blotted out. **27** And they that remain shall know that there is nothing better than the fear of the Lord, and that there is nothing sweeter than to take heed unto the commandments of the Lord. **28** It is great glory to follow the Lord, and to be received of him is long life.

24

1 Wisdom shall praise herself, and shall glory in the midst of her people. **2** In the congregation of the most High shall she open her mouth, and triumph before his power. **3** I came out of the mouth of the most High, and covered the earth as a cloud. **4** I dwelt in high places, and my throne is in a cloudy pillar. **5** I alone compassed the circuit of heaven, and walked in the bottom of the deep. **6** In the waves of the sea and in all the earth, and in every people and nation, I got a possession. **7** With all these I sought rest: and in whose inheritance shall I abide? **8** So the Creator of all things gave me a commandment, and he that made me caused my tabernacle to rest, and said, Let thy dwelling be in Jacob, and thine inheritance in Israel. **9** He created me from the beginning before the world, and I shall never fail. **10** In the holy tabernacle I served before him; and so was I established in Sion. **11** Likewise in the beloved city he gave me rest, and in Jerusalem was my power. **12** And I took root in an honourable people, even in the portion of the Lord's inheritance. **13** I was exalted like a cedar in Libanus, and as a cypress tree upon the mountains of Hermon. **14** I was exalted like a palm tree in En-gaddi, and as a rose plant in Jericho, as a fair olive tree in a pleasant field, and grew up as a plane tree by the water. **15** I gave a sweet smell like cinnamon and aspalathus, and I yielded a pleasant odour like the best myrrh, as galbanum, and onyx, and sweet storax, and as the fume of frankincense in the tabernacle. **16** As the turpentine tree I stretched out my branches, and my branches are the branches of honour and grace. **17** As the vine brought I forth pleasant savour, and my flowers are the fruit of honour and riches. **18** I am the mother of fair love, and fear, and knowledge, and holy hope: I therefore, being eternal, am given to all my children which are named of him. **19** Come unto me, all ye that be desirous of me, and fill yourselves with my fruits. **20** For my memorial is sweeter than honey, and mine inheritance than the honeycomb. **21** They that eat me shall yet be hungry, and they that drink me shall yet be thirsty. **22** He that obeyeth me shall never be confounded, and they that work by me shall not do amiss. **23** All these things are the book of the covenant of the most high God, even the law which Moses commanded for an heritage unto the congregations of Jacob. **24** Faint not to be strong in the Lord; that he may confirm you, cleave unto him: for the Lord Almighty is God alone, and beside him there is no other Saviour. **25** He filleth all things with his wisdom, as Phison and as Tigris in the time of the new fruits. **26** He maketh the understanding to abound like Euphrates, and as Jordan in the time of the harvest. **27** He maketh the doctrine of knowledge appear as the light, and as Geon in the time of vintage. **28** The first man knew her not perfectly: no more shall the last find her out. **29** For her thoughts are more than the sea, and her counsels profounder than the great deep. **30** I also came out as a brook from a river, and as a conduit into a garden. **31** I said, I will water my best garden, and will water abundantly my garden bed: and, lo, my brook became a river, and my river became a sea. **32** I will yet make doctrine to shine as the morning, and will send forth her light afar off. **33** I will yet pour out doctrine as prophecy, and leave it to all ages for ever. **34** Behold that I have not laboured for myself only, but for all them that seek wisdom.

25

1 In three things I was beautified, and stood up beautiful both before God and men: the unity of brethren, the love of neighbours, a man and a wife that agree together. **2** Three sorts of men my soul hateth, and I am greatly offended at their life: a poor man that is proud, a rich man that is a liar, and an old adulterer that doateth. **3** If thou hast gathered nothing in thy youth, how canst thou find any thing in thine age? **4** O how comely a thing is judgment for gray hairs, and for ancient men to know counsel! **5** O how comely is the wisdom of old men, and understanding and counsel to men of honour. **6** Much experience is the crown of old men, and the fear of God is their glory. **7** There be nine things which I have judged in mine heart to be happy, and the tenth I will utter with my tongue: A man that hath joy of his children; and he that liveth to see the fall of his enemy: **8** Well is him that dwelleth with a wife of understanding, and that hath not slipped with his tongue, and that hath not served a man more unworthy than himself: **9** Well is him that hath found prudence, and he that speaketh in the ears of them that will hear: **10** O how great is he that findeth wisdom! yet is there none above him that feareth the Lord. **11** But the love of the Lord passeth all things for illumination: he that holdeth it, whereto shall he be likened? **12** The fear of the Lord is the beginning of his love: and faith is the beginning of cleaving unto him. **13** [Give me] any plague, but the plague of the heart: and any wickedness, but the wickedness of a woman: **14** And any affliction, but the affliction from them that hate me: and any revenge, but the revenge of enemies. **15** There is no head above the head of a serpent; and there is no wrath above the wrath of an enemy. **16** I had rather dwell with a lion and a dragon, than to keep house with a wicked woman. **17** The wickedness of a woman changeth her face, and darkeneth her countenance like sackcloth. **18** Her husband shall sit among his neighbours; and when he heareth it shall sigh bitterly. **19** All wickedness is but little to the wickedness of a woman: let the portion of a sinner fall upon her. **20** As the climbing up a sandy way is to the feet of the aged, so is a wife full of words to a quiet man. **21** Stumble not at the beauty of a woman, and desire her not for pleasure. **22** A woman, if she maintain her husband, is full of anger, impudence, and much reproach. **23** A wicked woman abateth the courage, maketh an heavy countenance and a wounded heart: a woman that will not comfort her husband in distress maketh weak hands and feeble knees. **24** Of the woman came the beginning of sin, and through her we all die. **25** Give the water no passage; neither a wicked woman liberty to gad abroad. **26** If she go not as thou wouldest have her, cut her off from thy flesh, and give her a bill of divorce, and let her go.

26

1 Blessed is the man that hath a virtuous wife, for the number of his days shall be double. **2** A virtuous woman rejoiceth her husband, and he shall fulfil the years of his life in peace. **3** A good wife is a good portion, which shall be given in the portion of them that fear the Lord. **4** Whether a man be rich or poor, if he have a good heart toward the Lord, he shall at all times rejoice with a cheerful countenance. **5** There be three things that mine heart feareth; and for the fourth I was sore afraid: the slander of a city, the gathering together of an unruly multitude, and a false accusation: all these are worse than death. **6** But a grief of heart and sorrow is a woman that is jealous over another woman, and a scourge of the tongue which communicateth with all. **7** An evil wife is a yoke shaken to and fro: he that hath hold of her is as though he held a scorpion. **8** A drunken woman and a gadder abroad causeth great anger, and she will not cover her own shame. **9** The whoredom of a woman may be known in her haughty

looks and eyelids. 10 If thy daughter be shameless, keep her in straitly, lest she
abuse herself through overmuch liberty. 11 Watch over an impudent eye: and
marvel not if she trespass against thee. 12 She will open her mouth, as a thirsty
traveller when he hath found a fountain, and drink of every water near her: by
every hedge will she sit down, and open her quiver against every arrow. 13 The
grace of a wife delighteth her husband, and her discretion will fatten his bo-
nes. 14 A silent and loving woman is a gift of the Lord; and there is nothing so
much worth as a mind well instructed. 15 A shamefaced and faithful woman is
a double grace, and her continent mind cannot be valued. 16 As the sun when
it ariseth in the high heaven; so is the beauty of a good wife in the ordering of
her house. 17 As the clear light is upon the holy candlestick; so is the beauty
of the face in ripe age. 18 As the golden pillars are upon the sockets of silver;
so are the fair feet with a constant heart. 19 My son, keep the flower of thine
age sound; and give not thy strength to strangers. 20 When thou hast gotten
a fruitful possession through all the field, sow it with thine own seed, trusting in
the goodness of thy stock. 21 So thy race which thou leavest shall be magnified,
having the confidence of their good descent. 22 An harlot shall be accounted
as spittle; but a married woman is a tower against death to her husband. 23 A
wicked woman is given as a portion to a wicked man: but a godly woman is given
to him that feareth the Lord. 24 A dishonest woman contemneth shame: but
an honest woman will reverence her husband. 25 A shameless woman shall be
counted as a dog; but she that is shamefaced will fear the Lord. 26 A woman
that honoureth her husband shall be judged wise of all; but she that dishonoureth
him in her pride shall be counted ungodly of all. 27 A loud crying woman and
a scold shall be sought out to drive away the enemies. 28 There be two things
that grieve my heart; and the third maketh me angry: a man of war that suffereth
poverty; and men of understanding that are not set by; and one that returneth
from righteousness to sin; the Lord prepareth such an one for the sword. 29 A
merchant shall hardly keep himself from doing wrong; and an huckster shall not
be freed from sin.

27

1 Many have sinned for a small matter; and he that seeketh for abun-
dance will turn his eyes away. 2 As a nail sticketh fast between the
joinings of the stones; so doth sin stick close between buying and selling. 3 Un-
less a man hold himself diligently in the fear of the Lord, his house shall soon be
overthrown. 4 As when one sifteth with a sieve, the refuse remaineth; so the
filth of man in his talk. 5 The furnace proveth the potter's vessels; so the trial
of man is in his reasoning. 6 The fruit declareth if the tree have been dressed;
so is the utterance of a conceit in the heart of man. 7 Praise no man before
thou hearest him speak; for this is the trial of men. 8 If thou followest righte-
ousness, thou shalt obtain her, and put her on, as a glorious long robe. 9 The
birds will resort unto their like; so will truth return unto them that practise
in her. 10 As the lion lieth in wait for the prey; so sin for them that work
iniquity. 11 The discourse of a godly man is always with wisdom; but a fool
changeth as the moon. 12 If thou be among the indiscreet, observe the time;
but be continually among men of understanding. 13 The discourse of fools
is irksome, and their sport is the wantonness of sin. 14 The talk of him that
sweareth much maketh the hair stand upright; and their brawls make one stop
his ears. 15 The strife of the proud is bloodshedding, and their revilings are
grievous to the ear. 16 Whoso discovereth secrets loseth his credit; and shall
never find friend to his mind. 17 Love thy friend, and be faithful unto him:
but if thou betrayest his secrets, follow no more after him. 18 For as a man
hath destroyed his enemy; so hast thou lost the love of thy neighbor. 19 As
one that letteth a bird go out of his hand, so hast thou let thy neighbour go, and
shalt not get him again 20 Follow after him no more, for he is too far off; he is
as a roe escaped out of the snare. 21 As for a wound, it may be bound up; and
after reviling there may be reconcilement: but he that betrayeth secrets is without
hope. 22 He that winketh with the eyes worketh evil: and he that knoweth him
will depart from him. 23 When thou art present, he will speak sweetly, and
will admire thy words: but at the last he will writhe his mouth, and slander thy
sayings. 24 I have hated many things, but nothing like him; for the Lord will
hate him. 25 Whoso casteth a stone on high casteth it on his own head; and a
deceitful stroke shall make wounds. 26 Whoso diggeth a pit shall fall therein:
and he that setteth a trap shall be taken therein. 27 He that worketh mischief,
it shall fall upon him, and he shall not know whence it cometh. 28 Mockery
and reproach are from the proud; but vengeance, as a lion, shall lie in wait for
them. 29 They that rejoice at the fall of the righteous shall be taken in the snare;
and anguish shall consume them before they die. 30 Malice and wrath, even
these are abominations; and the sinful man shall have them both.

28

1 He that revengeth shall find vengeance from the Lord, and he will
surely keep his sins [in remembrance.] 2 Forgive thy neighbour the
hurt that he hath done unto thee, so shall thy sins also be forgiven when thou
prayest. 3 One man beareth hatred against another, and doth he seek pardon
from the Lord? 4 He sheweth no mercy to a man, which is like himself: and
doth he ask forgiveness of his own sins? 5 If he that is but flesh nourish hatred,
who will intreat for pardon of his sins? 6 Remember thy end, and let enmity ce-
ase; [remember] corruption and death, and abide in the commandments. 7 Re-
member the commandments, and bear no malice to thy neighbour: [remember]
the covenant of the Highest, and wink at ignorance. 8 Abstain from strife, and
thou shalt diminish thy sins: for a furious man will kindle strife, 9 A sinful man
disquieteth friends, and maketh debate among them that be at peace. 10 As
the matter of the fire is, so it burneth: and as a man's strength is, so is his wra-
th; and according to his riches his anger riseth; and the stronger they are which
contend, the more they will be inflamed. 11 An hasty contention kindleth a
fire: and an hasty fighting sheddeth blood. 12 If thou blow the spark, it shall
burn: if thou spit upon it, it shall be quenched: and both these come out of thy
mouth. 13 Curse the whisperer and doubletongued: for such have destroyed
many that were at peace. 14 A backbiting tongue hath disquieted many, and
driven them from nation to nation: strong cities hath it pulled down, and over-
thrown the houses of great men. 15 A backbiting tongue hath cast out virtuous
women, and deprived them of their labours. 16 Whoso hearkeneth unto it shall
never find rest, and never dwell quietly. 17 The stroke of the whip maketh
marks in the flesh: but the stroke of the tongue breaketh the bones. 18 Many
have fallen by the edge of the sword: but not so many as have fallen by the ton-
gue. 19 Well is he that is defended through the venom thereof; who hath not
drawn the yoke thereof, nor hath been bound in her bands. 20 For the yoke
thereof is a yoke of iron, and the bands thereof are bands of brass. 21 The
death thereof is an evil death, the grave were better than it. 22 It shall not
have rule over them that fear God, neither shall they be burned with the flame
thereof. 23 Such as forsake the Lord shall fall into it; and it shall burn in them,
and not be quenched; it shall be sent upon them as a lion, and devour them as a
leopard. 24 Look that thou hedge thy possession about with thorns, and bind
up thy silver and gold, 25 And weigh thy words in a balance, and make a door
and bar for thy mouth. 26 Beware thou slide not by it, lest thou fall before him
that lieth in wait.

29

1 He that is merciful will lend unto his neighbour; and he that
strengtheneth his hand keepeth the commandments. 2 Lend to
thy neighbour in time of his need, and pay thou thy neighbour again in due
season. 3 Keep thy word, and deal faithfully with him, and thou shalt always
find the thing that is necessary for thee. 4 Many, when a thing was lent them,
reckoned it to be found, and put them to trouble that helped them. 5 Till he
hath received, he will kiss a man's hand; and for his neighbour's money he will
speak submissly: but when he should repay, he will prolong the time, and return
words of grief, and complain of the time. 6 If he prevail, he shall hardly receive
the half, and he will count as if he had found it: if not, he hath deprived him
of his money, and he hath gotten him an enemy without cause: he payeth him
with cursings and railings; and for honour he will pay him disgrace. 7 Many
therefore have refused to lend for other men's ill dealing, fearing to be defrau-
ded. 8 Yet have thou patience with a man in poor estate, and delay not to shew
him mercy. 9 Help the poor for the commandment's sake, and turn him not
away because of his poverty. 10 Lose thy money for thy brother and thy friend,
and let it not rust under a stone to be lost. 11 Lay up thy treasure according to
the commandments of the most High, and it shall bring thee more profit than
gold. 12 Shut up alms in thy storehouses: and it shall deliver thee from all
affliction. 13 It shall fight for thee against thine enemies better than a mighty
shield and strong spear. 14 An honest man is surety for his neighbour: but he
that is impudent will forsake him. 15 Forget not the friendship of thy surety,
for he hath given his life for thee. 16 A sinner will overthrow the good estate
of his surety: 17 And he that is of an unthankful mind will leave him [in dan-
ger] that delivered him. 18 Suretiship hath undone many of good estate, and
shaken them as a wave of the sea: mighty men hath it driven from their houses,
so that they wandered among strange nations. 19 A wicked man transgressing
the commandments of the Lord shall fall into suretiship: and he that undertaketh
and followeth other men's business for gain shall fall into suits. 20 Help thy
neighbour according to thy power, and beware that thou thyself fall not into the
same. 21 The chief thing for life is water, and bread, and clothing, and an house
to cover shame. 22 Better is the life of a poor man in a mean cottage, than de-
licate fare in another man's house. 23 Be it little or much, hold thee contented,
that thou hear not the reproach of thy house. 24 For it is a miserable life to
go from house to house: for where thou art a stranger, thou darest not open thy
mouth. 25 Thou shalt entertain, and feast, and have no thanks: moreover thou
shalt hear bitter words: 26 Come, thou stranger, and furnish a table, and feed
me of that thou hast ready. 27 Give place, thou stranger, to an honourable man;
my brother cometh to be lodged, and I have need of mine house. 28 These
things are grievous to a man of understanding; the upbraiding of houseroom, and
reproaching of the lender.

30

1 He that loveth his son causeth him oft to feel the rod, that he
may have joy of him in the end. 2 He that chastiseth his son shall
have joy in him, and shall rejoice of him among his acquaintance. 3 He that
teacheth his son grieveth the enemy: and before his friends he shall rejoice of
him. 4 Though his father die, yet he is as though he were not dead: for he hath
left one behind him that is like himself. 5 While he lived, he saw and rejoiced in
him: and when he died, he was not sorrowful. 6 He left behind him an avenger
against his enemies, and one that shall requite kindness to his friends. 7 He
that maketh too much of his son shall bind up his wounds; and his bowels will

be troubled at every cry. **8** An horse not broken becometh headstrong: and
a child left to himself will be wilful. **9** Cocker thy child, and he shall make
thee afraid: play with him, and he will bring thee to heaviness. **10** Laugh not
with him, lest thou have sorrow with him, and lest thou gnash thy teeth in the
end. **11** Give him no liberty in his youth, and wink not at his follies. **12** Bow
down his neck while he is young, and beat him on the sides while he is a child,
lest he wax stubborn, and be disobedient unto thee, and so bring sorrow to thine
heart. **13** Chastise thy son, and hold him to labour, lest his lewd behaviour be
an offence unto thee. **14** Better is the poor, being sound and strong of consti-
tution, than a rich man that is afflicted in his body. **15** Health and good estate
of body are above all gold, and a strong body above infinite wealth. **16** There is
no riches above a sound body, and no joy above the joy of the heart. **17** Death
is better than a bitter life or continual sickness. **18** Delicates poured upon a
mouth shut up are as messes of meat set upon a grave. **19** What good doeth the
offering unto an idol? for neither can it eat nor smell: so is he that is persecuted of
the Lord. **20** He seeth with his eyes and groaneth, as an eunuch that embraceth
a virgin and sigheth. **21** Give not over thy mind to heaviness, and afflict not
thyself in thine own counsel. **22** The gladness of the heart is the life of man,
and the joyfulness of a man prolongeth his days. **23** Love thine own soul, and
comfort thy heart, remove sorrow far from thee: for sorrow hath killed many, and
there is no profit therein. **24** Envy and wrath shorten the life, and carefulness
bringeth age before the time. **25** A cheerful and good heart will have a care of
his meat and diet.

31

1 Watching for riches consumeth the flesh, and the care thereof dri-
veth away sleep. **2** Watching care will not let a man slumber, as a
sore disease breaketh sleep, **3** The rich hath great labour in gathering riches
together; and when he resteth, he is filled with his delicates. **4** The poor la-
boureth in his poor estate; and when he leaveth off, he is still needy. **5** He that
loveth gold shall not be justified, and he that followeth corruption shall have
enough thereof. **6** Gold hath been the ruin of many, and their destruction was
present. **7** It is a stumblingblock unto them that sacrifice unto it, and every fool
shall be taken therewith. **8** Blessed is the rich that is found without blemish, and
hath not gone after gold. **9** Who is he? and we will call him blessed: for won-
derful things hath he done among his people. **10** Who hath been tried thereby,
and found perfect? then let him glory. Who might offend, and hath not offended?
or done evil, and hath not done it? **11** His goods shall be established, and the
congregation shall declare his alms. **12** If thou sit at a bountiful table, be not
greedy upon it, and say not, There is much meat on it. **13** Remember that a
wicked eye is an evil thing: and what is created more wicked than an eye? therefore
it weepeth upon every occasion. **14** Stretch not thine hand whithersoever it
looketh, and thrust it not with him into the dish. **15** Judge not thy neighbour
by thyself: and be discreet in every point. **16** Eat as it becometh a man, those
things which are set before thee; and devour note, lest thou be hated. **17** Leave
off first for manners' sake; and be not unsatiable, lest thou offend. **18** When
thou sittest among many, reach not thine hand out first of all. **19** A very little
is sufficient for a man well nurtured, and he fetcheth not his wind short upon his
bed. **20** Sound sleep cometh of moderate eating: he riseth early, and his wits are
with him: but the pain of watching, and choler, and pangs of the belly, are with an
unsatiable man. **21** And if thou hast been forced to eat, arise, go forth, vomit,
and thou shalt have rest. **22** My son, hear me, and despise me not, and at the
last thou shalt find as I told thee: in all thy works be quick, so shall there no sick-
ness come unto thee. **23** Whoso is liberal of his meat, men shall speak well of
him; and the report of his good housekeeping will be believed. **24** But against
him that is a niggard of his meat the whole city shall murmur; and the testimonies
of his niggardness shall not be doubted of. **25** Shew not thy valiantness in wine;
for wine hath destroyed many. **26** The furnace proveth the edge by dipping: so
doth wine the hearts of the proud by drunkeness. **27** Wine is as good as life to
a man, if it be drunk moderately: what life is then to a man that is without wine?
for it was made to make men glad. **28** Wine measurably drunk and in sea-
son bringeth gladness of the heart, and cheerfulness of the mind: **29** But wine
drunken with excess maketh bitterness of the mind, with brawling and quarrel-
ling. **30** Drunkenness increaseth the rage of a fool till he offend: it diminisheth
strength, and maketh wounds. **31** Rebuke not thy neighbour at the wine, and
despise him not in his mirth: give him no despiteful words, and press not upon
him with urging him [to drink.]

32

1 If thou be made the master [of a feast,] lift not thyself up, but be
among them as one of the rest; take diligent care for them, and so
sit down. **2** And when thou hast done all thy office, take thy place, that thou
mayest be merry with them, and receive a crown for thy well ordering of the
feast. **3** Speak, thou that art the elder, for it becometh thee, but with sound
judgment; and hinder not musick. **4** Pour not out words where there is a musi-
cian, and shew not forth wisdom out of time. **5** A concert of musick in a ban-
quet of wine is as a signet of carbuncle set in gold. **6** As a signet of an emerald
set in a work of gold, so is the melody of musick with pleasant wine. **7** Spe-
ak, young man, if there be need of thee: and yet scarcely when thou art twice
asked. **8** Let thy speech be short, comprehending much in few words; be as
one that knoweth and yet holdeth his tongue. **9** If thou be among great men,
make not thyself equal with them; and when ancient men are in place, use not
many words. **10** Before the thunder goeth lightning; and before a shamefaced
man shall go favour. **11** Rise up betimes, and be not the last; but get thee
home without delay. **12** There take thy pastime, and do what thou wilt: but
sin not by proud speech. **13** And for these things bless him that made thee,
and hath replenished thee with his good things. **14** Whoso feareth the Lord
will receive his discipline; and they that seek him early shall find favour. **15** He
that seeketh the law shall be filled therewith: but the hypocrite will be offended
thereat. **16** They that fear the Lord shall find judgment, and shall kindle justice
as a light. **17** A sinful man will not be reproved, but findeth an excuse accor-
ding to his will. **18** A man of counsel will be considerate; but a strange and
proud man is not daunted with fear, even when of himself he hath done without
counsel. **19** Do nothing without advice; and when thou hast once done, repent
not. **20** Go not in a way wherein thou mayest fall, and stumble not among
the stones. **21** Be not confident in a plain way. **22** And beware of thine own
children. **23** In every good work trust thy own soul; for this is the keeping of
the commandments. **24** He that believeth in the Lord taketh heed to the com-
mandment; and he that trusteth in him shall fare never the worse.

33

1 There shall no evil happen unto him that feareth the Lord; but in
temptation even again he will deliver him. **2** A wise man hateth
not the law; but he that is an hypocrite therein is as a ship in a storm. **3** A
man of understanding trusteth in the law; and the law is faithful unto him, as
an oracle. **4** Prepare what to say, and so thou shalt be heard: and bind up in-
struction, and then make answer. **5** The heart of the foolish is like a cartwheel;
and his thoughts are like a rolling axletree. **6** A stallion horse is as a mocking
friend, he neigheth under every one that sitteth upon him. **7** Why doth one day
excel another, when as all the light of every day in the year is of the sun? **8** By
the knowledge of the Lord they were distinguished: and he altered seasons and
feasts. **9** Some of them hath he made high days, and hallowed them, and some
of them hath he made ordinary days. **10** And all men are from the ground,
and Adam was created of earth: **11** In much knowledge the Lord hath divided
them, and made their ways diverse. **12** Some of them hath he blessed and exal-
ted and some of them he sanctified, and set near himself: but some of them hath
he cursed and brought low, and turned out of their places. **13** As the clay is in
the potter's hand, to fashion it at his pleasure: so man is in the hand of him that
made him, to render to them as liketh him best. **14** Good is set against evil,
and life against death: so is the godly against the sinner, and the sinner against the
godly. **15** So look upon all the works of the most High; and there are two and
two, one against another. **16** I awaked up last of all, as one that gathereth after
the grapegatherers: by the blessing of the Lord I profited, and tred my winepress
like a gatherer of grapes. **17** Consider that I laboured not for myself only, but
for all them that seek learning. **18** Hear me, O ye great men of the people, and
hearken with your ears, ye rulers of the congregation. **19** Give not thy son and
wife, thy brother and friend, power over thee while thou livest, and give not thy
goods to another: lest it repent thee, and thou intreat for the same again. **20** As
long as thou livest and hast breath in thee, give not thyself over to any. **21** For
better it is that thy children should seek to thee, than that thou shouldest stand
to their courtesy. **22** In all thy works keep to thyself the preeminence; leave
not a stain in thine honour. **23** At the time when thou shalt end thy days, and
finish thy life, distribute thine inheritance. **24** Fodder, a wand, and burdens,
are for the ass; and bread, correction, and work, for a servant. . **25** If thou set
thy servant to labour, thou shalt find rest: but if thou let him go idle, he shall seek
liberty. **26** A yoke and a collar do bow the neck: so are tortures and torments for
an evil servant. **27** Send him to labour, that he be not idle; for idleness teacheth
much evil. **28** Set him to work, as is fit for him: if he be not obedient, put on
more heavy fetters. **29** But be not excessive toward any; and without discretion
do nothing. **30** If thou have a servant, let him be unto thee as thyself, because
thou hast bought him with a price. **31** If thou have a servant, entreat him as a
brother: for thou hast need of him, as of thine own soul: if thou entreat him evil,
and he run from thee, which way wilt thou go to seek him?

34

1 The hopes of a man void of understanding are vain and false: and
dreams lift up fools. **2** Whoso regardeth dreams is like him that
catcheth at a shadow, and followeth after the wind. **3** The vision of dreams is the
resemblance of one thing to another, even as the likeness of a face to a face. **4** Of
an unclean thing what can be cleansed? and from that thing which is false what
truth can come? **5** Divinations, and soothsayings, and dreams, are vain: and
the heart fancieth, as a woman's heart in travail. **6** If they be not sent from the
most High in thy visitation, set not thy heart upon them. **7** For dreams have
deceived many, and they have failed that put their trust in them. **8** The law shall
be found perfect without lies: and wisdom is perfection to a faithful mouth. **9** A
man that hath travelled knoweth many things; and he that hath much experience
will declare wisdom. **10** He that hath no experience knoweth little: but he that
hath travelled is full of prudence. **11** When I travelled, I saw many things; and
I understand more than I can express. **12** I was ofttimes in danger of death: yet
I was delivered because of these things. **13** The spirit of those that fear the Lord
shall live; for their hope is in him that saveth them. **14** Whoso feareth the Lord
shall not fear nor be afraid; for he is his hope. **15** Blessed is the soul of him that

feareth the Lord: to whom doth he look? and who is his strength? **16** For the eyes of the Lord are upon them that love him, he is their mighty protection and strong stay, a defence from heat, and a cover from the sun at noon, a preservation from stumbling, and an help from falling. **17** He raiseth up the soul, and lighteneth the eyes: he giveth health, life, and blessing. **18** He that sacrificeth of a thing wrongfully gotten, his offering is ridiculous; and the gifts of unjust men are not accepted. **19** The most High is not pleased with the offerings of the wicked; neither is he pacified for sin by the multitude of sacrifices. **20** Whoso bringeth an offering of the goods of the poor doeth as one that killeth the son before his father's eyes. **21** The bread of the needy is their life: he that defraudeth him thereof is a man of blood. **22** He that taketh away his neighbour's living slayeth him; and he that defraudeth the labourer of his hire is a bloodshedder. **23** When one buildeth, and another pulleth down, what profit have they then but labour? **24** When one prayeth, and another curseth, whose voice will the Lord hear? **25** He that washeth himself after the touching of a dead body, if he touch it again, what availeth his washing? **26** So is it with a man that fasteth for his sins, and goeth again, and doeth the same: who will hear his prayer? or what doth his humbling profit him?

35

1 He that keepeth the law bringeth offerings enough: he that taketh heed to the commandment offereth a peace offering. **2** He that requiteth a goodturn offereth fine flour; and he that giveth alms sacrificeth praise. **3** To depart from wickedness is a thing pleasing to the Lord; and to forsake unrighteousness is a propitiation. **4** Thou shalt not appear empty before the Lord. **5** For all these things [are to be done] because of the commandment. **6** The offering of the righteous maketh the altar fat, and the sweet savour thereof is before the most High. **7** The sacrifice of a just man is acceptable. and the memorial thereof shall never be forgotten. **8** Give the Lord his honour with a good eye, and diminish not the firstfruits of thine hands. **9** In all thy gifts shew a cheerful countenance, and dedicate thy tithes with gladness. **10** Give unto the most High according as he hath enriched thee; and as thou hast gotten, give with a cheerful eye. **11** For the Lord recompenseth, and will give thee seven times as much. **12** Do not think to corrupt with gifts; for such he will not receive: and trust not to unrighteous sacrifices; for the Lord is judge, and with him is no respect of persons. **13** He will not accept any person against a poor man, but will hear the prayer of the oppressed. **14** He will not despise the supplication of the fatherless; nor the widow, when she poureth out her complaint. **15** Do not the tears run down the widow's cheeks? and is not her cry against him that causeth them to fall? **16** He that serveth the Lord shall be accepted with favour, and his prayer shall reach unto the clouds. **17** The prayer of the humble pierceth the clouds: and till it come nigh, he will not be comforted; and will not depart, till the most High shall behold to judge righteously, and execute judgment. **18** For the Lord will not be slack, neither will the Mighty be patient toward them, till he have smitten in sunder the loins of the unmerciful, and repayed vengeance to the heathen; till he have taken away the multitude of the proud, and broken the sceptre of the unrighteous; **19** Till he have rendered to every man according to his deeds, and to the works of men according to their devices; till he have judged the cause of his people, and made them to rejoice in his mercy. **20** Mercy is seasonable in the time of affliction, as clouds of rain in the time of drought.

36

1 Have mercy upon us, O Lord God of all, and behold us: **2** And send thy fear upon all the nations that seek not after thee. **3** Lift up thy hand against the strange nations, and let them see thy power. **4** As thou wast sanctified in us before them: so be thou magnified among them before us. **5** And let them know thee, as we have known thee, that there is no God but only thou, O God. **6** Shew new signs, and make other strange wonders: glorify thy hand and thy right arm, that they may set forth thy wondrous works. **7** Raise up indignation, and pour out wrath: take away the adversary, and destroy the enemy. **8** Sake the time short, remember the covenant, and let them declare thy wonderful works. **9** Let him that escapeth be consumed by the rage of the fire; and let them perish that oppress the people. **10** Smite in sunder the heads of the rulers of the heathen, that say, There is none other but we. **11** Gather all the tribes of Jacob together, and inherit thou them, as from the beginning. **12** O Lord, have mercy upon the people that is called by thy name, and upon Israel, whom thou hast named thy firstborn. **13** O be merciful unto Jerusalem, thy holy city, the place of thy rest. **14** Fill Sion with thine unspeakable oracles, and thy people with thy glory: **15** Give testimony unto those that thou hast possessed from the beginning, and raise up prophets that have been in thy name. **16** Reward them that wait for thee, and let thy prophets be found faithful. **17** O Lord, hear the prayer of thy servants, according to the blessing of Aaron over thy people, that all they which dwell upon the earth may know that thou art the Lord, the eternal God. **18** The belly devoureth all meats, yet is one meat better than another. **19** As the palate tasteth divers kinds of venison: so doth an heart of understanding false speeches. **20** A froward heart causeth heaviness: but a man of experience will recompense him. **21** A woman will receive every man, yet is one daughter better than another. **22** The beauty of a woman cheereth the countenance, and a man loveth nothing better. **23** If there be kindness, meekness, and comfort, in her tongue, then is not her husband like other men. **24** He that getteth a wife beginneth a possession, a help like unto himself, and a pillar of rest. **25** Where no hedge is, there the possession is spoiled: and he that hath no wife will wander up and down mourning. **26** Who will trust a thief well appointed, that skippeth from city to city? so [who will believe] a man that hath no house, and lodgeth wheresoever the night taketh him?

37

1 Every friend saith, I am his friend also: but there is a friend, which is only a friend in name. **2** Is it not a grief unto death, when a companion and friend is turned to an enemy? **3** O wicked imagination, whence camest thou in to cover the earth with deceit? **4** There is a companion, which rejoiceth in the prosperity of a friend, but in the time of trouble will be against him. **5** There is a companion, which helpeth his friend for the belly, and taketh up the buckler against the enemy. **6** Forget not thy friend in thy mind, and be not unmindful of him in thy riches. **7** Every counsellor extolleth counsel; but there is some that counselleth for himself. **8** Beware of a counsellor, and know before what need he hath; for he will counsel for himself; lest he cast the lot upon thee, **9** And say unto thee, Thy way is good: and afterward he stand on the other side, to see what shall befall thee. **10** Consult not with one that suspecteth thee: and hide thy counsel from such as envy thee. **11** Neither consult with a woman touching her of whom she is jealous; neither with a coward in matters of war; nor with a merchant concerning exchange; nor with a buyer of selling; nor with an envious man of thankfulness; nor with an unmerciful man touching kindness; nor with the slothful for any work; nor with an hireling for a year of finishing work; nor with an idle servant of much business: hearken not unto these in any matter of counsel. **12** But be continually with a godly man, whom thou knowest to keep the commandments of the Lord, whose, mind is according to thy mind, and will sorrow with thee, if thou shalt miscarry. **13** And let the counsel of thine own heart stand: for there is no man more faithful unto thee than it. **14** For a man's mind is sometime wont to tell him more than seven watchmen, that sit above in an high tower. **15** And above all this pray to the most High, that he will direct thy way in truth. **16** Let reason go before every enterprize, and counsel before every action. **17** The countenance is a sign of changing of the heart. **18** Four manner of things appear: good and evil, life and death: but the tongue ruleth over them continually. **19** There is one that is wise and teacheth many, and yet is unprofitable to himself. **20** There is one that sheweth wisdom in words, and is hated: he shall be destitute of all food. **21** For grace is not given, him from the Lord, because he is deprived of all wisdom. **22** Another is wise to himself; and the fruits of understanding are commendable in his mouth. **23** A wise man instructeth his people; and the fruits of his understanding fail not. **24** A wise man shall be filled with blessing; and all they that see him shall count him happy. **25** The days of the life of man may be numbered: but the days of Israel are innumerable. **26** A wise man shall inherit glory among his people, and his name shall be perpetual. **27** My son, prove thy soul in thy life, and see what is evil for it, and give not that unto it. **28** For all things are not profitable for all men, neither hath every soul pleasure in every thing. **29** Be not unsatiable in any dainty thing, nor too greedy upon meats: **30** For excess of meats bringeth sickness, and surfeiting will turn into choler. **31** By surfeiting have many perished; but he that taketh heed prolongeth his life.

38

1 Honour a physician with the honour due unto him for the uses which ye may have of him: for the Lord hath created him. **2** For of the most High cometh healing, and he shall receive honour of the king. **3** The skill of the physician shall lift up his head: and in the sight of great men he shall be in admiration. **4** The Lord hath created medicines out of the earth; and he that is wise will not abhor them. **5** Was not the water made sweet with wood, that the virtue thereof might be known? **6** And he hath given men skill, that he might be honoured in his marvellous works. **7** With such doth he heal [men,] and taketh away their pains. **8** Of such doth the apothecary make a confection; and of his works there is no end; and from him is peace over all the earth, **9** My son, in thy sickness be not negligent: but pray unto the Lord, and he will make thee whole. **10** Leave off from sin, and order thine hands aright, and cleanse thy heart from all wickedness. **11** Give a sweet savour, and a memorial of fine flour; and make a fat offering, as not being. **12** Then give place to the physician, for the Lord hath created him: let him not go from thee, for thou hast need of him. **13** There is a time when in their hands there is good success. **14** For they shall also pray unto the Lord, that he would prosper that, which they give for ease and remedy to prolong life. **15** He that sinneth before his Maker, let him fall into the hand of the physician. **16** My son, let tears fall down over the dead, and begin to lament, as if thou hadst suffered great harm thyself; and then cover his body according to the custom, and neglect not his burial. **17** Weep bitterly, and make great moan, and use lamentation, as he is worthy, and that a day or two, lest thou be evil spoken of: and then comfort thyself for thy heaviness. **18** For of heaviness cometh death, and the heaviness of the heart breaketh strength. **19** In affliction also sorrow remaineth: and the life of the poor is the curse of the heart. **20** Take no heaviness to heart: drive it away, and member the last end. **21** Forget it not, for there is no turning again: thou shalt not do him good, but hurt thyself. **22** Remember my judgment: for thine also shall be so; yesterday for me, and to day for thee. **23** When the dead is at rest, let his remembrance rest; and be comforted for him, when his Spirit is departed from him. **24** The wisdom of a learned man cometh by opportunity of leisure: and

he that hath little business shall become wise. **25** How can he get wisdom that
holdeth the plough, and that glorieth in the goad, that driveth oxen, and is occu-
pied in their labours, and whose talk is of bullocks? **26** He giveth his mind to
make furrows; and is diligent to give the kine fodder. **27** So every carpenter and
workmaster, that laboureth night and day: and they that cut and grave seals, and
are diligent to make great variety, and give themselves to counterfeit imagery, and
watch to finish a work: **28** The smith also sitting by the anvil, and considering
the iron work, the vapour of the fire wasteth his flesh, and he fighteth with the
heat of the furnace: the noise of the hammer and the anvil is ever in his ears, and
his eyes look still upon the pattern of the thing that he maketh; he setteth his
mind to finish his work, and watcheth to polish it perfectly: **29** So doth the
potter sitting at his work, and turning the wheel about with his feet, who is alway
carefully set at his work, and maketh all his work by number; **30** He fashioneth
the clay with his arm, and boweth down his strength before his feet; he applieth
himself to lead it over; and he is diligent to make clean the furnace: **31** All
these trust to their hands: and every one is wise in his work. **32** Without these
cannot a city be inhabited: and they shall not dwell where they will, nor go up and
down: **33** They shall not be sought for in publick counsel, nor sit high in the
congregation: they shall not sit on the judges' seat, nor understand the sentence of
judgment: they cannot declare justice and judgment; and they shall not be found
where parables are spoken. **34** But they will maintain the state of the world, and
[all] their desire is in the work of their craft.

39 1 But he that giveth his mind to the law of the most High, and is
occupied in the meditation thereof, will seek out the wisdom of all
the ancient, and be occupied in prophecies. **2** He will keep the sayings of the
renowned men: and where subtil parables are, he will be there also. **3** He will
seek out the secrets of grave sentences, and be conversant in dark parables. **4** He
shall serve among great men, and appear before princes: he will travel through
strange countries; for he hath tried the good and the evil among men. **5** He
will give his heart to resort early to the Lord that made him, and will pray before
the most High, and will open his mouth in prayer, and make supplication for
his sins. **6** When the great Lord will, he shall be filled with the spirit of under-
standing: he shall pour out wise sentences, and give thanks unto the Lord in his
prayer. **7** He shall direct his counsel and knowledge, and in his secrets shall he
meditate. **8** He shall shew forth that which he hath learned, and shall glory in
the law of the covenant of the Lord. **9** Many shall commend his understanding;
and so long as the world endureth, it shall not be blotted out; his memorial shall
not depart away, and his name shall live from generation to generation. **10** Na-
tions shall shew forth his wisdom, and the congregation shall declare his prai-
se. **11** If he die, he shall leave a greater name than a thousand: and if he live, he
shall increase it. **12** Yet have I more to say, which I have thought upon; for I am
filled as the moon at the full. **13** Hearken unto me, ye holy children, and bud
forth as a rose growing by the brook of the field: **14** And give ye a sweet savour
as frankincense, and flourish as a lily, send forth a smell, and sing a song of praise,
bless the Lord in all his works. **15** Magnify his name, and shew forth his praise
with the songs of your lips, and with harps, and in praising him ye shall say after
this manner: **16** All the works of the Lord are exceeding good, and whatsoever
he commandeth shall be accomplished in due season. **17** And none may say,
What is this? wherefore is that? for at time convenient they shall all be sought
out: at his commandment the waters stood as an heap, and at the words of his
mouth the receptacles of waters. **18** At his commandment is done whatsoever
pleaseth him; and none can hinder, when he will save. **19** The works of all
flesh are before him, and nothing can be hid from his eyes. **20** He seeth from
everlasting to everlasting; and there is nothing wonderful before him. **21** A man
need not to say, What is this? wherefore is that? for he hath made all things for
their uses. **22** His blessing covered the dry land as a river, and watered it as a
flood. **23** As he hath turned the waters into saltness: so shall the heathen inherit
his wrath. **24** As his ways are plain unto the holy; so are they stumblingblocks
unto the wicked. **25** For the good are good things created from the beginning:
so evil things for sinners. **26** The principal things for the whole use of man's life
are water, fire, iron, and salt, flour of wheat, honey, milk, and the blood of the
grape, and oil, and clothing. **27** All these things are for good to the godly: so
to the sinners they are turned into evil. **28** There be spirits that are created for
vengeance, which in their fury lay on sore strokes; in the time of destruction they
pour out their force, and appease the wrath of him that made them. **29** Fire,
and hail, and famine, and death, all these were created for vengeance; **30** Te-
eth of wild beasts, and scorpions, serpents, and the sword punishing the wicked
to destruction. **31** They shall rejoice in his commandment, and they shall be
ready upon earth, when need is; and when their time is come, they shall not
transgress his word. **32** Therefore from the beginning I was resolved, and thou-
ght upon these things, and have left them in writing. **33** All the works of the
Lord are good: and he will give every needful thing in due season. **34** So that a
man cannot say, This is worse than that: for in time they shall all be well appro-
ved. **35** And therefore praise ye the Lord with the whole heart and mouth, and
bless the name of the Lord.

40 1 Great travail is created for every man, and an heavy yoke is upon the
sons of Adam, from the day that they go out of their mother's womb,
till the day that they return to the mother of all things. **2** Their imagination of
things to come, and the day of death, [trouble] their thoughts, and [cause] fear of
heart; **3** From him that sitteth on a throne of glory, unto him that is humbled
in earth and ashes; **4** From him that weareth purple and a crown, unto him that
is clothed with a linen frock. **5** Wrath, and envy, trouble, and unquietness, fear
of death, and anger, and strife, and in the time of rest upon his bed his night sleep,
do change his knowledge. **6** A little or nothing is his rest, and afterward he is
in his sleep, as in a day of keeping watch, troubled in the vision of his heart, as if
he were escaped out of a battle. **7** When all is safe, he awaketh, and marvelleth
that the fear was nothing. **8** [Such things happen] unto all flesh, both man and
beast, and that is sevenfold more upon sinners. **9** Death, and bloodshed, strife,
and sword, calamities, famine, tribulation, and the scourge; **10** These things are
created for the wicked, and for their sakes came the flood. **11** All things that
are of the earth shall turn to the earth again: and that which is of the waters doth
return into the sea. **12** All bribery and injustice shall be blotted out: but true
dealing shall endure for ever. **13** The goods of the unjust shall be dried up like
a river, and shall vanish with noise, like a great thunder in rain. **14** While he
openeth his hand he shall rejoice: so shall transgressors come to nought. **15** The
children of the ungodly shall not bring forth many branches: but are as unclean
roots upon a hard rock. **16** The weed growing upon every water and bank of
a river shall be pulled up before all grass. **17** Bountifulness is as a most fruitful
garden, and mercifulness endureth for ever. **18** To labour, and to be content
with that a man hath, is a sweet life: but he that findeth a treasure is above them
both. **19** Children and the building of a city continue a man's name: but a
blameless wife is counted above them both. **20** Wine and musick rejoice the
heart: but the love of wisdom is above them both. **21** The pipe and the psaltery
make sweet melody: but a pleasant tongue is above them both. **22** Thine eye
desireth favour and beauty: but more than both corn while it is green. **23** A
friend and companion never meet amiss: but above both is a wife with her hu-
sband. **24** Brethren and help are against time of trouble: but alms shall deliver
more than them both. **25** Gold and silver make the foot stand sure: but counsel
is esteemed above them both. **26** Riches and strength lift up the heart: but the
fear of the Lord is above them both: there is no want in the fear of the Lord, and
it needeth not to seek help. **27** The fear of the Lord is a fruitful garden, and
covereth him above all glory. **28** My son, lead not a beggar's life; for better it is
to die than to beg. **29** The life of him that dependeth on another man's table is
not to be counted for a life; for he polluteth himself with other men's meat: but a
wise man well nurtured will beware thereof. **30** Begging is sweet in the mouth
of the shameless: but in his belly there shall burn a fire.

41 1 O death, how bitter is the remembrance of thee to a man that liveth
at rest in his possessions, unto the man that hath nothing to vex him,
and that hath prosperity in all things: yea, unto him that is yet able to receive
meat! **2** O death, acceptable is thy sentence unto the needy, and unto him who-
se strength faileth, that is now in the last age, and is vexed with all things, and to
him that despaireth, and hath lost patience! **3** Fear not the sentence of death,
remember them that have been before thee, and that come after; for this is the
sentence of the Lord over all flesh. **4** And why art thou against the pleasure of
the most High? there is no inquisition in the grave, whether thou have lived ten,
or an hundred, or a thousand years. **5** The children of sinners are abominable
children, and they that are conversant in the dwelling of the ungodly. **6** The
inheritance of sinners' children shall perish, and their posterity shall have a per-
petual reproach. **7** The children will complain of an ungodly father, because
they shall be reproached for his sake. **8** Woe be unto you, ungodly men, which
have forsaken the law of the most high God! for if ye increase, it shall be to your
destruction: **9** And if ye be born, ye shall be born to a curse: and if ye die, a
curse shall be your portion. **10** All that are of the earth shall turn to earth again:
so the ungodly shall go from a curse to destruction. **11** The mourning of men
is about their bodies: but an ill name of sinners shall be blotted out. **12** Have
regard to thy name; for that shall continue with thee above a thousand great
treasures of gold. **13** A good life hath but few days: but a good name endureth
for ever. **14** My children, keep discipline in peace: for wisdom that is hid, and
a treasure that is not seen, what profit is in them both? **15** A man that hideth
his foolishness is better than a man that hideth his wisdom. **16** Therefore be
shamefaced according to my word: for it is not good to retain all shamefacedness;
neither is it altogether approved in every thing. **17** Be ashamed of whoredom
before father and mother: and of a lie before a prince and a mighty man; **18** Of
an offence before a judge and ruler; of iniquity before a congregation and people;
of unjust dealing before thy partner and friend; **19** And of theft in regard of
the place where thou sojournest, and in regard of the truth of God and his cove-
nant; and to lean with thine elbow upon the meat; and of scorning to give and
take; **20** And of silence before them that salute thee; and to look upon an har-
lot; **21** And to turn away thy face from thy kinsman; or to take away a portion
or a gift; or to gaze upon another man's wife. **22** Or to be overbusy with his
maid, and come not near her bed; or of upbraiding speeches before friends; and
after thou hast given, upbraid not; **23** Or of iterating and speaking again that
which thou hast heard; and of revealing of secrets. **24** So shalt thou be truly
shamefaced and find favour before all men.

42 **1** Of these things be not thou ashamed, and accept no person to sin thereby: **2** Of the law of the most High, and his covenant; and of judgment to justify the ungodly; **3** Of reckoning with thy partners and travellers; or of the gift of the heritage of friends; **4** Of exactness of balance and weights; or of getting much or little; **5** And of merchants' indifferent selling; of much correction of children; and to make the side of an evil servant to bleed. **6** Sure keeping is good, where an evil wife is; and shut up, where many hands are. **7** Deliver all things in number and weight; and put all in writing that thou givest out, or receivest in. **8** Be not ashamed to inform the unwise and foolish, and the extreme aged that contendeth with those that are young: thus shalt thou be truly learned, and approved of all men living. **9** The father waketh for the daughter, when no man knoweth; and the care for her taketh away sleep: when she is young, lest she pass away the flower of her age; and being married, lest she should be hated: **10** In her virginity, lest she should be defiled and gotten with child in her father's house; and having an husband, lest she should misbehave herself; and when she is married, lest she should be barren. **11** Keep a sure watch over a shameless daughter, lest she make thee a laughingstock to thine enemies, and a byword in the city, and a reproach among the people, and make thee ashamed before the multitude. **12** Behold not every body's beauty, and sit not in the midst of women. **13** For from garments cometh a moth, and from women wickedness. **14** Better is the churlishness of a man than a courteous woman, a woman, I say, which bringeth shame and reproach. **15** I will now remember the works of the Lord, and declare the things that I have seen: In the words of the Lord are his works. **16** The sun that giveth light looketh upon all things, and the work thereof is full of the glory of the Lord. **17** The Lord hath not given power to the saints to declare all his marvellous works, which the Almighty Lord firmly settled, that whatsoever is might be established for his glory. **18** He seeketh out the deep, and the heart, and considereth their crafty devices: for the Lord knoweth all that may be known, and he beholdeth the signs of the world. **19** He declareth the things that are past, and for to come, and revealeth the steps of hidden things. **20** No thought escapeth him, neither any word is hidden from him. **21** He hath garnished the excellent works of his wisdom, and he is from everlasting to everlasting: unto him may nothing be added, neither can he be diminished, and he hath no need of any counsellor. **22** Oh how desirable are all his works! and that a man may see even to a spark. **23** All these things live and remain for ever for all uses, and they are all obedient. **24** All things are double one against another: and he hath made nothing imperfect. **25** One thing establisheth the good or another: and who shall be filled with beholding his glory?

43 **1** The pride of the height, the clear firmament, the beauty of heaven, with his glorious shew; **2** The sun when it appeareth, declaring at his rising a marvellous instrument, the work of the most High: **3** At noon it parcheth the country, and who can abide the burning heat thereof? **4** A man blowing a furnace is in works of heat, but the sun burneth the mountains three times more; breathing out fiery vapours, and sending forth bright beams, it dimmeth the eyes. **5** Great is the Lord that made it; and at his commandment runneth hastily. **6** He made the moon also to serve in her season for a declaration of times, and a sign of the world. **7** From the moon is the sign of feasts, a light that decreaseth in her perfection. **8** The month is called after her name, increasing wonderfully in her changing, being an instrument of the armies above, shining in the firmament of heaven; **9** The beauty of heaven, the glory of the stars, an ornament giving light in the highest places of the Lord. **10** At the commandment of the Holy One they will stand in their order, and never faint in their watches. **11** Look upon the rainbow, and praise him that made it; very beautiful it is in the brightness thereof. **12** It compasseth the heaven about with a glorious circle, and the hands of the most High have bended it. **13** By his commandment he maketh the snow to fall aplace, and sendeth swiftly the lightnings of his judgment. **14** Through this the treasures are opened: and clouds fly forth as fowls. **15** By his great power he maketh the clouds firm, and the hailstones are broken small. **16** At his sight the mountains are shaken, and at his will the south wind bloweth. **17** The noise of the thunder maketh the earth to tremble: so doth the northern storm and the whirlwind: as birds flying he scattereth the snow, and the falling down thereof is as the lighting of grasshoppers: **18** The eye marvelleth at the beauty of the whiteness thereof, and the heart is astonished at the raining of it. **19** The hoarfrost also as salt he poureth on the earth, and being congealed, it lieth on the top of sharp stakes. **20** When the cold north wind bloweth, and the water is congealed into ice, it abideth upon every gathering together of water, and clotheth the water as with a breastplate. **21** It devoureth the mountains, and burneth the wilderness, and consumeth the grass as fire. **22** A present remedy of all is a mist coming speedily, a dew coming after heat refresheth. **23** By his counsel he appeaseth the deep, and planteth islands therein. **24** They that sail on the sea tell of the danger thereof; and when we hear it with our ears, we marvel thereat. **25** For therein be strange and wondrous works, variety of all kinds of beasts and whales created. **26** By him the end of them hath prosperous success, and by his word all things consist. **27** We may speak much, and yet come short: wherefore in sum, he is all. **28** How shall we be able to magnify him? for he is great above all his works. **29** The Lord is terrible and very great, and marvellous is his power. **30** When ye glorify the Lord, exalt him as much as ye can; for even yet will he far exceed: and when ye exalt him, put forth all your strength, and be not weary; for ye can never go far enough. **31** Who hath seen him, that he might tell us? and who can magnify him as he is? **32** There are yet hid greater things than these be, for we have seen but a few of his works. **33** For the Lord hath made all things; and to the godly hath he given wisdom.

44 **1** Let us now praise famous men, and our fathers that begat us. **2** The Lord hath wrought great glory by them through his great power from the beginning. **3** Such as did bear rule in their kingdoms, men renowned for their power, giving counsel by their understanding, and declaring prophecies: **4** Leaders of the people by their counsels, and by their knowledge of learning meet for the people, wise and eloquent are their instructions: **5** Such as found out musical tunes, and recited verses in writing: **6** Rich men furnished with ability, living peaceably in their habitations: **7** All these were honoured in their generations, and were the glory of their times. **8** There be of them, that have left a name behind them, that their praises might be reported. **9** And some there be, which have no memorial; who are perished, as though they had never been; and are become as though they had never been born; and their children after them. **10** But these were merciful men, whose righteousness hath not been forgotten. **11** With their seed shall continually remain a good inheritance, and their children are within the covenant. **12** Their seed standeth fast, and their children for their sakes. **13** Their seed shall remain for ever, and their glory shall not be blotted out. **14** Their bodies are buried in peace; but their name liveth for evermore. **15** The people will tell of their wisdom, and the congregation will shew forth their praise. **16** Enoch pleased the Lord, and was translated, being an example of repentance to all generations. **17** Noah was found perfect and righteous; in the time of wrath he was taken in exchange [for the world;] therefore was he left as a remnant unto the earth, when the flood came. **18** An everlasting covenant was made with him, that all flesh should perish no more by the flood. **19** Abraham was a great father of many people: in glory was there none like unto him; **20** Who kept the law of the most High, and was in covenant with him: he established the covenant in his flesh; and when he was proved, he was found faithful. **21** Therefore he assured him by an oath, that he would bless the nations in his seed, and that he would multiply him as the dust of the earth, and exalt his seed as the stars, and cause them to inherit from sea to sea, and from the river unto the utmost part of the land. **22** With Isaac did he establish likewise [for Abraham his father's sake] the blessing of all men, and the covenant, And made it rest upon the head of Jacob. He acknowledged him in his blessing, and gave him an heritage, and divided his portions; among the twelve tribes did he part them.

45 **1** And he brought out of him a merciful man, which found favour in the sight of all flesh, even Moses, beloved of God and men, whose memorial is blessed. **2** He made him like to the glorious saints, and magnified him, so that his enemies stood in fear of him. **3** By his words he caused the wonders to cease, and he made him glorious in the sight of kings, and gave him a commandment for his people, and shewed him part of his glory. **4** He sanctified him in his faithfuless and meekness, and chose him out of all men. **5** He made him to hear his voice, and brought him into the dark cloud, and gave him commandments before his face, even the law of life and knowledge, that he might teach Jacob his covenants, and Israel his judgments. **6** He exalted Aaron, an holy man like unto him, even his brother, of the tribe of Levi. **7** An everlasting covenant he made with him and gave him the priesthood among the people; he beautified him with comely ornaments, and clothed him with a robe of glory. **8** He put upon him perfect glory; and strengthened him with rich garments, with breeches, with a long robe, and the ephod. **9** And he compassed him with pomegranates, and with many golden bells round about, that as he went there might be a sound, and a noise made that might be heard in the temple, for a memorial to the children of his people; **10** With an holy garment, with gold, and blue silk, and purple, the work of the embroidere, with a breastplate of judgment, and with Urim and Thummim; **11** With twisted scarlet, the work of the cunning workman, with precious stones graven like seals, and set in gold, the work of the jeweller, with a writing engraved for a memorial, after the number of the tribes of Israel. **12** He set a crown of gold upon the mitre, wherein was engraved Holiness, an ornament of honour, a costly work, the desires of the eyes, goodly and beautiful. **13** Before him there were none such, neither did ever any stranger put them on, but only his children and his children's children perpetually. **14** Their sacrifices shall be wholly consumed every day twice continually. **15** Moses consecrated him, and anointed him with holy oil: this was appointed unto him by an everlasting covenant, and to his seed, so long as the heavens should remain, that they should minister unto him, and execute the office of the priesthood, and bless the people in his name. **16** He chose him out of all men living to offer sacrifices to the Lord, incense, and a sweet savour, for a memorial, to make reconciliation for his people. **17** He gave unto him his commandments, and authority in the statutes of judgments, that he should teach Jacob the testimonies, and inform Israel in his laws. **18** Strangers conspired together against him, and maligned him in the wilderness, even the men that were of Dathan's and Abiron's side, and the congregation of Core, with fury and wrath. **19** This the Lord saw, and it displeased him, and in his wrathful indigna-

tion were they consumed: he did wonders upon them, to consume them with the
fiery flame. 20 But he made Aaron more honourable, and gave him an heritage,
and divided unto him the firstfruits of the increase; especially he prepared bread
in abundance: 21 For they eat of the sacrifices of the Lord, which he gave unto
him and his seed. 22 Howbeit in the land of the people he had no inheritance,
neither had he any portion among the people: for the Lord himself is his portion
and inheritance. 23 The third in glory is Phinees the son of Eleazar, because he
had zeal in the fear of the Lord, and stood up with good courage of heart: when
the people were turned back, and made reconciliation for Israel. 24 Therefore
was there a covenant of peace made with him, that he should be the chief of the
sanctuary and of his people, and that he and his posterity should have the dignity
of the priesthood for ever: 25 According to the covenant made with David son
of Jesse, of the tribe of Juda, that the inheritance of the king should be to his po-
sterity alone: so the inheritance of Aaron should also be unto his seed. 26 God
give you wisdom in your heart to judge his people in righteousness, that their
good things be not abolished, and that their glory may endure for ever.

46

1 Jesus the son a Nave was valiant in the wars, and was the successor
of Moses in prophecies, who according to his name was made great
for the saving of the elect of God, and taking vengeance of the enemies that rose
up against them, that he might set Israel in their inheritance. 2 How great glory
gat he, when he did lift up his hands, and stretched out his sword against the ci-
ties! 3 Who before him so stood to it? for the Lord himself brought his enemies
unto him. 4 Did not the sun go back by his means? and was not one day as
long as two? 5 He called upon the most high Lord, when the enemies pressed
upon him on every side; and the great Lord heard him. 6 And with hailstones
of mighty power he made the battle to fall violently upon the nations, and in
the descent [of Beth-horon] he destroyed them that resisted, that the nations
might know all their strength, because he fought in the sight of the Lord, and he
followed the Mighty One. 7 In the time of Moses also he did a work of mercy,
he and Caleb the son of Jephunne, in that they withstood the congregation, and
withheld the people from sin, and appeased the wicked murmuring. 8 And of
six hundred thousand people on foot, they two were preserved to bring them in
to the heritage, even unto the land that floweth with milk and honey. 9 The
Lord gave strength also unto Caleb, which remained with him unto his old age:
so that he entered upon the high places of the land, and his seed obtained it
for an heritage: 10 That all the children of Israel might see that it is good to
follow the Lord. 11 And concerning the judges, every one by name, whose
heart went not a whoring, nor departed from the Lord, let their memory be bles-
sed. 12 Let their bones flourish out of their place, and let the name of them that
were honoured be continued upon their children. 13 Samuel, the prophet of
the Lord, beloved of his Lord, established a kingdom, and anointed princes over
his people. 14 By the law of the Lord he judged the congregation, and the Lord
had respect unto Jacob. 15 By his faithfulness he was found a true prophet,
and by his word he was known to be faithful in vision. 16 He called upon the
mighty Lord, when his enemies pressed upon him on every side, when he offered
the sucking lamb. 17 And the Lord thundered from heaven, and with a great
noise made his voice to be heard. 18 And he destroyed the rulers of the Tyrians,
and all the princes cf the Philistines. 19 And before his long sleep he made
protestations in the sight of the Lord and his anointed, I have not taken any man's
goods, so much as a shoe: and no man did accuse him. 20 And after his death
he prophesied, and shewed the king his end, and lifted up his voice from the earth
in prophecy, to blot out the wickedness of the people.

47

1 And after him rose up Nathan to prophesy in the time of Da-
vid. 2 As is the fat taken away from the peace offering, so was David
chosen out of the children of Israel. 3 He played with lions as with kids, and
with bears as with lambs. 4 Slew he not a giant, when he was yet but young?
and did he not take away reproach from the people, when he lifted up his hand
with the stone in the sling, and beat down the boasting of Goliath? 5 For he
called upon the most high Lord; and he gave him strength in his right hand to
slay that mighty warrior, and set up the horn of his people. 6 So the people
honoured him with ten thousands, and praised him in the blessings of the Lord,
in that he gave him a crown of glory. 7 For he destroyed the enemies on every
side, and brought to nought the Philistines his adversaries, and brake their horn
in sunder unto this day. 8 In all his works he praised the Holy One most high
with words of glory; with his whole heart he sung songs, and loved him that
made him. 9 He set singers also before the altar, that by their voices they might
make sweet melody, and daily sing praises in their songs. 10 He beautified their
feasts, and set in order the solemn times until the end, that they might praise his
holy name, and that the temple might sound from morning. 11 The Lord took
away his sins, and exalted his horn for ever: he gave him a covenant of kings, and
a throne of glory in Israel. 12 After him rose up a wise son, and for his sake he
dwelt at large. 13 Solomon reigned in a peaceable time, and was honoured; for
God made all quiet round about him, that he might build an house in his name,
and prepare his sanctuary for ever. 14 How wise wast thou in thy youth and,
as a flood, filled with understanding! 15 Thy soul covered the whole earth, and
thou filledst it with dark parables. 16 Thy name went far unto the islands; and
for thy peace thou wast beloved. 17 The countries marvelled at thee for thy son-
gs, and proverbs, and parables, and interpretations. 18 By the name of the Lord
God, which is called the Lord God of Israel, thou didst gather gold as tin and
didst multiply silver as lead. 19 Thou didst bow thy loins unto women, and by
thy body thou wast brought into subjection. 20 Thou didst stain thy honour,
and pollute thy seed: so that thou broughtest wrath upon thy children, and wast
grieved for thy folly. 21 So the kingdom was divided, and out of Ephraim ruled
a rebellious kingdom. 22 But the Lord will never leave off his mercy, neither
shall any of his works perish, neither will he abolish the posterity of his elect, and
the seed of him that loveth him he will not take away: wherefore he gave a rem-
nant unto Jacob, and out of him a root unto David. 23 Thus rested Solomon
with his fathers, and of his seed he left behind him Roboam, even the foolishness
of the people, and one that had no understanding, who turned away the people
through his counsel. There was also Jeroboam the son of Nebat, who caused Israel
to sin, and shewed Ephraim the way of sin: 24 And their sins were multiplied
exceedingly, that they were driven out of the land. 25 For they sought out all
wickedness, till the vengeance came upon them.

48

1 Then stood up Elias the prophet as fire, and his word burned like
a lamp. 2 He brought a sore famine upon them, and by his zeal he
diminished their number. 3 By the word of the Lord he shut up the heaven,
and also three times brought down fire. 4 O Elias, how wast thou honoured in
thy wondrous deeds! and who may glory like unto thee! 5 Who didst raise up a
dead man from death, and his soul from the place of the dead, by the word of the
most High: 6 Who broughtest kings to destruction, and honorable men from
their bed: 7 Who heardest the rebuke of the Lord in Sinai, and in Horeb the ju-
dgment of vengeance: 8 Who annointedst kings to take revenge, and prophets
to succeed after him: 9 Who was taken up in a whirlwind of fire, and in a cha-
riot of fiery horses: 10 Who wast ordained for reproofs in their times, to pacify
the wrath of the Lord's judgment, before it brake forth into fury, and to turn the
heart of the father unto the son, and to restore the tribes of Jacob. 11 Blessed
are they that saw thee, and slept in love; for we shall surely live. 12 Elias it
was, who was covered with a whirlwind: and Eliseus was filled with his spirit:
whilst he lived, he was not moved with the presence of any prince, neither could
any bring him into subjection. 13 No word could overcome him; and after
his death his body prophesied. 14 He did wonders in his life, and at his death
were his works marvellous. 15 For all this the people repented not, neither
departed they from their sins, till they were spoiled and carried out of their land,
and were scattered through all the earth: yet there remained a small people, and
a ruler in the house of David: 16 Of whom some did that which was pleasing
to God, and some multiplied sins. 17 Ezekias fortified his city, and brought in
water into the midst thereof: he digged the hard rock with iron, and made wells
for waters. 18 In his time Sennacherib came up, and sent Rabsaces, and lifted
up his hand against Sion, and boasted proudly. 19 Then trembled their hearts
and hands, and they were in pain, as women in travail. 20 But they called
upon the Lord which is merciful, and stretched out their hands toward him: and
immediately the Holy One heard them out of heaven, and delivered them by the
ministry of Esay. 21 He smote the host of the Assyrians, and his angel destroyed
them. 22 For Ezekias had done the thing that pleased the Lord, and was strong
in the ways of David his father, as Esay the prophet, who was great and faithful in
his vision, had commanded him. 23 In his time the sun went backward, and he
lengthened the king's life. 24 He saw by an excellent spirit what should come
to pass at the last, and he comforted them that mourned in Sion. 25 He shewed
what should come to pass for ever, and secret things or ever they came.

49

1 The remembrance of Josias is like the composition of the perfume
that is made by the art of the apothecary: it is sweet as honey in all
mouths, and as musick at a banquet of wine. 2 He behaved himself uprightly in
the conversion of the people, and took away the abominations of iniquity. 3 He
directed his heart unto the Lord, and in the time of the ungodly he established the
worship of God. 4 All, except David and Ezekias and Josias, were defective: for
they forsook the law of the most High, even the kings of Juda failed. 5 Therefo-
re he gave their power unto others, and their glory to a strange nation. 6 They
burnt the chosen city of the sanctuary, and made the streets desolate, according to
the prophecy of Jeremias. 7 For they entreated him evil, who nevertheless was
a prophet, sanctified in his mother's womb, that he might root out, and afflict,
and destroy; and that he might build up also, and plant. 8 It was Ezekiel who
saw the glorious vision, which was shewed him upon the chariot of the cheru-
bims. 9 For he made mention of the enemies under the figure of the rain, and
directed them that went right. 10 And of the twelve prophets let the memorial
be blessed, and let their bones flourish again out of their place: for they comforted
Jacob, and delivered them by assured hope. 11 How shall we magnify Zoroba-
bel? even he was as a signet on the right hand: 12 So was Jesus the son of Jose-
dec: who in their time builded the house, and set up an holy temple to the Lord,
which was prepared for everlasting glory. 13 And among the elect was Neemias,
whose renown is great, who raised up for us the walls that were fallen, and set up
the gates and the bars, and raised up our ruins again. 14 But upon the earth
was no man created like Enoch; for he was taken from the earth. 15 Neither
was there a young man born like Joseph, a governor of his brethren, a stay of the

people, whose bones were regarded of the Lord. **16** Sem and Seth were in great
honour among men, and so was Adam above every living thing in creation.

50 **1** Simon the high priest, the son of Onias, who in his life repaired
the house again, and in his days fortified the temple: **2** And by him
was built from the foundation the double height, the high fortress of the wall
about the temple: **3** In his days the cistern to receive water, being in compass
as the sea, was covered with plates of brass: **4** He took care of the temple that it
should not fall, and fortified the city against besieging: **5** How was he honoured
in the midst of the people in his coming out of the sanctuary! **6** He was as the
morning star in the midst of a cloud, and as the moon at the full: **7** As the sun
shining upon the temple of the most High, and as the rainbow giving light in the
bright clouds: **8** And as the flower of roses in the spring of the year, as lilies by
the rivers of waters, and as the branches of the frankincense tree in the time of
summer: **9** As fire and incense in the censer, and as a vessel of beaten gold set
with all manner of precious stones: **10** And as a fair olive tree budding forth
fruit, and as a cypress tree which groweth up to the clouds. **11** When he put on
the robe of honour, and was clothed with the perfection of glory, when he went
up to the holy altar, he made the garment of holiness honourable. **12** When
he took the portions out of the priests' hands, he himself stood by the hearth
of the altar, compassed about, as a young cedar in Libanus; and as palm trees
compassed they him round about. **13** So were all the sons of Aaron in their
glory, and the oblations of the Lord in their hands, before all the congregation
of Israel. **14** And finishing the service at the altar, that he might adorn the
offering of the most high Almighty, **15** He stretched out his hand to the cup,
and poured of the blood of the grape, he poured out at the foot of the altar a swe-
etsmelling savour unto the most high King of all. **16** Then shouted the sons of
Aaron, and sounded the silver trumpets, and made a great noise to be heard, for
a remembrance before the most High. **17** Then all the people together hasted,
and fell down to the earth upon their faces to worship their Lord God Almighty,
the most High. **18** The singers also sang praises with their voices, with great va-
riety of sounds was there made sweet melody. **19** And the people besought the
Lord, the most High, by prayer before him that is merciful, till the solemnity of
the Lord was ended, and they had finished his service. **20** Then he went down,
and lifted up his hands over the whole congregation of the children of Israel, to
give the blessing of the Lord with his lips, and to rejoice in his name. **21** And
they bowed themselves down to worship the second time, that they might receive
a blessing from the most High. **22** Now therefore bless ye the God of all, whi-
ch only doeth wondrous things every where, which exalteth our days from the
womb, and dealeth with us according to his mercy. **23** He grant us joyfulness
of heart, and that peace may be in our days in Israel for ever: **24** That he would
confirm his mercy with us, and deliver us at his time! **25** There be two manner
of nations which my heart abhorreth, and the third is no nation: **26** They that
sit upon the mountain of Samaria, and they that dwell among the Philistines, and
that foolish people that dwell in Sichem. **27** Jesus the son of Sirach of Jerusalem
hath written in this book the instruction of understanding and knowledge, who
out of his heart poured forth wisdom. **28** Blessed is he that shall be exercised in
these things; and he that layeth them up in his heart shall become wise. **29** For
if he do them, he shall be strong to all things: for the light of the Lord leadeth
him, who giveth wisdom to the godly. Blessed be the name of the Lord for ever.
Amen, Amen. A Prayer of Jesus the son of Sirach.

51 **1** I will thank thee, O Lord and King, and praise thee, O God my
Saviour: I do give praise unto thy name: **2** For thou art my defender
and helper, and has preserved my body from destruction, and from the snare of
the slanderous tongue, and from the lips that forge lies, and has been mine helper
against mine adversaries: **3** And hast delivered me, according to the multitude
of they mercies and greatness of thy name, from the teeth of them that were ready
to devour me, and out of the hands of such as sought after my life, and from the
manifold afflictions which I had; **4** From the choking of fire on every side, and
from the midst of the fire which I kindled not; **5** From the depth of the belly of
hell, from an unclean tongue, and from lying words. **6** By an accusation to the
king from an unrighteous tongue my soul drew near even unto death, my life was
near to the hell beneath. **7** They compassed me on every side, and there was no
man to help me: I looked for the succour of men, but there was none. **8** Then
thought I upon thy mercy, O Lord, and upon thy acts of old, how thou deliverest
such as wait for thee, and savest them out of the hands of the enemies. **9** Then
lifted I up my supplications from the earth, and prayed for deliverance from de-
ath. **10** I called upon the Lord, the Father of my Lord, that he would not leave
me in the days of my trouble, and in the time of the proud, when there was no
help. **11** I will praise thy name continually, and will sing praises with thanksgi-
ving; and so my prayer was heard: **12** For thou savedst me from destruction,
and deliveredst me from the evil time: therefore will I give thanks, and praise
thee, and bless they name, O Lord. **13** When I was yet young, or ever I went
abroad, I desired wisdom openly in my prayer. **14** I prayed for her before the
temple, and will seek her out even to the end. **15** Even from the flower till the
grape was ripe hath my heart delighted in her: my foot went the right way, from
my youth up sought I after her. **16** I bowed down mine ear a little, and received
her, and gat much learning. **17** I profited therein, therefore will I ascribe glory
unto him that giveth me wisdom. **18** For I purposed to do after her, and ear-
nestly I followed that which is good; so shall I not be confounded. **19** My soul
hath wrestled with her, and in my doings I was exact: I stretched forth my hands
to the heaven above, and bewailed my ignorances of her. **20** I directed my soul
unto her, and I found her in pureness: I have had my heart joined with her from
the beginning, therefore shall I not be foresaken. **21** My heart was troubled in
seeking her: therefore have I gotten a good possession. **22** The Lord hath given
me a tongue for my reward, and I will praise him therewith. **23** Draw near
unto me, ye unlearned, and dwell in the house of learning. **24** Wherefore are
ye slow, and what say ye to these things, seeing your souls are very thirsty? **25** I
opened my mouth, and said, Buy her for yourselves without money. **26** Put
your neck under the yoke, and let your soul receive instruction: she is hard at
hand to find. **27** Behold with your eyes, how that I have but little labour, and
have gotten unto me much rest. **28** Get learning with a great sum of money,
and get much gold by her. **29** Let your soul rejoice in his mercy, and be not
ashamed of his praise. **30** Work your work betimes, and in his time he will give
you your reward

APOCRYPHA BOOK OF BARUCH

The Book of Baruch

1 **1** And these are the words of the book, which Baruch the son of Nerias, the son of Maasias, the son of Sedecias, the son of Asadias, the son of Chelcias, wrote in Babylon, **2** In the fifth year, and in the seventh day of the month, what time as the Chaldeans took Jerusalem, and burnt it with fire. **3** And Baruch did read the words of this book in the hearing of Jechonias the son of Joachim king of Juda, and in the ears of all the people that came to hear the book, **4** And in the hearing of the nobles, and of the king's sons, and in the hearing of the elders, and of all the people, from the lowest unto the highest, even of all them that dwelt at Babylon by the river Sud. **5** Whereupon they wept, fasted, and prayed before the Lord. **6** They made also a collection of money according to every man's power: **7** And they sent it to Jerusalem unto Joachim the high priest, the son of Chelcias, son of Salom, and to the priests, and to all the people which were found with him at Jerusalem, **8** At the same time when he received the vessels of the house of the Lord, that were carried out of the temple, to return them into the land of Juda, the tenth day of the month Sivan, namely, silver vessels, which Sedecias the son of Josias king of Jada had made, **9** After that Nabuchodonosor king of Babylon had carried away Jechonias, and the princes, and the captives, and the mighty men, and the people of the land, from Jerusalem, and brought them unto Babylon. **10** And they said, Behold, we have sent you money to buy you burnt offerings, and sin offerings, and incense, and prepare ye manna, and offer upon the altar of the Lord our God; **11** And pray for the life of Nabuchodonosor king of Babylon, and for the life of Balthasar his son, that their days may be upon earth as the days of heaven: **12** And the Lord will give us strength, and lighten our eyes, and we shall live under the shadow of Nabuchodonosor king of Babylon, and under the shadow of Balthasar his son, and we shall serve them many days, and find favour in their sight. **13** Pray for us also unto the Lord our God, for we have sinned against the Lord our God; and unto this day the fury of the Lord and his wrath is not turned from us. **14** And ye shall read this book which we have sent unto you, to make confession in the house of the Lord, upon the feasts and solemn days. **15** And ye shall say, To the Lord our God belongeth righteousness, but unto us the confusion of faces, as it is come to pass this day, unto them of Juda, and to the inhabitants of Jerusalem, **16** And to our kings, and to our princes, and to our priests, and to our prophets, and to our fathers: **17** For we have sinned before the Lord, **18** And disobeyed him, and have not hearkened unto the voice of the Lord our God, to walk in the commandments that he gave us openly: **19** Since the day that the Lord brought our forefathers out of the land of Egypt, unto this present day, we have been disobedient unto the Lord our God, and we have been negligent in not hearing his voice. **20** Wherefore the evils cleaved unto us, and the curse, which the Lord appointed by Moses his servant at the time that he brought our fathers out of the land of Egypt, to give us a land that floweth with milk and honey, like as it is to see this day. **21** Nevertheless we have not hearkened unto the voice of the Lord our God, according unto all the words of the prophets, whom he sent unto us: **22** But every man followed the imagination of his own wicked heart, to serve strange gods, and to do evil in the sight of the Lord our God.

2 **1** Therefore the Lord hath made good his word, which he pronounced against us, and against our judges that judged Israel, and against our kings, and against our princes, and against the men of Israel and Juda, **2** To bring upon us great plagues, such as never happened under the whole heaven, as it came to pass in Jerusalem, according to the things that were written in the law of Moses; **3** That a man should eat the flesh of his own son, and the flesh of his own daughter. **4** Moreover he hath delivered them to be in subjection to all the kingdoms that are round about us, to be as a reproach and desolation among all the people round about, where the Lord hath scattered them. **5** Thus we were cast down, and not exalted, because we have sinned against the Lord our God, and have not been obedient unto his voice. **6** To the Lord our God appertaineth righteousness: but unto us and to our fathers open shame, as appeareth this day. **7** For all these plagues are come upon us, which the Lord hath pronounced against us **8** Yet have we not prayed before the Lord, that we might turn every one from the imaginations of his wicked heart. **9** Wherefore the Lord watched over us for evil, and the Lord hath brought it upon us: for the Lord is righteous in all his works which he hath commanded us. **10** Yet we have not hearkened unto his voice, to walk in the commandments of the Lord, that he hath set before us. **11** And now, O Lord God of Israel, that hast brought thy people out of the land of Egypt with a mighty hand, and high arm, and with signs, and with wonders, and with great power, and hast gotten thyself a name, as appeareth this day: **12** O Lord our God, we have sinned, we have done ungodly, we have dealt unrighteously in all thine ordinances. **13** Let thy wrath turn from us: for we are but a few left among the heathen, where thou hast scattered us. **14** Hear our prayers, O Lord, and our petitions, and deliver us for thine own sake, and give us favour in the sight of them which have led us away: **15** That all the earth may know that thou art the Lord our God, because Israel and his posterity is called by thy name. **16** O Lord, look down from thine holy house, and consider us: bow down thine ear, O Lord, to hear us. **17** Open thine eyes, and behold; for the dead that are in the graves, whose souls are taken from their bodies, will give unto the Lord neither praise nor righteousness: **18** But the soul that is greatly vexed, which goeth stooping and feeble, and the eyes that fail, and the hungry soul, will give thee praise and righteousness, O Lord. **19** Therefore we do not make our humble supplication before thee, O Lord our God, for the righteousness of our fathers, and of our kings. **20** For thou hast sent out thy wrath and indignation upon us, as thou hast spoken by thy servants the prophets, saying, **21** Thus saith the Lord, Bow down your shoulders to serve the king of Babylon: so shall ye remain in the land that I gave unto your fathers. **22** But if ye will not hear the voice of the Lord, to serve the king of Babylon, **23** I will cause to cease out of the cites of Judah, and from without Jerusalem, the voice of mirth, and the voice of joy, the voice of the bridegroom, and the voice of the bride: and the whole land shall be desolate of inhabitants. **24** But we would not hearken unto thy voice, to serve the king of Babylon: therefore hast thou made good the words that thou spakest by thy servants the prophets, namely, that the bones of our kings, and the bones of our fathers, should be taken out of their place. **25** And, lo, they are cast out to the heat of the day, and to the frost of the night, and they died in great miseries by famine, by sword, and by pestilence. **26** And the house which is called by thy name hast thou laid waste, as it is to be seen this day, for the wickedness of the house of Israel and the house of Juda. **27** O Lord our God, thou hast dealt with us after all thy goodness, and according to all that great mercy of thine, **28** As thou spakest by thy servant Moses in the day when thou didst command him to write the law before the children of Israel, saying, **29** If ye will not hear my voice, surely this very great multitude shall be turned into a small number among the nations, where I will scatter them. **30** For I knew that they would not hear me, because it is a stiffnecked people: but in the land of their captivities they shall remember themselves. **31** And shall know that I am the Lord their God: for I will give them an heart, and ears to hear: **32** And they shall praise me in the land of their captivity, and think upon my name, **33** And return from their stiff neck, and from their wicked deeds: for they shall remember the way of their fathers, which sinned before the Lord. **34** And I will bring them again into the land which I promised with an oath unto their fathers, Abraham, Isaac, and Jacob, and they shall be lords of it: and I will increase them, and they shall not be diminished. **35** And I will make an everlasting covenant with them to be their God, and they shall be my people: and I will no more drive my people of Israel out of the land that I have given them.

3 **1** O Lord Almighty, God of Israel, the soul in anguish the troubled spirit, crieth unto thee. **2** Hear, O Lord, and have mercy; ar thou art merciful: and have pity upon us, because we have sinned before thee. **3** For thou endurest for ever, and we perish utterly. **4** O Lord Almighty, thou God of Israel, hear now the prayers of the dead Israelites, and of their children, which have sinned before thee, and not hearkened unto the voice of thee their God: for the which cause these plagues cleave unto us. **5** Remember not the iniquities of our forefathers: but think upon thy power and thy name now at this time. **6** For thou art the Lord our God, and thee, O Lord, will we praise. **7** And for this cause thou hast put thy fear in our hearts, to the intent that we should call upon thy name, and praise thee in our captivity: for we have called to mind all the iniquity of our forefathers, that sinned before thee. **8** Behold, we are yet this day in our captivity, where thou hast scattered us, for a reproach and a curse, and to be subject to payments, according to all the iniquities of our fathers, which departed from the Lord our God. **9** Hear, Israel, the commandments of life: give ear to understand wisdom. **10** How happeneth it Israel, that thou art in thine enemies' land, that thou art waxen old in a strange country, that thou art defiled with the dead, **11** That thou art counted with them that go down into the grave? **12** Thou hast forsaken the fountain of wisdom. **13** For if thou hadst walked in the way of God, thou shouldest have dwelled in peace for ever. **14** Learn where is wisdom, where is strength, where is understanding; that

thou mayest know also where is length of days, and life, where is the light of the
eyes, and peace. **15** Who hath found out her place? or who hath come into her
treasures ? **16** Where are the princes of the heathen become, and such as ruled
the beasts upon the earth; **17** They that had their pastime with the fowls of the
air, and they that hoarded up silver and gold, wherein men trust, and made no
end of their getting? **18** For they that wrought in silver, and were so careful, and
whose works are unsearchable, **19** They are vanished and gone down to the gra-
ve, and others are come up in their steads. **20** Young men have seen light, and
dwelt upon the earth: but the way of knowledge have they not known, **21** Nor
understood the paths thereof, nor laid hold of it: their children were far off from
that way. **22** It hath not been heard of in Chanaan, neither hath it been seen
in Theman. **23** The Agarenes that seek wisdom upon earth, the merchants of
Meran and of Theman, the authors of fables, and searchers out of understanding;
none of these have known the way of wisdom, or remember her paths. **24** O
Israel, how great is the house of God! and how large is the place of his posses-
sion! **25** Great, and hath none end; high, and unmeasurable. **26** There were
the giants famous from the beginning, that were of so great stature, and so expert
in war. **27** Those did not the Lord choose, neither gave he the way of knowle-
dge unto them: **28** But they were destroyed, because they had no wisdom, and
perished through their own foolishness. **29** Who hath gone up into heaven, and
taken her, and brought her down from the clouds? **30** Who hath gone over the
sea, and found her, and will bring her for pure gold? **31** No man knoweth her
way, nor thinketh of her path. **32** But he that knoweth all things knoweth her,
and hath found her out with his understanding: he that prepared the earth for
evermore hath filled it with fourfooted beasts: **33** He that sendeth forth light,
and it goeth, calleth it again, and it obeyeth him with fear. **34** The stars shined
in their watches, and rejoiced: when he calleth them, they say, Here we be; and so
with cheerfulness they shewed light unto him that made them. **35** This is our
God, and there shall none other be accounted of in comparison of him **36** He
hath found out all the way of knowledge, and hath given it unto Jacob his servant,
and to Israel his beloved. **37** Afterward did he shew himself upon earth, and
conversed with men.

4

1 This is the book of the commandments of God, and the law that en-
dureth for ever: all they that keep it shall come to life; but such as leave
it shall die. **2** Turn thee, O Jacob, and take hold of it: walk in the presence of
the light thereof, that thou mayest be illuminated. **3** Give not thine honour to
another, nor the things that are profitable unto thee to a strange nation. **4** O
Israel, happy are we: for things that are pleasing to God are made known unto
us. **5** Be of good cheer, my people, the memorial of Israel. **6** Ye were sold
to the nations, not for [your] destruction: but because ye moved God to wrath,
ye were delivered unto the enemies. **7** For ye provoked him that made you by
sacrificing unto devils, and not to God. **8** Ye have forgotten the everlasting God,
that brought you up; and ye have grieved Jerusalem, that nursed you. **9** For
when she saw the wrath of God coming upon you, she said, Hearken, O ye that
dwell about Sion: God hath brought upon me great mourning; **10** For I saw
the captivity of my sons and daughters, which the Everlasting brought upon
them. **11** With joy did I nourish them; but sent them away with weeping and
mourning. **12** Let no man rejoice over me, a widow, and forsaken of many,
who for the sins of my children am left desolate; because they departed from
the law of God. **13** They knew not his statutes, nor walked in the ways of his
commandments, nor trod in the paths of discipline in his righteousness. **14** Let
them that dwell about Sion come, and remember ye the captivity of my sons
and daughters, which the Everlasting hath brought upon them. **15** For he hath
brought a nation upon them from far, a shameless nation, and of a strange lan-
guage, who neither reverenced old man, nor pitied child. **16** These have carried
away the dear beloved children of the widow, and left her that was alone desolate
without daughters. **17** But what can I help you? **18** For he that brought these
plagues upon you will deliver you from the hands of your enemies. **19** Go your
way, O my children, go your way: for I am left desolate. **20** I have put off the
clothing of peace, and put upon me the sackcloth of my prayer: I will cry unto
the Everlasting in my days. **21** Be of good cheer, O my children, cry unto the
Lord, and he will deliver you from the power and hand of the enemies. **22** For
my hope is in the Everlasting, that he will save you; and joy is come unto me from
the Holy One, because of the mercy which shall soon come unto you from the
Everlasting our Saviour. **23** For I sent you out with mourning and weeping: but
God will give you to me again with joy and gladness for ever. **24** Like as now
the neighbours of Sion have seen your captivity: so shall they see shortly your sal-
vation from our God which shall come upon you with great glory, and brightness
of the Everlasting. **25** My children, suffer patiently the wrath that is come upon
you from God: for thine enemy hath persecuted thee; but shortly thou shalt see
his destruction, and shalt tread upon his neck. **26** My delicate ones have gone
rough ways, and were taken away as a flock caught of the enemies. **27** Be of
good comfort, O my children, and cry unto God: for ye shall be remembered
of him that brought these things upon you. **28** For as it was your mind to go
astray from God: so, being returned, seek him ten times more. **29** For he that
hath brought these plagues upon you shall bring you everlasting joy with your
salvation. **30** Take a good heart, O Jerusalem: for he that gave thee that name
will comfort thee. **31** Miserable are they that afflicted thee, and rejoiced at thy
fall. **32** Miserable are the cities which thy children served: miserable is she that
received thy sons. **33** For as she rejoiced at thy ruin, and was glad of thy fall: so
shall she be grieved for her own desolation. **34** For I will take away the rejoicing
of her great multitude, and her pride shall be turned into mourning. **35** For
fire shall come upon her from the Everlasting, long to endure; and she shall be
inhabited of devils for a great time. **36** O Jerusalem, look about thee toward the
east, and behold the joy that cometh unto thee from God.

APOCRYPHA LETTER OF JEREMIAH

The Epistle [or Letter] of Jeremiah [Jeremy]

1 1 A copy of an epistle, which Jeremy sent unto them which were to be led captives into Babylon by the king of the Babylonians, to certify them, as it was commanded him of God. **2** Because of the sins which ye have committed before God, ye shall be led away captives into Babylon by Nabuchodonosor king of the Babylonians. **3** So when ye be come unto Babylon, ye shall remain there many years, and for a long season, namely, seven generations: and after that I will bring you away peaceably from thence. **4** Now shall ye see in Babylon gods of silver, and of gold, and of wood, borne upon shoulders, which cause the nations to fear. **5** Beware therefore that ye in no wise be like to strangers, neither be ye and of them, when ye see the multitude before them and behind them, worshipping them. **6** But say ye in your hearts, O Lord, we must worship thee. **7** For mine angel is with you, and I myself caring for your souls. **8** As for their tongue, it is polished by the workman, and they themselves are gilded and laid over with silver; yet are they but false, and cannot speak. **9** And taking gold, as it were for a virgin that loveth to go gay, they make crowns for the heads of their gods. **10** Sometimes also the priests convey from their gods gold and silver, and bestow it upon themselves. **11** Yea, they will give thereof to the common harlots, and deck them as men with garments, [being] gods of silver, and gods of gold, and wood. **12** Yet cannot these gods save themselves from rust and moth, though they be covered with purple raiment. **13** They wipe their faces because of the dust of the temple, when there is much upon them. **14** And he that cannot put to death one that offendeth him holdeth a sceptre, as though he were a judge of the country. **15** He hath also in his right hand a dagger and an ax: but cannot deliver himself from war and thieves. **16** Whereby they are known not to be gods: therefore fear them not. **17** For like as a vessel that a man useth is nothing worth when it is broken; even so it is with their gods: when they be set up in the temple, their eyes be full of dust through the feet of them that come in. **18** And as the doors are made sure on every side upon him that offendeth the king, as being committed to suffer death: even so the priests make fast their temples with doors, with locks, and bars, lest their gods be spoiled with robbers. **19** They light them candles, yea, more than for themselves, whereof they cannot see one. **20** They are as one of the beams of the temple, yet they say their hearts are gnawed upon by things creeping out of the earth; and when they eat them and their clothes, they feel it not. **21** Their faces are blacked through the smoke that cometh out of the temple. **22** Upon their bodies and heads sit bats, swallows, and birds, and the cats also. **23** By this ye may know that they are no gods: therefore fear them not. **24** Notwithstanding the gold that is about them to make them beautiful, except they wipe off the rust, they will not shine: for neither when they were molten did they feel it. **25** The things wherein there is no breath are bought for a most high price. **26** They are borne upon shoulders, having no feet whereby they declare unto men that they be nothing worth. **27** They also that serve them are ashamed: for if they fall to the ground at any time, they cannot rise up again of themselves: neither, if one set them upright, can they move of themselves: neither, if they be bowed down, can they make themselves straight: but they set gifts before them as unto dead men. **28** As for the things that are sacrificed unto them, their priests sell and abuse; in like manner their wives lay up part thereof in salt; but unto the poor and impotent they give nothing of it. **29** Menstruous women and women in childbed eat their sacrifices: by these things ye may know that they are no gods: fear them not. **30** For how can they be called gods? because women set meat before the gods of silver, gold, and wood. **31** And the priests sit in their temples, having their clothes rent, and their heads and beards shaven, and nothing upon their heads. **32** They roar and cry before their gods, as men do at the feast when one is dead. **33** The priests also take off their garments, and clothe their wives and children. **34** Whether it be evil that one doeth unto them, or good, they are not able to recompense it: they can neither set up a king, nor put him down. **35** In like manner, they can neither give riches nor money: though a man make a vow unto them, and keep it not, they will not require it. **36** They can save no man from death, neither deliver the weak from the mighty. **37** They cannot restore a blind man to his sight, nor help any man in his distress. **38** They can shew no mercy to the widow, nor do good to the fatherless. **39** Their gods of wood, and which are overlaid with gold and silver, are like the stones that be hewn out of the mountain: they that worship them shall be confounded. **40** How should a man then think and say that they are gods, when even the Chaldeans themselves dishonour them? **41** Who if they shall see one dumb that cannot speak, they bring him, and intreat Bel that he may speak, as though he were able to understand. **42** Yet they cannot understand this themselves, and leave them: for they have no knowledge. **43** The women also with cords about them, sitting in the ways, burn bran for perfume: but if any of them, drawn by some that passeth by, lie with him, she reproacheth her fellow, that she was not thought as worthy as herself, nor her cord broken. **44** Whatsoever is done among them is false: how may it then be thought or said that they are gods? **45** They are made of carpenters and goldsmiths: they can be nothing else than the workmen will have them to be. **46** And they themselves that made them can never continue long; how should then the things that are made of them be gods? **47** For they left lies and reproaches to them that come after. **48** For when there cometh any war or plague upon them, the priests consult with themselves, where they may be hidden with them. **49** How then cannot men perceive that they be no gods, which can neither save themselves from war, nor from plague? **50** For seeing they be but of wood, and overlaid with silver and gold, it shall be known hereafter that they are false: **51** And it shall manifestly appear to all nations and kings that they are no gods, but the works of men's hands, and that there is no work of God in them. **52** Who then may not know that they are no gods? **53** For neither can they set up a king in the land, nor give rain unto men. **54** Neither can they judge their own cause, nor redress a wrong, being unable: for they are as crows between heaven and earth. **55** Whereupon when fire falleth upon the house of gods of wood, or laid over with gold or silver, their priests will flee away, and escape; but they themselves shall be burned asunder like beams. **56** Moreover they cannot withstand any king or enemies: how can it then be thought or said that they be gods? **57** Neither are those gods of wood, and laid over with silver or gold, able to escape either from thieves or robbers. **58** Whose gold, and silver, and garments wherewith they are clothed, they that are strong take, and go away withal: neither are they able to help themselves. **59** Therefore it is better to be a king that sheweth his power, or else a profitable vessel in an house, which the owner shall have use of, than such false gods; or to be a door in an house, to keep such things therein, than such false gods. or a pillar of wood in a a palace, than such false gods. **60** For sun, moon, and stars, being bright and sent to do their offices, are obedient. **61** In like manner the lightning when it breaketh forth is easy to be seen; and after the same manner the wind bloweth in every country. **62** And when God commandeth the clouds to go over the whole world, they do as they are bidden. **63** And the fire sent from above to consume hills and woods doeth as it is commanded: but these are like unto them neither in shew nor power. **64** Wherefore it is neither to be supposed nor said that they are gods, seeing, they are able neither to judge causes, nor to do good unto men. **65** Knowing therefore that they are no gods, fear them not, **66** For they can neither curse nor bless kings: **67** Neither can they shew signs in the heavens among the heathen, nor shine as the sun, nor give light as the moon. **68** The beasts are better than they: for they can get under a cover and help themselves. **69** It is then by no means manifest unto us that they are gods: therefore fear them not. **70** For as a scarecrow in a garden of cucumbers keepeth nothing: so are their gods of wood, and laid over with silver and gold. **71** And likewise their gods of wood, and laid over with silver and gold, are like to a white thorn in an orchard, that every bird sitteth upon; as also to a dead body, that is east into the dark. **72** And ye shall know them to be no gods by the bright purple that rotteth upon then**1** and they themselves afterward shall be eaten, and shall be a reproach in the country. **73** Better therefore is the just man that hath none idols: for he shall be far from reproach.

APOCRYPHA PRAYER OF AZARIAH

The Prayer of Azariah and Song of three Jews

1 1 And they walked in the midst of the fire, praising God, and blessing the
Lord. **2** Then Azarias stood up, and prayed on this manner; and opening
his mouth in the midst of the fire said, **3** Blessed art thou, O Lord God of our
fathers: thy name is worthy to be praised and glorified for evermore: **4** For thou
art righteous in all the things that thou hast done to us: yea, true are all thy works,
thy ways are right, and all thy judgments truth. **5** In all the things that thou hast
brought upon us, and upon the holy city of our fathers, even Jerusalem, thou hast
executed true judgment: for according to truth and judgment didst thou bring all
these things upon us because of our sins. **6** For we have sinned and committed
iniquity, departing from thee. **7** In all things have we trespassed, and not obeyed
thy commandments, nor kept them, neither done as thou hast commanded us, that
it might go well with us. **8** Wherefore all that thou hast brought upon us, and
every thing that thou hast done to us, thou hast done in true judgment. **9** And
thou didst deliver us into the hands of lawless enemies, most hateful forsakers of
God, and to an unjust king, and the most wicked in all the world. **10** And now
we cannot open our mouths, we are become a shame and reproach to thy servants;
and to them that worship thee. **11** Yet deliver us not up wholly, for thy name's
sake, neither disannul thou thy covenant: **12** And cause not thy mercy to de-
part from us, for thy beloved Abraham's sake, for thy servant Issac's sake, and for
thy holy Israel's sake; **13** To whom thou hast spoken and promised, that thou
wouldest multiply their seed as the stars of heaven, and as the sand that lieth upon
the seashore. **14** For we, O Lord, are become less than any nation, and be kept
under this day in all the world because of our sins. **15** Neither is there at this
time prince, or prophet, or leader, or burnt offering, or sacrifice, or oblation, or
incense, or place to sacrifice before thee, and to find mercy. **16** Nevertheless in
a contrite heart and an humble spirit let us be accepted. **17** Like as in the burnt
offerings of rams and bullocks, and like as in ten thousands of fat lambs: so let
our sacrifice be in thy sight this day, and grant that we may wholly go after thee:
for they shall not be confounded that put their trust in thee. **18** And now we
follow thee with all our heart, we fear thee, and seek thy face. **19** Put us not to
shame: but deal with us after thy lovingkindness, and according to the multitude
of thy mercies. **20** Deliver us also according to thy marvellous works, and give
glory to thy name, O Lord: and let all them that do thy servants hurt be asha-
med; **21** And let them be confounded in all their power and might, and let their
strength be broken; **22** And let them know that thou art God, the only God,
and glorious over the whole world. **23** And the king's servants, that put them in,
ceased not to make the oven hot with rosin, pitch, tow, and small wood; **24** So
that the flame streamed forth above the furnace forty and nine cubits. **25** And it
passed through, and burned those Chaldeans it found about the furnace. **26** But
the angel of the Lord came down into the oven together with Azarias and his fel-
lows, and smote the flame of the fire out of the oven; **27** And made the midst
of the furnace as it had been a moist whistling wind, so that the fire touched them
not at all, neither hurt nor troubled them. **28** Then the three, as out of one
mouth, praised, glorified, and blessed, God in the furnace, saying, **29** Blessed
art thou, O Lord God of our fathers: and to be praised and exalted above all for
ever. **30** And blessed is thy glorious and holy name: and to be praised and exalted
above all for ever. **31** Blessed art thou in the temple of thine holy glory: and to
be praised and glorified above all for ever. **32** Blessed art thou that beholdest
the depths, and sittest upon the cherubims: and to be praised and exalted above
all for ever. **33** Blessed art thou on the glorious throne of thy kingdom: and to
be praised and glorified above all for ever. **34** Blessed art thou in the firmament
of heaven: and above ail to be praised and glorified for ever. **35** O all ye works
of the Lord, bless ye the Lord : praise and exalt him above all for ever, **36** O ye
heavens, bless ye the Lord : praise and exalt him above all for ever. **37** O ye angels
of the Lord, bless ye the Lord: praise and exalt him above all for ever. **38** O all ye
waters that be above the heaven, bless ye the Lord: praise and exalt him above all
for ever. **39** O all ye powers of the Lord, bless ye the Lord: praise and exalt him
above all for ever. **40** O ye sun and moon, bless ye the Lord: praise and exalt him
above all for ever. **41** O ye stars of heaven, bless ye the Lord: praise and exalt him
above all for ever. **42** O every shower and dew, bless ye the Lord: praise and exalt
him above all for ever. **43** O all ye winds, bless ye the Lord: praise and exalt him
above all for ever, **44** O ye fire and heat, bless ye the Lord: praise and exalt him
above all for ever. **45** O ye winter and summer, bless ye the Lord: praise and exalt
him above all for ever. **46 0** ye dews and storms of snow, bless ye the Lord: praise
and exalt him above all for ever. **47** O ye nights and days, bless ye the Lord: bless
and exalt him above all for ever. **48** O ye light and darkness, bless ye the Lord:
praise and exalt him above all for ever. **49** O ye ice and cold, bless ye the Lord:
praise and exalt him above all for ever. **50** O ye frost and snow, bless ye the Lord:
praise and exalt him above all for ever. **51** O ye lightnings and clouds, bless ye
the Lord: praise and exalt him above all for ever. **52** O let the earth bless the
Lord: praise and exalt him above all for ever. **53** O ye mountains and little hills,
bless ye the Lord: praise and exalt him above all for ever. **54** O all ye things that
grow in the earth, bless ye the Lord: praise and exalt him above all for ever. **55** O
ye mountains, bless ye the Lord: Praise and exalt him above all for ever. **56** O ye
seas and rivers, bless ye the Lord: praise and exalt him above all for ever. **57** O ye
whales, and all that move in the waters, bless ye the Lord: praise and exalt him abo-
ve all for ever. **58** O all ye fowls of the air, bless ye the Lord: praise and exalt him
above all for ever. **59** O all ye beasts and cattle, bless ye the Lord: praise and exalt
him above all for ever. **60** O ye children of men, bless ye the Lord: praise and
exalt him above all for ever. **61** O Israel, bless ye the Lord: praise and exalt him
above all for ever. **62** O ye priests of the Lord, bless ye the Lord: praise and exalt
him above all for ever. **63** O ye servants of the Lord, bless ye the Lord: praise and
exalt him above all for ever. **64** O ye spirits and souls of the righteous, bless ye
the Lord: praise and exalt him above all for ever. **65** O ye holy and humble men
of heart, bless ye the Lord: praise and exalt him above all for ever. **66** O Ananias,
Azarias, and Misael, bless ye the Lord: praise and exalt him above all for ever: far he
hath delivered us from hell, and saved us from the hand of death, and delivered us
out of the midst of the furnace and burning flame: even out of the midst of the fire
hath he delivered us. **67** O give thanks unto the Lord, because he is gracious: for
his mercy endureth for ever. **68** O all ye that worship the Lord, bless the God of
gods, praise him, and give him thanks: for his mercy endureth for

APOCRYPHA BOOK OF BEEL AND THE DRAGON

The Book of Bel and the Dragon [in Daniel]

The History of the Destruction of Bel and the Dragon, Cut off from the end of Daniel.

1 **1** And king Astyages was gathered to his fathers, and Cyrus of Persia received his kingdom. **2** And Daniel conversed with the king, and was honoured above all his friends. **3** Now the Babylons had an idol, called Bel, and there were spent upon him every day twelve great measures of fine flour, and forty sheep, and six vessels of wine. **4** And the king worshipped it and went daily to adore it: but Daniel worshipped his own God. And the king said unto him, Why dost not thou worship Bel? **5** Who answered and said, Because I may not worship idols made with hands, but the living God, who hath created the heaven and the earth, and hath sovereignty over all flesh. **6** Then said the king unto him, Thinkest thou not that Bel is a living God? seest thou not how much he eateth and drinketh every day? **7** Then Daniel smiled, and said, O king, be not deceived: for this is but clay within, and brass without, and did never eat or drink any thing. **8** So the king was wroth, and called for his priests, and said unto them, If ye tell me not who this is that devoureth these expences, ye shall die. **9** But if ye can certify me that Bel devoureth them, then Daniel shall die: for he hath spoken blasphemy against Bel. And Daniel said unto the king, Let it be according to thy word. **10** Now the priests of Bel were threescore and ten, beside their wives and children. And the king went with Daniel into the temple of Bel. **11** So Bel's priests said, Lo, we go out: but thou, O king, set on the meat, and make ready the wine, and shut the door fast and seal it with thine own signet; **12** And to morrow when thou comest in, if thou findest not that Bel hath eaten up all, we will suffer death: or else Daniel, that speaketh falsely against us. **13** And they little regarded it: for under the table they had made a privy entrance, whereby they entered in continually, and consumed those things. **14** So when they were gone forth, the king set meats before Bel. Now Daniel had commanded his servants to bring ashes, and those they strewed throughout all the temple in the presence of the king alone: then went they out, and shut the door, and sealed it with the king's signet, and so departed. **15** Now in the night came the priests with their wives and children, as they were wont to do, and did eat and drinck up all. **16** In the morning betime the king arose, and Daniel with him. **17** And the king said, Daniel, are the seals whole? And he said, Yea, O king, they be whole. **18** And as soon as he had opened the dour, the king looked upon the table, and cried with a loud voice, Great art thou, O Bel, and with thee is no deceit at all. **19** Then laughed Daniel, and held the king that he should not go in, and said, Behold now the pavement, and mark well whose footsteps are these. **20** And the king said, I see the footsteps of men, women, and children. And then the king was angry, **21** And took the priests with their wives and children, who shewed him the privy doors, where they came in, and consumed such things as were upon the table. **22** Therefore the king slew them, and delivered Bel into Daniel's power, who destroyed him and his temple. **23** And in that same place there was a great dragon, which they of Babylon worshipped. **24** And the king said unto Daniel, Wilt thou also say that this is of brass? lo, he liveth, he eateth and drinketh; thou canst not say that he is no living god: therefore worship him. **25** Then said Daniel unto the king, I will worship the Lord my God: for he is the living God. **26** But give me leave, O king, and I shall slay this dragon without sword or staff. The king said, I give thee leave. **27** Then Daniel took pitch, and fat, and hair, and did seethe them together, and made lumps thereof: this he put in the dragon's mouth, and so the dragon burst in sunder : and Daniel said, Lo, these are the gods ye worship. **28** When they of Babylon heard that, they took great indignation, and conspired against the king, saying, The king is become a Jew, and he hath destroyed Bel, he hath slain the dragon, and put the priests to death. **29** So they came to the king, and said, Deliver us Daniel, or else we will destroy thee and thine house. **30** Now when the king saw that they pressed him sore, being constrained, he delivered Daniel unto them: **31** Who cast him into the lions' den: where he was six days. **32** And in the den there were seven lions, and they had given them every day two carcases, and two sheep: which then were not given to them, to the intent they might devour Daniel. **33** Now there was in Jewry a prophet, called Habbacuc, who had made pottage, and had broken bread in a bowl, and was going into the field, for to bring it to the reapers. **34** But the angel of the Lord said unto Habbacuc, Go, carry the dinner that thou hast into Babylon unto Daniel, who is in the lions' den. **35** And Habbacuc said, Lord, I never saw Babylon; neither do I know where the den is. **36** Then the angel of the Lord took him by the crown, and bare him by the hair of his head, and through the vehemency of his spirit set him in Babylon over the den. **37** And Habbacuc cried, saying, O Daniel, Daniel, take the dinner which God hath sent thee. **38** And Daniel said, Thou hast remembered me, O God: neither hast thou forsaken them that seek thee and love thee. **39** So Daniel arose, and did eat: and the angel of the Lord set Habbacuc in his own place again immediately. **40** Upon the seventh day the king went to bewail Daniel: and when he came to the den, he looked in, and behold, Daniel was sitting. **41** Then cried the king with a loud voice, saying, Great art Lord God of Daniel, and there is none other beside thee. **42** And he drew him out, and cast those that were the cause of his destruction into the den: and they were devoured in a moment before his face.

APOCRYPHA BOOK OF SUSANNA

The History of Susanna [in Daniel]

Set apart from the beginning of Daniel, beca*use it is not in the Hebrew, as neither the Narration of Bel and the Dragon.*

1 **1** There dwelt a man in Babylon, called Joacim: **2** And he took a wife, whose name was Susanna, the daughter of Chelcias, a very fair woman, and one that feared the Lord. **3** Her parents also were righteous, and taught their daughter according to the law of Moses. **4** Now Joacim was a great rich man, and had a fair garden joining unto his house: and to him resorted the Jews; because he was more honourable than all others. **5** The same year were appointed two of the ancients of the people to be judges, such as the Lord spake of, that wickedness came from Babylon from ancient judges, who seemed to govern the people. **6** These kept much at Joacim's house: and all that had any suits in law came unto them. **7** Now when the people departed away at noon, Susanna went into her husband's garden to walk. **8** And the two elders saw her going in every day, and walking; so that their lust was inflamed toward her. **9** And they perverted their own mind, and turned away their eyes, that they might not look unto heaven, nor remember just judgments. **10** And albeit they both were wounded with her love, yet durst not one shew another his grief. **11** For they were ashamed to declare their lust, that they desired to have to do with her. **12** Yet they watched diligently from day to day to see her. **13** And the one said to the other, Let us now go home: for it is dinner time. **14** So when they were gone out, they parted the one from the other, and turning back again they came to the same place; and after that they had asked one another the cause, they acknowledged their lust: then appointed they a time both together, when they might find her alone. **15** And it fell out, as they watched a fit time, she went in as before with two maids only, and she was desirous to wash herself in the garden: for it was hot. **16** And there was no body there save the two elders, that had hid themselves, and watched her. **17** Then she said to her maids, Bring me oil and washing balls, and shut the garden doors, that I may wash me. **18** And they did as she bade them, and shut the garden doors, and went out themselves at privy doors to fetch the things that she had commanded them: but they saw not the elders, because they were hid. **19** Now when the maids were gone forth, the two elders rose up, and ran unto her, saying, **20** Behold, the garden doors are shut, that no man can see us, and we are in love with thee; therefore consent unto us, and lie with us. **21** If thou wilt not, we will bear witness against thee, that a young man was with thee: and therefore thou didst send away thy maids from thee. **22** Then Susanna sighed, and said, I am straitened on every side: for if I do this thing, it is death unto me: and if I do it not I cannot escape your hands. **23** It is better for me to fall into your hands, and not do it, than to sin in the sight of the Lord. **24** With that Susanna cried with a loud voice: and the two elders cried out against her. **25** Then ran the one, and opened the garden door. **26** So when the servants of the house heard the cry in the garden, they rushed in at the privy door, to see what was done unto her. **27** But when the elders had declared their matter, the servants were greatly ashamed: for there was never such a report made of Susanna. **28** And it came to pass the next day, when the people were assembled to her husband Joacim, the two elders came also full of mischievous imagination against Susanna to put her to death; **29** And said before the people, Send for Susanna, the daughter of Chelcias, Joacim's wife. And so they sent. **30** So she came with her father and mother, her children, and all her kindred. **31** Now Susanna was a very delicate woman, and beauteous to behold. **32** And these wicked men commanded to uncover her face, (for she was covered) that they might be filled with her beauty. **33** Therefore her friends and all that saw her wept. **34** Then the two elders stood up in the midst of the people, and laid their hands upon her head. **35** And she weeping looked up toward heaven: for her heart trusted in the Lord. **36** And the elders said, As we walked in the garden alone, this woman came in with two maids, and shut the garden doors, and sent the maids away. **37** Then a young man, who there was hid, came unto her, and lay with her. **38** Then we that stood in a corner of the garden, seeing this wickedness, ran unto them. **39** And when we saw them together, the man we could not hold: for he was stronger than we, and opened the door, and leaped out. **40** But having taken this woman, we asked who the young man was, but she would not tell us: these things do we testify. **41** Then the assembly believed them as those that were the elders and judges of the people: so they condemned her to death. **42** Then Susanna cried out with a loud voice, and said, O everlasting God, that knowest the secrets, and knowest all things before they be: **43** Thou knowest that they have borne false witness against me, and, behold, I must die; whereas I never did such things as these men have maliciously invented against me. **44** And the Lord heard her voice. **45** Therefore when she was led to be put to death, the Lord raised up the holy spirit of a young youth whose name was Daniel: **46** Who cried with a loud voice, I am clear from the blood of this woman. **47** Then all the people turned them toward him, and said, What mean these words that thou hast spoken? **48** So he standing in the midst of them said, Are ye such fools, ye sons of Israel, that without examination or knowledge of the truth ye have condemned a daughter of Israel? **49** Return again to the place of judgment: for they have borne false witness against her. **50** Wherefore all the people turned again in haste, and the elders said unto him, Come, sit down among us, and shew it us, seeing God hath given thee the honour of an elder. **51** Then said Daniel unto them, Put these two aside one far from another, and I will examine them. **52** So when they were put asunder one from another, he called one of them, and said unto him, O thou that art waxen old in wickedness, now thy sins which thou hast committed aforetime are come to light. **53** For thou hast pronounced false judgment and hast condemned the innocent and hast let the guilty go free; albeit the Lord saith, The innocent and righteous shalt thou not slay. **54** Now then, if thou hast seen her, tell me, Under what tree sawest thou them companying together? Who answered, Under a mastick tree. **55** And Daniel said, Very well; thou hast lied against thine own head; for even now the angel of God hath received the sentence of God to cut thee in two. **56** So he put him aside, and commanded to bring the other, and said unto him, O thou seed of Chanaan, and not of Juda, beauty hath deceived thee, and lust hath perverted thine heart. **57** Thus have ye dealt with the daughters of Israel, and they for fear companied with you: but the daughter of Juda would not abide your wickedness. **58** Now therefore tell me, Under what tree didst thou take them companying together? Who answered, Under an holm tree. **59** Then said Daniel unto him, Well; thou hast also lied against thine own head: for the angel of God waiteth with the sword to cut thee in two, that he may destroy you. **60** With that all the assembly cried out with a loud voice, and praised God, who saveth them that trust in him. **61** And they arose against the two elders, for Daniel had convicted them of false witness by their own mouth: **62** And according to the law of Moses they did unto them in such sort as they maliciously intended to do to their neighbour: and they put them to death. Thus the innocent blood was saved the same day. **63** Therefore Chelcias and his wife praised God for their daughter Susanna, with Joacim her husband, and all the kindred, because there was no dishonesty found in her. **64** From that day forth was Daniel had in great reputation in the sight of the people

APOCRYPHA

1ST BOOK OF MACCABEES

The First Book of the Maccabees

1 1 And it happened, after that Alexander son of Philip, the Macedonian, who came out of the land of Chettiim, had smitten Darius king of the Persians and Medes, that he reigned in his stead, the first over Greece, **2** And made many wars, and won many strong holds, and slew the kings of the earth, **3** And went through to the ends of the earth, and took spoils of many nations, insomuch that the earth was quiet before him; whereupon he was exalted and his heart was lifted up. **4** And he gathered a mighty strong host and ruled over countries, and nations, and kings, who became tributaries unto him. **5** And after these things he fell sick, and perceived that he should die. **6** Wherefore he called his servants, such as were honourable, and had been brought up with him from his youth, and parted his kingdom among them, while he was yet alive. **7** So Alexander reigned twelves years, and then died. **8** And his servants bare rule every one in his place. **9** And after his death they all put crowns upon themselves; so did their sons after them many years: and evils were multiplied in the earth. **10** And there came out of them a wicked root Antiochus surnamed Epiphanes, son of Antiochus the king, who had been an hostage at Rome, and he reigned in the hundred and thirty and seventh year of the kingdom of the Greeks. **11** In those days went there out of Israel wicked men, who persuaded many, saying, Let us go and make a covenant with the heathen that are round about us: for since we departed from them we have had much sorrow. **12** So this device pleased them well. **13** Then certain of the people were so forward herein, that they went to the king, who gave them licence to do after the ordinances of the heathen: **14** Whereupon they built a place of exercise at Jerusalem according to the customs of the heathen: **15** And made themselves uncircumcised, and forsook the holy covenant, and joined themselves to the heathen, and were sold to do mischief. **16** Now when the kingdom was established before Antiochus, he thought to reign over Egypt that he might have the dominion of two realms. **17** Wherefore he entered into Egypt with a great multitude, with chariots, and elephants, and horsemen, and a great navy, **18** And made war against Ptolemee king of Egypt: but Ptolemee was afraid of him, and fled; and many were wounded to death. **19** Thus they got the strong cities in the land of Egypt and he took the spoils thereof. **20** And after that Antiochus had smitten Egypt, he returned again in the hundred forty and third year, and went up against Israel and Jerusalem with a great multitude, **21** And entered proudly into the sanctuary, and took away the golden altar, and the candlestick of light, and all the vessels thereof, **22** And the table of the shewbread, and the pouring vessels, and the vials. and the censers of gold, and the veil, and the crown, and the golden ornaments that were before the temple, all which he pulled off. **23** He took also the silver and the gold, and the precious vessels: also he took the hidden treasures which he found. **24** And when he had taken all away, he went into his own land, having made a great massacre, and spoken very proudly. **25** Therefore there was a great mourning in Israel, in every place where they were; **26** So that the princes and elders mourned, the virgins and young men were made feeble, and the beauty of women was changed. **27** Every bridegroom took up lamentation, and she that sat in the marriage chamber was in heaviness, **28** The land also was moved for the inhabitants thereof, and all the house of Jacob was covered with confusion. **29** And after two years fully expired the king sent his chief collector of tribute unto the cities of Juda, who came unto Jerusalem with a great multitude, **30** And spake peaceable words unto them, but all was deceit: for when they had given him credence, he fell suddenly upon the city, and smote it very sore, and destroyed much people of Israel. **31** And when he had taken the spoils of the city, he set it on fire, and pulled down the houses and walls thereof on every side. **32** But the women and children took they captive, and possessed the cattle. **33** Then builded they the city of David with a great and strong wall, and with mighty towers, and made it a strong hold for them. **34** And they put therein a sinful nation, wicked men, and fortified themselves therein. **35** They stored it also with armour and victuals, and when they had gathered together the spoils of Jerusalem, they laid them up there, and so they became a sore snare: **1** Maccabees Page **648** **36** For it was a place to lie in wait against the sanctuary, and an evil adversary to Israel. **37** Thus they shed innocent blood on every side of the sanctuary, and defiled it: **38** Insomuch that the inhabitants of Jerusalem fled because of them: whereupon the city was made an habitation of strangers, and became strange to those that were born in her; and her own children left her. **39** Her sanctuary was laid waste like a wilderness, her feasts were turned into mourning, her sabbaths into reproach her honour into contempt. **40** As had been her glory, so was her dishonour increased, and her excellency was turned into mourning. **41** Moreover king Antiochus wrote to his whole kingdom, that all should be one people, **42** And every one should leave his laws: so all the heathen agreed according to the commandment of the king. **43** Yea, many also of the Israelites consented to his religion, and sacrificed unto idols, and profaned the sabbath. **44** For the king had sent letters by messengers unto Jerusalem and the cities of Juda that they should follow the strange laws of the land, **45** And forbid burnt offerings, and sacrifice, and drink offerings, in the temple; and that they should profane the sabbaths and festival days: **46** And pollute the sanctuary and holy people: **47** Set up altars, and groves, and chapels of idols, and sacrifice swine's flesh, and unclean beasts: **48** That they should also leave their children uncircumcised, and make their souls abominable with all manner of uncleanness and profanation: **49** To the end they might forget the law, and change all the ordinances. **50** And whosoever would not do according to the commandment of the king, he said, he should die. **51** In the selfsame manner wrote he to his whole kingdom, and appointed overseers over all the people, commanding the cities of Juda to sacrifice, city by city. **52** Then many of the people were gathered unto them, to wit every one that forsook the law; and so they committed evils in the land; **53** And drove the Israelites into secret places, even wheresoever they could flee for succour. **54** Now the fifteenth day of the month Casleu, in the hundred forty and fifth year, they set up the abomination of desolation upon the altar, and builded idol altars throughout the cities of Juda on every side; **55** And burnt incense at the doors of their houses, and in the streets. **56** And when they had rent in pieces the books of the law which they found, they burnt them with fire. **57** And whosoever was found with any the book of the testament, or if any committed to the law, the king's commandment was, that they should put him to death. **58** Thus did they by their authority unto the Israelites every month, to as many as were found in the cities. **59** Now the five and twentieth day of the month they did sacrifice upon the idol altar, which was upon the altar of God. **60** At which time according to the commandment they put to death certain women, that had caused their children to be circumcised. **61** And they hanged the infants about their necks, and rifled their houses, and slew them that had circumcised them. **62** Howbeit many in Israel were fully resolved and confirmed in themselves not to eat any unclean thing. **63** Wherefore the rather to die, that they might not be defiled with meats, and that they might not profane the holy covenant: so then they died. **64** And there was very great wrath upon Israel.

2 1 In those days arose Mattathias the son of John, the son of Simeon, a priest of the sons of Joarib, from Jerusalem, and dwelt in Modin. **2** And he had five sons, Joannan, called Caddis: **3** Simon; called Thassi: **4** Judas, who was called Maccabeus: **5** Eleazar, called Avaran: and Jonathan, whose surname was Apphus. **6** And when he saw the blasphemies that were committed in Juda and Jerusalem, **7** He said, Woe is me! wherefore was I born to see this misery of my people, and of the holy city, and to dwell there, when it was delivered into the hand of the enemy, and the sanctuary into the hand of strangers? **8** Her temple is become as a man without glory. **9** Her glorious vessels are carried away into captivity, her infants are slain in the streets, her young men with the sword of the enemy. **10** What nation hath not had a part in her kingdom and gotten of her spoils? **11** All her ornaments are taken away; of a free woman she is become a bondslave. **12** And, behold, our sanctuary, even our beauty and our glory, is laid waste, and the Gentiles have profaned it. **13** To what end therefore shall we live any longer? **14** Then Mattathias and his sons rent their clothes, and put on sackcloth, and mourned very sore. **15** In the mean while the king's officers, such as compelled the people to revolt, came into the city Modin, to make them sacrifice. **16** And when many of Israel came unto them, Mattathias also and his sons came together. **17** Then answered the king's officers, and said to Mattathias on this wise, Thou art a ruler, and an honourable and great man in this city, and strengthened with sons and brethren: **18** Now therefore come thou first, and fulfil the king's commandment, like as all the heathen have done, yea, and the men of Juda also, and such as remain at Jerusalem: so shalt thou and thy house be in the number of the king's friends, and thou and thy children shall be honoured with silver and gold, and many rewards. **19** Then

Mattathias answered and spake with a loud voice, Though all the nations that are
under the king's dominion obey him, and fall away every one from the religion of
their fathers, and give consent to his commandments: 20 Yet will I and my sons
and my brethren walk in the covenant of our fathers. 21 God forbid that we
should forsake the law and the ordinances. 22 We will not hearken to the king's
words, to go from our religion, either on the right hand, or the left. 23 Now
when he had left speaking these words, there came one of the Jews in the sight of
all to sacrifice on the altar which was at Modin, according to the king's command-
ment. 24 Which thing when Mattathias saw, he was inflamed with zeal, and his
reins trembled, neither could he forbear to shew his anger according to judgment:
wherefore he ran, and slew him upon the altar. 25 Also the king's commissio-
ner, who compelled men to sacrifice, he killed at that time, and the altar he pulled
down. 26 Thus dealt he zealously for the law of God like as Phinees did unto
Zambri the son of Salom. 27 And Mattathias cried throughout the city with a
loud voice, saying, Whosoever is zealous of the law, and maintaineth the cove-
nant, let him follow me. 28 So he and his sons fled into the mountains, and left
all that ever they had in the city. 29 Then many that sought after justice and
judgment went down into the wilderness, to dwell there: 30 Both they, and
their children, and their wives; and their cattle; because afflictions increased sore
upon them. 31 Now when it was told the king's servants, and the host that was
at Jerusalem, in the city of David, that certain men, who had broken the king's
commandment, were gone down into the secret places in the wilder-
ness, 32 They pursued after them a great number, and having overtaken them,
they camped against them, and made war against them on the sabbath
day. 33 And they said unto them, Let that which ye have done hitherto suffice;
come forth, and do according to the commandment of the king, and ye shall
live. 34 But they said, We will not come forth, neither will we do the king's
commandment, to profane the sabbath day. 35 So then they gave them the
battle with all speed. 36 Howbeit they answered them not, neither cast they a
stone at them, nor stopped the places where they lay hid; 37 But said, Let us die
all in our innocency: heaven and earth will testify for us, that ye put us to death
wrongfully. 38 So they rose up against them in battle on the sabbath, and they
slew them, with their wives and children and their cattle, to the number of a
thousand people. 39 Now when Mattathias and his friends understood hereof,
they mourned for them right sore. 40 And one of them said to another, If we
all do as our brethren have done, and fight not for our lives and laws against the
heathen, they will now quickly root us out of the earth. 41 At that time there-
fore they decreed, saying, Whosoever shall come to make battle with us on the
sabbath day, we will fight against him; neither will we die all, as our brethren that
were murdered im the secret places. 42 Then came there unto him a company
of Assideans who were mighty men of Israel, even all such as were voluntarily
devoted unto the law. 43 Also all they that fled for persecution joined themsel-
ves unto them, and were a stay unto them. 44 So they joined their forces, and
smote sinful men in their anger, and wicked men in their wrath: but the rest fled
to the heathen for succour. 45 Then Mattathias and his friends went round
about, and pulled down the altars: 46 And what children soever they found
within the coast of Israel uncircumcised, those they circumcised valiant-
ly. 47 They pursued also after the proud men, and the work prospered in their
hand. 48 So they recovered the law out of the hand of the Gentiles, and out of
the hand of kings, neither suffered they the sinner to triumph. 49 Now when
the time drew near that Mattathias should die, he said unto his sons, Now hath
pride and rebuke gotten strength, and the time of destruction, and the wrath of
indignation: 50 Now therefore, my sons, be ye zealous for the law, and give
your lives for the covenant of your fathers. 51 Call to remembrance what acts
our fathers did in their time; so shall ye receive great honour and an everlasting
name. 52 Was not Abraham found faithful in temptation, and it was imputed
unto him for righteousness? 53 Joseph in the time of his distress kept the com-
mandment and was made lord of Egypt. 54 Phinees our father in being zealous
and fervent obtained the covenant of an everlasting priesthood. 55 Jesus for
fulfilling the word was made a judge in Israel. 56 Caleb for bearing witness
before the congregation received the heritage of the land. 57 David for being
merciful possessed the throne of an everlasting kingdom. 58 Elias for being
zealous and fervent for the law was taken up into heaven. 59 Ananias, Azarias,
and Misael, by believing were saved out of the flame. 60 Daniel for his innocen-
cy was delivered from the mouth of lions. 61 And thus consider ye throughout
all ages, that none that put their trust in him shall be overcome. 62 Fear not
then the words of a sinful man: for his glory shall be dung and worms. 63 To
day he shall be lifted up and to morrow he shall not be found, because he is retur-
ned into his dust, and his thought is come to nothing. 64 Wherefore, ye my
sons, be valiant and shew yourselves men in the behalf of the law; for by it shall ye
obtain glory. 65 And behold, I know that your brother Simon is a man of
counsel, give ear unto him alway: he shall be a father unto you. 66 As for Judas
Maccabeus, he hath been mighty and strong, even from his youth up: let him be
your captain, and fight the battle of the people. 67 Take also unto you all those
that observe the law, and avenge ye the wrong of your people. 68 Recompense
fully the heathen, and take heed to the commandments of the law. 69 So he
blessed them, and was gathered to his fathers. 70 And he died in the hundred
forty and sixth year, and his sons buried him in the sepulchres of his fathers at
Modin, and all Israel made great lamentation for him.

3 1 Then his son Judas, called Maccabeus, rose up in his stead. 2 And all
his brethren helped him, and so did all they that held with his father, and
they fought with cheerfulness the battle of Israel. 3 So he gat his people great
honour, and put on a breastplate as a giant, and girt his warlike harness about
him, and he made battles, protecting the host with his sword. 4 In his acts he
was like a lion, and like a lion's whelp roaring for his prey. 5 For He pursued the
wicked, and sought them out, and burnt up those that vexed his people. 6 Whe-
refore the wicked shrunk for fear of him, and all the workers of iniquity were
troubled, because salvation prospered in his hand. 7 He grieved also many kin-
gs, and made Jacob glad with his acts, and his memorial is blessed for ever. 8 Mo-
reover he went through the cities of Juda, destroying the ungodly out of them,
and turning away wrath from Israel: 9 So that he was renowned unto the ut-
most part of the earth, and he received unto him such as were ready to peri-
sh. 10 Then Apollonius gathered the Gentiles together, and a great host out of
Samaria, to fight against Israel. 11 Which thing when Judas perceived, he went
forth to meet him, and so he smote him, and slew him: many also fell down slain,
but the rest fled. 12 Wherefore Judas took their spoils, and Apollonius' sword
also, and therewith he fought all his life long. 13 Now when Seron, a prince of
the army of Syria, heard say that Judas had gathered unto him a multitude and
company of the faithful to go out with him to war; 14 He said, I will get me a
name and honour in the kingdom; for I will go fight with Judas and them that are
with him, who despise the king's commandment. 15 So he made him ready to
go up, and there went with him a mighty host of the ungodly to help him, and to
be avenged of the children of Israel. 16 And when he came near to the going up
of Bethhoron, Judas went forth to meet him with a small company: 17 Who,
when they saw the host coming to meet them, said unto Judas, How shall we be
able, being so few, to fight against so great a multitude and so strong, seeing we
are ready to faint with fasting all this day? 18 Unto whom Judas answered, It is
no hard matter for many to be shut up in the hands of a few; and with the God
of heaven it is all one, to deliver with a great multitude, or a small com-
pany: 19 For the victory of battle standeth not in the multitude of an host; but
strength cometh from heaven. 20 They come against us in much pride and
iniquity to destroy us, and our wives and children, and to spoil us: 21 But we
fight for our lives and our laws. 22 Wherefore the Lord himself will overthrow
them before our face: and as for you, be ye not afraid of them. 23 Now as soon
as he had left off speaking, he leapt suddenly upon them, and so Seron and his
host was overthrown before him. 24 And they pursued them from the going
down of Bethhoron unto the plain, where were slain about eight hundred men of
them; and the residue fled into the land of the Philistines. 25 Then began the
fear of Judas and his brethren, and an exceeding great dread, to fall upon the na-
tions round about them: 26 Insomuch as his fame came unto the king, and all
nations talked of the battles of Judas. 27 Now when king Antiochus heard the-
se things, he was full of indignation: wherefore he sent and gathered together all
the forces of his realm, even a very strong army. 28 He opened also his treasure,
and gave his soldiers pay for a year, commanding them to be ready whensoever he
should need them. 29 Nevertheless, when he saw that the money of his treasu-
res failed and that the tributes in the country were small, because of the dissension
and plague, which he had brought upon the land in taking away the laws which
had been of old time; 30 He feared that he should not be able to bear the char-
ges any longer, nor to have such gifts to give so liberally as he did before: for he
had abounded above the kings that were before him. 31 Wherefore, being gre-
atly perplexed in his mind, he determined to go into Persia, there to take the tri-
butes of the countries, and to gather much money. 32 So he left Lysias, a noble-
man, and one of the blood royal, to oversee the affairs of the king from the river
Euphrates unto the borders of Egypt: 33 And to bring up his son Antiochus,
until he came again. 34 Moreover he delivered unto him the half of his forces,
and the elephants, and gave him charge of all things that he would have done, as
also concerning them that dwelt in Juda and Jerusalem: 35 To wit, that he
should send an army against them, to destroy and root out the strength of Israel,
and the remnant of Jerusalem, and to take away their memorial from that pla-
ce; 36 And that he should place strangers in all their quarters, and divide their
land by lot. 37 So the king took the half of the forces that remained, and depar-
ted from Antioch, his royal city, the hundred forty and seventh year; and having
passed the river Euphrates, he went through the high countries. 38 Then Lysias
chose Ptolemee the son of Dorymenes, Nicanor, and Gorgias, mighty men of the
king's friends: 39 And with them he sent forty thousand footmen, and seven
thousand horsemen, to go into the land of Juda, and to destroy it, as the king
commanded. 40 So they went forth with all their power, and came and pitched
by Emmaus in the plain country. 41 And the merchants of the country, hearing
the fame of them, took silver and gold very much, with servants, and came into
the camp to buy the children of Israel for slaves: a power also of Syria and of the
land of the Philistines joined themselves unto them. 42 Now when Judas and
his brethren saw that miseries were multiplied, and that the forces did encamp
themselves in their borders: for they knew how the king had given commandment
to destroy the people, and utterly abolish them; 43 They said one to another,
Let us restore the decayed fortune of our people, and let us fight for our people
and the sanctuary. 44 Then was the congregation gathered together, that they
might be ready for battle, and that they might pray, and ask mercy and compas-
sion. 45 Now Jerusalem lay void as a wilderness, there was none of her children
that went in or out: the sanctuary also was trodden down, and aliens kept the
strong hold; the heathen had their habitation in that place; and joy was taken

from Jacob, and the pipe with the harp ceased. **46** Wherefore the Israelites assembled themselves together, and came to Maspha, over against Jerusalem; for in Maspha was the place where they prayed aforetime in Israel. **47** Then they fasted that day, and put on sackcloth, and cast ashes upon their heads, and rent their clothes, **48** And laid open the book of the law, wherein the heathen had sought to paint the likeness of their images. **49** They brought also the priests' garments, and the firstfruits, and the tithes: and the Nazarites they stirred up, who had accomplished their days. **50** Then cried they with a loud voice toward heaven, saying, What shall we do with these, and whither shall we carry them away? **51** For thy sanctuary is trodden down and profaned, and thy priests are in heaviness, and brought low. **52** And lo, the heathen are assembled together against us to destroy us: what things they imagine against us, thou knowest. **53** How shall we be able to stand against them, except thou, O God, be our help? **54** Then sounded they with trumpets, and cried with a loud voice. **55** And after this Judas ordained captains over the people, even captains over thousands, and over hundreds, and over fifties, and over tens. **56** But as for such as were building houses, or had betrothed wives, or were planting vineyards, or were fearful, those he commanded that they should return, every man to his own house, according to the law. **57** So the camp removed, and pitched upon the south side of Emmaus. **58** And Judas said, arm yourselves, and be valiant men, and see that ye be in readiness against the morning, that ye may fight with these nations, that are assembled together against us to destroy us and our sanctuary: **59** For it is better for us to die in battle, than to behold the calamities of our people and our sanctuary. **60** Nevertheless, as the will of God is in heaven, so let him do.

4

1 Then took Gorgias five thousand footmen, and a thousand of the best horsemen, and removed out of the camp by night; **2** To the end he might rush in upon the camp of the Jews, and smite them suddenly. And the men of the fortress were his guides. **3** Now when Judas heard thereof he himself removed, and the valiant men with him, that he might smite the king's army which was at Emmaus, **4** While as yet the forces were dispersed from the camp. **5** In the mean season came Gorgias by night into the camp of Judas: and when he found no man there, he sought them in the mountains: for said he, These fellows flee from us **6** But as soon as it was day, Judas shewed himself in the plain with three thousand men, who nevertheless had neither armour nor swords to their minds. **7** And they saw the camp of the heathen, that it was strong and well harnessed, and compassed round about with horsemen; and these were expert of war. **8** Then said Judas to the men that were with him, Fear ye not their multitude, neither be ye afraid of their assault. **9** Remember how our fathers were delivered in the Red sea, when Pharaoh pursued them with an army. **10** Now therefore let us cry unto heaven, if peradventure the Lord will have mercy upon us, and remember the covenant of our fathers, and destroy this host before our face this day: **11** That so all the heathen may know that there is one who delivereth and saveth Israel. **12** Then the strangers lifted up their eyes, and saw them coming over against them. **13** Wherefore they went out of the camp to battle; but they that were with Judas sounded their trumpets. **14** So they joined battle, and the heathen being discomfited fled into the plain. **15** Howbeit all the hindmost of them were slain with the sword: for they pursued them unto Gazera, and unto the plains of Idumea, and Azotus, and Jamnia, so that there were slain of them upon a three thousand men. **16** This done, Judas returned again with his host from pursuing them, **17** And said to the people, Be not greedy of the spoil inasmuch as there is a battle before us, **18** And Gorgias and his host are here by us in the mountain: but stand ye now against our enemies, and overcome them, and after this ye may boldly take the spoils. **19** As Judas was yet speaking these words, there appeared a part of them looking out of the mountain: **20** Who when they perceived that the Jews had put their host to flight and were burning the tents; for the smoke that was seen declared what was done: **21** When therefore they perceived these things, they were sore afraid, and seeing also the host of Judas in the plain ready to fight, **22** They fled every one into the land of strangers. **23** Then Judas returned to spoil the tents, where they got much gold, and silver, and blue silk, and purple of the sea, and great riches. **24** After this they went home, and sung a song of thanksgiving, and praised the Lord in heaven: because it is good, because his mercy endureth forever. **25** Thus Israel had a great deliverance that day. **26** Now all the strangers that had escaped came and told Lysias what had happened: **27** Who, when he heard thereof, was confounded and discouraged, because neither such things as he would were done unto Israel, nor such things as the king commanded him were come to pass. **28** The next year therefore following Lysias gathered together threescore thousand choice men of foot, and five thousand horsemen, that he might subdue them. **29** So they came into Idumea, and pitched their tents at Bethsura, and Judas met them with ten thousand men. **30** And when he saw that mighty army, he prayed and said, Blessed art thou, O Saviour of Israel, who didst quell the violence of the mighty man by the hand of thy servant David, and gavest the host of strangers into the hands of Jonathan the son of Saul, and his armourbearer; **31** Shut up this army in the hand of thy people Israel, and let them be confounded in their power and horsemen: Page 65 1 Maccabees **32** Make them to be of no courage, and cause the boldness of their strength to fall away, and let them quake at their destruction: **33** Cast them down with the sword of them that love thee, and let all those that know thy name praise thee with thanksgiving. **34** So they joined battle; and there were slain of the host of Lysias about five thousand men, even before them were they slain. **35** Now when Lysias saw his army put to flight, and the manliness of Judas' soldiers, and how they were ready either to live or die valiantly, he went into Antiochia, and gathered together a company of strangers, and having made his army greater than it was, he purposed to come again into Judea. **36** Then said Judas and his brethren, Behold, our enemies are discomfited: let us go up to cleanse and dedicate the sanctuary. **37** Upon this all the host assembled themselves together, and went up into mount Sion. **38** And when they saw the sanctuary desolate, and the altar profaned, and the gates burned up, and shrubs growing in the courts as in a forest, or in one of the mountains, yea, and the priests' chambers pulled down; **39** They rent their clothes, and made great lamentation, and cast ashes upon their heads, **40** And fell down flat to the ground upon their faces, and blew an alarm with the trumpets, and cried toward heaven. **41** Then Judas appointed certain men to fight against those that were in the fortress, until he had cleansed the sanctuary. **42** So he chose priests of blameless conversation, such as had pleasure in the law: **43** Who cleansed the sanctuary, and bare out the defiled stones into an unclean place. **44** And when as they consulted what to do with the altar of burnt offerings, which was profaned; **45** They thought it best to pull it down, lest it should be a reproach to them, because the heathen had defiled it: wherefore they pulled it down, **46** And laid up the stones in the mountain of the temple in a convenient place, until there should come a prophet to shew what should be done with them. **47** Then they took whole stones according to the law, and built a new altar according to the former; **48** And made up the sanctuary, and the things that were within the temple, and hallowed the courts. **49** They made also new holy vessels, and into the temple they brought the candlestick, and the altar of burnt offerings, and of incense, and the table. **50** And upon the altar they burned incense, and the lamps that were upon the candlestick they lighted, that they might give light in the temple. **51** Furthermore they set the loaves upon the table, and spread out the veils, and finished all the works which they had begun to make. **52** Now on the five and twentieth day of the ninth month, which is called the month Casleu, in the hundred forty and eighth year, they rose up betimes in the morning, **53** And offered sacrifice according to the law upon the new altar of burnt offerings, which they had made. **54** Look, at what time and what day the heathen had profaned it, even in that was it dedicated with songs, and citherns, and harps, and cymbals. **55** Then all the people fell upon their faces, worshipping and praising the God of heaven, who had given them good success. **56** And so they kept the dedication of the altar eight days and offered burnt offerings with gladness, and sacrificed the sacrifice of deliverance and praise. **57** They decked also the forefront of the temple with crowns of gold, and with shields; and the gates and the chambers they renewed, and hanged doors upon them. **58** Thus was there very great gladness among the people, for that the reproach of the heathen was put away. **59** Moreover Judas and his brethren with the whole congregation of Israel ordained, that the days of the dedication of the altar should be kept in their season from year to year by the space of eight days, from the five and twentieth day of the month Casleu, with mirth and gladness. **60** At that time also they builded up the mount Sion with high walls and strong towers round about, lest the Gentiles should come and tread it down as they had done before. **61** And they set there a garrison to keep it, and fortified Bethsura to preserve it; that the people might have a defence against Idumea.

5

1 Now when the nations round about heard that the altar was built and the sanctuary renewed as before, it displeased them very much. **2** Wherefore they thought to destroy the generation of Jacob that was among them, and thereupon they began to slay and destroy the people. **3** Then Judas fought against the children of Esau in Idumea at Arabattine, because they besieged Gael: and he gave them a great overthrow, and abated their courage, and took their spoils. **4** Also he remembered the injury of the children of Bean, who had been a snare and an offence unto the people, in that they lay in wait for them in the ways. **5** He shut them up therefore in the towers, and encamped against them, and destroyed them utterly, and burned the towers of that place with fire, and all that were therein. **6** Afterward he passed over to the children of Ammon, where he found a mighty power, and much people, with Timotheus their captain. **7** So he fought many battles with them, till at length they were discomfited before him; and he smote them. **8** And when he had taken Jazar, with the towns belonging thereto, he returned into Judea. **9** Then the heathen that were at Galaad assembled themselves together against the Israelites that were in their quarters, to destroy them; but they fled to the fortress of Dathema. **10** And sent letters unto Judas and his brethren, The heathen that are round about us are assembled together against us to destroy us: **11** And they are preparing to come and take the fortress whereunto we are fled, Timotheus being captain of their host. **12** Come now therefore, and deliver us from their hands, for many of us are slain: **13** Yea, all our brethren that were in the places of Tobie are put to death: their wives and their children also they have carried away captives, and borne away their stuff; and they have destroyed there about a thousand men. **14** While these letters were yet reading, behold, there came other messengers from Galilee with their clothes rent, who reported on this wise, **15** And said, They of Ptolemais, and of Tyrus, and Sidon, and all Galilee of the Gentiles, are assembled together against us to consume us. **16** Now when Judas and the people heard these words, there assembled a great congregation together, to consult what they should do for their brethren, that were in trouble, and assaulted of them. **17** Then said Judas unto Simon his brother, Choose thee out men, and go and deliver thy brethren that are in Galilee, for I and Jonathan my brother will go into the country of Galaad. **18** So he left Joseph the son of Zacharias, and Azarias, captains of the people, with the remnant of the host in Judea to keep it. **19** Unto whom he gave commandment, saying, Take ye the charge of this people, and see that ye make not war against the heathen until the time that we come again. **20** Now unto Simon were given three thousand men to go into Galilee, and unto Judas eight thousand men for the country of Galaad. **21** Then went Simon into Galilee, where he fought many battles with the heathen, so that the heathen were discomfited by him. **22** And he pursued them unto the gate of Ptolemais; and there were slain of the heathen about three thousand men, whose spoils he took. **23** And those that were in Galilee, and in Arbattis, with their wives and their children, and all that they had, took he away with him, and brought them into Judea with great joy. **24** Judas Maccabeus also and his brother Jonathan went over Jordan, and travelled three days' journey in the wilderness, **25** Where they met with the Nabathites, who came unto them in a peaceable manner, and told them every thing that had happened to their brethren in the land of Galaad: **26** And how that many of them were shut up in Bosora, and Bosor, and Alema, Casphor, Maked, and Carnaim; all these cities are strong and great: **27** And that they were shut up in the rest of the cities of the country of Galaad, and that against to morrow they had appointed to bring their host against the forts, and to take them, and to destroy them all in one day. **28** Hereupon Judas and his host turned suddenly by the way of the wilderness unto Bosora; and when he had won the city, he slew all the males with the edge of the sword, and took all their spoils, and burned the city with fire, **29** From whence he removed by night, and went till he came to the fortress. **30** And betimes in the morning they looked up, and, behold, there was an innumerable people bearing ladders and other engines of war, to take the fortress: for they assaulted them. **31** When Judas therefore saw that the battle was begun, and that the cry of the city went up to heaven, with trumpets, and a great sound, **32** He said unto his host, Fight this day for your brethren. **33** So he went forth behind them in three companies, who sounded their trumpets, and cried with prayer. **34** Then the host of Timotheus, knowing that it was Maccabeus, fled from him: wherefore he smote them with a great slaughter; so that there were killed of them that day about eight thousand men. **35** This done, Judas turned aside to Maspha; and after he had assaulted it he took and slew all the males therein, and received the spoils thereof and and burnt it with fire. **36** From thence went he, and took Casphon, Maged, Bosor, and the other cities of the country of Galaad. **37** After these things gathered Timotheus another host and encamped against Raphon beyond the brook. **38** So Judas sent men to espy the host, who brought him word, saying, All the heathen that be round about us are assembled unto them, even a very great host. **39** He hath also hired the Arabians to help them and they have pitched their tents beyond the brook, ready to come and fight against thee. Upon this Judas went to meet them. **40** Then Timotheus said unto the captains of his host, When Judas and his host come near the brook, if he pass over first unto us, we shall not be able to withstand him; for he will mightily prevail against us: **41** But if he be afraid, and camp beyond the river, we shall go over unto him, and prevail against him. **42** Now when Judas came near the brook, he caused the scribes of the people to remain by the brook: unto whom he gave commandment, saying, Suffer no man to remain in the camp, but let all come to the battle. **43** So he went first over unto them, and all the people after him: then all the heathen, being discomfited before him, cast away their weapons, and fled unto the temple that was at Carnaim. **44** But they took the city, and burned the temple with all that were therein. Thus was Carnaim subdued, neither could they stand any longer before Judas. **45** Then Judas gathered together all the Israelites that were in the country of Galaad, from the least unto the greatest, even their wives, and their children, and their stuff, a very great host, to the end they might come into the land of Judea. **46** Now when they came unto Ephron, (this was a great city in the way as they should go, very well fortified) they could not turn from it, either on the right hand or the left, but must needs pass through the midst of it. **47** Then they of the city shut them out, and stopped up the gates with stones. **48** Whereupon Judas sent unto them in peaceable manner, saying, Let us pass through your land to go into our own country, and none shall do you any hurt; we will only pass through on foot: howbeit they would not open unto him. **49** Wherefore Judas commanded a proclamation to be made throughout the host, that every man should pitch his tent in the place where he was. **50** So the soldiers pitched, and assaulted the city all that day and all that night, till at the length the city was delivered into his hands: **51** Who then slew all the males with the edge of the sword, and rased the city, and took the spoils thereof, and passed through the city over them that were slain. **52** After this went they over Jordan into the great plain before Bethsan. **53** And Judas gathered together those that came behind, and exhorted the people all the way through, till they came into the land of Judea. **54** So they went up to mount Sion with joy and gladness, where they offered burnt offerings, because not one of them were slain until they had returned in peace. **55** Now what time as Judas and Jonathan were in the land of Galaad, and Simon his brother in Galilee before Ptolemais, **56** Joseph the son of Zacharias, and Azarias, captains of the garrisons, heard of the valiant acts and warlike deeds which they had done. **57** Wherefore they said, Let us also get us a name, and go fight against the heathen that are round about us. **58** So when they had given charge unto the garrison that was with them, they went toward Jamnia. **59** Then came Gorgias and his men out of the city to fight against them. **60** And so it was, that Joseph and Azaras were put to flight, and pursued unto the borders of Judea: and there were slain that day of the people of Israel about two thousand men. **61** Thus was there a great overthrow among the children of Israel, because they were not obedient unto Judas and his brethren, but thought to do some valiant act. **62** Moreover these men came not of the seed of those, by whose hand deliverance was given unto Israel. **63** Howbeit the man Judas and his brethren were greatly renowned in the sight of all Israel, and of all the heathen, wheresoever their name was heard of; **64** Insomuch as the the people assembled unto them with joyful acclamations. **65** Afterward went Judas forth with his brethren, and fought against the children of Esau in the land toward the south, where he smote Hebron, and the towns thereof, and pulled down the fortress of it, and burned the towers thereof round about. **66** From thence he removed to go into the land of the Philistines, and passed through Samaria. **67** At that time certain priests, desirous to shew their valour, were slain in battle, for that they went out to fight unadvisedly. **68** So Judas turned to Azotus in the land of the Philistines, and when he had pulled down their altars, and burned their carved images with fire, and spoiled their cities, he returned into the land of Judea.

6 **1** About that time king Antiochus travelling through the high countries heard say, that Elymais in the country of Persia was a city greatly renowned for riches, silver, and gold; **2** And that there was in it a very rich temple, wherein were coverings of gold, and breastplates, and shields, which Alexander, son of Philip, the Macedonian king, who reigned first among the Grecians, had left there. **3** Wherefore he came and sought to take the city, and to spoil it; but he was not able, because they of the city, having had warning thereof, **4** Rose up against him in battle: so he fled, and departed thence with great heaviness, and returned to Babylon. **5** Moreover there came one who brought him tidings into Persia, that the armies, which went against the land of Judea, were put to flight: **6** And that Lysias, who went forth first with a great power was driven away of the Jews; and that they were made strong by the armour, and power, and store of spoils, which they had gotten of the armies, whom they had destroyed: **7** Also that they had pulled down the abomination, which he had set up upon the altar in Jerusalem, and that they had compassed about the sanctuary with high walls, as before, and his city Bethsura. **8** Now when the king heard these words, he was astonished and sore moved: whereupon he laid him down upon his bed, and fell sick for grief, because it had not befallen him as he looked for. **9** And there he continued many days: for his grief was ever more and more, and he made account that he should die. **10** Wherefore he called for all his friends, and said unto them, The sleep is gone from mine eyes, and my heart faileth for very care. **11** And I thought with myself, Into what tribulation am I come, and how great a flood of misery is it, wherein now I am! for I was bountiful and beloved in my power. **12** But now I remember the evils that I did at Jerusalem, and that I took all the vessels of gold and silver that were therein, and sent to destroy the inhabitants of Judea without a cause. **13** I perceive therefore that for this cause these troubles are come upon me, and, behold, I perish through great grief in a strange land. **14** Then called he for Philip, one of his friends, who he made ruler over all his realm, **15** And gave him the crown, and his robe, and his signet, to the end he should bring up his son Antiochus, and nourish him up for the kingdom. **16** So king Antiochus died there in the hundred forty and ninth year. **17** Now when Lysias knew that the king was dead, he set up Antiochus his son, whom he had brought up being young, to reign in his stead, and his name he called Eupator. **18** About this time they that were in the tower shut up the Israelites round about the sanctuary, and sought always their hurt, and the strengthening of the heathen. **19** Wherefore Judas, purposing to destroy them, called all the people together to besiege them. **20** So they came together, and besieged them in the hundred and fiftieth year, and he made mounts for shot against them, and other engines. **21** Howbeit certain of them that were besieged got forth, unto whom some ungodly men of Israel joined themselves: **22** And they went unto the king, and said, How long will it be ere thou execute judgment, and avenge our brethren? **23** We have been willing to serve thy father, and to do as he would have us, and to obey his commandments; **24** For which cause they of our nation besiege the tower, and are alienated from us: moreover as many of us as they could light on they slew, and spoiled our inheritance. **25** Neither have they stretched out their hand against us only, but also against their borders. **26** And, behold, this day are they besieging the tower at Jerusalem, to take it: the sanctuary also and Bethsura have they fortified. **27** Wherefore if thou dost not prevent them quickly, they will do the greater things than these, neither shalt thou be able to rule them. **28** Now when the king heard this, he was angry, and gathered together all his friends, and the captains of his army, and those that had charge of the horse. **29** There came also unto him from other kingdoms, and from isles of the sea, bands of hired soldiers. **30** So that the number of his army was an hundred thousand footmen, and twenty thousand horsemen, and two and thirty elephants exercised in battle. **31** These went through Idumea, and pitched against Bethsura, which they assaulted many days, making engines of war; but they of Bethsura came out, and burned them with fire, and fought valiantly. **32** Upon this Judas removed from the tower, and pitched in Bathzacharias, over against the king's camp. **33** Then the king rising very early marched fiercely with his host toward Bathzacharias, where his armies made them ready to battle, and sounded the trumpets. **34** And to the end they might provoke the elephants to fight, they shewed them the blood of grapes and mulberries. **35** Moreover they divided the beasts among the armies, and for every elephant they appointed a thousand men, armed with coats of mail, and with helmets of brass on their heads; and beside this, for every beast were ordained five hundred horsemen of the best. **36** These were ready at every occasion: wheresoever the beast was, and whithersoever the beast went, they went also, neither departed they from him. **37** And upon the beasts were there strong towers of wood, which covered every one of them, and were girt fast unto them with devices: there were also upon every one two and thirty strong men, that fought upon them, beside the Indian that ruled him. **38** As for the remnant of the horsemen, they set them on this side and that side at the two parts of the host giving them signs what to do, and being harnessed all over amidst the ranks. **39** Now when the sun shone upon the shields of gold and brass, the mountains glistered therewith, and shined like lamps of fire. **40** So part of the king's army being spread upon the high mountains, and part on the valleys below, they marched on safely and in order. **41** Wherefore all that heard the noise of their multitude, and the marching of the company, and the rattling of the harness, were moved: for the army was very great and mighty. **42** Then Judas and his host drew near, and entered into battle, and there were slain of the king's army six hundred men. **43** Eleazar also, surnamed Savaran, perceiving that one of the beasts, armed with royal harness, was higher than all the rest, and supposing that the king was upon him, **44** Put himself in jeopardy, to the end he might deliver his people, and get him a perpetual name: **45** Wherefore he ran upon him courageously through the midst of the battle, slaying on the right hand and on the left, so that they were divided from him on both sides. **46** Which done, he crept under the elephant, and thrust him under, and slew him: whereupon the elephant fell down upon him, and there he died. **47** Howbeit the rest of the Jews seeing the strength of the king, and the violence of his forces, turned away from them. **48** Then the king's army went up to Jerusalem to meet them, and the king pitched his tents against Judea, and against mount Sion. **49** But with them that were in Bethsura he made peace: for they came out of the city, because they had no victuals there to endure the siege, it being a year of rest to the land. **50** So the king took Bethsura, and set a garrison there to keep it. **51** As for the sanctuary, he besieged it many days: and set there artillery with engines and instruments to cast fire and stones, and pieces to cast darts and slings. **52** Whereupon they also made engines against their engines, and held them battle a long season. **53** Yet at the last, their vessels being without victuals, (for that it was the seventh year, and they in Judea that were delivered from the Gentiles, had eaten up the residue of the store;) **54** There were but a few left in the sanctuary, because the famine did so prevail against them, that they were fain to disperse themselves, every man to his own place. **55** At that time Lysias heard say, that Philip, whom Antiochus the king, whiles he lived, had appointed to bring up his son Antiochus, that he might be king, **56** Was returned out of Persia and Media, and the king's host also that went with him, and that he sought to take unto him the ruling of the affairs. **57** Wherefore he went in all haste, and said to the king and the captains of the host and the company, We decay daily, and our victuals are but small, and the place we lay siege unto is strong, and the affairs of the kingdom lie upon us: **58** Now therefore let us be friends with these men, and make peace with them, and with all their nation; **59** And covenant with them, that they shall live after their laws, as they did before: for they are therefore displeased, and have done all these things, because we abolished their laws. **60** So the king and the princes were content: wherefore he sent unto them to make peace; and they accepted thereof. **61** Also the king and the princes made an oath unto them: whereupon they went out of the strong hold. **62** Then the king entered into mount Sion; but when he saw the strength of the place, he broke his oath that he had made, and gave commandment to pull down the wall round about. **63** Afterward departed he in all haste, and returned unto Antiochia, where he found Philip to be master of the city: so he fought against him, and took the city by force.

7

1 In the hundred and one and fiftieth year Demetrius the son of Seleucus departed from Rome, and came up with a few men unto a city of the sea coast, and reigned there. **2** And as he entered into the palace of his ancestors, so it was, that his forces had taken Antiochus and Lysias, to bring them unto him. **3** Wherefore, when he knew it, he said, Let me not see their faces. **4** So his host slew them. Now when Demetrius was set upon the throne of his kingdom, **5** There came unto him all the wicked and ungodly men of Israel, having Alcimus, who was desirous to be high priest, for their captain: **6** And they accused the people to the king, saying, Judas and his brethren have slain all thy friends, and driven us out of our own land. **7** Now therefore send some man whom thou trustest, and let him go and see what havock he hath made among us, and in the king's land, and let him punish them with all them that aid them. **8** Then the king chose Bacchides, a friend of the king, who ruled beyond the flood, and was a great man in the kingdom, and faithful to the king, **9** And him he sent with that wicked Alcimus, whom he made high priest, and commanded that he should take vengeance of the children of Israel. **10** So they departed, and came with a great power into the land of Judea, where they sent messengers to Judas and his brethren with peaceable words deceitfully. **11** But they gave no heed to their words; for they saw that they were come with a great power. **12** Then did there assemble unto Alcimus and Bacchides a company of scribes, to require justice. **13** Now the Assideans were the first among the children of Israel that sought peace of them: **14** For said they, One that is a priest of the seed of Aaron is come with this army, and he will do us no wrong. **15** So he spake unto them, peaceably, and sware unto them, saying, we will procure the harm neither of you nor your friends. **16** Whereupon they believed him: howbeit he took of them threescore men, and slew them in one day, according to the words which he wrote, **17** The flesh of thy saints have they cast out, and their blood have they shed round about Jerusalem, and there was none to bury them. **18** Wherefore the fear and dread of them fell upon all the people, who said, There is neither truth nor righteousness in them; for they have broken the covenant and oath that they made. **19** After this, removed Bacchides from Jerusalem, and pitched his tents in Bezeth, where he sent and took many of the men that had forsaken him, and certain of the people also, and when he had slain them, he cast them into the great pit. **20** Then committed he the country to Alcimus, and left with him a power to aid him: so Bacchides went to the king. **21** But Alcimus contended for the high priesthood. **22** And unto him resorted all such as troubled the people, who, after they had gotten the land of Juda into their power, did much hurt in Israel. **23** Now when Judas saw all the mischief that Alcimus and his company had done among the Israelites, even above the heathen, **24** He went out into all the coasts of Judea round about, and took vengeance of them that had revolted from him, so that they durst no more go forth into the country. **25** On the other side, when Alcimus saw that Judas and his company had gotten the upper hand, and knew that he was not able to abide their force, he went again to the king, and said all the worst of them that he could. **26** Then the king sent Nicanor, one of his honourable princes, a man that bare deadly hate unto Israel, with commandment to destroy the people. **27** So Nicanor came to Jerusalem with a great force; and sent unto Judas and his brethren deceitfully with friendly words, saying, **28** Let there be no battle between me and you; I will come with a few men, that I may see you in peace. **29** He came therefore to Judas, and they saluted one another peaceably. Howbeit the enemies were prepared to take away Judas by violence. **30** Which thing after it was known to Judas, to wit, that he came unto him with deceit, he was sore afraid of him, and would see his face no more. **31** Nicanor also, when he saw that his counsel was discovered, went out to fight against Judas beside Capharsalama: **32** Where there were slain of Nicanor's side about five thousand men, and the rest fled into the city of David. **33** After this went Nicanor up to mount Sion, and there came out of the sanctuary certain of the priests and certain of the elders of the people, to salute him peaceably, and to shew him the burnt sacrifice that was offered for the king. **34** But he mocked them, and laughed at them, and abused them shamefully, and spake proudly, **35** And sware in his wrath, saying, Unless Judas and his host be now delivered into my hands, if ever I come again in safety, I will burn up this house: and with that he went out in a great rage. **36** Then the priests entered in, and stood before the altar and the temple, weeping, and saying, **37** Thou, O Lord, didst choose this house to be called by thy name, and to be a house of prayer and petition for thy people: **38** Be avenged of this man and his host, and let them fall by the sword: remember their blasphemies, and suffer them not to continue any longer. **39** So Nicanor went out of Jerusalem, and pitched his tents in Bethhoron, where an host out of Syria met him. **40** But Judas pitched in Adasa with three thousand men, and there he prayed, saying, **41** O Lord, when they that were sent from the king of the Assyrians blasphemed, thine angel went out, and smote an hundred fourscore and five thousand of them. **42** Even so destroy thou this host before us this day, that the rest may know that he hath spoken blasphemously against thy sanctuary, and judge thou him according to his wickedness. **43** So the thirteenth day of the month Adar the hosts joined battle: but Nicanor's host was discomfited, and he himself was first slain in the battle. **44** Now when Nicanor's host saw that he was slain, they cast away their weapons, and fled. **45** Then they pursued after them a day's journey, from Adasa unto Gazera, sounding an alarm after them with their trumpets. **46** Whereupon they came forth out of all the towns of Judea round about, and closed them in; so that they, turning back upon them that pursued them, were all slain with the sword, and not one of them was left. **47** Afterwards they took the spoils, and the prey, and smote off Nicanors head, and his right hand, which he stretched out so proudly, and brought them away, and hanged them up toward Jerusalem. **48** For this cause the people rejoiced greatly, and they kept that day a day of great gladness. **49** Moreover they ordained to keep yearly this day, being the thirteenth of Adar. **50** Thus the land of Juda was in rest a little while.

8

1 Now Judas had heard of the the Romans, that they were mighty and valiant men, and such as would lovingly accept all that joined themselves unto them, and make a league of amity with all that came unto them; **2** And that they were men of great valour. It was told him also of their wars and noble acts which they had done among the Galatians, and how they had conquered them, and brought them under tribute; **3** And what they had done in the country of Spain, for the winning of the mines of the silver and gold which is there; **4** And that by their policy and patience they had conquered all the place, though it were very far from them; and the kings also that came against them from the uttermost part of the earth, till they had discomfited them, and given

them a great overthrow, so that the rest did give them tribute every year: **5** Be-
side this, how they had discomfited in battle Philip, and Perseus, king of the
Citims, with others that lifted up themselves against them, and had overcome
them: **6** How also Antiochus the great king of Asia, that came against them in
battle, having an hundred and twenty elephants, with horsemen, and chariots,
and a very great army, was discomfited by them; **7** And how they took him
alive, and covenanted that he and such as reigned after him should pay a great
tribute, and give hostages, and that which was agreed upon, **8** And the country
of India, and Media and Lydia and of the goodliest countries, which they took
of him, and gave to king Eumenes: **9** Moreover how the Grecians had deter-
mined to come and destroy them; **10** And that they, having knowledge thereof
sent against them a certain captain, and fighting with them slew many of them,
and carried away captives their wives and their children, and spoiled them, and
took possession of their lands, and pulled down their strong holds, and brought
them to be their servants unto this day: **11** It was told him besides, how they
destroyed and brought under their dominion all other kingdoms and isles that at
any time resisted them; **12** But with their friends and such as relied upon them
they kept amity: and that they had conquered kingdoms both far and nigh, inso-
much as all that heard of their name were afraid of them: **13** Also that, whom
they would help to a kingdom, those reign; and whom again they would, they
displace: finally, that they were greatly exalted: **14** Yet for all this none of them
wore a crown or was clothed in purple, to be magnified thereby: **15** Moreover
how they had made for themselves a senate house, wherein three hundred and
twenty men sat in council daily, consulting alway for the people, to the end they
might be well ordered: **16** And that they committed their government to one
man every year, who ruled over all their country, and that all were obedient to
that one, and that there was neither envy nor emmulation among them. **17** In
consideration of these things, Judas chose Eupolemus the son of John, the son of
Accos, and Jason the son of Eleazar, and sent them to Rome, to make a league of
amity and confederacy with them, **18** And to intreat them that they would take
the yoke from them; for they saw that the kingdom of the Grecians did oppress
Israel with servitude. **19** They went therefore to Rome, which was a very great
journey, and came into the senate, where they spake and said. **20** Judas Macca-
beus with his brethren, and the people of the Jews, have sent us unto you, to make
a confederacy and peace with you, and that we might be registered your confede-
rates and friends. **21** So that matter pleased the Romans well. **22** And this is
the copy of the epistle which the senate wrote back again in tables of brass, and
sent to Jerusalem, that there they might have by them a memorial of peace and
confederacy: **23** Good success be to the Romans, and to the people of the Jews,
by sea and by land for ever: the sword also and enemy be far from them, **24** If
there come first any war upon the Romans or any of their confederates throu-
ghout all their dominion, **25** The people of the Jews shall help them, as the time
shall be appointed, with all their heart: **26** Neither shall they give any thing
unto them that make war upon them, or aid them with victuals, weapons, mo-
ney, or ships, as it hath seemed good unto the Romans; but they shall keep their
covenants without taking any thing therefore. **27** In the same manner also, if
war come first upon the nation of the Jews, the Romans shall help them with all
their heart, according as the time shall be appointed them: **28** Neither shall
victuals be given to them that take part against them, or weapons, or money, or
ships, as it hath seemed good to the Romans; but they shall keep their covenants,
and that without deceit. **29** According to these articles did the Romans make a
covenant with the people of the Jews. **30** Howbeit if hereafter the one party or
the other shall think to meet to add or diminish any thing, they may do it at their
pleasures, and whatsoever they shall add or take away shall be ratified. **31** And
as touching the evils that Demetrius doeth to the Jews, we have written unto him,
saying, Wherefore thou made thy yoke heavy upon our friends and confederates
the Jews? **32** If therefore they complain any more against thee, we will do them
justice, and fight with thee by sea and by land.

9 **1** Furthermore, when Demetrius heard the Nicanor and his host were
slain in battle, he sent Bacchides and Alcimus into the land of Judea the
second time, and with them the chief strength of his host: **2** Who went forth by
the way that leadeth to Galgala, and pitched their tents before Masaloth, which is
in Arbela, and after they had won it, they slew much people. **3** Also the first
month of the hundred fifty and second year they encamped before Jerusa-
lem: **4** From whence they removed, and went to Berea, with twenty thousand
footmen and two thousand horsemen. **5** Now Judas had pitched his tents at
Eleasa, and three thousand chosen men with him: **6** Who seeing the multitude
of the other army to he so great were sore afraid; whereupon many conveyed
themselves out of the host, insomuch as abode of them no more but eight hun-
dred men. **7** When Judas therefore saw that his host slipt away, and that the
battle pressed upon him, he was sore troubled in mind, and much distressed, for
that he had no time to gather them together. **8** Nevertheless unto them that
remained he said, Let us arise and go up against our enemies, if peradventure we
may be able to fight with them. **9** But they dehorted him, saying, We shall never
be able: let us now rather save our lives, and hereafter we will return with our
brethren, and fight against them: for we are but few. **10** Then Judas said, God
forbid that I should do this thing, and flee away from them: if our time be come,
let us die manfully for our brethren, and let us not stain our honour. **11** With
that the host of Bacchides removed out of their tents, and stood over against
them, their horsemen being divided into two troops, and their slingers and ar-
chers going before the host and they that marched in the foreward were all mighty
men. **12** As for Bacchides, he was in the right wing: so the host drew near on
the two parts, and sounded their trumpets. **13** They also of Judas' side, even
they sounded their trumpets also, so that the earth shook at the noise of the ar-
mies, and the battle continued from morning till night. **14** Now when Judas
perceived that Bacchides and the strength of his army were on the right side, he
took with him all the hardy men, **15** Who discomfited the right wing, and
pursued them unto the mount Azotus. **16** But when they of the left wing saw
that they of the right wing were discomfited, they followed upon Judas and those
that were with him hard at the heels from behind: **17** Whereupon there was a
sore battle, insomuch as many were slain on both parts. **18** Judas also was kil-
led, and the remnant fled. **19** THen Jonathan and Simon took Judas their
brother, and buried him in the sepulchre of his fathers in Modin. **20** Moreover
they bewailed him, and all Israel made great lamentation for him, and mourned
many days, saying, **21** How is the valiant man fallen, that delivered Isra-
el! **22** As for the other things concerning Judas and his wars, and the noble acts
which he did, and his greatness, they are not written: for they were very
many. **23** Now after the death of Judas the wicked began to put forth their he-
ads in all the coasts of Israel, and there arose up all such as wrought iniqui-
ty. **24** In those days also was there a very great famine, by reason whereof the
country revolted, and went with them. **25** Then Bacchides chose the wicked
men, and made them lords of the country. **26** And they made enquiry and se-
arch for Judas' friends, and brought them unto Bacchides, who took vengeance of
them, and used them despitefully. **27** So was there a great affliction in Israel, the
like whereof was not since the time that a prophet was not seen among
them. **28** For this cause all Judas' friends came together, and said unto Jona-
than, **29** Since thy brother Judas died, we have no man like him to go forth
against our enemies, and Bacchides, and against them of our nation that are ad-
versaries to us. **30** Now therefore we have chosen thee this day to be our prince
and captain in his stead, that thou mayest fight our battles. **31** Upon this Jona-
than took the governance upon him at that time, and rose up instead of his
brother Judas. **32** But when Bacchides gat knowledge thereof, he sought for to
slay him **33** Then Jonathan, and Simon his brother, and all that were with him,
perceiving that, fled into the wilderness of Thecoe, and pitched their tents by the
water of the pool Asphar. **34** Which when Bacchides understood, he came near
to Jordan with all his host upon the sabbath day. **35** Now Jonathan had sent his
brother John, a captain of the people, to pray his friends the Nabathites, that they
might leave with them their carriage, which was much. **36** But the children of
Jambri came out of Medaba, and took John, and all that he had, and went their
way with it. **37** After this came word to Jonathan and Simon his brother, that
the children of Jambri made a great marriage, and were bringing the bride from
Nadabatha with a great train, as being the daughter of one of the great princes of
Chanaan. **38** Therefore they remembered John their brother, and went up, and
hid themselves under the covert of the mountain: **39** Where they lifted up their
eyes, and looked, and, behold, there was much ado and great carriage: and the
bridegroom came forth, and his friends and brethren, to meet them with drums,
and instruments of musick, and many weapons. **40** Then Jonathan and they
that were with him rose up against them from the place where they lay in ambush,
and made a slaughter of them in such sort, as many fell down dead, and the rem-
nant fled into the mountain, and they took all their spoils. **41** Thus was the
marriage turned into mourning, and the noise of their melody into lamenta-
tion. **42** So when they had avenged fully the blood of their brother, they turned
again to the marsh of Jordan. **43** Now when Bacchides heard hereof, he came
on the sabbath day unto the banks of Jordan with a great power. **44** Then Jona-
than said to his company, Let us go up now and fight for our lives, for it standeth
not with us to day, as in time past: **45** For, behold, the battle is before us and
behind us, and the water of Jordan on this side and that side, the marsh likewise
and wood, neither is there place for us to turn aside. **46** Wherefore cry ye now
unto heaven, that ye may be delivered from the hand of your enemies. **47** With
that they joined battle, and Jonathan stretched forth his hand to smite Bacchides,
but he turned back from him. **48** Then Jonathan and they that were with him
leapt into Jordan, and swam over unto the other bank: howbeit the other passed
not over Jordan unto them. **49** So there were slain of Bacchides' side that day
about a thousand men. **50** Afterward returned Bacchides to Jerusalem and re-
paired the strong cites in Judea; the fort in Jericho, and Emmaus, and Bethhoron,
and Bethel, and Thamnatha, Pharathoni, and Taphon, these did he strengthen
with high walls, with gates and with bars. **51** And in them he set a garrison, that
they might work malice upon Israel. **52** He fortified also the city Bethsura, and
Gazera, and the tower, and put forces in them, and provision of victuals. **53** Be-
sides, he took the chief men's sons in the country for hostages, and put them into
the tower at Jerusalem to be kept. **54** Moreover in the hundred fifty and third
year, in the second month, Alcimus commanded that the wall of the inner court
of the sanctuary should be pulled down; he pulled down also the works of the
prophets **55** And as he began to pull down, even at that time was Alcimus pla-
gued, and his enterprizes hindered: for his mouth was stopped, and he was taken
with a palsy, so that he could no more speak any thing, nor give order concerning
his house. **56** So Alcimus died at that time with great torment. **57** Now when
Bacchides saw that Alcimus was dead, he returned to the king: whereupon the
land of Judea was in rest two years. **58** Then all the ungodly men held a council,
saying, Behold, Jonathan and his company are at ease, and dwell without care:

now therefore we will bring Bacchides hither, who shall take them all in one ni-
ght. **59** So they went and consulted with him. **60** Then removed he, and
came with a great host, and sent letters privily to his adherents in Judea, that they
should take Jonathan and those that were with him: howbeit they could not, be-
cause their counsel was known unto them. **61** Wherefore they took of the men
of the country, that were authors of that mischief, about fifty persons, and slew
them. **62** Afterward Jonathan, and Simon, and they that were with him, got
them away to Bethbasi, which is in the wilderness, and they repaired the decays
thereof, and made it strong. **63** Which thing when Bacchides knew, he gathe-
red together all his host, and sent word to them that were of Judea. **64** Then
went he and laid siege against Bethbasi; and they fought against it a long season
and made engines of war. **65** But Jonathan left his brother Simon in the city,
and went forth himself into the country, and with a certain number went he for-
th. **66** And he smote Odonarkes and his brethren, and the children of Phasiron
in their tent. **67** And when he began to smite them, and came up with his for-
ces, Simon and his company went out of the city, and burned up the engines of
war, **68** And fought against Bacchides, who was discomfited by them, and they
afflicted him sore: for his counsel and travail was in vain. **69** Wherefore he was
very wroth at the wicked men that gave him counsel to come into the country,
inasmuch as he slew many of them, and purposed to return into his own coun-
try. **70** Whereof when Jonathan had knowledge, he sent ambassadors unto him,
to the end he should make peace with him, and deliver them the priso-
ners. **71** Which thing he accepted, and did according to his demands, and swa-
re unto him that he would never do him harm all the days of his life. **72** When
therefore he had restored unto him the prisoners that he had taken aforetime out
of the land of Judea, he returned and went his way into his own land, neither
came he any more into their borders. **73** Thus the sword ceased from Israel: but
Jonathan dwelt at Machmas, and began to govern the people; and he destroyed
the ungodly men out of Israel.

10

1 In the hundred and sixtieth year Alexander, the son of Antiochus
surnamed Epiphanes, went up and took Ptolemais: for the people had
received him, by means whereof he reigned there, **2** Now when king Demetrius
heard thereof, he gathered together an exceeding great host, and went forth
against him to fight. **3** Moreover Demetrius sent letters unto Jonathan with
loving words, so as he magnified him. **4** For said he, Let us first make peace with
him, before he join with Alexander against us: **5** Else he will remember all the
evils that we have done against him, and against his brethren and his peo-
ple. **6** Wherefore he gave him authority to gather together an host, and to pro-
vide weapons, that he might aid him in battle: he commanded also that the hosta-
ges that were in the tower should be delivered him. **7** Then came Jonathan to
Jerusalem, and read the letters in the audience of all the people, and of them that
were in the tower: **8** Who were sore afraid, when they heard that the king had
given him authority to gather together an host. **9** Whereupon they of the tower
delivered their hostages unto Jonathan, and he delivered them unto their paren-
ts. **10** This done, Jonathan settled himself in Jerusalem, and began to build and
repair the city. **11** And he commanded the workmen to build the walls and the
mount Sion and about with square stones for fortification; and they did
so. **12** Then the strangers, that were in the fortresses which Bacchides had built,
fled away; **13** Insomuch as every man left his place, and went into his own
country. **14** Only at Bethsura certain of those that had forsaken the law and the
commandments remained still: for it was their place of refuge. **15** Now when
king Alexander had heard what promises Demetrius had sent unto Jonathan:
when also it was told him of the battles and noble acts which he and his brethren
had done, and of the pains that they had endured, **16** He said, Shall we find
such another man? now therefore we will make him our friend and confedera-
te. **17** Upon this he wrote a letter, and sent it unto him, according to these
words, saying, **18** King Alexander to his brother Jonathan sendeth gree-
ting: **19** We have heard of thee, that thou art a man of great power, and meet to
be our friend. **20** Wherefore now this day we ordain thee to be the high priest
of thy nation, and to be called the king's friend; (and therewithal he sent him a
purple robe and a crown of gold:) and require thee to take our part, and keep
friendship with us. **21** So in the seventh month of the hundred and sixtieth
year, at the feast of the tabernacles, Jonathan put on the holy robe, and gathered
together forces, and provided much armour. **22** Whereof when Demetrius he-
ard, he was very sorry, and said, **23** What have we done, that Alexander hath
prevented us in making amity with the Jews to strengthen himself? **24** I also
will write unto them words of encouragement, and promise them dignities and
gifts, that I may have their aid. **25** He sent unto them therefore to this effect:
King Demetrius unto the people of the Jews sendeth greeting: **26** Whereas ye
have kept covenants with us, and continued in our friendship, not joining your-
selves with our enemies, we have heard hereof, and are glad. **27** Wherefore now
continue ye still to be faithful unto us, and we will well recompense you for the
things ye do in our behalf, **28** And will grant you many immunities, and give
you rewards. **29** And now do I free you, and for your sake I release all the Jews,
from tributes, and from the customs of salt, and from crown taxes, **30** And
from that which appertaineth unto me to receive for the third part or the seed,
and the half of the fruit of the trees, I release it from this day forth, so that they
shall not be taken of the land of Judea, nor of the three governments which are
added thereunto out of the country of Samaria and Galilee, from this day forth
for evermore. **31** Let Jerusalem also be holy and free, with the borders thereof,
both from tenths and tributes. **32** And as for the tower which is at Jerusalem, I
yield up authority over it, and give the high priest, that he may set in it such men
as he shall choose to keep it. **33** Moreover I freely set at liberty every one of the
Jews, that were carried captives out of the land of Judea into any part of my king-
dom, and I will that all my officers remit the tributes even of their cattle. **34** Fur-
thermore I will that all the feasts, and sabbaths, and new moons, and solemn days,
and the three days before the feast, and the three days after the feast shall be all of
immunity and freedom for all the Jews in my realm. **35** Also no man shall have
authority to meddle with or to molest any of them in any matter. **36** I will
further, that there be enrolled among the king's forces about thirty thousand men
of the Jews, unto whom pay shall be given, as belongeth to all king's for-
ces. **37** And of them some shall be placed in the king's strong holds, of whom
also some shall be set over the affairs of the kingdom, which are of trust: and I will
that their overseers and governors be of themselves, and that they live after their
own laws, even as the king hath commanded in the land of Judea. **38** And
concerning the three governments that are added to Judea from the country of
Samaria, let them be joined with Judea, that they may be reckoned to be under
one, nor bound to obey other authority than the high priest's. **39** As for Ptole-
mais, and the land pertaining thereto, I give it as a free gift to the sanctuary at
Jerusalem for the necessary expences of the sanctuary. **40** Moreover I give every
year fifteen thousand shekels of silver out of the king's accounts from the places
appertaining. **41** And all the overplus, which the officers payed not in as in
former time, from henceforth shall be given toward the works of the tem-
ple. **42** And beside this, the five thousand shekels of silver, which they took
from the uses of the temple out of the accounts year by year, even those things
shall be released, because they appertain to the priests that minister. **43** And
whosoever they be that flee unto the temple at Jerusalem, or be within the liberties
hereof, being indebted unto the king, or for any other matter, let them be at liber-
ty, and all that they have in my realm. **44** For the building also and repairing of
the works of the sanctuary expences shall be given of the king's accounts. **45** Yea,
and for the building of the walls of Jerusalem, and the fortifying thereof round
about, expences shall be given out of the king's accounts, as also for the building
of the walls in Judea. **46** Now when Jonathan and the people heard these words,
they gave no credit unto them, nor received them, because they remembered the
great evil that he had done in Israel; for he had afflicted them very sore. **47** But
with Alexander they were well pleased, because he was the first that entreated of
true peace with them, and they were confederate with him always. **48** Then
gathered king Alexander great forces, and camped over against Demetri-
us. **49** And after the two kings had joined battle, Demetrius' host fled: but
Alexander followed after him, and prevailed against them. **50** And he conti-
nued the battle very sore until the sun went down: and that day was Demetrius
slain. **51** Afterward Alexander sent ambassadors to Ptolemee king of Egypt with
a message to this effect: **52** Forasmuch as I am come again to my realm, and am
set in the throne of my progenitors, and have gotten the dominion, and over-
thrown Demetrius, and recovered our country; **53** For after I had joined battle
with him, both he and his host was discomfited by us, so that we sit in the throne
of his kingdom: **54** Now therefore let us make a league of amity together, and
give me now thy daughter to wife: and I will be thy son in law, and will give both
thee and her as according to thy dignity. **55** Then Ptolemee the king gave an-
swer, saying, Happy be the day wherein thou didst return into the land of thy
fathers, and satest in the throne of their kingdom. **56** And now will I do to thee,
as thou hast written: meet me therefore at Ptolemais, that we may see one another;
for I will marry my daughter to thee according to thy desire. **57** So Ptolemee
went out of Egypt with his daughter Cleopatra, and they came unto Ptolemais in
the hundred threescore and second year: **58** Where king Alexander meeting
him, he gave unto him his daughter Cleopatra, and celebrated her marriage at
Ptolemais with great glory, as the manner of kings is. **59** Now king Alexander
had written unto Jonathan, that he should come and meet him. **60** Who the-
reupon went honourably to Ptolemais, where he met the two kings, and gave
them and their friends silver and gold, and many presents, and found favour in
their sight. **61** At that time certain pestilent fellows of Israel, men of a wicked
life, assembled themselves against him, to accuse him: but the king would not
hear them. **62** Yea more than that, the king commanded to take off his garmen-
ts, and clothe him in purple: and they did so. **63** And he made him sit by
himself, and said into his princes, Go with him into the midst of the city, and
make proclamation, that no man complain against him of any matter, and that no
man trouble him for any manner of cause. **64** Now when his accusers saw that
he was honored according to the proclamation, and clothed in purple, they fled
all away. **65** So the king honoured him, and wrote him among his chief friends,
and made him a duke, and partaker of his dominion. **66** Afterward Jonathan
returned to Jerusalem with peace and gladness. **67** Furthermore in the; hun-
dred threescore and fifth year came Demetrius son of Demetrius out of Crete into
the land of his fathers: **68** Whereof when king Alexander heard tell, he was ri-
ght sorry, and returned into Antioch. **69** Then Demetrius made Apollonius the
governor of Celosyria his general, who gathered together a great host, and camped
in Jamnia, and sent unto Jonathan the high priest, saying, **70** Thou alone liftest
up thyself against us, and I am laughed to scorn for thy sake, and reproached: and
why dost thou vaunt thy power against us in the mountains? **71** Now therefore,
if thou trustest in thine own strength, come down to us into the plain field, and
there let us try the matter together: for with me is the power of the cities. **72** Ask

and learn who I am, and the rest that take our part, and they shall tell thee that
thy foot is not able to to flight in their own land. **73** Wherefore now thou shalt
not be able to abide the horsemen and so great a power in the plain, where is
neither stone nor flint, nor place to flee unto. **74** So when Jonathan heard these
words of Apollonius, he was moved in his mind, and choosing ten thousand men
he went out of Jerusalem, where Simon his brother met him for to help
him. **75** And he pitched his tents against Joppa: but; they of Joppa shut him out
of the city, because Apollonius had a garrison there. **76** Then Jonathan laid
siege unto it: whereupon they of the city let him in for fear: and so Jonathan won
Joppa. **77** Whereof when Apollonius heard, he took three thousand horsemen,
with a great host of footmen, and went to Azotus as one that journeyed, and
therewithal drew him forth into the plain. because he had a great number of
horsemen, in whom he put his trust. **78** Then Jonathan followed after him to
Azotus, where the armies joined battle. **79** Now Apollonius had left a thousand
horsemen in ambush. **80** And Jonathan knew that there was an ambushment
behind him; for they had compassed in his host, and cast darts at the people, from
morning till evening. **81** But the people stood still, as Jonathan had comman-
ded them: and so the enemies' horses were tired. **82** Then brought Simon forth
his host, and set them against the footmen, (for the horsemen were spent) who
were discomfited by him, and fled. **83** The horsemen also, being scattered in
the field, fled to Azotus, and went into Bethdagon, their idol's temple, for sa-
fety. **84** But Jonathan set fire on Azotus, and the cities round about it, and took
their spoils; and the temple of Dagon, with them that were fled into it, he burned
with fire. **85** Thus there were burned and slain with the sword well nigh eight
thousand men. **86** And from thence Jonathan removed his host, and camped
against Ascalon, where the men of the city came forth, and met him with great
pomp. **87** After this returned Jonathan and his host unto Jerusalem, having any
spoils. **88** Now when king ALexander heard these things, he honoured Jona-
than yet more. **89** And sent him a buckle of gold, as the use is to be given to
such as are of the king's blood: he gave him also Accaron with the borders thereof
in possession.

11

1 And the king of Egypt gathered together a great host, like the sand
that lieth upon the sea shore, and many ships, and went about through
deceit to get Alexander's kingdom, and join it to his own. **2** Whereupon he took
his journey into Spain in peaceable manner, so as they of the cities opened unto
him, and met him: for king Alexander had commanded them so to do, because he
was his brother in law. **3** Now as Ptolemee entered into the cities, he set in every
one of them a garrison of soldiers to keep it. **4** And when he came near to Azo-
tus, they shewed him the temple of Dagon that was burnt, and Azotus and the
suburbs thereof that were destroyed, and the bodies that were cast abroad and
them that he had burnt in the battle; for they had made heaps of them by the way
where he should pass. **5** Also they told the king whatsoever Jonathan had done,
to the intent he might blame him: but the king held his peace. **6** Then Jonathan
met the king with great pomp at Joppa, where they saluted one another, and lod-
ged. **7** Afterward Jonathan, when he had gone with the king to the river called
Eleutherus, returned again to Jerusalem. **8** King Ptolemee therefore, having
gotten the dominion of the cities by the sea unto Seleucia upon the sea coast,
imagined wicked counsels against Alexander. **9** Whereupon he sent ambasadors
unto king Demetrius, saying, Come, let us make a league betwixt us, and I will
give thee my daughter whom Alexander hath, and thou shalt reign in thy father's
kingdom: **10** For I repent that I gave my daughter unto him, for he sought to
slay me. **11** Thus did he slander him, because he was desirous of his king-
dom. **12** Wherefore he took his daughter from him, and gave her to Demetrius,
and forsook Alexander, so that their hatred was openly known. **13** Then Ptole-
mee entered into Antioch, where he set two crowns upon his head, the crown of
Asia, and of Egypt. **14** In the mean season was king Alexander in Cilicia, becau-
se those that dwelt in those parts had revolted from him. **15** But when Alexan-
der heard of this, he came to war against him: whereupon king Ptolemee brought
forth his host, and met him with a mighty power, and put him to flight. **16** So
Alexander fled into Arabia there to be defended; but king Ptolemee was exal-
ted: **17** For Zabdiel the Arabian took off Alexander's head, and sent it unto
Ptolemee. **18** King Ptolemee also died the third day after, and they that were in
the strong holds were slain one of another. **19** By this means Demetrius reigned
in the hundred threescore and seventh year. **20** At the same time Jonathan ga-
thered together them that were in Judea to take the tower that was in Jerusalem:
and he made many engines of war against it. **21** Then came ungodly persons,
who hated their own people, went unto the king, and told him that Jonathan
besieged the tower, **22** Whereof when he heard, he was angry, and immediately
removing, he came to Ptolemais, and wrote unto Jonathan, that he should not lay
siege to the tower, but come and speak with him at Ptolemais in great ha-
ste. **23** Nevertheless Jonathan, when he heard this, commanded to besiege it
still: and he chose certain of the elders of Israel and the priests, and put himself in
peril; **24** And took silver and gold, and raiment, and divers presents besides,
and went to Ptolemais unto the king, where he found favour in his sight. **25** And
though certain ungodly men of the people had made complaints against
him, **26** Yet the king entreated him as his predecessors had done before, and
promoted him in the sight of all his friends, **27** And confirmed him in the high
priesthood, and in all the honours that he had before, and gave him preeminence
among his chief friends. **28** Then Jonathan desired the king, that he would
make Judea free from tribute, as also the three governments, with the country of
Samaria; and he promised him three hundred talents. **29** So the king consen-
ted, and wrote letters unto Jonathan of all these things after this man-
ner: **30** King Demetrius unto his brother Jonathan, and unto the nation of the
Jews, sendeth greeting: **31** We send you here a copy of the letter which we did
write unto our cousin Lasthenes concerning you, that ye might see it. **32** King
Demetrius unto his father Lasthenes sendeth greeting: **33** We are determined to
do good to the people of the Jews, who are our friends, and keep covenants with
us, because of their good will toward us. **34** Wherefore we have ratified unto
them the borders of Judea, with the three governments of Apherema and Lydda
and Ramathem, that are added unto Judea from the country of Samaria, and all
things appertaining unto them, for all such as do sacrifice in Jerusalem, instead of
the payments which the king received of them yearly aforetime out of the fruits of
the earth and of trees. **35** And as for other things that belong unto us, of the
tithes and customs pertaining unto us, as also the saltpits, and the crown taxes,
which are due unto us, we discharge them of them all for their relief. **36** And
nothing hereof shall be revoked from this time forth for ever. **37** Now therefore
see that thou make a copy of these things, and let it be delivered unto Jonathan,
and set upon the holy mount in a conspicuous place. **38** After this, when king
Demetrius saw that the land was quiet before him, and that no resistance was
made against him, he sent away all his forces, every one to his own place, except
certain bands of strangers, whom he had gathered from the isles of the heathen:
wherefore all the forces of his fathers hated him. **39** Moreover there was one
Tryphon, that had been of Alexander's part afore, who, seeing that all the host
murmured against Demetrius, went to Simalcue the Arabian that brought up
Antiochus the young son of Alexander, **40** And lay sore upon him to deliver
him this young Antiochus, that he might reign in his father's stead: he told him
therefore all that Demetrius had done, and how his men of war were at enmity
with him, and there he remained a long season. **41** In the mean time Jonathan
sent unto king Demetrius, that he would cast those of the tower out of Jerusalem,
and those also in the fortresses: for they fought against Israel. **42** So Demetrius
sent unto Jonathan, saying, I will not only do this for thee and thy people, but I
will greatly honour thee and thy nation, if opportunity serve. **43** Now therefore
thou shalt do well, if thou send me men to help me; for all my forces are gone
from me. **44** Upon this Jonathan sent him three thousand strong men unto
Antioch: and when they came to the king, the king was very glad of their co-
ming. **45** Howbeit they that were of the city gathered themselves together into
the midst of the city, to the number of an hundred and twenty thousand men, and
would have slain the king. **46** Wherefore the king fled into the court, but they
of the city kept the passages of the city, and began to fight. **47** Then the king
called to the Jews for help, who came unto him all at once, and dispersing them-
selves through the city slew that day in the city to the number of an hundred
thousand. **48** Also they set fire on the city, and gat many spoils that day, and
delivered the king. **49** So when they of the city saw that the Jews had got the
city as they would, their courage was abated: wherefore they made supplication to
the king, and cried, saying, **50** Grant us peace, and let the Jews cease from as-
saulting us and the city. **51** With that they cast away their weapons, and made
peace; and the Jews were honoured in the sight of the king, and in the sight of all
that were in his realm; and they returned to Jerusalem, having great spoils. **52** So
king Demetrius sat on the throne of his kingdom, and the land was quiet before
him. **53** Nevertheless he dissembled in all that ever he spake, and estranged
himself from Jonathan, neither rewarded he him according to the benefits which
he had received of him, but troubled him very sore. **54** After this returned
Tryphon, and with him the young child Antiochus, who reigned, and was crow-
ned. **55** Then there gathered unto him all the men of war, whom Demetrius
had put away, and they fought against Demetrius, who turned his back and
fled. **56** Moreover Tryphon took the elephants, and won Antioch. **57** At that
time young Antiochus wrote unto Jonathan, saying, I confirm thee in the high
priesthood, and appoint thee ruler over the four governments, and to be one of
the king's friends. **58** Upon this he sent him golden vessels to be served in, and
gave him leave to drink in gold, and to be clothed in purple, and to wear a golden
buckle. **59** His brother Simon also he made captain from the place called The
ladder of Tyrus unto the borders of Egypt. **60** Then Jonathan went forth, and
passed through the cities beyond the water, and all the forces of Syria gathered
themselves unto him for to help him: and when he came to Ascalon, they of the
city met him honourably. **61** From whence he went to Gaza, but they of Gaza
shut him out; wherefore he laid siege unto it, and burned the suburbs thereof with
fire, and spoiled them. **62** Afterward, when they of Gaza made supplication
unto Jonathan, he made peace with them, and took the sons of their chief men for
hostages, and sent them to Jerusalem, and passed through the country unto Da-
mascus. **63** Now when Jonathan heard that Demetrius' princes were come to
Cades, which is in Galilee, with a great power, purposing to remove him out of
the country, **64** He went to meet them, and left Simon his brother in the coun-
try. **65** Then Simon encamped against Bethsura and fought against it a long
season, and shut it up: **66** But they desired to have peace with him, which he
granted them, and then put them out from thence, and took the city, and set a
garrison in it. **67** As for Jonathan and his host, they pitched at the water of
Gennesar, from whence betimes in the morning they gat them to the plain of
Nasor. **68** And, behold, the host of strangers met them in the plain, who, ha-
ving laid men in ambush for him in the mountains, came themselves over against
him. **69** So when they that lay in ambush rose out of their places and joined

battle, all that were of Jonathan's side fled; **70** Insomuch as there was not one of
them left, except Mattathias the son of Absalom, and Judas the son of Calphi, the
captains of the host. **71** Then Jonathan rent his clothes, and cast earth upon his
head, and prayed. **72** Afterwards turning again to battle, he put them to flight,
and so they ran away. **73** Now when his own men that were fled saw this, they
turned again unto him, and with him pursued them to Cades, even unto their
own tents, and there they camped. **74** So there were slain of the heathen that
day about three thousand men: but Jonathan returned to Jerusalem.

12 1 Now when Jonathan saw that time served him, he chose certain
men, and sent them to Rome, for to confirm and renew the friendship
that they had with them. **2** He sent letters also to the Lacedemonians, and to
other places, for the same purpose. **3** So they went unto Rome, and entered
into the senate, and said, Jonathan the high priest, and the people of the Jews,
sent us unto you, to the end ye should renew the friendship, which ye had with
them, and league, as in former time. **4** Upon this the Romans gave them letters
unto the governors of every place that they should bring them into the land of
Judea peaceably. **5** And this is the copy of the letters which Jonathan wrote to
the Lacedemonians: **6** Jonathan the high priest, and the elders of the nation,
and the priests, and the other of the Jews, unto the Lacedemonians their brethren
send greeting: **7** There were letters sent in times past unto Onias the high priest
from Darius, who reigned then among you, to signify that ye are our brethren,
as the copy here underwritten doth specify. **8** At which time Onias entreated
the ambassador that was sent honourably, and received the letters, wherein de-
claration was made of the league and friendship. **9** Therefore we also, albeit
we need none of these things, that we have the holy books of scripture in our
hands to comfort us, **10** Have nevertheless attempted to send unto you for the
renewing of brotherhood and friendship, lest we should become strangers unto
you altogether: for there is a long time passed since ye sent unto us. **11** We the-
refore at all times without ceasing, both in our feasts, and other convenient days,
do remember you in the sacrifices which we offer, and in our prayers, as reason
is, and as it becometh us to think upon our brethren: **12** And we are right glad
of your honour. **13** As for ourselves, we have had great troubles and wars on
every side, forsomuch as the kings that are round about us have fought against
us. **14** Howbeit we would not be troublesome unto you, nor to others of our
confederates and friends, in these wars: **15** For we have help from heaven that
succoureth us, so as we are delivered from our enemies, and our enemies are brou-
ght under foot. **16** For this cause we chose Numenius the son of Antiochus, and
Antipater he son of Jason, and sent them unto the Romans, to renew the amity
that we had with them, and the former league. **17** We commanded them also to
go unto you, and to salute and to deliver you our letters concerning the renewing
of our brotherhood. **18** Wherefore now ye shall do well to give us an answer
thereto. **19** And this is the copy of the letters which Oniares sent. **20** Areus
king of the Lacedemonians to Onias the high priest, greeting: **21** It is found in
writing, that the Lacedemonians and Jews are brethren, and that they are of the
stock of Abraham: **22** Now therefore, since this is come to our knowledge, ye
shall do well to write unto us of your prosperity. **23** We do write back again to
you, that your cattle and goods are our's, and our's are your's We do command
therefore our ambassadors to make report unto you on this wise. **24** Now when
Jonathan heard that Demebius' princes were come to fight against him with a
greater host than afore, **25** He removed from Jerusalem, and met them in the
land of Amathis: for he gave them no respite to enter his country. **26** He sent
spies also unto their tents, who came again, and told him that they were appoin-
ted to come upon them in the night season. **27** Wherefore so soon as the sun
was down, Jonathan commanded his men to watch, and to be in arms, that all the
night long they might be ready to fight: also he sent forth centinels round about
the host. **28** But when the adversaries heard that Jonathan and his men were
ready for battle, they feared, and trembled in their hearts, and they kindled fires
in their camp. **29** Howbeit Jonathan and his company knew it not till the mor-
ning: for they saw the lights burning. **30** Then Jonathan pursued after them,
but overtook them not: for they were gone over the river Eleutherus. **31** Whe-
refore Jonathan turned to the Arabians, who were called Zabadeans, and smote
them, and took their spoils. **32** And removing thence, he came to Damascus,
and so passed through all the country, **33** Simon also went forth, and passed
through the country unto Ascalon, and the holds there adjoining, from whence
he turned aside to Joppa, and won it. **34** For he had heard that they would
deliver the hold unto them that took Demetrius' part; wherefore he set a garrison
there to keep it. **35** After this came Jonathan home again, and calling the elders
of the people together, he consulted with them about building strong holds in
Judea, **36** And making the walls of Jerusalem higher, and raising a great mount
between the tower and the city, for to separate it from the city, that so it might
be alone, that men might neither sell nor buy in it. **37** Upon this they came
together to build up the city, forasmuch as part of the wall toward the brook on
the east side was fallen down, and they repaired that which was called Caphena-
tha. **38** Simon also set up Adida in Sephela, and made it strong with gates and
bars. **39** Now Tryphon went about to get the kingdom of Asia, and to kill An-
tiochus the king, that he might set the crown upon his own head. **40** Howbeit
he was afraid that Jonathan would not suffer him, and that he would fight against
him; wherefore he sought a way how to take Jonathan, that he might kill him.
So he removed, and came to Bethsan. **41** Then Jonathan went out to meet him
with forty thousand men chosen for the battle, and came to Bethsan. **42** Now
when Tryphon saw Jonathan came with so great a force, he durst not stretch
his hand against him; **43** But received him honourably, and commended him
unto all his friends, and gave him gifts, and commanded his men of war to be
as obedient unto him, as to himself. **44** Unto Jonathan also he said, Why hast
thou brought all this people to so great trouble, seeing there is no war betwixt
us? **45** Therefore send them now home again, and choose a few men to wait
on thee, and come thou with me to Ptolemais, for I will give it thee, and the
rest of the strong holds and forces, and all that have any charge: as for me, I will
return and depart: for this is the cause of my coming. **46** So Jonathan belie-
ving him did as he bade him, and sent away his host, who went into the land of
Judea. **47** And with himself he retained but three thousand men, of whom he
sent two thousand into Galilee, and one thousand went with him. **48** Now as
soon as Jonathan entered into Ptolemais, they of Ptolemais shut the gates and
took him, and all them that came with him they slew with the sword. **49** Then
sent Tryphon an host of footmen and horsemen into Galilee, and into the great
plain, to destroy all Jonathan's company. **50** But when they knew that Jonathan
and they that were with him were taken and slain, they encouraged one another;
and went close together, prepared to fight. **51** They therefore that followed
upon them, perceiving that they were ready to fight for their lives, turned back
again. **52** Whereupon they all came into the land of Judea peaceably, and there
they bewailed Jonathan, and them that were with him, and they were sore afraid;
wherefore all Israel made great lamentation. **53** Then all the heathen that were
round about then sought to destroy them: for said they, They have no captain, nor
any to help them: now therefore let us make war upon them, and take away their
memorial from among men.

13 1 Now when Simon heard that Tryphon had gathered together a great
host to invade the land of Judea, and destroy it, **2** And saw that the
people was in great trembling and fear, he went up to Jerusalem, and gathered the
people together, **3** And gave them exhortation, saying, Ye yourselves know what
great things I, and my brethren, and my father's house, have done for the laws
and the sanctuary, the battles also and troubles which we have seen. **4** By reason
whereof all my brethren are slain for Israel's sake, and I am left alone. **5** Now
therefore be it far from me, that I should spare mine own life in any time of trou-
ble: for I am no better than my brethren. **6** Doubtless I will avenge my nation,
and the sanctuary, and our wives, and our children: for all the heathen are gathe-
red to destroy us of very malice. **7** Now as soon as the people heard these words,
their spirit revived. **8** And they answered with a loud voice, saying, Thou shalt
be our leader instead of Judas and Jonathan thy brother. **9** Fight thou our batt-
les, and whatsoever, thou commandest us, that will we do. **10** So then he gathe-
red together all the men of war, and made haste to finish the walls of Jerusalem,
and he fortified it round about. **11** Also he sent Jonathan the son of Absolom,
and with him a great power, to Joppa: who casting out them that were therein re-
mained there in it. **12** So Tryphon removed from Ptolemaus with a great power
to invade the land of Judea, and Jonathan was with him in ward. **13** But Simon
pitched his tents at Adida, over against the plain. **14** Now when Tryphon knew
that Simon was risen up instead of his brother Jonathan, and meant to join battle
with him, he sent messengers unto him, saying, **15** Whereas we have Jonathan
thy brother in hold, it is for money that he is owing unto the king's treasure, con-
cerning the business that was committed unto him. **16** Wherefore now send
an hundred talents of silver, and two of his sons for hostages, that when he is at
liberty he may not revolt from us, and we will let him go. **17** Hereupon Simon,
albeit he perceived that they spake deceitfully unto him yet sent he the money
and the children, lest peradventure he should procure to himself great hatred of
the people: **18** Who might have said, Because I sent him not the money and
the children, therefore is Jonathan dead. **19** So he sent them the children and
the hundred talents: howbeit Tryphon dissembled neither would he let Jonathan
go. **20** And after this came Tryphon to invade the land, and destroy it, going
round about by the way that leadeth unto Adora: but Simon and his host marched
against him in every place, wheresoever he went. **21** Now they that were in the
tower sent messengers unto Tryphon, to the end that he should hasten his coming
unto them by the wilderness, and send them victuals. **22** Wherefore Tryphon
made ready all his horsemen to come that night: but there fell a very great snow,
by reason whereof he came not. So he departed, and came into the country of Ga-
laad. **23** And when he came near to Bascama he slew Jonathan, who was buried
there. **24** Afterward Tryphon returned and went into his own land. **25** Then
sent Simon, and took the bones of Jonathan his brother, and buried them in
Modin, the city of his fathers. **26** And all Israel made great lamentation for
him, and bewailed him many days. **27** Simon also built a monument upon the
sepulchre of his father and his brethren, and raised it aloft to the sight, with hewn
stone behind and before. **28** Moreover he set up seven pyramids, one against
another, for his father, and his mother, and his four brethren. **29** And in these
he made cunning devices, about the which he set great pillars, and upon the pillars
he made all their armour for a perpetual memory, and by the armour ships carved,
that they might be seen of all that sail on the sea. **30** This is the sepulchre which
he made at Modin, and it standeth yet unto this day. **31** Now Tryphon dealt
deceitfully with the young king Antiochus, and slew him. **32** And he reigned
in his stead, and crowned himself king of Asia, and brought a great calamity
upon the land. **33** Then Simon built up the strong holds in Judea, and fenced

them about with high towers, and great walls, and gates, and bars, and laid up victuals therein. **34** Moreover Simon chose men, and sent to king Demetrius, to the end he should give the land an immunity, because all that Tryphon did was to spoil. **35** Unto whom king Demetrius answered and wrote after this manner: **36** King Demetrius unto Simon the high priest, and friend of kings, as also unto the elders and nation of the Jews, sendeth greeting: **37** The golden crown, and the scarlet robe, which ye sent unto us, we have received: and we are ready to make a stedfast peace with you, yea, and to write unto our officers, to confirm the immunities which we have granted. **38** And whatsoever covenants we have made with you shall stand; and the strong holds, which ye have builded, shall be your own. **39** As for any oversight or fault committed unto this day, we forgive it, and the crown tax also, which ye owe us: and if there were any other tribute paid in Jerusalem, it shall no more be paid. **40** And look who are meet among you to be in our court, let then be enrolled, and let there be peace betwixt us. **41** Thus the yoke of the heathen was taken away from Israel in the hundred and seventieth year. **42** Then the people of Israel began to write in their instruments and contracts, In the first year of Simon the high priest, the governor and leader of the Jews. **43** In those days Simon camped against Gaza and besieged it round about; he made also an engine of war, and set it by the city, and battered a certain tower, and took it. **44** And they that were in the engine leaped into the city; whereupon there was a great uproar in the city: **45** Insomuch as the people of the city rent their clothes, and climbed upon the walls with their wives and children, and cried with a loud voice, beseeching Simon to grant them peace. **46** And they said, Deal not with us according to our wickedness, but according to thy mercy. **47** So Simon was appeased toward them, and fought no more against them, but put them out of the city, and cleansed the houses wherein the idols were, and so entered into it with songs and thanksgiving. **48** Yea, he put all uncleanness out of it, and placed such men there as would keep the law, and made it stronger than it was before, and built therein a dwellingplace for himself. **49** They also of the tower in Jerusalem were kept so strait, that they could neither come forth, nor go into the country, nor buy, nor sell: wherefore they were in great distress for want of victuals, and a great number of them perished through famine. **50** Then cried they to Simon, beseeching him to be at one with them: which thing he granted them; and when he had put them out from thence, he cleansed the tower from pollutions: **51** And entered into it the three and twentieth day of the second month in the hundred seventy and first year, with thanksgiving, and branches of palm trees, and with harps, and cymbals, and with viols, and hymns, and songs: because there was destroyed a great enemy out of Israel. **52** He ordained also that that day should be kept every year with gladness. Moreover the hill of the temple that was by the tower he made stronger than it was, and there he dwelt himself with his company. **53** And when Simon saw that John his son was a valiant man, he made him captain of all the hosts; and he dwelt in Gazera.

14 **1** Now in the hundred threescore and twelfth year king Demetrius gathered his forces together, and went into Media to get him help to fight against Tryphone. **2** But when Arsaces, the king of Persia and Media, heard that Demetrius was entered within his borders, he sent one of his princes to take him alive: **3** Who went and smote the host of Demetrius, and took him, and brought him to Arsaces, by whom he was put in ward. **4** As for the land of Judea, that was quiet all the days of Simon; for he sought the good of his nation in such wise, as that evermore his authority and honour pleased them well. **5** And as he was honourable in all his acts, so in this, that he took Joppa for an haven, and made an entrance to the isles of the sea, **6** And enlarged the bounds of his nation, and recovered the country, **7** And gathered together a great number of captives, and had the dominion of Gazera, and Bethsura, and the tower, out of the which he took all uncleaness, neither was there any that resisted him. **8** Then did they till their ground in peace, and the earth gave her increase, and the trees of the field their fruit. **9** The ancient men sat all in the streets, communing together of good things, and the young men put on glorious and warlike apparel. **10** He provided victuals for the cities, and set in them all manner of munition, so that his honourable name was renowned unto the end of the world. **11** He made peace in the land, and Israel rejoiced with great joy: **12** For every man sat under his vine and his fig tree, and there was none to fray them: **13** Neither was there any left in the land to fight against them: yea, the kings themselves were overthrown in those days. **14** Moreover he strengthened all those of his people that were brought low: the law he searched out; and every contemner of the law and wicked person he took away. **15** He beautified the sanctuary, and multiplied vessels of the temple. **16** Now when it was heard at Rome, and as far as Sparta, that Jonathan was dead, they were very sorry. **17** But as soon as they heard that his brother Simon was made high priest in his stead, and ruled the country, and the cities therein: **18** They wrote unto him in tables of brass, to renew the friendship and league which they had made with Judas and Jonathan his brethren: **19** Which writings were read before the congregation at Jerusalem. **20** And this is the copy of the letters that the Lacedemonians sent; The rulers of the Lacedemonians, with the city, unto Simon the high priest, and the elders, and priests, and residue of the people of the Jews, our brethren, send greeting: **21** The ambassadors that were sent unto our people certified us of your glory and honour: wherefore we were glad of their coming, **22** And did register the things that they spake in the council of the people in this manner; Numenius son of Antiochus, and Antipater son of Jason, the Jews' ambassadors, came unto us to renew the friendship they had with us. **23** And it pleased the people to entertain the men honourably, and to put the copy of their ambassage in publick records, to the end the people of the Lacedemonians might have a memorial thereof: furthermore we have written a copy thereof unto Simon the high priest. **24** After this Simon sent Numenius to Rome with a great shield of gold of a thousand pound weight to confirm the league with them. **25** Whereof when the people heard, they said, What thanks shall we give to Simon and his sons? **26** For he and his brethren and the house of his father have established Israel, and chased away in fight their enemies from them, and confirmed their liberty. **27** So then they wrote it in tables of brass, which they set upon pillars in mount Sion: and this is the copy of the writing; The eighteenth day of the month Elul, in the hundred threescore and twelfth year, being the third year of Simon the high priest, **28** At Saramel in the great congregation of the priests, and people, and rulers of the nation, and elders of the country, were these things notified unto us. **29** Forasmuch as oftentimes there have been wars in the country, wherein for the maintenance of their sanctuary, and the law, Simon the son of Mattathias, of the posterity of Jarib, together with his brethren, put themselves in jeopardy, and resisting the enemies of their nation did their nation great honour: **30** (For after that Jonathan, having gathered his nation together, and been their high priest, was added to his people, **31** Their enemies prepared to invade their country, that they might destroy it, and lay hands on the sanctuary: **32** At which time Simon rose up, and fought for his nation, and spent much of his own substance, and armed the valiant men of his nation and gave them wages, **33** And fortified the cities of Judea, together with Bethsura, that lieth upon the borders of Judea, where the armour of the enemies had been before; but he set a garrison of Jews there: **34** Moreover he fortified Joppa, which lieth upon the sea, and Gazera, that bordereth upon Azotus, where the enemies had dwelt before: but he placed Jews there, and furnished them with all things convenient for the reparation thereof.) **35** The people therefore sang the acts of Simon, and unto what glory he thought to bring his nation, made him their governor and chief priest, because he had done all these things, and for the justice and faith which he kept to his nation, and for that he sought by all means to exalt his people. **36** For in his time things prospered in his hands, so that the heathen were taken out of their country, and they also that were in the city of David in Jerusalem, who had made themselves a tower, out of which they issued, and polluted all about the sanctuary, and did much hurt in the holy place: **37** But he placed Jews therein. and fortified it for the safety of the country and the city, and raised up the walls of Jerusalem. **38** King Demetrius also confirmed him in the high priesthood according to those things, **39** And made him one of his friends, and honoured him with great honour. **40** For he had heard say, that the Romans had called the Jews their friends and confederates and brethren; and that they had entertained the ambassadors of Simon honourably; **41** Also that the Jews and priests were well pleased that Simon should be their governor and high priest for ever, until there should arise a faithful prophet; **42** Moreover that he should be their captain, and should take charge of the sanctuary, to set them over their works, and over the country, and over the armour, and over the fortresses, that, I say, he should take charge of the sanctuary; **43** Beside this, that he should be obeyed of every man, and that all the writings in the country should be made in his name, and that he should be clothed in purple, and wear gold: **44** Also that it should be lawful for none of the people or priests to break any of these things, or to gainsay his words, or to gather an assembly in the country without him, or to be clothed in purple, or wear a buckle of gold; **45** And whosoever should do otherwise, or break any of these things, he should be punished. **46** Thus it liked all the people to deal with Simon, and to do as hath been said. **47** Then Simon accepted hereof, and was well pleased to be high priest, and captain and governor of the Jews and priests, and to defend them all. **48** So they commanded that this writing should be put in tables of brass, and that they should be set up within the compass of the sanctuary in a conspicuous place; **49** Also that the copies thereof should be laid up in the treasury, to the end that Simon and his sons might have them.

15 **1** Moreover Antiochus son of Demetrius the king sent letters from the isles of the sea unto Simon the priest and prince of the Jews, and to all the people; **2** The contents whereof were these: King Antiochus to Simon the high priest and prince of his nation, and to the people of the Jews, greeting: **3** Forasmuch as certain pestilent men have usurped the kingdom of our fathers, and my purpose is to challenge it again, that I may restore it to the old estate, and to that end have gathered a multitude of foreign soldiers together, and prepared ships of war; **4** My meaning also being to go through the country, that I may be avenged of them that have destroyed it, and made many cities in the kingdom desolate: **5** Now therefore I confirm unto thee all the oblations which the kings before me granted thee, and whatsoever gifts besides they granted. **6** I give thee leave also to coin money for thy country with thine own stamp. **7** And as concerning Jerusalem and the sanctuary, let them be free; and all the armour that thou hast made, and fortresses that thou hast built, and keepest in thine hands, let them remain unto thee. **8** And if anything be, or shall be, owing to the king, let it be forgiven thee from this time forth for evermore. **9** Furthermore, when we have obtained our kingdom, we will honour thee, and thy nation, and thy temple, with great honour, so that your honour shall be known throughout the world. **10** In the hundred threescore and fourteenth year went Antiochus into

the land of his fathers: at which time all the forces came together unto him, so that
few were left with Tryphon. **11** Wherefore being pursued by king Antiochus, he
fled unto Dora, which lieth by the sea side: **12** For he saw that troubles came
upon him all at once, and that his forces had forsaken him. **13** Then camped
Antiochus against Dora, having with him an hundred and twenty thousand men
of war, and eight thousand horsemen. **14** And when he had compassed the city
round about, and joined ships close to the town on the sea side, he vexed the city
by land and by sea, neither suffered he any to go out or in. **15** In the mean sea-
son came Numenius and his company from Rome, having letters to the kings and
countries; wherein were written these things: **16** Lucius, consul of the Romans
unto king Ptolemee, greeting: **17** The Jews' ambassadors, our friends and con-
federates, came unto us to renew the old friendship and league, being sent from
Simon the high priest, and from the people of the Jews: **18** And they brought
a shield of gold of a thousand pound. **19** We thought it good therefore to write
unto the kings and countries, that they should do them no harm, nor fight against
them, their cities, or countries, nor yet aid their enemies against them. **20** It
seemed also good to us to receive the shield of them. **21** If therefore there be
any pestilent fellows, that have fled from their country unto you, deliver them
unto Simon the high priest, that he may punish them according to their own
law. **22** The same things wrote he likewise unto Demetrius the king, and Atta-
lus, to Ariarathes, and Arsaces, **23** And to all the countries and to Sampsames,
and the Lacedemonians, and to Delus, and Myndus, and Sicyon, and Caria, and
Samos, and Pamphylia, and Lycia, and Halicarnassus, and Rhodus, and Aradus,
and Cos, and Side, and Aradus, and Gortyna, and Cnidus, and Cyprus, and
Cyrene. **24** And the copy hereof they wrote to Simon the high priest. **25** So
Antiochus the king camped against Dora the second day, assaulting it continually,
and making engines, by which means he shut up Tryphon, that he could neither
go out nor in. **26** At that time Simon sent him two thousand chosen men to
aid him; silver also, and gold, and much armour. **27** Nevertheless he would not
receive them, but brake all the covenants which he had made with him afore, and
became strange unto him. **28** Furthermore he sent unto him Athenobius, one
of his friends, to commune with him, and say, Ye withhold Joppa and Gazera;
with the tower that is in Jerusalem, which are cities of my realm. **29** The borders
thereof ye have wasted, and done great hurt in the land, and got the dominion
of many places within my kingdom. **30** Now therefore deliver the cities which
ye have taken, and the tributes of the places, whereof ye have gotten dominion
without the borders of Judea: **31** Or else give me for them five hundred ta-
lents of silver; and for the harm that ye have done, and the tributes of the cities,
other five hundred talents: if not, we will come and fight against you **32** So
Athenobius the king's friend came to Jerusalem: and when he saw the glory of
Simon, and the cupboard of gold and silver plate, and his great attendance, he
was astonished, and told him the king's message. **33** Then answered Simon, and
said unto him, We have neither taken other men's land, nor holden that which
appertaineth to others, but the inheritance of our fathers, which our enemies had
wrongfully in possession a certain time. **34** Wherefore we, having opportunity,
hold the inheritance of our fathers. **35** And whereas thou demandest Joppa and
Gazera, albeit they did great harm unto the people in our country, yet will we
give thee an hundred talents for them. Hereunto Athenobius answered him not
a word; **36** But returned in a rage to the king, and made report unto him of
these speeches, and of the glory of Simon, and of all that he had seen: whereupon
the king was exceeding wroth. **37** In the mean time fled Tryphon by ship unto
Orthosias. **38** Then the king made Cendebeus captain of the sea coast, and gave
him an host of footmen and horsemen, **39** And commanded him to remove his
host toward Judea; also he commanded him to build up Cedron, and to fortify
the gates, and to war against the people; but as for the king himself, he pursued
Tryphon. **40** So Cendebeus came to Jamnia and began to provoke the people
and to invade Judea, and to take the people prisoners, and slay them. **41** And
when he had built up Cedrou, he set horsemen there, and an host of footmen, to
the end that issuing out they might make outroads upon the ways of Judea, as the
king had commanded him.

16

1 Then came up John from Gazera, and told Simon his father what
Cendebeus had done. **2** Wherefore Simon called his two eldest sons,
Judas and John, and said unto them, I, and my brethren, and my father's house,
have ever from my youth unto this day fought against the enemies of Israel; and
things have prospered so well in our hands, that we have delivered Israel often-
times. **3** But now I am old, and ye, by God's mercy, are of a sufficient age: be
ye instead of me and my brother, and go and fight for our nation, and the help
from heaven be with you. **4** So he chose out of the country twenty thousand
men of war with horsemen, who went out against Cendebeus, and rested that
night at Modin. **5** And when as they rose in the morning, and went into the
plain, behold, a mighty great host both of footmen and horsemen came against
them: howbeit there was a water brook betwixt them. **6** So he and his people
pitched over against them: and when he saw that the people were afraid to go over
the water brook, he went first over himself, and then the men seeing him passed
through after him. **7** That done, he divided his men, and set the horsemen in
the midst of the footmen: for the enemies' horsemen were very many. **8** Then
sounded they with the holy trumpets: whereupon Cendebeus and his host were
put to flight, so that many of them were slain, and the remnant gat them to the
strong hold. **9** At that time was Judas John's brother wounded; but John still fol-
lowed after them, until he came to Cedron, which Cendebeus had built. **10** So
they fled even unto the towers in the fields of Azotus; wherefore he burned it
with fire: so that there were slain of them about two thousand men. Afterward he
returned into the land of Judea in peace. **11** Moreover in the plain of Jericho
was Ptolemeus the son of Abubus made captain, and he had abundance of silver
and gold: **12** For he was the high priest's son in law. **13** Wherefore his heart
being lifted up, he thought to get the country to himself, and thereupon consul-
ted deceitfully against Simon and his sons to destroy them. **14** Now Simon was
visiting the cities that were in the country, and taking care for the good ordering
of them; at which time he came down himself to Jericho with his sons, Mattathias
and Judas, in the hundred threescore and seventeenth year, in the eleventh month,
called Sabat: **15** Where the son of Abubus receiving them deceitfully into a
little hold, called Docus, which he had built, made them a great banquet: how-
beit he had hid men there. **16** So when Simon and his sons had drunk largely,
Ptolemee and his men rose up, and took their weapons, and came upon Simon
into the banqueting place, and slew him, and his two sons, and certain of his
servants. **17** In which doing he committed a great treachery, and recompensed
evil for good. **18** Then Ptolemee wrote these things, and sent to the king, that
he should send him an host to aid him, and he would deliver him the country
and cities. **19** He sent others also to Gazera to kill John: and unto the tribunes
he sent letters to come unto him, that he might give them silver, and gold, and
rewards. **20** And others he sent to take Jerusalem, and the mountain of the
temple. **21** Now one had run afore to Gazera and told John that his father and
brethren were slain, and, quoth he, Ptolemee hath sent to slay thee also. **22** He-
reof when he heard, he was sore astonished: so he laid hands on them that were
come to destroy him, and slew them; for he knew that they sought to make him
away. **23** As concerning the rest of the acts of John, and his wars, and worthy
deeds which he did, and the building of the walls which he made, and his doin-
gs, **24** Behold, these are written in the chronicles of his priesthood, from the
time he was made high priest after his father.

APOCRYPHA

2ST BOOK OF MACCABEES

The Second Book of the Maccabees

1 1 The brethren, the Jews that be at Jerusalem and in the land of Judea,
wish unto the brethren, the Jews that are throughout Egypt health and pea-
ce: 2 God be gracious unto you, and remember his covenant that he made with
Abraham, Isaac, and Jacob, his faithful servants; 3 And give you all an heart to
serve him, and to do his will, with a good courage and a willing mind; 4 And
open your hearts in his law and commandments, and send you peace, 5 And
hear your prayers, and be at one with you, and never forsake you in time of
trouble. 6 And now we be here praying for you. 7 What time as Demetri-
us reigned, in the hundred threescore and ninth year, we the Jews wrote unto
you in the extremity of trouble that came upon us in those years, from the time
that Jason and his company revolted from the holy land and kingdom, 8 And
burned the porch, and shed innocent blood: then we prayed unto the Lord, and
were heard; we offered also sacrifices and fine flour, and lighted the lamps, and set
forth the loaves. 9 And now see that ye keep the feast of tabernacles in the mon-
th Casleu. 10 In the hundred fourscore and eighth year, the people that were
at Jerusalem and in Judea, and the council, and Judas, sent greeting and health
unto Aristobulus, king Ptolemeus' master, who was of the stock of the anointed
priests, and to the Jews that were in Egypt: 11 Insomuch as God hath delive-
red us from great perils, we thank him highly, as having been in battle against a
king. 12 For he cast them out that fought within the holy city. 13 For when
the leader was come into Persia, and the army with him that seemed invincible,
they were slain in the temple of Nanea by the deceit of Nanea's priests. 14 For
Antiochus, as though he would marry her, came into the place, and his friends
that were with him, to receive money in name of a dowry. 15 Which when
the priests of Nanea had set forth, and he was entered with a small company
into the compass of the temple, they shut the temple as soon as Antiochus was
come in: 16 And opening a privy door of the roof, they threw stones like thun-
derbolts, and struck down the captain, hewed them in pieces, smote off their
heads and cast them to those that were without. 17 Blessed be our God in all
things, who hath delivered up the ungodly. 18 Therefore whereas we are now
purposed to keep the purification of the temple upon the five and twentieth day
of the month Casleu, we thought it necessary to certify you thereof, that ye also
might keep it, as the feast of the tabernacles, and of the fire, which was given
us when Neemias offered sacrifice, after that he had builded the temple and the
altar. 19 For when our fathers were led into Persia, the priests that were then
devout took the fire of the altar privily, and hid it in an hollow place of a pit
without water, where they kept it sure, so that the place was unknown to all
men. 20 Now after many years, when it pleased God, Neemias, being sent
from the king of Persia, did send of the posterity of those priests that had hid it
to the fire: but when they told us they found no fire, but thick water; 21 Then
commanded he them to draw it up, and to bring it; and when the sacrifices were
laid on, Neemias commanded the priests to sprinkle the wood and the things laid
thereupon with the water. 22 When this was done, and the time came that the
sun shone, which afore was hid in the cloud, there was a great fire kindled, so
that every man marvelled. 23 And the priests made a prayer whilst the sacrifice
was consuming, I say, both the priests, and all the rest, Jonathan beginning, and
the rest answering thereunto, as Neemias did. 24 And the prayer was after this
manner; O Lord, Lord God, Creator of all things, who art fearful and strong, and
righteous, and merciful, and the only and gracious King, 25 The only giver of
all things, the only just, almighty, and everlasting, thou that deliverest Israel from
all trouble, and didst choose the fathers, and sanctify them: 26 Receive the
sacrifice for thy whole people Israel, and preserve thine own portion, and sanctify
it. 27 Gather those together that are scattered from us, deliver them that serve
among the heathen, look upon them that are despised and abhorred, and let the
heathen know that thou art our God. 28 Punish them that oppress us, and with
pride do us wrong. 29 Plant thy people again in thy holy place, as Moses hath
spoken. 30 And the priests sung psalms of thanksgiving. 31 Now when the
sacrifice was consumed, Neemias commanded the water that was left to be poured
on the great stones. 32 When this was done, there was kindled a flame: but it
was consumed by the light that shined from the altar. 33 So when this matter
was known, it was told the king of Persia, that in the place, where the priests that
were led away had hid the fire, there appeared water, and that Neemias had puri-
fied the sacrifices therewith. 34 Then the king, inclosing the place, made it holy,
after he had tried the matter. 35 And the king took many gifts, and bestowed
thereof on those whom he would gratify. 36 And Neemias called this thing
Naphthar, which is as much as to say, a cleansing: but many men call it Nephi.

2 1 It is also found in the records, that Jeremy the prophet commanded
them that were carried away to take of the fire, as it hath been signi-
fied: 2 And how that the prophet, having given them the law, charged them not
to forget the commandments of the Lord, and that they should not err in their
minds, when they see images of silver and gold, with their ornaments. 3 And
with other such speeches exhorted he them, that the law should not depart from
their hearts. 4 It was also contained in the same writing, that the prophet, being
warned of God, commanded the tabernacle and the ark to go with him, as he
went forth into the mountain, where Moses climbed up, and saw the heritage
of God. 5 And when Jeremy came thither, he found an hollow cave, wherein
he laid the tabernacle, and the ark, and the altar of incense, and so stopped the
door. 6 And some of those that followed him came to mark the way, but they
could not find it. 7 Which when Jeremy perceived, he blamed them, saying, As
for that place, it shall be unknown until the time that God gather his people again
together, and receive them unto mercy. 8 Then shall the Lord shew them these
things, and the glory of the Lord shall appear, and the cloud also, as it was shewed
under Moses, and as when Solomon desired that the place might be honourably
sanctified. 9 It was also declared, that he being wise offered the sacrifice of dedi-
cation, and of the finishing of the temple. 10 And as when Moses prayed unto
the Lord, the fire came down from heaven, and consumed the sacrifices: even so
prayed Solomon also, and the fire came down from heaven, and consumed the
burnt offerings. 11 And Moses said, Because the sin offering was not to be
eaten, it was consumed. 12 So Solomon kept those eight days. 13 The same
things also were reported in the writings and commentaries of Neemias; and how
he founding a library gathered together the acts of the kings, and the prophets,
and of David, and the epistles of the kings concerning the holy gifts. 14 In
like manner also Judas gathered together all those things that were lost by reason
of the war we had, and they remain with us, 15 Wherefore if ye have need
thereof, send some to fetch them unto you. 16 Whereas we then are about
to celebrate the purification, we have written unto you, and ye shall do well, if
ye keep the same days. 17 We hope also, that the God, that delivered all his
people, and gave them all an heritage, and the kingdom, and the priesthood, and
the sanctuary, 18 As he promised in the law, will shortly have mercy upon us,
and gather us together out of every land under heaven into the holy place: for he
hath delivered us out of great troubles, and hath purified the place. 19 Now as
concerning Judas Maccabeus, and his brethren, and the purification of the great
temple, and the dedication of the altar, 20 And the wars against Antiochus Epi-
phanes, and Eupator his son, 21 And the manifest signs that came from heaven
unto those that behaved themselves manfully to their honour for Judaism: so that,
being but a few, they overcame the whole country, and chased barbarous multitu-
des, 22 And recovered again the temple renowned all the world over, and freed
the city, and upheld the laws which were going down, the Lord being gracious
unto them with all favour: 23 All these things, I say, being declared by Jason
of Cyrene in five books, we will assay to abridge in one volume. 24 For consi-
dering the infinite number, and the difficulty which they find that desire to look
into the narrations of the story, for the variety of the matter, 25 We have been
careful, that they that will read may have delight, and that they that are desirous to
commit to memory might have ease, and that all into whose hands it comes might
have profit. 26 Therefore to us, that have taken upon us this painful labour of
abridging, it was not easy, but a matter of sweat and watching; 27 Even as it is
no ease unto him that prepareth a banquet, and seeketh the benefit of others: yet
for the pleasuring of many we will undertake gladly this great pains; 28 Leaving
to the author the exact handling of every particular, and labouring to follow the
rules of an abridgement. 29 For as the master builder of a new house must care
for the whole building; but he that undertaketh to set it out, and paint it, must
seek out fit things for the adorning thereof: even so I think it is with us. 30 To
stand upon every point, and go over things at large, and to be curious in parti-
culars, belongeth to the first author of the story: 31 But to use brevity, and
avoid much labouring of the work, is to be granted to him that will make an
abridgment. 32 Here then will we begin the story: only adding thus much to

that which hath been said, that it is a foolish thing to make a long prologue, and
to be short in the story itself.

3 **1** Now when the holy city was inhabited with all peace, and the laws
were kept very well, because of the godliness of Onias the high priest, and
his hatred of wickedness, **2** It came to pass that even the kings themselves did
honour the place, and magnify the temple with their best gifts; **3** Insomuch that
Seleucus of Asia of his own revenues bare all the costs belonging to the service of
the sacrifices. **4** But one Simon of the tribe of Benjamin, who was made gover-
nor of the temple, fell out with the high priest about disorder in the city. **5** And
when he could not overcome Onias, he gat him to Apollonius the son of Thraseas,
who then was governor of Celosyria and Phenice, **6** And told him that the trea-
sury in Jerusalem was full of infinite sums of money, so that the multitude of their
riches, which did not pertain to the account of the sacrifices, was innumerable,
and that it was possible to bring all into the king's hand. **7** Now when Apollo-
nius came to the king, and had shewed him of the money whereof he was told,
the king chose out Heliodorus his treasurer, and sent him with a commandment
to bring him the foresaid money. **8** So forthwith Heliodorus took his journey;
under a colour of visiting the cities of Celosyria and Phenice, but indeed to fulfil
the king's purpose. **9** And when he was come to Jerusalem, and had been cour-
teously received of the high priest of the city, he told him what intelligence was
given of the money, and declared wherefore he came, and asked if these things
were so indeed. **10** Then the high priest told him that there was such money
laid up for the relief of widows and fatherless children: **11** And that some of it
belonged to Hircanus son of Tobias, a man of great dignity, and not as that wicked
Simon had misinformed: the sum whereof in all was four hundred talents of silver,
and two hundred of gold: **12** And that it was altogether impossible that such
wrongs should be done unto them, that had committed it to the holiness of the
place, and to the majesty and inviolable sanctity of the temple, honoured over all
the world. **13** But Heliodorus, because of the king's commandment given him,
said, That in any wise it must be brought into the king's treasury. **14** So at the
day which he appointed he entered in to order this matter: wherefore there was no
small agony throughout the whole city. **15** But the priests, prostrating themsel-
ves before the altar in their priests' vestments, called unto heaven upon him that
made a law concerning things given to he kept, that they should safely be preser-
ved for such as had committed them to be kept. **16** Then whoso had looked the
high priest in the face, it would have wounded his heart: for his countenance and
the changing of his colour declared the inward agony of his mind. **17** For the
man was so compassed with fear and horror of the body, that it was manifest to
them that looked upon him, what sorrow he had now in his heart. **18** Others
ran flocking out of their houses to the general supplication, because the place was
like to come into contempt. **19** And the women, girt with sackcloth under their
breasts, abounded in the streets, and the virgins that were kept in ran, some to the
gates, and some to the walls, and others looked out of the windows. **20** And
all, holding their hands toward heaven, made supplication. **21** Then it would
have pitied a man to see the falling down of the multitude of all sorts, and the
fear of the high priest being in such an agony. **22** They then called upon the
Almighty Lord to keep the things committed of trust safe and sure for those that
had committed them. **23** Nevertheless Heliodorus executed that which was
decreed. **24** Now as he was there present himself with his guard about the trea-
sury, the Lord of spirits, and the Prince of all power, caused a great apparition, so
that all that presumed to come in with him were astonished at the power of God,
and fainted, and were sore afraid. **25** For there appeared unto them an horse
with a terrible rider upon him, and adorned with a very fair covering, and he ran
fiercely, and smote at Heliodorus with his forefeet, and it seemed that he that sat
upon the horse had complete harness of gold. **26** Moreover two other young
men appeared before him, notable in strength, excellent in beauty, and comely
in apparel, who stood by him on either side; and scourged him continually, and
gave him many sore stripes. **27** And Heliodorus fell suddenly unto the ground,
and was compassed with great darkness: but they that were with him took him
up, and put him into a litter. **28** Thus him, that lately came with a great train
and with all his guard into the said treasury, they carried out, being unable to
help himself with his weapons: and manifestly they acknowledged the power of
God. **29** For he by the hand of God was cast down, and lay speechless without
all hope of life. **30** But they praised the Lord, that had miraculously honoured
his own place: for the temple; which a little afore was full of fear and trouble,
when the Almighty Lord appeared, was filled with joy and gladness. **31** Then
straightways certain of Heliodorus' friends prayed Onias, that he would call upon
the most High to grant him his life, who lay ready to give up the ghost. **32** So
the high priest, suspecting lest the king should misconceive that some treachery
had been done to Heliodorus by the Jews, offered a sacrifice for the health of the
man. **33** Now as the high priest was making an atonement, the same young
men in the same clothing appeared and stood beside Heliodorus, saying, Give
Onias the high priest great thanks, insomuch as for his sake the Lord hath gran-
ted thee life: **34** And seeing that thou hast been scourged from heaven, declare
unto all men the mighty power of God. And when they had spoken these words,
they appeared no more. **35** So Heliodorus, after he had offered sacrifice unto
the Lord, and made great vows unto him that had saved his life, and saluted
Onias, returned with his host to the king. **36** Then testified he to all men the
works of the great God, which he had seen with his eyes. **37** And when the
king Heliodorus, who might be a fit man to be sent yet once again to Jerusalem,
he said, **38** If thou hast any enemy or traitor, send him thither, and thou shalt
receive him well scourged, if he escape with his life: for in that place, no doubt;
there is an especial power of God. **39** For he that dwelleth in heaven hath his
eye on that place, and defendeth it; and he beateth and destroyeth them that come
to hurt it. **40** And the things concerning Heliodorus, and the keeping of the
treasury, fell out on this sort.

4 **1** This Simon now, of whom we spake afore, having been a betrayer of the
money, and of his country, slandered Onias, as if he ha terrified Heliodo-
rus, and been the worker of these evils. **2** Thus was he bold to call him a traitor,
that had deserved well of the city, and tendered his own nation, and was so zealous
of the laws. **3** But when their hatred went so far, that by one of Simon's faction
murders were committed, **4** Onias seeing the danger of this contention, and
that Apollonius, as being the governor of Celosyria and Phenice, did rage, and
increase Simon's malice, **5** He went to the king, not to be an accuser of his
countrymen, but seeking the good of all, both publick and private: **6** For he saw
that it was impossible that the state should continue quiet, and Simon leave his
folly, unless the king did look thereunto. **7** But after the death of Seleucus,
when Antiochus, called Epiphanes, took the kingdom, Jason the brother of Onias
laboured underhand to be high priest, **8** Promising unto the king by interces-
sion three hundred and threescore talents of silver, and of another revenue eighty
talents: **9** Beside this, he promised to assign an hundred and fifty more, if he
might have licence to set him up a place for exercise, and for the training up of
youth in the fashions of the heathen, and to write them of Jerusalem by the name
of Antiochians. **10** Which when the king had granted, and he had gotten into
his hand the rule he forthwith brought his own nation to Greekish fa-
shion. **11** And the royal privileges granted of special favour to the Jews by the
means of John the father of Eupolemus, who went ambassador to Rome for ami-
ty and aid, he took away; and putting down the governments which were accor-
ding to the law, he brought up new customs against the law: **12** For he built
gladly a place of exercise under the tower itself, and brought the chief young men
under his subjection, and made them wear a hat. **13** Now such was the height
of Greek fashions, and increase of heathenish manners, through the exceeding
profaneness of Jason, that ungodly wretch, and no high priest; **14** That the
priests had no courage to serve any more at the altar, but despising the temple,
and neglecting the sacrifices, hastened to be partakers of the unlawful allowance
in the place of exercise, after the game of Discus called them forth; **15** Not
setting by the honours of their fathers, but liking the glory of the Grecians best of
all. **16** By reason whereof sore calamity came upon them: for they had them to
be their enemies and avengers, whose custom they followed so earnestly, and unto
whom they desired to be like in all things. **17** For it is not a light thing to do
wickedly against the laws of God: but the time following shall declare these thin-
gs. **18** Now when the game that was used every faith year was kept at Tyrus, the
king being present, **19** This ungracious Jason sent special messengers from Jeru-
salem, who were Antiochians, to carry three hundred drachms of silver to the sa-
crifice of Hercules, which even the bearers thereof thought fit not to bestow upon
the sacrifice, because it was not convenient, but to be reserved for other char-
ges. **20** This money then, in regard of the sender, was appointed to Hercules'
sacrifice; but because of the bearers thereof, it was employed to the making of
gallies. **21** Now when Apollonius the son of Menestheus was sent into Egypt
for the coronation of king Ptolemeus Philometor, Antiochus, understanding him
not to be well affected to his affairs, provided for his own safety: whereupon he
came to Joppa, and from thence to Jerusalem: **22** Where he was honourably
received of Jason, and of the city, and was brought in with torch alight, and with
great shoutings: and so afterward went with his host unto Phenice. **23** Three
years afterward Jason sent Menelaus, the aforesaid Simon's brother, to bear the
money unto the king, and to put him in mind of certain necessary mat-
ters. **24** But he being brought to the presence of the king, when he had magni-
fied him for the glorious appearance of his power, got the priesthood to himself,
offering more than Jason by three hundred talents of silver. **25** So he came with
the king's mandate, bringing nothing worthy the high priesthood, but having the
fury of a cruel tyrant, and the rage of a savage beast. **26** Then Jason, who had
undermined his own brother, being undermined by another, was compelled to
flee into the country of the Ammonites. **27** So Menelaus got the principality:
but as for the money that he had promised unto the king, he took no good order
for it, albeit Sostratis the ruler of the castle required it: **28** For unto him apper-
tained the gathering of the customs. Wherefore they were both called before the
king. **29** Now Menelaus left his brother Lysimachus in his stead in the priestho-
od; and Sostratus left Crates, who was governor of the Cyprians. **30** While tho-
se things were in doing, they of Tarsus and Mallos made insurrection, because
they were given to the king's concubine, called Antiochus. **31** Then came the
king in all haste to appease matters, leaving Andronicus, a man in authority, for
his deputy. **32** Now Menelaus, supposing that he had gotten a convenient time,
stole certain vessels of gold out of the temple, and gave some of them to Androni-
cus, and some he sold into Tyrus and the cities round about. **33** Which when
Onias knew of a surety, he reproved him, and withdrew himself into a sanctuary
at Daphne, that lieth by Antiochia. **34** Wherefore Menelaus, taking Androni-
cus apart, prayed, him to get Onias into his hands; who being persuaded thereu-
nto, and coming to Onias in deceit, gave him his right hand with oaths; and

though he were suspected by him, yet persuaded he him to come forth of the sanctuary: whom forthwith he shut up without regard of justice. **35** For the which cause not only the Jews, but many also of other nations, took great indignation, and were much grieved for the unjust murder of the man. **36** And when the king was come again from the places about Cilicia, the Jews that were in the city, and certain of the Greeks that abhorred the fact also, complained because Onias was slain without cause. **37** Therefore Antiochus was heartily sorry, and moved to pity, and wept, because of the sober and modest behaviour of him that was dead. **38** And being kindled with anger, forthwith he took away Andronicus his purple, and rent off his clothes, and leading him through the whole city unto that very place, where he had committed impiety against Onias, there slew he the cursed murderer. Thus the Lord rewarded him his punishment, as he had deserved. **39** Now when many sacrileges had been committed in the city by Lysimachus with the consent of Menelaus, and the fruit thereof was spread abroad, the multitude gathered themselves together against Lysimachus, many vessels of gold being already carried away. **40** Whereupon the common people rising, and being filled with rage, Lysimachus armed about three thousand men, and began first to offer violence; one Auranus being the leader, a man far gone in years, and no less in folly. **41** They then seeing the attempt of Lysimachus, some of them caught stones, some clubs, others taking handfuls of dust, that was next at hand, cast them all together upon Lysimachus, and those that set upon them. **42** Thus many of them they wounded, and some they struck to the ground, and all of them they forced to flee: but as for the churchrobber himself, him they killed beside the treasury. **43** Of these matters therefore there was an accusation laid against Menelaus. **44** Now when the king came to Tyrus, three men that were sent from the senate pleaded the cause before him: **45** But Menelaus, being now convicted, promised Ptolemee the son of Dorymenes to give him much money, if he would pacify the king toward him. **46** Whereupon Ptolemee taking the king aside into a certain gallery, as it were to take the air, brought him to be of another mind: **47** Insomuch that he discharged Menelaus from the accusations, who notwithstanding was cause of all the mischief: and those poor men, who, if they had told their cause, yea, before the Scythians, should have been judged innocent, them he condemned to death. **48** Thus they that followed the matter for the city, and for the people, and for the holy vessels, did soon suffer unjust punishment. **49** Wherefore even they of Tyrus, moved with hatred of that wicked deed, caused them to be honourably buried. **50** And so through the covetousness of them that were of power Menelaus remained still in authority, increasing in malice, and being a great traitor to the citizens.

5

1 About the same time Antiochus prepared his second voyage into Egypt: **2** And then it happened, that through all the city, for the space almost of forty days, there were seen horsemen running in the air, in cloth of gold, and armed with lances, like a band of soldiers, **3** And troops of horsemen in array, encountering and running one against another, with shaking of shields, and multitude of pikes, and drawing of swords, and casting of darts, and glittering of golden ornaments, and harness of all sorts. **4** Wherefore every man prayed that that apparition might turn to good. **5** Now when there was gone forth a false rumour, as though Antiochus had been dead, Jason took at the least a thousand men, and suddenly made an assault upon the city; and they that were upon the walls being put back, and the city at length taken, Menelaus fled into the castle: **6** But Jason slew his own citizens without mercy, not considering that to get the day of them of his own nation would be a most unhappy day for him; but thinking they had been his enemies, and not his countrymen, whom he conquered. **7** Howbeit for all this he obtained not the principality, but at the last received shame for the reward of his treason, and fled again into the country of the Ammonites. **8** In the end therefore he had an unhappy return, being accused before Aretas the king of the Arabians, fleeing from city to city, pursued of all men, hated as a forsaker of the laws, and being had in abomination as an open enemy of his country and countrymen, he was cast out into Egypt. **9** Thus he that had driven many out of their country perished in a strange land, retiring to the Lacedemonians, and thinking there to find succour by reason of his kindred: **10** And he that had cast out many unburied had none to mourn for him, nor any solemn funerals at all, nor sepulchre with his fathers. **11** Now when this that was done came to the king's car, he thought that Judea had revolted: whereupon removing out of Egypt in a furious mind, he took the city by force of arms, **12** And commanded his men of war not to spare such as they met, and to slay such as went up upon the houses. **13** Thus there was killing of young and old, making away of men, women, and children, slaying of virgins and infants. **14** And there were destroyed within the space of three whole days fourscore thousand, whereof forty thousand were slain in the conflict; and no fewer sold than slain. **15** Yet was he not content with this, but presumed to go into the most holy temple of all the world; Menelaus, that traitor to the laws, and to his own country, being his guide: **16** And taking the holy vessels with polluted hands, and with profane hands pulling down the things that were dedicated by other kings to the augmentation and glory and honour of the place, he gave them away. **17** And so haughty was Antiochus in mind, that he considered not that the Lord was angry for a while for the sins of them that dwelt in the city, and therefore his eye was not upon the place. **18** For had they not been formerly wrapped in many sins, this man, as soon as he had come, had forthwith been scourged, and put back from his presumption, as Heliodorus was, whom Seleucus the king sent to view the treasury. **19** Nevertheless God did not choose the people for the place's sake, but the place far the people's sake. **20** And therefore the place itself, that was partaker with them of the adversity that happened to the nation, did afterward communicate in the benefits sent from the Lord: and as it was forsaken in the wrath of the Almighty, so again, the great Lord being reconciled, it was set up with all glory. **21** So when Antiochus had carried out of the temple a thousand and eight hundred talents, he departed in all haste unto Antiochia, weening in his pride to make the land navigable, and the sea passable by foot: such was the haughtiness of his mind. **22** And he left governors to vex the nation: at Jerusalem, Philip, for his country a Phrygian, and for manners more barbarous than he that set him there; **23** And at Garizim, Andronicus; and besides, Menelaus, who worse than all the rest bare an heavy hand over the citizens, having a malicious mind against his countrymen the Jews. **24** He sent also that detestable ringleader Apollonius with an army of two and twenty thousand, commanding him to slay all those that were in their best age, and to sell the women and the younger sort: **25** Who coming to Jerusalem, and pretending peace, did forbear till the holy day of the sabbath, when taking the Jews keeping holy day, he commanded his men to arm themselves. **26** And so he slew all them that were gone to the celebrating of the sabbath, and running through the city with weapons slew great multitudes. **27** But Judas Maccabeus with nine others, or thereabout, withdrew himself into the wilderness, and lived in the mountains after the manner of beasts, with his company, who fed on herbs continually, lest they should be partakers of the pollution.

6

1 Not long after this the king sent an old man of Athens to compel the Jews to depart from the laws of their fathers, and not to live after the laws of God: **2** And to pollute also the temple in Jerusalem, and to call it the temple of Jupiter Olympius; and that in Garizim, of Jupiter the Defender of strangers, as they did desire that dwelt in the place. **3** The coming in of this mischief was sore and grievous to the people: **4** For the temple was filled with riot and revelling by the Gentiles, who dallied with harlots, and had to do with women within the circuit of the holy places, and besides that brought in things that were not lawful. **5** The altar also was filled with profane things, which the law forbiddeth. **6** Neither was it lawful for a man to keep sabbath days or ancient fasts, or to profess himself at all to be a Jew. **7** And in the day of the king's birth every month they were brought by bitter constraint to eat of the sacrifices; and when the fast of Bacchus was kept, the Jews were compelled to go in procession to Bacchus, carrying ivy. **8** Moreover there went out a decree to the neighbour cities of the heathen, by the suggestion of Ptolemee, against the Jews, that they should observe the same fashions, and be partakers of their sacrifices: **9** And whoso would not conform themselves to the manners of the Gentiles should be put to death. Then might a man have seen the present misery. **10** For there were two women brought, who had circumcised their children; whom when they had openly led round about the city, the babes handing at their breasts, they cast them down headlong from the wall. **11** And others, that had run together into caves near by, to keep the sabbath day secretly, being discovered by Philip, were all burnt together, because they made a conscience to help themselves for the honour of the most sacred day. **12** Now I beseech those that read this book, that they be not discouraged for these calamities, but that they judge those punishments not to be for destruction, but for a chastening of our nation. **13** For it is a token of his great goodness, when wicked doers are not suffered any long time, but forthwith punished. **14** For not as with other nations, whom the Lord patiently forbeareth to punish, till they be come to the fulness of their sins, so dealeth he with us, **15** Lest that, being come to the height of sin, afterwards he should take vengeance of us. **16** And therefore he never withdraweth his mercy from us: and though he punish with adversity, yet doth he never forsake his people. **17** But let this that we at spoken be for a warning unto us. And now will we come to the declaring of the matter in a few words. **18** Eleazar, one of the principal scribes, an aged man, and of a well favoured countenance, was constrained to open his mouth, and to eat swine's flesh. **19** But he, choosing rather to die gloriously, than to live stained with such an abomination, spit it forth, and came of his own accord to the torment, **20** As it behoved them to come, that are resolute to stand out against such things, as are not lawful for love of life to be tasted. **21** But they that had the charge of that wicked feast, for the old acquaintance they had with the man, taking him aside, besought him to bring flesh of his own provision, such as was lawful for him to use, and make as if he did eat of the flesh taken from the sacrifice commanded by the king; **22** That in so doing he might be delivered from death, and for the old friendship with them find favour. **23** But he began to consider discreetly, and as became his age, and the excellency of his ancient years, and the honour of his gray head, whereon was come, and his most honest education from a child, or rather the holy law made and given by God: therefore he answered accordingly, and willed them straightways to send him to the grave. **24** For it becometh not our age, said he, in any wise to dissemble, whereby many young persons might think that Eleazar, being fourscore years old and ten, were now gone to a strange religion; **25** And so they through mine hypocrisy, and desire to live a little time and a moment longer, should be deceived by me, and I get a stain to mine old age, and make it abominable. **26** For though for the present time I should be delivered from the punishment of men: yet should I not escape the hand of the Almighty, neither alive, nor dead. **27** Wherefore now, manfully changing this life, I will shew myself such an one as mine age requireth, **28** And leave a notable example to such as be young to die willingly and courageously for the honourable and holy laws. And when he had said these words, immediately he went to the torment: **29** They that led him changing the good will they bare him a little before into hatred, because the foresaid speeches proceeded, as they thought, from a desperate mind. **30** But when he was ready to die with stripes, he groaned, and said, It is manifest unto the Lord, that hath the holy knowledge, that whereas I might have been delivered from death, I now endure sore pains in body by being beaten: but in soul am well content to suffer these things, because I fear him. **31** And thus this man died, leaving his death for an example of a noble courage, and a memorial of virtue, not only unto young men, but unto all his nation.

7 **1** It came to pass also, that seven brethren with their mother were taken, and compelled by the king against the law to taste swine's flesh, and were tormented with scourges and whips. **2** But one of them that spake first said thus, What wouldest thou ask or learn of us? we are ready to die, rather than to transgress the laws of our fathers. **3** Then the king, being in a rage, commanded pans and caldrons to be made hot: **4** Which forthwith being heated, he commanded to cut out the tongue of him that spake first, and to cut off the utmost parts of his body, the rest of his brethren and his mother looking on. **5** Now when he was thus maimed in all his members, he commanded him being yet alive to be brought to the fire, and to be fried in the pan: and as the vapour of the pan was for a good space dispersed, they exhorted one another with the mother to die manfully, saying thus, **6** The Lord God looketh upon us, and in truth hath comfort in us, as Moses in his song, which witnessed to their faces, declared, saying, And he shall be comforted in his servants. **7** So when the first was dead after this number, they brought the second to make him a mocking stock: and when they had pulled off the skin of his head with the hair, they asked him, Wilt thou eat, before thou be punished throughout every member of thy body? **8** But he answered in his own language, and said, No. Wherefore he also received the next torment in order, as the former did. **9** And when he was at the last gasp, he said, Thou like a fury takest us out of this present life, but the King of the world shall raise us up, who have died for his laws, unto everlasting life. **10** After him was the third made a mocking stock: and when he was required, he put out his tongue, and that right soon, holding forth his hands manfully. **11** And said courageously, These I had from heaven; and for his laws I despise them; and from him I hope to receive them again. **12** Insomuch that the king, and they that were with him, marvelled at the young man's courage, for that he nothing regarded the pains. **13** Now when this man was dead also, they tormented and mangled the fourth in like manner. **14** So when he was ready to die he said thus, It is good, being put to death by men, to look for hope from God to be raised up again by him: as for thee, thou shalt have no resurrection to life. **15** Afterward they brought the fifth also, and mangled him. **16** Then looked he unto the king, and said, Thou hast power over men, thou art corruptible, thou doest what thou wilt; yet think not that our nation is forsaken of God; **17** But abide a while, and behold his great power, how he will torment thee and thy seed. **18** After him also they brought the sixth, who being ready to die said, Be not deceived without cause: for we suffer these things for ourselves, having sinned against our God: therefore marvellous things are done unto us. **19** But think not thou, that takest in hand to strive against God, that thou shalt escape unpunished. **20** But the mother was marvellous above all, and worthy of honourable memory: for when she saw her seven sons slain within the space of one day, she bare it with a good courage, because of the hope that she had in the Lord. **21** Yea, she exhorted every one of them in her own language, filled with courageous spirits; and stirring up her womanish thoughts with a manly stomach, she said unto them, **22** I cannot tell how ye came into my womb: for I neither gave you breath nor life, neither was it I that formed the members of every one of you; **23** But doubtless the Creator of the world, who formed the generation of man, and found out the beginning of all things, will also of his own mercy give you breath and life again, as ye now regard not your own selves for his laws' sake. **24** Now Antiochus, thinking himself despised, and suspecting it to be a reproachful speech, whilst the youngest was yet alive, did not only exhort him by words, but also assured him with oaths, that he would make him both a rich and a happy man, if he would turn from the laws of his fathers; and that also he would take him for his friend, and trust him with affairs. **25** But when the young man would in no case hearken unto him, the king called his mother, and exhorted her that she would counsel the young man to save his life. **26** And when he had exhorted her with many words, she promised him that she would counsel her son. **27** But she bowing herself toward him, laughing the cruel tyrant to scorn, spake in her country language on this manner; O my son, have pity upon me that bare thee nine months in my womb, and gave thee such three years, and nourished thee, and brought thee up unto this age, and endured the troubles of education. **28** I beseech thee, my son, look upon the heaven and the earth, and all that is therein, and consider that God made them of things that were not; and so was mankind made likewise. **29** Fear not this tormentor, but, being worthy of thy brethren, take thy death that I may receive thee again in mercy with thy brethren. **30** Whiles she was yet speaking these words, the young man said, Whom wait ye for? I will not obey the king's commandment: but I will obey the commandment of the law that was given unto our fathers by Moses. **31** And thou, that hast been the author of all mischief against the Hebrews, shalt not escape the hands of God. **32** For we suffer because of our sins. **33** And though the living Lord be angry with us a little while for our chastening and correction, yet shall he be at one again with his servants. **34** But thou, O godless man, and of all other most wicked, be not lifted up without a cause, nor puffed up with uncertain hopes, lifting up thy hand against the servants of God: **35** For thou hast not yet escaped the judgment of Almighty God, who seeth all things. **36** For our brethren, who now have suffered a short pain, are dead under God's covenant of everlasting life: but thou, through the judgment of God, shalt receive just punishment for thy pride. **37** But I, as my brethren, offer up my body and life for the laws of our fathers, beseeching God that he would speedily be merciful unto our nation; and that thou by torments and plagues mayest confess, that he alone is God; **38** And that in me and my brethren the wrath of the Almighty, which is justly brought upon our nation, may cease. **39** Than the king' being in a rage, handed him worse than all the rest, and took it grievously that he was mocked. **40** So this man died undefiled, and put his whole trust in the Lord. **41** Last of all after the sons the mother died. **42** Let this be enough now to have spoken concerning the idolatrous feasts, and the extreme tortures.

8 **1** Then Judas Maccabeus, and they that were with him, went privily into the towns, and called their kinsfolks together, and took unto them all such as continued in the Jews' religion, and assembled about six thousand men. **2** And they called upon the Lord, that he would look upon the people that was trodden down of all; and also pity the temple profaned of ungodly men; **3** And that he would have compassion upon the city, sore defaced, and ready to be made even with the ground; and hear the blood that cried unto him, **4** And remember the wicked slaughter of harmless infants, and the blasphemies committed against his name; and that he would shew his hatred against the wicked. **5** Now when Maccabeus had his company about him, he could not be withstood by the heathen: for the wrath of the Lord was turned into mercy. **6** Therefore he came at unawares, and burnt up towns and cities, and got into his hands the most commodious places, and overcame and put to flight no small number of his enemies. **7** But specially took he advantage of the night for such privy attempts, insomuch that the fruit of his holiness was spread every where. **8** So when Philip saw that this man increased by little and little, and that things prospered with him still more and more, he wrote unto Ptolemeus, the governor of Celosyria and Phenice, to yield more aid to the king's affairs. **9** Then forthwith choosing Nicanor the son of Patroclus, one of his special friends, he sent him with no fewer than twenty thousand of all nations under him, to root out the whole generation of the Jews; and with him he joined also Gorgias a captain, who in matters of war had great experience. **10** So Nicanor undertook to make so much money of the captive Jews, as should defray the tribute of two thousand talents, which the king was to pay to the Romans. **11** Wherefore immediately he sent to the cities upon the sea coast, proclaiming a sale of the captive Jews, and promising that they should have fourscore and ten bodies for one talent, not expecting the vengeance that was to follow upon him from the Almighty God. **12** Now when word was brought unto Judas of Nicanor's coming, and he had imparted unto those that were with him that the army was at hand, **13** They that were fearful, and distrusted the justice of God, fled, and conveyed themselves away. **14** Others sold all that they had left, and withal besought the Lord to deliver them, sold by the wicked Nicanor before they met together: **15** And if not for their own sakes, yet for the covenants he had made with their fathers, and for his holy and glorious name's sake, by which they were called. **16** So Maccabeus called his men together unto the number of six thousand, and exhorted them not to be stricken with terror of the enemy, nor to fear the great multitude of the heathen, who came wrongly against them; but to fight manfully, **17** And to set before their eyes the injury that they had unjustly done to the holy place, and the cruel handling of the city, whereof they made a mockery, and also the taking away of the government of their forefathers: **18** For they, said he, trust in their weapons and boldness; but our confidence is in the Almighty who at a beck can cast down both them that come against us, and also all the world. **19** Moreover, he recounted unto them what helps their forefathers had found, and how they were delivered, when under Sennacherib an hundred fourscore and five thousand perished. **20** And he told them of the battle that they had in Babylon with the Galatians, how they came but eight thousand in all to the business, with four thousand Macedonians, and that the Macedonians being perplexed, the eight thousand destroyed an hundred and twenty thousand because of the help that they had from heaven, and so received a great booty. **21** Thus when he had made them bold with these words, and ready to die for the law and the country, he divided his army into four parts; **22** And joined with himself his own brethren, leaders of each band, to wit Simon, and Joseph, and Jonathan, giving each one fifteen hundred men. **23** Also he appointed Eleazar to read the holy book: and when he had given them this watchword, The help of God; himself leading the first band, **24** And by the help of the Almighty they slew above nine thousand of their enemies, and wounded and maimed the most part of Nicanor's host, and so put all to flight; **25** And took their money that came to buy them, and pursued them far: but lacking time they returned: 2 Maccabees Page **684** **26** For it was the day before the sabbath, and therefore they would no longer pursue them. **27** So when they had gathered their armour together, and spoiled their enemies, they occupied themselves about the sabbath, yielding exceeding praise and thanks to the Lord, who had preserved them unto that day, which was the beginning of mercy distilling upon

them. 28 And after the sabbath, when they had given part of the spoils to the
maimed, and the widows, and orphans, the residue they divided among themsel-
ves and their servants. 29 When this was done, and they had made a common
supplication, they besought the merciful Lord to be reconciled with his servants
for ever. 30 Moreover of those that were with Timotheus and Bacchides, who
fought against them, they slew above twenty thousand, and very easily got high
and strong holds, and divided among themselves many spoils more, and made the
maimed, orphans, widows, yea, and the aged also, equal in spoils with themsel-
ves. 31 And when they had gathered their armour together, they laid them up
all carefully in convenient places, and the remnant of the spoils they brought to
Jerusalem. 32 They slew also Philarches, that wicked person, who was with Ti-
motheus, and had annoyed the Jews many ways. 33 Furthermore at such time
as they kept the feast for the victory in their country they burnt Callisthenes, that
had set fire upon the holy gates, who had fled into a little house; and so he recei-
ved a reward meet for his wickedness. 34 As for that most ungracious Nicanor,
who had brought a thousand merchants to buy the Jews, 35 He was through
the help of the Lord brought down by them, of whom he made least account;
and putting off his glorious apparel, and discharging his company, he came like a
fugitive servant through the midland unto Antioch having very great dishonour,
for that his host was destroyed. 36 Thus he, that took upon him to make good
to the Romans their tribute by means of captives in Jerusalem, told abroad, that
the Jews had God to fight for them, and therefore they could not be hurt, because
they followed the laws that he gave them.

9

1 About that time came Antiochus with dishonour out of the country of
Persia 2 For he had entered the city called Persepolis, and went about
to rob the temple, and to hold the city; whereupon the multitude running to
defend themselves with their weapons put them to flight; and so it happened, that
Antiochus being put to flight of the inhabitants returned with shame. 3 Now
when he came to Ecbatane, news was brought him what had happened unto
Nicanor and Timotheus. 4 Then swelling with anger. he thought to avenge
upon the Jews the disgrace done unto him by those that made him flee. Therefo-
re commanded he his chariotman to drive without ceasing, and to dispatch the
journey, the judgment of GOd now following him. For he had spoken proudly
in this sort, That he would come to Jerusalem and make it a common burying
place of the Jews. 5 But the Lord Almighty, the God of Isreal, smote him with
an incurable and invisible plague: or as soon as he had spoken these words, a
pain of the bowels that was remediless came upon him, and sore torments of the
inner parts; 6 And that most justly: for he had tormented other men's bowels
with many and strange torments. 7 Howbeit he nothing at all ceased from his
bragging, but still was filled with pride, breathing out fire in his rage against
the Jews, and commanding to haste the journey: but it came to pass that he fell
down from his chariot, carried violently; so that having a sore fall, all the mem-
bers of his body were much pained. 8 And thus he that a little afore thought
he might command the waves of the sea, (so proud was he beyond the condi-
tion of man) and weigh the high mountains in a balance, was now cast on the
ground, and carried in an horselitter, shewing forth unto all the manifest power
of God. 9 So that the worms rose up out of the body of this wicked man, and
whiles he lived in sorrow and pain, his flesh fell away, and the filthiness of his
smell was noisome to all his army. 10 And the man, that thought a little afore
he could reach to the stars of heaven, no man could endure to carry for his into-
lerable stink. 11 Here therefore, being plagued, he began to leave off his great
pride, and to come to the knowledge of himself by the scourge of God, his pain
increasing every moment. 12 And when he himself could not abide his own
smell, he said these words, It is meet to be subject unto God, and that a man that
is mortal should not proudly think of himself if he were God. 13 This wicked
person vowed also unto the Lord, who now no more would have mercy upon
him, saying thus, 14 That the holy city (to the which he was going in haste to
lay it even with the ground, and to make it a common buryingplace,) he would
set at liberty: 15 And as touching the Jews, whom he had judged not worthy
so much as to be buried, but to be cast out with their children to be devoured
of the fowls and wild beasts, he would make them all equals to the citizens of
Athens: 16 And the holy temple, which before he had spoiled, he would gar-
nish with goodly gifts, and restore all the holy vessels with many more, and out
of his own revenue defray the charges belonging to the sacrifices: 17 Yea, and
that also he would become a Jew himself, and go through all the world that was
inhabited, and declare the power of God. 18 But for all this his pains would
not cease: for the just judgment of God was come upon him: therefore despairing
of his health, he wrote unto the Jews the letter underwritten, containing the form
of a supplication, after this manner: 19 Antiochus, king and governor, to the
good Jews his citizens wisheth much joy, health, and prosperity: 20 If ye and
your children fare well, and your affairs be to your contentment, I give very great
thanks to God, having my hope in heaven. 21 As for me, I was weak, or else I
would have remembered kindly your honour and good will returning out of Per-
sia, and being taken with a grievous disease, I thought it necessary to care for the
common safety of all: 22 Not distrusting mine health, but having great hope
to escape this sickness. 23 But considering that even my father, at what time
he led an army into the high countries. appointed a successor, 24 To the end
that, if any thing fell out contrary to expectation, or if any tidings were brought
that were grievous, they of the land, knowing to whom the state was left, might
not be troubled: 25 Again, considering how that the princes that are borderers
and neighbours unto my kingdom wait for opportunities, and expect what shall
be the event. I have appointed my son Antiochus king, whom I often committed
and commended unto many of you, when I went up into the high provinces;
to whom I have written as followeth: 26 Therefore I pray and request you to
remember the benefits that I have done unto you generally, and in special, and
that every man will be still faithful to me and my son. 27 For I am persuaded
that he understanding my mind will favourably and graciously yield to your de-
sires. 28 Thus the murderer and blasphemer having suffered most grievously,
as he entreated other men, so died he a miserable death in a strange country in
the mountains. 29 And Philip, that was brought up with him, carried away
his body, who also fearing the son of Antiochus went into Egypt to Ptolemeus
Philometor.

10

1 Now Maccabeus and his company, the Lord guiding them, recove-
red the temple and the city: 2 But the altars which the heathen had
built in the open street, and also the chapels, they pulled down. 3 And having
cleansed the temple they made another altar, and striking stones they took fire out
of them, and offered a sacrifice after two years, and set forth incense, and lights,
and shewbread. 4 When that was done, they fell flat down, and besought the
Lord that they might come no more into such troubles; but if they sinned any
more against him, that he himself would chasten them with mercy, and that they
might not be delivered unto the blasphemous and barbarous nations. 5 Now
upon the same day that the strangers profaned the temple, on the very same day it
was cleansed again, even the five and twentieth day of the same month, which is
Casleu. 6 And they kept the eight days with gladness, as in the feast of the taber-
nacles, remembering that not long afore they had held the feast of the tabernacles,
when as they wandered in the mountains and dens like beasts. 7 Therefore they
bare branches, and fair boughs, and palms also, and sang psalms unto him that
had given them good success in cleansing his place. 8 They ordained also by
a common statute and decree, That every year those days should be kept of the
whole nation of the Jews. 9 And this was the end of Antiochus, called Epipha-
nes. 10 Now will we declare the acts of Antiochus Eupator, who was the son of
this wicked man, gathering briefly the calamities of the wars. 11 So when he
was come to the crown, he set one Lysias over the affairs of his realm, and appoin-
ted him his chief governor of Celosyria and Phenice. 12 For Ptolemeus, that
was called Macron, choosing rather to do justice unto the Jews for the wrong that
had been done unto them, endeavoured to continue peace with them. 13 Whe-
reupon being accused of the king's friends before Eupator, and called traitor at
every word because he had left Cyprus, that Philometor had committed unto
him, and departed to Antiochus Epiphanes, and seeing that he was in no honou-
rable place, he was so discouraged, that he poisoned himself and died. 14 But
when Gorgias was governor of the holds, he hired soldiers, and nourished war
continually with the Jews: 15 And therewithall the Idumeans, having gotten
into their hands the most commodious holds, kept the Jews occupied, and re-
ceiving those that were banished from Jerusalem, they went about to nourish
war. 16 Then they that were with Maccabeus made supplication, and besought
God that he would be their helper; and so they ran with violence upon the strong
holds of the Idumeans, 17 And assaulting them strongly, they won the holds,
and kept off all that fought upon the wall, and slew all that fell into their hands,
and killed no fewer than twenty thousand. 18 And because certain, who were
no less than nine thousand, were fled together into two very strong castles, having
all manner of things convenient to sustain the siege, 19 Maccabeus left Simon
and Joseph, and Zaccheus also, and them that were with him, who were enough
to besiege them, and departed himself unto those places which more needed his
help. 20 Now they that were with Simon, being led with covetousness, were
persuaded for money through certain of those that were in the castle, and took
seventy thousand drachms, and let some of them escape. 21 But when it was
told Maccabeus what was done, he called the governors of the people together,
and accused those men, that they had sold their brethren for money, and set their
enemies free to fight against them. 22 So he slew those that were found traitors,
and immediately took the two castles. 23 And having good success with his
weapons in all things he took in hand, he slew in the two holds more than twenty
thousand. 24 Now Timotheus, whom the Jews had overcome before, when he
had gathered a great multitude of foreign forces, and horses out of Asia not a few,
came as though he would take Jewry by force of arms. 25 But when he drew
near, they that were with Maccabeus turned themselves to pray unto God, and
sprinkled earth upon their heads, and girded their loins with sackcloth, 26 And
fell down at the foot of the altar, and besought him to be merciful to them, and
to be an enemy to their enemies, and an adversary to their adversaries, as the
law declareth. 27 So after the prayer they took their weapons, and went on
further from the city: and when they drew near to their enemies, they kept by
themselves. 28 Now the sun being newly risen, they joined both together; the
one part having together with their virtue their refuge also unto the Lord for a
pledge of their success and victory: the other side making their rage leader of their
battle 29 But when the battle waxed strong, there appeared unto the enemies
from heaven five comely men upon horses, with bridles of gold, and two of them
led the Jews, 30 And took Maccabeus betwixt them, and covered him on every
side weapons, and kept him safe, but shot arrows and lightnings against the ene-
mies: so that being confounded with blindness, and full of trouble, they were

killed. 31 And there were slain of footmen twenty thousand and five hundred,
and six hundred horsemen. 32 As for Timotheus himself, he fled into a very
strong hold, called Gawra, where Chereas was governor. 33 But they that were
with Maccabeus laid siege against the fortress courageously four days. 34 And
they that were within, trusting to the strength of the place, blasphemed exceedin-
gly, and uttered wicked words. 35 Nevertheless upon the fifth day early twenty
young men of Maccabeus' company, inflamed with anger because of the blasphe-
mies, assaulted the wall manly, and with a fierce courage killed all that they met
withal. 36 Others likewise ascending after them, whiles they were busied with
them that were within, burnt the towers, and kindling fires burnt the blasphemers
alive; and others broke open the gates, and, having received in the rest of the
army, took the city, 37 And killed Timotheus, that was hid in a certain pit, and
Chereas his brother, with Apollophanes. 38 When this was done, they praised
the Lord with psalms and thanksgiving, who had done so great things for Israel,
and given them the victory.

11

1 Not long after the, Lysias the king's protector and cousin, who also
managed the affairs, took sore displeasure for the things that were
done. 2 And when he had gathered about fourscore thousand with all the hor-
semen, he came against the Jews, thinking to make the city an habitation of the
Gentiles, 3 And to make a gain of the temple, as of the other chapels of the
heathen, and to set the high priesthood to sale every year: 4 Not at all consi-
dering the power of God but puffed up with his ten thousands of footmen, and
his thousands of horsemen, and his fourscore elephants. 5 So he came to Judea,
and drew near to Bethsura, which was a strong town, but distant from Jerusalem
about five furlongs, and he laid sore siege unto it. 6 Now when they that were
with Maccabeus heard that he besieged the holds, they and all the people with
lamentation and tears besought the Lord that he would send a good angel to
deliver Israel. 7 Then Maccabeus himself first of all took weapons, exhorting
the other that they would jeopard themselves together with him to help their
brethren: so they went forth together with a willing mind. 8 And as they were
at Jerusalem, there appeared before them on horseback one in white clothing,
shaking his armour of gold. 9 Then they praised the merciful God all together,
and took heart, insomuch that they were ready not only to fight with men, but
with most cruel beasts, and to pierce through walls of iron. 10 Thus they mar-
ched forward in their armour, having an helper from heaven: for the Lord was
merciful unto them 11 And giving a charge upon their enemies like lions, they
slew eleven thousand footmen, and sixteen hundred horsemen, and put all the
other to flight. 12 Many of them also being wounded escaped naked; and Ly-
sias himself fled away shamefully, and so escaped. 13 Who, as he was a man of
understanding, casting with himself what loss he had had, and considering that
the Hebrews could not be overcome, because the Almighty God helped them,
he sent unto them, 14 And persuaded them to agree to all reasonable con-
ditions, and promised that he would persuade the king that he must needs be
a friend unto them. 15 Then Maccabeus consented to all that Lysias desired,
being careful of the common good; and whatsoever Maccabeus wrote unto Lysias
concerning the Jews, the king granted it. 16 For there were letters written unto
the Jews from Lysias to this effect: Lysias unto the people of the Jews sendeth
greeting: 17 John and Absolom, who were sent from you, delivered me the
petition subscribed, and made request for the performance of the contents there-
of. 18 Therefore what things soever were meet to be reported to the king, I have
declared them, and he hath granted as much as might be. 19 And if then ye will
keep yourselves loyal to the state, hereafter also will I endeavour to be a means of
your good. 20 But of the particulars I have given order both to these and the
other that came from me, to commune with you. 21 Fare ye well. The hundred
and eight and fortieth year, the four and twentieth day of the month Dioscorin-
thius. 22 Now the king's letter contained these words: King Antiochus unto his
brother Lysias sendeth greeting: 23 Since our father is translated unto the gods,
our will is, that they that are in our realm live quietly, that every one may attend
upon his own affairs. 24 We understand also that the Jews would not consent
to our father, for to be brought unto the custom of the Gentiles, but had rather
keep their own manner of living: for the which cause they require of us, that we
should suffer them to live after their own laws. 25 Wherefore our mind is, that
this nation shall be in rest, and we have determined to restore them their temple,
that they may live according to the customs of their forefathers. 26 Thou shalt
do well therefore to send unto them, and grant them peace, that when they are
certified of our mind, they may be of good comfort, and ever go cheerfully about
their own affairs. 27 And the letter of the king unto the nation of the Jews
was after this manner: King Antiochus sendeth greeting unto the council, and
the rest of the Jews: 28 If ye fare well, we have our desire; we are also in good
health. 29 Menelaus declared unto us, that your desire was to return home,
and to follow your own business: 30 Wherefore they that will depart shall have
safe conduct till the thirtieth day of Xanthicus with security. 31 And the Jews
shall use their own kind of meats and laws, as before; and none of them any
manner of ways shall be molested for things ignorantly done. 32 I have sent
also Menelaus, that he may comfort you. 33 Fare ye well. In the hundred forty
and eighth year, and the fifteenth day of the month Xanthicus. 34 The Romans
also sent unto them a letter containing these words: Quintus Memmius and Ti-
tus Manlius, ambassadors of the Romans, send greeting unto the people of the
Jews. 35 Whatsoever Lysias the king's cousin hath granted, therewith we also
are well pleased. 36 But touching such things as he judged to be referred to the
king, after ye have advised thereof, send one forthwith, that we may declare as it is
convenient for you: for we are now going to Antioch. 37 Therefore send some
with speed, that we may know what is your mind. 38 Farewell. This hundred
and eight and fortieth year, the fifteenth day of the month Xanthicus.

12

1 When these covenants were made, Lysias went unto the king, and
the Jews were about their husbandry. 2 But of the governours of
several places, Timotheus, and Apollonius the son of Genneus, also Hieronymus,
and Demophon, and beside them Nicanor the governor of Cyprus, would not
suffer them to be quiet and live in peace. 3 The men of Joppa also did such an
ungodly deed: they prayed the Jews that dwelt among them to go with their wives
and children into the boats which they had prepared, as though they had meant
them no hurt. 4 Who accepted of it according to the common decree of the
city, as being desirous to live in peace, and suspecting nothing: but when they
were gone forth into the deep, they drowned no less than two hundred of
them. 5 When Judas heard of this cruelty done unto his countrymen, he com-
manded those that were with him to make them ready. 6 And calling upon God
the righteous Judge, he came against those murderers of his brethren, and burnt
the haven by night, and set the boats on fire, and those that fled thither he
slew. 7 And when the town was shut up, he went backward, as if he would re-
turn to root out all them of the city of Joppa. 8 But when he heard that the
Jamnites were minded to do in like manner unto the Jews that dwelt among
them, 9 He came upon the Jamnites also by night, and set fire on the haven and
the navy, so that the light of the fire was seen at Jerusalem two hundred and forty
furlongs off. 10 Now when they were gone from thence nine furlongs in their
journey toward Timotheus, no fewer than five thousand men on foot and five
hundred horsemen of the Arabians set upon him. 11 Whereupon there was a
very sore battle; but Judas' side by the help of God got the victory; so that the
Nomades of Arabia, being overcome, besought Judas for peace, promising both to
give him cattle, and to pleasure him otherwise. 12 Then Judas, thinking indeed
that they would be profitable in many things, granted them peace: whereupon
they shook hands, and so they departed to their tents. 13 He went also about
to make a bridge to a certain strong city, which was fenced about with walls, and
inhabited by people of divers countries; and the name of it was Caspis. 14 But
they that were within it put such trust in the strength of the walls and provision
of victuals, that they behaved themselves rudely toward them that were with Ju-
das, railing and blaspheming, and uttering such words as were not to be
spoken. 15 Wherefore Judas with his company, calling upon the great Lord
of the world, who without rams or engines of war did cast down Jericho in the
time of Joshua, gave a fierce assault against the walls, 16 And took the city by
the will of God, and made unspeakable slaughters, insomuch that a lake two
furlongs broad near adjoining thereunto, being filled full, was seen running with
blood. 17 Then departed they from thence seven hundred and fifty furlongs,
and came to Characa unto the Jews that are called Tubieni. 18 But as for Ti-
motheus, they found him not in the places: for before he had dispatched any
thing, he departed from thence, having left a very strong garrison in a certain
hold. 19 Howbeit Dositheus and Sosipater, who were of Maccabeus' captains,
went forth, and slew those that Timotheus had left in the fortress, above ten
thousand men. 20 And Maccabeus ranged his army by bands, and set them
over the bands, and went against Timotheus, who had about him an hundred and
twenty thousand men of foot, and two thousand and five hundred horse-
men. 21 Now when Timotheus had knowledge of Judas' coming, he sent the
women and children and the other baggage unto a fortress called Carnion: for the
town was hard to besiege, and uneasy to come unto, by reason of the straitness of
all the places. 22 But when Judas his first band came in sight, the enemies,
being smitten with fear and terror through the appearing of him who seeth all
things, fled amain, one running into this way, another that way, so as that they
were often hurt of their own men, and wounded with the points of their own
swords. 23 Judas also was very earnest in pursuing them, killing those wicked
wretches, of whom he slew about thirty thousand men. 24 Moreover Ti-
motheus himself fell into the hands of Dositheus and Sosipater, whom he besou-
ght with much craft to let him go with his life, because he had many of the Jews'
parents, and the brethren of some of them, who, if they put him to death, should
not be regarded. 25 So when he had assured them with many words that he
would restore them without hurt, according to the agreement, they let him go for
the saving of their brethren. 26 Then Maccabeus marched forth to Carnion,
and to the temple of Atargatis, and there he slew five and twenty thousand per-
sons. 27 And after he had put to flight and destroyed them, Judas removed the
host toward Ephron, a strong city, wherein Lysias abode, and a great multitude of
divers nations, and the strong young men kept the walls, and defended them
mightily: wherein also was great provision of engines and darts. 28 But when
Judas and his company had called upon Almighty God, who with his power bre-
aketh the strength of his enemies, they won the city, and slew twenty and five
thousand of them that were within, 29 From thence they departed to Scytho-
polis, which lieth six hundred furlongs from Jerusalem, 30 But when the Jews
that dwelt there had testified that the Scythopolitans dealt lovingly with them,
and entreated them kindly in the time of their adversity; 31 They gave them
thanks, desiring them to be friendly still unto them: and so they came to Jerusa-
lem, the feast of the weeks approaching. 32 And after the feast, called Pente-

cost, they went forth against Gorgias the governor of Idumea, **33** Who came out with three thousand men of foot and four hundred horsemen. **34** And it happened that in their fighting together a few of the Jews were slain. **35** At which time Dositheus, one of Bacenor's company, who was on horseback, and a strong man, was still upon Gorgias, and taking hold of his coat drew him by force; and when he would have taken that cursed man alive, a horseman of Thracia coming upon him smote off his shoulder, so that Gorgias fled unto Marisa. **36** Now when they that were with Gorgias had fought long, and were weary, Judas called upon the Lord, that he would shew himself to be their helper and leader of the battle. **37** And with that he began in his own language, and sung psalms with a loud voice, and rushing unawares upon Gorgias' men, he put them to flight. **38** So Judas gathered his host, and came into the city of Odollam, And when the seventh day came, they purified themselves, as the custom was, and kept the sabbath in the same place. **39** And upon the day following, as the use had been, Judas and his company came to take up the bodies of them that were slain, and to bury them with their kinsmen in their fathers' graves. **40** Now under the coats of every one that was slain they found things consecrated to the idols of the Jamnites, which is forbidden the Jews by the law. Then every man saw that this was the cause wherefore they were slain. **41** All men therefore praising the Lord, the righteous Judge, who had opened the things that were hid, **42** Betook themselves unto prayer, and besought him that the sin committed might wholly be put out of remembrance. Besides, that noble Judas exhorted the people to keep themselves from sin, forsomuch as they saw before their eyes the things that came to pass for the sins of those that were slain. **43** And when he had made a gathering throughout the company to the sum of two thousand drachms of silver, he sent it to Jerusalem to offer a sin offering, doing therein very well and honestly, in that he was mindful of the resurrection: **44** For if he had not hoped that they that were slain should have risen again, it had been superfluous and vain to pray for the dead. **45** And also in that he perceived that there was great favour laid up for those that died godly, it was an holy and good thought. Whereupon he made a reconciliation for the dead, that they might be delivered from sin.

13

1 In the hundred forty and ninth year it was told Judas, that Antiochus Eupator was coming with a great power into Judea, **2** And with him Lysias his protector, and ruler of his affairs, having either of them a Grecian power of footmen, an hundred and ten thousand, and horsemen five thousand and three hundred, and elephants two and twenty, and three hundred chariots armed with hooks. **3** Menelaus also joined himself with them, and with great dissimulation encouraged Antiochus, not for the safeguard of the country, but because he thought to have been made governor. **4** But the King of kings moved Antiochus' mind against this wicked wretch, and Lysias informed the king that this man was the cause of all mischief, so that the king commanded to bring him unto Berea, and to put him to death, as the manner is in that place. **5** Now there was in that place a tower of fifty cubits high, full of ashes, and it had a round instrument which on every side hanged down into the ashes. **6** And whosoever was condemned of sacrilege, or had committed any other grievous crime, there did all men thrust him unto death. **7** Such a death it happened that wicked man to die, not having so much as burial in the earth; and that most justly: **8** For inasmuch as he had committed many sins about the altar, whose fire and ashes were holy, he received his death in ashes. **9** Now the king came with a barbarous and haughty mind to do far worse to the Jews, than had been done in his father's time. **10** Which things when Judas perceived, he commanded the multitude to call upon the Lord night and day, that if ever at any other time, he would now also help them, being at the point to be put from their law, from their country, and from the holy temple: **11** And that he would not suffer the people, that had even now been but a little refreshed, to be in subjection to the blasphemous nations. **12** So when they had all done this together, and besought the merciful Lord with weeping and fasting, and lying flat upon the ground three days long, Judas, having exhorted them, commanded they should be in a readiness. **13** And Judas, being apart with the elders, determined, before the king's host should enter into Judea, and get the city, to go forth and try the matter in fight by the help of the Lord. **14** So when he had committed all to the Creator of the world, and exhorted his soldiers to fight manfully, even unto death, for the laws, the temple, the city, the country, and the commonwealth, he camped by Modin: **15** And having given the watchword to them that were about him, Victory is of God; with the most valiant and choice young men he went in into the king's tent by night, and slew in the camp about four thousand men, and the chiefest of the elephants, with all that were upon him. **16** And at last they filled the camp with fear and tumult, and departed with good success. **17** This was done in the break of the day, because the protection of the Lord did help him. **18** Now when the king had taken a taste of the manliness of the Jews, he went about to take the holds by policy, **19** And marched toward Bethsura, which was a strong hold of the Jews: but he was put to flight, failed, and lost of his men: **20** For Judas had conveyed unto them that were in it such things as were necessary. **21** But Rhodocus, who was in the Jews' host, disclosed the secrets to the enemies; therefore he was sought out, and when they had gotten him, they put him in prison. **22** The king treated with them in Bethsum the second time, gave his hand, took their's, departed, fought with Judas, was overcome; **23** Heard that Philip, who was left over the affairs in Antioch, was desperately bent, confounded, intreated the Jews, submitted himself, and sware to all equal conditions, agreed with them, and offered sacrifice, honoured the temple, and dealt kindly with the place, **24** And accepted well of Maccabeus, made him principal governor from Ptolemais unto the Gerrhenians; **25** Came to Ptolemais: the people there were grieved for the covenants; for they stormed, because they would make their covenants void: **26** Lysias went up to the judgment seat, said as much as could be in defence of the cause, persuaded, pacified, made them well affected, returned to Antioch. Thus it went touching the king's coming and departing.

14

1 After three years was Judas informed, that Demetrius the son of Seleucus, having entered by the haven of Tripolis with a great power and navy, **2** Had taken the country, and killed Antiochus, and Lysias his protector. **3** Now one Alcimus, who had been high priest, and had defiled himself wilfully in the times of their mingling with the Gentiles, seeing that by no means he could save himself, nor have any more access to the holy altar, **4** Came to king Demetrius in the hundred and one and fiftieth year, presenting unto him a crown of gold, and a palm, and also of the boughs which were used solemnly in the temple: and so that day he held his peace. **5** Howbeit having gotten opportunity to further his foolish enterprize, and being called into counsel by Demetrius, and asked how the Jews stood affected, and what they intended, he answered thereunto: **6** Those of the Jews that he called Assideans, whose captain is Judas Maccabeus, nourish war and are seditious, and will not let the rest be in peace. **7** Therefore I, being deprived of mine ancestors' honour, I mean the high priesthood, am now come hither: **8** First, verily for the unfeigned care I have of things pertaining to the king; and secondly, even for that I intend the good of mine own countrymen: for all our nation is in no small misery through the unadvised dealing of them aforersaid. **9** Wherefore, O king, seeing knowest all these things, be careful for the country, and our nation, which is pressed on every side, according to the clemency that thou readily shewest unto all. **10** For as long as Judas liveth, it is not possible that the state should be quiet. **11** This was no sooner spoken of him, but others of the king's friends, being maliciously set against Judas, did more incense Demetrius. **12** And forthwith calling Nicanor, who had been master of the elephants, and making him governor over Judea, he sent him forth, **13** Commanding him to slay Judas, and to scatter them that were with him, and to make Alcimus high priest of the great temple. **14** Then the heathen, that had fled out of Judea from Judas, came to Nicanor by flocks, thinking the harm and calamities ot the Jews to be their welfare. **15** Now when the Jews heard of Nicanor's coming, and that the heathen were up against them, they cast earth upon their heads, and made supplication to him that had established his people for ever, and who always helpeth his portion with manifestation of his presence. **16** So at the commandment of the captain they removed straightways from thence, and came near unto them at the town of Dessau. **17** Now Simon, Judas' brother, had joined battle with Nicanor, but was somewhat discomfited through the sudden silence of his enemies. **18** Nevertheless Nicanor, hearing of the manliness of them that were with Judas, and the courageousness that they had to fight for their country, durst not try the matter by the sword. **19** Wherefore he sent Posidonius, and Theodotus, and Mattathias, to make peace. **20** So when they had taken long advisement thereupon, and the captain had made the multitude acquainted therewith, and it appeared that they were all of one mind, they consented to the covenants, **21** And appointed a day to meet in together by themselves: and when the day came, and stools were set for either of them, **22** Ludas placed armed men ready in convenient places, lest some treachery should be suddenly practised by the enemies: so they made a peaceable conference. **23** Now Nicanor abode in Jerusalem, and did no hurt, but sent away the people that came flocking unto him. **24** And he would not willingly have Judas out of his sight: for he love the man from his heart **25** He prayed him also to take a wife, and to beget children: so he married, was quiet, and took part of this life. **26** But Alcimus, perceiving the love that was betwixt them, and considering the covenants that were made, came to Demetrius, and told him that Nicanor was not well affected toward the state; for that he had ordained Judas, a traitor to his realm, to be the king's successor. **27** Then the king being in a rage, and provoked with the accusations of the most wicked man, wrote to Nicanor, signifying that he was much displeased with the covenants, and commanding him that he should send Maccabeus prisoner in all haste unto Antioch. **28** When this came to Nicanor's hearing, he was much confounded in himself, and took it grievously that he should make void the articles which were agreed upon, the man being in no fault. **29** But because there was no dealing against the king, he watched his time to accomplish this thing by policy. **30** Notwithstanding, when Maccabeus saw that Nicanor began to be churlish unto him, and that he entreated him more roughly than he was wont, perceiving that such sour behaviour came not of good, he gathered together not a few of his men, and withdrew himself from Nicanor. **31** But the other, knowing that he was notably prevented by Judas' policy, came into the great and holy temple, and commanded the priests, that were offering their usual sacrifices, to deliver him the man. **32** And when they sware that they could not tell where the man was whom he sought, **33** He stretched out his right hand toward the temple, and made an oath in this manner: If ye will not deliver me Judas as a prisoner, I will lay this temple of God even with the ground, and I will break down the altar, and erect a notable temple unto Bacchus. **34** After these words he departed. Then the priests lifted up their hands toward heaven, and besought him that was ever a defender of their nation, saying in this manner; **35** Thou, O Lord of all things, who hast need

of nothing, wast pleased that the temple of thine habitation should be among
us: **36** Therefore now, O holy Lord of all holiness, keep this house ever unde-
filed, which lately was cleansed, and stop every unrighteous mouth. **37** Now
was there accused unto Nicanor one Razis, one of the elders of Jerusalem, a lover
of his countrymen, and a man of very good report, who for his kindness was
called a father of the Jews. **38** For in the former times, when they mingled not
themselves with the Gentiles, he had been accused of Judaism, and did boldly
jeopard his body and life with all vehemency for the religion of the Jews. **39** So
Nicanor, willing to declare the hate that he bare unto the Jews, sent above five
hundred men of war to take him: **40** For he thought by taking him to do the
Jews much hurt. **41** Now when the multitude would have taken the tower, and
violently broken into the outer door, and bade that fire should be brought to burn
it, he being ready to be taken on every side fell upon his sword; **42** Choosing
rather to die manfully, than to come into the hands of the wicked, to be abused
otherwise than beseemed his noble birth: **43** But missing his stroke through ha-
ste, the multitude also rushing within the doors, he ran boldly up to the wall, and
cast himself down manfully among the thickest of them. **44** But they quickly
giving back, and a space being made, he fell down into the midst of the void pla-
ce. **45** Nevertheless, while there was yet breath within him, being inflamed with
anger, he rose up; and though his blood gushed out like spouts of water, and his
wounds were grievous, yet he ran through the midst of the throng; and standing
upon a steep rock, **46** When as his blood was now quite gone, he plucked out
his bowels, and taking them in both his hands, he cast them upon the throng, and
calling upon the Lord of life and spirit to restore him those again, he thus died.

15 1 But Nicanor, hearing that Judas and his company were in the strong
places about Samaria, resolved without any danger to set upon them
on the sabbath day. **2** Nevertheless the Jews that were compelled to go with
him said, O destroy not so cruelly and barbarously, but give honour to that day,
which he, that seeth all things, hath honoured with holiness above all other
days. **3** Then the most ungracious wretch demanded, if there were a Mighty
one in heaven, that had commanded the sabbath day to be kept. **4** And when
they said, There is in heaven a living Lord, and mighty, who commanded the se-
venth day to be kept: **5** Then said the other, And I also am mighty upon earth,
and I command to take arms, and to do the king's business. Yet he obtained not
to have his wicked will done. **6** So Nicanor in exceeding pride and haughtiness
determined to set up a publick monument of his victory over Judas and them that
were with him. **7** But Maccabeus had ever sure confidence that the Lord would
help him: **8** Wherefore he exhorted his people not to fear the coming of the
heathen against them, but to remember the help which in former times they had
received from heaven, and now to expect the victory and aid, which should come
unto them from the Almighty. **9** And so comforting them out of the law and
the prophets, and withal putting them in mind of the battles that they won afore,
he made them more cheerful. **10** And when he had stirred up their minds, he
gave them their charge, shewing them therewithall the falsehood of the heathen,
and the breach of oaths. **11** Thus he armed every one of them, not so much
with defence of shields and spears, as with comfortable and good words: and be-
side that, he told them a dream worthy to be believed, as if it had been so indeed,
which did not a little rejoice them. **12** And this was his vision: That Onias, who
had been high priest, a virtuous and a good man, reverend in conversation, gentle
in condition, well spoken also, and exercised from a child in all points of virtue,
holding up his hands prayed for the whole body of the Jews. **13** This done, in
like manner there appeared a man with gray hairs, and exceeding glorious, who
was of a wonderful and excellent majesty. **14** Then Onias answered, saying, This
is a lover of the brethren, who prayeth much for the people, and for the holy city,
to wit, Jeremias the prophet of God. **15** Whereupon Jeremias holding forth his
right hand gave to Judas a sword of gold, and in giving it spake thus, **16** Take
this holy sword, a gift from God, with the which thou shalt wound the adver-
saries. **17** Thus being well comforted by the words of Judas, which were very
good, and able to stir them up to valour, and to encourage the hearts of the young
men, they determined not to pitch camp, but courageously to set upon them,
and manfully to try the matter by conflict, because the city and the sanctuary and
the temple were in danger. **18** For the care that they took for their wives, and
their children, their brethren, and folks, was in least account with them: but the
greatest and principal fear was for the holy temple. **19** Also they that were in
the city took not the least care, being troubled for the conflict abroad. **20** And
now, when as all looked what should be the trial, and the enemies were already
come near, and the army was set in array, and the beasts conveniently placed, and
the horsemen set in wings, **21** Maccabeus seeing the coming of the multitude,
and the divers preparations of armour, and the fierceness of the beasts, stretched
out his hands toward heaven, and called upon the Lord that worketh wonders,
knowing that victory cometh not by arms, but even as it seemeth good to him,
he giveth it to such as are worthy: **22** Therefore in his prayer he said after this
manner; O Lord, thou didst send thine angel in the time of Ezekias king of Judea,
and didst slay in the host of Sennacherib an hundred fourscore and five thou-
sand: **23** Wherefore now also, O Lord of heaven, send a good angel before us
for a fear and dread unto them; **24** And through the might of thine arm let tho-
se be stricken with terror, that come against thy holy people to blaspheme. And he
ended thus. **25** Then Nicanor and they that were with him came forward with
trumpets and songs. **26** But Judas and his company encountered the enemies
with invocation and prayer. **27** So that fighting with their hands, and praying
unto God with their hearts, they slew no less than thirty and five thousand men:
for through the appearance of God they were greatly cheered. **28** Now when
the battle was done, returning again with joy, they knew that Nicanor lay dead in
his harness. **29** Then they made a great shout and a noise, praising the Almighty
in their own language. **30** And Judas, who was ever the chief defender of the
citizens both in body and mind, and who continued his love toward his country-
men all his life, commanded to strike off Nicanor's head, and his hand with his
shoulder, and bring them to Jerusalem. **31** So when he was there, and called
them of his nation together, and set the priests before the altar, he sent for them
that were of the tower, **32** And shewed them vile Nicanor's head, and the hand
of that blasphemer, which with proud brags he had stretched out against the holy
temple of the Almighty. **33** And when he had cut out the tongue of that ungo-
dly Nicanor, he commanded that they should give it by pieces unto the fowls, and
hang up the reward of his madness before the temple. **34** So every man praised
toward the heaven the glorious Lord, saying, Blessed be he that hath kept his own
place undefiled. **35** He hanged also Nicanor's head upon the tower, an evident
and manifest sign unto all of the help of the Lord. **36** And they ordained all
with a common decree in no case to let that day pass without solemnity, but to ce-
lebrate the thirtieth day of the twelfth month, which in the Syrian tongue is called
Adar, the day before Mardocheus' day. **37** Thus went it with Nicanor: and from
that time forth the Hebrews had the city in their power. And here will I make
an end. **38** And if I have done well, and as is fitting the story, it is that which I
desired: but if slenderly and meanly, it is that which I could attain unto. **39** For
as it is hurtful to drink wine or water alone; and as wine mingled with water is
pleasant, and delighteth the taste: even so speech finely framed delighteth the ears
of them that read the story. And here shall be an end

APOCRYPHA

1ST BOOK OF ESDRAS

The First Book of Esdras

1 1 And Josias held the feast of the passover in Jerusalem unto his Lord, and offered the passover the fourteenth day of the first month; **2** Having set the priests according to their daily courses, being arrayed in long garments, in the temple of the Lord. **3** And he spake unto the Levites, the holy ministers of Israel, that they should hallow themselves unto the Lord, to set the holy ark of the Lord in the house that king Solomon the son of David had built: **4** And said, Ye shall no more bear the ark upon your shoulders: now therefore serve the Lord your God, and minister unto his people Israel, and prepare you after your families and kindreds, **5** According as David the king of Israel prescribed, and according to the magnificence of Solomon his son: and standing in the temple according to the several dignity of the families of you the Levites, who minister in the presence of your brethren the children of Israel, **6** Offer the passover in order, and make ready the sacrifices for your brethren, and keep the passover according to the commandment of the Lord, which was given unto Moses. **7** And unto the people that was found there Josias gave thirty thousand lambs and kids, and three thousand calves: these things were given of the king's allowance, according as he promised, to the people, to the priests, and to the Levites. **8** And Helkias, Zacharias, and Syelus, the governors of the temple, gave to the priests for the passover two thousand and six hundred sheep, and three hundred calves. **9** And Jeconias, and Samaias, and Nathanael his brother, and Assabias, and Ochiel, and Joram, captains over thousands, gave to the Levites for the passover five thousand sheep, and seven hundred calves. **10** And when these things were done, the priests and Levites, having the unleavened bread, stood in very comely order according to the kindreds, **11** And according to the several dignities of the fathers, before the people, to offer to the Lord, as it is written in the book of Moses: and thus did they in the morning. **12** And they roasted the passover with fire, as appertaineth: as for the sacrifices, they sod them in brass pots and pans with a good savour, **13** And set them before all the people: and afterward they prepared for themselves, and for the priests their brethren, the sons of Aaron. **14** For the priests offered the fat until night: and the Levites prepared for themselves, and the priests their brethren, the sons of Aaron. **15** The holy singers also, the sons of Asaph, were in their order, according to the appointment of David, to wit, Asaph, Zacharias, and Jeduthun, who was of the king's retinue. **16** Moreover the porters were at every gate; it was not lawful for any to go from his ordinary service: for their brethren the Levites prepared for them. **17** Thus were the things that belonged to the sacrifices of the Lord accomplished in that day, that they might hold the passover, **18** And offer sacrifices upon the altar of the Lord, according to the commandment of king Josias. **19** So the children of Israel which were present held the passover at that time, and the feast of sweet bread seven days. **20** And such a passover was not kept in Israel since the time of the prophet Samuel. **21** Yea, all the kings of Israel held not such a passover as Josias, and the priests, and the Levites, and the Jews, held with all Israel that were found dwelling at Jerusalem. **22** In the eighteenth year of the reign of Josias was this passover kept. **23** And the works or Josias were upright before his Lord with an heart full of godliness. **24** As for the things that came to pass in his time, they were written in former times, concerning those that sinned, and did wickedly against the Lord above all people and kingdoms, and how they grieved him exceedingly, so that the words of the Lord rose up against Israel. **25** Now after all these acts of Josias it came to pass, that Pharaoh the king of Egypt came to raise war at Carchamis upon Euphrates: and Josias went out against him. **26** But the king of Egypt sent to him, saying, What have I to do with thee, O king of Judea? **27** I am not sent out from the Lord God against thee; for my war is upon Euphrates: and now the Lord is with me, yea, the Lord is with me hasting me forward: depart from me, and be not against the Lord. **28** Howbeit Josias did not turn back his chariot from him, but undertook to fight with him, not regarding the words of the prophet Jeremy spoken by the mouth of the Lord: **29** But joined battle with him in the plain of Magiddo, and the princes came against king Josias. **30** Then said the king unto his servants, Carry me away out of the battle; for I am very weak. And immediately his servants took him away out of the battle. **31** Then gat he up upon his second chariot; and being brought back to Jerusalem died, and was buried in his father's sepulchre. **32** And in all Jewry they mourned for Josias, yea, Jeremy the prophet lamented for Josias, and the chief men with the women made lamentation for him unto this day: and this was given out for an ordinance to be done continually in all the nation of Israel. **33** These things are written in the book of the stories of the kings of Judah, and every one of the acts that Josias did, and his glory, and his understanding in the law of the Lord, and the things that he had done before, and the things now recited, are reported in the book of the kings of Israel and Judea. **34** And the people took Joachaz the son of Josias, and made him king instead of Josias his father, when he was twenty and three years old. **35** And he reigned in Judea and in Jerusalem three months: and then the king of Egypt deposed him from reigning in Jerusalem. **36** And he set a tax upon the land of an hundred talents of silver and one talent of gold. **37** The king of Egypt also made king Joacim his brother king of Judea and Jerusalem. **38** And he bound Joacim and the nobles: but Zaraces his brother he apprehended, and brought him out of Egypt. **39** Five and twenty years old was Joacim when he was made king in the land of Judea and Jerusalem; and he did evil before the Lord. **40** Wherefore against him Nabuchodonosor the king of Babylon came up, and bound him with a chain of brass, and carried him into Babylon. **41** Nabuchodonosor also took of the holy vessels of the Lord, and carried them away, and set them in his own temple at Babylon. **42** But those things that are recorded of him, and of his uncleaness and impiety, are written in the chronicles of the kings. **43** And Joacim his son reigned in his stead: he was made king being eighteen years old; **44** And reigned but three months and ten days in Jerusalem; and did evil before the Lord. **45** So after a year Nabuchodonosor sent and caused him to be brought into Babylon with the holy vessels of the Lord; **46** And made Zedechias king of Judea and Jerusalem, when he was one and twenty years old; and he reigned eleven years: **47** And he did evil also in the sight of the Lord, and cared not for the words that were spoken unto him by the prophet Jeremy from the mouth of the Lord. **48** And after that king Nabuchodonosor had made him to swear by the name of the Lord, he forswore himself, and rebelled; and hardening his neck, his heart, he transgressed the laws of the Lord God of Israel. **49** The governors also of the people and of the priests did many things against the laws, and passed all the pollutions of all nations, and defiled the temple of the Lord, which was sanctified in Jerusalem. **50** Nevertheless the God of their fathers sent by his messenger to call them back, because he spared them and his tabernacle also. **51** But they had his messengers in derision; and, look, when the Lord spake unto them, they made a sport of his prophets: **52** So far forth, that he, being wroth with his people for their great ungodliness, commanded the kings of the Chaldees to come up against them; **53** Who slew their young men with the sword, yea, even within the compass of their holy temple, and spared neither young man nor maid, old man nor child, among them; for he delivered all into their hands. **54** And they took all the holy vessels of the Lord, both great and small, with the vessels of the ark of God, and the king's treasures, and carried them away into Babylon. **55** As for the house of the Lord, they burnt it, and brake down the walls of Jerusalem, and set fire upon her towers: **56** And as for her glorious things, they never ceased till they had consumed and brought them all to nought: and the people that were not slain with the sword he carried unto Babylon: **57** Who became servants to him and his children, till the Persians reigned, to fulfil the word of the Lord spoken by the mouth of Jeremy: **58** Until the land had enjoyed her sabbaths, the whole time of her desolation shall she rest, until the full term of seventy years.

2 1 In the first year of Cyrus king of the Persians, that the word of the Lord might be accomplished, that he had promised by the mouth of Jeremy; **2** The Lord raised up the spirit of Cyrus the king of the Persians, and he made proclamation through all his kingdom, and also by writing, **3** Saying, Thus saith Cyrus king of the Persians; The Lord of Israel, the most high Lord, hath made me king of the whole world, **4** And commanded me to build him an house at Jerusalem in Jewry. **5** If therefore there be any of you that are of his people, let the Lord, even his Lord, be with him, and let him go up to Jerusalem that is in Judea, and build the house of the Lord of Israel: for he is the Lord that dwelleth in Jerusalem. **6** Whosoever then dwell in the places about, let them help him, those, I say, that are his neighbours, with gold, and with silver, **7** With gifts, with horses, and with cattle, and other things, which have been set forth by vow, for the temple of the Lord at Jerusalem. **8** Then the chief of the families of Judea

and of the tribe of Benjamin stood up; the priests also, and the Levites, and all
they whose mind the Lord had moved to go up, and to build an house for the
Lord at Jerusalem, **9** And they that dwelt round about them, and helped them
in all things with silver and gold, with horses and cattle, and with very many free
gifts of a great number whose minds were stirred up thereto. **10** King Cyrus
also brought forth the holy vessels, which Nabuchodonosor had carried away
from Jerusalem, and had set up in his temple of idols. **11** Now when Cyrus
king of the Persians had brought them forth, he delivered them to Mithridates
his treasurer: **12** And by him they were delivered to Sanabassar the governor of
Judea. **13** And this was the number of them; A thousand golden cups, and a
thousand of silver, censers of silver twenty nine, vials of gold thirty, and of silver
two thousand four hundred and ten, and a thousand other vessels. **14** So all the
vessels of gold and of silver, which were carried away, were five thousand four hun-
dred threescore and nine. **15** These were brought back by Sanabassar, together
with them of the captivity, from Babylon to Jerusalem. **16** But in the time
of Artexerxes king of the Persians Belemus, and Mithridates, and Tabellius, and
Rathumus, and Beeltethmus, and Semellius the secretary, with others that were
in commission with them, dwelling in Samaria and other places, wrote unto him
against them that dwelt in Judea and Jerusalem these letters following; **17** To
king Artexerxes our lord, Thy servants, Rathumus the storywriter, and Semellius
the scribe, and the rest of their council, and the judges that are in Celosyria and
Phenice. **18** Be it now known to the lord king, that the Jews that are up from
you to us, being come into Jerusalem, that rebellious and wicked city, do build
the marketplaces, and repair the walls of it and do lay the foundation of the tem-
ple. **19** Now if this city and the walls thereof be made up again, they will not
only refuse to give tribute, but also rebel against kings. **20** And forasmuch as the
things pertaining to the temple are now in hand, we think it meet not to neglect
such a matter, **21** But to speak unto our lord the king, to the intent that, if it be
thy pleasure it may be sought out in the books of thy fathers: **22** And thou shalt
find in the chronicles what is written concerning these things, and shalt under-
stand that that city was rebellious, troubling both kings and cities: **23** And that
the Jews were rebellious, and raised always wars therein; for the which cause even
this city was made desolate. **24** Wherefore now we do declare unto thee, O lord
the king, that if this city be built again, and the walls thereof set up anew, thou
shalt from henceforth have no passage into Celosyria and Phenice. **25** Then the
king wrote back again to Rathumus the storywriter, to Beeltethmus, to Semellius
the scribe, and to the rest that were in commission, and dwellers in Samaria and
Syria and Phenice, after this manner; **26** I have read the epistle which ye have
sent unto me: therefore I commanded to make diligent search, and it hath been
found that that city was from the beginning practising against kings; **27** And
the men therein were given to rebellion and war: and that mighty kings and
fierce were in Jerusalem, who reigned and exacted tributes in Celosyria and Phe-
nice. **28** Now therefore I have commanded to hinder those men from building
the city, and heed to be taken that there be no more done in it; **29** And that
those wicked workers proceed no further to the annoyance of kings, **30** Then
king Artexerxes his letters being read, Rathumus, and Semellius the scribe, and
the rest that were in commission with them, removing in haste toward Jerusalem
with a troop of horsemen and a multitude of people in battle array, began to
hinder the builders; and the building of the temple in Jerusalem ceased until the
second year of the reign of Darius king of the Persians.

3 **1** Now when Darius reigned, he made a great feast unto all his subjects,
and unto all his household, and unto all the princes of Media and Per-
sia, **2** And to all the governors and captains and lieutenants that were un-
der him, from India unto Ethiopia, of an hundred twenty and seven provin-
ces. **3** And when they had eaten and drunken, and being satisfied were gone
home, then Darius the king went into his bedchamber, and slept, and soon after
awaked. **4** Then three young men, that were of the guard that kept the king's
body, spake one to another; **5** Let every one of us speak a sentence: he that shall
overcome, and whose sentence shall seem wiser than the others, unto him shall
the king Darius give great gifts, and great things in token of victory: **6** As, to
be clothed in purple, to drink in gold, and to sleep upon gold, and a chariot with
bridles of gold, and an headtire of fine linen, and a chain about his neck: **7** And
he shall sit next to Darius because of his wisdom, and shall be called Darius his
cousin. **8** And then every one wrote his sentence, sealed it, and laid it under
king Darius his pillow; **9** And said that, when the king is risen, some will give
him the writings; and of whose side the king and the three princes of Persia shall
judge that his sentence is the wisest, to him shall the victory be given, as was ap-
pointed. **10** The first wrote, Wine is the strongest. **11** The second wrote, The
king is strongest. **12** The third wrote, Women are strongest: but above all things
Truth beareth away the victory. **13** Now when the king was risen up, they took
their writings, and delivered them unto him, and so he read them: **14** And sen-
ding forth he called all the princes of Persia and Media, and the governors, and the
captains, and the lieutenants, and the chief officers; **15** And sat him down in
the royal seat of judgment; and the writings were read before them. **16** And he
said, Call the young men, and they shall declare their own sentences. So they were
called, and came in. **17** And he said unto them, Declare unto us your mind
concerning the writings. Then began the first, who had spoken of the strength of
wine; **18** And he said thus, O ye men, how exceeding strong is wine! it causeth
all men to err that drink it: **19** It maketh the mind of the king and of the fa-
therless child to be all one; of the bondman and of the freeman, of the poor man
and of the rich: **20** It turneth also every thought into jollity and mirth, so that a
man remembereth neither sorrow nor debt: **21** And it maketh every heart rich,
so that a man remembereth neither king nor governor; and it maketh to speak
all things by talents: **22** And when they are in their cups, they forget their love
both to friends and brethren, and a little after draw out swords: **23** But when
they are from the wine, they remember not what they have done. **24** O ye men,
is not wine the strongest, that enforceth to do thus? And when he had so spoken,
he held his peace.

4 **1** Then the second, that had spoken of the strength of the king, began to
say, **2** O ye men, do not men excel in strength that bear rule over sea
and land and all things in them? **3** But yet the king is more mighty: for he is
lord of all these things, and hath dominion over them; and whatsoever he com-
mandeth them they do. **4** If he bid them make war the one against the other,
they do it: if he send them out against the enemies, they go, and break down
mountains walls and towers. **5** They slay and are slain, and transgress not the
king's commandment: if they get the victory, they bring all to the king, as well the
spoil, as all things else. **6** Likewise for those that are no soldiers, and have not to
do with wars, but use husbundry, when they have reaped again that which they
had sown, they bring it to the king, and compel one another to pay tribute unto
the king. **7** And yet he is but one man: if he command to kill, they kill; if he
command to spare, they spare; **8** If he command to smite, they smite; if he
command to make desolate, they make desolate; if he command to build, they
build; **9** If he command to cut down, they cut down; if he command to plant,
they plant. **10** So all his people and his armies obey him: furthermore he lieth
down, he eateth and drinketh, and taketh his rest: **11** And these keep watch
round about him, neither may any one depart, and do his own business, neither
disobey they him in any thing. **12** O ye men, how should not the king be mi-
ghtiest, when in such sort he is obeyed? And he held his tongue. **13** Then the
third, who had spoken of women, and of the truth, (this was Zorobabel) began to
speak. **14** O ye men, it is not the great king, nor the multitude of men, neither
is it wine, that excelleth; who is it then that ruleth them, or hath the lordship over
them? are they not women? **15** Women have borne the king and all the people
that bear rule by sea and land. **16** Even of them came they: and they nourished
them up that planted the vineyards, from whence the wine cometh. **17** These
also make garments for men; these bring glory unto men; and without women
cannot men be. **18** Yea, and if men have gathered together gold and silver, or
any other goodly thing, do they not love a woman which is comely in favour and
beauty? **19** And letting all those things go, do they not gape, and even with
open mouth fix their eyes fast on her; and have not all men more desire unto her
than unto silver or gold, or any goodly thing whatsoever? **20** A man leaveth his
own father that brought him up, and his own country, and cleaveth unto his
wife. **21** He sticketh not to spend his life with his wife. and remembereth nei-
ther father, nor mother, nor country. **22** By this also ye must know that women
have dominion over you: do ye not labour and toil, and give and bring all to the
woman? **23** Yea, a man taketh his sword, and goeth his way to rob and to steal,
to sail upon the sea and upon rivers; **24** And looketh upon a lion, and goeth in
the darkness; and when he hath stolen, spoiled, and robbed, he bringeth it to his
love. **25** Wherefore a man loveth his wife better than father or mother. **26** Yea,
many there be that have run out of their wits for women, and become servants for
their sakes. **27** Many also have perished, have erred, and sinned, for wo-
men. **28** And now do ye not believe me? is not the king great in his power? do
not all regions fear to touch him? **29** Yet did I see him and Apame the king's
concubine, the daughter of the admirable Bartacus, sitting at the right hand of the
king, **30** And taking the crown from the king's head, and setting it upon her
own head; she also struck the king with her left hand. **31** And yet for all this the
king gaped and gazed upon her with open mouth: if she laughed upon him, he
laughed also: but if she took any displeasure at him, the king was fain to flatter,
that she might be reconciled to him again. **32** O ye men, how can it be but
women should be strong, seeing they do thus? **33** Then the king and the princes
looked one upon another: so he began to speak of the truth. **34** O ye men, are
not women strong? great is the earth, high is the heaven, swift is the sun in his
course, for he compasseth the heavens round about, and fetcheth his course again
to his own place in one day. **35** Is he not great that maketh these things? there-
fore great is the truth, and stronger than all things. **36** All the earth crieth upon
the truth, and the heaven blesseth it: all works shake and tremble at it, and with
it is no unrighteous thing. **37** Wine is wicked, the king is wicked, women are
wicked, all the children of men are wicked, and such are all their wicked works;
and there is no truth in them; in their unrighteousness also they shall peri-
sh. **38** As for the truth, it endureth, and is alwaYs strong; it liveth and conque-
reth for evermore. **39** With her there is no accepting of persons or rewards; but
she doeth the things that are just, and refraineth from all unjust and wicked thin-
gs; and all men do well like of her works. **40** Neither in her judgment is any
unrighteousness; and she is the strength, kingdom, power, and majesty, of all ages.
Blessed be the God of truth. **41** And with that he held his peace. And all the
people then shouted, and said, Great is Truth, and mighty above all thin-
gs. **42** Then said the king unto him, Ask what thou wilt more than is appointed
in the writing, and we will give it thee, because thou art found wisest; and thou
shalt sit next me, and shalt be called my cousin. **43** Then said he unto the king,

Remember thy vow, which thou hast vowed to build Jerusalem, in the day when thou camest to thy kingdom, **44** And to send away all the vessels that were taken away out of Jerusalem, which Cyrus set apart, when he vowed to destroy Babylon, and to send them again thither. **45** Thou also hast vowed to build up the temple, which the Edomites burned when Judea was made desolate by the Chaldees. **46** And now, O lord the king, this is that which I require, and which I desire of thee, and this is the princely liberality proceeding from thyself: I desire therefore that thou make good the vow, the performance whereof with thine own mouth thou hast vowed to the King of heaven. **47** Then Darius the king stood up, and kissed him, and wrote letters for him unto all the treasurers and lieutenants and captains and governors, that they should safely convey on their way both him, and all those that go up with him to build Jerusalem. **48** He wrote letters also unto the lieutenants that were in Celosyria and Phenice, and unto them in Libanus, that they should bring cedar wood from Libanus unto Jerusalem, and that they should build the city with him. **49** Moreover he wrote for all the Jews that went out of his realm up into Jewry, concerning their freedom, that no officer, no ruler, no lieutenant, nor treasurer, should forcibly enter into their doors; **50** And that all the country which they hold should be free without tribute; and that the Edomites should give over the villages of the Jews which then they held: **51** Yea, that there should be yearly given twenty talents to the building of the temple, until the time that it were built; **52** And other ten talents yearly, to maintain the burnt offerings upon the altar every day, as they had a commandment to offer seventeen: **53** And that all they that went from Babylon to build the city should have free liberty, as well they as their posterity, and all the priests that went away. **54** He wrote also concerning. the charges, and the priests' vestments wherein they minister; **55** And likewise for the charges of the Levites, to be given them until the day that the house were finished, and Jerusalem builded up. **56** And he commanded to give to all that kept the city pensions and wages. **57** He sent away also all the vessels from Babylon, that Cyrus had set apart; and all that Cyrus had given in commandment, the same charged he also to be done, and sent unto Jerusalem. **58** Now when this young man was gone forth, he lifted up his face to heaven toward Jerusalem, and praised the King of heaven, **59** And said, From thee cometh victory, from thee cometh wisdom, and thine is the glory, and I am thy servant. **60** Blessed art thou, who hast given me wisdom: for to thee I give thanks, O Lord of our fathers. **61** And so he took the letters, and went out, and came unto Babylon, and told it all his brethren. **62** And they praised the God of their fathers, because he had given them freedom and liberty **63** To go up, and to build Jerusalem, and the temple which is called by his name: and they feasted with instruments of musick and gladness seven days.

5 1 After this were the principal men of the families chosen according to their tribes, to go up with their wives and sons and daughters, with their menservants and maidservants, and their cattle. **2** And Darius sent with them a thousand horsemen, till they had brought them back to Jerusalem safely, and with musical [instruments] tabrets and flutes. **3** And all their brethren played, and he made them go up together with them. **4** And these are the names of the men which went up, according to their families among their tribes, after their several heads. **5** The priests, the sons of Phinees the son of Aaron: Jesus the son of Josedec, the son of Saraias, and Joacim the son of Zorobabel, the son of Salathiel, of the house of David, out of the kindred of Phares, of the tribe of Judah; **6** Who spake wise sentences before Darius the king of Persia in the second year of his reign, in the month Nisan, which is the first month. **7** And these are they of Jewry that came up from the captivity, where they dwelt as strangers, whom Nabuchodonosor the king of Babylon had carried away unto Babylon. **8** And they returned unto Jerusalem, and to the other parts of Jewry, every man to his own city, who came with Zorobabel, with Jesus, Nehemias, and Zacharias, and Reesaias, Enenius, Mardocheus. Beelsarus, Aspharasus, Reelius, Roimus, and Baana, their guides. **9** The number of them of the nation, and their governors, sons of Phoros, two thousand an hundred seventy and two; the sons of Saphat, four hundred seventy and two: **10** The sons of Ares, seven hundred fifty and six: **11** The sons of Phaath Moab, two thousand eight hundred and twelve: **12** The sons of Elam, a thousand two hundred fifty and four: the sons of Zathul, nine hundred forty and five: the sons of Corbe, seven hundred and five: the sons of Bani, six hundred forty and eight: **13** The sons of Bebai, six hundred twenty and three: the sons of Sadas, three thousand two hundred twenty and two: **14** The sons of Adonikam, six hundred sixty and seven: the sons of Bagoi, two thousand sixty and six: the sons of Adin, four hundred fifty and four: **15** The sons of Aterezias, ninety and two: the sons of Ceilan and Azetas threescore and seven: the sons of Azuran, four hundred thirty and two: **16** The sons of Ananias, an hundred and one: the sons of Arom, thirty two: and the sons of Bassa, three hundred twenty and three: the sons of Azephurith, an hundred and two: **17** The sons of Meterus, three thousand and five: the sons of Bethlomon, an hundred twenty and three: **18** They of Netophah, fifty and five: they of Anathoth, an hundred fifty and eight: they of Bethsamos, forty and two: **19** They of Kiriathiarius, twenty and five: they of Caphira and Beroth, seven hundred forty and three: they of Pira, seven hundred: **20** They of Chadias and Ammidoi, four hundred twenty and two: they of Cirama and Gabdes, six hundred twenty and one: **21** They of Macalon, an hundred twenty and two: they of Betolius, fifty and two: the sons of Nephis, an hundred fifty and six: **22** The sons of Calamolalus and Onus, seven hundred twenty and five: the sons of Jerechus, two hundred forty and five: **23** The sons of Annas, three thousand three hundred and thirty. **24** The priests: the sons of Jeddu, the son of Jesus among the sons of Sanasib, nine hundred seventy and two: the sons of Meruth, a thousand fifty and two: **25** The sons of Phassaron, a thousand forty and seven: the sons of Carme, a thousand and seventeen. **26** The Levites: the sons of Jessue, and Cadmiel, and Banuas, and Sudias, seventy and four. **27** The holy singers: the sons of Asaph, an hundred twenty and eight. **28** The porters: the sons of Salum, the sons of Jatal, the sons of Talmon, the sons of Dacobi, the sons of Teta, the sons of Sami, in all an hundred thirty and nine. **29** The servants of the temple: the sons of Esau, the sons of Asipha, the sons of Tabaoth, the sons of Ceras, the sons of Sud, the sons of Phaleas, the sons of Labana, the sons of Graba, **30** The sons of Acua, the sons of Uta, the sons of Cetab, the sons of Agaba, the sons of Subai, the sons of Anan, the sons of Cathua, the sons of Geddur, **31** The sons of Airus, the sons of Daisan, the sons of Noeba, the sons of Chaseba, the sons of Gazera, the sons of Azia, the sons of Phinees, the sons of Azare, the sons of Bastai, the sons of Asana, the sons of Meani, the sons of Naphisi, the sons of Acub, the sons of Acipha, the sons of Assur, the sons of Pharacim, the sons of Basaloth, **32** The sons of Meeda, the sons of Coutha, the sons of Charea, the sons of Charcus, the sons of Aserer, the sons of Thomoi, the sons of Nasith, the sons of Atipha. **33** The sons of the servants of Solomon: the sons of Azaphion, the sons of Pharira, the sons of Jeeli, the sons of Lozon, the sons of Israel, the sons of Sapheth, **34** The sons of Hagia, the sons of Pharacareth, the sons of Sabi, the sons of Sarothie, the sons of Masias, the sons of Gar, the sons of Addus, the sons of Suba, the sons of Apherra, the sons of Barodis, the sons of Sabat, the sons of Allom. **35** All the ministers of the temple, and the sons of the servants of Solomon, were three hundred seventy and two. **36** These came up from Thermeleth and Thelersas, Charaathalar leading them, and Aalar; **37** Neither could they shew their families, nor their stock, how they were of Israel: the sons of Ladan, the son of Ban, the sons of Necodan, six hundred fifty and two. **38** And of the priests that usurped the office of the priesthood, and were not found: the sons of Obdia, the sons of Accoz, the sons of Addus, who married Augia one of the daughters of Barzelus, and was named after his name. **39** And when the description of the kindred of these men was sought in the register, and was not found, they were removed from executing the office of the priesthood: **40** For unto them said Nehemias and Atharias, that they should not be partakers of the holy things, till there arose up an high priest clothed with doctrine and truth. **41** So of Israel, from them of twelve years old and upward, they were all in number forty thousand, beside menservants and womenservants two thousand three hundred and sixty. **42** Their menservants and handmaids were seven thousand three hundred forty and seven: the singing men and singing women, two hundred forty and five: **43** Four hundred thirty and five camels, seven thousand thirty and six horses, two hundred forty and five mules, five thousand five hundred twenty and five beasts used to the yoke. **44** And certain of the chief of their families, when they came to the temple of God that is in Jerusalem, vowed to set up the house again in his own place according to their ability, **45** And to give into the holy treasury of the works a thousand pounds of gold, five thousand of silver, and an hundred priestly vestments. **46** And so dwelt the priests and the Levites and the people in Jerusalem, and in the country, the singers also and the porters; and all Israel in their villages. **47** But when the seventh month was at hand, and when the children of Israel were every man in his own place, they came all together with one consent into the open place of the first gate which is toward the east. **48** Then stood up Jesus the son of Josedec, and his brethren the priests and Zorobabel the son of Salathiel, and his brethren, and made ready the altar of the God of Israel, **49** To offer burnt sacrifices upon it, according as it is expressly commanded in the book of Moses the man of God. **50** And there were gathered unto them out of the other nations of the land, and they erected the altar upon his own place, because all the nations of the land were at enmity with them, and oppressed them; and they offered sacrifices according to the time, and burnt offerings to the Lord both morning and evening. **51** Also they held the feast of tabernacles, as it is commanded in the law, and offered sacrifices daily, as was meet: **52** And after that, the continual oblations, and the sacrifice of the sabbaths, and of the new moons, and of all holy feasts. **53** And all they that had made any vow to God began to offer sacrifices to God from the first day of the seventh month, although the temple of the Lord was not yet built. **54** And they gave unto the masons and carpenters money, meat, and drink, with cheerfulness. **55** Unto them of Zidon also and Tyre they gave carrs, that they should bring cedar trees from Libanus, which should be brought by floats to the haven of Joppa, according as it was commanded them by Cyrus king of the Persians. **56** And in the second year and second month after his coming to the temple of God at Jerusalem began Zorobabel the son of Salathiel, and Jesus the son of Josedec, and their brethren, and the priests, and the Levites, and all they that were come unto Jerusalem out of the captivity: **57** And they laid the foundation of the house of God in the first day of the second month, in the second year after they were come to Jewry and Jerusalem. **58** And they appointed the Levites from twenty years old over the works of the Lord. Then stood up Jesus, and his sons and brethren, and Cadmiel his brother, and the sons of Madiabun, with the sons of Joda the son of Eliadun, with their sons and brethren, all Levites, with one accord setters forward of the business, labouring to advance the works in the house of God. So the workmen built the temple of the Lord. **59** And the priests stood arrayed in their vestments with musical instruments and trumpets; and the Levites the sons of Asaph had cymbals, **60** Singing songs of thanksgiving, and praising the Lord, according as David the king of

Israel had ordained. **61** And they sung with loud voices songs to the praise of
the Lord, because his mercy and glory is for ever in all Israel. **62** And all the
people sounded trumpets, and shouted with a loud voice, singing songs of thank-
sgiving unto the Lord for the rearing up of the house of the Lord. **63** Also of the
priests and Levites, and of the chief of their families, the ancients who had seen
the former house came to the building of this with weeping and great
crying. **64** But many with trumpets and joy shouted with loud voice, **65** In-
somuch that the trumpets might not be heard for the weeping of the people: yet
the multitude sounded marvellously, so that it was heard afar off. **66** Wherefore
when the enemies of the tribe of Judah and Benjamin heard it, they came to know
what that noise of trumpets should mean. **67** And they perceived that they that
were of the captivity did build the temple unto the Lord God of Israel. **68** So
they went to Zorobabel and Jesus, and to the chief of the families, and said unto
them, We will build together with you. **69** For we likewise, as ye, do obey your
Lord, and do sacrifice unto him from the days of Azbazareth the king of the As-
syrians, who brought us hither. **70** Then Zorobabel and Jesus and the chief of
the families of Israel said unto them, It is not for us and you to build together an
house unto the Lord our God. **71** We ourselves alone will build unto the Lord
of Israel, according as Cyrus the king of the Persians hath commanded
us. **72** But the heathen of the land lying heavy upon the inhabitants of Judea,
and holding them strait, hindered their building; **73** And by their secret plots,
and popular persuasions and commotions, they hindered the finishing of the bu-
ilding all the time that king Cyrus lived: so they were hindered from building for
the space of two years, until the reign of Darius.

6

1 Now in the second year of the reign of Darius Aggeus and Zacharias
the son of Addo, the prophets, prophesied unto the Jews in Jewry and
Jerusalem in the name of the Lord God of Israel, which was upon them. **2** Then
stood up Zorobabel the son of Salatiel, and Jesus the son of Josedec, and began
to build the house of the Lord at Jerusalem, the prophets of the Lord being with
them, and helping them. **3** At the same time came unto them Sisinnes the
governor of Syria and Phenice, with Sathrabuzanes and his companions, and said
unto them, **4** By whose appointment do ye build this house and this roof, and
perform all the other things? and who are the workmen that perform these thin-
gs? **5** Nevertheless the elders of the Jews obtained favour, because the Lord had
visited the captivity; **6** And they were not hindered from building, until such
time as signification was given unto Darius concerning them, and an answer re-
ceived. **7** The copy of the letters which Sisinnes, governor of Syria and Phenice,
and Sathrabuzanes, with their companions, rulers in Syria and Phenice, wrote and
sent unto Darius; To king Darius, greeting: **8** Let all things be known unto our
lord the king, that being come into the country of Judea, and entered into the city
of Jerusalem we found in the city of Jerusalem the ancients of the Jews that were
of the captivity **9** Building an house unto the Lord, great and new, of hewn and
costly stones, and the timber already laid upon the walls. **10** And those works
are done with great speed, and the work goeth on prosperously in their hands,
and with all glory and diligence is it made. **11** Then asked we these elders,
saying, By whose commandment build ye this house, and lay the foundations
of these works? **12** Therefore to the intent that we might give knowledge unto
thee by writing, we demanded of them who were the chief doers, and we required
of them the names in writing of their principal men. **13** So they gave us this
answer, We are the servants of the Lord which made heaven and earth. **14** And
as for this house, it was builded many years ago by a king of Israel great and
strong, and was finished. **15** But when our fathers provoked God unto wrath,
and sinned against the Lord of Israel which is in heaven, he gave them over into
the power of Nabuchodonosor king of Babylon, of the Chaldees; **16** Who pul-
led down the house, and burned it, and carried away the people captives unto
Babylon. **17** But in the first year that king Cyrus reigned over the country of
Babylon Cyrus the king wrote to build up this house. **18** And the holy vessels
of gold and of silver, that Nabuchodonosor had carried away out of the house at
Jerusalem, and had set them in his own temple those Cyrus the king brought for-
th again out of the temple at Babylon, and they were delivered to Zorobabel and
to Sanabassarus the ruler, **19** With commandment that he should carry away
the same vessels, and put them in the temple at Jerusalem; and that the temple
of the Lord should be built in his place. **20** Then the same Sanabassarus, being
come hither, laid the foundations of the house of the Lord at Jerusalem; and
from that time to this being still a building, it is not yet fully ended. **21** Now
therefore, if it seem good unto the king, let search be made among the records of
king Cyrus: **22** And if it be found that the building of the house of the Lord
at Jerusalem hath been done with the consent of king Cyrus, and if our lord the
king be so minded, let him signify unto us thereof. **23** Then commanded king
Darius to seek among the records at Babylon: and so at Ecbatane the palace, whi-
ch is in the country of Media, there was found a roll wherein these things were
recorded. **24** In the first year of the reign of Cyrus king Cyrus commanded that
the house of the Lord at Jerusalem should be built again, where they do sacrifice
with continual fire: **25** Whose height shall be sixty cubits and the breadth sixty
cubits, with three rows of hewn stones, and one row of new wood of that country;
and the expences thereof to be given out of the house of king Cyrus: **26** And
that the holy vessels of the house of the Lord, both of gold and silver, that Nabu-
chodonosor took out of the house at Jerusalem, and brought to Babylon, should
be restored to the house at Jerusalem, and be set in the place where they were befo-
re. **27** And also he commanded that Sisinnes the governor of Syria and Phenice,
and Sathrabuzanes, and their companions, and those which were appointed rulers
in Syria and Phenice, should be careful not to meddle with the place, but suffer
Zorobabel, the servant of the Lord, and governor of Judea, and the elders of the
Jews, to build the house of the Lord in that place. **28** I have commanded also
to have it built up whole again; and that they look diligently to help those that be
of the captivity of the Jews, till the house of the Lord be finished: **29** And out
of the tribute of Celosyria and Phenice a portion carefully to be given these men
for the sacrifices of the Lord, that is, to Zorobabel the governor, for bullocks, and
rams, and lambs; **30** And also corn, salt, wine, and oil, and that continually
every year without further question, according as the priests that be in Jerusalem
shall signify to be daily spent: **31** That offerings may be made to the most
high God for the king and for his children, and that they may pray for their
lives. **32** And he commanded that whosoever should transgress, yea, or make
light of any thing afore spoken or written, out of his own house should a tree be
taken, and he thereon be hanged, and all his goods seized for the king. **33** The
Lord therefore, whose name is there called upon, utterly destroy every king and
nation, that stretcheth out his hand to hinder or endamage that house of the Lord
in Jerusalem. **34** I Darius the king have ordained that according unto these
things it be done with diligence.

7

1 Then Sisinnes the governor of Celosyria and Phenice, and Sathrabuza-
nes, with their companions following the commandments of king Dari-
us, **2** Did very carefully oversee the holy works, assisting the ancients of the Jews
and governors of the temple. **3** And so the holy works prospered, when Aggeus
and Zacharias the prophets prophesied. **4** And they finished these things by
the commandment of the Lord God of Israel, and with the consent of Cyrus,
Darius, and Artexerxes, kings of Persia. **5** And thus was the holy house finished
in the three and twentieth day of the month Adar, in the sixth year of Darius
king of the Persians **6** And the children of Israel, the priests, and the Levites,
and others that were of the captivity, that were added unto them, did according
to the things written in the book of Moses. **7** And to the dedication of the
temple of the Lord they offered an hundred bullocks two hundred rams, four
hundred lambs; **8** And twelve goats for the sin of all Israel, according to the
number of the chief of the tribes of Israel. **9** The priests also and the Levites
stood arrayed in their vestments, according to their kindreds, in the service of
the Lord God of Israel, according to the book of Moses: and the porters at every
gate. **10** And the children of Israel that were of the captivity held the passover
the fourteenth day of the first month, after that the priests and the Levites were
sanctified. **11** They that were of the captivity were not all sanctified together:
but the Levites were all sanctified together. **12** And so they offered the passover
for all them of the captivity, and for their brethren the priests, and for themsel-
ves. **13** And the children of Israel that came out of the captivity did eat, even
all they that had separated themselves from the abominations of the people of the
land, and sought the Lord. **14** And they kept the feast of unleavened bread se-
ven days, making merry before the Lord, **15** For that he had turned the counsel
of the king of Assyria toward them, to strengthen their hands in the works of the
Lord God of Israel.

8

1 And after these things, when Artexerxes the king of the Persians reigned
came Esdras the son of Saraias, the son of Ezerias, the son of Helchiah, the
son of Salum, **2** The son of Sadduc, the son of Achitob, the son of Amarias, the
son of Ezias, the son of Meremoth, the son of Zaraias, the son of Savias, the son
of Boccas, the son of Abisum, the son of Phinees, the son of Eleazar, the son of
Aaron the chief priest. **3** This Esdras went up from Babylon, as a scribe, being
very ready in the law of Moses, that was given by the God of Israel. **4** And the
king did him honour: for he found grace in his sight in all his requests. **5** There
went up with him also certain of the children of Israel, of the priest of the Levites,
of the holy singers, porters, and ministers of the temple, unto Jerusalem, **6** In
the seventh year of the reign of Artexerxes, in the fifth month, this was the king's
seventh year; for they went from Babylon in the first day of the first month, and
came to Jerusalem, according to the prosperous journey which the Lord gave
them. **7** For Esdras had very great skill, so that he omitted nothing of the law
and commandments of the Lord, but taught all Israel the ordinances and judg-
ments. **8** Now the copy of the commission, which was written from Artexerxes
the king, and came to Esdras the priest and reader of the law of the Lord, is this
that followeth; **9** King Artexerxes unto Esdras the priest and reader of the law
of the Lord sendeth greeting: **10** Having determined to deal graciously, I have
given order, that such of the nation of the Jews, and of the priests and Levites
being within our realm, as are willing and desirous should go with thee unto Jeru-
salem. **11** As many therefore as have a mind thereunto, let them depart with
thee, as it hath seemed good both to me and my seven friends the counsel-
lors; **12** That they may look unto the affairs of Judea and Jerusalem, agreeably
to that which is in the law of the Lord; **13** And carry the gifts unto the Lord of
Israel to Jerusalem, which I and my friends have vowed, and all the gold and silver
that in the country of Babylon can be found, to the Lord in Jerusalem, **14** With
that also which is given of the people for the temple of the Lord their God at Je-
rusalem: and that silver and gold may be collected for bullocks, rams, and lambs,
and things thereunto appertaining; **15** To the end that they may offer sacrifices

unto the Lord upon the altar of the Lord their God, which is in Jerusa-
lem. **16** And whatsoever thou and thy brethren will do with the silver and gold,
that do, according to the will of thy God. **17** And the holy vessels of the Lord,
which are given thee for the use of the temple of thy God, which is in Jerusalem,
thou shalt set before thy God in Jerusalem. **18** And whatsoever thing else thou
shalt remember for the use of the temple of thy God, thou shalt give it out of the
king's treasury. **19** And I king Artexerxes have also commanded the keepers of
the treasures in Syria and Phenice, that whatsoever Esdras the priest and the rea-
der of the law of the most high God shall send for, they should give it him with
speed, **20** To the sum of an hundred talents of silver, likewise also of wheat even
to an hundred cors, and an hundred pieces of wine, and other things in abundan-
ce. **21** Let all things be performed after the law of God diligently unto the most
high God, that wrath come not upon the kingdom of the king and his sons. **22** I
command you also, that ye require no tax, nor any other imposition, of any of the
priests, or Levites, or holy singers, or porters, or ministers of the temple, or of any
that have doings in this temple, and that no man have authority to impose any
thing upon them. **23** And thou, Esdras, according to the wisdom of God or-
dain judges and justices, that they may judge in all Syria and Phenice all those that
know the law of thy God; and those that know it not thou shalt teach. **24** And
whosoever shall transgress the law of thy God, and of the king, shall be punished
diligently, whether it be by death, or other punishment, by penalty of money, or
by imprisonment. **25** Then said Esdras the scribe, Blessed be the only Lord God
of my fathers, who hath put these things into the heart of the king, to glorify his
house that is in Jerusalem: **26** And hath honoured me in the sight of the king,
and his counsellors, and all his friends and nobles. **27** Therefore was I encoura-
ged by the help of the Lord my God, and gathered together men of Israel to go up
with me. **28** And these are the chief according to their families and several di-
gnities, that went up with me from Babylon in the reign of king Artexer-
xes: **29** Of the sons of Phinees, Gerson: of the sons of Ithamar, Gamael: of the
sons of David, Lettus the son of Sechenias: **30** Of the sons of Pharez, Zacharias;
and with him were counted an hundred and fifty men: **31** Of the sons of Paha-
th Moab, Eliaonias, the son of Zaraias, and with him two hundred men: **32** Of
the sons of Zathoe, Sechenias the son of Jezelus, and with him three hundred
men: of the sons of Adin, Obeth the son of Jonathan, and with him two hundred
and fifty men: **33** Of the sons of Elam, Josias son of Gotholias, and with him
seventy men: **34** Of the sons of Saphatias, Zaraias son of Michael, and with him
threescore and ten men: **35** Of the sons of Joab, Abadias son of Jezelus, and
with him two hundred and twelve men: **36** Of the sons of Banid, Assalimoth
son of Josaphias, and with him an hundred and threescore men: **37** Of the sons
of Babi, Zacharias son of Bebai, and with him twenty and eight men: **38** Of the
sons of Astath, Johannes son of Acatan, and with him an hundred and ten
men: **39** Of the sons of Adonikam the last, and these are the names of them,
Eliphalet, Jewel, and Samaias, and with them seventy men: **40** Of the sons of
Bago, Uthi the son of Istalcurus, and with him seventy men. **41** And these I
gathered together to the river called Theras, where we pitched our tents three days:
and then I surveyed them. **42** But when I had found there none of the priests
and Levites, **43** Then sent I unto Eleazar, and Iduel, and Masman, **44** And
Alnathan, and Mamaias, and Joribas, and Nathan, Eunatan, Zacharias, and Mo-
sollamon, principal men and learned. **45** And I bade them that they should go
unto Saddeus the captain, who was in the place of the treasury: **46** And com-
manded them that they should speak unto Daddeus, and to his brethren, and to
the treasurers in that place, to send us such men as might execute the priests' offi-
ce in the house of the Lord. **47** And by the mighty hand of our Lord they
brought unto us skilful men of the sons of Moli the son of Levi, the son of Israel,
Asebebia, and his sons, and his brethren, who were eighteen. **48** And Asebia,
and Annus, and Osaias his brother, of the sons of Channuneus, and their sons,
were twenty men. **49** And of the servants of the temple whom David had ordai-
ned, and the principal men for the service of the Levites to wit, the servants of the
temple two hundred and twenty, the catalogue of whose names were
shewed. **50** And there I vowed a fast unto the young men before our Lord, to
desire of him a prosperous journey both for us and them that were with us, for our
children, and for the cattle: **51** For I was ashamed to ask the king footmen, and
horsemen, and conduct for safeguard against our adversaries. **52** For we had
said unto the king, that the power of the Lord our God should be with them that
seek him, to support them in all ways. **53** And again we besought our Lord as
touching these things, and found him favourable unto us. **54** Then I separated
twelve of the chief of the priests, Esebrias, and Assanias, and ten men of their
brethren with them: **55** And I weighed them the gold, and the silver, and the
holy vessels of the house of our Lord, which the king, and his council, and the
princes, and all Israel, had given. **56** And when I had weighed it, I delivered
unto them six hundred and fifty talents of silver, and silver vessels of an hundred
talents, and an hundred talents of gold, **57** And twenty golden vessels, and
twelve vessels of brass, even of fine brass, glittering like gold. **58** And I said unto
them, Both ye are holy unto the Lord, and the vessels are holy, and the gold and
the silver is a vow unto the Lord, the Lord of our fathers. **59** Watch ye, and keep
them till ye deliver them to the chief of the priests and Levites, and to the princi-
pal men of the families of Israel, in Jerusalem, into the chambers of the house of
our God. **60** So the priests and the Levites, who had received the silver and the
gold and the vessels, brought them unto Jerusalem, into the temple of the
Lord. **61** And from the river Theras we departed the twelfth day of the first
month, and came to Jerusalem by the mighty hand of our Lord, which was with
us: and from the beginning of our journey the Lord delivered us from every
enemy, and so we came to Jerusalem. **62** And when we had been there three
days, the gold and silver that was weighed was delivered in the house of our Lord
on the fourth day unto Marmoth the priest the son of Iri. **63** And with him was
Eleazar the son of Phinees, and with them were Josabad the son of Jesu and Mo-
eth the son of Sabban, Levites: all was delivered them by number and wei-
ght. **64** And all the weight of them was written up the same hour. **65** More-
over they that were come out of the captivity offered sacrifice unto the Lord God
of Israel, even twelve bullocks for all Israel, fourscore and sixteen rams, **66** Thre-
escore and twelve lambs, goats for a peace offering, twelve; all of them a sacrifice
to the Lord. **67** And they delivered the king's commandments unto the king's
stewards' and to the governors of Celosyria and Phenice; and they honoured the
people and the temple of God. **68** Now when these things were done, the rulers
came unto me, and said, **69** The nation of Israel, the princes, the priests and
Levites, have not put away from them the strange people of the land, nor the
pollutions of the Gentiles to wit, of the Canaanites, Hittites, Pheresites, Jebusites,
and the Moabites, Egyptians, and Edomites. **70** For both they and their sons
have married with their daughters, and the holy seed is mixed with the strange
people of the land; and from the beginning of this matter the rulers and the great
men have been partakers of this iniquity. **71** And as soon as I had heard these
things, I rent my clothes, and the holy garment, and pulled off the hair from off
my head and beard, and sat me down sad and very heavy. **72** So all they that
were then moved at the word of the Lord God of Israel assembled unto me, whilst
I mourned for the iniquity: but I sat still full of heaviness until the evening sacri-
fice. **73** Then rising up from the fast with my clothes and the holy garment rent,
and bowing my knees, and stretching forth my hands unto the Lord, **74** I said,
O Lord, I am confounded and ashamed before thy face; **75** For our sins are
multiplied above our heads, and our ignorances have reached up unto hea-
ven. **76** For ever since the time of our fathers we have been and are in great sin,
even unto this day. **77** And for our sins and our fathers' we with our brethren
and our kings and our priests were given up unto the kings of the earth, to the
sword, and to captivity, and for a prey with shame, unto this day. **78** And now
in some measure hath mercy been shewed unto us from thee, O Lord, that there
should be left us a root and a name in the place of thy sanctuary; **79** And to
discover unto us a light in the house of the Lord our God, and to give us food in
the time of our servitude. **80** Yea, when we were in bondage, we were not for-
saken of our Lord; but he made us gracious before the kings of Persia, so that they
gave us food; **81** Yea, and honoured the temple of our Lord, and raised up the
desolate Sion, that they have given us a sure abiding in Jewry and Jerusa-
lem. **82** And now, O Lord, what shall we say, having these things? for we have
transgressed thy commandments, which thou gavest by the hand of thy servants
the prophets, saying, **83** That the land, which ye enter into to possess as an
heritage, is a land polluted with the pollutions of the strangers of the land, and
they have filled it with their uncleanness. **84** Therefore now shall ye not join
your daughters unto their sons, neither shall ye take their daughters unto your
sons. **85** Moreover ye shall never seek to have peace with them, that ye may be
strong, and eat the good things of the land, and that ye may leave the inheritance
of the land unto your children for evermore. **86** And all that is befallen is done
unto us for our wicked works and great sins; for thou, O Lord, didst make our sins
light, **87** And didst give unto us such a root: but we have turned back again to
transgress thy law, and to mingle ourselves with the uncleanness of the nations of
the land. **88** Mightest not thou be angry with us to destroy us, till thou hadst
left us neither root, seed, nor name? **89** O Lord of Israel, thou art true: for we
are left a root this day. **90** Behold, now are we before thee in our iniquities, for
we cannot stand any longer by reason of these things before thee. **91** And as
Esdras in his prayer made his confession, weeping, and lying flat upon the ground
before the temple, there gathered unto him from Jerusalem a very great multitude
of men and women and children: for there was great weeping among the multitu-
de. **92** Then Jechonias the son of Jeelus, one of the sons of Israel, called out, and
said, O Esdras, we have sinned against the Lord God, we have married strange
women of the nations of the land, and now is all Israel aloft. **93** Let us make an
oath to the Lord, that we will put away all our wives, which we have taken of the
heathen, with their children, **94** Like as thou hast decreed, and as many as do
obey the law of the Lord. **95** Arise and put in execution: for to thee doth this
matter appertain, and we will be with thee: do valiantly. **96** So Esdras arose, and
took an oath of the chief of the priests and Levites of all Israel to do after these
things; and so they sware.

9 **1** Then Esdras rising from the court of the temple went to the chamber of
Joanan the son of Eliasib, **2** And remained there, and did eat no meat
nor drink water, mourning for the great iniquities of the multitude. **3** And there
was a proclamation in all Jewry and Jerusalem to all them that were of the capti-
vity, that they should be gathered together at Jerusalem: **4** And that whosoever
met not there within two or three days according as the elders that bare rule
appointed, their cattle should be seized to the use of the temple, and himself cast
out from them that were of the captivity. **5** And in three days were all they of
the tribe of Judah and Benjamin gathered together at Jerusalem the twentieth day
of the ninth month. **6** And all the multitude sat trembling in the broad court
of the temple because of the present foul weather. **7** So Esdras arose up, and
said unto them, Ye have transgressed the law in marrying strange wives, thereby

to increase the sins of Israel. **8** And now by confessing give glory unto the Lord
God of our fathers, **9** And do his will, and separate yourselves from the heathen
of the land, and from the strange women. **10** Then cried the whole multitude,
and said with a loud voice, Like as thou hast spoken, so will we do. **11** But
forasmuch as the people are many, and it is foul weather, so that we cannot stand
without, and this is not a work of a day or two, seeing our sin in these things is
spread far: **12** Therefore let the rulers of the multitude stay, and let all them of
our habitations that have strange wives come at the time appointed, **13** And
with them the rulers and judges of every place, till we turn away the wrath of the
Lord from us for this matter. **14** Then Jonathan the son of Azael and Ezechias
the son of Theocanus accordingly took this matter upon them: and Mosollam
and Levis and Sabbatheus helped them. **15** And they that were of the captivity
did according to all these things. **16** And Esdras the priest chose unto him the
principal men of their families, all by name: and in the first day of the tenth mon-
th they sat together to examine the matter. **17** So their cause that held strange
wives was brought to an end in the first day of the first month. **18** And of the
priests that were come together, and had strange wives, there were found: **19** Of
the sons of Jesus the son of Josedec, and his brethren; Matthelas and Eleazar, and
Joribus and Joadanus. **20** And they gave their hands to put away their wives
and to offer rams to make reconcilement for their errors. **21** And of the sons
of Emmer; Ananias, and Zabdeus, and Eanes, and Sameius, and Hiereel, and
Azarias. **22** And of the sons of Phaisur; Elionas, Massias Israel, and Nathana-
el, and Ocidelus and Talsas. **23** And of the Levites; Jozabad, and Semis, and
Colius, who was called Calitas, and Patheus, and Judas, and Jonas. **24** Of the
holy singers; Eleazurus, Bacchurus. **25** Of the porters; Sallumus, and Tolba-
nes. **26** Of them of Israel, of the sons of Phoros; Hiermas, and Eddias, and
Melchias, and Maelus, and Eleazar, and Asibias, and Baanias. **27** Of the sons of
Ela; Matthanias, Zacharias, and Hierielus, and Hieremoth, and Aedias. **28** And
of the sons of Zamoth; Eliadas, Elisimus, Othonias, Jarimoth, and Sabatus, and
Sardeus. **29** Of the sons of Babai; Johannes, and Ananias and Josabad, and
Amatheis. **30** Of the sons of Mani; Olamus, Mamuchus, Jedeus, Jasubus, Jasa-
el, and Hieremoth. **31** And of the sons of Addi; Naathus, and Moosias, Lacu-
nus, and Naidus, and Mathanias, and Sesthel, Balnuus, and Manasseas. **32** And
of the sons of Annas; Elionas and Aseas, and Melchias, and Sabbeus, and Simon
Chosameus. **33** And of the sons of Asom; Altaneus, and Matthias, and Baanaia,
Eliphalet, and Manasses, and Semei. **34** And of the sons of Maani; Jeremias,
Momdis, Omaerus, Juel, Mabdai, and Pelias, and Anos, Carabasion, and Enasi-
bus, and Mamnitanaimus, Eliasis, Bannus, Eliali, Samis, Selemias, Nathanias: and
of the sons of Ozora; Sesis, Esril, Azaelus, Samatus, Zambis, Josephus. **35** And
of the sons of Ethma; Mazitias, Zabadaias, Edes, Juel, Banaias. **36** All these had
taken strange wives, and they put them away with their children. **37** And the
priests and Levites, and they that were of Israel, dwelt in Jerusalem, and in the
country, in the first day of the seventh month: so the children of Israel were in
their habitations. **38** And the whole multitude came together with one accord
into the broad place of the holy porch toward the east: **39** And they spake unto
Esdras the priest and reader, that he would bring the law of Moses, that was given
of the Lord God of Israel. **40** So Esdras the chief priest brought the law unto
the whole multitude from man to woman, and to all the priests, to hear law in the
first day of the seventh month. **41** And he read in the broad court before the
holy porch from morning unto midday, before both men and women; and the
multitude gave heed unto the law. **42** And Esdras the priest and reader of the
law stood up upon a pulpit of wood, which was made for that purpose. **43** And
there stood up by him Mattathias, Sammus, Ananias, Azarias, Urias, Ezecias, Ba-
lasamus, upon the right hand: **44** And upon his left hand stood Phaldaius,
Misael, Melchias, Lothasubus, and Nabarias. **45** Then took Esdras the book of
the law before the multitude: for he sat honourably in the first place in the sight of
them all. **46** And when he opened the law, they stood all straight up. So Esdras
blessed the Lord God most High, the God of hosts, Almighty. **47** And all the
people answered, Amen; and lifting up their hands they fell to the ground, and
worshipped the Lord. **48** Also Jesus, Anus, Sarabias, Adinus, Jacubus, Sabateas,
Auteas, Maianeas, and Calitas, Asrias, and Joazabdus, and Ananias, Biatas, the Le-
vites, taught the law of the Lord, making them withal to understand it. **49** Then
spake Attharates unto Esdras the chief priest. and reader, and to the Levites that
taught the multitude, even to all, saying, **50** This day is holy unto the Lord; (for
they all wept when they heard the law:) **51** Go then, and eat the fat, and drink
the sweet, and send part to them that have nothing; **52** For this day is holy unto
the Lord: and be not sorrowful; for the Lord will bring you to honour. **53** So
the Levites published all things to the people, saying, This day is holy to the Lord;
be not sorrowful. **54** Then went they their way, every one to eat and drink, and
make merry, and to give part to them that had nothing, and to make great cheer;
55 Because they understood the words wherein they were instructed, and for the
which they had been assembled.

APOCRYPHA

2ST BOOK OF ESDRAS

The Second Book of Esdras

1 1 The second book of the prophet Esdras, the son of Saraias, the son of
Azarias, the son of Helchias, the son of Sadamias, the sou of Sadoc, the
son of Achitob, **2** The son of Achias, the son of Phinees, the son of Heli, the son
of Amarias, the son of Aziei, the son of Marimoth, the son of And he spake unto
the of Borith, the son of Abisei, the son of Phinees, the son of Eleazar, **3** The
son of Aaron, of the tribe of Levi; which was captive in the land of the Medes, in
the reign of Artexerxes king of the Persians. **4** And the word of the Lord came
unto me, saying, **5** Go thy way, and shew my people their sinful deeds, and
their children their wickedness which they have done against me; that they may
tell their children's children: **6** Because the sins of their fathers are increased in
them: for they have forgotten me, and have offered unto strange gods. **7** Am
not I even he that brought them out of the land of Egypt, from the house of bon-
dage? but they have provoked me unto wrath, and despised my counsels. **8** Pull
thou off then the hair of thy head, and cast all evil upon them, for they have not
been obedient unto my law, but it is a rebellious people. **9** How long shall I
forbear them, into whom I have done so much good? **10** Many kings have
I destroyed for their sakes; Pharaoh with his servants and all his power have I
smitten down. **11** All the nations have I destroyed before them, and in the east
I have scattered the people of two provinces, even of Tyrus and Sidon, and have
slain all their enemies. **12** Speak thou therefore unto them, saying, Thus saith
the Lord, **13** I led you through the sea and in the beginning gave you a large
and safe passage; I gave you Moses for a leader, and Aaron for a priest. **14** I
gave you light in a pillar of fire, and great wonders have I done among you; yet
have ye forgotten me, saith the Lord. **15** Thus saith the Almighty Lord, The
quails were as a token to you; I gave you tents for your safeguard: nevertheless
ye murmured there, **16** And triumphed not in my name for the destruction
of your enemies, but ever to this day do ye yet murmur. **17** Where are the
benefits that I have done for you? when ye were hungry and thirsty in the wilder-
ness, did ye not cry unto me, **18** Saying, Why hast thou brought us into this
wilderness to kill us? it had been better for us to have served the Egyptians, than
to die in this wilderness. **19** Then had I pity upon your mournings, and gave
you manna to eat; so ye did eat angels' bread. **20** When ye were thirsty, did I
not cleave the rock, and waters flowed out to your fill? for the heat I covered you
with the leaves of the trees. **21** I divided among you a fruitful land, I cast out
the Canaanites, the Pherezites, and the Philistines, before you: what shall I yet do
more for you? saith the Lord. **22** Thus saith the Almighty Lord, When ye were
in the wilderness, in the river of the Amorites, being athirst, and blaspheming my
name, **23** I gave you not fire for your blasphemies, but cast a tree in the water,
and made the river sweet. **24** What shall I do unto thee, O Jacob? thou, Juda,
wouldest not obey me: I will turn me to other nations, and unto those will I give
my name, that they may keep my statutes. **25** Seeing ye have forsaken me, I
will forsake you also; when ye desire me to be gracious unto you, I shall have no
mercy upon you. **26** Whensoever ye shall call upon me, I will not hear you:
for ye have defiled your hands with blood, and your feet are swift to commit
manslaughter. **27** Ye have not as it were forsaken me, but your own selves, saith
the Lord. **28** Thus saith the Almighty Lord, Have I not prayed you as a father
his sons, as a mother her daughters, and a nurse her young babes, **29** That ye
would be my people, and I should be your God; that ye would be my children,
and I should be your father? **30** I gathered you together, as a hen gathereth
her chickens under her wings: but now, what shall I do unto you? I will cast
you out from my face. **31** When ye offer unto me, I will turn my face from
you: for your solemn feastdays, your new moons, and your circumcisions, have
I forsaken. **32** I sent unto you my servants the prophets, whom ye have taken

and slain, and torn their bodies in pieces, whose blood I will require of your hands, saith the Lord. **33** Thus saith the Almighty Lord, Your house is desolate, I will cast you out as the wind doth stubble. **34** And your children shall not be fruitful; for they have despised my commandment, and done the thing that is an evil before me. **35** Your houses will I give to a people that shall come; which not having heard of me yet shall believe me; to whom I have shewed no signs, yet they shall do that I have commanded them. **36** They have seen no prophets, yet they shall call their sins to remembrance, and acknowledge them. **37** I take to witness the grace of the people to come, whose little ones rejoice in gladness: and though they have not seen me with bodily eyes, yet in spirit they believe the thing that I say. **38** And now, brother, behold what glory; and see the people that come from the east: **39** Unto whom I will give for leaders, Abraham, Isaac, and Jacob, Oseas, Amos, and Micheas, Joel, Abdias, and Jonas, **40** Nahum, and Abacuc, Sophonias, Aggeus, Zachary, and Malachy, which is called also an angel of the Lord.

2

1 Thus saith the Lord, I brought this people out of bondage, and I gave them my commandments by menservants the prophets; whom they would not hear, but despised my counsels. **2** The mother that bare them saith unto them, Go your way, ye children; for I am a widow and forsaken. **3** I brought you up with gladness; but with sorrow and heaviness have I lost you: for ye have sinned before the Lord your God, and done that thing that is evil before him. **4** But what shall I now do unto you? I am a widow and forsaken: go your way, O my children, and ask mercy of the Lord. **5** As for me, O father, I call upon thee for a witness over the mother of these children, which would not keep my covenant, **6** That thou bring them to confusion, and their mother to a spoil, that there may be no offspring of them. **7** Let them be scattered abroad among the heathen, let their names be put out of the earth: for they have despised my covenant. **8** Woe be unto thee, Assur, thou that hidest the unrighteous in thee! O thou wicked people, remember what I did unto Sodom and Gomorrha; **9** Whose land lieth in clods of pitch and heaps of ashes: even so also will I do unto them that hear me not, saith the Almighty Lord. **10** Thus saith the Lord unto Esdras, Tell my people that I will give them the kingdom of Jerusalem, which I would have given unto Israel. **11** Their glory also will I take unto me, and give these the everlasting tabernacles, which I had prepared for them. **12** They shall have the tree of life for an ointment of sweet savour; they shall neither labour, nor be weary. **13** Go, and ye shall receive: pray for few days unto you, that they may be shortened: the kingdom is already prepared for you: watch. **14** Take heaven and earth to witness; for I have broken the evil in pieces, and created the good: for I live, saith the Lord. **15** Mother, embrace thy children, and bring them up with gladness, make their feet as fast as a pillar: for I have chosen thee, saith the Lord. **16** And those that be dead will I raise up again from their places, and bring them out of the graves: for I have known my name in Israel. **17** Fear not, thou mother of the children: for I have chosen thee, saith the Lord. **18** For thy help will I send my servants Esau and Jeremy, after whose counsel I have sanctified and prepared for thee twelve trees laden with divers fruits, **19** And as many fountains flowing with milk and honey, and seven mighty mountains, whereupon there grow roses and lilies, whereby I will fill thy children with joy. **20** Do right to the widow, judge for the fatherless, give to the poor, defend the orphan, clothe the naked, **21** Heal the broken and the weak, laugh not a lame man to scorn, defend the maimed, and let the blind man come into the sight of my clearness. **22** Keep the old and young within thy walls. **23** Wheresoever thou findest the dead, take them and bury them, and I will give thee the first place in my resurrection. **24** Abide still, O my people, and take thy rest, for thy quietness still come. **25** Nourish thy children, O thou good nurse; stablish their feet. **26** As for the servants whom I have given thee, there shall not one of them perish; for I will require them from among thy number. **27** Be not weary: for when the day of trouble and heaviness cometh, others shall weep and be sorrowful, but thou shalt be merry and have abundance. **28** The heathen shall envy thee, but they shall be able to do nothing against thee, saith the Lord. **29** My hands shall cover thee, so that thy children shall not see hell. **30** Be joyful, O thou mother, with thy children; for I will deliver thee, saith the Lord. **31** Remember thy children that sleep, for I shall bring them out of the sides of the earth, and shew mercy unto them: for I am merciful, saith the Lord Almighty. **32** Embrace thy children until I come and shew mercy unto them: for my wells run over, and my grace shall not fail. **33** I Esdras received a charge of the Lord upon the mount Oreb, that I should go unto Israel; but when I came unto them, they set me at nought, and despised the commandment of the Lord. **34** And therefore I say unto you, O ye heathen, that hear and understand, look for your Shepherd, he shall give you everlasting rest; for he is nigh at hand, that shall come in the end of the world. **35** Be ready to the reward of the kingdom, for the everlasting light shall shine upon you for evermore. **36** Flee the shadow of this world, receive the joyfulness of your glory: I testify my Saviour openly. **37** O receive the gift that is given you, and be glad, giving thanks unto him that hath led you to the heavenly kingdom. **38** Arise up and stand, behold the number of those that be sealed in the feast of the Lord; **39** Which are departed from the shadow of the world, and have received glorious garments of the Lord. **40** Take thy number, O Sion, and shut up those of thine that are clothed in white, which have fulfilled the law of the Lord. **41** The number of thy children, whom thou longedst for, is fulfilled: beseech the power of the Lord, that thy people, which have been called from the beginning, may be hallowed. **42** I Esdras saw upon the mount Sion a great people, whom I could not number, and they all praised the Lord with songs. **43** And in the midst of them there was a young man of a high stature, taller than all the rest, and upon every one of their heads he set crowns, and was more exalted; which I marvelled at greatly. **44** So I asked the angel, and said, Sir, what are these? **45** He answered and said unto me, These be they that have put off the mortal clothing, and put on the immortal, and have confessed the name of God: now are they crowned, and receive palms. **46** Then said I unto the angel, What young person is it that crowneth them, and giveth them palms in their hands? **47** So he answered and said unto me, It is the Son of God, whom they have confessed in the world. Then began I greatly to commend them that stood so stiffly for the name of the Lord. **48** Then the angel said unto me, Go thy way, and tell my people what manner of things, and how great wonders of the Lord thy God, thou hast seen.

3

1 In the thirtieth year after the ruin of the city I was in Babylon, and lay troubled upon my bed, and my thoughts came up over my heart: **2** For I saw the desolation of Sion, and the wealth of them that dwelt at Babylon. **3** And my spirit was sore moved, so that I began to speak words full of fear to the most High, and said, **4** O Lord, who bearest rule, thou spakest at the beginning, when thou didst plant the earth, and that thyself alone, and commandedst the people, **5** And gavest a body unto Adam without soul, which was the workmanship of thine hands, and didst breathe into him the breath of life, and he was made living before thee. **6** And thou leadest him into paradise, which thy right hand had planted, before ever the earth came forward. **7** And unto him thou gavest commandment to love thy way: which he transgressed, and immediately thou appointedst death in him and in his generations, of whom came nations, tribes, people, and kindreds, out of number. **8** And every people walked after their own will, and did wonderful things before thee, and despised thy commandments. **9** And again in process of time thou broughtest the flood upon those that dwelt in the world, and destroyedst them. **10** And it came to pass in every of them, that as death was to Adam, so was the flood to these. **11** Nevertheless one of them thou leftest, namely, Noah with his household, of whom came all righteous men. **12** And it happened, that when they that dwelt upon the earth began to multiply, and had gotten them many children, and were a great people, they began again to be more ungodly than the first. **13** Now when they lived so wickedly before thee, thou didst choose thee a man from among them, whose name was Abraham. **14** Him thou lovedst, and unto him only thou shewedst thy will: **15** And madest an everlasting covenant with him, promising him that thou wouldest never forsake his seed. **16** And unto him thou gavest Isaac, and unto Isaac also thou gavest Jacob and Esau. As for Jacob, thou didst choose him to thee, and put by Esau: and so Jacob became a great multitude. **17** And it came to pass, that when thou leadest his seed out of Egypt, thou broughtest them up to the mount Sinai. **18** And bowing the heavens, thou didst set fast the earth, movedst the whole world, and madest the depths to tremble, and troubledst the men of that age. **19** And thy glory went through four gates, of fire, and of earthquake, and of wind, and of cold; that thou mightest give the law unto the seed of Jacob, and diligence unto the generation of Israel. **20** And yet tookest thou not away from them a wicked heart, that thy law might bring forth fruit in them. **21** For the first Adam bearing a wicked heart transgressed, and was overcome; and so be all they that are born of him. 2 Esdras Page **710** **22** Thus infirmity was made permanent; and the law (also) in the heart of the people with the malignity of the root; so that the good departed away, and the evil abode still. **23** So the times passed away, and the years were brought to an end: then didst thou raise thee up a servant, called David: **24** Whom thou commandedst to build a city unto thy name, and to offer incense and oblations unto thee therein. **25** When this was done many years, then they that inhabited the city forsook thee, **26** And in all things did even as Adam and all his generations had done: for they also had a wicked heart: **27** And so thou gavest thy city over into the hands of thine enemies. **28** Are their deeds then any better that inhabit Babylon, that they should therefore have the dominion over Sion? **29** For when I came thither, and had seen impieties without number, then my soul saw many evildoers in this thirtieth year, so that my heart failed me. **30** For I have seen how thou sufferest them sinning, and hast spared wicked doers: and hast destroyed thy people, and hast preserved thine enemies, and hast not signified it. **31** I do not remember how this way may be left: Are they then of Babylon better than they of Sion? **32** Or is there any other people that knoweth thee beside Israel? or what generation hath so believed thy covenants as Jacob? **33** And yet their reward appeareth not, and their labour hath no fruit: for I have gone here and there through the heathen, and I see that they flow in wealth, and think not upon thy commandments. **34** Weigh thou therefore our wickedness now in the balance, and their's also that dwell the world; and so shall thy name no where be found but in Israel. **35** Or when was it that they which dwell upon the earth have not sinned in thy sight? or what people have so kept thy commandments? **36** Thou shalt find that Israel by name hath kept thy precepts; but not the heathen.

4

1 And the angel that was sent unto me, whose name was Uriel, gave me an answer, **2** And said, Thy heart hath gone to far in this world, and

thinkest thou to comprehend the way of the most High? **3** Then said I, Yea, my
lord. And he answered me, and said, I am sent to shew thee three ways, and to
set forth three similitudes before thee: **4** Whereof if thou canst declare me one,
I will shew thee also the way that thou desirest to see, and I shall shew thee from
whence the wicked heart cometh. **5** And I said, Tell on, my lord. Then said he
unto me, Go thy way, weigh me the weight of the fire, or measure me the blast
of the wind, or call me again the day that is past. **6** Then answered I and said,
What man is able to do that, that thou shouldest ask such things of me? **7** And
he said unto me, If I should ask thee how great dwellings are in the midst of the
sea, or how many springs are in the beginning of the deep, or how many springs
are above the firmament, or which are the outgoings of paradise: **8** Peradventu-
re thou wouldest say unto me, I never went down into the deep, nor as yet into
hell, neither did I ever climb up into heaven. **9** Nevertheless now have I asked
thee but only of the fire and wind, and of the day wherethrough thou hast passed,
and of things from which thou canst not be separated, and yet canst thou give me
no answer of them. **10** He said moreover unto me, Thine own things, and such
as are grown up with thee, canst thou not know; **11** How should thy vessel then
be able to comprehend the way of the Highest, and, the world being now outwar-
dly corrupted to understand the corruption that is evident in my sight? **12** Then
said I unto him, It were better that we were not at all, than that we should live still
in wickedness, and to suffer, and not to know wherefore. **13** He answered me,
and said, I went into a forest into a plain, and the trees took counsel, **14** And
said, Come, let us go and make war against the sea that it may depart away before
us, and that we may make us more woods. **15** The floods of the sea also in like
manner took counsel, and said, Come, let us go up and subdue the woods of the
plain, that there also we may make us another country. **16** The thought of the
wood was in vain, for the fire came and consumed it. **17** The thought of the
floods of the sea came likewise to nought, for the sand stood up and stopped
them. **18** If thou wert judge now betwixt these two, whom wouldest thou begin
to justify? or whom wouldest thou condemn? **19** I answered and said, Verily it
is a foolish thought that they both have devised, for the ground is given unto the
wood, and the sea also hath his place to bear his floods. **20** Then answered he
me, and said, Thou hast given a right judgment, but why judgest thou not thyself
also? **21** For like as the ground is given unto the wood, and the sea to his floods:
even so they that dwell upon the earth may understand nothing but that which
is upon the earth: and he that dwelleth above the heavens may only understand
the things that are above the height of the heavens. **22** Then answered I and
said, I beseech thee, O Lord, let me have understanding: **23** For it was not my
mind to be curious of the high things, but of such as pass by us daily, namely,
wherefore Israel is given up as a reproach to the heathen, and for what cause the
people whom thou hast loved is given over unto ungodly nations, and why the
law of our forefathers is brought to nought, and the written covenants come to
none effect, **24** And we pass away out of the world as grasshoppers, and our
life is astonishment and fear, and we are not worthy to obtain mercy. **25** What
will he then do unto his name whereby we are called? of these things have I
asked. **26** Then answered he me, and said, The more thou searchest, the more
thou shalt marvel; for the world hasteth fast to pass away, **27** And cannot com-
prehend the things that are promised to the righteous in time to come: for this
world is full of unrighteousness and infirmities. **28** But as concerning the thin-
gs whereof thou askest me, I will tell thee; for the evil is sown, but the destruction
thereof is not yet come. **29** If therefore that which is sown be not turned upside
down, and if the place where the evil is sown pass not away, then cannot it come
that is sown with good. **30** For the grain of evil seed hath been sown in the he-
art of Adam from the beginning, and how much ungodliness hath it brought up
unto this time? and how much shall it yet bring forth until the time of threshing
come? **31** Ponder now by thyself, how great fruit of wickedness the grain of
evil seed hath brought forth. **32** And when the ears shall be cut down, which
are without number, how great a floor shall they fill? **33** Then I answered and
said, How, and when shall these things come to pass? wherefore are our years
few and evil? **34** And he answered me, saying, Do not thou hasten above the
most Highest: for thy haste is in vain to be above him, for thou hast much exce-
eded. **35** Did not the souls also of the righteous ask question of these things in
their chambers, saying, How long shall I hope on this fashion? when cometh the
fruit of the floor of our reward? **36** And unto these things Uriel the archangel
gave them answer, and said, Even when the number of seeds is filled in you: for
he hath weighed the world in the balance. **37** By measure hath he measured
the times; and by number hath he numbered the times; and he doth not move
nor stir them, until the said measure be fulfilled. **38** Then answered I and said,
O Lord that bearest rule, even we all are full of impiety. **39** And for our sakes
peradventure it is that the floors of the righteous are not filled, because of the
sins of them that dwell upon the earth. **40** So he answered me, and said, Go
thy way to a woman with child, and ask of her when she hath fulfilled her nine
months, if her womb may keep the birth any longer within her. **41** Then said
I, No, Lord, that can she not. And he said unto me, In the grave the chambers
of souls are like the womb of a woman: **42** For like as a woman that travaileth
maketh haste to escape the necessity of the travail: even so do these places haste
to deliver those things that are committed unto them. **43** From the beginning,
look, what thou desirest to see, it shall be shewed thee. **44** Then answered I and
said, If I have found favour in thy sight, and if it be possible, and if I be meet
therefore, **45** Shew me then whether there be more to come than is past, or
more past than is to come. **46** What is past I know, but what is for to come I
know not. **47** And he said unto me, Stand up upon the right side, and I shall
expound the similitude unto thee. **48** So I stood, and saw, and, behold, an hot
burning oven passed by before me: and it happened that when the flame was gone
by I looked, and, behold, the smoke remained still. **49** After this there passed
by before me a watery cloud, and sent down much rain with a storm; and when
the stormy rain was past, the drops remained still. **50** Then said he unto me,
Consider with thyself; as the rain is more than the drops, and as the fire is greater
than the smoke; but the drops and the smoke remain behind: so the quantity
which is past did more exceed. **51** Then I prayed, and said, May I live, thinkest
thou, until that time? or what shall happen in those days? **52** He answered me,
and said, As for the tokens whereof thou askest me, I may tell thee of them in
part: but as touching thy life, I am not sent to shew thee; for I do not know it.

5 **1** Nevertheless as coming the tokens, behold, the days shall come, that
they which dwell upon earth shall be taken in a great number, and the way
of truth shall be hidden, and the land shall be barren of faith. **2** But iniquity
shall be increased above that which now thou seest, or that thou hast heard long
ago. **3** And the land, that thou seest now to have root, shalt thou see wasted
suddenly. **4** But if the most High grant thee to live, thou shalt see after the
third trumpet that the sun shall suddenly shine again in the night, and the moon
thrice in the day: **5** And blood shall drop out of wood, and the stone shall give
his voice, and the people shall be troubled: **6** And even he shall rule, whom
they look not for that dwell upon the earth, and the fowls shall take their flight
away together: **7** And the Sodomitish sea shall cast out fish, and make a noise
in the night, which many have not known: but they shall all hear the voice there-
of. **8** There shall be a confusion also in many places, and the fire shall be oft sent
out again, and the wild beasts shall change their places, and menstruous women
shall bring forth monsters: **9** And salt waters shall be found in the sweet, and all
friends shall destroy one another; then shall wit hide itself, and understanding wi-
thdraw itself into his secret chamber, **10** And shall be sought of many, and yet
not be found: then shall unrighteousness and incontinency be multiplied upon
earth. **11** One land also shall ask another, and say, Is righteousness that maketh
a man righteous gone through thee? And it shall say, No. **12** At the same time
shall men hope, but nothing obtain: they shall labour, but their ways shall not
prosper. **13** To shew thee such tokens I have leave; and if thou wilt pray again,
and weep as now, and fast even days, thou shalt hear yet greater things. **14** Then
I awaked, and an extreme fearfulness went through all my body, and my mind was
troubled, so that it fainted. **15** So the angel that was come to talk with me held
me, comforted me, and set me up upon my feet. **16** And in the second night
it came to pass, that Salathiel the captain of the people came unto me, saying,
Where hast thou been? and why is thy countenance so heavy? **17** Knowest thou
not that Israel is committed unto thee in the land of their captivity? **18** Up
then, and eat bread, and forsake us not, as the shepherd that leaveth his flock in
the hands of cruel wolves. **19** Then said I unto him, Go thy ways from me, and
come not nigh me. And he heard what I said, and went from me. **20** And so
I fasted seven days, mourning and weeping, like as Uriel the angel commanded
me. **21** And after seven days so it was, that the thoughts of my heart were very
grievous unto me again, **22** And my soul recovered the spirit of understan-
ding, and I began to talk with the most High again, **23** And said, O Lord that
bearest rule, of every wood of the earth, and of all the trees thereof, thou hast
chosen thee one only vine: **24** And of all lands of the whole world thou hast
chosen thee one pit: and of all the flowers thereof one lily: **25** And of all the
depths of the sea thou hast filled thee one river: and of all builded cities thou hast
hallowed Sion unto thyself: **26** And of all the fowls that are created thou hast
named thee one dove: and of all the cattle that are made thou hast provided thee
one sheep: **27** And among all the multitudes of people thou hast gotten thee
one people: and unto this people, whom thou lovedst, thou gavest a law that is
approved of all. **28** And now, O Lord, why hast thou given this one people over
unto many? and upon the one root hast thou prepared others, and why hast thou
scattered thy only one people among many? **29** And they which did gainsay
thy promises, and believed not thy covenants, have trodden them down. **30** If
thou didst so much hate thy people, yet shouldest thou punish them with thine
own hands. **31** Now when I had spoken these words, the angel that came to me
the night afore was sent unto me, **32** And said unto me, Hear me, and I will
instruct thee; hearken to the thing that I say, and I shall tell thee more. **33** And
I said, Speak on, my Lord. Then said he unto me, Thou art sore troubled in mind
for Israel's sake: lovest thou that people better than he that made them? **34** And
I said, No, Lord: but of very grief have I spoken: for my reins pain me every hour,
while I labour to comprehend the way of the most High, and to seek out part of
his judgment. **35** And he said unto me, Thou canst not. And I said, Wherefore,
Lord? whereunto was I born then? or why was not my mother's womb then my
grave, that I might not have seen the travail of Jacob, and the wearisome toil of the
stock of Israel? **36** And he said unto me, Number me the things that are not yet
come, gather me together the dross that are scattered abroad, make me the flowers
green again that are withered, **37** Open me the places that are closed, and bring
me forth the winds that in them are shut up, shew me the image of a voice: and
then I will declare to thee the thing that thou labourest to know. **38** And I said,
O Lord that bearest rule, who may know these things, but he that hath not his
dwelling with men? **39** As for me, I am unwise: how may I then speak of these
things whereof thou askest me? **40** Then said he unto me, Like as thou canst

do none of these things that I have spoken of, even so canst thou not find out my
judgment, or in the end the love that I have promised unto my people. **41** And
I said, Behold, O Lord, yet art thou nigh unto them that be reserved till the end:
and what shall they do that have been before me, or we that be now, or they that
shall come after us? **42** And he said unto me, I will liken my judgment unto
a ring: like as there is no slackness of the last, even so there is no swiftness of the
first. **43** So I answered and said, Couldest thou not make those that have been
made, and be now, and that are for to come, at once; that thou mightest shew
thy judgment the sooner? **44** Then answered he me, and said, The creature
may not haste above the maker; neither may the world hold them at once that
shall be created therein. **45** And I said, As thou hast said unto thy servant, that
thou, which givest life to all, hast given life at once to the creature that thou hast
created, and the creature bare it: even so it might now also bear them that now be
present at once. **46** And he said unto me, Ask the womb of a woman, and say
unto her, If thou bringest forth children, why dost thou it not together, but one
after another? pray her therefore to bring forth ten children at once. **47** And I
said, She cannot: but must do it by distance of time. **48** Then said he unto me,
Even so have I given the womb of the earth to those that be sown in it in their
times. **49** For like as a young child may not bring forth the things that belong
to the aged, even so have I disposed the world which I created. **50** And I asked,
and said, Seeing thou hast now given me the way, I will proceed to speak before
thee: for our mother, of whom thou hast told me that she is young, draweth
now nigh unto age. **51** He answered me, and said, Ask a woman that beareth
children, and she shall tell thee. **52** Say unto her, Wherefore are unto they
whom thou hast now brought forth like those that were before, but less of statu-
re? **53** And she shall answer thee, They that be born in the the strength of youth
are of one fashion, and they that are born in the time of age, when the womb
faileth, are otherwise. **54** Consider thou therefore also, how that ye are less of
stature than those that were before you. **55** And so are they that come after you
less than ye, as the creatures which now begin to be old, and have passed over the
strength of youth. **56** Then said I, Lord, I beseech thee, if I have found favour
in thy sight, shew thy servant by whom thou visitest thy creature.

6

1 And he said unto me, In the beginning, when the earth was made,
before the borders of the world stood, or ever the winds blew, **2** Before
it thundered and lightened, or ever the foundations of paradise were laid, **3** Be-
fore the fair flowers were seen, or ever the moveable powers were established,
before the innumerable multitude of angels were gathered together, **4** Or ever
the heights of the air were lifted up, before the measures of the firmament were
named, or ever the chimneys in Sion were hot, **5** And ere the present years were
sought out, and or ever the inventions of them that now sin were turned, before
they were sealed that have gathered faith for a treasure: **6** Then did I consider
these things, and they all were made through me alone, and through none other:
by me also they shall be ended, and by none other. **7** Then answered I and
said, What shall be the parting asunder of the times? or when shall be the end
of the first, and the beginning of it that followeth? **8** And he said unto me,
From Abraham unto Isaac, when Jacob and Esau were born of him, Jacob's hand
held first the heel of Esau. **9** For Esau is the end of the world, and Jacob is the
beginning of it that followeth. **10** The hand of man is betwixt the heel and the
hand: other question, Esdras, ask thou not. **11** I answered then and said, O
Lord that bearest rule, if I have found favour in thy sight, **12** I beseech thee,
shew thy servant the end of thy tokens, whereof thou shewedst me part the last
night. **13** So he answered and said unto me, Stand up upon thy feet, and hear
a mighty sounding voice. **14** And it shall be as it were a great motion; but the
place where thou standest shall not be moved. **15** And therefore when it spea-
keth be not afraid: for the word is of the end, and the foundation of the earth is
understood. **16** And why? because the speech of these things trembleth and is
moved: for it knoweth that the end of these things must be changed. **17** And
it happened, that when I had heard it I stood up upon my feet, and hearkened,
and, behold, there was a voice that spake, and the sound of it was like the sound
of many waters. **18** And it said, Behold, the days come, that I will begin to
draw nigh, and to visit them that dwell upon the earth, **19** And will begin to
make inquisition of them, what they be that have hurt unjustly with their unri-
ghteousness, and when the affliction of Sion shall be fulfilled; **20** And when the
world, that shall begin to vanish away, shall be finished, then will I shew these
tokens: the books shall be opened before the firmament, and they shall see all
together: **21** And the children of a year old shall speak with their voices, the
women with child shall bring forth untimely children of three or four months
old, and they shall live, and be raised up. **22** And suddenly shall the sown places
appear unsown, the full storehouses shall suddenly be found empty: **23** And tha
trumpet shall give a sound, which when every man heareth, they shall be suddenly
afraid. **24** At that time shall friends fight one against another like enemies,
and the earth shall stand in fear with those that dwell therein, the springs of the
fountains shall stand still, and in three hours they shall not run. **25** Whosoever
remaineth from all these that I have told thee shall escape, and see my salva-
tion, and the end of your world. **26** And the men that are received shall see
it, who have not tasted death from their birth: and the heart of the inhabitants
shall be changed, and turned into another meaning. **27** For evil shall be put
out, and deceit shall be quenched. **28** As for faith, it shall flourish, corruption
shall be overcome, and the truth, which hath been so long without fruit, shall
be declared. **29** And when he talked with me, behold, I looked by little and
little upon him before whom I stood. **30** And these words said he unto me;
I am come to shew thee the time of the night to come. **31** If thou wilt pray
yet more, and fast seven days again, I shall tell thee greater things by day than I
have heard. **32** For thy voice is heard before the most High: for the Mighty
hath seen thy righteous dealing, he hath seen also thy chastity, which thou hast
had ever since thy youth. **33** And therefore hath he sent me to shew thee all
these things, and to say unto thee, Be of good comfort and fear not **34** And
hasten not with the times that are past, to think vain things, that thou mayest
not hasten from the latter times. **35** And it came to pass after this, that I wept
again, and fasted seven days in like manner, that I might fulfil the three weeks
which he told me. **36** And in the eighth night was my heart vexed within me
again, and I began to speak before the most High. **37** For my spirit was greatly
set on fire, and my soul was in distress. **38** And I said, O Lord, thou spakest
from the beginning of the creation, even the first day, and saidst thus; Let heaven
and earth be made; and thy word was a perfect work. **39** And then was the
spirit, and darkness and silence were on every side; the sound of man's voice was
not yet formed. **40** Then commandedst thou a fair light to come forth of thy
treasures, that thy work might appear. **41** Upon the second day thou madest
the spirit of the firmament, and commandedst it to part asunder, and to make a
division betwixt the waters, that the one part might go up, and the other remain
beneath. **42** Upon the third day thou didst command that the waters should
be gathered in the seventh part of the earth: six pats hast thou dried up, and kept
them, to the intent that of these some being planted of God and tilled might serve
thee. **43** For as soon as thy word went forth the work was made. **44** For im-
mediately there was great and innumerable fruit, and many and divers pleasures
for the taste, and flowers of unchangeable colour, and odours of wonderful smell:
and this was done the third day. **45** Upon the fourth day thou commandedst
that the sun should shine, and the moon give her light, and the stars should be
in order: **46** And gavest them a charge to do service unto man, that was to be
made. **47** Upon the fifth day thou saidst unto the seventh part, where the wa-
ters were gathered that it should bring forth living creatures, fowls and fishes: and
so it came to pass. **48** For the dumb water and without life brought forth living
things at the commandment of God, that all people might praise thy wondrous
works. **49** Then didst thou ordain two living creatures, the one thou calledst
Enoch, and the other Leviathan; **50** And didst separate the one from the other:
for the seventh part, namely, where the water was gathered together, might not
hold them both. **51** Unto Enoch thou gavest one part, which was dried up
the third day, that he should dwell in the same part, wherein are a thousand
hills: **52** But unto Leviathan thou gavest the seventh part, namely, the moist;
and hast kept him to be devoured of whom thou wilt, and when. **53** Upon the
sixth day thou gavest commandment unto the earth, that before thee it should
bring forth beasts, cattle, and creeping things: **54** And after these, Adam also,
whom thou madest lord of all thy creatures: of him come we all, and the people
also whom thou hast chosen. **55** All this have I spoken before thee, O Lord,
because thou madest the world for our sakes **56** As for the other people, which
also come of Adam, thou hast said that they are nothing, but be like unto spittle:
and hast likened the abundance of them unto a drop that falleth from a ves-
sel. **57** And now, O Lord, behold, these heathen, which have ever been reputed
as nothing, have begun to be lords over us, and to devour us. **58** But we thy
people, whom thou hast called thy firstborn, thy only begotten, and thy fervent
lover, are given into their hands. **59** If the world now be made for our sakes,
why do we not possess an inheritance with the world? how long shall this endure?

7

1 And when I had made an end of speaking these words, there was sent
unto me the angel which had been sent unto me the nights afore: **2** And
he said unto me, Up, Esdras, and hear the words that I am come to tell
thee. **3** And I said, Speak on, my God. Then said he unto me, The sea is set in
a wide place, that it might be deep and great. **4** But put the case the entrance
were narrow, and like a river; **5** Who then could go into the sea to look upon it,
and to rule it? if he went not through the narrow, how could he come into the
broad? **6** There is also another thing; A city is builded, and set upon a broad
field, and is full of all good things: **7** The entrance thereof is narrow, and is set
in a dangerous place to fall, like as if there were a fire on the right hand, and on
the left a deep water: **8** And one only path between them both, even between
the fire and the water, so small that there could but one man go there at
once. **9** If this city now were given unto a man for an inheritance, if he never
shall pass the danger set before it, how shall he receive this inheritance? **10** And
I said, It is so, Lord. Then said he unto me, Even so also is Israel's portion. **11** Be-
cause for their sakes I made the world: and when Adam transgressed my statutes,
then was decreed that now is done. **12** Then were the entrances of this world
made narrow, full of sorrow and travail: they are but few and evil, full of perils,:
and very painful. **13** For the entrances of the elder world were wide and sure,
and brought immortal fruit. **14** If then they that live labour not to enter these
strait and vain things, they can never receive those that are laid up for
them. **15** Now therefore why disquietest thou thyself, seeing thou art but a
corruptible man? and why art thou moved, whereas thou art but mor-
tal? **16** Why hast thou not considered in thy mind this thing that is to come,
rather than that which is present? **17** Then answered I and said, O Lord that
bearest rule, thou hast ordained in thy law, that the righteous should inherit these

things, but that the ungodly should perish. **18** Nevertheless the righteous shall suffer strait things, and hope for wide: for they that have done wickedly have suffered the strait things, and yet shall not see the wide. **19** And he said unto me. There is no judge above God, and none that hath understanding above the Highest. **20** For there be many that perish in this life, because they despise the law of God that is set before them. **21** For God hath given strait commandment to such as came, what they should do to live, even as they came, and what they should observe to avoid punishment. **22** Nevertheless they were not obedient unto him; but spake against him, and imagined vain things; **23** And deceived themselves by their wicked deeds; and said of the most High, that he is not; and knew not his ways: **24** But his law have they despised, and denied his covenants; in his statutes have they not been faithful, and have not performed his works. **25** And therefore, Esdras, for the empty are empty things, and for the full are the full things. **26** Behold, the time shall come, that these tokens which I have told thee shall come to pass, and the bride shall appear, and she coming forth shall be seen, that now is withdrawn from the earth. **27** And whosoever is delivered from the foresaid evils shall see my wonders. **28** For my son Jesus shall be revealed with those that be with him, and they that remain shall rejoice within four hundred years. **29** After these years shall my son Christ die, and all men that have life. **30** And the world shall be turned into the old silence seven days, like as in the former judgments: so that no man shall remain. **31** And after seven days the world, that yet awaketh not, shall be raised up, and that shall die that is corrupt **32** And the earth shall restore those that are asleep in her, and so shall the dust those that dwell in silence, and the secret places shall deliver those souls that were committed unto them. **33** And the most High shall appear upon the seat of judgment, and misery shall pass away, and the long suffering shall have an end: **34** But judgment only shall remain, truth shall stand, and faith shall wax strong: **35** And the work shall follow, and the reward shall be shewed, and the good deeds shall be of force, and wicked deeds shall bear no rule. **36** Then said I, Abraham prayed first for the Sodomites, and Moses for the fathers that sinned in the wilderness: **37** And Jesus after him for Israel in the time of Achan: **38** And Samuel and David for the destruction: and Solomon for them that should come to the sanctuary: **39** And Helias for those that received rain; and for the dead, that he might live: **40** And Ezechias for the people in the time of Sennacherib: and many for many. **41** Even so now, seeing corruption is grown up, and wickedness increased, and the righteous have prayed for the ungodly: wherefore shall it not be so now also? **42** He answered me, and said, This present life is not the end where much glory doth abide; therefore have they prayed for the weak. **43** But the day of doom shall be the end of this time, and the beginning of the immortality for to come, wherein corruption is past, **44** Intemperance is at an end, infidelity is cut off, righteousness is grown, and truth is sprung up. **45** Then shall no man be able to save him that is destroyed, nor to oppress him that hath gotten the victory. **46** I answered then and said, This is my first and last saying, that it had been better not to have given the earth unto Adam: or else, when it was given him, to have restrained him from sinning. **47** For what profit is it for men now in this present time to live in heaviness, and after death to look for punishment? **48** O thou Adam, what hast thou done? for though it was thou that sinned, thou art not fallen alone, but we all that come of thee. **49** For what profit is it unto us, if there be promised us an immortal time, whereas we have done the works that bring death? **50** And that there is promised us an everlasting hope, whereas ourselves being most wicked are made vain? **51** And that there are laid up for us dwellings of health and safety, whereas we have lived wickedly? **52** And that the glory of the most High is kept to defend them which have led a wary life, whereas we have walked in the most wicked ways of all? **53** And that there should be shewed a paradise, whose fruit endureth for ever, wherein is security and medicine, since we shall not enter into it? **54** (For we have walked in unpleasant places.) **55** And that the faces of them which have used abstinence shall shine above the stars, whereas our faces shall be blacker than darkness? **56** For while we lived and committed iniquity, we considered not that we should begin to suffer for it after death. **57** Then answered he me, and said, This is the condition of the battle, which man that is born upon the earth shall fight; **58** That, if he be overcome, he shall suffer as thou hast said: but if he get the victory, he shall receive the thing that I say. **59** For this is the life whereof Moses spake unto the people while he lived, saying, Choose thee life, that thou mayest live. **60** Nevertheless they believed not him, nor yet the prophets after him, no nor me which have spoken unto them, **61** That there should not be such heaviness in their destruction, as shall be joy over them that are persuaded to salvation. **62** I answered then, and said, I know, Lord, that the most High is called merciful, in that he hath mercy upon them which are not yet come into the world, **63** And upon those also that turn to his law; **64** And that he is patient, and long suffereth those that have sinned, as his creatures; **65** And that he is bountiful, for he is ready to give where it needeth; **66** And that he is of great mercy, for he multiplieth more and more mercies to them that are present, and that are past, and also to them which are to come. **67** For if he shall not multiply his mercies, the world would not continue with them that inherit therein. **68** And he pardoneth; for if he did not so of his goodness, that they which have committed iniquities might be eased of them, the ten thousandth part of men should not remain living. **69** And being judge, if he should not forgive them that are cured with his word, and put out the multitude of contentions, **70** There should be very few left peradventure in an innumerable multitude.

8 **1** And he answered me, saying, The most High hath made this world for many, but the world to come for few. **2** I will tell thee a similitude, Esdras; As when thou askest the earth, it shall say unto thee, that it giveth much mould whereof earthen vessels are made, but little dust that gold cometh of: even so is the course of this present world. **3** There be many created, but few shall be saved. **4** So answered I and said, Swallow then down, O my soul, understanding, and devour wisdom. **5** For thou hast agreed to give ear, and art willing to prophesy: for thou hast no longer space than only to live. **6** O Lord, if thou suffer not thy servant, that we may pray before thee, and thou give us seed unto our heart, and culture to our understanding, that there may come fruit of it; how shall each man live that is corrupt, who beareth the place of a man? **7** For thou art alone, and we all one workmanship of thine hands, like as thou hast said. **8** For when the body is fashioned now in the mother's womb, and thou givest it members, thy creature is preserved in fire and water, and nine months doth thy workmanship endure thy creature which is created in her. **9** But that which keepeth and is kept shall both be preserved: and when the time cometh, the womb preserved delivereth up the things that grew in it. **10** For thou hast commanded out of the parts of the body, that is to say, out of the breasts, milk to be given, which is the fruit of the breasts, **11** That the thing which is fashioned may be nourished for a time, till thou disposest it to thy mercy. **12** Thou broughtest it up with thy righteousness, and nurturedst it in thy law, and reformedst it with thy judgment. **13** And thou shalt mortify it as thy creature, and quicken it as thy work. **14** If therefore thou shalt destroy him which with so great labour was fashioned, it is an easy thing to be ordained by thy commandment, that the thing which was made might be preserved. **15** Now therefore, Lord, I will speak; touching man in general, thou knowest best; but touching thy people, for whose sake I am sorry; **16** And for thine inheritance, for whose cause I mourn; and for Israel, for whom I am heavy; and for Jacob, for whose sake I am troubled; **17** Therefore will I begin to pray before thee for myself and for them: for I see the falls of us that dwell in the land. **18** But I have heard the swiftness of the judge which is to come. **19** Therefore hear my voice, and understand my words, and I shall speak before thee. This is the beginning of the words of Esdras, before he was taken up: and I said, **20** O Lord, thou that dwellest in everlastingness which beholdest from above things in the heaven and in the air; **21** Whose throne is inestimable; whose glory may not be comprehended; before whom the hosts of angels stand with trembling, **22** Whose service is conversant in wind and fire; whose word is true, and sayings constant; whose commandment is strong, and ordinance fearful; **23** Whose look drieth up the depths, and indignation maketh the mountains to melt away; which the truth witnesseth: **24** O hear the prayer of thy servant, and give ear to the petition of thy creature. **25** For while I live I will speak, and so long as I have understanding I will answer. **26** O look not upon the sins of thy people; but on them which serve thee in truth. **27** Regard not the wicked inventions of the heathen, but the desire of those that keep thy testimonies in afflictions. **28** Think not upon those that have walked feignedly before thee: but remember them, which according to thy will have known thy fear. **29** Let it not be thy will to destroy them which have lived like beasts; but to look upon them that have clearly taught thy law. **30** Take thou no indignation at them which are deemed worse than beasts; but love them that always put their trust in thy righteousness and glory. **31** For we and our fathers do languish of such diseases: but because of us sinners thou shalt be called merciful. **32** For if thou hast a desire to have mercy upon us, thou shalt be called merciful, to us namely, that have no works of righteousness. **33** For the just, which have many good works laid up with thee, shall out of their own deeds receive reward. **34** For what is man, that thou shouldest take displeasure at him? or what is a corruptible generation, that thou shouldest be so bitter toward it? **35** For in truth them is no man among them that be born, but he hath dealt wickedly; and among the faithful there is none which hath not done amiss. **36** For in this, O Lord, thy righteousness and thy goodness shall be declared, if thou be merciful unto them which have not the confidence of good works. **37** Then answered he me, and said, Some things hast thou spoken aright, and according unto thy words it shall be. **38** For indeed I will not think on the disposition of them which have sinned before death, before judgment, before destruction: **39** But I will rejoice over the disposition of the righteous, and I will remember also their pilgrimage, and the salvation, and the reward, that they shall have. **40** Like as I have spoken now, so shall it come to pass. **41** For as the husbandman soweth much seed upon the ground, and planteth many trees, and yet the thing that is sown good in his season cometh not up, neither doth all that is planted take root: even so is it of them that are sown in the world; they shall not all be saved. **42** I answered then and said, If I have found grace, let me speak. **43** Like as the husbandman's seed perisheth, if it come not up, and receive not thy rain in due season; or if there come too much rain, and corrupt it: **44** Even so perisheth man also, which is formed with thy hands, and is called thine own image, because thou art like unto him, for whose sake thou hast made all things, and likened him unto the husbandman's seed. **45** Be not wroth with us but spare thy people, and have mercy upon thine own inheritance: for thou art merciful unto thy creature. **46** Then answered he me, and said, Things present are for the present, and things to cometh for such as be to come. **47** For thou comest far short that thou shouldest be able to love my creature more than I: but I have ofttimes drawn nigh unto thee, and unto it, but never to the unrighteous. **48** In this also thou art marvellous before the most High: **49** In that thou hast humbled thyself, as it becometh thee, and hast not judged thyself worthy to be much glorified among the righteous. **50** For many great miseries shall be done to them that in the latter time shall dwell in the world, because they have walked in great pride. **51** But understand thou for thyself, and seek out the glory for such as be like thee. **52** For unto you is paradise opened, the tree of life is planted, the time to come is prepared, plenteousness is made ready, a city is builded, and rest is allowed, yea, perfect goodness and wisdom. **53** The root of evil is sealed up from you, weakness and the moth is hid from you, and corruption is fled into hell to be forgotten: **54** Sorrows are passed, and in the end is shewed the treasure of immortality. **55** And therefore ask thou no more questions concerning the multitude of them that perish. **56** For when they had taken liberty, they despised the most High, thought scorn of his law, and forsook his ways. **57** Moreover they have trodden down his righteous, **58** And said in their heart, that there is no God; yea, and that knowing they must die. **59** For as the things aforesaid shalt receive you, so thirst and pain are prepared for them: for it was not his will that men should come to nought: **60** But they which be created have defiled the name of him that made them, and were unthankful unto him which prepared life for them. **61** And therefore is my judgment now at hand. **62** These things have I not shewed unto all men, but unto thee, and a few like thee. Then answered I and said, **63** Behold, O Lord, now hast thou shewed me the multitude of the wonders, which thou wilt begin to do in the last times: but at what time, thou hast not shewed me.

9

1 He answered me then, and said, Measure thou the time diligently in itself: and when thou seest part of the signs past, which I have told thee before, **2** Then shalt thou understand, that it is the very same time, wherein the Highest will begin to visit the world which he made. **3** Therefore when there shall be seen earthquakes and uproars of the people in the world: **4** Then shalt thou well understand, that the most High spake of those things from the days that were before thee, even from the beginning. **5** For like as all that is made in the world hath a beginning and an end, and the end is manifest: **6** Even so the times also of the Highest have plain beginnings in wonder and powerful works, and endings in effects and signs. **7** And every one that shall be saved, and shall be able to escape by his works, and by faith, whereby ye have believed, **8** Shall be preserved from the said perils, and shall see my salvation in my land, and within my borders: for I have sanctified them for me from the beginning. **9** Then shall they be in pitiful case, which now have abused my ways: and they that have cast them away despitefully shall dwell in torments. **10** For such as in their life have received benefits, and have not known me; **11** And they that have loathed my law, while they had yet liberty, and, when as yet place of repentance was open unto them, understood not, but despised it; **12** The same must know it after death by pain. **13** And therefore be thou not curious how the ungodly shall be punished, and when: but enquire how the righteous shall be saved, whose the world is, and for whom the world is created. **14** Then answered I and said, **15** I have said before, and now do speak, and will speak it also hereafter, that there be many more of them which perish, than of them which shall be saved: **16** Like as a wave is greater than a drop. **17** And he answered me, saying, Like as the field is, so is also the seed; as the flowers be, such are the colours also; such as the workman is, such also is the work; and as the husbandman ls himself, so is his husbandry also: for it was the time of the world. **18** And now when I prepared the world, which was not yet made, even for them to dwell in that now live, no man spake against me. **19** For then every one obeyed: but now the manners of them which are created in this world that is made are corrupted by a perpetual seed, and by a law which is unsearchable rid themselves. **20** So I considered the world, and, behold, there was peril because of the devices that were come into it. **21** And I saw, and spared it greatly, and have kept me a grape of the cluster, and a plant of a great people. **22** Let the multitude perish then, which was born in vain; and let my grape be kept, and my plant; for with great labour have I made it perfect. **23** Nevertheless, if thou wilt cease yet seven days more, (but thou shalt not fast in them, **24** But go into a field of flowers, where no house is builded, and eat only the flowers of the field; taste no flesh, drink no wine, but eat flowers only;) **25** And pray unto the Highest continually, then will I come and talk with thee. **26** So I went my way into the field which is called Ardath, like as he commanded me; and there I sat among the flowers, and did eat of the herbs of the field, and the meat of the same satisfied me. **27** After seven days I sat upon the grass, and my heart was vexed within me, like as before: **28** And I opened my mouth, and began to talk before the most High, and said, **29** O Lord, thou that shewest thyself unto us, thou wast shewed unto our fathers in the wilderness, in a place where no man treadeth, in a barren place, when they came out of Egypt. **30** And thou spakest saying, Hear me, O Israel; and mark my words, thou seed of Jacob. **31** For, behold, I sow my law in you, and it shall bring fruit in you, and ye shall be honoured in it for ever. **32** But our fathers, which received the law, kept it not, and observed not thy ordinances: and though the fruit of thy law did not perish, neither could it, for it was thine; **33** Yet they that received it perished, because they kept not the thing that was sown in them. **34** And, lo, it ls a custom, when the ground hath received seed, or the sea a ship, or any vessel meat or drink, that, that being perished wherein it was sown or cast into, **35** That thing also which was sown, or cast therein, or received, doth perish, and remaineth not with us: but with us it hath not happened so. **36** For we that have received the law perish by sin, and our heart also which received it **37** Notwithstanding the law perisheth not, but remaineth in his force. **38** And when I spake these things in my heart, I looked back with mine eyes, and upon the right side I saw a woman, and, behold, she mourned and wept with a loud voice, and was much grieved in heart, and her clothes were rent, and she had ashes upon her head. **39** Then let I my thoughts go that I was in, and turned me unto her, **40** And said unto her, Wherefore weepest thou? why art thou so grieved in thy mind? **41** And she said unto me, Sir, let me alone, that I may bewail myself, and add unto my sorrow, for I am sore vexed in my mind, and brought very low. **42** And I said unto her, What aileth thee? tell me. **43** She said unto me, I thy servant have been barren, and had no child, though I had an husband thirty years, **44** And those thirty years I did nothing else day and night, and every hour, but make my, prayer to the Highest. **45** After thirty years God heard me thine handmaid, looked upon my misery, considered my trouble, and gave me a son: and I was very glad of him, so was my husband also, and all my neighbours: and we gave great honour unto the Almighty. **46** And I nourished him with great travail. **47** So when he grew up, and came to the time that he should have a wife, I made a feast.

10

1 And it so came to pass, that when my son was entered into his wedding chamber, he fell down, and died. **2** Then we all overthrew the lights, and all my neighbours rose up to comfort me: so I took my rest unto the second day at night. **3** And it came to pass, when they had all left off to comfort me, to the end I might be quiet; then rose I up by night and fled, and came hither into this field, as thou seest. **4** And I do now purpose not to return into the city, but here to stay, and neither to eat nor drink, but continually to mourn and to fast until I die. **5** Then left I the meditations wherein I was, and spake to her in anger, saying, **6** Thou foolish woman above all other, seest thou not our mourning, and what happeneth unto us? **7** How that Sion our mother is full of all heaviness, and much humbled, mourning very sore? **8** And now, seeing we all mourn and are sad, for we are all in heaviness, art thou grieved for one son? **9** For ask the earth, and she shall tell thee, that it is she which ought to mourn for the fall of so many that grow upon her. **10** For out of her came all at the first, and out of her shall all others come, and, behold, they walk almost all into destruction, and a multitude of them is utterly rooted out. **11** Who then should make more mourning than she, that hath lost so great a multitude; and not thou, which art sorry but for one? **12** But if thou sayest unto me, My lamentation is not like the earth's, because I have lost the fruit of my womb, which I brought forth with pains, and bare with sorrows; **13** But the earth not so: for the multitude present in it according to the course of the earth is gone, as it came: **14** Then say I unto thee, Like as thou hast brought forth with labour; even so the earth also hath given her fruit, namely, man, ever since the beginning unto him that made her. **15** Now therefore keep thy sorrow to thyself, and bear with a good courage that which hath befallen thee. **16** For if thou shalt acknowledge the determination of God to be just, thou shalt both receive thy son in time, and shalt be commended among women. **17** Go thy way then into the city to thine husband. **18** And she said unto me, That will I not do: I will not go into the city, but here will I die. **19** So I proceeded to speak further unto her, and said, **20** Do not so, but be counselled. by me: for how many are the adversities of Sion? be comforted in regard of the sorrow of Jerusalem. **21** For thou seest that our sanctuary is laid waste, our altar broken down, our temple destroyed; **22** Our psaltery is laid on the ground, our song is put to silence, our rejoicing is at an end, the light of our candlestick is put out, the ark of our covenant is spoiled, our holy things are defiled, and the name that is called upon us is almost profaned: our children are put to shame, our priests are burnt, our Levites are gone into captivity, our virgins are defiled, and our wives ravished; our righteous men carried away, our little ones destroyed, our young men are brought in bondage, and our strong men are become weak; **23** And, which is the greatest of all, the seal of Sion hath now lost her honour; for she is delivered into the hands of them that hate us. **24** And therefore shake off thy great heaviness, and put away the multitude of sorrows, that the Mighty may be merciful unto thee again, and the Highest shall give thee rest and ease from thy labour. **25** And it came to pass while I was talking with her, behold, her face upon a sudden shined exceedingly, and her countenance glistered, so that I was afraid of her, and mused what it might be. **26** And, behold, suddenly she made a great cry very fearful: so that the earth shook at the noise of the woman. **27** And I looked, and, behold, the woman appeared unto me no more, but there was a city builded, and a large place shewed itself from the foundations: then was I afraid, and cried with a loud voice, and said, **28** Where is Uriel the angel, who came unto me at the first? for he hath caused me to fall into many trances, and mine end is turned into corruption, and my prayer to rebuke. **29** And as I was speaking these words behold, he came unto me, and looked upon me. **30** And, lo, I lay as one that had been dead, and mine understanding was taken from me: and he took me by the right hand, and comforted me, and set me upon my feet, and said unto me, **31** What aileth thee? and why art thou so disquieted? and why is thine understanding troubled, and the thoughts of thine heart? **32** And I said, Because thou hast forsaken me, and yet I did according to thy words, and I went into the field, and, lo, I have seen, and yet see, that I am not able to express. **33** And he said unto me, Stand up manfully, and I will advise thee. **34** Then said I, Speak on, my lord, in me; only forsake me not, lest I die frustrate of my hope. **35** For I have seen that I knew not, and hear that I do not know. **36** Or is my sense deceived, or my soul in a dream? **37** Now therefore I beseech thee that thou wilt

shew thy servant of this vision. 38 He answered me then, and said, Hear me,
and I shall inform thee, and tell thee wherefore thou art afraid: for the Highest
will reveal many secret things unto thee. 39 He hath seen that thy way is right:
for that thou sorrowest continually for thy people, and makest great lamenta-
tion for Sion. 40 This therefore is the meaning of the vision which thou lately
sawest: 41 Thou sawest a woman mourning, and thou begannest to comfort
her: 42 But now seest thou the likeness of the woman no more, but there appe-
ared unto thee a city builded. 43 And whereas she told thee of the death of her
son, this is the solution: 44 This woman, whom thou sawest is Sion: and whe-
reas she said unto thee, even she whom thou seest as a city builded, 45 Whe-
reas, I say, she said unto thee, that she hath been thirty years barren: those are
the thirty years wherein there was no offering made in her. 46 But after thirty
years Solomon builded the city and offered offerings: and then bare the barren a
son. 47 And whereas she told thee that she nourished him with labour: that
was the dwelling in Jerusalem. 48 But whereas she said unto thee, That my son
coming into his marriage chamber happened to have a fail, and died: this was the
destruction that came to Jerusalem. 49 And, behold, thou sawest her likeness,
and because she mourned for her son, thou begannest to comfort her: and of
these things which have chanced, these are to be opened unto thee. 50 For
now the most High seeth that thou art grieved unfeignedly, and sufferest from
thy whole heart for her, so hath he shewed thee the brightness of her glory, and
the comeliness of her beauty: 51 And therefore I bade thee remain in the field
where no house was builded: 52 For I knew that the Highest would shew this
unto thee. 53 Therefore I commanded thee to go into the field, where no foun-
dation of any building was. 54 For in the place wherein the Highest beginneth
to shew his city, there can no man's building be able to stand. 55 And therefore
fear not, let not thine heart be affrighted, but go thy way in, and see the beauty
and greatness of the building, as much as thine eyes be able to see: 56 And then
shalt thou hear as much as thine ears may comprehend. 57 For thou art blessed
above many other, and art called with the Highest; and so are but few. 58 But
to morrow at night thou shalt remain here; 59 And so shall the Highest shew
thee visions of the high things, which the most High will do unto them that
dwell upon the earth in the last days. So I slept that night and another, like as he
commanded me.

11

1 Then saw I a dream, and, behold, there came up from the sea an
eagle, which had twelve feathered wings, and three heads. 2 And
I saw, and, behold, she spread her wings over all the earth, and all the winds of
the air blew on her, and were gathered together. 3 And I beheld, and out of
her feathers there grew other contrary feathers; and they became little feathers
and small. 4 But her heads were at rest: the head in the midst was greater than
the other, yet rested it with the residue. 5 Moreover I beheld, and, lo, the eagle
flew with her feathers, and reigned upon earth, and over them that dwelt the-
rein. 6 And I saw that all things under heaven were subject unto her, and no
man spake against her, no, not one creature upon earth. 7 And I beheld, and,
lo, the eagle rose upon her talons, and spake to her feathers, saying, 8 Watch not
all at once: sleep every one in his own place, and watch by course: 9 But let the
heads be preserved for the last. 10 And I beheld, and, lo, the voice went not out
of her heads, but from the midst of her body. 11 And I numbered her contrary
feathers, and, behold, there were eight of them. 12 And I looked, and, behold,
on the right side there arose one feather, and reigned over all the earth; 13 And
so it was, that when it reigned, the end of it came, and the place thereof ap-
peared no more: so the next following stood up. and reigned, and had a great
time; 14 And it happened, that when it reigned, the end of it came also, like as
the first, so that it appeared no more. 15 Then came there a voice unto it, and
said, 16 Hear thou that hast borne rule over the earth so long: this I say unto
thee, before thou beginnest to appear no more, 17 There shall none after thee
attain unto thy time, neither unto the half thereof. 18 Then arose the third,
and reigned as the other before, and appeared no more also. 19 So went it with
all the residue one after another, as that every one reigned, and then appeared no
more. 20 Then I beheld, and, lo, in process of time the feathers that followed
stood up upon the right side, that they might rule also; and some of them ruled,
but within a while they appeared no more: 21 For some of them were set up,
but ruled not. 22 After this I looked, and, behold, the twelve feathers appeared
no more, nor the two little feathers: 23 And there was no more upon the eagle's
body, but three heads that rested, and six little wings. 24 Then saw I also that
two little feathers divided themselves from the six, and remained under the head
that was upon the right side: for the four continued in their place. 25 And I
beheld, and, lo, the feathers that were under the wing thought to set up them-
selves and to have the rule. 26 And I beheld, and, lo, there was one set up, but
shortly it appeared no more. 27 And the second was sooner away than the
first. 28 And I beheld, and, lo, the two that remained thought also in themsel-
ves to reign: 29 And when they so thought, behold, there awaked one of the
heads that were at rest, namely, it that was in the midst; for that was greater than
the two other heads. 30 And then I saw that the two other heads were joined
with it. 31 And, behold, the head was turned with them that were with it, and
did eat up the two feathers under the wing that would have reigned. 32 But this
head put the whole earth in fear, and bare rule in it over all those that dwelt upon
the earth with much oppression; and it had the governance of the world more
than all the wings that had been. 33 And after this I beheld, and, lo, the head
that was in the midst suddenly appeared no more, like as the wings. 34 But
there remained the two heads, which also in like sort ruled upon the earth, and
over those that dwelt therein. 35 And I beheld, and, lo, the head upon the right
side devoured it that was upon the left side. 36 Then I head a voice, which said
unto me, Look before thee, and consider the thing that thou seest. 37 And I
beheld, and lo, as it were a roaring lion chased out of the wood: and I saw that he
sent out a man's voice unto the eagle, and said, 38 Hear thou, I will talk with
thee, and the Highest shall say unto thee, 39 Art not thou it that remainest of
the four beasts, whom I made to reign in my world, that the end of their times
might come through them? 40 And the fourth came, and overcame all the be-
asts that were past, and had power over the world with great fearfulness, and over
the whole compass of the earth with much wicked oppression; and so long time
dwelt he upon the earth with deceit. 41 For the earth hast thou not judged with
truth. 42 For thou hast afflicted the meek, thou hast hurt the peaceable, thou
hast loved liars, and destroyed the dwellings of them that brought forth fruit, and
hast cast down the walls of such as did thee no harm. 43 Therefore is thy wron-
gful dealing come up unto the Highest, and thy pride unto the Mighty. 44 The
Highest also hath looked upon the proud times, and, behold, they are ended, and
his abominations are fulfilled. 45 And therefore appear no more, thou eagle,
nor thy horrible wings, nor thy wicked feathers nor thy malicious heads, nor thy
hurtful claws, nor all thy vain body: 46 That all the earth may be refreshed,
and may return, being delivered from thy violence, and that she may hope for the
judgment and mercy of him that made her.

12

1 And it came to pass, whiles the lion spake these words unto the ea-
gle, I saw, 2 And, behold, the head that remained and the four wings
appeared no more, and the two went unto it and set themselves up to reign, and
their kingdom was small, and fill of uproar. 3 And I saw, and, behold, they ap-
peared no more, and the whole body of the eagle was burnt so that the earth was in
great fear: then awaked I out of the trouble and trance of my mind, and from great
fear, and said unto my spirit, 4 Lo, this hast thou done unto me, in that thou se-
archest out the ways of the Highest. 5 Lo, yet am I weary in my mind, and very
weak in my spirit; and little strength is there in me, for the great fear wherewith I
was afflicted this night. 6 Therefore will I now beseech the Highest, that he will
comfort me unto the end. 7 And I said, Lord that bearest rule, if I have found
grace before thy sight, and if I am justified with thee before many others, and if
my prayer indeed be come up before thy face; 8 Comfort me then, and shew me
thy servant the interpretation and plain difference of this fearful vision, that thou
mayest perfectly comfort my soul. 9 For thou hast judged me worthy to shew
me the last times. 10 And he said unto me, This is the interpretation of the
vision: 11 The eagle, whom thou sawest come up from the sea, is the kingdom
which was seen in the vision of thy brother Daniel. 12 But it was not expoun-
ded unto him, therefore now I declare it unto thee. 13 Behold, the days will
come, that there shall rise up a kingdom upon earth, and it shall be feared above
all the kingdoms that were before it. 14 In the same shall twelve kings reign,
one after another: 15 Whereof the second shall begin to reign, and shall have
more time than any of the twelve. 16 And this do the twelve wings signify, whi-
ch thou sawest. 17 As for the voice which thou heardest speak, and that thou
sawest not to go out from the heads but from the midst of the body thereof, this is
the interpretation: 18 That after the time of that kingdom there shall arise great
strivings, and it shall stand in peril of failing: nevertheless it shall not then fall, but
shall be restored again to his beginning. 19 And whereas thou sawest the eight
small under feathers sticking to her wings, this is the interpretation: 20 That
in him there shall arise eight kings, whose times shall be but small, and their
years swift. 21 And two of them shall perish, the middle time approaching:
four shall be kept until their end begin to approach: but two shall be kept unto
the end. 22 And whereas thou sawest three heads resting, this is the interpreta-
tion: 23 In his last days shall the most High raise up three kingdoms, and renew
many things therein, and they shall have the dominion of the earth, 24 And of
those that dwell therein, with much oppression, above all those that were before
them: therefore are they called the heads of the eagle. 25 For these are they
that shall accomplish his wickedness, and that shall finish his last end. 26 And
whereas thou sawest that the great head appeared no more, it signifieth that one
of them shall die upon his bed, and yet with pain. 27 For the two that remain
shall be slain with the sword. 28 For the sword of the one shall devour the
other: but at the last shall he fall through the sword himself. 29 And whereas
thou sawest two feathers under the wings passing over the head that is on the
right side; 30 It signifieth that these are they, whom the Highest hath kept unto
their end: this is the small kingdom and full of trouble, as thou sawest. 31 And
the lion, whom thou sawest rising up out of the wood, and roaring, and speaking
to the eagle, and rebuking her for her unrighteousness with all the words which
thou hast heard; 32 This is the anointed, which the Highest hath kept for them
and for their wickedness unto the end: he shall reprove them, and shall upbraid
them with their cruelty. 33 For he shall set them before him alive in judgment,
and shall rebuke them, and correct them. 34 For the rest of my people shall he
deliver with mercy, those that have been pressed upon my borders, and he shall
make them joyful until the coming of the day of judgment, whereof I have spoken
unto thee from the the beginning. 35 This is the dream that thou sawest, and
these are the interpretations. 36 Thou only hast been meet to know this secret
of the Highest. 37 Therefore write all these things that thou hast seen in a book,

and hide them: **38** And teach them to the wise of the people, whose hearts
thou knowest may comprehend and keep these secrets. **39** But wait thou here
thyself yet seven days more, that it may be shewed thee, whatsoever it pleaseth
the Highest to declare unto thee. And with that he went his way. **40** And it
came to pass, when all the people saw that the seven days were past, and I not
come again into the city, they gathered them all together, from the least unto the
greatest, and came unto me, and said, **41** What have we offended thee? and
what evil have we done against thee, that thou forsakest us, and sittest here in
this place? **42** For of all the prophets thou only art left us, as a cluster of the
vintage, and as a candle in a dark place, and as a haven or ship preserved from
the tempest. **43** Are not the evils which are come to us sufficient? **44** If thou
shalt forsake us, how much better had it been for us, if we also had been burned
in the midst of Sion? **45** For we are not better than they that died there. And
they wept with a loud voice. Then answered I them, and said, **46** Be of good
comfort, O Israel; and be not heavy, thou house of Jacob: **47** For the Highest
hath you in remembrance, and the Mighty hath not forgotten you in tempta-
tion. **48** As for me, I have not forsaken you, neither am I departed from you:
but am come into this place, to pray for the desolation of Sion, and that I might
seek mercy for the low estate of your sanctuary. **49** And now go your way home
every man, and after these days will I come unto you. **50** So the people went
their way into the city, like as I commanded them: **51** But I remained still in
the field seven days, as the angel commanded me; and did eat only in those days
of the flowers of the field, and had my meat of the herbs

13 **1** And it came to pass after seven days, I dreamed a dream by ni-
ght: **2** And, lo, there arose a wind from the sea, that it moved all
the waves thereof. **3** And I beheld, and, lo, that man waxed strong with the
thousands of heaven: and when he turned his countenance to look, all the things
trembled that were seen under him. **4** And whensoever the voice went out of
his mouth, all they burned that heard his voice, like as the earth faileth when it
feeleth the fire. **5** And after this I beheld, and, lo, there was gathered together a
multitude of men, out of number, from the four winds of the heaven, to subdue
the man that came out of the sea **6** But I beheld, and, lo, he had graved himself
a great mountain, and flew up upon it. **7** But I would have seen the region or
place whereout the hill was graven, and I could not. **8** And after this I beheld,
and, lo, all they which were gathered together to subdue him were sore afraid, and
yet durst fight. **9** And, lo, as he saw the violence of the multitude that came, he
neither lifted up his hand, nor held sword, nor any instrument of war: **10** But
only I saw that he sent out of his mouth as it had been a blast of fire, and out
of his lips a flaming breath, and out of his tongue he cast out sparks and tempe-
sts. **11** And they were all mixed together; the blast of fire, the flaming breath,
and the great tempest; and fell with violence upon the multitude which was pre-
pared to fight, and burned them up every one, so that upon a sudden of an innu-
merable multitude nothing was to be perceived, but only dust and smell of smoke:
when I saw this I was afraid. **12** Afterward saw I the same man come down
from the mountain, and call unto him another peaceable Multitude. **13** And
there came much people unto him, whereof some were glad, some were sorry, and
some of them were bound, and other some brought of them that were offered:
then was I sick through great fear, and I awaked, and said, **14** Thou hast shewed
thy servant these wonders from the beginning, and hast counted me worthy that
thou shouldest receive my prayer: **15** Shew me now yet the interpretation
of this dream. **16** For as I conceive in mine understanding, woe unto them
that shall be left in those days and much more woe unto them that are not left
behind! **17** For they that were not left were in heaviness. **18** Now understand
I the things that are laid up in the latter days, which shall happen unto them, and
to those that are left behind. **19** Therefore are they come into great perils and
many necessities, like as these dreams declare. **20** Yet is it easier for him that is
in danger to come into these things, than to pass away as a cloud out of the world,
and not to see the things that happen in the last days. And he answered unto me,
and said, **21** The interpretation of the vision shall I shew thee, and I will open
unto thee the thing that thou hast required. **22** Whereas thou hast spoken of
them that are left behind, this is the interpretation: **23** He that shall endure the
peril in that time hath kept himself: they that be fallen into danger are such as
have works, and faith toward the Almighty. **24** Know this therefore, that they
which be left behind are more blessed than they that be dead. **25** This is the
meaning of the vision: Whereas thou sawest a man coming up from the midst of
the sea: **26** The same is he whom God the Highest hath kept a great season,
which by his own self shall deliver his creature: and he shall order them that are
left behind. **27** And whereas thou sawest, that out of his mouth there came as a
blast of wind, and fire, and storm; **28** And that he held neither sword, nor any
instrument of war, but that the rushing in of him destroyed the whole multitude
that came to subdue him; this is the interpretation: **29** Behold, the days come,
when the most High will begin to deliver them that are upon the earth. **30** And
he shall come to the astonishment of them that dwell on the earth. **31** And one
shall undertake to fight against another, one city against another, one place against
another, one people against another, and one realm against another. **32** And the
time shall be when these things shall come to pass, and the signs shall happen whi-
ch I shewed thee before, and then shall my Son be declared, whom thou sawest
as a man ascending. **33** And when all the people hear his voice, every man shall
in their own land leave the battle they have one against another. **34** And an
innumerable multitude shall be gathered together, as thou sawest them, willing
to come, and to overcome him by fighting. **35** But he shall stand upon the
top of the mount Sion. **36** And Sion shall come, and shall be shewed to all
men, being prepared and builded, like as thou sawest the hill graven without
hands. **37** And this my Son shall rebuke the wicked inventions of those nations,
which for their wicked life are fallen into the tempest; **38** And shall lay before
them their evil thoughts, and the torments wherewith they shall begin to be tor-
mented, which are like unto a flame: and he shall destroy them without labour
by the law which is like unto me. **39** And whereas thou sawest that he gathered
another peaceable multitude unto him; **40** Those are the ten tribes, which were
carried away prisoners out of their own land in the time of Osea the king, whom
Salmanasar the king of Assyria led away captive, and he carried them over the
waters, and so came they into another land. **41** But they took this counsel
among themselves, that they would leave the multitude of the heathen, and go
forth into a further country, where never mankind dwelt, **42** That they mi-
ght there keep their statutes, which they never kept in their own land. **43** And
they entered into Euphrates by the narrow places of the river. **44** For the most
High then shewed signs for them, and held still the flood, till they were passed
over. **45** For through that country there was a great way to go, namely, of a year
and a half: and the same region is called Arsareth. **46** Then dwelt they there
until the latter time; and now when they shall begin to come, **47** The Highest
shall stay the springs of the stream again, that they may go through: therefore
sawest thou the multitude with peace. **48** But those that be left behind of thy
people are they that are found within my borders. **49** Now when he destroyeth
the multitude of the nations that are gathered together, he shall defend his people
that remain. **50** And then shall he shew them great wonders. **51** Then said I,
O Lord that bearest rule, shew me this: Wherefore have I seen the man coming up
from the midst of the sea? **52** And he said unto me, Like as thou canst neither
seek out nor know the things that are in the deep of the sea: even so can no man
upon earth see my Son, or those that be with him, but in the day time. **53** This
is the interpretation of the dream which thou sawest, and whereby thou only
art here lightened. **54** For thou hast forsaken thine own way, and applied thy
diligence unto my law, and sought it. **55** Thy life hast thou ordered in wisdom,
and hast called understanding thy mother. **56** And therefore have I shewed thee
the treasures of the Highest: after other three days I will speak other things unto
thee, and declare unto thee mighty and wondrous things. **57** Then went I forth
into the field, giving praise and thanks greatly unto the most High because of his
wonders which he did in time; **58** And because he governeth the same, and
such things as fall in their seasons: and there I sat three days.

14 **1** And it came to pass upon the third day, I sat under an oak, and,
behold, there came a voice out of a bush over against me, and said,
Esdras, Esdras. **2** And I said, Here am I, Lord And I stood up upon my
feet. **3** Then said he unto me, In the bush I did manifestly reveal myself unto
Moses, and talked with him, when my people served in Egypt: **4** And I sent
him and led my people out of Egypt, and brought him up to the mount of whe-
re I held him by me a long season, **5** And told him many wondrous things,
and shewed him the secrets of the times, and the end; and commanded him,
saying, **6** These words shalt thou declare, and these shalt thou hide. **7** And
now I say unto thee, **8** That thou lay up in thy heart the signs that I have
shewed, and the dreams that thou hast seen, and the interpretations which thou
hast heard: **9** For thou shalt be taken away from all, and from henceforth
thou shalt remain with my Son, and with such as be like thee, until the times
be ended. **10** For the world hath lost his youth, and the times begin to wax
old. **11** For the world is divided into twelve parts, and the ten parts of it are
gone already, and half of a tenth part: **12** And there remaineth that which is
after the half of the tenth part. **13** Now therefore set thine house in order, and
reprove thy people, comfort such of them as be in trouble, and now renounce
corruption, **14** Let go from thee mortal thoughts, cast away the burdens of
man, put off now the weak nature, **15** And set aside the thoughts that are most
heavy unto thee, and haste thee to flee from these times. **16** For yet greater
evils than those which thou hast seen happen shall be done hereafter. **17** For
look how much the world shall be weaker through age, so much the more shall
evils increase upon them that dwell therein. **18** For the time is fled far away,
and leasing is hard at hand: for now hasteth the vision to come, which thou hast
seen. **19** Then answered I before thee, and said, **20** Behold, Lord, I will go,
as thou hast commanded me, and reprove the people which are present: but they
that shall be born afterward, who shall admonish them? thus the world is set in
darkness, and they that dwell therein are without light. **21** For thy law is burnt,
therefore no man knoweth the things that are done of thee, or the work that shall
begin. **22** But if I have found grace before thee, send the Holy Ghost into me,
and I shall write all that hath been done in the world since the beginning, which
were written in thy law, that men may find thy path, and that they which will
live in the latter days may live. **23** And he answered me, saying, Go thy way,
gather the people together, and say unto them, that they seek thee not for forty
days. **24** But look thou prepare thee many box trees, and take with thee Sarea,
Dabria, Selemia, Ecanus, and Asiel, these five which are ready to write swift-
ly; **25** And come hither, and I shall light a candle of understanding in thine
heart, which shall not be put out, till the things be performed which thou shalt
begin to write. **26** And when thou hast done, some things shalt thou publish,

and some things shalt thou shew secretly to the wise: to morrow this hour shalt
thou begin to write. **27** Then went I forth, as he commanded, and gathered
all the people together, and said, **28** Hear these words, O Israel. **29** Our fa-
thers at the beginning were strangers in Egypt, from whence they were delive-
red: **30** And received the law of life, which they kept not, which ye also have
transgressed after them. **31** Then was the land, even the land of Sion, parted
among you by lot: but your fathers, and ye yourselves, have done unrighteousness,
and have not kept the ways which the Highest commanded you. **32** And fora-
smuch as he is a righteous judge, he took from you in time the thing that he had
given you. **33** And now are ye here, and your brethren among you. **34** There-
fore if so be that ye will subdue your own understanding, and reform your hearts,
ye shall be kept alive and after death ye shall obtain mercy. **35** For after death
shall the judgment come, when we shall live again: and then shall the names of the
righteous be manifest, and the works of the ungodly shall be declared. **36** Let
no man therefore come unto me now, nor seek after me these forty days. **37** So
I took the five men, as he commanded me, and we went into the field, and remai-
ned there. **38** And the next day, behold, a voice called me, saying, Esdras, open
thy mouth, and drink that I give thee to drink. **39** Then opened I my mouth,
and, behold, he reached me a full cup, which was full as it were with water, but
the colour of it was like fire. **40** And I took it, and drank: and when I had drunk
of it, my heart uttered understanding, and wisdom grew in my breast, for my
spirit strengthened my memory: **41** And my mouth was opened, and shut no
more. **42** The Highest gave understanding unto the five men, and they wrote
the wonderful visions of the night that were told, which they knew not: and they
sat forty days, and they wrote in the day, and at night they ate bread. **43** As for
me. I spake in the day, and I held not my tongue by night. **44** In forty days they
wrote two hundred and four books. **45** And it came to pass, when the forty
days were filled, that the Highest spake, saying, The first that thou hast written
publish openly, that the worthy and unworthy may read it: **46** But keep the
seventy last, that thou mayest deliver them only to such as be wise among the
people: **47** For in them is the spring of understanding, the fountain of wisdom,
and the stream of knowledge. **48** And I did so.

15

1 Behold, speak thou in the ears of my people the words of prophecy,
which I will put in thy mouth, saith the Lord: **2** And cause them to
be written in paper: for they are faithful and true. **3** Fear not the imaginations
against thee, let not the incredulity of them trouble thee, that speak against
thee. **4** For all the unfaithful shall die in their unfaithfulness. **5** Behold, saith
the Lord, I will bring plagues upon the world; the sword, famine, death, and de-
struction. **6** For wickedness hath exceedingly polluted the whole earth, and
their hurtful works are fulfilled. **7** Therefore saith the Lord, **8** I will hold my
tongue no more as touching their wickedness, which they profanely commit, nei-
ther will I suffer them in those things, in which they wickedly exercise themselves:
behold, the innocent and righteous blood crieth unto me, and the souls of the just
complain continually. **9** And therefore, saith the Lord, I will surely avenge
them, and receive unto me all the innocent blood from among them. **10** Behold,
my people is led as a flock to the slaughter: I will not suffer them now to dwell in
the land of Egypt: **11** But I will bring them with a mighty hand and a stretched
out arm, and smite Egypt with plagues, as before, and will destroy all the land
thereof. **12** Egypt shall mourn, and the foundation of it shall be smitten with
the plague and punishment that God shall bring upon it. **13** They that till the
ground shall mourn: for their seeds shall fail through the blasting and hail, and
with a fearful constellation. **14** Woe to the world and them that dwell the-
rein! **15** For the sword and their destruction draweth nigh, and one people shall
stand up and fight against another, and swords in their hands. **16** For there shall
be sedition among men, and invading one another; they shall not regard their
kings nor princes, and the course of their actions shall stand in their power. **17** A
man shall desire to go into a city, and shall not be able. **18** For because of their
pride the cities shall be troubled, the houses shall be destroyed, and men shall be
afraid. **19** A man shall have no pity upon his neighbour, but shall destroy their
houses with the sword, and spoil their goods, because of the lack of bread, and for
great tribulation. **20** Behold, saith God, I will call together all the kings of the
earth to reverence me, which are from the rising of the sun, from the south, from
the east, and Libanus; to turn themselves one against another, and repay the thin-
gs that they have done to them. **21** Like as they do yet this day unto my chosen,
so will I do also, and recompense in their bosom. Thus saith the Lord
God; **22** My right hand shall not spare the sinners, and my sword shall not ce-
ase over them that shed innocent blood upon the earth. **23** The fire is gone
forth from his wrath, and hath consumed the foundations of the earth, and the
sinners, like the straw that is kindled. **24** Woe to them that sin, and keep not
my commandments! saith the Lord. **25** I will not spare them: go your way, ye
children, from the power, defile not my sanctuary. **26** For the Lord knoweth all
them that sin against him, and therefore delivereth he them unto death and de-
struction. **27** For now are the plagues come upon the whole earth and ye shall
remain in them: for God shall not deliver you, because ye have sinned against
him. **28** Behold an horrible vision, and the appearance thereof from the
east: **29** Where the nations of the dragons of Arabia shall come out with many
chariots, and the multitude of them shall be carried as the wind upon earth, that
all they which hear them may fear and tremble. **30** Also the Carmanians raging
in wrath shall go forth as the wild boars of the wood, and with great power shall
they come, and join battle with them, and shall waste a portion of the land of the
Assyrians. **31** And then shall the dragons have the upper hand, remembering
their nature; and if they shall turn themselves, conspiring together in great power
to persecute them, **32** Then these shall be troubled bled, and keep silence
through their power, and shall flee. **33** And from the land of the Assyrians shall
the enemy besiege them, and consume some of them, and in their host shall be
fear and dread, and strife among their kings. **34** Behold clouds from the east
and from the north unto the south, and they are very horrible to look upon, full
of wrath and storm. **35** They shall smite one upon another, and they shall smi-
te down a great multitude of stars upon the earth, even their own star; and blood
shall be from the sword unto the belly, **36** And dung of men unto the camel's
hough. **37** And there shall be great fearfulness and trembling upon earth: and
they that see the wrath shall be afraid, and trembling shall come upon
them. **38** And then shall there come great storms from the south, and from the
north, and another part from the west. **39** And strong winds shall arise from the
east, and shall open it; and the cloud which he raised up in wrath, and the star
stirred to cause fear toward the east and west wind, shall be destroyed. **40** The
great and mighty clouds shall be puffed up full of wrath, and the star, that they
may make all the earth afraid, and them that dwell therein; and they shall pour
out over every high and eminent place an horrible star, **41** Fire, and hail, and
flying swords, and many waters, that all fields may be full, and all rivers, with the
abundance of great waters. **42** And they shall break down the cities and walls,
mountains and hills, trees of the wood, and grass of the meadows, and their
corn. **43** And they shall go stedfastly unto Babylon, and make her
afraid. **44** They shall come to her, and besiege her, the star and all wrath shall
they pour out upon her: then shall the dust and smoke go up unto the heaven,
and all they that be about her shall bewail her. **45** And they that remain under
her shall do service unto them that have put her in fear. **46** And thou, Asia, that
art partaker of the hope of Babylon, and art the glory of her person: **47** Woe be
unto thee, thou wretch, because thou hast made thyself like unto her; and hast
decked thy daughters in whoredom, that they might please and glory in thy lo-
vers, which have always desired to commit whoredom with thee. **48** Thou hast
followed her that is hated in all her works and inventions: therefore saith
God, **49** I will send plagues upon thee; widowhood, poverty, famine, sword,
and pestilence, to waste thy houses with destruction and death. **50** And the
glory of thy Power shall be dried up as a flower, the heat shall arise that is sent over
thee. **51** Thou shalt be weakened as a poor woman with stripes, and as one
chastised with wounds, so that the mighty and lovers shall not be able to receive
thee. **52** Would I with jealousy have so proceeded against thee, saith the
Lord, **53** If thou hadst not always slain my chosen, exalting the stroke of thine
hands, and saying over their dead, when thou wast drunken, **54** Set forth the
beauty of thy countenance? **55** The reward of thy whoredom shall be in thy
bosom, therefore shalt thou receive recompence. **56** Like as thou hast done
unto my chosen, saith the Lord, even so shall God do unto thee, and shall deliver
thee into mischief **57** Thy children shall die of hunger, and thou shalt fall
through the sword: thy cities shall be broken down, and all thine shall perish with
the sword in the field. **58** They that be in the mountains shall die of hunger, and
eat their own flesh, and drink their own blood, for very hunger of bread, and
thirst of water. **59** Thou as unhappy shalt come through the sea, and receive
plagues again. **60** And in the passage they shall rush on the idle city, and shall
destroy some portion of thy land, and consume part of thy glory, and shall return
to Babylon that was destroyed. **61** And thou shalt be cast down by them as
stubble, and they shall be unto thee as fire; **62** And shall consume thee, and thy
cities, thy land, and thy mountains; all thy woods and thy fruitful trees shall they
burn up with fire. **63** Thy children shall they carry away captive, and, look,
what thou hast, they shall spoil it, and mar the beauty of thy face.

16

1 Woe be unto thee, Babylon, and Asia! woe be unto thee, Egypt and
Syria! **2** Gird up yourselves with cloths of sack and hair, bewail your
children, and be sorry; for your destruction is at hand. **3** A sword is sent upon
you, and who may turn it back? **4** A fire is sent among you, and who may quen-
ch it? **5** Plagues are sent unto you, and what is he that may drive them
away? **6** May any man drive away an hungry lion in the wood? or may any one
quench the fire in stubble, when it hath begun to burn? **7** May one turn again
the arrow that is shot of a strong archer? **8** The mighty Lord sendeth the plagues
and who is he that can drive them away? **9** A fire shall go forth from his wrath,
and who is he that may quench it? **10** He shall cast lightnings, and who shall
not fear? he shall thunder, and who shall not be afraid? **11** The Lord shall thre-
aten, and who shall not be utterly beaten to powder at his presence? **12** The
earth quaketh, and the foundations thereof; the sea ariseth up with waves from
the deep, and the waves of it are troubled, and the fishes thereof also, before the
Lord, and before the glory of his power: **13** For strong is his right hand that
bendeth the bow, his arrows that he shooteth are sharp, and shall not miss, when
they begin to be shot into the ends of the world. **14** Behold, the plagues are
sent, and shall not return again, until they come upon the earth. **15** The fire is
kindled, and shall not be put out, till it consume the foundation of the ear-
th. **16** Like as an arrow which is shot of a mighty archer returneth not backward:
even so the plagues that shall be sent upon earth shall not return again. **17** Woe
is me! woe is me! who will deliver me in those days? **18** The beginning of sor-
rows and great mournings; the beginning of famine and great death; the begin-

ning of wars, and the powers shall stand in fear; the beginning of evils! what shall
I do when these evils shall come? **19** Behold, famine and plague, tribulation
and anguish, are sent as scourges for amendment. **20** But for all these things
they shall not turn from their wickedness, nor be always mindful of the scour-
ges. **21** Behold, victuals shall be so good cheap upon earth, that they shall think
themselves to be in good case, and even then shall evils grow upon earth, sword,
famine, and great confusion. **22** For many of them that dwell upon earth shall
perish of famine; and the other, that escape the hunger, shall the sword de-
stroy. **23** And the dead shall be cast out as dung, and there shall be no man to
comfort them: for the earth shall be wasted, and the cities shall be cast
down. **24** There shall be no man left to till the earth, and to sow it **25** The
trees shall give fruit, and who shall gather them? **26** The grapes shall ripen, and
who shall tread them? for all places shall be desolate of men: **27** So that one
man shall desire to see another, and to hear his voice. **28** For of a city there shall
be ten left, and two of the field, which shall hide themselves in the thick groves,
and in the clefts of the rocks. **29** As in an orchard of Olives upon every tree
there are left three or four olives; **30** Or as when a vineyard is gathered, there are
left some clusters of them that diligently seek through the vineyard: **31** Even so
in those days there shall be three or four left by them that search their houses with
the sword. **32** And the earth shall be laid waste, and the fields thereof shall wax
old, and her ways and all her paths shall grow full of thorns, because no man shall
travel therethrough. **33** The virgins shall mourn, having no bridegrooms; the
women shall mourn, having no husbands; their daughters shall mourn, having no
helpers. **34** In the wars shall their bridegrooms be destroyed, and their hu-
sbands shall perish of famine. **35** Hear now these things and understand them,
ye servants of the Lord. **36** Behold, the word of the Lord, receive it: believe not
the gods of whom the Lord spake. **37** Behold, the plagues draw nigh, and are
not slack. **38** As when a woman with child in the ninth month bringeth forth
her son, with two or three hours of her birth great pains compass her womb,
which pains, when the child cometh forth, they slack not a moment: **39** Even
so shall not the plagues be slack to come upon the earth, and the world shall
mourn, and sorrows shall come upon it on every side. **40** O my people, hear my
word: make you ready to thy battle, and in those evils be even as pilgrims upon
the earth. **41** He that selleth, let him be as he that fleeth away: and he that
buyeth, as one that will lose: **42** He that occupieth merchandise, as he that hath
no profit by it: and he that buildeth, as he that shall not dwell therein: **43** He
that soweth, as if he should not reap: so also he that planteth the vineyard, as he
that shall not gather the grapes: **44** They that marry, as they that shall get no
children; and they that marry not, as the widowers. **45** And therefore they that
labour labour in vain: **46** For strangers shall reap their fruits, and spoil their
goods, overthrow their houses, and take their children captives, for in captivity
and famine shall they get children. **47** And they that occupy their merchandise
with robbery, the more they deck their cities, their houses, their possessions, and
their own persons: **48** The more will I be angry with them for their sin, saith the
Lord. **49** Like as a whore envieth a right honest and virtuous woman: **50** So
shall righteousness hate iniquity, when she decketh herself, and shall accuse her to
her face, when he cometh that shall defend him that diligently searcheth out every
sin upon earth. **51** And therefore be ye not like thereunto, nor to the works
thereof. **52** For yet a little, and iniquity shall be taken away out of the earth, and
righteousness shall reign among you. **53** Let not the sinner say that he hath not
sinned: for God shall burn coals of fire upon his head, which saith before the Lord
God and his glory, I have not sinned. **54** Behold, the Lord knoweth all the
works of men, their imaginations, their thoughts, and their hearts: **55** Which
spake but the word, Let the earth be made; and it was made: Let the heaven be
made; and it was created. **56** In his word were the stars made, and he knoweth
the number of them. **57** He searcheth the deep, and the treasures thereof; he
hath measured the sea, and what it containeth. **58** He hath shut the sea in the
midst of the waters, and with his word hath he hanged the earth upon the wa-
ters. **59** He spreadeth out the heavens like a vault; upon the waters hath he
founded it. **60** In the desert hath he made springs of water, and pools upon the
tops of the mountains, that the floods might pour down from the high rocks to
water the earth. **61** He made man, and put his heart in the midst of the body,
and gave him breath, life, and understanding. **62** Yea and the Spirit of Almighty
God, which made all things, and searcheth out all hidden things in the secrets of
the earth, **63** Surely he knoweth your inventions, and what ye think in your
hearts, even them that sin, and would hide their sin. **64** Therefore hath the
Lord exactly searched out all your works, and he will put you all to sha-
me. **65** And when your sins are brought forth, ye shall be ashamed before men,
and your own sins shall be your accusers in that day. **66** What will ye do? or
how will ye hide your sins before God and his angels? **67** Behold, God himself
is the judge, fear him: leave off from your sins, and forget your iniquities, to med-
dle no more with them for ever: so shall God lead you forth, and deliver you from
all trouble. **68** For, behold, the burning wrath of a great multitude is kindled
over you, and they shall take away certain of you, and feed you, being idle, with
things offered unto idols. **69** And they that consent unto them shall be had in
derision and in reproach, and trodden under foot. **70** For there shall be in every
place, and in the next cities, a great insurrection upon those that fear the
Lord. **71** They shall be like mad men, sparing none, but still spoiling and de-
stroying those that fear the Lord. **72** For they shall waste and take away their
goods, and cast them out of their houses. **73** Then shall they be known, who are
my chosen; and they shall be tried as the gold in the fire. **74** Hear, O ye my
beloved, saith the Lord: behold, the days of trouble are at hand, but I will deliver
you from the same. **75** Be ye not afraid neither doubt; for God is your gui-
de, **76** And the guide of them who keep my commandments and precepts,
saith the Lord God: let not your sins weigh you down, and let not your iniquities
lift up themselves. **77** Woe be unto them that are bound with their sins, and
covered with their iniquities like as a field is covered over with bushes, and the
path thereof covered with thorns, that no man may travel through! **78** It is left
undressed, and is cast into the fire to be consumed therewith.

APOCRYPHA PRAYER OF
MANASSEHOR

The Prayer of Manassehor, The Prayer of Manasses King of Judah

1 **1** O Lord, Almighty God of our fathers, Abraham, Isaac, and Jacob, and of their righteous seed; who hast made heaven and earth, with all the ornament thereof; who hast bound the sea by the word of thy commandment; who hast shut up the deep, and sealed it by thy terrible and glorious name; whom all men fear, and tremble before thy power; for the majesty of thy glory cannot be borne, and thine angry threatening toward sinners is importable: but thy merciful promise is unmeasurable and unsearchable; for thou art the most high Lord, of great compassion, longsuffering, very merciful, and repentest of the evils of men. Thou, O Lord, according to thy great goodness hast promised repentance and forgiveness to them that have sinned against thee: and of thine infinite mercies hast appointed repentance unto sinners, that they may be saved. Thou therefore, O Lord, that art the God of the just, hast not appointed repentance to the just, as to Abraham, and Isaac, and Jacob, which have not sinned against thee; but thou hast appointed repentance unto me that am a sinner: for I have sinned above the number of the sands of the sea. My transgressions, O Lord, are multiplied: my transgressions are multiplied, and I am not worthy to behold and see the height of heaven for the multitude of mine iniquities. I am bowed down with many iron bands, that I cannot life up mine head, neither have any release: for I have provoked thy wrath, and done evil before thee: I did not thy will, neither kept I thy commandments: I have set up abominations, and have multiplied offences. Now therefore I bow the knee of mine heart, beseeching thee of grace. I have sinned, O Lord, I have sinned, and I acknowledge mine iniquities: wherefore, I humbly beseech thee, forgive me, O Lord, forgive me, and destroy me not with mine iniquites. Be not angry with me for ever, by reserving evil for me; neither condemn me to the lower parts of the earth. For thou art the God, even the God of them that repent; and in me thou wilt shew all thy goodness: for thou wilt save me, that am unworthy, according to thy great mercy. Therefore I will praise thee for ever all the days of my life: for all the powers of the heavens do praise thee, and thine is the glory for ever and ever. Amen.

Made in the USA
Columbia, SC
18 July 2024

38976901R00405